A SUPPLEMENT TO THE

OXFORD ENGLISH
DICTIONARY

A SUPPLEMENT TO THE
OXFORD ENGLISH DICTIONARY

EDITED BY
R. W. BURCHFIELD

———

VOLUME II · H–N

OXFORD
AT THE CLARENDON PRESS
1976

Oxford University Press, Walton Street, Oxford OX2 6DP

OXFORD LONDON GLASGOW NEW YORK
TORONTO MELBOURNE WELLINGTON CAPE TOWN
IBADAN NAIROBI DAR ES SALAAM LUSAKA ADDIS ABABA
KUALA LUMPUR SINGAPORE JAKARTA HONG KONG TOKYO
DELHI BOMBAY CALCUTTA MADRAS KARACHI

© *Oxford University Press 1976*

British Library Cataloguing in Publication Data

The Oxford English dictionary.
  Supplement. Vol. 2 : H–N
  ISBN 0–19–861123–4
  1 Burchfield, Robert William.
  423 PE 1625
  English language – Dictionaries

Printed in Great Britain by William Clowes & Sons, Limited, London, Beccles and Colchester

This Supplement to the Oxford English Dictionary

is respectfully dedicated to

HER MAJESTY THE QUEEN

by her gracious permission

PREFACE

DRYDEN remarks in his *Preface to the Fables* (1700):

> 'Tis with a Poet, as with a Man who designs to build, and is very exact, as he supposes, in casting up the Cost beforehand: But, generally speaking, he is mistaken in his Account, and reckons short of the Expence he first intended: He alters his Mind as the Work proceeds, and will have this or that Convenience more, of which he had not thought when he began. So has it hapned to me; I have built a House, where I intended but a Lodge.

This comment came into my mind when it became apparent that the material in the letters after G could not easily be contained in the two further volumes that were promised when Volume I (A–G) was published in 1972. This second volume of the Supplement ends with N, and there will be two further volumes. The fourth volume will include an extensive Bibliography of works cited in the new Supplement.

The main lines of policy laid down in the first volume are retained in this one, but the material in our quotation files has continued to expand and this expansion is reflected in the vocabulary included in the present volume. It would be difficult to describe every aspect of 'this or that Convenience more' included in the range H–N. Some of the new areas explored are mentioned in papers that I delivered to the Philological Society in 1973[1] and to the Royal Society of Arts in 1975.[2] Others have been dealt with more briefly in several papers on miscellaneous topics.[3] The main conclusions of these papers are, among others, that (i) offensiveness to a particular group, minority or otherwise, is unacceptable as the sole ground for the exclusion of any word or class of words from the *O.E.D.*; (ii) it is therefore desirable to enter new racial and religious terms however opprobrious they may seem to those to whom they are applied and often to those who have to use them, or however controversial the set of beliefs professed by the members of minority sects; (iii) it is also desirable, in order to avoid misunderstanding and consequent hostility, that the somewhat antiquated historical record of words like *Jesuit*, *Jew*, *Negro*, *nigger*, and others already treated in the *O.E.D.* should be brought up to date. These things we have done. Proprietary terms are of more than routine concern to lexicographers and I have endeavoured to establish a policy which safeguards scholarly standards while not doing anything to imperil the proprietary rights of the owners of such terms. It gave me particular pleasure that the United States Trademark Association reprinted my 1973 comments on the subject as part of a regular issue of *The Trademark Reporter*.[4]

For new general vocabulary we have repeatedly and profitably turned to North American sources, including long runs of regional American and Canadian newspapers as well as more traditional sources like the *New York Times* and the *New Yorker*, in addition to the principal publications of the United Kingdom. We have given somewhat more attention in this volume

---

[1] 'The Treatment of Controversial Vocabulary in the *Oxford English Dictionary*', *Transactions of the Philological Society 1973* (1974), pp. 1–28.

[2] 'The Art of the Lexicographer', *Journal of the Royal Society of Arts*, Vol. CXXIII, May 1975, pp. 349–61.

[3] 'Data Collecting and Research', *Annals of the New York Academy of Sciences* Vol. CCXI (1973), pp. 99–103; 'Some Aspects of the Historical Treatment of Twentieth-Century Vocabulary', *Tavola Rotonda sui Grandi Lessici Storici* (Florence, 3–5 May 1971), Accademia della Crusca, Firenze, 1973,

pp. 31–5; (with Valerie Smith) 'Adzuki to Gun: Some Japanese Loanwords in English', *The Rising Generation* (Tokyo) Dec. 1973, pp. 524–6, and Jan. 1974, pp. 593–5; 'Acid to Downer: Some Words for O.E.D.', *Words*, Wai-te-ata Studies in Literature, No. 4 (Jan. 1974) (Wellington, N.Z.); and 'The Prosodic Terminology of Anglo-Saxon Scholars', *Old English Studies in Honour of John C. Pope* (1974), pp. 171–202. See also Sandra Raphael, 'Natural History and the *Oxford English Dictionary*', *Jrnl. Soc. Bibliography Nat. Hist.* Vol. VI (1973), pp. 229–35.

[4] Vol. 65, No. 4, July–August 1975, pp. 291–317.

than in the last to the special vocabulary of the West Indies and, nearer home, of Scotland. The rapid expansion of work in all the sciences has been fully taken into account: anyone interested in the history of scientific words will find much of permanent value in the pages that follow. The terms of the printing industry and the names of plants and animals have continued to yield lexical material of considerable interest. The historical treatment of words again provides many surprises: for example, *minibus* is recorded from 1845, and *mugging*, in its now current sense, turns out to be much older than most people supposed.

Most people, at one time or another, treat words 'as if they are people—beautiful, delinquent, degenerate, regal'.[5] My colleagues and I, who prepared this volume, are no exceptions to the general rule. We do not personally approve of all the words and phrases that are recorded in this dictionary nor necessarily condone their use by others. Nevertheless, in our function as 'marshallers of words',[6] we have set them all down as objectively as possible to form a permanent record of the language of our time, the useful and the neutral, those that are decorous and well-formed, beside those that are controversial, tasteless, or worse.

The late Professor Atcheson L. Hench (University of Virginia, Charlottesville, Virginia) let it be known before his death in 1974 that he wished us to have access to the Hench Collection, a large miscellaneous collection of quotations from Virginian and other newspapers from about 1930 onward. As a result, the *Sun* (Baltimore) and the *Richmond News-Leader*, together with some other daily papers from various cities in the Eastern and Southern United States, appear fairly frequently in entries from the letter M onward. Professor W. R. G. Branford and the staff of the forthcoming *Dictionary of South African English*, especially Mr. John Walker, made valuable contributions to our South African English items, as did also Professor N. G. Sabbagha and Mr. N. van Blerk. Professor K. Koike (especially) and other Japanese scholars have assisted us with the entries for words of Japanese origin, and Dr. L. V. Malakhovski with words from Russian. In 1975 Professor G. A. Wilkes (University of Sydney) allowed us to copy his valuable collection of quotations for Australian colloquialisms and there was time to add some of these to the relevant Australian items in the later letters of this volume. Our indebtedness to G. & C. Merriam Co., described in Volume I, was as great as ever, and I should like to restate our gratitude to Dr. H. B. Woolf and to his successor Dr. F. Mish for their continuing co-operation. Mr. Clarence L. Barnhart and Professor F. G. Cassidy have also made important contributions to this volume by supplying quotations from their dictionary files.

The major libraries in Oxford, London, and Washington, and numerous other libraries in other cities in various parts of the world, continued to give us every possible support as we continued with our work of research and verification. We were able to overcome the difficulties naturally resulting from the dispersal of books and periodicals to new areas distant from the main centres. Special mention should be made of the access to temporary book-stacks allowed to my scientific assistants by the Librarian of the Radcliffe Science Library in Oxford during a period of great upheaval while new sections of the main library were being built.

Sadly not all those who were associated with the Supplement survived to see the publication of this volume. Of members of staff, Miss Elizabeth Brommer died in 1972, a few months before the publication of A–G. Mrs. Joan Blackler (my secretary from 1966 to 1974) and Mrs. Peggy Kay (part-time library researcher from 1967 onward) both died in 1975. The following Contributors or Outside Consultants have also died since Volume I was published in 1972: Professor

---

[5] A remark (slightly adapted) by the New Zealand writer Janet Frame in *Islands* (Christchurch, N.Z.), Vol. 2, No. 3 (1973), p. 252.

[6] Adopting Joseph Trapp's description of Dryden as 'the best Marshaller of words' as a phrase that comes as near as possible to a description of the perfect historical lexicographer, bearing in mind the *O.E.D.* definition of *marshal*, v. (sense 5) as 'to dispose, arrange or set (things, material or immaterial) in methodical order'.

Sir Godfrey Driver, Mr. W. Granville, Professor A. L. Hench, Dr. M. D. W. Jeffreys, Dr. D. Lack, Mr. J. C. Maxwell, Dr. L. F. Powell, Mrs. Stefanyja Ross, and Miss Phyllis Trapp.

To the list of Contributors in Volume I the name of Dr. D. S. Brewer should be added. Major contributors of quotations in the period 1972–75 included the following: Professor W. S. Avis, D. J. Barr, G. Chowdharay-Best, C. Collier, Professor M. Eccles, R. Hall, T. F. Hoad, Dom Sylvester Houédard, Miss M. Laski, Dr. D. Leechman, Dr. J. Lyman, Professor J. B. McMillan, Mrs. J. M. Marson, Mrs. M. Y. Offord, and D. Shulman. Of these, Miss Laski, Dr. Leechman, Mrs. Offord, Mrs. Marson, and Mr. Chowdharay-Best contributed altogether approximately 70,000 quotations and all the others named supplied between 1,000 and 3,000 quotations each. Smaller, but valuable, sets of quotations were received from numerous others, including the Revd. H. E. G. Rope, R. E. Hawkins, and Mrs. Daphne McColl.

To the list of outside Proof-Readers the names of M. W. Grose, T. F. Hoad, and Dr. Kendon Stubbs should now be added.

The following new Outside Consultants have assisted us in addition to most of those named in Volume I: A. D. Alderson, Professor W. S. Avis, Dr. R. P. Beckinsale, Professor T. Burrow, Sir Alexander Cairncross, Professor Elizabeth Carr, Miss P. Cooray, Dr. S. T. Cowan, M. P. Furmston, B. Greenhill, Professor O. R. Gurney, R. Hall, Professor C. Hart, P. A. Hayward, Dr. R. Hunter, Dr. Russell Jones, Professor J. B. McMillan, Dr. C. I. McMorran, E. Mendelson, Professor G. B. Milner, D. D. Murison, P. H. Nye, Dr. K. P. Oakley, Dr. A. B. Paterson, Professor Dr. I. Poldauf, and N. G. Phillips.

This second volume contains about 13,000 Main Words divided into some 22,000 senses. There are a little under 8,000 defined Combinations within the articles and just over 5,000 undefined Combinations. The illustrative quotations number 125,000.

Finally, the Editor would like to record his personal indebtedness to the following for assistance on many matters: Dr. J. B. Sykes, Deputy Chief Editor of the Oxford English Dictionaries and Editor of the *Concise Oxford Dictionary* (1976), for valuable advice and co-operation at all times; Mr. A. J. Augarde, who has now moved across to the smaller Oxford dictionaries after a long period of service on the *Supplement to the O.E.D.*; the Managers and staff of the branches of the Oxford University Press for their efficiency and encouragement during the Editor's lecture tours of the Far East, the United States, South Africa, and elsewhere in 1972 and in 1974; his colleagues at St. Peter's College in Oxford; and, most particularly, his colleagues and assistants on the Dictionary staff itself, especially for their endurance and perseverance at many times when industrial and economic difficulties had their impact upon the O.E.D. Department as upon every other section of the community.

R.W.B.

Oxford
January 1976

CONTENTS

VOLUME II

EDITORIAL STAFF

The dates given after the names indicate when each person joined the editorial staff of this dictionary. The letter ᴾ precedes the names of those who worked as part-timers.

Senior Assistant Editor: A. J. AUGARDE 1960–76
Assistant Editor (Science): A. M. HUGHES 1968–
Assistant Editor (Natural History): SANDRA RAPHAEL 1969–
Assistant Editor (Bibliography): G. D. HARGREAVES 1973–5

Editorial Assistants:

E. C. DANN	1963–	JEAN H. BUCHANAN	1971–6
VERONICA M. SALUSBURY	1966–	VALERIE SMITH	1972–5
ADRIANA P. ORR	1966–	A. B. BUXTON	1972–5
ᴾ†PEGGY E. KAY	1967–75	GILLIAN A. RATHBONE	1973–6
ᴾFRANCES M. WILLIAMS	1968–76	R. E. ALLEN	1974–
W. H. C. WATERFIELD	1970–5	LESLEY S. BURNETT	1974–
DEBORAH M. COWEN	1970–	J. CLAIRE NICHOLLS	1974–
ᴾJOYCE L. HARLEY	1970–	ᴾMARGUERITE Y. OFFORD	1974–

Miss Salusbury and Mrs. Offord (based in London), Mrs. Orr (in Washington), and Miss Buchanan, Miss Harley, Miss Nicholls, and Miss Rathbone were mainly concerned with research (especially for 'first uses') and with the verification of quotations; Mrs. Orr was rejoined by Mrs. Daphne Gilbert-Carter (working part-time) in Washington in 1975. Mr. Waterfield and Mr. Buxton dealt with scientific terms, and Mrs. Cowen with terms in the Social Sciences. Miss Williams assisted with the reading of the proofs. All other Editorial Assistants named above undertook general editorial work.

Among those who assisted at various stages with the editorial work of Volume II as part of the regular staff were the following: ᴾL. B. Firnberg (1962–74), ᴾJelly K. Williams (1967–74), J. P. Barnes (1969–72), M. W. Grose (1969–72), Deirdre McKenna (1969–74), Juliet Field (1973–4), P. E. Davenport (1970–71), Gillian Bradshaw (1972–4), and L. M. Matheson (1974–5).

New members of the Editorial Staff, all of whom joined in 1975 and all of whom assisted with the final stages of Volume II, are D. R. Howlett, J. Paterson, ᴾE. Joan Pusey, Rosemary J. Sansome, W. R. Trumble, and N. S. Wedd.

Members of the Editorial Staff received valuable part-time assistance from the following outside helpers: Grace M. Briggs (1959–) and Rita G. Keckeissen (1968–).

Secretarial and Clerical Assistants: †Joan Blackler (Editor's Secretary, 1966–74), Pamela Bendall (1968–), Kathleen Johnston (1970–), Beta Cotmore (Editor's Secretary, 1974–), and Anne Whear (1975–).

KEY TO THE PRONUNCIATION

T HE pronunciations given are those in use in the educated speech of southern England (the so-called 'Received Standard'), and the keywords given are to be understood as pronounced in such speech.

I. *Consonants and Semi-Consonants*

b, d, f, k, l, m, n, p, t, v, z *have their usual English values*

g as in *go* (gōᵘ).
h ... *ho!* (hōᵘ).
r ... *run* (rʋn), *terrier* (te·riəɹ).
ɹ ... *her* (həɹ), *farther* (fā·ɹðəɹ).
s ... *see* (sī), *success* (sʋkse·s).
w ... *wear* (wēəɹ).
hw... *when* (hwen).
y ... *yes* (yes).

þ as in *thin* (þin), *bath* (baþ).
ð ... *then* (ðen), *bathe* (bēⁱð).
ʃ ... *shop* (ʃọp), *dish* (diʃ).
tʃ ... *chop* (tʃọp), *ditch* (ditʃ).
ʒ ... *vision* (vi·ʒən), *déjeuner* (deʒōne).
dʒ ... *judge* (dʒʋdʒ).
ŋ ... *singing* (si·ŋiŋ), *think* (þiŋk).
ŋg ... *finger* (fi·ŋgəɹ).

(FOREIGN AND NON-SOUTHERN)

ṅ as in French nasal, *environ* (aṅviroṅ).
lʸ ... It. *serraglio* (serā·lʸo).
nʸ ... It. *signore* (sinʸō·re).
χ ... Ger. *ach* (aχ), Sc. *loch* (lọχ), Sp. *frijoles* (frī·χoles).
χʸ ... Ger. *ich* (iχʸ), Sc. *nicht* (niχʸt).
γ ... North Ger. *sagen* (zā·γĕn).
γʸ ... Ger. *legen, regnen* (lē·γʸĕn, rē·γʸnĕn).
kʸ ... Afrikaans *baardmannetjie* (bā·rtmanəkʸi).

The reversed r (ɹ) and small 'superior' letters (pe·rĕmᴾtəri) are used to denote elements that may be omitted either by individual speakers or in particular phonetic contexts.

II. *Vowels*

The symbol ‾ placed over a vowel-letter denotes length.

The incidence of main stress is shown by a raised point (·) after the vowel-symbol, and a secondary stress by a double point (:) as in *callithumpian* (kæ:līþʋ·mpiăn).

The stressed vowels a, æ, e, i, o, u become obscured with loss of stress, and the indeterminate sounds thus arising, and approximating to the 'neutral' vowel ə, are normally printed ă, ǽ, ĕ, ĭ, ŏ, ŭ.

A break ˌ is used to indicate syllable-division when necessary to avoid ambiguity.

ORDINARY	LONG	OBSCURE
a as in Fr. *à la mode* (a la mod').	ā as in *alms* (āmz), *bar* (bāɹ).	ă as in *amœba* (ămī·bă).
ai ... *aye*=yes (ai), I*saiah* (əizai·ă).		ǽ ... *accept* (ǽkse·pt), *maniac* (mēⁱ·niǽk).
æ ... *man* (mæn).		
a ... *pass* (pas), *chant* (tʃant).		
au ... *loud* (laud), *now* (nau).		
ʋ ... *cut* (kʋt), *son* (sʋn).	v̄ ... *curl* (kv̄ɹl), *fur* (fv̄ɹ).	v̆ ... *datum* (dēⁱ·tv̆m).
e ... *yet* (yet), *ten* (ten).	ē (ēə)... *there* (ðēəɹ), *pear, pare* (pēəɹ).	ĕ ... *moment* (mōᵘ·mĕnt), *several* (se·vĕrăl).
‖e ... Fr. *attaché* (ataʃe).	ē (ēⁱ)... *rein, rain* (rēⁱn), *they* (ðēⁱ).	ĕ ... *separate* (*adj*.) (se·părĕt).
‖ę ... Fr. *chef* (ʃęf).	‖ę̄ ... Fr. *faire* (fę̄r').	
ə ... *ever* (e·vəɹ), *nation* (nēⁱ·ʃən).	ə̄ ... *fir* (fə̄ɹ), *fern* (fə̄ɹn), *earth* (ə̄ɹþ).	ė ... *added* (æ·dėd), *estate* (ėstēⁱ·t).
əi ... *I, eye* (əi), *bind* (bəind).		
‖ə ... Fr. *tour de force* (tūrdəfors).		
i ... *sit* (sit), *mystic* (mistik).	ī (īə) ... *bier* (bīəɹ), *clear* (klīəɹ).	ĭ ... *vanity* (væ·nĭti).
i ... *Psyche* (səi·ki), *react* (riˌæ·kt).	ī ... *thief* (þīf), *see* (sī).	i ... *remain* (rĭmēⁱ·n), *believe* (bĭlī·v).
o ... *achor* (ēⁱ·koɹ), *morality* (moræ·līti).	ō (ōə)... *boar, bore* (bōəɹ), *glory* (glō·ri).	ŏ ... *theory* (þi·ŏri).
oi ... *oil* (oil), *boy* (boi).		
o ... *hero* (hiə·ro), *zoology* (zoˌọ·lŏdʒi).	ō (ōᵘ)... *so, sow* (sōᵘ), *soul* (sōᵘl).	ŏ ... *violet* (vəi·ŏlėt), *parody* (pæ·rŏdi).
ọ ... *what* (hwọt), *watch* (wọtʃ).	ọ̄ ... *walk* (wọ̄k), *wart* (wọ̄ɹt).	ǫ ... *authority* (ǫþǫ·rĭti).
ọ,ǫ *... *got* (gọt), *soft* (sǫ̇ft)*.	ǭ ... *short* (ʃǭɹt), *thorn* (þǭɹn).	ǫ̇ ... *connect* (kǫ̇ne·kt), *amazon* (æ·măzǫ̇n).
‖ö ... Ger. *Köln* (köln).	‖ȫ ... Fr. *cœur* (kȫr).	
‖ȫ ... Fr. *peu* (pȫ).	‖ȫ̄ ... Ger. *Goethe* (gȫ̄tĕ), Fr. *jeûne* (ʒȫ̄n).	
u ... *full* (ful), *book* (buk).	ū (ūə)... *poor* (pūəɹ), *moorish* (mūə·riʃ).	
iu ... *duration* (diurēⁱ·ʃən).	iū, ⁱū... *pure* (piūⁱɹ), *lure* (lⁱūⁱɹ).	iŭ, ⁱŭ verdure (və̄·ɹdiŭɹ), *measure* (me·ʒⁱŭɹ).
u ... *unto* (ʋ·ntu), *frugality* (fru-).	ū ... *two moons* (tū mūnz).	ŭ ... *altogether* (ọ̄ltŭge·ðəɹ).
iu ... *Matthew* (mæ·þiu), *virtue* (və̄·ɹtiu).	iū, ⁱū... *few* (fiū), *lute* (lⁱūt).	iŭ ... *circular* (sə̄·ɹkiŭlăɹ).
‖ü ... Ger. *Müller* (mü·lĕr).		
‖ü ... Fr. *dune* (dün).	‖ǖ ˙ ... Ger. *grün* (grǖn), Fr. *jus* (ʒǖ).	

ə (see īə, ēə, ōə, ūə) ⎫ see Vol. I of Dict., p.
ⁱ, ᵘ (see ēⁱ, ōᵘ) ⎭ xxxiv, note 3.

' as in *able* (ēⁱ·b'l) ,*eaten* (ī·t'n) = voice-glide.

* Words such as *soft, cloth, cross* are often still pronounced with (ǭ) by Southern speakers in England but the pronunciation with ǫ is now more usual.

‖ Only in foreign (or earlier English) words.

LIST OF ABBREVIATIONS, SIGNS, ETC.

Some abbreviations here listed in italics are occasionally, for the sake of clarity,
printed in roman type, and vice versa.

a. (in Etym.)	adoption of, adopted from	Cryst.	in Crystallography
a (as a 1850)	ante, 'before', 'not later than'	Da.	Danish
a.	adjective	D.A.	Dictionary of Americanisms
abbrev.	abbreviation (of)	D.A.E.	Dictionary of American English
abl.	ablative	dat.	dative
absol.	absolute, -ly	def.	definite, -ition
Abstr.	Abstract(s)	deriv.	derivative, -ation
acc.	accusative	dial.	dialect, -al
ad. (in Etym.)	adaptation of	Dict.	Dictionary; spec., the Oxford English Dictionary
Add.	Addenda	dim.	diminutive
adj.	adjective	D.O.S.T.	Dictionary of the Older Scottish Tongue
adv.	adverb		
advb.	adverbial, -ly	Du.	Dutch
(Advt.),	advertisement	E.	East
Aeronaut.	in Aeronautics	Eccl.	in Ecclesiastical usage
AF., AFr.	Anglo-French	Ecol.	in Ecology
Afr.	Africa, -n	Econ.	in Economics
Agric.	in Agriculture	ed.	edition
Alb.	Albanian	E.D.D.	English Dialect Dictionary
Amer.	American	Educ.	in Education
Amer. Ind.	American Indian	e.g.	exempli gratia, 'for example'
Anat.	in Anatomy		
Anglo-Ind.	Anglo-Indian	Electr.	in Electricity
Anglo-Ir.	Anglo-Irish	ellipt.	elliptical, -ly
Anthrop., Anthropol.	in Anthropology	Embryol.	in Embryology
Antiq.	in Antiquities	e. midl.	east midland (dialect)
aphet.	aphetic, aphetized	Eng.	English
app.	apparently	Engin.	in Engineering
Arab.	Arabic	Ent.	in Entomology
Aram.	Aramaic	erron.	erroneous, -ly
Arch., Archit.	in Architecture	esp.	especially
arch.	archaic	et al.	et alii, 'and others'
Archæol.	in Archæology	etc.	et cetera
Arm.	Armenian	Ethnol.	in Ethnology
assoc.	association	etym.	etymology
Astr.	in Astronomy	euphem.	euphemistically
Astrol.	in Astrology	exc.	except
attrib.	attributive, -ly	f. (in Etym.)	formed on
Austral.	Australian	f. (in subordinate entries)	form of
A.V.	Authorized Version		
bef.	before	F.	French
Bibliogr.	in Bibliography	fem. (rarely f.)	feminine
Biochem.	in Biochemistry	fig.	figurative, -ly
Biol.	in Biology	Finn.	Finnish
Bot.	in Botany	fl.	floruit, 'flourished'
Bulg.	Bulgarian	Fr.	French
c (as c 1700)	circa, 'about'	freq.	frequent, -ly
c. (as 19th c.)	century	Fris.	Frisian
Canad.	Canadian	Funk's Stand. Dict.	Funk and Wagnalls Standard Dictionary
Cat.	Catalan		
catachr.	catachrestically	G.	German
Celt.	Celtic	Gael.	Gaelic
Cent. Dict.	Century Dictionary	Gaz.	Gazette (in names of newspapers)
Cf., cf.	confer, 'compare'		
Ch.	Church	gen.	genitive
Chem.	in Chemistry	gen.	general, -ly
Cinemat., Cinematogr.	in Cinematography	Geogr.	in Geography
cl. L.	classical Latin	Geol.	in Geology
cogn. w.	cognate with	Geom.	in Geometry
collect.	collective, -ly	Geomorphol.	in Geomorphology
colloq.	colloquial, -ly	Ger.	German
comb.	combined, -ing	Gmc.	Germanic
Comb.	Combinations	Goth.	Gothic
Comm.	in Commercial usage	Gr.	Greek
Communic.	in Communications	Gram.	in Grammar
comp.	compound, composition	Heb.	Hebrew
compar.	comparative	Her.	in Heraldry
compl.	complement	Herb.	among herbalists
Conch.	in Conchology	Hind.	Hindustani
concr.	concrete, -ly	Hist.	in History
conj.	conjunction	hist.	historical
cons.	consonant	Hort.	in Horticulture
const.	construction, construed with	Ibid.	Ibidem, 'in the same book or passage'
corresp.	corresponding (to)	Icel.	Icelandic
cpd.	compound	Ichthyol.	in Ichthyology

id.	idem, 'the same'
i.e.	id est, 'that is'
IE.	Indo-European
imit.	imitative
Immunol.	in Immunology
imp.	imperative
impers.	impersonal
impf.	imperfect
ind.	indicative
indef.	indefinite
inf.	infinitive
infl.	influenced
int.	interjection
intr.	intransitive
Introd.	Introduction
Ir.	Irish
irreg.	irregular, -ly
It.	Italian
J., (J.)	Johnson's Dictionary (quoted from)
(Jam.)	Jamieson, Scottish Dict.
Jap.	Japanese
joc.	jocular, -ly
l.	line
L.	Latin
lang.	language
Let., Lett.	letter, letters
LG.	Low German
lit.	literal, -ly
Lit.	Literary
Lith.	Lithuanian
LXX	Septuagint
Mal.	Malay, Malayan
Manuf.	in Manufacture, -ing
masc. (rarely m.)	masculine
Math.	in Mathematics
MDu.	Middle Dutch
ME.	Middle English
Mech.	in Mechanics
Med.	in Medicine
med.L.	medieval Latin
Metaph.	in Metaphysics
Meteorol.	in Meteorology
MHG.	Middle High German
midl.	midland (dialect)
Mil.	in military usage
Min.	in Mineralogy
MLG.	Middle Low German
mod.	modern
mod.L.	modern Latin
(Morris),	E. E. Morris's Austral English (quoted from)
Mus.	in Music
Mythol.	in Mythology
N.	North
N. Amer.	North America, -n
N. &. Q.	Notes and Queries
Nat. Hist.	in Natural History
Naut.	in Nautical language
Neurol.	in Neurology
neut. (rarely n.)	neuter
NF., NFr.	Northern French
nom.	nominative
north.	northern (dialect)
Norw.	Norwegian
N.T.	New Testament
Nucl.	Nuclear
Numism.	in Numismatics
N.Z.	New Zealand
obj.	object
obl.	oblique
Obs., obs.	obsolete
occas.	occasional, -ly
Oceanogr.	in Oceanography
OE.	Old English (=Anglo-Saxon)
OF., OFr.	Old French
OFris.	Old Frisian
OHG.	Old High German

OIr.	Old Irish
ON.	Old Norse (Old Icelandic)
ONF.	Old Northern French
Ophthalm.	in Ophthalmology
opp.	opposed (to), the opposite (of)
Opt.	in Optics
orig.	origin, -al, -ally
Ornith.	in Ornithology
OS.	Old Saxon
OSl.	Old (Church) Slavonic
O.T.	Old Testament
p.	page
Palæogr.	in Palæography
Palæont.	in Palæontology
pa. pple.	passive or past participle
(Partridge),	E. Partridge's *Dictionary of Slang and Unconventional English* (quoted from)
pass.	passive, -ly
pa. t.	past tense
Path.	in Pathology
perh.	perhaps
Pers.	Persian
pers.	person, -al
Petrogr.	in Petrography
Petrol.	in Petrology
(Pettman),	C. Pettman's *Africanderisms* (quoted from)
pf.	perfect
Pg.	Portuguese
Pharm.	in Pharmacology
Philol.	in Philology
Philos.	in Philosophy
phonet.	phonetic, -ally
Photogr.	in Photography
phr.	phrase
Phys.	in Physics, physical; (*rarely*) in Physiology
Physiol.	in Physiology
pl.	plural; plate
poet.	poetic, -al
Pol.	Polish
Pol.	in Politics
Pol. Econ.	in Political Economy
pop.	popular, -ly
poss.	possessive
ppl. a., ppl. adj.	participial adjective
pple.	participle
Pr.	Provençal
prec.	preceding (word or article)

pred.	predicative
pref.	prefix
pref., Pref.	preface
prep.	preposition
pres.	present
priv.	privative
prob.	probably
pron.	pronoun
pronunc.	pronunciation
prop.	properly
Pros.	in Prosody
Prov.	Provençal
pr. pple.	present participle
Psych., *Psychol.*	in Psychology
Q.	Quarterly (in names of periodicals)
quot(s).	quotation(s)
q.v.	*quod vide*, 'which see'
R.	Royal (in names of periodicals, etc.)
Radiol.	in Radiology
R. C. Ch.	Roman Catholic Church
redupl.	reduplicating
refash.	refashioned, -ing
refl., refl.	reflexive
reg.	regular
rel.	related (to)
repr.	representative, representing
Rhet.	in Rhetoric
Rom.	Roman, Romance, Romanic
Rum.	Rumanian
Russ.	Russian
S.	South
S. Afr.	South Africa, -n
sb.	substantive
sc.	*scilicet*, 'understand' or 'supply'
Sc., *Scot.*	Scotch, Scottish
Sci.	(in) Science, scientific
Sc. Nat. Dict.	*Scottish National Dictionary*
Ser.	series
sing.	singular
Skr.	Sanskrit
Slav.	Slavonic
S.N.D.	*Scottish National Dictionary*
Sociol.	in Sociology
Sp.	Spanish
sp.	spelling
spec.	specific, -ally
(Stanf.),	*Stanford Dictionary of Anglicised Words and Phrases* (quoted from)

subj.	subject, subjunctive
subord. cl.	subordinate clause
subseq.	subsequent, -ly
subst.	substantively
suff.	suffix
superl.	superlative
Suppl.	Supplement
Surg.	in Surgery
s.v.	*sub voce*, 'under the word'
Sw.	Swedish
s.w.	south-western (dialect)
syll.	syllable
Syr.	Syrian
techn.	technical, -ly
Tel.	Telegraph (in names of newspapers)
Telegr.	in Telegraphy
Teleph.	in Telephony
(Th.),	Thornton's *American Glossary* (quoted from)
Theatr.	in the Theatre, theatrical
Theol.	in Theology
Tokh.	Tokharian
tr., transl.	translation (of)
trans.	transitive
transf.	transferred sense
Trig.	in Trigonometry
Turk.	Turkish
Typog., *Typogr.*	in Typography
ult.	ultimate, -ly
unkn.	unknown
U.S.	United States
usu.	usual, -ly
v., vb.	verb
var(r)., vars.	variant(s) of
vbl. sb.	verbal substantive
Vet., *Vet. Sci.*	in Veterinary Science
viz.	*videlicet*, 'namely'
v. str., or *w.*	verb strong, or weak
vulg.	vulgar
W.	Welsh; West
wd.	word
Webster	*Webster's* (*New International*) *Dictionary*
WGmc.	West Germanic
w.midl.	west midland (dialect)
WS.	West Saxon
(Y.),	Yule & Burnell's *Hobson-Jobson* (quoted from)
Zoogeogr.	in Zoogeography
Zool.	in Zoology

Signs and Other Conventions

Before a word or sense	In the listing of Forms	In the etymologies
† = obsolete	1 = before 1100	* indicates a word or form not actually found, but of which the existence is inferred
‖ = not naturalized, alien	2 = 12th c. (1100 to 1200)	:– = normal development of
¶ = catachrestic and erroneous uses (see Dict., Vol. I, p. xxi)	3 = 13th c. (1200 to 1300), etc.	
	5–7 = 15th to 17th century. (See General Explanations, Dict., Vol. I, p. xxx)	

The printing of a word in SMALL CAPITALS indicates that further information will be found under the word so referred to.

In cross-references * indicates that the word or sense referred to is in the Supplement.

After the number of a sense * and ** (etc.) indicate new senses which are not directly related to the senses so numbered in the main body of the Dictionary, but which have to be inserted within the existing numerical sequence because of the custom in the Dictionary of placing the Combinations at the conclusion of each article.

.. indicates an omitted part of a quotation.

PROPRIETARY NAMES

THIS Supplement includes some words which are or are asserted to be proprietary names or trade marks. Their inclusion does not imply that they have acquired for legal purposes a non-proprietary or general significance nor any other judgement concerning their legal status. In cases where the editorial staff have established in the records of the Patent Offices of the United Kingdom and of the United States that a word is registered as a proprietary name or trade mark this is indicated, but no judgement concerning the legal status of such words is made or implied thereby.

H

H. Add: **I. 2.** *H girder, iron. H hinge,* a type of hinge which when open has the form of an H.

1726 in *Maryland Hist. Mag.* (1912) VII. 278 H hinges at 8s per pair. **1836** L. Hebert *Engin. & Mech. Encycl.* I. 674 Another sort, called H..hinges, from their resemblance to those letters, are extensively employed for common purposes. **1888** *Lockwood's Dict. Mech. Engin., H iron,* rolled wrought-iron bar whose section is that of the letter I. Used extensively for building up engineering structures. **1902** A. C. Harmsworth et al. *Motors* vi. 90 The roof of the house is strengthened at certain points by cross timbers which support two small H girders, and carry iron frames to which are attached pulley blocks. **1960** H. Hayward *Antique Coll.* 142/1 *'H' hinge,* like the cock's head hinge, an early external type of hinge in the form of the letter 'H' extensively used on cupboards of the 16th and 17th cent.

II. 3. b. Designation of a strong Fraunhofer line at 3969 Å, caused by calcium ions; † orig., (the position occupied by) the H and K lines as a pair. [Named by J. Fraunhofer 1817, in *Ann. d. Physik* LVI. 286.]

1823 tr. Fraunhofer in *Edin. Philos. Jrnl.* IX. 297 The two bands at H are of a very singular nature. **1865** *Phil. Trans.* CLIV. 149 A pair of strong lines..near the extreme refrangible end of the spectrum..may coincide with those of Fraunhofer's H. **1879, 1967** [see *K 3 c].

8. *Math., Physics. H* denotes the Hamiltonian function of classical mechanics or the Hamiltonian operator of quantum mechanics.

1835 W. R. Hamilton in *Phil. Trans. R. Soc.* LXXV. 98 If then we introduce, for abridgement, the following expression H. **1935** Pauling & Wilson *Quantum Mech.* i. 16 Involving a function *H*..called the Hamiltonian function. **1965** W. Hauser *Introd. Princ. Mech.* vi. 194 Whenever the Lagrangian is not explicitly a function of time, the function *H*..referred to as the *Hamiltonian* of the system, is a constant of the motion. *Ibid.* 195 This can be verified by considering the variation of *H*.

9. *Physics. h* denotes Planck's constant, the elementary quantum of action (M. Planck 1900, in *Verh. d. Deutsch. Physik. Ges.* II. 245). In more recent usage, the quantum of angular momentum $h/2\pi$ has been represented by $\hbar$.

1901 *Sci. Abstr.* IVa. 230, $\epsilon = h\nu$, where *h* is a constant. **1934** *Physical Rev.* XLVI. 925/2, $\hbar$. **1935** Pauling & Wilson *Quantum Mech.* ii. 25 The constant of proportionality, *h*, is a new constant of nature,..called *Planck's constant*... $h/2\pi$ [is] a natural unit or quantum of angular momentum. **1955** L. I. Schiff *Quantum Mech.* (ed. 2) i. 7 The product of the uncertainties of the..position and momentum components is at least of the order of magnitude of $\hbar$.

III. H., henry (*Electr.*), heroin; H, designating *horror* films; h., hot, as h. and c., hot and cold (water); H, hydrogen (bomb); so *H-bomb, -test,* etc.; H (on lead pencils) (examples); H. and D. (see quots. 1918, 1930); HB (on lead pencils) (examples); H.E., His Eminence, His (or Her) Excellency, high explosive; HF, H^{F}, Hꜰ, Hf, healthy female(s); H.F., h.f., high frequency; *H-Hour,* the hour at which an operation is to begin; cf. *D-Day; H.K., Hong Kong (in currency notation); HM, H^{M}, Hᴍ, Hm, healthy male(s); H.M.C., Headmasters' Conference; H.M.G., His (or Her) Majesty's Government; H.M.I.(S.), His (or Her) Majesty's Inspector of Schools; H.M.S.O., His (or Her) Majesty's Stationery Office; H.N.C., Higher National Certificate; H.O., Hostilities Only (see quots.); H.P., high pressure, hire purchase, hybrid perpetual; *H.P. Sauce,* the proprietary name of a type of spiced brown sauce; H.Q., Headquarters; H.T., h.t., high tension; HUAC, House [of Representatives] Un-American Activities Committee; Hz, hertz (unit of frequency).

1910 N. Hawkins *Electr. Dict.,* H. The symbol of nduction. The Henry. h. An abbreviation for the henry, the practical unit of induction. **1926** *Clues* Nov. 161/2 *H,* heroin. **1929** *Sat. Even. Post* 13 Apr. 54/3 Heroin is referred to as H. **1933** C. de Lenoir *Hundredth Man* iv. 61, I opened the packet of H. and took a generous sniff. **1962** K. Orvis *Damned & Destroyed* v. 42 Suppose I..ask you where to connect for H? **1938** *Ann. Reg. 1937* 339 In June, Lord Tyrell, President of the British Board of Film Censors, introduced a new film classification called 'H' to apply to horror films. Pictures so labelled will not be shown to children under 16, whether accompanied by an adult or not. **1958** *Times* 4 Aug. 10/2 'H' used to, and now 'X' does, among other things, stand for Horror, and the two new films this week..are rich in those qualities [etc.]. **1960** *Spectator* 1 July 20 *The Visit* is old-style *grand guignol* with a few modern H-certificate props. **1901** *Punch* 24 July 64/1 Bathroom (h. and c.). **1930** *Morning Post* 17 June 20/7, 4 bed-rooms (h. and c. in each). **1937** 'G. Orwell' *Road to Wigan Pier* xiii. 250 The literary gent in his Tudor cottage with bathroom h. and c. **1950** *Hansard, Commons* 6 Nov. 114, I am not one who criticised the right hon. Gentleman..for drawing attention to the H-bomb. **1952** *Manch. Guardian Weekly* 20 Nov. 2/2 The first test model of the H-bomb will be followed shortly by even more violent versions. **1955** *Bull. Atomic Sci.* June 226/2 He asserts that H-war, terrible as it will be, is still better than Communist domination. **1957** *Observer* 8 Sept. 9/3 With bovine stolidity Western man carries on with his H-bomb tests. **1958** 'P. Bryant' *Two Hours to Doom* 96 Their phoney ending of H-tests. **1959** *Listener* 16 July 88/2 United States H-bombers. **1968** *Times* 29 Oct. 7/3 The first Chinese H-bomb, tested in June last year, probably contained zinc in its construction. **1852** C. H. Weigall *Art of Figure Drawing* (Advts.) 14 H. Moderately hard (used for light sketching). HH. A degree harder (for outlines and fine Drawing). HHH. Very hard (for Architectural Drawing). **1895** *Army & Navy Co-op. Soc. Price List* 563/2 The 'Kohinoor', a high-class drawing Pencil..H, HH, HHH. **1926** R. Macaulay *Crewe Train* ii. xii. 211 She purchased a packet of notepaper and envelopes and a pencil (H.H.) at the post office. **1934** M. V. Hughes *London Child of Seventies* xiv. 167 'I say, Molly, lend us your Scripture pencil,' Dym would say, for he knew that was an H, and good for his geometry figures. **1948** H. Missingham *Student's Guide Commerc. Art* ii. 57 The degree markings on pencils are:..6H, 4H, 3H—Extra Hard. **1903** A. Watkins *Photogr.* (ed. 2) 29 A box of one maker's plates marked H & D 100. **1918** *Photo-Miniature* XV. Mar. (Gloss.), H. & D. (Hurter and Driffield)—used as a prefix to numbers signifying the speed of plates measured by the system devised by these investigators. Fastest plates, H. & D. 400 to 500. **1930** *Sel. Gloss. Motion Pict. Techn.* (*Acad. Motion Pict., Hollywood*), *H and D curve,* the characteristic curve of a photographic emulsion. **1852** C. H. Weigall *Art of Figure Drawing* (Advts.) 14 H.B. Hard and Black (deeper shade than F). **1962** L. Deighton *Ipcress File* xxv. 165, I took his wooden HB pencil. **1732** *Let.* 19 Feb. in *Calendar State Papers, Amer. & West Indies* (1939) 64 That H.E. and less than five of the Council could not hold Courts of Chancery. **1848** Thackeray *Van. Fair* li. 453 H.E. Papoosh Pasha, the Turkish Ambassador (attended by Kibob Bey, dragoman of the mission). *Ibid.* lxiii. 571 H.E. Madame de Burst received once a week. **1946** Koestler *Thieves in Night* 198 He thought that H.E. went indeed a bit far in demonstrating his dislike of the Hebrew community. **1970** *Catholic Directory* 43 (*heading*) Ireland. The hierarchy at the present time... Armagh. H.E. Cardinal William Conway. **1901** *Daily Chron.* 27 June 3/2 To introduce a very much larger proportion of H.E. shell. **1915** D. O. Barnett *Let.* 23 May 153 H.E. is the shell for attacking, because you blow the defenders out of their trenches. **1955** *Bull. Atomic Sci.* Feb. 55/3 The thoroughness of an atomic bombardment's 'area coverage' exceeds that of HE carpet bombing beyond comparison. **1880** H^{F} [see *HM* below]. **1913** *Year-Bk. Wireless Telegr.* 289 To make the current-distribution over the cross-section more uniform for H.F. currents. **1923** *Popular Wireless* (Suppl.) 13 Oct. 10 'Plug-in' H.F. Transformers. **1924** *Exper. Wireless* Apr. 397/2 The atmospheric band frequencies which penetrate the H.F. filter. **1942** *Electronic Engin.* XV. 168 A hair-pin filament heated by h.f. current. **1967** *New Scientist* 25 May 455/3 All the frequencies in the HF band that are needed by the many transmitters at the station are produced by processing the 'master' frequency. **1918** in *Amer. Speech* (1944) XIX. 302 'Over the top' is now 'the jump off' and 'zero hour' has changed to 'H hour'. **1927** J. M. Saunders *Wings* (1928) v. 210 The word went out that 'D' day was to be Sept. 12, and that 5 a.m. was to be 'H' hour. **1945** *Hutchinson's Pict. Hist. War 12 Apr.–26 Sept. 1944* 342 No fewer than 13 companies landed on the first tide, at H hour plus 25 minutes to be precise. **1952** *Hong Kong Trade Returns* Jan. 1 The unit of value is the Hong Kong dollar, the official rate of exchange being H.K. $16 = £1 sterling. **1964** *Asia Mag.* 12 July 24/1 According to official figures, on average nearly HK $1 million went into land and building every day in 1963. **1880** *Encycl. Brit.* XIII. 170/2 Table H^{MF}, comprising all the healthy lives, male and female, included in the observations...Table H^{M}, comprising the healthy male lives only...Table H^{F}, comprising the healthy female lives. **1898** *Westm. Gaz.* 14 Nov. 8/1 With its premiums and its reversionary bonuses, and its Hm tables and its surrender values. **1905** in *Rep. Headmasters' Conf. 1905* (1906) 97 The 1903 recommendations of the H.M.C. favoured solution (*b*) as more in harmony with the existing practice and principles of the Universities. **1966** *Rep. Comm. Inquiry Univ. Oxf.* II. 48 Among men from independent schools, the great majority are from H.M.C. schools. **1938** E. Waugh *Scoop* ii. xii. 137 We don't quite know what he's up to; whatever it is, it doesn't suit H.M.G.'s book. **1971** *Guardian* 28 July 11/1 Any deal with Ian Smith..would make it impossible for Labour men to support HMG on Europe. **1908** E. M. Sneyd-Kynnersley (*title*) H.M.I.: Some passages in the life of one of H.M. Inspectors of Schools. **1963** S. Marshall *Exper. in Education* ii. 40 The modern H.M.I. sniffs the atmosphere of a school the moment he opens the door. **1905** F. H. Collins *Author & Printer* 164/1 *H.M.S.O.,* (His or Her Majesty's) Stationery Office. **1969** *Listener* 20 Feb. 255/3 *Britain: An Official Handbook,* published by HMSO two or three weeks ago at 32s. 6d. **1949** *Educ. in 1948* (Cmd. 7724) 44 (*caption*) H.N.C. **1967** *Times Rev. Industry* Aug. 70/3 The rising failure rate of the HNC candidates. **1942** Partridge *Dict. Abbrev.* 48/2 *H.O.,* Hostilities only; applied to a man that has joined for the duration of the war. (Naval.) **1961** B. Fergusson *Watery Maze* i. 55 H.O. ('Hostilities Only') ratings—men who had joined the Royal Navy for the duration of the war. **1902** *Encycl. Brit.* XXXII. 151 The H.-P. valves are worked by means of a simple lever from the L.-P. valve-rods. **1930** *Engineering* 9 May 599/1 Since both the H.P. and L.P. rotors have their own thrust blocks, the two are connected by a Wellmann-Bibby coupling, which permits of free axial expansion. **1945** *Daily Mirror* 6 Sept. 3/2 'Stop H.P. babies'... Mothers..have to pay for their babies on the hire-purchase system because of the high charges of maternity homes. **1958** *Spectator* 13 June 759/2 They cannot keep up the HP payments. **1959** *New Statesman* 17 Oct. 494/2 The artisan class lives in new houses and pays off the telly and the car on HP. **1869** S. R. Hole *Bk. about Roses* xi. 174 Marguerite Dombrain, H.P...an early, reliable, vigorous, bright carmine Rose. **1893** W. Robinson *Eng. Flower Garden* (ed. 3) 644/2 Gabriel Luizet, General Jacqueminot and many other H.Ps do not usually bloom after the month of August. **1912** *Trade Marks Jrnl.* 22 May 768 HP..Sauce and pickles. Edwin Samson Moore, trading as 'The Midland Vinegar Company', 'The Trade Malt Vinegar Company', and as F. G. Garton & Co.,..Aston Cross,..Warwickshire, vinegar brewer and sauce and pickle manufacturer. **1926–7** *Army & Navy Stores Catal.* 37/1 Sauces..H.P.— -/9. **1940** J. Betjeman *Coll. Poems* (1958) 83, I pledge her in non-alcoholic wine And give the H.P. Sauce another shake. **1971** P. Worsthorne *Socialist Myth* viii. 171 He [*sc.* Mr. Harold Wilson] manages to retain a little of the working-class-lad-made-good appeal... The H.P.-Sauce style of leadership is a style, so long as it is abnormal. **1909** Webster, H.Q. **1915** D. O. Barnett *Let.* 18 Jan. 39 After reporting at Brigade H.Q. we went on to our regiments. **1958** M. Shaara in 'E. Crispin' *Best SF Three* 23 To heck with the rest. We'll let HQ worry about that. **1931** *Daily Express* 18 Mar. 13/2 Fuller 100 volt H.T. and G.B. Battery. **1966** *Economist* 27 Aug. 817/1 HUAC, even in its very name, implies an inquisitiveness about individual political beliefs that is unconstitutional. **1968** *Listener* 31 Oct. 566/3 HUAC is trying to investigate how far the Chicago violence was the result of a communist conspiracy. **1958** *Quantities & Units Periodic Phenom.* (ISO Recommendation R 31) 5, 1 Hz is the frequency of a periodic phenomenon of which the periodic time is 1 s. **1966** *Wireless World* Sept. 50 (Advt.), In order to extend the flat response below 40 Hz the rear of the bass driver is loaded with an acoustic transmission line. **1969** *Sears Catal.* Spring/Summer 8 Frequency response of 35 to 18,000 Hz. Crossover is at 2500 Hz.

haanepoot, haanepot, varr. *hanepoot.

Haarlem (hā·ɹləm). The name of a town in Holland, used *attrib.* in **Haarlem blue,** a variety of blue containing alumina; **Haarlem oil,** 'a proprietary diuretic and stimulant oil' (Dorland 1900).

1885 *Spons' Mech. Own Bk.* 407 Slight differences in the manufacture [of Prussian Blue] cause considerable variation in tint and colour, which leads to the material being known by different names—such as 'Antwerp', 'Berlin', 'Haerlem', 'Chinese' Blue. **1885** *Encycl. Brit.* XVIII. 720/1 Barbados tar, Haarlem oil, Seneca oil, and American oil, all consisting wholly or in large part of crude petroleum, were sold by apothecaries for years before petroleum was obtained by boring. **1906** *Practitioner* Dec. 852 Methyloids.—These are an improved combination of methylene blue, Santal oil, copaiba, Haarlem oil, and cinnamon oil, and are supplied in capsoid form.

habanera (hæbănēᵊ·ră). Also **habanero.** [Sp., short for *danza habanera* Havanan dance, f. *Havana,* capital of Cuba.] A slow Cuban dance and song in $\frac{2}{4}$ time. Also *attrib.*

1878 tr. *Bizet's Carmen* i 'Love the Vagrant', the celebrated Habanera, with English words. **1887** F. C. Gooch *Face to Face with Mexicans* viii. 289 The *danza* is the most distinctively national of all the dances, and bears a strong resemblance to the *Habanero,* as known in Cuba. **1926** Whiteman & McBride *Jazz* xi. 231 A fox trot was played in a rhythm exactly that of the Habanera or Tango, but much swifter in time. **1958** P. Gammond *Decca Bk. Jazz* xv. 176 He uses..often the minimum outline of a tango or habanera bass.

habara (hæ·bără). Also **habarah, habareh, habra, khabarah.** [Arab. *ḥabara.*] A woman's outdoor silk garment. Also *attrib.*

a **1817** J. L. Burckhardt *Trav. Arabia* (1829) I. 339 The women of Mekka and Djidda dress in Indian silk gowns, and very large blue striped trowsers..; over these they wear the wide gown called *habra,* of black silk stuff, used in Egypt and Syria. **1839** E. W. Lane tr. *Thousand & One Nights* (1859) I. 190 It [*sc.* the izár] is now generally made of white calico, but a similar covering of black silk for the married, and of white silk for the unmarried, is now worn by females of the higher and middle classes, and is called a 'ḥabarah'. **1851** *Illustr. Catal. Gt. Exhib.* v. ii. 1410 Habara veil, in black silk, for females. **1923** *Sunday at Home* Oct. 51/2 A black Egyptian habareh and veil.

habdabs (hæ·bˌdæ:bz). *slang.* Also **abdabs.** [Orig. obscure.] Nervous anxiety, the heebie-jeebies, esp. in phr. *to give* (a person) *the screaming habdabs.*

1946 *Penguin New Writing* XXVIII. 177 Come on, kid. This joint gives me the hab-dabs. **1962** *Spectator*

8 June 761/3 *Treasure Island* gives pleasure and excitement to some and the screaming habdabs to others. **1963** *Ibid.* 19 July 72 A desperate tension which the slightest crisis will transform into the screaming abdabs once more. **1966** L. Davidson *Long Way to Shiloh* ii. 28 Uri's whimsy-shrouded secrecy, strenuously maintained throughout the journey, had already brought on a severe attack of the habdabs.

Habdalah (hævdā·lă). Also **Habdala, Havdal(l)ah, Hovdoloh.** [a. Heb. *habhdālāh* separation, division.] A Jewish religious ceremony celebrating the end of the Sabbath; a prayer said at this ceremony.

1733 tr. *B. Picart's Ceremonies & Relig. Customs* I. 62 The Festival concludes with the Ceremony which they call Habdala, as it is observed on the Sabbath. *Ibid.* 65 The Repetition of the Habdala. **1891** M. Friedländer *Jewish Relig.* II. ii. 254 On Sabbath evening, after the close of the Sabbath, we recite the *Habdalah*, in which God is praised for the distinction made between Sabbath and the six week-days. **1892** I. Zangwill *Childr. Ghetto* (1893) I. xvi. 151 On Saturday night, immediately after *Havdalah*, Sugarman went to Mr. Belcovitch. *Ibid.* 409 *Havdalah*, ceremony separating conclusion of Sabbath or Festival from the subsequent days of toil. **1941** G. G. Scholem *Major Trends in Jewish Mysticism* ii. 67 An extremely interesting..magical text, the '*Havdalah* of Rabbi Akiba'. **1957** L. Stern *Midas Touch* III. xx. 150 His other treasures..a silver spice box and two *Hovdoloh* cups. **1960** *Commentary* June 500/2 To observe the ceremonies of.. the Sabbath meal, the blessing of children, and Havdallah. **1962** B. Abrahams tr. *Life Glückel of Hameln* iv. 102 At the close of Sabbath, while my husband was reciting the *Habdalah*.

haberdasher. Add: **b.** Formerly also a drink-seller (as a dealer in 'tape' = spirituous liquor).

1821 P. Egan *Life in London* II. viii. 354 The Haberdasher is busily employed in measuring out tape for his customers. **1828** 'W. T. Moncrieff' *Tom & Jerry* III. v. 76 The haberdasher is the whistler, otherwise the spirit-merchant, Jerry—and tape the commodity he deals in. **1893** Farmer & Henley *Slang* III. 243/1 *Haberdasher*, (humorously) a publican.

haberdashery. Add: **1.** Also *fig.*

1773 G. Steevens *Let.* 8 Dec. in *Garrick's Corr.* (1831) I. 588 He might have made many discoveries of consequence to us who deal in the haberdashery of words. **1923** Kipling *Independence* 31 He may be festooned with the whole haberdashery of success.

habit, *sb.* Add: **9. e.** *spec.* in *Psychol.* An automatic, 'mechanical' reaction to a specific situation which usually has been acquired by learning and/or repetition.

1859 A. Bain *Emotions & Will* ix. 519 Some natures are distinguished by plasticity or the power of acquisition, and therefore realize more closely the saying that man is a bundle of habits. **1871** E. B. Tylor *Primitive Culture* I. i. 1 Custom, and any other capabilities and habits acquired by man as a member of society. **1890** W. James *Princ. Psychol.* I. iv. 104 The moment one tries to define what habit is, one is led to the fundamental properties of matter. The laws of Nature are nothing but the immutable habits which the different sorts of elementary matter follow in their actions and reactions upon each other. **1956** E. R. Hilgard *Theories of Learning* (ed. 2) i. 10 The stimulus-response theorist and the cognitive theorist come up with different answers to the question, What is learned? The answer of the former is 'habits'; the answer of the latter is 'cognitive structures'.

f. The practice of taking addictive drugs (see also quot. 1914). *colloq.* (orig. *U.S.*).

1887 in *Amer. Speech* (1948) XXIII. 246/2 May he continue to wage war against them [*sc.* Chinese opium dens] until the habit has been swept entirely out of existence. **1894** [see Opiumate]. **1914** Jackson & Hellyer *Vocab. Criminal Slang* 41 *Habit*, current amongst dope fiends. Necessity for opiates; a craving; the condition produced by habitual indulgence in drugs... Example: 'I must drop into the hotel donegan (lavatory) and fire (take a hypodermic injection), for I feel my habit coming on.' **1926** J. Black *You can't Win* xii. 161 The sufferings they would undergo when there was no more and the 'habit' came on. **1959** *Daily Mail* 17 Oct. 7/3 'Do you have the habit?' He knew she meant 'Do you take drugs?'

12. (sense 9, esp. *9 e) *habit-bound* (examples), *-breaker*, *-formation*; *habit-forming* vbl. sb. and adj., *-worn* adj.; **habit-memory,** one of the two kinds of memory first distinguished by H. Bergson, which consists of motor mechanisms or 'habits' fixed in the organism and which acts in response to an appropriate stimulus, e.g. when repeating a lesson learnt by heart; **habit-neurosis,** a neurosis caused by habit-bound behaviour; **habit pattern,** a pattern of behaviour created by habit; **habit-response,** a response induced by habit; **habit spasm** *Med.*, = Tic 1; **habit strength** (see quot. 1958); also called sHr; **habit-training,** the training of an infant or child in regular habits of behaviour, often specifically referring to hygiene, sleeping, and eating.

1863 J. G. Whittier *Poetical Wks.* (1874) 412/2 But what if, habit-bound, thy feet Shall lack the will to turn? **1922** W. B. Yeats *Trembling of Veil* 140 Old and habit-bound. **1932** *Brit. Jrnl. Psychol.* July 54 Box 7 [in set of boxes designed for intelligence testing] was introduced as a habit breaker. **1913** *Lancet* 27 Sept. 964/2 (*title*) A preliminary note on habit-formation in guinea-pigs. **1936** *Mind* XLV. 290 All habit-formation under the example, instruction, command, influence, of others is propaganda. **1961** *Lancet* 27 Aug. 485/1 Narcotics had not been used for fear of habit-formation. **1899** W. James *Talks to Teachers on Psychol.* p. viii, Maxims relative to habit-forming. **1913** A. E. Leach *Food Inspection & Analysis* (ed. 3) xxi. 955 (*heading*) Habit-forming drugs in beverages. **1958** J. Cannan *And be a Villain* vii. 151, I didn't take any [sleeping pills] last night because if you keep on they might become habit-forming. **1911** Paul & Palmer tr. *Bergson's Matter & Memory* ii. 99 (*marginal note of translators*) Automatism has a wide range, and representative memory is often superseded or masked by habit memory. **1912** *Mind* XXI. 226 M. Bergson, in contrasting these two forms of memory, makes the motor or habit-memory *too* mechanical. **1925** C. Fox *Educ. Psychol.* 140 Take two processes, habit-memory and image-memory respectively. **1907** W. James *Mem. & Stud.* (1911) x. 239 There seems no doubt that we are each and all of us to some extent victims of habit-neurosis. **1960** G. Sanders *Mem. Professional Cad* II. iv. 133 Once a man has acquired this habit pattern it will be intolerable for him to stay home at night. **1964** *Word Study* Feb. 2/2 *Finalize* and *dollar-wise* were deep-seated habit patterns long before Webster's Third displayed them. **1960** B. Malinowski *Sex & Repress. Savage Soc.* 194 The zoologist deals with specific instinctive behaviour, the anthropologist with a culturally fashioned habit-response. **1888** W. R. Gowers *Man. Dis. Nervous Syst.* II. v. 586 Children often..present spasmodic movements such as winking, twitching the mouth, jerking the head..which the individuals are unable to control... This condition has been termed 'habit-chorea'..but..'habit-spasm' is, I think, a better name. **1940** S. A. K. Wilson *Neurology* II. 1629 In France the word 'tic' has been employed for centuries to denote a habitual, unpleasing gesture; but only within the last 30 years has it been current in English neurology, replacing the incorrect 'habit-spasm' or 'habit-chorea' of prior date. **1948** E. R. Hilgard *Theories of Learning* iv. 83 Habit strength increases when receptor and effector activities occur in close temporal contiguity. **1951** C. L. Hull *Essentials of Behavior* xiv. 57 We have presented evidence..to indicate the quantitative molar law according to which habit strength (sHr), primary motivation or drive (D), incentive motivation (K).. and the delay in reinforcement (J) respectively operate as functions in the determination of reaction potential. **1958** H. B. & A. C. English *Dict. Psychol. Terms* 235/2 *Habit strength or sHr*, (*C. Hull*) an inferred part of the organism that is determined by variation in four empirical determinants: number of reinforcements, amount of reinforcing agents, time between stimulation and response, time between response and reinforcement. **1959** Lambert & Fillenbaum in Saporta & Bastian *Psycholinguistics* (1961) vii. 455/1 An important paper by Pitres ..offered a different generalization in order to account for..the effect of aphasia on polyglots. In essence, Pitres' is a habit strength principle which states that the language or languages most used before the aphasic insult will be the first to recover. **1927** A. Gesell in C. W. Kimmins *Mental & Physical Welfare of Child* iii. 40 Wholesome habit training in infancy lays the foundation of mental health...Feeding, sleeping, bladder control, bowel control—these are not physical matters. They are 'mental'. **1939** E. R. Boyce *Infant School Activities* 240 Habit-training. The nursery school and class has been closely associated with training in good physical habits and with attention to the health of the child. **1960** I. Bennett *Del. & Neur. Childr.* v. 181 Difficulties in habit-training may be expected in both delinquent and neurotic children. Both types..are likely to express early difficulties in the form of sleep disturbances, feeding disturbances, or disturbances in bladder or bowel control. **1890** W. James *Princ. Psychol.* I. xvi. 655 These habit-worn paths of association are a clear rendering of what authors mean by 'predispositions', 'vestiges', 'traces', etc., left in the brain by past experience.

habitant. B. 2. (Earlier and later examples.)

1789 *Quebec Gaz.* 5 Feb. 4/1 My Brother Habitants will be..convinced of the expediency of the regulation. **1791** J. Long *Voy. & Trav. Indian Interpr.* 167 The Canadians are particularly fond of dancing, from the *seigneur* to the *habitant*. **1909** *Westm. Gaz.* 10 Apr. 6/2 From school Drummond became a clerk in a telegraph office at Bord-à-Plouffe, a little village on the Rivière des Prairies, where he was in the midst of habitants, lumbermen, and voyageurs. **1966** *Kingston* (Ont.) *Whig-Standard* 27 Aug. 4/3 As the old habitant joke had it, it's okay to t'row out de hank [*sc.* anchor], but suppose there's no rope on the hank?

habitat. Add: **2.** *Comb.* **habitat form,** the form developed by a race or organism in response to its habitat; **habitat group,** any group of species whose members favour a similar habitat.

1902 F. E. Clements in *Beiblatt zu den Botanischen Jahrbüchern* LXX. 17 A habitat form is the modified form of a species common to two or more formations produced by a particular formation, i.e. habitat, such as the alpine meadow habitat form of *Campanula rotundifolia*. **1916** B. D. Jackson *Gloss. Bot. Terms* (ed. 3) 169/1 *Habitat-form*, the impress given to the plant by the habitat. **1898** Pound & Clements *Phytogeogr. Nebraska* iv. 93 A habitat group is a group of species, which are subject to similar physical conditions, and frequent like habitats. **1959** E. F. Linssen *Beetles Brit. Is.* I. 57 This 'bionomic classification', as the method is called, is based on habitat-groups. **1962** *Conservationist* June–July 20/2 Four new life-size dioramas (natural habitat groups) of four types of fish areas in Rochester and Munroe County are featured in permanent exhibitions in the Hall of Natural Science at the Rochester Museum of Arts and Sciences.

habitation. Add: **5.** *Comb.* **habitation name,** a place-name in which at least one of the elements denotes an inhabited place; **habitation site** *Archæol.*, a site where there has been a settlement.

1936 *Oxf. Dict. Eng. Place-Names* p. xv, Near habitation-names stand names that originally denoted a pasture-ground or a shelter for the protection of animals, a cowhouse, a cattle-fold, etc. **1962** H. R. Loyn *Anglo-Saxon England* i. 9 There are more British habitation names in the region. **1925** *Antiquaries Jrnl.* Apr. 182 The author has more leisure to examine Meare, a similar habitation-site three miles distant. **1942** *Oxoniensia* VII. 106 The B-beaker and neolithic sherds were drift-sherds from one of the many habitation-sites..in the neighbourhood. **1962** H. R. Loyn *Anglo-Saxon England* ii. 15 This is not to deny the possibility of continuity in habitation sites at places such as London or York. **1971** *World Archaeol.* III. 141 Some of the shelters may have been habitation sites in the past.

habitative, *a.* Delete *rare* and add earlier and later examples; now esp. in place-name studies.

1578 [see Possessive *a.* 2]. **1929** A. Mawer *Probl. Place-Name Study* iii. 124 By the time that *tun* had become the great habitative suffix there were probably few such groups left. **1961** K. Cameron *Eng. Place-Names* ii. 27 Place-names..can be divided into two main types, habitative and topographical. **1967** A. H. Smith *Place-Names of Westmorland* I. p. xxxviii, The older English settlements are represented by some 30 or more habitative names of parishes and villages.

habituation. 1. Delete † *Obs.* and add: Esp. the formation of such habits as dependence on drugs. (Later examples.)

1929 *Jrnl. Pharmacol. & Exper. Therap.* XXXVI. 466 'Habituation' we interpret to mean a condition wherein one becomes accustomed to but not seriously dependent upon a drug. **1960** *Times* 21 Jan. 6/7 The two drugs specifically mentioned in this context are carbromal and bromvaletone. The committee state that cases of habituation arising from the widespread use of these by the public, largely without medical guidance, have been 'numerically very few, but individually serious'. **1962** *Jrnl. Amer. Med. Assoc.* 14 July 93/1 The inherent difficulty in establishing a uniform cut-off point where 'habituation' becomes 'addiction'. **1973** G. G. Nahas *Marihuana* v. 188 In Egypt 65% of the consumers of hashish declared they were unable to stop although they expressed a wish to discontinue their habituation.

2. esp. in *Psychol.* The diminishing of response to a frequently repeated stimulus. (Further examples.)

1895 *Amer. Jrnl. Psychol.* VII. 82 Gewöhnung, habituation. **1934** H. C. Warren *Dict. Psychol.* 120/1 *Habituation*, the process of becoming adapted to a given stimulus, situation, or general environment. [A pop. and rather loose term.] **1967** S. Arieti *Intrapsychic Self* iii. 47 Loss of awareness in the phenomenon of habituation is a parsimonious device used constantly by the nervous system. **1973** S. Rose *Conscious Brain* ix. 194 The habituation process is..both a behavioral and a physiological phenomenon.

habitudinal (hæbitiū·dinăl), *a.* [f. L. *habitūdo, -inis* Habitude + -al.] Of or pertaining to habit; habitual.

c **1380** Wyclif *Sel. Eng. Wks.* (1869) I. 78 But clerkes witen þat þer ben two manere of seyngis, þat ben personel seynge, and habitudinel seynge. **1925** *Glasgow Herald* 12 Apr. 12 Disease.., biologically considered, is of three great kinds—(a) constitutional, (b) occupational or habitudinal, and (c) parasitic and microbic. **1932** J. A. Thomson *Scientific Riddles* IV. 324 Deeply saturating changes, whether environmental, nutritional, or habitudinal.

haboob (habū·b). Also **haboub, habub,** etc. [Arab. *habūb* blowing furiously.] A violent and oppressive wind which blows at certain seasons in the Sudan, and which brings with it sand from the desert. Also *transf.*

1897 *Daily News* 2 Oct. 2/1 This was a real haboob—a tornado of sand and small stones. *Ibid.* 4/6 A soldier that had been swept into the river by the merciless haboob. **1928** *Blackw. Mag.* Feb. 259 May is the month of 'haboobs'. **1936** *Jrnl. R. Aeronaut. Soc.* XL. 91 Our captains pay the greatest respect to the 'haboobs' of the Sudan. **1959** R. E. Huschke *Gloss. Meteorol.* 268 *Haboob* (many variant spellings, including *habbub, habub, haboub, hubbob, hubbub*), a strong wind and sandstorm or duststorm in the northern and central Sudan, especially around Khartum, where the average number is about 24 a year. **1973** *Sci. Amer.* Jan. 46/3 The American haboobs are not so frequent as the Sudanese (two or three a year at Phoenix as compared with perhaps 24 a year at Khartoum).

habu (hā·bu). [Jap.: see quot. 1818.] A venomous pit-viper, *Trimeresurus flavoviridis*, native to the Ryukyu Islands and neighbouring areas.

[**1818** B. Hall *Acc. Voy. Discovery to Great Loo-Choo Island* App., Vocabulary of English and Loo-Choo Words...Snake—Háboo.] **1895** *Geogr. Jrnl.* V. 299 The poisonous Trimeresurus.., called *habu* by the natives, is 4 or 5 feet long by 2 inches in diameter, and is an object of universal fear. **1955** *Sci. News Let.* 15 Jan. 36/1 The habu and mamushi, native to certain islands of the Pacific and parts of the Asiatic mainland.

habutai (hā·butəi). Also **-aye, -ae.** [Jap.] A fine soft Japanese silk.

[**1822** F. Shoberl tr. *Titsingh's Illustr. Japan* 17 Tchouya followed, dressed in two robes of light blue, made of the stuff called *fabita*, with his hands tied behind him.] **1895** *Montgomery Ward Catal.* 12/3 Habutai Silk.. is a very soft, light weight of silk of Japanese make. **1902** *Encycl. Brit.* XXIX. 725/1 Pictures so elaborate and.. accurate as those produced by the *yuzen* process on silk crape or *habutaye*. **1921** *Daily Colonist* (Victoria, B.C.) 7 Apr. 13/6 Black Waists of heavy quality Habutai silk, with tucked fronts and neat collars. **1931** *Stud. Eng. Lit.* (Tokyo) XI. 515 *Habutae*, a kind of silk. This word is regularly used in newspaper advertisements in England. **1950** '*Mercury' Dict. Textile Terms* 254/2 A pure dye spotproof silk of the Habutai order, finished with a little lustre.

hacendado (ɑːsendā·do). Also **haciendado.** [Sp.] The owner of an hacienda.

1840 D. Turnbull *Trav. in West* 98 In the unexpected case of the confiscation of the rural property of a Hacendado, the civil judge of the district..is directed to proceed to the spot. **1862** Mayne Reid *Tiger Hunter* xix, To the haciendado he hired himself out a part of the year. **1897** *Blackw. Mag.* Nov. 685 The polity of the Mexican haciendado remains unchanged. **1897** *Outing* (U.S.) XXIX. 593/2 The plantation homes of the *hacien-dados*. **1920** *Glasgow Herald* 22 Sept. 8 The Chilean haciendado. **1934** A. Huxley *Beyond Mexique Bay* 284 These lands were once the property of rich *hacendados*. **1962** *Economist* 13 Oct. 157/3 The Constitutionalists [of Mexico] led by Carranza, a *hacendado*, and Villa, a former bandit.

hacienda. Add: Also *attrib.*

1860 *Ure's Dict. Arts* (ed. 5) III. 676 Working it on their own account, or, as it is termed, hacienda account. **1897** *Blackw. Mag.* Nov. 685/2 The pleasant picture of hacienda life in the land of the Aztecs. **1944** *Harper's Mag.* Aug. 201/2 The Rio Blanco textile works set up in Mexico..were designed to produce cloth for sale at hacienda stores.

hack, *sb.*¹ Add: **6.** An act of hacking; a hacking blow. Also *fig.*, now esp. (*U.S.*) a try, attempt.

1836 D. Crockett *Exploits & Adv. Texas* 79 Better take a hack by way of trying your luck at guessing. **1873–4** *Rep. Vermont Board Agric.* II. 238, I have a chance to have several hacks at the weeds before the crop is sown. **1898** M. Deland *Old Chester Tales* 244, I get more men in a saloon, that's why; and when the show's done I get a hack at 'em. **1969** *New Yorker* 12 Apr. 95/1 We go into the second order of testing,..which would give us a better hack, a better indication of what we are dealing with.

hack, *sb.*³ Add: **7. b.** *hack-cab* (example). **c.** *hack writer* (earlier example); so *hack-writing*.

1851 *London at Table* i. 31, I..started in a hack cab for the scene of action. **1826** *Blackw. Mag.* XX. 296/2 You forget the effrontery of the hack-writer in the shame-facedness of the would-be gentleman. **1850** Kingsley *Alton Locke* II. ii. 14 My hack-writing was breaking down my moral sense, as it does that of most men. **1933** E. Pound *Let.* 24 Sept. (1971) 247 Teaching damn sight easier way of earning living than hackwriting.

8. (Earlier U.S. examples.)

1812 *Boston Gaz.* 10 Sept., Advt. (Th.), Hack Stand. **1835** in *Southern Lit. Messenger* IV. 197/1 My hack-driver..assured [me] that there was no other tavern in the city.

hack, *v.*¹ Add: **2. b.** Also in *Rugby Football*. Const. *over, up*.

1864 *Blackheathen* 9/1 'Hacking first man up'.. remains at present quite a Rugby rule. **1887** M. Shearman *Athletics & Football* 395 No hacking, or hacking over, or tripping up shall be allowed under any circumstances. **1897** *Encycl. Sport* I. 404/1 *Rugby Football*... Not only was it legal to hack over the carrier of the ball, but also the first on side, and I have seen as many as four of the van brought to earth by this means. **1963** *Times* 24 Jan. 3/1 It had been agreed [when the laws of Rugby Union were drawn up] that hacking-over and tripping-up should not be permitted.

c. To embarrass, annoy; to disconcert, confuse. Freq. as **hacked** *ppl. a. U.S. slang* or *dial.*

1892 J. C. Harris *Uncle Remus & Friends* 349 When you once git 'em hacked dey er hacked fer good; dey des give right up en roll der eyes. **1908** *Dialect Notes* III. 318 We tried to hack the pitcher. **1917** *Ibid.* IV. 413 That joke hacks Steve to this day. **1969** *Rolling Stone* 28 June 19/1 The big word down there is *commercial*...I wouldn't be so hacked off about it if I didn't love country music.

d. To cope with, manage, accomplish; to tolerate, accept; to comprehend; freq. *to hack it. slang* (orig. *U.S.*).

1955 *Antioch Rev.* XV. 379, I can't hack something like stealing. **1968** *Maclean's Mag.* Dec. 29/1, I just couldn't hack teaching any more, it was as simple as that. **1970** *Globe Mag.* (Toronto) 26 Sept. 9/2 You know, they're shooting people at Kent State and we talk about amendments to the Warble Fly Act. I can't hack that; it drives me crazy. **1972** *Sunday Mirror* 16 Apr. 23/3 Now, suddenly and bewilderingly since President Nixon has ordered his legions home, the Arvin is a great little guy who *can* hack it. **1972** *Newsweek* 7 Aug. 18/2, I had proved to the world during my four years in the Senate..that I can hack it.

hackamore. Add: (Earlier and later examples.) Also, a headstall.

1850 W. R. Ryan *Upper & Lower California* I. 152 He overtook me, mounted on a well saddled horse, and leading another by the hackamore. **1926** D. Branch *Cowboy & his Interpreters* 39 But having the 'hackimore' rope fastened to my belt I held to him until help arrived. **1971** A. P. McInnes *Dunlevy* 86 Her only riding equipment was a rawhide hackamore already on the horse's head.

hackia (hæ·kiă). = Guaiacum 2.

1851 *Illustr. Catal. Gt. Exhib.* iv. i. 983/2 Hackia, lignum vitæ, transverse and vertical sections, from River Demerara. **1858** Simmonds *Dict. Trade, Hackia*, a wood ..used for mill cogs and shafts. **1969** S. M. Sadeek *Windswept & Other Stories* 36 The dark East Indian.. flicked a piece of paper before him with his hackia stick.

hackie (hæ·ki). *U.S. colloq.* Also **hacky.** [f. Hack *sb.*³ 2.] A taxi-driver.

1937 *Daily Express* 10 Mar. 6/7 'Hackie' is taxi-driver. **1946** Mezzrow & Wolfe *Really Blues* (1957) viii. 114 Weaving..like an expert hackie in heavy traffic. **1959** 'M. Neville' *Sweet Night for Murder* xiii. 129 And now.. unearth some other blasted hacky that drove me there.

hacking, *vbl. sb.* Add: **1. c.** [After G. *hackung*; cf. F. *hachement*.] Massage with the edge of the hand.

1890 A. Kellgren *Ling's Syst. Man. Treatm.* 25 Tapotement means hacking or beating. **1893** A. S. Eccles *Sciatica* 64 Thorough rubbing, kneading, hacking, and passive movements are practised.

5. [Hack *v.*³ 3.] **hacking coat, jacket,** a sports coat suitable for use when riding, often tailored in a tweed with vents at the side or at the back; **hacking length,** the length of a hacking jacket.

1948 'E. Crispin' *Buried for Pleasure* vi. 38 He wore jodhpurs, riding-boots, a violent check hacking coat, and a yellow tie. **1954** *New Yorker* 13 Nov. 168/2 A jacket with a center vent and four buttons, or a hacking coat with side vents and slanted flap pockets, is from $125 to $135. **1954** *Irish Digest* Nov. 40 Resplendent in cloth cap, tweed hacking jacket, [etc.].., Huston squires it happily among his beloved Irish. **1959** H. Hobson *Mission House Murder* ii. 11 My Harris tweed hacking-jacket. **1965** *Punch* 22 Dec. 933/3 Leo McKern's irascible Baron is a splendid comic creation, wrapped in a loud-checked hacking jacket (checks any larger and they wouldn't have fitted on to the material). **1966** *Guardian* 27 July 6/4 Jackets are hacking length.

hackle, *sb.*² Add: **1. b.** *Hairdressing.* (See quot. 1957.)

1903 A. M. Sutton *Boardwork* (ed. 2) i. 9 A 'card' or 'hackle', used for disentangling combings, smoothing and mixing hair, is a magnified comb composed of steel spikes or prongs. **1957** V. J. Kehoe *Technique Film & T.V. Make-Up* iii. 34 *Hackle*, a multi-spiked tool which is clamped to a bench and used for combing or carding skeins of hair.

3. Also, the feathers on the saddle of a cock.

1850 D. J. Browne *Amer. Poultry Yard* 22 The hackles of the lower part of the back. *Ibid.* 253 In capons..the hackle, the tail feathers, and the spurs grew to a much greater length than in cocks. **1970** H. E. Smith *Bantams* i. 9 Feathers towards the stern are correctly called 'saddle hackles'. *Ibid.* iii. 19 The colours of a Red Jungle Fowl.. male are neck hackle, golden; saddle hackle, orange.

hackle, *v.*³ Add to def.: Also used of dressing the hair in wigmaking.

1931 G. A. Foan *Art & Craft of Hairdressing* i. 11/1 When dry the hair is ready for drawing off into roots and points. Taking each section separately the student should lightly hackle the extreme ends. **1966** J. S. Cox *Illustr. Dict. Hairdressing* 68/1 *Hackle*, to draw hair through a hackle to disentangle it.

hackling, *vbl. sb.*¹ *attrib.* Add: *hackling house.*

1849 E. Chamberlain *Indiana Gazetteer* (ed. 3) 132 A brick building, erected for a hackling house.

hackman. Add: (Earlier and later examples.) Also *Canada.*

1796 *Boston Directory*, passim. **1806** *Repertory* (Boston) 3 Oct. (Th.), Died, in this town, Mr. Daniel Henry, hackman. **1819** *N.Y. Gaz.* in *Massachusetts Spy* 16 June 3/1 The horses were stopt by the hackmen on the stand. **1898** H. E. Hamblen *Tom Benton's Luck* 56 The line of vociferous hackmen who formed a gauntlet across the exit from the railroad station. **1906** *Daily Colonist* (Victoria, B.C.) 9 Jan. 5/4 A hack case is being heard in the city police court, in which one of the local hackmen is being charged with overcharging.

hackmanite (hæ·kmănəit). *Min.* [ad. Sw. *hackmanit* (L. H. Borgström 1901, in *Geol. Föreningens Stockholm Förh.* XXIII. 563), f. the name of Victor A. *Hackman* (1866–1941), Finnish geologist: see -ite¹.] A pink or reddish violet variety of sodalite which loses its colour when exposed to daylight but regains it in the dark.

1903 *Jrnl. Chem. Soc.* LXXXIV. ii. 304 Hackmanite, a new member of the sodalite group. **1941** *Amer. Mineralogist* XXVI. 441 The induced color change of hackmanite when exposed to ultra-violet light was first observed.. on hackmanite from Bancroft, Ontario, which changed from pink to a raspberry shade or deep violet on exposure to ultra-violet light. The induced color faded rapidly and nearly completely on exposure to strong light. **1970** *Physics Bull.* Nov. 487/1 Geologists had found that freshly cleared rocks of a naturally occurring form of sodalite, hackmanite, exhibited a pink colour.

hackney-carriage. (Earlier U.S. example.)

1796 *Mass. Acts & Laws* (1896) 62 The said Selectmen are hereby authorized to grant licences for such number of Hackney Coaches & Carriages..as they shall judge proper.

hackneydom (hæ·knidəm). [f. Hackney(ed *ppl. a.* 2 + -dom. Cf. Hackney *v.* 7.] A state of commonplaceness.

1897 G. B. Shaw *Our Theatres in Nineties* (1932) III. 235 The latest attempt to escape from hackneydom and cockneydom is the Chinatown play. **1959** *Times* 30 Nov. 14/3 Again this was a performance that shook the dust of hackneydom from the symphony.

hadada(h (hā·dadā). Also **hadadaw, haddada, hadeda, hadida.** [Onomatopœic from the bird's raucous call.] A large brown-green ibis, *Hagedashia hagedash.*

1801 J. Barrow *Trav. S. Afr.* I. iv. 264 The Egyptian black *ibis* (*niger*) and another species of *tantalus*, called by the farmers the *haddadas*, were procured at this place. **1846** tr. *Arbousset & Daumas's Narr. Tour Cape G.H.* 190 A large ibis of a brown lustre commonly called by onomatopy *addada*. **1862** J. S. Dobie *S. Afr. Jrnl.* 10 Oct. (1945) 40 Missed a hadadaw. **1907** *African Monthly* Oct. 445 Flocks of 'ha-di-da' grub silently and unconcernedly in close proximity to the camp. **1952** Mackworth-Praed & Grant *Birds E. & N.E. Afr.* I. 59 Key to the Adult Storks, Ibises...Back bronzy brown, no crest on nape, ridge of bill only red, bare skin confined to front of eye: Hadada *Hagedashia hagedash.* **1953** Bannerman *Birds W. & Equat. Afr.* I. 184 West African Hadada. *Hagedashia hagedash brevirostris*...The best guide to the Hadada's identity lies in its loud note—*kah-a-a-a*— uttered frequently, both in flight and on the ground. **1953** R. Campbell *Mamba's Precipice* v. 48 To the forest, on the left bank, flocks of hadadah ibis were flying back to roost. **1957** McLachlan & Liversidge *Roberts's Birds S. Afr.* 39 Hadeda...At a distance it appears dull olive-grey, but metallic reflections on back and wing-coverts may be seen. **1964** C. Willock *Enormous Zoo* vii. 120 Hadada ibises rise with the horrible complaining cry from which they get their title.

Hadassah (hădæ·să). [Heb., = myrtle, name of the Biblical Esther (Esther 2:7).] An American Zionist women's organization, founded in 1912, which contributes to welfare work in Israel.

1913 H. Szold *Let.* 15 July in M. Lowenthal *H. Szold Life & Lett.* (1942) 79 If we can keep up this folder propaganda as the winter's work of Hadassah, we shall be doing admirably. **1952** S. Spender *Learning Laughter* vii. 100 In 40 years Hadassah has grown from being a small organization for training a few nurses, into a main channel for transfusing life-blood into a young nation. **1964** D. Greenburg in *Playboy* Sept. 170/2 Your family ..will expect you to be able to relate amusing stories which you have heard..at a meeting of the Hadassah. **1966** H. Kemelman *Saturday the Rabbi went Hungry* (1967) i. 8 It fell off and I sewed it on myself. You were at a Hadassah meeting. **1972** *Times* 16 Oct. 6/1 The letter ..was addressed to a member of Hadassah, a women's Zionist organisation.

hadda (hæ·dă), repr. colloq. pronunc. of *had to* or *had a.*

1945 A. Kober *Parm Me* 34, I hadda do a lotta talking to get her to come here to-night. **1967** 'L. Egan' *Nameless Ones* xv. 192 Well, she hadda lot of trouble. *Ibid.* 193 She hadda give up an apartment, couldn't afford it. **1969** *Coast to Coast 1967–68* 4 There was that Alsatian they hadda shoot because it wouldn't leave a kid's grave and kept scrabbling at the loose dirt. **1971** 'A. Blaisdell' *Practice to Deceive* x. 138 'Did you hit her?' 'Naw, ..I never hadda chance.'

haddada, hadeda, varr. *hadada(h.

Hades. Add: **2. b.** Used trivially as a substitute for *hell* in imprecations, etc.

1912 A. Bennett *Matador* ii, What the hades are you waiting there for? **1917** [see *blind *sb.* 11]. **1942** T. Bailey *Pink Camellia* xxvii. 196 What in Hades is he doing here? **1972** G. Bell *Villains Galore* i. 4 Damn protocol to Hades!

hadida, var. *hadada(h.

Hadith (hæ·diþ). Also **Hadis, Hadithah.** Pl. **Hadithat.** [a. Arab. *ḥadīṯ* a tradition.] The body of traditions relating to Mohammed, which now form a supplement to the Koran, called the Sunna.

a **1817** J. L. Burckhardt *Trav. Syria & Holy Land* (1822) 326 An Olema thinks he has attained the pinnacle of knowledge if he can recite all the Koran together with some thousand of Hadeath, or sentences of the Prophet. **1880** *Encycl. Brit.* XI. 367/2 Rejecting the *Hadith*, or traditional sayings of Mahomet. **1883** *Ibid.* XVI. 594/2 The traditions of Mohammed, or *Hadith*, the collective body of which constitutes the *Sunna*, or custom. **1922** *Blackw. Mag.* Mar. 375/2, I treasured this like a *hadis*, an authentic tradition of which I was the custodian. **1924** A. Guillaume *Trad. Islam* 15 The hadith literature

as we now have it provides us with apostolic precept and example covering the whole duty of man. *Ibid.* 150 Many of the hadith already cited will have shown the good sense, amiability, and liberality of the prophet. **1951** 'N. SHUTE' *Round Bend* v. 137 Legacies are governed by *hadith*, based upon the Koran.

hadj. Add: Also **haj, hajj.** Also *transf.*

1910 *Encycl. Brit.* XII. 827/1 The word *hajj* is sometimes loosely used of any Mahommedan pilgrimage to a sacred place or shrine, and is also applied to the pilgrimages of Christians of the East to the Holy Sepulchre at Jerusalem. **1930** KIPLING *Limits & Renewals* (1932) 217 He had forbidden music because it was a *haj*.

hadjeen, var. *HYGEEN, HAJEEN.

hadji, hajji. Substitute for def.: The title given to one who has made the greater pilgrimage (on the 8th to 10th day of the 12th month of the Muslim year) to Mecca.

Hadrianic (hēⁱdriæ·nik), *a.* [f. L. *Hadriān(us* + -IC.] Of or pertaining to the Roman emperor Hadrian (A.D. 76–138).

1886 W. P. DICKSON tr. *Mommsen's Provinces of Roman Empire* I. v. 189 In the time of Diocletian we find the district between the two walls evacuated, but the Hadrianic wall occupied still as before. **1897** *Trans. Cumberland & Westmorland Antiquarian & Archæol. Soc.* XIV. 419 Hadrianic inscriptions occur at Chesterholm and Greatchesters. **1911** *Ibid.* New Ser. XI. 390 Vindolana and Magna, although occupied in Hadrianic times as Wall stations, differ from the others in Northumberland. **1921** *Jrnl. Roman Stud.* XI. 51 The idea of a single camp extending from sea to sea is a bold flight of imagination... It became..a cardinal feature in the 'Hadrianic Theory' of the nineteenth century. **1935** *Burlington Mag.* Feb. 97/1 Hadrianic art was certainly Greek in its nature. **1962** *Guardian* 11 July 5/7 The rampart and ditch of a small Hadrianic fort. **1972** *Daily Tel.* 5 Dec. 12/5 Coins and Antiquities gave £6,800 for a Hadrianic/Early Antonine period Roman marble figure called Paris.

hadrome (hæ·drōᵘm). *Bot.* [ad. G. *hadrom* (G. Haberlandt *Physiologische Pflanzenanatomie* (1884) VII. v. 265), f. Gr. ἁδρ-ός thick, bulky + *-OME.] The conducting tissue of the xylem, excluding fibres.

1898 H. C. PORTER tr. *Strasburger's Text-bk. Bot.* 102 Other terms often used to designate the vascular bundles are folio-vascular bundles and mestome. The vascular portion is also termed the xylem or hadrome. **1914** M. DRUMMOND tr. *Haberlandt's Physiol. Plant Anat.* vii. 347 The water-conducting vessels and tracheides constitute..the resistant hadrome portion [of the conducting strand]...The xylem includes the hadrome with its associated wood-fibres...Where..no wood-fibres are developed, xylem is the exact equivalent of hadrome. **1965** K. ESAU *Plant Anat.* (ed. 2) xii. 272 The parallel term for the xylem is *hadrom*, which refers to the conducting part of the xylem..excluding the fibers.

Hence **hadroce·ntric** *a.*, having the hadrome surrounded by the leptome; **ha·dromal** [a. G. *hadromal* (F. Czapek 1899, in *Zeitschr. f. physiol. Chem.* XXVII. 163], a hydrolysis product of lignin; *para*-coniferyl aldehyde, $C_6H_2(OH)(OCH_3)CH{:}CHCHO$; **ha:dromyco·sis**, a fungal disease of plants in which the xylem is the part most affected.

1899 *Jrnl. Chem. Soc.* LXXVI. I. 560 A substance termed hadromal has been isolated from different woody tissues; it has the properties of a phenol and of an aldehyde. **1900** B. D. JACKSON *Gloss. Bot. Terms* 310/1 *Hadrocentric*, having the hadrome in the centre surrounded by the leptome. **1914** M. DRUMMOND tr. *Haberlandt's Physiol. Plant Anat.* vii. 349 If the hadrome is central and the leptome peripheral, the bundle may be termed *hadrocentric.* **1916** G. H. PETHYBRIDGE in *Sci. Proc. Roy. Dublin Soc.* XV. 87 The fungus mycelium is, at any rate in the early stages of the disease, confined to the wood vessels.. and I, therefore, suggest the word 'hadromycosis' for use in this connexion. **1917** *Nature* 22 Feb. 500/2 Plants suffering from the choking of their vessels [by fungi] (hadromycosis). **1928** *Chem. Abstr.* XXII. 399 Czapek's hadromal.., which he considers responsible for the characteristic red color given by wood tissues with phloroglucinol-HCl. **1931** *Hilgardia* V. 197 (*title*) Verticillium hadromycosis. **1952** F. E. BRAUNS *Chem. Lignin* iv. 37 Hadromal occurs in wood as a coniferyl aldehyde cellulose ester. **1971** G. C. AINSWORTH *Ainsworth & Bisby's Dict. Fungi* (ed. 6) 254 Hadromycosis, a disease of plants in which the pathogen is confined to the xylem, e.g. *Verticillium* wilt of potato and tomato.

hadron (hæ·drǫn). *Physics.* [f. Gr. ἁδρ-ός thick, bulky + *-ON¹; first used in Russian, with the spelling *adron*.] Any strongly interacting sub-atomic particle. Hence **hadro·nic** *a.*

1962 L. B. OKUN' in *Proc. Internat. Conf. High-Energy Physics* 845/2 In this report I shall call strongly interacting particles hadrons, and the corresponding decays hadronic. **1966** *New Scientist* 26 May 500/1 The particles, so-called baryons and mesons, collectively called hadrons. **1968** *Sci. Jrnl.* Nov. 34/2 Weak decays of hadrons—which are nucleons (neutrons and protons) and their heavy partners. **1969** *Physics Bull.* Jan. 32/1 In high energy hadron collisions, the fraction of the total cross section going into two-body final states decreases rapidly with energy.

Haeckelian (hekī·liăn), *a.* [f. the name of E. H. *Haeckel* (1834–1919), German biologist: see -IAN.] Of or pertaining to the opinions of Haeckel; also as *sb.*, a believer in Haeckel's theories. So **Haeckelism** (he·kəliz'm), **-i·smus**, the opinions and theories of Haeckel.

1894 *Natural Sci.* Mar. 162 We are well content to cease from controversy, to let Calcareous sponges, the Gastrula, and..Haeckelismus take care of themselves. **1897** *Ibid.* Jan. 31 The typical form of the Haeckelian genealogical tree. **1899** E. J. CHAPMAN *Drama of Two Lives* 88 Thus, hæckelism's wondrous gleam Makes clear, to all, how all arose. **1930** G. R. DE BEER *Embryol. & Evol.* xv. 102 There is then no recapitulation in the Haeckelian sense of accelerated repetition of adult stages. **1971** *Nature* 11 June 400/2 The German Monist League..was neither a 'scientific' nor a 'political' body but rather one devoted to Haeckelian naturalism.

hæm, heme (hīm). [Back-formation from HÆM(OGLOBIN.] **a.** A chelation compound, $C_{34}H_{32}O_4N_4Fe$, of ferrous ion and protoporphyrin, obtained on reduction of hæmatin: the red-coloured non-protein constituent of hæmoglobin.

1925 ANSON & MIRSKY in *Jrnl. Physiol.* LX. 50 Haemoglobin is a conjugated protein consisting of globin and a non-protein part, containing pyrrol nuclei and iron, which we shall call haem. **1939** *Jrnl. Biol. Chem.* CXXXI. 661 Coryell..has applied the Pauling equation..to the oxidation of hemoglobin..and has shown that interaction among the four heme groups will account for the occurrence of an *n* which is not integral. **1956** *Nature* 11 Feb. 275/1 The angular variation of the *g* values enables an accurate determination to be made of the orientation of the hæm and porphyrin planes with respect to the external crystalline axes. *Ibid.* 275/2 Detailed information on the orientation of the hæm planes can be combined with X-ray measurements to calculate the polypeptide chain directions. **1970** R. W. MCGILVERY *Biochem.* ii. 13 The biological function of hemoglobin is therefore derived from both the heme and the peptides... Each of the four peptide chains has its own heme.

b. Any of various compounds of a ferrous or ferric ion and a porphyrin, present in biological pigments.

1948 *Biochem. Jrnl.* XLII. p. xlvii/2 The phase separation of haems has been applied to ox heart muscle. **1962** RIMINGTON & KENNEDY in Florkin & Mason *Comprehensive Biochem.* IV. xii. 563 By far the most important metalloporphyrins..are the iron complexes or hemes. In these nature has exploited the valency change from the ferric to ferrous state and vice versa to establish an electron transport system connecting the intracellular dehydrogenases with atmospheric oxygen. **1966** K. OKUNUKI in Florkin & Stotz *Comprehensive Biochem.* XIV. 233 Four types of haem have so far been known to occur in cytochromes...These are haem *a*, protohaem, haem *c* and so-called haem a_2.

hæmachromatosis, hem-, varr. *HÆMOCHROMATOSIS.

hæmagglutinate, hem- (hī:m,ăgliū·tinēⁱt), *v.* [f. Gr. αἷμ-α blood + AGGLUTINATE *v.*] *trans.* To cause (red blood cells) to agglutinate. So **hæ:magglu·tinating** *ppl. a.*

1921 *Jrnl. Immunol.* VI. 423 In..experiments with normal and 'immune' hemagglutinating sera we have used the slide method. **1922** *Jrnl. Amer. Med. Assoc.* 11 Nov. 1684/1 (*title*) The hemagglutinating fraction of human serums. *Ibid.* 1685/1 The hemagglutinating property is contained in the pseudoglobin fraction. **1936** *Nature* 26 Sept. 554/1 The haemagglutinating substance is present in the cotyledons of the seed of the runner bean. **1956** *Ibid.* 4 Feb. 234/2 Under the conditions of assay, five hæmagglutinating units were regularly inhibited by a minimum of 10–20μ gm. of preparation *IL-1*. **1961** *Lancet* 23 Sept. 718/1 Only 6 strains were found to hæmagglutinate the red cells of more than 5 species.

Also **hæ:magglutina·tion**, the action or process of hæmagglutinating.

1907 *Jrnl. Med. Res.* XVII. 323 Repeated controls have convinced me that the presence and degree of hemagglutination may be detected quite as accurately macroscopically as microscopically. **1919** *Jrnl. Immunol.* IV. 284 The use of hypertonic solutions of sodium chlorid are of no practical value in preventing hemagglutination in complement fixation tests. **1946** *Nature* 27 July 119/1 Vaccinia hæmagglutination is inhibited by appropriate immune sera either of animal or human origin. **1949** *Poultry Sci.* XXVIII. 622 (*title*) A plate hemagglutination-inhibition test for Newcastle disease antibodies in avian and human serums. *Ibid.* 622/1 Virus isolation and neutralization tests are carried out in embryonating chicken eggs; the hemagglutination-inhibition test is done in test tubes. **1969** *New Scientist* 30 Jan. 171/1 The basis of a simple laboratory test—the haemagglutination test—which is widely used in the study of influenza.

hæmagglutinin, hem- (hī:m,ăgliū·tinin). [f. Gr. αἷμ-α + *AGGLUTININ.] A substance that causes agglutination of red blood cells.

1904 *Amer. Jrnl. Med. Sci.* CXXVIII. 669 (*title*) Concerning haemagglutinins of bacterial origin and their relation to hyaline thrombi and liver necroses. *Ibid.* 670 The observations of Hueter..are of interest in connection with our recently acquired knowledge of bacterial haemagglutinins. **1946** *Nature* 27 July 119/1 Work on the hæmagglutinin of vaccinia virus was initiated by an observation by Burnet in October 1941 that a chorioallantoic membrane emulsion agglutinated fowl cells to a low titre. **1969** *New Scientist* 23 Jan. 171/1 The presence of haemagglutinin on the virus surface enables the influenza virus to adhere firmly to the surface of chicken erythrocytes.

hæmangioma, hem- (hī:mændʒi,ōᵘ·mă). *Path.* Pl. **-ata, -as.** [f. Gr. αἷμ-α blood + *ANGIOMA.] (See quot. 1900.)

1890 in BILLINGS *Nat. Med. Dict.* **1900** DORLAND *Med. Dict.* 291/2 *Hemangioma*, angioma containing blood-vessels, but not lymph-vessels; true angioma. **1913** C. P. WHITE *Path. Growth Tumours* vi. 86 Angeiomata..are formed in connection with blood vessels (haemangeioma) or with lymphatic vessels (lymphangeioma). **1961** *Lancet* 22 July 211/2 (*table*) Hæmangiomata. *Ibid.* 26 Aug. 492/2 Patients with coarctation of the abdominal aorta..or large hæmangiomas. **1962** *Ibid.* 6 Jan. 46/1 A capillary hæmangioma of the upper lips, nose, and frontal area seems to be highly pathognomonic of this syndrome. **1970** PASSMORE & ROBSON *Compan. Med. Stud.* II. xxx. 16 It is difficult to draw a dividing line between fibrous xanthomata..and the sclerosing haemangiomata.

Hence **hæ:mangiomato·sis**, a condition characterized by the presence of many hæmangiomata.

1912 *Jrnl. Amer. Med. Assoc.* 27 Apr. 1311/1 (*title*) General hemangiomatosis of placenta. **1913** DORLAND *Med. Dict.* (ed. 7) 415/2 Hemangiomatosis, a condition in which multiple hemangiomata are developed. **1970** *Gut* XI. 515 Radiotherapy has been reported..to be of some benefit in..hepatic haemangiomatosis.

hæmanthus, hem- (hīmæ·nþŏs). *Bot.* [mod.L. (Linnæus *Hortus Cliffortianus* (1737) 127), f. Gr. αἷμ-α blood + ἄνθος flower.] A bulbous plant of the genus so called, belonging to the family Amaryllidaceæ, native to southern and tropical Africa, and bearing umbels of red, pink, or white flowers.

1771 R. WESTON *Universal Botanist* II. 375 Hæmanthus, Blood flower, or African Tulip... Spotted-stalked Guinea Hæmanthus. **1834** *Curtis's Bot. Mag.* LXI. 3373 (*heading*) Hairy, Pink Hæmanthus. **1885** T. BAINES *Greenhouse & Stove Plants* 199/1 Hæmanthus are increased like Amaryllis by offsets which the strong bulbs produce. **1961** *Amateur Gardening* 14 Oct. 29/1 Bulbs of haemanthus can be potted now.

hæmarthrosis, hem- (hīm,arþrōᵘ·sis). *Path.* Pl. **-oses.** [f. Gr. αἷμ-α + ἄρθρο-ν joint + -OSIS.] Hæmorrhage into a joint.

1883 *Brit. Med. Jrnl.* 22 Sept. 561/2, I diagnosed the case as one of hæmarthrosis. **1891** C. W. M. MOULLIN *Surg.* III. vi. 613 In cases..in which the hæmorrhage is often considerable and the swelling immediate, it may be almost pure blood (hæmarthrosis). **1908** *Practitioner* Apr. 521 Other cases are given..of the association of fatal hæmorrhages from the bowels together with the hæmarthrosis. **1962** *Lancet* 27 Jan. 174/1 Their bleeding is similar to that seen in mild hæmophilia; they have had hæmarthroses, deep intramuscular hæmorrhage, and hæmaturia.

hæmato-, hemato-. Add: **hæ·matocri:t** [Gr. κριτ-ής judge], a centrifuge used to estimate the volume occupied by the red blood cells in a sample of blood; the value obtained, expressed as a percentage of the volume of the sample; also earlier **hæmatokrit**; †**hæ·matoge:n** [a. G. *hämatogen* (G. Bunge 1885, in *Zeitschr. f. physiol. Chem.* IX. 56)], a yellow powder obtained from egg yolk and supposed to be the precursor of hæmoglobin (*Obs.*); **hæmatolytic** *a.* (earlier example); **hæ:matomye·lia** [Gr. μυελ-ός marrow + -IA¹], hæmorrhage into the substance of the spinal cord; **hæ:matopo·rphyrin** [a. G. *haematoporphyrin* (F. Hoppe-Seyler *Med.-chem. Untersuch.* (1871) IV. liii. 533): see *PORPHYRIN], a dark violet porphyrin compound, $C_{34}H_{38}O_6N_4$, obtained by the action of concentrated acids on hæm or its derivatives; **hæ:matosa·lpinx** [SALPINX 2] (see quot. 1890).

1894 *Med. News* 29 Sept. 348/2 (*heading*) A modification of Hedin's hematokrit. *Ibid.* 350/2 States of comparative health..seem to be of the least importance of all the data necessary for the present status of the hematokrit. **1946** *Nature* 31 Aug. 304/1 These patients had,..because of the low hæmatocrit, a significantly reduced blood volume. **1958** *Immunology* I. 206 Blood samples were centrifuged in Wintrobe haematocrit tubes. **1966** *Lancet* 24 Dec. 1381/2 Chamberlain and Millard (1963) reduced the hæmatocrit and red-blood-cell volume (R.C.V.) in their patients with polycythæmia by means of oxygen. **1890** L. C. WOOLDRIDGE tr. *Bunge's Text-bk. Physiol. & Pathol. Chem.* vi. 102 The iron is more firmly fixed in the nuclein of the yolk of egg than in the albuminates of iron. ..The nuclein which contained iron..is doubtless the precursor of hæmoglobin, for there is no considerable quantity of any other compound of iron in the yolk. I have therefore proposed that this compound should receive the name hæmatogen (blood-former). **1934** J. F. MCCLENDON *Man. Biochem.* 112 Bunge..supposed that mammals are born with a store of iron. That led him to look for iron in the eggs of birds, and he found an iron compound which he called hematogen. **1875** R. FOWLER *Med. Vocab.* (ed. 2) 222/1 Hæmatolytic...1. Accompanied with the escape of blood from distended capillaries. 2. Applied adj. and subs. to medicines, said

to, by long continued use, impoverish the blood. **1881** *Brit. Med. Jrnl.* 28 May 852/2 A case of haematomyelia in a man aged 19. **1940** H. G. Wells *Babes in Darkling Wood* III. iii. 275 He was equal to hæmatomyelia, a sort of temporary stroke just at the back of the head. **1970** *Archiv. für Toxikol.* XXVI. 56 The apparent sudden onset, the lack of progression,..and the relatively advanced age of manifestation all point to hematomyelia as the cause of the lesion, which in turn follows as a consequence of the increased bleeding tendency associated with benzene poisoning. **1885** *Jrnl. Physiol.* VI. 27 The filtrate was reddish and shewed a spectrum which is that of acid haematoporphyrin. **1902** *Encycl. Brit.* XXXI. 726/2 By mineral acids the iron may be removed, leaving a purplish pigment, Hæmatoporphyrin, which has no power of taking up or giving off oxygen. **1928** J. Pryde *Recent Adv. Biochem.* (ed. 2) x. 315 It would seem that neither hæmatoporphyrin nor mesoporphyrin is formed in the human body. *Ibid.*, Hæmatoporphyrin has a very powerful light-sensitising action. **1955** *Sci. News Let.* 9 Apr. 240/3 Cancer tissue can be made to glow a bright red under ultraviolet light when a powder called hematoporphyrin is introduced intravenously before surgery. **1955** *Endeavour* XIV. 126/2 Haematoporphyrin..is accordingly described as 1,3,5,8-tetramethyl-2,4-di-(α-oxyethyl)-porphin-6,7-dipropionic acid. **1884** *Lancet* 2 Feb. 207/2 Haematosalpinx...Tumours were discovered to the left and right of the uterus. These..proved to be the tubes, full of tar-like blood and firmly adherent. **1890** Billings *Nat. Med. Dict.* 614/1 *Hæmatosalpinx*, collection of blood in the Fallopian tube. **1923** J. M. M. Kerr et al. *Combined Text-bk. Obstetr. & Gynæcol.* xli. 612 The fluid..may extend to the uterine cavity, forming a hæmatometra, and in the most extreme cases it may distend the Fallopian tubes, forming hæmatosalpinges. **1972** C. J. Dewhurst *Integrated Obstetr. & Gynaecol. Postgrad.* i. 12/2 Haematosalpinx is most uncommon except in cases of very long-standing [imperforate membrane], or in association with retention of blood in a fragment of upper vagina.

hæmatology. Add: Also **hem-. hæmatological** *a.* (examples). So also **hæmatolo·gic** *a.*; **hæmatolo·gically** *adv.*; **hæmato·logist**, one who specializes in hæmatology.

1904 *Lancet* 25 June 1790/2 The next method was demonstrated by Stengel some ten years ago and has since rapidly gained favour amongst hæmatologists, who frequently re-discover it. **1939** *Jrnl. Clin. Invest.* XVIII. 543/2 The serum or plasma iron fluctuations which occur in hematologically equilibrated subjects. **1946** *Nature* 6 July 24/2 We would like to take this opportunity of expressing our thanks to Dr. R. A. Kekwick for advising us on the hæmatological technique. *Ibid.* 21 Sept. 412/1 An International Hematology and *Rh* Conference will be held in Dallas, Texas, on November 15. **1947** *Radiology* XLIX. 286/2 The hematologic constituents of the peripheral blood were the most sensitive indicators of radiation effect. **1956** A. H. Compton *Atomic Quest* 333 Nuclear chemists,.. metallurgists, hematologists, and meteorologists. **1965** *Math. in Biol. & Med.* (*Med. Res. Council*) III. 90 (*title*) Digital computer as aid to differential diagnosis; use in hematologic diseases.

hæmerythrin, hem- (hīːmeri·þrin). *Biochem.* [f. Gr. αἷμ-α blood + Erythrin.] A red respiratory pigment in the blood of certain invertebrates.

1903 *Jrnl. Chem. Soc.* LXXXIV. II. 741 Haemerythrin, the pink colouring matter in the blood of *Sipunculus* and a few other worms, is contained in the blood corpuscles. **1950** *Sci. News* XV. 103 A..rare red respiratory pigment is hæmerythrin possessed by certain marine animals. **1963** R. P. Dales *Annelids* iii. 70 Amongst other peculiar features they have enucleate corpuscles containing the respiratory pigment haemerythrin, unique in the Annelida, and found elsewhere only in the sipunculids.

hæmiglobin, hem- (hīmiˌglōu·bin, hīməi-). *Biochem.* [ad. G. *hämiglobin* (Kiese & Kaeske 1942, in *Biochem. Zeitschr.* CCCXII. 122), f. *hämoglobin* haemoglobin, by alteration.] = Methæmoglobin.

1944 *Chem. Abstr.* XXXVIII. 1537 In expts. dealing with the mechanism of chlorate poisoning, H. and J. [Heubner and Jung] found that hemiglobin (hitherto termed methemoglobin)..served to accelerate its own formation. **1965** *Clin. Chim. Acta* XI. 571 (*heading*) The formation of haemiglobin using nitrites. **1966** *Biol. Abstr.* XLVII. 5186/1 The rate of hemiglobin formation was measured in human blood during drying in air.

hæmo-, hemo-. Add: **hæːmochromato·sis** (erron. **hæma-**) *Path.* [see Chromato- and -osis] = **bronze diabetes*; **hæːmochro·mogen** [Chromogen], a product obtained from hæmoglobin by hydrolysis; **hæːmoconcentra·tion** (see quot. 1949); **hæːmodia·lysis** *Med.* = *dialysis 5 b; hence **hæːmodi·alyser**, an artificial kidney; **hæːmodyna·mic** *a.*, of or belonging to hæmodynamics; **hæ·mogram** [-gram], a systematic description of a patient's blood cells; **hæːmogre·garine** [ad. mod.L. generic name *Hæmogregarina* (B. Danilewsky 1885, in *Archiv für mikroskopische Anatomie* XXIV. 589], a member of a group of coccidian parasites which infest the blood of vertebrates and are transmitted by invertebrates; **hæːmopoie·sis**, var. Hæmatopoiesis; **hæmopoietic** *a.* (later examples); **hæːmopoie·tin, -ine** [ad. F. *hémopoïétine* (Carnot & Deflandre 1906, in *Compt. Rend.* CXLIII. 386)], = *erythropoietin; **hæːmosi·derin** [a. G. *hämosiderin* (E. Neumann 1888, in *Arch. f. Path. Anat. u. Physiol.* CXI. 27), f. Gr. σίδηρ-ος iron: see -in[1]], a brownish-yellow granular iron-protein substance used to store iron in the body; **hæːmosidero·sis** [Siderosis], accumulation of hæmosiderin in body tissues; **hæmo·stasis** [cf. Stasis], stoppage of the flow of blood; **hæ·mostat** [cf. -stat], † **a.** (see quot. 1900). *Obs.*; **b.** an instrument for retarding hæmorrhage.

1899 *Brit. Med. Jrnl.* 9 Dec. 1595/1 In the general haemochromatosis associated with cirrhosis of the liver, the pigment is the haemosiderin and has an ochre yellow colour, which gives to the organs..a most remarkable and characteristic appearance. **1907** *Practitioner* Aug. 214 Haemochromatosis is a rare disease; the pigmentation is often, but not invariably, associated with glycosuria and cirrhosis of the liver. **1932** *Sunday Pictorial* 17 Jan. 6/4 The cause of death was hæmachromatosis, an extremely rare disease of metabolism. **1964** L. Martin *Clin. Endocrinol.* (ed. 4) v. 179 In hæmochromatosis the pigmentation is primarily a slaty-grey colour and there is hepatic enlargement with glycosuria. **1885** *Jrnl. Physiol.* VI. 28, I have seen in the lobule of the liver of a pigeon..in one part haemochromogen, in another biliverdin. **1957** *New Biol.* XXIV. 65 Another possible route for haemoglobin loss is the follo.wing In the gut there is found a compound known as a haemochromogen, which is related to haemoglobin. *Ibid.*, In the laboratory haemochromogen is a breakdown product of haemoglobin. **1940** *Acta Med. Scand.* CIII. 548 We shall be able to find hyperglobulinemia without any displacement of the ratio of albumin to globulin in those cases where there is a hemo-concentration on account of desiccation. **1947** *Radiology* XLIX. 302/2 These dogs also showed a terminal hemoconcentration. **1949** *New Gould Med. Dict.* 453/1 *Hemoconcentration*, an increase in the concentration of blood cells resulting from the loss of plasma or water from the blood stream; anhydremia. **1964** L. Martin *Clin. Endocrinol.* (ed. 4) v. 170 Shock is a complex syndrome manifested by hæmoconcentration. **1959** Kupfer & Rosenak in *Jrnl. Laboratory & Clin. Med.* Nov. 746 (*title*) A new parallel tube continuous hemodialyzer. **1963** *Lancet* 12 Jan. 82/2 The dialysing area of the particular hæmodialyser employed is given, together with the urea clearance achieved by its use. **1947** *Q. Cumulative Index Medicus* XLII. 1186/1 Attempted therapy of anuria by intraperitoneal hemodialysis. **1962** *Lancet* 19 May 1055/1 Hæmodialysis is now commonly applied in acute renal failure. **1968** Hæmodialysis [see *dialysis 5 b]. **1907** *Practitioner* Aug. 217 Although fully recognising the importance of the diastolic pressure, when working at hæmodynamic problems,..I did not consider it essential. **1961** *Lancet* 12 Aug. 331/1 (*title*) Hæmodynamic effects of guanethidine. **1929** R. B. H. Gradwohl tr. *Schilling's Blood Picture* 17 With the aid of..simple measures the 'hemogram' is constructed; by its brevity and capacity to express many things it constitutes the basis for the practical usage of the blood picture. **1961** *Lancet* 9 Sept. 568/1 Other studies showed a normal hæmogram and urine analysis. **1908** *Practitioner* Feb. 226 (*heading*) Piroplasmosis, hæmogregarines and Leishman-Donovan body. **1961** C. H. Pope *Giant Snakes* (1962) 189 No one knows just what hæmogregarines do to their reptile hosts. This technical name for such parasites derives from the fact that they live in red blood cells. **1900** Dorland *Med. Dict.* 296/1 Hemopoiesis. **1948** *Amer. Jrnl. Med. Sci.* CCXV. 411/1 We have noted that a number of chemical substances stimulated hemopoiesis in persons with Addisonian pernicious anemia...One of these, thymine.., is a pyrimidine base. **1964** D. Nichols in *Oceanogr. & Marine Biol.* II. 398 Most of the vessels are composed of large, loosely-packed connective tissue cells with scattered regions of haemopoiesis. **1947** *Radiology* XLIX. 291/2 These studies indicate a sensitivity of the hemopoietic system of man. **1956** *Nature* 10 Mar. 452/1 Adult mice irradiated with an expectedly lethal dose of X-rays could recover if grafted or injected with hæmopoietic tissue from a normal mouse. **1926** *Chem. Abstr.* XX. 1839 Hemopoëtin, a substance which appears in the serum of organisms exposed to reduced pressure and has a marked stimulating effect on the bone marrow resulting in increased regenerative capacity of the blood. **1932** Wilkinson & Klein in *Lancet* 2 Apr. 721/1 Hæmopoietin may be identified with or allied to Castle's 'intrinsic factor' of normal human gastric juice. *Ibid.* 721/2 This 'enzyme' acting on the proteins in a normal diet may produce a substance which is stored as the active principle in liver until it is required for haemopoietic regeneration... It is proposed temporarily to term this substance in hog's stomach 'haemopoietin'. **1960** *Blood* XVI. 1407 Up to the present the only reproducible sources of hemopoietine are plasma and urine of animals made severely hypoxic. **1970** Krantz & Jacobson *Erythropoietin* i. 4 The plasma factor that increased erythropoiesis had been termed hemopoietine by Carnot and Deflandre; however, as work proceeded, it appeared to be involved exclusively in red cell production.., and erythropoietin became the adopted name. **1896** F. W. Mott in T. C. Allbutt *Syst. Med.* I. i. 196 When blood corpuscles undergo destruction, as in large extravasations of blood, two substances may be formed—(*a*) *Haemosiderin* and (*b*) *Haematoidin*...Haemosiderin may also be found in the renal epithelium. **1964** S. Duke-Elder *Parsons' Dis. Eye* (ed. 14), xvi. 221 A brownish ring, probably due to hæmosiderin, may form in the epithelium encircling the cone (Fleischer's ring). **1972** Balcerzak & Wheby in C. E. Mengel et al. *Hematol.* ii. 41 At physiologic levels of tissue iron, slightly more ferretin iron is present than hemosiderin iron. Hemosiderin predominates when excess iron develops. **1909** *Cent. Dict.* Suppl., Hemosiderosis. **1942** M. M. Wintrobe *Clin. Hematol.* x. 435 Enlargement of the liver with hemosiderosis has been noted in a number of instances [of acute hemolytic anemia]. **1963** H. Burn *Drugs, Med. & Man* (ed. 2) xvi. 159 Among the Bantu in Africa, who use cooking utensils of iron, some of the iron of the pan gets into the food, so that the intake of iron is very high. The absorption of iron continues, and the amount of iron in the liver and other tissues becomes very large. The condition is known as haemosiderosis. **1971** Leavell & Thorup *Fund. Clin. Hematol.* (ed. 3) v. 149 Post-transfusional hemosiderosis is an important development in some patients with chronic bone marrow failure or hemolytic anemia who require frequent blood transfusions. Usually the iron is stored in the reticuloendothelial cells. **1843** *Maryland Med. & Surg. Jrnl.* III. 265 (*heading*) On hæmostasis, and the physical phenomenon of circulation. **1848** Dunglison *Med. Lex.* (ed. 7) 411/1 Hæmostasis. **1907** *Practitioner* Aug. 302 Simple serum contains all the coagulating ferments necessary for haemostasis. **1914** *Brit. Med. Jrnl.* 4 July 8/2 (*heading*) Note on haemostasis by application of living tissue. *Ibid.*, I found that a muscle haemostasis would resist as much as 60 to 80 mm. Hg blood pressure. **1962** *Lancet* 27 Jan. 177/1 It is interesting to speculate whether the control could be so low that defective hæmostasis would result despite a normal total prothrombin content. **1900** Dorland *Med. Dict.* 296/2 *Hemostat*, a proprietary remedy for nose-bleed, containing tannin, quinin sulphate, lard, and benzoic acid: used externally. **1904** F. P. Foster *Appleton's Med. Dict.* 1033/2 *Hæmostat*. 1. A hæmostatic forceps or other appliance. **1929** F. A. Pottle *Stretchers* (1930) 110 The assistant mops it up with a gauze sponge, discovers the point where the blood vessel is severed, and the surgeon clips it with a haemostat, another variety of pincers with handles like manicure scissors. **1969** Troup & Schwartz in S. I. Schwartz *Princ. Surg.* iii. 106/1 The finger has the advantage of being the least traumatic vascular hemostat.

hæmoglobin. In def. for 'a solid substance.. globulin' read 'a protein which is resolvable into hæm and globin'. Add later examples. Also *attrib.* and *Comb.*

1907 *Yesterday's Shopping* (1969) 510/1 Hæmoglobin Tablets. **1950** *Sci. News* XV. 96 But these lake-dwelling *Daphnia*, if deprived of abundant oxygen in the laboratory, also become pink with newly-formed hæmoglobin in their blood. Thus they have the capacity of hæmoglobin synthesis when stimulated by lack of oxygen, although they do not profit by this gift in nature. *Ibid.* 103 Hæmoglobin is unusual among proteins in having a coloured part of its molecule, a coloured part with characteristic absorption bands in its spectrum which can be measured. **1956** *Nature* 17 Mar. 524/1 There was a drop in the hæmoglobin-level from 81 to 70 per cent when tested by the Sahli method. **1956** *New Biol.* XXI. 55 Sickle-cell haemoglobin is the best known of the abnormal haemoglobins in man, but several other types can be distinguished by electrophoretic and solubility tests. These are known as haemoglobin types C, D, E, G, H, I, J, K, and M. **1957** *Ibid.* XXIV. 61 The mean of the twenty values on the scale gives the 'haemoglobin index' of the population. **1963** R. P. Dales *Annelids* iv. 81 Haemoglobin-containing corpuscles are distributed in the coelomic fluid. **1964** G. H. Haggis et al. *Introd. Molecular Biol.* v. 115 In the red blood cell it is the only structure observed between the haemoglobin-laden cytoplasm and the blood plasma. **1968** H. Harris *Nucleus & Cytoplasm* vi. 118 The failure of high concentrations of actinomycin D to inhibit decisive events in the differentiation of colonial myxamoebae, of pancreatic cells in the mouse embryo, and of haemoglobin-forming cells in the chick embryo. **1968** *Times* 17 May (*heading*) Structure of hæmoglobin solved.

Hence **hæmoglobinometry** (later example); **hæːmoglobino·pathy**, any condition in which the quality of the hæmoglobin in the blood is defective.

1961 *B.S.I. News* Dec. 27 (*heading*) Sealed glass cells for photometric hæmoglobinometry. **1957** A. W. Woodruff et al. in *Brit. Med. Jrnl.* 25 May 1235/1 (*heading*) Terminology of the hereditary haemoglobinopathies with haemoglobin variants. *Ibid.* 1235/2 The term haemoglobinopathy should be used to denote a condition in which the production of normal adult haemoglobin..is partly or wholly suppressed and it is partly or wholly replaced by one or more haemoglobin variants. **1962** *Lancet* 12 May 1006/2 As the hæmoglobinopathies grow in importance, a monograph taking stock of what we know of thalassæmia is welcome. **1966** *Ibid.* 31 Dec. 1435/1 The situation with respect to diabetes reminds one of attempts to analyse the hæmoglobinopathies before chemical techniques were available for the identification of hæmoglobins to discriminate between possible genotypes.

hæmolymph. (Later examples.)

1964 O. Kinne in *Oceanogr. & Marine Biol.* II. 302 Autoradiographs of *Asellus aquaticus* indicate that some 20 to 30% of the total body Na is located outside the haemolymph. **1968** H. Harris *Nucleus & Cytoplasm* iv. 79 Some authors believe that the proteins of the salivary secretion are not synthesized in the gland, but are simply extracted from the haemolymph.

hæmolysis, hem- (hīmǫ·lisis). *Med.* [f. Hæmo- + *-lysis.] The dissolution or lysis of red blood cells with the consequent liberation of their hæmoglobin.

1890 F. Taylor *Man. Pract. Med.* 663 The immediate cause of the anæmia is the destruction of red corpuscles in the blood (hæmolysis). **1892** Osler *Princ. Med.* 725 Increased hæmolysis and dissolution of the hæmoglobin in the blood-serum. **1901** *Jrnl. Chem. Soc.* LXXX. II. 325 Hæmolysis produced by Solanine. **1906** *Practitioner* Nov. 591 The jaundice of the newly born..is dependent upon changes, probably toxic in character, with excessive hæmolysis. **1947** *Radiology* XLIX. 307/2 Increased red

cell hemolysis is indicated by elevated excretion of fecal urobilinogen and urinary bilirubin. **1966** *Lancet* 24 Dec. 1382/1 Pyridium also causes hæmolysis.

Hence **hæmo·lysate**, any preparation obtained from hæmolysed blood; **hæ·molyse, -lyze** *v. trans.*, to lyse (red blood cells); also *intr.* (of red blood cells or a preparation of them) to undergo hæmolysis; **hæ·molysed, -lyzed, hæmoly·sing, -ly·zing** *ppl. adjs.*; **hæmolysin** (hīmǫ·lisin, hīmolǝi·sin) [see *LYSIN], any substance which causes hæmolysis; **hæmolytic** *a.* (in Dict. s.v. HÆMO-) (examples); **hæmoly·tically** *adv.*

1893 *Funk's Stand. Dict.*, Hemolytic. **1897** *Allbutt's Syst. Med.* II. 1044 Pointing to a hæmolytic as well as a simple hæmorrhagic origin for the anæmia. **1900** *Proc. Roy. Soc. Med.* LXVI. 435 Certain blood poisons, viz., the hæmolysines,..exercise a solvent action only on such red blood corpuscles as are able to unite chemically with them. **1901** *Lancet* 14 Dec. 166/31 Since the discovery of tetanolysin by Ehrlich a series of hæmolysins have been described. **1901** *Trans. Path. Soc. London* LXII. 212 A substance is present in the serum which dissolves or hæmolyses the blood-corpuscles of the rabbit *in vitro*. *Ibid.*, In general every serum that acts hæmolytically on a number of different kinds of erythrocytes possesses a corresponding number of immune bodies and of complements. **1902** *Jrnl. Chem. Soc.* LXXXII. II. 464 Hæmolysin of Bacillus Megatherium...In cultures of *B. megatherium* a specific lysin occurs which hæmolyses the corpuscles of guinea-pig, monkey, and man. **1903** *Ibid.* LXXXIV. II. 443 Influence of Cold on the Action of some Hæmolytic Agents. **1908** *Practitioner* Feb. 249 To yield substances which have similar hæmolysing properties to the hæmolytic agent found in tape-worms. **1911** *Jrnl. Amer. Med. Assoc.* 23 Dec. 2059/2 The amboceptor should be used in twice the strength sufficient to hemolyze the corpuscles in from fifteen to twenty minutes. *Ibid.*, The delay in hemolysis with tuberculous serums is striking in contrast to the promptness with which the controls hemolyze. **1916** *Jrnl. Immunol.* I. 37 The hemolyzed cells do not give up an effective hemolysin. **1920** *Nature* 13 May 347/2 The anti-coagulating and hæmolysing action of sodium nucleinate. **1946** *Ibid.* 24 Aug. 269/2 It was found possible to rear first instar bugs to the adult stage by feeding them on defibrinated hæmolysed blood through a mouse skin membrane. **1952** *Q. Jrnl. Exper. Physiol.* XXXVII. 163 The methaemoglobin (MHb) formation which occurs spontaneously in haemolysates of red blood cells occurs much faster when these have been treated so as to remove the posthaemolytic residue. **1957** *Times* 3 Sept. 15/4 Dr. Coombs, whose laboratory test for the diagnosis of haemolytic disease of the new-born infant is in worldwide use. **1962** *Lancet* 8 Dec. 1184/2 The hæmolysate of unfractionated whole-blood cells obtained from the same subject was diluted in the same way. **1967** *Jrnl. Gen. Microbiol.* XLVII. 153 Two haemolysins may be produced by *Escherichia coli*. **1968** *Sci. Jrnl.* Nov. 65/2 The cells are completely disrupted—haemolysed. *Ibid.* 65/3 The cells will haemolyse when subsequently exposed to some mild form of stress. **1972** *Science* 2 June 1030/2 After 72 hours, the tissue culture media were removed and assayed for hemolytically active C4 and C2.

hæmophilia. Add: **hæmophiliac** (-fi·liæ̆k) *a.*, affected with hæmophilia; also as *sb.*, a person so affected; **hæmophilic,** also as *sb.*, a hæmophiliac.

1896 *Lancet* 18 Jan. 153/2 An arrest of severe hæmophiliac bleeding from the gums was obtained by an application of calcium phosphate. **1897** *Boston Med. & Surg. Jrnl.* 11 Mar. 227/1 In hemophiliacs, leeching, extraction of the teeth and circumcision are very hazardous operations. **1897** *Lippincott's Med. Dict.* 454/1 *Hæmophilic*... 2. A person affected with hæmophilia. **1935** WHITBY & BRITTON *Disorders of Blood* xiv. 272 On Mendelian principles a female may be a true hæmophilic if she is the daughter of a hæmophilia-transmitting woman and a hæmophilic male. **1936** *Discovery* Dec. 388/2 A preparation from egg-white, which reduces the clotting time of blood, provides new hope for haemophiliacs. **1938** *New Statesman* 2 July 7/2 Between thirty-five and seventy haemophilics are alive in Greater London to-day. **1946** *Nature* 28 Sept. 447/1 We have been able to study the effect, in some hæmophiliac patients, of a product containing 82 per cent fibrinogen. **1962** *Lancet* 27 Jan. 194/1 A pharmacist who is a hæmophiliac had noted that by taking hesperidin chalcone (a flavonoid) he could ward off hæmorrhagic episodes. **1966** DUNLOP & ALSTEAD *Textbk. Med. Treatm.* (ed. 10) 496 In centres with suitable facilities, a supply of this plasma specifically for use in hæmophilics serves a useful purpose. **1967** M. M. WINTROBE *Clin. Hematol.* (ed. 6) xviii. 937/1 Karyotype analysis has been carried out in several of the hemophiliac women and only in 2 instances has the karyotype been abnormal.

hæmorrhoid[1], **hemorrhoid.** Add: Hence **hæ:morrhoide·ctomy**, the surgical removal of hæmorrhoids.

1917 V. C. DAVID in *Surg. Clinics Chicago* I. 543 (*title*) Local anesthesia for hemorrhoidectomy. *Ibid.* 552 Infiltration anesthesia with novocain offers a safe and technically simple method for hemorrhoidectomy. **1949** M. LOWRY *Let.* Oct. (1967) 182 I'm glad you're better now after your operation—the combination of a haemorrhoidectomy with a Catholic institution sounds sadistic. **1967** S. TAYLOR et al. *Short Textbk. Surg.* xxiii. 319 In third degree piles.., haemorrhoidectomy is indicated.

hæmostatic. A. *adj.* (Earlier example.)

1834 *Lancet* 8 Mar. 889/2, I have resolved upon giving such a view of it [*sc.* torsion of arteries] as will connect it with the other hæmostatic processes now in use in surgury.

haenapod, var. *HANEPOOT.

haeremai (hā·ǝrǝmāi, *anglicized* hǝiǝ·rėmǝi). *New Zealand.* Also **haere mai, haire mai, horomai.** [Maori, lit. = come hither.] A Maori term of welcome.

1769 J. BANKS *Jrnl.* 12 Nov. (1962) I. 432 As soon as they [*sc.* the Maoris] came near enough they wav'd and calld *horomai* and set down in the bushes near the beach (a sure mark of their good intentions). **1832** H. WILLIAMS *Jrnl.* in H. Carleton *Life* (1874) I. 112 They were very glad to see us, and gave us the usual welcome, '*haere mai!! haere mai!!*' **1845** E. J. WAKEFIELD *Adv. N.Z.* I. 249 No shouts of *haeremai*, so universal a welcome to the stranger, were to be heard. **1883** F. S. RENWICK *Betrayed* 34 (Morris), Haire mai ho! 'tis the welcome song Rings far on the summer air. **1938** R. D. FINLAYSON *Brown Man's Burden* 9 As the visitors splashed across the ford, that time-honoured cry of welcome broke from every throat. 'Haere mai!' **1943** N. MARSH *Colour Scheme* iii. 55 The Maori people..would like me to greet him with a cordial *haeremai*.

‖ **haff** (hæf). [G., f. (M)LG. *haf* sea, corresp. to ON. *haf*, OE. *hæf* sea.] A shallow fresh-water lagoon found at a river mouth, esp. one of those on the Baltic coast.

1859 S. O. BEETON *Dict. Univ. Information* 582/2 *Haff, haf*, an extensive bay or gulf of Pomerania... 2. Of East Prussia... 3. A very extensive bay of the Baltic. **1875** *Encycl. Brit.* III. 294/1 The shore of the Baltic is generally low. Along the southern coast it is for the most part sandy...Where streams come down, there are often fresh-water lakes termed *haffs*, which are separated from the sea by narrow spits called *nehrungs*. **1879** *Ibid.* X. 447/1 The 'haffs' or lagoons on the Baltic. **1933** *Discovery* June 203/1 He writes from experience of fishing in general—on Exmoor, in a Prussian haff, in Cornwall, on Scottish waters, and in Ireland.

haffle (hæ·f'l), *v. dial.* [cf. Du. (local) *haffelen* (of a suckling baby) to pull and push at the breast; (of women) to talk a lot, argue.] *intr.* To speak in a hesitant or stammering manner; to prevaricate, shilly-shally. Cf. *CAFFLE *v.*

1790 GROSE *Provincial Gloss.* (ed. 2) *Haffle*, to prevaricate. **1825** J. T. BROCKETT *Gloss. N. Country Words* 88 *Haffle*, to waver, to speak unintelligibly. **1869** R. B. PEACOCK *Gloss. Lonsdale* 39/1 *Haffle*, to stammer, to prevaricate, to falter. **1902** in *E.D.D.* s.v., [Nottingham] The doctor, he haffled and caffled, he didn't rightly know what war wrong wi' her himself. **1913** [see *CAFFLE *v.*]. **1913** D. H. LAWRENCE *Let.* 3 Mar. (1962) I. 191 The Nottingham people are still haffling and caffling about the children.

hafiz (hā·fiz). Also 7 **hafis,** 9 **hafeez.** [Pers., f. Arab. *ḥāfiẓ* watch, guard.] A Muslim who knows the Koran by heart.

1662 J. DAVIES tr. *Olearius' Voy. Ambass.* 314 [The] Turbants..of their Priests, and particularly, of the Hafis, are white. **1819** T. HOPE *Anastasius* (1820) I. x. 192 Who, to obtain the epithet of hafeez, had learnt his whole koran by heart unto the last stop. **1927** *Blackw. Mag.* May 574/2 A hafiz chanted the Koran for the rest of her soul. **1965** *Encycl. Islam* (new ed.) III. 55/2 Ḥāfiẓ..no doubt in youth..earned the right to use the title *ḥāfiẓ* (Ḳur'ān-memorizer), which became his pen-name.

hafnium (hæ·fniǝ̆m). *Chem.* [f. *Hafnia* (f. Da. *Havn* harbour (see HAVEN *sb.*), orig. name of Copenhagen (Da. *København*)), mod.L. name of Copenhagen: see -IUM.] A metallic element with a silver lustre usually found associated with zirconium, which it closely resembles chemically, and used in nuclear reactor control rods. Symbol Hf; atomic number 72. Earlier called *CELTIUM.

1923 COSTER & HEVESY in *Nature* 20 Jan. 79/2 For the new element we propose the name Hafnium (Hafniae = Copenhagen). **1955** *Sci. Amer.* Oct. 35 In its ores zirconium is invariably accompanied by hafnium, which absorbs neutrons all too readily. **1957** *Bull. Amer. Physical Soc.* II. 269/1 Hafnium's thermionic efficiency in terms of grams evaporated per unit electron emission is slightly greater than that of Th metal. **1967** W. H. KOHL *Handbk. Materials & Techniques for Vacuum Devices* xii. 329/2 The high neutron absorption of hafnium, its excellent corrosion resistance in high-temperature water, and its adequate strength at reactor operation temperatures make this metal suited as a control material.

hafod (ha·vǫd). [W., = summer dwelling.] In Wales = SHIEL.

[**1781** T. PENNANT *Tour in Wales* II. 161 This mountainous tract scarcely yields any corn. Its produce is cattle and sheep, which, during summer, keep very high in the mountains, followed by their owners,..who reside.. in *Havodtys*, or summer dairy-houses.] **1952** *Proc. Prehist. Soc.* XVIII. 74 The evidence therefore points to summer pastures, the older pound being used as a corral for cattle, while the lowland farmer set up his hafod within or just outside the wall. **1958** *Rep. R. Comm. Common Land* 274 in *Parl. Papers 1957–8* (Cmnd. 462) X. 1 *Hafod*,..the upland pastures in Wales to which transhumance took place in the summer months. **1963** *Times* 19 Apr. 6/1 Reminiscent of the earliest dwellings in Wales, the 'hafod' or summer home in the mountains, these will be available this season at a peak rental of 12 guineas a week.

haft, *sb.*[1] Add: **1. c.** *Bot.* Of an iris: the narrow part, or claw, at the base of the petal.

1924 W. R. DYKES *Handbk. Garden Irises* i. 1 An Iris flower consists usually of three outer segments called falls and of three inner segments called standards...The lower part of both the falls and the standards is usually called the haft. **1948** G. ANLEY *Irises* 113 *Haft*, the narrowed portion at the base of a perianth segment.

haft, *sb.*[2] **2.** See also *HEFT *sb.*[3]

hafta (hæ·ftă), repr. colloq. pronunc. of *have to* (see HAVE *v.* 7 c). Chiefly *N. Amer.*

1941 B. SCHULBERG *What makes Sammy Run?* v. 80 That's a honey... I'll hafta remember that one. **1945** A. KOBER *Parm Me* 58, I see...You don't hafta explain. **1952** E. WILSON *Equations of Love* 275 'I don't *haf*ta marry the Aldridge girls,' he said urgently. **1968** N. BENCHLEY *Welcome to Xanadu* vi. 133 You'll hafta carry him.

haftara, haftarot(h): see *HAPHTARAH.

hag, *sb.*[1] Add: **6.** *hag-like*, also adj.

1824 J. MORIER *Adv. Hajji Baba* I. xiii. 148 There was also..an old woman of a hag-like and decrepit appearance.

Haganah (hāgānā·). Also **Hagana.** [ad. Heb. *hᵃgannāh* defence.] A group of Jewish settlers in Palestine who, as an underground defence force, played a leading part in the creation of the state of Israel in 1948.

1923 *Daily Mail* 29 Jan. 6 He knows more about the 'Haganah', the Zionist Self-Defence force, than the authorities in Palestine like. **1949** KOESTLER *Promise & Fulfilment* 96 Specially picked anti-terrorist Haganah squads. **1960** *Guardian* 26 Aug. 5/3 The Hagana was transformed from an underground guerilla force into a regular army. **1973** *Jewish Chron.* 19 Jan. 12/4 The Haganah (Jewish self-defence) movement..ultimately became Israel's army.

hagden, hagdown. Add: Also **hagdel, hagdon.**

1832 W. D. WILLIAMSON *Hist. State Maine* I. 150 The Hagdel [is] of a dark brown colour, about as large as a Murr, though its feathers are longer. **1954** FISHER & LOCKLEY *Sea-Birds* i. 26 The Tristan great shearwater also probably reaches its greatest abundance on the North American coast,..where it is known as the 'hagdon'. **1959** BANNERMAN *Birds Brit. Isles* VIII. 141 Wynne-Edwards reminds us that it [*sc.* the sooty shearwater] is known to the fishermen as the hagdown or black hagdon.

hagfish, hag-fish. (In Dict. s.v. HAG *sb.*[1] 5.) Add later examples.

1931 J. R. NORMAN *Hist. Fishes* iii. 41 The related Hagfish (*Myxine*) possesses still more singular habits, and bores right into the fishes it attacks. **1967** *Oceanogr. & Marine Biol.* V. 291 Aqua-lung diving is beginning to provide exact data about the natural habitats of such animals, for example, the hagfish, *Myxine glutinosa*. **1968** *Times* 19 Dec. 4/8 Lampreys, like hagfish, are surviving members of the jawless fishes, the first group of vertebrates to evolve.

haggadah. Add: **2.** The Jewish ritual for the first two nights of the Passover. Also the book containing the text of the service.

1733 tr. *B. Picart's Ceremonies & Relig. Customs* I. 61 Then each of them holding a Glass of Wine in his Hand, says the Hagada. [**1887** JACOBS & WOLF *Catal. Anglo-Jew. Hist. Exhib.* 194 Haggadah Pesach, or Liturgy of the Passover.] **1891** M. FRIEDLANDER *Jewish Relig.* II. iv. 379 The first two evenings of Passover are..called '*seder*-evenings', and the book which contains this Service is generally called *Haggadah*. **1896** W. H. GREENBURG *Haggadah* 6 Upon the first cup one says the benediction... Upon the second cup one recites the Haggada. **1904** *Daily Chron.* 30 Mar. 7/5 Perhaps the whole genius of the celebration of the Passover may be summed up in the words of the Hagadah: 'In every generation each Israelite shall bethink himself as though he had been delivered from Egypt.' **1904** *Jewish Encycl.* VI. 142/2 The opinion of Friedmann..that special books containing the Passover service existed in Talmudic times, is based on a judgment of Raba in favor of a man who claimed a Haggadah..from an estate under the plea that he had lent it to the deceased. **1922** JOYCE *Ulysses* 708 An ancient hagadah book. **1972** *Publishers Weekly* 7 Feb. 16 (Advt.), We have created what we feel is the most unusual Haggadah for Passover 1972... A functional Haggadah with the complete Passover Seder service in both English and Hebrew.

haggadically (hægæ·dikăli), *adv.* [f. HAGGADICAL *a.* + -LY[2].] As in the haggadah.

1920 OESTERLEY & BOX *Lit. Rabbinical Judaism* 78 The Scriptural lesson..is haggadically developed.

haggis. Add: **1. d.** A mixture, hodge-podge; a mess.

1899 *Daily News* 13 Sept. 7/6 They cheerfully go through the curious haggis of social and philanthropic duties served up to them each week. **1928** W. A. J. ARCHBOLD (*title*) Bengal haggis. **1929** H. MARWICK *Orkney Norn* 66/1 He'll just mak a haggis o' the job.

haggy, *a.*[1] [f. HAG *sb.*[1] + -Y[1].] Of or pertaining to a hag.

The sense of quot. 1654 is uncertain: it may belong to HAG *sb.*[1] 1 or 2.

1654 M. STEVENSON *Occasions Off-spring* 83 Didst

thou devise This haggy look, to be thought weather wise? **1964** S. BELLOW *Herzog* (1965) 159 That bitch, Madeleine, whose face looks either beautiful or haggy.

haggy, *a.*[2] Chiefly *Sc.* [f. HAG *sb.*[4] + -Y[1].] Boggy and full of holes.

1794 *Scots Mag.* Oct. 624/1 The night was neither warm not [*sic*] dry, The road was rough and haggy. **1881** D. THOMSON *Musings among Heather* 62 He thocht he had yet tae cross, A haggy, benty, splashy moss. **1959** D. D. C. P. MOULD *Peter's Boat* vii. 113 This country of bare peat cut with haggy trenches.

haham (hā·hăm). Also **hakam;** *Yiddish* **chochem** (khō̜·khĕm), **cacham, chacham, -em.** [ad. Heb. *ḥākām* wise, wise man.] One learned in Jewish law; a wise man, savant; *spec.* a Jewish rabbi among Sephardic Jews.

1676 L. ADDISON *Present State of Jews* (ed. 2) xxvi. 216 In the first rank march the Chachams or Priests. **1733** tr. *B. Picart's Ceremonies & Relig. Customs* I. 46 A Man who hath made the Oral Law his principal Study, he is looked upon by the Generality amongst them as a Doctor, and is therefore called Cacham, or Wise Man. **1892** I. ZANGWILL *Childr. Ghetto* II. xix. 103 The *Gemorah* says ve muz be vise, *chocham.* **1894** —— *King of Schnorrers* 106 The Haham himself, the Sage or Chief Rabbi of the [Sephardic] congregation. **1901** *Daily Chron.* 23 Nov. 3/2 The vice-presidents include...Mrs. Gaster, wife of the Haham—the spiritual head of the Spanish and Portuguese [Jewish] congregation. **1960** *Jewish Chron.* 8 Apr. 16/1 The Haham or such other person as may for the time being constitute the Ecclesiastical Authority of the Spanish and Portuguese Jews of Great Britain. **1967** D. T. KAUFFMAN *Dict. Relig. Terms* 221/2 *Hakam,* wise one. Chief rabbi in sephardim communities, and among Palestinian Jews in talmudic times. **1968** L. ROSTEN *Joys of Yiddish* 63 A proud young *chachem* told his grandmother that he was going to become a doctor of philosophy. **1973** *Jewish Chron.* 18 May 8/3 The memorial service was organised by the Haham.

hahnium (hā·niə̆m). *Chem.* [f. the name of Otto *Hahn* (1879–1968), German radiochemist + -IUM.] An artificially produced radioactive element, atomic number 105. Symbol Ha.

1970 A. GHIORSO et al. in *Physical Rev. Let.* XXIV. 1503/1 In honor of the late Otto Hahn we respectfully suggest that this new element be given the name hahnium. **1971** *Nature* 26 Feb. 607/2 The present multi-detector shuttle apparatus is quite a complicated instrument.. and its value as a research tool has been proved by the quality of the nuclear spectroscopic data obtained for.. hahnium.

Haida (hai·dă), *a.* and *sb.* Also **Haidah, Hydah.** [Native word meaning 'people'.] **A.** *adj.* Of or pertaining to a North American Indian people living on the Queen Charlotte Islands, British Columbia, and on Prince of Wales Island, Alaska. **B.** *sb.* **a.** A member of this people; also in collective sense. **b.** The language of this people.

1841 *Jrnl. R. Geogr. Soc.* XI. 219 The *Haidah* tribes of the Northern Family inhabit Queen Charlotte's Island. *Ibid.*, Since the sea-otter has been destroyed, the Haidahs have become poor. **1862** F. POOLE *Diary* 5 Aug. in *Queen Charlotte Islands* (1871) vi. 73 Two Hydah chiefs and four of their women. *Ibid.* 75 He reciprocated by initiating me into the mysteries of the Hydah tongue. **1869** *Mainland Guardian* (New Westminster, B.C.) 30 Oct. 3/2 We bought a large Hydah canoe for $50, and hired ten siwashes (nine Hydahs and one bog-will Indian), for $10 a month. **1890** J. G. FRAZER *Golden Bough* I. i. 26 When a Haida Indian wishes to obtain a fair wind, he..shoots a raven. **1914** W. H. RIVERS *Kinship & Soc. Organisation* ii. 54 The only people among whom it has been recorded are the Haidahs of Queen Charlotte Island. **1921** E. SAPIR *Lang.* iii. 56 Haida, the Indian language spoken in the Queen Charlotte Islands. **1959** E. TUNIS *Indians* 136/1 In the north the Tlingit and the Haida were related to the Dené. *Ibid.* 136/2 A Haida house. **1969** *Times* 22 Sept. 14/2 A Haida amulet from the Queen Charlotte Islands has a bilaterally symmetrical design.

haikal (hai·kăl). [Coptic.] The central chapel of three forming the sanctuary of a Coptic church. Also *attrib.* in **haikal screen,** a screen, often elaborately carved or decorated, which separates the haikal from the body of the church.

1884 A. J. BUTLER *Anc. Coptic Churches* I. i. 28 The screen of the haikal, instead of aligning with that of the side chapels, projects out three or four feet into the choir. **1902** *Encycl. Brit.* XXVII. 238/1 The central division is called the haikal or sanctuary...Haikal screen and choir screen are often sumptuously carved and inlaid. **1935** D. ATTWATER *Catholic Eastern Churches* vi. 139 A church of the Coptic rite has a distinctive arrangement... Within the triple-domed sanctuary (*haikal*) are three altars... On the *haikal*-screen are a few pictures. **1961** O. MEINARDUS *Monks & Monasteries Egyptian Deserts* 302 Part of the haikal screen of the old church can still be seen.

‖ **haiku** (hai·ku). Also **haikai, hokku.** [Jap.] A form of Japanese verse, developed in the mid-16th century, usually consisting of 17 syllables and originally of jesting character; an English imitation of one.

The *hokku* was originally the opening hemistich of a linked series of *haiku* poems, but is now synonymous with *haiku* and *haikai*. An earlier meaning of *haikai*, an abbreviation of the phr. *haikai no renga* ('jesting linked-verse'), was a succession of *haiku* linked together to form one poem.

1899 W. G. ASTON *Hist. Jap. Lit.* iv. 289 In the sixteenth century a kind of poem known as Haikai, which consists of seventeen syllables only, made its appearance. **1899** *Trans. Asiatic Soc. Japan* XXVII. IV. p. xiv, The *hokku* must be an exceedingly compact bit of word and thought skill to be worth anything—as literature. **1902** *Ibid.* XXX. II. 243 The poets of Japan have produced thousands of these microscopic compositions...Their native name is *Hokku* (also *Haiku* and *Haikai*), which, in default of a better equivalent, I venture to translate by 'Epigram', using that term..as denoting any little piece of verse that expresses a delicate or ingenious thought. **1904** *Westm. Gaz.* 19 Apr. 10/1 The perfect haikai is a Lilliputian lyric of but three unrhymed lines of five, seven, and five syllables respectively—seventeen in all—in which is deftly caught a thought-flash or swift impression...An example..is the following: The west wind whispered And touched the eyelids of Spring: Her eyes, Primroses. **1957** C. BROOKE-ROSE *Lang. Love* 47 Her translations of *haiku* were elegant. **1969** *Radio Times* 15 May 9/1 A sequence of twenty-one sonnets and two haiku on the first American landing in Japan in the mid-nineteenth century.

Haileybury (hē̆i·libə̆ri). The name of a school (Haileybury College) in Hertfordshire, orig. owned by the East India Company, used to designate the system of providing civil servants, or the civil servants themselves, for service in India.

1864 in F. C. Danvers et al. *Mem. Old Haileybury Coll.* (1894) 95, I trust the new men will be found to furnish persons qualified to sustain the character of the Service.. [and] also worthily to fill those high posts of trust.. which we now see so happily filled by Haileybury civilians of the old school. **1902** *Encycl. Brit.* XXIX. 451/2 Towards the latter years of the 19th century the last of the old Haileybury civilians, who entered the service as nominees of the East India Company's directors under the system abolished in 1857, were leaving India. **1931** L. S. S. O'MALLEY *Ind. Civil Service* 241 A system of pass examinations, such as the Haileybury entrance examination. **1931** *Times Lit. Suppl.* 18 June 474/3 The modern Civilian is the descendant of the Haileybury students of the early nineteenth century. Whatever the merits or demerits of the Haileybury system, it at least 'led to a tradition of service handed down from generation to generation'.

hair, *sb.* Add: **8. b.** *in one's hair*: (*c*) being a nuisance or encumbrance, in one's way; usu. with *get* and *have*; so *out of one's hair*: out of one's way, not encumbering (see sense 8 r below). orig. *U.S.*

1851 *Oregon Statesman* (Oregon City) 30 Sept. 1/2, I shall depend on your honor..that you won't tell on me, cause if you did, I should have Hetty Gawkins in my hair in no time. **1880** 'MARK TWAIN' *Tramp Abroad* I. xx. 193 What you learn here, you've got to know..or else you'll have one of these..spectacled..old professors in your hair. **1935** S. LEWIS *It can't happen Here* xiii. 123 Maybe there'll be a few Communist cells around here now, when Fascism begins to get into people's hair. **1936** 'J. TEY' *Shilling for Candles* x. 115 She got in my hair until I couldn't bear it another day. **1945** M. LOWRY *Let.* (1967) 49 We had them in our hair all summer. **1951** C. FRY *Sleep of Prisoners* 4 You know what Absalom Said to the tree? 'You're getting in my hair.' **1957** R. WATSON-WATT *Three Steps to Victory* 255 His endurance of a bunch of untidy civilians constantly 'in his hair'.

l. *to put up one's hair* (examples); *let down her hair*, also *fig.*; and of both men and women, *to let* (*take*) *one's* (*back*) *hair down*, to throw off reserve, to become confidential.

1662 [see PUT *v.*[1] 53 a]. **1850** G. H. LEWES in *Leader* 7 Dec. 882/3, I am well aware that a little ranting and 'letting down the back hair' would have 'told' upon the audience with more noisy effect. **1921** W. DE LA MARE *Mem. Midget* iii. 15 On my seventeenth birthday I put up my hair, and was confirmed. **1925** N. COWARD *Vortex* II. 66 Helen and I have just had a grand heart-to-heart talk; we've undone our back hair. **1933** WODEHOUSE *Heavy Weather* vii. 116 You needn't be coy, Beach...No reporters present. We can take our hair down and tell each other our right names. **1951** AUDEN *Nones* (1952) 31 To let their hair down and be frank about The world. **1959** *Listener* 15 Oct. 608/1 Mr. Fredric Warburg has reminded us of this in a volume of autobiography..in which he lets down his hair. **1967** *Guardian* 3 Jan. 2/7 Lively young thing, I recall—but she'll have put her hair up by now. **1967** C. FREMLIN *Prisoner's Base* ix. 67 After you'd gone, Mother—he really let his back hair down. I was right, you know—he *has* been in prison. **1967** B. WOOTTON *In World I never Made* i. 36 Before it became customary for women of all ages to wear their hair short, one of the marks of entering upon adult status was to put one's hair 'up'.

p. *to get* (a person) *by the short hairs* (formerly *to get* (a person, etc.) *where the hair is short*): to have complete control over.

1872 G. P. BURNHAM *Mem. U.S. Secret Service* 207 You've got me where the ha'r is short! What a cursed fool I have been. **1880** 'MARK TWAIN' *Tramp Abroad* I. xx. 184, I had to tackle this miserable language...I've got it where the hair 's short, I think. **1888** KIPLING *Wee Willie Winkie* 67 Then they'll rush in, and then we've got 'em by the short hairs! **1928** *Blackw. Mag.* Feb. 150/1 Those Chinhwan really did seem to have got the rest of the world by the short hairs. **1930** SAYERS & EUSTACE *Docts. in Case* I. 25 She's evidently got her husband by the short hairs.

q. *to make one's hair curl*: see *CURL *v.*[1] 4.

r. *out of one's hair*: opp. *in one's hair* (sense *8 b (*c*)).

1902 KIPLING in *Sat. Even. Post* 6 Dec. 2/3 Get out o' my back-hair! **1949** 'J. TEY' *Brat Farrar* x. 81 They wouldn't bother to look for him. They would be too relieved to have him out of their hair. **1959** J. MASTERS *Fandango Rock* 173 He wouldn't want to interfere with her big moment, and he'd even managed to keep Peggy out of her hair. **1967** *Boston Sunday Globe* 23 Apr. 18/2 Two vice presidents of the First Pennsylvania Banking and Trust Co., the city's largest and most respected, said the bank paid Karafin and an associate $12,000 a year 'to keep him out of our hair'. **1971** WODEHOUSE *Much Obliged, Jeeves* xvi. 177 He wanted to get Florence out of his hair without actually telling her to look elsewhere for a mate.

s. *to lose one's hair* (or *to get one's hair off*): to lose one's temper.

c **1920** D. H. LAWRENCE *Phoenix II* (1968) 120 'Nay—nay,' said Lewis testily. 'Don't get your hair off, Mrs. Goddard.' **1931** T. R. G. LYELL *Slang* 356 *To lose one's hair*, to lose one's temper. 'Last night Jones quite lost his hair and made an awful fool of himself.' **1938** E. BOWEN *Death of Heart* III. ii. 343 *This* is what one gets for being so nicely nonchalant, for saving people's faces, for not losing one's hair.

9. a. *hair-chain, -combing, craft, crêpe, -fashion, fetishism, fetishist, -shaft, -work* (examples).

1895 *Montgomery Ward Catal.* 158 Hair Chains made to order. Send us the hair and we will braid. **1907** N. MUNRO *Daft Days* xxx, The lockets are large and strong, and hair-chains much abound. **1940** G. GREENE *Power & Glory* II. iv. 178 There was a hair-slide,..and a ball of hair-combings. **1962** *John o' London's* 4 Jan. 14/1 The haircraft women..used to tour the Swedish countryside..selling their products. **1957** V. J. KEHOE *Technique Film & T.V. Make-Up* xv. 203 *Hair crepe*..may be human hair (Caucasian, Chinese or Indian), yak or a combination of any or all of these types. **1944** KOESTLER in *Horizon* Mar. 162 There are..certain typical attitudes to life including clothing, hair-fashion, drink and food. **1951** C. BERG *Unconscious Significance of Hair* vii. 65 The universality of hair fetishism may be brought into relief by this short instance of its negative aspect: A young woman patient of mine, who had become completely bald,..had an indescribable horror of her predicament being seen or.. suspected by anyone. *Ibid.* 61 The hair fetishist loves the women's hair but frequently has the impulse to despoil or 'castrate' it. **1954** KOESTLER *Invisible Writing* xxiv. 284 The hair-fetishists who loiter in tube-stations with scissors in their pockets. **1906** *Practitioner* Nov. 692 Complete removal..of the hair-shaft, together with the root-sheath or papilla. **1924** *Chambers's Jrnl.* 668/2 The process flattens the almost spherical hairshaft and causes it to lean inwards. **1790** *Columbian Centinel* 13 Oct. 36/4 The Artists' ability in Painting and Hair-Work may be seen. **1959** *Times* 7 Mar. 9/4 Hairwork jewelry was already popular in the late seventeenth century.

b. *hair appointment, -clasp, -clip, conditioner, -cream, -dye* (examples), *-grip, lotion, -oil* (earlier examples), *-ornament, preparation, -slide* (SLIDE *sb.* 6), *-spray, -tonic, -wash* (earlier and later examples).

1938 D. DU MAURIER *Rebecca* xxiv. 402 Mrs. de Winter had a hair appointment from twelve until one thirty. **1894** A. M. EARLE *Costume Colonial Times* 121 *Hair-clasps.* These ornaments for the hair—clasps to hold up the braided back hair—were advertised for sale in the New York newspapers and in the *Connecticut Courant* of January, 1791, and were worn until a simpler form of hair-dressing appeared about the year 1800. **1957** J. FRAME *Owls do Cry* 55 Hairclips have been taken from them. **1951** *Catal. Exhibits, S. Bank Exhib., Festiv. Brit.* 63/2 Hair Conditioner. **1926–7** *Army & Navy Stores Catal.* 491/1 Hair Cream, for fixing the hair. **1843** *Ainsworth's Mag.* III. 554 Invent a new hair-dye expressly to accommodate his wife. **1933** W. S. MAUGHAM *Sheppey* I. 20, I don't believe there's another man in the business could 'ave sold Mr Bolton a bottle of 'air-dye. **1896** *Woman's Life* III. 462/2 Hair-Bow (Fitted with New Safety Hair-Grip). **1938** 'J. BELL' *Port of London Murders* vi. 91 The jug..contained..half a bootlace and two rusty hair grips. **1955** *Sci. News Let.* 5 Mar. 150/3 Hair-grips and kirbi-grips are known in America as bobby pins. **1906** T. D. LISTER *Chavasse's Advice to Mother* (ed. 16) III. 370 Avoid grease, pomatum, hair lotions, and all abominations of that kind. **1962** N. MARSH *Hand in Glove* vii. 221 Mr. Period's bedroom smelt of hair lotion. **1810** E. WEETON *Let.* 25 Feb. in *Jrnl. of Governess* (1969) I. 233 A small phial of hair oil. **1853** MRS. GASKELL *Cranford* xii. 174 The delusive lady was off upon..the merits of cosmetics and hair oils in general. **1895** *Montgomery Ward Catal.* 183 Real Tortoise Shell Hair Ornaments. **1967** H. PORTER in *Coast to Coast 1965–6* 178 They were not discussing the weather or hair-ornaments. **1897** *Sears, Roebuck Catal.* 779/5 Hair Preparation. **1909** in A. Adburgham *Shops & Shopping* (1964) xiii. 273 A handsome sales-room where are sold..Hair Preparations, ..Hair nets, etc. **1895** *Army & Navy Co-op. Soc. Price List* 15 Sept. (Index), Hair Slides. **1927** *Glasgow Herald* 6 Oct. 11 Her hair-slide was found some distance from the body. **1968** J. IRONSIDE *Fashion Alphabet* 166 A hair slide..is a clip for keeping the hair in place. **1959** *Sears, Roebuck Catal.* Spring & Summer 280/4 Glow Hair Spray. **1966** *Vogue* Nov. 81 Creamy Skin Perfume..and a hair spray. **1967** W. PINE *Protectors* i. 10 He smelt the scent of her hair-spray. **1895** *Montgomery Ward Catal.* Index, Hair Tonic. **1897** Hair tonic [see TONIC *sb.* 1]. **1938** AUDEN & ISHERWOOD *On Frontier* I. i. 28 Surely he's the man who does the hair-tonic advertisements? **1869** D. G. ROSSETTI *Let.* (1965) II. 707 Certainly a hair-wash would be the unkindest cut of all to bring against

the Absalom of modern poetry. **1938** H. Nicholson *Let.* 18 May (1966) 342 My hairwash comes from Floris.

c. *hair-clipper, -curler* (examples), *-cutter* (later example), *-dryer, -remover, -straightener, -waver; hair-colouring, -conditioning, -cutting* (earlier examples), *-doing, -drying, -lifting, -straightening* vbl. sbs. and/or ppl. adjs.

1895 *Montgomery Ward Catal.* 444/1 The very best hair clipper in the market. **1930** *Daily Express* 6 Nov. 19/3 A display of the latest type of electrical hair-clippers. **1972** G. Durrell *Catch me a Colobus* iii. 58 The next thing was carefully to shave the area...This was done with an electric hair-clipper. **1959** *Punch* 3 June 752/1 Hair-colouring (modern usage for hair-dyeing) has become part of a woman's normal routine. **1966** J. S. Cox *Illustr. Dict. Hairdressing* 70/2 *Hair-conditioning*, external treatment designed to improve the condition of the hair by means of lotions, creams, massage and the application of steam to the head and hair. **1753** in E. Singleton *Social N.Y. under Georges* (1902) 176 Hair-curler and peruke-maker from London. **1872** *Rep. Comm. Patents 1870* (U.S.) II. 779/1 Hair-Curler... [A] combination, with a curling-iron tube [etc.]. **1929** *Bookman* May 270/1 A woman's steel hair curlers. **1936** *Discovery* Aug. 250/2 A long ivory rod with a pomegranate finial is probably a hair curler. **1889** *Monthly Packet* Christmas 102, I suppose—there—ain't no hair-cutters up in Heaven? **1832** *Chambers's Edin. Jrnl.* I. 60/2 The announcement 'Hair-cutting rooms' in the window. **1850** Dickens *Dav. Copp.* vii. 77 My recollectons of..canings, rulerings, hair-cuttings, rainy Sundays. **1875** C. M. Yonge *My Young Alcides* I. vii. 232 In the midst of my hair-doing.. Viola's running in to me. **1895** *Army & Navy Co-op. Soc. Price List* 15 Sept. 180/1 The Princess Patent Hair Dryer and Burnisher. **1909** *Installation News* III. 7 This Hair-Dryer works..by means of a small..electric fan. **1909** *Westm. Gaz.* 13 Oct. 7/4 One ounce of hair, which she was drawing through the hair-dryer in her hands. **1961** *Times* 26 Apr. 25/4 Domestic appliances such as..hair-driers. **1902** M. Barnes-Grundy *Thames Camp* viii. 159 You dive into the sparkling river.., forgetting all about hair-drying. **1906** *Chambers's Jrnl.* 30 June 495/2 In my lady's room may be found electrically heated curling-irons and an ingenious hair-drying machine. **1889** 'Mark Twain' *Connecticut Yankee* 354, I flung out a hair-lifting, soul-scorching thirteen-jointed insult. **1907** *Yesterday's Shopping* (1969) 532/3 Hair Remover. **1951** M. McLuhan *Mech. Bride* 60/2 Hair removers..are backed by long-standing national advertising campaigns. **1898** *Today* 5 Nov. 18/1 'The Hair Straightener Company manufactures an instrument that will at once remove the curl from the most stubborn hair. ..' It would be a waste of money..to advertise its wares in a climate like ours, where the moisture of the atmosphere does more hair straightening than is conducive to feminine happiness. **1966** J. S. Cox *Illustr. Dict. Hairdressing* 74/2 *Hair-straightener*, (1) A preparation to straighten frizzy or over-curly hair. (2) An implement that straightens frizzy hair. **1966** *B.B.C. Handbk.* 25 Could we broadcast something about a new hair straightening cream? **1892** *Queen* 27 Feb. in L. de Vries *Vict. Advts.* (1968) 42/1 Automatic hair waver and curler.. Price 2s. 6d. **1895** *Army & Navy Co-op Soc. Price List.* 15 Sept. 180/2 Hair Wavers (Patent). **1966** J. S. Cox *Illustr. Dict. Hairdressing* 75/1 *Hair-waver*, (1) An implement such as waving irons by the use of which hair can be waved. (2) Any apparatus such as a permanent waving machine which heats the hair wound on curlers during the permanent waving process. (3) A person who waves hair.

d. *hair-bottomed* adj. **e.** *hair-stripe.*

1818 Keats *Let.* 5 July (1958) I. 319 Hair bottomed chairs. **1920** *Blackw. Mag.* Aug. 161/2 They would, I understand, be described by tailors as 'fine cachemire with hair-stripe suitable for gents' morning wear'.

10. hair bag, (*a*) a bag made of hair or of very thin thread; (*b*) a bag in which human hair is kept; (*c*) (see quot. 1966); **hair-colour,** (*b*) the colour of a person's hair; **hair-cord** (examples); (*b*) a cord made of human hair; **hair crack** *Metallurgy* = *hair-line 7; **hair-cut, haircut,** (*a*) an act of cutting the hair by a hairdresser; (*b*) the shape or style in which the hair is cut; (*c*) a customer for a hair-cut; **hair-mattress,** a mattress stuffed with hair; **hair-net** (see Net *sb.*[1] 3); so **hair-netted** *a.*; **hair-pencil** (earlier and later examples); **hair-piece,** a length of false hair used to augment the natural hair; **hair-point** *Bot.*, an extension of the nerve at the top of some moss leaves, forming a fine tip; **hair-raising** *a.*, capable of causing the hair to 'stand on end' through fear or excitement; so **hair-raiser; hair-raisingly** *adv.*; **hair-restorer** (earlier example); **hair-seal** (earlier examples); **hair-slip,** a place on a green hide where the grain has decayed causing the hair to slip; so **hair-slipped** *a.*, marked with decayed places; **hair-spring,** (*b*) of a trap (perhaps Spring *sb.*[3] rather than *sb.*[1]); **hair-style,** a particular way of dressing the hair; hence **hair-styling** *vbl. sb.*; **hair-stylist; hair-tidy,** a tidy [Tidy *sb.* c] for hair-combings; **hair-trim** [Trim *sb.* 3 d]; **hair-tuft** (see quots.).

1712 Mortimer *Husb.* II. 2 Haws put in a Hair-bag, and soaked in Water all Winter..will come up the first Year. **1723** J. Nott *Cook's & Confectioner's Dict.* § 136 To make cider..stamp your Apples, press them in a Hair Bag. **1747** H. Glasse *Art of Cookery* vi. 65 Strain it through a coarse Hair-bag..then strain it through a Hair-sieve. **1824** J. Morier *Adv. Hajji Baba* xvii. 188 The different operations of rubbing with the hand, and of the friction with the hair bag. **1911** R. G. Anderson in *4th Rep. Wellcome Tropical Res. Lab.* B. 253 By Blood-brotherhood is meant a mutual coalition... The rite.. consists in incising the other's forehead..drinking the outflow of blood, smearing an adjacent lock of hair in its residue, and cutting this off to keep..in a neatly woven hair bag as a charm. **1966** J. S. Cox *Illustr. Dict. Hairdressing* 69/2 *Hair-bag*,..a bag to hold the queue of a bag-wig. **1885** J. Beddoe *Races of Brit.* xiii. 144 The division of hair-colours..into red, fair, brown, dark, and black. **1906** *Jrnl. Anthropol. Inst.* XXXVI. 325 Such statistics as those..of eye colour, hair colour, as in many anthropological works. **1972** *Woman* 22 Jan. 17 Do you know that British women spend a staggering £10 million a year on changing their hair colour? **1866** in A. Adburgham *Shops & Shopping* (1964) xii. 133, 1 White hair cord dressing jacket. **1899** T. Watts-Dunton *Aylwin* ii. 46 'This is her hair,' he said, taking the hair-cord between his fingers and kissing it. **1920** L. Harmuth *Dict. Textiles* (ed. 2), *Haircord*, English dress muslin made with thick warp cords. **1923** *Weekly Dispatch* 18 Feb. 12 (Advt.), Useful Shirt in White Haircord Voile. **1951** *Good Housek. Home Encycl.* 34/1 For a..hair cord carpet, herring-bone the raw edges on the underside. **1960** *Textile Terms & Defs.* (ed. 4) 76 *Haircord carpet*, a hair carpet produced by weaving over unbladed wires. **1896** *Trans. Inst. Naval Archit.* XXXVII. 215 A 10 in. steel shaft..had shown fine hair cracks on the surface near the propeller. **1925** *Jrnl. Iron & Steel Inst.* CXI. 113 A defect known as *snow-flakes* or *flakes* (America), *hair-cracks* or *hair-lines* (Great Britain), *Flocken* (Germany), and *cassures ligneuses* (France), has received much attention among manufacturers and inspectors of alloy steel forgings. **1959** J. H. Thornley *Foundation Design & Pract.* xiii. 103/2 The test for hair cracks consists merely of cleaning the pile and washing or immersing it in a tinted fluid. **1899** *Westm. Gaz.* 5 Dec. 8/1 The trade in Pretoria was kept very busy for about ten days giving the burghers a commando hair-cut. **1900** *Ibid.* 22 Jan. 2/3 He won mainly on his promise that he would reform the city barber into charging two dollars fifty cents for a hair-cut. **1904** *Daily Chron.* 8 Apr. 4/7 The barbers of Bethlehem, Pa., have raised the price of haircuts from sevenpence to tenpence. **1923** *Glasgow Herald* 10 Feb. 8/8 Commenting upon how few of his customers in recent days had been 'haircuts', he remarked... 'The change of the moon always brings more haircuts out.' **1924** R. Macaulay *Orphan Island* xviii. § 2. 241 They were interrupted by Mr. Albert Edward Smith, who had come for a shave and a hair-cut. **1836** in *Mass. Hist. Soc. Proc.* (1892) 2nd Ser. VII. 276 Mine an upper berth; a hair mattress to lie on. **1863** J. Nash *Brit. Pat. 2681*, I..take an ordinary wool, hair, or other mattrass, and fasten it..to the top of the spring frame. **1931** *Times* 16 Mar. 2/7 Box-springs, hair mattresses. **1865** M. Eyre *Lady's Walks* xv. 185 Quilts, mittens, hair-nets, and other articles knitted, of Pyrenean wool. **1873** *Young Englishwoman* Jan. 38/2 Hair nets..may either be worked with coloured silk or, if intended for night wear, with white cotton. **1958** C. Fremlin *Hours before Dawn* ii. 22 The wisps of untidy grey hair protruding from her hairnet. **1950** J. Cannan *Murder Included* ii. 21 Elizabeth Hudson,..high-collared, hair-netted. **1951** E. Coxhead *One Green Bottle* vi. 164 The hair-netted lady at the next table. **1763** *Gentl. Mag.* XXXIII. 83/2 Let the spots be gently rubbed with a hair pencil. **1965** *Listener* 26 Aug. 316/2 Modelling, carving and engraving, prowess with the inked hair-pencil: these complete the specifically aesthetic skills of the Chinese. **1939** *Time* 25 Dec. 2/3 He wears a toupee (hairpiece or divot in Hollywood) for cinema and most public appearances. **1957** V. J. Kehoe *Technique Film & T.V. Make-Up* vi. 78 Incidentally, a wig covers not only the hair line, but the entire area of the hair on the head, while hairpieces are used to supplement the natural hair growth. **1969** *Times* 20 Mar. 27/1 The man sitting next to you may be wearing a hairpiece. **1818** Hooker & Taylor *Muscologia Brit.* 25 *P[olytrichum] juniperinum*... Except in the want of the hair-points to the leaves..we can find no essential difference between this and the preceding species [sc. *P[olytrichum] piliferum*]. **1893** H. G. Jameson *Illustr. Guide Brit. Mosses* 10 The single nerve [of the leaf] may either cease below..or in..the apex, or may run out beyond it so as to be *excurrent*, forming a *mucro*.., *cusp*.., or *hair-point*. **1966** *Oxf. Bk. Flowerless Plants* 74/2 In the form [of *Grimmia apocarpa*] shown here the leaves are tinged reddish-brown and have white 'hair points'. **1897** *Westm. Gaz.* 16 Nov. 3/2 The writer being put on his mettle merely to throw in what an American has felicitously called 'hair-raisers' by the way. **1900** *Daily News* 24 Apr. 7/5 The hair-raising, long, steep descent of Box Hill. **1902** *Daily Chron.* 16 Sept. 3/4 Marvellous yarns of hair-raising perils. **1928** *Daily Express* 17 Aug. 9/1 There were a few hair-raising mishaps, but nobody was hurt. **1957** *Times* 30 Aug. 8/6 A runaway 70-ton Army transporter..careered downhill into the village of Carlton, Notts., to-day at 60 m.p.h. after its brakes had failed... 'It was a hair-raising experience..' said Driver Lee. **1960** *Times* 15 Feb. 15/2 England had left it hair-raisingly late, but it was enough. **1873** *Young Englishwoman* Aug. 414/1 Helena has heard 'hair restorers' so much condemned. **1824** *Pettigrew Papers Shipping & Commercial List* 31 July (D.A.E.), About 500 hair Seal Skins, ..were sold by auction. **1846** R. B. Sage *Scenes Rocky Mts.* vi. 56 A hair-seal cap and a frock-coat. **1903** L. A. Flemming *Pract. Tanning* 265 Grading and Classification of Green Calf-Skins... Second, regular No. 1. .. Scores are allowed in this grade, but there must be no holes, hair slips or other bad imperfections. *Ibid.*, Third, good No. 2. This term designates those skins that are slightly hair slipped. **1707** Mortimer *Husb.* xi. 244 With the small Stick (gently put into the hole to stop the knot of the Hair-spring,..) place it in the Earth in the Moles passage. **1854** Thoreau *Walden* 37 With consummate skill he has set his trap with a hair springe.. and then..got his own leg into it. **1913** *Vanity Fair* (N.Y.) Oct. 91/1 Mme. Fried is prepared to show all of the latest..Hair Styles. **1944** M. Laski *Love on Supertax* ix. 84 She longed for some new perfume, a new hair-style. **1963** V. Nabokov *Gift* ii. 139 He had a remarkable hair style that was also somehow indecent. **1936** *Harper's Bazaar* Mar. 88/4 They specialise particularly in 'Hair Styling', which of course means designing coiffures to fit the individual, as well as carrying them out. **1960** *Guardian* 19 Apr. 2/5 The Princess had led the world's hair-styling fashion. She had been 'an ambassadress' of British hair-styling. **1935** 'Madame Louise' *Mod. Hair Cutting & Styling* 15 A hair stylist is a hairdresser who has the artistic ability to suggest and create a new hair fashion. **1950** 'P. Quentin' *Follower* i. 6 One of her clients at Maurice's, where she worked as a hair-stylist. **1907** *Yesterday's Shopping* (1969) 1164 Silver-mounted Hair Tidy. **1918** 'K. Mansfield' *Prelude* 11 She.. found nothing except a hair-tidy with a heart painted on it. **1935** *Punch* 15 May 592/1 The whole affair of the rejection of Miss Rinse's beaded hair-tidy from our Institute Exhibition has been most unfortunate. **1960** B. Snook *Eng. Hist. Embroidery* 116 It suddenly became genteel to embroider..hair tidies, pin-cushions, spectacle and comb cases and what-nots. **1957** S. Beckett *All that Fall* 30 Hairtrims and shaves. **1905** E. Phillpotts *Secret Woman* I. ii. 21 The hair-tufts of his eyebrows had been tawny, but they were now turning. **1923** G. A. Gaskell *Dict. Sacred Lang.* 335/2 Hair tuft between the eyebrows of Buddha: An emblem of spiritual truth within the soul.

hair, *v.* Add: **4.** *trans.* To fit hairs to (a violin-bow).

1898 H. R. Haweis *Old Violins* 116 Most violinists prefer to pay a small sum and get their bows haired.

hairbrush. Add: **2.** Used (chiefly *attrib.*) of a kind of hand-grenade.

1916 J. N. Hall *Kitchener's Mob* ix. 132 Ten or a dozen varieties of bombs were in use... The 'hairbrush', the 'lemon bomb', the 'cricket ball', and the 'policeman's truncheon' were the most important of these, all of them so-called because of their resemblance to the articles for which they were named. **1919** J. Masefield *Battle of Somme* 9 Just before they got us we found some hairbrush bombs. **1923** Kipling *Irish Guards in Great War* I. 75 The 'stick' hand-grenade of the hair-brush type. **1925** Fraser & Gibbons *Soldier & Sailor Words* 113 *Hair-brush grenade*, the name for a type of hand-grenade used in the early part of the War, with a handle, the shape of which suggested a lady's hair-brush.

hair-do (hēə·ɹdū). Also **hairdo.** [f. Hair *sb.* + Do *sb.*[1] 2.] **a.** A way or style of dressing the hair (orig. *U.S.*). **b.** A cutting and setting of the hair.

[**1917** *Ladies' Home Jrnl.* May 100/2, I had Madame Lily come out and do my hair.] **1932** E. Ferber *They brought their Women* (1933) 24 Why don't we wait until I get the new hair-do. **1935** *Mademoiselle* Oct. 42 He shows you how to achieve an evening look with the same hair-do, by drawing up the side curls high above the ears and clipping them with stones. **1941** *Illustrated* 6 Sept. 14/2 (*caption*) Judy tries a new hair-do. **1942** *Chicago Sunday Tribune* 5 July 1. 12/2 Spurts of rain inspired feminine picnickers eager to protect holiday hair-dos. **1946** 'S. Russell' *To Bed with Grand Music* iv. 55 Nail-varnish and perfumes and hair-do's. **1959** *Daily Tel.* 31 Dec. 9/7 The 'hair-do' took an hour and a half. **1971** *Petticoat* 17 July 2/2 Why do girls spend pounds on clothes, makeup and hairdos?

hairdressing. Add: (Later *attrib.* examples.) Also, a dressing (see Dressing *vbl. sb.* 4) for the hair.

1856 W. Ferguson *Amer. by River & Rail* 67, I.. resigned myself into the hands of one of the assistants in 'Phalon's Hair-dressing Saloon'. **1876** J. S. Ingram *Centenn. Exposition* 701 It contained..ladies' hair-dressing rooms. **1892** *York Co. Hist. Rev.* 60 William Schreiber's Fashionable Shaving and Hair-Dressing Parlors. **1907** *Yesterday's Shopping* (1969) 532/1 Paraffin Hair Stimulant...As a hair dressing it is unrivalled. **1908** *Westm. Gaz.* 29 Feb. 3/2 The hair-dressing sketch shows the Greek silhouette..inspired by Greek ideas. **1909** in A. Adburgham *Shops & Shopping* (1964) xxiii. 273 (*heading*) Ladies Hairdressing Courts. **1966** J. S. Cox *Illustr. Dict. Hairdressing* 71/1 *Hair-dressing*, a liquid preparation of a creamy consistency used to anoint the hair of the head to improve its condition, impart a sheen, facilitate its dressing or hold it in position. *Ibid.*, *Hair-dressing academy*, in the 18th cent. in Paris these academies were described as follows: 'The academy for teaching the art of female hair-dressing'.

haire mai, var. *haeremai.

hairily (hēə·rili), *adv.* [f. Hairy *a.* + -ly[2].] With hair or hairiness.

1925 W. Deeping *Sorrell & Son* xxx, A lone, grim, anthropoid creature, hairily grotesque.

hair-line. Add: **4.** = *hair-cord* (Hair *sb.* 10).

1862 *Catal. Internat. Exhibit., Brit.* II. No. 4104, Claret, drab, grey, and fancy hairlines. **1950** *'Mercury' Dict. Textile Terms* 256/1 An imitation hairline fabric, woven from woollen warp and worsted weft.

5. *Typogr.* The thin stroke in a letter form (as distinguished from the stem and the serifs). Also *attrib.*

1896 T. L. De Vinne in J. Moxon *Mech. Exerc. Printing* 415 No defined width is made for the thin-stroke, which is now called the hair-line. **1932** *Paper & Print* Dec. 326/2 Finely cut serifs, not the hair lines of Bodoni, but cut to a point, are characteristic of some of the latest types. **1970** W. P. Jaspert et al. *Encycl. Type Faces* (ed. 4) p. x, All book types show some variation of thick and thin; in the fifteenth century it was slight, and gradually became more pronounced, until it reached the extreme in the nineteenth century when they became called hair lines. **1972** P. Gaskell *New Introd. Bibliogr.* 29 Didot's

first neo-classic type did not show marked contrast, but later developments of the form, by Didot himself and by Bodoni in Italy, resulted by 1800 in faces of great contrast combined with vertical stress and unbracketed, hair-line serifs.

6. The limit-line of the hair on the head.

1922 S. Lewis *Babbitt* i. 8 A tremendous forehead, arching up two inches beyond the former hair-line. **1936** L. C. Douglas *White Banners* x. 225 The forward curve of the hair-line on the temples. **1959** A. Salkey *Quality of Violence* viii. 128 The rope round his neck was cutting into the hair-line at the back of his head.

7. *Metallurgy.* In full *hair-line crack*: see quot. 1949.

1923 J. A. Jones *Woolwich Res. Dept. Rep. no.* 55 51 The occurrence of hair-line cracks at one end of the forgings suggests that trouble might be experienced. **1925** [see *hair crack* s.v. *hair *sb.* 10]. **1949** R. T. Rolfe *Dict. Metallogr.* (ed. 2) 121 *Hair-line cracks* (or *hair c[racks]*), (1) very fine short cracks occurring in the interior of some steel forgings which have not been allowed to cool sufficiently slowly from the working temperature... (2) The term is also applied to any fine cracks which may occur in metals and alloys. **1962** G. R. Bashforth *Manuf. Iron & Steel* IV. ii. 31 When once this [hydrogen-rich] constituent has been formed, its breakdown at low temperatures must result in the formation of hairline cracks, but hairline cracks will not be formed if the breakdown..is brought about at higher temperatures. **1968** *Times* 28 Aug. 21/6 The South of England Electricity Board has had to take its newest.. power station..out of commission because of a discovery.. of hair-line cracks in welding.

8. In various technical uses: see quots.

1935 *Burlington Mag.* Sept. 109/2 The hair-line sprays with delicate gold leaves. **1955** *Sci. Amer.* May 124/1 Its operation resembles that of a slide rule. You first position the hairline of the slider over the caret between the first four balls. **1960** *Times* 25 Oct. 15/5 He has recovered from a hairline fracture of the wrist. **1961** T. Landau *Encycl. Librarianship* (ed. 2) 160/1 *Hair-line rule*, a fine line of varying length used for division of text matter. **1962** *Gloss. Terms Glass Ind.* (*B.S.I.*) § 72 *Hair line*, fine cord on the surface of glass. **1967** *Gloss. Paper/Ink Terms for Letterpress Printing* (*B.S.I.*) 12 *Hair lines*, fine filaments of foreign matter which forms barriers preventing the felting of many of the fibres and often leading to web breaks.

9. *fig.* A very thin dividing line. Also *attrib.*

1940 F. Scott Fitzgerald *Let.* 21 Sept. (1964) 124, I don't know how this job is going... Things depend on such hairlines here. **1959** *New Statesman* 29 Aug. 235/3 It is this hair-line compromise that Dr Stockwood has now challenged..in his statements, though not in his action, at Carshalton. **1962** *Times* 22 Mar. 3/3 It looked a hairline decision indeed.

hairpin. Add: **2.** A jocular word for: a person. Also, a thin person. *slang* (orig. *U.S.*).

1879 R. Grant *Little Tin Gods* 8 That is the kind of a hairpin that he is! **1884** E. W. Nye *Baled Hay* 103 That's the kind of hair pin he is. He never works. **1910** W. M. Raine *B. O'Connor* 214 Collins ain't that kind of a hairpin. **1959** I. & P. Opie *Lore & Lang. Schoolch.* ix. 168 The names [for thin people]..are merely descriptive, as..hairpin, [etc.].

3. In full *hairpin bend, corner*, etc. A sharp bend in a road or course likened to a hairpin in form.

1906 *Daily Chron.* 15 June 6/5 The length and steepness of the rise complicated by a double-hairpin corner. **1906** *Amer. Mag.* LXIII. 176/1 At hairpin turn, perhaps the worst of all, where the course doubles itself, were 500 machines and at least 10,000 people. **1912** *Motor* 23 Apr. Suppl. 2 As we dropped down the gentle 'hairpins' into Voreppe. **1912** G. B. Shaw *Let.* 9 Aug. (1952) 33 A journey of 800 miles includes crawls up endless hairpin zigzags. *Ibid.* 17 Sept. 148 Reversing at impossible hairpin corners. **1914** *Auto-Motor Jrnl.* 410/2 It is not unlike the higher part of Birdlip Hill, starting with a long and steep gradient and ending with a sharp hairpin bend just below the summit. **1923** *Motor Cycle* 13 Sept. 373/1 There is only one acute hair-pin bend, but there are several corners. *Ibid.* 374/1 A rather tricky and loose-surfaced left-hand hairpin was the principal feature of Chinnor Hill. **1957** P. Kemp *Mine were of Trouble* iii. 36 Its sudden ascents and declivities, its blind curves and hairpin bends flanked by unguarded precipices. **1971** D. O'Connor *Eye of Eagle* iii. 20, I..was driving up the hairpins that mark the beginning of the Simplon Pass.

4. Other *attrib.* uses.

1887 Bury & Hillier *Cycling* xiii. 344 In many tangent wheels very fine spokes are used, and their most delicate point is at the bend in the hub, where the double spoke is bent 'hair-pin' fashion. **1895** *Montgomery Ward Catal.* 195 Fancy Chased Hairpin Box. **1906** *Westm. Gaz.* 29 Dec. 15/2 Joined to the ninon with coarse hairpin stitch. **1917** W. Owen *Let.* 10 Jan. (1967) 426 Celluloid hair-pin box from Boots. **1932** D. C. Minter *Mod. Needlecraft* 104 (*heading*) Hairpin Work. *Ibid.* 104/1 Hairpin-work D'oyley.

hair-splitting, *vbl. sb.* (Earlier example.)

1826 *Blackw. Edin. Mag.* XX. 854/2 A sort of game at hair-splitting.

hair-trigger. Add: *fig.* (Earlier U.S. example.)

1876 'Mark Twain' *Tom Sawyer* 226 The inmates were asleep, but it was a sleep that was set on a hair-trigger.

b. (Earlier and later examples.)

1834 M. Edgeworth *Tour Connemara* (1950) 4, I had been much amused by my father's account of Dick Martin—'Hairtrigger Dick'. **1948** C. Day Lewis *Poems 1943–1947* 60 The quick-set ears, the hair-trigger nerves. **1968** *Observer* 1 Sept. 8/7 A hair-trigger laugh.

Hence **hair-triggered** *a.* (earlier and later examples); also **hair-triggerish, -triggery** *adjs.*

1806 *Balance* 7 Jan. (Th.), I know not whether hair-triggered pistols are in use in Penn. **1937** L. C. Douglas *Forgive our Trespasses* xv. 304 Intolerant, irascible, pig-headed, hair-triggered. **1945** *Daily Express* 4 June 2/7 The A.A. gunners..had become so hair-triggered that no Allied pilot dare come anywhere near. **1928** Galsworthy *Swan Song* ii. vi. 162 'I admit,' said Michael, unhappily, 'it's all hair-triggerish.' **1937** L. C. Douglas *Forgive our Trespasses* ii. 41 He is always so autocratic and hair-triggery.

hairworm. Substitute for def.: An aquatic, nematomorph worm of the order Gordioidea, which, in its larval stages, is a parasite of insects, worms, or fishes. (Later examples.)

1897 [see *horsehair snake* (*horsehair c)]. **1930** E. C. Faust *Human Helminthology* xxix. 483 (*heading*) Gordiacea or 'hairworms'. **1951** G. Lapage *Parasitic Animals* vi. 175 The larvae of the hairworms may also develop in freshwater worms or fish. **1963** J. B. Goodey *T. Goodey's Soil & Freshwater Nematodes* (ed. 2) 522 The hairworms or gordiids..occur in freshwater ponds, ditches, streams, lakes, etc.

hairy, *a.* Add: **1. c.** In names of animals (further examples): **hairy armadillo,** an edentate mammal (*Chaetophractus villosus*) found in Argentina; **hairy frog,** a West African frog (*Trichobatrachus robustus*), the male of which shows filaments of skin on sides and thighs during the breeding season; **hairy woodpecker** *U.S.*, a common woodpecker (*Dendrocopus auduboni* or *D. villosus*) of the eastern parts of North America.

1840 E. Blyth tr. *Cuvier's Animal Kingdom* 125 The *Pichiy* of Azzara, and an allied species, the Hairy Armadillo (*Tatou velu*, Az.), resemble the Encoubert. **1892** W. H. Hudson *Naturalist in La Plata* i. 17 The fourth..is the hairy armadillo, with habits which are in strange contrast to those of its perishing congeners, and which seem to mock many hard-and-fast rules concerning animal life. **1956** G. Durrell *Drunken Forest* ii. 47 The hairy armadillo is the vulture of the Argentine pampa. **1925** *Jrnl. Morphol. & Physiol.* XL. 342 The occurrence in a frog of long, hair-like processes covering the sides of the body and part of the thighs with a thick growth has excited the curiosity of biologists since the first discovery of this 'hairy frog' nearly twenty-five years ago. **1960** H. W. Parker *tr. Mertens's World of Amphibians and Reptiles* viii. 138 The male of the large, West African, Hairy Frog..shows hairlike proliferations of the skin 10–15 mm. (0·4–0·6 of an inch) long, at the breeding season; they are completely absent in the female. **1731** M. Catesby *Nat. Hist. Carolina* I. 19 *Picus medius, quasi villosus.* The Hairy Woodpecker, weighs two ounces. **1808** A. Wilson *Amer. Ornith.* I. 150 [The] Hairy Woodpecker..is another of our resident birds,..a haunter of orchards, and lover of apple trees, an eager hunter of insects. **1839** J. J. Audubon *Ornith. Biogr.* V. 164 The Hairy Woodpecker, *P[icus] villosus*, is a constant resident in our maritime and inland districts. **1880** *Harper's Mag.* Oct. 672/2 *Picus auduboni* is not now recognized as a valid species, but only as a local variety of the hairy woodpecker. **1896** Hairy woodpecker [in Dict.]. **1956** L. W. Wing *Nat. Hist. Birds* ii. 26 The Downy and Hairy Woodpeckers of North America bear striking resemblances to each other.

d. *hairy at* (*about, in, round*) *the heel*(*s*) (*fetlocks*): deficient in breeding or manners. So *hairy-heeled* adj., and simple *hairy*, in the same sense. *slang.* Cf. Hair *sb.* 8 d.

1890 R. L. Stevenson *Mem. & Portr.* 100 That hairy man of business knew his errand well. **1899** A. Conan Doyle *Duet* 212, I couldn't stand that chap at any price. A bit too hairy in the fetlocks for my taste. **1905** H. A. Vachell *Hill* xii, The Rev. Septimus scowled also, because he had always maintained that any Harrovian could accept defeat like a gentleman... 'I always said he was hairy at the heel.' **1906** *Macm. Mag.* Nov. 9, I would join you and cry *Viva Pio Nono!* with the hairiest. **1922** J. Buchan *Huntingtower* xi. 213, I can't say I ever liked him... Bit hairy about the heels. **1927** *Blackw. Mag.* Oct. 488/2 He took refuge in..the display..of an honest but slightly hairy heel. **1928** *Observer* 22 Jan. 10/7 (Advt.), There is an Atlantic [locomotive] over there..—a bit hairy about the heel.., but quite sporting on gradients. **1930** A. E. W. Mason *Dean's Elbow* xi, What would those people say..if they knew? Hairy-heeled, eh? **1962** N. Marsh *Hand in Glove* ii. 47, I always say that when people start fussing about family and all that, it's because they're a bit hairy round the heels themselves.

e. Excited, angry, 'out of temper'.

1914 J. Joyce *Dubliners* 54 She doesn't know my name. I was too hairy to tell her that. **1927** W. E. Collinson *Contemp. Eng.* 116 He got shirty or hairy.

f. *hairy ape*: a person of a low mental or social type.

[**1922** E. O'Neill (*title*) The Hairy Ape.] **1931** *Times Lit. Suppl.* 1 Oct. 750/3 The submerged tenth, the hairy apes of society.

g. In various *fig.* and slang senses: difficult (quot. 1848); out-of-date, passé; frightening, hair-raising; crude, clumsy, rough, erratic.

Some examples belong equally under sense 1 b. *transf.*

1848 A. H. Clough *Bothie* ix. 53 He..never once had brushed up his *hairy* Aldrich. **1914** D. O. Barnett *Let.* 25 Nov. (1915) 13, I..threw a hairy salute! *Ibid.* 2 Dec. 16 It's top-hole fun, with four hairy captains teaching us things. **1934** H. G. Wells *Exper. Autobiogr.* II. ix. 783 They were not throwing themselves into their parts as the hairy young Italians they were aping would have done. **1946** B. Marshall *George Brown's Schooldays* 7 There you go again using great long hairy words. **1950** Wentworth & Flexner *Dict. Amer. Slang* 239/1 *Hairy*, old, already known, passé; usu. said of a joke or story. **1962** D. Slayton in *Into Orbit* 22 If you happen to be pulling a lot of Gs..it might get a little hairy trying to manipulate the controls with all the finesse you'd need. **1966** 'W. Cooper' *Mem. New Man* iii. iv. 239 The problem was of the kind that Mike described in his up-to-date slang as 'hairy', meaning complex in surface detail and involving more parameters than anybody would want to cope with simultaneously. In a word, messy. **1966** J. Miles in T. Wisdom *High-Performance Driving* v. 45 You can go just as quickly if you brake and accelerate smoothly... If it's hairy its bad. **1966** *Surfer* VII. iv. 48 One of the fastest, hairiest waves I've ever ridden. **1967** *Autocar* 5 Oct. 24/1 This Healey had all the works racing mods which brought the engine power up to 210 b.h.p. and turned what is a hairy and perhaps a slightly clumsy road car into a Ferrari-beating racer. **1968** *Listener* 20 June 816/1 Khe Sanh wasn't too bad. They had good bunkers there, but most places since Tet have been pretty hairy. **1968** *Sun* 12 Nov. 8/5 *Hairy*: a fast driver is a hairy driver. **1968** H. C. Rae *Few Small Bones* i. iv. 39 'Were you ever at one of his parties?'..'Just one. .. It wasn't my style really. In fact it was pretty hairy... Too many jumped-up gentry.' **1969** J. Morris *Fever Grass* xvii. 154 Things may be rough now, baby, but they could get really hairy if you try to cross me. **1971** *New Yorker* 21 Aug. 39 And do you, Elizabeth, take this man, John, to have and to hold, to love and to cherish, until the going gets hairy? **1972** *Times* 14 Oct. 6/2 Lord Snowdon said during a break for an orange juice: 'I was a bit frightened. Some bends are a bit hairy.'

4. *hairy-arsed, -chested, -nosed* adjs.

1885 *Encycl. Brit.* XIX. 518/2 The Hairy-nosed Porcupine *H[ystrix] leucura.* **1911** *Ibid.* XXVIII. 782/1 In the hairy-nosed wombat (*P[hascolomys] latifrons*) of Southern Australia the fur is smooth and silky. **1937** C. W. Ferguson *Fifty Million Brothers* vii. 96 What is this thing that has..drawn the admiring gaze alike of dictators and hairy-chested novelists? **1944** A. Russell *Bush Ways* xliv. 192, I found there were numberless burrows of the hairy-nosed wombat. **1960** G. Sanders *Mem. Professional Cad* i. v. 44 Meanwhile the man will applaud in a manner that he feels will demonstrate a fine balance between hairy-chested virility and sensitive intellectuality. **1964** L. MacNeice *Astrol.* ii. 62 Saturn makes you hairy-chested. **1965** J. S. Gunn *Terminol. Shearing Industry* i. 31 *Hairy-arsed learner*, a man who has probably shorn hundreds of thousands of sheep..but whose skill has been much reduced by age or infirmity. **1967** Partridge *Dict. Slang* 1164/1 *Hairy-arsed*, no longer young... Mature and hirsute and virile.

B. *sb.* A heavy artillery draught horse, so called from its hairy fetlocks. *Army slang.*

1899 A. Conan Doyle *Duet* 215 The hairies—trooper's chargers, you know. **1924** *Blackw. Mag.* Mar. 365/2 We had the bar placed as high as possible and put the old 'hairies' as hard at the jumps as they could travel. **1930** *Even. Standard* 15 Feb. 15/1 Whipping up the lumbering hairies to a desperate canter. **1959** *Times* 31 Dec. 10/7 No longer should I be dependent on 'hairies' hired from the local cavalry regiment.

Haitian (hē¹·tiăn, həi·tiăn, -ʃăn), *a.* and *sb.* Also 9 **Haytian.** [f. *Haiti* + -an.] Of or pertaining to the island of Haiti or Hispaniola in the West Indies, or to the Republic of Haiti situated in the western part of that island. Also as *sb.*, a native or inhabitant of Haiti, or of the Republic of Haiti.

1805 M. Rainsford *Hist. Acct. Black Empire of Hayti* 448 Where is that Haytian so vile, Haytian so unworthy of his regeneration, who thinks he has not fulfilled the decrees of the Eternal, by exterminating these blood-thirsty tygers? **1811** *Gentl. Mag.* Sept. 275/1 After the ceremony, their Haytian Majesties..received the sacrament. **1828** J. Franklin *Pres. State Hayti* 6 The partial eulogists of the Haytians go to the length of asserting that they have arrived at a high degree of moral improvement. *Ibid.*, Instances of intelligence have been discovered in the Haytian citizen. **1863** *Chambers's Encyl.* V. 274/1 The inhabitants of the eastern or Spanish portion of Hayti, rising against their Haytian oppressors. **1880** *Encycl. Brit.* XI. 546/1 Haytian Republic. **1964** E. A. Nida *Towards Sci. Transl.* viii. 181 For Haiti, the Scriptures are published in Haitian Creole, which is essentially a colloquial dialect of French. **1966** G. Greene *Comedians* i. iii. 75 The walls were hung with pictures by Haitian artists. *Ibid.* 83 The little houses the Haitians constructed for their dead. **1972** *Daily Tel.* (Colour Suppl.) 10 Nov. 23/2 The Haitian government is encouraging the hotel boom with generous concessions.

haka (hā·kă). *N.Z.* [Maori.] A Maori ceremonial posture dance accompanied by chanting; one danced by members of a sports team, etc.

1832 H. Williams *Jrnl.* 13 Jan. in H. Carleton *Life H. Williams* (1874) I. 113 They now prepared for their *haka*, or dance. **1845** E. J. Wakefield *Adv. N.Z.* I. 98 A *haka* was now performed by about one hundred and fifty men and women. **1872** A. Domett *Ranolf* xv. vi. 19 The *hâka*-dances where she shone supreme. **1907** *Macm. Mag.* Sept. 855 The Maoris are a people with grand manners, and the *haka* is an amusement wherewith they beguile for their guests the long dark evening hours. **1920** *Glasgow Herald* 30 Apr. 9 At the close of the oration the warriors performed the 'Haka' war dance. **1934** *Bulletin* (Sydney) 15 Aug. 11/4 The haka is kept going by Maoriland footballers and hockey players. **1938** R. D. Finlayson *Brown Man's Burden* 13 Afterwards there were pois and there were hakas, and there was sure to be a dance. **1957** *N.Z. Listener* 22 Nov.

4/2 One common group..of Maori words has come right over into New Zealand English—whare, haka and mana (e.g.) have all acquired (when used in English) overtones and extra meanings that were not in the original Maori. They are true New Zealandisms. **1963** *Evening Post* (Wellington) 12 Oct., 'Kamate! Kamate!' the fierce Maori haka rang out today as the 1963–64 All Blacks for Britain had their first haka practice.

hakam, var. *HAHAM.

‖ **hakama** (ha·kamă). Also **hakkama.** [Jap.] Loose trousers with many folds in the front, worn in Japan.

1859 A. STEINMETZ *Japan & her People* I. iii. 152 A very peculiar sort of trousers called *hakkama*, which may be called an immensely full-plaited petticoat sewed up between the legs. **1871** A. B. MITFORD *Tales Old Japan* II. 264 The *hakama*, or loose trousers worn by the Samurai. **1893** A. M. BACON *Jap. Interior* vii. 119 The Japanese costume of purple hakama, or kilt-plaited divided skirt, which forms the uniform of the little school-girls. **1963** 'G. BLACK' *Dragon for Christmas* iv. 67 Mr. Kishimura opened the door wearing heavy grey-black silk robes, with the *hakama* over-garment.

‖ **Hakenkreuz, hakenkreuz** (ha·kənkroits). [G.] The Nazi swastika. Also *attrib.*

1931 *Times* 23 Dec. 7/4 A large Nazi Hakenkreuz flag, 'which can be seen for miles', flies from the tallest chimney. **1935** C. ISHERWOOD *Mr. Norris changes Trains* xi. 165 Hitler's negotiations with the Right had broken down; the Hakenkreuz was even flirting mildly with the Hammer and Sickle. **1966** 'M. ALBRAND' *Door fell Shut* xvi. 115 His eyes fell on a large hakenkreuz. To come upon the Nazi insignia so unexpectedly made Bronsky feel slightly sick. **1972** *Oxford Times* 28 July 9 Perhaps he [*sc.* Hitler] hoped the Hakenkreuz would bring bad luck to his enemies.

haker (hēⁱ·kəɹ). [f. HAKE *sb.*[1] + -ER[1].] A fisherman or a fishing-boat engaged in catching hake.

1880 *Harper's Mag.* Aug. 340/1 The man who fished for hake, and also his boat, was a 'haker'.

Hakka (hæ·kă). [Chinese.] A member of a people now dwelling in parts of southern China, especially in the province of Kwangtung or Canton, and in Taiwan, Hong Kong, etc.; also the dialect spoken by this people. Also *attrib.* or as *adj.*

1867 *N. & Q. on China & Japan* I. 66/2 It is a common saying among the Hakkas, that a Punti may study Hakka for many years, and yet not be able to speak it correctly. **1878** H. A. GILES *Gloss. of Reference* 56 *Hakkas*, strangers. A race said to have migrated from the North of China (Kiangsu or Shantung) to the Kuang-tung province at the time of the Yuan dynasty AD 1206–1368. **1879** *Encycl. Brit.* IX. 416/2 Hakkas from the vicinity of Swatow. **1881** J. D. BALL *Easy Sentences Hakka Dial.* p. i, While engaged in my studies in the Hakka dialect I put the sentences in Giles' *Handbook of the Swatow Dialect* into Hakka. **1921** *Outward Bound* July 17/1 He converses freely in Hakka, Cantonese, Mandarin [etc.]. **1926** *Blackw. Mag.* Nov. 628/1 The Hakkas, as wood-cutters and hunters, had already penetrated into the foothills. **1964** *Asia Mag.* 30 Aug. 5/1 (*caption*) Below is a Hakka woman in a work gang in K.L. **1968** 'B. MATHER' *Springers* xviii. 196 The old man at the helm.. looked like a Hakka to me. They are fishermen, and nobody's fools. **1971** K. HOPKINS *Hong Kong* 235 Cantonese is very much the predominant language but there are minorities who speak Hakka. **1971** *Nat. Geographic* Oct. 550/1 (*caption*) Curtained hat identifies a Hakka farm-woman. A distinctive group of immigrant Chinese, Hakkas till hillsides in the New Territories.

Halafian (hălā·fiăn), *a. Archæol.* [f. Tell *Halaf* in north-eastern Syria + -IAN.] Denoting the chalcolithic culture which existed in northern Syria and Iraq, characterized by polychrome pottery, evidence of which was first discovered at Tell Halaf.

1937 G. E. WRIGHT *Pottery of Palestine* ii. 30 Painted motifs used by the Palestinian potters are common in the region of the Halâf pottery... When it comes to the farms, however, the Ghassulian has very little in common with the Halafian. *Ibid.* 31 A type of small bowl with gently rounded sides seems also to be popular in the Halafian culture. **1947** *Iraq* IX. 45 It is evident that there must have been an extensive prehistoric settlement of the T. Halaf period. This Halafian culture has been found throughout the whole of Northern Syria from Ugarit in the west across the Upper Euphrates valley as far as the district of Nineveh on the Tigris. **1950** G. DANIEL *100 Yrs. Archaeol.* vi. 204 The Tell Halaf culture or the Halafian as it was called, could be accurately dated.

halal (hălā·l), *v.* Also **hallal.** [f. Arab. *ḥalāl* lawful.] *trans.* To kill (an animal) in the manner prescribed by Muslim law. Hence **halal** *sb.*, lawful food; also *attrib.* and as *adj.*

1855 R. F. BURTON *Personal Narr. Pilgrimage to El-Medinah* I. xiii. 377 To '*halál*' is to kill an animal according to Moslem rites: a word is wanted to express the act, and we cannot do better than to borrow it from the people to whom the practice belongs. **1858** W. JESSE tr. *Ferrier's Hist. Afghans* xxi. 289 They will not eat meat unless it is *halal* (lawful), that is, the animal must have its face turned towards Mecca, and its throat cut in a particular part of the neck. **1877** R. A. STERNDALE *Seonee* 454 *Hălāl.* Slaughtered according to religious law. **1879** F. T. POLLOK *Sport in Brit. Burmah* I. 142 My Mahouts, when they have got down to halal, or cut the throat of a stag, have had a narrow escape. *Ibid.* 179 The mahouts would not eat the stag as it had not been hallaled, so my Madrass servants and the Burmese had it all to themselves. **1883** E. H. AITKEN *Tribes on my Frontier* 167 To allow Peer Khan to make it halal, by cutting its throat in the name of Allah, and dividing the webs of its feet. **1895** *Daily News* 1 June 5/5 The special 'Halál' meal, ordained for the I'd [*i.e.* I'd-uz'zubá Festival] in question, will be provided. **1910** *Scribner's Mag.* Apr. 404/1 Wherever possible the game being hal-lalled in orthodox fashion by the Mahometans. **1952** J. MASTERS *Deceivers* xvii. 193 So the two black goats died, one in the Mohammedan manner, the halal, and one in the Hindu manner, its head struck off at a single blow. **1966** *Guardian* 9 Dec. 8/6 Nuts, spices, curries, meat (avowedly halal at that!). **1970** *Listener* 9 July 44/2 You can get kosher meat next to halal meat.

halation. Add: **b.** A similar effect in television (see quots.).

1937 A. T. WITTS *Television Cycl.* 56 *Halation*, the reflection of image rays by the back of a screen or film. Such reflection produces a blurring of the image as viewed by the observer, or is reproduced on the film. **1940** [see *BLOOMING *vbl. sb.*[1] 3]. **1958** *Chambers's Techn. Dict.* Suppl. 983/2 *Halation*, bright annular area around the cathode-ray tube phosphor spot, arising from internal reflection within the glass support.

halawi (hălā·wi). Also 9 **khalaweh.** [Arab.] A kind of sweetmeat; = *HALVA, *HULWA.

1836 E. W. LANE *Acct. Manners & Customs Mod. Egyptians* II. 14 The seller of a kind of sweetmeat (*khala'weh*), composed of treacle fried with some other ingredients. **1911** T. E. LAWRENCE *Lett.* (1938) 129 About halawi—I hope you remember the particular sticky sweetmeat of which Thompson & myelf used to eat pounds last year. **1913** —— *Home Lett.* (1954) 248 Eat that halawi in my house.

halch, *v.* Add: **3. b.** *Cotton-spinning*, etc. (see quots.). Also **halch-band.**

1892 J. NASMITH *Cotton Spinning* 286 As yarn is always wound off a cop by drawing it upwards,..any such condition of the cop nose results in a number of coils being drawn off simultaneously in an entangled condition. In this case the cop is said to be 'halched', and a good deal of waste is produced when the unwinding takes place. **1901** *N. & Q.* 9th Ser. VIII. 81/1 'Halsh'.—This word is in every-day use in various ways. So far as the cotton trade goes it refers to the band of coloured 'tie yarn' that encircles the 'knot', in addition to the ordinary tie yarn that holds each lea in the knot separately. This is called the 'halsh-band', and when the band is tied the knot is said to be 'halshed'...The 'halsh' is also—in the case of a necktie in the form of a bow, for example—that part in the centre that runs in a vertical or slightly oblique direction, embracing the whole bow...Saddlers also use the word, and possibly it is known in the woollen and worsted industries.

haldu (hæ·ldu). [Hindi.] A tree, *Adina cordifolia*, of the family Rubiaceæ, found in Burma, India, and Thailand; also its yellowish hardwood timber.

[**1881** J. S. GAMBLE *Man. Indian Timbers* 220 ADINA ..*A. cordifolia*..Vern. *Haldu.*] **1920** *Nature* CV. 693/1 *Haldu* (*Adina cordifolia*) is a bright canary-coloured wood notable for the smooth and even regularity of the grain. **1934** *Jrnl. R. Aeronaut. Soc.* XXXVIII. 51 Other timbers used for carving on account of their even structure are Pear (*Pyrus communis*) and the Indian wood known as Haldu (*Adina cordifolia*). **1958** CHOWDHURY & GHOSH *Indian Woods* I. p. xxxvi, In woods like axlewood (*Anogeissus latifolia*), haldu (*Adina cordifolia*) and sandalwood (*Santalum album*), the texture is fine giving a smooth feel.

hale, *a.* Add: **3.** Often in phr. *hale and hearty.*

1860 *Leisure Hour* 174/2 As hale and as hearty..as ever. **1863** *Good Words* IV. 295/2 He..was hale and hearty though upwards of a hundred years old. **1899** *Captain* I. 124/2 Dr. Grace is close on fifty-one, hale and hearty. **1903** T. HARDY *Dynasts* I. I. i. 14 We be the King's men, hale and hearty, Marching to meet one Buonaparty. **1928** A. B. CALLOW *Food & Health* 7 In the past many people have been perfectly hale and hearty without having any clear ideas about the science of nutrition.

half, *sb.* Add: **6. d.** Also in Rugby Union, Rugby League, etc. Cf. *fly-half* (*FLY *sb.*[2] 8), **scrum-half.*

1896 B. F. ROBINSON *Rugby Football* v. 90 The half 'working' the scrummage should rarely try to run himself. **1906** GALLAHER & STEAD *Compl. Rugby Footballer* iv. 64 A new line of attack and defence between the halves and the three-quarters. **1951** *Men's Hockey* (Know the Game Series) (1965) 17/2 At long corners..the halves go out behind them. **1960** E. S. & W. J. HIGHAM *High Speed Rugby* vii. 55 Give me a good pair of halves and I will give you a team.

f. *Golf.* A hole or point which is halved.

1881 [see *DEAD *a.* 21 b]. **1908** J. BRAID *Advanced Golf* 213 Halves ought rarely to be agreed upon unless the balls are so close to the hole that it is next to impossible for the putts to be missed. **1931** *Daily Tel.* 22 May 18/1 He..secured the necessary 5 for the half and the match. **1959** *Times* 29 May 5/1 Sewell got a brave half at the 18th.

g. In Old English prosody = *half-line* (*HALF- II. n).

1892 S. A. BROOKE *Hist. Early Eng. Lit.* I. p. x, The Anglo-Saxon line is divided into two halves by a pause. The first half has two 'measures'. **1940** J. R. R. TOLKIEN in J. R. C. Hall tr. *Beowulf* p. xxvii, The Old English line was composed of two opposed word-groups or 'halves'. Each half was an example, or variation, of one of six basic patterns.

h. A half-holiday.

1909 P. TRAHERNE *Diary* Nov. (1918) i. 28 By getting up this entertainment on a 'half' when there was nothing else to do I found myself launched into about six rows. **1934** *Neuphilol. Mitt.* XXXV. 130 He will acquire prep-school slang (words such as..*half* 'half holiday').

i. Ten shillings, half of £1. *slang.*

1931 W. F. BROWN in *Police Jrnl.* IV. 502 They speiled first for stakes of a sprazey,..increasing it..later to a half... This narrative..would in plain English read.. They played first for stakes of a sixpence..increasing.. later to ten shillings. **1938** G. GREENE *Brighton Rock* I. ii. 30 She's just a buer—he gave her a half.

j. A fare or ticket at a reduced (usu. half) rate. Also quasi-*adv.*

1935 *Punch* 30 Jan. 137 You two can't go half. You're over age. **1965** *New Statesman* 9 Apr. 567/2 Two adults and three halves, please.

7. e. Esp. in phr. *too clever by half*: trying too hard to be clever.

1858 [in Dict.]. **1889** W. WESTALL *Birch Dene* II. vi. 89 'Nobody can deny as he's clever.' 'Ay, too clever by half.' **1944** L. MACNEICE *Christopher Columbus* 8 Constant ingenuity..often leads to an appearance of being too clever by half. **1961** *Listener* 2 Nov. 717/1 A bad one [*sc.* documentary], whether dull through laziness, or self-conscious or pretentious or too-clever-by-half, can be a real catastrophe.

h. *and a half* (following a sb.): and more; of an exceptional kind. Cf. HEART *sb.* 39 b. *colloq.*

1636, etc. [see HEART *sb.* 39 b]. **1832** J. K. PAULDING *Westward Ho!* II. i. 7 Bushfield, too, was here in all his glory, and was not only a whole team, but a team and a half, good measure, as he affirmed. **1837** DICKENS *Pickw.* xlvi. 501, I raythe think the gov'ner vants to have a vord and a half vith you. **1911** T. E. LAWRENCE *Lett.* (1938) 118 Last night was paradise and a half. **1917** *Strand Mag.* LIII. 606/2 Golly! He took a toss and a half! **1959** 'M. M. KAYE' *House of Shade* x. 128 Roaring Rory must have been a hell-raiser and a half in his day.

i. *the half of it*: a significant or more important part of something. Usu. in negative contexts.

1932 WODEHOUSE *Hot Water* i. 27 It makes me sick. And that's not the half of it... She told me I've got to be American Ambassador to France. **1947** 'N. BLAKE' *Minute for Murder* i. 2 'We've not seen the half of it yet,' said the Messenger darkly. 'The half of what?' 'You mark my words, sir. When peace comes, as you might say real peace, there'll be chay-oh in this country.' **1966** M. BREWER *Man against Fear* xi. 117 'You haven't heard the half of it yet.' I went on to tell him about the Carver Street ambush. **1971** M. BABSON *Cover-up Story* x. 109 'How awful,' she said...I nodded, without telling her she didn't know the half of it.

half, *a.* Add: **1. a.** *half sheet* (earlier examples). See also *half-sheet* s.v. HALF- II. n in Dict. and Suppl.

1723 J. NOTT *Cook's & Confect. Dict.* 261c Lay every Cutlet on a half Sheet of Paper. **1852** E. RUSKIN *Let.* 17 Apr. in M. Lutyens *Effie in Venice* (1965) II. 296, I was very grateful for..Papa's half sheet about the Ruskins.

b. (Later examples.)

1849 [see BATTLE *sb.* 4]. **1864** TROLLOPE *Can you forgive Her?* I. xxxviii. 301 If you are half the woman that I take you to be, you will understand this. **1867** —— *Claverings* I. iii. 38 Though the lord might be only half a man, Julia walked out from the church every inch a countess. **1936** *Discovery* Dec. 397/2 The author has undoubtedly the gift of winning the confidence of his African hosts, which is half the battle. **1944** *Living off Land* i. 15 The correct mental approach to a lesson is often half the battle.

c. Also *half a bar* (see *BAR *sb.*[1] 3 c); *half a bull* [BULL *sb.*[1] 7], half a crown (*slang*).

1812 J. H. VAUX *Flash Dict.*, *Half a bull*, half a crown.

half, *adv.* Add: **1. c.** (Later examples.)

1910 W. DE LA MARE *Three Mulla-Mulgars* 63 Half-hiding his face in his jacket. **1918** D. H. LAWRENCE *New Poems* 13 One side shadow, half in sight, Half-hiding the pavement-run.

3. *not half* (further examples): 'not half a bad fellow' = a good fellow; 'not half long enough' = not nearly long enough; also (*slang*), extremely, violently, as 'he didn't half swear'.

1851 MELVILLE *Moby Dick* II. xxxi. 215, I don't half like that chap, Stubb. **1914** H. ASHTON *First from Front* xiv. 99 It wasn't half all right, I tell you. **1919** V. WOOLF *Night & Day* xv. 195, I could live on fifteen shillings a week... It wouldn't be half bad. **1920** GALSWORTHY *Foundations* III, in *Plays* (1929) 498 Talk of your sacrifices in the war—they put you on your honour, and you got stout on it. Rations—not 'arf! **1953** L. P. HARTLEY *Go-Between* xiv. 165 And we didn't half enjoy your songs. **1955** E. BOWEN *World of Love* ii. 19 He had no plans: he in fact would not be half sorry if someone said to him he was back for good. **1962** PARKER & ALLERTON *Courage of his Convictions* iii. 143 It doesn't half nark them.

half-. Add: **I. 1. a.** in the predicate. (Further examples.)

1844 J. R. LOWELL *Poems* 12 A youth half-smiling.

1846 'A LADY' *Jewish Manual* II. v. 216 Dresses made half high are..unbecoming; they should either be cut close up to the throat or low. **1849** THOREAU *Week on Concord* 399 They are half forgotten ere we have learned the language. **1858** BAGEHOT *Coll. Works* (1965) II. 55 Half-crazed as she [Meg Merrilies] is described to be. **1881** 'MARK TWAIN' *Prince & Paup.* 162 He was half-minded to resign. **1893** —— *Man corrupted Hadleyburg* (1900) 269 The station-master..became pleasant and even half-apologetic. **1904** W. DE LA MARE *Henry Brocken* 76, I glanced at the shock-haired creature, alert, half-human, beside me. **1910** J. MORLEY *Cromwell* (ed. 2) iii. 54 Never more were fish caught there, and the neighbouring town was half ruined. **1923** D. H. LAWRENCE *Birds, Beasts & Flowers* 41 The dim light of full, healthy life That is always half-dark. **1936** *Mind* XLV. 252 What were the views concealed or half-concealed, expressed or half-expressed? **1937** *Brit. Birds* XXX. 240 We have two records of single adults spending one day in the nest when their young were half-fledged. **1961** M. W. BARLEY *Eng. Farmhouse & Cottage* IV. ii. 196 Roofs gabled and half-hipped.

b. as attribute. (Further examples.)

c **1827** J. S. MILL in *Adelphi* (1924) I. 689 A half-cultivated taste is always caught by gaudy, affected, and meretricious ornament. **1833** —— *Lett.* (1910) I. 41 It looks like the production of some half-fledged pupil of yours. **1843** —— *Syst. Logic* II. v. ii. 345 It is in those steps of the reasoning which are made in this tacit and half-conscious, or even wholly unconscious manner, that the error oftenest lurks. **1851** MELVILLE *Moby Dick* I. xvii. 132 Their half crazy conceits on these subjects. *Ibid.* II. viii. 60 Some sort of a half-hinted influence. **1853/4** J. S. MILL *Draft Autobiogr.* (1961) 116, I had a half formed intention of writing a History of the French Revolution. **1854** THOREAU *Walden* 286 Thus, with half-shut eyes, looking out from the land of dreams. **1858** BAGEHOT *Coll. Works* (1965) II. 72 The undefined, half-expressed..feelings. **1869** D. G. ROSSETTI *Let.* 27 June (1965) II. 704 A half-crazed charwoman. **1877** WHITMAN *Specimen Days* 104 Some good people may think it a feeble or half-cracked way of spending one's time and thinking. **1895** W. ROBINSON *Eng. Flower Garden* (ed. 4) viii. 118 Shade is not essential, though we think the best effects are attained in half-shady spots. **1897** *Essex Antiquarian* I. 27 When neither stones nor timber were plenty the half-high wall..was early used, and is still common. **1904** W. H. HUDSON *Green Mansions* xv. 208 Leaving her half-human child to play her malicious pranks in the wood. **1907** *Daily Chron.* 6 Feb. 4/6 Is he really a half-sexed personage? **1908** *Westm. Gaz.* 23 Jan. 2/3 Some trivial gossip in the half-lit hall. *Ibid.* 29 July 3/2 The forces of Free-Trade may be confidently reckoned on to squash the half-believed-in promises of Tariff Reform. **1910** W. DE LA MARE *Three Mulla-Mulgars* 120 Her half-blind whitening eyes. **1923** D. H. LAWRENCE *Birds, Beasts & Flowers* 37 Wavering men of old Etruria ..Going with insidious, half-smiling quietness. *Ibid.* 41 The half-secret gleam of a passion-flower hanging from the rock. **1925** T. DREISER *Amer. Trag.* (1926) II. II. xi. 234 He achieved a..half-apologetic smile. **1927** *Daily Tel.* 15 Nov. 11/7 Most of the ploughing is done with a pair of horses of the half-legged class. **1929** V. WOOLF *Room of one's Own* 127 Those unsaid or half-said words. **1931** W. RIPMAN *Eng. Phonetics* 30 Intermediate positions give half-open and half-close vowels. **1932** D. JONES *Outl. Eng. Phonetics* (ed. 3) viii. 38 Half-close vowels are those in which the tongue occupies a position about one-third of the distance from 'close' to 'open'. *Ibid.*, Half-open vowels are those in which the tongue occupies a position about two-thirds of the distance from 'close' to 'open'. *a* **1930** D. H. LAWRENCE *Last Poems* (1932) 307 Invisible Between the half-visible hordes. **1934** E. LINKLATER *Magnus Merriman* 270 In the country of the blind the half-canned man is king. **1937** *Burlington Mag.* Nov. 234/2 Such half-forgotten artists. **1937** *Mind* XLVI. 83 There is a scale of 'standing-outness' (Abhebung) which reaches from intense experiential clarity to half-conscious habituation. **1941** *Mind* L. 10 Some [statements] which would usually be called 'half-joking' or 'not serious', as when the father says, 'The wolves are gaining.' **1949** K. S. WOODS *Rural Crafts Eng.* IV. xiii. 200 The delightfully plump and comfortable curves of old Devon roofs are partly due to the 'hipped' or 'half-hipped' form of the supporting timbers. **1951** W. F. LEOPOLD in Saporta & Bastian *Psycholinguistics* (1961) 355/1 The half-open fricatives were satisfactory as terminal consonants.

2. *half-apologetically, -consciously, -jokingly.*

1913 J. LONDON *Let.* 17 Oct. (1966) 408 He..is..half-apologetically explaining that it is the first time. **1807** COLERIDGE *Notebk.* (1962) II. 2998, I still half-consciously expect to awake from the night-mair. **1923** J. M. MURRY *Pencillings* 271, I was, half-consciously, anxious to be reassured. **1949** M. MEAD *Male & Female* ii. 22 It is often said half-jokingly.

3. *half-believe* (examples), *-laugh.* Also **half-inch** *v.* (*Rhyming slang*), to 'pinch', to steal; so **half-inching** *vbl. sb.*; **half-lap** [LAP *sb.*³ 2 b] *v.*, to make a half-lap joint.

1825 NICHOLSON *Oper. Mech.* 653 The reason for making the joints half-lapped, or scarfed, [etc.]. **1844** H. STEPHENS *Bk. Farm* II. 296 They are half-lapped in pairs at the centre. **1849** THOREAU *Week on Concord* 192, I half believed that I should get above it. **1924** J. M. MURRY *Voyage* viii. 152 'I can't help it,' she said, half-laughing at her own confession. **1925** FRASER & GIBBONS *Soldier & Sailor Words* 114 *Half-inch*, to steal. **1948** W. CLEWES *Journey into Spring* ii. 30 We can half-inch those [eggs] from the huts. **1950** T. E. LAWRENCE *Mint* 130 Half-inching is venial, in certain lines of goods. **1952** C. P. BLACKER *Eugenics* 293 The problem family is half-believed to be the product of the capitalistic system. **1972** *Times* 24 Aug. 12/1 If people are going to go around half-inching planets the situation is pretty serious.

4. half-cut *a.* (*slang*), half-drunk; **half-shaved** *a.* (*Obs. U.S. slang*), drunk.

1893 FARMER & HENLEY *Slang* III. 250/1 *Half-cut*, half-drunk. **1971** *Radio Times* 18 Nov. 80 Inebriation..is the sport of all ranks. How many executives can work reasonably effectively unless they are half-cut? **1818** M. L. WEEMS *Lett.* (1929) III. 225 One night, getting half shaved, he was easily over-persuaded (a common curse of whiskey) to try his luck at All Fours. *a* **1852** F. M. WHITCHER *Widow Bedott Papers* (1856) xxviii. 354 I've seen that man half shaved on cider afore breakfast in the mornin'.

II. In attributive relation to a sb.

a. In names of *Coins, Measures*, etc. *half-bottle, -caser* [*CASER²], *-litre*; *half-pint* (earlier and later *attrib.* uses); also *ellipt.*, a half-pint of beer; (see also *half-pint* under sense n below).

1877 E. S. DALLAS *Kettner's Bk. of Table* 287 Where are these bottles and half-bottles of Madeira to be found? **1927** E. HEMINGWAY *Men without Women* (1928) 172 The American lady bought..a half bottle of Evian water. **1950** T. S. ELIOT *Cocktail Party* I. ii. 51, I found some champagne—Only a half-bottle, to be sure. **1907** H. LAWSON in *Austral. Short Stories* (1951) 70 Felt under his pillow for two half-crowns. 'Here,' he said, 'here's two half-casers.' **1921** W. J. LOCKE *Mountebank* i. 7 A thick half-litre glass of beer. **1967** 'G. CARR' *Lewker in Tirol* iv. 56 He..ordered a half-litre of wine. **1611** J. DONNE in *Coryat's Crudities* Pref. verse, Can all carouse up thee? No: thou must fit Measures; and fill out for the half-pinte wit. **1728** E. SMITH *Compleat Housewife* (ed. 2) 151 Pour it into half-pint Basons. **1899** R. WHITEING *No. 5 John St.* xi. 107, I..fell upon roast pork..and a foaming half-pint. **1937** *Discovery* Sept. 277/1 Fill a half-pint mug. **1966** E. MCGIRR *Funeral was in Spain* 101 The barman..was morosely polishing half-pint glasses.

i. In *Games.* **half-back** (examples in other games, e.g. American Football, Rugby Football, Australian Rules); **half-blast** *Golf*, a shot which is played with half the force of a 'blast' (explosive shot); **half-blue**, the 'colours' (see BLUE *sb.* 9) awarded to a player chosen to represent his university in inter-university contests as second choice to a 'full blue', or to any chosen representative in sports or games not recognized by the Blues Committee as sufficiently important for the award of a 'full blue'; also, a competitor who has gained this award; **half-brassy shot** *Golf*, a brassy shot played with a half swing; **half-captain**, in women's colleges in Oxford, one who has attained a certain degree of proficiency in the management of a boat; so **half-captaincy**; **half-colour**, a badge showing that a stage of proficiency half-way towards getting one's colours has been reached (see *COLOUR *sb.*¹ 6 c); **half-court** *Tennis* and *Rackets*, half the court divided by a line (the *half-court line*) parallel with the side lines; **half-fifteen, -forty** *Tennis* (see quot.); **half-forward, half-forward flanker** *Austral.* (see quot. 1968); so *half-forward flank*; **half-hit** *Cricket* (read:), a faulty hit, the ball falling short of the distance it would have travelled if properly hit; **half-iron shot** *Golf*, an iron shot played with a half swing; **half nelson** *Wrestling*, a hold in which one arm is thrust under the corresponding arm of the opponent and the hand placed on the back of his neck; also *fig.* in phr. *to get a half-nelson on*, to hold in a crippling position, gain a complete hold over; hence as *v. trans.* with the sense of this phr.; **half-one** *Golf* (see quot.); **half-pin** *Chess*, that position in which a defending man lies between an attacking piece and the defended king and in the line of attack of the attacking piece, but has liberty to move along the line of attack; also, that position in which two defending men lie between the attacking piece and the king so that if either moves the other man becomes pinned; so **half-pinned** *a.*; **half-pinner**, a half-pin problem; **half-shot** *Golf*, a stroke made with a half swing, intended to carry less far than the full shot; **half-stroke** *Golf* = **half-one*; **half swing** *Golf*, a swing of half the usual amount of distance; **half-thirty** *Tennis* (see quot. s.v. **half-fifteen*); **half-topped** *a. Golf*, designating a shot in which the ball is partly topped; **half-volley** *Cricket* (earlier and later examples); also, a ball which pitches just in front of a fieldsman; (*b*) *Lawn Tennis*, a stroke made when the ball has just left the ground; so *half-volleyer*; also *half-volley* vb.

1887 *Century Mag.* Oct. 892 Behind the quarter-back, and covering the two sides of the field, are the 'half-backs', the cavalry of the team. **1906** GALLAHER & STEAD *Compl. Rugby Footballer* v. 71 The half back as we know him in New Zealand is the donkey man of the team. **1959** N. MAILER *Advts. for Myself* (1961) 53 He paused, crouched into a halfback's position, waiting for the ball. **1965** *Sun-Herald* (Sydney) 4 July 51 Sydney's half-back flanker Bob Sterling won the President's trophy. **1965** *Advertiser* (Adelaide) 17 July 25 Its half-forward line.. was over-run by the powerful South Adelaide half-back line. **1968** EAGLESON & MCKIE *Terminol. Austral. Nat. Football* II. 14 There are three half-backs in each team: left, centre, and right half-back. **1969** *Australian* 24 May 39/2 Ian Bremner, Norm Bussell and Peter Chilton constitute a tight-checking half-back line for Hawthorn. **1928** *Weekly Dispatch* 24 June 21/6 He played a superb 'half-blast' out of a trap to lay the ball one foot from the cup. **1908** *Westm. Gaz.* 29 July 10/4 The half-blue for billiards. **1909** *Ibid.* 26 Feb. 12/2 For some time players of lacrosse at Oxford have been urging the Blues Committee to grant them the Half-Blue. **1963** *Times* 5 Feb. 3/3 J. S. Grinalds (Brasenose), an old half-Blue, came back into the defence for the first time this season. **1903** *Westm. Gaz.* 28 Aug. 3/1 The half-brassy shot approach. **1928** *Daily Express* 7 May 5/2 She may not go on the river unless she is accompanied by a half-captain or is one herself. Half-captaincies may be had either in rowing, canoeing, or punting. **1929** *Evening News* 18 Nov. 13/5 The player who appears in future bowls international trial matches, but who fails to be selected for the English team, is to receive a 'half-colour'. **1888** *Encycl. Brit.* XXIII. 182/2 A space bounded by the net, the side line, the half-court line, and the service line. **1895** H. W. W. WILBERFORCE *Lawn Tennis* 62 The half-court-line dividing the space on each side of the net into two equal parts, called the right and left courts. **1898** *Encycl. Sport* II. 462/2 The half court nearest the dedans is called the 'service side'. *Ibid.*, The half-court line..dividing the court lengthways into practically two equal parts. **1961** *Times* 13 Jan. 16/3 Half-court drive down the wall. **1888** *Encycl. Brit.* XXIII. 182/2 Half-fifteen is one stroke given at the beginning of the second and every subsequent alternate game of a set...Half-thirty is one stroke given at the beginning of the first game, two strokes at the beginning of the second game; and so on, alternately, in all the subsequent games of a set...Half-forty is two strokes given at the beginning of the first game, three strokes at the beginning of the second game; and so on, alternately, in all the subsequent games of a set. **1963** *Courier-Mail* (Brisbane) 21 Nov. 7/5 A typical commentary from Australian Rules, 'a long drop-kick from the half-forward flank'. **1968** EAGLESON & MCKIE *Terminology Austral. Nat. Football* II. 14 *Half-forward*, a player occupying a half-forward position, which comes between the centre and full-forward positions. *Ibid.*, Half-forwards in the side position are generally referred to as *half-forward flankers*. **1969** *Australian* 24 May 39/2 Bremner will probably be given the task of watching Geelong's mercurial Ken Newland, who will start on a half-forward flank. **1888** Half-hit [in Dict.]. **1888** A. G. STEEL in Steel & Lyttleton *Cricket* iii. 112 Extra cover-point..may be..placed for half-hits wide on the on—i.e. about half the distance from the batsman that a deep field would stand. **1899** W. CAFFYN *Seventy-one not Out* 18 Fielder placed [behind the bowler] for half-hit. **1900** W. A. BETTESWORTH *Walkers of Southgate* 41 Mr. R. D. Walker, who was fielding in a nondescript sort of place for a half hit, brought off a brilliant catch. **1928** *Daily Tel.* 17 July 17/5 Freeman..had two half-hit fieldsmen. **1895** H. G. HUTCHINSON *Golf* (ed. 5) iv. 143 The attitude ..for the half-iron stroke. **1905** *Westm. Gaz.* 10 Nov. 4/2 The half-iron shot..cannot be played properly unless turf is taken. **1889** W. ARMSTRONG *Wrestling* 230 Half Nelson, Lancashire. **1896** ADE *Artie* xvii. 154 This thing got the half-Nelson on me before I know it. **1898** *Encycl. Sport* II. 548/2 The half Nelson and heave. **1901** *Black & White Budget* 30 Nov. 315/1 The half-nelson... You grasp your opponent by the right wrist with your left hand, thrust your right hand quickly under his arm at the same time seizing his neck and pressing his head forward. **1903** P. LONGHURST *Wrestling* 77 The arm that has the half-nelson hold. **1912** *Daily Chron.* 6 Mar., And Radicals in sunshine bask with Delight to see the clever Asquith Half-Nelson Bonar Law. **1961** *Observer* 26 Nov. 27/1 He gives an exquisite demonstration of the half-nelson generally used to make the unwilling talk. **1966** *New Statesman* 15 July 74/2 He knew..that Sir Alec Douglas-Home had to be..half-nelsoned and regularly thrown out of the ring. **1887** in J. L. Stewart *Golfiana Miscellanea* 299 *Half-one*, a handicap of a stroke deducted every second hole. **1922** HUME & WHITE *Good Companion Two-Mover* 245 The term 'half-pin' arose in 1915, in correspondence between Comins Mansfield and Murray Marble anent No. 122 D, a surprising example, with six half-pins... Greenwood, the composer of this problem, had published a complete half-pinner in 1859. **1926** H. WEENINK *Chess Problem* 71 By a Half-pin is understood an arrangement where two Black pieces stand in line in such a way that if either one moves the other becomes pinned by a White piece which has been standing behind both of them waiting to exert its pinning powers. **1928** *Observer* 24 June 25 These three variations are highly complex, the first two illustrating the unpin of the White Q by half-pinned Black Kt's; the third is a half-pin line combined with Black interference. **1891** H. G. HUTCHINSON *Golf* 26 The principle of the cutting stroke, on the other hand, lies in bringing the head of the iron across that line. It may be applied to a full shot, half shot, quarter shot or shortest wrist shot. **1893** —— *Golfing* 41 When the distance is less than that for which the three-quarter stroke is used, it is commonly called a half-shot distance. **1896** W. PARK *Game of Golf* v. 107 Three-quarter and half strokes are..much more difficult to play than full shots. **1897** *Encycl. Sport* I. 461 A half-stroke or over, both in singles and foursomes, shall count as one. **1891** H. G. HUTCHINSON *Golf* 30 Take pains in all half-swing shots to bring the club-head well and slowly away from the ball before striking. **1896** W. PARK *Game of Golf* ii. 39 A club lying on its heel would, in playing through the green, be apt to get away a half-topped ball. *Ibid.* x. 204 Hazards..should be placed at such distances from the teeing-grounds that, while a well-hit shot will carry them, a topped or half-topped stroke will get in. **1905** *Westm. Gaz.* 23 Aug. 5/1 A lucky half-topped shot. **1953** H. SIMMONS *Golfers' ABC*, The chip shot not as ought to be, The half-topped seven, scuttled three. **1843** 'A WYKEHAMIST' *Pract. Hints Cricket* 12 All balls pitching between the first line and the crease..are technically termed half vollies. *Ibid.* 17 A leg half-volley..may be.. 'dropped into' now and then. **1851** J. PYCROFT *Cricket Field* viii. 168 Every one knows the difficulty of making a good half-volley hit off a slow ball. *Ibid.* x. 189 If a bowler has half volleys returned to him, by stretching

and stooping after them, he gets out of his swing. **1867** G. H. SELKIRK *Guide Cricket Ground* v. 83 The half volley..requires practice to ensure its being picked up properly. **1870** *London Society* Nov. 425/1 The mode of playing a ball so well known at tennis, not quite half-volley. **1897** *Encycl. Sport* I. 621/2 *Half-volley*, a stroke made the moment the ball leaves the ground. **1960** *Times* 21 June 16/1 Taylor half-volleyed a return into the net. **1963** A. ROSS *Australia 63* iii. 76 He played at nothing he did not have to, leaving Davidson to flash the odd half-volley through the covers. **1969** *New Yorker* 14 June 45/1 Players call it a half-volley drop shot. Ashe reaches down, lightly touches the rising ball, and sends it on a slow, sharply angled flight toward the net. *Ibid.* 45/3 Ashe, moving up, is again confronted with the need to half-volley. **1912** *Daily News* 11 July 2 A famous half-volleyer.

l. *half-bath, -bathroom, -blind, -door* (later example), *-hoop* [cf. HOOP *sb.*[1] 7], *-tester* (examples).

1879 A. VON HARLINGEN in A. H. Buck *Treat. Hygiene & Public Health* I. 373 The half-bath, in which the bather sits in a tub filled with water to the depth of from ten to twelve inches,..is adapted to invalids. **1953** R. CHANDLER *Long Good-Bye* xxvii. 171 There was a half-bath off the study. **1959** *News Chron.* 19 June 4/3 A half-bathroom ..has a shower, wash-basin and lavatory, but no bath. **1763** BOSWELL *London Jrnl.* 22 July (1951) 382, I was disturbed by the light..at the earliest dawn, as the windows have only half-blinds. **1936** J. TICKELL *See how they Run* ii. 19 The sort of horse's face that looks out over the half-door of a loose-box. **1882** *Times* 31 Jan. 16/6 (Advt.), Single-stone, half-hoop, and cluster rings. **1892** KIPLING *Lett. of Travel* (1920) 94 His wife..wears half-hoop diamond rings. **1902** *Daily Chron.* 14 June 10/4 The hair..is surmounted by a half-hoop diadem encrusted with precious stones. **1928** R. HALL *Well of Loneliness* xxi. 198 'I made your mother's engagement ring for him; a large half-hoop of very fine diamonds.' **1960** R. COLLIER *House called Memory* x. 150 Uncle William Henry bought Dora a half hoop of diamonds as an engagement ring. **1803** T. SHERATON *Cabinet Dict.* 44 As to the particular management of beds, and the articles required in mounting them, together with their various classes; these..will most conveniently come under their respective names, as..Half-tester,..&c. **1859** *Blackw. Mag.* Aug. 229/1 We approached the bed and examined it—a half-tester, such as is commonly found in attics devoted to servants. **1960** H. HAYWARD *Antique Coll.* 279/2 At this period [*sc.* late 17th cent.] a new type of bedstead without footposts was introduced, known as a 'half-tester'.

m. Further examples: *half-believer* (earlier example), *-consciousness, -dark, -darkness, -dream, -education, -hint, -humour, -laugh, -lengthening, -lie, -literate, -look* (examples), *-mind, -power, -savage, -spacing* (on a type-writer), *-whisper* (earlier example).

1814 JANE AUSTEN *Mansf. Park* II. vii. 148 A certain half-look attending the..expression of his hope. **1816** —— *Emma* II. xvii. 320 Much that passed between them was in a half-whisper. **1836** J. S. MILL in *Westm. Rev.* XXV. 5 See how incapable half-savages are of co-operation. **1838** —— *Ibid.* XXVIII. 454 The sceptics and half-believers of the story. —— *Ibid.* XXXI. 484 Almost all rich veins of original and striking speculation have been opened by systematic half-minds. **1862** G. BORROW *Wild Wales* II. xxxii. 370 'In truth I am,' said she, with a half laugh. **1881** 'MARK TWAIN' *Prince & Paup.* 208 His senses struggled to a half-consciousness. **1895** KIPLING *Day's Work* (1898) 344 Leading him on to see, more by half-hints than by any direct word, how boys and men are all of a piece. **1898** *Pearson's Mag.* May 539/1 With a half-power steamer which had only one man all told upon her decks. **1900** *Daily News* 18 Aug. 6/1 How she did it she didn't know, she said, in a half-humour manner. **1904** W. DE LA MARE *Henry Brocken* 13 The half-dream [which] weariness brings. **1904** W. B. YEATS *Tables of Law* 9 The formalisms of half-education. **1905** *Westm. Gaz.* 25 Mar. 11/2 The inaccuracies do not matter very much unless they are so gross as to shock the great half-literate. **1926** FOWLER *Mod. Eng. Usage* 399/2 The uneasy half-literates who like to prove that they can spell. **1927** A. CLARKE *Son of Learning* II. 44 In the half-darkness his cowled figure suggests demonic possession. **1928** D. H. LAWRENCE *Lady Chatterley* xvi. 278 She could still see on Connie's face.. the half-dream of passion. *a* **1930** —— *Last Poems* (1932) 257 A half-lie causes the immediate contradiction of the half-lie. **1934** BLUNDEN *Choice or Chance* 40 Possessions too,—part fungus and part flower,—Forced on him their half-power. **1934** E. POUND *Eleven New Cantos* xxxix. 45 From star up to the half-dark. **1937** *Mind* XLVI. 101 Postulating a sort of extra, separate half-mind—entelechy—like Driesch. **1938** *Times Lit. Suppl.* 8 Oct. 638/3 The curious delicate half-humour which smiled at his own hypersensitiveness. **1941** T. S. ELIOT *Dry Salvages* ii. 11 The backward half-look Over the shoulder, towards the primitive terror. **1948** —— *Notes Def. Culture* 105 But what is important is to remember that 'half-education' is a modern phenomenon. **1949** KOESTLER *God that Failed* 31 Once or twice she spoke on the telephone to comrades of hers—always in half-words and half-hints. **1953** K. JACKSON *Lang. & Hist. Early Brit.* 342 Half-lengthening of penultimates could not have arisen until after the accent-shift. **1959** E. PULGRAM *Introd. Spectrogr. Speech* viii. 64 The half-power points, whose power is..proportional to the square of the amplitude. **1961** *Imperial Type Faces* 10 A half-spacing device lends itself to display work. **1962** *Which?* Dec. 359/2 If you leave out a letter, it should be possible, after rubbing out the word, to fit in the extra letter by using half-spacing.

n. half-Abo *Austral.*, a person having one Aboriginal parent (cf. *ABO *a.* and *sb.*); **half-adder** [*ADDER[1] 3], a unit in an electronic computer (see quot. 1962); **half-arsed, -ass, -assed** *adjs. slang* (orig. *U.S.*), ineffectual, inadequate, mediocre; stupid, inexperienced; **half-belt** (see quot. 1957); **half-bull,** (*b*) [BULL *sb.*[1] 7] *slang*, a half-crown; **half-cell** *Electr.* (see quot. 1943); **half-centre** (see quot.); **half-commission** *attrib.*, working for or based on half commission; **half-compression** *attrib.*, designating a device for lessening the compression of the explosive mixture in an internal-combustion engine; **half-day,** half a working day (cf. *DAY *sb.* 8 d); **half-dress** (see quot. 1960); **half-duck** = HALF-BIRD; **half-evergreen** *a.*, of a plant that is evergreen in a mild climate; also as *sb.*; **half-foot** (see quot. 1880); **half-frame,** (*a*) *pl.* reading-spectacles consisting of only the lower half of the frames and lenses; also in sing. *attrib.*; (*b*) (*Photogr.*) half the standard 35 mm. picture size; **half-gerund** (see quot. 1924); **half-hose** (see HOSE *sb.* 1 a γ); **half inferior** *a. Bot.* (see quots.); **half-integer,** any member of the set of numbers obtained by dividing the odd integers by two; hence **half-integral** *a.*; **half-landing,** a landing half-way up a flight of stairs; **half-lap** (see LAP *sb.*[3] 2 b); **half-lattice girder,** one consisting of a single system or row of triangles; **half-lift** [*LIFT *sb.*[2] 5 f], a medium-stressed lift in O.E. verse; **half-line** *Pros.* [LINE *sb.*[2] 23 e], half of a line of verse, used esp. of O.E. and related verse; **half-pass** (see quot. 1948); **half-period,** the *HALF-LIFE of a substance; see also quot. 1904; **half-pint** [cf. sense II. a] *fig.*, a small or insignificant person; also *attrib.*; **half-plane** *Math.* (see quot. 1959); **half-plate** *Photogr.* (see PLATE *sb.* 5 c), also *attrib.*; **half-portion,** a half of a portion; *fig.*, a small or insignificant person; **half-race** *Bot.* (see quots.); **half-rhyme,** an imperfect or near rhyme; hence **half-rhymed** *ppl. a.*; **half-ripper, half-rip saw,** a finer-toothed ripping saw (see RIPPER 2, RIP-SAW *sb.*); **half-roll** *Aeronaut.*, a manœuvre in which the aircraft turns through 180° about the longitudinal axis; hence **half-roll** *v. intr.*; **half-secret dovetail** (see quot.); **half-sheet,** (*b*) (see quots.); **half-sibling,** each of two or more individuals having one parent in common; **half-slip,** the lower half of a slip (see SLIP *sb.*[3] 4 c); a petticoat; **half-sole** *v.* (earlier U.S. example); **half-speed shaft,** the cam shaft of a four-stroke cycle internal-combustion engine, which rotates at half the speed of the crank shaft; **half-stress** *Pros.*, a secondary stress; **half-stuff** (later example); **half-term,** a period approximately half-way through a school or other term, often made the occasion of a holiday; freq. *attrib.* as in *half-term holiday*; **half-thickness** *Physics* = *HALF-VALUE *thickness*; **half-turning bolt** (see quot.); **half-uncial,** writing which combines the characters of uncial and cursive; semi-uncial; also *attrib.*; **half-valve** *Mus.* (see quot. 1955); hence **half-valved** *ppl. a.*; **half-valving** *vbl. sb.*; **half-verse** *Pros.*, = *half-line* (above); **half-virgin** = *DEMI-VIERGE; **half-watt** *a. Electr.*, applied to a gas-filled incandescent lamp consuming approximately a half-watt per candle-power; **half-wave,** one-half of a complete wave, esp. of electricity or radiation; freq. *attrib.*, utilizing only alternate halves of a sequence of waves, as *half-wave rectification* (*Chambers's Techn. Dict.* 1940); half a wave-length long, as *half-wave antenna, dipole*, etc.; **half-white** = HALF-BREED 2; **half-word, halfword,** a group of consecutive bits, which can be handled as a unit, occupying half a word storage unit of a computer; **half-world,** the demi-monde (earlier and later examples); also *transf.*

1945 C. MANN in B. James *Austral. Short Stories* (1963) 72 Little black half-abo. piccaninnies. **1954** *Electronic Engin.* XXVI. 288 Numbers always enter the accumulator loop via the two half-adders and are therefore automatically added to the previous contents. **1962** *Gloss. Terms Autom. Data Processing* (*B.S.I.*) 60 *Half-adder*, a logic element with two outputs and two inputs to which may be applied signals representing a digit or a number and a single addend or carry digit. **1961** A. WEST *Trend is Up* ix. 386 You don't know what it is to worry about what half-arsed thing your own son is going to pull on you next. **1972** *Observer* 24 Sept. 35/2 The sort of half-arsed dottiness they dish out in West End comedies. **1959** N. MAILER *Advts. for Myself* (1961) 399 He spent years hobnobbing with gentlemanly shits and half-ass operators. **1932** *Amer. Speech* VII. 333 *Half-assed*, mediocre; insignificant. **1955** W. GADDIS *Recognitions* I. v. 183 A half-assed critic..thinks he has to make you unhappy before you'll take him seriously. **1957** M. B. PICKEN *Fashion Dict.* 19 *Half b[elt]*, belt which extends only half-way around body; especially one across back section of garment, as on sports jackets or coats. **1960** *Farmer & Stockbreeder* 9 Feb. Suppl. 5/1 A..jacket with a half-belt at the back. **1789** Half bull [see *BOB *sb.*[8]]. **1852** Halfbull [see BULL *sb.*[1] 7]. **1906** E. DYSON *Fact'ry 'Ands* xvi. 216 I've gotter get that 'arf-bull 'r somethin' dangerous may set in. **1940** *Chambers's Techn. Dict.* 399/1 Half-cell. **1943** *Gloss. Terms Electr. Engin.* (*B.S.I.*) v. 93 *Half cell*, of an electrolytic cell: an electrode and that part of the electrolyte with which it is in contact. **1888** *Lockwood's Dict. Mech. Engin.*, *Half-centre*, half-centre is sometimes used to denote the position of the crank-pin of an engine when midway between the two dead centres or dead points. **1909** *Westm. Gaz.* 16 Feb. 7/4 He became a half-commission man with a firm of stockbrokers. **1927** *Sunday Express* 13 Mar. 2 A half-commission stockbroker. **1931** *Times* 16 Mar. 18/1 The Half Commission Practice. **1901** *Motor-Car World* II. 317/1 To facilitate starting the engine a half-compression device is fitted which operates on the exhaust valve through the medium of a second or subsidiary cam attached to the main cam working the exhaust. **1907** *Westm. Gaz.* 11 Nov. 7/2 The simple half-compression gear. **1791** F. BURNEY *Jrnl.* 31 July (1972) I. 2 One precious half Day I was indulged with my kindest Mr. Lock. **1876** LADY C. SCHREIBER *Jrnl.* (1911) I. 477 We found that we could not execute all our little shoppings.., because the Saturday is but a half-day. **1932** *Discovery* Mar. 71/2 Now the minimum wage [for farm workers] is 30s. per week of five shorter days and a half day. **1973** *Daily Tel.* 8 Feb. 1/1 The Shadow Cabinet decided to give up a half-day of its Parliamentary time to complete the debate in the Commons. **1788** E. SHERIDAN *Jrnl.* (1960) 138 Great coats made very open before to shew the peticoat—in Undress—half dress, Night gown and peticoat with fine muslin Aprons—full dress I have not seen. *c* **1810** W. HICKEY *Mem.* (1918) II. xx. 261 A tailor named Knill..advised my having a dark green with gold binding..and for half dress a Bon de Paris with gold frogs. **1815** *Belle Assemblée* Sept. Pl., Autumnal Walking Dress...The head dress must be either a half-dress cap, or a white satin gipsy, or Wellington hat. **1850** *Ladies' Gaz. Fashion* Aug. 255/1 Plain *mousseline de soie*.. begins to be a good deal seen in half-dress. **1960** CUNNINGTON & BEARD *Dict. Eng. Costume* 100/2 *Half dress*, late 18th and 19th c's...The costume worn at day functions and at informal evening ones. **1892** W. J. GORDON *Our Country's Birds* 10 Local and Popular Names...Half Duck. **1903** J. A. HAMILTON *MS. in Red Box* 329 Good sport among the half-duck and mussel-duck which abounded at Tudworth. **1934** WEBSTER, Half-evergreen. **1952** A. G. L. HELLYER *Sanders's Encycl. Gardening* (ed. 22) 131 Glaucophylla, half-evergreen. **1814** J. SINCLAIR *Agric. Scot.* App. II. 396 *Half foot*, is another method of occupying a farm, equally barbarous in itself, and adverse to improvement. It is not so prevalent in the Highlands, as in some of the Western Isles. **1873** *Trans. Highland Soc.* 298 *Out* or *led* farms like the *metayers* of France, or the *half-foot* tenants of the Hebrides. **1880** W. SKENE *Celtic Scot.* III. 370 A kind of tenancy called half-foot, where the possessor of the farm furnished the land and seed corn,..the produce being divided. **1961** *Colour Photogr.* VI. 249/3 The normal 20-exposure cassette gives 40 half-frame exposures and the 36-exposure cassette gives 72 so that each colour transparency would cost less than 6d. **1967** A. FLOWERS in L. Deighton *London Dossier* 170 Buy one of the half-frame cameras such as the Olympus Pen D2 or the Canon Dial. **1968** J. HUDSON *Case of Need* I. i. 10 'Call me,' Sanderson said, peering over his half frames. **1968** L. DEIGHTON *Only when I Larf* ii. 17 Strange half-frame spectacles that he peered over abstractedly. **1898** H. SWEET *New Eng. Gram.* II. 121 The absence of a distinction between common case and genitive in the plural often makes it impossible in the spoken language to distinguish between gerund and half-gerund, as in *to prevent the ladies leaving us, I generally ordered the table to be removed..*, where the..alteration of *ladies* into *ladies'* would make *leaving* into a full gerund. *Ibid.*, There seems little doubt that the colloquial half-gerunds in such causal constructions as *she caught cold sitting on the damp grass*..have arisen through dropping a preposition. **1924** H. E. PALMER *Gram. Spoken Eng.* 168 In certain constructions the ing form has a function intermediate between that of the present participle and the gerund. Sweet suggests for such cases the term *half-gerund*. **1900** B. D. JACKSON *Gloss. Bot. Terms* 118/1 *Half inferior*, used of an ovary when the stamens are perigynous. **1940** *Chambers's Techn. Dict.* 399/1 *Half inferior*, said of a flower in which the receptacle forms a cup which is adherent to the base of the ovary and partly up its side. **1928** *Proc. Physical Soc.* XL. 332 The number *m* can take only certain discrete values (either integers or half-integers). **1971** P. HLAWICZKA *Introd. Quantum Electronics* xvi. 247 The quantum numbers j_1 and j_2 may be either integers or half integers. **1930** RUARK & UREY *Atoms, Molecules & Quanta* vii. 187 Many authors use $j+\frac{1}{2}$ instead, when j is half-integral. **1968** M. S. LIVINGSTON *Particle Physics* ii. 24 Nuclei with an odd number of protons plus electrons, each with half-integral spin, should result in half-integral nuclear angular momenta. **1910** *Daily Chron.* 1 Feb. 1/1, I saw the proprietor, ..perched on the half-landing of the stairs. **1965** 'T. HINDE' *Games of Chance* I. i. 16 The black and lemon half-landing bathroom. *a* **1877** KNIGHT *Dict. Mech.*, II. 1049/2 *Half-lattice girder*, a form of girder..consisting of horizontal upper and lower bars, and a series of diagonal bars, sloping alternately in opposite directions, and dividing the space between the bars into a series of triangles. **1894** H. SWEET *Anglo-Saxon Reader* (ed. 7) p. xc, To make up for the want of an accompanying dip, an extra medium-stressed half-lift is made obligatory. **1967** C. L. WRENN *Study O.E. Lit.* 38 Five basic combinations of stress or lift of the voice, half or secondary stress or half-lift, and unstressed syllables. **1864** H. MORLEY *Eng. Writers* I. 251 The most important is a heroic poem.. extending..to 6357 of the short Anglo-Saxon lines, or half lines, as they are usually printed. **1900** A. S. COOK *Christ of Cynewulf* 70 Half-line space. **1910** F. TUPPER *Riddles of Exeter Bk.* 220 The half-line is of the A-type..

common in the *Riddles*. **1927** E. V. Gordon *Introd. Old Norse* 293 In ON. tradition the unit verse was not the long line, but the half-line, which was called a *visa* or line. **1964** *English Studies* XLV. 38 The patronymic epithet is separated from its antecedent by at least a full half-line. **1965** *Ibid.* XLVI. 420 In Germanic the basic principle is stress, together with a division into half-lines. **1929** *Man. Horsemastership, Equitation & Driving* ii. 115 The bending lesson includes..the 'half passage' or 'half pass'... In all lateral movements the forehand must slightly precede the hind quarters. **1948** E. Schmit-Jensen *Equestrian Olympic Games* App. 95 At the Half Pass the horse moves on two tracks... The outside legs pass and cross in front of the inside legs... The legs on the side to which the horse is moving are the inside legs; those on the opposite side the outside legs. **1904** Goodchild & Tweney *Technol. & Sci. Dict.* 277/2 The area included in this curve is the first half period element. *Ibid.*, The effect of the whole wave can be expressed in terms of these half period components. **1905** *Nature* 13 Apr. 574/1 Different samples gave for the half-period of decay from 52 to 55 seconds. **1942** J. D. Stranathan *'Particles' of Mod. Physics* xi. 448 One product of the nuclear disruption was a Ba isotope having a half period of 86 minutes. **1926** Maines & Grant *Wise-Crack Dict.* 9/1 *Half pint*, stunted individual. **1929** W. R. Burnett *Little Caesar* iv. ii. 117 'Here's the half-pint,' said Killer Pepi, pushing Joe Sansone forward. **1930** G. C. Myers *Mod. Parent* ix. 165 Here are types of remarks which some parents..will stoop to make: 'What do you think of our half-pint?' **1938** Wodehouse *Summer Moonshine* xvii. 200 That wonder girl in whose half-pint person were combined all the lovely qualities of woman of which he had so often dreamed. **1943** C. H. Ward-Jackson *Piece of Cake* 35 *Half-pint hero*, swaggerer. **1948** 'N. Shute' *No Highway* iii. 82 The little half-pint size, with thick glasses? **1891** Half-plane [see Orthomorphic *a.* 2]. **1927** H. G. Forder *Found. Euclidean Geom.* iii. 68 The regions into which a line *a* separates a plane *ω* in which it lies are the 'half-planes from *a* in *ω*'. **1959** G. & R. C. James *Math. Dict.* 182/1 *Half-plane*, the part of a plane which lies on one side of a line in the plane. **1968** P. A. P. Moran *Introd. Probability Theory* x. 473 In the cases considered the domain is a rectangle, an infinite strip, a half-plane, or infinite quadrant. **1877** *Design & Work* III. 451/1 Half-plate portrait lens. **1892** *Photogr. Ann.* II. 58 On your slide you require to get all the view on the half-plate negative. **1903** A. Watkins *Photogr.* (ed. 2) 13 Half-plate is the favourite amateur size. **1907** F. H. Burnett *Shuttle* xxxviii. 379 Adroit manipulation of 'portions' and 'half portions' ..enabled them to add variety to their bill of fare. **1919** Wodehouse *Coming of Bill* (1920) i. v. 59 He certainly is a kind o' half-portion, ma'am! **1967** —— *Company for Henry* vii. 130 Even when calling her a squirt and a half-portion he had thought of her as a comely squirt and a half-portion with plenty of sex appeal. **1967** L. Deighton *Expensive Place* ii. 14 [He] did not like orders for..*charcuterie* as a main dish or half-portions of anything. **1906** R. H. Lock *Variation, Heredity & Evolution* v. 141 In the case of a half-race a small percentage only of seedlings is found to produce plants which show the racial character. *Ibid.* 145 A half-race might have been defined as a strain in which the character of the complete race is usually latent, and only rarely appears. **1928** B. D. Jackson *Gloss. Bot. Terms* (ed. 4) 169/2 *Half-race*, a form intermediate between a species and a variety of it, producing but few seedlings of the racial character, the majority reverting to the specific type. **1830** B. Thorpe tr. *Rask's Gram. Anglo-Saxon Tongue* 139 Line-Rime is when two syllables, in the same line of verse, have their vowels and the consonants following them alike, which is called perfect rime (consonances), or unlike vowels, and only the following consonants the same, which is called half rime (assonances). **1860** G. P. Marsh *Lect. Eng. Lang.* xxv. 553 In Icelandic poetry,..imperfect rhyme is regularly employed, and..is called skothending,..which we may conveniently translate by *half-rhyme*. *Ibid.* 560 Although half-rhyme may be said to be peculiar to Icelandic poetry, ..yet there are examples of the employment of both full and imperfect line-rhymes in modern English. **1873–4** G. M. Hopkins *Note-Bks.* (1937) 243 In Icelandic verse an opposite kind of alliteration (skothending) is made use of, namely ending with the same consonant but after a different vowel, as *'bad' 'led'*, *'find' 'band'*, *'sin' 'run'* (from Marsh, who calls it *half-rhyme*). **1886** J. M. D. Meiklejohn *Eng. Lang.* ii. 186 The English language is very poor in rhymes, when compared with Italian or German. Accordingly, half-rhymes are admissible..: sun/gone, love/move, allow/bestow, etc. **1936** M. Roberts *Faber Bk. Mod. Verse* 28 In Owen's war poetry, the half-rhymes almost invariably fall from a vowel of high pitch to one of low pitch. **1960** D. S. R. Welland *Wilfred Owen* vi. 115 Only in 'Arms and the Boy', 'Wild with All Regrets', and 'Strange Meeting' does he [*sc.* Wilfred Owen] write in half-rhymed couplets throughout. **1841** *Penny Cycl.* XX. 476/2 The ripping-saw, half-ripper, hand-saw..are saws for the use of one person. **1846, 1875** Half-rip saw [see Rip-saw *sb.*]. **1926** J. M. Grider *War Birds* 206, I half rolled on top of him, he half rolled too. **1934** V. M. Yeates *Winged Victory* i. iii. 29 The same with the half-roll. Nothing would half-roll like a Camel. A twitch of the stick and flick of the rudder and you were on your back. **1904** Goodchild & Tweney *Technol. & Sci. Dict.* 277/2 *Half secret dovetail*, a dovetail of the form used in a drawer front; it is concealed in a front view, but visible in the side of the drawer when drawn out. **1683–4** J. Moxon *Mech. Exerc. Printing* (1962) 227 In Half-sheets, all the Pages belonging to the White Paper and Reteration are Imposed in one Chase, and are plac'd, as you see by the Drafts..of Half-sheet Forms. **1888** C. T. Jacobi *Printers' Vocab.* 56 Book-work is sometimes printed in 'half-sheet' fashion. When thus printed there are two copies on one sheet. **1914** T. L. De Vinne *Mod. Book Composition* ix. 336 It is called half-sheet because this larger sheet must be cut in halves before either half can be folded. **1952** E. J. Labarre *Dict. Paper* (ed. 2) 122/1 *Half-sheet*, printing a whole sheet of a book so that all the pages of a signature are in one forme. **1964** F. Bowers *Bibliogr. & Textual Crit.* iv. ii. 109 The work-and-turn method of printing by half-sheet imposition. **1903** *Biometrika* Nov. 391 The high values, however, found for half-siblings in the case of the thoroughbreds. **1938** *Jrnl. R. Anthrop. Inst.* 213 The mother allows the children to invite their half-siblings. **1959** B. Wootton *Social Sci. & Social Pathol.* iii. 85 Some authors state whether deceased, half- or step-siblings are included, or whether the delinquent himself is counted in the total of family members. **1952** H. Waugh *Last seen Wearing* (1953) 31 'What about her..undergarments?' 'Half-slip, pants, and bra.' **1957** M. B. Picken *Fashion Dict.* 313/1 *Half slip*, any of the various types of slips starting at the waistline. **1795** J. & E. Pettigrew *Let.* 5 Apr. (MS.) (D.A.E.), I have not got my shoes halfsoaled yet, as shewmakers are very scarce. **1902** A. C. Harmsworth et al. *Motors* viii. 152 A crank, operated by a connecting rod from the half-speed shaft on the engine. **1905** Goodchild & Tweney *Technol. & Sci. Dict.* s.v. *Motor Cycles*, The half speed shaft, rotating at one half the speed of the crank shaft. **1938** A. Campbell *Battle of Brunanburh* 24 Graz..regarding *butu* as having a half-stress on the second syllable. **1961** *Rev. Eng. Stud.* XII. 345 Long and short syllables must be distinguished in scansion, when they bear either a strong stress or a half-stress. **1912** *Chambers's Jrnl.* Oct. 671/2 The pulp—at this stage commonly called half-stuff—is fed into beating-engines. **1888** *Boy's Own Paper* Summer No. 16/2 At half-term it was Hoskyn's custom to write letters to all the parents with reports of their sons' progress. **1944** L. A. G. Strong *All fall Down* 55 It's half term, as even you must have realised. **1950** Hodgkinson & Muir in R. M. Scrimgeour *North London Collegiate Sch. 1850–1950* v. 101 Miss Drummond spent a half-term morning in her Sussex cottage trying to see whether, if girls spent the whole day at Canons, they could be supplied with adequate teaching there. **1950** Glasstone *Sourcebk. Atomic Energy* vii. 170/2 The mass half-thickness, i.e., the actual..half-thickness multiplied by the density, is almost independent of the material absorbing the gamma rays. **1958** W. K. Mansfield *Elem. Nucl. Physics* v. 45 To compare the penetrating power of the *γ*-rays with that of *α* and *β*-rays, it is necessary to estimate the half-thickness. **1960** J. N. Gregory *World of Radioisotopes* i. 9 The shorter the wavelength of the *γ*-radiation the greater the half-thickness. *a* **1877** Knight *Dict. Mech.* II. 1050 *Half-turning bolt*, one with a thread occupying one half of its cylindrical surface. **1885** *Encycl. Brit.* XVIII. 153/2 Examples of half-uncial writing. **1897** H. W. Johnston *Lat. MSS.* 70 Half-Uncials are derived from the uncials and represent the last efforts of the book hand to differentiate itself from the improved business hand of the time... It is also called the Roman Uncial and Pre-Caroline Minuscule. **1912** E. M. Thompson *Introd. Gr. & Lat. Palaeogr.* 305 It is the Half-uncial hand which we find employed as far back as the fifth century as a literary hand in the production of formally written MSS. **1926** E. A. Lowe in Crump & Jacob *Legacy of Middle Ages* 209 Before developing a minuscule Irish calligraphers had created a majuscule, the Irish half-uncial as it is styled, of which the Book of Kells, a work of unsurpassed skill and artistry, is the most eminent example. **1946** Mezzrow & Wolfe *Really Blues* i. 12 Yellow's half-valve inflections and slurs. **1955** L. Feather *Encycl. Jazz* vii. 292 *Boy meets Horn*, a showpiece displaying the novel style and tone he popularized using 'half-valve' effect (a squeezed tonal sound obtained by depressing the valve halfway). **1958** S. Dance in P. Gammond *Decca Bk. Jazz* xxiii. 297 Original creations like *Boy meets horn* with its stifled, half-valved statements. **1956** S. Traill *Play that Music* viii. 87 Some players achieve a sort of 'blue note' effect by 'half-valving', which would mean, in our particular example, pressing the middle valve (for a correct E♭) half down. The distortion of tone which this produces is not very attractive, and I would discourage 'half-valving' altogether. **1711** Half Verse [see Hemistich]. **1876** H. Sweet *Anglo-Saxon Reader* p. xcviii, There is often only one alliterative letter in the first half verse. **1907** F. A. Blackburn *Exodus & Daniel* p. x, Uncorrected errors are few, though occasional omissions occur, generally of a half-verse. **1938** A. Campbell *Battle of Brunanburh* 16 It will be convenient to group its half-verses in the 'five types' of Sievers. **1946** Koestler *Thieves in Night* 165 As obscene and shocking to me as a petting party with a half-virgin. **1965** N. Freeling *Criminal Conversation* ii. xv. 164, I imagined, being full of valuable premedical catch-phrases, that she was 'half-virgin' and therefore despicable. **1913** *Lighting Jrnl.* I. 207/1 (*heading*) A half watt lamp!..The types which it is expected to first develop..operate at an efficiency of half a watt per candlepower. **1915** *Nature* XCVI. 407/1 With electricity generated in modern power-houses, and ordinary metal filament lamps, 750,000 candle-power-hours are generated per ton of coal, compared with 260,000 C.P. per ton of coal when gas and modern gas mantles are used. The extended use of so-called 'half-watt' lamps will soon double this 750,000. **1932** N. Royde-Smith *Incredible Tale* 57 The white glare of the half-watt lamp hanging from the studio roof. **1904** Goodchild & Tweney *Technol. & Sci. Dict.*, *Half wave plate*, a plate of doubly refracting crystal, capable of splitting up a plane polarised ray into two portions, one of which is retarded half a wave length with respect to the other. **1912** *Motor Man.* (ed. 14) ii. 33 When the platinum contacts at the end of the armature touch, one-half of every complete wave flows into the accumulator, and when the contacts separate, the reverse wave of the current is interrupted at the zero or no-voltage line; thus only the half-waves of current flowing in the same direction are used. **1926** R. W. Hutchinson *Wireless* viii. 145 If the first half-wave is positive the grid will become positive. *Ibid.*, The next half-wave is negative and this still further lowers the potential of the grid. **1928** *Morning Post* 6 Feb. 3/4 A half wave rectifier. **1943** *Gloss. Terms Telecommunications* (*B.S.I.*) 67 *Half-wave dipole*, a straight aerial symmetrical in regard to its standing-wave current and usually approximately half a wavelength long. **1962** Simpson & Richards *Junction Transistors* xii. 276 The same is true of any amplifier, such as the Class AB, whose output is asymmetrical and consists of pulses that are larger than one half-wave. **1962** Corson & Lorrain *Introd. Electromagn. Fields* xiii. 446 After having mastered the electric dipole, we shall be able to study the radiation field of the half-wave antenna—the type commonly used for transmitting radio waves. **1866** 'Mark Twain' *Lett. fr. Hawaii* (1967) 26 Foreigners and the better class of natives, and 'ha whites' in carriages. **1897** —— *Following Equator* 63, I asked after 'Billy' Ragsdale, interpreter to the Parliament in my time—a half-white. **1901** *Daily Colonist* (Victoria, B.C.) 23 Oct. 8/3 In this boat's crew..was Charlie Diamond... He was a Bonin island half-white and is well known to old time sealers. **1959** J. Jeenel *Programming for Digital Computers* ii. 60 One might choose a 12-digit word size for the calculator and have a word represent either one number or a pair of instructions. The single-address instructions would be represented by 'half words'. **1964** Halfword [see *byte]. **1970** O. Dopping *Computers & Data Processing* vi. 105 Some machines pack two instructions per cell, and there are different addresses for each half-word, e.g. even addresses for left half-words, odd addresses for right half-words. **1870** D. J. Kirwan *Palace & Hovel* xliii. 613 'Baby Hamilton' is another celebrity of the Half-World. Many stories are told about the recklessness of this girl. **1874** *Porcupine* 21 Feb. 742/1 Those moral magistrates who have so distinctly set their faces against Cremorne and other outdoor haunts of the 'half-world'. **1950** Half-world [see *folk-jazz* s.v. *folk 6]. **1972** *Times* 6 Apr. 7/5 Away from his chosen half-world, Munby's social life was passed in the first literary and artistic circles of his day.

half-and-half. Add: **2. b.** A half-breed or half-caste.

1827 J. F. Cooper *Prairie* iii. 58 The half-and-halfs, that one meets in these distant districts, are altogether more barbarous than the real savage. **1922** Joyce *Ulysses* 315 Pity about her... Or any other woman marries a half and half.

half-baked, *a.* Add: Hence as *sb.*, a half-baked person. *colloq.* and *dial.*

1866 J. Sleigh in *Reliquary* VI. 160 *Half-char* or *half-baked*, a foolish fellow. **1923** U. L. Silberrad *Lett. J. Armiter* ix. 192, I believe girls were better off really with the old lock-and-key, guard-the-girls sort than with these half-bakeds, who let 'em have their heads.

half-binding. (Earlier U.S. example.)

1821 M. L. Weems *Lett.* III. 325 [Books] in neat half binding, red backs, and corners.

half-blood. Add: **4.** *attrib.* Half-blooded.

1830 in *Wisconsin State Hist. Soc. Coll.* (1892) XII. 185 He is a halfblood St. Regis, with a halfblood Menomonie wife. **1835** C. F. Hoffman *Winter in West* I. 215 The driver was also accompanied on the box by a well made young half-blood Chippeway. **1837** H. Colman *Rep. Agric. Mass.* (1838) 52, I have slaughtered two half-blood heifers, which have weighed at four years old over 700 lbs. **1873** J. H. Beadle *Undevel. West* xxi. 406 A handsome half-blood daughter married to a white man. **1943** *Sun* (Baltimore) 4 Dec. 12/6 A further sprinkling of transactions is noted in fine and half-blood wool.

half-bred, *a.* Add: **1. b.** Of a sheep. *Austral.* and *N.Z.*

1891 R. Wallace *Rural Econ. Austral. & N.Z.* xviii. 265 The half-bred sheep, being the various crosses between Merino ewes and long-woolled rams. **1959** Baker *Drum* ii. 116 *Halfbred sheep*, orig. a sheep by a longwool ram from a merino ewe; now loosely applied to the type.

B. *sb.* A half-bred sheep. *Austral.* and *N.Z.*

1848 E. G. Wakefield *Let.* in *N.Z. Jrnl. Agric.* (1950) Feb. 136/3 The want of the more prolific and hardy constitution of the half-bred. **1891** R. Wallace *Rural Econ. Austral. & N.Z.* xviii. 265 The half-breds, or first crosses, are the most profitable sheep. **1930** L. G. D. Acland *Early Canterbury Runs* i. 7 Corriedales and Half-breds have displaced the Merinos except on the lightest and highest country. **1956** G. Bowen *Wool Away!* (ed. 2) xii. 134 Half-breds are recognised in New Zealand as a cross between Merinos and one of the English longwool breeds.

half-breed. Add: **1.** (Later example.)

1858 C. L. Flint *Milch Cows & Dairy Farming* (1860) ii. 69 Qualities which are, in a measure, artificial.. change not only with the breed of one species, but with the different individuals of the same breed, of the same half-breed, and often of the same family.

2. (Earlier U.S. example.)

1760 *Newport* (R.I.) *Mercury* 22 Apr. 2/1 On the 18th a Half-Breed, who is a Leader and Head Warrior.. came..to Fort Augusta.

b. *transf.* and *fig.*

1846 *Quincy* (Ill.) *Whig* 27 Jan. 2/4 All the Jacks in the county, consisting of T. H. Owen, John Harper, Backenstos, Bedell, and a few 'half breeds'. **1883** 'Mark Twain' *Life on Mississippi* xliv. 402 This reminds me that a remark of a very peculiar nature was made here in my neighbourhood (in the North) a few days ago: 'He hadn't ought to have went.' How is that? Isn't that a good deal of a triumph? One knows the orders combined in this half-breed's architecture without inquiring: one parent Northern, the other Southern. **1952** A. Stevenson *Speeches* (1953) 179 I'm a half-breed myself. My father was from an old, staunch Democratic family, and he was a Presbyterian. My mother was from an equally old and staunch Republican family and she was a Unitarian.

4. (Earlier U.S. example.)

a **1762** S. Niles *Wars* in *Mass. Hist. Soc. Coll.* (1861) 4th Ser. V. ii. 538 One Molton, a half-breed fellow,.. seized the fellow that wounded Mr. Atkins.

half-cock, *sb.* Add: **3.** *attrib.*, as **half-cock shot** or **stroke** *Cricket*, a stroke begun as a forward stroke but checked half-way, the ball being allowed to hit the bat.

1888 R. H. Lyttelton in Steel & Lyttelton *Cricket* ii. 52 He may, after he has got forward and perceived his error, effect a compromise and perform what is sometimes called a 'half-cock stroke'. **1909** *Westm. Gaz.*

17 Apr. 16/2 He may occasionally use a half-cock stroke with the left leg well up to the bat. **1959** *Times* 29 May 4/4 Hallam..made a half-cock shot to be caught and bowled.

half-cocked, *ppl. a.* and *pa. pple.* [See HALF-COCK v.] **a.** Of a gun: at half-cock.
1809 [see COCKED *ppl. a.*² 2]. **1833** [see HALF-COCK v.]. **b.** Partly intoxicated. *dial.* and *slang.*
c **1830** T. WILSON *Pitman's Pay* (1843) 54 Half-cock'd and canty, hyem we gat. **1886** W. H. LONG *I.O.W. Dial.* 120 All on 'em was about half cocked. **1888** [see COCKED *ppl. a.*² 2]. **1910** *Dial. Notes* III. vi. 453 *Half-cocked,..* Half drunk.
c. *to go off half-cocked:* to speak or act prematurely. *U.S. colloq.*
1833 *Deb. Congress U.S.* 31 Jan. 1521 The gentleman from Maryland has gone off half cocked. **1877** J. HABBERTON *Jericho Road* xvi. 152 Just like you, always goin' off half-cocked. **1920** S. LEWIS *Main St.* 349 Well—I don't suppose I ought to have gone off half-cocked, and not jollied him along. **1940** E. POUND *Let.* 14 Mar. (1971) 340 No use my going off half-cocked on large subjects whereon I have not yet arrived at conclusion.
d. Incompletely prepared or realized. Also quasi-*advb.*
1946 M. SHULMAN *Zebra Derby* (1947) viii. 45 You know, we're not going into this thing half cocked. **1953** A. UPFIELD *Murder must Wait* xxi. 186 I've a half-cocked kind of idea.

half-crown. Add: (From 1970 no longer legal tender.)
Hence **half-crowner,** a person who pays a half-crown for a seat at a performance, etc.; a publication costing a half-crown.
1886 H. BAUMANN *Londinismen* 71/2 Half-crowner. **1890** G. B. SHAW *London Music 1888–89* (1938) 288 The half-crowners energetically cried 'Hear, hear'. **1893** FARMER & HENLEY *Slang* III. 250/1 *Half-crowner,* a publication costing 2s. 6d. **1959** *New Statesman* 25 July 106/2 One can watch the half-crowners filing..before the country-house displays of things properly designed and well made.

half-eagle. *U.S.* (Examples.)
1786 in *Amer. Museum* (1789) II. 182/2 There shall be two gold coins; one..equal to five dollars, to be stamped in like manner [to the eagle], and to be called a half-eagle. **1841** *Congress. Globe* 30 July 269/2 It was an open declaration of war upon the half eagles, the gold currency. ..This gold, in half eagles, was too good for us. **1852** *Knickerbocker* XL. 323 He was about to contribute a half eagle to the funds.

half-god. Delete † *Obs.* and add later examples.
1901 JOYCE *Day of Rabblement* 8 The *Adoration of the Magi*..shows what Mr. Yeats can do when he breaks with the half-gods. **1916** 'Æ' *National Being* ii. 14 The gods departed, the half-gods also. **1951** L. MACNEICE tr. *Goethe's Faust* I. 56 A half-god has dashed it asunder!

ha·lf-ha·rdy, *a.* [See HALF- 1 b and HARDY *a.* 4 b.] Of a plant: needing some protection from cold winter weather. Also as *sb.*
1824 LOUDON *Encycl. Gard.* 881 Half-hardy annual border-flowers. **1852** [see HARDEN v. 7]. **1862** [see HALF-1 b]. **1904** *Westm. Gaz.* 6 May 10/1 The fuchsias, the heliotrope, the geraniums..are half-hardies. **1960** *Guardian* 25 June 2/6 Most half-hardy plants are..a bit of a nuisance. *Ibid.,* The true alpine enthusiast will turn his nose up at some of these half-hardies **1972** *Suttons Seeds* (Catal.) 18 Dahlias..Can be treated as an annual or as a half-hardy perennial. *Ibid.* 37 The annual phlox. One of the best half-hardy annuals.

half horse. *U.S.* [HALF adv. 2.] Formerly used in the phr. *half horse and half alligator* (see quots.). Usu. *attrib.*
[**1809** 'D. KNICKERBOCKER' *Hist. N.Y.* (1820) IV. ii. 360 The backwood-men of Kentucky are styled half man, half horse, and half alligator, by the settlers on the Mississippi.] **1820** J. HALL *Lett. fr. West* (1828) 47 Eight or ten of those half-horse and half-alligator' gentry, commonly called Ohio boatmen. **1847** T. B. THORPE *Big Bear of Arkansas* 14 The half horse and half alligator species of men, who are peculiar to 'Old Mississippi'. **1860** *Oregon Argus* 13 Oct. (Th.), These half horse and half alligator sort of politicians are becoming a stench in the nostrils of the American people. **1948** E. N. DICK *Dixie Frontier* 241 More than once a 'half-horse and half-alligator' possessed accurate information on politics and government.

half joe. *N. Amer.* [f. HALF- II. a + JOE *sb.*¹] A Portuguese gold coin, worth 3,200 reis, formerly current in North America. (Cf. *Half Johannes,* s.v. JOHANNES.)
[**1772** [see JOE *sb.*¹].] **1775** in *New Hampshire Hist. Soc. Coll.* IX. 88 A Gentleman yesterday gave me a half Jo. **1809** in P. Horry *Life Marion* (1833) 29 He offered..a half joe a-piece for Marion and me to let the recruits go. **1955** E. POUND *Section: Rock-Drill* lxxxix. 53 Doubloons, guineas, half-Joes.

half-leg. *U.S.* Half the height of a man's leg. In phr. *half-leg deep, high.*
1752 J. HEMPSTEAD *Diary* (1901) 599 A great Snow knee deep..last night & this morning half Leg deep & more. **1825** J. NEAL *Bro. Jonathan* I. 112 Natty, makin' his way, through the bushes, half-leg deep. **1832** J. P. KENNEDY *Swallow Barn* II. i. 13 The snow was lying

about half-leg deep. **1852** G. N. JONES *Florida Plant. Rec.* (1927) 65, I have a little corn half leg high. **1855** *Ibid.* 133 The spring branch newground [is] knee high, spring branch cut half leg.

half-length. 1. (Later examples.)
1812 *Theatrical Inquisitor* I. 21 *Resolved...* That the armorial bearings of the society be a half-length of the American critic, Mr. Snarler. **1911** *Encycl. Brit.* XXII. 128/2 The small half-length of young Martin van Nieumenhoven.

ha·lf-life. Also **half life. 1.** A life of half the full length; an unsatisfactory way of life. Also *attrib.,* denoting a size of painting half life-size.
1864 *Atlantic Monthly* XIII. 157 (*title*) A half-life and half a life. **1867** D. G. ROSSETTI *Let.* 25 July (1965) II. 624 He would prefer a half-life scale. **1963** *Times Lit. Suppl.* 31 May 393/4 The half-life which men were leading.
2. The time in which the quantity of a substance (or the number of similar objects) in a sample decreases by half, *spec.* (*a*) in *Physics* of a radioactive substance, (*b*) in *Med.* and *Biol.* of a substance accumulated in (an organ of) the body. Also *half-life period.*
1907 *Jrnl. Chem. Soc.* XCI. II. 1281 Rutherford and others have shown that whilst radium A, B, and C have a life-period of only a few hours, radium D has a half-life-period of forty years. **1954** H. SEMAT *Introd. Atomic & Nucl. Physics* (ed. 3) xi. 363 The value of the half-life of the neutron was calculated from a determination of the density of the neutron beam and the number of neutrons decaying per unit time per unit volume. **1955** *Metabolism* IV. 419 Two patients convalescing from recently active rheumatic fever..had hydrocortisone half-life values which were similar to those seen in the control subjects. **1955** *Sci. Amer.* Aug. 37/1 So the hazard of a given radio-isotope depends basically on a composite quantity called the 'biological half-life'—a measure of the duration of its activity within the body. **1964** *Times* 31 Mar. 11/4 The extension of the half-life concept, familiar in the field of radioactivity, to the break-down of pesticide residues is very welcome. **1971** MURPHY & MUSTARD in J.-M. Paulus *Platelet Kinetics* ii. 26 The slope of the regression curve divided into −0·30103..is the estimated platelet half-life. **1971** *Nature* 26 Nov. 233/3 The holes made in leaves by herbivorous insects, the half-life of leaves (four to nine months in most species) and a mass of interesting information about the roots and buttresses of tropical trees. **1972** *Ibid.* 22 Dec. 465/1 Because ²⁴⁴Pu has an 82 m.y. half life, its presence today, 56 half lives after the formation of the Earth, is a most impressive accomplishment.

half-man. Add: **a, b.** (Later examples.) **c.** In Carlyle's use, one of two eminent men whose knowledge and attainments complement those of the other.
1832 CARLYLE in *Fraser's Mag.* VI. 413/2 They were the two half-men of their time: whoso should combine the intrepid Candour, and decisive scientific Clearness of Hume, with the Reverence, the Love, and devout Humility of Johnson, were the whole man of a new time. **1838** MILL in *Westm. Rev.* XXXI. 484 He [sc. Bentham] could be a systematic and accurately logical half-man; hunting half-truths to their consequences and practical applications, on a scale both of greatness and of minuteness not previously exemplified. **1932** R. KNOX *Broadcast Minds* vii. 160 We are introduced to a pack of half-men doing a maypole-dance round the Tree. **1941** V. WOOLF *Between Acts* 90 My child's not my child... I'm a half-man. **1953** R. P. ANSCHUTZ *Philos. J. S. Mill* iv. 61 As Carlyle had regarded Hume and Dr. Johnson as the two half-men of their time, so did Mill regard Bentham and Coleridge as the 'great seminal minds' who succeeded them. To Bentham it was given, Mill considered, to discern the truths with which existing doctrines and institutions were at variance; to Coleridge the neglected truths which lay *in* them. Since moreover it was in these terms also that the generality of early Victorians thought about politics, Mill and Carlyle in their turn came to be regarded as the two half-men of that age. **1954** P. H. JOHNSON *Impossible Marriage* 299 A lot of half-men who don't wash.

half-mast. Add: **b.** *transf.*
1940 L. A. G. STRONG *Sun on Water* 139 With his trousers at half-mast. **1966** *Listener* 10 Feb. 210/1 Its [*sc.* a dog's] tail at half-mast.

half-mile. *attrib.* [f. HALF- II. a.] Extending to, comprising or covering, half a mile. Hence **half-miler,** one who competes in a half-mile race; **half-miling,** the running of such a race.
1799 *Steele Papers* I. 176 The Purse is one hundred and fifty Dollars the first day 3 ½-mile heats. **1901** *Encycl. Sport* I. 48/2 The Amateur Championship meeting has..a Half Mile Race. **1934** T. O. BEACHCROFT *Young Man in Hurry* 49 'All out for the half-mile!'..Why did none of the other half-milers move? **1959** *Times* 18 May 3/3 Down the last back straight Valentin went like a half-miler. **1963** *Times* 27 May 5/6 British half-miling, which has been experiencing something of a renaissance this season, was further strengthened over the weekend.

half-moon, *sb.* Add: **2.** On a finger-nail.
1883 M. MORRIS *Bk. of Health* 912 The laminæ in the half moon, or lunula, near the root, are not supplied so abundantly with blood-vessels as those beneath the rest of the nail. **1914** JOYCE *Dubliners* 84 The half-moons of

his nails were perfect. **1952** E. GRIERSON *Reputation for Song* xvii. 144 The nails trimmed short, the half-moons only crescents, almost swallowed by the encroaching skin.
6. half-moon spectacles (or **glasses, specs**), spectacles having lenses shaped like half-moons, used esp. for reading.
1952 B. MALAMUD *Natural* 73 Pop, wearing half-moon specs. **1969** 'G.' NORTH *Procrastination of Sergeant Cluff* xiv. 133 The Duty-constable's reading glasses, wire-framed, half-moon, perched on the tip of his nose. **1969** C. BOOKER *Neophiliacs* viii. 207 Lord Home..looked out over his half-moon spectacles and read the message. **1972** P. TOWNEND *Zoom!* xi. 190 He put on his half-moon spectacles and glanced over them.

halfpenny. Add: Also **ha'penny, hapenny.**
1. Since 1969 used with reference to the 'new penny'.
1969 *Guardian* 30 July 16/1 The halfpenny ceases to be legal tender on Friday [i.e. 1 August]. **1975** *Daily Tel.* 5 May 1/4 Bread prices go up today.., sending the standard loaf up by a halfpenny to 16p.
d. A halfpenny stamp.
1881 *Stamp-Collector's Ann* 9 The penny adhesive stamp of the new type..appeared on the 1st of January, and was followed by the halfpenny and three-halfpence on the 14th October. **1908** *Daily Chron.* 20 Feb. 4/7 Many people..think it necessary to fortify themselves with penny stamps. Others cram on a couple of half-pennies.
2. *not a halfpenny the worse; a bad halfpenny.* (Cf. PENNY.)
1603 S. HARSNET *Declar. Egreg. Popish Impostures* 17 Syluester, Bonifacius, and some other Popes, haue beene errand deuill-coniurers, and yet theyr holinesse not an halfpeny the worse. **1819** J. H. VAUX *Mem.* II. 154 When a man has been upon any errand, or attempting any object which has proved unsuccessful or impracticable, he will say on his return, It's a bad halfpenny; meaning he has returned as he went. **1850** HAWTHORNE *Scarlet Let.* 22 It was not the first time, nor the second, that I had gone away—as it seemed, permanently—but yet returned, like the bad halfpenny. **1895** *Brewer's Dict. Phr. & Fable* (new ed.) 571/2 *I am come back again, like a bad ha'penny.* A facetious way of saying 'More free than welcome'. As a bad ha'penny is returned to its owner, so have I returned to you, and you cannot get rid of me.
3. b. A form of ear-mark on cattle and horses. *U.S.*
Cf. *halfpenny slit,* 'an ear-mark given to pigs or sheep' (E.D.D.).
1658 *Rec. East Hampton, N.Y.* (1887) I. 151 John Woodroff marked a horse colt with a hapenny under the left eare. **1666** *Early Rec. Portsmouth, R.I.* (1901) 266 A halfpeny from the route [of the ear]. **1667** *Ibid.* 269 A halfpeney out of the r[ight ear]. **1702** *Town Rec. Topsfield, Mass.* (1917) I. 124 A..horse..[with] a half penny cut out of the right Ear. **1845** *Early Rec. Portsmouth, R.I.* (1901) 387 The Ear Mark of the Creatures of David Baker is two half pennys before the near or left ear.
4. a. (Further examples.)
1729 E. SMITH *Compleat Housewife* (ed. 3) 86 Slice a halfpenny Loaf. **1747** H. GLASSE *Art of Cookery* xv. 140 Your Oven must be as hot as for Halfpenny Bread. **1762** BOSWELL *London Jrnl.* 21 Dec. (1950) 99 A halfpenny roll,..which I had bought at a baker's. **1903** G. B. SHAW *Man & Superman* II. 54 Here comes the New Man, demoralizing himself with a halfpenny paper as usual. **1908** *Chambers's Jrnl.* Jan. 62/1 It..marks as great advance upon the latter as does the incandescent gas-burner upon the halfpenny dip. **1909** H. G. WELLS *Tono-Bungay* III. iv. 423, I lost three pounds..at ha'penny nap and euchre. **1914** 'SAKI' *Beasts & Super-Beasts* 116 The office of one of the halfpenny dailies. *a* **1930** D. H. LAWRENCE *Last Poems* (1932) 169 Oh carcase with a board-school mind and a ha'penny newspaper intelligence.
b. (Later examples.)
1908 H. L. MENCKEN *Philos. Nietzsche* 284 Reich.. has attained the ha'penny celebrity he seems to crave in much the same manner. **1911** G. B. SHAW *Getting Married* 221 To lie down and let..every halfpenny journalist walk over us.

half-pie (hā·f,pəi), *a.* *N.Z. slang.* Also occas. **half-pi.** [perh. ad. Maori *pai* good.] Halfway towards, imperfect, mediocre. Also *absol.* or as *sb.*
c **1926** 'MIXER' *Transport Workers' Song Bk.* 11 There's no half-pie about this kid. **1938** R. FINLAYSON *Brown Man's Burden* 16 She would rather have a Maori who was a real man than a half-pie Pakeha who talked too much. *Ibid.* 78 A few straggling houses and a half-pie store. **1949** H. WADMAN *Life Sentence* I. i. 8 New Zealanders who go home on scholarships and come back half-pi Englishmen. **1952** R. FINLAYSON *Schooner came to Atia* x. 58 Half-pie commie and the gospel-thumpers together! **1955** *Landfall* IX. 274 He hadn't been a real officer, only a half-pie one.

half-round, *a.* and *sb.* Add: **A.** *adj.* *half-round bead, channel, chisel, gutter, screw.*
1888 *Lockwood's Dict. Mech. Engin.* (1918) 169 Half-round chisel. **1934** *Burlington Mag.* Nov. 209/2 Chinese details, such as the half-round beads ending in small volutes. **1940** *Chambers's Techn. Dict.* 122/2 *Button-headed screws,* screws having hemispherical heads, slotted for a screwdriver; known also as half-round screws. **1967** *Gloss. Sanitation Terms* (B.S.I.) 13 *Half-round channel,* a channel (def. 2) of semi-circular cross section. *Ibid.* 23 *Half round gutter,* an eaves gutter having a half round cross section.
B. *sb.* (Later example.)
1867 *Common Sense Cook Bk.* 38 Half-Round of Beef should be put into cold water.

half-shell. orig. *U.S.* Half an oyster shell. In phr. *on the half-shell*, served in this manner. Also *fig.*

1860 in *Amer. Speech* (1947) XXII. 203/1 Democrats fried,..roasted, or on the half shell. **1861** *Vanity Fair* 30 Mar. 148/1 Hard Shell,..and on the Half Shell Bapt-*ists*,..and all other *ists*. **1872** E. EGGLESTON *End of World* 155 The eggs..were not roasted on the half-shell. **1880** 'MARK TWAIN' *Tramp Abroad* xlix. 574 Blue points, on the half shell. **1940** A. SIMON *Conc. Encycl. Gastron.* II. 70/1 *Bluepoints* are one of the most popular varieties on the half shell. **1972** E. HARGREAVES *Fair Green Weed* iii. 49 They..ate..broiled lobster on the half-shell.

half-shot, *a. colloq.* (orig. *U.S.*). [f. HALF- 1; cf. SHOOT *v.* 32 d.] Half drunk.

1838 J. C. NEAL *Charcoal Sks.* 13 Moseying is only to be done when a gemman's half shot. **1943** N. MARSH *Colour Scheme* x. 187 'The chap was half-shot,' said Simon. 'They all say he smelt of booze.' **1948** J. M. CAIN *Moth* 64 Stuff for guys in college to gag about when they were half shot with beer.

half-time. Add: **1. d.** (See quot., also 3 below.)

1904 A. B. F. YOUNG *Compl. Motorist* iv. 118 All six valves are interchangeable and mechanically operated by rods worked from a cam shaft which is geared at half-time from the crank-axle.

e. Half the tempo of the performer; an accompaniment at half the tempo of the performer (see quot. 1961).

1938 D. BAKER *Young Man with Horn* iv. 265 They went into half-time together for a short coda. **1961** A. BERKMAN *Singers' Gloss. Show Business* 27 *Half-time*, while the singer continues singing the melody in the normal manner, the rhythmic complement is beat only half as fast as the original count.

f. *Chem.* (See quot.)

1957 *A.S.M.E. Gloss. Terms Nuclear Sci.* (1958) 72/2 *Half-time of exchange*, the time required for half the net realizable exchange of atoms in a chemical exchange reaction to take place.

3. half-time shaft = *half-speed shaft* (see *HALF- II. n).

1904 A. B. F. YOUNG *Compl. Motorist* iii. 49 The projecting part of a cam fixed on the half-time shaft. **1908** *Westm. Gaz.* 15 Oct. 4/2 The lubrication of the engine is carried out by a Dubrulle mechanical lubricator, fitted on the dash-board, and operated by an eccentric on the half-time shaft.

half-tone, *sb.* **2.** Delete 'used esp...*attrib.*' and read 'esp. in *Printing* and *Photogr.*, a photo-mechanical illustration printed from a block in which the tones are broken up into small or large dots by the interposition of a glass screen, ruled with fine cross-lines, between the camera and the object; this process. Also *attrib.*' Add earlier and later examples.

1867 G. W. SIMPSON *Photographs in Pigments* 51 The imperative condition upon which half-tone depends, the exposure of one side of the film to light..seemed to present an insuperable difficulty. **1911** *Encycl. Brit.* XIV. 325/1 Half-tone blocks..were used in the *Graphic* from 1884. **1937** E. J. LABARRE *Dict. Paper* 155/1 *Halftone paper*, a printing paper suitable for printing half-tone blocks. **1940** *Chambers's Techn. Dict.* 399/2 *Half-tone process*, a process of photographic reproduction in which the varying tones of the original are photographically translated into dots of uniform tone but varying size. **1958** *Times Lit. Suppl.* 17 Jan. 35/2 Such subjects as colour correction by masking, three-colour half-tone printing. **1959** *House & Garden* July 92/4 The publisher has had the sensible idea of backing his colour-plates..with half-tones in black-and-white. **1961** T. LANDAU *Encycl. Librarianship* (ed. 2) 160/2 *Half-tone screens*, transparent plates ruled diagonally with opaque lines at right angles to each other. **1967** KARCH & BUBER *Offset Processes* 541 *Halftone screen*, the ruled, plate glass dot-forming device used to translate continuous tones into halftones.

half-track. 1. [*TRACK *sb.*] A vehicle, usu. military, with wheels in front and caterpillar bands in the rear; also *attrib.* Also *half-tracked* adj., of such a vehicle.

1927 *Daily Express* 7 Mar. 1/2 Though armoured cars are still tied to roads, the introduction of the half-tracked and the six-wheel carriage will..enable them to move over normal field land. **1935** *Sun* (Baltimore) 9 Feb. 2/3 This force would necessitate acquisition of 285 lightweight tanks..and 76 half-track cars. **1943–4** *Hutchinson's Pict. Hist. War* 27 Oct.–11 Apr. 236 Manned by American infantrymen, this half-track vehicle is stolidly ploughing its way through thick mud. **1945** *Times* 24 Mar. 4/1 Infantry with the task-force dropped off the half-tracks in which they travelled and flushed the woods. *Ibid.* 12 May 4/2 There were a few mechanical vehicles, including some of the standard half-tracked troop-carriers. **1955** *Ibid.* 6 June 5/1 Israel forces made use of machine-guns and half-tracked vehicles in an attack on Egyptian positions. **1973** *Jewish Chron.* 19 Jan. 1/1 (*caption*) An Israeli Army half-track vehicle carries civilians across a main square in Jerusalem as the capital lies under the heaviest fall of snow for 21 years.

2. Half the width of a magnetic tape.

1956 G. A. BRIGGS *High Fidelity* xi. 127 A full-width single track tape can always be played on a half-track machine. Half-tracks can, of course, be played with full-width heads only when the adjacent track is unrecorded. **1959** W. S. SHARPS *Dict. Cinematogr.* 101 *Half-track recorder*, a magnetic tape recorder using a recording head covering half the tape width, so that double the playing time is obtained with any given length of tape and speed. **1962** A. NISBETT *Technique Sound Studio* 273 The standard width for the recording of sound programmes is ¼-inch and this may be recorded full, half or quarter track.

half-value. A value of a physical property that is half an earlier value; used esp. *attrib.*, as *half-value period* = *HALF-LIFE 2; *half-value thickness* (see quot. 1938).

1903 *Phil. Mag.* V. 578 The activity of the radium emanation decays to half-value in four days. **1908** *Amer. Jrnl. Sci.* XXV. 506 The half-value period of radium is..about 2000 years. **1910** *Nature* 6 Oct. 431/1 It is proposed that the term 'half-value period' should be used in all cases to represent the term required for a substance to be transformed to half its original value. **1922** *Times Lit. Suppl.* 18 May 318/2 The rate of decay of an element is measured by the 'half-value' period, which may vary from 10^{10} years to 10^{-11} of a second. **1938** R. W. LAWSON tr. *Hevesy & Paneth's Man. Radioactivity* (ed. 2) iii. 37 The intensity of the radiation is reduced to half its value in its passage through a layer of thickness 0·16 mm. Al... Accordingly, the 'half-value thickness' of aluminium for the β-rays from RaE has the value 0·16 mm. **1955** C. CROXSON in W. C. Newell *Casting of Steel* xii. 531 Some half-value thicknesses for steel are shown in the following table. **1962** F. I. ORDWAY et al. *Basic Astronautics* xii. 500 A useful concept in physical shielding is that of the *half value layer* (HVL) or the thickness of a specific material required to reduce a particular quantity of radiation by half. **1963** W. E. BURCHAM *Nucl. Physics* ii. 30 The interval..during which half the atoms disappear by decay (half-value period or half-life).

half-way, halfway. Add: **A.** *adv.* (Later examples.)

1926 J. BLACK *You can't Win* (1927) v. 60 She had cleaned up the room till it looked halfway decent. **1938** *Times* 25 May 17/3 He shows how much remains to be done before the standard of life of the West Indian labourer and of the West Indian peasant is raised to a level which can be regarded as halfway tolerable. **1942** *R.A.F. Jrnl.* 16 May 12 There is a drill which must be followed if the voyage is going to be halfway comfortable for everybody. **1960** H. PINTER *Caretaker* III. 77 He's nutty, he's half way gone.

B. *adj. half-way house* (earlier and later examples).

1694 W. BURNABY tr. *Petronius's Satyricon* 21 We could not reach Lycurgus's that Night, and therefore he brought us to a half-way House. **1901** S. E. WHITE *Westerners* xix. 164 Copper Creek had begun as a half-way house, and had ended as a camp. **1967** *Canad. Ann. Rev.* 1966 92 There was still need for such things as halfway group homes, preventive delinquency programs [etc.]. **1970** 'T. COE' *Wax Apple* (1973) iii. 24 Halfway houses are places for people returning to society but unable or unwilling to make the plunge all at once. There are halfway houses for ex-drug addicts, former convicts. **1973** *Canadian Antiques Collector* Jan.–Feb. 26/2 The buildings known as half-way houses..were the inns stationed halfway between the larger centres to accommodate weary travellers.

2. (Later examples.)

1903 *Daily Chron.* 3 Nov. 4/4 The halfway state between maidenhood and womanhood. **1909** *Ibid.* 31 Dec. 1/5, I am no halfway burglar, and I would kill a man for 2½d. **1962** *Guardian* 19 Nov. 16/1 These buildings are used by the LCC as 'halfway housing' for homeless families.

C. *sb.* **b.** The half-way line in a football field.

1960 V. JENKINS *Lions down Under* 202 New Zealand brought the ball back to half-way.

half-wit. Add: **2.** Also *attrib.*

1938 F. SCOTT FITZGERALD *Let.* Spring (1964) 29 We are setting it aside till we think of a way of half-witting halfwit Hayes and his Legion of Decency. **1960** *Times* 24 Sept. 10/7 Their half-wit uncle.

halide (hē·ləid). *Chem.* [f. HAL(OGEN + -IDE.] A binary compound formed from a halogen and a metal or radical. Also *attrib.*

1876 *Encycl. Brit.* V. 571/2 Acid Halides..may be regarded as the haloid ethers of acid radicles. **1927** N. V. SIDGWICK *Electronic Theory Valency* vi. 88 The halides of the elements show a similar differentiation into volatile non-salts and non-volatile salts. **1938** *Jrnl. R. Aeronaut. Soc.* XLII. 363 An attempt is made to explain the photolysis of silver halides in terms of the concepts of atomic physics. **1948** *Electronic Engin.* XX. 20 If a thin layer of alkali-halide crystals is bombarded with electrons, some electrons are displaced from the halides and secondaries are produced. **1957** *Jrnl. Chem. Soc.* 2071 (*title*) A new preparation of steroid halides.

Halifax (hæ·lifæks). [The name of a town in the West Riding of Yorkshire.] *Go to Halifax*: see GO *v.* 30 b. (Now regarded as a euphemism for *hell.*) Also in phr. *from Hell, Hull, and Halifax, Good Lord, deliver us* (see quot. *a* 1661).

In U.S., sometimes with supposed allusion to Halifax, Nova Scotia.

1630 J. TAYLOR *Works* 115/2 Now if my Whore or Thiefe play well their parts, Give them their due, applaud their good deserts. If ill, to Newgate hisse them, or Bridewell, To any place, Hull, Halifax or Hell. ***a* 1661** T. FULLER *Worthies* (1662) Yorks. 189 From Hell, Hull, and Halifax, —— deliver us... This is part of the Beggars and Vagrants Letany... Halifax, is formidable unto them for the Law thereof, whereby Theeves taken..in the very Act of stealing of cloath, are instantly beheaded with an Engine, without any further Legal Proceedings. **1669** [see GO *v.* 30 b]. **1807** *Deb. Congress U.S.* (1852) 11 Dec. 1169 Instead of sending it [*sc.* a ship] where he wished it had gone, to Halifax, or to the bottom. **1875–** in *Eng. Dial. Dict.* s.v. **1876** *Congress. Rec.* 4 Aug. 5185/1 'Go to Halifax' was a substitute for a more impious, but not more opprobrious expression. **1882** *Ibid.* 13 July 6015/1 He told them..that he had no further use for them, and they could go home, ashore, or to Halifax. **1920** H. J. JENNINGS *Chestnuts & Small Beer* xiii. 140, I refused to admit that I had made a *faux pas*, and told my critics to go to Halifax.

haliotis. Add: Also *attrib.*

1845 E. J. WAKEFIELD *Adv. N. Zealand* I. 241 These hooks..take their name from the *haliotus*[sic]-shell, with pieces of which they are lined. **1931** *Oxf. Univ. Gaz.* 17 June 715/2 Toe-bone with carved face and *haliotis* eyes.

halitosis (hælitōᵘ·sis). *Med.* [mod.L., f. L. *halitus* breath + -OSIS.] An abnormally odorous condition of the breath; foul breath.

1874 J. W. HOWE *Breath & Dis.* i. 20 Chronic poisoning from lead, arsenic, or mercury, may also be enumerated as a common cause of halitosis. **1928** *Punch* 17 Oct. 427/1, I shall become a mere mass of degenerate tissues, and flaccid muscles,..with probably a touch of halitosis and lethargy. **1934** S. ROBERTSON *Develop. Mod. Eng.* (1936) XI. 447 Thus *halitosis*, the happy discovery of purveyors of mouth-washes, has found a wider usefulness, and *bad breath* is taboo. **1957** *Times Lit. Suppl.* 12 July 426/4 The dismissed Mulcahy, sadly proud of his porous complexion, bad teeth and occasional morning halitosis.

hall¹. Add: **7.** Also in *pl.* (occas. in *sing.*), abbrev. of *music-hall.*

1862 A. J. MUNBY *Diary* 29 Mar. in D. Hudson *Munby* (1972) 119 Socially speaking, the audience were a good deal higher than those I have seen in similar Halls at Islington & elsewhere. **1895** CHEVALIER & DALY *A. Chevalier* 115 He was one of the few actors of any prominence who had migrated to the halls. **1898** J. D. BRAYSHAW *Slum Silhouettes* 29 He've tried every small 'all in town, even the pubs wot gits up 'smokers'. **1905** MORTON & NEWTON (*title*) Sixty years' stage service, being a record of the life of Charles Morton, 'the Father of the Halls'. **1923** N. COWARD *Coll. Sk. & Lyrics* (1931) 75 Doing a turn of me own on the halls—very trying work—and so cosmopolitan. **1934** T. S. ELIOT *Rock* i. 25 Robey's on the 'alls; but this gentleman..used to hentertain the toffs. **1942** E. BLOM *Mus. in Eng.* x. 168 The 'halls' were the last places where anybody would have thought of going for the sake of music. **1967** *Listener* 8 June 760/2 The vital and self-confident art of the halls..a London Sound to set beside the Liverpool sort.

13. *hall-chair* (examples), *-porter* (examples); **hall-bedroom** *U.S.*, a small bedroom partitioned off at one end of a hall; **hall-bed roomer** *U.S.*, one who sleeps in this; **hall-boy,** a page-boy in a large house; a call-boy in the hall of a hotel or the like; **hall-man** (example); **hall-room** *U.S.*, a room at the end of and of the width of a hall; also *v. intr.*, to live in such a room; **hall stand,** a piece of furniture used to receive umbrellas, hats, coats, and brushes usually situated near the front door in the hall of the house; **hall-table** (def. and further examples), (*a*) a large, solid table belonging to the hall in a mansion; (*b*) a small table situated in the hall near the front door; **hall-tree** *U.S.*, a hall stand or hat rack.

1738 *New Hampsh. Probate Rec.* II. 280 Samuel Brewster shall have..ye Hall Bed Room. **1886** H. JAMES *Bostonians* II. xxi. 44 One of his rooms was directly above the street-door of the house; such a dormitory, when it is so exiguous, is called in the nomenclature of New York a 'hall bedroom'. **1922** A. BENNETT *Lilian* I. vi. 57 In New York it would have been termed a hall-bedroom. **1934** L. MUMFORD in W. Frank et al. *Amer. & Alfred Stieglitz* ii. 35 Lonely young men and women from the country..faced their first year in the city from hall bedrooms on the top-floor rear of unamiable boarding-houses. **1899** J. L. WILLIAMS *Stolen Story* 230 Like many an other lonely hall-bed roomer. **1884** *N.Y. Herald* 27 Oct. 2/2 Janitors and hall boys in attendance. **1885** C. M. YONGE *Nuttie's Father* II. xiii. 158 The hall boy, an alert young fellow, had already dashed down the steps. **1892** —— *That Stick* I. ii. 23 He had been hall boy to a duke, footman to a viscountess, valet to an earl. **1912** L. J. VANCE *Destroying Angel* xx, The hall-boys said you were busy on the telephone. **1864** DICKENS *Mut. Fr.* I. ii. 5 The Veneering establishment, from the hall-chairs..to the grand pianoforte. **1939** A. CLARKE *Sister Eucharia* i. 7 The stage is seen to be quite bare except for two high hall chairs. **1883** D. COOK *On Stage* I. ix. 204 There is no situation in the world where a man can better study his kind than the hall-porter's chair of a London theatre. **1934** *Punch* 5 Aug. 164/2 The hall-porter moved wearily across the floor to take my luggage. **1859** *Ladies' Repository* XIX. 466/2 The little hall-room is just large enough for the boys to sleep in. **1919** T. K. HOLMES *Man fr. Tall Timber* i. 3 'Shucks! why didnt you say H. Harvey Stafford?' interrupted the hall-man. **1886** S. W. MITCHELL *R. Blake* (1895) v. 39 Miss Darnell had for her own use a like space on the third floor, leaving to Miss Wynne a bed-chamber..known as a hall-room. **1906** 'O. HENRY' *Four Million* (1916) xiv. 139 The restaurant was next door to the old red brick in which she hall-roomed. *Ibid.* 140 Schulenberg was to send three meals per diem to Sarah's hall-room. **1882** *Times* 31 Jan. 16/6 (Advt.), A very fine carved oak bookcase, two cabinets, a ditto hall

stand and table. **1897** R. Kron *Little Londoner* (1917) 28 Not far from the door, there are an umbrella-stand, a hat-rack, with several pegs on it, and a large looking-glass; if the three are combined, such a piece of furniture is called a hall-stand. **1911** *Daily Colonist* (Victoria, B.C.) 4 Apr. 19/1 (Advt.), Oak Hall Stand, Brussels Rugs. **1943** K. Tennant *Ride on Stranger* iii. 23 By applying her eye to one of the coloured panes in the front door, she could make out the dim bulk of a hall-stand. **1952** J. Gloag *Short Dict. Furnit.* 282 Hall stands were often made wholly of cast iron. **1869** L. M. Alcott *Little Women* II. xxiii. 327 He..never..expressed..surprise at seeing the Professor's hat on the Marches' hall-table. **1902** H. James *Wings of Dove* II. iv. 82, I shan't leave mine [*sc.* my letters] on the hall-table. *a* **1941** V. Woolf *Haunted House* (1943) 44 She touched the letters on the hall table. **1891** *Harper's Mag.* June 79/1 One could distinguish..the hall tree, whereon Rhodes's hat swung in its place. **1900** E. E. Peake *Darlingtons* ix. 79 She..walked back to the sitting-room, stopping to touch up her hair before the glass in the hall-tree. **1954** J. Steinbeck *Sweet Thursday* xviii. 108 He busted two windows and run off with the deer-antler hall-tree.

Hall². *Physics.* The name of Edwin H. Hall (1855–1938), American physicist, used attrib. to designate an effect discovered by him and various quantities associated therewith (see quot. 1958).

1902 Hall effect [see *electric potential* s.v. *electric *a.* 2 b]. **1922** Glazebrook *Dict. Appl. Physics* II. 468/2 The effect of a magnetic field upon the electrical conductivity of metals, first discovered by Lord Kelvin in 1856 and known as the Hall effect, is very marked in the case of bismuth wire or plates. **1940** *Chambers's Techn. Dict.* 400/1 *Hall effect*, a change in the distribution of current in a strip of metal, due to a magnetic field. **1958** *Van Nostrand's Sci. Encycl.* (ed. 3) 784/1 In 1879 Hall..discovered that if a strip of gold-leaf, carrying an electric current longitudinally was placed in a magnetic field with the plane of the strip perpendicular to the direction of the field, points directly opposite each other on the edges of the strip acquired a difference of electric potential...The transverse electric potential gradient per unit magnetic field intensity per unit current density is called the 'Hall coefficient' for the metal in question...The Hall angle is the ratio of E_y..to the field E_x... The Hall mobility is the mobility of the electrons or holes in a semiconductor as measured by the Hall effect. **1965** Phillips & Williams *Inorg. Chem.* I. vi. 195 Other methods which measure the mobility of the electrons, e.g. measurement of the Hall effect, also permit a distinction to be made between the two mechanisms of electron migration.

hallal, var. *halal *v.*

hallali (hæ·ləli). [Echoic.] A bugle call. Also *fig.*

1885 G. Meredith *Diana of Crossways* II. ii. 55 He knew enough to blow his huntsman's horn...His hallali rang high. **1898** —— *Reading of Life* 77 Right loud the bugle's hallali elate Rang forth. **1920** *Q. Rev.* July 13 The hallali was sounded in a famous letter to Lord Grey de Wilton, the candidate for Bath, in which Disraeli accused the Ministers of having for five years harassed every trade. **1923** W. J. Locke *Moordius & Co.* x. 140 On the stroke of four the orchestra of French hunting horns blew the *hallali.*

Hallé (hæ·le). Applied *attrib.* to an orchestra, concerts, and other musical events which owe their inception to Charles *Hallé* (orig. Carl Halle) (1819–1895). Also used *absol.*

1852 Mrs. Gaskell *Let.* 7 Dec. (1966) 217 We have 3 Hallé tickets for Thursday. *c* **1860** —— *Lett.* (1966) 614 Beautiful Hallé last night. **1936** R. C. K. Ensor *England 1870–1914* x. 327 Outside the metropolis..the chief purveyor of orchestral concerts [was] the Hallé orchestra. **1954** *Grove's Dict. Music* (ed. 5) V. 542/2 In 1895 the Hallé concerts had become a national institution. *Ibid.* 544/1 Philip Godlee, the former Chairman of the Hallé. *Ibid.*, The Hallé Choir had also had its vicissitudes. *Ibid.*, Concerts outside the Hallé series. **1957** *Times Lit. Suppl.* 1 Nov. 652/3 There is something wrong with a system of public finance that rewards hard work and the enterprise to secure solvency with a cut in the next year's subvention, as was the Hallé's experience. **1968** *Guardian* 29 Mar. 10/6 Our North Midlands scout, driving hard to attend a Hallé concert in Hanley, had to pause at a garage for repairs...'I'm going to the Hallé in Hanley.'

hallelujah, *sb.*¹ Add: **1. c.** hallelujah-lass (examples).

1886 F. Hume *Myst. Hansom Cab* (1887) xvi. 109 It appears that she had been in the Army as a hallelujah lass. **1967** W. S. Smith *London Heretics* III. v. 238 In 1879 ..more than 2,000 fellow citizens packed into Livingston Hall nightly to listen to the 'Hallelujah Lasses'.

2. A semi-Christian religion practised among the Carib-speaking peoples of Guyana.

1946 F. W. Kenswil *Childr. Silence* vi. 13 Aboriginal Indians are a very religious set of people...Those of the hinterland of this colony [British Guiana] have their own religion which they call 'Hallilieujah'. This Hallilieujah is said to have been conceived, in the dim past, by an Indian whose name was Bi-chi-wung. **1955** *Times* 22 June 11/7 The most primitive religion which they still practise is a debased version of Christianity called Hallelujah... It..seems to date from some time in the nineteenth century.

hallelujah, *sb.*² (Further examples.)

1920 *Sunday at Home* June 569/2 Oxalis, the wood-sorrel, was known as hallelujah,..from its blossoming between Easter and Whitsuntide, when psalms were sung ending in the word hallelujah. **1923** *Times Lit. Suppl.* 3 May 293/3 How happy is the country polyonymosity that hails it also as sheep-sorrel,..hallelujah,..and God Almighty's bread-and-cheese?

hallful (hǭ·lful). [f. Hall *sb.* + -ful 2.] As many or as much as will fill a hall.

1905 *Daily Chron.* 17 Feb. 3/6 The entertainment of a whole hallful of poor children. **1909** *Westm. Gaz.* 26 Sept. 6/3 What a hallful it was that received him with ringing, rousing, rollicking cheers!

halling (hæ·liŋ). [Norw., from *Hallingdal*, a valley in southern Norway.] A Norwegian country-dance in triple rhythm; also, the music for such a dance.

1866 Plesner & Rugeley-Powers tr. *Björnson's Arne* ii. 13 Nils played; and the two gentlemen each gave a dollar for him, and then asked for the *halling.* **1924** *Glasgow Herald* 31 May 4 We have no space here to describe the wonderful Halling dance. **1947** A. Einstein *Mus. Romantic Era* xvii. 320 Many of these dances show evidence of great age and uninterrupted tradition—the leaping dance (*springar*) in $\frac{3}{4}$ meter and the *halling* in duple meter.

hall-mark, *sb.* Delete def. and substitute: The official mark or stamp used by the three statutory Hall-marking Authorities in England (Birmingham, London, Sheffield) or by the one in Scotland (Edinburgh), in marking the standard of gold and silver articles assayed by them, without which articles of these metals may not legally be sold.

hall-mark, *v.* (Earlier example.)

1773 *Rep. Comm. Assay Offices* 25 He bought the Knives and Forks..and believed at that Time they had been Hall marked,..and refused selling them when he found they were not Hall marked.

hallo, *int.* Add: Used as a greeting, etc., on a telephone. Also, repeated, as a locution indicating surprise. Cf. *hello *int.* b, *hullo *int.*

1932 *N. & Q.* 6 Aug. 105/2 The telephonic 'hallo'. **1942** A. Christie *Body in Library* ii. 24 Hallo, 'allo, 'allo, what's this? **1972** *Police Rev.* 10 Nov. 1473/2 You could have a walking, talking plastic Policeman..saying 'Allo, allo, allo.'

Hallstatt (ha·lʃtat). The name of a village in Upper Austria, the site of an ancient necropolis, where rich archæological finds have been made, used *attrib.* to denote a phase of the early Iron Age, and the type of civilization of that period. So **Hallsta·ttian** *a.*

1866 J. Lubbock *Addr. Primæval Antiquities Archæol. Inst.* 17 The significance of the absence of silver in the Hallstadt find is greatly increased when we see that in the true Iron age..silver was used. **1869** —— *Pre-Historic Times* (ed. 2) i. 24 M. Ramsauer..director of the salt mines at Hallstadt, near Salzburg, in Austria, has discovered an extensive cemetery belonging to this transitional period. *Ibid.* 25 Another interesting point in the Hallstadt bronze, as in that of the true Bronze Age, is the absence of silver, lead, and zinc. **1893** *Funk's Stand. Dict.* I. 812/3 Hallstattian. **1900** tr. *Deniker's Races of Man* 315 The so-called 'Hallstattian' period lasted in Central Europe, France, and Northern Italy from the tenth or ninth to the sixth century B.C. The Hallstattian civilisation flourished chiefly in Carinthia, Southern Germany, Switzerland, Bohemia, Silesia, Bosnia, the south-east of France, and Southern Italy. **1905** *Brit. Mus. Guide Antiq. Early Iron Age* 36 The drum-shaped brooch..is also not uncommon in the Hallstatt period. *Ibid.* 39 The Hallstatt stage of culture is well represented at Glasinatz. **1931** *Times Lit. Suppl.* 1 Oct. 753/3 Scanty traces of Hallstatt immigrants. **1958** *Ibid.* 19 Sept. 526/2 The general reader..will meet..the well-known cultures of Hallstatt and La Tène.

hallucinant (hæli*ū*·sinănt), *sb.* and *a.* [f. Hallucin(ate *v.* + -ant¹.] **A.** *sb.* **a.** Someone who experiences hallucinations. **b.** A drug that induces hallucinations. **B.** *adj.* Producing or experiencing hallucinations.

1895 tr. *Nordau's Degeneration* I. iii. 32 The women devotees..did not merely believe that the hallucinant maiden had herself seen the vision, but all of them saw the Holy Virgin with their own eyes. **1910** A. W. Verrall *Bacchants of Euripides* 72 In a hallucinant working by suggestion..such effects are perfectly natural. **1932** A. Huxley *Brave New World* iii. 63 Euphoric, narcotic, pleasantly hallucinant. **1964** *Punch* 30 Dec. 1013/2 Someone who knew her potions, her febrifuges and hallucinants.

hallucinate, *v.* **2.** Delete *Obs.* or *arch.* and add later examples. Also, to have a hallucination or hallucinations. Now chiefly *U.S.*

1847 Webster, Hallucinate. **1930** C. Spearman *Creative Mind* x. 135 A man hallucinated that the clothes of the girls 'flew off them'. **1958** E. Dundy *Dud Avocado* III. vi. 270 My first thought was that I had gone stark raving mad..and that I was now hallucinating in a looney bin. **1964** A. Cross *In last Analysis* iii. 31 Had such an idea crossed her mind, Kate would have decided that..she was 'hallucinating'. **1973** *Publishers Weekly* 19 Mar. 61/3 He describes her and is told, bluntly, that he is hallucinating.

hallucinating *ppl. a.* (later examples).

1903 E. Wharton *Sanctuary* II. iv. 137 That hallucinating distinctness which belongs to the midnight vision. **1966** *New Statesman* 18 Feb. 233/2 Jennifer Dawson writes about the surface pain of living—with hallucinating effect.

hallucinatory, *a.* Add: Hence **hallucina·torily** *adv.*

1917 C. R. Payne tr. *Pfister's Psychoanalytic Method* xvii. 467 Then every time, out of hate and expiation, he changed hallucinatorily the feared one into the death's head. **1959** G. D. Painter *Marcel Proust* I. 178 They were irresistibly comic, and at the same time hallucinatorily accurate.

‖ **hallucinė** (hăliū·sine). *rare.* [Fr.] A person who regularly suffers from hallucinations.

1886 *Buck's Hand-bk. Med. Sci.* III. 481/1 Nowadays the hallucinés hear voices through the telephone, and feel electric shocks. **1898** *Daily News* 20 Sept. 4/5 Genius goes somehow with what we call hysteria, most persons of genius being epileptic, or 'hallucinés'. **1909** W. James *Let.* 19 Sept. in R. B. Perry *Thought & Char. W. James* (1935) II. lviii. 123, I strongly suspect Freud, with his dream-theory, of being a regular *halluciné.*

hallucinogen (hæli*ū*·sinŏdʒen). [f. Hallucin(ation + -o + -gen.] A drug which causes hallucinations (see Hallucination 2).

1954 A. Hoffer et al. in *Jrnl. Mental Sci.* C. 30 When the literature is examined to catalogue these hallucinatory substances, which for convenience we have called the hallucinogens, one is struck by their small number. **1954** A. Huxley *Doors of Perception* 6 Lysergic acid, an extremely potent hallucinogen derived from ergot. **1955** *Jrnl. Mental Sci.* CI. 318 There are so few hallucinogens known that we must study intensively the types of subgroups and molecules which cause hallucinations. **1958** *New Scientist* 28 Aug. 715/3 More recently..several hallucinogens have been observed which produce, in addition to other symptoms of schizophrenia, auditory hallucinations. **1969** *Times* 24 Jan. 6/6 The fly agaric fungus yields one of the most potent and anciently used hallucinogens, inducing a slight trembling followed by illusions.

So **hallu:cinoge·nic** *a.*, being or containing such a drug; causing hallucinations.

1952 *Jrnl. Mental Sci.* XCVIII. 311 There are many other hallucinogenic drugs, but none has either such striking properties or such a simple chemical constitution as mescaline. **1958** *Sci. News* XLVII. 36 Other lines of research..include the search for substances that antagonize the hallucinogenic drugs. **1959** *Times Lit. Suppl.* 27 Feb. 113/4 We believe our evidence points to a role for the hallucinogenic mushroom in the origins of the religious idea in primitive society. **1960** *Times* 31 Dec. 9/7 A liana of which the boiled juice has hallucinogenic effects. **1965** *Listener* 23 Sept. 465/1 It is a powerful mind-changer of the hallucinogenic variety. **1968** *Times* 13 Nov. 16/1 Many well known hallucinogenic drugs, such as LSD and mescaline, cause mice to exhibit the curious behaviour pattern of head twitching.

hallucinosis (hæli*ū*:sinōᵘ·sis). *Psychiatry.* [f. Hallucin(ation + -osis.] A disorder of the nervous system associated particularly with alcoholism, marked by persistent hallucinations, commonly auditory, with little if any impairment of consciousness.

1905 S. Paton *Psychiatry* xi. 300 Acute alcoholic hallucinosis. **1908** *Practitioner* Jan. 9 The acute hallucinosis and paranoidal forms of alcoholic insanity. **1912** Osler & McCrae *Princ. & Pract. Med.* (ed. 8) III. i. 399 Alcoholism...There is a condition termed *acute hallucinosis*, in which auditory hallucinations are marked..and the mental disturbances are fixed. Ideas of persecution are common. There are intermediate forms between this and the ordinary delirium tremens. **1914** *Amer. Jrnl. Insanity* LXX. II. 369 (*title*) Study of hallucinosis. **1962** Henderson & Gillespie *Text-bk. Psychiatry* xii. 291 Accompanied by..clear and orderly thinking, willing and acting; there is no real or genuine hallucinosis. **1964** Landis & Mettler *Varieties Psychopathol. Experience* xiv. 312 The horror, torture, and pain experienced during delirium tremens or alcoholic hallucinosis have been described many times.

hallway. For *U.S.* read orig. *U.S.* and add earlier and later examples.

1877 J. Habberton *Jericho Road* 173 It passed through the narrow hallway which separated the cell from the jailor's apartments. **1920** B. Cronin *Timber Wolves* ii. 41 He stood hesitating at the entrance to the musty hallway. **1953** L. Kuper *Living in Towns* ii. 13 The front doors..give direct access to hallway and staircase. **1959** *Shropsh. Mag.* Mar. 9/2 He has a beautiful wooden chest in his hallway. **1971** *Real Estate Rev.* Fall 104/2 A woman who had been attacked in the common hallway of her apartment house.

halo, *sb.* Add: **1. e.** A style in women's hats (worn at the back of the head with the brim thus framing the face). Also *attrib.* and *Comb.*, as *halo-brim(med)*, *hat*, *style*, etc.

1899 *Daily News* 22 Apr. 8/4 Some of the new models [*sc.* hats] are intended to be put on in the halo style. **1903** *Daily Chron.* 24 Oct. 8/4 The hat makes a halo in front. **1934** *Times* 22 June 17/4 A brown halo hat. **1935** *Times* 17 June 11/3 Felt halos are made with a velvet cap in front, and cost 3½ guineas. *Ibid.* 2 Oct. 17/4 A pale blue halo-brimmed hat. **1952** E. Grierson *Reputation for Song* xxvii. 244 Laura..wore a little black halo-hat to frame her pallid face.

f. A more or less circular bright or dark area formed in various photographic processes (see quots.).

1941 *Amer. Speech* XVI. 316/2 *Halo,* the effect obtained in portraiture when a strong back-light is used. **1961** G. MILLERSON *Technique Telev. Production* iii. 49 *Haloes* (throw-off). A black aureole surrounding an over-bright high-contrast area, and obliterating the nearby picture. **1967** KARCH & BUBER *Offset Processes* 541 *Halo,* a luminous circle or aura around the halftone dot.

4. halo blight, spot, either of two bacterial diseases caused by species of *Pseudomonas, P. coronafaciens* affecting oats, and *P. phaseolicola* affecting beans of the genus *Phaseolus;* characterized by brown spots surrounded by yellowish-green rings on leaves; **halo effect** *Psychol.*, the favourable bias in interviews, intelligence tests, and the like generated by an atmosphere of approbation; also *transf.*

1920 C. ELLIOTT in *Jrnl. Agric. Res.* XIX. 139 This 'halo-blight' is a disease which occurs to at least some extent each year throughout the oat-growing sections of the central and eastern States. **1930** W. H. BURKHOLDER in *Mem. Cornell Univ. Agric. Exper. Station* No. 127 37 The most striking symptom [of *Phytomonas medicaginis phaseolicola*] arises from a local infection, and is the spot to which Miss Hedges has applied the term *halo blight.* **1954** A. G. L. HELLYER *Encycl. Garden Work & Terms* 115 *Halo blight,* a disease of beans also sometimes known as halo spot. **1955** *Sci. Amer.* June 83 Bacterial blight of beans..embraces a group of diseases: common blight, fuscous blight and halo blight, each caused by a different bacterium. **1971** M. NOBLE in J. H. Western *Dis. Crop Plants* iii. 33 In New South Wales an inspection scheme for bean (*Phaseolus*) seed has been in operation..for control of halo blight. **1971** J. COLHOUN in *Ibid.* x. 211 Halo blight of oats..is not regarded as constituting an economic problem in the British Isles. [**1926** E. H. MAGSON in *Brit. Jrnl. Psychol. Mon. Suppl.* 9 89 It must be pointed out that it is quite unnecessary to employ a new technical term such as 'halo' or 'aura' to cover these cases.] **1938** *Brit. Jrnl. Psychol.* Jan. 285 Such general impressions, often called 'halo effects', have already been noted to affect the diagnosis of personal qualities. **1940** R. S. WOODWORTH *Psychol.* (ed. 12) v. 143 Another error [in rating intelligence tests] is known as the 'halo effect'. If an individual creates a favourable impression by his excellence in one trait, you are apt to rate him near the top in every trait. **1967** *Guardian* 20 Dec. 1/6 Mrs. Castle.. agreed that the new Act had a 'halo' effect in that it made drivers more careful. **1928** *Jrnl. Agric. Res.* 1 Mar. 428 Halo spot is known to occur in Georgia, Florida, and Connecticut.

halo- (hælo), combining form of Gr. ἅλς, ἁλός sea, salt, as in **ha·lobiont** *Ecol.*, an organism that lives in a saline habitat; hence **ha:lobio·ntic** *a.*; **ha:lobio·tic** *a. Ecol.*, living in the sea; **ha:lochro·mism** *Chem.* [ad. G. *halochromie* (Baeyer & Villiger in *Ber. d. Deut. Chem. Ges.* (1902) XXXV. 1190)], the property possessed by certain colourless or faintly coloured compounds of becoming brilliantly coloured in the presence of acids or of certain other compounds; **haloli·mnic** *a. Biol.*, living in fresh water but having an affinity with marine forms; **halomo·rphic** *a. Soil Sci.*, (of a soil) containing, or developed under the influence of, large quantities of salts other than calcium carbonate; **ha·lophyte** *Ecol.* [ad. mod. L. *halophyta* (J. F. Schouw *Grundtræk til en almindelig Plantegeographie* (1822) 138], a plant which is adapted to grow in saline conditions; so **halophy·tic** *a.*, growing, or adapted to grow, in saline conditions; **halopla·nkton,** marine plankton; **ha·losere** *Ecol.* (see quot. 1930[1]); **ha·lowax** [HALO(GEN + WAX *sb.*[1]] (see quots.).

1928 K. E. CARPENTER *Life Inland Waters* ix. 228 Other halobionts are: all known species of *Ephydra* (Diptera)..and several species of *Ochthebius, Philydrus,* and *Paracymus* (Coleoptera). **1937** ALLEE & SCHMIDT *Hesse's Ecol. Animal Geogr.* xix. 370 'Halobionts' are limited to water of rather high salt content, and are more or less salt-tolerant stenohaline forms. **1928** K. E. CARPENTER *Life Inland Waters* ix. 228 Above this concentration, species rapidly diminish in numbers, and above 10 per cent. are only found the true 'halobiontic' forms, which rarely, or never, occur in waters other than saline. **1909** WEBSTER, Halobiotic. **1927** R. S. LULL *Org. Evol.* (rev. ed.) v. 70 Halobiotic or Marine Realm. **1902** *Rep. Brit. Assoc.* 119 Reference may be made to some recent work of v. Baeyer and Villiger on dibenzylidene acetone and triphenyl methane. They refer to the constitution of colourless substances which form highly coloured salts, and term the phenomenon *halochromism.* **1944** *Hackh's Chem. Dict.* (ed. 3) 395/1 *Halochromism,* the formation of colored salts from colorless organic bases by the addition of acids. **1952** K. VENKATARAMAN *Chem. Synthetic Dyes* I. viii. 326 In the phenomenon of halochromism, the neutral organic compounds, which become brilliantly colored on the addition of hydrogen ion, are colored to about the same depth and intensity by the addition of neutral substances such as boron trichloride or stannic chloride instead of hydrogen ion. **1898** J. E. S. MOORE in *Proc. R. Soc.* LXII. 453 They probably belong to the same quasi-marine, or what I shall in future call the Halolimnic group. **1903** —— *Tanganyika Probl.* vii. 141 The animals forming the invertebrate section of this peculiar group have an obviously marine aspect, and on that account I have spoken of them elsewhere as forming a halolimnic series in Lake Tanganyika—that is to say, they form a group of animals which, although living in a freshwater lake, have at the same time the characters of animals that are typical of the sea. **1904** *Westm. Gaz.* 26 May 5/2 The shells of the halolimnic gasteropods. **1922** *Nature* 5 Jan. 28/1 The halolimnic forms..exhibit a marine-like appearance. **1938** *U.S. Dept. Agric. Yearbk.* 1169 *Halomorphic soils,* a suborder of intrazonal soils, the properties of which are determined by the presence of neutral or alkali salts, or both. **1968** R. W. FAIRBRIDGE *Encycl. Geomorphol.* 273/1 Other desert soils are intrazonal..and either contain appreciable amounts of calcium carbonate (the pedocal soils) or have relatively high concentrations of other soluble salts (the halomorphic soils). **1886** WEBSTER Add., Halophyte. **1894** F. W. OLIVER et al. tr. *Kerner's Nat. Hist. Plants* I. 74 Plants which only flourish abundantly on soils rich in alkaline salts are called halophytes. The same name has also been applied to plants which only thrive in sea-water. **1903** W. R. FISHER tr. *Schimper's Plant-Geogr.* 90 Halophytes can thrive on ordinary soil..without any addition of common salt. **1909** GROOM & BALFOUR tr. *Warming's Oecol. Plants* liv. 219 A halophyte..is one form of xerophyte. **1966** *New Scientist* 2 June 575/1 Because of the removal of water by transpiration or in the harvested crop, the concentration of salts in the system will rise so that even halophytes will suffer. **1895** G. HENSLOW *Orig. Plant Struct.* 83 Halophytic plants, and others yielding ethereal oils. **1950** *Engineering* 26 Mar. 610/3 While.. salt..is being washed out of the soil..the vegetation will still be halophytic. **1909** GROOM & BALFOUR tr. *Warming's Oecol. Plants* xxxviii. 160 The plankton of salt water may be subdivided into neritic and oceanic haloplankton. **1927** R. S. LULL *Org. Evol.* (rev. ed.) iii. 43 Marine or halo-plankton. **1929** WEAVER & CLEMENTS *Plant Ecol.* iv. 74 Hydroseres in saline areas are distinguished as (salt) haloseres. **1930** *Jrnl. Ecol.* XVIII. 201 *Halosere,* the sere commencing in saline water or upon saline soil. *Ibid.* 229 (*heading*) Communities developing within the halosere. **1964** K. A. KERSHAW *Quantitative & Dynamic Ecol.* iii. 39 Clements similarly termed the stages of salt marsh succession a halosere. **1922** *Halowax* (*Condensite Co. of America*) 3 Halowax for impregnating paper round electrical condensers. *Ibid.* 4 Halowax is a trade name for chloro-naphthalene substitution products, i.e., products in which chlorine atoms are substituted for those of hydrogen in the naphthalene. **1928** *Daily Express* 10 Jan. 3/7 The..Anti-Knock Compound..is a liquid consisting of tetra-ethyl lead, ethylene dibromide, halowax oil and red aniline dye. **1947** J. C. RICH *Materials & Methods of Sculpture* vi. 157 *Halowax* is a synthetic wax with a high melting point. It is a strong and hard material and imparts a milky opaqueness to a cool wax formula. **1963** R. F. WEBB *Motorist's Dict.* 121 *Halowax,* a type of oil, blended with a tetra-ethyl lead compound used to lubricate the working parts of some mechanical superchargers.

halogen. Add: In mod. use, any of the elements of group 7 of the periodic table, viz. fluorine, chlorine, bromine, iodine, and astatine. (Further examples.)

1867 C. L. BLOXAM *Chem.* 10 A salt-radical or halogen is a substance which forms an acid when combined with hydrogen. Examples.—Chlorine, which forms hydrochloric acid (HCl); Cyanogen (C_2N), which forms hydrocyanic acid (HC_2N). **1884** T. S. HUMPIDGE tr. *Kolbe's Short Text-bk. Inorg. Chem.* 96 The halogens or salt-producers. The four elements chlorine, bromine, iodine, and fluorine are grouped together under this name. **1959** *Nomencl. Inorg. Chem.* (I.U.P.A.C.) 6 The use of the collective names: halogens (F, Cl, Br, I, and At),..may be continued.

Hence **halogena·tion**, the introduction of an atom of a halogen into a molecule of a compound by addition or substitution.

1911 *Chem. Abstr.* V. 1436 (*heading*) Halogenation of benzene monohalides...The expts...were carried out at 55–75° without a diluent. **1965** PHILLIPS & WILLIAMS *Inorg. Chem.* II. xii. 463 Some of the interhalogens provide convenient solvents for halogenation reactions, particularly in view of their partial ionization.

haloid. Add: Now rare as adj. and superseded by *halide* as sb.

haloing, *ppl. a.* Add: Also *vbl. sb.*

1967 *Gloss. Paper/Ink Terms for Letterpress Printing* (*B.S.I.*) 9 *Haloing,* the appearance of vehicle from the ink round half-tone dots or characters.

halonate (hēi·lonĕt), *a. Bot.* [f. mod.L. *halōn-*, HALO *sb.* + -ATE[2].] Surrounded by an outer ring.

1911 CROMBIE & SMITH *Brit. Lichens* II. 359 Halonate ..surrounded by an outer circle. **1921** A. L. SMITH *Handbk. Brit. Lichens* 102 Spores ellipsoid or oblong.. usually with a hyaline mucilaginous epispore (halonate). **1959** U. K. DUNCAN *Guide to Study of Lichens* 64 Th. Fries..cited the halonate character of the spores [of *Rhizocarpon*] as the distinguishing factor.

halophile, *sb.* Add: **2.** *Ecol.* An organism which grows in or can tolerate saline conditions.

1928 K. E. CARPENTER *Life Inland Waters* ix. 229 These 'halophiles' are true freshwater species endowed with powers of resistance. **1965** B. E. FREEMAN tr. *Vandel's Biospeleol.* xiii. 196 The Pogoninae are for the most part halophiles. **1966** T. D. BROCK *Princ. Microbial Ecol.* iii. 47 Halophiles are in ionic equilibrium with their environment.

B. *adj. Ecol.* Growing in or tolerating saline conditions.

1909 *Cent. Dict.* Suppl., Halophile. **1961** *Times Rev. Industry* June 82/1 A gradual increase of the halophile (or, better, salt-resisting) plants..at the fringe of the oasis and the great desert beyond.

halophilic (hæ:lofi·lik), *a. Ecol.* [f. HALOPHIL(OUS *a.* + -IC.] Growing in or tolerating saline conditions, halophilous.

1919 *Jrnl. Bacteriol.* IV. 177 (*title*) A preliminary report upon some halophilic bacteria. **1964** *Oceanogr. & Marine Biol.* II. 161 Few studies have been made of the role of detritus as a food for halophilic Crustacea. **1971** M. ALEXANDER *Microbial Ecol.* viii. 181 Some populations are obligately halophilic.

halosaurus (hæ:losǭ·rŏs). [mod.L. (see quot. 1863); see HALOSAURIAN.] A deep-water marine fish of the genus so called, characterized by an elongated body and long tapering tail. Hence **ha·losaur,** a member of the family Halosauridæ, which includes both fossil and living fishes; **ha:losau·roid** *a.*, of, pertaining to, or resembling a fish of this kind; also as *sb.*

[**1863** J. Y. JOHNSON in *Proc. Zool. Soc.* 406 *Halosaurus,* gen. nov. Body elongated, clothed with cycloid scales;..tail compressed and tapering to a point.] **1893** *Funk's Stand. Dict.*, Halosauroid, a. & n. **1897** *Proc. Zool. Soc.* 268 On *Echidnocephalus,* a Halosauroid Fish from the Upper Cretaceous Formation of Westphalia.. Thanks to..new specimens of *Halosaurus* obtained by the 'Challenger' Expedition, it is now possible to demonstrate that..the strange Halosauroid type was already completely developed before the end of the Cretaceous period. **1904** G. A. BOULENGER in *Cambr. Nat. Hist.* VII. xxii. 622 The conformation of the pectoral arch has much in common with that of the Halosaurs. *Ibid.* 624 In *Halosaurus* the scales of the lateral line..are scarcely enlarged. **1957** R. CAMPBELL *Portugal* iv. 68 In the depth of Setúbal they were visited by many weird monsters,.. notably, the *halosaurus* with a long undulating tail. **1963** *New Scientist* 10 Jan. 80 The deeper-living benthic fishes, those that live at depths beyond 2,000 metres, are.. halosaurs (Halosauridae). **1971** *Nature* 2 Apr. 279/1 They include the halosaurs, which are known to develop from leptocephalus larvae, and the spiny eels or notacanths.

halothane (hæ·lǒþēin). [f. HALO(GEN + E)THANE.] A volatile liquid, $CF_3CHBrCl$, with a characteristic odour, used as a general anæsthetic.

1957 *Lancet* 8 June 1196/1 Dr Foster has done a grea service by his letter of June 1, if only by drawing attention to errors in the use of 'Fluothane' (halothane). *Ibid.* 7 Sept. 493 To date, cardiac arrest has been reported in five patients anæsthetised with halothane. **1961** *Brit. Med. Dict.* 653/1 *Halothane,* B.P. Commission approved name for 2-bromo-2-chloro-1:1:1-trifluoroethane, a volatile, non-explosive anaesthetic, more powerful than ether. **1971** *Nature* 1 Oct. 353/1 Cats anaesthetized with 50% nitrous oxide in oxygen and 1% halothane.

halt, *sb.*[1] Add: **b.** A small railway station without the ordinary accommodation or staff, at which only local trains normally stop.

1910 *Offic. Guide L.N.W.R.* (ed. 15) 410 Rail motor car halts at Wendlebury, Charlton, and Oddington. **1914** *Railway Mag.* Aug. 152/2 The provision of the 'halts' on the new line has been much appreciated locally. **1921** *Dict. Occup. Terms* (1927) § 706 *Halt attendant;* a porter who attends at roadside halt, where there is no proper station staff. **1973** *Country Life* 7 June 1612/4 A halt or unstaffed stopping place where trains called only if required.

halt, *v.*[2] Add: **1. b.** Also formerly used as a command in traffic regulations and on road signs. So *halt notice, sign.* Also *transf.*

1932 E. WALLACE *When Gangs came to London* xx. 175 He caught Terry's eye and abruptly changed the subject. When they were outside: 'What was that halt sign?' demanded Jiggs. **1935** *Highway Code* 21 (*caption*) Halt sign. **1958** A. WILSON *Middle Age of Mrs. Eliot* II. 153 David, recognizing the Grimm quotation as a halt sign, laughed too. **1965** D. M. DEVINE *His Own Appointed Day* I. ii. 17 Left, here. Then turn right at the halt sign. **1967** M. SUMMERTON *Memory of Darkness* ii. 21 He had driven through a halt sign, and collided with an on-coming tanker. **1969** *Times* 15 July 7/3 What are the advantages of the Give Way signs? Why cannot the Ministry go back to the old safer Halt notices?

halter, *sb.*[1] Add: **1. b.** A strap attached to the top of a backless bodice and looped round the neck; also, a bodice with such a strap or cut so as to give a similar effect. Hence *attrib.* and *Comb.*, as *halter neck(line), top.*

1935 *Mademoiselle* Aug. 1/2 (*caption*) Trunks with halter top. **1936** *New Yorker* 18 Jan. 50/2 When a dress terminates in a halter neck, they have an ingratiating habit of putting a little bolero jacket over it. **1939** M. B. PICKEN *Lang. Fashion* 102/3 Halter neckline.. introduced about 1933. Used in sports and evening clothes. **1948** N. MAILER *Naked & Dead* (1949) II. vii. 229 In the brothel the girls wear halters and trim panties with a tropical print. **1953** BERG *Dict. New Words* 91/1 *Halter,* a woman's bodice, held in place by straps around the neck and across the back, so as to leave the arms and the back free. **1958** J. D. MACDONALD *Executioners* (1959)

iv. 59 Nancy wore very short red shorts..and a yellow linen halter. **1959** *Vogue Pattern Book* June/July 23 A full, floating skirt and bare back halter top for a sun dress. **1971** *Vogue* Dec. 64/1 Black silk jersey halter-neck dress.. £70.

3. halter-break *v. U.S.* (earlier examples); **halter hitch** (see quot. 1944).

1837 *N.Y. Mirror* 28 Oct. 140/3 The moose has been frequently tamed, and unlike the common deer, can be halter-broken as easily as a horse. **1860** J. G. HOLLAND *Miss Gilbert's Career* xix. 350 You want to halter-break 'em when they're little and get 'em kind o' wonted to the feel of the harness. **1868** *Rep. Iowa Agric. Soc. 1867* 117 My colts are halter-broken as soon as foaled. **1944** C. W. ASHLEY *Bk. Knots* ii. 44 *Halter hitch.* Horses are hitched with this knot the world over. The end is stuck loosely through the loop, which is not tightened. The knot is easily slipped after removing the end from the loop. **1947** *Times Lit. Suppl.* 15 Nov. 594/4 When he was seven he was given a pony on condition that he mastered a halter hitch.

halteridium (hæltĕri·diŏm). *Zool.* Pl. **-ia.** [mod.L. (A. Labbé 1894, in *Archives de Zoologie expérimentale et générale*, 3e série, II. 129), f. Gr. ἁλτήρ weight used in leaping.] A name for the gametocytes of the protozoan genus *Hæmoproteus*, which is parasitic in birds, used when the gametocytes were erroneously considered to be a separate genus.

1901 G. M. STERNBERG in *Pop. Sci. Monthly* LVIII. 367 The mosquito..could not transmit the malarial parasite of man or another similar parasite of birds (halteridium). **1901** *Practitioner* Mar. 278 One of the malaria-like organisms of birds, namely, halteridium. **1962** J. D. SMYTH *Introd. Animal Parasitol.* ix. 107 These gametocytes [of *Hæmoproteus columbæ*] are shaped like a curved sausage and encircle the nucleus in a halter-fashion, and are sometimes referred to as *Halteridia*, as they were at one time called by the generic name of *Halteridium*.

haluka: see *KHALUKAH.

halutzim (hālū·tsim), *sb. pl.* Also **chalutzim, haluzim.** [Heb. *ḥălûṣ.*] Jewish pioneers entering Palestine in order to build up their future national home.

1921 *Daily Mail* 11 Apr. 6/5 The 'Haluzim' are the Jewish pioneers who are flocking into Palestine to help in building up the Jewish National Home. **1923** *Daily Mail* 18 July 7 Tel Aviv..is the headquarters of the Rutenberg Company and also of a number of co-operative building societies run by young Jewish halutzim pioneers. **1923** W. P. LIVINGSTONE *Galilee Doctor* 261 The halutzim, or 'pioneers'. **1971** D. MEIRING *Wall of Glass* ix. 71 A few other Second Aliyah men from Russia, calling themselves Chalutzim, pioneers.

halva (halvā·, χ-). Also **halvah, halwa.** [Yiddish *halva*, f. Turk. *helva*, f. Arab. *ḥalwa* *HULWA.] A sweetmeat made of sesame flour and honey.

1846 I. F. ROMER *Pilgrimage* II. ii. 33 The vender of sweetmeats with a tempting array of *halva* and 'lumps of delight' set out upon a wooden tray borne upon his head. **1908** *Daily Chron.* 12 June 4/7 A Greek merchant in the East-end, who..would sell you..black olives, rose leaf jam, and halvas. *a* **1916** 'SAKI' *Toys of Peace* (1919) 134 A tin of the best Smyrna halva. **1917** KIPLING *Eyes of Asia* (1918) 80, I eat..halwa and puri (native dishes). **1945** A. KOBER *Parm Me* 5 'Halvah', a Turkish confection. **1953** H. MILLER *Plexus* (1963) x. 352, I see Halvah and Baklava too. **1962** *Listener* 24 May 931/2 *Halva cake.* Many of the Greek cakes and pastries are beyond the scope of the home cook, but here is a simple one. **1964** W. MARKFIELD *To Early Grave* (1965) ii. 34 He brought a bagful of Hershey bars and Charms and sour balls and chocolate-covered halvah. **1973** *Sunday Express* 23 Sept. 7/1 From the first time he tasted halva as a child Gholamali Rastegar was obsessed by the traditional Arabic sweetmeat made from honey.

halver[1]. **2.** Delete *Obs.* exc. *dial.* and add U.S. examples: used esp. in phr. *do by halvers, go halvers (with).*

1865 'MARK TWAIN' *Celebr. Jumping Frog* (1867) 36 No man can say he ever see him do anything by halvers. **1873** J. H. BEADLE *Undevel. West.* iv. 93 'I'll go halvers with him,' shouts the conservative-looking chap. **1932** W. FAULKNER *Light in August* xviii. 394 Byron Bunch, that weeded another man's laidby crop, without any halvers.

halwa, var. *HALVA.

ham, *sb.*[1] Add: **3.** *ham-curing, -sandwich;* **hamfatter** *U.S. slang*, an ineffective actor or performer; (also *hamfat*) a mediocre jazz musician; so *hamfat man*, etc.; **ham-fisted** *a.*, having large or clumsy hands, heavy-handed, awkward; bungling; hence **ham-fistedly** *adv.*, **ham-fistedness; ham-footed** *a.*, clumsy, awkward, stupid; **ham-handed** *a.*, = **ham-fisted;* hence **ham-handedly** *adv.*, **ham-handedness; ham loaf** orig. *U.S.*, a shaped mass of chopped cooked ham intended to be cut into slices.

1907 *Daily Chron.* 23 Oct. 4/4 Spinning, or bread-baking, or ham-curing. **1880** G. A. SALA *America Revisited* (1882) I. iv. 66 Every American who does not wish to be thought 'small potatoes' or a 'ham-fatter' or a 'corner loafer'. **1889** *Cent. Dict., Hamfatter*,..a term of contempt for an actor of a low grade, as a negro minstrel. Said to be derived from an old-style negro song called 'The Ham-fat Man'. **1932** 'SPINDRIFT' *Yankee Slang* 20 *Hamfatter*, loudly-dressed and loudly-decorated dude. **1938** *N.Y. Amsterdam News* 12 Mar. 17 The Harlem Hamfats grind out the tune. **1946** MEZZROW & WOLFE *Really Blues* 58 A lot of beat up old hamfats..sang and played. **1959** S. B. CHARTERS *Country Blues* 86 The singing of these little 'hamfat' bands never reached the artistic intensity of men like Blind Lemon. **1966** *New Yorker* 11 June 160/2 Most of the musicians playing in these clubs are old men. ..They're hamfat musicians. In the old days, the rough musicians kept pieces of ham fat in their pockets to grease the slides of their trombones. **1928** *Daily Mail* 7 May 6/4 Ham Fisted.—Applied to pilots who are heavy on controls, or generally clumsy. **1928** *Sunday Express* 24 June 8/3 Two thousand lumber-jacks were in town, ham-fisted great fellows with hair on their chests and pine needles growing out of their ears. **1938** C. S. FORESTER *Ship of Line* 51 God damn and blast all you hamfisted yokels. **1942** H. ALLEN in Forbes & Allen *Ten Fighter Boys* 15 A dog-fight with a Hun very rarely entails a considered aerobatic movement as an evasive action. In fact, the more ham-fisted the movement, the better its effect. **1960** *Times* 20 Oct. 8/1 The play's basic idea implies a less ham-fisted humour than the authors can supply. **1964** *Punch* 2 Sept. 355/1 Some ham-fistedly insensitive moments. **1963** *Times* 16 Feb. 9/3 The campaign cannot be written off because of the hamfistedness of its beginnings. **1960** E. S. & W. J. HIGHAM *High Speed Rugby* 26 One 'ham-footed' forward ..makes a present of the ball to the other side. **1961** *Sunday Express* 7 May 14 Is he so thick-soled, ham-footed? **1918** W. A. BISHOP *Winged Warfare* 30 First the instructor would tell me I was 'ham-handed'—that I gripped the controls too tightly with every muscle tense. **1918** *Punch* 3 Apr. 222/2 *Second P[ilot]*...I was getting ham-handed and mutton-fisted, flapping the old things every day. **1930** C. DIXON *Parachuting* 93 The pilot with sensitive hands is a better pilot than one with non-sensitive hands. The latter are bluntly called 'ham-handed'. **1934** E. LINKLATER *Magnus Merriman* 98 Are you trying to insult me, or is that your ham-handed idea of a compliment? **1946** *Times* 3 Dec. 8/3 There should be no ham-handed bulk purchasing of stuff which was not really wanted. **1958** *New Statesman* 12 Apr. 458/3 Much of the recipient's pleasure is taken away by the very ham-handed invitation. **1964** *Economist* 11 Apr. 168/1 The FMC has gone a bit hamhandedly about its job. **1928** O. STEWART *Aerobatics* 50 One of the main objectives in finesse is the development of good 'hands'. ..Ham-handedness is not often a gift of unkind fate; it is not necessarily incurable. **1963** *Economist* 8 June 1046/1 The Kennedy Administration has contributed its own moments of hamhandedness. **1902** *Encycl. Brit.* XXVI. 558/2 Hamburger steak with onions, veal loaf, ham loaf. **1907** *Daily Chron.* 23 Sept. 7/5 Veal loaf, ham loaf, beef loaf. *c* **1847** J. S. COYNE in M. R. Booth *Eng. Plays of 19th Cent.* (1973) IV. 186 We used to go together to Greenwich, with a paper of ham sandwiches in my basket. **1866** 'MARK TWAIN' *Lett. fr. Hawaii* (1967) 68 The Sandwich Islanders always squat on their hams, and who knows but they may be the old original 'ham sandwiches'? **1872** 'L. CARROLL' *Through Looking-Glass* vii, I fed him with—with—with Ham-sandwiches and Hay. **1880** RUSKIN *Fathers have told Us* I. i, If he has bought his ham-sandwich, and is ready for the 'En voiture, messieurs'. **1972** B. EVERITT *Cold Front* xv. 145 The boy.. sat between us, polishing off a gigantic ham sandwich.

4. Phr. **ham and beef** *Rhyming slang*, the chief warder in a prison; **ham and eggs**, a dish consisting of fried ham and eggs.

1941 J. PHELAN *Murder by Numbers* iv. 46 There's the ham-and-beef and tickety-boo making rounds. **1962** *John o' London's* 25 Jan. 82/2 A chief warder or prison officer is known in rhyming slang as a *ham and beef.* **1837** W. H. WILLS *Jrnl.* in *S. Hist. Assoc. Pub.* VI. 473 They gave me fryed ham and eggs and biscuit, bread & Coffee. **1838** DICKENS *Let.* 1 Feb. (1965) I. 366 We have had for breakfast,..ham and eggs. **1967** C. DRUMMOND *Death at Furlong Post* iii. 31 'Get me ham and eggs,' he said.

II. 5. [App. short for **hamfatter*.] An inexpert performer; (also *ham actor, actress*) an ineffective or over-emphatic actor, one who rants or overacts. *slang* (orig. *U.S.*).

1882 *Illustr. Sport. & Dram. News* 23 Dec. 355/2 'Banjo Hams' are held up to scorn. *Ibid.*, One writer proudly describes himself as 'no ham, but a classical banjo player'. **1903** S. A. CLAPIN *New Dict. Amer.* 220 *Ham*, in theatrical parlance, a tenth-rate actor or variety performer. **1911** *Hampton's Mag.* Aug. 178/1 It was the voice of what is known as a 'ham', because Shakespeare once wrote a play. A 'ham' actor. **1926** H. C. WITWER *Roughly Speaking* 223 Ham actors get a extra split week at a picture house if their fearful monologs put the ladies on the broiler. **1928** *Daily Express* 20 June 9/4 Sophie Tucker will, in all probability, appear in a revue next autumn... 'You have never seen me in revue,' Sophie reminded me, 'I am a ham actor too, you know.' **1933** 'HAY' & 'ARMSTRONG' *Orders are Orders* II. 51 'We'd better have Harvey..to double for him.'..'*That* old ham actor?' **1936** WODEHOUSE *Laughing Gas* xviii. 200 Just one of these ham actors that's jealous of a fellow's screen genius. **1941** E. WILSON *Wound & Bow* i. 61 Dickens had a strain of the ham in him, and, in the desperation of his later life, he gave in to the old ham and let him rip. **1947** N. MARSH *Final Curtain* xii. 179 A squalid little ham actress. **1957** V. J. KEHOE *Technique Film & T.V. Make-Up* i. 15 The expression 'ham' actor originated from those performers who rubbed ham rind on their faces as a base for their colored powders when they could not afford the more expensive and less odoriferous oils. **1958** *Times* 16 Apr. 3/2 'He thought I was an old ham,' says Miss Seyler indulgently.

b. An inexpert or over-theatrical performance; ham acting. *slang.*

1942 R. CHANDLER *High Window* (1943) xxx. 195 Don't feed me the ham. I've been in pictures. I'm a connoisseur of ham. **1959** *Times Lit. Suppl.* 20 Feb. 95/3 Charles Dickens..saw Lemaître in his late period and was swept off his feet, but what he says might apply equally well to ham acting. In fact, it sounds suspiciously like ham. **1959** *Listener* 28 May 954/2 The mummer who thinks that all acting before his time was 'ham'.

6. An amateur telegraphist; now esp., an amateur radio operator. *slang* (orig. *U.S.*).

1919 C. H. DARLING *Jargon Bk.* 17 *Ham*, a student telegraph operator. **1922** *Glasgow Herald* 18 Aug. 6 Any person who passes a test prescribed by the Government can obtain a licence to 'send' radio messages in the United States, and in popular parlance one who has qualified and taken this 'Radio Operator Amateur—First Grade' certificate is dubbed a 'ham'. **1928** *Collier's* 22 Sept. 26 The amateur radio 'hams' have the ends of the earth for neighbors. **1929** *Amer. Speech* IV. 288 At either end of a wire an unskillful operator is a 'lid', 'ham', 'bum' or 'plug'. **1936** *Daily Herald* 19 Sept. 7/5 (Advt.), Do you ever hear the 'hams'? It appears that 'hams' is American for amateur radio transmitters... Of course, the 'hams' use the short wavelengths. **1955** *Sci. News Let.* 19 Mar. 188/2 Now it will be easier for a blind person to qualify for a license as a radio 'ham'. **1957** *Oxford Mail* 9 Nov. 4/5 The Russians invited radio 'hams' throughout the world to send details to Radio Magazine, Moscow, of reception from their satellites. **1967** *New Scientist* 11 May 322/3 The army of radio 'hams', who reach out over fantastic distances with their single sideband transmitters and receivers, are about to be reinforced. **1973** D. LEES *Rape of Quiet Town* vi. 90 He'd heard the radio ham speaking into a microphone.

III. 7. [Partly from **ham-fisted, -handed* adjs.] An incompetent boxer or fighter. *U.S. slang.*

1888 *Missouri Repub.* 27 Mar. (Farmer), He is a good fighter but will allow the veriest ham to whip him. **1929** *Sat. Even. Post* 14 Dec. 144/3 They want me to slug with this big ham.

B. *attrib.* or as *adj.* **1.** Characteristic of or relating to a ham actor or an inexpert performer; self-consciously theatrical. *slang.*

1935 H. WILLIAMS *4 Yrs. Old Vic* xi. 186 Young players to-day are scared of being what they call 'ham', which I suppose is an abbreviation of what used to be termed 'ham-bone'. **1938** *Evening Standard* 26 July 7/2 We hear a great deal about 'ham' acting nowadays. As far as I can judge, 'ham' acting is the habit of rolling sonorous speeches round the tongue and delivering them with extravagant relish to the gallery. **1944** AUDEN *Sea & Mirror* in *For Time Being* iii. 56 The schmalz tenor never quite able at his big moments to get right up nor the ham bass right down. **1958** B. NICHOLS *Sweet & Twenties* xvii. 231 His conception of aristocracy was strangely out of date, and more than a little 'ham'. **1958** *Observer* 4 May 15/7 It is one of the most extraordinary exhibitions of ham acting I've ever seen.

2. [Partly from **ham-fisted, -handed* adjs.] Clumsy, ineffective, incompetent. *slang.*

1941 M. ALLINGHAM *Traitor's Purse* xii. 133 Campion's thin hands remained expressionless and Lugg's great ham-fists did not stir. **1942** FORBES & ALLEN *Ten Fighter Boys* p. xv, What he obviously intended to do on overshooting me was to flick over and spin down, but being a little ham, he overdid the manœuvre and came the right way up. *Ibid.* 84, I didn't stay to argue, but went bowling down in the hammest manner possible. **1949** 'J. TEY' *Brat Farrar* xiv. 124 He was..reluctant to submit that tender mouth to the ham hands of a Westerner. **1963** *Times Lit. Suppl.* 1 Feb. 71/1 Nothing he hated more than 'ham' writing and 'prefabricated' characters.

ham (hæm), *v.*[2] *slang.* [f. HAM *sb.*[1]] To act in a 'hammy' manner, to over-act. Freq. const. *up.* Hence **ha·mmed-up** *ppl. a.*; **ha·mming** *vbl. sb.* and *ppl. a.*

1933 STANLEY & MAXFIELD *Voice* 268 Hamming. **1937** *Printers' Ink Monthly* Apr. 54 *Ham it*, overacts [*sic*] for emphasis—bluster. **1944** L. A. G. STRONG *Director* xxii. 166 What with toning my voice down to that kid's mewing, and then trying to balance that hamming bloody idiot. **1946** *Daily Tel.* 18 Nov. 6/6 Thomas Mitchell, after a deal of recent hamming, is a convincing detective. **1955** A. HUXLEY *Genius & Goddess* 16 The performance was on the corny side; but it was a sympathetic part and, though she dearly loved to ham it up, Beulah was not merely a treasure. **1955** T. STERLING *Evil of Day* ix. 110 'Any actor would give twenty years of his life to play the part.'..'I thought if I told you what it was you'd ham it.' **1957** *Listener* 12 Sept. 402/3 Nor does he purvey anything of Wales as it is—rather the hammed-up version of Wales that the stupider sort of Englishman prefers. **1957** *Observer* 10 Nov. 19/2 The temptation of second-feature hamming. **1958** M. DICKENS *Man Overboard* ii. 27 She had hammed her scene with the seducer at the final run through. **1960** S. H. COURTIER *Gently dust Corpse* iii. 38 Hamming it now, thought Birch, and it's time they were brought to their senses. **1965** *Listener* 18 Nov. 795/1 Marie Bell..hams it up in a smugly self-conscious cameo portrayal. **1973** E. PAGE *Fortnight by Sea* xii. 132 A hammed-up impression of a military man.

hamada(h), varr. *HAMMADA.

Hamadan (hā·mădān). The name of a town in north-west Iran, used *attrib.* or *ellipt.* to denote a kind of carpet or rug (see quot. 1960).

1901 J. K. MUMFORD *Oriental Rugs* xi. 199 There is little difficulty in distinguishing the Hamadan carpet from all other weavings. **1932** P. SELVER tr. *Čapek's Tales from Two Pockets* 184 By Jove, if it isn't a Hamadan. ..and sometimes there are some fine Karavams and Kelims to be picked up. **1960** H. HAYWARD *Antique Coll.* 138/1 Hamadan is the marketing centre for Kurdish rugs and they are often known by this name. Heavy, long pile of great durability, rather coarse in stitch but well coloured, designs often embellished with animal

figures. Hamadan rugs are frequently described as 'Persian'.

hamadryas. *hamadryas baboon* = HAMADRYAD 2 b.

1932 S. ZUCKERMAN *Soc. Life Monkeys & Apes* xii. 200 The barks of the Chacma are almost indistinguishable from those of the Hamadryas baboon. **1967** *Listener* 6 Apr. 459/3 The gelada baboon and the hamadryas baboon.

hamal, var. HAMMAL (Later examples.)

1962 J. FLEMING *When I grow Rich* iii. 44 Heavily disguised as *hamals*, or human mules. **1967** J. RATHBONE *Diamonds Bid* xii. 105 Grey-clad hamals, porters who will carry anything anywhere.

hamamelis (hæmămī·lis). [mod.L. (J. F. Gronovius in Linnæus *Genera Plantarum* (ed. 2, 1742), a. Gr. ἁμαμηλίς medlar.] A shrub or small tree of the genus so called, which is native to North America and Eastern Asia, belongs to the family Hamamelidaceæ, and includes several species bearing yellow flowers late in winter before the leaves appear; a witch-hazel. Also, the extract made from the leaves and bark of *Hamamelis virginiana*. So **hamame·lin**, the dried extract.

1743 J. BARTRAM *Observ. Trav. Pensilvania to Canada* 19 July (1751) 35 Now we came to most excellent level ground..full of tall timber..and shrubs, as opulus, green maple, hornbeam, hamamelis. **1760** J. LEE *Introd. Bot.* 332 Witch Hazel, *Hamamelis.* **1890** BILLINGS *Med. Dict.*, *Hamamelin*, name given to a dry powdered extract of hamamelis. **1898** *Rev. Brit. Pharm.* 10 Fresh hamamelis-leaves are macerated in a little more than double their volume of water and alcohol. **1900** M. THORN in W. D. Drury *Bk. Gardening* xi. 386 The Hamamelis here mentioned may be propagated by grafting in February or early March. **1910** *Practitioner* July 128 Dry skins..must be cleaned with cold cream,..Any teleangiectasis must be treated with very hot water, to which is added hamamelis. **1911** J. U. LLOYD in *Bull. Lloyd Libr.* XVIII. 47 The preparation known as distilled hamamelis, or distilled extract of hamamelis, introduced by Pond about the middle of the nineteenth century. **1941** R. C. WREN *Potter's Cycl. Bot. Drugs* (ed. 5) 376 The concentration 'Hamamelin' is used for piles mostly in form of suppositories. **1949** *National Formulary* (B.M.A.) 79 Suppositories, each containing 3 gr of dry extract of hamamelis, to be dispensed. **1969** *Jrnl. Roy. Hort. Soc.* XCIV. 85 Hamamelis should be planted, if possible, not too far from the house.

Haman (hēⁱ·mæn). **1.** The name of the chief minister of Ahasuerus who was hanged on the gallows prepared for Mordecai, as related in the Book of Esther, used allusively (phr. *to hang as high as Haman*). So **Hama·nic** *a.*

1644 R. BROWNE *Ld. Digbies Designe to betray Abingdon* 7 When their blinded Party shall..see him in his colours, they will at last pity..a Prince that makes use of such a wicked head..: And..may know who is that Haman which blasts Mordecai's petition. **1647** *Mercurius Melanchol.* No. 3. 13 What is honour, but another Haman? This day a companion with a King, on the morrow hanging on the gallowes. **1650** J. TRAPP *Comm. O.T.* Isa. lxi. 2 All Hamans be hanged up at that feast-royal, at the last day especially. **1816** SCOTT *Old Mort.* xxvii, The whig Captain Balfour..swore..that if the garrison was not gi'en ower the morn by daybreak, he would hing up the young lord, poor thing, as high as Haman. **1842** BARHAM *Ingol. Leg.* 2nd Ser. 57 I'll hang you, like Haman! **1881** H. ADLER in *19th Cent.* Dec. 813 Prof. Goldwin Smith renews his onslaughts upon Jews and Judaism with an acerbity and virulence which I may be permitted to term Hamanic.

2. Haman's ears, formerly **Haman's fritters,** fritters or cakes eaten by the Jews at the festival of Purim.

1846 'A LADY' *Jewish Man.* vii. 123 Haman's Fritters. **1949** *Housewife* May 50/1 The pudding that we ate..on Purim was appropriately called Hamaan's Ears—lovely crisp flaps of thin pastry sprinkled with sugar and cinnamon. **1961** *Times* 23 Dec. 9/1 'Haman's ears': a cake eaten by Jewish people at the festival of Purim, to commemorate the downfall of Haman, their persecutor.

hamartia (hămā·ɹtiă). [a. Gr. ἁμαρτία fault, failure, guilt.] The fault or error which entails the destruction of the tragic hero (with particular reference to Aristotle's *Poetics*).

[**1789** T. TWINING *Aristotle's Treat. Poetry* 308 Dacier confounds himself and his readers in his note about *Thyestes.* He mistakes Aristotle's sense of ἁμαρτια.] **1895** S. H. BUTCHER *Aristotle's Theory Poetry & Fine Art* viii. 300 But with him [*sc.* Macbeth] the ἁμαρτία, the primal defect, is the taint of ambition. **1927** F. L. LUCAS *Tragedy* iv. 102 If we seek the *hamartia* in more modern tragedy like Ibsen's, it becomes clearer than ever that an intellectual mistake is all that the term need mean. **1956** H. HOUSE *Aristotle's Poetics* vi. 94 All serious modern Aristotelian scholarship agrees..that 'hamartia' means an error which is derived from 'ignorance of some material fact or circumstance'. **1968** D. W. LUCAS in *Aristotle's Poetics* 302 The essence of *hamartia* is ignorance combined with the absence of wicked intent.

hamartoma (hæmaɹtōᵘ·mă). *Path.* [mod.L., ad. G. *hamartom* (E. Albrecht 1904, in *Verh. d. deutsch. path. Ges.* VII. 153), f. Gr. ἁμαρτ-άνω to go wrong: see *-OMA.] A tumour-like mass resulting from the faulty growth or development of normal cells or tissue.

1904 *Index Med.* II. 142/2 (*index*) Hamartoma. **1909** J. G. ADAMI *Princ. Path.* I. III. xxiii. 749 We must be governed here by our conception of the meaning of the word *angioma*..If we restrict it to mean a tumor, due to the independent growth of vessels, they [*sc.* other tumors having vessels as their main constituent] must be cast out of this class. To provide a class for them Albrecht has suggested the term *Hamartoma.* **1950** G. P. WRIGHT *Introd. Path.* xxvii. 479 Striking examples of the vascular hamartomas may be seen in the simple, cavernous, or more complicated plexiform, overgrowths of blood vessels that form congenital nævi, birth-marks,..or vascular warts. **1970** S. D. KOBERNICK tr. *Masson's Human Tumors* I. ii. 77 In one category, heterotopia consists of tissues which belong to the region where they are encountered, but have escaped the organization of this region and are found in excess: these are Hamartomas.

Hamathite (hēⁱ·măþəit). [f. *Hamath*, the biblical name for Hama in western Syria + -ITE[1].] An inhabitant of the ancient Syrian city of Hamath; also, a script found in the Taurus mountains, now called 'Hittite'. Also *attrib.*

1611 BIBLE *Gen.* x. 18 The Aruadite, the Zemarite, and the Hamathite. **1880** *Encycl. Brit.* XII. 26/1 Professor Sayce's view that the Hittites were the authors of the Hamathite hieroglyphics. **1926** D. G. HOGARTH *Kings of Hittites* 2 Hamathite territory is..the nearest to Galilee in which any sure evidence of occupation by Hittite civilization..has yet appeared. **1952** O. R. GURNEY *Hittites* 3 The same script had been noticed by E. J. Davis on the great rock-carving over a stream at Irriz in the Taurus mountains. Davis had then called the script 'Hamathite'.

hambergite (hæ·mbəɹgəit). *Min.* [ad. G. *hambergit* (W. C. Brögger 1890, in *Zeitschr. f. Kryst. und Min.* XVI (Specieller Th.). 65), f. the name of A. *Hamberg* (1863–1933), Sw. mineralogist, who discovered it: see -ITE[1].] A basic borate of beryllium, $Be_2(OH)BO_3$, occurring in colourless orthorhombic crystals that have strong double refraction.

1890 *Jrnl. Chem. Soc.* LVIII. II. 1078 Hambergite, discovered by A. Hamberg in 1889, and named after him by the author, crystallises in the rhombic system. **1962** R. WEBSTER *Gems* I. xvi. 265 Hambergite..was originally found in southern Norway in material of non-gem quality, but a discovery has now been made of large colourless crystals in central Madagascar.

hambo (ha·mbu). [f. *Hambo*, name of a parish in Hälsingland, Sweden.] A Swedish folk dance in ¾ time.

1925 *Blackw. Mag.* Jan. 79/1 We had been dancing in the Nylocks barn—dancing polskas and hambos. *Ibid.* Feb. 196/2 We only play old Swedish tunes..only old peasant polskas, hambos, and waltzes.

ha·m-bone. 1. The bone in a ham of hog meat; also, such a bone with the meat attached. Also (in *pl.*) *transf.*

1855 W. G. SIMMS *Forayers* 340 He had..brought with him the ham-bone and bread which he had so hastily appropriated. **1866** 'MARK TWAIN' in *Harper's Mag.* Dec. 111/1 We have only left a lower end of a ham-bone, with some of the outer rind and skin on. **1908** J. LONDON *Let.* 22 Dec. (1966) 275, I have to get down on my hambones and beg forgiveness. **1972** P. DICKINSON *Lizard in Cup* vi. 97 He found a bone in a trash-can—a bit of hambone.

2. An inferior or amateur actor, esp. one who speaks in a spurious Negro accent; a mediocre musician. *U.S. slang.*

1893 P. H. EMERSON *Signor Lippo* v. 11 Hambones! I told you so. I could vardy that when I heard them joggering. **1905** W. MELVILLE *No Wedding Bells for Her* II. iii, You are green, Ham bones means them as pays to act, which they can't do, and so saves the manager engaging deserving actors. **1942** BERREY & VAN DEN BARK *Amer. Thes. Slang* § 583/18 *Hambone*, an unconvincing blackface dialectician. **1960** B. KEATON *Wonderful World of Slapstick* (1967) 13 Because I was also a born hambone, I ignored any bumps..I may have got at first on hearing audiences gasp.

3. A sextant. *Naval slang.*

1938 F. A. WORSLEY *First Voy. in Square-Rigged Ship* viii. 144 What altitude have you got on that hambone, Stringer? **1962** GRANVILLE *Dict. Sailor's Slang* 58/1 *Hambone*, sextant which is of much the same shape.

hambro, hambro-line, vars. HAMBER-LINE.

1793 J. MACDONELL *Diary* in C. M. Gates *Five Fur Traders* (1933) 75 The canoe line..consists of fine Hambro lines loosely twisted upon one another. **1867** [see HAMBER-LINE]. **1961** F. H. BURGESS *Dict. Sailing* 108 *Hambro, Hambroline*, a small line, made of three strands of hemp, hard laid, sometimes tarred, and used for lacings, seizings, etc.

Hamburger. Also **-burgher, †-bourger.** [G. *Hamburger* a native or inhabitant of Hamburg in Germany.] **1.** A native or inhabitant of Hamburg. Also *attrib.* or as *adj.*

1616 G. CAREW *Let.* Jan. (1860) 81 The Kinge of Denmarke..purposeth to build a stronge fort vppon the River of Elbe, requiringe the Hambourgers to permitt 3,000 of his men to passe throughe there towne. **1653** W. GEE *Let.* 16 June in M. M. Verney *Memoirs* (1894) III. ii. 56 They had been fired upon by an English ship, and had pursued 'a Hamburger'. **1737** *London Mag.* Feb. 81/2 (*heading*) Of the City of Hamburgh, with several Observations on the Hamburghers, and other Germans. **1798** D. WORDSWORTH *Jrnl. Visit to Hamburgh* (1941) I. II. 21 Hamburgher girls with white caps. **1856** GEO. ELIOT in *Westm. Rev.* IX. 14 The fair Hamburghers acted in the spirit of Johnson's advice to Hannah More. **1932** L. GOLDING *Magnolia St.* II. iv. 314 The stolid young Hamburgers who went out rowing on Sundays on the Alster. **1966** *Guardian* 5 Nov. 7/3 He had the welfare of the sleeping Hamburghers in mind.

2. (Now freq. with lower-case initial.) In full *Hamburger steak* = *Hamburg steak* (see STEAK 2 c); also, a kind of sausage. Now, chopped beef, spiced and flavoured, formed into a cake and fried, often served between two halves of a toasted bun. So *hamburger bar*, etc. orig. *U.S.*

1889 *Walla Walla* (Wash.) *Union* 5 Jan. 2/4 You are asked if you will have 'porkchopbeefsteakhamandegg-hamburgersteakorliverandbacon'. **1901** ADE *40 Mod. Fables* 285 After the kid had been carried out of the Ring looking like a Hamburger Steak. **1902** *Encycl. Brit.* XXVI. 558/2 Hamburger steak with onions. **1908** 'YESLAH' *Tenderfoot S. Calif.* xiv. 118 Out of date eggs, last year's hamburger and over ripe limburger. **1912** I. COBB *Back Home* 147 A vendor..sold to the same customers..odorous hamburger and flat slabs..of striped ice-cream. **1920** *Chambers's Jrnl.* 348/2 Hamburger steaks and German pot roasts. **1929** E. HEMINGWAY *Farewell to Arms* II. xv. 106 They had the look of not too freshly ground hamburger steak. **1931** B. STARKE *Touch & Go* iv. 58 A truck driver transporting two huge draft horses took us to Bryan, where he grandly 'set 'em up' to hamburgers and coffee. **1943** *R.A.F. Jrnl.* Aug. 10 She held a pair of..gloves in one hand and a hamburger sandwich in the other. **1950** *Manch. Guardian Weekly* 6 Apr. 3 After much pleasantry over the hamburgers and hot dogs. **1957** *London Mag.* Dec. 19 There is a pier with all the usual sideshows, hot dog, hamburger and ice-cream stands. **1960** *Times* 30 Jan. 11/7 The mounting number of hamburger bars suggests that it is here to stay.

Hamburg parsley: see PARSLEY 1, 2.

hame[2]. Add: **b.** *hame-rein.*

1902 *Daily Chron.* 9 July 3/6 Why a tight hame rein should be used on so many builders' and other carts is..a puzzle. **1908** *N. & Q.* 10th Ser. X. 106 At the foot of a hill leading from Blackrock, near Brighton, to Rottingdean is a board with the inscription: 'Please slacken hame-rein on going uphill.'

hamel (hā·məl, ‖ha·məl). *S. Afr.* [Afrikaans = Du. *hamel*, G. *hammel* castrated ram; cf. HAMBLE *v.*] A wether.

1835 A. SMITH *Diary* 22 Apr. (1939) I. 376 If relatives rich, sometimes kill ten oxen and ten hamels. **1871** H. H. DUGMORE *Remin. Albany Settler* 14 A dozen of startled hamels, just separated from a large flock, would be likely to try a driver's legs, and lungs too, in crossing it. **1895** W. C. SCULLY *Kafir Stories* 28 Would your father have let me die rather than take a hamel from the flock of a rich, lazy boer, who never counts his sheep? **1896** R. WALLACE *Farm. Ind. Cape Col.* xvii. 346 Ram lambs are..'sorted' to make wethers or hamels. **1950** *Cape Times* 14 Dec. 13/6 At an auction sale..hamels fetched £6 11s.—the highest price for hamels in this district.

‖ **hamerkop** (hā·məɹkǫp, ha·məɹkǫp). *S. Afr.* Also semi-anglicized **hammerkop** (hæ·-). [Afrikaans, f. *hamer* hammer + *kop* head.] = HAMMER-HEAD 4.

1834 A. SMITH *Diary* 7 Dec. (1939) I. 163 A Basutu said the hammerkop gives rain. **1887** *Encycl. Brit.* XXII. 578/1 It [*sc. Scopus umbretta*]..is the 'Hammerkop' (Hammerhead) of the Cape colonists. **1890** [see HAMMER-HEAD 4]. **1895** *Funk's Stand. Dict.*, Hamerkop. **1946** *Cape Argus* 7 Dec. 2 Hamerkops are remarkable fowl... The hamerkop's nest is a huge affair, generally in a tree. **1952** *Cape Times Week-end Mag.* 8 Nov. 6 A solitary hamerkop flies homeward every evening. **1964** C. WILLOCK *Enormous Zoo* vii. 120 Hammerkops, the queer brown bird with the blunt head that gives it its name, pick over scraps in the rotting papyrus stems. **1966** E. PALMER *Plains of Camdeboo* xi. 195 We never saw the hamerkop in numbers. **1971** *Country Life* 28 Oct. 1127/2 Hammercops, curious bulky brown birds with crests and thick bills, flew about in pairs.

‖ **hametz** (hā·mets, χ-). Also **chametz, chometz,** etc. [Heb. *ḥāmēṣ.*] Leaven, or food that has been mixed with leaven, prohibited during the Passover.

1891 M. FRIEDLÄNDER *Jewish Relig.* 377 The head of the family..examines his residence thoroughly, and keeps the *chametz*, which he has found, in a safe place till the next morning. *Ibid.* 378 All the *chamets* that is left after the first meal on the 14th of *Nisan* must be removed. **1892** I. ZANGWILL *Childr. Ghetto* II. xxiv. 124 'Where is the Rabbi?' 'Up in the bedrooms gathering the *Chomutz*..hunting with a candle for stray crumbs.' **1960** *Jewish Chron.* 8 Apr. 35/1 The Rev. S. Black..told the boys and girls of Pesach and its meaning. Of the search for chametz (leavened bread). **1960** *Commentary* June 499/2 Removing bread (but not other *hametz*) from the house on Passover. **1973** *Jewish Chron.* 9 Feb. 12/5 He is convinced that no one eats *hametz* during Passover.

Ham Hill stone, Ham stone, a Somerset stone, representative of the lower part of the Upper Lias, quarried in the Ham Hill quarry

near Yeovil and used widely for building purposes in the area.

1889 H. B. Woodward in *Proc. Bath Nat. Hist. & Antiquarian Club* VI. 182 The celebrated building-stone of Ham Hill, near Yeovil..is not without geological interest... The Ham Hill stone is mainly composed of sand and comminuted shells. **1918** *Q. Jrnl. Geol. Soc.* LXXIV. 169 At Ham Hill..the portion of *moorei* date is exposed in the big quarry on the hill and the main mass of it is a 'freestone'—the celebrated Ham-Hill Building-Stone. In the big quarry the sequence is as follows: 1. Sand.. 2. 'Riddings'..3. Ham-Hill Stone. **1936** G. Pollett *Song for Sixpence* ix. 76 This grey Ham stone is most satisfying to the eye. **1961** *Countryman* LVIII. III. 439 Sophisticated strangers are not yet trying to buy the lovely old Hamstone farmhouses.

Hamidian (hæmi·dĭăn), *a.* [f. the name of Abdul *Hamid* II + -ian.] Pertaining to or resembling the rule of Abdul Hamid, Sultan of Turkey from 1876 to 1909. Hence **Hami·dianism.**

1908 *Westm. Gaz.* 1 Aug. 2/3 Thirty years of wandering in the Hamidian wilderness. **1908** *Daily Chron.* 24 Oct. 4/4 The Hamidian rule. *Ibid.* 18 Dec. 4/4 A reversion to Hamidianism. **1930** *Times Lit. Suppl.* 4 Dec. 1047/3 His spy-system appears to have been Hamidian in its extent and efficiency.

Hamidieh (hæmi·die). [f. the name of Abdul *Hamid* II + *-ieh* adj. suffix.] A body of Kurdish cavalry formed by the Turks in 1891.

1898 H. A. G. Percy *Diary Asiatic Turkey* 83 Zekki,..the reputed founder of the Hamidieh System. **1901** *Westm. Gaz.* 27 Aug. 2/2 The Hamidie Cavalry..defy the Porte by ignoring its commands. **1902** *Encycl. Brit.* XXV. 665/2 A tribal militia force (Hamidieh), consisting of 48 regiments, is formed somewhat on the lines of Cossacks.

Hamite, *sb.*[1] Add: Hence **Ha:miticiza·tion,** the action of becoming Hamitic; **Hami·ticized** *a.*, having become Hamitic; **Ha·mitoid** *a.*, resembling the Hamitic type.

1884 *Nature* 17 Apr. 581/1 These peoples should apparently be regarded rather as Negroes affected by Hamitic than as Hamites affected by Negro elements. In other words, they are Negroid rather than Hamitoid. **1911** H. H. Johnston *Opening up of Africa* iii. 91 The earlier and more elaborate of these works were inspired by Semites and executed by Hamiticized negroes. **1923** G. W. Murray *Eng.-Nubian Dict.* Introd., In the case of Nubian, the process of Hamiticization has gone so far that it has borrowed Hamitic personal-endings for its verb, Hamitic case-endings for its noun, and possesses a vocabulary largely Hamitic. **1936** *Discovery* June 171/1 The first great group of hamiticised Negroes, the Nilotes, constitute a well-defined physical type.

Hami·to-Semi·tic, *a.* Of or pertaining to a language, people, etc., having both Hamitic and Semitic features. Also as *sb.* Also **Hami·tic-Semi·tic** *a.* and *sb.*

1909 *Cent. Dict.* Suppl., *Hamito-Semitic*, relating to the peoples speaking Hamitic and Semitic languages which are considered members of one linguistic stock. **1936** *Science & Society* I. 25 He records similarities..between pronouns in Hamitic-Semitic. **1939** L. H. Gray *Foundations of Lang.* 357 Second in importance only to the Indo-European linguistic family comes the Hamito-Semitic group. **1964** R. H. Robins *Gen. Ling.* viii. 307 The Hamito-semitic family, represented by classical Arabic and the Arabic languages and dialects of the Middle East and North African coast.

Hamlet[2] (hæ·mlėt). The name of the prince of Denmark who is the hero of Shakespeare's play of this name, in allusive phr. *Hamlet without the Prince* (*of Denmark*): a performance without the chief actor or a proceeding without the central figure.

[**1775** *Morning Post* 21 Sept., Lee Lewes diverts them with the manner of their performing Hamlet in a company that he belonged to, when the hero who was to play the principal character had absconded with an inn-keeper's daughter; and that when he came forward to give out the play, he added, 'the part of Hamlet to be left out, for that night.'] **1818** Byron *Let.* 26 Aug. (1830) II. 445 My autobiographical essay would resemble the tragedy of Hamlet.., recited 'with the part of Hamlet left out by particular desire'. **1820** Lady Granville *Let.* 22 Aug. (1894) I. 161, I am not used to be newsmonger and perhaps I leave out Hamlet. **1825** Scott *Talisman* (1883) 5 The title of a 'Tale of the Crusaders' would resemble the playbill, which is said to have announced the tragedy of Hamlet, the character of the Prince of Denmark being left out. **1859** G. Meredith *Ordeal R. Feverel* I. vii. 109 'What have you been doing at home, Cousin Rady?' 'Playing Hamlet, in the absence of the Prince of Denmark.' **1902** *Daily Chron.* 22 Apr. 3/1 Of what avail is it to promise 'entirely new scenery' for 'Die Meistersinger', if the part of Hans Sachs is to be practically eliminated from the performance? And yet this 'Hamlet-without-the-Prince' method is consistently pursued season after season at Covent Garden. **1910** *Times Weekly* 17 June 452 The army without Kitchener is like Hamlet without the Prince of Denmark. **1918** L. Strachey *Emin. Victorians* 86 The Catholic Church without the absolute dominion of the Pope might resemble the play of Hamlet without the Prince of Denmark. **1967** J. Prescot *Case Counterfeit* viii. 96 Without Drax one can't do a thing. Hamlet without the Prince of Denmark, I guess. **1972** *Publishers Weekly* 3 Apr. 22/3 The article..in the March 6th *PW* was an attempt to stage Hamlet without the Dane.

Hence **Ha·mletish** *a.*; **Ha·mletism,** an attitude resembling that of Hamlet; **Ha·mletize** *v. rare*, to soliloquize or meditate after the manner of Hamlet.

1844 Hebbe & MacKay tr. *Sealsfield's Life in New World* 267 Halloo! Mr. Howard! Hamletizing? **1852** H. Melville *Pierre* VII. vi. 191 In this plaintive fable we find embodied the Hamletism of the antique world. **1854** 'G. Greenwood' *Haps & Mishaps in Europe* iii. 53 Herr Devrient is a handsome, Hamlet-ish man, with a melancholy refinement of voice. **1905** *Daily Chron.* 11 Apr. 4/7 Let us forget Hamletism and all its ills. **1920** D. H. Lawrence *Women in Love* xiv. 205 One shouldn't talk when one is tired and wretched.—One Hamletises, and it seems a lie. **1923** —— *Stud. Classic Amer. Lit.* ix. 180 So Dana sits and Hamletizes by the Pacific—chief actor in the play of his own existence. **1936** *Times Lit. Suppl.* 5 Sept. 711/2 Adams's madness is, indeed, a trifle Hamletish. **1945** W. Fowlie in *Mod. Reading* XII. 210 He is the one contemporary writer who has driven out from his nature all traces of hamletism, and yet he writes constantly about Hamlet. **1952** A. R. D. Fairburn *Strange Rendezvous* 25 He has played the gravedigger to many a Hamletish posture of my soul.

hammada (hæ̆mā·dă). *Geol.* Also **hamada(h).** [f. Arab *ḥammāda*.] A flat rocky area of desert blown free of sand by the wind, typical of the Sahara.

1853 J. Richardson *Narr. Mission Cent. Afr.* II. iv. 60 Aghadez is situated on a hamadah, or lofty plateau of sandstone and granite formation. **1857** H. Barth *Trav. N. & Cent. Afr.* I. v. 133 Overweg and I had no time to lose in preparing for our journey over the hammáda, or plateau. **1886** *Encycl. Brit.* XXI. 149/2 Nearly all the rest of the Sahara consists..of undulating surfaces of rock (distinguished as *hammada*),..and regions of sandy dunes. **1934** W. Fitzgerald *Africa* I. ii. 60 Rocky wastes with the bare exposure of fissured rocks as dominant features of the scene, form the 'hamada' type of the Sahara. **1966** *McGraw-Hill Encycl. Sci. & Technol.* IV. 76/2 Ordinarily, a hammada is a bare rock surface composed of relatively flat-lying consolidated sedimentary rocks from which overlying softer sediments have been stripped, principally by wind erosion.

hammel, var. Hemel.

1812 J. Sinclair *Syst. Husb. Scot.* I. 21 Small open sheds, or what, in Berwickshire, are called *Hammels* or *Hemmels*, with separate straw-yards attached. **1851** H. Stephens *Bk. Farm* (1855) I. 242 The hammels [are occupied] by the two-year-olds, or such as are fattening for the butcher. **1893** W. Fream *Youatt's Compl. Grazier* (ed. 13) 171 The litter used in hammels is..less by one-third than that required for stall-feeding.

hammer, *sb.* Add: **6.** *hammer and sickle*: an emblem consisting of a crossed hammer and sickle, used as a symbol of the industrial worker and the peasant, e.g. on the national flag of the U.S.S.R.; hence used allusively of Soviet-type Communism.

1921 *Times* 20 Sept. 4/6 The subjects of the..designs [of Bolshevist postage stamps] are symbolical of Labour.. the 20 roubles a shield charged with the device of a hammer and sickle crossed. **1933** H. G. Wells *Shape of Things to Come* III. § 11. 330 There was still no discord with Russia; there the blazon of the wings was put up side by side with the old hammer and sickle. **1935** E. Weekley *Something about Words* 27 A new ideal in literature and poetry, a kind of 'hammer and sickle' conception of artistic composition. **1937** H. G. Wells *Brynhild* v. 65 It might be possible to indicate whether the flavouring [of a book] were sexual, intellectual, left, right, or detective, by some variation in the general design, an obelisk, for example, the hammer and sickle, the swastika or what-not. **1958** *Listener* 5 June 928/2 An Algiers broadcast said the choice was 'between the Hammer and Sickle and the Cross of Lorraine'.

7. *hammer-boy, -shed*; **hammer-action,** (*a*) action of or as of a hammer; (*b*) those parts of a piano which compose and control the hammers; **hammer-axe** (later example); **hammer-block,** the steel face of a steam-hammer; **hammer-dress** *v.* (later examples); **hammer drill,** a percussion drill; **hammer-lock** *Wrestling*, a position in which a wrestler is held with one arm bent behind his back; also *fig.*; so **hammer-lock** *v. trans.*; **hammer-price** *Stock Exchange*, the price realized for shares (of a defaulter) closed at the hammer; **hammer-rifle,** a rifle fired by means of a hammer; **hammer-thrower** (see sense 1, note).

1885 *Encycl. Brit.* XIX. 71/2 An altered German harpsichord, the hammer action of which..may have been taken from Schroeter's diagram. *Ibid.* 72/1 In Frederici's upright grand action..the movement is practically identical with the hammer action of a German clock. **1906** *Westm. Gaz.* 22 Mar. 7/2 The explosion, which was probably caused by the hammer action of the water. **1927** Peake & Fleure *Priests & Kings* 165 Perforated hammer-axes..are said to have been found [at Tripolye]. **1861** W. Fairbairn *Iron* 121 The hammer-block is guided in its vertical descent by two planed guides or projections. **1881** *Instr. Census Clerks* (1885) 42 Forge and Hammer Boy. **1909** *Westm. Gaz.* 19 Aug. 9/4 There has been a considerable shortage of hammer boys in most of the mining districts. **1939** J. D. S. Pendlebury *Archaeol. Crete* iii. 98 The stones are invariably hammer-dressed, the saw not yet being used for masonry. **1940** *Chambers's Techn. Dict.* 401/1 *Hammer-dressed*, a term applied to stone surfaces left with a rough finish produced by the hammer. **1908** R. Peele *Compressed Air Plant for Mines* xx. 249 Numerous small air hammer drills..have come into favor in the past few years... The hammer drill strikes a light blow. **1922** *Encycl. Brit.* XXXI. 958/1 Machine drills underwent important changes during 1910–20, especially in the development of the 'hammer' drills... In the hammer drill, the bit is held stationary..and is struck a rapid succession of blows by the reciprocating piston-like hammer. **1897** *Pearson's Mag.* III. 638 Hammer lock and Nelson on the ground. **1905** *Daily Chron.* 21 Feb. 7/4 The very thought of being 'hammer-locked' should be enough to deter the most confirmed 'disorderly'. **1906** E. Dyson *Fact'ry 'Ands* vi. 72 Jest you take a 'ammerlock holt iv yerself, 'n' 'ave some dam consideration fer others. **1907** G. B. Shaw *Let.* 23 Sept. (1956) 107 Short of giving Phyllis a leading part, and thus giving you the hammer lock on him, I dont know what to do. **1944** *Infantry Jrnl.* (U.S.) June 25 He got his Jap in a hammerlock. **1965** *Economist* 4 Dec. 1072/2 These are fuzzy far-off dreams, considering the right wing's hammerlock on the Republican party today. **1900** *Westm. Gaz.* 4 June 7/1 He can have the stock closed at the hammer price. **1901** *Ibid.* 13 May 9/1 The actual dealings in the shares being between £6 and £8 per share and the hammer price £2. **1907** *Yesterday's Shopping* (1969) 634 Hammer rifles. **1920** G. Burrard *Notes on Sporting Rifles* 15 Hammerless ejectors are better than non-ejectors and hammer rifles. **1890** W. J. Gordon *Foundry* 13 The blast-furnaces that stand near the hammer-shed. **1899** *Daily News* 18 July 7/2 The hammer-throwers were out in the morning. **1968** *Listener* 11 July 49/2 There have been a number of marriages..between hammer-throwers and female discus-throwers.

hammer, *v.* Add: **1. a.** (Later examples.)

1907 F. H. Burnett *Shuttle* xxxviii. 379 Jem Belter, who 'hammered' a typewriter. **1959** M. Shadbolt *New Zealanders* 26 The Potoki boys hammered the piano and banged the drums.

2. e. To inflict heavy defeat(s) on, in war, games, etc.; to strike forcefully; to beat up. *colloq.*

1948 Partridge *Dict. Forces' Slang 1939–45* 90 *Hammer*, to shell severely. To inflict a heavy defeat on. **1959** *Times* 28 May 4/6 Smith hammered Slade for two fours and a six. **1973** *Times* 5 Jan. 17/5 Challenging the well-entrenched leaders in the United Kingdom car rental industry seems to hold no fears for Crook. He is hoping to hammer them on both quality and price. **1973** *Courier & Advertiser* (Dundee) 14 Feb. 5/3 He was severely injured about the face and his dentures were broken. He had no doubt that he had been 'hammered'.

3. b. Of a pipe: to make a knocking noise, as when a flow of liquid is suddenly stopped by turning a tap. (Cf. Water-hammer 2.)

1889 P. Hasluck *Model Engin. Handybk.* 108 The pump, owing to its not being filled properly at each stroke, will hammer very much.

hammerer. 1. Add: As a specific occupation.

1909 *Westm. Gaz.* 8 Feb. 3/1 The man was a 'hammerer'—i.e., a driver of rivets into boilers, &c. **1921** *Dict. Occup. Terms* (1927) § 278 *Hammerer*,..flattens saw blades,..by..striking any curved part with hammer.

hammer-head. 2. Delete † and add later example.

1947 R. Taylor *Bar Nothing Ranch* (1949) xvi. 151 The meanest old hammerheads under her tutelage became as cooing doves.

5. *hammer-head crane* = **hammer-headed crane*.

1910 *Encycl. Brit.* VII. 371/1 The Titan is portable and the hammer-head crane fixed. **1938** *Jane's Fighting Ships* 37 Fitting out berth equipped with giant 25 ton Hammer-head Crane.

hammer-headed, *a.* Add: **1. b.** *hammer-headed crane* (see quot. 1910).

1908 A. Tolhausen tr. *Böttcher's Cranes* IX. 492 (*title*) Hammer-headed crane of 150 tons, constructed by the Duisburger Maschinenbau-A.-G. **1910** *Encycl. Brit.* VII. 370/2 The so-called 'hammer-headed' crane consists of a steel braced tower, on which revolves a large horizontal double cantilever; the forward part of this cantilever or jib carries the lifting crab, and the jib is extended backwards in order to form a support for the machinery and counter-balance.

hammerkop: see *Hamerkop.

hammerman. c. (Later example.)

1880 *Harper's Mag.* Dec. 59 The hammer-man, in a swinging seat, times the turning of his rod of steel to the quick stroke of the hammer.

hammily: see *Hammy *a.*

hammock[1]. Add: **4. hammock chair,** a folding reclining-chair with canvas support for the body, suitable for use in a sitting-room or garden; a deck-chair; **hammock-moth** (see quot.).

1881 *Graphic* 18 June in L. de Vries *Vict. Advts.* (1968) 127/1 The Yankee hammock chair..costs but 17s. 6d. complete. **1885** *Army & Navy Co-op. Soc. Price List* II. 1478 Portable Hammock Chairs. **1971** *Country Life* 1 Apr. (Suppl.) 44/2 (Advt.), Early 19th century hammock chair in mahogany upholstered in deep-buttoned Havana brown leather. **1899** *Cambr. Nat. Hist.* VI. 379 The Hammock-moth, *Perophora sanguinolenta*, of the centre of South America, the larva of which constructs its portable habitations out of its own excrement.

Hammond organ (hæ·mənd ǭ·ɹgăn). *Mus.* [See quot. 1960.] The proprietary name of an

electric organ produced by the Hammond Organ Company, in which sounds are produced by generating and combining electric currents of suitable frequencies; applied also to similar instruments; also *ellipt.* as *Hammond*.

1935 *Electronics* VIII. 156 (*caption*) The Hammond electric organ. **1936** *Proc. Inst. Radio Engin.* XXIV. 1446 The amount of agreement and departure from this tempered scale of frequencies found in the Hammond organ have been listed in his [*sc.* Hammond's U.S.] patent No. 1,956,350. **1957** *Gramophone* Apr. 426/3, I confess that the Hammond organ is an instrument which I find hard to accept in the field of popular music. **1960** GAMMOND & CLAYTON *Guide Pop. Mus.* 100 *Hammond organ*, an electrical instrument invented by Laurens Hammond in 1929. The Hammond Instrument Company of Chicago was formed in this year and began marketing the instrument in 1935... In 1938 the Aeolian-Hammond Player-Organ was produced, an entirely mechanical instrument. **1970** *Melody Maker* 3 Oct. 15/1 Having squeezed every possible sound from his Hammonds, the Moog was the natural progression.

hammy, *a.* Add: Also, resembling ham.

1877 E. S. DALLAS *Kettner's Bk. of Table* 413 It was a grand hit this—the introduction of the hammy taste.

2. Of, pertaining to, or characteristic of a ham actor or ham acting. *slang.*

1929 T. WOLFE *Look Homeward, Angel* (1930) xxvii. 367 With fat hammy sonority he welcomed them. **1933** STANLEY & MAXFIELD *Voice* II. iii. 80 In particular, the prolongation of the vowel sounds associated with the consonants m, n and l is cheap and 'hammy'. **1946** *Penguin New Writing* XXVIII. 182 Toni..put on a hammy deep-in-thought act. **1965** G. MCINNES *Road to Gundagai* vi. 106 His part..was..hammy enough, but Carson managed to ham it up a good deal further. **1973** 'D. JORDAN' *Nile Green* xxxv. 171 Condon raised an eyebrow in a hammy attempt to be supercilious.

Hence (sense 2) **ha·mmily** *adv.*

1942 *Time* 27 Apr. 61 The talented author..has told one of the most hackneyed of all sentimental yarns, and told it hammily. **1958** *Spectator* 7 Feb. 175/2 Rather hammily acted but extremely well sung. **1961** *John o' London's* 14 Sept. 307/1 The plot is hackneyed to the point of imbecility, the slapstick hammily archaic.

Hampshire (hæ·mpʃəɪ). **a.** The name of a county in the south of England, used (chiefly *attrib.*) to designate a breed of sheep; also *Hampshire Down*; also designating a breed of pig.

a **1661** T. FULLER *Worthies* (1662) Hants. 2 Hantshire Hoggs, are allowed by all for the best Bacon. **1813** C. VANCOUVER *Gen. View Agric. Hampshire* 371 The.. common Hampshire ewe will cost from 25*s.* to 40*s.* each. **1825** LOUDON *Encycl. Agric.* 1123/2 The heath sheep, old Hampshire, or Wilts breeds. **1875** *Encycl. Brit.* I. 392/2 These sheep are now usually classed as Sussex Downs and Hampshire Downs, the former being the most refined type of the class.., and the latter..having a heavier fleece, stronger bone, and somewhat coarser and larger frame. *Ibid.* 400/2 The Berkshire and Hampshire hog seems originally to have been from the same stock, but by some early cross acquired the thicker carcase, prick-ears, shorter limbs, and earlier maturity of growth, by which they are characterised. **1886** C. SCOTT *Sheep-farming* 12 The Hampshire Down, though a larger sheep than the Southdown, does not mature so early. **1957** *Encycl. Brit.* XVII. 920/1 The Hampshire breed [of pig] originated in England and was later introduced into the United States... Hampshires possess good growing and fattening qualities. **1962** J. N. WINBURNE *Dict. Agric.* 361/1 *Hampshire swine*, an American, lard-type breed of black, white-belted swine. **1971** *Farmers Weekly* 19 Mar. 77/4 It was a risky step to take from the viewpoint of..Hampshire Down enthusiasts.

b. *Hampshire hog*: a colloq. or derogatory term for a native of Hampshire; also, a dish of boiled bacon and vegetables.

[**1622** DRAYTON *Polyolbion* II. xxiii. 70 As Hamshire long for her, hath had the tearme of Hogs.] *c* **1720** *Vade Mecum for Malt-Worms* I. 50 Now to the Sign of Fish let's jog, There to find out a Hampshire Hog. **1861** C. M. YONGE *Stokesley Secret* i. 9 'You could not be more right if you were a Hampshire hog,' said Sam. **1937** J. RAYNER *Shell Guide to Hampshire* 26/1 Hampshire Hog. You boil 4 to 5 lb. of bacon..in an iron saucepan, keep the extracted bacon hot on the hob, and put..cabbages..into the water. ..You can put potatoes in as well. *Ibid.* 30 There are three sorts of Hampshire hog, and they have given the county the subsidiary name of *Hoglandia*. One, the inhabitant of the county. Two, the less domestic animal from whose frequency the inhabitant gets his name...And three, the dish. **1944** in A. Wykes *Royal Hampshire Regiment* (1968) v. 104, I reckon us little lot of Hampshire Hogs have done well for his nibs Adolf in this invasion. **1963** C. MACKENZIE *My Life & Times* II. 169 She was a Dorset woman, and both she and her husband had a profound contempt for what they called the Hampshire hogs with whom they were condemned to live.

c. *pl.* The Royal Hampshire Regiment.

1904 *Westm. Gaz.* 14 June 8/2 The Hampshires, who mustered ten officers and 484 men. **1968** A. WYKES *Royal Hampshire Regiment* v. 107 The Hampshires, with..the Dorsets and Devons, were the three battalions of infantry forming one of the spearheads that was to land on the Arromanches beach.

Hampstead Heath (hæ·mpsted hīþ). The name of a district in north London, (*a*) used in *Rhyming Slang* to designate the teeth; also *Hampsteads*; (*b*) *Hampstead Heath sailor* (see quot. 1889).

1887 *Referee* 6 Nov. 7/3 She'd a Grecian 'I suppose', And of 'Hampstead Heath' two rows In her 'sunny south' that glistened Like two pretty strings of pearls. **1889** BARRÈRE & LELAND *Dict. Slang* I. 444/2 *Hampstead Heath sailor*.., a term of ridicule—no sailor at all. **1932** *Daily Express* 25 Jan. 6/6 (*heading*) 'Hampsteads' and 'Yobs'. A common expression for the feet is 'plates o' meat' and for the teeth 'Hampstead Heath'... These become simply 'plates' for feet and 'Hampsteads' for teeth. **1962** R. COOK *Crust on its Uppers* (1964) ii. 23 The rot had set in something horrible with her hampsteads and scotches.

hamseen, var. KHAMSIN.

1923 F. S. MARVIN *Sci. & Civiliz.* 29 Physical contrasts of seasonal and regional fertility are abrupt; solar heat contends with Nile water, sea breeze with scorching 'hamseen'.

Han[1] (hæn). Designating a Chinese dynasty (206 B.C.–220 A.D.) marked by the introduction of Buddhism, the extension of Chinese rule over Mongolia, the revival of letters, and increase of wealth and culture.

1736 R. BROOKES tr. *Du Halde's Gen. Hist. China* I. 346 (*heading*) The Fifth Dynasty, called *Han*, which had twenty-five Emperors in the Space of 426 Years. **1837** *Penny Cycl.* VII. 81/1 About the year 201 B.C., the race of Tsin was succeeded by that of Hân, which filled one of the most celebrated periods of Chinese history. **1876** *Encycl. Brit.* V. 644/1 Lew Pang was then proclaimed emperor (206 B.C.) under the title of Kaou-te, and the new line was styled the Han dynasty. **1930** *Times Lit. Suppl.* 2 Oct. 774/3 The majority seem to reflect the Han style... Two famous homonymous generals who flourished under the Han dynasty. **1935** A. TOYNBEE *Study of Hist.* (ed. 2) II. 373 The Han Empire and the Kushan Empire marched with one another in Central Asia for at least a century. **1971** *Ashmolean Mus. Rep. of Visitors 1970* 51 Imperial seals of the 17th and 18th centuries as well as some early Han types.

han[2]: see KHAN[2].

1903 *Westm. Gaz.* 10 Feb. 3/1 The *hans* are large, rambling inns, with a courtyard in the middle. **1920** *Q. Rev.* Apr. 395 Four hundred emaciated forms, the remnant of such convoys, are lying in one of the hans.

‖ **hanami** (hanami). [Jap.] (See quots.).

1891 A. M. BACON *Jap. Girls & Women* x. 295 The *hanami*, or picnic to famous places to view certain flowers as they bloom in their season. **1902** L. HEARN *Kottō* x. 97 All of us..should make up a party, and enjoy our *hanami* together. **1965** W. SWAAN *Jap. Lantern* iv. 47 This collection is suitable for such festive occasions as *hanami* (flower- and more particularly cherry-blossom-viewing).

hanapoot, var. *HANEPOOT.

‖ **hanashika** (hanaʃika). [Jap.] A professional story-teller.

1891 A. M. BACON *Jap. Girls & Women* x. 294 Public halls, where professional story-tellers, the *hanashika*, night after night, relate long stories to crowded audiences. **1936** K. NOHARA *True Face of Japan* v. 120 A *hanashika*, or story teller, is telling innocent stories.

hancockite (hæ·nkǫkəit). *Min.* [f. the name of E. P. *Hancock* (*c* 1834–1916), American artist and amateur mineralogist, who discovered it: see -ITE[1].] A variety of epidote rich in strontium and lead.

1899 PENFIELD & WARREN in *Amer. Jrnl. Sci.* CLVIII. 339 (*heading*) Hancockite. *Ibid.* 343 A considerable quantity of hancockite was taken from the mine at one time, and it is the most abundant of the new species described in this paper. It is named after Mr. E. P. Hancock of Burlington, N.J. **1900** *Jrnl. Chem. Soc.* LXXVIII. II. 88 Hancockite. This occurs as brownish-red, cellular masses of minute, lath-shaped crystals, which are monoclinic. **1968** I. KOSTOV *Mineral.* 309 Hancockite contains Pb and Sr.

hand, *sb.* Add: **1. f.** *pl.* In Association Football, the illegal handling of the ball.

1894 BRANSCOMBE & 'ROSS' *Morocco Bound* II. 28 The statute demands A free kick for hands! **1897** [see *HANDLING *vbl. sb.* 1 c]. **1967** *Assoc. Football* (Know the Game Series) 28 (*caption*) Area covered by 'Hands'.

5. Also as a symbol of acceptance of an invitation to dance.

1813 JANE AUSTEN *Pride & Prej.* I. xviii. 208 When the dancing recommenced..and Darcy approached to claim her hand. *a* **1817** —— *Northanger Abbey* (1818) II. i. 15 After aspiring to my hand, there was nobody else in the room he could bear to think of.

7. b. (Later example.)

1965 *Listener* 3 June 835/3 A major document of the post-Symbolist movement in Spain, with English versions by eleven hands, the 'hands' including W. S. Merwin,.. and James Wright.

14. b. A member of a cricket eleven.

1731 in H. T. Waghorn *Cricket Scores* (1899) 4 The Duke's hands came in first. **1874** *Baily's Monthly Mag.* Dec. 155 Seven of the eleven..were new hands.

† **c.** A score in cricket. *Obs.*

1833 J. NYREN *Young Cricketer's Tutor* 104 He would often get long hands. **1836** *New Sporting Mag.* Oct. 361 [Which number] added to the byes they stole, and the wide balls bowled, sufficed to make a hands of eighty-six runs. **1875** *Baily's Monthly Mag.* Sept. 273 Let me see him make a good hand against good bowling.

15. (Later examples.) Esp. in present-day use in phr. *to give* (or *get*, etc.) *a big* (or *good*) *hand*: to give, etc., a large round of applause. orig. *U.S.*

1838 DICKENS *Nickleby* xxix. 284 He has gone on night after night, never getting a hand and you getting a couple of rounds at least. **1849** *Theatrical Programme* 18 June 30 Buskin's part goes without a hand—Lamp carries off all the honours. **1883** G. B. SHAW *How to become Mus. Critic* (1960) 48 The dance-tunes, played by an indifferent band, went almost without a hand. **1886** *Lantern* (New Orleans) 6 Oct. 4/3 Their act always pulls a big hand. **1896** *Punch* 10 Oct. 180/2 Aeschylus..wrote tragedies in blank verse, but they are not now played at any London theatre. He would not get a 'hand' nowadays. **1922** C. SANDBURG *Slabs of Sunburnt West* 39 It's a good act—we got a good hand. **1924** H. A. VACHELL *Quinney's Adv.* 179 The second curtain fell without 'a hand'. **1927** PRINCE OF WALES in *Even. News* 7 Oct. 6/5 They both do a great deal of hard work for the British Legion. It may be I am more the fellow who travels about and gets the hands. **1932** A. J. WORRALL *Eng. Idioms* 40 He always gets a good hand when he appears in a London theatre. **1948** *Prairie Club Bull.* June 14 Three lusty cheers and a big hand for Charles, Our Star Square Dance Host! **1959** *Listener* 28 May 958/3 A deed which earned what our Quiz compères insist on calling 'a big hand'.

18. c. A device shaped like a hand.

1830 M. EDGEWORTH *Let.* 6 Dec. (1971) 439 Mr. Turner ..had shewn me the bank of England and the famous machine-*hand* which weighs the guineas without assistance from mortal touch. **1873** *Young Englishwoman* Jan. 52/1 Will any one.. tell her how to clean white..gloves. She possesses wooden hands for stretching them on. **1926–7** *Army & Navy Stores Catal.* 1008/2 Dairy utensils... Scotch hands [for shaping butter].

21. d. (Earlier example.)

1756 P. BROWNE *Civil & Nat. Hist. Jamaica* II. ii. 119, I have sometimes seen a hand of ginger weigh near half a pound... The larger spreading roots are called Hands in Jamaica.

23. Also, the cards held at any stage of such a game as Poker.

1889 R. GUERNDALE *Poker Bk.* 25 To fill your hand, to improve it by the draw. **1913** 'A. B. LOUGHER' *Poker* 13 The next process is that of drawing to fill the hands.

d. *to declare one's hand* (fig.): to reveal one's circumstances or aims. (Cf. DECLARE *v.* 11.)

1922 D. H. LAWRENCE *England, my England* 271 Upstairs Fanny evaded all the thrusts made by his mother, and did not declare her hand.

29. in hand. k. *Billiards.* Of the cue-ball: having been retrieved by hand, after being pocketed, and having been placed on any selected spot within the D preliminary to the next stroke.

1860 'R. CRAWLEY' *Handy Bk. Games* xiii. 106 Your ball being in hand, you must play for the hazard that shall bring the object-ball back to the opposite cushion. **1904** S. A. MUSSABINI *Mannock's Billiards* v. 228 The cue-ball is 'in hand' with the red ball, presenting a straightaway winning hazard into the right middle pocket.

l. *N.Z.* (See quots.)

1930 L. G. D. ACLAND *Early Canterbury Runs* i. 5 Until wire fences were introduced about 1862, all sheep on the plains were kept more or less in hand. The practice was for a shepherd to go round the boundary once or twice a day. **1933** —— in *Press* (Christchurch) 28 Oct. 15/7 Sheep are in hand when you have them in a mob near you.

33. c. *to eat* (or *feed*) *out of one's hand* (see *EAT *v.* 3 d).

1958 HAYWARD & HARARI tr. *Pasternak's Dr. Zhivago* I. vii. 212 'Well, have they had their tails twisted yet? Are they keeping quiet now?' 'The shopkeepers, you mean?.. Feed out of your hand!'

44. c. *to give a hand*: to help a person. Also, *to lend a hand* (see LEND *v.*[2] 2 e).

1860 in A. F. Ridgway *Voices from Auckland* 71 His young wife..will readily give him a hand at the crosscut for a few hours. **1880** *Daily Tel.* 26 Nov., A policeman gave him a hand up. **1949** J. ROUTH in *Granta* Christmas ed., 'Here, let me give you fellows a hand,' I suggested.

45*. put (one's) hand. a. *to put one's hand*: to exert oneself, use one's energies; now always with *to*: to set about, undertake (a piece of work).

1388 WYCLIF *Luke* ix. 62 No man that puttith his hoond to the plouȝ, and biholdynge bacward, is able to the rewme of God. **1439** in *Fenland N. & Q.* (1905) July 222 And yat..ye wole at yis tyme..putte youre handes and ese us by wey of lone of ye somme of C marc. *c* **1450** *St. Cuthbert* (Surtees) 6056 Þat to þi seruyce puttys þair hands. **1535** COVERDALE *Deut.* xii. 18 All yͭ thou puttest thine hande vnto. **1631** J. PRESTON *Treat. Effect. Faith* 45 If God himselfe put not his hand to the worke no man is able to believe. **1633** J. HALL *Hard Texts* Zech. xi. 9, I will not put my hand to redresse it. **1879** M. J. GUEST *Lect. Hist. Eng.* ix. 80 Whatever he put his hand to, he did it 'with all his might'.

b. *to put* (one's) *hand(s) on*, († *in*, † *unto*): to lay hands on (see LAY *v.*[1] 21 c); † to do violence to (*Sc. Obs.*); to get hold of, seize (also *fig.*).

1535 COVERDALE *Exod.* xxii. 8 ([He] shal sweare) that he hath not put his hande vnto his neghbours good. **1837** C. M. GOODRIDGE *Voy. S. Seas* (1843) 44 [We] got into her with such articles as we could immediately put our hands on. **1842** J. H. NEWMAN *Par. Serm.* VI. viii. 111 Perhaps..we can put our hand, as it were, on a time in our childhood [when, etc.]. **1972** L. HENDERSON *Cage until Tame* vii. 57 Right now he couldn't put his hands on a hundred quid.

53. hands off! Also *attrib.*

1902 *Daily Chron.* 23 Jan. 7/1 A protest must be made against the hands-off policy. **1908** *Times Lit. Suppl.*

3 Sept. 283/3 The hopelessly *doctrinaire* character of the old 'hands-off' individualism.

b. *Aeronaut.* Used as *adj.* and *adv.* in connection with an automatically controlled aircraft.

1932 *Flight* 20 May 443/1 By means of the adjustable tail plane the machine can be trimmed to fly 'hands off'. **1935** *Jrnl. R. Aeronaut. Soc.* XXXIX. 1041 Control of this airplane when operating on one engine was carefully studied with the result that it can be flown 'hands off'. **1959** *Times* 18 Sept. 7/3 Some 4,000 'hands off' landings have been made. **1966** *Electronics* 3 Oct. 134 On the last orbit, it guided Gemini 11 into a hands-off reentry and landing virtually down the stacks of the recovery ships. **1968** *New Scientist* 1 Feb. 251/1 Several companies have developed artificial stabilization systems which enable the helicopter to be flown 'hands-off'.

54. hands up! Also in *Curling* (see quot. 1897).

1873 J. Miller *Life amongst Modocs* 193 Hands up, gentlemen! **1897** *Encycl. Sport* I. 264/1 *Hands up*, the command of the Skip..to stop sweeping. **1910** *Encycl. Brit.* VII. 646/1 Curling has a language which contains many curious terms... *Hands up!* stop sweeping.

55. hand..fist. a. (Later examples.) Also, esp., *fig.* of the making of money.

1825 W. N. Glascock *Naval Sketch-Bk.* (1826) I. 26 The French..weathered our wake, coming up with us, 'hand over fist', in three divisions. **1833** S. Smith *Life Major J. Downing* (1834) 116 They..clawed the money off of his table, hand over fist. **1861** M. B. Chesnut *Diary* 8 Aug. (1949) 107 Fitzhugh Lee and Roony are being promoted hand over fist. **1888** 'R. Boldrewood' *Robbery under Arms* xxvii, We..made money hand over fist. **1901** *Daily Chron.* 27 Dec. 3/3 To use a phrase common to the Anglo-Saxon, they have been making money hand-over-fist. **1929** J. B. Priestley *Good Companions* II. vii. 445 She lost money hand-over-fist for weeks and weeks—and not a murmur—and now she is beginning to get a little back again. **1963** *Times* 12 June 13/4 It pays hand over fist always to take the secondary roads that run along the 'wrong' sides of rivers in preference to the main roads that run along their 'right' sides.

56. hand and foot (further example).

1955 L. P. Hartley *Perfect Woman* x. 96 He has everything he wants and servants who wait on him hand and foot.

59*. hands-across-the-sea, used *attrib.* of an act, etc., performed by one country as a gesture of friendship to an overseas country.

1899 *Westm. Gaz.* 1 Feb. 1/4 Mr. Tree has a new drama in his mind—an old-time hands-across-the-sea subject. **1955** *Sci. News Let.* 5 Feb. 88/3 The Missouri Commission is interested in the experiments, not only as a 'hands-across-the-sea gesture'..but because the Missouri bunny might also be susceptible to the dread disease, and advance knowledge would permit more effective preventive action. **1957** *Times Lit. Suppl.* 25 Oct. 635/2 What is this but empty rhetoric of the 'hands-across-the-sea' brand? **1971** C. Fick *Danziger Transcript* (1973) 88 It was supposed to be a hands-across-the-sea sort of thing.

60. h. *hands down*: with ease, with little or no effort; unconditionally, submissively; orig. in the racing phr. *to win hands down*, referring to the jockey dropping his hands, and so relaxing his hold on the reins, when victory appears certain.

1867 'Pips' *Lyrics & Lays* 155 There were good horses in those days, as he can well recall, But Barker upon Elepoo, hands down, shot by them all. **1882** *Moonshine* 3 June 265 (*caption*) Won!! 'Hands Down'. **1913** Mrs. H. Ward *Mating of Lydia* II. xii, That I should surrender, hands down, to a lot of trumpery complaints and grievances. **1920** W. B. Money *Humours of Parish* 126, I started off in the race in full nigger costume, and won hands down. **1958** *Times* 14 Aug. 9/7 Double this speed, however, and the submarine wins hands down.

61. a. *hand-gesture, -kiss, -movement, -rest.*

1930 R. Paget *Babel* ii. 56 The large number of ideas which cannot be symbolized directly by hand-gesture. **1962** *Listener* 1 Mar. 382/2 The energy and urgency of hand gesture, visible in his recent drawings, has extended itself on the larger scale of these paintings. **1861** C. Reade *Cloister & Hearth* ii. 32 A sweet little coaxing hand-kiss. **1958** F. Harris *My Life & Loves* V. i. 28 She sent me back with an imperious hand-kiss. **1924** R. M. Ogden tr. *Koffka's Growth of Mind* v. 254 During the hand-movements, the gaze is directed fixedly upon the object. **1904** Goodchild & Tweney *Technol. & Sci. Dict.* 279/1 *Hand rest*, the T-shaped support for supporting hand-turning tools in working at a lathe when a slide rest is not used. **1922** Joyce *Ulysses* 225 Two carfuls of tourists passed slowly, their women sitting fore, gripping frankly the handrests.

c. *hand-baggage, -camera* (earlier and later examples); so *hand-camerist*; *hand-lamp* (earlier and later examples), *-luggage, -microphone, -mike, -props.*

1902 *Daily Chron.* 27 Feb. 3/3 The Boer delegates have only brought with them hand-baggage. **1889** *Photogr. News* 15 Nov. 755/1 For the hand camera there is, I believe, a great and wide field of usefulness. **1910** *Chambers's Jrnl.* Sept. 588/1 Hand-cameras are made in a thousand patterns. **1892** *Photogr. Ann.* II. 52 It is this ungentlemanly abuse of the hand camera which brings the whole class of hand camerists into disrepute. **1897** C. M. Hepworth *Animated Photogr.* xiii. 96 Subjects which are suitably lighted and otherwise 'possible' for the hand camerist may be safely attempted with a cinematographic camera. **1831** Carlyle *Sart. Res.* I. x, Thou..wilt walk through thy world by the sunshine of what thou callest Truth, or even by the hand-lamp of what I call Attorney-Logic. **1836** *Mechanics' Mag.* XXV. 317 The fact is that no *unguarded* light should ever be permitted in any stable, warehouse, cellar, or bed chamber; cheap, convenient, and even elegant hand lamps and lanterns suited to these uses, are met with in abundance. **1940** *Chambers's Techn. Dict.* 401/2 *Hand-lamp*, a portable electric-light fitting suitable for carrying in the hand. Also called *inspection-lamp, portable-lamp.* **1965** 'Lauchmonen' *Old Thorn's Harvest* x. 134 They all sit down near to their handlamps. **1888** Ld. Macnaghten in *Law Rep. Ho. Lords* xiii. 55 Passengers take the lighter articles of luggage—or 'hand-luggage' as it is called,—in the carriage with them. **1908** *Daily Chron.* 8 Jan. 4/4 Glancing furtively at that terrible piece of hand-luggage, a New York Sunday newspaper. **1924** W. J. Locke *Coming of Amos* iv, Maxime possessed himself of her hand-luggage. **1970** *New Yorker* 16 May 41/3 'Any hand luggage?' says the clerk, peering over the top of the counter. **1968** *Radio Times* 20 June 58/1 For long I have been puzzled about the use of hand microphones. **1968** *Punch* 3 Jan. 29/1 He does know precisely what he's about when he clutches a handmike and sings. **1933** P. Godfrey *Back-Stage* iii. 34 'Props' is an abbreviation of 'stage properties', and therefore 'hand-props' are things handled by the actors, such as fans, snuff-boxes, etc.

d. *hand-brake* (later examples), *-brush, -carriage, -drum, -feed, -machine, -punch* (example; hence as vb.), *puppet, sewing-machine, -sled, -sledge* (earlier example), *-sleigh, -wheel* (examples).

1913 *Autocar Handbk.* (ed. 5) xiv. 216 In some Coventry Daimler cars the hand brake can be caused either to withdraw the clutch or not when it is applied. **1959** *Times* 15 Dec. 13/5 Consternation clutches at the heart while the driver clutches the handbrake. **1968** *Sun* 12 Nov. 8/5 *Handbrake turn*, the technique involving using the handbrake instead of reverse gear, for negotiating 'impossible' hairpins. **1747** H. Glasse *Art of Cookery* xvii. 150 Let them be scrubed clean with a Hand-Brush and Sand, and Fuller's Earth. **1904** J. Vaizey *More about Pixie* (1910) i. 7 She went down on her knees, and swept up the dust with a small hand-brush. **1745** Ellis *Mod. Husb.* VI. II. 14 This Farmer..carried his Wheat-sheaves into his Barn on a Sunday, by Hand-carriage. **1859** Dickens in *All Year Round* (1860) 11 Aug. 422/2 A hand-carriage, drawn by a man... I saw within it an old man. **1864** J. A. Grant *Walk across Africa* viii. 144 A band of hand-drums is near the sultan's hut, giving lighter dance-music for the amusement of the boys and girls. **1958** E. Borneman in P. Gammond *Decca Bk. Jazz* xxi. 275 A male leader and a small group.. who accompanied themselves on..hand drums,..and gong-gong. **1940** *Chambers's Techn. Dict.* 401/1 *Hand feed*, the hand operation of the feed mechanism of a machine tool, as distinct from an automatic feed. **1962** *Gloss. Autom. Data Proc.* (*B.S.I.*) 91 *Hand-feed punch*, a key punch into which punched cards have to be fed manually one at a time. **1873** *Young Englishwoman* Mar. 131/1 A most useful..hand-machine..at the low price of 39 s. **1927** T. Woodhouse *Artificial Silk* 81 Practically coincident with the hand knitting of jumpers and the like came the hand-machine knitting. **1962** *Gloss. Autom. Data Proc.* (*B.S.I.*) 91 *Hand punch*, a key punch into which punched cards have to be fed manually one at a time. *Ibid.* 96 *Hand punch*, a tape punch operated directly by hand. **1967** A. Battersby *Network Analysis* (ed. 2) xv. 264 Their decisions are hand-punched on to special cards. **1950** *Dryad Handicraft Catal.* 74 Hand puppets and string puppets. **1957** *Encycl. Brit.* XIV. 906/1 Hand puppets can be of wood, plaster,..or stuffed cloth. *a* **1877** Knight *Dict. Mech.* II. 1058/1 *Hand sewing-machine*, a form of sewing-machine in which the parts are pivoted jaws, operated in the manner of scissors. **1746** *Coll. New H. Hist. Soc.* IX. 141 [I] went to mill with a hand sled. **1780** in *Coll. Mass. Hist. Soc.* (1905) 7th Ser. V. 6 [They] hall their wood on hand sleds. **1843** *Knickerbocker* XXII. 294 The serjeant's hand-sled, piled with wood. **1871** *Rep. Vermont Board Agric.* IV. 92 Provided with a handsled, the boy would first roll on to it the back log. **1848** R. M. Ballantyne *Hudson's Bay* (1890) 83 The hand-sledge is a thin flat slip or plank of wood... Indians invariably use it when visiting their traps, for the purpose of dragging home the animals or game they may have caught. **1829** G. Head *Forest Scenes* 203 [The trees] had been..removed by means of small hand sleighs purposely prepared for them. **1836** C. P. Traill *Backwoods of Canada* 110 We were overtaken on our return by S— with a handsleigh, which is a sort of wheelbarrow, [etc.]. **1841** G. Powers *Hist. Sk. Coos* 70 A rude hand sleigh. **1936** D. McCowan *Anim. Canad. Rockies* xii. 103 An experienced trapper..delivered it on a hand sleigh. **1931** *Engineering* 9 Jan. 62/3 The roll adjusting gear is operated by a single handwheel, through an arrangement of steel bevel and spur gears. **1940** *Chambers's Techn. Dict.* 402/1 *Hand wheel*, a grooved pulley provided with a cranked handle and mounted on a universal form of vice, used for driving a lathe or other tool by hand. **1948** *Brit. Jrnl. Psychol.* Mar. 149 The pointer..moved steadily away from the line, and required a compensatory movement of the handwheel at a rate of 1 r.p.m. to keep it on the line.

62. a. *hand-holding* (hence as a back-formation *hand-hold* vb.), *-washing* (later example).

1963 *Movie* Apr. 12/1 Newsreel photographers were often forced to hand-hold their cameras. **1908** *Daily Chron.* 13 Mar. 4/6 Hand-holding ensures a rapid means of communication between the hand and the heart or brain. **1960** C. Day Lewis *Buried Day* v. 94 Hand-holdings and childish kisses. **1964** M. Hynes *Med. Bacteriol.* (ed. 8) ii. 22 Nevertheless the main sterilizing action of hand-washing is the mechanical removal of epithelial scales and surface bacteria.

b. *hand-done, -drawn* ppl. adjs.; *hand-feeding*; *hand-fired* ppl. adj. (so *hand-firing*); *hand-fisher*; *hand-flung, -held, -hewn* (ppl.) adjs.; *hand-knit* adj. (also as *sb.*), *-knitted* ppl. adj.; *hand-knitting*; *hand-milker, -milking*; *hand-operated, -set* ppl. adjs.; *hand-sew* vb. (so *hand-sewing, -sewn*); *hand-thrown, -tooled* ppl. adjs.; *hand-tufted* pa. pple. and ppl. adj.; *hand-washing* (see also 62 a); *hand-woven* (examples).

1907 N. Munro *Daft Days* xvii. 151 Another hand-done bill upon the counter. **1908** *Westm. Gaz.* 28 Dec. 5/2 Insets of hand-done crochet form one of the newest designs. **1907** *Yesterday's Shopping* (1969) 737/1 Hand-drawn linen. **1937** *Evening News* 15 Mar. 3/6 (Advt.), Hand-drawn top collar. **1957** Manvell & Huntley *Technique Film Music* iii. 167 Attempts at creating hand-drawn sound-tracks have been in progress since the coming of the sound film. *Ibid.*, He built up a sound-track of hand-drawn musical effects, mixing them occasionally with normal orchestral instruments to give variety. **1960** *Farmer & Stockbreeder* 29 Mar. 65/1 To the busy shepherd, hand-feeding may not seem worth while. **1968** *Gloss. Terms Offset Lithogr. Printing* (*B.S.I.*) 24 *Hand feeding*, the manual placing of single sheets of paper or other material to the machine lays. **1963** *Times* 23 May 7/3 Existing hand-fired plant still in fair condition. **1908** *Chambers's Jrnl.* Aug. 624/1 Owing to the fact that unscreened British coal is extensively employed in Hamburg hand-firing is more generally adopted. **1961** *Listener* 12 Oct. 583/2 'Hand-firing', or the fact that the fuel has to be brought to the boiler, is the drawback of all solid-fuel boilers. **1855** 'P. Paxton' *Captain Priest* 147 In the deeper places of such streams must the handfisher seek his prey. **1913** Kipling *Songs from Books* 113 But Tubal fashioned the hand-flung spears. **1923** Glazebrook *Dict. Appl. Physics* IV. 393/2 The hand-held camera implies 'exposures' of brief duration. **1969** *Daily Tel.* (Colour Suppl.) 10 Jan. 18 (*caption*) The photograph was taken by astronaut Anders with hand-held Hasselblad. **1969** *Jane's Freight Containers 1968–69* 584/1 All four motors are controlled from a single hand-held push-button control unit. **1938** M. K. Rawlings *Yearling* xiv. 143 The thick hand-hewn slabs of the shingled roof. **1969** *Computers & Humanities* III. 240 The work of Hagelman and Barnes is born into competition with one of the last of the hand-hewn concordances. **1920** F. Scott Fitzgerald *This Side of Paradise* (1921) I. ii. 63 The hand-knit, sleeveless jerseys were stylish. **1958** Handknit [see *bawneen]. **1959** *Manch. Guardian* 29 July 5/1 Woollens fall into two classes, the cashmere jerseys, sweaters, and cardigans..and the Scottish handknits. **1967** *Harper's Bazaar* Sept. 49 The neck, High-polo-ed, hand-knit. **1881** *Sylvia's Home Jrnl.* in A. Adburgham *Shops & Shopping* (1964) xvii. 189 The largest stock in the kingdom of hand-knitted socks and stockings. **1952** M. Laski *Village* viii. 135 A skirt and a hand-knitted jumper. **1902** *Daily Chron.* 20 Dec. 5/2 Another ancient industry is at its last gasp—viz., the hand-knitting of Kilmarnock bonnets. **1961** J. G. Davis *Dict. Dairying* (ed. 2) 740 The War of 1914–18, because of the acute shortage of hand milkers, gave an unexpected impetus to the adoption of machine milking. **1915** J. London *Let.* 26 Jan. (1966) 446 Get Timms' experience with hand-milking labor conditions. **1960** *Farmer & Stockbreeder* 8 Mar. 55/2 In the past when hand-milking was the rule. **1936** *Discovery* Nov. 350/1 The Electrotor meter has a hand-operated pump movement. **1908** *Daily Chron.* 23 Oct. 9/4 All hand-set [type] becomes unnecessary. **1938** *Times Lit. Suppl.* 26 Mar. 204/3 Hand-set in most attractive type. **1895** *Montgomery Ward Catal.* 318/3 Hame Strap, hand sewed. **1919** Barrie *Alice Sit-by-the-Fire* I. 21 You hand-sew them and stretch them over a tin cylinder. **1946** *Nature* 14 Dec. 868/1 The speed of expert hand-sewing, thirty stitches per minute, is slow and laborious compared with that of machine work. **1961** T. Landau *Encycl. Librarianship* (ed. 2) 161/1 *Hand sewing*, usually sewing through the fold by hand on the sewing frame, to suspended cords or tapes arranged across the back of a book. **1887** *Col. & Indian Exhib., Rep. Col. Sect.* 401 A handsome pair of men's hand-sewn Wellingtons. **1911** *Rep. on Labour & Social Conditions in Germany* III. vi–vii. 101, I could have my boots soled and heeled with this quality of leather, and hand-sewn for 3s. 5d. **1959** *Times* 7 Mar. 9/2 A pigskin-covered whip, tightly stretched and handsewn, makes a pleasing and serviceable article. **1909** *Westm. Gaz.* 22 Oct. 4/2 The barbed spear used..is a hand-thrown weapon. **1933** *Archit. Rev.* LXXIV. 38/1 (*caption*) These are hand-thrown pieces on the wheel. **1895** 'Mark Twain' in *North Amer. Rev.* July 2 An illustrated, gilt-edged, tree-calf, hand-tooled, seven-dollar Friendship's Offering. **1931** *Times Lit. Suppl.* 25 June p. vii/2 The Swiss hand-tooled bindings are disappointing. **1906** *Daily Chron.* 5 June 4/5 Killybegs carpets, which are hand-tufted by the peasants. **1922** Joyce *Ulysses* 697 Handtufted Axminster Carpet. **1962** *BSI News* Feb. 17/1 Methods for the determination of colour fastness of textiles to a number of agencies, for example, soda boiling, handwashing, [etc.]. **1880** L. Higgin *Handbk. Embroidery* 62 Neutral-tinted hand-woven linen. **1925** A. Huxley *Let.* 2 Nov. (1969) 258 We bought..twelve yards of hand woven material.

63. hand-bag, (*a*) a light travelling-bag, (*b*) a lady's bag for accessories; **hand-balancer,** an acrobat; **hand-bible** *slang* = Holy stone *sb.*; **hand block** (see Block *sb.* 7), a block used in printing textiles by hand; also *attrib.*; hence **hand-blocked** *a.* (cf. *block-printed* adj.); **hand-blown** *ppl. a.*, of glass blown by a craftsman; **hand-board** *U.S.*, a board in front of a preacher or speaker; **hand-fives,** the usual game of fives as distinguished from bat-fives (see Fives[2] 1); **hand-hole** (examples); **hand-jam** *v.* (*Mountaineering*), to wedge a hand in a crack as a handhold; hence as *sb.*; also **hand-jamming** *vbl. sb.*; **hand-jive** (see quot. 1961); hence **hand-jiving** *vbl. sb.*; **hand-laid** *ppl. a.* (cf. *laid paper*); **hand-letter** *v.* (see quots.); hence *hand-lettered* ppl. adj., *hand-lettering* vbl. sb.; **hand-light** (earlier example); **hand-pick** *v. trans.*, to pick by hand; also *fig.*; so **hand-picked** *ppl. a.*; **hand-piece, handpiece,** (*a*)

the part of a dental drill that is held in the hand; (*b*) the part of a sheep-shearing machine that is held in the shearer's hand; **hand-plate,** (*a*) = *finger-plate*; (*b*) a small plate to pass over the surface of work to be tested; **hand-pollinate** *v. trans.*, to pollinate by hand; so *hand-pollination*; **hand-print,** the mark left by the impression of a hand; also (quot. 1886), a representation of a hand; **hand-reading,** palmistry; so *hand-reader*; **hand signal,** a manual indication by the driver of a motor vehicle, pedal cycle, etc., of his intention to stop, turn, etc.; **hand-stand,** an act in gymnastics in which the body is supported by the hands while the feet are in the air; also *attrib.*; **hand-towel,** a small towel for wiping the hands after washing; **hand traverse** *Mountaineering* (see quots. 1897, 1957).

1862 *Englishwoman's Domestic Mag.* July 143 Portable umbrellas..may easily be carried in the hand-bag. **1867** A. D. Whitney *L. Goldthwaite* ii. 32 Their hand-bags were hung up. **1880** Hand-bag [see Hand *sb.* 61 c]. **1896** G. B. Shaw *Let.* 9 Nov. (1965) 700, I want to buy a handbag for the journey. **1899** O. Wilde *Importance of being Earnest* i. 37 'Where did the charitable gentleman who had a first-class ticket for this seaside resort find you?..' 'In a handbag.'..'A handbag?' **1913** *Vanity Fair* Dec. 79/2 The latest novelty in hand bags. **1923** *Weekly Dispatch* 13 May 14 Crocodile Calf handbag. **1937** *Discovery* Dec. 374/2 Ladies' shoes and hand-bags. **1968** *New Society* 22 Aug. 266/1 Non-U handbag/U bag (the thing carried by women). **1927** *Daily Tel.* 30 Aug. 12/6 Masu, the Japanese hand-balancer and juggler. [*a* **1865** Smyth *Sailor's Word-Bk.* (1867) 98 *Bible*,..a squared piece of freestone to grind the deck with sand in cleaning it; a small holystone, so called from seamen using them kneeling.] **1908** O. Onions *Pedlar's Pack* 109 That was Ben, and i' the Dolphin, where all they knew o' Bibles was the hand-bibles they holystoned the decks wi'. **1839** Ure *Dict. Arts* I. 215 The hand blocks are made of sycamore or pear-tree wood, or of deal faced with these woods. **1936** *Archit. Rev.* LXXIX. 291/1 Any artist of decorative faculties can create patterns for printed cretonnes or linens,..provided he is sufficiently familiar with the advantages and drawbacks of roller-printing, screen-printing and handblock-printing. **1928** *Daily Express* 9 Jan. 5/2 The new..hand-blocked linens are a boon. **1931** *Ibid.* 21 Sept. 5/2 Pure silks, whose hand-blocked patterns have all been designed by famous..British artists. **1928** *Ibid.* 28 May 7/2 An exhibition of hand-blown and enamelled glass. **1958** *Archit. Rev.* CXXIV. 256 These fittings are made of thick handblown glass in white or dark grey-green with inner shades masking the bulbs. **1734** *Col. Rec. Georgia* III. 130 Part of the Twenty one Pieces of Mahogany, Ash, Sycamore, Ilex and Red Bay Timber the Growth of Georgia used in the Experiments for making Hand Boards &c. **1845** A. Wiley in *Indiana Mag. Hist.* (1927) XXIII. 165 Behold the..awkward man arise and place his chair before him for his pulpit and hand-board. **1857** P. Cartwright *Autobiogr.* xx. 203 They drove a stake down, and nailed a board to it,.. and this was my hand board. **1905** *Westm. Gaz.* 17 Mar. 4/1 Our game of hand-fives is perhaps the closest approach we have to the central type of the games. *a* **1877** Knight *Dict. Mech.* II. 1055/1 *Hand-hole*, a small hole at or near the bottom of a boiler, for the insertion of the hand in cleaning, etc. It is closed by a hand-hole plate. **1967** *Gloss. Sanitation Terms* (*B.S.I.*) 24 *Handhole*, a small opening with an access cover to provide for the inspection, repair or cleaning of the inside of a vessel or pipe. **1948** H. C. Parker *Climbs on Gritstone* I. 37 The crack facing the Pinnacle is climbed, with the use of an awkward hand jam, to the second chockstone. **1937** *Mountaineering Jrnl.* V. 138/1 A crack in the right-hand corner of the rectangular grass platform was climbed with the aid of small holds and hand jamming. **1957** Clark & Pyatt *Mountaineering in Brit.* xvi. 237 A new method of hand-jamming, enabling a hold to be obtained in a cleft with far more flexibility and far less pain than the previously accepted method. **1958** M. Pugh *Wilderness of Monkeys* 33 There was no room for dancing but here and there couples were hand-jiving and one girl expressed ecstasy by pulling her hair down into her eyes. **1958** *Radio Times* 14 Feb. 5/1 The world of skiffle, rock 'n' roll, jazz, and the hand-jive. **1961** Partridge *Dict. Slang* Suppl. 1125 *Hand-jive*, system of rhythmic hand-movements in time to music where floor is too crowded to allow people present to jive (dance), esp. as in coffee bars. **1958** *Punch* 12 Feb. 288/3 Hand-jiving only employs the dancer from the waist up and affords a great saving on Espresso space, the calf muscles and shoe-leather. **1899** Hand-laid [see *deckle 2]. **1889** *Century Dict.*, *Hand-letter*, an impress on a book-cover by movable types from a hand-stamp. **1960** G. A. Glaister *Gloss. Bk.* 171/1 *Hand-letters*, brass letters, mounted in wooden handles, which are used by the finisher for lettering the title, etc., on the cover of a hand-bound book. **1907** N. Munro *Daft Days* xvii. 150 A large hand-lettered bill was in each window. **1969** 'I. Drummond' *Man with Tiny Head* xv. 171 A hand-lettered sign. **1967** Karch & Buber *Offset Processes* iv. 117 A few Filmotype lettering styles unlike the usual type faces appear to be special handlettering. **1824** M. R. Mitford *Our Village* 13 A melon bed!—fie! What a grand pompous name was that for three melon plants under a hand-light! **1831** *Sutherland Farm Rep.* 72 in *Brit. Husb.* (1840) III, A few boys and girls hand-pick the whole. **1881** *Chicago Times* 4 June, Good to choice mediums [*sc.* beans] were quotable at $2.25 & 2.40 per bu. for hand-picked. **1898** *Advance* (Chicago) 3 Mar. 282/1 [Loyola] face to face with individuals, hand-picking souls from the fire. **1907** *Westm. Gaz.* 12 Sept. 5/1 The most expensive of the ordinary coals—'large hand-picked coal'. **1918** *Times* 23 Jan. 6/3 True, there has been a widespread feeling that the Irish Convention was handpicked. **1925** J. Gregory *Bab of Backwoods* xii. 157 An able-bodied trio, hand-picked by William Badger. **1928** *Daily Express* 11 July 1/2 A handpicked 'National' Assembly for Parliament. **1949** I. Deutscher *Stalin* 353 Its members, though they had all been hand-picked by Stalin..differed on means and methods. **1959** *Manch. Guardian* 1 July 4/5 The director ..hand-picks his best students for design jobs in the potteries. **1889** C. A. Harris *Princ. & Pract. Dentistry* (ed. 12) 526 Its use will also keep the hand-piece in good condition. **1914** J. B. Parfitt in N. G. Bennett *Sci. & Pract. Dental Surg.* 326 Hand-pieces..are often liable to get very much soiled. **1949** F. Sargeson *I saw in my Dream* 115 The whirring of the hand-pieces. **1950** *N.Z. Jrnl. Agric.* May 463/3 Thorough scrubbing of the shearing board with disinfectant and the cleansing of handpieces are also worthwhile practices. **1960** *Farmer & Stock-breeder* 23 Feb. 67/2 Entrants for the final at the Royal Show..will be judged using their own handpieces. **1963** J. Osborne *Dental Mechanics* (ed. 5) x. 212 For these purposes..small rotary stones in a handpiece are advisable. **1900** H. Lawson *Over Sliprails* 49 Scraping old splashes of paint off the brass and hand-plate. **1918** *Nature* 15 Aug. 470/2 To hand-pollinate the flowers of a soft-shelled tree with pollen from a tree of similar character. **1954** A. G. L. Hellyer *Encycl. Garden Work* 130/2 As a result of the hand-pollination, seed may be formed. **1886** R. Tuck *Handbk. Biblical Difficulties* ii. 324 This hand-print is made in order to avert the 'evil eye'. **1894** 'Mark Twain' in *Cent. Mag.* Feb. 553 The hand-print of one twin is the same as the hand-print of the fellow-twin. **1966** *New Scientist* 3 Mar. 539/3 The use of handprints has spread from the charge room to the clinic. Three paediatricians..have reported..that newborn babies with congenital defects frequently have abnormal palm and fingerprints. **1902** *Daily Chron.* 28 Nov. 6/3 S.S.,..'hand reader',..appeared..to answer a charge of pretending to tell fortunes by palmistry. **1867** A. R. Craig *Bk. of Hand* 31 In obedience to the stern dictates of the hand-reading art. **1960** C. Storr *Marianne & Mark* ii. 29 She asked if I wanted the cards or the crystal or a hand reading. **1922** *Collier's* 7 Jan. 8/1, I am asked by Collier's to suggest a simple, universal, and almost automatic system of hand signals for the automobile driver. **1934** *Amer. Speech* IX. 114/2 On the way to business [by car],..those who drive have to make allowances for..hand signals. **1960** E. H. Clements *Honey for Marshal* v. 94 He made the hand-signal impatiently..as the lorry still seemed shackled by its own indecision. **1965** Priestley & Wisdom *Good Driving* vi. 47 The Highway Code..lists the three hand signals. **1899** H. Butterworth *How To* iv. 15 (*heading*) Hand stand. **1909** W. Skarstrom *Gymnastic Kinesiology* 74 But in raising the legs and inverting the body to the 'Hand stand' there is at first a considerable bend at the hips and more flexion in the elbows than occurs in 'Free Front Rest'. **1946** 'J. Tey' *Miss Pym Disposes* vi. 111 When she goes out from thees [*sic*] plaace [*sic*] it will not matter any longer that she can do a handstand better than anyone else. **1951** *Swimming* (E.S.S.A.) v. 87 Before attempting handstand dives, you must be able to maintain a steady hand balance..grip the end of the board with the hands,..you can then throw up or press up into the armstand position. **1959** *Times* 17 Feb. 3/2 The little girl with upraised arms about to perform a handstand. **1598** Florio *Worlde of Wordes* 355/1 *Sciugatóio*, a hand-towell, a wiper, a rubbing cloth. **1778** in P. Ziegler *King William IV* (1971) ii. 26, 2 Dozen of Hand Towels. **1972** M. Kenyon *Shooting of Dan McGrew* iv. 32 In the.. men's room he was drying his face on a hand-towel. **1897** O. G. Jones *Rock-Climbing* xvii. 268 We each in turn ventured on the *hand-traverse* from above...It is so named because the climber hangs by his hands,..and traverses across the face by sheer strength of his arms. **1935** D. Pilley *Climbing Days* i. 17 Above this the 'hand traverse' faced us. A crack..offers sloping and not very good holds to the hands..the slab gives a little friction to the knees, but not very much. **1957** Collomb *Dict. Mountaineering* 84 *Hand traverse*, a horizontal movement across a broad flake of rock, the body being supported entirely on the hands which grip the edge of the flake.

hand, *v.* Add: **4. a.** *spec.* To deliver or serve (food) at a meal. Also with passive force: to be served, to be delivered. Also with *round*.

1802 C. Wilmot *Let.* 3 Jan. (1920) 27 Cakes,..Lemonade, &c., continually handing about the Room. **1803** M. Wilmot *Let.* 13 May in *Russ. Jrnls.* (1934) i. 13 Soup was handed round. **1844** 'J. Slick' *High Life N.Y.* II. 250 The niggers..dodged about, fillin plates and a handin em round. **1851** *London at Table* ii. 44 Don't omit to hand the vegetables and sauces. **1901** F. H. Burnett *Making of Marchioness* i. iv. 134 'I ought to go and help hand cake,' she said. **1945** M. Allingham *Coroner's Pidgin* i. 11 I'm going to 'and round at the reception. **1964** S. H. Nowell-Smith *Edwardian England* iv. 183 At smart tables, dishes were now handed by the servants —service *à la russe*, as it was called.

c. To give, convey: often with implication of palming-off or imposing. *U.S.*

1901 Merwin & Webster *Calumet 'K'* ii. 21, I told him he ought to give it to somebody else, and he handed me a lot of stuff about my experience. **1908** 'O. Henry' *Options* (1916) 30 I've had it handed to me in the neck, too. **1925** F. Lonsdale *Spring Cleaning* 11 You ought to have heard the stuff they have handed over to her about you! **1926** J. Black *You can't Win* vi. 75 You'll.. maybe get grabbed off a train and handed thirty days at Colorado Springs. **1970** *Morning Star* 17 Feb., The American Civil Liberties Union has condemned sentences for contempt handed down by Judge Julius Hoffman.

d. *to hand it to*: to acknowledge the superiority of; to congratulate; freq. in phr. *you have* (*got*) *to hand it to* (someone). orig. *U.S.*

c **1906** J. F. Kelly *Man with Grip* 14 You must hand it to the Jap. **1923** H. L. Foster *Beachcomber in Orient* xiv. 377, I do not like John [Chinaman]... But, to use the vernacular, you have to hand it to him. **1923** *Harper's Mag.* Apr. 558 You've got to hand it to that kid... He's stood everything and never squealed a yelp. Some young tough, believe me! **1926** G. D. H. & M. Cole *Blatchington Tangle* xli. 279 'I must hand it to you, sir,' the pseudo-American acknowledged. **1926** E. Wallace *Ringer* i. 11 The Ringer's clever. I hand it to him. **1927** 'A. Berkeley' *Mr. Priestley's Problem* ii. 30 'Guy, I hand it to you,' Laura was shrieking. **1965** *Listener* 30 Sept. 498/1 You've got to hand it to the Jerries, they know how to make cars. **1973** D. Jordan *Nile Green* xxi. 85, I had to hand it to him: he hadn't missed a trick.

hand-ax, -axe. Add: **b.** A prehistoric stone implement, *esp.* a bifacially worked cutting tool typical of certain Lower and Middle Palæolithic industries. (Cf. *coup de poing.)

1878 *Brooklyn Monthly* May 143/2 Another pattern have the groove extending partly round; others are wholly without a groove, and are of a pattern sometimes called hand axes. **1914** J. Geikie *Antiquity of Man in Europe* ii. 44 The *coup de poing* or hand-axe still occurs, but is rare, and would seem to have gone out of use in early Mousterian times. **1955** J. S. Weiner *Piltdown Forgery* xiii. 185 At Olorgesailie in Kenya Leakey found some good examples of these spherical stone balls with the Hand-axe culture. **1959** J. D. Clark *Prehist. S. Afr.* ii. 41 *Handaxe*, a heavy all-purpose tool, often pear-shaped and some 8–9 inches in length. Believed to have been used in the hand without hafting. **1972** *Times Lit. Suppl.* 31 Mar. 371/2 The chopper and biface core tools generally known as hand-axes.

hand-ball. Add: **4.** A game resembling fives.

1886 G. H. Benedict *Spaldings Hand Bk. Sporting Rules* 45 A game of hand ball shall consist of twenty-one aces, to be played with a ball about two inches in diameter. **1910** *Encycl. Brit.* X. 450/2 Handball, of ancient popularity in Ireland and much played in the United States, is practically identical with fives. **1957** *Ibid.* IX. 339/1 Certain forms of the games [of fives] in the United States, in Ireland and in some parts of the north of England are known as handball. *Ibid.* XI. 141/1 There is evidence that handball originated in Ireland about a thousand years ago. *Ibid.* 142/1 The game of Irish handball..was played on a hard clay floor, with one wall of stone,..against which the ball was struck. **1961** J. S. Salak *Dict. Amer. Sports* 215 *Handball*, a wall game in which a black rubber ball is struck with the hand against a wall, or walls, the ball being struck alternately by opposing players. **1968** *Globe & Mail* (Toronto) 17 Feb. 48/1 (Advt.), Regulation-size squash and handball courts.

handbook. Add: **c.** A betting-book; *handbook man*, a bookmaker. Also *hand-booking*, bookmaking. *U.S.*

1894 *Voice* 20 Sept., In every saloon which boasts a ticker are to be found men who will register a bet to any amount. These 'handbook' men are all [etc.]. **1903** *N.Y. Evening Post* 14 Sept., A case where an officer arrested a handbook man. **1904** *N.Y. Times* 13 June 1 The handbooking possibilities on the Derby. **1946** *Chicago Daily News* 26 June 14/2 The mob was..operating handbooks with full knowledge of your police department.

handclap. Add: (Later example.)

1962 A. Nisbett *Technique Sound Studio* ii. 33 You can use a hand-clap to give a rough guide to the reverberation.

b. Applause.

1907 *Daily Chron.* 1 Oct. 4/5 The curtain goes up..to some feeble handclaps from invited guests. **1908** *Westm. Gaz.* 13 Mar. 7/3 The chairman of the company.., with the directors, entered the room, a hand-clap greeting them.

c. *slow handclap*: slow applause expressing disapproval. Also (with hyphen) as vb. Hence *slow hand-clapping* vbl. sb.

1953 *Britannica Bk. of Year* 638/2 The freedom of usage seen in the formation of compounds also allows frequent changes in function, so that verbs, for example, may be formed from nouns. Examples are: to slow-handclap. **1955** Miller & Whitington *Cricket Typhoon* 215 Indeed, they jeered and slow-handclapped Cowdrey. **1958** F. C. Avis *Boxing Ref. Dict.* 103 *Slow handclap*, ironic applause expressed by means of a very slow clapping of the hands. **1959** *News Chron.* 13 July 4/6 Some cynical dons..were giving the slow hand-clap to the end of the procession. **1961** *Guardian* 3 Apr. 1/7 All the slow hand-clapping and hysterical cheering. **1966** *Listener* 20 Jan. 88/2 This destructive criticism was nothing compared with the..slow-handclaps and final booing.

Hence **hand-clapping** *vbl. sb.*

1838, 1888 [see Hand *sb.* 62 a]. **1948** B. G. M. Sundkler *Bantu Prophets S. Afr.* vi. 189 After the hymn..sung with gusto and more handclapping, the testimonies begin. **1959** I. & P. Opie *Lore & Lang. Schoolch.* vi. 94 Bangor children find that an innocent hand-clapping game goes neatly to the words.

handcraft. Delete †*Obs.* and add later examples. Hence **handcraft** *v. trans.*; **hand-crafted** *ppl. a.*

1933 *Catholic News* (Johannesburg) Mar. 15 (Advt.), Hand-craft tailored suits. **1965** *Punch* 3 Nov. 645/3 The stone, being hand-crafted and set, remained in place for more than a month before it was washed away in a rainstorm. **1967** *Listener* 5 Jan. 21/2 The bowls appear hand-crafted instead of factory-manufactured. **1968** C. Leader *Angry Darkness* iv. 39 The tiny shops were filled..with old silver and hand-crafted copper and brass. **1968** J. Arnold *Shell Book of Country Crafts* 59 Machine- and mass-production, together, have had a tremendous impact..on hand-crafts. **1971** *Daily Colonist* (Victoria, B.C.) 24 Oct. 4/2 All the fuel injection parts had to be handcrafted.

handcraftsman. Delete †*Obs.* and add later examples. Hence **handcraftsmanship.**

1923 *Daily Mail* 22 Jan. 6 (Advt.), A specialised handcraftsmanship places these brushes as a blessing [etc.]. **1933** *Archit. Rev.* LXXIII. 253/1 The subject of handcraftsmanship and mass production has been touched upon. **1954** B. Griffiths *Golden String* ix. 137

If a society is to be really human, there will always be a need for the hand-craftsman. **1961** *John o' London's* 7 Sept. 275/2, I think no one today, save a few incurable rustic-romantics and starry-eyed handcraftsmen, will imagine that a solution is to be found.

handedness (hæ·ndèdnes). [f. HANDED *a.* + -NESS.] The tendency to, or the preference for, the use of either the right or the left hand. Also *transf.*

1921 *Trans. Utah Acad. Sci.* II. 59 (*title*) The problem of handedness. *Ibid.* 62 It is argued by some that a child's handedness is a result of imitating its parents. **1936** F. A. E. CREW in *Jrnl. Genetics* XXXIII. 67 It seemed to me necessary to examine each rat. .for evidence of this right-hand and left-hand turning habit,... [68] In any examination of handedness the experimentation must not be complicated by the presence of an alternating light. **1937** *N. & Q.* 10 July 32/1 The First Series of an exhaustive scientific work on the subject of 'Handedness'. **1961** *Lancet* 12 Aug. 363/1 The left hemisphere is usually dominant for speech regardless of the handedness of the individual. **1962** *Listener* 10 May 814/3 Proteins. .contain amino acids (all of one particular handedness) joined together. **1973** *Sci. Amer.* May 27/3 Background data, including. .length of postpartum separation from siblings and handedness of the mother.

Handelian (hændī·liăn), *a.* and *sb.* [f. the name of Georg Friedrich *Handel*, originally *Händel* (1685–1759), German musician + -IAN.] **A.** *adj.* Of, pertaining to, or characteristic of Handel, or his style of composition. **B.** *sb.* One who favours or imitates the style of Handel.

1770 *Priv. Lett. 1st Ld. Malmesbury* (1870) I. 205 Tenducci is amazingly improved; in his part the old Handelian songs were left out. **1788** F. BURNEY *Diary* (1842) IV. IV. 231 The concert was very Handelian. **1808** S. WESLEY *Lett.* (1875) 9 This would nettle the Handelians devilishly. **1825** LAMB *Lett.* (1888) II. 132 My sister's cold is as obstinate as an old Handelian, whom a modern amateur is trying to convert to Mozart-ism. **1865** J. HULLAH *Transition Per. Music* 244 It 'bears so genuine a Handelian impress'. **1885** *Athenæum* 28 Feb. 288/1 Revivals of Handelian oratorio. **1911** LADY GUTHRIE in R. L. Orr *Ld. Guthrie* (1923) 258 Those dusky simple souls interpreting the glorious Handelian strains. **1966** K. AMIS *Anti-Death League* 349 The series of florid, rather Handelian amens swung to its close.

handful. Add: **5.** *slang.* A five years' prison sentence.

1930 J. LAIT *Big House* i. 6 A five-year sentence is a 'handful'. **1953** M. GILBERT *Fear to Tread* ix. 118 He's had a two-stretch... He'll collect a handful next time. **1966** *New Society* 31 Mar. 22/2 Going up for a handful (receiving a sentence of five years' imprisonment).

hand-glass. **2.** (Earlier examples.)

1788 G. WHITE *Selborne* lxv. 304 The hail broke. .all my garden-lights and hand-glasses. **1824** LOUDON *Encycl. Gardening* (ed. 2) 287 The wrought-iron hand-glass is composed of solid iron sash-bars, and may therefore be formed of any shape or height.

handgun. Delete †*Obs.* exc. *Hist.* and add later *U.S.* examples. Hence **handgunner** (later example). Also **handgunning** *vbl. sb.*

1957 *Amer. Speech* XXXII. 190 It is inevitable. .that colloquialisms of the handgunner overlap with those of the rifleman. *Ibid.* 191 The word handgun is very old... Since the 1930s its use as a generic term in place of pistol [etc.]... Recent use has made familiar, at least in writing, such derivatives as. .handgun work,. .applied to shooting the handgun at paper targets. *Ibid.*, Handgunning offers a great diversity of matches (slow, timed, and rapid fire). **1961** WEBSTER, *Handgun*, a firearm held and fired with one hand. **1968** *Economist* 22 June 43/3 California's Department of Justice estimates that there are 3·5 million concealable hand-guns (pistols and revolvers) within the state.

handicap, *v.* Add: Hence **ha·ndicapped** *ppl. a.*, of persons, esp. children, physically or mentally defective. Also *absol.* as *sb.*

1915 L. D. WALD *House on Henry St.* 117 (*caption*) The Handicapped Child. **1919** *School & Society* 29 Aug. 256/2 There are, of course, other types of mentally handicapped children who should be sharply differentiated. **1942** *Q. Jrnl. Speech* Feb. 81/1 The child who is still babbling, lisping, stuttering. .at thirty-six months of age is just as handicapped. .as the child with a misshapen back. **1958** *Times Lit. Suppl.* 21 Nov. p. xiii/2 The approach is strictly a practical one and even extends to the needs of handicapped children. **1958** P. TOWNSEND in N. Mackenzie et al. *Conviction* 118 The handicapped. .still are treated too often as second-class citizens. **1959** *Housewife* June 33 Chronically sick or handicapped people.

handicapper. Add: **b.** A horse running in a handicap race.

1895 *Starting Price* 23 Mar. 1/3 *Barbary.*—A second-rate handicapper, but bad-tempered and disappointing. **1955** *Times* 25 Aug. 2/6 That fine handicapper Durante put up a splendid performance under 9 st. 7 lb. in coming away in the last two furlongs to beat Naval Patrol by five lengths.

handie-talkie (hæ·ndi,tǭ:ki). Also **Handie-Talkie, handy-talky.** [After *WALKIE-TALKIE.] Name of a light form of walkie-talkie two-way radio set, easily carried in the hand.

1942 *Nat. Geogr. Mag.* Nov. 680 Churchill. .is holding a 'handie-talkie' radio used for conversation between ground points and planes in the air. **1943** *Time* 27 Sept. 83/2 (Advt.), He'll talk his way out. .with his two-way 'handy-talkie'... The 'handy-talkie' is only one of many radio communication devices of our armed forces. **1960** *Times* 8 Mar. 15/3 The equipment is known as a Handie-Talkie and has been produced to replace the heavier walkie-talkie sets used during the last war. **1969** S. GREENLEE *Spook who sat by Door* xiii. 113 Cops spoke busily into their car radios and handy-talkies.

handkerchief. Add: (Additional examples of sense 'kerchief worn about the neck'.) Phr. *to drop the handkerchief* (example); *to throw* (or *fling*) *the handkerchief* (earlier and later examples).

1749 H. WALPOLE *Let.* 20 July (1903) II. 396 Till all the juries of matrons have finished their inquest, one shall not care to make one's choice—I was going to say—*throw one's handkerchief*, but at present that term would be a little equivocal. **1764** —— *Let.* 5 June (1904) VI. 78 Lord Tavistock has flung his handkerchief to Lady Elizabeth Keppel. **1786** E. SHERIDAN *Jrnl.* 21–23 Jan. (1960) 79 The hankerchiefs are not so much puff'd out and there is now a very pretty sort of hankerchief much worn open at the neck and exactly made and trim'd like a Boy's shirt. **1825** H. WILSON *Mem.* II. 11 The system at White's Club. .is. .never to black ball any man, who ties a good knot in his handkerchief. **1870** *Brewer's Dict. Phr. & Fable* 384/1 '*The committee was at a loss to know whom to throw the handkerchief to*' (*The Times*). .the allusion is to the game called in Norfolk 'Stir up the dumplings', and by girls 'Kiss in the ring'. **1897** *Outing* (U.S.) Apr. 71/2, I was hoping that they would have an English May-pole dance, but instead they played 'drop the handkerchief', which Philip said, though not so ancient, was more fun. **1932** *Times Lit. Suppl.* 16 July 506/3 If he hesitate today whether he shall throw the handkerchief to Germany or Russia, does not such an embarrassment prove his power?

b. *handkerchief blouse, -case, -cloth, dress, -hat, -pin, pocket, sachet, table, -turban*, etc.; **handkerchief-head** (see quot. 1942).

In several of the collocations applied to parts of costume made up of squares resembling or suggesting handkerchiefs.

1790 E. WYNNE *Diary* 17 Jan. (1935) I. ii. 30 Betzy bought. .a handkerchief pin. **1880** L. HIGGIN *Handbk. Embroidery* 106 (Advt.), Handkerchief sachets, from £3. 3s. **1890** LD. LUGARD *Diary* 27 Mar. (1959) I. iv. 161, I. .presented the women with a return present viz. a dhoti of 'handkerchief cloth'. **1893** 'MARK TWAIN' in *Cent. Mag.* Dec. 238/2 She took off her handkerchief-turban. **1895** *Montgomery Ward Catal.* Index, Handkerchief Boxes and Cases. **1896** E. TURNER *Little Larrikin* x. 106 She had conceived the idea of making Ruffy a present of a handkerchief-sachet. **1899** *Daily News* 1 July 4/3 The revival of the handkerchief dress. **1900** *Westm. Gaz.* 9 Aug. 3/2 The handkerchief blouse. **1903** *Daily Chron.* 18 July 8/4 The sleeves are handkerchief ones. **1922** JOYCE *Ulysses* 99 His inner handkerchief pocket. **1932** D. C. MINTER *Mod. Needlecraft* 246/1 *Handkerchief case.* .oblong folded to form pocket and flap. **1942** *Amer. Mercury* LV. 95 *Handkerchief-head*, sycophant type of Negro; also an Uncle Tom. **1950** A. LOMAX *Mr. Jelly Roll* (1952) v. 231 This corny old handkerchief-head would assert that Count Basie did not know piano. **1956** S. LONGSTREET *Real Jazz* 147 A 'handkerchief-head' is an old-fashioned Negro who doesn't know his rights. **1960** *Encounter* XIV. II. 39 The Negro officer isn't a 'handkerchief head', an Uncle Tom. **1960** H. HAYWARD *Antique Coll.* 138/2 *Handkerchief table*, an American term for a single-leaf table with leaf and top triangular in shape. Closed, the table fits in a corner, opened it is a small square. **1963** *Sunday Express* 3 Nov. 19/1 A group of handkerchief hats in pastel glove leather. **1971** P. D. JAMES *Shroud for Nightingale* v. 170 An embroidered handkerchief sachet with a dozen handkerchiefs carefully folded.

handky, var. *HANKY[1].

handle, *sb.*[1] Add: **1. b.** *to fly off the handle* (later examples; no longer restricted to the U.S.); now usually = 'to lose one's temper'. Also, in same sense, *to go* (or *be*) *off the handle.*

1888 KIPLING *Phantom Rickshaw* 2 Pansay went off the handle,. .all that nonsense about ghosts developed. **1898** —— *Day's Work* 78 How are we to do our work if you fly off the handle that way? **1908** C. E. MULFORD *Orphan* xxii. 271 He reckoned you would. .get good and mad, fly off the handle, and raise h—l generally. **1915** A. CONAN DOYLE *Valley of Fear* I. v. 82 A kind of wave of jealousy would pass over him and he would be off the handle and saying the wildest things in a moment. **1932** KIPLING *Limits & Renewals* 157 Jimmy went off the handle at once; and Nicol kept patting him on the back. **1958** *Times* 3 Nov. 11/7 Montgomery flew off the handle and told the Minister of Defence. .that he must find out whether Bevin still stood by what he said. **1964** L. NKOSI *Rhythm of Violence* 64 Calm down, for God's sake! Everybody 's flying off the handle. What 's the matter with everybody?

c. *to the handle, up to the handle*: thoroughly, completely, up to the hilt. *U.S. colloq.*

1833 *Louisville Publ. Adv.* 9 May, He is determined to carry the contest 'to the handle'. **1835** A. B. LONGSTREET *Georgia Scenes* 234 We'll all go in for you here up to the handle. **1843** T. C. HALIBURTON *Attaché* 1st Ser. I. viii. 119 Give me your figgery-four, Squire, I'll go in up to the handle for you. **1855** *Knickerbocker* XLV. 435 (Th., s.v. *Up*), He was enjoying his trip 'up to the handle'. **1860** *Ibid.* LV. 415 He had for the last few years used a boy and dog as fencing material; he found it 'a good institution'; they did the thing up to the handle. **1877** J. HABBERTON *Jericho Road* xi. 101 If he isn't playin' possum right up to the handle, then he is a fool.

d. *to give, use, the long handle* (Cricket): to hit freely and continuously.

1888 STEEL & LYTTLETON *Cricket* ii. 77 Hold the bat nearer the top and give her the long handle. **1903** WARNER in H. G. Hutchinson *Cricket* 71 As a rule the hitting or 'long-handle game', as it has been called, pays best under these circumstances [*sc.* on a sticky wicket]. **1928** *Daily Express* 20 Dec. 3/2 Ryder set about the bowlers unmercifully, using the long handle.

2. b. A small basket with a handle, in which soft fruit is packed for the market.

1900 *Daily Express* 30 June 5/5 French red currants reached 1s. 3d. a basket or 'handle'.

c. A measure of beer, approx. 1 pint. *N.Z.*

1938 R. D. FINLAYSON *Brown Man's Burden* 40 'A handle of beer,' Mr Puttle was saying easily to the barman. **1943** J. A. W. BENNETT in *Amer. Speech* XVIII. 89 [In New Zealand] beer is dispensed in *handles* (in Australia, *pots*) or *half-handles*. **1947** 'A. P. GASKELL' *Big Game* 57 'He gets one handle every day,' said George [barman]. **1956** *N.Z. Listener* 8 June in J. Reid *Kiwi Laughs* (1961) 204 They still drink beer out of handles, sixpence a pop.

4. b. A person's name; a nickname. *slang* (orig. *U.S.*).

1870 J. C. DUVAL *Adv. Big-Foot Wallace* xxxviii. 236, I would rather be called 'Big-Foot Wallace' than 'Lying Wallace'. . .Such handles to my name would not be agreeable. **1927** *Dialect Notes* V. 449 Whut's yer handle? **1935** *Amer. Speech* X. 18/2 *Monicker*, a genuine name, as distinguished from an alias. Modern *handle*. **1964** D. VARADAY *Gara-Yaka* xx. 180 One was Toothless Annie... She had come by her 'handle' when a hysterical grass-eater had kicked her teeth in. **1969** C. F. BURKE *God is Beautiful, Man* (1970) 82 One night Jesus met a guy named Nicodemus. How 's that for a handle?

5. handle-bar, a transverse bar, usually curved, with a handle at each end, connected with the driving- or steering-wheel of a cycle, by which the vehicle is guided by hand; *pl.* the right- and left-hand parts of which this is composed. Also *attrib.*, *spec.* of a (usually large) moustache of handle-bar shape.

1887 *Graphic* 3 Dec. 619 These machines. .are fitted with adjustable handles and seat rod. Well finished in black enamel, with plated hubs, handle bars, &c. **1894** *Million* V. 377/1 Pick up your dress with your right hand, take hold of the handle bar with your left. **1898** *Science Siftings* XV. 170/1 Handle-bars in which the drop is greater than four inches below the seat are. .dangerous. **1908** *Westm. Gaz.* 15 Apr. 10/2 A contributor to the *Motor Cycle* advises motor-cyclists to carry handle-bar mirrors on their machines. **1908** *Daily Chron.* 21 Nov. 9/4 One cannot effect this unobserved change when other than handle-bar control is fitted. **1909** *Captain* Aug. 448/2 Home-made Handlebar-grips. **1923** H. L. WILSON *Oh, Doctor!* xxiv. 333 [He] threw a confident leg across the saddle and worshipfully grasped the spreading handle bars. **1933** G. P. JACKSON *White Spirituals* 65 An elderly man with handle-bar moustache. **1941** *Penguin New Writing* VIII. 17 One man was huge and swarthy, with a handlebar moustache. **1953** M. DICKENS *No More Meadows* vii. 295 Chap with the handlebar moustache. Real Pilot-Officer Prune type. **1968** *Which?* Aug. 231/2 Turn the handlebars—the steering should not be too tight or too loose. *Ibid.* 232/1 If the brake levers are too far from the handlebar grips, a child with small hands might find it difficult to work them. **1972** J. ROSSITER *Rope for General Dietz* ii. 23 We both had the enormous handlebar moustaches *de rigueur* in the RAF at that time.

handle (hæ·nd'l), *sb.*[2] [f. HANDLE *v.*[1] I.] The feel of or sensation produced by goods, especially textiles, when handled.

1884 W. S. B. MCLAREN *Spinning* 19 It is not merely the coarseness or fineness of the fibre which guides him, but also the softness and kind 'handle', as it is called. **1898** *Daily News* 7 Mar. 2/1 For softness and beautiful handle they have no equal. **1927** T. WOODHOUSE *Artificial Silk* 2 The handle of many artificial silk articles of commerce compares favourably with that of most of the corresponding textures in the other branches of the textile industry. **1961** *Times* 26 Oct. p. iv, A new type of paper. . which had all the qualities—good surface and opacity, good colour and crispness of 'handle'. **1962** *Which?* Aug. 240/2 The blanket. .felted considerably and had a harsh 'handle'. **1968** J. IRONSIDE *Fashion Alphabet* 210 The filaments are 'crimped' to resemble wool, giving a warm, soft 'handle'. **1970** *Nature* 17 Oct. 212/1 The 'handle' and 'feel' of fabrics.

handle, *v.*[1] Add: **1. b.** (Later examples.)

1946 *Mod. Lang. Notes* LXI. 443 The use, in advertising, of the 'potential intransitive', in such examples as 'this car *operates*, *handles* smoothly'. **1958** *Times* 23 Sept. 14/2 Sceptre, handling excellently, rounded the mark to the sound of loud hootings. **1962** *Which? Car Suppl.* Oct. 142/1 It [*sc.* the car] handled very securely. **1972** *Country Life* 23 Mar. 703/3 The machine handles well, and I discovered no snags.

2. c. (Earlier example.)

1839 URE *Dict. Arts* 764 They [*sc.* the hides]. .are successively transferred into other pits with stronger ooze; all the while being daily *handled*, that is, moved up and down in the infusion.

d. *Cricket.* (See quots.)

1788 in H. T. Waghorn *Dawn of Cricket* (1906) 98 Their opponents were superior to them in handling [*sc.* fielding] the ball. **1797** in G. B. Buckley *Fresh Light on 18th Cent. Cricket* (1935) 184 Handling b. in play. **1841** *Manchester Chron.* 24 July, John Ogden. .handled the ball well [i.e. as bowler].

handleability (hæ:nd'lăbi·lĭti). [f. HANDLE-ABLE *a.*: see -ITY.] Ease of handling.

1947 N. BALCHIN *Aircraft Builders* v. 31 The problem

was one of combining performance with 'handleability' and toughness of condition. **1949** *Jrnl. R. Aeronaut. Soc.* LIII. 962/1 The general 'handleability' of an aeroplane must not be lost sight of in a welter of requirements which might lead to excessive stability. **1970** *Amat. Photographer* 22 Apr. 55/2 An indefinable quality of a camera is its 'handleability'.

handler. Add: **2.** One who shows the points of dogs at a trial, etc.

1897[in Dict.]. **1931** *Our Dogs* 23 Oct. 296 Handlers and Breakers. Gun dogs wanted for training or boarding. **1959** *Times* 18 Sept. 7/5 Of the nine handlers who took part in the opening event—the hired shepherds' championship—only two failed to complete the course.

b. A police officer who is in charge of a trained dog.

1959 B. J. FARMER *Murder Next Year* xxi. 134, I know Sergeant Cristobel... He's handler for a trained Alsatian. **1962** *Times* 29 Dec. 6/7 Minivans..containing two highly trained police dogs with their handlers. **1971** B. CALLISON *Plague of Sailors* 10 They're not dogs, they're bloody werewolves. What d'you handlers do for leave, spend it in the bloody jungle?

c. *Boxing.* (See quot. 1961.)

1950 J. DEMPSEY *Championship Fighting* 9 His handlers threw in the towel. **1960** *Times* 1 Sept. 4/4 It took several seconds of rough first aid by his handlers before he was able to regain his seat. **1961** J. S. SALAK *Dict. Amer. Sports* 216 *Handlers*, the chief second and assistant seconds of a boxer during a contest. **1973** *Sunday Express* (Trinidad & Tobago) 8 Apr. 29/2 (*caption*) One of his handlers..is near tears after Ali lost a 12 round non-title bout.

hand-line. Add: Hence **hand-line** *v.*, to fish with a hand-line; to pull in a fishing-line by hand.

1935 A. J. CRONIN *Stars look Down* II. xix. 437 Old Macer..had to make the best of it by hand-lining off shore for whiting. **1969** *Islander* (Victoria, B.C.) 7 Sept. 6/1 Peter began commercial fishing, handlining for cod. **1972** *Shooting Times & Country Mag.* 24 June 15/3, I was at one stage handlining in like fury to keep in touch and then suddenly as the fish passed us, was slipping line out to the running fish.

handling, *vbl. sb.* Add: **1. c.** In games, the illegal touching of the ball.

1882 in Charles-Edwards & Richardson *They saw it Happen* (1958) 300 For a breach of rule, which forbids handling, a free kick was awarded against the Etonians. **1897** *Encycl. Sport* I. 429/1 *Handling*, or *Hands*, touching the ball with any part of the arm when in play. Only the goal-keeper can do so without a penalty. 'Hands' is given against the offender.

d. [HANDLE *v.*¹ 1 b.] The way in which a motor vehicle handles.

1962 *Which? Car Suppl.* Oct. 143/1 Its handling was very secure, but the car was badly affected by side winds. **1967** *Autocar* 28 Dec. 5/3 In general the handling of the car was satisfactory.

5. *attrib.* (Additional examples.)

1927 *Observer* 27 Mar. 28 In spite of the progress Rugby has made, the Association game at the Schools..has fully held its own with the handling code. **1949** *Archit. Rev.* CV. 218 The east bay includes..the polymer handling bay. **1954** *Economist* 11 Sept. 8/2 The central terminal area, which will hold the permanent control tower and the passenger handling buildings, is now being completed. **1955** *Times* 6 July 4/4 A long handling rush by Britain looked dangerous and from a loose scrum in the opposing twenty-five their backs gained possession for O'Reilly to cut in and score. **1962** *Which?* Dec. 367/1 Labour costs were covered, but there was a 'handling charge' of 2s. 6d. **1969** *Times* 13 Jan. 11/2 The increase in the handling margins would be nearer to 100 than 10 per cent.

hand-loom. Add: Hence **ha·nd-loomed** *a.*

1928 *Daily Express* 13 July 3/6 Hand-loomed leathers.. are a vogue in exclusive handbags. **1966** A. ADBURGHAM *View of Fashion* 135 Hand-loomed skirts.

hand-made, *a.* Add: (Later examples.)

1959 HALAS & MANVELL *Technique Film Animation* vi. 69 The animated film is essentially a hand-made art. **1968** *Times* 31 Aug. 19/4 Some biographical facts (including the..item of her using the blue hand-made paper fabricated for Colette).

b. *fig.*

1936 *Punch* 7 Oct. 418/2 (*heading*) The hand-made short story. **1937** B. H. L. HART *Europe in Arms* iv. 49 The fortified region..is garrisoned by units of varying composition which are 'hand-made' to suit the sector allotted to them. **1958** *Listener* 9 Oct. 549/2 By the very terms of his [*sc.* de Gaulle's] own newly adopted hand-made constitution, the President must not be anything but an arbitrator.

ha·nd-me-down, *sb.* and *a. dial.* and *colloq.* [f. the verbal phr. *to hand down* (see HAND *v.* 4 b).] **A.** *sb.* That which is handed down, as an heirloom, a second-hand garment, etc.; also, a ready-made garment. **B.** *adj.* Having been handed down or passed on; = REACH-ME-DOWN *a.* So *hand-me-down shop*, etc. Also *fig.*

1874 HOTTEN *Dict. Slang* 187 *Hand-me-downs*, second-hand clothes. **1882** G. W. PECK *Peck's Sunshine* 213 A hand bill for a Chicago hand-me-down clothing store. **1888** *New York World* 5 Mar. (Farmer), A twelve-dollar suit of hand-me-downs. **1889** *Sporting Times* 29 June (Farmer), Trousers..which all over proclaim themselves entitled to the epithet of hand-me-down. **1896** ADE *Artie* xviii. 70 They'll be workin' for some Reub that come into town wearin' hand-me-downs. **1897** *Congress. Rec.* 25 Mar. 274/1 These cheap-johns, ready-made, 'hand-me-down' statesmen. **1904** *Boston Herald* 15 Oct. 2 He wears a cheap suit of 'hand-me-down' clothing. **1909** *Daily Chron.* 2 July 7/4 He got it from a lady admirer..and he wanted me to 'ave it as a hand-me-down. **1914** JOYCE *Dubliners* 150 His little old father kept the hand-me-down shop in Mary's Lane. **1925** S. LEWIS *Martin Arrowsmith* viii. § 2 A dirty old office, with hand-me-down chairs and a lot of second-hand magazines. **1935** A. J. CRONIN *Stars look Down* II. xiii. 375 A little hand-me-down factory. **1954** M. MEAD *Growing up in New Guinea* 188 Their myths are dull hand-me-downs. **1960** *Economist* 31 Dec. 1382/1 Many large corporations are still flying converted bombers and hand-me-down transports, but these are being supplemented by the newer, smaller light models. **1966** *New Yorker* 5 Nov. 197 To dramatize this hand-me-down truth.

hand-off (hæn·dǫ·f), *v. Rugby Football.* [f. HAND *v.* + OFF *adv.*] *intr.* To push off an opponent with the hand. Also *trans.* Hence **ha·nd-off** *sb.*, the action of pushing off an opponent.

1897 *Encycl. Sport* I. 429 *Handing-off*, pushing off an opponent who endeavours to impede a player running with the ball. **1920** *Times* 8 Nov. 6/2 The wings ran well and were not afraid to 'hand-off'. **1922** *Daily Mail* 8 Dec. 12 A dangerous scoring wing with a powerful hand-off and an elusive swerve. **1923** W. J. A. DAVIES *Rugby Football* 135 Coates..ran with his head half turned to the right.. which gave one the impression that he was waiting and was anxious to hand-off some one. **1928** *Observer* 19 Feb. 27/1 [He] has a fine kick, with a strong hand-off. **1959** *Times* 21 Sept. 3/5 Gray, who used his hand-off effectively.

hand-out. [f. HAND *v.* + OUT *adv.*]

1. *Tennis.* (See HAND *sb.* 63.)

2. a. That which is handed out; *spec.* (*a*) food or alms given to a beggar at the door; (*b*) a gift of money. orig. *U.S.*

1882 SWEET & KNOX *Texas Siftings* 195 If I can't get a 'hand-out' for it I can at least expatiate on its merits. **1887** M. ROBERTS *Western Avernus* 71 'Bummers' is American for beggars, and a 'hand out' is a portion of food handed out to a bummer or a tramp at the door when he is not asked inside. **1896** *Dialect Notes* I. 418 *Hand-out*, clothes such as a tramp asks for. **1896** ADE *Artie* vi. 50, I see barrel-house boys goin' around for hand outs that was more on the level than you was. **1903** *Daily Chron.* 4 Apr. 5/2 The weekly hand-out for the butcher. **1904** 'O. HENRY' *Trimmed Lamp* (1916) 32 Pretty soon I was in the free-bed line and doing oral fiction for hand-outs among the food bazaars. **1925** W. CATHER *Professor's House* 195 He soon drank up all his wages. When Rapp picked him up there he was living on hand-outs. **1931** C. MASSIE *Confessions of Vagabond* vii. 74 Tramps will often travel a hundred miles to one particular spot where they are sure to get a 'hand-out'. **1946** WODEHOUSE *Joy in Morning* vi. 45, I can well imagine a man of conservative views recoiling from one which might come asking for handouts for the rest of its life. **1959** *Daily Tel.* 27 July 12/6 The report in yesterday's newspapers that Mr Nixon, on an early morning visit to a Moscow market, had tried to give a 100-rouble note as a 'hand-out' to a worker. **1968** *Globe & Mail* (Toronto) 3 Feb. B4/3 Poor countries realize part of the burden lies on them... They're no longer just looking for handouts.

b. *attrib.*; *spec.* providing light refreshments in a handy form.

1910 *Salt Lake Tribune* 27 Nov. 32/7 On the first floor 'hand-out' luncheons were being served. **1928** F. N. HART *Bellamy Trial* viii. 277, I would take a good walk, get a bite to eat at one of the hand-out places in the vicinity of the station. **1960** *Farmer & Stockbreeder* 22 Mar. 79/3 The future of our industry is going to rely much more on capital grants than on hand-out grants.

3. Matter handed out to or by the newspaper press; more generally, matter handed out from any source to convey information, guidance, etc.

1927 *Amer. Speech* II. 242/1 To get pictures and 'hand-outs', that is, prepared statements given to the press by officials or other prominent persons. **1929** *Literary Digest* 12 Oct. 7/1 Mr. Shearer told..how he gave the newspaper men at Geneva 'hand-outs' to help them in preparing their despatches. **1929** *Sat. Even. Post* 7 Dec. 213/2 We have public-relations experts who do their stuff by means of propaganda in the press and hand-outs to the newspaper boys and girls. **1942** *Punch* 8 July 8/2 An N.C.O. distributes hand-outs in which we are warned that the information given on this course is going to be the most secret. **1942** *Gen* 15 Sept. 24/2 White feather hand-outs..to men and women not in uniform have now reached epidemic proportions. **1945** *Ann. Reg. 1944* 251 The Spanish official 'hand-out'..was a masterpiece of nebulous verbiage. **1951** *Manch. Guardian Weekly* 23 Nov. 2 Fakes a handout to several of his team. **1958** *Punch* 8 Jan. 84/2 B.O.A.C. hadn't given me a free briefcase full of handouts for nothing. **1959** 'H. HOWARD' *Deadline* viii. 66 A little loose-leaf notebook issued as a free handout by Hopalong Cassidy Enterprises. **1965** *Spectator* 22 Jan. 92/2 The handout is a (necessary) curse of modern political life. It shackles the speaker and bores his audience, but it delights the reporter. **1972** 'G. BLACK' *Bitter Tea* (1973) iv. 63 Not a handout likely to satisfy a newspaper reporter, Inspector.

hand over hand. Add: **c. hand-over-hand stroke**, a style of swimming in which each arm is alternately brought out of the water from behind and with a circular sweep returned to the water in front. Also as *adv. phr.*

1856 'STONEHENGE' *Brit. Sports* 516/2 The Hand-over-Hand style is a very rapid mode of swimming. **1872** H. GURR *Art of Swimming* 25 To Swim Hand-over-hand. **1904** R. THOMAS *Swimming* 139 The hand-over-hand is the most ancient stroke, at all events that is recorded.

Hence **ha:nd-over-ha·nder.**

1924 R. CLEMENTS *Gipsy of Horn* vi. 104 Sending the royal yards aloft to a rattling hand-over-hander.

hand over head. Add: **2. b.** *Cricket.* Designating a style of bowling (see OVERHAND *a.* 2).

1899 A. LANG in *Daily News* 22 July 4/2 The modern hand-over-head style.

hand-press. (Later example.)

1967 E. CHAMBERS *Photolitho-Offset* i. 3 The operation of printing consists, first, in damping the stone—with a wet sponge in hand-press printing or with a wet roller in power-press work.

handraulic (hændrǭ·lik), *a.* [f. HAND *sb.* + HYD)RAULIC *a.*] Of something done by hand rather than by machine. Hence **handrau·li-cally** *adv.*

1948 PARTRIDGE *Dict. Forces' Slang* 90 *Handraulic power*,..with a pun on hydraulic. *Ibid.* 103 *Johnny Armstrong*, the elementary motive power known in the Navy as 'handraulic', used for 'pully-haully' work. **1962** *Times* 4 Aug. 8/6 The ease with which even a battleship could be set in motion 'handraulically' was once vividly demonstrated. *Ibid.* 8/7 'Rolling ship' is more than just a spectacular display of 'handraulic' power. It is a good way of getting refloated. **1963** *Flight International* LXXXIII. 291/3 There are two general approaches to automation of the complex organisation of a traffic control centre: either a complete system is designed and tested more or less in isolation and transferred as an entity from the experimental stage into the working, or the existing 'handraulic' system is improved step-by-step until a clearer picture of an ultimate requirement emerges.

handset (hæ·nd,set). Also **hand-set.** [HAND *sb.* + SET *sb.*²] A telephone transmitter and receiver combined in a single instrument.

[**1914** SMITH & CAMPBELL *Automatic Teleph.* vi. 131 The telephone instrument follows the general form which is so popular on the Continent, making large use of the combined transmitter and receiver, sometimes known as the hand microphone set.] **1930** *Electr. Commun.* VIII. 265/2 The tendency towards more comfortable and convenient apparatus has been evidenced..finally by the development of handsets, or as they are sometimes called, 'micro-telephones'. **1955** 'N. SHUTE' *Requiem for Wren* 283 They repeated it and booked the call, and I put down the handset. **1962** A. NISBETT *Technique Sound Studio* 176 For telephones a standard hand-set can be similarly adapted, so that the bell may be worked by a press-button. **1972** C. DRUMMOND *Death at Bar* v. 127 There was a call box... He had to wait ten minutes while a young citizen..quacked into the handset.

handshake, *sb.* Add: **b.** A gift of money.

1960, etc. [see *golden handshake]. **1968** *Times* 3 July 26/6 (*headline*) Dockers told of handshake. *Ibid.*, An offer of bigger 'golden handshakes'. **1971** *Financial Mail* (Johannesburg) 26 Feb. 649/2 (Advt.), However you invest with the United, you get a handsome handshake.

handshake (hæ·ndʃēik), *v.* [Back-formation from HAND-SHAKING.] *intr.* To shake hands. So **ha·ndsha:ker.**

1898 H. JAMES *Two Magics* 8 We handshook and 'candlestuck', as somebody said, and went to bed. **1905** *Westm. Gaz.* 2 Nov. 12/1 As the line moves forward each hand-shaker is steadily pushed along. **1928** *Daily Express* 28 Aug. 8/3 Hearty handshakers. **1940** *Amer. Speech* XV. 211/2 Those who try to get promotions by pull with officers are called handshakers or suction kids. **1964** G. B. SCHALLER *Year of Gorilla* x. 240 The Belgians are the most confirmed handshakers I have ever met.

hand-shaking. (Later and *attrib.* examples.)

1964 ROSE & ZIMAN *Camford Observed* vii. 129 *Handshaking*: at Oxford the Master of a College interviews every undergraduate at the end of each term and hears a report on his progress by his Tutor. **1965** *Listener* 16 Sept. 425/2 A hand-shaking tour of the Soviet Union.

handsome, *a.* Add: **6. b.** Used, sometimes ironically, to address, or as a designation of, a handsome person. *colloq.* (orig. *U.S.*).

1921 J. DOS PASSOS *Three Soldiers* (1922) VI. ii. 334 'Teach him how to salute,' the officer had said and Handsome had stepped up to him and hit him. **1940** S. LEWIS *Bethel Merriday* i. 13 'Hya, Toots. Hya, handsome,' said her brother. **1945** E. WAUGH *Brideshead Revisited* I. v. 104 Be a sport, handsome: no one 's seen anything but you. **1963** 'H. CALVIN' *It's Different Abroad* ii. 7 Laurent turned to him and sneered. 'Okay, handsome,' he said.

B. *adv.* Now usu. in phr. *handsome is as handsome does.*

1847 F. A. DURIVAGE in W. T. Porter *Quarter Race in Kentucky* 48 She aint no Wenus, Sir,..but handsome is as handsome does. **1950** A. CHRISTIE *Murder is Announced* xiii. 139 'Such a handsome young man.'..'Handsome is as handsome does... Much too fond of poking fun at people.' **1963** *Times* 5 June 4/3 But handsome is as handsome does, and his job was done when he was caught off the last ball, when Kent still had a wicket to spare. **1970** G. GREER *Female Eunuch* 56 Men were slipping into relative anonymity and 'handsome is as handsome does'.

hands-up (hæ·ndz,ʋp), *v.* [f. the order *hands up!* (see HAND *sb.* 54).] *intr.* To put up the hands in token of surrender. Also *trans.*, to cause to surrender. So **ha·nds-up** *sb.*, the

action of putting up the hands (in quot. *attrib.*); **ha·nds-u:pper**, one who surrenders. Also **ha·nd-up** *sb.*, one who throws up his hands.

1901 *Contemp. Rev.* Mar. 327 A small patrol..went..to the farm of a 'hands upper', *i.e.*, one who had surrendered his arms. **1901** *Daily Chron.* 12 Nov. 5/4 They regard themselves as quite the aristocrats of the camp, and much superior to the 'hands-uppers', as they have delighted in calling the children of less obstinate patriots. **1901** 'LINESMAN' *Words by Eyewitness* 239 The refugee camps within the British lines, wherein dwell the hundreds of Dutchmen who have surrendered, or 'hands-upped'. **1902** *Westm. Gaz.* 20 Mar. 7/1 Trooper Long..was grabbed by the throat by a 'hands-up' prisoner, who threw down his rifle. **1902** *Appleton's Ann. Cycl.* 629/2 The Boers who had accepted British sovereignty at various times since the fall of Bloemfontein and Pretoria, contemptuously called 'handups' by the others. **1915** *Observer* 4 Apr. 7/2 We have now a case of 'hands-upping', the first in this war, by a whole unit of Germans. **1923** *Daily Mail* 9 Mar. 10 The Germans after 'hands-upping' Rumania proceeded literally to turn out their pockets. **1928** *Observer* 17 June 7 Those faint-hearted ones who are 'hands-uppers' in regard to aviation. **1929** J. BUCHAN *Courts of Morning* III. 307 They hands-upped like lambs. We've gotten a nice little bag—fourteen hundred and seventy-three combatant soldiers.

handwrite (hæ·nd,rəit), *sb. Sc., Ir.*, and *U.S.* [f. HAND *sb.* + WRITE *sb.*[1] 5. Cf. HANDWRIT and *hand of writ or write* (HAND *sb.* 16 b).] Handwriting.

1483– in *Dict. Older Scot. Tongue.* **1617** in W. K. Tweedie *Sel. Biogr.* (1847) I. 95, I receaved a letter..whilk albeit it wanted a subscription, yet by the handwrite..I knew to be yours. **1638** S. RUTHERFORD *Lett.* (1664) 14 His hand write, & his seal. **1688** in R. Wodrow *Hist. Suff. Ch. Scot.* (1722) II. 633 You..adhered to your preaching Book, and declared the same to be your own Hand-write. **1836** B. TUCKER *Partisan Leader* (1861) 16 (Th.), He has got a paper in the captain's hand-write to show him the way. **1856** W. G. SIMMS *Eutaw* 429 (Th.), Thar's his name in handwrite! Hyar's a boy that reads this handwrite. **1880** W. H. PATTERSON *Gloss. Antrim* 49 Whose hand write is that? **1907** N. MUNRO *Daft Days* xv, She knew she could never sustain the standard of hand-write, spelling, and information Bud had established in her first epistle. **1923** *Dialect Notes* V. 209, I know his hand write.

handwriting. Add: **2.** (Later *fig.* examples.)

1928 R. FRY in *S.P.E. Tract* XXXI. 331 *Ecriture.* Has a special sense in regard to painting, and refers to the rhythm of the handling of paint. *Handwriting* has hardly acquired this use, but perhaps might be adequate. **1959** *Sunday Times* 10 May 19/5 Certain designers possess an accuracy of taste and a precision of expression which produce an identifiable handwriting... Dior's was a great handwriting. **1959** *Observer* 20 Sept. 18/4 A style policy which is recognisably the 'handwriting of the store'. **1960** *Observer* 28 Feb. 5/3 Leonardo's left-handedness, his preoccupation with things observed..contribute to what Sir Kenneth [*sc.* Clark] calls his 'handwriting'. **1961** R. SETH *Anat. Spying* vi. 97 The individual's use of the morse-key is as distinctive as his handwriting—in fact, it is referred to as 'handwriting'.

3. *attrib.*, as **handwriting expert**, one who makes a study of handwriting in order to determine the authorship of disputed documents, to detect forgeries, etc.

1894 *Strand Mag.* VIII. 293/1 The methods employed by handwriting experts. **1897** *Westm. Gaz.* 2 Dec. 5/1 M. Bertillon, the famous handwriting expert, one of the witnesses at the Dreyfus trial. **1898** *Ibid.* 17 Jan. 7/2 The testimony of hand-writing 'experts'. **1967** G. B. MAIR *Girl from Peking* iv. 52 Our handwriting experts say that they *could* have been written by the same person.

handy, *sb.* Add: **2.** A hand-bier.

1909 *Daily Chron.* 8 June 2/5 Hearses, Handys, Biers, &c. **1922** *Daily Mail* 4 Nov. 10 The charges for licences on motor-hearses and handies.

handy, *a.* Add: **2. b.** Phr. *handy by, to*: conveniently situated for. *dial.* and *U.S.* So *handy for* (general colloq.).

1825 J. JENNINGS *Observ. Dial. W. Eng.* 133 I've hir'd 'twar handy ta tha zea. **1893** 'O. THANET' *Stories of Western Town* 136 It is customary in the Lossing Building to say, 'We are so handy to the cars.' **1934** H. G. WELLS *Exper. Autobiogr.* II. viii. 602 A miscellany of people came and went there and to lodgings handy-by the smaller house at Dymchurch. **1968** *Globe & Mail* (Toronto) 17 Feb. 45 (Advt.), Not one street to cross to get to public school. Handy to shopping plaza. Beautiful view over park.

3. b. *handy dog* (see quots.). *N.Z.*

1933 L. G. D. ACLAND in *Press* (Christchurch) 25 Nov. 15/7 Some dogs will both head and huntaway and are called handy dogs. **1968** *N.Z. News* 28 Aug. 16/1 A pack usually has several 'huntaways', a 'heading' dog and a 'handy' dog... The handy dog is generally versatile at all jobs.

5. b. handy-billy (later example); **handy-man,** (*b*) a sailor; **handy-sized** *a.*, of a convenient or suitable size.

1933 J. MASEFIELD *Bird of Dawning* 56 We handed up the handy billy, they made it fast to the davit-head. **1899** H. BEGBIE *Handy Man* iii, And the babe sleeps sound in her cot o' nights, and the trader may plot and plan, For under the stars on the rolling deep stands the vigilant Handy Man. **1900** *People* 1 Apr. (Ware), The handy man. High praise for the naval brigade. **1927** *Scots Observer* 19 Mar. 15/3 The need for a handy-sized and attractive edition of the Gospels. **1961** *Times* 7 Feb. 17/5 Few owners are building handy-sized tankers these days.

handy-dandy. 1. c. (Later examples.)

1965 *New Statesman* 3 Dec. 879/3 Change places, handy-dandy and the tone..could almost be Peter Simple on Dr Castrumba. **1966** *Ibid.* 15 Apr. 539/3 Handy-dandy, which is the Underground Man and which is the complacent bourgeois?

hanepoot (hā·nəpōːt, -pūəːt). *S. Afr.* Also **haanepoot, haanepot, haenapod, hanapoot,** and (corruptly) **honeypot.** [Afrikaans, f. Du. *haan* cock + *poot* foot.] **1.** The grape-variety Muscat of Alexandria, a table grape often also used for making wine and for raisins.

c **1798** LADY A. BARNARD in A. W. C. Lindsay *Lives of Lindsays* (1849) III. 403 The Honipot grape.., a fleshy white grape, which is of the Muscatel nature and excellent. **1801** J. BARROW *Trav. S. Afr.* I. 65 A large white Persian grape, called here the haenapod. **1855** W. R. KING *Campaigning in Kaffirland* (ed. 2) 190 The most deliciously flavoured grapes, one sort, called the 'honeypot',.. of immense size. **1878** T. J. LUCAS *Camp Life* 36 A fine fleshy well-favoured variety called hanne poot. **1887** *Colonial & Indian Exhib., Rep. Col. Sect.* 136 Raisins are made from the Haanepot grape. **1896** R. WALLACE *Farm. Ind. Cape Col.* x. 202 Of grapes the Haanepoot..and the Barbarossa are considered the best for the British market. **1927** *Daily Express* 8 Apr. 5 The Cape grapes..either the gros Colmars or the white Hanapoots. **1945** *Cape Times* 30 Mar. 4/7 The hanepoots are golden-brown and sweet. **1946** *Ibid.* 11 Feb. 6/5 In 1938–39 it was easy to buy good hanepoots at six or eight lb. for a shilling. **1971** *Rand Daily Mail* 28 July 15 The Spanish variety was thought to be the forebear of the Hanepoot grapes of today.

2. A sweet white wine made from hanepoot grapes.

1804 R. PERCIVAL *Acct. Cape of Good Hope* xi. 188 The Hanepod made from a large white grape is very rich, but scarce and dear. **1952** C. L. LEIPOLDT *300 Yrs. Cape Wine* xv. 203 A more common Hanepoot wine is a golden coloured, fairly sweet wine, of which several kinds are on the market. **1966** C. DE BOSDARI *Wines of Cape* (ed. 3) vi. 66 There are also the Muscadels,..from Hanepoot..to Frontignac.

hang, *v.* Add: **1.** (Later examples.)

1896 R. FRY *Lett.* (1972) I. 168 Tonks's *Broadstairs* is a terrible thing to hang: it is so spotty and brilliant that it knocks the other things to pieces. **1967** *Listener* 2 Mar. 296/2 More rewarding, and better hung,..is the loan exhibition of graphics.

6. b. *fig.* To reduce to, or hold in, a state of indecision or inaction; *esp.* in phr. *to hang a jury*, to prevent (as a juryman) a jury from reaching a verdict (cf.*17 c). *U.S.*

1778 G. WASHINGTON *Let.* 15 June in *Writings* (1834) V. 405, I am hung in suspense. **1848** E. BRYANT *California* xxvi. 291 The jury, after the case was referred to them, were what is called 'hung'; they could not agree. **1868** *Harper's Mag.* Mar. 542/2 The jury..returned with a verdict in favor of the *plaintiff!* On remonstrating with the Mexican why he did not 'hang' the jury, the lawyer asked him, 'Why did you bring in a verdict against yourself?' **1967** *Guardian* 3 Apr. 2/7 The lone juror who finally hangs the jury will not emerge,..unless at the start his view has some support.

7. b. To tie or hitch up (a horse). (Cf. 28 e.) Chiefly *U.S.*

1835 *Southern Lit. Messenger* I. 581 Having arrived at Blank, we *hung* our horses, as Virginians always do after riding them. **1843** 'R. CARLTON' *New Purchase* xxvi, While *hanging* Dick to a gate post. **1900** H. LAWSON *On Track* 30 He got down, wondering what was up, and hung his horse to the last post but one. **1916** J. B. COOPER *Coo-oo-ee!* xii. 164 You made the remark that 'you'd tie up your horse'—an Australian 'hangs' his horse to a fence.

10. Delete *arch.* and add further examples. Now usu. in phr. *to go hang*: to go and be hanged; to 'go to the devil'; to be dismissed or rejected; freq. *let* (*it*, etc.) *go hang*.

1921 R. HICHENS *Spirit of Time* xii. 203 Hold on to the best in yourself and let all the rest go hang. **1937** J. BETJEMAN *Coll. Poems* (1958) 41 Other cars all go hang My little bus is enough for us. **1960** M. SHARP *Something Light* xix. 174 Louisa instantly resolved to let the room go hang. **1973** *Physics Bull.* June 345/3 It would even be proper for SRC to decide to support (say) only 20 postgraduate schools of chemistry and to let the rest go hang.

b. To be in desperate difficulties. *slang.*

1874 HOTTEN *Slang Dict.* 187 *Hanging*, in difficulties. A man who is in great straits, and who is, therefore, prepared to do anything desperate to retrieve his fortunes, is said, among sporting men, to be 'a man hanging', i.e. a man to whom any change must be for the better. **1889** BARRÈRE & LELAND *Dict. Slang* I. 446/2 *To hang* (popular and sporting), to be in a desperate state.

d. Of a horse: to veer towards one side.

1951 E. RICKMAN *Come racing with Me* ii. 16 Sarda II 'hanging' towards Native Heath..who won by a short head. **1958** J. HISLOP *From Start to Finish* xi. 128 Courses such as Epsom and Lewes, where the ground slopes towards the rails and horses tend to hang that way. **1965** *Observer* (Colour Suppl.) 30 May 34 If he starts to hang before he tires a jockey can generally straighten him up.

11. c. *Iron-founding.* = SCAFFOLD *v.* 5.

1878 *Jrnl. Iron & Steel Inst.* XII. 202 When a furnace 'hangs' on one side, a more common occurrence with small old furnaces than with large modern ones, a system prevailed in some works of putting half a pig of lead in above the part that was fast. **1908** R. FORSYTHE *Blast Furnace* 242 When the stock becomes wedged so tightly that it can no longer descend, the furnace is said to 'hang'.

17. c. Of a jury: to fail to agree. (Cf. *6 b and *HUNG *ppl. a.* 3.) *U.S.*

1859 BARTLETT *Dict. Amer.*, *To hang*, to stick fast, come to a stand still; as, the jury hung, and 'the man got a new trial'. **1929** *Randolph Enterprise* (W.Va.) 24 Oct. 5/1 The jury hung up on the case and were discharged.

19. b. To slacken motion perceptibly; *spec.* in *Cricket* (see quots.) and *Baseball.* Occas. *trans.*

1838 *Bell's Life* 8 July 4/4 The dead state of the ground, which prevented the balls from working, and caused them to hang considerably. **1897** K. S. RANJITSINHJI *Jubilee Bk. Cricket* 77 The ball is made to hug the ground when it pitches, and to rise slowly afterwards, or 'hang', as it is called by cricketers... With some bowlers it either 'hangs' or more often comes fast off the pitch owing to something in their regular action. **1897** *Encycl. Sport* I. 246/1 A ball 'hangs' which rises unexpectedly slowly from the pitch. **1906** JEPHSON in H. G. Hutchinson *Cricket* 103 He ran up and delivered the ball, to all appearances, exactly similarly each time; but one found now that the ball was hanging in the air, now that it was on to one surprisingly soon. **1928** *Funk's Stand. Dict.* I. 1112/1 *Hang* (Sport), to slacken speed perceptibly and unexpectedly: said of a ball in flight in various games, and of a boat between strokes, in rowing. **1967** *Boston Globe* 5 Apr. 51/6 'It was a bad pitch,' Bennett admitted. 'I was trying to pitch low and instead I hung a high curve ball for him to hit.'

c. *to hang to* (see quot.).

1888 *Lockwood's Dict. Mech. Engin.* 172 *Hang to*, a term having several applications. A file hangs to its work when it cuts without slip. A saw hangs to, when it feels as though being drawn into the timber. A pattern hangs to the sand when it delivers with difficulty.

20. (Earlier and additional examples.) Also, esp. *U.S.*, *to hang around* (a person, place, etc.). So *hang-arounder*.

1830 *Corrector* (Sag Harbor, N.Y.) 26 June 1/3 What a number of young gentlemen you have in this city—hanging round the corners—standing in hotel doors. **1847** J. S. ROBB *Streaks of Squatter Life* 133 Every time I come up from Lusiane, I found Jess hangin' round that gal. **1885** 'C. E. CRADDOCK' *Prophet Gt. Smoky Mts.* 8, I hev seen that critter, that thar preacher, a-hangin' round you-uns house a powerful deal lately. **1897** S. T. CLOVER *Paul Travers' Adv.* 51, I guess I can fix you out if you hang around here, but keep shady. **1915** N. L. MCCLUNG *In Times like These* vi. 72 Although the polls are only open every three or four years, if women once get into the way of going to them, they will hang around there all the rest of the time. **1938** O. NASH *I'm Stranger Here Myself* 234 The hang-arounders' cheerful chirrups. **1939** I. BAIRD *Waste Heritage* xi. 136 He hung around the window then he stopped in the doorway and tried the door in case there was anyone inside the store could say whether Eddy had been hanging around. **1950** A. LOMAX *Mr. Jelly Roll* 57 Buddy Bolden, the most powerful trumpet player I've ever heard..and the absolute favourite of all the hangarounders in the Garden District. **1970** G. F. NEWMAN *Sir, You Bastard* viii. 244 He didn't hang around afterwards. **1973** *Melody Maker* 25 Aug. 27 In a front room in Shepherds Bush, however, plots are being hatched—and hang about, because I'm not going to bore you with yet another..yarn.

25. hang on. a. (Later examples.)

1899 G. B. SHAW *Let.* 20 Apr. (1931) 260 She is always hanging on by her eyebrows, whereas the German is comfortably seated in a solid, permanent, broadbottomed engagement. **1931** *Times Lit. Suppl.* 12 Mar. 193/1 Lacking roots in the soil of any particular country, Whistler had always to 'hang on by his eyebrows'. **1935** *Yachting* Dec. 82/3 *Hanging on by the eyelids*, the seaman's vivid description of his situation during a very heavy gale. **1958** *Listener* 21 Aug. 259/2 Each aircraft hangs on to the tail of the one directly in front.

c. To wait. Freq. in *imp.*, be patient, be reasonable!

1939 J. B. PRIESTLEY *Let People Sing* x. 262 I'd better hang on and have a word with her. **1941** BAKER *Dict. Austral. Slang* 34 *Hang on!*, be reasonable! Not so fast. **1971** *Woman's Own* 27 Mar. 26/1 Hang on a minute...I'm coming with you.

d. Used in a telephone conversation in the sense of 'hold the line'.

1936 R. LEHMANN *Weather in Streets* I. iv. 70 Hang on a moment...Mummy wants to speak to you. **1960** *Daily Tel.* 15 Aug. 17/5 Switchboard operators have been trained not to keep any caller 'hanging on'. **1969** S. HYLAND *Top Bloody Secret* i. 37 'Shall I tell him you're coming?' 'Yes please. Tell him to hang on.'

e. *to hang on to* (something): to retain.

1871 TROLLOPE *Eustace Diamonds* (1873) I. xvi. 220 It was manifest enough that she meant 'to hang on to them' [*sc.* the diamonds]. **1936** 'M. INNES' *Death at President's Lodging* ix. 166 He had in his possession certain valuable documents... Umpleby simply hung on to them. **1971** 'D. HALLIDAY' *Dolly & Doctor Bird* ii. 16 The hotel wouldn't let her hang on to her room.

f. *to hang one on*: to deal (someone) a blow.

1908 K. MCGAFFEY *Sorrows of Show-Girl* 200 Hauling off wifey hangs one on Alla's map. **1960** B. CRUMP *Good Keen Man* 44 I'd thought for a moment he was going to hang one on me. The idea..had got his goat all right. **1966** *Punch* 19 Jan. 69/1 There are moments when most of us have felt the keenest desire to hang one on the boss's chin and walk out.

g. Used in various technical senses (see quots.).

1963 *Amer. Speech* XXXVIII. 118 *Hang on*, to maintain a proper position for the receiver while it is coupled to the tanker's air refueling boom. 'Dingbat 27, can you hang on if I start a slow turn to the left?' **1967** *Gloss. Mining Terms* (*B.S.I.*) x. 7 *Clip on* or *hang on*, to attach a tub or tubs to a haulage rope by a clip or shackle.

26. b. Also, *to hang out to dry*: to suspend (wet washing) on a clothes-line in the open so that it can dry. Hence *transf.* in *Cricket*: *hang one's bat out to dry* (see quots.).

1893 [in Dict., in def. of *clothes-line*]. **1895** C. B. FRY in

Badminton Mag. Aug. 132 He [*sc.* the young player on hard wickets] gets into the habit of moving his right leg, leaving his bat hanging out to dry, and playing crooked. **1925** *Country Life* 25 July 142/1 In playing forward.. never 'hang your bat out to dry' by not advancing your left foot to the pitch of the ball; if you do, you have neither power nor control.

c. hang out. (Later examples.) Also, of a job: to be available, to be found.

c **1926** 'Mixer' *Transport Workers' Song Book* 69 When there is a job hanging out. **1931** T. Lyell *Slang* 364, I hear you've got a job in Foster's factory. Where does it actually hang out? **1931** D. Runyon *Guys & Dolls* (1932) ii. 35 He cannot have a whole lot of sense, or he will not be hanging out with Handsome Jack. **1935** *Forres, Elgin & Nairn Gaz.* 6 Nov. 4/5 (*heading*) Later American word-imports... Phrases are very numerous:—Where do you hang out? **1936** Wodehouse *Laughing Gas* ii. 23 The head of the family has always hung out at the castle.

d. Also without *it*: to endure, hold out. Chiefly *Austral.* and *N.Z.*

1939 J. Dell *Nobody ordered Wolves* ii. 14 B. and P. offered her twelve thousand..but I told her to hang out and sure enough Bill sold her to M.B.G. for fourteen thousand flat. **1941** Baker *Dict. Austral. Slang* 34 *Hang out*, to endure: to delay (a matter). **1944** J. Fullarton *Troop Target* xi. 87 I've been pretty crook for the last hour. But I wanted to hang out till we saw a house. **1946** K. Tennant *Lost Haven* ix. 132 The old punt had broken down at last. He had been hoping against hope that it would hang out until the war ended, but the luck was against him.

e. Slang phr. *to let it all hang out*: to be uninhibited or relaxed; to be candidly truthful. orig. *U.S.*

1970 C. Major *Dict. Afro-Amer. Slang* 76 *Let it all hang out*, to be uninhibited, free. **1972** *National Observer* (N.Y.) 27 May 17/3 Give it expression, they say, 'Let it all hang out.' If it 'all hangs out', it is bound to do some good. **1972** *Village Voice* (N.Y.) 1 June 51/1 No names, of course, will be used; he doesn't expect everyone will be as willing as he is to let it all hang out.

28. hang up. a. Also *absol.* = to hang up the receiver of a telephone at the end of a conversation; *to hang up on*: to break off telephonic communication with.

1911 A. B. Smith *Mod. Amer. Teleph.* xxvi. 759 When the subscribers are through talking, they hang up their receivers. **1928** E. Wallace *Double* viii, 'Oh, Mr. Staines! ..What a dull life yours must be!' And then she hung up on him, and left him feeling like a spanked child. **1928** F. N. Hart *Bellamy Trial* iii. 101 He'd hung up, I guess. Anyway he didn't answer. **1952** A. Baron *With Hope, Farewell* 103 He managed to say, 'Thank you,' and was about to hang up. **1960** *Daily Tel.* 15 Aug. 17/5 Several directors and secretaries of firms told me that they hung up within a minute if they could not get through. **1968** 'P. Barrington' *Accessory to Murder* vii. 125 Mrs. Lindley heard the click of the receiver and became indignant. He'd almost hung up on her.

b. *to hang up one's boots*, to give up playing a game; *to hang up the spoon*, to die; *to hang up one's hat* (further examples in various senses); *to hang up a record*, to set up a record.

1925 O. Jespersen *Mankind, Nation & Individ.* ix. 166 There are countless variants [for 'to die']..take an earth bath, hang up the spoon, snuff the candle, snuff it. **1930** *Publishers' Weekly* 15 Mar. 1508/2 A record sale was hung up..on Tuesday... Four hundred and ten copies of the book were sold in one hour. **1938** D. Runyon *Take it Easy* xv. 283 Professor D. says he has no doubt that under the old rule Nicely-Nicely will hang up a record that will endure through the ages. **1942** Berrey & Van den Bark *Amer. Thes. Slang* 44 *Reside*, hang up one's hat. *Ibid.* 132 *Die*, hang up one's hat. *Ibid.* 242 *Hang up one's hat*,..to be perfectly at ease, make oneself at home. **1949** F. Sargeson *I saw in my Dream* II. xiii. 113 Some said that..he'd have had more self-respect if he'd told the girl to go and hang her hat up somewhere else. **1963** *Times* 23 Jan. 3/4 Johnson, Miller, and Johnston hung up their boots soon afterwards and two years later Benaud began to build the side.

d. Also *to hang it up*, to chalk it up, to give credit. *slang.*

1841 *Swell's Night Guide* Gloss., *Hang it Up*, to go on Credit. **1874** 'Mark Twain' & Warner *Gilded Age* I. xiii. 172 The Colonel muttered something to the barkeeper about 'hanging it up'. **1942** S. H. Adams *Tambay Gold* xiv. 191 They hung me up for the parking fee.

e. (Earlier and later examples.)

1858 W. Kelly *Life in Victoria* (1860) 49 In Melbourne there are posts sunk in the ground almost opposite every door... Fastening your horse to one of these posts is called 'hanging him up'. **1966** 'J. Hackston' *Father clears Out* 118 On the Saturday many good hacks were hung up at the hotel.

f. Also, to suspend movement or action; to stop or stay.

1845 *Greenfield Fish. Rec., Chowan, N.C.* 6 May in N. E. Eliason *Tarheel Talk* (1956) 276 Made 2 hauls & hung up [for the fishing season]. **1854** *Congress. Globe* App. 108 (Th.), In reading the President's message,..he got befogged, and, in the language of the Kentucky boatman, 'hung up for the night'. **1874** E. Eggleston *Circuit Rider* xvi, You mou't get a place 'bout a mile furder on whar you could hang up for the night. **1895** *Dialect Notes* I. 372 A mower, when rain was coming on: 'I reckon we'll have to hang up for all day.'

g. *Cab-drivers' slang.* (See quots.)

1930 'A. Armstrong' *Taxi* xii. 164 'Hanging it up' is loitering past a theatre to snatch a fare away from the recognized rank. **1939** H. Hodge *Cab, Sir?* i. v. 50 Policemen in these outer districts are more easy-going than in the West End. So I chance 'hanging it up' as we call it, near the door, keeping my engine running in case the policeman looks too nasty.

hang, *sb.* Add: **1. b.** Also in *Cricket* (see *Hang *v.* 19 b).

1888 R. H. Lyttelton in Steel & Lyttelton *Cricket* ii. 48 Any break, hang, or rise that the bowler or the ground may impart to the ball must almost inevitably produce a bad stroke. **1897** K. S. Ranjitsinhji *Jubilee Bk. Cricket* 78 The ideal bowler..should do his best to acquire a command of off-break and leg-break, 'top' and 'hang'. **1901** [see *Bump *sb.*[1] 1 c].

2. a. Of a painting or work of art.

1959 *Listener* 5 Mar. 422/3 The Secretary of the Society, with no previous experience of the compromise necessary in rooms so unsuited to the display of very modern painting, has achieved a remarkably successful hang. **1964** *Guardian* 21 Apr. 9/1 At the great Tate Gallery exhibitions ..the brilliance of the hang has invariably been cancelled out by the failure of..the lighting engineers.

3. For *U.S. colloq.* read orig. *U.S. colloq.* and add further examples.

1890 *Daily Chron.* 4 Apr. 7/2 He gets what some call 'the hang' of the place. **1895** R. Kipling in *Century Mag.* Dec. 271/1 I'm getting the hang of the geography of that place. **1918** *War Illustr.* 13 July 372/3 On the second day I had a 'flip' round the aerodrome to get the 'hang' of the country. **1931** H. G. Wells *Work, Wealth & Happiness of Mankind* (1932) 1 Never before has there been this need and desire to 'get the hang' of the world as one whole. **1957** *Listener* 17 Oct. 606/1 Children..in their desire to get the hang of their surroundings.

6. (*a*) *hang of a*: an Australian and N.Z. intensive phrase, variously spelt (*hangava*, *hanguva*, etc., and in altered forms, e.g. *hangashun*), used informally, sometimes with adverbial force, of something big, bad, vexatious, etc., of its kind. Also *like hang*, like hell. Cf. *Hellishing, hellishun.

1941 Baker *N.Z. Slang* vi. 51 Expressions..in constant use by our youngsters..hangava, hangashun. **1943** J. A. W. Bennett in *Amer. Speech* XVIII. 90 The intensives hanguva, hangershun. **1945** F. Sargeson *When Wind Blows* ii. 14 They got down in a hang of a hurry. *Ibid.* iii. 16 All this was because Charlie was hang of a funny to be with. **1949** *Landfall* III. 145 Gosh, Dad's hangava crabby with you! **1950** B. Sutton-Smith *Our Street* ii. 33 It's a hang of a wet day. **1960** N. Hilliard *Maori Girl* 64 It hurts like hang.

hang-. Add: **hang-five, -ten** *Surfing* = *hanging five, ten* (*Hanging *ppl. a.* 6); so *to hang five, ten*; **hang-glider,** a suspension glider, controlled and stabilized by deliberate movements of the operator's body, which is suspended upright in the framework of the machine; hence *hang-gliding*; **hang-out** (further examples); **hang-up** *slang*, drawback, fault; difficulty, fixation, 'thing'; also *attrib.*

1962 D. Muirhead *Surfing in Hawaii* viii. 80 (*caption*) Film-maker Walt Phillips hangs five at Halewia, Hawaii. **1969** *Observer* 3 Aug. 35/1 He may 'nose ride', balancing on the very front of the board to achieve a 'hang five' or 'hang ten', with five or ten toes over the tip of the board. **1930** V. W. Pagé *Henley's ABC of Gliding & Sailflying* (1931) 202 On 'hang' gliders the lateral and longitudinal stability and the angle of attack are controlled by shifting the weight of the pilot. **1969** K. Munson *Pioneer Aircraft 1903–14* 125/2 The unpowered D.1 was launched from a 4-wheel trolley chassis for its first take-off in 1907 with Colonel Capper aboard. However, when it was damaged in a crash-landing further tests were abandoned in favour of the D.3 'hang-glider'. **1972** *Daily Tel.* 7 June 13/8 Considerable interest is being revived in hang gliders and at least four groups are now working on prototype flying wings... They rely on the pilot's leg-work to become airborne and span and performance is limited by the power of the human shoulder. **1973** *Daily Colonist* (Victoria, B.C.) 21 Aug. 16/3 She was flying a Black Hawk hang glider made of black plastic sheeting stretched on aircraft tubing and cable. It has a 38-foot wingspan and a 15-foot keel. **1972** *Daily Tel.* (Colour Suppl.) 13 Oct. 10/3 In America the sport of 'hang gliding'..is becoming extremely popular. **1973** *Daily Colonist* (Victoria, B.C.) 6 July 15/1 Hang gliding is the closest you can get to flying free. **1895** *Century Mag.* Oct. 943/1 In the afternoon some thirteen boys appeared at the 'hang-out'. **1896** *Atlantic Monthly* Jan. 67/2 His wanderings ended..oftener in some distracting vagabond's 'hang-out' in a neighboring city. *a* **1911** D. G. Phillips *Susan Lenox* (1917) II. x. 248 She avoided the tough places, the hang-outs of the gangs. **1951** R. Campbell *Light on Dark Horse* 244 But I had still another hang-out. That was the Harlequin Restaurant. **1957** *New Yorker* 5 Oct. 66/3 The most energetic dancer of her day, gyrating nightly at the Stork Club and other hangouts of the quality. **1960** *Guardian* 9 Nov. 8/6 Basement hangouts which have a vogue and then disappear. **1968** *Globe & Mail Mag.* (Toronto) 13 Jan. 7/3 It is 3 a.m. in a steam bath known as an after-midnight homosexual hangout. **1963** *Pix* 28 Sept. 62/2 *Hang ten*, ten toes over the nose of the board. **1967** *New Yorker* 25 Feb. 18/1 *The endless Summer*—A hang-ten documentary about surfing in various parts of the world. **1959** *Daily Colonist* (Victoria, B.C.) 16 Apr. 2/6 Man—Omnibus salutation extended to men, women, domestic animals—saves cool cat hangup of remembering names. **1967** A. Diment *Dolly Dolly Spy* ii. 27 Hash..is non-narcotic but whether..it leads you on to the hang up drugs I don't know. **1967** *Melody Maker* 27 May 10/6 All these hang-ups are eliminated by the truth—this is a great record. *Ibid.* 29 July 10/5 There are all sorts of hang-up noises going on in the background. **1967** *Ottawa Jrnl.* 31 May 39/2 Your husband's hang-up dates back to childhood and you must treat it as an illness, which it is most assuredly. **1967** *Crescendo* Dec. 27/4 He was always very kind and patient with me, as he was..with all people. A great degree of sensitivity to people's hang-ups, you know—he'd never put you on a spot. **1968** *Melody Maker* 22 June 2 The group didn't want the hang up of worrying about recording specific singles. **1968** *Observer* 22 Dec. 21/1 People have this hang-up about art. A woman will worry for days about spending money on a painting: is it a good investment, can she trust her own judgment? The same woman will spend $150 on a dress..without giving it a thought. **1973** *Black World* Apr. 17/1 Depressing piece about pushers, junkies, whores and their hang-ups.

hangar. Add, with pronunciation (hæ·ŋəɹ): **b.** A shed for the accommodation of aircraft or spacecraft.

1902 *Daily Chron.* 31 Oct. 5/3 Mr. Santos Dumont.. will construct a hangar in the Bois de Boulogne. **1935** H. G. Wells *Things to Come* ix. 48 Inside an aeroplane hangar. **1962** A. Shepard in *Into Orbit* 97, I tried to avoid moving into Hangar S—our quarters at the Cape—for as long as I could. **1962** V. Grissom *Ibid.* 119 On 1 July the capsule was taken from the hangar to the launching pad to be mated to the Redstone.

hangarage (hæ·ŋərėdʒ). [Blend of *hangar* and *garage*.] Accommodation for aircraft in a hangar.

1932 *Flight* 10 Nov. 1044/1 When I thought I was almost beaten, I suddenly won, and hangarage was granted. **1961** R. Higham *Brit. Rigid Airship* vii. 121 This caused a tremendous demand for hangarage and other means of storing gear under cover. **1970** M. Kelly *Spinifex* iii. 54 Hangarage for twenty planes. Full servicing workshops.

hangashun, hangava, etc.: see *Hang *sb.* 6.

hangbird. (Earlier examples.)

1789 J. Morse *Amer. Geogr.* 59 Upwards of one hundred and thirty American Birds have been enumerated.. [including the] Hangbird, Heron, Little white Heron. **1794** S. Williams *Hist. Vermont* 118 Hangbird, *Oriolus icterus*. **1824** Z. Thompson *Gazetteer Vermont* 18 The singing birds are the robin, thrush,.. springbird, goldfinch and hangbird. **1831** J. Q. Adams *Mem.* (1867) VIII. 426 The oriole of Baltimore is the fiery hang-bird.

hang-down (hæ·ŋ,daun), *sb.* and *a.* [f. phrase *to hang down* (see Hang *v.* 8).] **A.** *sb.* That which hangs down, *spec.* in certain technical uses. **B.** *adj.* That hangs down.

1888 *Lockwood's Dict. Mech. Engin.* 172 *Hang down*, or *hanger*, a bearing suspended from a roof or beam for the journal of a shaft. **1904** Goodchild & Tweney *Technol. & Sci. Dict.* 279/2 *Hang down* (Eng.), a frame for suspending a bearing from a roof or beam.—(Foundry), the sling which supports heavy weights in the foundry; the upper ends of the rods of the sling are attached to the travelling crane. **1906** Kipling *Actions & Reactions* (1909) 212 As Guiseppe [*sic*] unshipped the working mechanism of the organ (it developed a hang-down leg) from its wheels. **1967** *Punch* 31 May 804/2 Vintage varieties of [cider] apples (with names such as Dabinett, Woodbine, Slack-Ma-Girdle, Hangdown, Sheep's Nose) can be used for no other purpose.

hanger[2]. Add: **2. g.** (See quot. 1905.)

1905 Calkins & Holden *Art Mod. Advertising* 352 Hangers are printed or lithographed cards of various shapes and sizes, to be hung up in a store. **1927** in *John Edwards Mem. Foundation Q.* (1969) V. iv. 144 Inclosed find a folder... Also we have a large hanger and dealers order blank.

4. e. A coat- or dress-hanger.

1873 *Young Englishwoman* Feb. 91/1 The two different kinds of hangers..will be found very advantageous for hanging up heavy articles of dress, as winter cloaks, etc. **1908** *Daily Chron.* 26 Feb. 8/5 Every coat and every skirt should have a hanger to itself. **1934** L. A. G. Strong *Corporal Tune* II. iv. 151 It does clothes no good to stay all folded up. The sooner they're out and on hangers the better. **1955** M. Allingham *Beckoning Lady* iii. 38 She was carrying a newly pressed dress on a hanger. **1970** *New Yorker* 28 Feb. 34/3 There are no hangers for suits which have always had hangers.

6. *Comb.* **hanger-back,** one who hangs back (see Hang *v.* 22); **hanger-board** (see quot. 1893).

1923 *Q. Register* May 583 He never..played the calculating hanger-back. **1962** *Times* 10 Aug. 9/4 Young novelists..must realize..that, however many people will unwisely refrain from reading their daring first novels, their own mothers, and even their own grandmothers, will not be among the hangers-back. **18..** *Electr. Rev.* (U.S.) XII. 8 (Cent. Dict.), Electrical connection between the conducting-wires and lamps must be made through a suitable hanger-board. **1893** T. O'C. Sloane *Stand. Electr. Dict.*, *Hanger board*, a board containing two terminals, a suspending hook, and a switch, so that an arc lamp can be introduced into a circuit thereby, or can be removed as desired.

hang-fire (hæ·ŋ,fəiəɹ). [f. phrase *to hang fire* (see Hang *v.* 6).] A delay in the explosion of the charge of a gun or of a blasting charge. Also *transf.*

1892 W. W. Greener *Breech-Loader* 170 Nothing is more tantalising to the sportsman than miss-fires; hang-fires, too, are a great nuisance. **1899** *Kynoch Jrnl.* Oct.–Nov. 6/2 Hang fires, soft shots, high pressures, and other defects. **1936** L. B. Lyon *Bright Feather Fading* 40 Dove's hang-fire height A long way fails. **1955** *Times* 16 May 12/5 There is..no hang-fire in a story which..lacks the long dramatic suspense of the year before.

hangi (hæ·ŋi). *N.Z.* [Maori.] A Maori earth-oven in which food is placed on heated stones.

1861 *Richmond-Atkinson Papers* I. 697 They had made a 'hangi' just before the front windows. **1882** W. D. HAY *Brighter Britain* II. iii. 153 Fish and meat were frequently roasted on the clear side of the fire..but the great national culinary institution was the earth-oven, the kopa or hangi. **1905** W. SATCHELL *Toll of Bush* xxx. 343 At least the recipients of the hangi should partake of his hospitality. **1905** W. BAUCKE *Where White Man Treads* 16 For in their season he [*sc.* the Maori] could supplement his dry fare.. with the tender bulbous shoots of the tii (cabbage tree), at heart white and delicate, baked in a haangi. **1959** *Weekly News* (Auckland) 30 Dec. 42 Recently, 3404 guests sat down in relays to the wedding breakfast, cooked Maori style, in a hangi—a stone-lined pit—and served in woven flax. **1963** B. PEARSON *Coal Flat* xxii. 372 Yesterday..we had the *hangi* ready.

hanging, *vbl. sb.* Add: **5. b.** *Iron-founding.* = SCAFFOLDING *vbl. sb.* 2 a.

1878 *Jrnl. Iron & Steel Inst.* XII. 202 The modern system of putting the material round the in-wall and allowing it to roll to the centre, has diminished the heat at the in-wall of the furnace and greatly reduced the hanging and scaffolding. **1948** G. R. BASHFORTH *Manuf. Iron & Steel* I. x. 165 Hanging, which is sometimes referred to as wedging, is similar to scaffolding, but is due to carbon deposition.

8. *hanging day* (examples).

1795 tr. *Moritz's Travels* 60 Last Tuesday was (what is here called) hanging day... I only heard tolling at a distance the death-bell of the sacrifice to justice. **1806** *Balance* (Hudson, N.Y.) 11 Nov. 355 (Th.), Next Friday [the newspaper] promises to make its debut. Friday—that's hanging day—but no matter. **1857** D. G. ROSSETTI *Let.* June (1965) I. 325 *Friday* is the hanging day.

hanging, *ppl. a.* Add: **2. b.** *hanging gardens* (later examples).

1815 J. FERNIE *Hist. Dunfermline* 16 On the sides or slopes of the mound, and at the back of the houses are hanging gardens. **1931** H. CRANE *Let.* 21 Sept. (1965) 381 Dense tropical foliage and veritable hanging gardens. **1971** R. RUSSELL tr. *Ahmad's Shore & Wave* i. 13 He had conjured up a picture of the hanging gardens of Malabar Hill in Bombay, overlooking the sea.

5. *hanging judge* (later examples). Also *transf.*

1929 J. B. PRIESTLEY *Good Companions* II. iv. 339 Your Bruddersfordian is a hanging judge of anything that costs money. **1937** 'G. ORWELL' *Road to Wigan Pier* ix. 178 The worst criminal..is morally superior to a hanging judge. **1963** *Times* 9 Mar. 9/6 He became an advocate of reform and a hanging judge of the powers that be in politics, commerce and agriculture. **1972** M. GEE *In my Father's Den* 121 Price..is a combination public relations man and hanging judge.

6. hanging-block (see quot. *a* 1884); **hanging-bowl** *Archæol.*, name given to certain Celtic or Saxon bowls that were suspended from the roof; **hanging bridge,** a suspension-bridge; see also quot. *a* 1877; **hanging-compass** (see quot. *a* 1865); **hanging drop** *Biol.*, a drop of liquid suspended from a cover glass fitting on to a special transparent cell or microscope slide, by means of which living microorganisms or cells in the drop may be examined microscopically; usu. *attrib.*; **hanging five, ten** *Surfing*, used, freq. *attrib.*, with reference to the placing of all the toes of one foot (or of both feet) over the front edge of a surfboard; **hanging glacier** (see quot. 1940); **hanging glider** = *hang-glider* (see *HANG-); **hanging inden(ta)tion,** *(a) Printing* (see INDENTATION 3 and INDENTION 2); *(b) Librarianship* (see quot. 1941); **hanging lie** *Golf*, the position of a ball when it rests on ground sloping downwards in the direction of play; **hanging paragraph** = **hanging indent(at)ion*; **hanging pawn** *Chess*, one of two advanced pawns which are side by side with no pawns on the adjacent files that can support them; **hanging shelf,** a suspended shelf; **hanging steps** (see quot. 1904); **hanging ten,** see *hanging five* above; **hanging valley,** a valley which is abruptly cut across by the steep side of a larger valley or a sea-cliff; **hanging wall** (earlier and later examples); **hanging wardrobe,** *(a)* a wardrobe designed to accommodate clothes hanging at full length; *(b)* a row of hooks on which clothes may be hung.

a **1865** SMYTH *Sailor's Word-bk.* (1867) 366 *Hanging-blocks*..are sometimes fitted with a long and short leg, and lash over the eyes of the topmast rigging; when under, they are made fast to a strap. *a* **1884** KNIGHT *Dict. Mech.* Suppl. 436/2 *Hanging block*, a block through which the top-sail tye is rove, then through the tye-block on the yard, and the standing part made fast to the mast head. **1940** *Burlington Mag.* Dec. 180/2 The two bronze hanging-bowls (believed to be lamps) with enamelled escutcheons and mounts. **1956** I. S. MAXWELL in D. L. Linton *Sheffield* 122 The presence of three hanging-bowls from this same area may perhaps indicate that Celtic art survived for a long time in this remote district. **1962** H. R. LOYN *Anglo-Saxon England* i. 14 In the case of.. hanging-bowls, some of the richest work culturally of the whole settlement period may be attributed to Celtic craftsmen. **1815** *Niles' Weekly Register* IX. 92/1 The main post-road..crosses the Brandywine on a hanging bridge. *a* **1877** KNIGHT *Dict. Mech.* II. 1060/2 *Hanging-bridge.* 1. A hollow, vertical partition depending from the bottom of a boiler and serving to deflect the flame... 2. *a.* A suspension bridge. *b.* A truss-frame bridge. *a* **1865** SMYTH *Sailor's Word-bk.* (1867) 366 *Hanging-compass*, a compass so constructed as to hang with its face downwards. **1885** *Jrnl. R. Miscrosc. Soc.* V. 117 The 'hanging drop'..has some great..disadvantages. **1892** *Phil. Trans. R. Soc.* B. CLXXXIII. 130 Cultures in hanging drops, made in sterilised cells under the microscope. *Ibid.* 136, I..prepared a hanging drop culture of this. **1908** *Practitioner* Aug. 264 By observation of hanging-drop preparations from growth in glucose broth. **1970** PASSMORE & ROBSON *Compan. Med. Stud.* II. xviii. 13/1 The presence of flagella is usually inferred by observing..motility in hanging drop preparations of fluid cultures. **1963** *Sunday Mail Mag.* (Brisbane) 5 May 12/5 *Hanging five*, five toes over the nose of the board for maximum speed. **1965** P. L. DIXON *Compl. Bk. Surfing* vi. 78 Riding forward is a term used here to cover all sorts of nose-riding styles like hanging five and ten toes over. **1894** J. W. GREGORY in *Q. Jrnl. Geol. Soc.* L. 515 The 'corrie' or 'hanging glaciers'. **1902** *Encycl. Brit.* XXXI. 23/1 Hanging glaciers (*i.e.*, glaciers perched on steep slopes) often discharge themselves over steep rock-faces, the snout breaking off at intervals. **1940** C. M. RICE *Dict. Geol. Terms* 168/1 *Hanging glacier*, a glacier of small size on so steep a slope that the ice breaks off and falls from its lower end. **1932** J. MANCHOT tr. *Kronfeld's On Gliding & Soaring* 254 'Hanging Glider' is the literal translation of the German 'Hängegleiter'. **1956** *Flight* LXIX. 270/1 This also was a 'hanging' glider. **1927** *Amer. Speech* II. 239/2 The hanging indention is built just the opposite of a paragraph. **1941** *A.L.A. Catalog Rules* (ed. 2) p. xxv, *Hanging indention*, a form of indention in which the first line begins at author indention and succeeding lines at title indention. **1961** T. LANDAU *Encycl. Librarianship* (ed. 2) 161/1 Hanging indentation. **1909** P. A. VAILE *Mod. Golf* pl. 96 The stance and address for a hanging lie. **1959** L. M. HARROD *Librarians' Gloss.* (ed. 2) 140 Hanging..paragraph. **1964** T. L. KINSEY *Audio-Typing & Electric Typewriters* vii. 66 New paragraph to be typed as a hanging paragraph. **1927** *Brit. Chess Mag.* XLVII. 269/2 The fact that Black has completed his development so early with no other disadvantage than being saddled with the 'hanging Pawns' goes to show that the nightmare..is ended. **1943** R. FINE *Ideas Chess Openings* iv. 131 The hanging Pawns need not be feared by White because of his excellent development. **1726** SWIFT *Gulliver* I. II. ii. 179 The Cradle was put into a small Drawer..and the Drawer placed upon a Hanging-shelf for fear of the Rats. **1825** J. NEAL *Bro. Jonathan* I. 188 A hanging shelf..loaded with cheeses; ropes of onions; dried apples, [etc.]. **1881** S. P. MCLEAN *Cape Cod Folks* ii. 31 In one dark recess I came into forcible contact with a hanging-shelf of pies. **1962** *Williamsburg Reproductions Catal.* 12 An approved reproduction of a hanging shelf of English design, about 1760. **1876** *Notes Building Construction* II. 108 Hanging steps are fixed at one end only. **1904** GOODCHILD & TWENEY *Technol. & Sci. Dict.* 279/2 *Hanging steps*, stone steps having one end built into a wall. **1962** *Austral. Women's Weekly* Suppl. 24 Oct. 3/2 *Hanging ten*, a trick method of riding with toes tucked over the front of the surfboard. **1963** *Observer* 13 Oct. 15/4 The critical 'hanging ten' stance, in which the surfer speeds across the wave with his 10 toes actually hanging over the nose of the 10-ft. surfboard. **1900** W. M. DAVIS in *Proc. Boston Soc. Nat. Hist.* XXIX. 288 In the spring of 1899, I sent a brief note..to..Mr. G. K. Gilbert of Washington, telling him that all the lateral valleys seemed to be 'hung up' above the floors of the trunk valleys. His reply was long in coming..and he suggested that such laterals should be called 'hanging valleys'—a term I have since then adopted. He fully agreed that hanging valleys presented unanswerable testimony for strong glacial erosion. **1932** AUDEN *Orators* I. 22 Arguments from the other side of the lake on the formation of hanging valleys. **1938** *Sat. Rev. Lit.* 1 Jan. 17/3 We go..to hear a well-informed ranger explain how a glacier makes a U-shaped valley, leaving hanging valleys to dump waterfalls over the edge. **1952** H. W. TILMAN *Nepal Himalaya* II. xii. 149 In a sort of hanging valley, where the slope eased off.. we began searching for a camp site. **1963** D. W. & E. E. HUMPHRIES tr. *Termier's Erosion & Sedimentation* v. 126 It may have tributaries, but these are often 'hanging valleys' with waterfalls. **1968** R. W. FAIRBRIDGE *Encycl. Geomorphol.* 522 Interesting examples of hanging valleys may also be seen entering fjords, notably in Norway and New Zealand. Hanging valleys also occur sometimes along non-glaciated coasts where the rate of cliff retreat is higher than the adjustment potential of the smaller streams, e.g., in the chalk cliffs in the south of England. They are also to be seen along youthful fault scarps. **1778** W. PRYCE *Mineralogia Cornubiensis* II. i. 79 When the Miners dig down.., then the roof, i.e. the upper, the hanging wall, or incumbent wall of the Lode or Fissure, is.. over their heads. **1901** *Daily Colonist* (Victoria, B.C.) 31 Oct. 6/3 The quartz in the hanging wall here assayed $39.60 and that on the footwall $4.80. **1970** W. SMITH *Gold Mine* iv. 9 Rod pondered the unfortunate choice of mining terminology that had named the roof of an excavation 'the hanging wall'. **1896** *Heal & Son Catal.* 169 The 'Eversfield' Suite..consisting of 2 ft. 9 in. Hanging Wardrobe, [etc.]. **1907** *Yesterday's Shopping* (1969) 278/2 Hanging Wardrobe, in oak, teak and mahogany—6 hooks. **1972** *Country Life* 25 May (Suppl.) 37/1 Full length, Hanging Wardrobe in the Chippendale style. It is 4 feet 3 inches wide, 7 feet 2 inches high and 21 inches deep.

hang-over, hangover (hæ·ŋōu:vəɹ). orig. *U.S.* [HANG *v.* 17.] **1.** A thing or person remaining or left over; a remainder or survival, an after-effect. (Later quots. influenced by sense 2.)

1894 *Outing* (U.S.) XXIV. 67/2 Then there are a few 'hang-overs' who have tried before, and two or three green candidates. **1920** C. SANDBURG *Smoke & Steel* 153 A hangover of summer song. **1922** H. CRANE *Let.* 23 June (1965) 77 Since I have been writing ads a certain amount of hangover work to be done evenings. **1930** L. DENNY *Amer. conquers Brit.* 9 That easily inspired hatred of Germany remained as a hang-over in America long after it had been thrown over by the British. **1939** C. DAY LEWIS *Child of Misfortune* 136 At the beginning of his second University year, he was still suffering a little from the hang-over of public-school education. **1941** *Ann. Reg. 1940* 232 Owing to shortage of labour..as much as any hang-over from the Civil War, the..harvests were all unsatisfactory. **1958** *Economist* 20 Dec. 1054/2 There has been a slight move away from the previous invariable association of every increase in unemployment with a mental picture of lean and hungry men, in hangover from the grim thirties. **1959** *Times Rev. Industry* Dec. 54/3 Only just recovered from the ghastly hangover of that [buying] spree. **1963** *Times Lit. Suppl.* 8 Feb. 87/2 The bitter taste of the humanitarian hangover. **1973** *Daily Tel.* 19 Feb. 6/4 The oversized dormitories..are hang-overs from the old lunatic asylums.

2. The unpleasant after-effects of (esp. alcoholic) dissipation.

1904 'G. WURDZ' *Foolish Dict.*, *Brain*,..usually occupied by the Intellect Bros.,—Thoughts and Ideas—as an Intelligence Office, but sometimes sub-let to Jag, Hang-Over & Co. **1912** W. IRWIN *Red Button* 93 This was the first time in his life that Tommy North had ever admitted a 'hangover'. **1935** D. L. SAYERS *Gaudy Night* viii. 161 'How's Miss Cattermole?' 'Bad hang-over. As you might expect.' **1942** *New Statesman* 11 July 26/1 But the use of myths has a similar effect to the use of alcohol: an inevitable hang-over follows the original elation. **1957** *Listener* 18 July 105/2 Its [*sc.* coffee's] ability to quicken the spirits, and, above all, to remove the vestiges of those severe hang-overs which afflicted our hard-drinking forefathers. **1959** N. MAILER *Advts. for Myself* (1961) 220 It was the only good writing I ever did directly from a drug, even if I paid for it with a hangover beyond measure. **1962** K. ORVIS *Damned & Destroyed* ix. 59 Her eyes were walled in panic, flaming with hangover pain.

3. *Electr.* (See quots.)

1940 *Chambers's Techn. Dict.* 402/1 *Hang-over*, the delay in restoration of speech-operated switches, as in the *Vodas*, to ensure the non-clipping of weak final consonants of words. **1943** *Gloss. Terms Telecommun.* (*B.S.I.*) 12 *Hangover time*, of an echo-suppressor, the interval of time that elapses between the instant when the operating signal ceases to be applied at the input terminals of the echo-suppressor and the instant when the suppression loss is reduced to 6 db. **1961** G. A. BRIGGS *A to Z in Audio* 95 A perfect loudspeaker would cease to vibrate immediately any applied signal is cut off. Failure to do so is mainly due to resonance, and the unwanted output is sometimes referred to by the unpleasant word hangover. Its effect is to colour the reproduction and spoil the transient response. The worst offender is often the cabinet. **1967** W. E. PANNETT *Dict. Radio & Telev.* 125 *Hangover*, lack of 'attack' and extended decay in sound reproduction. It is most apparent with transients and is usually due to a resonance or insufficient damping in the system.

Hence **ha·ng-o:verish** *a.*, somewhat affected by a hang-over.

1936 'P. QUENTIN' *Puzzle for Fools* viii. 62, I felt a bit hang-overish, but that was nothing new.

hangul[1] (hɒ·ŋgŭl). Also **hungal.** [Kashmiri *hăngul.*] A deer, *Cervus cashmiriensis*, related to and perhaps a race of the red deer.

1858 A. L. ADAMS in *Proc. Zool. Soc.* XXVI. 529 *Cervus cashmereensis*..*Barra Singa* and *Hanglu* of the Cashmerees. **1869** A. A. A. KINLOCH *Large Game Shooting* 44 Cashmeerie hangul. **1898** R. LYDEKKER *Deer of all Lands* 83 The Hangul—*Cervus cashmirianus.* **1922** *Blackw. Mag.* Mar. 334/1 The hungal or Kashmir stag, found on the western side of Chamba. **1955** I. T. SANDERSON *Living Mammals of World* 251/1 The real Red Deer... include..the Hangul of Kashmir. **1973** *Times* 20 Feb. (India Suppl.) p. xi/3 The lordly Hangul, the most magnificent of deer, also dwell here.

‖**hangul**[2] (ha·nˌgul). Also **hankul.** [Korean, f. *Han* Korea + *kul* script, alphabet.] The Korean national phonetic alphabet (formerly called *ONMUN).

1951 C. OSGOOD *Koreans & their Culture* xvi. 323 Books were printed in the native alphabet, ŏnmun (or hangŭl), with the innovation of having the characters run horizontally from left to right instead of vertically. **1953** D. PORTWAY *Korea* vii. 122 Sino-Korean words can be transcribed into hangul. **1966** S. MCCUNE *Korea* xiii. 182 One of the benefits of the Korean phonetic writing system, *hangul*..has been that it could be quickly learned by those who speak Korean. **1972** P. M. BARTZ *S. Korea* iv. 39/1 In its modern form, *Hangul* consists of 24 phonetic symbols and is considered one of the most ingenious writing systems ever devised. **1972** *Computers & Humanities* VI. 264 The entries are transcriptions of the Korean syllabary (hangul) used to annotate those Chinese characters.

‖ **haniwa** (ha·niwa). [Jap.] A clay image or cylinder of a type anciently placed outside Japanese sepulchres.

1931 G. B. SANSOM *Japan* I. i. 7 Outside the mounds, but evidently associated with them, are found clay figures (known as *haniwa*). **1960** B. LEACH *Potter in Japan* vi. 136 Haniwa figures from A.D. 600. **1970** *Oxf. Compan. Art* 607/1 'Tomb figures' or *haniwa*, clay cylinders some of which were decorated with human or other figures. **1972** *Mainichi Daily News* (Japan) 7 Nov. 5/5 Shards of cylindrical Haniwa had been found at the site.

hanjee, var. KHANJEE.

1920 *Cornhill Mag.* Oct. 438 The hanjee was taking down his shutters.

hank, *sb.* Add: **2.** (Later examples.)

1880 *Harper's Mag.* Sept. 534/2 The ceilings [were] hung with hanks of blue yarn. **1888** *Century Mag.* XXXVI.

768/2 These little silken 'hanks' were sometimes..prettily colored. **1957** *Vogue Knitting Bk.* L. 70/2 (Advt.), 3, 4 & 2-ply Super Botany Wool. oz. hanks 1/5. **1966** *Which?* Feb. 53/2 Most yarns are sold in balls nowadays; we tested only nine still sold in the hank.

4. c. *Wrestling.* In the Cumberland and Westmorland style, a throw made by putting the left leg between the legs of an opponent, catching his left leg, and leaning or pulling backwards. Also *back-hank.*

1870 W. ARMSTRONG *Wrestliana* 44 Robinson lifted him up like a cat lifting a mouse, when, Plaskett immediately put in the hank. **1888** *Encycl. Brit.* XXIV. 690/2 Each man tries to throw his adversary by using the 'buttock',.. the 'crossbuttock',..or the 'back-hank'. **1898** *Encycl. Sport* II. 547/2 The hank, when manipulated by an expert wrestler, becomes one of the hardest and most dangerous falls of all.

hank, *v.* Add: **1. b.** *Wrestling.* To throw (an opponent) by means of the hank (see *HANK *sb.* 4 c).

1881 *Sportsman's Year-Bk.* 314 The next fall resulted in favour of Pooley, who hanked his adversary. **1894** *Carlisle Patriot* 13 July 7/4 (Cumbld. Gloss. 1899), J— was hanked, S— trying the inside click.

hankul, var. *HANGUL[2].

hanky[1] (hæ·ŋki). Also **handky, hankie.** Nursery and colloquial name for HANDKERCHIEF.

1895 J. DAVIDSON *Earl Lavender* iv. 73 They..sighed, and looked up, and the schoolmaster's wife used her handky. **1902** *Westm. Gaz.* 17 Dec. 8/2 Lovely ladies' hankies in dainty lawn. **1924** E. MARSH tr. *La Fontaine's Fables* 52 Every occurrence was referred to her; Whether one lost a hanky or a lover. **1939** [see *ACCESSORIZE *v.*]. **1953** [see *fly-whisk* s.v. *FLY *sb.*[1] 11]. **1967** N. FREELING *Strike Out* 133 Janine was snuffling in a silly little hanky.

hanky[2]. = HANKY-PANKY. *rare.*

1924 GALSWORTHY *White Monkey* II. iv, On our floor, with Michael outside the door, one would know there couldn't be any hanky.

Hannibal (hæ·nibăl). The name of the famous Carthaginian general, who fought against Rome in the third century B.C. Hence, *allusively*, a great general. (Also, in Shakes., humorously confounded with CANNIBAL.) †*Hannibal eye*, a blind eye.

1585 T. WASHINGTON tr. *Nicholay's Navig.* Ded. ¶ iii b, Were it not that I feare the censure of some politike Hanniball. **1603** SHAKES. *Meas. for M.* II. i. 187 Proue this, thou wicked Hanniball. *a* **1652** R. BROME *New Acad.* III. ii. in *Wks.* (1873) II. 58, I passe For a brisk youth, but for my Hannibal eye here.

Hence **Hannibalian** (hænibē·liăn), **Hannibalic** (-bæ·lik) *adjs.*, of, pertaining to, or characteristic of Hannibal.

1678 J. D. (*title*) The History of Appian..In Two Parts. The First consisting of the Punick..and Hannibalick Wars. **1862** W. P. DICKSON tr. *Mommsen's Hist. Rome* II. III. vi. 189 Thus ended the second Punic, or as the Romans more correctly called it, the Hannibalic, war. **1880** *Encycl. Brit.* XI. 444/2 In the year 202 B.C. the Second Punic, or, more properly, the Hannibalian War was at an end. **1886** H. F. LESTER *Under two Fig Trees* 135 And baby had registered a Hannibalic vow. **1934** A. TOYNBEE *Study Hist.* II. v. 162 The advance of the Roman frontier..was a direct..consequence of the Hannibalic War itself.

Hanover. Add: **2.** Phr. *what the Hanover*, an expression of irritation or impatience. *dial.* or *colloq.*

1902 *Eng. Dial. Dict.* III. 56/2 What the Hanover do I care about it? **1914** D. H. LAWRENCE *Prussian Officer* 223 'What the Hanover's got you?' asked Whiston. 'Nothing. Can't I get up?' **1915** —— *Rainbow* i. 27 He went home..wondering What the Hanover!

Hansen (hæ·nsən). *Med.* The name of G. H. A. *Hansen* (1841–1912), Norwegian physician, used *attrib.* and in the possessive to designate *Mycobacterium leprae*, the causative agent of leprosy, which he discovered, and occas. leprosy itself, as *Hansen('s) bacillus, Hansen's disease.*

1903 *Jrnl. Path. & Bacteriol.* VIII. 260 These bacilli had some resemblance in form to Hansen's bacilli. **1914** *Jrnl. R. Microsc. Soc.* 569 (*heading*) Behaviour of the Hansen bacillus in vitro. **1938** DORLAND *Med. Dict.* (ed. 18) 430/1 *Hansen's disease*, leprosy. **1947** *Amer. Jrnl. Public Health* Mar. 313 (*title*) Education in Hansen's disease. **1955** *Sci. News Let.* 21 May 322/3 Changes in the proteins in the blood of patients with Hansen's disease (leprosy) were reported. **1970** A. W. WOODRUFF *Alimentary & Haematol. Aspects Trop. Dis.* i. 3 Hansen's bacilli will readily be found in the second [disease].

hant, ha'nt. Revived as a variant of HAUNT *sb.* 5.

1933 M. EMMONS in B. A. Botkin *Treas. S. Folklore* (1949) III. ii. 540 One never knows when the most sociable of cats may turn out to be a witch or a 'ha'nt'. **1934** B. A. BOTKIN in W. T. Couch *Culture in South* xxvi. 589 A Bible or a sharp object under the pillow will keep away both 'hants' and witches. **1935** *Scribner's Mag.* XCVII. 121/2 Old Joe's daid an' gone But his hant blows de hawn. **1943** W. C. HENDRICKS *Bundle of Troubles* 98 Then the wife told the hant who her husband is, and the hant began at the start and told it all over agin. **1965** 'MALCOLM X' *Autobiogr.* i. 20 It was spooky, with ghosts and spirituals and 'ha'nts' seeming to be in the very atmosphere when finally we all came out of the church.

‖ **hantu** (hæ·ntu). [Malay.] An evil spirit, a ghost.

1821 J. LEYDEN tr. *Malay Annals* vi. 54 He saw a hantu, or spectre. **1839** T. J. NEWBOLD *Straits of Malacca* II. xii. 191 The Hantu Ribut is the storm fiend that howls in the blast. **1900** W. W. SKEAT *Malay Magic* iv. 101 *Hantu* and *sheitan* are generic terms for evil spirits, the former being the Malay term. *Ibid.* 103 The Hantu Kubor (Grave Demons) are the spirits of the dead, who are believed to prey upon the living. **1927** H. M. TOMLINSON *Gallions Reach* xxx. 239 They tell me this land is full of hantus, things that ought not to be about; souls now stowed safely away in Gehenna. **1959** *Listener* 8 Oct. 579/3 The spirits, or *hantus*, as they were called in Malay, were not always of human beings. **1962** *Times* 30 June 10/6 There was the *hantu* that brings the lightning.

Hanukkah, var. *CHANUKAH, CHANUKKAH.

hanum: see *KHANUM.

Hanuman (hʌnumā·n). Also **hoonoomaun, huniman,** etc. [Hind., Hindi *hanumān* (Skr. *hanumant*, f. *hanumat* large-jawed).] **1.** *Hindu Mythology.* Proper name of a monkey-chief; a semi-divine monkey-like creature, to whom extraordinary powers were attributed in legend.

1814 SOUTHEY in J. W. Robberds *Mem. W. Taylor* (1843) II. 427 For the last ten years..Buonaparte..was the God Hanuman—the monkeys, whom he commanded, did the mischief. **1883** *Trans. Asiatic Soc. Japan* XI. 270 For greater safety Râmachandra..stationed Hanuman, the monkey-god..to guard the palace. **1886** YULE & BURNELL *Hobson-Jobson* s.v. *Lungoor*, The monkey-god Hunimān. **1936** E. G. BOULENGER *Apes & Monkeys* ix. 215 The uncanny revenge taken by priests..upon an Englishman, who..insulted the image of Hanuman in a wayside temple. **1965** P. C. JAY in I. DeVore *Primate Behavior* vii. 197 One kind of monkey, the langur, has also had an important part in the traditions and epics of India and is often referred to in its role as the monkey deity Hanuman.

2. (with small initial) An Indian monkey, *Presbytis entellus*, venerated by Hindus.

1843 E. BLYTH in *Jrnl. Asiatic Soc. Bengal* XII. 174 The Hoonumans are strictly protected. *Ibid.*, I know of one locality where the whole numerous community of Bengal Hoonumans appears to consist of males only. **1867** T. HUTTON in *Proc. Zool. Soc.* 944 The particular species of Monkey to which the name of Hoonoomaun now more especially and properly applies is known to naturalists as the *Semnopithecus entellus.* **1891** J. L. KIPLING *Beast & Man in India* iii. 65 Of late years the tradesmen who form the bulk of the members of our municipalities have felt that there are too many Hanumāns abroad. **1897** *Q. Rev.* Oct. 395 No visitor to Hindostan..can have failed to see the sacred Monkey or Hanuman. **1936** E. G. BOULENGER *Apes & Monkeys* ix. 215 The sacred langur, or hanuman..ranges over India from the Deccan northward to the south bank of the Ganges. In its *rôle* of a sacred animal, dedicated to the god Hanuman, it is unique.

Hanunóo (hānŭnō͞u). [Native name.] A member of a people inhabiting southern Mindoro in the Philippines; also, the language of this people.

1949 *Amer. Anthropologist* LI. 269 The Hanunóo raise their own cotton and indigo, and weave and dye skirts, blankets, and other fabrics with considerable skill. *Ibid.*, While visiting in dingy Hanunóo huts, large piles of bamboo poles, four to six feet long, were found. *Ibid.* 271 The ambāhan 'literary' language is either an archaic form of Hanunóo, or a rarer type known as *binúkid.* **1963** J. LYONS *Structural Semantics* iii. 38 Hanunóo color categories.

haole (hau·li, ha·ōli). *Hawaiian.* [Native word.] One who is not a native Hawaiian; a white man. Also *attrib.* or as *adj.*

[**1825** W. ELLIS *Jrnl. Tour Hawaii* vii. 151 We had escaped, only because we were *haore*, (foreigners.) No Hawaiian..would have done so with impunity.] **1843** J. J. JARVES *Scenes Sandwich Islands* iii. 104 One brings vegetables, another fish..in short, any thing and every thing which they suppose the *haole*, (foreigner,) to want. **1866** 'MARK TWAIN' *Lett. fr. Hawaii* (1967) 161 But the thing was tabu..to foreigners—haoles. *Ibid.* 202 To the natives all whites are haoles—how-ries—that is, strangers, or more properly, foreigners. **1905** *Daily Chron.* 24 June 3/1 Stevenson 'fell in love' with the Polynesians,..and was consequently unjust to the *haoles*, or white people. *c* **1938** L. MUMFORD *Report on Honolulu* in *City Development* (1946) 75 A lasting link between their ancient ways and the less primitive life lived by the various haole groups that have followed. **1954** *Ellery Queen's Myst. Mag.* Oct. 8/2 The *haole*—white—characters are fiction. The Hawaiians..are authentic. **1970** *Language* XLVI. 981 Ever-increasing pressure for the use of English from 'haoles' (main-land whites) and others.

haoma (hō͞u·mă). [Zend.] = HOM.

1890 *Ann. Rep. Smithsonian Inst.* 91 On the position of the Haoma in the Avesta of the Parsees. **1953** *Trans. Philol. Soc.* 22 Old Ind. *durōṣa-*, Avestan *dūraoša-*, the epithet of soma and haoma.

haori (hā·ori). [Jap.] A short loose coat worn in Japan.

1877 *Trans. Asiatic Soc. Japan* V. i. 8 A *haōri*,—the upper mantle worn by the military class. **1880** F. V. DICKINS tr. *Chiushingura* (new ed.) iii. 16 Badge or device on the sleeves and back of the *haori* or mantle. **1896** L. HEARN *Kokoro* vi. 94 Haori, a sort of upper dress, worn by men as well as women. **1897** J. LA FARGE *Artist's Lett. from Japan* 274 Women under their umbrellas wore the graceful short overcoat they call *haori*, and tottered over the wet ground on high wooden pattens. **1907** *Daily Chron.* 15 May 3/5 The little ornament on his haori (the gown) was the family crest. **1922** J. STREET *Mysterious Japan* ii. 19 One or two of them wore the graceful and dignified *hakama* and *haori*—the silk skirt and coat of formal native dress. **1970** J. KIRKUP *Japan behind Fan* 125 There are even some small garments, jackets called *haori*, made from decorated paper. **1972** *National Geographic* CXLI. 692/2 In a quiet way several of the men were equally impressive in somber-hued kimonos complete with *haori*, the elegant outer jacket of dark silk.

‖ **hapax legomenon** (hæ·pæks lĕgǫ·mĕnǫn). Pl. **hapax legomena.** Also simply **hapax.** [Gr. ἅπαξ λεγόμενον (thing) once said.] A word or form of which only one instance is recorded in a literature or an author.

[**1654** J. TRAPP *Minor Prophets* 605 'Tis ἅπαξ λεγόμενον read only here: and hence this variety of interpretations. **1801** W. MAGEE *Atonement & Sacrifice* 336 [The book of Job's] very great antiquity, and uncommon sublimity of elevation, which has occasioned a greater number of ἅπαξ λεγομενα, and expressions difficult to be understood.] **1882** FARRAR *Early Chr.* I. xi. 236 The number of the *hapax legomena* is remarkable, and some of them are full of picturesqueness. **1931** *English Studies* XIII. 124 An article that should certainly find a place in a miscellany in honour of the brave defender of Wulfila as a translator: Collitz on two hapax legomena in Wulfila's translation. **1956** J. WHATMOUGH *Poetic, Scientific & other Forms of Discourse* ii. 37 The *hapax legomenon*, although statistically it hardly differs from a word of very low occurrence.. is nevertheless anomalous, just like the scazon in Greek comedy. **1957** C. BROOKE-ROSE *Langs. Love* iv. 34 She saw herself go through the minutiæ of scansion, dialect forms, emendation, haplography, *hapax legomena* and *anacolutha* in Beowulf. **1962** *Amer. Speech* XXXVII. 54 He..rejects a Middle English *hapax* as a genuine idiom unless he can trace it back to an Old Norse..word.

ha'pence, var. *halfpence* s.v. HALFPENNY.

ha'penny, hapenny, varr. HALFPENNY.

haphazard, *sb.*, *a.*, and *adv.* Add: Hence **hapha·zardry.**

1932 V. WOOLF *Common Reader* 2nd Ser. 63 But with all this haphazardry, the *Letters*..provide their own continuity. **1949** *Scrutiny* Sept. 196 *Antony and Cleopatra* has none of the haphazardries of *Pericles.* **1959** *Times Lit. Suppl.* 7 Aug. 459/1 A tape-recorder..that can reproduce in all their haphazardry the jumbled rhythms of modern conversation.

haphtarah. Add: Also **haftara, haftarot(h), haphtara, hapht(h)orah.** (Further examples.)

1891 M. FRIEDLÄNDER *Jewish Relig.* II. 347 The lesson from the Prophets is called *haphtarah*, 'conclusion'. **1907** I. ZANGWILL *Ghetto Comedies* 141 You shall read the *Haphtorah* (prophetic section) next *Shabbos.* **1932** C. ROTH *Hist. Marranos* xiii. 326 A translation of the Bible.. contained a list of the *Haftarot* (Prophetical lessons). **1973** *Jewish Chron.* 2 Feb. 23/4 During the reading I sat with anticipation awaiting his rendering of the haftara.

haplo-. Add: **ha·plophase** *Biol.*, the phase in the life-cycle of an organism when the nuclei are haploid; **ha·plopore** *Zool.*, an isolated pore on the surface of the theca of certain cystoids (order Diploporita) in which the pores usu. occur in pairs; also, a thecal canal that ends in one of these pores.

1925 E. B. WILSON *Cell* (ed. 3) 1132 *Haplophase*, that phase of the life-history, particularly in the antithetic alternation of generations in plants, in which the nuclei are haploid. **1957** FISCHER & HOLTON *Biol. & Control Smut Fungi* vii. 245 The point at which the haploid nuclei are reunited in conjugate association determines the duration of the haplophase. **1899** *Rep. Brit. Assoc. 1898* 917 The simple or irregular haplopores become connected in pairs (diplopores). **1962** D. NICHOLS *Echinoderms* xi. 138 The diploporite *Aristocystites*..is flask-shaped, with a theca composed of many irregularly arranged plates pierced by haplopores and diplopores.

b. *Genetics.* Used as a prefix to designate the presence of only one of a pair of homologous chromosomes.

1924 T. H. MORGAN in E. V. Cowdray *Gen. Cytol.* xi. 720 The offspring are of two kinds, one kind normal with two chromosome IV's, the other kind with only one IV. These haplo-IV flies also give an interesting result if crossed out to a stock that carries a recessive factor in chromosome IV. **1932** SINNOTT & DUNN *Princ. Genet.* (ed. 2) ix. 185 One whole IV chromosome is missing from the 'Diminished' flies; they have only one of the pair of small chromosomes and are thus known as haplo-IV individuals.

haploid (hæ·ploid), *a.* (and *sb.*). *Biol.* [a. G. *haploid* (E. Strasburger 1905, in *Jahrb. f. wissensch. Bot.* XLII. 62), f. Gr. ἁπλό-ος single: see *-PLOID.] Having a single set of

unpaired chromosomes, as in a gamete or germ-cell; made up of cells the nuclei of which contain such a set of chromosomes. (Distinguished from *DIPLOID, etc.) Also as *sb.*, a haploid individual. Hence **ha·ploidy**, the state or condition of being haploid.

1908 W. H. LANG tr. *Strasburger's Text-Bk. Bot.* (ed. 3) I. i. 165 The organism with the single number of chromosomes may be termed the haploid, or haploid generation, that with the double number the diploid, or diploid generation. **1914** G. N. CALKINS *Biol.* ix. 209 The chromatin of the nucleus collects in a thick fibrous mass on one side of the nucleus (synapsis stage) and from it emerge one-half as many chromosomes as are formed at ordinary vegetative divisions (in modern terminology this is called the haploid number). **1922** *Amer. Naturalist* LVI. 57 There is one striking difference between haploidy for X and haploidy for an autosome. **1925** *Nature* 10 Oct. 537/2 (*heading*) Haploidy in the male sawfly. **1926** T. H. MORGAN *Theory Gene* x. 139 A cell with one set of chromosomes is said to be haploid, and an individual made up of such cells is..called.., by extension, a haploid. **1946** *Nature* 17 Aug. 239/2 Since the basic haploid number of *Artemia salina* is known to be 21, the present race must be considered as decaploid with a slight augmentation of the number of 105 tetrads. **1957** C. P. SWANSON *Cytol. & Cytogenetics* vi. 159 In plants, where haploidy has been more commonly observed as an abnormality than in animals, the haploid individuals can generally be characterized as being smaller than their diploid progenitors. **1968** J. A. SERRA *Mod. Genetics* III. xx. 150 The course of meiosis is expected to be different in haploids derived from diploids than it is in haploids derived from polyploids.

haplont (hæ·plǫnt). *Biol.* [a. G. *haplont*, f. HAPLO- + Gr. ὤν, ὀντ- being: see ONTO-.] A sexual organism that is haploid at all stages of its life cycle other than the zygote, which is diploid; an organism at a stage, or during the stages, in its life cycle at which it is haploid. So **haplo·ntic** *a.*, characteristic of, or having the characteristics of, a haplont.

1920 *Bot. Abstr.* V. 214 (*heading*) Biology and morphology of the male haplonts of some Oenotheras. **1925** E. B. WILSON *Cell* (ed. 3) vi. 492 The spores..receive the haploid number of chromosomes and develop without fertilization into a haploid, gamete-producing 'sexual' generation, known as the haplont (in plants the gametophyte) which intervenes between meiosis and the gamete-formation. **1929** *Hereditas* XIII. 311, I propose the terms haplontic and diplontic sterility. **1938** *Bot. Rev.* IV. 135 It is more probable that the above-described diplohaplontic Ulvaceae and Cladophoraceae arose from a haplontic ancestor than from a primitive ancestral type with alternating unicellular haploid and diploid phases. **1951** M. O. P. IYENGAR in G. M. Smith *Man. Phycol.* iii. 59 *Protosiphon* is another member of the Siphonales which is a haplont and not a diplont like the majority of the Siphonales. **1964** PRIESTLEY & SCOTT *Introd. Bot.* (ed. 4) xxxiii. 499 If this is confirmed the nuclei in the Vaucheria thallus would be haploid and the life-cycle haplontic with the zygote (and zygospore) the only cell representing the diploid stage.

happen, *v.* Add: **1. a.** Said ominously of an accident or some serious thing (*spec.* death) happening to a person, with vague subject, *anything*, *something*.

1795 H. NELSON *Let.* 10 Mar. (1945) II. 18 A glorious death is to be envied; and if anything happens to me, recollect that death is a debt we must all pay. **1811** PRINCESS CHARLOTTE *Let.* 11 Oct. (1949) 9, I am going again on Monday at 1, unless anything should happen between this time & that. **1829** *Blackw. Mag.* June 719/1 In the event of 'any thing happening to his father', as the modern phrase for the termination of man's mortal career runs. **1862** *Cornhill Mag.* (1863) VIII. 574 Doctor says I shall not last long, so I don't think I shall be removed before anything happens. **1884** G. C. DAVIES *Peter Penniless* x, It isn't a night for any man to be left out in if anything has happened to him. **1885** RIDER HAGGARD *K. Solomon's Mines* ii, I will..arrange that in the event of anything happening to us or to you, that your son shall be suitably provided for. **1965** N. DUNN *Talking to Women* 40 Lots of people they plan and they put this away for when they get old and that type of thing and then anything happens and who has it, their kids, don't they?

3. b. Used with varying degrees of intensity to support or imply an assertion, const. *inf.* Also used impersonally, in which case it is sometimes followed by a subordinate clause.

1933 F. BALDWIN *Innocent Bystander* (1935) v. 95 She happens to be my only sister's child and I have an interest in her. **1937** S. LEWIS in *Colophon* Feb. 220 *Main Street*, which is always put down as my first book, happens to have been my seventh. **1956** N. COWARD *South Sea Bubble* II. i, *Ch.* You have got it in for her, haven't you? *C.* Certainly not. I just don't happen to like the way she goes on. **1957** B. & C. EVANS *Dict. Contemp. Amer. Usage* 217/1 We happen to like her. *Ibid.*, It happens we like her. **1973** 'M. INNES' *Appleby's Answer* vii. 74 You don't happen to have any cigarettes?

4. d. Also *happen along, around, back, by, over*. (Earlier and other U.S. examples.)

1749 in G. O. Seilhamer *Hist. Amer. Theatre* (1888) I. 29 Joseph Morris and I happened in at Peacock Bigger's and drank tea there. **1838** J. F. COOPER *Homeward Bound* viii. 112, I only happened in..to make a first call. **1845** C. M. KIRKLAND *Western Clearings* 116 He could hardly have 'happened in' at a more fortunate juncture. **1872** E. EGGLESTON *Hoosier Schoolmaster* xxxiii, Miss Nancy just happened over at Mrs. Thomson's humble home. **1882** A. PERCY *Twice Outlawed* 101 Under-sheriff Knight, of Pepin county, happened along that way. **1893** R. D. WIGGIN *Polly Oliver's Problem* (1894) ii. 20 A swarm of horrid insects might happen along and devour the plants. **1901** W. CHURCHILL *Crisis* III. ii. 366. I happened around at Colonel Carvel's this afternoon. **1930** R. FROST *Coll. Poems* 67, I go nowhere on purpose: I happen by. **1931** D. RUNYON *Guys & Dolls* (1932) 261 There we are away over by the East River in the early morning, with no other taxis in sight, and a cop liable to happen along any minute. **1953** H. MILLER *Plexus* (1963) viii. 228 We were literally without a cent when he happened along. **1970** G. F. NEWMAN *Sir, You Bastard* viii. 246 She had decided she would just happen back. **1970** *New Yorker* 26 Sept. 35/3 She held the paper in place with her left arm..and to any of the girls who happened in before she fell asleep she explained that she was taking forty-winks.

6. *intr.* To be successful; esp. in *it's all happening*, there is much activity or success. *slang.*

1949 A. SHAW *Vocab. Tin-Pan Alley* in *Music Libr. Assoc. Notes* Dec. 44/1 A song happens..when the preparatory work results in a successful bid for popularity. **1962** *Down Beat* 8 Nov. 38 It sounded like they were all striving to create..but it didn't really happen. **1966** *Crescendo* Mar. 2/3 'It's all happening' was one of the more tiresome items in the pseudo-hip phrase books of the recent past. It seldom meant much while it was in fashion, but there has now arisen a situation which it describes exactly. For it really *is* all happening for Stan Tracey this year. **1967** *Ibid.* Feb. 19/1 It's all been happening at the Village Vanguard lately. *Ibid.* Dec. 27/4 We could either go back to New York with a flop show, or try to stay over and make a band happen. **1971** *Melody Maker* 9 Oct. 18/5 The guitar solo didn't happen.

happenchance: see *HAPPENSTANCE.

happening, *vbl. sb.* Add: **2.** Also in *sing.*

1896 S. R. CROCKETT *Grey Man* xxviii, I could not find it in my heart to tell him of the happening. **1896** *Black & White* 27 June 824/2 Before the final coorious happening, there was a fire in a croft of auld Applebird's. **1899** *Daily News* 5 Apr. 2/4 Such a happening would almost certainly have had much more serious results had it been a horsed carriage. **1907** *Westm. Gaz.* 30 Dec. 2/2 The Denshawi incident is not viewed by all exactly alike, but it was decidedly a regrettable happening. **1921** E. E. CUMMINGS *Let.* 22 Apr. (1969) 75 The feria is..a double happening. There were the grounds..and there were the torros.

3. a. An improvised or spontaneous theatrical or pseudo-theatrical entertainment. Also in extended use, any spontaneous or 'vital' display. orig. *U.S.*

1959 *Nation* (N.Y.) 24 Oct. 260/2 The first exhibition is not of painting but is an 'event' consisting of eighteen 'happenings' by Allan Kaprow. **1962** *Listener* 5 Apr. 604/1 It was with their series of 'happenings' that these artists first reached the public. Happenings, usually staged in downtown lofts, were performances, improvised round basic ideas that left a good deal to chance and action on the night. Actors and décor mingled intimately with the audience. **1963** *Guardian* 13 Mar. 8/7 The latest form of 'way out' entertainment in Washington, DC, is a Happening..a goofy party. **1963** *Observer* 15 Sept. 27/6 The last day..gave us our notorious nude, who was towed across the musicians' gallery as part of a rehearsed 'Happening'. **1966** *Ibid.* 17 Apr. 11/4 Here are the long-term..effects of having the television cameras in the House... Politics comes to be regarded as a series of dramatic scenes. A Budget or a Bill is seen..as a happening. **1969** *Listener* 13 Mar. 339/2 The Japanese city is not a design that has been done badly: it's the negation of design, an urban happening with its own special vitality. **1970** *Daily Tel.* 29 Dec. 10 Tomorrow the 1,600 delegates will see a 'happening' called 'Thank God We're Normal' performed by 70 boys and girls from..comprehensive schools in London.

b. *Art.* (See quot. 1962.)

1962 *Listener* 5 Apr. 604/2 The room-sized collages called happenings or situations are works of art that actually simulate the environment. *Ibid.* 605/1 In his happenings, he [*sc.* Dine] used cheap materials and found objects, lifted from the city's waste. **1965** *Times Lit. Suppl.* 25 Nov. 1044/2 Happenings may be seen as the logical extension of the collage principle.

happen-so (hæ·p'n sōᵘ). Chiefly *U.S.* [f. HAPPEN *v.* + SO *adv.*] A chance event.

1904 *Westm. Gaz.* 13 Sept. 1/3 Politics..may or may not be mixed up in it. It is just a happen-so if they are. **1938** M. K. RAWLINGS *Yearling* xxiv. 310 Gittin' that buck was pure happen-so. **1962** M. & G. GORDON *Journey with Stranger* (1963) ix. 62 That Japanese girl—didn't have anything to do with us... It was just a happen so.

happenstance (hæ·p'nstăns). Chiefly *U.S.* [Amalgam of HAPPEN(ING + CIRCUM)STANCE *sb.*] A chance event; a coincidence. Occas. in altered form **happenchance**. Also *attrib.*

1897 *Outing* (U.S.) XXX. 557/1, I guess it was just a 'happenstance'. **1911** *Dialect Notes* III. 544 *Happenchance, happenstance*, happening, circumstance. Used facetiously. Blend-formations. **1937** *John o' London's* 12 Mar. 986/3 The buyer of *Human Psychology*..will be given the opportunity to defile his vocabulary with such terms as 'happenstance'. **1941** *Sat. Even. Post* 22 Mar. 24/3 Even if by happen-chance a hailstorm didn't come along and ruin the crop, there was always something to fight. **1946** M. C. SELF *Horseman's Encycl.* 306 The introduction of polo to England was pure happen-chance. **1960** *Listener* 7 Jan. 17/2 They shrewdly refused to attribute this to happenstance. **1963** D. B. HUGHES *Expendable Man* (1964) v. 149 The abortionist hadn't killed her, he would have no need of the happenstance tool. **1965** *Observer* (Colour Suppl.) 13 Apr. 27/2 Balloon races have a fixed beginning, all right, but their finishing ine is a matter of happenstance. **1966** OGILVY & ANDERSON *Excurs. Number Theory* x. 117 Again the last fraction, which we wish to discard, is ½ (it need not have been—that was just happenstance). **1969** *Sci. Jrnl.* May 9/3 Berry could say little, beyond suggesting that the use of seconal sleeping pills by both Schweickart and Frank Borman, who suffered a vomiting attack on the *Apollo 8* flight, was probably a 'happenstance'. **1973** *Tablet* 17 Feb. 155/2 'Falsifiability' is duly recorded—not long after fall-out', with which some might think positivism has a more than happenchance..connection.

happi-coat (hæ·pikōᵘt). Also **happy-**, (ellipt.) **happi.** [Jap. *happi* a kind of coat.] A Japanese loose outer coat of various materials; a similar fashion garment.

1880 *Trans. Asiatic Soc. Japan* VIII. 344 Young men often wore a red *Happi* with large sleeves. **1890** B. H. CHAMBERLAIN *Things Japanese* 94 But *jinrikisha*-men wear the *happi*. **1931** E. V. GATENBY in *Studies Eng. Lit.* (Tokyo) XI. Oct. 515 *Happi-coat*, often misspelt 'happy' coat. **1933** 'R. CROMPTON' *William—the Rebel* vi. 121 'Go and put on my happi coat, William,' she said. **1948** M. ALLINGHAM *More Work for Undertaker* (1949) vi. 70 She wore a gay little happi-coat. **1970** J. KIRKUP *Japan behind Fan* 127 Here there was a crowd of men in *happi* coats. **1971** *Daily Tel.* 1 Nov. 11/1 They want to trot around in tuxedo trouser outfits, Japanese happi coats, or pedal-pusher pants. **1971** *Catal. Exhib. C. Beaton's Fashion* (V. & A. Mus.) 54/1 A beige suede 'happi coat'..worn with tapering suede trousers.

happify, *v.* Delete (Now unusual.) and substitute (Now *U.S.*).

1875 M. B. EDDY *Science & Health* vi. 315 To happify existence by constant intercourse with those adapted to elevate it is the true motive for marriage. **1905** *Daily Chron.* 13 July 4/4 Her jargon about 'happifying existence' jars upon one after the Scriptural phrase, 'making glad the hearts of men'. **1945** L. SHELLY *Jive Talk Dict.* 12/2 *Happify*, to make happy. **1955** *Watchtower* 15 Mar. 182/2 Keeping these happifying thoughts in mind, we are determined to maintain our integrity faithfully.

happily, *adv.* Add: **4.** *happily ever after*: see *HAPPY *a.* 7 b.

happy, *a.* Add: **2. c.** *happy land*, a prosperous, favourable, etc., land; *spec.*, heaven.

1787 S. STENNETT in J. Rippon *Selection of Hymns* 584, I stand, And cast a wishful Eye, To Canaan's fair and happy Land. **1806** T. G. FESSENDEN *Democracy Unveiled* (ed. 3) I. 85 Such principles, alas, will flood Columbia's 'happy land' with blood. **1845** C. H. BATEMAN *Children's Hymn-Bk.* 36 There is a happy land Far far away. **1893** M. DANVERS *Grantham Myst.* xiii, The old 'un will soon join the young 'un in the happy land. **1902** *Daily Chron.* 6 Feb. 5/2 During the great..strike..a rhyme went round beginning 'There is a happy land, far, far way [*sic*], Where no blacklegs ever go'. **1943** M. KANTOR (*title*) Happy land. **1959** I. & P. OPIE *Lore & Lang. Schoolch.* xvii. 365 There is a happy land by the 'Red School' Where Miss Macdonald stands, preaching like a fool.

3. (Earlier examples of *many happy returns*.) Also in certain familiar or conventional special collocations: *happy day*, wedding day; *happy days!*, a drinking toast; similarly, esp. in aviation circles, *happy landings!*; *happy ending*, an ending in a novel, play, etc., in which the characters acquire spouses, money, do not die, etc.; *happy event*, the birth of a baby; *happy pair*, an engaged or newly wedded couple; *happy release*, (esp.) death.

1697 DRYDEN *Alexander's Feast* I The Lovely Thais by his side, Sate like a blooming Eastern Bride..Happy, happy, happy Pair! **1702** C. SEDLEY (*title*) The happy pair: or, a poem on matrimony. **1739–40** S. RICHARDSON *Pamela* (1740) II. 151 May I hope, my Pamela, said he, that next Thursday shall certainly be the happy Day? **1789** G. PARKER *Life's Painter* xiv. 115 (*title*) The happy pair. **1789** LADY NEWDIGATE *Let.* 2 June in A. E. Newdigate-Newdegate *Cheverels* (1898) vi. 84 Many happy returns of yᵉ day to us my Dʳ Love. **1821** [See RETURN *sb.* 2 b]. **1838** DICKENS *Nickleby* (1839) xiv. 124 Many happy returns of the day, my dear. [**1848** MRS. GASKELL *Mary Barton* I. xi. 205 So anticipating a happy ending to the course of her love, however distant it might be, she fell asleep.] **1850** THACKERAY *Pendennis* II. xxxvii. 357 The ardent Foker pressed onwards the happy day. **1850** DICKENS in *Househ. Words* 19 Oct. 74/1 His wife unfortunately took to drinking..before happy release in every point of view. **1864** —— in *All Year Round* 1 Dec. 7/2 Then I shouldn't have the agonies of trying to understand him which was a happy release. **1884** H. JAMES in *Longman's Mag.* Sept. 506 Another would say that it depends for a 'happy ending' on a distribution at the last of prizes, pensions, husbands, wives, babies, millions, appended paragraphs and cheerful remarks. **1913** G. B. SHAW *Quintessence of Ibsenism* (rev. ed.) 192 The substitution of a sentimental happy ending for the famous last scene. **1929** E. BOWEN *Joining Charles* 122 She was such a good soul—it seemed quite a happy release. **1934** *Evening News* 25 July 4/5 Ronnie swallowed half the whisky... 'Happy landings, Phyllis..dear!'.. The powder left his fingers, missed the glass. **1934** R. S. LAMBERT *For Filmgoers Only* 68 'Happy endings' are in much greater evidence on the screen than, for instance, in the play. **1934** E. WHARTON *Backward Glance* vii. 147 The American public always wants..a tragedy with a happy ending. **1935** G. GREENE *Basement Room* 106 'Your health, my dear. You look younger than ever.' 'Happy days,' Amy said. **1938** —— *Brighton Rock* v. v. 213 'When 's the happy day?' Cubitt said and they all smiled. **1940** PARTRIDGE *Dict. Clichés* 100 *Happy event*, *a* or *the*, the birth of a child; esp. the first in a family: mostly lower-middle class: from ca. 1880. **1946** T. RATTIGAN *Winslow Boy* I. 29 Happy pair, I think, is the phrase

that is eluding you. **1951** J. B. PRIESTLEY *Festival at Farbridge* II. i. 199 'Happy days!' cried Mobbs. 'Cheers!' said the Major gloomily. **1953** P. FRANKAU *Winged Horse* III. ii. 199 The glass lifted. 'Happy Landings,' Carey said. **1957** N. FRYE *Anat. Criticism* 104 Most students of literature prefer to keep in the middle distance..run-of-the-mill Elizabethan sonnets and love lyrics,..nineteenth-century happy-ending novels. **1960** *Times* 9 Jan. 7/7 The further analysis of 'happy events' that occurred in 1959.. reveals 7,070 births. **1966** T. WALSH *Face of Enemy* (1968) 62 Another drink was handed to him... 'Happy days, old boy.' **1969** *Times* 20 Mar. 16/2 Aunt Juju, in her harping upon 'happy events'..knows more about life and death than Hedda.

4. b. Freq. with neg., as *not* (*at all*), *not entirely*, *not quite happy about* (or *with*), usually indicating substantial dissatisfaction. Cf. NOT *adv.* 10 b.

1947 *People* 22 June 7/5 The receiving club were not at all happy about this. **1967** N. FREELING *Strike Out* 21, I dropped a monstrous clanger, letting anybody see I wasn't happy, but..I'm still not happy. **1971** *Guardian* 2 Dec. 11/2 She says, with some delicacy, that the studio, Paramount, was 'not happy with it' and failed to promote it.

c. *happy family*: (*a*) a conventional description of a harmonious family; also *fig.*; (*b*) (see FAMILY *sb.* 2 b); (*c*) *Austral.*, a popular name of the grey-crowned babbler (*Struthidea cinerea*); also called *happy jack*.

1868 F. HARRISON *Let.* 11 Nov. in *Geo. Eliot's Lett.* (1955) IV. 484, I know of no worse instance of the monkey-like criticism of the day, than the way in which the hedge-sparrows of the reviews (forgive this 'happy family' of metaphors) chirrup out their blame or praise. **1901** [see *APOSTLE III]. **1927** T. E. LAWRENCE *Lett.* (1938) 539 The happy family is the squadron or flight, and the misery of discipline..is resident in depots and workshops. **1932** *Week-end Rev.* 30 July 139/2 You just treat 'em like one big, happy family. **1939** *Times Lit. Suppl.* 14 Jan. 27/1 In spite of the title she has given to her book, Miss Stevenson's heroine comes from anything but a happy family. **1945** BAKER *Austral. Lang.* xii. 211 The Grey-crowned Babbler is known ..as the..happy family, happy jack. **1946** VISCT. MONTGOMERY *El Alamein* Foreword, The Eighth Army was a very happy family. **1958** N. W. CAYLEY *What Bird is That?* (ed. 2) 69 Also called Grey Jumper, Happy Family. **1963** *Austral. Encycl.* I. 385/1 Babblers..commonly known as catbirds (or caties), chatterers, happy families, and apostle-birds.

d. *happy families*: a game played with a pack of special cards, each card depicting on its face a member of a tradesman's family of four; it is the aim of each player to make as many complete families as he can.

1881 *Cassell's Bk. In-Door Amusem.* 142 The well-known game of Happy Families is nothing but a variation of Spade the Gardener. **1918** 'C. DANE' *First Blade* xxv, An early passion for Happy Families. **1954** E. HYAMS *Stories & Cream* 50 'Play cards, pal?'..The other man said, in a rather nasty way, 'Ah, 'appy families, I suppose?' **1955** J. LEHMANN *Whispering Gallery* IV. 225 We were like a pack of cards for Happy Families.

5. a. spec. *happy warrior*, applied conventionally to an excellent soldier; also *fig.*

1806 [see WARRIOR II. 2]. **1915** D. O. BARNETT *Let.* 1 July 200 The 'happy warrior' who did the deed is in my platoon, one Finlay, and his hair is red. **1924** F. D. ROOSEVELT in *N.Y. Times* 27 June 4/3 He [*sc.* Alfred E. Smith] is the 'Happy Warrior' of the political battlefield. **1959** *Listener* 12 Nov. 843/3 Ernest Jones was a happy warrior.

c. *happy medium* = *golden mean* (GOLDEN *a.* 5 c).

1778 *English Mag.* Feb. 59/2 All extremes are ridiculous: the happy medium is to be aimed at. **1782** J. PRIESTLEY *Hist. Corrupt. Chr.* I. II. viii. 272 Other persons..were able..to hit the happy medium between the popish doctrine of merit..and that of the total insignificance of good works. **1901** ADE *Forty Modern Fables* 51 Moral: only one in a thousand ever strikes the happy medium. **1920** *Ladies' Home Jrnl.* Oct. 163/2 There is a happy medium. **1947** K. TENNANT *Lost Haven* (1968) x. 164 Ain't there no bloody happy medium?

d. Exhibiting harmony or co-operation, esp. *happy ship*, a ship on which the crew work together harmoniously; also *transf.* of the conduct of any organization.

1905 *Westm. Gaz.* 9 Dec. 16/1 There never was a 'happier ship', and from captain to cabin-boy all worked cordially together. **1916** 'TAFFRAIL' *Pincher Martin* iii. 43 The *Belligerent* was notoriously a happy ship. **1929** T. E. LAWRENCE *Home Lett.* (1954) 375 The camp is comfortable, & the airmen say it is a happy place. **1950** W. J. M. MACKENZIE in G. F. M. Campion *Brit. Govt. since 1918* 83 A branch or a department may be a theoretical monstrosity and yet be a 'happy ship'; and traditionally a 'happy ship' is the only efficient ship. **1955** *Times* 10 May 5/6 A visit to our Combined Training team recently gave the pleasant impression of a thoroughly 'happy ship' and, without undue confidence, that it will take a very good team indeed to beat them. **1958** P. KEMP *No Colours or Crest* iii. 26 *Fidelity* was not a happy ship. **1958** *Observer* 31 Aug. 19/3 The team was an undeniably happy one with immense spirit.

e. Of drugs: in certain colloquial phrases with the sense 'intended to produce or induce happiness', e.g. *happy dust*, cocaine; *happy pill*, a tranquillizer.

1922 E. MURPHY *Black Candle* I. vii. 67 The boxes were found to contain cocaine, or 'happy-dust'. **1929** H. MILES tr. *Morand's Black Magic* I. i. 12 Cocaine (or 'happy-dust', as Congo said). **1937** E. ST. V. MILLAY *Conversation at Midnight* IV. 114 Your head's So full of dope, so full of happy-dust..you're just a drug Addict. **1956** A. HUXLEY *Let.* 14 Mar. (1969) 791 The present mass consumption of 'Happy Pills', (Miltown-Equanil). **1964** E. DUNDY *Old Man & Me* xviii. 176 Those heart-shaped 'happy-pills' of soft musty mauve, pale blue, or apple-green, with that faint incision down their middles. **1966** I. ASIMOV *Fantastic Voyage* i. 11 You've got that tranquillizer gleam in your eye, doctor. I don't need any happy pills.

7. *happy-natured*, *-seeming*.

1921 D. H. LAWRENCE *Sea & Sardinia* 56 Old wood.. happy-seeming as iron never can be. **1924** M. A. LOWNDES *Terriford Myst.* iii. 35 Yet she looked so happy-natured. **1946** E. SITWELL *Fanfare for Elizabeth* xv. 155 Katherine Parr, a happy-natured, placid woman. **1952** S. SPENDER *Learning Laughter* 103, I never noticed such a happy-seeming family.

b. Used in certain comparative or hyperbolical phrases, e.g. (*as*) *happy as the day* (*is long*); *as happy as Larry* (see *LARRY *sb.*[3]). Also, with reference to the happy endings of fairy tales, novels, etc., *happy* (also *happily*) *ever after*(*wards*).

1786 COWPER *Let.* 9 Feb. (1904) II. 462 We will be as happy as the day is long. **1823** C. LAMB *Let.* 6 Jan. (1935) II. 361 May your granaries be full..and you as idle and as happy as the day is long! **1853** C. M. YONGE *Heir of Redclyffe* II. xii. 187 Guy..and Amy..were in a course of living very happy ever after. **1858** LYTTON *What will he Do?* IV. VIII. iii. 61 And then they would live happy ever afterward as in fairy tales. **1864** GEO. ELIOT *Let.* 23 Nov. (1956) IV. 168 He is as happy as the day is long—and very good—one of those creatures to whom goodness comes naturally. **1873** L. TROUBRIDGE *Life amongst Troubridges* (1966) viii. 67 The hero and heroine.. marry comfortably off in the end and live happily ever after. **1905** *Westm. Gaz.* 1 July 7/1 This, of course, is the so-called 'happy-ever-after' ending: in most cases the comedies of this type are..artificial. **1925** R. HALL *Saturday Life* xi. 122 Eight weeks ago she had seemed as happy as the day. **1938** *Times Lit. Suppl.* 15 Jan. 43/3 Thus a story which..ends on a happily-ever-after note. **1963** *Harper's Bazaar* May 11 The happy-ever-after heroine is you! **1960** *Observer* 8 Feb. 14/7 There's a nasty rumour in some studios that the next fad will be 'happy ever after' endings.

-happy. Used freely during and since the 1939–45 war as the second element in many combinations: **a.** In a dazed, nervous, or light-headed state as a result of excessive strain, e.g. by exposure to bombs (*bomb-happy*), anti-aircraft fire (*flak-happy*), the desert (*sand-happy*), etc. **b.** Acting in an irresponsible, obsessive, or precipitate manner, e.g. *gadget-happy* (= obsessed with the acquisition of gadgets), *trigger-happy* (= liable to shoot at anything at any time). Cf. also *slap-happy*. (Examples are entered under the first elements in this Supplement.)

happy-go-lucky, *adv.*, *a.* (and *sb.*). Add: Hence **happy-go-luckiness.**

1893 YONGE & COLERIDGE *Strolling Players* xxii. 187 Her Irish happy-go-luckiness. **1928** *S.P.E. Tract* XXIX. 269 The fertility and happy-go-luckiness of Elizabethan English. **1952** G. RAVERAT *Period Piece* iii. 49 The casual happy-go-luckiness..which was one of her most attractive qualities.

hapten (hæ·ptĕn). *Immunol.* Also **-ene.** [ad. G. *hapten* (K. Landsteiner 1921, in *Biochem. Zeitschr.* CXIX. 303), f. Gr. ἅπτειν to fasten.] A substance, usu. of low molecular weight, which cannot by itself elicit an antibody, but which can do so when combined with another substance, usu. a protein, the antibody thus produced being capable of reacting either with the free or the combined hapten.

1921 *Chem. Abstr.* XV. 3317 (*heading*) Heterogeneous antigens and haptenes. **1926** *Proc. Soc. Exper. Biol. & Med.* XXIII. 343 Active fractions of the specific part of the heterogenetic antigen, haptene, were obtained by fractional precipitation with alcohol. **1928** *Jrnl. Immunol.* XV. 595 Specifically reacting non-antigenic substances—so-called haptens—play a great part in the constitution of the antigens of animal cells and bacteria. **1931** C. H. BROWNING in *Syst. Bacteriol.* (*Med. Res. Council*) VI. 206 These non-protein substances when isolated do not by themselves cause antibody production *in vivo*; therefore Landsteiner has classed them as 'haptens' in contrast to true antigens. **1969** *New Scientist* 12 June 575/1 Low molecular weight chemicals (haptens) which are themselves non-antigenic but become antigenic when conjugated to 'carrier' proteins.

Hence **hapte·nic** *a.*

1932 *Dorland's Med. Dict.* (ed. 16) 616/2 *Haptenic*, pertaining to or caused by haptens. **1966** *Lancet* 24 Dec. 1419/1 The capacity to manifest contact allergy to a haptenic substance is impaired in persons with leprosy.

hapteron (hæ·ptĕrǫn). Pl. **haptera.** [mod.L., badly f. Gr. ἅπτειν to fasten.] An organ of attachment by which certain aquatic plants or algæ fasten themselves to rocks.

1895 M. C. POTTER tr. *Warming's Handbk. Syst. Bot.* I. 10 Hairs and organs of attachment (rhizoids and haptera), which biologically serve as roots, are developed. **1909** GROOM & BALFOUR tr. *Warming's Oecol. Plants* lxii. 241 Lithophytes require *haptera* by which they can attach themselves to rock, unless the thallus itself adheres closely to this. **1967** C. D. SCULTHORPE *Biol. Aquat. Vasc. Plants* v. 111 It creeps over the rocks to which it adheres by hairs or by exogenous projections known as haptera, which secrete a cement from their discoid tips.

haptic (hæ·ptik), *a.* (and *sb.*). [ad. Gr. ἁπτικ-ός able to come into contact with, f. ἅπτειν to fasten.] **a.** Of, pertaining to, or relating to the sense of touch or tactile sensations. **b.** Having a greater dependence on sensations of touch than on sight, esp. as a means of psychological orientation. Also *absol.*, a haptic person.

1890 in BILLINGS *Med. Dict.* **1904** *Amer. Jrnl. Relig. Psychol.* May 33 The scourging, thorns, spear and other tactile or haptic sensations come next. **1939** *Mind* XLVIII. 360 There is the notion of pure 'touch', and there are 'kinæsthetic experiences', and we can have the one without the other; but when we speak of 'the world of touch', or 'tactile æsthetics', we are referring to the data provided by an intimate combination of them both and for this sense Prof. Révész uses the adjective 'haptic'. *Ibid.* 364 How does Prof. Révész find out whether the blind have tactile æsthetic experiences? Does he treat haptics seriously in their own right? **1954** *Archit. Rev.* CXVI. 400/3 Some of his ugly, tumescent pots are brutally haptic, and if it were not for the paintings on them, might be the work of primitive men, moulding bulbous petitions for fruitful wives. **1964** *Listener* 30 July 156/2 Sight becomes such a preponderant source of information as the child grows, that even those who are basically haptic types come to have a secondary dependence on visual imagery. **1966** *Publ. Amer. Dial. Soc.* 1964 XLII. 41 A complete record of the segmental, paralinguistic, kinesic, and haptic systems, none of which is within the grasp of the linguist today. **1971** *Which?* Oct. 304/1 Scleral (sometimes called haptic) lenses, about the size of a 5p piece, cover the whole front of the eye.

So **ha·ptical** *a.*, **ha·ptically** *adv.*; **ha·ptics** *Psychol.* and *Linguistics* [ad. G. *haptik* (M. Dessoir 1892, in *Arch. f. Physiol.* 242)], the study of touch and tactile sensations, esp. as a means of communication.

1895 E. B. TITCHENER in *Amer. Jrnl. Psychol.* VIII. 82 (*heading*) A psychological vocabulary..*haptik*, haptics. **1899** *Amer. Jrnl. Psychol.* XI. 25 Haptical images, beside being vague and ill-defined, offer peculiar difficulties. **1904** G. S. HALL *Adolescence* II. ix. 5 Haptics is thus a paleopsychic field *par excellence*, and the exploration of this most extended of all senses involves a study of the entire dermal area. **1964** *Listener* 30 July 156/2 Those who are..essentially haptically minded—in other words, who primarily orientate themselves by means of touch, and their own bodily feelings and muscular sensations. **1966** *Publ. Amer. Dial. Soc.* 1964 XLII. 48 Haptics is that sub-system of nonlanguage communication which conveys meaning through physical contact. **1972** W. M. AUSTIN in A. L. Davis *Culture, Class, & Lang. Variety* viii. 147 The highly social animals..greet each other haptically by briefly holding each other's muzzles in their mouths.

haptine (hæ·ptin, -īn). *Immunol.* [a. G. *haptine* (Ehrlich & Morgenroth 1900, in *Berlin. klin. Wochenschr.* 30 July 683/2), f. Gr. ἅπτειν to fasten: see -INE[5].] In Ehrlich's theory of immunization, a receptor detached from the parent-cell, circulating freely in the blood-stream, and acting as a protection against infection by combining with the foreign substance which would produce it. Cf. *HAPTOPHORE *a.* (and *sb.*).

1900 E. F. BASHFORD tr. P. Ehrlich in *Proc. R. Soc.* LXVI. 448 The sifting of the material obtained by observation is rendered more difficult by the occurrence under normal conditions of a great number of quite unlooked for bodies furnished with haptophore groups and arising from diverse organs, and which we may designate collectively as haptines. **1902** *Brit. Med. Jrnl.* 12 Apr. 918/1 Every normally functionating cell throws off large numbers of side chains, either as isolated complexes, or in connection with complement. These side chains are spoken of as haptines (Ehrlich). **1932** HEWLETT & MCINTOSH *Man. Bacteriol.* (ed. 9) v. 168 Ehrlich termed the diverse free receptors which occur in the body fluids in various circumstances 'haptines'.

haptoglobin (hæptoglōᵘ·bin). *Biochem.* [ad. F. *haptoglobine* (Polonovski & Jayle 1940, in *Compt. Rend.* CCXI. 518), f. Gr. ἅπτειν to fasten + HÆM)OGLOBIN.] Any of several proteins of the α_2-globulin group that occur in blood serum and are able to combine with free hæmoglobin to form fairly stable complexes.

1941 in *Index Medicus* XXIX. 190/2. **1956** *Nature* 29 Sept. 695/1 Since differences in the haptoglobins of individuals determine their inherited serum groups, we suggest that the system comprising these groups be known as the 'haptoglobin system'. **1961** *Lancet* 23 Sept. 722/1 Normal sera contain three types of haptoglobins, which are now known to occur in three genetically controlled combinations. **1966** E. S. WEST et al. *Textbk. Biochem.* (ed. 4) xv. 573 Only the haptoglobins of types 1–1 and 2–2 have been shown to be homogeneous compounds...Type 2–1 haptoglobin has been found to be heterogeneous by ultracentrifugation.

haptophore (hæ·ptofōəɹ), *a.* (and *sb.*). *Immunol.* Also **-phor.** [a. G. *haptophor* (P.

Ehrlich 1898, in *Deutsch. med. Wochenschr.* 22 Sept. 599/2), f. Gr. ἅπτειν to fasten + -o + -PHORE.] Applied, in Ehrlich's theory of immunization, to that group of atoms in the molecule of a toxin or other substance which enables it to combine with the corresponding receptors of a cell. Also *absol.* So **haptopho·ric, hapto·phorous** *adjs.*

1899 tr. P. Ehrlich in *Trans. Jenner Inst. Prevent. Med.* (2nd Ser.) 11, I have already..touched upon the question whether..the toxin molecule contains two independent groups, of which the one (the toxophore) conditions the toxicity, and the other (the haptophore) the combining property. *Ibid.* 12 With the help of the haptophore groups, the toxin molecule becomes 'anchored' to the cell. **1902** VAUGHAN & NOVY *Cellular Toxins* (ed. 4) 182 Both the toxophil groups of the cell, and the cytophil groups of the toxin may be designated as haptophorous bodies. **1902** *Brit. Med. Jrnl.* 29 Mar. 785 The atom arrangement, or group in the toxin, which corresponds to the receptor, he [*sc.* Ehrlich] calls the 'haptophoric group'. **1904** *Ibid.* 10 Sept. 574 Although the toxophoric group may be similar, the haptophor is dissimilar. **1938** W. BULLOCH *Hist. Bacteriol.* xi. 275 Of the two, the haptophore is the more stable. Ehrlich considered that the toxophoric atom group can deteriorate to a non-toxic state although the haptophoric group may at the same time remain unchanged. **1960** *New Biol.* XXXI. 104 It was very hard to conceive that 'haptophores' could pre-exist.

haptotropism (hæ:ptotrōu·piz'm, -trǫ·piz'm, hæptǫ·trǒpiz'm). *Bot.* [ad. G. *haptotropismus* (L. Errera 1884, in *Bot. Zeitung* 5 Sept. 564), f. Gr. ἅπτειν to fasten: see TROPISM.] The phenomenon whereby plant organs, as the tendrils of climbing plants, exhibit tropic movements in response to the stimulus of touch. Hence **haptotro·pic** *a.*

1892 L. ERRERA in *Ann. Bot.* VI. 373 Thus, the geotropic, heliotropic, hydrotropic, haptotropic curvatures arise, which are familiar to vegetable physiologists. **1900** B. D. JACKSON *Gloss. Bot. Terms* 118/2 *Haptotropism*, curvature induced in climbing plants by the stimulus of a rough surface. **1924** M. SKENE *Biol. Flowering Plants* iv. 298 The response to contact stimulus is termed haptotropism. **1934** WEBSTER, Haptotropic. **1953** FRITSCH & SALISBURY *Plant Form & Funct.* (rev. ed.) xxix. 263 Certain tropic growth-curvatures result from direct contact with a foreign body and are described as haptotropic. **1965** BELL & COOMBE tr. *Strasburger's Textbk. Bot.* (new ed.) 375 Many plants..are sensitive to touch...This phenomenon is termed haptotropism (thigmotropism).

hapu (hā·pu). *N.Z.* Also (erron.) **harpu.** [Maori.] A clan, sub-tribe, or small community.

1843 E. DIEFFENBACH *Trav. N.Z.* II. III. ix. 361/2 Hapu—tribe, family. **1857** C. F. HURSTHOUSE *New Zealand* I. 162 The 70,000 semi-civilized natives now in New Zealand are divided into some dozen chief tribes, and into numerous sub-tribes and 'Harpu'. **1873** *Jrnls. Ho. Reps. N.Z.* III. App. G. vii. 87 (Morris), Were not all your hapu present when the money was paid? **1891** *Rep. Australas. Assoc. Adv. Sci.* III. G. 378 (Morris), Tribes or nations, each of which was divided into hapus, and the hapus into families. **1921** H. GUTHRIE-SMITH *Tutira* viii. 52 In sympathy with this *hapu* or sub-tribe and its old-world ways. **1949** P. BUCK *Coming of Maori* (1950) III. i. 333 To denote the groupings in English, the *iwi* has been termed tribe and the *hapu* a sub-tribe. **1960** N. HILLIARD in C. K. Stead *N.Z. Short Stories* (1966) 241 He's East Coast, he don't know the *hapus* up our way.

hapuku, hapuka (hā·puku, -kă). *N.Z.* Also formerly **whapuku,** etc. [Maori *hapuku.*] A large marine food fish, *Polyprion oxygeneios*; = COD *sb.*³ 2 b and *GROPER².

1838 J. S. POLACK *New Zealand* I. ix. 322 Some deep banks lie off the east coast, on which the *kanai*, or mullet, *wapuka*, or cod-fish, and..salmon abound. **1844** W. WAKEFIELD in *N.Z. Co. Rep.* XXXVI. 31 Aug. 137 The habouka is taken in great quantities near the fishing town. *c* **1845** in C. F. Hursthouse *New Zealand* (1857) I. 217 We've..lowing herds on every side, Hapuka in every tide. **1855** R. TAYLOR *Te Ika a Maui* 411 *Hapuku*, or *whapuku* commonly called the cod, but a much richer fish in flavor. **1859** A. S. THOMSON *Story N.Z.* I. 30 The Hapuku is the largest New Zealand salt-water fish. **1944** *Mod. Jun. Dict.* (Whitcombe & Tombs) (ed. 7) 193 *Hapuka, hapuku*, the Maori name for a large edible fish, also called 'groper'. Often mispronounced 'ha-pu'-ka'. **1960** DOOGUE & MORELAND *N.Z. Sea Anglers' Guide* 209 *Groper* or *Hapuku*... Other names: *Polyprion oxygeneios*; whapuku (Maori)...The word 'hapuka' is a corruption of hapuku. **1966** *Encycl. N.Z.* I. 907/1 Hapuku or groper (*Polyprion oxygeneios*)..is a large, heavy, deep-sea fish closely related to the bass.

‖ **harai goshi** (hā·rəi gǫ·ʃi). [Jap., f. *harai, harau* to sweep + *goshi, koshi* loin, waist.] A throw in Judo.

1941 M. FELDENKRAIS *Judo* vi. 114 Japanese experts are generally smaller than their foreign opponents, and still they find no difficulty in throwing them by *Haraï-Goshi*, for example. **1954** E. DOMINY *Teach yourself Judo* 190 *Harai Goshi*,..Sweeping Loin Throw. **1957** TAKAGAKI & SHARP *Techniques of Judo* II. iii. 31 Techniques such as *harai-goshi*. **1965** *New Statesman* 14 May 760/2 My son..has applied the old Harai Goshi, a very effective throw in judo.

harambee (hăræ·mbi). [Swahili.] Pulling or working together; co-operation; the slogan of the Kanu government of Kenya at the time of independence. Also *attrib.*

1963 *Times* 13 Aug. 6/4 The farmers..joined him in the shout of 'Harambee'—the rallying call to the people of Kenya. *Ibid.* 12 Dec. (Kenya Suppl.) p. ii/7 They ran an effective Kanu government on the theme of *harambee* (working together) and at the pre-independence talks..they broadly won..all their main objectives. **1969** *Reporter* (Nairobi) 16 May 40/1 The farmers of Nyanza Province..are giving an example to the rest of the country in launching *harambee* self-help schemes. **1971** *E. Afr. Standard* (Nairobi) 13 Apr. 2/4 The self-help work carried out by the people on a harambee basis was intended to make them join hands together in the development of a strong nation. *Ibid.*, Harambee groups should offer co-operation to one another in giving donations to fund-raising meetings.

harassing, *vbl. sb.* Add: Also *attrib.*, as **harassing agent,** a gas intended for use in harassing or incapacitating an enemy, a rioting crowd, etc., without being lethal; also *harassing gas.*

1968 R. CLARKE *We All fall Down* iii. 40 No weapons of any kind are manufactured at Porton, although the harassing agent known as CS was developed there in the early 1950s. **1972** W. F. BIDDLE *Weapons Technology & Arms Control* xix. 286 The object of a harassing agent is to make it impossible for opposing troops either to stay in an area or to carry out their military duties. Harassing agents are not necessarily intended to be lethal. **1969** *New Scientist* 30 Jan. 219/2 The other major class of agents in use are the harassing gases CS, CN and DM. They are supposedly non-lethal.

harbour, *sb.*¹ Add: **3. b.** An airship shed or hangar.

1909 *Chambers's Jrnl.* Oct. 659/2 Work in connection with the other Zeppelin air-ships is so far advanced that as soon as the halls, or harbours, as they are called, are ready it will only be necessary to put the parts together. **1912** C. B. HAYWARD *Pract. Aeronaut.* 36 To the only two airship sheds or 'harbors' exceeding 400 feet in length..no less than nine had been added [in France].

c. (See quot. 1948.)

1935 *Jrnl. R. United Service Inst.* Nov. 747 The aeroplane cannot hit a moving tank with a bomb, but when the tanks harbour, the aircraft will make every effort to locate and bomb them...The bombing of tanks in harbour will cause immediate dispersion. **1948** PARTRIDGE *Forces' Slang* 91 *Harbour*, halting place for the night for guns and tanks. Also a verb.

5. harbour seal *N. Amer.*, the common seal, *Phoca vitulina*, found along the shores of northern oceans; **harbour-side; harbour stow,** furling in a body (cf. FURLING *vbl. sb.* 1); so **harbour-stowed** *a.*

1766 J. BANKS *Diary* Oct. in A. M. Lysaght *Joseph Banks in Newfoundland & Labrador* (1971) II. 145 They [*sc.* the fishermen] divide them [*sc.* the seals] into five sorts which they call Square Phipper Hooded Seal Heart or houke Bedlamer and harbour seal, which last stays in the Countrey all the year. **1832** J. MCGREGOR *British America* I. iii. 107 The harbour seal (phoca vitulina)..does not seem to be migratory. **1958** A. W. CAMERON *Canad. Mammals* 55 Apart from the grey seal, the harbour seal is the only member of the tribe that ordinarily spends the summer in southern Canada. **1964** E. P. WALKER et al. *Mammals of World* II. 1302 (*caption*) Hair or harbor seals (*Phoca vitulina*). **1947** CROWTHER & WHIDDINGTON *Science at War* 180 Larger explosive charges can be used, and their effects registered by electrical recording on the harbour-side. **1962** *Daily Tel.* 11 Aug. 14/5 It was then decided to take Coweslip, still low in the water, to the nearby harbourside home of Mr. B. A. L. **1969** *Jane's Freight Containers 1968–69* 56/2 D & F Harborside Terminal. **1886** R. BROWN *Spunyarn & Spindrift* xxv. 311 Every rope in its place and hauled taut, every sail neatly furled in a harbour-stow. **1924** R. CLEMENTS *Gipsy of Horn* v. 98 A 'harbour stow' we gave them, rolling the canvas into a neat skin as though it were covered with a jacket and passing the gaskets at regular intervals like seizings. **1924** J. MASEFIELD *Sard Harker* 24 She was in lovely order; yards squared, harbour-stowed.

harbour, *v.* Add: **9. b.** Of tanks, military forces, etc.: to shelter; to halt for the night. Cf. senses 7 and 9 in Dict.

1935, 1948 [see *HARBOUR *sb.*¹ 3 c]. **1956** W. SLIM *Defeat into Victory* 498 That night our leading troops harboured two hundred and forty miles from Rangoon.

hard, *a.* (*sb.*). Add: **I. 1.** *hard egg* (earlier and later examples).

1607 E. TOPSELL *Hist. Foure-footed Beastes* 188 Prescribing him a diet; which is to drink water, and to eat hard Egs. **1962** L. DEIGHTON *Ipcress File* xxi. 143, I was loaded with anchovy,..hard egg and salmon.

e. Of a lawn tennis court: made of asphalt or other hard material, as distinguished from a grass court.

1889 H. W. W. WILBERFORCE *Lawn Tennis* v. 19 Most people on a dry ground or a 'hard' court use brown leather or buck-skin shoes with thick, smooth, red rubber soles. **1909** *Westm. Gaz.* 30 Mar. 12/3 It is possible to place too much significance on hard-court results, grass conditions in England being so materially different. **1959** *Daily Tel.* 1 June 1/4 The French hard-court championships. **1973** G. MITCHELL *Murder of Busy Lizzie* i. 10 A sunken garden, a hard tennis court, miniature golf.

f. Of silk: retaining its natural gum. Also applied to a worker in hard silk.

a **1877** KNIGHT *Dict. Mech.* 2180/2. **1878** A. BARLOW *Hist. Weaving* 395 Before the gum has been boiled off the silk it is said to be hard silk. **1921** *Dict. Occup. Terms* (1927) § 399 *Hard hand* (silk); general term for any worker engaged in treating silk while still hard, *i.e.*, before it is degummed.

g. Of porcelain: made of hard paste; *hard paste*: see PASTE *sb.* 3 b, PORCELAIN 1 note.

1814 REES *Cycl.* XXVIII. Dd 4/2 Porcelain made of the best proportions of these two substances..is called hard porcelain. **1832** G. R. PORTER *Treat. Porcelain & Glass* iii. 43 This paste is not so cohesive or viscous as that which forms hard porcelain. **1848** H. R. FORSTER *Stowe Catal.* 6 The celebrated Porcelain of Dresden, or more properly, Meissen,..is the most choice..of German fabrication. The material is termed 'hard paste'. **1869** LADY C. SCHREIBER *Jrnl.* (1911) I. 44 A bird on a raised sort of foot, *possibly* hard paste English. **1879** Hard-paste [see PASTE *sb.* 3 b]. **1881** *Harper's Mag.* Feb. 368/1 There are now hard or true porcelain manufactories in New York. **1885** *Encycl. Brit.* XIX. 642/1 Bristol porcelain is of interest as being the first hard natural porcelain made in England. **1909** *Chambers's Jrnl.* Nov. 751/1 China manufactured in the eighteenth century was of two kinds—namely, 'hard' paste or true porcelain, and 'soft' paste or artificial china. **1968** *Canad. Antiques Collector* Aug. 27/1 Hard-Paste porcelain is unaffected by the file where it is 'free from the glaze'. **1968** J. ARNOLD *Shell Bk. Country Crafts* 234 Hard porcelain, already glazed, is fired at 1300°–1400°C., causing complete fusion.

h. In many specific collocations, e.g. *hard brass, cheese, coke, cure, glaze, lights, mixture, pavior, pitch, solder, solderer, soldering, stock.*

Also *hard coal* = ANTHRACITE; *hard rubber* = EBONITE, VULCANITE 2; *hard soap*, see SOAP *sb.* 2.

1873 E. SPON *Workshop Rec.* 1st Ser. 10 Hard Brass, for Casting.—25 parts copper, 2 zinc, 4.5 tin. **1888** *Lockwood's Dict. Mech. Engin., Hard Brass.*—(1) Brass which has not been annealed after drawing or rolling... (2) Hammered brass, and brass which contains a large proportion of tin. **1902** *Encycl. Brit.* XXVII. 355/1 A perfect Leicester is perhaps the most attractive of all the so-called 'hard' cheese. **1957** 'K. CURRAGH' *Lady into Cook* 68 Cheese Soufflé... 4 tablespoons grated cheese (Parmesan or any hard cheese). **1846** *N.Y. Morning Express* 2 Oct. 4/2 Hard Coal is a little higher owing to the increased traffic and freight. **1855** J. PHILLIPS *Man. Geol.* 190 'Hard' coal, in which the divisional structures are chiefly derived from the planes of stratification. **1960** *Gloss. Coal Terms* (*B.S.I.*) 8 *Hard coal*, all coal of higher rank than lignite. In the U.S.A. the term is restricted to anthracite. **1888** *Lockwood's Dict. Mech. Engin., Hard coke*, oven coke. **1907** Hard cure [see *CURE *sb.*¹ 12]. **1909** *Westm. Gaz.* 9 Nov. 12/1 Fine Hard Cure Para Rubber. **1962** J. T. MARSH *Self-Smoothing Fabrics* vi. 80 Another feature of the treatment with triazones is the necessity for a 'hard cure', e.g. for 2 to 3 min. at 150° C or 1 to 2 min. at 165° C. **1814** REES *Cycl.* XXVIII. Ee 2/2 The hard and less fusible glaze of the hard porcelain, which is mostly feldspar. **1839** URE *Dict. Arts* II. 1016 The hard glaze of pipeclay ware. **1930** *Sel. Gloss. Motion Pict. Techn.* (*Acad. Motion Pict., Hollywood*), *Hard lights.* (1) Arc lights. (2) Illumination from arcs, in general. Refers to the sharp shadows cast. **1909** *Practitioner* Feb. 266 The mixture of the cocculus with beer..was kept by brewers' druggists, and sold to brewers under the name of 'multum' or 'hard mixture'. **1904** GOODCHILD & TWENEY *Technol. & Sci. Dict.* 280/1 *Hard paviors*.., malm bricks, over-burnt and slightly blemished in colour, used for paving, coping, etc. **1879** *Encycl. Brit.* X. 100/1 If the heat is forced, and the distillation [sc. of coal-tar] continued, a large amount of 'heavy' or 'dead oils' is obtained, and the mass left in the still is 'hard pitch'. **1860** Hard rubber [see VULCANITE 2]. **1846** *Pat. Jrnl.* 1 Aug. 174/2 Hard solder. Melt together two pounds of copper and one pound of tin. **1873** E. SPON *Workshop Rec.* 1st Ser. 364, 2 parts of good silver and 1 of ordinary brass pins, well melted, is a good, useful jewellers' hard solder. *a* **1877** KNIGHT *Dict. Mech.* II. 1061/2 *Hard solder*, the solder used for uniting the more infusible metals. Spelter solder and silver solder are the two principal varieties. **1879** *Spon's Encycl. Industr. Arts* I. 324 Alloys employed for joining metals together are termed 'solders' and they are commonly divided into two classes: hard and soft solders. **1902** *Young Engineer* I. 104 The art of soldering may be divided into two distinct classes—soft soldering,..and hard soldering, in which the solders are composed of gold, silver, copper, zinc, or brass. **1921** *Dict. Occup. Terms* (1927) § 262 *Brazer, brazier; hard solderer*; joins together parts of steel, iron, brass or copper articles by brazing or hard soldering. **1836** *Penny Cycl.* V. 409/1 The bricks are now separated for sale; the hard sound stocks are the best, and are worth from 1*l.* 10*s.* to 2*l.* a thousand. **1879** *Notes Building Constr.* III. 105 Hard Stocks are overburnt bricks, sound, but considerably blemished both in form and colour. **1904** GOODCHILD & TWENEY *Technol. & Sci. Dict.* 69/2 Those [bricks] which are less overburnt are termed 'hard stock', and are useful for many building purposes.

5. c. *hard of hearing* (later examples).

1950 *Lancet* 11 Nov. 532/2 Practical courses..on audiometry and hearing-aids, hard-of-hearing children, [etc.]. **1968** *Brit. Med. Bull.* XXIV. 256/2 There may be a real problem in distinguishing the hard of hearing from those with organic intellectual impairment or autism.

d. (*to do something*) *the hard way*: (to do it) by one's own unaided efforts, through bitter experience, or by the most difficult method.

1931 D. RUNYON *Guys & Dolls* (1932) xiii. 276 'Charley,' he says, 'do you make it the hard way?' **1938** *Collier's* 2 Apr. 16 (*title*) The hard way. **1945** N. L. MCCLUNG *Stream runs Fast* ix. 80 You learned everything the hard way. **1951** 'N. SHUTE' *Round Bend* I, I came into aviation the hard way. **1954** M. CROFT *Spare Rod* I. ii. 12 I'm starting you off the hard way. **1958** *Observer* 26 Jan. 15/8 Making a movie the hard way spiritually and intellectually is the thing that really matters. **1958** *Listener* 28 Aug. 292/1 Unqualified men who come up what used

to be called 'the hard way'. **1959** *Times Lit. Suppl.* 4 Dec. 701/4 The Japanese failed to recognize it in the 1930s, and learnt it the hard way. **1971** D. LEES *Rainbow Conspiracy* ix. 135 In the end I nearly found the reservoir the hard way.

6. b. *hard word,* used *dial.* in various senses, e.g. pass-word, abuse, scandal, marriage proposal, refusal. Phr. *to put the hard word on* (someone) *Austral.* and *N.Z. slang,* to ask for a favour or a loan, esp. to ask a woman for her favours.

1831 S. LOVER *Legends & Stories of Ireland* 1st Ser. p. xxiii, *Hard word,* hint. **1843** W. CARLETON *Traits & Stories Irish Peasantry* I. 78 So I gives Jack the hard word [*sc.* pass-word]. **1891** B. STOKER *Snake's Pass* xvi, He would send the hard word round the country about me and my leman. **1899** SOMERVILLE & 'ROSS' *Exper. Irish R.M.* vi. 123, I had said what is called in Ireland 'the hard word' [*sc.* marriage proposal]. **1905** *Eng. Dial. Dict.* III. 63/1 Ah assed him for a shillin', an' he gev mi t'hard-word.

1919 W. H. DOWNING *Digger Dial.* 28 *Hard word,* an outrageous demand. (Put the hard word on.) **1927** J. DEVANNY *Old Savage* 144 He thinks she is putting the 'hard word' on him. **1943** *Coast to Coast 1942* 215 A tradesman notorious for putting the hard word on his typists. **1947** I. DOUGLAS *Opportunity in Australia* 89 *Put the hard word on,* to cadge for a loan or favour. **1959** BAKER *Drum* iv. 38 Establishing a suitable vantage point to 'put the hard word on' her. **1960** D. LOCKWOOD *Fair Dinkum* ii. 11 He didn't put the hard word on me once, and my credit is still good. **1969** *N.Z. News* 28 May 1/1 (*headline*) Pilots put hard word on airline. **1970** *N.Z. Listener* 21 Dec. 8/3 'Don't you think hitching 's a little dangerous for females?' 'Well, some sheilas I know have had the hard word put on them.'

7. *hard case*: delete *U.S.* and add earlier and later examples; also *attrib.*, hardened, tough. In Australia and New Zealand, an amusing or eccentric but adventurous person, a 'character'; also called *hard doer* (see *DOER 5), *hard shot, hard thing.* See also sense 11 below.

1836 W. T. PORTER *Quarter Race Kentucky* (1854) 38 A 'hard case' called Emanuel Allen. **1842** *Life in West* 323 A canoe full of 'hard cases' (vagabonds) had passed up the river. **1920** *Punch* 7 Apr. 266/1 The hard-case mates a-bawlin'. **1928** *Sunday Express* 8 Jan. 4 With memories that go back to the days of 'cracker-hash', 'lobscouse', and hard-case, blue-nose, Nova Scotia mates. **1928** *Sunday Dispatch* 29 July 2 Half a dozen particularly hard-case units of the Flying Squad. *a* **1936** KIPLING *Something of Myself* (1937) ii. 22 It [*sc.* a school]..had been made up..by drafts from Haileybury..and, I think, a percentage of 'hard cases' from other schools.

1896 H. LAWSON *In Days when World was Wide* (1900) 197 Cause of half the fun that's started—'Hard-case' Dan—Isn't like a broken-hearted, Ruined man. **1896** —— *While Billy Boils* in *Wks.* (1948) 54 Steelman was a hard case...There was no shaking off Steelman. **1900** —— *Over Sliprails* in *Ibid.* 273 After dinner a humorous old hard case mysteriously took us aside. **1918** *Chrons. N.Z.E.F.* 7 June 204 Without a smoke he was a hard thing. **1938** 'R. HYDE' *Nor Years Condemn* ix. 184 Fred's a hard shot. **1940** F. SARGESON *Man & Wife* (1944) 64 He was the hardest case bloke you ever came across. **1943** —— in *Penguin New Writing* XVII. 66 He looked a bit of a hard-shot. **1950** 'A. P. GASKELL' in *Landfall* IV. 18 Cliff was a hard case.

b. Of facts: incapable of being denied or explained away, 'stubborn'.

1887 *Graphic* 29 Jan. 123/1 Hard Facts. **1906** *Daily Chron.* 11 Apr. 3/4 A few more hard-fact letters and less of this soft imagining might have made the body of the book as interesting as the appendix. **1929** CHESTERTON *Poet & Lunatic* iv, Thank God for hard stones; thank God for hard facts. **1956** A. H. COMPTON *Atomic Quest* 311 The hard fact is that war, like business, reduces to a question of gain versus cost. **1973** *Daily Tel.* 8 May 7/2 We have been unable to substantiate the allegations. We have few hard facts to go on but are continuing our investigations.

c. Of news or information: factual, real, objective, reliable, substantiated.

1938 E. WAUGH *Scoop* II. i. 117 There isn't any hard news. **1948** *Newsweek* 16 Aug. 51/1 The bulk of the broadcast time is given over to so-called 'hard news'—that is, straight newscasts of what is going on in the world and in the United States. **1956** A. J. AYER *Probl. of Knowl.* iii. 92 Those who have sought to erect an edifice of knowledge on the basis of what Bertrand Russell..has called 'hard data', have commonly agreed that such data were yielded by sense-perception. **1958** *Listener* 16 Aug. 239/2 This would yield some interesting and some relatively 'hard' evidence. **1958** *Economist* 13 Sept. 815/2 Two hard items for the agenda. **1959** DUKE OF BEDFORD *Silver-Plated Spoon* ix. 185 Newspapers do not encourage telephone calls to the other side of the world unless they are in possession of pretty hard information. **1963** *Ann. Reg. 1962* 520 Upon receiving the first preliminary hard information of this nature..I directed that our surveillance be stepped up.

11. *hard case*: applied to a sailing-ship on which conditions are rough; *hard luck*: see LUCK *sb.* 1; also *attrib.*; *hard-lying money*: corruption of *hard line money* (see LINE *sb.*[2] 6); hence *hard lyer*; (joc.) *hard-liar.*

1920 *Blackw. Mag.* Mar. 322/2 The mate of a Yankee hard-case. **1924** R. CLEMENTS *Gipsy of Horn* vi. 111 He signed away as Third Mate on a hard-case Yankee barque. **1900** ADE *More Fables in Slang* (1902) 18 Her Hard-luck story. **1906** B. VON HUTTEN *What became of Pam* II. viii, Learning..something of..his hard-luck story. **1919** H. L. WILSON *Ma Pettengill* iv. 109 She said it [*sc.* the letter] would tell a new hard-luck tale for non-payment of a note. *Ibid.* 134 It was another hard-luck letter. **1959** P. H. JOHNSON *Humbler Creation* v. 32 The hard-luck stories of all parsons whose luck would never get any better. **1916** 'TAFFRAIL' *Pincher Martin* iv. 56 'They ain't so bad,' he murmured. 'You gits a tanner a day, 'ard lyers in 'em.' **1920** —— *H.M.S. Anonymous* xv. 291 What d'you think the government pay us one and six hard lyers for? Twenty seven extra bloomin' pounds per annum. **1916** —— *Pincher Martin* iv. 56 Men serving in destroyers receive sixpence a day extra pay. It is known as 'hard-lying money'. **1925** FRASER & GIBBONS *Soldier & Sailor Words, Hard-lying money,* the extra allowance granted to officers and men for service in destroyers and torpedo boats, and as compensation for wear and tear of uniform and clothing, etc. Extended in the War to the crews of motor launches and other auxiliary small craft. (Abolished in 1923.) **1927** *Daily Express* 10 Oct. 3 Sometimes, in recompense for discomforts endured, the crews of drifters draw what is termed 'hard-lying money' (those who receive this are naturally known as 'hard liars').

12. c. (Later example.)

1968 *Times* 26 Aug. 7/2 The House of Commons today must take a hard look at British defence policy.

14. c. For *U.S.* read orig. *U.S.* and add earlier and later examples.

1789 F. ASBURY *Jrnl.* (1821) II. 304 [A] drink made of one quart of hard cider, [etc.]. **1810** M. L. WEEMS *Lett.* (1929) III. 13 What could possibly have kept me from hard drink? **1840** *Congress. Globe* 13 Feb. 197/3 He had heard..the same arguments preached nine hundred and ninety-nine times over a barrel of hard cider. **1848** *Ibid.* 27 Apr. 688/2 They had charged him [*sc.* President Harrison] with drinking hard cider. **1857** *Spirit of Times* 3 Jan. 281/1 It was not infrequent, as late as the hard-cider campaign of 1840,..that [etc.]. **1861** H. W. HARPER *Lett. from N.Z.* (1914) iv. 67 Order up some hard stuff to give them something to drink. **1946** F. SARGESON *That Summer* 35 They all started on hard stuff and went on to beer later. **1964** C. WILLOCK *Enormous Zoo* ix. 169 With a hard drink in the hand the day lengthens and softens. **1965** O. A. MENDELSOHN *Dict. Drink* 90 *Cider,*... If fermented and therefore alcoholic, the term hard cider is frequently used.

d. Of oil (see SOFT *a.* 23 d).

e. Of drugs: dangerous and habit-forming, addictive, e.g. heroin and cocaine.

1955 *Amer. Speech* XXX. 87 *Hard stuff,* opium. **1965** 'MALCOLM X' *Autobiogr.* vii. 110 As the pros did, I too would key myself to pull these jobs by my first use of hard dope. I began with..sniffing cocaine. **1967** *Listener* 10 Aug. 169/2 Nothing on earth would persuade me to try LSD or the hard drugs. **1967** *Times* 7 Oct. 5/3 The Court said that anyone supplying a child with a hard drug was doing a terrible deed which called for grave punishment. ..The Court refused an application..for leave to appeal against..conviction..of supplying a dangerous drug (six tablets of heroin). **1969** J. GARDNER *Compl. State of Death* ix. 167 You start on pot and straight off you're mixing with people who've graduated to the hard stuff.

f. Of nuclear sites and structures (see quot. 1960). Also applied to nuclear missiles.

1958 R. D. BOWERS in *Air Univ. Q. Rev.* X. 91 It would be useful to know how the cost of a hard base compares to that of a soft base if they have equal measures of merit (cost per surviving missile). **1960** *Amer. Speech* XXXV. 302 The adjective *hard* is now used in certain parts of the Air Force..to refer to the resistance to atomic explosions of airfields, missile launching pads, command posts, and other structures, their resistance coming from underground location or toughness of structure or both. **1962** *Listener* 29 Mar. 547/2 The American development of missiles such as Minuteman which can be fired from strongly protected pits in the ground—the so-called hard missile sites—as well as the Polaris submarines. **1965** H. KAHN *On Escalation* vii. 136 Let the reader assume.. that both the Soviet Union and the United States have 10,000 hard and dispersed missiles on each side.

15. (Earlier U.S. example.)

1838 D. WEBSTER *Private Corr.* (1856) II. 37 Money is very hard, all along the coast, from here [i.e. Washington, D.C.] North.

16*. *Physics.* **a.** Of radiation: having great penetrating power.

1902 *Encycl. Brit.* XXVIII. 52/2 If the exhaustion of the bulb is carried further, so that there is a considerable increase in the potential difference between the cathode and anode and therefore in the velocity of the cathode rays, the Röntgen rays have much greater penetrating power and are often called 'hard rays'. **1938** R. W. LAWSON tr. *Hevesy & Paneth's Man. Radioactivity* (ed. 2) iv. 49 The wave-length of the 'hard' γ-radiation is so small that even crystals are of no avail here as diffraction gratings. **1940** *Nature* 8 June 903/2 (*title*) Absorption of hard cosmic rays and mesotron decay. **1943** *Electronic Engin.* XVI. 54 Short wave, or hard, radiation penetrates more deeply into the tissues. **1955** *Gloss. Terms Radiology* (*B.S.I.*) 12 *Hard radiation,* a term used to describe qualitatively the more penetrating types of X-rays, beta rays and gamma rays.

b. Of a vacuum: complete or almost complete. Of a vacuum tube or thermionic valve: containing a high vacuum.

1899 W. CROOKES in *Rep. Brit. Assoc. Adv. Sci. 1898* 23 Röntgen suggests a convenient phraseology; he calls a low vacuum tube, which does not emit the highly penetrating rays, a 'soft' tube, and a tube in which the exhaustion has been pushed to an extreme degree, in which the highly penetrating rays predominate, a 'hard' tube. **1919** R. STANLEY *Textbk. Wireless Telegr.* (ed. 2) II. 22 With a hard vacuum none of these varying effects are present... The hard valve, made by Langmuir, was called by him a Pliotron. **1923** E. W. MARCHANT *Radio Telegr.* v. 61 *Hard Valves.*—The only way in which this can be achieved is by exhausting the air so completely from the bulb that there is nothing but a pure electron discharge. **1931** DUNCAN & DREW *Radio Telegr. & Telephony* (ed. 2) 214 The degree of vacuum in the tube would change and some tubes became *soft* (having less vacuum) while others became *hard* (having a higher vacuum, with little or no gas present). **1940** *Chambers's Techn. Dict.* 403/1 *Hard tube,* a high-vacuum discharge tube. **1943** *Gloss. Terms Telecomm.* (*B.S.I.*) 28 *Hard vacuum tube,* a vacuum tube evacuated to such a degree that its electrical characteristics are essentially unaffected by ionisation of included gas. **1953** *Electronic Engin.* XXV. 241 A blocking oscillator was first used as a hard-valve time-base in 1923. **1962** F. I. ORDWAY et al. *Basic Astronautics* xi. 449 The hard-vacuum condition of space.

18. b. *hard labour*: also *attrib.*

1905 *Daily Chron.* 10 July 5/2 Hard-labour convicts. *Ibid.* 6 Nov. 5/6 Hard-labour prisoners. **1908** *Ibid.* 7 Jan. 4/6.

20. *hard at it* (cf. HARD *a.* 19); *hard cases make bad law* (see quot. 1903); *to play hard to get* (cf. PLAY *v.* 34), to pretend to remain aloof, to act or behave as if unapproachable or uninterested; also *hard-to-get* attrib. phr., aloof, unapproachable.

1749 FIELDING *Tom Jones* III. VII. v. 32 Pray who hath been the Occasion of putting her into those violent Passions? Nay, who hath actually put her into them? Was not you and she hard at it before I came into the Room? **1811** JANE AUSTEN *Let.* 30 Apr. (1932) 278 By this time I suppose she is hard at it, governing away—poor creature! **1923** J. S. HUXLEY *Ess. Biologist* iii. 119 The two are hard at it, shaking their heads. **1964** C. WILLOCK *Enormous Zoo* i. 13 The circular saws were soon hard at it. **1854** G. HAYES in W. S. Holdsworth *Hist. Eng. Law* (1926) IX. App. 423 Sur. B. [*i.e.* Baron Surrebutter] A hard case. But hard cases make bad law. **1903** V. S. LEAN *Collectanea* III. 479 Hard cases make bad law, i.e. lead to legislation for exceptions. **1909** *Spectator* 22 May 809/1 'Hard cases make bad law', and also bad policy. **1945** A. KOBER *Parm Me* 32 'I played "hard to get". Y' know,' he amplified, 'like I couldn't be bothered.' **1951** WODEHOUSE *Old Reliable* xi. 132 Why are you pulling this hard-to-get stuff on Joe? **1951** AUDEN *Nones* (1952) 18 But that Miss Number in the corner Playing hard to get. **1959** P. CAPON *Amongst those Missing* 194 To be blunt, you sort of strike me as playing hard to get. **1959** J. FLEMING *Miss Bones* xv. 168 Is she playing hard-to-get? he thought angrily. **1961** *Times* 26 Oct. 18/1 Miss Nancie Jackson's Millamant is a statuesque blonde, playing hard-to-get while keeping our sympathy. **1962** *Guardian* 8 Feb. 7/4 The wish to create a hard-to-get atmosphere for the coming negotiations.

21. *hard-backed, -based, -edged* (examples), *-faced* (examples), *-glazed, -leaved, -lipped, -nailed, -textured.*

1853 MRS. GASKELL *Cranford* xvi. 312 Mr. Peter said he was tired of sitting upright against the hard-backed uneasy chairs. **1959** Hardbacked [see *HARDBACK 2]. **1959** *Listener* 31 Dec. 1140/1 Within a few years it [*sc.* the American Strategic Air Command] will have at its disposal enough 'hard-based' missiles—that is, either housed in protected subterranean sites or mounted on mobile carriers—to make it impossible for any surprise attack to succeed at all. **1954** J. R. R. TOLKIEN *Two Towers* 22 Long slopes they climbed, dark, hard-edged against the sky. **1964** *English Studies* XLV. 28 Nor are registers hard-edged pigeon-holes. **1871** J. G. WHITTIER *Marguerite* in *Wks.* (1898), By her bed the hard-faced mistress sat. **1958** B. NICHOLS *Sweet & Twenties* 145 Harding was a hardfaced provincial politician. **1928** *Daily Express* 6 Oct. 11/7 A hard-glazed lacquer work upon tin-plate. **1926** J. MASEFIELD *Odtaa* xiii. 223 Hi crackled through some hard-leaved scrub. **1849** ROSSETTI *Let.* 27 Sept. (1965) I. 60 Hunt reads Dumas, hard-lipped. **1961** *John o' London's* 6 July 57/2 One of his virtuoso essays in hard-lipped sensitivity. **1879** G. M. HOPKINS *Sermons* (1959) 18 Christ has..made us deaf here,..with his hands hardnailed out and appealingly stretched on the cross. **1910** W. DE LA MARE *Three Mulla-Mulgars* xvii. 232 Long, hairy, hard-nailed toes. **1937** E. SITWELL *I live under Black Sun* 141 A sour hard-textured unripe plum.

22. a. hard fescue (see FESCUE *sb.* 4); **hard-grass** (later examples); **hard wheat,** any wheat having a hard grain rich in gluten; also *attrib.* **b. hard bop** (see *BOP *sb.*[2]); **hard-bread** (U.S. examples); **hard cheddar, cheese** *colloq.*, hard luck (see also sense 1 h above); **hard chine** [CHINE *sb.*[3] 2] (see quot. 1961); so **hard-chined** *a.*; **hard copy** (see quots.); **hard core,** (*a*) (see CORE *sb.*[1] 7 d); (*b*) an irreducible nucleus or residuum; also a stubborn or reactionary minority; something blatant or intractable; freq. *attrib.*; **hard cover** orig. *U.S.*, (of a book) a stiff binding case, chiefly (with hyphen) *attrib.*; also **hard-covered** *a.* = *hard-bound* (*HARD *adv.* 8 d); **hard currency,** (*a*) in specie as opposed to paper currency, metallic currency (*Obs.*); (*b*) (see quot. 1949); **hard dot** *Printing* (see quot. 1968); **hard-edge,** a style of painting (see quot. 1962[1]); also freq. *attrib.*; **hard facing** *Metallurgy*, the application to the surface of a metal of a protective hard material resistant to wear, corrosion, etc.; hence **hard-faced** *a.*; **hard glass,** a borosilicate glass (cf. *PYREX); **hard hat,** (*a*) a hat made of hard or stiffened felt; a bowler hat; (*b*) a tin helmet; (*c*) a person who wears a tin helmet, *spec.* a construction worker; (*d*) a person who is reactionary or conservative; also *attrib.*; **hard-hitter** (hat) *Austral.* and *N.Z. colloq.*,

= BOWLER³; **hard landing** *Astronaut.*, an uncontrolled landing in which the vehicle is destroyed; so **hard lander**; **hard-line** *attrib.*, adhering to a hard or firm policy without abatement or concession (cf. sense 12 c); so **hard-liner**; **hard-nosed** *a.*, (*a*) (see quot. 1889); (*b*) *U.S. slang*, obstinate, stubborn; **hard pad**, a form of distemper in dogs and sometimes other animals; **hard pear**: see *HARDPEER; **hard-rock,** (*a*) *attrib.* or as *adj.* (*N. Amer.*), 'experienced in underground work in hard massive formations;—said of a miner' (Webster 1934); (*b*) (*N. Amer. slang*) as noun phr., a hard, craggy person; also *attrib.*; (*c*) a type of strident music; **hard sell** orig. *U.S.*, aggressive salesmanship or advertising; also *attrib.*; **hard-sell** *v.*; **hard-selling; hard-sold** *ppl. a.*; **hard shoulder** (see quot. 1955); **hard-standing** (occas. **hard-stand**) (see quots. 1951, 1956); **hard top,** (*a*) a rigid or fixed roof of a motor-car (as opposed to one of soft material); also a car so fitted; (*b*) (see quot. 1957); **hard tube** (see sense 16* b); **hard twist,** a hard-spun yarn, a yarn with more than the usual amount of twist; **hard valve** (see sense 16* b); **hard waste** (see quot.).

1781 HEATH in R. Putnam *Mem.* (1903) 187 The major is gone to the commissary to obtain some hard bread if possible. **1835** in J. B. Thoburn *Stand. Hist. Oklahoma* (1916) vi. 74 The ration of bread shall be one pound of wheat flour, Indian meal, or hard bread. **1857** W. CHANDLESS *Visit Salt Lake* ii. 11 What we call rolls, in America are ycleped biscuits, and biscuits in their turn hard bread. **1905** G. E. COLE *Early Oregon* i. 12 Having no salt junk or hard bread left. **1931** 'N. BELL' *Life & Andrew Otway* 464 'He knew all about cutting throats. Seen a bit in his time.' 'Hard cheddar. I reckon a bullet'd be my mark if I wanted to pass in my checks.' *Ibid.* 465 No, I don't see how you can blame the bleedin' government. Hard cheddar on you but—. **1876**, etc. Hard cheese [see *CHEESE *sb.*¹ 2 d]. **1913** C. MACKENZIE *Sinister St.* I. II. i. 149, I thought it hard cheese on her. **1973** J. I. M. STEWART *Mungo's Dream* xxii. 270 It was hard cheese on him coming up against another top-class specimen. **1912** *Motor Boat Man.* (ed. 5) v. 44 'Miranda IV'..has a single step... The hard chine or angular bilge is not an essential feature. **1951** *Engineering* 8 June 680/2 In general, the appraisal of the respective merits and demerits of round-bilge, hard-chine and stepped hulls is fair and temperate. **1961** F. H. BURGESS *Dict. Sailing* 110 *Hard chine*, a feature of a boat in which the topsides and bottom meet at an angle instead of curving to a round bilge. **1967** *Jane's Surface Skimmer Systems 1967–68* 86/2 A small sports hydrofoil, the ST-1 has a typical hard-chine type hull of wooden construction. **1966** *Amer. Speech* Oct. 235 *Lightning*, a wood-planked, hard-chined boat made for racing. **1964** *Gloss. Automated Typesetting* (C.I.S.) 17 *Hard copy*, a printed (typewritten) record or copy of machine output. **1964** T. W. MCRAE *Impact of Computers on Accounting* vi. 165 An intermediate device, the computer, is necessary to translate the 'magnetic' records into a 'hard copy' format suitable for audit. **1936** *Nature* 12 Sept. 441/2 Possibly 200,000 would be practically unemployable on any ordinary basis—the 'hard core' as it is called. **1940** *Economist* 3 Feb. 193/2 One of the more encouraging developments of the last few months is a substantial loosening of what has hitherto been regarded as the 'hard core' of unemployment. **1951** J. CORNISH *Provincials* 24 The party was acknowledged even by the hard-core cynics to be a credit to the Dunseith brothers. **1955** *Treatm. Brit. P.O.W.'s in Korea* (H.M.S.O.) 25 This camp..was the home of the hard core of Other Rank reactionaries—men who had distinguished themselves by their heroic resistance to all Chinese brutality. **1956** *Ann. Reg. 1955* 300 A hard core of Karens in both zones maintained resistance. **1958** *Daily Mail* 15 Aug. 2/1 More than 100 hardcore EOKA terrorists have been netted in the anti-terrorist operation. **1958** *Listener* 11 Dec. 982/1 In seven 'hard core' States, no Negro child attends a white school. **1959** F. VAN P. BRYAN in Ernst & Schwartz *Censorship* (1964) xix. 130 A work of literature..stands on quite a different footing from hard core pornography. **1961** R. KEE *Refugee World* iii. 26 Weiss, the Frankfurt jeweller..was a 'hard-core' case in 1950. **1968** *Times* 2 Sept. 2/7 Heathrow airport..could, perhaps, be called the hard core of Britain's noise problem. **1973** *Times Lit. Suppl.* 20 Apr. 451/5 The leading modern writer of hard-core science fiction. **1949** in *Amer. Speech* (1952) XXVII. 148 Hard-cover reprints. *Ibid.*, Hard-cover reprint house. **1951** *Sat. Rev. Lit.* 12 May 31/1 Much of the reading involves books whose quality does not justify any particular consideration just because the pages are bound inside a hard cover. **1951** *Publishers' Weekly* 12 May 1949 Each issue will be a hard-cover book. **1957** *Economist* 5 Oct. 45/1 Critics of mass market publishing suspect that it spreads mediocrity, even to the hardcover business. **1960** *News Chron.* 10 Jan. 3/7 The Heinemann group..published..an expurgated version of 'Lady Chatterley'..in hard cover in this country. *Ibid.* 3/8, I would immediately bring out a hard-cover edition. **1968** *Times* 14 Sept. 21/4 The whole inquiry relates exclusively to hard-cover sales. **1952** *Amer. Speech* XXVII. 147 (*heading*) Books: hard-bound, hard-cased, hard-covered, limp-covered. **1851** J. H. GREEN *Twelve Days in Tombs* 33 The politicians were fiercely discussing the 'hard' and 'soft' currency question. **1940** *Economist* 6 Apr. 609/1 The phenomenon of a 'free' rate diverging from the 'official' rate occurs only in respect of those so-called 'hard' currencies for which official rates are fixed by the Bank of England (notably American dollars). **1948** *Hansard Commons* 29 Jan. 1247 As a hard-currency market, the United States is of great importance. **1948** *Ibid.* 9 Mar. 1003 Does the Chancellor of the Exchequer think it right to spend over £60 million a year in hard currency? **1949** *Times* 10 Sept., *Hard currency*, a term without precise meaning. In general, when used in relation to this country, it means the currency of any country with which this country has an adverse balance of payments in current transactions which has to be settled in gold or dollars...Hard currency is..a relative rather than an absolute term, reflecting as it does the relation between one currency and another. **1950** *Engineering* 10 Feb. 144/1 Vehicles for export to hard-currency countries. **1957** *Time* 2 Sept. 27/2 Canadians last week enjoyed the mixed blessing of having the world's hardest currency. **1969** *Listener* 20 Feb. 229/3 Arthritis would have helped me break into the hardest of hard-currency resort areas. **1961** DUGAN & PINE in *Penrose Ann.* LV. 135 (*title*) The hard-dot positive in gravure. *Ibid.*, The need for a 'hard-dot' in the positive plates. **1968** *Gloss. Terms Offset Lithogr. Printing* (*B.S.I.*) 15 *Hard dot*, a half-tone dot with a high edge density. **1961** *Times* 6 June 16/5 The 'hard-edge' abstractions of recent years. **1962** *Guardian* 18 Jan. 7/7 During the last three years.. a new branch-line in British painting has opened up and been loosely labelled the 'hard-edge school'..The paintings tend to be precisely geometric, crisp..and totally withdrawn from any personal emotive content. *Ibid.* 12 July 6/4 Hard-edge is socially useful..but it is neither art nor painting. **1962** *Listener* 21 June 1080/2 Kelly is a 'hard-edge' abstractionist. He balances simple areas of sharply defined flat colour one against the other. **1965** *New Statesman* 30 Apr. 693/2 The exhibition effects an uneasy marriage between, on the one hand, hard-edge abstraction and stain painting, fields in which the Americans easily excel, and, on the other, optical art. **1960** *Jrnl. Iron & Steel Inst.* CXCIV. 269/3 Hard-faced rolls had a useful service life five times as long as the usual steel rolls. **1930** *Ibid.* CXXII. 542 Welded-on overlays or 'hard facings' have been applied to drill bits and other tools to combat abrasion. **1931** *Ibid.* CXXIV. 634 The author cites a number of applications of hard facing and indicates the economy of the process. **1904** S. P. MULLIKEN *Method Identification Pure Org. Compounds* I. 10 Prepare an ignition-tube 8–10 cm. in length from a piece of hard-glass combustion tubing. **1937** *Discovery* Nov. 360/2 Pyrex and other hard glasses. **1965** PHILLIPS & WILLIAMS *Inorg. Chem.* II. xiv. 545 Hard glass or pyrex is made from mixed boron (30 per cent) and silicon oxides. **1961** R. W. BUTCHER *Brit. Flora* II. 978 *Parapholis* (*Lepturus*) *incurva*. The curved hard-grass is a small, tufted annual with many erect, curved stems 1–6 in. high. *Ibid.* 979 *Parapholis strigosa*. The sea hard-grass is a small, tufted annual with many slender, solitary, erect or bent stems 6–18 in. high. **1935** A. J. POLLOCK *Underworld Speaks* 51/1 *Hard hat*, a derby. **1945** BAKER *Austral. Lang.* 181 The Australian equivalents of what the Englishman calls a bowler and the American a derby. Here are our contributions: boxer,..hard hat, [etc.]. **1953** *Collective Bargaining Agreement Giant Yellowknife Gold Mines* 3 Protective devices..shall be provided by the Company, but this shall not include personal necessities such as hard hats, hard toed boots and gloves. **1956** H. M. NEWELL *Dam* xvii. 84 Workmen were cocooned in clothing till he couldn't recognize them...Beneath their hard-hats, stocking caps or scarves or kerchiefs tied under their chins. **1963** A. LUBBOCK *Austral. Roundabout* 21, I was given a white tin hat, as it is a regulation that these safety helmets must be worn in the 'hard hat' areas of the mines. **1970** *Sunday Tel.* 14 June 12/7 All the dangerous implications of 'hard-hat' demonstrations by flag-waving workers who see the anti-war movement as a betrayal. **1970** *Sunday Mail* (Brisbane) 14 June 21/2 A 'Hard Hat' is a construction worker, but his helmet symbolises all those beefy blue-collar workers who have suddenly become the knuckleduster on the strong right arm of President Nixon's silent majority. **1972** D. E. WESTLAKE *Cops & Robbers* (1973) v. 63 It was one of those huge office buildings being constructed there, and the hardhats kept steady working away at it. **1895** J. ROBERTS *Diary* 7/2, I had long ere this put on my own clothes..of the 'masher' type—white shirt, hard-hitter, tight trousers, etc. **1907** H. LAWSON *Romance of Swag* (1948) 478 Jim sat in his shirt-sleeves, with his flat-brimmed, wire-bound, 'hard-hitter' hat on. **1924** H. T. GIBSON *That Gibbie Galoot* i. 1, I didn't mind so much when my former mates sat on my hard-hitter hat. **1932** N. SCANLAN *Pencarrow* xxiv. 242 Then hats. Of course they must have hard hitters..black bowler hats—hard hitters as they were usually called in the colony. **1962** F. I. ORDWAY et al. *Basic Astronautics* v. 176 (*caption*) Exterior view of Ranger lunar hard lander. **1958** *Times* 28 Mar. 10/3 The first [*sc.* landing on the moon] would be a simple shot, ending either in a 'hard' (uncontrolled) landing or a circling of the moon. **1967** *Technology Week* 23 Jan. 61/1 (Advt.), Grumman is engaged in major application research to develop vehicles for soft and hard landings on Mars. **1962** *Times Lit. Suppl.* 21 Dec. 992/5 The 'hard-line' periodical *Literatura i zhizn*, which has up to now dealt exclusively with the literature of the Russian Federation, will close down. **1964** *Economist* 18 Jan. 206/1 CIA's..reputation as a 'hard-line' agency. **1965** *New Statesman* 7 May 710/3 Among those whose toughness stiffened the rebels' will to resist were.. the 50 or 60 'hard line' communists. **1970** *Guardian* 28 Oct. 4/6 He has not concealed his hardline views, but has avoided coming into direct public confrontation with the party leadership. **1963** *Sat. Rev.* 25 May 22/2 The fact that war has now become an instrument of mutual suicide..has made no dent in the thinking of hardliners. **1966** *Observer* 17 Apr. 2/8 Vice-President Humphrey—widely regarded as a hard-liner on Asia. **1969** *Guardian* 5 Mar. 8/1 Hardliners of the Right and the Left will say..that there is no middle way in Latin-American politics. **1889** *Cent. Dict.*, *Hard-nosed*, in hunting, having little or no sense of smell: said of dogs. **1927** *Hollis St. Theatre Prog.* (Boston) 19 Sept. Gloss., *Hard nosed*, stubborn. **1949** *Penguin New Writing* XXXVIII. 49 And *there* there is a lock, too, with the saint who welched three times in charge of the keys, who can be trusted not to be too hard-nosed. **1965** *Economist* 3 Apr. 27/2 Washington has got pretty 'hard-nosed' about criticism of its Congo policy. **1971** *New Society* 7 Jan. 26/1 A whole host of prophetic ravers and hard-nosed technocrats. **1973** *Times* 8 Feb. 23/2 Dolly's hard-nosed business approach to publishers probably did not have universal support. **1948** MACINTYRE et al. in *Vet. Rec.* 28 Feb. 103/1 We now recognise a condition which we have tentatively called 'hard pad disease'. **1950** A. C. SMITH *Dogs since 1900* 35 The disease should be more properly termed canine encephalitis...It became known as 'hard-pad' because a curious symptom.. is a hardening of the pads. **1958** *New Yorker* 22 Feb. 31/3 Even the fact that foxes are now carrying a disease called hardpad is insufficient reason for shooting a fox. **1923** 'B. M. BOWER' *Parowan Bonanza* iv. 56 Tommy's an old, hard-rock man. **1926** *Amer. Speech* II. 87/1 The old hardrock miners (now nearly extinct) were either single jackers or double jackers. **1949** *Chicago Daily News* 9 Apr. 1/6 A machinist drilling with a crew of hardrock miners 75 feet below the surface. **1950** W. R. BIRD *This is Nova Scotia* 19 One night..he ran up against a hardrock from Spencer's Island, and when the fracas ended he had been completely thrashed. **1962** K. ORVIS *Damned & Destroyed* xvi. 119 A hard-rock by the name of Welch. **1965** *Globe & Mail* (Toronto) 6 Jan. 24/9 Page [is] a hard-rock defensive back. **1967** *Boston Sunday Herald* 26 Mar. I. 11/2 'Sing-Out' shook Saunders Theater with its mesmeric hard-rock beat. **1969** *Rolling Stone* 28 June 38/2 Drummer, hard-rock, blues, heavy, wants dependable group with horns. **1952** *Business Week* 9 Aug. 40 A few months ago everyone had keyed himself up to the 'hard sell'. **1957** 'E. MCBAIN' *Con Man* (1960) iii. 31 It's the hard sell and the soft sell, anywhere you go. **1958** D. DELMAN (*title*) The hard sell. **1959** *Times Lit. Suppl.* 13 Nov. 662/3 One does not see any examples..of what is called 'hard-sell' advertising. **1961** *Economist* 14 Jan. 114/2 The need for the 'hard sell' is evident. **1963** *Guardian* 16 Nov. 14/7 It is difficult to hard-sell the honest song the way they do the contemporary counterfeit. **1963** *New Scientist* 19 Sept. 613/1 The reader cannot miss the hard-sell line of advertising copy. **1966** *Ibid.* 21 July 125/1 Whatever one may think of the 'hard-sell' methods employed by big American corporations, they obviously work. **1960** *Economist* 8 Oct. 158/2 The current slump in sales has also prompted many firms to return to the 'hard-selling' practices of earlier recessions. *Ibid.* 172/1 The fuel-economy services offered by the coal and oil industries to sell their products may not prove serious competition for an independent organisation like Nifes, which may end up refereeing between them for hard-sold firms. **1955** *Times* 6 July 10/1 The motorways are to be constructed to modern standards, with hard shoulders of 9 ft. (land hardened and laid down for vehicles to get safely off the running lanes). **1959** *Ibid.* 4 Nov. 9/7 The hard shoulder, used by vehicles for emergency stops, has collapsed at one point under the weight of a heavy lorry. **1973** *Scotsman* 12 Jan. 11/4 Twenty-six of the accidents were on the inside lane or hard shoulder. **1944** *R.A.F. Jrnl.* Aug. 259 Our lorries, drawn up on the hardstanding ground, beside lines of gliders. **1951** *Gloss. Aeronaut. Terms* (*B.S.I.*) III. 22 *Hard standing*, a prepared hard surface for parking aircraft or heavy vehicles. **1956** W. A. HEFLIN *U.S.A.F. Dict.* 245/1 *Hardstand*, any paved, compacted, or otherwise specially-prepared surface or area set up either for parking an airplane or ground vehicle, or for storing supplies and equipment. *Ibid.* 245/2 *Hardstanding*, the facility provided by hardstands. **1957** *Times* 1 Mar. 9/6 These are certainly the aircraft which one sees on the hardstanding. **1960** *Guardian* 19 May 1/6 The rural council intends to provide hard-standing for caravans. **1968** *Bucks Examiner* 2 Aug. 2/7 Hardstanding for the parking of one coach or coaches. **1949** FRAZEE & BEDELL *Automotive Fundamentals* 82 The convertible sedan features the same entrance and seating arrangements as are found in the regular hard-top sedan. **1951** *Amer. Automobile* Mar. 78/3 Plymouth has adopted entirely new designations... The coming hardtop will be called Belvidere. **1952** *Autocar* 12 Dec. 1663/1 The hardtop style of roof is now used on all bodies, whether they have two or four doors. **1956** *Sat. Rev.* 7 Apr. 40/2 The number of enclosed theatres now colloquially known as 'hard tops' declines. **1957** *Amer. Speech* XXXII. 239 The conventional movie house under a roof is now referred to as a hardtop. **1959** 'S. RANSOME' *I'll die for You* iv. 43 Two Burt Fishers ..driving two identical Chevy hard-tops. **1967** *Guardian* 3 Oct. 5/3 The price of the hard top has gone up to £1,255. **1897** *Sears, Roebuck Catal.* 186/1 This suit is made from genuine Michigan hard twist cassimere. **1921** T. WOODHOUSE *Yarn Counts* vii. 87 There are..exceptional degrees of twist, some..of which might exceed the value of the so-called hard twist. **1963** A. J. HALL *Textile Sci.* iii. 114 In a similar manner much the same considerations apply in a multi-ply yarn if the two or more single yarns present are only slightly or highly twisted (often referred to as soft and hard twist) together. **1921** *Dict. Occup. Terms* (1927) § 362 *Breaker, hard waste*; *hard waste tenter*; feeds and operates machine which opens out hard cotton waste (waste from ring frames and from reeling and winding machines, cop bottoms and other thready waste) in preparation for re-spinning, or for use in manufacture of gun cotton. **1812** in H. Davy *Elem. Agric. Chem.* (1813) 133 Hard wheat always sells at a higher price in the market than soft wheat. *Ibid.*, The flour of hard wheat is in general superior to that made from soft. **1843** *Penny Cycl.* XXVII. 301/2 There are three principal varieties...These are the hard wheats, the soft wheats, and the Polish wheats. **1856** J. C. MORTON *Cycl. Agric.* II. 1005 *T*[*riticum*] *vulgare durum*, hard African wheat. **1908** *Westm. Gaz.* 1 July 6/3 The hard-wheat lands of Canada. **1971** *Times* 23 Jan. 21/4 Britain should take commodities like oil, wine, hard wheat.

B. *sb.* **1. a.** Delete † *Obs.* and add later examples.

1795 A. SHIRREFS *Sale Catal.* 3 (E.D.D.), A plain North-country bard, Who fain would cripple through the hard. **1808** JAMIESON *Dict. Scot. Lang.*, *Hard*, difficulty, hardship. *To come through the hard*, to encounter difficulties, to experience adverse fortune. **1858** G. ROY *Generalship* vi. 101 The bits o' bairns run a great risk o' coming through the hard. **1902** *Westm. Gaz.* 10 July 10/1 He had 'come through the hards' himself. **1904** *Daily Chron.* 27 May 3/4 She is a lady who..has given her life to nursing, and has gone through its hards.

c. In various technical applications.

1855 *First Rep. Adulteration of Food* 2 in *Parl. Papers 1854–5* VIII. 221 Bread is adulterated with mashed

potatoes, alum, 'hards', and sometimes..with sulphate of copper. **1921** *Dict. Occup. Terms* (1927) § 238 *Sider, hard* (needles); burnishes sides of sewing machine needles in the hard, *i.e.*, after hardening on revolving bob with oil and emery. **1937** *Archit. Rev.* LXXXI. 269/2 Scrap lead may contain other metals, such as the tin in solder, resulting in what is known as 'hards'. **1956** F. S. Atkinson in D. L. Linton *Sheffield* 268 The 'hards' of the Barnsley seam and, to a lesser extent, of the Parkgate or Deep Hard, make an excellent locomotive coal. **1960** *Gloss. Coal Terms* (*B.S.I.*) 12 *Hards*, a commercial term for the larger sizes of dull hard coal, in contrast to 'brights'.

d. Also *hard-on* sb. (and as adj.). An erection of the penis. *slang.*

1893 Farmer & Henley *Slang* III. 269/1 *Hard-bit* (or *bit of hard*). 1. The *penis* in erection. *Ibid.* 270/1 *Hard-on* adj. phr., prick-proud. **1922** Joyce *Ulysses* 527 What, boys? That give you a hardon? **1937** Partridge *Dict. Slang* 375/2 *Have a hard up*, to have a priapism. **1966** N. Behn *Kremlin Let.* I. iv. 56 When he wasn't plundering I suppose he was raping. He was more like a dog with a hard-on than a man with a mission. **1967** A. Wilson *No Laughing Matter* III. 377 He pulled up her red woollen dress..but still no hard. **1971** B. W. Aldiss *Soldier Erect* 44 The bromide damped down desire—you really had to work to get a hard on, whereas before it always flipped up naturally. **1971** B. Thornberry tr. Hansen & Jensen's *Little Red School-Bk.* (ed. 2) 95 When boys get sexually excited, their prick goes stiff. This is called having an erection or 'getting a hard on'. **1972** *Screw* 12 June 10/2 Billy and I talked down our hardons and..went downstairs to load the truck.

8. Tobacco in a cake.

1865 T. Archer *Pauper, Thief & Convict* v. 83 Peaceable companions..smoking pipefuls of 'hard' which they cut from a flat cake with their clasp-knives. **1898** G. Bartram *White-headed Boy* iv. 102 Packages of shag tobacco, lumps of sweetened 'hard'. *Ibid.* 105 Lind me a hand..with this lump o' harrd. **1898** *Daily News* 24 Feb. 3/1 Mr. Atkins..pulled at his pipe until he floated off into dreamland on a whiff of 'hard'.

hard, *adv.* Add: **1. c.** Very, extremely. *U.S. colloq.*

1850 N. Kingsley *Diary* (1914) 97 Mr. Hopkins is hard sick. *a* **1910** 'O. Henry' *Trimmed Lamp* (1916) 16 He isn't a millionaire so hard that you could notice it, anyhow.

8. a. *hard-bit, hard-driven, hard-driving* (example), *hard-hitting* (earlier and later examples), *hard-hurled, hard-running, hard sought, hard-worked* (examples); **b.** *hard-lived, -looking, -pressing, -tried, -used* (example); **hard-hit,** severely stricken by misfortune, grief, or disaster; deeply in love; **hard-pushed,** in difficulties; **hard run** *U.S.*, in difficulties or want, esp. with regard to money; **hard-wearing,** able to stand a considerable amount of wear; **d.** *hard-pressed* (examples); **hard-bound** orig. *U.S.*, (of books) bound in boards; **hard-cased** *U.S.* = **hard-bound*; **e. hard-spun** (example); also *hard-twisted.*

1886 Kipling *Dep. Ditt.* (ed. 2) 108 What a hard-bit gang were we. **1946** *Publishers' Weekly* 5 Oct. 1971/1 Several publishers of hard-bound reprints offer new series or expanded ones. **1952** *Amer. Speech* XXVII. 148 The ubiquitous 'paper-back'..is undoubtedly the cause of a reversal in bookbinding nomenclature. Whereas the board-bound used to be the normal and expected kind of book it is now necessary to use the qualifying adjectives *hard-bound, hard-cased,* or *hard-covered* when one refers to any book not in paper covers. **1959** *Times Lit. Suppl.* 6 Nov. p. xxxviii/4 It is estimated that more than 233,000,000 copies were sold in 1957, as against 32,000,000 hard-bound adult trade books. **1951** *Publishers' Weekly* 2 June 2357 Using the conventional method, eight to ten hours is a fair estimate of the time required to build in each batch of hard-cased books. It takes that long for paste to set and hinges to be formed. **1902** 'Mark Twain' in *North Amer. Rev.* Dec. 762 The poor and the hard-driven. **1949** R. K. Merton *Social Theory* (1951) 17 A small, hard-driven group of professors. **1951** M. McLuhan *Mech. Bride* 157/1 The cowboy is as non-erotic as the hard-driving executive. **1860** 'Old Shekarry' *Hunting Grounds of Old World* i. 19, I feel sure he is hard hit. *Ibid.* 20 A bright crimson pool..showed that he was hard hit. **1884** G. C. Davies *Peter Penniless* xix. 145 Hard Hit. **1891** M. E. Braddon *Gerard* xxix, You've been hard hit. **1909** H. G. Wells *Ann Veronica* ix, She saw her aunt in tears, her father white-faced and hard hit. **1839** *Q. Rev.* LXIII. 25 Our hard-hitting Irish labourers. **1955** *Times* 16 July 5/3 His plea was for an immediately available joint military force of hard-hitting character. **1962** *Christian Cent.* 26 Sept. 1164/1 Hard-hitting new book and films to help you combat communism. **1876** G. M. Hopkins *Poems* (1918) 22 A released shower, let flash to the shine, not a lightning of fire hard-hurled. **1921** Galsworthy *To Let* II. i, A look of life hard-lived. **1884** 'Mark Twain' *Huck. Finn* 89 A couple of mighty hard-looking strangers. **1915** A. Conan Doyle *Valley of Fear* v. 79 They were a mighty hard-looking crowd. **1825** Mill *Speech* in *Autobiogr.* (1924) 282 The Lion, finding himself hard-pressed, called together the aristocracy of the forest. **1891** Hard-pressed [see Pressed *ppl. a.*[1]]. **1961** *New Scientist* 16 Mar. 664/3 Hard-pressed managers and engineers can hope to read only a tiny fraction of it. **1938** *New Statesman* 20 Aug. 282/1 Mr. Lennox Robinson..said that..it was not fair to press the lecturer. But the S.J...was a hard-pressing man. **1950** D. Gascoyne *Vagrant* 43 And the heart's slowly dulled By the hard-pressing years. **1807** J. Barlow *Columb.* VII. 259 To aid her hard-pusht powers. **1834** [Asa Greene] *Perils of Pearl St.* 123 (Bartlett), We began to be hard pushed. Our credit, however was still fair. **1822** J. Fowler *Jrnl.* 22 June (1898) 163 We have left them all behind, and will be hard run for meat. **1834** *Deb. Congress U.S.* 10 Mar. 848 Men, I say, who, to use the mercantile phrase, are 'hard run' to make ends meet, and only wanting an honorable excuse to fail. **1845** *N.Y. Tribune* 1 Nov. (Bartlett), We knew the Tammany party were hard run; but we did not know it was reduced to the necessity of stealing the principles of Nativism. **1865** Rossetti *Let.* 27 July (1965) II. 562 I'm dreffle hard run for tin till the end of next week when I shall have some. **1939** C. Morley *Kitty Foyle* 324 Everybody there looked so hard-run it cheered me up. **1952** C. Day Lewis tr. *Virgil's Aeneid* v. 98 The hard-running waves off Malea. **1963** *Times* 29 May 3/5 Hard-running fairways and small, sometimes tricky greens. **1909** J. Jusserand *Lit. Hist. Eng. People* III. 162 His [*sc.* Shakespeare's] most wonderful inventions were not hard-sought finds. **1906** Goodchild & Tweney *Technol. & Sci. Dict.* 864/2 s.v. *Yarn*, The yarn is defined as soft spun, medium spun, hard spun, according to the amount of twist it has received. **1906** *Daily Chron.* 1 Oct. 3/2 Its purpose of helping the hard-tried bookseller. **1906** Goodchild & Tweney *Technol. & Sci. Dict.* 833/1 s.v. *Warp*, The term applied to the series of spun threads, usually stronger and harder twisted than the weft. **1962** J. T. Marsh *Self-Smoothing Fabrics* xi. 168 Cotton voiles with their hard-twisted yarns may be impregnated on a mangle whose bowls have been wrapped with a fine cloth. **1950** *Mind* LIX. 407 Difficulties which can in one sense of a hard-used word be called 'philosophical'. **1909** *Daily Chron.* 11 June 7/5 Everything possible to be done is achieved in the endeavour to make it hard-wearing. **1928** *Observer* 1 Apr. 13 [This] Lingerie is amazingly hard-wearing. **1894** 'Mark Twain' in *Century Mag.* Jan. 330/1 He was coarsely fed and hard worked. *a* **1930** D. H. Lawrence *Phoenix* (1936) 74 The busy, hard-worked-looking woman.

hard-and-fa·stness. The condition of being hard and fast; hard and fast character.

1903 *Daily Chron.* 5 Mar. 3/3 The 'hard-and-fastness' of experience. **1904** *Westm. Gaz.* 18 June 13/2 By denying the hard-and-fastness and asserting the strictly provisional character of the forms or categories.

Hardanger (hā·ɹdæŋəɹ). The name of a district in west Norway used *attrib.* or *absol.* in names of things connected with Hardanger, as *Hardanger cloth, embroidery, fiddle, violin.*

1883 J. M. Fleming *Old Violins & their Makers* v. 177 In the Exhibition of 1862, a specimen of their class of work—a Hardanger violin—was exhibited. **1900** Grove *Dict. Mus.* (ed. 2) IV. 663/1 The Halling...is accompanied on the Hardanger fiddle.., a violin strung with four stopped and four sympathetic strings. **1908** *Sears, Roebuck Catal.* 527/5 Hardinger [*sic*] Canvas. **1928** *Funk's Stand. Dict.*, *Hardanger*, ornamental needlework in the pattern of diamonds or squares, made at Hardanger. **1930** tr. *T. de Dillmont's Encycl. Needlework* 580 This border is a specimen of the Norwegian openwork known under the name of 'Hardanger' embroidery. **1957** M. B. Picken *Fashion Dict.* 159/1 *Hardanger cloth*, soft cotton cloth of excellent quality. *Ibid.*, *Hardanger embroidery*, heavy, symmetrical, Norwegian needlework done in elaborate diamond or square pattern. **1972** P. A. Whitney *Listen for Whisperer* vii. 120 What you heard was one of our Hardanger fiddles.

hardback. Add: **a.** (Later examples.)

1958 J. Carew *Wild Coast* ii. 22 Hector..watched a hardback beetle crawling up the wall..'Boy, if you kill all the hardbacks that come in here you will make a mess of my clean floor.' **1959** P. Capon *Amongst those Missing* 66 The insects..whirred and buzzed..and the noise made by the hardbacks..kept Harry's nerves on the stretch.

2. A book bound in stiff boards; cf. *paperback(ed). Also *attrib.* So **hard-backed** *a.* (see also *hard *a.* 21).

1954 *New Republic* 26 Apr. 18 (*heading*) New novels: hardbacks or paperbacks. **1957** *Harper's Mag.* Sept. 94/3 Is it not possible that he may come away reading nothing but paperback books, that he will have become attuned to never spending $4.50 on a hardback? **1958** *Economist* 8 Nov. Suppl. 1/1 The retailer's margin on paperbacks is just as profitable as on hardbacks... A hardback order may well be topped up with a couple of 'quality paperbacks'. **1959** *Times* 24 Nov. 6/4 Most 'respectable' American publishers respect the British publisher's hardbacked and paperbacked book rights. **1960** *Times* 3 Feb. 17/4 The big paperback publishers are not hardback publishers but specialists in what is virtually a new genre. **1970** G. Greer *Female Eunuch* 170 Love affairs whether in cheap 'romance' comic-papers or in hard-back novels.

hardboard. [Board *sb.* 3.] A stiff type of board made from wood-pulp fibre. Also *attrib.*

1929 C. J. West *Bibliogr. Pulp & Paper Making 1900–1928* 157 (*heading*) Preparation of hard boards. **1934** *House Building 1934–1936* xxvii. 264 (Advt.), Insulite is an ideal material for the lining of walls and ceilings... Insulite products include Hardboard and Boards for Roof Insulation. **1939** *Chem. Abstr.* 2675 A process of making dense hardboard sheet products, which consists in subjecting fibrous wood or woody lignocellulose material..to a heat treatment. **1959** *Times* 18 May 10/4 Composite hardboard..is displacing traditional panelled construction in many buildings. **1959** *Housewife* June 32 Many of the huts are divided..by hardboard partitions.

hard-boil, *v.* [Back-formation f. next.] *trans.* To boil (an egg) until hard-boiled. Also *transf.*

1895 'Mark Twain' in *Harper's* Nov. 886 No more time to decide it than it takes to hard-boil an egg. *a* **1930** D. H. Lawrence *Etruscan Places* (1932) 16 He [*sc.* a shepherd] is the faun escaping again out of the city precincts... You cannot hard-boil him. **1963** *Listener* 10 Jan. 103/3 Hard-boil the eggs. **1973** *Nature* 23 Mar. 258/2 Considerably less than 12 h is required, either at 91° or 86° C, to hard-boil an egg.

hard-boiled, *a.* [f. *to boil hard,* where *hard* is a predicative adj. Cf. Hard *adv.* 8.]

1. Of an egg: boiled till the white and yolk are solid.

1723 J. Nott *Cook's & Confect. Dict.* No. 21, Mince.. the Yolks of hard boil'd Eggs. **1747** H. Glasse *Cookery* (1784) 71 Chop two or three hard-boiled eggs fine. **1833** [see Hard *adv.* 8 d]. **1846** A. Soyer *Gastron. Regen.* 445 Prepare a border of hard-boiled eggs. **1968** C. Roden *Bk. Middle Eastern Food* 99 (*heading*) Fried hard-boiled eggs.

2. Of articles of clothing: stiff, hard. *U.S.*

1903 A. Adams *Log of Cowboy* ix. 58 That fellow in front of the drug store over there with the hard boiled hat on. **1919** S. Lewis *Free Air* 86 To Claire, traveling men were merely commercial persons in hard-boiled suits.

3. Hardened, callous; hard-headed, shrewd. orig. *U.S.* Hence, of measures, practical.

1886 'Mark Twain' *Speeches* (1923) 137 Hard-boiled, hide-bound grammar. **1915** in *Amer. Speech* (1937) 260 Hard boiled egg who wouldn't bid 90 on 100 aces. **1919** in F. A. Pottle *Stretchers* (1930) 354 We are too hard-boiled to make much of a demonstration. *Ibid.* 358 Two hardboiled Irish sergeants are terrorizing the barrack. **1926** *Publishers' Weekly* 10 July 120/1 Stone..being hard-boiled, waited a few days to notice any appreciable increase in sales. **1926** *Ladies' Home Jrnl.* 26 Aug., The hard-boiled cynic has a shell it [*sc.* satire] can never penetrate. **1928** *Weekly Dispatch* 3 June 10/3 From its obscure beginning down in the 'tough' section of New York, up through the 'hard-boiled' wards of the great city, into municipal politics and thence into the Governor's chair. **1929** A. Conan Doyle *Maracot Deep* vi. 153 The hard-boiled Scanlan actually fell down in a faint. **1931** Buck & Anthony *Bring 'Em Back Alive* 163 It is all a hard-boiled proposition of not treading on the other fellow's feet for fear he may rise up and poke his big toe in your eye. **1932** E. Wilson *Devil take Hindmost* viii. 80 That man of iron..a drastic-minded and hard-boiled Dane. *Ibid.* 82 There is a Detroit type which..has some of the energy and hard-boiled bluffness of the Chicagoans. **1934** *Archit. Rev.* LXXV. 116/2 Yet those old houses are safe and kind and probably better employed in modifying some hard-boiled business man's mentality. **1942** *Mind* LI. 274 It certainly is difficult to remain a stoic or a cynic, to be 'hard-boiled', for a long time. **1959** *Encounter* Sept. 62/2 The disregard of truth in favour of hard-boiled scientific ideals. **1968** *Times* 27 Sept. 2/3 Mr. Heath's hard-boiled image is beginning to crack.

Hence **hard-boi·ledly** *adv.*; **hard-boi·ledness.**

1933 H. J. Massingham *London Scene* iv. 76 No other quarter of London is so consciously, hard-boiledly, shamelessly middle-class [*sc.* as Kensington]. **1934** Webster, Hard-boiledness. **1936** *Times Lit. Suppl.* 28 Mar. 255/2 Pareto apprehended the essential 'hardboiledness' of politics by personal and bitter experience. **1939** A. Huxley *After many a Summer* I. vii. 86 He dreaded for her the influence of so much cynicism and hardboiledness.

ha·rd-burned, -burnt, *a.* [Hard *adv.* 8 d.] Made hard by intensified firing.

1851 C. Cist *Cincinnati* 214 Walls of hard-burnt brick. **1869** *Rep. Comm. Agric. U.S. 1868* 360 Hard-burned terra cotta pipes. **1893** Kate Sanborn *Truthf. Wom. S. California* 45 Half-cylindrical plates of hard-burnt clay.

harden, *v.* Add: **1. b.** *spec.* of metals.

1797 *Encycl. Brit.* VIII. 310/1 There are several ways of hardening iron and steel, as by hammering them, quenching them in cold water, &c. *a* **1877** Knight *Dict. Mech.* II. 1060/2 Iron is surface hardened by heating to a bright red, sprinkling with prussiate of potash, allowing to cool to a dull red, and cooling with water. **1957** *Encycl. Brit.* VI. 906/2 After the blades are forged or cut out they are hardened by heating in a suitable furnace to the correct temperature and then quenched.

7. *to harden off*: to inure (plants) to cold by gradually reducing the temperature of a hot-bed or forcing-house or by increasing the time of exposure to wind and sunlight.

1873 *Young Englishwoman* May 238/1 Everything which has been kept in the house during winter for summer planting, or raised in a frame..should be gradually hardened to endure the changes of life in the open air... This 'hardening off', as the gardeners term it [etc.]. **1905** *Terms Forestry & Logging* 13 *Harden off*, to prepare seedlings in the seedbed for transplanting by gradually exposing them to wind and sunlight. **1909** *Daily Chron.* 5 June 9/5 This cool treatment or 'hardening off' process. **1912** *Chambers's Jrnl.* Dec. 848/1 Plants raised in this frame require no hardening off. **1933** *Jrnl. R. Hort. Soc.* LVIII. 117 Such young plants are generally well hardened-off, and receive but little check when transferred to their new quarters. **1970** C. Lloyd *Well-Tempered Garden* ii. 54 When they [*sc.* the cuttings] have rooted, they can be ..returned to a close atmosphere but then gradually hardened off by the admission of more air.

b. To render (a nuclear missile or base) hard (see *hard *a.* 14 f).

1958 R. D. Bowers in *Air Univ. Q. Rev.* X. 90 Another possibility..might be to harden our sites. *Ibid.* 92 Repeating the analyses and assigning various values to the parameters should provide a good feeling for the payoff in hardening missile sites. **1960** *Times* 11 Feb. 11/6 Though land-based missiles can be 'hardened' by burying them and surrounding them with concrete they are still vulnerable to..nuclear attack. **1972** *Sci. Amer.* June 15/3 Attempts to 'harden' such fixed missile-launchers (that is, to increase their resistance to the effects of nuclear explosions) are in the long run doomed to futility.

ha:rdenabi·lity. *Metallurgy.* [f. HARDEN *v.*: see -ITY.] The extent to which a metal may be hardened (see also quot. 1954).

1932 *Jrnl. Iron & Steel Inst.* CXXVI. 609 (*heading*) Factors affecting the inherent hardenability of steel. **1950** J. H. BATEMAN *Materials of Construction* 411 The surface hardness and the distance from the surface of the hardening effect are measures of the hardenability of steel. **1951** *Engineering* 14 Dec. 764/2 He said that in some circumstances an alloy content was necessary in order to achieve the necessary hardenability of the steel. **1954** *Gloss. Terms Iron & Steel (B.S.I.)* 1. 16 *Hardenability*, the property which determines the depth and distribution of hardness after quenching under specified conditions. *Ibid.*, *Hardenability test*, a test to assess hardenability. A common example is the Jominy test.

hardened, *ppl. a.* Add: **1.** (Additional example.)

1730 [see QUENCHING *vbl. sb.* 1].

3. Rendered hard (see *HARD *a.* 14 f).

1960 *Aeroplane* XCIX. 588/2 In the case of Atlas, this hurried development has resulted in four different types of operational launch site—unprotected, semi-protected, semi-hardened and hardened—and immense cost has been a feature of the programme. **1962** *Listener* 5 Apr. 605/2 A relatively small number of 'hardened', invulnerable, I.C.B.M.s.

hardener. Add: **2.** That which hardens. **a.** *Photogr.* Any chemical used in the making of gelatine negatives to prevent the melting or frilling of the film in warm weather.

1909 *Cent. Dict.* Suppl., Hardener [Photogr.]. **1930** *Sel. Gloss. Motion Techn.* (*Acad. Motion Pict., Hollywood*), *Hardener*, solution used to harden photographic emulsion. **1948** A. L. M. SOWERBY *Dict. Photogr.* (ed. 17) 362 A hardener containing 1½ per cent. of potash alum, used at this *p*H value, may be expected to raise the melting point of the gelatine.

b. In various technical applications (see quots.).

1903 *Westm. Gaz.* 30 Nov. 2/1 The hardening temperature for the steel called 'high carbon' is difficult to define; for the personal equation comes into play, and with different hardeners the variation in hardening temperature often reduces the quality of the steel. **1945** R. T. ROLFE *Dict. Metallogr.* 101 *Hardeners*, alloys prepared for the purpose of adding small quantities of additional elements to molten metals. **1951** *Gloss. Terms Plastics (B.S.I.)* 17 *Hardener*, a material used to promote the setting of certain types of synthetic resin. **1959** *Gloss. Packaging Terms (B.S.I.)* 13 *Hardener*, a chemical used to promote the setting of adhesive. **1966** A. W. LEWIS *Gloss. Woodworking Terms* 43 *Hardener*, liquid used to speed up the setting of resin glue. **1967** E. CHAMBERS *Photolitho-Offset* ix. 130 Potassium alum is recommended as a *hardener* in preference to chrome alum which, although more potent, loses its hardening power after short use and forms a sludge.

hardening, *vbl. sb.* and *ppl. a.* (Further examples: see Dict. s.v. HARDEN *v.*)

1877 *Encycl. Brit.* VI. 734/1 The hardening is accomplished by heating the blade to a cherry-red heat and suddenly quenching it in cold water. **1902** *Daily Chron.* 18 Jan. 5/4 The hardening of new-arrived drafts [of troops] is most noticeable. **1902** A. BENNETT *Anna of Five Towns* viii. 176 The 'hardening-on' kiln, a minor oven where for twelve hours the oil is burnt out of the colour in decorated ware. **1908** *Westm. Gaz.* 15 Apr. 1/3 The inexorable and hardening passage of twenty years. *Ibid.* 21 Aug. 5/4 There has been a great hardening on the part of the merchants, who were formerly placing the stones [*sc.* diamonds] on the market for anything they could fetch. **1930** *Economist* 5 Apr. 758/2 The hardening of bill rates, which put a further reduction of the Bank Rate out of court for the time being. **1936** *Forestry* X. 124 By exposure to suitable, but not damagingly low, temperatures plants are rendered more resistant to frost; this is the process known as hardening, and takes place naturally during the autumn. **1940** *Economist* 6 Jan. 12/2 These difficulties have already had as their effect a general hardening of prices. **1959** *Chambers's Encycl.* X. 686/2 Most fixing solutions also contain a tanning or hardening agent which unites with the gelatin of the emulsion layer, increases its melting-point and reduces its swelling in water. **1970** *New Yorker* 17 Oct. 171/1 These maneuvers have all added up to what one astute observer of the talks has described as 'a hardening of the arteries'.

harder (hā·ɹdəɹ). *S. Afr.* Also 8 **harter,** 20 **haarder.** [a. Afrikaans *harder*, Du., LG. *harder*, OE. *heardhara, heardra.*] Any of various species of the grey mullet family (Mugilidæ), of which *Liza ramada* and *M. cephalus* are well known.

1731 G. MEDLEY tr. *Kolben's Pres. State Cape Good-Hope* II. 193 Theris..about the Cape a Sort of Herrings the Cape-Europeans call Harters. **1838** D. MOODIE tr. *Record* 13 We..caught and salted 400 large steenbrass, and about 2,000 harders. **1892** SIMMONDS *Dict. Trade* (new ed.), *Harder*, a kind of mullet about twelve inches long, caught near the coasts of the Cape colony. **1947** K. H. BARNARD *Pict. Guide S. Afr. Fishes* 81 The family of Grey Mullets, called in South Africa Harders or Springers (*Mugilidae*) is economically very important. **1962** *Cape Argus* (Mag. Sect.) 11 Aug. 1/7 Bunches of harder, maasbanker and pilchards and many other kinds of fish. **1971** *Daily Dispatch* (East London, Cape Province) 8 Mar., There were hundreds of haarders (mullet) in the bay itself.

hardhack. (Earlier and later examples.)

1832 W. D. WILLIAMSON *Hist. State Maine* I. 116 The Hardhack, a barren bush, usually chooses poor cold ground for its residence and growth. **1880** *Harper's Mag.* Dec. 85 Them mulleins an' hardhacks in the buryin'-ground. **1968** E. R. BUCKLER *Ox Bells & Fireflies* vi. 95 The hardhacks, with roots like the roots of wisdom teeth, to be kept back from the edges of the cleared land.

hardhead[1]**, hard-head.** Add: **1.** (Later example.)

1967 P. JONES *Fifth Defector* xiii. 190 I'd advise you to keep your mouth shut and let the hardheads handle it at embassy level.

b. A person not easily affected by alcohol.

1860 E. COWELL *Diary* 19 Mar. (1934) 41 Mr. Van Orden a very pleasant, but, to Sam, very dangerous companion being a great drinker, and one of the 'Hard Heads' whom drink does not seem to hurt.

Hardian: see *HARDYAN *a.* and *sb.*

hardie, var. HARDY *sb.*

1957 R. LISTER *Decorative Wrought Iron-Work* ii. 13 The square hole through the heel is called a *hardie hole*. *Ibid.* 228 *Hardie*, a small chisel, used in the anvil. **1964** [see *hot set* s.v. *HOT *a.* 12 c]. **1965** A. F. SHIRLEY *Metalwork Techniques* vi. 84 Metal..should be heated where it is to be cut and this part placed on the hardie and hammered to form a vee cut.

hardly, *adv.* Add: **10.** *hardly-used* (earlier example), *-won.*

1866 TROLLOPE *Belton Est.* II. vi. 158 The hardly-used groom had returned from his futile afternoon's inquiry. **1937** *Discovery* Aug. 240/2 The hardly-won natural gem. **1952** C. P. BLACKER *Eugenics* 282 Each hardly-won improvement in human conditions.

hard metal. 1. Any of various alloys valued for their hardness.

1729, 1845 [see METAL *sb.* 5]. **1911** *Encycl. Brit.* XXI. 339/1 Hard metal (96 parts of tin, 8 of antimony and 2 of copper), a mixture very closely resembling..'Britannia metal'.

2. (See quot. 1967.)

1936 *Jrnl. Iron & Steel Inst.* CXXXIV. 66A The author discusses the application of hard metal alloys and of diamond substitutes (such as tungsten carbide) to the hard-facing of tools. **1960** *Ibid.* CXCIV. 532/1 The final section is devoted to a consideration of materials used for cutting tools, namely unalloyed tool steels, alloyed tool steels,..hard metals, i.e. sintered tungsten carbide and the like. **1967** A. K. OSBORNE *Encycl. Iron & Steel Industry* (ed. 2) 195/1 *Hard metals*, powdered carbides of tungsten, tantalum, or titanium, cemented into solid masses by mixing with powdered cobalt or nickel, then cold pressing and sintering. Used for cutting tools, wire drawing dies, and parts subjected to heavy wear and abrasion.

hardness. Add: **c.** *spec.* The degree of resistance of a mineral to abrasion or scratching.

1784 R. KIRWAN *Elem. Mineral.* 1. App. 171 (*heading*) Table of the comparative hardness of different Species of Stones, extracted chiefly from the Memoirs of Stockholm, for 1768. Mr. Quist, the author of this Memoir determined the hardness of most of the following stones. **1904** GOODCHILD & TWENEY *Technol. & Sci. Dict.* 279/2 *Hardness*, the hardness of a mineral is determined by noting which of the standard minerals the specimen may be scratched by, and which of the ten it will scratch.

d. Of radiation (cf. *HARD *a.* 16* a).

1926 R. W. LAWSON tr. *Hevesy & Paneth's Man. Radioactivity* iv. 1. 45 The shorter the wave-length of the γ-rays, the greater is their penetrating power through matter, or the greater their 'hardness'.

hardometer (hāɹdǫ·mɪtəɹ). [f. HARD *a.* + -O + -METER.] An instrument for measuring the hardness of metals.

1934 H. O'NEILL *Hardness of Metals* iii. 90 The 'Firth Hardometer'..is an excellent bench instrument. **1940** *Jrnl. R. Aeronaut. Soc.* XLIV. 845 The following chapter carries on the hardness tests with details of the Rothwell test, the Firth hardometer, the Firth-Brown variable load hardometer and notched bar impact testing. **1946** *Firth Brown Gloss. Metall. Terms* 26 *Firth hardometer*,... For testing harder materials a pyramid diamond indenter is recommended and can be supplied with the [Brinell] machine in addition to the hardened steel ball. **1958** *Oxf. Univ. Gaz.* 10 Mar. 772/1 Mr. Allen also completed the examination of about 40 Bronze Age implements of copper and bronze by hardometer.

hard-on: see *HARD *sb.* 1 d.

hard-pan. For *U.S.* read orig. *U.S.* Add: **1.** (Earlier and later examples.)

1817 T. DWIGHT *Trav. New Eng.* (1821) I. 374 What is here called hard pan, a very stiff loam, so closely combined, as wholly to prevent the water from passing through it. **1963** D. W. & E. E. HUMPHRIES tr. *Termier's Erosion & Sedimentation* 406 *Hardpan*, an English agricultural term (used mainly in the U.S.A., Africa and Australia) for a horizon in podsolic and lateritic soils hardened by precipitation and cementation. **1968** *New Scientist* 10 Oct. 79/3 The number of rice paddies under cultivation in some Far Eastern countries could be doubled using an asphalt 'hardpan'.

3. *attrib.* and *Comb.*

1870 J. K. MEDBERY *Men & Myst. Wall St.* 212 Hard pan is soon reached, and both old world and new are full of hard-pan capitalists. **1889** K. MUNROE *Golden Days* xi. 122 To tell the honest hard-pan truth. **1907** R. W. SERVICE *Songs of Sourdough* (1908) 77 When a man gits on his uppers in a hard-pan sort of town. **1928** *Bull. Amer. Soil Survey Assoc.* IX. 33 Immaturely developed soils may have a hardpan-like horizon.

hardpeer (hā·ɹtpīəɹ). *S. Afr.* Also **hardepeer,** and anglicized **hard pear.** [Afrikaans; f. Du. *hard* hard + *peer* pear.] A small tree of the Cape, *Olinia cymosa*, having hard wood; also applied to other trees (see quot. 1913).

1801 J. BARROW *Trav. S. Afr.* I. 340 Hard peer...Uses.. Sometimes in waggons. **1851** *Catal. Gt. Exhib.* IV. 1. 951 Pear (hard). **1874** LINDLEY & MOORE *Treas. Bot.* Suppl. s.v. *Olinia*, The plant grows in rocky thickets and woods at the Cape, where it is known as Hardpeer. **1880** Hard Pear [see PEAR *sb.* 3]. **1887** C. A. MOLONEY *Sk. Forestry W. Afr.* 354 Hardpeer of the Cape..Shrub 4 to 10 feet high. **1913** PETTMAN *Africanderisms*, *Hard Pear.* (1) In Natal this name is given to *Pleurostylia capensis*. (2) In the Cape Colony it is applied to *Strychnos Henningsii.* **1961** PALMER & PITMAN *Trees S. Afr.* lii. 297 *Strychnos Henningsii. Hard pear*, hardepeer... This tree should not be confused with the 'hard pear' of the Knysna forests, which is *Olinia cymosa*, and which belongs to a different family.

hard scrabble (hāɹd skræ·b'l). *U.S. colloq.* [cf. SCRABBLE *v.* 4.] **1.** 'A place thought of as the acme of barrenness where a livelihood may be obtained only with great difficulty. Also attrib. Often as a proper name.' (*Dict. Americanisms.*)

1804 LEWIS & CLARK *Orig. Jrnls.* (1905) VII. 38 Got on our way at hard Scrable Perarie. **1904** *Pittsburgh Gaz.* 7 July 4 In the early days of my ministry..I was sent to take charge of a little hard-scrabble circuit. **1949** *Sat. Even. Post* 30 Apr. 22/3 She was the daughter of a hard-scrabble rancher. **1972** *Science* 26 May 891/1 The reservoir would back up along the creek and inundate 125 small, hardscrabble farms that lay along 24 miles of the stream's flood-plain.

2. 'A vigorous effort made under great stress.' (*Dict. Americanisms.*)

1812 *Salem Gaz.* 29 May 2/3 Presidential Hard Scrabble! **1851** H. MELVILLE *Moby Dick* II. xxx. 205 While taking that hard-scrabble scramble upon the dead whale's back. **1854** S. HALE *Lett.* (1919) 7 By a well-organised hard-scrabble, Luc. and I get the breakfast things washed by nine o'clock. **1972** *Sat. Rev.* 26 Feb. 31/3 [Ulster] Catholics..enjoy the benefits of..an economy that may be hardscrabble but is still substantially more prosperous than the South's.

hardshell, *a.* and *sb.* Add: **A.** *adj.* **1.** (U.S. examples.) Also applied to the fruit of a nut-tree.

1798 *Spectator* (N.Y.) 7 Nov. 2/5 Hardshell almond trees. **1818** *Amer. Monthly Mag.* II. 296 The hard shell clam..is cooked by roasting. **1855** *Knickerbocker* XLVI. 222 'Hard-shell' clam-catchers. **1942** M. K. RAWLINGS *Cross Creek Cookery* xvii. 190 We have four turtles, the gopher;..the hard-shell cooter; the soft-shell; and the alligator cooter.

2. (Earlier examples.)

1838 W. Y. ALLEN *Diary* 17 July in *S.W. Hist. Q.* (1914) XVII. 54 Was introduced to Daddy Spraggins, a Hardshell Baptist preacher. **1846** J. J. HOOPER *Adv. Simon Suggs* i. 13 He lived with his father, and an old 'hard shell' Baptist preacher.

B. *sb.* **1.** Also *fig.*, a stubborn or unemotional person.

1858 *South. Cultivator* XVI. 187/2 We have, however, one or two specimens in our eye of the genus, *hard shell*, who still do as their *daddies* did. **1916** H. L. WILSON *Somewhere in Red Gap* iv. 135 A grouchy old hardshell with white hair and whiskers whirling about his head. **1919** T. K. HOLMES *Man fr. Tall Timber* xiii. 156 I've ridden up here from Tall Timber Junction to get acquainted with you hardshells.

2. (Earlier and later examples.)

1845 *Knickerbocker* XXVI. 285 A 'Hard-Shell' recently turned a 'Soft-Shell' out of church. **1855** *Putnam's Monthly* V. 190 The claim of 'Hard-Shells', touching their familiarity with the Bible. **1872** E. EGGLESTON *Hoosier Schoolmaster* xii, Of course the Hardshells are prodigiously illiterate. **1908** *Dialect Notes* III. 319 *Hardshell*, a Primitive Baptist.

hardshelled, *a.* **1.** Having a hard shell; = HARDSHELL *a.* 1.

1611 [in Dict.]. **1782** J. H. ST. J. DE CRÈVECŒUR *Lett. Amer. Farmer* iv. 135 The shores..abound with the soft-shelled, the hard-shelled, and the great sea clams. **1796** B. HAWKINS *Lett.* (1916) 17 A grove of dwarf hard shelled hickory trees. **1839** C. F. BRIGGS *Adv. H. Franco* II. i. 2 Close by, was a negro opening hard-shelled clams. **1865** *Trans. Ill. Agric. Soc.* V. 408 Beetles, or, as they are sometimes called, 'hard-shelled bugs'. **1942** M. K. RAWLINGS *Cross Creek Cookery* xvii. 191 Why does a hard-shelled cooter lay a soft-shelled egg, and a soft-shelled cooter lay a hard-shelled egg?

2. *fig.* = HARDSHELL *a.* 2. Also, hardened, callous.

1842 J. S. BUCKINGHAM *Slave States Amer.* I. 197 The Baptists [in Macon, Georgia] are of the order called here 'Hardshelled Baptists'. **1872** W. MATHEWS *Getting on in World* xi. 153 There is no man so 'hard-shelled' that his soul cannot be reached by kindness. **1904** *N.Y. Herald* 23 Oct. 16 There are a good many hard shelled Bryan men who intend to vote for Roosevelt. **1909** R. A. WASON *Happy Hawkins* 108 It was a hard-shelled book. **1941** J. STUART *Men of Mountains* 331 If you could see all of us Republicans, Democrats, Methodists, Forty-Gallon Baptists, Hard shelled Baptists,..shaking hands and asking the other how he is after the long night o' sleep. **1965** *Times Lit. Suppl.* 25 Nov. 1046/1 Various forms of hard-shelled Establishment versus dissent.

hard stone, ha·rdstone. a. Any type of hard stone. **b.** A precious or semi-precious stone.

The earliest examples are instances of the informal union of *hard* adj. and *stone*.

1568 [see HARD *a.* 1]. **1613** [see STONE *sb.* 2]. **1733** W. TOWNESEND *Let.* 28 Aug. in *Archit. Rev.* (1945) XCVIII. 105/3 Eight feet below the top of ye hardstone plinth. **1905** *Daily Chron.* 11 July 5/7 The hard-stone works. **1921** *Dict. Occup. Terms* (1927) § 572 *Banker hand, hewer* or *mason*; *hard-stone banker mason*; cuts, and if necessary saws, blocks of stone at 'banker'. **1931** *Times* 16 Mar. 22/4 Chinese hard-stone carvings. **1935** *Burlington Mag.* June 299/1 (*title*) An exhibition of hardstone carvings. **1936** *Ibid.* Aug. 91/2 A few jades and hardstones. **1958** *Times* 2 Dec. 12/5 Chinese porcelain and hardstones realized £9,585 at Christie's yesterday.

hard-tack. Add: (Earlier and later examples.) Also, hard bread or biscuits generally. Also *fig.* and *attrib.*

1836 *Knickerbocker* VIII. 203 When I was the size of that monkey there, who knows how to do nothing but gnaw hard tack. **1888** *Century Mag.* XXXVI. 614/1 A little rabbit that kept..nibbling at our bread and hard-tack. **1899** T. HALL *Tales* 108 A meal of raw bacon, hard-tack and cold water. **1909** *Daily Chron.* 8 July 9/2 Of all the hard-tack breads..I have found..the small ringed bread of Siberia the most substantial. **1931** *Economist* 5 Dec. 105/1 It has paved the way..for the real hard-tack committee work on the thousand practical problems of the constitution builder. **1955** W. FOSTER-HARRIS *Look of Old West* ii. 56 Hardtack..was hard, unleavened bread, baked in cakes..about 3 inches square, decorated with what looked like nail punctures. **1960** *Economist* 15 Oct. 219/1 Some of those who raised left-wing political rather than hard-tack organisational questions being shouted down by genuine party workers.

hardtail (hā·ɹd,tē[i]l). *U.S.* [f. HARD *a.* + TAIL *sb.*[1]] **a.** A marine fish, *Caranx crysos*, found in the western parts of the Atlantic Ocean.

1884 G. B. GOODE *Fisheries U.S.* I. 324 The Jurel—Caranx Pisquetus. This fish, known about Pensacola as the 'Jurel', 'Cojinua', and 'Hard-tail'. **1902** JORDAN & EVERMANN *Amer. Food & Game Fishes* 306 The runner, hard tail, or jurel, reaches a foot or more in length..and is a food-fish of considerable importance. **1968** *OECD Multiling. Dict. Fish* 139 *Caranx crysos*...Also called runner, hardtail, crevalle.

b. *slang.* A mule.

1917 A. G. EMPEY *Over Top* 294 *Hard tails*, mules. **1931** 'D. STIFF' *Milk & Honey Route* 207 *Hard tails*, mules, usually old ones. So named because they show little response to the skinner's whip. Young mules are shavetails. **1966** *Publ. Amer. Dial. Soc.* XLVI. 26, I was driving an old pair of hard tails.

hard up. Add: Also *sb.* (see quots.).

1851 MAYHEW *Lond. Labour* I. 3/2 The cigar-end finders, or 'hard-ups', as they are called. **1905** *Daily Chron.* 17 May 6/7 In tramp phrase they [*sc.* cigar and cigarette ends] are known as 'hard-ups', and are smoked along the road. **1933** 'G. ORWELL' *Down & Out* xxxii. 236 Hard-up—tobacco made from cigarette ends. **1959** *Listener* 5 Mar. 406/1 We roll a couple of 'hard-ups' to smoke. Hard-ups are made of tobacco we collect from cigarette ends.

hard-upishness. (Earlier example.)

1859 D. G. ROSSETTI *Let.* 23 June (1965) I. 353 As for hardupishness..I have been literally penniless for two days.

hardware. Add: **1. b.** Weapons.

1865 L. N. BEAUDRY *Hist. Rec. 5th N.Y. Cavalry* (1868) 38 Capt. Hammond..charged upon the rebels.., crying as he flew forward, 'give them your hardware, boys!' **1885** *Daily News* 12 Nov. 5/4 The chances are that the authorities..may have had an eye on such kind of 'hardware' [*sc.* torpedoes]. **1914** JACKSON & HELLYER *Vocab. Criminal Slang* 42 *Hardware*,..weapons; knives; razors; tools and paraphernalia used by safe-crackers [etc.]. **1929** *Amer. Speech* V. 59 His [*sc.* a Nebraska cowboy's] fire arms are frequently called his 'hardware'. **1955** *Bull. Atomic Sci.* Apr. 168/2 How much does our superiority in hardware contribute to our over-all security? **1966** *New Yorker* 29 Oct. 236 Oh, put your hands up, dear. He's got the hardware. **1967** *Observer* 11 June 11/2 The wholesale destruction this week of expensive hardware has brought home to some Arabs the folly of an extravagant armament policy.

c. The physical components of a system or device as opposed to the procedures required for its operation; opp. **software*.

1947 D. R. HARTREE *Calculating Machines* 14 The ENIAC... I shall give a brief account of it, since it will make the later discussion more realistic if you have an idea of some 'hardware' and how it is used, and this is the equipment with which I am best acquainted. **1953** A. D. & K. H. V. BOOTH *Automatic Digital Calculators* xv. 169 The engineering difficulties encountered in this type of machine are great, and a considerable increase in the size and complexity of the 'hardware' seems inevitable. **1960** [see *ALGORITHMIC *a.*]. **1960** *Times* 21 Mar. 13/6 Academician Sedov..knows the hazards of 'hardware' projected into space. **1960** *Times* (Computer Suppl.) 4 Oct. p. iii/7 Both punched card and computer 'hardware' will continue to develop very rapidly. **1962** J. GLENN in *Into Orbit* 6 The engineers and technicians had to start from scratch to develop the capsule and some of the other pieces of hardware which we are using. **1963** *Engineering* 23 Aug. 246/1 Hardware means the apparatus or machinery of computing, both the main instrument and its peripheral or ancillary equipment. **1964** *Daily Tel.* 14 Feb. 29/8 Engineers are leaving because..they cannot rely on..early development being continued to the 'hardware' stage. **1965** *New Scientist* 4 Nov. 331/1 All necessary hardware [for computers] exists today and is in production, but getting a comprehensive system off the ground requires the creation of a great deal of software. **1968** *Lebende Sprachen* XIII. 3/1 The practical requirements for the manned lunar landing program are being translated into hardware, experiments and programs. **1968** *Brit. Med. Bull.* XXIV. 198/2 Elaborate hardware is not a substitute for a thoroughgoing analysis of the whole area of medical vocabularies, procedures, information and systems for the care of patients. **1969** *Computers & Humanities* III. 139 Hardware refers to the physical apparatus while software describes the program languages that permit efficient use of the hardware.

d. Various slang and colloquial senses.

1839 *Spirit of Times* 1 June 153/3 He prepared to swallow his fifth invoice of 'hardware' [*sc.* whisky]. **1945** L. SHELLY *Jive Talk Dict.* 12/2 *Hardware*, flashy jewelry. **1951** I. SHAW *Troubled Air* vii. 105 When the rating goes up, I buy my hardware [*sc.* jewellery] at Cartier's. **1963** *Amer. Speech* XXXVIII. 206 *Hardware*, slang for a medal or trophy won in a skiing competition. **1968** *Times* 9 Sept. 6/7 Prince William has some useful leisure hardware—like a private aircraft.

2. hardware paper, a make of durable wrapping-paper; **hardware store** orig. *U.S.*, an ironmongery shop.

1789 *Boston Directory*, Whitwell,..hardware store. **1886** *Harper's Mag.* June 48/1 Wrapping the stem [of the peach-tree]..with strong hardware or sheathing paper. **1964** M. GALLANT in R. Weaver *Canad. Short Stories* 2nd Ser. (1968) 60 Across the Alps was the name of a hardware store and its address on the other side of Montreal. **1972** *P.O. Telephone Directory, London Yellow Pages Classified* (North) 152/1 Barker's Hardware Stores Ltd, 43 High St.

hardwood. Add: **1.** (Later examples of attrib. use.)

1840 *Knickerbocker* XXVIII. 337 Most unexceptional 'hardwood' land. **1869** *Trans. Ill. Agric. Soc.* VII. 578 Some elevated ridges..called technically, hard wood ridges..escaped wholly, or in part the effects of the fire. **1903** S. E. WHITE *Forest* viii. 89 The trunks of the hardwood forest. **1911** *Daily Colonist* (Victoria, B.C.) 15 Apr. 18/1 We mail on request an illustrated catalogue of plain and fancy hardwood floors with prices attached. **1968** E. R. BUCKLER *Ox Bells & Fireflies* xxi. 297, I stand on top of the hardwood hill.

b. *ellipt.* A hardwood tree.

1905 J. NISBET *Forester* I. III. iv. 419 Pit-planting is the usual method of growing Oak and all other kinds of hardwoods. **1908** *Westm. Gaz.* 15 Aug. 15/3 The tender colours of the hardwoods bursting towards summer glory. **1972** *Country Life* 16 Mar. 653/3 The number of trees by species..together with some idea of their quality (in the case of hardwoods, veneer, good or..low-grade mining and fencing timber).

hardy, *a.* **4. b.** (Earlier examples); *hardy annual* (earlier examples); *hardy perennial*, a herbaceous plant with a perennial rootstock; also *fig.*

1664 EVELYN *Kalendarium Hortense* in *Sylva* 59 Auriculas..need not be hous'd; it is a hardy Plant. **1783** T. BLAIKIE *Diary of Scotch Gardener* (1931) 187 A little way from St Germains..ther is a Curious Gentelman one Mr. Trochereau who has a curious collection of hardy exotick plants. **1813** [see BORECOLE]. **1831** *Athenæum* 5 Nov. 718 This, truly, is 'a hardy Annual'! **1852** R. BUIST *Amer. Flower-Garden Directory* (ed. 5) 29 Hardy Annuals..are possessed of much beauty of hue. **1900** J. M. ABBOTT in W. D. Drury *Bk. Gardening* viii. 260 Hardy herbaceous perennials are a very popular set of plants. **1916** 'TAFFRAIL' *Pincher Martin* xiv. 248 The subjects most often brought under discussion, however—the hardy perennials, so to speak—were: [etc.]. **1944** A. HUXLEY *Let.* 9 Apr. (1969) 502, I am very glad to hear the good news of *The Art of Seeing*. The book has all the appearance of a hardy perennial. **1967** C. O. SKINNER *Madame Sarah* vii. 132 Thousands of playgoers travelled thousands of miles to sob over Marguerite Gauthier's departure from life..in that hardy perennial whose actual title is *La Dame aux Camélias*. **1967** C. LLOYD *Hardy Perennials* i. 9 The hardy perennial possesses every virtue that you could require of a plant, except for a permanently visible structure.

Hardyan, Hardian (hā·ɹdiăn), *a.* and *sb.* [f. the name of Thomas *Hardy* (1840–1928), novelist and poet + -IAN.] Characteristic of the works of T. Hardy. Also *sb.*, an admirer or follower of Hardy. Similarly **Hardye·sque** *a.*

1910 R. BROOKE *Let.* Jan. (1968) 216 That abysmal darkness..inspired me with thousands of Hardyesque short poems about people whose affairs went dismally wrong. **1927** H. CRANE *Let.* 29 May (1965) 300 A footnote of Hardian doom. **1929** *Sat. Rev.* 24 Aug. 221/2 But in the dialogue of the rustics it shows a delicious Hardyesque sense of humour. **1931** *Times Lit. Suppl.* 28 May 423/1 Confirmed and receptive Hardians..will know how many ..approach it with preconceptions of various degrees of falseness. **1941** BLUNDEN *Thomas Hardy* 271 It can be admitted by almost any Hardyan that the poor passages in his work are an offering to the wanton or the unsympathetic critic. **1944** —— *Cricket Country* 142 An unspoken Hardyan complaint. **1960** C. DAY LEWIS *Buried Day* vi. 111 The rich Dorset accents and the Hardy-esque names.

hare, *sb.* Add: **2.** *to make a hare of* (examples).

1830 W. CARLETON *Traits & Stories* II. 111 What a hare Mat mad iv 'im;..and did not lave him a leg to stand upon. **1938** J. CARY *Castle Corner* x. 562 That fella thought he'd made a hare of me, but I knew one trick better.

3. b. *hare and hounds* (= *paper chase* s.v. PAPER *sb.* 12): also *fig.*

1920 T. S. ELIOT *Sacred Wood* 11 Coleridge is apt to take leave of the data of criticism, and arouse the suspicion that he has been diverted into a metaphysical hare-and-hounds. **1938** PARTRIDGE *World of Words* ix. 261 Well worth the hare-and-hound chase through the dictionary. **1963** *Daily Tel.* 5 Feb. 20/6 Throughout his speech he was constantly heckled and interrupted, but the scene cannot be described as 'Hare and hounds'.

6. hare-coursing: see COURSING *vbl. sb.*[1] 2; **hare-pocket**, a pocket in a shooting-coat, made of a size to hold a hare; **hare's fur** *Ceramics*, a brown or black glaze streaked with silvery white or yellow used on some Chinese pottery.

1840 D. P. BLAINE *Encycl. Rural Sports* v. i. 562 The credit of the organisation of the sport of hare coursing.. [is] without all doubt the undisputed property of the English. **1972** *Times* 5 Feb. 1/2 The House of Commons ended its Friday sitting in uproar and confusion when the Hare Coursing (Abolition) Bill was talked out. **1925** G. BURRARD *Big Game Hunting* 281 Two 'hare' or 'poacher' pockets will be found most useful on occasions. **1950** *Q. Jrnl. Forestry* XLIV. 60 The map should be made ..to fit into the forester's hare pocket. **1899** S. W. BUSHELL *Oriental Ceramic Art* xxvii. 724 The most highly appreciated ware at the tea-testing parties..was the dark-colored pottery of the province of Fuchien..the tea-bowls of which were known to Chinese virtuosos as 'hare's-fur bowls'. **1934** *Burlington Mag.* May 214/1 *Temmoku* tea bowls with the 'hare's fur' glaze...They have a blackish stone-ware body, and a thick, lustrous black glaze streaked with hair lines of brown and silver. **1959** G. SAVAGE *Antique Coll. Handbk.* 52 The black glazed wares of Honan are of great interest, and tea-bowls with a variegated dark brown glaze, known as 'hare's fur', came from Chien-an in Fukien Province.

hare, *v.*[2] [f. HARE *sb.*] *intr.* †**a.** To double like a hare. **b.** To run or move with great speed. Also with *it.*

1893 FARMER & HENLEY *Slang*, *To hare it*, to retrace one's steps; to double back. **1908** D. COKE *House Prefect* xi. 141 He had heard..the order, 'Hare'! Now 'Hare'! is Seftonian for 'Run—and run jolly quick'! *a* **1914** J. E. RAPHAEL *Mod. Rugby Football* (1918) 262 Receiving the ball well inside his own half-way, Palmer commenced to 'hare' for the touch-line. **1917** P. GIBBS *Battles of Somme* 173 There were other trenches ahead, and the men 'hared' off to these. **1923** WODEHOUSE *Inimitable Jeeves* xiv. 178, I..hared it rapidly to the spot. **1957** *Listener* 19 Dec. 1046/1 The producer..can't go haring about collecting the items. **1958** *Woman* 11 Jan. 47/1, I hared up to London, left my book with the publishers and went to my flat. **1963** *Times* 13 June 5/1 Boulter took over by the backstraight and went haring away past 660 yards in 1 min. 21.1 sec.

harebell. Add: **3.** *attrib.*, as *harebell blue.*

1909 *Daily Chron.* 15 June 7/5 The dress linens..have been prepared in many exquisite shades of leaf-green, pale primrose, hare-bell blue. **1925** T. DREISER *Amer. Trag.* III. xvi. 647 His harebell eyes showing only cold..practical logic. **1940** C. DAY LEWIS *Poems in Wartime* 8 This harebell height of calm. *Ibid.* 9 The climb To a tremulous, hare-bell crest. **1969** R. GODDEN *In this House of Brede* (1970) i. 39 Dame Veronica of the wistful hare-bell blue eyes.

harefoot. Restrict ? *Obs.* to senses 2, 3, 4 in Dict. and add examples to sense 1. Also *hare's foot.*

1901 *Encycl. Sport* I. 329/2 *Harefoot*, a long, narrow foot, carried far forward. **1945** C. L. B. HUBBARD *Observer's Bk. Dogs* 161 American standards permit hare-feet. **1952** R. LEIGHTON *Compl. Bk. Dog* (ed. 6) v. 80 Faults: [in Boxer]..hare's feet.

5. Used adverbially: swiftly. *poet.*

1939 T. S. ELIOT *Family Reunion* I. ii. 60 What of the terrified spirit Compelled..To rise toward the violent sun.. Harefoot over the moon?

Hare Krishna (hā·re kri·ʃnā). [f. Hindi *hare* O God! + *Krishṇā* name of an incarnation of the god Vishnu.] The title of a love-chant or mantra based on a name of the Hindu deity Vishnu; used esp. as an incantation by members of a religious cult in the U.S. and elsewhere; hence *attrib.* or *absol.* to designate this cult or its members.

1968 *New Yorker* 17 Aug. 36 Newspaper pictures of the poet [*sc.* Ginsberg] chanting '*Hare Krishna*' at one of Leary's psychedelic celebrations. **1970** *Time* 3 Aug. 31 He [*sc.* David Hoyt] became a member of the Hare Krishna cult and custodian of the Radha Krishna temple. **1971** *Times* 5 July 3/6 The founder of the Hare Krishna Movement, his Divine Grace A. C. Bhakividanta, did not make his expected appearance. **1971** E. LARSEN *Strange Sects & Cults* viii. 164 Small groups of smiling English youngsters..could be seen slowly dance-marching in file through London's West End..to the accompaniment of some tinkling Oriental instruments, chanting 'Hare Krishna' and offering passers-by literature on their 'Krishna Consciousness Movement'. **1972** G. V. HIGGINS *Friends of Eddie Coyle* xi. 68 Near the first subway kiosk the Hare Krishnas sang and danced, wearing saffron robes and tattered gray sweaters.

harem. Add: **2. b.** Applied *spec.* to the family units of various animals.

1898 D. S. JORDAN *Fur Seals* I. 57 The average size of a harem..is about thirty females to a single bull. **1932** S. ZUCKERMAN *Soc. Life Monkeys & Apes* xi. 178 Sokolowsky's account of sexual life in a chimpanzee harem is by far the best that has hitherto appeared. **1948** A. L. RAND *Mammals E. Rockies* 26 In the autumn..the bull

elk come down from the mountains to gather their harems. **1955** L. DARLING *Seals & Walruses* 24 There are an average of forty cows in a fur seal's harem. **1964** G. DURRELL *Menagerie Manor* i. 32 The peacock..leading his vacant-eyed harem towards their roosting place.

4. harem dress, a dress with a harem hem; **harem hem**, a hem which draws in the material which then billows over it; **harem skirt**, a loose trouser-like skirt as worn in a harem, or an imitation of one; hence *harem-skirted* adj.

1911 *Sphere* 11 Mar. 219 The opinions of London and Paris over the harem skirt seem to be as divided as is the costume itself. **1927** *Delineator* June 21 *Chéruit* was the first to make taffeta frocks in great puffs with harem hems. **1952** *California Stylist* May, The harem dress.. mushrooming fullness on a delicate stem. **1957** *Punch* 14 Aug. 191/1 His cocktail and evening dresses are harem skirted, and there was a bright yellow harem trouser-dress. **1958** J. LAVER *Edwardian Promenade* vii. 163 Two symbolic kinds of skirt: the harem skirt and the hobbleskirt. **1958** *Vogue* Mid-Sept. Extra Issue 77/4 Electric blue chiffon softly wrapping a tiny waist and gently curving into a harem hem. **1966** *Sunday Times* (Colour Suppl.) 27 Feb. 32/4 Paul Poiret's harem dress.. was inspired by Bakst's designs.

haremlik (hēə·rĕm-, hărī·mlik). [Turk., f. HAREM + *-lik* place.] = HAREM I.

1920 *Blackw. Mag.* Nov. 661/2 High above their bench and entered from the Haremlik, is an iron grille or cage, in which the Padishah could overhear unseen his Ministers' deliberations. **1936** N. M. PENZER *Harēm* i. 16 Relations with European powers soon gave rise to the coining of a word that would embrace not only the *harēmlik* and the *serāmlik* but the entire Royal buildings as a whole... The word *seraglio* was chosen. **1941** *Archit. Rev.* XC. 101/2 The houses were divided vertically into two parts—the *Haremlik* or women's quarters, and the *Selamlik* for the men.

hare's-foot. Add: **2*.** A hare's foot used in applying rouge, etc., to the face.

c **1800** [see *burnt cork* s.v. *BURNT *ppl. a.* 7]. **1827** L. T. REDE *Road to Stage* 38 Burn a cork to powder, wet it with beer (which will fix the colouring matter), and apply it with a hare's-foot, or a cloth. **1835** DICKENS *Sk. Boz* (1836) II. 206 The young lady with the liberal display of legs, who is kindly painting his face with a hare's foot. **1859** E. WINSTANLEY *Shifting Scenes Theatr. Life* xxi. 200 There are pots of rouge, hare's feet, powder-boxes. **1877** 'HARESFOOT & ROUGE' *How to 'Make-up'* 13 Then with a hare's foot apply a colouring of Rouge to the cheeks. **1939–40** *Army & Navy Stores Catal.* 1097/1 Theatrical make-up...Hares' feet.

harewood (hēə·ɹwud). Also **hairwood, air-wood** (8 aire-); and simply 7 **ayer, ayre.** [ad. dial. G. *aehre, ehre,* or its apparent source Friulian, etc. *ayar, ayer, aire* :- Rom. **acre* = L. *acer* maple.] Stained sycamore wood, used by cabinet-makers.

1664 EVELYN *Sylva* I. x. 28 The Timber [of Maple] is far superiour to Beech for all uses of the Turner...Also for the lightness (under the name Ayer) imploy'd often by those who make Musical-instruments. **1676** T. MACE *Musick's Mon.* 49 Next, what Wood is Best for the Ribbs. The Air-wood is absolutely the Best. *Ibid.* 64 A Lute made of Ayre. **1723** *Evening Post* 30 May, He has..some fine Aire-wood for furnishing the Insides [of harpsichords]. **1843** HOLTZAPFFEL *Turning* etc. I. 107 A variety of sycamore, which is called harewood, is richer in figure and sometimes striped. **1873** E. SPON *Workshop Rec.* 1st Ser. 414/1 Have the veneers ready, which must be air-wood. *Ibid.* 423/2 Hair-wood. **1899** *Daily News* 22 June 8/7 A cabinet..of inlaid satin, hare, and other woods. **1901** *Westm. Gaz.* 9 May 1/3 On satin and harewood banded with rosewood. **1947** J. C. RICH *Materials & Methods of Sculpture* x. 296 English sycamore, or Harewood, is actually a variety of maple. It is a light-colored, fine-grained, figured wood and is generally available in the form of thin planks. **1968** *Times* 26 Nov. 13/6 A pair of George III satinwood and harewood commodes. **1973** *Country Life* 7 June 1587/1 A pembroke table in the silvery green of harewood.

Hargrave (hā·ɹgrēⁱv). The surname of Lawrence *Hargrave* (1850–1915), an Australian pioneer in Aeronautics, used *attrib.* to designate a cellular box-kite invented by him in 1894.

1900 R. S. BAKER *Boy's Bk. Inventions* vi. 210 Those [tailless kites] of the Hargrave model giving the impression of a number of big pasteboard boxes with the bottoms knocked out. **1908** W. H. STORY tr. *Hildebrandt's Airships* x. 117 (*caption*) Hargrave kite. *Ibid.* x. 121 Four Hargrave kites were used. **1945** BAKER *Austral. Lang.* x. 200 Hargrave box kite.

haricot, *sb.* Add: **2.** Also *haricot blanc, pod, vert.*

1845 E. ACTON *Mod. Cookery* xv. 328 The haricot blanc is the seed of a particular kind of French bean. **1877** E. S. DALLAS *Kettner's Bk. Table* 242 (*heading*) Haricot pods, what the French call haricots verts; called also French beans. **1907** *Yesterday's Shopping* (1969) 45/1 Vegetables, preserved, in Tins..Haricots Verts, extra fins—tin, 0/7½. **1941** A. SIMON *Conc. Encycl. Gastron.* III. 46/2 In the U.S.A...there is a variety of canned String Beans..marketed under the name of *Haricots verts.* **1966** *Harrod's Food News* Sept. 2/1 Haricot Verts—8 oz. 3/3. **1967** *Listener* 20 Apr. 533/3 Chefs who bite the *haricots verts* or spit on the icing sugar. **1970** *Sat. Rev.* 3 Oct. 44/3 *Cassoulet*..usually includes goose..sausages, and *haricots blancs* or white beans.

Harijan (hæ·ridʒăn). [a. Skr. *harijan(a)* person devoted to the god Vishnu, f. *Hari* Vishnu + *jana* person.] The name given by Gandhi to the Untouchables in India. Also as *adj.*

1931 M. K. GANDHI *Bleeding Wound* (1932) ix. 40 Only the other day a friend suggested to me that the word Harijana (man of God) be substituted for the word 'antyaja' (the 'lastborn') that is being used for 'untouchables'... I am delighted to adopt that word. **1932** *Ibid.* App. 186, I would like to assure my Harijan friends, as I would like henceforth to name them, that..I am wedded to the whole..agreement. **1958** G. MIKES *East is East* 162 But the untouchables—the *harijans*—are still not regarded as human beings. **1960** *Times* 23 May 13/7 Many more Harijan children are now attending the village schools. **1966** *New Statesman* 11 Feb. 190/1 Already the leader of the untouchables..has won a seat in the cabinet ..in recognition of the 70-odd Harijan votes cast against Desai. **1969** *Times* 13 Oct. (India Suppl.) p. vi/2 In Porbander, in spite of Gandhi's dream and work to eradicate untouchability and the Government's enlightened policy during the past 22 years, Harijans must still draw water from separate taps. **1973** *Times* 20 Aug. 12/1 Harijans, or 'Children of God', the name coined by Mahatma Gandhi—and now generally used—for the Untouchables.

hark, *v.* Add: **2. a.** Also const. *at.*

1887 G. M. FENN *Dick o' the Fens* vii, Hark at him!.. young squire ar'n't going to eat any more bacon, 'cause it's cruel to kill the pigs. **1895** 'G. MORTIMER' *Like Stars that Fall* xiii, 'You're so spry, I can't trust you for a grass widow.' 'Hark at him!' laughed Mrs. Larpenti.

4. d. *to hark after*: to go after, to follow.

1899 B. TARKINGTON *Gentleman fr. Indiana* vii. 109 Men were running around a corner of the court-house, and the women and children were harking after.

harka (hā·ɹkă). [a. Moroccan Arab. *ḥarka* military expedition, classical Arab. *ḥaraka* movement.] A body of Moroccan irregular troops.

1903 *Daily Chron.* 18 Sept. 4/6 The regions in the Sahara affected by the recent incursions of the Moorish harkas. **1909** *Ibid.* 26 July 1/5 The harka..consisted of about 15,000 Kabyles. **1925** *Blackw. Mag.* Nov. 624/1 [He] led out a harka to fight in the national cause.

harl, *sb.*³ Add: **5.** A composition of lime and gravel or sand; roughcast.

1869 R. L. STEVENSON *Let.* 18 June in *Scribner's Mag.* (1899) XXV. 42/1 The houses, white with harl. **1898** J. J. BURGESS *Tang* ii. 23 The gable was white, for the 'harl' had been picked off in the spring. **1940** 'M. INNES' *Secret Vanguard* ix. 92 The walls of the sort of rough-cast which in Scotland is called harl.

Harlem (hā·ɹlĕm). The name of a predominantly Negro area in Manhattan, New York, used *subst., attrib.* or in *Comb.* to designate a strongly swinging jazz style. Also as quasi-*adj.*

1934 C. LAMBERT *Music Ho!* III. vii. 201 By jazz, of course, I mean the whole movement roughly designated as such, and not merely that section of it known as Afro-American, or more familiarly as 'Harlem'. *Ibid.* viii. 224 American jazz is either too Hollywood or too Harlem—it rarely suggests the dusty panorama of American life. **1946** R. BLESH *Shining Trumpets* xiii. 315 Harlem piano was, more than any other style, akin to the player piano, no doubt because many Harlem pianists made early player rolls. **1947** R. DE TOLEDANO *Frontiers of Jazz* p. ix, Harlem Jazz is..much more commercial, there's less going on, and therefore it's easier to understand. **1958** C. FOX in P. Gammond *Decca Bk. Jazz* vii. 87 A percussive, striding style of playing..still called ..'Harlem Piano'. **1959** M. T. WILLIAMS *Art of Jazz* (1960) iii. 17 The Harlem style of James P. Johnson and Fats Waller.

Harlemese (hāɹlĕmī·z). [f. prec. + -ESE.] A regional type of speech used by the inhabitants of Harlem. Also *attrib.* or as *adj.*

1928 *Opportunity* VI. xi. 346/2 Dr. Fisher writes with equal authority and zest of..his Harlemese version of a sermon on the battle of Jericho, the technique of piano moving, [etc.] **1932** *Ibid.* X. x. 320/2 The escapades of these two roustabouts and the 'Harlemese' which they use so glibly. **1942** *Amer. Mercury* July 84 She offers a sketch of Harlem life couched in Harlemese. **1963** A. BONTEMPS *Amer. Negro Poetry* p. xvi, Hughes's art can be likened to that of Jelly Roll Morton and the other creators of jazz. His sources are street music. His language is Harlemese. **1972** *Listener* 27 Jan. 125/3 [They] assume we know Brooklynese..and Harlemese, and Bronxese. **1973** *Black World* Mar. 81 His [*sc.* Langston Hughes'] language has been appropriately called Harlemese: vibrant, rhythmic, direct, and racy.

Harlemite (hā·ɹlĕmait). [f. *HARLEM + -ITE¹.] A person born in or residing in the Harlem area in the city of New York.

1890 *Harlem Local Reporter* 1 Mar. 2/5 The average Harlemite is in a continuous swim of development and prosperity. **1896** *N.Y. Dramatic News* 4 July 6/3 With music nightly the place will be of great benefit to Harlemites. **1897** *Outing* (U.S.) XXX. 488/1 As a contrast to the scope and aim of the Harlemites,..the Riverside Wheelmen, of New York, may be quoted. **1926** A. NILES in W. C. Handy *Blues* 22 His satire on the prissy and citified Harlemite. **1950** A. LOMAX *Mr. Jelly Roll* II. 78 The passionate enthusiasm of a Harlemite for baseball. **1958** C. FOX in P. Gammond *Decca Bk. Jazz* vii. 86 The 'twenties found many Harlemites..throwing parlour-socials (or rent parties). **1971** *Black Scholar* June 18/1 The Harlemites appearing in the simple stories are..'like the knights and courtiers in *Le Morte d'Arthur*'.

harlequin, *sb.* Add: **6. harlequin bug** *Austral.*, either of two bugs with brightly-coloured markings, *Dindymus versicolor* or *Tectocoris diophthalmus*; **harlequin (Great) Dane,** a Great Dane having a black and white coat; **harlequin fish,** (*a*) *Rasbora heteromorpha*, a small cypriniform fish found in Thailand, Malaya, and Sumatra; (*b*) *Othos dentex*, the scarlet rock cod, a perciform fish found along the coasts of south and west Australia; **harlequin fly,** a fly of the genus *Chironomus*; **harlequin (eye)glasses, spectacles,** spectacles with the frame tilted upwards at the corners (named from their resemblance to a harlequin's mask); **harlequin opal** = HARLEQUIN *sb.* 4; **harlequin smiler,** *Merogymnus eximius*, a small Australian perciform fish.

1945 K. C. MCKEOWN *Austral. Insects* xv. 81 The commonest and best known species [of Pyrrhocoridæ] is the striking red and black insect popularly known as the Harlequin Bug (*Dindymus versicolor* Sch.), found throughout Australia, and attacking apples and other fruits. **1970** T. E. WOODWARD et al. in *Insects of Australia* (C.S.I.R.O.) xxvi. 450/1 *Tectocoris diophthalmus* (Thunb.), the 'harlequin bug' of Queensland, attacks the bolls of cotton, and is common on other malvaceous plants. **1800** Harlequin Dane [see DANE 2]. **1909** *Daily Chron.* 28 July 7/1 A black and white or harlequin Great Dane. **1948** 'SIGMA' in B. Vesey-Fitzgerald *Bk. Dog* II. 420 When smart men drove a well-appointed turnout, a Dalmatian or harlequin Great Dane was necessary to complete the picture. **1956** M. WEST *Gallows on Sand* x. 115 A school of harlequin fish flirted away from my descent, their tube-like bodies flashing blue and gold, their ugly faces smiling like a circus clown's. **1959** *Times* 3 Mar. 7/1 The 'guinea pigs' in these experiments are inch-long harlequin fish .. from south-east Asia. **1900** MIALL & HAMMOND (*title*) The structure and life history of the harlequin fly (*Chironomus*). **1956** *Nature* 17 Mar. 534/1 The family Chironomidae has scarcely been studied at all in New Zealand...Known colloquially as the 'Harlequin fly', they are, it seems, almost ubiquitous. **1945** 'L. LEWIS' *Birthday Murder* (1951) i. 7 Her harlequin eyeglasses became crooked on her pointed face. **1961** WODEHOUSE *Service with Smile* ix. 130 She was regarding him austerely through her harlequin glasses. **1887** *Col. & Indian Exhib., Rep. Col. Sect.* 70 Some specimens are of a rare kind, known as 'Harlequin' opals. **1955** A. ROSS *Australia 55* ix. 118 Sharks..whose presence causes.. coral trout and Harlequin Smilers suddenly to evaporate. **1964** T. C. MARSHALL *Fishes of Great Barrier Reef* 326 Harlequin Smiler *Merogymnus eximius.* **1940** *Optometric Weekly* 19 Dec. 1262 The Harlequin spectacle frame is protected by patents. **1962** J. BRAINE *Life at Top* xii. 154 Her harlequin spectacles didn't make her expression any less severe.

harlequin, *v.* Restrict *rare* to senses in Dict. and add: **c.** To colour, decorate with contrasting colours. So **ha·rlequined** *ppl. a.*

1941 'R. WEST' *Black Lamb* II. 304 A slope of long grass harlequined with flowers. **1959** *Housewife* June 5 The two colours daringly harlequinned. **1963** *Harper's Bazaar* July 44 Shetland jumper—white, harlequinned in different greys. **1965** D. FRANCIS *For Kicks* iv. 49 She wore a black and white harlequined ski-ing jacket.

Harley (hā·ɹli). *Harley Street*: name of a street in London associated with eminent physicians and surgeons; hence used allusively for the specialists of the medical profession.

1830 *New Monthly Mag.* II. 220 Harley-street was..in an uproar at these monstrous stipulations. **1905** G. B. SHAW *Shaw on Shakes.* (1962) I A regular company.. holding itself as exclusively above the casual barnstormer as a Harley Street consultant holds himself above a man with a sarsaparilla stall. **1958** B. NICHOLS *Sweet & Twenties* xi. 138 The sort of people who always contribute to symposiums—a bishop, a general..an 'eminent Harley Street surgeon'. **1961** L. MUMFORD *City in History* iv. 105 'Harley Street', 'Madison Avenue', 'State Street', are shorthand expressions not just for occupations, but for a whole way of life that they embody. **1972** M. GILBERT *Body of Girl* xvii. 156 Two Harley Street surgeons discussing a difficult case.

harm, *sb.* Add: **1.** Often in the set phrase 'to do more harm than good'. Cf. quot. 1875 in sense 1 in Dict.

1809 *Q. Rev.* May 305 The story should be suppressed altogether, as one which will do more harm than good. **1857** DICKENS *Dorrit* II. xxix. 723, I should have done you more harm than good, at first. **1914** G. B. SHAW *Misalliance* p. xxix, These rare cases actually do more harm than good.

harmattan. (Later examples.)

1906 F. B. ARCHER *Gambia Colony* i. 27 This excessive dryness is undoubtedly due to the severe 'harmattan' experienced in the locality. **1963** W. SOYINKA *Lion & Jewel* 22 The dew-moistened leaves on a Harmattan morning.

harmonic, *a.* and *sb.* Add: **A.** *adj.* **1.** *harmonic telegraph* (earlier example). Also, *harmonic telegraphy.*

1878 *Telegraphic Jrnl.* VI. CXXXIII. 348/1 Gray's

harmonic telegraph can now be seen in operation at the Paris Exhibition. **1902** *Westm. Gaz.* 8 Jan. 6/2 The extensive adoption of..harmonic telegraphy. **1925** *Telegr. & Teleph. Jrnl.* XI. cxxii. 152/2 Mr. Cromwell Varley, who seems to have been the first to get hold of the fundamental idea of harmonic telegraphy, of sending into the telegraph line a number of different frequencies of signalling current at the same time and sorting them out at other stations.

4. *harmonic minor mode* or *scale*: see quot. 1884. Also *harmonic series* = *harmonic scale.*

1884 Maitland in Grove *Dict. Mus.* IV. 666/2 Harmonic minor is the name applied to that version of the minor scale which contains the minor sixth together with the major seventh, and in which no alteration is made in ascending and descending. **1889** E. Prout *Harmony* (ed. 10) vii. § 171 This form is known as the Harmonic Minor Scale, the other two being called Melodic Minor Scales. **1910** *Encycl. Brit.* XIII. 1/1 The unisonous quality of octaves is easily explained when we examine the 'harmonic series' of upper partials.

5. a. *Math. harmonic average* = *harmonic mean*; *harmonic ratio* = *harmonic proportion*; *harmonic series* = *harmonic progression*; esp. the series $1+\frac{1}{2}+\frac{1}{3}+\frac{1}{4}+\ldots$

1866 Brande & Cox *Dict. Sci., Lit., & Art* II. 96/1 *Harmonic Progression or Series*, a series of numbers such that any three consecutive terms are in harmonic proportion. **1942** G. James *Math. Dict.* 199/1 *Harmonic ratio.* If the cross ratio of four points (or four lines) is equal to -1, it is called a harmonic ratio and the last two points are said to divide the first two harmonically. **1949** G. & R. C. James *Math. Dict.* 23/2 The harmonic average is the reciprocal of the arithmetic average of reciprocals of the observations. **1964** Crowder & McCuskey *Topics in Higher Analysis* iv. 193 Since $\sqrt{(n+1)}/n>1/n$ for all $n>0$, and

$$\sum_{n=1}^{\infty} 1/n$$

is the harmonic series that diverges,

$$\sum_{n=1}^{\infty} \sqrt{(n+1)}/n$$

also diverges.

b. *harmonic analyser* (example); *harmonic current*, an alternating current the variations of which, graphically represented, follow a harmonic curve.

1908 *R. Soc. Catal. Sci. Papers 1800–1900* I. *Pure Math.* 402/1 (*title*) Harmonic analyser. **1910** *Hawkins's Electr. Dict.* 193/1 Harmonic current.

c. *Electr.* Of or relating to harmonics (*harmonic *sb.* 2 b), as *harmonic distortion*, non-linear distortion of a wave-form in which harmonics of the original frequencies are introduced into it; *harmonic generator*, a device that generates and combines harmonics of one or more sinusoidal oscillations to produce a complex wave-form; *harmonic interference*, interference caused by the reception of harmonics of a transmitted signal of some other frequency; *harmonic selective signalling* (see quot.).

1929 K. Henney *Princ. Radio* xvii. 450 We determined the percentage of harmonic distortion that occurred in an amplifier when it worked over a curved characteristic. **1930** *Terms & Def. Telegr. & Teleph.* (*B.S.I.*) 21 *Harmonic selective signalling*, signalling a number of stations on one circuit by means of alternating or pulsating currents of different frequencies, each individual station being tuned to one frequency only. A calling station can call any selected station independently of the others by employing the frequency particular to the selected station. **1930** *Proc. Inst. Radio Engin.* XVIII. 31 If a receiver with poorly designed selective circuits is subjected to relatively high local field intensities one of the radio-frequency tubes may be overloaded and may then function as a modulator or harmonic generator. *Ibid.*, Complaints of harmonic interference are, at times, received by the operators of broadcast stations which can be traced directly to deficiencies in the design of the receivers employed. **1931** *Trans. Amer. Inst. Electr. Engin.* L. 811/1 The vacuum-tube harmonic generators of present practise are fundamentally amplifiers operated under conditions of input voltage and grid bias. **1962** A. Nisbett *Technique Sound Studio* 249 Harmonic distortion is most easily caused by flattening of peaks in the waveform. *Ibid.*, 1% harmonic distortion is not usually noticeable.

B. *sb.* **2. b.** *Electr.* In an alternating circuit, a component current whose frequency is a multiple of the fundamental; also, a corresponding electro-magnetic oscillation.

1894 *Amer. Jrnl. Sci.* CXLVIII. 379 The presence of upper harmonics in an alternating current wave. *Ibid.* 383 For every harmonic of the inducing current we shall have a harmonic electromotive force of the same frequency in the resonant circuit. **1919** R. Stanley *Text-bk. Wireless Telegr.* (ed. 2) II. 164 When the fundamental oscillations in a circuit are accompanied by other subsidiary oscillations the latter are called harmonics. **1955** *Sci. Amer.* June 43/3 They act like radio transmitters, emitting radio waves at the critical frequency and at harmonics of this frequency.

harmonica. 1. c. (Examples.)

1895 *Montgomery Ward Catal.* 241/1 Concert harmonica, 10 double holes, 40 reeds, brass reed plates, celluloid covers, absolutely perfect in tone. **1938** S. G. Hedges *Hohner Harmonica Band Bk.* iii. 15 Harmonicas are made in several keys, the principal being G and C. **1966** L. M. Fox *Instruments Pop. Mus.* xiii. 84 Some harmonicas have a slider stop which can switch into play a second row of reeds tuned a semitone higher. **1973** *Advocate-News* (Barbados) 24 Feb. 3/6 (Advt.), Attention all musicians... Just arrived:—..Harmonica Holders.

harmonization. Add: **1. b.** Agreement in colour.

1897 R. Kearton *Nature & Camera* 252 Their wonderful harmonisation with the sand upon which they lay stretched. **1925** R. W. G. Hingston in E. F. Norton *Fight for Everest, 1924* 262 We are attracted by their example of harmonization, the pale grey colour of their fur blending well with the upland soil.

harmonize, *v.* Add: **3. d.** To form a harmonious combination *with.*

1852 *Art-Jrnl.* Apr. 117/3 If it is necessary that the colours of the different articles of dress should..harmonise with each other. **1862** *Englishwoman's Domestic Mag.* May 60/1 Flowers, and shells, and coloured fabrics that harmonise admirably with themselves and with the tropical scenery among which she lives. **1925** R. W. G. Hingston in E. F. Norton *Fight for Everest, 1924* 265 Then unexpectedly the bird alights, the crimson colour vanishes, the white spots disappear, and the bird again harmonizes with the hill. **1949** *Oxf. Jun. Encycl.* II. 72/1 Colour is used in one of the following ways: to break up the outline of the body, or to make it harmonize completely with the background, or to provide obliterative shading.

harmon mute (hā·ɹmǫ̆n miūt). [perh. f. Harmonica.] A type of mute for a trumpet or trombone, also called *wa-wa mute.* Hence **harmon-muted** *a.*

1955 L. Feather *Encycl. Jazz* ii. 64 The sounds produced by both trumpet and trombone were changed by..a variety of mutes, including the straight, cup and Harmon mutes and the rubber plunger. **1966** *Crescendo* Dec. 29/2 A slow, moody piece, with flute and Harmon-muted trumpet. **1967** *Ibid.* Feb. 26/2 Pull out the tube on your harmon mute.

harmonogram (haɹmǫ·nŏgræm). [f. as Harmonograph: see -gram.] A figure or curve drawn by a harmonograph.

1902 *Pearson's Mag.* Apr. 445/1 Not only can an infinity of varying harmonograms be produced with one ratio of pendulum length, but the ratio can be altered. **1962** R. Quirk *Use of English* (*dust jacket*), The Harmonogram illustrated on this jacket is Crown Copyright, Science Museum, London.

harness, *sb.* Add: **2. e.** (See quot. 1940.) Also called *ignition harness.*

1938 R. Keen *Wireless Direction Finding* (ed. 3) xiii. 523 To reduce the capacity of the screening of the cables, and to avoid the bulk and inconvenience of large numbers of separately screened leads, the whole wiring system of an engine may be built into a unit known as 'screening harness'. Fig. 405 shows such a harness..for a Bristol 'Pegasus' radial engine. **1940** *Chambers's Techn. Dict.* 404/1 *Harness*, the entire system of screened ignition leads enclosed within their screening tubes to prevent electromagnetic radiation from affecting the radio-receiving equipment. **1956** W. A. Heflin *U.S.A.F. Dict.* 262/2 *Ignition harness*, a system or assembly of wires, together with any shielding or conduits inclosing them, for conducting electric current from the distributor to the spark plugs of an aircraft engine.

4. a. *double harness*, harness for two draught horses working side by side; *single harness*, harness for a draught horse working alone; *in harness*, side by side, together. Often *fig.*

1838 *Lexington Observer & Rep.* 2 June, We soon hitch'd traces to trot in double harness. **1846** R. Ford *Gatherings from Spain* viii. 88 Those who have a friend with whom they feel they can venture to go in double harness, had better do so. **1862** *Catal. Internat. Exhib., Brit.* II. No. 4732 Double and single harness, pads, collars, round reins, pole pieces. **1873** 'Mark Twain' & Warner *Gilded Age* 373 He and I are sworn brothers on that measure; we work in harness. **1901** 'M. Gray' *Four-Leaved Clover* i, And it's about time you went in double harness. I go better in single. To confess the solid truth, I was born an old maid. **1907** G. B. Shaw *John Bull's Other Island* i. 20 In the main it is by living with you and working in double harness with you that I have learnt to live in a real world and not in an imaginary one. **1937** D. L. Sayers *Busman's Honeymoon* vii. 152 It was her own feelings that didn't seem to be quite pulling in double harness with her intelligence. **1967** *Listener* 2 Feb. 177/3 Prokofiev enthusiasts will be delighted to see that Milstein has now recorded the two violin concertos in harness.

c. From their resemblance to the harness of a horse (see sense 4 a above): straps so arranged that they can be fitted for the protection of travellers in an aeroplane or car. Also used of straps fitted (*a*) on a dog, instead of a collar; (*b*) on a parachute; (*c*) in a perambulator; (*d*) round a child and held by an adult as a safety lead or leash. Also called *safety harness.*

1895 *Montgomery Ward Catal.* 484/2 Pug dog harness, black or russet leather. **1897** H. Dalziel *Brit. Dogs* (ed. 2) III. 43 A kind of dog-harness to mitigate the evils of..choking by the collar. **1935** C. G. Burge *Compl. Bk. Aviation* 538/1 Safety belts and safety harness have been specially designed for use in aircraft...Harness must hold the wearer firmly in his seat against upward accelerations. **1939** *Sewing Machine & Pram Gaz., Buyers' Guide* Apr. 30 (*caption*) This firm have a very wide selection of reins and safety belts... A typical model of Safety harness is illustrated **1945** C. H. Ward-Jackson *Piece of Cake* (ed. 2) 38 *Harness*, strap holding one to one's seat in an aircraft. **1951** *Gloss. Aeronaut. Terms* (*B.S.I.*) iii. 13 *Harness*, an assembly of straps or cords worn by a parachutist or employed to suspend an inanimate load to which the parachute is attached. **1962** *Times* 23 Jan. 5/6 Every approved harness [in a motor-car] has a quick-release catch. **1962** *Which?* Jan. 8/1 The buckles of the three harnesses that survived the test crash intact were easy to release. **1963** *B.S.I. News* May 34 Safety harness for babies...The types dealt with will be suitable for attachment to perambulators, push chairs and high chairs. Provision will also be made for use of reins with the harness, when the child is able to walk. **1971** J. Philips *Escape a Killer* (1972) i. ii. 24 She unbuckled the dog's harness. **1972** P. Cleife *Slick & Dead* xviii. 233 Tripping the quick-release of my harness, I leapt from my seat.

5. b. Uniform, clothes. *harness bull, cop*, a policeman in uniform. *U.S. slang* (chiefly *criminals*').

1891 'Mark Twain' *What is Man?* (1917) 225 At the Metropolitan in New York they sit in a glare, and wear their showiest harness. **1899** B. W. Green *Word-bk. Virginia Folk-Speech* 178 *Harness*,..clothing, dress garments. **1903** A. H. Lewis *Boss* 262 [The] Captain sends along a couple of his harness bulls from Mulberry Street. **1914** Jackson & Hellyer *Vocab. Criminal Slang* 42 *Harness*, general currency. A uniform...A 'harness bull' is the commonest form of the term's use. **1926** J. Black *You can't Win* iv. 31 The 'harness cop' who had been at the front door went back to his beat. *Ibid.* xii. 165 We're bang up against the city prison when a big, flat-footed, harness bull steps out an' yaffles us. **1930** E. H. Lavine *Third Degree* ii. 12 'Wise detectives', who dread going back into 'harness', or uniform,..sail along the lines of least resistance. **1931** 'D. Stiff' *Milk & Honey Route* iv. 45 Any harness bull can tell you where the municipal lodging house..is to be found. **1972** J. Godey *Three Worlds* (1973) iii. 32 The cops. From the chief on down to the harness bulls.

6. (Later U.S. example.)

1888 Eggleston in *Century Mag.* XXXVI. 529/2 When Barbara had tied a broken string in the 'harness' of the loom, she resumed her seat on the bench.

9. *harness-horse* (earlier example); **harness (horse) racing**, a race between horses harnessed to vehicles; also **harness race** (Webster, 1909).

1861 Walsh & Lupton *Horse* xv. 272 Hacks and Harness-horses demand nearly as much time and care to prepare them for their work. **1901** *World Almanac* 266 Harness racing. **1909** *Ibid.* 213 Harness horse racing. **1947** *Newsweek* 8 Sept. 71/1 Harness racing is doing very well in keeping up with the flashy bankrolls of the times. **1968** *Globe & Mail* (Toronto) 3 Feb. 36/2 About the only sure thing in harness racing is that Russ Miller..will come up with something special each year. *Ibid.* 17 Feb. 44 (Advt.), Nine harness races today. **1971** *Guardian* 9 June 6/5 Trotting or harness racing, which has become a major sporting attraction in Australia and the United States, is making a comeback in its place of origin, the Yorkshire dales and fells.

harness, *v.* Add: **3.** *fig.* (Later examples.) Now chiefly 'to utilize (a river, waterfall, natural forces, atomic energy) for motive power'.

1927 A. Christie *Big Four* xvii. 258, I believe that she has, to a certain extent, succeeded in liberating atomic energy and harnessing it to her purpose. **1935** *Discovery* Feb. 41/1 The business of harnessing cosmic rays, of forcing them to do the work of electricity, is proceeding apace. **1955** *Times* 19 May 3/6 This monster is, of course, the huge underwater vessel Nautilus..propelled by 'the dynamic force of the universe', which somehow he has succeeded in harnessing. **1965** *Listener* 3 June 823/1 This seems..to make sense: harnessing individual and group enthusiasm to enrich the region.

harnessed, *ppl. a.* Add: **4. harnessed antelope.** Also called *bushbuck.* (Earlier and later examples.)

c **1789** *Encycl. Brit.* IV. 149/1 The scipta or harnessed antelope..has straight horns nine inches long, pointing backwards. **1899** H. A. Bryden *Great & Small Game of Africa* 453 (*heading*) The bushbucks. Genus Tragelaphus. The harnessed antelopes, or bushbucks,..may be arranged as follows:— A... 1. The Bongo (*T. eurycerος*). 2. The Nyala (*T. angasi*)... 3. West African Bushbuck (*T. gratus*). 4. Situtunga (*T. Spekei*)... 5. Lesser Bushbuck (*T. scriptus*). The last is represented by several local races. **1960** *Times* (Nigeria Suppl.) 29 Sept. p. xxi/4 The bushbuck, also called harnessed antelope from the pattern of white stripes on its coat, remains widespread.

harnser, dial. form of Heronsew.

haroses, haroset(h, varr. *charoset(h.

harp, *sb.*[1] Add: **1.** *spec.* One used by Anglo-Saxon minstrels.

1767 Percy *Ess. Anc. Eng. Minstrels* 9 In the early times it was not unusual for a Minstrel to have a servant to carry his harp. **1807** S. Turner *Hist. Anglo-Saxons* (ed. 2) II. 407 Of the harp, Bede mentions, that in all festive companies it was handed round, that every one might sing in turn. **1898** S. A. Brooke *Eng. Lit. fr. Beginnings to Norman Conq.* iv. 82 We should place ourselves..in the hall..when the benches are filled..and hear the Shaper strike the harp to sing this heroic lay. **1903** L. F. Anderson *Anglo-Saxon Scop* 36 The harp was the instrument most used by the scop. **1942** J. C. Pope *Rhythm of Beowulf* 91 If the harp were keeping time, the voice might omit the first accent of a verse..without causing the slightest confusion. **1957** *Rev. Eng. Stud.* VIII. 7 The clear song of the bard is accompanied by the music of the harp.

e. *U.S. colloq.* Also **mouth harp** = Mouth-organ, harmonica. *colloq.* (orig. *U.S.*).

1887 *Scribner's Mag.* Oct. 481/1 She displayed a flimsy

red silk handkerchief and a child's harp. **1903** Ade *In Babel* 40 I'd walked from Loueyville over to Terry Hut with a nigger that played the mouth harp. **1963** *Amer. Speech* XXXVIII. 246 *Harp* or *mouth harp* 'harmonica'. **1965** *Melody Maker* 10 July 12/6 For the best blues sound you have to..play the harp in a transposed manner.

f. An Irishman. *U.S. slang.*

1904 'No. 1500' *Life in Sing Sing* xiii. 249/1 *Harp*, an Irishman. **1926** T. Beer *Mauve Decade* iv. 162, I sewed up his head for a young Italamerican who had been trying to impress the haughty Harps on his street. **1936** J. Dos Passos *Big Money* 75 The foreman was a big loudmouthed harp.

harpacticid (hāɹpæ·ktisid). *Zool.* [f. Gr. ἁρπακτικ-ός rapacious + -id³.] One of the family Harpacticidæ, tiny copepod crustacea. Also as *adj.*

1909 G. Smith in *Cambr. Nat. Hist.* IV. iii. 62 *Euterpe acutifrons*..exhibits the structure of a typical Harpacticid. **1932** *Discovery* Sept. 287/2 The Cyclopids and Harpacticids are, of course, represented in ponds and streams on the surface. **1957** *New Biol.* XXIV. 70 Yet other free-living copepods belong to the group called harpacticids. **1961** J. Green *Biol. Crustacea* iii. 45 Some crustaceans (e.g. harpacticid copepods) do not have a heart.

harpacticoid (hāɹpæ·ktikoid). *Zool.* [f. as prec. + -oid.] One of the order Harpacticoida, very small worm-like copepod crustacea. Also as *adj.*

1946 *Nature* 28 Dec. 935/1 Its [sc. *Bathynella*'s] habitat ..is analogous to that of the interstitial harpacticoid copepods. **1952** J. Clegg *Freshwater Life Brit. Isles* xii. 176 There are about forty-six species of Harpacticoids in Britain. **1956** *Nature* 11 Feb. 289/2 The sample contained ..one harpacticoid copepod and numerous nematodes. **1961** J. Green *Biol. Crustacea* v. 72 There may be one sac, as in many calamoids and harpacticoids, or two sacs as in most cyclopoids. **1970** *Nature* 24 Oct. 323/2 These fish use their gill rakers to strain off the minute animals such as harpacticoid copepods.

harper¹. Add: **1.** *spec.* in the Anglo-Saxon period.

1767 Percy *Ess. Anc. Eng. Minstrels* 7 Much greater honours seem to have been heaped upon the northern scalds..than appear to have been paid to the minstrels and harpers of the Anglo-Saxons. **1883** Vigfusson & Powell *Corpus Poeticum Boreale* p. lv, In England an innovation appears, the harper who sits at the king's feet. **1912** W. M. Dixon *Eng. Epic & Heroic Poetry* 61 The braggart, the coward, the bard or harper, cunning with the glee-wood..all are there.

harpist. Add: *spec.* in the Anglo-Saxon period.

1898 S. A. Brooke *Eng. Lit. fr. Beginnings to Norman Conq.* ii. 41 As far as we can go back with certainty we find the Teutonic..harpists and singers. **1948** K. Malone in A. C. Baugh *Lit. Hist. England* I. 46 Whether Scilling was Widsith's harpist or a fellow scop..we cannot tell.

harpoon, *sb.* Add: **2. b.** *Med.* A trocar-like surgical instrument for removing small pieces of living tissue for examination.

1876 J. S. Bristowe *Theory & Pract. Med.* (1878) 719 The extraction by means of a suitable instrument (harpoon) of fragments of striped muscular tissue. **1897** *Allbutt's Syst. Med.* II. 1057 The harpoon designed..for this purpose produces an unsurgical wound.

‖ **harpuisbos** (harpö̆ü·sbǫs). Also 9 **harpuisbosje** (-bǫsi) and (semi-anglicized) **harpuis, arpuse,** or **rapuis bush.** [Afrikaans, f. *harpuis* resin + *bos* bush.] An evergreen shrub belonging to the genus *Euryops*, esp. the resin-bush, *E. multifidus.*

[**1793** tr. *C. P. Thunberg's Trav. Europe, Afr., & Asia* I. 211 A species of *Coccus*, called *Harpuys*, that was found on the branches of trees, was said to prove mortal to sheep.] **1811** W. J. Burchell *Trav. S. Afr.* (1822) I. xii. 259 The inhabitants of this district, when in want of resin, use as a substitute, a gum which exudes from different species of shrubs; which they therefore call *Harpuis bosch* (Resin bush). **1815** A. Plumptre tr. *Lichtenstein's Trav.* II. 176 A shrub, which grows from two feet to three feet and a half high, called by the colonists *harpuisbosjes*, the rosin tree. **1846** H. H. Methuen *Life in Wilderness* 112 We again were in danger of being burnt; a sea of flame raging on one side of the road, and consuming the resinous *arpuse* bushes with a roaring noise, audible a long way off. [**1912** *East London Dispatch* 22 Aug. 5 (Pettman), Mr. Moffatt (Tarka) brought up the question of the noxious *rapuis* which had hitherto baffled their efforts.] **1926** O. Schreiner *From Man to Man* xi. 353 They burnt harpuis bushes on the lands at home. **1952** *Cape Argus* (Mag. Section) 1 Nov. 1/7 The yellow of the harpuisbos.

Harrian, var. *Hurrian *sb.* and *a.*

Harriet Lane (hæ:riĕt lēⁱ·n). *slang* (chiefly *Naut.*). [f. the name of a famous murder victim; cf. *Fanny Adams.] Preserved meat, esp. Australian tinned meat.

1896 in Farmer & Henley *Slang* IV. 153/2. **1909** B. Lubbock *Deep Sea Warriors* ix. 117 I'd rayther eat this here than the Harriet Lane we get served out for our Sunday dinner. **1909** J. R. Ware *Passing Eng.* 150/2 *Harriet Lane*, Australian canned meat—because it had the appearance of chopped up meat; and Harriet Lane was chopped up by one Wainwright. **1916** 'Taffrail' *Carry On!* 28 'Fanny Adams' and 'Harriet Lane' were the names once given to the preserved meat issued to seamen. **1932** J. W. Harris *Days of Endeavour* viii. 134 A meal of pantiles and cold 'Harriet Lane' is provided. **1938** W. E. Dexter *Rope-Yarns* 30 On Sunday we were allowed 1 lb. of preserved meat, known as 'Harriet Lane', from the name of a woman who had disappeared.

Harris (hæ·ris). The name of the southern section of the island of Lewis with Harris in the Outer Hebrides, used (chiefly *attrib.*) to designate the hand-woven tweed produced by the inhabitants of this region. Also *ellipt.* (*Harris* is a proprietary term in relation to tweed manufactured in the island of Lewis with Harris.)

1892–3 *T. Eaton & Co. Catal.* Fall & Winter 11/2 The finest Harris tweed with detachable cape. **1894** *Strand Mag.* VIII. 661/2 My tailor tells me that Harris tweed cannot wear out. **1898** *Daily News* 5 July 2/4 The delightful 'Harris', 'Shetland', and 'Sutherland' tweeds that were being shown. **1924** Galsworthy *White Monkey* II. ii. 131 Very elegant in smoke-grey Harris tweeds. **1939** 'N. Blake' *Smiler with Knife* ii. 33 Her trim, green Harris-tweed suit. **1949** H. Wadman *Life Sentence* 5 We have no tailors who know how to handle Harris. **1971** *Stornoway Gaz.* 21 Aug. 6/7 (Advt.), Gent's Harris heavy knit crew necks.

Harrogate (hæ·rogĕⁱt). Name of a borough in the West Riding of Yorkshire used *attrib.* to designate (*a*) a medicinal water originating in Harrogate, (*b*) the proprietary name of a kind of toffee.

1771 Smollett *Humph. Cl.* I. 229 Harrigate-water, so celebrated for its efficacy in the scurvy..is supplied from a copious spring. **1867** Bloxam *Chem.* 45 The Harrowgate water is eminently sulphureous. *Ibid.* 654/1 (*index*) Harrogate water. **1890** in A. Davis *Package & Print* (1967) 64 (Advt.), Farrah's Original Harrogate Toffee. **1910** *Trade Marks Jrnl.* 28 Dec. 2069 Farrah's Harrogate Toffee...John Farrah, Limited..Harrogate; Toffee Manufacturers. **1931** W. Holtby *Poor Caroline* vii. 278 Eleanor came..bringing..the caramels and Harrogate toffee that Caroline loved. **1938** *Harrogate Spa Med. Jrnl.* Apr. 17 All the Harrogate waters are chemically unstable in contact with oxygen, indicating a measure of activity not common to most mineral springs. **1967** H. Johnson in C. Ray *Compleat Imbiber* IX. 141 Harrogate water is bottled to this day. **1967** E. S. Turner *Taking Cure* iii. 40 Knaresborough..was to become eclipsed in reputation by the near-by 'stinking' wells, the source of 'Harrogate water'.

Harrow, *sb.³* *Cricket.* The name of a public school at Harrow in Middlesex, used *attrib.* to designate: a bat of less than full size (also *ellipt.*); 'a stroke by which the ball is driven in the direction of mid-off' (Lewis); also, an ineffectual attempt at such a stroke; 'the position of the fieldsman placed for the Harrow drive' (Lewis).

1851 J. Pycroft *Cricket Field* ix. 171 'I beg your pardon, sir,' he..said.., 'but ain't you Harrow?'—'Then we shan't want a man down there,'..; 'stand for the "Harrow drive", between point and middle wicket.' **1877** C. Box *Eng. Game Cricket* 451 *Harrow drive.* Some persons define this phrase to mean a fluke in the slips, after an ineffectual attempt to play forward. **1887** J. Lillywhite *Cricketers' Ann.* (Advt.), 7 Youth's Cane-handled Bats. Harrow size. **1922** D. J. Knight *First Steps to Batting* i. 13 For a boy of 14 or 15 who has chosen a Harrow 2 lbs. 2½ oz. should be satisfactory. **1958** *Times* 22 May 15/4 It was pure pantomime with Chinese cuts and Harrow drives flying off Lobb's bat. **1970** *Times* 6 Mar. 16/8 His one escape was from a 'Harrow' drive, off McKenzie, which narrowly missed his leg stump.

harrumph (hə̆rʌ·mf). Chiefly *U.S.* Also **harrump.** [Imitative.] A guttural sound made by clearing the throat. Also *fig.* So as *vb.*, to make this sound; to speak in a rasping or guttural voice; to make a comment implying disapproval.

1936 'J. Tey' *Shilling for Candles* iv. 34 'Howdyudo. Harrump!' He cleared his throat. **1941** *Time* 16 June 29/2 This touching appeal evoked a harrumph from the New York *Times*. **1942** *N.Y. Herald Tribune Books* 11 Jan. 13 He seems to be a figure of fun, with his..fairly continuous harrumphing. **1943** *Time* 11 Oct. 86 The State Department harrumphed and other U.S. oil companies stood on their legal, unenforceable rights. **1957** *Ibid.* 2 Sept. 23/2 Harrumphed one official: 'The best way of putting it would be to say at this point we are tolerant of Dr. Nkrumah's actions.' **1965** G. McInnes *Road to Gundagai* ii. 33 The Captain harrumphed. **1967** *New Yorker* 25 Feb. 99 My goodness, Henry, you're much too young to be going *har-rumph, har-rumph* all the time! **1970** *Times Lit. Suppl.* 29 Jan. 113 Across the room he'd go, singing and harrumphing.

Harry, *sb.²* Add: **2. c.** *Flash Harry*: an ostentatious, loudly-dressed, and usually ill-mannered man; cf. Flash *a.³* Also *attrib.*

1960 J. Rae *Custard Boys* II. xiii. 158 'They're just a lot of smart Alecs.' 'Flash Harrys,' suggested Peter. **1960** *Times* 31 Oct. 16/4 He registers emotional upset by a slightly raised eyebrow, and then briskly readjusts his flash-Harry tie. **1962** *Times* 22 May 15/4 Her flash-Harry boy-friend.

7*. *to box Harry*: see *box *v.²* 3 b.

8. b. In arbitrary appositive uses of which a few have emerged as set expressions, e.g. **Harry Flakers** *Naut. slang*, exhausted; **Harry Flatters** *Naut. slang*, (of the sea) calm; **Harry Freeman's** (also **Harry Frees**) chiefly *Naut. slang*, a gift; also as *adj.*, free; **Harry James** *slang*, nose.

1925 Fraser & Gibbons *Soldier & Sailor Words* 115 *It's Harry Freeman's*, a gift. Something gratis. (Navy.) **1929** F. C. Bowen *Sea Slang* 64 *Harry Frees*, the name given in the Grand Fleet to the very welcome fruit and vegetables sent up as gifts by the public. **1935** 'L. Luard' *Conquering Seas* xii. 139, I don't expect to supply cigarettes Harry Freemans. **1941** C. Graves *Life Line* 154 Fortunately, the sea has dropped and it is Harry Flatters. Harry Flatters means flat calm, and Harry is used as a predicate for almost any expression. **1946** *Lancet* 2 Feb. 177/1 Get in there, and strip off Harry Nuders. **1950** T. E. Lawrence *Mint* 32 Sort of thing the civvies in London pay fifty quid for, we get harry-freeman's. **1958** F. Norman *Bang to Rights* 36 Plenty of dust floating about in the air, which gets..up your Harry James. **1962** *John o' London's* 14 June 571/2 'Harry Flakers' to mean worn out after a party or heavy work. *Ibid.*, 'Harry Flatters' for a flat calm sea. **1962** P. Purser *Peregrination 22* xxii. 99 It's okay for our kind of thing but it would be Harry Grimmers for ordinary civilians. **1966** F. Shaw et al. *Lern Yerself Scouse* 58, *I wuz lookin fer some Arry Freeman's*, I was looking for something for nothing. **a 1966** M. Allingham *Cargo of Eagles* (1968) viii. 103 Get me a Harry pinkers—a large one. **1969** *Guardian* 14 Mar. 10/5 It's derisory, old boy, they'll turn it down harry nem-conners. *Ibid.*, Harry shambles, old boy... In the old Imperial Aircraft days.. the engineer would bring the old kite down harry plonkers on the grass.

Harry Tate (hæ·ri tēⁱ·t). [Stage-name of R. M. Hutchison (1872–1940), music-hall comedian.] Used *attrib.* or in the possessive to designate anything incompetent or disorderly. Also (by *Rhyming slang*), a state, usually of nervous excitement or irritability.

1925 Fraser & Gibbons *Soldier & Sailor Words* 115 *Harry Tate's Cavalry*, a nickname occasionally applied in jest to Yeomanry. *Ibid.*, *Harry Tate's Navy*, a nickname occasionally used in jest for the Royal Naval Volunteer Reserve. **1929** F. C. Bowen *Sea Slang* 64 *Harry Tate's Navy*, before the war a term of derision applied to the Royal Naval Volunteer Reserve generally, but dropped completely since they showed their value. During the War it was generally applied to the Auxiliary patrol, particularly the Motor Boat Reserve. **1932** 'P. P.' *Rhyming Slang* ii. 21 *Harry Tate*, state. **1935** *Brit. Jrnl. Psychol.* Jan. 359 Native courts have been established [in Uganda]... Their methods have been described as 'Harry Tate' procedure; but they are generally successful in arriving at the facts.

hartal (hā·ɹtæl, ‖hɒ·rtāl). *India.* [Hind. *hartāl* for *haṭtāl* lit. 'locking of shops' (Skr. *haṭṭa* shop, *tālaka* lock, bolt).] Organized shutting of shops and cessation of business, to serve, usually, as a protest against government legislation or a political situation, or as an act of mourning.

1920 *Blackw. Mag.* Apr. 441/1 What I had seen there of the crowds at the Hartal..had made me nervous. **1921** *Q. Rev.* July 54 He proclaimed a universal 'hartal', or cessation from business, as a protest against the Rowlatt legislation. **1922** *Ibid.* Oct. 417 Gandhi was preparing a *Hartal* at Bombay. **1931** *Daily Tel.* 6 Jan. 9/5 The Moslems enforced a complete 'hartal' (day of mourning or strike). **1955** *Times* 18 Aug. 8/5 A hartal to be observed throughout India on Friday was called here to-day by the Goa liberation committee in memory of the Indians killed by Portuguese fire on Monday. **1958** J. V. Bondurant *Conquest of Violence* iii. 36 Non-cooperation may include strike, walk-out, *hartal*, and resignation of offices and titles. *Ibid.* iv. 119 The *hartal* is usually of short duration—a day or two. Shops close and work ceases. *Hartal* is also employed at times of national mourning. **1962** A. Carter *Direct Action* 8 At the beginning of the Rowlatt Act Satyagraha Gandhi called on his followers for a 'hartal'—a day of abstention from work and of fasting and prayer.

hartebeest. Add: Also in Afrikaans form **hartebees.** Also *attrib.*, as **hartebeest house,** hut, 'a frail structure of "wattle and daub", so called, apparently, because a similar primitive structure was often erected by the earlier hunters' (Pettman); also **hartebeeste house.**

[**1815** A. Plumptre tr. *Lichtenstein's Trav.* II. 95 Not far from this wretched cabin stood a somewhat more spacious, but very ruinous straw hut, of the sort which is here called *hartebeesthuisje*.] **1818** B. H. Latrobe *Jrnl.* 256 A hartebeest-house, being a roof, put upon a wall about two feet in height. **1863** W. C. Baldwin *Afr. Hunting* i. 16 What is called a hartebeest house, of very tall reeds, stuck close together in a kind of trench dug for them in bundles, and meeting over head. **1873** F. Boyle *To Cape for Diamonds* 242 A colony of Hottentot women had seized possession of our 'hartebeest's hut'. **1898** W. C. Scully *Vendetta of Desert* iv. 23 Uncle Diederick lived in a structure known in South Africa as a 'hartebeeste house'. **1959** *Cape Times* 27 Jan. 2/6 Rare kinds of buck, such as eland and red hartebees. **1961** L. van der Post *Heart of Hunter* III. xiv. 178 Once, the story says, Mantis appeared to the children of the early race as a dead Hartebees.

harumfrodite (hĕᵊrʌ·mfrŏdəit). *Jocular slang.* Also **harumphrodite, herumfrodite.** [After *hermaphrodite.*] = Hermaphrodite *sb.* and *a.*

So **haru:mphrodi·tic** *a.*, characteristic of an hermaphrodite.

1896 [see *GIDDY *a.* 3 b]. **1924** *Blackw. Mag.* Aug. 235/1 Take the young Jot from the plough and turn him to Pope's 'Rape of the Lock' or Shelley's 'Adonais', and you will make a comfortless harumphroditic amphibian of him. **1953** *Essays & Studies* VI. 103 A Welsh writer writes in Welsh..and those others who make articulate some two-thirds of the nation are, according to taste, 'lost to the English' or base harumphrodites.

Harveian (haɹvī·ăn, hā·ɹviăn), *a.* [f. the name of William *Harvey* (1578–1657), English physician, who discovered how the blood circulated + -AN.] Pertaining or relating to, expounded by, or commemorating Harvey.

1755 T. LEMAN *Some Mem. Life & Writings Late Dr. Richard Mead* 27 In 1723, Dr. Mead was appointed to speak the anniversary Harveian oration, before the members of the college of physicians. **1837** *London Med. Gaz.* 8 July 565/1 The College of Physicians continues to show their classic taste in the Harveian Oration. **1839** J. TURNER *Reg. Exper. Living Animals* 34 As a sceptic of the Hunterian and Harveian doctrines, I here take my stand. **1880** *Encycl. Brit.* XI. 505/1 Caspar Hoffmann,.. admitting the truth of the lesser circulation in the full Harveian sense. *Ibid.* 506/2 The Harveian Orations. **1903** *Lancet* 6 June 1608/1 The Harveian Lectures of the Harveian Society of London. **1928** *Daily Tel.* 15 May 14/3 MSS., books, pictures, and other objects of Harveian interest. **1972** *Times Lit. Suppl.* 7 Apr. 403/3 (Advt.), Qualified cataloguer (temporary) urgently required... Applications..to: Harveian Librarian, Royal College of Physicians of London.

harvest, *v.* Add: **1. c.** *trans.* To kill or remove (wild animals belonging to a local population) so as to provide food (or other useful product) or sport, or to reduce the population.

1947 *Biol. Abstr.* XXI. 1602/2, 14 tagged fish were recaptured later by anglers, suggesting that only a small % of the sauger crop is being harvested. **1948** *Jrnl. Wildlife Managem.* XII. 78/1 In 13 years of harvesting the surplus, 546 deer have been taken. **1960** *Biol. Abstr.* XXXV. 2529/1 *Aeromonas* caused heavy mortality of golden shiners..when these fish were harvested and moved to holding tanks. **1961** *Listener* 7 Sept. 348/2 Now 500 to 1,000 hippo are being harvested annually for food. **1970** *Daily Tel.* 30 Oct. 4/8 The tablets were made from the livers of seals harvested in Alaska in 1964. **1973** *Times* 10 Oct. 6/8 Shellfish in Italian waters can be harvested again after a month-long ban brought about by cholera.

d. To remove (cells) from a culture made *in vitro* or *in vivo*; to remove (cells, tissues, organs, or embryos) from an animal for experimental purposes.

1946 *Nature* 9 Nov. 677/2 Table 2 shows the general metabolic activities of normal cells compared with those of cells harvested from a culture grown for 90 min. in the presence of 10 units [of] penicillin per ml. medium. **1957** *Jrnl. Cellular & Compar. Physiol.* XLIX. 369 Various numbers of HeLa cells were added to duplicate Warburg flasks and oxygen consumption was measured for 68·5 hours. The results..indicated that..the rate of oxygen consumption was related linearly to number both of cells inoculated and cells harvested. **1960** *Biol. Abstr.* XXXV. 460/2 (*heading*) Effects of 2,4-dinitrophenol on endogenous respiration of yeast harvested during the first budding cycle. **1971** *Nature* 17 Dec. 385/3 The lymphoid organs are always harvested 24 h after the injection of labelled cells. **1972** *Ibid.* 24 Mar. 169/1 Macrophages were harvested from the peritoneal cavity 10 days after the second immunization. **1972** *Science* 5 May 519/1 Pregnant animals were killed 3 days later and the embryos were harvested.

harvester. Add: **3.** (Earlier and later examples.) Cf. **combine harvester*. **harvester-thresher**, a machine for both harvesting and threshing.

1848 *U.S. Pat.* 21 Nov., Harvester. **1851** C. CIST *Sk. Cincinnati* 161 Harvesters and mowing-machines. **1858** SIMMONDS *Dict. Trade, Harvester*, an American machine for cutting clover and timothy seed, &c. **1911** *Daily Colonist* (Victoria, B.C.) 5 Apr. 1/3 Large shipments of harvester machinery are arriving from overseas points. **1929** NEWMAN & BLACKABY (*title*) Report of the trials of the combined harvester-thresher in Wiltshire, 1928. **1950** *Engineering* 17 Nov. 391/3 Attempts to solve the potato-harvester problem. **1971** *Farmers Weekly* 19 Mar. 83/3 One man with the buckrake comfortably kept pace with a double-chop harvester.

harvesting, *vbl. sb.* **b.** (Earlier example.)

1836 *U.S. Pat.* 28 June, Harvesting machine.

Harvey, *sb.* Add: **2.** The name of Peter *Harvey* (see quot. 1959), English publican, in *Harvey's Sauce* (now a proprietary trademark). Also *Harvey Sauce* and *ellipt.*

1817 [see KETCHUP]. **1856** DICKENS in *Household Words* XIII. 555/2 The grocer's hot pickles, Harvey's Sauce, Doctor Kitchener's Zest. **1870** —— *E. Drood* xi. 80 A condiment of a profounder flavor than Harvey. **1876** *Trade Marks Jrnl.* 28 June 198 Harvey's Sauce for Fish, Game, Steaks etc. Prepared from the Original Receipt, only at E. Lazenby's Fish Sauce Warehouse. *Ibid.* 199 Harvey's Sauce—Caution: The admirers of this celebrated Sauce are..requested to observe that each bottle bears the well-known Label signed 'Elizabeth Lazenby'. **1905** E. WHARTON *House of Mirth* I. xiv. 243 A bottle of Harvey sauce on the sideboard. **1959** *Tradition* (*E. Lazenby & Co.*) Jan. 2/1 The history of Elizabeth Lazenby can really be dated from 1760. In that year, a Mr. Peter Harvey, owner of an inn called the 'Black Dog' in Bedfont, Middlesex, invented a thin sauce known as 'Harvey's Sauce'. So good was it that many of his customers endeavoured to obtain the recipe, and one of them, a certain London grocer named M. Lazenby, offered to buy it, but Peter Harvey refused to part with his secret. Mr. Lazenby.. married Harvey's sister, Elizabeth. As a wedding present, Peter Harvey gave Elizabeth..the recipe for his famous sauce. **1967** A. DAVIS *Package & Print* 44 It is likely that by the end of the eighteenth century Burgess's essence of anchovies..and Lazenby's Harvey's sauce were on the market in labelled bottles not noticeably different from those in which they were to enter the twentieth.

harzburgite (hā·ɹtsbɒ̄ɹgəit). *Petrogr.* [ad. G. *harzburgit* (H. Rosenbusch *Mikrosk. Physiogr. d. Min. u. Gesteine* (ed. 2, 1887) II. i. 270), f. *Harzburg*, name of a town in Saxony: see -ITE[1].] A rock of the peridotite group consisting basically of orthopyroxene and olivine.

1890 *Mineral. Mag.* IX. 41 The typical norite has 49·23 *per cent.* of silica,..the well-known 'schillerfels' or bastite-serpentine-rock (Harzburgite of Rosenbusch) 42·36. **1922** *Mineral. Abstr.* I. 396 The rocks of Mansjö Mtn. (61½°N., 15⅜°E.), Sweden, include crystalline limestone and gneiss with intruded amphibolites and later harzburgite and eulysite. **1924** *Trans. Geol. Soc. S. Afr.* XXVI. 14 The recognisable harzburgites exhibit fairly considerable differences in composition and grain. **1965** G. J. WILLIAMS *Econ. Geol. N.Z.* x. 149/1 Hutton (1942) identified chromite grains in dunite-serpentinite and harzburgite-serpentinite in a tributary of Gentle Annie Creek in western Otago. **1970** *Nature* 28 Mar. 1227/2 Most of the volcanics were basic, but during the upper Cretaceous ultrabasics (harzburgite, lherzolite, dunite and anorthosite) were intruded.

has-been, *sb.* Add: (Further examples.) Also **hasbeen.**

1853 B. F. TAYLOR *Jan. & June* (1871) 206 Dilapidated 'has-beens', and despised 'used-to-be's'. **1879** G. F. JACKSON *Shropsh. Word-bk.* 180 'Er's a good owd 'as bin. **1904** *Philadelphia Even. Tel.* 9 Nov. 5 Parker and his party are among the has beens. **1905** B. TARKINGTON *In Arena* 3 I'll potter along trying to look knowing and secretive, like the rest of the has-beens. **1914** G. ATHERTON *Perch of Devil* I. 70 The obsolete notions that made most of our relations a sort of premature has-beens. **1929** *Psyche* Apr. 27 The age when physicians are divided into Has-beens and Neverwozzers. **1972** J. WAMBAUGH *Blue Knight* (1973) vii. 104 When I retire I'm just a has-been.

2. *pl.* Old times. *U.S.*

1904 W. H. SMITH *Promoters* v. 91, I met old Bishop Slosher..and just for has-beens I took him to lunch with me.

hasenpfeffer (hā·zĕn(p)fefeɹ, hā·s-). [G.] A highly seasoned rabbit stew.

1892 *Sun's Guide to New York* 16 Pork and beans, *hassenpfeffer*, and corned beef and cabbage are equally palatable over there. **1909** L. MEIER *Art of German Cooking* vii. 142/2 (*heading*) Hasenpfeffer. **1967** P. McGERR *Murder is Absurd* x. 127 There's a restaurant in Baltimore that has a real knack with Hasenpfeffer.

hash, *v.* Add: **2.** (Later examples.) Also *hash over.*

1920 F. S. FITZGERALD *This Side of Paradise* (1921) iv. 129 The things..they had hashed and rehashed for many a frugal conversational meal. **1931** LOEB & SCHENKER *Please stand By* I. iv. 45 But drop up anyway, I have something I want to hash over with you. **1950** *New Yorker* 16 Dec. 26/1 Asked him in to hash over a point or two. **1958** *Times Lit. Suppl.* 5 Sept. 493/3 It is the classic film formula, the sort of thing that dead-beat script-writers hash up for B. pictures.

Hence **hasher**, also *U.S. slang*, a waiter or waitress in a restaurant; **ha·shery** *U.S. slang*, a hash-house, a cheap eating-house.

1916 A. B. DUNN in *Editor* 11 Mar. 297/2 Hasher, meaning waitress. **1960** *Listener* 18 Aug. 250/2 When it came to making an impression on the 'hashers' in the railroad 'beaneries', the boomers really let themselves go... The 'hashers' were girls chosen for their looks. **1961** *Amer. Speech* XXXVI. 271 Somewhere on your run you will spend some time at a truck stop..while the hasher serves your diesel. **1870** *Alaska Times* (Sitka) 8 Jan. 1/3 Having lately opened a hashery, I send you this my rules and regulations. **1901** *Munsey's Mag.* XXIV. 568/2 The salary was ten times what she was getting at the hashery. **1957** J. KEROUAC *On Road* (1958) 172 Her honest labors in the hashery.

hash, *sb.*[1] Add: **3. b.** (Earlier and later examples.)

1803 I. CRUIKSHANK *Olympic Games* 16 June (*caption*), I think the first round will settle his hash. **1807** *Massachusetts Spy* 14 Oct. 4/1 This settles all the hash. **1809** T. G. FESSENDEN *Pills Poetical* 114 We therefore mean to make a dash, To settle fighting Europe's hash. **1822** [see SETTLE *v.* 21 b]. **1930** R. H. MOTTRAM *Europa's Beast* xii. 292 He's settled my hash, right enough. **1933** C. ST. J. SPRIGG *Fatality in Fleet St.* x. 124 What are you going to do? Settle his hash and drop him overboard?

6. hash-house chiefly *U.S. colloq.*, a cheap eating-house, boarding house, etc.; also *attrib.*; **hash-joint** *U.S. slang* = **hash-house*; **hash-mark** *U.S. slang*, a military service stripe; **hash-slinger** *U.S. slang*, a waiter or waitress; **hash-up** *slang*, a hastily cooked meal; also *fig.*, something concocted afresh from existing material; a reworking.

1869 *Territorial Enterprise* (Virginia, Nev.) 21 Sept. 3/1 The Mayor proposes to double the tax on all 'hash houses'. **1875** *Scribner's Monthly* July 277/1 In the slang vernacular, an eating place is a 'hash house'. **1883** *Daily Tel.* 10 Jan. 5/4 (Farmer), Fifteen-cent restaurants, commonly called hash-houses. **1895** W. C. GORE in *Inlander* Dec. 116 *Hash-house*, boarding house. **1897** *Outing* (U.S.) XXX. 362/1 It has its swell hotels..and its 'hash-houses'. **1900** H. LAWSON *On Track* in *Prose Wks.* (1948) 223 Fourpenny hash-houses (good beds, 6d.). **1903** A. H. LEWIS *Boss* xx. 273 His is this deadfall on Barclay Street, with that hash-house keeper to give him th' dough for his checks. **1936** I. L. IDRIESS *Cattle King* xviii. 170 Sid Kidman found every hotel, every boarding-house, every hash-house, every room crowded. **1946** 'P. QUENTIN' *Puzzle for Fiends* (1947) xxiv. 171 You'll have to take that job in a hashhouse after all. **1960** N. HILLIARD *Maori Girl* 221, I see the hotels and the hash-houses. **1895** W. C. GORE in *Inlander* Dec. 116 *Hash-joint*, boarding-house. **1930** J. DOS PASSOS *42nd Parallel* 101 Passing the same Chink hashjoint for the third time. **1909** *Man-o' Warsman* Dec. 24/1 First Sergeant John J. Maloney earned another hash-mark. **1935** G. & S. LORIMER *Heart Specialist* vi. 168 Slim and Shorty each had two gold stripes on their left sleeve that Slim called hash marks because they were service stripes and stood for the number of years of free food they'd had on Uncle Sam, he said. **1868** *Gold Hill News* (Nevada) 6 May, The nice young man of Washoe may or may not be some kind of a clerk, a hash-slinger, or a check-guerrilla. **1895** W. C. GORE in *Inlander* Dec. 116 *Hash-slinger*, table waiter. **1946** *Amer. Speech* XXI. 86 The cooks and 'hashslingers' of former years went off to war or to the shipyards. **1895** A. W. PINERO *Second Mrs. Tanqueray* II. 71 Dreams are only a hash-up of one's day-thoughts. **1902** *N.Z. Illustr. Mag.* VI. 452 While sharing their 'hash-up', he had [determined] to pitch camp on the [gum] field. **1914** *Auto-motor Jrnl.* 816/2 The so-called 'motoring notes' in the daily press are a thinly disguised hash-up of the best stuff in the motor press proper. **1970** *Times* 28 Feb. p. iv, A style perilously close to certain Colour Supplement hash-ups and clearly aligned for Overground consumption.

hash, *sb.*[2] Colloq. abbrev. of HASHISH.

1959 N. MAILER *Advts. for Myself* (1961) 245 Drawing upon hash, lush, Harlem, Spanish wife, Marxist culture [etc.]. **1967** *Listener* 31 Aug. 262/2 If people use dangerous machinery..while they are high on hash, the consequences may be..brash. **1968** A. DIMENT *Gt. Spy Race* viii. 143 What do you and Riordan do for a living—I thought he was just another part-time hash pusher? **1972** P. DICKINSON *Lizard in Cup* x. 157 'It's morphine she's been on?' said Pibble. But Tony shook her head. 'Just grass. Hash.'

Hashimite (hæ·ʃimǝit), *a.* and *sb.* Also **Hashemite.** [f. the name of *Hāšim*, great-grandfather of Mohammed + -ITE[1].] **A.** *adj.* Of, pertaining to, or characteristic of the Hashimites. **B.** *sb.* A member of an Arabian princely family claiming descent from Hashim.

1697 H. PRIDEAUX *True Nature of Imposture in Life Mahomet* 5 From him [*sc.* Hashem] the Kindred of Mahomet are called Hashemites. **1757** S. OCKLEY *Hist. Saracens* (ed. 3) I. 6 Hashem the great grandfather of Mahomet, whose descendants were from him called Hashemites. **1883** *Encycl. Brit.* XV. 672/1 Native princes claiming descent from the Prophet—the Háshimite emírs of Mecca.—attained to great authority and aimed at independence. **1949** KOESTLER *Promise & Fulfilment* xvi. 177 Transjordan was and is as interested in a solution on these lines as the Jews, in view of the age-old rivalry between the Hashimite and Saudite dynasties. **1958** *Spectator* 7 Feb. 159/2 The Hashemites of Transjordan or Iraq. **1973** *Times* 22 Sept. 5/1 Despite a spiritual attachment to the guerrillas and a distaste for Hashemite rule, Jordan's Palestinian majority view any guerrilla return with far less enthusiasm than Arabs elsewhere.

Hashimoto (hæʃimōᵘ·tō). *Med.* The name of H. *Hashimoto* (1881–1934), Japanese surgeon, used in the possessive to designate struma lymphomatosa, a disease (described by him in 1912), usu. of women and probably of autoimmune origin, in which the thyroid is enlarged, usu. symmetrically, and infiltrated by lymphoid tissue, as *Hashimoto's disease, goitre, struma* (*lymphomatosa*), *thyroiditis.*

1935 *Arch. Surg.* XXXI. 424 No cervical adenitis is present in association with Hashimoto's struma. **1936** STEDMAN *Med. Dict.* (ed. 13) 475/2 *Hashimoto's disease*, struma lymphomatosa. **1937** J. H. MEANS *Thyroid & its Dis.* xix. 503 The histology of Hashimoto's goiter is that of extensive lymphoid infiltration. **1956** *Jrnl. Clin. Endocrinol.* XVI. 1570 (*title*) An unusual iodinated protein of the serum in Hashimoto's thyroiditis. **1962** *Times* 30 Nov. 19/4 Hashimoto's disease, in which there is a gradual destruction of the thyroid gland. **1968** *Brit. Med. Bull.* XXIV. 224/2 Shown are the observed frequencies of occurrence of signs, symptoms and results of laboratory tests in three diseases: Hashimoto's disease, simple goitre and thyroid cancer. **1972** BASTENIE & ERMANS *Thyroiditis & Thyroid Function* v. 110 The formal criteria of Hashimoto's goitre, namely a recently developed symmetrical and homogeneous goitre, the presence of very high thyroid antibody titres, and the diffuse lesions characteristic of the disease. *Ibid.* 118 The progress of untreated Hashimoto's thyroiditis is variable.

hashmagandy (hæ:ʃmăgæ·ndi). *Austral.* and *N.Z. slang.* Also **hash-me-gandy, hash magandy.** [f. HASH *sb.* 1.] A type of stew.

1919 W. H. DOWNING *Digger Dial.* 28 *Hashmagandy*, an

insipid and monotonous army dish. **1941** BAKER *N.Z. Slang* vi. 54 Terms bequeathed to us by shearers and tramps and farmers..that appear to have originated this century..*hash-me-gandy*, station stew. **1945** —— *Austral. Lang.* 81 For stews our only original contributions appear to be *hash-me-gandy* and *mulliga stew*. **1951** L. G. D. ACLAND *Early Canterbury Runs* 381 *Hash-me-gandy*, station stew.

Hasid, -ic, -im, -ism: see *CHASID, CHASSID.

haskinize (hæˑskinəiz), *v.* [f. the name of S. E. *Haskin*, the inventor of the process + -IZE.] *trans.* To submit (green timber) to a process by which it becomes hard and durable through the application of heat of over 212°F. under a pressure of 200 pounds to the square inch. So **ha:skinizaˑtion.**

1897 S. E. HASKIN (*title*) Haskinizing—Vulcanizing—for the preservation of wood from decay. **1908** W. R. FISHER tr. *Gayer's Forest Utiliz.* (ed. 2) 509 The process is termed Haskinisation or Vulcanisation, and has given good results on the Manhattan Railway, New York.

Hasmonean (hæzmonīˑăn), *sb.* and *a.* Also **Ash-, -æan, Asmonean, -æan.** [f. mod.L. *Asmōnæus*, f. Ἀσαμωναῖος (Josephus) = *ḥašmōnây*, name of the reputed grandfather of Mattathias.] **A.** *sb.* A member of a Jewish dynasty or family to which the Maccabees belonged. **B.** *adj.* Of or pertaining to this dynasty.

1620 LODGE tr. *Josephus* XIV. xxviii. 381 Thus ended the estate of the Asmoneans, after 120. and sixe yeeres. *Ibid. marg.*, The end of the Asmonean family. **1832** H. COTTON *Five Bks. Maccabees* 50 Ashmonæan princes. **1834** *Penny Cycl.* II. 485 Asmonæans. **1880** *Encycl. Brit.* XIII. 421/2 A certain priest Mattathias, of the family of the Hasmonæans. **1898** *Expositor* Apr. 273 The Hasmonean priestly dynasty. **1926** E. F. SCOTT *1st Age Christianity* i. 16 In virtue of his priestly descent the Asmonaean king could also hold the office of high-priest. **1956** A. TOYNBEE *Historian's Approach to Religion* x. 134 A short-lived Hasmonaean successor-state. **1973** *Sci. Amer.* Jan. 80/2 We would know nothing of the political fortunes of the Hasmonean dynasty, which followed the Maccabean revolt.

Hassid, -ic, -im, -ism: see *CHASID, CHASSID.

hassle (hæˑs'l). *colloq.* (chiefly *N. Amer.*). Also **hassel.** [Eng. and U.S. dial.: see *E.D.D.* and Wentworth *Amer. Dial. Dict.*] A quarrel, argument, fuss; a difficulty, problem; trouble. Also as *vb.*, to quarrel, argue; to worry, harass.

1945 *Down Beat* 15 Feb. 1/5 Building bands is getting to be a habit with Freddie Slack. He broke up his last few after booking hassels. **1946** *Sat. Even. Post* 31 Aug. 72/2 'Hassle' is a gorgeously descriptive word which lately has won wide usage in show business. **1950** B. SHULBERG *Disenchanted* (1951) ix. 102 She's actually a society girl.. who's had a hassel with her family and wants to prove she can get by on her own. **1957** J. KEROUAC *On Road* (1958) 50 We'll both understand purely and without any hassle that we are simply stopping talking. **1959** F. W. HOUSEHOLDER in Saporta & Bastian *Psycholinguistics* (1961) 18/1 The chief metaphysical bones hassled over in recent years concern such points as 'biuniqueness'. **1967** *Boston Sunday Globe* 23 Apr. 25/1 Now the zoning hassle has switched across the city to..where the Greek Orthodox Church is petitioning for a rezoning to allow a developer to erect..a $1.8 million office building complex. **1969** *Rolling Stone* 17 May 11/2 All others [*sc.* dancing clubs] had collapsed or been hassled to death. **1971** *Frendz* 21 May 16/1 The Edgar Broughton Band toured Germany earlier this year and were involved in some heavy hassles with the promoters of the various gigs.

‖ **hasta la vista** (aˑsta la viˑsta). [Sp.] Good-bye, au revoir (used chiefly in Spanish contexts).

1935 C. MORLEY (*title*) Hasta la vista, or, A postcard from Peru. **1940** A. HUXLEY *Let.* 5 Jan. (1969) 449 Well, bless you both. Give our loves to the love-worthy. Hasta la vista. **1967** C. ARMSTRONG *Gift Shop* ix. 76 Dorinda had bade him a gay *hasta la vista* in Copenhagen and gone off. **1967** K. GILES *Death in Diamonds* ix. 168 'Come and stay with us...' 'I hope to. Hasta la vista.'

haste, *sb.* Add: **5.** *to make haste.* **b.** *to make haste slowly*, after L. *festina lente* (Suet. *Aug.* 25).

1744 B. FRANKLIN *Poor Richard* (1890) Apr. 146 Make haste slowly. **1831** *Deb. Congress U.S.* 4 Feb. 98 Thus far the committee have 'made haste slowly'. **1938** M. TEAGLE *Murders in Silk* iii. 22 Easy, son. Let's make haste slowly. Does Conner know where the knife came from?

c. *Cricket.* Of a ball: to come up from the pitch with increased speed.

1888 A. G. STEEL in Steel and Lyttelton *Cricket* iii. 123 Every now and then one of their balls will, in cricket slang, 'make haste from the pitch'. **1904** P. F. WARNER *How we recovered Ashes* ix. 177 The ball made haste off the pitch, kept a little low, and clean beat Duff. **1920** —— *Cricket Reminisc.* ii. 19 Australia, where the bowler who makes haste off the pitch is the most useful type.

hasten, *v.* Add: **2.** *to hasten slowly*: cf. *HASTE *sb.* 5 b.

1907 *Spectator* 12 Jan. 43 'Hasten slowly' is a very good motto in Imperial politics. **1958** *Oxford Mail* 14 Aug. 1/3 The Government is still hastening slowly on re-expansion.

hastener. Add: **1. a.** *Services' slang.* (See quot. 1946.)

1943 C. H. WARD-JACKSON *Piece of Cake* 35 *Hastener*, a letter asking for a reply to a previous letter. **1946** J. IRVING *Royal Navalese* 92 *Hastener*, a letter or a 'Minute' asking for a reply to some previous correspondence. **1955** *Times* 12 May 11/4 Those who were once temporary soldiers may recall how they used to send 'hasteners' for the stores they wanted.

hasty pudding. (Later U.S. examples.)

1879 B. F. TAYLOR *Summer-Savory* i. 7 Their green knapsacks are growing plump with rations of samp, hasty-pudding, and Indian bread. **1881** *Harper's Mag.* Jan. 227/1 Cod-fish balls for breakfast on Sunday morning, ..and fried hasty-pudding. **1948** *Newsweek* 5 Jan. 66/1 Cook in an iron pot; turn out on a dish and the result: hasty pudding.

hat, *sb.* Add: **3. a.** An office, position, occupation; esp. in phr. *to wear two hats*, to hold two appointments concurrently; *wearing one's —— hat*, in one's capacity as ——.

[**1869** S. R. HOLE *Bk. about Roses* viii. 111, I never remember to have seen a scientific botanist and a successful practical florist under the same hat.] **1961** WEBSTER *Hat*, an office symbolized by or as if by the wearing of a special hat. **1963** *Times* 25 Apr. 13/7 They..would perform that precarious feat known in the Whitehall idiom as wearing two hats. **1965** *Observer* 31 Oct. 21/4 Even when he is wearing his ecumenical hat he is reported to be speaking as Archbishop of Canterbury. **1966** *Rep. Comm. Inquiry Univ. Oxf.* I. 27 Members of the colleges have accustomed themselves 'to wear two hats' and to act both as lecturers paid by the University and as fellows paid by their colleges. **1967** *Even. Standard* 29 Aug. 1/1 Wearing his new 'economic overlord' hat the Prime Minister summoned three key figures to Downing Street today. **1968** *Listener* 8 Feb. 177/2 Cecil Day-Lewis has two hats: one has laurel in it, the other is that of Nicholas Blake, who writes detective stories. **1972** *Village Voice* (N.Y.) 1 June 17/5, I wear two hats. Are you asking me this question as president of the Bartenders Union or as chairman of the ABC?

5. a. *to take off one's hat*: to doff or remove the hat, as a salute or sign of respect. Hence *hats off to..*, as a command or exhortation.

1856 *Punch* 5 Jan. 3/2 *Quaker*, a friend who..in the art of making inflammatory speeches, takes his hat off to no man. **1857** D. LIVINGSTONE *Miss. Trav.* viii. 272 This being the only hill we had seen since leaving the Bamangwato, we felt inclined to take off our hats to it. **1863** A. J. MUNBY *Diary* 7 Mar. in D. Hudson *Munby* (1972) 151 The populace..caught fire all at once. 'Hats off!' shouted the men: 'Here she is!' cried the women. **1881** *Harper's Mag.* Jan. 206/1 Over in Greenwood there is a stately monument, to the New York fireman,..before which I take off my hat. **1886** *Ibid.* June 45/2 We should take off our hats to them [*sc.* the 'lady-bugs'] and wish them godspeed. **1923** *Daily Mail* 22 Jan. 6, I say in all sincerity: 'Hats off to France!' **1947** 'P. WOODRUFF' *Wild Sweet Witch* iv. 106, I take off my hat to that boy. **1972** M. FARHI *Pleasure of your Death* vii. 198 'Hats off to them.' 'Yes, of course. Hats off to all the dead.'

b. (Earlier examples.)

1857 KINGSLEY *Two Y. Ago* I. v. 137 A little packet, containing not one five pound note, but four... The Mumpsimus men..had 'sent round the hat' for him. **1863** W. H. GOODE *Outposts of Zion* xxi. 182 The hat for the collection was carried around by a hand disabled by a gunshot.

c. *bad hat* (later examples); *to be in a (the) hat* (later example); also *to make a hat of*, to make a mess of; *to hang one's hat*: to take up one's quarters (in a certain place); *to hang one's hat on*: to depend upon; *to talk through one's hat*: to make unsupported or 'wild' assertions, to talk nonsense; *to throw one's hat into the ring*: to take up a challenge; *under one's hat*: secret, sub rosa; *my hat!*, a trivial exclamation of surprise. See also *HIGH HAT.

1847 *Sporting Life* V. 224/2 Warren threw his hat in the ring. **1848** *Ibid.* 1 Jan. 237/1 Curtis..threw his hat into the ring. **1875** TROLLOPE *Prime Minister* (1876) I. II. xx. 335 Lopez can come in and hang up his hat whenever it pleases him. **1880** A. A. HAYES *New Colorado* (1881) viii. 118 Why that's *my* preacher. I hang my hat on him every time. **1885** C. M. YONGE *Nuttie's Father* I. xviii. 220 Nuttie..was taking in all these revelations with an open-eyed, silent horror... It was all under her hat, however, and the elder ladies never thought of her. **1888** *N.Y. World* 13 May 12/3 Dis is only a bluff dey're makin'—see! Dey're talkin' tru deir hats. **1899** KIPLING *Stalky & Co.* 174 My Hat!..That's pretty average heroic. **1902** W. N. HARBEN *Abner Daniel* 81 All this talk about the devil makin' the bad an' the Lord the good is talk through a hat. **1904** 'O. HENRY' *Cabbages & Kings* vi. 117 The governor man had a bit of English under his hat, and when the music was choked off he says: 'Ver-r-ree fine.' **1904** *N.Y. American* 18 July 2 If the Tammany leader expects to hang his hat inside Judge Parker's political headquarters, he must come here voluntarily. **1912** *Nation* 7 Mar. 226/1 When Mr. Roosevelt threw his hat into the ring the other day, he gave the signal for a contest the like of which has not been seen before in this country. **1914** C. MACKENZIE *Sinister St.* II. III. viii. 661 'My hat, what a frowst,' exclaimed Maurice. **1916** *Chambers's Jrnl.* May 302/2 Now, Joshua Billings, A.B., though officially a bad hat, was one of the best seamen in the ship. **1916** *Chums* 30 Sept. 37/2 I'm in no end of a hat, chauffeur. Can you give me a hand? **1917** W. J. LOCKE *Red Planet* xxiv, 'You dashed young idiot,' I cried, 'do you think I'm in the habit of talking through my hat?' **1923** WODEHOUSE *Inimitable Jeeves* xviii. 249 She kept it under her hat. She meant to spring it on me later, she said. **1925** J. BUCHAN *John Macnab* xv. 312 Palliser-Yeates lost at Glenraden..and now I've made a regular hat of things at Haripol. **1928** *Observer* 4 Mar. 11/2 Mr. Secretary Hoover has been forced to throw his hat into the ring for the Presidency, but he does not mean to follow it there. **1929** GALSWORTHY *Roof* iv, *Mr. B.* I suppose you think you never snore. *Mrs. B.* I know I don't. *Mr. B.* My hat! **1939** 'A. BRIDGE' *Four-Part Setting* 155 One couldn't just sit by and watch a person..make a complete hat of her life and herself and her character. **1945** M. ALLINGHAM *Coroner's Pidgin* xiv. 118 My hat! was it only last night? **1953** 'N. SHUTE' *In Wet* viii. 251 'Nothing about that in the papers, is there?' 'Not yet. Keep it under your hat.' **1956** 'A. GILBERT' *Death came Too* xiv. 152 'You,' suggested Frank, politely, 'are talking through your hat.' **1958** *Daily Mail* 6 Sept. 4/2 Some of them innocent hard-working people, others petty thieves and bad hats. **1963** N. MARSH *Dead Water* (1964) vi. 148 I'd be very grateful ..if you'd keep the whole affair under your hat.

Also, in contexts referring to the drawing of names from (or the putting of names into) a hat in selecting opponents in a competition, etc.; also with reference to the conjuring trick of producing a rabbit from a hat.

1929 *Evening News* 18 Nov. 13/2 Dagenham..will be amongst the distinguished clubs to go into the hat. **1958** *Listener* 18 Sept. 404/1 Mr. Dulles first pulled indirect aggression out of the hat in mid-July. **1963** A. ROSS *Australia 63* v. 110 Simpson's five [wickets] were simply out of the hat. **1966** H. WAUGH *Pure Poison* (1967) xv. 93 He picked Roger out of a hat as a victim? **1971** J. MCCLUNE *Steam Pig* ii. 26, I must say you've really pulled one out of the hat this time.

6. d. The creamy top of hatted kit.

1831 [see HATTED *ppl. a.* c]. **1946** *Farmhouse Fare* (new ed.) 124 Hatted Kit..can..be made without milking the cow into it, although direct milking puts a better 'hat' on the Kit. **1952** F. WHITE *Good Eng. Food* IV. ii. 180 *Hatted Kit*..fresh good butter-milk, and a pint of milk hot from the cow. Mix well by jumbling... It will now firm, and gather a hat.

7. b. *dial.* A clump of trees.

1895 DE CRESPIGNY & HUTCHINSON *New Forest* 113 The term 'hat' is still in use for a little wood crowning a hill. **1895** G. PATTERSON in *Jrnl. Amer. Folk-Lore* VIII. 29 A hat of trees. **1936** C. R. ACTON *Sport & Sportsmen of New Forest* ii. 43 A clump of trees is known as a 'Hat'; two examples being 'Crab Hat' and 'King's Hat'.

8. *hat-securer.*

1892 A. CONAN DOYLE in *Strand Mag.* III. 75/1 It was pierced in the brim for a hat-securer, but the elastic was missing.

9, 10. *hat-raising, -trimming*; **hat-check boy, girl** *U.S.*, a cloakroom attendant; **hat-guard** (examples); **hat leather** (see quot. 1888); **hat-pad,** a pad usually of velvet for wiping the dust off or smoothing the nap of a hat; **hat-rack,** (*a*) a rack to hold hats; (*b*) *slang*, a scraggy animal; (*c*) *slang*, the head; **hat-tip,** the circular piece of stuff used to line the crown of a hat; **hat-tree,** (*b*) *Austral.* (see quot.).

1917 *N.Y. Tribune* 19 June 8/4 How about the hat check boys? **1921** WODEHOUSE *Indiscretions of Archie* xiv. 159 He paid no attention to the hat-check boy. **1959** *Guardian* 22 Dec. 5/1 He found work as a hatcheck boy. **1920** WODEHOUSE *Jill the Reckless* (1922) xv. 223 When a burglar marries a hat-check girl, their offspring goes into the theatrical business automatically. **1938** *Times Lit. Suppl.* 3 Sept. 572/4 He..has included all the important information..even to..the name of the hat-check girl in the New York restaurant. **1899** *Catal.* in A. Adburgham *Shops & Shopping* (1964) xxii. 261 Hat guards. **1912** A. BENNETT *Matador* 131 William Henry commanded her to buy a hat-guard. The hat-guard cost sixpence. **1888** *Lockwood's Dict. Mech. Engin.*, *Hat leather*, the leather ring packing used for hydraulic pistons. **1940** *Chambers's Techn. Dict.* 405/1 *Hat-leather packing*, an L-section leather ring, gripped between discs to form a piston, or similarly attached to the ram of a hydraulic machine to prevent leakage. **1902** W. W. JACOBS *Lady of Barge* 221 At the hall he paused, and busied himself with the clothes-brush and hat-pad. **1872** Hat-rack [in Dict., sense 8]. **1935** *Amer. Speech* X. 269/1 If he should try to hang his hat on the hatrack he will probably find that he will have to catch it first, for the hatrack will be found milling about in one of the pens. *Ibid.* 271/1 *Hatrack*, an old, thin cow, a nellie or canner. **1942** BERREY & VAN DEN BARK *Amer. Thes. Slang* § 121/56 *Head*,..hat rack. **1957** R. CAMPBELL *Portugal* v. 73 One trick is to deprive a hatrack of an old horse of water, and let him have a good lick of salt. **1964** L. HAIRSTON in J. H. Clarke *Harlem* 286 If you spent half as much time tryin' to put something *inside* that worthless hat-rack as you did having your brains fryed. **1905** *Westm. Gaz.* 11 Aug. 7/1 At Trafalgar-square there was much hat-raising. **1908** *Ibid.* 30 Jan. 12/2 The hat-raising habit. **1921** *Dict. Occup. Terms* (1927) § 549 *Hat tip sizer*, prints hat tip with size before gold leaf or bronze dust is applied by hat tip printer. **1898** MORRIS *Austral Eng.*, *Hat-tree*, name given to a species of *Sterculia*, the Bottle-trees. **1895** *Montgomery Ward Catal.* Index, Hat trimmings. **1905** *Daily Chron.* 23 Dec. 6/5 The success of the hat-trimming competition.

hat, *v.* Add: **c.** *intr.* To work alone. (Cf. HATTER *sb.* 2.) *Austral.*

1891 *Age* 25 Nov. 6/7 (Morris), Two old miners have been..hatting for gold amongst the old alluvial gullies. **1900** H. LAWSON *On Track* 88 And he 'hatted' and brooded over it till he went ratty.

‖ **hatamoto** (hætămōᵘˑto). [Jap.] In the

Japanese feudal system, a vassal or member of the household troops of a Shogun.

1871 A. B. MITFORD *Tales of Old Japan* I. 95 *Hatamoto.* This word means 'under the flag'. The Hatamotos were men who..rallied round the standard of the Shogun, or Tycoon, in war-time. **1899** L. HEARN *In Ghostly Japan* vi. 74 The *hatamoto* were samurai forming the special military force of the Shōgun. **1904** —— *Japan: Attempt at Interpretation* xii. 267 These two bodies of samurai formed the special military force of the Shōgun; the hatamoto being greater vassals with large incomes. **1968** J. W. HALL *Japan fr. Prehist. to Mod. Times* x. 166, 5,000 'bannermen' (*hatamoto*), who were privileged to come into the Shogun's presence.

hatch, *sb.*[1] Add: **3. d.** fig. *down the hatch*: a toasting or drinking phrase.

1931 *Amer. Mercury* Mar. 357/2 The boys didn't pester her to drink. 'Down the hatch!' they said. **1933** M. LOWRY *Ultramarine* iii. 120 'Well, let's shoot a few whiskies down the hatch, and you'll see three,' I remarked fatuously. **1935** *Yachting* Dec. 32/2 'Down the hatch!' is a toast well known ashore. **1942** T. RATTIGAN *Flare Path* I. 110 That went down the old hatch pretty quick, didn't it? **1958** B. HAMILTON *Too Much of Water* xii. 272 And so now, down the hatch, and let's..see what we can do with the pudding and souse. **1972** *House & Garden* Mar. 130/1 Unlike the professionals, who take a small sip ..and then spit it out..we, as amateurs, adopted the 'down the hatch' technique.

e. *Aeronaut.* An opening or door in an aeroplane or space capsule. See also quot. 1948.

1940 [see *escape hatch* s.v. *ESCAPE *sb.*[1] 8]. **1943** *Coastal Command* (Ministry of Information) ix. 89 At 1.55, after the rigger has reported that all hatches are closed, the klaxon sounds. The Catalina moves slowly at first... The take-off has begun. **1943** E. V. RICKENBACKER *Seven came Through* i. 13, I helped Sergeant Alex pry open the bottom hatch in the tail and between us we dumped all that high-priority mail into the blue Pacific. **1948** PARTRIDGE *Dict. Forces' Slang* 92 *Hatch*, a bomb-hatch—the bomb-aimer's compartment, at the front of the kite, especially in 'Lanks' and 'Wimpeys'. **1956** W. A. HEFLIN *U.S.A.F. Dict.* 246/1 *Hatch*, a ship term sometimes applied to an opening or door in an aircraft, esp. one in the deck of an aircraft or in the top and bottom of the fuselage. **1962** D. SLAYTON in *Into Orbit* 26 We asked them to adapt the entry hatch and convert it into an exit, too. **1969** *Times* 23 May 1/2 The two craft are linked by a 3 ft. connecting tunnel, sealed at each end by a hatch.

hatch, *sb.*[2] Add: Also in phr. *hatches, matches, and dispatches* (occas. in *sing.*), a newspaper list of births, marriages, and deaths.

1878 J. PAYN *By Proxy* I. xix. 217 First came the Births, Deaths, and Marriages... The female mind.. takes an interest in the 'Hatch, Match, and Despatch' of its fellow-creatures. **1880** *Times for Year 1980* 1/1 Hatches... Matches... Despatches. **1953** M. STEEN *Anna Fitzalan* viii. 215 Dismissing reviews..Lin turned to what Mummy called Hatches, Matches and Despatches. **1959** F. KING *So Hurt & Humiliated* 128 Glancing through the 'Hatches, Matches, Despatches' columns in *The Times* at breakfast, Emily suddenly interrupted my reading of the *Economist*. **1966** 'H. HOWARD' *Counterfeit* iii. 57 He might even be a registrar of births, marriages and deaths—the man who issued certificates for what people used to call Hatches, Matches and Despatches.

hatch, *v.*[1] Add: Hence **hatchabi·lity**, the condition or state of being likely to hatch, or able to produce eggs which will hatch.

1916 *Experiment Station Rec.* Feb. 178 The hatchability of eggs which are produced. **1950** *N.Z. Jrnl. Agric.* Jan. 14/1 Work is involved in keeping data about the hatchability of the eggs from each pen. **1956** *New Biol.* XXI. 116 There is evidence that the presence of earthworms in soil increases the hatchability of the cysts of the potato root eelworm. **1960** *Farmer & Stockbreeder* 9 Feb. 87 Greater egg production, better grading, increased hatchability.

hatchel, *sb.* See also *HETCHEL *sb.*

hatchel, *v.* Add: **1. b.** *transf.*

1845 [see *HETCHEL *v.*].

2. (Earlier U.S. example.)

1800 *Aurora* (Phila.) 20 Oct. (Th.), They have..hatchelled them with prosecutions, fines, and imprisonments.

hatchery. Add: (Later examples.) Also *fig.*

1932 A. HUXLEY *Brave New World* i. 1 Central London hatchery and conditioning centre. **1932** M. A. JULL *Poultry Breeding* xi. 347 Sanitary conditions at hatcheries must be approved by the hatchery inspector. Only eggs from approved hatchery flocks may be incubated. **1942** D. MITRANY in *Agenda* I. 305 The T.V.A. is itself a hatchery of public enterprise. **1952** *Oxf. Jun. Encycl.* VI. 360/2 Some poultry-farmers do not hatch eggs from their own birds but buy day-old chicks from 'hatcheries', which are places that do nothing but incubate eggs on a very large scale.

hatchet, *sb.* Add: **2.** See also BURY *v.* 2 a in Dict. and Suppl.

3. hatchet fish, a member of the family Gasteropelecidæ, South American flying characins which are often kept in aquaria, or one of the family Sternoptychidæ, deep-sea clupeiform fishes found in most of the oceans of the world; also *hatchet* ellipt.; **hatchet-job, -work** (see *HATCHET-MAN 3).

1931 J. R. NORMAN *Hist. Fishes* xii. 231 (*caption*) Hatchet-fish (*Argyropelecus* sp.). **1959** P. CAPON *Amongst those Missing* 196 Hatchet-fish skimmed the water. **1960** M. BURTON *Under Sea* xi. 198 Another consumer of small prey is the 'hatchet' fish, so called because its body is flattened from side-to-side... For the most part hatchets are only a few inches long. **1962** K. F. LAGLER et al. *Ichthyology* ii. 36 Family Sternoptychidae—deepsea hatchet fishes.

hatchet, *v.* Restrict *Obs.* to sense in Dict. and add: **2.** *transf.* To act as a hatchet-man against (someone), to do down.

1959 'B. O'BRIEN' *Operators & Things* (1960) i. 34 Even the Knoxes were willing to hatchet each other.

ha·tchet-man. [f. HATCHET *sb.* + MAN *sb.*[1]] † **1.** A pioneer or axeman serving in a military unit. *U.S. Obs.*

1755 [see *hatchet-man* s.v. HATCHET *sb.* 3].

2. In the U.S., a hired Chinese assassin. Also *transf.*

1880 G. B. DENSMORE *Chinese in California* xii. 94 Some of them are called hatchet-men. They carry a hatchet with the handle cut off. **1888** *Boston Jrnl.* 3 May 1/2 The work of the hatchetmen among the enemies of the organization. **1913** J. LONDON *Valley of Moon* III. xx, Chan Chi, had been a hatchet-man of note, in the old fighting days of the San Francisco tongs. **1957** P. FRANK *Seven Days to Never* III. iii. 90 He was a hatchet man for the NKVD... He may have delivered Beria over to Malenkov and Krushchev.

3. (Now the usual sense.) A person, especially a journalist, employed to attack and destroy other people's reputations. So *hatchet job, work*. orig. *U.S.*

1944 *Time* 23 Oct. 20 Exuberant hatchet jobs were.. done on Foster Dulles because of his Wall Street connections. **1952** *Manch. Guardian Weekly* 3 Apr. 15/4 Republican hatchet-men. **1961** M. McCARTHY *On Contrary* (1962) I. 87 The literary Communists..doing the hatchet work on artists' reputations. **1959** *Encounter* July 83/1 One has no difficulty in recognising the familiar tones of Dr. Leavis' hatchet-men when he is attacked. **1959** *Guardian* 13 Oct. 7/4 One critic..was the meanest son of a bitch that ever lived. His criticism was a hatchet job on every book. **1960** *News Chron.* 14 July 1/5 The Kennedy family went into action with a commando team of political hatchet-men. **1962** *Listener* 21 June 1089/1 It was difficult enough to sympathise with the hero once we'd seen him doing his hatchet work.

hatching, *vbl. sb.*[1] Add: **a.** Also, that which is hatched, a brood.

1905 *Kynoch Jrnl.* Apr.–June 108 The hatchings at the present time are quite up to the average of a good year.

hatchling (hæ·tʃliŋ). [f. HATCH *sb.*[2] + -LING[1].] A very young fish or bird, etc., usually artificially hatched and not old enough to take care of itself.

1899 *19th Cent.* Sept. 399 The ova hatched out *en route*, and the hatchlings died. **1899** *Field* 16 Sept. 496 This assertion may be verified by throwing some hatchlings into a tank where fish of all sizes are mixed together. It will be seen that the strangers are at once devoured. **1955** *Sci. Amer.* Oct. 98/3 It is curious that, although the young hatchling in the nest is in great hazard of its life, once it has begun to fly it is extremely unlikely to be lost during the remainder of the dependence period. **1957** *New Scientist* 24 Oct. 9 The female octopus..laid eggs..on 6 September. ..The first hatchlings appeared on 16 October.

hatch-out (hæ·tʃˌaut). [f. the verbal phr. *to hatch out* (see HATCH *v.*[1] 2).] The action of hatching out; also, the brood hatched out.

1898 *Westm. Gaz.* 13 May 4/1 It only depends upon climatic conditions to ensure a good hatch out. **1908** *Ibid.* 5 June 4/2 While the hatch-out is in progress the number of the fly is marvellous. *Ibid.* 14 Aug. 4/2 Partridges are more faithful to a fixed date for the hatch-out of their eggs than grouse.

hate, *sb.*[1] Add: **1. c.** In the war of 1914–18, a bombardment, a 'strafe'. *slang.*

A jocular use based upon the German 'Hymn of Hate', which was ridiculed in *Punch* 24 Feb. 1915, p. 150, in the legend of a drawing, 'Study of a Prussian household having its morning hate'.

[**1914** *Punch* 30 Dec. 530/1 Kaiser, what vigil will you keep tonight?.. While your priesthood chants the Hymn of Hate, Like incense will you lift to God your breath?] **1915** D. O. BARNETT *Lett.* 204 There are some unhealthy spots, 'Suicide Corner', 'Deadman's Alley' and others, where they drop shells regularly, trying to catch our transport at night. We call it the 'Evening Hate'. **1926** F. M. FORD *Man could stand up* II. v. 174 There is not going to be a *strafe*. This is only a little extra Morning Hate. **1927** E. THOMPSON *These Men thy Friends* 112 He was watching a spasmodic 'hate' of some violence. **1968** D. REEMAN *Pride & Anguish* x. 180 I'm going to turn in, Sub. I want a couple of hours before the night's 'hate' gets going.

d. Phr. *to have a hate on* or *against* (a person) (see quot. 1941).

1941 BAKER *Dict. Austral. Slang* 38 *Have a hate against*, actively to dislike a person or thing. **1966** 'S. WOODS' *Let's choose Executors* 62 Things have been perfectly horrid, ever since Mark started to have a hate against her. *Ibid.* 220 She seemed to have a complete hate on him.

2. *hate-maddened* adj.; **hate-love**, a conflicting emotion combining hate and love (cf. **love-hate*).

1915 J. C. POWYS *Visions & Revisions* 244 This monstrous *hate-love*, caressing the bruises itself has made, and shooting forth a forked viper-tongue of cruelty from between the lips that kiss. **1962** *Listener* 5 July 11/2 He consciously contrasts his teaching with that of the object of his hate-love. **1921** R. GRAVES *Pier-Glass* 25 It beams on set jaw and hate-maddened eye. **1937** B. H. L. HART *Europe in Arms* xxii. 284 To use force without limit and without calculation of cost may be instinctive in a hate-maddened mob, but it is the negation of statesmanship.

b. Used *attrib.* or as quasi-*adj.*: designed to stir up hate, e.g. *hate campaign*; marked or characterized by hate.

1916 *Daily Colonist* (Victoria, B.C.) 21 July 12/7 The official Cologne Gazette published the following excellent example of 'hate literature': 'Among those who are guilty of involving Europe in a bath of blood Lord Northcliffe is perhaps the guiltiest of all.' **1949** 'G. ORWELL' *Nineteen Eighty-Four* I. 5 The economy drive in preparation for Hate Week. **1959** *Daily Tel.* 18 May 6/2 Hence, perhaps, the decision to revert to 'Western imperialism' as target of a fresh hate-campaign in Iraq. **1966** H. WAUGH *Pure Poison* (1967) xii. 71 Have you or your wife ever received hate phone calls or hate messages before? **1969** *N.Y. Rev. Books* 16 Jan. 36/1 Mr Epstein reaches the heights..of absurdity by stating that the hate literature distributed in the Ocean Hill-Brownsville teacher mail boxes may have been fraudulent.

hateworthy (hēⁱ·tˌwɒ̄:ɹði), *a.* [f. HATE *sb.*[1] + WORTHY *a.*] Worthy of hate, hateful.

1901 A. SYMONS *Poems* (1907) I. 180, I tremble lest a wrath so just avenge On him a mother so most hateworthy. **1924** *Public Opinion* 9 May 450/3 There is nothing sinister or hateworthy in Mrs. Carlyle's slowly and deliberately formed judgement.

hatha-yoga (ha·tăyōu·gă). [Skr., f. *haṭha* force, violence, forced meditation + YOGA.] A system of exercises and control of breathing forming part of the Hindu religious philosophy of yoga. So **hatha-yogi(n)**, a devoteee of hatha-yoga.

1911 *Encycl. Brit.* XXVI. 791/1 The physical methods and spiritual exercises recommended by theosophists are those inculcated in the systems known in Hindu philosophy as Râjâ Yoga in contradistinction to the Hatha Yoga system, which is most commonly to be met with in India, and in which the material aspects are given greater prominence. **1937** A. HUXLEY *Ends & Means* xiii. 234 The methods of Hatha Yoga, as they are called in India, are said to result in heightened mental and physical powers. *Ibid.* 247 It is possible for meditation to be practised by those who are neither extreme ascetics nor Hatha-Yogis. **1956** E. WOOD *Yoga Dict.* 62 *Hatha-yoga*, a form of yoga which is concerned chiefly with the regulation of breathing, and secondarily with other bodily disciplines or training. **1956** A. HUXLEY *Adonis & Alphabet* 32 The training of the dervish or the hatha-yogin is a long laborious affair. **1963** *Times Lit. Suppl.* 11 Jan. 29/3 It may be observed that even Indian Buddha figures ..by no means express the strenuous constrictions of mediaeval Hindu Hatha-yoga. **1967** *Daily Tel.* 1 Feb. 13/5 Hatha yoga, he explained, deals with the mastery of thought and breath. 'If we control our breath we control our thought. When we control our thought we begin to understand the full meaning of life.'

hathi (hā·ti). *India.* Also **hotty, huttee**, etc. [Hind. *hāthī* (also Marathi, etc. *hattī*), f. Skr. *hastin* elephant, f. *hasta* elephant's trunk, hand.] An elephant. Also *attrib.*: **hathi tractor**, a kind of tractor used in the war of 1914–18.

[**1826** LEYDEN & ERSKINE tr. *Mem. Zehir-Ed-Din* 315 As for the animals peculiar to Hindustân, one is the elephant, the Hindustânis call it *Hathi*.] **1831** TYERMAN & BENNET *Voy. & Trav.* II. 375 Our bearers suddenly set up the cry of 'Huttee! huttee!' **1838** in E. Eden *Up Country* (1866) I. 269 You are of course aware that we habitually call elephants Hotties. **1860** W. H. RUSSELL *Diary India* I. 392 We came to the Ramgunga, a deep stream, which our elephant waded across... The hathi nearly floated his driver off his neck. **1890** KIPLING *Barrack-r. Ballads* (1892) 51 An' the *hathis* pilin' teak. **1922** *Glasgow Herald* 11 Feb. 10 Golden also was the head of the 'hathi' selected for this honour. **1926** *Glasgow Herald* 27 Aug. 11 There was the Hathi tractor, constructed in the first place largely from German spare parts, captured during the war. The Hathi—its title is the Indian word for elephant—had besides the strength of the elephant qualities which that intelligent animal does not possess.

Hathor (hā·þǫɹ). Also **Athor.** [ad. Gr. Ἀθώρ, f. Egypt. *Ḥet-Ḥerh* the house above, or *Ḥet-Ḥeru* house of Horus.] The name of an Egyptian divinity, the goddess of love, often represented with the head or ears of a cow, used *attrib.* or *Comb.* to designate a type of column surmounted by a capital on which are carved one or more representations of the head of Hathor. So **Hathoric** (hăþǫ·rik), *a.* Hence **Hathore·sque** *a.*, in the style of a Hathor figure.

1786 tr. *C. E. Savary's Lett. on Egypt* II. xlviii. 351 Athor, or the night, in the opinion of the Egyptian priests, represented the darkness which enveloped the chaos before the creation. **1851** W. S. W. VAUX *Handbk. Antiq. B.M.* 355 The Venus of the Egyptians was called Athor, Hathor, or Athyr, and her name implied the abode of Horus. **1857** J. GARDNER WILKINSON *Egyptians* 273 His hair is that of the milky way..his eyes, the symbolical eyes of Athor.

1896 W. M. F. PETRIE *Koptos* i. 4/2 Below the scene is a frieze of *dad* signs alternating with figures, the lower parts of which are like the Isiac girdle tie, while above they have the human Hathor head, with cows' ears and horns.. They seem as if they might be copies of some primitive Hathor idol. **1901** R. STURGIS *Dict. Archit.* I. 854/2 The columns are easily divisible into a few general types, such as the single and the clustered lotus-bud, the campaniform, the palm-capped, and the Hathor-headed. *Ibid.* II. 366/2 *Hathoric*, having to do with the Egyptian goddess Hathor. **1934** E. POUND *Eleven New Cantos* xxxix. 44 When Hathor was bound in that box afloat on the sea wave. **1960** *Times* 7 Mar. 8/3 A handsome jewelry box with an ivory inlay of Hathor beads. **1962** D. HARDEN *Phoenicians* xiii. 198 A peculiar multiple vase for offerings has..a Hathoresque head above a long-horned cow's head.

hatikvah (hati·kvā). [ad. Heb. *ha-tiḳwāh* hope]. A national song, of which the words were written by N. H. Imber (1856–1909), adopted by the Zionist movement in 1907; since 1948 the Israeli national anthem.

1925 P. GUEDALLA *Napoleon & Palestine* 63 The proceedings concluded with the singing of the Hatikvah by some of the audience. **1932** L. GOLDING *Magnolia St.* I. viii. 130 The Jewish guests thought it would balance things nicely if they sang the Jewish anthem, *Hatikvah*. **1965** *Times Lit. Suppl.* 30 Dec. 1210/5 The Jewesses of Salonika singing the Hatikvah, the Jewish anthem. **1970** I. SIEFF *Memoirs* vi. 111 We sang *Hatikvah*, and also 'God Save the King'.

hatless, *a.* Add: Hence **ha·tlessly** *adv.*; **ha·tlessness,** hatless condition.

1890 E. DOWSON *Let.* 1 June (1967) 149 We sat & smoked for some hours hatlessly on the balcony. **1881** R. G. WHITE *Eng. Without & Within* 271 The hatlessness, the shoelessness, the rags, and the dirt. **1902** *Westm. Gaz.* 17 Oct. 2/3 Hitherto hatlessness was only *de rigueur* in the stalls and the front row of the dress circle. **1924** *Glasgow Herald* 29 May 6 Many people, who advocate hatlessness during the summer months. **1933** E. A. ROBERTSON *Ordinary Families* x. 229 He did not mind my looking out of place through hatlessness. **1960** *Guardian* 15 July 8/2 The prevailing..hatlessness of Frenchwomen.

hatter, *sb.* **2.** For def. read: One who lives or works alone, orig. a miner; a solitary bushman. *Austral.* and *N.Z.* Add earlier and additional examples.

1853 J. ROCHFORT *Adv. Surveyor* viii. 66 The Bendigo diggings are suitable for persons working singly... Such persons are humorously called 'hatters'. **1865** B. L. FARJEON *Shadows on Snow* II. 76, I was working as a 'hatter'. **1889** E. WAKEFIELD *N.Z. after 50 Yrs.* vi. 165 Miners who work alone are called 'hatters', one explanation of the term being that they frequently go mad from the solitude of their claim away in the bush, exemplifying the proverb 'As mad as a hatter'. **1903** 'S. RUDD' *Our New Selection* iv. 37 A weird, silent 'hatter' was there,.. the strange man who lived..away from everybody. **1914** J. M. BELL *Wilds of Maoriland* vi. 135 At times one comes across an old hatter [near Karamea]. **1924** H. T. GIBSON *That Gibbie Galoot* xxvii. 124 The skipper [of a timber scow] I seldom saw, for he was a 'hatter' and kept to his cabin and keg. **1943** V. PALMER in *Coast to Coast 1942* 21 People on the mainland said that McGowan was a cranky old hatter who had gone off his head because his home was broken up and was now letting his mind rot in isolation. **1944** F. CLUNE *Red Heart* 66 The 'hatter' was mumbling to himself in the manner of lonely outback prowlers. **1966** *Southerly* XXVI. 108 Rueben McGrath was..a bush 'hatter', a loner.

Hattic (hæ·tik), *a.* Also **Kh-**. [f. Assyrian and Hittite *Ḫatti* + -IC.] Of or pertaining to the Hatti or their language, formerly regarded as conterminous with the Hittites, now as a section of them. Hence as *sb.*, their language. So **Ha·ttian** *sb.* and *a.* **a.** One of the race of Hatti or their language. **b.** = *Hattic* adj. above. **Ha·ttism,** the social and political system of the Hatti.

[**1874** *Trans. Soc. Bibl. Arch.* III. 245 The king of the Khati. **1880** CHEYNE in *Encycl. Brit.* XII. 25/1 Hittites, a warlike and powerful nation... In the Egyptian inscriptions they are called the Khita or Kheta; in the Assyrian, the Khatti; in the Hebrew Scriptures, the Khittim.] **1924** D. G. HOGARTH in *Cambr. Anc. Hist.* II. 253 Boghaz Keui..is the site of the Hattic capital. **1926** —— *Kings of Hittites* 3 The Hittite civilization of Hamath was but an outlier of 'Hattism', advanced southward along a trunk-road. *Ibid.* 8 Have any remains been revealed which manifestly are Cappadocian Hattic, wholly or in part? **1928** C. DAWSON *Age of Gods* 302 The official language of the empire has been named by its discoverers Nashili or Kanesian; but since the ruling people have always been known as the Hittites, it seems better to retain the same name for their language and to describe the native Hattic tongue as Old Hittite. **1929** J. GARSTANG *Hittite Empire* ii. 39 The suggestion of language..would seem to indicate an original movement or series of movements from or affecting the Caucasian area, which at the same time peopled Armenia, northern Mesopotamia, and Elam, and won for the Hattians and other Hittite tribes a footing on the eastern mountains and plateau of Asia Minor. *Ibid.* 40 The Hattians themselves were an inland and not a seafaring people. **1933** E. H. STURTEVANT *Compar. Gram. Hittite Lang.* i. 29 Fortunately our use of the biblical name Hittite leaves the ancient stem free for use in its original sense; we shall call the predecessor language Hattic. **1952** O. R. GURNEY *Hittites* ii. 64 The original (Hattian?) form of the name. *Ibid.* 69 This conclusion agrees well with the linguistic evidence, according to which a group of Indo-European immigrants became dominant over an aboriginal race of 'Hattians'. **1958** *Archivum Linguisticum* X. II. 82 Bilinguals whose native language was Hattic. **1963** *Times Lit. Suppl.* 1 Feb. 72/3 The fully prehistoric 'Hattian' period.

hat trick. Add: **2.** *Cricket.* (Earlier example.)

1877 J. LILLYWHITE *Cricketers' Compan.* 181 Having on one occasion taken six wickets in seven balls, thus performing the hat-trick successfully.

b. Hence *gen.*, a threefold feat in other sports or activities.

1909 *Daily Chron.* 12 Aug. 9/2 It is seldom that an apprentice does the 'hat trick', but the feat was accomplished by..an apprentice... His three successes were gained on Soldier.., Lady Carlton.., and Hawkweed. **1930** *Morning Post* 16 July 17/2 Wragg's mount..enabled his jockey to complete the so-called 'hat-trick'. **1931** *Statesman* (Calcutta) 5 Dec., British aircraft constructors are hoping that an official attempt will shortly be made on the world's height record, and the 'hat trick' accomplished by the annexation of all three of the records which really matter in aviation. **1958** *Economist* 13 Sept. 819/1 The Tories are excited because it looks as if they may flout all precedents and complete a hat-trick of wins. **1967** J. POTTER *Foul Play* (1968) ix. 100 Apart from a hat trick by our centre forward it wasn't much of a game.

hatty (hæ·ti), *a.* [f. HAT *sb.* + -Y[1].] Wearing showy hats; interested in wearing hats.

1909 H. G. WELLS *Tono-Bungay* III. ii. 294 They all sat about in the summer-house and in garden-chairs, and were very hatty and ruffley and sunshadey. **1959** *Star* 29 Jan. 4/2 'I'm not a hatty person really,' she confessed. 'They always take so long to put on when I'm rushing out shopping.'

hau (hau). *Bot.* Also **hau-tree.** The Hawaiian name for a tropical shrub or tree, *Hibiscus tiliaceus*, belonging to the family Malvaceæ.

1843 J. J. JARVES *Scenes & Scenery Sandwich Islands* iii. 117 Groves of dark-leaved *hau*. **1866** 'MARK TWAIN' *Lett. fr. Hawaii* (1967) 99 Large tracts were covered with large hau (how) bushes, whose sheltering foliage is so thick as to be almost impervious to rain. **1888** W. HILLEBRAND *Flora Hawaiian Islands* 49 A small freely branching tree... Occurs in all tropical countries and is abundant in all Pacific islands. Native name: 'Hau'. **1913** R. BROOKE *Let.* 12 Oct. (1968) 518 I'm sitting under a busy 'Hau-Tree' (pronounced 'How'). **1915** W. A. BRYAN *Nat. Hist. Hawaii* xv. 201 One of the most common, persistent and useful of the native trees.. is the hau. **1935** F. B. H. BROWN *Flora S.E. Polynesia* III. 174 The native name [of *Hibiscus tiliaceus*] is..hau in the northern islands of the Marquesas,..and in Hawaii.

hauchecornite (haukĕkǭ·ɹnəit). *Min.* [ad. G. *hauchecornit* (R. Scheibe 1893, in *Jahrb. d. Preuss. geol. Landesanst. und Bergakademie zu Berlin, 1891* XII. 91), f. the name of Wilhelm *Hauchecorne* (1828–1900), German geologist: see -ITE[1].] A bronze-coloured sulphide of nickel, bismuth, and antimony, $Ni_9(Bi,Sb)_2S_8$.

1893 *Jrnl. Chem. Soc.* LXIV. II. 418 Hauchecornite is of a light, bronze-yellow colour. **1950** *Amer. Mineralogist* XXXV. 440 Study of a specimen..from the original locality, Friedrich mine, Hamm a. d. Sieg, Westphalia, confirms the individuality of hauchecornite. **1968** I. KOSTOV *Mineral.* 117 (*table*) Hauchecornite.

Hau Hau (hau·hau). *N.Z.* Also **Hauhau, Hau-hau, hau hau.** [Maori.] A follower of the Pai-Marire religion during the nineteenth-century Maori Wars. Also *attrib.* Hence **Hau·-hauism.**

1865 *Richmond-Atkinson Papers* II. iii. 171 The excitement among the Hau-hau and other hostile natives was reviving. **1871** C. L. MONEY *Knocking about in N.Z.* x. 137 A large village..said to be a nest of Hau-haus. **1875** *Official Handbk. N.Z.* (ed. 2) 28/2 Many who eagerly adopted Hau-hauism at first, have since given it up. **1884** M. MARTIN *Our Maoris* xi. 169 Early in 1865 came the terrible news from the East Cape, of the Rev. Carl Volkner's murder by the fanatical Hauhaus there. [*Ibid.* 173 He proclaimed a new religion, though indeed it was a mixture of wild applications of Old Testament history with spells and incantations. A pole was set up in the pah, round which the people danced. They drew in their breaths all at once, somewhat in the way paviours used to do. This deep groan at the end of each sentence, 'Hau', gave a name to the fanatical movement which lasts to this day.] **1914** *Chambers's Jrnl.* Mar. 173/2 In religion he follows 'Hau-hauism', a strange intermingling of ideas, based largely on the Old Testament. **1930** J. COWAN in J. Reid *Kiwi Laughs* (1961) 97 They would have had his head to decorate the end of a Hauhau pole had they discovered the particular potato-pit in which he was hiding. **1949** P. BUCK *Coming of Maori* (1950) IV. iii. 474 Possession was practised by the fanatical followers of the late post-European sect known as *hauhau*, when dancing around a pole termed the *niu*. **1959** M. SHADBOLT *New Zealanders* 237 The great-grandfather was eaten in the latter stage of the Maori wars by the *Hau Hau*, that fanatic group which combined Christianity and cannibalism with apparent success.

hau-hau (hǭ,hǭ), *v.* [Echoic.] *intr.* To utter the cry of a hyena.

1924 *Other Lands* Jan. 43/1 A hyena went hau-hauing down the path between the tent and the garden.

haul, *v.* Add: **1. e.** To transport by cart or other conveyance; to cart, carry.

1741 *New Hampshire Probate Rec.* III. 43 Her fire wood from time to time shall be haul'd to Said house. **1787** [in Dict., sense 1 a]. **1814** H. M. BRACKENRIDGE *Views Louisiana* 141 They are sometimes employed in hauling lead from the mines. **1852** *Trans. Mich. Agric. Soc.* III. 179, I haul it [*sc.* manure] out in the fall, spread it and plow it in immediately after. **1880** *Harper's Mag.* Sept. 619/2 In winter I haul logs, and in summer I haul mealers. **1887** *Congress Rec.* 10 Jan. 484/1 There is not one-tenth part of the risk in hauling dressed beef that there is in hauling live animals. **1918** F. HACKETT *Ireland* ii. 46 The more fish was caught..the less any one of them was worth. And when it came to salting them or hauling them, the same curse was in it. **1970** *Washington Post* 30 Sept. B13/4 The company sought a million-dollar contract with Ft. Rucker, Ala., to haul gasoline.

absol. **1871** R. L. DASHWOOD *Chiploquorgan* viii. 117 We had fifteen miles to haul along a lumber road to the mouth of Rocky brook. **1883** J. HAY *Bread-winners* vi. 96 You know Clinsty Fore, that hauls for the Safe Company? **1933** E. MERRICK *True North* 338 We hauled across lots of yellow, slushy places.

f. *intr.* With *out, up.* Of bachelor seals: to come out of the water to rest on the hauling-grounds.

1869 *Overland Monthly* III. 39 To ascertain if any elephant-seal had 'hauled up' on the beach. **1894** KIPLING *Jungle Bk.* 98 I've often thought we should be much happier if we hauled out at Otter Island. **1902** *Encycl. Brit.* XXXII. 488/1 The young males, or bachelors, haul out to rest and sleep on beaches adjacent to, but distinct from, the breeding-grounds. **1967** *Listener* 6 Apr. 459/1 Adult male seals hold territories on beaches where a population hauls out for breeding.

3. c. *to haul off* (chiefly *U.S.*), to withdraw or draw back a little before completing an action of any kind; *to haul out* (*U.S.*), to go out, depart.

1866 W. H. JACKSON *Diary* 30 July in *Nebr. Hist. Mag.* (1932) XIII. 156 Hauled out before sunrise and corralled at the Springs by 9 o'clock. **1870** 'MARK TWAIN' in *Galaxy* Oct. 572/2 Suppose he should take deliberate aim and 'haul off' and fetch me with the butt-end of it [*sc.* a gun]? **1902** A. D. MCFAUL *Ike Glidden* xxv. 282 The train hauled out while the officer was taking him into custody. **1930** D. RUNYON in *Collier's* 20 Dec. 32/3 Then Lily hauls off and gives me a big kiss right in the smush. **1961** M. MCLUHAN *Mech. Bride* 60/2 Looks like he's going to haul off and kiss her. **1960** WODEHOUSE *Jeeves in Offing* vi. 63, I shall have no alternative but to haul off and bop *him* one. *Ibid.* vii. 71 A cow that looked as if it were planning, next time it was milked, to haul off and let the milkmaid have it in the lower ribs.

haul, *sb.* Add: **1. c.** *spec.* The distance over which something is hauled, freq. in phr. *long* (or *short*) *haul.* Also *fig.*

1877 W. ROCKEFELLER *Let.* 17 Oct. in *Philadelphia Inquirer* (1879) 8 Mar. 2/c We will endeavor to deliver the oil to you at points from which you will have short hauls. **1884** *Congress. Rec.* 18 June 5314/2 The farmer has to pay for short hauls just about what they ask him [etc.]... We must study the effect..of short hauls and long hauls. **1905** *Terms Forestry & Logging* 39 *Haul*, in logging, the distance and route over which teams must go between two given points, as between the yard or skid way and the landing. **1909** H. N. CASSON *Life C. H. McCormick* 213 Today it is not the long haul of wheat, but the short haul, that is more expensive. **1936** L. C. DOUGLAS *White Banners* vi. 123 Florid, peaches-and-cream blondes weren't intended for long hauls of worry. **1957** *Sunday Times* 13 Oct. 5/6 A new building for long-haul traffic is recommended. **1962** *Listener* 15 Feb. 307/1 Both points of view are necessary at different times, but the C.R.O. one is designed for the long haul. **1968** *Times* 1 Nov. 10/3 Improvements would be certainly possible; but he gave a warning: 'This is a long haul. You cannot suddenly change the existing systems.' **1973** *Daily Tel.* 15 Jan. 19/1 Everyone knows that you don't just buy investment trusts for the short haul.

haulabout (hǭ·lăbaut). *U.S.* [f. the verbal phrase *to haul about* (HAUL *v.* 1).] A vessel, resembling a barge, used for coaling ships.

1903 *Trans. Inst. Naval Archit.* XLV. 221 These vessels, ..like the smaller barges, or 'coal haulabouts' as they are termed, have no means of propelling themselves.

haulage. Add: **4.** *haulage-engine.*

1909 *Daily Chron.* 16 Sept. 1/3 A haulage engine..was taking a load of bricks up the steep gradient. *Ibid.* 30 Sept. 1/5 The flood carried away the haulage engine at the entrance of the level.

haulier. Add: **2.** A firm or a person engaged in road transport.

1919 *Commercial Motor* 1 May 199/1 We do not find a motor haulier keeping his vehicles in the garage because his repair department informs him that this is the best way of reducing the cost of maintenance. **1951** *Oxf. Jun. Encycl.* IV. 277/1 Hauliers often have to transfer loads from one vehicle to another at the state border. **1959** *Times Rev. Industry* May 44/3 Hauliers are afraid to work out costs properly. **1967** *Listener* 20 Apr. 539/3 Interviews with drivers and hauliers.

hauling. Add: **b. hauling-ground,** a place where bachelor seals congregate, distinguished from the rookery or ground occupied by breeding seals.

1898 D. S. JORDAN *Fur Seals* I. 36 Adjoining the breeding grounds and an essential part of each rookery are what are known as the 'hauling grounds' of the bachelors, frequented by the young males of the ages of 5 years and under. **1960** *Canad. Audubon* Jan.–Feb. 2/2 Localities

where sea lions come ashore for purposes other than breeding or pupping are called 'hauling grounds'.

haunch, *sb.*[1] Add: **3. b.** The side of a made-up road.

1937 [see *HAUNCHING 2].

4. c. The end of a tenon reduced in width. So **haunched** *a.*, (of a tenon) having its end reduced in width; **haunching,** a recess in a style for the end of a tenon.

1885 *Spons' Mech. Own Bk.* 276 The haunched tenon [is used] when the edge of the piece on which the tenon is formed is required to be flush with the end of the piece containing the mortice. **1904** A. C. PASSMORE *Handbk. Techn. Terms, Haunch,* the wide part left close to the root when part of a tenon is cut away. **1904** GOODCHILD & TWENEY *Technol. & Sci. Dict.* 282/1 *Haunched tenon,* a tenon cut back in its width to allow for wedging. **1964** W. L. GOODMAN *Hist. Woodworking Tools* 53 The joints themselves are stub tenons, haunched and pinned in a very modern manner.

haunching. Add: **2.** (See quot.)

1937 *Times* 13 Apr. p. viii/2 In such cases (of excessive camber) the process known as 'haunching' should be carried out. The haunches or sides of the road are made up with stone,..and the whole road is then dressed with a new surface dressing.

haunk-haunk (hǭŋk,hǭŋk). [Echoic.] The cry of a hyena. Cf. *HAU-HAU *v.*

1895 B. M. CROKER *Village Tales* (1896) 208 Another sound that made his heart beat very fast—the 'haunk-haunk' of a hyena.

haunt, *sb.* Add: **5.** (Earlier and later examples.) Also (occas.) in wider use. Cf. *HANT, HA'NT.

1843 WINNEMORE & REPS *Cudjo's Wild Hunt* (song) 3 It am de hunt ob Cudjo dat nigger so bold. **1896** MRS. STOWE *Oldtown Folks* vi. 80 But this 'ere's a regular haunt,..they both on 'em said..they'd seen a figger of a man. **1902** *Westm. Gaz.* 5 Feb. 2/1 This is the 'haunt' that troubles all our minds, and, especially, that comes forth..when the question is of peace by arrangement. **1952** W. R. TITTERTON in *Columba* Aug. 102/1 We had a haunt in our flat. Father Vincent came home with us that day, and blessed the place, and the haunt was no more.

haunted, *ppl. a.* Add: **3. b.** In wider use.

1906 *Daily Chron.* 23 Feb. 3/4 The beauty-haunted eyes of such painters as Gainsborough, Romney, Botticelli. **1906** RIDER HAGGARD *Benita* vii, Staring at the white Benita and at her haunted eyes. **1908** *Westm. Gaz.* 17 Aug. 3/1 He paces the garden in this haunting, haunted fashion. **1910** A. C. BENSON *Silent Isle* xv, You become aware that some exquisite haunted quality has slipped away from the later work.

c. *Comb.*, as *haunted-looking* adj.

1883 LD. R. GOWER *My Remin.* II. 26 A low, long, damp, haunted-looking gallery. **1918** MRS. BELLOC LOWNDES *Out of the War?* xx. 257 Haunted-looking eyes.

Hausa (hau·să). Also **Haussa, Hous(s)a.** [Native name.] A widespread Negroid people of the Sudan and N. Nigeria, of the Bantu family with some Hamitic mixture; also, the language of this people, used, esp. in commerce, over much of W. Africa. Also *attrib.* or as *adj.*

1820 J. G. JACKSON (*title*) Account of Timbuctoo and Housa. **1853** E. NORRIS (*title*) Dialogues and a small portion of the New Testament, in the English, Arabic, Haussa, and Bornu languages. **1879** *Encycl. Brit.* X. 59/1 An armed police force, recruited..from the Mahometan tribe of the Houssas. **1923** F. W. TAYLOR *Pract. Hausa Gram.* i. 9 Hausa occupies a position midway between the tone languages, such as Yoruba, and the stress languages, such as English. **1926** *Blackw. Mag.* Nov. 666/1 The troops were Hausas—I don't think we had begun to call them 'Waffs' then. **1957** M. BANTON *W. Afr. City* viii. 158 Some blind Hausa beggars come from Nigeria to Freetown to sing in the streets. **1959** R. C. ABRAHAM *Lang. Hausa People* i. 3 In Hausa..each word has its fixed tone, no matter what the emotional context. **1962** *Listener* 22 Feb. 335/1 A Hausaman, clad in a scarlet tarbush and flowing white robes. **1967** *Listener* 24 Aug. 230/1 There have been several uprisings already among Hausas and Yorubas trying to take revenge on Ibos. **1971** *E. Afr. Jrnl.* Mar. 8/1, I haven't worked and slaved..to have you give me a Hausa grandson.

‖ **hausfrau** (hau·sfrau). Also **house-frau.** [G.] A housewife. Also **hausvrow, huisvrouw** [after Du. *huisvrouw*].

1798 LADY A. BARNARD *S. Afr. Cent. Ago* (1901) 157 This, as a careful haus-vrow, devolved on me. **1843** E. HALL *Diary* in O. A. Sherrard *Two Victorian Girls* (1966) ix. 92 [On my way] to do the haus-frau, dear Mr. Shore met me. **1848** *Wesleyan-Meth. Mag.* Aug. 886 You find the *huis-vrouw*, or 'mistress', seated at a small table. **1866** C. M. YONGE *Dove in Eagle's Nest* i. 29 Hausfrau Johanna adjured her father..to be a true guardian and protector to the child. **1873** —— *Pillars of House* II. xiii. 40 A simple painstaking businesslike man, who had married a German hausfrau. **1918** R. WILSON *Martin Schüler* xi. 120 My sister Bertha was charming: now she is a house-frau. **1925** 'E. BARRINGTON' *Divine Lady* II. xv. 213 Her Majesty Queen Charlotte, the prim German hausfrau. **1930** *Observer* 20 Apr. 8/4 The big German newspapers, cognisant of the power of the hausfrau. **1962** *Punch* 9 May 706/2 Women in West Germany appear to have taken a tremendous leap forward from *hausfrau* to high executive positions.

‖ **hausmaler** (hau·smāləɹ). [G., = house-painter.] One who paints undecorated china in his own house or private workshop. Hence **hau·smalerei** (-əi), the painting and decorating of such china.

1935 *Burlington Mag.* June 271/1 The painting on this jug bears the signature of the well-known *Hausmaler* Abraham Helmhack. *Ibid.*, Johann Schaper, the first great master of *Hausmalerei* on faience. **1938** *Ibid.* Dec. p. xviii/2 Some interesting *Hausmalerei* from the same region. **1959** G. SAVAGE *Antique Coll. Handbk.* 68 The work of outside decorators (or *Hausmaler*), who bought white porcelain and decorated it in their homes. **1959** *Times* 6 Jan. 16/7 A Meissen hausmaler bowl. **1971** *Times* 30 Nov. 24/3 (Advt.), An important German faience Hausmaler tankard.

haustellation (hǭstĕlēi·ʃən). [f. HAUSTELLATE *a*: see -TION.] The action of sucking.

1901 *Practitioner* Mar. 278 If a mosquito be killed on the second day after haustellation.

haustrum (hǭ·strǒm). *Anat.* Pl. **haustra.** [mod. use of L. *haustrum* bucket, scoop, f. *haurīre, haust-* to draw (water).] Each of the small sacs enclosed by folds in the colon. Hence **hau·stral** *a.*

[**1826** J. LIZARS *Syst. Anat. Plates.* Descriptions of Plates. xi. 30 These bands purse the colon into these peculiar pouches or cells ([*Footnote*] Syn. Cellulæ seu haustra) so characteristic of this intestine.] **1889** A. MACALISTER *Text-bk. Human Anat.* § 257. 405 Its [the colon's] cavity is to some extent sacculated, the haustra, or pouches being separated by crescentic plicæ sigmoideæ. **1913** DORLAND *Med. Dict.* (ed. 7), *Haustral,* pertaining to the haustra of the colon. **1936** *Med. Rec.* 1 Jan. 28/1 The loss of haustral markings with and without dilatation, was found much less frequently. **1959** R. D. LOCKHART et al. *Anat. Human Body* 522 Compared with the smooth small intestine, the large is sacculated along its length, the sacculations or haustra bulging between three equidistant longitudinal bands.

Haut-Brion (obrī·oṅ). Also 7 **Hobriant, Ho Bryan,** 9 **Obryan.** [Fr., f. the name of an estate, Château *Haut-Brion,* in the commune of Pessac, near Bordeaux.] In full *Château Haut-Brion.* A variety of fine quality claret.

1663 PEPYS *Diary* 10 Apr. (1893) III. 89 Here drank a sort of French wine, called Ho Bryan, that hath a good and most particular taste that I never met with. **1670** W. HUGHES *Compl. Vineyard* (ed. 2) 65 A sort of Claret called Hobriant-wine, of a deep red colour. *a* **1700** [see VIGNOBLE]. **1792** T. JEFFERSON *Let.* in A. Lichine *Encycl. Wines* (1967) 4/2 Bordeaux red wines. There are four crops of them more famous than the rest. These are Chateau-Margau, Tour de Segur, Hautbrion & De La Fitte. **1833** C. REDDING *Hist. Mod. Wines* 145 The first growth of this noted commune [*i.e.* Pessac] is Château Haut Brion. **1845** *Encycl. Metrop.* XXV. 1287/2 The following are the principal wines, or those most celebrated in the different countries where the vine has long been cultivated:—France... Bordeaux. Lafitte, red... Haut Brion, ditto. **1851** C. REDDING *Hist. Mod. Wines* (ed. 3) 174 In 1710, a wine called Obryan claret was sold in London at three shillings the bottle. **1888** *Encycl. Brit.* XXIV. 605/1 Château Haut-Brion, Pessac. **1935** *Punch* 28 Aug. 238/2 The Old Yquem which was not too sweet, And the Old Haut Brion so round and neat. **1959** W. JAMES *Word-Bk. Wine* 93 Haut Brion for some odd reason has always been regarded by Englishmen with a peculiar tenderness.

‖ **haute Bohème** (ot bo͞ɛm). [Formed by M. Baring after *HAUTE BOURGEOISIE.] A name applied to members of any fast or high-class Bohemian set.

1925 M. BARING *Cat's Cradle* I. xvii. 216 You see quite different people..people like the Svensens and all those musicians and archaeologists... *La Haute Bohème*... You never went near them before. **1939** O. LANCASTER *Homes Sweet Homes* 46 The cult of æstheticism..was only accepted whole-heartedly by..the *haute Bohème* of the day. **1954** *Design & Industries Assoc. Yearbk.* 37 The intelligentsia is..becoming, in Maurice Baring's phrase, an Haute Boheme. **1964** M. LASKI in S. Nowell-Smith *Edwardian England* iv. 196 A fast Bohemian set, what Maurice Baring had called the *haute Bohème.*

‖ **haute bourgeoisie** (ot burʒwazī). [Fr.] The French upper middle class; also extended to the upper middle class of other countries. Cf. BOURGEOISIE in Dict. and Suppl.

1888 *Athenæum* 4 Aug. 153/2 The haute bourgeoisie and the humble shopkeeper, citizens by nature and condition, have interests as indivisible. **1901** G. B. SHAW *Sixteen Self-Sketches* (1949) ix. 51 On the down grade from the zenith of *haute bourgeoisie* and landed gentry. **1924** A. D. SEDGWICK *Little French Girl* I. ii. 12 Alix was to tell her whether they were *petite noblesse* or *haute bourgeoisie.* **1934** A. HUXLEY *Beyond Mexique Bay* 7 A collection of the elderly *haute bourgeoisie.* **1940** F. SCOTT FITZGERALD *Let.* 14 Aug. (1964) 420 My father and Aunt Elise struggling to keep their children in the *haute bourgeoisie.* **1962** *Listener* 22 Feb. 350/1 A rich residential district for the prosperous Glasgow *haute bourgeoisie.* **1969** *N.Y. Rev. Books* 16 Jan. 34/3 The Business Council —which is about as close to an executive committee of the American *haute bourgeoisie* as one can get.

‖ **haute boutique** (ot būtīk). [Fr., f. *haute* (fem.) high + *BOUTIQUE.] (See quot. 1969.)

1966 *Guardian* 25 July 6/2 Simonetta is said to be presenting a much bigger haute boutique collection this season. **1969** *Ibid.* 14 Jan. 7/6 The class that the French call *haute boutique*—midway between couture and ready-to-wear.

haute couture: see *COUTURE.

‖ **haute cuisine** (ot kwizīn). [Fr., f. *haute* (fem.) high + CUISINE.] High-class (French) cooking.

1926 *Time* 5 July 12 In France, perhaps in France alone, the traditions of *la haute cuisine* survive from the days of the great gastronomes. **1928** S. BROWNE tr. *T. H. Varo de Velde's Ideal Marriage* xv. 277 The most effective dish in the *haute cuisine* is supposed to be crayfish soup. **1930** A. BENNETT *Imperial Palace* xxxvi. 246 *La Haute cuisine.* Not fifty people in the world were equipped by education and natural taste to comprehend it. **1935** *Time* 11 Mar. 22/1 If only English landladies spoke French, and if only their English cooks knew something of *haute cuisine,* Frenchmen with gold francs would be tempted across the Channel. **1951** E. DAVID *French Country Cooking* 172 Their use in what was regarded as *Haute Cuisine* became ridiculously excessive, and no dish was considered really refined without a garnish of sliced truffle. **1959** *Listener* 30 Apr. 776/3 The miracles of *haute cuisine* often arrive from a kitchen where the scales are faulty! **1962** AUDEN *Dyer's Hand* 75 It is difficult to imagine a *haute cuisine* based on algae and chemically treated grass. **1966** *Observer* 25 Sept. 46/2 An egg-based haute cuisine dinner for 6.

‖ **haute école** (ot ekol). [Fr., = high school. Cf. SCHOOL *sb.*[1] 3 d.] The more difficult feats of horsemanship. Also *attrib.* and *transf.* (esp. in *Mus.*).

1858 *Rarey's Art of Taming Horses* i. 5 The accomplished Colonel Greenwood, who was equally learned in the *manége* of the *Haute Ecole,* and skilled in the style of the English hunting-fields. **1864** G. A. SALA *Quite Alone* I. xi. 191 She was doing the haute école. **1889** G. B. SHAW *London Mus. 1888–89* (1937) 215 The haute-école acts of the prima donna and tenor. **1896** *Strand Mag.* Mar. 334/2 Five other 'artistes'—trapezists, *haute école,* and 'bare-back' ladies. **1931** *Times Lit. Suppl.* 26 Mar. 247/3 The excellent *haute-école* rider seen at the Kingsway Opera House. **1953** G. BROOKE *Introd. Riding* vii. 69 Genuine 'Haute École', as maintained and demonstrated today. **1955** *Times* 15 Aug. 5/5 An energetic circus performer of the haute école. **1959** *Listener* 30 Apr. 776/2 Balakirev's *Islamey* is written in close imitation of Liszt's *haute école.* **1959** [see *gun-dog* (*GUN *sb.* 15)]. **1960** *Times* 4 June 9/3 It is even more gratifying to hear the superbly groomed *haute école* pianism on the disc.

hautefeuillite (otfö·yəit). *Min.* [a. F. *hautefeuillite* (L. Michel 1893, in *Bull. de la Soc. française de Min.* XVI. 40), f. the name of P. G. *Hautefeuille* (1836–1902), French chemist.] A hydrous phosphate of magnesium and calcium that occurs in colourless crystals; possibly the same as bobierrite, the calcium being due to contamination with apatite.

1896 *Jrnl. Chem. Soc.* LXX. II. 112 (*heading*) Hautefeuillite, a new mineral from Bamle, Norway. **1937** *Amer. Mineralogist* XXII. 337 Michel..introduces the name *hautefeuillite* for a bobierrite-like mineral which, according to his analysis, differs from bobierrite..in its optical orientation. However, the redetermined optical properties of bobierrite correspond to those of hautefeuillite as given by Michel. *Ibid.* 338 Until more evidence is produced ..it seems best to discard hautefeuillite as a mineral name. **1955** M. H. HEY *Index Min. Species* (ed. 2) 232 *Hautefeuillite.* (Mg, Ca)$_3$PO$_4$.8H$_2$O... Has been interpreted as a mixture of Bobierrite..and Apatite..but the H$_2$O is very high for this interpretation, and further study is desirable.

‖ **haute noblesse** (ot nobles). [Fr., f. *haute* (fem.) high + NOBLESSE.] The upper stratum of the aristocracy.

1787 W. BECKFORD *Let.* 8 Nov. in *Italy* (1834) II. xxx. 146 The famous tenor singer, who entertained us..with many private anecdotes of the *haute noblesse.* **1907** M. E. BRADDON *Dead Love has Chains* ii. 23 She had friends among the *haute noblesse*..in the old St. Germain faubourg. **1934** A. WOOLLCOTT *While Rome Burns* 220 The panic among the English *haute noblesse* during the Oscar Wilde trial.

‖ **haute vulgarisation** (ot vŭlgarizasyoṅ; also freq. with (quasi-)anglicized pronunc. of second word). [Fr., f. *haute* (fem.) high + VULGARIZATION.] The popularization of abstruse or complex matters.

[**1943** *Mind* LII. 178 Mr. Skemp would refer us..to the *Timaeus* of which he regards the utterances of *Laws X* as only a 'popularised' version, in the nature of what the French call an *œuvre de haute vulgarisation.*] **1946** *Christian Sci. Monitor* 21 Dec. (Mag. Sect.) 10 Mr. Van Doren has written a work of '*haute vulgarization*'. **1958** *Times* 6 Dec. 7/7 This can only be achieved if some of the scholars themselves transform their knowledge into the *haute vulgarisation* of which Cicero himself, far more even than H. G. Wells, was the master. **1960** *Cambr. Rev.* 16 Jan. 232/3 Is the *haute-vulgarization* of archaeology, which we see happening.., a good thing? **1966** *Listener* 13 Oct. 544/2 Mrs. Thomson's edition is a model of *haute vulgarisation.* It is based on her father's..standard edition..but modernized and abridged. **1968** *Times* 9 Nov. 23/6 This book is an extraordinary mixture of

lucid demonstration, mathematical wizardry and ebullient high spirits, which the two American authors define as 'haute vulgarisation'.

|| **haut monde** (*o* mõñd). [Fr., lit. high world.] The fashionable world: cf. BEAU-MONDE.

1864 MRS. BEETON *Jrnl.* in N. Spain *Mrs. Beeton & her Husband* (1948) II. vi. 215 Her dress would have been the envy of many of our *haute monde* [sic]. **1894** M. BEERBOHM in *Yellow Bk.* III. 253 A certain lack of tone had crept into the amusements of the *haut monde*. **1930** *Aberdeen Press & Jrnl.* 22 Apr. 4 The Aberdeen Lido scene which depicts *haut monde* life..at the glorified Aberdeen beach of the future. **1931** *Times Lit. Suppl.* 28 May 429/1 Several ladies of the *haut monde*. **1935** *Punch* 30 Jan. 114/2 And top-hats at breakfast? Are these the manners of the *haut monde*? **1969** C. IRVING *Fake!* (1970) iii. 32 All of the *haut monde* of New York was there...You couldn't move, it was so packed.

Havana. Add: **a.** *Havana cigar* (earlier and later examples).

1802 *Deb. Congress U.S.* 31 Mar. 229 The greater part of what we have imported came..in the shape of Havana cigars. **1972** 'A. YORK' *Expurgator* iv. 69 They lunched..on ham..on real coffee and Havana cigars.

c. ellipt. for *Havana-brown*.

1873 *Young Englishwoman* July 338/1 Two shades of brown—Havana and maroon. **1922** *Daily Mail* 12 Dec. 7 In delightful shades of Saxe, Heliotrope, Dove Grey, or Havana. **1967** N. FREELING *Strike Out* 27 A large complicated overcheck of fuchsia, havana and off-white.

d. Havana rabbit, a variety of domesticated rabbit distinguished by its dark brown fur, bred near Utrecht about 1898, and kept for both fur and meat. Also *ellipt*.

1912 G. A. TOWNSEND *Pract. Rabbit Keeping* xx. 273 The Havana rabbit..was first introduced..into England in 1910...The originals, born in Holland, were obtained accidentally. **1953** W. K. WILSON *Mod. Rabbit Husb.* i. 14 Other fur breeds were imported, e.g. Champagnes and Havanas.

Havdal(l)ah, varr. *HABDALAH.

have, *v.* Add: **7. d.** *to have to be*: must be. *colloq.* Cf. *GET *v.* 24, *JOKE *v.* 1 b.

1967 *Weekend Mag.* 2 Dec. 2/1 That had to be the most bizarre Grey Cup game ever. **1969** V. CANNING *Queen's Pawn* ii. 8 The car had a Kent number plate MKE 800F. The woman had to be a stranger. **1971** 'A. GILBERT' *Tenant for Tomb* viii. 146 'Even your famous Mr Crook can't disprove evidence,' Ponting pointed out. 'You have to be joking,' said Gray. **1972** *Student Movement* 7 Dec. 13/2 My heart goes out to the performers who watched ⅓ to ½ of their audience leave during what had to be the most tragic selection for a Christmas program I have ever heard.

8. *to have it in one*: to have the ability (to do something). Cf. IN *prep.* 25.

c **1600** [see IN *prep.* 25]. **1887** A. CONAN DOYLE *Study in Scarlet* (1893) I. ii. 32, I know well that I have it in me to make my name famous. **1889** [see IN *prep.* 25].

13. a. (Later examples.)

1955 *Times* 18 June 6/1 One report had it that Rosario ..was still in rebel hands. **1967** *Listener* 13 Apr. 485/1 The party, as the classic socialist phrase has it, is the means of activating the masses.

c. To represent as doing something. *U.S. colloq.*

1928 *Amer. Speech* June 379 William De Morgan, in *Alice for Short*, has the 'toffs' say *daw* and *flaw* for 'door' and 'floor'.

14. a. *to be had* (*of*): to be obtained (from).

1429 *Will of Gerard de Braybroke* in *Trans. Essex Archæol. Soc.* (1873) V. 298 And xij poure men clothed in Russet fryse yif hit may be had or ellis in other. **1582** [in Dict.]. **1663** PEPYS *Diary* 12 Apr. (1971) IV. 101 Creede and I took a turn at White-hall; but no coach to be had and so I returned to them. **1736** *Gentl. Mag.* VI. *title-p.*, Sold by the Booksellers..; of whom may be had compleat setts, or any single Number. **1765** H. GLASSE *Art of Cookery* (ed. 9) Index, Advt., Thomson's Works... N.B. *The Seasons* may be had alone. **1803** *Watering & Sea-Bathing Places* Term. Advt., And which may be had of the Booksellers. **1861** [in Dict.]. **1930** *Times Lit. Suppl.* 19 June 513/3 (Advt.), All these books may be had of any bookseller. **1946** *New Statesman* 1 June 402/2 A thousand customers have I told this day there is never a fowl to be had.

e. To have sexual intercourse with, to possess sexually. Also in *colloq.* phrases *to have it away, off* (*with*), *to have* (a person) *away, off*.

1594 SHAKES. *Richard III* I. ii. 230 Was ever woman in this humour woo'd? Was ever woman in this humour won? I'll have her;—but I will not keep her long. **1596** —— *1 Henry IV* III. iii. 133 Why, she's neither fish nor flesh; a man knows not where to have her. **1743** FIELDING *J. Wild* III. IV. vii. 336 'None of your Coquet Airs, therefore, with me, Madam,' said he, 'for I am resolved to have you this Night.' **1762** BOSWELL *London Jrnl.* 28 Nov. (1950) 54 In the midst of divine service I was laying plans for having women. **1820** KEATS *Let.* 1 Nov. (1931) II. 568, I should have had her when I was in health, and I should have remained well. **1894** H. JAMES *Notebks.* (1947) 170 The idea of the physical possession, the brief physical, passionate rapture..the incongruity, the nastiness, *en somme* of the man's 'having' a sick girl. **1937** in Partridge *Dict. Slang Suppl.* (ed. 6, 1967) 1169 *Have it off*..'is also used..by a man that has contrived to seduce a girl'. **1952** S. J. KAUFFMANN *Philanderer* (1953) xi. 182 It's the first time I ever had a girl from Kentucky. **1962** *Times* 23 Oct. 15/2 My wife went to France and had it off with everyone in sight. **1965** G. MELLY *Owning-Up* iv. 29, I derived iconoclastic pleasure from having it off in the public parks where fifteen years before my brother and I..accompanied our nurse on sunny afternoons. **1967** S. BECKETT *Eh Joe* 19 You've had her, haven't you?.. You've laid her? **1967** A. WILSON *No Laughing Matter* III. 304 Having it off may make you feel very good but a diamond bracelet lasts for ever. **1968** A. DIMENT *Gt. Spy Race* ii. 28 In future please check with the duty officer if I am free. For all you knew I might be having my secretary off on the desk. *Ibid.* viii. 141 It had crossed my mind I was going to be asked to have the old fart away. **1970** G. GREER *Female Eunuch* 265 The vocabulary of impersonal sex is peculiarly desolating. Who wants to.. 'have it away'? **1970** *Private Eye* 13 Mar. 16 He's had more sheilahs than you've had spaghetti breakfasts. **1972** R. PERRY *Fall Guy* iii. 52 No one would dream of having it away with his mistress.

f. *to have it in for*: to have something unpleasant in store for; to have a grudge against or dislike for (app. modelled on *to be in for*: see IN *adv.* 8).

1849 'A. HARRIS' *Emigrant Family* II. vi. 122 In consequence of a former disagreement, the speaker already '*had it in for him*' whenever a drinking bout should afford opportunity for the said 'it' becoming a transferable possession. **1888** 'R. BOLDREWOOD' *Robbery under Arms* II. xviii. 283 He 'had it in' for more than one of the people who helped the police. **1927** *Daily Mirror* 10 Dec. 2/1 If it was not for the prejudice of a certain detective-sergeant who has had it in for me since I left the police force, I should be found not guilty. **1927** WODEHOUSE *Meet Mr. Mulliner* iii. 92, I have had it in for that dog since the second Sunday before Septuagesima. **1934** A. CHRISTIE *Murder on Orient Express* II. ix. 136 A few people had it in for Cassetti all right. **1942** A. L. ROWSE *Cornish Childhood* 112 He was very unpopular with the big boys..and they had it in for him. **1961** D. G. JAMES *M. Arnold* iii. 71 He has it in for the Romantic writers, certainly. **1967** *Punch* 9 Aug. 194/2 If and when the law catches up with them, I hope it has it in for them.

g. *to have it*: to have a solution.

1856 C. M. YONGE *Daisy Chain* I. xxvi. 275 'V.V.,' continued Meta, 'what can that mean?' 'Five, five, of course,' said Flora. 'No, no! I have it, *Venus Victrix*,' said Ethel. **1897** A. TWEEDIE *Through Finland* xviii. 307 'I have it,' said the student, after a long pause, during which we had all sought an excuse to enable us to depart without hurting the farmer's feelings. 'I will tell them.'

h. *to have it on* or *over* (a person): to have the advantage of, to be superior to; to have 'the pull' of or over. *to have nothing on*, (*a*) to have no advantage of or superiority over; conversely *to have something on* (occas. *over*), to have an advantage over (a person); (*b*) to know nothing discreditable or incriminating about (a person), whence conversely *to have something on* (a person). Cf. *GET *v.* 5 b.

[**1906** H. GREEN *At Actors' Boarding House* 27 I'll show 'em the Waldoff ain't got nothin' on Maggie de Shine.] **1910** S. E. WHITE *Rules of Game* v. xxiv, They think they have it on us straight enough. **1912** C. MATHEWSON *Pitching in a Pinch* 7 'Hans' Wagner of Pittsburg, has always been a hard man for me, but in that I have had nothing on a lot of other pitchers. **1917** S. MERWIN *Temperamental Henry* 31 He had it all over the banjo-strumming Thomas P. of the unpleasantly rasping voice. **1919** F. HURST *Humoresque* 298 Baby Ella herself had nothin' on you. **1922** H. TITUS *Timber* vii. 65 You know he has it on you. There is no use trying to fight the law. **1924** A. CHRISTIE *Man in Brown Suit* 6 Every one of us incriminated..and not one of us has anything on him. **1928** *Daily Express* 19 June 12 Kerensky, who tried to do what Napoleon said no man could do: run a revolution and a war simultaneously. Kerensky thought Napoleon had nothing on him. **1928** *Observer* 22 July 28/3, I have carefully analysed the pre-Olympic performances of Liddell, who won in 1924, and J. W. J. Rinkel, who we hope is going to win this year. Liddell had nothing on Rinkel in preliminaries. **1928** *Daily Express* 27 Aug. 15/3 America's heavy-weight champion of the world has nothing on Great Britain's Prime Minister. **1929** 'G. DAVIOT' *Man in Queue* iii. 30 If he thinks he has anything on me..he has another guess coming. **1930** *Publisher's Weekly* 5 July 27 Deciding that the antique hussies of history in spite of their hot reputations have nothing on her. **1936** T. S. ELIOT *Essays Anc. & Mod.* 68 Huysmans' fee-fi-fo-fum *décor* of mediævalism has nothing on Mr. Symons's 'veiled altar'. **1938** E. BOWEN *Death of Heart* I. v. 94 While you had it on me, it made it more difficult. **1941** *Punch* 9 Apr. 341/1 It has never been finally worked out which system is the more disappointing, but it is generally admitted that each has something over the other. **1947** *Penguin New Writing* XXXI. 67 He..took out his best clothes. Going to the barracks, he had to look smart, he had to show the soldiers they had nothing on him. **1960** K. HOPKINS *Dead against my Principles* xix. 129 'She is the daughter of a criminal.' ..'Yes. But we have nothing on her.' **1962** J. BRAINE *Life at Top* x. 122, I wasn't Mark, I never could be Mark; but there at least I had it over him. **1963** M. MCCARTHY *Group* iii. 63 The *Tribune*'s typography has it all over the *Times*'s. **1967** *Listener* 28 Dec. 857/1 For a picture of sheer bloodcurdling hatred and human degradation, our playwrights have nothing on this 60-year-old music-drama inspired by Sophocles' play.

i. *to have it off*: to rob or burgle. *Criminals' slang.*

1931 A. R. L. GARDNER *Art of Crime* 233 Bill has had it off last night. **1936** J. CURTIS *Gilt Kid* ii. 20 'I had it off last week,' he said with a wink, 'not a big job, just a little snout gaff, but I earned myself a score.' **1939** J. PHELAN *In Can* ii. 14 'Denny 's 'ad it orf again,' commented one of the patrons.

j. *to have oneself* (something): to provide (something) for oneself, to indulge oneself with (something). *colloq.* (orig. and chiefly *U.S.*).

1929 E. WILSON *I thought of Daisy* iii. 155 Ray seems to be having himself a time with Rita Cavanagh! **1936** R. CHANDLER *Killer in Rain* (1964) iv. 49 I'm going to have me a short nap now. **1939** C. MORLEY *Kitty Foyle* 263, I went and had myself a small brandy. **1940** O. LA FARGE in *55 Short Stories fr. New Yorker* (1952) 265 He had himself two good highballs. **1957** J. OSBORNE *Entertainer* 44 We're going to have ourselves a hero, you can see that. **1966** *New Yorker* 6 Aug. 71 (Advt.), Come to Portugal and have yourself a good cry.

k. *to have had it*: to have no chance whatever of having or doing something; to have had one's (adverse) fate finally decided, to be defeated; to be dead, to have been killed; to be ruined, broken down, useless; to have had enough. *colloq.*

1941 *New Statesman* 30 Aug. 218/3 *To have had it*, to miss something pleasant, e.g. leave. **1943** *Time* 22 Mar. 51 'You've had it,' in R.A.F. vernacular, means 'You haven't got it and you won't get it.' **1946** S. GIBBONS *Westwood* vi. 78 *That* could not be got over..as Hilda's boys would say, 'You've had it', and there was nothing she could do. **1951** L. P. HARTLEY *My Fellow Devils* 277 That was the ghastly moment, coming back fo find you gone. Then I did feel I'd had it. **1952** N. COWARD *Relative Values* II. vi. 64 Of course they're still alive, but I never see a telegram come into the house without saying.. 'Sarah 's had it!' **1954** J. B. PRIESTLEY *Magicians* ix. 175 Two more 'ave 'ad it, mate... Two-seater goes off the road an' straight over the bloody edge to Kingdom Come. **1954** D. UNWIN *Governor's Wife* 34 Conversation with an educated African is like walking a tightrope. One slip and you've had it. **1956** 'M. INNES' *Appleby plays Chicken* I. iv. 39 The heart wasn't beating... Whoever he was, the chap had had it. **1956** 'J. WYNDHAM' *Seeds of Time* 163, I was thinking: 'Well, that's that. I've had it', and deciding that I was now in..heaven. **1957** *Listener* 13 June 945/2 Here are the men who matter—the highly paid white artisan has had it, but he'll put up a big rearguard action. **1958** P. SCOTT *Mark of Warrior* 41 He was so weary he just let the men bunch up. They'd all had it. **1959** *N.Z. Listener* 12 June 21/3 He re-wound the cord and tried again: no spark. 'It's had it, I think.' **1959** *News Chron.* 10 July 4/2 In private, Labour politicians admit that they have had it. **1971** J. KILLENS in A. Chapman *New Black Voices* (1972) 58, I mean, I'd had it, for a time, with that traveling-is-broadening shit.

l. *to have had* (a person or thing): to have had enough of, to be fed up with. *colloq.*

1943 *N.Z.E.F. Times* 21 June, I've had the club. **1947** N. MARSH *Final Curtain* xvi. 249 We'd all..just about *had* Cedric. **1953** G. HEYER *Detection Unlimited* ii. 23 He's just about had Warrenby, muscling into every damned thing here. **1956** A. WILSON *Anglo-Saxon Att.* I. iii. 60 When you resigned in November, I'd about had politics, as much as the Labour Party 'd about had you. **1965** *Sunday Mail Mag.* (Brisbane) 15 Aug. 11/1 By October..N. Dixon Campbell had utterly had that little old white schoolhouse at Pallawalla, and stamped out of it never to return.

m. *to have it* (*so*) *good*: to possess (so many) advantages. Chiefly in neg. contexts. *colloq.* (orig. *U.S.*).

1946 *Amer. Speech* XXI. 243 *You never had it so good.* This is a sardonic response to complaints about the Army; it is probably supposed to represent the attitude of a peculiarly offensive type of officer. **1957** *Times* 22 July 4/6 [Mr. Macmillan's speech at Bedford on 20 July] Let us be frank about it: most of our people have never had it so good. **1957** *Glasgow Herald* 16 Nov. 5/1 Mr. Harold Macmillan, at Maidstone last night..repeated ..'They have never lived so well; they have never had it so good.' **1958** *Times* 8 May 11/5 When one boy said, 'My dad says we never had it so good', he was expressing a very general acceptance of what the 'past' really meant in East London. **1958** *Times* 12 July 7/7 How long can women's magazines have it so good? **1958** *Listener* 13 Nov. 776/2 They have it so good in their garden-world. **1959** *Times Lit. Suppl.* 3 Apr. 198/2 James Bond is having it good again. **1960** J. RAE *Custard Boys* I. vii. 87 'I've never had it so good,' he told me..'during the blitz I had more business than I could handle.' **1961** C. MCCULLERS *Clock without Hands* vii. 158 From then on I never had it so good. Nobody ever had it so good. **1969** *Times* 4 Oct. 7/7 The last phrase borrowed from that campaign [*sc.* the American Presidential campaign of 1952] by a British Prime Minister was from the Democrat Party's campaign slogan of that year. The words 'never had it so good' were first used by Mr. Macmillan two years before his party won its third election in a row.

n. *to have on*: to be prepared to accept (a person, proposition, etc.); also, to attack or fight (a person). *Austral.* and *N.Z. colloq.*

1941 BAKER *Dict. Austral. Slang* 34 *Have* (*someone*) *on*, to be prepared to fight a person: to accept a challenge to a contest or fight. **1945** —— *Austral. Lang.* vi. 120 A man who attacks another is said..to have him on. **1946** F. SARGESON *That Summer* 54 A girl came past that I thought might have me on. **1965** —— *Memoirs of Peon* vii. 252, I didn't see why we shouldn't introduce you... But John Morgan wouldn't have it on.

o. *have* —, *will* —: in numerous expressions of the type illustrated indicating willingness to travel, etc., because one possesses an essential object, etc.

1954 B. HOPE *Have Tux, will Travel* 1 Hoofers, comedians and singers used to put ads in *Variety*. Those ads read: 'Have tuxedo, will travel.' This meant they were ready to go any place at any time. **1960** *Daily Mail* 13 July 6/2 Never in the whole history of moving pictures has film-making been such a mobile and international industry. 'Have talent, will travel' is the watchword now. **1961**

John o' London's 18 May 567/3 (*heading*) Have towel, will strip. **1961** *Sunday Times* 25 June 21/2 Have honours degree, will travel. **1965** *Harrods Xmas Catal.* 43/1 *Have iron, will travel*—featherweight iron weighs only 2¼ lbs. and travels..complete with universal adapters for use with any voltage..£4. 4. 0. **1966** *Listener* 16 June 889/1 *Have Gun Will Travel* was a much better western..than the ones they are making now. **1968** *Times* 29 Nov. p. vi/4 Have portable, will play. **1969** *Times* 14 July 5/5 The..scene has now gone one step further towards the American dream with the opening of Have Typewriter, Will Travel.

15. b. (Earlier example.)

1816 SCOTT *Old Mort.* in *Tales of Landlord* IV. vii. 125 He has you there, I think, my Lord Duke.

d. *to have on*: to puzzle or deceive intentionally; to chaff, tease; to hoax. orig. *dial.*

1867 J. T. STATON *Rays fro' Loominary* 117 It looks as if somebuddy wur havin me on. **1893** FARMER & HENLEY *Slang, To have on*, to secure a person's interest, attention, sympathy: generally with a view to deceiving him (or her). **1895** M. MATHER *Lancs. Idylls* 46, I were nobbud hevin' her on a bit. **1928** *Daily Express* 31 Aug. 7 Speaking unjudicially and in ordinary language you are 'having him on'. **1951** L. P. HARTLEY *Travelling Grave* 52 'Of course,' said Dickie, when the boy had gone off with his *mancia*, whistling, 'he's having us on.'

16. b. *to have it out*: see OUT *adv.* 7 b.

c. *to have it away*: to escape from prison or custody. *Criminals' slang.*

1958 F. NORMAN *Bang to Rights* 48 The P.O. who was in charge of the escort that was going to..make sure no one had it away. **1965** *New Statesman* 30 July 152/3 One thing broke the monotony of this dreary sentence and that was the occasion when a geezer, three peters away from me, had it away. **1969** T. PARKER *Twisting Lane* 196 After I'd had it away three times, they decided it was no use bothering with me in these open places.

18. a. *to have it coming to one*: see *COME *v.* 9 b.

21. The following phrases are also treated under the indicated words: *to h.* *EVERYTHING, *h. a* *HEART, *as* *LUCK *would h. it*, *WHAT *h. you.*

24. d. (*I*) *have and* (*I*) *haven't*: a phrase indicating that a statement is true in some respects but not in others.

1858 TROLLOPE *Dr. Thorne* II. xiv. 282 'Have you spoken to my niece about this, Sir Louis?' 'Well, I have, and yet I haven't; I haven't, and yet in a manner I have.' **1910** J. BUCHAN *Prester John* vi. 108 'Had the man any news?' I asked. 'He had and he hadn't.' **1933** A. CHRISTIE *Ld. Edgware Dies* iii. 31 'You have a problem for me—yes?'..'Well,..I have and I haven't.' **1967** 'L. BRUCE' *Death of Commuter* v. 58 'You haven't got any suspicions about Mr. Parador's death, have you?'..'Well, I have and I haven't.'

26. ¶ (Later U.S. examples.)

1816 U. BROWN *Jrnl.* in *Maryland Hist. Mag.* (1915) X. 282 If this forest had never have been fired it would have been a vast..Timbered country. **1869** *Trans. Ill. Agric. Soc.* VII. 444 If said hogs had, in style of Hanlon Brothers, have stood one on the other. **1911** J. F. WILSON *Land Claimers* i. 17 'If the fire hadn't have gone out,' he mused.

27. have-got: see *HAVE *sb.* 2; **have-on** *slang* = HAVE *sb.* 3 (cf. sense *15 d).

1931 T. R. G. LYELL *Slang* 372 *Have* or *have on*, a swindle; a mild joke to deceive a person. **1967** *Listener* 16 Feb. 237/3 Puns, tropes, polyglot have-ons, batty new coinings.

have, *sb.* Add: **2.** Also, a nation or country that *has* or possesses; one of the wealthier nations. Also *attrib.* and (occas.) *have-got.* (Usu. opp. *have-not.*)

1919 J. L. GARVIN *Econ. Found. Peace* xvi. 375 They contemplate a World-Federation when the international League of the Have-Nots has conquered all the Haves. **1937** E. SNOW *Red Star over China* VI. iii. 227 The Reds..radically changed the situation for..all the 'have-not' elements. **1949** KOESTLER *Insight & Outlook* xvi. 227 The equalization of the steep gradients..between have and have-not nations. **1955** *Bull. Atomic Sci.* Jan. 3/2 The proposal is for the atomic 'haves' to contribute crucial materials and at least some limited amount of technical information to the 'have nots'. **1959** *Times* 29 Sept. 18/5 Algerian oil is expected to change France from an oil 'have-not' to a 'have'. **1962** *Listener* 5 July 29/3 The greatest of the 'have' powers. *Ibid.* 30/1 The Soviet Union is a 'have' society that ought to be more generous. **1959** *Brno Studies* I. 70 The sharp distinction..between the 'have-gots' and the 'have-nots' was soon felt in politics. **1963** *Listener* 21 Mar. 487/1 Russia was becoming a 'have-got' power herself with a productive capacity second only to that of the United States. **1965** H. KAHN *On Escalation* xiii. 244 A 'have' nation might perceive a situation that threatened its possessions as a crisis. **1968** *Punch* 22 May 757/3 The country had a one-crop economy; the more cocoa it exported, the less the 'have' nations were willing to pay for it.

havelock. Add: *havelock cap*, a military cap provided with a havelock.

1880 *Harper's Mag.* Oct. 399 A poncho and havelock cap comprise the rubber clothing outfit.

haver, *v.* Add: **2.** Orig. *Sc. dial.* but now in general English use: to hesitate, to be slow in deciding.

1866 W. GREGOR *Dial. Banffshire* 73 *Haiver*, to hesitate and make much ado about doing anything. **1955** J. BAYLEY *In Another Country* 75 It was a classic moment for polite havering, but the sensible girl did not haver: he was holding the front door open and she climbed in without more ado. **1957** *Times* 14 Nov. 13/3 No doubt the Government, in deciding to institute an inquiry.., might appear at first sight to have been havering and shifting their ground.

havoc, *sb.* Add: **2.** Also in weakened sense: confusion and disorder, disarray; *to play havoc* (examples); freq. const. *with.* The phrases *to work havoc, create havoc* are also common.

1812 M. E. BICKNELL *Let.* 28 Oct. in *J. Constable's Corr.* (1964) II. 91 You perfectly well know, what terrible havoc it [*sc.* meeting often] makes with your time. **1900** J. MORLEY *Cromwell* I. 3 The thirst after broad classifications works havoc with truth. **1908** E. J. BANFIELD *Confessions of Beachcomber* iv. 129 Terrestrial storms work as much if not greater havoc in the shallow places of the sea as on the land. **1910** G. D. ABRAHAM *Mountain Adv.* vi. 115 The hot sun, reflected off the snow, played havoc with his complexion. **1934** G. G. COULTON *H. W. Fowler* 156 He..displayed..anxiety about the havoc made in the projected festivities. **1949** *Times Lit. Suppl.* 4 Nov. 715/2 History has played havoc with their hopes. **1961** J. E. MANSION *Harrap's French-Eng. Dict.* 705/2 The storm..played havoc with the crops. **1961** WEBSTER s.v. *havoc*, Several small children can create havoc in a house. **1964** *Times* 5 Sept. 9/5 Surely one can make up one's mind as to which [political party] would create less havoc if they came to power. **1965** A. NICOL *Truly Married Woman* 24, I have created enough havoc in one afternoon as it is. **1966** B. KIMENYE *Kalasanda Revisited* 86 The fine, dust-like substance enveloped him in a cloud which played havoc with the delicate membranes of his eyes and nose. **1969** *Times* 25 Mar. 16/1 The noise and clatter of high-revving engines can play havoc with a driver's nerves. **1971** B. PATTEN *Irrelevant Song* 32 This creature singled out creates Havoc with intelligence.

haw, *int.*[2] and *sb.*[5] *dial.* and *U.S.* A call used to direct a horse or team to turn to the left.

1843 *Knickerbocker* XXI. 494 He admonishes them with his goad, and ejaculates, 'Haw'. **1843** 'R. CARLTON' *New Purchase* xxvi. 239 Whoas, gees and haws. **1856** J. C. MORTON *Cycl. Agric.* II. 723/2 Horses—terms used in directing—...Cheshire...To left. Haw. **1864** WEBSTER s.v., *Haw, haw here*;—words used by teamsters in guiding their teams. **1930** *Amer. Speech* V. 419 *Haw*, direction given to oxen to turn to the left. **1972** *Even. Telegram* (St. John's, Nwfndl.) 24 June 14/3 'Gee' tells the dogs to take a right turn, and 'Haw' means left.

haw, *v.*[2] *U.S.* (but *Eng. dial.* in quot. 1911). [f. prec.] **a.** *intr.* Of a horse or team: to turn to the left. Also *fig.* (see quot. 1864).

1846 *Knickerbocker* XXVII. 119 The plough-boy has hardly energy to cry out..'Gee-haw, there, I tell you to haw, now.' **1861** *Trans. Ill. Agric. Soc.* IV. 99 They were required to plow lands of about fifteen rods in length, and 'haw' about. **1864** WEBSTER s.v., *To haw and gee*, or *haw and gee about*, to go from one thing to another without good reason; to have no settled purpose; to be irresolute or unstable. (*Colloq.*) **1911** J. MASEFIELD *Everlasting Mercy* 86 Now and then he seems to stoop To clear the coulter with the scoop, Or touch an ox to haw or gee.

b. *trans.* To direct (a horse, etc.) to turn to the left. Also *fig.*

1864 WEBSTER s.v., *To haw and gee*, or *haw and gee about*, to lead this way and that at will; to lead by the nose; to master or control. (*Colloq.*) **1867** [see *GEE *v.*[2] b].

Hence **hawing** *vbl. sb.*

1843 'R. CARLTON' *New Purchase* xvi. 119 After performing wonders on the journey from Philadelphia to the West in hawing and geeing. **1867** [see *GEE *v.*[2] b].

Hawaiian (hăwai·ăn), *a.* and *sb.* Also **Hawaian.** [f. *Hawaii* + -AN.] **A.** *adj.* Of or pertaining to the island of Hawaii, or to the whole group of the Sandwich Islands in the North Pacific. **B.** *sb.* **1.** A native or inhabitant of Hawaii. **2.** The language of Hawaii, belonging to the Malayo-Polynesian group.

1825 W. ELLIS *Jrnl. Tour Hawaii* 205 The account given this evening of the Hawaiian *hades.* **1859** [see *inter-island* s.v. INTER- 5]. **1864** W. D. ALEXANDER *Hawaiian Gram.* 20 What would form a long sentence in English, in Hawaiian is generally broken up into several independent propositions. **1877** T. H. STREETS *Nat. Hist. Hawaiian & Fanning Isl.* 8 The Fanning group, with the exception of the Hawaiian, were the only islands visited in the Pacific. **1877** L. H. MORGAN *Anc. Society* III. ii. 404 These are terms in Hawaiian for grandparent. **1893** *Funk's Stand. Dict.* I. 825/1 *Hawaiian*, a native..of Hawaii. **1913** R. BROOKE *Coll. Poems* (1918) 28 And new stars burn into the ancient skies, Over the murmurous soft Hawaian sea. **1921** *Nature* 20 Jan. 673/1 Some broad features of Hawaiian petrology. **1929** C. H. SMITH *Bridge of Life* ii. 29 White men, Chinese, Japanese, Hawaiians and many others slept in the common dormitory. **1936** *Discovery* June 198/2 He is bold enough to believe that the Hawaiian native practitioners can handle elemental spirits 'like tame animals'. **1957** P. WORSLEY *Trumpet shall Sound* i. 30 Sects..have also appeared amongst the..Hawaiians. **1970** *Western Folklore* XXIX. 234 The slider occasionally covers several strings at once to produce different chords in the 'Hawaiian' style.

II. *Special Combs.* **Hawaiian goose,** a rare bird, *Branta sandvicensis*, formerly called the Sandwich Island goose; **Hawaiian guitar,** a type of guitar, usually held in a horizontal position, in which the pitch is obtained by placing a small metal bar on the strings and moving it up and down to produce *glissando* effects; hence *Hawaiian guitarist, orchestra*; **Hawaiian** (or **Hawaii**) **shirt,** a highly coloured and gaily patterned shirt.

[**1834** *Proc. Zool. Soc.* 41 A specimen was exhibited of the young of the *Sandwich Island Goose.*] **1915** W. A. BRYAN *Nat. Hist. Hawaii* xxv. 336 The nene or Hawaiian goose..is confined to the Island of Hawaii, where it leads a life of seclusion, high up on the mountainside. **1958** E. T. GILLIARD *Living Birds of World* 80/2 One of the rarest is the néné or Hawaiian Goose (*Branta sandvicensis*) of which less than 70 wild birds are thought to survive. **1964** *Listener* 23 July 125/1 The Hawaiian goose..had it not been for special breeding studies..would have already become extinct. **1972** G. DURRELL *Catch me a Colobus* x. 219 The Hawaiian goose... This beautiful bird was almost extinct but, due to the sensible attitude of the Hawaiian authorities and the far-sightedness of Peter Scott, it has been saved from certain extinction. **1926** H. O. OSGOOD *So this is Jazz* 97 Practice with it..will enable the trumpeters..to imitate the violin, Hawaiian steel guitar, oboe [etc.]. **1928** *Melody Maker* Feb. 188/2, I was at first very surprised at the 'Hawaiian guitar' solos in some of the waltzes. **1935** L. MACNEICE *Poems* 13 Jazz-weary of years of drums and Hawaiian guitar. **1968** *Blues Unlimited* Nov. 20 He cannot play standard guitar, but plays a hawaiian guitar on a stand. **1959** 'F. NEWTON' *Jazz Scene* xii. 203 As he played, he pressed a knife on the strings of the guitar in a manner popularised by Hawaiian guitarists who used steel bars. **1955** L. FEATHER *Encycl. Jazz* vii. 79 The Decca company began to record him..in duets with pop singers, and even with Hawaiian orchestras. **1955** G. GREENE *Quiet American* II. i. 90, I noticed that he was wearing a Hawaii shirt, even though it was comparatively restrained in colour and design. **1962** L. DEIGHTON *Ipcress File* xviii. 114 Dalby had changed into a red Hawaiian shirt with large blue and yellow flowers across it. **1968** R. CLAPPERTON *No News on Monday* xi. 129 He was wearing a red Hawaiian shirt, unbuttoned.

haw-haw. C. *adj.* Add: Further examples: freq. applied to what is taken to resemble upper-class speech.

1900 *Daily News* 8 Oct., The Censor was one of those haw-haw officers, who look down upon men like me as unnecessary upon this earth. *Ibid.* 20 Nov. 3/5 The answer I got was in Mr. Hales's 'haw-haw' style. 'Ah've nothing to dah with Mafeking.' **1913** R. BROOKE *Let.* 22 Nov. (1968) 535 Weedy Australian clerks, uncertain whether they most despise a 'haw-haw Englishman', or a 'dam nigger'. **1941** *Time* 27 Jan. 22/1 Declaring that BBC announcers were 'too haw haw' in their diction, he is responsible for the nickname 'Lord Haw-Haw' given to Nazi propagandist William Joyce. **1953** K. JACKSON *Lang. & Hist. Early Brit.* 108 The language..must have seemed..upper-class and 'haw-haw'. **1968** *Listener* 9 May 615/2 Kuo-yü spoken in the next room can sound just like somewhat haw-haw English.

haw-haw, *v.* Add: **b.** *trans.* To laugh at.

1862 THACKERAY *Adv. Philip* III. xxxi. 30 It's good to see him haw-haw Bickerton. **1922** Z. GREY *To Last Man* x. 226 Some of the gang haw-hawed him.

hawk, *sb.*[1] Add: **3.** Also in *Politics*, a person who advocates a hard-line or warlike policy, opp. to a *dove* (cf. *DOVE *sb.* 2 f). Also *attrib.* or as quasi-*adj.*

1962, 1964 [see *DOVE *sb.* 2 f]. **1965** *Economist* 25 Sept. 1189/2 President Ayub's difficulties in curbing the 'hawks' in his country. **1966, 1967** [see *DOVE *sb.* 2 f]. **1967** D. BOULTON *Objection Overruled* iii. 85 The committee seems to have become immersed immediately in a struggle between doves and hawks. **1969** *Guardian* 21 Feb. 10/2 The hawks at the Treasury..want to have one more hack at consumption.

4. a. *hawk-faced* adj.

1889 O. WILDE in *19th Cent.* Jan. 47 She has hawk-faced gods that worship her. **1932** WODEHOUSE *Louder & Funnier* 68 Just one more of those curt, hawk-faced amateur investigators. **1936** *Discovery* Dec. 380/2 A hawk-faced negro of Benin type. **1954** 'R. CROMPTON' *William & Moon Rocket* iv. 101 Trying to look keen-eyed and hawk-faced, the two made their way round the cottage to the little back garden.

b. hawk-cuckoo, an Indian cuckoo, *Cuculus* (*Hierococcyx*) *varius*, resembling a hawk in appearance; **hawk-eye,** (*a*) *U.S.* (examples); (*b*) (a person with) a keen eye like that of a hawk. Cf. HAWK'S EYE 1. Also *transf.*

1862 T. C. JERDON *Birds of India* I. 329 The Common Hawk-Cuckoo..is the common Cuckoo of the plains of India. **1901** *Westm. Gaz.* 8 Aug. 8/2 The Zoological Society have lately received..a specimen of the hawk-cuckoo. **1960** M. MACDONALD *Birds in my Indian Garden* 41 It was the Common Hawk-cuckoo, whose monotonously, maddeningly reiterated phrase..gives it the nickname of Brainfever Bird. **1823** J. F. COOPER *Pioneers* II. 44 Hawk-eye. **1826** —— *Last of Mohicans* III. vii. 160, I am the man..that got..the compliment of Hawk-eye from the Delawares. **1833** [see HAWK'S EYE 1]. **1839** (*title*) Hawk-eye and Iowa Patriot. **1845** [see *CORN-CRACKER 1]. **186.** in F. Moore *Songs of Soldiers* (1864) 114 We have come from the prairies Of the young Hawkeye State. **1901** *Lady's Realm* X. 552/2 The most contemptuous glances of her hawk-eyes. **1911** C. HARRIS *Eve's Second Husband* 244 When he ran for Congress the hawkeye of more than one newspaper in the state was turned..upon him. **1913** D. H. LAWRENCE *Love Poems* 45 'Er black hawk-eyes as I've Mistrusted all along! **1960** *Ottawa Citizen* 18 Nov. 5/4 Across..Canada,..74 federal hawkeyes keep a watch on hundreds of millions of dollars being paid out to unemployed persons. **1966** *Listener* 2 June 796/2 The head's wife was known behind her back as Hawk-eye from her habit of seeing everything.

hawkish, *a.* Add: Also, inclined to favour hard-line or warlike policies. Cf. *HAWK *sb.*[1] 3. Hence **haw·kishness.**

1965 *New Statesman* 17 Sept. 386/2 The very hawkish chairman of the House of Representatives Armed Services Committee..hankers to bomb Communist China. **1967** *Guardian* 15 Feb. 6/2 Hawkishness in Bonn could undo the promise of everything that has so far been achieved. **1967** *Listener* 21 Sept. 365/2 It is..inevitable for the newspaper to take a strong—or, as we would now say, hawkish—stand in any international dispute. **1968** *Guardian* 9 July 8/6 Sir Henry Johnson, chief of BRB, was a true hard-liner, most hawkish of hawks. **1968** *Times* 4 Nov. 1/1 President Thieu agreed to the bombing halt in advance and..his present performance is directed at hawkish opinion within South Vietnam. **1969** *Guardian* 13 Feb. 10/1 At yesterday's student meeting [at LSE] there were signs of a new hawkishness among the moderates. **1970** *Ibid.* 4 Aug. 2/6 Withdrawal may be political dynamite, but so is hawkishness. **1972** *Listener* 6 Jan. 8/1 Pakistan's hawkish enemies in New Delhi.

hawkshaw (hǭ·kʃǭ). Also **Hawkshaw.** [Name of a detective in *The Ticket-of-Leave Man* (1863), a play by Tom Taylor, English dramatist (1817–1880); also in the comic strip *Hawkshaw the Detective,* by Gus Mager, American cartoonist (d. 1956).] A detective; also *attrib.*

[*c* **1863** T. TAYLOR in M. R. Booth *Eng. Plays in 19th Cent.* (1969) II. 77 *The Ticket-of-Leave Man...* Cast.. Hawkshaw, a detective.] **1903** 'H. MCHUGH' *Back to Woods* iii. 59 He didn't even whimper when the village Hawkshaw snapped the bracelets on his wrist. **1942** BERREY & VAN DEN BARK *Amer. Thes. Slang* § 460/18 Hawk, hawkshaw, heavy foot, hot hand. **1967** N. MAILER *Cannibals & Christians* I. 40 The hawkshaw *geist* of the F.B.I. **1968** *Listener* 15 Feb. 214/1 A 'Treasury hawkshaw', charged with seizing and selling up Confederate cotton. **1973** R. TRAVERS *Murder in Blue Mountains* x. 96 The 'Hawkshaws from the Antipodes' as the [San Francisco] *Bulletin* called Roche and his men.

hawthorn. Add: **3. hawthorn jar, pot, vase,** etc., a jar made of hawthorn china.

1905 *Daily Chron.* 18 May 4/6 The enormous sum paid yesterday at Christie's for a 'hawthorn' jar. **1906** S. W. BUSHELL *Chinese Art* II. viii. 35 A typical 'hawthorn ginger jar'..decorated with rising and falling sprays of prunus blossom. **1866** D. G. ROSSETTI *Let.* 3 Aug. (1965) II. 601, I went yesterday to see Mr. Huth's hawthorn pot at Kensington, and really after that I could not become the possessor of the one you brought me, good as it is. **1969** M. G. EBERHART *Message from Hong Kong* xix. 169 A Hawthorn vase..its beautiful glaze, its incredible blue, the pure, amazing white of its blossoms.

hay, *sb.*[1] Add: **1. b.** *the hay*: colloq. phr. for 'bed'; esp. in phrases *to roll in the hay* (sense *3); *to hit the hay* (*HIT *v.* 11 c).

1903 ADE *People you Know* 13 When he had put in a frolicsome Hour or so with the North American Review, he crawled into the Hay at 9.30 p.m. **1930** WODEHOUSE *Very Good, Jeeves* vi. 160 My experience of women has been that the earlier they leave the hay the more vicious specimens they are apt to be. **1959** N. MAILER *Advts. for Myself* (1961) 334 Al had the reputation of being great in the hay.

3. *that ain't hay* (U.S. colloq.), that is a lot of money; similarly in other negative contexts; *to roll in the hay* (colloq.), to make love; hence *a roll in the hay,* love-making; also *concr.*, a person making, or willing to make, love.

1943 R. CHANDLER *Lady in Lake* (1944) vii. 44 Job pays eighty a month, cabin, firewood...That ain't hay. **1945** 'L. LEWIS' *Birthday Murder* (1951) iii. 39 He gets something out of it...Maybe just a good roll in the hay. **1948** C. PORTER *Always True to you in my Fashion* (song) p. 4 Mis-ter Thorne once cor-nered corn—and that ain't hay. **1949** M. MILLER *Sure Thing* (1950) 79, I thought here's a kind of pretty girl..and I bet she'd be a good roll in the hay. **1952** P. BONNER *SPQR* (1953) xxvi. 233, I had fancied her as a desirable bit for a roll in the hay. **1958** R. STOUT *Champagne for One* (1959) iv. 42 Fresh figs in March, by air from Chile, are not hay. **1959** G. FISHER *Hospitality for Murder* xvii. 137 Just over a million bucks per day, to be exact—and that ain't hay. **1963** M. MCCARTHY *Group* xiv. 332 We had a few rolls in the hay...Then for him it was over. **1966** J. PORTER *Sour Cream* xiii. 166 There she was, rolling around in the hay with enough evidence for a dozen divorces. **1968** *Times* 9 Nov. 23/3 Peterson's marriage is collapsing... He..rolls in the hay with..a plump little thing. **1969** 'H. PENTECOST' *Girl Watcher's Funeral* (1970) II. i. 73, I will come into a cool two and a half million dollars... I will also collect executor's fees which won't be hay. **1973** *Times* 9 Mar. 18/2 A quiet girl librarian, on vodka, has fantasy dreams of rolling in the hay in frilly drawers.

4. a. *hay-bale*; *hay-bond* (dial.); *hay paddock* (Austral. and N.Z.); *hayshed.* **b.** *hay-baler* (U.S.), *-cutter* (mechanical contrivance or person). **c.** *hay-cutting* (orig. U.S.).

1851 A. O. HALL *Manhattaner* 5 It was a modest commercial plain..with bits of machinery, and ploughs, and oat bags, and hay bales. **1911** *Daily Colonist* (Victoria, B.C.) 14 Apr. 3/4 The sentence was duly carried out, the young Indian being bound to a stake with hay-bale wire. **1962** *Times* 31 May 14/7 We use haybales to build mothering-up pens. **1895** M. GRAHAM *Stories of Foot-Hills* 209 The song of the haybalers and the whir of the threshing machine had died out of the valley. **1936** *Scrutiny* IV. iv. 443 Mark Twain's presentation of Mississippi pilots and Nevada pioneers is comparable with Davis's accounts of timber-line settlers and haybalers. **1874** HARDY *Far fr. Madding Crowd* x. 89 Tending thrashing-machine, and wimbling haybonds. **1953** A. JOBSON *Household & Country Crafts* xvi. 163 In the old days the thatcher made his own broaches, as he made his own hay-bonds. **1653** in *Mayflower Descendant* XI. 200 One haycutter,..00–01–06. **1838** W. B. DEWEES *Lett. fr. Texas* (1852) xxiii. 226 As it chanced there was a hay-cutter, who was at work a short distance from where the scene took place. **1867** J. N. EDWARDS *Shelby* xx. 352 Shelby marked the hay-cutters struggling over stubble and wind row. **1873** J. M. BAILEY *Life in Danbury* 21 It did seem as if I never would get out from under that hay-cutter. **1972** *Country Life* 30 Mar. 769/1 The hay-cutter or hay-knife was the proper tool for cutting into a rick. **1665** *Rowley Rec.* (Mass.) (1894) 163 John Trumble for hay cutting. **1869** J. R. BROWNE *Adv. Apache Country* 443 Twenty settlers,.. most of whom are engaged in stock-raising and hay-cutting. **1906** 'MARK TWAIN' *Autobiogr.* (1924) II. 48 Hay-cutting time was approaching. **1933** R. TUVE *Seasons & Months* iv. 165 The eleventh-century Julius A vi has..hay-cutting for July. **1966** *Te Reo* IX. 53 Is it not the case that wheat [in N.Z.] is grown in a wheatfield but hay is grown in a hay paddock? **1967** *Landfall* XXI. 127 The cock pheasant strutting in a hay paddock. **1865** *Atlantic Monthly* XV. 516, I used to notice her..about Easter day, proclaiming her arrival..from the peak of the barn or hay-shed. **1920** *Glasgow Herald* 12 Nov. 8 Farmhouses and haysheds were also fired between Killarney and Tralee. **1936** *Brit. Birds* XXX. 108 The other Martins' nests were in haysheds or under eaves.

5. hay-bag *slang*, a woman; **hay-box,** (*a*) *dial.* a hay-loft; (*b*) a box filled with hay in which food after being brought to boiling-point in a saucepan is placed to finish cooking; also *attrib.*; (*c*) a box containing hay; **hay-home supper,** a meal to celebrate the successful bringing home of the hay; cf. HARVEST HOME; **hay-hut** [tr. G. *heuhütte*], a wooden hut covering a hay-stack on the mountainside; **hay-press** *U.S.*, a press for baling hay; **hayride** *U.S.*, a pleasure ride in a hay-wagon; **hay-scales** *U.S.*, a public weighing-machine for weighing loads of hay, etc.

1851 MAYHEW *Lond. Labour* I. 217/2 Haybag, a woman. **1925** F. G. BOND *Flatboating on Yellowstone, 1877* 12, I asked a passing corporal the way to the haybag quarters. He was a married man and lived in haybag row. **1931** D. RUNYON *Guys & Dolls* (1932) viii. 159 She is nothing but an old haybag. **1939** ABBOTT & SMITH *We pointed them North* 143 A woman they called Big Ox, who was one of those haybags that used to follow the buffalo camps. **1967** *Spectator* 10 Nov. 565/3 The weary certainty that one more stranger has paused to inspect her casually and to depart calling her a haybag. **1885** B. BRIERLEY *Tales Lancs. Life* iii. 45 There's a hay-boax theere ut I've bin in afore. **1908** *Chambers's Jrnl.* Jan. 119/2 The receptacle with its boiling contents is placed in the hay-box. **1915** *Queen* 13 Nov. 897/2 Boiled beef should be allowed thirty minutes' boiling for a large joint and three to four hours in the hay-box. **1927** *Daily Express* 6 Aug. 9/4 To feed the personnel of the force by means of new mobile hay-box cookers. **1960** *Farmer & Stockbreeder* 19 Jan. Suppl. 39/2 The hay-box fold is most useful for carrying on chicks during the spring and summer months. **1860** C. M. YONGE *Friarswood Post-Office* ii. 34 Mrs. King would not let him go to the hay-home supper in the barn. **1943** F. THOMPSON *Candleford Green* iv. 69 That was the hay-home supper, a survival, though perhaps not more ancient than a couple of hundred years or so. **1903** *Daily Chron.* 23 Mar. 3/7 One sees the bright green mountain where the hay-huts hang like birds' nests on the steep slope. **1912** D. H. LAWRENCE *Let.* 2 Sept. (1932) 56 We take rucksacks.., cook our meals by some stream—and twice we have slept in hay-huts. *c* **1912** —— *Love among Haystacks* (1930) 63 There must be a hay hut somewhere near. We *can't* sleep here. **1829** *20th Congress 2 Sess.* State P. No. 59, 3 [Improvement] in the hay press [patented Jan.] 26 [1828 by] Moses B. Bliss. **1835** J. H. INGRAHAM *South-West* II. 221 A large building resembling a northern hay-press. **1872** E. EGGLESTON *Hoosier Schoolmaster* xxvi. 127 To see his new red barn with its large 'Mormon' hay-press..consumed, was too much for the Hawkins' heart to stand. **1897** *Sears, Roebuck Catal.* 151/3 Our $235,000 Belt Power Hay Press. [**1856** *Spirit of Times* 8 Nov. 154/2 The invitations he had at first received to join pic-nics, boating excursions on the river, and haywagon rides, after a while became intermittent.] **1896** *Advance* (Chicago) 19 Mar. 414/2 Everybody being as comfortable as hay-ride etiquette permitted, the word was given, and away they went. **1906** 'MARK TWAIN' *Autobiogr.* (1924) II. 50 The remembrance of poor Susy's lost hay-ride still brings me a pang. **1915** J. WEBSTER *Dear Enemy* (1916) 274 We have had hay-rides and skating-parties and candy-pulls. **1966** *Punch* 21 Dec. 921/2 Hay-rides, an American indulgence by no means confined to Texas, are laid on by riding academies and picnic area operators. **1973** *Sat. Rev. Soc.* May 64/1 She's..become a steady patron of..hayrides..and Ladies' Nights. **1773** *Rec. Early Hist. Boston* (1893) XXIII. 204 The Ground on which the Hay Scales stands. **1844** G. W. KENDALL *Narr. Santa Fé Exped.* II. xvii. 327 They might as well say that the natives can tell the time by consulting..a pair of hay-scales. **1855** M. M. THOMSON *Doesticks* v. 34 The writer,.. wearied of..the same unvarying prospect of ox-teams, hay-scales,..took the roving fever. **1893** *Citizen Guide to Brooklyn & Long Island* 8 The old hay-scales stood there, and on its roof was the first fire-bell owned by Brooklyn.

hay, *sb.*[5] [tr. F. *foin.*] The choke of an artichoke.

1877 E. S. DALLAS *Kettner's Bk. of Table* 43 Some French cooks, before sending the artichoke to table, are careful to remove the choke, or as they call it, the hay. **1958** W. BICKEL tr. *Hering's Dict. Classical & Mod. Cookery* 558 *Artichoke Béarnaise style,* blanched, hay removed, braised in white wine, [etc.]. **1960** *News Chron.* 6 July 6/6 In the middle of the vegetable is the hay or choke (what would be the flower itself if it were not an artichoke but a thistle).

Hay (hēi). The name of William Howard *Hay* (1866–1940), U.S. physician, used *attrib.* to designate various methods of medical and dietary treatment advocated by him, as *Hay diet,* a diet based on the belief that proteins and carbohydrates should not be eaten at the same meal.

1925 *Jrnl. Amer. Med. Assoc.* 20 June 1938/2 Hay rest cure. **1933** *Ibid.* 25 Feb. 595/2 Can you give me any information on Dr. Hay and the Hay diet which has become so popular in certain sections of our country? I believe that it is based on the idea of not eating meats and starches in the same meal! **1936** D. POWELL *Turn, Magic Wheel* II. 142, I wish you'd let me put you on a Hay diet. All proteins at once, all starches. **1937** W. H. HAY *Human Ailments* xix. 136 If you wish to end colds for all time, then merely follow the directions for building health that you will find stressed continually by the Hay System. **1937** M. OSBORNE (*title*) Meatless dishes for Hay dieters. **1969** SINCLAIR & HOLLINGSWORTH *Hutchison's Food & Princ. Nutrition* (ed. 12) viii. 193 Gastric digestion of protein is not indispensible and its importance can easily be overestimated, as in the fallacious rationale underlying the Hay diet.

hay·-foot. [HAY *sb.*[1]] *hay-foot, straw-foot*: with right and left foot alternately (at the word of command). Also as *vb.*

In allusion to the alleged use of hay and straw to enable a rustic recruit to distinguish the right foot from the left.

1851 *Knickerbocker* XXXVIII. 79 At company-training and general-training..it was all 'hay-foot, straw-foot' with him. **1887** J. D. BILLINGS *Hardtack & Coffee* 208 Scores of men..would 'hay-foot' every time when they should 'straw-foot'. **1898** J. MACMANUS *Bend of Road* 40 Poor fool, he's off, hay foot straw foot, an' small grass grows round his heels till he's there. **1911** R. D. SAUNDERS *Col. Todhunter* vii. 98 You never got in a thousand miles of one of 'em for all your 'heppin' and 'hay-foot' and 'straw-foot' drillin'. **1911** H. S. HARRISON *Queed* i. 12 They march like little lambs when I say the word. Hay-foot—straw-foot.

haylage (hēi·lėdʒ). *Agric.* [Portmanteau word f. HAY *sb.*[1] + SI)LAGE *sb.*] Silage made from grass which has been partially dried.

1960 *Times* 5 July (Agric. Suppl.) p. i/1 The preservation and mechanical feeding of grass as haylage. **1962** *Outlook on Agric.* III. 259/1 Both hay and haylage, cut at the same stage of growth, give better live weight gains in cattle than silage does. **1973** *Country Life* 28 June 1863/2 Some of the best silage, or haylage as this system is known, is made in towers.

hay-maker. Add: **4.** A swinging blow. *slang* or *colloq.*

1912 ADE *Knocking Neighbors* 87 Every time he landed a crushing Hay-Maker on her Family History, she countered with a short-arm Jolt. **1918** *Amer. Mag.* Apr. 113/3 'Gitteloutahere,' panted Slough, aiming a hay-maker at Doug. **1924** *Glasgow Herald* 18 July 10 It was not at all improbable that Eagan would bring over a 'haymaker' and put the Englishman out. **1925** J. J. CORBETT *Roar of Crowd* 87, I deliberately pulled my right back and swung 'hay-makers' at Choinyski, intending to miss him. **1938** I. KUHN *Assigned to Adventure* xxix. 305 Mrs. Medvedeff..emerged once more and landed a haymaker on her husband's chin. **1961** J. HELLER *Catch-22* (1962) xlii. 442 'I'm going to punch Captain Black right in the nose the next time I see him,' gloried the chaplain, throwing two left jabs in the air and then a clumsy haymaker. 'Just like that.' **1972** 'E. LATHEN' *Murder without Icing* (1973) xxii. 189 Rising from a collision, he had thrown off his glove and landed a haymaker.

b. *Cricket.* A sweeping stroke with the bat.

1954 J. FINGLETON *Ashes crown Year* 117 Davidson tried his luck with a hay-maker off Tattersall and Graveney..took a splendid catch. **1955** *Times* 24 June 14/2 There were only a few haymakers from Wardle left.

hay-making. Add: Also *fig.* and *transf.* The action of 'making hay' (see HAY *sb.*[1] 3).

1882 *Daily News* (Ware), A number of men go into a friend's room, find him absent, and testify to their chagrin by disturbing the arrangements of his furniture. But hay-making of this sort is comparatively harmless and inoffensive. **1924** W. R. INGE *Lay Thoughts* (1926) 193 The hay-making of the profiteer after the war. **1971** *Weekend World* (Johannesburg) 9 May 1/2 The unrated Mexican shattered the..boxing champion's hopes of a crack at the world title with a hay-making left hook in the ninth of their..10 round fight.

hay-seed, hayseed. Add: **3.** (Earlier example.) Also *Canada, Austral.*, and *N.Z.*

1851 H. MELVILLE *Moby Dick* I. vi. 52 Ah, poor Hay-Seed! how bitterly will burst those straps in the first howling gale! **1883** *Prince Albert Times* (Sask.) 28 Dec. 3/1 Where the hay seeds may work at their farming. **1901** *Daily Colonist* (Victoria, B.C.) 11 Oct. 4/2 It is the habit of the comic journals to print pictures about the 'hay-seeds' who are gulled by confidence men. **1916** C. J. DENNIS *Songs Sentimental Bloke* 117 *'Ayseed* (Hayseed), a rustic. **1965** F. SARGESON *Memoirs of Peon* ix. 271 He might be identified as either peasant or hayseed. *Ibid.*, Exhibiting something of the hayseed character which he lacked.

haystack. Add: *to look for a needle in a haystack*: see NEEDLE *sb.* 1 c.

hay·wire, *sb.* and *a.* [f. HAY *sb.*[1] + WIRE *sb.*] **A.** *sb.* Wire for binding bales of hay, straw, etc. *N. Amer.*

1917 *Deb. House of Commons Canada* 5351/2 But the 'hay wire' did not hold. **1921** *Outing* (U.S.) Dec. 101/1 You can't run a logging camp without snuff and hay wire. **1936** D. McCOWAN *Anim. Canad. Rockies* xii. 103 A thick mesh of hay wire. **1942** E. PAUL *Narrow St.* v. 41 The tenants bought kindling wood in little bundles... These neat little sticks had been dipped in resin at one end, and were bound with haywire.

B. *adj.* **1.** Poorly equipped, roughly contrived, inefficient, esp. *hay-wire outfit* (from the practice of using hay-wire for makeshift repairs). orig. *U.S.*

1905 *Forestry Bureau Bull.* (U.S.) 61B, *Hay wire outfit*, a contemptuous term for loggers with poor logging equipment. **1931** 'D. STIFF' *Milk & Honey Route* 207 A haywire outfit is something that is all tied and patched together. **1934** *N. & Q.* CLXVI. 13/1, I first heard 'haywire' in the summer of 1929, when I was living in northern New York State. There is also the expression 'haywire outfit', a job on which poor living accommodations are provided for the workers. Also an inefficient factory or shop. **1959** *Listener* 26 Feb. 388/2 A haywire, unpredictable, one-man business. **1968** R. D. PATTERSON *Finlay's River* 145 The..irritating, because man-made, chaos attendant on the intrusion of a haywire railroad into the ordered life of the frontier now lay behind them.

2. Of a person, circumstances, etc.: in an emotional state, tangled, involved, confused, crazy. *colloq.* (orig. *U.S.*).

1934 J. O'HARA *Appointment in Samarra* vii. 226 A married man..and absolutely haywire on the subject of another woman. **1939** W. FAULKNER *Wild Palms* 223 Now you can eat something. Or do you think that will send you haywire again? **1942** D. POWELL *Time to be Born* (1943) xiv. 330 Everything seems so haywire, lately. **1955** 'E. C. R. LORAC' *Ask Policeman* viii. 89 The time element's all haywire.

b. *spec.* in phr. *to go haywire*, to go wrong; to become excited or distracted, to become mentally unbalanced. *colloq.* (orig. *U.S.*).

1929 *N.Y. Times* 13 Oct., When some element in the recording system becomes defective it is said to have gone haywire. **1933** *Daily Express* 16 Nov. 6/4 *Haywire*, epithet applied currently in U.S. to man of confused ideas... New York's newly elect mayor La Guardia is said by his enemies to have gone all haywire. **1936** M. ALLINGHAM *Flowers for Judge* i. 15, I suppose some wives would have gone haywire by this time. **1940** N. MARSH *Surfeit of Lampreys* (1941) vii. 103 Some nice homicidal maniac..going all haywire. **1942** *Tee Emm* (Air Ministry) II. 88 If the Governor Unit should go haywire then you merely pull the little switch down to the fixed position and all is well. **1942** E. WAUGH *Put out More Flags* 42 'If anyone so much as mentions concentration camps again,' said Ambrose Silk, 'I shall go frankly haywire.' **1945** *Times* 28 May 2/1 The compasses acted normally, but over the magnetic pole, where the weather was more favourable, they 'went haywire'. **1951** M. KENNEDY *Lucy Carmichael* III. i. 149 They go haywire because they haven't had any love affair at all. **1962** *Cath. Herald* 26 Oct. 1/5 Architecture has gone haywire. Music is without harmony. **1962** A. NISBETT *Technique Sound Studio* xii. 214 Everything..going haywire at the same time.

Haytian, var. *HAITIAN *a.* and *sb.*

hazan, hazzan, varr. *CHAZZAN.

hazard, *v.* Add: **5. c.** With quoted words as obj.

1881 C. E. L. RIDDELL *Sen. Partner* III. xxxiii. 110 'I met Mr. Robert the other day,' hazarded the clerk. **1903** R. LANGBRIDGE *Flame & Flood* vii. 108 'Love is so rare in this world,' she hazarded.

haze, *v.*[1] Add: **6.** *trans.* To drive an animal (while on horseback).

1890 L. C. D'OYLE *Notches on Rough Edge of Life* 68 Bill 'hazed' 'em again, and they ran up and stood about opposite to me. **1897** *Westm. Gaz.* 8 Oct. 2/1 The beast may trip or run for dangerous ground, and it is then that a well-mounted companion is necessary to haze or ride him off. **1949** P. NEWTON *High Country Days* 95 As each raceful was finished, the calves were hazed through the gate and out into a clean yard. **1962** A. FRY *Ranch on Cariboo* xxiv. 242 A fine dust rose behind the cattle as we hazed them along the wagon tracks between the scattered trees.

hazel[1]. Add: **4. a.** *hazel-brush, -rod* (earlier and later examples).

1822 J. WOODS *2 Yrs. Res. Eng. Prairie Illinois* 206, I dug a piece of prairie-land to sow it on; part of it had some hazle-brush on it. **1932** F. L. WRIGHT *Autobiogr.* I. 46 With scattered hazel-brush and trees. *c* **1786** T. BLAIKIE *Diary of Scotch Gardener* (1931) 205 They have had here the famous Charlatain Lebreton who pretends by means of a hazel rod to discover Springs..; he pretend[s] to be taken with a trembling and the rod to turn round upon his hands. **1904** GOODCHILD & TWENEY *Technol. & Sci. Dict.* 282/2 *Hazel rods*. Thin rods of hazel are often used for the handles of smiths' tools..which have to be struck by a hammer.

c. hazel-hoe (see quot. 1953); **hazel-splitter** *U.S.*, a breed of pigs; **hazel-wizard,** a diviner by means of a hazel-twig; a water-finder.

1895 *Montgomery Ward Catal.* 391/2 Hazel Hoes, weight, 3 pounds, length, 10 in...Hazel Hoe Handles. **1953** *Brit. Commonw. Forest Terminol.* I. 75 s.v. *Hoe*, *Hazel hoe*, a fire trenching or digging tool, resembling a grub hoe but having a shorter, broader and lighter blade, a round or oval eye, and usually a straight pick-like head. **1867** *Trans. Ill. Agric. Soc.* VI. 334 [Those] who prefer the active, energetic 'hazel splitters' to the lazy Berkshire. **1930** *Amer. Speech* V. 18 *Hazel splitter*, a wild, lean range hog, a razor-back. **1843** 'R. CARLTON' *New Purchase* lii. 206 We had ceased from digging a well, after finding no water at twenty-five feet, although we had employed a great hazel-wizzard.

hazer. Add: **2.** (See quots.) Chiefly *U.S.* Cf. *HAZE *v.*[1] 6.

1897 E. HOUGH *Story of Cowboy* 90 Two other men, sometimes known in these days of modern ranching as 'hazers', now mount and ride up..ready to drive on the horse that is to be broken. **1965** *Wanganui* (N.Z.) *Photo News* 13 Feb. 23 In bulldogging the rider and a hazer chase the bull. **1968** *Chicago Tribune* 7 July VII. 16/2 He was the first cowboy ever to bulldog a steer. In this event, two cowboys work as a team. One, called the hazer, rides parallel with the running steer, forcing him close to the dogger.

Hazlittian (hæzli·tiăn), *a.* and *sb.* Also **-ean.** [f. the name of W. *Hazlitt* (1778–1830), English critic + -IAN.] **a.** *sb.* An admirer of Hazlitt. **b.** *adj.* Of, pertaining to, or characteristic of Hazlitt or his work.

1923 *Nation* (N.Y.) 17 Jan. 75 [The essay] on Antony and Cleopatra is Hazlittian in its enthusiasm and its opulence of phrase. **1930** *Times Lit. Suppl.* 18 Dec. 1082/4 We know that we are in the hands of a true Hazlittian. **1931** *Ibid.* 10 Sept. 669/4 His Hazlittian freedom in misquotation. **1962** *John o' London's* 19 July 59/3, I like a certain Hazlittean waywardness to my journeyings.

H-bomb: see *H III.

he, *pers. pron.* Add: **6. b.** = *IT *pron.* 1 f. Also a game of this type.

1810 *Gammer Gurton's Garland* III. 31 One-ery, two-ery, Ziccary zan; Hollow bone, crack a bone, Ninery ten:.. Stick, stock, stone dead, Blind man can't see, Every knave, will have a slave, You or I must be *He*. **1863** *Boy's Handy Bk. of Sports* I. 8 Touch is a very simple game...One of the ten or twelve..is chosen..to use the approved schoolboy expression..'*he*'. **1893** *Funk's Stand. Dict.*, *He*, sometimes, the leader of a game, or one who takes some special part in it. **1900** E. V. & E. LUCAS *What shall we do Now?* 113 For a short time 'He' is a good warming game. It is the simplest of all games. The 'He' runs after the others until he touches one. The one touched then becomes 'He'. **1902** *Little Folks* Aug. 113/1 Let's play 'Touch last'. Look out, I'm 'He'! **1924** W. DE LA MARE *Ding Dong Bell* 23 'Twas life's bright game And Death was 'he'. **1937** HULL & WHITLOCK *Far-Distant Oxus* ii. 40 It was not real hide-and-seek..but..a wild game of 'he'. **1960** S. H. COURTIER *Gently dust Corpse* iv. 43 The youngsters had played a game of hide-and-seek. In the course of one of Pete's turns as 'he'..he sallied into the hall. **1969** I. & P. OPIE *Children's Games* ii. 64 We played He and I was had, so I had to be he.

8. a. *spec.* **he-man** orig. *U.S.*, a particularly strong, virile, or masterful man. Also *attrib.* So **he-male; he-mannish** *a.*

1832 J. K. PAULDING *Westward Ho!* I. 101 A young fellow who could..tree a rackoon with any he man that ever breathed in all out of doors. **1909** J. R. WARE *Passing Eng.*, *He-male*, a full shape of male, and resulting from calling female she-male. **1922** C. E. MULFORD *Tex* xiv. 207 Yo're about th' best he-man I've seen since I looked into a looking-glass. **1924** A. J. SMALL *Frozen Gold* vii, He's such a great big he-male-masculine man. **1926** *Times Lit. Suppl.* 25 Feb. 147/4 That was in the late nineties, when the 'real he-men'..had not attained the softer exterior of the civilization they despised. **1926** S. LEWIS *Mantrap* v. 48 Woodbury was a zealot at showing how lusty and he-mannish he could be. **1931** W. HOLTBY *Poor Caroline* vi. 111 'And how was our friend Johnson?' asked Basil. 'More he-mannish, dirty and businesslike than ever.' **1931** L. STEFFENS *Autobiogr.* I. 406 The rulers of his city, who knew what he knew and knew also what a he man was, held him to be the First Citizen of Pittsburgh. **1931** *Punch* 22 July 60/1 One of their [*sc.* the Americans'] hundred-per-cent he-men. **1934** *N.Z. Alpine Jrnl.* V. XXI. 412 Mt Whitcombe is the 'he-man' peak of the Ramsay and Lyell Valleys. **1937** D. L. SAYERS *Busman's Honeymoon* v. 93 Strong, he-man stuff. **1955** W. GADDIS *Recognitions* I. vi. 204 That wonderful he-man aroma that girls really go for. **1961** *Times* 2 Mar. 15/5 Why is the American way of life now so infantilist..when it was notoriously he-mannish?

d. *He Bible*: the first of the two issues of the Bible printed in 1611, so called from its rendering of Ruth iii. 15.

1878 [see *she bible* (SHE *pers. pron.* 13)]. **1888** J. R. DORE *Old Bibles* (ed. 2) 329 A 'He' Bible used as 'copy' at one printing office, and a 'She' Bible at another. **1911** A. W. POLLARD *Records English Bible* 11. 72 The first edition of the translation is frequently called the He-Bible and the second the She-Bible.

head, *sb.* Add: **1. c.** (Earlier examples.)

13.. *Sir Gawain & Green Knight* 333 Þe stif mon hym bifore stod vpon hyȝt, Herre þen ani in þe hous by þe hede and more. **14..** *ME. Metrical Paraphrase Old Testament* 5160 He was cumly to ken, of breyd and heyghnes als, A bowe all oþer men both be þe hede and þe hals. **1800** *Sporting Mag.* XVI. 104/2 The first heat was..won by Omen, beating Play or Pay by only half a head. **1805** *Ibid.* XXVI. 270/2 He [*sc.* a race-horse]..won his race by a head. **1823** 'J. BEE' *Slang* 94 *Head* (turf), 'won by a head', or 'half-a-head':..is by so much that one horse comes in before another.

d. A headache, esp. such a condition caused by a blow or over-indulgence in liquor.

[**1857** G. A. LAWRENCE *Guy Liv.* iii. 23 Pale men with splitting heads..after a heavy drink.] **1869** TROLLOPE *Phineas Finn* I. xxiii. 189 Don't you know how one feels sometimes that one has got a head? And when that is the case one's armchair is the best place. **1888** KIPLING *Plain Tales fr. Hills* 15 The 'head' that followed after drink. **1889** E. DOWSON *Let.* 18 Feb. (1967) 36, I have not felt myself since my generous allowance of the potent green on Thursday... To day for the first time I awoke without a head. **1889** *St. James's Gaz.* 10 Aug. 3/2 He is decidedly feverish, and, in the pleasing vernacular of the modern youth about town, he has a 'head' on him. **1906** *'Varsity* 17 May 323/3 One has not gone to bed over-night to wake up with a 'head' consequent on over-indulgence in the flowing bowl. **1919** *Punch* 22 Jan. 67 *Sailor.* The only time I smoked it [*sc.* opium] was in China, an' for three days I 'ad an 'ead on me like a smoke barrage. **1928** R. MACAULAY *Keeping up Appearances* xxv. 291 'God, I've got a head.' 'You look rotten..better go straight to bed.' **1938** D. SMITH *Dear Octopus* II. ii. 64 She was lying down with a head. **1954** I. MURDOCH *Under Net* x. 131 It was no use..my trying to think it all out,.. especially with the head I still had. **1961** J. WADE *Back to Life* xi. 164, I get one of those blinding heads. **1973** B. GRAEME *Two & Two make Five* ii. 12 'How long have you been suffering these heads?' 'For months now..they have become more frequent.'

e. *a good* or *strong head*: see STRONG *a.* 2 d; *a good* (or *bad*, etc.) *head for heights*: a feeling of security (insecurity) when at an unaccustomed distance above the ground.

c **1810** W. HICKEY *Mem.* (1960) ii. 36, I replied that I could drink as much as the best of them and..I had, for such a youngster, a tolerable strong head. **1822** [see STRONG *a.* 2 d]. **1932** E. BOWEN *To North* xiii. 131 Markie had a good head; if he had been very drunk he was not drunk now. **1935** *Discovery* Dec. 351/2 A silly old man who tried to please a ridiculous enthusiast of a girl by climbing about on towers when he had no head for heights. **1947** A. MENEN *Prevalence of Witches* ix. 159 Most people have a bad head for heights. **1954** I. MURDOCH *Under Net* vi. 98, I..looked at the drop, and decided that I was not a daring fellow. I have no head for heights.

2. c. *to have a* (*good*) *head* (*up*)*on one's shoulders*: to be sensible, able, proficient; *to have a head for* (figures, etc.): to be adept at; *to have an old head on young shoulders*: see SHOULDER *sb.* 2 c.

1812 M. EDGEWORTH *Absentee* in *Tales Fash. Life* (1848) II. xvi. 244 Lady Dashfort, who had always.. 'her head upon her shoulders'. **1883** [see SHOULDER *sb.* 2 c]. **1886** [in Dict., sense 2 a]. **1930** J. B. PRIESTLEY *Angel Pavement* vi. 301 You say I haven't a head for business. **1931** *Times Lit. Suppl.* 1 Oct. 742/2 He had a head for figures. **1932** A. J. WORRALL *Eng. Idioms* 42 Young Brown will go far; he has a good head on his shoulders. **1939** G. B. SHAW *Good King Charles* I. 61 It is not your fault that you have no head for politics.

3. b. *heads I win,* (*and*) *tails you lose*, I win whatever happens.

1832 A. FONBLANQUE *Eng. under 7 Admin.* (1837) II. 302 They would play the toss up with the creditor on the terms 'Heads I win, tails you lose'. **1846** [in Dict.]. **1909** F. M. FORD *Let.* 29 Jan. (1965) 33 This is an arrangement for Wells of an entirely 'Heads, I win. Tails, you lose'. **1958** *Times* 17 Oct. 17/1 The heads-I-win, tails-you-lose sort of argument between the conscious and the unconscious.

c. A postage-stamp: so called from the figure of the sovereign's head. (Cf. *queen's head*, QUEEN *sb.* 14 b.) *colloq.* or *dial.*

1840 R. H. BARHAM *Let.* 30 July in R. H. D. Barham *Life* (1870) II. viii. 99 One of those abominable little heads which the wisdom of our Post Office people has invented. **1854** R. S. SURTEES *Handley Cross* (rev. ed.) xix. 147 Take that to the Post, and mind you don't pick the 'ead off. **1859** *Punch* 17 Dec. 243/1 We signed it and sealed it, and put it into a hangvelop, and stuck a ned on it, and put it into the Post. **1927** G. STURT *Small Boy in Sixties* i. 2 One very curious request would sometimes come from a villager; the man or woman asking for 'a head'.

7. e. A drug-addict or drug-taker; freq. with defining word prefixed, as *HOPHEAD, *pot-head*; also *transf. slang* (orig. *U.S.*).

1911 [see *HOPHEAD 1]. **1936** L. DUNCAN *Over Wall* i. 21, I saw the more advanced narcotic addicts.., laudanum fiends, and last but not least, the veronal heads. **1955** *U.S. Senate Hearings* (1956) VIII. 4164 Terms for morphine addicts: 'Hype', 'Hygelo', 'Head', [etc.]. **1959** N. MAILER *Advts. for Myself* (1961) 438 There was a horde: movie stars who left early,.. councillors, potheads (discreet to be sure), hoodlums, [etc.]. **1966** *Observer* 25 Sept. 21/6 You've been to the delicatessen, of course, that's where the acid-heads and pot-heads assemble. **1969** *It* 11–24 Apr. 3/3 Berlin is alive with heads, dropping acid and STP in cinemas, parks, buses. *Ibid.* 18–31 July 9/4 Nightride was taken from a spot so convenient to many music heads and put on at an awkward hour. **1970** K. PLATT *Pushbutton Butterfly* xiii. 149 A punchy Hell's Angel tea-head. **1973** *Daily Mail* 3 Apr. 19/4 *Heads*, habitual users of drugs, divided into acid heads (LSD) and potheads (cannabis).

8. q. = POMMEL *sb.* 5. Cf. *leaping-head* (LEAPING *vbl. sb.* b).

1850 S. C. WAYTE *Equestrian's Manual* VI. 166 There are people who say *no* to the off head being cut off, as if in case a lady is nervous she cannot steady herself so well as when the head is left on. *Ibid.*, The saddler must have the head (or what we call the pummel) of the saddle to begin upon, and the further that can be carried forward the better. **1891** A. T. FISHER *Through Stable & Saddle-Room* xiii. 117 In some provincial, but nowadays in no well-made London saddles, the head of the saddle is cut back towards the seat. **1963** E. H. EDWARDS *Saddlery* xiv. 96

The head and gullet are strengthened with steel plates and there is also a steel reinforcement laid on to the underside of the tree from the head to the cantle.

r. The closed end of a cylinder of a pump or engine, esp. an internal-combustion engine; a cylinder-head or cylinder-cover.

1884, 1895 [see *cylinder head* s.v. *CYLINDER *sb.* 9 b]. **1904** A. B. F. YOUNG *Compl. Motorist* iv. 111 The cylinders consist of two separate parts. The body of the cylinder proper is a cast-iron liner... The head—containing the vertical valves and ignition-plug—is a separate casting. **1907** R. B. WHITMAN *Motor-Car Princ.* i. 5 While in the great majority of steam engines the steam acts first on one side of the piston and then on the other, in an automobile gasoline engine the pressure is exerted on only one side, the combustion of the mixture taking place between the piston and the closed end, or head, of the cylinder. **1965** P. H. SMITH *High-Speed Two-Stroke Petrol Engine* xiii. 258 On air-cooled engines, non-detachable heads are generally confined, in the case of iron castings, to the simplest and cheapest industrial engines.

s. Of a bicycle frame (see quot. 1904). Also *attrib.*

1887 BURY & HILLIER *Cycling* (1889) xiv. 321 Beneath the head and between the forks is placed the trouser guard. **1902** *Captain* VII. 82/1 That going from the head to the crank bracket is made duplex. **1904** GOODCHILD & TWENEY *Technol. & Sci. Dict.* 282/2 *Head* (Cycles), the socket or hollow tube through which the tube carrying the front fork runs. **1959** *Sears, Roebuck Catal.* Spring & Summer 1017/1 Universal Head Bearing Set... Fits all bicycles.

t. Of an explosive shell.

1898 [see *war-head* (WAR *sb.*[1] 11)]. **1899** *Kynoch Jrnl.* Oct.–Nov. 17/1 The head [of a shrapnel shell] is attached to the body by means of small rivets.

11. c. (Additional examples.)

1930 L. M. DAVIES in P. O'Connell *Science of To-Day* (1959) II. xii. 75 'Head' is a term applied to this rubble-drift where it masks an old raised beach. **1934** *Antiquity* VIII. 305 The angular deposit..corresponds to what is termed 'head' in Devon and Cornwall.

f. *Curling* and *Bowls*. (See quots. 1897.)

1828 *Kilmarnock Treat. Curling* (1883) 79 Head (probably a corruption of *heat*,) that portion of the game in which both parties play all their stones once. **1877** *Encycl. Brit.* VI. 713 [Curling Rules.] All matches to be of a certain number of heads. **1897** *Encycl. Sport* I. 129/1 (Bowls) *End*—One delivery of all the bowls upon the two sides, after which the jack is again 'set'. Also called Head. *Ibid.* 264/1 (Curling) *Head*, the portion of the game in which all the players have delivered their stones, and have counted the winning shot or shots. **1969** R. WELSH *Beginner's Guide Curling* xvi. 104 All matches shall be of a certain number of Heads, or Shots, or by Time as may be agreed on, or as fixed by the Umpire at the outset.

g. A device designed to convert variations in an electrical signal into variations in the motion of a stylus (in the making of a gramophone record) or *vice versa* (in the playing of one). Also, a device in which a small electromagnet is similarly used to produce or respond to variations in the magnetization of magnetic tape as the tape is moved past it. Freq. with defining word(s), as *cutting head, erase head, magnetic head* (see the defining words in Supplement).

1951 *Catal. Exhibits S. Bank Exhib., Festival of Brit.* 143/1 Gramophone pick-up with interchangeable heads. **1960** COOKE & MARKUS *Electronics & Nucleonics Dict.* 207/1 *Head.* 1. The photoelectric unit that converts the sound track on motion-picture film into corresponding audio signals in a motion-picture projector. 2. Cutter. 3. Magnetic head. **1962** L. DEIGHTON *Ipcress File* xxvii. 172 He laid a huge shiny L.P. on the..turntable and delicately applied the diamond head. **1962** A. NISBETT *Technique Sound Studio* 255 *Head*, transducer which converts electrical energy into magnetic or mechanical energy, or vice versa. Thus we have a tape recording and reproducing heads and disc cutter and pick-up heads. The electromagnet used for erasing tape is also called a head. **1963** *Which?* Jan. 8/2 The pick up is composed of two parts—an arm, and at the end of the arm..a head. The head contains the cartridge, and set into the cartridge is the stylus. **1964** *Honeywell Gloss. Data Proc.* 29/1 *Head*, a device that reads, records or erases information in a storage medium, e.g., a small electromagnet used to read, write or erase information on a magnetic drum or tape, or the set of perforating, reading or marking devices and block assembly used for punching, reading or printing on paper tape. **1964** F. L. WESTWATER *Electronic Computers* (ed. 2) iv. 68 Each track must have its read/write head.

13. b. The top of a book. Cf. HEADBAND 3.

1835 J. HANNETT *Bibliopegia* 26 The book is now taken between the hands and well beaten up at the back and head on a smooth board, to bring the sheets level and square. **1876** *Encycl. Brit.* IV. 43/1 The object of the binder in this operation is to make every page of uniform size, presenting a smooth and equal 'head', 'tail', and 'fore-edge'. **1930** *Godfrey's Catal.* No. 134. 26/1 Folio, old sheep (roughly repaired at head and heel).

c. A headline in a newspaper.

1911 H. S. HARRISON *Queed* xviii. 230 The Chronicle that afternoon shrieked it under a five-column head. **1915** J. WEBSTER *Patty & Priscilla* xi. 170 A life-size portrait of her..appeared in a New York evening paper, and scare-heads three inches high announced..that the champion athlete..was at death's door. **1962** *Amer. Speech* XXXVII. 200 A *Saturday Evening Post* editorial head: 'Good News.' **1967** *Guardian* 2 Nov. 8/7 'Ebullient Mr Brown hits out,' said the (changed) head on the last edition.

19. c. (*a*) *Phonetics.* The initial stressed element(s) in a sequence of sounds before the nucleus. (*b*) *Linguistics.* (See quot. 1964[1].)

1922 H. E. PALMER *Eng. Intonation* v. 17 Any syllable or syllables preceding the nucleus in the same Tone-Group is termed the 'Head' of the group. **1961** R. B. LONG *Sentence & its Parts* i. 20 Headed units are made up of (1) contained heads and (2) contained modifiers which attach to these heads. **1964** R. H. ROBINS *Gen. Ling.* vi. 236 The word or group sharing the syntactic functions of the whole of a subordinative construction is called the head, and the other components are subordinate. Thus in English adjective noun groups, the noun is head and the adjective subordinate. In adverb adjective groups the adjective is head and the adverb subordinate..; in *reasonably clever boys*, *boys* is head and *reasonably clever* is subordinate, and within this latter group *clever* is head and *reasonably* is subordinate. **1964** M. SCHUBIGER in D. Abercrombie et al. *Daniel Jones* 263, I am using the term head for the first stressed element pitched high. **1964** *Amer. Speech* XXXIX. 37 Nice city home... All the ten fine old stone houses. In these sequences the noun is more intimately tied to the head than is the adjective. *Ibid.* 38 A noun that has 'widespread' use as attributive to many different heads is an adjective.

21. d. A ship's latrine (in the bows). Often (in the U.K., usually) in *pl.* In the U.S. also used of W.C.s ashore.

1748 SMOLLETT *R. Random* I. xxviii. 253 The madman ..took an opportunity, while the centinel attended him at the head, to leap over-board. **1905** *Trans. Inst. Naval Archit.* XLVII. I. 29 The W.C.s for officers, and the seamen's head for the crew, are to be fitted where shown on the drawings. **1938** C. S. FORESTER *Ship of Line* 21 You'll clean out the heads of this ship every day. **1952** 'E. BOX' *Death in Fifth Position* (1954) iv. 85, I saw Louis coming out of the head with a blond footman. **1957** *Partisan Rev.* 328 Yet it had happened and here I was, talking about algebra to a lot of boys who might..be popping off needles every time they went to the head. **1965** J. R. HETHERINGTON *Selina's Aunt* 48 The rating who cleans them is Captain of the Heads. **1972** *Daily Colonist* (Victoria, B.C.) 20 Jan. 28/2 The head, or shipboard bathroom, for women crew members is to be the same one that male crew members now use exclusively.

26. c. *Rugby Football.* In full *loose head*: in the front row of the scrummage the forward closest to the scrum half as he puts the ball into the scrummage; *to win the ball against the head*, to hook the ball notwithstanding the fact that the opposition front row holds the advantage by having a player in the loose-head position.

1917 in P. Jones *War Lett.* (1918) 259 We used to spend hours arguing over anything, from free-will to the 'loose-head'. **1959** *Times* 7 Sept. 16/2 A heel against the loose head was a prelude to Coventry's next try. **1960** *Times* 30 Nov. 3/6 He even managed to win the ball against the head in a five-yard scrummage.

35. on..head. e. *to do it* (*standing*) *on one's head*: to do it with ease. *slang.*

1896 G. B. SHAW *Our Theatres in Nineties* (1932) II. 227 Of course, Mr Waring does the thing on his head, so to speak; but how can I compliment an actor who has done what he has done on stuff like that? **1897** CONRAD *Nigger of Narcissus* i. 7 It's a 'omeward trip... Bad or good I can do it hall on my 'ed. **1922** A. A. MILNE *Red House Myst.* xvi, Right, old boy. Leave it to me. I can do this on my head. **1923** *Westm. Gaz.* 19 Mar., Mr. Wells, assuming the best Cockney accent, intimated that he could 'do it on 'is 'ead'. **1944** M. SHARP *Cluny Brown* xvi. 109 If there was one thing Betty could do on her head, it was handle a compliment. **1968** J. M. WHITE *Nightclimber* viii. 60 The climb he wanted me to attempt was a simple one. At Cambridge I could have done it standing on my head.

36. out of one's head. b. Out of one's mind. Chiefly *U.S.*

1825 J. NEAL *Bro. Jonathan* I. 267 You are out o' your head, I guess. **1878** H. JAMES *Fr. Poets & Novelists* 428 Pathelin pretends to be out of his head. **1902** C. E. JEFFERSON *Quiet Hints Preachers* xiii. 103 If they could not understand what was going on they..might think Christians out of their head.

38. b. *to go to* (some)one's *head*: (*a*) to intoxicate; cf. Go *v.* 37 b; (*b*) to make one vain or proud.

1912 A. LUNN *Oxf. Mountaineering Essays* ix. 233 The delight of watching distant hills..went to my head like wine. **1939** A. CHRISTIE *Ten Little Niggers* x. 143 He's played God Almighty for a good many months every year. That must go to a man's head eventually. **1942** —— *Body in Library* xii. 108 He settled a large sum of money on Frank... It went to Frank's head.

39. ¶ *head over ears* (later example).

1912 G. B. SHAW *Let.* 22 Dec. in *Times* (1968) 19 Oct. 19/5, I plunged in head over ears and..wrote off my 56 years.

39*. head in the air. *to go about with one's head in the air*: to assume a pose of superiority. Hence *head-in-air*, designating either one who is absent-minded and dreamy or one who is a snob or a 'highbrow', or the actions of such persons.

1848 *English Struwwelpeter* (ed. 4) 21 (*title*) The story of Johnny Head-in-Air. **1903** *Trawl* May 7 The Laureate crost over the lawn with the dreamy head-in-air gait that was known through five parishes round. **1906** RIDER HAGGARD *Benita* iv, On the ship I always thought him rather a head-in-air kind of swell, but he was a splendid fellow. **1942** J. PUDNEY *Dispersal Point* 24 Do not despair For Johnny-head-in-air; He sleeps as sound As Johnny underground.

41*. head and girth. See GIRTH *sb.*[1] 1 b.

43. head to head. Delete † *Obs. rare* and add later examples. Also *transf.*

1799 *Sporting Mag.* XIII. 311/1 The contest here commenced,..the horses never being more than a length asunder, and generally head to head. **1950** J. DEMPSEY *Championship Fighting* 63 Short range. That's the head-to-head slugging range. **1956** *Nature* 4 Feb. 206/2 There is the so-called head-to-head or head-to-tail arrangements. **1966** *B.B.C. Handbk. 1966* 14 Much of the time the BBC's competition is merely head-to-head. **1972** *Time* 17 Apr. 24/1 Until December the Gallup poll did not even pit McGovern in head-to-head polls with President Nixon and Wallace.

44. b. Also *fig.* (In quot. 1924 with contextual omission of *heels.*)

1834 D. CROCKETT *Narr. Life* i. 20, I soon found myself head over heels in love with this girl. **1924** GALSWORTHY *White Monkey* II. vi. 158 They were head over— the family feud stopped that [marriage].

c. *head over tip* = *head over heels.*

1824 P. EGAN *Boxiana* IV. 260 A first-rate *swell*, who was extremely eager to get on board, lost his footing, and went *head* over *tip* into the water. **1906** E. DYSON *Fact'ry 'Ands* xv. 202 Er stream iv water..sluices ther red-'eaded girl..'ead-over-tip down ther front stairs.

46*. heads and posts. Leather heads placed on posts for use in cavalry exercises.

1895 *Army & Navy Co-op. Soc. Price List* 15 Sept. 1456 Heads and Posts. For Military Tournaments. **1902** *Encycl. Brit.* XXVI. 156/1 Courses for jumping and 'heads and posts' exercise. **1907** *Yesterday's Shopping* (1969) 1017/2 Heads and Posts..for Military Tournaments.

47. head and shoulders. c. A portrait in which only the head and shoulders are shown. Freq. *attrib.*

1865 D. G. ROSSETTI *Let.* 30 July (1965) II. 562, I fear all I could undertake with prospect of bringing it to a conclusion without unreasonable delay would be a 'head and shoulders' portrait. **1897** H. B. WHEATLEY *Hist. Portraits* viii. 173 Stoop himself made an etching of this portrait... The picture is described as 'Head and shoulders'. **1902** *Daily Chron.* 7 July 3/5 A head and shoulders portrait of Lady Morshead in white dress and fichu. **1968** R. SAWKINS *Snow along Border* xv. 121 The picture was a head-and-shoulders portrait of a man of about thirty.

d. *head-and-shoulder target*, a target representing a head and shoulders.

1899 *Westm. Gaz.* 23 Nov. 2/2 A hostile force in entrenchments is represented by rows of 'head and shoulder' targets. **1901** *Ibid.* 11 Sept. 3/1 Not only were there the usual head-and-shoulder dummies, but there were several 'surprise' targets.

49*. get one's **head down.** To have a sleep.

1943 in Hunt & Pringle *Service Slang* 35. **1958** 'N. SHUTE' *Rainbow & Rose* 61 I'll have to get my head down for a bit, though, before going out again.

49. have** one's **head examined** (or need one's **head examining**). A jocular phrase suggesting that one is 'off one's head'.

1949 'J. TEY' *Brat Farrar* xxvi. 239 Of all the 'old soldier' tricks to fall for!..I ought to have my head examined. **1954** J. SYMONS *Narrowing Circle* xxxii. 145 Giue me credit for a bit of sense...If I'd behaved in the way you suggest I should need my head examining. **1965** R. MCDOWELL *Hound's Tooth* (1967) vii. 69, I let Bowman persuade me to call in the state police...I should've had my head examined. **1966** J. BINGHAM *Double Agent* ii. 25 If you think these chaps know nuclear secrets..you want your head examined. **1972** *N.Y. Times* 3 Nov. 22/6 Anyone who votes for Nixon ought to have his head examined.

52*. open one's **head.** To speak. *U.S. slang.*

1849 *Neal's Sat. Gaz.* (Phila.) 17 Feb. 1/1 But don't you open yer head about it to no other indiwiddiwal—for I want to supprise the Wiggletown folks, and make 'em open ther eyes a leetle. **1885** H. JACKSON *Zeph* ii. 44 He never opens his head to nobody. **1895** *Century Mag.* Sept. 674/1 I'm glad you didn't open your head about it. **1898** M. DELAND *Old Chester Tales* 307 Jones said..that he hardly opened his head for the whole twenty-one miles.

53*. put a head on. 'To punch or assault another, and figuratively to silence, or shut up another' (Clapin). *U.S. slang.* (Cf.*1 d.)

1868 F. WHYMPER *Trav. Alaska* 283 One calls the other a 'regular dead beat!' at which he, in return, threatens to 'put a head on him!' **1869** *Overland Monthly* III. 63 The gentlemanly proprietor of the premises had kindly volunteered to 'put a head' on the man who fired the pistol. **1876** *Scribner's Monthly* Nov. 142/2 Threats, profanely emphasized, 'to put a head on' me! **1911** R. W. CHAMBERS *Common Law* ii. 46 Kelly will put a head on you!

61. (Further examples.)

1894 G. B. SHAW *Let.* 3 Dec. (1965) 467 You could, at your worst, talk the heads off most of them. **1931** H. CRANE *Let.* 11 Sept. (1965) 379 Yesterday we..worked our heads off digging into the side of a small hill. **1951** J. CORNISH *Provincials* 11 As term progressed, Saturdays and Sundays..we would sit in our den..talking our heads off. **1965** W. SOYINKA *Road* 17 The bishop sermonized his head off.

62*. *to put a pistol to* one's *head*: to commit suicide by shooting; *to put a pistol to* (someone's) *head*: to coerce (someone). Also *fig.*

1841 C. DICKENS *Let.* 26 Feb. (1969) II. 220 Put a penny pistol to Chapman's head, and demand the blocks of him. **1853** THACKERAY *Newcomes* (1854) I. ix. 91 I'm blowed if I don't put a pistol to my 'ead, and end it, Mrs. G. **1896** A. E. HOUSMAN *Shropshire Lad* xliv. 67 And early wise and brave in season [you] Put the pistol to your head.

63. a. *head-waiter* (earlier and later examples).

1805 G. COLMAN *John Bull* I. i. 17 *Dan.*..I be head-

waiter and hostler:—only we never have no horses, nor customers. **1823** L. Minor *Jrnl.* 29 Nov. in *Atlantic Monthly* (1870) XXVI. 171/1 It is a singular spectacle to see a man, who has occupied such high and varied stations, bustling about a tavern at once as landlord, barkeeper, and head waiter. **1971** *Good Food Guide* 484 Rich, male, business customers..will receive highly skilled attention from everybody, starting with the headwaiter and sommelier and going down to the busboy.

64. *head sea* (later example).

1886 R. Brown *Spunyarn & Spindrift* ix. 167 A head-sea began to heave up.

65. a. *head-flannel, -wrap.*

1861 Mrs. Beeton *Bk. Househ. Managem.* 1021 The infant..must not be exposed to strong light, or too much air; and in carrying it about the passages, stairs, &c., the nurse should always have its head-flannel on. **1880** Advt. in L. Higgin *Handbk. Embroidery* 106 Babies' Headflannels, from £1 3s. **1896** *Godey's Mag.* Feb. 202/1 Fastening..a sombre head-wrap over her..hair. **1905** *Daily Chron.* 15 May 3/3 A hood of this kind..will obviate any necessity for the wearing of those head-wraps.

b. *head-scratching* (also *fig.*), *-shaking* (additional examples), *-splitting*; *head-scratcher* (also *fig.*), *-shaker*. Cf. Shake *v.* 6 b.

1936 J. B. Priestley *They walk in City* 375 A pair of tweezers and a head-scratcher from Ur of the Chaldees. **1969** E. H. Pinto *Treen* ii. 26 The plain lignum vitae, English head scratcher..was typical of that 18th-century elegance which accepted public poking of wigs and itching heads as normal. **1971** *Daily Colonist* (Victoria, B.C.) 22 July 1/1 Now, the head-scratcher is how interest rates can be going up. **1926** J. S. Huxley *Ess. Biologist* v. 178 It was a hard nut for them, and there was much head-scratching. **1958** *Times* 22 Oct. 14/3 It is now that the Rugby football captains get down to their real head-scratching. **1973** *Times* 3 July 23/4 If it is cleared without reference, then there will be more head scratching. **1927** H. G. Wells in *Sunday Express* 1 May 12/3 The Gummidge chorus is never silent; the thoughtful headshaker moping for a return to medievalism casts his daily shadow on every patch of sunshine. **1958** *Times Lit. Suppl.* 14 Mar. 140/3 Even the contemplative Henry James became a head-shaker. **1869** Geo. Eliot *Lett.* (1955) V. 54 Best love to Sara—and some headshaking at her tendency to work too hard. **1961** *Times* 11 Mar. 3/3 Both new works caused widespread discussion and much head-shaking. **1903** W. J. Locke *Where Love Is* (1904) i. 3 Discussing the functions of art and other such head-splitting matters. **1953** W. Stevens *Let.* 8 Dec. (1967) 804, I sat..listening to platitudes propounded as if they were head-splitting perceptions.

66. head arrangement *Jazz* (see quot. 1946); **head-ball** *Cricket*, a cunningly-bowled ball; so **head bowler, bowling**; **head-carry** *v.*, to carry (a load) on one's head; **head-cheese** (earlier and later examples); **head-clause** *Gram.*, the principal clause; **head-cover** *Mil.*, protection for the head, *spec.* a shield for protection against gun-fire; *Fortif.* (see quot. 1892); **head dip** *Surfing* (see quots.); **head doctor** *slang*, a psychiatrist; **head-feast**, a feast in celebration of successful head-hunting; **head-fold** (see quots.); **head-form**, (*a*) the form of the head, *spec.* in reference to the ratio of its breadth to its length; (*b*) the first word in a dictionary or glossary entry, lemma; **head girl** (see quot. 1963); also *transf.*; **headlamp**, one of the headlights of a (motor) vehicle; **head-load**, a load carried on the head; so **head-load** *v.*; **head-lock, -locking**, (*a*) (see quots.); (*b*) *Wrestling* (see quot. 1961); **head metal** *Founding*, the head of metal at the upper end of a cylindrical casting (see Dead-head 2 a); **head-reach** *v.* (later example); also *trans.*; **head-register** (see quots. and Register *sb.*[1] 8 b); also *attrib.*; **head resistance**, resistance of a fluid to the movement of a body through it; **head-right** *U.S.*, an inheritable right to land, formerly granted by the state of Texas to the heads of immigrating families; **head-ring**, (*b*) (examples); **head-scarf, headscarf**, a scarf worn instead of a hat; hence **head-scarved** *a.*; **headset**, (*a*) a pair of earphones; (*b*) a combination of earphones and a microphone as worn by a telephone exchange operator; **head-shaking**, a display by certain birds at mating or egg-laying (see also sense 65 b in Dict. and Suppl.); so **head-shake** *v.*; **head-shrinker**, (*a*) a head-hunter who preserves and shrinks human heads; (*b*) *slang* (orig. *U.S.*) a psychiatrist; so (sense (*a*)) **head-shrinking** *vbl. sb.*; **head-shy** *a.*, of animals: afraid of having the head touched; so **head-shyness**; **head start**, an advantage at the beginning of a race; also *transf.*; *spec.* (with capitals) the name of an educational and welfare programme in the United States; **head-station** (further examples); also *N.Z.*; **head-stream, -tributary**, a head-water stream or tributary; **head-tie**, a head-band or scarf worn by women, esp. among peoples of African origin; **head-up** *Aeronautics*, used *attrib.* of a visual display system by which the pilot is able to read his instruments without averting his eyes from the aircraft's course; also, such a system in a motor vehicle; **head-wall** *Phys. Geogr.*, the steep slope at the head of a glaciated valley, esp. a cliff that rises abruptly from the floor of a cirque; **head-word**, (*b*) *Gram.* a word modified by another word or words; (*c*) = **head* *sb.* 19 c (*b*); = **head-form* (*b*).

1946 R. Blesh *Shining Trumpets* (1949) xi. 251 'Head' arrangement. *footnote.* A memorized, not written arrangement, that leaves ample room for improvisation. **1949** L. Feather *Inside Be-bop* iii. 21 He'd help to set up ideas for head arrangements. **1958** N. D. Hinton in *Publ. Amer. Dialect Soc.* xxx. 46 Head arrangement, a musical arrangement which is not written down and never has been, but is known by all the members of the ensemble. **1968** *Jazz Monthly* Feb. 21/1 The functional scoring of *John's idea, Shorty George* and *Cherokee* was the work of Jimmy Mundy,..the remainder probably being head arrangements. **1870** *Baily's Monthly Mag.* July 295 Alfred Shaw..is one of the few bowlers..qualified to attempt a 'head ball'. **1902** *Westm. Gaz.* 11 Aug. 7/1 Self-restraint that not even the most tempting 'head-balls' of Lockwood and of Rhodes could overcome. **1870** F. Gale in *New Sporting Mag.* New Ser. LX. 35, I must.. see another little square man..before I believe that a better head bowler ever lived than Lillywhite. **1867** G. H. Selkirk *Guide Cricket Ground* ii. 28 Head Bowling. **1957** R. Campbell *Portugal* 84 Trundling, head-carrying, or pedalling their various contraptions. **1968** *Times* (Pakistan Suppl.) 6 Apr. p. v/5 For eight or more hours a day, he head-carries his dish of earth from one spot to another and his pay is about three rupees, or roughly 4s. **1841** *Southern Lit. Messenger* VII. 39/2 The animal..may be traced in the stewed chine and souse, the head cheese and sausages. **1891** H. Frederick *Copperhead* (1894) 255 Reducing what remained of the [pig's] head into small bits, to be seasoned..and then fill other pans as head-cheese. **1942** C. Morley *Thorofare* (1943) xli. 159 Yes, Ma'am, over here we call it headcheese, but I remember my old gramp called it brawn. **1970** C. Major *Dict. Afro-Amer. Slang* 65 *Headcheese*, various cheap grades of pork meat prepared and sold as lunch meat. **1928** H. Poutsma *Gram. Late Mod. Eng.* (ed. 2) 38 A subordinate statement with modal *may* often stands with a head-clause containing *possible.* **1957** R. W. Zandvoort *Handbk. Eng. Gram.* I. iv. 62 The *perfect of experience*..is not unknown in other languages, at least in head-clauses, though an adjunct expressing repetition is usually added. **1890** Ld. Lugard *Diary* 26 Mar. (1959) I. iv. 160 Along the top [of the Stockade] a log for head cover, and line below it for firing. **1892** F. Irwin *Fortification* (ed. 2) 37 Always place head-cover on wall when firing over the top. **1916** 'Boyd Cable' *Action Front* 229 It's a good foot and a half I have of head-cover. **1923** Kipling *Irish Guards in Gt. War* I. 24 The Battalion..next day quietly improved trenches and head-cover. **1962** *Austral. Women's Weekly* Suppl. 24 Oct. 3/2 *Head dip*, trick riding—putting head in and out of a wave while riding it. **1963** *Observer* 13 Oct. 15/5 The 'head dip', in which the rider bends double and dips his head into the wave at his feet. **1956** 'E. McBain' *Cop Hater* (1958) xxi. 177 'What's the matter with this guy?' 'Nothing that a head doctor couldn't cure,' Byrnes said. **1959** M. Dolinsky *There is no Silence* vii. 114, I was impressed in spite of my previous opinions about 'head doctors'. **1971** 'A. Blaisdell' *Practice to Deceive* xiv. 210 Getting let loose by some damn-fool head doctor. **1882** H. De Windt *On Equator* 82 These 'Head Feasts' are general among the aboriginal tribes throughout the island of Borneo. **1890** Billings *Med. Dict.*, *Head-fold*, a fold of the blastoderm under the cephalic end of the embryo. **1893** A. M. Marshall *Vert. Embryol.* 226 The head of the embryo is lifted up above the yolk-sac by an anterior constriction or head fold. **1885** J. Beddoe *Races of Britain* xiii. 259 The principal ethnical elements in Britain are too much alike in headform to yield their differences to an average constructed on but a few living heads. **1903** *Biometrika* II. 505 We are ignorant..of the characters of such a race, of its variability, for instance in head-, nose- or hair-form. **1927** Peake & Fleure *Peasants & Potters* 128 There can be little doubt that profile and head-form have subtle..interrelations. **1935** *Proc. Prehist. Soc.* I. 4 The particulate inheritance of the several genes determining head-form. **1962** K. Malone in Householder & Saporta *Probl. Lexicogr.* 112 Here such verbs are listed in full, and the irregular forms of each verb are entered against the head-form. **1846** C. M. Yonge in *Mag. for Young* 2 Sept. 196 At school..she went to.. the head girl. **1919** A. Brazil (*title*) The Head Girl at the Gables. **1941** *Brit. Jrnl. Psychol.* Jan. 194 The 'head-girls' [in a factory] wear an overall different in colour. **1963** Barnard & Lauwerys *Handbk. Brit. Educ. Terms* 104 *Head boy/girl*, a boy or girl appointed or elected as a leader of the other pupils, and who traditionally in public schools has considerable responsibilities for the maintenance of discipline acting through prefects. **1964** M. Drabble *Garrick Year* xii. 179, I was a prefect, but I wasn't head girl. **1885** Kipling *Phantom 'Rickshaw* in *Quartette* 96 It [*sc.* a rickshaw] lay in readiness in the Mall, and..with a lighted head-lamp. **1912** *Motor Man.* (ed. 14) iii. 123 Paraffin Head-lamps. **1961** *Times* 25 Apr. 17/3 The first British production car to be fitted with two pairs of twin headlamps. **1972** *Country Life* 7 Dec. 1592/3 The brakes were effective..and wipers and headlamps very good. **1927** W. H. Todd *Tiger, Tiger!* 20 Carrying head-loads of sand. **1957** M. Banton *W. Afr. City* iv. 67 Head-loading someone's baggage or helping to take goods out of a lorry. **1959** *Times* (Ghana Suppl.) 9 Nov. p. iv/1 Much of the cocoa starts its journey to the coast by being head-loaded along the bush tracks. **1971** J. Spencer *Eng. Lang. W. Afr.* 29 *Head-load* (a term now surely becoming obsolescent with the advent of mechanical modes of transport). **1901** Dorland *Med. Dict.* (ed. 2), *Head-lock*, the locking together of the chins in twin labor. **1905** F. R. Toombs *How to Wrestle* (1906) 107 Secure a head lock by putting your left forearm..on the defensive man's head. **1934** J. M. Cain *Postman always rings Twice* x. 109 He's the only one in this town can throw the headlock on Sackett. **1957** *Encycl. Brit.* XXIII (*caption*, facing p. 804), Jim Browning..with a headlock on Danno O'Mahoney. **1961** J. S. Salak *Dict. Amer. Sports* 220 *Headlock*, a hold in which the wrestler encircles the opponent's head with one or both arms. **1973** *Times* 16 Mar. 2/2 They dragged me out of the house and struck me on the head and legs, holding me in a headlock. **1890** Billings *Med. Dict.*, *Head-locking*, in twin labor, one child being born by the breech, its chin catches upon the chin of the second child presenting by the head. **1888** *Lockwood's Dict. Mech. Engin.* s.v., When the casting is removed from the mould the head metal is turned off, leaving the actual casting smooth and free from these foreign impurities. **1960** R. Lister *Decorative Cast Ironwork* 229 *Head metal*, the metal in a feeding head. **1892** *Outing* (U.S.) Apr. 57/1 Soon she had head-reached them all, *Shadow* included, and showed to the front of the fleet. **1938** C. S. Forester *Ship of Line* 276, I want to hear instantly if they alter course, or if they headreach upon us. **1890** Billings *Med. Dict.*, *Head-register*, register in which the pitch is raised by shortening the vocal chords; second falsetto in females. **1909** H. Klein *Phono-Vocal Method* 37 The blending of the medium and head registers will be practised upon the same plan. **1966** H. L. Shorto in C. E. Bazell *In Memory of J. R. Firth* 407 Henderson found that in Cambodian a sequence of head-register consonant and chest-register vowel..was the mark of a secondary pattern. **1889** J. J. Welch *Text Bk. Naval Archit.* iii. 53 This [fluid] resistance is due:—..(2) To the opposition offered to the passage through the water..of projections such as the keel and bilge keels, and of the comparatively flat parts of the ship at the ends: this is known as direct or head resistance. **1891** *Railroad & Engin. Jrnl.* LXV. 465/1 The head or hull resistance will probably be found to be the chief element which will limit the possible speed of flying machines. **1909** *Westm. Gaz.* 1 July 4/1 Allowing a coefficient of ·3 for the pointed ends, the total head-resistance would be reduced to 3,324 lb. **1922** R. Glazebrook *Dict. Appl. Physics* I. 717/1 A second form of eddy resistance developed by a ship, sometimes called 'head resistance', is due to such features as..web supports to the propeller shafts, thick stems, and stern posts. **1934** *Discovery* Dec. 352/2 Another cowl known as a Townend Ring..produces ..a reduction in head resistance. **1959** J. L. Nayler *Dict. Aeronaut. Engin.* 128 *Head resistance*, a term used for the resistance, or drag at no yaw, of the front part of a projectile, the remainder of the drag being due to skin friction and base drag. **1703** in *Amer. Speech* (1961) XXXVI. 152 Head-right. **1799** in O. A. Rothert *Hist. Muhlenberg County* (1913) 45 Colonel William Campbell's head-right.. adjoining the lands [etc.]. **1828** *Laws of Texas* Nov. (Bartlett, 1860), So much of the vacant lands..shall be surveyed and sectionized..as will be sufficient to satisfy all claims for scrip sold, soldier's claims, and head-rights. **1898** H. S. Canfield *Maid of Frontier* i. 13 He owned the headright of 160 acres on which his house was built. **1866** C. Barter *Alone among Zulus* v. 51 When a [Zulu] soldier has attained a certain standing he receives the royal permission to marry, and adopt the head-ring as a mark of manhood. **1952** S. G. Millin *Burning Man* xxv. 227, I have worn the head-ring of a married man for three years. **1921** G. B. Shaw *Back to Methuselah* iii. 101 (*stage direction*) A handsome negress is trying on a brilliant head scarf. **1955** G. Freeman *Liberty Man* i. i. 18 Maureen came out adjusting her headscarf. **1962** D. Harden *Phoenicians* vii. 103 A bearded priest with a head-scarf. **1960** M. Sharp *Something Light* ii. x. 91 A head-scarved plumpish figure. **1970** *Guardian* 13 July 9/3 Head-scarfed refugees. **1921** *Telegr. & Teleph. Jrnl.* Dec. 46/2 Supervisor (speaking on head-set of bewildered learner). **1942** *Tee Emm* (Air Ministry) II. 84 The pilot..should see that his headset plug is firmly in. **1955** 'N. Shute' *Requiem for Wren* 64 A telephone headset strapped across his beret. **1957** *Spaceflight* I. 71/2 Each seat in the auditorium was fitted with a headset and switchbox, by means of which one could select the language one desired. **1970** N. Armstrong et al. *First on Moon* iii. 63 They had to be checked out: the communications consoles, the technician headsets, the purge ventilators. **1930** J. S. Huxley *Bird-Watching & Bird Behaviour* iv. 70 It is doubtless very enjoyable to head-shake together. *Ibid.* v. 95 The head-shaking ceremony. **1959** Bannerman *Birds Brit. Isles* VIII. 217 The second important display is 'head-shaking'. The bird..waggles its head from side to side at another... Birds already paired together frequently head-shake together. **1926** G. M. Dyott *On Trail of Unknown* xii. 173 (*heading*) The head shrinkers. *Ibid.* 190 In the process of head-shrinking, the hair retains its original length and..looks longer than it did on the original man. **1950** *Time* 27 Nov. 19 Anyone who had predicted that he would end up as the rootin'-tootin' idol of U.S. children would have been led instantly off to a headshrinker. **1957** A. Maney in G. Oppenheimer *Passionate Playgoer* (1958) 381 Marcus Heiman, head of the United Booking Office, turned the play over to his psychiatrist. That headshrinker said a play glorifying a drunkard conflicted with public interest. **1958** *Spectator* 22 Aug. 241/2 The head-shrinkers would doubtless say it is the universal human search for a father-figure that is behind it. **1959** T. B. Morris *Death among Orchids* xiii. 121 There are still cannibals... But the worst of them are now..the head-shrinkers. **1968** *New Scientist* 8 Feb. 289/1 Dr. Louis West..may eventually be taking the caviare out of headshrinkers' mouths with his development of the robot psychiatrist. **1970** I. Reed in A. Chapman *New Black Voices* (1972) 516 A vocabulary that calls things by their names: 'headshrinker' and 'egghead'. **1900** M. H. Hayes *Among Horses in Russia* iv. 82 They weren't head-shy, and liked their manes to be scratched. *Ibid.*, Every horseman knows that 'head-shyness' is one of the worst of vices. **1952** J. Steinbeck *East of Eden* 384 A few strokes on the nose will make a puppy head-shy. **1886** in *Amer. Speech* (1950) XXV. 34/1 Fifteen paces, head start. **1911** W. James *Some Probl. Philos.* xi. 180 Owing to the tortoise's head-start, the tortoise's path is only a part of the path of Achilles. **1935** F. Scott Fitzgerald *Let.* (1964) 6 You and Peaches (who isn't selfish, I think) had a superficial head-start with prettiness. **1962** *Economist* 18 Aug. 620/2 The research data needed to give them a head-start in the market. **1965** Mrs. L. B. Johnson *White House*

Diary 3 Feb. (1970) 235 Sarge [Shriver] asked me if I would consider and sponsor the program Head Start. **1968** *Times* 9 Oct. 10/7 If we can give them a head start—..they're going to do as well as other children. **1970** *Washington Post* 30 Sept. 133/1 Volunteers are urgently needed for Head Start and day care programs throughout the Washington area. **1973** *Black World* Mar. 37 Effective or not, the Poverty Program, Headstart, compensatory education programs,..and so on were efforts toward establishing justice for Blacks. **1973** J. Pattinson *Search Warrant* ii. 37 He decided to spend the night in Philadelphia...The other man had a head start anyway. **1862** R. Henning *Let.* 19 Oct. (1966) 111 It is a most eligible spot for a head-station, and the two carpenters have already begun putting up the store. **1895** G. Chamier *South-Sea Siren* xi. 161 [The house] was used as the head-station for a sheep run. **1936** A. Russell *Gone Nomad* iii. 14, I had left the head station at sunrise and ridden all day. **1817** S. R. Brown *Western Gaz.* 8 Navigation..can be pursued up the Coose to one of its head streams. **1899** A. H. Keane *Man Past & Present* 190 Northwards..about the Irawadi head-streams. **1908** *Athenæum* 11 Apr. 456/3 From its head-streams in the glens. **1956** D. L. Linton *Sheffield* p. xxiv, Turning southwards round the headstreams of the Don our boundary passes above the long Woodhead tunnel. **1857** M. Griffith *Autobiogr. Female Slave* i. 17 One gave a yard of ribbon, another a half-paper of pins, a third presented a painted cotton head-tie. **1956** in Cassidy & Le Page *Dict. Jamaican Eng.* (1967) 222/2 [*Head-tie*] a head scarf. **1967** W. Soyinka *Kongi's Harvest* 52 You see yourself How the courtesan is one hour escalating Her brocade head-tie. **1973** *Trinidad Guardian* 1 Feb. 11/1 She was wearing black shoes, a flowered dress and headtie. **1925** N. E. Odell in E. F. Norton *Fight for Everest, 1924* iii. 292 A far-flung head tributary of the Dzakar Chu. **1960** *Times* 15 Dec. 4/3 Mr. Naish said that some 1,200 hours of laboratory 'flying' with the head-up device used in conjunction with the flight simulator had shown that accuracy in following flight directions was twice as good as with the normal instruments. **1968** *New Scientist* 8 Aug. 273/1 A new term has found its way into the cockpits of military aircraft in the past few years. It is 'head-up display'. It connotes a system whereby the pilot can see what tale his instruments are telling without taking his eyes off the scene ahead. *Ibid.* 273/2 Head-up flying is a bonus derived from the application of electronics in many new ways. **1972** *Drive* Spring 43/2 Road-speed reflected in the windscreen glass by the safety-first 'head up' display. **1972** *Times* 14 Sept. 31/1 At present only the drivers of a handful of experimental cars (and the pilots of supersonic aircraft) get the benefit of head-up displays... Smiths are working on head-up displays for family cars. **1904** *Jrnl. Geol.* XII. 570 The canyons, at their heads, were abnormally deep..and their head walls..stood as nearly upright, apparently, as scaling of the rock would permit. **1910** *Geogr. Jrnl.* XXXV. 154 Perhaps because of their small size these cliff glaciers have not developed cirques, though a Bergschrund parallels the generally straight headwall. **1954** W. D. Thornbury *Princ. Geomorphol.* xv. 367 A cirque headwall may be as much as 2000 to 3000 feet high and is notably steep and free from talus at its base, even in empty cirques. **1898** Sweet *New Eng. Gram.* II. § 1759 Thus pre-adjunct or pre-adjective position means that the adjunct-word precedes its head-word. **1939** *English Studies* XXI. 71 It [*sc.* the genitive] was pinned down..to its head-word, first either in front or in post-position, eventually only in front position. **1940** *Ibid.* XXII. 88 *Headwords, attributes* and *adjuncts*, the terms representing their relative importance or ranks within the sentence, headwords coming first. **1957** S. Potter *Mod. Ling.* v. 115 In the phrase *good men* there are two ranks: *men* is the head-word or primary and *good* is the attribute or secondary. **1957** R. W. Zandvoort *Handbk. Eng. Gram.* II. ii. 104 The headword need not be repeated if it occurs earlier or later in the sentence: She put her arm through her mother's. **1961** R. B. Long *Sentence & its Parts* v. 121 But in true phrasal passives the auxiliaries set the time for actions whose semantic centers are the head-word participles. **1964** M. Schubiger in D. Abercrombie et al. *Daniel Jones* 258 Restrictive relative clauses preceded by their head-words. **1966** *English Studies* LXVII. 211 Head-words..appear in their West-Saxon variant. **1967** *Listener* 26 Oct. 545/3 (Advt.), 97,000 headwords.

Head (hed). The name of Sir Henry *Head* (1861–1940), English neurologist, used *attrib.* and in the possessive with reference to his work on sensation, etc.

1908 *Jrnl. Nerv. & Mental Dis.* XXXV. 576 (*title*) On the hyperesthetic areas (Head's zones) in visceral disease. *Ibid.* 577 His experience would not corroborate Dr. Bloomfield's as to the great value of Head's test. *Ibid.*, Dr. McCarthy asked in what percentage of tuberculous cases Dr. Ludlum found the distinct Head sign. *Ibid.* 578 Head's lines cannot be elicited in chronic cases. *Ibid.*, That patient still shows Head's lines. **1910** *Practitioner* Jan. 119 Some of the headache of pyorrhœa alveolaris may be reflex (*cf.* Head's areas). **1913** Dorland *Med. Dict.* (ed. 7) s.v. *Zone*, *Head's zones*, areas of cutaneous sensitiveness associated with diseases of the viscera: called also zones of hyperalgesia. **1941** *Brit. Jrnl. Psychol.* XXXII. i. 6 Physiological experiments upon the action of the vagus nerve in respiratory movements..[which were recorded] by the use of a strip of the diaphragm (known henceforth as 'Head's strip'). **1961** *Brain* LXXXIV. 530 He [*sc.* Head] devised the preparation which is known as the 'Head's diaphragm slip preparation'. *Ibid.* 533, I suggest the possibility that this gasping response in the newborn baby is in fact Head's Paradoxical Reflex. *Ibid.* 532 The Head Reflex is carried in small unmyelinated fibres.

head, *v.* Add: **9.** Also with *up*. Chiefly *N. Amer.*

1959 E. Lipsky *Scientists* 178 Bronco and I feel you're the logical one to head up a committee. **1968** *Globe & Mail* (Toronto) 17 Feb. B7 (Advt.), Company..requires capable and professional person..to head up real estate department. **1971** *Daily Tel.* 21 Oct. 10 (Advt.), We need women who can head up the book department of several of our branches throughout England and Wales.

12. *intr.* Also *fig.*

1903 G. B. Shaw *Man & Superman* II. 56, I rather think Rhoda is heading for a row with Ann. **1922** H. Crane *Let.* 7 Nov. (1965) 104 Matty's trans[lations] from Soupault in the last *Broom* are undoubtedly clever, but I don't see how he can rave so...Where is he headed for, anyway?

13. b. (Earlier example of *head off*.)

1841 J. F. Cooper *Deerslayer* v. 29 But 'head him off', as you say of the deer.

c. *N.Z.* (See quot. 1933.)

1933 L. G. D. Acland in *Press* (Christchurch, N.Z.) 28 Oct. 15/7 A dog goes round to the far side of a mob of sheep and stops them. This is called heading... The owner would also say 'I can head with him'. **1934** J. Lilico *Sheep Dog Mem.* 27 [The dogs] would head, lead, huntaway, force and back, though, of course, they were best at rouseabout work. **1947** P. Newton *Wayleggo* (1949) v. 52 This dog would 'head a nor'wester'.

head, colloq. abbrev. of *headlight.

1959 I. Jefferies *13 Days* vi. 75 He..flashed his heads just as I got abreast. **1969** 'A. Hall' *Striker Portfolio* ix. 112 My undipped heads catching the Mercedes full across the screen. **1971** —— *Warsaw Document* xxii. 279 The patrol-car coming at us with the heads full on.

headache. Add: **1. b.** Phr. *to be no more use than* (or *as good as*) *a* (*sick*) *headache*: said of something quite useless. *colloq.*

1915 D. O. Barnett *Lett.* 153 Shrapnel is for defenders, to stop an advance of infantry, but no more use against prepared positions than a sick headache. **1927** D. L. Sayers *Unnatural Death* I. v. 50 That woman..was no more use than a headache—to use my brother's rather vigorous expression. **1931** W. Holtby *Poor Caroline* vi. 225 The Tona Perfecta's no more use to any company today than a sick headache. **1963** *Guardian* 3 Dec. 5/5 The car's contract of sale gives no undertaking or guarantee except the usual one—and that is as good as a sick headache.

c. A troublesome or annoying problem. *colloq.* (orig. *U.S.*).

1934 M. Weseen *Dict. Amer. Slang* 347 *Headache*, anxiety; worry. **1937** *Punch* 1 Dec. 610/1 My headache is this—the Big Guy, my boss, won't go to the movies and see for himself what a newspaper girl can do. **1939** G. B. Gilbert *Forty Years a Country Preacher* 77 The new rectory was both beautiful and expensive, but it proved to be a great headache. **1942** 'H. Habe' *Thousand shall Fall* ix. 181, I asked him how we were expected to transport all these goods. He shrugged his shoulders. 'That's your headache!' **1945** *Times* 11 Jan. 2/4 Commander Bower continued: 'The biggest headache of all is undoubtedly Poland.' **1952** N. Streatfeild *Aunt Clara* 251 They're my headache, not yours. **1968** *New Scientist* 25 Jan. 205/1 The single-celled organism *Euglena* is rather a headache for those who would like to divide living things neatly into plants and animals.

headachiness. (Earlier example.)

1862 Geo. Eliot *Let.* 1 May (1956) IV. 28 In a moment of feverish headachiness I transgressed my own rule.

headachy, *a.* **1.** (Earlier examples.)

1795 Lady Newdigate *Let.* Aug. in A. E. Newdigate-Newdegate *Cheverels* (1898) xi. 154 Want of sleep..makes me feel Languid & headachy in a Morning. **1813** Jane Austen *Let.* 29 Jan. (1952) 298, I was rather headachey that day & could not venture on anything sweet except jelly.

headage (he·dèdʒ). [f. Head *sb.* 7 c + -age.] The number of animals; = Head *sb.* 7 c. Also *attrib.*

1957 *Liverpool Daily Post* 30 Jan. 5/9 Abbey-Cwm-Hir..Fox Destruction Society have decided to pay headage money on rabbits and carrion crows, as well as foxes, that are killed in the society's area. **1960** *Farmer & Stockbreeder* 5 Jan. 91/1 A headage price [for a steer] of 22,356 dollars. **1962** *Times* (Agric. Suppl.) 3 July p. ii/3 Winter reserves of fodder to carry a greatly increased headage of stock. **1972** *Guardian* 30 Dec. 4/7 'Headage' subsidies for sheep flocks are ruled out by the EEC commission.

headband. Add: **1. c.** The band connecting a pair of receivers or ear-phones.

1913 *Work* 17 May 145/3 Double Receivers, with adjustable head-band. **1962** A. Nisbett *Technique Sound Studio* 256 *Headphones*, a pair of electro-acoustic transducers..held to the ears by a headband.

head-block. Add: **4.** (See quot. 1905.)

1853 *Trans. Mich. Agric. Soc.* IV. 35 G. S. Snyder, Lancaster O. improved head block for setting logs on saw mills. **1905** *Terms Forestry & Logging* 39 *Head block*, the log placed under the front end of the skids in a skidway to raise them to the desired height.

head-chief. *U.S.* [Head *sb.* 63.] The paramount chief of an Indian tribe.

1806 J. Ordway in *Jrnls. Lewis & O.* (1916) 355 The head chief..informd us that the most of our horses and pack Saddles were Safe. **1837** R. M. Bird *Nick of Woods* I. 236 From the head-chief to the commoner. **1881** *Harper's Mag.* Apr. 670/2 White Eagle, head-chief of the Poncas. *a* **1918** G. Stuart *40 Yrs. on Frontier* (1925) I. 96 The head chief proposed to meet the interpreter unarmed and talk with him.

hea·d-dresser. = Hairdresser. Also, one who makes head-dresses (*Obs.*).

1727 Defoe *Compl. Eng. Tradesman* II. ii. v. 166 Now we see..the Millenary Trade separated into innumerable little Commode Shops, Head Dressers and such like People. **1859** Trollope *Bertrams* ix. 81 No stray jagged ends would show themselves if by chance she removed her bonnet, nor did it even look as though it..required to be afresh puffed out by some head-dresser's mechanism. **1927** *Daily Tel.* 24 May 17/3 The 'head-dressers'' shops are nests of decoy birds.

header. Add: **4. c.** = *heading dog* (*heading *vbl. sb.* 4 b). *N.Z.*

1938 R. M. Burdon *High Country* x. 107 Dogs are usually kept in the proportion of three or four huntaways to one header now. **1958** *Landfall* XII. 17 Watching him work the new sheep dog, I see the taut thread of his whistle run from his mouth to the pricked quivering ears of the header. **1973** *Times* 13 Oct. 14/4 Early British sheep dogs were less versatile, They were divided into those which fetched the sheep and those which drove them away, as still occurs in New Zealand with header and hunt-away.

5. b. A top layer. *U.S.*

1867 *Trans. Ill. Agric. Soc.* VI. 641 Prime Pork—Shall be packed with a header of side cuts, the regular width, three half heads.

c. *Engin.* (See quot. 1940.)

1930 *Engineering* 25 July 121/1 They contain four headers, which are turned from solid mild-steel forgings. **1940** *Chambers's Techn. Dict.* 406/2 *Header*, a box or manifold supplying fluid to a number of tubes or passages, or connecting them in parallel. **1958** W. Hryniszak *Heat Exchangers* vii. 132 The function of the headers is either to distribute the gas over the matrix (inlet header), or to collect it from the matrix (outlet header) with the minimum possible loss of pressure not used for heat transfer purposes.

d. *Hedging.* (See quot.)

1941 *Archit. Rev.* LXXXIX. 85/2 The 'pleaches' too are rammed down, and when several yards are ready the two men work in the headers, which are slender and straight rods, twisted over and across, in and out of the stakes.

9. b. = Heading *vbl. sb.* 11.

1877 R. W. Raymond *Statistics of Mines* 165 The header had reached..a length of 12,259 feet.

11. *Association Football.* A ball which is headed. Also, one who heads the ball (see Head *v.* 15).

1906 L. V. Lodge in B. O. Corbett *Ann. Corinthian Football Club* 188 A back must be not only a good kick and sound tackler, but at the same time an accurate header. *Ibid.* 189 A really high-class header, by a skilful movement of the neck.., can move the ball a surprising distance. **1927** *Daily Express* 20 Apr. 13/2 Trotter gave the home club the lead with a beautiful header, following a free kick well taken by Leach. **1955** *Times* 13 Aug. 4/3 Yashin brought off a wonderful one-handed save to push out Wilshaw's header, which looked a certain goal. **1969** *Times* 8 Oct. 13/3 It was Marsh who came closest to scoring, when Kelly, using his left arm like a scythe, turned a header over the bar.

12. *attrib.* and *Comb.*: **header-board,** a diving-board; **header brick** = Header 5; so **heading brick.**

1913 E. F. Benson *Thorley Weir* i, The nude figure of a boy on the header-board in the act of springing from it into the water. **1897** F. C. Moore *How to build Home* vii. 110 A 'header' brick is one laid in the wall so that only its end shows. **1901** J. Black *Illustr. Carp. & Build., Scaffolding* 24 Cavities in the brickwork obtained by leaving out 'header' bricks at proper intervals. *Ibid.* 26 A 'heading' brick.

heading, *vbl. sb.* Add: **4. b.** *N.Z.* Of a farm dog: see quot. 1933. Hence *heading dog.* Cf. *head *v.* 13 c.

1913 A. I. Carr *Country Work & Life N.Z.* xix. 33 A new hand, if he intends to qualify for the work [as shepherd] is wise in investing in a good huntaway or a heading dog. **1933** L. G. D. Acland in *Press* (Christchurch, N.Z.) 28 Oct. 15/7 A dog goes round to the far side of a mob of sheep and stops them. This is called heading. Hence heading dog, one whose work this is. **1947** P. Newton *Wayleggo* (1949) 13 The heading dog is bred to run out silently, cast round sheep, and bring them back to his master. **1968** *N.Z. News* 28 Aug. 16/1 The heading dog brings sheep up to the shepherd and holds them at one spot. **1972** P. Newton *Sheep Thief* v. 40 He told her of his successes on the dog trial grounds. His old huntaway, Sam, was his particular pride, and he also had high hopes for his little heading dog, Smoke.

c. *Aeronaut.* (See quot. 1951.)

1935 T. C. Lyon *Pract. Air Navigation* 29 *Compass heading*, the true course plus or minus variation and deviation, and *including* allowance for wind. **1951** *Gloss. Aeronaut. Terms* (*B.S.I.*) III. 7 *Heading*, the direction of the longitudinal axis of an aircraft defined by the angle it makes with a specified meridian. **1968** *New Scientist* 18 Apr. 133/1 The aircraft's heading is defined by the localizer's two overlapping beams.

7. (Earlier examples.)

1682 T. A. *Carolina* 6 With this [cedar] they make Heading for their Cask. **1752** J. MacSparran *Amer. Dissected* (1753) 26 Barrel and Hogshead Staves and Heading.

headlight (heˑdləit). orig. *U.S.* Also with hyphen. [HEAD *sb.* 66.] A powerful light carried on the front of a locomotive or on the mast-head of a vessel; each of two powerful lamps carried on the front of a motor vehicle. Also *attrib.* and *fig.*

1861 *Remin. Life Railroad Engineer* 124, I saw the glimmer of his head-light when he first turned the curve. **1862** in *U.S. Pat. 35486*. **1891** C. ROBERTS *Adrift Amer.* iii. 55 The great head-light which forms such a noticeable feature of American engines at night. **1904** A. B. F. YOUNG *Compl. Motorist* (ed. 2) xii. 257 On dark nights it is advisable, when driving in the country, to carry on such cars a single head-light of greater power... On very fast cars two of these head-lights should be carried. **1907** *Autocar* 28 Dec. 1067/2 The thief calmly took the large valuable head light off and disappeared. **1929** *Evening News* 18 Nov. 4/4 He had almost reached the high road when the headlights of an automobile swung round a corner. **1959** *Sears, Roebuck Catal.* Spring & Summer 1103/3 Chrome-plated headlight shields. **1963** *Times* 13 Mar. 10/6 It has transistorised ignition, a.c. electrical generator, automatic headlight dipper, [etc.]. **1971** *Daily Tel.* 11 Feb. 11/2 It is only when they commit some offence that they are caught in the headlights of history. **1973** 'M. INNES' *Appleby's Answer* IV. xx. 172 The sound of a motor engine..and the sudden appearance of wavering headlights.

head-line. Add: Now usu. **headline. 2. c.** *to make* or *hit the headlines*: to be given prominent notice in the newspapers.

1934 M. WESEEN *Dict. Amer. Slang* (1935) xvii. 257 *Hit the headlines*, to become famous; to gain notoriety. **1939** *War Illustr.* 21 Oct. 181 He [*sc.* Winston S. Churchill] 'hit the headlines' in 1899 with a dramatic escape from captivity in a Boer armoured train. **1944** F. CLUNE *Red Heart* 12 It was just another tragedy of the Outback, the sort of thing that doesn't make headlines in the City newspapers, but it wrings the hearts of people who really know. **1948** *Manch. Guardian Weekly* 29 Jan. 11 The publication..hit the headlines here last night. **1957** 'J. WYNDHAM' *Midwich Cuckoos* 12 Before that it [*sc.* the village] hit the headlines—well, anyway, the broadsheets—when Black Ned, a second-class highwayman, was shot on the steps of The Scythe and Stone Inn by Sweet Polly Parker. **1968** *Globe & Mail* (Toronto) 3 Feb. 35/1 Anybody who gets his picture on the cover of the magazine [sc. *Time*] immediately breaks a leg, or hits the headlines in embarrassing fashion about the date of publication.

d. *Broadcasting.* Usu. in *pl.* A summary of important news items, given at the beginning or end of a news bulletin.

1908 'O. HENRY' *Gentle Grafter* 39 He shows me a machine..with two things for your ears..I puts it on and listens. A female voice starts up reading headlines of murders, accidents and other political casualties. 'What you hear,' says the farmer, 'is a synopsis of to-day's news..wired in to our Rural News Bureau and served hot to subscribers.' **1934** *B.B.C. Year-Bk.* 82 They [*sc.* Topical Talks] were given five minutes every evening in which to deal with the 'head line' of the day, and were tacked on like a tail to the news bulletins. **1941** *B.B.C. Gloss. Broadc. Terms* 14 Headline News: Brief statements giving, within the space of not more than five minutes, salient news items without comment or background material. **1971** 'D. HALLIDAY' *Dolly & Doctor Bird* i. 6, I watched the news headlines on television.

3. b. A line fastening the head of a vessel to the shore.

1876 'MARK TWAIN' *Tom Sawyer* ii. 29 Get out that headline! **1877** J. HABBERTON *Jericho Road* i. 9 The headline was cast off as the pilot's bell rang. **1958** E. S. LAND *Winning War with Ships* 105, I 'went ashore with the headline', contacted the Italian Admiral, and cooled off somewhat.

4. A base-line in surveying.

1656 *Doc. & Rec. New Hampshire* I. 221 From the said head lyne we measured for the length..6 miles & a halfe. **1704** *New Hampshire Probate Rec.* I. 514 All my land.. up as far as the southern hills, viz. as far as to butt against Andrews head line.

5. *Palmistry.* A line of the head (cf. LINE *sb.*[2] 8 b).

1867 A. R. CRAIG *Bk. of Hand* xxiii. 189 If a line sets out from the head line, and rises straight to the mount of Jupiter, crosses it, and cuts the roots of the forefinger, it is excessive pride. **1894** 'MARK TWAIN' in *Century Mag.* Feb. 554/2 Wilson began to study Luigi's palm, tracing life lines, heart lines, head lines, and so on. [**1911** *Encycl. Brit.* XX. 650/1 s.v. *Palmistry*. A line starting above the head of the second metacarpal bone and crossing the hand to the middle of its ulnar border is the line of the head.] **1934** *Cassell's Mod. Encycl.* 733/1 The principal lines on the palm are named life line, head line, heart line, fate line, and line of Apollo.

6. *attrib.* and *Comb.*

1909 *Daily Chron.* 19 Aug. 3/1 His ingenuity is amazing, ..and not merely amazing in the headline sense of that ill-used word. **1933** *Amer. Speech* Dec. 6/2 'Headline English' has become almost a menace to standard English usage nowadays. **1958** *Times* 11 Aug. 11/3 She.. is usually to be seen..at Broadway first nights,.. at headline parties. **1963** *Times* 11 June 17/4 The headline-maker, of course, has been the contract from United Airlines, of the United States, which has taken delivery of its 20-plane medium-range jet fleet from France. **1965** *Economist* 2 Oct. 57/3 He still uses that unfortunate American headline-verb 'to score' (meaning 'to attack').

head-line, *v.* Now usu. headline. Add later examples. Hence **heaˑdlined** *ppl. a.*, furnished with a headline.

1891 [in Dict.]. **1912** *Out West* Apr. 237/2 A big headlined, illustrated .. story, the pride of some reporter's heart. **1953** *Manch. Guardian Weekly* 12 Feb. 3 The 'New York Herald Tribune' headlined this story to-day. **1958** *Listener* 20 Nov. 811/2 The answer.. faithfully reported and perhaps headlined the next day in the local press. **1964** *Melody Maker* 28 Nov. 4/2 Nashville Teens, Kinks and Hullaballoos will be headlined in the 10-day Christmas holiday show..at Brooklyn's Fox Theatre.

headliner. Add: One whose name appears in a headline; a chief personage or performer. *U.S.*

1896 *N.Y. Dramatic News* 4 July 10/3 That clever pair..were the headliners..last week. **1905** *Daily Chron.* 11 Feb. 3/5 They..secure good 'head-liners' or 'stars' at paralysing salaries. **1907** *Chicago Tribune* 8 May 7 The 'Headliners' on the program will be James Whitcomb Riley, George Ade, etc. **1914** *Boston Herald* 23 June 8/4 The headliner at B. F. Keith's. **1966** R. STOUT *Death of Doxy* (1967) xii. 140 Julie's dressing room..was about six by eight, par for a headliner in a place with a four-dollar cover charge. **1970** *Globe & Mail* (Toronto) 26 Sept. 35/1 He is the centre on a checking line, a headliner on the penalty-killing unit.

2. One engaged in head-lining (HEAD *sb.* 66).

1963 *Times* 5 Mar. 13/1 A typical example were the head-liners, who fitted the roof linings in vehicles.

headlineˑse. [*-ESE.] The elliptical style of language characteristic of the headlines, esp. in popular newspapers.

1927 C. G. MARSHALL *Private Let.* (G. & C. Merriam Co. files) 12 Aug., In the headlines of general newspapers you see time after time such words as 'Probe', 'Quiz', 'Tilt', 'Pact', etc. In Newspaper offices such language is referred to as 'Headlinese'. We banned it from the headlines of The [United States] Daily. **1934** *Times Lit. Suppl.* 1 Feb. 66/3 They recognize that the difficulty nowadays is to keep the headline 'from shouting too loudly', and they cannot condemn too heartily mere 'headlinese'. **1935** H. STRAUMANN *Newspaper Headlines* 256 An essential feature of present-day headlinese is the typographical make-up. **1966** *Listener* 2 June 811/3 In headlinese you don't marry, you wed... You don't advance arguments against, you score.

head master, head-master. Add: Hence **headmaˑster** *v.*, to act as headmaster; also *transf.*; **headmaˑsterly** *a.*

1940 J. H. JAGGER *English in Future* vi. 73 No novelist has *headmastered* his countrymen as frequently as Mr. H. G. Wells. **1959** R. FULLER *Ruined Boys* 154 The school..so brilliantly headmastered. **1964** *English Studies* XLV (Suppl.). 9 Further headmasterly duties took him to Klagenfurt. **1965** G. HOUSEHOLD *Olura* 175 A headmasterly grief that there should be nigger-lovers in the upper forms. **1967** *Guardian* 4 Oct. 1/4 A headmasterly chat.

head-note. Add: **3.** A note or comment inserted at the head of the text.

1863 D. G. ROSSETTI *Let.* (1965) II. 472 Alteration of the last part to suit the new plan of head-notes to Part II. *Ibid.* 479, I am glad you like the headnote plan. **1965** *Listener* 17 June 905/3 A headnote to each poem. **1972** *Times* 4 Mar. 12/7 Since performance details for individual [crossword] puzzles are likely to interest many more readers than they may distress, it is hoped that those in the latter category will agree to turn a blind eye to headnotes to puzzles.

head office. [f. HEAD *sb.* 63 + OFFICE *sb.* 8.] The principal, controlling office of a firm or organization, where the chief administration is carried out, policy decisions made, etc. Also *attrib.*

1869 *Bradshaw's Railway Man.* XXI. (Advt.), London & County Banking Company... Head Office. 21, Lombard Street. *Ibid.* 390 Head office accounts, local. **1933** A. G. MACDONELL *England, their England* vi. 70, I was warned by telephone, my Lord, from our Head Office. **1941** F. THOMPSON *Over to Candleford* xiv. 214 I'll speak to Head Office. **1952** A. BRIGGS *Hist. Birmingham* II. 54 In 1881 an export representative was sent out to Australia and New Zealand with his first head office in Sydney, and later on new offices were opened at Melbourne, Adelaide, and Brisbane. **1972** *Woman* 4 Mar. 10/2 If you ever feel you have been badly treated [by the bank], *complain*—first to the branch and, if that's no good, then wake up head office. **1972** C. WATSON *Broomsticks over Flaxborough* xi. 150 In this trade you get used to being buggered about a bit by head office.

head-on, *adv.* and *a.* orig. *U.S.* [HEAD *sb.* 21 b.] **A.** *adv.* (*heaˑd-oˑn*). With the head pointed directly towards or running full against or towards something. Also *fig.* **B.** *adj.* (*heaˑd-on*). Of a collision: involving the direct meeting of the fronts of two vehicles in the same track, or of the head of a vehicle with an object. Also *fig.*

1840 R. H. DANA 2 *Yrs. bef. Mast* ii. 15 The two vessels stood 'head on', bowing and curveting at each other. **1903** C. E. MERRIMAN *Lett. from Son* 33 It's a case of head-on collision with your pride. **1904** *N.Y. Evening Post* 11 May 2 A head-on collision between north and southbound passenger trains. **1907** *Westm. Gaz.* 16 Sept. 5/2 New York, September 16.—A head-on collision between two passenger trains. **1916** H. BARBER *Aeroplane Speaks* 46 Gliding just over the trees and head on to the wind. **1930** *Daily Express* 8 Sept. 1/3 When the vehicles collided head-on. **1932** *Economist* 20 Feb. 400/2 At the same time, a head-on collision between the chamber and the Senate is an unusual occurrence. **1952** *Manch. Guardian Weekly* 15 May 2 The General will here run head-on into the irony of the destiny he has chosen. **1954** J. STEINBECK *Sweet Thursday* 166 Despair and humour crashed head-on in Doc. **1957** *Economist* 9 Nov. 492/1 He is known to be working..to present foreign aid next year in a way that will meet head-on and in good time any indiscriminate renewal of the economy drive. **1958** E. L. MASCALL *Recovery of Unity* i. 4 It shows directly how a head-on theological conflict can arise from the unquestioned assumption of a common premiss. **1961** *Lancet* 5 Aug. 325/1 The Government had a head-on collision with the medical profession in 1956. **1973** *Listener* 14 June 790/3 The coming of the Renaissance..was a head-on collision with the medieval system.

headphone (heˑdfōᵘn). [f. HEAD *sb.* + *phone* of TELEPHONE (see *-PHONE).] = *ear-phone* (*a*) and (*c*), s.v. *EAR *sb.*[1] 16.

1914 *Work* 7 Mar. 506/1 Electrolite Head-phones. *Ibid.* 28 Mar. 576 We..consider our Headphones a perfect treat. **1926** C. SIDGWICK *Sack & Sugar* xxi. 250 At present they only had head-phones. **1926** *Proc. Musical Assoc.* 1926–7 19 Many seem to have the headphones permanently attached to themselves. **1929** *Strand Mag.* Aug. 152 Women whose head-phones appear so appropriate. **1965** *Listener* 20 May 743/2 These side plaits were gathered into nets..in something like our headphone style. **1970** J. EARL *Tuners & Amplifiers* iii. 76 Headphones..can nowadays give a subjective impression of quality, spaciousness and stereo effect equally as good as the best loudspeakers.

headquarter (heˑdkwǭːɹtəɹ), *v.* Usu. in *pass.*: to be provided with headquarters.

1903 *Daily Mail* 3 Sept. 4/4 The off-scourings of civilisation which are headquartered in Constantinople. **1958** P. SCOTT *Mark of Warrior* III. 203 We can take it that Blake's headquartered on the ridge. **1963** *Time & Tide* 28 Mar. 24/2 The society is headquartered in Westminster. **1971** W. TUCKER *This Witch* (1972) v. 55 The refugee camps..are really terrorist camps as well. The Al Fatah are headquartered there.

head-quarters. Add: Also **headquarters. 2.** (Earlier and additional examples.)

1780 A. YOUNG *Tour in Ireland* 382 A good line in which to view these objects is..to make Dobbin's inn, at Ballyporeen, the head quarters, and view them from thence. **1809** J. M'MAHON in G. L. Wardle *Charges against Duke of York* 235 Although he has returned to town for the season as his head-quarters, he makes two or three days excursions from it as often as he can. **1834** G. CRABBE Jun. *Life G. Crabbe* ix. 270 Mr. Crabbe, in subsequent years, made Hampstead his head-quarters on his spring visits. **1836** DICKENS *Let.* ?22 Aug. (1965) I. 168, I shall be at head quarters by 12 Wednesday Noon. **1922** E. WALLACE *Crimson Circle* v. 34, I didn't think that head-quarters had much use for private men like you. *Ibid.* vi. 37 We view with consternation the seeming helplessness of police head-quarters to deal with this criminal gang. **1929** A. CHRISTIE *Partners in Crime* xi. 107 The local Inspector of Police had unemotionally arrested the second footman who proved to be a thief well known at headquarters.

head-rail[1]**.** Add: **3.** Usu. in *pl.* Teeth. *slang.*

1785 GROSE *Dict. Vulg. T.*, *Head rails*, teeth; sea phrase. **1854** 'C. BEDE' *Verdant Green* II. iv. 31 Your head-rails were loosened there, wasn't they? **1935** A. J. POLLOCK *Underworld Speaks* 52/1 *Head rails*, the teeth.

headroom. Restrict †*Sc. Obs.* to sense in Dict., and add: **2.** Room above the head; overhead space. Also *fig.*

1851 [see HEAD *sb.* 65 a]. **1876** *Encycl. Brit.* IV. 267/2 Sufficient light, and headroom of at least 48 inches, being provided. **1902** *Eng. Dial. Dict.* s.v. *Head* sb. II, *Headroom*, of ceilings, staircases, etc.: sufficient height overhead. **1908** *Installation News* II. 68/1 Arrangements are being made to provide 15 feet headroom. **1933** *Punch* 18 Oct. 421/1 In the two-decker Underground trains.. the upper deck would have less than six feet of head-room. **1958** *Economist* 20 Dec. 1103/2 Greater 'headroom' to make..increases in passenger fares..was the main object of the application by the Transport Commission. **1960** *Farmer & Stockbreeder* 15 Mar. 157, 14 ft. clear headroom.

head-rope. Add: **4.** Also for other animals.

1936 P. FLEMING *News from Tartary* 328 The camels' headropes were fixed not to nose-pegs but to gaily decorated halters. **1957** P. KEMP *Mine were of Trouble* viii. 137 Hold on to the mules' head-ropes!

headstock. Add: **1. g.** The horizontal end members in the under-frame of a railway carriage or truck.

1888 *Lockwood's Dict. Mech. Engin.*, *Headstock*. (2) The end timbers in the under frame of a railway truck. **1928** *Daily Express* 29 Dec. 9/4 The interval between headstocks of coaches should be as small..as practicable for necessary freedom of movement.

h. (See quot.[1])

1927 T. WOODHOUSE *Artificial Silk* 108 Occasionally both reeds are placed on what is termed a dividing head or headstock. *Ibid.* 112 Fig. 50 illustrates the delivery or headstock end with the weaver's beam partially filled with the sheet of sized and dried threads.

headward. Add: **C.** adj. *headward erosion*: erosion of a stream at its head, in such a way that the length of the stream is increased.

1916 H. F. CLELAND *Geol.* iv. 99 A valley is lengthened

at its upper end and is cut back by the water which flows in at its head... This is called headward erosion. **1922** C. A. COTTON *Geomorphol. N.Z.* I. 72 They [*sc.* insequent streams] rapidly eat their way back into the interfluves by headward erosion. **1937** WOOLDRIDGE & MORGAN *Physical Basis Geogr.* xii. 162 With the progress of time it [*sc.* down-cutting] proceeds backwards, *i.e.* headwards, from the lowest point. The grading of a stream course thus involves headward erosion. **1944** A. HOLMES *Princ. Physical Geol.* II. x. 153 The torrent tract..evolves into the valley tract, and each gradually migrates inland as the source continues to recede by headward erosion. **1965** F. J. MONKHOUSE *Dict. Geogr.* 154/2 *Headward erosion*, the cutting back upstream of a valley above its original source by rainwash, gullying and spring-sapping. **1968** [see *DISSECTION 6*].

head-water. Add: **1. b.** *ellipt.* = *head-water-mark.*

1908 *Westm. Gaz.* 29 Apr. 6/3 The Thames has risen rapidly during the night, and is now 2 ft. 6 in. above head-water at Windsor.

headway. Add: **6.** The interval of time or the distance between two consecutive trains, trams, buses, etc., running on the same route and in the same direction. orig. *U.S.*

1895 in *Funk's Standard Dict.* **1900** *Jrnl. Soc. Arts* 2 Mar. 315/1 The headway between the carriers is fixed say at ten or twenty seconds. **1930** *Oxford Times* 21 Mar. 17/4, I think Route 2 should have a six-minute headway between 8 a.m. and 10.30 a.m. *Ibid.*, Until the headway was closed to 15 minutes in the morning, and 12 minutes in the afternoon, serious inadequacy existed. **1970** *Courier-Mail* (Brisbane) 17 Dec. 1/3 The 30-minute headway between each bus reduced to a 50-minute headway. **1971** *Mod. Railways* May 193/3 Page 105 of the March *Modern Railways* indicates a new 17.11 Paddington to Bristol, first stop Didcot, thus providing a second 3 min headway to Didcot East Junction with the existing 17.15 to Worcester.

headwear (he·dwēəɹ). [f. HEAD *sb.* + WEAR *sb.* 3.] = HEAD-GEAR I.

1896 J. C. HARRIS *Sister Jane* 39 Gi' me my bonnet. It's all the head-wear I've got left. **1900** *Daily News* 27 Mar. 4/2 They were most easily classified by their headwear. Caps, bowlers, and felt hats were there in almost equal proportions. **1904** W. M. GALLICHAN *Fishing & Trav. Spain* vii. 76 He was much interested in my wife's hat. Such headwear had never been seen in Coria. **1937** *Discovery* Apr. 106/2 The head wear is the Kalpak, a tall cap, not unlike a busby in principle. **1939–40** *Army & Navy Stores Catal.* p. xxxviii/5 Headwear, Naval, Military and Tropical.

headwork. Add: **1.** (Earlier example.)

1837 DICKENS *Pickw.* liv. 587 How the blazes you can stand the head-work you do, is a mystery to me.

b. The practice of carrying loads on the head.

1840 R. H. DANA *2 Yrs. bef. Mast* xiv, For we soon found that..'head-work' was the only system for California.

c. Skill in games and sports.

1851 J. PYCROFT *Cricket Field* ii. 22 There is a deal of head-work in bowling. **1898** B. J. ANGLE in W. A. Morgan *'House' on Sport* 42 His quickness of foot and tricky head-work quickly demoralised the majority of his opponents. **1898** K. S. RANJITSINHJI *With Stoddart's Team* (ed. 3) iv. 84 The English bowling..aimed at steadiness, rather than head work and sting. **1958** F. C. AVIS *Boxing Ref. Dict.* 52 *Headwork*, craftiness in boxing.

3. *pl.* **a.** Apparatus for controlling the flow of water in a river or canal. **b.** (See quot. 1905.)

1891 *Scribner's Mag.* X. 468 The river flowing between firm banks, could be permanently controlled by head-works of masonry. **1903** *Sci. Amer. Suppl.* 10 Jan. 22597/3 Headworks can be placed more easily along the banks of smaller streams, or dams built across their beds, raising and controlling the waters. **1905** *Terms Forestry & Logging* 40 *Headworks*, a platform or raft, with windlass or capstan, which is attached to the front of a log raft or boom of logs, for warping, kedging, or winding it through lakes and still water, by hand or horse power. **1963** *Times* 19 Apr. 14/6 Smoothly it flowed, the head-works of a carefully planned series of canals. **1971** N. SMITH *Hist. Dams* i. 10 The headworks of the irrigation canal.

heady, *a.* Add: **2.** Also, that affects or turns the head; that turns one giddy.

1898 *Atlantic Monthly* Apr. 501/1 He would sit on a heady scaffold. **1924** A. I. I. FINCH in G. I. Finch *Making of Mountaineer* xii. 177 Up and down we seemed to go, and once round a little natural balcony that hung out over space but proved not in the least heady.

c. Headachy (cf. *HEAD *sb.* 1 d).

1872 GEO. ELIOT *Let.* 4 June (1956) V. 277 George, being a little heady, and unable to occupy his mornings with writing, is going tomorrow to see the aquarium. **1934** *Air Rev.* Nov. 60, I was feeling a little 'heady' as.. a good sea was running, and I was making an effort to eat some nice fat, greasy beef. **1955** E. HILLARY *High Adventure* 69 In the morning I felt thick and heady and a sharp cough rasped my sore throat. **1965** 'J. LYMINGTON' *Green Drift* iv. 63, I was feeling very heady and tired. *Ibid.* 64 'Do you still have this heady feeling?' 'Yes, I think it must be the heat. Thundery.'

heah. A representation of a *colloq.* pronunciation of HERE *adv.* Freq. used in Black English.

1927 A. P. RANDOLPH in A. Dundes *Mother Wit* (1973) 200 Bin heah too long. **1937** C. HIMES *Black on Black* (1973) 139 A nickel victrola in the rear blared a husky, negroid bellow: 'Anybody heah wanna buy.' **1970** R. D. ABRAHAMS *Positively Black* p. ix, Everybody 'round heah is talkin' 'bout 'ligion, gittin' happy an' shoutin'. **1973** *Black World* June 61 Yo ole man in heah?

healder (hī·ldəɹ). [f. HEALD + -ER[1].] An operative who draws the warp yarn through the eyes of a heald. So **hea·lding** *vbl. sb.*

1881 *Instr. Census Clerks* (1885) 64 Woollen cloth manufacture... Healder. **1888** R. BEAUMONT *Woollen & Worsted Cloth Manuf.* 138 After healding the work of loom mounting is comparatively simple, the only operation requiring attention being that of sleying.

health, *sb.* Add: **1. b.** Colloq. phr. *for one's health*, used esp. in neg. contexts or with negative implication, e.g. *to be not doing* (something) *for one's health*: to have a serious purpose in doing something, to be doing something for one's material advantage. orig. *U.S.*

1887 G. H. DEVOL *Forty Yrs. a Gambler* 133 We called it ours, for we had fitted it up just to suit us; and for fear someone would use it when we were out traveling for our health we paid for it all the time. **1900** *Congress. Rec.* 5 Feb. 1520/2, I am not making this speech for fun, nor for my health, nor as an oratorical exercise. **1900** J. K. JEROME *Three Men on Bummel* iv. 96 What d'ye think I'm running this shop for—my health? **1909** *Westm. Gaz.* 5 July 2/2 We..doubt if it can really be said that Tariff Reformers are 'in it for their health' (to use a very expressive Americanism) or anybody else's. **1914** WODEHOUSE *Man Upstairs* 229 What is it that makes men do perilous deeds? Why does a man go over Niagara Falls in a barrel? Not for his health. **1927** G. K. CHESTERTON *Coll. Poems* 90 He will learn..Whether the Health Ministry Are in it for their health. **1944** L. A. G. STRONG *Director* 31 I'm not in this job for my health, any more than you are. **1955** L. P. HARTLEY *Perfect Woman* ix. 86 You ought to have sold several hundredweight, at least, or several tons if you want to persuade the Inspector that you're not in business for your health.

8. a. *health-card, certificate.* **b.** *health-biscuit; health-screening, -seeker* (examples). **d. health camp** *N.Z.*, a camp open (for exercise, outdoor life, etc.) to children below the average in physique, etc.; **health centre** (cf. *CENTRE *sb.* 6 a), a local headquarters of medical services, *spec.*, a local centre for a group practice; **health club**, an establishment where one can do exercises, have massage, etc.; **health farm** orig. *U.S.*, a place to which people resort in the hope of improving their health; **health food**, food chosen for its dietary or health-giving properties; **health insurance**, insurance against financial loss through illness; **health physics**, that branch of radiology which is concerned with the health of those working with radioactive material; **health salt**, freq. in *pl.*, name given to a number of salts, sold under various brand-names, obtained from or mixed with mineral water or other beverages; **health service**, name given generally or specifically to the aggregate of public (as opposed to private) medical facilities available to members of a community; **health visitor**, a specially trained nurse concerned with the welfare of sick or old people, expectant mothers, etc., in their homes.

1905 *Daily Chron.* 25 Apr. 4/5 An uneatable health biscuit..stood by his bedside. **1925** *N.Z. Educ. Gaz.* 1 May 68/1 The teachers decided to hold a 'health camp' for the twenty-six children. **1963** *Evening Post* (Wellington) 26 Oct., A woman doctor whose name will always be remembered in New Zealand as the pioneer of the health camp movement, Dr. Elizabeth Catherine Gunn, M.B.E., died in Wellington today. **1940** AUDEN *Another Time* 96 And his Health-card shows he was once in hospital but left it cured. **1970** T. LILLEY *Projects Section* x. 123 You will not..have inoculations to bring your Health Card up to date. **1916** *Public Health Nurse Q.* (U.S.) Jan. 27 Historically the first Health Center started under that name was begun by the New York Health Committee in 1913. *Ibid.* 33 This Health Center..illustrates two fundamental principles, namely a definite area is selected for the field of operation; [etc.]. **1918** *Lancet* 29 June 922/2 With the removal of the medical officer of health from the jurisdiction of the borough council that official will need a new office in the town, with laboratories, museum, library, and lecture hall. This I call for want of a better title the future 'Health Centre' of the borough. **1934** T. S. ELIOT *Rock* ii. 72 Libraries and health centres and milk for the children. **1968** *Brit. Med. Bull.* XXIV. 198/1 With the era of the medical team and health centre upon us, the necessity for adequate documentation already exists. **1972** *Times* 22 Feb. 3/1 Some 3,000 family doctors will be practising from more than 500 health centres by the end of 1974. **1938** F. G. HOBSON *Med. Pract. Residential Schools* p. xv (*heading*) Organization of medical services. A. Health Certificates. B. Records. **1960** J. BETJEMAN *Summoned by Bells* vii. 66 My health certificate, photographs of home. **1961** *Economist* 27 May 872/1 The active gymnasia ('health clubs') are much of a type. **1962** *Which?* Oct. 303/1 These health clubs, which have been fashionable in the United States for many years, have appeared in this country over the last three. **1964** S. BELLOW *Herzog* (1965) 84 Herzog had met him in the steam bath at Postl's Health Club. **1970** L. SANDERS *Anderson Tapes* xliv. 121 We were in the steam room of that health club the Doc's got on West Forty-eighth Street. **1927** E. HEMINGWAY *Men without Women* (1928) 115 Jack started training at Danny Hogan's health farm over in Jersey. **1928** WODEHOUSE *Money for Nothing* ix. 196 What if that health-farm was a mere blind for more dastardly work? **1966** G. B. MAIR *Kisses from Satan* v. 55 He was going to enter one of the most fashionable health farms in the world. **1969** *Guardian* 18 Aug. 7/5 Their health farm..is the place where they go once a year ..and..lose 10 lb. or 15 lb. in two weeks. **1882** W. D. HOWELLS *Mod. Instance* xxviii, I put the camp on a health-food basis. **1884** E. W. NYE *Baled Hay* 75, I have had occasion to thoroughly investigate the subject of so-called health food, such as gruels, beef tea. **1939** 'G. ORWELL' *Coming up for Air* IV. v. 261 Health-food cranks. **1962** J. B. PRIESTLEY *Margin Released* I. iii. 26 Another shop, specialising in health foods, had a line in mashed dates and coconut. **1965** *Observer* 18 Apr. 45/2 Health food shops, where everything is free range, unsprayed, naturally fertilized. **1972** *New York* 8 May 49 *Health Food*. As used to describe stores, this term has taken on a generic meaning, encompassing everything from organic, natural, and specialized diet foods to whole wheat and other products mass-produced and refined. **1901** *Index-Catal. Library Surg.-General's Office U.S. Army* Ser. 2. VI. 849/1 (*heading*) Health-insurance. **1911** *Act* 1 & 2 *Geo. V* c. 55. 1 (*heading*) National Health insurance...All persons so insured..shall be entitled..to the benefits in respect of health insurance and prevention of sickness. **1916** *Machinery* July 1018/1 Booklet entitled 'Health Insurance'. **1941** J. S. HUXLEY *Uniqueness of Man* p. ix, Subsidized housing..health insurance..free education..are all symptoms of..change. **1946** R. S. STONE in *Proc. Amer. Philos. Soc.* XC. 13/2 The term 'Health-Physics' has been used..to define that field in which physical methods are used to determine the existence of hazards to the health of personnel. *Ibid.* 16/1 The instrument development problems that faced the Health-Physics section were numerous. **1961** *Engineering* 26 May 734/2 The syllabus will include lectures..with..instruction in health physics. **1900** *Confectioners' Union Hand-bk.* 169 Gums, jellies, lozenges..health salt, etc. **1921** D. H. LAWRENCE *Sea & Sardinia* 46 Like a health-salts..advertisement. **1962** A. NISBETT *Technique Sound Studio* x. 177 Health salts do fine for fizzy drinks. **1966** *New Scientist* 1 Dec. 499/2 Whether Britain goes ahead with an intensive programme of health screening is a decision for the politicians. **1968** *Daily Tel.* 22 Nov. 25 A £250,000 health-screening centre aided by computers in a new building..adjoining Harley Street. **1832** *Chambers's Edinb. Jrnl.* I. 113/2 When a health-seeker takes a walk, he keeps his coat wide open. **1953** DYLAN THOMAS *Under Milk Wood* (1954) 23 There is little to attract the hillclimber, the healthseeker, [etc.]. **1935** *Economist* 7 Sept. 456/2 Twenty-five years ago only the germ of our present health services existed, in the form of the old Poor Law and a rudimentary Old-Age Pension scheme. **1938** B. WEBB *Let.* Jan. in K. Martin *Editor* (1968) iii. 73 The organisation of a public Health Service. **1958** *Times Lit. Suppl.* 12 Dec. 717/2 The Health Service and the welfare state...have brought appalling drabness into the doctor's life. **1901** Health visitor [see VISITOR 1 c]. **1905** *Westm. Gaz.* 3 Apr. 12/2 An audience of health visitors, district visitors, charity organisation visitors. **1917** *New Witness* 28 June 202/1 The bare idea that a Health Visitor should attempt to force her way into a Frenchwoman's house would be regarded with horror. **1965** *Listener* 30 Sept. 483/1, I would think it most important by means of..the health visitor..to make assessments of the food which they require. **1970** G. GREER *Female Eunuch* 19 The revolutionary woman must know her enemies, the doctors, psychiatrists, health visitors.

healthy, *a.* Add: **2. b.** In ironical use.

1831 S. SMITH *Life & Writings Major J. Downing* 149 Major Eaton, it won't be healthy for you to come on to these steps to-night. **1902** C. HYNE *Mr. Horrocks Purser* 251, I want to impress on them that they'll find it more healthy not to try for more. **1916** 'BOYD CABLE' *Action Front* 179 'Additional artillery support would be useful a—a—a.' 'Sounds healthy, don't it?' said the sergeant reflectively.

4. *healthy-minded* adj. (earlier example); *healthy-mindedness.*

a **1882** H. JAMES *Lit. Remains* (1885) 117 In a pluralistic philosophy the healthy-minded moralist will always feel himself at home. *Ibid.*, The feeling of *action*..makes us turn a deaf ear to the thought of *being*; and this deafness and insensibility may be said to form an integral part of what in popular phrase is known as 'healthy-mindedness'. **1906** *Westm. Gaz.* 25 Jan. 12/2 The spirit which animated Japan was chivalry and healthy-mindedness. **1931** *Times Lit. Suppl.* 19 Feb. 122/1 So well supplied is the Victorian era with names standing for stability, sanity and healthy-mindedness.

heap, *sb.* Add: **1. e.** Usually preceded by a defining word: a slovenly woman. *colloq.* (orig. *dial.*).

1806 A. DOUGLAS *Poems* 125 She jaw'd them, misca'd them For clashin' claikin' haips. **1810** J. COCK *Simple Strains* II. 91 Foul fa' the sly bewitchin' heap Cou'd turn hersel' in ony shape. **1922** JOYCE *Ulysses* 300 The fat heap he married is a nice old phenomenon with a back on her like a ball-eye. **1957** J. FRAME *Owls do Cry* 106, I may be *forced* to [sell-out], if that lazy heap doesn't help me.

f. A battered old motor vehicle. *colloq.* (orig. *U.S.*).

1926 *Clues* Nov. 161/1 *Heap*, automobile. **1928** R. J. TASKER *Grimhaven* iii. 28 Once in a while some fellow who really did own a good car would come up to be topped, but, as a rule, I've noticed that kind never have much to say about their heaps. **1935** R. CHANDLER *Killer in Rain* (1964) 7, I got out of the Chrysler... I went back to my heap. **1951** J. KEROUAC *On Road* (1958) 79 He gunned the heap to eighty. **1959** J. BRAINE *Vodi* xiv. 190 Bought two old heaps today. Just junk really, a '28

Chrysler and a '27 Essex. **1967** A. Hunter *Gently Continental* xi. 166 Stody too has driven away in his modest heap. **1969** C. F. Burke *God is Beautiful, Man* (1970) 56 You will be like a guy who paid no attention to his heap and it broke down in the traffic.

4. d. In the representation of the speech of North American Indians used adverbially and as quasi-adj.: very, very much, a great deal.

1832 W. Irving *Jrnl.* (1919) III. 180 'Look at these Delawares,' say the Osages, 'dey got short legs—no can run—must stand and fight a great heap.' **1848** *Blackw. Mag.* LXIII. 719 An Indian is always a 'heap' hungry or thirsty—loves a 'heap'—is a 'heap' brave—in fact, 'heap' is tantamount to very much. **1850** 'M. Tensas' *Louisiana 'Swamp Doctor'* 42 Whoop! whiskey lour! Injun big man, drunk heap. **1867** *Harper's Mag.* July 137/1 Disturb the game and you make the Indian 'heap big mad'. **1872** 'Mark Twain' *Roughing It* (1873) xxxix. 276 'Heap' is 'Injun-English' for 'very much'. **1902** —— in *Harper's Mag.* Jan. 270/2 Billy explained.. 'she heap much hungry'. **1958** B. Cerf *Shake well before Using* 17 President Coolidge posed later in the regalia of a heap-big chief. **1968** Mrs. L. B. Johnson *White House Diary* 21 June (1970) 688 His favorites among the presents were.. the gift wrappings, or maybe the rubber canoe that said 'Heap Big Indian Lyn'.

e. *a heap sight* (U.S. *dial.* and *colloq.*): see Heap *sb.* 4 c and Sight *sb.*[1] 2.

1874 E. Eggleston *Circuit Rider* i. 14 He 'lows there was a heap sight more corn. **1888** G. W. Cable *Bonaventure* 49 He's..a heap sight happier than us. **1906** *Smart Set* June 107/1, I care a heap sight too much for Ummy to let him go through what I know 's comin'. **1911** R. D. Saunders *Col. Todhunter* x. 152 You're a heap-sight smarter man than I gave you credit for bein'.

5. e. Also, *to knock all of a heap*.

1898 W. J. Locke *Idols* xiii, It knocked the prosecution all of a heap. **1928** *Manch. Guardian Weekly* 7 Sept. 183/3 Its owner's anxiety to knock the critics all of a heap.

heaping, *ppl. a. U.S.* [f. Heap *v.*] Of a spoonful: heaped. Also *fig.* mounting up.

1838 *Congress. Globe* June 470/2 App., The amount of money..is a very high and heaping price. **1868** L. M. Alcott *Lit. Women* xi, Amy..took a heaping spoonful, choked..and left the table precipitately. **1908** *Smart Set* June 25/1 Aunt Natica waddled off..to fetch Thorndyke a heaping portion of the *dulce*. **1965** C. D. Eby *Siege of Alcázar* (1966) xi. 221 He had just been served a heaping ration of rice and beans, a special treat.

hear, *v.* Add: **3. e.** *to like to hear oneself speak, talk* (and similar phrases): to be fond of talking; *to hear oneself think*: usu. in neg. contexts, not to be able to think because there is too much noise going on.

1592 Shakes. *Rom. & Jul.* ii. iv. 156 Pray what sawcie Merchant was this?.. *Rom.*: A Gentleman Nurse that loves to heare himselfe talke. **1781** George III *Lett.* (1927) V. 304 Considering the great love modern Orators have of hearing themselves speak. **1920** R. Macaulay *Potterism* vi. iii. 226, I wish everyone would shut up, so that we could hear ourselves think. **1927** H. T. Lowe-Porter tr. *Mann's Magic Mountain* II. vii. 779 You won't be able to hear yourselves think. **1934** J. E. Mansion *Harrap's French & Eng. Dict.* 272/1 *Discoureur... C'est un grand d.*, he likes to hear himself talk. **1962** *New Yorker* 12 May 38/1 You have to wear earplugs to hear yourself think.

4. b. *to hear out*: also, to distinguish (the sounds of something heard).

1922 R. S. Woodworth *Psychol.* x. 230 By careful attention and training we can 'hear out' the separate overtones from the total blend.

7. c. *to hear to*, to listen to, to hear of. *U.S.*

1833 H. Barnard in *Maryland Hist. Mag.* (1918) XIII. 379, I made a move to depart—but they would not hear to that. **1869** Mrs. Stowe *Oldtown Folks* xx. 243 She has her own ways and doings, and she won't hear to reason. **1915** E. Poole *Harbor* 202 When I tried at last to turn our talk to our affairs at home, at first she would not hear to it.

11. *to hear from*: (also, pregnantly) to receive a reprimand from.

1907 *Munsey's Mag.* Dec. 307/1 If those louts up at the castle neglected to have dinner ready.., they would hear from him... If they didn't [spring at his word] they always heard from him.

hearing, *vbl. sb.* Add: **7. hearing aid**, a sound-amplifier for the hard of hearing.

1922 *Lancet* 11 Mar. 462/2 These electrical instruments should go far towards destroying the too general prejudice against the use of hearing aids. **1950** *Lancet* 11 Nov. 532/2 Practical courses..on audiometry and hearing-aids. **1951** *Consumer Reports* Jan. 13/1 Hearing aids and batteries are..supplied without charge. **1960** 'H. Carmichael' *Seeds of Hate* ii. 18 A grey-haired woman who wore a hearing aid. **1969** B. Patten *Notes to Hurrying Man* 57 Much later on in life I wear my hearing-aid.

hearse, *sb.* Add: *hearse-driver*.

1829 G. Griffin *Collegians* III. xxxiii. 60 ''Twill be a great funeral,' said the hearse-driver. **1841** J. S. Buckingham *Amer.* II. 322 The Whig authorities of New-Haven, have removed Mr. Willoughby..from the place of hearse-driver, and appointed another person in his place. **1851** H. Melville *Moby Dick* III. xiii. 90 The old hearse-driver, he must have been. **1922** Joyce *Ulysses* 590 Sober hearse-drivers a speciality.

hearsy (hɔ̄·ɹsi), *a.* [f. Hearse *sb.* 8 + -y[1].] Resembling or characteristic of a hearse; funereal.

1901 'A. Hope' *Tristram of Blent* v. 57 Mr. Gainsborough was obviously a man who would not waste his chance of a funeral;..it would need startling measures to keep him from a funeral. 'I hate hearsey people,' grumbled Harry as he threw the letter down. **1908** Hardy *Dynasts* iii. vi. vi. 476 Full-clothed in black, with nodding hearsy plumes.

heart, *sb.* Add: **1. c.** A diseased or disordered heart: often with defining word; as *athletic heart*, simple hypertrophy of the heart with no disease of the valves; *fatty heart* (see Fatty *a.* 5); *smoker's heart* (see 1 b).

1862 W. H. Walshe *Pract. Treat. Dis. Heart* (ed. 3) ii. 320 Patients..often express themselves, 'they have a heart', (the mildest form of cardiac paræsthesia). **1871** Da Costa in *Amer. Jrnl. Med. Sci.* LXI. 17, I noticed cases of a peculiar form of functional disorder of the heart, to which I gave the name of irritable heart. **1886** Fagge & Pye-Smith *Princ. Med.* II. 41 Rather more than a century ago Haller described the 'hairy' heart as occurring especially in bold and adventurous men. **1888** Smoker's heart [in Dict., sense 1 b]. **1902** *Daily Chron.* 3 Nov. 8/4 [He] has been forbidden to row again.. owing to his having developed 'a heart'. **1908** *Westm. Gaz.* 29 Oct. 14/1 [He] failed to qualify before the Medical Board of the police on the ground that he had an 'athletic heart'. **1929** E. Bowen *Joining Charles* 125 Cottesby the cow-herd, a greyish-faced man, had 'a heart'. **1965** 'W. Haggard' *Hard Sell* i. 4 He's got a heart, by the way, and I'm afraid this might finish him. **1971** *Current Slang* (Univ. S. Dakota) VI. 6 Slow down or you'll give me a *heart*.

10. d. *to have a heart* colloq., to be merciful. Freq. in *imp.*: come off it, be reasonable, show some pity!

1917 Wodehouse & Bolton (*play title*) Have a heart. **1928** *Observer* 1 Jan. 4 We only sigh for old delights, and in homely phrase beseech him..to 'have a heart'. **1936** P. Bottome *Level Crossing* xviii. 225 'Have a heart!' Nelly told her crossly. **1950** W. Stevens *Let.* 28 June (1967) 683 If you use the things..I shall have to go out and drown myself... Have a heart. **1967** J. B. Priestley *It's Old Country* xix. 209 'You haven't made any plans for him, have you?' 'How could I?..Have a heart!' **1970** *New Yorker* 12 Sept. 50/3 Spare us a reefer, beautiful. Have a heart.

24. b. *Hearts*, a card-game for three or four players, similar in principle to whist but without partners or a trump suit: the object of the game is to avoid taking a trick containing a Heart or the Queen of Spades.

1886 'The Major' (*title*) The game of hearts. Rules of the game. How to play hearts. **1907** *Yesterday's Shopping* (1969) 361/1 *Invitation Cards*... At Home, Progressive Hearts —— o'clock. R.S.V.P. **1930** W. S. Maugham *Writer's Notebk.* (1949) 231 In the evening the guests collect and play hearts for infinitesimal sums. **1943** 'C. Dickson' *She died a Lady* viii. 67 You don't call playing bridge or hearts on Saturday night a very Bohemian sort of life, do you? **1946** A. Christie *Hollow* viii. 75 Do you think Hearts or Bridge or Rummy? **1959** J. D. Salinger in *New Yorker* 6 June 101 At all card games, without exception—Go Fish, poker, cassino, hearts, old maid..—he was absolutely intolerable.

51. c. *heart-to-heart*: used to denote conversation, discussion, etc. of real frankness and sincerity; usually *attrib.* but also *absol.* as *sb.*

1867 *Mission Life* 1 Mar. 190 The visitation of an Australian Bishop..is a hand-to-hand and heart-to-heart visit to each Clergyman, and to his people with him. **1894** *Advance* 11 Oct., A kind of public religious 'orphanage', where no true heart-to-heart 'mothering'..was possible. **1902** A. H. Lewis *Wolfville Days* xi. 152 He don't own no real business to transact; he's out to have a heart-to-heart interview with the great Southwest. **1902** Kipling *Traffics & Discov.* (1904) 22 He began by a Lydia Pinkham heart-to-heart talk about my health. **1906** *Daily Chron.* 5 Mar. 6/4 A heart-to-heart discussion of the solar plexus and its part in the emotional economy of man. **1910** S. E. White *Rules of Game* v. xvi. 444 Let's have a heart-to-heart, and find out how we stand. **1918** E. M. Roberts *Flying Fighter* 201 After a heart-to-heart talk, I induced him to let me remain in the Flying Service. **1925** Wodehouse *Carry on, Jeeves* ix. 221 He and Jeeves had had a heart-to-heart chat in the kitchen. **1934** J. E. Neale *Queen Eliz.* ii. 31 Parry came back to have heart-to-heart talks with Mistress Ashley and to probe Elizabeth's mind. **1948** A. Waugh *Unclouded Summer* xv. 252, I have the girls up there in the evenings for 'heart-to-hearts'. **1951** L. MacNeice tr. *Goethe's Faust* 50 All this needs a little explaining And will keep till our next heart-to-heart. **1955** W. Gaddis *Recognitions* i. v. 180 Baby, I just make a few notes on them and write these heart-to-heart confessions.

55. a. (*a*) *heart attack, condition, failure* (examples), *rate, -shape* (earlier example), *-strain, -tube, -valve* (examples); (*b*) *heart-burst, -lift* (so *-lifter*), *-springs, -wound*; *heart-sinking* (earlier example).

1935 D. L. Sayers *Gaudy Night* xxi. 444 She's had rather a nasty heart-attack, but she's better now. **1845** P. J. Bailey *Festus* (ed. 2) 258 Like a horse Put to his heart-burst speed, sobbing up hill. **1896** A. Morrison *Child of Jago* xiii. 134 Dicky..had been afflicted to heart-burst by his father's dodging and running. **1946** *Mod. Lang. Notes* Nov. 442 Heart condition. **1958** *Listener* 13 Nov. 778/2 Before cleaning a car..be certain you haven't a heart condition. **1971** D. O'Connor *Eye of Eagle* viii. 53 He has a heart condition—nothing very serious. **1894** 'O. Henry' *Compl. Wks.* (1928) 797 'Read this,' he said, 'here is proof that Marie Cusheau died of heart failure.' **1906** *Lancet* 13 Jan. 96/2 Dr. C. Bolton..read a paper entitled 'The Treatment of Heart Failure in Diphtheria'. **1960** I. A. Stanton *Dict. for Med. Secretaries* 68/1 Occasionally heart failure denotes a sudden cessation of heart action, but generally it merely means insufficient circulation. **1893** 'Mark Twain' in *Cosmopolitan* Nov. 61/2 Oh, the heart-lift that was in those words! **1967** 'La Meri' *Sp. Dancing* (ed. 2) 7 Yet who can reflect in the immutable phrase the heartlift in watching emotion in motion? **1901** Kipling *Kim* x. 260 You will find one small silver amulet..a heart-lifter. **1959** *New Statesman* 25 Apr. 576/3 The heart-lifter that I chanced to hear was well up to her standard. **1936** *Discovery* 291/2 Adrenalin, by increasing the heart rate..facilitates the passage of the current. **1961** *Lancet* 22 July 190/1 An increase in heart-rate may also increase potassium efflux. **1842** W. Howitt *Rural & Dom. Life Germany* v. 62 The gingerbread was all made up into heart-shapes. **1743** D. Brainerd *Let.* 30 Apr. in J. Edwards *Life D. B.* (1765) There seems to be little of the special workings of the divine Spirit among them yet; which gives me many a heart-sinking hour. **1969** B. Harraden *Kath. Frensham* xviii. 278 She, with ..perseverance, dug a hole in their frozen heart-springs. **1907** Kipling *Bk. of Words* (1928) 36 A people..whose heart-springs go down deep into the fabric. **1906** *Med. Ann.* 241 Heart-strain in growing boys. **1909** *Daily Chron.* 21 Aug. 6/2 Heartstrain and contraction of the joints. **1881** *Trans. Obstetr. Soc. Lond.* XXII. 78 An abnormal amount of tension on the primitive heart-tube. **1932** *Gray's Anat.* (ed. 25) 1437 Heart valves. **1963** *Daily Tel.* 21 Sept. 9/5 (*heading*) Heart valve operation. *Ibid.*, The limited number of heart valve replacement operations so far carried out. **1839** P. J. Bailey *Festus* 269 Her heart-wound. **1902** *Temple Bar* CXXVI. 111 It rained upon his bleeding heart-wound like balm. **1906** *Westm. Gaz.* 3 Aug. 10/2 The faint, fine smell of new-mown grass Stabs like a heart-wound as I pass.

b. *heart-holding, -shaking, -sickening, -swelling, -tearing, -warming, -wringing* adjs.

1897 J. L. Allen *Choir Invisible* xvi. 240 Universal fellowship with seeding grass and breeding herb and every heart-holding creature of the woods. **1913** E. F. Benson *Thorley Weir* iv, Things fairer and more heart-holding. **1907** *Tatler* 22 May 132/2 A heart-shaking tragedy. **1911** Kipling *Diversity of Creatures* (1917) 130 The heart-shaking jests of Decay. **1918** V. Woolf in *Times Lit. Suppl.* 31 Jan. 55/1 Effective and heart-shaking ghost stories. **1945** W. S. Churchill *Victory* (1946) 223 The decision..remained nevertheless a heart-shaking risk. **1820** *Edin. Monthly Rev.* Apr. 449 Can anything be more heart-sickening to such a philanthropist? **1902** *London Mag.* VIII. 432/2 It was heart-sickening, as his great form with its yellow skin and black stripes, as his blazing eyes, his flashing teeth and his outspread claws rose toward us through the air. **1814** Jane Austen *Mansf. Park* III. vi, Her happiness was of a quiet, deep, heart-swelling sort. **1884** W. James *Coll. Ess. & Rev.* (1920) 258 In listening to poetry..we are often surprised at the..heart-swelling and the lachrymal effusion that unexpectedly catch us. **1916** 'Boyd Cable' *Action Front* 149 Thirty-six solid hours of physical stress and heart-tearing strain. **1920** *Glasgow Herald* 21 Oct. 6 The latest phases of the heart-tearing Irish tragedy. **1899** *Daily News* 20 Apr. 5/7 They are a heart-warming cordial. **1966** *Times* (Austral. Suppl.) 28 Mar. p. viii/4 Perth..friendly enough to give..migrants..a heartwarming impression of their new country. **1932** H. Crane *Let.* 12 Apr. (1965) 408 The Mexican singer..is generally shrill but capable of heart-wringing vibrations.

c. *heart-wrung* adj. (earlier and later examples).

1791 Burns *Ae Fond Kiss* in *Wks.* (1871) 294 Deep in heart-wrung tears I'll pledge thee. **1948** C. Day Lewis *Poems 1943–47* 70 One heart-wrung phantom still.. Shadows my noontime still.

56. heart-balm, (*a*) something that soothes a person's emotions; (*b*) *U.S. slang*, alimony; **heart-block** [*block *sb.* 19 d] *Med.* (see quot. 1906); **heart brass**, a brass sepulchral tablet in which a heart is represented (see quot. 1912); **heart-hurry** *Med.*, tachycardia (see also quot. 1897); **heart-line** *Palmistry* = *line of the heart* (Line *sb.*[2] 8 b); **heart-lung** *attrib.*, involving or consisting of the heart and the lungs, esp. when removed together for physiological experimentation; *heart-lung machine*, a machine to which a patient's blood supply is connected during an operation and which by-passes and takes over the functions of the heart and the lungs; **heart-rot**, a disease which causes decay in the heart of a tree; also, a fungous disease of beetroots etc.; **hearts-and-flowers** orig. *U.S.*, undue sentimentality, cloying sweetness; also *attrib.*; **heart-talk**, a heart-to-heart talk; **heart-throb**, (*a*) lit. a pulsation of the heart; (*b*) *colloq.* (orig. *U.S.*) something or (esp.) someone that thrills the heart, a lover: freq. used of film stars and other entertainers; also *attrib.*; **heart transplant**, an operation in which a heart from one person is transplanted into the body of another; similarly of two animals; a heart so transplanted; also *attrib.* and *fig.*; **heart-worm**, a parasitic nematode worm which infests the hearts of some carnivores, or the disease caused by this worm; also *transf.*

1922 Joyce *Ulysses* 352 There were wounds that wanted healing with heartbalm. **1938** Wodehouse *Summer Moonshine* x. 126 This Miss Prudence Whittaker

issuing this T. P. Vanringham for breach of promise and heart balm. **1903** *Lancet* 22 Aug. 523/1 The jugular pulsations correspond to independent auricular contractions which are not propagated to the ventricles—a state of 'heart-block'. **1906** *Brit. Med. Jrnl.* 27 Oct. 1107/1 The term 'heart-block' is applied to that condition where the stimulus for contraction passing from auricle to ventricle, is stopped or 'blocked' on account of some defect in those muscle fibres. **1966** *Lancet* 31 Dec. 1441/1 Patients who had partial heart block while on P.G.I. therapy alone.. reverted to sinus rhythm. **1971** *Jrnl. Gen. Psychol.* Jan. 13 Magnesium sulphate was superior to sodium amytal and ether. Its main drawback was its tendency to produce heart block. **1907** H. W. MACKLIN *Brasses of England* VIII. 205 The typical form of a heart brass is seen when this device is placed by itself in the midst of a monumental slab. **1912** J. S. M. WARD *Brasses* 80 Heart brasses proper fall into two main divisions: (*a*) plain, sometimes inscribed or with scrolls, (*b*) held by hands, usually coming out of a cloud. **1956** A. C. BOUQUET *Church Brasses* VII. 114 There is a large heart brass at Melton Mowbray, Leicestershire. **1891** *Lancet* 18 July 118/2 (*title*) Paroxysmal heart hurry associated with visceral disorders. **1897** *Med. Times & Hosp. Gaz.* XXV. 33/2 By acceleration of the heart or 'heart-hurry', is meant a persistent increase of the pulse above eighty in a woman, well above seventy beats per minute in a man, and above ninety in a child. Heart-hurry is divided into two kinds; they are tachycardia and palpitation. **1893** BEERBOHM *Let.* 14 Oct. (1964) 76 He has no heart-line on his right hand. **1894** 'MARK TWAIN' in *Century Mag.* Feb. 554/2 Wilson began to study Luigi's palm, tracing life lines, heart lines, head lines, and so on. **1956** N. D. FORD *Life in your Hands* v. 40 The Head and Heart lines join in forming one straight line... The Fate line begins well clear of the Heart line. **1912** *Jrnl. Physiol.* XLV. 213 The heart-lung preparation should serve therefore for investigations on the normal gaseous metabolism of the heart. *Ibid.* 214 The apparatus consisted of the heart-lung circulation apparatus as described by Knowlton and Starling, and of a respiration apparatus. **1925** *Ibid.* LX. 103 (*title*) A closed circuit heart lung preparation. **1945** *Amer. Jrnl. Physiol.* CXLIV. 191 No details of the experiments on the heart-lung preparation need be presented. *Ibid.*, The results of the thirty-two heart lung experiments can be summarized as follows. **1959** *Daily Tel.* 24 Apr. 13/3 In the party is Dr. Denis Melrose, inventor of the heart-lung machine which bears his name. This makes possible the by-passing of heart and lungs, and enables the operating surgeon to work on a heart which is bloodless, clear and stopped. **1961** *Lancet* 22 July 187/1 (*heading*) Variable atrial venting for the Melrose heart-lung machine. **1968** J. H. BURN *Lect. Notes Pharmacol.* (ed. 9) 37 Another way of demonstrating the action of ouabain on the ventricular contraction is in the heart-lung preparation of the dog. **1847** J. BROWN *Forester* v. 193 That disease, now so prevalent among our larch plantations, generally termed the *heart-rot*—or, as some writers term it, *dry-rot*. **1882** *Encycl. Brit.* XIV. 311/2 A far more formidable enemy [of larches] is the disease known as the 'heart-rot'. **1909** *Cent. Dict.* Suppl. 571/2 *Heart-rot*..of beets. **1919** W. E. HILEY *Fungal Dis. Common Larch* v. 80 Heart-rot of trees is caused by fungi which grow saprophytically on the dead wood. **1945** *New Biol.* I. 52 Heart rot of swedes. **1955** AUDEN *Shield of Achilles* i. 19 An oak with heart-rot. **1968** *Gloss. Terms Timber Preservation* (*B.S.I.*) 10 *Heart rot*, a type of decay characteristically confined to the heart-wood. [**1908** A. WOOLLCOTT *Lett.* (1946) 13 Taking dinner with the mother of the girl I hope to marry some day, and she played 'Hearts and Flowers' for me.] **1942** BERREY & VAN DEN BARK *Amer. Thes. Slang* § 265.1 *Sentimentality*, hearts and flowers. **1964** *Times* 16 Apr. 6/7 We are nearly betrayed into a hearts-and-flowers ending in domestic compromise. **1967** *Listener* 11 May 626/2 Hearts-and-flowers confrontations between..pop singer..and a girl friend. **1912** F. M. HUEFFER *Panel* i. ii. 31, I want a regular—what you might call—heart-talk with Miss Delamere. **1839** P. J. BAILEY *Festus* 62 We should count time by heart-throbs. **1846** [in Dict., sense 55 a]. **1908** *Modern Song Favorites: High Voices* 2 (*title*) Heart-Throbs. **1912** J. LONDON *Let.* 19 Nov. (1966) 368 I've not much heart-throb left for my fellow beings. **1914** G. BURGESS *Burgess Unabridged* 7 The 'jacket' of the 'latest' fiction.. tells of 'thrills' and 'heart-throbs'. **1926** *Atlantic Monthly* Mar. 390/1 Word has gone out to the writers..that the heart throb is what the reading world now pulsates to. **1928** J. P. McEVOY *Show Girl* (title-p.), Cast... Also..the Heart-throb Poet. **1930** WODEHOUSE *Very Good, Jeeves* ix. 227 She has got that way..from a lifetime of writing heart-throb fiction for the masses. **1943** 'A. A. FAIR' *Double or Quits* (1949) vii. 72 She's easy on the eyes, but she's a little too anxious to have it understood I'm her heart throb. **1958** G. MITCHELL *Spotted Hemlock* ii. 16 He was quite a heart-throb, you know. **1959** D. DU MAURIER *Breaking Point* 202 A heart-throb, a lover, someone with wide shoulders and no hips. **1966** *Listener* 23 June 911/2 Rudolph Valentino was the great heart-throb of the silent screen in the nineteen-twenties. **1952** *Surg. Forum 1951* 217 An arterial supply from the host was anastomosed to a pulmonary vein of the heart transplant and an outlet for the left ventricular output of the heart transplant was provided. **1960** *Ibid.* X. 103 Forty-eight puppy heart transplants are reported. **1963** *Surg. Gynecol. & Obstetrics* CXVII. 361/2 If a renal graft fails to function for several days after transplantation, the host can be supported by dialysis. A heart transplant at the present time enjoys no such privilege and must function vigorously immediately. **1967** *Times* 4 Dec. 1/7 The heart transplant operation, the first in the world, took Groote Schuur's surgical team five hours. **1968** *Guardian* 11 Sept. 1/5 Some of the gravest criticisms yet were yesterday levelled against the over-eagerness of heart-transplant surgeons to get hold of donors. **1973** *N.Y. Times Bk. Rev.* 21 Jan. 2 It is a real heart-transplant into English of the great Alexandrian love-poet and voluptuary. **1888** J. S. STALLYBRASS tr. J. Grimm's *Teut. Mythol.* IV. 1659 Stories of the heart-worm. *Ibid.* 1660 The miser's heart-worm. **1955** W. W. DENLINGER *Compl. Boston* 94 Heart worms..in dogs are rare. **1957** *Encycl. Brit.* XVI. 207/2 *Dirofilaria immitis* (cause of heartworm in dogs). **1959** *Listener* 5 Nov. 796/1 The professional intimate, the confidential heart-worm with the hypodermic technique, is one of the horrors of television. **1965** E. J. L. SOULSBY *Textbk. Vet. Clin. Path.* I. iv. 100 *Dirofilaria immitis* is the heartworm and is parasitic in the..dog, fox, wolf and various other wild carnivores.

hearth[1]. Add: **1. b.** (Later example.)

1845 E. ACTON *Mod. Cookery* vii. 191 The hot plates, or *hearths* with which the kitchens of good houses are always furnished.

4. hearth tidy, a pan for containing the ashes that fall from a fireplace.

1920 *Ironmonger* 18 Dec. 95 Saucepans, hearth tidies, curbs, plate racks.

b. hearth-bottom (examples).

1880 *Encycl. Brit.* XIII. 299/2 This is the hearth bottom, formerly made of one or more large slabs of sandstone. **1951** *Good Housek. Home Encycl.* (1956) 269/2 Sunk or hearth-bottom grates, in which the fuel rests on a bed of fire clay.

hearth-rug. Add: Also *attrib.* (*a*) fireside, domestic; (*b*) resembling a hearth-rug.

1901 *Daily Chron.* 31 July 7/2 Turning the hearthrug favourite into the streets is certainly better than shutting it up, slowly to starve in an unoccupied house. **1902** *Ibid.* 2 Sept. 5/2 The sparrow is far too 'fly' a bird for the hearth-rug-bred cat. **1909** *Westm. Gaz.* 20 July 5/1 The inelegant, cumbrous, and shaggy hearth-rug coats.

heartland (hā·ɹtlænd). [f. HEART *sb.* 17 + LAND *sb.*] A (usually extensive) central region of homogeneous (geographical, political, industrial, etc.) character. Also *transf.*

1904 H. J. MACKINDER in *Geogr. Jrnl.* XXIII. 434 But trans-continental railways are now transmuting the conditions of land-power, and nowhere can they have such effect as in the closed heart-land of Euro-Asia, in vast areas of which neither timber nor accessible stone was available for road-making. **1919** —— *Democratic Ideals & Reality* 96 Taken together, the regions of Arctic and Continental drainage measure nearly a half of Asia and a quarter of Europe, and form a great continuous patch in the north and centre of the continent..inaccessible to navigation from the ocean... Let us call this great region the Heartland of the Continent. **1947** *Landfall* I. 298 We are in the frontier West, the heartland of the American myth. **1949** 'G. ORWELL' *Nineteen Eighty-Four* II. 189 The territory which forms the heartland of each super-state always remains inviolate. **1959** A. J. TOYNBEE *Hellenism* 2 The matrix of the Indo-European languages, somewhere in the heartland of the Old World. **1966** *New Statesman* 13 May 674/3 Mr Heath..is right to make the attempt even if it means some ill-feeling in the Conservative heartlands. **1968** POWELL & WALLIS *House of Lords in Middle Ages* viii. 123 King John planned a concerted attack on the French heartland from east and west. **1972** *Observer* 30 July 9/8 Chobham Farm container depot and Midland Cold Storage nestling within a few hundred yards of each other, lie at the very heartland of British trade unionism.

heartwater (hā·ɹtwǭ:təɹ). *Vet.* [f. HEART *sb.* + WATER *sb.*: so called from the characteristic accumulation of straw-coloured fluid in the pericardium of the heart.] A febrile disease of sheep, goats and cattle, caused by the virus *Rickettsia* (= *Cowdria*) *ruminantium*, transmitted by the bont tick (or other closely related ticks), and occurring in various parts of Africa, esp. South Africa, and in Madagascar.

1882 S. HECKFORD *Lady Trader in Transvaal* xiv. 134 The Nell family..swore it had died of what they call here 'heart-water'. **1896** R. WALLACE *Farm. Ind. Cape Col.* xx. 380 Heart-water in sheep is another obscure disease of a specific nature, which seems to be unknown in other sheep countries. **1905** *Rep. Brit. Assoc.* 282 An old-time supposition that *A[mblyomma] hebræum* was associated with a disease called 'heartwater', which had practically put a stop to the farming of sheep and angora goats in several south-eastern districts. **1930** *Discovery* Aug. 265/2 Heartwater in sheep was..caused by the bite of a tick, *Amblyomma hebraeum*. **1949** *Cape Argus* 11 Aug. 3/6 They dealt with heartwater..in the Union.

heart-wood. Add: **2.** The Tasmanian ironwood, *Notelæa ligustrina*.

1889 J. H. MAIDEN *Useful Native Plants Austral.* 579 The heart-wood yields a very peculiar figure; it is a very fair substitute for Lignum-Vitæ. **1902** G. S. BOULGER *Wood* ii. 221 *Notelæa ligustrina*...South-eastern Australasia. Known also as 'Heartwood' in Tasmania...exceedingly hard and close-grained.

hearty, *a.* and *sb.* Add: **C.** *sb.* **3.** At some English universities, used to denote an extrovert who enters heartily into college life and sports; an athletic (as distinguished from an æsthetic) man. Also in more general use (see quot. 1955).

1925 *Weekly Dispatch* 22 Nov. 9/2 The leaders in the sport ['debagging'] are a band of 'hearties' who hail mostly from Magdalen and 'The House'. **1928** in L. MacNeice *Strings are False* (1965) 274 Capell was knocked down in the Broad the other day by a hearty. **1930** *Times Lit. Suppl.* 24 July 610/4 At English universities undergraduates classify themselves into the mutually exclusive categories of 'aesthetes' and 'hearties'. **1934** C. LAMBERT *Music Ho!* iii. 216 The sheer anger aroused in 'hearties' of the Beachcomber order by such different manifestations of contemporary depression as jazz songs and the poetry of Eliot. **1955** *Times* 12 May 11/4 A hearty has come to mean an oppressively cheerful, muscular and back-slapping personage who is prostrating company. **1959** *News Chron.* 19 Aug. 4/3 There is no trace of the horse-play hearty in his make-up. **1964** C. MACKENZIE *My Life & Times* III. iv. 130 To go back to the noise in Trinity quad on that Saturday evening in 1903. 'Oh, these hearties!' I said... From that moment, at first as a term for Trinity men and later more generally, 'hearties' became current.

heat, *sb.* Add: **11. a.** (Further examples.)

1958 *Listener* 30 Oct. 709/2 The heat is being pumped into utterly different quarrels. **1962** *Ibid.* 5 Apr. 587/1 His foreign minister..had set himself the task of taking the heat out of inter-Arab exchanges. **1964** *Ann. Reg. 1963* 100 This merely added more heat to the argument.

e. *U.S. slang.* A state of intoxication caused by alcohol or drugs, esp. in phr. *to have a heat on.*

1912 D. LOWRIE *My Life in Prison* vii. 77 A few years ago this dump was full of dope. Every other man y'r met had a heat on, an' lots o' young kids what came here strong an' healthy went out with a habit. **1931** D. RUNYON *Guys & Dolls* (1932) ii. 41 The party is going big along toward one o'clock when all of a sudden in comes Handsome Jack Maddigan with half a heat on, and in five minutes he is all over the joint, drinking everything that is offered him.

12. (Later examples.)

1944 'N. SHUTE' *Pastoral* ix. 206 He wants to get you both off the station on leave till the heat goes off. **1970** E. R. JOHNSON *God Keepers* (1971) xii. 132 There was a lot of merit in having the ranking man right where the heat was going to be.

b. *slang* (orig. *U.S.*), in various interconnected senses, notably (*a*) a gun (? as an instrument of 'heat'); also *heater*; (*b*) in phr. *to turn on* (or *give*) *the heat*, to use a gun, hence *fig.*, *to turn the heat on* (someone), to apply pressure on; (*c*) involvement with or pursuit by the police; a police officer, the police.

1928 *Amer. Mercury* May 80/1 The greatest difficulty for such a mob was to avoid another's *heat*. *Ibid.*, It's not so much your own heat you got to watch, but you're apt to run into a bunch of hoosiers out looking for another outfit just hot from some caper. **1929** *Sat. Even. Post* 13 Apr. 54/3 A pistol may be a heat... A man shooting a gun is fogging... 'I fogged away with my heat until I pooped that dummy.' **1929** *Detective Fiction Weekly* 9 Nov. 651/2 Aw, put up your heaters. If you bump me you don't git anywheres. **1930** *Amer. Mercury* Dec. 456/1 Either take our beer or it's plenty of heat for yours. **1931** G. IRWIN *Amer. Tramp & Underworld Slang* 96 *Heat*, the state of mind of the police or public following a crime or series of crimes, when the people are 'hot under the collar' or 'all heated up'. More lately, any trouble, as 'in hot water'. **1931** D. RUNYON *Guys & Dolls* (1932) iii. 58 Maybe you remember John the Boss, and the heat which develops around and about when he is scragged in Detroit? **1932** W. R. BURNETT *Silver Eagle* i. 7 'He don't even pack a heater.' 'Don't what?' 'He don't carry a gun.' **1934** H. N. ROSE *Thesaurus of Slang* iii. 16/2 Cover One with a Gun (v. phr.): to turn on the heat. **1936** J. G. BRANDON *Pawnshop Murder* xxv. 246 You planted yourself in a safe spot to give Lou the heat. **1936** H. COREY *Farewell, Mr. Gangster* xiv. 174 But the word went out that the government heat was on. The FBI was known to be relentless in its pursuit. *Ibid.* ii. 14 During the heat on the bank robbers the field agents almost lost the habit of sleep. **1937** E. H. SUTHERLAND *Professional Thief* 238 *Heat*, danger in general; an investigation; a policeman. **1938** J. CURTIS *They drive by Night* xix. 211 The bleeding heat's on here for me. **1939** R. CHANDLER *Big Sleep* xiv. 110 Then he leaned back..and held the Colt on his knee. 'Don't kid yourself I won't use this heat, if I have to.' **1944** W. R. BURNETT *Nobody lives Forever* xvii. 137 Jim.. took out his gun..and..tossed it down a manhole-grating... 'I was hoping that I'd never have to use that heater.' **1957** *Listener* 24 Oct. 637/2 The moment seemed opportune to 'turn the heat' on Turkey. **1967** W. MURRAY *Sweet Ride* x. 168 He got busted last week and he don't take that too kindly. Guess he figured you was heat. **1969** *New Yorker* 19 July 20 Out the door comes this great big porcine member of the heat, all belts and bullets and pistols and keys. **1970** C. MAJOR *Dict. Afro-Amer. Slang* 65 *Heat*, law-enforcement officer. **1972** WODEHOUSE *Pearls, Girls, & Monty Bodkin* xi. 178 And Dolly, drop the heater and leave that jewel case where it is, I don't want any unpleasantness.

14. a. *heat-capacity, -cloud, -flow, -haze, -insulation, -insulator, -isolation, -mist, -power, -radiator* (= RADIATOR b), *-retrogression, -shock, -test, -trap, -value*; also *heat-labile, -regulating, -resistant, -resisting, -sensitive, -stable* adjs. **b.** *heat-absorption, -evolution, -loss, -producer, -production, -storage*. **c.** *heat-crazed, -hazed, -killed, -misted, -set* adjs. (so *heat-setting* vbl. sb. and adj.); *heat-seal* vb. (so *heat-sealed, -sealing* ppl. adjs.); also with meaning 'against or from heat', as *heat-insulated, -isolated, -proof* adjs.

1902 *Encycl. Brit.* XXXIII. 280/1 Heat-evolution is reckoned as positive, heat-absorption as negative. *Ibid.* 279/2 The heat-capacity of the water. **1895** KIPLING *2nd Jungle Bk.* 140 When the heat-cloud sucks the tempest. **1926** *Daily Colonist* (Victoria, B.C.) 23 July 1/4 In Jersey City, three heat-crazed dogs attacked two young boys. **1902** *Encycl. Brit.* XXXIII. 297/1 Heat-flow due to Conduction. **1925** J. JOLY *Surface-Hist. Earth* vi. 104 Steady heat-flow to the surface. **1955** *Times* 11 July 2/6 A research group investigating problems of heat flow in supersonic aircraft. **1971** I. G. GASS et al. *Understanding*

Earth iii. 67/1 The 'heat flow'—the rate of escape of interior heat from the Earth's surface. **1899** *Daily News* 12 Jan. 6/2 The flat, endless continent, fading away in the heat-haze. **1901** 'Linesman' *Words by Eyewitness* (1902) 30 The ranks of little kopjes across the river slumbered in the heat-haze. **1960** C. Day Lewis *Buried Day* ii. 43 Summer lanes Whose sound quivers like heat-haze endlessly. **1913** E. F. Benson *Thorley Weir* iii, Over all lay a grey heat-hazed sky. **1963** A. J. Hall *Textile Sci.* v. 221 The pin or clip chains over the greater part of their travel run through a heat-insulated chamber. **1902** *Encycl. Brit.* XXXIII. 283/2 Expansion or compression under the condition of heat-insulation, represented by curves called Adiabatics. **1937** *Discovery* Feb. 35/1 Double walls of canvas enclosing an air space, which acted as a perfect heat insulator. **1902** *Encycl. Brit.* XXXIII. 288/1 If the system is heat-isolated. *Ibid.*, The difficulty of realizing experimentally the condition of heat-isolation. **1946** *Nature* 27 July 121/1 In heat-killed grain there was no change in nucleolar size. *Ibid.*, One vital heat-labile system in the earliest stages of the chain of activity preceding cell division. **1964** *Oceanogr. & Marine Biol.* II. 342 A hot-water extract (containing the substrate but not the heat-labile enzyme). **1899** Callendar & Barnes in *Rep. Brit. Assoc.* 626 The external heat loss is more regular and certain. **1902** *Encycl. Brit.* XXVI. 508/1 The heat-loss can be reduced to a minimum. **1935** *Archit. Rev.* LXXVIII. 129 A double window was evolved with central heating between the two glass lines to minimize the heat loss occasioned by the lavish use of glass. **1964** R. F. Ficchi *Electr. Interference* viii. 151 As ground current flows through the ground rod electrode, heat is generated that follows the well known I^2R heat-loss pattern. **1901** H. W. Wilson *With Flag to Pretoria* I. vi. 91 Indistinct lines of Boer entrenchments, flickering through the heat-mist. **1940** W. Empson *Gathering Storm* 48 The heat-mists that my vision hood Shudder precisely with the throng. **1894** M. Dyan *All in Man's Keeping* I. vi. 98 The deep heat-misted valley. **1905** *Westm. Gaz.* 26 Aug. 13/2 The practical science of heat-power-production. **1956** A. H. Compton *Atomic Quest* 52, 10,000 kilowatts of heat-power. **1905** *Daily Chron.* 14 July 4/4 Animal foods rich in fat..are heat-producers of the first order. **1884** *Jrnl. Nerv. & Mental Dis.* XI. 141 He believed the central nervous system to have an immediate influence on heat-production. **1927** Haldane & Huxley *Animal Biol.* iii. 87 If we put our man..into a calorimeter for a day and measure his heat-production. **1906** *Daily Colonist* (Victoria, B.C.) 6 Jan. 5/6 Get a 34-inch poker for your air-tight heater; they are nicely made and have the Alaska heat-proof handle. **1909** *Daily Chron.* 21 Jan. 4/7 Glasses treated in this manner become heat-proof, and may last for years. **1920** H. G. Wells *Outline Hist.* 21 This novel covering of feathers, this new heat-proof contrivance that life had chanced upon. **1867** *Trans. Ill. Agric. Soc.* VI. 53 Heat Radiator [exhibited]. **1904** Goodchild & Tweney *Technol. & Sci. Dict.* 283/2 *Heat radiator*, a device by which the cooling of the cylinder of a motor cycle or of the condenser of a car is promoted. **1897** *Allbutt's Syst. Med.* II. 26 The paralysis of the heat-regulating centres. **1904** *Daily Chron.* 29 Nov. 4/5 The heat-regulating mechanism of the body. **1964** L. Martin *Clinical Endocrinol.* (ed. 4) vii. 227 A varicocœle may also upset the heat-regulating mechanism and this is aggravated by a suspensory bandage. **1960** *Farmer & Stockbreeder* 22 Mar. Suppl. 11/3 The steel-reinforced, heat-resistant handle. **1961** Whitby & Hynes *Med. Bact.* (ed. 7) ii. 17 The ultimate test of a sterilizer is to show that live spores are killed. The spores must be carefully chosen—soil bacteria are often too heat-resistant for the purpose. **1899** *Daily News* 21 July 4/4 A heat-resisting alloy. **1934** *Archit. Rev.* LXXV. 24/2 With the removal of weight from partitions and external walls came a reduction in thickness of material, with a consequent loss of sound and heat-resisting qualities. **1962** *Gloss. Terms Glass Industry* (*B.S.I.*) 8 *Heat-resisting glass*, a glass able to withstand high thermal shock. **1880** S. Haughton *Phys. Geogr.* vi. 312 Periods of heat-retrogression (such as the glacial). **1961** *Lancet* 9 Sept. 592/1 This is heat-sealed across its width. **1964** *Discovery* Oct. 17/1 So impervious to water-vapour is the laminate, even along heat-sealed seams, that less than 0.012 grams per square metre can be leaked through samples every 24 hours. **1952** E. J. Labarre *Dict. Paper* (ed. 2) 125/2 Heat-sealing papers include several types of paper coated with wax, varnish..which will adhere when pressed together with heat. **1946** *Nature* 10 Aug. 194/1 Electronics have brought a contribution in the evaporation of solutions of heat-sensitive materials such as penicillin. **1964** N. G. Clark *Mod. Org. Chem.* i. 5 This may cause the decomposition of one or more of the heat-sensitive components. **1963** A. J. Hall *Textile Sci.* iii. 130 The yarn becomes bulky, with each filament having heat-set small loops closely but irregularly spaced. **1957** *Textile Terms & Defs.* (ed. 3) 88 (s.v. *Setting*), In order to ensure that the crimp is not readily removed..the fibre may be set to impart permanency of crimp, and the operation is known as heat-setting. **1962** J. T. Marsh *Self-Smoothing Fabrics* ii. 8 During the early investigations into the finishing of nylon fabrics, it was found that a heat-setting process had a stabilising effect. **1946** *Nature* 23 Nov. 763/1 The production in certain varieties of apples, of diploid pollen by heat-shock treatment of the pollen mother cells. **1956** *Ibid.* 4 Feb. 227/2 In *Drosophila*, heat-shock at an appropriate stage results in the development of the cross-veinless phenotype. **1946** *Ibid.* 23 Nov. 760/1 Heat-stable enzyme. **1964** M. Hynes *Med. Bacteriol.* (ed. 8) xxiii. 339 *R. prowazeki* and *R. mooseri*..are differentiated by specific heat-labile major antigens, but share a common heat-stable antigen. **1951** *Good Housek. Home Encycl.* 263/1 All heat-storage cookers have insulated hot-plate covers. **1901** *Kynoch Jrnl.* Feb.–Mar. 57/1 The Heat-Test of Nitro Explosives. **1906** W. De Morgan *Joseph Vance* xviii, I think of the *sole di marzo* blazing on the roses in that Tuscan heat-trap. **1887** *Chambers's Jrnl.* 24 Sept. 623/1 The exact heat-value of different kinds of liquid fuel. **1962** *Economist* 21 July 256/1 The main use of this gas should be to fuel power stations (at a 'heat value' parity price with coal or oil).

d. heat balance, the distribution of the flow of heat and other forms of energy into and out of a system in which there is no change in internal energy; also, an account or record of such a distribution, esp. as a means of evaluating the efficiency of boilers, etc.; **heat barrier** *Aeronaut.*, the limitation on the speed of aircraft, etc., due to heating by air friction; **heat bump,** a protuberance on the skin supposed to be due to heat; **heat-centre** *Physiol.*, any of several areas within the central nervous system which control the regulation of the body temperature; **heat coil** *Electr.*, a device fitted in a telephone exchange to protect the lines against small harmful currents; **heat cycle,** a cycle of operations or states in a heat engine; **heat-death** (see quot. 1930[2]); **heat-energy,** that form of energy which is manifested in heat; **heat equator** = *thermal equator* (see *Equator 3 b); **heat exchanger,** a device used for the transference of heat from one medium to another; so **heat exchange, heat exchanging; heat filter,** any device that selectively removes heat radiation but permits the passage of light; **heat flash** (see quot. 1958); **heat-lightning** (earlier examples); **heat-pipe,** a closed, evacuated tube containing around its inner surface a wire mesh or other wick saturated with a working liquid, which through the capillary action of the wick and the higher vapour pressure of the liquid when heated makes possible the rapid conduction of heat away from a source; **heat-pump,** a heat-engine working in reverse (such as a refrigerator), in which work supplied to it is used to transfer heat from a colder to a hotter body; **heat-set, heat-setting ink** (see quots.); see also *heat-set* adj., *-setting* vbl. sb. and adj. sense 14 c above; **heat-shield** (see quots.); **heat-sink** (see quot. 1965[2]); **heat sponge,** a type of heat sink; **heat tinting** (see quot. 1958); **heat tonality, tone, toning** *Physical Chem.* [tr. G. *wärmetönung*], the sum of the heat produced in a chemical reaction and of the work done by the system, expressed in heat-units; the heat of reaction at constant volume (*disused*); **heat transfer,** the transfer of heat from one medium to another.

1898 B. Donkin *Heat Efficiency of Steam Boilers* xiv. 239/2 An approximate 'heat balance', or statement of the distribution of the heating value of the coal among the several items of heat utilised and heat lost, may be included in the report of a test. **1954** *Jrnl. Meteorol.* XI. 8/1 The heat balance between the surface of the earth and the atmosphere..involves a flux of latent heat and of sensible heat, in addition to the radiational items. **1971** *Nature* 25 June 540/1 Ecologists are therefore interested in ways of inferring the temperature of a leaf from a knowledge of its heat balance. **1953** H. Haber *Man in Space* 66 The designers of the Sky-rocket had to be on guard against not only the sonic barrier. With its high rate of speed their craft might run into an obstacle more serious than buffeting shock waves: the heat barrier. **1953** *Sci. Amer.* Dec. 80/1 This is the heat barrier: the heating of a plane by the friction and piling up of air on aircraft surfaces at supersonic speeds. **1954** *Times* 5 Mar. 11/5 They might well find that [the ultimate limits of manned aircraft] were very high and that in the same way as the sound barrier had been overcome the problems of the heat barrier would be solved also. **1957** [see *Barrier *sb.* 4 b]. **1970** J. Chaplin *Wings & Space* 146/1 There is no way to break through the heat barrier as there is with sound. **1927** W. E. Collinson *Contemp. Eng.* 57 Spots, which, it is hoped, are heat-bumps. **1884** *Jrnl. Nerv. & Mental Dis.* XI. 141 Tscheschichin was the first to announce the existence of an inhibitory heat-centre in the nervous system. **1907** *Practitioner* June 771 The action of the heat-centres being sluggish. **1968** M. Monnier *Functions Nerv. Syst.* I. xv. 422 Successful protection from cold is possible through the central nervous co-ordination of several biophysical and chemical mechanisms. This is accomplished by the so-called heat center in the posterior hypothalamus. **1900** K. B. Miller *Amer. Telephone Pract.* (ed. 3) xxiii. 275 A device to afford protection against currents such as these [*sc.* sneak currents]..is termed a heat coil. **1971** *Gloss. Electrotechnical Power Terms* (*B.S.I.*) III. ii. 13 *Heat coil*, a thermal device to protect apparatus from damage by external currents. **1894** B. Donkin *Text-bk. Gas, Oil, & Air Engines* I. ii. 13 (*heading*) Heat 'cycles' and classification of gas engines... Engineers have agreed to designate as a 'cycle' the successive operations taking place in a heat motor. **1930** *Engineering* 8 Aug. 187/3 The following..trends were..observable:..design and operation on more efficient heat cycles [etc.]. **1930** J. Jeans *Mysterious Universe* i. 13 The second law of thermodynamics predicts that there can be but one end to the universe—a 'heat-death' in which the total energy of the universe is uniformly distributed, and all the substance of the universe is at the same temperature. **1959** J. Blish *Clash of Cymbals* iii. 73 Any cyclical theory of the universe, any continuous and eternal systole/diastole from monobloc to heat-death and back again. **1973** *Nature* 11 May 65/1 What lies ahead is, in Clausius's later term, 'a heat death'. **1876** P. G. Tait *Rec. Adv. Phys. Sci.* 138 We are led to speak of the availability of an amount of heat-energy. **1893** *Jrnl. Soc. Arts* 8 Sept. 897/1 The practically unavoidable waste of heat energy. **1902** *Encycl. Brit.* XXXIII. 283/2 The whole of its intrinsic heat energy might theoretically be recovered in the form of external work. **1915** *Chambers's Jrnl.* Jan. 43/1 For all the heat-energy wasted..the consumer has had to pay. **1968** R. A. Lyttleton *Mysteries Solar Syst.* ii. 77 The release exceeds the gentle loss of heat-energy arising from the very slow processes of conduction within the Earth. **1904** Goodchild & Tweney *Technol. & Sci. Dict.* 283/2 Heat Equator. **1911** M. I. Newbigin *Mod. Geogr.* iv. 87 Those regions of the earth which are directly beneath the vertical rays of the sun are heated most intensely... This belt of high temperature is called the heat equator. **1902** G. E. Davis *Handbk. Chem. Engin.* II. ii. 132 (*caption*) Diagrammatic sketch of heat-exchanging tanks. *Ibid.* 133 (*heading*) Heat exchangers... In no case would the cold water be heated to the temperature of the original hot water. **1908** *Sci. Abstr.* A. XI. 203 For snow the average total daily heat-exchange is 19 gm. cals. per cm.[2] **1915** *Chem. Abstr.* IX. 2332 (*heading*) Heat exchange apparatus wherein the one agent flows through one tube and the other agent flows through an annular chamber surrounding the said tube. **1924** R. Seligman *Brit. Pat.* 223,033, In some.. descriptions of heat exchanging or sterilising apparatus.. it has been proposed in order to obtain a tight jointing to groove and tongue the rims. *Ibid.*, The plates should be working in parallel and the heat exchange effected by counter current. **1947** *Science News* IV. 33 A heat exchanger, then, is merely a means whereby the heat which would normally be wasted is used for combustion. **1952** *Ibid.* XXV. 87 This is done by means of the heat exchanger, which by various means effects the transfer of heat from the gases leaving the turbine to the air entering the combustion chamber. **1958** *Engineering* 28 Feb. 284/1 As an aid in securing high thermal efficiency from gas-turbine plants, use is frequently made of a heat exchanger, whereby the turbine exhaust heat is used to preheat the combustion gas. **1959** *Listener* 29 Oct. 732/3 Twelve heat exchangers for the new Bradwell (Essex) nuclear power station. **1967** M. Chandler *Ceramics in Mod. World* v. 157 Where refractories are used to store and transfer heat, as in heat exchangers, the most important property required is high heat capacity. **1898** W. E. Woodbury *Encycl. Dict. Photogr.* 367, I have taken a powerful projection lantern and set it as near to the microscope as the intervening heat-filter will permit. **1962** *Which?* Mar. 68/2 The heat filter prevents much of the heat radiated from the lamp, from reaching the slide. **1958** *Chambers's Techn. Dict.* Suppl. 984/1 *Heat flash*, intense heat radiation from an elevated A or H bomb, detection of which, by heat-sensitive paint, gives the precise indication of ground-zero. **1961** 'C. E. Maine' *Man who owned World* x. 118 Central London was a wilderness of fused stone and leaning skeletal buildings, blackened and oxidised by nuclear heat flash. **1834** C. A. Davis *Lett. J. Downing* ii. 17 You may just as well try to paint a flash of heat-lightning in dog-days. **1849** Thoreau *Week Concord Riv.* 275 Friendship is..remembered like heat lightning in past summers. **1964** G. M. Grover et al. in *Jrnl. Applied Physics* XXXV. 1990/1 We will refer to devices of this general class, for brevity, as 'heat pipes'. *Ibid.* 1991/1 A liquid sodium heat pipe for operation at about 1100°K was constructed. **1969** *New Scientist* 19 June 641/1 A heat pipe is one of the major components of the most powerful and efficient radioisotope-heated power generator yet built. *Ibid.*, The advantage of the heat pipe is that the outside surface is at the same temperature along the whole of its length. **1894** J. A. Ewing *Steam-Engine* iv. 118 By a refrigerating machine or heat-pump is meant a machine which will carry heat from a cold to a hotter body. *Ibid.*, Any heat-engine will serve as a heat-pump if it be forced to trace its indicator diagram backwards. **1948** E. F. Obert *Thermodynamics* xiv. 520 The reversed heat-engine cycle is called a refrigerator (and, also a heat pump) when the evaporator is used for cooling purposes..; the same cycle is called a heat pump (but not a refrigerator) when the condenser is used for heating purposes. **1957** *Encycl. Brit.* XIX. 55/2 The heat-pump system..is a conventional refrigeration system where the heat rejected by the refrigerant at the condenser is utilized for heating during the winter while the evaporator absorbs heat from..any..low-grade heat source. **1966** *McGraw-Hill Encycl. Sci. & Technol.* VI. 369/1 Unless the price of electric energy is low..the heat pump cannot be justified solely as a heating device. However, if there is also need for comfort cooling..in the summer, the heat pump, to do both the cooling and heating, becomes attractive. **1941** *Inland Printer* Nov. 42/1 The new presses..would enable us to print the body of the magazine entirely with the improved heat-set inks. **1947** R. Burns *Printing Inks* v. 249 (*heading*) Heat-setting inks. The fresh prints are exposed to intense heat from gas flames or radiant surfaces for a very short period. **1963** Kenneison & Spilman *Dict. Printing* 91 *Heat-set inks*, printing inks manufactured in a special way to induce quicker drying... The vehicle of these inks is such that it vaporizes rapidly when the paper is heated after printing. **1957** W. E. Clason *Elsevier's Dict. Electronics* 226 *Heat shield*, a metallic surface surrounding a heat radiating element e.g. a hot cathode in order to reduce the radiation loss. **1962** J. Glenn et al. in *Into Orbit* 245 *Heatshield*, as used in Project Mercury missions ..consists of a coating of ablative material on the rounded base of the capsule which evaporates during re-entry and carries off much of the heat in the form of a gas. **1968** *Times* 16 Dec. 7/3 Reentry speed was slightly faster than expected for Apollo 8 and the heat shield on the spacecraft was charred to a depth of three-quarters of an inch. **1956** *Jrnl. Brit. Interplan. Soc.* XV. 302 The determination of optimum sink temperature is beyond the scope of this paper, particularly since thorough analysis of the entire radiant heat sink problem has been previously presented. **1957** W. E. Clason *Elsevier's Dict. Electronics* 226 *Heat sink*, used with power transistors to dissipate heat. **1959** *Listener* 28 May 930/1 By mounting the transistor on a relatively large piece of metal, which in turn is fixed to what is called a heat sink—something into which unwanted heat can be shot—the powers that transistors can handle..have been greatly increased. **1961** *Aeroplane* C. 372/2 For the Mach 2 aircraft the air supply from the main engines can be cooled by using the fuel as a heat sink. **1965** *New Scientist* 20 May 507/1 Satisfactory control of the rate and extent of cooling of the patient is obtained by regulating the temperature of the heat sink.

1965 W. H. ALLEN *Dict. Technical Terms for Aerospace Use* 132/2 *Heat sink*, (1) in thermodynamic theory, a means by which heat is stored, or is dissipated or transferred from the system under consideration; (2) a place toward which the heat moves in a system; (3) a material capable of absorbing heat; a device utilizing such a material and used as a thermal protection device on a spacecraft or reentry vehicle; (4) in nuclear propulsion, any thermodynamic device, such as a radiator or condenser, that is designed to absorb the excess heat energy of the working fluid. **1972** *Sci. Amer.* Mar. 118/2 All power transistors.. must be mounted on heat sinks that have large cooling fins. **1949** A. R. WEYL *Guided Missiles* 15 For short ranges, cooling of the heated walls may be avoided, either by the 'heat sponge' principle (absorption and conduction of heat through walls of substantial thickness) [etc.]. **1958** A. G. HALEY *Rocketry* iii. 57 The American Rocket Society..developed a 'heat sponge' motor, wherein blocks of aluminum absorbed large amounts of heat. **1910** C. H. DESCH *Metallogr.* vii. 149 Stead has devised an electrical heater, by means of which the heat-tinting can be carried on on the stage of the microscope. **1958** A. D. MERRIMAN *Dict. Metallogr.* 121/2 *Heat tinting*, a method of distinguishing and of identifying the micro-constituents of a polished surface of a metallographic specimen. The method is based on the fact that temper colours or heat tints..appear when oxidation begins on a polished surface that is being heated. **1895** C. S. PALMER tr. *Nernst's Theoret. Chem.* III. iv. 435 Instead of using the 'heat-toning' (heat tonality) to determine the ratio of distribution, one may employ..the changes in the volumes..of the solutions, on neutralisation. *Ibid.* IV. i. 491 The sum of the heat produced in the reaction, and of the external work performed,..we will call the 'heat-toning' (Wärmetönung) of the reaction... This 'heat-toning' represents the change of the total energy..of the system. **1902** H. C. JONES *Elem. Physical Chem.* 286 Since we have reactions which evolve heat.., and also reactions in which heat is absorbed.., the heat tone may be positive or negative. **1934** A. J. MEE *Physical Chem.* xv. 608 The term 'heat tonality' is sometimes used to denote the amount of heat associated with a chemical reaction. **1940** GLASSTONE *Physical Chem.* iii. 192 At one time the heat of reaction at constant volume was called the 'heat tone' (Wärmetönung) of the reaction; although this term is still used in German scientific literature, its significance is now equivalent to the general expression 'heat of reaction', the qualification of constant volume or pressure being added. **1937** *Jrnl. R. Aeronaut. Soc.* XLI. 121 He had been very interested in discovering the relationship between heat transfer and friction. *Ibid.*, It was well known that a flat plate and a rough surface produced comparatively the same rate of heat transfer. **1958** *Times Rev. Industry* Apr. 9/1 The relative virtues of..heat-transfer media. **1966** W. A. HEFLIN *Second Aerospace Gloss.* 60/2 *Heat transfer*, the transfer of heat within a substance or structure by radiation, conduction, or convection.

heated, *ppl. a.* Add: **1. b.** *heated term*, the hot season of the year. *U.S.*

1855 *N.Y. Herald* 26 Dec. 3/4 Our 'heated terms' are over, and we now begin to look out for the approach of the 'northers'. **1867** *Congress. Globe* 5 July 487/1, I think we could go on now during the heated term.. better than..during the cold season. **1873** J. H. BEADLE *Undevel. West* 793 The average of the 'heated term', one day with another, is there recorded at eighty-four degrees. **1949** *Chicago Tribune* 11 Sept. 43/5 What a month ago appeared to be a trivial item of conversation during the heated term has become a raging topic among scientists.

heater. Add: **1. b.** *slang.* A gun (see *HEAT *sb.* 12 b).

2. a. (Earlier examples.) **c.** Also, a usual name for a domestic electric or gas fire.

1666 in *Essex Inst. Hist. Coll.* XXV. 147 It. boxe Iron & heaters. **1744** B. FRANKLIN *Acc. Fire-Places* 27 You.. may..warm the Flat-Irons, heat Heaters [etc.].

f. A triangular structure resembling in form the heater of a box-iron.

1797 J. A. GRAHAM *Descr. Sk. Vermont* 119 There are two arches..with a pier in the centre..with the addition of a heater, or triangular front. **1899** DICKINSON & PREVOST *Cumbld. Gloss.* 379 *Heater bit* is the triangular piece of ground, generally grass-grown, at the junction of three roads; so called because of resemblance to the iron heater in a box-iron.

g. A device used for the indirect heating of the cathode of a thermionic valve.

1940 *Chambers's Techn. Dict.* 407/2 *Heater*, the conductor carrying the current for heating an equipotential cathode, generally enclosed by the cathode. **1945** *Electronic Engin.* XVII. 454 Radio receivers and other electronic devices may have the valve heaters connected in series.

h. A device used for heating the interior of a motor car. Also *attrib.* and *Comb.*, as *heater-demister, -fan.*

1939–40 *Army & Navy Stores Catal.* 266/1 *Car heater*... A robust and reliable heater. **1948** *Motor Man.* (ed. 33) xii. 232 (*heading*) Car heaters. The use of car heaters has spread in recent months, largely owing to the spur of the export trade. **1961** *Which?* (Reports on Cars) 14 Heater efficiency is measured and compared, and the results analysed for average interior temperatures and effective distribution of heat. **1962** *Ibid.* Oct. 310/2 Most modern cars can have a built-in heater-demister which blows warmed air into the car. **1969** S. HYLAND *Top Bloody Secret* ii. 163 The [car] engine was silent, but the heater-fan was still humming.

3. heater-shaped (examples); **heater-piece** *U.S.* (examples).

1859 BARTLETT *Dict. Amer.*, *Heater piece*, a gore or triangular piece of land, so called probably, from a flat iron, the form of which it resembles. **1863** D. G. MITCHELL *My Farm* 243 Waal—kinder like to have a little 'heater' piece, the boys, you see, hoe it out in odd spells. **1847** C. BOUTELL *Monumental Brasses* 37 The shield is small, flat, and heater-shaped. **1917** A. C. FRYER in *Trans. Bristol & Glouc. Archaeol. Soc.* XL. 41 A half angel vested in alb and holding a heater-shaped shield.

heath, *sb.* **4. a.** *heathland* (later examples).

1936 *Discovery* Jan. 25/1 Only about 50,000 acres of Breckland remain at the present moment as heathland. **1954** M. BERESFORD *Lost Villages* vi. 200 This was forest, scrub or rough heathland. **1966** M. R. D. FOOT *SOE in France* xii. 407 Bourgoin was too wily a fighter to be rounded up methodically in his heathland base.

heather. 3. a. *heather-honey* (earlier and later examples.).

1826 *Blackw. Edin. Mag.* XX. 412/1 Heather-honey of this blessed year's produce. **1935** *Jrnl. Physical Chem.* XXXIX. 213 The term 'heather honey' is used to describe any honey derived largely from the nectar of *Calluna vulgaris, Erica cinerea*, and allied species. **1971** *Country Life* 28 Oct. 1107/2 The drawback to heather honey is that it is difficult to extract. **1971** *Harrod's Xmas Catal.* 59/3 'Double Scotch' Honey is a unique blend of Scottish heather honey and rare old malt whisky.

Heath Robinson (hīþ rǫ·binsǒn). [f. the name of the humorous artist W. *Heath Robinson* (1872–1944).] Used *attrib.* or *ellipt.* of any absurdly ingenious and impracticable device of the kind illustrated by this artist. Hence **Hea:th-Robinsone·sque, Hea:th-Ro·binsonish** *adjs.*; **Hea:th Ro·binsonism.**

1917 'CONTACT' *Airman's Outings* i. 12 The movable mounting for the observer's gun in the rear cockpit... We called it the Christmas Tree, the Heath Robinson, the Jabberwock, the Ruddy Limit, and names unprintable. **1930** *Telegr. & Teleph. Jrnl.* June 180/2 The tour commenced at the principal machine shop. Here one is introduced to what on first acquaintance appears to be a Heath Robinson nightmare. **1931** D. L. SAYERS *Five Red Herrings* xiii. 137 'Not very lively,' he mused; 'better, I think, for a Heath Robinson picture.' **1934** *Discovery* Nov. 328/2 This 'Heath-Robinson' jumble of wooden sheds, sluices, and water troughs looks ridiculous, yet it works all right. **1951** R. CAMPBELL *Light on Dark Horse* xiii. 175 In the bay was the Heath-Robinsonesque, palm-crested fortress of Goree. **1960** L. DAVIDSON *Night of Wenceslas* xiii. 207 It was surely a bit of a Heath-Robinsonish way of passing valuable secrets. **1962** *New Scientist* 29 Mar. 762/2 Certain general principles of heathrobinsonism. **1963** *Times* 26 Feb. 9/5 Some of the devices look somewhat Heath Robinson and rather like a film set, but of their serious purpose the visitor is left in no doubt. **1968** N. FREELING *This is Castle* III. iii. 163 The English talked about things being 'Heath-Robinson' to this day, quite rightly—he recalled the man from his own childhood, a caricaturist who filled his drawings with wonderful complicated mechanisms made out of every kind of rubbish-tip junk held together with knotted bits of string.

heating, *vbl. sb.* Add: **b.** *heating arrangement(s)*; **heating element** (see *ELEMENT *sb.* 4 c).

1873 *Leisure Hour* 18 Jan. 48/1 Cisterns in the upper parts of a house should be emptied, if the heating arrangement has been neglected. **1902** *Encycl. Brit.* XXVI. 510/2 It [*sc.* a temperature of 20°C] is readily attainable at any time in a modern laboratory with adequate heating arrangements. **1923** R. G. COLLINGWOOD *Roman Brit.* 54 The discovery of skeletons huddled inside the heating-arrangements beneath the floors.

heatronic (hītrǫ·nik), *a.* [f. HEAT *sb.* + *ELECT)RONIC *a.*] (See quot. 1943.)

1943 *Plastics Engin.* Mar. 87/1 Heatronic molding is announced as a most significant advance in the art of molding plastics. This process is the result of..research involving the application of electronics to the molding of thermosetting materials. **1944** *Electronic Engin.* XVII. 40 Space is devoted to discussing the physical properties of heatronic mouldings.

heat treatment. a. The specialized application of heat to various substances to produce a desired metallurgical or physical condition, e.g. hardness, softness, toughness. Hence **heat-treat** *v.*; **heat-treatable** *a.*; **heat-treated** *ppl. a.*; **heat-treating** *vbl. sb.*

1895 H. M. HOWE in *Trans. Amer. Inst. Mining Engin. 1894* XXIV. 746, I..call your attention to two directions in which very important progress may be..hoped for—pyrometry and the heat-treatment of steel. *Ibid.* 747 In the hardening and tempering of tools, in the annealing of steel castings,..and in the manufacture of guns, projectiles, and armor, we have already extensive and careful if empirical heat-treatment. **1899** *Jrnl. Iron & Steel Inst.* LIV. 147 The simple heat treatment had converted the more or less brittle annealed material into tough and strong steel. **1904** F. W. HARBORD *Metallurgy of Steel* xxxix, (*title*) Heat treatment of steel. **1908** *Chem. Abstr.* II. 1121 The Structure of Metals. Changes Produced by Working and by Heat Treatment. **1908** *Westm. Gaz.* 2 June 4/2 The wonderful effect of heat-treating [of steel]. *Ibid.*, With these alloying materials added to steel small gears can be made that, if properly heat-treated, they will be so tough and strong as to make it impossible to break out a tooth even with a sledge-hammer. **1946** *Nature* 27 July 120/2 Plants from heat-treated grain were..somewhat shorter in the straw. **1947** *Hansard, Commons* 4 Dec. 559 Mr. Lambert asked the Minister of Education the number of rural schools..in which the children are supplied with heat-treated milk. **1947** *Food & Drugs Statut. Rules & Orders* DCXII. (*heading*) The ice cream (heat treatment, etc.) regulations, 1947. *Ibid.*, The mixture shall be subjected to heat treatment as follows [etc.]. **1950** J. G. DAVIS *Dict. Dairying* 332 *Heat treatment of milk.* The term is a general one covering any of the ordinary commercial heating methods by which the keeping quality of milk is enhanced and pathogenic organisms destroyed. **1956** *Nature* 25 Feb. 360/1 He invented the heat-treatment which has for decades been applied as compulsory routine at every ginnery in the country. *Ibid.* 3 Mar. 436/2 The specimen [of an alloy] had been heat-treated. **1960** *Farmer & Stockbreeder* 5 Jan. 64 All seed grown from heat-treated stocks. **1960** *Times* (Roy. Soc. Number) 19 July p. xxi/3 Heat-treatable aluminium alloys. **1963** *B.S.I. News* Feb. 17/1 Fifteen different steels..were heat-treated by the National Engineering Laboratory. **1971** *Nature* 26 Nov. 231/1 Heat treatment (57°C for 30 s in summer) disrupted the layer into irregular globules.

b. The therapeutic use of heat, esp. radiant and infra-red heat.

1934 J. E. MANSION *Harrap's Fr. & Eng. Dict.* 837/2 *Thermothérapie*, heat cure, heat treatment, thermotherapy. **1967** *Listener* 5 Oct. 427/2 He asked for..heat treatment, which my wife should apply herself.

heave, *sb.* Add: **1. c.** *Wrestling.* A chip performed by bringing the right arm round the opponent's right shoulder preparatory to a throw. *Cornwall heave*, a heave in which a wrestler places one hand in front and one behind his adversary, and falls with him.

1889 W. ARMSTRONG *Wrestling* 224 The Heave, Cornwall and Devon. *Ibid.* 230 The principal Cornish and Devon chips are..the Back-heave, the Belly-heave, the Heaving-toe. **1898** *Encycl. Sport* II. 548/2 One way to stop the heave is to cross click your man and then ply the crossbuttock.

5. *Comb.*: **heave-gate** *local*, a gate which is opened by being lifted out of the sockets or mortises.

1736 PEGGE *Kenticisms* (1876), *Heave-gate*, when the rails, with the pales nailed to them, may be taken out of their mortises, and then put in again. **1876** in G. L. Gower *Surrey Provincialisms.* **1887** I. R. *Lady's Ranche Life Montana* 27, Instead of gates out here, they generally have bars, which you have to let down,..like the 'heave gates' in Sussex. **1907** 'J. HALSHAM' *Lonewood Corner* 149, I perched myself on the heave-gate between the two fields. **1959** F. DONALDSON *Child of Twenties* vii. 107 A very easy hunting country, mainly a question of jumping the local Sussex heave-gates and small fences.

heave ho. Add: **b.** orig. *U.S. slang.* A snub or dismissal.

1944 D. RUNYON *Runyon à la Carte* (1946) vi. 107 A most obnoxious character..tries to claim the deuce as a sleeper and gets the heave-o from Nathan Detroit. **1952** B. CERF *Good for Laugh* (1953) 152 I'll bet that new girl.. gave you the heave-ho. **1962** WODEHOUSE *Service with Smile* vii. 112 If I were you, I think I would reconsider this idea of yours of giving Bill Bailey the old heave-ho. **1966** *New Yorker* 22 Oct. 52 Do we keep him on or give him the heave-ho? **1973** *Guardian* 20 Jan. 1/5 Mr Heath's prices and incomes package was given the old heave-ho by..the TUC Economic Committee.

heave-ho *v.* (later example); also *v. trans.*, to heave or lift with force.

1964 *New Yorker* 18 Jan. 84 A groaning mass of men heave-ho'd the snow car up the ramp. **1968** *Listener* 5 Dec. 768 During a rehearsal of *Billy Budd*, a singer was asked why he was just lolling about in the wings, not heave-hoing with the rest of them. **1971** *Guardian Weekly* 7 Aug. 17 The [Congolese] women who, apparently 12 months pregnant, nonetheless are constantly hauling and heave-hoing on this packing case of merchandise or that basket full of provisions.

heaven, *sb.* **6. d.** Also, *Heavens above, alive!*; *Heavens to Betsy!* (U.S.).

1892 R. T. COOKE *Huckleberries fr. New England Hills* 173 'Heavens to Betsey!' gasped Josiah. **1895** A. W. PINERO in M. R. Booth *Eng. Plays of 19th Cent.* (1969) II. 275 They say Orreyed has taken to tippling at dinner. Heavens above! **1913** 'S. ROHMER' *Mystery of Fu-Manchu* xix. 205 The eyes—heavens above, the huge green eyes! **1914** *Dialect Notes* IV. 74 *Heavens to Betsy!* Common Exclamation among women. **1957** M. SUMMERTON *Sunset Hour* i. 56 Heavens alive, it's ten past one. I haven't been up so near dawn for years. **1958** HAYWARD & HARARI tr. *Pasternak's Dr. Zhivago* II. viii. 246 But Heavens above! You misunderstood us. What are we talking about? **1968** 'E. V. CUNNINGHAM' *Cynthia* (1969) xi. 130 'Oh, heavens to Betsy, I am scared, Harvey,' Lucille whispered.

e. *Heaven knows.* (*a*) Used to emphasize the truth of a statement. (*b*) Used to imply that something is unknown to the speaker, and probably also to others. Freq. with *what, where, who.* Cf. GOD 10.

[**1605** SHAKES. *Macbeth* v. i. 52 Shee ha's spoke what shee should not, I am sure of that: Heauen knowes what shee ha's knowne.] **1711** [in Dict., sense 6 a]. **1805** WORDSWORTH *Prelude* XI. 141 Not in Utopia—subterranean fields,—Or some secreted island, Heaven knows where! **1872** GEO. ELIOT *Middlemarch* IV. VIII. lxxiv. 198 She invites clergymen and heaven-knows-who. *a* **1916** 'SAKI' *Square Egg* (1924) 125 From privates in the Regular Army to Heaven-knows-what in some intermediate corps. **1936** *Delineator* CXXIX. 48/3 It was clearly apart from the spirituals..and heaven knows, was unlike any music that America had been playing before. **1967** *Listener* 26 Jan. 117/1 Heaven knows, there are old excuses for it. **1969** *Ibid.* 13 Mar. 351/2 Heaven knows, he'd been through this often enough in the past.

heavenly, *a.* Add: **4. b.** *colloq.* Excellent, particularly enjoyable.

1874 L. TROUBRIDGE *Life amongst Troubridges* (1966) ix. 88 We had a most heavenly bathe. **1931** R. LEHMANN *Let. to Sister* 11 The heavenly mixing of paints and distempers. **1940** N. MITFORD *Pigeon Pie* viii. 127 Sophia felt at once extremely dowdy. 'You are lucky,' she said, 'the way you always have such heavenly things.'

heavens, *adv. dial.* and *colloq.* (Earlier examples.)

1858 DICKENS in *Househ. Words* Xmas no. 21/1 A shy company though its raining Heavens hard. **1870** —— *E. Drood* i. 2, I got Heavens-hard drunk for sixteen years afore I took to this.

hea:vier-than-ai·r, *attrib. phr. Aeronautics.* Designating a flying-machine whose weight is greater than the weight of the air which it displaces, and whose lift is not dependent on light gases; also applied to the use of such a machine or machines in flight.

[**1870** tr. *Marion's Wonderful Balloon Ascents* II. ix. 162 To form a 'Free Association for Aerial Navigation by means of Machines heavier than Air'. **1879** *Encycl. Brit.* IX. 309/2 Weight, however paradoxical it may appear, is necessary to flight. Everything which flies is vastly heavier than the air.] **1903** *Westm. Gaz.* 18 Sept. 9/3 The only example of the heavier-than-air machine. [**1904** *Chambers's Jrnl.* 1 Oct. 699/1 All who have sought to sail the skies divide themselves..into..the 'lighter-than-airites. and the 'heavier-than-airites'.] **1908** H. G. WELLS *War in Air* viii. § 2 The most efficient heavier-than-air fliers. **1909** A. BERGET *Conquest of Air* II. ii. 155 Many persons ask aviators why their 'heavier-than-air' apparatus is not provided with parachutes. **1909** *Flight* 19 June 356/1 Any heavier-than-air type of machine. **1909** *Daily Chron.* 9 Sept. 1/6 For a long time, Mr. Cody has practised heavier-than-air flying on Laffan's Plain. **1927** C. L. M. BROWN *Conquest of Air* 21 When heavier-than-air flight was an accomplished reality. **1961** C. B. SMITH *Testing Time* ii. 27 The War Office instructed O'Gorman to concentrate entirely on airships. They admitted that 'heavier-than-air dirigibles' might one day have military uses.

heavily, *adv.* Add: **6.** *Comb.*: often equivalent to parasynthetic comb. of the adj., as *heavily-booted*, having heavy boots.

1883 A. THOMAS *Mod. Housewife* 131 Trodden by heavily-booted feet. **1883** LD. R. GOWER *My Remin.* II. 79 A large and heavily-veined nose. **1904** *Westm. Gaz.* 27 Aug. 6/2 This heavily-scented, image-laden atmosphere. **1905** *Daily Chron.* 20 Oct. 8/5 Those heavily-jetted waistbelts. **1906** *Ibid.* 11 June 5/2 A good deal of heavily-jewelled..speech. **1907** B. VON HUTTEN *Halo* I. i, Very long, half-closed, heavily-lashed eyes. **1927** A. CONAN DOYLE *Case Bk. S. Holmes* xi. 293 A strong, heavily-moustached face and angry eyes. *c* **1909** D. H. LAWRENCE *Collier's Friday Night* (1934) i. 9 Then he drags his heavily-shod feet to the door on right. **1938** *Daily Tel.* 18 Jan. 6/3 As the heavily-policed funeral was marched down the street every window was flung open and red flowers showered down. **1961** *B.S.I. News* Feb. 6/1 Fast heavily-trafficked roads.

Heaviside (he·visəid). *Physics.* The name of O. *Heaviside* (1850–1925), English physicist, used attrib. to designate concepts proposed by him; esp. *Heaviside layer*, an ionized layer in the upper atmosphere able to reflect long radio waves (now usu. called *E layer of the ionosphere*); *Heaviside–Lorentz units* (H. A. Lorentz, 1853–1928, Dutch physicist), or *Heaviside rational units*, units of electric charge or magnetic pole defined in a certain manner which simplifies many formulæ; *Heaviside unit function*, a function which is zero when its argument is negative, and unity when its argument is positive; used esp. in *Electr. Communication*.

1911 *Encycl. Brit.* XXVII. 744/2 It will be seen..that the Heaviside rational units are all incommeasurable with the practical units. **1912** *Proc. R. Soc.* A. LXXXVII. 95 Both long and short waves are propagated through the lower and middle atmosphere in straight lines to great heights and reflected at the Heaviside layer. **1913** *Year-Bk. Wireless Telegr.* 395 The conductivity, and consequently the reflecting power, of the Heaviside layer depends greatly on the presence of local electromotive forces. **1926** R. W. HUTCHINSON *Wireless* vii. 131 It is clear that if the earth were surrounded by a spherical conductor some distance away from it the waves would travel between this conducting surface and the conducting surface of the earth, and they would follow the curvature of the earth... Such a conductor does exist and it is known as the Heaviside layer. **1937** *Discovery* Mar. 65/2 The well known Heaviside and Appleton layers which play such an important part in carrying broadcasting to long distances. **1940** *Chambers's Techn. Dict.* 407/2 *Heaviside unit function*, a step in which the change in amplitude is unity. **1955** O. KLEIN in W. Pauli *N. Bohr* 99 The units are the usual ones, $\hbar = c = 1$ and Heaviside–Lorentz units for the electromagnetic quantities. **1963** JERRARD & MCNEILL *Dict. Sci. Units* 14 The Heaviside–Lorentz units were the earliest rationalized units, they were proposed by Heaviside in 1883 and used by him in a classical paper on electrical theory published nine years later.

heavy, *a.*[1] (*sb.*) Add: **A. 1. c.** Also of timber: consisting of large trees. *U.S.*

1843 *Yale Lit. Mag.* VIII. 406 In this patch of 'heavy timber'. **1853** B. F. TAYLOR *Jan. & June* (1871) 252 [The storm] went crashing on, into the heavy timber.

2. c. Applied to elements whose specific gravity is relatively great; *heavy metal* (see also sense 6 b in Dict.), a metal of high specific gravity (see quot. 1955).

1864 *Jrnl. Chem. Soc.* XVII. 126 In support of the view that thallium is one of the heavy metals, the following reasons may be given. **1868** [in Dict., sense 2 a]. **1903** *Jrnl. Physiol.* XXIX. 165 Most of the heavy metals when injected directly into the circulation give rise to increased movements of plain muscle throughout the body. **1922** F. W. ASTON *Isotopes* viii. 101 The nucleus of the atom of an ordinary element (not hydrogen)..is very small compared with the atom itself. Its dimensions can be roughly determined by actual experiment in the case of the heavy elements. **1936** *Discovery* Feb. 36/1 Heavy elements, such as gold, silver, and lead. **1936** R. P. BELL tr. *Bjerrum's Inorg. Chem.* 213 The metals fall naturally into two groups: the light metals with densities below four, and the heavy metals with densities above seven... The heavy metals have their electrons more firmly bound and are less electropositive than the light metals. **1946** *Monthly Notices R. Astron. Soc.* CVI. 357 Material at any point.. on the other side of the curve is composed almost entirely of heavy elements, the main mass of the elements in the latter case having atomic weight greater than 50. **1955** *Chem. & Engin. News* 2 May 1902/2 Karl F. Heumann wonders what is meant by 'heavy metal'. One authority says it is any metal having a specific gravity greater than 4.0. Another says it is sometimes applied to those of sp. gr. 5.0 or over... Has 'heavy metal' ever been officially defined? **1961** *Jrnl. Chem. Educ.* XXXVIII. 67/1 The present treatment will be restricted to the main process responsible for the heavy elements, of mass number *A* greater than 70. **1972** *Science* 14 Apr. 161 (*title*) Enrichment of heavy metals and organic compounds in the surface microlayer of Narragansett Bay, Rhode Island.

d. *Physics.* Of hydrogen: consisting of the isotope deuterium (which is of greater mass than protium, the normal isotope). Of a compound of hydrogen: having some or all of the hydrogen isotope present as deuterium. So **heavy water,** deuterium oxide, D_2O, or a mixture of this with ordinary water; **heavy-water-moderated** *a.*, of a nuclear reactor: employing heavy water as a moderator; **heavy water reactor,** a nuclear reactor in which the moderator is heavy water.

This usage is occas. extended to the isotopes of other elements to designate an isotope that is of greater mass than the normal isotope.

1933 *Nature* 22 Apr. 590/2 Heavy water freezes when surrounded by melting ice. **1933** *Jrnl. Chem. Physics* June 344/2 Let us make an estimate of the amount of the heavy hydrogen isotope in ordinary water. **1933** *Discovery* July 211/1 For the first time in history a chemical element has been divided into two completely different parts. A new 'heavy' hydrogen has been separated from the old. **1933** *Science* 29 Dec. 602/1 In fact, if there were only two waters, two ammonias, and so forth, the names 'light water', 'heavy water', 'light ammonia' and 'heavy ammonia' would be very satisfactory indeed. **1934** *Discovery* Jan. 1/1 There is one part only of heavy hydrogen to 35,000 parts of light hydrogen. **1934, 1935** [see *DEUTERIUM]. **1936** *Punch* 23 Sept. 337/1 'Heavy-water', the newly-discovered fluid, costs £120 a teaspoonful. **1937** *Discovery* Oct. 317/1 The value of heavy nitrogen for research in physiological chemistry is inestimable. **1938** *Encycl. Brit. Bk. of Year* 320/1 'Heavy water' or deuterium oxide is now manufactured commercially and is an article of commerce. **1938** R. W. LAWSON tr. *Hevesy & Paneth's Man. Radioactivity* (ed. 2) xx. 187 The properties of 'heavy hydrogen' or 'deuterium'..differ..strongly from those of the much more abundant ordinary hydrogen. **1941** in M. Gowing *Britain & Atomic Energy* (1964) App. ii. 395 We know that Germany has taken a great deal of trouble to secure supplies of the substance known as heavy water. **1945** H. D. SMYTH *Gen. Acct. Devel. Atomic Energy Mil. Purposes* i. 11 A frequently used 'beam' source of neutrons results from accelerated deuterons impinging on 'heavy water' ice. **1946** *Electronic Engin.* XVIII. 142 The deuteron..which is the nucleus of heavy hydrogen, or deuterium. **1947** CROWTHER & WHIDDINGTON *Science at War* 145 The slow neutrons produced by the uranium and heavy-water system would transmute many uranium atoms into the new element plutonium. **1955** *Ann. Reg. 1954* 393 Dimple (deuterium moderated pile, low energy) was Britain's first heavy water reactor. **1956** *Nature* 4 Feb. 205/2 Three enriched-uranium heavy-water-moderated..reactors are under construction. **1958** *Listener* 28 Aug. 294/2 Producing heavy water from electricity from the proposed Aswan High Dam. **1964** M. GOWING *Britain & Atomic Energy* ii. 73 Meanwhile doubts grew about the wisdom of pressing the Americans too hard about the heavy water project.

5. b. Esp. in phr. *heavy industry*. Hence *heavy-industrial* adj. Also *heavy chemicals*: see *CHEMICAL *a.* 6 b.

1932 *Times* 5 Jan. 11/2 The Central Committee of the Communist Party has decided to reorganize the Union Supreme Economic Council, which is to be styled Commissariat of Heavy Industries. **1938** *Archit. Rev.* LXXXIII. 117/2 The majority of 'heavy' industries are of the latter type. **1938** *Times* 17 Feb. 16/1 The comparatively high price of iron and steel in Japan (a result of the artificial character of heavy-industrial growth in a country with insufficient ore and unsuitable coal). **1944** J. S. HUXLEY *On Living in Rev.* I. iii. 6 The deliberate encouragement of heavy industry under a Five Year Plan, at the expense of all other kinds of enterprise which would have flourished in a *laisser-faire* economy, is the most clear-cut example. **1957** L. F. R. WILLIAMS *State of Israel* 44 The raw materials required by her expanding heavy and light industries.

6. Also applied to aerial bombs.

1917 'CONTACT' *Airman's Outings* 206 A line of narrow-nosed buses, with heavy bombs fitted under the lower planes, ready to leave for their objective.

7. Also of military aircraft, descriptive of a large type of bombing aeroplane.

1921 *Flight* XIII. 615/2 The S.E.5's made the first attack, and dropped about 40 25-lb Cooper bombs, with the object of..preparing the way for the heavy bombers. **1939** *War Illustr.* 18 Dec. 459 Described as modern heavy bombers, these 'planes of the Red Air Force are certainly larger than any standard bomber in the British Air Force.

9. b. *Golf.* Of a ball: lying in sand.

1886 H. HUTCHINSON *Hints Game Golf* 39 When lying 'heavy'..bear in mind that it is better to hit the ball with the iron than to miss it with a spoon.

13. Of an amatory relationship: intense, intensive; spec. *heavy petting*, non-coital physical contact between two people, involving sexual stimulation of the genitals.

1952 M. R. RINEHART *Pool* xii. 111 He has a sort of heavy date here with a girl called Janey. **1959** 'M. NEVILLE' *Sweet Night for Murder* vii. 76 Duncan was making a very heavy pass at Cathy. **1960** 'M. CAINE' *S Man* 126 What is called 'heavy petting' in which frank exploration of each other's bodies is permitted. **1968** M. RICHLER *Cocksure* xviii. 111 His thirteen-year-old daughter was the only girl in the fifth form to stop at.. *heavy* petting. **1972** *Daily Tel.* 29 Jan. 2/6 Heavy petting between boys and girls is not discouraged and intercourse is described in some detail.

14. b. *fig.*, esp. in phr. *to make heavy weather of*: to make (unnecessary) fuss or labour over.

1915 [see WEATHER *sb.* 2 c]. **1955** *Times* 21 July 8/5 The Geneva conference ran into heavy weather this morning, but made some ground later. **1957** *Listener* 24 Oct. 664/1 He makes rather heavy weather of the difference. **1960** V. GIELGUD *To Bed at Noon* I. xii. 92 Aren't you making rather heavy weather out of nothing?

15. *heavy face* (*type*): see FACE *sb.* 22.

1891 [see FACE *sb.* 22]. **1898** J. SOUTHWARD *Mod. Printing* I. xxii. 140 The first would be called a *light face*, and the second a *heavy face*.

17. b. Of a line in Old English verse: containing more than the normal number of stressed elements. Also, more generally, opp. to LIGHT *a* 12.

1893 J. LAWRENCE *Chapt. Allit. Verse* 46 Verses with double alliteration are as a rule heavier than those with single. **1948** *Mod. Philol.* XLVI. 81 These heavy and extra-heavy verses, are the exceptions. **1958** A. J. BLISS *Metre of Beowulf* 8 There are also many verses which contain three stressed elements instead of the normal two: blæd | wide | sprang 18 b... All verses of this kind are here termed 'heavy' verses.

19. a. (Further examples.)

1962 *Which?* (Car Suppl.) Oct. 117/1 The Riley 4/72's steering was somewhat heavy and imprecise. *Ibid.* 119/2 The Ford Taunus foot brake was not too heavy at 30 mph but needed a great deal of pressure for gentle stops at 60 mph.

d. Of market conditions.

1831 [in Dict., sense 19 b]. **1843** *Times* 20 May 7/3 The English securities were heavy again to-day. **1935** *Economist* 2 Feb. 261/2 Japanese bonds were heavy. **1962** S. STRAND *Marketing Dict.* 339 *Heavy market*, a market of declining prices.

e. *heavy going*: see *GOING *vbl. sb.* 4 a.

20. b. Of newspapers, journals, etc.: serious, addressed to the serious-minded.

1874 TROLLOPE *Way we live Now* (1875) I. xxx. 187 Old Splinter,..who had written for the heavy quarterlies any time this last forty years, professed that he saw through the article. **1967** *Listener* 7 Dec. 743/1 The editors of the heavy dailies.

c. orig. in Jazz and popular music, used in various senses to designate something profound, serious, etc. *colloq.*

1937 B. GOODMAN *This Thing called Swing* 9 *Mugging heavy*: soft swing with a heavy beat. **1940** *Swing* July 17 Very fast semi-boogie blues in Gabriel with nasty, heavy off-beat drumming. **1958** BLESH & JANIS *They all played Ragtime* vi. 117 *Victory Rag*, a 'heavy' number of great difficulty, went on the market in 1921. **1959** 'F. NEWTON' *Jazz Scene* xiv. 261 Jazz is not simply an ordinary music, light or heavy. **1969** *Rolling Stone* 28 June 38/4 Bass player wanted for heavy blues-rock band. **1969** *It* 4–17 July 10/2 The Rolling Stones..are well supported by such swingin' outfits as..the very heavy Third Ear Band. **1970** *Time* 17 Aug. 32 Marcuse is heavy stuff. **1971** *It* 2–16 June 2/1 The Bournemouth drug squad (reputed to be one of the heaviest squads in the country). **1972** *Last Whole Earth Catalog* (Portola Inst.) 30/1 Not heavy stuff about what is terrible or what should happen, but how to remake life and stay alive in the process. **1972** *Southerly* XXXII. 101 We talk about this and that and where's the heavy dope scene now.

21. (Earlier and additional examples.)

1814 JANE AUSTEN *Mansf. Park* I. xv. 301 'Anhalt' is a heavy part. **1823** *Drama* IV. 209 Mr. Hillington takes the heavy line of business. *a* **1828** J. BERNARD *Retrosp. Stage* (1830) I. 13 The Company consisted of a heavy man, who played the tyrants in tragedy. **1833** R. DYER *9 Yrs. of Actor's Life* 237 This gentleman possesses natural requisite and acquired talents of the first order in heavy tragedy. **1858** H. J. BYRON *Maid & Magpie* 35 Such a heavy villin. **1860** G. VANDENHOFF *Dramatic Rem.* 176 There was no heavy lady for the Emilias and Lady Macbeths. **1870** T. A. BROWN *Hist. Amer. Stage* 54/1 In California she played all lines of business, from walking ladies to heavy, and juvenile leading. **1884** [see LEAD *sb.*[2] 7]. **1901** C. MORRIS *Life on Stage* 40 Then came the

leading lady, the first old woman (who was sometimes the heavy woman). **1909** J. R. Ware *Passing Eng.* 151/2 *Heavy merchant*, man who plays the villain. **1941** *Picturegoer* 26 July 6/1 John [Barrymore] started off in heavy drama.

b. Also, ponderously dignified; stern, repressive, unbending: esp. *heavy father, heavy uncle*, which are also used as attrib. phrases (= sternly paternal or avuncular). orig. *Theatrical slang*.

1849 Thackeray *Pendennis* I. xxix. 281 Those parts in the drama, which we called the heavy fathers. **1853** 'C. Bede' *Verdant Green* v. 42 He took an affectionate farewell of his son, somewhat after the manner of the 'heavy fathers' of the stage. **1858** H. J. Byron *Maid & Magpie* 4 A Fine Specimen of the good old Heavy Father of Melodrama. **1864** H. Morley *Jrnl.* (1866) 339 A heavy father in broad farce. **1898** Rider Haggard *Doctor Therne* iii, Sir John..received me in his best 'heavy-father' manner. **1931** *Daily Express* 31 Jan. 15/2 The heavy uncle attitude. **1931** *Times Lit. Suppl.* 13 Aug. 613/4 The Venetian Pantalone becomes the Atellane 'heavy father' Pappus. **1956** 'M. Westmacott' *Burden* II. iii. 83 Really, Laura dear, you might be at least fifty. A heavy Victorian father rather than a sister.

22. c. *heavy man*: a criminal or law-breaker. *U.S. slang*.

1926 J. Black *You can't Win* xx. 302 It was the kind of safe that discouraged the 'heavy man' (safe breaker). **1963** H. L. Mencken *Amer. Lang.* (ed. 4) 730 *Heavy man*, one transporting narcotics.

24. b. *heavy-duty* (see Duty 6), used *attrib.*, of a machine, material, etc., designed to deal with heavy materials or to be suitable to stand up to hard wear. Also *transf.*

1914 *Engineering* 4 Dec. 670/2 (*caption*) Heavy-Duty Drilling-Machine. **1935** *Discovery* July 202/1 Fireproof materials can be substituted for practically every form of heavy duty cloth. **1958** *Listener* 20 Nov. 839/3 The heavy-duty rubber tyre. **1964** *English Studies* XLV. 426 Special attention has been given to 'heavy-duty' words such as *have*. **1969** *Computers & Humanities* III. 137 A stand-alone device which consists of a magnetic tape unit, keyboard, and heavy-duty selectric typewriter.

30. heavy bag, a punch-bag; **heavy franc**, name given to the new franc, equivalent to 100 old francs, introduced in France in 1960; **heavy mineral** (see quot. 1971); **heavy oil**, any oil of high specific gravity, orig. such an oil obtained from the distillation of coal-tar (cf. *dead oil* s.v. Dead *a.* D. 2); **heavy sugar** *U.S. slang*, 'big money' (see Sugar *sb.* 2 c); **heavy swell** (earlier example); **heavy-wooded pine**, the western yellow pine, *Pinus ponderosa*.

1950 J. Dempsey *Championship Fighting* 41 Canvas or leather 'dummy bag'—sometimes known as the 'heavy bag'. **1958** *Times* 29 Dec. 6/4 (*headline*) The 'Heavy' Franc. *Ibid.*, A new monetary unit is to be created [in France] worth 100 francs. It will be introduced gradually during the next 12 months. **1959** *Observer* 11 Oct. 3/8 The new 'heavy franc', which officially comes into use next January. **1893** A. Geikie *Text-bk. Geol.* (ed. 3) II. ii. 129 These heavy minerals constitute sometimes as much as 4 per cent of the Bagshot sand. **1939** *Proc. Prehist. Soc.* V. 109 A heavy-mineral analysis of a sample of the sand. **1971** I. G. Gass et al. *Understanding Earth* xiii. 166/2 Rather more satisfactory from the point of view of recognising parent rocks is the presence of a small proportion (often less than 1%) of what are known as 'heavy minerals'. These have a greater specific gravity than the common minerals quartz and feldspar (hence the name), and are separated by breaking up the rocks and floating off the lighter minerals in a heavy liquid (bromoform, S.G. 2.89 is commonly used). Assemblages of heavy minerals may be characteristic of certain groups of parent rocks. **1849** Heavy oil [see *dead oil* s.v. Dead *a.* D. 2]. **1913** V. B. Lewes *Oil Fuel* 129 The heavy tar oil, or 'creosote oil' forms a fairly good liquid fuel. The specific gravity is usually in the neighbourhood of 1.1, hence its name of 'heavy-oil', being heavier than water. *Ibid.* 180 Heavy oil engines. **1936** *Discovery* Feb. 37 Locomotives driven by heavy oil and electricity. **1926** Maines & Grant *Wise-Crack Dict.* 9/2 *Heavy sugar papa*, sweet old man with fat purse. **1928** *Flynn's* 4 Feb. 437/1 Johns with heavy sugar. **1819** Heavy swell [see Swell *sb.* 9 a]. **1836** P. & C. Lawson *Agriculturalist's Manual* 354 Pinus ponderosa—Heavy Wooded Pine... Introduced by Mr. Douglas from the west coast of North America in 1828. **1858** J. A. Warder *Hedges & Evergreens* II. 250 *Pinus ponderosa*, or Heavy-wooded Pine, has leaves from nine inches to a foot long. **1866** 'Senilis' *Pinaceæ* 125 *Pinus Ponderosa*: The Heavy-Wooded Pine. Introduced from North America nearly forty years ago. **1923** Dallimore & Jackson *Handbk. Coniferæ* 437 *Pinus ponderosa*, Douglas. Western Yellow Pine... Big Pine; Bull Pine; Heavy Pine; Heavy-wooded Pine.

31. *heavy-footed* (later example), *-framed, -jowled, -lidded* (example; so *heavy-liddedness*), *-scented, -set*; **heavy-faced**, having a heavy face (see Face *sb.* 22 and sense 15 above); **heavy-timbered,** (*a*) thickly furnished with growing trees; (*b*) large-limbed.

1917 F. S. Henry *Printing for School & Shop* vii. 90 Heavy-faced types are appropriate in printed matter for the iron and steel industry. **1957** T. Gunn *Sense of Movement* 13 Here is a room with heavy-footed chairs. **1898** *Daily News* 14 Mar. 7/2 A heavy-framed colt. *a* **1963** J. Fountain in B. James *Austral. Short Stories* (1963) 2nd Ser. 274 His heavy-framed bike loaded with packages. **1944** A. L. Rowse *Eng. Spirit* 88 That earlier Tudor type ..clean-shaven and heavy-jowled. **1919** V. Woolf *Night & Day* xxvii. 390 Camels slanted their heavy-lidded eyes at her. **1961** *New Yorker* 25 Feb. 129/1, I remember experiencing spells of heavy-liddedness during a fairly recent stage presentation of this talkfest. **1906** *Westm. Gaz.* 4 Jan. 2/1 The heavy-scented buds. **1908** *Ibid.* 7 Aug. 3/1 Never was such clover!..heavy-scented, rich, and generous. **1938** D. Runyon *Furthermore* vii. 130 He is a heavy-set guy. **1831** J. W. Peck *Guide for Emigrants* II. 40 The wide, level, and heavy timbered alluvions, are.. unhealthy. **1861** Whyte Melville *Market Harb.* 7 Deep-ribbed, heavy-timbered hounds. **1903** S. E. White *Conjuror's House* iv. 39 The fort itself, a medley of heavy-timbered stockades and square block-houses. **1908** *Westm. Gaz.* 25 Aug. 7/1 A dark, heavy-timbered wood.

B. *sb.* **1. b.** *the heavies*, the heavy artillery.

1908 *Daily Chron.* 6 Aug. 6/4 The excellent firing of the 4·7 guns by the First and Seconds (or, as they are more familiarly called, 'the Heavies'). **1916** 'Boyd Cable' *Action Front* 113 The Heavies as well as the Field guns were to bombard. **1918** E. M. Roberts *Flying Fighter* 57 Soon the field artillery and the 'heavies' woke up again.

c. A heavy bomber.

1943 *Time* 15 Nov. 26/2 Another co-ordinated series of punches..cost the Allies only ten heavies, two Marauders and five fighters. **1944** *Even. Standard* 16 Dec. 1/4 Heavy bombers could be heard massing for an attack... Wave after wave of 'heavies' went out. **1961** W. Vaughan-Thomas *Anzio* viii. 164 In cold blood the heavies may not have done vital damage to the Germans forming up on the ground.

d. *the heavies*, the serious newspapers, journals, etc. (see sense *A. 20 b).

1950 C. Woodham-Smith *F. Nightingale* 310 In 1857 great influence was exercised by 'the heavies'—the quarterlies and the reviews. **1962** *Guardian* 5 Dec. 7/4, I was reading the Sunday papers... I picked up one of the two Heavies. **1962** 'O. Mills' *Headlines make Murder* viii. 89 All three 'heavies', *The Times, Telegraph* and.. *Guardian*. **1971** *Author* LXXXII. 101 The popular press, thrown off balance and uncertain of its role, lost out to the heavies and the provincials.

2. b. Anything particularly large and weighty of its kind.

1897 *Daily News* 25 Nov. 5/1 Amongst the elephantine heavies is Mandarin, who killed a keeper during his last residence at Olympia. **1908** *Pall Mall Gaz.* 27 Mar. 12/3 Firms..which have specialised in the manufacture of 'heavies' [*sc.* motor vehicles]. **1935** *Amer. Speech* X. 271/1 *Heavies*, very heavy beef cattle, more than two years old. **1960** *Farmer & Stockbreeder* 15 Mar. 6/2 Of the uncertified beasts, lightweights were more plentiful than heavies. **1965** *Listener* 8 Apr. 537/1 The 'heavies' are on the march. By 1970 there will be 120 trucks for every 100 there are now on our inadequate roads. **1968** *Times* 25 Oct. 25/3 (*heading*) 60 mph for 'heavies' [*sc.* motor vehicles].

c. A heavyweight boxing-match or boxer.

1913 J. G. B. Lynch *Compl. Amat. Boxer* 221, I remember in the finals of the heavies at the All-India Championship of 1909 seeing Private Clohessy..take on Bombardier Wells. **1950** J. Dempsey *Championship Fighting* 16 Top-flight heavies like Frank Moran.

d. *pl. Racing.* Heavy horseshoes.

1930 *Times* 24 Mar. 4/2 It is almost impossible to tell by watching a horse walk in the parade ring whether he is plated, or whether he is carrying, to use a racing term, 'the heavies'.

e. A strongly built person, usu. of violent disposition.

1936 [see *come *v.* 13 d]. **1962** R. Cook *Crust on its Uppers* i. 22 A good solid heavy like Chas to deal with the writ-servers. **1970** G. Greer *Female Eunuch* 194 Cherry is surrounded by threatening creatures, mostly the nightclub heavies. **1972** *Catholic Herald* 28 Jan. 2/5 Sit down, we want to talk to you... We are going out to get the 'heavies'. **1973** *Times* 12 July 4/1 Prostitutes were threatened with 'heavies' working for a man named Kenny Lynch.

5. esp. *Theatr.* Short for *heavy actor, villain*, etc. Cf. sense A. 21 in Dict. and Suppl.

1880 F. Belton *Random Recoll. Old Actor* viii. 132 Robertson (the celebrated author of 'Caste' 'School' etc. for 'second heavies'). **1906** S. Ford *Shorty McCabe* (1908) 70 So far it's as good as playin' leading heavy in 'The Shadows of a Great City'. **1928** *Observer* 22 July 15/2 The fun succumbed to a bucolic lethargy that was only partially shaken off by the retreat to Half Moon Street and the assault of the sentimental heavies. **1937** 'C. McCabe' *Face on Cutting-room Floor* vii. 53, I asked..who the man was... 'That's Vic's new heavy.' **1961** J. McCabe *Mr. Laurel & Mr. Hardy* (1962) ii. 49, I always played a 'heavy'—you know, the villain. *Ibid.* ii. 57 The villains in those days were always called 'heavies'. Their trademark was usually *heavy* eyebrows and moustache makeup. **1962** J. D. Salinger *Franny & Zooey* 143 I'm sick to death of being the heavy in everybody's life... They're as happy as pigs till I show up. I feel like those dismal bastards Seymour's beloved Chuang-tzu warned everybody against. **1966** *Listener* 15 Dec. 890/2 Two of the chief characters are avowed communists, and yet are not the heavies plotting to overthrow the free world. **1973** J. Wainwright *Pride of Pigs* i. 178 Two of the heavies dived for Tallboy.

6. *pl.* The heavy trades or industries (see Heavy *a.* 5); also, stocks or shares in such a trade or industry.

1900 *Westm. Gaz.* 26 Jan. 11/1 Hope for the Heavies. **1902** *Daily Chron.* 20 May 3/6 The ratio of working expenses for the past half-year on the North British railways was 49 per cent., compared with 65 per cent., or more, on the four 'heavies'. **1922** *Daily Tel.* 12 June 2/3 The prices of the other comparable 'heavies'—Great Western and London and North-Western—have also gone ahead.

heavy-handed, *a.* Add: **3. b.** Of a joke, humour, etc.: clumsy.

1910 A. C. Benson *Diary* 7 Dec. (1926) 199 Their jokes are very heavy-handed, and generally involve discomfort for the victim. **1934** *Amer. Speech* IX. 158/2 The work of heavy-handed humorists.

heavy-weight. Also **heavyweight. a.** Substitute for def.: A person or animal of more than the average weight; *spec.* a jockey, etc., of more than the average weight; a professional boxer weighing over 12 st. 7 lb., or *transf.*, a horse which carries more than the average weight.

1877 'Pugnus' *Hist. Prize Ring* II. 104 For such a heavy weight, Hooper had a particularly small foot, of which he was very proud. **1888** *Encycl. Brit.* XXIV. 691/1 Heavy weights [amateur] to be over 11 stone 4 lb. **1889** [see Feather-weight 3]. **1910** [see Welter weight 2]. **1917** *Sat. Rev.* 10 Nov. 373/2 Thanks to the muscle, he has become a champion heavy-weight. **1928** [see *cruiser 4]. **1954** F. C. Avis *Boxing Dict.* 52 *Heavyweight*, a standard weight division for professional boxers weighing more than 12 st. 7 lb.; for amateurs, 12 st. 10 lb.

c. A work of large size or serious content. Cf. Heavy *a.*[1] 20 a (in Dict), b (in Suppl.).

1928 Blunden *Undertones of War* x. 111 When I saw scattered about the porch and the doorstep,..a number of volumes,.. I could not but snatch up four or five... The heavyweight was..a treatise on Country Houses. **1963** *Punch* 3 Apr. 488/2, I have managed to convert my wisp of a *conte* into a heavyweight.

d. *attrib.* Also as *adj.*, particularly heavy of its kind.

1895 *Montgomery Ward Catal.* 283/1 Ladies' jersey knit ribbed vests, heavy weight Egyptian cotton. **1909** *Westm. Gaz.* 2 Mar. 5/2 In a variety of cloths, serges, and heavy-weight cashmere. **1931** *Bombay Chron.* 14 Oct. 1 Heavy-weight championship. **1934** G. B. Shaw *Too True to be Good* I. 40 Oh, sweetest, why did you tell me that this heavyweight champion was a helpless invalid? **1958** *Times* 26 Sept. 6/3 Heavyweight American and Continental trucks and buses are not being exhibited. **1963** *Times Lit. Suppl.* 4 Jan. 16/5 Figgins's heavyweight version of Caslon's (1816) Sanserif in 1832. **1972** *Guardian* 31 Oct. 11/5 Underwear: Heavy-weight tights in nylon.

hebdomadarian (hebdǫmădēə·riăn). [f. Hebdomadary *sb.* and *a.* + -ian.] = Hebdomadary *sb.*

1898 W. St. Clair Baddeley *Cotteswold Shrine* 75 At a signal given by the hebdomadarian of the week they returned to the Cloister. **1949** M. Baldwin *I leap over Wall* vi. 139 The 'hebdomadarian' (such was the official title of the 'Great Week' keeper in the *Ceremonial*) was continually in evidence.

hebe[1]. Add: **2*.** *Bot.* [mod.L. (P. Commerson in A. L. Jussieu *Genera Plantarum* (1789) 105).] A member of a large genus of shrubs so called, mostly native to New Zealand, belonging to the family Scrophulariaceæ, and formerly included in the genus *Veronica*.

[**1921** F. W. Pennell in *Rhodora* XXIII. 2 The austral distribution, with its suggestion of genetic remoteness, emphasizes *Hebe's* claim to recognition as a genus. **1927** Cockayne & Allan in *Trans. N.Z. Inst.* LVII. 13 A species is usually transferred to *Hebe* only when..we are pretty well convinced it is valid.] **1961** *Amat. Gardening* 21 Oct. 5/1 The hebes, as the shrubby veronicas are now called. **1972** *Country Life* 23 Mar. 690/1 Our hebes have come through remarkably well: even the tenderest kinds like Simon Deleaux and Andersonii Variegata.

Hebe, hebe[2] (hīb). Also **Heeb.** [abbrev. of Hebrew *sb.* 1.] A derogatory term for a Jew.

1932 J. T. Farrell *Studs Lonigan* (1936) iv. 71 He should've been a nigger or a hebe instead of Irish. **1946** Mezzrow & Wolfe *Really the Blues* 374/2 *Heeb*, Jewish person. **1950** T. Sugrue in M. Hay *Foot of Pride* p. xx, He might go through the whole of his life without expressing more than a casual distaste for 'the Hebes'. **1953** E. F. Russell *Somewhere a Voice* (1965) 11 Lastly there was Sammy Finestone... A typical Hebe. **1972** *National Observer* (U.S.) 27 May 17/4 They will be followed close upon their heels by miserly Hebes, and cheating kikes.

hebe-. Add: **b. hebephrenia** (examples); **hebephreniac** *sb.* (examples); also **hebephre·nic** *a.* and *sb.*

1883 W. A. Hammond *Treat. Insanity* 556 Hebephrenia..is the term applied to the insanity of pubescence. **1948** *Brit. Jrnl. Psychol.* XXXIX. 89 Hebephrenia is featured by silliness, incongruity, mannerisms etc. **1956** C. P. Snow *Homecomings* 348 He lay on his back, his legs relaxed, like a figure on a tomb or one in a not disagreeable state of hebephrenia. **1884** *Jrnl. Nerv. & Mental Dis.* XI. 303 Imperative conceptions are relatively frequent among hebephreniacs. **1885** *Ibid.* XII. 516 (*heading*) Autopsy findings in a hebephreniac. **1908** *Practitioner* Jan. 12 The patient may gradually become imbecile and demented—the hebephrenic type. **1915** C. R. Payne tr. *Pfister's Psychoanalytic Method* 542 Dementia praecox (in catatonic, hebephrenic and paranoid forms). **1938** S. Beckett *Murphy* 168 A hebephrenic playing the piano intently. **1973** 'E. McBain' *Let's hear It* v. 59 He considered them [*sc.* the police] obsolete and essentially hebephrenic.

Heberden's nodes (he·bəɹdenz nōᵘdz). *Med.* [f. the name of William *Heberden*, Eng. physician (1710–1801), who described the condition.] Nodular enlargements of the terminal joints of the fingers due to osteoarthritis.

1889 D. Duckworth *Treat. Gout* iv. 72 (*heading*) Heberden's nodes in a case of gout—..patient has noticed a gradual increase in size of the joints of the

fingers... Heberden's nodes, both hands. **1911** *Encycl. Brit.* XXIII 239/1 What are termed 'Heberden's nodes' are small hard knobs about the size of a pea frequently found upon the fingers near the terminal phalangeal joints...These nodes are..a manifestation of arthritis. **1961** R. D. Baker *Essent. Path.* xxi. 578 In the hands the hypertrophy of the bones about the distal interphalangeal joints is known as Heberden's nodes. **1972** H. L. Jaffe *Metabolic, Degenerative & Inflammatory Dis. Bones & Joints* xxv. 757 With advancing age, the incidence of Heberden's nodes increases.

hebetude. (Later examples.)

1918 E. Pound *Let.* 3 Apr. (1971) 133 There is *something* in his [*sc.* Jules Romains's] work. It is not the hebetude of a lignified cerebrum. **1955** W. Gaddis *Recognitions* ii. vi. 564 The robe was too big. Nevertheless, the pattern was so conservative, and the material so fine, that this seemed rather a mark of luxuriance than some deliberate hebetude on the part of the giver.

hebra (he·bră). Also **chevra(h).** Pl. **hebras, hebroth, chevroth.** [Heb. *ḥeḇrāh*, association, society; group as small religious community.] (See quot. 1959.)

1880 *Jewish Chron.* 6 Feb. 9/2 The poorer classes prefer to belong to one of the numerous *Hebras* which.. abound in the East End. *Ibid.* 4/1 Many of these unattached Jews are not wealthy...They..have their *Hebras*, their customs and peculiarities. **1892** I. Zangwill *Childr. Ghetto* I. i. ii. 44 Even in the smallest *Chevrah* the high hat comes next in sanctity to the Scroll of the Law. **1918** C. G. Montefiore *Liberal Judaism & Hellenism* v. 259 This oligarchic tendency is counteracted by the little Synagogues and the *Chevras*. **1959** F. M. Wilson *They came as Strangers* iii. iii. 195 Thousands of Jews were too poor to be seat-holders in the synagogue, so they formed *chevras*, which were partly Friendly Societies, and partly groups for public worship and the study of the Talmud. **1960** *Economist* 25 June 1331/1 Here and there are the little *chevras* or conventicles whose continued existence so much annoyed the big synagogues. **1960** L. P. Gartner *Jewish Immigrant* vii. 186 In the *hebra*..a Jew associated himself with fellow Jews..for..worship and study and conviviality.

Hebraist. Add: **4.** One who maintains that the New Testament was written in Greek that contained Hebrew idioms.

1859 E. Masson tr. *Winer's Gram. N.T. Diction* i. i. 25 Various..scholars (the Purists) perseveringly endeavoured to demonstrate that the style of the N.T. entirely reaches the standard of classical Greek purity..while others (the Hebraists) maintained..that it exhibits a..predominant Hebrew tincture. **1906** J. H. Moulton *Gram. N.T. Greek* (1908) 3 The Hebraist went absurdly far in recognising Semitic influence where none was really operative. **1907** [see Purist 2].

Hebrid (he·brid), *a.* [ad. *Hebrides*: see next.] = ***Hebridean** *a.* Also **He·bridal** *a.*

1748 Thomson *Cast. Indol.* i. xxx, A shepherd of the Hebrid Isles. **1841** W. Yarrell *Brit. Fishes* (ed. 2) II. 133 The Hebridal Smelt, *Osmerus Hebridicus*..is at once clearly distinguishable from our long-known and highly-esteemed favourite, the common Smelt. **1923** *United Free Ch. Mission Rec.* July 275 From many a Hebrid isle ..from plain manses and luxurious mansions these men and women have come.

Hebridean (hebridī·ăn, hĕbri·dĭăn), *a.* and *sb.* Also 6–9 **-ian.** [f. *Hebrides*, an alteration, said to have originated in an accidental misprint, of L. *Hebudes* (Pliny), Gr. Ἕβουδαι (Ptolemy).] **A.** *adj.* Of or pertaining to the Hebrides, a group of islands off the west coast of Scotland. **B.** *sb.* A native or inhabitant of the Hebrides.

1623 Cockeram, *Hebridean wave*, the Irish sea. **1632** Lithgow *Trav.* 494 The desperate courage of these awfull Hebridians. **1641** in J. Sylvester tr. *Du Bartas's Weeks* 331/1 *Hebridian Wave*, the Sea about the Isles Hiberides, to the North from Ireland. **1775** Johnson *West. Isl.* 221 Such intelligence the Hebridians probably receive from their transmarine correspondents. **1780** J. Johnstone (*title*) Anecdotes of Olave the Black, King of Man, and the Hebridian Princes of the Somerled Family. **1810** Scott *Fam. Lett.* 10 June (1894) I. 181, I intend to take the Hebridian character and scenery..for my subject. **1828** J. Tytler *Hist. Scot.* I. i. 29 Dugal and other Hebridean chiefs. **1833–4** J. Phillips *Geol.* in *Encycl. Metrop.* VI. 561/1 The Zetland Isles, which are in some measure to be viewed as a prolongation to the Hebridian group. *a* **1856** H. Miller *Cruise Betsey* (1858) vi. 90 The penetrating powers of a true Hebridean drizzle. **1887** H. B. Woodward *Geol. Eng. & Wales* (ed. 2) 38 The Lewisian (or Hebridean) group. **1897** R. H. Story *Apostolic Ministry Scot. Church* v. 154 The beehive cells, the remains of which may still be seen in Eilean Naomh and other Hebridean isles. **1911** *Encycl. Brit.* XXIV. 416/1 The oldest rocks of Scotland and of the British Isles are known..as Archean, and consist chiefly of gneiss (called..Lewisian and Hebridean). **1926** *Chambers's Jrnl.* Sept. 577/2 Our comely Hebridean. **1972** *Daily Tel.* 29 Jan. 16/5 The Hebridean processes of cloth-treatment are in danger of falling into oblivion.

hechima (hetʃī·mă). [Jap.] The sponge-gourd (see Sponge *sb.*[1] 13 c).

1883 *Trans. Asiatic Soc. Japan* XI. 13 (*heading*) Luffa petola, Ser. Hechima... Young fruit as food: and fibres of ripe fruit as brushes and sponges. **1889** J. J. Rein *Industries of Japan* i. 72 (*heading*) 21. *Luffa petola*, Ser., Jap. Hechima, Tô-guwa. The long cylindric fruit resembles a long straight cucumber.

heck (hek), *sb.* and *int. dial.* and *colloq.* Euphemistic alteration of *hell.* (Also *hecky* in dial. use.)

[**1865** [J. A. Ferguson] *Wot Aw seed ut th' Preston Eggsibishun* 88 (E.D.D.), Well, aw'll go to ecky, he cried. **1878** J. Almond *Bunch of Watercresses* 21 Where the hecky could he go to?]

1887 T. Darlington *Folk-sp. S. Cheshire* s.v., What the heck are yŏ up to? **1922** S. Lewis *Babbitt* xiv. 178 How it feels, by heck, to be up at five-thirty. **1925** *Blackw. Mag.* Oct. 545/1, I couldn't make out what in heck was going on. **1928** M. Walsh *While Rivers Run* ii. § 3 By heck! what a kick he must have in that right of his. **1930** *Daily Express* 23 May 10/3 Does the borough council care? By heck, it doesn't! **1932** J. T. Farrell *Studs Lonigan* (1936) iii. 68 He would have the heck of a time explaining his shiner to the old lady. **1933** *Punch* 11 Jan. 52/1 He insisted on St. Isinglas because he thought everything here was so well organised. The heck it is. **1936** M. H. Bradley *Five Minute Girl* xiii. 236 He had certainly played heck with that party. **1956** E. Pound tr. *Sophocles' Women of Trachis* 17 That fellow was lying, one time or the other, One heck of a messenger! **1957** I. Cross *God Boy* (1958) i. 12 Heck now, I started off with Dad talking to me..and here we are no further on. *Ibid.* xii. 95 People go all the way the heck over to France. **1966** *Guardian* 5 Feb. 6/4 Sometimes he sings for sheer fun and the heck of it. **1973** D. Westheimer *Going Public* i. 15 It's a heck of a responsibility.

heckelphone (he·kəlfōᵘn). Also **-phon.** [ad. G. *heckelphon*, f. name of *Heckel*, an instrument-maker of Biberich, after *saxophone*.] A baritone oboe.

1905 *Westm. Gaz.* 14 Dec. 8/2 A new instrument, called appropriately the 'Heckelphon', answered from the orchestra. **1914** C. Forsyth *Orchestration* 228 Strauss has made use of the Heckelphon in..*Salome*. **1940** G. Jacob *Orchestral Technique* (ed. 2) i. 3 Some very fully scored modern symphonic and operatic works employ quadruple woodwind, such exotics as the bass flute and heckelphone sometimes being added to the flute and oboe group respectively. **1966** *Guardian* 22 Apr. 12/5 A heckelphone (a kind of outsize 'baritone' oboe).

heckle, *sb.* Add: **4. b.** The action of heckling.

1905 *Westm. Gaz.* 29 Apr. 3/2 Our congratulations to.. Mr. Davies on his..successful heckle. **1944** H. van Zeller *Ezechiel* viii. 69 We again look for some sort of an apologia, an objection or two, a mild heckle, a question.

hecogenin (hekodʒe·nin). *Chem.* [f. mod.L. *Hec*(*htia*, name of a genus of plants + -o + ***genin**.] A steroid glycoside (see quot. 1965) occurring in various plants, as *Hechtia texensis* and *Agave* species, obtained commercially from sisal waste and used commercially as a precursor in the manufacture of cortisone and other steroid hormones.

1943 R. E. Marker et al. in *Jrnl. Amer. Chem. Soc.* LXV. 1199/2 We first isolated from *Hechtia texensis* (S. Wats.) a new steroidal sapogenin having the composition $C_{27}H_{42}O_4$..which we have named hecogenin. **1952** *Sci. News* XXV. 115 More than 100,000 tons of fibre are produced yearly from sisal,..and..approximately the same amount of waste material, containing 0.04 per cent to 0.1 per cent of hecogenin, are available. **1965** Pollock & Stevens *Dict. Org. Compounds* (ed. 4) III. 1809/1, 3β-Hydroxy-5α-spirostan-12-one (Hecogenin). **1972** *Materials & Technol.* V. xx. 752 Hecogenin is extracted from sisal waste.

hecte, var. ***hekte.**

hectic, *a.* Add: **4.** Stirring, exciting, disturbing; characterized by a state of feverish excitement or activity. *colloq.*

1904 Kipling *Traffics & Discov.* 210 Didn't I say we never met in pup-pup-puris naturalibus, if I may so put it, without a remarkably hectic day ahead of us? **1922** *Westm. Gaz.* 19 Aug., The hectic undulations of the mark. *Ibid.* 7 Nov., Those hectic inconsidered actions which kept the country in a state of crisis for some ten days. **1922** *Daily Mail* 21 Nov. 11 As additional excitements to the hectic finishes one horse was killed and the judge mistook the winner of the Leycester Nursery. **1925** Fraser & Gibbons *Soldier & Sailor Words* 117 *Hectic show*, an Air Force expression for flying very low. **1968** *Daily Mirror* 20 Aug. 9/2 Stretch bikini bottoms and loose towelling tops in hectic colours.

hectically. Add: **b.** With feverish activity. *colloq.*

1908 *Daily Chron.* 18 May 3/5 So many pictures in the Salons look as if they had been painted hectically a month before the exhibitions opened. **1972** *Daily Tel.* 15 Jan. 11 A hectically social couple of my acquaintance.

hectography (hektǫ·grăfi). [f. Hectograph *sb.*: see -graphy.] The use of the hectograph.

1889 J. H. Scrine *Mem. E. Thring* 31 Splice 3 pens together,..and execute the task..by fraudulent hectography.

hector, *v.* Add: Hence **he·ctoringly** *adv.*, in a hectoring manner.

1913 W. J. Locke *Stella Maris* xx. 251 He..questioned her further, almost hectoringly. **1963** *Punch* 27 Feb. 315/3 His adopting a hectoringly superior manner.

hedebo (he·debo). [ad. Dan. *hedebobroderi*, f. *hede* heath + *bo* dwelling + *broderi* embroidery.] (See quots.)

1932 D. C. Minter *Modern Needlecraft* 49/2 The drawing of threads..forms the basis of various interesting forms of embroidery. This network..is sometimes used as a contrast for parts of a richly embroidered surface. This kind of work is known as *Hedebo work*, and is usually executed almost entirely in white. **1957** M. B. Picken *Fashion Dict.* 171/1 *Hedebo embroidery*, Danish embroidery of cut and drawn work.

heder, var. ***cheder.**

hedge, *sb.* Add: **5.** Also *Commercial, Financial*, and *transf.* (cf. ***hedge** *v.* 8 c).

1917 A. W. Atwood *Exchanges & Speculation* xiv. 196 The local elevator companies..place their hedges as soon as they begin to accumulate supplies of grain. **1955** *Times* 8 June 9/2 Your board are keenly aware of the need that the group should continue to build up, in the form of profitable interests elsewhere, 'hedges' against catastrophe in British Guiana. *Ibid.* 29 June 11/3 As for the hedge of going into television itself that may save the property but it will not save the Press. **1957** *Economist* 12 Oct. 152/2 In France, wool was probably taken into stock as a hedge against currency devaluation and the pressure of credit restriction is also at work there. **1958** *Punch* 19 Nov. 669/2 A good unit trust group..provides the best way of combining the safety of numbers with the promise of participating in the economic growth that lies before us and of providing a hedge against inflation. **1959** *Ibid.* 19 Aug. 54/2 The share of these companies would seem to be a perfect election hedge.

7. *hedge-cricket, -cutter, -cutting*: examples; *hedge-wren.*

1820 Keats *To Autumn* in *Lamia*, etc. 139 Hedge-crickets sing. **1881** *Encycl. Brit.* XII. 234/1 A new instrument for clipping hedges, Ridgway's hedge-cutter. **1960** *Farmer & Stockbreeder* 2 Feb. 80/1 There was a record entry of nearly 100 mechanical hedge-cutters. **1971** P. Gresswell *Environment* 125 The mechanical hedge-cutter clears the young saplings. **1899** *Westm. Gaz.* 22 Dec. 1/3 Hedge-cutting competitions have a..useful effect in checking the use of barbed wire. *Ibid.* 21 July 2/3 The swallow does not fear us, the hedge-wren does not flout us. **1907** *Academy* 9 Feb. 131/2 The hedge-wren..Is out in the open.

9. hedge-clause *U.S.*, a safeguarding clause in a contract; **hedge-fence**, a hedge serving as a fence; **hedge-grown** *a.* (see quots.); **hedge-hop** *v. colloq.*, to fly in an aircraft at low levels so as to suggest hopping over hedges; so **hedge-hopper, -hopping** *vbl. sb.* and *ppl. a.*; also *fig.*; **hedge selling** (see 5 above and ***hedge** *v.* 8 c); **hedge trimmer** (see Trimmer 3); **hedge trimming,** (*a*) (see Trimming *vbl. sb.* 1 b); (*b*) (see Trimming *vbl. sb.* 1 c).

1928 *Sat. Even. Post* 10 Mar. 185/2 In the Wall Street language..hedge clauses..signify that if the representations turn out to be wrong the banker shall not be held accountable. **1662** *Portsmouth* (R.I.) *Rec.* 396 The said fence..provided that it be a hedge fence. **1778** *Essex Inst. Hist. Coll.* LII. 13 Seeing this hedge fence, they might take it to be a breastwork thrown up to annoy them. **1826–44** Hedge fence [in Dict., sense 7 a]. **1820** Keats *Fancy* in *Lamia*, etc. 124 The first Hedge-grown primrose that hath burst. **1900** *Daily Express* 3 Aug. 2/7 Barley is not so good this year, for it has come up irregularly..; barley of this character is known with us as a 'hedge-grown crop'. **1926** *Nat. Geogr. Mag.* Jan. 18/2 Back he'd go 'upstairs' under a 200-foot ceiling, and hedge-hop along 20 miles or so, to the next emergency field. **1928** *Daily Express* 21 May 10/3 They can 'hedge-hop' with skill or fly to the greater heights with as much impunity as a man pilot. **1940** 'Gun Buster' *Return via Dunkirk* ii. xi. 171 A German plane hedge-hopped right over us. **1962** L. Deighton *Ipcress File* vii. 49 The machine [*sc.* a helicopter]..hedge-hopped in 100 m.p.h. gallops towards the sea. **1940** H. E. Baughman *Aviation Dict.* 96/1 *Hedge-hopper airplane* (slang), any small, under-powered plane with enough power and lift to get off the ground a few feet for a brief period of time. **1957** R. W. Zandvoort et al. *Wartime Eng.* 127 *Hedge-hopper*, a low-flying aircraft. **1919** R. H. Reece *Night Bombing with Bedouins* 23 The British sport of 'hedge-hopping', i.e., flying close to the ground and 'zooming' up over trees. **1939** *War Illustr.* 11 Nov. 286 The German pilot's story of his eventful pursuit of a hedge-hopping English 'plane. **1955** *Amer. Speech* XXX. 72 Hedge-hopping..took on a special meaning in the 1952 presidential campaign—using an airplane in political campaigning. **1957** L. Durrell *Bitter Lemons* 100 My own ambitions were more hedge-hopping and my means forbade me to indulge in such delightful fantasies. **1920** J. Stephenson *Princ. Commercial Corr.* ii. xiii. 151 Further liquidation and some hedge selling caused another decline. **1930** *Daily Express* 8 Sept. 2/7 A reaction occurred owing to liquidation, hedge selling, a bearish crop estimate. **1964** *Financial Times* 12 Mar. 2/7 Selling was stop loss, together with some hedge selling. **1870** *Trans. Ill. Agric. Soc.* VIII. 18 For want of opportunity there had been no test made of the Hedge Trimmer, entered by D. Oliver, of Galesburg, Ill. **1961** *Times* 26 May 16/7 Hedge-trimmers and verge-cutters are a common part of the roadside scene. **1859** *Trans. Ill. Agric. Soc.* III. 362, I believe that the men are..here present, who will live to see..hedge trimming &c., done by steam. **1960** *Farmer & Stockbreeder* 12 Jan. 63/2 Disposing of hedge-trimmings.

10. hedge-cactus *U.S.*, a cactus (*Cereus peruvianus*) grown as a hedge-plant; **hedge-nettle** (later example).

1883 J. H. Beadle *Western Wilds* xxxvi. 593 There is.. the hedge cactus, with which Mexicans fence their fields. **1869** J. G. Fuller *Flower Gatherers* 277 There are several other species of the Hedge-nettle, some of them without hairs.

hedge, *v.* Add: **8. c.** To insure against risk of loss by entering into contracts which

balance one another. Also *trans.*, to operate in (a commodity) in this way.

1909 I. FISHER *Elimination of Risk* 12 An important method of shifting risks is 'hedging', whereby a dealer, for instance in transporting wheat, may be relieved of the risk of a change of price. **1917** A. W. ATWOOD *Exchanges & Speculation* xiv. 195 Hedging..consists in matching a purchase with a sale, or vice versa; in other words, it consists in making a purchase or sale for future delivery to offset and protect an actual merchandising transaction. *Ibid.* xiv. 197 It makes little difference to an elevator if wheat rises or falls fifty cents a bushel, provided its holdings have been hedged. **1957** *Times* 19 Dec. 16/1 We have drawn the attention of the stockholders to the difficulty in hedging our unsold stocks against a fall in cotton content value.

hedge-bank. (Later examples.)

1900 *Daily News* 21 Sept. 3/2 Deeply laid roads and high, steep hedge banks. **1909** *Westm. Gaz.* 6 Mar. 16/3 A network of tiny marks..crossing and recrossing from hedge-bank to stack. **1937** *Discovery* Apr. 120/2 Feverfew, commonly found about hedgebanks.

hedgehog. Add: **4. e.** (Earlier example.)

1838 *Civil Engin. & Archit. Jrnl.* Dec. 391/1 (*title*) A machine called a hedgehog for removing mud etc. in rivers.

f. (Earlier and later examples.)

1723 J. NOTT *Cook's & Confect. Dict.* 28 (*heading*) To make a hedge-hog. *Ibid.*, Almonds,..Eggs,..Cream,.. Butter..stirring, till it is stiff enough to be made in the Form of a Hedge-hog; then stick it full of blanch'd Almonds,..like the Bristles of a Hedge-hog. **1960** *Good Housek. Cook. Bk.* 405/2 Hedgehog cake.

g. A fortified position 'bristling' with guns pointing in all directions.

1942 *Daily Tel.* 22 May 1/2 The German infantry has been used to being led by tanks and, throughout the past winter, to holding strong points called 'hedgehogs'. **1943** *Times* 16 Dec. 4/1 The Germans fought with the utmost ferocity for their old 'hedgehog' position. **1952** *Time* 29 Sept. 18/1 Holdfast's strategists had developed their plan after studying German tactics in the long retreat from Stalingrad (in which the Germans first used the word 'hedgehog').

h. (See quot. 1947.)

1947 *Jane's Fighting Ships 1946–7* 6 Anti-Submarine Weapons..include the 'hedgehog', a salvo of 24 depth charges each containing 32 lb. of explosive fired ahead of a ship from a spigot mortar. **1968** D. MCLACHLAN *Room 39* xiv. 329 The dangers of underwater hedgehogs to the Mulberry floating harbours [had not] been closely examined.

6. *hedgehog roller.*

1930 *Engineering* 14 Nov. 615/2 An elevator..delivered the clay into small hedgehog rollers.

7. b. hedgehog converter, transformer *Electr.*, a type of transformer (no longer used) with open magnetic circuit, in which the ends of the iron wire core assume a bristling appearance; **hedgehog fish,** = *porcupine fish*; **hedgehog wheat,** a race of hardy dwarf wheats, grown in mountainous districts of Europe, having dense short ears and awned glumes.

1851 P. H. GOSSE *Nat. Sojourn Jamaica* 244 Specimens of the Hedgehog-fish, or Sea Porcupine (*Diodon*), are frequently carried home by mariners. **1902** *Encycl. Brit.* XXVIII. 117/2 The wire..used..to form the core of his 'hedgehog' transformers. **1909** WEBSTER, Hedgehog wheat. **1921** J. PERCIVAL *Wheat Plant* 307 Club, Dwarf, Cluster or Hedgehog Wheat, *Triticum compactum.*

hedging, *vbl. sb.* Add: **3.** (Later examples.)

1917 [see *HEDGE *v.* 8 c]. **1940** *Economist* 11 May 863/1 Much of the apparent speculation taking place in markets..is, in fact, justifiable hedging either against receipts of sterling..or against the holding of sterling assets... But over and above such hedging some outright speculation is also proceeding. **1954** *Ibid.* 22 May 642/2 The Liverpool market should..offer Lancashire a satisfactory hedging medium. **1958** *Spectator* 13 June 785/1 The tenacity of the 'inflation hedging' investor.

5. *hedging-glove* (later example).

1906 KIPLING *Puck of Pook's Hill* 235, I was cheated.. over a pair of hedging-gloves.

hedgy, *a.* Add: **c.** Of behaviour (see HEDGE *v.* 9).

1928 D. H. LAWRENCE *Lady Chatterley* iv. 38 Clifford was much more hedgey and nervous. **1955** 'C. H. ROLPH' *Women of Streets* 154 *Personality*: Suspicious, hedgy, aggressively defensive.

hedonal (hī·dŏnăl). *Chem.* [a. G. *hedonal* (H. Dreser 1899, in *Verh. d. Ges. deutsch. Naturf. und Ärzte* II. 48), f. Gr. ἡδονή pleasure + -AL.] A white crystalline compound, $C_6H_{13}O_2N$, that has been used as a hypnotic and an anæsthetic; methyl-propyl-carbinol urethane.

1900 *Brit. Med. Jrnl.* epit. 21 July 12/1 (*heading*) Hedonal. Schüler..publishes 21 cases in which this new hypnotic was used in Krafft-Ebing's clinic. Hedonal is methyl-propyl-carbinol-urethan, a white crystalline body. **1905** *Med. Ann.* 191 Hedonal has been used by Varges in the treatment of chorea. **1927** *Observer* 27 Mar. 13/1 Drugs such as hedonal may be injected..to facilitate or produce surgical anaesthesia. **1971** MCCOMISH & BODLEY *Anaesthesia for Neurol. Surg.* i. 15 The vogue for hedonal [as an anæsthetic] did not last long because the war in 1914 stopped supplies from Germany, and toxic effects later became apparent.

hedonic, *a.* and *sb.* Add: **A.** *adj.* In wider use, chiefly in *Psychol.*: of, pertaining to, or involving pleasurable or painful sensations or feelings, considered as affects. Spec. *hedonic tone*, the degree of pleasantness or unpleasantness associated with an experience or state, esp. considered as a single quantity that can range from extreme pleasure to extreme pain.

1901 G. F. STOUT *Man. Psychol.* (ed. 2) I. i. 63 When we wish to say that pleasure or displeasure belongs to this or that mental process, we say that the process is pleasantly or unpleasantly toned. Hedonic-tone is a generic term for pleasure and the reverse, considered as attributes of this or that mental process. *Ibid.*, Anger has hedonic-tone, mostly of an unpleasant kind. **1932** J. G. BEEBE-CENTER *Psychol. Pleasantness & Unpleasantness* i. 6 In the present volume..the general algebraic variable, whose positive values correspond to pleasantness and whose negative values correspond to unpleasantness, will be called hedonic tone. **1940** *Jrnl. Exper. Psychol.* XXVI. 233 The oscillations of hedonic tone in his case are slight, and the tone rises continuously from the beginning, in spite of pain and fatigue. *Ibid.* 227 While Ss worked Es took their tapping rate every minute..and in a number of cases called at stated intervals for a rating on a previously agreed hedonic scale. **1952** D. J. O'CONNOR *John Locke* 51 By pleasure and pain Locke..is referring to what the psychologists nowadays call the hedonic tone of our experiences which can be roughly measured on a scale ranging from very pleasant through mildly pleasant, neutral, mildly unpleasant to very unpleasant. **1961** P. T. YOUNG *Motivation & Emotion* v. 153 The sign, intensity, and temporal changes of affective processes can be represented upon the hedonic continuum.

2. *Zool.* Of or pertaining to sexual activity; *hedonic gland*, any of various specialized glands found in many reptiles and amphibia that serve, apparently by secreting an attractive-smelling substance, to attract members of the opposite sex.

1901 H. GADOW *Amphibia & Reptiles* x. 443 All the recent Crocodilia possess two pairs of skin-glands, both secreting musk... The use of these strongly scented organs, which are possessed by both sexes, is obviously hedonic. *Ibid.* 658/2 (*index*) Hedonic glands (ἡδονή, lust). **1931** G. K. NOBLE *Biol. Amphibia* vi. 137 The secretions of the hedonic glands of newts and plethodontid salamanders have no recognizable odor and yet they seem to function in holding the attention of the female during courtship. **1960** H. M. SMITH *Evol. Chordate Struct.* xiii. 344 A large number of integumentary glands of spotty distribution among vertebrates are of hedonic function.

So **hedo·nically** *adv.*

1951 H. A. MURRAY in Parsons & Shils *Toward Gen. Theory Action* IV. iii. 456 The kinds of events that are hedonically negative and the kinds that are hedonically positive. *Ibid.* 457 The aim of all needs is hedonically positive (in the imagination). **1961** P. T. YOUNG *Motivation & Emotion* ii. 49 It is reasonable to assume that playful behavior is generally enjoyable, hedonically positive.

hedonical, *a.* (Example.)

1897 B. RUSSELL *Essay Foundations Geom.* iii. 158 They would leave Geometry in a position no better than that of the Hedonical Calculus, in which we depend on a purely subjective measure.

hedrumite (he·drŭ̆məit). *Petrogr.* [a. G. *hedrumit* (W. C. Brögger 1890, in *Zeitschr. f. Kryst. und Min.* XVI. 40), f. *Hedrum*, the name of a village north of Larvik, Norway + -ITE[1].] A hypabyssal porphyritic igneous rock having a trachytic texture and consisting essentially of a potash-feldspar with small amounts of pyribole and usu. also nepheline.

1896 J. F. KEMP *Handbk. Rocks* 141 *Hedrumite*, a name proposed by Brögger for certain syenitic rocks that are poor or lacking in nepheline, but that have a trachytic texture. **1920** A. HOLMES *Nomencl. Petrol.* 116 *Hedrumite*... A leucocratic variety of alkali-syenite containing accessory nepheline. **1938** A. JOHANNSEN *Descr. Petrogr. Igneous Rocks* IV. I. 25 Hedrumites..are essentially pulaskite-porphyries with a coarse trachytic texture. Brögger defined them as the mineralogical and chemical hypabyssal-trachytoid-equivalents of the pulaskites. **1964** *Mineral. Abstr.* XVI. 574/1 Senonian hedrumites cutting somewhat earlier andesites and pyroclastics have been found..in Bulgaria.

hedychium (hĕdi·kiə̆m). [mod.L. (J. G. Koenig in A. J. Retzius *Observationes Botanicæ* (1785) III. 73), f. Gr. ἡδύς sweet + χιών snow, in allusion to the fragrant white flowers of one species.] A perennial herb of the genus so called, belonging to the family Zingiberaceæ, native to tropical Asia, and bearing showy flowers in a terminal spike; the garland-flower. Also, a fibre obtained from a species of this plant.

1822 *Curtis's Bot. Mag.* XLIX. 2300 Roots of this undescribed species of *Hedychium* were sent by Dr. Wallich of Calcutta, to our friend Mr. Kent. **1894** A. K. NAIRNE *Flowering Plants W. India* 339 *Hedychium*, with long and slender filament and broad lateral staminodes, is..a garden plant with pure white, fragrant flowers. **1920** CROSS & BEVAN *Text-bk. Paper-Making* (ed. 5) 171 *Hedychium coronarium.* Hedychium has lately come into prominence as a paper-making fibre. **1952** F. KINGDON-WARD *Plant Hunter in Manipur* 237 During the long summer..Hedychium, with several species and in many bright colours, comes into bloom.

Heeb, var. *HEBE, HEBE[2].

heebie-jeebie(s (hī·bi,dʒī·bi(z. *slang* (orig. *U.S.*). Also **heebies, heeby-jeebies,** etc. A feeling of discomfort, apprehension, or depression; the 'jitters'; delirium tremens; also, formerly, a type of dance.

1923 W. DE BECK in *N.Y. American* 26 Oct. 9/3 You dumb ox—why don't you get that stupid look offa your pan—you gimme the heeby jeebys! *Ibid.* 10 Nov. 10/1, 31,000 shares! Worthless stock of 'the Belgian Hair Tonic Company' wiped out! Every cent I had in the world... It gives me the heebie jeebies. **1924** H. C. WITWER in *Cosmopolitan* Oct. 114/2 That discovery gave my new found friend the hibby jibbys. **1926** MAINES & GRANT *Wise-Crack Dict.* 9/2 *Heebie-jeebies*, alcoholic shimmy. **1926** *Bulletin* 13 Dec. 5/5 The latest dance, the 'Heebie-Jeebies' is said to represent the incantations made by Red Indian witch doctors before a human sacrifice. **1927** *Punch* 2 Feb. 116/1 It is interesting to observe that in spite of artificial sunlight, television, winter sports and the heebie-jeebie there are still some stalwarts who stand by the old traditional amusements of the English people. **1927** *Weekly Dispatch* 1 May 8 The Heebie Jeebies is rich in haunch movements. *Ibid.* 3 May 3/7 A terrible girl in the next gallery, painted in the fearsome and fashionable 'pink and putty' manner, had given him what an American present might have called the 'heeby-jeebies'. *Ibid.* 17 Aug. 3/2 Does this work never give you the heeby-jeebies? Does it never depress you? **1929** R. C. ANDREWS *Ends of Earth* 89, I thought I had the 'hebe-jibies' and stepped up very gingerly. **1934** R. NICHOLS *Fisbo* 37 It would have given the downright heebee-jeebee To even the dullest of the dull *amœbæ*. **1959** J. FLEMING *Miss Bones* viii. 94 You've given me the heeby jeebies... It'll be the end of me. **1971** R. DENTRY *Encounter at Kharmel* iii. 57 That little creep..gives me the screaming heebies. **1972** WODEHOUSE *Pearls, Girls & Monty Bodkin* ix. 138 He was suffering from an ailment known to the medical profession as the heeby-jeebies, and anything having the appearance of a hitch in the programme might lead to a total collapse.

heel, *sb.*[1] Add: **1. e.** *heel of Achilles, Achilles' heel*: the only vulnerable spot (in allusion to the story of the dipping of Achilles in the river Styx: cf. *tendon of Achilles* s.v. TENDON a).

1810 COLERIDGE *Friend* 431 Ireland, that vulnerable heel of the British Achilles! **1864** CARLYLE *Fredk. Gt.* IV. XVII. ii. 522 Hanover,..the Achilles'-heel to invulnerable England. **1897** G. B. SHAW *Let.* 2 July (1965) 777 Divorce is the Achilles heel of marriage. **1930** L. D. BRONSHTEIN tr. *Trotsky's Life* xxv. 262 By his verbal artifices, he only discloses his own Achilles' heel. **1944** *Times* 19 June 5/6 Military observers have dubbed Viipuri the Achilles' heel of the Finnish defences. **1957** A. E. COPPARD *It's Me, O Lord!* ii. 17 The three R's, the third of which..was..my Achilles heel. **1972** *Catholic Herald* 28 Jan. 1/5 It is this refusal to condemn which is the Achilles heel of contemporary Christian psychology.

f. *Horsemanship.* Management by the heel, esp. the spurred heel.

1728 CHAMBERS *Cycl.* s.v., This horse understands the Heels well.

3. a. In *Rugby Football*: a heeling of the ball from the scrummage. Cf. HEEL *v.*[1] 5 b.

1937 *Times* 15 Feb. 5/3 A quick heel and the ball went through the hands of [etc.].

5. b. *high heel* (earlier and later examples).

1671 A. WOOD *Life & Times* (1892) II. 226, 4*d* given to see a man at the King's Head 7 foot and an half high... He had a night gowne on, which made him seem taller, and high heels. **1950** G. BARKER *News of World* 10 Heavy my heart walks ahead on the pavements With her high-heel shoe my martyrdom on stone.

7. b. (Further example.)

1933 L. G. D. ACLAND in *Press* (Christchurch) 28 Oct. 15/7 *Heel*, the corner of a shear blade, next the grip.

k. The lower part of the back of a book.

1930 *Godfrey's Catal.* No. 134. 26 Small piece gone from heel, and joint becoming tender.

l, m. (See quots.)

1880 E. D. COPE in *Amer. Naturalist* XIV. 836 Stages in the following modification of parts:—..(6) In the obliteration of the inner tubercle of the lower sectorial. (7) In the extinction of the heel of the same. **1888** *Lockwood's Dict. Mech. Engin.*, *Heel*, the thick or broad end of a wedge-shaped piece, the broad end of a railway switch for example. **1957** R. LISTER *Decorative Wrought Ironwork* i. 12 The anvil's parts are known by special names... The part of the face and body that terminates in a thick wedge-shaped end is the *heel.*

11. (Further examples.) Also **down-at-heels** *attrib.*; **down-at-heeledness.**

1906 *Daily Chron.* 22 Dec. 3/2 A down-at-heels party hailed him as a countryman, and asked 'the lend of the loan of twopence'. **1919** C. ORR *Glorious Thing* iv. 37 The old down-at-heel slippers she kept for working. **1956** E. C. HISCOCK *Around World in Wanderer III* vi. 68 To hear once more the shrill scream of pigs protesting their passage aboard some down-at-heel schooner. **1963** A. LUBBOCK *Austral. Roundabout* 31 The usual two-storey bush pub, rather scruffy and down-at-heel. **1924** Down-at-heeledness (see *DAVERDY *a.*).

13. Also as a word of command: *heel!*

1878 C. HALLOCK *Amer. Club List & Sportsman's Gloss.* p. vi, *Heel*, the order to dogs to come behind the gunner. **1923** D. L. SAYERS *Whose Body?* ix. 200 The dog..barked. .. 'Heel,' said the man in velveteen, violently. The animal sidled up, ashamed. **1935** G. HEYER *Death in Stocks* ii. 13 She..was chiefly occupied in keeping

back a powerful bull-terrier... 'Shut up, you fool!' commanded the girl. '*Heel!*' **1971** M. TRIPP *Five Minutes with Stranger* I. vi. 64 She was saying 'Heel' in a voice that would have quelled a riot in hell.

14. c. Of motoring. Also as *vb.* (see quot. 1962). So **heeling-and-toeing** *vbl. sb.*

1937 O. STEWART *Learn to Drive* viii. 63 A method of gear changing..is that which employs heel-and-toe operation of clutch and accelerator pedals at the same time. **1962** *Which?* (Suppl.) July 96/2 If you want to, you can 'heel-and-toe'—work brake and accelerator at the same time. **1966** T. WISDOM *High-Performance Driving* viii. 73 Use of the 'heel-and-toe' technique.. reduces the time and distance taken to complete the slowing-down and gear-change operations. **1966** R. MAXWELL in T. Wisdom *High-Performance Driving* viii. 72 Heeling and toeing..involves double-declutching into a lower gear while braking. **1973** 'J. ASHFORD' *Double Run* xiv. 114 With heel-and-toe braking and gear changing he flicked down through the gears.

16*. dig in one's heels: see ***DIG** *v.* 11 c.

22. (Earlier example.)

1751 FIELDING *Amelia* III. IX. vii. 283 Instead..of attempting to follow her, he turned on his Heel, and addressed his Discourse to another Lady.

24. c. *to run heel.* Delete † and add later examples.

1923 *Times* 17 Jan. 5/5 The old Melbreak hounds will never run heel. **1946** M. C. SELF *Horseman's Encycl.* 455 When hounds hit the line and run it backwards they are said to 'run heel'.

25. *heel-back, -chaser, -dance, -kicker; heel-clacking, -clicking* vbl. sbs. and ppl. adjs.; *heel-free* adj.

1936 *Times* 9 Jan. 4/1 A quick heel-back from a loose scrummage. **1938** DYLAN THOMAS *Let.* 1 June (1966) 199 It's the dog among the fairies..the wizard's heel-chaser. **1922** JOYCE *Ulysses* 515 A firm heelclacking is heard. **1928** BLUNDEN *Undertones of War* 155 Strutting with redoubled vanity and heel-clicking. **1970** R. PARKES *Death Mask* v. 64 The abrupt, heel-clicking return of Castilla. **1951** KOESTLER *Age of Longing* I. iv. 58 Loose, springy limbs which seemed specially designed for the Kaukasian heel-dance. **1948** B. VESEY-FITZGERALD *Bk. Dog* 223 Ten minutes a day for three days and most puppies will be 'heel-free' in the pen. **1926** D. H. LAWRENCE *Let.* 19 Jan. (1932) 647 Murry..wrote me impertinently..that I was a professional heel-kicker.

26. a. heel-breast, in a shoe, the inside edge of the heel, adjoining the waist; so **heel-breaster,** an operator who cuts heel-breasts; also, the tool used; **heel-breasting,** the cutting of heel-breasts; **heel-parer,** one who shapes and trims heel-blanks; **heel-scourer,** one who scours the surface of heels.

1921 *Dict. Occup. Terms* (1927) § 429 *Scourer*..designated according to parts upon which he works, *e.g.* bottom or naumkeag scourer, heel scourer, heel-breast scourer. **1905** *Westm. Gaz.* 30 Oct. 7/3 The same firm have several other novelties, including an automatic Louis heel-breaster. The uninitiated may like to know that 'heel-breasting' is the operation of bevelling out the curve on the inside edge of the heel to the familiar half-moon or other shape. **1921** *Dict. Occup. Terms* (1927) § 414 *Heel breaster*; cuts breast on front of heel square. **1881** *Instr. Census Clerks* (1885) 76 Heel Parer. **1904** *Daily Chron.* 11 June 8/6 Boot Trade.—Wanted good heel parers and heel scourers. **1921** Heel scourer [see *bottom-scourer* s.v. *BOTTOM *sb.* 19].

c. heel bug, a harvest mite, *Trombicula autumnalis*, or the skin disease it causes in horses.

1920 *Vet. Rec.* 6 Nov. 218/1 Heel bug, or harvester, *Leptus autumnalis*, is an annual source of trouble to thoroughbreds in training. **1931** *Daily Tel.* 22 May 19/7 Lady Marjorie is suffering from lameness in the off-hind heel, due to variola, which is a similar complaint to heel-bug. **1950** W. E. LYON *First Aid Hints Horse Owner* (rev. ed.) iv. 87 Heel Bug. As a rule only well-bred horses with thin skins are affected. The heels will be swollen and painful: lameness may also be present. **1954** P. SMYTHE *Jump for Joy* v. 83 She had contracted a heel bug disease. **1968** G. LAPAGE *Vet. Parasitol.* (ed. 2) xxxii. 771 *T*[*rombicula*] *autumnalis* may be the cause of 'heel-bug' of racehorses.

heel (hīl), *sb.*³ *slang* (orig. *U.S.*). [Of doubtful origin though prob. f. HEEL *sb.*¹ (cf. sense 3).] Among criminals: a double-crosser, a sneak-thief; more generally: a dishonourable or untrustworthy person, a rotter.

1914 JACKSON & HELLYER *Vocab. Criminal Slang* 43 *Heel*,..An incompetent; an undesirable; an inefficient or pusillanimous pretender to sterling criminal qualifications. **1916** *Lit. Digest* 19 Aug. 425/1 She..is said to be running a respectable 'scatter' in Dayton, Ohio, for reformed pickpockets and 'heels' or 'pennyweighters', the argot for sneak-thieves and shoplifters. **1929** *Sat. Even. Post* 13 Apr. 54/4 If a crook becomes an informer, then he is a rat or a heel. **1932** J. T. FARRELL *Studs Lonigan* xvi. 354 Studs watched him give the college handshake, thought what a heel O'Brien had turned into. **1949** 'J. TEY' *Brat Farrar* xvii. 157 Signing a paper didn't make him any more of a heel than he was being at the moment. **1949** R. GRAVES *Seven Days in New Crete* 67 She had not only treated me foully but managed at the same time to put me in the wrong and make me feel a thorough heel. **1957** L. P. HARTLEY *Hireling* 225 It doesn't matter how she feels, does it, when she's lost her fiancé—though he was a heel and she's well rid of him? **1958** *Times Lit. Suppl.* 26 Dec. 749/5 John Augustus Grimshawe was a heel about money and women.

heel, *v.*¹ Add: **2. b.** (Further example.)

1873 J. MILLER *Life amongst Modocs* 301 This was his signal to 'heel' himself and come upon the ground.

4. Read: To follow at the heels of, chase by running or nipping at the heels; also *absol.* to follow at a person's heels. (Further examples.)

1940 E. C. STUDHOLME *Te Waimate* (1954) xvi. 138 Two good dogs, one of which frightened the beasts by heeling them up (biting their heels) and the other by pulling their tails. **1947** R. B. KELLEY *Sheep Dogs* (ed. 2) xv. 178 Dogs that heel when forcing can be made relatively harmless by removing their canine..teeth. **1966** 'J. HACKSTON' *Father clears Out* 14 Our half-bred sheep-dog, which for years had poked about the kindly heels of callers' nags, got it in the ribs. 'No mong's going to heel that horse.'

5. b. (Further example.) Also *trans.*

1930 R. CAMPBELL *Poems* 11 See the fat nouns like porky forwards sprawl Into a scrum that never heels the ball. **1936** *Times* 9 Jan. 4/3 In the earlier scrummages the Navy's forwards heeled the ball with commendable cleanness. **1955** *Times* 22 Aug. 3/2 One of the those [*sc.* abilities] is to heel out sufficiently cleanly to offer the halves a chance to open up the play.

7. *intr.* To run back on the scent, to run heel.

1898 *Daily News* 5 Oct. 6/6 One or two of the best hounds showed a disposition to heel—i.e.—go back on the line if they chanced to lose it.

heel (hīl), *v.*³ [A corruption of earlier HELE, HEAL *v.*²] With *in* = HELE *v.*² 2 (*a*). Hence **hee·ling-i·n** *vbl. sb.*

1857 *Rep. Comm. Patents 1856* (U.S.): *Agric.* 93 In nurseries, fruit-trees are often taken up and 'heeled in'. **1882** [see HELE *v.*² 2 (*a*)]. **1928** *Forestry* II. 54 A group of thirty young elms which had been 'heeled-in' temporarily in the nursery. **1953** H. L. EDLIN *Forester's Handbk.* iv. 59 The bundles [of plants] are then *heeled in* —that is, set in a trench to keep their roots moist—until needed. **1957** *N.Z. Timber Jrnl.* Aug. 59/1 *Heeling in*, placing plants temporarily in a shallow trench, the roots covered with soil to prevent loss of moisture before planting.

heelaman, -oman, varr. HIELAMAN.

1848 H. W. HAYGARTH *Recoll. Bush Life Austral.* x. 113 The heeloman is a sort of shield, made of the toughest wood procurable, about three feet in length, and six inches in breadth at the centre, whence it gradually tapers off to a point at either extremity.

heeled, *ppl. a.* **2.** For *U.S. slang* read *slang* (orig. *U.S.*). (Add earlier and later examples.)

1866 'MARK TWAIN' *Lett. fr. Hawaii* (1967) 86 In Virginia City, in former times, the insulted party..would lay his hand gently on his six-shooter and say, 'Are you heeled?' **1873** J. H. BEADLE *Undevel. West* 351 To travel long out West a man must be, in the local phrase, 'well heeled'. **1915** A. CONAN DOYLE *Valley of Fear* II. i. 153 'Halloa, mate!' said he. 'You seem heeled and ready.' **1928** 'I. HAY' *Poor Gentleman* xvii. 284 A scattered shot or two rang out—doubtless some of the defenders were 'heeled'. **1956** 'E. MCBAIN' *Cop Hater* (1958) v. 47 'Were you heeled when they pulled you in?'..'We didn't even have a water pistol between us.'

b. Provided with money. Usu. preceded by *well. slang* (orig. *U.S.*).

1880 *Pacific Metropolis* (San Francisco) 12 June 8/4 His friends want him to go 'heeled' and so they've got up the biggest sort of a bill for..next Wednesday night. **1897** E. W. BRODHEAD *Bound in Shallows* 153, I ain't so well-heeled right now. **1936** J. CURTIS *Gilt Kid* v. 51 He had done a gaff and was well heeled with dough. **1965** G. MCINNES *Road to Gundagai* x. 176 Dr. Crapp was a prominent dentist...He was therefore obviously well heeled. **1968** *Daily Tel.* (Colour Suppl.) 19/1 Though the million and a quarter left by his grandfather has been spread among a large family he is still well-heeled enough.

4. *heeled bet*: in card games (see quot.).

1923 L. H. DAWSON *Hoyle's Games Modernized* 274 A 'heeled Bet' is said to be one in which the counters of the stake are placed diagonally across from one card to another signifying that the punter is playing both cards to win.

heeler. Add: **3. b.** (See quots.)

1929 F. BOWEN *Sea Slang* 66 *Heeler*, a fast sailing ship. **1961** F. H. BURGESS *Dict. Sailing* 114 *Heeler*, a light fast sailing boat with a good performance; it is said to possess a good, or clean, pair of heels.

4. b. A working dog that urges animals, esp. cattle, onwards by nipping at their heels. Also (quot. 1888), a nip on the heels. Also *blue heeler* (*BLUE *a.* 12 a). *Austral.*

1888 'R. BOLDREWOOD' *Robbery under Arms* xii, He fetches him [*sc.* the horse] such a 'heeler' as gave him something else to think of for a few miles. **1928** 'BRENT OF BIN BIN' *Up Country* 11 Bert's heelers and kangaroo dogs chased the packhorses ahead. **1940** F. D. DAVISON *Woman at Mill* III. 214 As thick as the hair on a heeler's back. **1945** [see *Australian cattle-dog* s.v. *AUSTRALIAN B *adj.* b]. **1959** A. UPFIELD *Bony & Black Virgin* vii. 58 Bluey, the heeler dog, laid himself in the trough. **1966** 'J. HACKSTON' *Father clears Out* 116 Patting the Queensland heeler..that was..to be rechristened later on, 'lousy mongrel'. **1968** K. WEATHERLY *Roo Shooter* 139 He [*sc.* a dog] was a heeler, and it was his nature to attack from the rear.

5. (Later examples.)

1901 *Daily Chron.* 6 Nov. 6/2 The assurance of the Tammany 'Heelers' was less blatant than usual. **1933** H. G. WELLS *Shape of Things to Come* III. 311 The specialist demagogue, sustained by his gang and his heelers, his spies and secret police.

6. One who heels (cf. HEEL *v.*¹ 5 b).

1898 MACLAGAN & JEFFERY in W. A. Morgan *'House' on Sport* 157 An English [Rugby football] team is an amalgam of heelers, wheelers, pushers (scarce), and sprinters.

heeler². *colloq.* [f. HEEL *v.*² + -ER¹.] A lurch to one side; also, a boat inclined to lurch.

1894 *Times* 6 Aug. 5/2 The wind came off in hard puffs. Each took a regular heeler as they crossed the mouth of the Medina. **1926** R. CLEMENTS *Stately Southerner* 106 The ship herself was a heeler.

heeling, *vbl. sb.*¹ Add: **1.** (Further example.)

1963 *Times* 14 Feb. 3/4 They were helped, it is true, by the quicker heeling, although perhaps hindered by their stand-off half's unwillingness to part with the ball until too late.

3. *heeling dog*, a heeler (*HEELER 4 b).

1947 P. NEWTON *Wayleggo* 101 Jim had the severest heeling dog I have seen.

heel-piece. Add: **1. d.** *Shipbuilding.* An angle-bar joining the heels of a frame across the keel. **e.** *Electr.* The iron bar connecting the soft iron cores in an electro-magnet.

1904 A. C. HOLMS *Pract. Shipbuilding* I. 471 The frame heel pieces are usually fitted when the frames are screwed up ready for riveting. **1904** M. M. KIRKMAN *Telegr. & Telephone* 29 The magnet is constructed of a bar or heel piece of soft iron, into which are screwed two pencil-shaped pieces of iron which form the cores of the magnets.

heel-plate. Add: **2.** (Examples.)

1895 *Montgomery Ward Catal.* 526/1 Star heel plates, for preventing boots and shoes from wearing off at the heels. **1905** *Daily Chron.* 27 Dec. 4/7 The accident was through A wicked heel-plate on my shoe. **1959** *Sears, Roebuck Catal.* Spring & Summer 565/1 Home shoe repair outfit, includes ..6 pairs of heel plates.

3. A plate to support the heel of the boot in a metal skate; also, 'a slotted plate fixed on a boot-heel, to which a skate may be locked' (*Funk's Standard Dict.* 1893).

1890 D. ADAMS *Skating* 5 A metal sole and heel-plate screwed on to the boot with ordinary screws, is unquestionably the best and firmest. **1895** G. A. MEAGHER *Figure & Fancy Skating* 19 A perfect skate should be all of one piece. This is effected by welding the toe and heel plates on to the blade itself.

heel-tap, *sb.* Add: **1.** (Later example.)

1954 J. STEINBECK *Sweet Thursday* 136 Run up the street to Wildock's and get new heel-taps on these [shoes].

2. (Later example.)

1933 C. ST. J. SPRIGG *Fatality in Fleet St.* v. 55 Wait, I have still a heel-tap. I must drink a toast.

heel-tap, *v.* Add: (Later example); also (*b*) to delay. So **heel-tapping** *vbl. sb.*

1909 *Westm. Gaz.* 15 May 2/3 He riveted china, and clumped or heel-tapped boots. **1958** M. MCMINNIES *Visitors* 491 Twenty-four hours to git—and no heel-tapping. **1968** *Daily Colonist* (Victoria, B.C.) 19 Dec. 4/8 To put it bluntly the government is heel-tapping and will continue to do so until and unless all those affected make themselves heard.

Heemrad (hī·mrat, hēⁱ·mrād). *Hist.* Also **-raad, -raat.** Pl. **-ra(a)den.** [Du., f. *heem* village, home + *raad* council.] A local petty court or council assisting the landdrost in South Africa and also formerly in Holland; also, a member of this council.

1801 J. BARROW *Trav. S. Afr.* i. 12 A civil magistrate called a *Landrost*, who, with his *Hemraaden*, or a council of country burghers, is vested with powers to regulate the police of his district, [etc.]. **1823** W. W. BIRD *State of Cape of Good Hope in 1822* ii. 23 An Englishman has been rarely called to the office of heemrad. **1876** *Encycl. Brit.* V. 47/2 Prior to 1827 there existed in the several districts of the colony an institution established by the Dutch called the Board of Landrost and Heemraaden. **1888** THEAL in J. P. Fitzpatrick *Transvaal* (1899) 10 The abolition in 1827 of the courts of landdrost and heemraden. **1900** *Westm. Gaz.* 19 Dec. 3/2 Lord Caledon, after our second annexation of the Cape, revived an old kind of elected Councils, named Heemraden, for the government of the inland districts. **1970** *S. Afr. Panorama* Feb. 45/2 In 1682 local administration was set up in the form of four Heemraden.

heffalump (he·fălʊmp). A child's word for 'elephant'.

Now commonly in adult use.

1926 A. A. MILNE *Winnie-the-Pooh* v. 66 He would go up very quietly to the Six Pine Trees now, peep very cautiously into the Trap, and see if there *was* a Heffalump there. **1928** —— *House at Pooh Corner* iii. 43 He guessed what had happened. He and Piglet had fallen into a Heffalump Trap. **1958** *Spectator* 22 Aug. 241/1 The Conservatives are not going to leap into the heffalump-trap in which their opponents..reside. **1959** *Manch. Guardian* 14 July 6/3 Hannibal's heffalumps can hardly have had any such protection against the weather.

Hefner (he·fnəɹ). *Physics.* The shortened name of F. F. von *Hefner*-Alteneck (1845–1904), German electrical engineer, used *attrib.* to designate esp. a lamp devised by him and formerly used as a photometric standard and the intensity of light obtained from it, as **Hefner candle** (see quot. 1943); **Hefner (amyl** or **amyl-acetate) lamp,** a lamp of standard

dimensions and with standard parts burning amyl acetate. Also *Hefner flame*, *kerze* (G., = candle), *standard*, *unit*. Also occas. in full *Hefner-Alteneck lamp* etc.

1891 *Jrnl. Soc. Chem. Industry* X. 685/2 A discussion on the subject of amyl acetate, the fuel of the Hefner lamp, has recently taken place. **1896** *Electrician* 2 Oct. 738/2 The standard of light will be either the Vernon-Harcourt or the Hefner-Amyl-Acetate. **1898** *Electr. Rev.* XLII. 795/1 As a result of the investigations of the German Reichsanstalt, the Hefner lamp alone fulfils all technical requirements. The light of the Hefner lamp is designated a Hefner candle. *Ibid.*, The Hefner candle was accepted as the international unit of light by the Electrical Congress at Geneva in 1896. **1901** *Phil. Trans. R. Soc.* A. CXCVI. 26 Knowing the value of the energy of the visible light of the Hefner standard, the heating effect of the rays can be deduced. *Ibid.* 37 The chief source of difficulty in the comparison is the difference in colour between the light from the Hefner lamp and a fluorescent screen. **1902** *Encycl. Brit.* XXX. 235/2 For accurate scientific purposes the best standard is the Hefner-Alteneck or amyl-acetate lamp. **1911** *Ibid.* XXI. 526/2 Various experimental investigations into the properties of the Hefner flame. **1914** S. E. Sheppard *Photo-Chem.* 23 Viollé's unit was found by Lummer to equal 26 Hefner units. *Ibid.* 24 The light-unit 1 HK (Hefner-Kerze or Hefner candle) is taken as the mean of protracted observations on a Hefner lamp at the Physik. Techn. Reichsanstalt in Charlottenburg. **1917** G. Martin *Industr. & Manuf. Chem.* II. 357 The Hefner candle power is equal to about 0·9 British standard candle. **1943** *Gloss. Terms Electr. Engin.* (*B.S.I.*) 112 *Hefner candle*, a unit of luminous intensity equal to that of the Hefner lamp burning under specified conditions of atmospheric pressure and humidity. It is the official unit of luminous intensity in Germany and is accepted internationally as equivalent to 0·9 candle. **1963** Jerrard & McNeill *Dict. Sci. Units* 30 Germany, however, continued to use the Hefner candle (Hefnerkerze HK) unit which was derived from the Hefner lamp and had a luminous intensity of about 0·9 International candles.

heft, *sb.*¹ **1.** (Further examples.)

1864 'E. Kirke' *Down in Tennessee* viii. 107 I's six foot three,..weigh a hun'red an' eighty, kin whip twice my heft in Secesh, bars, or rattlesnakes. **1966** H. Roth *Button, Button* (1967) iv. 84 He was more on the lean side than supplied with heft. **1972** *Sci. Amer.* Dec. p. ii/2 Go ahead, pick it up. The heft tells you it's solid sterling silver.

‖ **heft** (heft), *sb.*² Pl. **hefte.** [G.] A number of sheets of paper fastened together to form a book; *spec.* a division of a serial work; a part of a serial publication, a fascicle.

1886 *Athenæum* 9 Oct. 464/1 This treatise forms the fifth *Heft* of the second volume. **1892** *Rev. Reviews* Jan. 58/1 There is another interesting article..in Heft 14 of the *Gartenlaube*.

heft, *sb.*³ *local.* [Var. of Haft *sb.*² 2.] (The sheep in) a settled or accustomed pasture-ground.

1960 Williamson & Boyd *St. Kilda Summer* 84 The Hirta flock is divided into hefts, more or less discrete groups each restricted to its own particular range. **1961** *New Scientist* 9 Nov. 341/2 The natural unit in hill sheep farming is the heft—the group of sheep that habitually graze within the confines of a particular area of hill ground. **1971** *Country Life* 28 Oct. 1166/1 Anticipated difficulties from depriving the hefted sheep of their age-old hefts or heafs have not occurred.

heft, *v.*¹ Add: **1.** (Later examples.) Also *absol.*

1913 R. W. Service *Rhymes of Rolling Stone* 40 And here they must make the long *portage*, and the boys sweat in the sun; And they heft and pack, and they haul and track, and each must do his trick. **1932** W. Faulkner *Light in August* xiv. 308 He was hefting the bench leg. **1960** J. Maclaren-Ross *Until Day she Dies* ii. 36 'Can't see anybody,' I said, hefting the case.

3. (Further example.)

1893 C. M. Yonge *Treasures in Marshes* ii. 11, I do believe it is [gold]. Brass never would heft so much.

hefty, *a.* Add: **1.** Now in general colloq. use; also, large or significant in size. Also *advb.*, 'powerfully', exceedingly.

1871 *N.Y. Tribune* 21 Jan., He is, as a Yankee would say, a little hefty for the ideal lover. **1890** P. H. Emerson *Diary* 25 Nov. in *On Eng. Lagoons* (1892) xxii. 100 Rum night this, hefty weather, don't it blow and snow. **1898** Kipling *Land & Sea T.* (1923) 135 What are we going to do? It's hefty damp here. **1905** *Daily Chron.* 18 Sept. 8/2 When an American girl does that, you can guess there's something 'mighty hefty' weighing her down. **1908** *Daily Chron.* 1 July 3/3 Mr. Barnes of New York was hefty with the trigger. **1925** E. F. Norton *Fight for Everest, 1924* 39 The bucolic bumpkin with coarse features and slow brain fails no less than the 'hefty' giant. **1930** J. B. Priestley *Angel Pavement* ii. 85 It's a hefty commission all right. **1930** *Diary of Public School Girl* 32 Played in a game with Highlands. Got some good hefty bangs. **1958** *Oxf. Mag.* 22 May 461/1 Slighter than Hitchcock but heftier than Chaplin. **1959** *Manch. Guardian* 29 Jan. 5/5 You may protect yourself in respect of the very hefty bill for any medical treatment if someone falls ill..while you are abroad. **1972** *Sunday Times* 30 Jan. 63/5 On top of the hefty basic wage is a bonus system from the pool of tips. **1972** *Sunday Tel.* 6 Feb. 14/6 This hefty book, written in brisk journalese, brings Capone to life.

Hegelian. B. *sb.* (Earlier and later examples.)

1843 Mill *Logic* V. iii. 364 Whether in the Vedas, in the Platonists, or in the Hegelians, mysticism is neither more nor less than ascribing objective existence to the subjective creations of the mind's own faculties. **1891** [see Thing *sb.*¹ 14 e].

Hegelianism. Add: (Earlier example.)

1846 J. D. Morell *Hist. View Philos.* II. ii. v. 160 It is in the department of theology chiefly, that the great battle of Hegelianism has been, and is still being fought.

Hegelese (earlier example); **Hegelism** (further example). Also **Hege·lianizing** *ppl. a.* and *vbl. sb.*, rendering Hegelian; **He·gelizer** = Hegelian *sb.*

1879 W. James *Let.* 3 Sept. in R. B. Perry *Tht. & Char. of W. J.* (1935) II. 15 Poor Palmer has gone abroad to steep himself I suppose still more deeply in that priggish English Hegelism. **1886** *Mind* XI. 258 The chief point about the law of development is its containing what in Hegelese might be called *Aufgehobensein*. **1890** W. James *Princ. Psychol.* I. vi. 163 The Hegelizers amongst them will take high ground at once, and say that the glory and beauty of the psychic life is that in it all contradictions find their reconciliation. *Ibid.* xii. 464 A conception, according to the Hegelizers in philosophy, 'develops its own significance'. **1910** *Mind* XIX. 123 The Hegelianising of poetry. **1945** K. R. Popper *Open Society* II. xxii. 196 These Hegelianizing theories. **1970** A. MacIntyre *Marcuse* ii. 35 The counterpart to Marcuse's Hegelianizing of Marx is a total neglect of Engels.

hegemon (hī·dʒĭmǫn, he·-). [a. Gr. ἡγέμων leader.] A leading or paramount power.

1904 *Forum* Jan.–Mar. 347 (Cent. Dict. Suppl.), The *hegemon* of the western hemisphere is the United States. **1920** *Public Opinion* 2 July 6/1 Japan..asserting her ambition to become hegemon of a far East on which white influence shall be reduced to a vanishing point. **1936** W. J. Entwistle *Spanish Lang.* v. 135 He was king of León as others were sovereigns elsewhere in the Peninsula, but he alone was hegemon and the successor of those who had ruled all Spain from Toledo.

hegemonist (hĭdʒe·mǒnist). [f. Hegemon(y + -ist.] An advocate of hegemony. Also **hege·monizer.**

1898 *Pall Mall Gaz.* 12 Feb. 4/1 This Prince Kraft was also, it would seem, the earliest Prussian hegemonist, who has so far, and as such, revealed himself to us. **1921** *Pilgrim* Apr. 273 It does not..follow that the resistance of England to the previous hegemonisers would be condemned.

Hehner (hēi·nəɹ). The name of the chemist Otto *Hehner* used attrib. in *Hehner number*, *value* (see quots.).

1909 Webster *Hehner value*, a number expressing the percentage of insoluble fatty acids in an oil or fat. **1913** G. Martin *Industr. & Manuf. Chem.* I. iv. 64 Hehner Value.—This test devised by Hehner indicates the percentage of insoluble fatty acids which can be separated from oil or fat... Thus butter usually has a Hehner value ranging from 85–88. **1915** *Chem. Abstr.* IX. 531 (*heading*) A new modification for making the Hehner number determination. **1918** T. H. Pope tr. *Villavecchia's App. Anal. Chem.* I. 382 Insoluble, Fixed Fatty Acid Number. (Hehner Number.)

Heian (hēi·ăn), *a.* [Jap.] Of or pertaining to a period in Japanese history from the late 8th to the late 12th century A.D.

1893 F. Brinkley tr. *Hist. Empire Japan* iii. 104 The people called the new capital 'Heian-kyo'... The interval ..from 794 to 1186 A.D.—is known in history as the 'Heian Epoch'. **1909** *Westm. Gaz.* 30 Dec. 9/1 It has been decided to arrange the pictures in strict historical sequence, commencing with examples of the Heian period. **1911** *Encycl. Brit.* XV. 259/1 All the pastimes of the Nara epoch were pursued with increased fervour and elaboration in the Heian (Kiōto) era. **1959** *Chambers's Encycl.* VIII. 41/2 (*title*) The Heian Period. *Ibid.*, A new capital was built on the site of the present city of Kyoto. It was given the auspicious name of Heian-kyō (the 'city of peace and tranquillity'). **1960** *Times* 1 Mar. 9/7 Professor Sakamoto..in Heian court robes. **1967** *Listener* 14 Dec. 791/2 In Japan quite a lot of Heian literature has been preserved. **1970** *Oxf. Compan. Art* 609 During the later Heian or Fujiwara period an easier, milder Buddhist sect prevailed. **1973** *Times Lit. Suppl.* 2 Mar. 237/2 The Heian period, perhaps the apogee of Japanese culture, was essentially peaceful.

heiau (hēi·ɑu). [Hawaiian.] A temple.

1825 W. Ellis *Jrnl. Tour Hawaii* 51 Tamehameha.. finished the heiau, dedicated it to his god of war. **1920** *Nature* 15 July 628/1 There are shorter notes on heathen prayers and the ceremonial erection of the *heiau* or god's house. **1954** J. Sheridan in J. Macdonald *Lethal Sex* (1962) 160 Sacred regions where ancient *heiaus* still stand.

Heidelberg (həi·dəlbəɹg, ‖ hai·delbēɹχ). The name of a German city used *attrib.* to denote a jaw found at Mauer near Heidelberg in 1907, or the type of prehistoric man (*Homo heidelbergensis*) indicated by this jaw.

1911 A. Keith in *Nature* 25 May 414/1 The Heidelberg mandible was found in 1907 embedded in the Mauer sand beds. **1912** W. L. H. Duckworth *Prehistoric Man* 10 The Heidelberg or Mauer jaw. **1927** R. S. Lull *Org. Evol.* xxxviii. 677 The Heidelberg man represents the oldest recorded European race, geologically speaking. **1964** K. P. Oakley *Frameworks for Dating Fossil Man* 108 He considered that the horizon of the Heidelberg jaw was at the base of the 30-m terrace which he equated with the Mindel-Riss Interglacial.

Heidsieck (həi·dsīk). [Name of the original producer and exporter.] The proprietary name of a brand of champagne.

1853 E. K. Kane *U.S. Grinnell Exped.* ix. 64 We tapped a bottle of Heidsiek.., and all hands spliced the main-brace. **1877** *Trade Marks Jrnl.* 29 Jan. 249/1 Charles Heidsieck. Charles Heidsieck, Reims (Marne), France; champagne merchant... Wine. **1890** Kipling *Life's Handicap* (1891) 163 The King's Peg..liqueur brandy for whisky, and Heidsieck for soda-water. **1904** A. Bennett *Great Man* xxv. 284 He was intoxicated..though not with the Heidsieck. **1920** G. Saintsbury *Notes on Cellar-Bk.* v. 70 The earliest pages of my book show Pommery itself and Heidsieck Monopole. **1956** A. L. Simon *Know your Wines* 82 Heidsieck & Co. are a firm of producers and shippers of Reims. It started as a man's name. **1959** *Trade Marks Jrnl.* 26 Aug. 731/1 Heidsieck... Champagne wines. Kunkelmann et Compagnie.., Reims, France; wine shippers. **1965** O. A. Mendelsohn *Dict. Drink* 163 *Heidsieck*, old-established champagne of Reims, not to be confused with Piper-Heidsieck.

heifer. Add: **1. d.** A woman, a girl. *depreciatory slang.*

1835 A. B. Longstreet *Georgia Scenes* 143 He rushed into the Kitchen in a fury. 'You infernal heifer!' said he to Aunt Clory. **1853** T. C. Haliburton *Sam Slick's Wise Saws* II. xii. 282, I have half a mind to marry that heifer, tho' wives are bothersome critters when you have too many of them. **1940** M. Marples *Pub. Sch. Slang* 115 Charwomen were satirically known as heifers at Charterhouse. **1964** O. E. Middleton in C. K. Stead *N.Z. Short Stories* (1966) 201 Was that heifer of Blackie's the same one he had a fortnight ago? **1973** *Black World* Jan. 62/2 That heifer that been trying to get next to my man Lucky since the year one.

2. heifer dust *slang*, (*a*) nonsense (see also quot. 1927²); (*b*) (see quot. 1945); **heifer-paddock** *Austral. slang*, a girls' school.

1927 'J. Barbican' *Confess. Rum-Runner* xxiii. 256 Even if they do get pinched, they always have some heifer dust ready about laying a trap for a ship. **1927** *Dialect Notes* V. 449 *Heifer dust act, the*, an arrest and cross-questioning by the police. **1941** Baker *Dict. Austral. Slang* 35 *Heifer dust*, nonsense. **1945** —— *Austral. Lang.* vi. 123 Other Australianisms for girls or young women include:..a bit of heifer dust. **1885** Mrs. C. Praed *Sketches Austral. Life* ii. 50 Next year I shall look over a heifer-paddock in Sydney, and take my pick.

height, *sb.* Add: **1. c.** Of type: the distance from the foot to the face, called by printers *height to paper*.

1683–4 J. Moxon *Mech. Exerc. Printing* (1962) 157 If he finds that the edge of the Liner just touch..as well all the parts of his Proof-Letters as they do upon his old Letters, He concludes his Matrice is Sunk to a true Height against Paper. **1771** P. Luckombe *Hist. Printing* 243 They [*sc.* imperfections] are seldom exact to the prior sorts, but differ from them, sometimes in thickness, height to paper, or depth of Body. **1888** *Encycl. Brit.* XXIII. 698/2 The height of type varies slightly with different founders, the mean being $\frac{29}{32}$ in. **1890** A. Oldfield *Pract. Man. Typogr.* xxii. 164 Each letter should be of exactly the same height to paper; the height of type being 11-12ths of an inch. **1900** H. Hart *Cent. Typogr.* 23 Five packets of types of the same face, but cast on a Pica body and Dutch 'height-to-paper', were found at the Oxford Press in 1898.

12. (Later example.)

1923 T. E. Lawrence *Lett.* (1938) 407 Knewstub.. thinks it's the height of John.

14. *height of land*, a watershed or ridge of high land dividing two river basins. *N. Amer.*

1725 in G. Sheldon *Hist. Deerfield* (1895) I. 559 They told us they wd travel to the hight of land by black river. **1805–9** J. J. Henry *Camp. agst. Quebec* (1812) 36 On this lake, we obtained a full view of those hills which were then, and are now, called the 'Heighth of land'. **1860** H. Y. Hind *Narr. Canad. Red River Exped.* II. 225 The Vermilion Pass, which was traversed by Dr. Hector presents on the whole the greatest natural facilities for crossing the mountains without the aid of engineering work, as the rise to the height of land is gradual from both sides. **1875** *Encycl. Brit.* II. 201/1 In the north it [*sc.* the watershed] is found in a stretch of country, called the Height of Land, that lies between the White and the Green Mountains, and gives birth to the Connecticut and a number of smaller streams. **1902** *Ibid.* XXXI. 330/2 Beyond the Height-of-Land the Winnipeg and English rivers flow westward to Lake Winnipeg. **1918** H. Bindloss *Agatha's Fortune* xxv, It was hardly a range of hills, but rather what prospectors call a 'heighth' of land. **1930** G. L. Wood *Pacific Basin* 5 Behind the peninsula of California the height of land is a thousand miles from the sea.

19. For †*Obs.* read *Obs.* exc. in literary use.

1820 Lamb *Elia* (1823) 8 While he held you in converse, you felt strained to the height in the colloquy. **1871** Tennyson *Last Tournament* 658 For once—ev'n to the height—I honour'd him.

heik, var. *Hike *v.* and *sb.*

‖ **heil** (həil), *int.* [G., = hail!] Used in the expression *Heil Hitler!* by the Germans during the Nazi regime. Also *transf.*, and as *sb.* So heil *v.*, to give the Nazi salute; **heiled** *ppl. a.* *Ski-heil!*: good skiing!

1927 E. Hemingway *Men without Women* (1928) 182 'Ski-heil!' said the innkeeper. 'Heil!' we said. **1937** *Nation* 31 July 114/2 The weekly scene of heiling. **1937** A. S. Neill *That Dreadful School* i. 20 In the absence of a government I herewith declare myself Dictator. Heil Neill! **1938** [see *Click *v.*¹ 2 a]. **1939** *Journal* (Topeka, Kans.) 20 Apr. 1/7 Germany heils Hitler on fiftieth birthday. **1939** S. Spender tr. *Toller's Pastor Hall* i. 48 Extending your arm like a crane and yelling, 'Heil Hitler.' **1940** *Time* 15 Apr. 43/1 One of the most widely heiled of German sculptors. **1942** E. Waugh *Put out More Flags* iii. § 5. 234 An obnoxious young man..said 'Heil Mosley.'

1961 J. HELLER *Catch-22* (1962) xxiii. 241 When the Germans marched into the city, I danced in the streets..and shouted, '*Heil* Hitler!' until my lungs were hoarse. **1965** EVA-LIS WUORIO *Z for Zaborra* VI. v. 175 The man..gave ..a sharp salute. 'Leader and blood brother,' he heiled.

‖ **Heilsgeschichte** (həi·lzgĕʃi·χʏtə). *Theol.* [G.] Sacred history, *spec.* the history of God's saving work among men; history seen as the working out of God's salvation. So **hei·lsgeschichtlich** *a.*

1938 C. H. DODD *History & Gospel* v. 168 The whole of history is in the last resort sacred history, or *Heilsgeschichte*. **1952** G. E. WRIGHT *God who Acts* v. 115 Biblical faith may be treated in such a way as to preserve its history-centred (or as the Germans call it, *heilsgeschichtlich*) nature. **1957** D. M. BAILLIE *Theol. Sacraments* ii. 69 It is bound up with the rediscovery that the Christian message is a *Heilsgeschichte*, a sacred story, running on from eternity through history to eternity again, with Christ as its central and determinative point. **1959** GUTHRIE & HALL tr. *Cullmann's Christology N.T.* i. 9 There can be no *Heilsgeschichte* without Christology; no Christology without a *Heilsgeschichte* which unfolds in time.

heimin (hē̆i·min). [Jap., f. *hei* level (horizontal), common + *min* people.] In Japanese society of the feudal period, the common people, including the peasantry, craftsmen, and traders, as contrasted with the court aristocracy and samurai (the warrior class).

1875 *Trans. Asiatic Soc. Japan* (1884) III. II. 104. **1891** A. M. BACON *Jap. Girls & Women* ix. 228 The great héimin class includes not only the peasants of Japan, but also the artisans and merchants. **1904** *Daily Chron.* 30 Mar. 4/5 Of those not Samurai, the heimin, or commoners, the peasantry ranked first. **1904** L. HEARN *Japan: Attempt at Interpretation* xii. 271 The Buddhist (like the Shintō) priests, though forming a class apart, ranked with the samurai, not with the heimin. **1951** D. H. JAMES *Rise & Fall Jap. Empire* iii. 119 The profession of arms, previously the privilege of Samurai, was extended to heimin (commoners).

‖ **heimisch** (həi·miʃ), *a.* orig. *U.S.* Also **haimish, heimische, heimishe, heymish.** [a. G. *heimisch* domestic, homelike.] Homely; unpretentious. Hence **hei·mischness**, homeliness.

1964 S. BELLOW *Herzog* (1965) 35 A politician..still found me good company, *heimisch*, and took me along to the races. **1968** L. ROSTEN *Joys of Yiddish* 148 *Haimish, haimisher,..haimisheh,..*informal, cozy,..having the friendly characteristics..that exist inside a happy home, ..unpretentious; putting on no airs... Jews put a high value on being *haimish*. **1970** L. M. FEINSILVER *Taste of Yiddish* II. 111 *Heymish*, homey, friendly, informal. *Ibid.* 279 This conveys the sense of good talk in congenial company—the 'Heymishness' of herd warmth. **1970** 'E. QUEEN' *Last Woman* I. 8, I own..a guest cottage... It's all terribly *heimisch*. **1973** *Times* 3 Feb. 13/4 Another word that may confuse is *heimishe*, which is Yiddish, and means roughly..'home cooking' or 'traditional' cooking. *Ibid.*, The heimishe cooking at Leslie's is only part of a large suburbanized menu.

‖ **Heimweh** (həi·mvē̆i). [G.] Home-sickness.

a **1721** PRIOR *Essay upon Opinion* in *Dialogues of Dead* (1907) 199 The Swiss are remarked to have a Distemper, which they call the Hemvie, a desire of going home, and where ever They are in Service they get leave to return to their Canton at least once in Some Years, and certainly desire to Dye there. **1756, 18..** [see HOME-SICKNESS]. **1845** R. FORD *Handbk. Trav. Spain* II. 695 If debarred a hope of return, they [*sc.* the Asturians] pine from Nostalgia or Heimweh. **1850** GEO. ELIOT *Let.* 9 Feb. (1954) I. 328, I have a little *Heimweh* 'as it regards' my friends. **1912** R. BROOKE *Let.* 24 June (1968) 389 Writing about Grantchester gave me a bit of *Heimweh*. **1920** D. H. LAWRENCE *Let.* in C. Mackenzie *My Life & Times* (1966) V. 170 Heimweh or nostalgia there, for the North. **1971** *Guardian* 25 Nov. 13/4 The *Heimweh* of absences.

‖ **Heimwehr** (həi·mvēəɹ). [G., f. *heim* home + *wehr* defence.] Formerly, the German or the Austrian Home Defence Force. Also *attrib.*

1931 *Ann. Reg. 1930* 184 The usual collisions between Heimwehr and Socialists recommenced, in consequence of the revival of the Heimwehr policy of holding provocative marches. **1938** *Times Lit. Suppl.* 15 Jan. 34/4 A *Heimwehr* officer in the late twenties. **1939** *War Illustr.* 2 Dec. 384/2 Prince von Starhemberg, formerly leader of the Austrian Heimwehr, has been deprived of German citizenship. **1957** *Times Lit. Suppl.* 20 Dec. 771/4 He was later in charge of several *Heimwehr* newspapers—the organs of Austrian Fascism.

Heinesque (həine·sk), *a.* [f. the name of H. *Heine* (1799–1856), German poet + -ESQUE.] Of, pertaining to, or resembling the style of Heine.

?**1892** E. DOWSON *Let.* ?Jan. (1967) 222 Where would appreciation of the Heinesque style come in? **1899** *Academy* 24 June 677/1 A grimly tragic vignette of peasant life, with a Heinesque turn at the close. **1907** *Daily Chron.* 2 Aug. 3/3 His Heinesque moods are steeled through with a strong man's virility. **1915–16** *Musical Assoc. Proc.* 158 Beethoven is never sinister, never even Heinesque, if I may use the word.

Heinie (həi·ni). *N. Amer. slang.* Also **Heine, Hiney.** [f. the German Christian name *Heinrich.*] A German (soldier).

1904 'No. 1500' *Life in Sing Sing* xiii. 249/1 *Hiney*, a German. **1917** *Daily Chron.* 25 Aug. 1/7 The Canadians call their enemy Heine and not Fritz. **1918** *Daily Mirror* 12 Nov. 6/4 An Irish terrier of my acquaintance was perfectly certain that the maroons meant a visit from Heinie. **1925** FRASER & GIBBONS *Soldier & Sailor Words, Heine* (or *Hiney*). **1929** E. W. SPRINGS *Above Bright Blue Sky* 227 'There, you're all right,' the sergeant soothed him. 'Those yellow-bellied Heinies can't kill you. We got ten of 'em this morning.' **1931** [see *DUTCHMAN 1 a]. **1961** *Listener* 20 Apr. 684/1 It's not the Russians we should be congratulating..but the Heinies. Sure, we got Von Braun, but the Russians grabbed all the rest of the German rocket guys.

heintzite (həi·ntsəit). *Min.* [ad. G. *heintzit* (O. Luedecke 1890, in *Zeitschr. f. Kryst. und Min.* XVIII. 485), f. the name of W. H. *Heintz* (1817–80), German chemist: see -ITE[1].] A borate of potassium and magnesium, at first also called *HINTZEITE and now regarded as the same as kaliborite.

1891 *Jrnl. Chem. Soc.* LX. I. 528 For the new borate, Milch proposes the name of *hintzeite*, after Professor Hintze, of Breslau; whilst Luedecke proposes that of *heintzite*, after Heintz, the discoverer of pinnoite. **1892** *Ibid.* LXII. II. 791 The author [*sc.* O. Luedecke]..admits that the chemical composition of kaliborite and heintzite is practically identical, both containing about the same percentage of boric acid, potash, magnesia, and water. This does not, however, prove them to be the same mineral. Whilst kaliborite occurs in badly-formed, crystalline crusts on the surface of pinnoïte, heintzite, which is found on the inside, forms well-made crystals with shining faces, and is readily cleavable in three directions. **1951** C. PALACHE et al. *Dana's Syst. Min.* (ed. 7) II. 368 Heintzite (and hintzeite, the two names being proposed simultaneously for the mineral) was later shown to be identical with kaliborite.

heir, *sb.* Add: **1. b.** *heir-designate*, one who has been designated as a person's heir.

1909 *Daily Chron.* 6 Sept. 3/3 Her relatives, heirs-designate of Charles Dorrien in the scrap of paper lying in his widow's writing-desk. **1961** B. FERGUSSON *Watery Maze* xii. 311 The meeting in Carthage on Christmas Day, with Churchill presiding, and Eisenhower and Wilson as his heir-designate.

heir, *v.* Add: **b.** *intr.* To inherit. *rare.*

1900 J. HASTINGS *Dict. of Bible* III. 270 The younger brother, instead of himself heiring, raises up heirs to the deceased.

Heisenberg (həi·zənbəɹg). The name of Werner *Heisenberg* (b. 1901), German physicist, used esp. with reference to his matrix theory of quantum mechanics, and to the 'uncertainty principle' deduced by him in 1927.

1932 W. T. STACE *Theory of Knowl. & Existence* xiv. 381 Heisenberg's Principle of Indeterminacy..lays it down that an electron may have a determinate position or a determinate velocity, *but not both*. **1951** *Physical Rev.* LXXXII. 922/1 Note that these Schrödinger equations have been obtained from the Heisenberg picture. **1955** W. PAULI *Niels Bohr* 38 We..restrict ourselves to the discussion of the field operators (Heisenberg-representation). **1965** PHILLIPS & WILLIAMS *Inorg. Chem.* I. i. 3 As this [*sc.* wave mechanics] provides a relatively simple method of representing atoms and molecules in pictorial terms, we use it in preference to such alternatives as Heisenberg's matrix mechanics which can be shown to be equivalent. **1968** *Peace News* 18 Oct. 6/3 A kind of Heisenberg effect which is far more serious than anything in the physical or biological sciences: the very act of observation distorts that which is being observed. **1968** J. J. C. SMART *Betw. Sci. & Philos.* 12 Some scientific results (Heisenberg's uncertainty principle, for example) do *not* bear on the problem of free will.

heist (həist). *slang* (orig. *U.S.*). [Repr. U.S. local pronunc. of HOIST *v.* and *sb.*] A hold-up, a robbery; also *attrib.* and *Comb.* Also as *vb.*, to hold up, rob, steal. So **hei·ster**, a robber, a hijacker; a shoplifter. Cf. *HIST *v.* 2, *HOIST *v.* 6 and *sb.* 5.

1927 *Dialect Notes* V. 449 *Heister*, n. (1) A nickname. Suggested etymon, Ger. 'heissen'. (2) A shoplifter. **1930** E. D. SULLIVAN *Chicago Surrenders* (1931) xiv. 229 Any such giant 'heist'. **1931** [see *HOIST *v.* 6]. **1943** P. CHEYNEY *You can always Duck* xi. 170 If you think I'm gonna be heisted by a cheap thug like you, you made a mistake. **1947** S. J. PERELMAN *Westward Ha!* (1949) x. 123 His new ballpoint fountain pen..had been heisted by the attendants. **1953** 'S. RANSOME' *Drag Dark* (1954) ii. 22 Any heister..would face a bit of a problem in moving his loot. **1955** D. W. MAURER in *Publ. Amer. Dial. Soc.* XXIV. 18 Very peaceful when he ain't on the heist. *Ibid.* 92 Thus a *heist mob* is one which brooks no interference and robs the victim willy-nilly. **1965** *Punch* 11 Aug. 199/2 Six years ago Jim Tempest was one of a bunch of tearaways heisting cars round the North Circular. **1967** 'D. SHANNON' *Chance to Kill* (1968) i. 7 The pair of heist boys had been busy... Since ten days they had..hit four liquor stores, three small markets, two bars, and a drugstore, for a total take of around eighteen hundred bucks. **1968** 'E. TREVOR' *Place for Wicked* ii. 22 A heist was when you took a motor with the idea of doing a repaint and flogging it with a bent log-book you'd got from a breaker.

‖ **hei-tiki** (hē̆iti·ki). *New Zealand.* [Maori, f. *hei* to hang + *tiki* the first created being.] A greenstone neck-ornament worn by Maoris.

1835 W. YATE *Acc. N.Z.* (ed. 2) 151 The *hei-tiki* being taken off the neck, laid down..and then wept and sung over. **1843** E. DIEFFENBACH *Trav. N.Z.* II. iv. 55 Around the neck both sexes generally wear a figure cut out of jade. This they call E' Tiki: it has an enormous head, very large eyes, and monstrous and disproportionate arms and legs. **1880** *Encycl. Brit.* XIII. 540/1 The hideous breast ornament termed *hei tiki*. **1887** *Col. & Indian Exhib., Rep. Col. Sect.* 74 Heitikis or native deities. **1936** 'R. HYDE' *Check to your King* 153 Queer little amulets, some of which, the hei-tikis, were in the shape of the human embryo. **1949** P. BUCK *Coming of Maori* (1950) II. xii. 295 The term *tiki* was applied to the carved human figures set up at the gable end of important houses. When the ornaments in human form were made, they were also termed *tiki* but, to distinguish them from the larger wooden *tiki*, the nephrite ornaments were termed *hei tiki*, *hei* meaning to tie around the neck.

hejeen, var. *HYGEEN, HAJEEN.

hekistotherm (hĭki·stoþəɹm). *Bot.* [ad. F. *hékistotherme* (A. de Candolle 1874, in *Archives des Sciences physiques et naturelles* L. 14), f. Gr. ἥκιστο-ς smallest + θέρμη heat.] A plant which can grow in very cold environments, as the arctic and antarctic lichens and mosses. Hence **hekistothe·rmic** *a.*

1875 J. H. BALFOUR *Man. Bot.* (ed. 5) 817 Hekistotherms, plants requiring a very small amount of heat, as arctic or antarctic plants. **1909** GROOM & BALFOUR tr. *Warming's Oecology of Plants* 36 Hekistothermic: plants living beyond the limits of tree-growth, where the annual mean temperature sinks below 0° C. **1934** H. GILBERT-CARTER tr. *Raunkiaer's Life Forms of Plants* ii. 6 A fourth group, Hecistotherms, comprises plants belonging to the cold regions. They have the lowest heat demand of all plants, will grow where the summer is short, and are able to endure a long and very cold winter. **1965** F. J. MONKHOUSE *Dict. Geogr.* 155/2 *Hekistotherm*, a plant such as reindeer moss or lichen, which can exist where the mean temperature of the warmest month is under 50°F.

hekte (he·kti). Also **hecte.** [Gr. ἕκτη the sixth (of a stater), fem. (sc. μοῖρα part) of ἕκτος sixth.] A Greek silver coin.

1872 B. V. HEAD in *Synopsis Contents Brit. Museum* (Dept. Coins & Medals) 37 The work upon many of these staters and hektæ is exceedingly fine. **1906** G. F. HILL *Hist. Greek Coins* 17 A few specimens of an electrum *hekte*, or sixth of the stater. **1921** *Brit. Mus. Return* 79 An electrum hecte with the type of a crouching lion and a hemihecte with the type of a winged monster. **1933** C. SELTMAN *Greek Coins* vii. 113 The staters of Cyzicus, and her *hektai*, or 'sixths',..testify..to the large issues of these states.

HeLa (hī·lă). [f. the name, *He*nrietta *La*cks, of the patient from whom the original tissue was taken (cf. *Obstetr. & Gynecol.* XXXVIII (1971). 945).] Designating a strain of human epithelial cells maintained in tissue culture and derived originally from tissue from a carcinoma of the cervix. Occas. *absol.*

1953 W. F. SCHERER et al. in *Jrnl. Exper. Med.* XCVII. 695 This cellular strain, designated as strain HeLa by one of the authors (G. G[ey]) when he obtained it from an epidermoid carcinoma of the cervix has been maintained in continuous serial culture passage *in vitro* from February 8, 1951, until the present. *Ibid.* 705 Cultures of strain HeLa cells are capable of producing large quantities of poliomyelitis virus. **1959** *Laboratory Invest.* VIII. 278 Since the human cancer cell strain HeLa is in such wide use as an in vitro system for the study of cell processes, it appeared to be of value to study..aspects of DNA physiology in these cultures. *Ibid.* 283 The variability in DNA synthesis in HeLa is small in this medium. **1965** C. H. ANDREWES *Common Cold* viii. 65 A few lines of cells..have been growing happily for years and these have been sent all round the world, so that the best-known lines, such as HeLa cells from a human cancer..are used in hundreds of laboratories.

Helanca (helæ·ŋkă). [Proprietary term.] (See quot. 1964.)

1944 *Trade Marks Jrnl.* 15 Nov. 544/2 Helanca. Textile yarns. Heberlein & Co. A.G. (a Joint Stock Company organized under the laws of Switzerland), Wattwil, Canton of St. Gallen, Switzerland. **1946** J. V. & S. L. SHERMAN *New Fibers* xii. 229 An interesting new type of viscose rayon, known as 'Helanca', was used extensively in Switzerland during the war as a substitute for wool. It is a yarn mechanically and chemically treated to produce a permanent wool-like effect. *Ibid.* 230 Helanca yarns are available in a wide variety of colors. **1959** *Times* 7 Dec. 13/2 Elasticised cloth (generally wool and Helanca) gives the greatest comfort as well as best and smartest fit. **1960** *Guardian* 26 Aug. 6/5 The brown and white Helanca bikini was lovely. **1964** *Which?* Sept. 286/1 *Helanca*, wide range of bulked and stretched yarns (made from a number of man-made fibres).

held, *ppl. a.* Add: Also with adverbs.

c **1611** CHAPMAN *Iliad* xxiv. 275 With held vp hands. **1906** *Westm. Gaz.* 28 Dec. 7/2 A long string of 'held-up' cars.

‖ **Heldentenor** (he·ldĕntenōə·ɹ). [G.] A powerful tenor voice suited to the singing of heroic roles in opera; a person with such a voice.

1926 *Times* 18 May 6/3 Herr Melchior..has..the physical energy of voice and action which is the essential qualification of the *helden* tenor. **1931** *Gramophone* Suppl. Oct. 16/1 A *Heldentenor* whose career..has been almost exclusively restricted to the embodiment of Wagner's

greatest heroes. **1947** N. Cardus *Autobiogr.* III. 234 A fearsome imitation of the latest Heldentenor at Covent Garden. **1962** J. B. Priestley *Margin Released* III. iii. 175 The help he gave the *Heldentenor* Melchior. **1962** *Listener* 5 Apr. 617/1 Mr Thomas has the commanding quality of a real *Heldentenor*, not a pushed-up baritone as are many Wagnerian tenors. **1973** *Times* 20 Mar. 16/8 Mr Lauritz Melchior, whom English opera goers remember as the greatest Wagnerian *Heldentenor* of his generation between the wars, died in Santa Monica, California.

Helderberg (he·ldəɹbɜːg). *Geol.* The name of a range of hills in New York State, used *attrib.* to designate a group of strata found there and later also the lower division of the Lower Devonian in North America and the fossils, etc., typical of it. Hence **Helderbe·rgian** (-bɜːg-, -bɜːdʒ-), *a.*

1840 W. W. Mather in *Geol. Surv. State N.Y.* (Assembly No. 50) 212 The subjoined nomenclature of these rock groups is presented as local, and one of convenience merely... (3) The next in order is the Helderberg group, which is composed of various strata of common and hydraulic limestones..interstratified with grits and shales. **1880** J. Dana *Man. Geol.* (ed. 3) III. ii. 236 The Lower Helderberg period..is so named because its beds are well displayed in the Helderberg Mountains, south of Albany, beneath Devonian beds called the 'Upper Helderberg'. *Ibid.*, The Helderberg rocks outcrop also over a large area in western Ohio. **1906** Chamberlin & Salisbury *Geol.* II. 454 From this intermediate or transitional assemblage the Helderberg fauna seems to have taken its origin. *Ibid.* 455 The capulid shells which abound at some localities in the Helderbergian.. faunas. **1949** C. O. Dunbar *Hist. Geol.* x. 207 Two stages [of the American Devonian] are recognized, the Helderbergian and the Deerparkian, each with several formations. The Helderberg stage includes only limestone and calcareous shales.

helenium (helī·niəm). [mod.L., f. Gr. ἑλένιον, possibly commemorating Helen of Troy.] **1.** An early name for elecampane, the European herb *Inula helenium*, of the family Compositæ.

1608 Topsell *Serpents* 5 Helen..planted the same there..called..after her owne Name Helenium, which the skilfull Herborists at this day affirme to grow in Pharus. **1777** R. Weston *Universal Botanist* II. 380 Many of the Varieties of the Helenium of Vaillant, are arranged under Aster and Inula. **1931** M. Grieve *Mod. Herbal* I. 279/1 Elecampane was known to the ancient writers on.. natural history... *Inula*, the Latin classical name for the plant, is considered to be a corruption of the Greek word *Helenion*, which in its Latinized form *Helenium*, is also now applied to the same species.

2. [Adopted by Linnæus in *Hortus Cliffortianus* (1737) 418.] A plant of a large genus of North American annual or perennial herbs so called, belonging to the family Compositæ; a sneezeweed.

1789 W. T. Aiton *Hortus Kewensis* III. 227 (*heading*) Smooth Helenium. *Nat[ive]* of North America. **1900** J. M. Abbott in W. D. Drury *Bk. Gardening* viii. 272 Heleniums are valuable composite plants for back positions in mixed borders. **1961** *Amateur Gardening* 16 Sept. 7/2 Despite the epithet 'autumnale', many of the heleniums are summer-flowering plants.

helgramite: see Hellgrammite.

1878 C. Hallock *Amer. Club List & Sportsman's Gloss.* p. vi, *Helgramite*, the dobson. **1894** *Outing* (U.S.) XXIV. 228/2 Helgramites (purchasable at most any of the tackle stores during the bass season). **1957** *Times* 11 Oct. 12/6 A helgramite net—a flat wire tray that will catch any insects swept down by the current.

heli-, combining form, repr. the first element of *helicopter (cf. Gr. ἕλιξ), used (*a*) in the names of types of helicopters or aircraft resembling helicopters, as **helibus**, a helicopter with accommodation for a large number of passengers; (*b*) = 'helicopter', as **heliborne** *a.*, carried by helicopter; **heli-lift** *v.*, to transport by helicopter; **helipad**, a 'pad' or landing-ground for a helicopter; **helipod**, a 'pod' or container borne by a helicopter and carried e.g. to forward battle-areas for use as an operating theatre, workshop, etc. See also *helidrome, *heliport.

1949 *News-Age-Herald* (Birmingham, Ala.) 13 Nov. A18/3 There is much work..to be done before the combination of the jetliner and the helibus can be fully utilized. **1956** *Britannica Bk. of Year* 493/1 Helicar, a combination of automobile and helicopter. **1960** *Times* 29 Oct. 4/5 A Rotodyne helicopter lifting the 'helipod', which contains two operating theatres. **1961** *New Scientist* 8 June 583/3 The principles of the helicopter and the ducted air flying platform are combined in a vehicle named 'Helipod' and designed by an American business man. **1961** *Aeroplane* CI. 822/2 There are now 487 established heliports or helipads in the U.S.A., Canada and Puerto Rico. **1966** *Guardian* 2 Apr. 14/2 Military requests for a hard 'helipad' that could be laid swiftly in jungles on mud, sand, grass, or dusty surfaces. **1966** *Atlantic Monthly* Oct. 14 Man for man, the U.S. troops may lack some of their enemies' jungle skill, but the rapid availability of firepower and heliborne mobility have tipped the scales decisively in their favor. **1966** *New Statesman* 14 Oct. 549/1 Heli-lifted Medivac Attends the WIA. **1968** *Guardian* 29 Feb. 5/5 Hovercraft and helibuses would transport people and goods. **1968** *Courier-Mail* (Brisbane) 5 June 2/6 Because of the heliborne capability of the Government forces it was no longer possible for the Viet Cong to concentrate anywhere in company strength. **1969** I. Kemp *Brit. G.I. in Vietnam* xii. 197 A 'heliborne' assault in the jungle near Song Be mountain. **1970** *Guardian* 12 Sept. 11 The Israelis..could heli-lift a half brigade to Dawsons Field. **1973** *Observer* (Colour Suppl.) 3 June 34/2 Units of the elite First Cav, the new heliborne division.

helianthemum (hīliˌæ·nþĭməm). *Bot.* [mod. L. (J. P. de Tournefort *Elemens de Botanique* (1694) I. vi. 214), f. Gr. ἥλι-ος sun + ἄνθεμον flower.] A plant of the very large, widely-distributed genus of evergreen shrubs or herbs so named, belonging to the family Cistaceæ; also called *rock-rose, sun-rose*, or *frost-weed.*

1822 Loudon *Encycl. Gard.* 1406/1 *Helianthemum*, sun-rose..and cistineæ..grow in sandy loam and peat. **1827** R. Sweet *Cistineæ* 43 They were both sent from the Brazils..as two distinct species, one marked *Helianthemum*, 19, the other 48. **1900** M. Thorn in W. D. Drury *Bk. Gardening* xi. 436 Helianthemums (Sun Roses)..are charming plants of dwarf habit. **1934** V. Rendall *Wild Flowers in Lit.* 67 The flower was called *Helianthemum*, 'sun-flower' in Greek, because the blossoms open out in sunshine. **1958** *Listener* 26 June 1058/3 Helianthemums are ideal plants for a new garden.

helical, *a.* Add: *helical gear, tube* (see quots.). Also *Comb.*, as *helical-cut* adj.

1888 *Lockwood's Dict. Mech. Engin.*, *Helical gear*, toothed gear in which the wheel-teeth instead of being at right angles with their faces are set at some other angle therewith. **1904** Goodchild & Tweney *Technol. & Sci. Dict.* s.v. *Cycles*, A form of tube known as 'helical', which is formed from a thin steel band or ribbon, wrapped into the form of a tube and brazed at the edges. **1908** *Westm. Gaz.* 28 May 4/2 The live axle is chiefly noticeable for its helical-cut driving pinion. *Ibid.* 18 Nov. 5/1 Several of the wheels have helical-cut teeth. **1958** *Which?* I. III. 30 The new..[drill] has..helical gears, which give quieter running and longer life.

B. *sb.* = *helical gear.*

1913 *Lockwood's Dict. Mech. Engin.* (ed. 4) s.v. *Helical gear cutting*, Double helicals are cut in the same way if the teeth are staggered and divided at the apex.

helically, *adv.* Add: Also *Comb.*

1908 *Westm. Gaz.* 14 Nov. 14/2 Helically-cut half-time gear-wheels to ensure silence. **1962** [see *delay *sb.* 3].

helicity (hīli·siti). [f. L. *helix, helic-em* (see Helix) + -ity.] **1.** *Physics.* The projection of the spin angular momentum of an elementary particle on the direction of its linear momentum.

1958 *Physical Rev.* CIX. 1017/1 Our result seems compatible with..100% negative helicity of the neutrinos emitted in orbital electron capture. **1968** M. S. Livingston *Particle Physics* vii. 142 Helicity must be defined relative to a particular coordinate system. For example, if an electron is emitted from a beta decay process with velocity $v = 0{\cdot}95c$ and is observed in the laboratory to have left-handed helicity, its helicity would be reversed if viewed from a coordinate system moving parallel to the particle with velocity $v = 0{\cdot}99c$. **1970** *New Scientist* 19 Mar. 545/2 A particle has helicity + 1 if it is seen as spinning counter-clockwise while approaching an observer, while if the observer sees the particle as spinning clockwise, it has helicity − 1.

2. *Biochem.* Helical character.

1965 *Biochem. & Biophys. Res. Communications* XIX. 231 We observe that the degree of helicity in native and denatured α lactalbumin are the same. **1970** *Nature* 25 July 336/2 The side chains in a series of water-soluble glutamine derivatives, the helicity of which can be controlled.

helico- (he·liko), comb. form of Gr. ἕλιξ Helix, in names of chemical substances occurring in snails.

1914 J. A. Mandel tr. *Hammarsten & Hedin's Physiol. Chem.* (ed. 7) 174 Another phosphoglycoprotein is helicoproteid, obtained by Hammarsten from the glands of the snail Helix pomatia. **1917** *Jrnl. Chem. Soc.* CXII. I. 421 Helicorubin is thus closely related to hæmoglobin, and acts without doubt in the intestine of the snail as a respiratory pigment.

helicoid. B. *sb.* Delete †*Obs. rare* and add later example.

1959 *New Scientist* 5 Mar. 515/2 Inside the silencer cylinders there are two helicoids which have the effect of mincing the air flow passing through the cylinder.

helicon. Add: **2. b.** (Later example.)

1961 J. Richardson tr. *'Ilf' & 'Petrov's' Twelve Chairs* (1965) 257 The most powerful machine in the band was the helicon, encircled three times by a brass serpent.

3. In various techn. senses (see quots.).

[**1961** P. Aigrain in *Proc. Internat. Conf. Semiconductor Physics* (*Prague 1960*) 225 Le temps d'atténuation des ondes basse fréquence..que nous proposons d'appeler 'hélicon'.] **1962** *Electronics* 9 Feb. 26/1 He'll talk about active homogenous semiconductor developments including the Ecole [Normale Supérieure, Paris]'s helicon. Defined as devices without p-n junctions that amplify or oscillate by an action similar to that of a traveling-wave tube, these devices are expected to have a bright future. **1966** *New Scientist* 20 Jan. 155/3 The type of plasma-wave currently exciting most attention is called a helicon. It is transverse and circularly polarized..and moves along the direction of a magnetic field. **1968** *Ibid.* 17 Oct. 13/2 One might also single out for their promise the intriguing 'helicon waves' which result from the interaction between electromagnetic radiation and a 'gas' of electrons within a solid.

helicopter (he·likǫptəɹ). [ad. F. *hélicoptère*, f. Gr. ἕλικος, ἕλιξ spiral, Helix + πτερόν wing.] A flying machine sustained by one or more lifting screws revolving horizontally. Also *attrib.* and *Comb.* Also formerly in Fr. form.

[**1861** G. L. M. de Ponton *Brit. Pat. 1929*, The required ascensional motion is given to my aerostatical apparatus (which I intend denominating aeronef or helicoptere,) by means of two or more superposed horizontal helixes combined together.] **1887** tr. *Verne's Clipper of Clouds* iv, We can look forward to such contrivances..which we can call streophores, helicopters, orthopters..by means of which man will become the master of space. **1908** O. & W. Wright in *Century Mag.* Sept. 641/2 Several years later we began building these hélicoptères for ourselves. **1909** *Westm. Gaz.* 28 Jan. 4/2 Mr. Howard Wright's helicopter, with which flying tests have been satisfactorily carried out, is now *en route* for Italy. *Ibid.* 2 Mar. 4/1 The Gobron engined Breguet helicopter aeroplane. **1921** *Glasgow Herald* 11 Nov. 6 Recently the Aero Club of France..offered a prize..to the first helicopter pilot in France to take a machine 25 metres up in the air. **1923** *Ibid.* 5 May 8 (*heading*) Helicopter Flight. **1927** C. L. M. Brown *Conquest of Air* 39 The helicopter method of flight. **1958** *Jane's Fighting Ships 1957–8* 9 Official illustrations of the new..helicopter carrier. **1959** *Daily Tel.* 24 Apr. 20/7 He was opening the helicopter station built in Battersea. *Ibid.*, It is intended primarily to be experimental and to assist in the development of helicopter services for London rather than as a permanent station. **1961** *Ibid.* 11 Oct. 25/7 The men are normal infantry, not specialist helicopter-borne troops. **1963** *Economist* 30 Mar. 1213/1 Several helicopter-carriers and three anti-submarine hunter-killer air groups. **1967** *Courier-Mail* (Brisbane) 17 Mar. 4 The petrol drums.. were blasted alight by tracer bullets from R.A.A.F. helicopter gunships hovering 60 ft. above the treetops. **1973** *Guardian* 24 Feb. 2/2 Three helicopter carriers had arrived in the Gulf of Tonkin to join the US naval fleet.

Hence **he·licopt, he·licopter** *vbs. trans.* and *intr.*, to fly with or as with a helicopter; to transport by helicopter; **helico·pterist** (now *rare*), one who uses a helicopter.

1923 *Daily Mail* 12 Feb. 7 M. Raoul de Pescara, the helicopterist. **1926** *Spectator* 10 Apr. 665/1 An albatross, helicoptering over the masthead, signalled the land. **1959** *Time* 23 Mar. 15 He might be helicoptered up to Camp David. **1961** *Aeroplane* CI. 121/2 The sequence is then: brakes off..and helicopt away. **1962** *New Scientist* 3 May 230/1 The rotor on its long spindle helicoptered up and out of its case into the air. **1965** *Sunday Times* 10 Oct. 44/3 They build it on deck, and then helicopt it ashore. **1968** *Radio Times* 10 Oct. 31/1 We joined her [*sc.* the aircraft-carrier] off Singapore, helicoptering over the rubber forest.

helictite (heli·ktəit). [f. Gr. ἑλικτός twisted: after Stalactite.] A distorted twig-like form of stalactite.

1882 H. C. Hovey *Celebrated Amer. Caverns* xi. 186 The term 'Helictite' has been suggested as appropriate to these contorted growths. **1941** *Illustr. London News* CXCIX. 186 (*caption*) The roof of the first grotto or chamber, festooned with stalactites of varied shapes and structure, some tree-like, termed helictites. **1954** W. D. Thornbury *Princ. Geomorphol.* xiii. 337 There is found in portions of some caves a form known as a helictite. It is unusual in that its growth does not necessarily extend along vertical lines. **1971** *Islander* (Victoria, B.C.) 24 Jan. 5/3 Helictites are the amazing coral-like stalactites which grow in every direction, seemingly to defy the law of gravity.

helidrome (he·lidrōᵘm). [f. *heli- after *aerodrome.] A landing-site for helicopters.

1951 *Daily Tel.* 5 June 4/6 Helidrome, rotorport, helistop and helihalt are among recent verbal coinage[s] to signify a helicopter station. **1952** *Times* 10 Oct. 7/4 What ..is a 'helidrome'? So far as I can see it is either a place where marsh-meadows run..or a place where [s]nails run ..But in either case the word ought to be 'helodrome'. **1953** *Listener* 25 June 1040/2 One can almost hear the sound of rockets being fired from the space ships moored at the South Bank helidrome to herald in the twenty-first century. **1966** *Punch* 6 July 8/2 The Director..with a personal helidrome at Great Yarmouth.

Heligoland trap (he·ligolænd træp). [f. *Heligoland*, a German island in the North Sea: see Trap *sb.*[1]] A type of trap used to catch birds for banding or ringing.

1935 *Brit. Birds* XXVIII. 310 The few hundred Pipits which have been caught since a Heligoland trap was put into operation on Skokholm in August, 1933. **1960** E. Ennion *House on Shore* iv. 40 Variety in the design of Heligoland and crow traps at the various Observatories is as nothing compared with the diversity found among their smaller..types of trap.

helio[1]. Add: **b.** = *heliograph *sb.* 4 b.

1886 Kipling *Departm. Ditties* (1904) 23 All honour unto Bangs, for n'er did Jones thereafter know By word or act official who read off that helio. **1901** 'Linesman' *Words by Eyewitness* (1902) 32 Then another helio, spelt out painfully by the frowning, staring signallers, 'Very hard pressed'.

helio[2]. [colloq. abbrev. of HELIOTROPE.] = HELIOTROPE 1 d.

1894 *T. Eaton & Co. Catal.* Spring & Summer 31/3 Pink, sky and helio. printed pique vest. **1922** *Daily Mail* 22 Nov. 5 Very exceptional value with Blue or Black or Helio border. **1928** *Ibid.* 31 July 1/3 Dainty..Dressing Jackets in Pink, Apple and Helio.

helio-. Add: **helio·phyllite** *Min.* [ad. G. *heliophyllit* (G. Flink 1888, in *Öfversigt af kongl. Vetenskaps-Akad. Förh.* XLV. 575), f. Gr. φύλλον leaf: so called because of its colour and structure], a yellowish oxychloride of lead and arsenic, probably dimorphous with ecdemite; **heliopo·lar** *a.*, pertaining to the pole of the sun's rotation; **heliota·ctic** *a.*, responding to sunlight by movement; characterized by heliotaxis; **heliota·xis**, phototaxis due to the rays of the sun; **heliothe·rapy**, the treatment of disease by exposure to the sun's rays; **he:liozinco·graphy** (see quots.).

1890 *Jrnl. Chem. Soc.* LVIII. I. 459 On specimens of the so-called rhodotilite from Pajsberg a yellow mineral has been observed... The author names this mineral heliophyllite. **1968** I. KOSTOV *Mineral.* II. vii. 467 Ekdemite is tetragonal, dimorphous with heliophyllite which is orthorhombic pseudotetragonal. **1902** *Science* 7 Feb. 223/2 The vector diagram in heliopolar coordinates takes the form of a conical surface around the Sun. **1898** *Jrnl. R. Microsc. Soc.* 422 The progressive movements of the larvæ of the gooseberry mite (*Bryobia ribis* Th.) are always positively heliotactic. **1904** *Biol. Bull.* VI. 253 The mating habits of these highly heliotactic males and wingless females. **1898** *Jrnl. R. Microsc. Soc.* 422 (*heading*) Heliotaxis of larval mites. **1890** BILLINGS *Med. Dict.* I. 627/2 *Heliotherapy*, treatment of disease by exposure to sunlight. **1903** *Lancet* 11 July 104/1 The fundamental principles and practical applications of heliotherapy and phototherapy. **1921** *Glasgow Herald* 15 July 10 For the information of medical practitioners interested in heliotherapy. **1928** A. HUXLEY *Let.* 23 May (1969) 297 My medical uncle..says that he has known TB of the intestine greatly benefited by heliotherapy. **1903** *Nature* 19 Nov. 60 Two new methods have now superseded photozincography; one of these, 'heliozincography', was worked out by the Ordnance Survey... The first method consists in reproduction direct on a sensitised zinc plate in contact with a reversed negative. **1936** H. S. L. WINTERBOTHAM *Key to Maps* xix. 196 We have seen above how work from paper may go direct to the zinc by a process known as vandyking. To do the same with a negative and a sensitized sheet of zinc is known as heliozincography.

heliocentrically, *adv.* (Later example.)

1960 V. NABOKOV *Bend Sinister* ii. 18 They of the solar side saw heliocentrically what you telurians [*sic*] saw geocentrically.

heliodon (hī·liodǫn). [f. HELI(O- + Gr. ὁδός way, path.] A mechanical apparatus for demonstrating the sun's apparent motion, used in astronomy or in architectural design.

1909 in WEBSTER. **1932** DUFTON & BECKETT in *Jrnl. Sci. Instrum.* IX. 253 In the Heliodon, the apparatus which is the subject of the present paper, the representation of the motion of the sun is simplified. **1964** *New Scientist* 30 Jan. 288/1 Models of a building..with an artificial Sun would be of immense value... Although individual machines were given such names as 'sunshine analyser' or 'solarometer', the generic name for them is 'heliodon'.

heliodor (hī·liodōᵊɹ). *Min.* Also **-dore.** [a. G. *heliodor*, f. Gr. ἥλιο-ς sun + δῶρον gift.] A richly coloured variety of golden beryl found in South West Africa.

1913 *Mineral. Mag.* XVI. 362 *Heliodor*... Trade-name for a golden beryl of gem-quality from German South-West Africa. **1952** L. G. GREEN *Lords of Last Frontier* (1953) xviii. 185 Heliodore is found only on the barren slopes of Rossing Mountain... Apparently it does not exist anywhere else in the world. German prospectors discovered the first deposit..and the lovely greenish-yellow opalescent stones were set in the form of a cross. **1959** *Chambers's Encycl.* II. 281/2 The pink morganite, the golden heliodor and the green emerald are among the most attractive of coloured gems.

Heliogabalus (hī:liogæ·bălɒ̆s). [Latinized f. *Elagabal*, Syro-Phœnician sun-god.] The adopted name of Varius Avitus Bassianus, Roman Emperor A.D. 218–222, famed for folly and profligacy, used allusively. Also **He:liogaba·lian** (-găbēi·liăn) *a.*, resembling the character or tastes of Heliogabalus. **He:lioga·balize** *v. intr.*, to act like Heliogabalus.

1589 GREENE *Menaphon* (1880) 71 For his dissolute life he seemed another Heliogabalus. **1618** J. TAYLOR (Water P.) *Pennilesse Pilgr.* sig. F3ʳ Had I beene a Sardanapalus, or a Heliogabalus, I thinke that..the great trauell ouer the Mountaines had tamed me. **1624** BURTON *Anat. Mel.* (ed. 2) I. ii. II. ii. 63 What Fagos, Epicures, Apitios, Heliogables our times affourd? **1859** *National Mag.* V. 142/1 In California..the Celestials..make a Heliogabalian [*sic*] kind of dish of rats' brains. **1893** W. S. GILBERT *Utopia Ltd.* I. 5 His Majesty is one of the most Heliogabalian profligates that ever disgraced an autocratic throne. **1930** D. H. LAWRENCE *Phoenix II* (1968) 492 Perhaps the mentality of a boy of fourteen..is more wholesome than the mentality of the young cocktaily person..whose mind has nothing to do but play with the toys of life... Heliogabulus [*sic*], indeed!

heliograph, *sb.* Add: **4. b.** A message sent by heliograph.

1899 *Pall Mall Mag.* Nov. 319, I have just received a heliograph that the Basutos have bands out through.. the valley.

heliolithic (hī:lioli·þik), *a.* [f. HELIO-, after *eolithic*, etc.] Designating a civilization characterized by megaliths and sun-worship.

1915 G. E. SMITH *Migr. Early Culture* 4 The habit of megalithic building and sun-worship (a combination for which it is convenient to use Professor Brockwell's distinctive term 'heliolithic culture'). **1916** *Church Q. Rev.* Jan. 283 The world-wide migration of this 'heliolithic culture'. **1925** *Bull. John Rylands Libr.* IX. 402 There is no known heliolithic temple in the Thames Valley. **1929** W. DEEPING *Roper's Row* xxxvi, But assuredly Ruth belonged to the old heliolithic people. She had something of the south in eyes, hair, temperament.

heliometer. Add: **1.** (Further example.) Also *attrib.*

1874 *Monthly Not. R. Astron. Soc.* XXXIV. 279 The planet Juno at the opposition of 1874 appears to be very favourably situated for a trial of this method..and the Repsold Heliometer, with which the transit is to be observed, a suitable instrument. **1893** D. GILL (*title*) Heliometer observations for determination of stellar parallax made at the Royal Observatory, Cape of Good Hope. **1905** *Astrophysical Jrnl.* XXII. 103 The heliometer measures made in connection with transits of Venus in 1874 and 1882.

So **heliometry** (hīlio·mètri), the art or practice of using the heliometer.

helion (hī·liǫn). *Nuclear Physics.* [ad. F. *hélion* (G. Fournier 1930, in *Jrnl. de Physique et le Radium* I. 196, f. HELI(UM + *-ON[1].] **a.** The nucleus of the normal helium isotope ^{4}(He), consisting of two protons and two neutrons; an alpha-particle. **b.** The nucleus of the helium isotope ^{3}He, consisting of two protons and one neutron.

1930 *Sci. Abstr.* A. XXXIII. 969 Equilibrium tends to be conserved between the number of helions (helium nuclei) in the nucleus and the number of free nuclear electrons. **1964** L. PAULING in *Nature* 4 Jan. 61/1, I suggest that the word helion be used for the α-particle, the nucleus of the helium atom. **1965** *New Scientist* 14 Oct. 87/2 The helium nucleus, or helion, consisting of two neutrons and two protons. **1972** *Nature* 8 Dec. 325/1 In the case of deuterons, the low binding energy makes it easy to calculate the deuteron-nucleus potential from the constituent neutron-nucleus and proton-nucleus optical potentials, but for the more tightly bound helions, tritons and α particles this cannot yet be done wiih sufficient accuracy.

heliotrope. Also with pronunc. (he·liotrōᵘp).

heliotropin (hīliotrōᵘ·pin). *Chem.* Also **-ine.** [f. HELIOTROP(E 1: see -IN[1].] A colourless crystalline compound, $C_8H_6O_3$, present in the heliotrope and other plants, that has a strong smell of heliotropes and is made synthetically for use in perfumes. Also called *piperonal.*

1881 *Chemist & Druggist* 15 Sept. 396/2 (*heading*) Heliotropine... Messrs. Schimmel & Co., of Leipsic, now prepare pure heliotropine in crystals... The heliotropine prepared by them is..suitable for preparing perfumes. **1943** *Thorpe's Dict. Appl. Chem.* (ed. 4) VI. 191/1 Most of the artificial heliotrope perfumes contain modifiers of the geraniol type, the basic ingredients being heliotropin, with a little vanillin, coumarin and dimethylhydroquinone. **1963** *New Scientist* 4 Apr. 30/3 Two Japanese scientists have produced..aromas for cosmetics and foodstuffs similar to the heliotropin..obtained by chemical synthesis.

helipad, helipod : see *HELI-.

heliport (he·lipōᵊɹt). [f. *HELI- after *AIRPORT.] A landing-place for helicopters.

1948 *Amer. Aviation* 1 June 20 The helicopter is a marvelous vehicle. It just plops down anywhere. All but three of the 12 stops were made right inside towns on small fenced-off portions of vacant lots which have been designated by the super-name of 'heliports'. **1950** *N.Y. Times* 28 Nov. 46/3 (*heading*) Construction of City's first aerial heliport begun atop Port Authority's headquarters. **1955** *Economist* 5 Mar. 813/2 Plans for the first commercial heliport on Manhattan Island in New York City now await only the final approval of the city and port authorities. **1958** *Times* 15 May 16/5 A committee appointed by the Helicopter Association of Great Britain have come to the conclusion that there is an immediate need for a London 'heliport'. **1959** *Daily Tel.* 24 Apr. 20/7 'Guinea pig' heliport is opened. **1971** *Guardian* 17 Nov. 15/1 A public inquiry into a proposal for a heliport at Shadwell Basin on the Thames..opens today.

helipterum (heli·pterɒ̆m). *Bot.* [mod.L. (A. P. de Candolle *Prodromus* (1837) VI. 211), f. Gr. ἥλι-ος sun + πτερόν wing, in allusion to the feathery pappus.] A shrub or herb of the genus so called, belonging to the family Compositæ, native to South Africa and Australia, and including several plants described as everlastings or immortelles (q.v. in Dict.).

1862 *Curtis's Bot. Mag.* LXXXVIII. 5350 Major Sandford's Helipterum... Whether it be a true *Helipterum* or a *Helichrysum* I will not venture to say. **1886** G. NICHOLSON *Illustr. Dict. Gardening* II. 131/2 Helipterums may be raised from seeds. **1962** *Amateur Gardening* 7 Apr. 3/1 Catalogues may list the attractive little rhodanthes either separately or under helipterum, which is their proper name.

helium. Add: (Earlier and later examples.)

1872 W. THOMSON in *Rep. Brit. Assoc.* p. xcix, Frankland and Lockyer find the yellow prominences to give a very decided bright line not far from D, but hitherto not identified with any terrestrial flame. It seems to indicate a new substance, which they propose to call Helium. **1955** *Sci. Amer.* Oct. 61/1 Helium is an ideal cooling gas, because it has a high specific heat and does not capture neutrons, but it is very expensive and is not available in large quantities in Great Britain. **1958** *Chambers's Techn. Dict.* 984/2 *Helium*, proposed coolant for reactors because of negligible cross-section for neutrons.

b. *attrib.* and *Comb.*, as *helium atom, content,* etc.; **helium star**, a star which exhibits the helium lines in its spectrum.

1903 A. M. CLERKE *Probl. Astrophysics* 93 A helium-envelope surrounds the sun to a depth of five thousand miles. *Ibid.* 94 Now that the helium-spectrum has been unravelled. **1904** GOODCHILD & TWENEY *Technol. & Sci. Dict.* 284/2 *Helium stars*, stars the spectra of which show prominently the lines of the gas helium. **1920** *Discovery* Apr. 111/1 Helium determinations never can provide data for more than a *minimum* estimate [of the age of a mineral]. All that the helium-ratio can tell us is that the age of the mineral to which it refers is greater than a certain minimum value. **1921** *Ibid.* Sept. 236/1 The B or helium stars are on the crest of the evolutionary curve, at the meridian of stellar life. **1926** R. W. LAWSON tr. *Hevesy & Paneth's Man. Radioactivity* xxvi. 216 (*heading*) Age determination from the helium content. **1938** *Ibid.* (ed. 2) xxv. 267/2 When the 'helium method' was first applied to minerals, it gave values for the age which were mostly only about one-half or one-third of the values found by the 'lead method'. **1940** *Chambers's Techn. Dict.* 409/1 *Helium diving bell*, a diving bell in which the nitrogen in the compressed-air is replaced by helium, thus reducing tendency to the bends. **1956** A. H. COMPTON *Atomic Quest* iii. 163 The only plans for a production plant..were those of Moore's helium-cooled reactor. **1957** *Gloss. Terms Nucl. Sci.* (Nat. Res. Council U.S.) 7/1 s.v. *Age*, If the age is calculated from the relative number of atoms of a stable radiogenic end product and radioactive parent present, the method is designated by the name of the end product. Examples are the lead age and helium age of a uranium-containing and/or thorium-containing mineral. **1957** *Technology* Mar. 14/2 In the hydrogen bomb the energy generated is derived from the fusion of hydrogen atoms into helium atoms. **1958** F. E. ZEUNER *Dating Past* (ed. 4) 329 Were there not certain difficulties connected with the gaseous nature of helium, age estimates could be carried out with the helium generated by radioactive substances just as well as with the lead. The amount of helium present is determined and compared with the amount of uranium (and thorium) contained in the mineral, in other words, the helium-ratio is determined. *Ibid.* 427 A sample of magnetite from Larder Lake District..has yielded a helium-age of 2,400 million years. **1960** *Nature* 24 Sept. 1077/1 At the meeting of the International Committee of Weights and Measures held in Sevres, during September 29–October 3, 1958, the recommendation was adopted that the '1958 Helium-4 Vapour Pressure Scale of Temperatures'..should be used as the international standard scale of temperature between 1° and 5·2°K.

helixin (hī·liksin). [f. HELIX + -IN[1].] **1.** *Chem.* A crystalline glucoside found in the seeds and leaves of ivy, *Hedera helix*, later called *hederin.* **2.** An antibiotic produced from species of *Streptomyces*, a genus of actinomycete fungi.

1894 C. E. SOHN *Dict. Active Princ. Plants* 56/2 (*heading*) Hedera helix (Ivy);..Helixin G. (Hedera Glucoside). *Ibid.*, Fehling's solution not reduced till the Helixin has been boiled with acid. **1952** C. LEBEN et al. in *Mycologia* XLIV. 160 A name, helixin, is tentatively proposed for the antibiotic produced... The name was suggested by the helical nature of the spore chains produced by the antibiotic organism. *Ibid.* 167 Helixin appears to be an antibiotic potent primarily against fungi.

hell, *sb.* Add: **4. a.** (Further examples.)

1903 KIPLING *Five Nations* 51 Yes, we shall be perfectly pleased with our work, And that is the perfectest Hell of it! **1944** *Living off Land* v. 103 A boggy area is hell to plough through with a wheeled vehicle. **1951** N. BALCHIN *Way through Wood* viii. 111, I should think he'd be pretty average hell to live with. **1971** H. E. BATES *Blossoming World* xv. 176 If the times had been bad for writers in 1926,..they were now hell.

d. *a hell of a* —: also, an exceedingly bad, great, loud, etc. Also *the hell of a* —. Cf. *HELLUVA.

1776 J. LEACOCK *Fall Brit. Tyranny* IV. vii, This is a hell of a council of war. **1778** in S. CURWEN *Jrnl.* (1842) x. 207 After travelling in the heat of the season in a hell of a climate. **1806** M. L. WEEMS *Lett.* (1929) II. 354 I've had a hell of a time in your service. **1897** 'MARK TWAIN' *Following Equator* xxxi, It's a charming town, with a hell of a hotel... It's the worst hotel in Australia. **1910** R. W. SERVICE *Ballads of Cheechako* 133 Lord! it's a hell of a night. *a* **1918** MCCUDDEN *Five Yrs. R.F.C.* (1919) 232 There was immediately a Hell of a yell. **1920** C. E. MULFORD *J. Nelson* xii. 126 You must 'a' had one h—l of a time gettin' out. **1923** —— *Black Buttes* ii. 24 He was a hell of a trail-boss, an' he had a hell of an outfit, if you leave it to me! **1931** J. BETJEMAN *Mount Zion* 20 And we each had a couple of toy balloons and made the hell of a din. **1942** N. COWARD *Blithe Spirit* I. ii. 34 Pedalling off down the drive at the hell of a speed. **1944** *Living off Land* vii. 155 The Abo thinks himself a hell of a feller, the same as you do. **1947** 'N. SHUTE' *Chequer Board* i. 3, I had the hell of a headache. **1964** E. A. NIDA *Toward Sci. Transl.* ix. 215 In Bassa, a language of Liberia, the English phrase *hell of a* has been borrowed through Pidgin

English as an attributive meaning 'tremendous, great, and important', so that a Bassa churchgoer can quite appropriately tell the pastor that his latest message was 'a helava sermon'. **1969** *New Yorker* 14 June 44/3 His forehand is a hell of a weapon.

e. Used in the genitive (esp. with *own*), or as *hells* quasi-adverbially, with intensive force.

1926 E. Hemingway *Fiesta* (1927) I. vii. 65 You've got hell's own drag with the concierge. **1962** 'J. Le Carré' *Murder of Quality* i. 10 He's entertaining every don... Hells extravagant. **1963** C. Bingham *Coronet among Weeds* ii. 25 They sit about and..talk about their ancestors. Ancestors are hell's boring. **1968** 'M. Underwood' *Man who killed too Soon* ix. 84, I had a puncture. I had hell's own time changing the wheel.

7. b. Also designating similar receptacles for waste.

1872 *Saddl. Harn. & Carriage Builder's Gaz.* 1 Dec. 207/2 Each smith shop has what is termed the 'hell', and in cutting off a set of tires, if the farmer is not present, the largest half of the end cut off finds its way to the 'hell'. **1886** *Encycl. Brit.* XXI. 345/2 A useful adjunct to the many saw-mills, which produce more waste than can be consumed in raising the necessary steam, is the 'slab-burner' or 'hell'.

9. (Further examples.) *hell's bells!*: an expression of anger or annoyance. *what the hell!*, = what does it matter?, who cares? Also used in expressions of strong disagreement of the type 'Will I hell!' = 'I won't'.

1872 Geo. Eliot *Middlemarch* II. III. xxiii. 21 But, what the hell! the horse was a penny trumpet to that roarer of yours. **1893** *St. Louis Republic* 8 July 16/3 The dealer..said: 'Say, Rick, do you know this gentleman? He's been playing mighty lucky.' Rickebaugh glanced at the great stack of chips..and sarcastically remarked: 'Lucky h—!' **1902** R. H. Davis *Capt. Macklin* 295 'Then why in hell didn't you say so!' he roared. **1912** Z. Grey *Riders of Purple Sage* i. 10 To hell with your Mormon law! **1912** E. Hubbard *Age of Rubber* 11 Goshity gosh, helzbelz, there ain't no such animile. **1913** *Maclean's Mag.* Mar. 45/1 'To hell with 'em,' he grated. **1919** *Thrill Bk.* 1 May 13/1 '*Mister!*' I corrected him in his own tone... 'Mister, was it?' he rumbled... 'Mister—hell!' **1920** S. Lewis *Main Street* 352 Hell's bells,..no harm in being polite. **1925** N. Coward *Fallen Angels* III. 83 *Maurice*: We are great friends—they confide in me. *Fred*: The hell they do! **1925** *New Yorker* 22 Aug. 5/1 Where the hell is my comb? **1927** D. L. Sayers *Unnatural Death* III. xxi. 244 Hell's bells. Here's somebody at the door. **1931** E. Linklater *Juan in Amer.* II. xvii. 183 'We'll all see her,' shouted the Snake's Hips. 'Will you hell!' said Rosy. **1931** G. B. Shaw *Too True to be Good* (1934) I. 46 *The Patient*... Doesnt that tempt you? *The Nurse*. Tempt me hell! I'll see you further first. **1932** J. Maxwell (*title*) Hell's bells and mademoiselles. **1933** *Atlanta Jrnl.* 21 Jan., I've abandoned it completely. The hell with it. **1936** R. Lehmann *Weather in Streets* II. 235 As if she'd decided to say at last, 'Oh, what the hell! Let them rip.' **1942** N. Coward *Blithe Spirit* I. ii. 42 *Mrs. Bradman*: Ought we to pick it up or leave it where it is? *Dr. Bradman*: How the hell do I know? **1943** F. J. Bell *Condition Red* 38 Carrier, hell! It's a goddamn submarine! **1957** *New Yorker* 5 Oct. 37/2 'The hell with organization,' Todd said. **1958** *Engineering* 4 Apr. 424/3 If *we* can't do it how the hell can I expect Government to do it? *Ibid.* 425/1 Why the hell haven't we got a computer? **1959** M. Hastings *Hour-Glass to Eternity* II. i. 154 Hell's bells! You talk and I'll spill the beans. **1961** *John o' London's* 18 May 567/3 The hell with realism. **1962** P. Gregory *Like Tigress at Bay* vi. 70, I wish to hell I was out of it. **1962** *Sunday Express* 1 Apr. 19/5 Am I dressed for ease and comfort? Am I *hell*? **1968** *Landfall* XXII. 195 Why in hell didn't you get John to build it for you? **1968** A. MacLeod *Dam* xiv. 140 'Hell's teeth!' he swore furiously.

10. Phrases. **With another substantive.*

b. not a chance, hope, in hell: no possibility; also, *a snowball's chance in hell* and similar phrases.

1923 O. Onions *Peace in Our Time* iii. 37 'I rather fancied Lovelightly.' 'Lovelightly? Not a hope in Hell!' **1931** *Amer. Speech* VI. 435 As much chance as a snowball in hell. **1961** K. Vonnegut *Sirens of Titan* (1962) v. 129 The Army of Mars didn't have the chance of a snowball in hell. **1963** J. T. Story *Something for Nothing* iii. 79 'What are the chances of a job here, then?' Albert asked. 'For you—not a chance in hell.' She spoke matter-of-factly. **1966** J. Porter *Sour Cream* vii. 94 One telephone call from Melkin..and Babak wouldn't have a snowball's chance in hell. **1972** *Listener* 27 Jan. 126/2 Poor Robert's empirical doubts don't stand a snowflake's chance in hell.

c. hell and (or **or**) **high water**: any great difficulty or obstacle.

1915 *Everybody's Mag.* June 69/2 He'll be one of us in spite of hell and high water. **1918** C. E. Mulford *Man fr. Bar-20* xii. 120 Logan found out that he was a *real* man, a *gun*-man, an' not scared of h—l an' high water. **1939** A. Keith *Land below Wind* I. ii. 26 'Let empires be built!'—and, come hell or high water, they build 'em. **1939** P. I. Wellman *Trampling Herd* viii. 93 'In spite of hell and high water'..is a legacy of the cattle trail when the cowboys drove their horn-spiked masses of longhorns through high water at every river and continuous hell between. **1962** *Sunday Times* 12 Aug. 27/7 A superb instinct for working with the camera guided her to rough out a public image which, come hell or high water, she was not going to change.

d. hell for leather: at breakneck speed, orig. used with reference to riding on horseback; also (usu. with hyphens) *attrib.* or as *adj.*

1889 Kipling *Story of Gadsbys* (1891) 116 Here, Gaddy, take the note to Bingle and ride hell-for-leather. **1893** —— *Many Invent.* 47, I perceived a gunner-orf'cer in full rig'mentals perusin' down the road, hell-for-leather, wid his mouth open. **1915** D. O. Barnett *Lett.* 176 The little English plane went humming back, hell-for-leather. **1927** *Sunday Express* 10 July 4 A long line of stage coaches starting on a hell-for-leather race. **1928** H. W. Freeman *Joseph & His Brethren* vi. 48 Charging down hell for leather with your sabres all flashing in the sun. **1930** *Daily Express* 6 Sept. 8/7 That magnificent, hell-for-leather, boiling verse. **1963** *Times* 21 Feb. 3/2 Australia's plan was to make 90 during the afternoon, if they could, without losing too many wickets and to go hell for leather afterwards.

e. hell on wheels: someone or something regarded as resembling hell; also *attrib.* or quasi-*adj.*

1843 *Quincy* (Ill.) *Herald* 10 Mar. 1/4 Hell-upon-Wheels!..the most appropriate name for that craft [*sc.* a steam-boat]. **1868** S. Bowles in F. L. Paxson *Hist. Amer. Frontier* (1924) lii. 497 'Hell on Wheels' was the appropriate name that Samuel Bowles of the Springfield *Republican* bestowed upon the town he visited in 1868. **1897** P. Warung *Tales of Old Regime* 50 To look up an' know heaven's above, an' not the roof of a hell-on-wheels —oh, that'll be grand! **1945** Wyndham Lewis *Let.* 13 Mar. (1963) 381 We learn here that the 'Hell-on-wheels' outfit has reached the Elbe. Hooray! **1966** J. Pearl *Crucifixion P. McCabe* (1967) ii. 24 He's hell on wheels on Monday mornings. **1968** S. Challis *Death on Quiet Beach* xii. 174 You don't pull any imitation disease over the immigration doctors. Those guys are hell on wheels.

f. hell's delight: pandemonium.

1823 'J. Bee' *Slang* 95 Kicking up hell's delights. **1835** *Sessions Paper* Apr. 959 She said if I went out, she would kick up *hell's delight*. **1888** 'R. Boldrewood' *Robbery under Arms* II. xix. 287 If these fellows are half drunk they'll..play hell's delight. **1918** W. J. Locke *Rough Road* xi. 131 Just listen to the hell's delight that's going on over yonder. **1958** L. A. G. Strong *Light above Lake* 26 Once let anything bad go wrong with them, and you'd hell's delight to mend it. **1961** M. Kelly *Spoilt Kill* iii. 134 There'll be hell's delight ringing round all the hotels till we find him.

***With a verb.*

g. to beat, blast, knock, etc., **hell out of** (a person): to pound heavily, thrash, 'beat up'; also *fig.* to achieve supremacy over.

1922 Joyce *Ulysses* 247 His old fellow welted hell out of him. **1925** [see *gang *v.*[2] 2 b]. **1937** E. Ambler *Uncommon Danger* viii. 110 Are you going to be sensible or do I knock hell out of you first? **1945** C. Isherwood *Prater Violet* 95 If anybody says you're not, I'll help you beat the hell out of him. **1958** P. Scott *Mark of Warrior* II. 166 How did we interrogate Mr Baksh? Beat the hell out of him, I hope? **1965** *Times* 15 Apr. 12/1 Given the response of which our people are capable..we shall be ready to knock hell out of you.

h. when, till, until hell freezes (over): advb. phr. indicating a date in the impossibly distant future, for ever.

1919 J. A. Fisher *Let.* 13 June in *Henry Bristow Ltd. Catal.* (1973) No. 203.9 Yours till hell freezes. **1931** *Amer. Speech* VI. 435 Till hell freezes over. **1949** *Romance Philol.* II. 105 We have the meaning 'forever' in 'I'll wait until Hell freezes over' and the meaning 'never' in 'I'll do it when Hell freezes over'. **1961** 'A. A. Fair' *Stop at Red Light* (1962) ii. 36 If their suspicions once get aroused, they'll investigate until hell freezes over. **1962** *Listener* 1 Nov. 704/1 'I am prepared,' Mr Stevenson rasped out, 'to wait for an answer till hell freezes over.' **1966** *Guardian* 17 Aug. 9/2 The Texan chairman..declared that he would..open the hearing today even if it meant going to gaol 'until hell freezes'.

i. to get hell: to be given hell, to be reprimanded, dressed down.

1938 E. Bowen *Death of Heart* III. iv. 382 'I was using the telephone in Miss Paullie's study, and she came in and caught me...' 'So then you got hell, I suppose.' **1951** Wodehouse *Old Reliable* ii. 32, I would only get hell from Emily Post.

j. to get the (or **to**) **hell out** (of a place): to make a hasty retreat.

a **1911** D. G. Phillips *Susan Lenox* (1917) II. x. 257 Get the hell out... I want to sleep. **1929** E. Linklater *Poet's Pub* vii. 83 Get to hell out of this, you accidental offspring of a Marine sentry. **1934** W. Saroyan *Daring Young Man* (1935) 262 Get the hell out of here, I reply quietly. **1944** 'Brahms' & 'Simon' *Titania has Mother* xiii. 147 'Get to hell out of here,' he roared. **1952** 'J. Tey' *Singing Sands* ix. 139 You want her to get the hell out of here. **1961** J. Heller *Catch-22* (1962) vi. 57 He.. felt that any who did not share this confidence he had placed in them could get the hell out. The only way they could get the hell out, though..was by flying the extra ten missions. **1972** Wodehouse *Pearls, Girls, & Monty Bodkin* v. 67 You ought to be in bed. Get the hell out of here, Bodkin.

k. to give (a person) **hell**: to give him 'a bad time'.

1851 *Harper's Mag.* III. 461/1 Riley shouted, 'Forward and give them h–ll.' **1863** O. W. Norton *Army Lett.* (1903) 161 We have met the enemy and given them hell. *a* **1917** E. A. Mackintosh *War, the Liberator* (1918) 141 You swine, I'll give you hell for this. **1940** N. Marsh *Surfeit of Lampreys* (1941) xv. 235 Gabriel would give me hell and we would both get rather angry with each other.

l. hell to pay: great trouble, discord, pandemonium.

1807 Ld. Paget *Let.* 29 July in A. Paget *Paget Papers* (1896) II. 311 Did you not know..that there has been hell to pay between the Dukes of York and Cumberland. **1811** [in Dict.]. **1956** Wallis & Blair *Thunder Above* (1959) iv. 42, I got you all in this mess... There'll be hell to pay.

m. to play hell (with): to upset, confuse; to alter for the worse; to make a fuss (cf. quots. 1832–4 and 1879 in Dict.).

1803 G. Colman *John Bull* III. ii. 39 I'll be good to the landlord, but I'll play hell with his wife! *a* **1911** D. G. Phillips *Susan Lenox* (1917) I. xiii. 218 Don't drink..it'll play hell—excuse me—it'll spoil your looks. **1927** H. Crane *Let.* 19 Dec. (1965) 312 Port every night for dinner is playing hell with my waistline. **1937** T. Rattigan *French without Tears* I. 22 As a matter of fact it would rather amuse me to see you play hell with the Commander. **1959** *Listener* 4 June 979/1 Wingate and his Chindits would play hell with the Japanese communications. **1960** 'A. Burgess' *Right to Answer* xix. 201 E talks about gross neglect..and e plays ell. **1960** L. Cooper *Accomplices* II. v. 119 The firm..wanted delivery and were playing hell about it.

n. to raise hell: to create a disturbance; to cause great trouble. (The slogan 'Kansas should raise less corn and more hell' is attributed to Mrs Mary Ellen Lease (1853–1933) but proof is lacking. See *Kansas Quarterly* Fall 1969, 52–58.)

1896 *Emporia Weekly Gaz.* 20 Aug., We have decided to send three or four harpies out lecturing, telling the people that Kansas is raising hell and letting the corn go to weeds. *a* **1911** D. G. Phillips *Susan Lenox* (1917) II. viii. 214 What hell Jim will raise when he finds I spent the night working in this house. **1959** M. Scott *White Elephant* iii. 24 He would go home, ring Bert and 'raise hell'.

****Other phrases.*

o. (**just**) **for the hell of it**: out of (pure) devilry, (merely) for fun.

1934 'J. Spenser' *Limey breaks In* x. 166 Both of them were of the mischievous type that misbehaves 'just for the hell of it'. **1939** R. Chandler in *Sat. Even. Post* 14 Oct. 74/3, I wouldn't be telling you just for the hell of it. **1951** W. Stevens *Let.* 7 Sept. (1967) 726, I assume that he is merely doing it for the hell of it. **1959** P. McCutchan *Storm South* xiii. 197 The kind of bloke you'd expect to find taking passage in a venture like ours, just for the hell of it.

p. like hell: recklessly, desperately; extremely, very much: freq. as a mere intensive; also ironically, to indicate emphatic contradiction: not at all, on the contrary.

1855 [in Dict.]. **1892** Kipling *Lett. of Travel* (1920) 66 'Hit, old man?' 'Like hell,' he said. **1922** D. H. Lawrence *England, my England* 231 'And I shall miss thee, Jack.'..'Miss you like hell.' **1925** F. Lonsdale *Last of Mrs. Cheyney* I. 19 *Maria*: Enjoying the concert, Willie? *Willie*: Like hell! **1930** D. Hammett *Maltese Falcon* xx. 260 'You can't say that.' 'Like hell I can't,' Spade said. **1941** H. MacInnes *Above Suspicion* ix. 76 'I've quite enjoyed it here.' Like hell I have, she added under her breath.

q. merry hell: a disturbance, upheaval, great trouble; severe pain.

a **1911** D. G. Phillips *Susan Lenox* (1917) II. xi. 279 We don't dare let you off...They'd send down along the line, to have merry hell raised with us. **1922** S. Lewis *Babbitt* xix. 229 I've come to raise particular merry hell. *c* **1926** 'Mixer' *Transport Workers' Song Bk.* 13 We don't get drunk to fight the boss Or kick up merry hell. **1931** D. L. Sayers *Five Red Herrings* xxii. 248, I am supposed to have faked an alibi, suborned my friends and played merry hell generally. **1938** S. V. Benét *Thirteen O'Clock* IV. 268 If you think it was all romance..you're wrong. A lot of it was merry hell. **1944** J. H. Fullarton *Troop Target* 86 This arm's giving me merry hell. **1961** B. Fergusson *Watery Maze* iv. 102 The Special Boat Squadron..was to play merry hell in the Eastern Mediterranean during the next two years. **1963** M. Duggan in *Landfall* Mar. 9 Watching mum with a shoehorn wedging nines into sevens and suffering merry hell.

r. to hell and gone: used hyperbolically = 'a long way', 'for ever', etc.

1938 S. J. Perelman in *New Yorker* 15 Oct. 17/2 Zarah Trenwick just got blasted to hellangone in her tepee at the Gayboy. **1944** N. Mailer in *Cross-Section* 332 Picking up two-foot piles of plates and lugging them to hell and gone. **1957** M. Millar *Soft Talkers* 39 That's my business. I can contradict myself to hell and gone if I feel like it. **1972** R. Lockridge *Preach No More* ii. 24 Name's Manuel something...Lives to-hell-and-gone downtown.

11. a. *hell-brew, -pack, -pride, -queen, -rake, -rook, -spurge.*

1923 Wodehouse *Inimitable Jeeves* viii. 69 'Have some lemon squash,' I said... The hell-brew appeared to buck him up, for he resumed in a slightly more pally manner. **1935** *Discovery* Sept. 264/2 The dart poison..is indeed a hell-brew. **1923** R. Graves *Whipperginny* 56 Twenty swans glide out With hell-packs loathlier yet to amaze the night. **1944** Blunden *Shells by Stream* 50 Passions armed with horror and hell-pride. **1918** D. H. Lawrence *New Poems* 63 Out of the hell-queen's cup, the heaven's pale wine. **1794** R. F. Greville *Diary* 28 Aug. (1930) 309 His M. order'd Me to call at Farmer Sherring's where I order'd two of those Broad Rakes called Hell Rakes. **1879** G. M. Hopkins *Poems* (1918) 44 The hell-rook ranks. **1849** D. G. Rossetti *Let.* 18 Oct. (1965) I. 74 Hell-spurge of geomaunt and teraphim.

b. *hell-buster, -raiser; hell-raising, -raking, -roaring, -tearing.* Also *hell-rake* vb.

1929 J. B. Priestley *Good Companions* III. iii. 2 They're all damned good, but the last two are real hell-busters. **1914** *Emporia* (Kans.) *Gaz.* 13 Jan., He is a..rip-snorting hell-raiser. **1925** S. Lewis *Martin Arrowsmith* iii. 20 Young men technically known as 'hell-raisers' looked forward to his lectures on physiology. **1928** *Daily Express* 1 June 9 She dislikes the 'hell-raiser' that he likes to make the public believe he is. **1971** *Guardian* 24 July 10/6 The ex-hell raiser of the Bevanite group [*sc.* Michael Foot]..seemed to have settled comfortably into the new role of Left-wing Whip. **1922** S. Lewis *Babbitt* iii. 25 When it comes to..a lot of hell-raising all the while.., it's too rich for my blood! **1936** W. Stevens *Let.* 27 Jan.

(1967) 307 Any form of hell raising is simply out. **1966** WODEHOUSE *Plum Pie* ix. 215 She's the hell-raising type, always apt to be starting something. **1915** J. E. FLECKER *Old Ships* 5 The pirate Genoese Hell-raked them till they rolled Blood, water, fruit and corpses up the hold. **1960** *Spectator* 17 June 870 Chatter nostalgically but amusingly about the hellraking times at Balliol. **1920** J. GREGORY *Man to Man* iv, Your hell-roaring old grand-dad. **1915** W. J. LOCKE *Jaffery* xxi, These hell-tearing fellows.

c. and **d.** *hell-black* (later example), *-purple*; *hell-mouthed*, *-plumed*.

1904 SWINBURNE *Poems* VI. 392 Till murder dawns Blood-red from hell-black treason's heart of hate. **1934** DYLAN THOMAS *Let.* 11 May (1966) 126 Today I complain again for a hell-mouthed mist is blowing. **1876** G. MEREDITH *Vittoria* iii. 35 Those hell-plumed Tyrolese. **1923** D. H. LAWRENCE *Birds, Beasts & Flowers* 57 At her white ankles Hell rearing its husband-splendid, serpent heads, Hell-purple, to get at her.

12. hell-box (examples); **hell-diver** *U.S.*, the dabchick; **hell-driver**, delete sense (*b*) and substitute: (*b*) one who drives a motor vehicle in a very fast or dare-devil manner; hence *hell-driving*; **hell-hole** (further examples); **hell's angel** (usu. in *pl.*), name given in the 1950s in the U.S. (later to similar people elsewhere) to a member of a group of lawless, usually leather-jacketed, motor-cyclists notorious for their disturbances of civil order in California (featured, but there called 'Black Rebels', in a 1954 film entitled 'The Wild One'); also earlier casual uses, e.g. (in *pl.*) as the name of a film about air-battles in the 1914–18 war (quot. 1930) and (in *sing.*) as the name of a Flying Fortress aeroplane (quot. 1943); **hell-ship**, a hell-afloat (cf. HELL *sb.* 4 a).

1889 BARRÈRE & LELAND *Dict. Slang* I. 458/1 *Hell-box*, the receptacle for bad, broken, or 'battered' letters, which are eventually melted down. **1909** 'MARK TWAIN' *Is Shakes. Dead?* vii. 73 If a man should..say '..empty.. the imposing stone into the hell-box..' I should..know that the writer was only a printer theoretically, not practically. **1839–40** Hell-diver [in Dict.]. **1940** E. T. SETON *Trail of Artist-Naturalist* 89, I traced them to the pied-bill grebe, or little helldiver. **1942** BERREY & VAN DEN BARK *Amer. Thes. Slang* § 723/2 *Automobile racer*,..hell driver. **1971** *Cape Times* 13 Feb. 7/6 The helldriver with the 99-to-1 chance of becoming the first Cape Times hell-driving champion. *Ibid.*, One of the hottest nights of helldriving. **1866** J. C. GREGG *Life in Army* xxi. 184 All the whiskey shops, even down to the lowest hell-hole, adopt the decent name..of a 'Coffee-house'. **1891** G. M. HOPKINS *Let.* 15 June (1956) 63 Liverpool too, 'hellhole' though it is. **1945** J. B. PRIESTLEY *Three Men in New Suits* ii. 26 Go and drudge in some hell-hole of an office. **1930** (*film title*) Hell's Angels. **1943** *Examiner* (San Francisco) 8 Aug. 3/1 The ten-man crew which manned the flying fortress, 'Hell's Angel', on her thirty-three raids across the English channel. **1957** *Chronicle* (San Francisco) 3 June 5/1 It also attracted several hundred cyclists who are not American Motorcycle Association members, but who belong to such clubs as the Vampires, Scavengers and Hell's Angels group that rides in the Bay Area. **1957** *Call-Bulletin* (San Francisco) 9 Aug. 3/4 Police raiders cracked down last night on the Hell's Angels, a hard-riding motorcycle outfit whose members have had brushes with the law in the past. **1958** *Ibid.* 1 Aug. 11/1 The main wheel of the 'Hell's Angels' motorcycle club is a more or less conservative delivery man during the week, but Fridays he..combs his hair into a wild mane, gets into black denims and motorcycle boots, plus a red-fringed vest with the club's death's-head emblem, fastens his pierced ear-lobe and dyes his blonde handlebar mustache with heliotrope pencil. **1967** G. LEGMAN *Fake Revolt* 21 The hoodlum drug-addicts and homosexual motorcyclists..who've had two 'Hell's Angels' movies already exposing (*read*: glorifying) them. **1968** *Listener* 22 Feb. 253/2 The Hell's Angels—those much-publicised outlaw motor-cyclists, noted for their wearing of leather jackets and Nazi insignia, whose hunting ground is mainly California. **1969** *Oz* Apr. 3/2 Hell's Angels were moved in on the 3rd floor as a protection against external aggression. **1971** *New Scientist* 11 Feb. 331/2 The Hell's Angels created rather than prevented disorder when Mick and the Stones were dispensing their magic. **1927** *Observer* 21 Aug. 15/2 Hell-ships they must be if three and four months' passages..is anything from which to form an opinion. **1934** *Times Lit. Suppl.* 18 Oct. 713/2 The Dovenby Hall, a notorious hell-ship in her day. **1971** D. NIVEN *Moon's a Balloon* (1972) vii. 93 The troopship was a hell-ship of about 11,000 tons.

hell, *v.*² Add: Revived in various, chiefly *slang*, uses: **a.** to make into a hell. **b.** to give (a person) hell. **c.** to hurry, to go 'hell for leather', to 'fly' *around* (esp. in some activity disapproved of by the speaker).

1897 O. WISTER *Lin McLean* (1898) 60 A man was liable to go sporting and helling around till he waked up. **1903** P. F. ROWLAND *New Nation* 34 The raging bush-fires that hell the Australian plains. **1924** KIPLING *Debits & Credits* (1926) 242 *That's* not his real trouble... I wonder what's really helling him. **1928** J. P. MCEVOY *Show Girl* 166 You were in the show business and throwing your best years away helling around. **1929** W. FAULKNER *Sound & Fury* 243 She had to come helling in there at twelve, worrying me about that letter. **1929** —— *Sartoris* (1933) II. 53 Men can't stand anything... Can't even stand helling around with no worry. **1959** E. FENWICK *Long Way Down* x. 83 Had his supper..just like he always did. I missed *mine*, helling up here this way. **1960** F. SULLIVAN *Let.* 9 Jan. in *Groucho Lett.* (1967) 147 That oppressed and downtrodden share-cropper, Massa Nunnally Johnson, is hellin' around with Ava Gardner, making a picture. **1969** 'E. LATHEN' *Come to Dust* xvii. 172 'If he did any helling around, it wasn't here,' the janitor continued.

Helladic, *a.* Add: **b.** *Archæol.* Denoting the Bronze Age cultures of Greece, lasting from about 2800 to 1200 B.C. Also *absol.*

1921 WACE in *Jrnl. Hellenic Studies* XLI. II. 260 Early Helladic pottery. *Ibid.* 265 With the Third Late Helladic Period Mycenae reached the zenith of its dominion and riches. **1925** V. G. CHILDE *Dawn Europ. Civilization* v. 74 The first metal-using culture therefore is called Early Helladic. **1927** PEAKE & FLEURE *Priests & Kings* 113 The sub-periods range from Early Helladic I to Late Helladic III. **1940** *Antiquity* XIV. 244 Deposits earlier than the beginning of Late Helladic III, the fourteenth century B.C. **1971** J. L. CASKEY in *Cambr. Anc. Hist.* (ed. 3) I. II. xxvi(*a*). 783 There has been a question whether material elements of the latest Stone Age culture persisted for a time alongside the earliest Helladic, since pottery of both types was found together.

hellandite (he·lăndəit). *Min.* [ad. G. *hellandit* (W. C. Brögger 1903, in *Nyt Mag. f. Naturvid.* XLI. 213), f. the name of A. *Helland* (1846–1918), Norwegian geologist: see -ITE¹.] A hydrous borosilicate of the rare earths and calcium, samples of which also contain aluminium, manganese, and iron, perhaps as impurities, that is found in pegmatite veins in Norway.

1903 *Jrnl. Chem. Soc.* LXXXIV. II. 657 Both in crystalline form and chemical composition, hellandite is analogous to guarinite. **1924** J. W. MELLOR *Inorg. & Theoret. Chem.* V. 512 Brownish-red hellandite from Lindvikskollan near Kragerö, Norway. **1964** *Mineral. Abstr.* XVI. 644/2 Hellandite is a boro-silicate with more than 10% B_2O_3 in addition to the known major constituents.

he·ll-bent, *a.* and *adv. colloq.* (orig. *U.S.*). [HELL *sb.* 11 d, BENT *ppl. a.* 3.] 'Fiendishly', doggedly, or recklessly determined (*on* or *upon* a certain course). Also *advb.* determinedly, recklessly.

1835 *Knickerbocker* VI. 12 A large encampment of savages,..'hell-bent on carnage'. **1840** *Pol. Song* (Cent. Dict.), Maine went Hell-bent For Governor Kent. **1904** *Boston Herald* 2 Aug. 6 The Populist Democrats are going 'hell-bent', as the old song says, for Roosevelt. **1910** W. M. RAINE *B. O'Connor* ii. 21, I know your kind—hell-bent to spend what you cash in. **1910** C. E. MULFORD *Hopalong Cassidy* xxviii. 184 As soon as we lick this aggregation of trouble-hunters, what's left will ride hell-bent for that valley. **1912** L. J. VANCE *Destroying Angel* ix, Unless you're hell-bent upon sticking around here. **1918** C. E. MULFORD *Man fr. Bar-20* xv. 152, I was hell-bent to get down here,..an' now I'm hell-bent to get back again. **1926** B. CRONIN *Red Dawson* vi, Shaw sending the coach hell-bent round the curve of Jumping Lead. **1935** A. SQUIRE *Sing Sing Doctor* iii. 32 We'll always have people hell bent on doing what they want to. **1957** *Times* 27 Dec. 6/1 Sir Edmund Hillary's message.. went on to say: 'We are heading hellbent for the Pole, God willing and crevasses permitting.' **1967** *Spectator* 24 Nov. 633/1 This report has been widely used to sustain the charge that the French government was hell-bent on feeding speculation against the pound. **1968** *Times* 31 Oct. 11/3 It is now becoming..clear that an intelligent plan may have to be drawn, according to which those elements hell-bent on..embarrassing the School will have to be expelled from it. **1973** *Times* 31 July 1/3 A minority of Unionist Party members..feel obliged to vote with those who are hell-bent on destroying the first democratically elected assembly the Ulster people have had since the dissolution of Stormont.

helleborine. (Later examples.)

1833 SMITH & SOWERBY *Eng. Bot.* 2775 Purple-leaved Helleborine..was discovered in Worcestershire in 1807. **1900** *Daily Express* 22 June 2/7, I was surprised..to find the large white helleborine..flowering in plenty. **1951** V. S. SUMMERHAYES *Wild Orchids Brit.* vii. 123 The helleborines have rather tall slender stems.

Hellenian. B. *sb.* (Later example.)

a **1846** B. R. HAYDON *Autobiogr.* (1927) III. xvi. 308 Two complete subjects of combat,—viz. between the Centaurs and Lapithæ, and between the Amazons and Hellenians.

Hellenic, *a.* Add: (Additional examples.)

1936 A. THIRKELL *August Folly* viii. 240 Everyone had a suggestion to make for spending the gift... Mrs. Tebben thought an Icelandic or Hellenic cruise. **1971** A. CHRISTIE *Nemesis* vii. 76 They had been on an Hellenic cruise last year and a tour of bulbs in Holland the year before.

2. *Typogr.* Designating a variety of Greek type.

1927 *Greek Printing Types* (Exhib. B.M.) 3 It is thus only natural that the Graeco-Latin founts should now make way for more directly Hellenic styles of type. *Ibid.* 21 Thucydides, Funeral Oration of Pericles (part). Printed with 12-point 'New Hellenic' type.

Hellenophile (he·lĕnŏfəil), *a.* and *sb.* Also **Hellenophil** (-fil). [f. HELLENE + -O + -PHIL, -PHILE.] = PHILHELLENE *a.* and *sb.* Also **Hellenophi·lic** *a.*

1897 E. A. BARTLETT *Battlefields of Thessaly* iii. 60 A little splutter of Hellenophile and Radical agitation in this country. **1898** [see *ARMENO-]. **1959** *Encounter* July 48/1 A few Greek and hellenophil critics acclaimed Kazantzakis's poem as a masterpiece. **1966** *Listener* 6 Jan. 34/3 Another Hellenophile's reluctant conversion to the spell of the old Turkey. **1970** *Nature* 21 Nov. 711/1 Travers reports the discovery of another such protein, which in the Hellenophilic tradition of Harvard he duly names psi.

heller² (he·ləɹ). *U.S. slang.* [f. *HELL *v.*² + -ER¹.] One who 'hells around'.

1895 W. C. GORE in *Inlander* Nov. 67 Heller, a remarkable person. 'He is a heller at foot-ball.' **1933** *Amer. Speech* VIII. I. 81/2 *Heller*, one who is unusually daring or aggressive, intensified usually as *a regular heller*. **1939** J. STEINBECK *Grapes of Wrath* viii. 107 Tom grinned affectionately at him. 'Ain't he a heller?' he said. **1959** *Listener* 17 Dec. 1086/1 Jack Harrick, the old hillbilly satyr or 'heller'.

hell-fire. Add: **1.** (Later examples.)

1915 W. S. MAUGHAM *Of Human Bondage* xxviii. 122 He could go his way without the intolerable dread of hell-fire. **1972** P. M. HUBBARD *Whisper in Glen* vi. 59 Abomination was one of the devalued words. No one had used it wholly seriously. Mrs Haskell did, so that there was the reek of hell-fire to it.

3. (Further examples.)

1952 R. CAMPBELL *Lorca* 10 The hell-fire sermons of the local priest. **1957** J. S. HUXLEY *Relig. without Revelation* (new ed.) ii. 31 A Hell-fire revivalist preacher. **1957** *Economist* 21 Dec. 1046/3 He reacted violently..against the hellfire faith which had laid waste his childhood. **1972** P. M. HUBBARD *Whisper in Glen* xviii. 175 The old woman tried to purge her own indiscretions by giving her daughter a hell-fire upbringing.

hell-fired, *a.* **2.** (Further examples.)

1833 J. NEAL *Down-Easters* I. 79 See what a hell fired noise it [*sc.* the watch] makes. **1972** J. S. HALL *Sayings from Old Smoky* 80 It was the hell-firedest wreck I've ever seen!

hell-gate. (Later examples.)

1892 KIPLING *Barrack-Room Ballads* 195 He yearned to the flare of Hell-gate there as the light of his own hearth-stone. **1934** T. S. ELIOT *Rock* i. 47 The Heart of Man.. Swinging between Hell Gate and Heaven Gate.

hellgrammite, helgramite. Add: (Earlier example.) Also *transf.*

1866 *Wilkes' Spirit of Times* 14 July 315/3 There is another bait for bass called *kill-devil*—a sort of indescribable Barnum-what-is-it thing... An old friend of mine denominated them hell gramites. **1935** O. NASH *Primrose Path* (1936) 122 This human hellgramite that I think we could all dispense with.

hellion, hellyon (he·lyən). *U.S. colloq.* [prob. variant of HALLION, HALLYON, with assimilation to HELL *sb.*] A troublesome or disreputable person; a mischievous child.

1846 J. J. HOOPER *Adv. Simon Suggs* i. 18 The 'oudacious' little hellions! **1857** *Jrnl. Discourses* V. 135/2 We are going to dig a cache..and put all the whining men and women into it... We want to be released from such poor hellyons. **1896** J. C. HARRIS *Sister Jane* 136 If dey ever was a hellian he wuz one. **1906** 'O. HENRY' *Four Million* 8 Jawn, did ye ever see a straighter-nosed gang of hellions in the days of your life? **1919** H. L. WILSON *Ma Pettengill* vii. 225 Three children that was known to be hellions. **1941** H. G. WELLS *You can't be too Careful* III. xxii. 218 That vision of Swedenborg's where all the damned and blessed fly of their own accord to the particular places appointed for them, hellions of every sort to their hells and the blessed to their heavens. **1957** M. MEZZROW in S. Traill *Concerning Jazz* 26 Baby Dodds, our drummer in Nice, is a wonderful person, but in his younger days he was a real hellion, and would fight at the drop of a hat. **1973** J. WAINWRIGHT *Pride of Pigs* 83 They were young animals..pure, down-to-earth hellions.

he·llishing, he·llishun. *slang* (chiefly *Austral.* and *N.Z.*). Used as intensive adj. or adv.: terrible; very. Cf. *hangashun* s.v. *HANG *sb.* 6.

1931 *Amer. Speech* VI. 434 He seems to be in a hellishin' hurry about something. This is a hellishin' fine time to tell us about it. **1941** BAKER *Dict. Austral. Slang* 35 *Hellishun*, an intensive used widely by children. **1950** *Landfall* IV. 38 It's hellishun funny. **1967** K. GILES *Death & Mr. Prettyman* vii. 145 The journey was as hellishing as he remembered. **1968** E. MCGIRR *Lead-Lined Coffin* iii. 114, I don't know that anybody..has any knowledge of how hellishing thorough we are.

hello. Add: **A.** *int.* (Further examples.) Also as a greeeting.

1967 *Listener* 5 Oct. 427/2 'Hello,' I thought, 'Now she's overdoing it.' **1971** *Farmer & Stockbreeder* 23 Feb. 3/3 Next week..we shall say hello again to most of you, and to 100,000 new readers as well.

b. Used as an answer to a telephone call.

1892 KIPLING *Lett. of Travel* (1920) 94 A..millionaire ..clawing wildly at the telephone... 'Hello!.. Yes. Who's there?' **1922** S. LEWIS *Babbitt* iv. 41 On the telephone they said only: '..Oh, Hello, 343?' **1973** J. WAINWRIGHT *Pride of Pigs* 169 She..picked up the receiver, waited for the S.T.D. pips to stop, said 'Hello?' and..recognised her brother's voice.

B. *sb. Comb.* (Earlier and later examples.)

1889 'MARK TWAIN' *Connecticut Yankee* 176 The humblest..hello-girl..could teach the highest duchess. **1928** *Daily Chron.* 4 Feb. (*headline*) Brave Hello Girls. **1971** *New Scientist* 17 June p. iv, That was the day we said Goodbye to the Hello girls.

helluva: used freq. to represent 'hell of a'. Cf. *HELL *sb.* 4 d.

1910 C. E. MULFORD *Hopalong Cassidy* xxvi. 176, I got money—helluva lot of money. **1934** E. POUND *Eleven*

New Cantos xxxv. 24 It must be one helluva country. **1959** 'H. CARMICHAEL' *Stranglehold* ii. 25 Be a helluva thing of I've left it just too late. **1959** 'M. M. KAYE' *House of Shade* ii. 26 It looks like saving you a helluva headache. **1967** *Crescendo* Dec. 33/1 Although she may not be as good a jazzer as Humph, she's certainly one helluva lot prettier. **1968** *Times* 23 Oct. 10/8 It's very unfortunate looking like him: he must have a helluva life.

helly, *a.* Revived in literary example.

1934 DYLAN THOMAS *Let.* 11 May (1966) 127 Every doubt and misgiving that an hereditary..imagination, an hereditary thirst..are capable of conjuring up out of their helly deeps.

Helmholtz (heˈlmhǫlts). *Physics.* The name of H. L. F. von *Helmholtz* (1821–1894), German scientist, used attributively with reference to various devices and theories invented by him. Also **Helmhoˈltzian** *a.*

1890 W. JAMES *Princ. Psychol.* II. xx. 170 The Helmholtzian theory is probably not the last word in the physiology of hearing. **1920** G. B. SHAW *How to become Mus. Critic* (1960) 311 The Helmholtzian chords of Scriabin. **1930** R. PAGET *Human Speech* 8 The ocarina is, I believe, the only well-known wind instrument which operates on the principle of the 'Helmholtz' resonator. **1940** *Chambers's Techn. Dict.* 409/2 Helmholtz galvanometer, Helmholtz resonance, Helmholtz resonator. **1962** CORSON & LORRAIN *Introd. Electromagn. Fields* v. 215 A pair of Helmholtz coils consists of two identical circular current loops placed coaxially so as to obtain uniformity of the magnetic induction *B* in the region midway between the loops.

helmitol (heˈlmitǫl). [a. G. *helmitol* (E. Eichengrün 1902, in *Pharm. Zeitschr.* XLVII. 866/2).] A proprietary name of a derivative of hexamethylenetetramine that has been used as a urinary antiseptic and in the treatment of rheumatism.

1903 *Jrnl. Chem. Soc.* LXXXIV. I. 195 Helmitol.. forms colourless crystals. **1908** *Practitioner* Jan. 64 The newer drugs, urotropine, hetraline, helmitol, are useless in gleet. **1933** A. J. CLARK *Appl. Pharmacol.* (ed. 5) ii. 50 Hexamethylenetetramine anhydromethylene citrate (helmitol) yields formaldehyde with alkalis as well as with acids, but it is doubtful whether it yields formaldehyde in alkaline urines. **1967** *Martindale's Extra Pharmacopoeia* (ed. 25) II. 1524/1 Proprietary preparations of formamol were formerly marketed in Great Britain under the name helmitol (Bayer Products).

helophyte (heˈlǒfəit). *Bot.* [mod. f. Gr. ἕλος marsh + φυτ-όν plant.] A marsh plant.

[**1902** F. E. CLEMENTS *Syst. Nomencl. Phytogeogr.* 6 Helium, a marsh formation; helia, a group of marsh formations; helophyta, marsh plants; helophilus, marsh-loving.] **1909** GROOM & BALFOUR tr. *Warming's Oecology of Plants* xxxiv. 131 There is a group of plants, marsh plants (*helophytes*), which..develop their lower parts.. in water or at least in soaking soil, but have their assimilatory organs mainly adapted to existence in the air. **1913** *Jrnl. Ecol.* I. 17 Another division [of plants] is characterised by semi-aquatic dormant buds—helophytes and hydrophytes. The helophytes or marsh-plants do not include all so-called marsh species. **1926** TANSLEY & CHIPP *Study of Vegetation* ii. 22 The marsh plants (*Helophytes*) and water-plants (*Hydrophytes*), whose [perennating] buds are situated at the bottom of the water or in the subjacent soil. **1960** N. POLUNIN *Introd. Plant Geogr.* xv. 505 Marsh-plants (*helophytes*..) and water-plants (*hydrophytes*) are much alike in their morphological and anatomical characteristics.

helotage. (Later examples.)

1957 K. A. WITTFOGEL *Oriental Despotism* 414 The helotage-based societies of ancient Greece. **1962** *Listener* 27 Sept. 478/3 Spartan helotage barely lasted into the second century B.C.

helotism. Add: **2.** *Biol.* [ad. Sw. *helotisme* (E. Warming *Plantesamfund* (1895) II. iv. 85), prob. after G. *helotenthum* (S. Schwendener *Die Algentypen der Flechtengonidien* (1869) 4).] A form of symbiosis in which one organism makes use of another as if it were a slave, by causing it to function to its own advantage; used *esp.* of the relationship of the fungus and alga in a lichen by those who regard it as neither mutualism nor parasitism.

1900 B. D. JACKSON *Gloss. Bot. Terms* 119/2 *Helotism*, Warming's term for the relation of the symbionts in the Lichen thallus. **1909** GROOM & BALFOUR tr. *Warming's Oecology of Plants* 85 The symbiosis between lichen-fungi and algae is obviously most correctly interpreted as helotism. **1932** FULLER & CONARD tr. *Braun-Blanquet's Plant Sociol.* i. 6 The original individualities of fungus and alga are lost and merged in a new and more aggressive organism, so that the term helotism does not seem any more fortunate than the term mutual parasitism. **1962** C. J. ALEXOPOULOS *Introd. Mycology* (ed. 2) xxii. 539 Botanists of a middle-of-the-road group..state that the fungus holds the alga imprisoned in a state of slavery, helotism being the word used, thus granting that the fungus has the upper hand.

help, *v.* Add: **1. c.** Also ellipt. *so help me,* and as a variant *so help me bob.* Cf. SWELP.

1821 P. EGAN *Life in London* II. iii. 229 She tripped me up, my Lord, so help me bob, it is true. **1869** TROLLOPE *Vicar of Bullhampton* (1870) iii. 20 Just go home to father's, sir; not a foot else, s' help me. **1936** L. C. DOUGLAS *White Banners* iv. 69 That he would never again ..so help him..fritter away precious time.

5. a. Delete 'this is now *dial.* or *vulgar*' and read 'this is now a common *colloq.* form'.

1941 *Punch* 2 July 13/3 Sir Kingsley Wood..asked the House for another £1,000,000,000, to help pay for the next three months of war.

b. (Further examples.)

1936 *Punch* 1 Apr. 375/1, I suppose you two fellows wouldn't help me get the stuff into the coal-cellar, would you? **1940** *Ibid.* 5 June 620/3 The collection of waste-paper that's going to help us win the war. **1971** D. E. WESTLAKE *I gave at Office* (1972) 121 None of the locals.. had any desire to help us off-load the plane.

6. d. To render assistance in dealing *with.*

1924 A. D. SEDGWICK *Little French Girl* I. v, If he sat there..not helping with the water-cans, the baskets of flowers, the scissors, it was because he loved her and wanted to watch her. **1933** *Punch* 26 July 104/2 'Poetry. I believe people use it in exams to remember rules.. and things...' 'That wouldn't help with Greek and Latin,' said Charles.

e. Phr. *to help the police in* (or *with*) *their inquiries*: to be questioned by the police in connection with a crime, often regarded as having the implication of being the chief suspect; also *to help the police, to help with inquiries.*

1957 *Times* 3 Sept. 4/3 The police are anxious to trace an itinerant photographer... It is believed that he may be able to help them in their inquiries. **1970** *Guardian* 10 Nov. 20/4 A man was helping police last night after the body of Susan Young, aged 12..was found. **1971** 'J. FRASER' *Death in Pheasant's Eye* xxvi. 162 What's the deadline for arresting Stanley Robinson? At the moment he's 'helping with enquiries'. **1972** V. C. CLINTON-BADDELEY *To study Long Silence* ii. 72 In newspaper language..the man who is 'helping the police' is the chap who's being badgered into a confession. **1973** *Sunday Times* 14 Oct. 1/1 A 17-year-old girl..was found battered to death... Later, a man was helping police with their inquiries.

8. b. (Later examples.)

1919 V. WOOLF *Night & Day* xxxi. 2 She behaves very oddly. She forgets to help the pudding. **1938** M. K. RAWLINGS *Yearling* i. 11 Ma Baxter sat at the table waiting for them, helping their plates.

c. help-yourself, used *attrib.* esp. of a restaurant or cafeteria where one serves oneself, or of the meal obtained there; also as *sb.* Also *transf.*

1894 M. FRY *Let.* in E. H. Jones *Margery Fry* (1966) v. 37 Then at 1 is lunch..a help-yourself meal and you get up and come away as soon as you've done without waiting for anyone else. **1923** [see *CAFETERIA]. **1955** T. H. PEAR *Eng. Social Diff.* 183 The 'help yourself' cafeteria system. **1959** R. POSTGATE *Good Food Guide* 280 There is an à la carte menu and a 'help-yourself' lunch for the hasty at 6/6. **1961** *Times Lit. Suppl.* 13 Oct. 712/5 Up to a point he has invented the help-yourself novel. **1967** 'A. GILBERT' *Visitor* iii. 38, I got a cup of coffee and a sandwich at a help-yourself, and went back to the flat.

11. a. (Later example.)

1963 *Sunday Express* 3 Mar. 2/5 You are aware that the archdeacon swears that he never wears pyjamas?— I can't help that.

b. (Later examples.)

1928 *Manch. Guardian Weekly* 5 Oct. 263/4 If clairvoyants are to be attached to police stations they can hardly help but become officials. **1952** G. SARTON *Hist. Sci.* I. xxi. 526 They were brutally raped by conquistadors ..who could not help increase geographic knowledge.

help, *sb.* Add: **3. c.** (Further examples.)

1743 ELLIS *Mod. Husb.* III. II. 2 Next to them [*sc.* hired servants] we should be provided with auxiliary Helps. **1807** C. W. JANSON *Stranger in Amer.* 87, I am Mr —'s *help.* I'd have you know..that I am no *sarvant.* **1815** *Massachusetts Spy* 23 Aug. (Th.), Our lady and gentleman 'hired helps' do not understand who is meant when their master is inquired for. **1818** H. B. FEARON *Sk. Amer.* 80 Servants, let me here observe, are called 'helps'. If you call a servant by that name they leave you without notice. **1838** J. F. COOPER *Amer. Democrat* 122 Those who aid their masters in the toil may be deemed 'helps', but they who perform all the labor do not assist..but they do it themselves. **1899** *Westm. Gaz.* 4 Aug. 2/3 Judge: What is a 'help'? Plaintiff: Well, she's a cook-housemaid-barmaid. **1949** 'J. TEY' *Brat Farrar* xi. 84 Lana, their 'help'..'obliged' only because her 'boy friend' worked in the stables. **1971** [see *DAILY *a.* 1 b].

d. For *U.S.* read orig. *U.S.* Add examples.

1959 S. GIBBONS *Pink Front Door* xviii. 221 The months when she had been without help had established Molly's unexpected visits as a habit. **1962** P. MORTIMER *Pumpkin Eater* xi. 106 'We got help. I don't know why it's called help.' 'You mean servants?' 'We don't call them servants.'

7. *help-girl*; **help-mate** *Chess*, a type of chess problem in which Black is required to play so that White may give mate in a certain number of moves.

1863 MRS. GASKELL *Cousin Phillis* in *Cornhill Mag.* Nov. 633 Betty..carried off the great dish to the kitchen, where an old man..and a help-girl, were awaiting their meal. **1897** ROWLAND & ROWLAND *Problem Art* 91 Another class of problems..in which *both players concur* in endeavouring to effect the speediest mate—..which we term Help-mate Problems. **1913** A. C. WHITE *Sam Loyd* 31 Whether Loyd was the inventor of the Help-mate problem..I do not know. **1966** *New Statesman* 11 Nov. 718/3 'Help-mate'..Black moves first and helps White to mate in a given number of moves.

helpable. (Earlier example.)

1833 J. S. MILL *Lett.* (1910) I. 48, I believe I am the least *helpable* of mortals.

helped (helpt), *ppl. a.* [f. HELP *v.* + -ED[1].] That has been helped, aided, or assisted. Also with advs., as *helped-out.*

1905 *Daily Chron.* 15 May 3/5 The dowagers of to-day, with their helped-out complexions and Venetian red hair. **1910** E. M. ALBANESI *For Love of Anne Lambart* 104 But this is no helped success, this is real.

helter-skelter. Add: **C.** *sb.* **b.** (Also *helter-skelter lighthouse.*) A tower-like structure used in fun fairs and pleasure-grounds, with an external spiral passage for sliding down on a mat.

1906 *Westm. Gaz.* 1 June 10/2 The World's Manufacturing Company, examples of whose 'helter-skelter' lighthouses are at Earl's Court, Blackpool, Southport, and other places. **1907** *Daily Chron.* 4 Sept. 2/7 All sorts of fearsome things..from a helter-skelter..to a smashing saloon and a 'coker nut' alley. **1927** *Sunday Express* 5 June 4 They will travel on the merry-go-rounds... They will go down with the mats on the helter-skelter, and up with the swings. **1945** G. MILLAR *Maquis* i. 8, I began to feel that I was sitting on a mat on top of a helter-skelter. That somebody would give me a push and I would be away with..nobody at the bottom to pick me up. **1968** D. BRAITHWAITE *Fairground Archit.* 24 Vertical features like the 'Big Wheel', 'Helter Skelter' and 'Chair-o-Planes'..are valuable advertising symbols.

helvellic (helveˈlik), *a.* [tr. G. *helvellasäure* helvellic acid (Boehm & Külz 1885, in *Arch. f. exper. Path. u. Pharm.* XIX. 414), f. mod.L. *Helvella*, a genus of ascomycetous fungi: see -IC.] *helvellic acid*, a poisonous acid, $C_{12}H_{20}O_7$, present in some fungi of the sub-family Helvellæ.

1906 H. B. SHAW in Allbutt & Rolleston *Syst. Med.* (ed. 2) II. I. 871 Helvellic acid and extracts of the Helvella produce nausea, vomiting, hæmoglobinuria, icterus,.. and uræmia. **1947** F. A. & F. T. WOLF *Fungi* II. xv. 351 There occurs in *Helvella esculenta* a water-soluble, heat-labile, hemolytic principle that has been identified as helvellic acid, $C_{12}H_{20}O_7$. **1953** J. RAMSBOTTOM *Mushrooms & Toadstools* vi. 54 *Gyromitra esculenta, Helvella crispa*..and several other Discomycetes contain helvellic acid, which has a strong dissolving action on the red corpuscles of the blood.

helvetium (helvīˈʃiǝm). *Chem.* [ad. G. *helvetium* (W. Minder 1940, in *Helvetica Physica Acta* XIII. 152), f. mod.L. *Helvet(ia* Switzerland + -IUM.] Earlier name for *ASTATINE. Cf. also *ALABAMINE and *ANGLO-HELVETIUM. (*Disused.*)

1940 *Times* 13 Aug. 3/2 The Swiss scientist, Dr. W. Minder, of Berne University, has now succeeded in isolating element '85', which, in honour of his Fatherland, he has named 'Helvetium'. He has proved that 'Helvetium' is produced in small quantity from the decomposition of actinium, which is radio-active.

helvolic (helvǫˈlik), *a.* *Biochem.* [f. mod.L. *helvola* yellowish, the name of the mutant variety of fungus, characterized by its buff colour, from which the acid was first isolated: see -IC.] *helvolic acid*, an antibiotic with the probable formula $C_{32}H_{42}O_8$ produced by some strains of the fungus *Aspergillus fumigatus.* Also called *fumigacin.*

1943 E. CHAIN et al. in *Brit. Jrnl. Exper. Path.* XXIV. 119 A new antibiotic has been isolated in the crystalline state from culture filtrates of *Aspergillus fumigatus*, mut. *helvola* Yuill. It has been named helvolic acid. **1944** *Jrnl. Bacteriol.* XLVII. 392 Helvolic acid is apparently identical with the fumigacin from which the gliotoxin fraction has been removed. **1949** H. W. FLOREY et al. *Antibiotics* i. 66 Helvolic acid..had some protective action against streptococcal infection in mice, but its other properties made it unsuitable for use in man. **1953** J. RAMSBOTTOM *Mushrooms & Toadstools* xxiii. 289 Fumigacin (helvolic acid) produced by *Aspergillus fumigatus* has all the necessary qualities except that bacteria readily acquire resistance to it. **1965** P. K. C. AUSTWICK in Raper & Fennell *Genus Aspergillus* vii. 106 *Aspergillus fumigatus* is known to produce three antibiotics that are toxic to experimental animals: fumigatin,..helvolic acid,..and gliotoxin.

helxine (helksəiˈni, helzəiˈni). *Bot.* [mod.L. (E. Requien 1825, in *Annales des Sciences Naturelles* V. 384), f. Gr. ἑλξίνη pellitory, a related plant.] *Soleirolia soleirolii*, a creeping, perennial herb of the family Urticaceæ, native to Corsica and Sardinia, formerly called by the generic name *Helxine.*

1873 MRS. HOOKER tr. *Le Maout & Decaisne's Gen. Syst. Bot.* II. 667 Flowers [of Urticaceæ]..very rarely solitary and axillary (*Helxine*). **1924** L. H. BAILEY *Man. Cultivated Plants* 241 Helxine..making a matted moss-like covering. **1964** M. FISH *Ground Cover Plants* v. 44 If one happened to have a dark, dank courtyard which needed the softening influence of tender green, nothing could be more charming than helxine. **1969** O. POLUNIN *Flowers of Europe* 58 *Soleirolia soleirolii*..(*Helxine*).. Native of Mediterranean islands; naturalized in Western Europe.

hem, *sb.*[1] Add: **5.** *Comb.* **hem-line,** the outline of the hem, hence the height from the ground, of a woman's skirt.

1923 *T. Eaton & Co. Catal.* Spring & Summer 34 The modish uneven hemline. **1927** *Vanity Fair* Sept. 4/3 Liberty of opinion, in skirt lengths, hemlines, waistlines, ..was convincingly demonstrated. **1929** *Daily Tel.* 16 Jan. 8/4 It is admitted that the hem lines of 1928 changed the whole contour of the evening mode as they flounced and floated in uneven length to the ground. **1957** *New Yorker* 30 Mar. 98/3 This year, she puts a minute and completely absurd circular godet, only three inches deep, at the hemline in front—to allow for striding, they say. **1958** *T.V. Times* 10 Oct. 21/2 Other girls put up their hem-lines a couple of inches as Paris dictates. **1971** R. Garrett *Spiral* x. 94 She fidgeted with the hemline of her skirt.

he-man: see *HE *pers. pron.* 8 a.

heme, var. *HÆM.

hemera² (heˑmĕră). *Palæont.* and *Geol.* Pl. **-æ.** [mod.L., f. Gr. ἡμέρα day.] A period of geological time in which any particular species was most abundant as represented in strata; an interval between times when two successive species were dominant. Hence **heˑmeral** *a.*

1893 S. S. Buckman in *Q. Jrnl. Geol. Soc.* XLIX. 481 For a palaeontological purpose... I propose the term 'hemera'... I wish to use it as the chronological indicator of the faunal sequence. **1898** —— *Ibid.* LIV. 443 The hemeral names are taken from the names of ammonites. *Ibid.*, The shortest geological time-division is a hemera: that is, the time during which a particular species..had dominant existence. *Ibid.* 448 The genera *Dactylioceras* and its allies..almost disappear with the close of the hemera *bifrontis.* **1902** —— in *Geol. Mag.* Dec. 555 A 'hemera' was designed to mark the time from..when one species or set of species becomes dominant to the time when another..does so. **1920** *Q. Jrnl. Geol. Soc.* LXXVI. 63 The range of strata which Mr. Richardson has divided into seven or at the most eight hemeræ cover, according to my more detailed subdivisions, thirty-two hemeræ, and should afford a good test as to whether this more detailed method of dating makes for greater precision. **1933** W. J. Arkell *Jurassic Syst. Gt. Brit.* i. 20 Nine years later, finding that there were still some who considered that a hemera was simply a subdivision of a zone, Buckman published a fresh explanation. *Ibid.* 27 In the course of an argument with Buckman over his insertion of an excessive number of hemeræ into the time-table of the Corallian rocks, I attempted to justify my view..that many of his hemeral indices lived side by side on the same sea-bed. **1966** D. T. Donovan *Stratigr.* vii. 160 Several other time terms have been proposed but have never achieved general recognition. Perhaps the most notorious is the *hemera.* *Ibid.* 161 Hemerae were much used by English Jurassic workers for about forty years, but hardly at all by anyone else.

hemerocallis. For etym. and def. read: [mod.L., ad. L. *hemerocalles*, Gr. ἡμεροκαλλές a kind of lily, f. Gr. ἡμέρα day + κάλλος beauty, adopted by Linnæus in his *Hortus Cliffortianus* (1737) 128 as the name of a genus.] A herbaceous perennial plant of the genus so called, belonging to the family Liliaceæ, mostly native to temperate, eastern Asia, and bearing corymbs of yellow or orange, trumpet-shaped, short-lived flowers; a Day-lily. (Later examples.)

1900 L. H. Bailey *Cycl. Amer. Hort.* II. 728/1 The flowers of Funkia are borne in racemes; of Hemerocallis in corymb-like panicles. **1938** F. Perry *Water Gardening* xvi. 271 Hemerocallis have some economic qualities, for in the Orient the flower petals are gathered. **1970** *Observer* 23 Aug. 25/4 In the Orient hemerocallis flowers are often used for food.

hemi-. Add: **hemi-aˑcetal** *Chem.*, any of a class of compounds having the general formula R·CH(OH)(OR′), differing from an acetal in having an -OH group in place of one of the -OR groups; **he:miamblyoˑpia** *Ophthalm.*, amblyopia of half of the field of vision; hence **he:miamblyoˑpic**, one suffering from hemiamblyopia; **he:miangiocaˑrpic, -caˑrpous** *adjs.*, designating a fungus in which the hymenium is enclosed during the early part of its development; characteristic of such a fungus; **he:micoleˑctomy** *Surg.*, excision of part of the colon, *esp.* of the right or left half; **hemidemisemiquaver** (later example); **hemihydrate** (examples); **hemihypeˑrtrophy**, unilateral or partial hypertrophy; **hemikaˑryon** *Cytol.* [a. G. *hemikaryon* (T. Boveri 1905, in *Jenaische Zeitschr. f. Naturwiss.* XXXIX. 447), f. Gr. κάρυον: see Karyo-] (see quot.); so **he:mikaryoˑtic** *a.*; **hemimeˑllit(h)ene, -ine** *Chem.* = *trimethylbenzine*; **hemiobole:** also **hemiobol;** **hemipaˑrasite** *Bot.* [G. (F. Johow 1890, in *Verhandl. Deutsch. Wissensch. Ver. Santiago* II. ii. 67)], a facultative parasite, e.g. certain fungi; also a plant which is partially parasitic, drawing water and mineral nutrients but not synthesized foods from its host, e.g. certain higher plants, as the mistletoe; hence **he:miparasiˑtic** *a.*; **hemiparesis** (examples); **hemipeˑnis** *Zool.*, one of the paired eversible copulatory organs in snakes and lizards; **hemisaˑprophyte** *Bot.* [ad. G. *hemisaprophyt* (F. Johow 1889, in *Jahrb. f. wissensch. Bot.* XX. 479)], a facultative saprophyte, being alternatively either parasitic or autotrophic; hence **he:misaprophyˑtic** *a.*

1893 *Jrnl. Chem. Soc.* LXIV. i. 563 (*heading*) Hemi-acetals derived from substituted chloranils. **1964** N. G. Clark *Mod. Org. Chem.* xiv. 273 Hemi-acetals are generally unstable intermediates in the formation of true acetals. **1890** W. James *Princ. Psychol.* I. ii. 44 According to Loeb, the defect is a dimness of vision ('hemiamblyopia') in which (however severe) the centres remain the best seeing portions of the retina. **1947** F. B. Walsh *Clin. Neuro-Ophthalm.* i. 56/1 Along with hemiamblyopia, hemiachromatopsia is evidence for early and partial involvement of the primary visual pathways. **1960** H.-L. Teuber et al. *Visual Field Defects* vi. 64 (*caption*) The hemiamblyopia was more disturbing to this patient than an outright hemianopia. **1933** *Mind* XLII. 386 In hemiamblyopics there is a tendency for a displacement, towards the sound side, of stimuli falling on the amblyopic area. **1902** *Encycl. Brit.* XXVIII. 558/2 Gymnocarpic and Hemiangiocarpic:—*Hymenomycetes.* **1900** B. D. Jackson *Gloss. Bot. Terms, Hemiangiocarpous*, when the hymenium of some Fungi is for some time covered with a membrane, the gonidiophore is so termed. **1902** *Encycl. Brit.* XXVIII. 561/1 The Discomycetes and their immediate allies are termed Hemiangiocarpous, because however much their fructifications are closed at first, they ultimately open and expose the layers of asci. **1928** C. W. Dodge tr. *Gäumann's Compar. Morphol. Fungi* xxv. 410 In the second, or hemiangiocarpous, stage.. the sporiferous tissue is differentiated from the tissue in the interior of the fundaments. **1967** M. E. Hale *Biol. Lichens* ii. 32 Henssen has recently traced consistent hemiangiocarpous development in a group of genera. **1926** R. J. E. Scott *Gould's Med. Dict.* 596/1 Hemicolectomy. **1963** *Lancet* 19 Jan. 133/1 A man, aged 53, had had right hemicolectomy performed eight months previously on account of carcinoma of the cæcum. **1959** D. Cooke *Lang. Mus.* iii. 133 A bass of rushing hemi-demi-semi-quavers. **1909** Webster, Hemihydrate. **1946** *Nature* 6 July 13/2 Calcium sulphate exists in three states of hydration, anhydrite, gypsum, and the lower hydrate, generally known as hemihydrate or plaster of Paris. **1965** *New Scientist* 18 Mar. 709/2 Gypsum is calcined to form the hemi-hydrate which sets after wetting to re-form gypsum. **1900** Dorland *Med. Dict.* 294/1 Hemihypertrophy. **1922** *Proc. R. Soc. Med.* XV Child. 51 Forty cases..of complete hemihypertrophy where all the structures on one side of the body were involved. **1964** S. Duke-Elder *Syst. Ophthalm.* III. xvii. 1028 Facial hemihypertrophy is a much rarer condition which may involve the whole of one side of the body. **1925** E. B. Wilson *Cell* (ed. 3) 1132 *Hemikaryon*, a nucleus containing the haploid number of chromosomes. *Ibid.* ix. 728 (*caption*) Karyoplasmic relation in embryos of the sea-urchin..stage of haploid (hemikaryotic) dwarf, from merogonic egg-fragment. **1889** Muir & Morley *Watts' Dict. Chem.* (rev. ed.) 671/1 *Hemimellithene*,..formed by distilling (*a*)-cuminic acid with lime. *Ibid.*, Hemimellithene may also be isolated from coal-tar oil. **1956** *Nature* 18 Feb. 301/2 The great variety of organic compounds contained in this latest issue [of a text-book] may be indicated by mentioning azelanitrile,..hemimellitine, [etc.]. **1921** *Brit. Mus. Return* 81 A gold hemiobol of the fourth century B.C. **1941** *Antiquity* XV. 302 Issues of tetrobols and hemiobols. **1891** *Jrnl. R. Microsc. Soc.* 70 Each of these classes, except the last, may be again divided into Holoparasites and Hemiparasites. **1900** B. D. Jackson *Gloss. Bot. Terms* 120/1 *Hemiparasite*, a facultative saprophyte, a parasite which can exist as a saprophyte. **1927** Hemiparasite [see *facultative *a.* 1 c]. **1960** N. Polunin *Introd. Plant Geogr.* xiv. 437 There are..two main synusiae in the tropical rain forest—the root-parasites growing on the ground..and the semi-parasites (often termed hemi-parasites) growing epiphytically on the trees. **1970** *Nature* 21 Mar. 1162/1 Annual hemiparasites characteristically form haustorial connexions (root grafts) with most of the plants that surround them. **1902** *Encycl. Brit.* XXV. 439/2 Loranthaceæ and Santalaceæ are chiefly hemiparasitic. **1970** *Nature* 21 Mar. 1161/2 The hemiparasitic flowering plants that live in annual grasslands are of special interest. **1893** *Funk's Stand. Dict.*, Hemiparesis. **1952** M. E. Florey *Clin. Appl. Antibiotics* ii. 37 One patient developed hemiparesis and prolonged convulsions. **1909** Webster, Hemipenis. **1913** G. A. Boulenger *Snakes of Europe* ix. 83 Each hemipenis is lodged in a cavity on each side of the base of the tail. **1965** R. & D. Morris *Men & Snakes* viii. 190 Male snakes possess two hemipenes. Only one hemipenis is inserted at a time and apparently males do not switch from one to the other during the same mating bout. **1895** *Ann. Bot.* IX. 337 The structure of the stele in absorbing rhizome-axes of hemi- and holo-saprophytes is frequently remarkably like that of a root. **1900** B. D. Jackson *Gloss. Bot. Terms* 120/2 *Hemisaprophyte*, a facultative parasite. **1909** Groom & Balfour tr. *Warming's Oecology of Plants* ii. xxv. 90 *Hemisaprophytes* have the external appearance and structure of normal plants. **1927** Hemisaprophyte [see *facultative *a.* 1 c]. **1895** *Ann. Bot.* IX. 337, I have already shown that in a hemisaprophytic Orchid (*Corysanthes*) there is an atrophy in the leaves of the absorbing rhizome.

hemianopia (he:miănōˑpiă). *Ophthalm.* [mod. L., f. Hemi- + Gr. ἀν priv. + -ωπία sight.] = Hemianopsia. Hence **hemianoˑpic** *a.*, of, pertaining to, or characterized by hemianopia; also as *sb.*, a person with hemianopia.

1882 *Ophthalmic Rev.* I. 253 The more exactly the cause of a homonymous hemianopia can be localised in the cortex of one occipital lobe, the more improbable becomes the theory of Charcot and Landolt. **1889** G. A. Berry *Dis. Eye* xi. 340 Hemianopia may be to the right or left, and partial or complete. *Ibid.* 341 Ferrier's experiments, which led him to localise the visual centres in the angular gyri, have given rise to the hemianopic symptoms. **1891** F. Taylor *Man. Pract. Med.* (ed. 2) 161 A transient hemianopia may occur in cerebral hæmorrhage. **1898** *Nature* 13 Jan. 255/1 Hallucinations connected with hemianopia. **1908** *Practitioner* Oct. 558 Hysterical hemianopia. **1943** *Mind* LII. 363 This seems ruled out by the experiments of Gelb and Goldstein on hemianopics, who saw a field of vision of the normal shape, though the receptive area had been severely damaged. **1964** S. Duke-Elder *Parsons' Dis. Eye* (ed. 14) iv. 37 A lesion in the optic tract will produce a hemianopic reaction involving both eyes. **1966** D. G. Cogan *Neurol. Visual Syst.* xiv. 265 The most common complaint of patients with hemianopia, aside from collision with objects on the blind side, is the difficulty with reading.

hemianopsia. Add: (Earlier and later examples.) Also **hemianopsy.**

1883 *Ophthalmic Rev.* II. 82 The above named recent works on hemianopsia and the decussation of the optic nerve contain much of interest. **1884** *Encycl. Brit.* XVII. 785/1 Hemianopsia means loss of one-half of the visual field. **1908** *Practitioner* Jan. 15 Attacks of aphasia, monoplegias, hemiplegias, word-blindness, and word-deafness, or hemianopsy. **1962** L. S. Sasieni *Optical Dispensing* viii. 200 Hemianopsia spectacles.

hemicellulose (hemiseˑliulōus). [a. G. *hemicellulose* (E. Schulze 1891, in *Ber. d. Deut. Chem. Ges.* XXIV. 2286), f. Hemi- + Cellulose *sb.*] Any of various non-cellulosic polysaccharides, of simpler composition than cellulose, that are major constituents of the cell walls of many plants and are characterized by undergoing hydrolysis by acids more readily than cellulose to give a variety of simple sugars and other carbohydrates and by being extractable with dilute alkaline solutions.

1891 *Jrnl. Chem. Soc.* LX. 1179 Those constituents of the cell which dissolve easily in dilute mineral acids, with formation of glucose, he [*sc.* E. Schulze] calls hemicelluloses. **1921** A. L. Smith *Lichens* v. 212 In *Cladonia rangiferina*..the cell-membranes of the hyphae contained, as hemicelluloses, pentosans in small quantities and galactan. **1948** *New Biol.* IV. 87 Interspersed in the meshes of the cellulose, which constitutes approximately 50 per cent of the weight of the dry wood, are a number of other substances which apparently serve to stiffen the framework, principally hemicelluloses..and the more complex carbohydrate lignin. **1963** R. R. A. Higham *Handbk. Papermaking* ii. 33 Hemi-celluloses are found in two main groups, i.e., those associated mainly with the plant cellulose and centred largely in the structure of the fibre and those associated with lignin, in the middle lamella and primary walls of fibres. *Ibid.*, The presence of hemi-celluloses in papermaking pulps is very important, as they assist in internal fibrillation of the fibres, but owing to their short chain structure they easily become broken down during digestion and are lost in the form of by-products.

hemicryptophyte (hemikriˑptofəit). *Bot.* [ad. Da. *hemikryptofyte* (C. Raunkiaer 1904, in *Bot. Tidsskrift* XXVI, p. xiv), f. Hemi- + Crypto-: see -phyte.] (See quot. 1932.) Also *attrib.* Hence **he:micryptophyˑtic** *a.*

1913 *Jrnl. Ecol.* I. 24 The *Anemone nemorosa* facies of the beech-wood is geophytic since the 0·1 sq. m. readings show geophytes 82 per cent., hemicryptophytes 18 per cent. *Ibid.* 25 The contrast between spruce hemicryptophytic wood and beech geophytic wood. **1932** Fuller & Conard tr. *Braun-Blanquet's Plant Sociol.* xii. 291 Hemicryptophytes..plants with perennial shoots and buds close to the earth's surface. **1938** J. R. Carpenter *Ecol. Gloss.* 130 *Hemicryptophyte climate*, the climate of the greater part of the cold temperate zone. **1964** V. J. Chapman *Coastal Veget.* vi. 150 A hemicryptophyte flora.

hemicyclic, *a.* (Later example.)

1878 [see Acyclic *a.*].

heˑmi-de:mi-seˑmi: used as adj. and sometimes as a combining form in imitation of the use in *hemidemisemiquaver* (s.v. Hemi-).

1929 J. Laird *Idea of Value* ix. 302 Even believers in the 'unconscious'..seem commonly to hold that the 'unconscious' is at least hemi-demi-semi conscious. **1958** *Spectator* 3 Jan. 14/3 What is the point of ideological compromises and hemi-demi-semi pro-Soviet hedging? **1965** O. Barfield in J. Gibb *Light on C. S. Lewis* p. xiii, Hemi-demi-semitone of alteration in the pitch of his voice.

hemidesmus (hemideˑsmɒ̆s). *Bot.* [mod.L. (R. Brown, 1809) f. Hemi- + Gr. δεσμός bond; so named in allusion to the incomplete coherence of the anthers with the stigma.] A small, swimming herb of the genus so named, belonging to the family Asclepiadaceæ, and native to India and Ceylon; *esp.* a plant of *Hemidesmus indicus*, the root of which is used as a substitute for sarsaparilla; also, a syrup prepared therefrom. Hence **hemideˑsmic** *a.*

1809 R. Brown in *Mem. Wernerian Nat. Hist. Soc.* I. 56 Hemidesmus..whose name is derived from the partial connection of the stamina, is composed of *Periploca Indica*, and two very nearly related unpublished species. **1844** *Pharm. Jrnl.* III. 239 The root of hemidesmus indicus has for some years been sold in this

country under the name of Smilax Aspera. **1880** Garrod & Baxter *Mat. Med.* 311 Hemidesmus Root.. It.. contains a peculiar volatile, crystallizable substance, with acid properties: this has been called hemidesmic acid. **1898** *Revised Brit. Pharmacop.* 4 The retention of hemidesmus is noteworthy, and a tribute to the St. Bartholomew's school of physic. **1968** D. C. Gunawardena *Genera et Species Plantarum Zeylaniae* 122 Hemidesmus... Anther connective prolonged, covering over stigma.

hemimorphite. (In Dict. s.v. Hemimorphic *a.*) Add: Now generally used in place of earlier names such as *calamine*. (Examples.)

1868 J. D. Dana *Syst. Min.* (ed. 5) v. 409 Unfortunately, Brooke & Miller, in 1852, reversed Beudant's use of these names [sc. *calamine* and *smithsonite* for the silicate and carbonate of zinc], with no good reason; and in 1853, Kenngott, on account of the confusion of names, as he says, introduced for the silicate the new name *Hemimorphite*, and so added to the confusion. **1910** *Encycl. Brit.* VII. 583/1 Two hemihedral or hemimorphic crystals (e.g. of diamond or of hemimorphite) are often united in twinned positions. **1951** A. N. & H. Winchell *Elem. Optical Mineral.* (ed. 4) II. x. 482 Hemimorphite is found in veins with smithsonite and sphalerite.

hemin, var. Hæmin.

1955 *Sci. News Let.* 29 Oct. 274/1 Hemin, a chemical related to the red color chemical of blood, and protein. **1963** *New Scientist* 25 July 182 Biliverdin is formed by biological degradation of the red blood pigment hemin.

Hemingwayesque (he:miŋwēˌe·sk), *a.* [f. the name of Ernest *Hemingway* (1898–1961), American novelist + -esque.] Characteristic of the works of E. Hemingway. So **He:mingwa·yan** *a.*; **He:mingwaye·se**; **He·mingwayish** *a.*

1942 H. Haycraft *Murder for Pleasure* viii. 171 Hemingwayesque courage and fatalism. **1957** J. Kerouac *On Road* (1958) vii. 41 Composing his latest Hemingwayan short story. **1959** *Times Lit. Suppl.* 4 Sept. 505/3 His father, a Hemingwayish figure. **1964** *Listener* 28 May 882/2 Plain unvarnished Hemingwayese looks decidedly mannered. **1970** *English Studies* LI. 491 In *Ernest Hemingway, A Life Story*..Carlos Baker has adopted his subject's deliberately simple declarative style. The opening and closing of the book are archly Hemingwayesque; some parts of the 640 pages that come between are simply Hemingwayese.

hemiopia. Add: So **hemio·pic** *a.*

1873 *Arch. Sci. & Pract. Med.* I. 293 (*title*) Hemiopic and sector-like defects in the field of vision. **1890** W. James *Princ. Psychol.* I. ii. 42 A hemiopic disturbance of vision is one in which neither retina is affected in its totality, but in which, for example, the left portion of *each* retina is blind, so that the animal sees nothing situated in space towards its right.

hemiplegic, *a.* Add: Also *sb.*, one who is affected by hemiplegia (see also quot. 1970).

1890 *Retrospect Med.* CII. 155 Convalescent hemiplegics. **1970** *New Scientist* 3 Sept. 473/1 It would enable amputees and hemi-plegics—persons paralyzed below the waist—to walk about under their own power.

hemispherectomy (he:misfere·ktŏmi). *Surg.* [f. Hemispher(e 5 + *-ectomy.] Excision of a cerebral hemisphere.

1950 *Jrnl. Neurol. & Psychiatry* XIII. 243/1 Over a period of five years..12 hemispherectomies were performed on patients suffering from infantile hemiplegia. *Ibid.* 263/1 Because of the ventricular distortion, hemispherectomy was carried out. **1956** E. L. Mascall *Christ. Theol. & Nat. Sci.* vi. 252 There are no *theoretical* problems for Christian faith..in the remarkable psychological effects of operations such as pre-frontal leucotomy, lobotomy and hemispherectomy.

hemistich. Add: *spec.* such a half-line or line in Old English verse.

1823 J. Bosworth *Elem. Anglo-Saxon Gram.* 246 The question, as to whether the two hemistichs shall be regarded as one or two lines, is evidently that of a writer or printer, not of a singer or reciter. **1857** C. Patmore in *North Brit. Rev.* XXVII. 148 Each hemistich contains two accented syllables. **1888** A. S. Cook *Judith* p. l, The line of poetry consists of two hemistichs, separated by the cæsura. **1925** M. D. Clubb *Christ & Satan* p. xv, The mark most consistently..employed is the metrical point, indicating the pause between hemistichs. **1970** *Jrnl. Eng. & Gmc. Philol.* LXIX. 86 One would not expect *þā* to provide the only alliteration in the second hemistich.

hemixis (hemi·ksis). *Biol.* Also **hemimixis.** [f. Hemi- + Gr. μίξις mixing, f. μ(ε)ίγνυμι to mix: see Mixo-.] In *Paramecium*, any of several types of change in the macronucleus, such as fission or elimination of chromatin, which take place without involving the micronucleus. So **hemi·ctic** *a.*, of, pertaining to, or characterized by hemixis.

1936 W. F. Diller in *Jrnl. Morphol.* LIX. 18 The attempt at interpreting the varied cytological conditions which P. aurelia exhibits under different circumstances has led to the discovery of a hitherto undescribed sexual reproductive process which corresponds to autogamy as it is known in other animals, and to a group of asexual phenomena which will be called 'hemixis'. *Ibid.* 36 It is proposed to group these reorganizations together.. and refer to them collectively by the term 'hemixis'. By this term is meant a series of autonomous changes which the macronucleus undergoes in vegetative life, exclusive of binary fission. *Ibid.*, No genetic relationships are necessarily implied between the varieties of hemictic phenomena. **1940** L. H. Hyman *Invertebrates* I. iii. 176 In hemimixis the macronucleus undergoes degenerative changes. **1953** R. Wichterman *Biol. Paramecium* iii. 90/2 Hemictic animals with the two micronuclei may show variable numbers and sizes of macronuclear fragments. **1961** Mackinnon & Hawes *Introd. Study Protozoa* iv. 292 A variety of nuclear changes may occur [in *Paramecium*] without the intervention of a micronucleus; they are collectively known as hemixis..and their significance is uncertain.

hemizygous (hemizəi·gəs), *a. Biol.* [f. Hemi- + *homo)zygous *a.*] Having a single unpaired allele at a particular genetic locus, as at all the loci in an XO pair of sex-chromosomes and some of the loci in an XY pair, rather than having two paired alleles, one on each homologous chromosome, as normally occurs in a diploid. So **hemizy·gote**, a hemizygous organism; **hemizygo·tic** *a.*, hemizygous; **hemizy·gously** *adv.*, in a manner characteristic of a hemizygote.

1921 W. A. Lippincott in *Amer. Naturalist* LV. 570, I should like to suggest the noun *hemizeuxis* (a half yoking) and the corresponding adjective *hemizygous* (half yoked). Should such a suggestion prove acceptable there would be the three adjective series: homozygous, heterozygous, and hemizygous, referring to the three possible conditions with respect to any single gene, namely, 'like mates', 'differing mates', and 'no mate'. **1935** H. J. Muller in *Jrnl. Genetics* XXX. 407 The terms 'hemizygous' and 'hemizygote' (Serebrovsky) refer to the condition of being haploid for a given gene when the genome as a whole is diploid; its usual usage is in connection with sex-linked genes in the sex in which they are haploid. *Ibid.*, The normal gene, although apparently quite dominant to white and to the other mutants, must in reality be incompletely so, and the heterozygotes, being like uncompensated hemizygotes, must have a definitely lower average survival rate. **1939** C. H. Waddington *Introd. Mod. Genetics* ii. 62 Muller has suggested that it would be better to speak of factors in haploid organisms such as male bees as hemizygous; and this word can also be used for factors (e.g. in an unpaired *X* chromosome) for which there is no allelomorph in a normal diploid. **1961** *Lancet* 16 Sept. 626/2 In a hemizygous XO female, a recessive gene could express itself as in a heterozygous XY male. **1965** J. A. Serra *Mod. Genetics* I. iv. 103 The genes for haemophilia and for colour-blindness have no allele in the Y chromosome, that is the males are hemizygotic for these factors. *Ibid.* 109 The yellow-black pair of alleles in cats producing either yellow or black hemizygous males but giving patched black and yellow or 'tortoise-shell' females when these are heterozygous. *Ibid.* 111 Such a character is transmitted from father to son and because there is no corresponding allele in the X chromosome, it manifests itself hemizygously.

hemlock, *sb.* Add: **2.** (Later examples.)

1927 M. de la Roche *Jalna* xviii. 213 She stood.. looking at the sombre shapes of the hemlocks. **1932** *Atlantic Monthly* Mar. 331/2 We come to that hidden glade, under the beeches, under the hemlocks.

hemlock (he·mlǫk), *v.* [f. the sb.] *trans.* To poison with hemlock. Hence **he·mlocked** *ppl. a.*

1846 Thackeray *Cornhill to Cairo* v. 66 Of the race of Englishmen who come wondering about the tomb of Socrates, do you think the majority would not have voted to hemlock him? **1908** L. Abercrombie *Interludes & Poems* 18 The slave Fate who serves Gods..fetched Skill'd poison,..and with this stew Hemlock'd the wine of Heaven. **1934** Dylan Thomas *Let.* 11 May (1966) 129 A twisted veil of evil..coils up from the pit to the top of the hemlocked world.

hemming, *vbl. sb.*[1] Add: Also *hemming-in.*

1905 *Fabian News* Mar. 14/2 It is enacted that 'he who receives relief must submit to the hemmings in of his personal liberty which the law imposes'.

b. *attrib.*

1858 *U.S. Patent 21,355* (*title*) Improvement in hemming guides for sewing machines. *a* **1865** in M. Johnson *Amer. Advertising* (1960), Patent binding folders and hemming guides on hand. **1932** D. C. Minter *Mod. Needlecraft* 196/2 *For Machining Hems.*—Screw on the hemming foot in place of the presser foot. **1972** *Canad. Antiques Collector* Mar.–Apr. 32/2 A hemming bird, ornate and beautifully made..brought over..one hundred and fifty years ago from Scotland.

hemp-agrimony. (Earlier and later examples.)

1760 J. Lee *Introd. Bot.* 304 Hemp agrimony, Eupatorium. **1908** *Westm. Gaz.* 31 Aug. 2/3 Nature had.. enriched the banks with..meadow-sweet and hemp-agrimony. **1971** *Country Life* 17 June 1520/1 The muzzy mauve hemp-agrimony (*Eupatorium purpureum*).

hen, *sb.* Add: **1. b.** *like a hen with one chick*(*en*): indicating extreme solicitude or fussiness about a small matter; (*as*) *mad as a wet hen*: very angry; (*as*) *scarce* (occas. *rare*) *as hen's teeth* (orig. *U.S.*): very scarce.

1595 G. Delamothe *Treasure French Toung* 19 He is as busie as a henne that hath but one chicken. **1670** J. Ray *Coll. Eng. Prov.* 203 As busie as a hen with one chicken. **1732** T. Fuller *Gnomologia* 25 As busy as a Hen with one Chick. **1823** J. Doddridge *Logan* 42 Every body that was not ax'd was mad as a wet hen. **1854** A. E. Baker *Gloss. Northampt.* I. 320 'As busy as a hen with one chick.' Unnecessarily solicitous or active over trifles. **1858** in N. E. Eliason *Tarheel Talk* (1956) 276 As scarce as hen's teeth. **1863** 'E. Kirke' *Southern Friends* 250 [Horses are] scarcer than hen's teeth round here. **1881** A. Parker *Oxfordshire Words* (Suppl.) s.v., To be as busy as a hen with one chick is to make a great fuss over a little work. They also say 'as proud as a hen with one chick'. **1893** *Congress. Rec.* 2 Oct. 2044/1 North of Mason and Dixon's line, colored county officials are scarce as hen's teeth. **1904** E. F. Benson *Challoners* x, Karl is devoted to him, just like a beautiful old hen in spectacles with one chicken. **1907** *Amer. Mag.* Feb. 339/1 He just looked at me and then flounced out, mad as a wet hen. **1962** *Listener* 5 July 8/2 A good guide for Western leaders, among whom communiqués were 'as scarce as hens' teeth'. **1969** *Times* 12 June 3 (Advt.), Stoppages are as rare as hen's teeth.

4. (Earlier example.)

1747 H. Glasse *Art of Cookery* xxi. 164 Cock Lobster is known by the narrow back Part of the Tail... The Hen is soft, and the back of her Tail broader.

8. *hen-run, -yard; hen-brained, -headed, -housed, -toed* adjs.; **hen-and-egg**, used *attrib.* of the unresolvable problem of the 'first cause' (freq. in somewhat trivial contexts); cf. *chicken *sb.*[1] 6 b; **hen-cackle** *N.Z. slang* (see quots.); **hen-fruit** chiefly *U.S. slang*, eggs; also *hen's fruit*; **hen-party** (later example); **hen scratch** *U.S.*, 'a chicken feed made from grain for scattering in litter or on the ground to induce chickens to scratch' (*Dict. Americanisms*); **hen-scratch** *v.*, to scratch in the manner of a hen; also *transf.*; **hensure** *a.* [joc. formation after Cock-sure *a.*], = Cock-sure *a.* 5; so **he:nsu·reness.**

1931 A. L. Rowse *Politics & Younger Generation* 146 It is the old hen-and-egg argument, that there is no knowing which comes first. **1951** W. Empson *Struct. Complex Words* 436 But firstly, there is a typical hen-and-egg problem. *a* **1963** L. MacNeice *Astrology* (1964) ii. 39 The old hen-and-egg dilemma (did god or planet come first?). **1923** W. de la Mare *Riddle* 93 Poor hen-brained things, they came to be fed. **1965** A. Garner *Elidor* xix. 147 You landed us in enough trouble yesterday with your hen-brained ideas. **1939** J. Pascoe *Unclimbed N.Z.* ii. 33 All the lasting Alpine partnerships in Canterbury have been formed on the easy expeditions. 'Hen-cackles' we call these expeditions. **1941** Baker *N.Z. Slang* vi. 57 Hen-cackle..is applied by mountaineers to a mountain that is easy to climb. Doubtless there is a wider application of the term since a mere hen-cackle, a trifle, seems to have been the origin of the application. **1854** *Harper's Mag.* Jan. 280/2 A young lady is said to have asked a gentleman at the table of a hotel 'down East' to pass her the 'hen fruit'. She pointed to a plate of eggs. **1873** C. G. Leland *Egypt. Sketch-Bk.* 71 Their 'hen-fruit', as it is elegantly termed in America. **1887** *Boston Guide* (Farmer), If he confines his Hen Fruit to the vintage of '87. **1942** *Sunday Chron.* 1 Mar. 1/1 To him [*sc.* a ward-room steward] egg and bacon is 'hen's fruit and hog's body'. **1912** *Dialect Notes* III. 578 *Hen-headed*, brainless. 'That hen-headed cuss can't do anything you tell him.' **1938** A. H. Bill *Astrophel* iv. 76 Elizabeth, always short of money.., railed against the required outlay like a hen-headed housewife over a coal bill. **1960** *Farmer & Stockbreeder* 16 Feb. 152/1 A hen-housed average of 104·4 eggs per bird in 112 days. **1960** *Guardian* 15 Feb. 4/3 A hen-party can be a very pleasant, relaxing affair, particularly for the older woman. **1897** Hen-run [in Dict.]. **1929** J. B. Priestley *Good Companions* i. i. 20 He was now 'on his own' at Wabley, the proud proprietor of a large hen-run. **1887** V. Pyke *Hist. Early Gold Discoveries in Otago* 35 Peter was only *hen-scratching* on the edges of the creek. **1921** D. H. Lawrence *Sea & Sardinia* 267 It was a small, stony, hen-scratched place of poor people. **1931** *Daily News-Jrnl.* (Murfreesboro, Tenn.) 15 Apr. 4/2 Corn,..White oats,..Hen Scratch. **1957** V. J. Kehoe *Technique Film & T.V. Make-Up* vii. 86 Facial lining for old age and other character make-ups should not look like 'hen scratchings'. **1929** D. H. Lawrence *Assorted Articles* (1930) 72 There are the women who are cocksure, and the women who are hensure. *Ibid.* 76 The lovely henny surety, the hensureness which is the real bliss of every female, has been denied her. **1951** M. McLuhan *Mech. Bride* 64/1 The old age reserved for the hensure types. **1937** Partridge *Dict. Slang* 388 *Hen-toed*, with one's feet turned in as one walks. **1955** I. Peebles *Ashes* 36 He stands at the wicket rather hen-toed. **1816** M. L. Weems *Lett.* (1929) III. 166 Yr. Bible carts had been here as thick as weasels in a hen yard selling Bibles at nearly half price. **1876** *Scribner's Monthly* Apr. 813/2 The best places in which to look for Jacobean sideboards..are found to be the hen-yard. **1960** *Farmer & Stockbreeder* 2 Feb. 121/1 The breeders have been housed in the henyard previously used for layers.

hen and chickens. Add: **3.** The name of a children's game.

1894 A. B. Gomme *Trad. Games Eng. Scot. & Irel.* I. 201 Hen and Chicken... The game is played in the usual manner of 'Fox and Goose' games. One is chosen to be the Hen, and one to be the Fox. The rest are the Chickens. **1969** I. & P. Opie *Children's Games in Street & Playground* xi. 311 It was played..under the names 'Fox and Chickens'..and 'Hen and Chickens'.

hence, *sb. U.S.* [Hence *adv.* 3 b and 4 c.] **a.** The other world. **b.** The future.

1884 E. W. Nye *Baled Hay* 26 All-wool delaine that was worn by one who is now in the golden hence. **1904** F. Lynde *Grafters* xviii. 233 Now suppose you hint.. that more..developments may be safely predicted in the immediate hence.

hen-coop. Add: **b.** *attrib.*

1898 *Daily News* 28 Sept. 5/3 The huge hen-coop crinoline disfigured the women. **1937** E. SITWELL *I live under Black Sun* 296 There came a sound of crazy hen-coop laughter.

hendeca-. Add: **b.** *Organic Chem.* Occas. used in place of the synonymous and more usual prefix *undeca-* to denote the presence in a molecule of eleven carbon atoms, as in **he·ndecane**, undecane; **hendeco·ic acid**, undecoic acid.

1889 MUIR & MORLEY *Watts' Dict. Chem.* II. 673/1 n-*Hendecane* $C_{11}H_{24}$... Formed by the action of HI and phosphorus at 230° upon hendecoic (undecylic) acid. **1943** *Thorpe's Dict. Appl. Chem.* (ed. 4) VI. 204/1 (*heading*) Hendecoic acids (undecoic acids), $C_{11}H_{22}O_2$. **1960** *Handbk. Chem. Soc. Authors* iii. 49 Greek numeral roots are used, except that 9 (alone or in combination) is rendered by the Latin nona (not the Greek ennea) and 11 by the Latin undeca (not the Greek hendeca).

hen-egg. (Additional examples.)

1900 *Daily News* 23 July 5/1 When they [*sc.* hailstones] attain the size of hen-eggs..the matter is beyond a joke. **1961** *Ann. Reg. 1960* 508 The guaranteed prices for..hen eggs..were reduced.

heneicosane (henəi·kosēⁱn). *Chem.* Also **henicosane.** [f. Gr. ἑν-, εἷς one + εἴκοσι twenty + -ANE.] Any of the hydrocarbons of the paraffin series having twenty-one carbon atoms, *esp.* the unbranched isomer (n-*heneicosane*). Hence **heneicosa·nic, -cosano·ic, -coso·ic acid,** the saturated fatty acid, $C_{20}H_{41}COOH$, derived from *n*-heneicosane.

1889 MUIR & MORLEY *Watts' Dict. Chem.* II. 674/1 *Henicosane* $C_{21}H_{44}$... Formed by reduction of the dichloride..of the ketone. **1915** *Jrnl. Chem. Soc.* CVII. 738 Heneicosoic acid, $CH_3{\cdot}[CH_2]_{19}{\cdot}CO_2H$, is readily soluble in ether. **1924** *Jrnl. Biol. Chem.* LIX. 920 n-Heneicosanic Acid..melted at 75–76°C. **1945** A. N. SACHANEN *Chem. Const. Petroleum* iv. 232 The heneicosanes substituted in position 11 ($C_{10}H_{21}.CHR.C_{10}H_{21}$) have low melting points (below −7°C). **1951** KIRK & OTHMER *Encycl. Chem. Technol.* VI. 257 Heneicosanoic acid, $C_{21}H_{42}O_2$, has been reported to occur in Japanese wax and earth-nut oil, but the evidence presented indicates that it is not found in natural fats and waxes.

henge[2] (hendʒ). [f. STONE)HENGE.] **1.** In particular reference to the name *Stonehenge*: something 'hanging' or in suspense. **2.** *Archæol.* A term (first applied by T. D. Kendrick) for classes of monuments more or less akin to the stone circle of Stonehenge. Also *attrib.*

1740 W. STUKELEY *Stonehenge* ii. 8 Pendulous rocks are now called henges in Yorkshire, and I have been informed of another place there called Stonehenge, being natural rocks. So that I doubt not, Stonehenge in Saxon signifies the hanging stones. **1742** in Defoe *Tour Gt. Brit.* (ed. 3) I. v. 257 The present Name [*sc.* Stonehenge] is Saxon, tho' the Work is beyond all Comparison older, signifying a hanging Rod or Pole, *i.e.* a Gallows, from the hanging Parts, Architraves, or rather Imposts; and pendulous Rocks are still in Yorkshire called Henges. **1932** KENDRICK & HAWKES *Archæol. in Eng. & Wales* vii. 83 (*heading*) The 'henge' monuments. **1936** *Proc. Prehist. Soc.* II. 1 A new monument of the 'henge' class. **1951** *Field Archæol.* (*Ordnance Survey*) (ed. 3) 17 The critical event in the modern study of 'henges' was the discovery of the site known as 'Woodhenge' from the air, two miles east-north-east of Stonehenge... The term henge monument..is an unsatisfactory term since, on strict etymological grounds, it should only be applied to sites which contain a 'hanging' element like the lintels of Stonehenge. **1967** *Antiquaries Jrnl.* XLVII. 166 The term 'henge' is applied to those monuments which enclose a circular or oval area by means of a bank and *internal* ditch and which possess one or two opposed entrances (Atkinson, Piggott, and Sandars, 1951, p. 82).

hen-hawk. (Earlier examples.)

1806 W. CLARK in Lewis & Clark *Orig. Jrnls.* (1905) IV. 131, I have observed..a hawk of an intermediate size with a long tail and blewish coloured wings, remarkably swift in flight and very ferce. Sometimes called in the Un. States the hen Hawk. **1819** D. THOMAS *Trav. W. Country* 210 The Hen-Hawk is not very numerous.

hen-house. Add: **b.** *fig.* A house or establishment inhabited chiefly by women.

1785 GROSE *Dict. Vulg. T., Hen house,* a house where the woman rules. **1931** W. FAULKNER *Sanctuary* xxi. 193 She's got two daughters... I'm heading for the hen-house. **1963** P. MOYES *Murder à la Mode* ii. 29 'You know what this place is, don't you, sir?' The sergeant was plunged in gloom. 'Fashion magazine. Ruddy hen-house.'

henid (he·nid). *Philos.* [ad. G. *henide,* coined by Weininger on the basis of Gr. ἑν- one; cf. HENISM.] In the philosophy of Otto Weininger (1880–1903): see quots. Hence **heni·dical** *a.*

1906 tr. *O. Weininger's Sex & Character* II. iii. 99, I propose for psychical data at this earliest stage of their existence the word Henid (from the Greek ἕν, because in them it is impossible to distinguish perception and sensation as two analytically separable factors, and because, therefore, there is no trace of duality in them)... The very idea of a henid forbids its description; it is merely a something. **1909** J. LONDON *Martin Eden* xxxvii. 322 By some henidical process—henidical, by the way, is a favourite word of mine which nobody understands—by some henidical process you persuade yourself that you believe in the competitive system and the survival of the strong. **1914** —— *Let.* 10 Sept. (1966) 428 The word henid was coined by a crazy German philosopher... All persons possess henids. **1915** —— *Jacket* xiv. 160 'I'll—' he began explosively, proving, by his inability to conclude the remark, that he thought in henids. **1946** D. ABRAHAMSEN *Mind & Death of Genius* 112 Weininger introduces a special name for the psychological data at the earliest stage, before clarification has begun. He calls the vague perception the henid. *Ibid.* 113 According to Weininger, the henid is the form of perception known to the lower types of organism. In mankind development from the henid to the completely differentiated form of perception and idea is possible.

Henle (he·nli). *Anat.* The name of F. G. J. *Henle* (see HENLEAN *a.*) used in the possessive and with *of* adjunct to designate numerous anatomical structures, as: **a.** *Henle's layer* (or *layer of Henle*), a single layer of cubical cells in the inner root sheath of the hair follicle, between Huxley's layer and the outer root sheath. Formerly also called *Henle's sheath* etc. (cf. sense c).

1853 BUSK & HUXLEY tr. *Kölliker's Man. Human Histol.* I. 186 The outermost layer [of the inner root-sheath of the hair], which alone was formerly known, the inner root-sheath of Henle, is formed of elongated cells without nuclei. **1860** G. BUCHANAN tr. *Kölliker's Man. Human Microsc. Anat.* 109 (*caption*) A portion of the root of a dark hair..f. outer fenestrated layer (*Henle's* layer). **1892** H. E. CLARK *Wilson's Anatomist's Vade Mecum* (ed. 11) 70 The inner root-sheath [of a hair] is again divisible into..an outer layer (Henle's sheath). **1970** T. S. & C. R. LEESON *Histol.* (ed. 2) xiii. 263/2 Henle's layer..is a single layer of flattened, clear cells which contain hyaline fibrils.

b. *Henle's loop* (or *loop of Henle*), a portion of a uriniferous tubule from where it passes from the cortex of the kidney into the medulla to where it returns into the cortex, also *spec.* the central part of this where it forms a distinct loop at its deepest point in the medulla. Also called *Henle's* (*looped*) *tube* or *tubule* etc.

1867 *Quain's Elem. Anat.* (ed. 7) II. 930 The tubes in question have been designated looped tubes of Henle. **1877** W. TURNER *Introd. Human Anat.* II. xi. 785 Each intermediary tube..descends..into the medullary pyramid, where it turns on itself, forms a loop, known as the looped tube of Henle, and reenters the cortex as the ascending limb of the looped tube. **1885** [see LOOP *sb.*[1] 4 a]. **1890** BILLINGS *Med. Dict.* I. 631/2 *Henle's loop,* loop of Henle. *Ibid., Henle's tubules,* looped tubules of Henle. **1970** T. S. & C. R. LEESON *Histol.* (ed. 2) xvi. 374/2 The loop of Henle consists of the straight part of the proximal tubule in the descending limb, a thin segment in descending and ascending limbs, and the straight part of the distal tubule in the ascending limb.

c. *Henle's sheath* (or *sheath of Henle*) (see quot. 1942). Cf. sense a.

[**1878** M. L. RANVIER *Lecons Histol. Syst. Nerveux* I. x. 159 Nous pouvons vous montrer sous un de ces microscopes des nerfs composés d'un seul tube nerveux qui possèdent une membrane enveloppante; j'appellerai cette membrane, gaîne [= sheath] de Henle, du nom de l'auteur qui l'a découverte.] **1887** *Buck's Handbk. Med. Sci.* V. 145/1 The sheath in this form has been named the sheath of Henle (Ranvier). There is a space between the nerve-fibre and the sheath. **1890** BILLINGS *Med. Dict.* I. 631/2 *Henle's sheath,* a continuation of the fibrous tissue of the perineurium. **1942** O. LARSELL *Anat. Nervous Syst.* iv. 48 A delicate sheath of connective tissue fibers, continuous with the endoneurium of the nerve trunk, is intimately associated with and surrounds the neurolemma of most individual peripheral fibers. This is usually called the sheath of Henle.

d. *Henle's gland* (or *gland of Henle*), any of numerous gland-like structures in the conjunctiva of the eye-lid (see quot. 1933).

1890 BILLINGS *Med. Dict.* I. 631/2 *Henle's glands,* short tubular glands said to be found on the palpebral conjunctiva. **1933** E. WOLFF *Anat. Eye & Orbit* iii. 105 Henle's 'Glands' occur in the palpebral conjunctiva between the tarsal plates and the fornices. They are probably not true glands, but folds of mucous membrane cut transversely. **1961** S. DUKE-ELDER *Syst. Ophthalm.* II. iii. 115 The epithelial depressions between them were originally described by Henle (1866) as glands (the *glands of Henle*) and were termed conjunctival crypts by Dubreuil (1908).

Henley (he·nli). The name of a town on the Thames, in Oxfordshire, used alone or *attrib.* to designate the annual regatta held there since 1839. Hence **He·nleyite,** a Henley enthusiast.

1839 *Times* 6 June 3/5 Henley Regatta..takes place on Friday, the 14th. **1861** T. HUGHES *Tom Brown at Oxf.* II. 218 You know the Leander are to be at Henley... There will be a splendid race for the cup. **1868** *Broadway* I. 104/2 Roland rowed his man—a Henley winner—down. **1887** [see REGATTA 2 *attrib.*]. **1893** *Isis* 29 Apr. 130/2, I have heard nothing more about the Henley arrangements. *Ibid.* 3 June 207/2 The Oxford arrangements for Henley are now getting into rather a more settled condition. **1901** *Westm. Gaz.* 2 July 7/2 Henleyites..will be depressed to hear that the Meteorological Office forecasts..rainy and colder weather. **1902** *Encycl. Brit.* XXXII. 307/1 A motion was proposed at the October meeting of the Henley Stewards to exclude foreign crews from the regatta. **1959** *Chambers's Encycl.* VII. 13/2 Henley Royal Regatta (1851—formerly Henley Regatta, 1839).

henna. b. Add: (with reference to dyeing or staining with henna) *henna-dyeing*; *henna-coloured, -dyed, -haired, -tipped, -tressed* adjs.

1954 M. MEAD *Growing up in New Guinea* 143 Henna-coloured betel juice. **1920** *Chambers's Jrnl.* May 299/1 He..showed a handful of his henna-dyed beard. **1906** *Daily Chron.* 27 June 6/4 From tight-lacing to henna-dyeing the frisky matron is a study in successful artifice. **1907** *Ibid.* 31 Dec. 3/1 His American trotting-car and his henna-haired wife. **1923** *Chambers's Jrnl.* 306/2 Their henna-tipped fingers are loaded with rings. **1939** R. CAMPBELL *Flowering Rifle* I. 24 Amongst her Modern Southeys, henna-tressed.

hennaed (he·năd). [f. HENNA + -ED[2].] Dyed or stained with henna.

1924 *Countries of World* II. 1145/1 A slim hand with hennaed nails. **1925** H. V. MORTON *Heart of London* 53 Maud's hennaed hair. **1961** A. WILSON *Old Men at Zoo* vii. 309 Her dark hennaed hair.

Henoch (hī·noχ). The name of E. H. *Henoch* (1820–1910), German pædiatrician, used in the possessive and occas. *attrib.* to designate esp. purpura associated with abdominal symptoms, as *Henoch('s) purpura*; also used *attrib.*, in combination with the name of Schönlein (see *SCHÖNLEIN), to designate purpura associated with both the abdominal symptoms of Henoch's purpura and the articular symptoms of Schönlein's purpura, as *Henoch–Schönlein* (or *Schönlein–Henoch*) *purpura, syndrome.*

1893 DUNGLISON *Dict. Med. Sci.* (ed. 21) 522/1 *Henoch's purpura,* purpura complicated with infection of the intestines. **1896** *Intercolonial Med. Jrnl. Australasia* I. 364 (*title*) A case of Henoch's purpura hæmorrhagica. **1897** *Brit. Med. Jrnl.* 18 Dec. 1800/1 Henoch's purpura. Dr. Dreschfeld made some observations on the symptoms, pathology, and treatment of this disease, cases of which, though not under that name, had been repeated, observed and described in English journals. **1908** *Practitioner* June 824 Gastro-intestinal crises are common with both Henoch's purpura and angioneurotic oedema. **1947** *Gastroenterology* IX. 610 My working diagnosis in this case was Henoch's Purpura. **1948** *Q. Jrnl. Med.* XLI. 95 (*title*) The Schönlein-Henoch syndrome (anaphylactoid purpura). **1952** *Arch. Dis. Childhood* XXVII. 480 (*title*) The Schoenlein-Henoch syndrome in childhood with particular reference to the occurrence of nephritis. **1959** *Brit. Med. Jrnl.* 19 Dec. 1385/2 (*heading*) Familial incidence of the Henoch-Schönlein syndrome. **1966** DUNLOP & ALSTEAD *Textbk. Med. Treatm.* (ed. 10) 502 (*heading*) Henoch-Schönlein purpura. *Ibid.*, In this condition,..abdominal symptoms,..(Henoch purpura), and pain and swelling in joints (Schönlein purpura), may occur together. **1967** A. C. ALLEN *Skin* (ed. 2) xvii. 661/1 In Henoch's purpura..the prominent symptoms are recurrent abdominal pain..and colic, associated with moderate fever and with melena, tenesmus, and mucus in the stools. **1968** *Gastroenterology* LIV. 260 (*title*) Gastro-intestinal and roentgenological manifestations of Henoch-Schoenlein purpura.

henpeck, *sb.* Add: **1. b.** A husband so domineered.

1765 GARRICK *Let.* 23 May in *Corr. Garrick* (1831) I. 185 More of the sneaking hen-peck, than of the tender enamoured husband.

hen-peckery. (Later examples.)

1869 *Harper's Mag.* Mar. 508/2 Husbands flee from hen-peckery, and wives desert bearish husbands. **1958** *Daily Mail* 15 July 3/4 Charmian Eyre..remains disarmingly human at the height of henpeckery.

hen-pecked, *ppl. a.* (Later examples.)

1923 D. H. LAWRENCE *Kangaroo* i. 4 A little red-faced man, rather beery and hen-pecked looking. **1930** G. B. SHAW *Apple Cart* Interlude 57 *Orinthia*: Why are you so afraid of your wife? You are the laughing stock of London, you poor henpecked darling. **1939** —— *In Good King Charles's Golden Days* I. 57 What! that henpecked booby! *Ibid.* 58 He may be henpecked: what married man is not?

Henrician, *sb.* Add: **3.** A supporter of the ecclesiastical policy of Henry VIII. Hence **Henricianism** (henri·ʃⁱăniz'm), the ecclesiastical policy of Henry VIII.

1828 E. NARES *Mem. Ld. Burghley* I. IV. 53 The king's supremacy, which, like a true *Henrician,* he was very careful to maintain. **1900** F. W. MAITLAND *Coll. Papers* (1911) III. 159 Calvin had spoken ill of Henricianism. **1903** —— in *Camb. Mod. Hist.* II. 555 A Reformed religion, or some northern version of Henricanism [*sic*]. **1946** A. L. ROWSE *Use Hist.* 180 Yet we cannot be grateful enough to the (sometimes unattractive) Henricians and Elizabethans who pushed us through it.

Henri Deux (aṅri dȫ). [Fr., = Henri II.] Designating the style of Renaissance architecture or art developed in France during the reign of Henri II, king of France 1547–59; *spec.* the purest style of the French Renaissance.

1863 W. CHAFFERS *Marks Pott. & Porc.* 89 The following is a list of all the pieces of Henri II. ware now known to be extant. **1873** *Young Englishwoman* May 234/2 The

Henri II. hat is very becoming to a young face. **1881** C. C. HARRISON *Woman's Handiwork* II. 104 Modern English potters have put within our reach reproductions of that exquisite (so-called 'Henri Deux') faïence bequeathed to the world by the lady Hélène de Hangest-Genlis—the ware of the Chateau d'Oiron. **1884** KNIGHT *Dict. Mech.* Suppl. s.v., Henri-Deux Ware (*Faïence d'Oiron*). **1960** R. G. HAGGAR *Conc. Encycl. Cont. Pott. & Porc.* 397 Saint-Porchaire earthenware *tazza* with inlaid decoration in coloured clays (so-called Henri Deux Ware), c. 1540.

Henrietta (henrie·tă). *Disused.* [Female name.] Designating a light-weight dress fabric, sometimes with a silk warp.

1851 *Illustr. Catal. Gt. Exhib.* III. 494/2 Henrietta cloths, with silk warp and worsted weft. **1862** *Illustr. Catal. Internat. Exhib., Industr. Dept., Brit. Div.* II. No. 4018 Paramatta, or Henrietta Cloth, twill. **1890** *Advt.* (Ann Arbor, Mich.) 1 Mar., We offer a 46-inch Black Silk Warp Henrietta. **1901** *Daily News* 23 Feb. 6/7 Henrietta cloths, which wear so well and drape so charmingly. **1908** *Sears, Roebuck Catal.* 933/1 Cotton henrietta cloth..having all the appearance and touch of an imported all wool henrietta.

hen-roost. Add: **b.** *fig.* A source of plunder: in allusion to a political speech referring to 'the robbing of hen-roosts'.

1909 *Westm. Gaz.* 16 Apr. 5/1 Mr. Lloyd George's now historic reference to 'hen-roosts'. **1928** *Britain's Industr. Future* (*Lib. Ind. Inq.*) v. xxix. § 2. 420 Apart from the public hen-roosts which Mr. Churchill has raided, it is impossible for an outsider to estimate what private henroosts inside the Treasury he has also helped himself to.

Henry[1] (he·nri). The name of Benjamin Tyler *Henry* (1821–98), American inventor, used attrib. to designate a breech-loading magazine rifle or parts thereof, subsequently used in the Martini-Henry rifle. Also *ellipt.*

1859 G. A. JACKSON *Diary* 25 Jan. in F. Hall *Hist. Colorado* (1890) II. 522 Packed up our things for the trip and got Oakes' Henry rifle for Phil. **1869** in *Frontier* (1929) IX. 157 One of them..lost one of our Henry carbines. **1880** *Encycl. Brit.* XI. 282/1 In the Henry action the barrel does not move, but is closed at the breech end by a sliding vertical block. *Ibid.* 282/2 The combination of the Martini breech action with the Henry barrel. *Ibid.* 283/2 Henry rifling. **1902** *Ibid.* XXXII. 242/1 In 1861 the Henry grooving for a cylindrical bullet, a modification of the Whitworth, first appeared. **1927** C. M. RUSSELL *Trails plowed Under* 71, I guess his weapon's a Henry. **1964** H. L. PETERSON *Encycl. Firearms* 180 (*caption*) Iron-frame Henry rifle and brass-frame Henry rifle.

Henry[2] (he·nri). The name of William *Henry* (1774–1836), English chemist, used in *Henry's law* (see quot. 1940).

1886 *Syd. Soc. Lex.*, H[enry]'s law. **1910** *Encycl. Brit.* XIII. 302/1 The conclusion he reached ('Henry's law') being that 'water takes up of gas condensed by one, two or more additional atmospheres, a quantity which, ordinarily compressed, would be equal to twice, thrice, &c. the volume absorbed under the common pressure of the atmosphere'. **1940** *Chambers's Techn. Dict.* 411/1 *Henry's Law.* The amount of a gas absorbed by a given volume of a liquid at a given temperature is directly proportional to the pressure of the gas. **1966** PHILLIPS & WILLIAMS *Inorg. Chem.* II. xix. 43 Oxygen dissolves as atoms (obeying Henry's law) in molten silver.

henry[3] (he·nri). *Physics.* The name of Joseph *Henry* (1797–1878), American physicist, used (pl. *henrys, henries*) to designate the practical unit of inductance, now incorporated in the International System of Units, i.e. the inductance of a circuit in which an electromotive force of one volt is produced by a current changing at the rate of one ampere per second. Abbrev. H or (*rare*) h. Also **he·nrymeter** (see quot. 1940).

1893 *Electrician* 29 Sept. 577/2 There was the proposal [at the International Electrical Congress] to christen the unit of self-induction as the *henry* in honour of Joseph Henry its discoverer. **1915** *Proc. IRE* III. 223 The transformer is made up of coils having an inductance of the order of a henry or more. **1929** K. HENNEY *Princ. Radio* iv. 62 The coils used in radio apparatus vary from inductances of the order of microhenries to very large ones having over 100 henries in inductance. **1940** *Chambers's Techn. Dict.* 411/1 *Henrymeter*, an obsolete apparatus for measuring inductance; in it an alternating current was passed through the inductance under test and a standard inductance in series, the voltage drop across the two being compared. **1947** *Jrnl. Inst. Electr. Engin.* XCIV. 342/1 From the 1st January the units employed [at the National Physical Laboratory] will be those derived from the centimetre, gramme and second, i.e. the so-called 'absolute' units. The effects of this change may be seen from the following table:..One international henry = 1·00049 'absolute' henrys. **1952** *Electronic Engin.* XXIV. 465 A 10 henry A.F. choke has been provided in the cathode circuit.

Henry Clay. The name of an American statesman (1777–1852) used to designate a type of cigar.

1867 in *Amer. Speech* (1965) XL. 130. **1884** *Harper's Mag.* Sept. 647/1 The dealer..asked him if he would 'like to 'ave a 'Enry Clay'. **1888** KIPLING *Departmental Ditties* (1890) 105 There's peace in a Laranaga, there's calm in a Henry Clay. **1893** *Harper's Mag.* Dec. 34/1 And bring some cigars—Henry Clays. *Ibid.*, My father was always a Henry Clay man. **1922** JOYCE *Ulysses* 243 He removed his large Henry Clay decisively. **1969** L. GROW tr. *Davidoff & Lambert's Connoisseur's Bk. Cigar* 71 Henry Clay (now planted in the Canary Islands) has changed its name; its owners have struck the new name of Don Miguel.

Hentenian (hentī·niăn), *a.* [f. the name of John *Henten* or *Hentenius* (1499–1566), a theologian of the Dominican order at Louvain: see -IAN.] Of or pertaining to Henten, or to the editions of the Vulgate (Louvain 1547, often reprinted) prepared by him.

1902 H. J. WHITE in J. Hastings *Dict. Bible* IV. 880/2 The various Hentenian editions remained for some years as the standard text of the Roman Church, but were still private publications. **1930** S. ANGUS in *Internat. Stand. Bible Encycl.* V. 3061/2 Hentenian critical ed. (Louvain, 1547).

hentriacontane (he:ntraiăkǫ·ntēⁱn). *Chem.* [f. Gr. ἑν-, εἷς one + τριάκοντα thirty + -ANE.] A hydrocarbon of the paraffin series, $C_{31}H_{64}$, *esp.* the solid unbranched hydrocarbon $CH_3\cdot(CH_2)_{29}\cdot CH_3$ present in petroleum and many natural waxes.

1887 *Jrnl. Chem. Soc.* LII. I. 124 The most soluble portion of the extract melting..at 67°, is probably identical with normal hentriacontane, $C_{31}H_{64}$. **1950** J. BONNER *Plant Biochem.* xxiv. 366 Commercial candelilla wax (*Euphorbia* sp.) contains..50–60% of a paraffin, *n*-hentriacontane.

heortology (hī,ǫɹtǫ·lŏdʒi). [ad. G. *heortologie*, F. *héortologie*, f. Gr. ἑορτή feast: see -OLOGY.] The science or study of the origin, meaning, growth, and history of the religious feasts and seasons of the Christian year. Hence **heortolo·gical** *a.*, of or pertaining to heortology; **heorto·logist**, one who studies heortology.

1900 *Expositor* Nov. 348 We are to regard the statement of the calendars as the conjecture of a heortologist. **1901** J. R. HARRIS in *Soc. Hist. Theology* 31 Oct. 5 The Study of Christian Heortology... The problems that belong to the region of Christian Heortology. **1913** J. R. MCKEE (*title*) The Church's year, a handbook of heortology. **1918** E. BISHOP *Liturg. Hist.* 258 Recalling too how the recent heortologist Dr. Kellner considers that the mention of the feast in the Irish calendars does not prove the celebration of the feast.

hep (hep), *a. slang* (orig. *U.S.*). [Of unknown origin.] Well-informed, knowledgeable, 'wise *to*', up-to-date; smart, stylish. Hence as *sb.*, the state of being 'hep'. Also as *vb.*, to pep *up*; **hepped** *ppl. a.* (often with *up*); *to be hepped on*, to be enthusiastic about, 'bitten with'. Cf. *HEP-CAT, *HIP *a.*

1908 *Sat. Even. Post* 5 Dec. 17/1 What puzzles me is how you can find anybody left in the world who isn't hep. **1914** JACKSON & HELLYER *Vocab. Criminal Slang* 43 *Hep*,... Sapiency; understanding... Derived from the name of a fabulous detective who operated in Cincinnati. **1918** WODEHOUSE *Piccadilly Jim* xi. 118 'You see in me a confidant. I am hep.' 'You know—' 'Everything.' **1923** —— *Adv. Sally* xiii. 148 He was aware that women were seldom hep to the really important things in life. **1927** P. MARKS *Lord of Himself* 47 You're pleased because the top-notchers wanted me, but that doesn't make you think I'm a top-notcher. I'm just getting hep. There you have it. **1938** 'J. SPENSER' *Crime against Society* xxiv. 235 The coppers are hep and we've got to stage a cover-up. **1941** *Amer. Speech* XVI. 154/1 'Tis said that back in the 1890's Joe Hep ran a saloon in Chicago... Although he never quite understood what was going on, he thought he did... Hence his name entered the argot as an ironic appellation for anyone who thought he knew but didn't. The ironic sense has now largely disappeared..in..to get hep to. **1951** M. MCLUHAN *Mech. Bride* 68/2 His failure to be hep to success doctrines. **1956** D. KARP *All Honorable Men* 107 You know how hepped on the matter of wasting time the whole Board is. **1957** C. MACINNES *City of Spades* I. iii. 19 Where can I get a shirt like that?.. It's hep. Jumble style, but hep. **1958** N. D. HINTON in *Publ. Amer. Dial. Soc.* XXX. 40 In the swing period, 'hep' was widely used by musicians to mean 'in the know', 'possessed of good taste', or to indicate simple understanding... The boppers quickly changed the word to 'hip'. Use of 'hep' was then regarded as a sign that the speaker was not the right sort. **1958** *Punch* 27 Aug. 270/1 And when I stood up and he began to get hep I noticed that his shoes were cunningly low cut. **1959** 'M. M. KAYE' *House of Shade* xviii. 246 Are you, in the distressing jargon of the age, 'hep'? **1959** *Guardian* 16 Oct. 10/6 Columns of drug-hepped, ragged men. **1959** *News Chron.* 14 July 4/4 A slightly hepped-up version of the old deck chair and concert party formula. *Ibid.* 21 July 1/6 The pills were being taken..to give the addicts a form of 'hep'. **1959** T. GRIFFITH *Waist-high Culture* (1960) 238 A California chemist who is hep to every current allusion and is an asset to any party. **1960** *News Chron.* 6 July 3/1 Even some of the classics..have been hepped up to circus style. **1960** *Guardian* 12 Aug. 8/3 Not even its bitterest critics could accuse the Labour party of being 'hep'. **1962** *Listener* 6 Sept. 350/2 'I wasn't hepped on becoming a painter,' he [*sc.* Henry Miller] said. **1970** *Cape Times* 28 Oct. 1/8 Are you hep to what the Beatles are saying? **1972** J. L. DILLARD *Black English* iii. 119 It is, of course, a commonplace of the jazz language that *hep* is a white man's distortion of the more characteristically Negro *hip.*

hep (hep), *int.* [Said to be f. the initials of *H*ierosolyma *E*st *P*erdita; or, the cry of a goatherd.] Usu. *hep, hep!* The cry of those who persecuted Jews in the 19th century. Also *attrib.*

1839 *Penny Cycl.* XIII. 122/1 They [*sc.* the Jews] were massacred at the cry of 'Hep', 'Hep', the initials of the words 'Hierosolyma est perdita'. **1879** GEO. ELIOT *Impressions of Theophrastus Such* xviii. 313 (*heading*) The Modern Hep! Hep! Hep! **1930** D. PHILIPSON *Reform Movement in Judaism* (rev. ed.) i. 25 The *hep hep* cry resounded in the streets of..Frankfort and Würzburg. *Ibid.* vi. 108 A violent anti-Jewish literary campaign ensued..which culminated in the..disgraceful hep-hep outbreaks of the year 1819. **1971** *Encycl. Judaica* VII. 1227/1 Hamburg Jews were molested during the Hep! Hep! riots of 1819.

heparin (he·părin). *Biochem.* [f. HEPAR + -IN[1].] A sulphated polysaccharide present in various body tissues and organs, esp. the liver, lungs, and muscles, and used therapeutically as an anti-coagulant.

1918 HOWELL & HOLT in *Amer. Jrnl. Physiol.* XLVII. 328 A phosphatid, not previously described, which exists in various tissues but is found in greatest abundance in the liver. This phosphatid is designated as *heparin* to indicate its origin from liver... This substance was [previously] described under the name of antiprothrombin. **1933** *Jrnl. Biol. Chem.* CII. 435 Dog liver contains approximately twice as much heparin as does beef liver. **1946** *Nature* 24 Aug. 270/1 Even drastic blood changes brought about by the injection of dicoumarol or heparin had only a slight effect on the rate of growth of the bugs. **1968** A. WHITE et al. *Princ. Biochem.* (ed. 4) xxxi. 732 Many tissues of the body contain heparin since it specifically originates in the metachromatic granules of mast cells.

Hence **he:pariniza·tion**, the process of heparinizing; **he·parinize** *v. trans.*, to treat with heparin and thus reduce the clotting power of the blood; **he·parinized** *ppl. a.*

1940 J. E. R. MCDONAGH *Universe through Med.* 24 Snake venom has the same action in this condition as has calcium in making heparinised blood coagulate. **1943** *Science* 2 July 20/1 In all experiments in which heparinized whole blood or plasma was administered the lipemia was abolished. **1956** *New Eng. Jrnl. Med.* 29 Nov. 1027/2 General heparinization carries with it the risk of serious hemorrhage from bleeding lesions elsewhere in the body as well as at the operative site. **1959** *Lancet* 11 July 25/1 The risk of heparinising a patient who is receiving a coumarin drug. **1961** *Ibid.* 14 Oct. 858/1 The principle of regional heparinisation is to supply anticoagulated blood to the artificial kidney, whilst not interfering with the normal coagulation of blood in the patient.

hepat-. Add: **hepate·ctomy**, excision of (a part of) the liver; also **hepate·ctomized** *ppl. a.*; **hepato·ma**, a tumour of the liver (see quot. 1934).

1900 DORLAND *Med. Dict.* 296/2 Hepatectomy. **1910** *Practitioner* Mar. 383 Hepatectomy under these conditions does not appear to add to the gravity of the prognosis. **1946** *Nature* 31 Aug. 310/2 The so-called xanthorubin, a yellow compound present in the serum of hepatectomized dogs. **1905** H. D. ROLLESTON *Dis. Liver* 457 The term 'hepatoma' was suggested by Sabourin to describe the transitional stage between adenoma and carcinoma. **1912** *Ibid.* (ed. 2) 474 This condition [*sc.* primary carcinoma developing in a cirrhotic liver] was described..as Hepatoma by Rénon, Géraudel, and Monier-Vinard who insist that it is not a carcinoma. 'Hepatoma', also employed by Sabourin..is a confusing title. **1934** *Brit. Jrnl. Surg.* XXI. 684 The next advance of note was made by Yamagiura in 1911. He..made two simple divisions: (1) Hepatoma, i.e., carcinoma of hepatic cells; and (2) Cholangioma, i.e., carcinoma of bile-ducts. The term 'hepatoma' had previously been used by Sabourin in reference to a condition of nodular hyperplasia which in his opinion was a transitional stage between adenoma and carcinoma. Most modern writers, however, accept Yamagiura's interpretation, and use it as a term for primary carcinoma of the liver cells. **1971** *New Scientist* 17 June 668/3 From one strain of a mouse hepatoma they have a factor which they describe as being 'a heat stable molecule of low molecular weight'.

hepatic, *a.* and *sb.* Add: **B.** *sb.* (Later examples.)

1908 *Chambers's Jrnl.* Sept. 671/2 An East Indian Aloes used to..be quoted in trade papers under the distinction of 'Hepatic'.

2. *Bot.* Usu. in *pl.* = HEPATICA.

1939 *Nature* 2 Sept. 416/2 The three smallest plants which have left recognizable fragments are a fungus and two liverworts or, as they are often called, hepatics, a group allied to the mosses but of simpler construction. **1964** V. J. CHAPMAN *Coastal Veget.* vi. 152 It is here also that some hepatics..can be found.

hepatico- (hĭpæ·tiko), combining form of HEPATIC, = HEPATO-.

For further examples see medical dicts.

1910 *Practitioner* Mar. 384 The hepatico-cystic confluence. *Ibid.* 385 Vautrin put a drain in the hepatic duct, thus making a hepaticostomy. **1933** *Med. Rec.* 18 Jan. 52/2 Hepaticocholangiogastrostomy..should be used only when other methods are impracticable.

hepatin (he·pătin). *Biochem.* Also (sense 1) **-ine.** [f. HEPAT- + -IN[1].] †**1.** = GLYCOGEN. *Obs.*

1858 F. W. Pavy in *Guy's Hosp. Rep.* IV. 316 [In calling it glucogenic] we are giving a name..to a substance which implies a purpose to which the facts..show it does not naturally administer in the living animal.. I therefore propose to call it hepatine—a term which.. cannot convey an erroneous impression..and which, nevertheless, is strictly pertinent. **1860** —— in *Phil. Trans. R. Soc.* CL. 608, I have made some analyses to show..how much sugar is formed for the hepatine that disappears. **1865** W. B. Carpenter *Man. Physiol.* (ed. 4) I. iii. 108 The conversion of hepatine into sugar seems to be promoted by the presence of a 'ferment' not merely in the liver itself, but also in the blood circulating through it. *Ibid.* II. viii. 454 There is evidence that Hepatin may be formed in the Liver at the expense of Albuminous substances.

2. [a. G. *hepatin* (S. S. Zaleski 1886, in *Zeitschr. f. physiol. Chem.* X. 494)], an iron-containing protein reported to occur in liver.

1886 *Jrnl. Chem. Soc.* L. 1054 Iron..is found in all the morphological constituents of the liver tissue in organic combinations, both with albuminates and with nucleïn. In the iron-nucleïn group of compounds, one is present which gives the ordinary tests for iron in contradistinction to the others which do not; from this latter group one compound, hepatin, has been isolated. **1891** W. D. Halliburton *Text-bk. Chem. Physiol. & Path.* xxv. 551 The quantity of iron in the blood-free liver was found to vary between wide limits, but it was constantly found in organic combinations in the liver-cells, especially with nuclein; and one of the iron-nuclein compounds named hepatin was isolated. **1914** G. M. Niles *Diagn. & Treatm. Digestive Dis.* xiv. 357 Other somewhat vaunted preparations are gasterin and hepatin, which are obtained from the gastric juice of dogs through gastric fistulas.

hepatitis. Delete ‖. Substitute for def.: Inflammation of the liver. (Later examples.)

1879 A. Flint *Clinical Med.* III. 370 Diffuse, or parenchymatous hepatitis and yellow atrophy of the liver are considered as one affection. **1938** Yater & Ault in W. M. Yater *Fund. Internal Med.* IV. 375 The differential diagnosis of the various types of hepatitis brings into consideration the differentiation of the causes of jaundice. **1955** Gaiger & Davies *Vet. Path. & Bacteriol.* (ed. 4) xxxiii. 644 Apart from the specific forms of hepatitis met with in tuberculosis,..the two main forms of inflammation met with are suppurative hepatitis due to bacterial activity within the liver tissue and chronic interstitial hepatitis due to blood-borne toxins and other agents. **1959** *Chambers's Encycl.* VII. 23/2 Acute infective hepatitis is the newer name for a condition long known in medical practice as catarrhal jaundice. **1963** L. Schiff *Dis. Liver* (ed. 2) xii. 370/1 At least two forms of viral hepatitis are recognized: the naturally occurring type referred to as infectious hepatitis (catarrhal jaundice, infectious jaundice, etc.), and homologous serum hepatitis (transfusion jaundice, yellow fever vaccine jaundice, syringe jaundice, postarsphenamine jaundice, etc.). *Ibid.* xiv. 453 (*heading*) Toxic and drug-induced hepatitis.

hepato-. Add: **he:patoce·llular** *a.*, of or pertaining to hepatic cells; **hepatofla·vin** *Biochem.*, a substance first isolated from liver and later found to be the same as *riboflavin; **hepato-lenticular degeneration** [tr. F. *dégénérescence hépato-lenticulaire* (H. C. Hall, 1921)], a progressive disease of the nervous system (see quot. 1955); Wilson's disease; **he:patomega·lia, -me·galy,** abnormal enlargement of the liver; **hepatoscopy** (later examples); hence **hepato·scopist**, one who practises hepatoscopy; **he:patosple:nomega·lia, -me·galy,** abnormal enlargement of the liver and spleen; **hepatoto·xic** *a.*, having a toxic effect on the liver; so **he:patotoxi·city; hepatoto·xin,** (*a*) any substance which has a toxic effect on the liver; (*b*) an antibody produced by injecting liver tissue into an animal.

1940 E. Rosenthal *Dis. Digestive Syst.* iii. 212 Jaundice may be i. Mechanical ii. Functional (hepatocellular) iii. Hæmolytic. **1949** Kantor & Kasich *Handbk. Digestive Dis.* (ed. 2) xvii. 415 The hepatocellular and the obstructive forms of jaundice make up more than 95 per cent of the cases encountered in clinical practice. **1962** *Lancet* 13 Jan. 67/1 Patients with hepatocellular disease are faced with the prospect of hepatic coma and death every time they have a haemorrhage. **1933** K. G. Stern in *Nature* 18 Nov. 784/1 The isolation in a crystalline state of the lyochrome from horse liver, to be designated as 'hepatoflavin', has been achieved. **1936** *Jrnl. Nutrition* XI. 75 Fractions prepared from liver extract which were rich in vitamin G (B_2) and from which the hepatoflavin had been removed..were very active in the cure of black tongue. **1943** M. E. Rehfuss *Indigestion* xxiv. 392 The terms lactoflavin, ovoflavin, hepatoflavin, and so on serve to indicate the source of the particular riboflavin under discussion. **1960** A. E. Bender *Dict. Nutrition* 62/1 *Hepatoflavin*, name given to substance isolated from liver, shown later to be riboflavin. **1922** *Lancet* 29 Apr. 849/2 This is an account of the disease known as progressive lenticular degeneration, which Dr. Hall christens hepato-lenticular degeneration. **1925** *Brain* XLVIII. 332 It would be better to adopt Hall's terminology, and refer to the condition as hepato-lenticular degeneration... This title fails to indicate the peculiar type of the disease in the liver..but it indicates.. that the lenticular disease is a sequel to liver damage. **1945** *Archives Internal Med.* LXXV. 151/1 Wilson in 1912 ..first clearly defined the condition now most widely known as hepatolenticular degeneration. **1955** S. Sherlock *Dis. Liver & Biliary Syst.* xiii. 339 Hepatolenticular degeneration is a rare disease of young people characterised by portal cirrhosis of the liver, bilateral softening and degeneration of the lenticular nuclei of the basal ganglia of the brain, and greenish-brown pigmented rings in the periphery of the cornea. **1893** Dunglison *Dict. Med. Sci.* (ed. 21) 524/1 Hepatomegalia. **1910** Collins & Liebmann tr. *Dieulafoy's Text-bk. Med.* II. viii. i. 1916 He [*sc.* Glénard] found that hepatomegalia is the most frequent of the organic changes in diabetes. **1904** Stedman *Dunglison's Dict. Med. Sci.* (ed. 23) 527/1 Hepatomegaly. **1937** J. L. Kantor *Synopsis Digestive Dis.* xxi. 230 Cancer of the liver must be differentiated from other conditions causing hepatomegaly. **1969** Hepatomegaly [see **hepatotoxicity* below]. **1947** Auden *Age of Anxiety* (1948) vi. 121 Peace was promised by the public hepatoscopists. **1928** C. Dawson *Age of Gods* xiii. 307 The practice of Hepatoscopy or divination from the liver of the sacrificial victim, which reached Asia Minor from Mesopotamia, was carried by the Etruscans to Italy. **1957** *Encycl. Brit.* XI. 451/1 The theory underlying hepatoscopy consists of the belief (1) that the liver is the seat of life, or the soul of the animal; and (2) that the liver of the sacrificial animal..took on the same character as the soul of the god to whom it was offered. **1930** *Chem. Abstr.* XXIV. 886 In hepatosplenomegalia and hepatic cirrhosis, the urobilin increased in the urine and feces. **1939** Stedman *Med. Dict.* (ed. 14) 496/2 Hepatosplenomegaly. **1961** *Lancet* 19 Aug. 434/2 Physical examination revealed considerable hepatosplenomegaly. **1940** *Jrnl. Amer. Med. Assoc.* 28 Dec. 2264/2 (*heading*) Alleged hepatotoxic action of stilbestrol. **1961** *Lancet* 16 Sept. 623/1 Each of the drugs which has caused jaundice is a derivative of hydrazine, itself a potent hepatotoxic agent in laboratory animals. **1972** *Nature* 4 Feb. 279/1 Both compounds..have been reported to be hepatotoxic, carcinogenic, teratogenic and neurotoxic. **1952** *New Eng. Jrnl. Med.* 20 Nov. 797 (*heading*) The hepatotoxicity of intravenous aureomycin. **1969** *Nature* 19 Apr. 223/2 Increase in size of the liver (hepatomegaly) is not a reliable indication of hepatotoxicity. **1904** Stedman *Dunglison's Dict. Med. Sci.* (ed. 23) 527/1 *Hepatotoxin*, a cytotoxin having a specific action on the cells of the liver. **1909** J. G. Adami *Princ. Path.* I. III. viii. 489 Ciliated epithelium was shown to have its cytotoxin.., as have kidney cells (nephrotoxin), liver cells (hepatotoxin), pancreatic, adrenal, and, in fact, every form of animal cell that has been tested. **1929** *Chem. Abstr.* XXIII. 5509 Hepatotoxins, prepd. by immunizing rabbits with emulsions of rabbit and rat livers, were injected into rabbits and rats. **1951** A. Grollman *Pharmacol. & Therapeutics* xxvii. 607 Because of their lipotropic action, choline and, to a lesser extent, methionine..have been used therapeutically in cirrhosis of the liver,..and as a prophylactic in poisoning by hepatotoxins. **1963** G. Klatskin in L. Schiff *Dis. Liver* (ed. 2) xiv. 453/1 Hepatotoxins, a heterogeneous group of naturally occurring and synthetic chemical agents, produce a variety of lesions in the liver that are classified as forms of toxic hepatitis.

Hepburn (he·pbɒ̄ɹn, he·bɒ̄ɹn). The name of J. C. *Hepburn* (1815–1911), Amer. physician and missionary, used *attrib.* in *Hepburn system*, a Romanized transcription of Japanese characters. So **Hepbu·rnian** *a.*

[**1867** J. C. Hepburn (*title*) A Japanese and English dictionary.] **1937** *Mélanges Ling. et Phil. offerts à J. van Ginneken* 357 The Nipponsiki or Japanese system versus the Hepburnian system. *Ibid.* 358 It was this Hepburn system..which was adopted by the Romajikai. **1950** D. Jones *Phoneme* 38 The old (Hepburnian) Roman writing of Japanese. **1961** T. Landau *Encycl. Librarianship* (ed. 2) 369/1 These [Japanese] sounds are transcribed into Roman letters, either by the Hepburn system ..or by the Japanese system of 'New spelling'... The outside world sticks to the Hepburn system.

hep-cat (he·pkæt). *slang* (orig. *U.S.*). [f. *hep *a.* + *cat *sb.*[1] 2 c.] An addict of jazz, swing music, etc.; one who is 'hep'; = *hipster[1].

1938 in *Amer. Speech* (1939) XIV. 140 *Hep cat*,..guy who knows what it's [*sc.* swing music is] all about. *a* **1940** F. Scott Fitzgerald *Last Tycoon* (1949) v. 127 Suddenly they were at work again—taking up this new theme in turn like hepcats in a swing band and going to town with it. **1955** *Sci. News Let.* 1 Oct. 221/2 This is not cool chatter between some young hep-cats in a smoke-filled jazz joint. **1957** C. MacInnes *City of Spades* II. xii. 184 You 's the hep-cat what stole Mr. Vial's puss-cat! **1959** *Listener* 9 Apr. 646/2 The lament at a local hep-cat's funeral. **1959** *News Chron.* 14 Oct. 8/6 The jazz-loving 'hep-cat'. **1961** *Times* 20 May 5/1 Mr. Louis Armstrong and his fellow hepcats.

Hepialid (hī·piæ·lid), *a.* and *sb.* *Zool.* Formerly also **epialid**. [ad. mod.L. *Hepialidæ*, f. *Hepialus* (J. C. Fabricius, *Systema Entomologiæ* (1775) 589), a. Gr. ἠπίολος moth; sometimes *Epialidæ*, *Epialus*, perhaps through confusion with Gr. ἠπίαλος nightmare: see -id[3].] (Of or pertaining to) a moth of the family Hepialidæ, the ghost-moths or swifts.

1888 *Proc. Linnean Soc. N.S.W.* II. 1015 We have drawn up a description of the finely coloured Hepialid which was exhibited at the June meeting. **1895** *Funk's Stand. Dict.*, *Ghost-moth*, an epialid moth, especially *Epialus humuli*. *Ibid.*, *Swift*, n... 2. An epialid or ghost-moth. **1900** *Trans. Ent. Soc.* III. 411 (*title*) Life histories in the Hepialid group of Lepidoptera. **1931** *Ann. Appl. Biol.* XVIII. 54 The larva of a Hepialid moth, *Oncopera intricata*.

Hepplewhite (he·p'lˌwəit). The name of George *Hepplewhite* (died 1786), who was succeeded by A. *Hepplewhite* and Co., used *attrib.* to designate an English style of furniture of the latter part of the eighteenth century, characterized by lightness, delicacy, and graceful curves, being an adaptation of current French styles.

1897 K. W. Clouston *Chippendale Period Eng. Furnit.* vii. 177 The Hepplewhite commode has long been obsolete or transformed into the modern cabinet with mirror back. **1900** *Jrnl. Soc. Arts* 23 Mar. 380/1 Hepplewhite and Sheraton furniture should be studied by designers for *motifs*. **1901** *Connoisseur* Dec. 272/2 Six Hepplewhite arm-chairs. **1903** *Chambers's Jrnl.* 20 June 460/1 Three.. ball-and-claw Hepplewhite chairs. **1957** *Encycl. Brit.* XI. 453/1 The smaller Hepplewhite pieces are much prized by collectors.

hepster (he·pstəɹ). *slang* (orig. *U.S.*). Now *rare*. [f. *hep *a.* + -ster.] = *hep-cat. Cf. *hipster[1].

1938 in *Amer. Speech* (1939) XIV. 140/2 Cab Calloway's Cat-alogue, a 'hepster's' dictionary. **1948** [see *bop *sb.*[2]]. **1958** *Spectator* 21 Nov. 702/1 Yet although jazz seems to have burst out of the locked treasure casket over which an egghead minority of hepsters crooned for so many years, it still remains a curiously unreal cult.

hepta-. Add: **he·ptachlor** *Chem.*, a chlorinated hydrocarbon, $C_{10}H_5Cl_7$, used as an insecticide; **hepta(i)co·sane** *Chem.* [Gr. εἴκοσι twenty: see -ane], any of the hydrocarbons of the paraffin series having twenty-seven carbon atoms, *esp.* the unbranched isomer, which is present in tobacco oil and many natural waxes; **heptade·cane** *Chem.* [Gr. δέκα ten: see -ane], any of the hydrocarbons of the paraffin series having seventeen carbon atoms, *esp.* the unbranched isomer; **he:ptahydra·ted** *a.* *Chem.*, containing seven molecules of water; **heptahy·dric** *a.* *Chem.*, containing seven hydroxyl groups; **he·ptastyle** *Archit.* [-*style*, a. Gr. στῦλος pillar], (a building or portico) having seven columns in front; **he·ptose** [a. G. *heptose* (E. Fischer 1890, in *Ber. d. Deut. Chem. Ges.* XXIII. 934): see -ose[2]], any of a group of monosaccharides, $C_7H_{14}O_7$, present in some plants and as constituents of some bacterial polysaccharides.

1949 *Jrnl. Econ. Ent.* XLII. 328/1 Heptachlor, a close relative of chlordan, gave results superior to chlordan. **1961** *New Scientist* 6 July 9/2 British manufacturers of agricultural chemicals have agreed with the Government to restrict the use of three pesticides..aldrin, dieldrin and heptachlor. **1963** R. Carson *Silent Spring* x. 140 Heptachlor, after a short period in the tissues of animals or plants or in the soil, assumes a considerably more toxic form known as heptachlor epoxide... The Food and Drug Administration took action which had the effect of banning any residues of heptachlor or its epoxide in food. **1968** M. Pyke *Food & Society* viii. 119 [They] found not only DDT and its breakdown products, but BHC, heptachlor and dieldrin as well in the tissues of penguins. **1889** Muir & Morley *Watts' Dict. Chem.* II. 675/1 *n*-Heptaicosane $C_{27}H_{56}$. **1901** *Jrnl. Chem. Soc.* LXXIX. I. 96 The results of the analysis..indicate that the second hydrocarbon is in all probability heptacosane, $C_{27}H_{56}$. **1961** L. F. & M. Fieser *Adv. Org. Chem.* iv. 110 Beeswax contains heptacosane ($C_{27}H_{56}$) and hentriacontane ($C_{31}H_{64}$). **1882** *Jrnl. Chem. Soc.* XLII. 1272 Heptadecane (from margaric acid, or from the ketone $C_{17}H_{34}O$, obtained from barium palmitate) crystallizes in large hexagonal plates. **1895** G. Lunge *Sulphuric Acid* (ed. 2) II. 22 The anhydrous salt..if protected from the air is changed into heptahydrated..salt. **1892** E. F. Smith tr. *V. von Richter's Chem. Carbon Compounds* (ed. 2) 49 The heptahydric aldehydes, $C_7H_{14}O_7$, resemble the sugars in their behavior. **1968** J. A. Monick *Alcohols* v. 442 Perseitol..is a heptahydric alcohol with a 7-carbon atom straight-chain that contains seven hydroxyl groups. **1843** *Civil Engin. & Archit. Jrnl.* VI. 167/1 The temple of the giants, at Agrigentum (heptastyle). **1909** A. Marquand *Greek Archit.* vi. 313 Another classification of temples notes merely the number of columns exhibited in the façade... The Theseion at Athens was hexastyle; the Temple at Thorikos, heptastyle. **1890** *Jrnl. Chem. Soc.* LVIII. I. 598 The author proposes to employ the terms pentose, heptose, octose, &c., for the sugars..and heptonic acid, octonic acid, &c., for the acids of the series, according to the number of carbon-atoms in the compounds. **1916** Heptose [see *biose]. **1952** J. K. N. Jones in E. M. Rodd *Chem. Carbon Compounds* IB. xx. 1264 Heptose sugars may exist in ketose and aldose forms. **1960** *Adv. Carbohydrate Chem.* XV. 288 Whereas, in the Enteric group of bacteria, there is as yet no evidence for the presence of heptoses other than L-*glycero*-D-*manno*-heptose, this is not true of other Gram-negative groups.

heptane. Add: **heptano·ic acid,** œnanthic acid, $CH_3\cdot(CH_2)_5\cdot COOH$; **hepteno·ic acid,** any of several monocarboxylic acids, $C_6H_{11}COOH$, having one double bond.

1928 *Chem. Abstr.* XXII. 5909 (*index*) Heptanoic acid. See Enanthic acid. **1964** N. G. Clark *Mod. Org. Chem.* xvi. 317 By heating the heptonic acid with hydriodic acid and red phosphorus, (*n*-)heptanoic acid is produced. **1889** Muir & Morley *Watts' Dict. Chem.* II. 676/1 Heptenoic acid $C_7H_{12}O_2$. **1948** A. W. Ralston *Fatty Acids* ii. 86 None of the heptenoic acids has been identified in the naturally occurring fats and oils.

heptarch (he·ptaɹk), *a.* *Bot.* [f. Gr. ἑπτά seven + ἀρχή beginning, origin: cf. Diarch, Monarch, Octarch, Polyarch, Tetrarch, Triarch *adjs.*] Arising from seven distinct

points of origin, as the xylem of the root of some plants.

1884 [see DECARCH *a.*]. 1914 M. DRUMMOND tr. *Haberlandt's Physiol. Plant Anat.* vii. 353 (*caption*) The heptarch radial bundle [*sc.* stele] of an adventitious root. 1951 MCLEAN & IVIMEY-COOK *Textbk. Theoretical Bot.* I. xx. 791 Dicotyledons usually have two..four..or five xylem groups, less frequently three (triarch) or seven (heptarch), and rarely more.

heptode (he·ptōᵘd). *Radio.* [f. HEPT(A- + *-ODE.] A valve with seven electrodes. Also *attrib.*

1932 *Post Office Electr. Engin. Jrnl.* XXIV. IV. 299/2 A complete electrode assembly of this type includes seven electrodes—hence the name 'Heptode' for the double-acting balanced thermionic valve. 1934 *Times* 11 Aug. 7/3 The days when one could speak simply of a screen-grid valve or a pentode are almost gone, for now there are in general use the double-diode-triode, the heptode, and many others with a double and even treble purpose. 1942 *Electronic Engin.* XIV. 629 The frequency changer follows normal practice..a separate triode with hexode or heptode comprising the local oscillator. 1943 *Gloss. Terms Telecomm.* (*B.S.I.*) 30 *Heptode*, a vacuum tube with seven electrodes normally comprising a hexode with an auxiliary anode between the first grid and the first screen grid or with a suppressor grid between the second screen grid and the (main) anode. 1945 *Electronic Engin.* XVII. 648 A circuit composing a heptode oscillator.

heptose: see *HEPTA-.

Heracleid. Add: **c.** A poem describing the exploits of Heracles.

1725 [see *Theseid* s.v. THESEAN *a.*]. 1904 T. R. GLOVER *Stud. Virgil* iii. 75 Poets who have composed a Herakleid, a Theseid, or other poems of the kind.

heracleum (heræ·kliŏm, herăklī·ŏm). *Bot.* [mod.L. (C. Linnæus *Systema Naturæ* 1735), f. Gr. Ἡρακλεία, the plant named after Heracles.] A plant of a genus of large herbs of this name, belonging to the family Umbelliferæ and native to northern temperate regions; COW-PARSNIP or HOGWEED.

1787 W. WITHERING *Bot. Arrangem. Brit. Plants* (ed. 2) I. 287 Heracleum. 1824 J. E. SMITH *Eng. Flora* II. 101 Heracleum. Cow-parsnep. 1847 H. C. WATSON *Cybele Britannica* I. 451 This [*Angelica sylvestris*] and the Heracleum are the two most widely distributed species of their order. 1864 D. OLIVER *Less. Elem. Bot.* II. 175 (*caption*) Vertical section of flower of Common Heracleum. 1894 W. ROBINSON *Wild Garden* (ed. 4) xiii. 133 Such plants as Heracleum, Willow Herb, and many others..should be planted only in outlying positions. 1951 *Dict. Gardening* (R. Hort. Soc.) II. 986/1 The Heracleums are sometimes grown in shrubberies or the rougher parts of the pleasure grounds.

Heraclitean, *a.* Add: (Earlier and additional examples.) Also **Heracleitean.**

1791 W. ENFIELD *Hist. Philos.* I. 443 Plato himself, when he was young, learned the Heraclitean philosophy from Cratylus, and adopted that part which treated of the nature and motion of matter. 1875 [in Dict.]. 1955 J. K. BAXTER *Fire & Anvil* 65 A Heracleitean cosmos.

Heracliteanism: also **Heracleiteanism.**

1932 *Times Lit. Suppl.* 21 July 531/1 Professor Laird yet finds it in him to relax his comity when dealing with the epistemological Heracleiteanism of Gentile.

herald, *sb.* Add: **5. herald-snake,** the southern African snake, *Crotaphopeltis hotambœia hotambœia*, which has red or yellow lips and is also called the red-lipped snake.

1910 F. W. FITZSIMONS *Snakes S. Afr.* iii. 57/2 The Red-lipped or Herald Snake..is one of the best-known and most widespread snakes in Africa. 1947 J. STEVENSON-HAMILTON *Wild Life S. Afr.* xxxvi. 330 The red-lipped or herald snake (*Leptodira hotamboea*).—This is distinguished by its upper lip being of bright red colour; it carries large light-brown scales and a black headband. 1970 V. F. M. FITZSIMONS *Field Guide to Snakes S. Afr.* 118 *Herald* or *Red-lipped Snake*.., according to the prevailing colour on the upper lips, it is variously known as the White- or Yellow-lipped Snake.

Herat (herā·t). The name of a city in north-western Afghanistan, used to designate a kind of carpet and rug made there, and the small, close design of leaf and rosette patterns characteristic of such rugs. Also **Hera·ti.**

1917 in R. Storrs *Orientations* (1937) x. 261 Some fine old carpets, including a brilliant Herāt. 1931 A. U. DILLEY *Oriental Rugs & Carpets* Pl. 51 (*caption*) Herat rugs... Herat borders. *Ibid.* iv. 118 Herat, applied both to the 'Ispahan' weaving of the sixteenth century and to the blue Herati-patterned rug of the nineteenth century, is, rightly or wrongly, the outstanding name in rugs. 1957 *Encycl. Brit.* XIX. 622/1 (*caption*) The Herati pattern. *Ibid.* 628C/2 The Ferraghan [rugs], with their so-called Herati pattern—an all-over, rather dense design with a light green border on a mordant dye that leaves the pattern in relief. 1960 H. HAYWARD *Antique Coll.* 141/2 *Herat carpets*, fine quality Persian carpets... Knot: Ghiordes or Sehna. 1967 'W. HAGGARD' *Conspirators* ix. 99 There was..fine old mahogany furniture and a Herati rug. 1969 —— *Doubtful Disciple* xv. 166 The dealers call them Isfahans and most of the time they know they're Heratis. 1972 *Observer* 8 Oct. 14/1 (Advt.), A central panel leading to the reception panel shows the Herati pattern on a light red ground.

herb, *sb.* Add: **6.** *herb-lore, -master.*

1955 J. R. R. TOLKIEN *Return of King* 145 A chance of talking herb-lore with me. *Ibid.* 140, I will go and ask of the herb-master.

7. herb-doctor *local U.S.*, one who treats or cures ailments by means of herbs. So **herb-doctress.**

1854 THOREAU *Walden* 150 Hygeia, who was the daughter of that old herb-doctor Aesculapius. *a* 1864 HAWTHORNE *S. Felton* (1871) 113 [Aunt Keziah was] a mixture of an Indian squaw and herb doctress. 1881 *Harper's Mag.* July 305/2 The herb-doctor was not so fortunate as another practitioner of his own class who came to England some years ago. 1891 *Ibid.* Jan. 220/1, I would say that Mr. Pettingill has behaved very strangely —sending for a herb doctor.

herbaceous, *a.* Add: **4.** *herbaceous border*, a border filled with herbaceous perennial plants (so, as nonce-wd., *herbaceous borderer*); *herbaceous perennial*, a plant whose roots live for several years, although stem and leaves die down to the ground each year, after flowering.

[1822 LOUDON *Encycl. Gard.* III. 993 (*heading*) Species and Varieties of..Herbaceous Border-flowers. 1868 D. THOMSON *Handy Bk. of Flower Garden* 6 There is enough in a border of hardy herbaceous plants..to gratify the keenest sensibility.] 1881 T. MOORE *Epitome of Gardening* vi. 190 The herbaceous border should be a distinct compartment, and not less than 10 ft. in width. 1883 F. MILES in W. Robinson *Eng. Flower Garden* p. xl/2 What cannot be done with an herbaceous border edge when that edge is the green grass? 1909 H. G. WELLS *Tono-Bungay* III. ii. § 1 An ardent rose grower and herbaceous borderer. 1931 C. ST. JOHN *Ellen Terry & Bernard Shaw* 132 Miss Audrey Campbell: an enthusiastic amateur actress, and a plant of 'vigorous habit' in Ellen Terry's herbaceous border of friends. 1968 R. HAY *Gardener's Round* 213 A friend, anxious to replant a fairly large herbaceous border, asked me to mark a catalogue for him. 1868 D. THOMSON *Handy Bk. Flower Garden* vi. 153 Herbaceous perennials are a class of plants distinct in their nature. 1871 W. ROBINSON *Hardy Flowers* III. 277 (*heading*) A choice selection of the very finest herbaceous perennials. 1959 C. H. POTTER *Perennials in Garden* i. 8 The term perennial..refers to hardy herbaceous perennials which tend to live year after year without replanting.

herbarium. Add: Also *attrib.*

1849 J. H. BALFOUR *Man. Bot.* 616 This [*sc.* the vasculum] should be of sufficient length to receive a plant of the full size of the herbarium paper. 1887 C. A. MOLONEY *Sk. Forestry W. Afr.* 319 He compared the available herbarium material of the two plants. 1898 B. TORREY in *Atlantic Monthly* Apr. 461/2 A comparison with herbarium specimens. 1962 D. B. O. SAVILE *Coll. & Care Bot. Specimens* i. 50 (*heading*) Herbarium sequence. The operation of the phanerogamic herbarium of the Plant Research Institute may serve as an example of herbarium management. *Ibid.* 52 Ideally the herbarium units should be built like library stack rooms.

Herbartian (həɹbā·ɹtiăn), *a.* and *sb.* [f. the name of J. F. *Herbart* (1776–1841), German philosopher + -IAN.] **A.** *adj.* Of or pertaining to Herbart, or to the system of psychology and teaching originated by him. **B.** *sb.* A disciple or follower of Herbart. Hence **Herba·rtianism,** the doctrines of Herbart.

1884 W. JAMES *Coll. Ess. & Rev.* (1920) 267 The Herbartian psychologists have tried to distinguish feelings due to the *form* in which ideas may be arranged. 1886 *Encycl. Brit.* XX. 41/1 The whole Herbartian psychology. *Ibid.* 62/2 This difference between a conflict of presentations to enter consciousness..and that opposition or incompatibility of presentations which is only possible when they are in consciousness has been strangely confused by the Herbartians. 1903 HAYWARD & THOMAS (*title*) The critics of Herbartianism. 1904 C. I. DODD (*title*) Introduction to the Herbartian principles of teaching. 1908 H. G. WELLS *New Worlds for Old* (1912) v. § 1. 91 This change in the circle of ideas (as the Herbartians put it) is the essence of the Socialist project. *Ibid.* x. § 1. 225 The majority of Socialists still fail to grasp completely the Herbartian truth. 1932 L. BLOOMFIELD in *Language* VIII. 225 Interpreting their methods in terms of Herbartian or Wundtian psychology. 1952 J. A. PASSMORE in G. F. Stout *God & Nature* p. xxix, The Herbartian ethnographic psychologists—Waitz, Lazarus, Steinthal—were at this time exerting a powerful influence upon him. 1971 *Language* XLVII. 980 The choice was between Herbartian and Wundtian doctrines.

herbicide (hə̄·ɹbisəid). [f. L. *herba* grass, green crops + -CIDE.] † **a.** Proprietary name for a preparation, prob. of sodium arsenite, used as a weed-killer. *Obs.* **b.** Any chemical agent that is toxic to some or all plants and is used to destroy unwanted vegetation. Hence **he·rbicidal** *a.*

1899 *Vermont Agric. Exper. Station Ann. Rep. 1898–99* 185 Carbolic acid is a valuable herbicide..but..the herbicidal action is of short duration. 1906 *U.S. Trade-mark 48,757* My [*sc.* W. J. Reade's] trade-mark consists of the coined word 'Herbicide'. The trade-mark has been continuously used in my business since 1894. 1915 *Chem. Abstr.* IX. 1973 (*caption*) Herbicides with arsenical base. 1942 W. W. ROBBINS et al. *Weed Control* xiii. 229 Studies of herbicides in soils show that the following factors determine the herbicidal effects of any chemical: (1) inherent toxicity of the chemical; (2) adsorption of the chemical by the soil; (3) decomposition..tending to reduce toxicity;..and (6) species tolerance. 1947 *New Biol.* II. 109 During recent years various organic compounds have been tested for their possible herbicidal value. 1954 *Sci. News* XXXI. 104 Weeds, therefore, could easily get life insurance were it not for the modern technique of chemical weed-killing, in particular by selective herbicides. 1959 *New Scientist* 5 Nov. 894/2 In abstracting and indexing the world's literature on weed control at Oxford [Department of Agriculture] we are constantly faced with difficulties caused by there being no agreement on what to call a herbicide. 1969 N. W. PIRIE *Food Resources* ii. 65 In Britain nearly all farms of more than 100 acres use herbicides on cereals. 1971 *Nature* 22 Jan. 224/1 Herbicidal attack appears to prevent the re-establishment of any new plant community..for at least six years.

Hercynian, *a.* Delete the phr. beginning 'esp.' and add: **1.** (Later examples.)

1890 J. G. FRAZER *Golden Bough* I. i. 56 Down to the first century before our era the Hercynian forest stretched eastward from the Rhine for a distance at once vast and unknown. 1935 W. G. EAST *Hist. Geogr. Europe* ii. 51 The Hercynian forest, as Caesar described it, could be crossed in nine days by a fast runner.

2. In *Geol.* used by different writers in various senses, with allusion to the Harz Mountains.

The word was first used in geology as the G. *hercynisch* (according to Suess by von Buch) in sense c, and was adopted by several writers, chiefly German and French, in sense a; in 1887 Bertrand (*Bull. de la Soc. géol. de France* XV. 438) used it in sense b to replace the *variscisch und armoricanisch* of Suess, and this has become the usual sense in English.

a. Designating one of the Devonian formations of the Harz Mountains; so *Hercynian fauna* (after Kayser, 1879), *gneiss* (after Gümbel, 1868).

1880 J. D. DANA *Man. Geol.* (ed. 3) III. i. 151 In Europe, the Archæan system has been distinctly recognized in.. Bavaria (Hercynian and Bojie Gneiss). 1885 Hercynian gneiss [in Dict.]. 1893 P. LAKE tr. *Kayser's Text Bk. Compar. Geol.* II. 101 First described by H. Römer and Giebel as Silurian, this Hercynian fauna of the Lower Harz has more recently been compared by E. Beyrich with the fauna of the Bohemian stages F, G, H of Barrande, and was afterwards described by Kayser..as Lower Devonian. 1895 J. D. DANA *Man. Geol.* (ed. 4) IV. ii. 570 Kayser concluded..that the Lower Helderberg formation of America was Hercynian, that is, lowest Devonian. 1906 CHAMBERLIN & SALISBURY *Geology* II. viii. 450 The Hercynian fauna which characterizes this stage of the Devonian in southern Europe has much in common with the Helderberg fauna of America. 1955 G. G. WOODFORD tr. *Gignoux's Stratigr. Geol.* iv. 128 The Hercynian facies of the Lower Devonian appears in the Kellerwald.

b. Of, pertaining to, or contemporaneous with the mountain-building movements that occurred in Europe in late Carboniferous and early Permian times, or the mountains then formed; hence, late Palæozoic; = *ARMORICAN *a.* 2.

1895 J. D. DANA *Man. Geol.* (ed. 4) IV. iii. 734 The 'Hercynian system' of Bertrand includes a long range of dislocated Devonian and Carboniferous rocks extending from Brittany to the Vosges and Ardennes, and beyond along the Black Forest, the Harz to Bohemia. 1926 *Publ. Carnegie Inst. Washington* No. 375. v. 69 The movements in late Stephanian and in Permian time can best be considered as the final effects of the Hercynian movement. 1935 E. B. BAILEY *Tectonic Ess.* i. 5 The Ardennes of Belgium and much of the Appalachians of America are alike members of the Hercynian System. *Ibid.* 8 Hercynian in Bertrand's sense has established itself apparently for all time in the literature of France, Switzerland, Britain, and America. 1948 R. L. SHERLOCK *Permo-Triassic Formations* iv. 40 Like the present Alps, the Hercynian Mountains were the result of the squeezing of the sediments deposited in a Mediterranean Sea, the Palaeozoic Tethys. 1967 D. H. RAYNER *Stratigr. Brit. Isles* i. 27 Extending down the centre of England..there are various Carboniferous outcrops whose structures are largely Hercynian in age but which follow older directions.

c. Applied (rarely in English) to those faults, folds, and other geological features in Europe with a predominantly north-western direction.

1904 H. B. SOLLAS tr. *Suess's Face of Earth* I. I. iii. 121 This..does not exclude the existence in Central Europe of two different directions, which have produced folds and mountain chains striking more to the north-east in the one case, in the other more to the north-west. The former is known as the direction of the Netherlands, the latter as the Hercynian direction. 1909 *Ibid.* IV. v. i. 2 The important point for L. von Buch, when he created the 'Hercynian system', was the (orographical) north-westerly direction, for Marcel Bertrand it was the tectonic age. *Ibid.* 33 These fractures..determine L. von Buch's 'Hercynian system', which embraces all the mountains striking to the north-west; many eminent German geologists still describe these long lines as Hercynian. 1935 E. B. BAILEY *Tectonic Ess.* i. 5 For von Buch, the Hercynian character was a west-north-westerly, or north-westerly, *trend*... Accordingly, among German-speaking tectonists, Hercynian is still commonly employed to group together a very important set of more or less north-westerly fractures and folds that characterize much of Czechoslovakia, Germany, and Scania.

herd, *sb.*[1] Add: **4. a. herd-testing** *vbl. sb.*, testing of the butterfat content of the milk from cows of a specified herd and their productivity; so **herd-tester**; also *herd test.*

1962 J. N. WINBURNE *Dict. Agric.* 374/2 *Herd test*, a

type of semiofficial testing for milk production in which the whole herd of cows of milking age are included. **1960** B. CRUMP *Good Keen Man* 94 He told me..all about one of his sisters who was training to be a herd-tester. **1966** G. W. TURNER *Eng. Lang. Austral. & N.Z.* vii. 149 A herd-tester is a man or woman who goes from farm to farm sampling milk to test cows for their productivity and the fat content of their milk. **1911** *Jrnl. Dept. Agric.* (N.Z.) 15 July 26 A striking case of the value of testing the individual members of a herd is reported from a district where a herd-testing association has been established. **1956** AMESS & JOHNSON *Dairying* (ed. 4) xv. 195 All herd-testing is now done by the New Zealand Herd Improvement Associations under direction from the Dairy Board.

b. *Psychol.* Denoting feelings, actions, thoughts, etc., common to a large company of people; esp. **herd instinct**, an instinctive tendency to think and act as one of a crowd. (Cf. sense 3.)

1908 W. TROTTER in *Sociol. Rev.* I. 227 (*title*) Herd instinct and its bearing on the psychology of civilised man. **1908** *Westm. Gaz.* 22 Aug. 16/1 The fundamental assumptions of the Liberal and the Conservative are hostile, and are the outcome of herd tradition. **1912** J. LONDON *Let.* 18 Jan. (1966) 359 There is a sort of herd psychology in this. **1914** G. B. SHAW *Androcles & Lion* (1916) 46 That herd instinct which makes men abhor all departures from custom. **1919** M. K. BRADBY *Psycho-anal.* 113 Not even abandonment to 'herd enthusiasm' could destroy the terrible loneliness of death. **1920** B. RUSSELL *Pract. & Theory Bolshevism* I. 125 The Marxian assumes that a man's 'herd' from the point of view of herd-instinct, is his class. **1922** *Brit. Jrnl. Psychol.* Oct. 118 The love complex, the religion complex, the herd complex and many others. **1923** J. S. HUXLEY *Ess. Biologist* vii. 275 The herd ideas..may be those of a nation or of a stratum within the nation. **1924** W. B. SELBIE *Psychol. Relig.* 148 Man is a gregarious animal, and even in his civilized condition never quite loses his herd consciousness. **1927** N. P. WILLIAMS *Ideas of Fall & Orig. Sin* p. xxix, We therefore identify the 'inherited infirmity' of theology with 'inherited weakness of herd-complex'. **1927** M. SADLEIR *Trollope* ii. 49 She was.. lacking in that pride of individuality which throws persons of a different type into automatic opposition to herd-bias. **1928** G. B. SHAW *Intell. Woman's Guide Socialism* v. 11 Our minds are mostly herd minds, with only a scrap of individual mind on top. **1932** Q. D. LEAVIS *Fiction & Reading Public* I. iii. 67 These writers are using the technique of Marie Corelli..to work upon and solidify herd prejudice. **1939** J. MASEFIELD *Live & Kicking Ned* 344 What saved us was the fact that Mimbo is an animal passion or herd-madness, which blinds each of the herd to all other things than the herd-enemy. **1942** R. A. KNOX *In Soft Garments* xxi. 162 There is such a thing as herd-morality. You notice it especially in matters like divorce, where social considerations necessarily apply. **1960** C. DAY LEWIS *Buried Day* ii. 43 At the age of eight or nine the herd instinct begins to operate.

herd, *v.*[2] **1. b.** Delete *rare* and add further examples. Also *transf.*, spec. (*U.S. slang*) to drive (a car, aircraft, etc.).

1895 KIPLING *Second Jungle Book* 67 Who is Man that we should care for him..? I have followed him all day—at noon—in the white sunlight. I herded him as the wolves herd buck. **1927** W. FAULKNER *Mosquitoes* 261 'Come on here, you men.' He named over his depleted watch and herded it forward. He herded it down to his cabin and nourished it with stimulants. **1954** —— *Fable* (1955) 100 He saw the two-seater..the two S.E.'s above and behind it, herding it down. **1955** *Sunday Times* 25 Sept. 3/3 (*heading*) Herd that beast!.. I append an up-to-the-minute glossary of motoring terms..*herd*, to drive a car. **1971** M. TAK *Truck Talk* 82 *Herd*, to drive a truck.

herdsman. Add: So **he·rdsmanship**, the performance or occupation of a herdsman.

1889 J. M. ROBERTSON *Christ & Krishna* xvi. 113 The theory of Krishna's herdsmanship being derived from the cloud-cows of the Vedas is new. **1960** *Farmer & Stockbreeder* 8 Mar. 120 (*caption*) Good herdsmanship, prompt veterinary attention and close liaison between the herdsman and the farm staff are essential.

here, *adv.* Add: **1. e.** *here today and gone tomorrow*: a catch-phrase indicating a constant change of events or someone (or something) remaining in a place for a short time.

1687 A. BEHN *Luckey Chance* iv. 47 Faith Sir, we are here to Day and gone to Morrow. **1776** H. NEWDIGATE *Let.* in A. E. Newdigate-Newdegate *Cheverels* (1898) i. 10 Going over for a day to Arbury to beat for Wood Cocks.. as they are birds of passage, here today and gone tomorrow. **1895** KIPLING *Day's Work* (1898) 172 Here today and gone tomorrow. Didn't come to stay for ever. **1944** W. S. MAUGHAM *Razor's Edge* IV. iv. 132 Even in the old days you could never count on his being where you expected him to be. He was here today and gone tomorrow. **1972** *Listener* 23 Nov. 690/2 We [*sc.* the TUC] put forward proposals for a general rise in pensions—not a 'Christmas Box' that is here today and gone tomorrow.

2. b. *here's hoping, how, looking* (*at you*), *luck*, formulas used in drinking healths.

1888 KIPLING *Soldiers Three* (1889) 51 He opened a bottle... 'Here's luck!' **1896**, etc. [see How *adv.* 18 in Dict. and Suppl.]. **1910** W. M. RAINE *B. O'Connor* iii. 40 'Here's hoping,' Bucky nodded gaily. 'I bet there will be a right lively wolf hunt.' **1933** M. LOWRY *Ultramarine* 164 Here's looking at you! **1938** E. HEMINGWAY *Fifth Column* (1939) 184 Here's looking at you... Here's how. **1973** E. LEMARCHAND *Let or Hindrance* xii. 142 Pollard..raised his glass to her. 'Here's hoping.'

5. b. *here's where..*, this is the point at which. *U.S. colloq.*

1923 R. D. PAINE *Comr. Rolling Ocean* xii. 203 'It makes me feel sick at my stomach', declared Briscoe. 'Here's where you feel sicker. Great Scott, look at that.' *Ibid.* xiv. 250 Here's where I slip it out to the old gink.

13. b. here we go again: we are off on the same undesirable course, project, etc., as before. Also used as *attrib. phr.*

1954 R. BISSELL *High Water* (1955) xix. 161 'Time to get up, Mister Duke.' 'Oh, hell,' I thought. 'Here we go again.' **1958** B. MALAMUD *Magic Barrel* (1960) 72 'Ah, there I can't help you,' said the portiere. 'I haven't got the key.' 'Here we go again,' Carl muttered. **1962** J. BALDWIN *Another Country* (1963) II. iii. 270 'Oh, shit,' he said, 'here we go again.' **1969** *Listener* 12 June 836/1 One of William Glock's most difficult tasks in planning each year's series of Promenade Concerts is to write that desperate here-we-go-again introduction to the prospectus.

B. as *sb.* Delete (*nonce-uses*) and add: (Instances of objective uses.) *here and now* (later examples); also as *advb. phr.*; so *here-and-nowness*. Also *here and there* sb. phr.

1816 M. E. BICKNELL *Let.* 26 Sept. in J. Constable *Corr.* (1964) II. 210, I know of no other plan but of my leaving here early on Monday. **1838** DICKENS *O. Twist* II. xxxiv. 269, I—I—ought to have left here before. **1839** —— *Let. c* 24 July (1965) I. 567, I dine in town tomorrow and shall leave *for here* at 10 at night. **1857** —— *Dorrit* II. xxxiv, You would rather not leave here till to-morrow morning. **1874** GEO. ELIOT in *Macm. Mag.* XXXVIII. July 177 Widening his consciousness from Here and Now to larger wholes. **1887** RIDER HAGGARD *A. Quatermain* xvi. 188 Here and now for thy dear sake I will forget my people and my father's house. **1922** W. S. MAUGHAM *On Chinese Screen* xliii. 172 Your thoughts travel through time and space, far from the Here and Now. **1933** P. GODFREY *Back-Stage* xiv. 176 Its romantic appeal is an escape from here and now into an artificial world of somewhere else or some time past. *a* **1943** R. G. COLLINGWOOD *Idea of Hist.* (1946) 248 The detail of the here-and-now as given him in perception. **1957** C. DAY LEWIS *Pegasus* 56 The truant here-and-there of the Stour. **1959** *Listener* 26 Feb. 385/1 Whether Condorcet or Huxley is right is an undecidable question for us here and now. **1959** *Times Lit. Suppl.* 11 Sept. 522/3 All combine to form a subtle escape-route from the unwelcome here-and-now of the twentieth century. **1961** I. MURDOCH *Severed Head* x. 85 She was all gentleness and filled with so genuine a concern to save me here and now from distress and anxiety. **1962** *Listener* 26 Apr. 717/2 Here and now Russia, while she does not want a war with us, is nevertheless our antagonist. **1963** *Times* 27 Feb. 13/1 They came, it seems, to a realization of the here-and-nowness of life. **1971** *New Scientist* 27 Apr. 263/1 Cocking's group have *their* minds firmly concentrated on the here-and-now.

hereditary, *a.* Add: **2. a.** (Further examples.)

1833 *Destructive* 22 June 166/3 (*heading*) Absurdity of 'hereditary wisdom'. **1899** W. JAMES *Talks to Teachers* xiv. 164 The foreign terms 'déséquilibré', 'hereditary degenerate', and 'psychopathic' subject, have arisen in response to the same need. **1928** B. D. JACKSON *Gloss. Bot. Terms* (ed. 4) 176/1 *Hereditary symbiosis*, the presence of mycobacteria in the tissues, including seeds. **1941** J. S. HUXLEY *Uniqueness of Man* ii. 48 The latter [*sc.* fraternal twins] will have hereditary outfits as different as those of members of the same family born at different times. **1967** MAHLOUDI & PIKIELNY in *Brain* XC. 672 With such divergence of opinion, it may be wise to drop the term paramyoclonus multiplex altogether. Instead we suggest the term *hereditary essential myoclonus*.

B. as *sb.* A hereditary ruler; in *pl.*, the House of Lords.

1836 *Radical* 13 Mar. 4/1 The debate, or rather debates in the House of Commons, on the question of justice to the Irish, are but a sad augury of its ever passing the 'Hereditaries' unemasculated. **1932** G. B. SHAW *Platform & Pulpit* (1962) 246 The hereditaries are brought up to exercise their personal power conventionally and leave the rest to their ministers.

Hereford (he·rĭfǝɹd). The name of the county town of Herefordshire, a county in the west of England, used to designate a breed of cattle originating there, distinguished by their reddish-brown colour and white faces. Also **He·refordshire.**

1789 W. MARSHALL *Rural Econ. Glouc.* II. 226 The Herefordshire breed of cattle..may..be deemed the finest breed of cattle in this island... In general appearance the Herefordshire cattle resemble very much those of Sussex. **1805** J. LAWRENCE *Gen. Treat. Cattle* 46 Are we to conjecture, that the Herefords owe their bald face to the smoky white faces of the red cattle of Montgomery? *Ibid.* 48 The distinguishing qualities of Hereford oxen. **1805** J. DUNCUMB *Agric. Hereford* 118 The Leicestershire cow..will never breed a rival to the Herefordshire ox... There is an extraordinary difference between the weight of a Herefordshire cow and the ox bred from her. **1807** R. SOUTHEY *Lett. from Eng.* (1951) lxxi. 452 Here people will apply to..a Herefordshire bull, the same epithets of praise..which a sculptor would bestow upon the Venus de Medici. **1834** W. YOUATT *Cattle* iii. 31 The Herefordshire white-faced breed... The Hereford oxen are considerably larger than the North Devons... The old Herefords were brown or red-brown. **1836** *Penny Cycl.* VI. 379/2 The Herefordshire oxen are best suited to the rich pastures of their native county. **1844** H. STEPHENS *Bk. Farm* III. 1273 Another breed ..is the Hereford, which has long been famed for its excellent steers. **1862** J. C. MORTON *Farmer's Cal.* 578 The Herefords, another leading breed of cattle, characterized by red body and white or mottled face, come almost as early to maturity as the short-horn. **1875** *Encycl. Brit.* I. 388/1 The Hereford is the breed which in England contests most closely with the short-horns for the palm of excellence. **1889** R. WALLACE *Farm Live Stock* (ed. 2) vi. 74 *A Cross*, bred from a Galloway cow by a bull of one of the favourite or improved breeds, such as short-horn or Hereford, is usually an excellent butchers' animal... The Hereford crosses are..polled, with a white head and a red or dark grey body. **1931** *Times Lit. Suppl.* 20 Aug. 625/3 The fat Herefords that graze lazily in English meadows. **1960** *Farmer & Stockbreeder* 15 Mar. 95 A yardful of well-finished Hereford-cross beef. **1973** *Country Life* 8 Mar. 654 Cattle Societies... The Hereford herd book society.

herem, var. *CHEREM.

Herero (herēǝ·ro). One of a negroid people in South-West Africa, also called *Cattle Damara*; also their Bantu language, called *Otshi-Herero* by the Hereros themselves.

1862 W. H. I. BLEEK *Comp. Gram. S. Afr. Langs.* I. 8 The language of *Benguela*..is quite distinct..from the Herero species. *Ibid.* ii. 22 Kongo *bhobha* (to speak, talk) is Hereró *póp͡a* (to warn, persuade). **1868** F. W. KOLBE (*title*) A brief statement of the discovery of the laws of the vowels in Herero. **1880** *Encycl. Brit.* XI. 731/2 *Hereroland*..so called from the native race known to the Namaqua as Herero and to the Cape colonists as Damara. **1904** *Westm. Gaz.* 30 Jan. 2/2 The Kaffirs are joining the Hereros in attacking the Germans. **1952** L. G. GREEN *Lords of Last Frontier* (1953) ii. 18 Midway in the sixteenth century those forceful Bantu, the Hereros, reached the end of a long migration, and settled in the cattle country. *Ibid.* xv. 148 Hereros are tall people, especially the men... Features are almost European, with well-shaped noses, high foreheads and oval faces. **1961** L. VAN DER POST *Heart of Hunter* I. iii. 64 The black man, the Herero, the Bastaards, had kraals and lands of their own. **1972** *Cape Times* 10 Mar. 1/1 Mr. John Garvey Muundjua, a Herero who is the South West Africa National Union's 'Secretary for External Affairs'. **1973** *Times* 8 Mar. 6/2 Herero tribal leaders have rejected an invitation from the Government to appoint representatives to sit on the advisory council.

heresy. Add: **4.** *heresy-hunter*.

1765 A. MACLAINE tr. *Mosheim's Eccl. Hist.* (1844) I. xiii. 344 This new set of heresy-hunters. **1831** CARLYLE in *Edin. Rev.* LIII. Mar. 168 Scenting out Infidelity with the nose of an ancient Heresy-hunter, though for opposite purposes. **1902** *Westm. Gaz.* 7 May 12/1 A proceeding quite in harmony with the usual methods of heresy-hunters. **1906** *Daily Chron.* 16 Oct. 3/3 The heresy-hunter made him his quarry.

herewith, *adv.* Add: **B.** *adj.* Accompanying.

1917 'CONTACT' *Airman's Outings* p. xii, It was a squadron that possessed..the herewith testimonial.

Hering (hē·riŋ, he·-). The name of Karl Ewald Konstantin *Hering* (1834–1918), German psychologist and physiologist, used *attrib.* or in the possessive to designate certain physiological effects observed, and principles enunciated, by him.

1891 M. FOSTER *Textbk. Physiol.* (ed. 5) IV. III. iii. 1232 Hering's theory attempts to reconcile..the various facts of colour vision with the supposition that we possess ..six fundamental sensations. **1902** *Encycl. Brit.* XXI. 749/2 Hering's theory proceeds on the assumption of chemical changes in the retina under the influence of light. *Ibid.*, Hering's theory accounts satisfactorily for the formation of coloured after-images. **1911** GOULD *Pocket Med. Dict.* (ed. 6) 415 *Hering's Law.* The distinctness or purity of any sensation or conception depends upon the proportion existing between their intensity and the sum total of the intensities of all simultaneous sensations and conceptions. **1934** H. C. WARREN *Dict. Psychol.* 123/2 *Hering after-image*, the first positive after-image, or after-sensation, which occurs following a brief light-stimulus. *Ibid.*, *Hering illusion*, an illusion, or distorted perception of visual form, observed when a number of lines radiating from a point are crossed by two parallel lines on opposite sides of the point and equidistant from it; the parallel lines appear to bow outward, i.e. away from the central point. *Ibid.*, *Hering theory of vision*, the theory..according to which visual sensations are due to three pairs of antagonistic processes in the optic system. **1971** *Jrnl. Gen. Psychol.* LXXXIV. 164 The Zöllner and Hering illusions are examples of phenomena in which the overall pattern dominates the geometry and leads to the perceptual distortion of straight lines into curved lines.

herit. Delete †*Obs.* and add *rare.* (Later examples.)

1876 'INDIAN CHAPLAIN' *Mahabuleshwar Hills* 40 Each hallow'd spirit Hath gone the land of life and love to herit. **1922** JOYCE *Ulysses* 401 To herit the tradition of a proper breeding.

hermeneut and related words: (Earlier and later examples.)

1678 R. BURTHOGGE *Organum Vetus & Novum* 70 Ratiocination Speculative, is either Euretick or Hermeneutick, Inventive or Interpretative. **1906** *Westm. Gaz.* 19 Jan. 4/2 More than could be expected from the most practical and most skilful hermeneutist. **1965** *Listener* 3 June 820/1 The word-event which once happened and in happening became the text..must become a word-event again through the interpretation of the 'hermeneut', who transposes it into the thought-mode of his own day. **1967** J. MACQUARRIE *God-Talk* vii. 148 We could say that history is the hermeneutic of historical existence, or even that physics..is the hermeneutic of nature. **1968** C. E. BRAATEN *History of Hermeneutics* vi. 138 Preaching today is the goal of exegesis and hermeneutical reflection. **1972** *Times Lit. Suppl.* 20 Oct. 1262/1 The quest for a hermeneutics.

Hermesianism. (Earlier example.)
1847 J. H. NEWMAN *Let.* 10 Jan. (1962) XII. 8, I dread Hermesianism.

hermetic, *a.* **2. a, b.** *fig.* and *transf.* Further examples, esp. in senses 'unaffected by external influences, recondite'.
1954 *Ann. Reg. 1953* 204 From the published texts [of the Spanish agreement with America] might be inferred the existence of certain secret clauses, guardedly described as 'hermetic'. **1965** *Listener* 2 Sept. 351/2 Poems ranging from the hermetic to the directly obscene. **1966** *Ibid.* 5 May 663/2 It is hermetic music and solely concerned with problems of formal design, structure, and instrumental texture. **1972** *Times Lit. Suppl.* 25 Aug. 984/3 The poetry which he had written between the wars was considered hermetic by some.
3. a. (Examples.)
a **1891** J. R. LOWELL *Old Eng. Dramatists* (1892) 17 They [*sc.* the Elizabethans] had the Hermetic gift of buckling wings to the feet of their verse. **1951** AUDEN *Nones* (1952) 60 In fake Hermetic uniforms. *Ibid.* 61 Keep well the Hermetic Decalogue.

hermetism (hɜ·ɹmĭtiz'm). [f. HERMET(IC *sb.* + -ISM.] Hermetic or theosophical philosophy; hermetics. So **hermeto·logist**, a hermetist.
1894 G. S. HALL in *Forum* Aug. 719 (Cent. D. Suppl.), Its teachings..make the doctrine of sin as vital as with the most ardent of the old hermetologists. **1898** H. C. BOLTON in *Smithsonian Rep. 1897* 213 Traditions of the kabala, the mysteries of hermetism, and the practice of transmutation. **1927** *Contemp. Rev.* July 59 M. Valéry's poetics have been accused of hermetism and of preciousness.

hermit, *sb.* Add: **3.** *spec.* of a sheep. Also *hermit sheep*. *Austral.* and *N.Z.*
1874 A. BATHGATE *Colonial Experiences* xv. 212 A sheep which has been badly tutued and recovers, loses its gregarious habits, and becomes what the shepherds call a 'hermit'. **1917** E. GLEN *Six Little N.Zers* vii. 95 They brought in a 'hermit' sheep which lived by itself, and had been overlooked in the last muster. **1933** L. G. D. ACLAND in *Press* (Christchurch, N.Z.) 28 Oct. 15/7 *Hermit*, a single sheep which for some reason takes to living by himself, away from the mob. **1966** G. W. TURNER *Eng. Lang. Austral. & N.Z.* viii. 165 Sheep that recovered [from eating tutu] sometimes became hermit sheep, losing their gregarious habits.

hermithood (hɜ·ɹmithud). [f. HERMIT *sb.*: see -HOOD.] The state or condition of a hermit.
1915 C. C. MARTINDALE *In God's Army* I. ii. 62 Vocations to hermithood are few. **1938** *Times Lit. Suppl.* 19 Nov. 745/2 Sentenced to a compulsory hermithood in a hideous African desert, the convict contrives to be brought back to Constantinople.

Hermitian (hɜɹmi·ʃăn), *a.* *Math.* Also **herm-, -ean.** [ad. F. *hermitien* sb. and adj. (L. Autonne 1902, in *Rendiconti d. Circolo matem.* XVI. 104), f. the name of C. *Hermite* (1822–1905), French mathematician: see -IAN.] Applied to a matrix in which pairs of elements symmetrically placed with respect to the principal diagonal are complex conjugates, and to other quantities (such as a self-adjoint operator or transformation, or a bilinear form) whose coefficients or elements form such a matrix; *Hermitian conjugate*, the complex conjugate of the transpose of a matrix.
1927 *Proc. R. Soc.* A. CXIII. 628 If *b* commutes with H, the new matrix..will be a diagonal matrix, and if in addition the elements of the matrices *b* and b^{-1} satisfy the condition that $b(\alpha'\alpha'')$ and $b^{-1}(\alpha''\alpha')$ are conjugate imaginaries, each matrix G will be Hermitian when the corresponding matrix *g* is Hermitian. **1935** P. A. M. DIRAC *Princ. Quantum Mech.* (ed. 2) ii. 29 These are just the relations required for the matrix formed by the α_{rs} to be what is called a Hermitian matrix. A linear operator that satisfies this condition may conveniently be called a Hermitian operator. **1940** E. T. BELL *Devel. Math.* xiv. 285 From Hermite's arithmetical theory of these forms..evolved the extensive theory of Hermitian forms and matrices, which after 1925 became familiar to physicists through the revised quantum theory. **1951** J. A. SCHOUTEN *Tensor Analysis for Physicists* x. 241 For co- or contravariant hermitian tensors the following theorem holds. **1961** POWELL & CRASEMANN *Quantum Mech.* ix. 295 Other matrices related to $A = (a_{ij})$, which occur frequently in the theory, are the transpose of *A*,.. and the Hermitian conjugate of *A*, $A^{\dagger} = (a^{*}_{ji})$. **1965** *Czech. Math. Jrnl.* XV. 37 Let *A*, *H* be *n*-by-*n* hermitian matrices. **1967** G. G. HALL *Appl. Group Theory* iii. 33 A less obvious example is that complex Hermitean 2×2 matrices form a four-dimensional real Euclidean space. **1969** T. F. JORDAN *Linear Operators Quantum Mech.* ii. 23 A Hermitian operator *A* is characterized by the equation $(\phi, A\psi) = (A\phi, \psi)$ or $(\phi, A\psi) = (\psi, A\phi)^{*}$ holding for all vectors ψ and ϕ. **1973** *Physics Bull.* July 449/2 The analogous results for hermitean matrices.

herniation (hɜɹniēⁱ·ʃən). *Path.* [f. HERNIA + -TION.] Protrusion as in a hernia.
1897 *Allbutt's Syst. Med.* III. 712 A series of herniations of the intestinal walls. **1962** *Lancet* 22 Dec. 1332/2 Powell and Johnstone have reported the case of a mother who had taken phenmetrazine during two of her pregnancies and produced both times an infant with a defect of the left diaphragm and herniation of abdominal organs into the thoracic cavity.

hernio-. Add: **herniorrha·phy** *Surg.* [*-RRHAPHY], the operation of repairing a hernia and suturing the opening.
1919 *Surg., Gynec. & Obstetr.* XXIX. 201 Treatment of the sac in herniorrhaphy... High ligation and amputation of the hernial sac is a point..on which most surgeons are agreed. **1962** *Lancet* 27 Jan. 221/1 This problem engaged our interest in 1959 when we reviewed 762 patients who had had herniorrhaphies performed in the previous ten years. **1963** *Ibid.* 19 Jan. 133/1 A man, aged 62, who had a large indirect inguinal hernia with an associated undescended testis, underwent right inguinal herniorrhaphy and orchidectomy.

hero, *sb.* Add: **5.** *hero-cult, -fantasy, -figure, -image*; **hero sandwich** *U.S. slang*, a very large sandwich; also *ellipt.* **hero.**
1945 KOESTLER *Yogi & Commissar* III. ii. 197 His famous speech on the 24th anniversary of the Soviet Revolution..which started the new hero-cult. **1960** C. DAY LEWIS *Buried Day* 22 Nor..did I indulge in the hero-fantasies of the only child. **1958** *Punch* 23 July 102/3 But surely his agent..built up an image of this untalented scallywag as a top-line genius and hero-figure for millions who little guessed? **1963** *Times Lit. Suppl.* 11 Jan. 29/3 The bodily posture adopted by Japanese hero-figures. **1951** M. MCLUHAN *Mech. Bride* 63/1 Li'l Abner himself is a cluster of the swarming hero images. **1955** *Sat. Even. Post* 1 Jan. 16 When he got back to Brooklyn, the first thing he asked for was an Italian hero sandwich.., two inches thick and eighteen inches long. **1957** *Britannica Bk. of Year* 512/1 *Hero-sandwich*, a sandwich made with a whole loaf of bread. **1959** R. CONDON *Manchurian Candidate* v. 91 She wiped her mouth with the back of her hand like a labourer who had just finished a hero sandwich and a bottle of beer. **1963** M. SCHERF *Death & Diplomat* (1964) v. 62 They have hot and cold heros next door. **1972** *New Yorker* 1 July 21/2 An office just above a hero-sandwich shop.

Herodotean (hĭrǫdǫ̆tī·ăn), *a.* [f. the name of *Herodotus* (Gr. Ἡρόδοτος), Greek historian of the fifth century B.C.: see -AN.] Of, pertaining to, characteristic of, or mentioned by Herodotus.
1856 K. H. DIGBY *Lover's Seat* II. xiii. 67 They are remarkably Herodotean in their style of operation. **1857** DUFFERIN *Lett. High Lat.* 54 The Herodotean work of Sturleson. **1872** W. MINTO *Man. Eng. Prose Lit.* II. vi. 413 A Herodotean knack of giving numerical measures of extent. **1881** *Athenæum* 2 Apr. 456/2 Some of the reports which he received he recounts with Herodotean incredulity. **1883** *Macm. Mag.* May 67/2 This is what I mean by calling him Herodotean. Nothing was too small nor too apparently remote from the main studies of his life to escape him or be without interest for him.

heroic, *a.* Add: **2.** *heroic age*: also *transf.*
1897 W. P. KER *Epic & Romance* i. 7 What the 'heroic age' of the modern nations really was, may be learned from what is left of their heroic literature, especially from three groups or classes,—the old Teutonic alliterative poems on native subjects; the French *Chansons de Geste*; and the Icelandic Sagas. **1912** H. M. CHADWICK *Heroic Age* v. 105 This carries us back..to what we may call the Russian Heroic Age. **1927** E. V. GORDON *Introd. Old Norse* p. xxix, The Germanic heroic age of the fourth to seventh centuries. **1928** W. W. LAWRENCE *Beowulf & Epic Trad.* 24 This was the usual procedure of a minstrel of the Heroic Age, who knew of all notable men about the circle of the seas. **1948** K. MALONE in *English Studies* XXIX. 170 All these passages serve to make our hero part and parcel of the heroic age of Germanic antiquity. **1965** K. SISAM *Struct. Beowulf* 7 The doors of Heorot opened into the Heroic Age.

heroin (he·roˌin; formerly also hĭrōᵘ·in). [a. G. *heroin*, f. Gr. ἥρως HERO; said to be so derived because of the inflation of the personality consequent upon taking the drug: see -INE⁵.] A white crystalline alkaloid prepared from morphine by acetylation, which is administered usu. in the form of its hydrochloride as a hypnotic and analgesic (though many countries prohibit this medical use), and which is illicitly used as a powerful and addictive drug producing intense euphoric sensations. Also *attrib.*
1898 *Lancet* 3 Dec. 1511/1 A new hypnotic, to which the name of 'heroin' has been given, has been tried in the medical clinic of Professor Gerhardt in Berlin. According to a communication made by Dr. Strube to the *Berliner Klinische Wochenschrift* it is a product of the di-acetic ester of morphia, and it was discovered by Professor Dreser, chief of the chemical department of the Elberfeld Farben Fabriken. **1908** *Practitioner* Apr. 436 Subcutaneous injections of morphia or heroin locally. **1910** *Ibid.* Apr. 542 A sedative may be prescribed... Heroin hydrochloride is the best drug for this purpose. **1920** A. B. BAXTER *Parts Men Play* xviii, She..took to opium cigarettes, and then to heroin. She disappeared one night. **1955** *Sci. News Let.* 2 Apr. 219/2 Morphine and heroin, for example, do not give normal persons the 'kick' and pleasant sensations they are supposed to give. **1962** K. ORVIS *Damned & Destroyed* iv. 30 One would be compelled to rush wildly off in search of heroin-relief. *Ibid.* xi. 76 A heroin-party. **1968** *Lancet* 7 Dec. 1239/2 The cost of treating heroin addiction is particularly great. **1968** *Even. News* 11 Dec. 13/1 The 'erratic and unsatisfactory life' of a 19-year-old heroin addict ended when he took a barbiturate overdose. **1969** *Times* 9 July 2/3 (*headline*) Heroin 'black market' in West End. *Ibid.* 2/4 Scotland Yard's Drug Squad..have been raiding premises..for a gang of heroin 'pushers'. **1972** *Listener* 27 Jan. 125/3 The Marseilles–New York heroin traffic.

heroine, *sb.* Add: **5.** *heroine-worship, -worshipper* (cf. HERO-WORSHIP).
1900 *Westm. Gaz.* 1 May 4/2 Mrs. Cock has succeeded in giving a true and striking portraiture, without falling into mere heroine-worship. **1916** A. BENNETT *Lion's Share* xxiii. 165 'Jenny!' Audrey protested, full of heroine-worship. **1943** BEERBOHM *Lytton Strachey* 11 He was not a hero-worshipper, or even a very gallant heroine-worshipper. **1970** R. RENDELL *Guilty Thing Surprised* ix. 111 It was a case of heroine worship on one side and a sort of flattered acceptance on the other.

herola (herōᵘ·lă). Also **hirola.** [Galla name.] A small, rare antelope, *Damaliscus hunteri*, native to Kenya and Somalia, and more frequently called Hunter's hartebeest.
1894 H. C. V. HUNTER in Sclater & Thomas *Bk. Antelopes* I. 57 Their Galla name is 'Herola', not 'Horonta'. **1915** *Chambers's Jrnl.* Nov. 700/2 Then follows the curious Hunter's hartebeest or herola, having horns which somehow suggest a connecting link with the fleet and supremely graceful impala. **1957** *Encycl. Brit.* II. 22/2 In *Damaliscus*, the bastard hartebeeste,..the horns arise directly from the head. The hirola or Hunter's hartebeeste (*D. hunteri*) has a white chevronlike marking on the forehead; it is found only on the north side of Tana valley in Jubaland, east Africa.

heron. Add: **2.** *heron pie*; *heron-billed, -built, -feathered, -haunted* adjs.
1932 W. B. YEATS *Words for Music* 12 The heron-billed pale Cattle-birds. **1851** H. MELVILLE *Moby Dick* III. xxii. 153 Tall, heron-built captains. **1935** C. DAY LEWIS *Time to Dance* 21 The heron-feathered sky. **1903** *Daily Chron.* 10 Dec. 3/2 It [*sc.* a mist]..hid all the heron-haunted flats and marshes. **1723** J. NOTT *Cook's & Confect. Dict.* 32 H, To make a Hern Pye. **1963** V. CRONIN *Comp. Guide Paris* iv. 67 Where else but in Paris would a king raise a restaurateur to the nobility simply because he enjoyed his heron-pies?

heroon (hĭrōᵘ·ǫn). *Gr. Antiq.* Pl. **-a.** Also **heröon, heroum.** [L. *heroum*, a. Gr. ἡρῷον, f. ἡρώιος of a hero, f. ἥρως HERO.] A sepulchral monument in the form of a small temple; orig. a temple or sanctuary dedicated to a hero, often over his supposed tomb.
1775 R. CHANDLER *Trav. Asia Minor* 111 Searching about, we found..an inscription, which has belonged to an heroum or sepulchre. **1820** T. S. HUGHES *Trav. Sicily* I. 298 The Heroa of Theseus and Pirithous. **1883** A. S. MURRAY *Hist. Greek Sculpture* II. 289 The heröon at Gjölbaschi in Lycia. **1904** T. R. GLOVER *Stud. Virgil* iv. 89 A hêrôon of Aeneas in Ambracia. **1950** *Antiquity* XXIV. 131 Dyggve himself has excavated such a Heroon at Kalydon.

hero-worship, *v.* Delete (*nonce-wd.*) and add examples. Also **he·ro-wo:rshipful** *a.*
1914 G. B. SHAW *Pygmalion* (1916) 195 The weak may not be admired and hero-worshipped; but they are by no means disliked and shunned. **1918** BEERBOHM *And even Now* (1920) 203 The hero-worshipful gaze. **1936** N. MARSH *Death in Ecstasy* vii. 86 Maurice hero-worshipped Father Garnette. **1948** 'J. TEY' *Franchise Affair* xix. 224 The centre of an adoring family—secure, loved, hero-worshipped. **1960** C. DAY LEWIS *Buried Day* i. 21, I hero-worshipped him.

herpes. Add: **1.** Now recognized as a group of virus diseases, the chief of which are **herpes si·mplex**, ordinary or 'simple' herpes (as contrasted with *herpes zoster*), distinguished as *herpes facialis, genitalis, labialis*, etc., according to the part of the body affected, and caused by *Herpesvirus hominis*; **herpes zo·ster**, shingles, caused by *H. varicellæ*.
1807 MORRIS & KENDRICK *Edin. Med. & Physical Dict.* II, Herpes zoster. **1813** T. BATEMAN *Pract. Synopsis Cutaneous Dis.* vi. 233 The Herpes labialis..occurs most frequently in the course of diseases of the viscera. **1886** FAGGE & PYE-SMITH *Princ. & Pract. Med.* II. 670 His [*sc.* Willan's] species of herpes included (1) *Herpes zoster* or zona... (2) *Herpes circinatus*, which..is now classed with *Tineæ*. **1907** *Jrnl. Amer. Med. Assoc.* 2 Mar. 746/2 (*heading*) The nature of herpes simplex. *Ibid.* 750/1 Herpes zoster and herpes simplex—both facial and genital varieties—while not clinically identical, are closely related. *Ibid.* 749/2 Another form of simple herpes..is herpes genitalis. **1946** G. C. ANDREWS *Dis. Skin* (ed. 3) xx. 537 Certain types of herpes zoster have received descriptive terms, the more important of which is herpes zoster frontalis, which is an involvement of the area supplied by the upper branches of the trigeminal nerve. **1962** *Lancet* 13 Jan. 105/1, I have often been impressed by the frequent association of herpes zoster with stress and anxiety, especially in the elderly. **1967** A. C. ALLEN *Skin* (ed. 2) viii. 335/2 Herpes simplex (fever blisters, cold sores, herpes facialis, herpes labialis) is..a mild, extremely recurrent, eruption.
b. *herpes virus* (also as one word), any of a group of related viruses that includes those causing shingles and chicken-pox, esp. *Herpesvirus hominis*, the cause of herpes simplex.
1925 *Amer. Jrnl. Path.* I. 337 (*heading*) Studies on filterable viruses... Cultivation of herpes virus. *Ibid.*, We have used herpes virus and a note on the cultivation of this virus is given below. **1955** *Sci. Amer.* May 33/1

The benign but recurrent lesions known as fever blisters or cold sores, caused by the herpes virus. **1968** A. ROOK et al. *Textbk. Dermatol.* I. xxiv. 763/2 The particles of herpesvirus are first found in the nucleus and later appear in the cytoplasm from which the virus is gradually released with destruction of the cell.

Herr (hĕr). Pl. **Herren**. [G., master, lord; Mr. Cf. HER, HERE *sb.*] The German equivalent of Mr.; a German gentleman.

1653 R. CREIGHTON *Let.* 28 Jan. in M. M. Verney *Mem. Verney Fam.* (1894) III. iii. 81 Herr Skatt hath undertaken the cure. **1828** T. CARLYLE *Let.* 16 Apr. (1887) 81 How is it that the Author of *Faust* and *Meister* can *tryste* himself with such characters, as 'Herr ——' (the simplest and stupidest man of his day, a Westmoreland Gerundgrinder and *Cleishbotham*)? **1849** THACKERAY *Pendennis* I. xiv. 124 Herr Garbage's lions and tigers had drawn for a little time, until one of the animals had bitten a piece out of the Herr's shoulder. **1879** C. M. YONGE *Magnum Bonum* (1882) xxi. 294 He..was a decided favourite with Fraülein Rosalie, who would do anything for her dear young Herr. **1940** W. S. CHURCHILL *Speech* 21 Oct. in *Second World War* (1949) II. xxvi. 452 But Herr Hitler is not thinking only of stealing other people's territories. **1954** 'M. COLES' *Not for Export* iii. 34 Life was difficult for the poor in Berlin, as the *Herr* would understand. **1959** *Times* 30 Jan. 11/2 The possibility that Herr Alfred Krupp may be allowed to retain his main holdings in coal, iron, and steel. **1967** 'G. CARR' *Lewker in Tirol* iii. 36 Your glass, *mein Herr*. *Ibid.* 53 It was in the corner of the big bar..the guides..meet their *Herren* there. **1970** E. PACE *Saberlegs* (1971) xii. 109 *Herrgott*, he was tired.

‖ **Herrenvolk** (hḗrənfǫlk, -fōᵘk). Also **h-**. [G., master-race.] The Nazi conception of the German people as born to mastery; also *transf.* as an appellation of other 'superior' groups. Also *attrib.* or as *adj.*

1940 *New Statesman* 17 Feb. 198/1 Show how German industry can enjoy prosperity without rearmament and no German worker will accept the starvation wages of a *Herrenvolk* pursuing the mirage of a closed imperialism. **1941** *Amer. Guardian* 15 Oct. 6/1 Hitler's race program was stolen from the White Trash Herrenvolk of Dixie. **1941** M. TREADGOLD *We couldn't leave Dinah* xii. 184 The representative of the Herrenvolk nodded. **1941** H. G. WELLS *You can't be too Careful* v. ii. 245 A people.. who were united in their dislike to the German *herrenvolk*. **1941** D. WILSON *Germany's 'New Order'* 22 A *Herrenvolk* to dominate other peoples. **1943** W. S. CHURCHILL *End of Beginning* 103 Forms of warfare which, according to the German view, should be the strict monopoly of the *Herrenvolk*. **1944** G. B. SHAW *Everybody's Political What's What?* x. 82 Nations each of which regards itself as The Chosen Race or *Herrenvolk* appointed by God to own and rule all the others. **1944** H. G. WELLS *'42 to '44* 187 The evil suggestion of inherently inferior peoples, predestined hewers of wood and drawers of the water for some imaginary *Herrenvolk*. **1947** *Penguin New Writing* XXXI. 157 He referred to them [*sc.* Sinhalese] in their presence as 'wogs'..and forced them to admit his herrenvolk creed. **1958** *Listener* 9 Oct. 566/2 The *Herrenvolk* ideas, against which so many of us..fought and suffered during the seven terrible years of the war. **1960** *Guardian* 28 June 10/5 A.. Portuguese..cursing an African..in that unmistakable way which those who know Africa cannot fail to recognise—the herrenvolk attitude. **1964** *Punch* 1 July 31/3 Brutality and *herrenvolk* arrogance.

herring. Add: **1. b.** *fat herring* (*FAT *a.* 2 f).
2. Phrase (local): *every herring should hang by its own head, gills, neck, tail.*

1639 J. CLARKE *Paroemiologia Anglo-Latina* 20 Every herring must hang by th'owne gill. **1672** W. WALKER *Parœmiologia Anglo-Latina* 23/1 Every herring must hang by its own neck; gill. **1694** T. D'URFEY *Comical Hist. D. Quixote* I. III. ii. 32 Let not the fault of the Ass be laid upon the Pack-Saddle, every Herring must hang by its own tail. **1721** J. KELLY *Compl. Coll. Scot. Prov.* 240 Let every Herring hing by its own Head. **1818, 1824** [in Dict.]. **1890** HALL CAINE *Bondman* II. ii, Adam, thinking as little of pride, said No, that every herring should hang by its own gills.

3. a. *herring-spawn* (examples).

1906 *Daily Colonist* (Victoria, B.C.) 11 Jan. 3/4 The practice of using herring spawn..has been the habit of the Indians all over British Columbia for many years. **1972** *Guardian* 1 Apr. 7/8 Herring spawn is relatively vulnerable and relatively few survive.

b. herring choker *slang*, (*a*) *Canad.* a nickname for a native or inhabitant of the Maritime Provinces; (*b*) *U.S.* a Scandinavian.

1899 *Yarmouth Telegram* (Nova Scotia) 20 Oct. 1/1, I am down among the 'herring chokers' and 'blue noses' for a few weeks. *Ibid.*, Happy the wearied globe-trotter and denizen of the 'herring chokers' of Nova Scotia. **1944** H. WENTWORTH *Amer. Dial. Dict.* 290/1 *Herring-choker.* 1. A Prince-Edward-Islander, or native of any of the Provinces 'down east'. 2. A Scandinavian. **1954** *Fundy Fisherman* (Black's Harbour, N.B.) 3 Mar. 4/4 These Herring Choker senators point out that Duplessis has already peddled a lot of horse power to Ontario and indeed is selling plenty to Premier Frost et al. right now. **1968** *Word Study* Dec. 3/2 The Roman Catholic is frequently called a *fish*, short for *fish-eater*... Similar is the term *herring-choker*, another name for a Scandinavian.

herring-bone, *sb.* Add: **1. b.** *pl.* Small cirrocumulus clouds (cf. *mackerel sky*).

1905 *Westm. Gaz.* 22 Apr. 4/2 The sky was sunny, but mottled in the north-west with 'herring-bones', which prophesied wind.

c. *pl.* The herring-bone-line hatching used to represent mountains on a map.

1900 E. T. FOWLER *Farringdons* v, 'I see. And please what are the mountain-ranges that you are drawing now?' 'These,' replied Elisabeth, covering her map with herring-bones, 'are your scruples.'

d. *Furniture.* (See quot. 1952.)

1937 *Burlington Mag.* July 45/2 All the ornament required is to be found in the finely figured wood, the craftsmanship displayed in the herringbone and cross-banded borders. **1952** J. GLOAG *Short Dict. Furniture* 285 *Herringbone*, patterns in the form of a herring bone were used on the banding of drop fronts on early 18th century walnut furniture. **1960** H. HAYWARD *Antique Coll.* 142/1 *Herring-bone banding*, a decorative veneer border much used on walnut furniture of the late 17th and early 18th cent. consisting of two narrow strips of veneer laid together diagonally forming a pattern resembling a herring-bone or feather [etc.].

e. *Skiing.* (See quot. 1924.) Also *attrib.*

1904 E. C. RICHARDSON *Ski-Running* 35 A short, steep bit of slope may be overcome by the methods illustrated in Figs. 12 and 13, but both are fatiguing,.. especially the 'herring bone'. **1924** *Tourist* Winter Sports No. 12/1 *Herring-bone*, a method of climbing without kick-turns which leaves tracks like the well-known stitch. **1972** M. YORKE *Silent Witness* iii. 58 [Her] muscles always screamed after..side-stepping or herring-bone climbing.

2. e. *herring-bone coralline* (see quots.).

1755 J. ELLIS *Ess. towards Nat. Hist. Corallines* 17 Herring-bone Coralline. This Coralline is often found sticking to Oysters as they are brought to the London Market, during the Winter-season. **1850** A. PRATT *Common Things Sea-side* 258 The Herring-bone Coralline ('Halecium halecinum') which grows on stones and shells, in the deep parts of the sea. **1915** E. R. LANKESTER *Divers. Nat.* 97 Very minute jelly-fish,..[which] originate as buds from small branching polyps, one kind of which is common on oyster-shells, and is called 'the herring-bone coralline'.

f. Designating a type of milking parlour in which the stalls are arranged in a herring-bone pattern.

1957 *Farmer & Stockbreeder* 9 Apr. 45/1 The yard and parlour system obviously attracts those changing over to dairying and the main interest centred on the..herring-bone parlour design. **1963** *Ibid.* 5 Mar. 33/2 (Advt.), Gascoigne milking systems. Herringbone parlour for batch milking. **1970** *Times* 9 Mar. 13/5 Another innovation costs £120 a milking stall, or £600 for this item alone in the five-point herringbone parlour.

herring-bone, *v.* Add: **3.** To make (a wall, floor, etc.) of herring-bone work. Hence **he·rring-boned** *ppl. a.*

1907 W. DE MORGAN *Alice-for-Short* ix, A 'erring-boned brick floor.

4. *Skiing.* (See *HERRING-BONE *sb.* 1 e.) Hence **herring-boning** *vbl. sb.*

1904 E. C. RICHARDSON *Ski-Running* 35 (*caption*) Herring-boning. **1914** *Queen* 17 Jan. 128/2 He climbed very quickly, looking uncommonly like a monkey up a stick as he herring-boned in jerks up the slope. **1919** *Century Mag.* May 43/1 'You're herring-boning!' shouted Dean. 'Don't herring-bone! We'll come to that later.' **1946** H. CROOME *Faithless Mirror* 55 Half a dozen boys herringboning up from the road. *Ibid.* 67 Half a dozen skiers herringboned up the trail towards them.

hers, *poss. pron.*[1]: see *HIS *absolute poss. pron.* b.

Herschel. Add: **2.** Used *attrib.* or in the possessive to designate certain phenomena or principles discovered by or related to the work of Sir William or Sir John *Herschel* (see HERSCHELIAN *a.*), as *Herschel('s) condition*, a condition that must be satisfied by a system of lenses if spherical aberration is to be absent in the images of two neighbouring objects; *Herschel effect*, the partial destruction of the latent image on a photographic negative by the action of infra-red radiation; *Herschel's fringes*, spectral fringes observed in a prism standing on a plane mirror at the line of separation between the brighter field, due to incident light internally reflected by the prism, and the darker field, due to light externally reflected by the mirror, first observed by Sir William Herschel.

1890 T. PRESTON *Theory of Light* viii. 153 (*heading*) Herschel's fringes. **1909** *Jrnl. Chem. Soc.* XCVI. II. 141 Warnerke's modification of the Herschel Effect and the Preparation of the Substance of the Latent Image. **1910** J. P. C. SOUTHALL *Princ. & Methods Geom. Optics* xii. 394 It has..been suggested that the other requirement should be the so-called Herschel-Condition; that is, that the function $\phi_1 Z_1 + \phi_2 Z_2$ should vanish not only for the particular value of x_1 but also for object-points on the axis very near to the point M_1 to which the value x_1 belongs. **1932** HARDY & PERRIN *Princ. Optics* vi. 98 The condition that $n \sin \frac{1}{2}\theta / n' \sin \frac{1}{2}\theta' =$ a constant must be satisfied for all values of θ. This is commonly called the Herschel condition although it had not been formulated mathematically when Herschel constructed his objective. *Ibid.* xi. 233 This Herschel effect has a very important significance in connection with theories of the latent image but has not been found very useful as a technique for infrared photography. **1957** R. S. LONGHURST *Geom. & Physical Optics* xiv. 280 Herschel's condition is the condition that must be satisfied if the system is to form, simultaneously, a good image of a neighbouring axial object point.

Hertz (hɜːts, ‖ hḗrts). **1.** The name of H. R. *Hertz* (1857–1894), German physicist, used *attrib.* to denote apparatus used or invented, phenomena discovered, or concepts elaborated by him.

1890 *Nature* Feb. 368 By separating the coats of the jar as far as possible we get a typical Hertz vibrator. **1892** O. LODGE *Mod. Views Electr.* 361 Hertz waves can get through deal doors and stone walls. **1898** *Science Siftings* XIV. 117/2 A Hertz-wave 'detector'. **1898** *Westm. Gaz.* 12 May 9/2 Experiments in Hertz-wave space telegraphy. **1902** *Encycl. Brit.* XXXIII. 230/2 This aerial being used as a Hertz oscillator or radiator. **1962** CORSON & LORRAIN *Introd. Electromagn. Fields* xiii. 488 The Hertz vector Π is defined by the equation

$$A = \epsilon\mu \frac{\partial \Pi}{\partial t}.$$

2. *Physics.* (Usu. *hertz.*) A unit of frequency, equal to one cycle per second. Abbrev. Hz.

1928 *B.B.C. Handbk.* 270/1 *Hertz*, a term sometimes used to designate frequency, meaning one cycle per second. **1934** *Electr. Engin.* (U.S.) LIII. 403/2 It was proposed by the Italian committee that the name *hertz* be given to the unit of frequency—one cycle per second... The *hertz* is used almost universally in German technical literature. **1967** *Electronics* 6 Mar. 325/1 Markus continues to use 'cycles per second' instead of 'hertz'. **1967** *New Scientist* 5 Oct. 6/2 The frequency band between about 10 megahertz and 20 gigahertz is technically suitable for space communication.

Hertzian (hɜ·ɹtsiăn), *a.* [f. the name *Hertz* (see prec.) + -IAN.] Of or pertaining to Hertz or to the phenomena discovered by him.

Hertzian telegraphy: wireless telegraphy. *Hertzian waves* (see WAVE *sb.* 5 a).

1890 A. E. BOSTWICK in *Appleton's Ann. Cycl.* 716/1 (Funk), Trouton..found that glass absorbs Hertzian vibrations with comparative rapidity. **1897** RUTHERFORD in *Phil. Trans. R. Soc.* A. CLXXXIX. 1 They were also found to be a sensitive means of detecting electrical radiation from Hertzian vibrators at long distances from the vibrator. *Ibid.* 8 A detector for electrical waves was devised, which proved to be a sensitive means of detecting Hertzian waves. **1898** *Daily News* 3 May 5/3 The General Post Office..is also carrying out experiments in wireless Hertzian telegraphy. **1900** *Jrnl. Soc. Arts* XLVIII. 788/1 The sensation created in 1897 by Mr. Marconi's application of Hertzian waves. **1900** J. J. FAHIE *Hist. Wireless Telegr.* 197 Sir William Crookes..was..the first to distinctly foresee the applicability of Hertzian waves to practical telegraphy. **1907** J. ERSKINE-MURRAY *Handbk. Wireless Telegr.* 36 The transmitter consisted of a Hertzian oscillator placed in the focal line of a parabolic mirror. **1908** J. A. FLEMING *Elem. Man. Radiotelegr.* 132 An arrangement of two rods.. with a spark gap in the centre constitutes the simplest form of linear radiator or Hertzian Oscillator for the production of damped electro-magnetic waves. **1914** R. STANLEY *Textbk. Wireless Telegr.* 91 Using a suitable length of spark gap the discharge of this Hertzian open circuit is oscillatory. **1922** A. N. WHITEHEAD *Princ. Relativ.* xiv. 117 Now consider the internal vibration of a molecule which radiates light of period *T*..as capable of being represented as the vibration of a variable electric Hertzian doublet with this period. **1940** *Chambers's Techn. Dict.* 412/2 *Hertzian waves*, electromagnetic waves having frequencies between zero and approximately ten thousand million cycles per second; especially those towards the upper limit of this range. **1971** *Gloss. Electrotechnical Power Terms (B.S.I.)* III. vii. 7 *Hertzian waves*, electromagnetic waves having frequencies below those of infra-red waves.

herumfrodite, var. *HARUMFRODITE.

Herzegovinian (hɜːɹtsəgǒvi·niăn), *a.* and *sb.* Also **Herzo-**. [f. *Herzegovina*: see -IAN.] (Of or pertaining to) a native or inhabitant of Herzegovina, a region to the south of Bosnia, now forming part of Bosnia-Herzegovina, a constituent republic of Yugoslavia. So **Herz(e)govine·se** *a.* and *sb.*

1876 *Fraser's Mag.* May 541/2 The Herzgovinese insurgents. **1880** *Encycl. Brit.* XI. 775/2 Much of the old Slavonic customs..still holds among the Herzegovinian Mussulmans. *Ibid.*, The Herzegovinians are tall, broad, and darker..than the Bosnians. **1900** tr. *Deniker's Races of Man* 345 The southern [Slav] group.. comprises the Herzogovinians, Bosnians, Montenegrins. **1904** M. E. DURHAM *Through Lands of Serb* 6 These Herzegovinese migrated to Montenegro. **1918** R. J. KERNER *Jugo-Slav Movement* 4 The Herzegovinian Serbs of the Narenta. **1935** HUXLEY & HADDON *We Europeans* vii. 213 The Herzegovinian type has a broad head, and is rather tall and inclined to be fair.

Heshvan, var. *HESVAN.

Hesiodic (hīsiǫ·dik), *a.* [f. the name of *Hesiod* (Gr. Ἡσίοδος), Greek poet of about the eighth century B.C. + -IC.] Of, pertaining to, or resembling the poetical style of Hesiod, or the school of poetry which followed him. Also **Hesio·dian** *a.*

1838 *Penny Cycl.* XII. 186/2 Ulrici considers..the story of Prometheus and that of the Five Ages as much altered from their original Hesiodic form. **1847** J. LEITCH tr. *Müller's Anc. Art* § 77 The Hesiodic bards

come down to about the 40th Ol[ympiad]. **1873** J. Davies *Hesiod & Theognis* i. 19 Under one or other of these heads it is easy to group the Hesiodic poems. *Ibid.* ii. 23 The Hesiodian rhapsodists. **1908** A. W. Mair *Hesiod* p. xi, The Hesiodic epic is the antithesis of the Homeric. **1970** G. E. Evans *Where Beards wag All* xx. 223 In literature there was little beyond a Hesiodic theogony or some Orphic hymns to exhibit.

hesitate, *v.* Add: **1. a.** Const. various preps.

a **1849** Poe *Tales* (1884) I. 93 At the baptismal font I hesitated for a name. **1856** De Quincey *Confess.* (1896) 216 This..surgeon saw no reason whatever in the simple practice of opium-eating for hesitating upon a life-insurance proposal. **1860** W. Collins *Woman in White* I. iv. 33, I hesitated about answering it. **1908** *Grand Mag.* Dec. 612/2 I'm only hesitating over the price.

d. *spec.* in *Dancing* (see quot. 1919).

1914 V. Castle *Mod. Dancing* iv. 72 In my opinion it is much better to hesitate when the music hesitates. **1919** E. Scott *All about Latest Dances* 87 The term 'hesitate', as regards the waltz we are now considering, implies merely that you pause, or move in what appears a faltering manner at a given juncture.

e. To move in an indecisive, faltering manner.

1908 H. G. Wells *War in Air* v. 168 He hesitated towards the door of the cabin. **1917** T. S. Eliot *Prufrock* 27 Regard that woman Who hesitates toward you in the light of the door.

3. b. With sentence as quasi-obj.

1816 Scott *Tales my Landlord* II. xii. 311 'I am not sure,' hesitated Edith. **1881** C. E. L. Riddell *Sen. Partner* xvi, 'It looks awful like the stuff last night,' hesitated Mr. McCullagh.

hesitation. Add: **2. b.** *hesitation-form*, a sound or form, e.g. (ə), used deliberately or accidentally when faltering or stammering in speech. So *hesitation-vowel*, etc. (Cf. *er.)

1933 Bloomfield *Lang.* xii. 186 When a speaker hesitates, English and some other languages offer special parenthetic *hesitation-forms*, as [əː] or [ɛ] in *Mr.—ah—Sniffen.* **1957** S. Potter *Mod. Ling.* v. 122 He may even inflict indeterminate *hesitation-forms* [əː] or [ɑː] upon his suffering hearers. **1965** *Canad. Jrnl. Ling.* XI. I. 36 This is often called the 'hesitation vowel' although it is not a vowel qua vowel at all.

3. In full *hesitation waltz* or *valse*: a variety of waltz, characterized by the *hesitation step* (see quot. 1919). Also *fig.* So **hesitation-valse** (*nonce-wd.*) *v. intr.*

1914 V. Castle *Mod. Dancing* iv. 71 It is the Hesitation Waltz. **1918** J. M. Grider *Diary* 29 Jan. (1927) 71 It's a long jump from the Boston and the hesitation to the giant swing, but we had them all fox-trotting in no time. **1919** E. Scott *All about Latest Dances* 86 As you lift the left foot..from the floor, count a short one, two; and on three drag the other foot along the floor, bringing it over in front of the first foot, which is by this time on the floor... That is the hesitation step. **1920** A. M. Cree *Ball-Room Dancing* 41 The Hesitation Valse is a variety of the true valse that can very easily be performed once the valse is known. **1924** 'L. Malet' *Dogs of Want* v. § 2 For over four hours a mixed multitude..had one-stepped, two-stepped, hesitation-valsed, and fox-trotted. **1927** *Daily Express* 31 Oct. 11/6 The foxtrot, tango, and the hesitation. **1959** *Chambers's Encycl.* IV. 364/1 During the first world war.. the occasional waltzes..were danced with a slight hesitation movement. **1972** R. Mayne *Europeans* v. 136 Britain's slow hesitation waltz with European unity.

Hesped (heˑsped). [Heb.] A funeral oration pronounced over the dead at a Jewish memorial service.

1650 E. Chilmead tr. *Leon Modena's Hist. Rites of Jews* v. ix. 242 If he were a Rabbine that is dead, or a person of quality, they then have Sermons, and Funeral Orations, which they call..*Hesped*, made for him. **1892** I. Zangwill *Childr. Ghetto* I. I. xiv. 295 Moses Ansell was at *Shool*, listening to a *Hesped* or funeral oration. **1970** L. M. Feinsilver *Taste of Yiddish* 131 *Hesped*, eulogy.

Hesperian. B. *sb.* **2.** (U.S. examples.)

1869 *Rep. U.S. Commissioner Agric. 1868* 314 The family of skippers, Hesperians, are rather small, thick-bodied butterflies. **1881** *Papilio* I. 132 (*title*) Two new Hesperians.

Hesperid. Add: **2.** *Ent.* (Also **Hesperiid.**) One of the family Hesperidæ or Hesperiidæ of lepidopterous insects; a Hesperian butterfly; a skipper. Also *attrib.*

1889 in *Cent. Dict.* **1912** *Entomologist* XLV. 5 (*title*) A Supplementary Note on Hesperiid Classification. **1930–1** *Proc. Ent. Soc.* V. 88 Similar observations had been made on African Hesperiids. **1931** *Oxf. Univ. Gaz.* 17 June 704/1 The Hesperid butterfly *Parnara zelleri cinhara.* **1957** Richards & Davies *Imms's Gen. Textbk. Ent.* (ed. 9) III. 560 Its larvae and pupae exhibit definite Hesperiid characters.

Hessian, *a.* and *sb.*[1] **B.** *sb.* **1.** (Earlier examples.)

1729 A. Irwin *Let.* 1 Feb. in *15th Rep. Hist. MSS. Commission* App. VI. (1897) 56 The House..voted 30,000 English and 12,000 Hessians, which is the same number I think we had last year. **1776** *Jrnls. Continental Congress* (1906) V. 640 The Hessians, and other foreigners, employed by the King of Great Britain. **1846** *Knickerbocker* XXVII. 559 A Montreal editor [noted] the demise at that city of an old Hessian who was in Burgoyne's army when he surrendered.

hessonite (heˑsŏnəit). *Min.* Also **essonite.** [ad. F. *essonit* (R. J. Haüy *Traité Pierres Préc.* (1817) 51), f. Gr. ἥσσων less + -ite[1]: so called because it is less hard and heavy than some minerals, such as hyacinth, which it resembles.] A variety of garnet containing calcium and aluminium. Also called *cinnamon-stone, grossularite.*

1820, 1884 [see Essonite]. **1892** E. S. Dana *Dana's Syst. Min.* (ed. 6) 440 Cinnamon-stone, or essonite (more properly hessonite), included a cinnamon-colored variety from Ceylon, there called hyacinth. **1895** *Amer. Jrnl. Sci.* L. 128 (*heading*) Apatite and hessonite in a pegmatite from Canaan, Ct. **1933** *Mineral. Abstr.* V. 281 The other [belt], from Ramona to Jacumba, is in granodiorite and the gem minerals in the pegmatites are mainly hessonite, beryl, and topaz. **1959** C. S. Hurlbut *Dana's Man. Min.* (ed. 17) v. 403 *Grossularite* (*Essonite, Cinnamon Stone*). Often contains ferrous iron replacing calcium and ferric iron replacing aluminium.

Hesvan (heˑsvăn). Also **Chesvan, Heshvan,** etc. [Heb. *ḥešwān*, f. earlier *marḥešwān* (recorded in the Mishnah, 2nd cent. B.C.), ad. Akkadian *Araḫ samna* eighth month.] The eighth month of the Jewish ecclesiastical year and the second month of the civil year, corresponding to parts of October and November; also formerly called Bûl.

1833 H. Nicolas *Chronol. Hist.* 167 Marchesvan, Chesvan, or Bul 29 or 30 [Days]. **1838** E. H. Lindo *Jewish Cal.* 5 The perfect [year] has 355 days, and is when the months of Hesvan and Kislev have each 30 days. **1876** *Encycl. Brit.* IV. 678/1 The signs + and – are respectively annexed to Hesvan and Kislev to indicate that the former of these months may sometimes require to have one day more, and the latter sometimes one day less, than the number of days shown in the table. **1903** M. Joseph *Judaism as Creed & Life* 310 The ordinary Jewish year consists of twelve months... Cheshvan or Marcheshvan (November). **1927** G. F. Moore *Judaism* II. 67 If by the seventeenth of Marḥeshvan the autumn rains had not begun, the religious heads of the community began to fast in a mitigated fashion. **1956** Pearl & Brookes *Guide Jewish Knowledge* 2 (*heading*) Cheshvan (Oct.–Nov.).

het, *ppl. a.* **1.** Add to def.: also *transf.*, and for 'Now *dial.*' read 'Orig. *dial.* and *U.S.* Also with *up. colloq.*'

[**1886** S. W. Mitchell *R. Blake* ii. 17, I don't het up easy.] **1894** Kipling *Day's Work* (1898) 46 You look consider'ble het up. Guess you'd better..cool off a piece. **1902** G. H. Lorimer *Lett. Merchant* v. 59 But you mustn't get yourself all 'het up' before you take the plunge. **1930** W. de la Mare *On Edge* 244 You must have been overdoing it. You look quite het up. **1932** C. Williams *Greater Trumps* x. 182 Yours is a remarkable family, Henry; you get all het up over your hobbies. **1945** L. A. G. Strong *Othello's Occupation* ii. 43 The poor chap gets terrifically het up. **1967** *Listener* 20 Apr. 518/3 One thing that I think endears him to the normal young intellectual, is that he can get tremendously het-up about a cause.

hetærio: see *etærio.

hetærolite (hetīᵊˑroləit). *Min.* [f. Gr. ἑταῖρο-ς companion (see quot. 1877) + -lite.] A black oxide of zinc and manganese, $ZnMn_2O_4$, isostructural with hausmannite and found in New Jersey associated with franklinite and with chalcophanite.

The mineral of quot. 1913 was later regarded as a separate species and named *hydrohetærolite*.

1877 G. E. Moore in *Amer. Jrnl. Sci. & Arts* XIV. 423 From its invariable association with and close genetic relation to chalcophanite, I propose for the species the name *Hetærolite.* **1913** *Amer. Jrnl. Sci.* XXXV. 601 The hetærolite from Leadville was found..about 700 feet below the surface. **1928** [see *hydrohetærolite* s.v. *hydro-]. **1942** *Amer. Mineralogist* XXVII. 50 It was..proposed by Palache to adopt Moore's name hetaerolite for the anhydrous mineral, analogous to hausmannite,..since this was the sense of the original definition. The actual material of Moore..was separated under the name hydrohetaerolite as a distinct species. The hydrous mineral from Leadville..also is to be classed as hydrohetaerolite.

hetchel, *sb. dial.* and *U.S.* = Hatchel *sb.*

1869 Mrs. Stowe *Oldtown Folks* xlii. 530 She don' know no more 'bout religion than an old hetchel. **1929** J. Shelton *Salt-box House* xvii. 143 Mops were made of corn-husks bound to a handle, the husks having been drawn through a hetchel which shredded them.

hetchel, *v. dial.* and *U.S.* = Hatchel *v.*

1845 S. Judd *Margaret* I. xiii. 100 The clouds hung low, and their floating skirts seemed to be pierced and hetchelled by the trees. **1878** *Harper's Mag.* LVII. 576 She'll hetchel the old woman mortally, I be afraid. **1897** [see Hatchel *v.* 2]. **1906** C. H. Parkhurst *Lower than Angels* 18 Mercilessly hetchelled by some prosecuting attorney.

hetero, colloq. abbrev. of Heterosexual *a.* and *sb.*

1933 E. A. Robertson *Ordinary Families* xiii. 272 The odd thing about me is that..I should be so purely 'hetero' in spite of lack of opportunity. **1957** J. Osborne *Look Back in Anger* II. i. 50 I'm tired of being hetero. **1960** I. Jefferies *Dignity & Purity* ii. 28 Is that really a fact about Proust being a secret hetero? **1968** J. R. Ackerley *My Father & Myself* xii. 117 Almost the first mischievous question he shot at me was 'Are you homo or hetero?' **1970** *Sunday Times* 6 Sept. 24 Talking.. about homosexual life and letters..I meant to ask him.. why homos found it so much easier to find sleeping partners than heteros.

hetero-. Add: heːteraromaˑtic *a.* = **hetero-aromatic* adj.; **heterauxesis,** now applied to animals as well as plants, with a more specialized meaning (see quot. 1941); **heːtero-agglu:tinabiˑlity,** the ability to undergo heteroagglutination; **heːtero-agglutinaˑtion,** agglutination of cells due to the action of a hetero-agglutinin; so **heːtero-aggluˑtinating** *vbl. sb.*; **heːtero-aggluˑtinative** *a.*, producing heteroagglutination; **heːtero-aggluˑtinin,** an agglutinin that causes agglutination of foreign cells, esp. red blood cells of another group or from an animal of another species; **heːteroaˑlbumose** *Biochem.*, an albumose insoluble in water but soluble in solutions of sodium chloride; **heːteroaromaˑtic** *a. Chem.*, heterocyclic and aromatic; also as *sb.*; **heˑtero-atom** *Chem.*, an atom in the ring of a cyclic compound other than a carbon atom (also as two words); so **heːtero-atoˑmic** *a.*; **heːtero-aˑxial** *a.* [a. G. *heteroaxial* (V. Goldschmidt *Index d. Krystallformen d. Mineralien* (1891) III. 136)], having a structure based on two axes or sets of axes; *spec.* of a geological feature: having an external symmetry that does not correspond with the symmetry of the individual components of the fabric; **heteroblastic** *a.*, (*b*) *Bot.*, (characterized by) having a marked difference between the immature and adult forms; (*c*) *Petrol.*, composed of grains of two or more distinct sizes; opp. *homœoblastic*; **heːteroblaˑstically** *adv.*, in a heteroblastic manner; **heˑterocharge,** the charge on an electret that is polarized in the opposite direction to that of the original polarizing field; hence **heˑterocharged** *a.*; **heːterochlamyˑdeous** *a. Bot.* [Gr. χλαμύς, χλαμυδ- cloak], having a perianth in which the calyx and corolla are of a different colour or texture; **heˑterochrome** *a.* = *heterochromatic *a.* (sense 1); **heːterochroˑmia** (-krōᵘˑmiă) *Med.*, a difference in colour between two organs (esp. the eyes), or between different parts of the same organ, that are usually the same colour; so **heːterochroˑmic** *a.*; **heːterochroˑmosome** *Cytol.*, a modified or differentiated chromosome, *esp.* a sex-chromosome; **heterochthonous** (-ǫˑkþŏnəs) *a. Path.* [after Autochthonous *a.*], originating in or derived from another organism; **heˑteroclin, -cline** *sb. Min.* [ad. G. *heteroklin* (A. Breithaupt 1840, in *Ann. Physik und Chem.* XLIX. 205), f. Gr. ἑτεροκλινής leaning to one side] = Marceline[2]; **heːterocœˑlous** *a. Zool.* [Gr. κοῖλος hollow], applied to vertebrae in which the articular facets are saddle-shaped, as in certain birds; **heterocyst** (earlier example); **heːterocyˑstous** (-siˑstəs) *a. Biol.*, containing heterocysts; **heterodeˑsmic** *a. Chem.* [Gr. δεσμός bond], containing chemical bonds of more than one type; **heterodu·plex** *a. Biochem.*, containing or consisting of polynucleotide strands derived from two different parent molecules; also as *sb.*, a heteroduplex molecule; **heːterodynaˑmic, -dyˑnamous** *adjs. Ent.* [ad. F. *hétérodyname* (E. Roubaud 1922, in *Bull. Biol. de la France et de la Belg.* LVI. 471)], (of an insect, its life cycle, etc.) characterized by having a continuous succession of generations only during the favourable part of the year; **heterœˑcious** *a.* [first formed as G. *heterőcisch* (A. de Bary 1866, in *Monatsber. d. K. Preuss. Akad. d. Wissensch. zu Berlin 1865* 32)]; **heːtero-immuˑne** *a.*, immune to the cells or cell-products of an animal of a different species, or producing such immunity; **heːtero-inoculaˑtion,** inoculation from another organism; **heːtero-inoˑculable** *a.*; **heˑterojunction** *Electronics* [*junction 2 b], an area of contact between different semiconducting materials; **heːterokineˑsis** *Cytol.*, the division of a cell into cells having dissimilar hereditary tendencies; opp. *homœokinesis*; **heːteroleˑcithal** (-leˑsiþăl) *a. Embryol.* [Gr. λέκιθος yolk of an egg], (of an egg cell) having the yolk unevenly distributed in the cytoplasm;

he:terone·reid *a.*, of, pertaining to, or of the character of a heteronereis; also as *sb.*, a heteronereis; **he:terone·reis** *Zool.*, a dimorphic sexual form of certain worms of the genus *Nereis*, so called because originally regarded as a distinct genus; also *attrib.*; **he:teropho·ria** *Ophthalm.*, a latent tendency to squint; hence **heteropho·ric** *a.*; **heterophtha·lmic** *a.*, characterized by heterophthalmy; **he:teropolymeriza·tion** *Chem.* [a. G. *heteropolymerisation* (T. Wagner-Jauregg 1930, in *Ber. d. Deut. Chem. Ges.* LXIII. 3213)], a reaction in which a polymer is formed from two or more different molecules, esp. such a reaction when one of the monomers will not polymerize by itself; so **he:teropo·lymer**, a polymer so formed; **he:teropolysa·ccharide** *Chem.*, any polysaccharide composed of molecules of two or more different monosaccharides; **he:teropro·teose** *Biochem.*, any of a class of proteoses that are insoluble in water but soluble in dilute salt solutions and are formed during gastric digestion; **he:terosceda·stic** *a. Statistics* [Gr. σκέδαστ-ός capable of being scattered (σκεδάννυμι I scatter)], of unequal scatter or variation; having different variances; so **he:teroscedasti·city; heterosome,** (*b*) *Cytol.*, a sex chromosome; **heterospeci·fic** *a.*, (*a*) said of blood or serum of different blood groups; *heterospecific pregnancy*, one in which the red blood cells of the fœtus would be agglutinated by the serum of the mother; (*b*) derived from an organism of a different species; **heterospo·ric** *a.* = *heterosporous* adj.; **hetero·spory** *Bot.*, the condition of being heterosporous; **he:terosugge·stion** *Psychol.*, suggestion from another person, contrasted with *AUTO-SUGGESTION; **he:terosylla·bic** *a. Philol.*, belonging to a different syllable (opp. to *tautosyllabic*); **he:terosy·llis** *Zool.*, a breeding form of worms of the family Syllidæ; **he:terote·lic** *a.*, having or being an external end or purpose; **he:terotha·llic** *a. Biol.*, (of a fungus) having an incompatibility system by which only genetically different strains can undergo nuclear fusion during sexual reproduction; so **he:terotha·llism, -tha·lly,** the condition of being heterothallic; **he·terotope** *Physics* and *Chem.* [Gr. τόπος place], each of two or more elements the atoms of which have different atomic numbers and so occupy different positions in the periodic table; **he·terotype, heteroty·pic, heteroty·pical** *adjs. Cytol.* [ad. G. *heterotypisch* (W. Flemming 1887, in *Arch. f. mikrosk. Anat.* XXIX. 400)], designating the first division of meiosis; **heteroxa·nthine** *Biochem.* [ad. G. *heteroxanthin* (G. Salomen 1885, in *Ber. d. Deut. Chem. Ges.* XVIII. 3407)], 7-methylxanthine, $C_6H_6O_2N_4$, a purine sometimes found in human urine; **heterozoœcium** (-zōu,ī·siɒm) *Zool.* [Gr. ζῷον animal + οἰκία house] = **heterozooid*; so **heterozoœ·cial** *a.*; **he·terozooid** (-zōu,oid) *Zool.*, any reduced or modified form of the typical bryozoan zooid, found chiefly in the class Gymnolæmata.

1960 *Tetrahedron Lett.* XXIII. 8 (*heading*) New heteraromatic compounds containing two boron atoms. **1940** NEEDHAM & LERNER in *Nature* 9 Nov. 618/1 We welcome a suggestion..by Dr. Arthur L. Peck..that for relative *growth*, in contradistinction to relative *proportions*, the word *heterauxesis* should be used... It is true that the terms auxesis, heterauxesis,..etc., were formerly employed in plant physiology, but they have long been obsolete there. **1941** *Ibid.* 23 Aug. 225/1 *Heterauxesis*, the relation of the growth-rate of a part of a developing organism (whether morphological or chemical) to the growth-rate of the whole or of another part; a comparison between organisms of the same group but of different ages and hence sizes. **1964** *Biol. Abstr.* XLV. 946/1 Hetero-agglutinability of goat erythrocytes by zebu serum. **1913** *Jrnl. Exper. Zool.* XIV. 564 The iso-agglutinating action was noted as undiminished, whereas the hetero-agglutinating action was entirely lost. *Ibid.* 561 (*heading*) Hetero-agglutination and the question of specificity: reactions between Nereis and Arbacia. **1949** *Biol. Abstr.* XXIII. 156/2 Lecithin suppresses the auto-agglutination as well as heteroagglutination of rabbit erythrocytes by bovine plasma. **1938** BELDING & MARSTON *Textbk. Med. Bacteriol.* lx. 451 The demonstration of the M and N antigens in human cells requires the production of heteroagglutinative immune sera by the injection of human cells into some experimental animal. **1906** DORLAND *Med. Dict.* (ed. 4) 332/1 Hetero-agglutinin. **1913** *Jrnl. Exper. Zool.* XIV. 564 The egg-extract contained two agglutinating substances at least, namely: An iso-agglutinin and a hetero-agglutinin. **1945** *Biol. Bull.* LXXXIX. 193 Lobster-serum contains at least ten hetero-agglutinins for sperm or blood cells of various animals. **1956** *Nature* 18 Feb. 329/2 The injections caused no increase in the titre of natural heteroagglutinin against human red cells. **1884** KÜHNE & CHITTENDEN in *Amer. Chem. Jrnl.* VI. 33 We name..No. II. Heteroalbumose. *Ibid.* 103 Nothing characterises heteroalbumose more than its alteration by boiling and the properties of the coagulum thus formed. **1908** J. R. BRADFORD in Allbutt & Rolleston *Syst. Med.* (ed. 2) IV. I. 561 Albumoses, and especially hetero-albumoses, which are the kind commonly present in the urine, form a precipitate on the addition of nitric acid. **1958** A. ALBERT *Trends Heterocyclic Chem.* iv. 20 (*heading*) Addition to double-bonds in N-heteroaromatic six-membered rings. **1958** *Jrnl. Chem. Soc.* 3076 A wide range of new heteroaromatic systems should exist, derived from normal aromatic compounds by replacing pairs of carbon atoms, one by boron and one by nitrogen. **1959** A. ALBERT *Heterocyclic Chem.* iii. 31 (*heading*) A general discussion on heteroaromatics. **1900** E. F. SMITH tr. *von Richter's Org. Chem.* (ed. 3) II. 435 The basal element of these rings is carbon, and accordingly the members not produced by C-atoms are designated as hetero-atoms. **1949** G. B. BACHMAN *Org. Chem.* xxvii. 336 O-, S-, and NH-containing rings undergo substitution practically exclusively at the carbons holding the hetero atom. **1966** *McGraw-Hill Encycl. Sci. & Technol.* VI. 427/2 The number of heteroatoms in any one ring is commonly one or two, less commonly three or more. **1967** KATRITZKY & LAGOWSKI *Princ. Heterocyclic Chem.* v. 144 (*heading*) Four or five heteroatoms. Tetrazoles are formed by the action of nitrous acid on amidrazones, and pentazoles from the reaction of diazonium cations with azide anions. **1968** *New Scientist* 31 Oct. 268/3 Heterocyclic compounds containing nitrogen, sulphur and oxygen as the heteroatom. **1900** E. F. SMITH tr. *V. von Richter's Org. Chem.* (ed. 3) II. 435 Hetero-atomic rings. **1926** *Mineral. Abstr.* III. 186 A study of the directions of optical extinction in the lamellae, the striations on the faces, and the etch figures on the basal plane, leads to the conclusion that the twinning is of the 'heteroaxial' type. **1938** E. B. KNOPF in *Mem. Geol. Soc. Amer.* VI. vi. 84 An example of heteroaxial orienting in two phases of the deformation is the fabric of certain pencil gneisses in which the symmetry of the grain fabric in the pencils does not conform with the fabric axes of the external form of the pencils. **1894** S. H. VINES *Stud. Text-bk. Bot.* I. i. 14 In certain cases the embryo produced by the spore differs more or less widely from the adult form, and does not directly develope into it, but bears it as a lateral outgrowth; this mode of embryogeny is indirect or heteroblastic. **1932** A. HARKER *Metamorphism* xiii. 202 To rocks in which the essential constituents are of two distinct orders of magnitude Becke gave the name 'heteroblastic', in contradistinction to 'homoeoblastic'. **1954** R. L. PARKER tr. *Niggli's Rocks & Min. Deposits* vi. 237 Crystalloblastic structures: homeoblastic, heteroblastic, porphyroblastic, with porphyroblasts or possibly crystalloid phenocrysts. **1963** DAVIS & HEYWOOD *Princ. Angiosperm Taxon.* x. 342 Heteroblastic development results in the formation of adult and juvenile leaves. **1888** *Nature* 13 Dec. 151/1 Tenontogenous or desmogenous [sesamoids], like the patella, are formed heteroblastically inside of a tendon. **1935** A. GEMANT in *Philos. Mag.* XX. 933 We observe both kinds of charges on electrets. One has the opposite sign to that of the adjacent polarizing electrode, and for the sake of shortness will be denoted as heterocharge. **1965** *New Scientist* 27 May 590/2 Under a certain critical applied field the heterocharge decays to a constant value. **1965** *Jrnl. Chem. Physics* 1 Feb. 967 Both heterocharged and homocharged electrets have been made from common ice at reduced temperatures. **1895** S. H. VINES *Stud. Text-bk. Bot.* III. 512 When the calyx and corolla clearly differ from each other in colour, texture, etc., the flower is said to be heterochlamydeous. **1965** BELL & COOMBE tr. *Strasburger's Textbk. Bot.* III. 621 Perianths are of two kinds: (*a*) Homoiochlamydeous..or (*b*) heterochlamydeous, i.e. with dissimilar members, namely an outer, generally green calyx and an inner, mostly brightly coloured corolla. **1933** *Nature* 6 May 667/1 A solution of the problem of heterochrome photometry of incandescent lamps. **1889** *Ophthalmic Rev.* July 205 Liability to disease on the part of the lighter eye in heterochromia. **1964** F. C. BLODI in A. Sorsby *Mod. Ophthalmol.* III. iii. 375 There will be a gradual change in colour of the iris giving one of the varieties of heterochromia. **1911** *Ophthalmoscope* 1 July 501 Heterochromia iridium is found in two forms. In one the heterochromia is merely an anomaly, and in the other it is a symptom of a definite disease... This latter variety is best designated heterochromic cyclitis. **1940** W. S. DUKE-ELDER *Text-bk. Ophthalmol.* III. xxxviii. 3229 Heterochromic cataract..is associated with an exceedingly slow and benign inflammation of the uveal tract. **1904** T. H. MONTGOMERY in *Biol. Bull.* VI. 145 The Heterochromosomes. I offer this name to include those peculiarly modified chromosomes to which have been given the names 'accessory chromosomes'.., 'small chromosomes'..and 'chromatin nucleoli'. **1926** *Nature* 9 Jan. 50/2 Cytological investigations in the Salicaceæ, undertaken to demonstrate the presence or absence of sex- or heterochromosomes in certain species of Salix. **1968** J. A. SERRA *Mod. Genetics* III. xxiii. 552 In haploid organisms or the haploid phase the heterochromosomes are found separately in the mitoses of each sex. **1891** FOSTER *Med. Dict.* III, *Heterochthonous*, originating from without the organism. **1921** BEATTIE & DICKSON *Text-bk. Gen. Path.* (ed. 2) ix. 273 Some have defined teratomata as heterochthonous tumours derived from the inclusion of *another* individual..or the ovum or germ-cell from which such twin would have been developed. **1950** G. P. WRIGHT *Introd. Path.* xx. 374 Chorion carcinomas are not derived from the tissues of the mother, but from the tissues of a different, though at the same time fœtal, individual. For this reason such tumours are sometimes termed 'heterochthonous'. **1844** J. D. DANA *Syst. Min.* (ed. 2) vi. 443 Heteroclin..was first instituted by Breithaupt, and named..in allusion to its oblique form of crystallization. **1898** E. S. DANA *Textbk. Min.* (ed. 2) IV. 343 Marceline (heterocline) from St. Marcel, Piedmont, is impure braunite. **1884** E. COUES *N. Amer. Birds* (ed. 2) 138 Both ends of each vertebra are saddle-shaped; ..a condition which may be called heterocœlous. **1933** H. F. GADOW *Evol. Vertebral Column* xxxv. 311 The embryonic vertebrae of all Birds are at first amphicoelous, then they change through opisthocoelous into the heterocoelous or saddle-shaped type, which..represents the highest stage of interaxial joint, allowing of most excursion. **1872** *Q. Jrnl. Microsc. Sci.* XII. 367 Its minute size calls to mind *Nostoc minimum* (Currey), but in it..the heterocysts are large, whilst here..the heterocysts are but slightly wider, though longer than the ordinary cells. **1887** *Jrnl. R. Microsc. Soc.* 793 (*heading*) Heterocystous Nostocaceæ. **1951** *Proc. Linnean Soc. Lond.* CLXII. II. 195 Heterocystous blue-green algae. **1939** R. C. EVANS *Introd. Crystal Chem.* i. 8 Crystals..in which two or more different types of bond are in operation between different parts of the structure are termed heterodesmic. **1952** B. MASON *Princ. Geochem.* iv. 67 In heterodesmic structures the physical properties ..are in general determined by the weakest bonds. **1963** A. H. DOERMAN in W. J. Burdette *Methodol. Basic Genet.* 34 The heterozygote is imagined to consist of a heteroduplex molecule in which every genetic site is represented twice. **1966** *Progress Nucleic Acid Res.* V. 319 The exposed polynucleotide chains can be thought to anneal during the act of rejoining to produce a heteroduplex region lying between the two recombinant segments. **1968** *Proc. Nat. Acad. Sci.* LX. 243 Each heteroduplex should thus contain a single-stranded loop in the wild-type DNA strand at the point where the deletion occurs. **1968** *Sci. Jrnl.* Nov. 5/1 The mixture [of DNA] now contains some 'heteroduplex' molecules consisting of a wild-type and a mutant strand. **1931** *Trans. Entomol. Soc. London* LXXIX. 105 Essentially different is the heterodynamic type, in which the annual cycle bears a more or less definite relation to the season. **1964** BORROR & DELONG *Introd. Study Insects* (rev. ed.) iii. 44 Most insects in temperate regions have what is called a heterodynamic life cycle; that is, the adults appear for a limited time during a particular season, and some life stage passes the winter in a state of dormancy. **1929** Heterodynamous [see *homodynamous* s.v. *HOMO-]. **1903** *Lancet* 4 Apr. 944/2 The introduction of the hetero-immune serum. **1967** C. W. H. HAVARD *Lect. Med.* vi. 147 Individuals respond immunologically to tissues of other species (hetero-immune) or to tissues of another individual of the same species (iso-immune). **1894** J. C. DACOSTA *Man. Mod. Surg.* xv. 168 Primary syphilis is not auto-inoculable, but is hetero-inoculable. **1888** E. L. KEYES *Surg. Dis. Genito-Urinary Organs* II. ii. 494 Few at the present day can be found who..consider as gonorrhœa a urethral discharge producing syphilitic chancre by hetero-inoculation. **1960** [see *homojunction* s.v. *HOMO-]. **1971** *New Scientist* 16 Sept. 628/1 The light produced in the active [region] travels into the n-type region between the two heterojunctions. **1893** Heterokinesis [see *homœokinesis* s.v. *HOMŒO-]. **1896** E. B. WILSON *Cell* ix. 305 In the second case ('heterokinesis', qualitative or differential division), the daughter-cells receive different groups of chromatin-elements, and hence become differently modified. **1892** Heterolecithal [see *homolecithal* s.v. *HOMO-]. **1896** E. B. WILSON *Cell* 336 *Heterolecithal*..having unequally distributed deutoplasm (includes telolecithal and centrolecithal). **1896** W. B. BENHAM in *Cambr. Nat. Hist.* II. x. 277 There are then three different kinds of males and of females in this one species [sc. *Nereis*], some being found at the bottom of the sea, as the large Heteronereid form, while the small Heteronereid swims on the surface. **1963** R. P. DALES *Annelids* vi. 124 In heteronereids the parapodia are greatly increased in surface area and musculature. **1875** *Encycl. Brit.* II. 67/1 Another [sexual form] which becomes transformed into a *Heteronereis* before the sexual elements are developed. **1880** F. M. BALFOUR *Compar. Embryol.* I. xii. 284 Claparède traced the passage of large asexual examples of the Nereis form into the large Heteronereis form. **1886** Heterophoria [see *exophoria* s.v. *EXO-]. **1957** *New Scientist* 9 May 38/2 Treatment aims at restoring normal functioning of the eyes, especially in what is popularly known as 'lazy' eyes and squint, but also in the more common condition of heterophoria—a tendency to squint. **1894** GOULD *Dict. Med.*, Heterophoric. **1970** *Jrnl. Gen. Psychol.* LXXXII. 109 The mean duration of lateral AM was not systemically affected by heterophoric change from zero to 28 prism diopters. **1924** *Jrnl. Genetics* XIV. 365 (*heading*) Heterophthalmic cats. **1931** *Chem. Abstr.* XXV. 2419 Benzalfluorene (IV) and I give in good yield in the fused mixt. at 130°..a white amorphous heteropolymer. **1948** C. E. H. BAWN *Chem. High Polymers* iii. 85 The individual monomers undergoing copolymerization may not polymerize alone. A copolymer formed with the latter type of monomer is often called a heteropolymer. **1952** *Jrnl. Polymer Sci.* VIII. 260 It is..recommended that the word 'heteropolymer' not be used for a copolymer in which one of the units does not polymerize by itself. **1971** *Nature* 23 July 254/2 The requirements of the RNA-DNA reaction indicate that a heteropolymer is formed, for the omission of any one of the triphosphate substrates suppresses synthesis almost completely. **1931** *Chem. Abstr.* XXV. 2418, 2 unlike units of low mol. wt., each contg. a C:C union, can ..be combined into a large mol. by polymerizing addn. The name additive heteropolymerization is suggested for such a process. **1958** *Van Nostrand's Sci. Encycl.* 132/1 Heteropolymerization is an addition polymerization. **1948** W. PIGMAN *Chem. Carbohydrates* xii. 513 The second class (heteropolysaccharides), which consists of polysaccharides giving after hydrolysis more than one monosaccharide type. **1970** Heteropolysaccharide [see *homopolysaccharide* s.v. *HOMO-]. **1891** *Jrnl. Physiol.* XII. 21 There are at least three normal proteoses formed in gastric digestion. Of these, proto and heteroproteose are first formed. **1916** A. P. MATHEWS *Physiol. Chem.* ix. 361 There are three divisions of the group: namely, the primary proteoses, including the protoproteoses and hetero-proteoses, and the secondary, or deutero-proteoses. **1905** Heteroscedastic [see *homoscedastic* s.v. *HOMO-]. **1937** YULE & KENDALL *Introd. Theory Statistics* (ed. 11) xi. 214 Arrays in which the standard deviations are equal are sometimes said to be 'homoscedastic'; in the contrary case 'heteroscedastic'. **1965** M. G. BULMER *Princ. Statistics* xii. 215 The variance of Y may not be constant but may depend on x; the regression is then said to be heteroscedastic. **1905** K. PEARSON in *Drapers' Company Res. Mem.* (Biometric Ser.) II. 23, I am thus inclined to speak of $\chi_1 - 1$ and χ_2 as measures of heteroscedasticity and heteroclisy. **1964**

JOHNSON & LEONE *Statistics & Exper. Design* II. xvii. 321 Replication at each vertex does provide some information on possible heteroscedasticity of the residual variation. **1938** A. F. SHULL *Heredity* (ed. 3) x. 92 The spermatozoa of a mammal are of two kinds, half of them containing an X chromosome, half of them a Y (or no heterosome at all in species in which Y has been lost). **1966** D. M. KRAMSCH tr. *Grundmann's Gen. Cytol.* ii. 102 Man has 22 autosomes and one heterosome in a haploid set. **1929** R. R. GATES *Heredity in Man* ix. 191 In 12·5 per cent. of heterospecific pregnancies an agglutinin passed from the mother's blood to that of the child. **1958** STRATTON & RENTON *Pract. Blood Grouping* i. 14 A mother of group O would have an incompatible or heterospecific pregnancy if the child were group A or group B. **1962** *Lancet* 5 May 965/1 Two of these components could agglutinate red cells in the presence of heterospecific serum by a mechanism previously unknown among viruses. **1969** *Nature* 6 Sept. 1021/2 The possible use of hybrids of tumour cells and heterospecific cells to stimulate an immune response. **1895** D. H. CAMPBELL *Struct. & Devel. Mosses & Ferns* i. 6 In all of the heterosporic Pteridophytes the reduction of the vegetative part of the gametophyte is very great. **1967** M. E. HALE *Biol. Lichens* iii. 46 The identity of this heterosporic mat. **1898** *Nat. Science* June 375 Its independent appearance in distinct groups may be compared with the appearance of heterospory. **1959** *Chambers's Encycl.* XI. 613/1 Heterospory..is well developed in the seed plants, where the microspores are the pollen grains. **1901** BALDWIN *Dict. Philos.* I. 96/1 Wundt uses the term Fremdsuggestion for the contrasted and usual process of suggestion from another person. The analogous Greek formation would be Heterosuggestion. **1921** *Spectator* 19 Mar. 364/2 A portion of the doctors and men of science.. began to perceive that it was primarily not their suggestions, but the patient's own suggestions to his subconscious self, which produced the wonderful results... It was auto-suggestion, not hetero-suggestion. **1951** F. HOPKINS in E. N. Chamberlain *Text-bk. Med.* ix. 660 The terms autosuggestion and heterosuggestion are used according as to whether the suggestion is made by oneself or others. **1913** J. M. JONES *Welsh Gram.* 72 In N. W[ales] the vowel is medium in *aw, ew, iw* before a vowel, that is the *w* is heterosyllabic. **1896** *Cambr. Nat. Hist.* II. 278 In some genera [of the family Syllidae]..there occur changes quite similar to those characterising 'Heteronereis'—that is, the posterior segments in which the genital organs exist become altered, so that the worm consists of two distinct regions, and is termed a 'Heterosyllis'. **1967** H. W. & L. R. LEVI tr. *Kaestner's Invertebr. Zool.* I. xix. 496 Reproduction is complicated by alternation of sexual and asexual generations... *Syllis*, 1–5 cm. change [*sic*] to heterosyllis. **1901** BALDWIN *Dict. Philos.* I. 96/1 *Heterotelic*, having or serving a foreign or external end. **1902** *Ibid.* II. 668/1 To the deist the world process is heterotelic;..to the thoroughgoing monistic idealist it is autotelic. **1904** A. F. BLAKESLEE in *Science* 3 June 865 According to their method of zygospore formation, the various species among the Mucorineæ may be divided into two main categories, which may be designated as homothallic and heterothallic... In the heterothallic group..zygospores are developed from branches which necessarily belong to thalli or mycelia diverse in character, and can never be obtained from the sowing of a single spore. **1959** *Chambers's Encycl.* VI. 117/1 *Sporodinia grandis* is homothallic, and a single spore from a sporangium will give rise both to sporangia and to zygospores, whereas *Mucor* is heterothallic, and a single spore gives rise only to sporangia. **1906** Heterothallism [see *homothallism* s.v. *HOMO-]. **1952** *New Biol.* XIII. 107 The discovery of heterothallism proved to be of fundamental importance since it has now been shown to occur in a modified form in all the major groups of fungi. **1940** *Bot. Rev.* VI. 74 There has been progressive sexual differentiation beginning with the gametes..and extending outward from them to the gametangia and prothallia, as indicated by the successive acquirement of heterogametangy and heterothally. **1942** Heterothally [see *homothally* s.v. *HOMO-]. **1919** F. SODDY in *Jrnl. Chem. Soc.* CXV. 11 Boyle's practical definition of the element.. became replaced by a theoretical conception, to which.. I propose to apply the term 'heterotope', meaning the occupant of a separate place in the periodic table of elements. **1959** L. W. H. HULL *Hist. & Philos. Sci.* viii. 267 It is now known that there are atoms of different weights having the same chemical properties. These are called isotopes. There are also 'isobaric heterotopes', which have the same weight but different chemical properties. **1895** *Ann. Bot.* IX. 479 The indifference manifested in the second mitosis in animals..as to whether it be heterotype or homotype, is of some theoretical interest. **1920** L. DONCASTER *Introd. Study Cytol.* vi. 89 When the heterotype chromosomes split longitudinally, part of one longitudinal half of one chromosome may exchange places with a similar part of the corresponding longitudinal half of the other. **1889** *Q. Jrnl. Microsc. Sci.* XXX. 203 In another deviation, which Flemming describes as the 'homöotypic Form' (that is to say, 'a form more like the usual one than the one just described, which he names "heterotypic"'), it would appear..that longitudinal splitting may be entirely absent. **1931** W. SHUMWAY *Gen. Biol.* vi. 149 The first maturation division is sometimes called the heterotypic division because of its novel features of synapsis and tetrad-formation. **1969** Heterotypic [see *homœotypic* s.v. *HOMŒO-]. **1888** Heterotypical [see *homœotypical* s.v. *HOMŒO-]. **1896** E. B. WILSON *Cell* ii. 60 (*caption*) Heterotypical mitosis in spermatocytes of the salamander. **1886** *Jrnl. Chem. Soc.* L. 266 These..researches have led to the isolation of another constituent of human urine, which it is proposed to call heteroxanthine. **1943** *Thorpe's Dict. Appl. Chem.* (ed. 4) VI. 206/1 Heteroxanthine appears to be a product of the metabolism of theobromine and caffeine, for when these alkaloids are administered to rabbits, dogs or men, heteroxanthine appears in the urine. **1909** G. M. R. LEVINSEN *Cheilostomatous Bryozoa* 74 The same heterozoœcium may appear in the same genus, even occasionally in the same species, sometimes as an avicularium, sometimes as a vibraculum... The genus *Microporella* as well as the genus *Escharina* may serve as examples of such a variable development of the two heterozoœcial forms. *Ibid.* 46 We can distinguish between four main forms of individuals (Bryozooids):.. *Heterozoœcia* (*Heterozooids*), which have no intestinal canal, and at most have a trace of a polypide in a small cell-body, furnished with a circle of fine bristles. The chamber contains a strong muscular apparatus for moving the operculum. **1959** L. H. HYMAN *Invertebrates* V. xx. 325 Other types of zooids are termed collectively heterozooids and are characterized by the reduction of the polypide, which loses its nutritive and reproductive function.

heteroauxin (he:tĕro͵ǭ·ksin). *Biochem.* [a. G. *hetero-auxin* (F. Kögl et al. 1934, in *Zeitschr. f. physiol. Chem.* CCXXVIII. 94), f. HETERO- + *AUXIN.] A growth-promoting hormone, $(C_8H_6N)CH_2\cdot COOH$, that occurs in some plants and micro-organisms; also called *β-indolyl acetic acid, 3-indoleacetic acid.*

1935 *Chem. Abstr.* XXIX. 195 Normal individuals excrete auxins and heteroauxin in the proportions of about 4:1. **1940** W. R. FEARON *Introd. Biochem.* (ed. 2) 446 It was found that urine was very rich in a growth-promoting factor, which on isolation proved to be chemically unrelated to auxin *a* or *b*, and was termed hetero-auxin. **1949** *New Biol.* VII. 69 Two principal plant hormones..have actually been isolated from plant tissues, viz. auxin and hetero-auxin. **1966** NOWAKOWSKI & CLARKE tr. *Kretovich's Princ. Plant Biochem.* v. 175 Heteroauxin is used for accelerating root formation in cuttings of various plants e.g. citrus.

heterocaryon, -caryosis, -caryotic: see *HETEROKARYON, etc.

heterochromatic (he:tĕrǝkromæ·tik), *a.* [f. HETERO- + CHROMATIC *a.* 1 in sense 1; in sense 2, f. next + -IC.] **1.** Relating to or possessing more than one colour; relating to light or other radiation of more than one wavelength. Also *fig.*

1895 F. W. OLIVER et al. tr. *Kerner's Nat. Hist. Plants* II. 569 Contrasting with these heterochromatic species are those with homochromatic flowers, which..invariably present the same colour and pattern. **1924** *Nature* 30 Aug. 329/2 The use of absorbing screens in heterochromatic photometry. **1932** W. S. DUKE-ELDER *Text-bk. Ophthalmol.* I. xxii. 861 The comparison of the luminosities of lights of different colours comprises the science of heterochromatic photometry. **1937** *Archit. Rev.* LXXXI. 198/2 Heterochromatic harmonies, or harmonies of different hue. **1969** *Nature* 11 Oct. 162/2 Along each heterochromatic channel there is..a positional as well as a wavelength variation which must be taken into account in the interpretation of line profiles.

2. *Cytol.* Of chromosome material: becoming heteropycnotic at some stage in the nuclear cycle.

1936 [see *EUCHROMATIC *a.*]. **1942** *Nature* 17 Jan. 66/2 The two properties of inertness and abnormality of nucleic acid cycle are combined in the same genes or chromomeres... These are then said to be heterochromatic as opposed to the active or euchromatic genes. **1951** G. H. BOURNE *Cytol. & Cell Physiol.* (ed. 2) v. 195 On the one hand the heterochromatic regions may be thicker and more dark-staining than the euchromatic ones. ..On the other hand, a heterochromatic region or chromosome may appear thinner and stain more weakly than euchromatic regions in the same nucleus. **1956** *Nature* 10 Mar. 452/2 It usually appears as three dots arranged in a triangle, suggesting the presence of an under-stained ('heterochromatic') region close to the centromere. **1969** *Ibid.* 16 Aug. 684/2 In plants.. supernumerary heterochromatic chromosomes may make pollen grains undergo additional divisions and quicken cell division.

heterochromatin (he:tĕrǝkrōᵘ·mătin). *Cytol.* [a. G. *heterochromatin* (E. Heitz 1928, in *Jahrb. f. wissenschaftliche Bot.* LXIX. 764), f. HETERO- + CHROMATIN.] Heterochromatic chromosome material.

1932 [see *EUCHROMATIN]. **1941** *Ann. Bot.* V. 203 Large distal segments which appear as heterochromatin in mitosis, that is to say they are overstained in resting nuclei and, after freezing, understained in metaphase. **1951** G. H. BOURNE *Cytol. & Cell Physiol.* (ed. 2) v. 196 Probably there are many varieties of heterochromatin and euchromatin, constituting a continuous 'spectrum', to the two ends of which the terms heterochromatin and euchromatin are somewhat arbitrarily applied. **1969** *Nature* 16 Aug. 683/1 The observations that heterochromatin formation is a variable property and represents cyclical physiological states of chromosome segments.. led to a shift of emphasis from heterochromatin as a substance to heterochromatin as a state.

heterochromatization (he:tĕrǝkrōᵘ:mătəizēɪ·ʃən). *Cytol.* Also **he:terochro:matiniza·tion.** [f. prec. + -IZATION.] A change of state of chromosome material in which it becomes heterochromatic and the action of the genes is modified or suppressed; also, the extent to which such a change has occurred. So **he:terochro·mat(in)ized** *ppl. a.*

1941 *Cold Spring Harb. Symp. Quant. Biol.* IX. 158/2 When extra heterochromatin..is added to a cell, the heterochromatization..is lessened. *Ibid.*, The euchromatic regions which have been transferred into the vicinity of heterochromatic ones are themselves partly..'heterochromatized'. **1944** *Amer. Naturalist* LXXVIII. 207 Variable 'heterochromatinization' takes place not only in salivary gland cells but in other body cells as well. **1948** *Jrnl. Genetics* XLVIII. 80 The process of heterochromatization (heteropycnosis) is reversible. *Ibid.* 83 The active section is sometimes so highly heterochromatized that it becomes quite indistinguishable from the neighbouring inert region. **1957** C. P. SWANSON *Cytol. & Cytogenetics* xiv. 469 This proposes that heterochromatin is formed from euchromatin by a process of genic degeneration... The end point of such an evolutionary trend..would be heterochromatinization of the entire Y. **1964** *Science* 10 July 130/1 Tissue..in which the heterochromatized *X* is of paternal origin. **1969** *Nature* 16 Aug. 683/2 The *X* chromosome that forms the sex-chromatin mass of normal females..is clearly heterochromatic when it forms (by facultative heterochromatization) a distinct chromocentre in the interphase nucleus.

heterochronous, *a.* Add: **b.** *Palæont.* [ad. G. *heterochron* (E. Mojsisovics *Die Cephalopoden der Hallstätter Kalke* (1893) II. 5).] Originating or formed at different periods.

1895 [see *HOMŒOMORPHY]. **1913** *Q. Jrnl. Geol. Soc.* LXIX. 166 Isochronous and heterochronous homœomorphy state whether the homœomorphous species lived in the same or at different times. **1952** R. C. MOORE et al. *Invert. Fossils* vi. 218 The other category includes two or more shells of different geologic age, in which one simulates the other. These are termed heterochronous homeomorphs.

he·terocy:clic, *a.* and *sb.* [f. HETERO- + CYCLIC *a.*] **1.** *Bot.* = HETEROMEROUS *a.* 2 b.

1895 S. H. VINES *Text-bk. Bot.* 500 When the whorls are heteromerous the flowers are said to be heterocyclic. **1924** HOLMAN & ROBBINS *Textbk. Gen. Bot.* vii. 228 The flowers of the great majority of plants are heterocyclic.

2. *Chem.* Pertaining to or containing a ring of atoms of more than one kind. Opp. to *homocyclic, isocyclic.* Also as *sb.*, a heterocyclic compound.

1899 E. F. SMITH tr. *V. von Richter's Org. Chem.* (ed. 3) I. 78 In the case of many heterocyclic compounds..the substances with open chains from which they may be theoretically deduced do not really exist. **1900** *Proc. Chem. Soc.* 6 Feb. 11 The action of bases on ethyl phenylpropiolate gives rise to heterocyclic compounds. **1936** L. J. DESHA *Org. Chem.* xxiv. 479 In the most typical heterocyclic compounds, the ring systems are extremely stable. **1956** *Nature* 16 June 1116/2 The oxygenated heterocyclics were discussed with emphasis on the biochemical aspects. **1966** *McGraw-Hill Encycl. Sci. & Technol.* VI. 427/2 Heterocyclic systems are encountered in many groups of organic compounds, both synthetic and natural. **1968** *New Scientist* 31 Oct. 268/3 Classification of heterocyclics into suitable groups is somewhat of a problem.

Hence **he·terocycle,** a heterocyclic ring or compound.

1909 WEBSTER, *Heterocycle*, a heterocyclic compound. **1931** *Jrnl. Amer. Chem. Soc.* LIII. 806 Ethylene oxide, the simplest oxygen heterocycle. **1957** E. H. RODD *Chem. Carbon Compounds* IVA Introd. 1 Compounds containing these heterogeneous rings (heterocycles) are classed as heterocyclic.

heterodyne (he·tĕrǝdəin), *a.* *Electr.* [f. HETERO- + *-DYNE.] Pertaining to, involving, or designating the production of a beat frequency by the combination of two oscillations of slightly different frequency, esp. as a method of radio detection in which one oscillation is the incoming signal and the other is produced in the receiver. Also (now *rare*) as *sb.*, a heterodyne receiver or its local oscillator.

1908 J. ERSKINE-MURRAY tr. *Ruhmer's Wireless Teleph.* 201 One of the most interesting of Professor Fessenden's many inventions is what he has called the 'Heterodyne' receiver. **1915** W. H. ECCLES *Wireless Telegr.* 151 In receiving signals sent out by the spark sets..the heterodyne produced a telephone current variation averaging 4·65 times that due to the liquid barretter alone. **1919** *Wireless World* Mar. 663 (*heading*) Heterodyne reception. **1922** A. F. COLLINS *Bk. Wireless Telegraph* III. ii. 174 The oscillations set up by the incoming waves from the distant sending stations and those set up by the separate oscillator tube, or heterodyne..have a slightly different frequency. **1931** *B.B.C. Yearbk.* 442/2 *Heterodyne interference*, interference caused to broadcast reception by the carrier wave of an unwanted station beating with that of the wanted station. *Ibid.*, *Heterodyne reception*, a method of receiving C.W. wireless signals in which use is made of a local oscillator to 'beat' with or 'Heterodyne' the incoming C.W. **1946** *Nature* 6 July 33/1 The usual heterodyne methods of measuring a frequency..can be extended to the highest frequencies now in general use. **1957** W. FRASER *Telecommunications* xxii. 735 The heterodyne waveform when rectified produces a current which varies in amplitude at the beat frequency.

fig. **1930** *Musical Assoc. Proc.* 97 To write atonally in a harmonic form at present is to produce a thought 'heterodyne'.

Hence **he·terodyne** *v. trans.*, (*a*) to produce heterodyne interference with (a radio station) (*obs.*); (*b*) to change the frequency of (a signal) by a heterodyne process; *intr.*, to combine so as to produce beat oscillations or a difference frequency; **he·terodyning** *vbl. sb.* and *ppl. a.*; **he·terodyned** *ppl. a.*

1923 *Glasgow Herald* 15 Oct. 6 A spark station previously heterodyned by a carrier. **1925** *Ibid.* 10 Nov. 8

Glasgow can be as effectively 'heterodyned' by a German station as Radio Paris can be by a Spanish one working on an almost identical wave-length. **1926** *Encycl. Brit.* III. 1044/2 If the signal current has a frequency of 10^5 cycles (3,000 metres), to give it an audible frequency of c″–512 the heterodyning current must have a frequency of 10^5 plus or minus 512. **1933** K. HENNEY *Radio Engin. Handbk.* x. 274 The frequencies in this selected range are made to heterodyne with an oscillator at a frequency of 42,000 cycles. **1934** *Proc. IRE* XXII. 1269 The oscillator operated at a higher frequency than the incoming carriers and heterodyned them to 6 and 7 megacycles. **1943** C. L. BOLTZ *Basic Radio* xiv. 223 This sound is called the heterodyne note, and the process is called heterodyning. **1965** WOZENCRAFT & JACOBS *Princ. Communication Engin.* vi. 493 At the receiver the signals are heterodyned back down from passband to baseband. **1967** *Electronics* 6 Mar. 288/3 In this coherent conversion system, heterodyning converts incoming reference and test signals to 45 Mhz and then to 1 kilohertz. *Ibid.* 291/1 A comparison is made between the phase of a heterodyned 1-khz test signal and the phase of a second 1-khz signal. **1972** *Science* 20 Oct. 252/2 It arises because the emission heterodynes with the collinear laser beam.

fig. **1931** T. H. PEAR *Voice & Personality* iv. 44 The rudeness..heterodynes the shyness. So, while an unselective receiver, or strange listener, perceives a jumbled mixture of both, the ear which is sensitised to rudeness hears it only, while you hear only shyness.

heterogamete (heˈtĕrogæːmīt). *Biol.* [f. HETERO- + GAMETE.] Either of a pair of conjugating gametes that differ in character or form.

1897 *Ann. Bot.* XI. 120 The stage of *Aphanochaete* is..the intermediate step between two motile heterogametes and the true sexuality realized in the higher types. **1949** B. B. MUNDKUR *Fungi & Plant Dis.* vi. 49 While the gametes are motile isogametes in *Synchytrium endobioticum*, they are non-motile heterogametes in *Olpidiopsis*.

heterogametic (heːtĕrogămīˈtik), *a. Biol.* [f. HETERO- + *GAMETIC *a.*] (Of a sex or its individual members) producing gametes that differ with respect to a sex chromosome. Opp. *HOMOGAMETIC *a.* So **heːterogaˈmety**, the state or condition of being heterogametic.

1910 E. WILSON in *Science Progress* IV. II. 572 If the two kinds of spermatozoa be designated as the 'X-class' and the 'Y-class', respectively, the eggs are all of the X-class. The male may, accordingly, be designated as the *heterogametic* sex, the female as the *homogametic*. **1932** SINNOTT & DUNN *Princ. Genet.* (ed. 2) x. 215 Two kinds of sperm (male heterogamety) are formed in equal numbers, half with X, and half with Y. **1966** *Amer. Naturalist* C. 122 The fact that heterogametic males do occur suggests..that *P. nubifer* is probably in the process of changing from male to female heterogamety. **1971** [see *HOMOGAMETIC *a.*]. **1971** *Nature* 18 June 432/2 In animals with female heterogamety, many authors refer to the chromosome which is present only in females as *W* and the paired sex chromosomes of males as *ZZ*.

heterogamous, *a.* Add: **1.** (Earlier example.)

1839 J. LINDLEY *Introd. Bot.* (ed. 3) I. ii. 157 If all the flowers are hermaphrodite in the capitulum, it is homogamous; if the outer are neuter, or female, and the inner hermaphrodite, or male, it is heterogamous.

4. *Biol.* Involving, having the character of, or producing heterogametes.

1895 J. R. GREEN *Man. Bot.* I. I. ii. 215 The smaller are held..to be male, and the larger female. Plants with such gametes are called heterogamous. **1900** *Ann. Bot.* XIV. 662 The union of heterogamous walled aplanogametes. **1925** E. B. WILSON *Cell* (ed. 3) vii. 593 In true heterogamous forms the macrogamete becomes a large, non-motile cell. **1957** H. C. BOLD *Morphol. Plants* iii. 55 These plants are the male and female gametophytes which liberate the heterogamous gametes at maturity. **1969** G. W. PRESCOTT *Algae* i. 42 Sexual reproduction may include isogamous, anisogamous, or heterogamous methods, with or without special sex organs.

heterogamy. Add: **3.** *Biol.* **a.** The condition of having or producing heterogametes; reproduction involving heterogametes. **b.** Heterogamous reproduction.

1894 S. H. VINES *Text-bk. Bot.* III. 275 Heterogamy:—*a.* Oogamy: sexual cells, oospheres and undifferentiated male cells... *b.* Carpogamy: no differentiated female cell. **1897** *Ann. Bot.* XI. 106 Isogamy, heterogamy, and conjugation have been observed. *Ibid.* 118 The curious heterogamy of *Aphanochaete.* **1925** E. B. WILSON *Cell* (ed. 3) vii. 584 A third type is true heterogamy... The gametes are here widely different from each other. **1966** *McGraw-Hill Encycl. Sci. & Technol.* III. 83/2 Heterogamy is also characteristic of land plants and is regarded as the most advanced type of sexual reproduction.

Hence **heterogaˈmic** *a.*, characterized by heterogamy (sense *3).

1904 *Science* 3 June 866/1 In the heterogamic subdivision of the homothallic group, a distinct and constant differentiation exists between the zygophoric hyphæ and the gametes derived from them. **1904** *Proc. Amer. Acad. Arts & Sci.* Aug. 210 Two genera of the homothallic group..are heterogamic in that their gametes show a certain constant inequality in size. **1927** GWYNNE-VAUGHAN & BARNES *Struct. & Devel. Fungi* 112 None of the heterothallic forms among the mucors is known to be heterogamic.

heterogeneous, *a.* Add: **4. a.** In various other technical usages, as *heterogeneous fusion, radiation, strain, stream.* Also *heterogeneous reactor*, a nuclear reactor in which the fuel is not uniformly mixed with the moderator and/or coolant (opp. 'homogeneous reactor'); also *heterogeneous pile.*

1883 *Encycl. Brit.* XV. 693/1 Heterogeneous strain. **1902** *Ibid.* XXVIII. 567/2 In the case of crystalline fusion it is necessary to distinguish two cases, the Homogeneous and the Heterogeneous... In the second case, the solid and liquid phases differ in composition; that of the liquid phase changes continuously, and the temperature does not remain constant during the fusion. *Ibid.* XXIX. 257/1 The nuclear divisions are what Weismann calls 'differentiating' or heterogeneous divisions. In them the microcosms of the germ-plasm are not doubled, but slowly disintegrated. **1922** W. B. SCOTT *Physiogr.* vi. 154 Heterogeneous streams are those which have two or more different kinds of courses, and most rivers, including almost all the longer ones, are of this class. **1947** C. GOODMAN *Sci. & Engin. Nucl. Power* I. ix. 320 (*caption*) Heterogeneous reactor with circulating liquid fuel. **1949** M. L. OLIPHANT *Atomic Age* 23 The arrangement used is a so-called 'heterogeneous pile', consisting of some tens of tons of uranium rods or slugs disposed in a calculated 'lattice' throughout a mass of some hundreds of tons of graphite. **1958** O. R. FRISCH *Nucl. Handbk.* xii. 2 By far the largest number of reactors built to date have been thermal, heterogeneous reactors. **1958** *Chambers's Techn. Dict.* (ed. 3) 984/2 *Heterogeneous radiation*, that having particles of various energies and/or wavelengths.

b. Denoting the presence of more than one phase (solid, liquid, or gas) in a system or process.

1878 J. W. GIBBS in *Trans. Connecticut Acad. Arts & Sci.* III. 108 (*heading*) On the equilibrium of heterogeneous substances. **1895** *Jrnl. Chem. Soc.* LXVIII. II. 72 (*heading*) Graphical representation of heterogeneous systems. **1928** J. K. ROBERTS *Heat & Thermodynamics* xviii. 356 Heterogeneous reactions in which solids and vapours take part. **1950** *Sci. News* XV. 65 Much research had been carried out on heterogeneous catalysts, that is, catalysts at whose surfaces reactions between gases are brought about.

heterogenetic, *a.* Add: **1.** (Earlier example.)

1872 *Proc. R. Soc.* XX. 264 The living units combine, they undergo molecular rearrangements, and the result of such a process of heterogenetic biocrasis is the appearance of larger and more complex organisms.

2. b. *Med.* Of a disease: produced by infection from outside the body.

1890 in BILLINGS *Med. Dict.*

3. *Path.* [ad. G. *heterogenetisch* (Friedberger & Schiff 1913, in *Berl. klin. Wochenschr.* 25 Aug. 1558/1).] = *HETEROPHILE *a.* 1.

1918 C. H. BROWNING *Appl. Bacteriol.* x. 175 'Heterogenetic' antibodies (Friedberger). *Ibid.* 176 The capacity to produce a positive Wassermann reaction is probably a somewhat similar heterogenetic phenomenon. **1920** *Jrnl. Path. & Bacteriol.* XXIII. 364 The injection of organs of certain animals into rabbits leads to the development of 'heterogenetic' immune body for sheep's blood corpuscles. The tissues which act in this way are called 'heterogenetic antigens'. **1944** *Jrnl. Exper. Med.* LXXIX. 556 A heterogenetic antibody showing fixation of complement with human liver and agglutination of sheep erythrocytes was found in certain cases of acute infective hepatitis.

heterogenic (heːtĕrodʒeˈnik), *a.*[1] [f. Gr. ἑτερογεν-ής (see HETEROGENE *a.*) + -IC; in sense 2 prob. directly f. *HETEROGENY 3 b.]

1. 'Occurring in the wrong sex, as a beard upon a woman' (Dorland, 1900).

2. *Biol.* Characterized by an alternation of generations; = HETEROGENETIC *a.* 1.

1901 *Jrnl. Exper. Med.* VI. 80 These various forms were but different phases in the cycle of a single heterogenic parasite.

3. *Med.* Derived from animals of a different species.

1911 *Jrnl. Exper. Med.* XIV. 245 Fetal tissues of the chicken grew extensively in human, rabbit, and dog plasma. In general, however,..the development of the tissues is slighter..in heterogenic than in autogenic and homogenic plasma. **1920** *Jrnl. Path. & Bacteriol.* XXIII. 366 There is established the existence of an apparently specific relationship between the lipoids of heterogenic organs and the heterogenetic antibody. **1922** *Jrnl. Exper. Med.* XXXV. 17 It would be of advantage to cultivate chicken tissue in heterogenic serum because it is much more difficult to keep alive *in vitro* permanently a strain of mammal fibroblasts than of chicken fibroblasts.

heterogenic (heːtĕrodʒīˈnik), *a.*[2] *Genetics.* [f. HETERO- + *GEN(E + -IC.] Having more than one allele of a particular gene.

1947 D. LEWIS in *Heredity* I. 86 Pollen grains with such different alleles are described as heterogenic. *Ibid.* 88 Some types of heterogenic pollen were fully compatible on a style carrying only one of the alleles present in the pollen, but were incompatible on styles carrying the other allele only. **1967** *Hereditas* LVIII. 25 There is lack of interaction in all the twelve allelic pair constellations which are possible in the heterogenic pollen of the tetraploid.

heterogenist. (Earlier example.)

1870 *Nature* 14 July 224/1 M. Pasteur's researches.. have..strongly influenced the opinions of very many scientific men on the question of the truth or falsity of the doctrines of the heterogenists.

heterogenite (hetĕrǫˈdʒīnəit). *Min.* [ad. G. *heterogenit* (A. Frenzel 1872, in *Jrnl. f. prakt. Chem.* V. 404), f. Gr. ἑτερογεν-ής of different kinds, in allusion to the fact that the mineral differs in composition from some manganese oxides, which it outwardly resembles: see -ITE[1].] A name applied to various hydrous oxides of cobalt.

1872 *Jrnl. Chem. Soc.* XXV. 991 Heterogenite is a product of the decomposition of smaltine or tin-white cobalt (speiss-kobalt). **1922** *Amer. Mineralogist* VII. 195 It is therefore recommended that the prior name heterogenite be applied to *all cobalto-cobaltic hydroxides*, of varying purity. **1962** *Mineral. Mag.* XXXIII. 258 Of the many names proposed for natural cobaltic hydroxide, heterogenite has a clear priority over transvaalite, stainierite, mindigite, trieuite, and boodtite. Heubachite is a nickelian and schulzenite a cuprian heterogenite.

heterogenous, *a.* Delete † *Obs.* and add later examples. (In mod. use prob. repr. the pronunc. (hetĕrǫˈdʒīnəs) given by some speakers to *heterogeneous*: cf. *homogenous* (*HOMOGENEOUS *a.* ¶).)

1916 [see *club necktie* (*CLUB *sb.* 19)]. **1961** WEBSTER, *Heterogenous* = Heterogeneous. **1971** *Nature* 20 Aug. 586/1 A very heterogenous collection of twenty articles discusses basic physiology of the small intestine. **1972** *Ibid.* 10 Mar. 78/1 A heterogenous population of schizophrenic patients.

2. *Surg.* [prob. directly f. Gr. γένος race.] Of transplanted tissue: † **a.** = *HOMOGENOUS *a.* 2, *HOMOPLASTIC *a.* 2. *Obs.*

1909 *Boston Med. & Surg. Jrnl.* 23 Dec. 916/1 Whether heterogenous grafts are taken from a living or from a dead subject, there is with them some likelihood of failure to form *permanent* skin.

b. = *HETEROPLASTIC *a.* 3.

1939 S. FOMON *Surg. Injury & Plastic Repair* ii. 107 Failure of heterogenous transplants. **1949** EICHELBAUM & TURNER in M. Thorek *Mod. Surg. Technic* (ed. 2) II. xxix. 1149/1 The heterogenous graft..has been abandoned in favor of the homogenous graft which as an autogenous graft is now in the widest use. **1965** *Jrnl. Amer. Med. Assoc.* 2 Aug. 380/1 Results with the processed heterogenous bone transplants closely parallel those with autogenous and homogenous bone transplants.

heterogeny. Add: **2.** Delete *rare.* (Later examples.)

1921 *S.P.E. Tract* v. 10 We find a heterogeny of words in use. **1927** *Sunday Express* 29 May 5/1 Every conceivable kind of article which forms the heterogeny of the shops patronised by women.

3. b. Alternation of generations, *esp.* of a sexual and a parthenogenetic generation.

1886 W. E. HOYLE tr. *Leuckart's Parasites of Man* 25 The theory of the heterogeny of Entozoa. *Ibid.* 96, I have for some time been accustomed to call such an alternate succession of dimorphous sexual generations by the name 'Heterogeny'. **1889** E. B. POULTON et al. tr. *Weismann's Ess. Heredity* 325 In the *Daphnidae*, heterogeny may pass into pure parthenogenesis by the non-appearance of the sexual generations. **1931** BLACKLOCK & SOUTHWELL *Guide Human Parasitol.* xii. 105 Where one egg produces more than one adult, asexual multiplication has obviously followed the sexual multiplication, *i.e.* alternation of generations, or heterogeny, exists. **1946** B. DAWES *Trematoda* xiv. 501 Heterogeny, namely, the alternation of a parthenogenetic with a sexual generation.

heterogonic (heːtĕrogǫˈnik), *a.* [f. HETEROGON(Y + -IC; in sense 1 ad. F. *hétérogonique* (A. Pézard 1918, in *Bull. biol. de la France et de la Belg.* LII. 25).] **1.** = *ALLOMETRIC *a.*

1924 *Nature* 20 Dec. 895/1 Whereas in the male the ratio *abdomen-breadth : carapace-breadth* remained constant, in the female it increased continuously... Pézard (1918) has styled the growth of such an organ *heterogonic.* **1935** *Ibid.* 14 Sept. 433/2 Heterogonic growth clearly involves a regularly continuous change of proportions. **1964** H. W. MANNER *Elem. Compar. Embryol.* xi. 216 Differential growth is referred to as heterogonic growth.

2. Exhibiting heterogony (sense *1 b); applied to a life-cycle in which free-living organisms alternate with parasites, and to the free-living generation of such a cycle.

1926 J. H. SANDGROUND in *Amer. Jrnl. Hygiene* VI. 338 In the genus Strongyloides [of nematodes] heterogony may be involved in the life-cycle, but in many instances there is only one multiplicative generation and this mode of development has been called *direct* or, if we may introduce a new term to express this, homogonic in contradistinction to heterogonic or indirect. **1936** *Amer. Jrnl. Hygiene* XXIV. 83 No obvious necessity for the interpolation of a heterogonic generation in the reproductive cycle of *S. ratti* has manifested itself. **1951** L. H. HYMAN *Invert.* III. xiii. 304 The eggs..may develop into free-living males and females, the offspring of which proceed to the parasitic phase so that the cycle is indirect or heterogonic.

So **heːterogoˈnically** *adv.*

1932 J. S. HUXLEY *Probl. Rel. Growth* II. ii. 53 The trunk grows heterogonically with reference to the head.

heterogony. Add: **1. b.** *Biol.* Alternation of generations, *esp.* of a diœcious and a hermaphroditic generation.

1906 P. FALCKE tr. *Braun's Anim. Parasites Man* 273 In a number of Nematodes..heterogony occurs. **1908**

BEATTIE & DICKSON *Textbk. Gen. Path.* vi. 395 In other nematodes what is known as Heterogony occurs, in which there may be alteration [ed. 2, 1921, alternation] of fully developed sexual generations. **1936** *Nature* 9 May 780 Heterogony has been widely used to denote a certain type of reproductive cycle.

2. *Biol.* = *ALLOMETRY.

1927 *Jrnl. Genetics* XVII. 309 (*heading*) Discontinuous variation and heterogony in Forficula. **1938** [see *ALLOMETRY].

3. Phr. *heterogony of ends*: a principle enunciated by Wundt (*Ethik* 1886), according to which the development of religion and of codes of moral and social behaviour produced results that are to be distinguished from the cause of the development and were not intended at its outset; e.g. moral customs are regarded as (unforeseen) outgrowths from religious ceremonial.

1887 *Mind* XII. 286 The most general results of the author's [*sc.* Wundt's] investigation are a 'law of three stages' of moral development and a 'law of the heterogony of ends'. **1897** J. H. GULLIVER et al. tr. *Wundt's Ethik* I. 330 The law of the *heterogony of ends*. We mean to express by this name what is a matter of universal experience: that manifestations of will, over the whole range of man's free voluntary actions, are always of such a character that the effects of the actions extend more or less widely beyond the original motives of volition, so that *new* motives are originated for future actions, and again, in their turn, produce new effects. **1911** *Encycl. Brit.* XVIII. 241/2 Each particular will is directed to particular ends, but..beyond these ends effects follow as unexpected consequences, and..this heterogony produces social effects which we call custom.

heterograft (he·tĕrŏgrɑft). *Med.* and *Biol.* [f. HETERO- + GRAFT *sb.*[1]] A graft taken from an individual of a species different from that of the recipient; a heterotransplant.

Quot. 1909 is in the sense of *HOMOGRAFT.

1909 *Boston Med. & Surg. Jrnl.* 23 Dec. 918/2 Autografts succeed better than hetero-grafts. **1923** STEDMAN *Med. Dict.* (ed. 7) 449/2 *Heterograft*, a graft taken from an animal—not from another person, *isograft*, or from another part of the same individual, *autograft*. **1927** H. T. KARSNER *Human Path.* xi. 313 The fact that chemical conditions must be nicely adjusted is indicated by the failure of heterografts and the relatively higher degree of success of autografts over homeografts. **1948** *Endeavour* VII. 165 In simpler organisms, such as *Hydra*, the graft can be of different species (heterograft). **1972** *Daily Colonist* (Victoria, B.C.) 12 Mar. 22/5 The Brooke research team looked to animals as a source of possible heterografts.

Hence **he·terografted** *ppl. a.*; **he·terografting** *vbl. sb.*

1927 H. T. KARSNER *Human Path.* xi. 312 Heterografting..would throw open a large field for transplantation of various tissues and organs which cannot be removed from human donors..until death has occurred. **1961** *Biol. Abstr.* XXXVI. 2017/2 Regeneration of homografted and heterografted limbs in the stick insects. **1968** J. C. NORMAN et al. *Organ Perfusion & Preservation* xxviii. 382 Heterografted fox livers. *Ibid.* 383 The loss of perfusion immediately after heterografting.

heterography. **1.** (Later examples.)

1908 *Daily Chron.* 6 May 4/6 On the subject of 'howlers', we all make them at times, being victims of heterophasia (or heterography). **1920** W. PERRETT *Peetickay* 15 There is a pretty general consensus that unconventional spelling or heterography is bad spelling.

heterokaryotic (he:tĕrokæri,ǫ·tik), *a. Bot.* Also **-caryotic.** [ad. G. *heterocaryotisch* (H. Burgeff 1913, in *Ber. d. Deut. Bot. Ges.* XXX. 680), f. HETERO- + KARY(O- + -OTIC.] Exhibiting or resulting from heterokaryosis. Hence **he:teroka·ryon** (-kæ·ri,ǫn), a heterokaryotic cell, structure, or organism; **he:terokaryo·sis** (-kæri,ōu·sis), the condition, prevalent among fungi, in which two or more genetically different nuclei are maintained in a common cytoplasm.

1916 B. D. JACKSON *Gloss. Bot. Terms* (ed. 3) 178/1 *Heterokaryotic*,..the character of spores in which both male and female nuclei exist (Burgeff); *Heterokaryosis* is the condition. **1932** *Phytopathology* XXII. 955 The term 'heterocaryosis' precisely describes the condition of a cell containing 2 or more genetically different nuclei. **1935** *Ibid.* XXV. 285 The very young spore already contains several nuclei; hence it is quite possible that each may carry different factors for cultural characters and pathogenicity. The organism may then be truly heterocaryotic. **1942** *Bull. Torrey Bot. Club* LXIX. 75 (*heading*) Heterocaryotic vigor in Neurospora. **1945** *Genetics* XXX. 13 The natural heterokaryon in *Neurospora crassa* generally contains both plus and minus nuclei. **1952** S. EMERSON in J. W. Gowan *Heterosis* xii. 200 (*caption*) Heterocaryon formation resulting from hyphal fusion. **1955** *New Biol.* XIX. 20 Heterokaryosis has this advantage over sex that a single organism can contain genes from more than two parents. **1969** *Nature* 30 Aug. 961/2 The diploid nuclei were produced by rare nuclear fusion in a balanced heterokaryon formed from two different uninucleate colour mutants.

heterological (he:tĕrolǫ·dʒikăl), *a.* [ad. G. *heterologisch* (Grelling & Nelson 1907, in *Abhandl. Fries'schen Schule* II. 307), f. HETERO- + Gr. λόγος word: see LOGOS.] Of an adjective or other predicate: not having the property it denotes. Hence **he:terologica·lity**, the property of being heterological.

1926, 1952 [see *AUTOLOGICAL *a.*]. **1940** B. RUSSELL *Inquiry Meaning & Truth* v. 79 'Long' is heterological because it is not a long word, but 'short' is homological. **1950** *Analysis* X. 79 When one is asked, 'Is "heterological" heterological?' no answer need be given until the notion of heterologicality is further analyzed.

heterologous. Add: **c.** (See quot. 1889.)

1889 V. H. W. WINGRAVE *Dunman's Gloss. Anat. Terms, Heterologous stimuli*, stimuli which will excite a sensory nerve when applied either to its termination or in its continuity. **1913** *Amer. Jrnl. Physiol.* XXXII. 230 Aronsohn..declared that substances in solution when poured into the nose, could be smelled... This conclusion was confirmed by Vaschide (1901), and by Veress (1903), though the latter showed that the solutions tested were rather in the nature of heterologous than homologous stimuli.

d. *Path.* and *Bacteriol.* Deriving from, associated with, or belonging to another species or type of organism or an antigen or antibody of different constitution.

1893 PARKER & RÖNNFELDT tr. *Weismann's Germ-Plasm* ix. 265 In the crosses between different species, the idioplasm of a cell in many stages will be composed of homologous as well as of heterologous ids. **1910** *Jrnl. Path. & Bacteriol.* XIV. 30 We have endeavoured to determine whether..the inoculation of heterologous bacteria..affects the production of specific agglutinins in animals previously immunised against the *Bacillus coli*. **1915** *Lancet* 3 Apr. 701/2 (*heading*) Heterologous transplantation: mouse tumours in rats. **1916** *Jrnl. Path. & Bacteriol.* XX. 214 Heterologous resistance as exemplified in the reactions of the sera of animals immunised with transplanted new growths from alien species. **1933** W. W. C. TOPLEY *Outl. Immunity* vi. 91 A serum that agglutinates the same bacterium but has been produced by the inoculation of some other bacterium, differing in one or more of its antigenic components, is termed a heterologous serum. **1958** *Nature* 13 Dec. 1678/2 The multiplication of extraneous viruses in tumours grown in homologous and heterologous hosts depends on the host animal.

heterolysin (he:tĕrolǝi·sin). [a. G. *heterolysin* (Ehrlich & Morgenroth 1900, in *Berl. klin. Wochenschr.* XXXVII. 455/1), f. HETERO- + *LYSIN.] A hæmolysin formed in the bloodstream of an animal when blood cells from one of a different species are introduced.

1901 in DORLAND *Med. Dict.* (ed. 2). **1903** *Science* 3 July 9/1 Many observations upon the effects of iso- and hetero-lysins—as for kidney and liver cells—about which there is no reasonable doubt. **1934** ZINSSER & BAYNE-JONES *Textbk. Bacteriol.* (ed. 7) xvi. 212 The blood cells of one animal, injected into an animal of another species, give rise to a hemolytic substance in the blood serum of the second animal, which is strictly specific for the variety of cells injected. Such hemolysins..are spoken of as *heterolysins*.

heterolysis (hetĕrǫ·lisis). [f. HETERO- + *-LYSIS.] **1. a.** The dissolution of blood cells by a heterolysin. **b.** The dissolution of cells of one kind by an enzyme of cells of another kind.

1902 VAUGHAN & NOVY *Cellular Toxins* (ed. 4) vii. 129 Ehrlich suggests that the hemolytic action of the blood serum of one animal upon the corpuscles of another species be designated as 'heterolysis'. **1909** ALLBUTT & ROLLESTON *Syst. Med.* (ed. 2) VI. 783 The autolysis of bland infarcts is..due to enzymes derived from the cytoplasm..and is a much slower process than the heterolysis due to the leucocytic invasion seen in infective infarcts. **1924** R. MUIR *Text-bk. Path.* i. 14 The term autolysis has been applied to the digestive softening of tissues produced by their own organisms. Such enzymes ..may be produced by other cells, especially leucocytes —heterolysis. **1962** H. HANSON in A. Pirie *Lens Metabolism Rel. Cataract* 470 More significant for the specification of intracellular proteases are experiments on heterolysis, i.e. the action of cell proteases on proteins or peptides that are foreign to the cell.

2. *Chem.* The splitting of a molecule into two oppositely charged ions.

1938 C. K. INGOLD in *Trans. Faraday Soc.* XXXIV. 227, I would suggest that we may as well have two [new words] and be done with it: *viz.*, 'heterolysis' and 'homolysis', defined as follows: A:B→A+:B (*Heterolysis*) [and] A:B→A.+.B (*Homolysis*). Here the dots represent electrons. **1946** *Nature* 28 Sept. 448/2 A slow heterolysis of nitric acid cannot depend only on proton transfers. **1965** PHILLIPS & WILLIAMS *Inorg. Chem.* I. x. 344 Due to the high energy of production of A^+A^-, heterolysis..of homonuclear species is not very probable, except in the presence of catalysts.

So **heteroly·tic** *a.*, characterized by or of the nature of heterolysis (in either sense).

1909 *Chem. Abstr.* III. 1766 Cancer tissue itself possesses no heterolytic properties. **1919** J. EWING *Neoplastic Dis.* iii. 67 A heterolytic action of tumor ferments has been actively claimed. **1941** *Trans. Faraday Soc.* XXXVII. 604 It is necessary to distinguish between two main types of bond-fission, *viz.*, symmetric or homolytic fission and dissymmetric or heterolytic fission, defined as follows (the dots representing electrons): R.|.X (homolytic fission) [and] R|..X (heterolytic fission). *Ibid.* 608 The heterolytic substitutions under discussion are characterised by important electrical transferences in the reactant species. **1964** N. G. CLARK *Mod. Org. Chem.* xxv. 514 This process is called heterolysis, and reactions involving it are termed heterolytic reactions.

heteromorphic, *a.* Add: **1. a.** In wider use in *Biol.*

1935 F. E. FRITSCH *Struct. & Reprod. Algae* I. 52 The last type of life-cycle..exhibits an alternation of a large sporophyte and a generally small gametophyte. This heteromorphic (antithetic) alternation is encountered solely among Phaeophyceae. **1967** ALEXOPOULOS & BOLD *Algae & Fungi* iv. 23 In heteromorphic alternation, the two sequential organisms differ morphologically.

c. *Cytology.* Applied to homologous chromosomes that differ in size or form.

1917 E. E. CAROTHERS in *Jrnl. Morphology* XXVIII. 449 The unusual conditions of the chromosomes in this group have made advisable the introduction of four new terms... Heteromorphic—used to designate those tetrads made up of morphologically different homologues. **1925** E. B. WILSON *Cell* (ed. 3) vi. 571 The so-called heteromorphic chromosome-pairs in which the synaptic mates are visibly distinguishable by the eye by differences of size, form, mode of spindle-attachment or structure. **1955** *Jrnl. Genetics* LIII. 593 Symmetrical separation of the pair of heteromorphic X- and Y-chromosomes in the first anaphase of meiosis.

d. *Min.* [tr. F. *hétéromorphe* (A. Lacroix 1917, in *Compt. Rend.* CLXV. 486).] (See quot. 1920.)

1920 A. HOLMES *Nomencl. Petrol.* 117 *Heteromorphic*, a term applied to rocks of similar chemical composition, but of different mineral composition. **1921** —— *Petrogr. Methods* x. 410 Each of these rocks is a heteromorphic type of theralite.

e. *Zool.* (See quots.)

1931 W. C. ALLEE *Animal Aggregations* ii. 16 Heteromorphic colonies are formed when the divisions are unequal, as is the case with the strobila of the Scyphozoa, or during the processes of asexual reproduction of certain worms, such as *Autolytus*. *Ibid.* 23 Heteromorphic and polymorphic colonies are formed when there is a differentiation between the different members of the colony, as occurs in the hybrid Hydractinia, in which feeding, reproductive, and protective zoöids may be recognized.

3. *Biol.* Resulting from heteromorphosis.

1898 *Arch. f. Entwickelungsmech. d. Organismen* VII. 481 Neither the present nor other experiments indicate, that the influence of the organism as a whole upon the regenerating part is able to bring forth a heteromorphic structure..out of material which would normally produce something else. **1932** J. S. HUXLEY *Probl. Rel. Growth* vi. iii. 175 The regenerated heteromorphic appendage almost invariably is of a type which normally belongs to a more posterior segment—e.g. antenna regenerated instead of eye-stalk (Palaemon). **1966** E. D. HAY *Regeneration* ii. 75 The heteromorphic growths..may result because an insufficient mass of cells is present for correct differentiation of the skeletal pattern.

Hence **he:teromo·rphically** *adv.*, by means of heteromorphosis.

1959 *Jrnl. Biophysical & Biochem. Cytol.* V. 25 Cultures of subcutaneous areolar fibroblasts..are changed heteromorphically so as to resemble cultures of nervous tissue.

heteromorphism. Add: **2.** 'The property of replacing lost parts by new parts which are different from those that have been lost' (*Cent. Dict.* Suppl. 1909); = *HETEROMORPHOSIS b.

3. Examples relating to additional senses of *HETEROMORPHIC *a.*

1895 F. W. OLIVER tr. *Kerner's Nat. Hist. Plants* II. 469 One branch of the colony is concerned in the acquiring of nutrition, another in reproduction... To this differentiation among equivalent members we may apply the term Heteromorphism. **1921** A. HOLMES *Petrogr. Methods* x. 407 (*heading*) Heteromorphism in igneous rocks. **1954** R. L. PARKER tr. *P. Niggli's Rocks & Min. Deposits* iv. 125 Variations in primary mineralogical composition..can result from the bulk chemical composition (heteromorphism).

heteromorphosis (he:tĕromǭ·ɹfŏsis, -mǭɹfōu·sis). [f. HETERO- + MORPHOSIS; in sense b ad. G. *heteromorphose* (J. Loeb *Untersuchungen z. physiol. Morphologie d. Thiere* (1891) I. i. 10), f. Gr. ἕτερο-ς different + μόρφωσ-ις formation.] **a.** Abnormal tissue, or tissue formed at the wrong place; heteroplasia.

1891 FOSTER *Med. Dict.* III, *Heteromorphosis*, a malformation. The *heteromorphoses*..in Fuchs's classification of skin diseases are a genus..including nævus, ochthiasis, polytrichia, and polonychia. **1922** *Guy's Hosp. Rep.* LXXII. 200 Cells differing in structure from those characteristic of the part of the body are produced. Here we have a heteroplasia or heteromorphosis.

b. The regeneration of an organ or structure that is different from the one lost.

1894 *Jrnl. Morphology* IX. 418 To this phenomenon of the reproduction of an organ typically different from the one which had originally occupied that position, he [*sc.* Jacques Loeb] has given the name heteromorphosis. **1901** J. LOEB *Compar. Physiol. Brain* xiv. 203 The processes of heteromorphosis—that is, the transformation or substitution of one organ for a morphologically different one by means of certain external influences—force us to the same view. **1932** J. S. HUXLEY *Probl. Rel. Growth* vi. iii. 172 The production of axial heteromorphosis in regeneration, such as biaxial heads or tails, can also be satisfactorily interpreted in terms of the gradient hypothesis. **1940, 1966** [see *HOMŒOSIS].

heteronomous, *a.* Add: **3.** (Earlier and later examples.)

a **1871** G. GROTE *Eth. Fragm.* (1876) ii. 47 The will

is..in a certain sense *autonomous*, not *heteronomous*. **1932** W. L. GRAFF *Lang.* vi. 221 These are *conditioned* sound changes, also called *dependent* or *heteronomous* because they appear to depend upon the extraneous influence of their phonetic surroundings.

Hence **hetero·nomously** *adv.*

1909 *Cent. Dict.* Suppl., *Heteronomously*, in a heteronomous manner. **1948** J. L. ADAMS tr. *Tillich's Protestant Era* iii. 46 Religion, if it acts heteronomously, has ceased to be the substance and life-blood of a culture and has become itself a section of it. **1966** J. A. SERRA *Mod. Genetics* II. xii. 118 In a few cases, however, the colour developed heteronomously; in such cases the host influenced the colour of the implanted eye.

heteronomy. 2. (Earlier example.)

1798 WILLICH *Elem. Crit. Philos.* 160 Heteronomy, or a foreign legislation, is that, in which not the will itself, but something else determines us to act in a certain manner.

heteronuclear (he:tĕroniū·klĭăɹ), *a.* [f. HETERO- + NUCLEAR *a.*] **a.** *Chem.* Taking place on different rings in a polycyclic molecule.

1900 E. F. SMITH tr. *V. von Richter's Org. Chem.* (ed. 3) II. 390 It can first be ascertained whether the substituents are in the same nucleus (isonuclear) or in different nuclei (heteronuclear). **1951** I. L. FINAR *Org. Chem.* I. xxix. 586 When NO_2 or SO_3H is in the 1- or 2-position, heteronuclear substitution occurs in position 5 or 8.

b. *Physics* and *Chem.* Of a molecule: composed of atoms whose nuclei are unlike, i.e. atoms of different elements or of different isotopes of the same element.

1930 *Physical Rev.* XXXVI. 617 The words even and odd are applied..to the *complete* ψ function of any molecule, homonuclear or heteronuclear. **1940** *Ibid.* LVII. 684/2 The HD molecule is heteronuclear and there is no quantum number of total spin. **1950** J. W. T. SPINKS tr. *Herzberg's Molecular Spectra & Molecular Structure* (ed. 2) I. iii. 94 This agrees with the observed infrared spectrum of HCl..and of other heteronuclear molecules.

heterophile (he·tĕrofəil), *a.* and *sb.* Also **heterophil.** [a. G. *heterophil* (U. Friedemann 1917, in *Biochem. Zeitschr.* LXXX. 334), f. HETERO- + -PHIL(E).] **1.** *adj.* Able to react immunologically with sera, etc., from organisms of another species.

1920 *Jrnl. Path. & Bacteriol.* XXIII. 366 The term heterogenetic is not altogether appropriate in this connection, since the important character is not that the antibody is generated by a different kind of antigen, but that it has an affinity for receptors of a species other than that in response to which it was developed, *heterophile* describes this property better. **1929** TOPLEY & WILSON *Princ. Bacteriol. & Immunity* II. li. 748 It is now known that the so-called 'heterophile', or 'Forssman' antigen..is widely distributed among the animal species which have been examined, and in a curiously random fashion. **1935** *Arch. Path.* XIX. 841 Heterophile phenomena embrace those immunologic reactions in which the interaction of antigen and antibody is seemingly not specific in the strictly orthodox conception of the term. **1950** J. V. DACIE *Pract. Hæmatol.* xi. 150 The limits of the titre of heterophile antibodies present in health are ill-defined. **1960** I. A. STANTON *Dict. Med. Secretaries* 70/2 *Heterophile agglutination test..*, a method of testing for the presence of infectious mononucleosis. The blood of patients with this disease contains antibodies for the red blood cells of sheep.

2. *adj.* and *sb.* A polymorphonuclear leucocyte found in the blood of mammals and stained by both acidic and basic dyes; usu. as *sb.*

1938 H. DOWNEY *Handbk. Hematol.* I. ii. 167 The special or 'heterophile' leucocytes of the animals commonly used in experimental research resemble the human neutrophile quite closely in size and morphology, but with slight variations in nuclei, and in the size and staining of the specific granules which make them distinctive. **1941** CALKINS & SUMMERS *Protozoa Biol. Research* xviii. 835 The heterophils are functional in immunity by virtue of their obvious phagocytic activities and probably because of their secretion of enzymes. **1965** P. D. STURKIE *Avian Physiol.* (ed. 2) i. 13 The heterophils in the blood of children are usually round and have a diameter of approximately 10 to 15 microns.

heterophilic (he:tĕrofi·lik), *a.* [f. prec. + -IC.] = *HETEROPHILE *a.*

1929 *Jrnl. Exper. Med.* XLIX. 497 Horse serum is known to contain a heterophilic antigen. **1966** *Jrnl. Cell Biol.* XXIX. 309 (*caption*) Thin section of heterophilic myelocyte found in rabbit bone marrow.

heterophony (hetĕrǫ·fŏni). [Gr. ἑτεροφωνία: see Plato *Leges* VII. 812D.] Simultaneous performance by two or more singers or instrumentalists of different versions of the same melody. Also **heteropho·nic, hetero·phonous** *adjs.*, different in sound.

1919 *Musical Q.* V. 599 Two forms of instrumental accompaniment were known to the Greeks, namely the homophonic and heterophonic. **1936** *Amer. Speech* XI. 299 Any phonic difference found between comparably situated sounds in heterophonous words in a given language constitutes a phonemic contrast. **1939** *Scrutiny* VII. 402 Ruth Crawford writes heterophonic music in which the various linear strands bear no relation to one another except that of proximity in time-space. **1945** *Times* 16 Mar. 6 The name for this simultaneous variation with its permitted dissonance is heterophony. **1962** *Listener* 21 June 1091/2 The pianos are brilliantly used as percussion instruments, sometimes in harp-like arpeggiated pentatonics, sometimes in wildly clashing heterophony. **1970** *Daily Tel.* 16 Nov. 9/4 Heterophony was..only just round the corner from the virelais, 'Se Ma Dame' and 'Comment qu'a moy', as treated here with instrumental doubling of the voice parts. **1971** *Guardian* 22 Feb. 8/4 The work was somewhat discursive, there being too few landmarks in the prevailing heterophonic texture to compel the listeners' attention throughout.

heteroplastic, *a.* Add: **3.** *Surg.* Said of a graft between two individuals of different species.

[**1889**: see *HOMOPLASTIC *a.* 2.] **1898** *Arch. f. Entwickelungsmech. d. Organismen* VII. 471 There were obtained a number of larvae of normal external form, but which were composed of parts derived from two distinct species. ..The general biological interest attaching to such heteroplastic combinations is naturally great. **1908** A. CARREL in *Jrnl. Amer. Med. Assoc.* 14 Nov. 1664/1 There are several varieties of heteroplastic transplantations according to the zoologic distance which separates the host and the owner of the transplanted tissue. **1909** [see *HOMOPLASTIC *a.* 2]. **1917** *Brit. Jrnl. Surg.* V. 199 Heteroplastic grafts—i.e. bones transferred from one animal to another of a different species—..show neither vitality nor proliferative capacity. **1923** [see *HETEROPLASTY 1 b]. **1924** *Proc. Nat. Acad. Sci.* X. 69 The heteroplastic transplantation of limbs. **1959** *Arkiv f. Zool.* XII. 183 Heteroplastic transplantation would be a most valuable means of demonstrating the role of movable cells during a regeneration, because the chromosome number and morphology reveals the origin of the cells.

So **heteropla·stically** *adv.*

1928 *Proc. Soc. Exper. Biol. & Med.* XXV. 686 (*heading*) Growth of heteroplastically transplanted eyes and limbs in Amblystoma. **1932** J. S. HUXLEY *Probl. Rel. Growth* II. ii. 53 Eyes and other organs when heteroplastically transplanted. **1960** B. I. BALINSKY *Introd. Embryol.* vi. 167 Hilde Mangold transplanted heteroplastically (from *Triturus cristatus* to *Triturus taeniatus*) a piece of the dorsal lip of the blastopore of an early gastrula.

heteroplasty (he·tĕroplæsti). [f. HETERO- + -PLASTY.] **1.** *Med.* and *Biol.* [ad. F. *hétéroplastie* (P. F. Blandin *Autoplastie* (1836) 7)] The operation of grafting tissues between different individuals. **a.** Between two individuals of the same species.

1855 DUNGLISON *Dict. Med. Sci.* (ed. 12) 440/2 *Heteroplasty*, irregular plastic or formative operations, that do not admit of exact classification. **1874** *English Mechanic* 321 The name heteroplasty has been adopted for the operation of taking pieces of skin from amputated limbs, and using them to produce cicatrisation on the bodies of other subjects. **1901** A. G. GERSTER in R. Park *Treat. Surgery* liv. 1154 Heteroplasty..is the operation wherein living tissues foreign to the bearer of the defect are employed. The transfer of a skin-flap from one individual to another constitutes heteroplasty. **1909** *Boston Med. & Surg. Jrnl.* 23 Dec. 915/1 (*heading*) Heteroplasty. (Grafting from another person.)

b. Between two individuals of different species.

1923 H. NEUHOF *Transplantation of Tissues* i. 3 By heterotransplantation (heteroplasty, heteroplastic transplantation, zoöplasty) is meant the transference of a tissue from an individual of one species to an individual of a different species. **1929** *Ann. Surg.* XC. 929 In grafting skin derived from other animal species (heteroplasty), that of dogs, chickens or the internal pellicle of an egg may be used.

2. *Path.* = HETEROPLASIA.

1886 *Syd. Soc. Lex.*, Heteroplasty, same as Heteroplasia.

heteroploid (he·tĕroploid), *a.* (and *sb.*). [a. G. *heteroploid* (H. Winkler 1916, in *Zeitschr. f. Bot.* VIII. 422), f. HETERO- + *-PLOID.] Having a chromosome number that is neither the haploid nor the diploid number characteristic of the species; freq., in restricted sense, = *ANEUPLOID *a.* (see quot. 1928); also as *sb.*, a heteroploid organism. Hence **he·teroploidy**, the condition of being heteroploid.

1926 T. H. MORGAN *Theory Gene* xii. 172 In so far as the addition of one or more chromosomes to, or loss from, a given group produces a new number, the word heteroploid has been used. *Ibid.* 176 In contrast to these triplo-types of Drosophila there is another heteroploid type..in which one of the small chromosomes is absent. *Ibid.* 188 The heteroploids are not so viable as the balanced types from which they arise. *Ibid.*, The occurrence of heteroploidy must be regarded as a significant genetic event. **1928** C. A. JØRGENSEN in *Jrnl. Genetics* XIX. 135 The term heteroploid was introduced by Winkler in 1916 to designate..not only the straight numbers $3n$, $4n$, $5n$, etc., but also $2n+1$, $2n+2$, $3n-1$, etc. The heteroploid numbers were divided by Täckholm (1922) into euploid..and aneuploid... I prefer to restrict the term heteroploid to the series n, $3n$, $4n$, $5n$, etc... and to use the term *aploid* for the irregular numbers. **1934** *Nature* 3 Nov. 708/2 In the heteroploid series, all having 25 chromosomes, the anatomical differences..were due to the genic constitution of the extra chromosome. **1955** J. B. & H. D. HILL *Genetics & Human Heredity* xvii. 331 Although rare in animals, heteroploidy occurs frequently in plants. **1956** *Nature* 25 Feb. 384/2 It is of interest to try to find whether the heteroploid cells appear only in certain tissues or if they can arise anywhere in the young embryos.

heteropolar (he:tĕropōu·lăɹ), *a.* [f. HETERO- + POLAR *a.*] **1.** *Bot.* [In Dict. s.v. HETERO-, where read 844 for 843.] **2.** *Electr.* Of an electric generator or its operation: using armature conductors that pass alternate north and south magnetic poles, so that the current generated is periodically reversed. Cf. *HOMOPOLAR *a.* 2.

1896 S. P. THOMPSON *Dynamo-Electric Machinery* (ed. 5) 475 In cases where it [*sc.* a conductor] passes from being opposite a N-pole to being opposite a S-pole, the operation is said to be heteropolar. **1946** *Nature* 28 Sept. 455/1 For the majority of applications the modern heteropolar inductor alternator is the most suitable machine.

3. *Chem.* [a. G. *heteropolar* (R. Abegg 1906, in *Zeitschr. f. anorg. Chem.* L. 309).] Formed by ions of opposite sign, between which there is electrostatic attraction. Cf. *HOMOPOLAR *a.* 3.

1922 [see *homœopolar* adj. s.v. *HOMŒO-]. **1930** *Engineering* 5 Dec. 700/3 There were, further, different types of cohesive forces...(3) Ionic or heteropolar cohesion. In the rock-salt atom, for instance, the valency electron of the sodium migrated into the chlorine structure, giving rise to electrostatic action. **1964** J. W. LINNETT *Electronic Struct. Molecules* ix. 143 Values which bring the results for these heteropolar molecules to the same scale as that for homopolar molecules.

heteropycnosis (he:tĕropiknōu·sis). *Cytol.* Also **-pyknosis.** [ad. G. *heteropyknose* (S. Gutherz 1907, in *Arch. f. mikrosk. Anat.* LXIX. 495), f. HETERO- + Gr. πυκν-ός thick, dense: see -OSIS.] The persistence of greater than average staining in chromosomal material; the character or condition, exhibited by some chromosomes or chromosomal regions in any particular nucleus, of being more (or, for negative heteropycnosis, less) condensed and hence appearing to take up more (or, less) stain than do the majority of chromosomes or chromosomal regions. Hence **heteropycno·tic** *a.*

1925 E. B. WILSON *Cell* (ed. 3) x. 759 In the greater number of cases heteropycnosis first takes place after the final spermatogonial division. **1934** *Genetics* XIX. 467 In the latter species [*sc. Drosophila melanogaster*] he finds that about half of the X chromosome is heteropycnotic in the interphase. **1952** G. H. BOURNE *Cytol. & Cell Physiol.* (ed. 2) v. 195 This property of heteropycnosis is especially characteristic of sex-chromosomes, such as the Y-chromosome of *Drosophila* species and the X-chromosomes of grasshoppers, but is also shown by many autosomal chromosome regions, and sometimes by whole autosomes. **1962** *Lancet* 19 May 1075/1 Once isopyknosis or heteropyknosis of a given X chromosome has been established, it is irreversible. **1963** LEWIS & JOHN *Chromosome Marker* 1. i. 18 This positive heteropycnosis is later reversed and by metaphase-I the X has become negatively heteropycnotic and stains faintly. **1968** H. HARRIS *Nucleus & Cytoplasm* iv. 75 It is probable that other highly condensed heterochromatic or heteropyknotic regions in interphase nuclei also synthesize very much less RNA than the euchromatic regions.

heterosexual (hetĕrose·ksiuăl), *a.* and *sb.* [See HETERO- and SEXUAL.] **1. a.** Characterized by a sexual interest in members of the opposite sex. **b.** Pertaining to sexual relations between people of opposite sex. Also as *sb.*, a heterosexual person.

1892 C. G. CHADDOCK tr. *Krafft-Ebing's Psychopathia Sexualis* iii. 324 The object of post-hypnotic suggestion is to remove the impulse to masturbation and homosexual feelings and impulses, and to encourage heterosexual feelings with a sense of virility. **1920** J. RIVIERE et al. tr. *Freud's Coll. Papers* (1924) II. 207 To convert a fully developed homosexual into a heterosexual. **1927** *Scots Observer* 1 Oct. 15/3 A certain proportion of people.. are as instinctively homosexual as the normal individual is heterosexual. **1935** *Discovery* Oct. 313/2 Homosexuality under the homosexual period of Greek life was not a sin, but it became so under heterosexual Christianity. **1966** K. WALKER *Sexual Behaviour* xxv. 222 Homosexuals vary as much in physique and in temperament as do heterosexuals. **1969** *Daily Tel.* 21 Jan. 17/3 Co-educational schools probably tend to hasten heterosexual experimentation. **1972** *Sat. Rev.* (U.S.) 12 Feb. 27/1 Homosexuals, like heterosexuals, should be treated as individual human beings.

2. Pertaining to, characteristic of both sexes.

1918 *Genetics* III. 287 Studies..on ablation of the gonads in birds, combined with hetero-sexual transplantation, show that both the testes and ovary in birds produce substances that have a profound regulatory effect on growth. **1963** *Cytogenetics* II. 332 The corresponding ovaries, generally atrophied owing presumably to male testicular hormones, contained no heterosexual cells.

Hence **he:terosexua·lity**, the condition of being heterosexual; heterosexual characteristics.

1900 H. BLANCHAMP tr. *Féré's Sexual Instinct* viii. 183 Psycho-sexual hermaphroditism, in which there are traces of hetero-sexuality, though homo-sexuality predominates. **1965** *New Statesman* 30 Apr. 677/2 Many people are made unhappy by their heterosexuality, but I do not believe the psychotherapist exists who would try to cure that.

heterosis. Add: **2.** *Zool.* Segmentation in which the parts are different.

1902 E. R. Lankester in *Encycl. Brit.* XXV. 691/2 It becomes apparent from this enumeration that there are a good many important elements or 'meromes' in an Arthropod metamere or somite which can become the subject of heteromerism or, to use a more apt word, of 'heterosis'. *Ibid.*, The Fourth Law of metamerism (autoheterosis of the meromes).

3. *Genetics.* The tendency of cross-breeding to produce an animal or plant with a greater hardiness and capacity for growth than either of the parents; hybrid vigour.

1914 G. H. Shull in *Zeitschr. f. induktive Abstammungs- und Vererbungslehre* XII. 127, I suggest that instead of the phrases, 'stimulus of heterozygosis', 'heterozygotic stimulation', 'the stimulating effects of hybridity', 'stimulation due to differences in uniting gametes', etc...the word 'heterosis' be adopted. The corresponding adjective 'heterotic' may also be useful in such expressions as 'heterotic effects'. **1938** *Nature* 3 Dec. 1002/2 The expression of heterosis is much influenced by various external factors. **1959** *New Biol.* XXVIII. 75 Less severe departures from normal growth in hybrids may.. involve slower development and poorer growth co-ordination, or..higher growth rates and seemingly enhanced vigour—the latter the phenomenon of heterosis, or hybrid vigour.

heterosite (he·tĕrosəit). *Min.* Formerly also **heteposite, heterozite.** [ad. F. *hétérosite, -zite* (named by F. Alluaud aîné: see L. N. Vauquelin 1825, in *Ann. de Chim. et de Phys.* XXX. 294, where the word is spelt *hétépozite*), irreg. f. Gr. ἕτερος different + -ite[1].] A phosphate of iron and manganese, differing from purpurite in containing more iron.

1834 R. Allan *Man. Min.* 309 Heteposite. **1835** C. U. Shepard *Treat. Min.: Second Part* I. 258 Heterosite. (See Triplite). **1854** J. D. Dana *Syst. Min.* (ed. 4) II. 407 Heterosite, by Rammelsberg's analysis. **1858** J. Nicol *Elem. Min.* 241 Heterozite. **1951** C. Palache et al. in *Dana's Syst. Min.* (ed. 7) II. 676 Heterosite and purpurite are secondary minerals formed by oxidation of triphylite and lithiophilite.

heterotic (hetĕrǫ·tik), *a.* [f. Heter(osis + -otic; in sense 1 f. directly on Gr. ἑτέρωσις alteration.] **1.** Pertaining to the manipulation of differences (*nonce-use*).

1905 G. M. Fisher tr. *Höffding's Probl. Philos.* ii. 99 The advance of knowledge consists in a reduction of differences (to a 'heterotic minimum') and in an approximation to a pure description of a continuous process.

2. *Genetics.* Pertaining to or exhibiting heterosis (sense *3).

1914 *Zeitschr. f. induktive Abstammungs- und Vererbungslehre* XII. 127 A highly heterotic plant..because of its unusual vigor may develop branches from buds which in a weaker plant would remain dormant. **1944** *Bull. Torrey Bot. Club* May 267 (*heading*) Heterotic hybrids. **1967** *Amer. Naturalist* CI. 189 (*heading*) Opposite heterotic effects on male weights of reciprocal species hybrids.

heterotopy. Add: Hence **he:teroto·pically** *adv.*, with the result of becoming heterotopic.

1923 *Guy's Hosp. Rep.* LXXIII. 328 They re-acquired ..the prospective fate of being differentiated heterotopically into squamous epithelium.

heterotransplant (he:tĕrotra·ns,plɑnt), *sb.* *Med.* and *Biol.* [f. Hetero- + Transplant *sb.*] A piece of tissue or an organ taken from one individual and transplanted (or intended for transplantation) to another individual of a different species.

1918 *Jrnl. Med. Res.* XXXVII. 378 It is..improbable that the preponderance of lymphocytes in the heterotransplants..was altogether due to the bacterial infection. **1935** *Amer. Jrnl. Cancer* XXIII. 284 One of the growing heterotransplants of mouse sarcoma 37 was removed from a normal rat. **1959** *Ann. R. Coll. Surgeons* XXV. 45 So far with heterotransplants of human tissue the sex of the recipient has not appeared to influence the survival of the graft.

heterotransplant (he:tĕrotrɑns,plɑ·nt), *v.* *Med.* and *Biol.* [f. prec. sb.] *trans.* To transplant from one individual to another of a different species. So **he:terotranspla·nted** *ppl. a.*

1920 *Jrnl. Exper. Med.* XXXI. 767 The greater part of the heterotransplanted thyroid suffered..through lack of suitability of the body fluids of the host. **1959** *Cancer Res.* XIX. 633 (*heading*) Heterotransplanted choriocarcinomas. **1962** *Ibid.* XXII. 563 Two choriocarcinomas ..were successfully heterotransplanted to cortisone-treated hamsters.

heterotransplantable (he:tĕrotrɑns,plɑ·ntăb'l), *a.* *Med.* and *Biol.* [f. prec. vb., after *transplantable*.] Capable of being successfully transplanted from one individual to another of a different species. So **he:terotransplantabi·lity.**

1943 *Cancer Res.* III. 809/1 An interpretation of the significance of this demonstration necessitated a more accurate definition of the limits of heterotransplantability. **1947** Ackerman & del Regato *Cancer* iii. 70 Greene believes that failure in transplanting benign tumors suggests that heterotransplantability is a characteristic property of cancer. **1952** *Cancer Res.* V. 41/1 The heterotransplantable phase of the tumor's existence was of relatively short duration. **1971** *Nature* 16 Apr. 455/1 The newborn hamster treated with ALS seems to be more sensitive than the cortisone-treated adult for the purposes of testing heterotransplantability of cultured cells.

heterotransplantation (he:tĕrotrɑns,plɑntē^i·ʃən). *Med.* and *Biol.* [f. Hetero- + Transplantation.] The operation of transplanting tissue from one individual to another of a different species.

1905 [see *homotransplantation]. **1907** *Jrnl. Exper. Med.* IX. 226 These heterotransplantations were attempted with the aim of ascertaining whether the vessels, in spite of the toxic action of the cat's blood on the dog's tissue, could..take over the function of the vessels removed. **1940** *Amer. Jrnl. Cancer* XXXIX. 170 The direct heterotransplantation of tissues is rarely, if ever, successful among higher mammals. **1971** [see *homotransplantation].

heterotropal, *a.* (Earlier example.)

1832 J. Lindley *Introd. Bot.* I. ii. 193 The radicle will point neither to the apex nor to the base of the seed, but the embryo will lie, as it were, across it, or be heterotropal, as is the case in the primrose.

heterotroph (he·tĕrotrǭ^uf). *Biol.* Also **-trophe.** [f. Hetero- + Gr. τροφός feeder.] Any organism which requires an external supply of energy contained in complex organic compounds to maintain its existence.

1900 B. D. Jackson *Gloss. Bot. Terms* 311/1 *Heterotroph*, employed by Pfeffer to denote a pure saprophyte. **1959** *New Scientist* 7 May 1002/3 The evolutionary steps.. were first, the formation of what he calls heterotrophes, organisms that absorbed as their nutrients organic substances dissolved in the seas in which they lived. **1971** Hawker & Linton *Micro-organisms* v. 145 Fungi, most protozoa, and many bacteria are heterotrophs.

heterotrophic (he:tĕrotrǭ^u·fik), *a.* *Biol.* [f. Hetero- + Gr. τροφικός nursing.] Characterized by or exhibiting heterotrophy (in various senses: now only in the sense of *heterotrophy 1 c); living as a heterotroph. So **he:terotro·phically** *adv.*

1893 *Jrnl. R. Microsc. Soc.* 665 According as lichens carry on their existence with or without these lodgers, the author [*sc.* Minks] places them respectively under the head of 'autotrophic' or 'heterotrophic' lichens. **1896** *Ibid.* 326 Prof. J. Wiesner proposes the general term *Trophy* for all unilateral excesses of growth in tissues or in organs which are dependent on the position of the organ in question, the term position being understood in a wide sense, as the relation in space of the heterotrophic organ to the horizon and to its parent-shoot. **1900** A. J. Ewart tr. *Pfeffer's Physiol. Plants* I. vii. 363 Plants which are unable to assimilate carbon dioxide must obtain all their organic food-materials from without (heterotrophic or allotrophic nutrition). **1935** W. H. Brown *Plant Kingdom* xvii. 378 Some of the autotrophic bacteria can live heterotrophically. **1969** *Ecology* L. 88/1 Eleven heterotrophic aerobic bacterial types were isolated from the microcosm. **1971** I. G. Gass et al. *Understanding Earth* ix. 139/1 Fox has been able to show that proteinoid microspheres will..come into existence spontaneously on innumerable occasions. If the correct foods are available, they can proliferate heterotrophically indefinitely.

heterotrophism (he:tĕrotrǭ^u·fiz'm). *Biol.* [f. next: see -ism.] = *heterotrophy 1 c.

1900 A. J. Ewart tr. *Pfeffer's Physiol. Plants* I. vii. 364 All stages of transition between pure autotrophism and heterotrophism are exhibited among obligate or facultative mixotrophic plants. **1936** W. Stiles *Introd. Princ. Plant Physiol.* xiii. 285 Some autotrophic plants..when kept in the dark and provided with such organic nutrients ..exhibit a degree of heterotrophism. **1951** Werkman & Wilson *Bacterial Physiol.* 407 (*heading*) Carbon dioxide assimilation and concepts of autotrophism and heterotrophism.

heterotrophy (he·tĕrotrǭ^ufi). [f. Hetero- + Gr. τροφή nourishment.] **1.** *Biol.* † **a.** [ad. G. *heterotrophie* (A. B. Frank 1885, in *Ber. d. Deut. Bot. Ges.* III. 143).] (In Dict. s.v. Hetero-.) (Example.) *Obs. rare.*

1891 F. P. Foster *Med. Dict.* III. 1867/2 *Heterotrophy*, the quality of obtaining nutrition adventitiously by means of a Fungus whose mycelium takes the place of root-hairs.

† **b.** [ad. G. *heterotrophie* (A. Minks 1893, in *Verhandl. d. zool.-bot. Ges. in Wien* XLII. 402).] (See quot. 1900.) *Obs. rare.*

1900 B. D. Jackson *Gloss. Bot. Terms* 123/1 *Heterotrophy*, (1) used by Minks for those Lichens living symbiotically.

c. The state or quality of living as a heterotroph; heterotrophism.

1930 W. H. Lang tr. *Strasburger's Text-bk. Bot.* (ed. 6) 259 The heterotrophy is not always..complete... Some heterotrophic Phanerogams can construct their organic carbon-compounds in the normal fashion... The converse case is frequently met with. **1949** A. Nelson *Introd. Bot.* xxv. 387 There are degrees of morphological adaptation for heterotrophy.

† **2.** *Bot.* [ad. G. *heterotrophie* (J. Wiesner 1895, in *Ber. d. Deut. Bot. Ges.* XIII. 482).] (See quot. 1900.) *Obs. rare.*

1896 *Jrnl. R. Microsc. Soc.* 326 (*heading*) Heterotrophy and anisophylly. **1900** B. D. Jackson *Gloss. Bot. Terms* 123/1 *Heterotrophy*..(2) [used] by Wiesner for the compound position of a shoot with regard to the horizon and of the mother-shoot.

heterotropic, *a.* Add: **2.** *Genetics.* Applied to chromosomes that are not paired at meiosis.

1905 E. B. Wilson in *Jrnl. Exper. Zool.* II. 508 Since there is no reason for considering the 'accessory chromosome' as in any sense accessory to the others,.. I suggest that..chromosomes of this type may provisionally be called *heterotropic* chromosomes (in allusion to the fact that they pass to one pole only of the spindle in one of the maturation-divisions). **1920** L. Doncaster *Introd. Study Cytol.* xi. 155 When..the heterotropic or *X*-chromosome passes undivided to one pole of the first spermatocyte division-figure, it divides equationally in the division of those secondary spermatocytes which contain it.

heterozygote (he:tĕrozəi·gǭ^ut). *Biol.* [f. Hetero- + Zygote.] **1.** A diploid individual that has different alleles at one or more genetic loci. Also *attrib.* or as *adj.*, = **heterozygous.*

1902 Bateson & Saunders *Rep. Evol. Comm. R. Soc.* I. 126 The zygote formed by the union of a pair of opposite allelomorphic gametes, we shall call a heterozygote. **1902** W. Bateson *Mendel's Princ. Hered.* 23 This *Aa* is the hybrid or 'mule' form, or as I have elsewhere called it, the heterozygote, as distinguished from *AA* or *aa* the homozygotes. **1906** R. H. Lock *Variation, Heredity, & Evolution* vii. 186 *Plate*, Cobs borne by heterozygote plants pollinated with the recessive. **1930** R. A. Fisher *Genet. Theory Nat. Selection* 8 The heterozygote when mated to either kind of homozygote would produce both heterozygotes and homozygotes. **1949** Darlington & Mather *Elem. Genetics* v. 110 The original form of any heterozygote must be a mutation. **1971** J. Z. Young *Introd. Study Man* iii. 60 Apparently the heterozygotes have an increased resistance.

2. A bacteriophage that carries two different copies of some of its genetic information and produces two kinds of progeny when it infects a bacterial cell.

1952 Hershey & Chase in *Cold Spring Harbor Symp. Quant. Biol.* XVI. 474/1 Since there is adequate reason to call these markers allelic genes, the mottling particles are appropriately termed heterozygotes. **1968** D. S. Ray in Fraenkel-Conrat *Molec. Basis Virol.* ii. 247 The purified heterozygotes are twice the length of normal phage particles and apparently contain two DNA molecules.

Hence **he:terozygosis** (-zəigǭ^u·sis), the fusion of two genetically different gametes; the state or condition of being heterozygous; **he:terozygo·sity** (-zəigǫ·sĭti), the state or condition of being heterozygous; the degree or extent to which an individual is heterozygous with respect to its complement of genetic loci; **he:terozygo·tic** *a.*, resulting from or pertaining to heterozygosis; **he:terozy·gous** (-zəi·gəs) *a.*, having different alleles at one or more genetic loci.

1902 Bateson & Saunders *Rep. Evol. Comm. R. Soc.* I. 130 The determination from statistical study of zygotes must be exceedingly difficult, seeing that both resulting forms may be heterozygous. **1905** *Rep. Brit. Assoc.* 1904 585 Appearances have been seen..suggesting at first sight that a heterozygosis between two gametes, *both* extracted, may give, *e.g.*, dominance. **1911** *Amer. Naturalist* XLV. 142 The surprises of heterozygotic 'constructions' or of new combinations in F_2 may..be responsible for the case of De Vries's buttercups. **1912** East & Hayes *Heterozygosis in Evol. & Plant Breeding* 37 Decrease in vigor due to inbreeding lessens with decrease in heterozygosity. **1914** Heterozygotic [see *heterosis 3]. **1949** Darlington & Mather *Elem. Genetics* xiii. 280 (*caption*) The potential variability existing in the differences between homozygotes..must first be converted into heterozygotic potential by intercrossing. *Ibid.* xii. 261 It is only when a heterozygous species is crossed with another, heterozygous or homozygous, that its heterozygosity is shown by the mixture in the progeny. **1965** T. Dobzhansky *Heredity & Nature of Man* v. 156 Although persons who inherit this gene from both parents (homozygotes) die of fatal anemia, the heterozygous carriers may be said to show a hybrid vigor..in malaria-ridden environments.

heuchera (hoi·kərə). *Bot.* [mod.L., f. the name of J. H. *Heucher* (1677–1747), German botanist (C. Linnæus *Hortus Cliffortianus* (1737) 82).] A plant of a large genus of perennial herbs, of the family Saxifragaceæ, native to North America. Hence **heuchere·lla,** a member of a group of bigeneric hybrids between heuchera and tiarella.

1772 R. Weston *Universal Botanist* III. 387 American Heuchera or Sanicle. **1829** *Bot. Reg.* XV. 1302 Small-flowered Heuchera. **1884** J. Wood *Hardy Perennials* 143 The Heucheras bloom from May to August. **1924** R. Wright *Pract. Bk. Outdoor Flowers* II. i. 99 The newer hybrid Heucheras. **1949** L. H. Bailey *Man. Cultivated Plants* 481 Heucherella: from heuchera and tiarella. **1961** *Amateur Gardening* 23 Sept. 2/2 Hybrids, between heuchera and *Tiarella wherryi*, listed as heucherella. **1962** *Ibid.* 21 Apr. 4/2 Heucheras like open soil and an open position.

heumite (hiū·məit). *Petrol.* [a. G. *heumite, heumit* (W. C. Brögger 1898, in *Skr. udg. af Videnskabsselsk. i Christiania* (*Math.-naturv. Klasse*) *1897* VI. 46), f. the name of *Heum* in southern Norway: see -ITE[1].] A brownish-black hypabyssal dike-rock containing alkali feldspars, biotite, and barkevikite, with nepheline, sodalite, and other rocks.

1901 *Jrnl. Chem. Soc.* LXXX. II. 169 Heumite is the name given to a dyke-rock from Heum, consisting of hornblende and felspar, with some biotite, and smaller amounts of nephelite, sodalite, diopside, &c. **1938** A. JOHANNSEN *Descr. Petrogr.* IV. 170 The heumite from Brathagen..contains essential soda-microcline and soda-orthoclase with a little andesine.

‖**heurige** (hoi·rigə). Also (representing G. declined forms) **heurigen, heuriger.** [South G. and Austrian G., = (adj.) new, (sb.) new wine, from the latest harvest; vintner's establishment.] **1.** The wine from the latest harvest, produced in and near Vienna.

1935 SCHOONMAKER & MARVEL *Compl. Wine Bk.* vi. 152 Grinzing, now part of Vienna, is famous for its *vin nouveau* (*Heuriger*), served in picturesque rustic cafés to the music-loving population. **1941** 'R. WEST' *Black Lamb* (1942) II. 490 It is delightful to drink the heuriger wine in the gardens of Grinzing. **1964** F. BOWERS *Bibliogr. & Textual Crit.* I. 3 Experts..testify that a headache can be especially acute the morning after tasting *Heurige*, the new wine. **1967** A. LICHINE *Encycl. Wines* 115/2 The stinging new *heurige* wine served in their wine-garden is, for the tourists who flock there, the essence of Viennese gaiety.

2. An establishment or wine-garden where this wine is served.

1934 P. BOTTOME *Private Worlds* iii. 27 One hot summer night at a *Heurigen*, he had met a beautiful young dancer. **1939** N. MONSARRAT *This is Schoolroom* III. xvii. 400 We might..row across the lake to the tiny *Heuriger* and there drink a bottle of Niersteiner. **1965** *Daily Tel.* 23 Sept. 15/6 To be in Vienna and not visit a heuriger is like seeing Naples and not dying.

heurism (hiūᵊ·riz'm). [f. HEUR(ISTIC + -ISM.] The educational principle or practice of placing a pupil, as far as possible, in the position of a discoverer.

1919 *Times Educ. Suppl.* 17 Apr. 181/3 The whole trend of modern educational improvement is to give the pupils just the benefits that Professor Laurie demanded. Boy-scouting.., direct methods, heurism, and..'the play way'. **1920** T. P. NUNN *Education* 91 Dr. M. W. Keatinge, ..a severe critic of heurism and of the general idea of freedom in education. **1925** C. FOX *Educ. Psychol.* 214 The second general principle of method [in teaching] is that known as heurism, i.e. the method of placing the pupil..in the position of the discoverer. This method had a great vogue a generation ago. **1959** *Chambers's Encycl.* VII. 80/2 All teaching is balanced between the poles of heurism and of didactic suggestion.

heuristic, *a.* Add: **a.** (Earlier and later examples.)

1821 COLERIDGE *Let.* 8 Jan. (1971) V. 133, I am.. getting regularly on with my LOGIC—in 3 parts—..3. Organic or Heuristic (εὑριστικόν). **1853** *N. & Q.* 1. Ser. VII. 320 *Heuristic,*..as an English scholar would write it, or *Heuristisch*, as it would be written by a German. **1955** *Sci. Amer.* July 72/3 Einstein's 1905 paper, for which (nominally) he had been awarded the Nobel prize, did not contain the word 'theory' in the title, but referred instead to considerations from a 'heuristic viewpoint'. **1967** *Listener* 28 Sept. 386/2 His [*sc.* M. McLuhan's] style is jargon-ridden—all this talk of 'heuristic probes', as if a probe could be anything but heuristic. **1973** *N.Y. Times* 2 May 36/2 The kind of criticism being written now is looser, more fluid, more ad hoc and heuristic.

b. *Educ.* (See quot. 1898.) Also **heuri·stical** *a.*

1848 W. ROSS *Teacher's Man.* v. 92 The Heuristical method. **1884** in *Spec. Rep. Educ.* II. 390 in *Parl. Papers 1898* (C. 8943) XXIV. 1 The heuristic method is the *only* method to be applied in the pure sciences; it is the best method in the teaching of the applied sciences. **1898** H. E. ARMSTRONG *Ibid.*, Heuristic methods of teaching are methods which involve our placing students as far as possible in the attitude of the discoverer—methods which involve their *finding out*, instead of merely being told about things. **1959** *Chambers's Encycl.* VII. 80/2 Science-teaching should always be permeated by a heuristic bias (i.e. methods of investigation must be used whenever possible).

c. *Computers.* (See quot. 1964.)

1960 *Information Processing: Proc. Internat. Conf., 1959* (Unesco) 275/1 The technique of heuristic programming is under detailed investigation as a means to the end of applying large-scale digital computers to the solution of a difficult class of problems currently considered to be beyond their capabilities. **1964** T. W. MCRAE *Impact of Computers on Accounting* 297 Under an 'heuristic' programming procedure the computer searches through a number of possible solutions at each stage of the programme, it evaluates a 'good' solution for this stage and then proceeds to the next stage. Essentially heuristic programming is similar to the problem solving techniques by trial and error methods which we use in everyday life. **1969** P. B. JORDAIN *Condensed Computer Encycl.* 235 The heuristic program should be able to judge whether the problem is closer to solution after each attempt.

Hence **heuri·stically,** in a heuristic manner; using heuristic processes.

1935 *Jrnl. Theol. Stud.* XXXVI. 314 The belief that the world's orderedness or knowability is an expression of mind, and that the category of purpose..is applicable to it otherwise than heuristically. **1963** J. LYONS *Structural Semantics* ii. 17 What is not made clear is the purpose served by the semantic criterion (except heuristically) in the first place. **1965** *Language* XLI. 507 Nonlinguistic context may be heuristically useful in establishing lexical fields. **1965** N. CHOMSKY *Aspects of Theory of Syntax* i. 52 It is historically accurate as well as heuristically valuable to distinguish these two very different approaches to the problem of the acquisition of knowledge. **1968** P. A. P. MORAN *Introd. Probability Theory* ix. 441 On solving this problem heuristically it is found that *u*(*t*), also, is a random process.

B. *sb.* **1. a.** (Later examples.)

1945 G. POLYA *How to solve It* p. vii, The subject of heuristic has manifold connections; mathematicians, logicians, psychologists, educationalists, even philosophers may claim various parts of it. *Ibid.* 102 The aim of heuristic is to study the methods and rules of discovery and invention. **1957** *Proc. Western Joint Computer Conf.* XV. 218 (*heading*) Empirical explorations of the logic theory machine. A case study of heuristic.

b. A heuristic process or method for attempting the solution of a problem; a rule or item of information used in such a process.

1957 A. NEWELL et al. in *Proc. Western Joint Computer Conf.* XV. 223 A process that *may* solve a given problem, but offers no guarantees of doing so, is called a heuristic for that problem. *Ibid.*, For conciseness, we will use 'heuristic' as a noun synonymous with 'heuristic process'. **1958** *IBM Jrnl. Res. & Devel.* II. 337/1 For the moment..we shall consider that a heuristic method (or a heuristic, to use the noun form) is a procedure that may lead us by a short cut to the goal we seek or it may lead us down a blind alley. **1962** LEDLEY & WILSON *Programming & utilizing Digital Computers* viii. 349 Such criteria are called the heuristics of the problem. The field of heuristic programming is concerned with the investigation and understanding of various aspects of heuristics, such as how they are discovered, what kinds there are. **1967** A. BATTERSBY *Network Analysis* (ed. 2) xii. 192 It would..seem more reasonable to recalculate the float next time (6,14) was a candidate for limited resources. Some heuristics do this.

2. *pl.* The study and use of heuristic techniques in data processing.

1963 *Times* 8 June 11/2 Whether every manager needs to know about cybernetics, econometrics, and heuristics is arguable, but cost analysis, market research, production control, and other developing subjects should be within his purview. **1967** *Observer* 9 Apr. 21/3 This branch of artificial intelligence—building machines to take short cuts to a solution—is known as 'heuristics' and is being actively pursued at the moment.

hevea (hī·viă). *Bot.* [mod.L., f. native name *hevé* (F. Aublet, *Histoire des Plantes de la Guiane Françoise* (1775) II. 871).] A South American tree of the genus so called, belonging to the family Euphorbiaceæ, and having milky sap which provides rubber.

1878 W. T. THISELTON-DYER *Let.* 17 Apr. in *Indian Forester* (1879) IV. 42 The climate of Calcutta did not prove very favorable to the Heveas, which require the conditions of growth met with in hot and moist tropical forests. **1899** *Hooker's Icones Plantarum* XXVI. 2575 The seeds of *Hevea* are..incorrectly described. **1909** J. C. WILLIS *Agric. in Tropics* xiii. 129 Hevea certainly forms 95% of all cultivated rubber. **1927** *Daily Tel.* 11 May 3/4 The rest would be dug up after the present season, and rubber planted in its stead, as the hevea trees remaining were widely spaced. **1935** *Nature* 16 Mar. 417/1 The exudation..is known as hevea-latex, since *Hevea brasiliensis* is only one of some four hundred plant species which elaborate juices containing rubber. **1964** J. HUTCHINSON *Ess. Crop Plant Evol.* viii. 167 Such an evolutionary phenomenon as *Hevea* rubber, of which some individuals of the original domestication are said to be still alive.

hew, *v.* **B. 1. b.** (Later U.S. examples.)

a **1861** T. WINTHROP *John Brent* (1883) xxviii. 298, I saw a vista in new life, hewed in and took in and took up a 'claim' which I have held good. **1891** *Harper's Mag.* Aug. 451/1 How closely they hewed to the line in this respect is attested by the dying remarks of one of the men hanged.

hewed (hiūd), *ppl. a.* (under HEW *v.*). (Modern U.S. examples. Also of *hewed-log* in attrib. use.)

1793 in L. Collins *Hist. Sk. Kentucky* (1847) 517 Every purchaser or purchasers of lotts..shall build thereon a hued log house, with a brick or stone chimney. **1805** D. MCCLURE *Diary* (1899) 14 There was a small church made of hewed logs. **1843** *Amer. Pioneer* II. 148 Two small hewed-log houses had been erected, and several cabins. **1849** *President's Mess. Congress* II. 1089 One hewed-log dwelling,..comfortably furnished cost $351. **1883** E. EGGLESTON *Hoosier School-boy* xvi. 106 There's the old hewed-log house..where we used to live.

hewettite (hiū·ĕtəit). *Min.* [f. the name of Donnel Foster *Hewett* (1881–1971), American geologist: see -ITE[1].] A deep red hydrated calcium vanadate, $CaV_6O_{16}\cdot 9H_2O$, occurring in nodules and as the coating of fibres or needles (see also quot. 1955).

1914 W. F. HILLEBRAND et al. in *Proc. Amer. Philos. Soc.* LIII. 31 The Peruvian mineral..we are pleased to name hewettite, after Mr. D. Foster Hewett, now of the U.S. Geological Survey, who has done so much to make the Minasragra occurrence known. **1955** *Amer. Mineralogist* XL. 691 There appear to be three types of material variously labelled 'hewettite' or 'metahewettite', namely, (I) hewettite, $CaO\cdot 3V_2O_5\cdot nH_2O$.., which exists in at least three hydrate forms,..(II) the unnamed sodium analogue of hewettite in the trihydrate form,..and (III) the material,..possibly a mixed sodium-calcium variety of the sodium analogue, represented by specimen 4.

hewgag. *U.S.* (Earlier and later examples.)

1850 *California Courier* (San Francisco) 6 Sept. 2/3 Beat the hong-gong; sound the hew-gag! **1855** *Vermont Free Press* 8 June (Th.), The T.I.N. Horn-et Band, with Sackbut, Psaltery, Dulcimer,..and Hugag, marched next. **1905** B. TARKINGTON *In Arena* 152 He had *all* the honours..; professors and students all kow-towed and sounded the hew-gag before him.

hewn, *ppl. a.* **1.** (Later example.)

1869 'MARK TWAIN' *Innoc. Abr.* xix. 196 A massive hewn-stone affair.

hex (heks), *v.* Chiefly *U.S.* [ad. Pennsylvanian G. *hexe*, f. G. *hexen*.] *intr.* To practise witchcraft. Also *trans.*, to bewitch, to cast a spell on.

1830 J. F. WATSON *Ann. Philad.* 232 A decent storekeeper once got him to hex for his wife, who had conceited that an old Mrs. Wiggand had bewitched her, and made her to swallow a piece of linseywoolsey. **1932** B. A. DE VOTO *Mark Twain's Amer.* iii. 74 The cat is hexen: it is approved by Mother Hawkins, a witch. **1935** *Language* XI. 147 Belief in witchcraft is fast disappearing and with it the word [hɛks] *to bewitch* or *a witch* or *wizard*. A countryman may still say: *My pigs are hext.* **1956** H. GOLD *Man who was not with it* (1965) xi. 97, I stood hexing the cars on Route One.

hex (heks), *sb.* Chiefly *U.S.* Also **hexe.** [Pennsylvanian G., ad. G. *hexe*. Cf. HAG *sb.*[1]] **1.** A witch. Also *transf.*, a witch-like female.

1856 G. HENDERSON *Pop. Rhymes* 43 'An old hexe', means an old witch, and is often applied, in a bad sense, to females of the present day. **1920** S. LEWIS *Main Street* xiii. 159, I couldn't talk to you without twenty old hexes watching, whispering. **1928** *Daily Express* 10 Dec. 11/1 York County's early settlers were Germans, and their present-day descendants still remain under the spell of medieval German necromancy. One of their sacred words is 'hex', said to be corrupt German for witch. **1935** *Amer. Speech* X. 170/1 *Hex*, a witch..the *hex* trial at Lancaster.

2. A magic spell or curse.

1909 *Sat. Even. Post* 16 Jan. 7/1 'Old pal,' agreed J. Rufus, 'the hex is sure on me.' **1942** D. POWELL *Time to be Born* (1943) xiii. 326 She could count on winning him... Unless Julian really could put a hex on her. **1951** M. LOWRY *Let.* Apr. or May (1967) 234 Everything from how to put the hex on your more troublesome pupils [etc.]. **1952** M. MCCARTHY *Groves of Academe* (1953) xii. 237 She hoped..that the hex signs on the neighbouring barns would serve to ward off all evil influences from the vicinity and not, as the ignorant sometimes thought, to attract them or indicate their presence. **1958** *Times* 4 Oct. 8/7 If Ladan stayed Shehu would gather up his robes and depart, leaving a hex on us all. **1966** *Punch* 30 Mar. 458/3 'What?' says the young man, picking it up gingerly and nervously, half afraid she's put a hex on it. **1968** *Word Study* Oct. 6/1 Each of us carries around a set of shibboleths..with..totemic reverence..; meanwhile we trample blithely on spells and hexes we have never heard of.

hex (heks). Abbrev. of 'uranium hexafluoride'.

1956 S. GLASSTONE *Princ. Nuclear Reactor Engin.* viii. 449 For use in nuclear energy work, uranium is generally required either in the form of uranium metal, for fabrication into fuel elements, or as hexafluoride ('hex') to constitute the feed for the separation of the isotopes by the gaseous-diffusion method. **1964** M. GOWING *Britain & Atomic Energy* ii. 63 Secrecy in the project now and later was aided by the elaborate code systems used. These were different in different groups... Hexafluoride was known variously as 'V1', 'hex' and 'the working gas'. **1971** *New Scientist* 16 Sept. 617/2 Uranium hexafluoride ('hex' for short) is pumped through a cascade of.. thousands of membranes.

hexa-. Add: **he:xachlor(o)be·nzene,** C_6Cl_6, an agricultural fungicide used as a seed-dressing; **he:xachlor(o)cyclohe·xane** = **benzene hexachloride*; **he:xachlor(o)ethane** (-klōᵊrōᵘᵢī·þēⁱn, -klōᵊrī·þēⁱn), a toxic crystalline compound, $Cl_3C\cdot CCl_3$, having uses as an insecticide and anthelmintic and as an ingredient in smoke-producing mixtures; **hexachlo·rophane, -phene,** a diphenylmethane derivative, $CH_2(C_6HCl_3OH)_2$, a white crystalline powder used as a disinfectant, esp. for the skin; **he·xact** *a.* and *sb.* = *hexactine*; **hexactine** *a.*, also as *sb.*, a sponge-spicule having six rays; **hexactine·llidan** *a. Zool.* = HEXACTINELLID *a.*; **hexade·canol** = *cetyl alcohol*; **he:xadeceno·ic acid,** an unsaturated fatty acid, $C_{16}H_{30}O_2$, occurring naturally in several isomeric forms one of which is widespread in many animal and vegetable fats and oils; it has also been known as *palmitoleic, physetoleic,* and *zoomaric acid*; **hexae·thyl tetrapho·sphate** (heksă,eþil), a viscous brownish liquid capable of irreversibly inhibiting mammalian cholinesterase; orig. used to

designate an insecticide later found to be a mixture of organic phosphates containing tetraethyl pyrophosphate as the chief active ingredient; **hexahy·drate,** a hydrate that contains six molecules of water; so **hexa-hydra·ted** *a.*; **hexahy·dric** *a.*, containing six hydroxyl groups in a molecule; **he·xamer** *Chem.* [*-MER], a polymeric unit or molecule made up of six monomers; **hexame·ric** *a. Chem.*, consisting of a hexamer; **hexa·merous** *a. Biol.* [Gr. μέρος part], having members in groups of six, or multiples of six; hence **hexa·merism; he:xametapho·sphate,** a phosphate regarded as being a salt of hexametaphosphoric acid, $(HPO_3)_6$; used loosely to designate a glassy, water-soluble sodium salt (also known as Graham's salt) having an approximate empirical formula $Na_2O \cdot P_2O_5$ and used industrially to soften water; **hexa-metho·nium,** a quaternary ammonium ion, $[(CH_3)_3N(CH_2)_6N(CH_3)_3]^{++}$; also, any of the salts of this ion, some of which have been used as ganglionic blocking drugs in the treatment of severe hypertension; **hexa-me·thylene,** CYCLOHEXANE; **hexame:thy-lenediamine** (-dəi,æ·mīn), a white crystalline solid, $H_2N(CH_2)_6NH_2$, used in the manufacture of nylon; **hexame:thylenete·tramine,** a colourless crystalline compound, $(CH_2)_6N_4$, having various industrial uses, esp. in the manufacture of phenol-formaldehyde resins and in many antiseptic preparations; **he·xamine** = **hexamethylenetetramine*; **hexa-petalous** *a.* (earlier example); **he·xarch** *a. Bot.*, having six rays, formed from six points of origin, as in some vascular bundles; **he·xasome** *Biol.*, a set of six homologous chromosomes; so **hexaso·mic** *a.*, having six of one or more chromosomes in a nucleus that is not hexaploid.

1885 I. REMSEN *Introd. Org. Chem.* 253 As the final products, hexa-chlor-benzene, C_6Cl_6, and hexa-brom-benzene C_6Br_6 are obtained. **1961** *Lancet* 22 July 176/2 Recently, several thousand cases of human porphyria have been seen in Turkey after the consumption of wheat containing 0·1–0·2% of hexachlorobenzene. **1908** *Chem. Abstr.* II. 793 Hexachlorcyclohexanes.—On continuing the action of chlorine in the sunlight, a viscous liquid is obtained. **1945** R. E. SLADE *Gamma Isomer of Hexa-chlorocyclohexane* ('*Gammexane*') 11 The hexachloro-cyclohexanes possess considerable chemical stability. **1898** *Jrnl. Chem. Soc.* LXXIV. I. 626 When a current of chlorine is passed into a mixture of pentachlorethane and aluminium chloride heated at 100°, hexachlorethane is obtained. **1936** *Discovery* Aug. 255/2 A new way of killing mosquitoes..involves the use of hexachloroethane. **1960** *Farmer & Stockbreeder* 16 Feb. 109 (Advt.), In the Nicholas Liver Fluke Drench, hexachloroethane particles are suspended in a free-flowing liquid and this ensures *accurate* dosing. Result: greater fluke kill than ever before! **1960** *Which?* Feb. 32/2 One can attempt to prevent the sweat from decomposing by using an anti-septic, such as *hexachlorophane*. **1948** *Jrnl. Amer. Med. Assoc.* 14 Feb. 471/2 The Council [on Pharmacy and Chemistry] considered the proposal of a pharmaceutical manufacturer for the use of the term hexachlorophene as a generic designation for *bis*(2-hydroxy-3,5,6-trichloro-phenyl) methane... The Council voted to recognize hexa-chlorophene as the generic, or common, designation. **1953** *Jrnl. Parasitol.* XXXIX. 79 Hexachlorophene..is effective in removing *Raillietina cesticillus* from chickens. **1886** R. VON LENDENFELD in *Proc. Zool. Soc.* 590 The Recent Families of Sponges... With hexact spicules and thimble-shaped chambers. **1887** tr. F. E. Schulze in *Challenger Rep., Zool.* XXI. 29 Regular Hexacts are all spicules in which the rays lie at right angles to one another, and are of equal length and similar form. **1940** L. H. HYMAN *Invertebrates* I. vi. 327 They [*sc.* triacts] may show their origin from a hexact by the presence near the middle of knobs or branches of the axial fibre. **1900** E. A. MINCHIN in E. R. Lankester *Treat. Zool.* II. iii. 117 One or more rays of the hexactine..may become modified in various ways. **1940** L. H. HYMAN *Invertebrates* I. vi. 327 The basic regular hexactine consists of three axes crossing at right angles, forming six rays of approximately equal length. **1887** tr. F. E. Schulze in *Challenger Rep., Zool.* XXI. 37 Certain Hexactinellidan families have typical and regular *Uncinata*, while in others they are absent. **1914** *Jrnl. Chem. Soc.* CV. II. 2251 Acetate of *l*-γ-Hexa-decanol, $C_2H_5 \cdot CH(O \cdot CO \cdot CH_3) \cdot C_{13}H_{27}$. **1964** *Oceanogr. & Marine Biol.* II. 177 The higher aliphatic alcohols of the wax esters [found in fish lipids] usually contain hexadecanol (cetyl alcohol) and octadec-9-enol (oleyl alcohol) as main components. **1901** *Jrnl. Chem. Soc.* LXXX. I. 252 The product was found to yield a hexa-decenoic acid, $C_{16}H_{30}O_2$, melting at 36°, when fused with potassium hydroxide. **1948** A. W. RALSTON *Fatty Acids* ii. 98 The fats of fresh water fish contain somewhat less 9-hexadecenoic acid than those of marine origin. **1946** *Jrnl. Econ. Ent.* XXXIX. 812/1 Hexaethyl tetraphos-phate merits considerable attention as a commercial control for numerous insects causing serious damage to agricultural and garden crops. **1951** A. W. JOHNSON et al. in E. H. Rodd *Chem. Carbon Compounds* IA. iv. 342 A mixture of phosphates, known commercially as 'hexa-ethyl tetraphosphate', is formed when $POCl_3$ reacts with triethyl orthophosphate or with ethanol. **1965** A. & E. F. GROLLMAN *Pharmacol. & Therapeutics* (ed. 6) xxxi. 823 Hexaethyltetraphosphate..is highly toxic, exerting a potent anticholinesterase action. **1908** H. C. COOPER tr. *Holleman's Text-bk. Inorg. Chem.* (ed. 3) 487 Two hexa-hydrates of chromic chloride, $CrCl_3 \cdot 6H_2O$, are known. **1951** C. PALACHE et al. *Dana's Syst. Min.* (ed. 7) II. 493 [Pentahydrite is] obtained in crystals together with the hexahydrate and tetrahydrate by evaporation..of a solution of magnesium sulfate. **1880** G. LUNGE *Sulphuric Acid* II. III. i. 277 (*heading*) Hexahydrated salt has been obtained by Mitscherlich from a solution of Na_2S in the air. **1951** C. PALACHE et al. *Dana's Syst. Min.* (ed. 7) II. 493 The minerals of this group..are isostructural with the monoclinic artificial hexahydrated sulfates and selenates of Mg, Co, Ni, and Zn. **1885** *Jrnl. Chem. Soc.* XLVIII. II. 1046 (*heading*) Reduction in hexahydric alcohols. **1964** N. G. CLARK *Mod. Org. Chem.* xvi. 315 The pro-duct, sorbitol, is a hexahydric alcohol (one of the 'sugar alcohols'), which occurs naturally in many fruits. **1953** R. G. R. BACON in E. H. Rodd *Chem. Carbon Compounds* IIA. xi. 403 A mixture of polymers..was separated, by means of a molecular still, into fractions ranging from trimers to hexamers. **1969** *Nature* 1 Nov. 493/2 The insulin hexamer..is a compact, oblate spheroid, formed by the coordination of three insulin dimers around the two zinc ions. **1940** *Jrnl. Chem. Soc.* 1169 The trimeric, tetrameric, and pentameric portions of the polymeride have been separated from one another by molecular distillation, leaving as residue a highly viscous liquid of mainly hexameric complexity. **1903** *Science* 17 July 80/2 In some species [of corals] the hexamerism becomes much obscured in later stages, while in others it is more or less distinctly preserved. **1877** T. H. HUXLEY *Man. Anat. Invertebr. Animals* iii. 159 The finally hexamerous Antho-zoon passes through a tetramerous and an octomerous stage. **1905** I. B. BALFOUR tr. *Goebel's Organogr. Plants* II. 538 The first flowers of some Caryophylleae are hexamerous. **1940** L. H. HYMAN *Invertebrates* I. vii. 579 In typical hexamerous anemones, the number of pairs of septa in the various cycles is then: 6 (primaries), 6, 12, 24, 48, etc. **1891** W. RAMSAY *Syst. Inorg. Chem.* xxiii. 370 *Hexametaphosphates.*—These are the salts prepared by the usual methods from ordinary metaphosphoric acid. **1892** *Jrnl. Chem. Soc.* LXII. II. 1050 The uncrystal-lisable hexametaphosphates, $Na_6(PO_3)_6$ and $Ag_6(PO_3)_6$, are obtained from Graham's soluble sodium metaphos-phate.., which is a mixture of the foregoing sodium salt with several other hexametaphosphates. **1963** A. J. HALL *Textile Sci.* vi. 292 Important sequestering agents.. include sodium pyrophosphate $Na_4P_2O_7$, and especially hexametaphosphate $(NaPO_3)_6$. **1949** *Jrnl. Pharmacy & Pharmacol.* I. 603 An antidote exists for decamethonium iodide in hexamethonium iodide..and..this substance has been suggested for use in hypertension and vascular diseases. **1964** S. DUKE-ELDER *Parsons' Dis. Eye* (ed. 14) xxi. 300 The operation is most conveniently done under basal anæsthesia, and the systemic administration of sympatholytic drugs such as hexamethonium may be of value in relieving congestion by lowering the general blood pressure. **1887** *Abstr. Proc. Chem. Soc.* III. 96 Hitherto all attempts to synthesise hexamethylene-derivatives have been unsuccessful. **1909** C. A. KEANE *Mod. Org. Chem.* v. 64 The six carbon atom analogue of these alicyclic compounds is hexamethylene, C_6H_{12}. **1894** *Jrnl. Chem. Soc.* LXVI. I. 410 Hexamethylenedia-mine nitrite. **1896** *Ibid.* LXX. I. 464 Hexamethylene-diamine, $C_6H_{12}(NH_2)_2$, melts at 40° and boils at 192–195°. **1962** J. K. STILLE *Introd. Polymer Chem.* vi. 93 Nylon 66 is formed from the reaction of adipic acid (a six-carbon dibasic acid) and hexamethylenediamine (a six-carbon diamine). **1888** *Jrnl. Chem. Soc.* LIV. 1268 A well-cooled solution of hexamethylenetetramine. **1940** *Thorpe's Dict. Appl. Chem.* (ed. 4) IV. 27/2 The inodorous solid product, hexamethylenetetramine, $C_6H_{12}N_4$ (hexamine, urotropine), is a serviceable antiseptic in cystic affections, and is administered to typhoid 'carriers' to destroy the bacilli of the disease in the urine. **1961** *Encycl. Brit.* IX. 524/1 Nitration of hexamethylenetetramine gives the explosive, RDX. **1914** *Brit. Pharmacopœia* 171 Hexa-mine may be obtained by the interaction of ammonia with formic aldehyde. **1956** LD. AMULREE in A. Pryce-Jones *New Outl. Mod. Knowl.* 222 Others have used hexamine with glucose and vitamin B_1 but this treatment, again, does not seem to be generally applicable [in cases of senile dementia]. **1707** H. SLOANE *Voy. Jamaica* I (Pref.), I have followed mostly the Method of Mr. Ray in his History of Plants, joining his Genera or Tribes together by the Method of Rivinus, or Number of the Petala or Leaves of the Flowers; As those which are Monopetalous first, those Dipetalous next, then the Tripetalous, Tetrapetalous, Pentapetalous, Hexapetalous, and such as have no exact Numbers of Coloured Leaves in their Flowers. **1900** B. D. JACKSON *Gloss. Bot. Terms* 123/2 Hexarch. **1914** M. DRUMMOND tr. *Haberlandt's Physiol. Plant Anat.* vii. 352 It is customary to discriminate be-tween diarch, tetrarch, pentarch, hexarch and polyarch bundles. **1965** BELL & COOMBE tr. *Strasburger's Textbk. Bot.* I. iv. 170 Pentarch..and hexarch roots also occur. **1921** A. F. BLAKESLEE in *Amer. Naturalist* LV. 259 The following terms are suggested to designate sets with numbers of chromosomes from 1 to 12: monosome, disome, trisome, tetrasome, pentasome, hexasome, heptasome, oktasome, enneasome, dekasome, hendeka-some, dodekasome. **1922** *Genetics* VII. 527 If..the chromosomes of a tetrasomic or hexasomic set assort at random in an F_1 hybrid a 35:1 or 399:1 ratio will be found in the F_2. **1930** *Jrnl. Genetics* XXII. 146 Doubly and trebly hexasomic tetraploids are more likely to come from the derivatives of a tetraploid-hexaploid cross. **1955** J. B. & R. D. HILL *Genetics & Human Heredity* xviii. 363 Hexasomic tetraploid Globe: 4x+*21 · 22*+*21 · 22*.

hexagonal, *a.* Add: **3.** *hexagonal close-packed* adj., applied to a type of crystal structure or lattice with hexagonal symmetry in which each ion or atom has twelve equi-distant neighbours; so *hexagonal close-pack-ing* (see quot. 1917); *hexagonal symmetry*, the symmetry of a figure or body that coincides with its original position after rotation about an axis through an angle of 60° or any multiple of this.

1878 Hexagonal symmetry [in Dict.]. **1917** *Physical Rev.* X. 678 The so-called hexagonal close-packing.. is one of the two alternative arrangements which the atoms would assume if they were hard spheres and were forced by pressure into the closest possible packing. **1920** *Science* 3 Sept. 228/1 The arrangement of atoms in zinc is like that in magnesium, namely: hexagonal close packed. **1966** L. G. BASSETT et al. *Princ. Chem.* iii. 171 The difference between hexagonal close packing and face-centered close packing arises from the two arrange-ments for atoms in the third layer.

hexahydrite (heksăhəi·drəit). *Min.* [f. **hexahydr*(*ate* + -ITE[1].] The hexahydrate of magnesium sulphate, $MgSO_4 \cdot 6H_2O$.

1911 R. A. A. JOHNSTON in *Sum. Rep. Geol. Surv. Br. Dept. Mines 1910* (Canada) 257 As this is the first instance in which this salt has been recorded as occurring in a state of nature, this substance is entitled to be regarded as a new mineral, and the name hexahydrite is proposed for it, in allusion to the six molecules of water which enter into its composition. **1959** BERRY & MASON *Mineralogy* xiii. 437 In dry air at ordinary temperatures epsomite loses up to $1H_2O$, changing to hexahydrite.

hexamitiasis (heksămitəi·ăsis). *Med.* [f. the generic name *Hexamita*: see *-IASIS.] A disease caused by protozoa of the genus *Hexamita*; *esp.* an infectious catarrhal enteritis in turkeys often fatal to poults and caused by *H. meleagridis*.

1941 *Jrnl. Parasitol.* XXVII. 186 One essential difference in the pathology of hexamitiasis of pigeons [from that of turkeys] is the consistent catarrhal inflam-mation with a heavy mucous deposit in the rectum of young pigeons. **1966** T. DALLING *Internat. Encycl. Vet. Med.* III. 1432 In Great Britain, hexamitiasis appears to have been confined to a number of localized outbreaks and..the disease at present is not of great economic importance.

hexane. Add: **hexano·ic** *a.* = CAPROIC *a.*; **he·xanoyl** [*-OYL], the radical $C_5H_{11}CO-$ of hexanoic acid; also called *caproyl*.

1926 *Chem. Abstr.* XX. 4598/1 *Hexanoic acid*, see *Caproic acid*. **1927** *Jrnl. Amer. Chem. Soc.* XLIX. 1828 (*heading*) Some bromine derivatives of pentanoic and hexanoic acids. **1949** *Union Internat. Chim. pure et appl., Compt. Rend.* XV. 144 Rule 58.3. The Commission [of nomenclature of organic chemistry]..recommends that the carboxyl carbon be always numbered as 1 whether the name be a Geneva name or a trivial name, but not when it is a 'carbonyl' name. *Examples of numbering*: hexanoyl, caproyl [etc.]. **1952** *Ibid.* XVI. 101 Change: 'Caproyl' to 'Hexanoyl replacing caproyl'..[rule] 58.3. **1967** *Canad. Jrnl. Chem.* XLV. 2600/2 When a cyclo-hexane solution of hexanoyl azide and acetophenone was irradiated with light of wavelength over 3000 Å, nitrogen was rapidly evolved.

hexaploid (he·ksăploid), *a.* and *sb.* *Biol.* [f. HEXA- + *-PLOID.] (Made up of somatic cells) containing six sets of chromosomes. Also as *sb.*, a hexaploid organism.

1920 G. TÄCKHOLM in *Svensk Bot. Tidskr.* XIV. 302 The diploid and tetraploid forms [of roses] of the types 1 and 2 are represented in about equal frequence in my material, the hexaploid (type 3) being rarely met with. **1921** *Ann. Bot.* XXXV. 185 The remainder of the tetra-ploids, the whole of the pentaploids and hexaploids, showed a partial reduction involving fourteen or twenty-eight chromosomes. **1952** *New Biol.* XIII. 32 The common bread-wheats which have 42 chromosomes, or 6 sets, are hexaploids. **1956** *Nature* 25 Feb. 384/2 Hexaploid cells in mouse blastocysts. **1970** *Watsonia* VIII. 130 Two other differences between the rhizome scales of the diploid and hexaploid were noticed.

Hence **he·xaploidy,** the state or condition of being hexaploid.

1922 *Genetics* VII. 540 There is evidence that does not support the view that tetraploidy and hexaploidy in wheat is actually due to chromosomal duplication. **1925** *Jrnl. Genetics* XV. 263 Tetraploidy and hexaploidy may play a part in the striking changes of the chromosome group from species to species.

hexatone (he·ksătōun). *Mus.* [f. HEXA- + TONE; cf. PENTATONE.] 'A gapped scale con-taining six notes within an octave' (Grove, 1954).

hexatonic (heksătǫ·nik), *a.* *Mus.* Character-ized by hexatones.

1930 *Times Lit. Suppl.* 6 Feb. 95/1 Another good tune ..has additional sources of strength in being constituted as a ten bar sentence without any repetition of phrase, and being hexatonic in mode. **1946** R. BLESH *Shining Trumpets* (1949) ii. 44 The scalar concept scarcely enters into African music although it is constantly referred to as predominantly pentatonic and hexatonic, i.e., five and six-toned.

hexestrol, var. *HEXŒSTROL.

hexite (he·ksəit). [See HEXA- and -ITE[1] 4.]
1. *Chem.* [ad. G. *hexit.*] = *HEXITOL.

1899 E. F. SMITH tr. *V. von Richter's Org. Chem.* (ed. 3) I. 540 Certain hexites have been prepared by the reduc-tion of the corresponding glucoses..with sodium amalgam. **1938** G. H. RICHTER *Textbk. Org. Chem.* xx. 395 The

relationship of the aldohexoses to the corresponding hexites and dicarboxylic acids.

2. A high explosive, hexanitrodiphenylamine, $[C_6H_2(NO_2)_3]_2NH$.

1931 J. F. NORRIS *Princ. Org. Chem.* (ed. 3) xxvi. 483 Hexite or hexil..was the high explosive used in bombs which were dropped on London. **1944** *Jrnl. Amer. Med. Assoc.* 20 May 189/2 Hexite is now being made and used but not in as large quantities as trinitrotoluene. **1951** KIRK & OTHMER *Encycl. Chem. Technol.* VI. 54 Hexite is only slightly less sensitive to impact than Tetryl, but is distinctly less sensitive to the impact of a rifle bullet.

hexitol (he·ksitǫl). *Chem.* [f. HEX(OSE + *-ITOL.] Any of a class of hexahydric alcohols that are closely related to the hexoses.

1894 *Jrnl. Chem. Soc.* LXVI. I. 395 According to theory, 10 stereoisomeric forms of hexitol should exist. **1913** T. H. POPE tr. *Molinari's Org. Chem.* II. 433 With hydrogen the hexoses form hexitols, which are not aldehydic but only alcoholic in character. **1959** A. WHITE et al. *Princ. Biochem.* (ed. 2) xviii. 423 The cyclic hexitol *myo*inositol..occurs abundantly in nature, and is present chiefly in the form of polyphosphates in plants.

hexobarbital (heksobā·ɹbităl). *Pharm.* [f. as next: see *BARBITAL.] The equivalent in the U.S. Pharmacopœia of *HEXOBARBITONE.

1941 [see next]. **1943** WOOD & OSOL *Dispensatory of U.S.A.* (ed. 23) 511/2 Hexobarbitonum solubile... Soluble Hexobarbital; Soluble Evipal; Cyclural Sodium. **1957** T. SOLLMANN *Man. Pharmacol.* (ed. 8) 942/1 Hexobarbital sodium ('Evipal', 'Evipan') was introduced especially for intravenous anesthesia, as its action is brief.

hexobarbitone (heksobā·ɹbitōᵘn). *Pharm.* [f. HEX- (in *hexenyl*) + -O- + *BARBITONE.] A short-acting barbiturate, $C_{12}H_{16}N_2O_3$, with hypnotic properties; also known by proprietary names, as *Evipal, Evipan*; *loosely*, = **hexobarbitone sodium**, the monosodium derivative of hexobarbitone, a very short-acting and soluble anæsthetic usu. given intravenously or intramuscularly; also called *hexobarbitone soluble*.

1941 *Brit. Pharmacopœia 1932* (Add. 3) 8 (*heading*) Hexobarbitonum... Hexobarbitone. *Synonym.* Hexobarbital... Hexobarbitone is 5-Δ′-*cyclo*hexenyl-5-methyl-N-methyl-barbituric acid. **1943** *Brit. Med. Jrnl.* 5 June 714/2 Hexobarbitone given by mouth is an excellent hypnotic when there is no pain. *Ibid.* 20 Nov. 646/1 Cyanosis rapidly became extreme; 0·5 g. of hexobarbitone soluble (evipan sodium) was dissolved in 5 c.cm. of distilled water and administered intravenously. **1952** *Martindale's Extra Pharmacopœia* (ed. 23) I. 260 Hexobarbitone sodium has largely been superseded by thiopentone sodium which gives greater muscular relaxation. **1962** H. BURN *Drugs, Med. & Man* ix. 98 The substance hexobarbitone could be injected into a vein and the patient went to sleep with no more warning than he had when going to sleep in his own bed.

hexode, *a.* and *sb.* Add: **A.** *adj.* (Earlier example.)

1886 W. H. PREECE in *Jrnl. Soc. Telegr.-Engin. & Electr.* XV. 231 A two-way mode of working, or a mode by which two messages are practically sent at the same time, will be diode working, three-way triode, four-way tetrode, five-way penthode, and six way [*sic*] hexode.

B. *sb. Radio* [a. G. *hexode*]. A valve with six electrodes. Also *attrib.* or as *adj.*

1933 *Electronics* Mar. 76/2 The special tube which was selected..is a hexode..having a fourth grid and a redesign of all the grids. **1933** *Pract. Wireless* 27 May 358 (*caption*) Superhet circuit employing new Hexode single valve frequency changer. **1944** *Electronic Engin.* XVII. 60/1 In hexode valves the mutual conductance between the first grid potential and the anode current varies in a linear manner with the voltage applied to the third grid. **1955** J. THOMSON *Electronics* vi. 90 The simplest practical form of mixer valve, but one which is not much used nowadays is the hexode. *Ibid.* 91 The hexode may be regarded as a screen-grid tetrode with two control grids.

hexœstrol (heksī·strǫl). *Pharm.* Also **hexestrol.** [f. HEX(ANE + ŒSTR(US + -OL 2.] A synthetic œstrogen, $C_{18}H_{22}O_2$, related to stilbœstrol and used in hormone therapy.

1939 N. R. CAMPBELL et al. in *Lancet* 5 Aug. 312/1 The œstrogenic activity of the synthetic substance 4:4′-dihydroxy-γ:δ-diphenyl-*n*-hexane (hexœstrol) has been described. **1954** *Thorpe's Dict. Appl. Chem.* (ed. 4) XI. 370/2 Hexœstrol dipropionate is of particular value for inhibiting lactation, owing to its speed of action. **1960** *Farmer & Stockbreeder* 19 Jan. 62/3 Between the two most popular synthetic oestrogens—stilboestrol and hexoestrol—the latter was to be preferred as it was less toxic to man. **1971** *New Scientist* 8 Apr. 104/1 Potent drugs—for example the hormone hexoestrol.

hexogen (he·ksŏdʒĕn). Also **hexogene.** [a. G. *hexogen*.] = *CYCLONITE.

1923 *Chem. Abstr.* XVII. 2364 Nitrated hexamethylenetetramine (hexogen)..and mannitol hexanitrate occupy the highest places in the order of effectiveness. **1945** *Industr. & Engin. Chem.* XXXVII. 666/2 Increasing the weight of charge in a mercury fulminate detonator ..is not nearly so effective as substituting a composition having a higher rate of detonation, such as PETN or hexogen. **1960** *Guardian* 19 Aug. 10/4 Hexogen, he added, was a very powerful explosive used by the US Army.

hexokinase (heksokəi·nēis, -z). *Biochem.* [f. *HEXO(SE + *KINASE.] Any of various enzymes that catalyse the transfer of a phosphate group from adenosine triphosphate to glucose or other hexoses as the first step in glycolysis.

1930 O. MEYERHOF in *Lancet* 27 Dec. 1418/1 By itself this activator can do nothing, but its addition to the muscle extract induces hexoses to split even more rapidly than glycogen... I propose the name 'hexokinase' for it, since it acts just as other auxiliary enzymes designated as kinases. **1954** A. WHITE et al. *Princ. Biochem.* xvii. 404 There exists a hexokinase for fructose in yeast and brain apparently independent of the hexokinase for glucose. **1964** G. H. HAGGIS *Introd. Molecular Biol.* ii. 28 The breakdown of glucose to CO_2 and water involves a large number of enzymes, the first in the sequence being hexokinase.

hexone (he·ksōᵘn). Formerly also **hexon.** *Chem.* [See HEX- and -ONE; in sense 1, ad. G. *hexon*, *hexonbase* (A. Kossel 1898, in *Zeitschr. f. physiol. Chem.* XXV. 175).] **1.** In full, *hexone base*: any of the three basic amino-acids arginine, histidine, and lysine.

Kossel distinguished between *hexon* and *hexonbase* (see quot. 1898[2]).

1898 *Jrnl. Chem. Soc.* LXXIV. I. 612 The substances.. are called protones; these are, by the prolonged action of pancreatic juice, partially broken up into hexones (lysine, histidine, arginine). *Ibid.* 715 By the further hydrolysis of the protamines the hexon bases, histidine, arginine, and lysine, are produced, the name hexon being retained for nitrogenous substances, and obtained by the decomposition of proteids containing six atoms of carbon. **1905** J. WADE *Introd. Org. Chem.* (ed. 2) lxxiii. 555 Histidine, the principal representative of the 'hexone' bases, is an important degradation product of proteïns. **1953** *Biochem. Jrnl.* LIII. 435/2 A new technique for the estimation and isolation of the hexone bases in protein hydrolysates.

2. The name for **methyl isobutyl ketone* as used industrially.

1938 T. H. DURRANS *Solvents* (ed. 4) II. iii. 126 Methyl isobutyl ketone, or 2-methyl pentanone 5, known industrially as hexone, is a medium boiling solvent for nitrocellulose. **1966** *McGraw-Hill Encycl. Sci. & Technol.* X. 423/1 In the industrial process employing hexone (the Redox process), the uranium fuel is dissolved in nitric acid.

hexose (he·ksōᵘs, -z). *Chem.* [f. HEX- + -OSE.] A monosaccharide that contains six carbon atoms; *hexose phosphate*, a phosphate derivative of a hexose, as *hexose monophosphate, diphosphate*, substances important as intermediates in many metabolic processes.

1892 E. F. SMITH tr. *V. von Richter's Org. Chem.* (ed. 2) 499 The hexoses occur frequently in plants, especially in ripe fruits. **1909** *Proc. R. Soc.* B. LXXXI. 528 (*heading*) The hexosephosphate formed by yeast-juice from hexose and phosphate. **1916** A. P. MATHEWS *Physiol. Chem.* iv. 169 All true nucleic acids, or polynucleotides, of animal origin..have been found to contain a hexose group, or several of them. **1926** *Biochem. Jrnl.* XX. 854 Blood-plasma contains small amounts of a phosphatase similar to that found in bone. Like the latter it hydrolyses sodium glycerophosphate, hexosemonophosphate and hexosediphosphate. **1935** TIPSON & STILLER in Harrow & Sherwin *Textbk. Biochem.* ii. 63 The naturally occurring hexoses (*d*-glucose, *d*-mannose, *d*-galactose and *d*-fructose) are the only sugars which undergo fermentation by yeast. **1956** *Nature* 11 Feb. 274/1 In algae it is considered that the oxidative assimilation of hexose follows the same glycolytic pathway as in higher organisms. **1960** *McGraw-Hill Encycl. Sci. & Technol.* II. 460/1 The principal alternative pathways by which sugars are dissimilated.. are known as the hexose monophosphate pathways. **1965** *New Scientist* 17 June 761/1 Food sugars absorbed from the gut are hexoses.

So **hexo·nic** *a.* [*-ONIC], designating an acid formed from an aldohexose by oxidation of the aldehyde group to a carboxyl group; **hexosamine** (heksōᵘ·sămīn) [AMINE], a derivative of a hexose in which a hydroxyl group is replaced by an amino group; so **hexosami·nic** *a.*, designating the acid derived from hexosamine; **he·xosan** [-AN], a polysaccharide of which the constituent monosaccharides are hexoses.

1894 G. M'GOWAN tr. *Bernthsen's Org. Chem.* (ed. 2) ix. 236 By the conversion of the hexonic acids (through the hexoses) into the corresponding alcohols (mannite, etc.), the number of possible stereo-isomers is diminished. **1894** *Amer. Chem. Jrnl.* XVI. 227 If hexosans are gradually oxidized with chromic acid and afterwards distilled with acids, large amounts of furfurol are obtained. **1914** *Jrnl. Biol. Chem.* XVIII. 123 The hexosamine..was obtained directly on concentration of the product of hydrolysis of chondroitin sulphuric acid. **1915** *Ibid.* XX. 441 (*heading*) Hexosaminic acid from ribose. **1921** A. L. SMITH *Lichens* v. 211 Besides these [carbohydrates], which rank as hexosans, Ulander found small quantities of pentosans and methyl pentosans. **1957** E. V. MILLER *Chem. Plants* i. 7 The hexosan cellulose is the fundamental constituent of the plant cell wall. **1958** FRUTON & SIMMONDS *Gen. Biochem.* (ed. 2) xxi. 536 The oxidation of D-galactose by *Pseudomonas saccharophila* also appears to involve the intermediate formation of hexonic acids. **1961** *New Scientist* 5 Jan. 15/1 In chronic brain diseases and manic psychoses the macromolecular hexosamine was elevated.

hex-radiate (heks,rēⁱ·diĕt), *a.* [f. Gr. ἕξ six + L. *radiatus* rayed, RADIATE.] = HEXIRADIATE.

1883 W. S. KENT in A. J. Adderley *Fisheries Bahamas* 37 The glass-rope, birds'-nest, and hat sponges share..the circumstance that the silicious spicules of which their skeletons are composed belong..to what is known as the hex-radiate type.

hexuronic (heksiūᵊrǫ·nik), *a.* [f. *HEX(OSE + *URONIC *a.*] *hexuronic acid*, any of a class of uronic acids derived from hexose; *spec.* = **ascorbic acid*.

1928 A. SZENT-GYÖRGYI in *Biochem. Jrnl.* XXII. 1409 The substance is a hitherto unknown, highly reactive isomer of glycuronic acid, so that the substance is a hexuronic acid. *Ibid.*, The isolation of the hexuronic acid from oranges and cabbages is described. **1933** *Times Lit. Suppl.* 16 Nov. 798/3 They have discovered hexuronic acid to be identical with vitamin C. **1957** *Science News* XLV. 82 Monosaccharides include hexoses such as glucose, ..hexuronic acids such as glucuronic acid and galacturonic acid with the molecular formula $C_6H_{10}O_7$, and hexosamines. **1963** D. M. DOUGLAS *Wound Healing & Managem.* vi. 49 Szent-Györgi is credited with the chemical isolation of ascorbic acid, which he first called hexuronic acid... Szent-Györgi renamed hexuronic acid, ascorbic acid.

hexyl. Add: **hexylreso·rcinol** (also as two words), a crystalline derivative of resorcinol, $C_6H_3(OH)_2\cdot(CH_2)_5CH_3$, used as an anthelmintic and a urinary antiseptic.

1924 *Jrnl. Amer. Med. Assoc.* 20 Dec. 2007/1 Unlike a great many antiseptics and germicides, hexyl resorcinol retains its bactericidal power when dissolved in urine of either acid or alkaline reaction. **1949** KRANTZ & CARR *Pharmacol. Princ. Med. Pract.* xviii. 247 Hexylresorcinol capsules are composed of a solution of the drug dissolved in olive oil. **1968** J. H. BURN *Lect. Notes Pharmacol.* (ed. 9) 125 Oil of chenopodium and hexylresorcinol (by mouth) are also used for ascaris infections.

hey, *int.* (*sb.*). Add: **2. e. hey, Rube!** A rallying call or a cry for help used by circus people. As *sb.*, a fight between circus workers and the general public. *U.S. slang.* (Cf. *REUB.)

1882 *Times* (Chicago) 3 Dec. Suppl. 12/4 A canvasman watching a tent is just like a man watching his home. He'll fight in a minute if the outsider cuts the canvas, and if a crowd comes to quarrel he will yell, 'Hey Rube!' That's the circus rallying cry, and look out for war when you hear it. **1935** *Amer. Mercury* XXXV. 229/2 Heyrube: general uprising of spectators. **1939** *Sat. Even. Post* 25 Mar. 75/2 The expression disappeared forty years ago, along with the old rallying cry, 'Hey, Rube!' **1956** H. GOLD *Man who was not with It* (1965) i. 6 We found ourselves with an old-fashioned hey-rube and obliged to move the show on that night. **1962** E. S. GARDNER *Case of Blonde Bonanza* (1967) xv. 182 And 'Hey Rube' is a rallying cry for the circus people to unite in a fight against the outsiders? **1973** *Daily Colonist* (Victoria, B.C.) 12 Oct. 2/2 There..could be a very interesting hey Rube between incumbent Frances Elford and Ald. Brian Smith.

hi, *int.* Add: **2.** A word of greeting. *colloq.* (chiefly *N. Amer.*).

1862 M. D. COLT *Went to Kansas* ix. 143 When out on the prairie, up galloped an Indian on his pony with his saluting 'hi!' **1885** 'P. PERKINS' *Familiar Lett.* (1886) 33 We would have had to walk, I believe, if a *man* hadn't come along and let out the most satisfactory 'Hi, there!' you've ever heard, and stopped a car. **1920** F. SCOTT FITZGERALD *This Side of Paradise* (1921) II. i. 199 *Alec*: Hi, Amory! *Amory*: Hi, Alec! Tom said he'd meet you at the theatre. **1951** J. D. SALINGER *Catcher in Rye* iii. 26 He.. came in the room. 'Hi,' he said..like he was terrifically bored. **1953** H. CLEVELY *Public Enemy* xviii. 111 Tillie nodded to the uniformed commissionaire..and said: 'Hi, Charlie,' and they entered. **1959** I. & P. OPIE *Lore & Lang. Schoolch.* vii. 116 Hi, Roy Rogers! How about a date? **1963** H. GARNER in R. Weaver *Canad. Short Stories* 2nd Ser. (1968) 50 'Hi, Eric!' shouted Pete Adams..from where he was standing at the drinking fountain. **1972** WODEHOUSE *Pearls, Girls & Monty Bodkin* ii. 28 A musical voice in his left ear said 'Hi'. **1973** *Black Panther* 11 Aug. 2/2 (*letter to editor*), Hi, I've been following serialization of Operation Gemstone in the Panther Paper.

hi (həi), abbrev. of HIGH *a.*, freq. used in advertising and commercial slogans. (Cf. *HI-FI.) Chiefly *U.S.*

1911 *T. Eaton & Co. Catal.* Spring & Summer 179/4 Hi-up battery. A very powerful cell for all forms of ignition work. **1930** *Engineering* 10 Jan. 63/3 This embodies the form of motor known as the Hicycle motor, that is, an alternating current induction motor, using a supply of a frequency of 180 cycles to 200 cycles. **1959** *Sears, Roebuck Catal.* Spring & Summer 87/4 Hi-Society—a glamorous new idea in lipstick! **1963** *Times* 12 Mar. p. xii/4 A new use for ball and chain. Known as the Hi-ball method, 100 acres of lightly timbered country can be cleared in a day. **1972** *Guardian* 3 Feb. 13/4 Kids prefer 'hi-riser' bicycles..with their apehanger handlebars and their drag style saddles.

hiaqua (həi·ăkwa). Also **haiqua, haigua,** etc. [Chinook jargon, f. Nootka.] An ornament or necklace composed of tooth-shells,

formerly used as money by the Indians of the north Pacific coast of North America.

1824 G. SIMPSON *Jrnl.* in *Fur Trade* (1931) 96 The Ears are perforated all round and Beads or Hyaques suspended therefrom. **1862** *Nor' Wester* (Red River Settlement) 5 Mar. 4/3 Instead of the nose jewels being 'of tin' they were composed of the Hyaqua shells. *a* **1861** T. WINTHROP *Canoe & Saddle* (1883) vii. 95 Tribes..among whom hiaqua is plenty as salmon-berries are in the woods. **1881** E. B. TYLOR *Anthropol.* xi. 282 The Indians of British Columbia, whose strings of haiqua-shells..serve them..as currency. **1923** *Canad. Hist. Rev.* IV. 37 The shell *dentalium indianorum,* commonly called hiquia, is much esteemed by the coast Indians, and amongst them has fulfilled some of the functions of money. **1953** E. E. CLARK *Indian Legends* 220 Hiaqua..—shell money and ornaments highly prized by the Indians of the Pacific Northwest Coast.

hiatal (həiˌēⁱ·tăl), *a.* [f. HIAT(US + -AL.] Of or pertaining to a hiatus.

1909 J. P. IDDINGS *Ign. Rocks* I. vi. 198 Hiatal fabrics being those in which variations in the sizes of crystals are not in continuous series, but in broken series with hiatuses, it follows that the most characteristic feature of such fabrics is the marked contrast between the sizes of some of the crystals. **1923** R. KNOX *Radiogr. & Radio-Ther.* (ed. 2) I. 319 Cardiospasm (Hiatal Oesophagismus). **1957** [see *FIXATION 3 c]. **1961** *Lancet* 7 Oct. 810/1 In hiatus hernia, if the hiatal slit is small enough, the mucosal surfaces of the stomach may be adequately opposed.

hiatus. Add: **1. b.** Also *attrib.*, as **hiatus hernia,** a hernia in which an organ, esp. the stomach, protrudes through the œsophageal opening in the diaphragm.

1928 *Acta Radiologica* IX. 301 Diaphragmatic hiatus-hernia and oesophageal diverticulum were roentgenologically diagnosed. **1934** *Jrnl. Amer. Med. Assoc.* 24 Feb. 586/1 A hiatus hernia should always be considered as a possible diagnosis when upper abdominal symptoms of doubtful origin occur chiefly or only at night. **1958** *Sunday Times* 28 Sept. 27/3 A condition known medically as hiatus hernia..occurs when something goes wrong with the diaphragm. **1971** *Brit. Med. Bull.* XXVII. 34/1 Difficulty in swallowing is associated with..hiatus hernia.

3. Also *attrib.* and *Comb.*, as *hiatus-consonant, -filler, -glide*; *hiatus-filling* adj.

1945 *Mod. Lang. Notes* Dec. 550 The spelling *donmore* for *Dunmowe* may indicate the development of a hiatus-filling *r* in sandhi. **1948** D. DIRINGER *Alphabet* II. vi. 350 The letters..were also used as 'hiatus-consonants'. **1953** K. JACKSON *Lang. & Hist. Early Brit.* 278 The hiatus-glide with native *e* was..ị. *Ibid.* 367 The hiatus-filler here is ụ rather than ị. **1968** *Language* XLIV. 454 The general outlines of this 'hiatus diphthongization' have been known for more than three-quarters of a century.

‖ **hibachi** (hi·batʃi, hibā·tʃi). Also formerly **hebachi.** [Jap. *hibachi, hi-hachi,* f. *hi* fire + *hachi* bowl, pot.] A large earthenware pan or brazier in which charcoal is burnt esp. in order to warm the hands or heat a room.

1863 R. ALCOCK *Capital of Tycoon* II. xvi. 379 There were also some fifty *Hebachis,* or vessels for burning charcoal and warming the rooms, corresponding with the Spanish *Brazeiro.* **1874** *Trans. Asiatic Soc. Japan* II. 132 Boys and girls assemble around the *hibachi.* **1921** *Outward Bound* Apr. 22/1 The little *kimori* [sic, for *komori* nurse-maid] was bidden to join the family circle around the *hibachi.* **1959** R. KIRKBRIDE *Tamiko* iv. 28 The small.. mat room was bare except for..the hibachi, and a scattering of china on the shelf. **1965** *Austral. Women's Weekly* 20 Jan. 27/1 The other indispensable came from a prolonged stay in Yokohama, a small serviceable iron *hibachi,* the original of the Western barbecue grill, but portable.

Hiberno-. (Further examples.)

1907 *Daily Chron.* 6 Sept. 3/1 Hiberno-Egyptian. **1908** *Westm. Gaz.* 20 Aug. 5/2 A Hiberno-Romanesque church. **1939** *Burlington Mag.* Jan. 43/1 The brilliance and precocity of the Hiberno-Saxon arts. **1953** K. JACKSON *Lang. & Hist. Early Brit.* I. v. 175 This family of remote Hiberno-British princelings wished to make clear its claim to Roman status.

hibschite (hi·bʃəit). *Min.* [ad. G. *hibschit* (F. Cornu 1905, in *Tschermaks min. und petrogr. Mitt.* XXIV. 327), f. the name of J. E. *Hibsch* (1852–1940), Bohemian mineralogist: see -ITE¹.] A calcium aluminosilicate hydroxide, a member of the garnet family.

1907 *Mineral. Mag.* XIV. 400 Hibschite... Minute, octahedral, optically isotropic crystals of contact-metamorphic origin, occurring in enclosures of chalk-marl in phonolite at Aussig, Bohemia. **1942** *Amer. Mineralogist* XXVII. 783 *X*-ray powder patterns of hibschite from the type locality..closely resemble patterns of grossularite and plazolite. **1962** W. A. DEER et al. *Rock-Forming Min.* I. 79 Hibschite, $Ca_3Al_2Si_2(OH)_4O_8$, has a cell side of 12.16Å..and eight molecules to the unit cell. **1966** [see *hydrogrossular* s.v. *HYDRO-].

hiccoughy, var. HICCUPY *a.*

1911 J. C. LINCOLN *Cap'n Warren's Wards* i. 2 The train slowed down, in a jerky hiccoughy sort of way.

hiccup, *sb.* Add: **c.** *attrib.* **hiccup-nut** *S. Afr.*, the fruit of an ornamental shrub, *Combretum* (*Poivrea*) *bracteosum,* belonging to the family Combretaceæ; also, the plant itself; **hiccup strike** [It. *sciopero a singhiozzi*] *colloq.*, a strike normally of short duration which forms part of a series of similar and irregularly spaced strikes.

1862 HARVEY & SONDER *Flora Capensis* II. 512 *P*[*oivrea*] *bracteosa*... Fruit oval or slightly obovate, indistinctly 5-angled, glabrous, 1-seeded. Called 'Hiccup-nut' in the colony. **1868** J. CHAPMAN *Trav.* II. App. 447 The exquisite heads of scarlet flowers of the Hiccup-nut. **1899** WOOD & EVANS *Natal Plants* I. II. 63 The fruit is known locally as 'Hiccup Nut' and is palatable, but usually produces violent hiccough. **1951** *Dict. Gardening* (R. Hort. Soc.) II. 531/1 C. bracteosum. Hiccup-nut. **1950** *Times* 27 Jan., In the meantime the 'hiccup' strikes go on in the Paris region. where 12 'bus lines were out of action. **1962** *Daily Tel.* 28 June 26/3 Most are on what are known in Italy as 'hiccup strike', two-day stoppages at irregular intervals.

hiccupy *a.* (earlier and later examples).

1853 LYTTON *My Novel* II. VII. x. 225 Long and loud talk recommenced, Burley's great voice predominant, Mr. Douce chiming in with hiccupy broken treble. **1968** *Listener* 11 July 55/2 Chopped-up, hiccupy sentences, often one word long. **1971** *Daily Tel.* 16 Oct. 7/6 The old Japanese anemone, mentioned in catalogues..as having the hiccupy name of Anemone hupehensis.

‖**hic et nunc** (hīk et nuŋk), *phr.* [L., 'here and now'.] At the present time and place; in this particular situation; spatio-temporal nature of a phenomenon (see quot. 1948).

1935 *Studies in Hist. of Ideas* III. 469 One must distinguish between the *type* or *kind* of a sign, and its *hic et nunc* spatio-temporal exemplification. **1948** L. SPITZER *Linguistics & Lit. Hist.* 14 An explanation of the concrete *hic et nunc* of a historical phenomenon. **1950** I. SILONE in Koestler et al. *God that Failed* 103 A political revolution, *hic et nunc.* **1966** *Listener* 20 Oct. 580/1 The presence of God in the world, *hic et nunc,* at man's level.

hick, *sb.*¹ Delete †*Obs.* and add later U.S. examples.

1916 H. L. WILSON *Somewhere in Red Gap* iii. 113 So I yelled out back to an old hick of a gardener..and he comes running. **1923** R. D. PAINE *Comrades of Rolling Ocean* vi. 106, I come from a small town and that makes me a hick. My opinions aren't worth much. **1925** *Glasgow Herald* 16 Sept. 4 In the United States the 'Hicks' are still for the most part tenacious of that doctrine which assigns to speculations a 'bearish' or depressing influence on the markets. **1927** *Observer* 1 May 10/2 It is ..much easier to write a good play about hicks, boobs, hayseeds, highbrows,..and sentimentalists than about decent English people. **1928** *World's Work* Apr. 628 Broadway humorists, only a few years ago, used to make fun of Long Islanders by calling them 'hicks'. **1929** A. CONAN DOYLE *Maracot Deep* 18 He could not make these country hicks understand. **1970** W. BURROUGHS JR. *Speed* ii. 39 The proprietor was a knobby, obliging old hick and he watched us all real close to make sure we didn't try to lift any fertilizer. **1970** J. HANSEN *Fadeout* (1972) ii. 10 He was killed... They just stopped playing him. As though we was such hicks we didn't know there's such a thing as tapes these days.

b. *attrib.* or as *adj.* Like a hick, unsophisticated, provincial. *colloq.* (chiefly *N. Amer.*).

1920 S. LEWIS *Main Street* xiv. 164 He graduated from a hick college in Pennsylvania. **1920** —— in *Sat. Even. Post* 11 Dec. 92/2 Why the plates turned over? That's hick-town stuff. **1921** H. C. WITWER *Leather Pushers* ix. 216 His..features wasn't bad looking in a hick way. **1936** J. DOS PASSOS *Big Money* 256 Tad was sitting there hanging his head, his hick hands dangling between his knees. **1952** M. MCCARTHY *Groves of Academe* (1953) xii. 243 He..nodded triumphantly at his friend,.. who had been trying to persuade him that science fantasy was hick. **1958** *Punch* 27 Aug. 283/3 Why stick with some depressing Yank writer who takes a cool six hundred pages to chronicle the twenty-four-hour doings of a single character in a hick town? **1967** *Listener* 17 Aug. 218/3 Telly was still rather a hick affair back in 1951.

†**hickboo** (hi·kbū). *Air Force slang.* Also **hickaboo.** An air raid. *Obs.*

1919 *Athenæum* 23 May 360/2. **1925** FRASER & GIBBONS *Soldier & Sailor Words* 119 *Hickaboo*.., an Air Force term for an Air Raid.

hickey (hi·ki), *sb.* Chiefly *U.S.* Also **hickie.** [Origin unknown.] **1.** Any small gadget or device; something of little consequence; = *DOOHICKEY.

Quot. 1909 is more specific than is warranted by the available evidence.

1909 WEBSTER, *Hickey* (a), a device for bending a conduit, consisting of an iron pipe used as a handle fitted at one end with a tee through which the conduit is passed; (b) a small fitting used in wiring for electric lights, a fixture piped for gas. **1913** in WENTWORTH *Amer. Dial. Dict.* 291/1 S.C. Rock Hill. Common. 'Hand me that hickey.' **1928** *Papers Michigan Acad. Sci. Arts & Lett.* X. 298 *Hickie,* a word applicable to anything whose name one does not remember; 'what's its name'. **1932** *Atlantic Monthly* CXLIX. 665 We have little hickeys beside our seats to regulate the amount of air admitted through a slot in each window. **1935** *Hearst's International* Oct. 24/2 The chances are the management will be putting hickeys in their keyholes. **1940** *Sat. Even. Post* 15 June 38/2 There was a violent distaste for the fraction-of-a-cent tokens, disks of aluminum with a hole in the center. These were variously called 'Chinese money', 'hickeys', 'monkey money' and 'agony money'.

2. A pimple. *U.S. dial.* or *colloq.*

Said by Wentworth and Flexner to be *c* 1915 but printed evidence is lacking.

1934 *Amer. Ballads & Folk Songs* (1960) 19 Godamighty made a 'gator wid hickies all over his Tail. **1937** *Ten-Story Love Mag.* May 2 (Advt.), Hickies spoil everything. I know. I had 'em until I began eating Fleischmann's yeast. **1946** *Publ. Amer. Dial. Soc.* Nov. 17 *Hickey,* a small festered spot on the skin of a person. Salem. Reported 1942. **1956** H. GOLD *Man who was not with It* (1965) xviii. 158 A woman is not just soul and hickie-squeezing. *Ibid.* xxv. 235 Tall..skinny, big blue hickie on the face.

3. *Printing.* (See quots.)

1940 *Correct English* (Chicago) Mar. 63/3 *Hickey,* printer's slang term for ornament. **1961** H. B. JACOBSON *Mass Communications Dict.* 163 *Hickey.* 1. Slang term for slight tears or rips in wet collodion or stripfilm negatives, or for small 'runs' or blemishes in sensitized coatings. 2. A speck on the printing area of an engraving that remains after the etch. Must be routed off. **1967** E. CHAMBERS *Photolitho-Offset* 273 *Hickeys,* faults in the printed result which show as irregular spots with white surrounding haloes, caused by dirt or hardened specks of ink.

4. See *JIM-HICKEY.

hickey (hi·ki), *a. slang.* [? f. HICK *v.*] Tipsy.

Recorded in dictionaries of slang: Grose (1788), Matsell (1859), Barrère & Leland (1889), Berrey & Van den Bark (1942), etc.

hickory. Add: **2. c.** (Examples.)

1827 *Hallowell* (Maine) *Gaz.* 20 June 2/2 He was in favor of amending the Constitution, so as to let the people vote for Old Hickory. **1860** J. PARTON *Life A. Jackson* I. xxxiv. 381 It was on this homeward march that the nick-name of 'Old Hickory' was bestowed on the General. **1907** *Springfield* (Mass.) *Republ.* 24 Oct. 8, I should not say that Old Hickory was faultless, but Andrew Jackson was as upright a patriot as ever any nation had. **1949** B. A. BOTKIN *Treas. S. Folklore* p. xx, In this land..men put daring above discipline and etiquette to give us heroes like the 'Swamp Fox', 'Old Hickory', [etc.]. **1967** *Oxf. Compan. Eng. Lit.* (ed. 4) 592/1 *Old Hickory,* a nickname of Andrew Jackson.

4. a. Also applied *fig.* to members of various religious sects.

1831 *Boston* (Mass.) *Transcript* 12 Dec. 1/1 This assemblage of *Shaking* Quakers, for so many of them proved, who were only *hickory* ones till they joined the sett. **1855** *Jrnl. Discourses* II. 322 If there are any Gentiles, or hickory 'Mormons'..write it down. **1859** BARTLETT *Dict. Amer.* s.v., A 'hickory Catholic'..is a flexible, yielding one. **1872** E. EGGLESTON *End of World* xxxix. 249 Any member of your class would do better to marry a good, faithful, honest New Light than to marry a hickory Methodist. **1940** *Sat. Even. Post* 30 Mar. 37/4 He is..referred to by the neighbors as a 'hickory Amish' because of some infraction not publicly mentioned, but most likely that of going to a movie.

b. hickory shad, the gizzard-shad (*Dorosoma cepedianum*); also, the fall-herring; **hickory shirt** (earlier examples).

1800 B. HAWKINS *Sk. Creek Country* in *Georgia Hist. Soc. Colls.* (1848) III. 53 The fish taken here are, the hickory shad, [etc.]. **1871** *Amer. Naturalist* V. 398 The 'Hickory Shad'..were also filled with comminuted Crustacea. **1947** B. W. DALRYMPLE *Panfish* 341 Then suddenly a big buck Shad of four or five pounds, or a small Alewife or Hickory Shad. **1836** D. HARRIS in *Texas Hist. Assoc. Q.* (1900–1) IV. 160 Mother..made two striped hickory shirts and bags to carry provisions. **1850** L. H. GARRARD *Wah-To-Yah* xii. (1927) 58 Hickory shirts. *a* **1861** T. WINTHROP *Canoe & Saddle* (1883) iii. 33 Hickory shirts and woolen blankets are worn instead of skin raiment.

hi-coc(k)alorum, -olorum, occas. sp. of *high cockalorum*: see COCKALORUM 1 and 3.

1860 *Illustr. London News* 7 Jan. 24/2 The little innocents, however, chiefly devote their energies to mud-pie manufacture and the games of Mulberry-bush, I-spy-I, Hi Cockolorum, Hopscotch, or Buttons. **1926** FOWLER *Mod. Eng. Usage* 164/2 Mock Latin: bonus, bogus, hocus-pocus, hi-cocalorum (hic, hoc, horum?). **1950** C. FRY *Venus Observed* 82 The seven seas, and the milky way And morning, and evening, and hi-cockalorum are in it. **1969** I. & P. OPIE *Children's Games* viii. 257 Croydon boys call it [*sc.* the game] not only 'Hi Jimmy Knacker', but 'Bung the Barrel', 'Hi Cockalorum', [etc.].

Hidatsa (hidæ·tsă). [Native name *hiratsa* willow wood lodge (Dr. Sturtevant).] A member of a group of N. American Indians; also, the language of this people. Also *attrib.*

1873 W. MATTHEWS *Gram. & Dict. Lang. Hidatsa* p. xvi, The origin of the word Hidatsa is obscure, yet it is the name by which these Indians now designate themselves... One of their villages on Knife River was named Hidatsa; and probably when they were reduced by small-pox the majority of survivors came from that village, which then lent its name to the whole Tribe... The name Hidatsa is said by some to mean 'willows'. **1890** J. G. FRAZER *Golden Bough* II. iv. 339 Some of the Hidatsa Indians explain the phenomena of gradual death..by supposing that man has four souls. **1911** —— *Ibid.* (ed. 3) I. iii. 55 Similar practices are reported among the Illinois, the Mandano, and the Hidatsas of North America. **1964** E. BACH *Introd. Transformational Gram.* v. 89 Languages..Arabic, Hidatsa. **1969** *Observer* (Colour Suppl.) 18 May 22/2 A special development in the warrior societies was found among the Mandan, Hidatsa,..and Blackfoot, which had a hierarchy of societies.

hidden, *ppl. a.* Add: **1. b.** (*the*) *hidden hand,* secret or occult influence, esp. of a malignant character.

1870 T. TAYLOR (*title*) The hidden hand. **1879** *Scribner's Monthly* July 326/2 Mr. Chaufrau played..the negro Wool in a dramatization of Mrs. Southworth's '*Hidden Hand*'. **1932** *Ann. Reg. 1931* II. 21 One Labour member

attributed the appointment to the influence of a 'hidden hand' which was forcing the Labour Party to act against its principles. **1969** *Daily Tel.* 8 Mar. 20/3 Government action was being urgently considered against the 'hidden hand type of pressure' in public relations.

c. Gram. *hidden quantity* (see quot. 1898).

1898 G. M. Lane *Latin Gram.* § 2459 A vowel which stands before two consonants, or a double consonant, belonging to the same word, so that its natural quantity cannot be determined from the scansion of the word, is said to possess Hidden Quantity. **1965** W. S. Allen *Vox Latina* 65 A long vowel in such a position is sometimes said to have 'hidden quantity'.

d. *hidden reserve*: (*a*) in *Econ.* (see quot. 1965); (*b*) in general or transf. use, something kept in reserve in a concealed form.

1930 *Economist* 30 Aug. 408/1 Many of the assets in the balance sheet contain substantial hidden reserves. **1935** *Discovery* Oct. 290/2 It was not until the 'hidden reserve' of radioactivity was discovered that it was possible for the prolonged youth of the Earth to be explained. **1965** J. L. Hanson *Dict. Econ.* 213/1 If the assets of a firm have been deliberately undervalued, perhaps because the value of these assets has increased, the difference between their value as shown in the firm's balance sheet and their real value provides the firm with a 'hidden reserve', of which most shareholders will be unaware.

e. *hidden persuaders*, a term used, orig. by the Amer. writer Vance Packard (b. 1914), to describe those involved in the organization and practice of advertising; hence *hidden persuasion*.

1957 V. Packard (*title*) The hidden persuaders. **1959** *Daily Mail* 2 Apr. 1/4 This is the diet with the hidden persuader and the built-in will-power. **1960** *Guardian* 28 Dec. 8/4 The hidden persuasions. **1962** *Sunday Express* 30 Dec. 17/1 At sales time the hidden persuasion works harder—'15½ guineas slashed to £5'.

hide, *sb.*[1] Add: **2. c.** Impudence, effrontery, 'nerve'. (App. an elliptical use of 'thick hide'.)

Freq. in Australia and N.Z. but also occurs elsewhere.

1916 J. B. Cooper *Coo-oo-ee* xi. 150 Don't you think you have a hide to ask me? **1926** 'J. Doone' *Timely Tips for New Australians*, *Hide*, a slang term denoting impudence. **1947** K. Tennant *Lost Haven* ii. 37 He *might* have told me. Just springing it on me..out of the blue... Like his hide! For two pins I'd tell him where to go. **1949** H. Wadman *Life Sentence* 9 Talk about self-confidence... What a hide! **1959** P. H. Johnson *Unspeakable Skipton* v. 34 The beast has had the hide..to dictate that to a secretary. **1961** *Coast to Coast 1959–60* 120 He wants to be a farmer. A farmer! Had the hide to try and tell *me* what farm life's like—me, born and bred on one.

hide, *sb.*[3] **II. 2.** (Later examples.) Also *attrib.*

1920 *Nature* CV. 146/2 The cock bird discovered Mr. Brook leaving the 'hide'. **1934** *Brit. Birds* XXVIII. 97, I had just seen my companion into his hide tent..when a small wader came off her nest at my feet. **1935** *Discovery* Aug. 228/1 We built our first hide..four feet away from one nest. **1940** 'Gun Buster' *Return via Dunkirk* II. i. 85 The guns and vehicles went into a 'hide' in a large orchard. **1952** E. F. Davies *Illyrian Venture* xi. 220 The others had been sealed into a hide in the camp and were not discovered for four days. **1965** P. Wayre *Wind in Reeds* iv. 43 He had already started work on the construction of permanent observation huts or hides built into the sea-wall itself, from which it was possible to watch the wild geese in comfort.

hide, *v.*[1] Add: **1.** Further examples of *to hide away*. Also const. *up*. (Cf. sense 2 b.)

1854 W. Collins *Hide & Seek* III. xxiii. 227, I shall find him! I don't care where he's hid away from me. *Ibid.* xxiv. 271 She..hid it away in her bosom. **1884** 'Mark Twain' *Huck. Finn* xxiv. 241 It's reckoned he left three or four thousand in cash hid up som'ers. **1891** C. Graves *Field of Tares* 109 There was a fresh canvas upon the easel, the tattered one had been carefully hidden away. **1928** E. Wallace *Flying Squad* xvi. 169 Bradley's fond of her. He hid her up once: why shouldn't he hide her up again? **1948** 'N. Shute' *No Highway* vi. 168 It was impossible to hide up evidence like that.

2. c. *to hide out*: to go into hiding; to hide from the authorities. *U.S.*

1884 J. C. Harris *Mingo* 124 The revenue fellers better not git too clost ter Hog Mountain, bekaze the hidin'-out bizness is done played. **1885** 'C. E. Craddock' *Prophet Gt. Smoky Mts.* ii. 44 Loneliness had made his sensibilities tender and 'hiding out' affected his spirits more than dodging the officers. **1911** R. D. Saunders *Col. Todhunter* i. 19 You got to hide out when that word is delivered, suh. **1924** F. R. Bechdolt *Tales Old-Timers* 345 A man..could hide out and hold up his herd. **1969** C. F. Burke *God is Beautiful, Man* (1970) 25 So he tries to find a pad where he can hide out.

hide-and-coop. *U.S.* = Hide-and-seek.

1850 S. Judd *R. Edney* 128 (Th.), As if religion were a game of hide and coop, each called out from his secret place a faint, long-drawn 'c-o-o-p'. **1909** *N. & Q.* 10th Ser. XII. 371/1 In 'hide and coop', each called out from his secret place a faint, long-drawn 'c-o-o-p'. **1910** S. E. White *Rules of Game* III. xii. 258 The herders grinned as the rangers came in sight. They had been 'tagged' in this 'game of hide and coop'. **1923** K. D. Wiggin *My Garden of Memory* 14 The board-piles afforded the best possible place for playing 'Hide and Coop'.

hide-and-seek. (Earlier and later (chiefly) U.S. examples of **hide-and-go-seek.**)

1724 *Essex Inst. Hist. Coll.* XXXVI. 333 At night was at Madam Brownes playing hide and goe seek with Olive Parker, Wibird, &c. **1821** J. F. Cooper *Spy* (1831) xxxvi. 405 Since when, we have been playing hide-and-go-seek with the ships. **1908** T. Roosevelt *Lett. Children* 2 Jan. (1919), Do you recollect how we all used to play hide-and-go-seek in the White House? **1925** F. Scott Fitzgerald *Great Gatsby* v. 82 At first I thought it was another party, a wild rout that had resolved itself into 'hide-and-go-seek'. **1969** I. & P. Opie *Children's Games* iv. 154 In Scotland it is often 'Hide and Go Seek'—as also in the United States. **1971** A. Bailey *In Village* (1972) xx. 202 There are games of prisoner's base and hide-and-go-seek.. with the parked cars providing a forest of hiding places.

hideaway, *sb.* Add: **2.** A small, quiet restaurant, etc., or a secluded place of entertainment.

1929 *World's Work* Nov. 40/2 The vaudeville performer on the two-a-day has played to punks in the hideaways who turned his riot into an oil can. **1939** C. Morley *Kitty Foyle* xviii. 171 He took me to a French hideaway up on Pine Street. **1962** *Times* 9 May 7/1 Dozens of inexpensive hideaways where the entertainment ranges from progressive jazz quartets to the folk songs of the South and West. **1971** *New Yorker* 11 Sept. 99/2 (Advt.), We can take you on a tour of romantic little hideaways, golden beaches and the excitement of the bullring.

3. A place of concealment or retreat.

1930 'E. Queen' *French Powder Myst.* II. xiii. 104 This is also the conference room for directors' meetings, the Old Man's hideaway, et cetera. **1941** 'R. West' *Black Lamb* II. 12 A Bulgarian leader who was lying wounded in a hideaway. **1959** *Times Lit. Suppl.* 20 Nov. 680/5 They meet in his hideaway to discuss the state of the world.

hi-de-hi (həi·ˌdiˌhəi·), *int.* An exclamation, used chiefly by army instructors to greet, or attract the attention of, their troops. Also *transf.* and *attrib.*

1941 G. Kersh *They die with their Boots Clean* II. 67 'Now, when I say *Hi-de-Hi Squad!* you shout *Ho-de-Ho!*—and shout it loud! Now: *Hi-de-Hi Squad!*' We roar: 'Ho-de-Ho!' **1943** *N. & Q.* CLXXXV. 83/2 A reviewer in *The Listener* (27 May) writes:..the hi-de-hi qualities of Dr. I. A. Richards's latest book should..make our minds spring to attention with the appropriate ho-de-ho. **1944** *N. & Q.* CLXXXVI. 57/1 It was the C.O. of a training camp who instructed his officers on seeing their men in the street to come to attention and say hi-de-hi, whereupon the men came to attention and replied ho-de-ho. **1950** J. Vedey *Band Leaders* iv. 29 He [*sc.* Harry Roy] made them sing Hi-de-hi at the May Fair.

hi-de-ho (həi·ˌdiˌhōu·), *int.* An exclamation of joy used chiefly by jazz and dance bands. Also *attrib.* and as *sb.*

1936 *Delineator* Nov. 10/6 They have not come here to dance and drink away an evening in the usual night-club hi-de-ho. **1946** Mezzrow & Wolfe *Really Blues* viii. 120 The hi-de-ho, vo-de-o-do and boop-boop-a-doo howlers that later sprouted up. **1949** L. Feather *Inside Be-Bop* iii. 23 There was plenty going on in the band besides hi-de-ho.

hideling, *a.* and *sb.* Add: Also **hidling.** **A.** *adj.* (Earlier examples.)

1834 R. Mudie *Feathered Tribes Brit. Isles* I. 327 The lesser white-throat is, however, a more hidling bird than the white-throat. **1839** W. MacGillivray *Hist. Brit. Birds* II. 334 So hideling are its habits that one seldom obtains a glimpse of it.

hideosity. (Earlier and later examples.)

1807 C. Wilmot *Let.* 15 May in *Russ. Jrnls.* (1934) II. 245 Nothing before our eyes but Minerals & Fossils & Animals in every State of Hideosity. **1841** C. Ridley *Lett.* (1958) 69 Never in my life have I seen such frightful hideosities of beds as they are. **1970** *New Yorker* 12 Sept. 56/1 Don't speak to me of caravans... Such hideosities.

hide-out (həi·dˌaut). orig. *N. Amer.* Also **hideout.** A hiding-place. Also *attrib.*

1885 *Century Mag.* Mar. 684/2 They guv my place the name o' Hide-out, an' they didn't conscrip' me, nuther. **1913** A. B. Emerson *R. Fielding at Snow Camp* 174 Meanwhile, the wind shrieked through the forest above their 'hideout'. **1920** B. Cronin *Timber Wolves* 76 'In rough country like this a man could bury himself for years.'..'This coast is full of hide-outs, as they call them.' **1933** *Amer. Speech* VIII. 49/2 *Hide-out country*, any trackless wilderness. **1935** G. Gorer *Africa Dances* III. iv. 225 Even if they are inspected by the local authorities..they have..neighbouring hide-outs. **1940** *Economist* 11 May 848/1 The long coastline of Norway provides innumerable hide-outs for German submarines. **1958** *Listener* 25 Dec. 1074/2 The National Gallery pictures, tucked away in their air-conditioned, thermostatically controlled, war-time hideout in the Welsh mountains. **1963** *Daily Tel.* 14 Aug. 20/6 Special squads combed the hideout house. **1973** J. Cleary *Ransom* iii. 71 She had made a mistake in choosing this place as their hide-out, but nowhere else had seemed better.

hidey (həi·di), *int.* Chiefly *Austral.* and *U.S.* Also **hidy, highdey.** [Blend of Hi and *howdey* (see How-do-ye).] A word of greeting.

1941 Baker *Dict. Austral. Slang* 35 *Hidey! Highdey!*, Hail!, How are you! **1959** I. Jefferies *13 Days* xi. 182 'Hidey,' I said. **1962** E. B. Atwood *Regional Vocab. Texas* iii. 70 *Hidy*, probably a blend of the old and new.

hiding, *vbl. sb.*[1] Add: **4.** *hiding power*, the capacity of paint or other colouring materials to obliterate certain surfaces.

1951 R. Mayer *Artist's Handbk.* 433 *Hiding power*, degree of opacity in a paint or pigment; ability to mask or conceal an underpainting. The term *covering power* is sometimes confused with it. **1966** J. S. Cox *Illustr. Dict. Hairdressing* 79/1 *Hiding power*, the power of an opaque dye or other colouring material, when applied to hair, to cover or hide its existing colour. **1967** *Gloss. Paper Ink Terms Letterpress Printing* (*B.S.I.*) 11 *Hiding power*, the capacity of an ink to obliterate the previously printed ink film.

hidy-hole (həi·diˌhōul). orig. *Sc.* Also **hidey-, hidie-.** [Alteration of *hiding-hole*: see Hiding *vbl. sb.*[1] 4.] A hiding-place.

1817 *Blackw. Mag.* Nov. 158/2 They're darned in some o' the queer hidy-holes about the rocks there. **1828** D. M. Moir *Mansie Wauch* ix. 79 We got James..hauled out of his hidy-hole. **1870** R. Chambers *Pop. Rhymes* 91 He had not been long in his hidy-hole, before the awful Etin came in. **1896** S. R. Crockett *Cleg Kelly* iii. 18 Tim Kelly's 'hidie holes', where he kept the weapons of his craft. **1920** *Glasgow Herald* 6 Dec. 10 The story of the Ballantrae smugglers' 'hidie-hole'. **1927** *Hutchinson's Myst. Story Mag.* IX. XLVIII. 50/2 So it's obvious that there may quite easily be another snug little hidy-hole which none of us knows of. **1934** D. L. Sayers *Nine Tailors* 261 A nice little six-inch hidey-hole where nobody would ever dream of looking for it. **1955** J. Thomas *No Banners* xxxiii. 330 There's a concrete hidey-hole underneath. **1959** P. H. Johnson *Humbler Creation* xlii. 286 So this was where he came,..into this snugness, this hidey-hole. **1969** I. & P. Opie *Children's Games* iv. 157 Those who are still searching..rush to the places where they were last seen, thinking that they will be near the hidy-hole.

hielaman. b. **hielaman tree** (examples).

1884 A. Nilson *Timber Trees N.S.W.* 136 Heelaman tree. **1889** J. H. Maiden *Useful Native Plants Austral.* 426 *Heilaman tree.* The wood is soft, and used by the aborigines for making their 'heilamans' or shields.

hien, hsien (hyen, ʃyen). Pl. uninflected. Also **heen.** [Chinese.] An administrative division of a fu or department, or of an independent chow or district; also, the seat of government of such a division. Also *attrib.*

1837 *Penny Cycl.* VII. 77/1 The subordinate cities and districts of each province in the three ranks of Foo, Chow, and Hien, are under the charge of their respective magistrates, who take their rank and titles from the cities they govern. **1901** *Westm. Gaz.* 23 Aug. 8/2 Among the candidates was a man who has the hsien B.A. degree. During the examination it was found that he had some books with him. The examiner at once ordered his expulsion from the hall, but the men from his hsien objected. **1909** *Ibid.* 24 May 8/2 A circular has been sent to all viceroys and governors by the Pekin Cabinet ordering that a stop be put to the old custom of levying benevolences on the governors of hien cities. **1938** *New Statesman* 15 Jan. 74/1 This means in practice control of the whole administrative machine down to the smallest units, the hsien. **1959** *Chambers's Encycl.* III. 439/2 The provincial health administration..supervised the work of the *hsien* and municipal authorities. **1971** *N.Y. Times* 27 June 20 Each hsien [in China] has been given the target of becoming self-sufficient in food and light industrial products.

hierarchize, *v.* Add: (Later examples.) Hence **hierarchiza·tion.**

1931 C. Williams *Place of Lion* ii. 26 These hierarchized celsitudes are but the last traces..of the ideas which Plato taught his disciples existed in the spiritual world. **1954** B. & R. North tr. *Duverger's Pol. Parties* II. iii. 405 Party hierarchization becomes more theoretical than practical. **1961** *New Left Rev.* May–June 34/2 Management..is not so amalgamated or hierarchised. **1967** D. Cooper *Psychiatry & Anti-Psychiatry* v. 100 We have eliminated formal hierarchization to a point beyond which no similar experiment in the literature of the subject has gone. **1971** *Jrnl. Gen. Psychol.* LXXXIV. 202 By hierarchization Piaget means that there is a constant order of succession of different levels of functioning constituting a genetic sequence. **1971** G. Steiner *In Bluebeard's Castle* iv. 88 An explicit grammar is an acceptance of order: it is a hierarchization..of the forces and valuations prevailing in the body politic.

hierarchy. 4. (Later examples.)

1932 Von Wiese & Becker *Systematic Sociology* 355 Whenever persons join or otherwise enter into a plurality pattern they almost invariably take their places in an implicit or explicit hierarchy, and consciously or unconsciously expect the fact that there are ranks above and below them. **1947** *Soc. Research* XIV. 165 This hierarchy, like any other, is a social order in which human relations are determined by the degree of authority exercised by one group over another. **1961** G. G. Simpson *Princ. Animal Taxon.* i. 13 A hierarchy is a systematic framework for zoological classification with a sequence of classes (or sets) at different levels in which each class except the lowest includes one or more subordinate classes. **1963** Davis & Heywood *Princ. Angiosperm Taxon.* iii. 75 Before we go on to discuss the taxonomic hierarchy, it will be as well to list the ranks.. which are accepted in the *International Code of Botanical Nomenclature.*

hieratite (həi·ĕrătəit). *Min.* [a. It. *hieratite* (A. Cossa 1882, in *Atti d. R. Accad. dei Lincei* (*Trans.*) VI. 141), f. *Hiera*, ancient name of Vulcano, one of the Lipari Islands: see -ite[1].] A colourless or greyish fluoride of potassium and silicon, K_2SiF_6, occurring in

stalactitic concretions in the crater of Vulcano and on Vesuvius.

The abstract cited in quot. 1882 consistently spells the word *hieralite*, although Cossa's form was *-tite*.

1882 *Jrnl. Chem. Soc.* XLII. 705 For this natural fluosilicate he proposes the name *hieralite*, from *Hiera*, the Greek name for the island Vulcano. Hieralite is associated in the concretions with selensulphur, realgar, mirabilite, [etc.]. **1951** C. Palache et al. *Dana's Syst. Min.* (ed. 7) II. 104 Hieratite is isostructural with the corresponding salts of Rb, Cs, Tl, and NH_4.

hieroglyphic, *sb.* **2. b.** (Further example.)

1853 Mrs. Gaskell *Cranford* xv. 296 About a year after Miss Matty set up shop, I received one of Martha's hieroglyphics, begging me to come to Cranford very soon.

hieromonach. Add: Also **hieromo·nk.**

1932 *Pax* Oct. 161 These are divided as follows: Maronite Antonians: 520 hieromonks, 221 monks. **1964** P. F. Anson *Bishops at Large* i. 37 Almost any alien calls himself..hieromonk..or any other Oriental ecclesiastical title.

hi-fi (həi·fəi·). [colloq. abbrev. of *high fidelity.] That part of acoustics and electronics that deals with the design, construction, and use of equipment for the recording and reproduction of sound to a fairly high standard. Also *attrib.* or as *adj.*, esp. **hi-fi equipment, set, system,** equipment for the home designed to reproduce (and sometimes to record) sound to such a standard, consisting often of several distinct units. Also *ellipt.* for *hi-fi equipment*, etc.

1950 *Audio Engin.* Aug. 24 (*title*) Hi-fi at seven-and-a-half. **1952** *Time* 22 Dec. 62/2 Until last week, most 'hi-fi' sets, which reproduce music in the home with the clarity and realism of the concert hall, were custom-made from standard parts by small radio and phonograph shops at a cost of from $150 to $2,000. **1953** *House & Garden* Dec. 132 (*heading*) What do they mean when they talk about hi-fi? **1953** *Life* 15 June 146/1 The name most generally used for this new kind of sound reproduction is high fidelity or 'hi-fi'. **1958** *Observer* 20 Apr. 10/6 The choice of a loudspeaker system is quite the most important task confronting those in search of 'Hi-Fi'. **1958** *Gramophone* June 35/1 The latest hi-fi developments. **1959** E. Fenwick *Long Way Down* x. 93 They had spent the evening working on their hi-fi system: three speakers, at different points, and miles of wiring. **1959** C. MacInnes *Absolute Beginners* 26, I put a disc on to his hi-fi. **1959** *Spectator* 20 Nov. 708/1 As recordings, they may not command the velvety tone, sumptuous presence and richly defined detail of the best of modern hi-fi. **1962** A. Nisbett *Technique Sound Studio* iii. 69 The full hi-fi treatment (in the sense, that is, of extended frequency response). *Ibid.* iv. 76 Hi-fi (a term which covers any sound equipment from medium quality upwards). *Ibid.* v. 98 Wide-range hi-fi, demanding not only high-quality transmissions but also a wide dynamic range. **1963** *Which?* Jan. 3/2 People may also want to consider hi-fi equipment. **1971** *Ibid.* June 187/1 Look for discounts in tape and hi-fi magazines. **1971** *Daily Tel.* 27 Aug. 17/6 The study thinks there is a continuing swing to quality but the lack of standards of what constitutes Hi-Fi is felt to be a disadvantage.

higgle (hi·g'l), *sb.* [f. the vb.] The adjusting of prices so that demand and supply are equal.

1908 *Daily Chron.* 5 Dec. 4/6 If they were abolished altogether the 'higgle of the market' would level freights correspondingly down.

hi:ggledipi·ggledness. Also **higgledy-piggledyness.** The quality or condition of being higgledy-piggledy.

1854 *Punch* 18 Nov. 204/1 That structural higgledipiggledness. **1918** A. Bennett *Roll-Call* I. i. 12 An agreeable and original higgledy-piggledyness!

higgledy. Abbrev. of Higgledy-piggledy.

a **1953** Dylan Thomas *Quite Early One Morning* (1954) 30 Neat and silly..they helped in the higgledy kitchen.

higgler. Add: **2. d.** (See quot.)

1930 M. Clark *Home Trade* 176 The term 'higgler' is applied in the Covent Garden market to a dealer who buys his supplies of fruit with a view to selling what he buys at a profit to any buyer, either on that market or on any other; to wholesalers or to retailers.

high, *a.* Add: **1. c.** Of clothes: high-necked.

1827 [see *canezou]. **1857** Mrs. Gaskell *Let.* 13 & 14 Sept. (1966) 471 My grey carmelite, & black moiré, high, & next to no collars. **187**– L. Troubridge *Life amongst Troubridges* (1966) x. 102, I had a chemisette to make my gown high, and no ornaments. **1937** J. Laver *Taste & Fashion* xiii. 185 In the early [eighteen-] sixties, it is interesting to note, there was less *décolletage* in good families in France than in England. The high dress was worn at dinner parties even of a formal kind. **1957** M. B. Picken *Fashion Dict.* 230/2 Boat-shaped neckline..high in front and back, wide at sides.

d. *Typogr.* (See quots.).

1683–4 J. Moxon *Mech. Exerc. Printing* (1962) 37 Head sticks..are Quadrat high, straight, and of an equal thickness all the length. **1888** C. T. Jacobi *Printers' Vocab.* 59 *High spaces*, spaces specially cast nearly type-high. **1904** Goodchild & Tweney *Technol. & Sci. Dict.* 287/2 *High*, a term applied to type or blocks which stand out in front of the rest of the type in the forme; *e.g.* new type stands higher than worn type. **1963** Kenneison & Spilman *Dict. Printing* 92 *High quads* (or *spaces*), spaces cast to the height of the shoulder of type.

4. a. Further examples of specialized meanings, esp. in *Athletics*. (Cf. sense * 17 i.)

1895 High hurdle, jump [see Jump *sb.*[1] 1 b]. **1897** *Encycl. Sport* I. 50/2 High jumping may be..a gift. *Ibid.* 51/2 High kicking is very useful during the off-season. **1924** C. W. Mason *Chinese Confessions* xliv. 326 The high-jump and hurdles were my specialities. **1955** *Athletics* ('Know the Game' Series) 15 High jumping: Western roll; straddle; Eastern cut-off. **1964** M. Watman *Encycl. Athletics* 83/1 Britain possessed two world class high hurdlers in the 1930s.

b. Hence in numerous adjectival *Combs.*, as *high-back, -central, -front, -mid, -mixed, -narrow, -rising.*

1888 H. Sweet *Hist. Eng. Sounds* i. 2 So we have altogether nine positions [of the tongue]: high-back.. high-mixed..high-front [etc.]. **1924** H. E. Palmer *Gram. Spoken Eng.* I. 13 High-Rising. Nucleus-tone. **1934** J. J. Hogan *Outl. Eng. Philol.* 15, *u*: high-back rounded, as in *wolf*. *Ibid.* 16, *oi*: mid-back rounded + high-front. **1934** Webster I. xxviii/2 In English a high-central vowel is not usual. **1951** Z. S. Harris *Methods in Struct. Ling.* 57 High-rising [intonation] for impatient question. **1961** R. B. Long *Sentence & its Parts* xix. 422 (*heading*) High-back /u/. **1962** *Amer. Speech* XXXVII. 169 This diphthong may be described as beginning at a somewhat retracted low-front position and terminating at an open, slightly rounded, high-central position. **1964** Jakobson & Halle in D. Abercrombie *Daniel Jones* 98 The 'high-narrow' vowels are particularly short. **1964** *Language* XL. 100 The sounds..are high-mid. **1965** *Canad. Jrnl. Linguistics* Fall 65 In each case the checked high-front, high-back..and mid-back vowels are paired with phonically similar free vowels. **1966** *Publ. Amer. Dial. Soc.* XLVI. 32 Long, unrounded, high-mid front vowel.

c. *high breast wheel* (see quots.).

1880 *Encycl. Brit.* XII. 522/2 Overshot and High Breast Wheels. *Ibid.* 523/2 With greater variation of head-water level, a pitch-back or high breast wheel is better. **1888** *Lockwood's Dict. Mech. Engin.* s.v. *Breast wheel*, When the water flows in at a point above the horizontal line, the wheel is termed high breast, and when at a point below, low breast.

5. *high life* (later examples). Also *high society*.

1801 M. Edgeworth *Belinda* I. ix. 277 He had merely considered her ladyship as an object of amusement, and an introduction to high life. **1853** Mrs. Gaskell *Cranford* viii. 140 One would not have Lady Glenmire think we were quite ignorant of the etiquettes of high life in Cranford. **1892** C. M. Yonge *That Stick* I. x. 106 Utterly inexperienced as she was, even in domestic, not to say high life. **1920** D. Parker (*title*) High society. **1955** 'E. C. R. Lorac' *Ask Policeman* iii. 28 Perhaps wealthy Australians were sent back to high-life schools in England in her day. **1971** 'D. Halliday' *Dolly & Doctor Bird* xi. 155 The police..would spoil the leisurely high-society image. Dirty little men running over the Begum's nice holiday island.

6. a. *high art* (earlier and later examples). Also *high comedy, culture.*

1817 B. Haydon *Autobiogr.* (1926) I. xvii. 266, I had, by my public devotion to High Art, a claim on all the nobility and opulent in the kingdom. **1848** Geo. Eliot *Let.* 11 Feb. (1954) I. 247, I cannot recognize the truth of all that is said about the necessity of religious fervour to high art. **1849** —— *Let.* 20 Sept. (1954) I. 308 She is a person of high culture according to the ordinary notions of what feminine culture should be. **1856** —— in *Westm. Rev.* IX. 3 High culture demands more complete harmony with its moral sympathies in humor than in wit. **1883** 'V. Lee' in P. Gunn *Vernon Lee* (1964) vii. 88 A long pseudo-medieval ballad... It felt so completely high art. **1895** G. B. Shaw *Our Theatres in Nineties* (1932) I. 106 After the exasperatingly bad acting one constantly sees at the theatres where high comedy and 'drama' prevail, it is a relief to see even simple work creditably done. **1906** E. Garnett in Defoe *Capt. Singleton* p. viii, Rembrandt's choice of beggars..for his favourite subjects seemed a low and reprehensible taste in 'high art'. **1919** G. B. Shaw *Heartbreak House* p. viii, The only part of our society in which there was leisure for high culture. **1963** *Observer* 12 May 28/3 Miss Murdoch is one of the sharpest writers of high comedy at present active in the theatre. **1964** Hall & Whannel *Popular Arts* I. ii. 55 These popular arts..were not objects of contemplation like the works of high art, but communal artifacts. **1966** D. Jenkins *Educated Society* ii. 50 High culture..tries to be creative in relation to the future and responsible in relation to the past.

d. Having a highly developed or complex organization; spec. *Biol.*, phylogenetically advanced or developed; often in the comparative degree, as *the higher apes, the higher plants.*

[**1807** W. Wood *Zoography* I. p. xii, If we ascend to a higher class of beings, and contemplate the extensive range of the animal creation.] **1848** J. Lindley *Introd. Bot.* (ed. 4) xvi. 323 Plants have no circulation of their fluids analogous to that of blood in the higher animals. **1867** H. Spencer *Princ. Biol.* § 364 Every type that is best adapted to its conditions, which on the average means every higher type, has a rate of multiplication that insures a tendency to predominate. **1875** *Encycl. Brit.* II. 168/1 As man is the highest animal. **1902** *Ibid.* XXVI. 366/1 The first is an amyloïn of a 'high', the second an amyloïn of a 'low' type. *Ibid.* XXVIII. 343/1 The gorilla and the chimpanzee, the highest members of the apes. *Ibid.*, The embryonic stages of higher forms. **1936** E. G. Boulenger *Apes & Monkeys* 15 The apes and higher monkeys are quite as much reliant for their various needs upon the ground as among the tree-boughs. **1954** H. I. Featherly *Taxon. Terminol. Higher Plants* 157 In the evolution of the higher plants, the greatest number of changes has come about in the reproductive organs. **1964** E. Becker in I. L. Horowitz *New Sociol.* 114 Separation anxiety of the helpless higher-primate infant is the pivot for his early learning. **1966** R. & D. Morris *Men & Apes* vi. 165 This is the point at which we pass from the lower primates (the prosimians) to the higher primates (the anthropoids), and consider the evolution of monkeys, apes and man.

8. b. Of the condition of an animal or of soil: resulting from over-feeding or from too great an application of manure. Also of a crop: produced by an over-manured soil.

1834 W. Youatt *Cattle* xvi. 553 This occurs particularly in young cows after their first calving, and when they are in a somewhat too high condition. **1886** C. Scott *Sheep Farming* 116 Hill ewes are never in too high condition; the danger is all the other way. **1902** *Encycl. Brit.* XXVI. 361/1 It is better not to grow barley after roots fed off by sheep, as this rotation leaves the land..in too 'high' a condition... By taking barley as a second corn crop, the latter following roots fed off, or a 'high' crop, [etc.].

9. a. (Earlier example.)

c **1807** Jane Austen *Watsons* (1954) 344 As the partridges were pretty high, Dr Richards would have them sent away to the other end of the Table.

b. Of tobacco: moist. *U.S.*

1850 *Rep. U.S. Comm. Patents, Agric. 1849* 322 Tobacco should not be too moist, or 'high' as it is termed, when put in the stalk-bulks. **1865** *Trans. Ill. Agric. Soc.* V. 669 Care must be taken that the tobacco does not imbibe too much moisture, or get too high in case before it is bulked.

10. a. *high explosive*: see *explosive *sb.* 2.

e. Of money: lent out at a high rate of interest; dear.

1899 *Daily News* 31 Mar. 3/5 New York... Higher money.

g. *Naut.* Near the wind: designating a vessel or its head when pointing close to the wind, as in the command *no higher.*

a **1865** Smyth *Sailor's Word-bk.* (1867), No Higher! **1948** R. de Kerchove *Internat. Maritime Dict.*, No higher!

h. In card-playing: *ace high* (*king high*, etc.): having the ace (king, etc.) as highest card: said of the hand or suit, also *occas.* of the person. Cf. *ace 4.

1887 S. Cumberland *Queen's Highway* 276 Had I a 'flush' with 'king high' some one would be sure to rake in the shekels with 'ace high'. **1964** N. Squire *Bidding at Bridge* xxi. 172 You may rely upon two defensive tricks when your partner opens the bidding. These may not be in the actual suit he mentions, because it might, for example, be Knave high. **1973** D. Westheimer *Going Public* v. 79 Margo drew the low hand, a nine-high nothing. 'Poker never was my game,' he said cheerfully.

11. b. *spec.* Of a period of time: fully developed, at its peak.

1930 Baedeker *Northern Italy* (ed. 15) 622 The fine *Palazzo Larderel*.., formerly *Palazzo Giacomini*, in the High Renaissance style, by Giovanni Antonio Dosio (1558–80). **1934** *Burlington Mag.* Jan. 14/1 The usual technique of the high renaissance outside Venice. **1944** *Ibid.* Jan. 13/2 He was sufficiently adaptable to learn..some later developments of the High Renaissance. **1956** K. Clark *Nude* ix. 341 The root of high-renaissance taste. **1961** Webster (s.v. *high* adj. 1 b), The high middle ages. **1962** *Listener* 18 Oct. 601/1 This happened during the mid-sixteenth century, in the aftermath of the High Renaissance. **1964** C. S. Lewis *Discarded Image* vii. 182 Hence a modern finds those [chronicles] of the Dark Ages suspiciously epic and those of the High Middle Ages suspiciously romantic. **1965** K. Charlton *Educ. Renaissance Eng.* ii. 21 Such was the education of the High Middle Ages. **1972** *Country Life* 23 Mar. 696/3 The high Victorian Gothic style.

16. (Further examples of *high* (*old*) *time*, etc.)

1833 C. A. Davis *Lett. J. Downing* (1834) 177 Just after breakfast yesterday, I and the gineral had a high time [i.e. a heated argument] together. **1858** *Spirit of Times* 30 Jan. 345/1 Our friends..are having a real 'high old time' generally, just now, in trotting on the ice. **1869** B. Harte *Luck of Roaring Camp* (1871) 226 These are high old times, ain't they? **1870** D. J. Kirwan *Palace & Hovel* xxxi. 470 That's a werry 'igh old game is the Canteen; sort of priveet like. **1873** J. H. Beadle *Undevel. West* xxiii. 451 Santa Fe De San Francisco—so the old Spaniards named it—is a high old city. **1899** R. Whiteing *No. 5 John St.* III. xxi. 215 'Ah, they was 'igh old times!' is his final word. **1941** E. Bowen *Look at Roses* 255 Those two will be having a high old time, with the cat away. **1955** J. Potts *Death of Stray Cat* ii. 11 You probably had a high old time chasing blondes. **1962** N. Marsh *Hand in Glove* vii. 235 We picked him up ..having a high old time with the boxer bitch.

b. Phr. *high as a kite*: very drunk.

1939 *Amer. Speech* XIV. 90/2 *High as a kite*, completely drunk. *a* **1966** M. Allingham *Cargo of Eagles* (1968) iv. 54 He..gave them a champagne lunch in a marquee..and held a sale. By then everyone was as high as a kite.

c. Under the influence of, stimulated by, a drug or drugs. Freq. const. *on.*

1932 *Evening Sun* (Baltimore) 9 Dec. 31/4 *High*, under the influence of a narcotic. **1940** *Amer. Speech* XV. 337/1 *To be high*, to be contented from the drug. **1951** *N.Y. Times* 13 June 24/5 We would go out together and get high. I used to sleep with him whenever we got high. **1951** *San Diego Even. Tribune* 28 June a-1/4 He'd been 'getting high' on heroin week-end after week-end. **1957** C. MacInnes *City of Spades* I. x. 72 Hamilton's acquaintances.. rocking high with charge. **1961** *Spectator* 17 Nov. 712 The momentary kick when the drug is taken, when you're 'high'. **1969** *New Scientist* 29 May 455/1 It is far safer to drive a car when high on marihuana than when drunk. **1970** 'D. Shannon' *Unexpected Death* (1971) i. 9 He an

his pal Roderick Drover had had some boyish fun last week sniping at an innocent driver—probably while high on something.

d. Highly interested in, keen *on*. *slang.*

1942 Berrey & Van den Bark *Amer. Thes. Slang* § 274/5 *Enthusiastic about*..high on. **1966** L. Deighton *Billion-Dollar Brain* xxii. 240 It 's about Signe... She 's high on you, you know. **1972** *Guardian* 30 Oct. 2/5 'I am not high on the Thieu brand of Government,' he [*sc.* McGovern] said, noting that 40,000 people had been executed..by it.

17. a. *high and dry*: further *fig.* examples. Also used in sense 'safe'. Also earlier example of the ecclesiastical sense.

1838 Dickens *Let.* 26 July (1965) I. 421, I no sooner get myself up, high and dry, to attack him [*sc.* Oliver Twist] manfully than up come the waves of each month's work. **1853** Bunsen *Let.* in *Life & Wks. Kingsley* (1901) II. 112 You know of the persecution of the Evangelicals, and High and dry against Maurice. **1881** E. W. Hamilton *Diary* 18 June (1972) I. 146 Meanwhile, Dr. Flood's successor had been appointed, and Dr. Flood was left high and dry without preferment owing to an undoubted breach of faith on the part of Duckworth. **1927** J. Galsworthy *Castles in Spain* 169 A true work of art remains beautiful and living, though an ebb tide of fashion may leave it for the moment high and dry on the beach. **1941** W. S. Maugham *Writer's Notebk.* (1949) 305 The river has flowed on and left him high and dry on the bank. The writer has his little hour..but an hour is soon past. **1960** *Times* 30 Aug. 11/6 Cella's back-heel, so deceptive, so utterly unexpected, left Rossano high and dry.

f. *high-and-mighty*: also used *absol. high-and-mightiness* (earlier example).

1804 M. Wilmot *Let.* 24 Apr. in *Russ. Jrnls.* (1934) I. 94 The High and Mighty then go into..another little room well heated. **1852** C. M. Yonge *Two Guardians* xiii. 246 That touch of Edmund's, which had shown her how he regarded her 'high-and-mightiness', had made her..ashamed. **1905** G. B. Shaw in *Grand Mag.* Feb. 116 Our high and mighties didn't exactly see the point. **1924** J. Galsworthy *White Monkey* II. ii, Mr. Mont 's a gent.. no high-and-mighty about *him*.

i. *to be for the high jump*: see *jump *sb.*[1] 7 and *high *a.* 4 a.

j. *high, wide, and handsome* (and similar phrases), in a carefree manner, in good style (see also quot. 1971). orig. *U.S.*

1907 S. E. White *Arizona Nights* 35 Tim could talk high, wide, and handsome when he set out to. **1932** 'Spindrift' *Yankee Slang* 21 *High, wide and handsome*, in good or great style. Common shout at a rodeo: 'Ride him, Cowboy, high, wide and handsome.' **1939** Wodehouse *Uncle Fred in Springtime* iii. 50 He has a nasty way of lugging Pongo out into the open and..proceeding to step high, wide and plentiful. **1958** L. van der Post *Lost World of Kalahari* (1961) vii. 155 The day was riding high, wide and handsome into the deeps of the incredible blue sky. **1971** J. Wainwright *Last Buccaneer* II. 234 The cops 'll be high, wide and helpless. They won't know what in hell's hit 'em.

21. high camp, 'camp' (**sb.*[5]) of a sophisticated kind (in quot. 1963 used adjectivally); also (with hyphen) *attrib.*; so *high campery*; **high command** (see *command *sb.* 7 b); **high commission** (see Commission *sb.*[1] 7); **high commissioner** (see *commissioner 1 c); **high contrast** *Photogr.* (see quot. 1940); also (with hyphen) *attrib.*; **high country** *N.Z.*, hilly country that is difficult of access; freq. *attrib.*; *Canada* [tr. Canad. F. *haut pays*], the hinterland, the forests of N. and North-west Canada; hence **high countryman**; **high dilutionist** *Homœopathy*, an advocate of extreme dilution of medicine; **high farming,** the extensive use of fertilizers in land cultivation; **high finance,** finance concerned with large sums of money; **high forest,** a forest composed wholly or chiefly of trees raised from seed; also, in more general use, a forest of lofty trees (cf. G. *hochwald*); also *attrib.*; **high-fusing** *a.* (see quot. 1940); **high grinding** = *high milling* (Milling *vbl. sb.* 1 a); **high hook** *colloq.* or *slang*, the angler of a party who hooks the largest fish; **high-key** *Photogr.* (see quots.); **high kick** *Dancing*, a kick in the air, esp. one executed simultaneously by a row of female dancers and repeated by raising each leg in turn; also (with *high* used adverbially) **high-kick** *v.*, **high-kicking** *vbl. sb.* and *ppl. a.*; so *high-kicker*; **high lead** *Forestry* (see quot. 1957); also (with hyphen) *attrib.*, as *high-lead logging*; **high life,** a West African dance; also (with hyphen) *attrib.*; **high line,** (*a*) *Fishing* (*N. Amer. colloq.* or *slang*), the person who, or the boat which, has the best haul during a specified time; occas. a good catch; also *attrib.*; so **high liner**; (*b*) *Forestry*, an overhead cable attached to a spar tree in logging; so *high-line logging*; **high-lining** *vbl. sb.*; **high-low bed** (see quot. 1964); **high mass** (see Mass *sb.*[1] 3 a, High *a.* 19 b); **high milling** (see Milling *vbl. sb.* 1 a); **high place,** also, in *pl.*, the upper echelon of any organization; **high polymer,** a polymer with a high molecular weight; also (with hyphen) *attrib.*; **high-rise** *a.*, of a building, tall, multi-storey; also *transf.*; as *sb.*, a tall building; also occas. **hi-rise**; **high sign** *colloq.*, a surreptitious sign indicating **that all** is well or that the coast is clear; so **high-sign** *v.*; **high spot** (freq. in *pl.*) *slang*, the outstanding part or feature of something; *to hit the high spots*, to go to excess or extremes; to rise to a very high level; to include or touch on the most important points or places; cf. *high light 2; **high step,** (*a*) a military step in which the feet and knees are raised high; also (with hyphen) *attrib.*; (*b*) in *pl.*, a step-ladder; **high stool,** a tall stool; **high tea** (earlier and later examples); **high-tensile,** used *attrib.* of steel or other metals possessing great tensile strength; **high wine,** wine containing a high percentage of alcohol; **high wire,** a high tight-rope; **high yaller, yellow,** a half-caste of light yellow complexion; also as *adj. phr.*; **high-yield, -yielding,** designating something that furnishes or produces a large or valuable, etc., product or return.

1954 High camp [see *camp *a.* (and *sb.*[5])]. **1963** *Punch* 5 June 830/1 Gerda Charles..makes her young, with-it, high camp. **1964** *New Statesman* 6 Mar. 373/2 The..show starts depressingly, and the aura of high camp threatens to asphyxiate. **1968** *Listener* 27 June 843/2 The melodramatic trappings might have had a certain aesthetic high-camp value. **1967** *Spectator* 1 Dec. 690/3 Witness in this exhibition the high campery of the Coldstream Guards in 1821. **1940** A. L. M. Sowerby *Dict. Photogr.* (ed. 15) 157 A negative is said to have high contrast if tones but slightly different in the original subject show marked differences in the negative. **1961** G. Millerson *Technique Telev. Production* iii. 47 Subject contrast must be kept down, by preventing high-contrast surfaces appearing in the same shot. **1967** Karch & Buber *Offset Processes* iii. 64 High-contrast photography may be used. **1874** A. Bathgate *Colonial Experiences* xv. 212 Squatters whose runs include high country. **1903** S. E. White *Forest* 278 The base-line..was the only evidence of man we saw in the high country. **1930** L. G. D. Acland *Early Canterbury Runs* 1st Ser. i. 8 The severe snow storms..used up several years' profits of high country runholders. **1942** G.Campbell *Thorn-Apple Tree* 152 Some time again we winter in the high country, maybe. **1947** D. McEldowney in D. M. Davin *N.Z. Short Stories* (1953) 379 The grass was sharp and scanty on the unfertilised high country soil. **1950** *N.Z. Jrnl. Agric.* Apr. 364/1 The merino..bred..for sale to high-country runs [in Canterbury]. **1972** P. Newton *Sheep Thief* xiv. 110 He was full of questions about the country and it was obvious that his one ambition was to become a high country musterer. **1922** C. G. Turner *Happy Wanderer* 51 The high-countryman may drink his cheque. **1847** *Brit. Jrnl. Homœopathy* V. 154 We can no more reject the conclusions of the high dilutionists than we can despise those of their opponents. **1892** High dilutionist [see Dilutionist]. **1848** Mill *Pol. Econ.* I. 215 To apply the high farming of Europe to any American lands. **1894** G. B. Shaw in *Fortn. Rev.* LXI. 480 High farming cannot increase the natural rent of an acre. **1931** C. S. Orwin (*title*) High farming. **1966** *Listener* 1 Sept. 307/2 By 1939 British agriculture..had ceased to rely on the high farming we had developed in our own land. **1905** *McClure's Mag.* XXV. 48 In other words, we could eat our cake and have it, too—which is one secret of high finance. **1934** L. Mumford in W. Frank *Amer. & Alfred Steglitz* ii. 50 Advertising, insurance, and high finance, the divine trinity that rules the world of industry. **1936** *Discovery* Sept. 280/2 It is not big guns nor even high finance that ultimately rules the world. **1879** *Encycl. Brit.* IX. 398/2 In..Germany..care is always taken that in high forest there is a good stock of self-sown trees before the old crop is entirely removed. **1927** *Forestry* I. 1. 24 The three main forestry systems, High Forest, Coppice-with-Standards, and Coppice. **1938** C. P. Ackers *Pract. Brit. Forestry* 9 High forest may be subdivided into..clear felling..and..the selective system. **1953** *Brit. Commonw. Forest Terminol.* I. 151 *High Forest Systems*, crops normally of seedling origin, either natural or artificial or a combination of both. Rotation usually long. **1955** *Jrnl. Ecol.* XLIII. 572 It will be referred to in this paper simply as 'High Forest', the adjective 'high' being used in a double sense to indicate that both the trees themselves are lofty and in the more specialized sense of the forester, to indicate that they have grown uninterrupted by coppicing or pollarding. **1959** *Times* 2 June 12/6 Growing conifers as high forest. **1911** G. H. Wilson *Man. Dental Prosthetics* viii. 313 The high fusing porcelains are practically insoluble. **1940** J. Osborne *Dental Mechanics* xxii. 412 Porcelains used in dentistry may be divided into two types according to their fusing temperatures: (1) *High fusing*, those whose fusing temperature is above the melting point of gold. (2) *Low fusing*, those whose fusing point is below 1065°C. **1956** J. N. Anderson *Appl. Dent. Mat.* xxiv. 330 For high-fusing porcelains, the furnace may be preheated. **1875** *Miller* May 55/1 (*title*) The Hungarian system of high grinding. *Ibid.*, In such mills..the whole of the high-grinding system was carried out. *a* **1884** Knight *Dict. Mech.* Suppl. 457/2 *High grinding*, a process of gradual reduction of the wheat by a succession of partial crushings, alternating with sifting and sorting the product. **1945** J. F. Lockwood *Flour Milling* xvii. 283 The wheat could either be rapidly and roughly reduced to flour by setting the two stones very close together, a process called low grinding, or the reduction could be made slowly and carefully with the stones further apart; this was called high grinding. **1848** in *D.A.E.*, *High hook*, the one who catches the largest or the greatest quantity of fish. **1894** *Outing* (U.S.) XXIV. 259/2 F. was high hook with a five and a half pounder. **1918** *Photo-Miniature* XV. Mar. (Gloss.), *High-key*, a style of photographic print (portrait or landscape) consisting entirely of light tones, differing little from each other in depth. **1919** *Brit. Jrnl. Photogr. Alm.* 250 Photographs consisting almost entirely of light tones are said to be high-key. **1967** E. Chambers *Photolitho-offset* xi. 158 For high-key work, such as pencil sketches where delicate high-light detail has to be retained in offset printing, the Sears method of making a continuous tone negative..is used. **1898** G. B. Shaw *Our Theatres in Nineties* (1932) III. 336 The four beauteous ladies who, though apparently competent dancers, persist in punctuating their evolutions with graceless high kicks. **1906** E. Dyson *Fact'ry 'Ands* vii. 89 He came out on ther John's arm, 'igh kickin', 'n' singin' fit t' split. **1914** R. Brooke *Let.* 3 Sept. (1968) 613 The play was too foolish for words... Not a high-kick or a wriggle or a ragtime song in the whole thing! **1933** P. Godfrey *Back-Stage* xv. 194 Their white-washed legs..are doing energetic high-kicks and splits. *Ibid.* xviii. 224 They tap-dance, high-kick, turn cartwheels, and do the splits. **1962** A. Huxley *Island* xiii. 223 'What sort of dancing does he teach?' Mrs Narayan tried to describe it. No leaps, no high kicks, no running. **1966** 'J. Hackston' *Father clears Out* 92 He had high-kicked the boss at the ..store for a fiver and had won by an ankle. **1896** W. Stevens *Let.* 31 July (1967) 9 A plain little horse though a high-kicker. **1897** Kipling *Capt. Cour.* iv. 103 There's somethin' of a sea to-night... She *is* a high-kicker. **1897** G. B. Shaw *Our Theatres in Nineties* (1932) III. 12 Cancanist high-kickers. **1922** Joyce *Ulysses* 359 Skirt-dancers and highkickers. **1895** High-kicking [see Split *sb.*[1] 4 b]. **1901** *Daily Chron.* 11 Dec. 6/5 Several dancers of the high-kicking and other schools. **1925** A. Philip *Crimson West* 144 He yawned sleepily. 'Got to fix a "spar-tree" for a "high-lead" to-morrow, so I better hit the hay.' **1939** Beaulieu & Barton *Appl. Lumber Sci.* (ed. 2) 35 The High-Lead is the most common method of yarding by steam. **1951** W. F. Heald *Scenic Guide to Oregon* 17 Modern 'high lead' and 'skidder' logging whisks tree sections. **1957** *N.Z. Timber Jrnl.* Aug. 59/1 *High lead*, extraction of timber by means of overhead cable attached to a high spar at hauler end. This gives the front end of logs sufficient lift to clear obstructions during haul. **1955** *Times* 23 Aug. 10/6 'High lifes', marches, songs in the vernacular of dubious propriety. **1959** A. Abbs *Ashanti Boy* vi. 212 He has a big collection of high-life records. **1959** *Guardian* 22 Dec. 5/2 Man, I've got a..West African band... They play high life. **1963** *Listener* 14 Mar. 456/1 A Ghanaian band was playing 'highlife' music for dancing. *Ibid.*, Highlife is as distinctively New African as the Kwela music played and danced to in Johannesburg at the other end of the continent. **1856** C. Nordhoff *Whaling & Fishing* xviii. 354 Several had at different times been 'high line' from Harwich. **1864** *Harper's Mag.* Feb. 367/2 Captain Aleck was determined to fish for 'high line'. **1885** J. S. Kingsley *Stand. Nat. Hist.* III. 196 The emulation to be 'high-line' for the day and for the season is extreme. *Ibid.*, In a single day a high-line fisherman has caught from ten to fifteen barrels. **1890** *Grip* (Toronto) 5 Apr. 233/2 Always 'high line', he was always 'filled up' with the split mackerel of the North Bay. **1929** F. C. Bowen *Sea Slang* 66 *High line*, on the Grand Banks a particularly good catch, also applied to the most successful fishing boat or clipper of the season. **1931** *Amer. Speech* VII. 49 The man who..attaches the 'high line' is called a 'skyrigger'. *Ibid.*, A 'high line', which is of one-inch steel, extends, often one-half mile, to either end of the 'set'. **1965** *Brit. Columbia Digest* Sept.–Oct. 19/1 Mobile spar trees, which are monstrous self-propelled cranes whose thick booms bear a multiplicity of sheaves and cables, are used in modern high-line logging to replace the spar trees used until recently as the focal point for the complicated system of cables and pulley-blocks. **1893** in *Funk's Stand. Dict.*, High-liner. **1914** W. D. Steele *Storm* 56 On the grounds he was a great 'killer', an unmerciful 'driver', and for three years running now the 'high liner' of the Old Harbor fleet. **1916** F. W. Wallace *Shack Locker* 65, I ain't a highliner this season, but we've got one thing to brag about when it comes to fishin'. **1965** *Brit. Columbia Digest* Sept.–Oct. 20/1 But many [high-riggers] just disappeared, as did the giant trees they had topped, limbed and rigged for high-lining. **1964** G. D. Cherescavich *Textbk. Nursing Assistants* vii. 52 *High-low bed*, an electrically or manually operated bed which can be raised to the height of the regular hospital bed and lowered to the height of the home bed. **1967** *Nursing Times* 18 Aug. 1088/2 There are many types of variable height beds (sometimes called high-low beds). **1918** L. Strachey *Eminent Victorians* 245 There were rumours of debaucheries in high places. **1922** G. M. Trevelyan *Brit. Hist. 19th Cent.* iii. 54 Evangelicalism brought rectitude, unselfishness and humanity into high places. **1931** F. W. Crofts *Myst. in Channel* xviii. 227 Persons in high places made comments. **1931** *Economist* 10 Oct. 656/1 Any talk at this moment in 'high places' of the abandonment of the gold standard would be quite likely to result in a stampede. **1938** *Archit. Rev.* LXXXIII. p. lvi, It is to be hoped that the contents..have percolated through to the authorities and those in 'high places' whose responsibility it is to plan ahead for the future of road transport in this country. **1971** G. Household *Doom's Caravan* ii. 54 'It was her mother's correspondence which I feared might be of interest to enemy agents.' 'That has already been taken care of in high places.' **1946** *Nature* 27 July 122/1 The most important new dielectrics are usually of the high-polymer type. *Ibid.* 19 Oct. 553/1 (*heading*) Effect of environment on the reactivity of high polymers. **1968** Greenwood & Banks *Synthetic High Polymers* i. 3 A high polymer is simply a chemical substance which is made up of giant molecules. **1954** *Archit. Rev.* CXVI. 414/2 In general form—podium and high-rise accommodation—this scheme follows the general pattern of current thought. **1958** *Listener* 20 Nov. 827/1 A point block of government offices is now going up at Wellington..and other high-rise slabs for offices and flats. **1961** *Observer* 7 Jan. 17/4 When one high-rise building is surrounded by many similar structures, height alone loses this special distinction. **1965** in *Amer. Speech* (1967) XLII. 159 Roosevelt

Grier: the high-rise football star of the L. A. Rams. 1967 Boston Sunday Herald 26 Mar. I. 41/4 (Advt.), The convenience and prestige of a luxury high-rise. 1967 Time 20 Oct. 60 She likes the high-rise boots because 'they give my legs a sleek stocking look'. 1968 Globe & Mail (Toronto) 13 Jan. 45 (Advt.), Adult hi-rise building. Ibid. 17 Feb. 12 Block-heeled pump with high-rise vamp. 1903 R. L. McCardell Conversat. Chorus Girl 111 When who should peek-a-boo in but my friend!..I gave him the high sign, but he passed me up. 1928 Sunday Dispatch 29 July 2 He gave the pawnbroker the high-sign. 1946 Wodehouse Joy in Morning xxv. 229 As soon as he is in a melting mood, you give me the high sign, and I carry on from there. 1957 Amer. Ballads & Folk Songs 135 She was pleadin' with him, her eyes all teary and dim, As I high-signed the barkeep for mine. 1962 L. Deighton Ipcress File xii. 72 He gave us the high sign with thumb touching forefinger. 1962 K. Orvis Damned & Destroyed xxv. 185, I high-signed him to follow. 1910 W. M. Raine B. O'Connor 12 Here comes your train a-foggin'—also and likewise hittin' the high spots. 1926 Spectator 11 Sept. 373/1 Chicago was the 'high-spot' of the trip. 1927 Daily Express 15 Sept. 9/5 The 'high spot' of the production—cinematic equivalent to the chariot-racing scenes in 'Ben-Hur'. 1928 Sunday Dispatch 22 July 23/4 It looks as though the standard of racing is going to hit the high spots. 1936 Economist 29 Feb. 483/1 The 'high-spot' was the 20 per cent. dividend (against 10 per cent.) announced by Associated Portland Cement. 1936 'J. Tey' Shilling for Candles iv. 48 Two years of hitting the high spots must have educated you to something. 1961 J. Carter ABC for Book-Collectors 111 'High spot' collecting is a sort of dictated eclecticism. 1964 Publishers' Weekly 28 Sept. 59 (heading), Religious books. Some Fall highspots, September through December. 1889 Infantry Drill I. I. 32 The High Step. 1894 Mrs. Alexander Choice of Evils II. viii. 199 He was exceedingly busy with hammer and nails, and the 'high steps', putting up fresh curtains. 1969 Daily Tel. (Colour Suppl.) 10 Jan. 32/1 The music [of the Celts] is the wail of the bagpipe, played to the jig and the fling and the high-step whirl. 1825 H. Wilson Mem. III. 76 The Duchess of Beaufort..appears never so happy nor so comfortable as when he is perched upon a high stool by her side. 1837 Dickens Pickw. l. 538 A high stool, four chairs, a table, and an old eight-day clock. 1892 C. M. Yonge That Stick I. xiii. 139 Whatever promise there may have been..must have been nipped upon the top of a high stool. 1935 G. Greene England made Me I. 1 For half an hour she had sat on the same high stool, half turned from the counter. 1961 Guardian 14 Nov. 10/3 He sat on a high stool [at a bar]. 1831 F. A. Kemble Rec. Girlhood 14 June (1878) III. 49 We did not return home till near nine, and so, instead of dinner, all sat down to high tea. 1922 W. S. Maugham Chinese Screen xlix. 193 He thought of the high tea to which he sat down when he came home from school.., a slice of cold meat, a great deal of bread and butter and plenty of milk in his tea. 1957 London Mag. Nov. 53 We ate high-tea made of fresh salmon, or mushrooms we'd risen at dawn to gather. 1923 Man. Seamanship (H.M.S.O.) II. 263 All material contributing to the longitudinal strength [of a ship's hull] is of high tensile steel. 1932 Discovery May 146/2 High tensile irons, corrosion-resisting irons, and growth-resisting irons are now made in large quantities. 1937 Archit. Rev. LXXXI. 268 (caption) Right, a welded tubular bus frame seat, utilizing the strength of high-tensile alloy tube. c 1384 Heiȝe wynes [see High a. 8]. 1542 Boorde Dyetary (1870) x. 254 Hyghe wynes, as malmyse, maye be kepte longe. 1871 Trans. Ill. Agric. Soc. VIII. 143 The necessity would still exist for converting..corn into beef and pork and highwines. a 1884 Knight Dict. Mech. Suppl. 458/1 High wines, crude alcohol of higher proof than singlings. 1958 J. Carew Black Midas vi. 112 They drank highwine and bush rum from half-pint tumblers. 1961 Webster, High wire. 1962 Listener 10 May 822/3 The bulk of the poems go all out for intellectual sophistication... He is not at his ease on the intellectual high wire. 1962 Observer 23 Sept. 26/5 A clown picking dust off his suit on the high wire. 1923 J. Dos Passos Streets of Night 133 Ought to see them high yallers down there if you're stuck on girls. 1929 Variety 17 Apr. 51/3 She looks like a genuine high-yaller (that being her make-up in buxom mammy fashion). 1929 T. Wolfe Look Homeward, Angel (1930) II. xxii. 318 There's a High Yaller in here... You can have that if you want it. 1937 Wyndham Lewis Blasting & Bombardiering IV. viii. 241 At present I should be living in a villa just outside Paris with a Japanese cook and a Zulu butler, with three highyaller kids getting ready to go to Eton. 1947 'N. Shute' Chequer Board iii. 61 [He] had played and danced with various mulatto and 'high yaller' girls back home in Nashville. 1951 M. Kennedy Lucy Carmichael I. iii. 25 She isn't exactly black... She's high yellow. 1969 'J. Morris' Fever Grass xviii. 158 The big high yellow nodded at him with impersonal cordiality. 1957 High yield [see low-yield adj. s.v. *low a. 23]. 1958 Times 12 Sept. 10/1 A high yield nuclear device was successfully exploded. 1959 Britannica Bk. of Year 546/1 Another new term was high-yield explosion, an atomic explosion powerful enough to produce various widely felt and easily registered phenomena. 1960 Farmer & Stockbreeder 16 Feb. 66/3 He was no 'high-yield' merchant, but he would compare his profits..with any..breeder. 1970 Daily Tel. 16 Feb. 17 (Advt.), The aim of High-Yield Units is to give the highest return consistent with reasonable security of capital. 1946 Nature 12 Oct. 522/1 High-yielding herds. 1956 Ibid. 3 Mar. 416/1 The cocoa trade has accepted the very high-yielding Upper Amazon selections..as conforming to its quality requirements.

b. high-liver, (*a*) (earlier example); **high-ranker,** a person of high rank.

1881 J. W. Buel Border Outlaws 166 All the band were known to be high livers during their periods of plenty. 1953 P. C. Berg Dict. New Words 93/1 High-ranker, a person of high rank, esp. in one of the Services. 1958 W. J. H. Sprott Human Groups ix. 147 When he played against a gang high-ranker, he was seldom 'on form'. 1973 J. Wainwright Pride of Pigs 18 High-rankers and C.I.D. wallahs bobbing in and out.

22. a. *high-accuracy, -amplitude, -carbon, conductivity, -cost, -current, -density, -efficiency, -energy, -fat, -field, -gain, -hurdle, -impedance, -income, -intensity, -investment, -nitrogen, -octane, -order, -output, -performance, -permeability, -potency, -potential, -power, -precision, -pressure* (further examples; also as *vb.*), *-prestige, -price, -protein, -purity, -quality, -resistance, -resolution, -risk, -stability, -status, -strength, -tension, -test, -tone, -vacuum, -value, -wage*; **high-altitude,** occurring, working, or carried out at high altitudes; **high-angle** *Gunnery*, denoting the fire from guns, mortars, etc., at a high angle of elevation; hence *high-angle gun*, etc.; also *transf.*, as of a camera; **high-board,** of or relating to diving from a high diving-board; **high-duty,** (*a*) subject to heavy customs duty; (*b*) designed to perform heavy tasks; = *heavy-duty* (*HEAVY *a.*[1] 24 b); **high-fashion** (see *FASHION *sb.* 9 c); **high-flash,** denoting oil whose vapour ignites only at a relatively high temperature; **high-flux,** denoting (*a*) a high density of magnetic flux; (*b*) a large number of elementary particles per second; **high-humidity** *Forestry*, of the treatment of timber by exposing it to high humidity for a specified purpose; **high-level,** situated, built, etc., in, or carried out from, a high position; denoting talks, a meeting, etc., of an exalted status or grade; in the field of *Computers*, applied to a programming language that is largely independent of any particular kind of computer and bears some resemblance to an existing language (as English) or symbolism; **high-lift,** of something that is raised high or that lifts something up high; **high-pass** *Electr.*, denoting a filter that attenuates components with a frequency less than some cut-off frequency and passes components of higher frequency; **high-sea(s),** operating or carried out on the high seas; *High Sea Fleet* = G. *Hochsee Flotte*; **high-velocity,** of high speed; *spec.* denoting a gun capable of discharging a projectile with great force and speed; also denoting the projectile so fired; **high-warp,** denoting a manner of weaving or tapestry in which the warp is vertical.

1958 Listener 13 Nov. 779/1 The manufacture of high-accuracy gyroscopes. 1963 B. Fozard Instrumentation Nuclear Reactors ix. 105 (heading) High-accuracy ratemeters. 1925 E. F. Norton Fight for Everest, 1924 86 [They] were both suffering from very bad high-altitude throat. Ibid. 106 This hateful duty of high-altitude cooking. 1955 E. Hillary High Adventure 58 We signed on ten Sherpas to act as high-altitude porters. 1966 Electronics 3 Oct. 181 Also in the national space lineup is project '621', aimed at developing recoverable high-altitude sounding rockets. 1956 Nature 21 Jan. 121/1 High-amplitude effects in reflexion amplifiers. 1879 Man. Artill. Exerc. I. v. 23 High-angle fire from howitzers and mortars. 1890 G. S. Clarke Fortification xiv. 205 Large numbers of high-angle guns which would prove most formidable to ships. 1915 Pearson's Mag. XXXIX. 66 High-angle trajectory. 1928 C. F. S. Gamble N. Sea Air Station ix. 122 The addition of some motor-cars equipped with machine-guns on 'high-angle mountings'. 1956 Nature 17 Mar. 502/2 (caption) High-angle photographs from a carbonized coking coal. 1963 Listener 28 Mar. 569/2 The mere novelty (for television drama) of the high-angle viewpoint gave the shot a sly edge. 1936 Southern Counties' Amat. Swimming Assoc. Handbk. 12 The positions in National championships are..C. D. Tomalin..Highboard diving..1st. 1959 Times 22 Sept. 3/3 Phelps is the European and national highboard title-holder. 1937 Discovery May 156/1 High carbon (hyper-eutectoid) steel. 1958 Aspects of Translation 84 The melting of the high-carbon cast iron. 1909 Proc. R. Soc. A. LXXXII. 232 A small, adjustable, open, high-conductivity, self-induction spiral. 1940 Chambers's Techn. Dict. 415/2 High conductivity copper, metal of high purity, having an electrical conductivity not much below that of the international standard. 1931 G. B. Ford Building Height, Bulk & Form Title-p., Uneconomic types of buildings on high-cost land. 1964 Ann. Reg. 1963 259 German farmers were high-cost producers. 1949 Nature 17 Sept. 485/2 (heading) High-current betatron conditions. 1952 Ann. Reg. 1951 401 High-density..central city areas. 1960 Times 28 Sept. 21/7 New plastics such as high-density polyethylene. 1962 Listener 15 Nov. 806/2 The high density life of the town. 1964 M. A. Johnson in Oceanogr. & Marine Biol. II. 33 The possibility of high-density turbidity currents in the ocean. 1973 Times 14 Aug. 2/5 Housewives doing their washing yesterday stopped the pumping of high density foam into the damaged Liberian tanker. 1920 Ham's Yearbk. I. Customs 173 In the case of high-duty goods.. the issuing officer will send an advice..to the Inspector-General of Waterguard. 1923 R. T. Kent Kent's Mech. Engin. Handbk. (ed. 10) ix. 692 (heading) Table 44.—Direct-connected, electrically-driven, two-stage compressors,.. Sea level high duty. Air pressure of 100–115 lb. 1937 Times 13 Apr. p. xxii/2 A high-duty lubricant has been introduced to deal with high tooth pressures now usual in rear axle mechanism. 1947 Nature CLIX. 51 The production of still stronger high-duty irons. 1962 Simpson & Richards Junction Transistors ix. 202 A high-efficiency hole injector. 1938 Nature 29 Oct. 781/1 Excitation..is..due..to the production of numbers of fairly high-energy electrons. 1958 Listener 27 Nov. 871/1 Hoyle and Gold are convinced that the radio waves in these regions are emanating from high-energy particles moving in extensive magnetic fields. 1972 Physics Bull. Apr. 215/1 Bubble chambers are amongst the most widely used instruments in high energy physics for the detection of the tracks of ionizing particles. 1946 Nature 7 Sept. 350/1 A high-fat diet. 1943 Rep. Progress Physics IX. 184 Thermionic emission under the Schottky high-field condition. 1968 C. G. Kuper Introd. Theory Superconductivity vii. 130 Most of the Type II superconducting materials used for high-field magnets are rather 'dirty' metallurgically, and probably do contain normal inclusions. 1899 Westm. Gaz. 14 Feb. 4/3 A fourth high-flash oil. 1904 Goodchild & Tweney Technol. & Sci. Dict. 278/2 High flash point, oil whose vapour is only ignited at a high temperature. 1949 Wireless World Apr. 137/1 A high-flux version (Type R22) of the single diaphragm T2 is now available with a density of 17,500 gauss in the $1\frac{3}{4}$ in diameter gap. 1955 Bull. Atomic Sci. Mar. 93/2 A high-flux heavy water reactor primarily intended to investigate radiation damage in reactor building materials. 1971 New Scientist 3 June 579/1 The Franco-German high-flux reactor in Grenoble. 1936 Nature 11 July 87/1 The apparatus was designed to detect the presence of destructive insects in timber, and consists of a sound-proof chest, a sensitive microphone and a high-gain amplifier. 1962 F. I. Ordway et al. Basic Astronautics v. 176 (caption) High-gain communications antenna. 1925 H. L. Henderson in Bull. N.Y. State College Forestry XXV. xvi. 65 Another method is to use the high humidity treatment... This process will balance up the moisture percentages in less than 24 hours. 1957 N.Z. Timber Jrnl. Aug. 59/1 High humidity treatment, temporarily raising the humidity of the circulating air in a kiln when drying wood requiring special treatment. 1893 Outing (U.S.) XXII, The following fall..Harding was third in the high-hurdle race. 1949 Wireless World Apr. 136/1 There seems to be a trend towards the use of high-impedance windings in high-fidelity pickups. 1937 Amer. Speech XII. 315/2 His store..makes little attempt to attract a high-income clientele. 1937 Discovery Feb. 45/1 For production of the screen image a high intensity automatic arc is being used. 1962 F. I. Ordway et al. Basic Astronautics iii. 68 High-intensity solar ultraviolet radiation. 1960 Encounter XV. iv. 10 The average rate of profit..need not be lower in a high-investment than a high-consumption economy. 1876 Q. Jrnl. Geol. Soc. XXXII. 185 The altitude of high-level drift on the western slopes of the Pennine chain. a 1890 High-level [in Dict., sense 22 a]. 1936 Discovery May 132/2 The high-level gravels in which Harrison discovered those eoliths that gave proof of the oldest human culture in this island. 1943 Aeronaut. Engin. Rev. Apr. 59/3 The removal of objections against high-level daylight raids..[is] specified. 1951 Ann. Reg. 1950 45 It was the will that was lacking, and high-level meetings would not alter that. 1951 Sci. Amer. Sept. 42/1 Some, though they have obtained degrees, can hardly be classed as capable of high-level mental work. 1959 Daily Tel. 8 July 10/3 The proposed policy of continual high-level talks with Russia, extending over the next few years, has its opponents. 1964 Jrnl. Assoc. Computing Machinery XI. 21 Emphasis has been placed on simplicity and intuitiveness while maintaining so far as possible the inherent power of a high-level programming language. 1964 K. L. Pike in D. Abercrombie Daniel Jones 425 High-level phonological units. 1965 N. Chomsky Aspects of Theory of Syntax iv. 153 Deviation from selectional rules involving high-level features is apparently more serious than deviation from selectional rules involving lower-level features. 1969 H. Perkin Key Profession v. 209 A long-term high-level demand for university places. 1972 Computer Jrnl. XV. 195/1 The main purpose of a high-level language is to make programs and programming more intelligible to human beings. 1921 Discovery Apr. 96/2 High-lift wings are, of course, those that give the highest lift–drift ratio. 1933 Jrnl. R. Aeronaut. Soc. XXXVII. 79 The Hall high-lift wing is an application of the same principle... Similar results are obtained, namely, a large increase in maximum lift and a shift backwards of the centre of pressure. 1958 Times Rev. Industry June 20/1 A new, high-lift boom machine. 1902 Encycl. Brit. XXV. 208/1 High-nitrogen foods. 1960 Farmer & Stockbreeder 15 Mar. 113/1, 3 cwt per acre of the high-nitrogen compound in the seedbed should not affect it. 1932 Chem. Abstr. XXVI. 3097 Changes in design of cracking units to enable them to produce high-octane gasoline. 1958 Times 6 Nov. 7/5 All high compression engines respond to high-octane, highly anti-knock fuel. 1972 M. Gilbert Body of Girl iv. 43 Filling the tank of an old Bentley with high-octane petrol. 1938 S. Chase Tyranny of Words i. 6 We.. allow our language forms or symbolic machinery to fashion a demonology of absolutes and high-order abstractions. 1968 Fox & Mayers Computing Methods for Scientists & Engineers vii. 134 Economization was effected just by removing successive high-order terms. 1960 Farmer & Stockbreeder 8 Mar. 48/2 (Advt.), The best high-output combine in the world. 1963 Listener 14 Mar. 466/2 A living-room fire with a high-output back boiler. 1925 Post Office Electr. Engin. Jrnl. XVII. 311 Tests on high pass filters of three sections. 1946 Nature 13 July 47/1 Figures 1, 2 and 3..were taken with a high-pass filter in the circuit which attenuated the low-frequency response of the microphone. 1940 War Illustr. 19 Jan. 620 (caption) The introduction into the Fleet Air Arm of high-performance monoplanes like the Blackburn 'Skua'. 1966 T. Wisdom High-Performance Driving ii. 17 You need more skill for high-performance road-driving than you do for competitive motoring. 1930 Wireless World 21 May 538 (heading) High permeability alloys. 1963 B. Fozard Instrumentation Nucl. Reactors viii. 102 In general a tube must be placed..at least four inches away from another trochotron, a strong magnet, or a high-permeability screen. 1944 Mod. Lang. Notes Dec. 515 High-potency capsule. 1962 F. I. Ordway et al. Basic Astronautics xiii. 526 High-potency drugs such as the phenothiazines..could be incorporated. 1934 Webster, High-potential. 1954 Essays in Criticism IV. 313 The value of high-potential person-to-person situations. 1962 Simpson & Richards Junction Transistors

iv. 68 A particle such as an electron can pass through a high-potential barrier if the barrier is sufficiently thin. **1892** A. CONAN DOYLE *Adv. Sherlock Holmes* i. 2 A crack in one of his own high-power lenses. **1898** *Westm. Gaz.* 28 May 2/1 Modern high-power guns. **1901** *Kynoch Jrnl.* June–July 108/2 Modern high-power smokeless propellants. **1934** *Discovery* Dec. 341/2 Here the microscope is set up vertically for high-power work. **1971** *Gloss. Electrotechnical, Power Terms (B.S.I.)* III. vii. 21 *High-power modulation*, modulation of the carrier of a radio transmitter. **1946** *Nature* 19 Oct. 537/2 For high-precision measurements, as for observing wind-tunnel forces, the current is limited to 5 milliamp. **1960** *Times* 18 Nov. 4/6 The first essential..is a network of high-precision stations. **1872** F. W. ROBINSON *Wrayford's Ward* III. 207 A high-class, high-priced, high-pressure seminary. **1907** *Westm. Gaz.* 15 Oct. 1/1 The high-pressure life which he led in London. **1928** D. BRUNT *Meteorol.* iv. 30 These high and low-pressure systems. **1933** *Archit. Rev.* LXXIV. 183/2 To launch a high-pressure salesmanship offensive. **1936** *Discovery* Feb. 38/2 Steam undergoes expansion in both high-pressure and low-pressure cylinders. **1940** *Topeka Jrnl.* 4 May 2 Photographers..hipressuring portrait sales. **1941** *Sat. Even. Post* 8 Feb. 54, I did not attempt to high-pressure the man too much. **1946** MEZZROW & WOLFE *Really Blues* viii. 128 He began to high-pressure us with a Chamber-of-Commerce spiel. **1958** J. CANNAN *And be a Villain* vii. 165, I get so confused by high-pressure salesmen. **1962** 'A. GARVE' *Prisoner's Friend* ii. 105 She didn't want to. Laurence high-pressured her into it. **1972** *Mod. Law Rev.* XXXV. I. 24 It is surely desirable to prevent abuses in marketing, particularly fraud, high pressure techniques, and the deliberate sale of defective goods. **1956** C. W. MILLS *Power Elite* xii. 282 High-prestige organizations to which the elite usually belong. **1959** V. PACKARD *Status Seekers* (1960) vi. 84 A few old high-prestige neighbourhoods manage..to maintain their status. **1906** *Daily Chron.* 27 Sept. 3/6 The benefits of the high-price policy which they choose to pursue. **1944** *Mod. Lang. Notes* Dec. 515 High-protein foods. **1964** 'D. SHANNON' *Root of all Evil* (1966) v. 66 Sure, she gives me the high-protein diet, and I'm still learning to drink coffee without sugar. **1936** *Metals Handbk.* 925 (*heading*) Electrical properties of high-purity annealed aluminium wire. **1910** *Westm. Gaz.* 21 Apr. 12/1 Until plenty of high-quality beet is procurable. **1913** V. B. LEWES *Oil Fuel* 180 High-quality coal-gas. **1939** W. S. CHURCHILL *Into Battle* (1941) 85 High-quality war materials. **1948** *Wireless World* Jan. 2/1 Most high-quality radio receiver units will provide an output of well over 4 volts. **1884** High resistance [see RESISTANCE 6]. **1962** SIMPSON & RICHARDS *Junction Transistors* xi. 259 When feeding a high-resistance load from a relatively low-resistance source..the potentiometer should be connected as a voltage divider. **1946** *Nature* 19 Oct. 550/2 Using the high-resolution system of the R.C.A. type E.M.U. microscope as a diffraction camera, we have attempted to find some feature of the diffraction by oxides of this type. **1970** G. K. WOODGATE *Elem. Atomic Struct.* 217 High-resolution optical spectroscopy. **1951** S. A. STOUFFER in Parsons & Shils *Toward General Theory Action* IV. v. 494 In a high-risk cheating situation. **1963** *Economist* 14 Dec. 1175/2 All the 'high-risk' mothers. **1969** *Times* 3 Apr. 28/6 Many companies ..had cancelled policies in high-risk areas such as the ghettoes. **1907** *Daily Chron.* 9 Oct. 4/6 The German high-sea fleet. **1931** *Times Lit. Suppl.* 10 Sept. 673/3 A lack of familiarity with the naval idiom can alone account..for calling..the fleet under Cornwallis 'the high seas fleet'. **1961** A. J. MARDER *From Dreadnought to Scapa Flow* I. ix. 243 While the High Seas Fleet had concentrated.., the British Fleet was in a very different condition. **1949** *Wireless World* Mar. 16a (Advt.), High stability capacitors. **1963** B. FOZARD *Instrumentation Nucl. Reactors* ix. 108 High-stability, close-tolerance components are required in the measuring circuits. **1959** V. PACKARD *Status Seekers* (1960) ix. 129 Some women said it made them 'feel good' just to go into a high-status store. **1965** *Language* XLI. 295 An honored or high-status person. **1940** *Chambers's Techn. Dict.* 416/1 High-strength brass. **1961** *Times* 13 Dec. 21/6 High-strength..paper bags. **1969** *Jane's Freight Containers 1968–69* 111/3 Aimed at providing a high-speed, high-strength route for 'jumbo' freight cars. **1911** *Daily Colonist* (Victoria, B.C.) 11 Apr. 10/5 Harry Gillis..was killed and ten bricklayers narrowly escaped death today when Gillis came in contact with a 30,000 volt high tension wire. **1970** *New Yorker* 10 Oct. 64/1 The denizens of the ocean, some of whom learned to produce high-tension electricity long before man. **1936** *Metals Handbk.* 439 The curves marked 'High Test' and 'Nickel' Irons in Fig. 21 were stressed to 10,000 psi. **1955** *Jrnl. Brit. Interplanetary Soc.* XIV. 159 Developments throughout the world have resulted in the production of hydrogen peroxide up to 90 per cent. strength, known as high-test peroxide or H.T.P. **1958** A. D. MERRIMAN *Dict. Metallurgy* 126/1 *High-test cast iron*, cast iron possessing a tensile strength not less than some arbitrary value, varying with different authorities. **1959** *Chambers's 20th Cent. Dict.* Suppl. 1378/2 *High-test*, (of petrol) boiling at comparatively low temperature and so of high performance. **1923** *Bull. Sch. Orient. & Afr. Stud.* III. I. 125 This significant tone of the future of all high tone verbs need not be specially marked in broad transcriptions. **1964** J. CARNOCHAN in D. Abercrombie *Daniel Jones* 403 All these examples have a high-tone initial syllable. **1965** *Language* XLI. 347 A toneless base..to which I would add..three affixes (the high-tone superfix, the suffix *-a*, and the mid-tone superfix) to produce the noun. **1893** *Jrnl. Soc. Arts* 5 May 624/1 The phosphorescent glow of the novel high-frequency, high-voltage, high-vacuum lamps. **1927** *Nature* 8 Oct. 510/1 We have made a further study of the phenomena exhibited by these high-vacuum tubes, with especial reference to the spectra of the discharge. **1971** *Gloss. Electrotechnical, Power Terms (B.S.I.)* II. ii. 8 High-vacuum diode. **1963** *Rep. Comm. Decimal Curr.* iii. 17 in *Parl. Papers 1962–3* (Cmnd. 2145) XI. 1 Because workable cent systems with high-value major units are available..we preferred cent systems to mil ones. **1966** *Listener* 1 Sept. 307/2 High value perishable foods such as milk and meat and vegetables. **1892** F. IRWIN *Fortification* (ed. 2) 43 Modern high-velocity guns. **1898** *Engineering Mag.* XVI. 112/2 These high-velocity bullets. **1934** *Discovery* June 155/2 The jet of high-velocity air is about 8 feet across, and an expenditure of energy at the rate of 400 horse-power is necessary to maintain it. **1946** *Nature* 28 Dec. 932/2 Anomalously short travel-time signifies the approach towards the surface, along the radius concerned, of a high-velocity medium. **1962** F. I. ORDWAY et al. *Basic Astronautics* viii. 334 The venturi principle is applied..in the aerodynamic wind tunnel to achieve high-velocity flow. **1964** CRYSTAL & QUIRK *Syst. Prosodic & Paralinguist. Features Eng.* iii. 38 Turbulent flow, with projection of high-velocity jet into pharynx. **1956** J. M. MOGEY *Family & Neighbourhood* 5 Before 1920 Oxford had not been a high-wage town. **1964** S. M. MILLER in I. L. Horowitz *New Sociol.* 294 The high-wage..occupations. *a* **1877** KNIGHT *Dict. Mech.* II. 1103/1 *High-warp loom*, a tapestry loom in which the warp-frame is vertical and the weaver works standing. **1904** GOODCHILD & TWENEY *Technol. & Sci. Dict.* 287/2 *High warp*, tapestry in which the warp takes a vertical position, *e.g.* Gobelins tapestry. **1934** *Archit. Rev.* LXXV. *caption* facing 95 For instance, Burne-Jones drew cartoons for the revival of high-warp tapestry weaving which Morris initiated.

b. *high-banked, -bosomed, -bridged, -ceilinged, -hedged, -hilled, -pooped* (examples), *-pressured, -priced* (later example), *-sided, -souled* (later examples); **high-coloured,** also *fig.*, exaggerated, forced; as, *a high-coloured description*; **high-geared,** having high gears; also *transf.*, fast-moving, active; **high-horsed** (delete † and add examples).

1899 *Daily News* 25 Dec. 5/2 A dangerous high-banked river. **1900** *Westm. Gaz.* 26 Jan. 4/3 The broad-faced, high-bosomed model is the palpable grandmother of many Rubenses. **1961** *Times* 25 Apr. 20/7 The white high-bosomed dress of Empire style. **1871** 'M. LEGRAND' *Cambr. Freshm.* 138 A Quixotic gentleman, of ancient lineage, in whose high-bridged and defiant nose the Indian saw a resemblance to an eagle's beak. **1907** *Daily Chron.* 30 July 4/4 It was a high-ceilinged, sombre room. **1960** *Farmer & Stockbreeder* 9 Feb. Suppl. 3/2 A high-ceilinged, rather sunless sittingroom. **1925** F. M. FORD *No More Parades* 309 There were two girls who kept a tea-shop in Poperinghe... High coloured. **1899** *Daily News* 13 Feb. 5/3 Our high-geared population. **1906** A. BENNETT *Whom God hath Joined* v. 169 Gater's high-geared bicycle. **1924** H. CRANE *Let.* 12 Jan. (1965) 169 Working at high speed as one does in such high geared agencies. **1904** *Westm. Gaz.* 3 Aug. 2/3 In the shady high-hedged garden. **1906** KIPLING in *Tribune* 15 Jan. 2/3 A high-hedged road. **1807** J. BARLOW *Columbiad* VI. 224 Gates in their van, on high-hilled Bemus rose. **1896** A. E. HOUSMAN *Shropshire Lad* 83 Westward on the high-hilled plains Where for me the world began. **1900** *Westm. Gaz.* 6 Feb. 3/2 To..ride off high-horsed on the theory that the battle had to be fought. **1928** *Observer* 22 Jan. 14/5 The high-horsed fanatics of universal Communism. **1889** O. WILDE in *19th Cent.* Jan. 54 The high-pooped galleys. **1921** W. DE LA MARE *Veil* 74 That midnight-stealing, high-pooped galliass, *Sleep*. **1947** *Horizon* XVI. 202 Muggleton was high-pressured and loud. **1961** *Times* 15 Nov. 19/1 High-pressured modern life. **1962** *B.S.I. News* July 19/1 It was no use building a high-priced article for 20–30 years' service if it was to be outmoded by advancing techniques. **1960** *Farmer & Stockbreeder* 26 Jan. 65/3 Force the lacerated trimmings up a delivery chute into a high-sided trailer. **1905** *Westm. Gaz.* 6 Dec. 5/2 There was no more high-souled, high-minded man than the man who was now Prime Minister. **1930** A. HUXLEY *Let.* 14 June (1969) 337 English reviews..have been rather snorty and high-souled about the book.

B. *sb.* **1. b.** An area of high barometric pressure. Also *transf.*

1878 *Pop. Sci. Monthly* July 310 These high and low areas, or 'highs' and 'lows' as they are technically known, travel. **1901** *Yearbk. U.S. Dept. Agric. 1900* 332 The hot wave..seemed to join forces with the permanent high over the ocean. **1958** 'N. SHUTE' *Rainbow & Rose* 290 A high had come along that the Met had not been able to forecast. **1966** *New Statesman* 27 May 759/1 There are..highs and lows of political intensity: right now, we are approaching a moderate high.

c. = the 'High Street' in Oxford.

1853 'C. BEDE' *Verdant Green* 1st Ser. x. 88 He at once sallied forth to 'do the High', and display his new purchases. **1912** A. QUILLER-COUCH in *Oxf. Bk. Victorian Verse* 860 Yet if at last not less her lover You in your hansom leave the High [etc.]. **1921** C. S. LEWIS *Let.* 10 May (1966) 59 It is still pleasant to see fewer foreign visitors pacing the High with guide books. **1955** *Times* 11 Aug. 7/6 A proposal..to close Magdalen Bridge,..preventing the High from being used as a motor thoroughfare.

d. = *high gear* (*GEAR *sb.* 7 b).

1921 A. F. HALL *Handbk. Yosemite Nat. Park* 308 You may hear a driver boast that he made such and such a grade on 'high', but that is merely an admission of poor judgment. **1931** *Kansas City Star* 8 Aug., Now [all they talk about is] whether or not they were able to go up Pikes Peak on high. **1934** J. M. CAIN *Postman always rings Twice* ix. 89, I went into high. **1970** *Globe Mag.* (Toronto) 26 Sept. 7/1 Lewis moved into high, knowing, but really knowing that Walter would be in the race.

e. A record, a high level exceeding that previously attained.

1926 *Chicago Tribune* 23 Jan. II. 9/1 Wheeling and Lake Erie issues resumed their advance, the common toward a new high at 49⅝. **1928** *Weekly Dispatch* 3 June 7/2 When he buys, they buy; the lot of them can create..a new 'high' in any share in which Mr. Durant fancies. **1937** *Lit. Digest* 20 Mar. 3 (*heading*) Nazi epithets at U.S. set new high. **1939** [see *all-time* (*ALL *a.* 13)]. **1951** W. STEVENS *Let.* 25 June (1967) 720 The whole thing has brought my morale up to an all-time high. **1953**, etc. [see *LOW *sb.* 3 c]. **1959** *Encounter* Sept. 59/1 Beckett's stock has reached a steady high at Langham Place. **1964** R. D. HOPPER in I. L. Horowitz *New Sociol.* 317 The gross national product has reached an all-time high. **1968** *Listener* 22 Feb. 228/2 The series manifestly represented a new high in the adaptation of fiction to film.

f. = High School (SCHOOL *sb.*[1] I j). *N. Amer. colloq.*

1928 *Boston Even. Transcript* 30 Mar. 15/7 I'm hardly more than a schoolboy, not so very long out of Dorchester High. **1930** H. CRANE *Let.* 29 Nov. (1965) 359, I left East High without even a diploma—in my junior year. **1963** H. GARNER in R. Weaver *Canad. Short Stories* 2nd Ser. (1968) 49 He had graduated from technical high, and was going to university in the fall. **1968** *New Yorker* 18 May 56, I started playing drums in junior high.

g. *pl.* The higher range of audio-frequencies.

1940 in *Chambers's Techn. Dict.* 415/2. **1962** A. NISBETT *Technique Sound Studio* ii. 46 Such screens have the advantage of being dual purpose: used dead side to the microphone, they will damp down the highs: with the bright side forward, the highs will be emphasized.

h. A euphoric state induced by the taking of a drug or drugs. *slang.* (Cf. *HIGH *a.* 16 c.)

1953 W. BURROUGHS *Junkie* (1972) xv. 149 Finally, the peyote came up solid like a ball of hair,..clogging my throat. As horrible a sensation as I ever stood still for. After that, the high came on slow. Peyote high is something like benzedrine high. **1956** H. GOLD *Man who was not with It* (1965) i. 6 Dreamy in my high, I floated down ..to kick the smaller mark. **1967** *Listener* 3 Aug. 130/1 It is not easy..to describe the effect of a trip on LSD or a marijuana high. **1967** *Spectator* 4 Aug. 131/1, I was a drug addict..for two years. I was in an almost permanent state of high. **1969** *Times* 21 May 7/3 The two cigarettes smoked by each subject were intended to produce a 'normal social cannabis high'.

3. a. Also, the highest card in cutting for deal. *high-low-jack* (*and the game*): = ALL-FOURS I. (See quots.)

[**1674** C. COTTON *Compl. Gamester* x. 111 This Game I conceive is called All-Fours from Highest, Lowest, Jack and Game, which is the Set as some play it. *Ibid.* 113 Sometimes you are highest, lowest, Jack, and Game.] **1814** C. JONES *Hoyle's Games Impr.* 170 All-fours..derives its name from the four chances therein, for each of which a point is scored, namely, *high*, the best trump out; *low*, the smallest trump dealt; *jack*, the knave of trumps; *game*, the majority of pips reckoned from such of the following cards as the respective players have in their tricks; viz. every ace is counted as 4; king 3; queen 2; knave 1; and ten for 10. **1818** TODD s.v. *All-fours*, The all-four are high, low, Jack, and the game. **1843** 'J. SLICK' *High Life N.Y.* II. 214 Under the table..was a hull squad of playin cards..as if somebody had got beat a playing high-low-jack and the game. **1895** *Funk's Stand. Dict.*, *High-low-jack*. Same as All-fours. **1898** B. KIRKBY *Lakeland Words* 72 *High-low*, a card game. High-low, Jack an' t' gam. **1911** R. F. FOSTER *Compl. Hoyle* 328 As High, Jack, and Game are always counted by the player holding those points at the end of the play, there can be no question about them: but serious disputes sometimes arise as to who played Low... It is even possible, if there is no other trump or counting card in play, for the Jack to be High, Low, Jack, and the Game. **1963** G. F. HERVEY *Handbk. Card Games* 16 The players then turn up their tricks and score for High, Low, Jack and Game.

b. Phr. *how is that for high?*: an exclamation inviting admiration; in allusion to the card called the high in the game of high-low-jack. *U.S. colloq.*

1872 SCHELE DE VERE *Americanisms* 326 The phrase 'How is that for high?' borrowed from a low game known as Old Sledge, where the *high* depends, not on the card itself but on the adversary's hand. Hence the phrase means, What kind of an attempt is that at a great achievement? **1887** F. FRANCIS *Saddle & Mocassin* xviii. 315 'How's that for high, boys?' concluded the narrator, when he had told his tale. 'That's on top,' declared Black Jack; 'that takes the cake.' **1922** JOYCE *Ulysses* 122 What about that, Simon?..How's that for high?

high, *adv.* Add: **2. c.** (Later examples.)

1894 *Vermont Agric. Rep.* XIV. 102 Will a colt do well..if fed high in winter? **1965** T. CAPOTE *In Cold Blood* (1966) iii. 135 Him and Carol lived too high, kept buying stuff they couldn't nohow afford. **1967** L. J. BRAUN *Cat who ate Danish Modern* xv. 137 David lived high, and he gave every thing away.

9. b. *to live* (or *eat*) *high off* (or *on*) *the hog*: to live (etc.) in luxury. orig. *U.S.*

1946 *Call-Bulletin* (San Francisco) 27 May Edit. page, I have to do my shopping in the black market because we can't eat as high off the hog as Roosevelt and Ickes and Joe Davis and all those millionaire friends of the common man. **1946** *Time* 27 May 22/2 Eatin' on the Hog. In the years of political wars the Organization had grown and resistance diminished. **1956** 'E. S. AARONS' *Assignment Treason* (1967) ii. 27 He lives high off the hog. He needs money. **1966** A. PRIOR *Operators* vi. 69 That had been a good year, a year of living high off the hog. **1967** *Observer* 30 Apr. 11/5 Die..for what? So that the Saigonese and other civilians can live high off the hog? **1967** K. GILES *Death in Diamonds* iii. 47, I hope these Uppings eat high on the hog. **1969** *New Scientist* 6 Mar. 511/1 A cod lives quite high on the hog—until he turns up on someone else's menu.

10. a. *high-dried* (also as *sb.*), *-laced, -lying, -perched, -piled, -reared* (later examples); **high-keyed** *Mus.*, of a high pitch; also *fig.*; **high-sniffing** *colloq.*, contemptuous, disdainful; **high-strung** (further examples: now used esp. in the sense 'in a state of nervous tension').

1818 SCOTT *Heart of Midlothian* in *Tales of My Landlord* III. x. 265, I have always a chat with Mrs Glass when I purchase my Scots high-dried. **1858** GEO. ELIOT

Scenes Clerical Life I. 48 If Mr. Barton had shaken into that little box a small portion of Scotch high-dried, he might have..[etc.]. **1893** *Funk's Stand. Dict.* I. 848/1 *High-keyed*, 1. *Mus.* high-pitched. 2. Sensitive, spirited; as, a *high-keyed* woman. **1906** *Daily Chron.* 18 June 6/3 Mr. P. Wilson Steer has several examples of his familiar high-keyed method, including a not too happy portrait of himself in a grey tweed suit. **1938** *Burlington Mag.* Feb. 75/2 Painted in thick and high-keyed colours. **1938** M. K. Rawlings *Yearling* xvi. 181 There was an excitement..that made him nervous and high-keyed. **1851** J. G. Whittier *Works* (1898) 210 Madam in her high-laced ruff. **1880** 'Mark Twain' *Tramp Abroad* II. xxxiv. 26 These wore..hob-nailed high-laced walking-shoes. *a* **1930** D. H. Lawrence *Phoenix II* (1968) 46 Even then, I lack high-laced boots and one stocking. **1934** *Discovery* June 166/2 The more high-lying burials.. contained 'reserved slip' pottery. **1958** *Times* 19 Dec. 7/1 The difficult is intonation in high-lying passages. **1969** *Daily Tel.* 12 Mar. 21/3 High-lying solos in the Mozart finale. **1863** Longfellow *Tales Wayside Inn* 45 High-perched upon the back of which there stood The image of a falcon carved in wood. **1906** *Westm. Gaz.* 16 June 12/2 Each high-perched farmhouse was changed by sunset glamour to a magic castle. **1945** W. S. Churchill *Victory* (1946) 207 Flags from high-perched windows. **1862** W. C. Bryant *Poet. Wks.* (1883) II. 312 Clouds, High-piled. **1932** V. Woolf *Common Reader* 2nd Ser. 226 Its high-piled metaphors. **1952** C. Day Lewis tr. *Virgil's Aeneid* xi. 257 Treading the high-piled embers as we perform your rites. **1896** A. E. Housman *Shropshire Lad* xxxvii. 53 The high-reared head of Clee. **1922** Joyce *Ulysses* 422 The swancomb of the gondola, high-reared, forges on. **1906** *Daily Chron.* 12 July 3/3 High-sniffing pretenders..affect to find in Mr. Meredith's poetry naught that is obscure. **1863** *Country Gentleman* 7 May 300/2 When the sire and the dam of a colt possess much spirit and are 'high strung'. **1868** W. James in *North Amer. Rev.* CVII. 322 That high-strung attitude of vigilance, suspicion, and suspended judgment. **1902** A. Bennett *Anna of Five Towns* xi. 283 You're so sensitive and high-strung. **1946** M. Lowry *Let.* 15 Sept. (1967) 125 Writers often tend to be high-strung creatures. **1956** A. H. Compton *Atomic Quest* 125 He could keep a group of high-strung specialists working smoothly together.

high altar. [OE. *heah-altar*.] The principal altar of a church.

c **950** in T. Wright *Vol. Vocab.* (1873) II. 23 *Cibborium*, þæs heahalteres ofergeweorc. **13..** *Gaw. & Gr. Knt.* 592 So harnayst as he was he herknez his masse, Offred and honoured at þe heȝe auter. *c* **1460** *Oseney Reg.* 137 Reynolde, By the grace of god Bisshop of Clone,..halowed the Chapell of Saunforde and the high auter. *c* **1553** in *Diary of H. Machyn* (1848) 399 The highe altar table. *a* **1700** Evelyn *Diary* 25 Oct. 1644, On the large high altar is a brazen vessel of admirable invention. *c* **1777** in *Cath. Rec. Soc. Publ.* VIII. 173 He lays buried in our Church at the foot of the High Altar. **1826** [see Altar 2]. **1894** C. M. Church *Chapters Early Hist. Ch. Wells* App. W. 419 High altar dedicated to St. Andrew. **1927** W. Cather *Death comes for Archbishop* ix. viii. 299 The next morning the old Archbishop lay before the high altar in the church he had built. **1954** *Oxf. Jun. Encycl.* XII. 8/2 Large churches often have subsidiary chapels with their own altars, and then the principal one is called the High Altar.

highball. Add: Also **high ball, high-ball.**
1. (Earlier example.)

1882 C. M. Chase *Editor's Run in New Mexico* 134 Mexican monte, keno, faro, high ball, etc., are the prevailing games.

2. (In full *highball signal*.) A signal to proceed given to a locomotive driver, formerly by hoisting a ball aloft. Also *gen.*, a signal to go ahead, a clear way, a straight course. *U.S.*

1897 *Chicago Record* 1 Mar. 6/1 'Milk trains'..have 'rights' over the rails and get nothing but 'high balls'. **1909** *Sat. Even. Post* 26 June 9/1, I gave 'em the highball signal to go ahead. **1920** J. M. Hunter *Trail Drivers of Texas* 68 We had a high ball trail from there on. *Ibid.* 354 Mr. Butler and I told them [*sc.* cowboys]..to strike a high ball to town. **1931** 'D. Stiff' *Milk & Honey Route* 207 *High ball*, signal for a train to pull out of town. **1938** A. E. Parkins *South* 168 We are informed that the signal the conductor waves to the engineer to go ahead is still known as the 'high ball' on most lines. **1940** *Sat. Even. Post* 16 Nov. 18 Picking up the highball as he drifted out of the freight yards, Engineer Joe De Nobel gave her the throttle. **1959** J. Thurber *Years with Ross* iv. 63 The parlance of railroading—deadhead, highball, whistle stop, gandy dancer.

3. A drink of whisky and soda or other mineral water served with ice in a tall glass. *U.S.* Also *attrib.*

1898 *N.Y. Jrnl.* 16 Sept. 4/2 Evening dress and khaki talked much sport and a little war over 'high balls' or chicken livers. **1899** Ade *Doc. Horne* ii. 11 Lush..drank two magnificent 'high balls'. **1909** Eaton & Underhill *Runaway Place* 128 The pleasant occupation of consuming three chocolate éclairs and a high ball. **1915** Wodehouse *Something Fresh* iii. 59 Beyond Baxter, a cigar in his mouth and a weak high-ball at his side, the Earl of Emsworth took his ease. **1925** H. L. Foster *Trop. Tramp Tourists* 109 The crowd from Ohio..celebrated by drinking several highballs. **1933** N. Coward *Design for Living* iii. i. 1 Who'd like a highball? **1949** F. Maclean *Eastern Approaches* i. vii. 82 The crystal chandeliers shed a cheerful light on the silver trays of highballs and old-fashioneds. **1959** *Sears, Roebuck Catal.* Spring & Summer 1394/3 Highball glasses. **1965** *Amer. Speech* XL. 77 In sophisticated drinking circles the term *high-ball* has become practically archaic... The illuminati ask for 'whiskey and water' or 'Scotch and soda'. **1973** H. Nielsen *Severed Key* viii. 92 A soiled highball glass on the counter.

hi·ghball, *v. U.S. slang.* [f. the sb.] **a.** *intr.* To give a locomotive driver a signal to proceed; also *transf.* **b.** To go or travel at speed (const. *it* or with *adv.*). **c.** *trans.* To drive (a locomotive or vehicle) at speed.

1912 *Railroad Man's Mag.* XVII. 493 The con high-balled, and the manifest freight Pulled out on the stem behind the mail. *Ibid.*, She whistled twice and high-balled out, They were off—down the Gila Monster Route. **1931** 'D. Stiff' *Milk & Honey Route* v. 53 Often they highball the cops and you get raided. **1935** Partridge *Slang To-Day* (ed. 2) 442 *Highball*, to travel swiftly; to depart, esp. hastily. **1941** *Amer. Speech* XVI. 233/1 *High ball*, to speed up operations. **1941** *Pop. Sci. Monthly* May 76 Its smooth power..is fully available, whether the giant is pulling away from a dead stop or highballing along at its maximum governed speed. **1943** S. K. Farrington *Railroading from Head End* 48 We highballed out at 5:05. No hurry, no lost motion, no excitement—just clocklike precision by every man jack of them. **1945** *This Week Mag.* 14 July 19/2 He highballed the big locomotive down the tracks. **1946** *Sat. Even. Post* 11 May 27/3 Everyone else had highballed..out of there. **1961** *Amer. Speech* XXXVI. 271 Imagine yourself on the seat of an enormous freighter, high-balling it down a West Coast highway. **1962** *Ibid.* XXXVII. 131 A logging train that is highballing or making a fast run. **1971** M. Tak *Truck Talk* 82 *Highball it*, to drive a tractor-trailer at or near its top speed.

high-binder. 2. (Earlier example.)

1876 *San Francisco Call* 27 Mar. 1/7 Refined ladies could no longer submit to be jostled at the church door by the Mongolian *chiffonier* or high-binder.

3. Delete def. and substitute: *transf.* Used abusively to denote a swindler, esp. a fraudulent politician.

1903 A. H. Lewis *Boss* 136 He's goin' to take copies of th' accounts that show what th' Chief an' them other high-binders at the top o' Tammany have been doin'. **1908** G. H. Lorimer *J. Spurlock* xii. 324 That's what I do mean—it [*sc.* the railroad] 's been stolen by that Bonsall bunch of high-binders. **1916** H. L. Wilson *Somewhere in Red Gap* i. 21 So I left these two lady highbinders and went on into the retail side of the Family Liquor Store. **1952** in Wentworth & Flexner *Amer. Dict. Slang* (1960) 255/2 The winter meeting of the grand inner circle of high-binders at Miami Beach.

high-boy. Add: **3.** = Tallboy 2. *U.S.*

1891 *Scribner's Mag.* X. 353 In the top drawer of a high chest of drawers, a 'high boy'. **1902** L. V. Lockwood *Col. Furnit. Amer.* 56 The common form of the flat-topped bandy-legged high-boy is made of cherry, maple or walnut. **1909** J. C. Lincoln *Keziah Coffin* i. 10 Removing towels, tablecloths, and the like from the drawers in a tall 'high-boy'. **1926** *Bulletin* 29 June 10/2 The..lady.. belonged against a background of mahogany highboys, old china..and an Adams' mantel. **1972** *Town & Country* Mar. 106/1 (*caption*) American William and Mary high-boy.

highbrow, high-brow (həi·brau), *sb.* and *a. colloq.* orig. *U.S.* [Back-formation from *high-browed *a.* 2.] **A.** *sb.* A person of superior intellectual attainments or interests: occas. with derisive implication of conscious superiority to ordinary human standards.

1908 *Sat. Even. Post* 29 Aug. 27/1 It takes all sorts of men to make a party, and Mr. Hearst apparently led in a few prize-fighters with the other high-brows and reformers he accumulated. **1911** H. S. Harrison *Queed* iv. 41 Who knew but what this little highbrow was the very man they were looking for? **1914** G. Atherton *Perch of Devil* i. 41 I'll be a real high-brow in less than no time. **1921** H. S. Walpole *Young Enchanted* iii. vi. 301 There was the theatre (so much better than the highbrows asserted), there were concerts. **1922** D. H. Lawrence *Phoenix II* (1968) 240 Then the highbrows come and say: 'Poor Indian, dear Indian! why, *all* America ought to belong to him!' **1925** A. P. Herbert *Laughing Ann* 86 I'll be a high-brow, but I'll look hearty, And I won't laugh at the Liberal Party. **1934** S. R. Nelson *All about Jazz* i. 18 The strangely disreputable lady 'Jazz'—disreputable because she was not sponsored by the highbrows. **1955** *Times* 23 June 11/4 The highbrows in those parts all go up in smoke or mist if you confess to liking those among their native artists who seem most typically Scottish.

B. *adj.* Of, pertaining to, or characteristic of a highbrow; intellectually superior.

1884 L. Troubridge *Life amongst Troubridges* (1966) xii. 169 Mr. Hope had suggested that we would be at some highbrow part of the Exhibition—looking at pictures I think, but Jo had said firmly, 'If I know the Troubridges they will be at the Chocolate Stall', and we were! **1914** S. Lewis *Our Mr. Wrenn* 42 All them high brow sermons. **1916** S. Leacock in 'O. Henry' *Waifs & Strays* (1919) 161 Shakespeare, except as revived at twenty-five cents a seat with proper alterations in the text, is 'highbrow'. **1917** W. J. Locke *Red Planet* xxiv. 306 She'd die of culture in the mater's highbrow establishment. **1925** *Punch* 22 Apr. 437/2 'The programmes are too highbrow,' I maintained. 'They are hopelessly beyond the intelligence of the mass, at any rate.' **1931** R. Church *High Summer* 12 Mother insists on my being highbrow and visiting all the historical places. **1943** C. Gray *Contingencies* (1942) i. 41 The choice of programme was uncompromisingly what it is customary to describe as 'highbrow', but the house was packed on both occasions. **1963** Auden *Dyer's Hand* 408 All high-brow–lowbrow frontiers of taste.

So **hi·ghbrowish** *a.*, fairly, or extremely, highbrow; **hi·ghbrowism**, the condition of being highbrow, intellectual superiority.

1921 *Glasgow Herald* 22 Jan. 4/2 This doctrine is tainted with high-browism. **1923** A. Bennett *Things that have interested Me* II. 207 The audiences were artistic and earnest, with a dash of high-browism. **1926** Whiteman & McBride *Jazz* viii. 108 Does the very word 'classical' make you nervous because it sounds so high-browish? **1927** D. H. Lawrence *Let.* 19 May in E. & A. Brewster *Reminisc. & Corr.* (1934) 132, I can't stand high-browish..people any more. **1937** *John o' London's* 1 Jan. 585/1, I am incapable of 'highbrowism', I make no pretensions to be a literary critic. **1947** N. Cardus *Autobiogr.* i. 16 The..Bloomsbury-Chelsea highbrowism which does not understand that genius is a miracle to be revered. **1953** *Harper's Mag.* Mar. 48/2 Articles. Books. Highbrowish stories.

high-browed (həi·braud), *a.* [f. High *a.* + Brow *sb.*[1] + -ed[2].]
1. Having a lofty forehead.

1848 'Geo. Eliot' *Let.* 23 Nov. (1954) I. 273 We have brought you [*sc.* Mother Nature] many gentle maidens and high-browed, brave men. **1875** *Brit. Q. Rev.* Apr. 500 One can conjure up a vision of them: the one fair, pale, high-browed. **1891** Flügel *Eng.-German Dict.*

2. = *highbrow *a.* orig. *U.S.*

1906 'O. Henry' in Davis & Morris *Caliph of Bagdad* (1931) xiv. 238 That, in addition to the $150 that I screwed out of the high-browed and esteemed B. Merwin during your absence. **1908** R. W. Chambers *Firing Line* ix, You were very much amused, I suppose—to see me sitting bras-dessus-bras-dessous with the high-browed and precious. **1909** H. G. Wells *Ann Veronica* vii. 121 Their very furniture had mysteriously a high-browed quality. *Ibid.* viii. 144 Goopes, she was sure, was always high-browed and slow and Socratic. **1916** —— *Mr. Britling* ii. iv. § 10, I was too high-browed about this war business. **1923** A. Bennett *Things that have interested Me* II. 207 If artistic, earnest, and high-browed women only knew how to dress! **1927** *Daily Express* 3 May 3/7 Meeting a highbrowed friend.

high chair. [High *a.* 3.] A child's chair with high legs, usually fitted with a movable tray and footrest.

1848 Thackeray *Van. Fair* xliv. 400 Little Rawdon ..was perched on a high chair by the baronet's side. **1853** C. Brontë *Villette* I. ii. 23 The demure little person.. perched now on a high chair. *Ibid.* 25 She relinquished the high chair for a low stool. **1885** C. M. Yonge *Two Sides of Shield* II. i. 8 Mrs. Halfpenny [*sc.* the nanny] always put us on the high chair with our faces to the wall when we were jealous. **1913** C. Mackenzie *Sinister St.* I. i. 7 Stella was fitted into her high chair; the circular top was brought over from behind and thumped into its place with a click. **1943** C. McCullers *Heart is Lonely Hunter* ii. ix. 214 Ralph banged his spoon on his high-chair tray. **1959** *Sunday Times* 25 Oct. 20/6 Spoon overboard: the tyrant in the high chair makes a point.

higher. Add: **A.** *adj.* **2.** *higher education* (examples); *Higher* (*School*) *Certificate*, an examination instituted in 1917 and replaced in 1951 by the Advanced level General Certificate of Education, taken by pupils of about 18; *Higher Thought* = *New Thought.

1866 E. Davies (*title*) The higher education of women. **1868** *Rep. Sch. Inqu. Comm.* I. 115 in *Parl. Papers 1867–8* (C. 3966) XXVIII. 1, [Endowed] Schools have been regarded as the subjects of special trusts..not as local contributions to the higher education of the country. **1877** *Encycl. Brit.* VII. 674/1 Every Jesuit college was divided into two parts, the one for higher the other for lower education. **1884** C. Bird *Higher Educ. in Germany & England* i. 5 Few [*sc.* people] realise to what an extent we are surpassed by Germany..as regards the liberal provision made for higher education. **1896** *Spectator* 30 May 767/1 The great feature of the higher education should be a very well-marked revolt of the body against the mind. **1909** Chesterton *Orthodoxy* v. 136 Of all conceivable forms of enlightenment the worst is..the Inner Light... Anyone who knows anyone from the Higher Thought Centre knows how it does work. **1909** H. G. Wells *Ann Veronica* vi. 124 Jim is up to the neck in Mahatmas and Theosophy and Higher Thought and rot. **1918** *Univ. Cambridge Local Exam. Synd. Higher School Certificate Exam. List* 6 (*heading*) Exemption from the Previous examination by means of the higher school certificate examination. **1931** (*title*) Report of the Commission on Christian Higher Education in India. **1933** *Discovery* Sept. 271/2 He is best known for his researches on the Higher Thought Processes. **1945** *Guide Educ. Syst.* Gloss. 58 *Higher School certificate* (*higher certificate*), certificate awarded on results of the examination taken at about 18 by grammar school pupils. **1949** H. McLennan *Cross-country* 169 So much for higher education in Canada. **1961** *Sunday Times* 26 Feb. 12/6 By 1970 there could be 140,000 children applying for the 70,000 places there will then be in higher education. **1963** Barnard & Lauwerys *Handbk. Brit. Educ. Terms* 106 The Higher School Certificate examination, which came into operation in 1917 and was conducted by certain university boards, was taken by pupils in grammar schools at about the age of 18. It was primarily intended to be a test of a two-years sixth form course of a somewhat specialised nature. **1968** *Listener* 6 June 723/1, I use the expression 'higher education' in the same sense as the Robbins Committee. Broadly, it covers courses for students of 18 and over which reach a standard above A-level in GCE and for which the normal entry qualifications are at least five O-level passes or the equivalent. Degree courses account for a big proportion of the field.

4. (Further examples.)

1955 *Internat. Survey Programmes Social Devel.* (U.N.) 8 Training abroad on fellowships has made an important though necessarily limited contribution to the supply of higher-level technical and professional workers in some countries. **1958** B. Abel-Smith in N. Mackenzie *Conviction* 59 The middle classes..participate with the higher

income groups in special benefits from their employment. **1960** *Amer. Speech* XXXV. 230 English open internal juncture..is defined as the boundary point between two higher level phonological units (bounded sequences). **1962** CORSON & LORRAIN *Introd. Electromagn. Fields* i. 24 The sum of these four terms (neglecting higher-order differentials because we are interested in the limit S→O) is equal to the right-hand side of Eq. *1–109*. **1964** CRYSTAL & QUIRK *Prosodic & Paralinguist. Features Eng.* iv. 52 One might set up the existence of higher-order patterns as a hypothesis. **1965** C. H. SPRINGER et al. *Adv. Methods & Models* iii. 76 We might as well finish the job by deriving formulas for these *higher-order* differences. **1967** *Computers & Automation* Feb. 30/1 The single most important tool is what has become known as a 'programming language', sometimes called a 'higher level language' (to distinguish it from the normal machine codes or assembly languages..). **1968** FOX & MAYERS *Computing Methods for Scientists & Engineers* iii. 32 It is..possible to start with a very accurate y_0 and use double or higher precision arithmetic, but this is lengthy.

B. *adv.* **2.** (Further examples.)

1883 'MARK TWAIN' *Life on Mississippi* li. 502 Explosion followed explosion..reports grew steadily sharper and higher-keyed. **1923** H. CRANE *Let.* 21 July (1965) 142 Being with the largest advertising agency in the world.. will get me higher-paid positions in other places after awhile. **1969** *Punch* 15 Jan. 91/3 Allied Breweries, the International Compressed Air Corporation or other proclaimed seekers of higher-educated manpower.

higher-up. orig. *U.S.* [HIGH *a.* 5.] One occupying a superior position or post.

1911 *McClure's Mag.* Aug. 351 Resolved to get those dynamiters and to get the 'higher-ups', if there were any behind them. **1916** C. SANDBURG *Chicago Poems* 61 Higher-ups among the con men of Jerusalem. **1929** *Literary Digest* 12 Oct. 7/1 He is..insists the New York Telegram—'only the henchman of higher-ups'. **1931** L. STEFFENS *Autobiogr.* II. x. 254 Other 'higher-ups' confessed. **1939** 'G. ORWELL' *Coming Up for Air* II. viii. 145 The mysterious higher-ups who were running the war. **1953** K. TENNANT *Joyful Condemned* v. 47 She's in with all the higher-ups. **1960** H. L. LAWRENCE *Children of Light* iv. 63 Tell them the War Office is scared of a scandal and that the—er—higher-ups are willing to help them. **1970** K. GILES *Death in Church* ii. 38 The higher-ups were all chartered accountants from Krupps who did not like waste.

highfalutin, -ing. B. *adj.* (Earlier and later examples.)

1839 *Spirit of Times* 18 May 123/3 Them high-faluting chaps. **1941** *Coast to Coast 1941* 49 And then hear some announcer in his highfalutin voice, telling her summer was coming. **1948** *Manch. Guardian Weekly* 30 Sept. 9 When all the highfalutin and magical jargon of diplomacy is removed, you'll find the diplomats like a group of children aged about three or four. **1962** *New Statesman* 2 Mar. 308/2 This is..a pleasing unsententious compilation, not really a lecture at all. Sir Compton is never highfalutin.

high fide·lity. [f. HIGH *a.* + *FIDELITY 2 c.] In equipment used in the recording and reproduction of sound, the property of producing little distortion in the signal, so that the sound produced bears as close a resemblance as possible to the original. Also applied to the recording of electrical signals generally (quots. 1938, 1957). Also *attrib.* or as *adj.* So *higher fidelity*. Cf. *HI-FI.

1934 *Electronics* July 223/2 If the term 'high-fidelity' is to mean anything the predicated performance should be kept at a reasonably high level. **1934** *Wireless World* 19 Oct. 318/2 With the introduction of the 'high fidelity' receiver the broadcasters, who have repeatedly criticised the manufacturers for low-quality receivers which cut off the extreme notes, now make the admission that improvement is necessary in their own transmitters. **1937** *Time* 8 Mar. 62/1 (Advt.), Victor records: higher fidelity. **1938** *Jrnl. R. Aeronaut. Soc.* XLII. 1049 Present-day high fidelity 441-line television demands modulation frequencies as high as 4 megacycles. **1940** *Chambers's Techn. Dict.* 415/2 *High-fidelity*, an inexact term generally meaning sound reproduction of a superior, but undefined, quality. **1946** *Electronic Engin.* XVIII. 54 It has not been possible up to the present to obtain full advantage of the high fidelity of the moving coil pick-up. **1955** PRIESTLEY & HAWKES *Journey down Rainbow* 27 There was talk; there were high-fidelity records. **1957** *Times* 7 Oct. 8/3 The power of the transmitters guarantees high fidelity reception of the wireless signals. **1958** *Times* 17 May 9/5 This search for the elusive 'high fidelity' is pursued with an avidity only limited by the depth of his pocket. **1972** *Sci. Amer.* Sept. 100/3 If one wishes to transmit music with high fidelity, the required bandwidth is 15,000 hertz.

high-flyer, -flier. Add: **1. c.** A variety of walnut.

1822 *Trans. Lond. Hort. Soc.* IV. 517 The Highflyer Walnut. **1824** LOUDON *Encycl. Gardening* 742 Walnut... Highflyer of Thetford, the best variety known. **1866** LINDLEY & MOORE *Treas. Bot.* 640/2 A variety called the Highflyer Walnut, is considered the best English variety. **1880** *Encycl. Brit.* XII. 278/1.

5. d. = FLYER 5 b.

1961 in WEBSTER. **1964** *Economist* 22 Feb. 722/1 Stocks, variously called 'glamour' issues or 'high flyers'. **1969** *Daily Tel.* 8 Feb. 6/4 The other fund may have been lucky—or clever—enough to have a number of real 'high-fliers' in its portfolio and so has had to do comparatively little switching to achieve its 100 p.c. growth. **1969** *Times* 16 July 22/4 Another of last year's high flyers came unstuck yesterday when Qualitex Yarns revealed that it had missed its forecast.

high fre·quency. [f. HIGH *a.* + FREQUENCY 4.] **1. a.** A frequency (see FREQUENCY 4 b in Dict. and Suppl.) having a relatively large number of cycles in a second. Applied esp. to an electric current or voltage, an electromagnetic wave or a sound wave. Abbrev. *H.F., esp. in radio and telecommunications, where it also refers specifically to electromagnetic waves of 3–30 MHz. Often *attrib.*

1893 [see FREQUENCY 4 b]. **1923** *Nature* 7 July 12/2 The vibrations are of frequency 200,000 per second, such as are commonly used in wireless telegraphy and telephony. Such high frequencies are neither seen nor heard, but can be detected by special methods. **1934** S. G. B. STUBBS *Electr. Encycl.* II. 612/2 *High frequency (H.F.)*, refers to alternating currents, the frequency of which is reckoned in thousands. There is no definite line of demarcation between high and low frequency, but in general an alternating current is reckoned as of high frequency when the number of periods is greater than 10,000 per second. **1960** H. CARTER *Dict. Electronics* 127 *High frequency.* (1) A general term used to distinguish signals of radio frequency from those of audio frequency. (2) A relative term used to describe frequencies at the upper end of a particular frequency band. (3) Term of specific application to radio waves in the frequency range between 3 and 30 Mc/s, i.e. of wavelengths from 100 m down to 10 m. **1962** A. NISBETT *Technique Sound Studio* iii. 79 High frequencies can be lost in a variety of ways. **1962** M. G. SAY *Newnes' Conc. Encycl. Electr. Engin.* 360/1 Fig. 1 (*b*) and (*c*) show that at high frequencies above 1,000 c/s there is an increasing tendency for the current to flow in a shallow surface layer of the conductor.

b. *transf.* A high rate of occurrence, in space or in time.

1935 HUXLEY & HADDON *We Europeans* ix. 267 Our picture of the human species will be like a contour-map, a region of high frequency for, say, round-headedness being separated from another similar peak by a 'valley' of low frequency. **1971** *Sci. Amer.* Oct. 21/1 A high frequency of kwashiorkor is now being found among the East Pakistan refugees in India.

2. *attrib.* (usu. with hyphen). **a.** In sense 1 a, implying an applicability to an oscillation with a high frequency, as *high-frequency formula*, or an action or manner of working that involves such an oscillation.

1892 HEAVISIDE *Electr. Papers* II. 279 The high-frequency formulae are not so generally applicable as in the case of cores. **1893** *Jrnl. Soc. Arts* 5 May 624/1 The phosphorescent glow of the novel high-frequency, high-voltage, high-vacuum lamps. **1902** *Proc. R. Soc.* LXX. 341 The special manner in which a core or rod of iron or steel placed in a varying magnetic field is affected by high-frequency oscillations transmitted from considerable distances. **1903** *Daily Chron.* 14 Nov. 5/2 High-frequency apparatus and superb laboratories are beside the point compared with air and light. **1914** R. STANLEY *Text-bk. Wireless Telegr.* xii. 149 Do high and low frequency waves travel at the same speed? **1921** *Jrnl. Industrial & Engin. Chem.* July 639/2 High frequency voltage (10,000 to 20,000 cycles) is applied at the terminals of the coil. **1928** *Nature* 21 Apr. 623/1 High frequency sound waves of low intensity passed through these cells cause the protoplasm to rotate. **1955** F. E. TERMAN *Electronic Radio Engin.* (ed. 4) xxiv. 937 These requirements are usually more difficult to meet at the high-frequency end of the modulation range. **1960** R. W. MARKS *Dymaxion World of B. Fuller* 23/1 The high-frequency hiss of the surf. **1962** A. NISBETT *Technique Sound Studio* iv. 80 Another example of high-frequency attenuation will occur in recording if the tape is in imperfect contact with the head. *Ibid.*, Where the high frequency losses are progressive, measures may be taken to equalize for them. *Ibid.* 81 For a recording head the effect of high-frequency bias is to narrow the effective gap width.

b. In sense 1 b, meaning 'occurring often or involving a rapid succession of events'.

1957 D. L. BOLINGER in *Publ. Amer. Dialect Soc.* XXVIII. 89 Contrast the high-frequency *suppose* with the lower-frequency *suspect*. **1965** *English Studies* Feb. 75 It is hard to judge of the size of the corpus..but it seems to be adequate at least for high-frequency items.

3. *Comb.*, as *high-frequency amplifier, choke, cinematography, condenser microphone, current, photography, response, transformer*; **high-frequency alternator**, any of several kinds of alternator designed to give an alternating current with a frequency greater than about 10 kHz; **high-frequency amplification**, amplification of signals of high frequency; in *Radio* applied *spec.* to amplification at the carrier frequency in a radio receiver; **high-frequency heating**, the heating of a substance by placing it in an alternating electric field (dielectric heating) or magnetic field (induction heating) with a frequency above that of the mains electricity supply; **high-frequency induction furnace** (see quot. 1958); **high-frequency resistance**, (*a*) the increased electrical resistance of a conductor at high frequencies, owing to the **skin effect*; (*b*) a resistance for use at high frequencies; **high-frequency treatment**, (*a*) *Med.* (see quot. 1931); (*b*) *Metallurgy*, the hardening of metals by heating them inductively and quenching.

1901 *Proc. R. Soc.* LXVIII. 514 (*heading*) The high frequency alternator. **1935** J. B. MOORE in K. Henney *Radio Engin. Handbk.* (ed. 2) 564 The high-frequency alternator is one of the most used types of transmitter for long-wave transoceanic code communication. **1919** *Wireless World* Nov. 448 An eight valve amplifier, comprising five stages of high-frequency amplification, one stage of rectification, and two stages of audio-frequency amplification with transformer coupling. **1934** S. O. PEARSON in S. G. B. Stubbs *Electr. Encycl.* II. 612/1 The magnification of electrical variations at the signal—or radio—frequency of the received oscillations, that is, before they are applied to the detector of a wireless receiver, is termed high-frequency amplification. **1919** *Wireless World* Feb. 628 (*heading*) The use of impedance, capacity and resistance couplings in high-frequency amplifiers. **1928** [see *CHOKE 6]. **1958** *Van Nostrand's Sci. Encycl.* (ed. 3) 812/1 High-frequency photography includes both still and motion-picture photography... In high-frequency (slow-motion) cinematography the exposing rate may range from 32 to several thousand frames per sec. *Ibid.* 813/1 High-frequency photography which consists of a number of high-speed photographs made in rapid succession. **1940** *Chambers's Techn. Dict.* 188/1 *High-frequency condenser microphone*, a condenser microphone in which the polarising voltage is alternating at a high radio-frequency, amplitude modulation of which is detected by a de-modulator and used for audio-frequency transmission. **1896** *McClure's Mag.* VI. 414/2 A high frequency current. **1923** E. W. MARCHANT *Radio Telegr.* ii. 13 When we come to deal with the high-frequency currents that are employed in Radio, their behaviour is quite different. **1925** *Jrnl. Iron & Steel Inst.* CXII. 73 High-frequency heating may be found useful in the forging and heat treatment of steel. **1967** A. K. OSBORNE *Encycl. Iron & Steel Ind.* (ed. 2) 218/1 The polarity of this field changes many times per second with the alternation of the current necessary for high frequency heating. **1920** *Trans. Amer. Electrochem. Soc.* XXXV. 158 Since the presentation of the above paper a development into commercial form of high-frequency induction furnaces of the oscillatory current type has been actively continued. **1958** A. D. MERRIMAN *Dict. Metallurgy* 125/1 A high-frequency induction furnace is a melting furnace in which currents at a frequency above 500 c./sec. are used to induce eddy currents in the charge, which in turn generate heat in the material. **1958** High-frequency photography [see **high-frequency cinematography*]. **1892** HEAVISIDE *Electr. Papers* II. 193 The high-frequency resistance is independent of the steady resistance, and must be much greater than it. **1951** A. HUND *High-Frequency Measurements* (ed. 2) ii. 96 Any amplitude differences are balanced out by properly chosen high-frequency resistances. *Ibid.* ix. 310 In *all* cases, the high-frequency resistance is that quantity which, when multiplied by the square of the effective value of the high-frequency current, gives the energy dissipated in the conductor. **1930** *Wireless World* 17 Dec. 686/2 (*heading*) High frequency response. **1923** E. W. MARCHANT *Radio Telegr.* iv. 56 This change in voltage may be passed on..by means of a small high-frequency transformer, to the grid of a second valve. **1931** S. R. ROGET *Dict. Electr. Terms* (ed. 2) 146/2 *High frequency treatment*, curative treatment involving the use of interrupted trains of damped high frequency oscillations. **1967** A. K. OSBORNE *Encycl. Iron & Steel Industry* (ed. 2) 202/2 High-frequency treatment.

Highgate (hɒi·gĕt). The name of a hill in London, used *attrib.* in *Highgate resin*, a mineral resin similar to copal found in Highgate Hill. Also called *copalin(e), copalite, fossil copal.*

1813 T. THOMSON in *Ann. Philos.* II. 9 The colour of Highgate resin is of a dirty yellowish light brown. **1815** A. AIKIN *Man. Min.* (ed. 2) 64 Fossil Copal. Highgate Resin. Colour light yellowish dirty brown. **1839** *Phil. Mag.* XIV. 91 The Highgate resin has much resemblance to copal. **1898** E. S. DANA *Textbk. Min.* (rev. ed.) IV. 543 Copalite, or Highgate resin, is from the London blue clay. **1968** *Encycl. Brit.* VI. 462/2 *Copalite*.., also termed 'fossil resin' and 'Highgate resin', a naturally occurring organic substance found as irregular pieces of pale-yellow colour in the London clay at Highgate hill.

hi·gh-grade, *a.* and *sb.* [HIGH *a.* 22 a.] **A.** *adj.* Of a high grade or quality; *spec.* **a.** (See quot. 1909.) **b.** Denoting ores rich in metal value; *spec.* in commercial use denoting those which, owing to convenience in situation and transport facilities, can be worked at a large profit.

1878 R. J. HINTON *Handbk. Arizona* 161 The Metallic Accident is a large lode of low-grade ore, with a number of high-grade feeders. **1880** 'MARK TWAIN' *Tramp Abroad* I. xxiv. 230 Only the few are educated up to a point where high-grade music gives pleasure. **1890** [see HIGH *a.* 22 a]. **1902** *Daily Chron.* 10 Apr. 7/2 Great Britain is becoming very short of high-grade ores. **1907** *Springfield Republ.* 13 May 3 (Advt.), Auction sale of high grade household furniture. **1909** *Cent. Dict.* Suppl., *High-grade*,..specifically, having more than three quarters pure blood: applied by stockbreeders to animals. **1910** *Westm. Gaz.* 4 Jan. 5/2 The high-grade nature of the material and workmanship. **1919** *Empire Rev.* 79 Its products are high-grade steels. **1929** *Daily Express* 7 Nov. 8/4 The high-grade private car. **1932** *Discovery* Nov. 357/2 The institute conducts genetical studies leading to the breeding and selection of high-grade wheats. **1939** R. R. SNAPP *Beef Cattle* (ed. 3) xviii. 252 Their color indicates that they are high grade and purebred individuals of strictly beef type. **1940** *War Illustr.* 12 Apr. 360 A view of a Nazi petrol-substitute refinery where the raw material is converted into high-grade spirit suitable for use in the specially designed aeroplane engines. **1946** *Mind* LV. 114 Some human being in his right mind, that is to say, a human agent capable of relatively high-grade action. **1958** *Times Lit. Suppl.* 23 May 279/4 But, unlike other fellow-travellers, he was actually engaged in high-grade espionage.

B. *sb.* **a.** High-grade stock. **b.** (See quot. 1904 and cf. the vb.)

1882 *Rep. Maine Board Agric.* XXVI. 253 High-grades of either breed [Jersey or Guernsey]. **1904** *N.Y. Sun* 14 Aug. 11 One of the pests of gold mining in Colorado is the high grades, which is a polite term for the ore thief. The term high grades comes from the fact that they steal only high grade ore.

Hence **hi·gh-grade** *v. intr.* and *trans.*, to steal high-grade ore.

1907 *Westm. Gaz.* 6 June 10/1, I had been 'high grading' in the Vindicator mine. **1923** 'B. M. Bower' *Parowan Bonanza* vi. 73 He..could not leave his claims and let Al Freeman..'high grade' his gold the minute his back was turned. **1927** *Blackw. Mag.* June 833/1 In Cobalt..'high-grading' was rigorously dealt with. **1963** *Time* (Canad. ed.) 18 Jan. 10/2 Some Timmins stores have been known to accept high-graded ore in payment for grocery bills.

high-ha·ndedly, *adv.* [f. High-handed *a.* + -ly².] In a high-handed manner.

1898 N. Munro *John Splendid* xxi. 206 Seven fugitives of the clan that had come so high-handedly through their neighbourhood. **1927** *Daily Express* 26 Oct. 1/2 High-handedly putting a pistol to the heads of his opponents. **1948** A. L. Kroeber *Anthropol.* (rev. ed.) 617 Freud.. treated the findings of psychology almost as high-handedly as he did those of prehistory and culture history.

high hat, hi·gh-hat. [High *a.* 1.] **1.** A tall hat; *fig.* a person of affected superiority. Also *attrib.* or as *adj.*, superior, lofty.

1889 in C. W. & P. Cunnington *Handbk. Eng. Costume 19th Cent.* (1959) 309 Is it not considered bad taste to wear anything else but a high hat with a Frock coat? **1899** A. H. Quinn *Pennsylvania Stories* 39 Houston..was under strong suspicion of having worn a high hat out to college that morning. **1923** *N.Y. Times* 9 Sept. vii. 2/1 (Stage Gloss.), High Hat—swelled head. **1924** P. Marks *Plastic Age* 149 Christmas Cove's a nice place; not so high-hat as Bar Harbor. *Ibid.* 196 We're a lot of low-brows pretending to be intellectual high-hats. **1927** *Cleveland Press* 29 Jan., We see no point in assuming a high hat attitude towards what one doesn't know. **1930** *Publishers' Weekly* 22 Mar. 1674 The shop is not 'high hat'. **1931** G. B. Stern *Shortest Night* xvi. 263 That hot-tempered young high-hat. **1932** E. Wallace *When Gangs came to London* xxi. 186 Eddy was getting high-hat..now this new and irritating situation had arisen. **1932** E. Wilson *Devil take Hindmost* xviii. 205 He gets high-hat and speaks with scorn of the Mexicans. **1953** R. Lehmann *Echoing Grove* iii. 199 Forgive me if I sound high-hat—I don't think you can possibly understand it. **1969** in Halpert & Story *Christmas Mumming in Newfoundland* 197 They looked very smart in their trimmed pants, white shirts and high hat with ribbons and tassles.

2. *Photogr.* (See quot. 1930.)

1930 *Sel. Gloss. Motion Pict. Techn.* (*Acad. Motion Pict., Hollywood*) 16/1 *High hat*, a very low camera stand. **1953** *Time* 2 Nov. 35/2 *High-hat*, low camera support for 'worm's eye' pictures.

3. *Jazz.* A pair of cymbals worked by the foot. Also **hi-hat.**

1934 E. Little *Mod. Rhythmic Drumming* I. xxii. 21 The 'High-Hat' pedal brings the cymbals within reach of the snare drum sticks. Rhythm can be played on them. **1948** *Metronome* Nov. 28 I'd rather use the high-hat as a back beat and break up the bass rhythms. **1949** L. Feather *Inside Be-bop* ii. 58 In the old days the drummer frequently played high hat cymbal for the second and fourth beat accents. **1956** S. Traill *Play that Music* v. 56 Keep your hi-hat cymbals flat. **1956** M. Stearns *Story of Jazz* (1957) xviii. 234 The left foot played the high-hat, and the right foot exploded the bass drum. **1966** *New Yorker* 11 June 153/1 Barbarin..uses a high hat and ride cymbals to excellent effect. **1966** *Crescendo* Dec. 27/2 A tambourine on the hi-hat..makes a jingle sound every time the hi-hat cymbals come down. **1968** *Ibid.* Apr. 29/1 An intriguing hi-hat backing from the excellent drummer.

hi·gh-hat, *v.* Chiefly *U.S.* [f. prec.] *intr.* To wear a high hat; to assume a superior attitude. *trans.* To treat condescendingly. So **high-hatted** *a.*

1924 H. C. Witwer in *Cosmopolitan* Apr. 68/1 'Why high hat me?' he complains. 'I'm harmless and I may be able to do you a lot of good.' **1924** H. Crane *Let.* 24 Jan. (1965) 171 It's become fashionable for the high-hatted uptowners now to buy Matisse's paintings. **1925** S. Lewis *Martin Arrowsmith* xxxix. 455 If I blew in and old Mart high-hatted me, I'd just about come nigh unto letting him hear the straight truth. **1927** *Sat. Even. Post* 24 Dec. 22/3 What made me so sore..was her thinkin' she could high-hat me. **1929** C. E. Merriam *Chicago* 292 Dever's dignity was mistaken by some for 'high-hatting'. **1941** N. Coward *Australia Visited* iii. 15 The true representative American..is unpretentious... He dislikes being 'ritz'd' or 'high-hatted'. **1941** Belloc *Silence of Sea* xxxi. 193 The Americans..say of a proud man that 'he wears a high hat'... 'If you talk like that,' he was told, 'they will think you are high-hatting them.' **1965** *New Statesman* 7 May 730/2 Her ineffective efforts to make her sons 'high-hat the neighbours' and join the élite.

high-headed (stress variable), *a.* orig. *U.S.* [High *a.* 22 b.] Carrying the head high; proud, arrogant.

1837 *Southern Lit. Messenger* III. 86 One of them high-headed Roanoke planters. **1903** W. B. Yeats *In Seven Woods* 43 And that high-headed even-walking queen. **1909** R. A. Wason *Happy Hawkins* i. 10 The most obstinate, high-headed, bull-intellected thin-skin 'at ever drew down top wages fer punchin' cows. **1955** W. W. Denlinger *Compl. Boston* 112 A dog cannot display a high-headed style without well laid back shoulders.

high jinks: see Jink *sb.*¹ 3.

Highland, *a.* and *sb.* Add: **B.** *adj.* **2. a.** *Highland bonnet* = Scotch cap; *Highland Boundary Fault*, a geological fault extending across Scotland from the Firth of Clyde on the west coast to Stonehaven on the east; also called *Great Highland Fault*; (*West*) *Highland cattle*, a breed of small cattle from the Highlands, characterized by thick, shaggy hair and long curved horns set wide apart; *Highland dress* (examples); *Highland fling* (see Fling *sb.* 4 a); *Highland games* (see *game *sb.* 4 d); *Highland honours* (see quot. 1858); *Highland kilt* = Kilt *sb.*; *Highland pony*, one of a breed of ponies originating in the Highlands; *Highland terrier*, a variety of terrier descended from the working terrier of the Scottish Highlands; also called *West Highland white terrier, White West Highlander.*

1760 *Aberdeen Jrnl.* 22 Jan., His Grace..appears every Day in the Highland Dress, which becomes him extremely well. **1771** [see Kilt *sb.*]. **1818** Scott *Rob Roy* II. xiv. 192 The Baillie, thus refreshed, was mounted on a small Highland poney. **1819** *Observer* 25 July 4/4 A parcel of these children dressed in the Highland kilt. **1819** *Edin. Even. Courant* 31 July 1 Lost, A Highland Terrier, that answers to the name of Brogach. **1821** *Edin. Star* 2 Feb., There is something so hearty and rapturous in the Highland honours which follow the toasts. **1822** D. Wordsworth *2nd Tour Scotl.* in *Jrnls.* (1941) II. 373 Boys dressed in their glossiest and best—little ones in Tartan with Highland bonnets. **1825** Loudon *Encycl. Agric.* § 6118 Along the eastern coast, north of the Firth of Forth, the Highland cattle are intermixed with various local breeds. **1831** W. Youatt *Horse* iv. 59 The Highland Pony is far inferior to the galloway. **1833** *Chambers's Edin. Jrnl.* II. 137/2 The popularity which Highland bonnets acquired from the glory of the Scottish regiments at Waterloo. **1834** W. Youatt *Cattle* iii. 66 The striking peculiarities of the Highland cattle. **1844** H. Stephens *Bk. Farm* III. 1274 The West Highland has long been famed in Scotland as a superior breed of cattle. **1846** C. St. John *Short Sk. Highlands* xiv. 113 Why do Highland terriers so often run on three legs?.. I never had a Highland terrier who did not hop along constantly on three legs. **1853** J. E. Millais *Let.* ? 8 Oct. in M. Lutyens *Millais & Ruskins* (1967) 93 He comes out in the Highland kilt and cap. **1858** Q. Victoria *Let.* 1 Apr. in R. Fulford *Dearest Child* (1964) 83 Alfred and Arthur in Highland dress. **1858** *Illustr. News of World* 12 June 300/3 All the loyal toasts were proposed and drunk with 'Highland honours'—a kind of demonstration which the polite reader may think somewhat ludicrous..since it consists of putting one leg on a chair and another on the table, elevating the right hand to its utmost stretch, and 'draining the wine cup to the very dregs'. **1875** *Encycl. Brit.* I. 389/1 The Kyloes or West Highland cattle. **1893** *Q. Jrnl. Geol. Soc.* XLIX. 354 The grey slate or phyllite, north of the Great Highland Fault. **1901** A. Geikie *Scenery Scotl.* (ed. 3) iii. 64 The line of the Highland boundary fault runs out to sea immediately to the north of Stonehaven. **1911** *Encycl. Brit.* VIII. 376/1 An application which was made (1900) by some of their admirers for separate classification was refused by the Kennel Club, but afterwards it was granted, the breed being classified as the West Highland white terrier. **1922** R. Leighton *Compl. Bk. Dog* xiv. 206 The Poltalloch, or White West Highlander. **1929** J. W. Gregory in Evans & Stubblefield *Handbk. Geol. Gt. Brit.* i. 10 The Middle Devonian age of the Highland Boundary Fault is shown near Loch Lomond. **1937** J. Macdonald *Highland Ponies* 39 For several years the Department of Agriculture for Scotland has been supplying Highland pony stallions for the use of the crofters. **1961** L. D. Stamp *Gloss. Geogr. Terms* 234/1 Geographically the 'Highlands of Scotland' is the name applied to the whole massif north of the Highland Boundary Faults. **1969** R. T. Wilcox *Dict. Costume* 305/2 *Scottish Highland dress*..: the kilt; a hill jacket..; the sporran. **1970** *New Yorker* 28 Feb. 44/2 Calvin was the little West Highland terrier she and Grandpa Nye had got on their wedding trip in Scotland in 1937. **1973** *Courier & Advertiser* (Dundee) 26 Feb. 1/1 (Advt.), Cattleman required for suckler herd and pedigree Highland cattle.

b. Resembling, having the characteristics of, or typical of the people of the Highlands of Scotland.

c **1780** J. R. (*song title*) The Highland character... No effeminate customs our sinews unbrace, No luxurious tables enervate our race. **1787** Burns in *Poems ascribed to Burns* (1801) 53 There's naething here but Highland pride, And Highland scab and hunger. **1792** —— *Poems & Songs* (1968) I. 358 In Heaven itself I'll ask no more Than just a Highland welcome. **1816** Scott *Antiquary* I. ix. 204 Rab Tull keepit a Highland heart, and bang'd out o' bed..and he did follow the thing up stairs and down stairs. **1818** —— *Rob Roy* II. v. 54 Ay, he has a kind o' Hieland honesty—he's honest after a sort, as they say. **1829** *Blackw. Mag.* Sept. 400 Yet still the blood is strong, the heart is Highland, And we in dreams behold the Hebrides. **1871** L. W. M. Lockhart *Fair to See* (1872) I. ii. 58 I'm as Highland as—as—anything. **1897** R. M. Ferguson *Village Poet* 172 They'll not jew us—we're no' sae hieland.

highlander. Add: **2. b.** Highland cattle.

1771 *Caled. Mercury* 17 Aug., One Hundred Cows, mostly Highlanders, laid early on the grass in the spring to fatten. **1787** W. H. Marshall *Rural Econ. Norf.* (1795) II. 381 Highlanders, Scotch cattle of the Highland breed. **1825** Loudon *Encycl. Agric.* § 6122 The other variety of Highland cattle is the Norlands, or North Highlanders. **1834** W. Youatt *Cattle* iii. 69 There is little or no variety of breeds of cattle in the Hebrides. They are pure West Highlanders. *Ibid.* 79 The character of the Highlander must still be, that he will pay better for his quantity of food than any other breed. **1875** *Encycl. Brit.* I. 389/1 They [*sc.* the Pembrokes] excel the West Highlanders in this respect, that they make good dairy cattle, the cows being peculiarly adapted for cottagers' purposes.

5. *White West Highlander*: see **Highland terrier*.

hi·gh-life, -lifed, *a. U.S.* [High *a.* 16.] Full of life or spirit. (Cf. *high life* s.v. *high *a.* 21.)

1861 *Trans. Ill. Agric. Soc.* IV. 376 A long narrow-headed high-lifed brainless animal. **1902** A. D. McFaul *Ike Glidden* ix. 70 Ike told him..to always drive on the bit, because the colt was a high-life fellow. **1935** *Archit. Rev.* LXXVII. 64/2 He was busy building for 'high-life' America.

high light, hi·gh-light. [High *a.* 10, Light *sb.* 12.] **1. a.** In painting, photography, and cinematography, any of the brightest parts of a subject or a representation of it; often *pl.* Also *attrib.*

1658, 1859 [see Light *sb.* 12]. **1892** A. Brothers *Photogr.* 335 In a portrait, if well lighted, there should be parts which are brighter than the rest of the face—on the forehead and nose, for instance; they are called *high lights.* **1903** A. Watkins *Photogr.* (ed. 2) 64 The tone D is called the 'high light', for although it is the blackest in the negative it represents white in the original. *Ibid.* 77 It may happen that there is no white part or high light in the subject you are developing. **1913** J. A. Sinclair *Handbk. Photogr.* (ed. 2) 226 To clear up high-lights or remove pressure marks from thick bromide papers. **1930** *Sel. Gloss. Motion Pict. Techn.* (*Acad. Motion Pict., Hollywood*), *High light*, object, scene, or picture having low color saturation, that is, containing a large proportion of white. **1931** Selden & Sellman *Stage Scenery* 158 In order to give interest to high lights and shadows. **1937** *Bell Telephone Q.* Apr. 110 The painter contributes highlight in the sense of accent. **1951** G. H. Sewell *Amateur Film-Making* (ed. 2) ii. 20 The high-light meter reads the intensity of the light falling upon the subject, instead of the light reflected from it. **1957** R. W. G. Hunt *Reprod. of Colour* vii. 73 A highlight mask is made by contact printing the transparency onto a very high contrast black and white negative material. **1968** *Gloss. Terms Offset Lithogr. Printing* (*B.S.I.*) 13 *Highlight stop*, a lens aperture used in half-tone photography which has a specific influence on the formation of highlight tones. *Ibid.* 17 *Highlight mask*, a mask used to retain or increase highlight contrast in the reproduction.

transf. **1929** K. H. Brown *Father* vi. 61 There were artless scarlet highlights cut from portions of the little boys' outgrown woolen underwear.

b. A bright tint in the hair; that portion of the hair that reflects the most light. Also *attrib.*

1941 *Hairdressers' Weekly Jrnl.* 1 Feb. 155/2 One can bring out high-lights on every shade of hair by the appropriate use of toning rinses. **1966** Cox *Illustr. Dict. Hairdressing* 79/2 *High-light cap*, a plastic head cap with holes in it used for drawing a strand or strands of hair through to bleach without bleaching the other hair.

2. *fig.* A 'bright', prominent, or outstanding feature or characteristic. Chiefly *pl.* Phr. *to hit the high lights*, = *to hit the high spots* (s.v. *high *a.* 21).

1855 *Knickerbocker* XLVI. 40 If we have chosen to speak of the shadows in the fair portrait, we have also neglected to point out the high lights. **1905** A. Adams *Outlet* 275 It was the recognized cattle centre of Montana .., but devoid of the high-lights which were a feature of the trail towns. **1922** A. Waugh *Public School Life* i. 16 It would be filled with high lights, with breathless escapades, with impossible heroics. **1923** *Weekly Dispatch* 21 Jan. 11 There is no 'hitting the high lights' when he is not in training. **1927** *Hutchinson's Myst. Story Mag.* Feb. 117 One by one, Dan and I met all the high lights of the town. **1931** *Times Lit. Suppl.* 15 Jan. 34/2 It is not readable in the sense that some modern biographies are readable; it has no 'high lights'. **1931** *Morning Post* 21 Aug. 11/7 These were the highlights of to-day's practice over the course. **1961** Baughman & Robinson *Secret Service Chief* (1963) ii. 23 Flipping the years like pages I see many interesting and instructive highlights—and some funny ones too. **1969** *Times* 10 Feb. 6/5 The highlight of the lunch will be a speech..on the vital relationship between the industrial leader and his executive secretary. *Ibid.* 19 Feb. 17/2 Highlights from one of tonight's top soccer matches.

hi·ghlight, hi·gh-light, *v.* [f. prec.] *trans.* **a.** To bring into prominence, to 'feature', to draw attention to.

1934 M. Weseen *Dict. Amer. Slang* x. 143 *Highlight*, to give one a prominent place on a program or a leading part in a show. *Highlighted*, marked by; featured by. **1945** Nelson & Wright *Tomorrow's House* iv. 43/2 This seemingly minor problem..highlights what should be the fundamental approach to planning. **1951** *Mind* LX. 23 The view is..made more plausible by highlighting.. aspects of scientific procedure. **1952** Granville *Dict. Theatr. Terms* (ed. 2) 97 *Highlight*, to give prominence to an artiste in the billing or newspaper publicity matter, the build-up of a show, or of an individual artiste. **1955** Priestley & Hawkes *Journey down Rainbow* p. xi, Football games, night clubs, TV programmes, hotel festivities, can be ignored and certainly should not be high-lighted by the serious social critic. **1957** *Economist*

19 Oct. 192/1 The genuineness with which each holds the belief was highlit during last week's..interview. **1958** *Listener* 2 Oct. 501/1 Statistics such as these are cold and dull and do little to highlight the tremendous importance of industrial organizations in modern society. **1965** *New Statesman* 30 Apr. 670/3 Thursday's polling is unlikely to highlight any notable national trends. **1967** SINGHA & MASSEY *Indian Dances* ii. 42 A tirmana is used to conclude a section of dance or highlight a portion in the middle.

b. *spec.* To tint or bleach portions of the hair in such a way that they catch and reflect the light. More widely in make-up: see quot. 1952. Also **hi·ghlighting** *vbl. sb.*

1942 D. POWELL *Time to be Born* (1943) vi. 132 'You've had your hair dyed.'..'Not dyed. High-lighted is the new word,' said Vickey. **1952** GRANVILLE *Dict. Theatr. Terms* (ed. 2) 97 *Highlight*, in make-up, to accentuate cheekbones and other features and effectively contrast the shade, on the face. **1959** *Punch* 3 June 752/2 For grey hair there is a treatment..which highlights the hair and dismisses yellow discoloration. **1972** *Vogue* 15 Mar. 3/2 New Pure Pearl-Light Everywhere Colour for highlighting round the eyes.

highly, *adv.* **6.** (Further examples.)

1831 J. S. MILL in *Examiner* 12 June 24 Indebted to men of highly-cultivated intellects. **1836** —— in *Lond. Rev.* II. 368 The feelings of a highly-educated and sensitive girl. **1910** *Busy Man's Mag.* July 88/1 He betrays a highly-strung temperament, which is seldom held in leash. **1964** S. DUKE-ELDER *Parsons' Dis. Eye* (ed. 14) xxiv. 362 Highly-strung people. **1969** *Jane's Freight Containers 1968–69* 143/1 There is considerable evidence of highly-integrated freight services being developed.

high-muck-a-muck (həi·mɒ:kəmɒk). *N. Amer. colloq.* Also **high-you-muck-a-muck.** [app. ad. Chinook Jargon *hiu* plenty + *muckamuck* food.] A self-important person, one who imagines he is more exalted than he is.

1856 *Democratic State Jrnl.* (Sacramento) 1 Nov. 3/1 The professors—the high 'Muck-a-Mucks'—tried fusion, and produced confusion. **1866** 'MARK TWAIN' *Lett. fr. Hawaii* (1967) 32 Not if I was High-You-Muck-a-Muck and King of Wawhoo. **1869** —— *Sk. New & Old* (1875) 69 High Muck-a-mucks, the paleface from the land of the setting sun greets you! **1879** C. E. S. WOOD *Jrnl.* 13 Feb. in *Oreg. Hist. Q.* (1969) LXX. 144 Go to Thompsons 2 bit house, no deception there, hi you muck a muck and here's your bill of fare. **1920** S. LEWIS *Main Street* 117 He looks at me like he wants me to remember he's a highmuckamuck and worth two hundred thousand dollars. **1927** A. PHILIP *Painted Cliff* 14 J. B. Smith is the high muck-a-muck, the tyee of the mining business of British Columbia. **1947** *Chicago Tribune* 21 Dec. (Comics section) 8 They's a highmuckymuck in th'radio business vacationin' here, so we gotta be good. **1965** *Time* (Canad. ed.) 16 Apr. 14/3 Not all the Liberal high muckamucks were as warmly defended as Favreau.

hi·gh-powered, *a.* [HIGH *a.* 22 b.] Having great power or drive (lit. and fig.); forceful, energetic; of good or high quality.

1903 *Daily Chron.* 1 Aug. 3/7 High-priced, high-powered cars. **1917** 'CONTACT' *Airman's Outings* p. xv, Modern two-seaters, high-powered, fast, and reliable. **1928** *Daily Mail* 16 Aug. 19/4 This class of fraud does not require so many high-powered salesmen as the old method of selling by personal canvas. **1934** T. S. ELIOT *Rock* ii. 51 Does the whole world stray in high-powered cars on a by-pass way? **1936** *Amer. Scholar* V. 83 The schools are failing, with all their high-powered modern pedagogy. **1944** *Living off Land* v. 114 High-powered microscopes. **1957** *Times Lit. Suppl.* 29 Nov. 724/2 American motor-cars that are always 'high-powered'. **1958** *Engineering* 14 Mar. 336/1 Automatic train control was developed.. early this century..and, in 1920, a high-powered committee..recommended its general adoption on all British railway lines. **1958** *Spectator* 25 July 138/1 High-powered promotion men. **1960** *News Chron.* 18 Mar. 6/4 The National Executive should..set up a high-powered inquiry into those industries which have already been nationalised. **1969** *Daily Tel.* 5 Feb. 15/1 The girl graduate, however high-powered her degree, is very often unemployable.

hi·gh-ranking, *a.* orig. *U.S.* [RANKING *ppl. a.* s.v. RANK *v.*[1]] Of an officer: of high rank. Also more widely: senior, important.

1922 S. LEWIS *Babbitt* xviii. 232 He ought to have been a high-ranking officer, he had that natural ability to command. **1924** *Amer. Mercury* II. 173/1 Wary Wade, a high ranking student at Ohio State, has the right angle on boxing. **1936** *Time* 13 Jan. 26 To this dinner come high ranking members of both political parties in the Senate and House of Representatives. **1946** G. H. SEWARD *Sex & Social Order* x. 127 Such women relieved the ennui of wealthy high-ranking men. **1953** *Times* 6 Mar. 7/7 She left him..a son, Vassili, now a high ranking officer in the Soviet Air Force. **1957** H. ROOSENBERG *Walls came tumbling Down* 19 We were intended as exchanges against some high-ranking Nazis. **1960** P. H. REANEY *Orig. Eng. Place-Names* vii. 163 Holderness (ERY), 'headland of the *hold*', a high-ranking officer in the Danelaw. **1961** NEW ENG. BIBLE *Acts* xxv. 23 Accompanied by high-ranking officers and prominent citizens. **1964** *Observer* 16 Aug. 1/3 Six sets of the master-key..in a prison..would be available..to a limited number of high-ranking officers.

hi·gh-roller. *U.S. slang.* [HIGH *a.*, ? ROLLER *sb.*[1] 15.] One who spends extravagantly; one who gambles for high stakes.

1881 *Reinbeck* (Iowa) *Times* 15 Sept. 1/6 California's Speculators who invest large sums are called 'high rollers'. **1903** A. H. LEWIS *Boss* xiv. 184 I'd like to learn how you moral an' social high rollers reconcile yourselves to things. **1909** 'O. HENRY' *Roads of Destiny* xx. 340 There comes a party of these high-rollers that are always hunting up new places to eat in and poke fun at. **1927** K. NORRIS *Barberry Bush* vi. 156 'Say,' said Link, slightly drawling the last word, 'that girl is a high-roller, believe me. She's full of the Old Nick!' **1968** L. BLACK *Outbreak* ii. 20 He's a high roller... A big gambler. **1972** *Sunday Mail* (Brisbane) 2 July 19/5 The Hughes places had included some of the chief centres for the big-money gamblers, or 'high-rollers'.

high school: see SCHOOL *sb.*[1] 1 j.

hi·gh-speed, *a.* [HIGH *a.* 22 a.] **a.** Able or fitted to work or travel at high speed. **b.** Produced by swift processes or machinery. **c.** Produced or caused by, or during, high speed.

high-speed steel, an alloy steel of such toughness and hardness that it can be used for tools cutting so rapidly as to become red-hot.

1873 [see HIGH *a.* 22 a]. **1888** *Lockwood's Dict. Mech. Engin.* s.v., High-speed engines may be considered to embrace any engines making over 200 to 300 revolutions per minute... High-speed belting applies to belts for fans, wood-working machinery, centrifugal pumps, &c., in opposition to those for line and counter, and other slowly driving shafts. *High speed bearings*, bearings whose length exceeds their diameter by from four to six times. **1898** *Daily News* 1 Oct. 2/8 A high-speed destroyer. **1904** *Chambers's Jrnl.* 142/1 High-speed tool-steel lathes. **1908** *Daily Chron.* 6 Feb. 3/1 The crude truths that we look for only in the high-speed camera. **1909** *Westm. Gaz.* 11 Mar. 4/2 The high-speed flier of the future. **1912** *Chambers's Jrnl.* June 367/1 Their [*sc.* British makers'] introduction of high-speed steel in 1900. **1920** J. L. MYRES in H. G. Wells *Outl. Hist.* v. xxvii. 249/1 The bow..discharges a high-speed arrow with a twang. **1926** *Jrnl. Iron & Steel Inst.* CXIII. 307 High-speed steels are well known to be very complex alloys, a fact readily grasped when it is considered that even simple types contain elements such as tungsten, chromium, and vanadium, in addition to those usually found in plain steels. **1943** T. HORSLEY *Find, Fix & Strike* 20 He can concentrate on hitting his target..in the sure knowledge that he's virtually safe from a high-speed stall. **1943** *Sci. News* VII. 29 The dynamics of high-speed flow. **1950** *Gloss. Aeronaut. Terms* (*B.S.I.*) I. 29 High-speed wind tunnel. **1952** *This Week* 1 June 8/1 A second danger on the superhighways is something called 'high-speed hypnosis'—a trance-like state induced by mile after mile of effortless driving. **1954** WEBSTER Add. p. cxiii/2 *Skiing*, High-speed turn. **1956** A. H. COMPTON *Atomic Quest* 86 The action of high-speed neutrons moving through uranium 235 and plutonium. **1957** *Technology* Mar. 3/2 A complete set of all equipment likely to be of use in research from high-speed and time-lapse cameras down to X-ray cinematographic equipment for biological work. **1960** COOKE & MARKUS *Electronics & Nucleonics Dict.* 211/2 *High-speed carry*, a carry that bypasses the normal adding circuit in a computer. **1964** S. CRAWFORD *Basic Engin. Processes* iv. 104 High-speed steel, fully heat treated. An alloy steel containing tungsten.., with small percentages of chromium, vanadium and cobalt. **1967** *Technology Week* 23 Jan. 11/1 (Advt.), Sigma 5.. does foreground real-time control..and high-speed input/output. **1969** *Times* 5 Feb. 13/6 The tracks are recorded by taking high-speed photographs. **1972** J. EASTWOOD *Henry in Silver Frame* ix. 95 The dentist's high-speed drill.

high-stepping, *a.* (Earlier and later examples.)

1848 THACKERAY *Van. Fair* li. 456 Splendid high-stepping carriage horses. **1973** D. RAMSAY *Deadly Discretion* 63 A millionaire..is pretty high stepping for a two-bit dancer.

highstrikes (həi·strəiks). *jocular colloq.*, orig. *dial.* or *vulgar.* ¶. Perverted form of HYSTERICS.

1838 C. SELBY *Jacques Strop* ii. 4 Didn't I do the *high-strikes* famously? **1846** D. CORCORAN *Pickings* 149 She's one of the dreadfullest cases of the highstrikes I ever did see. **1899** *Pall Mall Mag.* Jan. 82 [Mrs.] Flounce fell into the highstrikes at traipsing the roads after four o'clock. **1914** G. ATHERTON *Perch of Devil* I. 204 If you don't get us out of this quick I'll have high-strikes. **1922** GALSWORTHY *Windows* I. 19 They say she 'ad the 'ighstrikes after. **1945** L. A. G. STRONG *Othello's Occupation* iv. 102 Maisie just cavorts along..till things get too much. Then she has the highstrikes. **1957** H. CROOME *Forgotten Place* xvi. 193 There I was, all in among the bicycles, having hysterics—yes, I mean it, genuine old-fashioned high strikes.

hi·ghtail, hi·gh-tail, *v. colloq.* (orig. *U.S.*). [In allusion to the erect tails of animals in flight.] *intr.* To run (quickly) away, to move quickly. Freq. const. *it*.

1925 *Amer. Speech* I. 149/2 'I high-tailed out of there.'.. 'High-tail' comes straight from the plains where a mustang, when startled, erects his tail in a sudden, quick gesture and runs like the wind. So to make a sudden departure is to 'high-tail'. **1928** L. R. FREEMAN *Nearing North* 157 A string of red-brown bodies hightailing it through the bush. **1930** *Detective Fiction Weekly* 19 Apr. 566/2 We high-tailed it for the hideout. **1953** M. LOWRY *Let.* Nov. (1967) 349, I hightailed it thither anyhow, fire-extinguisher in hand. **1958** P. DE VRIES *Mackerel Plaza* v. 62, I was only always high-tailing it after everything in skirts, that's all. **1959** C. WILLIAMS *Man in Motion* ii. 29, I..high-tailed it in the other direction, and ducked into an alley. **1962** *Listener* 22 Mar. 524/2 The two of them high-tailed it for Oldham. **1971** *Nat. Geographic* May 721/2 Suddenly a Chinese goose, honking belligerently, high-tailed straight for me. **1973** *Caribbean Contact* Jan. 2/3 They get the point. Pronto. And high-tail it back home!

hi·gh-tone, *attrib.* or as *adj.* = next.

1897 E. W. BRODHEAD *Bound in Shallows* 105 They was high-tone lookin' fellers, and I'd like 'em to brag up the house. **1898** *Christian Herald* 19 Jan. 44/4 The infernal delusion that it was not high-tone for women to learn a profitable calling. **1925** F. SCOTT FITZGERALD *Let. c.* 27 Dec. (1964) 194 Saw Leslie also and went on some very high-tone parties. **1939** L. HELLMAN *Little Foxes* II. 66 Everybody going to be high-tone rich. Big rich.

high-toned, *a.* Add: **3.** (Earlier and later examples.) Also, stylish, pretentious. Also *absol.* Cf. *high-tone* (*HIGH *a.* 22 a).

1807 in *Western Pennsylvania Hist. Mag.* (1947) Mar.–June 56 The same editor also states that there were 'no Demo-Republicans in it, all high-toned gentlemen'. **1829** *Virginia Herald* (Fredericksburg) 28 May 2/3 He might be President if he liked; but this high-toned eulogy, he thought highly objectionable. **1854** GEO. ELIOT in *Westm. Rev.* Oct. 453 That blending of the high-toned chivalry of Spain with the caustic wit and refined irony of Italy. **1866** *Washoe* (Nevada) *Eastern Slope* 11 Aug. 2/2 It is [necessary] when the high toned meet..for the purpose of cutting off debate, that they should be ready to raise the previous question at any moment. **1876** 'MARK TWAIN' *Tom Sawyer* xxxvi. 272 A robber is more high-toned than what a pirate is..as a general thing. **1888** A. C. GUNTER *Mr. Potter* IV. xxiii. 278 The Democratic Party thought Sampson Potter a more high-toned name to run for Congress than Sammy Potts. **1912** BEERBOHM *Christmas Garland* p. v, Tripping off the pens of all higher-toned reviewers. **1956** AUDEN *Old Man's Road*, The smart crescent of a high-toned suburb. **1966** *Listener* 22 Sept. 426/1 The girls whose vicissitudes after graduating from a high-toned American college supply the film's story line.

hi·gh-up, *a. colloq.*, orig. *dial.* [f. HIGH *a.* + UP *adv.*[2]] In a high or elevated position, high above the ground; also *fig.*, of high place or rank.

1868 J. C. ATKINSON *Gloss. Cleveland* s.v., He's some desput high-up chap. **1899** S. MACMANUS *In Chimney Corners* 155 There was a lot of high-up folk being entertained. **1899** *Westm. Gaz.* 12 June 1/3 The gilt-edged lies of the high-up men. **1903** *Book Lover* May 3/1 In a high-up room in the Rue Lafayette. **1918** C. WELLS *Vicky Van* ii. 23 A high-up Publican. **1920** J. M. HUNTER *Trail Drivers of Texas* 219 Our 'high up' officers were.. somewhere in town. **1934** E. BOWEN *Cat Jumps* 74 The skies were disturbed by a high-up swift rustling sigh: the summer birds flying south. **1940** 'G. ORWELL' *Notebooks* 24 June in *World Review* (1950) June 27 High-up influences in England are preparing for a..sell-out. **1942** A. L. ROWSE *Cornish Childhood* iv. 82 Myself sitting in the high-up baby's chair with the little tray attached in front. **1961** *Guardian* 27 May 3/7 His penetrating assessment of high-up American attitudes to Cuba.

Also *colloq.* as *sb.*, a person of high rank or status. Cf. *HIGHER-UP.

1929 W. R. BURNETT *Little Caesar* VII. vi. 299 Rico got in touch with some of the high-ups. **1939** *News Review* 30 Nov. 13/1 As time went on, the Nazi high-ups took Admiral Raeder's advice. **1946** J. RICHARDSON *Phoney Phleet* 150 Two high-ups, lordly ones, or nobs. **1949** 'M. INNES' *Journeying Boy* i. 6 Only the high-ups had their heads substantially above the soapsuds. **1969** AUDEN *City without Walls* 84 How golden-tongued was Socrates, Who always spoke the truth, But high-ups do not like to think. **1971** *Physics Bull.* Dec. 735/2 Whitten and Poppoff, both high-ups in NASA's Ames Research Center, have filled the gap admirably despite their lack of academic background.

highveld (həi·felt, həi·velt). [Partial transl. of Afrikaans *hoëveld*, f. *hoog* high + VELD.] The inner plateau of the subcontinent of South Africa, which is from 5,000 to 6,000 feet above sea-level.

1878 A. AYLWARD *Transvaal To-day* 18 The High-veld... The large, bare, but healthy elevated plateau—the great watershed of the Transvaal. **1905** J. W. GREGORY in *Rep. Brit. Assoc.* 399 The old rocks that form the foundation of the present high veldt of Rhodesia. **1906** RIDER HAGGARD *Benita* v. 63 They were on the Transvaal high-veld. **1907** P. FITZPATRICK *Jock of Bushveld* 223 For perhaps a week the towering bulwarks of the Highveld were visible as we toiled along. **1954** D. D'EWES *Mydorp* 51 Sirius and the Southern Cross.. shining with the ecstatic brightness that only the high-veld sky can offer. **1961** L. VAN DER POST *Heart of Hunter* I. ii. 45 My first memories are of the incomparable starlight of the high-veld of Southern Africa and the far sea-sound that goes with it. *Ibid.* III. xii. 161 The light of a high-veld sunset. **1971** *World Archaeol.* III. 178 The highveld reaches an altitude of 5,500 feet at Johannesburg. **1972** *Stand. Encycl. S. Afr.* V. 522/1 *Highveld*, Tvl. and O.F.S... It lies about 1200 to 1800 metres above sea-level, more or less between 26° and 30° S.

high-water mark. Add: **c.** *jocular colloq.* A dirty mark showing the limit to which a person has washed.

1886 in BAUMANN *Londinismen.* **1899** *Daily News* 31 Jan. 6/4 The high-water mark is plainly visible above a tattered scarf tied loosely round his neck.

highway. Add: **1. c.** In allusion to Matt. xxii. 9, 10, Luke xiv. 23.

1843 H. BONAR *Hymn*, '*Go labour on*' vii, Go forth into

the world's highway, Compel the wanderer to come in. **1898** *Daily News* 6 Oct. 6/7 The South London officials of the Salvation Army have..been..gathering together of late from the highways and by-paths of Lambeth those who..are entitled to be ranked as 'Hooligans'. **1908** *Westm. Gaz.* 27 Jan. 1/3 It is highways and hedges work, and we shall need van for van and lecturer for lecturer. **1948** A. J. TOYNBEE *Civilization on Trial* vi. 111 The United States—who had previously not only welcomed European immigrants but whose employers of labour had sought them in the highways and hedges of Europe and compelled them to come in.

2. c. *Computers.* (See quot. 1962.)

1949 D. R. HARTREE *Calculating Instruments & Machines* (1950) viii. 107 A number of source-gates..on the right, and a number of destination-gates on the left, are connected by a single bus labelled 'Highway'. In this bus there is a further gate, labelled 'transfer gate', which exercises the main control over transfer of words between the various sources and destinations. *Ibid.* 108 An instruction..opens the corresponding S-gate and D-gate through selecting circuits; then at the appropriate time the main transfer gate in the highway opens. **1962** *Gloss. Automatic Data Processing Terms (B.S.I.)* 87 *Highway*, a major path along which signals travel from one of several sources to one of several destinations. **1964** F. L. WESTWATER *Electronic Computers* i. 7 The number..can either be allowed to pass on to one of the so-called 'highways' in the computer or it can be obliterated. *Ibid.* 9 Numbers are driven out on to the highways serially by admitting electronic pulses to the registers.

4. *highway robber* (later example), *robbery* (freq. in trivial use of something that is exorbitantly expensive); **Highway Code**, in Britain, an official publication containing the 'rules of the road', esp. for motor vehicles; first published in 1931, it has appeared subsequently in revised editions. Also *transf.*

1930 *Act* 20 & 21 *Geo. V* c. 45 § 1 The Minister shall..prepare a code (in this section referred to as the 'highway code') comprising such directions as appear to him to be proper for the guidance of persons using roads. **1935** *Archit. Rev.* LXXVIII. 110/3 The free issue of the Highway Code to all of his Majesty's lieges who have come (or are supposed to have come) to years of discretion is a portent. **1958** *Listener* 20 Nov. 835/1 The importance of reading the Highway Code. **1959** *Daily Tel.* 1 July 1/3 Highway Code revised for motorways. **1970** 'A. GILBERT' *Death wears Mask* x. 166 And then there's the Highway Code. **1972** *Listener* 23 May 375/3 Here was a book that..had broken the Highway Code of conventional English culture. **1904** KIPLING *Traffics & Discov.* 330 The other six hundred [acres] are nearly all let to folk who knew my folk..but this Turpin is a new man—and a highway robber. **1778** J. WEDGWOOD *Let.* 19 Mar. (1965) 218 On Monday night last there was three highway robberies between this place and Newcastle. **1853** MRS. GASKELL *Cranford* x. 181 She indeed inclined to the idea that, in some way, the French were connected with..the burglaries and highway robberies. **1886** *Lantern* (New Orleans) 3 Nov. 2/3 Highway robbery is no name for it. **1920** A. HUXLEY *Limbo* 122 The organized highway robbery of Red Cross collectors. **1941** 'R. CROMPTON' *William does his Bit* ii. 36 'I've heard people talk about highway robbery quite lately.' 'Yes, but they only mean people chargin' too much for meals,' explained Ginger, 'not the old sort.' **1967** J. B. PRIESTLEY *It's Old Country* ix. 107 Nothing on the wine list..under two-pound-ten. Highway robbery by candlelight.

highwayman. Add: **3.** Used *attrib.* or in the possessive designating a type of long loose coat or cape suggestive of the kind once worn by highwaymen.

1901 *Daily Chron.* 9 July 3/5 Sarah Bernhardt..looked very striking in a wonderful gown..half-concealed by a long paletot of white silk, made in the 'highwayman' shape, with a number of natty little capes. **1960** *Guardian* 29 July 7/1 A very dashing full length highwayman coat..with a huge cape collar. **1966** *Vogue* Nov. 88 (*caption*) Vogue's adventurers wear..highwaymen's coats.

highwood (həi·wud). [f. HIGH *a.* + WOOD *sb.*[1]; cf. *high forest* (*HIGH *a.* 21) and G. *hochwald.*] A forest of tall trees.

1900 J. NISBET *Our Forests & Woodlands* iii. 105 Data are not yet available to indicate anything like definitely what rotation of oak in highwoods will prove most remunerative. **1904** G. A. B. DEWAR *Glamour of Earth* v. 83 He turns bravely to the dripping highwood, to cut and lay in lands or rows the hazel and oak stems. **1905** J. NISBET *Forester* I. II. ii. 346 Highwood..woods..are not cleared..until..maturity. **1959** E. POUND *Thrones* cvii. 110 High-wood is called saltus.

higlif (*iglif*). [Repr. Fr. pronunc. of 'high life' (HIGH *a.* 5 in Dict. and Suppl.).] High society.

1911 'I. HAY' *Safety Match* xiv. 222 That variegated cosmos which..Gallic students of British sociology term 'Le Higlif'. **1925** A. HUXLEY *Along Road* IV. 256 English *Higlif*, as seen through the eyes of an Italian touring company, was worth coming for. **1960** *Harper's Bazaar* Oct. 141/1 Token names which evoke romance or the longed-for *higlif*. **1961** *John o' London's* 24 Aug. 235/2 It sees through this neurotic *hig-lif* caper to the fear and insecurity underneath.

hi-hat, var. *HIGH HAT 3.

hijack (həi·dʒæk), *v.* orig. *U.S. slang* (now passing into general use). Also **hi-jack,** (formerly) **highjack.** [Origin unknown.] *trans.* To steal (contraband or stolen goods) in transit, to rob (a bootlegger or smuggler) of his illicit goods; to hold up and commandeer (a vehicle and its load) in transit; to seize (an aeroplane) in flight and force the pilot to fly to a new destination. Also *transf.*

1923 *Lit. Digest* 4 Aug. 51/3 'I would have had $50,000,' said Jimmy, 'if I hadn't been hijacked.' **1927** 'J. BARBICAN' *Confess. Rum-Runner* xvii. 181 So we landed the cargo as quickly as we could, and took the chance of the cargo being seized or hijacked on shore. **1936** E. AMBLER *Dark Frontier* xi. 178, I still don't see how we're going to high-jack Groom's men. **1936** J. G. BRANDON *Pawnshop Murder* v. 47 Some one else has been on to this deal, given him the works and hi-jacked the stuff. **1959** A. W. SHERRING *Tip Off* i. 8 A stack of old banknotes leaves Central Post Office at three this afternoon. The van will be hijacked. **1961** *John o' London's* 12 Oct. 423/3 The plot concerns an attempt to hi-jack a million dollars. **1963** *Times* 4 Sept. 5/1 A lorry driver was beaten over the head and his load of cigarettes worth nearly £50,000 hi-jacked near Isleworth. **1968** *Daily Tel.* 7 Dec. 17/1 One of our planes with 35 on board was hi-jacked and flown to Cuba. **1970** *Daily Tel. Mag.* 16 Jan. 17/2 When a virus enters a cell it hijacks it, and makes it do what it wants.

So **hi·jacking** *vbl. sb.* and *ppl. a.* Also **hi·jack** *sb.*, an instance of hijacking; also *attrib.*

1923 *Lit. Digest* 4 Aug. 55/1 So much for hijacking on the high seas. **1924** *Daily Mail* 22 Dec. (N.Y. Corresp.), The duties of American coastguards are confined to seizing rum-ships; they cannot seize a Hi-Jacking ship unless it has pirated. **1927** *Observer* 16 Oct. 15/1 Playgoers here are not interested in the humours and results of Prohibition, boot-legging, and hi-jacking. **1928** *Hearst's International* Aug. 72/1 Some hi-jacking exploit. **1929** *Daily Express* 21 Jan. 2/7 A gang of 'hijack bootleggers' who had forced a restaurant owner to pay them £1,000. **1966** *Times* 22 Sept. 1/2 A £7,000 reward has been offered by an insurance company for information about the hi-jacking of two lorries. **1967** *Listener* 10 Aug. 179/1 The aerial hijacking of Moise Tshombe was commissioned..by the Congolese Government. **1968** *Sun* 14 Nov. 5 Hi-jack figures released by Scotland Yard. **1968** *Daily Tel.* 7 Dec. 17/1 Our airline has been hit harder by hi-jacks than any other. **1972** *Guardian* 17 Nov. 14/1 The problems of becoming a hijack haven have made their mark.

hi·jacker. Also **hi-jacker,** formerly occas. **highjacker.** [f. prec. + -ER[1].] One who hijacks (illicit liquor, a vehicle, an aeroplane, etc.).

1923 *Nation* 11 July 36 There was, of course, the rush of adventurers, oil promoters, highjackers (an oil-region term for murderous robbers). **1925** *Times* 26 Oct. 13/7 A shooting affray between bootleggers and 'hijackers' (men who prey on bootleggers) took place..in a lodging-house on the west side of New York. **1936** J. G. BRANDON *Pawnshop Murder* v. 43 Any lurking hi-jacker who might..have acquired an inkling of what he was carrying. **1969** *Guardian* 9 Sept. 8/1 The hijackers have put the lives of about 10,000 air passengers at risk.

‖ **hikayat** (hikai·yat). Also **Hikaiat, Hikayet.** [Malay, ad. Arab. *ḥikāya* story, narrative.] In classical Malay literature, a prose narrative combining romance and biography.

1808 *Asiatick Researches* X. iii. 177 The Cheritra or Hikaiat..is more generally written in prose, but frequently intermixed with verse. **1839** T. J. NEWBOLD *Straits of Malacca* II. xiv. 317 From Arabia and Persia, great part of that class of compositions termed Hikayet..are borrowed. **1887** H. N. VAN DER TUUK in *Misc. Papers relating to Indo-China* II. viii. 3 The Malay author says in the opening that his work..gives a great many beautiful tales in the beginning, and afterwards the tale named *Hikayat Pandawa Jaya.* **1894** N. B. DENNYS *Descr. Dict. Brit. Malaya* 152 There are several *Hikayats* extant. **1900** W. E. MAXWELL in W. W. Skeat *Malay Magic* ii. 16 This..Malay myth occurs in the 'Sri Rama', a Malay prose *hikayat.* **1964** M. TAIB BIN OSMAN in Wang Gungwu *Malaysia* III. xv. 211 In the written romances, we find princes and princesses bearing hindu and muslim names, hindu gods, muslim prophets and local heroes, indigenous beliefs, hindu ethics and muslim teachings: all blended together in the *hikayat* or story.

hike (həik), *v. colloq.* orig. *dial.* and *U.S.* Also † **hyke, heik.** [Of obscure origin. Cf. *HOICK *v.*[1]

A possible early example of this word may be seen in the following: **1736** *Applebee's Weekly-Jrnl.* 17 July 2/1 Gowing..stood Centry 'till the Cargo amounted to as much as they could conveniently yike off with.]

1. *intr.* **a.** To walk or march vigorously or laboriously. **b.** To walk for pleasure; to go for a long walk, or walking tour, *spec.* in the country. Also, to travel by any means.

1809 S. WESLEY *Lett.* (1875) 32 Adieu for the present,—we must Contrive one more Pull at Surry before I hyke over to Staffordshire. **1825** J. JENNINGS *Observ. Dial. W. Eng.*, *To hike off*, to go away; to go off. Used generally in a bad sense. **1868** S. HALE *Lett.* (1919) 39 This day we moved over to the Thebes side and were to have done Karnak..but..I was really sick with heiking. *a* **1872** J. M. BAILEY *Folks at Danbury* (1877) 55 You've got to hike aroun', and fling some style inter the victuals. **1884** *Daily Tel.* 2 Feb. 3/1 (Farmer), We three, not having any regler homes..hike about for a living. **1886** S. HALE *Lett.* (1919) 157 You see the Churches can't do much, but Mr. Warner is wild to be heiking about. *a* **1902** *Scribner's Mag.* (Webster 1902), It's hike, hike, hike (march) till you stick in the mud, and then you hike back again a little slower than you went. **1904** *Chicago Evening Post* 23 Aug. 7 These girls had hiked up the dizzy trail along the face of Glacier to the summit. **1910** S. E. WHITE *Rules of Game* III. xii, 'I'm going to hike out before breakfast,' said he before turning in, 'so if you'll just show me where the lantern is, I won't bother you in the morning.' *Ibid.* v. viii, No animal in its senses would hike uphill and then down again. **1920** *Contemp. Rev.* Sept. 341 To take stick and pack, and 'hike' away from these cities for hundreds or thousands of miles. **1926** *Glasgow Herald* 25 Aug. 8 Guides in gay girlhood will hike through the hollow. **1927** A. CONAN DOYLE *Case-bk. S. Holmes* 149, I told him I was a busy man and could not spend my life hiking round the world in search of Garridebs. **1936** F. CLUNE *Roaming round Darling* xi. 101 Upon returning to Sydney I hiked out to Watson's Bay. **1937** *Amer. Speech* XII. 162/1 High school students have used *hike* to mean going to a play spot, either by automobile, by hayrack, or on foot. **1971** *Sci. Amer.* June 16/3, I occasionally take time off to hike in the mountains and ski.

2. *trans.* **a.** To force to move or go; to convey forcibly or laboriously; to pull *on, up, over,* etc.; to 'drag out'; to increase (a price, etc.). Also *fig.*

1867 S. HALE *Lett.* (1919) 32 Our side-saddles were *heiked* on to them. **1869** *Punch* 9 Jan. 8/2 If they finds any sitch thing as a jemmy about yer,..they'll hike yer off to be tried for intendin' to commit a felony. **1870** F. P. VERNEY *Lettice Lisle* xxiii, I'd like to hike out the whole boiling o' um. **1886** S. HALE *Lett.* (1919) 163 Tuesday he heiked us all forth early in the morning to the lake. **1899** *Strand Mag.* Apr. 454/1 We'll join hands end lay ourselves flat on the rock so thet you can hike your head over, and look all you want to. **1904** *Topeka Capital* 10 June 4 City Center kept the price of ice cream sodas at five cents until the State Sunday School convention struck town, and then the scale was hiked to ten cents. **1915** T. BURKE *Nights in Town* 119 Two bare-armed ladies, with skirts hiked up most indelicately behind them. **1921** *Chambers's Jrnl.* Dec. 835/2, I hiked him into a taxicab. **1927** *Blackw. Mag.* July 11/1 We flitted across the road like ghosts in the moonlight, hiking our equipage, and deposited same at the door of a wooden inn. **1929** W. P. RIDGE *Affect. Regards* 117 Saw where I was paying attention..and then barged in... And apparently managed to hike me out! **1969** C. IRVING *Fake!* (1970) xii. 147 To provide a testimonial which..was also so classy that it hiked the price to its limit, they hit on a scheme. **1973** *Observer* 22 July 13/1 The Bank of England hiked its minimum lending rate..to 9 per cent.

absol. a **1902** KIPLING (Webster 1902), If you persist in heaving and hiking like this.

b. *intr.* To work upwards out of place. Const. *up.*

c **1873** SCHELE DE VERE *MS. Notes* 488 (D.A.E.), What makes y[ou]r dress hike up so? **1890** *Amer. Dialect Notes* I. 61 The curtain hikes or hikes up. **1902** G. H. LORIMER *Lett. Merchant* ix. 119 We boys who couldn't walk across the floor without feeling that our pants had hiked up till they showed our feet to the knee,..didn't like him. **1948** *Sat. Even. Post* 4 Dec. 127/2 When I sit down, it hikes up.

Hence **hiker** (həi·kəɹ), one who hikes or goes on a hike; **hi·king** *vbl. sb.* (also *attrib.*).

1901 *Princeton Alumni Weekly* 518/1 Here I got my first chance at 'hiking' in the Philippines. **1913** F. H. HARRIS *Dartmouth out o' Doors* 32 While building strong physiques for themselves, the cross-country 'hikers' are providing for happier possibilities for the generations to come. **1923** *T. Eaton & Co. Catal.* Spring & Summer 51 New styles for misses, including the hiking suit and costume skirt. **1926** *Daily Colonist* (Victoria, B.C.) 20 July 18/4 Women's Tweed Hiking Breeches..of good grade materials, smart fawn and grey mixtures; well tailored and buttoned at the knee. **1927** *Daily Express* 24 May 3/5 We [of the Camping Club] have 3,000 members... Most of these are solitary 'hikers', who carry all their kit with them. **1930** *Times Lit. Suppl.* 11 Sept. 710/4 A special kind of traveller, belonging to the class of 'hikers'. **1931** *Daily Tel.* 21 Jan. 8/6 'Hikers'' Hostels at 1s. a Night. **1931** *Times Lit. Suppl.* 7 May 368/1 The sturdy young 'heroes' who accompanied him on the hiking adventures. **1931** *Daily Tel.* 21 May 16/2 The widespread hiking movement in Germany and other Continental countries. **1959** M. SHADBOLT *New Zealanders* 71 He was used to hiking. **1972** *L. L. Bean, Inc. Catal.* (Freeport, Maine) Spring 8 *Sierra club cup* for hikers and campers. **1972** *Sci. Amer.* July 13/1, I enjoy cross-country skiing in the winter and hiking and bicycling the rest of the year.

hike (həik), *sb. colloq.* orig. *dial.* and *U.S.* Also † **heik.** [f. prec.] **1.** A vigorous or laborious walk; a tramp or march; a walking tour or expedition undertaken for exercise or pleasure. Also *fig.* *On hike*, on the tramp. hiking.

1865 S. HALE *Lett.* (1919) 15 I've been engaged this week in a pecunious *heik*; to wit, getting money from the ladies of the Parish to get a new gown for Dr. Hedge. **1868** *Ibid.* 45, *I* ascended the Grand Pyramid, Lucretia got half-way..and Susie didn't try. It is a fearful heik. *a* **1902** *Scribner's Mag.* (Webster 1902), With every hike there's a few laid out with their hands crossed. **1903** S. E. WHITE *Forest* ii. 18 All other utensils belong to permanent camps, or open-water cruises,—not to 'hikes' in the woods. **1907** R. W. SERVICE *Songs of Sourdough* (1908) 59 And I burrowed a hole in the glowing coal, and I stuffed in Sam McGee. Then I made a hike, for I didn't like to hear him sizzle so. **1907** R. BEACH *Barrier* (1908) iv. 53 He's the feller that killed the gold-commissioner. Of course that put him on the hike again. **1916** H. L. WILSON *Somewhere in Red Gap* ix. 369 What's the matter with him and Lon taking a swift hike down to New York? **1921** *Outward Bound* June 10/1 Chinese Boy Scouts..on 'hike' on the veldt of South Africa. **1921**

Blackw. Mag. Aug. 262/1 Dempsey had passed the afternoon in a 'limbering-up hike'. **1932** *News Chron.* 28 Apr. 1/2 He then began a non-stop hike up and down the corridors of the hospital that had lasted till late this afternoon. **1970** H. D. CORBIN *Recreation Leadership* (ed. 3) xxiii. 333 The craving for adventure can be nurtured by a hike or an exploration perhaps more than by any other activity.

2. An increase (in prices, wages, etc.). Chiefly *N. Amer.*

1931 *Kansas City Star* 5 Aug., The hike was occasioned by the fact that cigarette butts..are now only a half inch. **1948** *Herald-Press* (St. Joseph, Mich.) 14 Aug. 3/1 There is enough unfilled demand for new cars to absorb a lot more price hikes. **1966** *Economist* 28 May 986/1 A wave of spending at the end of last year in anticipation of hikes in indirect taxes. **1968** *Observer* 28 Jan. 12/3 A 7.25 per cent price hike in two months. **1969** *Eugene* (Oreg.) *Register-Guard* 3 Dec. 1A (*heading*) Senate votes hike in tax exemptions.

Hilaria (hilēə·riă). [L., neut. pl. of *hilaris* HILARIOUS.] A festival in honour of Cybele, celebrated at the vernal equinox. (See quots.)

1738 CHAMBERS *Cycl.*, The *Hilaria* were solemnized with great pomp, and rejoicing. **1842** W. SMITH *Dict. Gr. & Roman Antiq.* 482/2 The hilaria were..either private or public. Among the former..the day on which a person married, and on which a son was born; among the latter, those days of public rejoicings appointed by a new emperor. **1907** L. R. FARNELL *Cults Gk. States* III. 301 The Attis-festival of the Hilaria. **1968** *Encycl. Brit.* II. 147/1 *April Fool's Day*..resembles the Hilaria of ancient Rome (March 25) and the Huli festival of India.

Hilary. Delete 'At Oxford now more generally called *Lent term*'.

hill, *sb.* Add: **1. b.** *hill and dale*: also, applied to any markings or groovings likened to hills and dales; *spec.* used *attrib.* to denote that manner of making gramophone records, or the records themselves, in which the undulations are cut in a vertical plane by the recording stylus. Also, applied to the alternating ridges and hollows of waste rock, etc., which are created by open-cast mining or ironstone working; also *attrib.*

1918 in WEBSTER Add. **1929** WILSON & WEBB *Mod. Gramophones* ii. 34 This form of record has several advantages over the hill-and-dale cut. **1931** *News Chron.* 20 Mar. 15/2 A graph, whose hills and dales represent maximum and minimum velocity of each of a series of strokes. **1949** *Hansard, Commons* 6 Dec. 1835 The whole countryside is disfigured by deep cuttings and large tracts of what is known as hill and dale—impassable areas of heaped limestone. *Ibid.* 1844 We do not really know enough about hills and dales to be quite satisfied in all cases. **1964** A. NELSON *Dict. Mining* 218 *Hill-and-dale formation*.., a term applied to the ridges and hollows along the surface of dumped material (usually overburden) at an opencast mine.

e. *over the hill*: having passed the prime in professional ability, physical beauty, etc. Chiefly *U.S.*

1950 *N.Y. Herald Tribune* 6 Dec. 35/2 He has lost his punch... He's a lot farther over the hill than I was when I hung up the gloves in 1927. **1952** M. R. RINEHART *Pool* xxxii. 259 The flawless skin goes, the lovely eyes fade, and she knows she is over the hill. **1957** I. CROSS *God Boy* (1958) xxiii. 197 As they say about boxers who are getting on in years, she is over the hill. **1962** *N.Y. Times Bk. Rev.* 17 June 20/3 Must you feel 'over the hill' after 40? **1972** H. KEMELMAN *Monday Rabbi took Off* ii. 24 When a rabbi gets to be around fifty, his chances of getting another job are not so good. He's like over the hill.

3. b. (Further examples.) Also, the cluster of plants on level ground. Cf. *a hill of beans* (*BEAN *sb.* 6 e).

1775 B. ROMANS *Nat. Hist. Florida* 120 A man ought to go through the field, and pull up those plants that look least promising leaving only three plants in each hill. **1854** *Trans. Pennsylvania State Agric. Soc.* 79 The best corn planter..marks the ground so as to keep the hills in rows in all directions. **1873** J. H. BEADLE *Undevel. West* 570 Each field..contained some three hundred hills of corn. **1884** H. BUTTERWORTH *Zigzag Journ. Western States* 42 Jerry was working like a beaver, and only three hills of potatoes to the square now. **1964** A. H. BURGESS *Hops* vi. 82 If rooted sets..are unobtainable, cuttings can be used for planting the [hop] garden. When this is done two or three cuttings should be planted at each hill.

d. *Her.* A charge representing a hill, usually vert.

1828 in BERRY *Encycl. Her.* I. **1889** ELVIN *Dict. Her.* p. lii, Three Hills, as in the arms of Brinckman. **1966** SCOTT-GILES & BROOKE-LITTLE *Boutell's Heraldry* (rev. ed.) 301 *Hill, or Hillock*, a green mount.

e. A nitro-glycerine factory.

1897 *Pearson's Mag.* IV. 150/2 You have now reached the bottom of the 'hill'—all nitro-glycerine factories are called 'hills'. **1921** *Dict. Occup. Terms* (1927) § 149 *Nitroglycerine hillman*, an explosive worker engaged on repetition work in nitroglycerine manufacture.

4. a. *hill-brow, -name, -slope, -wash.* **b.** *hill-station* (later examples).

1913 D. H. LAWRENCE *Love Poems* 40 The warm hay from The hill-brow. **1954** J. R. R. TOLKIEN *Fellowship of Ring* 146 The north end of the hill-brow. **1922** E. EKWALL *Place-Names Lancs.* 28 Very few hill-names, apart from those which have given names to places, are found in early sources. **1872** TENNYSON *Gareth & Lynette* 181 The damp hill-slopes. **1908** *Daily Chron.* 14 May 5/4 On the north side of the valley the hill-slopes are fairly open. **1919** J. MASEFIELD *Reynard* 97 The hill-slope [seemed] steeper. **1958** P. KEMP *No Colours or Crest* iv. 43 March-Phillipps had served in India..where he had experienced..the glitter of social life in various hill stations. **1969** *Filmfare* (Bombay) 1 Aug. 31/4 Once, while shooting at a hill station, the entire R. K. unit was staying in a quaint hillside hotel. **1936** *Nature* 29 Aug. 357/2 A hill-wash, some 11 ft. in thickness, contained large numbers of flint artefacts. **1958** F. E. ZEUNER *Dating Past* (ed. 4) 158 The Middle Older Loess of the section is a complex of loessic hillwash material derived from higher up the slope.

c. Also, pertaining to the rearing and tending of sheep in hilly country.

1749 H. PUREFOY in *Purefoy Lett. 1735–53* (1931) I. 162, I desire you will buy for mee ten ewes & lambs of the little short-legged horned Hill Sheep. **1841** *Penny Cycl.* XXI. 358/1 The average weight of the fleece..is now at least 3 lbs. in the hill-sheep, and nearly 4 lbs. in the lowland-sheep. **1841** THOREAU *Jrnl.* 13 Feb. (1962) I. 211/2 His hill-farm is poor stuff. **1886** C. SCOTT *Sheep-farming* 101 Hill farms... Hill stocks should always be fixtures on the farm. *Ibid.* 103 Hill sheep farming. *Ibid.* 116 A successful hill lambing depends very much upon.. the condition of the ewes at that period. Hill ewes are never in too high condition. *Ibid.* 123 The science of hill-herding. **1946** *Act* 9 & 10 *Geo. VI* c. 73 § 1 'Hill farming land' means mountain, hill and heath land which is suitable for use for the maintenance of sheep of a hardy kind but not of sheep of other kinds, or which by improvement could be made suitable. **1962** *Coast to Coast 1961–62* 13 Nicholas wanted to..gambol as senselessly as the new lambs in the hill paddocks. **1963** *Times* 13 Feb. 14/7 Should lamb and hill wool continue to be treated as special cases on social grounds?

d. *hill-culture, -kangaroo, -town* (further examples), *-tribe, -village.*

1936 *Discovery* June 179/2 This midden culture, which we call Sotho, differs..in nearly every respect from our Shona or Hill culture. **1950** WEBSTER Add., *Hillculture*, a system of agriculture utilizing erosion-preventing crops that are ecologically and economically best suited for sloping or hilly (often sub-marginal) land. **1935** H. H. FINLAYSON *Red Centre* (1952) 40 The short-limbed, broad-chested, sturdy, hill kangaroos or euros. **1944** *Living off Land* ii. 27 A number of men are required to capture the wallaby or the euro (hill kangaroo). **1911** R. BROOKE *Poems* 24 Out of the white hill-town, High up I clamber. **1972** W. GARNER *Ditto, Brother Rat!* xxiii. 172 'Tell me about Vauban.'..'A dilapidated little hill town.' **1870** *Brewer's Dict. Phr. & Fable* 406/1 *Hill tribes*, the barbarous tribes dwelling in remote parts of the Deccan or plateau of Central India. **1946** *Nature* 6 July 35/1 Any hill-tribe tends to lead a more or less segregated life. **1972** *Nat. Geographic* Feb. 271/1 Although often labeled as a 'hill tribe', Thailand's Karens occupy both upland and lowland villages. **1905** *Daily Chron.* 9 Oct. 4/2 The picturesque little hill-village of Moniaive [in Dumfriesshire]. **1947** *Geogr. Jrnl.* CX. 79 By no means all hill villages..are in the pastoral zone and many are associated with a fully-developed system of common arable fields.

e. *hill-born* adj.; **hill-set** *a.* (after Matt. v. 14), 'set' or situated on a hill.

1911 E. POUND *Canzoni* 21 A swelling turbid sea Hill-born and tumultuous. *a* **1963** C. S. LEWIS *Poems* (1964) 35 The hill-born, earthy spring,..The ripe peach from the southern wall still hot. **1906** *Westm. Gaz.* 16 June 12/2 Brown-roofed, hill-set villages. **1906** *Macm. Mag.* July 695 Ruler of his tiny hill-set principality. **1907** *Westm. Gaz.* 9 Aug. 2/4 Our hillset house of prayer.

f. hill-climb, the action of climbing hills, esp. as a test for motor vehicles; so **hill-climbing,** also *attrib.*; **hill-engraver,** in map-making, one who makes the representations of elevations on an engraved plate; so **hill-engraving; hill-map,** a map showing elevations; **hill-spur** (see SPUR *sb.*[1] 11).

1905 *Westm. Gaz.* 6 June 4/2 At the hill-climb on May 27. **1907** *Ibid.* 26 Feb. 4/2 The club will organise competitions, hill-climbs, club-runs, and so on. **1971** I. WAGSTAFF in J. Walton *Castrol Guide Motoring Sport* x. 70 The object of a hill climb is for drivers..to reach the top of the hill in a shorter time than any other competitor. **1637** SHIRLEY *Hide Parke* IV. sig. G2, Hill climbing white-rose, praise doth not lacke. **1861** [see Dict. 4 e]. **1900** [see *CAR *sb.*[1] 1 e]. **1904** *Peel Guardian & Chron.* 23 Apr., The venue of the hill-climbing contest has not been fixed. **1908** *Westm. Gaz.* 19 Mar. 4/1 Its smooth and faultless running and wonderful hill-climbing abilities. **1931** [see *DECOKE *v.*]. **1900** *Geogr. Jrnl.* June 589 The employment of hill-engravers, who are, as already stated, so much required for the completion of the hill-engraving of the 1-inch map. *Ibid.* 578 Progress of the 1-inch Hill Map of the United Kingdom. **1871** W. MORRIS in Mackail *Life* (1899) I. 253, I went about looking for game about the hill spurs. **1887** MEREDITH *Ballads & P.* 88 Down the hillspurs.

hi·ll-bi:lly. Chiefly *U.S.* Also **hillbilly, hilly-billy, -billie.** [f. HILL *sb.* 4 + BILLY[1] 2.]

1. A person from a remote rural or mountainous area, *esp.* of the southeastern U.S. Also *attrib.* and *transf.*

1900 *N.Y. Jrnl.* 23 Apr. 2/5 In short, a Hill-Billie is a free and untrammelled white citizen of Alabama, who lives in the hills, has no means to speak of, dresses as he can, talks as he pleases, drinks whiskey when he gets it, and fires off his revolver as the fancy takes him. **1911** *N.Y. Sun* 10 Aug. (Funk), These two were farmers' boys and hillbillies and jayhawkers. **1932** E. WILSON *Devil take Hindmost* xxii. 236 A coarse-spoken frank humorous old hillbilly talking to neighbors. **1933** *Amer. Speech* VIII. III. 27/2 *Hill Billy*, a rube or uncouth and stupid fellow. **1952** *History Today* July 451/1 Most of his country-men give him no grander name than 'hillbilly', a term as contemptuous as comic. **1957** *Daily Mail* 26 Sept. 8/2 At 47 the hillbilly who used to scratch a living as a dirt farmer at Greasy Creek in the Ozark Mountains has come a long way. **1966** D. STEWART in 'J. Hackston' *Father clears Out* p. x, As lively a collection of Australian hill-billies as I have ever seen. **1967** *Boston Sunday Herald* 2–8 Apr. 9/2 An Air Force man who wants a missile site, and the hill-billy fighting progress.

2. A type of American folk music. Also *attrib.*

1924 *Talking Machine World* XX. 207/1 Hill Billie Blues..Banjo. **1925** *Ibid.* XXI. 186/2 The [rural] demand is largely for Blues, Coon songs, and Hilly-Billy numbers. **1932** *Daily Mirror* 1 July 10/3, I should not be surprised to hear that the hill-billy king and his suite visit the recording studio every morning of the week. **1953** A. MOOREHEAD *Rum Jungle* iv. 58 They wanted gramophones, and the music they liked best was hill-billy. **1955** L. FEATHER *Encycl. Jazz* (1956) 110 Piano with local hillbilly, Dixieland and swing bands from age 13. **1959** 'F. NEWTON' *Jazz Scene* x. 172 The full bag of hilly-billy melodies, or the like. **1971** M. BABSON *Cover-up Story* vi. 66 They may start out as Hillbilly, or Country and Western but they can be turned into Folk. **1972** *Jazz & Blues* Feb. 19/1 Fats Domino had done some real down home hillbilly-motown stuff.

hi·ll-cou:ntry. [HILL *sb.* 4.] A district composed of hills or elevated ground.

1582 [see HILL *sb.* 4]. **1789** G. WHITE *Selborne* I. i. 2 The down..is a pleasing park-like spot..jutting out on the verge of the hill-country. **1816** U. BROWN *Jrnl.* in *Maryland Hist. Mag.* (1915) X. 283 A handsome hill country in a good state of cultivation. **1865** A. D. WHITNEY *Gayworthys* xv. 133 The slow, ponderous vehicle went..creaking on, up into the hill-country. **1875** [see HILL *sb.* 4]. **1903** *Westm. Gaz.* 14 Jan. 2/1 The Surrey hill-country.

hilling, *vbl. sb.*[2] (Later U.S. examples.)

1814 J. TAYLOR *Arator* 233 How often he had passed over the land..in fallowing, hilling, cutting off hills, planting, replantings. **1833** B. SILLIMAN *Man. Sugar Cane* 17 It is advisable not to plough deep, especially for the last hoeing or hilling. **1887** *Harper's Mag.* Jan. 306/1 There is a broad hilling up so as to have a slope inward toward the plants as well as away from them.

hill-man, hillman. Add: Also **hillsman.**

1854 J. D. HOOKER *Himalayan Jrnls.* I. v. 136 Carriers and mountaineers...If they serve a good hills-man like themselves, they will follow him with alacrity, sleep on the cold, bleak mountain. **1920** *London Mag.* Apr. 187/2 This rain would hold. He knew it with a hillsman's knowledge. **1938** V. MCNABB *Life of Our Lord* iii. 42 The hillsman from Galilee..had to pass through the country of Samaria.

hill-top. Add: **hill-top novel,** the name given by Grant Allen to those of his novels in which he expressed his views on moral and social questions, especially views not generally acceptable to his contemporaries; **hill-top surface** (see quot. 1961).

1895 G. ALLEN *British Barbarians* p. xi, I propose in future to add the words, 'A Hill-top Novel', to every one of my stories which I write of my own accord, simply and solely for the sake of embodying and enforcing my own opinions. *Ibid.* p. xvi, Why, once more, this particular name, 'A Hill-top Novel'? For something like this reason. I am writing in my study on a heather-clad hill-top... Everything around is fresh and pure... But away below in the valley, as night draws on, a lurid glare ..marks the spot where the great wen of London heaves and festers. **1896** *Pearson's Mag.* May 556/1 Latterly he [*sc.* Grant Allen] has doubled up his social philosophy with his fiction, producing what he calls 'Hill Top' novels. **1901** *Sketch* XXV. 256/2 The lady sportswoman is the Colonel's abomination; he regards her as a monstrous product of the divided skirt and the 'Hill-top' novel. **1930** J. CHALLINOR in *Geography* Dec. 656 The object of the foregoing remarks is therefore to suggest that a hill-top surface, having a 'plateau quality' about it, need not necessarily be evidence of an uplifted peneplane. **1961** —— *Dict. Geol.* 100/1 *Hill-top surface*, an imaginary surface, as smooth as possible, touching the tops of the hills of a region.

hilo[1] (hī·lo). [Sp., = thread :— L. *fīlum.*] A thin vein of ore (see quot. 1908).

1848 *English & Foreign Mining Gloss.* 5/4 *Hilo*, a small vein or thread of ore in a lode. *hilo de la veta*, line or direction of the vein. *hilos altos*, threads or small veins of ore falling into or proceeding from the upper or hanging wall of a lode. *hilos baxos*, threads or small veins of ore proceeding from or falling into the lower wall of a lode. **1908** E. HALSE *Dict. Spanish Mining Terms* 188 *Hilo* (thread), (1) *h. de la veta* or *h. del criadero*, direction of the vein or deposit..(2) small vein or thread of ore in a lode, *e.g.*, *hilos altos*, threads falling into or proceeding from the hanging wall..; in the Cauca, the name is applied to small veins of gold-bearing quartz. *Ibid.* 186 *Hebra*, (1) a thread or yarn of a hempen or other rope..; several twisted together form the *hilo*.

Hilo[2] (hī·lo). [Hawaiian.] *Hilo grass*, a large and coarse grass, *Paspalum conjugatum.*

1888 W. HILLEBRAND *Flora Hawaiian Islands* 493 The well known *Hilo grass*, which first appeared about 1840 in the district of Hilo and soon spread there,..is a native of tropical America..but is found now also in tropical Africa, the Galapagos Islands, Australia, and India. **1915** W. A. BRYAN *Nat. Hist. Hawaii* 208 The well known and generally despised Hilo grass, occurs in moist, heavy soils in the lower zone. **1917** *Nature* 20 Sept. 57/2 In the moister portions of the islands large

areas have been occupied by Hilo grass. **1929** W. T. Pope *Man. Wayside Plants Hawaii* 27 Vigorous cultivation of fields keeps Hilo grass in control.

hilt, *sb.* Add: **3.** Also *to the hilt.*

1950 J. D. Carr *Below Suspicion* x. 122 You may trust me to the hilt! **1965** *New Statesman* 16 Apr. 604/1 The Prime Minister..backs their decisions to the hilt. **1965** *Listener* 20 May 742/2 Every event I attended was subscribed to the hilt, and the house was full.

Himalayan. Add: **1. Himalayan black bear,** *Selenarctos thibetanus.*

[**1858** *Proc. Zool. Soc.* 518 Black Bear of Europeans... The species is generally distributed over the lower ranges of the Western Himalayas.] **1869** A. A. A. Kinloch *Large Game Shooting* I. 49 The Himalayan Black Bear is pretty generally distributed throughout the Himalayas. **1925** G. Burrard *Big Game Hunting* iv. 73 The Himalayan black bear is one of the most widely distributed game animals of the Himalayas. **1966** R. & D. Morris *Men & Pandas* viii. 177 The Himalayan, or Asiatic black bear (*Selenarctos thibetanus*).

Himalo- (himā·lo), used as combining form of the *Himalayas*, as in *Himalo-Chinese* adj.

1873 Elwes in *Proc. Zool. Soc.* 654 Himalayan or Himalo-Chinese Subregion. **1910** *Encycl. Brit.* III. 976/1 The Himalo-Chinese or Transgangetic province.

himself, *pron.* **IV.** (Further examples.)

1901 M. Franklin *My Brilliant Career* xxxii. 273 Pa is goin' to write a whole letter all by hisself. **1945** A. Kober *Parm Me* 146 He sits and he *shuckles* hisself and is oney one thing he's saying all the time—nutting! **1965** T. Capote *In Cold Blood* (1966) iii. 166, I talked to the deputy. Then I told the warden hisself. **1969** Widdowson & Halpert in Halpert & Story *Christmas Mumming in Newfoundland* 149 A gentleman..made hisself up with burnt cork.

hina hina (hī·na hī·na). *N.Z.* Also **hinihini.** [Maori.] = Mahoe.

1867 J. D. Hooker *Handbk. N. Z. Flora* II. 765/1 Hina-hina, *Geolog. Surv. Melicytus ramiflorus.* **1868** J. Buchanan in *Trans. N.Z. Instit.* I. Essays III. 37 Hinihini or Mahoe (*Melicytus ramiflorus*). A very variable tree in size of leaves and shape of trunk, the latter angled or round. **1921** H. Guthrie-Smith *Tutira* xxii. 206 The Kowhai and fuchsia and hina hina..will have died out. **1946** J. C. Andersen in *Jrnl. Polynesian Soc.* June 151 *Hinahina*, alternative name for the tree mahoe.

hinaki (hī·nakī). *N.Z.* Pl. **hinaki.** [Maori.] A wicker eel-pot.

1845 E. J. Wakefield *Adv. N.Z.* I. viii. 252 They place eel-pots, called *hinaki*,..at the lower extremity of funnels formed by series of upright poles driven into the bed of the river. **1905** W. B. *Where White Man Treads* 256 My father and his younger brother went to lift a 'hinaki' (eel basket) into the canoe. **1921** H. Guthrie-Smith *Tutira* x. 86 The huge *hinaki* or wicker-work pot, where eels required for immediate consumption were placed. **1952** *Landfall* VI. 288 It was a well-kept looking net.. and with fine meshes. It made me feel shy about my old hinaki. **1966** *Encycl. N.Z.* II. 441/1 Traps for eels and lampreys, termed hinaki, were made from the slim stems of the mangemange.

hinau (hi·nɑu). Also **hino(u), inau.** [Maori.] A New Zealand evergreen tree, *Elæocarpus dentatus*, yielding a black dye; the wood of this tree. Also *attrib.*

1832 G. Bennett in *London Med. Gaz.* X. 794/2 This tree, the Elœocarpus dicera of Forster, the Inau of the natives, is found abundant on the hills of New Zealand. **1835** W. Yate *Account N.Z.* (ed. 2) ii. 49 Hinau (*Dicera dentata*)—This tree..grows to a height of sixty or seventy feet. **1845** E. J. Wakefield *Adv. N.Z.* II. 246 The *totara*, the *mai*, and the *hinau*, were found to work up into very handsome side-boards, tables, and book-shelves. **1859** A. S. Thomson *Story N.Z.* I. 156 The hinau berries are generally steeped for several days in a running stream... Hinau cakes are much esteemed. **1867** *Richmond–Atkinson Papers* (1960) II. 249 The board on the dead hinau tree announces that application for graves is to be made to E. Patten. **1883** J. Hector *Handbk. N.Z.* 130 (Morris), Hinau, a small tree about fifty feet high and eighteen inches thick in stem, with brown bark which yields a permanent blue-black dye, used for tanning. **1921** H. Guthrie-Smith *Tutira* xii. 99 Other large species in the mixed bush are hinau (*Elæocarpus dentatus*), tawa..and maire. **1968** M. Johnson *N.Z. Flowering Plants* 61 *E. dentatus*, hinau, the larger of our two species, reaches about 50 feet.

Hinayana (hīnăyā·nă). [Skr., f. *hīna* lesser, little + *yāna* vehicle.] The Lesser Vehicle, a name given to the system by the followers of the Mahāyāna, the Greater Vehicle; the Buddhism of Ceylon as distinguished from the northern or Mahāyāna Buddhism. Also *attrib.* Also **Hinaya·nism, Hinaya·nist; Hinaya·nian** *a.*

Hīnayāna was the pristine form of the faith, while the Mahāyāna represents the general one, followed by the majority of followers.

1868 J. Fergusson *Tree & Serpent Worship* 65 Mahâyâna, or as M. Julien translates it, the 'Grand Véhicule', as opposed to Hînayâna or the 'Petit Véhicule'; the distinction between the two being in almost every respect identical with that which exists between Evangelical and Mediæval Christianity. **1877** T. W. Rhys Davids *Buddhism* viii. 200 The system of the *Little Vehicle* (*Hînayâna*). **1882** *Encycl. Brit.* XIV. 229/1 These volumes [*sc.* the Kandjur] contain about a dozen works of the oldest school of Buddhism, the Hīnayāna. **1907** D. T. Suzuki *Outl. Mahayana Buddhism* 2 Buddhism was now split into two great systems, Mahâyânism and Hînayânism. *Ibid.* 8 The distinction of Mahâyânists and Hînayânists became definite. **1945** A. Huxley *Let.* 27 May (1969) 526 In later, Mahayana Buddhism much is said about the dangers of fixed, strained, rigid concentration of the attention (such as was practised by the Hinayanists). **1951** H. Zimmer *Philos. of India* 509 'The Big Ferryboat' (*mahāyāna*), the ferry in which all may ride, in contrast to 'The Little Ferryboat' (*hīnayāna*), the way of those lonely ones, 'lights unto themselves', who steer the difficult strait of individual release. **1956** A. Toynbee *Historian's Approach Relig.* 17 The Hinayanian Buddhist gospel of self-liberation through self-extinction. **1960** 'S. Harvester' *Chinese Hammer* xi. 110 The differences between Hinayana Buddhism, the original form, and the Mahayana version. **1973** *Times* 14 Apr. (Nepal Suppl.) p. ii/3 Buddhism in the Katmandu Valley subsequently forsook the ascetic path of Hīnayāna.

hincty (hi·ŋkti), *a.* *U.S. slang.* Also **hinkty.** [Origin unknown.] Conceited, snobbish, stuck-up.

Connection with clipped forms of 'handkerchief-head' (= an Uncle Tom Negro) has been suggested but the phonetic development is incapable of demonstration.

1924 in W. C. Handy *Treasury of Blues* (1949) 144 We'll I am hinkty and I'm low down too. **1936** *Esquire* (Chicago) May 192/3 '*She* couldn't be mixed up in no murder trial. She's too respectable.' 'A hinkty hussy!' said Sling. **1941** *Examiner* (San Francisco) 20 July PR 2 Jack, it ain't like me to be hincty so I'll be there with my boots laced tall. **1948** *Capitol News from Hollywood* Jan. 12/1 Patrons who dropped into the hincty, ultra-ultra Circus room of Santa Monica's lavish Hotel Ambassador. **1957** J. Kerouac *On Road* (1958) 86 Wetting their eyebrows with hincty fingertip. **1969** C. Himes *Blind Man with Pistol* vi. 72 All those hincty bitches fell on those whitey-babies like they was sugar candy.

hind, *a.* Add: **A. c.** *to get on one's hind legs*: see Leg *sb.* 2 c. *to talk the hind leg(s) off a donkey*, etc.: see *talk *v.*

C. a. *hind-wing.*

1932 E. Step *Bees, Wasps, Ants Brit. Isles* p. xxiv, In flight, the fore- and hind-wings of a side usually act as one.

Hindemithian (hindəmi·tiăn), *a.* and *sb.* [f. the name of Paul *Hindemith* (1895–1963), German musician + -ian.] **A.** *adj.* Of, pertaining to, or characteristic of Hindemith, or his style of composition. **B.** *sb.* One who favours or imitates the style of Hindemith.

1941 A. Copland *Our New Mus.* 159 This last contains remarkable Hindemithian premonitions. **1954** *Encounter* June 60/1 How refreshing..to meet a Hindemithian who does not think twelve-tone music a disease. **1958** *Listener* 18 Sept. 441/1 Reizenstein..continues in a gravely Hindemithian style. **1962** *Ibid.* 21 June 1091/2 A gayer, more elastic Hindemithian counterpoint.

hinder, *a.*[1] Add: **B.** *sb.* (usu. *pl.*). Hindquarters, buttocks; hind legs.

1857 J. Scholes *Tim Gamwattle* 20 (E.D.D.), Thir is nah a barro e Smobruff uts big anouff fur iz hoinders. **1880** J. F. S. Gordon *Bk. Chron. Keith* 55 Boasting of kissing, at their meetings, the Devil's 'hinder'. **1891** M. M. Dowie *Girl in Karpathians* xiii. 173 The painter spread his coat upon the hinders of the second horse. **1892** J. Lumsden *Sheep-head & Trotters* 268 A pull that brought the pony in a moment back upon its hinders. **1948** F. Brown *Dead Ringer* (1949) xi. 131 He stood up on his short little hinders and got himself a lawyer.

Hindki (hi·ndkī). Also **Hindeki, Hindkee.** The name of a people, and of their language, of north-west India and Afghanistan.

1815 M. Elphinstone *Acct. Kingdom of Caubul* II. xii. 309 It has been observed that there is scarcely any part of Afghaunistaun in which the whole population is Afghaun, and that the mixture is composed of Taujiks in the West, and of Hindkees in the East. **1875** *Encycl. Brit.* I. 235/2 *Hindkis.* This is the name given to people of Hindu descent scattered over Afghanistan. They are said to be of the *Kshatri* or military caste. **1886** Yule & Burnell *Anglo-Indian Gloss.* 315/2 *Hindki* or *Hindeki.* This modification of the name is applied to people of Indian descent, but converted to Islam, on the Peshawar frontier, and scattered over other parts of Afghānistān. They do the banking business and hold a large part of the trade in their hands. **1911** *Encycl. Brit.* XVI. 80/2 The principal varieties of the northern group are Hindki (the same in meaning as Hindko) and Pōthwārī. **1919** G. A. Grierson *Ling. Surv. India* VIII. I. 333 The Lahndā of Deva Ghazi Khan goes by several names, such as Hindī, Hindkī, Jatkī, and Dērāwāl... I call it Hindkī in these pages. **1964** S. K. Chatterji in D. Abercrombie et al. *Daniel Jones* 409 Languages like..Hindki (western Panjabi or Lahndi).

hindside (həi·ndsəid). [f. Hind *a.* A.] The back part of anything. Also in quasi-combs., as *hindside-foremost.*

1862 [see Hind *a.* C. a]. **1915** E. Pound *Lett.* (1951) 91 Objectivity and again objectivity, and expression: no hindside-beforeness. **1929** W. Faulkner *Sartoris* (1932) iv. 270 Negro in a hind-side-before collar. **1931** E. Wilson *Axel's Castle* iii. 88 His hindside-foremost presentations of thought. **1934** J. Marston *Andromeda* xiv. 194 That's crude sentimentality hindside up. **1942** *New Yorker* 10 Oct. 33 What's she doing out in this rain, shoving along the beach on her hindside?

hind-sight. Add: **1. b.** *to knock* (or *kick*) *the hindsight out* or *off*: to dispose of or demolish completely. *U.S. colloq.*

1834 W. A. Carruthers *Kentuckian in N.Y.* I. 21 As sure as you saw the fire at the muzzle of his gun, so sure he knocked the creter's hind sight out. **1850** L. H. Garrard *Wah-To-Yah* (1927) xx. 248 They backed their ears preparatory to kicking the hindsights off the first man that struck them. **1872** E. Eggleston *Hoosier Schoolmaster* x. 58 Ef its rendered right, it'll knock the hind sights off of any rheumatiz you ever see. **1892** *Congress. Rec.* 1 Apr. 2843/1 The American producer.. can knock the hindsights off the producer anywhere else on the face of the earth. **1954** in J. A. Weingarten *Amer. Dict. Slang* 186/2.

hinge, *sb.* Add: **I. 1. d.** In Philately: see quot. 1883.

1883 *Stamp-Collecting & Exchange* 8/2 There is only one really satisfactory process for mounting postage labels, viz., the now almost universal hinge-system. This consists of a piece of thin paper a little smaller than the stamp itself, and affixed to the album with a drop of gum, or, if the hinge be already prepared for adhesion,.. no inconvenience or trouble will be experienced. **1892** *Stamp Collector* Apr. 33 In the earlier days of stamp collecting, before such things as gummed hinges were offered to the collecting public. **1967** *Exchange & Mart* 20 July 19/4 (Advt.), Stamps stay put without stamp hinges, in our brand new plastic stamp album. **1971** D. Potter *Brit. Eliz. Stamps* xv. 163 At the turn of the century, hinges were monstrous things, designed for their sticking power.

III. 7. hinge-ligament (see quot. 1909).

1909 *Cent. Dict.* Suppl. 589/3 *Hinge-ligament*, in bivalve mollusks, a tough, uncalcified, elastic membrane which connects the two valves. **1945** E. Step *Shell Life* (rev. ed.) 56 The hinge-ligament exerts a pulling action which tends to separate the lower edges.

hinihini, var. *hina hina.

‖ **hinin** (hī·nin). [Jap.] A member of an outcast group in Japan. Also *collect.* and *attrib.* Cf. *Eta.

1884 tr. *J. J. Rein's Japan* II. i. 329 Geshas (female dancers and singers) and Jôrôs (prostitutes)..were despised, and considered..socially below the level of the Hinin. **1891** A. M. Bacon *Jap. Girls & Women* ix. 228 The éta and hinin—outcasts who lived by begging, slaughtering animals, caring for dead bodies, tanning skins, and other employments which rendered them unclean. **1904** L. Hearn *Japan: Attempt at Interpretation* vi. 110 The banished man was most often doomed to become a *hinin*—one of that wretched class of wandering pariahs who were officially termed 'not-men'. **1970** J. W. Hall *Japan* x. 179 Tohugawa society..was conceived of..as falling into the following categories: the *kuge*, the samurai (including daimyo), priests, peasants, urban residents, and pariah (*hinin* and *eta*).

hinkty, var. *hincty *a.*

‖ **hinoki** (hinǫ·ki). Also † **finoki.** [Jap.] A large conifer, *Chamæcyparis obtusa*, native to Japan, or the timber obtained from it.

1727 J. G. Scheuchzer tr. *Kæmpfer's Hist. Japan* I. I. 118 *Finoki* and *Suggi* are two sorts of Cypress-trees, yielding a beautiful light whitish wood. **1884** tr. *J. J. Rein's Japan* II. ii. 445 The pure and simple Shintô-temple ..is built of the white wood of the Hinoki. **1904** L. Hearn *Japan: Attempt at Interpretation* ix. 184 Such superior qualities of wood as *keyaki* or *hinoki.* **1964** *Illustr. Important Forest Trees Japan* (Japan Forest Technical Assoc.) 44/2 The hinoki cypress is abundantly found on ridges. **1965** J. Ohwi *Flora Japan* 117/1 *Chamaecyparis obtusa*...Hinoki...Much planted for timber. **1969** R. C. Bell *Board & Table Games* II. iii. 61 The best boards.. are also made of 'Gingko' (*Salisburia Adiantifolia*) and 'Hinoki' (*Thuya Obtusa*).

hino(u), varr. *hinau.

hint, *sb.* Add: **2. b.** A small piece of practical information.

1777 P. Thicknesse *Year's Journey* II. 221 (*heading*) General hints to strangers who travel to France. **1807** R. Southey *Lett. fr. England* (1951) 348 The Monthly is more miscellaneous in its contents... All sorts of heretical opinions are started here, agricultural hints thrown out, and queries propounded of all kinds. **1830** Coleridge & Southey *Devil's Walk* 24 The Devil was charm'd, for it gave him a hint For improving the prisons of Hell. **1841** S. Ellis (*title*) Family secrets; or, Hints to those who would make home happy. **1872** *Young Englishwoman* Nov. 598 Household hints for young housewives. **1926** R. Macaulay *Crewe Train* II. x. 181 Audrey gave them household hints, about how to keep the kettle from furring, and the stove and the milk jar from smelling. **1972** *Guardian* 29 Mar. 11/5 Angela Kay's Household Hints..has a pretty good selection of useful answers to some eight hundred possible problems.

hint, *v.* Add: **1. c.** With sentence as object.

1843 Dickens *Christmas Carol* iii. 107 'I'm sure he is very rich, Fred,' hinted Scrooge's niece. **1891** C. Graves *Field of Tares* 41 'I have been a stranger to the neighborhood,' returned the other, 'for years.' 'Many years?' hinted Mr. Brinnilow.

2. b. With other constructions; also *absol.*

1865 *Punch* 21 Jan. 32 If I wos allowed to 'int, Ladies, I shud say, Torse Hup! **1891** HARDY *Group of Noble Dames* 77 Her husband's tutor was found to hint very strongly against such a step. **1894** G. DU MAURIER *Trilby* III. VII. 178 The night above was dark, but 'star-dials hinted of morn'.

hinterland. Add: Also applied spec. to the area lying behind a port, and to the fringe areas of a town or city.

a **1910** in L. D. Stamp *Gloss. Geogr. Terms* (1961) 235 *Hinderland, Hinterland,* the region the seaborne trade of which belongs to a particular seaport or seaboard. **1922** *Geogr. Rev.* Apr. 260 The main factor which determined the selection of ports in prehistoric times was the presence of a populous hinterland of effective buyers. **1936** E. VAN CLEEF *Trade Centers & Trade Routes* iii. 34 The immediately contiguous territory within the continuous hinterland which in some instances contributes to the formation of the metropolitan city has been termed by the Germans, the 'Umland' or country about. **1938** A. J. SARGENT *Seaports & Hinterlands* 3 A port, essentially, is a transit area, a gateway through which goods and people move from and to the sea, by way of rail, inland waterway, or sometimes by road. The region to and from which this movement is directed is commonly and somewhat vaguely described as the hinterland. **1945** E. WAUGH *Brideshead Revisited* 7 Here the close, homogeneous territory of housing estates and cinemas ended and the hinterland began. **1950** *Geogr. Jrnl.* CXVI. 64 The approximate boundaries of urban spheres of influence or hinterlands. **1968** *Guardian* 23 Oct. 9 As Clydeside developed industrially so it attracted labour from its own hinterland and from famine-stricken Ireland.

2. *fig.* and *transf.*

1919 M. K. BRADBY *Psycho-Analysis* (1920) 75 Unexplored territories full of mystery and danger in the hinterland of their own minds. *Ibid.* 251 The individual who is introduced to the 'hinterland' of his own conscious being. *a* **1930** D. H. LAWRENCE *Last Poems* (1932) 182 We are mostly unexplored hinterland. **1965** *New Statesman* 23 Apr. 646/3 The council meets in that dour ecclesiastical hinterland of Westminster Abbey, where you can buy a second-hand cassock.

3. *Geol.* (See quot. 1961.)

1937 WOOLDRIDGE & MORGAN *Physical Basis Geogr.* vi. 76 The African 'hinterland' is believed to have moved northward towards the European 'foreland'. **1961** J. CHALLINOR *Dict. Geol.* 100/2 *Hinterland,* the moving block which compresses the sediments of a geosyncline and forces them towards the foreland.

hintzeite (hi·ntsəit). *Min.* [ad. G. *hintzeït* (L. Milch 1890, in *Zeitschr. f. Kryst. und Min.* XVIII. 480), f. the name of C. A. F. *Hintze* (1851–1916), German mineralogist: see -ITE^1.] = *HEINTZITE.

1891, 1951 [see *HEINTZITE].

hiortdahlite (hyǭ·ɹtdāləit). *Min.* [ad. G. *hiortdahlit* (W. C. Brögger 1888, in *Nyt Mag. f. Naturvidensk.* (1889) XXXI. III. 232), f. the name of Th. H. *Hiortdahl* (1839–1925), Norwegian chemist: see -ITE^1.] A rare mineral, essentially a fluoride-containing silicate of zirconium, sodium, and calcium, found in yellow triclinic crystals.

1892 E. S. DANA *Dana's Syst. Min.* (ed. 6) 377 (*heading*) Hiortdahlite. **1968** *Mineral. Abstr.* XVIII. 304/2 Hiortdahlite occurs as columnar crystals up to 3 and 4 cm long in pegmatite..in the Korgeredaba pluton in southeastern Sangilen, Tuva.

hip, *sb.*^{1} Add: **2. b.** *on the hip* (further example).

1967 *Listener* 16 Nov. 628/3 You have me on the hip here a bit because I think..that all these old ideas we had are as dead as the dodo.

4. a. *hip-boot.*

1893 *Outing* (U.S.) XXII. 124/2 Gossamer hip-boots are good if of reliable stock. **1922** S. LEWIS *Babbitt* x. 138 He gloated on fly-rods and gorgeous rubber hip-boots. **1969** *Sears Catal.* Spring/Summer 709 Ted Williams hip boots have nylon added to latex for long-lasting strength and comfort.

b. *hip-swaying, -swinging* adjs.; **hip-flask,** a flask for intoxicating liquor carried in a hip-pocket; **hip-hole,** a hollow dug in the ground to accommodate the hip (for greater comfort when sleeping on hard ground); **hip-huggers** *sb. pl.*, trousers that fit tightly to the hips; also **hip-hugger,** used *attrib.* of such trousers; **hip-hugging** *a.*, fitting closely to the hips; **hip-length** *a.*, denoting a garment which reaches down to the hips; **hip-line,** the outline or contour of the hips; **hip-pocket** (earlier and later examples); **hip throw,** a throw in Judo; **hip-yoke,** in dressmaking, a shaped piece extending from the waist to the hips, designed to fit the figure closely without gathers.

1923 E. MARBURY *My Crystal Ball* lxxi. 352 Let these same people frequent ballrooms..and they will find the hip flasks in evidence and the consequent conditions a sorry spectacle. **1928** *Sunday Dispatch* 2 Sept. 7/1 [American *loq.*] We have become a people who think 'likker', talk it, and lead a hip-flask life! **1944** BRAHMS & SIMON *Titania has Mother* xiii. 145 Merry moujiks drinking from hip flasks and lolling in all directions. **1973** D. LEES *Rape of Quiet Town* ii. 33 A hip-flask full of brandy. **1936** F. CLUNE *Roaming round Darling* xxv. 271 Then we made a fire, boiled the billy, gouged out hip-holes for ourselves, and camped till daylight. **1965** G. MCINNES *Road to Gundagai* x. 167, I tried digging a hip-hole. **1967** *Boston Sunday Herald* 26 Mar. (Advt.), Zowie prints and belted hip-huggers..striped and printed. **1967** *New Yorker* 26 Aug. 82 There are separates, too, such as long jackets, stovepipe hip-hugger trousers, [etc.]. **1973** *Houston* (Texas) *Chron. Mag. People, Places, Pleasures* 14 Oct. 24/5 Today the young women wear shorts and hip-huggers, the older sit in their traditional long black dresses. **1969** *Times* 7 Nov. 14/1 Hip-hugging..trousers. **1971** B. MALAMUD *Tenants* 43 Willie..was dolled up in hip-hugging yellow pants and two-tone brown-and-black shoes. **1921** Hip length [see *gum-boots* s.v. *GUM *sb.*^{2} 9]. **1931** *Daily Express* 18 Mar. 5/3 Hip-length coats. **1961** *Harper's Bazaar* Feb. 75 The hip-length cardigan. **1907** *Westm. Gaz.* 30 Mar. 14/1 It [*sc.* a skirt] blurs over the aggressive hip-line. **1935** *Times* 2 Dec. 19/4 The coat just reaches the hipline. **1973** *Country Life* 8 Mar. 635/2 Dress in black-and-white-check wool with smooth hipline. **1880** *Cimarron News & Press* 22 July 3/2 Lee snatched Armstrong's revolver from his hip pocket and pointed it at Armstrong. **1922** S. LEWIS *Babbitt* xviii. 228 Drinking together from hip-pocket flasks. **1972** *Guardian* 27 Oct. 12/1 A general election..is one option in Mr Heath's hip pocket list. **1920** *Glasgow Herald* 17 Apr. 6 The Hawaiian corps de ballet..began a..performance of rhythmical hip-swaying dances. **1965** *Midnight* 12 July 3/1 The hip-swinging wedding party was celebrated to the strains of the watusi and frug, pounded out by Christopher's group, the Wild Ones. **1966** *Word Study* Oct. 7/1 A hip-swinging, slender-bodied blonde. **1957** TAKAGAKI & SHARP *Techniques of Judo* II. iv. 50 Generally, when a hip throw is employed, the opponent turns his back into you and pulls you to the right front corner by your right arm which is pulled tightly across his chest. **1960** *Oxf. Mail* 10 Mar. 8/2 He..went on to win the match with another ankle throw, with which he countered an attempted hip throw. **1931** *Daily Tel.* 21 May 6/4 Small gathers at each side of the hip yoke in front.

hip, *v.*^{2} Add: **4.** To carry on the hip. *U.S.*

1818 H. C. KNIGHT *Lett. from South* 93 Some mothers here [*sc.* in Kentucky] hip their infants, as do the Sumatrans. **1843** 'R. CARLTON' *New Purchase* xx. 191 Still oftener each [log] is hipped and hipping is done by one man..who adroitly whips up the log on his hip.

hip (hip), *v.*^{5} *slang* (orig. *U.S.*). [f. *HIP *a.*] *trans.* To render 'hip'; to inform. (Freq. as pa. pple. in passive.) Hence **hipped** *ppl. a.* well-informed, 'with it'; (esp. with *on*) fond of, 'bitten with'.

1920 F. SCOTT FITZGERALD *This Side of Paradise* (1921) II. iii. 246 I'm hipped on Freud and all that. **1925** T. DREISER *Amer. Trag.* (1926) II. III. xv. 191 He is still hipped over this second girl. **1927** *Daily Express* 24 Oct. 8 'New York,' as the manager of one of the largest hotels remarked lately, 'is badly "hipped" on dining in public.' **1932** *Evening Sun* (Baltimore) 9 Dec. 31/4 *Hip,* to give information. **1938** *Amer. Speech* XIII. 314/1 *Hipped to the jive,* well informed on the latest slang expressions. **1944** D. BURLEY *Dan Burley's Orig. Handbk. Harlem Jive* 19 Uncle is hipping a whole lot of cats as to what to do when the action gets off the track. **1945** L. SHELLY *Jive Talk Dict.* 26 *Hipped spade,* smart Negro. **1947** *Esquire* Apr. 76 'Are there any squares in this outfit?' 'No, man, we're all hipped.' **1954** *Encounter* Feb. 55/1 If I admitted..to being a little bit hipped on the subject of Trotsky, I could sometimes gain an indulgent if flickering attention. **1958** J. KEROUAC *Subterraneans* 90 Sand must have hipped him quietly in a whisper somewhere what was happening with the lovers. **1962** *Spectator* 20 Apr. 511 Betjeman is absolutely hipped on his subject. **1973** *Black World* Jan. 64/2, I had just about decided to find some way to hip her to contraceptives.

hip (hip), *a. slang* (orig. *U.S.*). [Origin unknown.] = *HEP *a.* Hence **hi·p-cat** = *HEP-CAT; **hi·pness,** the condition or quality of being 'hip'.

1904 G. V. HOBART *Jim Hickey* i. 15 At this rate it'll take about 629 shows to get us to Jersey City, are you hip? **1926** *Detective Fiction Weekly* 16 Jan. 640/2, I sashayed for a legger an' run into a rube hip agent with a bottle and some jake which helped some. **1938** C. CALLOWAY *Hi De Ho* 16 *Hip,* wise, sophisticated, anyone with boots on. **1944** C. HIMES *Black on Black* (1973) 199 I'm a hipcat from way back. **1946** MEZZROW & WOLFE *Really Blues* xii. 226 Their hipness..bubbled up out of the brute scramble and sweat of living. **1951** *San Diego Even. Tribune* 28 June *a*–2/5 We did it because we thought it was 'hip' or smart. **1958** W. BRYANT *Jive in Hi-Fi* 13 The correct word is 'hip'. It comes from a story of a fisherman warning young fishermen never to wade in deep water without hip boots on because they could run into trouble. So, when you hear the words, 'I'm hip' or 'I'm booted' it's said to let you know they have no fear of trouble or that they understand what's shaking [i.e., happening]. **1957** J. KEROUAC *On Road* (1958) 10 Elmer Hassel, with that hip sneer. **1959** *Spectator* 31 July 134/2 He has a fast line of jive-patter and uses such hip endearments as 'angel-cake' and 'gorgeous'. *Ibid.* 7 Aug. 161/2 Audiences there are hip to the latest gossip. **1959** C. MACINNES *Absolute Beginners* 164 It was like getting a hip cat into a symphony concert, but I succeeded. **1959** *Observer* 4 Oct. 9/7 The only really hip Labour candidate. **1961** *New Left Rev.* May–June 47/1 The goofs of the second act did a lot to dispel the hipness of the first. **1961** *Listener* 9 Nov. 786/1 As Norman Mailer would say, it's 'hip' to use obscure terms and meaningless symbols. **1966** H. S. THOMPSON *Hell's Angels* (1967) 68 Frank was so completely hip that he went down to Hollywood and bought the blue-and-yellow striped sweatshirt that Lee Marvin wore in *The Wild One.* **1971** *Black Scholar* Jan. 22/2 As Cannonball Adderly has said 'Hipness is not a state of mind. It is a fact of life.' **1972** V. FERDINAND in A. Chapman *New Black Voices* 472 We sometimes..go in for that kind of living thinking it's hip.

hip-cat: see *HIP *a.*

hipe, *sb.*^{1} Also **hype.** Add quots. illustrating various kinds of hipe, as *left leg hipe, right leg hipe, swinging hipe,* etc.

1888 *Encycl. Brit.* XXIV. 690–1 The 'left leg hipe'.. consists in lifting and swinging him [*sc.* one's adversary] round to the right, then striking the inside of his right thigh with the outside of the left thigh, by which he gets off his balance and falls; the 'right leg hipe' is the same action *mutatis mutandis.* **1893** *Carlisle Patriot* 26 May 3/3 (Cumbld. Gloss.), In the third round S—— threw M—— after a tight bout with the inside hipe. In the next tussle J—— passed S—— by means of the outside hipe. **1893** ROBINSON & GILPIN *Wrestling* 56 Robley..has been credited with being the first introducer of the swinging hype.

So **hi·per,** one who uses the hipe in wrestling.

1823 W. LITT *Wrestliana* 168 As a hiper, he is certainly the quickest and best on the list.

hipe (həip), *sb.*^{2} *Army slang.* [From the sound of the substitute commonly used for the word *arms* in such commands as 'Slope arms!'] A rifle.

1917 P. MACGILL *Brown Brethren* vi. 89 He seemed to have lost all interest in his best friend, his ''ipe'. *Ibid.* xii. 173 The sun's catchin' the sniper's 'ipe. **1927** D. B. W. LEWIS *On Straw* 59 Brass-Hats rich and ripe Clicked their heels together, Sloped the Army's hipe. **1942** 'N. SHUTE' *Pied Piper* 107 It was full of muckin' Jerries. All loosing off their hipes at Bert and me.

hipe, var. *HYPE *v.* ^{1}

hipness: see *HIP *a.*

hippeastrum (hipíæ·strŏm). *Bot.* [mod.L. (see quot. 1821), f. Gr. ἱππεύς horseman, knight + ἄστρον star.] A member of the genus of South American bulbous plants so named, belonging to the family Amaryllidaceæ; the knight's star lily.

1821 W. HERBERT in *Bot. Reg.* VII. App. 7 Other points of agreement with Crinum separate them [*sc.* the plants] still more widely from the occidental bulbs which I have heretofore called Amaryllis, but in deference to the type of Linnæus, propose now to call Hippeastrum or Knight's-star-lily. **1866** [see AMARYLLIS]. **1899** *Daily News* 16 Mar. 9/2 An immense stand of hippeastrums.. carried off the palm in the shape of the society's gold medal. **1938** A. G. L. HELLYER *Your Garden Week by Week* 102 Start the remaining hippeastrum bulbs into growth now. **1961** *Amateur Gardening* 30 Sept. 6/2 Another plant to be rested is the hippeastrum—or, as many still prefer to call it, the amaryllis.

hipped, *ppl. a.*: see *HIP *v.*^{5}

hipper^2 (hi·pəɹ). *Austral.* [f. HIP *sb.*^{1} + -ER.] (See quots.) Cf. *hip-hole* (*HIP *sb.*^{1} 4 b).

1934 *Bulletin* (Sydney) 26 Sept. 20/3 A tired man usually contents himself with a ground-sheet and blanket after digging himself a 'hipper'—a small cavity to accommodate his hips. **1945** BAKER *Austral. Lang.* 106 The hipper, something soft—such as a piece of possum skin or a stuffed strip of bagging—to put under the hip when lying on hard ground.

hippety (hi·pėti). Also **-ity.** Jingling combination of HIP *v.*^{1} and HOP *v.*, as in *hippety-hop, hippety-hoppety.*

1825 J. JENNINGS *Observ. Dial. W. Eng.* 45 *Hippety-hoppety, adv.*, in a limping and hobbling manner. **1880** *West Cornwall Gloss.* s.v., 'He goes hippety-hoppety' (walks unevenly). **1886** F. T. ELWORTHY *W. Somerset Word-bk.*, *Hippety-hop, hippety-hoppety*.., lame, limping in a very marked manner: applied to both man and beast. **1920** *Cornhill Mag.* Sept. 332 A row of children playing hippety-hop across a broad lawn. **1925** D. H. LAWRENCE *Refl. Death Porcupine* 186 'I am the captain of my soul!' Are you, old boy? Then why hippety-hop? **1950** J. DEMPSEY *Championship Fighting* 58 Under no circumstances take any little half-step or hippity-hop.

hippie, hippy (hi·pi), *sb.* and *a. slang* (orig. *U.S.*). [f. *HIP *a.* + -Y *suffix*^{6}.] **A.** *sb.* A hipster; a person, usually exotically dressed, who is, or is taken to be, given to the use of hallucinogenic drugs; a beatnik. **B.** *adj.* Of, pertaining to, or characteristic of hippies.

1953 D. WALLOP *Night Light* 157 Man, I really get a bellyful of these would be hippies. **1959** *Village Voice* 18 Nov. 13 Imagine coming on so jaded,..so hippie,.. and fed up. **1965** *New Yorker* 24 July 27 All the hippies are leaving for the New World. **1967** *Daily Tel.* 21 Feb. 16/3 These people, 'writers, musicians, psychedelic popsters and hippies..' see London as a 'focal city for permissive experiments' in art and life. **1967** *Sunday Truth* (Brisbane) 2 Apr. 63/1 A hippie is the LSD Age's equivalent of a beatnik, and they turn on with marihuana, LSD, benzedrine or merely with the idea of turning-on. **1967** *Spectator* 7 July 32/3 Promises that in future they will live in accordance with the principles of love demanded by the hippies. **1967** *Guardian* 12 July 1/7 Have you ever been to the hippie district [of San Francisco]? **1967** *New Statesman* 27 Oct. 531/3 The

[demonstration] marches cannot end the war, whether they are moderate and middle-class, insurrectionist, hippy or whatever. **1968** *Times* 16 Dec. 5/3 About 1,000 Hippies from several countries have set up a 'Hippy Republic' here [S. José, Costa Rica]. **1969** *Times* 27 Mar. 1/1 Without..losing her cool, as the hippy idiom would put it. **1969** *Daily Mail* 26 Sept. 7/1 The estimated number of full-time Hippies in London is 2,000,..and more than 60,000 part-timers in Britain alone. **1969** *Times* 5 Dec. 7/1 Religion, in one form or another, is frequently a straw to which the lost generation of hippies clings. *Ibid.*, The members of the hippy commune charged with the Sharon Tate killings are no more typical of America's long-haired 'make love, not war' youth than the soldiers involved in the alleged My Lai massacre are typical of the United States Army. **1972** *New Society* 30 Nov. 496/2 The word 'hippy' is now in current usage throughout Uganda, Tanzania and Kenya, and often just refers to anyone with long hair, almost always a European. **1973** *Friend* 13 July 839/1 'Hippie' is rather a general term applied quite often to anyone young and unkempt in appearance, who is considered to have dropped out of 'straight' society, and who in general puts little premium on the values of contemporary society which he has rebelled against.

Hence **hi·ppiedom,** the condition or fact of being a hippie; the domain of hippies; **hi·ppieland,** the domain of hippies; **hi·ppi(e)ness,** the quality or characteristics of a hippie or hippies.

1967 *N.Y. Times* 5 May 42 There are two philosophical trends in hippiedom. **1967** *Economist* 15 July 217/2 Some of the music is attracting attention outside of hippieland. **1968** *Blues Unlimited* Dec. 9, I guess California, and psychedelia, and hippieness have had the influence. **1969** *Listener* 20 Feb. 250/1 *One Step Away*..is the most comprehensive documentary I have seen so far about West Coast hippiedom. **1969** *Times* 5 Dec. 7/1 The west coast with its sunshine and sparkling surf, cut off by the desert on one side and the Pacific on the other, is the hot-house of America's hippiedom. **1970** K. PLATT *Pushbutton Butterfly* (1971) iv. 41 A lot of girls disappear in hippieland. **1971** *Guardian* 17 June 9/4 A group like Exodus..with their veneer of Dutch hippiness. **1971** *Ibid.* 9 Sept. 9/3 Descriptions of hippiedom by well-meaning admirers.

hippo-. Add: **hippoma·nia** [-MANIA], excessive fondness for horses; so **hippoma·niac,** one affected by hippomania; **hippoma·nic** *a.*; **hippoti·grine** *a.*, pertaining to the striped members of the genus *Equus*, such as the zebra and the quagga; **hippotra·gine** *a.*, belonging to the sub-family Hippotraginæ of the family Bovidæ, a group of large African antelopes.

1961 *Spectator* 9 June 853 The combination of hippomania, secretarial-college chumship. **1963** *Daily Tel.* 8 Jan. 13/4 BBC television is to investigate present-day 'hippomania'... The word was apparently used by the Romans to describe excessive love by women for horses. **1940** V. WOOLF *Roger Fry* 126 He had been thrown riding 'with that hippo-maniac Goldie'. **1963** *Listener* 7 Feb. 260/3 The splendidly hippomanic girl..who met her future husband after a toss in the hunting-field. **1875** *Encycl. Brit.* I. 259/1 Of wild horses the asinine group is characteristic of Asia, and the hippotigrine of Africa. **1947** J. STEVENSON-HAMILTON *Wild Life S. Afr.* vi. 51 The Cape mountain zebra (*Equus zebra*) is the smallest of the group of hippotigrine equines, standing some 4 feet at the shoulder. **1891** FLOWER & LYDEKKER *Introd. Mammals* 342 Hippotragine Section.—Includes very large African Antelopes, with long horns. **1910** H. F. OSBORN *Age of Mammals* v. 337 (*caption*) A recent hippotragine type of Africa, the sable antelope (*Hippotragus niger*).

hippoboscid (hipobǫ·sid), *a.* and *sb.* [f. mod.L. *Hippoboscidæ*, f. HIPPO- + Gr. βόσκειν to feed: see -ID².] Of or pertaining to a member of the family Hippoboscidæ of blood-sucking flies, sometimes called louse-flies, parasitic on mammals and birds.

1891 *Insect Life* III. 357 Mr. Townsend read a paper on a remarkable new Hippoboscid..which had been taken on a bat. **1920** *Q. Rev.* July 91 Tsetse-flies..are the nearest living relations of the Hippoboscid family. **1962** W. R. HORSFALL *Med. Ent.* v. 171 Nycteribiidae and Streblidae ..live in the manner of the hippoboscid flies. **1972** *Nature* 4 Feb. 249/1 Hippoboscids are at best poor fliers, with a strong tendency to wing degeneration.

Hippocratic, *a.* Add: **1.** *Hippocratic oath,* an oath comprising the obligations and professional conduct of physicians, taken by those entering upon medical practice.

1747 J. BARKER *Essay Anc. Mod. Physicians* Dedication p. v, By the Hippocratic Oath, a Physician is bound to honour the Master who has instructed him in his Art. **1969** *Nature* 4 Jan. 2/1 The Hippocratic oath of the medical profession has excited the attention of several moralists.

hippodrome, *sb.* Add: **3.** A theatre used for various stage entertainments.

1899 *Daily News* 10 July 8/1 Hippodromes, as such strictly, have not hitherto been greatly in fashion in London, and they have had but a fitful existence since Mr. Batty started the memorable one known by his name, at the time of the Great Exhibition of 1851. **1902** *Encycl. Brit.* XXXI. 49/1 London in 1902 had..the 'Hippodrome' in Cranbourn Street. **1972** *Times* 8 Apr. 12/5 At the moment, 21 London theatres and halls are listed:.. they are the Duke of York's, Garrick, Her Majesty's, Coliseum, Hippodrome, Lyceum, [etc.].

hi·ppodroming, *vbl. sb.* (See HIPPODROME *sb.* 2 and *v.*)

a **1867** H. WOODRUFF *Trotting Horse* (1868) xxxv. 288 An arrangement was entered into by means of which the former and Lancet travelled together, to trot for purses and divide the profits. It was a new sort of thing, and was ..called 'Hippodroming'. **1946** *Chicago Tribune* 1 Feb. (Grafic Mag.) 13/1 Cynics argue there is a great deal of hippodroming [in ice hockey].

hippo fly (hi·po fləi). [prob. abbrev. of HIPPO(POTAMUS, in reference to the size of the fly.] A large blood-sucking fly of the family Tabanidæ, found in central Africa.

1901 *Geogr. Jrnl.* July 75 The large biting fly called the 'hippo' fly was a great annoyance. **1929** PATTON & EVANS *Insects, Ticks, Mites & Venomous Animals* I. 294 The Tabanidæ have received various local names such as horseflies, seroot flies, mangrove flies, hippo flies.

hippomobile (hi·pomōubīl). (*Disused.*) [f. HIPPO- + MOBILE *a.*] A word used in the early days of motor vehicles for a horse-drawn vehicle. So **hippomo·bilism,** the use of a hippomobile.

1904 in A. B. F. Young *Compl. Motorist* xiii. 275 A hippo-mobile was despatched. **1904** *Westm. Gaz.* 15 Nov. 4/2 A motor-van..would certainly do the journey more quickly..and presumably such a vehicle will supersede the hippomobile in time. **1905** *Ibid.* 20 June 4/2 How much longer, motorists may be tempted to ask, is such a dangerous mode of locomotion as the hippomobile to be tolerated? **1908** *Daily Chron.* 16 Jan. 4/4 Hippomobilism was out of the question. **1963** BIRD & HUTTON-STOTT *Veteran Motor Car* 26 Even in 1899 this contrivance had an air of hippomobile antiquity.

hippus (hi·pŏs). *Ophthalm.* [mod.L., f. Gr. ἵππος horse.] Tremor of the iris; *esp.* a rhythmic contraction and dilatation of the pupil independent of the light intensity; also, a complaint of the eyes, such that they are always winking.

1684 S. BLANCARD *Physical Dict.* 150 *Hippus* is an Affection of the Eyes, wherein they continually shake and tremble, and now and then twinkle. **1838** H. HOUSTON in S. Littell *Dis. Eye* 177 Oscillation of the iris is applied to the alternate contraction and expansion (hippus iridis), as well as to the trembling of the iris. **1904** L. W. FOX *Dis. Eye* xix. 428 Hippus is the term employed to designate a chronic spasm of the iris, as is seen in hysteria, neurasthenia,..and various spinal diseases. **1932** W. S. DUKE-ELDER *Text-bk. Ophthalmol.* I. xii. 563 In the condition of hippus a rhythmic contraction and dilatation of the pupil occurs regularly a definite number of times per minute. **1968** J. L. SMITH *Neuro-Ophthalmol.* IV. iv. 60 No satisfactory explanation has been given for hippus as yet.

hippy (hi·pi), *a.*² [f. HIP *sb.*¹] With large or prominent hips.

1919 F. HURST *Humoresque* 55, I seen you widening into a thirty-eight... You're getting hippy, girl. **1938** *Life* 5 Sept. 43 (*heading*) Hippy girls welcome the form-concealing flattery of hoopskirts. **1956** H. GOLD *Man who was not with It* (1965) xix. 172 She was getting a hippy and breasty look fast. **1969** 'M. FALLON' *Fine Night for Dying* ii. 21 A small hippy woman.

hippy, var. *HIPPIE *sb.* and *a.*

hipster¹ (hi·pstəɹ). *slang* (orig. *U.S.*). [f. *HIP *a.* + -STER.] One who is 'hip'; a hip- (or hep-)cat. Also *attrib.* Hence **hi·psterism,** the condition or fact of being a hipster; the characteristics of hipsters. Cf. *HEPSTER.

1941 J. SMILEY *Hash House Lingo* 31 *Hipster*, a know-it-all. **1946** MEZZROW & WOLFE *Really Blues* 374 *Hipster*, man who's in the know, grasps everything, is alert. **1948** *Partisan Rev.* XV. 722 Carrying his language and his new philosophy like concealed weapons, the hipster set out to conquer the world. **1956** *Observer* 23 Sept. 2/5 'Hipster' is modern jazz parlance for 'hep-cat'. **1958** *Listener* 3 July 16/1 This whole vexed question of hipsterism, anger, French new realism, and so forth. **1958** *New Statesman* 6 Sept. 292/3 The anthology is valuable for a speculative essay by Norman Mailer on 'beat' or hipster culture. **1959** 'F. NEWTON' *Jazz Scene* 291 *Jive-talk* or hipster-talk is..an argot or cant designed to set the group apart from outsiders. **1959** N. MAILER *Advts. for Myself* (1961) 303 The exchange was called 'Reflections on Hipsterism', when it appeared in *Dissent*. I did not choose the title, and so I have altered the name of the piece. **1967** *Lancet* 15 July 150/2 The 'hipster' movement in California..seemed to be an outright rejection of accepted standards and values.

hipster² (hi·pstəɹ). [f. HIP *sb.*¹ + -STER.] Used esp. *attrib.* of, or pertaining to, a garment, e.g. a skirt or trousers, that extends from the hips rather than the waist. In *pl.*, such a pair of trousers.

1962 *Sunday Express* 30 Dec. 16/4 Top girls are buying camel-hair hipsters with long matching braces. **1967** *Spectator* 14 July 53/3 A shop in the Chelsea Antique Market has neatly solved the male sartorial problem at a price level to fit any hipster pocket. **1968** J. IRONSIDE *Fashion Alphabet* 45 *Hipster*, a skirt which sits on the hips instead of the waist.

Hirado (hirā·do). Also **-ato.** The name of a small island off the west coast of the province of Hizen on the island of Kyushu in Japan, used *attrib.* to designate a rich elaborate (blue-and-)white porcelain.

The art was originally introduced from Korea about A.D. 1600.

1880 in A. W. Franks *Jap. Pottery* 96 The works were established..in accordance with the order of a prince of the Matsu-ura family residing at Hirato. Hence the articles made here are generally called Hirato ware. **1881** AUDSLEY & BOWES *Keramic Art Japan* 154 The productions of this kiln have commonly been called Hirado ware.

hiragana (hirăgā·nă). Also **firo-, -kana, -kanna.** [Jap., f. *hira* plain + *kana* (*kanna, kari-na*) borrowed letter(s).] The cursive form of the Japanese syllabary derived from the Tsau style of Chinese ideographs: intended for use by women. Cf. *KATAKANA.

1822 F. SHOBERL tr. *Titsingh's Illustr. Japan* 122 These two kinds of poems are composed in *firokanna*, or women's writing. **1859** A. STEINMETZ *Japan & her People* I. vii. 305 The other style, called *hiragana*, employs at least six characters, radically different from each other, for each sound. **1861** G. SMITH *Ten Weeks in Japan* vi. 92 Sentences written in..the irregularly flowing easy current style of the Japanese Hiragana character, are to be met with in every direction. **1863** *Chambers's Encycl.* V. 687/1 The phonetic alphabet, invented about the year 810 A.D., is known as the Hiragana form of character. **1880** *Encycl. Brit.* XIII. 585/1 Each character may be written in either the *katakana* or the *hiragana* style. **1883** I. TAYLOR *Alphabet* I. 35 The Hirakana syllabary was derived from a cursive form of the Chinese writing called the Tsau or 'grass' character. **1928** G. B. SANSOM *Hist. Gram. Jap.* 45 At some period in the development of the script, probably about the time when the *hiragana* and *katakana* syllabaries were contrived. **1973** *Physics Bull.* May 280/3 We have also extended the process by including, in addition to the 881 Chinese characters, the 50 Japanese Kata-Kana and 50 Hira-Gana characters.

hire, *sb.* Add: **5.** *hire-car, -carriage*; **hire-purchase** (further examples); used esp. *attrib.*; also as vb., and **hi·re-purchasing** *ppl. a.*; cf. *H.P.* (s.v. *H III).

1895 *Brit. Warehouseman* Feb. 30/2 The plaintiff let a piano to one Sullivan under an ordinary hire-purchase agreement. **1901** KIPLING *Kim* v. 122 The woman, she kept *kabarri* shop near where the hire-carriages are. **1909** *Chambers's Jrnl.* July 421/1 Not hire-purchased, you see; I'm not to be gulled by silly advertisements. No. I found my own shop and made my own choice. **1909** *Installation News* iii. 134/1 The hire and hire-purchase of cooking, heating, and other apparatus. **1923** 'BARTIMEUS' *Seaways* 36 If it wasn't for my daughter Annie bein' musical an' wantin' a pianner on the 'ire purchase, I wouldn't stop aboard 'er another night. **1930** *Economist* 25 Jan. 215/2 (Advt.), Bank of England and Hire Purchase. **1947** *E. Afr. Ann.* 1946–7 28/2 (Advt.), Largest fleet of hire cars in Kenya. **1960** *Author* Summer 64/2 All up-to-date readers are hire-purchasing electronic computors to read their library books for them. **1960** *Guardian* 9 May 6/7 The true-born, hire-purchasing Briton. **1964** R. BRADDON *Year Angry Rabbit* xi. 94 It was *her* hire car that rammed the car taking Dorfmann and Welch to the deportation ship. **1966** *Times* (Canada Suppl.) 28 Feb. p. ii, Planes and hire-cars whisk you to the magic. **1972** *Mod. Law Rev.* XXXV. 1. 38 All three hire-purchase agreements were illegal.

hire, *v.* Add: **1.** Also in phr. *hire and fire* [FIRE *v.*¹ 16]; also as *sb.* and *attrib.*

1958 *Listener* 23 Oct. 632/2 Men who can be hired and fired according to the current level of business. **1963** *Times* 6 Feb. 6/3 'Hire and fire' is no longer associated with the construction industries. *Ibid.* 24 Apr. 7/4 Sir Donald said a five-year building programme should be planned in the public sector to ensure continuity of work and stop the 'hire and fire' attitude. **1970** *Sci. Amer.* Mar. 35/3 The inability to hire and fire in order to vary the work force with fluctuations in the business cycle. **1973** *Advocate-News* (Barbados) 20 Feb. 4/2 The locals are in the 'hire and fire' positions.

3. b. (Canadian example and earlier U.S. examples.)

1776 S. CURWEN *Jrnl. & Lett.* (1864) 74 The inhabitants [of Sidmouth, Devon, England] chiefly hired out to the Newfoundland traders. **1833** C. A. DAVIS *Lett. J. Downing* (1834) 35, I had hired out here this summer. **1969** in Halpert & Story *Christmas Mumming in Newfoundland* 26 They hired out as fishing servants.

hi-rise, var. *high-rise* (*HIGH *a.* 21).

Hirmologion (hə̄ɹmolǭu·dʒiǭn). Also **Heirmologion, Hirmologium.** Pl. **-ia.** [med. Gr. εἱρμολόγιον or f. εἱρμός (see next) + λογ-, variant of λεγ- to say.] In the Eastern Church, a book containing eucharistic prayers, hirmoi, etc.

1850 in J. M. Neale *Eastern Church, Gen. Introd.* I. 890. **1952** *Monumenta Musicae Byzantinae* IV. 1 The final publication of the whole Byzantine Hirmologium is beyond the power of one man and must be based on a complete survey of all the sources. *Ibid.* VI. 1. p. xxxiv, We have a better knowledge of old Hirmologia than of old Sticheraria. **1961** E. WELLESZ *Hist. Byzantine Mus.* (ed. 2) p. v, Some authors..prefer the Latin form *Hirmologium*, others the Greek spelling *Heirmologion* or *Hirmologion*.

hirmos (hɜ̄·ɹmǫs). Also **heirmos, hirmus.** Pl. **-moi, -mi.** [Gr. εἱρμός series, connection.] In the hymnology of the Eastern Church, a model stanza forming a pattern for the other stanzas.

1850 J. M. NEALE *Eastern Church, Gen. Introd.* I. 830 There are a certain number of *Troparia*..called Hirmoi, on the model of which all other troparia, etc., are formed. *Ibid.* 835 Here we have the actual hirmos on which the third ode is arranged. **1863** R. F. LITTLEDALE *Offices East. Ch.* 214. **1880** *Encycl. Brit.* XII. 580/1 An *ode* is a song or hymn compounded of several similar 'troparia'. ..To these is always prefixed a typical or standard 'troparion', called the *hirmus.* **1959** *Chambers's Encycl.* VII. 348/2 A *contakion*, consisting (broadly speaking) of a *heirmos*, which set the pattern of what followed, succeeded by a series of *troparia.* **1961** E. WELLESZ *Hist. Byzantine Mus.* (ed. 2) 14 Dom Gaisser's article on the *Heirmoi*, the model strophes of the Easter Hymn, is the first detailed study of Byzantine hymnography.

hirola, var. *HEROLA.

Hirschsprung (hɪə·ɹʃsprʊŋ). The name of Harald *Hirschsprung* (1830–1916), Danish physician, used in the possessive in *Hirschsprung's disease*, congenital enlargement of the colon, occurring esp. in boys, *spec.* such enlargement due to the absence of the ganglion cells of a segment of the lower colon or rectum.

1900 DORLAND *Med. Dict* 208/2 *Hirschsprung's d[isease]*, congenital hypertrophic dilatation of the colon. **1908** *Practitioner* Sept. 456 An example of idiopathic dilatation of the colon, or—as it is called in Germany—Hirschsprung's disease, is recorded by Wagner. **1949** *Lancet* 1 Jan. 10/2 A considerable proportion of cases of megacolon (not being Hirschsprung's disease) remain in the residual 'idiopathic' group. **1966** B. C. MORSON in Wright & Symmers *Syst. Path.* I. xvii. 549/1 Idiopathic megacolon..has to be distinguished from congenital megacolon (Hirschsprung's disease), in which there is a characteristic underlying histological defect. **1968** F. A. JONES et al. *Clin. Gastroenterol.* (ed. 2) iv. 121 Confusion later arose because the term Hirschsprung's disease was applied to any megacolon.

hirsel, *sb.* Add: **1. c.** The ground occupied by a flock of sheep.

1822 SCOTT *Fortunes of Nigel* III. ii. 50 Being in a strange country, like a poor lamb that has wandered from its own native hirsel. **1856** J. C. MORTON *Cycl. Agric.* II. 723/2. **1886** C. Scott *Sheep-Farming* 122 He will be able to divide the hill into 'hirsels', and the hirsel again into 'cuts'. **1922** *Glasgow Herald* 16 Dec. 4 There they are fed for days ..till the hirsels are green again. **1944** G. HENDERSON *Farming Ladder* i. 28 A mountain sheep farm, or hirsel, is selected in such a manner that food and shelter can be obtained by the stock. **1965** *Punch* 3 Mar. 325/2 The Welsh fridd system, which keeps sheltered grazing fresh for lambing time, is so much better than the Scottish hirsel (where the flock grazes all the year round on one hill) that it is rapidly winning popularity.

hirsute, *a.* Add: Hence **hi·rsutism**, an abnormal degree of hairiness.

1926 in *Index-Catal. Library Surg.-General's Office, U.S. Army* VI. 753/2. **1927** *Jrnl. Amer. Med. Assoc.* 19 Mar. 969 Hirsutism and suprarenal virilism. **1959** *New Biol.* XXVIII. 132 Other serious abnormalities occur in these diseases, but hirsutism in female patients is a particularly distressing result.

hirudin (hirū·din). *Biochem.* [a. G. *her-, hirudin*, attributed to Jacobj (see F. Franz 1903, in *Arch. f. exper. Path. und Pharm.* XLIX. 362), f. L. *hirūdo* leech + -IN¹.] An anticoagulant protein produced by the salivary glands of leeches which acts by combining with thrombin in the blood.

1905 *Jrnl. Chem. Soc.* LXXXVIII. II. 339 The substance named hirudin separated from leech extract has a very variable activity. **1908** *Practitioner* Apr. 463 Coagulation is prevented by the use of 'hirudin'. **1963** R. P. DALES *Annelids* ii. 60 Leeches have one or more pairs of 'salivary' glands producing an anti-coagulant, 'hirudin', preventing the blood from clotting as it is ingested.

his, *absolute poss. pron.* Add: **b.** Used, normally in combination with or in opposition to *hers*, of an article, room (e.g. a W.C.), etc., intended for males. Occas. used before a following noun.

1949 *Good Housekeeping* June 26/2 With color contrasts in towels and washcloths, it's easy to distinguish 'his' from yours. **1950** *Charm* Apr. 82 Among your wedding gifts..may be a set of bath towels labelled with beautiful equity and foresight: 'His' and 'Hers'. **1953** *Imagination* June 115/1 Almost before Crae brought the car to a gravel-spraying stop..Ellena had the door open and was out and around the corner marked His and Hers. **1962** J. BLACKBURN *Gaunt Woman* x. 156 'His' was a gloomy little room, laid with dirty grey lino. **1964** *Guardian* 10 Oct. 5/2 We halve the available space..under the primitive his and hers law... There is usually a his chair and a her chair. **1965** *New Statesman* 21 May 790/3 What I call a His/Her double bedroom. **1967** *Guardian* 4 Jan. 7/4 *His and Hers.* J. R. L. Andersen reports on the Boat Show. Women's influence in the world of small boats is now almost dominant.

hislopite (hi·zlǫ̆pəit). *Min.* [f. the name of the Rev. Stephen *Hislop* (1817–63), Scottish missionary and naturalist: see -ITE¹.] An Indian variety of calcite coloured green by the presence of glauconite.

1859 S. HAUGHTON in *Phil. Mag.* XVII. 18, I propose to give the name of Hislopite to the remarkable combination of Calc-spar and Glauconite found by him [*sc.* Mr. Hislop] at Nágpur. **1893** *Rec. Geol. Surv. India* XXVI. 171 The name hislopite loses its specific value when the variation of the included so-called glauconite is..so great as the foregoing results show.

hisn, his'n. Add: (Further examples.) Also **hissn.**

1867 'MARK TWAIN' *Celebr. Jumping Frog* 15 It always makes me feel sorry when I think of that last fight of his'n. **1910** C. E. MULFORD *Hopalong Cassidy* xx. 130 Taking the button and looking it over. 'Yep, its hissn, all right.' **1923** 'R. CROMPTON' *William Again* x. 179 Well it isn't his'n—it's stole stuff.

hispa (hi·spă). *Ent.* [mod.L. (C. Linnæus *Systema Naturæ* (ed. 12, 1767) II. 603), f. L. *hispidus* bristly, hairy.] A tropical leaf-beetle of the genus so named. Hence **hi·spid, hi·spine** *adjs.*, of or pertaining to the family Hispinæ, which has *Hispa* as its typical genus.

1794 P. A. NEMNICH *Allgemeines Polyglotten-Lexicon der Naturgeschichte* III. 165 *Hispa.* [*Entomol.*]... *Engl.* The hispa. **1835** *Boston Jrnl. Nat. Hist.* I. 147, I found full grown larvæ of a Hispa in the leaves. **1889** E. C. COTES *Further Notes Indian Insect Pests* 37 The Bengal Rice Hispa. **1922** D. SHARP in *Cambr. Nat. Hist.* VI. v. 282 *Hispa* is one of the most extensive of the numerous genera of Hispides. **1924** *Bull. Entomol. Res.* XIV. 245 (*title*) A new Hispid beetle. **1933** *Proc. Zool. Soc.* 669 (*title*) On the structure of larvae of Hispine beetles. **1962** R. WYNIGER *Pests of Crops in Warm Climates* III. 179 Sugar-cane hispid miner.

Hispanic, *a.* Add: Also **Hi·spanism** = *Hispanicism.*

1949 S. DE MADARIAGA *Christopher Columbus* (ed. 2) 410 When he makes errors in Latin they are Hispanisms. **1964** Y. MALKIEL in *Archivum Linguisticum* XVI. 3 Differently developed Hispanisms in Arabic.

Hispanist, hispanist (hi·spănist). [f. HISPAN(IC *a.* + -IST.] A student of the literature, language, and civilization of Spain.

1934 WEBSTER, *Hispanist*, one versed in, or devoted to, the Spanish language or the study of Spanish. **1960** *Times* 17 Oct. 20/6 His untimely death is a grievous loss to hispanists in the University of London. **1964** *Archivum Linguisticum* XVI. 12 Such an approach predominates in the work of the contemporary Hispanist.

Hispano-. Add: **Hispa:no-Ame·rican** *a.*, Spanish and American; also as *sb.*; **Hispa:no-A·rab, -Ara·bian, -A·rabic** *adjs.*, Spanish and Arabian; **Hispa:no-Go·thic** *a.*, Spanish and Gothic; **Hispa:no-Maure·sque, -More·sco, -More·sque** *adjs.*, Spanish and Moorish; **Hispa·nophil(e)**, a lover of Spain and Spanish culture.

1823 T. Ross tr. *Bouterwek's Hist. Span. Lit.* 6 The nobles, who were of French or Hispano-Gothic origin. **1880** *N. & Q.* 16 Oct. 306/1 (*heading*) Hispano-Arabian poetesses. **1881** C. C. HARRISON *Woman's Handiwork* II. 104 A charm of Fortuny's studio was his Hispano-Moresco lustred pottery. **1904** W. H. HUDSON *Green Mansions* 4 The nervous olive-skinned Hispano-American of the tropics. [**1906** *Daily Chron.* 19 May 3/2 A Hispanofilo to the core.] **1909** *Ibid.* 18 Nov. 1/3 The eighteen-carat gold casket presented to the King of Portugal..is oblong in shape and in the Hispano Gothic style. **1910** *Ibid.* 4 Jan. 3/1 The true Hispanophil with the cult in his veins. **1920** *Glasgow Herald* 25 Nov. 6 All good British Hispanophils. **1933** *Archit. Rev.* LXXIII. 5/1 Most people would even be eager to concede that this hispano-arabian pastry was the reverse of a great art-form. *Ibid.*, And certainly nothing could be more unlike the structureless confections of the hispano-mauresque than the type of these Kasbahs. **1936** *Burlington Mag.* Apr. 198/2 The so-called mudéjar (Hispano-Moresque) style of the kingdoms of Aragon and Castile. **1942** *Ibid.* Feb. 41/1 The two pile carpets here reproduced..provide a further link in the chain of Hispano-American art. **1959** *Listener* 12 Mar. 471/2 He belonged to a distinguished Hispano-Arab family. **1960** *John o' London's* 14 Apr. 432 Many an English Hispanophile. **1964** *Archivum Linguisticum* XVI. 3 *Plomo* may similarly have had a Hispano-Arabic predecessor. **1964** *Punch* 29 July 173/3 Recommended to all Hispanophiles. **1973** *Daily Tel.* 12 Jan. 29/1, I see happy Hispanophiles streaming from Greenock and Blackburn to the Costa del Sol.

Hisperic (hispe·rik), *a.* [ad. med.L. *Hisperica* (see def.). Cf. G. *hisperisch.*] Epithet of a variety of mediæval Latin, of which *Hisperica Famina* (probably of the 6th century) is a notable example, characterized by a highly artificial vocabulary of which the use of borrowed words of Hebrew, Greek, and other origin is a salient feature.

1904 W. P. KER *Dark Ages* 35 The 'Hisperic' vocabulary, which is that of Apuleius, Florus, Martianus Capella, exaggerated out of all measure. **1907** *Cambr. Hist. Eng. Lit.* I. 69 The hymn..known as *Altus prosator* contains very marked specimens of Hisperic Latinity. **1931** E. J. JONES *Hist. Educ. Wales* I. 179 Hisperic words are included in the Anglo-Saxon glossaries of the tenth century. **1948** E. S. DUCKETT *Anglo-Saxon Saints & Scholars* i. 75 Rhyming eight-syllabled lines, again filled with uncouth Hisperic words.

hi-spy, var. HY-SPY.

1876 'MARK TWAIN' *Tom Sawyer* xxviii. 267 They had an exhausting good time playing 'hi-spy'.

hiss, *v.* Add: **1.** Also in *Electricity.* Cf. **hissing arc.*

1961 J. THEWLIS *Encycl. Dict. Physics* III. 703/1 If the current passing through a carbon arc exceeds a certain value depending on the length of the arc, the latter begins to 'hiss'.

hiss, *sb.* **1. b.** Add to def.: Now chiefly the sibilants [s] and [z].

1933 L. BLOOMFIELD *Language* vi. 100 Our gingival spirants [s, z] are hisses or sibilants. **1953** *Archivum Linguisticum* V. 68 The distinction between hiss- (Fr. *sifflantes*) and hush-sibilants (Fr. *chuintantes*).

his-self. Add: Also as one word, representing a *colloq.* or *dial.* pronunciation of HIMSELF.

Further examples s.v. *HIMSELF IV (above).

a **1876** E. LEIGH *Gloss. Words Dial. Cheshire* (1877) 103 'He is not hissell', *i.e.* 'He is out of his mind.' **1902** *Dialect Notes* II. 316 He has hurt *hisself* mighty bad. **1938** M. RICHARDSON in B. A. Botkin *Treas. S. Folklore* (1949) III. i. 443 He would chop a tree by hisself. **1969** R. PHARR in A. Chapman *New Black Voices* (1972) 69 If he wants something for hisself, let him get out and work for it like we do. **1972** 'J. & E. BONETT' *No Time to Kill* x. 133 He's earned hisself a medal. **1973** *Black World* July 64/1 He can take care of hisself.

hissing, *ppl. a.* Add: **1.** (Further examples.)

1922 [see *CLICK *sb.*¹ 1 b]. **1936** *Bell Syst. Techn. Jrnl.* XV. 197 If such a resistance element is in a current-carrying circuit associated with a telephone receiver or loud speaker..a steady hissing noise which sounds like that due to shot effect or thermal agitation of electric charge is heard.

d. *Comb.* **hissing adder, hissing sand-snake** (see quots.); **hissing arc,** an electric arc which emits a hissing sound.

1931 R. L. DITMARS *Snakes of World* vii. 72 *H[eterodon] contortrix* is the common eastern species [*sc.* of hognosed snake] found from Massachusetts to Florida and westward to Minnesota and Texas. It is known as the Flat-headed 'Adder', Hissing 'Adder', and other names in keeping with its antics. **1895** *Electrician* 18 Jan. 338/2 The potential difference for hissing arcs increases with length of arc, but appears to be fairly constant for a given length of arc... One talks of hissing, however, as if there were only one sort of hissing, whereas really there are at least two, with very different significations. **1941** J. D. COBINE *Gaseous Conductors* 293 The high-pressure carbon arc is seen to have two characteristics, one of hyperbolic shape for a silent arc, and the other, essentially linear, for a hissing arc. **1910** F. W. FITZSIMONS *Snakes S. Afr.* iii. 54/2 Psammophis sibilans. Hissing Sand Snake... Distribution: Tropical Africa and Egypt, Rhodesia, Transvaal, Zululand, Port Elizabeth. **1954** J. A. PRINGLE *Common Snakes* 20 Hissing Sand-Snake. *Psammophis sibilans*..occurs in all the provinces of the Union [*sc.* of South Africa] except the Cape.

hissy (hi·si), *a.* [f. HISS *sb.* + -Y¹.] Consisting of a hiss; of a sound, resembling that of a hiss.

1905 J. MASEFIELD *Tarpaulin Muster* (1907) 171 Snakes,..laughing in a sort of hissy chuckle. **1948** I. BROWN *No Idle Words* 42 Cypress, though rather a 'hissy' word.

hist (həist), *v.* Chiefly *U.S.* Also **h'ist, hyst.** [dial. form of HOIST *v.*; cf. *HEIST.]

1. To provide the key for singing (a hymn, etc.). *rare.*

1857 *Harper's Mag.* Sept. 572/1 As they have no choir in the congregation, any one who considers himself qualified has authority to hist the hymns.

2. To raise aloft; = HOIST *v.* 1; also, to steal, hijack. Cf. *HEIST *v.*, *HOIST *v.* 6.

1867 'MARK TWAIN' *Celebr. Jumping Frog* 18 Dan'l give a heave, and hysted up his shoulders. **1872** 'AGRIKLER' *Rhymes* 17 Hev a fresh cask ready histed. **1919** H. L. MENCKEN *Amer. Lang.* iii. 91 They still cling, in their common speech, to such forms as *h'ist* for *hoist.* **1930** *Amer. Mercury* Dec. 456/1 *Hist*, to hold up;to hyjack. 'We hist the mutt's plant for fifty cases of skee.' **1936** M. MITCHELL *Gone with Wind* xxxiv. 569 You'd better hist up your skirts a little. **1938** D. RUNYON *Furthermore* xiv. 290 This is one of the very first cases of histing a truckload of legal beer that comes off in this country. **1938** M. K. RAWLINGS *Yearling* viii. 70, I h'isted him over old Caesar's rump and away we goed.

Hence **hi·sting** *vbl. sb.*

1935 J. T. FARRELL *Judgment Day* x. 213 There's been too many histing jobs pulled off lately in this neighborhood, and the sergeant has been hopping on my tail about them.

Histadrut (hi·stadrūt). Also **Histadrud, Histadruth.** [mod.Heb. *ha-histadrūṯ* the federation: in full *ha-histadrūṯ ha-kᵉlālīṯ šel hā-ʿōḇᵉḏīm bᵉʾeres yisrāʾēl* the general federation of workers in the land of Israel.] The General

Federation of Labour in Israel, founded in 1920.

1923 P. GRAVES *Palestine* vii. 144 A young, idealistic party who work with the Ahaduth Ha-Avoda in the Histadrud Ha-Ovdim, or Workmen's Organization. **1925** L. STEIN *Zionism* v. 171 The *Histadruth* provides its members with evening classes, workmen's clubs, lectures, concerts, and travelling libraries. **1931** F. F. ANDREWS *Holy Land under Mandate* II. 26 The Histadruth has an active Press, its most influential paper being the daily, 'Davar', with a circulation of over four thousand. **1937** *Palestine Labour Studies* IV. 7 The Histadruth is—in aspiration and essence—an organization binding together the founders of a National Home, the builders of a country, the liberators of a people. **1952** S. SPENDER *Learning Laughter* xv. 196 The Histadrut (Trades Union Federation) is perhaps the most powerful Trades Union Organization in the world. **1972** *Times* 6 Apr. 15/7 He served in a number of senior posts in the Histadrut, the Israel Federation of Labour.

histamine (hi·stămīn). *Biochem.* Formerly also **-in.** [f. *HIST(IDINE + AMINE.] An amine formed from histidine by decarboxylation, widely found in both animal and plant tissues, and having a specific action as a stimulator of gastric secretion and as a dilator of the capillaries. Hence **hi·staminase** [see *-ASE], an enzyme which inhibits the action of histamine.

1913 DORLAND *Med. Dict.* (ed. 7), *Histamin*, betaimidazolylethylamin: used like pituitrin. **1913** *Jrnl. Chem. Soc.* CIV. I. 681 Histamine..is a base which Barger and Dale separated from the intestinal mucous membrane. **1918** *Jrnl. Amer. Chem. Soc.* XL. 1723 The first 3 extracts were pale yellow in color and contained practically all the histamine. **1918** *Jrnl. Physiol.* LII. 110 In earlier papers P. P. Laidlaw and one of us [*sc.* H. H. Dale] referred to it by its chemical name, β-Iminazolylethylamine (abbreviated for conveinience to β-I.), being unwilling to coin a new name for a substance long known... Several later investigators of its action, however, have used for it the name 'histamine', which is so obviously appropriate for this amine derived from histidine, that we have adopted it here. **1920** *Nature* 4 Mar. 11/2 A compound of known chemical structure, called 'histamine',.. which is able to produce a state of the circulation like that present in wound-shock. **1929** *Times* 28 Oct. 15/3 These products produce what is spoken of as 'histamine poisoning', the substance histamine being the principal toxic agent. **1930** BEST & MCHENRY in *Jrnl. Physiol.* LXX. 557 We suggest..that the substance, or system, which produces a change in structure responsible for the loss of physiological activity of histamine be designated histaminase. **1951** WHITBY & HYNES *Med. Bacteriol.* (ed. 5) 90 The hypothesis that histamine-release is the immediate cause of the symptoms of anaphylactic shock formerly rested largely on the close similarity between the symptoms of histamine poisoning and of anaphylactic shock in different animals and *in vitro*. **1957** *New Biol.* XXIV. 54 Histamine belongs to a group of substances known chemically as amines and physiologically as vasodilators, i.e. they dilate the blood vessels. **1965** LEE & KNOWLES *Animal Hormones* viii. 119 Histaminase, which destroys histamine, does not affect the potency of the extract and gastrin appears to be a true hormone. **1968** J. H. BURN *Lect. Notes Pharmacol.* (ed. 9) 24 Histamine is an amine which can be formed by removing the —COOH group from the amino-acid histidine.

hister (hi·stəɹ). [mod.L. (C. Linnæus *Systema Naturæ* (ed. 10, 1758) I. 358), f. L. *hister* = *histrio* actor.] A beetle of the genus so named of the family Histeridæ of clavicorn coleoptera. Also **hi·sterid** *a.*, belonging to this family; *sb.*, a beetle of this family.

1794 P. A. NEMNICH *Allgemeines Polyglotten-Lexicon der Naturgeschichte* III. 165 *Hister*. [Entoml. [*sic*]]... *Engl.* The hister. **1839** J. O. WESTWOOD *Introd. Class. Insects* I. 182 Cadet de Vaux, in his *History of the Mole*, observes that, almost as soon as it is dead, it is attacked by a number of Histers. **1874** J. G. WOOD *Insects Abroad* 89 The Giant Hister. **1915** W. A. BRYAN *Nat. Hist. Hawaii* 417 The histerid beetles. **1925** A. D. IMMS *Text-Bk. Entomol.* 483 Hister and its allies frequent dung and carrion. **1965** B. E. FREEMAN tr. *Vandel's Biospeleol.* xiii. 212 Patrizi..has described another hypogeous histerid. **1966** C. SWEENEY *Scurrying Bush* iv. 52 Two adult histerid beetles, black, shiny and oval, occurred.

histidine (hi·stidīn, -in). *Biochem.* Also **-in.** [ad. G. *histidin* (A. Kossel 1896, in *Zeitschr. f. physiol. Chem.* XXII. 176), f. Gr. ἱστ-ός web, tissue + *-IDINE c.] An amino-acid; see quot. 1940.

1896 *Jrnl. Chem. Soc.* LXX. I. 582 The sulphate from.. sturgeon sperm has rather different solubilities in sodium chloride solutions, and the names *salmine* and *sturine* are suggested by the two protamines. By decomposing the latter base with sulphuric acid, a new crystalline base was prepared, which is called *histidine*. **1900** DORLAND *Med. Dict.* 301/2 *Histidin*, a substance, $C_6H_9N_3O_2$, obtainable from any protamin by the action of sulphuric acid and water. **1919** *Nature* CIV. 322/2 The diamino-acids lysin, histidin, and arginin. **1940** *Chambers's Techn. Dict.* 417/2 *Histidine*, α-amino-β-imidazole propionic acid, a protein derivative belonging to the group of hexone bases. **1963** H. BURN *Drugs, Med. & Man* (ed. 2) vii. 73 Protein is a structure rather like a house which is built from bricks, each of which is chemically an amino-acid. One of these bricks is an amino-acid called histidine.

histiocyte (hi·stiosəit). *Physiol.* [ad. G. *histiozyt* (Aschoff & Kiyono 1913, in *Folia Haematologica: Arch.* XV. 386), f. Gr. ἱστίο-ν web, dim. form of ἱστός web, tissue + -CYTE.] A large, highly phagocytic cell found in connective tissue and becoming motile when stimulated; also called *adventitious cell, clasmatocyte, macrophage, resting wandering cell*. So **histiocy·tic** *a.*, of or pertaining to, of the nature of, histiocytes.

1924 *Jrnl. Infectious Dis.* XXXIV. 583 These resting wandering cells or histiocytes in all their modifications in the different organs and tissues..are the most active elements in the various inflammatory processes and in particular in tuberculosis. *Ibid.*, It is natural that the lymphocytes should also play an active rôle in the same inflammatory processes and join the polyblasts of histiocytic origin. **1961** *Lancet* 2 Sept. 523/2 The dark red spleen..was unremarkable microscopically except for an occasional large histiocyte in the red pulp with finely vacuolated cytoplasm. **1966** [see HISTIOCYTOSIS below].

Also **hi:stiocyto·sis** *Path.* [-OSIS], any condition characterized by a proliferation of histiocytes.

1925 W. BLOOM in *Amer. Jrnl. Path.* I. 623 For the want of a better name we would suggest 'lipoid-histiocytosis' as tending to convey the idea of a process involving the storing of lipoid material by the histiocytes throughout the body. **1953** L. LICHTENSTEIN in *A.M.A. Arch. Path.* LV. 102 The conditions previously designated eosinophilic granuloma of bone, 'Letter-Siwe disease' and 'Schüller-Christian disease' are interrelated manifestations of a single malady. The name 'histiocytosis X' is suggested as a provisional broad general description for this nosologic entity. **1966** *New Eng. Jrnl. Med.* 28 Apr. 929/1 The association of histiocytic proliferations with recurrent infections has been noted in histiocytosis X and in pigmented histiocytosis.

histo-. Add: **histoche·mically** *adv.*, by histochemical means; **hi:stocompatibi·lity,** compatibility (sense *2 b) between a grafted tissue and the recipient; so **hi:stocompa·tible** *a.*; **histo·genous** *a.*, formed by tissue; **hi·stolyse** *v.*, to subject to histolysis; so *hi·stolysing* ppl. adj.; **hi:stometa·basis** *Palæont.* [METABASIS], a state of complete fossilization in which the minute markings of grain and texture are preserved; **hi:stopatholo·gic, -ical** *adjs.*, characterized by diseased tissues; of or pertaining to histopathology; **hi:stopatho·logist,** one who specializes in histopathology; **hi:stopatho·logy,** (the study of) the tissue changes associated with a disease or disorder; **histopla·smin** [-IN[1]], a sterile preparation of a culture of the fungus *Histoplasma capsulatum*, used in skin tests for histoplasmosis; **hi:stoplasmo·sis** [-OSIS], an infection due to the fungus *Histoplasma capsulatum*, endemic in parts of the United States and taking the form of either a benign transient infection of the lungs or, rarely, a disseminated, usu. fatal, disease of the reticulo-endothelial system.

1955 *Brain* LXXVIII. 327 Lafora bodies (intracellular amyloid bodies) were encountered, and were examined histochemically. **1971** *Jrnl. Insect Physiol.* XVII. 862 Approximately 10 per cent of the histochemically identifiable lysosomal phosphatase remains in tissue fragments attached to the silk. **1948** G. D. SNELL in *Jrnl. Genetics* XLIX. 87 Genes of the type postulated in the genetic theory of tumour transplantation will be here referred to as histocompatibility genes. The prefix 'histo' is used because the same genes which determine susceptibility or resistance to tumour transplants probably also determine susceptibility or resistance to tissue transplants in general. **1969** N. A. MITCHISON et al. *Organ Transplantation Today* 26 The genetic system controlling histocompatibility is not too complicated to defy analysis. **1964** *Transplantation* II. 656/1 An inbred strain is a histocompatible donor to its F_1 offspring. **1907** *Practitioner* Sept. 455 The Histogenous Cells which originate locally as the result of local tissue proliferation. **1946** *Nature* 3 Aug. 147/2 Histogenous demarcation of infected tissue (for example, abscission in shot-hole disease of peach and demarcation by cork layer in black root rot of tobacco). **1963** R. P. DALES *Annelids* vi. 124 The muscles of the body wall are partly histolysed and those of the parapodia augmented. **1946** *Nature* 14 Sept. 367/2 The cutis acts as a physico-chemical barrier, inhibiting the penetration of the histolysing substances into the zone of amputation from the regenerating epithelium. **1893** C. A. WHITE in *U.S. Nat. Mus. Ann. Rep. 1892* 264 The term histometabasis is applied to that condition of fossilization in which an exchange of the original substance for another has occurred in such a manner as to retain or reproduce the minute and even the microscopic texture of the original. **1917** R. S. LULL *Org. Evol.* xxv. 412 The resultant fossil retains..not only the external form but the histologic characters (histometabasis,..) of the original structure as well. **1903** *Detroit Med. Jrnl.* Feb. 705/1 The histopathologic states of the finer structures of the labyrinth. **1947** *Radiology* XLIX. 292/2 Histopathologic changes in organs and tissue may occur in the absence of or prior to observable changes in the blood or blood-forming tissue. **1934** WEBSTER, Histopathological. **1940** E. VON HAAM in *Textbk. Clin. Path.* (ed. 2) xxii. 552 The histopathological change in the syphilitic lesion is a valuable addition to diagnostic methods. **1946** *Acta Med. Scand.* CXXIII. 445 Histopathological discoveries in amyotonia congenita. **1909** WEBSTER, Histopathologist. **1961** *Lancet* 30 Sept. 770/2 London histopathologists. **1966** *Ibid.* 31 Dec. 1450/1 The wealth of photomicrographs is likely to appeal more to the practising histopathologist than to the physicians, dentists, and students. **1896** N. WALKER tr. P. G. Unna (*title*) The histopathology of the diseases of the skin. **1908** *Practitioner* Jan. 27 The histo-pathology of the lesions. **1959** *Chambers's Encycl.* VI. 123/2 Fungi of this group cause systemic mycoses which may closely resemble tuberculosis in their symptomatology and histopathology. **1945** CHRISTIE & PETERSON in *Amer. Jrnl. Publ. Health* XXXV. 1135/2 Histoplasmin is the term we used to designate the antigen we were using for skin testing. It is to be hoped that this natural term will be used for any antigen which may be found satisfactory for the purpose of skin testing in relation to histoplasmosis. **1964** B. D. FALLIS *Textbk. Path.* ix. 242/1 Skin tests using histoplasmin (the counterpart of tuberculin) suggest that in endemic areas histoplasmosis is a common disease, which is not usually clinically apparent. **1907** S. T. DARLING in *Maryland Med. Jrnl.* L. 125 (*heading*) Notes on histoplasmosis—a fatal disorder met with in tropical America. **1955** *Sci. Amer.* Jan. 44/3 There has been a good deal of question about the mode of spread of histoplasmosis, a lung disease widely prevalent in the Middle West. **1973** *Daily Colonist* (Victoria, B.C.) 13 May 40/1 Pigeons on the roof are suspected as the source of an illness called histoplasmosis recently suffered by two law professors.

histogram (hi·stogræm). *Statistics.* [f. Gr. ἱστό-ς mast, web + -GRAM.] A diagram consisting of a number of rectangles or lines drawn (usu. upwards) from a base line, their position along this line representing the value or range of one variable and their height the corresponding value of a second variable.

1891 in E. S. Pearson *Karl Pearson* (1938) 143 The geometrical representation of statistics... D. By Columns. *Histograms.* Optical advantage of vertical over horizontal columns. **1895** K. PEARSON in *Philos. Trans. R. Soc.* A. CLXXXVI. 399 The histogram shows, however, the amount of deviation at the extremes of the curve. [*Note.* The word 'histogram' was] introduced by the writer in his lectures on statistics as a term for a common form of graphical representation, *i.e.*, by columns marking as areas the frequency corresponding to the range of their base. **1903** *Nature* 17 Dec. 149/2 We should like to protest against any such crude process of determining goodness of fit as that of placing a normal curve down on seven or eight blocks forming a 'histogram' and judging the look of the fit. **1949** *Jrnl. R. Aeronaut. Soc.* LIII. 974/2 In Fig. 4..the best exponential curve has been fitted to the histogram of the lengths of over 1,300 conversations on the London Airport R/T channel of frequency 118·1 Mcs. **1969** *Nature* 15 Nov. 655/2 The 178 *z*-values analysed are collected in bins of 0·01*z* and are then marked off as a histogram on a *z*-scale.

histomap (hi·sto,mæp). [f. HISTO(RY + MAP.] (See quot. 1956.)

1945 *Amer. Speech* XX. 76/2 A 'Histomap of Religion' was sent to customers and friends at Christmas time, 1943, by the Kalamazoo Vegetable Parchment Company. **1956** R. REDFIELD *Peasant Soc. & Cult.* 72 A picture of their relationships would be something like those 'histomaps' we sometimes see, those diagrams of the rise and change through time of religions and civilizations.

histone (hi·stōᵘn). Formerly also **-on.** *Biochem.* [ad. G. *histon* (A. Kossel 1884, in *Zeitschr. f. physiol. Chem.* VIII. 512), perh. f. Gr. ἱστ-άναι to arrest or ἱστ-ός HISTO-: see -ONE.] Any of a small class of simple, basic proteins which are soluble in water and dilute acids but insoluble in dilute ammonia and which are most commonly found in association with nucleic acids.

1885 *Jrnl. Chem. Soc.* XLVIII. I. 572 Extraction with dilute acid isolates a substance which belongs to the class of bodies called A-peptones by Meissner... The author names this substance *histon*. **1905** C. E. SIMON *Physiol. Chem.* (ed. 2) 194 The protamins are decomposed entirely like the albumoses and peptones, while the histons are only affected in part, which coincides with the position which the histons occupy midway between the protamins and the true albumins. **1952** *Sci. News* XXIV. 37 Histones..are present in appreciable amounts in the nuclei of the tissue cells of all animal species examined. **1968** *New Scientist* 7 Nov. 319/3 What now seems much more possible is that the histones are simply the tool needed to shut down genes, and that they are instructed which particular gene..to shut down by another, specific, molecule.

historic, *a.* **1.** (Further examples.)

1907 I. ZANGWILL *Ghetto Comedies* 391 'The unconditional historic necessity will carry us on of itself towards a better social state.' 'There you go with your Marx and your Hegel!' **1921** G. B. SHAW in *Nation* 19 Feb. 705/1 Mr. Hyndman falls back..on Historic Determinism, and declares that the Bolshevists must fail because the economic conditions are not ripe. **1940** 'G. ORWELL' *Inside Whale* 22 There is no perception here of what is now called historic necessity.

historical, *a.* Add: **1.** (Further examples.)

1937 A. HUXLEY *Ends & Means* vii. 66 One word is common to all the dictatorial vocabularies and is used for purposes of justification and rationalization by Fascists, Nazis and Communists alike. That word is 'historical'. *Ibid.* 67 The dictatorship of the proletariat is an 'historical necessity'. The violence of Communists is justified because..it is being used to forward an ineluctable 'historical' process. **1964** S. BELLOW *Herzog* (1965) 99 You must sacrifice your poor, squawking, niggardly individuality..to historical necessity.

2. d. Related to or connected with history;

considered from the historian's point of view; belonging to the past.

1881 E. A. FREEMAN *Hist. Geogr. Europe* I. i. 2 It is with political divisions that historical geography has to deal in the first place. **1894** G. A. SMITH *(title)* The historical geography of the Holy Land. **1923** L. D. STAMP *Introd. Stratigr.* i. 1 Stratigraphy is another name for Historical Geology. **1924** O. JESPERSEN *Philos. Gram.* ii. 31 Descriptive linguistics can never be rendered superfluous by historical linguistics. **1933** *Amer. Speech* VIII. III. 6/2 It is the paradox of linguistic geography that a method of research strictly limited to contemporary speech has proved to be the means of revitalizing the study of historical linguistics. **1964** R. H. ROBINS *Gen. Ling.* 5 Historical linguistics is the study of the developments in languages in the course of time.

3. (Further examples.)

1816 JANE AUSTEN *Let.* 1 Apr. (1952) 452, I am fully sensible that an historical romance, founded on the House of Saxe Cobourg, might be much more to the purpose of profit or popularity. **1826** *Blackw. Edin. Mag.* XX. 52/1 These historical novels may operate advantageously on the mind. **1874** GEO. ELIOT *Legend of Jubal* 193 Imagination... Aiming at fiction called historical. **1939** O. LANCASTER *Homes Sweet Homes* 18 The dashing cloak-flinging figure of historical fiction. **1951** *Observer* 28 Jan. 7/4 Philip Woodruff's *Colonel of Dragoons*..a very model of what historical fiction ought to be. **1972** *Guardian* 28 Mar. 12/5 The movie..is..a great deal more than a decently-handled historical pageant.

5. (Later example.)

1965 *English Studies* Feb. 60 An interesting paper on 'Chaucer's Historical Present, its Meaning and Uses' by L. D. Benson.

7. In *Comb.*, prefixed to an adj. to denote: **a.** 'historical and...', as *historical-comparative, -economic, -sociological*; **b.** 'historically, as applied to history', as *historical-lexicographical, -onomatological, -typological*; also *historical-minded* adj., *-mindedness*.

1933 L. BLOOMFIELD *Language* i. 19 These two streams of study, the historical-comparative and the philosophical-descriptive. **1948** J. TOWSTER *Political Power in U.S.S.R.* iv. 53 The historical-economic conditions of national movements. **1965** *Language* XLI. 138 Historical-lexicographical monographs. **1903** F. VON HÜGEL *Let.* 14 Mar. (1927) 117 Dr. Bigg, Dr. Bryce..are historical-minded also. **1964** *Language* XL. 115 Edgerton's linguistic work..historical-minded but not to the neglect of description. **1895** ACTON *Lect. Study History* 58 That influence for which the depressing names historicism and historical-mindedness have been devised. **1965** *Listener* 3 June 819/1 In one important aspect at least the change can be described as the growth of a new kind of historical-mindedness. **1960** *Amer. Speech* XXXV. 210 Four name maps described as a 'historical-onomatological record'. **1965** *English Studies* Feb. 73 The historical-sociological aspects of art. **1962** D. C. SWANSON in Householder & Saporta *Probl. Lexicogr.* 72 'Recent' refers to the other end of the (historical-typological) pole.

B. *sb.* (Further examples.)

1967 E. GRIERSON *Crime of one's Own* i. 7 The dreadful proliferation of Whodunnits and Historicals. **1967** H. HARRISON *Technicolor Time Machine* (1968) iv. 36 I've always been interested in doing a historical. **1971** 'A. BLAISDELL' *Practice to Deceive* iv. 55 Donaldson was yawning over a paper-back historical, when he was buzzed by the desk.

historically, *adv.* (Further examples.)

1937 A. HUXLEY *Ends & Means* vii. 67 No less 'historically' necessary and right are the brutalities of men in brown shirts. **1958** *Spectator* 27 June 849/1 Our undated and long-dated Government stocks are selling at historically low levels. **1959** *Brno Studies* I. 30 How rewarding the study of the written norm may be even for the historically-minded specialist. **1960** *Economist* 15 Oct. 285/3 The yields on copper shares are at historically high levels.

historicism (histǫ·risiz'm). [f. HISTORIC *a.* + -ISM; tr. G. *historismus*.] **1.** The attempt, found esp. among German historians since about 1850, to view all social and cultural phenomena, all categories, truths, and values, as relative and historically determined, and in consequence to be understood only by examining their historical context, in complete detachment from present-day attitudes.

1895 [see *historical-mindedness* s.v. *HISTORICAL *a.* 7]. **1920** *Contemp. Rev.* Oct. 536 If we find in him..some acute historical observation, the merit must be attributed to the historicism of the century. **1938** *Mind* XLVII. 114 Historicism..acknowledges truth only as valid in a special epoch. **1946** A. L. ROWSE *Use Hist.* v. 140 Marxism..brings us up against the question of historical relativism, or historicism. **1949** WELLEK & WARREN *Theory of Lit.* iv. 32 We must..enter into the mind and attitudes of past periods and accept their standards, deliberately excluding the intrusions of our own preconceptions. This view, called 'historicism', was elaborated consistently in Germany during the nineteenth century. **1972** *Sci. Amer.* Dec. 89/1, I was surprised, however, to find an eminent scientist embracing historicism (the theory championed by Hegel and Marx holding that history is determined by immutable forces rather than by human agency) as an explanation for the evolution of science.

2. A tendency in philosophy to see historical development as the most fundamental aspect of human existence, and historical thinking as the most important type of thought, because of its interest in the concrete, unique, and individual.

1939 I. BERLIN *Karl Marx* iii. 49 Against the scientific empiricism of the French and English, the Germans put forward the metaphysical historicism of Herder and of Hegel. **1940** *Mind* XLIX. 120 Hegel is right in teaching.. an 'absolute historicism'. **1964** C. S. LEWIS *Discarded Image* vii. 174 On this view the *differentia* of Christian historiography ought to be what I call Historicism; the belief that by studying the past we can learn not only historical but meta-historical or transcendental truth.

3. The belief that historical change occurs in accordance with laws, so that the course of history may be predicted but cannot be altered by human will; the resulting attitude to the social sciences, of regarding them as concerned mainly with historical prediction.

[**1901** C. S. PEIRCE *Coll. Papers* (1958) VIII. I. vii. 107 He may aim at hastening some result not otherwise known in advance than as that..to which some process seeming to him good must inevitably lead, such as.. whatever the historical evolution of public sentiment may decree (*historicism*).] **1940** K. R. POPPER in *Mind* XLIX. 423 Marx's emphasis on historical method in sociology, a tendency which I may call 'historicism'. **1943** F. A. HAYEK in *Economica* X. 50 *(title)* Scientism and the study of society: the historicism of the scientistic approach. **1957** K. R. POPPER *Poverty of Historicism* 3, I mean by 'historicism' an approach to the social sciences which assumes that *historical prediction* is their principal aim, and..that this aim is attainable by discovering the 'rhythms'..that underlie the evolution of history. **1959** G. D. MITCHELL *Sociol.* i. 5 When we speak of historicism we refer to the attempt to discern a law governing social development.

4. Excessive regard for the institutions and values of the past; *spec.* in *Architecture*, the use of historical styles in design.

1939 *Archit. Rev.* LXXXVI. 55 If she has, in the New York Fair, done little more than to turn away from historicism to a new kind of pastiche, we can hope at least that with the new school of architects now springing up..the real reform will not be long delayed. **1942** *Ibid.* XCI. 52 In between there came a wave of European historicism, all the varieties of Victorian period imitation. **1966** *New Statesman* 25 Feb. 260/2 His [*sc.* I. J. Tengbom's] Högalids Church of 1916–23 and Concert Hall of 1920–26, both in Stockholm, are among the key monuments in Europe of the transition from historicism.

Hence **histo·ricist**, an adherent or proponent of historicism (in various senses); also, one who specializes in the historical branch of a subject; also *attrib.* or as *adj.* So **historici·stic** *a.*

1937 J. ORR tr. *Iordan's Introd. Romance Ling.* iv. 298 His..field of research, namely, Indo-European philology, made him [*sc.* Meillet]..a historicist and comparatist. **1946** K. BURKE in W. S. Knickerbocker *XX. Cent. Eng.* 287 The modern historicist mode of thought. **1948** *Archit. Rev.* CIV. 226 Meldahl was the most important Danish historicist. **1949** *Mind* LVIII. 411 Guido de Ruggiero..avoided being committed to the amoralism inherent to any historicistic conception. **1954** *Word* X. ii. 123 A 'historicist' will be just as blind to the bundles of intimate connections which the synchronist points out between the different units of a language system. **1955** *Scott. Jrnl. Theol.* VIII. 181 The resurrection..cannot be proved by historicist methods, but it is an act. **1957** K. R. POPPER *Poverty of Historicism* ii. 41 Sociology, to the historicist, is theoretical history. **1959** G. D. MITCHELL *Sociol.* 5 The *historicist* tradition which we have seen in Comte. **1964** C. S. LEWIS *Discarded Image* vii. 175 The best medieval historians, like the best historians in other periods, are seldom Historicists.

historicizer (histǫ·risəizəɹ). [f. HISTORICIZE *v.* + -ER[1].] One who historicizes.

1956 *Scott. Jrnl. Theol.* IX. 406 Mark really sees Jesus and the Church as the historicisers of the Jewish eschatological hope.

historico-. Add further examples. Also used to form sbs., as *historico-novelese, -philology*.

1854 GEO. ELIOT tr. *Feuerbach's Essence Christ.* p. xli, This work is nothing but a faithful, rigid, historico-philosophical analysis of religion. **1900** W. A. ELLIS *Life Wagner* I. 225, I was wafted by the image of a great historico-political event. **1905** *Daily Chron.* 20 June 3/3 Pursuing his fascinating historico-biographic method, which gives to criticism the movement and charm of narrative. **1906** *Daily Chron.* 9 Oct. 3/3 'The King's Guerdon' is an historical romance, written in historico-novelese. **1926** *Year's Work in Eng. Stud.* 1924 58 The difficulties and toils of this historico-philology. **1929** S. HOOK in *Essays in Honor J. Dewey* 164 The historico-genetic method tends to minimize origins and beginnings, since it confessedly cannot explain them in terms of spatio-temporal continuity. **1931** *Times Lit. Suppl.* 26 Mar. 242/2 To study the Alsatian question from a historico-psychological standpoint. **1937** J. ORR tr. *Iordan's Introd. Romance Ling.* i. 48 Cases when the historico-comparative method may and must be dispensed with. *Ibid.* iii. 228 The whole applied from a historico-cultural angle. **1938** C. GRAY *Contingencies* (1947) 146 In..his invention of the historico-dramatic tableau he is the father of the Russian operatic composers.

historied, *a.* Add: **1.** (Example.)

1936 A. W. CLAPHAM *Romanesque Archit.* iii. 64 The historied capital, or capital carved with figure-subjects, appears first in minor features.

2. Now *literary* and chiefly *poet.*

1889 W. B. YEATS *Wanderings of Oisin* 122 You move in another dominion And hang o'er the historied stone. **1896** BELLOC *Verses & Sonnets* 63 November is some historied Emperor, Conquered in age. **1934** R. GRAVES *Claudius the God* 333 It will be a matter for laughter to you ..if your minds were ever dazzled by the historied glories of a remote past. **1943** S. SPENDER *Spiritual Exercises* 6 Within my shut skull flows a historied stream Of myths, fears, crimes.

historio-, combining form occurring in Greek (cf. Gr. ἱστοριογραφία HISTORIOGRAPHY) and now used to an increasing extent in English, as *historio-cultural, -patriotic, -pœic* adjs.

1958 W. STARK *Sociology of Knowledge* iv. 169 The historio-cultural sciences. **1967** *Listener* 16 Feb. 237/2 The story was tedious and repetitive as modern Russian historio-patriotic writing sometimes can be. **1953** *Antiquity* XXVII. 97 The abstract, age-long yearning of the Jewish nation in the Diaspora..found its historiopoeic expression in written history and poetry.

history, *sb.* Add: **2.** (Further examples.)

1928 *Daily Tel.* 14 Aug. 5/3 We have had enough of drum-and-trumpet history. **1967** *Listener* 16 Mar. 349/2 This is only one more step away from the older type of 'drum-and-trumpet' history.

3. *ancient history*: also applied *colloq.* to comparatively recent events which are regarded as nevertheless far back in a person's experience. (Further examples.)

1875 *Contemp. Rev.* XXVI. 870 The mutiny is now becoming an event of ancient history. **1908** *Busy Man's Mag.* Nov. 37/1 'Ancient history, governor,' said Woolford. 'We knew all that before.' **1910** BELLOC *Pongo* v. 73 He reminded Dolly of the days when Consols were at 92... All that was ancient history. **1939** C. DAY LEWIS *Child of Misfortune* III. vi. 350 Already the crisis through which they had passed was beginning to seem ancient history. **1946** J. B. PRIESTLEY *Bright Day* x. 320 I'm going to risk telling you something... It's all ancient history, but..we might as well get it straight. **1961** P. SPENCER *Full Term* i. 15 You won't get anywhere by fretting about it... It's ancient history by now, anyway. People do odd things in drink.

4. c. *to make history*: to influence or guide the course of history; also, to do something spectacular or worthy of remembrance (see *history-maker, -making*, sense 9 in Dict. and Suppl.).

1862 *Chambers's Jrnl.* 1 Mar. 139/1 People engaged in public transactions are sometimes said to be making history, because they occasionally perform actions to which history condescends to impart perpetuity. **1889** *Puck* XXV. 133/2 If the hero who thinks he 'makes history' could only wake from his sleep after three hundred years and read the works of half-a-dozen..historians, he wouldn't know his own face on their pages. **1890** WILDE in *19th Century* July 137 Anybody can make history. Only a great man can write it. **1907** *Edin. Rev.* Jan. 4 The average man is of the Centre; and history in the long run is made by the average man. **1915** 'I. HAY' *First Hundred Thousand* XX. 311 We shall have a chance of making history over this, old man. **1959** N. MAILER *Advts. for Myself* (1961) 208, I had been ready to..publish..at my own expense, and try to make a kind of publishing history.

7. Delete † and add later examples.

1958 *Listener* 19 June 1024/3 It was a race that.. converted the classical 'history' into a kind of privileged leg show. **1963** *Ibid.* 28 Feb. 384/3 He [*sc.* Degas] remains ..even when he is no longer a painter of 'histories', a profoundly reactionary figure.

9. *history-master, -mill, paper, -play*; **history-making** *a.* (examples); also *vbl. sb.*

1898 'MARK TWAIN' in *Harper's Mag.* Mar. 538/2 On Thanksgiving Day the sitting was a history-making one. **1949** WYNDHAM LEWIS *Let.* Apr. 491 Excuse me for breaking in upon your as it were private, and partisan, history-making. **1963** AUDEN *Dyer's Hand* 278 Man is a history-making creature. **1891** W. J. GREENSTREET tr. *Guyau's Educ. & Heredity* iii. 128 The history-master might have taken us to the National Library. **1889** 'MARK TWAIN' *Connecticut Yankee* iv. 39 Sir Kay..began to fire up on his history-mill, with me for fuel. **1963** *Times Lit. Suppl.* 11 Jan. 29/1 Grist to some history-mill. **1857** J. A. SYMONDS *Let.* 8 Feb. (1967) I. 90, I was so amused yesterday with hearing the answers of some of the Sixth Form to our History Paper. **1957** N. FRYE *Anat. Criticism* iv. 283 The Elizabethan secular *auto* eventually became the history-play.

hit, *v.* Add: **1. b.** (*b*) *to hit off* (earlier example).

1865 F. LILLYWHITE *Guide to Cricketers* 86 Messrs. Tritton and Wright hit off 25 in 20 minutes.

4. b. To strike exactly or at the proper point. Usually in phr. *to hit on* so many *cylinders*: (of an internal-combustion engine) to be running properly on so many cylinders; hence, *to be hitting on all four* or *six* (*cylinders*), to be running or working perfectly; *fig.* to be in good trim or form.

1912 [see *CYLINDER *sb.* 6]. **1928** *Sat. Even. Post* 10 Mar. 127/1 Modern science offers you a natural means to keep you 'hitting on all six'—every minute of the day.

8. *to hit home* (later example).

1938 *Times* 30 Apr. 11/4 Mr. Roosevelt says that the one lesson in events abroad that has 'hit home' is that 'the liberty of a democracy is not safe if the people tolerate the growth of private power to a point where it becomes stronger than their democratic State itself'.

c. To criticize, make fun of or ridicule (a person or thing): sometimes const. *at.*

1843 *Punch* 23 Sept. 131/2 Instead of an outburst of enthusiasm at the line 'Confound their politics', the

waltzer is supposed to execute a *pirouette*, which is supposed to hit at our wavering propensities. **1936** *S.P.E. Tract* XLV. 190 The member of a newspaper staff who is responsible for writing the headlines prefers..*hit*..to *criticize*. **1945** BAKER *Austral. Lang.* vi. 121 A man who has acquired a strong dislike of another person..hits or..criticizes him. **1969** *Pen* IX. 47 He could supply her with a list of synonyms for the verb 'savage', i.e...hit at.

d. To occur to (a person); to affect in a particular way, to appear to; to have an impact on.

1891 KIPLING *Light that Failed* v. 78 Look at their faces. It hits 'em. **1914** G. ATHERTON *Perch of Devil* I. xxx. 175 Lucky it hit him to buy the house and send that last five thousand. **1916** 'B. M. BOWER' *Phantom Herd* v. 68, I wanted to see how it would hit you. **1916** G. B. SHAW *Doctors' Delusions* (1932) 105 Their worthlessness would not hit us in the face as the worthlessness of Dr Saleeby's figures does. **1921** GALSWORTHY *To Let* II. xi. 212 Their manners now really quite hit you in the eye. **1937** *Even. News* 28 Jan. 7/1 (*headline*) Finding best colours for crossing that will 'hit the eye'. **1958** *Listener* 16 Oct. 600/2 This book..was published about two years ago, and it has not yet hit the architectural profession.

e. *not to know* (or *to wonder*) *what hit one*: to be killed; to be surprised or disconcerted.

1923 J. MINER *Jack Miner & Birds* viii. 27 He came to examine the decoys near me and while his attention was rivetted on them I raised up and fired, and he never knew what hit him. **1961** *Listener* 19 Oct. 589/1 Many of our less efficient firms would be hurt so hard that they could never quite know what had hit them. **1963** *Observer* 10 Feb. 24/3 They must have wondered what hit them in Paris last week, for almost every female member of the British Press made a dead set for the hosiery counter at Galeries Lafayette.

f. fig. *to hit for six* [cf. sense 1 b (*a*)]: to demolish an argument, scheme, etc., to vanquish; to deal a severe blow to.

1937 *Times Lit. Suppl.* 1 May 343/4 Lawrence..was chiefly concerned to hit swots and cads and foreigners for six. **1957** I. CROSS *God Boy* (1958) xiii. 109, I had really hit her for a six and made her change her tune properly. **1961** *Oxf. Mag.* 15 June 413/1 Mr. Sisam, the Secretary, hit most of the questioners for six. **1967** *Lancet* 1 July 41/1, I began to wonder if my massive and inexpert administration of chloroform had not hit his liver—perhaps not inappropriately—for six.

g. To give or administer a narcotic drug to (a person). Also *intr. slang* (orig. *U.S.*).

[**1949** N. ALGREN *Man with Golden Arm* 76 It [*sc.* a narcotic injection] hit all right. It hit the heart like a runaway locomotive, it hit like a falling wall.] **1953** W. BURROUGHS *Junkie* (1972) xiv. 144 'Hit me, will you, Ike?' Old Ike poked a gentle finger along the vein holding the dropper poised between thumb and fingers. **1959** —— *Naked Lunch* 67 The addict regards his body as an instrument to absorb the medium in which he lives, evaluates his tissue with the cold hands of a horse dealer. 'No use trying to hit there.' **1970** *N.Y. Times* 23 Feb. 26 How did he become an addict? 'You mean, who hit me first? My friend, Johnny.'

h. To kill; to rob. *slang* (orig. *U.S.*).

1955 *People* (Austral.) 19 Oct. 13/2 Dutch bellowed, 'Dewey's gotta go. He's gotta be hit.' **1968** N. GIOVANNI in A. Chapman *New Black Voices* (1972) 250, I have been robbed It looked like they knew That i was to be hit They took my tv My two rings. **1972** D. E. WESTLAKE *Cops & Robbers* (1973) xvi. 247 If they're cops, maybe it's not such a good idea to have them hit. **1973** *Publishers Weekly* 29 Jan. 229/2 A professional killer who has 'hit' 38 victims.

11. a. Freq. in modern (esp. U.S.) colloquial use in the sense 'to arrive at'; also, to go to (a place), go upon (a course). Phr. *to hit the trail* (less commonly *the grit, pike, road,* etc.): to take the road, to get on the way, to go away.

1873 W. F. BUTLER *Wild North Land* xviii. 208 In the morning 'Twa-poos', or the Three Thumbs, sets forth to look for a moose; he hits the trail and follows it. **1888** in *Amer. Speech* (1962) XXXVII. 76 *Hit the grit*, get going; get out of here. **1888** *Detroit Free Press* Oct. (Farmer), Professor Rose, who hit this town last spring, is around calling us a fugitive from justice. **1889** BARRÈRE & LELAND *Dict. Slang, Hit the flat, to* (cowboys), to go out on the prairies. **1893** P. H. EMERSON *On Eng. Lagoons* xii. 40, I have been hitting the road something to get here quick. **1896** ADE *Artie* xiv. 127 'A little more weather like this and we'll be hittin' the park,' he observed. **1897** *Outing* (U.S.) XXX. 374/1 Men can pass out the church door, shoulder their packs of general cussedness, and unconcernedly hit the trail to the lower [regions]. **1901** S. E. WHITE *Westerners* i. 7 Thought you wasn't no tenderfoot. Ever hit the trail? **1904** *Hartford Courant* 25 June 6 The..convention, whose delegates were so summarily ordered to hit the pike by the national committee-men. **1907** R. W. SERVICE *Songs of Sourdough* (1908) 65 It lies with thee—the choice is thine, is thine, To hit the ties or drive thy auto-car. **1918** C. E. MULFORD *Man fr. Bar-20* xiii. 131, I was a rich man until I hit town. **1925** WODEHOUSE *Carry on, Jeeves* v. 126 Jimmy Mundy.. has come to save New York from itself; to force it—in his picturesque phrase—to hit the trail. **1925** Z. A. TILGHMAN *Dugout* 70, I must hit the road. **1931** 'D. STIFF' *Milk & Honey Route* 207 *Hitting the grit*, to be forced off a fast moving train. **1932** T. S. ELIOT *Sweeney Agonistes* 18 We hit this town last night for the first time. **1948** G. H. JOHNSTON *Death takes Small Bites* ii. 54 Go down this corridor, up the stairway at the end, straight on until you hit the second court. **1950** T. LONGSTAFF *This my Voyage* v. 97 So on May 31st Mumm and I hit the trail once more. **1973** *Christian Sci. Monitor* 14 Apr. B16/2 These two hit the road together, modern pilgrims making very little progress.

c. *to hit the hay*, to go to bed. Also *to hit the sack*. *slang* (orig. *U.S.*).

1912 *Dialect Notes* III. 578 *Hit the hay*, to go to bed. **1922** S. LEWIS *Babbitt* xix. 245 You probably want to hit the hay. **1930** 'SAPPER' *Finger of Fate* 184 On those two nights we all hit the hay before midnight. **1943** in J. J. Fahey *Pacific War Diary* (1963) i. 74, I hit the sack at 8 P.M. I slept under the stars on a steel ammunition box two feet wide. **1957** J. KEROUAC *On Road* (1958) 93 Terry and I..got ready to hit the sack. **1961** A. MILLER *Misfits* x. 98 Well, I don't know about you educated people, but us ignorant folks got to hit the sack.

d. *to hit the bricks*: (*a*) (see quot. 1950); (*b*) to go on strike. *U.S. slang.*

1931 *Amer. Speech* VI. 439 *Hit the bricks, to*, to be released from prison. **1946** *Seafarers' Log* 1 Feb. 4/3 When you hit the bricks in those days you didn't expect to come back aboard real soon. *Ibid.* 17 May 6/4 The seamen responded almost unanimously to the strike call with organized and unorganized seamen alike tying up the ships and hitting the bricks. **1950** H. E. GOLDIN *Dict. Amer. Underworld Lingo* 97/2 *Hit the bricks*,..to be paroled, discharged, acquitted, or otherwise set free. 'Hawk's got a flat bit..so he's gotta hit the bricks.' **1964** *Time* 2 Oct. 111 The United Auto Workers hit the bricks against giant General Motors.

19. (Later U.S. examples.)

1905 R. BEACH *Pardners* (1912) i. 24 We hit for camp on the run. *Ibid.* ii. 48 So me and 'Kink' Martin..hit west. **1916** 'B. M. BOWER' *Phantom Herd* xiii. 218 When I hit for the land of orange blossoms and singing birds and sunshine.

b. *rare.* To go, pass. *U.S.*

1911 H. S. HARRISON *Queed* vii. 86 I've seen you hit by the window many's the time.

20. b. Also more widely, to become friendly, to be on good terms. (Further examples.)

1863 TROLLOPE *Rachel Ray* II. xiv. 297, I am so happy.. that you and he have hit it off. **1954** T. S. ELIOT *Confid. Clerk* i. 16 Mr. Kaghan is prejudiced. He's never hit it off with Lady Elizabeth.

d. To travel at speed. *U.S.*

1911 J. C. LINCOLN *Cap'n Warren's Wards* iii. 39 They nabbed us for speeding... Said we were hitting it at fifty an hour.

22. *hit or miss* (further examples).

1848 in *Amer. Speech* (1935) X. 40/2 Hit-or-miss-carpet, a carpet woven from strips of old cloth sewed together. **1864** *Harper's Mag.* June 60/1 My husband is Colonel of the Third Regiment in the Hit-or-Miss Brigade, United States Cavalry. **1927** J. ADAMS *Errors in School* 211 Hit-or-miss method. **1955** A. L. ROWSE *Expansion Eliz. Eng.* 399 They were impulsive, chancy, amateurish, very much hit-or-miss. **1959** P. BULL *I know Face* vii. 114 It was much a hit-or-miss part. **1967** KARCH & BUBER *Offset Processes* v. 168 Motor-driven lenses, or hit-or-miss methods involving tricky out-of-focus photographic and lighting techniques are used.

b. *hit and miss* = *hit or miss*. Also (with hyphens) *attrib.* and *spec.*, as **hit-and-miss governor**, a type of governor used in internal-combustion engines which causes the engine to miss one or more explosions when the speed is too great; **hit-and-miss ventilator** (see quots.).

1897 W. E. BARTON *Hero in Homespun* 377 They ripped up the new hit-an'-miss carpet for horse blankets. **1897** R. M. STUART *Simpkinsville* 156 Takin' 'em hit and miss, we wouldn't know the diff'rence hardly. **1902** A. C. HARMSWORTH et al. *Motors* viii. 162 Many of these engines have now the ordinary hit and miss exhaust governor as well. **1909** WEBSTER, *Hit-and-miss ventilator*, a window ventilator consisting of a perforated glass disk, lying flat against, and pivoted through its center to, a correspondingly perforated window. **1931** *Discovery* Sept. 298/1 [Without these criteria] the procedure would be unnecessarily hit-and-miss. **1940** *Chambers's Techn. Dict.* 417/2 *Hit-and-miss ventilator*, a ventilating device consisting of a slotted plate over which may be moved another slotted plate, so that the openings for access of air may be more or less restricted as required. **1955** W. W. DENLINGER *Compl. Boston* 156 Hit-and-miss, take-a-chance breedings are fewer. **1956** G. TAYLOR *Silver* iii. 53 A simple pattern, often seen on Communion Cups, consists of rows of 'hit and miss' ornament. **1970** *Morning Star* 11 July 2 The pedlars of such gifts are only worried about the wastage involved..and the general hit-and-miss aspect of the whole business.

22*. Various phrases.

a. *to hit the pipe*: to smoke opium. Also *to hit the gong, gow, stuff*: to take drugs. So *to hit cigarettes*: to smoke heavily. *U.S. slang.*

1886 T. F. BYRNES *Profess. Criminals of Amer.* 385 Joe did not 'hit the pipe'. **1902** *Chicago Record Herald* 7 Sept. vi. 5/2 On each bunk two almond-eyed devotees of the drug may be seen 'hitting the pipe', as opium smoking is termed. **1933** *Amer. Speech* VIII. II. 27/1 When one has contracted the [drug] habit..he is..hitting the gow. *Ibid.* 27/2 When the opium addict is smoking he is said to be hitting the gong. **1936** *Ibid.* XI. 122/2 To hit the stuff, to be addicted to narcotics... The act of taking dope. **1939** *Ibid.* (1942) XVII. 206/1 Bill is hitting cigarets some.

b. *to hit the booze, bottle, jug, pot*: to drink excessively. *slang* (orig. and chiefly *U.S.*).

1889 *Oregonian* (Portland) 14 Oct. 3/1 If Dasher gets a dozen or more customers with his own appetite for hitting the booze he will have no trouble making it go. **1908** J. M. SULLIVAN *Crim. Slang* 13 *Hitting the pots*, excessive drinking. **1942** BERREY & VAN DEN BARK *Amer. Thes. Slang* § 102.22 *Drink liquor, esp. intemperately*,..hit the booze,..bottle. **1942** R. CHANDLER *High Window* (1943) x. 78 We were kind of hitting the bottle a little. **1946** MEZZROW & WOLFE *Really Blues* 374 *Hit the jug*, drink heavily, often from the bottle; have a drink. **1956** A. CHRISTIE *Dead Man's Folly* iii. 40 The most incredible shirts..covered with crawling turtles and things—made me think I'd been hitting the bottle. **1957** *Landfall* XI. 38 Everyone knew he'd turn out a flop.. Hit the booze and got T.B. **1965** *Times Lit. Suppl.* 25 Nov. 1068/2 We are 'wild spiders crying together'..who must crack or hit the bottle.

c. *to hit the ceiling*: see *CEILING *vbl. sb.* 5 b.

d. *to hit the headlines*: see *HEADLINE 2 c.

e. *to hit the deck*: (*a*) to go to bed; (*b*) to land an aircraft; (*c*) to fall to the ground; (*d*) to get up (from bed). *colloq.*

1918 *Sat. Even. Post* 21 Dec. 29 The sergeants and corporals emphasized the command to rise with sharp injunctions to 'Snap out of it!', 'Hit the deck!' **1935** W. DE LA MARE in *Proc. Brit. Acad.* 247 He hit the deck; he slung his hammock; he went to bed;..they all signify much the same thing. **1943** C. H. WARD-JACKSON *Piece of Cake* 36 *Hit the deck*, to land [an aircraft]. **1954** *Manch. Guardian Weekly* 4 Mar. 2/1 The whole House fell on its knees or went prone behind desks, as one Pacific veteran shouted out: 'Hit the deck, you damn fools!' **1956** *Amer. Speech* XXXI. 193 *Hit the deck!*, wake up; begin working; jump to the floor. **1958** F. C. AVIS *Boxing Ref. Dict.* 53 *Hit the deck*, a slang expression meaning to fall to the ring floor. **1961** F. H. BURGESS *Dict. Sailing* 115 *Hit the deck*, take an upper-deck siesta. **1966** 'J. HACKSTON' *Father clears Out* 52 I'm going to hit the deck now, and I'm going to turn the lamp out.

f. *to hit the silk*: see quot. 1941. *colloq.*

1941 *Amer. Speech* XVI. 166/2 *Hit the silk*, use a parachute. **1958** 'P. BRYANT' *Two Hours to Doom* 104 If it came to the worst, they could always drop altitude and hit the silk.

23. c. *Polo.* (See quot. 1963.)

1906 T. B. DRYBROUGH *Polo* (rev. ed.) xiv. 279 A ball once over the side-boards is out, although it rebounds in or is hit in by a player before it touches the ground. **1930** *Hurlingham Club Rules of Polo* (ed. 43) III. 60 (*heading*) Explanation of terms... 'Hit in' means 'to hit the ball into the field of play'. **1963** BLOODGOOD & SANTINI *Horseman's Dict.* 104 *Hit in*, in polo to hit the ball into the field of play; not to bowl it in under-hand.

25*. hit up. a. To force up; to speed up. With *it*: to put on pressure; to make efforts in a certain direction.

1893 W. K. POST *Harvard Stories* 49, I could hear him objurgating Steve Hudson for hitting up the stroke. *Ibid.* 146 When you are doing better than three and a half [miles an hour], you are hitting it up pretty well. **1904** F. LYNDE *Grafters* xx. 257 Two days after the Universal's triumph in the Belmount field, the Argus began to 'hit it up' boldly toward the capital. **1912** MULFORD & CLAY *Buck Peters* iii. 49 Hit her up or you'll be late. **1918** in F. A. Pottle *Stretchers* (1930) 270 Back he went, while we waited. When he got back with his jam, we hit it up again. It seemed miles before we got anywhere.

b. To make or score (runs).

1895 [see UP *adv.*[1] 19 b]. **1899** *Daily News* 9 June 6/7 They were batting all day, and hit up 397 for the loss of seven wickets. **1928** *Evening News* 18 Aug. 10/5 Middlesex hit up 365 in the first day's play.

c. *to hit* (a person) *up for*: to ask (someone) for. *U.S.* and *N.Z. slang.*

1917 *Chrons. N.Z.E.F.* 5 Sept. 28/1 We hit him up for a loan for weeks afterwards and he always came to light too. **1935** C. W. THURLOW CRAIG *Paraguayan Interlude* xxv. 291, I..hit him up for a job, and here I am. **1936** J. STEINBECK *In Dubious Battle* 108 Don't hit 'im up for anything else but breakfast. **1957** I. CROSS *God Boy* (1958) xii. 98 'I'll have to hit my old man up for a new bike,' he said. **1972** M. J. BOSSE *Incident at Naha* iii. 135 She hit me up for bread.

hit, *sb.* Add: **1.** *hit-in* (in *Polo*), the hitting of the ball into the field of play. (Cf. *HIT *v.* 23 c.)

1930 *Hurlingham Club Rules of Polo* (ed. 43) III. 63 Penalty 2, *by the side fouled*—a hit in from behind by the other side..the defending side being free to place themselves where they choose. **1937** *Times* 16 July 5/5 Captain Morrison, after meeting a hit-in by Major Harrison put Adsdean further ahead with a stupendous shot under his pony's neck. **1959** *Times* 18 May 2/1 Lucas met a hit-in to score early in the second chukka.

b. A dose of a narcotic drug; the action of obtaining or administering such a dose. Also *attrib.*, as **hit-mark**, the scar from an injection of a drug. *slang* (orig. *U.S.*).

1951 *Nat. Educ. Assoc. U.S. Jrnl.* May 342/2 They are anxious to make a 'connection', 'score' or 'hit'. **1962** 'E. MCBAIN' *Like Love* (1964) ix. 119 A narcotics cop will insist on examining a prostitute's thighs for hit marks, even when he knows she couldn't possibly be a junkie. **1966** L. COHEN *Beautiful Losers* (1970) I. 106 They rustled among their veins for one that still carried blood, tapped the needles under the flesh, waited for the red signal of a 'hit', and then squirted the solution into circulation. **1970** *Daily Tel.* 27 Apr. 4/8 In San Francisco's Haight-Ashbury district, the hippie Mecca, the price of one 'hit' has dropped from 12s to 2s 6d. **1972** *Southerly* XXXII. 103 Somebody hands me a joint and I take a hit and hand it to Marlene who takes a hit. **1972** C. WESTON *Poor, Poor Ophelia* (1973) ii. 15 You're blind! You have to wait for a report to see the hit marks?

c. A killing; a robbery. Also *attrib.*, as **hit-man**, a hired murderer. *slang* (orig. *U.S.*).

1970 *Sunday Truth* (Brisbane) 8 Mar. 32/5 The Mafia cringe at the way our boys carry out their hits. **1970** J. PHILIPS *Nightmare at Dawn* (1971) II. 97 He was..a hired gun, a hit-man. **1971** D. MACKENZIE *Sleep is for Rich* vi. 186, I got scared and called the whole thing off. Someone else must have made the hit. **1973** *Daily Tel.* 25 July 4/8 Bryant is alleged to have been a 'hit man' (assassin) for drug traffickers and to have carried out a 'contract' to kill Finley.

4. Add to def.: esp. any popular success (a person, a play, a song, etc.) in public entertainment. (Earlier and later examples.) Also *attrib.* and *Comb.*, as **hit parade**, a programme or grouping of 'hits'; **hit tune** (or **song**), a tune that proves popular.

1811 C. MATHEWS *Let.* 22 June (1838) II. 123 Mawworm was a most unusual hit, I am told. **1835** DICKENS *Let.* 9 Dec. (1965) I. 103 The insertion of another Prison Paper would decidedly detract from the 'hit' of the first. **1908** *Sears, Roebuck Catal.* 199/1 Orchestra selections.. 'Broadway Hits'. **1918** *Talking Machine News & Jrnl. Amusements* Feb. 83 (Advt.), All the song-hits of the moment. *Ibid.* 89/2 (Advt.), When a title makes a hit, we are bound to have another something like it before long. *Ibid.* Mar. p. iv (Advt.), Always a hit!! A 'Record' in a Record. **1927** *Melody Maker* Aug. 800 (Advt.), The sensational hit. Sweeping the country like a cyclone. The Doll Dance. **1932** *Amer. Speech* Apr. 252 The motto of the song writers is..'A hit is not an aesthetic triumph, it is something that sells.' **1937** *Cinema Arts* June 22 (*caption*) The Hit Parade. **1937** W. S. MAUGHAM *Theatre* xxviii. 270 I'm very pleased with her. I think she'll make quite a hit. I've half a mind to give her a contract. **1942** BERREY & VAN DEN BARK *Amer. Thes. Slang* § 580/2 A popular song which has stood the test of time; hit song or tune. **1947** R. DE TOLEDANO *Frontiers of Jazz* xvi. 172 Hit tunes of his own composition. **1948** *Manch. Guardian Weekly* 1 Jan. 13/4 The box-office of any hit-show on Broadway. **1948** F. BROWN *Murder can be Fun* (1951) i. 18 She had big blue eyes that would have been a hit on television. **1957** *Observer* 29 Sept. 13/1 It must first be said that Miss Storm has written a resounding, self-evident hit. **1957** *Times Lit. Suppl.* 4 Oct. 593/1 Hollywood now makes its smash hits out of American self-criticism. **1958** *Times* 26 May 7/6 The numbers listed in the hit parade all have a structure of professionalism. **1959** G. FREEMAN *Jack would be Gent.* vi. 129 The first dozen of you lucky kids..will be presented with my latest hit disc. **1967** *Boston Sunday Globe* 23 Apr. A28/2 Lemons and peppermints have been 'hit items' from the very first fair, and so have rides on one of the Brookline Fire Department's engines. **1967** *Melody Maker* 29 July 7/3 I'm not chasing any hit records any more. **1968** *Brit. Med. Bull.* XXIV. 245/1 Fowler (1966), using a program in Elliot 803 Autocode, has explored the effect of combining models with varying distributions of hit numbers. **1969** *Punch* 29 Jan. p. v, Don Partridge, who shot from the pavement into the hit parade, is putting on a Buskers Concert.

hit and run. 1. *Baseball.* 'A play wherein a base runner starts with the pitcher's throw as the batter attempts a hit, a sacrifice hit' (*D.A.*).

1899 *Chicago Daily News* 2 May 7/1 A rare combination for the hit-and-run game. **1904** R. H. BARBOUR *Bk. Sch. & Coll. Sports* 188 *Team batting.* The best known example of this is what is called the sacrifice hit or 'hit and run'. *Ibid.* 191 The 'hit-and-run' play may also be used when there is a man on third and a run is badly needed. **1909** *Amer. Mag.* May 35/1 Evers and Kling analyzed and discovered every hit and run signal used by the Cincinnati club. **1957** *Encycl. Brit.* III. 164/1 Since the hit-and-run play involves two players, there is usually the exchange of a secret signal between them, or a signal to both of them by the manager or one of the coaches. **1967** [see *BUNT *v.*[2] 2].

2. *Motoring.* The action of the driver of a motor vehicle who fails to stop after an accident for which he is responsible. Freq. *attrib.* Also **hit-run.**

1924 *Sci. Amer.* Sept. 181/1 With the bumper in circuit with the ignition, there would be no more 'hit-and-run' driving. **1926** *Amer. Speech* I. 460/1 The hit-and-run driver. **1933** *Bulletin* (Sydney) 11 Jan. 9 The power to inflict the death penalty on the hit-run driver who kills. **1944** E. S. GARDNER *Case of Careless Kitten* xxiv. 217 Lunk's dead, found at a road intersection a couple of blocks from his house, a hit-and-run car. **1949** 'M. INNES' *Journeying Boy* ix. 109 If Soapy had been a bit nearer the kerb, I'd have felt like a little hit and run. **1955** C. S. FORESTER *Good Shepherd* 24 He had been in trouble with the civil authorities for a hit-run automobile offence. **1965** 'L. EGAN' *Detective's Due* (1966) xii. 129 There had been a hit-run yesterday. **1972** *Times* 14 Dec. 4/8 Professor Christiaan Barnard..will suffer no after-effects from injuries sustained when knocked down by a hit-and-run motorist.

3. Used *attrib.* to denote a raid, raider, etc., using swift action followed by an immediate withdrawal.

1940 *Hutchinson's Pict. Hist. War* 2 Oct.–26 Nov. 98 Two of the three trams blasted by bombs in a Nazi 'hit and run' raid on the morning of 25th October, 1940. **1941** *Ibid.* 14 May–8 July 71 The heavily armed raiding cruiser, or hit-and-run battleship. **1955** *Times* 20 Aug. 5/2 Some of them were indulging in violence and arson, adopting 'hit and run' tactics. **1957** L. F. R. WILLIAMS *State of Israel* 30 Arab forays, which often took the form of hit-and-run tactics. **1966** [see *fire-bombing* s.v. *FIRE *sb.* B 5].

hitch, *v.* Add: **3. b.** (Later U.S. examples.)

1868 H. WOODRUFF *Trotting Horse* iv. 59 When it was found that they began to hitch and hobble, a good let-up would do more to restore the stroke than anything else. **1889** *Century Mag.* 907/2, I do not know what would happen to a man who 'hitched' in his saddle.

4. b. = *HITCH-HIKE *v.* Also *trans.*, *to hitch a lift*, etc.: to obtain a lift in a vehicle.

1931 'B. STARKE' *Touch & Go* ix. 133 She told me she had hitched her way down to New Orleans a week before. *Ibid.* xii. 192 Two lads spoke to me, and asked if I were hitching it by myself. **1948** PARTRIDGE *Dict. Forces' Slang* 94 Hitch a lift, or ride. **1959** 'G. CARR' *Swing Away, Climber* i. 17 We hitched—got lifts, you know—from Birmingham. **1960** *Sunday Express* 6 Nov. 7/5 The car in which he had hitched a lift crashed into a lorry. **1963** *Guardian* 4 Feb. 6/5 They hitch there and back.

5. e. Also *to get hitched up*, to be married, to become married. Chiefly *dial.* and *N.Z.*

1890 S. S. BUCKMAN *John Darke's Sojourn in Cotteswolds* xxii, 'Twarn't long avor we got hitched up together. **1911** 'KIWI' *On Swag* vii. 14 Elsie and I got 'hitched up'. **1944** J. H. FULLARTON *Troop Target* iii. 24 That's the fifth o the old gang to get hitched up in five months.

hitch, *sb.* Add: **1. c.** A catch in or a turn at wrestling.

1834 H. M. BRACKENRIDGE *Recoll.* ix. 94 I'll stan iny mon a hitch in Butler county, if so be he'll clear me o' the la'. **1880** *Harper's Mag.* Mar. 525 How with 'ducking' heads and muffled screams you..saw them scrambling for a 'hitch'.

4. b. = **hitch-hike* sb. *colloq.*

1955 *Times* 27 Aug. 7/4 They are not asked in the middle of doing 200 miles in four hours for a half-mile 'hitch'. **1966** J. PHILIPS *Wings of Madness* (1967) II. iv. 132, I came down by bus. I thought maybe you'd give me a hitch back.

5. b. A mode of harnessing a horse or team; a vehicle with its horse or team. *U.S.*

1876 *Rep. Vermont Board Agric.* III. 143 If he can go best in one kind of a hitch, and, in that hitch, make the best time ever made by any horse. **1898** *Christian Herald* (N.Y.) 2 Mar. 167/2 Several hitches are a mule and steer together. **1905** *Springfield* (Mass.) *Weekly Republ.* 22 Sept. 12 There were also several other creditable displays, both single and double hitches. **1912** MULFORD & CLAY *Buck Peters* xxii. 201, I want a hitch of some kind,..something with speed and bottom, and the sooner the better.

8. A period of service, e.g. in the armed forces. Chiefly *U.S. slang.*

1835 *Novascotian* (Halifax) 12 Nov. 332/2 At last he said, which way are you from, Mr. Slick, this hitch. **1913** *Army & Navy Jrnl. Philippines* 4 Oct. 15/1, I had to go or else re-up For seven long years hitch. **1955** C. S. FORESTER *Good Shepherd* 24 He was new to the ship, a transfer made when they were in Reykjavik, serving his second hitch. **1957** J. KEROUAC *On Road* (1958) 257 Another hitch in prison and you'll be put away for life. **1959** *Listener* 15 Oct. 607/1 Newspapermen who did a hitch in Britain during the war. **1973** *Washington Post* 13 Jan. A3/2 In his work in intelligence, Pounder had many assignments, including a hitch as part of the White House security detail during President John F. Kennedy's Ireland trip.

9. *Comb.*: **hitch and kick, hitch-kick,** a form of high-kicking or long-jumping; **hitch-knot**= sense 6 b.

1898 *N.Y. Tribune* 6 Sept. 9/4 Michael Sweeney, the well-known jumper, broke a world's record in the hitch-and-kick by one inch. **1931** F. A. M. WEBSTER *Athletes in Action* 155 Numerous men using the 'hitch-kick', or 'mid-air-running' style, have beaten 25 ft. **1957** DUNCAN & BONE *Oxf. Pkt. Bk. Athletic Training* (ed. 2) 71 Do not spend time on learning the hitchkick at the expense of developing speed, etc. **1847** T. STODDART *Angler's Comp.* 69 In making large fly-hooks..I bring down the thread and fasten it, with a simple hitch-knot.

hitch-, in combs. = *hitching* vbl. sb. (see HITCH *v.*). *U.S.*

1899 ADE *Doc. Horne* i. 7, I jumped off my horse and threw him one end of my hitch-rein and pulled him out. **1903** A. ADAMS *Log of Cowboy* xxi. 138 Tying our horses in a group to a hitch-rack in the rear of a saloon. **1906** H. D. PITTMAN *Belle of Bluegrass C.* xiii. 187 A slim-legged yellow girl..swinging by her arms from a hitch rail. **1922** *Blackw. Mag.* June 714/1 It needs many a coat of paint, clean, and hitch-up. **1935** C. DAY LEWIS *Time to Dance* 61 A coast-to-coast hitch-up. **1954** *Encounter* Oct. 3/1 The hitch-rail enclosing the county court-house.

Hitchcock (hi·tʃkɒk). The name of L. H. *Hitchcock* (1795–1852) used *attrib.* to designate any one of various chairs made by him or produced in his chair factory at Barkhamsted, Conn.

c **1828** in M. R. Moore *Hitchcock Chairs* (1933) 5 Hitchcock chairs,..flag and wooden seats, warranted well manufactured. **1933** M. R. MOORE *Ibid.* 3 The first Hitchcock chairs probably had the rush seat, but very soon were added the cane and solid wood seats. **1959** L. BOGER *Compl. Guide Furnit. Styles* xxii. 373 The name Hitchcock is given to a particular type of painted American Empire open back chair. **1967** *Boston Sunday Herald* 30 Apr. I. 23/1 (Advt.), The charm of genuine Hitchcock Colonial chairs.

hitcher, *sb.* Add: **3.** One who hitch-hikes.

1960 *20th Cent.* Nov. 476 Do you often pick up hitchers? **1972** R. QUILTY *Tenth Session* 19 When the road seemed to stretch endlessly..Bill always felt he was doing the company a service by picking up a hitcher. **1973** *Daily Colonist* (Victoria, B.C.) 1 July 4/2 The film company.. advertised for hitchers to tell their stories of experiences good and bad.

hitch-hike (hi·tʃ,həik), *v.* orig. *U.S.* Also **hitchhike.** [f. HITCH *v.* + *HIKE *v.*] *intr.* To travel by means of lifts in vehicles. Also *fig.* Hence as *sb.*, such a journey. Also **hi·tch-hiker,** one who hitch-hikes; **hi·tch-hiking** *vbl. sb.*

1923 *Nation* 19 Sept. 297/2 Hitch-hiking is always done by twos and threes. **1927** *New Masses* June 15/1 Most young janes have their heads full of a trip to Paris, or a hitch-hike thru New England. **1927** *Glasgow Herald* 6 Sept. 10 There are apparently hitchhikers in the United States who boast they can travel 500 miles free of charge without walking more than 10. **1931** 'B. STARKE' *Touch & Go* iv. 58, I..wondered how Dot would ever dare..tell the people there that she had hitch-hiked home. *Ibid.* 64 We may charge this wicked hitch-hiker the ten cents extra that she deserves for asking for a bath towel. **1940** A. CHRISTIE *Buckle my Shoe* 182 He told amusing stories of his hitch-hikes and tramps in wild places. **1941** AUDEN *New Year Let.* 68 Kids When their imagination bids Hitch-hike a thousand miles to find The Hesperides that's on their mind. **1945** *Daily Mirror* 27 Sept., Hitch-hiking by air from London to Manila, five British Red Cross welfare sisters arrived in Canberra, Australia. **1958** *Manch. Guardian* 26 Sept. 4/4 He decided to hitch-hike around the world. **1959** *Times* 1 Oct. 9/6 Hitch-hiking appears to have replaced old-fashioned walking and has obviously graduated into a recognized pursuit, ready perhaps to be nurtured and protected by an international organization empowered to negotiate with transport ministers and police chiefs. **1973** *Black World* Apr. 80/1 Walton sees the need for people to realize their own cultural heritage and not hitchhike on somebody else's.

hitching (s.v. HITCH *v.* in Dict.), *vbl. sb.* (Further examples.)

1842 J. L. SCOTT *Jrnl. Missionary Tour Pennsylvania* (1843) vi. 68 When at the door they alighted, and he rode off to the '*hitching post*'. **1852** C. A. BRISTED *Upper Ten Thousand* 67 [He] pulled a hitching-strap from under the seat, and fastened his off-horse very neatly to a lamp-post. **1871** MRS. STOWE *Old Town Fireside Stories* 84 All the hitchin'-posts was full clean up to the tavern. **1884** W. D. HOWELLS *Silas Lapham* xviii. 336 He got the hitching-weight from under the buggy seat and made it fast to the mare's bit. **1920** J. GREGORY *Man to Man* ix. 103 A dozen saddle-horses were tied at the hitching-rail. **1926** J. BLACK *You can't Win* ix. 108, I..limped outside where I had an old 'swift' tied to a hitching rack. **1963** *Guardian* 4 Feb. 6/3 At weekends hitching..is widely practised. **1963** J. N. HARRIS *Weird World Wes Beattie* (1964) xviii. 216 'Oh, Gargoyle, darling,' she said, sitting down on an old hitching block at the edge of the Rosedale pavement, 'isn't it too gorgeous?'

hi·tchlessly, *adv.* [HITCH *sb.* 7.] Without a hitch.

1910 W. DE LA MARE *Private View* (1953) 26 Stealthily and hitchlessly the scenes clear, brighten, fade, and close. **1958** W. STARK *Sociology of Knowledge* viii. 325 It is thought which works in 'hitchlessly', as the Americans would say, with the established social pattern.

Hitler (hi·tləɹ). [Name of Adolf *Hitler* (1889–1945), chancellor of the German Reich and leader of the National Socialist (*NAZI) Party in Germany.] One who embodies the characteristics of Hitler; a dictatorial person. Also used in the possessive to designate the war of 1939–45; also *attrib.* and *Comb.*

1930 *Times* 27 Sept 10/1 The action of the Court was hailed in the Hitler camp as a great tactical success. **1931** WYNDHAM LEWIS *Hitler* I. i. 8 The Hitler Movement.. received so much advertisement in the English Press. **1932** *Times* 26 Mar. 9/5 General Groener has forbidden a rally of the Hitler Youth. **1934** E. WAUGH in *Ninety-Two Days* ii. 49 He was comic; huge feet and hands, huge mouth, and an absurd little Hitler moustache. **1934** J. SPENSER *Limey breaks In* v. 82 Sparkes wanted to be the Hitler of that kitchen. **1935** *Economist* 29 June 1478/1 Refusing to give the Hitler salute in his lecture-room. **1936** WODEHOUSE *Laughing Gas* xxiv. 257 The Hitlers and Mussolinis of the picture world. **1937** *Ann. Reg. 1936* II. 184 Membership of the Hitler Youth Movement became compulsory for all the young people of the country. **1939** *War Illustr.* 14 Oct. 138/3 Millions of leaflets warning the German people of the deadly consequences of 'Hitler's war' if it were prolonged. **1940** *Ibid.* 5 Jan. 574/3 This has been given public expression by Dr. Robert Ley.. addressing the Hitler Youth. **1940** M. P. PRICE (*title*) Hitler's war and eastern Europe. **1962** J. MAYO *Season of Nerves* iv. 12 A tiny chin and a sandy Hitler moustache. **1963** N. FREELING *Because of Cats* vii. 108 The building.. looks like nothing more than a Hitler-bunker. **1966** *Economist* 15 Oct. p. xii/1 The brief crop of 'Hitler babies', born in the 1930s..would soon be reaching working age—and the prospect was alarming.

So **Hitlere·sque, Hitlerian** (-lɪə·r-), **Hi·tlerish** *adjs.*, of, pertaining to, characteristic of, or (somewhat) resembling Hitler; **Hitleria·na,** objects, etc., owned by or connected with Hitler; **Hi·tlerism,** the political principles or policy of the Nazi party in Germany; **Hi·tlerist, Hi·tlerite,** a follower of Hitler; also (both words) *attrib.* or as *adj.*; **Hitleri·stic** *a.*; **Hi·tlerize** *v.*, to make subject to Hitler, to make Hitlerite.

1930 *Times* 26 Sept. 13/2 These Hitlerite outbursts may disturb German Liberals and Socialists. *Ibid.* 27 Sept. 11/3 The most effective antidote to Hitlerism. **1930** *New Statesman* 1 Nov. 106/1 One may magnify or minimise the role of the Hitlerites, but [etc.]. **1931** WYNDHAM LEWIS *Hitler* 4 An exponent..of German National Socialism, or Hitlerism. *Ibid.* 32 The militant nationalism of the Hitlerist. **1931** *Times Lit. Suppl.* 16 Apr. 296/2 Hitlerite anti-Semitism. **1933** *Business Week* 24 May 23/1 (*heading*) Hitlerizing industry. **1934** A. HUXLEY *Beyond Mexique Bay* 113 Dislike and fear of Hitlerian Germany. **1935** N. MARSH *Enter Murderer* iv. 55 Sorry to be a bit Hitlerish, but it'll save time. **1940** *Ann. Reg. 1939* 90 The cause they had undertaken till Hitlerism had been destroyed and a liberated Europe re-established. **1941** *Common Sense* (N.Y.) Jan. 30/1 For the Hitleristic reason of grabbing everything in sight. **1943** *Times* 27 Apr. 5/3 The inherent instability of its Hitlerized Europe publicly exposed by the defection of one of the members. **1944** J. S. HUXLEY

On Living in Revol. xii. 131 In a totalitarian, Hitlerian way, or in a democratic, co-operative way. **1944** G. B. SHAW *Everybody's Political What's What?* xlii. 352 Political ignorance and idolatry will produce not only Hitleresque dictatorships but stampedes led by liars or lunatics. **1960** *News Chron.* 9 June 1/2 Mass crimes committed by Hitlerite agents. **1966** *New Statesman* 17 June 874/3 The collection of Hitleriana is small but fascinating. **1969** *Daily Tel.* (Colour Suppl.) 14 Feb. 12/3 The German ethos that produced Hitlerism. **1973** *Daily Tel.* 24 Apr. 18 Both men and women could be..detained indefinitely, without charge and without trial, during the Hitlerian war.

Hittite (hi·təit), *sb.* and *a.* [f. Heb. *Ḥitt(īm*, Hittite *Ḫatti* + -ITE¹. The form *Hittite* occurs first in the Geneva version, 1560, of the Bible. The LXX has *Χέτταιοι* (identified as children of Heth (*Χέτ*), Heb. *benê Ḥêth*), the Vulgate *Hethæi*, whence *Ethei* in the Wycliffite versions, G. *Hethiter* (Luther), Eng. *Hethite* (Coverdale, etc.), F. *Héthéen.*] **A.** *sb.* **a.** In the Bible (Gen. xv. 20, etc.), one of a Canaanitic or Syrian tribe of greater or less extent, perh. an offshoot of the next. **b.** In modern archæology and philology, a member of a powerful and widespread ancient (non-Semitic) people, variously named *Khita* or *Kheta* in Egyptian, and *Khatti*, *Ḫatti* (see *HATTIC *a.*) in Hittite and Assyrian, whose history can be traced from *c* 1900 to 700 B.C. in Asia Minor and northern Syria, or a member of a people conquered by the Hittite empire. **c.** The Indo-European language (written in cuneiform and hieroglyphs) of this people. **B.** *adj.* Of or pertaining to this people or their language.

1608 TOPSELL *Hist. Serpents* 93 Most fierce & cruell enemies, which should put & cast forth the Cananites, Hettites, and Cheuits. **1614** RALEIGH *Hist. World* I. viii. 162 The second sonne of Canaan was Heth or Cethus: of whom came the Hethites, or Hittites. **1871** tr. *Ewald's Hist. Israel* III. 262 Among the petty Hittite (i.e. generally Canaanite), and Aramean kings. **1879** *Academy* 16 Aug. 124/1 The sculpture accompanied by inscriptions in Hittite (or Hamathite) characters..discovered at Ibreez in Lycaonia..proves that the Hittites had penetrated through the eastern barrier of Asia Minor formed by the Taurus range. **1880** *Encycl. Brit.* XI. 808/2 The discovery of a new hieroglyphic character in the Hittite inscriptions. *Ibid.* XII. 26/2 Our knowledge of the Hittite language is confined to the proper names mentioned in the Egyptian and Assyrian inscriptions. **1880** [see *HATTIC *a.*]. **1884** W. WRIGHT *Empire of Hittites* iv. 56 There can be little doubt that the Lycaonian *patois*, which continued to be the vernacular of the people till the days of Paul, was Hittite. **1884** A. H. SAYCE *Ibid.* xi. 170 The bilingual inscription of Tarkondêmos in cuneiform and Hittite. **1920** A. E. COWLEY *Hittites* i. 1 Until forty years ago, or less, the Hittites were still grouped with Hivites and Jebusites as an insignificant Syrian tribe unknown outside the Bible. **1926** *Year's Work in Eng. Stud.* 1924 38 We have in Hittite..the earliest Indo-European language recorded. **1952** O. R. GURNEY *Hittites* vi. 130 The original home of Hieroglyphic Hittite seems on present evidence most likely to have been Kizzuwatna [1961 ed., Cilicia]. **1962** *Times* 31 Oct. 14/6 Stone stairway flanked by modern but Hittite-type lions. **1972** C. RAPHAEL *Feast of History* i. 15 All the peoples—Amorites, Moabites, Hittites, Horites, and of course the familiar Philistines..with whom the Hebrews dealt constantly in the Old Testament.

So **Hittito·logy**, the study of Hittite philology, archæology, or history; **Hittito·logist.**

1948 D. DIRINGER *Alphabet* I. v. 89 Some Hittitologists accept the term *Nashili*. **1952** O. R. GURNEY *Hittites* 8 There developed an entirely German science of Hittitology devoted to the study of the cuneiform tablets. **1964** *Language* XL. 149, I am not a Hittitologist.

Hittorf (hi·tǫɹf). The name of Johann Wilhelm *Hittorf* (1824–1914), German scientist, used *attrib.* and occas. in the possessive to denote various phenomena, pieces of apparatus, techniques, and concepts observed or invented by him, as *Hittorf dark space* = **Crookes dark space*; *Hittorf method*, a method of finding the transport numbers of ions in an electrolyte by measuring the change in concentration of the ions near the electrodes during electrolysis; *Hittorf transport* (or *transference*) *number*, a transport number as found by the Hittorf method.

1893 T. O'C. SLOANE *Stand. Electr. Dict.* 289 *Hittorf's solution*, a solution sometimes used as a resistance. It is a solution of cadmium iodide in amylic alcohol. *Ibid.* 466 *Hittorf's resistance*, a high resistance, often a megohm, composed of Hittorf's solution. **1897** M. M. P. MUIR tr. *Lüpke's Elem. Electro-Chem.* I. iii. 41 (*heading*) Hittorf's transport-numbers. **1909** *Jrnl. Amer. Chem. Soc.* XXXI. 351 (*heading*) The relation between the true transference number and the Hittorf transference number. *Ibid.*, The ordinary transference number (T_H) for concentrated solutions, as obtained by the Hittorf method, is erroneous in cases where the ions are hydrated, since it is calculated on the assumption that the water remains stationary during the passage of the current. **1916** F. B. PIDDUCK *Treat. Electr.* xii. 487 The negative glow and the Hittorf dark space expand continually as the pressure is reduced. **1941** J. D. COBINE *Gaseous Conductors* viii. 213 Following the cathode glow is another dark space variously called the cathode dark space, the Crookes dark space, the Hittorf dark space. **1942** GLASSTONE *Introd. Electrochem.* vi. 114 Although the Hittorf method is simple in principle, accurate results are difficult to obtain.

hive, *sb.* Add: **7. hive-bound** *a.*, confined to a hive; **hive-moth**, an alternative name for the wax-moth or honeycomb moth.

1921 R. GRAVES *Pier-Glass* 30 A hive-bound bee. **1945** W. DE LA MARE *Burning-Glass* 67 As passive as the hive-bound bees. **1931** *Oxf. Univ. Gaz.* 17 June 703/1 Hive-moth (*Galleria*) at Nairobi.

hive, *v.* Add: **5.** (Further examples.) Now esp., to break away from, to separate from, a group. Also *trans.*, to remove from a group, a large unit, etc., to make separate.

1902 *Westm. Gaz.* 10 July 9/1 The Board is now hiving off to a mine with at least a promising name, the 'Baron Rothschild', in the Tati district. **1931** *Economist* 5 Dec. 1060/2 And even Syrai Proper has been made to hive off the autonomous Governments of the Jebel Druse and Alexandretta. **1937** *Nature* 16 Oct. 659/1 Experimental psychology..has hived off from physiology. **1951** *Engineering* 28 Sept. 403/2 The..firm..was 'hived off' from the parent company. **1957** *Economist* 30 Nov. 783/2 It will be remembered that, while part of the Moroccan Liberation Army..agreed to incorporation in the Royal Moroccan army, another part preferred to hive off and disappear into remote areas. **1959** HALAS & MANVELL *Technique Film Animation* xix. 257 Many animators with a flair for individual work have hived off from these studios. **1959** DUKE OF BEDFORD *Silver-Plated Spoon* x. 201 The trustees were slowly hiving off part of the family estates to meet the awful burden of taxation. **1961** T. LANDAU *Encycl. Librarianship* (ed. 2) 146/1 Large public library systems are increasingly 'hiving off' special sections dealing with foreign literature. **1963** *Times* 20 Apr. 7/6 The territorial wings of the U.F.P. in Northern and Southern Rhodesia and Nyasaland would now 'hive off' with 'full authority to act for themselves' under new names. **1969** *New Scientist* 1 May 262/2 The large machines are beginning to sprout small sideshoots on to which specialized tasks can be hived off. **1971** *Times* 21 Dec. 14/3 Strong opposition to the British Steel Corporation's plans to hive off part of the River Don works at Sheffield..is likely to be encountered.

hives. Add: **hive-syrup** *U.S.*, compound syrup of squills.

1839 *Southern Lit. Messenger* V. 65/2 There 's nothing there but a few drops of peppermint,..and some of the patent hive-syrup. **1901** T. H. SOLLMANN *Text-bk. Pharmacol.* 612 *Syrupus Scillæ Compositus* (U.S.P.) (*Hive Syrup*)... Used especially in whooping-cough. **1936** COOK & LAWALL *Remington's Pract. Pharm.* (ed. 8) 304 Syrupus Scillæ Compositus... Hive Syrup, Coxe's Hive Syrup.

hiya (həi·yă), *int.* Also **hi-ya, hiyah.** [App. shortened from *How are you?* and influenced by HI *int.* 2.] A word of greeting.

1940 'N. BLAKE' *Malice in Wonderland* I. ii. 31 'Hi-ya, boys and girls,' he cried. 'Hi-ya, Teddy,' the cry went back. **1940** R. CHANDLER *Farewell, My Lovely* xxxix. 309 Hiya, babe. Long time no see. **1946** P. QUENTIN *Puzzle for Fiends* (1947) 190 'Hiyah, baby,' I said. **1959** *Elizabethan* May 35/1 Robin Fawcett turned the grin on Friday and me and said 'Hi-ya'.

Hizen (hī̆ze·n). Also †**Fisen, Fizen.** The name of a province in the north-west of Kyushu in Japan used *attrib.* and *ellipt.* to denote a class of porcelains characterized by rich decoration, delicate colouring, and fine workmanship, and including Hirado, Imari, and Nabeshima ware. Cf. *HIRADO.

1727 J. G. SCHEUCHZER tr. *Kæmpfer's Hist. Japan* II. App. 61 In *Fisen* they have a certain white clay, of which they make all sorts of Porcellane-ware. **1859** L. OLIPHANT *Narr. Elgin's Miss. China & Japan* II. iii. 52 The egg-shell China is..made principally in the provinces of Fizen and Satsuma. **1875–80** AUDSLEY & BOWES *Keramic Art Japan* I. 26 The old red, blue and gold Hizen. *Ibid.*, Old Hizen ware..includes white porcelain. **1878** J. J. YOUNG *Ceramic Art* II. vii. 177 The rich beauty of the coloring of Hizen porcelain is indescribable. **1965** S. JENYNS *Jap. Porcelain* iii. 89 The early Hizen blue underglaze ware..was by far the most beautiful of all Japanese underglaze porcelains.

Hjelmslevian (hielmzle·viăn), *a.* [f. the name of Louis *Hjelmslev* (b. 1899), Danish linguist + -IAN.] Of, pertaining to, or characteristic of the writings, or style of writing, of Hjelmslev.

1950 *Archivum Linguisticum* II. 96 'Form' is not used here in its Hjelmslevian sense. **1961** *Amer. Speech* XXXVI. 160 An elaborate and opaque Hjelmslevian terminology. **1963** *Ibid.* XXXVIII. 139 Levin, resorting to a Hjelmslevian concept, considers two forms as 'semantically equivalent insofar as they overlap in cutting up the general "thought-mass"'. **1963** J. LYONS *Structural Semantics* vi. 113 The particular (Hjelmslevian) framework within which the analysis of the Greek system is presented.

hlonipa (hlǫ·nipă), *v.* Also **hlonipha.** [a. Zulu, Xhosa *hlonipa* vb.] Among south-east African Bantu peoples of the Nguni group: to avoid in conversation the radical of the name of certain persons to whom such respect is due. In English contexts often treated as a noun. In quot. 1850 *uku-* is the Xhosa infinitive prefix.

[**1850** J. W. APPLEYARD *Kafir Lang.* 70 The Kafir *women* have many words peculiar to themselves. This arises from a national custom, called *ukuhlonipa*.] **1913** PETTMAN *Africanderisms* 212 The word *hlonipa* means that they [*sc.* women] are too bashful or polite to use such names in common everyday speech. **1936** E. J. KRIGE *Social Syst. Zulus* ii. 30 The behaviour towards relatives-in-law is largely bound up with the custom of *hlonipha*. **1970** *Stand. Encycl. S. Afr.* II. 96/1 Among the Nguni peoples of South Africa the relationship [between parents-in-law and children-in-law] is clearly defined in a code of conduct known as *hlonipha*. A wife must *hlonipha* her in-laws, in other words she must act humbly and respectfully toward them and shun them.

Ho (hōᵘ), *sb.*⁴ [Native name, said to be a contraction of *horo* man.] **a.** One of the principal dialects of central India, belonging to the Kolarian group. **b.** One who speaks this language. Also *attrib.* or as *adj.*

1840 S. R. TICKELL in *Jrnl. Asiat. Soc.* IX. II. 997 The Ho language has no written character. **1860** F. MASON *Burmah* (ed. 2) 131 These Moondas now call themselves Hos. **1871** E. BALFOUR *Cycl. India* (ed. 2) II. 589/2 A Ho bridegroom buys his bride. **1905** P. WAGNER tr. *Nottrott's Gram. Kol-Language* 4 The dialect of the Larka-Kols or Hos. **1906** G. A. GRIERSON *Linguistic Surv. India* IV. 116. **1908** H. H. RISLEY *People of India* 94 The Hos of Singhbhum. **1926** *Encycl. Brit.* XV. 891/2 The Hos, who are closely akin to the Mundas, also inhabit the Chota Nagpur division; in 1901 they numbered 386,000.

Ho (hōᵘ), *sb.*⁵ [Native name, = a heap of dried peas.] Name of a tribe of the Ewe people living near the town of Ho in former Togoland, now part of Ghana.

1890 J. FRAZER *Golden Bough* I. v. 265 The Ho tribe of German Togoland.

Hoabinhian (hōᵘăbi·niăn), *a.* Also **Hoabinian.** [f. *Hoabinh*, the name of a village in Vietnam where the first major site was found + -IAN.] Of, pertaining to, or designating a Mesolithic or Neolithic culture found in parts of South-East Asia, particularly Vietnam, Laos, and Malaysia. Also *ellipt.* as *sb.*

1942 A. H. BRODRICK *Little China* 63 Last of all.. comes the Hoabinhian which may stretch back into the Old Stone Age, although nothing unquestionably Palaeolithic has been found. **1971** *Nat. Geographic* Mar. 339/1 The first domestication of plants in the world was done by people of the Hoabinhian culture, somewhere in South-east Asia. **1972** *Sci. Amer.* Apr. 36/2 Since the initial discovery, many other sites containing Hoabinhian artifacts have been found. *Ibid.* 39/3 Local cultures that were distinctly different from the late Hoabinhian evolved at the start of this period. **1972** M. SHEPPARD *Taman Indera* 3 The culture which these pre-historic cave dwellers followed probably preceded the end of the Ice Age. It has been named Hoabinhian, after a province in North Vietnam where this culture was first recognized.

Hoadlyism (hōᵘ·dli,iz'm). Also **Hoadleyism.** [f. name of Benjamin *Hoadly* (1676–1761), Bishop of Winchester + -ISM.] The opinions or policy characteristic of the latitudinarian clergy of whom Bishop Hoadly was typical. So **Hoa·dlyan** *a.*, **Hoa·dlyite.**

1800 J. MILNER *Lett. to Prebendary* viii. 233 This doctrine..is absurd in the highest degree on the principles of Hoadlyism. *Ibid.* 225, I know that the Hoadlyites deny the existence of such sacramental grace. *Ibid.* 238 The Hoadlyan system..incumbers it with a great number of perplexing consequences. **1863** J. S. BREWER *Eng. Studies* (1881) 300 He may write and preach as much Hoadleyism..as he pleases. **1896** E. S. PURCELL *Manning* I. 499 Its [*sc.* the Established Church's] Hoadleyism, if I may so speak, which prevailed before the Tractarian movement.

hoagie (hōᵘ·gi). *U.S. local.* [Origin unknown.] A sandwich made with a French loaf split lengthways and filled with lettuce and a variety of cold meats and cheeses. Cf. **submarine roll*, *sandwich*.

1967 *Amer. Speech* XLII. 280 Temporary residents of Philadelphia attending Temple University..had some knowledge of the sandwich, locally known as a *hoagie*. **1973** *Home & Store News* (Ramsey, N.J.) Mar., *Hoagies* include ham, salami, provolone cheese and shredded lettuce all stuffed into a seven-inch submarine roll. A packet of salad dressing is included with each hoagie. **1973** *Welcomat* (Philadelphia) 10 Oct. 1/1 The Council for Social Development profited from the Pine Street Sidewalk Fair, which is perhaps why five-inch 'hoagies' were sold for ninety cents.

Hoa Hao (hōᵘ:ă hau·). [Name of the village of birth of the founder, in Vietnam.] A form of nationalistic Buddhism, set up in 1939 in Indo-China by Huynh Phu So. Freq. *attrib.* Cf. *CAODAISM.

1955 *Times* 2 May 12/2 The Hoa Hao commander-in-chief. **1969** *New Yorker* 20 Sept. 110/3 The scattered religious elements in the South—the Buddhists, the Catholics,..the Hoa Hao sect. **1971** I. M. SACKS in R. F. Spencer *Relig. & Change in Contemp. Asia* 54 The Hoa Hao religion was founded by the so-called 'mad monk', Huynh Phu So. The doctrines of Hoa Hao are..to honor

one's parents; to love one's country; to respect Buddhism and its teachings; to love one's fellow man. ('Buddhism' ..means..the teachings of Huynh Phu So.)

hoar-frost. Add: In scientific use now distinguished from rime. (Later examples.)

Hoar-frost is a crystalline deposit of ice formed by the sublimation of water vapour; rime is a more amorphous deposit formed by the rapid freezing of supercooled droplets of water when they are brought by air currents into contact with a cold surface.

1895 T. RUSSELL *Meteorol.* iii. 53 Hoar-frost is a name given to the curious, regular figures resembling ferns that form on objects, especially on the window-panes in houses. ..Rime is a thick, heavy frost forming on objects from frozen rain or mist. **1921** A. E. M. GEDDES *Meteorol.* vi. 182 An examination of these crystals shows that they have not been deposited first as water drops, for they are not frozen drops of water. A deposit of this form is called hoar frost. **1967** R. W. FAIRBRIDGE *Encycl. Atmos. Sci.* 402/1 'Frost' has several meanings, most commonly implying hoar-frost or white frost which occurs when the air has been damp, leading to direct sublimation and the building of interlocking ice crystals on exposed surfaces.

b. hoar-frost curve or **line**: a line representing the conditions for equilibrium between the solid and the vapour phases of water in the absence of the liquid phase.

1879 *Encycl. Brit.* VIII. 731/2 At this point the steam line, ice line, and hoar-frost line intersect, and it has therefore been called the triple point. **1940** GLASSTONE *Text-bk. Physical Chem.* vi. 459 The vapor pressure curve of ice.. is often called the hoar-frost curve.

hoary, *a.* Add: **4. c.** In names of animals having a hoary appearance (see quots.).

1781 T. PENNANT *Hist. Quadrupeds* II. 398 Hoary M[armot] with the tip of the nose black..hair universally rude and long; that on the back, sides and belly cinereous at the root, black in the middle, whitish at the tip, so that the animal has a hoary appearance. **1829** [see sense 4 b in Dict.]. **1832** J. RENNIE *Butterfl. & Moths* 183 The Hoary Double Crescent..frequents ash-trees. **1903** *Bull. Amer. Mus. Nat. Hist.* XIX. 539 Marmotta caligata (Eschscholtz). Hoary marmot. **1948** W. J. STOKOE *Caterp. Brit. Moths* I. 151 (*heading*) The Hoary Footman. **1954** O. J. MURIE *Field Guide to Animal Tracks* 136 The hoary marmot has also sought the high mountains. **1959** HALL & KELSON *Mammals N. Amer.* I. 192/1 The hoary bat is solitary and roosts in trees and shrubs.

hob, *sb.*[1] Add: **2. b.** (Earlier and later examples.) Also *to raise hob.* Chiefly U.S.

1838 *N.Y. Mirror* 2 June 387/1 They say it's playing *hob* with the fellers in these here parts. **1905** B. TARKINGTON *In Arena* 23, I believe that idiot's right, he won't lose votes by playing hob with *us.* **1911** J. C. LINCOLN *Cap'n Warren's Wards* vi. 88 Theoph's been raising hob because the Odd Fellows built on to their building. **1916** H. L. WILSON *Somewhere in Red Gap* iii. 120 He looked like one of them silly little critters that play hob with Rip Van Winkle..before he goes to sleep. **1927** P. MARKS *Lord of Himself* xvi. 244 Carl parked the car and stowed the flask in the door-pocket before speaking, and then he murmured sympathetically, 'It [*sc.* liquor] played hob with you, didn't it, old girl?' **1935** M. DE LA ROCHE *Young Renny* xxv. 219 It's the food you eat without enjoyment that plays hob with your stomach. **1940** D. A. LORD *Our Lady in Mod. World* iii. 141 The revolutionists who are playing hob with our generation are really masters of the obsolete. **1949** *Chicago Tribune* 14 June II. 1/1 The change in time on the new quiz programs is raising hob with getting the evening chores finished. **1967** *Electronics* 6 Mar. 352/2 The Chinese presumably could raise hob..with vlf transmission to submarines from the base at North West Cape.

hob, *sb.*[2] Add: **1. b.** One of the level supports on the top of a stove over which pots and pans, etc., are placed to be heated, etc.

1962 *Listener* 13 Sept. 411/2 The gas-cooker hobs have four self-lighting burners. *Ibid.* 411/3 Centre hob-grill. **1969–70** *Catal. Belling Electric Heating & Cooking* 59 No need to worry if anything boils over...No need to.. take the pans off to lift the hob to get at the mess. Simply slide out the spillage tray from under the hob and clean it at the sink.

3. Also, a master tap.

1881 F. CAMPIN *Mech. Engin.* 49 The taps used for making screw tools and worm wheels are called hobs. *a* **1884** KNIGHT *Dict. Mech.* Suppl. 458/2 *Hob*, a hardened steel mandrel with a threaded portion which is fluted. **1888** *Lockwood's Dict. Mech. Engin.* 178 *Hob*, or *Hub*, a master tap.

6. *Comb.* **hob-grate,** a grate fitted with a hob or hobs.

1915 C. MACKENZIE *Guy & Pauline* i. 53 Guy sat by the small hob-grate. **1959** *Times* 27 Jan. 10/6 He sat erect in a tall wooden chair beside a hobgrate.

hob, *v.*[3] Add: (Later example.) Hence **ho·bber,** one employed in driving hobnails into boots; **ho·bbing** *vbl. sb.*, the action of hobnailing boots and shoes; **hobbing boot** = **hobbing foot*; **hobbing foot** *local*, a shoemaker's last.

1866 R. HALLAM *Wadsley Jack* vii. 36 Thie fooit.. weean't skar me—noa, not if it wor a hobbin fooit. **1907** *Daily Chron.* 8 Jan. 6/2 The woman was struck on the head by a shoemaker's 'hobbing foot'. **1907** *Daily Chron.* 31 Jan. 6/7 He struck his wife on the head with an iron foot—a shoemaker's hobbing boot. **1921** *Dict. Occup. Terms* (1927) § 429 *Hobber*..drives in hobnails round rims of soles of heavy boots, by hand with a hammer. **1922** G. BLAIR *Haunted Dominie* 43 There's some that skimp the hammerin' upon the hobbin'-feet. **1936** T. E. LAWRENCE *Mint* (1955) III. i. 166 Marching boots so hobbed that every pavement became a skating rink.

hob (hǫb), *v.*[4] [f. HOB *sb.*[2] 3.] *trans.* To cut or form by means of a hob or master tap. Hence **ho·bbing** *vbl. sb.* Also *hobbing machine,* a machine in which worm-wheels, spur and spiral gears are cut by means of a hob or master tap; *hobbing cutter* (see quot. 1940).

1892 *Lockwood's Dict. Mech. Engin.* App. 428. **1913** *Ibid.*, App. 439 *Hobbing Machines.* In these, spur and spiral gears as well as worm wheels are cut by a hob, the same hob serving for each type of gear by altering the angle of inclination of the thread. **1930** *Engineering* 17 Oct. 479/1 The defects of the present hobbing process of producing gear wheels. **1940** *Chambers's Techn. Dict.* 418/1 *Hobbing cutter*, a gear-cutting tool resembling a milling cutter or a worm gear, whose thread is interrupted by grooves so as to form cutting faces. **1943** *Jrnl. R. Aeronaut. Soc.* XLVII. 83 A hobbing machine with a properly designed solid master worm wheel will cut accurate and quiet-running gears. **1950** *Engineering* 18 Aug. 145/3 The majority of spur and helical gears are produced by hobbing.

hobbit (hǫ·bit). [See below.] In the tales of J. R. R. Tolkien (1892–1973): one of an imaginary people, a small variety of the human race, that gave themselves this name (meaning 'hole-dweller') but were called by others *halflings,* since they were half the height of normal men. Also *attrib.* and *Comb.* Hence **ho·bbitish** *a.*, resembling a hobbit, hobbit-like; **ho·bbitomane,** a devotee of hobbits; **ho·bbitry,** the cult of hobbits; hobbits collectively, or their qualities.

1937 J. R. R. TOLKIEN *Hobbit* i. 11 In a hole in the ground there lived a hobbit. **1947** C. S. LEWIS in *Ess. presented to C. Williams* 104 *The Hobbit* escapes the danger of degenerating into mere plot and excitement by a very curious shift of tone. As the humour and homeliness of the early chapters, the sheer 'Hobbitry', dies away we pass insensibly into the world of epic. **1954** J. R. R. TOLKIEN *Fellowship of Ring* 7 The memoirs of the renowned Hobbits, Bilbo and Frodo. *Ibid.* 11 A few notes..are here collected from Hobbit-lore. *Ibid.* 20 The Thain was..captain of the Shire-muster and the Hobbitry-in-arms. *Ibid.* 46 It was a tendency of hobbit-holes to get cluttered up. **1955** —— *Return of King* 416 *Hobbit* is an invention. In the Westron the word used, when this people was referred to at all, was *banakil* 'halfling'. But..the folk of the Shire and of Bree used the word *kuduk*... It seems likely that *kuduk* was a worn-down form of *kûd-dûkan* [= 'hole-dweller']. The latter I have translated..by *holbytla* ['hole-builder']; and *hobbit* provides a word that might well be a worn-down form of *holbytla*, if the name had occurred in our own ancient language. **1962** *Listener* 22 Nov. 881/3 The more ambitious hobbit saga, *The Lord of the Rings. Ibid.*, To those who are already hobbitomanes, this book is bound to be a delight. **1966** *New Statesman* 11 Nov. 701/2 The newest and richest site of hobbitry is the American campus, where students are said to greet each other with hobbitish salutations such as 'May your beard never grow less'. **1968** *Listener* 20 June 790/3 Professor Tolkien was thinking of the average, ambling Englishman when he wrote about his hobbits. **1970** H. PERRY *Human Be-In* i. 20 The consistently good people in the Tolkien books are Hobbits and they have the lowliest status of all the groups of characters in the books. The hippies thought of themselves as being or becoming Hobbits; from time to time as the winter wore on, a sign would appear in the window of one of their gathering places to this effect: Do not add to the street confusion this weekend... Be good little Hobbits and stay home.

hobble, *sb.* Add: **3.** Also (chiefly *Austral.*) *hobble chain.*

1901 'M. FRANKLIN' *My Brilliant Career* (1966) ix. 52 The sound of camp-bells and jingle of hobble chains.. had come to these men. **1928** 'BRENT OF BIN BIN' *Up Country* xv. 272 He remembered the hobble-chains behind the old stable. **1959** *Listener* 15 Jan. 113/1 In a brawl, they're deadly. Anything goes—spurs, hobble chains, the lot.

4. In full *hobble-skirt.* A close-fitting skirt usually confined by a wide band below the knees and above the ankles.

1911 *Smart Set* Mar. 40 A hobble skirt is an awful habit to get into. **1912** *Punch* 3 Apr. 255/1 The continued success of the hobble..has..restricted the use of textile material. **1918** *Wireless World* Oct. 372 A feminine atrocity in a cerise muslin sheath on 'hobble-skirt' lines. **1920** M. ASQUITH *Autobiog.* I. 221 From the hoop to the hobble is not a more violent change than from the riding-hats of 1894 to the riding-hats of 1917. **1921** C. TORR *Small Talk at Wreyland* II. 69, I said, 'You don't go in for hobble-skirts, I see.' **1969** H. E. BATES *Vanished World* vii. 71 Ladies in flowered hats and hobble skirts.

hobby, *sb.*[1] Add: **6.** Also *hobby farm, farmer, shop, show.*

1960 Hobby farm [see *golden handshake* s.v. *GOLDEN *a.* 10 a]. **1968** *Globe & Mail* (Toronto) 15 Jan. 24/2 (Advt.), 50 acres..ideal for retirement or hobby farm. **1961** *Ann. Reg. 1960* 16 Loss relief for 'hobby farmers' was terminated. **1945** *Time* 9 Apr. 82 Prison hobby shops are not unusual. **1966** 'D. SHANNON' *With a Vengeance* (1968) viii. 107 This is Mr. Seidenbaum from the hobby shop. **1967** 'W. WRIGHT' *Shadows don't Bleed* i. 20 A girl friend of Bridget's who owns a hobby shop here in town. **1921** *Daily Colonist* (Victoria, B.C.) 9 Apr. 10/1 The first annual boys' hobby show will be held at the Y.M.C.A. this afternoon and evening..The exhibition will consist of manual training work, working models of aeroplanes, boats, etc.

hobby-horse, *v. intr.* Add: (Earlier example.) Also, to move like a hobby-horse.

1819 KEATS *Let.* (1935) 315 He is not only reconcil'd to it but hobbyhorses upon it. **1958** M. PUGH *Wilderness of Monkeys* ii. 22 A sheep started at his cursing and went hobby-horsing down the hill. **1965** *Sunday Tel.* 19 Sept. 24/7 She started to hobby-horse and at the third bounce in the height of the gust of about 30 knots in went her bows. **1967** *Daily Tel.* 30 Mar. 18/6 A continual hobby-horsing which stopped it dead about every third wave it hit.

hobbyist. Add: (Further examples.) Sometimes used with a connotation of crankiness.

1935 W. DE LA MARE *Early One Morning* 582 Of such kind are nascent cranks and hobbyists, and some of them attain at last to the rank..of English 'characters'. **1937** AUDEN & MACNEICE *Lett. fr. Iceland* 105 A circle where one's known Of hobbyists and rivals. **1948** F. A. STAPLES *Water-Color Painting* 1 A non-technical manner suited to the hobbyist or art student. **1959** N. MAILER *Advts. for Myself* (1961) 137 'That's a nice Jap machine gun.' He looked at it with the professional curiosity of a hobbyist. **1971** *Guardian* 11 Aug. 10/4 The young hobbyist was encouraged to specialise.

hobday (hǫ·bdēi), *v.* [The name of F. T. *Hobday,* veterinary surgeon (1869–1939).] *trans.* To operate on (a horse) in order to improve its breathing. Chiefly as *vbl. sb.*, **ho·bdaying.**

1938 F. T. G. HOBDAY *50 Yrs. Vet. Surgeon* iv. 55, I contributed considerably to the successful establishment of an operation now familiarly known..as being 'Hobdayed'. **1958** J. HISLOP *From Start to Finish* 171 *Hobdaying*, an operation to help the breathing of horses who are wrong in the wind, but not by putting a tube in their throat. **1963** *Times* 2 Mar. 3/4 A wind infirmity handicapped King of Saba last year and he has now been hobdayed.

hobo. For '*Western U.S.*' read 'orig. *Western U.S.*' Add further examples.

1889 *Ellensburgh* (Wash.) *Capital* 28 Nov. 2/2 The tramp has changed his name, or rather had it changed for him, and now he is a 'Hobo'. **1918** *Let.* in F. A. Pottle *Stretchers* (1929) x. 295 We had been so long separated from our organization that we had pretty thoroughly acquired a hobo frame of mind. **1925** J. BUCHAN *John Macnab* vii. 157 The gillies have..gathered in some wretched hobo they found looking at the river. **1928** *Punch* 15 Feb. 196/1 Few dramatic critics..could display so adequate a working knowledge of..the ways of hobos in the United States. **1959** I. & P. OPIE *Lore & Lang. Schoolch.* iii. 55 Gipsies, usually known as 'gyppoes' or 'hoboes'. **1963** H. GARNER in R. Weaver *Canad. Short Stories* 2nd Ser. (1968) 40 Harvest hands are like hobos, their friendships as casual as the mating of a pair of flies.

Hence **ho·bo** *v. intr.* (and quasi-*trans.* with *way*), to act the hobo; to journey or travel as a tramp; also with *it.* Also **ho·bodom, ho·boism,** the realm or world of the hobo; **hobo·e·tte,** an occasional term for a female hobo.

1906 U. SINCLAIR *Jungle* xxv. 298 Then he explained how he had spent the last summer, 'hoboing it', as the phrase was. **1914** J. LONDON *Let.* 28 July (1966) 426 You can scarcely find a tramp today..who has not hoboed with me. **1918** *Dialect Notes* V. 5 Hoboettes of America. **1923** H. L. FOSTER *Beachcomber in Orient* ix. 183 Having hoboed my way thus far, I could afford to travel as a passenger the rest of the way. **1928** *Daily Mail* 9 Aug. 11/4, I sort of hoboed my way out to San Francisco. **1930** *Publishers' Weekly* 31 May 3736/2 Any hobo temporarily sober can find a publisher to place on the market with great éclat an epic of Hobodom, provided that there is sufficient of the hobo atmosphere. **1930** *19th Cent.* June 849 These were the high days of American hoboism. **1931** 'D. STIFF' *Milk & Honey Route* xv. 172 He can never understand why the hobos want to keep out the women, whom he labels..'the hoboettes'. **1949** *Landfall* III. 136 Have I.. hoboed through fifteen of these United States only to be jailed like a common criminal? **1966** *Punch* 4 May 671/1 They give us a fleeting glimpse into their world of pop, incipient careers, hoboism and love. **1967** K. ALLSOP *Hard Travellin'* xvii. 206 Typical of this idiom is Benson's *Hoboes of America* pamphlet in which he loudly warns boys—and 'hoboettes' too. **1972** *Village Voice* (N.Y.) 1 June 78/3 He and his brother were hoboing it in Missouri.

hobohemia (hōubohī·miă). Chiefly *U.S.* [Blend of HOBO and BOHEMIA.] A community of hoboes, or the district in which they live; the life of the hobo. Also **hobohe·mian** *a.* and *sb.*

1923 N. ANDERSON *Hobo* i. 4 This four-part concept, Hobohemia, is Chicago to the down-and-out. **1931** 'D. STIFF' *Milk & Honey Route* p. v, I have a good deal to say ..about Hobohemia, the habitat of hobos. *Ibid.* iii. 32 You will fall into your place in the Hobohemian pyramid of social status. **1936** F. CLUNE *Roaming round Darling* xx. 200 Nadbuck was a dinkum hobohemian. **1960** *Spectator* 2 Dec. 899 The New Lefties, the hobohemians, the *Encore* subscribers. **1973** *New Society* 3 May 257/3 An awareness of what aspects of hobohemia need consideration.

Hobson-Jobson (hǫ·bsən dʒǫ·bsən). *Anglo-Ind.* Also 7 **Hosseen Gosseen, Hossy Gossy;** 8 **Hossein Jossen, Hassan Hassan,** etc. [Corruption by British soldiers in India of Arab. *Yā Ḥasan! Yā Ḥusayn!* = O Hasan! O Husain!] **1.** Anglicized form of the repeated

wailings and cries of Muslims as they beat their breasts in the *Muharram* procession; hence this festal ceremony. Also *transf.*

Hasan and Husain, grandsons of Muhammad, were killed while fighting for the faith.

1634 T. HERBERT *Trav.* 167, I have seene them nine severall dayes..in the streets all together crying out *Hussan, Hussan.* **1698** J. FRYER *New Account E. India & Persia* 108 The Moors solemnize the Exequies of *Hosseen Gosseen. Ibid.* 357 That Liberty, which was chiefly used in their *Hossy Gossy.* **1773** E. IVES *Voy.* I. ii. 28 Their *Hassan Hassan*, in memory of the two sons of Ali by Fatima (Mahomet's daughter) being killed in one day fighting for the faith. **1817** T. S. RAFFLES *Hist. Java* II. 4 The ceremony of *húsen húsen*..here passes by almost without notice. **1829** *Oriental Sporting Mag.* (1873) I. 129/2 The folks makes sich a noise..shouting Hobson Jobson, Hobson Jobson. **1861** J. T. WHEELER *Madras* II. xxxii. 347 The Mussulman feast called '*Hossein Jossen*'. **1935** M. E. HOUTZAGER *Unconscious Sound- & Sense-Assimilations* ii. 52 Hobson-Jobson, suggestive of a proper name, is the name of a native festal excitement.

2. a. Used as the title of a famous collection of Anglo-Indian words.

1886 YULE & BURNELL (*title*) Hobson-Jobson, a glossary of colloquial Anglo-Indian words and phrases, and of kindred terms.

b. *the law of Hobson-Jobson*: a phrase sometimes used of the process of adapting a foreign word to the sound-system of the adopting language. So **Ho:bson-Jo·bsonism.**

1898 MORRIS *Austral Eng.* 287/2 The name of the shell is a corruption of this word, by the law of Hobson-Jobson. **1919** MENCKEN *Amer. Lang.* 41 Its variations show a familiar effort to bring a new and strange word into harmony with the language—an effort arising from what philologists call the law of Hobson-Jobson. **1934** *S.P.E. Tract* XLI. 21 There are the words ('Hobson-Jobsonisms') where the original [*sc.* Indian] form has been more or less modified in the process of Anglicization.

‖**hoc genus omne** (hǫk ge·nǖs ǫ·mni), phr. [L. (Horace, *Satires* I. ii. 2).] Usu. in phr. *et* (occas. *and*) *hoc genus omne*: and the whole of that class or group; and all that kind of thing (often as ornamental substitute for *et cetera*).

1748 CHESTERFIELD *Let.* 9 Mar. (1774) I. 271 All the shops, drolls, tumblers, rope-dancers, and *hoc genus omne.* **1834** C. C. F. GREVILLE *Mem.* (1874) III. xxiii. 95 He saw Newcastle, Winchelsea, Wetherell, and *hoc genus omne* as much the objects of idolatry as himself. **1867** ROSSETTI *Let.* 23 Oct. (1965) II. 641 When razzias occur on the part of organ-grinders, brass bands, *et hoc genus omne.* **1889** G. B. SHAW *London Mus. 1888–89* (1937) 94 Handfuls of earls, a dean..half-a-dozen members of Parliament, *et hoc genus omne.* **1953** *Essays in Criticism* III. 2 The Herbert Warrens and the Sidney Lees, *et hoc genus omne.*

hoch (hōχ), *sb.* [a. G. *hoch*, short for *hoch lebe* long live.] An instance of the ejaculation *Hoch!*; an exclamation of loyal approval; a cheer, hurrah. Hence **hoch** *v. intr.*, to utter a *hoch* or *hochs*; *trans.* to cheer with cries of *Hoch!*

1867 J. PAGET *Let.* 20 Sept. (1901) 232 The regular German 'festive dinner'; with the speeches and songs between the courses; songs by the whole 400 of us; uproarious 'hochs'; clinking of glasses. **1870** E. G. E. WARD *Jrnl.* 23 Sept. in *Outside Paris* (1871) 18 The General was giving a dinner..to his officers, and we could hear their 'Hoch!' 'Hoch!' after the toasts. **1907** *Daily Chron.* 13 Sept. 6/6 On the whole it will be prudent for the average Englishman not to attempt a 'Hoch!' in welcoming the Kaiser to London to-day. **1909** *Ibid.* 2 June 5/6 They 'hoched' us on our way, and cheered when they got tired of 'hoching'. **1920** *Chambers's Jrnl.* June 374/2 If Britain had had a million Australian troops, they, the present gathering, would be 'hoch, hoching' in Berlin. **1921** A. S. M. HUTCHINSON *If Winter Comes* III. i. 148 The 25th anniversary of the Emperor William's accession was 'Hoch'd' throughout the German Empire. *Ibid.*, Such fervent and sincere 'Hochs!' never boomed across the seas of the world.

hocheur (oʃœr). [Fr., f. *hocher* to nod the head.] *Cercopithecus nictitans*, the white-nosed monkey or spot-nosed guenon, found in tropical Africa.

1840 tr. *Cuvier's Anim. Kingd.* 57 Next follows a group of smaller species..consisting of the Talapoin M[onkey].. the Moustache M[onkey]..the Vaulting M[onkey]..the Hocheur. **1883** *List Vert. Anim. Zool. Soc.* (ed. 8) 12 *Cercopithecus nictitans* (Linn.), Hocheur Monkey. **1905** *Westm. Gaz.* 6 Feb. 6/3 A specimen of the Hocheur monkey is among the new inmates of the Monkey House.

‖**hochgeboren** (hǫ·χgĕbōᵊ:rĕn), *a.* and *sb.* Also **hochwohlgeboren.** [Ger.] **A.** *adj.* = HIGH-BORN *a.* **B.** *sb.* A high-born person; such people collectively.

1905 M. A. VON ARNIM *Princess Priscilla's Fortnight* i. 7 Was she not a *hochgeboren*, a member of an ancient house? **1930** W. S. MAUGHAM *Cakes & Ale* iii. 38 She was a simple old lady..but she had not..forgotten that she was *hochwohlgeboren.* **1933** D. C. PEEL *Life's Enchanted Cup* xviii. 238 The German ladies..were convinced that we had forced Germany to go to war, and the Hochgeboren..felt bitter towards us. **1949** O. NASH *Versus* 139 Do not overlook the fact, *hoch-geboren* Bretheren and Sisteren. **1951** J. C. FENNESSY *Sonnet in Bottle* v. v. 173 He probably thinks he's as *hochgeboren* as the half-caste descendant of an English knight and a Peruvian D.P. **1972** 'J. MELVILLE' *Ironwood* v. 74, I am *hoch geboren*, as my stuffy German grandaunts still like to put it.

hock, *sb.*⁴ Add: **b. hock-cup.**

1851 *London at Table* III. 50 (*heading*) Champagne, Hock, or Chablis cup. **1899** *Daily News* 20 May 8/7 There is a wonderful hock-cup 'made in Germany', which the knowing ones partake of. **1958** A. L. SIMON *Dict. Wines* 66/2 *Hock cup.* To a bottle of Hock add 3 wine-glasses of Sherry, 1 lemon sliced, and some balm or borage.

hock, *sb.*⁶ Add: (Examples.) *U.S.*

1859 G. W. MATSELL *Vocabulum* 113 *Hock*, the last card in the box. **1913** C. E. MULFORD *Coming of Cassidy* vii. 118 In his agitation he exposed the hock card before he realized what he was doing. **1931** G. F. WILLISON *Here They dug Gold* 217 The last card, the 'hock',..likewise pays nothing.

b. *from soda* (*card*) *to hock*: from the top card to the last in the dealing-box; hence, from beginning to end.

1902 H. L. WILSON *Spenders* v. 49 Young Bines played the deal from soda card to hock. **1918** C. E. MULFORD *Man fr. Bar-20* ii. 21 You got me beat from soda to hock. *Ibid.* xiii. 134 'Are you in?' 'Every d—d chip; from my hat to my worn-out boots; from soda to hock.' **1925** —— *Cottonwood Gulch* xvi. 219 You've got 'em all guessin', from soda to hock. Good for you! **1938** H. ASBURY *Sucker's Progress* 16 For many years a common expression was 'from soda to hock', meaning the whole thing, from soup to nuts.

hock (hǫk), *sb.*⁷ *U.S. slang.* [a. Du. *hok* hutch, hovel, prison, (*slang*) credit, debt.] **a.** Phr. *in* (occas. *the*) *hock*: (*a*) in the act (of gambling); (*b*) in prison; (*c*) in pawn; (*d*) in debt. So occas. *out of hock.*

1859 G. W. MATSELL *Vocabulum* 113 When one gambler is caught by another, smarter than himself, and is beat, then he is in hock. Men are only caught, or put in hock, on the race-tracks, or on the steamboats down South... Among thieves a man is in hock, when he is in prison...'If the cove should be caught in the hock he won't snickle,' if the fellow should be caught in the act, he would not tell. **1860** 'C. MARTEL' *Detective's Note-Bk.* 36 In about ten minutes from that time we had them 'in hock' (the cells). **1872** G. P. BURNHAM *Mem. U.S. Secret Service* p. vi, *In the hock*, in the act of commission; on the spot. **1883** H. C. LUKENS *Jets & Flashes* 146 We deeply regret that our india-rubber armor is in hock. **1896** ADE *Artie* xviii. 169 They go back home and leave all their stuff in hock. **1898** J. LONDON *Let.* 30 Nov. (1966) 7, I..got my watch out of hock. **1902** W. N. HARBEN *Abner Daniel* xxiii, I felt..ef they did git Jimmy out o' hock..without me a-chippin' in, I'd never be able to look at 'em without remorse. **1903** A. H. LEWIS *Boss* 31 Well..even a crook has got to go somewhere. That is,..when he ain't in hock. **1908** G. H. LORIMER *J. Spurlock* vii. 141 He made me feel that I was doing him a favour in consenting to have my evening clothes taken out of hock. **1911** C. E. MULFORD *Bar-20 Days* xiii. 141, I said pound, not pond. P-O-U-N-D; which means that it's pawned, in hock. **1913** —— *Coming of Cassidy* vii. 118 If the four lay under the Queen, Cassidy lost; if not, he either won or was in hock. **1926** J. BLACK *You can't Win* xxiv. 390, I was in hock to friends who saved me from a heavy sentence, provided me with work [etc.]. **1929** *Collier's* 5 Jan. 40/4 My cash was gone, and I was in hock for the next three years. **1956** B. HOLIDAY *Lady sings Blues* (1973) i. 1 She worked her way out of hock in the hospital and took me home to her folks. **1971** M. TAK *Truck Talk* 89 *In hock constantly*, humorous expression for the financial condition of any owner-operator who has a tractor manufactured by International Harvester Company.

b. *attrib.* and *Comb.*, as **hock-game** (see quot. 1859); **hock-shop,** a pawnshop.

1859 G. W. MATSELL *Vocabulum* 113 In a hock-game, if a man hits a card, he is obliged to let his money lie until it either wins or loses. **1871** *Sessions Papers* Apr. 485 That piece that I dropped in the *hock* shop. **1886** *Lantern* (New Orleans) 22 Sept. 2/3 Take the bed too, and run it into a hock shop. **1907** I. ZANGWILL *Ghetto Comedies* 296 The diamond necklace..stolen..and found afterwards..in a low 'hock-shop' in New Orleans. **1926** J. BLACK *You can't Win* xxi. 336 The average thief will walk by the hockshop and look in. The hockshop man..knows he has something 'hot', or crooked. **1969** C. IRVING *Fake!* (1970) xvi. 198 He had previously pawned one of the Matisse oils..to the Mont de Piété, the French national hockshop.

hock, *v.*³ *slang* (orig. *U.S.*). [f. *HOCK *sb.*⁷] *trans.* To pawn.

1878 *San Francisco Trade Herald* Aug. 2/2 To soak—to hock—Yer upper benjamin at yer uncle's, to get the 'sugar' for a good square meal. **1902** H. L. WILSON *Spenders* xxxiii. 397 The only thing I'll do..is to hock a few blocks of the stock I bought outright. **1904** G. H. LORIMER *Old Gorgon Graham* 184 You can hock your overcoat before marriage to buy violets for a girl. **1922** H. L. FOSTER *Adv. Trop. Tramp* xx. 354 I've just hocked my camera, and all I've got is two dollars. **1945** G. MILLAR *Maquis* i. 23 You might be able to hock them if you run out of money. **1969** C. F. BURKE *God is Beautiful, Man* (1970) 65 Then he went and he took everything he had—his automobile—and he hocked them.

hockelty. *U.S. slang.* Also **hocklety, hockley, hocly.** (See quots.) Cf. HOCK *sb.*⁶

1843 J. H. GREENE *Expos. Arts Gambling* 210 By hocklety and splitting, many men have experienced great disappointment on this same device of hocklety. *Ibid.* 166 *Hockley*, signifies the last card but one, the chance of which the banker claims, and may refuse to let any punter withdraw a card when eight or less remain to be dealt. **1867** *Bohn's Hand-bk. Games* 336 The last card but one is called holy, and forms part of the banker's gain. **1895** MANSON *Sporting Dict.* 58 (Faro), *Hock* or *Hockelty card*, the last card remaining in the box, after the deal has been made.

hockey². Add: **1. b.** In N. Amer. = **ice hockey*.

The older game is referred to as *field hockey*.

1895 *Rat Portage* (Ont.) *News* 11 Jan. 1/2 Hockey is the most popular winter sport in Canada, taking the place of lacrosse. **1906** *Daily Colonist* (Victoria, B.C.) 5 Jan. 2/1 The first hockey match of the season was played here between Rossland and Nelson teams. **1953** *Canad. Geogr. Jrnl.* XLVI. 138/2 The children maintain their own open air hockey rink on the ice of Green River. **1969** WIDDOWSON & HALPERT in Halpert & Story *Christmas Mumming in Newfoundland* 162, I dressed in a hockey suit.

3. *hockey-girl, -playing, -set, -type.*

1906 *Daily Chron.* 4 Oct. 4/4 The 'hockey set' are as a rule some of the healthiest girls in college. **1909** *Ibid.* 5 May 9/2 'Dear me, no, Miss Bulliphant,' she replied in what I call the downright, hockey-girl manner. **1915** V. WOOLF *Voyage Out* xiv. 211 Hockey-playing young women in Wiltshire. **1936** 'R. WEST' *Thinking Reed* xii. 435 You look awfully well now, well to the point of hockey-playing. **1959** *Times* 16 Feb. 11/5 The models are all looking much better fed, and without yet suggesting hockey-girls they don't any longer look like haughty hunger-strikers. **1961** *Times* 18 May 17/1 Miss Sian Reynolds as a hockey-girl St. Joan. **1963** J. T. STORY *Something for Nothing* i. 17, I like the hockey type...I can't stand these sex-pots.

ho·ckeyist. *Canad.* [f. *HOCKEY² 1 b + -IST.] A person who plays ice hockey.

1895 *Athletic Life* Mar. 121 In his stead was elected..an enthusiastic hockeyist and vice-president of the Victoria club. **1902** *Canadian Mag.* Mar. 435 The Montreal and Winnipeg Clubs for some years were acknowledged to excel all other hockeyists in Canada. **1963** *National Hockey Ann.* 36/2 Shack..was actually a reluctant hockeyist and was thrust into the game by his father.

hodad (hōᵘ·dæd). *Surfing slang.* [Origin obscure.] (See quots.)

1962 *Austral. Women's Weekly* Suppl. 24 Oct. 3/2 *Ho-dad*, anyone who annoys board-riders while they surf. **1963** *Pix* 28 Sept. 62/2 *Hodad*, non-surfing beach bum. **1965** *Daily Express* 16 Aug. 6/8, I could be a 'hodad' which means a man who talks big about his surfing exploits, but jibs at riding the big waves. **1965** *N.Z. Listener* 17 Dec. 4/5 Surfers..are..antagonistic towards..ill-mannered surf bums ('hodads'). **1971** *Studies in English* (Univ. Cape Town) Feb. 26 *Ho-dad* is a much misunderstood word. Basically, it is a double contraction from the American slang word *hood*, which in turn comes from *hoodlum*.

hoddy-doddy, *sb.* **2.** Delete † *Obs.* and add later examples.

Quot. *a* 1953 is perh. influenced by sense 3, noodle, 'dodderer'.

1877 E. LEAR *Laughable Lyrics*, You're such a Hoddy Doddy. *a* **1953** DYLAN THOMAS *Quite early one Morning* (1954) 64 Exhibitionists,.. theological rhetoricians, historical hoddy-doddies, balletomanes,..windbags. **1969** R. J. WHITE *Women of Peasen Hall* v. 56 Gardiner always refers to him as 'Dids', or a 'Hoddy-doddy'—which is Suffolk for a diminutive person.

hoddy-noddy. Delete † *Obs.* and add later examples.

1951 DYLAN THOMAS *Let.* 12 Apr. (1966) 356 No more of that beer-cheepened hoddy-noddy. **1970** 'M. HEBDEN' *Mask of Violence* (1971) xx. 183 They were..no end considerate. Shoved everybody out of the way. Damn near a punch-up with one lot of beer-cheepened hoddy-noddy.

Hodegetria (hōᵘdigī·triă). [f. Gr. ὁδηγήτρια (see below).] An iconographical variant of the Virgin and Child in which the Child is depicted on the Virgin's left arm while she indicates Him with her right hand as 'The Indicator of the Way' (the meaning of the Greek word).

According to tradition the arrangement follows that of a painting originally attributed to St. Luke, but the earliest surviving example is probably to be assigned to the 7th century. The composition was frequently copied in Italy, the Byzantine world, and Russia. Sometimes, in the process of copying, the Child was transferred from the Virgin's left arm to the right and she indicates Him with her left hand, but there is no particular significance in this variant.

1880 E. VENABLES in Smith & Cheetham *Dict. Chr. Antiq.* II. 1152/2 The famous *Hodegetria*..which was for so many centuries regarded with the deepest reverence by the Greeks. **1911** L. GILLET in *Cath. Encycl.* XI. 397/2 Mention must be made of the numerous icons, the various types of the Madonna (Panagia, Nicopœia, Hodegetria). **1937** *Burlington Mag.* July 18/2 The Madonna Enthroned in the central field of the Antwerp altarpiece belongs to the Hodegetria type common in Italy in the thirteenth century. **1952** D. T. RICE *Eng. Art 871–1100* v. 116 The most usual type of Virgin was that known as the *Hodegetria* or Indicator of the Way, where the Virgin holds the Child on her left arm while she points to Him with her right hand; the Child's right hand is extended in blessing. **1959** C. CECCHELLI et al. *Rabbula Gospels* 49 The Madonna is a Hodegetria type, that is, inspired by a famous image venerated since the 5th century in the Church of the Guides at Constantinople.

ho-de-ho (hōᵘ·ˌdiˌhōᵘ·), *int.* An exclamation, used as the appropriate response to *HI-DE-HI *int.* Also *transf.*

1941, 1943, 1944 [see *HI-DE-HI *int.*].

hoden (*ū*·dən), *a. Kentish dial.* Also **hooden.** [Origin uncertain: perh. from association with *wooden* from the wooden horse's head.] Of or pertaining to the horse with wooden head and clapping jaws featured in a masquerade which formerly took place, *spec.* in Kent, on Christmas Eve. **ho·dener,** a performer in this masquerade; **ho·dening,** the name of the performance; also *attrib.*

1807 *European Mag.* LI. 358 This [mumming] is called, *provincially,* a Hodening, and the figure above described a Hoden, or Woden horse. **1887** PARISH & SHAW *Dict. Kentish Dial.* 77 *Hoodening*.., the name formerly given to a mumming or masquerade. **1891** *Church Times* 2 Jan. 20/1 'Hodening' still goes on..at Deal and Walmer. **1909** P. MAYLAM *Hooden Horse* i. 2 Everyone springs up, saying, 'The hoodeners have come, let us go and see the fun.' *Ibid.* 7 A farm with more than one team would have a hooden horse to each team. *Ibid.* 9, I had intended to walk on to Deal and look for the hoodening parties there. **1966** G. E. EVANS *Pattern under Plough* xix. 193 The hobby-horses that appear in many countryside ceremonies and ritual dances, notably the *Hodening Horse.* **1971** *Country Life* 17 June 1533/1 The Hooden Horse, a mystic man-animal found only in East Kent, will be at large in Folkestone..June 19.

Hodgkin's disease. (Earlier example.)

1865 S. WILKS in *Guy's Hosp. Rep.* XI. 56 (*heading*) Cases of enlargement of the lymphatic glands and spleen (or, Hodgkin's disease).

hodja, var. KHOJA.

hodograph. Add: **1.** Hence extended to curves in which the radius represents other vector quantities.

1944 H. R. BYERS *Gen. Meteorol.* viii. 212 The details of the change of the geostrophic winds with height are studied by means of a hodograph. **1961** *Aero/Space Engin.* Feb. 24/2 (*title*) The hodograph and ballistic missile trajectory problems. **1966** *McGraw-Hill Encycl. Sci. & Technol.* XIII. 508/2 These [changes] are most readily described with the aid of a hodograph of the potential gradient vector...One vector only is shown..extending from the origin of coordinates to a point on the hodograph.

hodoscope (hǫ·doskōᵘp). [f. Gr. ὁδό-ς way + -SCOPE.] **1.** *Microscopy.* (See quot.)

1915 J. W. EVANS in *Jrnl. Quekett Microsc. Club* XII. 613 It is frequently desirable to examine simultaneously the optical properties of a number of different directions in a mineral... For this purpose the microscope is.. converted into an optical instrument in which every point in the image corresponds not to a point in the object under examination, but to a direction along which light traverses that object in parallel paths. Such an instrument may be conveniently described as a *hodoscope* or path viewer, a term which is to be preferred to the word 'konoscope' employed by some authors.

2. *Physics.* An assembly of particle detectors used for observing the paths of cosmic-ray and other particles.

1950 *Physical Rev.* LXXVIII. 715/1 For the purpose of analyzing the shower phenomena in a hodoscope set it would appear desirable to use as large a number of narrow counters as possible. **1967** *Nuclear Instruments & Methods* LI. 1/1 An experiment on mu meson pair production was performed..utilizing a 192 unit hodoscope. For each hodoscope counter only the detection or non-detection of a particle (and not pulse height) was recorded.

hoe, *v.* Add: **3.** See also ROW *sb.*[1] 6 b, c.

hoe (hōᵘ), *v.*[2] *U.S.* [f. HOE-DOWN.] To dance or play a hoe-down.

1835 *Gent's Vade-Mecum* (Phila.) 21 Mar. 3/5 'Pooh!' replied his panting rib, hoeing it off like a regular Juba, 'don't be a nigger all the days of your life.' **1909** *Cent. Dict.* Suppl.

hoe-cake. (Earlier examples.)

1745 W. LOGAN *Jrnl.* 12 Oct. in *Pennsylvania Mag. Hist.* (1912) XXXVI. 12 Breakfasted on Tea & Hoe Cake Bread, which we have done in common. **1745** *Ibid.* 21 Oct. 162 Got Breakfast on Tea & Hoe Cake. **1774** P. V. FITHIAN *Jrnl.* 15 Jan. (1900) 93 Sup'd on chocolate, & hoe-Cake, so Called because baked on a Hoe before the fire. **1780** W. FLEMING in N. D. Mereness *Trav. Amer. Col.* (1916) 641, I had lived for a constancy on poor dried buffalo bull beef cured in the smook..without any addition but a piece of Indian hoe-cake.

hoed, *ppl. a.* (s.v. HOE *v.*). (Amer. examples.)

1643 *New Plymouth Laws* 74 By ymproved lands are understood meddow land plowed land and howed lands. **1879** *Scribner's Monthly* Dec. 239/2 The owner has only to give it a year of ordinary cultivation, taking from it.. some profitable hoed crop.

hoe-down. (Earlier and later examples.)

[**1807** W. IRVING *Salmagundi* 7 Mar. 98 As to dancing, no Long-Island negro could shuffle you 'double trouble', or 'hoe corn and dig potatoes' more scientifically.] **1841** *Picayune* (New Orleans) 14 Jan. 2/1 He looks and walks the character to the life, and some of his touches are of the genuine 'hoe down', 'corn-field' order. **1849** T. T. JOHNSON *Sights Gold Region* iv. 38 One of our party commenced a regular hoe-down, knocking his shins with heavy boots. **1855** *Knickerbocker* XLVI. 227 Rude, high-legged reels and 'hoe-downs'. **1919** T. K. HOLMES *Man fr. Tall Timber* vii. 84 A medley of old-time hoe-downs and jig music. **1961** *Times* 30 Mar. 6/7 The hoe-down sequence in *Seven Brides for Seven Brothers.* **1963** *Punch* 3 July 23/3, I was invited to the last hoe-down. **1967** 'J. MUNRO' *Money that Money can't Buy* ix. 114 Two more cowboys appeared. ..They played hoe-down music. **1969** *Guardian* 2 Sept. 8/2 The atmosphere was that of..a hoedown in—well, perhaps in Hibbing, Minn.

hœrnesite (hō·ɹnēzəit). *Min.* Also **hörnesite.** [ad. G. *hörnesit* (W. Haidinger, reported in *Jahrb. d. k.-k. geol. Reichsanstalt: Verhandl.* (1860) XI. 41), f. the name of M. *Hörnes* (1815–68), Austrian mineralogist: see -ITE[1].] A white hydrated arsenate of magnesium $Mg_3(AsO_4)_2.8H_2O$.

1868 J. D. DANA *Syst. Min.* (ed. 5) 817 Hœrnesite... First distinguished by Kenngott in minerals from the Bannat, Hungary. **1903** *Jrnl. Chem. Soc.* LXXXIV. II. 655 (*heading*) Crystallised magnesium phosphate and arsenate: artificial production of bobierrite and hœrnesite. **1968** I. KOSTOV *Mineralogy* 448 (*table*) Hörnesite. **1969** *Mineral. Abstr.* XX. 229/1 Hoernesite..is monoclinic.

Hoffmann (hǫ·fmæn). **1.** The name of Friedrich *Hoffmann* (1660–1742), German physician, used in the possessive in *Hoffmann's anodyne* (in full *Hoffmann's mineral anodyne liquor*), compound spirit of ether, a mixture of alcohol and ether with ethereal oil.

1747 R. JAMES *New Univ. Eng. Dispensatory* 803/1 Liquor Mineralis Anodynus Hoffmanni. Frederic Hoffman's Anodyne Mineral Liquor. **1857** *Amer. Jrnl. Pharm.* May 200 For some years past the preparation sold under the name of Hoffman's anodyne has been forcibly dragged along by the materia medica list, supported alone by its unused formula and former character. **1878** W. B. WOODMAN tr. *von Ziemssen's Cycl. Pract. Med.* XVII. 442 The internal use of ether (Hoffmann's anodyne) may lead to poisoning. **1910** A. C. WOOTTON *Chron. Pharm.* I. xiii. 348 Hoffmann's 'Mineral Anodyne Liquor', the original of our Spiritus Ætheris Co., was a semi-secret preparation much prescribed by the famous inventor. **1945** D. GUTHRIE *Hist. Med.* xii. 217 One of his preparations, Hoffmann's anodyne (Spiritus Aetheris Co) still survives, although his extensive work..in nine volumes..has long since been forgotten.

2. The name of Friedrich *Hoffmann* (1818–1900), used *attrib.* and in the possessive to designate a form of continuous kiln consisting of a number of compartments with a common chimney, so arranged that the fire can be moved to each compartment in turn, with hot air from cooling bricks used for heating unburnt bricks.

1875 *Ure's Dict. Arts* III. 20 (*heading*) Hoffmann's continuous kiln. **1879** *Notes on Building Construction* III. 101 Hoffmann's Kiln is used chiefly in brick-manufactories on a large scale, where a great number of bricks is required annually. **1960** M. BOWLEY *Innovat. Building Mat.* III. viii. 163 The majority of kilns in the industry are variations of the Hoffman kiln.

3. The name of Johann *Hoffmann* (1857–1919), German neurologist, used *attrib.* and in the possessive to designate various signs, etc., discovered or described by him, as *Hoffmann('s) atrophy* = **Werdnig–Hoffmann('s) atrophy*; *Hoffmann('s) sign*: (*a*) increased sensitivity of the sensory nerves to mechanical stimulation; also called *Hoffman('s) phenomenon, symptom*; (*b*) a type of reflex action of the fingers; also called *digital reflex, Hoffmann('s) reflex*; also *ellipt.*

1900 DORLAND *Med. Dict.* 600/2 *Hoffmann's s[ign]*, increased mechanic irritability of the sensory nerves in tetany. **1908** A. GORDON *Dis. Nerv. Syst.* xxi. 399 Hoffmann's Sign.—Pressure upon sensory nerve produces marked pain. **1908** A. CHURCH *Dis. Nerv. Syst.* 916 (*heading*) Mechanical Hyperirritability (Chvostek's phenomenon, Hoffmann's phenomenon). **1910** OSLER & MACRAE *Syst. Med.* VII. 73 The sensory nerves may also be hypersensitive, and tapping at Valleix's points then calls forth abnormally intense sensations (Hoffmann's symptom). **1916** *Jrnl. Nervous & Mental Dis.* XLIV. 51 During a period spent at the Neurological Institute of New York, I was told of a reflex of the fingers which was designated by the term 'Hoffmann's Sign'. **1933** *Ibid.* LXXVII. 598 Of the 26 patients with the post-encephalitic Parkinson syndrome, the Hoffmann reflex was positive in 6 and the Babinski positive in 4. **1939** W. HAYMAKER tr. *Bing's Textbk. Nerv. Dis.* iv. 150 Increased galvanic irritability of sensory nerves, occurring at times in patients with tetany, is known as Hoffmann's phenomenon. **1950** R. N. DEJONG *Neurol. Exam.* xxxvi. 593 The Hoffmann is a positive sign of definite significance, even though it may occur on occasion in the absence of organic disease.

Hofmann (hǫ·fmæn). **1.** The name of August Wilhelm von *Hofmann* (1818–92), German chemist, used *attrib.* and in the possessive to designate dyestuffs discovered and chemical apparatus and procedures devised by him, as *Hofmann('s) degradation*: (*a*) the elimination of a carbonyl group from an acid amide when it is heated in a sodium hypohalite solution, giving a primary amine; (*b*) the pyrolysis of a quaternary ammonium hydroxide to give a tertiary amine and an olefin; *Hofmann('s) exhaustive methylation*: a method for determining the structure of amino compounds by methylation followed by pyrolysis, the resulting amine being subjected successively to the same procedure until trimethylamine and olefins are obtained; *loosely,* the Hofmann degradation (sense b); *Hofmann('s) method*: (*a*) a method for finding the vapour density of a liquid (see quot. 1902[2]); (*b*) the preparation of amines by means of the Hofmann degradation of amides; *Hofmann('s) reaction*: either of the Hofmann degradations; *Hofmann('s) rearrangement*: the Hofmann degradation of amides; *Hofmann('s) rule* (see quot. 1954); *Hofmann('s) violet* (also *Violet*): any of several basic dyes that are salts of ethyl and methyl derivatives of rosaniline and pararosaniline and were formerly used with wool, silk, and mordanted cotton.

1869 H. E. ROSCOE *Lessons Elem. Chem.* (new ed.) xxxix. 385 Triethylrosaniline, $C_{20}H_{16}(C_2H_5)_3N_3$, is manufactured for its splendid colour, and is known as Hofmann's violet. **1876** *Encycl. Brit.* V. 548/1 (*caption*) Hofmann's Vapour-Density Apparatus. *Ibid.*, Gay-Lussac and Hofmann's Methods. **1902** *Jrnl. Chem. Soc.* LXXXII. II. 663 Sodium hypochlorite is a more valuable reagent than the hypobromite in Hofmann's reaction. **1902** J. B. COHEN *Theoret. Org. Chem.* iii. 30 Victor Meyer's method and Hofmann's method consist in ascertaining the volume occupied by a given weight of the vaporised substance. *Ibid.* xiv. 195 If a primary amine is treated by Hofmann's method with an alkyl iodide in which the alkyl group is different from that present in the amine, a mixed amine is formed. **1902** *Encycl. Brit.* XXVII. 337/2 The basis of these methods consists in causing a swelling of the cell-wall..and subsequent staining with Hoffmann's blue. **1905** CAIN & THORPE *Synthetic Dyestuffs* xiv. 90 Hofmann's violet was the first violet dyestuff of this [rosaniline] series prepared, and is now merely of historical interest. **1910** *Chem. Abstr.* IV. 583 (*heading*) Acid properties of halogen amides. Hofmann's rearrangement. **1938** L. SMALL in H. Gilman *Org. Chem.* II. xii. 1024 The most generally applicable method for ascertaining structure is exhaustive methylation, also known as the Hofmann degradation. **1938** *Thorpe's Dict. Appl. Chem.* (ed. 4) II. 375/1 An important reaction of carboxylic acids is their conversion to amines by the Hofmann degradation, whereby the amide is treated with bromine and alkali. **1938** G. H. RICHTER *Textbk. Org. Chem.* xiv. 239 (*heading*) Hofmann's exhaustive methylation. *Ibid.* 241 The decomposition of these substances on heating to a high temperature has already been indicated in the Hofmann exhaustive methylation procedure. **1949** J. R. PARTINGTON *Adv. Treat. Physical Chem.* I. vii. 760 In Hofmann's method, a uniform glass tube about 1 m. long..is supported in a glass jacket through which the vapour of a liquid, boiling in a separate vessel, is passed. *Ibid.* 761 A modified Hofmann apparatus for accurate vapour-density determinations. **1950** L. F. & M. FIESER *Org. Chem.* (ed. 2) xxxv. 865 The correct structure of the lobelia alkaloids.. was first deduced from the result of Hofmann degradation of the quaternary hydroxide. **1951** E. D. HUGHES in E. H. Rodd *Chem. Carbon Compounds* IA. 183 The Hofmann rule refers to the preferential formation of that ethylene which bears the smallest number of alkyl groups. **1952** K. VENKATARAMAN *Chem. Synthetic Dyes* I. i. 3 In 1866 Bardy oxidized a mixture of mono- and dimethylanilines to Methyl Violet, which soon eliminated the Hofmann Violets. **1954** *Van Nostrand Chem. Dict.* 356/2 *Hofmann rule,* in the decomposition of a quaternary ammonium hydroxide containing different primary alkyl radicals, the products are such that the ethylene formed will contain the least number of alkyl substituents. **1968** R. O. C. NORMAN *Princ. Org. Synthesis* xiv. 446 (*heading*) Hofmann rearrangement.

2. The name of Georg von *Hofmann-Wellenhof* (d. *c* 1890), Austrian bacteriologist, used *attrib.* and in the possessive in *Hofmann('s) bacillus,* a non-pathogenic bacillus similar to the diphtheria bacillus and common in the nose and throat; variously known as *Corynebacterium pseudodiphtheriticum, C. hofmanni,* etc.

[**1891** *Johns Hopkins Hosp. Bull.* II. 143/2 Kolisko and Paltauf..were able to find the pseudo-diphtheritic bacillus of von Hoffmann only very rarely.] **1897** *Jrnl. Path. & Bacteriol.* IV. 190 The cases affected with Hofmann's bacillus unassociated with diphtheria bacilli, which have come under my notice, have always recovered. **1897** *Trans. Brit. Inst. Prev. Med.* 12 Peters..does not seem to have noticed any difference of growth of the Klebs-Löffler and von Hoffmann bacilli on alkaline potato. **1959** F. S. STEWART *Bigger's Handbk. Bacteriol.* (ed. 7) xviii. 307 *C. pseudodiphtheriticum* (Hofmann's bacillus)..is often present in the nose and less frequently in the throat.

hog, *sb.*[1] Add: **1. c.** (Earlier and later examples.)

1776 W. HOOPER in *Lett. James Murray* (1901) 239 That I might enjoy in my own Cabin, eat my Hogg & Hominee without anything to make me afraid. **1816** *Mass. Spy* 10 Jan. (Th.), [If a man] can be content with hog and hommany, he can live easier in Ohio. **1888** *Century Mag.* XXXVI. 261/2 Corn-bread and bacon, or, in purer vernacular, 'hog and hominy'. **1948** E. N. DICK *Dixie Frontier* 290 The monotonous diet was often referred to as 'hog and hominy'.

7. c. A person who behaves in a rude mannerless fashion without respect for the

safety or convenience of others; esp. in *road-hog* (ROAD *sb.* 12).

1906 *Daily Chron.* 2 Feb. 7/3 Showing to the astounded heathens (save the word) the latest game of 'hog-amok'. **1928** *Daily Mail* 25 July 17/4 So far we have met no 'canal hogs'. **1942** *Topeka* (Kan.) *Capital* 16 May 7/2 The Office of Price Administration made things unpleasant for 'gas hogs' tonight.

9. d. A railway locomotive used for hauling freight. *U.S. slang.*

1888 *Walla Walla* (Wash.) *Union* 24 Nov. 3/4 The 'hog' will haul nine loaded cars up the heavy Alto grade, while the ordinary road engine had a hard tussel to haul four or five. **1903** *Sci. Amer.* 23 May 392/2 In anthracite drifts steam locomotives of a small and peculiar type known as 'hogs' haul the trains. **1960** *Listener* 18 Aug. 250/2 A steam locomotive is a 'hog' or 'pig'.

e. *Forestry.* (See quots.)

1898 *Lumber Trade Jrnl.* 1 Jan. 31 (Advt.), The big slab grinding hog for grinding up slabs, edgings and mill refuse into fuel. **1904** *Dialect Notes* II. 398 *Hog*, a machine for grinding logs. **1913** WEBSTER, *Hog*, a machine with revolving knife cutters for grinding up edgings and slabs. **1957** *Brit. Commonw. Forest Terminol.* II. 93 *Hog*, a machine for reducing wood to coarse chips, usually for converting mill waste into fuel. **1969** *Timber Trades Jrnl.* 29 Nov. 57/3 Waste blocks..are often chuted.. on to a conveyor which automatically takes them to a refuse hog.

f. A large, often old, car or motor-cycle. *U.S. slang.*

1967 W. MURRAY *Sweet Ride* vii. 112 The heat was on so bad we couldn't ride our bikes... Get on our hogs and them mothers'd pick us up. **1968–70** *Current Slang* (Univ. S. Dakota) III–IV. 68 *Hog*,..an old, heavy Harley Davidson motor-cycle... 1956 or 1958 Cadillac; any large car which takes up all the road. **1971** *Black Scholar* Jan. 41/1 He bought him a 'Hog' with all the accessories on it. Man, this Cadillac had air horns, white-walls, [etc.]. **1971** P. L. CAVE *Chopper* v. 45 Pulling away, he swung the hog round in a wide U-turn and went after Ethel.

10. Also, the distance-line itself, the hog-score.

1824 J. MACTAGGART *Gallovid. Encycl.* 274 Sweeping is not allowed until the stone comes over the 'hogg', unless by the person who played it. **1853** W. WATSON *Poems* 63 Stan' back at the hog wi' a besom. **1897** *Encycl. Sport* I. 258 It [*sc.* a stone] must be over the Hog, but must not touch the Stone to be guarded.

11. *like* or *as a hog on ice*, denoting independence, awkwardness, or insecurity. *U.S. colloq.*

1857 *San Francisco Call* 19 Apr. 2/3 He don't appear to care nothing for nobody—he's 'as independent as a hog on ice!' **1894** *Vermont Agric. Rep.* XIV. 124 How would a Hackney look going around the track after old Highland Gray? 'Like a hog on ice.' **1922** C. SANDBURG *Slabs of Sunburnt West* 8 Chicago fished from its depths a text: Independent as a hog on ice. **1948** *Time* 9 Aug. 18/2 They like to think of themselves as independents—independent as a hog on ice.

b. (Earlier U.S. and further examples.)

1828 in G. T. Curtis *Life D. Webster* (1870) I. 337 [Andrew Jackson] will either go with the party, as they say in New York, or go 'the whole hog', as it is phrased elsewhere. **1829** *Virginia Herald* (Fredericksburg) 28 Mar. 2/3 We all know that of late he has shown a disposition to become 'a whole hog man', but if he can swallow this, he can swallow anything. **1835** H. C. TODD *Notes Canada & U.S.A.* 46 In Virginia originated *Go the whole hog*, a political phrase marking the democrat from a federalist. **1852** *Household Words* 31 July 474/1 When a Virginian butcher kills a pig, he is said to ask his customers whether they will 'go the whole hog', as, in such case, he sells at a lower price than if they pick out the prime joints only. **1914** D. H. LAWRENCE *Prussian Officer* 207 Do you mean to say you used to go—the whole hogger? **1928** *Daily Chron.* 3 Nov. 4 The whole-hoggers argue that that statement leaves the position more ambiguous than before. **1929** S. ANDERSON in *Mercury Story Book* 234, I went the whole hog. **1964** R. H. GERHARD in D. Abercrombie et al. *Daniel Jones* 283 Bloomfield who first adopted it 'whole hog'. **1973** *Times* 28 Mar. 4/4 He does not go the whole hog with his father in his belief in the arcane and ancient mysteries of [bacon-]smoking.

13. a. hog-head *U.S. slang*, the driver of a locomotive; **hog-Latin**, bad, spurious, or mongrel Latin; **hog-line** *Curling*, the distance-line (=HOG-SCORE); **hog-tight** *a.*, said of fences which are close enough to prevent swine from forcing their way through; **hog-wild** *a.*, wild in the manner of a hog; **hog-yoke** (later U.S. example); (*b*) a quadrant.

1907 *Sunset* XVIII. 290/2 The anxious gaze of the hoghead (*Anglice*: engineer). **1931** *Illinois Central Mag.* June 30/2 To the initiated, a 'tallow-pit' is a locomotive fire-man and a 'hoghead' is the engineer. **1960** *Listener* 18 Aug. 250/2 Engineers are 'hogheads' or 'eagle-eyes'. **1810** M. DWIGHT *Journey to Ohio* (1912) 53 He pass'd us on the road, singing & screaming, advising us to go back & learn hog-latin—alias German—or dutch. **1834** C. A. DAVIS *Lett. J. Downing* 19 You shall give the address after all, only just let Seth stick a little Hog-latin into it here and there. **1930** *Daily Express* 8 Sept. 8/6 The millions now being wasted in teaching bewildered youngsters hog Latin and piano and bad Greek. **1904** *Westm. Gaz.* 13 May 3/1 There is no reason in the world why you should not mark out a 'hog' line with whitewash. **1963** *Times* 25 Feb. p. xvi/2 Briefly, the rule allows a curler to keep his grip on his rock until the first hog line is reached—a distance of 32 feet from the hack in which the toe is placed. **1859** BARTLETT *Dict. Amer.* s.v., Hog-tight and horse-high, always used together, of fences that are sufficient to restrain trespassing stock. Maryland. **1879** A. W. TOURGÉE *Fool's Errand* xxx. 194 The split-board paling.. was 'horse-high, hog-tight, and bull-strong'. **1885** *Rep. Indian Affairs* 110 All of these tracts are enclosed with hog-tight fences. **1972** *Christian Sci. Monitor* 28 Sept. 16/4 The pioneers..tipped the stumps up with their roots in the air, and lined them along so they were, as the saying went, 'horse-high, hog-tight, and bull-strong'. **1904** *Dialect Notes* II. 418, I never saw such an excitement over a little thing in Arkansas as there was over that debate. They went *hog wild*. **1938** J. RICE *Somers Inheritance* III. x. 178 The fact is they're eaten up with envy because they're not getting some of the money. They're hog-wild, that's it, hog-wild. **1940** C. MCCULLERS *Heart is Lonely Hunter* (1943) I. ii. 21 This here white man had just gone hog wild. He were butting his head against the side of this brick wall. **1969** *Eugene* (Oreg.) *Register-Guard* 3 Dec. 2D/1 Arkansas has gone hog wild over its second-ranked Razorbacks this week. **1841** F. A. OLMSTED *Incidents Whaling Voy.* vi. 83 A quadrant receives the very undignified and unphilosophical name of a 'hog-yoke'. *a* **1852** F. M. WHITCHER *Widow Bedott Papers* (1883) x. 35, I ain't so fond o' pork as to eat hog yokes. **1897** KIPLING *Capt. Cour.* v. 107 The old green-crusted quadrant that they called the 'hog-yolk'. **1929** F. BOWEN *Sea Slang* 67 *Hog yoke*, the old fashioned wooden quadrant in American ships and Grand Bankers, so-called from its likeness to the wooden yoke put over hogs to prevent them breaking through fences.

b. hog-age *U.S.*, adolescence. ? *Obs.*

1848 J. MITCHELL in *Amer. Speech* (1935) X. 40 *Hog age*, between Boyhood & Manhood. **1893** FARMER & HENLEY *Slang*, *Hog-age*, the period between boyhood and manhood.

c. hog-sucker (examples.)

1883 *Bull. U.S. Nat. Mus.* XXVII. 478 *Catostomus nigricans*...Hog Sucker...United States from New York to Florida and westward to Alabama and Kansas; Great Lake region. **1888** GOODE *Amer. Fishes* 435 The..'Hog Sucker'..abounds in most waters from the great lakes southward.

hog, *v.*[1] Add: **1. a.** Also *transf.* and *absol.*

1860 R. F. BURTON *Lake Regions Central Africa* I. 85 They [*sc.* asses] hog and buck till they burst their frail girths. **1956** *Archit. Rev.* CXIX. 143/2 Owing to the eccentric placing of the prestressing wires, which cannot be avoided, there is always the tendency for the units to 'hog', i.e., to assume a permanent deflection upwards during stressing.

2. (Earlier U.S. example.)

1803 *Deb. Congr. U.S.* 19 Jan. (1851) 407/1 He did not.. believe that there would be any more danger of the ship's hogging, when lowered down..than when on the stocks.

5. For *U.S. slang* read orig. *U.S. slang* and add further examples.

1884 'MARK TWAIN' *Huck. Finn* xxvii. 275 S'pose somebody has hogged that bag on the sly? **1917** J. C. MCCORQUODALE *In Divers Moods* 16 What blinking luck! —Let's have a sup: Don't hog the lot. My Christ! it's cold. **1936** WODEHOUSE *Laughing Gas* xxii. 237 Maybe that will teach you not to go crawling to directors so that they will let you hog the camera! **1959** *Listener* 26 Mar. 566/1 He never hogs the limelight. **1960** *Woman* 9 Jan. 13/2 You've got a no-good wardrobe, piano, pram or bed, hogging precious space in the house. **1973** *Freedom* 7 July 1/4 The inquiry could go on without hogging the headlines from him.

b. *trans.* and *intr.* To behave as a road-hog; to monopolize the road. Also as *vbl. sb.*

1897 KIPLING *Capt. Cour.* vi. 129 You..go hoggin' the road on the high seas with no blame consideration fer your neighbours. **1914** 'I. HAY' *Knight on Wheels* xx. 200 Now I will really hog it a bit: this is a lovely piece of road. **1925** R. J. B. SELLAR *Sporting Yarns* 135 As they were hogging it through the country-side with the speedometer hovering over the sixty mark. **1925** *Punch* 22 Apr. 432 'Frightful rate that bike we just passed was going, wasn't it?' 'Yes. They ought to have the man for "hogging".' **1926** *Chambers's Jrnl.* Dec. 875/1 Why don't you sound your hooter before hogging round corners? **1956** W. GRAHAM *Sleeping Partner* iv. 35, I hogged the road to Lewes cutting in and out among all the family 8-horse powers.

c. *trans.* To interfere with in wireless transmission, as by a more powerful instrument. So also *to hog the ether.*

1914 *Pears' Christmas Annual* 21/2 They should be hogged till doomsday..if a single ship was on fire! *Ibid.*, The operator heard. He started up as if he had been hogged himself. **1959** *News Chron.* 14 Dec. 4/6 The B.B.C., according to Mr. Collins, 'hog the ether to a shocking extent'.

d. *trans.* To eat (something) greedily.

1928 M. LOWRY *Lett.* (1967) 4 Sometime..wdst hog it over the way somewhere with me? **1932** D. H. LAWRENCE *Last Poems* (1933) 50 The only way to eat an apple is to hog it down like a pig And taste nothing. **1946** B. MARSHALL *George Brown's Schooldays* v. 24 The Bruiser did not pause to observe it, hogging down the mashed up mess in front of him.

9. *trans.* To feed swine on (a crop or crop-covered land). Also with *down* or *off*. *U.S. colloq.*

1859 H. W. BEECHER *Pleasant Talk* 93 Some of the best farmers in this region hog their corn-lands. *Ibid.* 94 Land being hogged, will be free from cut-worms. **1863** *Rep. Comm. Agric. 1862* (U.S.) 82, I was forced to hog down my crop this year. **1937** *Amer. Speech* XII. 104 *To hog down corn* means to let hogs eat unharvested corn in the field. **1948** *Clarke Co. Democrat* (Grove Hill, Ala.) 19 Aug. 7/3 A good place to plant crimson clover and rye grass is where you hogged off peanuts.

hogan (hōᵘ·găn). [Navajo.] The rude hut of Navajo and other American Indian tribes of the south-western United States.

1872 *Rep. Indian Affairs 1871* (U.S.) 379 When a member of a family dies, in most cases they immediately leave their hogan (or wigwam) with the dead body in it. **1904** *New York Even. Post* 2 July 2 The North American Indians in their primitive state, living in the tepees, hogans, sod-lodges and grass houses. **1927** W. CATHER *Death comes for Archbishop* VII. iii. 217 For his lodging the Bishop was given a solitary hogan. **1955** PRIESTLEY & HAWKES *Journey down Rainbow* 242 This lot have come in from their lonely hogans, the little round wooden huts with a corral or two for horses. **1973** *Times* 15 May 19/8 At night the doors to the Navajo's huts, or hogans, were often covered by a blanket.

hogback. Add: **1. b.** The sunfish, a member of the genus *Lepomis*. *U.S.*

1832 *Coll. New H. Hist. Soc.* III. 86 The hogback or sunfish, as some call it, is a very attracting thing. It is about as large as the perch.

c. Any fish with a hog-like back.

1893 in *Funk's Stand. Dict.* **1923** *Chambers's Jrnl.* Dec. 791/2 Bill, said the latter, the hog-back run is come.

2. (Earlier U.S. examples of form.)

1840 J. P. KENNEDY *Quodlibet* 26 The farm where he now lives at the foot of the Hogback. **1847** in *31st Congress 1 Sess.* H.R. Ex. Doc. No. 5. II. 731 The banks [of a river].. worn in some places into hog-backs. **1888** *Harper's Mag.* Nov. 860/1, I pushed forward across deep gulches, over high peaks and 'hog-backs'.

c. *N.Z.* (See quot. 1940.)

1933 *N.Z. Alpine Jrnl.* V. xx. 180 Dark clouds..a bevy of 'hog-backs'. *Ibid.* 235 A 'hog's back' warned that further storms were brewing. **1940** W. S. GILKISON *Peaks, Packs & Mountain Tracks* 24 He showed me a hogsback... Term applied to a particularly unwelcome cloud only too well-known to climbers, and almost invariably heralding a north-west storm.

hogen, *sb.* **2.** (Later examples.)

1905 in *Chambers's Eng. Dict.* **1963** *Punch* 20 Feb. 282/1 Hogan..is a strong Norfolk beer.

hogg, var. HOG *sb.*[1] 4 a.

1842–4 [see HOG *sb.*[1] 4 a]. **1899** *Daily News* 21 Apr. 7/4 North hoggs and Yorkshire Wold hoggs are becoming scarce. **1963** *Times* 13 May 16/7 In six lamb crops, starting as a hogg, she has produced and reared 20 lambs.

hoggery. 3. (Later example.)

1933 J. CARY *Amer. Visitor* xx. 285 A dash of hoggery now and then may even improve and refine the artistic reactions.

ho·g-ki:lling. [HOG *sb.* 12 b.] The killing of a pig. *hog-killing time* U.S., the time when pigs are killed; a time of special enjoyment; also *absol.*

1817 in A. Royall *Lett. fr. Alabama* (1830) 36 It was hog-killing day at Wills. *a* **1883** G. W. BAGBY *Old Virginia Gentleman* (1910) 96 They are the fixtures used at hog-killing time. **1879** *Harper's Mag.* Nov. 812/1, I..was as big as a dog at hog-killing. **1903** A. ADAMS *Log of Cowboy* xiii. 83 According to their report the boys had had a hog-killing-time. **1927** H. A. VACHELL *Dew of Sea* etc. 259 When I ask my friends to have a hog-killing-time with me, I foot all bills. **1933** *Amer. Speech* VIII. 49/2 *Hog-killing*, any sort of hilarious celebration or jollification. We-all shore did have a hawg-killin' time over t' th' dance t'other night. **1951** *Publ. Amer. Dial. Soc.* XIV. 37 Hog killing time is a season of severe and lasting cold weather, required for the preserving of the meat; also a time of plenty and rejoicing.

hogo. 1. b. Delete † and add later example.

1922 JOYCE *Ulysses* 368 Come near. Then get a hogo you could hang your hat on.

ho·g-pen. *U.S.* [HOG *sb.* 13.] A pen or enclosure for swine.

1640 in *Maryland Hist. Mag.* (1910) V. 374 The Neck of Land called hog penn Neck. **1663** *Springfield* (Mass.) *Rec.* I. 312 There is granted to Rowland Thomas 6 acres of the low land on hog pen dingle below ye place where hog pen was. **1695** [see HOG *sb.* 13]. **1769** in *Maryland Hist. Mag.* (1917) XII. 285 If the bounds of the Hog pen cannot be found. **1837** *Southern Lit. Messenger* III. 238 Cornwallis's cave is converted to a hog-pen. **1874** *Rep. Vermont Board Agric.* II. 512 In said basement I have my hog-pen. **1964** *Publ. Amer. Dial. Soc.* XLII. 21 All [pigs] may live in a *pigpen* or a *hogpen*.

attrib. **1850** *Rep. U.S. Comm. Patents, Agric. 1849* 122 Leached ashes, hen-house and hog-pen refuse are very valuable fertilizers.

ho·g-round. *U.S.* (See quot. 1899.)

1819 *Amer. Farmer* (Baltimore) I. 142 Bacon the hog round, 12 to 13 [dollars]. **1835** *Louisville Publ. Adv.* 14 Feb., 8000 lbs bulk pork, hog round..for sale. **1886** *Harper's Mag.* 206/2 Lard, made from hog-round. **1899** B. W. GREEN *Word Bk. Virginia* 189 Hams, shoulders and middlings have different prices, but when taken altogether at one price, it is so much hog-round.

hog's back, var. HOGBACK.

1800 in *Vermont Hist. Soc. Proc. 1920–21* (1921) 168 Whats call'd the hogs back is a ridge of mountains on the north side (of the Onion river, Vt.). **1827** J. F. COOPER *Red Rover* i, The hog's back over which the water pitches. **1834–63** [see HOGBACK 2]. **1973** *Guardian* 23 Jan. 13/1 The Prime Minister ..will be there, in his retreat on the hogs-back of the Delimara peninsula.

hog-skin. 1. (Earlier Amer. example.)

1673 *Essex Inst. Hist. Coll.* L. 27 A meale trough..a hog-skin, a reele.

ho·g-tie, *v.* orig. *U.S.* [HOG *sb.*[1] 1.] *trans.* To secure by tying the four feet, or the hands and feet, together. Also *fig.*, to fetter.

1894 [see HOG *sb.*[1] 13]. **1903** A. ADAMS *Log Cowboy* xi. 75 We threw him, hog-tied him and rolled him into the water. **1905** A. H. LEWIS *Sunset Trail* i. 3 Something wherewith he might hogtie steers when in the course of duty he must rope and throw them. **1906** S. E. WHITE in *McClure's Mag.* Mar. 518/1 In time he got to be a fairly accurate and very quick shot. The same way with roping and hog-tying and all the rest. **1907** —— *Arizona Nights* III. xii. 300 With a short piece of hard rope the cow-boy always carries to 'hog-tie' cattle, he lashed her wrists together. **1910** W. M. RAINE *B. O'Connor* (1920) xx. 226 He's hogtied to the scenery long enough to do my business. **1924** C. E. MULFORD *Rustlers' Valley* xi. 136 However, just now we got to hog-tie our soarin' spirits. **1926** J. BLACK *You can't Win* xvii. 240 When I was caught in a burglary, overpowered, hog-tied, and waiting for the waggon. **1961** R. P. HOBSON *Rancher takes Wife* xv. 180 We hogtied the three..calves we were caring for and heaved them into the boat. **1968** *Word Study* Oct. 6/1 It often results in the present stupidly allowing itself to be hog-tied by the past. **1972** *Daily Tel.* 2 Nov. 19 Sir Stephen McAdden..said judges were hog-tied by stipulations banning sentences between six and 18 months on people under 21. **1973** J. ASHFORD *Double Run* xv. 132 They thought they'd got him hog-tied whereas in fact he was helping to play them for suckers.

ho·g-tie, *sb.* *U.S.* [f. the vb.] The form of securing or fettering produced by 'hog-tying'; a secure hold.

1910 W. M. RAINE *B. O'Connor* (1920) vi. 78 They sure do hate to turn loose a gringo when they have got the hog-tie on him. **1940** E. T. SETON *Trail of Artist-Naturalist* 321 The two cowmen jerked loose the hog-ties, the broncos sprang to their feet, and of course ran away.

hog-trough. (Later U.S. examples.)

1855 M. M. THOMSON *Doesticks* x. 83 After a long search [I] found him wrapped up in the colors, fast asleep with his head in a hog-trough. **1972** J. S. HALL *Sayings from Old Smoky* 87 Fifty years ago if a younger sister married first, folks would say the older sister 'had to dance in the hog trough'.

hog-wash. Add: (Further examples.) **b.** Esp. applied to inferior writings of any kind.

1773 GARRICK *Let.* 16 Nov. (1831) I. 583 The Fair Quaker, which we agreed to be *skimmed milk*, (nay, hogwash) whipped up into *syllabub*, and swallowed by a foolish audience as if substantial as *roast beef*. **1893** FARMER & HENLEY *Slang* III. 329/2 *Hogwash*..(journalists').—Worthless newspaper matter. **1912** G. B. SHAW in *Daily News* 22 May 6/5 Exactly the same 'hogwash'.. would have been lavished on the veriest dastards as upon a crew of Grace Darlings. **1930** WYNDHAM LEWIS *Apes of God* v. 161 Yes, man alive, a lousy limited edition of an intellectually-fraudulent book that no one could sell, that no one would want!..Not even as honest-to-goodness bookstall hogwash. **1939** L. DURRELL *Spirit of Place* (1969) 62 Only look at the faces of cabinet without reading their hogwash and you see that they are a pack of degenerates. **1955** A. HUXLEY *Genius & Goddess* 36 Tripe and hogwash dished out by the moulders of public opinion. **1965** *Spectator* 5 Mar. 293/1 The whole of the artistic world has been debauched by the hogwash of the do-it-yourself vogue.

Hohenzollernism (hōu·entsǫːləɹniz'm). [a. G. *Hohenzollern*, the name of a family originating from Hohenzollern in southern Germany which became successively electors of Brandenburg, kings of Prussia, and emperors of Germany (see PRUSSIAN B. *sb.* note) + -ISM.] The autocratic spirit or belligerent policies of the Hohenzollern dynasty. So **Ho·henzo:llernist** *a.*

1915 *Scotsman* 23 Jan. 12/2 The 'Prussianism' of to-day [is] merely 'Hohenzollernism' grafted on to a good people. **1919** J. L. GARVIN *Econ. Found. Peace* xi. 252 Let us not think for a moment that such thoughts were associated only with Hohenzollernism, Junkerism, and militarism, and must disappear of themselves if Germany becomes an advanced democracy. **1919** G. B. SHAW *Peace Conference Hints* ii. 19 They were..far more determined to overthrow the Hohenzollernist Junkerdom than the Jingos. **1930** —— *What I Really wrote about War* (1931) 2, I did not want Hohenzollernism to win.

hohmannite (hōu·mænəit). *Min.* [ad. G. *hohmannit* (A. Frenzel 1888, in *Min. und petrogr. Mittheil.* IX. 397), f. the name of Thomas *Hohmann*, mining engineer of Valparaiso, who discovered it: see -ITE[1].] A hydrous basic ferrous sulphate, $FeSO_4(OH).3H_2O$, occurring in triclinic crystals of a brownish red colour that rapidly dehydrate on exposure to air.

1888 *Jrnl. Chem. Soc.* LIV. 923 In a sample of copiapite, from Valparaiso, a new iron sulphate was found, to which the name Hohmannite has been given. **1900** E. S. DANA *Text-bk. Min.* 536 Amarantite. $Fe_2O_3.2SO_3.7H_2O$... Hohmannite is the same partially altered. **1938** *Amer. Mineralogist* XXIII. 745 On dehydration..hohmannite apparently loses the four loosely held molecules of water and forms what is here called metahohmannite. In this respect it differs from amarantite, which is much more stable under atmospheric conditions. **1968** I. KOSTOV *Mineral.* 499 Amarantite and hohmannite are triclinic-pinacoidal.

ho-ho (hoˌho). [Chin.] *ho-ho bird*, a mythical bird of pheasant-like appearance used frequently as an emblem of courage.

1901 C. MONKHOUSE *Hist. & Descr. Chinese Porc.* II. 158 It [*sc.* the phoenix] is referred to as the *fong-hoa* or *ho-ho* bird. **1927** W. B. HONEY *Guide Later Chinese Porcelain* 84 The phoenix (*fêng-huang*, the *ho-ho* bird of old catalogues) is apparently related to the sun-bird of Near Eastern and Indian mythology, and was an emblem of the empress. **1963** *Times* 7 May 7/2 A swordguard in silver formed as a Ho-ho bird and Kirin, undercut in the round with gilt details.

Hohokam (hohokā·m), *sb.* and *a.* [ad. Pima *húhukam*, old one.] **A.** *sb.* **a.** An extinct people of North American Indians. **b.** The culture of this people, centred in Arizona and flourishing after *c* 450, characterized by irrigated agriculture and houses built in pits. **B.** *adj.* Of or pertaining to this people or culture.

1884 A. F. BANDELIER in *Archæol. Inst. Amer. Rep.* V. 80 The Casa Blanca and all the ruins of the Gila were the abode of the fore-fathers of the Pimas, designated by them as 'Vi-pi-sĕt' (great-grandparents), or 'Ho-ho-q̄om' (the extinct ones). **1912** J. W. FEWKES *Casa Grande, Ariz.* 153 The Pima name Hohókam may be adopted to designate this ancestral stock, to whom may be ascribed the erection of the casas grandes on the Gila. **1937** *Southwestern Lore* Dec. 54 As a result of investigations conducted at Winona Village certain archaeological discoveries have definitely explained the affiliation with the Hohokam Culture. **1940** E. FERGUSSON *Our Southwest* 116 What happened to the early Hohokam people is still in dispute. **1948** A. L. KROEBER *Anthropol.* (ed. 2) xviii. 809 Parallel to the Anasazi development is the Hohokam one of lowland, desert, torrid southern Arizona. *Ibid.*, Ceremonial kivas did not develop among the Hohokam, but there were dugout courts for a ritual ball game.

ho-hum (hōu·hʌm), *int.* [f. HO *int.*[1] + HUM *int.*] = HUM *int.* (usu. as an expression of boredom). Also as *sb.* and *v.* As *adj.*, dull and routine.

1924 *Dialect Notes* V. 270 Oh ho hum (vex[ation] or dis[gust]). **1962** *Listener* 4 Oct. 536/3 Listing last week's dramas I find scarcely enough straw to make a useful brickbat:..the return, ho-hum, of *Maigret*. **1962** *John o' London's* 10 May 460/3 Mr. Ustinov sits there..blinking, double-talking and ho-humming. **1963** M. DUGGAN in C. K. Stead *N.Z. Short Stories* (1966) 101 His mouth served out its lying old hohums. **1969** *Daily Colonist* (Victoria, B.C.) 27 Sept. 2/3 People are pretty ho-hum on most parts of the [Vancouver] Island right now..but if anything does happen, they will be the first to cry for damages. **1973** *Jewish Chron.* 19 Jan. 14/1 So the Composers' Guild of Great Britain wants the Arts Council to twist the arms of orchestral managements to make them perform more works by British composers. Ho-hum.

hoick (hoik), *sb.* *colloq.* Also **hoik.** [See next.] **a.** *Rowing.* (See quot. 1898.) **b.** *Aeronaut.* A jerky pull (on the stick). (Cf. *HOICK *v.*[1] 2.) **c.** *Cricket.* A jerky, hoisted shot.

1898 *Encycl. Sport* II. 297/1 *Hoick*, a jerk with the arms at the beginning or end of the stroke, which prevents a steady leg drive from the stretcher. **1907** *Daily Chron.* 8 Mar. 9/1 Cambridge sacrifice everything to a terrible hoick at the finish. **1946** A. PHELPS *I couldn't care Less* vi. 43 The Magister responded to my wild hoik on the stick and came off. **1954** A. G. MOYES *Austral. Batsmen* xii. 164 He..gets a lot of runs with a stroke which Cheetham called a 'hoik'. **1956** R. ALSTON *Test Commentary* ix. 60 Lindwall's one scoring stroke was an ungainly 'hoick' for six.

hoick (hoik), *v.*[1] *slang* or *colloq.* Also **hoik.** [Perhaps orig. a local variant of *HIKE *v.*] **1.** *trans.* To lift up or hoist, often with a jerk or rapid movement. Also to haul or turn *out*. Also *transf.* and *fig.*

1898 G. NICKALLS in W. A. Morgan *'House' on Sport* 346 Until the finish, which, to be made really effective, must be honestly hoicked out. **1908** BELLOC *On Nothing* 136 Beneath him the sand sloped down until it met the sea... Every now and then Mahmoud would force a son or domestic of his to go down and hoick out a pearl. **1911** *Chambers's Jrnl.* Mar. 146/1 The patient Captain Croucher hoicked her from destruction in the nick of time. **1914** W. J. LOCKE *Fort. Youth* i. 20 He hoicked a bit of his shirt-tail from his breeches and proceeded to knot the cornelian heart secure therein. **1916** J. BUCHAN *Greenmantle* ii. 24, I had got myself adjusted to this trench business... And now you have hoicked me out. **1918** 'Q' *Foe-Farrell* vi, I dashed around to the rear of the cab, collared Farrell, and hoicked him inboard. **1931** C. MACKENZIE *Buttercups & Daisies* v, Blackbirds and thrushes hoicking worms out of the moist ground. **1930** BLUNDEN *De Bello Germanico* iii. 28 His cue to 'hoik out' the unwary scrimshankers. **1934** G. B. SHAW *Too True to be Good* II. 49 The noise stops; and the bicyclist, having hoiked his machine up on to its stand..comes past the pavilion. **1952** WODEHOUSE *Pigs have Wings* v. 99 'Mr. Galahad is in the amber drawing-room.'..'Then go and hoik him out of it.' **1954** W. FAULKNER *Fable* (1955) 66 No need for them to hunt down and hoick out and execute a mere thirteen men. **1962** M. MCLUHAN *Gutenberg Galaxy* 51 This process..hoicks societies of the world of 'sacred' or cosmic space and time into the detribalized or 'profane' space and time of civilized and pragmatic man. **1972** *Country Life* 9 Mar. 548/3 Is there anything conceivably related to the art of fly fishing in hoicking out trout that have had no chance to live a natural life?

2. To force (an aeroplane) to climb steeply to a higher level. Also *intr.*, to jerk oneself *out of*, etc.

a **1918** J. T. B. MCCUDDEN *Five Yrs. R.F.C.* (1919) 287 He..hoicked out of the dive with such vim that three wing-tips at once collapsed. **1919** *Glasgow Herald* 19 Dec. 10 The pilot yanks the joystick to hoick her up. **1928** *Daily Mail* 7 May 6/4 Hoiking.—Sweeping suddenly to avoid an obstacle or a dangerous approach to earth.

hoick, *v.*[2] [Prob. a dial. variant of HAWK *v.*[3]] = HAWK *v.*[3] Hence **hoi·cking** *vbl. sb.*

1926 A. HUXLEY *Essays New & Old* 5 These frightful hoickings in the throat. **1926** —— *Jesting Pilate* I. 43 The holy man woke up and began to hoick and spit.

‖**hoi polloi** (hoi pǫ·loi; also pǫloi·). [Gr. οἱ πολλοί, lit. 'the many'.] The majority; the masses. Also formerly in *Univ. slang*, candidates for a pass degree.

In English use normally preceded by the definite article even though *hoi* means 'the'.

[**1668** DRYDEN *Dram. Poesie* 65 If by the people you understand the multitude, the οἱ πολλοί. **1791** [see POLL *sb.*[3]]. *c* **1821–2** BYRON in *Lett.* (1830) I. 633 [We] put on masques, and went on the stage with the οἱ πολλοι.] **1837** J. F. COOPER *Europe* II. 94 After which the *oi polloi* are enrolled as they can find interest. **1855** *Read & Reflect* I. 60 The *hoi polloi* [of Mauritius], as we say at Oxford, are mindless—all blank. **1895** *Brewer's Dict. Phr. & Fable* (new ed.) 613/1 *Hoi Polloi (the)*, the poll-men in our Universities, that is, those who take their degrees without 'honours'. **1905** *Daily Chron.* 29 Aug. 4/4 A couple of immense swells..staring stiffly at 'hoy-polloy'. **1932** F. L. WRIGHT *Autobiogr.* (1945) III. 256 Now it all ended in this triumph for them, hoi-polloi, rag, tag, and bobtail.

hoist, *v.* Add: **6.** *Criminals' slang.* To break into (a building) (? *Obs.*); to steal, rob. Hence **hoister,** a housebreaker (? *Obs.*); a shoplifter; a pickpocket; **hoisting** *vbl. sb.*, (esp.) shoplifting. Cf. *HEIST.

1708 J. HALL *Mem.* (ed. 4) 6 *Hoisters*, such as help one another upon their Backs in the Night-time to get into Windows. **1790** H. T. POTTER *New Dict. Cant & Flash Lang.* (1795) (ed. 2) 34 *Hoister*, a shoplifter. **1796** GROSE *Dict. Vulgar T.* (ed. 2), *Hoist*, to go upon the hoist; to get into windows accidentally left open. **1931** *Amer. Speech* VII. 109 *Heist* (or *hoist*), to hold up a person, or to rob at the point of a gun. **1936** J. CURTIS *Gilt Kid* iv. 39 What did you get done for? Hoisting? **1938** F. D. SHARPE *Sharpe of Flying Squad* xiv. 154 Gangs of women shoplifters or 'Hoisters' are to be found in Hoxton. **1960** *Observer* 25 Dec. 7/6 Various petty fiddles and con games to which Christmas trading lent itself, and of course hoisting —shoplifting. **1962** *Coast to Coast 1961–62* 21 'I know where we can hoist a car,' Mick said. 'We'll carry the stuff in it.' **1966** *New Statesman* 23 Dec. 934/2 You know Annie Ward, well she's on the hoisting racket. **1970** M. KENYON *100,000 Welcomes* ii. 10 That half-world of hustlers, hoisters, screwsmen, bogeys, bird, bent gear and tom. **1970** G. F. NEWMAN *Sir, You Bastard* ii. 45 The hoister was held under a guard a dozen strong. **1971** L. GRIBBLE *Alias the Victim* viii. 140 Cop slang. A hoister is a pick-pocket or shoplifter.

hoist, *sb.* Add: **3.** Also preceded by a defining word.

a **1884** KNIGHT *Dict. Mech.* Suppl. 12/2 Pneumatic hoist. *Ibid.* 459/1 Builder's hoist. **1963** A. LUBBOCK *Austral. Roundabout* 195 Small bungalow homes with the sun-fresh washing blowing..from the rotary hoists in their back gardens. **1967** *Nursing Times* 18 Aug. 1091/2 The Winchester hoist has also an important use in home nursing.

5. Housebreaking (? *Obs.*); shoplifting. *Criminals' slang.*

1714 A. SMITH *Hist. Highwaymen* I. 143 He pursued his old Courses of going on the Top or Hoist, that is, breaking into a House in a dark Evening, by getting in at a Window one Story high, which they perform by one Thief standing on the Shoulders of another. *a* **1790** H. T. POTTER *New Dict. Cant & Flash Lang.* (1795) (ed. 2) 39 *Lift*, or *hoist*, shop-lifting, or robbing a shop. **1812** J. H. VAUX *Mem.* (1819) 180 *Hoist*. The game of shop-lifting is called the hoist; a person expert at this practice is said to be a good hoist. **1914** JACKSON & HELLYER *Vocab. Criminal Slang* 44 *Hoist*, the profession of shoplifting. **1938** F. D. SHARPE *Sharpe of Flying Squad* i. 15 Shoplifting as an art known as 'The Hoist', and its devotees are called 'Hoisters'. **1958** F. NORMAN *Bang to Rights* 72 My old woman's still out on the hoist now.

hoist-. Add: **hoist-door** (see quot.).

1881 *Harper's Mag.* Mar. 528/1 In the middle of the hall was the 'hoist-door', through which the wheat was hoisted up by a crane and stored in the loft.

Hokan (hōu·kăn). Name given to a group of languages of certain American Indian peoples inhabiting the west coast of the U.S. So **Ho·kanist,** one who is versed in these languages. Also *Comb.*, as *Hokan-Siouan*.

1913 DIXON & KROEBER in *Science* 7 Feb. 225/2 The new larger [native Indian language] families..are..Hokan, comprising Shasta, Chimariko and Pomo, probably Karok, and possibly Yana. **1920** *Internat. Jrnl. Amer. Ling.* Dec. 280/2 It is difficult for me to suggest any alternative to the hypothesis of a common origin of the Hokan and Coahuiltecan languages. **1965** *Language* XLI.

303 Two Hokanists..have examined the Sapir (1929) subgrouping labelled Northern Hokan. **1965** *Canad. Jrnl. Ling.* Spring 83 These..families had been placed in the Hokan–Siouan superstock.

hoke (hōᵘk), *v.* [Back-formation from *HOKUM.] On the stage or screen: to overplay (a part), to act (a part) in an insincere, sentimental, or melodramatic manner. Also *transf.* and with *up*.

1935 A. J. POLLOCK *Underworld Speaks* 57/1 *Hoke*, to string along; to jolly; to ridicule. **1938** M. MCCARTHY in *Partisan Rev.* Jan. 48 Actors who have been playing for a long time in the same play will..'hoke' their performances more and more. A giggle becomes a laugh; a catch in the throat, a sob. **1939** C. MORLEY *Kitty Foyle* xxv. 244 She had the guts to keep her stuff to exclusive outlets and hoke it up with all sorts of restrictions. **1940** S. LEWIS *Bethel Merriday* xxvii. 283 Mr. Nooks had ..overplayed—'hoked' is the technical word—the role of the Apothecary. **1961** *Punch* 22 Feb. 331/2 The average moviegoer..is pleased to see pictorial evidence, a little hoked up for added amusement. **1971** M. BABSON *Cover-up Story* iii. 33 Just *try* it straight..it's a mistake to hoke it up.

hokee-pokee. *rare*⁻¹. [Cf. HOKEY-POKEY.] (See quot.)

1873 J. MILLER *Life amongst Modocs* (1876) xiii. 192 One man..danced a sort of a savage hokee-pokee, and sang.

hokey, *sb.* Add: Also, *by the hokey fiddle*.

1922 JOYCE *Ulysses* 513 By the hoky fiddle, thanks be to Jesus. **1958** *Engineering* 4 Apr. 426/1 It may be five years before it pays dividends but by the hokey fiddle it'll shake us.

hokey (hōᵘ·ki), *a. slang* (orig. *U.S.*). Also **hokie, hoky.** [f. *HOKE *v.*, *HOKUM + -Y¹.] Characterized by hokum; sentimental, melodramatic, artificial.

1945 *N.Y. Times* 19 Aug. 3/8 Equally a part of America ..are the dull films, the tasteless, hoky confections that public taste ought to repudiate. **1968** *Surfer Mag.* Jan. 58/1 They know the films are hokie Hollywood products. **1969** *Northwest* (*Sunday Oregonian Mag.*) 14 Dec. 11/2 Not the 'hokey' set-ups I've been through a half dozen times, but a supervised transitional period. **1970** *New Yorker* 16 May 105/3 A funny and hokey reënactment of the pantomime pocket drama that Colette did in music halls all over France. **1971** *Rolling Stone* 24 June 31/4 A closing piece [on a record], 'Sometimes', is embarrassingly hokey.

hokey-cokey (hōᵘ·ki,kōᵘ·ki). [Cf. *HOKEE-POKEE.] A kind of dance.

[**1943** *Dancing Times* Sept. 570/2, I found a party-dance that was quite new to me. Locally it was (inaccurately) called the 'Hokey Pokey'...The correct name is 'Cokey Cokey'...The chorus runs:..You do the Cokey Cokey and turn around That's what it's all about.] **1966** *Crescendo* Jan. 23/1 'The next dance will be a Veleta' is about my lot, and even then I'm likely to say 'Hokey-Cokey'. **1967** *Ibid.* May 10/3 Your bandleader must present all the ritual party dances including, of course, an ever popular Hokey Cokey. **1967** *Listener* 2 Nov. 587/1 It turned out to be a strong dose of barn-dance and hokey-cokey. **1972** *Sunday Express* 2 Jan. 15/1 (*heading*) Hokey-cokey at the club forces family to sleep in tent. *Ibid.* 15/4 It was 1.30 a.m. at the county council's staff social club and they were dancing the hokey-cokey.

hokey-pokey. Add: **2.** (Later examples.)

1910 A. BENNETT *Clayhanger* II. 226 Three hokey-pokey ice-cream hand-carts, one after another, turned the corner of Trafalgar Road. **1955** *Times* 8 June 7/4 'Hokey-pokey', which, as children used to know, sold for a penny a lump and was (presumably because of its freezing touch on the tongue) the stuff to make you jump. **1970** J. BROWN *Unmelting Pot* i. 23 An Italian organ-grinder..who sold ice-cream or hokey-pokey at ½d a piece during the summer.

4. A toffee-like sweet. *N.Z.*

1939 'K. MANSFIELD' *Scrapbook* 3 We always gave him the same presents..three cakes of hoky-poky.

hokku: see *HAIKU.

Hokonui (hǫ·kǒnu,i). *N.Z.* [Maori place-name.] = MOONSHINE 4.

1947 D. M. DAVIN *Gorse blooms Pale* 29 The men outside..tasting the jar of Hokonui that Tom MacDonald had brought. **1963** *Truth* (Wellington) 17 Sept., Today's distillers of Hokonui can use electricity, smokeless fuels, to keep their spasmodic industry out of sight.

hokum (hōᵘ·kəm). orig. *U.S. Theatrical slang.* Also **hocum.** [? A blending of HOCUS-POCUS and BUNKUM.] Speech, action, properties, etc., on the stage, designed to make a sentimental or melodramatic appeal to an audience. Also *transf.* Hence *gen.*, bunkum.

1917 *Sun* (N.Y.) 5 Aug. III. 3/7 'Jasbo' is a form of the word common in the varieties, meaning the same as 'hokum', or low comedy verging on vulgarity. **1922** C. SANDBURG *Slabs of Sunburnt West* 25 Hokum—they lap it up. **1926** *N.Y. Times* 29 Aug., This may be grounding comedy, but it is not pure hokum. **1926** *Ladies' Home Jrnl.* Apr. 38 'What they tell is..bold and defiant realism.' 'Bold and defiant hokum, I should call it.' **1927** *Sunday Express* 17 Apr. 4 Channing Pollock believed that in 'The Fool' he had written a work of genius. Even when other people said it was hokum he still went on. **1928** *Publishers' Weekly* 16 June 2440 It is pure hokum to suggest that all authors are always interesting. **1928** *Sunday Dispatch* 15 July 15/1 The Adelphi..was occupied by a Mr. Sam Bernard with a musical play called 'The Belle of Bond Street'—what an outrage that 'Girl' and 'Belle' hokum must have become! **1930** *Publishers' Weekly* 15 Mar. 1559 In spite of the fact that the hokum of it all has been pointed out to them. **1937** *Daily Tel.* 26 Oct. 8/5 His story is what the film trade calls 'hokum', the recipe as before with inferior or stale ingredients. **1970** *New Yorker* 12 Dec. 125/1 Most people in Washington dismissed this statement as a piece of sentimental hokum. **1973** *Washington Post* 5 Jan. B7/4 *The Poseidon Adventure*..strictly formula hokum but reasonably diverting.

holard² (hǫ·laɹd). *Ecology.* [f. Gr. ὅλος whole + ἄρδειν to water.] The total water content of the soil.

1905 F. E. CLEMENTS *Res. Methods Ecol.* ii. 32 The total amount of water in the soil is divided into the available and the non-available water content. The terms suggested for these are respectively, holard.. chresard..and echard. **1926** TANSLEY & CHIPP *Study of Vegetation* vii. 127 If the echard is subtracted from the holard (total amount of water in the fresh soil) the difference is called the chresard. **1929** WEAVER & CLEMENTS *Plant Ecol.* ix. 182 Of the total water content or holard (whole amount) the larger portion can be absorbed by the plant and is consequently termed available water.

holaspidean (hǫlæspi·dĭăn), *a. Zool.* [f. mod.L. *Holaspideæ* (C. J. Sundevall *Methodi Naturalis Avium Disponendarum Tentamen* (1872) I. 53), f. Gr. ὅλος whole + ἀσπίς shield.] Pertaining to passerine birds that have a single series of large scutella on the posterior portion of the tarsus.

1885 J. S. KINGSLEY *Riverside Nat. Hist.* (1888) IV. 485 This peculiarity consists in the holaspidean tarsi, technically making them scutelliplantar, the hind surface of the tarsus being broken up into scutes similar to those covering the front part. **1907** R. RIDGWAY *Birds N. & Middle Amer.* IV. 329 In all Oscines except the Alaudidæ (in which the tarsus is holaspidean) [the tarsus] has the posterior margin contracted into a sharp or narrow ridge or edge. **1959** VAN TYNE & BERGER *Fund. Ornith.* ii. 48 Several types of passerine tarsal scutellation have been described... Holaspidean: With rear surface of tarsus covered by a single series of broad, rectangular scales.

Holbein (hōᵘ·lbəin, hǫ·l-). The name of the German painter Hans *Holbein* (1497–1543), used *attrib.* to designate embroidery, rugs, etc., embodying qualities or decoration characteristic of Holbein or his work. Hence **Holbeine·sque** *a.* [see -ESQUE], resembling the work of Holbein.

1881 C. C. HARRISON *Woman's Handiwork* I. 44 Holbein stitches appear the same on right and wrong sides of the material. **1882** CAULFEILD & SAWARD *Dict. Needlework* 252/2 *Holbein Stitch*, also known as Italian Stitch, and used in Holbein Embroidery to cover the outline patterns that form the work. *Ibid.* 253/1 *Holbein Work*..consists of an outline Embroidery executed with great care and exactitude, so that the right and wrong side of the work are alike. **1895** J. A. GRAY *At Court of Ameer* xxxi, The most skilful of the artists gave an almost Holbeinesque look to his drawings. **1904** *Westm. Gaz.* 14 Nov. 4/2 His fine Holbeinesque drawings. **1931** A. U. DILLEY *Oriental Rugs & Carpets* vi. 146 The oldest group of rugs remaining to us of the weavings of the Ottoman Turks..are the fifteenth-century products now handsomely called Holbein rugs in compliment to Hans Holbein the Younger. **1950** *Chambers's Encycl.* I. 612/2 The 'Holbein'..and 'Landsknecht' types..which are a German form of short dagger, the former so called from the sheaths being frequently decorated with Holbein's 'Dance of Death' in pierced and chased metal. **1960** *Times* 21 June 22/4 A Holbeinesque bracelet.

holcus (hǫ·lkŏs). *Bot.* [mod.L. (C. Linnæus *Hortus Cliffortianus* (1737) 468), f. Gr. ὁλκός a kind of grass.] A plant of a genus of annual or perennial grasses so called, native to Europe, Africa, and south-west Asia.

1771 P. MILLER *Abridgm. Gardeners Dict.* (ed. 6) s.v. *Holcus*..Holcus with hairy chaff, and bearded seeds. *Ibid.*, Holcus with smooth husks. **1806** J. BARROW *Voy. Cochin China* 392 All the houses were enclosed by a fence made of strong reeds, of the straw of *holcus*, or twigs of wood. **1859** [see UNHUSKED *ppl. a.*¹]. **1915** L. H. BAILEY *Stand. Cyclop. Hort.* III. 1496/2 The name Holcus was accepted by some botanists. **1947** J. G. DICKSON *Dis. Field Crops* ix. 169 The holcus spot is characterized by tan red-bordered round to elliptical lesions on the leaves.

hold, *v.* Add: **2. b.** (Earlier and later examples.)

1744 *Laws* [of Cricket] in *New Dict. Arts & Sci.* (1755) IV. 3459/1 If the ball be held before she touches ground, though she be hugged to the body, it is out. **1868** *Baily's Monthly Mag.* July 127 Mr. Miles would have got ten wickets had there been any man in the field capable of holding a catch. **1903** G. L. JESSOP in H. G. Hutchinson *Cricket* v. 130 'Dolly' catches are much more difficult to hold than those from hard drives.

d. To keep back, detain, delay.

1891 F. H. SMITH *Col. Carter* 135 'Where did you get this?' he asked, aghast. 'From the carrier. It [*sc.* a letter] was held for postage.' **1904** *New York Times* 20 Aug. 1 The railroad has issued an order..that trains shall not be held for the..taking of baggage after the regular time scheduled for stops has expired. **1970** G. F. NEWMAN *Sir, You Bastard* viii. 203 Sneed was greeted by Sergeant Waugh, who jumped back to try and hold the lift for him.

e. To detain in custody, keep under arrest. orig. *U.S.*

1903 *N.Y. Evening Post* 19 Aug., The men were held for felonious assault, and the woman as a witness. **1906** *Springfield* (Mass.) *Weekly Republican* 14 June 1 If the New York insurance officials cannot be held for larceny, they might evidently be held for forgery or perjury. **1922** H. TITUS *Timber* iii. 32 'Why did he arrest you?' 'Oh, I dropped a cigarette out here in summer an' started a fire,..an' he held me under the fire law.' **1966** J. BINGHAM *Double Agent* xii. 183 He spoke to the Maltese police inspector. 'You would do me a personal favour if you would hold him for twenty-four hours.' **1972** J. RATHBONE *Trip Trap* viii. 89 There were no convictions, but she had been held for questioning on three occasions.

f. *Boxing.* (See quot. 1954.)

1922 N. CLARK *How to Box* xii. 191 It must be understood that it takes two to make a clinch, and unless both men are holding, the referee has not the power to call 'break-away'. **1923** T. C. WIGNALL *Story of Boxing* 318 The referee shall have power to disqualify for..holding, butting, shouldering, [etc.]. **1954** F. C. AVIS *Boxing Ref. Dict.* 53 *Hold*, to grasp an opponent with the hands—not permitted. **1960** *Times* 28 Sept. 16/7 The referee had to speak to both men for holding. **1961** *Times* 8 Mar. 17/3 Spinks appeared to be palming and holding so flagrantly.

5. b. *spec.* Of a theatre: to have capacity for (freq. with reference to the size of a theatre's seating capacity expressed in terms of the takings).

1740 C. CIBBER *Apology for Life* xii. 240 Spectators, who may remember what Form the Drury-Lane Theatre stood in, about forty Years ago, before the old Patentee, to make it hold more Mony, took it in his Head to alter it. **1812** *Dramatic Censor 1811* Apr. 218 Which..will, at the old prices, hold as much money as the modern excessively large Theatres. **1894** G. B. SHAW *Let.* 20 Mar. (1965) 421 The Avenue [theatre] holds, when full, £200. **1946** —— *Matter with Ireland* (1962) 13 It [*sc.* the theatre] held more money per square foot of ground than the classical Royal.

6. g. Phr. *to hold the stage* (or *house*): to command the attention of a theatre audience.

1889 BARRÈRE & LELAND *Dict. Slang*, *Hold the stage, to* (theatrical), is said of an experienced actor who is fully at home on the stage, and always commands the attention of the audience. **1893** FARMER & HENLEY *Slang*, *To hold the stage*, to have the chief place on the boards and the eye of the audience. **1916** *To-day* 22 July 368/1 You do not need to be a very experienced playgoer to know when an actress is holding a house. **1967** 'LA MERI' *Sp. Dancing* (ed. 2) viii. 98 Many dancers assisted by only a pianist held the stage alone for the two hours of a complete evening's performance.

h. *to hold the line*: to maintain telephonic connection during a break in conversation. (Cf. *40 g.) Also *fig.*

1912 BEERBOHM *Christmas Garland* 6 It was with a certain sense of his rashness in the matter, therefore, that he now, with an air of feverishly 'holding the line', said 'Oh, as to that.' **1915** *Punch* 10 Nov. 390/1 Such are some of the miseries of holding the line. **1931** WODEHOUSE *Big Money* i. 24 'Hold the line,' he said in a low, strained voice.

7. Also *hold it!* : stay as you are; do not go on!; steady on!

1926 A. HUXLEY *Jesting Pilate* IV. 262 That's good. Hold it. **1930** AUDEN *Poems* 23 Moisten the lips and start afresh. Hold it. **1948** M. ALLINGHAM *More Work for Undertaker* xiii. 160 Oh, I say, hold it...I don't think you ought to go as far as that. **1962** A. CHRISTIE *Mirror Crack'd* xv. 167 'That'll do. Hold it. We'll have one more. ..It looks smashing,' said the photographer. **1973** E. BERCKMAN *Victorian Album* 20 'Let's go and talk to her quickly, quickly—.' 'Hold it, darling,' she interrupted.

f. *to hold the road*: to continue to occupy the road; to keep to the road without skidding, etc.

1926 T. E. LAWRENCE *Let.* 27 Sept. (1938) 500 The S.S. 100 holds the road extraordinarily. **1971** P. D. JAMES *Shroud for Nightingale* ii. 43 [She] wondered whether her small car would hold the road.

8. b. (Further example.)

1934 C. LAMBERT *Music Ho!* III. 205 When a guitar hung in every negro barber's shop, and a client who was waiting would vamp about on the instrument until at a lucky *trouvaille* everyone would shout 'Hold that chord'.

11. c. Phr. *to hold one's horses*: used esp. in *imper.* (*hold your horses!*) = be patient, hold on! orig. *U.S.*

1844 *Picayune* (New Orleans) 16 Sept. 241/4 Oh, hold your hosses, Squire. There's no use gettin' riled, no how. **1847** J. S. ROBB *Streaks of Squatter Life* 24 Jest hold your hosses, boys—he'll come out directly. **1917** *Woman's Home Compan.* Nov. 58 Now Phebe..you just hold your hosses and speak a little slower. **1939** *Chatelaine* Oct. 43/4 Hold your horses, dear. **1943** HUNT & PRINGLE *Service Slang* 39 *Hold your horses*, hold the job until further orders. (Comes from the Artillery.) **1945** S. LEWIS *Cass Timberlane* (1947) xl. 272 Hey, hold your horses, Cass. Don't get sore. **1967** N. FITZGERALD *Affairs of Death* vii. 119 'I'm going in to the station *now*,' he said. 'Hold your horses,' Marr said. 'The night's young.'

d. To keep (a person) from speaking; to prevent (a person) from being troublesome. *N. Amer. colloq.*

1901 ADE *Forty Modern Fables* 244 'And I guess that'll Hold you for a While,' added the Biggest Boy in the Room. **1922** S. LEWIS *Babbitt* v. 63 'I guess that'll hold you for a while, George!' said Finkelstein. **1935** N. L. MCCLUNG *Clearing in West* xvii. 136 Maybe that would hold Miss Adams! **1965** 'S. WOODS' *Though I know she Lies* xvi. 212 '*That* should hold him for a while,' said Derek with satisfaction.

e. *hold everything!*: wait! take no action! **1930** in *Amer. Speech* VI. 92. **1948** C. Day Lewis *Otterbury Incident* viii. 93 Hold everything now, this is the big bang coming. **1951** L. Hobson *Celebrity* (1953) xi. 155 Hold everything; let's see.

15. e. Only in pres. pple. *holding*: 'financial', in funds. *Austral.* and *N.Z. colloq.*

c **1926** 'Mixer' *Transport Workers' Song Bk.* 11 'What-ho, Jerry, how yer holding?'..'I haven't made enough this week For to pay the blooming rent.' **1930** *Bulletin* (Sydney) 29 Oct. 21/1 Whether a man was 'oldin' or whether a man was broke, Joe was a man you could bank on.

f. To be in possession of drugs for sale. *U.S. slang.*

1935 A. J. Pollock *Underworld Speaks* 3/2 *Are you holding?* Have you any dope to sell? **1953** W. Burroughs *Junkie* (1972) ii. 26 The connection was here about ten minutes ago. This character's holding, but he won't turn loose of any. **1961** R. Russell *Sound* (1962) i. i. 15 Don't jump the light, baby, mother's holding, you know. *Ibid.* ii. ix. 158 He was holding, just as Red had said. Santa had the sweets.

23. c. (Further examples.)

1818 Shelley *Let.* 30 Apr. (1964) II. 14 But this holds good, as I know, only to Milan. **1937** *Discovery* May 139/1 His words of seven years ago hold good today.

d. To continue fine, to keep from raining. (Cf. 44 i.)

1893 *Chambers's Jrnl.* 10 June 355/2 If the weather holds, we'll both take a trip.

29. d. *to hold someone's hand*, to give comfort or moral support to someone; to back someone up. *colloq.*

1935 C. Isherwood *Mr. Norris changes Trains* vi. 90, I shall need your moral support. You must come and hold my hand. **1961** A. Wilson *Old Men at Zoo* iv. 220 Martha's been holding his hand in California. **1972** B. Everitt *Cold Front* vii. 55, I 'held his hand' to the best of my ability with school-girl French and passable Italian.

30. b. *to hold up one's head* (further examples).

1808 Jane Austen *Let.* (1932) 205 Her Daughter..who says as little as ever, but holds up her head & smiles. **1859** Lytton *What will he do with It?* I. ii. v. 171 But they could never again hold up their heads with the noblemen and great squires in the county. **1900** E. Wharton *Gift from Grave* vi. 80 Why, you don't suppose if he were alive he could ever hold up his head again, with these letters being read by everybody? *a* **1953** E. O'Neill *Touch of Poet* (1957) 33 *Nora.* You have the fine opinion av yourself! *Sara...* I've had need to have, to hold my head up, slaving as a waitress and chambermaid.

34. hold back. c. With *on*: to refrain from disclosing (something to someone).

1956 E. Pound tr. *Sophocles' Women of Trachis* 22 I'll tell the truth, I won't hold back on you.

35. hold down. c. To remain in (a position or situation); to continue to occupy (a place or post) or succeed in discharging the duties of (one's employment). orig. *U.S. colloq.*

1891 C. Roberts *Adrift Amer.* 92 Jumping an east bound freight.., I managed to hold it down or keep on it till I got to Alameda. **1893** *Harper's Mag.* Dec. 80/2 If a man is to 'hold down' a big ranch in northern Mexico he has got to be 'all man'. **1896** Ade *Artie* xiv. 129 I'll bet that guy up in your place don't know nothin' on earth except how to hold down his measly job. **1902** G. H. Lorimer *Lett. Merchant* v. 60 The fellow who's got the right stuff in him is holding down his own place with one hand. **1910** S. E. White *Rules of Game* i. iii. 19, I didn't much think you could hold down a job here. You see there's too much doing here. **1913** F. H. Burnett *T. Tembarom* ii, I wonder, if I ever did get his job, if I could hold it down? **1931** G. D. H. Cole in W. Rose *Outl. Mod. Knowledge* xvi. 688 There are few pleasures in life equal to that of successfully holding down a difficult and responsible job. **1936** *Punch* 14 Oct. 439/2 He never could hold down a job. **1973** A. Behrend *Samarai Affair* i. 12 Captain Coldstream looked exactly what he was—an ex-sailor of quality now holding down an exacting shore job.

40. hold on. c. Also in jocular phrases.

1930 'Sapper' *Finger of Fate*, etc. 35 Having to hold on by one's eyebrows whenever one moves gets a bit monotonous after a time.

e. (Earlier examples.)

1846 C. M. Kirkland *Western Clearings* 45 'But hold on a little till I tell ye!' interposed Master George. [For **1860** read **1848**.]

g. *Telephony.* To keep the line open.

1892 Kipling in *Times* 29 Nov. 8/1 A..millionnaire,.. clawing wildly at the telephone..'Hello!..I *told* you to hold on. What? .. No. Hold on.' **1919** V. Woolf *Night & Day* xxiv. 327 'I'll look at my engagements...Hold on.' She dropped the machine. **1920** *Punch* 1 Sept. 176/3 'What is your number, please?'..'Just hold on a minute while I look it up.' **1920** R. Macaulay *Potterism* iii. i. 104 You mustn't ring off yet...Hold on while I tell daddy. **1949** J. B. Priestley *Home is Tomorrow* 38 (*into telephone*) Yes, I'll hold on. **1971** A. Cross *Theban Mysteries* (1972) xi. 165 She did go to the phone, but she got the doctor's exchange, which said, 'Hold on,' and then went off the line.

41. hold out. l. To keep back; to retain or detain; (also const. *on*) to withhold (information or the like). *colloq.* (orig. *U.S.*).

1907 E. S. Field *Six-Cylinder Courtship* 71 If it wasn't for Bellows and Rooker, we'd hold out on him every time. **1911** H. S. Harrison *Queed* v. 57 Surface, by clever juggling of his books had managed to 'hold out' a large sum of money in the enforced settlement of his affairs. **1916** H. L. Wilson *Somewhere in Red Gap* viii. 345, I wanted to send a postal card to the..Dye Works at Red Gap, for some stuff they had been holding out on me a month. **1923** R. D. Paine *Comrades of Rolling Ocean* i. 13 He dumped his wages upon the sitting-room table, holding out only the price of a new pair of shoes. **1926** J. Black *You can't Win* ix. 112 The thief who holds out a lady's watch on his pal to give to his girl has no character. **1932** Wodehouse *Hot Water* i. 21 And me who had split Even Stephen with her on every deal, never chiselling, never holding out on her, no, not so much as a dime. **1944** L. A. G. Strong *All fall Down* 99 The thought came to me that maybe the old cuss was just holding out on me. **1945** J. B. Priestley *Three Men in New Suits* v. 88 'Boss,' said Markinch, who liked to be American too, 'he's holding out on us.' **1972** 'G. Black' *Bitter Tea* (1973) v. 81 If I find out that you've been holding out on me over this identification, I'll come down on you like a pile driver.

42. hold over. c. *U.S. colloq.* (See quot. 1889.)

1872 'Mark Twain' *Innoc. at Home* 18 (Farmer), You ruther hold over me, pard. I reckon I can't call that hand. **1889** Farmer *Amer.*, *To hold over one* is to have an advantage in some way or other. This particular usage probably comes from poker phraseology. **1889** K. Munroe *Golden Days* xii. 127 Do we hold over Bowers?

44. hold up. d. (Later U.S. examples in sense 'keep back, withhold'.)

1889 *Kansas Times & Star* 4 Dec., Major Davenport is holding up the firemen's payroll for November owing to alleged irregularities. **1894** *Vermont Agric. Rep.* XIV. 70 When..a cow holds up her milk there is some disturbing element.

e. Also, to arrest the progress of, obstruct the passage of (*lit.* and *fig.*).

1904 *Philadelphia Even. Telegr.* 15 Nov. 1 Out of the 900 steerage passengers that came over on the Merion, 135 failed to pass the immigration inspectors, and were held up. **1905** *N.Y. Evening Post* 16 Mar. 1 Another landslide has occurred..and nine passenger trains are held up in the mountains. **1906** *N.Y. Herald* 5 Mar. 5 It is thought the Senate Finance Committee will seek to devise new excuses for holding up the investigation of the State Banking Department, which it has succeeded in smothering for five weeks. **1909** H. N. Casson *C. H. McCormick* 146 One bill for $15 was held up for a week because it was not properly drawn. **1972** *Daily Hampshire Gaz.* (Northampton, Mass.) 9 May 1/3 A passing motorist asked Witkos if he was 'going to let them hold up the traffic all day?'

hold, *sb.*[1] Add: **2. b.** Also in *Judo.*

1954 E. Dominy *Teach yourself Judo* iii. 39 Theoretically, a hold consists of nothing more than controlling your opponent's body with the weight of your own.

c. (*with*) *no holds barred*, (with) all restrictions relaxed. Also as *attrib. phr.*

1942 Berrey & Van den Bark *Amer. Thes. Slang* § 217/6. **1952** *Economist* 1 Nov. 313/1 An independent [broadcasting] agency..could talk back at the Russians with no holds barred. **1958** *Times* 28 Nov. 13/6 No holds were barred, so to speak, for the Prince's unorthodox education and his own reputedly emancipated views allowed almost every hypothesis. **1961** *Economist* 6 May 524/1 Waging..a sweaty, no-holds-barred tussle all around the world without benefit of parley. **1972** *Real Estate Rev.* Winter 29/1 This allows trust managers to compete on a no-holds-barred basis.

5. b. A delay, pause, postponement. Also *attrib.*

1961 *Observer* 28 May 4/2 The long countdowns, checks and 'holds' possible at Cape Canaveral would be suicide on the moon. **1968** *Time* 27 Dec. 13 The countdown schedule had been padded with enough precautionary hold time to enable technicians to replace the oxygen without delaying the launch. **1969** *New Scientist* 27 Feb. 439/1 Unless there has been a last-minute 'hold' at Cape Kennedy, the first of a pair of *Mariner* spacecraft should now be on its way. **1971** *Daily Tel.* 4 Jan. 2/4 Concorde, counting time for 'taxi-ing' and 'holds' could arrive in New York at 7 a.m. after taking off from Heathrow at eight. **1971** *Nature* 26 Nov. 181/2 Liquid-fueled rockets ..could not be kept in the launching tower in a 'hold' status to await a transient event.

14. *Cinemat.* (See quots.)

1918 H. Croy *How Motion Pictures are Made* vii. 179 If the story demands instantaneous materialization the effect is secured by a photographic means usually known as 'the hold'. It is so called by reason of the fact that all the other characters in such a scene must hold their positions while the trick character is made to materialize. **1940** *Chambers's Techn. Dict.* 418/2 *Hold*, the retention of an image on a screen longer than is natural.

hold-all. Add: **2.** *fig.*, esp. with reference to books of the omnibus or encyclopædic kind.

1903 *Daily Chron.* 9 Nov. 3/3 There is a little of everything in the hold-all. **1904** M. Davies (*title*) The housewife's what's what: a hold-all of useful information for the house. **1964** [see *ceteris paribus].

hold-back. Add: **2.** (Earlier example.)

1850 *N.H. Hist. Soc. Coll.* VI. 220 The hold-backs of his harness gave way, and precipitated his gig upon the horse.

3. The act of holding back. Also *attrib.*, unprogressive.

1852 *Trans. Mich. Agric. Soc.* III. 333 A few specimens of the hold-back and stand-still class. **1888** 'Buffalo Bill' *Story of Wild West* 627 There was no brake on the wagon, and the horses were not much on the hold back.

ho·ld-down. [f. phr. *hold down* (Hold *v.* 35).] **1.** A device to prevent material or apparatus from shifting or shaking. Also *attrib.*

1888 *Lockwood's Dict. Mech. Engin., Foundation Bolts.* ..Also termed hold-down bolts. **1962** J. Glenn in *Into Orbit* 188 Then the big hold-down clamps dropped away and I could feel us start to go. **1967** Karch & Buber *Offset Processes* x. 465 Set the rear pile hold-down..to hold the rear edge of the sheet to the pile.

2. A judo grip.

1954 E. Dominy *Teach yourself Judo* iii. 39 In judo contests, there are three recognised methods of obtaining a point. The first is by means of a clean throw, the second by means of a 'Hold Down'. **1956** K. Masuda tr. *Tomiki's Judo* iii. 91 In the practice of grappling, hold-downs, strangle-holds and bone-locks are connected with one another like the three sides of a triangle, the hold-downs being the base.

holder[1]**.** Add: **2.** Also, a shareholder.

1848 J. J. Ruskin *Let.* 22 Mar. in M. Lutyens *Effie in Venice* (1965) i. 17 A person of very sound Judgement on Railroad Shares...To Holders he says—if they have no other means of meeting Calls—sell.

b. *Sports.* The possessor for the time (as the winner) of a championship, cup, etc. which is open to competition.

1830 *Sporting Mag.* 2nd Ser. I. 337/1 The holder [of the sculls] shall row the best, or only, challenger, on the 10th of August. **1873** *Football Ann.* 54 Association Challenge Cup, 1872–73... Final Tie. Wanderers (holders) beat Oxford Association by two goals..to none. **1887** *Athletic Jrnl.* 9 Aug. 16 West Manchester (the winners and present holders of the Manchester Cup). **1900** *Field* 7 July 3/3 Hants County Public School Challenge Shield... This annual competition was held on the playgrounds of the holders, Churcher's College, Petersfield, on Thursday in last week. *Ibid.* 14 July 61/1 The holder of the challenge cup, Wadsley, was quite unable to do himself justice. **1928** *Daily Mail* 25 July 14/7 Middlesex, the holders, are..the only county to have won two matches in this group. **1955** *Times* 16 June 3/2 The effect on the players was clearly seen when L. Hoad, the holder, beat R. Bedard.

3. (Further examples.)

1846 R. Ford *Gatherings from Spain* xxiv. 338 A Spanish fore-finger and thumb are quite fire-browned and fire-proof, although some polished exquisites use silver holders. **1916** E. F. Benson *David Blaize* vi. 111 A magnificent present of twenty-five cigarettes and a cherry-wood holder. **1957** J. Osborne *Entertainer* 16 He unwraps the cigarettes and takes out an ivory holder from his waistcoat.

holderbat (hōu·ldəɹbæt). [f. Holder[1] + Bat *sb.*[2]] A type of bracket for fastening a pipe to a wall or other surface, consisting of two semicircular parts that are clamped round the pipe and a projection on one of the parts that is built into the wall.

1914 Sage & Fretwell *Text-bk. Elem. Building Constr.* xi. 225 The best method, however, is to dispense with ears and use 'holderbats' built into the wall. **1955** N. W. Kay *Mod. Building Encycl.* 331/2 The holderbat has two portions, a circular ring, with a jointed or removable portion,.. and a tail which is cemented into the wall.

holdfast, *sb.* Add: **4. b.** *Bot.* An organ for superficial attachment developed by some algæ and fungi.

1841 W. H. Harvey *Man. Brit. Algæ* p. xiv, Most Algæ are, at some period of their growth, found attached to other substances by means of a root, or at least a hold-fast. **1895** G. Murray *Introd. Study Seaweeds* 23 The sculpturing of outward form reaches its highest point in the differentiation..of a root-like holdfast. **1902** *Science* Jan. 59/2 Kelp hold-fasts, of which none grow in the immediate vicinity, were taken in abundance by the dredge. **1930** H. M. Fitzpatrick *Lower Fungi: Phycomycetes* iii. 45 In the typical epibiotic species (Rhizidiaceæ) the germ tube of the cytospore acts as a holdfast. **1931** L. Newton *Handbk. Brit. Seaweeds* p. vi, One of the main factors affecting the distribution of algæ is the securing of a suitable holdfast. **1962** C. J. Alexopoulos *Introd. Mycol.* (ed. 2) x. 213 The basal part of the hypha [of members of the order Eccrinales] is in the form of a disc-like holdfast by means of which the fungus is attached to the host. **1966** F. H. Brightman *Oxf. Bk. Flowerless Plants* 6/2 The holdfast is disc-shaped, but root-like structures also develop from the base of the stalk. **1971** *Where* July 202/2 They are the lovely coloured seaweeds or algae, with their interestingly-named parts: the 'holdfast' which forms the root, and the 'thallus' or fronds which make up the body.

holding, *vbl. sb.* Add: **1. d.** *holding up* (see quot. 1888).

1888 *Lockwood's Dict. Mech. Engin.* 178 *Holding up*, the maintaining of a firm pressure against the heads of rivets while their closing up is being effected, a holding-up hammer being used for the purpose. **1908** J. G. Horner *Plating & Boiler-making* (ed. 2) xii. 214 Holding-up dollies were shown in Figs. 56 and 57... In girder work a rig-up like that shown in Fig. 235 is used. It consists of a heavy holding-up hammer A, on the end of a long elastic handle B.

e. *Association Football.* The obstruction of a player by taking hold of his jersey, etc.

1866 *Cassell's Illustr. Fam. Paper* 17 Mar. 509/2 'Holding' includes the obstruction of a player by the hands, arms, or body without kicking or throwing. **1967** *Association Football* ('Know the Game' Series) 33 Should the obstruction take the form of a personal foul, e.g., pushing, holding, charging unfairly or tripping, then the foul is penalised by a direct free kick.

3. c. The cards held by a player.

1929 M. C. Work *Compl. Contract Bridge* iv. 38 With such holdings..the rebid should be made. **1959** *Listener* 10 Dec. 1054/2 The high card holding is weak.

6. b. holding ground (later example); (*b*) a site for storing floating timber; **holding operation**, an undertaking which prevents a

situation from worsening, but can do little or nothing to improve it; **holding paddock** *Austral.* and *N.Z.*, a paddock where sheep or cattle are kept until required (for droving, shearing, etc.); similarly **holding pen, yard.**

1957 *Brit. Commonw. Forest Terminol.* 2 *Holding ground*, a boom site for storing timber. **1961** F. H. BURGESS *Dict. Sailing* 116 *Holding ground*, the nature of the bottom and its holding quality for purposes of anchoring. **1962** *Listener* 8 Mar. 400/1 Whether it [*sc.* a White Paper] will achieve its immediate object of persuading the unions to help the economy over its next stile by holding down labour costs, we must wait and see... As a holding operation it may win some success. **1972** *Guardian* 9 Sept. 13/8 Mr Jenkins's last-minute scramble to satisfy the TUC..was only a holding operation to keep him sweet with Congress. **1933** L. G. D. ACLAND in *Press* (Christchurch) 28 Oct. 17/7 *Holding paddock*, a small paddock, close to yards, wool-shed, or mustering hut, for holding (not feeding) sheep. **1934** *Bulletin* (Sydney) 16 May 38/4 At midday the cattle, mad with thirst, broke out of the holding paddock and vanished in a wild stampede over a high hillcrest into the vast unfenced wilderness of the hills beyond. **1941** *Coast to Coast 1941* 22 Wiggins said some steers had got out of his holding paddocks. **1950** *N.Z. Jrnl. Agric.* Oct. 35 Cattle in a holding paddock before being drafted. **1923** *Ibid.* 20 Mar. 144 The holding-pens in the shed..should never be too large. **1965** J. S. GUNN *Terminol. Shearing Industry* I. 32 *Holding pen*, one of the small pens or yards in which sheep are held, usually within the shed, under shelter, while awaiting shearing. **1950** *N.Z. Jrnl. Agric.* Apr. 377/2 For handling large herds [of cows] a crush yard is recommended, with the main holding yard either in front or at one side. **1959** *Listener* 15 Jan. 115/1 There were some good holding yards where we could put the cattle for the night.

c. *Aeronaut.* Used *attrib.*, of or pertaining to the process of 'stacking' aircraft in the air above a landing site before they come down to land.

1948 *Shell Aviation News* No. 116. 19/3 Holding procedures as an integral part of the traffic control system for jet transports should be completely eliminated. **1958** *Chambers's Techn. Dict.* 985/1 *Holding pattern*, a specified flight track..which an aircraft may be required to maintain about a holding point. *Holding point*, an identifiable point, such as a radio beacon, in the vicinity of which an aircraft under air traffic control may be instructed to remain. **1969** *Daily Tel.* 14 Nov. 1/7 Stacking over a 'holding area' while waiting a turn to land, is not uncommon, especially in poor weather conditions. **1972** *New Yorker* 16 Sept. 26/1 He turned on the plane's radio, in order to hear the traffic controller at the..airport talking to several airliners stacked in a holding pattern overhead.

holding, *ppl. a.* Add: **1.** (Later examples.)

1930 *Daily Express* 6 Nov. 16/1 The keen east wind dried up the course, which was inclined to be on the holding side. **1955** *Times* 19 May 4/4 In August last year the going was extremely holding.

b. *holding company*: a trading company which possesses the whole of, or a controlling interest in, the share capital of one or more other companies.

1906 *Daily Colonist* (Victoria, B.C.) 18 Jan. 1/5 A bill to prohibit 'holding companies' such as have lately effected the merger of various corporations..was introduced in the legislature today. **1912** *Q. Rev.* Jan. 195 The Federal Steel Company, which is technically, like the Steel Corporation of to-day, a holding company. **1928** *Britain's Industr. Future* (*Liberal Ind. Inq.*) II. viii. 93 To treat trusts, cartels, combinations, holding companies, and trade associations as inexpedient abnormalities in the economic system. **1928** *Daily Mail* 7 Aug. 18/4 This conservative finance enables the Shell, as a holding company,..to maintain its dividends in times of depression. **1930** A. PALMER *Company Secretarial Pract.* xix. 255 The Act does not specifically define a holding company, but refers to it as a company holding shares, either directly or through a nominee, in a subsidiary company. **1958** *Times* 11 Aug. 11/2 Mrs. Roebling..is director or trustee of more than 16 organizations and president of a holding company. **1972** 'E. LATHEN' *Murder without Icing* (1973) xv. 131 Holland's other assets could take a long time to find. He's got everything wrapped up in holding companies.

3. *holding-down bolt, pin, ring.*

1846 *Patent Jrnl.* I. 226/2 On each side of the holding down bolts..an upright pillar is erected. *a* **1877** KNIGHT *Dict. Mech.* II. 1112/2 *Holding-down Bolt*,..one of twelve or more strong bolts, which are passed from the outside of a steam-vessel through the floor-timbers, sleepers, foundation-plate of the engine, and the bosses on the cylinders, condensers, and side-frames, and are secured by strong nuts. **1892** W. W. GREENER *Breech-Loader* 19 Every gun provided with a holding-down bolt. *Ibid.* 260 Certain accessories.., such as cords, planks, and holding-down pins. **1899–1900** *Kynoch Jrnl.* Dec.–Jan. 29/2 The cones are secured to ships' decks by holding-down rings. **1930** *Engineering* 4 Apr. 440/2 Checking parts for fit and tightening holding-down and other bolts.

holdless (hōᵘ·ldlės), *a. Mountaineering.* [f. HOLD *sb.*[1] + -LESS.] Affording no holds; having a smooth unbroken surface.

1922 E. R. EDDISON *Worm Ouroboros* xiii. 184 Cliffs smooth and holdless as a castle wall. **1933** [see *ABSEIL]. **1971** *Country Life* 25 Feb. 410/1 Alastair solved problem after problem..making short work finally of the hardest obstacle, an awkward holdless entry to a chimney at the start of the last tower.

hold-out. Add: **b.** The act of holding out; something that or someone who holds out; *spec.* (chiefly *U.S.*) a player, usu. in baseball, who refuses to play until he is promised higher pay.

1945 *Sun* (Baltimore) 17 Feb. 7/7 This is another year when any baseball holdouts will do their shouting in whispers. *Ibid.* (*heading*) Holdout is weapon. **1952** B. MALAMUD *Natural* (1963) 22 He was a holdout for $75,000 and was coming East to squeeze it out of his boss. **1964** *Amer. Speech* XXXIX. 91 Occasionally there was a hold-out, as in this lamentation: [etc.]. **1970** *Globe & Mail* (Toronto) 26 Sept. 35/1 Whatever became of another well-known holdout, Joe Kapp?..Kapp keeps waiting for the Minnesota Vikings to pay him more money.

c. Of paint or ink (see quot. 1965).

1965 *Gloss. Paint Terms* (*B.S.I.*) 32 *Hold out*, the ability of a paint film to dry to its normal finish on a somewhat absorptive surface. **1971** *Timber Trades Jrnl.* 21 Aug. 29/1 Golden Royal hardboard..was already accepted as a good painting medium, but application of a seal..meant that..certain properties, including paint hold-out, workability and strength, were improved. **1972** *Publishers Weekly* 4 Dec. 11 (Advt.), Its unique combination of high ink hold-out, high brightness, and high opacity.

hold-over. Add: **d.** Something left over; a remainder or survival. *U.S.*

1904 *Los Angeles Express* 11 Aug. 12 Doing the best it could on crackers and cheese and holdovers. **1909** 'O. HENRY' *Roads of Destiny* iv. 58 She was a hold-over from the Greek classics. **1929** *Atlantic Monthly* Mar. 298 The little village of Washington in Connecticut, one of the most charming holdovers of the past that state possesses. **1951** E. PAUL *Springtime in Paris* iii. 53 Like several other articles, it seemed to be a holdover from the previous tenant. **1969** *Times* 6 Mar. 23/1 Both the present assistant secretaries for international affairs in the Treasury..are Johnson hold-overs.

hold-up. (No longer restricted to *U.S. slang.*) Add: **b.** (Earlier and later examples.)

1878 F. M. A. ROE *Army Lett.* (1909) 206 The driver is their only protector, and the stage route is through miles and miles of wild forest, and in between huge boulders where a 'hold-up' could be so easily accomplished. **1904** *Daily Chron.* 23 Dec. 4/5 There are epidemics of robberies, murders and hold-ups in all the large cities. **1928** *Daily Express* 15 June 7/5 The 'hold-up' of a steamer crowded with holiday-makers on Lake Windermere. **1968** *Globe & Mail* (Toronto) 17 Feb. 2/2 Police said they had recovered $3,991 from yesterday's holdup.

c. A stoppage or check in the passage or progress of a person or thing; a temporary stoppage of traffic; a cessation, stop. orig. *U.S.*

1837 *Knickerbocker* X. 439 The wheels of the coach are shod with the preparation of iron slippers, which are essential to a hold-up. **1882** in G. H. Putnam *Mem. Publisher* (1915) 289 We don't have hold-ups [*sc.* strikes] in Leadville. **1904** *N.Y. Tribune* 15 May 2 A vote of thanks to the Tribune for its efforts to end the hold-up of the Port Chester Railroad's application for a permit to cross streets in the Bronx. **1907** *Putnam's Monthly* July 482/1 He cursed the luck of the hold-up. **1913** A. B. EMERSON *R. Fielding at Snow Camp* 154 We got to sit down and wait for a hold-up [of the storm]. **1918** 'Q' *Foe-Farrell* vii. 125 There was a hold-up as we [in a taxi] neared the bridge. **1928** *Daily Express* 14 July 2/1 There had been two or three hold-ups with the points prior to my arrival at 4.50 p.m. **1964** *Ann. Reg. 1963* 224 In connexion with the various hold-ups of Allied military convoys on the autobahn..it was recalled that the D.D.R. had only temporarily handed over control of military traffic to the Soviet military. **1973** 'H. CARMICHAEL' *Too Late for Tears* xi. 131, I nearly didn't get here. Ran into a traffic hold-up and was stuck. **1973** E. LEMARCHAND *Let or Hindrance* viii. 93 The hold-up over the Fortnight film while Paul King finished editing the last part.

d. An instance of extortion. Chiefly *U.S.*

1908 L. MITCHELL *New York Idea* I. 15 The people insisted on electing a desperado to the presidential office—they must take the hold-up that follows. **1910** *Sat. Even. Post* 27 Aug. 6/3 Our house..cost twenty-five thousand dollars, exclusive of the plumber's little hold-up and the Oriental rugs. **1939** J. MULGAN *Man Alone* i. 14 It never was farming land. It's a hold-up, and God help the poor bastards who have to take it at that price.

e. *Bridge.* (See quot. 1959.) Cf. HOLD *v.* 44 d.

1945 PHILLIPS & REESE *How to play Bridge* III. 101 The principal device available to the declarer to prevent the establishment of an opponent's long suit is hold-up play. **1959** REESE & DORMER *Bridge Player's Dict.* 113 *Hold-up play.* A player is said to hold up when for tactical reasons he declines to play a winning card. Usually, his object is to destroy communication between the enemy hands, but there can be other and more subtle reasons for the hold-up. **1962** *Listener* 22 Mar. 534/1 This uncommon hold-up play will prevent the defence from bringing in the suit unless North has two entries.

f. (See quot.)

1945 H. D. SMYTH *Gen. Acct. Devel. Atomic Energy Mil. Purposes* ix. 94 The total amount of material tied up in a separation plant is called a 'hold-up'. The hold-up may be very large in a plant consisting of many stages.

2. *attrib.* = Engaged in, involving, or characterized by forcible stopping and robbing of a person.

1881 E. W. NYE *B. Nye & Boomerang* 192, I did give him the grand bounce, and now he hath joined a hold-up outfit on the overland stage route. **1899** *Chicago Tribune* 16 Jan., The holdup gang who shot and killed policeman.. Wallner. **1930** [see *BAIL *v.*[3] 3]. **1959** *Times Lit. Suppl.* 20 Feb. 93/3 Unfortunately the stranger is not only a 'goy' and a drifter but he has been worse—a hold-up man, one of whose victims was once the grocer himself.

hole, *sb.* **2. b.** Delete *Obs.* and add later examples. Now usu. the cell used for solitary confinement, and hence solitary confinement itself.

1912 D. LOWRIE *My Life in Prison* iv. 39 'It's a case of spending the night at the springs if you're not at your cell for the count.' In answer to my hurried inquiry about 'the springs' he informed me that he referred to 'the hole'. **1964** *Amer. Speech* II. 282/1 *Hole*, dungeon or place for solitary confinement. **1935** N. ERSINE *Underworld & Prison Slang* 45 *Hole*,..the solitary confinement cells of a prison. 'Smitty just got tossed in the *hole*.' **1955** W. GADDIS *Recognitions* II. v. 488 He had..spent a fair amount of time in solitary confinement ('the hole', as it was called). **1970** G. JACKSON *Let.* 25 Mar. in *Soledad Brother* (1971) 197 They're out of the hole (isolation) already.

d. A shilling. *slang.*

1934 P. ALLINGHAM *Cheapjack* iv. 38 A penny is a 'clod', and 'sprasy' means sixpence. A shilling is also a 'hole', and a two-shilling piece is a 'two-ender'. **1939** [see *BAR *sb.*[1] 3 c].

3. (Later examples.)

1925 WODEHOUSE *Carry on, Jeeves!* iv. 81 'Mr Bickersteth is in a hole, Jeeves,..and wants you to rally round.' 'Very good, sir.' **1937** A. CHRISTIE *Murder in Mews* 218 Lawyers, even the most respectable, have been known to embezzle their client's money when they themselves are in a hole. **1970** G. F. NEWMAN *Sir, You Bastard* v. 154 Too bad if he has, I'll be in a great big hole.

4. a. *spec.* One of the (usu. nine or eighteen) strips of land on a golf-course, consisting of a tee, fairway (and bordering rough), green and hole (sense 4 a), over which a golfer plays his ball; the play which takes place between teeing off and holing the ball; *hole in one*, the driving of the ball from the tee into the hole with only one stroke. Also *fig.*

1874 J. BLACKWOOD *Let.* 4 Aug. in Geo. Eliot *Lett.* (1956) VI. 74 When we were a few holes out he exclaimed fervently, 'This is a great, glorious, and noble game.' **1887** J. L. STEWART *Golfiana Miscellanea* 100 The hole is won by the side holing at fewest strokes. **1891** H. G. HUTCHINSON *Famous Golf Links* 90 Point Garry is a long, hazardous hole. *Ibid.* 156 The third hole (135 yards) is an exact counterpart of the second. **1893** BARRIE & CONAN DOYLE *Jane Annie* II. 41, I give in! You have my word of honour! It's your hole. **1908** J. BRAID *Advanced Golf* 252 Holes of about 360 to 380 yards. **1935** GRAVES & LONGHURST *Candid Caddies* 28 There are all kinds of variants on the 'hole in one' story where the player has achieved this feat with a club other than the one selected by the caddie. **1971** *Daily Tel.* 12 June 1/5 (*heading*) Golfer gets two holes in one. *Ibid.*, Successive holes in one have been done only twice before in Britain. **1972** I. STUART *Golf in Hertfordshire* 67 There are six par-three holes, all of them fair and only one over 200 yards. **1973** *Country Life* 17 May 1369/3 The final rounds of a 72-hole event.

d. *Chess.* (See quots.)

1894 J. MASON *Princ. Chess* i. 24 *Hole*, a square on the third or fourth rank, neither commanded, nor liable to be commanded, by any friendly Pawn. **1895** H. E. BIRD *Chess Novelties* 115 KBP was followed by QP2, leaving at once a landing square (a nasty hole Steinitz would call it) for opponent's pieces. **1922** *Brit. Chess Mag.* Feb. 105/2 The net result of the two moves is to create a hole at White's Q Kt 4. **1955** *Chess* ('Know the Game' Series) 26/1 Another example of weakness in the pawn-formation is that of 'holes' or 'fore-posts' which may be occupied successfully by an opposing piece. **1968** O. HINDLE *Further Steps in Chess* iv. 49 Holes..are squares which the defender can no longer protect with his pawns. They are thus ideal posts for attacking pieces, which can settle on them without fear of being easily driven off.

e. *Eton Fives.* A small square portion of the floor enclosed by the pepper-box and step. Phr. *to be in holes*; hence *attrib.* in *holes innings*.

1897 *Encycl. Sport.* I 399 A, who begins serving, is bound to give C—who is said to be 'in holes'—the sort of service which he prefers. *Ibid.* 400 All alike differ from Eton Courts in having no pepper-box, hole, or step. *Ibid.* 402 In the first innings of a game A (who goes in first) is said to have 'holes innings', *i.e.*, when both A and B have been put out, A will be 'in holes'.

f. *Physics.* A position from which an electron is absent: orig. a concept in the theory of the positron, now esp. a position in a semiconductor which may be regarded as a mobile carrier of a positive charge. Also *attrib.* and *Comb.*

1930 P. A. M. DIRAC in *Proc. R. Soc.* A. CXXVI. 362 Only the small departures from exact uniformity, brought about by some of the negative-energy states being unoccupied, can we hope to observe. Let us examine the properties of the vacant states or 'holes'. **1933** *Ibid.* CXXXIX. 714 The few states which are unoccupied behave like ordinary particles with positive kinetic energy and with a positive charge. Dirac originally wished to identify these 'holes' with protons, but this had to be abandoned when it was found that the holes necessarily have the same mass as negative electrons. **1934** P. A. M. DIRAC in *Proc. Cambr. Phil. Soc.* XXX. 150 Any unoccupied negative-energy states would be observable to us, as holes in the distribution of negative-energy electrons, but these holes would appear as particles with positive kinetic energy... It seems reasonable..to identify these holes with the recently discovered positrons. **1936** W. HEITLER *Quantum Theory of Radiation* 188 Thus.. positive electrons are represented as holes in the distribution of electrons filling up the negative energy states. **1940** *Nature* 29 June 998/2 It is suggested..that in cuprous oxide the vacant lattice points and the points from which an electron is missing (positive holes) are dissociated. **1948** *Physical Rev.* LXXIV. 230/2 As a result, the current in the forward direction with respect to the block is composed in large part of holes, i.e., of carriers of sign opposite to those normally in excess in the body of the block. **1949**

[see *ACCEPTOR 3]. **1954** *Electronic Engin.* XXVI. 34 Positive charge carriers known as 'holes'.. These holes are thought to have different mean life-times and mobilities in different diodes. **1957** *Ibid.* XXIX. 3 As all transistors have a finite base width all transistors must show hole storage effects due to the time taken for holes to cross the base from emitter to collector. **1962** SIMPSON & RICHARDS *Junction Transistors* ii. 32 Also, because impurities or defects that trap electrons may have characteristics quite different from those of their hole-trapping counterparts, the lifetime of minority carriers may be quite different in *p*-type and *n*-type materials of similar quality. **1966** *New Scientist* 11 Aug. 317/3 Travel is limited to the distance covered before electron and hole annihilate one another.

7. b. *hole in the wall*, (an originally disparaging term for) any small, obscure place; *spec.* in the U.S., a place where alcoholic drinks are sold illegally. Applied, esp. *attrib.*, to a business that is very small, mean, dingy, or the like, or to a person running such a business.

1822 W. HAZLITT in *New Monthly Mag.* IV. 102, I had heard Mr. James Simpkins.. when the character of the *Hole in the Wall* was brought in question, observe—'The house is a very good house, and the company quite genteel.' **1856** *Iroquois Republican* (Middleport, Ill.) 25 Dec. 2/3 A 'grocery'—a 'doggery'—a 'hole-in-the-wall' —is an 'odious damned spot' in any community. **1870** DICKENS *E. Drood* xviii. 142 The Gate House, of which.. the Verger's hole in the wall was an appanage or subsidiary part. **1887** *Minnesota Gen. Statutes Suppl.* (1888) 248 Whoever shall attempt to evade or violate any of the laws of this state.. by means of the artifice or contrivance known as the 'Blind Pig', or 'Hole in the Wall'.. shall.. be punished. **1896** C. H. SHINN *Story of the Mine* 51 Many lived in 'dug-outs', which they called 'holes in the wall'. **1919** *Detective Story Mag.* 25 Nov. 129 He breakfasted at a hole-in-the-wall lunch room before starting out on his quest. **1923** D. SELLS *Brit. Trade Boards System* iv. ii. 259 The emphasis which reputable employers lay upon the benefit of Trade Boards in eliminating the 'hole in the wall' employer.. from the field of industry, can hardly be overstated. **1940** F. RIESENBERG *Golden Gate* 212 Craft that could go into the 'hole in the wall' along the ragged Pacific Coast. **1945** E. S. GARDNER *Case of Gold-Digger's Purse* (1948) xiii. 153 It's just a little place—just a little lunch counter. Sort of a hole in the wall. **1945** 'L. LEWIS' *Birthday Murder* (1951) iii. 37 Sawn scorned.. decadent play spots of the economically fortunate, and would insist on going to a hole in the wall infested by cockroaches, cocottes and cab drivers. **1951** C. W. MILLS *White Collar* I. ii. 30 The hole-in-the-wall business, also known as a Mom-and-Pop store. **1953** W. R. BURNETT *Vanity Row* viii. 60 A Bohemian section of the town.. dotted with little.. hole-in-the-wall cafés. **1958** *Time* 3 Feb. 23/1 To survive, most workers have to take second jobs, many of them in the innumerable hole-in-the-wall private enterprises that have sprung up. **1973** J. GOODFIELD *Courier to Peking* ix. 100 One of her favourite places was more a hole-in-the-wall than a shop.

c. *in holes*: perforated with holes, worn into holes.

1851 MAYHEW *London Labour* II. 470/2, I can't abide this muckydam [*sc.* macadam].. it's sloppy stuff, and goes so bad in holes. **1926** A. CHRISTIE *Murder R. Ackroyd* x. 127 He wouldn't even buy new face towels, though I told him the old ones were in holes.

d. Aeronautics. *hole in the air*: an old name for an *air-pocket* (*AIR *sb.*[1] III. 1).

1911 G. C. LOENING *Monoplanes & Biplanes* xiv. 305 The air is very variable, and even on a relatively calm day there are likely to be 'holes in the air'. **1916** H. BARBER *Aeroplane Speaks* 51 Now the Aeroplane is almost over the river, and the next instant it suddenly drops into a 'hole in the air'. **1917** C. C. TURNER *Aircraft of To-day* vi. 98 The terms 'air-pocket' and 'hole in the air' are frequently heard in flying circles.

e. colloq. *hole in* (*the*) *heart*: a congenital malformation of the heart in which there is an abnormal communication between the right and left sides.

1958 *Hammersmith Post* 25 July 1/4 (*heading*) Mother reassured over 'hole in heart' operation. *Ibid.*, A seven-year-old boy.. is due to have a 'hole in heart' operation. **1959** *Times Lit. Suppl.* 25 Sept. 549/5 The author describes the operation for a septal defect—the condition popularly known as a 'hole in the heart'. **1961** *Listener* 2 Nov. 693/1 The oxygenator took over the duties of heart and lung in the 'hole-in-the-heart' operation. **1966** *Guardian* 17 May 3/4 Oxygen 15.. is being used.. for the diagnosis of the hole-in-the-heart condition.

8. *spec.* (*slang*) The mouth, the anus, or the female external genital organs. (Add further examples.)

1592 SHAKES. *Rom. & Jul.* II. iv 94 This driveling Love is like a great Naturall, that runs lolling vp and downe to hid his bable in a hole. **1719** D'URFEY *Pills* IV. 72 It has a Head much like a Mole's, And yet it loves to creep in Holes: The Fairest She that e'er took Life, For love of this, became a Wife. *c* **1744** in *Oxf. Dict. Nursery Rhymes* (1951) 372 Little Robin red breast, Sitting on a pole, Niddle, Noddle, Went his head, And Poop went his Hole. **1922** JOYCE *Ulysses* 748 My hole is itching me. **1959** I. & P. OPIE *Lore & Lang. Schoolch.* iii. 49 Habitual grumblers in London's East End receive the poetic injunction: 'Oo, shut yer moanin' 'ole'. **1966** L. COHEN *Beautiful Losers* (1970) I. 9 Don't give me this all diamond shit, shove it up your occult hole.

11. Phrases. *to put in the hole* (slang): to swindle, defraud; *to make a hole in the water*: see WATER *sb.* 6 f; *to be in the hole* U.S.: to be in (usu. financial) difficulties (cf. 3); *a hole in the head*, esp. in phr. *to need* (*something*) *like a hole in the head* (cf. Yiddish *ich darf es vi a loch in kop*): applied to something not desired at all or something useless.

1812 J. H. VAUX *Vocab. Flash Lang.* in *Mem.* (1964) 243 *To put a person in the hole*, to defraud him of his due share of the booty by embezzling a part of the property, or the money, it is fenced for; this phrase also applies generally to defrauding anyone with whom you are confidentially connected of what is justly his due. **1833** *Session Papers* 3 Jan. 115/1 Miller.. said they had *put him in the hole*, and he.. would say where they were; by *putting him in the hole*, I understand they did not take the property away as he expected. **1890** *Centralia* (Wash.) *Chron.* 18 Sept. 3/2 His failure leaves a number of our local dealers in the hole for amounts ranging from $200 down. **1893** L. W. MOORE *His Own Story* xxi. 293 What was said at that time about his being 'put in the hole', I cannot say; but I do know he held me blameless, for none of the funds, except my own share, was ever in my possession. **1897** *Boston Jrnl.* 12 Mar. 10/1 The sporting-man was $40 in the hole. **1916** *Lit. Digest* 8 Jan. 87/1 The Wards were in the hole to the extent of close to $800,000. **1926** J. BLACK *You can't Win* ix. 104, I thought you put me in the hole for some coin, but I found out that the people lost just what you both said. **1939** WODEHOUSE *Uncle Fred in Springtime* iii. 45 How in the world did you manage to get in the hole for a sum like that? **1951** in M. McLuhan *Mech. Bride* 29/2 A smart operator needs a dame like he needs a hole in the head. **1951** J. D. SALINGER *Catcher in Rye* xiv. 91 The Disciples.. were about as much use to Him as a hole in the head. **1955** W. GADDIS *Recognitions* I. iii. 101, I need this drink like I need a hole in the head. **1971** D. CREED *Trial of Lobo Icheka* xiii. 133 He needed Petersen about as much as he needed a hole in the head.

12. *hole-punched*, *-puncher*; **hole-card,** in stud poker, a card which has been dealt face down; also *fig.*; **hole-high** *a.* (see quots.); **hole-mouth(ed)** *Archæol.*, said of pottery vessels without a neck; **hole-nester,** a bird that nests in a hole; so **hole-nesting** *ppl. a.*; **hole-proof** *a.*, that will not wear into holes; **hole saw** = *crown-saw* (CROWN *sb.* 35).

1908 *Sat. Even. Post* 5 Dec. 19/2 Scarcely glancing at his hole card Phelps let him take the pot, and it became Phelps' deal. **1926** C. E. MULFORD *Bar 20 rides Again* xxi. 282 Beginnin' with this hand I'm bettin' five hundred blind on th' hole-card, an' seein' if I can't bring this game to a finish. **1952** J. STEINBECK *East of Eden* ix. 79 The preacher turned over his hole-card, the sure-fire card. **1971** J. BALL *First Team* (1972) xxiii. 353 We may be playing with a bust hand; we don't know if our hole card has been stolen or not. **1897** *Encycl. Sports* I. 472/2 A ball is said to be hole high when it is played on to the putting green from a distance. **1961** J. S. SALAK *Dict. Amer. Sports* 228 *Hole-high* (golf), a point even with the hole but to one side or the other. **1909** *Cent. Dict.* Suppl., Hole-mouthed vase. **1960** K. M. KENYON *Archæol. in Holy Land* v. 124 The type of jar, known as the hole-mouth jar, neckless with a simple in-curved rim, which was used for cooking and storage, may be as much as 3 feet in height. **1938** *Brit. Birds* XXXI. 242 In the present experiments three hole-nesting species.. were selected. *Ibid.* XXXII. 31 In similar experiments with another hole-nester.. the male attacked the male mount but.. ignored the female mount. **1953** N. TINBERGEN *Herring Gull's World* x. 94 Territory in the Herring Gull most certainly has nothing to do with the reservation of a nesting site.. as it has in hole-nesting birds. **1913** *Work* 17 May 102 A.. cloth that will not tear—in fact, is hole-proof. **1915** *Truth* LXXVIII. 848/1 Another customer tells me her experience in regard to some 'hole-proof' hose. **1962** *Economist* 2 June 897/1 Stockings.. to be ladder-proof, although not holeproof. **1956** S. BELLOW *Seize Day* (1957) ii. 42 He put the hole-punched cards in his pocket. **1961** *Lebende Sprachen* VI. 70/1 Hole puncher. **1961** WEBSTER, Hole saw. **1967** *Catal. Black & Decker Powertools*, A drill with power to spare... Will drive holesaws up to $1\frac{1}{2}''$ dia.

hole, *v.*[1] Add: **1. c.** To fire a bullet into.

1847 TROLLOPE *Macdermots* I. iv. 59 We'll hole him till there ar'nt a bit left in him to hole. *a* **1882** —— *Land-leaguers* (1883) I. ii. 34 Keep yourself from being holed as they holed Muster Bingham the other day.

6. b. *to hole* (*out*) *in one*: to achieve a 'hole in one' (see *HOLE *sb.* 4 a). Also *fig.*

1894 [see HOLE *v.*[1] 6 c]. **1928** D. L. SAYERS *Unpleasantness at Bellona Club* xii. 141 'I say we shall find a long scratch on the paint,' said Parker... 'Holed it in one, Charles.' **1939** 'N. BLAKE' *Smiler with Knife* iii. 49 'Oh, E.B. The E.B. printed on the flag we found in that locker?' 'Holed out in one.' **1971** *Daily Tel.* 12 June 1/5 John Hudson made golfing history in the Martini tournament.. yesterday, holing in one at successive holes.

7. *to hole up*: also, to seek shelter, to seek (temporary) quarters; (*b*) to lie in wait or in ambush, to hide (chiefly *U.S. slang*).

1875 J. BURROUGHS *Winter Sunshine* 279 Only five days was I compelled to 'hole up' in my state-room. **1910** MRS. H. WARD *Canadian Born* ix. 181 I'm a poor old broken-down.. miner, who wants to hole-up somewhere, and get comfortable for his old age. **1912** MULFORD & CLAY *Buck Peters* xxvii. 235 Go slow, Tex; mebby he's holin' up on us, like he did on Buck. **1924** C. E. MULFORD *Rustlers' Valley* xii. 141 Now you'll mebby have to take to th' hills an' hole up just when I need you most. **1925** —— *Cottonwood Gulch* xvi. 218 It would have been only a matter of a few minutes before they would have forced him to abandon the horse and to hole up on the defensive, to make a losing fight. **1929** FAULKNER *Sartoris* IV. 282 Hole up here, you potlickin' fool. **1929** D. HAMMETT *Red Harvest* xviii. 179 You'll have to.. take a plant on Willsson's.. I hear whisper Thaler's holing-up there. **1939** R. CHANDLER *Big Sleep* xxvii. 240 That's the place where she's holed up. **1951** S. LEWIS *World so Wide* xii. 135 We've got to begin thinking about holing up for the night. **1952** WODEHOUSE *Pigs have Wings* ix. 178 The poltergeist, for such he assumed it to be, appeared to have holed up behind the door that led presumably to the kitchen. **1954** 'N. BLAKE' *Whisper in Gloom* II. xiv. 194, I bet you Elmer's holed up in Harwich, or somewhere near it. **1961** G. GREENE *Burnt-Out Case* II. iii. 37 Who would expect to find *the* Querry holed up in a leproserie? **1973** D. JORDAN *Nile Green* xlv. 234 We were holed up in the flat, drinking Gold Star beer.

9. *trans.* To record by punching a hole in an allotted space in a card.

1911 *Chambers's Jrnl.* May 335/2 Not only are the old-time data, such as age,.. 'holed' into the card, but whether you are married or single. *Ibid.* 336/2 In this machine the data 'holed' in every tag can be all or partly recorded on another form.

holeable (hōᵘ·lăb'l), *a.* *Golf.* Also **holable.** [f. HOLE *v.*[1] + -ABLE.] Of a stroke, esp. a putt: capable of sending the ball into the hole.

1909 *Westm. Gaz.* 30 Apr. 12/2 On the green Taylor failed at a holable putt for 5. *Ibid.* 10 June 12/3 Four holeable putts which he missed. **1927** *Sunday Express* 29 May 21/7 The short eleventh was halved in three, both players missing holeable putts. **1955** *Times* 1 June 4/1 Pattinson missed only one putt that looked holeable and holed a good number that were missable.

Holi, var. HOOLEE.

1910 *Encycl. Brit.* XIII. 507/2 The *Holi*, the Indian Saturnalia in the month of Phālguṇa (February to March). **1921** E. M. FORSTER *Let.* 1 Apr. in *Hill of Devi* (1953) 58 My painted escort (they had been celebrating Holi) were all that is polite. **1958** *Listener* 13 Nov. 768/1 The great spring game of Holi that they play all over northern India. *Ibid.*, Holi used to be the loveliest of festivals. **1969** *Eve's Weekly* (Bombay) 20 Dec. 67/3 When I was a young girl every year brought Holi with its gay colours.

holiday, *sb.* Add: **2. e.** Euphemistically used for: imprisonment.

1901 *Pall Mall Mag.* Feb. 197 A sentence of a month or two.. a little 'holiday' with food and shelter and warmth.

4. a. *holiday centre, job, ramble, resort, tutor*(*ship*); **holiday camp,** an informally run camp for a holiday; now esp. a complex of chalets, places of entertainment, etc., designed for family holidays; **holiday course** [= G. *ferienkurs*, F. *cours de vacances*, etc.], a series of lectures, classes, etc. which is held during a school or college vacation; **holiday home,** (*a*) a place where poor persons, or children whose parents cannot take charge of them, can be accommodated, sometimes at little or no cost to themselves, for a period of holiday; (*b*) a house where people spend their holidays; **holiday task,** homework to be done during the holidays.

1870 R. ST. J. CORBET (*title*) The holiday camp: three days' picnic: story for boys and girls. **1927** *Cornh. Mag.* Feb. 225 Of the many thousands of children who were sent into the country.. 25% stayed for two weeks or more in the Holiday Camps. These Camps are an interesting feature of the Copenhagen holiday system. *Ibid.* 226 Life in a Holiday Camp is always the simplest, and is spent, so far as possible, in the open air. *Ibid.* 231 The Danes do not regard the Holiday Camp system as an ideal system. **1940** *Manch. Guardian Weekly* 1 Nov. 320/1 Then there were the Holiday Camps, cheap, social, with every modern convenience and all the modern pleasures. Their official hosts and hostesses mapped out the day with a colossal time-table of delights. **1949** M. DICKENS *Flowers on Grass* vii. 181 I've got to go to a holiday camp to do some sketches of happy campers for publicity. **1958** *Times* 8 Sept. 6/1 A steel cabinet in the security block at Butlin's holiday camp at Ayr was forced at the weekend. **1944** J. S. HUXLEY *On Living in Rev.* I. iii. 6 The elaborate system of rest-houses and holiday centres and the equally elaborate arrangements for holiday transport. **1966** *Economist* 17 Sept. 1143/2 Very soon now a vast new 'holiday centre' will open in Aviemore itself, containing both accommodation of all kinds and prices and entertainments of a similarly wide variety. **1906** *Teacher* 30 June 616/3 The Greifswald Holiday Course.. the oldest of the German holiday courses.. has now been in existence for fifteen years. **1887** *Girl's Own Paper* 22 Oct. 48/3 A lady who has a large house and grounds would give a lady of small means a 'holiday home'. **1931** *Geography* Sept. 219 The hostel.. is more akin to the 'dak-bungalow' or the 'cold harbour' than to the rest-camp or holiday-home. **1937** *Discovery* June p. xlvi/2 (Advt.), Schools, coaching colleges, holiday homes. **1972** *Guardian* 1 Sept. 8/6 The 'white settlers' who buy croft houses for use as holiday homes. **1973** *Ibid.* 28 May 4/1 The Welsh Language Society is planning.. to try to prevent the sale of houses as second or holiday homes. **1866** 'MARK TWAIN' *Lett. fr. Hawaii* (1967) 91 In Honolulu it is not a holiday job to ship a crew. **1969** *Times* 14 June 18/4 (Advt.), Holiday job wanted.. by 6th form girl. **1854** SHERWOOD & KELLY *Boys will be Boys* ii. 31 That part of the country.. within the nearer reach of a holiday ramble. **1936** *Discovery* Sept. 263/1 A famous holiday-resort has been selected [as a meeting-place for the British Association]. **1827** J. LEECH *Let.* in W. P. Frith *John Leech* (1891) I. i. 12, I think I shall get promoted when Dr Russell sees my Holiday Task. **1899** KIPLING *Stalky & Co.* 180 They have a holiday task.. which.. none.. will ever look at. **1912** E. W. HORNUNG *Fathers of Men* xi. 130 So they give you saying-lessons for holiday tasks at your school? *Ibid.* xii. 137 He'd no right to set us a holiday task of his own like that. **1930** C. MACKENZIE *April Fools* vii. 138 I'm reading 'Homes without Hands' for a holiday task. **1900** *Captain* II. 375/1 When Mr. Soames asked the professor to come and be holiday tutor. *Ibid.*, Open to take a holiday tutorship.

b. *holiday-maker* (earlier example), *-making* (examples).

1792 W. B. STEVENS *Jrnl.* 27 May (1965) 24 Set out in the afternoon, holiday-making to Birmingham. **1836** DICKENS *Sk. 'Boz'* I. 323 The four clowns..may be all very well for the low-minded holiday makers. **1855** GEO. ELIOT in *Fraser's Mag.* LII. 60/1 The good people who come to take dinner..here, by way of holiday making. **1969** *Daily Tel.* 4 Jan. 18/6 There is one valuable holiday-making aid to the Gulf and the Bay of Naples.

holier-than-thou: see *HOLY *a.* 5 c.

holiness. Add: **4. b.** Used *attrib.* (usu. with capital initial) to denote any of various religious sects which emphasize sanctification, spiritual purity, and perfectionism, or members, churches, etc., of any of these sects. orig. and chiefly *U.S.*

1888 *California State Gaz.* 623/2 Pasadena..contains Methodist, Baptist,..Friends, and Holiness churches. **1913** H. KEPHART *Our Southern Highlanders* 271 In our day the same may be said of the Holy Rollers and Holiness People. **1928** *Amer. Mercury* Oct. 185/1 This..was first preached by the Straight Holiness sect in Kansas in the 1890's. **1940** J. B. HOLT in *Amer. Sociol. Rev.* V. 740 (*title*) Holiness religion: cultural shock and social reorganisation. **1947** J. WACH *Sociol. Relig.* II. v. 189 The Methodist and the Holiness movements are especially concerned with ethical perfection. **1957** J. M. YINGER *Relig., Soc. & Individual* I. x. 282 Any description of religious trends in the United States that did not refer to the strength of the 'holiness' sects..would be incomplete. **1958** M. ARGYLE *Relig. Behaviour* iv. 33 Many of these sects—the Pentecostal, Holiness, Nazarene churches and others—have increased enormously in proportion to their size during this period [*sc.* 1926–1953]. **1961** B. R. WILSON *Sects & Soc.* I. v. 98 Elim is in no way as extreme as some of the Holiness cults of Tennessee and North Carolina. *Ibid.* 105 In Britain it began..in such organisations as the Faith Mission, independent Holiness missions,..and among the Plymouth Brethren. **1968** W. PHILLIPS in P. Oliver *Screening Blues* ii. 63 Now the Holiness people, when they come in, They said, 'Boy we can make it by livin' above sin.'

holing, *vbl. sb.* Add: **1.** Also, the production of holes, e.g. in garments (cf. HOLE *v.*[1] 8).

1910 *Daily Chron.* 14 Mar. 6/4 The Stockings that are actually insured against holing.

c. *Golf.* The action of holing the ball; also *attrib.*, as *holing distance*, *holing-out putt*.

1875 'STONEHENGE' *Brit. Sports* (ed. 12) 695/1 He who succeeds in holeing in fewer strokes than his opponent wins that hole. **1901** *Scotsman* 11 Sept. 10/1 A nicely-played mashie stroke took his ball within holing distance. **1906** *Westm. Gaz.* 10 Aug. 4/2 The longer holing-out putts. **1972** *Country Life* 7 Dec. 1600/3 As often as not, the ball would finish within likely holing distance.

holism (hǫ·liz'm, hōu·liz'm). [f. Gr. ὅλος whole + -ISM.] A term coined by Gen. J. C. Smuts (1870–1950) to designate the tendency in nature to produce wholes (*i.e.* bodies or organisms) from the ordered grouping of unit structures. So **holist, holi·stic** *a.*, **holi·stically** *adv.*

1926 J. C. SMUTS *Holism & Evol.* 99 The whole-making, holistic tendency, or Holism, operating in and through particular wholes, is seen at all stages of existence. *Ibid.* 127 There is a synthesis which makes the elements or parts act as one or holistically. **1927** *Brit. Weekly* 20 Jan. 418/4 The real entities of the material world must, like organisms, be creative, self-transcending, functional. They must be Holistic unities. **1931** SMUTS in *Times* 2 Sept. 7/7 Instead of the animistic, or the mechanistic, or the mathematical universe, we see the genetic, organic, holistic universe. **1937** 'C. CAUDWELL' *Illusion & Reality* ix. 180 A large portion of reality will be conveniently removed to the sphere of religion, as among the vitalists, holists, entelechists and spiritualists generally. **1945** *Word* i. 109 Haldane suggested for this movement [in biology] the name 'holism'; others preferred to call it 'organicism'. To my mind, this new holism or organicism bears a close relationship to linguistic structuralism. **1952** C. P. BLACKER *Eugenics* x. 240 The principle of monism is much the same as that of General J. C. Smuts's holism. **1959** *Times* 11 Dec. 15/1 Holism has at last penetrated departments of nutrition, and a new school of nutrition has arisen which realizes that the integration of nutrition, health and disease is a problem that must be attacked on a wide front. **1961** J. WILSON *Reason & Morals* ii. 117 There may be sane people who do not 'appreciate' (i.e. respond holistically to) works of art or to nature. **1964** *Punch* 20 May 736/1 If..we view a person as a large..holistic, versatile, symbol processing system. **1964** *Listener* 21 May 825/1, I mentioned the unresolved conflict between the atomistic psychology of the Behaviourists and the somewhat schematic holism of the Gestalt school. **1970** *New Scientist* 9 July 96/1 Each level is equipped with its own 'laws of organization', 'intrinsic patterns' or whatever 'holistic' term you prefer to choose. **1971** *Nature* 13 Aug. 504/2 Professor J. S. Weiner has pioneered the modern holistic approach to the study of man. **1971** F. A. STAFLEU *Linnaeus & Linnaeans* ii. 39 'Canon' means here 'general rule or axiom' and has overtones of 'genuine and inspired', known instrictively by a holistic, not an analytical, approach to the phenomena of life.

holk, howk, *v.* Add: **1.** (Further examples.)

1899 A. WERNER *Captain of Locusts* 160 They howked a grave near the kraal, and buried their chief *pro tem.* **1926** D. H. LAWRENCE *Let.* 28 Dec. (1932) 676 We shall stay here if not howked out. **1950** B. MARSHALL *Every Man a Penny* xlix. 229 Deep in their trenches the hairy men stood, howking out the brown earth. **1955** E. POUND *Classic Anthol.* II. 90 Howk 'em up with a landing scoop.

2. (Later examples.)

1906 KIPLING *Puck of Pook's Hill* 69 Dan hiked and howked with a boat-hook (the brook was too narrow for sculls). **1950** *John o' London's* 24 Nov. 621/1 The solan goose..starts howking and pecking at the rope which sustains the climber.

Holland. 1. b. Add: *Holland sauce* = *HOLLANDAISE.

1877 E. S. DALLAS *Kettner's Bk. of Table* 162 Dutch or Holland Sauce: Sauce Hollandaise. **1892** [see *DUTCH *a.* 3 b].

Holland[2] (hǫ·lǎnd). The name of J. P. *Holland* (1840–1914), the designer of a class of submarines adopted by the American navy, used as the proper name of the first submarine of this type and afterwards generically.

1899 *Westm. Gaz.* 7 Dec. 2/3 The President of the official Naval Board, and several of its members have signed a statement declaring that their 'Holland' has fulfilled all requirements in her trial trip. **1902** *Encycl. Brit.* XXXII. 576/2 The *Holland*, a smaller boat, having a length of about 59 ft., though begun after the *Plunger*, has already been completed. *Ibid.*, The latest Holland design is shown in Fig. 95. **1906** *Daily Chron.* 8 Sept. 5/3 The original Holland class of submarine.

Hollandaise (hǫ·lǎndēⁱz, ‖olańdḗz). [Fr., fem. of *hollandais* Dutch, f. *Hollande* Holland.] *Hollandaise sauce* (see quot. 1907); *à la Hollandaise*, served with Hollandaise sauce.

1841 THACKERAY in *Fraser's Mag.* XXIII. 719/1 Turbot with lobster-sauce is too much; turbot *à la Hollandaise* vulgar. **1861** MRS. BEETON *Bk. Househ. Managem.* 195 Green Dutch sauce, or Hollandaise verte. **1899** N. NEWNHAM-DAVIS *Dinners & Diners* iv. 26 Artichokes good, though we preferred plain vinegar as a dressing to the *hollandais* one. **1907** ESCOFFIER *Mod. Cookery* 22 Hollandaise Sauce...One and one-half lbs. of butter, the yolks of six eggs, one pinch of mignonette pepper and one-quarter oz. of salt, three tablespoonfuls of good vinegar. *Ibid.* 23 The consistence of sauces whose processes are identical with those of the Hollandaise may be varied at will. **1964** C. WILLOCK *Enormous Zoo* ix. 169 Nile perch with Hollandaise sauce.

Hollander. Add: **b.** A South African colonist or immigrant of Dutch birth or descent. Also *attrib.*, or as *adj.*, and *Comb.*

1699 W. A. COWLEY *Voy.* in W. Hacke *Collect. Voy.* (1729) v. 34 The Village inhabited by the Hodmandods, so called by the Hollanders. **1897** in H. M. Stanley *Thro' S. Afr.* (1898) v. 75, I do not blame the Boers so much as I blame the Hollanders and our Jews here. **1899** *Westm. Gaz.* 16 Oct. 7/2 The Boers who have occupied Newcastle consist of both Transvaal and Free State commandos, with 400 Hollanders. **1899** *Daily News* 2 Nov. 5/2 It has not been he, but the 'Hollander', a most unfavourable specimen of the Dutch race, who has been concerned in all the doubtful intrigues..of the last few years. **1902** *Encycl. Brit.* XXXII. 721/1 The effect of this development was the production of a body of officials in the Transvaal, partly Hollander and German, partly Boer. **1903** G. W. T. OMOND *Boers in Eur.* 31 South Africa, big towns and seaports excepted, being Hollander-Boer to the core. **1934** [see *AFRICAN *sb.* b]. **1971** *Rand Daily Mail* (Home Owner) 27 Mar. 16/1 Developer-builder Gard Duys, a Hollander with a soft spot for progressive architecture, is delighted with the result.

2. *Paper-making.* A beating-engine, invented in Holland, for the conversion of the bleached rags into paper-pulp. Also called *Hollander-beater*.

1878 *Design & Work* 19 Jan. 88/3 About fifty years after the invention of the 'Hollander'..alkali began to be employed for boiling the rags. **1900** CROSS & BEVAN *Paper-Making* (ed. 2) 172 The ordinary form of beater is fitted with a single roll, and the general arrangement of its working parts is that..described..for a 'breaking' engine. This type of beater is known as the Hollander. **1902** *Encycl. Brit.* XXXI. 458/2 One of the various forms of beating engine or 'Hollander'. **1907** CROSS & BEVAN *Paper-Making* (ed. 3) 179 The Hollander consists of an oblong trough, with semi-circular ends, with a partition or mid-feather running down the centre so as to form a continuous channel round which the stuff can circulate. **1963** R. R. A. HIGHAM *Handbk. Papermaking* xiii. 266 In the middle of the eighteenth century, the development of the Hollander beater revolutionized stock preparation methods. This beater was invented in Holland—hence the name—and it replaced the old rag stampers.

3. A Dutch clinker.

1897 WEBSTER, *Hollander*. 2. A very hard, semi-glazed, green or dark brown brick, which will not absorb water;—called also Dutch clinker. Wagner.

4. (See quot.)

1879 *Encycl. Brit.* IX. 400/2 The largest spars [of timber] are called 'Hollander'.

hollandite (hǫ·lǎndəit). *Min.* [f. the name of Sir Thomas Henry *Holland* (1868–1947), British geologist: see -ITE[1] 2 b.] An oxide of barium and manganese occurring as brittle silvery grey to black crystals having a metallic lustre.

1906 L. L. FERMOR in *Trans. Mining, Geol. & Metall. Inst. India* I. II. 77 For this new mineral I propose the name of *hollandite*, after Mr. T. H. Holland, F.R.S., Director of the Geological Survey of India, and President of this Institute. **1943** *Amer. Mineralogist* XXVIII. 505 Cryptomelane, hollandite, and coronadite are isostructural and form isomorphous mixtures to some extent. **1952** *Nature* 6 Dec. 974/1 The formula of hollandite, deduced from that of the psilomelane used in this investigation, is $Ba_{1.01}(Mn,R)_8O_{16}$, in good agreement with that previously proposed by Byström and Byström, $Ba_{(2-x)}Mn_8O_{16}$, where *x* is approximately equal to one. It has been suggested that discrete water molecules may be present in hollandite as occupants of vacant sites of otherwise perfect sub-rows.

holler (hǫ·ləɹ), *v. dial.* and *U.S.* Also **holer,** † **hollar.** [var. HOLLO *v.*] *intr.* To cry out loud, to shout; to complain. In a fight: to give up, to cry 'enough'. Also, to sing a 'holler' (see next). Occas. *trans.*

1699 in *Cal. Virginia State Papers* (1875) I. 67 We gott to the River side oppisett to the ffort, & theire hollerd & Immediately they answered. **1834** S. SMITH *Sel. Lett. J. Downing* 37 All hollering 'stooboy'. **1843** 'R. CARLTON' *New Purchase* I. xiv. 101 Provided you knew how 'to holler', within hearing of both. **1845** W. T. PORTER *Big Bear Arkansas* 41 Who hollered? Which gave up? **1852** *N. & Q.* 14 Feb. 148/2 The village boys..get some halfpence given them for their 'hollering'. **1859** *Atlantic Monthly* Aug. 239/2 Here is a boy that loves to..'holler' Fire! on slight evidence. **1883** [see HOLLO *v.* 1 a]. **1898** C. M. YONGE *John Keble's Parishes* xv. 175 Curate. Have you heard the nightingale yet? Boy. Please, sir, I don't know how he hollers. Everything hollers, from a church bell to a mouse in a trap. **1901** MERWIN & WEBSTER *Calumet 'K'* viii. 155 I'll holler up to you, Max, when we're ready down below. **1904** 'No. 1500' *Life in Sing Sing* 249/2 *Hollar*, complain. **1926** J. BLACK *You can't Win* iv. 43 Holler before you're hurt; that's my motto. **1934** *Nat. Geographic* LXV. 624/2 Daybreak and sundown are favorite times for 'holerin''. It is an invariable accompaniment of driving the cattle home in the evening. **1936** J. A. & A. LOMAX *Negro Folk-Songs* II. iii. 113 He has hollered and moaned his troubles and his observations on the ways of the world. **1940** W. FAULKNER *Hamlet* IV. i. 343 And when I holler run, you run. You hear me? **1967** *Boston Globe* 30 Mar. 14/1 Everyone hollers about the damage to the children if the schools are shut one day because of a teacher–school committee disagreement. **1969** *Times* 22 July (Moon Report Suppl.) p. ii/3 When Colonel Aldrin jumped off the last step of the moon ladder..everyone in the Aldrin home was whooping and hollering. **1970** P. OLIVER *Savannah Syncopators* 66 (*caption*) Arthur Crudup 'hollers' with a high-pitched voice. **1973** J. THOMSON *Death Cap* xiii. 177 I'll holler you to come down.

holler (hǫ·ləɹ), *sb.*[1] *dial.* and *U.S.* Also † **hollar.** [var. HOLLO *sb.*] = HOLLO *sb.*; also, a complaint, a cry of protest; *spec.* in the Southern States of America, a work-song.

1825 J. JENNINGS *Obs. Dial. W. Eng.*, Hollar. **1886** F. T. ELWORTHY *W. Somerset Word-Bk.* 346 *Holler*,..the cry given when the quarry is seen; the view-halloo. **1896** ADE *Artie* xvi. 147, I put up a holler right at the jump. **1901** 'J. FLYNT' *World of Graft* 133 Some gamblers were particularly loud in making their 'hollers', and threatened to bring about an investigation. **1908** J. M. SULLIVAN *Criminal Slang* 13 *Holler*, plaint of a victim. **1936** J. A. & A. LOMAX *Negro Folk-Songs* II. iii. 113 The holler is a way of singing—free, gliding from a sustained high note down to the lowest register. **1939** *Congress Rec.* 5 Aug. App. 3975/1 [Will Rogers] came across the American scene with..a hoot and a 'holler', and a laugh. **1940** J. W. WORK *Amer. Negro Songs* 34 Approaching his house or that of his sweetheart in the evening, or sometimes out of sheer lonesomeness, he would emit his 'holler'. *Ibid.* 35 In these 'hollers' the idiomatic material found in the blues is readily seen. **1956** M. STEARNS *Story of Jazz* (1957) i. 10 The street-cry and field-holler of the American Negro are earlier examples of the same tradition. **1958** P. GAMMOND *Decca Bk. Jazz* i. 20 Solo work-songs of field-hands..took the form of 'hollers' or 'arwhoolies'—long meandering cries that were half-sung thoughts and half yodels. **1959** R. CONDON *Manchurian Candidate* (1962) vii. 137 If you're ever around Wainwright, Alaska, you'll give me a holler. **1968** P. OLIVER *Screening Blues* 4 The more primitive examples of field cries, hollers and work songs, of children's game songs and unaccompanied blues were only heard on record in the rarest of instances.

holler (hǫ·ləɹ), *sb.*[2] *U.S. colloq.* var. HOLLOW *sb.* 2.

1845 W. T. PORTER *Big Bear Arkansas* 151 [I] putt off emediately fur watur that I node waz klose down the holler. **1947** RANDOLPH & WILSON (*title*) Down in the holler: a gallery of Ozark folk speech. **1972** J. S. HALL *Sayings from Old Smoky* 8 Many of these stock boasts hinge on the steepness or wildness of the mountain country, the darkness of the 'hollers', even in midday, and the hardihood of the people.

Hollerith (hǫ·ləriþ). The name of Herman *Hollerith* (1860–1929), American inventor, used esp. *attrib.* in reference to the use of punched cards in accounting, statistics, etc. Hence as *sb.*, used *fig.* in reference to modern society viewed as a processing machine (see quot. 1957).

1890 *Jrnl. Franklin Inst.* XCIX. 306 The cost of compiling a census by the Hollerith system, would appear to be only one-third the cost of compiling the same census by the next best system. **1891** *Electrical Engineer* (U.S.) 11 Nov. 530/1 Not a little skill and judgment was necessary in perfecting the mechanical details of the Hollerith electric tabulating system. **1946** A. C. CLARKE in *Astounding Sci. Fiction* Sept. 24/1 That wonderful battery of almost human Hollerith analyzers. **1957** *London Mag.*

June 61 The writer needs his partial disengagement from the social hollerith so as to free the one incomparable tool that he can call his own. **1958** H. T. HIMMELWEIT et al. *Television & Child* 85 The number of Hollerith cards needed for each child. **1960** *Times* 31 Mar. 3/1 An internal Hollerith installation and external computing facilities are used extensively. **1970** *Computers & Humanities* V. 2 The first was the pre-computer phase of the 1950s, characterized by the use of Hollerith (IBM) cards and unit record equipment to sort and tally large bodies of information.

holliper, var. OLIVER².

hollow, *sb.* Add: **1. e.** (See quot. 1940.)
1885 J. G. HORNER *Pattern Making* iii. 26 Many of the best wheels are made with hollows at the roots of the teeth, for here the action of leverage on the tooth induces the greatest stress. **1924** J. McC. WILSON *Pattern-Making* iv. 28 In finishing the pattern all the angled corners are filled in either with Angled or Hollowed Fillets...Hollows are used in well-finished work. **1940** *Chambers's Techn. Dict.* 418/2 *Hollows*, fillets, or curves of small radius, uniting two surfaces intersecting at an angle.

hollow, *a.* and *adv.* Add: **7.** *hollow block, tile*; **hollow heart**, a disease of potatoes in which a cavity is formed in the centre of the tuber; **hollow-horn** *U.S.* (see quot. 1962); **hollow roll**: see ROLL *sb.*¹ 11 b; **hollow wall** = *cavity wall* (*CAVITY 4).
1964 J. S. SCOTT *Dict. Building* 167 *Hollow blocks* or *hollow tiles.* Concrete or burnt clay hollow building blocks are used for making partitions or external walls, or for forming reinforced concrete hollow-tile floors. Lightweight, thermally-insulating, hollow blocks are also made of foamed slag concrete, diatomite, gypsum, etc. **1926** F. D. HEALD *Man. Plant Dis.* v. 94 Hollow heart is most frequent in potatoes which have been stimulated to an excessive growth by abundant moisture. **1951** *Dict. Gardening* (R. Hort. Soc.) III. 1655/1 Hollow Heart is usually due to the tubers experiencing a dry period in which they mature and lose water so that when the rain comes the quick growth causes the inner tissues to split apart. **1805** R. PARKINSON *Tour Amer.* 87 There were a few half-starved cattle; in general standing shaking with cold, and many more complaining of what they call the hollow-horn. **1825** J. LORAIN *Pract. Husb.* 455 The hollow horn, a disease which seldom fails to attack half-famished cattle. **1868** *Rep. Iowa Agric. Soc. 1867* 129 Cattle have few diseases in this locality except the 'buck eye' and 'hollow horn'. **1962** J. N. WINBURNE *Dict. Agric.* 382/1 *Hollow horn*, an imaginary disease arising from the erroneous belief that loss of appetite and listlessness in a cow was due to hollow horns. The remedy was supposed to be (a) boring a hole in each horn ..(b) filling the cavity with salt, sugar, and pepper, and (c) plugging the hole with a wooden peg. The belief was that if the cow had hollow horn this remedy would cure her, and if she did not have hollow horn, the remedy would prevent her getting it. **1914** *Archit. Rec.* Feb. 142/2 Terra cotta hollow tile was employed in the exterior and interior bearing walls. *Ibid.* 144/2 The floor construction used was the combination system of hollow tile and reinforced concrete. **1936** *Archit. Rev.* LXXX. 144/1 Floors and roofs throughout are hollow tile and concrete, and internal walls in the ward block are of hollow partition blocks. **1823** *New Pract. Builder & Workman's Compan.* 586/2 *Hollow-wall*, a wall built in two thicknesses, leaving a cavity between, which may be either for saving materials or for preserving an uniform temperature in apartments. **1891** *Notes on Building Construction* II. 10 The hollow wall is often arranged to begin on the damp-proof course. **1942** J. A. MULLIGAN *Handbk. Brick Masonry Construction* 362 The building code of the City of New York uses the term 'hollow wall' instead of cavity wall.
8. *hollow-cheeked* (examples), *-chested*; **hollow-fronted, -nosed, -pointed** *adjs.*, said of a bullet with a hollow in the point to ensure expansion of the projectile on impact.
1598 FLORIO *Worlde of Wordes* 273/1 *Pettoruto*,..that is hollow chested. **1851** H. MELVILLE *Moby Dick* III. xlv. 255 'Look!' replied the hollow-cheeked captain from his taffrail. **1886** W. B. YEATS *Mosada* 6 Bright-eyed, and hollow-cheeked From fasting. **1899** *Kynoch Jrnl.* Oct.–Nov. 14/2 If the ·577 pure lead hollow-fronted bullet hit a man he knew it at once. **1902** *Encycl. Brit.* XXXII. 244/1 The hollow-pointed expanding bullet with soft lead nose. **1902–3** *Kynoch Jrnl.* Dec.–Jan. 43/1 Without the mutilation so commonly caused by hollow pointed bullets. **1909** *Daily Chron.* 26 June 1/4 The other cartridges..being of nickle steel and hollow-nosed. **1920** G. BURRARD *Notes on Sporting Rifles* 40 A hollow-nosed bullet. **1963** V. NABOKOV *Gift* iv. 240 He listened to these hollow-chested verses.
B. *adv.* **3.** **hollow-ground** *a.*, ground so as to have a concave surface; so *hollow-grinding.*
1885 *Army & Navy Co-op. Soc. Price List* 1048 The guaranteed razors. Cases containing 2 Hollow Ground. **1937** R. W. FAIRBROTHER *Text-bk. Med. Bacteriol.* ii. 10 In carrying out the examination by direct microscopy use is made of the hollow-ground slide, which is a slide with a hollow of approximately ½ in. ground out on one surface. **1951** R. H. HORDERN *Woodworking Industry Managem.* iv. 72 (*heading*) Hollow-grinding machine. *Ibid.* 73 This..will produce a hollow-ground bevel on the cutter. There are a number of reasons why hollow grinding is preferable to straight. **1968** *Gloss. Terms Mechanized & Hand Sheet Metal Work* (*B.S.I.*) 12 *Hollow grinding*, a method of grinding a tool to produce a concave face or faces behind a cutting edge.

holloware, var. HOLLOW-WARE.
1959 *Sears, Roebuck Catal.* Spring & Summer 575/4 Melmac Dinner Sets..Holloware in solid color. **1962** *Engineering* 22 June 819/2 Aluminium sheet clad with stainless steel..is intended basically for the domestic holloware trade. **1963** *Times* 28 May 1/7 Domestic holloware made from aluminium. **1972** *Daily Tel.* 25 Apr. 15 Pans, or 'holloware' as they are called in the trade.

Holloway (hǫ·lowēi). [f. the name of Thomas *Holloway* (1800–83), their inventor and manufacturer.] *Holloway's pill*, a patent medicine used principally for laxative purposes. Also *Holloway's ointment.*
1838 *Town* 16 June 440/1 (Advt.), Holloway's universal family ointment...Holloway's external disease pill. **1849** E. RUSKIN *Let.* 8 Nov. in M. Lutyens *Effie in Venice* (1965) I. 59, I get..a Holloway's Pill when I require such medicine. **1877** E. S. DALLAS *Kettner's Bk. of Table* 432 This is..suggestive of the African tribes mentioned by Sir Samuel Baker, who believed in Holloway's Pills because of their rapid and irrepressible results. **1885** *Trade Marks Jrnl.* 18 Nov. 1084 Holloway's Pills... The firm trading as Thomas Holloway,..London; patent medicine vendors... Pills for human use. *Ibid.*, Holloway's Ointment... The firm trading as Thomas Holloway,.. London; patent medicine vendors... Ointment. **1939–40** *Army & Navy Stores Catal.* 396/1 Holloway's Pills—box 1/3. **1951** *Chemist & Druggist Yearbk.* 196 Holloway's Pills, Ltd... King George's Avenue, Watford. *Ibid.* 457 (*heading*) Proprietary medicines advertised to the public. ..458/1 Holloway's ointment. Holloway's pills.

holluschickie (hǫ·lɒ̆sˌtʃiki), *collect. pl.* Also **holloschickie, holluschuckie.** [ad. Russ. *kholostyaki* pl., bachelors.] Young males of the northern, Pribilof, or Alaska fur seal, *Callorhinus ursinus*; = *BACHELOR 4 c.
1874, 1884 [see *BACHELOR 4 c]. **1893** KIPLING *Seven Seas* (1896) 70 But he'll lie down on the killing-grounds where the holluschickie go. **1894** —— *Jungle Bk.* 97 They [*sc.* seals] were called the holluschickie—the bachelors. **1901** *Munsey's Mag.* XXV. 355/1 The holluschickie who have reached the age when they contemplate matrimony. **1929** *Encycl. Brit.* IX. 952/1 The young males or bachelors (*holloschickie*).

holly. Add: **3. b. holly blue**, the azure blue butterfly *Celastrina argiolus.*
1853 F. O. MORRIS *Hist. Brit. Butterflies* 136 Holly Blue. Azure Blue... This plain but neat species is to be found..in places where the holly abounds. **1905** *Daily Chron.* 6 Apr. 3/2 The holly-blue often flies on days when there is more hail than sun. **1927** [see *CHALK *sb.* 7 b]. **1952** L. H. NEWMAN *Transformations of Butterflies & Moths* 46 Holly Blue caterpillars vary quite considerably, but the ground colour of the body is always a shade of green. **1970** *Times* 19 Aug. 9/6, I recently chased a Holly Blue around a holly tree for at least an hour before eventually retiring exhausted, with the total day's bag of one small butterfly.

hollyhock. Add: **2. b. hollyhock disease**, = **hollyhock rust*; also, blight caused by the parasitic fungus *Colletotrichum malvarum*; **hollyhock fungus**, a fungus, *Puccinia malvacearum*, parasitic on the hollyhock; **hollyhock rust**, hollyhock fungus or the disease caused by this.
[**1865** *Gardeners' Chron.* 2 Sept. 817/2 We have received ..some information with respect to a Disease with which Hollyhocks are affected to such a degree as almost to preclude their cultivation.] **1898** W. ROBINSON *Eng. Flower Garden* (ed. 6) 389/1 Owing to the Hollyhock disease it is often a better plan to abandon the named kinds increased from cuttings and resort to seedlings only for stock. **1951** *Dict. Gardening* (R. Hort. Soc.) II. 1006/1 Hollyhock disease is not seen in the neighbourhood of industrial towns. **1883** W. ROBINSON *Eng. Flower Garden* 13/2 The Hollyhock Fungus (*Puccinia malvacearum*)..is..destructive to the Hollyhock. **1899** G. MASSEE *Text-bk. Plant Dis.* 252 Hollyhock rust. **1910** T. W. SANDERS *Garden Foes* 227 Hollyhock Rust (Puccinia malvacearum). At one time this fungoid disease played great havoc with the hollyhock. **1951** *Dict. Gardening* (R. Hort. Soc.) II. 1005/2 The onset of Hollyhock rust..led to its almost complete disappearance as a florists' flower.

Hollywood (hǫ·liwud). [A region near Los Angeles in California, the chief production centre of the U.S. cinema business.] Generally, the American type of moving picture, its characteristics and background. Also *attrib.* (or as *adj.*) and *Comb.*
1926 A. HUXLEY *Jesting Pilate* II. 198 What is this famous civilisation of the white man which Hollywood reveals? **1928** H. CRANE *Let.* 27 Apr. (1965) 325 She ought to be a little different than the typical Hollywood hostess. **1929** E. WALLACE *Red Aces* i. 218 A high-class school at Brighton, where girls are taught to..use lipstick and adore the heroes of Hollywood. **1932** KIPLING *Limits & Renewals* 143 The standardised Hollywood screech of a Producer. **1933** *Punch* 30 Aug. 225/1 An American producer says that if he had his way he could make Elstree into an English Hollywood. **1934** H. G. WELLS *Exper. Autobiogr.* II. viii. 513 There was a vast editor's desk, marvellously equipped, like a desk out of Hollywood. **1935** R. MACAULAY *Personal Pleasures* 137 It is not..for mechanically recorded voices, however Hollywood, to mimic this universal terrestrial passion [love]. **1937** *N. & Q.* 13 Mar. 181/2 Unlike the Japanese, they [*sc.* the Chinese] do not ape Hollywood. **1939** C. MORLEY *Kitty Foyle* 319 Those black and white yachting shoes..were definitely Hollywood. **1940** *Writer's Digest* June 13/2 It is at this point that the Hollywood ingenue goes Hollywood. **1942** T. RATTIGAN *Flare Path* I. 23 Face the music? How beautifully Hollywood! What was your idea? To get Teddy alone and say 'I love your wife'? **1959** *Listener* 10 Dec. 1048/3 A revolt against Hollywood–bourgeois values. **1970** G. GREER *Female Eunuch* 294 Her Hollywood-interior lodge.
Hence **Hollywoode·se**, the style of language supposed to be characteristic of Hollywood films; **Hollywoode·sque** *a.*, characteristic of or resembling Hollywood films; **Ho:llywoo·dian, -ean** *a.*, of, pertaining to, or characteristic of Hollywood or its films; **Ho·llywoodish** *a.*, somewhat resembling Hollywood films; **Ho·llywoodism**, characteristic style or idiom of Hollywood films; **Ho·llywoodize** *v.*, to make typically Hollywoodian; so **Ho:llywoodi·zing** *vbl. sb.*
1927 *Daily Express* 4 May 4 The cottage is so picturesque and Hollywoodesque that..it is more like a 'set' than a real house. **1928** *Ibid.* 4 May 10/2 Mr. Douglas Fairbanks..is meditating..a slap-up, original Hollywoodish sequel of his own devising. **1934** A. HUXLEY *Beyond Mexique Bay* 23 What frills, what flounces!..The cut was a Hollywoodian adaptation from the French. **1941** *Scrutiny* IX. 346 Puccini, that voice pervasively symbolic of the Hollywoodizing of human emotions. **1950** *John o' London's* 7 July 419/1 The modern kind of roadhouse which might adopt a Spanish wear with self-conscious Hollywoodism. **1951** F. LAWRENCE *Let.* 20 Jan. in *Mem. & Corr.* (1961) 298 We have a very 'Hollywoodean' place, not far from the Huxleys. **1957** *Essays in Crit.* VII. 209 One scarcely needs to pursue the poem through the Hollywoodese of 'our hearts go round'. **1959** *Encounter* July 53/2 Some deep Hollywoodean reason. **1960** *House & Garden* July 36 There is nothing Hollywoodian about Miss Caron's decorative indulgences. **1962** *Listener* 6 Sept. 342/2 Those brawny, masculine, sunburnt figures of my youth..were Hollywoodish figures. **1963** *Sunday Express* 24 Feb. 23/3 *Nine Hours to Rama* is a lamentable failure because it is permeated with Hollywoodisms. **1965** *New Statesman* 19 Mar. 462/1 So far, only the cosmopolitan and European [behaviour] has been permitted..and that, all too often, heavily Hollywoodised. **1967** *Guardian* 11 Apr. 5/1 Such incredible Hollywoodising of Malcolm X did much to create an atmosphere in which he could only be killed.

Holmesian (hōu·mziăn), *a.* and *sb.* [f. Sherlock *Holmes*, name of the amateur detective who is the chief figure in the detective stories of A. Conan Doyle (1859–1931) + -IAN.] **A.** *adj.* Of, pertaining to, or in the manner of Sherlock Holmes. **B.** *sb.* A devotee of Sherlock Holmes.
1929 'G. DAVIOT' *Man in Queue* vi. 62 Grant disclaimed any such Holmesian qualities. **1934** J. CARTER *New Paths in Book Collecting* 34 Mr. Desmond MacCarthy is a prominent Holmesian scholar. **1940** E. BENTLEY *Those Days* ix. 250 If the nature of the detective-story, as of other things, is to be found in its complete development, that was the Holmesian saga. **1947** C. WAUGH *Comics* iii. 40 Hawkshaw's part is to uncover such fiendish plots with the aid of magnifying glass, pipe and Holmesian costume. **1958** *Times* 19 Feb. 10/4 In the belief no Holmesian had previously done so. **1972** *Times Lit. Suppl.* 7 Apr. 391/1 The great Holmesian game trundles along with unabated vigour.

Holmgren¹ (hōu·mgrĕn, hōu·lmgrĕn). The name of A. F. *Holmgren* (1831–97), Swedish physiologist, used in the possessive in *Holmgren's* (*wool*) *test*, a test for colour-blindness devised by Holmgren in which the subject is asked to match differently coloured pieces of wool; also *Holmgren's wools*, † *worsteds.*
1879 B. J. JEFFRIES *Color-Blindness* xviii. 195 Dr. Magnus of Breslau has lately proposed a modification of Holmgren's test by letting the examined pick out from bundles of colored worsteds those which match the colors of the solar spectrum shown them at the same time. *Ibid.* xxii. 241 To further test railroad employés or others, after having decided on their color-blindness by Holmgren's worsteds,..will be..of great value to examiners. **1890** Holmgren's wools [see GREEN-BLIND *a.*]. **1932** S. DUKE-ELDER *Text-bk. Ophthalm.* I. xxv. 987 Holmgren's wool test, despite the strictures which have been passed upon it, is of great service. **1964** —— *Parsons' Dis. Eye* (ed. 14) xxiv. 364 Holmgren's Wools. These consist of a selection of skeins of coloured wools from which the candidate is required to make a series of colour-matches.

Holmgren² (hōu·mgrĕn, hōu·lmgrĕn). The name of E. A. *Holmgren* (1866–1922), Swedish biologist, used *attrib.* to designate a system of canals discovered by him in the cytoplasm of some cells.
1921 *Anatomical Rec.* XXII. 78 Further work upon the Holmgren canals is required to clearly demonstrate the developmental stages. **1936** *Nature* 30 May 915/2 The relation of the vacuome system to the Golgi network or the Holmgren canals. **1952** G. H. BOURNE *Cytol. & Cell Physiol.* (ed. 2) vi. 250 Evidence obtained from ultra-centrifugation of cells..shows that the Holmgren canals become stratified in a different position from the Golgi apparatus.

holmia (hōu·lmiă). *Chem.* [mod.L., f. next after *erbia*, the oxide of erbium, *ceria*, the oxide of cerium, etc.; the oxide of holmium was not specifically named by either Cleve or

Soret in their papers of 1879.] The sesquioxide of holmium, Ho_2O_3, a pale yellow basic compound.

The substance obtained by Cleve was later shown (by de Boisbaudran, 1886) to be a mixture of the oxides of holmium and of a new element, dysprosium.

1880 *Jrnl. Chem. Soc.* XXXVIII. 7 The author [*sc.* J. L. Soret] considers that the new earth, holmia, discovered by Clève, is identical with an earth..to which Delafontaine gave the name philippia. **1886** [see *FRACTIONAL *a.* b]. **1924** J. W. MELLOR *Inorg. & Theoret. Chem.* V. xxxviii. 697 The fractional crystallization of the ethyl sulphates enables holmia to be separated from erbia, thulia, etc., and to be partially separated from dysprosia. **1968** C. A. HAMPEL *Encycl. Chem. Elem.* 268/2 Holmia was not isolated into a reasonably pure compound until 1911.

holmium (hō̆u·lmiəm). *Chem.* [mod.L. (P.T. Cleve 1879, in *Compt. Rend.* LXXXIX. 480), f. *Holmia* Stockholm (see quot. 1879) + -IUM.] A silvery, relatively soft, metallic element of the lanthanide series which is present in monazite, gadolinite, and other rare-earth minerals and forms a series of strongly paramagnetic salts, mostly of a brown or yellow colour, in which it is trivalent. Atomic number 67; symbol Ho.

1879 P. T. CLEVE in *Chem. News* 12 Sept. 126/2, I propose for this metal the name of Holmium, Ho, derived from the latinized name of Stockholm, in the neighbourhood of which so many minerals rich in yttria are to be found. **1886** [see *DYSPROSIUM]. **1893** *Jrnl. Chem. Soc.* LXIV. II. 467 The holmium oxides were obtained from strongly basic yttrium earths containing a large amount of yttrium oxide. **1924** J. W. MELLOR *Inorg. & Theoret. Chem.* V. xxxviii. 696 The four rare earth elements—dysprosium, Dy; holmium, Ho; erbium, Er; and thulium, Tm—are considered as a family or sub-group of the yttrium elements. **1940** *Nature* 20 Apr. 633/1 The investigation of holmium with the mass-spectrograph has shown that the element is composed of one type of atom only, with a mass of 165. **1967** [see *DYSPROSIUM].

holmquistite (hō̆u·mkwistəit, -kvist-). *Min.* [ad. G. *holmquistit* (A. Osann 1913, in *Sitzungsber. d. Heidelberger Akad. d. Wiss.* IVA. XXIII. 11), f. the name of P. J. *Holmquist*, Swedish mineralogist: see -ITE[1].] A rare basic alumino-silicate of lithium, magnesium, and aluminium that is an orthorhombic member of the amphibole group and typically occurs in light blue to dark violet masses.

1914 *Chem. Abstr.* VIII. 1556 The formation of the holmquistite was no doubt a pneumatolytic process, connected with the intrusion of the well known Li-pegmatites of the region. **1930** *Amer. Mineralogist* XV. 292 Holmquistite from the North Carolina locality is composed largely of the lithia member of the amphibole group and a minor amount of a deficient silica member commonly found in basic rocks. **1966** W. A. DEER et al. *Introd. Rock-Forming Min.* II. 159 Holmquistite typically occurs at the contact of lithium-rich pegmatites with country rocks.

holo-. Add: **holoaxial** (hǫlo,æ·ksiăl) *a. Cryst.*, having or exhibiting all the axes of symmetry compatible with one another but no plane or centre of symmetry; also, more widely, having one or more axes of symmetry but no plane or centre of symmetry; **holobasi·dium** *Bot.*, = *AUTOBASIDIUM; **holobe·nthic** *a. Biol.* [Gr. βένθος depth of the sea], living in the depths of the sea at all stages of the life cycle; **holoca·rpic** *a. Bot.* [Gr. καρπός fruit, seed], designating or (of a fungus) possessing a thallus the whole of which becomes transformed into a reproductive structure at maturity; **holocephalan** (-se·fălăn), **-cepha·lian** *sbs. Ichthyol.*, a fish of the sub-class Holocephali; *adjs.*, = *holocephalous* adj. (s.v. HOLO-); **ho·locrine** (-krəin), *a. Physiol.* [ad. F. *olocrine* (L. Ranvier 1887, in *Jrnl. de Micrographie* XI. 9), f. Gr. κρίν-ειν to separate], of, pertaining to, or designating a gland in which the secretion is produced by the complete disintegration of its cells; **holo-enzyme** (hǫ·lo,enzəim) *Biochem.* [a. F. *holoenzyme* (*Compt. Rend. XIIme Conf. Union Internat. de Chim.* 43)], the active form of an enzyme, consisting of the apoenzyme combined with its co-enzyme; **holomi·ctic** *a.* [ad. G. *holomiktisch* (I. Findenegg 1935, in *Internat. Rev. d. ges. Hydrobiol.* XXXII. 377), f. Gr. μικτός mixed], applied to a lake in which the full depth of water takes part in the circulation; **holomo·rphosis** *Biol.*, the perfect regeneration of a lost member or part; **holono·mic** *a. Mech.* [ad. G. *holonom* (H. Hertz *Ges. Werke* (1894) III. I. 91), f. Gr. νόμ-ος law], applied to a constrained system in which the equations defining the constraints are integrable or already free of differentials, so that each equation effectively reduces the number of coordinates by one; also applied to the constraints themselves; so **holo·nomous** *a.*, in same sense; **holopa·rasite** *Biol.* [ad. G. *holoparasit* (F. Johow 1890, in *Verhandl. Deutsch. wissensch. Ver. Santiago* II. II. 67)], an obligate parasite, unable to exist except in association with its host; so **ho:loparasi·tic** *a.*; **holopa·rasitism**, the condition of being a holoparasite; **holophytic** *a.*, substitute for def.: of, pertaining to, or designating a plant that is able to transform inorganic substances into food by photosynthesis, and so is neither parasitic nor saprophytic; (add earlier and later examples); **holopla·nkton** *Biol.* [back-formation from the adj.], a collective term for aquatic organisms that are holoplanktonic; **ho:loplankto·nic** *a.* [ad. G. *holoplanktonisch* (E. Haeckel *Plankton-Studien* (1890) iii. 25)], passing all stages of the life-cycle drifting or swimming weakly in the water; **holopneu·stic** *a. Ent.* [ad. G. *holopneustisch* (J. A. Palmén *Morphol. des Tracheensystems* (1877) vii. 78), f. Gr. πνευστικ-ός for breathing (πνεῖν to breathe)], having ten pairs of spiracles (in some cases eleven), all of which are functional; **holosa·prophyte** *Bot.* [ad. G. *holosaprophyt* (F. Johow 1889, in *Jahrb. f. wissensch. Bot.* XX. 479)], an obligate saprophyte; so **ho:losaprophy·tic** *a.*

1902 H. A. MIERS *Mineral.* I. i. 45 When an axis of *n*-fold symmetry is perpendicular to *n* digonal axes and there is no other element of symmetry, the crystal may be called 'holoaxial', since it possesses all the symmetry-axes compatible with each other, and only axes. **1903** H. HILTON *Math. Crystallogr.* v. 52 In this chapter we shall investigate those finite groups of the first sort—also called holoaxial groups—which contain only 2-al, 3-al, 4-al, and 6-al rotation-axes. **1961** TERPSTRA & CODD *Crystallometry* iv. 129 Crystals are divided according to their true symmetry into 32 crystal classes. Of these 32 classes, 11 have symmetry elements consisting exclusively of symmetry axes: these are called the eleven holoaxial classes. [**1900** B. D. JACKSON *Gloss. Bot. Terms* 124/2 *Holobasid*, an undivided basidium in Basidiomycetes (Van Tieghem).] **1928** Holobasidium [see *AUTOBASIDIUM]. **1970** J. WEBSTER *Introd. Fungi* 279 In the toadstools and their allies the basidium is a single cylindrical cell, undivided by septa, typically bearing four basidiospores at its apex... Such basidia are termed holobasidia. **1902** *Encycl. Brit.* XXXIII. 935/2 Another hindrance to the extension of many deep-sea species is that they are holobenthic. **1916** B. D. JACKSON *Gloss. Bot. Terms* (ed. 3) 181/2 Holocarpic. **1928** C. W. DODGE tr. *Gäumann's Compar. Morphol. Fungi* iii. 12 In the holocarpic forms, gametangial copulation naturally leads to the fusion of whole individuals. **1930** H. M. FITZPATRICK *Lower Fungi* ii. 24 In some of the lower families [of Phycomycetes] the entire thallus is transformed at maturity into a single reproductive organ (Olpidiaceae) or group (sorus) of them (Synchytriaceae). In such cases the organism is said to be holocarpic. **1970** J. WEBSTER *Introd. Fungi* 62 In the Lagenidiales..the thallus is holocarpic. **1934** WEBSTER, Holocephalan *adj.* & *n.* **1942** L. H. HYMAN *Compar. Vertebr. Anat.* (ed. 2) iv. 40 The chimaeras or holocephalans are peculiar-looking fish. **1934** WEBSTER, Holocephalian *adj.* & *n.* **1965** *Gen. & Compar. Endocrinol.* V. 434/2 The ratfish or chimera is a holocephalian. **1970** *Nature* 11 July 187/2 A holocephalian elasmobranch fish, *Hycholagus colliei*. **1905** GOULD *Dict. New Med. Terms* 296/1 *Holocrine*, applied to a gland the cell of which, after having elaborated the material of secretion, falls into disuse and disappears. **1928** E. V. COWDRY *Special Cytol.* I. ii. 36 In the sebaceous glands the secretory products are elaborated by the fatty metamorphosis, destruction and discharge of the cells themselves. These are the 'holocrine' glands of Ranvier. **1939** V. B. WIGGLESWORTH *Princ. Insect Physiol.* xi. 264 In Orthoptera, secretion is merocrine during continuous small meals, holocrine when a meal follows a period of fasting. **1949** *Gray's Anat.* (ed. 30) 1254 As the sebaceous glands produce their secretion by complete fatty degeneration of their central cells they are classed as holocrine glands. **1961** E. H. MERCER *Keratin & Keratinization* ii. 59 Some cutaneous holocrine glands of reptiles..are sac-like invaginations of the epidermis producing fatty materials. **1943** SUMNER & SOMERS *Chem. & Methods Enzymes* i. 32 A few examples of coenzymes and holoenzymes are given in Table II. **1950** Holoenzyme [see *CO-ENZYME]. **1971** *Nature* 15 Oct. 478/2 The rate of production of active holoenzyme from apoenzyme is enhanced by tryptophan about ten-fold. **1937** *Trans. Connecticut Acad. Arts & Sci.* XXXIII. 74 A normal (holomictic) thermally stratified lake consists of an epilimnion and a hypolimnion. **1957** G. E. HUTCHINSON *Treat. Limnol.* I. viii. 537 Most of the lakes discussed herein are holomictic; that is to say, when they circulate, the circulation is complete to the bottom. **1901** T. H. MORGAN *Regeneration* i. 24 Under this heading [*sc.* homomorphosis] we may distinguish two cases, in one of which the entire lost part is at once, or later, replaced—holomorphosis. **1904** E. T. WHITTAKER *Treat. Analyt. Dynamics* ii. 33 Holonomic systems are therefore characterised by the fact that the number of degrees of freedom is equal to the number of independent coordinates required to specify the configuration of the system. **1954** R. A. BECKER *Introd. Theor. Mech.* xiii. 318 Simple examples of holonomic constraints involving a single particle are those where the motion is confined to a single curve or surface. **1899** D. E. JONES & WALLEY tr. *Hertz's Princ. Mech.* iv. 80 A material system between whose possible positions all conceivable continuous motions are also possible motions is called a holonomous system. **1911** A. & J. G. GRAY *Treat. Dynamics* x. 555 Systems are now called holonomous or not holonomous, according as the constraints are or are not defined by finite equations. **1891** *Jrnl. R. Microsc. Soc.* 70 Each of these classes, except the last, may be again divided into Holoparasites and Hemiparasites. **1903** W. R. FISHER tr. *Schimper's Plant-Geogr.* 203 Holoparasites, which live entirely at the cost of the organic substance of their host, like holosaprophytes are devoid of chlorophyll. **1965** BELL & COOMBE tr. *Strasburger's Textbk. Bot.* I. iv. 197 While the semi-parasites can often at first glance hardly be distinguished from their green, wholly autotrophic relatives, the total or holo-parasites display a complete or almost complete loss of chlorophyll. **1902** *Encycl. Brit.* XXV. 439/2 Cytineæ, Balanophoreæ, Orobanchaceæ, Lennoaceæ, are families..which are characteristically holoparasitic. **1927** W. MCDOUGALL *Plant Ecol.* ix. 125 The family Scrophulariaceæ contains representatives of all gradations from complete independence to holoparasitism. **1885** Holophytic [see HOLOZOIC *a.*]. **1900** *Ann. Bot.* XIV. 669 Thus either a saprophytic or holophytic nutrition can be maintained. **1964** PRIESTLEY & SCOTT *Introd. Bot.* (ed. 4) xxxvii. 593 It is usual for flowering plants to be autotrophic (holophytic). **1909** E. WARMING *Oecol. Plants* xxxviii. 161 These terms 'neritic' and 'pelagic' or 'oceanic' plankton approximately correspond to Haeckel's 'neroplankton' and 'holoplankton' respectively. **1942** H. U. SVERDRUP et al. *Oceans* xvii. 816 The holoplankton is composed of forms representing nearly every phylum of the animal kingdom. **1955** C. C. DAVIS *Marine & Fresh-water Plankton* i. 29 The life history is completed without the animals ever leaving their planktonic life. Animals of this type are classified as the holoplankton. **1893** G. W. FIELD tr. *Haeckel's Planktonic Stud.* in *Rep. U.S. Comm. Fisheries 1889–91* 583 Numerous organisms pass their whole life..hovering in the ocean, while with others this is not the case. The first group we call holoplanktonic. **1963** J. E. G. RAYMONT *Plankton & Productivity in Oceans* xiv. 371 The holoplanktonic members are also subject to seasonal breeding. **1892** J. A. THOMSON *Outl. Zool.* xiii. 266 In adult aërial life, the tracheæ of the body acquire stigmata, and the insect becomes 'holopneustic'. **1947** *Trans. R. Ent. Soc.* XCVIII. 459 Aquatic holometabolous larvae which are holopneustic do not appear to exist. **1960** RICHARDS & DAVIES *Imms's Textbk. Ent.* (ed. 9) I. 134 The Holopneustic Respiratory System.—This is the most primitive arrangement found in living insects, 10 pairs of functional spiracles being present. **1890** *Jrnl. R. Microsc. Soc.* 205 Herr F. Johow describes the peculiarities of structure of the 'holosaprophytes', or saprophytes destitute of chlorophyll. **1902** *Encycl. Brit.* XXV. 439/1 Angiospermous holosaprophytes are not common. **1960** W. B. CROW *Synopsis Biol.* lxxxiv. 518 The completely saprophytic genera (holosaprophytes) in Britain are the orchids *Neottia* and *Corallorhiza* and the similar *Monotropa* which is allied to the heath family. **1895** *Ann. Bot.* IX. 327 A number of holosaprophytic forms found in the tropics..constitute the Burmanniaceous genus *Thismia*.

holocaine (hǫ·lokēin). *Pharm.* Also † -cain. [a. G. *holocaïn*, after *cocaïn* (now *kokain*) COCAINE.] The proprietary name of a synthetic derivative, $C_{18}H_{22}N_2O_2$, of *p*-phenetidine which resembles cocaine in its action and is used (in the form of the hydrochloride) as a surface anæsthetic for the eye; phenacaine.

1897 *Lancet* 29 May 1466/1 A new alkaloid called holocaine..described as an effective anæsthetic for ophthalmic purposes. **1899** *Amer. Jrnl. Med. Sci.* CXVII. 121 The bactericidal power of holocain gives it the advantage that solutions..will keep themselves sterile. **1910** L. W. FOX *Pract. Treat. Ophthalm.* x. 287 The pain caused by this injection is very severe, and to mitigate this the eye should be thoroughly anaesthetized with holocain, cocain being insufficient. **1955** J. ADRIANI *Selection of Anesthesia* x. 98 Holocaine is prepared from para-ethoxy aniline (phenetidin). **1968** J. H. BURN *Lect. Notes Pharmacol.* (ed. 9) 62 Phenacaine (holocaine) is prompt in action and is used especially for the eye.

holocaust, *sb.* **2. c.** Freq. applied to the mass murder of the Jews by the Nazis in the war of 1939–1945. Also *attrib.*

1965 A. DONAT (*title*) The holocaust kingdom. **1967** N. COHN *Warrant for Genocide* ix. 208 By the autumn of 1944 the holocaust was nearing its conclusion. **1968** *Manch. Guardian Weekly* 25 Apr. 10/4 There is now within modern history a compartment of 'holocaust studies'—dealing with the wholesale destruction by the Nazis of European Jewry. **1972** F. FORSYTH *Odessa File* 306 The mausoleum of Yad Vashem,..the shrine to six million of his fellow Jews who died in the holocaust.

holocellulose (hǫlose·liulōus, -z). *Chem.* [f. HOLO- + CELLULOSE *sb.*] A polysaccharide fraction obtained from plant material, esp. wood, by the removal of lignin and various extractives, and principally consisting of cellulose and hemicellulose.

1933 RITTER & KURTH in *Industr. & Engin. Chem.* XXV. 1250 The authors propose the word 'holocellulose' as preferable to *Skelettsubstanzen*, maintaining that the latter term does not describe the material correctly either from the physical or chemical point of view. **1946** *Nature* 14 Dec. 855/1 Holocellulose, now known to be a very important constituent of chemical pulps so far as their behaviour on beating is concerned. **1969** R. L. JANES in Macdonald & Franklin *Pulping of Wood* (ed. 2) I. ii. 52/2 In practice..all the holocellulose isolation procedures ..leave behind traces of degraded lignin and/or adsorbed solvents.

Holocene (hǫ·losīn), *a. Geol.* Also holo-. [ad. F. *holocène*, f. HOLO- + Gr. καιν-ός new, recent, after *Eocene*, etc.] Of, pertaining to, or designating the most recent geological epoch, which began approximately 10,000 years ago

and still continues and which together with the Pleistocene epoch makes up the Quaternary period; also *absol.*

[**1867** P. GERVAIS *Recherches sur l'Ancienneté de l'Homme et la Période quaternaire* ii. 32 Les dépôts récents que j'avais proposé, il y a plusieurs années, de nommer *holocènes*.] **1897** *Q. Jrnl. Geol. Soc.* LIII. 434 Mollusca from the Holocene deposits of the Kennet Valley at Newbury. **1927** PEAKE & FLEURE *Apes & Men* 14 The Holocene is more often called the Recent Period. **1935** *Nature* 7 Sept. 353/1 The pauses in the contraction of the lake must be due to increased rainfall, but nothing like a 'pluvial period' is admitted in holocene times. **1963** R. CARRINGTON *Million Years of Man* xiii. 164 In this Holocene epoch..the hunters and food-gatherers of Upper Palaeolithic and Mesolithic times adopted an entirely new mode of existence. **1971** *Nature* 24 Sept. 281/1 A considerable isostatic rise in the land must have occurred in the late Pleistocene with continuation in the Holocene.

holochoanite (hǫ:lokō͡u·ănəit). *Palæont.* Also **Holo-**. [f. mod.L. *Holochoanites*, altered form of *Holochoanoida* (see next): see -ITE[1] 2 a.] A nautiloid cephalopod in which the septal necks extend from the septum in which they originate as far as the next septum towards the apex; also, a member of the obsolete sub-order Holochoanites, of which such necks were characteristic.

1898 A. HYATT in *Proc. Amer. Assoc. Advancem. Sci.* XLVII. 364 The suborders..are as follows: I. Holochoanites with the funnels of the siphuncle reaching entirely across each air chamber completely shutting off the interior of each chamber from the interior of the siphuncle. **1929** *Bull. Geol. Soc. China* VIII. 119 Stages in development of the primitive Holochoanite. **1944** E. O. ULRICH et al. *Ozarkian & Canadian Cephalopods* III. 28 Most of the Early Paleozoic holochoanites that have long straight conchs can be referred to the Endoceratidae, but a few..are being placed in the Suecoceratidae. **1952** R. C. MOORE et al. *Invertebr. Fossils* ix. 342/1 Thin-section studies indicate that the elongate septal necks which are supposed to distinguish the Holochoanites occur only in a minority of them.

Hence **ho:lochoani·tic** *a.*, (having septal necks) characteristic of a holochoanite; (by some writers used to include *MACROCHOANITIC *a.*).

1905 *Bull. N.Y. State Mus.* LXXX. 339 *Piloceras newtonwinchelli* Clarke is by the structure of its ectosiphuncle not a holochoanitic form..but an orthochoanitic form. **1950** *Jrnl. Paleontol.* XXIV. 604/1 Only a small part of Hyatt's Holochoanites is actually holochoanitic. **1964** C. TEICHERT in R. C. Moore *Treat. Invertebr. Paleont.* K. 164/2 Endoceratidae with holochoanitic, and even macrochoanitic, septal necks and complete endocone systems also appeared in the late Early Ordovician.

holochoanoidal (hǫ:lokō͡uˌănoi·dăl), *a. Palæont.* [f. mod.L. *Holochoanoid-a* (A. Hyatt 1883, in *Proc. Boston Soc. Nat. Hist.* XXII. 260), f. HOLO- + Gr. χοάν-η funnel + *-oida* (see -OID): see -AL.] Originally, characteristic of the group Holochoanoida (now obsolete) of nautiloid cephalopods; hence, = *HOLOCHOANITIC *a.*

1883 *Proc. Boston Soc. Nat. Hist.* XXII. 267 The first three genera appear to have holochoanoidal siphons. **1933** *Biol. Rev.* VIII. 443 There is no essential difference in the structure of the siphuncle, holochoanoidal (Foerste) or orthochoanoidal (Troedsson).

hologamy (holǫ·gămi). *Biol.* [ad. F. *hologamie* (P. A. Dangeard 1900, in *Botaniste* VII. v. 265), f. HOLO- + *-GAMY.] **a.** A mode of reproduction found in certain protozoa and algæ, in which copulation consists in the fusion of whole organisms morphologically similar to the vegetative form.

1925 E. B. WILSON *Cell* (ed. 3) vii. 582 Hologamy or Macrogamy...This condition is seen in various flagellates, rhizopods, ciliates, diatoms, desmids and the Conjugatæ generally. **1940** L. H. HYMAN *Invertebrates* I. iii. 99 Sexual processes are absent except in *Scytomonas* where hologamy has been observed. **1965** V. A. DOGIEL *Gen. Protozool.* (ed. 2) vii. 308 Hologamy is characterized by an almost complete absence of the preparatory stage of gametocytes.

b. A mode of reproduction found in certain fungi, in which the entire thallus becomes a gametangium and fusion of two mature individuals occurs.

1928 C. W. DODGE tr. *Gäumann's Compar. Morphol. Fungi* iv. 12 This special case of gametangial copulation.. is called hologamy. **1965** J. WILKINSON tr. *Langeron's Outl. Mycol.* (ed. 2) ix. 378 Hologamy is gametangial copulation of holocarps.

Hence **ho·logamete**, a gamete that is morphologically similar to the vegetative cell and is not specially formed by fission; **hologa·mic**, **holo·gamous** *adjs.*

1925 E. B. WILSON *Cell* (ed. 3) vii. 583 Even when hologamous gametes are alike or closely similar in appearance they often display definite physiological differences that become evident at the time of conjugation. *Ibid.* 589 Gametes of the hologamic type. **1926** G. N. CALKINS *Biol. Protozoa* x. 498 In the case of *Scytomonas* (*Copromonas*) *subtilis*..the evidence appears to be fairly convincing that copulation of hologametes actually does occur. **1932** BORRADAILE & POTTS *Invertebrata* ii. 27 *Volvox*..and related forms have an anisogamy in which the female gamete is a hologamete. **1965** V. A. DOGIEL *Gen. Protozool.* (ed. 2) vii. 309 Hologamous copulation takes place also in some Phytomonadina belonging to the genus *Chlamydomonas*.

hologenesis (hǫloˌdʒe·nėsis). [ad. It. *ologenesi*: see HOLO- and -GENESIS.] The name of a theory of evolution first propounded by D. Rosa (in *Ologenesi* (1918)), and later adopted by G. Montandon (in *L'Ologenèse humaine* (1928)) to account for the origin of human races.

[**1929** *Nature* 11 May 709/1 The theory of evolution which he [*i.e.* G. Montandon] applies is that formulated by Prof. Rosa of Modêna in 1918 and named by its originator 'ologenesi'.] **1931** *Ibid.* 12 Sept. 430/1 Having reached maturation, the germ plasm of the species undergoes a sudden change whereby the mother species suddenly gives rise to two daughter species...The daughter species then set out to unfold their determinants, and if the environment is favourable—for environment and selection play their part in the theory of hologenesis—then maturation stages are again reached and a further dichotomy with the production of a new species takes place. **1959** R. ALTEVOGT tr. *Rensch's Evol. above Species Level* iv. 58 Rosa advanced a theory of 'hologenesis' according to which dichotomic branchings necessarily proceed in predetermined directions. **1959** B. WALL tr. *Teilhard de Chardin's Phenomenon of Man* III. i. 187 Man, according to these authorities, must have started simultaneously in several regions on the 'anthropoid layer' of the Pliocene era...The idea involves 'hologenesis' and therefore polycentricity.

Hence **hologene·tic** *a.*

1936 *Nature* 27 June 1055/1 An exposition of the hologenetic point of view in the origin and distribution of races. **1948** A. L. KROEBER *Anthropol.* (ed. 2) iv. 170 The hologenetic theory makes a blanket assumption in advance instead of trying genuinely to investigate each case and then seeing whether there is a common principle in them all.

hologram (hǫ·logræm). *Physics.* [f. HOLO- + -GRAM.] A pattern produced when light (or other radiation) reflected, diffracted, or transmitted by an object placed in a coherent beam is allowed to interfere with an undiffracted background or reference beam related in phase to the first (or identical with it); a photographic plate or film containing such a pattern.

When suitably illuminated a photographic hologram causes a two- or three-dimensional image of the original (two- or three-dimensional) object to form in space.

1949 D. GABOR in *Proc. R. Soc.* A. CXCVII. 456 The name 'hologram' is not unjustified, as the photograph contains the total information required for reconstructing the object, which can be two-dimensional or three-dimensional. **1952** *Sci. News* XXVI. 40 In the taking of the hologram, the amplitude of the wave scattered by the object is much smaller than that of the primary wave coming from the source. **1956** *Nature* 31 Mar. 613/2 The resultant hologram..was put on to the optical bench. **1964** *Electronics Weekly* 16 Dec. 6/1 A recent demonstration..showed a toy train in accurate three-dimensional representation, using a hologram illuminated from behind by a gas laser. **1966** *Observer* 15 May 13 Every bit of a hologram contains information about the whole scene. So you can snip it into pieces, shine a laser at one of the pieces, and you will see the original scene, only somewhat fuzzier. **1967** *Applied Physics Lett.* XI. 294/2 An investigation here has shown the feasibility of using a deformable film on a solid substrate to record an ultrasonic hologram in a way similar to that in which photographic film records an optical hologram. **1968** *Ultrasonics* VI. 81/1 There may be several intermediary stages before the ultrasound hologram is in the form of a photographic transparency which can be used in the reconstruction process. **1968** *Times* 12 Dec. 15/3 Scientists at the Bell Telephone Laboratories..claim that as many as 1,000 different holograms..can be stored in a crystal of lithium niobate. **1971** R. J. COLLIER et al. *Optical Holography* x. 298 Holograms can be recorded in a thermoplastic film by causing its surface to deform in accordance with the light intensity variations of holographic interference patterns.

holograph (hǫ·lograf), *v.* [Back-formation from *HOLOGRAPHY, after *photograph*, *telegraph* vbs.] *trans.* To record as a hologram, to make a holographic record of.

1968 *Ultrasonics* VI. 87/1 Although Greguss has demonstrated that ultrasound holograms can be visualized by this technique, he has not published results of any attempts to reconstruct images of the original objects holographed. **1970** *Sci. Jrnl.* Aug. 17/1 The light from a pulsed laser is split into two beams, one going direct to the metal film and the other going first to the object to be holographed and then to the metal film. **1970** *Physics Bull.* Nov. 493/2 In any sort of holography..the aim is to obtain an image of the object being 'holographed'.

holographic (hǫlogræ·fik), *a.* [f. *HOLOGRAPH(Y + -IC.] **1.** (In Dict. s.v. HOLOGRAPH *a.* and *sb.*)

2. *Physics.* Of or pertaining to holography; produced by, involving, or used in holography.

1964 *Physics Lett.* XIII. 306 High resolutions did not heretofore appear attainable in comparable image-forming X-ray microscopy using..holographic wavefront reconstruction methods. **1966** *Nature* 5 Mar. 1015/1 Fig. 1 shows the experimental arrangement used to produce holographic recording[s] of a piece of steel channel-section girder, and to demonstrate interference effects on distorting it. **1967** *Proc. Inst. Electr. Engin.* LV. 570/1 The extension of holographic techniques to radio frequencies offers new possibilities. **1967** DEVELIS & REYNOLDS *Theory & Applic. Holography* i. 6 Holographic interferometry shows promise in the areas of vibration and stress analysis and turbulence studies. **1971** R. J. COLLIER et al. *Optical Holography* x. 294 We describe here a method of film preparation which can be easily followed in a photographic or holographic laboratory.

Hence **hologra·phically** *adv.*, by means of holography; in a holographic manner.

1966 G. W. STROKE *Introd. Coherent Optics & Holography* v. 79 (*heading*) Optical filtering with holographically matched spatial filters. **1968** *Nature* 2 Nov. 474/2 Memory might behave holographically. **1968** *Physics Bull.* Dec. 423/1 An improved interferometer for comparing the shape of a diesel fuel injector cylinder against a holographically recorded master cylinder.

holography (hǒlǫ·grăfi). [f. HOLO- + -GRAPHY.] **1.** (In Dict. s.v. HOLOGRAPH *a.* and *sb.*)

2. *Physics.* [f. after *photography*, *telegraphy*, etc., on the basis of *HOLOGRAM.] The process or science of producing and using holograms.

1964 *Physics Lett.* XIII. 308 A well-resolved, magnified 'image' of the scattering object has been reproduced.. without losing the general simplicity and speed which are characteristic of holography. **1965** *New Scientist* 19 Aug. 431 The technique, known as holography, relies on the fact that an optical description of an object can be stored as a diffraction pattern instead of as a photograph. **1967** *Contemporary Physics* VIII. 153 Leith and Upatnieks (1963, 1964) were the first to demonstrate the very striking three-dimensional imaging that could be obtained by holography. **1967** *Sunday Times* 12 Feb. 8/8 Holography is currently a fashionable topic in the scientific world. **1967** *Applied Physics Lett.* XI. 294/1 The advantage of using acoustic holography to visualize, in three-dimensional fashion, objects in optically opaque material has been intriguing to many investigators. **1969** H. M. SMITH *Princ. Holography* i. 6 Further work on x-ray holography is still awaiting a small, monochromatic source of x-rays. **1971** *Sci. Amer.* Dec. 39 In the past 10 years holography has been used to study how objects change shape under strain, to record high-speed events in gas dynamics and to store information with high density.

holoku (holō͡u·ku). [Hawaiian.] A long gown with a train as worn in Hawaii.

1891 R. L. STEVENSON *Island Nights' Entertainments* (1893) 177 She..stood by the track-side in her red holoku. *Ibid.* 207 Kokua concealed the bottle under her holoku. **1923** C. CAMERON *Two Yrs. in Southern Seas* i. 20 Her gown was a 'holoku', the native robe of a long 'princess' style, loose and flowing with train of bright yellow. **1954** J. SHERIDAN in J. D. MacDonald *Lethal Sex* (1962) 155 A stately Hawaiian woman in a flowered *holoku*. **1960** *Guardian* 3 Nov. 10/4 Long-skirted dresses, called muumuus and holokus, that were adaptations of respectable female attire in Massachusetts. **1967** M. DAVIS *Strange Corner* (1968) xv. 111 He..dropped his eyes to the skin-tight white holoku and whistled.

holomorphic, *a.* Add: Hence **holomo·rphically** *adv.*, in such a way as to be or remain holomorphic (in sense 2); **holomorphy** (examples in *Math.*).

1957 *Pacific Jrnl. Math.* VII. 812 There exist domains ..such that all *G*-holomorphic functions can be continued *G*-holomorphically into a larger domain. *Ibid.* 820 If *D* is a domain of holomorphy, then the set *C*.. belongs to *D*. **1963** STANDRING & SHUTRICK tr. *Cartan's Elem. Theory of Analytic Functions* ii. 73 For functions of a complex variable, there is an equivalence between holomorphy and analyticity. **1966** *Mathematical Rev.* XXXI. 33/2 A closed holomorphic differential *p*-form in *x*, holomorphically varying with *y*.

Holophane (hǫ·lofēin). Also **holophane.** [f. HOLO- + Gr. φαίνειν to shine, appear.] A proprietary name used *attrib.* as *adj.* to designate a type of lamp-shade that encloses the bulb but is made of glass specially fluted to refract and reflect the light in the required manner with little loss; also applied to the glass itself.

1893 PSAROUDAKI & BLONDEL *Brit. Pat. 19,185*, Our invention has for object to replace the globes, shades, reflectors..in use, by others made of transparent or crystal glass giving the..following results:— 1st. They are shining on almost the whole of their visible surface and receive for this cause the name of 'holophane' (entirely shining). *Ibid.*, For making the globe appear 'holophane'. **1911** V. ZINGLER in L. Weaver *House & Equipment* 116 For general dispersed lighting, a bowl or hemisphere of holophane glass, mounted on the ceiling with the lamp inside, gives a soft and pleasing light. **1927** *Brit. Weekly* 14 Nov. 193/4 The modern electric lighting with soft light and clusters of Holophane globes is a marked improvement. **1956** L. E. JONES *Edwardian Youth* x. 245 An American inventor of a prismatic glass called 'Holophane' was looking for an assistant. **1964** S. DUKE-ELDER *Parsons' Dis. Eye* (ed. 14) xxxvii. 559 The distribution of light from artificial sources varies greatly. It can be modified by the use of reflectors and prismatic (holophane) globes.

holophrase (hǫ·lǫfrēiz). *Philol.* [f. HOLO- + PHRASE *sb.*: cf. HOLOPHRASIS.] A single word used instead of a phrase, or to express a combination of ideas (e.g. *ungetatable*).

1899 E. J. PAYNE *Hist. New World* II. 201 This multiplication of elements denoting personality, in combination with more and more elements denoting Things, tends to the dissolution of the holophrase.. The holophrase naturally follows the progression of the mind from point to point. **1914** W. R. M. LAMB *Clio Enthroned* 239 We can regard his periodic structures as a reversion..to the primitive holophrase. **1969** *Language* XLV. 325 *All gone* may be two words, or it may be a holophrase.

holophrastic, *a.* Add: Hence (as a back-formation, after *spasm, spastic*, etc.) **ho·lophrasm** = *HOLOPHRASE.

1862 D. WILSON *Preh. Man* II. xxv. 436 Holophrasms are common in all its [*sc.* the Algonquin] dialects. **1900** *Amer. Anthropologist* II. 615 A word-sentence may be called a 'holophrasm'.

holothuria (hǫlǫþiūə·riă). *Zool.* Pl. **-iæ, -ias.** = HOLOTHURIAN *sb.*

1792 M. RIDDELL *Voy. Madeira* 79 These holothuriae are singularly beautiful when floating on the surface of the water in a clear day. **1816** TUCKEY *Narr. Exped. R. Zaire* (1818) i. 11 The holothuria made its first appearance on the 4th instant. **1844** *Chambers's Edin. Jrnl.* 23 Nov. 323/2 It may be of small moment to you, who, mayhap, know nothing of holothurias. **1876** tr. *Beneden's Anim. Parasites* (1883) 5 Dr. Greef..found..a holothuria of a foot in length.

holotype (hǫ·lǫtəip). *Biol.* [f. HOLO- + *TYPE *sb.*[1] 8 e.] A specimen chosen as the basis of the first description of a new species.

1897 C. SCHUCHERT in *Science* 23 Apr. 637/2 A holotype in natural history is a particular individual deliberately selected by the author of a species, or it may be the only example of a species known at the time of original publication. **1946** *Nature* 23 Nov. 762/1 The holotype and only specimen of this was housed in the Bristol Museum. **1964** *Internat. Code Zool. Nomencl.* xvi. 77 If a nominal species is based on a single specimen, that specimen is the 'holotype'. **1966** *Internat. Code Bot. Nomencl.* ii. 18 As long as a holotype is extant, it automatically fixes the application of the name concerned.

holp, holpen, pa. t. and pple. of HELP *v.* Delete 'obs. or arch.' and add: Now *U.S. dial.* Also occas. used as pres. t. and infin.

1881 'MARK TWAIN' *Prince & Pauper* xix. 221 Of a truth I was right—he hath holpen in a kitchen. **1890** *Dialect Notes* I. 68 *Holp*.., for *helped*. 'He holp me out of the scrape.' **1917** *Ibid.* IV. 413 *Holp* v. tr., to help. 'I axed him to *holp* me out.' **1927** *Amer. Speech* II. 357/2 He holpen me over the creek. **1931** *Ibid.* VI. 230 Such old forms of English as..'holp' for 'help', and 'effen' for 'if' may be heard in the ordinary speech of the natives [of Oregon]. **1939** JOYCE *Finnegans Wake* 118 So holp me Petault, it is not a miseffectual whyacinthinous riot of blots and blurs. **1940** W. FAULKNER *Hamlet* I. ii. 47 'Help him up.' So the nigger holp Ab onto the horse. **1962** E. B. ATWOOD *Regional Vocab. Texas* vi. 118 Items of nonstandard 'grammer' are usually considerably more frequent..in the less-educated group: for example *clum* (climbed), *throwed, holp(ed)*.

hols (hǫlz), *sb. pl.* Colloq. (esp. schoolchildren's) abbrev. of *holidays* (HOLIDAY *sb.* 2 b).

1905 H. A. VACHELL *Hill* vi. 137 The governor pointed that out last hols. **1921** S. THOMPSON *Rough Crossing* ii. 105, I may be staying in Oxford in the spring hols. **1931** *Church Times* 25 Sept. 344/4 After next 'hols' it will be a very different little boy who will take the train at Waterloo or Victoria. **1958** *Spectator* 30 May 677/1 The House broke up for the hols.

Holstein (hǫ·lstəin, -stīn). [Name of a region in N.W. Germany.] A breed of black-and-white dairy cattle, orig. raised in Friesland. Also *attrib.*

1865 *Rep. Comm. Agric. 1864* (U.S. Dept. Agric.) 161 Holstein cattle..[have] not received that appreciation in this country to which they are entitled. **1872** *Rep. Vermont Board Agric.* I. 176 The Dutch cattle, or as I believe it is settled they are to be called, the 'Holsteins'. **1876** *Trans. Ill. Dept. Agric.* XIV. 296 S. W. Kingsley spoke in favor of Holsteins for the dairy. **1971** *Farmers Weekly* 19 Mar. 77/3 The Dutch paraded six top-grade show cows, which were not for sale, while Canada exhibited 16 Holsteins from French herds.

holster (hōu·lstəɹ), *v.* Chiefly *U.S.* [f. the sb.] *trans.* To put (a gun) into its holster. Hence **ho·lstered** *ppl. a.*

1930 *Argosy* 12 July 690/2 Both men had holstered rifles on their saddles. **1956** 'E. MCBAIN' *Cop Hater* (1958) iv. 36 'We won't need these,' Bush said. He holstered his gun. **1972** B. F. CONNERS *Don't embarrass Bureau* (1973) II. 113 He holstered his weapon. **1973** R. HAYES *Hungarian Game* xvii. 108 The guard snatched at his holstered gun.

holt[2]. Add: **1.** Also *U.S. colloq.* Cf. *a-holt* (s.v. *A-HOLD *adv. phr.*).

1825 J. NEAL *Bro. Jonathan* II. 60 [He cried] 'lay holt there; lay holt, every one o' you', throwing the reins behind him, into the carriage. **1848** BARTLETT *Dict. Amer., Holt*, for hold. Ex. 'Death has got holt of him.' **1898** E. N. WESTCOTT *David Harum* xxii. 199 Of course you've heard the things that some folk say of him, an'.. they got some holt on your mind. **1909** R. A. WASON *Happy Hawkins* iv. 52 He'd 'a' been killed that trip if you hadn't taken holt when you did. **1930** *Amer. Speech* V. 151 *Catch holt of*, grab. 'Catch holt of my hand, quickly.' **1940** W. FAULKNER *Hamlet* iv. i. 313 'Grab a holt,' the Texan said. Eck grasped the wire also.

holy, *a.* Add: **3. a.** *the holy souls*, the souls of the faithful departed, the blessed dead.

971 *Blickling Homilies* (1880) vi. 67 Drihten.. helle bereafode, & þa halgan sauwla þonon alædde, & hie generede of deofles anwalde. **1357** JOHN DE THORESBY *Lay Folks Catechism* (1901) 2 This maner of knawying ..shuld we have had..Noght so mikell als hali saules has now in heven, Bot mikel mare than man has now in erthe. **1720** G. STANHOPE tr. *St. Augustine's Pious Breathings* (ed. 5) I. xxiii. 48 (*heading*) The Happiness of Holy Souls at their departure out of this World. **1849** F. W. FABER *Jesus & Mary* 92 Pray for the Holy Souls that burn This hour amid the cleansing flames. **1898** A. G. MORTIMER *Cath. Faith & Practice* II. xiv. 361 The Intermediate State, where the holy souls are waiting until their purification is accomplished. *Ibid.* 371 The joys and consolations of the holy souls in their preparation for Heaven. **1958** G. MONTAGUE *Probl. Liturgy* v. 305 It is clear..that the Holy Souls could not be properly named as the titular of a church. The Souls in Purgatory are not an object of the public veneration of the church.

b. the Holy Name, the name of Jesus as an object of formal devotion among Catholics, as in the Litany of the Holy Name and the festival of the Holy Name of Jesus.

See also *M.E.D.* s.v. *holi* adj.[2] 2 a.

c **1440** *Thornton MS.* f. 192 Of the vertuz of the holy name of Ihesu. **1526** [see NAME *sb.* 3]. **1720** T.M. tr. *Horstius' Paradise of Soul* (1771) 409 Great are the Honours and Priviledges of the Holy Name, Jesus. **1851** J. B. PAGANI *Life A. Gentili* III. xi. 196 Singing along the way the Litany of the Holy Name of Jesus. **1884** ADDIS & ARNOLD *Cath. Dict.* s.v. *Jesus*, An office of the Holy Name. **1901** G. TYRRELL *Autobiogr.* (1912) I. vii. 94 Two of the boys..would bow their heads at the Holy Name at morning prayers. **1968** R. WOOLF *Eng. Relig. Lyric* v. 172 Both 'Luf es lyf' and 'My sange es in syhtyng' include verses expressing devotion to the Holy Name. *Ibid.* 173 In medieval spirituality..the devotion to the Holy Name becomes a form of devotion to Christ in His humanity. **1970** R. W. PFAFF *New Liturgical Feasts Later Med. England* iv. 63 The quite historical indulgences connected with the Name of Jesus from the thirteenth century are concerned not with the mass but with pious ejaculations mentioning the Holy Name.

4. c. Used trivially: (*a*) with *horror* or the like (orig. *U.S.*), expressing intensity; (*b*) with unfavourable implication of piety or sanctimoniousness (*colloq.*); (*c*) used with a following word as an oath or expletive, as *holy cow!, holy Moses!, holy smoke!*

Holy Joe: see quots.; *holy terror*: a person of exasperating habits or manners; *Holy Willie*: a hypocritically pious person.

[**1785** BURNS *Poems & Songs* (1968) I. 74 (*title*) Holy Willie's prayer. *Ibid.* 78 Here Holy Willie's sair worn clay Taks up its last abode.] **1837** *Southern Lit. Messenger* III. 668, I have a holy horror of gossips. **1855** [see MOSES I c]. **1860** S. MORDECAI *Virginia* xxxii. 317 The Virginia Legislature had such a holy horror of banks in 1803, that they refused a charter to the petitioners. **1874** HOTTEN *Slang Dict.* 193 *Holy Joe*, a sea-term for a parson. **1883** G. W. PECK *Mirth for Millions* p. viii, 'Have you read "Peck's Bad Boy"!'..News agents on the Railroad cars found it almost impossible to meet the demand of those who yearned to become acquainted with this 'holy terror'. **1886** J. M. THOMPSON *Banker of Bankersville* 265 To get it by means of such a holy terror of exhortation. **1889** BARRÈRE & LELAND *Dict. Slang* I. 469/1 *Holy Joe* (prison and nautical), the chaplain or any religious person. **1892** KIPLING & BALESTIER *Naulahka* i. 4 By the holy smoke, some one has got to urge girls to stand by the old machine. **1893** *Strand Mag.* VI. 105/1 Not excepting even the Dwarf, and he's, generally speaking, a holy terror. **1916** 'TAFFRAIL' *Pincher Martin* iii. 34 Even the chaplain, the Reverend Stephen Holiman, set an example by shedding his clerical garments and trundling a barrow. The men loved seeing Holy Joe 'sweatin' himself', as they put it. **1916** G. B. SHAW *Androcles* p. xciv, The imitators of the apostles, whether they are called Holy Willies or Stigginses in derision, or, in admiration, Puritans or saints. **1917** *Dialect Notes* IV. 341 *Holy horrors*, a fright. 'It gave me the *holy horrors*.' **1920** 'SAPPER' *Bull-Dog Drummond* v. 125 'Holy smoke! laddie,' he murmured. **1921** N. H. THORP *Songs of Cowboys* (ed. 2) 73 Holy Moses and the Prophets how we split the Texas air. **1924** *Dialect Notes* V. 265 *Cow*: holy — (vex[ation]: New York). **1933** J. MASEFIELD *Conway* 211 *Holy Joe*, one who is good at Scripture. **1934** J. A. LEE *Children of Poor* 130 The Holy Willies would throw a party. 'Come to our Sunday School?' **1941** BAKER *Dict. Austral. Slang* 35 *Holy Joes*, prudish, narrow-minded puritans. **1942** BERREY & VAN DEN BARK *Amer. Thes. Slang* § 194/6 Holy cow! **1941** A. L. ROWSE *Tudor Cornwall* vi. 121 He must have been a holy terror to the neighbourhood. **1949** M. LOWRY *Let.* 26 Mar. (1967) 177 Holy great cow, what prose is this? **1951** J. CORNISH *Provincials* 40 Quit showing off. Holy cow! **1951** J. D. SALINGER *Catcher in Rye* xiv. 120 They all have these Holy Joe voices when they start giving their sermons. **1958** *Listener* 18 Sept. 429/3, I cannot find justification for Mr. McCallion's term 'holy voice'. **1959** 'J. ROSS' *Boy in Grey Overcoat* viii. 94 She said again, in that holy voice, [etc.]. **1960** I. CROSS *Backward Sex* 40 'Holy smoke,' he gasped, 'That's a funny face.' **1967** V. CANNING *Python Project* vii. 135, I said.. 'Holy Moses!' **1973** J. WAINWRIGHT *Pride of Pigs* 104 Holy cow! I forgot to switch the bloody immersion heater off.

5. a. holy laugh *U.S.*, a laugh by a person in a state of religious fervour; **Holy Roller** (see ROLLER *sb.*[1] 17 b).

1829 *Western Monthly Rev.* II. 477 Dr. Roberts is very pointed in his testimony against the abominable practice of jumping, pointing, dancing, boreing... Might he not have added the 'holy laugh'? **1833** H. BARNARD *Let.* 27 Mar. in *Maryland Hist. Mag.* (1918) XIII. 328 The preacher in the midst of a fervent prayer, will all of a sudden burst out into a loud boisterous laugh... The most godly of his brethren join with him. This is called the 'Holy Laugh'. **1845** J. J. HOOPER *Some Adv. S. Suggs* x. 122 Near these last, stood a delicate woman in that hysterical condition in which the nerves are incontrollable, and which is vulgarly..termed the 'holy laugh'. **1948** E. N. DICK *Dixie Frontier* 198 When it got started in an audience, everybody would be seized with hearty natural laughter. It would last for hours sometimes. This was known as the 'holy laugh'.

b. holy basil, the common Indian species of basil, *Ocimum sanctum*.

1880 *Encycl. Brit.* XII. 720/2 The worship of the *tulsi* plant, or holy basil, by the Hindus. **1894** A. K. NAIRNE *Flowering Plants W. India* 251 *O[cimum] sanctum*. Holy basil... Very commonly cultivated, particularly about temples and in Brahmins' gardens. **1906** T. COOKE *Flora of Presidency of Bombay* (1908) II. 440 The Holy Basil, the most sacred plant in the Hindu religion, very doubtfully indigenous.

c. Compar. *holier* in colloq. phr. *holier-than-thou*: characterized by an attitude of superior sanctity. (Cf. Isaiah lxv. 5.)

1912 T. DREISER *Financier* lxvi. 684 The 'holier than thou' attitude, intentional or otherwise, is quite the last and most deadly offense within prison walls. **1918** *Maclean's Mag.* Jan. 45/1 His holier-than-thou attitude irritates the officials. **1922** S. LEWIS *Babbitt* xix. 239 But I don't want you to think you can get away with any holier-than-thou stuff. **1928** F. HURST *President is Born* xiii. 155 If the whole holier-than-thou house of Schuyler has got to be protected from me, dammit, I'm not going to do the protecting. **1957** R. HOGGART *Uses of Literacy* vi. 169 They counter-accuse their accusers of being 'holier than thou', of smugness, of 'hypocrisy'. **1958** *Listener* 23 Oct. 660/1 She distrusted high flights of emotion, any parade of spiritual inclinations, any holier-than-thou attitudes. **1973** *Ibid.* 4 Jan. 9/3 The Mormons were not only holier-than-thou; they were thriftier.

C. *Comb.* **b.** *holy-eyed, -minded* (example), *-rolling* adjs.

1922 JOYCE *Ulysses* 182 An ollav, holyeyed. **1957** J. KEROUAC *On Road* (1958) 221 A thin..holy-eyed..lost soul. **1902** W. JAMES *Var. Relig. Exper.* xi. 296 The holy-minded person finds..inner smoothness and cleanness. **1965** *Punch* 20 Oct. 583/1 Sister Margaret, formidable pastor of one of those holy-rolling Harlem churchlets.

holy cross. Add: **c. holy cross toad,** a frog of New South Wales, *Notaden bennettii*, so called from a dark cross-shaped marking on the back.

1891 J. H. ROSE in *Proc. Linn. Soc. N.S.W.* 2nd Ser. VI. 265 *Notaden bennettii*, the Catholic frog, or as I have heard it called the 'Holy Cross toad'. **1969** M. BURTON *Animals of Australia* xiv. 120 The holy cross toad is unusual among Australian amphibians in that it comes out during the day to feed.

homalographic, *a.* Add: **1.** The form *homolographic* is the usual one. (Further examples.)

1921 *Times Lit. Suppl.* 6 Oct. 646/3 This map of the Pacific, on Mollweide's homolographic projection. **1937** *Geogr. Jrnl.* XC. 569 Equal-area projections being desirable for distribution maps, a modification of Goode's Homolographic projection—called by the compilers the 'Interrupted Mollweide's Homolographic'—is employed.

Hence **ho:malogra·phically** *adv.*

1969 N. R. HANSON *Perception & Discov.* xix. 325 We never see it sinusoidally, orthogonally, or homolographically, we just represent that world this way.

homatropine (homæ·trŏpĭn). *Pharm.* Also † **-in.** [ad. G. *homatropin* (A. Ladenburg 1880, in *Ber. d. Deut. Chem. Ges.* XIII. 107), f. HOM(O- b + ATROPINE.] A synthetic alkaloid, $C_{16}H_{21}NO_3$, the tropine ester of mandelic acid, which is used chiefly as the hydrobromide in ophthalmology to dilate the pupil of the eye.

1880 *Jrnl. Chem. Soc.* XXXVIII. 410 Homatropine aurochloride..forms first as an oil, which becomes crystalline on standing. **1901** T. SOLLMANN *Text-bk. Pharmacol.* xi. 261 For ophthalmologic examinations the preference should be given to homatropin, since its effects set in and disappear more quickly. **1951** A. GROLLMAN *Pharmacol. & Therapeutics* xiv. 271 Homatropine methylbromide..was introduced as a substitute for atropine in the treatment of gastro-intestinal spasm. **1970** DUKE-ELDER & ABRAMS in S. Duke-Elder *Syst. Ophthalm.* V. ix. 388 Homatropine is weaker than atropine but has the advantage of wearing off more quickly.

hombre (ǫ·mbre). Chiefly *U.S.* [Sp.; cf. OMBRE.] A man of Spanish descent; by extension, a man.

1846 S. S. MAGOFFIN *Down Santa Fé Trail* (1926) 93 Not only the children, but.. *hombres* (men) swarmed around me like bees. **1851** N. KINGSLEY *Diary* 2 Feb. (1914) 172 [I] had a fine sing in the evening with three or four other 'hombres'. **1918** C. E. MULFORD *Man fr. Bar-20* viii. 79 'Friend of this hombre?' 'Yes; sort of.' **1930** [see *FIX *sb.* 5]. **1930** *London Mercury* Feb. 324 'Look here,' said Clytemnestra..'is this *hombre* worth it?' 'If you don't think so, leave him to me.' **1940** *Amer. Speech* XV. 220/2 Cowboys living a rough and hardy existence occasionally develop into 'tough hombres'. **1957** *Times Lit. Suppl.* 25 Oct. 646/4 This book describes the doings of the

bad hombre. **1972** P. CLEIFE *Slick & Dead* xxx. 250, I had to find a tough hombre with enough guts and initiative to act on his own.

Homburg (hǫ·mbɒɹg). [Name of a town near Wiesbaden, Germany.] In full *Homburg hat.* A soft felt hat with a curled brim and a dented crown, first worn at Homburg, once a fashionable health-resort.

1894 *Country Gentlemen's Catal.* 155/1 'The Homburg Hat', as worn by H.R.H. Prince of Wales—10/6. **1901** *Sketch* 4 Sept. 254/1 The quiet gentleman in dark clothes and a Homburg hat. **1904** *To-Day* 29 June 256/1 At one time any man who wore a 'Homburg' was popularly supposed to be either an actor or an artist. **1922** E. WALLACE *Valley of Ghosts* xv. 142 He..put his Homburg hat on the table. **1940, 1958** [see *ANTHONY EDEN]. **1972** WODEHOUSE *Pearls, Girls & Monty Bodkin* v. 68 Characters.. who kept getting locked up in cellars under the river by sinister men in Homburg hats and raincoats.

home, *sb.*[1] and *a.* Add: **A.** *sb.* **2.** In N. America and Australasia (and increasingly elsewhere), freq. used to designate a private house or residence merely as a building.

1879 M. J. LAMB (*title*) The homes of America. **1882** *Harper's Mag.* Dec. 58/1 A lovely drive..is bordered with homes, many of which make pretensions to much more than comfort. **1889** *Kansas Times & Star* 6 July, A fine stone-front home at Twenty-seventh and Troost. *Ibid.* 5 Dec., For rent, a fine home at 1223 Broadway. **1929** *Publishers' Weekly* 7 Dec. 2661/1 Then out to see the new Ranh Brauch, a stunning private home turned over to the library. **1930** *San Antonio* (Texas) *Light* 31 Jan., Wilson wounded Elliott and his wife in a dispute Wednesday at the Elliott home in Mendota. **1955** A. ROSS *Australia 55* 37 More houses (or 'homes' as a house is kindly called here) are needed. **1968** *Globe & Mail* (Toronto) 17 Feb. 1/1 Her three..sons were shot to death in their home. **1971** *Timber Trades Jrnl.* 14 Aug. 21/1 The June figures showed more private homes completed than in any month since December 1968. **1973** *Guardian* 18 May 1/6 Motorway schemes..often wipe out considerable numbers of reasonable homes in accessible areas. **1973** *Ibid.* 20 Oct. 11/6 In Beverly Hills and Bel Air, we saw the homes (never called houses) of Jane Withers, Greer Garson, and Barbra Streisand.

b. (Later example.)

1936 C. F. M. SWYNNERTON in *Trans. R. Ent. Soc.* LXXXIV. 520 *Home*..that portion of the tsetse-habitat used by the tsetse..for both resting and breeding.

3. *a home from home*, a place away from home which provides home-like accommodation or amenities. Also (outside Britain), *a home away from home*.

1872 in S. Walker *Whistling Commercial* (Advt.), The real comforts of a home from home. **1906** *Morning Post* 1 Feb. 7/2 To provide them with a 'home from home' while engaged in the studies which fitted them for the positions in life they were destined to fill. **1907** *Daily Chron.* 30 Nov. 3/3 The British man is a clubbable animal, and doesn't mind paying handsomely for his 'home from home'. *c***1926** 'MIXER' *Transport Workers' Song Bk.* 21 It's like a home-away-from-home. **1961** *Times* 26 May 9/6 Durrants Hotel in George Street, for years the home-from-home of English County families. **1961** M. BEADLE *These Ruins are Inhabited* (1963) xii. 165 The delicatessen that is the foreigners' home-away-from-home in Oxford. **1962** *Guardian* 6 Oct. 12/4 The idea is to provide a 'home from home' atmosphere for boys between 16 and 19.

6. (N.Z. example.)

1842 *N.Z. Govt. Gaz.* Suppl. II. 40 In accordance with instructions from home.

9. a. (Earlier example.)

1854 DICKENS *Let.* 12 July (1938) II. 566 The keeping up of a 'home' at rounders.

b. *Lacrosse.* Each of the three players stationed nearest their opponents' goal.

1869 W. G. BEERS *Lacrosse* (1875) xii. 191 It is essential that Goal-keeper,..and Home should be special men accustomed to those positions. *Ibid.* 195 *Home.* Should stand within eight or ten feet of the opposing goal. *Ibid.* App. 254 The players of each side shall be designated as follows:..'Home', nearest opponent's goal. **1892** *Lippincott's Mag.* XLIX. 746 Outside home, and inside home. *Ibid.* 748 To secure the ball in the 'draw-off'..and pass it to the home or attack men. **1897** *Encycl. Sport* I. 607/1 The three *Homes* must be adepts in taking short and high catches with absolute certainty. **1964** *Lacrosse* ('Know the Game' Series) 35 First Home should make moves to as far away as Third Home level, to the goal, and round it. **1973** *Sunday Tel.* 4 Mar. 38/6 First home, Janet Roberts, with her dynamic underarm flick, deserved more than the two she obtained.

11. b. (Further Australasian examples.)

1861 T. GILBERT *N.Z. Settlers & Soldiers* 33 The..cliffs of Mokau..call to mind the chalk cliffs of dear old England—Beachy Head, and other favourite localities at 'home'. **1908** E. J. BANFIELD *Confessions of Beachcomber* I. ii. 77 Australians cannot with justice complain when the good old folks at home blunder..the while..so much local misapprehension prevails.

e. *Cribbage.* (See quot. 1877.)

1796 C. JONES *Hoyle's Games Improved* 294 By attending to the above Calculation any Player may judge whether he is at Home or not. **1877** *Encycl. Brit.* VI. 577/1 (*Cribbage*) Each player ought to reckon slightly over six in hand and play and five in crib, or seventeen and a half in two deals to be *at home.* A player who scores more than the average and leaves his adversary six or seven points in arrear is *safe at home.* When at home it is best to play off; when the adversary is safe at home it is best to play on.

f. Used in colloq. phrases expressing (freq. scornful) doubt or a query about the identity of a person or thing, *e.g.* 'Who is he when he 's at home?'

1887 KIPLING *Plain Tales fr. Hills* (1888) 99 You.. dimonstrate to *my* frind here, where *your* frinds are whan they're at home? **1914** E. PUGH *Cockney at Home* 118 Who is Popkins when he's at home? **1930** J. B. PRIESTLEY *Angel Pavement* ii. 64 'And we can't all look like Mr. Ronald Mawlborough either.' 'Who's he when he's at home?' Mr. Smeeth inquired. **1957** M. KENNEDY *Heroes of Clone* III. ii. 165 'And what's existentialist, when it's at home?' she asked. **1960** R. COLLIER *House called Memory* viii. 112 *Peachy?* I have no idea what you mean. What's that when it's at home? **1972** A. ROSS *London Assignment* 20 'Farrow?' I said. 'Who 's he when he 's at home?'

g. Used of a match when the team referred to is playing on its own ground. (Cf. *AWAY *adv.* II.)

1898 *Football Telegraph* (Kettering) 1 Jan. 3/2 Last season,..a splendid victory was achieved at home, the locals winning by 2 goals to 0. **1930** *Daily Tel.* 5 Dec. 20/3 Clapton Orient, 'at home' to Luton Town at Highbury. **1967** *Listener* 17 Aug. 223/1 They had just lost three matches at home.

13. b. (Later examples.)

1863 QUEEN VICTORIA *Let.* 5 Aug. in R. Fulford *Dearest Mama* (1968) 254 No one saw the correspondence. I think the King should look nearer home for such things. **1886** C. M. YONGE *Chantry House* II. xiv. 138 'I meant something nearer home,' said Clarence, and proceeded to ask if I did not think Lawrence Frith..smitten with Emily. **1969** *Listener* 2 Jan. 22/2 It seemed thus to be about something both larger and nearer home than Cohn-Bendit's subject.

13*. **to home.** *dial.* (also *U.S.*) = At home.

1795 B. DEARBORN *Columbian Gram.* 139 Improprieties, commonly called Vulgarisms..[include] To home for At home. **1833** J. NEAL *Down-Easters* I. 62 When he's to home..he's match for gab with anybody 't ever you come across. **1839** *Knickerbocker* XIV. 153, I used to be quite good at reckoning, when I was to home, in the state of New Hampshire. **1868** LADY VERNEY *Stone Edge* ii, I'm main sorry Master Broom ain't to home. **1873** 'S. COOLIDGE' *What Katy Did* xii, 'Tain't every girl would know how to take care of a fat old woman, and make her feel to home. **1910** *Dialect Notes* III. 450 (Western New York) Is your father to home? **1935** Z. N. HURSTON *Mules & Men* (1970) I. ix. 192 Come on, Big Sweet, we got to go to home. **1972** J. GORES *Dead Skip* (1973) viii. 52 White meat don't turn me on. I got Maybelle and four cute kids to home.

14. *attrib.* and *Comb.* (The distinction made in the Dict. between senses A. 14 b and B. 1 is no longer valid, since present-day hyphening cannot be assumed to be a reliable guide to grammatical function.) **b.** In relation to domestic economy: *home art(s)*, *care* (later examples), *circle* (earlier examples), *daughter*, *girl*; **home-bird, homebody** orig. *U.S.*, a person, etc., who prefers staying at home to going out or travelling; **home boarder,** a day-boarder, day-boy; **homecraft,** an art or craft pursued in the home; also, the household arts; **home loan,** a loan granted to someone to assist in the purchase of a house, flat, etc., to live in; **home unit** *Austral.*, a flat or apartment, normally one owned by the occupant.

1821 J. F. COOPER *Spy* I. xi. 175 Marry him I don't think I will——unless he becomes steadier and more of a homebody. **1841** DICKENS *Let.* 16 Mar. (1969) II. 238 With love *to* all your home circle and *from* all mine. **1850** C. KINGSLEY *Alton Locke* vi. 97 To..live a life of sneaking and lying under petticoat government, as all home-birds were sure to do in the long-run. **1853** MRS GASKELL *Ruth* III. viii. 230 Leonard's remaining such a home-bird..with such a mother..will do him no harm. **1855** —— *Let.* *c* 20 Oct. (1966) 873 Thank you for your kind message to my home circle. **1857** A. J. SYMONDS *Let.* 24 May (1967) I. 110 There were two brothers homeboarders but belonging to the School. **1881** C. M. YONGE *More Bywords* (1890) 125 An excellent plan..for bringing the whole family together round our dear old mother and her home daughter. **1886** Home-bird [in Dict.]. **1902** *Encycl. Brit.* XXV. 686/1 The Home Arts and Industries Association. **1905** H. A. VACHELL *Hill* xi. 228 He wished to educate his only son at Harrow as a 'Home-Boarder', or day-boy. **1914** M. HILL (*title*) Homecraft in the classroom. **1924** WODEHOUSE *Bill the Conqueror* ii. 32 He said this girl was one of those domestic girls, a little home-body, and might be leaving the party any moment now. **1927** PEAKE & FLEURE *Hunters & Artists* 79 *Art mobilier*, which has been translated 'mobiliary art', 'portable art', or 'home art'. **1927** *Daily Express* 26 Feb. 5/2 Women who seek a pleasant paying homecraft. *Ibid.* 23 Mar. 5 Modern Homecraft Notions. **1934** T. WILDER *Heaven's My Destination* 53 Snappiest little home-girl in Oklahoma. **1941** *Brit. Jrnl. Psychol.* Apr. 306 Finally she had to leave her University post... 'I could no longer keep it and be a home daughter.' **1944** J. S. HUXLEY *On Living in Rev.* iii. 28 Ma Ferguson, pictured as a very motherly sort of home-body. **1959** S. GIBBONS *Pink Front Door* iv. 52 The daughter at home, 'the home bird'. **1959** *News Chronicle* 12 Aug. 6/8 She liked to be a homebody and..lie with her head on her master's foot. **1961** R. B. LONG *Sentence & its Parts* ii. 54 She isn't a home girl. **1961** *Spectator* 17 Mar. 352 The great increase of home-care cases that must follow the demolition of the mental hospitals. **1962** *Southerly* XXII. ii. 92 By 'standard words' is implied those which soberly indicate what they have to indicate (like home-unit and bombora). **1966** AUDEN *About House* 24 A cellar never takes umbrage; It takes us as we are, explorers, homebodies. **1966** *Times* 7 Apr. 12/1 The ban on home loans by local authorities has been lifted. **1967** *Guardian* 16 May 8/4 The one school with 'home boarders'—where some boys live in the town and take 'bed and breakfast' at home. **1967** *Canad. Ann. Rev. 1966* 92 Government support to develop a complex of services, including hospital-based home care programs. **1967** E. HUNT *Danger Game* viii. 151, I know Mrs Dell lived in a home unit in Coogee. **1969** T. PARKER *Twisting Lane* 48, I was a great home-bird myself. **1969** *West Australian* 5 July 48/2 (Advt.), Prestige loc[ality]..suitable flats or home units. *Ibid.*, Home unit Scarborough open for inspection...This spotless apartment..compr[ises] 2 good bedrms. [etc.]. **1972** *P.O. Telephone Directory* Sect. 102 (London Postal Area E–K) 513/3 Homecraft Supplies. **1972** *Publishers Weekly* 30 Oct. 33/2 A country of homebodies with the concerns of homebodies is quite different from an outgoing one. **1973** *Times* 27 June 23/1 (*headline*) Tempers fray in tussle between home loan chiefs and Government. **1973** *Sun-Herald* (Sydney) 26 Aug. 11/2 (*heading*) A bolt of lightning damaged a block of home units at Vaucluse.

c. (Further examples.)

1745 W. ELLIS *Mod. Husb.* VI. I. 33 My Rows of broad Beans in my Home-close. **1853** C. W. ADAMS *Spring in Canterbury Settlement* vii. 69 The home-station was situated at the mouth of the river Motunau. **1884** W. SHEPHERD *Prairie Experiences* 205 Stock are always restless at first on a drive, and are striving to get back on their home-ranges. **1902** *N.Z. Illustr. Mag.* VII. 117/2 We'll keep the home-block. **1903** 'T. COLLINS' *Such is Life* 170 In two seconds more, Cleopatra was stretching away..towards Yoongoolee home-station, distant about sixteen miles. **1904** 'G. B. LANCASTER' *Sons o' Men* 3 Lane's out-station was twelve rough miles from the home-block. **1915** D. H. LAWRENCE *Rainbow* i. 6 A confusion of sheds spread into the home-close. **1933** C. DAY LEWIS *Dick Willoughby* 9 The cowman and his herd moving into the home-meadow.

d. (Further examples.)

1797 NELSON *Let.* Apr. (1845) II. 374 Had there been no Fleet in the Channel, the French might have come up the Mediterranean and taken us all; therefore the Home Fleet certainly took care of us and covered us. **1883** *Peel City Guardian* 15 Sept., Our harbour is once more almost empty, as the Home Fleet are fishing off Douglas. **1903** *Westm. Gaz.* 30 Mar. 2/2 What military stations abroad are now reckoned as Home stations. **1904** *To-Day* 14 Dec. 162/1 The Present Home Fleet is to be called the Channel Fleet. **1906** *Daily Chron.* 24 Oct. 7/4 A distinct fleet will be constituted from the ships in commission in reserve, to be called the 'Home Fleet'. **1915** KIPLING *Fringes of Fleet* 35 From the peace of the German side he had entered our hectic home-waters. **1927** W. DEEPING *Kitty* i. 10 A home-service job with one of the home-service battalions. **1941** *Ann. Reg. 1940* 55 Small bodies of highly mobile and strongly armed troops, known as 'Ironsides', after the first Commander-in-Chief of the Home Forces. **1972** *Whitaker's Almanack 1973* 461/1 Sir Andrew Lewis K.C.B. (Commander-in-Chief Naval Home Command).

h. *home-breaker, -buyer, -owner* (so *-ownership*), *-seeker* (examples); *home influence, news*; *home-breaking* vbl. sb.

1928 *Sunday Dispatch* 2 Sept. 17/1 As a home-breaker woman is..as good as a man. **1936** N. COWARD *To-night at 8.30* II. 74 You mean you'd prefer to be implicated with a professional homebreaker as opposed to an amateur one? **1907** *Daily Chron.* 18 June 3/6 Home-breaking is a more serious offence against society than house-breaking. **1969** *Times* 20 May 28/3 (*headline*) S[elective] E[mployment] T[ax] hits home buyer. **1973** *Times* 6 Oct. 1/1 A plan to help young home-buyers is likely to be announced within the next week. **1847** G. AGUILAR (*title*) Home influence. **1852** C. M. YONGE *Two Guardians* xiv. 255 Marian had..weakened the only home influence..which held Caroline to the right. **1966** D. JENKINS *Educated Society* v. 208 Home influence..[is] a major factor in determining whether people will be able to take advantage of educational opportunities. **1852** MRS. GASKELL *Let.* 2 Mar. (1966) 181, I don't think there is much home news. Last week was very quiet; and very busy with writing. **1936** *Punch* 5 Aug. 144/3 It is one of our principles that our students should *earn while they learn*, and for this reason our first practical efforts will be in the realms of the easiest department of Romantic Journalism, namely Home News. **1945** NELSON & WRIGHT *Tomorrow's House* xvii. 203/1 There are almost 35,000,000 dwellings in the United States. Maybe you own one of them... To the homeowner who is intrigued by..tomorrow's house, several possibilities are open besides..selling the roof over his head. **1956** J. H. GREENBERG in Saporta & Bastian *Psycholinguistics* (1961) 474/1 Homeowners must pay real estate taxes. **1960** *Times* 21 Nov. (Canada Suppl.) p. v/6, Canadians are the greatest home-owners in the world. **1960** *Times* 24 Oct. (Financial Rev.) p. xi/5, Thrift and home-ownership. **1972** *Guardian* 6 July 24/7 Home ownership in cities averaged 42 per cent. **1889** *Advance* (Chicago) 7 Mar. 191 The home-seekers of the 19th Century Pilgrim Fathers. **1911** *Daily Colonist* (Victoria, B.C.) 1 Apr. 12/1 (Advt.), Pandora Avenue Homeseekers. We have the finest residential buy in Victoria today. **1937** *Sunday Dispatch* 14 Feb. 18/4 The scope for the homeseeker is, in fact, extremely wide. **1963** *Times* 12 Feb. 8/1 *A Homeseeker.* Once you have found the house you are looking for, talk.. about a loan to help you buy.

i. *home-baked* (earlier examples), *-based, -consumed, -cooked, -cured, -grown* (earlier and later examples; also *transf.* and *fig.*), *-killed, -produced*; *home-cooking, -curing, -dressmaking, -nursing, -sewing, -staying* (examples); *home-duty, -growth, nurse*; *HOME HELP; *home-dressmaker, -grower, -sewer.*

1766 H. BROOKE *Fool of Quality* (1870) I. 99 Nurse went upstairs with a most bountiful cut of home-baked bread and butter. **1816** JANE AUSTEN *Emma* II. ix. 186 The finest looking home-baked apples I ever saw in my life. **1944** *Ann. Reg. 1943* 8 British and American home-based bombers made..day or night raids. **1956** *Nature* 25 Feb. 366/2 Six..schemes, applicable to the tropics, which were for home-based work..were added. **1904** *Westm.*

Gaz. 27 Dec. 4/3 A considerable proportion of export tonnage besides home-consumed manufactures..is conveyed by horse-drawn vehicles. **1923** H. CRANE *Let.* 12 Oct. (1965) 150 A very fine home-cooked chicken dinner. **1968** M. KANE *Walk of Devil* iii. 27, I know what you need...A nice home-cooked dinner in pleasant surroundings. **1934** *Amer. Speech* IX. 113/2 The tourist who enjoys strange foods..will rarely escape the home-cooking and the home-made pies that emerge from tin cans and factory-like bakeries. **1937** 'M. HILLIS' *Orchids on Budget* (1938) vi. 94 Steaks and roasts are so well prepared in the best restaurants that you might..turn up your nose at them for home cooking. **1968** O. WYND *Sumatra Seven Zero* i. 5 The other patrons..all came often to get away from home cooking. **1973** H. NIELSEN *Severed Key* i. 6 Didn't I ever tell you how much I hate home cooking? **1863** MRS. GASKELL *Cousin Phillis* in *Cornh. Mag.* Nov. 619, I handled and weighed in my fancy the home-cured ham. **1959** R. POSTGATE *Good Food Guide* 236 Breakfast was home-cured ham, thick, well grilled, with eggs and tomato. **1960** *Farmer & Stockbreeder* 16 Feb. Suppl. 8/1 When Denmark entered the trade at the end of the nineteenth century, bacon was still being produced from the whole sides in an adaptation of the traditional home-curing method. **1960** *Sunday Express* 11 Sept. 15/6 The ideal fabric for the home dress-maker. **1971** *Guardian* 10 Aug. 9/2 These costly fabrics (up to £50 a yard) are..being displayed..as temptations to home dressmakers. **1896** *Woman's Life* 4 July 138/1 Many people put up with faults in home dressmaking which they would rate in a regular dressmaker. **1966** H. YOXALL *Fashion of Life* viii. 68 When I first joined *Vogue* the early demise of home-dressmaking was predicted. **1850** MRS. GASKELL *Let.* 14 May (1966) 117 Girls, having..the home-duties of parents dependent upon them. **1825** J. S. MILL in *Westm. Rev.* III. 418 The home-grower is subject to many taxes, from which foreign corn is exempt. **1827** —— *Ibid.* VII. 173 They consume *home-grown* corn. **1895** *Cricket Handbk.* 31 It is sincerely to be hoped that the means may yet be found of recruiting the eleven from home-grown cricketers. **1935** *Discovery* June 162/1 The Great War undoubtedly had a great influence in fostering the canning of home-grown foods. **1959** *Times* 31 Mar. 11/1 Yet there was nothing unprofessional about the timing, staging, or lighting of even these most home-grown numbers. **1966** *Times* 28 Feb. (Canada Suppl.) p. xiii/3, Last summer, with a home-grown production of a musical..it played a six weeks season. **1973** J. THOMSON *Death Cap* iv. 56 A board..announcing in crude, hand-painted letters: 'For Sale. Home-grown Produce. Flowers. Fruit. Vegetables. Eggs.' **1825** J. S. MILL in *Westm. Rev.* III. 413 If the new material..be of home growth, the production of that material would open a new channel for the profitable employment of agricultural capital. **1873** E. E. ESTCOURT *Question of Anglican Ordinations* ii. 15 All the preceding seems to have been the direct home-growth of Lollardism or of Wicliffe's teaching. **1906** *Daily Chron.* 20 Sept. 6/1 Not even an expert could tell the difference between home-bred and home-killed meat unless he were on the spot. **1958** Home nurse [see *HOME HELP]. **1963** *Times* 24 May 8/5 All the old public assistance buildings replaced by pleasant old people's homes, with sufficient home nurses or home helps. **1905** *Daily Chron.* 25 Oct. 7/4 Instruction of..future mothers.. in..home-nursing. **1959** *Sears, Roebuck Catal.* Spring & Summer 831/3 Illustrated family handbook of home nursing and medical care. **1905** *Westm. Gaz.* 21 Aug. 2/1 Out of deference to the agrarian interest, prohibitive Customs and 'sanitary' restrictions keep out the food which is ready on the frontiers, while the prices of home-produced flesh rise to a height hitherto unknown. **1966** *Times* 28 Mar. (Austral. Suppl.) p. v/6, Home-produced crude oil. **1964** *McCall's Sewing* ii. 19/2 Whether you are a beginner or an experienced home-sewer, every pattern should be carefully studied. **1908** *Westm. Gaz.* 13 June 13/2 Every home-sewing room should include..a skirt-board [etc.]. **1964** *McCall's Sewing* ii. 15 Without patterns, home-sewing would probably be a lost art. **1854** THOREAU *Walden* 170, I the home-staying, laborious native. **1905** *Daily Chron.* 9 June 8/5 The home-staying Englishman.

B. 1. *home comfort* (earlier and later examples).

a **1855** C. BRONTË *Professor* (1857) II. xxv. 223 To sit on a foot-stool at the fire-side—to enjoy home-comforts. **1922** JOYCE *Ulysses* 296 Their abodes were equipped with every modern home comfort. **1942** *R.A.F. Jrnl.* 13 June 15 Some have heard about the living-out system, and dream of feather beds and home comforts. **1973** 'B. MATHER' *Snowline* xix. 225 The place where we're staying—all home comforts and no questions asked.

2. a. (Further examples.)

1857 R. B. PAUL *Lett. fr. Canterbury, N.Z.* 89 If you have not decided on the site of your home station on a previous visit to the run, the first step will be to ride well over it. **1865** M. A. BARKER *Station Life in N.Z.* (1870) v. 31 By the time we reached the Home Station we were ready for luncheon. **1930** L. G. D. ACLAND *Early Canterbury Runs* v. 113 He arranged that his executors should bury him in one of the home paddocks at Cracroft. **1939** P. A. ROLLINS *Gone Haywire* 62 The ol' man's bin steadily enlargin' his home range till now it includes mos' all the headwaters o' Elk Prairie Crick. **1946** F. D. DAVISON *Dusty* ix. 95 The sheep were approaching the home paddock. **1966** *Te Reo* IX. 54 The home paddock and the night paddock which..must in the early years have been the same piece of land.

b. *Home Counties.* For def. read: the counties nearest to London, namely Surrey, Kent, Essex (and formerly Middlesex); sometimes with the addition of Hertfordshire, Buckinghamshire, Berkshire, and occasionally Sussex. Add examples.

1898 *Mddx. & Herts. N. & Q.* IV. 153 The publication, ..will..relate not only to London, Middlesex and Hertfordshire, but also to Essex, Buckinghamshire, Berkshire, Surrey and Kent; that is, to the Home Counties. **1959** I. & P. OPIE *Lore & Lang. Schoolch.* xii. 233 In London and the Home Counties the police now chase off the streets even the simple waits singing Christmas carols. **1966** *Listener* 11 Aug. 218/1 The chances are..small that a writer setting his play in outer suburbia or inner Home County will make of it more than a painful banality. **1972** J. BLACKBURN *For Fear of Little Men* ii. 29 Her accent clashed dramatically with the jargon of Home Counties suburbia.

c. (Further examples.)

1800 *Spokane Falls* (Wash.) *Globe* 26 July 1/3 Six hundred baseball cranks witnessed..one of the prettiest exhibitions of ball playing that ever took place on the home grounds. **1802** *Sporting Mag.* XIX. 219/2 They were willing to run a match with a leash of greyhounds..or six brace belonging to each county, running home and home, for a sum to be agreed on. *Ibid.* 221/2 He has refused to run you *home and home*, or in any *central county* between the two. **1887** F. GALE *Game of Cricket* 51 The principal innkeeper and a few good local players inaugurated occasionally good out and home matches, in the same season. **1889** *Seattle Post-Intelligencer* 3 July 1/8 The home team played an up hill game. **1916** E. F. BENSON *David Blaize* iv. 60 The home team took the visitors off to the dormitories to put on their flannels. *Ibid.* 62 The field was cleared for the match; the home side won the toss. **1930** H. G. WELLS *Autocr. Mr. Parham* II. iii. 109 That complete lack of information about the visitors attributed to the home team. **1955** L. A. G. STRONG *Dr. Quicksilver* 25 The creator of Zeal-of-the-Land Busy was on his home ground in the last two lines. **1962** *Listener* 4 Jan. 41/1 Three generations on my home ground were equally disgruntled. **1969** *Ibid.* 3 Apr. 473/3 The factual conclusion is that if Arsenal had fouled more in these two home games (amongst others), they might have won them. **1972** *Oxford Mail* 15 Feb. 12/6 Carlisle dropped an unexpected home point last weekend.

d. *home signal*: on railways, a stop signal marking the end of a block section, and controlling entry either to station limits or the block section ahead. (Cf. DISTANT *a.* 3 d.)

1874, 1889 Home signal [see DISTANT *a.* 3 d]. **1923** W. G. CHAPMAN *10.30 Limited* x. 79 The home signal is the second signal reached and is usually near a signal box. It is a stop signal and must not be passed at 'Danger'. **1940** A. E. TATTERSALL *Railway Signalling* i. 16 Home and starting signals only for each direction at stations on single lines which are staff or electric token posts will be necessary. **1963** KICHENSIDE & WILLIAMS *Brit. Railway Signalling* ii. 16 Stop signals are..divided into two types: 'home' signals, usually placed on the approach side of a signal box, and 'starting' signals, placed beyond or in advance of a signal box... Before a signalman can accept a train from the previous signal box, the line must usually be clear for ¼-mile beyond his home signal. **1968** L. T. C. ROLT *Railway Engin.* vi. 93 By exhibiting three, or in some cases four, 'aspects' they [*sc.* colour light signals] combine the function of home and distant signals.

e. *Home Service*, one of the programme services broadcast by the B.B.C. (see quot. 1966). Also *Home programme* and *ellipt.*, *the Home.* (On 30 Sept. 1967 the name was changed to 'Radio 4'.)

1939 *Radio Times* 8 Sept. 3/1 In addition to the Home Service..two other British programmes are going out every day. One is a short-wave service to the whole world,..the other a short-wave service meant primarily for Europe. **1947** 'G. ORWELL' *Let.* 25 Jan. (1968) IV. 276 It was done on the Eastern and African services, but in those days I wasn't well-connected enough to crash the Home. **1948** [see *BREAK *v.* 50 g]. **1960** *B.B.C. Handbk.* 238, 1939..Home Service replaced National and Regional Services. **1965** G. MELLY *Owning-Up* vi. 64 Loudspeakers in every bedroom with a control switch marked 'Light. Home. Room Service'. **1966** *B.B.C. Handbk.* 44 The Home Service serves the broad middle section of the community...It is the main vehicle for news and for the daily reporting of Parliamentary proceedings.

3. a. (Further examples.)

1765 J. WEDGWOOD *Let.* 2 Mar. (1965) 29 Our home consumption is very trifleing in comparison to what are sent abroad. **1765** in *Amer. Hist. Rev.* (1921) XXVI. 743 The planters..reside Mostely on the Borders of James and York rivers which is the best soil for tobacco Especially the Sweet sented which is so much Esteemed in England, where they keep it for their own use, or what they Call home Consumption. **1825** J. S. MILL in *Westm. Rev.* III. 418 A protecting duty, in that case, would be a premium on home production, and, therefore, injurious. **1842** *Niles' Reg.* 12 Feb. 384/2 A state convention is to be held..at Hartford, Connecticut, to adopt measures for laying before congress the claims of home industry. **1844** MILL *Ess. Pol. Econ.* i. 14 It would be for the interest.. of Germany herself, to keep her linen a little below the value at which it could be produced in England, in order to keep herself from being supplanted by the home producer. **1848** —— *Pol. Econ.* II. III. xviii. 122 The value.. of a foreign commodity, depends on the quantity of home produce which must be given to the foreign country in exchange for it. *Ibid.* v. iv. 400 It would seem that.. taxes on exports..fall entirely on foreigners, taxes on imports wholly on the home consumer. **1876** C. M. YONGE *Womankind* xiii. 97 Factories or small home industries, such as glove or lace making. **1926** A. HUXLEY *Jesting Pilate* I. 187 We shipped the best part of a thousand lacquered kettle-drums—for home consumption, I suppose. **1937** E. SNOW *Red Star over China* vii. 253 The bulk of manufacturing..was by handicraft and home industry. **1940** *Time* 1 Jan. 29/3 Entente Cordiale.. was probably intended as French propaganda for home consumption on the present Anglo-French alliance.

b. (Further examples.)

1828 *Home Missionary Mag.* May 1 The design of the American Home Missionary Society [founded 1819] is to promote..the religious benefit of a great and growing nation. **1836** *Ibid.* Sept. 37/1 Endeavour to engage Ministers..to promote the great cause of Home Missions. **1842** *Ainsworth's Mag.* I. 232, I had occasion to accompany a home missionary into a few of the dens of London. **1844** *Ibid.* VI. 113 The manœuvres by which certain county members manage to obtain audiences of the home secretary, or the colonial secretary. **1855** MRS. GASKELL *Let.* 27 July (1966) 363 Papa..finished up his Home Mission with an address to the Students in the Chapel. **1881** E. W. HAMILTON *Diary* 25 Dec. (1972) I. 204 An office established to register the decrees of the Home Secretary and other Ministers. **1886** H. C. E. CHILDERS *Let.* 11 Nov. in S. Childers *Life* (1901) II. 245 The prerogative of mercy inherent in the Crown is dispensed..by the Home Secretary. **1938** M. C. BOATRIGHT in B. A. Botkin *Treas. S. Folklore* (1949) I. iv. 96 A Presbyterian home missionary came to a cabin and engaged a woman in conversation. **1958** S. HYLAND *Who goes Hang?* viii. 44 Home Secretary. A question to the Home Sec. **1966** *Listener* 17 Mar. 373/1 The Ministry of Defence is classified as a 'home' rather than an 'overseas' department.

4. (Further examples.) Also *transf.*

1856 *Spirit of Times* 4 Oct. 86/1 He was headed off and put out on the home base. *Ibid.*, An injudicious attempt ..to get a home run. **1867** H. CHADWICK *Base Ball Player's Bk. Reference* 138 Standing at the home base. **1920** S. LEWIS *Main St.* 300 He invariably decided that coming confinement-cases or land-deals would prevent his 'getting away from home-base for very long this year'. **1926** *Daily Colonist* (Victoria, B.C.) 22 July 12/3 Thirteen hurlers appeared. There were ten home runs, seven two-baggers and four triples. **1962** *Listener* 22 Feb. 337/2 In a big hit, what the Americans call a 'home run', the wood of which the bat is made is called upon to sustain stress several times bigger than would be required to break it in two, if maintained for a longer time. **1966** *Ibid.* 3 Nov. 644/1 The correspondent who never gets to home base comes to believe he is identifying himself with the ordinary sensible Briton.

5. b. *home key*: in *Mus.*, the basic key in which a work is written.

1959 D. COOKE *Lang. Mus.* v. 269 'They finally decide on E minor, which is, after all, the home key.' It is obvious that a modern composer need not be concerned about ending in the 'home key', after the 'progressive tonality of Mahler, Nielsen and others'. **1968** *Listener* 22 Aug. 250/1 The 'home' key of Weill's original score..is C.

home, *adv.* Add: **1. b.** (Later examples.)

1954 *Ann. Reg. 1953* 286 Americans were the target of propaganda of the 'Go Home, Yank!' type. **1973** *Guardian* 9 June 13/7 Vauxhall car workers..were..shouting, 'Yankees Go home! Bloody Americans!'

d. Also with ellipsis of *drive*, esp. in *Home, James (, and don't spare the horses)!*

1927 E. WALLACE *Mixer* viii. 114 'All right, Paul,' returned Mr. Sparkes...'Home, James.' 'James' grinned in the darkness, and the car moved forward. **1934** F. HILLEBRAND (*song title*) Home James, and don't spare the horses. **1964** WODEHOUSE *Frozen Assets* xi. 213 Okay, Watson, drive on. Home, James, and don't spare the horses.

2. b. *transf.* Safely or successfully at the end of (usually something arduous). Esp. in phr. *home and dry.*

Baker also records *home and dried* (*on the pig's back*) from Australia.

1930 V. PALMER *Passage* I. x. 86 You've done it this time, Lew! Home and dry on the pig's back! **1938** 'N. SHUTE' *Ruined City* ii. 26 'That's the Finnish business, then,' he said. 'We're practically home on that.' **1951** L. G. D. ACLAND *Early Canterbury Runs* 382 *Home and dry*, out of trouble. **1958** *Times* 21 Apr. 5/4 It was a most exciting finish, for apart from Miss Willcox, who, bar accidents, was 'home and dry', any one of six could easily have come second. **1962** J. BRAINE *Life at Top* iii. 46, I was in. I was home and dry. I'd got the order. **1963** *Guardian* 8 Feb. 1/1 Labour members felt after the ballot that Mr Wilson was 'home and dry'. **1965** M. WEST *Ambassadors* xi. 253 We're home and dry... Small casualties. A new Government.

3. b. (Later examples.) Also used in sport, etc., in sense shown in 4.

1903 J. A. T. BRAMSTON in Benson & Miles *Bk. Golf* 114 Be content merely to return to the fair course, and to get 'home' with the next shot. **1920** H. S. BROWNING *How to play Cards* 110 When each has dealt once, they [*sc.* the players of cribbage] should stand abreast at seventeen to eighteen, and so on throughout the game. The player who has maintained this average is said to be 'home'. **1934** W. J. LEWIS *Lang. Cricket* 130 *Home*, in various terms and phrases with reference to the batsman's ground, i.e. within the popping crease, as *to get home* in completing a run; [etc.]. **1954** F. C. AVIS *Boxing Reference Dict.* 47 *Get home*, to hit an opponent with the blow intended. **1955** *Times* 30 June 4/1 Nielsen's strength, his power of service, but not least his tactical skill in attacking Rosewall's service at all costs, just and only just got him home, when the whole issue was in doubt until the very last point. **1973** *Country Life* 17 May 1369/3 No man has won or lost until he has played home from the 14th tee.

5. b. Also with *get.*

1931 *Punch* 4 Nov. 496/1 Yet we have to admit that these songs 'get home' on us: that, singing them, we become as little children. **1958** *Church Times* 29 Aug. 3/4, I know that a lot of this will not get home among those who do not want to resolve discord.

7. d. *to write home about*: to boast of, to 'make a song about'. Usu. in negative contexts.

1914 'I. HAY' *Knight on Wheels* xxix. 291 'Anything doing at present?' 'Nothing to write home about, thanks.' **1925** A. HUXLEY *Those Barren Leaves* II. 96 There is nothing in these virtues *à la* Dickens to 'write home about'. **1930** M. KENNEDY *Fool of Family* xix, I know Bach had twenty sons, but they weren't anything to write home about. **1950** A. BARON *There's no Home* 11 Oh, this is something to write home about, all right. **1958** *Times* 3 Nov. 3/6 But for much of the day there was little to write home about as M.C.C.'s last eight wickets fell for

125 runs. **1959** *Times* 10 Aug. 6/1 Student nurses.. dismiss their share of the award as not worth writing home about. **1967** V. CANNING *Python Project* ii. 25 He has a small place in the country... Don't run away with the idea of anything worth writing home about when I say 'place'. It's a crumby little cottage.

8. a. *home-goer, -going*, also as *adj.* (later examples); *home-come* adj.; also *home-deliver* vb.

1908 *Westm. Gaz.* 12 Dec. 6/3 Who holds up to her home-come soldier's lips The babe he hath not seen. **1910** *Daily Chron.* 21 Jan. 6/6 The newsboy..handing them out to the sleepy home-goers. **1918** W. J. LOCKE *Rough Road* xix, The home-come warrior. **1937** J. JOYCE *Let.* 1 Nov. (1966) III. 408 We are sorry to hear you had such a stormy homegoing. **1958** *Time* 8 Dec. 42/2 To home-deliver fully 85% of the Sunday papers. **1967** K. GILES *Death & Mr. Prettyman* viii. 146 With a small van we could home-deliver so they don't have to leave the telly. **1973** D. CRAIG *Bolthole* i. 9 They were beginning to reach thick home-going traffic.

c. In senses 'in or at one's home', 'in one's home country', as *home-living* ppl. adj. and vbl. sb.

1881 W. D. HAY *300 Years Hence* i. 48 The disabilities under which the home-living population laboured. **1963** F. F. LAIDLER *Gloss. Home Econ. Educ.* 42 *Home living*, life within the home and family.

home, *v.* Add: **4.** *intr.* Of a homing pigeon: to fly back to its 'home' or loft after being released at a distant point; to arrive at the loft at the end of such a flight. Hence of any animal: to return to some specific territory or spot after being removed by an external agent or leaving it of its own accord. Freq. const. *to*.

1875 *Live Stock Jrnl.* 23 Apr. 57/3 Pigeons home by sight and instinct. **1895** *Cambr. Nat. Hist.* III. ii. 35 Snails and slugs possess to a considerable extent the faculty of 'homing', or returning to the same hiding-place day after day, after their night excursions in search of food. **1899** *Westm. Gaz.* 12 Apr. 9/1 The first [pigeon] homed at nine o'clock. **1904** *Daily Chron.* 25 July 9/2 Out of this vast army of birds not one homed on the day of release. **1934** E. S. RUSSELL *Behaviour of Animals* iv. 71 Arey and Crozier..relate of *Chiton tuberculatus*..that it keeps to one limited area and does not wander very far, though it does not appear to 'home' to a particular spot as does the limpet. **1956** W. H. THORPE *Learning & Instinct in Animals* xvi. 412 In one case a dog homed a 'bee-line' distance of 6 kilometres. **1958** *Observer* 26 Jan. 18/2 Migrating birds, and birds that can 'home' over great distances. **1966** R. ARDREY *Territorial Imperative* (1967) iv. 134 No random hunting or zigzag uncertainties marred the voyages. Sunfish truly home, and home to territories. **1971** *Nature* 17 Sept. 218/2 Visual recognition of their external surroundings..was used to resettle birds to 'home' to new loft-sites in place of old ones.

b. *trans.* To train (a carrier-pigeon) to fly home.

1928 *Sunday Dispatch* 29 July 22 Leatham (Downpatrick) has achieved what many thought impossible—viz., homing a bird from San Sebastian (Spain), distance over 800 miles, to the Emerald Isle, 300 miles of which, supposing the bird crossed from the northern coast of France, is over water.

5. *intr.* Of a vessel, aircraft, missile, etc.: to be set, or guided, to its target or destination, by use of a landmark or by means of a radio beam, etc. Also *fig.* Freq. const. *on* or *in on*.

1920 *Wireless World* Mar. 728/2 The pilot can detect instantly from the signals, especially if 'homing' towards a beacon. **1940** *Jrnl. R. Aeronaut. Soc.* XLIV. 569 The tanker must be equipped with D.F. gear, so that the two aircraft may 'home' on each other if visibility is poor. **1947** CROWTHER & WHIDDINGTON *Science at War* 119 Torpedoes and bombs that follow or 'home' on to their targets. **1948** [see *A.D.F.* s.v. * A III]. **1948** *Ann. Reg. 1947* 458 The equipment [for automatic take-off and control of an aircraft], which can be fitted to a standard aircraft, homes on a beam sent out by a radio beacon. **1955** C. M. KORNBLUTH *Mindworm* 53 That was near. He crossed the street and it was nearer. He homed on the thought. **1956** *Amer. Speech* XXXI. 228 A good officer could even 'home in on a bottle of whisky' placed on the landing field. **1958** 'P. BRYANT' *Two Hours to Doom* 58 Infra-red missiles which homed on the radiations given off from jet engines. **1962** F. I. ORDWAY et al. *Basic Astronautics* ix. 386 The guided vehicle then homes on the reflected signals as in the active case. **1971** *Daily Tel.* 23 Aug. 1/5 The other helicopter located the dinghy by homing in on the bleeping of the emergency distress [call]. **1971** *New Scientist* 16 Sept. 629/1 Mexico's Professor S. F. Beltran homed in on education as a critical need. **1972** *Daily Tel.* 7 June 2/8 A killer satellite is one which can home in on other objects in earth orbit and destroy them.

ho·me-along, *adv. dial.* Homewards.

1874 HARDY *Far fr. Madding Crowd* I. iv. 44 So I'll take myself home-along. **1905** E. PHILPOTTS *Secret Woman* II. vi. 154 I'll take Salome home-along presently. **1912** C. MACKENZIE *Carnival* xxxiii. 343 Well, I'm going home-along myself in November month.

home boy. Also home-boy. [f. HOME *sb.* + BOY *sb.*] **a.** A boy who is fond of staying at home. **b.** *Canad.* A boy who has been brought up in an orphanage or institution. (See HOME *sb.*[1] A. 8.) **c.** *U.S.* (See quot. 1970.)

1886 [see HOME *sb.*[1] A. 14 b]. **1913** S. A. FRANCIS *Canadian Home Boy* iii, The Canadian reader will need no explanation of the title 'Home Boy', but to the British reader this term will convey little meaning...It denotes a boy who has been brought up in some charitable 'Home', and from whom little that is good is expected. **1932** N. M. JAMIESON *Cattle in Stall* 192 [A] lonesome little English home boy [was] playing his mouth organ softly in the dusk. **1967** *Amer. Speech* XLII. 238 *Home boy* is a slang expression particularly in vogue among students at Southern Negro colleges... *Home boy* and similar forms, such as *home girl* and *home people*, denote individuals who come from the same hometown as the speaker. **1970** C. MAJOR *Dict. Afro-Amer. Slang* 66 *Homeboy*, person from one's home town.

home-brew. Add: **2.** *Canad. Sport.* A player, *spec.* of professional football, who is native to the country, town, etc., which he or his team represents. Also *attrib.*

1957 *Star Weekly* (Toronto) 17 Aug. 9/1 The Leos still are short of homebrews and are plagued by a problem at quarterback they have never succeeded in solving. **1958** *Edmonton* (Alberta) *Jrnl.* 18 June 12/3 To make room for import talent en route from the States, Edmonton Eskimos announced the release of 16-year-old home-brew third sacker Gene Kinesewich today. **1964** *Winnipeg Free Press* 19 June 36/4 The chief economic factor is that American players, whether Canadianized or not, still draw more salary than homebrews. **1970** *Toronto Daily Star* 24 Sept. 18/2 So what has become of Mike Wadsworth..and Walt Balasuk, another homebrew tackle?

home center. *U.S.* [f. HOME *sb.*[1] 2 + *CENTRE 6 a.] A shop which sells building, hardware, and decorating materials for the home. Also *attrib.*

1966 *Building Materials Merchandiser* Dec. 59/2 Small towns everywhere can provide a good base for a modern, one-stop Home Center where hardware, paints and related items are sold together with lumber and building materials. **1971** *Hardware Retailer* June 41 Today's Home Center is a hardware store. **1972** *Hardware Retailing* May 298/2 That these products are hot sellers is borne out by the experience of thousands of home centers. **1972** *Home Center* June 14 Handyman, the Home Center chain with 26 stores in California, the northwest and Scottsdale, Ariz., will move into Texas this year. *Ibid.* 53 Today's Home Center *is* much more than a lumberyard, but building materials and hardware are the heart of every Home Center operation.

ho·me-co:mer. Add: [HOME *adv.* 8 a.] (Earlier and later examples.) Also in more recent use with special reference to the Isle of Man.

1540 PALSGRAVE tr. *Acolastus* sig. C1, The father reioyseth the sonne to be a safe home commer vnto hym. **1927** *Peel City Guardian* 27 May, The Homecomers will arrive at Montreal during the afternoon of June 2nd. **1930** *Ibid.* 21 June 6/1 The White Star liner, 'Doric', will anchor in Douglas Bay..with 279 'homecomers' on board. **1947** *Chicago Tribune* 1 Nov. 19/5 Illinois' embattled players..adjourned to the Champaign Country club..to escape a horde of homecomers who are flooding this university community.

home-coming, *sb.* Add: Also *attrib.*, and with special reference to the Isle of Man.

1903 *Westm. Gaz.* 11 Sept. 4/2 The only greens.. that there is any reasonable chance of getting on to at St. Andrews are the greens of the home-coming holes. **1926** *Peel City Guardian* 26 June 2/2 The Mayor of Douglas intends to do what he can..to promote a big home-coming of Manx people and their descendants for June of next year. **1927** *Ibid.* 7 May, A meeting of the Executive Committee in connection with the Manx Homecoming movement. **1935** *Chronicle-News* (Trinidad, Colo.) 16 Oct., A 'Homecoming Dance' at the Trinidad high school will be held Saturday evening following the Trinidad–Salida football game. **1947** R. ALLEN *Home made Banners* iii. 17 In the crowded beer parlors they tended to herd together, like old grads on the eve of a homecoming game.

home-coming, *a.* Add: **b.** That comes, or is coming, home.

1898 *Month* Nov. 487 The lowing of the home-coming cattle.

ho·me-croft. = CROFT *sb.*[1] 2. In accordance with a housing scheme for industrial workers, a detached cottage, with land and outbuildings for poultry and other small livestock. Also *attrib.* Hence **ho·mecrofter, ho·me-crofting** *vbl. sb.*

1859 [see HOME A. 14 c]. **1925** *Public Opinion* 7 Aug. 121/1 The industrial workers to spread out and become home-crofters as well as workers. **1925** *Spectator* 5 Dec. 1018/1 Dr. Hilda Clark, whose work in Vienna was of such immense importance, has also sent us a terse but comprehensive account of the work and its objects. We note the interesting fact that she now calls these Land Settlements 'Homecroft Holdings'. *Ibid.*, We do not think that the word 'homecrofting' had been heard of in Vienna three years ago. **1926** *Ibid.* 24 July 130/1 The land and buildings shall be used in perpetuity as 'home-crofts'. **1927** *Daily Express* 21 Nov. 3/1 Earl Beauchamp opened the first six cottages of a 'home-crofting' experiment.

home-defe·nce. [HOME *sb.*[1] 14 d.] The defence of one's native or home country; an armed force designed for this. Also *attrib.*

1642 [see HOME *sb.*[1] 14 d]. **1671** J. OGILBY *America* ii. 29 Lest if Carthage should be invaded by a foraign Enemy, it should want People for a Home-defence. **1885** *Marine Engineer* 1 July 89/2 With such a fleet.. we could dispense with the Channel Squadrons, for home defence. **1904** *Rep. R. Comm. Militia & Volunteers* in *Parl. Papers* XXX. 16 A home-defence army. **1917** 'CONTACT' *Airman's Outings* 189 Mention must also be made of the Home Defence groups, but for which wholesale Zeppelin raids on the country would be of common occurrence. **1922** *Encycl. Brit.* XXXI. 83/2 On the War Office taking over the responsibility for anti-aircraft defence from the Admiralty in Feb. 1916, a definite Home Defence organization was adopted. *Ibid.*, In June the Home Defence wing was formed to include all Home Defence units. **1934** S. BALDWIN in *Hansard Commons* 19 July 1275 Of these 41 squadrons, 33 will be allotted to Home Defence, raising the existing 42 squadrons at home to a total of 75 squadrons. **1939** *War Illustr.* 4 Nov. 237/1 Further openings for the older men will be given in two new directions..Home Defence Battalions..and an Auxiliary Pioneer Corps which will take over military pioneer work, both overseas and here. **1964** E. H. POWELL in I. L. Horowitz *New Sociol.* 342 The home-defense brigades partially filled this need.

home econo·mics. orig. *U.S.* [HOME *sb.*[1] B. 1.] The art or science of domestic economy. Hence **home eco·nomist.**

1899 (*title*) Lake Placid conference on home economics proceedings. **1926** *Chicago Drovers' Jrnl.* 5 May 3/3 Here all of the home economics work..will be housed. **1943** M. LYON *And so to Bedlam* 262 The young woman..was a graduate home economist. **1960** A. E. BENDER *Dict. Nutrition* p. v, Medical practitioners,..home economists, ..all, from time to time, step into the food field. **1963** *Weekly News* (Auckland) 27 Mar. 11/1 Miss Elsa Haglund, of Sweden, home economics officer of the [United Nations] Food and Agriculture Organisation, with headquarters in Rome. *Ibid.* 11/2 It is the job of the home economist to study..the..living patterns in any district. **1969** *Daily Nation* (Nairobi) 7 Nov. 32/1 A thorough knowledge of hygiene, nutrition and home economics is essential and applicants must be in possession of a valid driving licence. **1970** *Globe & Mail* (Toronto) 25 Sept. B 6/4 (Advt.), Applicants should have a diploma or a degree in Home Economics or Food Science and experience in the formulation of foods. **1973** *Jrnl. Genetic Psychol.* CXXII. 309 A home economics class composed of 28 eighth-grade girls.

home-fire. Used, like *hearth*, as symbolic of the home and family life, and especially popular during the war of 1914–18 in phr. *to keep the home-fires burning*: to keep the home going, to 'carry on' at home.

1892 I. ZANGWILL *Childr. Ghetto* I. I. xiii. 288 Happy fathers of happy children, men who warmed their hands at the home-fire of life. **1914** IVOR NOVELLO *Song*, Keep the home-fires burning, While your hearts are yearning. **1928** D. L. SAYERS *Unpleasantness at Bellona Club* iii. 29 Health gone—no money—heroic wife keeping the home fires burning. **1931** P. WILLIAMS *Word of To-Morrow* IV. i, When they were holding the line in France, and he and all the other old gollywogs were keeping the home fires burning, snug and comfortable. **1972** *Listener* 6 July 13/2 Famine, rapine, rape... All keep the home fires burning, spread good cheer.

ho·me-folk, -folks. *colloq.* [HOME *sb.*[1] 14 i.] The people from or near one's home, *i.e.* one's friends, relatives, or neighbours. Chiefly *U.S.*

1884 'C. E. CRADDOCK' *In Tenn. Mts.* 288 All the home-folks, an' everybody that kems hyar to sot an' talk. **1900** J. W. RILEY (*title*) Home-folks. **1907** *Westm. Gaz.* 21 Sept. 6/2 They wander from the home-folks' ken. **1909** *Ibid.* 2 Dec. 2/3 Of home-folk caught by crumbling walls. **1915** H. L. WILSON *Ruggles of Red Gap* (1917) v. 99 Then we tried his home-folks in Boston. **1955** E. POUND *Classic Anthol.* I. 19 When I come in from being out My home-folk don't want me about. **1964** MRS. L. B. JOHNSON *White House Diary* 7 Jan. (1970) 33, I greeted L. F. McCollum of Continental Oil of Houston as homefolks.

home front: see *FRONT *sb.* 5 f.

ho·me-guard, Home Guard. [HOME *sb.*[1] 14 a.] **a.** A member of a local volunteer force. *U.S.* **b.** *Hist.* In England, the Territorial Forces.

1861 *Richmond* (Va.) *Examiner* 6 Sept. 2/4 The Secessionists..attacked the..Home Guards. **1862** O. W. NORTON *Army Lett.* (1903) 123 Nothing would make me ready to fight sooner than to hear some home guard abuse McClellan. **1873** 'MARK TWAIN' & WARNER *Gilded Age* xviii. 170 He was captain of the home-guards in Hawkeye. **1891** *Century Mag.* Jan. 409 An unexpected musketry fire was opened from the Indiana side by a party of home-guards. **1896** *Congress. Rec.* 25 Apr., App. 298 Before Gen. Burnside came, the mountain men of East Tennessee organized themselves into companies called 'Home Guards'. **1909** *Westm. Gaz.* 7 Jan. 7/3 A movement has been set on foot which has for its object the presentation of colours to the 'Home Guard', as we call the Territorials. **1919** F. HURST *Humoresque* 245, I know half a dozen who have got in the home guard..and have saved themselves by volunteering from being sent to France. **1969** E. W. MORSE *Fur Trade Canoe Routes* I. ii. 15 With the Hudson's Bay Company it was the 'Home Guard' Indians, the Swampy Crees, who served as middlemen.

c. One who lives or works continuously in the same place; *spec.* (*a*) a resident logger; (*b*) a non-migrant beggar, hobo, or thief. Also *collect. N. Amer. colloq.*

1919 *Camp Worker* (Vancouver) 19 Sept. 8/3 Camp poorly organized; too many home guards. **1923** N. ANDERSON *Hobo* i. 7 The vagabond who has settled and retired, the 'home guard' as they are rather contemptuously referred to by the tribe of younger and more

adventurous men who still choose to take the road. *Ibid.* vii. 96 The home guard, like the hobo, is a casual laborer, but he works, often only by the day, now at one and again at another of the multitude of unskilled jobs in the city. **1926** J. Black *You can't Win* xvi. 219 The gangs [of thieves] are made up of natives and 'home guards'. **1931** 'D. Stiff' *Milk & Honey Route* iii. 37 At the other extreme from the ramblers we find a large variety of home guards who keep pretty much to one locality. **1942** R. E. Swanson *Rhymes of Western Logger* 35 You talk of your drums! you home-guard bums should have seen the size of her 'main'! **1955** *Publ. Amer. Dial. Soc.* xxiv. 98 They will say about home guards, they'll say, 'Pay no attention to him..he's just a local character.'

d. In form *Home Guard.* The military force organized in 1940 for the defence of Great Britain and Northern Ireland against possible invasion, orig. called Local Defence Volunteers. Also a member of this force. (Disbanded 31 July 1957.) Similarly in other countries.

1940 W. S. Churchill *Into Battle* (1941) 251 Behind the regular Army we have more than a million of the Local Defence Volunteers, or, as they are much better called, the 'Home Guard'. **1942** *Ann. Reg. 1941* 45 On May 14 the Home Guard celebrated its first anniversary. **1943** *N. & Q.* 10 Apr. 220/1 A company of a Home Guard battalion. **1945** *Daily Mirror* 15 Aug. 3/1 When an eighteen-year-old Home Guard decided to impersonate his brother and take his place in the Army he ran into trouble right away. **1970** *Daily Tel.* 21 Mar. 4/7 Lebanon is to establish a 'home guard' to police the border areas with Israel, where tension between Palestinian guerillas and the Lebanese Army has been high. **1970** *New Yorker* 19 Sept. 34/1 At the entrance to the hospital [in Israel], a Home Guard..sucked furiously on his unlit pipe.

home help. [Home *sb.*^{1} 14 b.] A domestic worker; *spec.* a woman made available by local authorities, etc., for help in the home.

1900 *Daily News* 13 June 8/6 The West Central Jewish Girls' Club... Its objects are educational, recreational, and religious. There are 221 members..home-helps, 17. **1939** M. Spring Rice *Working-Class Wives* 14 While women..go into hospital..trained home helps can be provided to look after the father and children. **1958** *Times* 24 Feb. 11/1 One obvious solution to the problem is for local authorities to provide a better service of home helps and home nurses. **1958** P. Townsend in N. Mackenzie *Conviction* 117 There is the nucleus of a home help service. **1973** *Times* 17 Jan. 4/2 Their response epitomizes some of the misconceptions about home helps which Mrs Clark..rebuts.

homeland. a. (Later examples.)

1941 W. S. Churchill in *Second World War* (1950) III. 583 We should therefore face now the problems..of driving Japan back to her homelands and regaining undisputed mastery in the Pacific. **1963** *Ann. Reg. 1962* 314 A series of 'independent' Bantu 'homelands', where each ethnic group would have a vote. **1968** G. Jones *Hist. Vikings* III. i. 145 The political and dynastic history of the Scandinavian homelands. **1970** *Caribbean Studies* July 90 With such chronological spacing for Homeland English..it is not surprising that..English usage in colonised places also had its period of graduation before being lexicographically chronicled, and..that such chronicles should be..modest imitations of the recognised Homeland product. **1970** *Nature* 24 Oct. 311/2 One of the regions of South Africa now set aside as a 'homeland' for the native population.

b. = Home *sb.*^{1} 6.

c **1892** C. Bingham *Song,* The Dear Home-Land. **1899** *Daily News* 26 Oct. 7/1 Looking..at the old Homeland through the eyes of Young Australia. **1905** *Daily Chron.* 22 June 6/6 We are here to-night..a body of Canadian business men, chiefly in order that we may learn to know the people of the homeland. **1907** Scott & Wallas *(title)* The call of the Homeland: a collection of English verse.

home language. [Home *sb.*^{1} B. 1 and 3.] The language spoken in one's home; one's native language; the mother-tongue.

1926 M. West *Bilingualism* I. i. 14 The Magh has Magh as his Home language. **1933** L. Bloomfield *Language* iii. 56 Ordinarily one language is the *home language,* while the other serves a wider range. **1934** *Cape Argus* 3 May 9/6 The only thing to do, therefore, is to define the words 'home language' as the language best known and understood by the child. **1957** R. MacNab *Emergence of Afrikaans* 4/1 Some of the descendants of those great Scottish churchmen now have Afrikaans as their home language, while their cousins have English. **1958** *Sunday Times* (Johannesburg) 21 Sept. 25/2 Applicants must be bilingual and preference will be given to those whose home language is Afrikaans.

ho·me-leave. [Home *sb.*^{1} 6.] Leave, often of fairly lengthy duration, granted to officials and others serving overseas.

1923 Kipling *Irish Guards in Gt. War* I. p. viii, Their short home-leaves gave them sudden changes to the tense home atmosphere. **1946** *Nature* 7 Sept. 320/2 Home-leave at regular intervals and free, or at least assisted, passages for themselves and their families..should be provided for officers whose homes are not in the Colony in which they serve. **1962** *Times* 6 Aug. 9/6 The parents' frequent home-leaves. **1973** *Guardian* 30 May 15 Lieutenant Mark Phillips ..was hurried off to Germany to join his regiment... Within the fortnight he was back again on weekend leave, prompting Mr Arthur Lewis to ask a Parliamentary question..about whether officers of the Queen's Dragoon Guards got special privileges for home leave.

ho·me-life. [Home *sb.*^{1} 14 b.] Life at home or in domestic surroundings.

1846 Queen Victoria *Jrnl.* 8 June in E. Longford *Victoria R.I.* (1964) I. xiii. 184 When one is so happy and blessed in one's home life, as I am, Politics..must take only a 2nd. place. **1859** C. Fox *Jrnl.* 5 Jan. (1882) xxv. 344 Settled once more into dear, beautiful home-life. **1867** 'T. Lackland' *Homespun* I. 39 The sincerest pleasures of the home-life are woven closely in with those of the garden. **1871** [see Home B. 1]. **1879** *Rep. Indian Affairs* 32 The absence of the example of the better home-life of our own people. **1898** T. N. Page *Red Rock* vii. 64 These men were thoroughly enjoying home life. **1906** J. London *Let.* 8 Apr. (1966) 199 In addition to home-life articles..I could furnish you other descriptive articles suitable for your pages. **1933** *Punch* 31 May 608/2 The kind of thing that might quite easily wreck one's home-life altogether. **1973** E. Lemarchand *Let or Hindrance* xii. 148 Most of my women are married, and one doesn't want to disrupt what home life they have.

home-made, *a.* Add: (Further examples.) Also *ellipt.* as *sb.*

1898 *Westm. Gaz.* 17 Nov. 7/1 There are two fogs familiar to the Londoner—the 'home-made fog', still, cold, anticyclonic, [etc.]. **1932** Blunden *Face of Eng.* 110 A box or two of popcorn and 'home-mades' in the front window of a cottage. **1934** H. G. Wells *Exper. Autobiogr.* II. ix. 808 He [*sc.* Stalin]..preferred that it [*sc.* criticism] should be home-made by the party. **1946** A. Huxley *Let.* 19 June (1969) 547 Whether there are powers of evil other than our own home-made devils is an open question. **1955** [see * farm-house b]. **1959** *Brno Studies* I. 24 The most important of such home-made digraphs is obviously *gh,* which replaced the old grapheme *h* in medial and word-final positions.

ho·me-maker. [Home *sb.*^{1} 14 h.] A housewife, esp. one in charge of the domestic arrangements (as opp. to a paid housekeeper); also, one who manages a household. So **ho·me-making** *sb.* and *a.*

1876 C. M. Yonge *Womankind* xxx. 266 Home-making is..her paramount earthly duty. **1886** [see Home *sb.*^{1} 14 h]. **1890** W. Booth *In Darkest Eng.* I. viii. 66 The general shiftlessness from the home-making point of view. **1895** J. R. Miller *(title)* Home-making, or the ideal family life. **1905** *Daily Chron.* 10 May 4/5 There could not be a greater boon to the many distressed home-makers of Canada than the advent of..domestic servants from the British Isles. **1934** *G. K.'s Weekly* 11 Jan. 306/1 The breathless never-can-we-catch-up feeling ..is essential to the happiness of the true homemaker. **1954** J. Steinbeck *Sweet Thursday* 88 It was real nice. She was a home-maker. **1963** A. Heron *Towards Quaker View of Sex* ii. 19 Home-making is a satisfying outlet for many women. **1968** *Ideal Home* Nov. 42/1 Homemaking young marrieds. **1973** *N.Y. Law Jrnl.* 31 Aug. 1/2 These services might include specialized centers which can provide extensive supervision and education during the day, twenty-four-hour home-maker services, and counselling.

home market. [Home *sb.*^{1} B. 3.] The market for goods or produce in the place or country of production.

1758 Hume *Ess.* II. vi. 188 A great number of commodities are raised and perfected for the home-market. **1776** Adam Smith *Wealth of Nations* I. I. xi. 243 The bounty.. may..have occasioned..a greater cheapness of corn in the home-market than what would otherwise have taken place there. **1794** [see Home B. 3]. **1813** *Niles' Reg.* IV. 274/1 Then shall the home market still the rage for foreign export. **1843** *Amer. Pioneer* II. 214 Money became plenty, and a cash home-market was established. **1847** C. Lanman *Summer in Wilderness* i. 14 This city is the home market for all the natural productions of a wilderness country. **1892** *Rep. Vermont Board Agric.* XII. 132 Furnishing a home market for their products. **1972** D. G. Rhys *Motor Industry* ii. 40 The immediate post-war concentration on export markets had repercussions on the home market.

home movie. [Home *sb.*^{1} B. 1.] A home-made movie; a film made of the activities of one's own circle. Also *attrib.*

1939–40 *Army & Navy Stores Catal.* 910 Home movie camera. **1941** *Time* 16 June 33/1 Once 'expense' might have been a reason for doing without home movies. **1967** *Listener* 27 July 123/2 Some home movies of a retired politician. **1968** M. Richler *Cocksure* x. 53 The usual home movie stuff. Mortimer mowing the lawn. **1969** *Listener* 1 May 594/1 Old newsreels, live film (as distinct from reconstructions) of men and events—home movies, for that matter—are primary sources.

home perm. [Home *sb.*^{1} B. 1.] A permanent wave in the hair produced by equipment designed for use in the home (as opp. to one prepared professionally in a hairdressing establishment). So **home-perm** *v.,* **home-permed** *ppl. a.*

1949 *Woman's Own* 29 Sept. 3/3 (Advt.), Give yourself a Toni Home Perm today! **1954** M. Allingham *No Love Lost* i. 129, I..bought..one of those cheap home perm outfits. **1955** G. Freeman *Liberty Man* III. vi. 173 The rows of industrious home-permed heads over the desks. **1959** [see *applicator]. **1959** *News Chron.* 11 Aug. 6/2 Home perms are now being used on many children. **1969** J. Fredman *Fourth Agency* i. 8 Her iron-grey hair had been home-permed.

ho·me place. *U.S.* [Home *sb.*^{1} 14 a.] The place or piece of ground where one's home is situated.

1736 in *N.H. Probate Rec.* II. 625, I give & bequeath.. my Dwelling and Devise to my Son..all my land..Known by the name of my home place. **1885** *Weekly New Mexican* 12 Feb. 4/3 They are connecting D.D.'s outlying ranches with the home place. **1931** *Amer. Speech* VII. 93 *Home-place,* the part of a farm on which the house and out-buildings are located. **1946** G. Foreman *Last Trek of Indians* 91 They continued in their attachment to the old home place. **1973** *Amer. Folklore Newslet.* Spring 2/2, I enjoy going back to the old home place, now deserted, and the double-log cabin falling into decay.

home plate. *Baseball.* [Home *sb.*^{1} B. 4.] The plate at the apex of the diamond on which the batter stands, and which must be touched by the base runner before a run is scored.

1875 *Chicago Tribune* 3 Aug. 7 He stole third..and reached the home-plate. **1889** 'Mark Twain' *Yankee* xxii. 245 No fault of hers that she couldn't fetch the home-plate. **1891** N. Crane *Baseball* 79 *Ball,* a pitched ball, which does not pass over the home plate [etc.]. **1957** *Encycl. Brit.* III. 160/2 The outfielders are called right fielder, centre fielder and left fielder with relation to a man standing on home plate. **1970** *Globe & Mail* (Toronto) 26 Sept. 51/5 Let's appoint the umpires...Porky, you take homeplate.

homer^{1}. Add: **2.** [Home *sb.*^{1} B. 4.] In *Baseball,* a home run. So **homer** *v.,* to hit a home run.

1868 *New Eng. Base Ballist* 6 Aug. 3/1 The second inning saw a change as the Champions went out for two runs, one of these a 'homer'. **1951** in Wentworth & Flexner *Dict. Amer. Slang* (1960) 265/1 Bobby Thomson, who homered..and Monte Irwin, who also homered. **1961** *Listener* 19 Oct. 594/2 A homer is a mighty hit at baseball: into the stands or out of the ground—the equivalent of a six at cricket. *Ibid.,* Babe Ruth hit his sixty homers in a season of 154 games. **1967** *Boston Herald* 8 May 16/2 Fregosi homered in the fifth and Knoop in the sixth off reliever Bob Humphreys for the only Angel extra-base hits. **1972** *N.Y. Times* 4 June v. 1/8 Johnny Bench had homered in the seventh.

3. [Home *sb.*^{1} 6.] (See quot. 1945.) *Austral.* and *N.Z. slang.*

1945 Baker *Austral. Lang.* viii. 156 *Homer,* a wound sufficiently serious to cause a man to be sent home. **1949** E. de Mauny *Huntsman in Career* 180 'Don't say you've got a "homer" already, mate.' He pointed to Peter's bandaged hand. **1950** G. Wilson *Brave Company* xi. 173, I nearly did get a homer that time.

4. [*Home *v.* 5.] A homing device.

1958 *Chambers's Techn. Dict.* Add. 985/1 *Homer,* any arrangement which provides signals or fields which can be used to guide a vehicle to a specific location, usually determined by a homer transmitter. **1959** *Daily Tel.* 1 June 9/3 Thunderbird is what is known as 'a semi-active homer'. It receives the echoes of the illuminating radar's beam in a set in its own nose and homes on to the target accordingly. **1959** 'J. Wyndham' & Parkes *Outward Urge* i. 29 Fix up one of the dispatch homers on it, and let it jet itself along.

ho·meroom. *U.S.* [Home *sb.*^{1} 5.] (See quot. 1961.)

1915 *Ann. Rep. Comm. Educ. 1914* (U.S. Office of Educ.) I. iii. 45 The regular or home-room teacher feels a definite responsibility for the class wherever it may be. **1928** *Bull. Nat. Assoc. Secondary-School Principals* XIX. 16 The foundations of all guidance within the school are found in the homeroom organization. Efficiency in secondary school administration is demanding that every teacher shall be a 'homeroom' teacher. **1930** *School Rev.* Apr. 300 The home-room organization..in Detroit may be defined as a large number of one-room schools.. gathered together under one roof with a central office to facilitate their proper functioning. *Ibid.,* The home room is the unit of organization of the school and is the center of the pupil's school activities. **1961** Webster, *Home-room.* 1. A schoolroom where pupils of the same class or grade but often with different academic programs report at the opening of school and meet informally under the guidance of a teacher to conduct class business, plan and organize group activities, and discuss individual and group problems. 2. A group of pupils assigned to the same homeroom. **1966** Bereiter & Engelmann *Teaching Disadvantaged Children* iv. 71 The homeroom should have at least 400 square feet of floor space, and should be equipped with a piano and (like the other rooms) a chalkboard. **1968** 'R. Macdonald' *Instant Enemy* i. 8, I got in touch with her homeroom teacher and found she'd been playing hookey all day.

home science. [Home *sb.*^{1} B. 1.] The art or science of domestic economy.

Term not used in Britain.

1912 *Calendar Univ. Otago* 79 The Home Science Department (opened in April, 1911) has been housed for the present in part of the old Mining School. **1943** J. H. Murdoch *High Schools N.Z.* vi. 362 Home science students may substitute arithmetic for mathematics. **1963** F. F. Laidler *Gloss. Home Econ. Educ.* 46 The term 'Home Science' as used in New Zealand is, in general, comparable with the terms 'Domestic Science' in the U.K. and 'Home Economics' in the U.S.A. **1969** *Australian* 24 May 31/5 (Advt.), Home Science Teacher required immediately for second term, Woodstock Presbyterian Girls' School. **1969** *Hindu* 3 Aug. 2/2 (Advt.), Good academic record..preferably a B.Sc. degree in Home Science.

ho·mesite. *N. Amer.* [*home *sb.*^{1} 2.] = House-lot.

1911 *Daily Colonist* (Victoria, B.C.) 2 Apr. 12/2 Saanich

Waterfront...Magnificent homesites of nearly two acres from $450. **1968** *Globe & Mail* (Toronto) 17 Feb. 46/6 (Advt.), Landscaped, fenced homesite.

homestead, *sb.* Add: **2. b.** Freq. in Australia and N.Z.: the residence of the owner of a sheep or cattle station; in later use also = STATION *sb.* 14 (quot. 1898).

1849 *Handbk. Suburban & Rural Districts Otago Settlement* 7 Sheep or cattle owners, who, establishing their temporary homesteads, or stations, near or in the bush, might run their flocks or herds amongst the hills. **1851** E. SHORTLAND *Southern Districts N.Z.* xiv. 263 Farmers and stock-keepers, however, who have their homesteads on the plain. **1853** C. W. ADAMS *Spring in Canterbury Settlement* vii. 70 This homestead much resembles a small English farm-house, save that the sleeping loft had seldom fewer than ten occupants. **1891** R. PRICE *Through Uriwera Country* 61 As an out-station is to the homestead of a sheep-run, so is this little fort to Te Teko. **1901** M. FRANKLIN *My Brilliant Career* (1966) viii. 39 Home to.. the dear old homestead I love so well. **1911** C. E. W. BEAN *'Dreadnought' of Darling* i. 4 Most homesteads are apt to consider themselves pretty well on the outskirts of things if they get only one mail a week. At this particular station they get two mails a year. **1930** L. G. D. ACLAND *Early Canterbury Runs* 1st Ser. i. 8 'Station' is being driven out of use in its original sense of 'a place from which to work a run' by 'homestead'... When an old fashioned squatter or station hand used the word 'homestead' he used it to signify the owner's residence as opposed to the men's quarters and other station buildings. **1933** —— in *Press* (Christchurch) 28 Oct. 15/7 *Homestead.* In the old days, the owner's residence, but only if it was some distance from the rest of the station buildings... When the Government began cutting up the runs in the 'nineties, they or their surveyors adopted the word to signify what had been formerly called *the station*, and the new settlers followed them, so that the new sense of the word is now widely used. **1941** I. L. IDRIESS *Great Boomerang* ii. 10 Fifty miles from the homestead, on the New South Wales–South Australian border. **1946** F. DAVISON *Dusty* ix. 97 People came from all over the settlement, camping in and around the old homestead. **1961** B. CRUMP *Hang on a Minute* 73 They arrived at the Paranui homestead in the late afternoon.

homestead, *v.* (Earlier and later N. Amer. examples.)

1872 *Newton Kansan* 12 Sept. 3/3 [He] had homesteaded the south-east quarter of sec. 14. **1877** H. RUEDE *Sod-House Days* (1937) 123 If he homesteads, you would have to be here inside of 6 months. **1879** *Congress. Rec.* 26 Apr. 952/1 To prove their right to pre-empt or 'homestead' their lands. **1912** J. SANDILANDS *West Canadian Dict.* 23 Any person who is the sole head of a family, or any male over 18.., may homestead a quarter-section of..land in Manitoba, [etc.]. **1952** J. STEINBECK *East of Eden* 6 There was still marginal land to be homesteaded. **1959** *Times Lit. Suppl.* 6 Nov. p. xii/4 Yoknapatawpha County is William Faulkner's just as much as if he had homesteaded there and proved his claim. **1972** *New York* 12 June 15/3 A couple who leave Lima to homestead in the jungle.

homesteader. (Further, incl. non-U.S., examples.)

1872 J. H. TICE *Over Plains* 80 As far as the eye can reach the plain is dotted with new shanties of the homesteaders and pre-emptioners. **1882** *Brandon Daily Mail* (Manitoba) 23 Dec. 4/3 Some of the neighbors found the old homesteader near his tent dead. **1906** *Daily Colonist* (Victoria, B.C.) 6 Jan. 5/5 Each route north was lined this summer and fall with homesteaders, timber cruisers and miners. **1909** *Daily Chron.* 30 June 4/4 For these homesteaders of the ultimate [*sc.* Canadian] wheatlands..the main ordeal will be..loneliness and monotony. **1928** W. BAUCKE *Where White Man Treads* (ed. 2) 307 The nation composed of a large salting of freehold homesteaders will be the staunchest and strongest. **1950** J. JENKS *From Ground Up* xix. 204 Those who have the qualities and the desire to become homesteaders.

homesteading. Add: **2.** The granting of land according to the Homestead Act of Congress, 1862 (see HOMESTEAD *sb.* 3). *U.S.* Also, a similar settlement in Canada.

1891 *Grip* (Toronto) 13 June 377/1 Mr. Dabin moved that certain settlers in the North-West be granted the privilege of second homesteading. **1906** *Daily Chron.* 1 Oct. 4/4 There is no more homesteading—viz., free grants of land—it has to be bought. **1925** *Glasgow Herald* 10 Aug. 4 Homesteading has been a great factor in the agricultural development of Western Canada. **1936** *Scrutiny* IV. IV. 441 *Honey in the Horn* is a detailed account of life in the state of Oregon during the homesteading period (1906–8).

ho·me-stretch. *U.S.* [HOME *sb.*[1] B. 4, STRETCH *sb.* 8.] The return stretch of a course; *esp.* the stretch of a racecourse on which a race finishes. Also *fig.*

1841 *Picayune* (New Orleans) 19 Jan. 1/6 At the head of the home stretch Cowboy overtook him and..beat him out by a length. **1860** [see *BEEF *v.* 2]. **1861** *Trans. Ill. Agric. Soc.* IV. 38 On the last home stretch the steam [of the plough] became so low that it required some minutes to get up sufficient to run the furrow through. **1864** *Congress. Globe* 12 Mar. 1069/3 Already we see the slave States ..on the home-stretch to become free. **1868** H. WOODRUFF *Trotting Horse* xxiv. 207, I passed first one and then the other, and came on the home-stretch with a clear lead. **1878** *Trans. Ill. Dept. Agric.* XIV. 146 Still, a fleet horse who gathers up handsomely on the home-stretch, is not to be sneezed at by any one. **1897** [see HOME *sb.*[1] B. 4]. **1903** [see *BREAK *sb.*[1] 8 b]. **1968** *Daily Tel.* 4 Nov. 17/1 It was a furious home-stretch spurt that will last until he reaches his home in Minnesota at five a.m. on Tuesday, election day.

ho·me-town. orig. *U.S.* [HOME *sb.*[1] 14 a.] The town in which one's home is, or was originally; one's native town. Also *attrib.*

1912 *Top-Notch Mag.* (U.S.) 1 Aug. 64/2 He was killed in a pool-room row in my home town up the State. **1919** H. L. WILSON *Ma Pettengill* xi. 307 Having got the thanks of the French nation and his home-town paper. **1935** R. FROST *Let.* 21 Aug. (1964) 262 The sordidness..of home-town society all over Russia. **1938** *Times Lit. Suppl.* 6 Aug. 514/4 'Home-town' mixture, Scandinavian, Italian, ..all, whatever the race, nationality, class or occupation, end..by being good fellows. **1948** *Oakhillian* Summer 12 The other dignitaries returned to their various hometowns. **1953** [see *FAKE *sb.*[2] 3]. **1971** *Nat. Geogr. Mag.* Oct. 551/2 They [*sc.* boats] hold about a dozen people each and introduce the visitor to some of the more interesting of the hometown folk.

ho·mework. [HOME *sb.*[1] 14 b.]

1. Work done at home, esp. as distinguished from work done in a shop or factory. Also *attrib.*

a **1683** B. WHICHCOTE *Sel. Serm.* (1698) 402 Wherefore let every Man, in the first place, look after his Home-work; what he hath to do at Home. **1856** [see HOME *sb.*[1] 14 b]. **1861** G. MOORE *Lost Tribes* xviii. 364 One [apartment] more open and larger is reserved for visitors, or..is used for spinning or other home-work. **1901** *Act 1 Edw. VII.* c. 22 § 110 Prohibition of home work in places where there is infectious disease. **1907** *Rep. Sel. Comm. Home Work* in *Parl. Papers* VI. 61/1 Any instance of sweating in home work in connection with such things as ladies' jackets. **1908** *Franco-Brit. Exhib., Women's Section* 64 Frame of Quilting and Embroidery, lent by Home Work Co-operative Society. **1935** *Times Lit. Suppl.* 21 Dec. 882/1 The particularly mean swindlers who prey on the unemployed, either by 'homework' or by salaried jobs.. are duly pilloried.

b. Phr. *to do one's homework*: to do the preparatory work for a meeting, discussion, etc.

1934 R. STOUT *Fer-de-lance* iii. 40 There's three things I want to know. Or am I supposed to go up front and do my home work? **1959** *Listener* 6 Aug. 200/2 The Soviet reporter had been 'doing his homework' to some effect. **1966** M. CATTO *Bird on Wing* ii. 36, I have taken the trouble to do my homework on him. I know more about him than he thinks! **1971** *Guardian* 25 Feb. 15/2 The Government, says the report, appears not to have done its homework in considering how local radio should be financed.

2. Lessons and exercises to be done by a school-child at home.

1889 A. E. FLETCHER *Sonnenschein's Cycl. Educ.* (ed. 2) 155/1 Written home-work. **1897** C. DUKES in P. A. Barrett *Teaching & Organisation* 366 The large amount of homework which is assigned to pupils for preparation alone in the evening. **1905** *Westm. Gaz.* 28 Jan. 5/2, I think it is a wrong principle altogether to help a child with his home-work. **1970** C. LACEY *Hightown Gram.* viii. 168 I've just caught two boys in the quad, copying homework.

3. *slang.* Petting; also concr., a girl-friend: used esp. in phr. *a bit* (or *piece*) *of homework*.

1942 BERREY & VAN DEN BARK *Amer. Thes. Slang* § 847/3 'Petting', 'Necking'..homework. **1945** L. LANE *How to become a Comedian* vii. 75 Bert Errol [a female impersonator], when on the stage, looks a ravishing and beautiful bit of home-work. **1948** PARTRIDGE *Dict. Forces' Slang* 95 *Homework*; a *piece of homework*,..one's sweetheart or temporary girl friend. **1953** E. AMBLER *Schirmer Inheritance* 177 'And that little bit of homework you've got with you?' 'Miss Kolin, you mean? She's an interpreter.' **1968** J. SYMONS *Man whose Dreams came True* III. v. 171 He produced a dog-eared snap of a girl in a bikini. 'How's that for a piece of homework?'

Hence **ho·me-worker, -working.**

1902 A. BALLANTYNE in T. Oliver *Dangerous Trades* vii. 98 The home-worker..has been left outside the protecting pale of the Factory Acts. **1907** *Rep. Sel. Comm. Home Work* in *Parl. Papers* VI. 19/1 The duty of seeing to the sanitary condition of home workers' premises. **1907** *Daily Chron.* 11 Feb. 4/4 The success of this home-working experiment under leasehold conditions. **1973** *Guardian* 17 Oct. 15/8 Most home workers are women..a classic case of powerless employees... They need..the flexibility of working hours that home work allows... The unions, understandably, are completely opposed to home working.

homey, homie (hōu·mi). *N.Z. slang.* [HOME *sb.*[1] 6.] An Englishman; a British immigrant, esp. one newly arrived.

1927 J. DEVANNY *Old Savage* 170 The crowd at the house were mostly 'homies'. **1939** A. E. BROWN *Farmer's Wife* III. v. 161 My fishman has a pleasant slow drawl that betrays the 'Homie'. **1939** J. MULGAN *Man Alone* 28 That Saturday night I met you and our homey here. **1953** M. SCOTT *Breakfast at Six* viii. 67 These Homies with money, they stick together. **1970** D. M. DAVIN *Not Here, Not Now* IV. i. 217 An English accent. How hard it was to remember that it was as natural to a homey as your own accent was to you.

homing, *vbl. sb.* **2.** (Further examples, *esp.* relating to animals other than pigeons.)

1901 *Cambr. Nat. Hist.* VIII. ix. 387 The same homing instinct has been observed in some females of the Green Turtle. **1907** G. B. SHAW *John Bull's Other Island* I. 16 *Broadbent*: Here you are, belonging to a nation with the.. most inveterate homing instinct in the world! and you pretend youd rather go anywhere than back to Ireland. **1922** FLATTELY & WALTON *Biol. Sea-Shore* viii. 178 There is evidence of a 'homing sense' in the common limpet and its relatives. **1939** *Copeia* III. 127 Most grown turtles (89·5 per cent) showed some homing instinct or tendency to return to territory from which they were moved. **1956** W. H. THORPE *Learning & Instinct in Animals* xvi. 412 Experiments on the homing of dogs. *Ibid.*, The homing performances of bats. **1967** GARDINER & FLEMISTER *Princ. Gen. Biol.* (ed. 2) xiv. 248 Insects respond to polarized light, and..this capacity is used in orientation and homing behavior.

3. (In sense of *HOME *v.* 5); also *attrib.*, esp. in *homing device*, an automatic device for guiding aircraft, missiles, etc.

1923 *Jrnl. Inst. Electr. Engin.* 803/2 As this method seriously affects the compass and takes a machine off its course, wing coils are only used for 'homing', i.e. flying along a radius towards a transmitting station, thus enabling the aircraft to return to its base. **1933** *Bureau of Standards Jrnl. Res.* XI. 740 In these tests the direction finder was used as a homing device. **1940** *Illustr. London News* CXCVII. 567 (*caption*) Direction-finding radio compass for work in connection with loop aerial and 'homing' beam. **1947** CROWTHER & WHIDDINGTON *Science at War* IV. 178 Another..success was gained against the acoustic homing torpedo. **1951** *Gloss. Aeronaut. Terms* (*B.S.I.*) III. 27 *Homing aids*, systems designed to guide an aircraft to an aerodrome or carrier. **1955** *Times* 28 June 8/6 There are..other means of detecting a camouflaged operations centre, such as high altitude vertical photography and 'homing' on to radio transmissions. **1957** *Oxford Mail* 20 Aug. 1/4 After launching, the weapon is guided to the target by a special homing head which picks up the ground radar beams reflected back from the enemy. **1962** *Gloss. Aeronaut. Terms* (*B.S.I.*) VI. 4 *Homing guidance*, a system wherein devices built into a missile enable it to detect and steer itself towards, or to intercept, a target.

hominid. Substitute for def.: **A.** *sb.* A member of the mammal family Hominidæ (J. E. Gray 1825, in *Ann. Philos.* XXVI. 338), of which *Homo sapiens*, man, is the only surviving species.

1889 *Cent. Dict.*, *Hominid*, one of the *Hominidæ*; a man. **1916** *Bull. Amer. Mus. Nat. Hist.* XXXV. 347 Some day..one will discover a hominid of small stature, and almost erect posture. **1925** *Glasgow Herald* 25 July 4 That the human race, with all its tentative as well as more or less realised Hominids, arose from an ancestral stock common to it and the Anthropoids. **1957** *Observer* 1 Sept. 11/1 This glittering..exhibition is..the latest in toyfairs for spoilt hominids. **1969** *Times* 17 Jan. 13/6 A fragment of the upper part of a thigh bone from a hominid which lived at least three million years ago has now been recovered from the Olduvai Gorge, in Tanzania.

B. *adj.* Of, belonging to, or characteristic of a hominid or the Hominidæ.

1916 *Bull. Amer. Mus. Nat. Hist.* XXXV. 347 The divergence of the Hominid branch occurred..from the anthropoid stem after the separation of the gibbons. **1939** C. S. COON *Races of Europe* ii. 51 During the Middle Pleistocene..a mixture took place between early white dolichocephals and one or more non-*sapiens* hominid species, including *Homo neanderthalensis*. **1971** J. Z. YOUNG *Introd. Study of Man* xxxii. 444 Hominid creatures existed a good deal earlier than had previously been supposed. **1971** *Nature* 30 July 308/1 So few identifiable parts were visible that it is remarkable it was recognized as hominid.

hominine, *a.* Add: Also pronounced (hǫ·minīn). **2.** Of, belonging to, or characteristic of a hominine or Homininæ.

1959 *Cold Spring Harbor Symp. Quant. Biol.* XXIV. 244/1 The earlier forms are the more hominine... This suggests the probability that the known Australopithecines represent a somewhat specialized offshoot from the mainline of hominine evolution.

B. *sb.* [f. mod.L. *Homininæ* (G. Heberer 1949, in *Die Umschau* 1 May 258/1), the subfamily including man.] A member of the subfamily Homininæ, which is sometimes used as a division of the family Hominidæ to comprise large-brained hominids, in contrast to the small-brained ones of the sub-family Australopithecinæ.

1961 K. P. OAKLEY in *Times* 5 Sept. 13/5 Three main points of emergence in man's evolution—the first toolmakers, the first hominines, and the first men of our own species. **1963** G. G. SIMPSON in S. L. Washburn *Classification & Human Evol.* (1964) i. 29 In the Hominidae, I see no sufficient reason for having two subfamilies, especially as each has only one known genus as I and, I believe, most others now define the genera. 'Australopithecine' and 'hominine' may still be used as strictly vernacular terms for structural levels. **1971** *Nature* 6 Aug. 383/1 The bones throw some light on the structure and function of the lower limb skeleton of Middle Pleistocene hominines in East Africa.

hominist (hǫ·minist). *rare.* [f. L. *homo*, *homin-em* man + -IST.] One who advocates for men the rights and privileges conventionally accorded to women. Also *attrib.* or as *adj.*

1903 G. B. SHAW *Man & Superman* p. xviii, The wildest hominist or feminist farce is insipid after the most commonplace 'slice of life'. **1914** R. BROOKE *Let.* 10 June (1968) 592 If feminists are 'women' trying to be men, I suppose 'men' trying to be women are hominists.

hominization (hǫminəizēi·ʃən). [a. F. *hominisation* (P. Teilhard de Chardin *Le Phénomène Humain* (1948) III. i. 199), f. L. *homo*,

homin- man + -IZATION.] The evolutionary development of characteristics, esp. mental or spiritual ones, that are held to distinguish man from other animals.

1953 J. S. HUXLEY *Evol. in Action* vi. 136 The original stock of pre-human apes differentiated into many species, all showing a trend towards what has been called hominization—the acquisition of more human characters. **1959** B. WALL tr. *Teilhard de Chardin's Phenomenon of Man* III. i. 180 Hominisation can be accepted in the first place as the individual and instantaneous leap from instinct to thought, but it is also..the progressive phyletic spiritualisation in human civilisation of all the forces contained in the animal world. **1962** W. HOWELLS *Ideas on Human Evol.* 295 (*heading*) The hominization of the masticatory apparatus, and modifications of diet.

Also **ho·minized** *ppl. a.*

1959 B. WALL tr. *Teilhard de Chardin's Phenomenon of Man* III. iii. 223 Are not the artificial, the moral and the juridical simply the hominised versions of the natural, the physical and the organic? **1973** *Times Lit. Suppl.* 27 Apr. 479/3 To supersede Rudolph Otto's notion of the holy as the numinous..and to do this for a hominized, secularized world.

hominoid (hǫ·minoid), *a.* and *sb.* [f. L. *homo, homin-* man + -OID.] **A.** *adj.* **a.** Of human form; man-like (rather than ape-like). Cf. *HUMANOID *a.* and *sb.*

1927 *Glasgow Herald* 3 Sept. 4/2 The divergence of the Hominoid and the Anthropoid branches. **1937** *Discovery* Feb. 62/1 He fixes the habitat for the first hominoid being as central Asia.

b. [ad. mod.L. *Hominoidea* (G. G. Simpson 1931, in *Bull. Amer. Mus. Nat. Hist.* LIX. 272).] Of, belonging to, or characteristic of a hominoid or the Hominoidea.

1950 *Q. Jrnl. Geol. Soc.* CV. 238 In all the hominoid species of Miocene and Pliocene age so far known..the canine is in the form of a strong pointed tooth. **1959** *Cold Spring Harbor Symp. Quant. Biol.* XXIV. 238/1 In 1949, Hürseler in Basel re-evaluated the..*Oreopithecus* material from the 19th century, and recognized it as being hominoid. **1973** *Nature* 3 Aug. 313/1 Species of *Ramapithecus* are among the few hominoid species currently considered as possibly close to the direct line of human ancestry.

B. *sb.* **a.** An animal resembling man.

1927 *Glasgow Herald* 3 Sept. 4/2 The early hominoids.

b. *spec.* [ad. mod.L. *Hominoidea* (see above)]: a member of the superfamily Hominoidea, which includes man and the anthropoid apes.

1949 W. E. LE GROS CLARK *Hist. Primates* 74 The earliest fossil records of *true* Man, that is, of hominoids which definitely come within the family of the Hominidae, have been found in the Far East. **1950** *Q. Jrnl. Geol. Soc.* CV. 231 A great many specimens of fossil hominoids.. were collected. **1963** R. CARRINGTON *Million Years of Man* iii. 26 The smallest and most primitive of all living hominoids are the gibbons. **1967** W. E. LE GROS CLARK *Man-Apes or Ape-Men?* i. 2 The human and anthropoid ape families are now usually included in a common group, a superfamily called the Hominoidea (or, colloquially, hominoids).

hominy. a. (Later examples.)

1860 S. MORDECAI *Virginia* xxxi. 314 Slow as the process of 'beating hominy' is, it was a great resource, as was the eating of it for lack of hoecake. **1888** *Rep. Vermont Board Agric.* X. 30 The refuse of white corn after what is termed the 'hominy' has been removed, is more valuable as a feed for stock than yellow corn. **1922** W. G. R. FRANCILLON *Good Cookery* (ed. 2) xiv. 251 Wash and soak the hominy in water, overnight. Boil gently for half-hour or more. Stir frequently, and serve as oatmeal porridge. **1926–7** *Army & Navy Stores Catal.* 21/2 Hominy, finest pearl—bag about 5 lb. 1/4. **1959** E. TUNIS *Indians* 43/1 Wherever corn was raised in the East, hominy was an important food. **1963** R. I. MCDAVID in Mencken *Amer. Lang.* 699 In South Carolina I was taught that hominy designated what the less fortunate called grits.

b. (Further examples.)

1711 in *Col. Rec. N. Carolina* (1886) I. 765 The planter here..dare not allow himself to partake of his own creatures except it be the corn of the country in hominy bread. **1827** J. F. COOPER *Prairie* ii, Others [were engaged] in plying the heavy pestle of a moveable hominy-mortar. *Ibid.* xvi, Giving her a morsel of venison, now and then, or a spoon around his hominy-dish. **1843** 'R. CARLTON' *New Purchase* I. xv. 111 Here were all the vulgar pots, kettles, frying-pans, homminy-block, and the like. **1876** M. N. HENDERSON *Pract. Cooking* 71 When the milk is salted and boiling, stir in the hominy grits, and boil twenty minutes. **1961** *Listener* 17 Aug. 234/2 In Dixie you are offered some strange dishes; one is called 'hominy grits'—..it tastes like a cross between porridge and tapioca.

‖ **homme** (ǫm). [Fr., man.] In Fr. combinations: **homme d'affaires** (ǫm dafẹ̄r), a business man, an agent, a lawyer; **homme fatal,** used jocularly as the masculine equivalent of a **femme fatale*; **homme moyen** (ǫm mwayẹ̃n), used in various phrases with defining adjective, esp. **homme sensuel moyen,** average sensual man (cf. *AVERAGE *a.* 2 b); also **homme moyen sensuel.**

1717 M. W. MONTAGU *Let.* 17 May (1837) I. 410 Every pashá has his Jew, who is his *homme d'affaires.* **1815** SCOTT *Guy M.* II. xviii. [*sic*=xvii.] 305 Dinmont..stood poking his large round face over the shoulder of the *homme d'affaires.* **1851** E. RUSKIN *Let.* 20 Dec. in M. Lutyens *Effie in Venice* (1965) II. 235 It would cost him nothing farther than a letter to his homme-d'affairs at Vienna to arrange. **1882** [see SENSUAL *a.* 4 a]. **1894** G. DU MAURIER *Trilby* III. VIII. 103 The good Taffy had constituted himself Trilby's secretary and *homme d'affaires.* **1922** C. E. MONTAGUE *Disenchantment* v. 66 Church parades, a ministration of which the average private, *l'homme moyen sensuel* of Matthew Arnold, had taken a long and glad farewell. **1928** A. HUXLEY *Point Counter Point* xiv. 266 Scientific eyes, economic eyes, *homme moyen sensuel* eyes. **1932** *N. & Q.* 8 Oct. 269/1 They represent the opinion of the *homme lettré moyen* of our day rather than give us examples of brilliant criticism. **1935** *Times Lit. Suppl.* 9 Nov. 724/4 She intrigues to interest Edward Hudson, an *homme fatal,* in her friend. **1936** C. S. LEWIS *Allegory of Love* iv. 173 Even so, long after the original reasons for the tradition have been forgotten, the *homme sensuel moyen* with his fair, large ears appears in the *Midsummer Night's Dream.* **1958** *Spectator* 7 Feb. 166/1, I find it difficult to imagine anything more nicely calculated to convince *l'homme moyen cynique* that the Parker Tribunal was an elaborate white-washing operation fixed up by the Government. **1959** *Encounter* XII. II. 32 Humbert Humbert, her *homme fatal.* **1959** *Times* 22 Sept. 11/3 A good family solicitor.. is very much the *homme d'affaires.* **1961** *Guardian* 16 Feb. 10/4 Camus finds his 'homme moyen sensuel' in Dr Rieux, who is not interested in the salvation of men but wishes to cure them. **1972** *Listener* 22 June 840/3 He works much too hard at being mysterious, at playing *l'homme fatal.*

homo. Add: (Also with pronunc. hǫ·mo.) **b.** For 'single species' read 'single living species' and add: Many other species of the genus *Homo* have been proposed, to include various fossils of extinct hominids (as *Homo neanderthalensis, H. erectus, H. habilis,* etc.). *Homo sapiens* (sẽⁱ·pienz, sæ·pienz) [mod.L. (Linnæus *Systema Naturæ* (ed. 10, 1758) I. 20), f. L. *sapiens* wise]: the human species; the form of man represented by the surviving races and varieties. (Examples.)

1797 *Encycl. Brit.* X. 507/2 In the *Systema Naturæ,* Man (*Homo*) is ranked as a distinct genus of the order *Primates.* **1802** W. TURTON tr. *Linnæus's Gen. Syst. Nature* I. 9 Homo. *Sapiens.* Diurnal; varying by education and situation. **1864** *Rep. Brit. Assoc. 1863* II. 82 The author [*sc.* W. King] is led to regard the Neanderthal skull as belonging to a creature cranially and psychically different from man; and he proposes to distinguish the species by the name of *Homo Neanderthalensis.* **1896** KIRKALDY & POLLARD tr. *Boas' Text-bk. Zool.* 536 All Men are usually regarded as one species, *Homo sapiens,* divided into a number of races. **1924** G. ELLIOT SMITH *Evol. Man* ii. 76 The Rhodesian species was the most primitive member of the genus *Homo* at present known. **1940** *Nature* 17 Feb. 261/1 Many anthropologists, disregarding the rules of nomenclature, relegate all forms of Homo that do not differ structurally from what they loosely term 'modern man' to the sole species *Homo sapiens.* **1964** L. S. B. LEAKEY et al. *Ibid.* 4 Apr. 8/1 Genus *Homo* Linnæus. Species *habilis* sp. nov. (Note: The specific name is taken from the Latin, meaning 'able, handy, mentally skilful, vigorous'. We are indebted to Prof. Raymond Dart for the suggestion that *habilis* would be a suitable name for the new species.) **1969** LEAKEY & GOODALL *Unveiling Man's Origins* (1970) p. xiv, The word *Homo* is the scientific name for the genus of man, and includes the species *sapiens,* which is man as we know him today, and other species such as *erectus* and *habilis.* Many other species names, in this genus, have been proposed from time to time (such as *heidelbergensis* and *neanderthalensis*) but these are not now generally recognized. **1971** J. Z. YOUNG *Introd. Study Man* xxxi. 444 Most of the characteristics of *Homo* seem to have evolved well within the Pleistocene. **1971** *Sci. Amer.* Dec. 42 In a heavy brow ridge and a low forehead, the Pyrenees fossils more closely resemble *Homo erectus,* the 500,000-year-old fossil man of Java and China.

c. Used with L. or mock-L. adjs. in names imitating *Homo sapiens,* etc., and intended to personify some aspect of human life or behaviour (indicated by the adj.). *Homo faber* (fẽⁱ·bəɹ) [H. Bergson *L'Evolution Créatrice* (1907) ii. 151], a term used to designate man as a maker of tools.

1911 A. MITCHELL tr. *Bergson's Creative Evolution* ii. 146 We should say perhaps not *Homo sapiens,* but *Homo faber.* **1934** A. TOYNBEE *Study Hist.* III. 229 As *Homo Belligerans,* he focuses his convergent beams upon a single point on an aerial plane that is determined by the momentary presence of a hostile piece of aircraft. **1944** H. G. WELLS *'42 to '44* II. 100 Since poor rambling *Homo insipiens* began to put facts together and ask questions about them, he has been accumulating a vast disorder of answers. **1946** M. L. ANDISON tr. *Bergson's Creative Mind* ii. 99, I believe that it is of man's essence to create materially and morally, to fabricate things and to fabricate himself. Homo faber is the definition I propose. **1948** *Education* (Boston) Oct. 80/2 The range of possible noises that homo loquens can produce is ultimately conditioned by the structure of the human vocal apparatus and hearing apparatus. **1956** A. HUXLEY *Adonis & Alphabet* 10 There are many anthropologists who prefer to think of man as *homo faber*—the smith, the maker of tools. **1959** *Encounter* July 46/1 The Stoic philosophers.. seem to have made much of these emblems of moral dangers, turning..Odysseus into the ideal *homo viator.* **1960** E. DELAVENAY *Introd. Machine Transl.* 1 We can therefore rely on the inventiveness of *homo faber.* **1961** *Times* 25 Apr. 15/7 Symbolizing..this concept of *homo turisticus,* the new Hilton hotel..will have 500 rooms—all with a view of the Parthenon. **1962** *Daily Tel.* 7 Apr. 13 The bustling homo-sapiens was becoming homo-sedentarius, a quiet animal who sat and used his intelligence to push buttons and pull switches. **1962** M. MCLUHAN *Gutenberg Galaxy* 70 As long as *homo sedens* avoids the more potent kinds of optical conditioning..the mere shades of sacral life, as between nomadic and sedentary man, do not faze Eliade. **1963** AUDEN *Dyer's Hand* II. 88 Something managers need to be reminded of, namely, that the managed are people with faces,..that *Homo Laborans* is also *Homo Ludens.* **1964** *English Studies* XLV. (Suppl.) 244 An arraignment of Walter Pater in his quality as homo aestheticus. **1972** *N.Y. Times Bk. Rev.* 26 Nov. 22/3 *Homo lexicographicus* is a chalcenterous species of mankind. **1973** HOLT & MARJORAM *Maths. in Changing World* ii. 21 On a more sophisticated level of appreciation, there seems to be evidence for an evolution of intelligence from *Homo faber,* the tool-user, to *Homo sapiens,* the wise one.

homo (hōᵘ·mo), *sb.*[2] and *a.* A colloq. abbrev. of *HOMOSEXUAL *a.* and *sb.*

A. *sb.*

1929 M. LIEF *Hangover* vi. 100 Do you think Will Hays will let that play get by—with all those homos and everything? **1933** C. MACKENZIE *Water on Brain* iv. 44 There's a nasty old homo at the next table trying to catch your eye. **1967** *Listener* 21 Sept. 381/2 Sally's breathless confession to Dr Dale about hubby being a homo must have caused many a benighted bigot's heart to stop. **1973** A. S. NEILL *Neill! Neill! Orange Peel!* (rev. ed.) II. 216, I never had any symptoms of homosexuality but I wonder if some homos could date their condition to some early incident that made a girl, and subsequently all girls, taboo.

B. *adj.*

1933 E. A. ROBERTSON *Ordinary Families* xiii. 271 Round about six, fifteen and twenty are the recognized 'homo' ages in women. **1957** F. KING *Man on Rock* iv. 120 Sometimes they muttered to each other that he was 'homo'.

Hence **ho·moism** (*nonce-wd.*), homosexuality; homosexual practices.

1949 WYNDHAM LEWIS *Let.* 3 Mar. (1963) 480 Homoism died down in the 'thirties, but is so prevalent now as to be the [word] among the student or intellectual young.

homo-. Add: **ho·mocharge,** the charge on an electret polarized in the same direction as the original polarizing field; **homochlamy·deous** *a. Bot.* [Gr. χλαμύς cloak], having the outer and inner layers of the perianth alike, not differentiated into sepals and petals; **homo·-chromy** *Zool.*, cryptic colouring (of an animal); **homocy·clic** *a. Chem.*, containing or designating a ring formed of atoms of a single element; **homode·smic** *a. Chem.* [Gr. δεσμ-ός bond], containing only a single kind of chemical bond; **homodyna·mic** *a. Ent.* [ad. F. *homodyname* (E. Roubaud 1922, in *Bull. Biol. de la France et de la Belg.* LVI. 470)], (of an insect, its life cycle, etc.) characterized by a continuous succession of generations throughout the year, so long as reasonably favourable conditions prevail; also **homody·namous** (*b*); **ho·modyne** [after *HETERODYNE], a name given to a radio receiver and a method of detection which employs a local oscillator tuned to the carrier frequency of the detected signal; **ho·mojunction** *Electronics* [*JUNCTION 2 b], an area of contact between different conductivity types of a single semiconducting material; **homola·teral** *a.*, on or affecting the same side of the body; **homole·cithal** *a. Embryol.* [Gr. λέκιθος yolk of an egg], (of an egg cell) having the yolk uniformly distributed throughout the cytoplasm; **homomo·rphosis** *Biol.*, the regeneration of an organ or part similar to the one lost; **homopo·lymer** *Chem.*, a polymer formed from only one kind of monomer; so **ho:mopolyme·ric** *a.*; **ho:mopolymeriza·tion** *Chem.* [a. G. *homopolymerisation* (T. Wagner-Jauregg 1930, in *Ber. d. Deut. Chem. Ges.* LXIII. 3213)], a reaction in which identical molecules become joined, forming a homopolymer; so **homopo·lymerize** *v. trans.* and *intr.*, to form a homopolymer (of); **ho:mopolysa·ccharide** *Chem.*, any polysaccharide composed of molecules of a single monosaccharide; **ho:mosceda·stic** *a. Statistics* [Gr. σκεδαστ-ός capable of being scattered (σκεδάννυμι to scatter)], of equal scatter or variation; having equal variances; so **ho:moscedasti·city**; **homosta·tic** *a. Med.* and *Biol.*, applied to transplant tissue which is inert and not actively growing in the donor's body; opp. **homovital* adj.; **homotha·llic** *a. Biol.*, (of a fungus) having no genetically controlled incompatibility system; not heterothallic; so **homotha·llism, -tha·lly,** the condition of being homothallic; **ho·motherm** *Zool.* = *homœotherm* (s.v. *HOMŒOTHERMIC *a.*); **homothe·rmic** *a. Zool.* = *HOMŒOTHERMIC *a.*; **homovi·tal** *a. Med.* and *Biol.*, applied to transplant tissue which in the donor's body con-

tains actively multiplying cells; opp. **homostatic* adj.

1935 A. Gemant in *Phil. Mag.* XX. 933 We observe both kinds of charges on electrets. One has the opposite sign to that of the adjacent polarizing electrode,..the other has the same sign as the adjacent polarizing electrode, and will be denoted as homocharge. **1965** *New Scientist* 27 May 590/2 Under a certain critical applied field the heterocharge decays to a constant value and a homocharge does not appear. **1895** S. H. Vines *Students' Text-bk. Bot.* II. 512 When the perianth-leaves are all alike, the flower is said to be homochlamydeous. **1899** *Natural Sci.* Dec. 396 Homochromy and other protective adaptations. **1967** *Oceanogr. & Marine Biol.* V. 470 The chiton *Middendorfia caprearum* shows a conspicuous homochromy with the substratum. **1903** *Nature* 17 Sept. 475/1 The rings may be either homocyclic or heterocyclic without the character of the spectra being altered. **1932** H. G. Rule tr. *Schmidt's Text-bk. Org. Chem.* (ed. 2) II. i. 347 These [*sc.* carbocyclic compounds] are sometimes called homocyclic or isocyclic compounds. **1961** G. M. Badger *Chem. Heterocyclic Compounds* i. 10 The systematic method for naming dicyclic and polycyclic compounds follows that used for homocyclic compounds. **1939** R. C. Evans *Introd. Crystal Chem.* i. 8 Crystals..in which only one type of force occurs, are said to be homodesmic. **1957** H. D. Megaw *Ferroelectr. in Crystals* 205 In a homodesmic structure it is incorrect to speak of 'molecule' or 'molecular weight', since the molecule is coextensive with the crystal. **1931** *Trans. Entomol. Soc.* LXXIX. 105 The outstanding characteristic of this homodynamic..type of development is the absence of a definite annual life-cycle, the number of generations in a year depending on the actual weather conditions. **1964** Borror & DeLong *Introd. Study Insects* (rev. ed.) iii. 44 Many insects, particularly those living in the tropics, have a homodynamic life cycle; that is, development is continuous and there is no regular period of dormancy. **1929** V. E. Shelford *Lab. & Field Ecol.* vi. 160 Roubaud separates the higher Diptera into two categories, homodynamous and heterodynamous. **1928** Sterling & Kruse *Radio Man.* iv. 149 If the local generated frequency is tuned to exactly the same frequency as the received signals..the condition of 'zero beat' is said to exist. This means of receiving has also been termed 'homodyne' method. **1965** *New Scientist* 11 Feb. 344/1 The approach adopted..is to stabilise the laser at a single frequency, using an 'optical homodyne' receiver. The system uses a helium-neon laser stabilised at 6328 angstroms as both transmitter and local oscillator. **1960** R. L. Anderson in *IBM Jrnl. Res. & Devel.* IV. 287 Junctions between two dissimilar semiconductors will be referred to as heterojunctions and those in the same semiconductor with different doping as homojunctions. **1966** *New Scientist* 11 Aug. 316/3 On bringing two conductivity types of the same material..into contact, in a homojunction, considerable border disturbances take place between the hordes of electrons and holes confronting each other. **1971** *Sci. Amer.* July 39/2 The structure therefore has a *p-n* junction in gallium arsenide (a homojunction). **1910** *Practitioner* July 98 Should the lesion be in or close to the red nucleus, the tremor will be on the opposite side of the body, while if any other part of the system be affected the tremor will be homolateral. **1919** *Jrnl. Exper. Zool.* XXIX. 255 At the sides of the body, those parts innervated by the pallial strands are conspicuously homolateral in their responses. **1956** *Nature* 17 Mar. 529/2 These thoracic responses also remained when the major portion of the homolateral corpora pedunculata was removed. **1892** E. L. Mark tr. *Hertwig's Text-bk. Embryol.* i. 28 The translator has been accustomed for several years to use the word homolecithal instead of alecithal, heterolecithal being employed as a coördinate term to embrace telolecithal and centrolecithal eggs. **1914** W. E. Kellicott *Textbk. Gen. Embryol.* iii. 93 It is often difficult to distinguish the telolecithal egg from the homolecithal type. **1958** B. M. Patten *Found. Embryol.* iv. 78 In the egg of *Amphioxus* the yolk is relatively meager in amount and fairly uniformly distributed throughout the cell. An ovum with such a yolk distribution is termed isolecithal (homolecithal). **1901** T. H. Morgan *Regeneration* 23 When the new part is like that removed, or like a part of that removed, as when a leg or a tail is regenerated in a newt, the process is one of 'homomorphosis'. **1967** Gardiner & Flemister *Princ. Gen. Biol.* (ed. 2) xxii. 464/1 The conditions of homo- and heteromorphosis make it apparent that in the construction of a new part the old exerts some kind of influence. **1946** A. M. Ross in Richardson & Wilson *Fund. Plastics* ix. 146 Neither the vinyl chloride–vinyl acetate copolymers nor the vinylidene chloride–vinyl chloride copolymers can be fractionated so as to yield either pure homopolymer. **1970** *New Scientist* 30 Apr. 230/3 Teflon homopolymers are good reinforcing fillers. **1971** *Nature* 26 Nov. 197/1 Combinations of synthetic primer oligomers with homopolymeric templates..allow one to distinguish the viral enzyme from other DNA polymerases. **1931** *Chem. Abstr.* XXV. 2419 The hydrocarbons which are well adapted to heteropolymerization show no marked tendency to homopolymerization. **1937** R. S. Morrell et al. *Synthetic Resins* x. 251 Products..not easily obtained by homopolymerization. **1963** A. J. Hall *Textile Sci.* ii. 88 It [*sc.* acrylonitrile] very readily undergoes polymerisation by itself (homopolymerisation) and with other polymerisable compounds (copolymerisation). **1952** C. E. Schildknecht *Vinyl & Related Polymers* iii. 173, 2-Isopropenyl thiophenes would not homopolymerize on heating with peroxide catalyst, but..copolymerized with butadiene. **1957** *Ann. N.Y. Acad. Sci.* LXIX. 334 Some amino acids..do not homopolymerize to linear peptides under the thermal conditions that were employed. **1970** *Nature* 3 Jan. 60/1 Bis-(betachloroethyl) vinyl phosphonate is difficult to homopolymerize by a free radical mechanism to high molecular weight polymers. **1948** W. W. Pigman *Chem. Carbohydrates* xii. 513 Members of the first class (homopolysaccharides) give only one monosaccharide type when completely hydrolyzed. **1970** G. O. Aspinall *Polysaccharides* i. 5 The first broad division in the classification of polysaccharides is between homopolysaccharides..and heteropolysaccharides. **1905** K. Pearson in *Drapers' Company Res. Mem.* (Biometric Ser.) II. 22 If..all arrays are equally scattered about their means, I shall speak of the system as a homoscedastic system, otherwise it is a heteroscedastic system. **1934** *Brit. Jrnl. Psychol.* XXIV. 337 It is essential for factor studies that the correlation surfaces of the pairs of variables should be comparable. This is the case when each is homoscedastic, homoclitic, with rectilinear regression lines. **1970** *Nature* 12 Dec. 1098/1 Although the compared sample groups appear to be homoscedastic (*F* test) and results from the *t* test are significant ($P < 0{\cdot}001$), the size of the sample population is so small that we have relied on the non-parametric Mann–Whitney *U* test. **1905** *Drapers' Company Res. Mem.* (Biometric Ser.) II. 22, $\chi_1 = 1$ is a necessary result of homoscedasticity. **1957** Dixon & Massey *Introd. Statistical Analysis* (ed. 2) xi. 199 The regression curve of *Y* on *X* and the regression curve of *X* on *Y* are both straight lines with homoscedasticity (constant variance) for both *X* and *Y* variables. **1952** W. P. Longmire in *Jrnl. Nat. Cancer Inst.* XIV. 669 The term *homostatic graft* might be applied to inert tissues such as bone and cartilage when transferred from one individual to another of the same species; and the term *homovital graft* might be used in reference to grafts whose cells must continue to grow and reproduce for the graft to be effective after similar transplantation. **1971** Billingham & Silvers *Immunobiol. Transplantation* vi. 93 The long-term preservation of homostatic grafts is relatively simple. **1904, 1959** Homothallic [see *heterothallic* adj. s.v. *hetero-]. **1967** M. E. Hale *Biol. Lichens* iii. 42 There is good reason..to suppose that lichens are homothallic. **1906** A. F. Blakeslee in *Science* 27 July 120/2 Homothallism and heterothallism therefore seem to be fixed conditions in the forms in which the sexual character has been determined. **1966** J. R. Raper *Genetics of Sexuality in Higher Fungi* iii. 40 Three types of homothallism are found among self-fertile species. **1942** *Nature* 10 Jan. 56/1 It is also possible that such behaviour exists as a stage in the transit between full homothally and full heterothally. **1949** Darlington & Mather *Elem. Genetics* xii. 240 In some fungi..two cells of a single haploid hypha fuse in sexual reproduction. This is called homothally. **1934** Webster, Homotherm. **1960** K. Schmidt-Nielsen *Animal Physiol.* iii. 42 As an example of temperature regulation in a homotherm, let us look at the situation in man. **1971** *Language* XLVII. 417 Homotherms—that is, warm-blooded vertebrates, such as birds and mammals. **1890** Billings *Med. Dict.* I, Homothermic. **1901** *Proc. R. Soc.* LXVIII. 353 Variation in production of heat is the ancestral method of homothermic adjustment. **1960** K. Schmidt-Nielsen *Anim. Physiol.* iii. 38 Homothermic animals maintain a constant body temperature. **1952** Homovital [see *homostatic* above]. **1959** P. B. Medawar in L. A. Peer *Transplantation of Tissues* II. ii. 41 Homovital grafts start alive and..remain so, but homostatic grafts are progressively revitalized by the tissues of their hosts.

homocaryon, -caryosis, -caryotic: see *homokaryotic *a.*

homocentric, *a.* and *sb.* Add: **A.** *adj.* (Later example.)

1952 G. Sarton *Hist. Sci.* I. xx. 510 The main achievement of the astronomers of this period, if not of Aristotle himself, was the completion of the theory of homocentric spheres.

2. Of rays of light or a beam of particles: diverging from or converging to a single focal point (or appearing to do so when produced).

1886 C. M. Culver tr. *Landolt's Refraction & Accommodation of Eye* i. 13 In order that the homocentric rays may remain homocentric, the surface must have such a form that the angles of incidence shall be everywhere the same. **1949** *Proc. R. Soc.* A. CXCVII. 456 An electron gun, combined with a suitable aperture and electron lens system, produces a coherent illuminating beam, as nearly homocentric as possible. **1969** G. A. Fry *Geom. Optics* vi. 41 As long as the wave fronts are spherical and concentric, the rays all converge at the center of curvature of the wave front and constitute a homocentric bundle of rays.

Hence **homocentri·city**, the condition of being homocentric.

1959 Born & Wolf *Princ. Optics* iv. 168 In general, the homocentricity of a pencil is destroyed on refraction or reflection.

homoclime (hǫ·mokləim). *Geogr.* [f. Homo- + Gr. κλίμα (see Climate) or Eng. Clime.] A region or place that has a similar climate to some given region.

Orig. defined more narrowly: see quot. 1916.

1916 T. G. Taylor *Control of Settlement* (Commonwealth Bur. Meteorol. Bull. XIV) 23 Those regions in which climate, topography, and industries, &c., are similar I call 'homoclimes'. *Ibid.*, Homo-climes are British Isles, North France, much of the German Empire, [etc.]. **1931** A. A. Miller *Climatology* ii. 14 Stations having similar climographs are described as 'homoclimes'. Alice Springs is the homoclime of Biskra (Algeria), Perth of Cape Town, Brisbane of Durban, etc. **1950** *New Biol.* VIII. 68 The first work to do..is to define the climate where the insects must be established, and to locate its homoclimes (i.e. areas of similar climate).

homocline (hǫ·mokləin). *Geol.* [f. Homo- + *cline*, as in *anticline, syncline,* etc.] A set of strata dipping throughout in the same general direction; *esp.* one over which the angle of dip is more or less uniform.

1915 R. A. Daly in *Geol. Survey Canada Mem.* LXVIII. 53 For convenience the word 'homocline' will here be used as a general name for any block of bedded rocks all dipping in the same direction... A 'homocline' may be a monocline, an isocline, a tilted fault-block, or one limb of anticline or syncline. **1942** M. P. Billings *Struct. Geol.* iii. 42 The term homocline..may be applied to strata that dip in one direction at a uniform angle. Although many homoclines are, if large areas are considered, limbs of folds, the term is useful to refer to the structure within the limits of a small area. **1965** G. J. Williams *Econ. Geol. N.Z.* xix. 344/1 The dominant structure of the Tertiary beds of the Taranaki region is that of a gently (about 4°) south or south-south-east dipping homocline.

Hence **homocli·nal** *a.*, of, pertaining to, or associated with a homocline.

1916 R. A. Daly in *Bull. Geol. Soc. Amer.* XXVII. 92 The broad, useful concept denoted by the 'monoclinal' of W. B. and H. D. Rogers needs a new name... They intended to name a body of strata showing throughout dip in the *same* direction and for that 'homocline' (or 'homoclinal'; adjective, 'homoclinal') is the appropriate word. **1922** C. A. Cotton *Geomorphol. N.Z.* I. viii. 98 A striking effect of homoclinal drifting is seen where a stream crosses the strike diagonally. **1941** —— *Landscape* x. 91 Moderately inclined strata now outcrop as homoclinal ridges. **1954** W. D. Thronbury *Princ. Geomorphol.* ix. 225 Homoclinal ridges develop upon the dipping beds on the flanks of anticlines and synclines.

homocysteine (hǫmosi·stīn, -si·stiˌin). *Chem.* [f. Homo- b + *cysteine.] An amino-acid, $HS{\cdot}CH_2{\cdot}CH_2{\cdot}CH(NH_2){\cdot}COOH$, which is important as an intermediate in the metabolism of methionine and cysteine.

1932 *Jrnl. Biol. Chem.* XCIX. 137 If the hydrolysis, however, should take place between the methyl group and the sulfur then methyl alcohol and homocysteine would result. **1935** *Ibid.* CXII. 149 (*heading*) The isolation of homocysteine and its conversion to a thiolactone. **1962** *Biochem. & Biophys. Res. Comm.* IX. 493 The normal pathway for the metabolism of methionine involves demethylation to homocysteine which in turn combines with serine to form cystathionine, an intermediate along the pathway to cysteine and cystine.

homocystine (hǫmosi·stīn). *Chem.* [f. Homo- b + Cystine.] An amino-acid $(-S{\cdot}CH_2{\cdot}\text{-}CH_2{\cdot}CH(NH_2){\cdot}COOH)_2$, which is the oxidized form of homocysteine.

1932 *Jrnl. Biol. Chem.* XCIX. 136 We have drawn the conclusion that the compound is bis-(γ-amino-γ-carboxypropyl) disulphide, the next higher symmetrical homologue of cystine. Because of this relationship we wish to suggest the name of homocystine for the compound. **1962** *Biochem. & Biophys. Res. Comm.* IX. 493 (heading) The identification of homocystine in the urine.

Hence **ho:mocystinu·ria** [-uria], a rare condition, caused by a hereditary enzyme deficiency, in which homocystine is present in the urine.

1962 Carson & Neill in *Arch. Dis. Childhood* XXXVII. 512/2 The following abnormalities were discovered... A so far undescribed abnormality in cystine metabolism, homocystinuria. **1969** *New Scientist* 3 July 10/1 Prevention of postnatal brain damage by dietary treatment has been reported in a number of other inborn errors of metabolism. Examples include galactosaemia, tyrosinosis, maple syrup urine disease and possibly homocystinuria.

Homœan (hǫmī·ăn), *a.* and *sb. Theol.* Also **Homoian** (hǫmoi·ăn). [f. mod.L. *homœ-us*, f. Gr. ὅμοιος like, similar + -an.] **A.** *adj.* Of or pertaining to the Homœans.

1833 J. H. Newman *Arians* iv. iv. 362 Furthering their splitting into the Homœan and Homœusian factions. **1888** *Encycl. Brit.* XXIII. 720/1 He appears to have joined the Homoian party, which took shape and acquired influence before the council of Constantinople in 360. *Ibid.*, The Homoian formula, 'filium similem esse patri suo'. **1950** J. N. D. Kelly *Early Chr. Creeds* ix. 290 It gave expression to the new 'Homœan' formula of compromise..—*like in all respects*—and strictly avoided technical terms.

B. *sb.* One of a group of Arians that developed *c* 355 and repudiated both the Homoousion and the Homoiousion, maintaining simply that in the Trinity the Son is 'like' the Father.

1896 G. P. Fisher *Hist. Chr. Doctrine* 142 The 'Homœans' would not go a step beyond the affirmation of a 'likeness',—meaning a likeness in will and active energy. **1912** *Eng. Hist. Rev.* Oct. 761 It was of course the Homoeusians, not the Homoeans, who inclined towards the Nicenes. **1957** *Oxf. Dict. Chr. Ch.* 81/1 The middle party, called 'Homoeans'.., aimed at avoiding dogmatic precision as far as possible. **1966** P. R. Coleman-Norton *Roman State & Chr. Ch.* II. 420 Probably the Homoeans, moderate Arians, are meant.

homœo-. Add: **homœarchon** (hǫmiˌā·ɹkǫn), **homœoa·rchon** = *homœoarchy* (s.v. Homœo-); **homœobla·stic** *a. Petrol.* [ad. G. *homoeoblastisch* (F. Becke 1904, in *Compt. Rend. IX. Session Congr. géol. internat.* II. 570)], composed of grains of equal size; **ho:mœo-chlamy·deous** *a. Bot.* = *homochlamydeous* adj. s.v. *homo-; **ho·mœograft** *Med.* and *Biol.* = *homograft; so **ho·mœografted** *ppl.a.*, **-grafting** *vbl. sb.*; **ho:mœokine·sis** *Cytol.*, the division of a cell into cells having similar hereditary tendencies; **ho:mœo-osmo·tic, homœosmo·tic**

adjs. Physiol. [OSMOTIC *a.*], (of an animal) maintaining a more or less constant concentration of solute in its body fluids regardless of fluctuations of the concentration in the surrounding medium; usu. spelt *homoi(o)-*; so **ho:mœo-osmo·sis, homœosmo·sis; homœopo·lar** *a. Chem.* [ad. G.: see *HOMOPOLAR *a.* 3] = *HOMOPOLAR *a.* 3; **ho·mœotype** *Taxon.* = *HOMOTYPE 2; **homœoty·pic, -ty·pical** *adjs. Cytol.* [ad. G. *homöotypisch* (W. Flemming 1887, in *Arch. f. mikrosk. Anat.* XXIX. 400)], designating the second division of meiosis.

1896 W. M. LINDSAY *Lat. Textual Emend.* 50 The homœoteleuton and homœarchon of these lines has led to omission. **1942** *Jrnl. Theol. Stud.* XLIII. 86 In ver. 39 it seems clear that ℵ* omitted was θερισμος..οι δε (by homoeoarchon [*printed* homoeoarcton]). **1920** A. HOLMES *Nomencl. Petrol.* 118 *Homœoblastic*, a term used instead of equigranular and applied to metamorphic rocks to indicate that the texture so described is due to recrystallisation. **1932, 1954** Homœoblastic [see *heteroblastic* s.v. *HETERO-]. **1900** B. D. JACKSON *Gloss. Bot. Terms* 125/1 *Homoiochlamydeous*, used by Engler and Prantl when the perianth is uniform. **1965** Homoiochlamydeous [see *heterochlamydeous* adj. s.v. *HETERO-]. **1913** *Arch. f. Entwicklungsmech. d. Organismen* XXXVII. 263 Desquamation is approximately equally marked in both auto and homöo grafts. **1915** *Jrnl. Exper. Med.* XXI. 174 In..the first 4 to 5 days after transplantation, there is no noticeable difference between the auto- and homeograft. **1952** *Cancer Res.* XII. 379/1 Tumor homoiografts between mice of unrelated inbred strains. **1920** *Jrnl. Exper. Med.* XXXII. 115 In a few instances..well established blood supply, and evidence of growth were found. This is observed generally with homeografted tissues. **1930** *Physiol. Rev.* X. 582 It has been maintained..that the result of homoiografting of skin largely depends upon whether donor and host do or do not belong to the same blood group. **1893** PARKER & RÖNNFELDT tr. *Weismann's Germ-Plasm* 34 These kinds of division we may speak of as homœokinesis and heterokinesis, that is, as a division into parts similar or dissimilar to each other with regard to the hereditary tendencies they contain. **1896** E. B. WILSON *Cell* ix. 305 Mitotic division is conceived [by Weismann] as an apparatus which may distribute the elements of the chromatin to the daughter nuclei either equally or unequally. In the former case ('homœokinesis', integral or quantitative division), the resulting nuclei remain precisely equivalent. **1939** A. KROGH *Osmotic Regulation in Aquatic Animals* 240 Homoiosmosis. **1964** *Oceanogr. & Marine Biol.* II. 307 Osmo-regulators exhibit an appreciable tendency towards homeo-osmosis. **1931** *Biol. Rev.* VI. 473 In contrast with these are the 'homoiosmotic' organisms which include typically estuarine animals such as *Carcinus maenas*. **1939** A. KROGH *Osmotic Regulation in Aquatic Animals* 8 When animals maintain a total concentration of their body fluids different from that of the surrounding water they can be termed 'homoiosmotic'. **1953** E. PALMER tr. *Ekman's Zoogeogr. Sea* vi. 118 Bony fishes and fresh-water animals in general are homoio-osmotic. **1967** G. E. HUTCHINSON *Treat. Limnol.* II. xviii. 153 Such animals have thus become at least to some extent osmotically independent of their environment; they are at least partly homoiosmotic. **1922** A. D. UDDEN tr. *Bohr's Theory of Spectra* III. iii. 93 The latter kind of compounds, to which the greater number of simple inorganic compounds belong, is frequently called 'heteropolar' and possesses a far more typical character than the first compounds which are called 'homoeopolar'. **1923** E. N. DA C. ANDRADE *Struct. Atom* xii. 232 We shall also make use of Abegg's terminology of homœopolar and heteropolar compounds. **1905** SCHUCHERT & BUCKMAN in *Science* 9 June 900/2 Homeotype..homotype... A specimen identified by a specialist after comparison with the holotype or lectotype. **1939** *Ann. Entomol. Soc. Amer.* XXXII. 694 Homoeotype: A specimen named by another than the author upon comparison with the type. The value of a homeotype is apparent. **1967** [see *HOMOTYPE 2]. **1889** Homœotypic [see *heterotypic* s.v. *HETERO-]. **1925** E. B. WILSON *Cell* (ed. 3) vi. 532 (*heading*) The interkinesis and the homeotypic division. **1969** BROWN & BERTKE *Textbk. Cytol.* xx. 436 Previously, meiosis I was called the heterotypic mitosis, implying that it is an atypical mitosis, which it certainly is; and meiosis II was called the homeotypic mitosis, implying that it is a fairly typical mitotic division, which it is. **1888** *Jrnl. R. Microsc. Soc.* 553 He [*sc.* Flemming] finds that these cells [*sc.* spermatocytes] exhibit a remarkable dimorphism of mitosis; in the heterotypical form the chromatic formations exhibit metakinesis. The two forms, the other of which may be called homœotypical, are sometimes found together.

homœomorph (hǫ·miomǭɹf). Also **homeo-**. [f. HOMŒO- + Gr. μορφ-ή form.] Something that is homœomorphous or homœomorphic.

a. (In Dict. s.v. HOMŒOMORPHOUS *a.*)

b. *Palæont.* One of two or more homœomorphous fossils or fossil species.

1898 S. S. BUCKMAN in *Q. Jrnl. Geol. Soc.* LIV. 453 The compressed species of the Arietidan Epoch, which are generally classed as *Oxynotoceras*, are, as their septal details show, certainly polygenetic homœomorphs. **1920** A. M. DAVIES *Introd. Palæont.* i. 29 The failure to discriminate between homoeomorphs has frequently led to mistakes in the correlation of strata. **1952** R. C. MOORE et al. *Invertebr. Fossils* i. 34 Two convergent species, so similar as hardly to be distinguished on superficial characters, are called homeomorphs.

c. (Usu. *homeo-*.) *Math.* A figure or a topological space that is homœomorphic to some other one.

1926 *Trans. Amer. Math. Soc.* XXVIII. 3 Such a C_n is he homeomorph of an *n*-dimensional polyhedron.. whose faces are all simplicial cells. **1951** M. H. A. NEWMAN *Topology of Plane Sets of Points* (ed. 2) iii. 61 Homeomorphism is an equivalence relation, and a space and its homeomorphs have all their topological properties in common. **1965** S. BARR *Exper. Topology* vi. 70 Perhaps it is a Moebius in disguise—the homeomorph of one?

homœomorphic (hǫmiomǭ·ɹfik), *a.* Also **homeo-**. [f. as next + -IC.] **1.** *gen.* Of the same kind or form.

1902 *Buck's Handbk. Med. Sci.* (rev. ed.) IV. 660/1 In a remarkable proportion of cases of mental and other nervous disturbances we find a history of antecedent nervous conditions, either homoeomorphic, i.e. of the same order, or heteromorphic, of different type.

b. *Palæont.* = *HOMŒOMORPHOUS *a.* c.

1923 H. H. SWINNERTON *Outl. Palæont.* x. 214 These forms presented homeomorphic resemblances to *Amaltheus*.

2. (Usu. *homeo-*.) *Math.* [ad. F. *homéomorphe* (H. Poincaré 1895, in *Jrnl. de l'École polytechn.* I. 9).] Related by a homœomorphism, topologically equivalent *to* a complex, figure, or topological space; that is a homœomorphism.

1918 O. VEBLEN *Analysis Situs* (Cambridge Colloq. Lect., Vol. 5, Pt. 2) i. 3 Two complexes related by a homeomorphism are said to be homeomorphic. **1926** *Trans. Amer. Math. Soc.* XXVIII. 4 The manifold condition is equivalent to demanding that all these complexes be homeomorphic to cell boundaries. **1932** *Ann. Math.* XXXIII. 550 The isomorphism..induces a homeomorphic (i.e., a one–one bi-continuous) correspondence between the points of the two group spaces. **1956** E. M. PATTERSON *Topology* i. 6 Topologically, the Möbius band is a different surface from the cylinder, which means that the two surfaces are not homeomorphic. **1967** F. HARARY *Seminar on Graph Theory* ii. 15 A subdivision of a graph *G* is any graph obtainable from *G* by replacing some line *uv* of *G* by a new point *w* and two new lines *uw* and *wv*. Two graphs are homeomorphic if there is a third graph which can be obtained from each by a sequence of subdivisions. **1967** D. W. BLACKETT *Elem. Topology* i. 13 Any two circles are homeomorphic and..any circle is homeomorphic to any square. On the other hand, a circle and a figure eight are not homeomorphic.

Hence **homœomo·rphically** *adv. Math.*, in a way that preserves all topological properties.

1927 *Trans. Amer. Math. Soc.* XXIX. 438 Two *h*-cells can be homeomorphically transformed into one another in such manner that two $(h-1)$-cells of their boundaries are similarly transformed. **1965** S. BARR *Exper. Topology* i. 6 If we draw a triangle on a lump of Plasticine, it is conceivably possible to distort it homeomorphically so as to get rid of the three angles and make it into a circle.

homœomorphism (hǫmiomǭ·ɹfiz'm). Also **homeo-**. [f. Gr. μορφ-ή shape + -ISM.] **1.** (In Dict. s.v. HOMŒOMORPHOUS *a.*)

2. (Usu. *homeo-*.) *Math.* [ad. F. *homéomorphisme* (H. Poincaré 1895, in *Jrnl. de l'École polytechn.* I. 7).] A one-to-one transformation of one complex or topological space on to another that is continuous and has a continuous inverse; a topological transformation; a topological equivalence between two figures.

1918 O. VEBLEN *Analysis Situs* (Cambridge Colloq. Lect., Vol. 5, Pt. 2) i. 3 A (1–1) continuous transformation of a complex into itself or another complex is called, following Poincaré, a homeomorphism. **1929** *Fundamenta Math.* XIV. 94 Let I_1 be the interval from (0, 1) to (0, 0) in a plane E_2, and let Φ be a homeomorphism between the arc x_1y_1 and the interval I_1. **1956** E. M. PATTERSON *Topology* i. 2 The fundamental type of equivalence in topology is called topological equivalence or homeomorphism. **1961** S. S. CAIRNS *Introd. Topology* iii. 54 Topology is the study of those properties of spaces which are preserved by homeomorphisms. **1965** S. BARR *Exper. Topology* vi. 77 There is one crossing of the edge with itself at *C*, which cannot be removed by distortion, or even the cutting and re-joining allowed by homeomorphism. **1969** LUNDELL & WEINGRAM *Topology CW Complexes* ii. 46 Since each cell σ of *X* is compact and *Y* is Hausdorff, $f|\sigma$ is a homeomorphism onto its image cell $\tau \subset Y$.

homœomorphous, *a.* Add: **c.** *Palæont.* Exhibiting or characteristic of homœomorphy; similar in general aspect but dissimilar in detail.

1895 S. S. BUCKMAN in *Q. Jrnl. Geol. Soc.* LI. 456 Biplicate *Terebratulæ* are, at any rate in the Jurassic rocks, independent, or heterogenetic, homœomorphous derivatives of non-plicate forms. **1913** —— *Ibid.* LXIX. 167 The two species..look like enough to be confused (are homœomorphous) until they are analysed ontogenetically. **1962** *Proc. Geologists' Assoc.* LXXIII. 12 It requires only sufficient skill and discernment..to see repeatedly, in one guise or another, homoeomorphous resemblances in many groups of organisms.

homœomorphy (hǫ·miomǭɹfi). *Palæont.* Also **homeo-**. [f. HOMŒO- + Gr. μορφ-ή shape + -Y³.] A superficial resemblance between two fossils or two fossil species sufficient to suggest a taxonomic identity that close examination shows not to exist; esp. a resemblance that is due to convergent evolution.

1895 S. S. BUCKMAN in *Q. Jrnl. Geol. Soc.* LI. 457 Mojsisovics has called such cases, between non-contemporaneous ammonites, 'heterochronous convergence'. I would rather apply the term 'heterochronous homœomorphy' to the phenomenon; and the term 'isochronous homœomorphy' would describe the resemblance between the contemporaneous *Buckmani* with its derivatives. **1952** R. C. MOORE et al. *Invertebr. Fossils* vi. 219 In spite of their resemblance, these two shells could hardly be farther apart in classification. They constitute remarkable examples of homeomorphy. **1969** *Nature* 4 Jan. 15/1 The problem of homoeomorphy—the production of similar morphologies in distantly related stocks either more or less contemporaneously or at different geological times.

homœoplastic, *a.* Add: **2.** (Also *homoio-*.) *Med.* and *Biol.* = *HOMOPLASTIC *a.* 2.

1913 *Arch. f. Entwicklungsmech. d. Organismen* XXXVII. 249 Loeb did not at that time distinguish between the results of auto- and homoeoplastic transplantation. Later he found a marked difference in the results obtained after auto- and homoeotransplantation in the case of tumors. *Ibid.* 250 The homoeoplastic transplants acted quite differently. **1938** *Amer. Jrnl. Physiol.* CXXI. 650 (*heading*) Homeoplastic transplantation of adrenal glands in rats of inbred strains. **1952** G. R. CAMERON *Path. Cell* xxvii. 527 Homoioplastic transplantation succeeds with some tissues, but it is doubtful whether success is prolonged or permanent.

Hence **homœopla·stically** *adv.*; **ho·mœoplasty** = *HOMOPLASTY.

1915 *Jrnl. Exper. Med.* XXI. 164 The difference in the growth of auto- and homeoplastically transplanted thyroid tissue. **1929** *Ann. Surg.* XC. 926 Homoplasty, homeoplasty and isoplasty mean tissue transplantation from one individual to another of the same species.

homœosis (hǫmi,ōᵘ·sis). *Biol.* Also **homeosis.** Pl. **homœoses.** [mod.L., ad. Gr. ὁμοίωσις a becoming like, f. ὅμοιος like.] The replacement in a metamerically segmented animal, esp. in the course of regeneration, of a structure forming part of one segment by a structure characteristic of another segment; also used of an analogous process in plants (e.g. the replacement of stamens by petals). So **homœo·tic** *a.*, exhibiting or characterized by homœosis; **homœo·tically** *adv.*

1894 W. BATESON *Study of Variation* i. 85 For the word 'Metamorphy' I therefore propose to substitute the term Homœosis. *Ibid.*, The distinction between Homœotic Variation and strictly Meristic Variation is sufficiently obvious. **1913** —— *Mendel's Princ. Heredity* (ed. 2) xi. 198 A simple homœosis of the stamens and carpels. **1913** —— *Prob. Genetics* iii. 68 When a lumbar vertebra varies homoeotically into the likeness of the last dorsal and bears a rib. *Ibid.*, The consequences of such homoeoses are sometimes very extensive. **1940** R. GOLDSCHMIDT *Material Basis Evol.* 326 For a long time the phenomenon of homoeosis (called heteromorphosis by some authors) has been known as an occasional monstrosity in arthropods...The classical example is the regeneration of an antenna after removal of the eyestalk in Decapods. **1962** D. J. MERRELL *Evol. & Genetics* x. 101 The homeotic mutants cause one of a series of parts to assume the character of another member of the series. **1966** E. D. HAY *Regeneration* i. 34 A unique kind of heteromorphosis called homeosis occurs occasionally in arthropod regeneration.

homœostasis (hǫmi,ǫ·stăsis, hǫmiostē̆ⁱ·sis). Also **homeo-**. [mod.L., f. HOMŒO- + Gr. στάσις standing still, stationariness.] The maintenance of a dynamically stable state within a system by means of internal regulatory processes that tend to counteract any disturbance of the stability by external forces or influences; the state of stability so maintained; *spec.* in *Physiol.*, the maintenance of relatively constant conditions in the body (e.g. as regards blood temperature) by physiological processes that act to counter any departure from the normal.

1929 W. B. CANNON in *Physiol. Rev.* IX. 400 The coördinated physiological reactions which maintain most of the steady states in the body are so complex, and are so peculiar to the living organism, that it has been suggested (Cannon, 1926) that a specific designation for these states be employed—homeostasis. **1941** —— in *Science* 3 Jan. 8/1 The functioning of the human brain has made social homeostasis differ markedly from physiological homeostasis...An upset of constancy necessarily results. Railways replace canals, automobiles crowd out the horse and buggy, [etc.]. **1949** KOESTLER *Insight & Outlook* xx. 279 The chemical balance of the body fluids (homeostasis). **1955** L. R. DICE *Man's Nature* ix. 113 The individual organism, to maintain its homeostasis (state of balance), will throw away not only water and salts, but even sugar if necessary. **1962** *Lancet* 6 Jan. 31/1 These clinical indications of defective renal homœostasis suggest the need for a more thorough exploration of renal function. **1962** V. C. WYNNE-EDWARDS *Animal Dispersion* xxiii. 561 The general concept of homeostasis in aquatic populations through growth-inhibitory substances..is complicated by the fact that, in some of the very same species, growth-*promoting* metabolites have also been discovered. **1964** M. MCLUHAN *Understanding Media* (1967) II. x. 109 The city, as a form of the body politic, responds to new pressures and irritations by resourceful new extensions—always in the effort to exert staying power, constancy, equilibrium, and homeostasis. **1964** N. WIENER *God & Golem* vi. 86 Science is an important contribution to the homeostasis of the community. **1971** *Nature* 20 Aug. 562/2 Drinking is essential for the homeostasis of body fluids.

homœostasy (hǫmi͵ǫ·stăsi), anglicized form of prec.

1945 S. BRODY *Bioenergetics & Growth* x. 250 A calcium hexose monophosphate is the important intermediary in.. calcium homeostasy. **1959** *Times Rev. Industry* Jan. 42/1 The human body contains a vast hierarchy of controls which help to maintain a constant and stable state. The American physiologist W. B. Cannon termed this condition homeostasy. **1971** D. WATTS *Princ. Biogeogr.* v. 223 This notion has also been criticized by Lack on the grounds that..the stability produced from homeostacy [*sic*] could equally well result from the density-dependent factors already described.

homœostat (hǫ·miostæt). Also **homeo-**. [Back-formation from *HOMŒOSTATIC *a.*, after words like *thermostat* (see -STAT).] A homœostatic apparatus or system; something that adapts itself (within limits) to changes in its environment in such a way as to preserve a state of internal stability.

1948 W. R. ASHBY in *Electronic Engin.* XX. 382 The homeostat will adapt not only to random changes in hand settings but to *any* change in the dynamic nature of the machine. **1959** S. BEER *Cybernetics & Management* iii. 23 In a homeostat a critical variable is held at a desirable level by a self-regulatory mechanism. **1960** *20th Cent.* Mar. 269 Something goes wrong with our lives; this puts our homeostat out of order; as a result we may be unable to digest properly (and so we get stomach ulcers). **1964** J. Z. YOUNG *Model of Brain* i. 3 When we say that living things have 'needs' we emphasize that they are self-maintaining systems; 'homeostats' in modern terminology. **1971** *Nature* 22 Jan. 233/2 Beer and others have shown how a large industrial company can usefully be considered as a homeostat.

homœostatic (hǫmiostæ·tik), *a.* Also **homeo-**. [f. *HOMŒOSTASIS, after *stasis, static.*] Maintained by, involving, or effecting homœostasis; of or pertaining to homœostasis.

1929 *Physiol. Rev.* IX. 401 The adjectival form, *homeostatic*, would apply to the physiological reactions or agencies or to the circumstances which relate to steady states in the organism. *Ibid.* 417 (*heading*) The homeostatic functions of hunger and thirst. **1955** J. Z. YOUNG in B. I. Evans *Studies in Communication* 93 Since man's special homeostatic machinery is mainly social, medicine may often be called upon to assist in correcting some social incapacity. **1959** S. DUKE-ELDER *Parsons' Dis. Eye* (ed. 13) ii. 22 The pressure within the eye is maintained at its homeostatic level despite considerable variations in the other factors which tend to alter it. **1961** *Lancet* 2 Sept. 551/1 A general disturbance of the homœostatic mechanisms regulating immune tolerance. **1963** R. P. DALES *Annelids* viii. 167 We are not yet certain about the nature of these homeostatic mechanisms which maintain the annelid body as a whole. **1964** A. RAPOPORT in I. L. Horowitz *New Sociol.* vi. 99 Man as a physico-chemical system in homeostatic equilibrium with the environment. **1964** N. WIENER *God & Golem* vi. 87 The difficulties of establishing a really homeostatic regulation of society are not to be overcome by replacing one set pattern..by an equal and opposed set pattern of the same sort. **1971** D. WATTS *Princ. Biogeogr.* v. 230 Many populations have homeostatic mechanisms within them which are designed to maintain stability through reducing the number of species which are overspecialized.

Hence **homœosta·tically** *adv.*

1959 S. BEER *Cybernetics & Management* xv. 140 These two systems are linked homeostatically as mutually vetoing systems against the two managerial criteria. **1962** J. C. WYNNE-EDWARDS *Animal Dispersion* xv. 363 It is social integration that supplies the means of controlling population-density homeostatically. **1971** *Nature* 22 Jan. 233/2 With the health sciences system and its environment homeostatically related.

homœothermic (hǫmiopə̄·ɹmik), *a.* *Zool.* Usu. **homoio-**; also **homeo-**. [ad. G. *homöotherm* (C. Bergmann 1847, in *Göttinger Studien* I. 613): see HOMŒO- and THERMIC *a.*] Maintaining an almost constant body temperature; warm-blooded; homothermous. Also **homœothe·rmal** *a.*, in the same sense.

1870 Homoeothermal [in Dict. s.v. HOMŒO-]. **1885** W. STIRLING tr. *Landois' Text-bk. Human Physiol.* I. vi. 426 Bergmann introduced the word homoiothermal animals for the warm-blooded animals. **1889** V. H. W. WINGRAVE *T. Dunman's Gloss. Anat. Terms* App. 175 *Homœothermic*,..of even temperature: applied to warm-blooded animals which maintain the same temperature, irrespective of that of the surrounding medium. **1891** *Ann. Rep. Smithsonian Inst. 1890* 407 Man, mammals, and birds are called creatures of equable temperature, homeothermic. **1903** *Phil. Trans. R. Soc.* B. CXCV. 37 Variation in production of heat is the ancestral method of homœothermic adjustment. **1928** PEARSE & HALL *Homoiothermism* v. 31 Homoiothermal animals. *Ibid.* 33 Homoiothermic marine animals. **1965** B. E. FREEMAN tr. *Vandel's Biospeleol.* xiv. 237 Not one true cavernicole is known among the homoiothermic vertebrates, that is to say the birds and mammals. **1966** *New Statesman* 11 Nov. 697/1 Man is a homoiothermic animal... When it is cold the body attempts to reduce heat loss.

Hence **ho·mœotherm**, a homœothermic animal.

1891 *Ann. Rep. Smithsonian Inst. 1890* 411 These phenomena, which are numerous and active in animals of the higher class (homeotherms), are much less so in cold-blooded animals. **1968** D. W. WOOD *Princ. Animal Physiol.* viii. 123 In contrast to poikilotherms, homeotherms maintain their body temperature at a more or less constant level, irrespective of the environmental temperature.

homœothermism (hǫmiopə̄·ɹmiz'm). *Zool.* Usu. **homoio-**; also **homeo-**. [f. prec. + -ISM.] The maintenance or possession of an almost constant body temperature. Also **ho·mœothermy**, in the same sense.

1903 *Phil. Trans. R. Soc.* B. CXCV. 36 During the cold weather Echidna abandons all attempts at homœothermism and hibernates for four months. **1928** PEARSE & HALL *Homoiothermism* xii. 91 Homoiothermism apparently had its origin at the time when the great dinosaurs were becoming extinct. **1961** WEBSTER, Homoiothermy, homeothermy. **1966** W. S. HOAR *Gen. & Compar. Physiol.* x. 321 Increasing complexity of organization (especially behavioral organization) makes homeothermy a necessity. **1972** *Sci. Amer.* June 71/2 Maintaining homeothermy is energetically expensive.

homœotransplant (hǫmiotrɑ·ns͵plɑnt), *sb.* *Med.* and *Biol.* Usu. **homoio-**; also **homeo-**. [f. HOMŒO- + TRANSPLANT *sb.*] = *HOMOTRANSPLANT *sb.*

1914 *Jrnl. Med. Res.* XXX. 115 A second piece [of the thyroid] was placed into the left ear of the second or control animal as a homeo-transplant. **1930** *Physiol. Rev.* X. 551 Regenerative processes are, as a rule, more extensive in autotransplants than in homoiotransplants. **1952** *Jrnl. Nat. Cancer Inst.* XIV. 692 Tumor homoiotransplants, i.e. tumors transplanted within the species but outside the strain of origin, fail to grow, or grow temporarily and then regress.

homœotransplant (hǫ:miotrɑns͵plɑ·nt), *v.* *Med.* and *Biol.* Usu **homoio-**; also **homeo-**. [f. prec. sb.] *trans.* = *HOMOTRANSPLANT *v.*

1926 *Amer. Jrnl. Path.* II. 117 Bone and bone marrow adjoining the xiphoid cartilage were homoiotransplanted together with the cartilage. **1930** *Physiol. Rev.* X. 561 Tumours differ from normal tissues in that they can be homoiotransplanted as well as autotransplanted.

So **homœotranspla·nted** *ppl. a.*; also **ho:mœotransplantabi·lity.**

1915 *Jrnl. Amer. Med. Assoc.* 27 Feb. 727/2 In the homoiotransplanted tissue the fibroblasts very soon form dense fibrous material. **1930** *Physiol. Rev.* X. 551 Directly around the homoiotransplanted cartilage there forms..a thick layer of fibrous tissue. **1954** *Cancer Res.* XIV. 1 (*heading*) The cytotoxicity of serum for mouse mammary cancer cells. I. The effects of admixture *in vivo* upon homoiotransplantability.

ho:mœotransplanta·tion. Usu. **homoio-**; also **homeo-**. *Med.* and *Biol.* [f. HOMŒO- + TRANSPLANTATION.] = *HOMOTRANSPLANTATION.

1913 [see *HOMŒOPLASTIC *a.* 2]. **1928** D. MARINE in E. V. Cowdry *Special Cytol.* I. xvii. 564 In man, by transplanting within the same blood group, it is probable that the average life of homeografts might be prolonged, but homeotransplantation at present has no permanent value. **1953** G. D. SNELL in Homburger & Fishman *Physiopath. Cancer* xiv. 355 It is more plausible to expect..serial transfer of normal tissue to occur in isotransplantation than in homoiotransplantation.

homo-erotic (hǫmo͵erǫ·tik), *a.* and *sb.* *Psychiatry.* Also **homoerotic**. [f. HOMO- + EROTIC *a.* and *sb.*] **A.** *adj.* Pertaining to or characterized by a tendency for erotic emotions to be centred on a person of the same sex; of or pertaining to a homo-erotic person. Freq. a synonym of *homosexual.*

1916 E. JONES tr. *Ferenczi's Contrib. Psycho-Analysis* xii. 268 The development of a homo-erotic obsessional neurosis. **1917** C. R. PAYNE tr. *Pfister's Psychoanalytic Method* ix. 178 After the damming up of the homoerotic instinctive activity, a physical symptom appeared. **1936** W. S. SADLER *Theory & Pract. Psychiatry* xxxviii. 626 Many notable individuals in history have been homoerotic, among them Alexander the Great and Michelangelo. *Ibid.* 627 On getting into the case, I found that she was homoerotic—homosexual. **1959** *Jrnl. Analytical Psychol.* IV. 11. 120 From his dreams in particular the repressed homo-erotic aspect of these clearly emerged. **1961** *Encounter* Mar. 75 The only enduring friendships are 'homoerotic'. **1969** *Listener* 20 Feb. 250/3 A slick, unreal, wisecracking comedy about New York homo-erotic life. **1971** M. ALTSCHULER in Marshall & Suggs *Human Sexual Behavior* ii. 48 One may see, in various houses, boys and young men..wrapped in each other's arms... This behavior is not specifically homosexual, but it may be called homoerotic. It is noticed only during fiestas.

B. *sb.* A homo-erotic person.

1936 W. S. SADLER *Theory & Pract. Psychiatry* xxxviii. 626 The congenital, full-fledged homoerotic is never really cured.

Hence **homo-ero·ticism, -e·rotism,** the concentration of erotic impulses on a person of the same sex.

1916 E. JONES tr. *Ferenczi's Contrib. Psycho-Analysis* xii. 253 Even superficial observation of these two kinds of homo-erotism shews that they belong..to quite different syndromes. **1936** W. S. SADLER *Theory & Pract. Psychiatry* xxxviii. 628 The well-known tendency toward a certain degree of homoeroticism in the Army and Navy. **1950** E. JONES tr. *Ferenczi's Sex in Psychoanalysis* xii. 299 Homo-erotism...The word..is in my opinion preferable to the ambiguous expression homosexuality, since it makes prominent the psychical aspect of the impulse in contradistinction to the biological term 'sexuality'.

homogametic (hǫmogămī·tik), *a.* *Biol.* [f. HOMO- + *GAMETIC *a.*] (Of a sex or its individual members) producing gametes that all have the same kind of sex chromosome. Opp. *HETEROGAMETIC *a.*

1910 [see *HETEROGAMETIC *a.*]. **1971** *Nature* 18 June 432/1 In the Lepidoptera, males are homogametic and females heterogametic.

Hence **homogame·ty**, the state or condition of being homogametic.

1939 C. H. WADDINGTON *Introd. Mod. Genetics* iii. 81 In a type with female homogamety, *Drosophila* for example, the non-disjunctional *XX* eggs with the extra chromosome when fertilized by *X* sperm give super-females. **1961** A. MÜNTZING *Genetic Res.* xiii. 98/2 The occurrence of homo- and hetero-gamety in dioecious plant species was first demonstrated by Correns in *Bryonia dioica*.

homogamous, *a.* Add: **c.** *Evolution.* Of or pertaining to homogamy (sense *b). Also **homogamy,** (*b*) *Evolution*, preferential breeding between individuals similar in some characteristic; inbreeding; **homoga·mic** *a.*, = *HOMOGAMOUS *a.* c.

1897 G. J. ROMANES *Darwin, & after Darwin* III. i. 5 For the sake..of securing more descriptive terms, I will coin the words Apogamy and Homogamy...Homogamy ..answers to discriminate isolation, or segregate breeding: only individuals belonging to the same variety or kind are allowed to propagate. **1903** *Biometrika* II. 481 If the male class of a given character tends to mate with a female class with generally like character, we have a tendency to homogamy. *Ibid.*, The whole range of effect from pure random matings to perfectly homogamous unions within a population is almost but not quite as important as the difference between self and cross fertilization in plants. **1907** *Fabian News* XVII. 55/2 Professor Pearson's theory of homogamic mating. **1947** *Evolution* I. 270/2 The concept of homogamy or associative mating states that within a population the most similar individuals will mate with each other. **1970** T. DOBZHANSKY *Genetics Evol. Process* iv. 100 There may, however, be assortative mating, such as some preference for mating of like (homogamy). *Ibid.* x. 328 If eggs of the two species of sea urchins..are exposed to mixtures of sperm of both species, homogamic fertilizations greatly outnumber heterogamic ones.

homogenate (hǒmǫ·dʒǐnēⁱt). [f. HOMOGEN(IZE *v.* + *-ate*, after *condensate, filtrate*, etc.] The suspension of cell fragments and cell constituents that is obtained when tissue is homogenized.

1941 V. R. POTTER in *Jrnl. Biol. Chem.* CXLI. 775 Rat liver which had been freshly homogenized and diluted.. was used unless otherwise indicated. This material will be referred to as a 'homogenate'. **1948** *Biochem. Jrnl.* XLII. 205/2 Stained smears of such homogenates consisted merely of amorphous material quite unrecognizable as belonging to the organ in question. **1962** *Lancet* 27 Jan. 191/2 Samples of lung were homogenised in 10 volumes of 0·85% saline, and the homogenate was allowed to stand for three hours. **1970** *Nature* 28 Mar. 1252/1 After homogenizing for 30 s in a chilled, loose-fitting, mechanically driven glass homogenizer, the homogenate was centrifuged at 3,000 r.p.m.

homogeneous, *a.* Add: **2. b.** *Physics.* Of light: not decomposable into light of other colours. Hence of radiation generally: monochromatic.

[**1671** NEWTON in *Phil. Trans. R. Soc.* VI. 3081 Light is not similar, or homogeneal, but consists of difform Rays, some of which are more refrangible than others.] **1783** *Phil. Trans. R. Soc.* LXXIII. 97 An oblique pencil of homogeneous rays. **1863** E. ATKINSON tr. *Ganot's Physics* VII. iv. 406 In optical researches it is frequently of great importance to procure homogeneous or monochromatic light. **1897** NICHOLS & FRANKLIN *Elem. Physics* III. vii. 73 Homogeneous light is sometimes called monochromatic light. **1913** *Proc. R. Soc.* A. LXXXIX. 246 The wave-length of a homogeneous beam of X-rays. **1942** W. B. BOAST *Illum. Engin.* i. 3 Radiant energy from a gaseous-discharge source, such as mercury vapor,..consists of..one or more homogeneous component radiations.

c. *Physical Chem.* Consisting of, occurring in, or involving a single phase.

1874 *Proc. R. Soc.* XXII. 30 The body may be either homogeneous throughout, as a continuous solid, or liquid, or gas; or it may be heterogeneous, as a mass of water and aqueous vapour (*i.e.* steam). **1878** J. W. GIBBS in *Trans. Connecticut Acad. Arts & Sci.* III. 116 By *homogeneous* is meant that the part in question is uniform throughout, not only in chemical composition, but also in physical state. **1930** W. T. HALL *Textbk. Quantitative Analysis* xi. 135 A mixture of two solid substances is not homogeneous. A solution, on the other hand, is homogeneous when it is thoroughly mixed. **1940** C. N. HINSHELWOOD *Kinetics Chem. Change* iv. 70 A reaction may be partly homogeneous and partly heterogeneous. **1947** S. GLASSTONE *Elem. Physical Chem.* xviii. 587 Homogeneous reactions..take place entirely in one phase, either gas or solution. **1966** *McGraw-Hill Encycl. Sci. & Technol.* II. 547/1 If the catalyst is in the same phase as the reactants, the process is homogeneous catalysis... A homogeneous catalyst is molecularly dispersed (dissolved) in the reactants which are, most commonly, in the liquid state.

d. *Nuclear Science.* Of a nuclear reactor: having the fuel intimately and uniformly mixed with the moderator (which if liquid may also serve as the coolant).

1947 C. GOODMAN *Sci. & Engin. Nuclear Power* I. ix. 273 The reactors are considered to be of two classes: heterogeneous and homogeneous. In the latter, the fissionable material is uniformly distributed throughout the

active portion of the reactor. **1955** *Times* 10 Aug. 8/4 The so-called 'homogeneous reactor', in which the nuclear fuel is circulated in solution. **1964** M. Gowing *Britain & Atomic Energy* x. 273 The possibilities of a homogeneous heavy water pile..were it is true not promising.

3. c. *homogeneous co-ordinates*, a system in which the ratios of the co-ordinates (one more than necessary) are substituted for the co-ordinates themselves, making the equations (all except one) homogeneous.

1879 *Encycl. Brit.* X. 408/1 For the proper development of the science [of analytical geometry] homogeneous coordinates..are required. **1934** D. M. Y. Sommerville *Analyt. Geom. Three Dimensions* ii. 18 If $[X, Y, Z]$ are the ordinary non-homogeneous coordinates..let $X = x/w$, $Y = y/w$, $Z = z/w$, then $[x, y, z, w]$ are called the homogeneous cartesian coordinates. **1965** H. Eves *Surv. Geom.* II. x. 71 Homogeneous coordinates enable us to establish the important principle of duality of plane projective geometry.

¶. The spelling **homogenous** is less common than the pronunc. (hǒmǫ·dʒǐnəs), which perh. owes its currency partly to the influence of the vb. *homogenize* and its derivs.

1956 J. N. Anderson *Appl. Dent. Mat.* xx. 243 Thorough mixing of the dry ingredients..and vigorous spatulation..help to produce a homogenous mix. **1961** Webster, *Homogenous* = Homogeneous. **1964** E. Palmer tr. *Martinet's Elem. Gen. Ling.* ii. 39 No linguistic community of any great size is homogenous. **1970** *Times* 2 June (Container Suppl.) p. i/6, As general cargo is homogenized into standard boxes, it will inevitably follow in the path of the homogenous bulk trades such as oil and ore. **1971** *Nature* 17 Sept. 203/1 Fractions which were homogenous by thin-layer chromatography..were used. **1972** *Ibid.* 21 Jan. 138/2 A procedure for purification has been described that gives a product which appears homogenous.

homogenic (hǫmǫdʒe·nik), *a.*[1] *Med.* [f. Gr. ὁμογεν-ής of the same kind + -ic.] Obtained from an animal, or from animals, of the same species.

1911 *Jrnl. Exper. Med.* XIV. 244 Autogenic and homogenic plasma constitute the best media, but heterogenic plasma can also be used. **1922** *Ibid.* XXXV. 18 The action of different dilutions of homogenic and heterogenic sera on the rate of growth of chicken fibroblasts.

homogenic (hǫmǫdʒī·nik), *a.*[2] *Genetics.* [f. Homo- + *gen(e + -ic.] Having only one allele of a particular gene; of or pertaining to organisms that have identical alleles of some gene.

1947 D. Lewis in *Heredity* I. 101 Heterogenic (S4.6) pollen grains in a style carrying S6 and not S4 should have the same incompatibility reaction as the homogenic (S6.6) pollen grain in a style carrying both these alleles. **1966** J. R. Raper *Genetics of Sexuality in Higher Fungi* i. 3 Homogenic incompatibility, in which mating is prevented between strains having the same factor(s). *Ibid.* 4 Outbreeding is enhanced by homogenic incompatibility. **1973** *Nature* 3 Aug. 305/1 Which reacted according to the tetrapolar mechanism of the homogenic incompatibility system in the same way as known in other Basidiomycetes.

homogenization (hǒmǫ:dʒǐnəizē¹·ʃən). [f. Homogeniz(e *v.* + -ation.] **1.** The process of making or becoming homogeneous; the action of homogenizing. Also *fig.*

1908 *Practitioner* June 830 Methods for concentrating the bacilli..depend mainly on the homogenisation of the sputum by means of dilute alkalies or of enzymes. **1915** *Jrnl. Physical Chem.* XIX. 225 The stability of an emulsion is tremendously enhanced by homogenization. **1936** W. L. Davies *Chem. Milk* xii. 256 The homogenisation of cream, especially coffee cream, is widely practised. **1962** *Lancet* 22 Dec. 1330/2 Tissues were similarly extracted by fourfold homogenisations at 0°C in perchloric acid. **1963** *Times* 30 May 13/2 This homogenization of political discourse presents the Labour Party with some difficulties. **1964** M. McLuhan *Understanding Media* (1967) ii. xxxi. 345 America long ago achieved its Common Market by mechanical and literate homogenization of social organization. **1965** P. G. Shewmon in R. W. Cahn *Physical Metall.* viii. 370 Rates of homogenization are of interest in many metallurgical problems.

2. The state produced in something that has been homogenized; uniformity of composition.

1938 D. K. Bullens *Steel & its Heat Treatment* (ed. 4) I. v. 131 When the more rapid cooling is to be used.. it is desirable to attain homogenization of the austenite. **1955** P. Becher *Princ. Emulsion Technol.* v. 76 In order to achieve complete homogenization of milk..it is often necessary to employ a two-stage machine. **1962** A. G. Guy *Physical Metall.* (1963) viii. 253 At a moderate temperature the rapid diffusion of zinc in copper produces effective homogenization of cast brasses.

homogenize, *v.* Delete *rare* and add: To unite or incorporate into a single whole of uniform composition; to make uniform or similar. Also *fig.* (Further examples.)

1908 *Practitioner* June 831 Nebel homogenises the sputum with lime-water. **1957** W. H. Whyte *Organization Man* xxiv. 323 In the new middle-class rhythm of life obligations are homogenized, for the overriding aim is to have oneself precommitted to regular, unvarying monthly payments on all the major items. **1964** M. McLuhan *Understanding Media* (1967) ii. x. 101 The new centralist power always takes action to homogenize as many marginal areas as possible. *Ibid.* xxiii. 244 Any community that wants to..maximize the exchange of goods..has simply got to homogenize its social life. **1965** *Times Lit. Suppl.* 25 Nov. 1063/3 To omit the commas..is in a sense to denature or homogenize the lines.

b. To subject (milk or another emulsion) to a process by which the suspended globules or droplets are broken up into smaller ones and distributed throughout the liquid, so that they have no tendency to collect into a cream.

1904 *Sci. Amer.* 16 Apr. 315/2 To the many methods of purifying, modifying, and preserving milk must now be added a process for homogenizing it so that it will keep almost indefinitely. **1913** *Pharmaceutical Jrnl.* 24 May 734/1 It has become the practice of the emulsion manufacturer to perfect his emulsions by the use of..the apparatus constructed for the dairyman and used..for homogenising milk. **1936** W. L. Davies *Chem. Milk* xii. 256 Gaulin..first conceived the idea of homogenising already existing emulsions, such as milk, so as to obtain greater stability. **1949** Kirk & Othmer *Encycl. Chem. Technol.* IV. 823 The purpose of homogenizing evaporated milk is to prevent fat separation in the manufactured product. **1971** *Nature* 29 Oct. 617/2 Machines with triple-piston pumps..are used extensively in..the dairy industry, for homogenizing milk, cream, ice-cream mix and other products.

c. To make (an alloy) more uniform in chemical composition by holding it at a high temperature for a period and then allowing it to cool slowly.

1924 [see *homogenizing* vbl. sb. and ppl. adj. below]. **1948** *Metals Handbk.* (Amer. Soc. Metals) 977/1 The [magnesium] alloys that contain aluminum may be homogenized in cast form. **1955** E. Johnson in W. C. Newell *Casting of Steel* x. 448 The practice of homogenizing alloy castings at 850°C to 950°C for one hour per inch of heaviest section is common. **1965** P. G. Shewmon in R. W. Cahn *Physical Metall.* viii. 372 This also indicates one reason why a wrought product is more easily homogenized..than a cast product.

d. To prepare a suspension of cell fragments and cell constituents from (tissue) by physical treatment in a liquid medium.

1936 *Jrnl. Biol. Chem.* XXXVI. 504 A new method for the study of tissue respiration is described in which the tissues are homogenized in a buffer medium by a high speed glass pestle. **1959** *Sci. News* LIII. 51 They killed the guinea-pig, rapidly dissected out its liver, and homogenized it in sugar solution in a Waring blendor. **1964** G. H. Haggis et al. *Introd. Molecular Biol.* ii. 31 The tissue is first homogenized, the cells being disrupted by the shearing forces of the homogenizer. **1971** *Nature* 10 Sept. 127/1 The brains were homogenized in cold distilled water (6 ml./brain) at 850 r.p.m. using a 'Teflon' pestle.

2. *intr.* To become homogeneous; to respond to homogenization.

1938 D. K. Bullens *Steel & its Heat Treatment* (ed. 4) I. v. 131 The same procedure of air cooling may be used even upon steels that would readily homogenize at ordinary annealing temperatures. **1949** Brick & Phillips *Structure & Properties of Alloys* (ed. 2) xi. 323 Small castings usually consist of very fine dendrites that homogenize quite readily with respect to C and Mn.

So **homo·genizing** *vbl. sb.* and *ppl. a.*

1913 *Pharmaceutical Jrnl.* 24 May 734/1 The actual homogenising section of the machine is a valve formed by an agate cone which is pressed into a gun-metal seating. **1924** Jeffries & Archer *Sci. of Metals* x. 353 The effect of a homogenizing treatment on the properties of an alloy. **1963** *Times* 14 Feb. 12/7 The curious homogenizing process of reaching a consensus. **1964** M. McLuhan *Understanding Media* (1967) ii. xxxi. 344 The homogenizing power of the literate process had gone further in America by 1800 than anywhere in Europe.

homogenized (hǒmǫ·dʒǐnəizd), *ppl. a.* [f. Homogeniz(e *v.* + -ed[1].] **1.** Rendered uniform throughout in composition or character; *loosely*, = Homogeneous *a.* 2.

1935 G. E. Doan *Princ. Physical Metall.* iv. 140 The true solidus line of alloys of this kind is..determined..by reheating specimens of a completely homogenized alloy. **1959** *Observer* 29 Mar. 15/4 As for his [*sc.* the novelist's] 1980s these are just a little more prefabricated and homogenised than our time. **1964** M. McLuhan *Understanding Media* (1967) i. v. 60 The fragmented man creates the homogenized Western world, while oral societies are made up of people differentiated..by their unique emotional mixes. **1967** *N.Y. Times* (Internat. ed.) 11–12 Feb. 4/7 The time for studying people in different environments is running out. The world is becoming homogenized.

b. *esp.* of milk, cream, etc.: having the globules of fat reduced in size and distributed throughout the liquid; also of other emulsions (see * homogenize *v.* 1 b).

1904 *Sci. Amer.* 16 Apr. 315 Homogenized milk, a trade-name for milk which has been heated to 185°F. and forced by heavy pressure through a number of very fine openings. **1913** *Pharmaceutical Jrnl.* 24 May 734/1 Homogenised oil emulsions are permanent for an almost indefinite time. **1923** W. Clayton *Theory Emulsions* viii. 123 In America homogenised cream is extensively used in the manufacture of ice-cream, where a smooth texture is demanded. **1951** *Good Housek. Home Encycl.* 509/1 Homogenised milk is considered more quickly digestible on account of the fineness of the fat globules. **1963** *Observer* 5 May 9/5 A sales drive by dairymen to popularise homogenised milk and collect an extra half-penny a pint is gathering momentum. **1969** *Daily Colonist* (Victoria, B.C.) 24 Sept. 9/3 (Advt.), Empress pure peanut butter. Homogenized, regular or chunk style.

2. Of various things in respect of each other: not readily differentiated; similar in nature, meaning, etc. (Used when an expected or desirable difference is not found.)

1958 *Vogue* Oct. 153 Beside this deeply particular tragedy, Mr Eliot's homogenized characters seem insufficient. **1959** N. Mailer *Advts. for Myself* (1961) 210 Each reference to yourself as individual as a carloading of homogenized words. **1970** *New York* 16 Nov. 50/2 Even these words have become murky, homogenized.

homogenizer (hǒmǫ·dʒǐnəizəɹ). [f. Homogeniz(e + -er[1].] A machine or apparatus designed to homogenize some kind of material (as milk or tissue). Also *fig.*

1886 [in Dict. s.v. Homogenize *v.*]. **1908** *N.Y. Produce Rev. & Amer. Creamery* 11 Nov. 92/2 (*heading*) A new homogenizer. **1910** *Ibid.* 9 Feb. 600/1 A machine of much interest to the dairy trade..is the Gaulin Homogenizer. **1936** *Jrnl. Biol. Chem.* XXXVI. 496 To prepare tissue for study, a measured volume of the desired buffer is placed in the homogenizer tube, which is then weighed. **1955** P. Becher *Princ. Emulsion Technol.* v. 74 A homogenizer is a device in which dispersion is effected by forcing the mixture to be emulsified through a small orifice under very high pressure. **1956** *Nature* 4 Feb. 233/2 Disintegration of spleen cells (grinding in a homogenizer at high speed) destroys their protective effect on antibody formation. **1969** J. G. Brennan et al. *Food Engin. Operations* v. 93 The many applications for ultrasonic homogenizers..include: the manufacture of salad creams, ice-cream mixes,..and baby foods. **1973** *Daily Tel.* 24 Mar. 14/4 The social and aesthetic attitudes have been passed through the homogeniser of the bureauctatic hive-mind.

homogenous, *a.* Add: **2.** *Surg.* Of transplanted tissue: = *homoplastic *a.* 2.

1919 *Ann. Surg.* LXIX. 123 It is possible that further experiments with homogenous transplants from young to old and from old to young animals would answer this question. **1939** S. Fomon *Surg. Injury & Plastic Repair* ii. 107 Homogenous transplants..are usually taken from members of the same family. **1964** R. Battle *Plastic Surg.* ii. 37 Any graft, either autogenous or homogenous, that is not immediately required can be stored for use at a later date.

homogenous, var. *homogeneous *a.*

homogentisic (hǫmǫdʒenti·sik), *a.* [tr. G. *homogentisinsäure* homogentisic acid (Wolkow & Baumann 1891, in *Zeitschr. f. physiol. Chem.* XV. 245), f. Homo- b + Gentisic *a.*] *homogentisic acid*: a crystalline compound, $C_8H_8O_4$, which oxidizes to a black compound in air, is an intermediate in the metabolism of aromatic amino-acids, and is excreted in large amounts by persons with alkaptonuria; alkapton, 2,5-dihydroxyphenylacetic acid. So **homoge·ntisate**, a salt or ester of this acid.

1891 *Jrnl. Chem. Soc.* LX. 1129 These [crystals] consisted of a substance very similar to, but not identical with, Kirk's uroleucic acid, and the name homogentisic acid is given to it. *Ibid.*, Lead homogentisate, $(C_8H_7O_4)_2Pb+3H_2O$, crystallises in colourless, brilliant, transparent needles and prisms. **1942** *Jrnl. Amer. Med. Assoc.* 11 July 882/1 Homogentisic acid isolated from one of the positive urines itself gave a strongly positive reaction. **1961** *Lancet* 5 Aug. 320/1 The homogentisate level in body fluids and urine. **1969** *Listener* 16 Jan. 74/3 It's now known that not only do one's genes decide whether one is to have red hair, double-jointed thumbs or a Hapsburg lip, but they also decide whether one is going to excrete homogentisic acid or not. **1970** C. N. Graymore *Biochem. Eye* vii. 478 Phenylalanine and tyrosine are converted through quinone intermediates to homogentisic acid.

homogonic (hǫmogǫ·nik), *a. Biol.* [f. Homo- + Gr. -γονος generating, γόνος offspring + -ic.] Applied to a life cycle of certain nematodes in which the offspring of a parasitic generation themselves develop into parasites, without the intervention of a free-living generation; also applied to organisms reproducing by such a cycle. Opp. * heterogonic *a.* 2.

1926 [see *heterogonic *a.* 2]. **1939** *Amer. Jrnl. Hygiene* XXX. d. 15 In those *Strongyloides* infections where both modes of larval development are commonly encountered, there is little constancy in the daily yields of heterogonic, i.e., indirect or free-living adult, in contrast to homogonic, or direct, progeny. **1951** L. H. Hyman *Invertebrates* III. xiii. 307 It is probable that any species of *Rhabdias* may employ either the homogonic or heterogonic type of life cycle. **1968** N. D. Levine *Nematode Parasites* ii. 75/1 Absence of food, too, led to homogonic development.

Hence **homogo·nically** *adv.*, by means of a homogonic life cycle.

1938 *Amer. Jrnl. Hygiene* XXVIII. 224 The production of these two types of progeny was related to the age of the single, homogonically derived parasite. **1968** N. D. Levine *Nematode Parasites* ii. 75/1 In a loam soil.. 40% of the larvae developed into females, 40% into males and 20% homogonically into infective larvae.

homograft (hǫ·mogrɑft). *Med.* and *Biol.* [f. HOMO- (in *homogenous, homologous,* and *homoplastic*) + GRAFT *sb.*[1]] A graft taken from another individual of the same species as the recipient; a homotransplant; *homograft reaction,* the immunological reaction that causes a homograft to be rejected by the recipient's body.

1923 H. NEUHOF *Transplantation of Tissues* ii. 32 Autografts of skin have a degree of permanency in both animal and clinical surgery whereas..occasional successes with homografts of skin have been more than counterbalanced by the frequent failures. **1944** *Jrnl. Anat.* LXXVIII. 182/2 The time-relations of the homograft reaction vary from one pair of animals—donor and recipient—to another. **1955** *Sci. News* XXXV. 105 Blood vessel homografts are now being used on an ever increasing scale. **1960** *News Chron.* 22 June 6/4 Within a decade, the homograft barrier will be penetrated and human 'spare-part' surgery will be a reality. **1961** *New Scientist* 15 June 632/3 Only identical twins can accept organ and tissue grafts from one another without exciting the homograft reaction. **1962** *Lancet* 27 Jan. 193/2 A woman who had received a homograft of bone-marrow from her brother. **1968** D. LONGMORE *Spare-Part Surg.* vi. 161 For the past three years my colleagues and I have been transplanting heart-lung homografts experimentally in animals.

Hence **ho·mografted** *ppl. a.*; **ho·mografting** *vbl. sb.* = *HOMOTRANSPLANTATION.

1923 H. NEUHOF *Transplantation of Tissues* i. 3 Homotransplantation (homoplasty, isoplasty, homografting, homoiotransplantation, homoplastic transplantation, isoplastic transplantation) is the transference of a tissue from one to another individual of the same species. **1937** *Surgery* I. 558 (*heading*) Homografting of skin: with report of success in identical twins. **1952** *Jrnl. Nat. Cancer Inst.* XIV. 669 Many surgeons..have found the results of grafting with autogenous tissues..superior to the results obtained by the use of similar homografted material. **1953** *Proc. Soc. Exper. Biol. & Med.* LXXXII. 523/2 Skin homograftings have been permanently successful only between identical twins..or between members of the same family.

homographically (hǫmogræ·fikăli), *adv.* *Math.* [f. HOMOGRAPHIC *a.*: see -ICALLY.] In a homographic manner.

1860 *Phil. Trans. R. Soc.* CXLIX. 67 Four or more tetrads of points in a line may be homographically related to the same number of tetrads in another line. **1947** HODGE & PEDOE *Methods Algebraic Geom.* I. vi. 217 A one-to-one correspondence..is set up between the ranges, ..and we say that these ranges are projectively, or homographically, related.

homography. 1. (Further examples.)

1959 E. M. PATTERSON *Topology* (ed. 2) ii. 21 Congruence and similarity in Euclidean geometry and homography in projective geometry are all equivalence relations. **1965** H. EVES *Surv. Geom.* II. xii. 203 A transformation of the form $z' = (az+b)/(cz+d)$, $ad-bc \neq 0$, is called a homography (or bilinear substitution).

Homoian, var. *HOMŒAN *a.* and sb.

Homoiousian, *a.* (Earlier example.)

1683 W. CAVE *Ecclesiastici* 167 The Synod was divided into two principal Factions, the one of the Semiarian or Homoiousian Party,..the other of the Heterousians.

Homoiousion (hǫmoi,ɑu·ziǫn, -ɑu·siǫn, -ū·-). *Theol.* [eccl. Gr. ὁμοιούσιον, neuter form of ὁμοιούσιος: see HOMOIOUSIAN *a.* and *sb.* and cf. *HOMOOUSION *sb.* and *a.*] *The Homoiousion,* the term used to express the doctrine put forward by the Semi-Arians, that the Son is 'of like substance' with the Father; the doctrine itself: opposed to the term ὁμοούσιον (see * HOMOOUSION *sb.* and *a.*). The masc. form **homoiousios** is also used.

[**1683** W. CAVE *Ecclesiastici* 164 They rejected both the ὁμοούσιον and the ὁμολουσιον [*sic*], as Expressions unknown to Scripture.] **1833** J. H. NEWMAN *Arians* iv. 369 Acacius..proposed a creed in which the Homoousion and Homoiousion, were condemned..and his own Homoion adopted. **1873** W. BRIGHT *Orations of St. Athanasius against Arians* p. lxvii, The Semi-arians.. insisted on their own formula of the 'Homoiousion'. **1969** A. RICHARDSON *Dict. Chr. Theol.* 347/2 In their manifesto of 358 they rejected the *Homoousios*..and proposed the *Homoiousios.*

homokaryotic (hǫ:mokæri,ǫ·tik), *a.* *Bot.* Also **-caryotic.** [ad. G. *homocaryotisch* (H. Burgeff 1913, in *Ber. d. Deut. Bot. Ges.* XXX. 680), f. HOMO- + KARY(O- + -OTIC.] Exhibiting homokaryosis. Hence **homokaryon** (-kæ·ri,ǫn), a homokaryotic cell, structure, or organism; **homokaryosis** (-kæri,ōu·sis), the condition, prevalent among fungi, in which two or more genetically identical nuclei are maintained in a common cytoplasm.

1916 B. D. JACKSON *Gloss. Bot. Terms* (ed. 3) 183/2 Homokaryotic. **1921** *Phil. Trans. R. Soc.* B. CCX. 111 The contamination may be purely cytoplasmic, and the progeny of such a cell will therefore still be homocaryotic. **1928** B. D. JACKSON *Gloss. Bot. Terms* (ed. 4) 443/1 Homocaryosis. **1939** *Mycologia* XXXI. 226 Although the conidia and ascospores of *B[otryosphaeria] Ribis* are multinucleate, all of the nuclei of a single conidium or ascospore have the same origin and hence are homocaryotic or genetically similar. **1949** H. W. FLOREY et al. *Antibiotics* II. xvi. 673 Heterokaryons are, in general, more vigorous than the homokaryons from which they originate. **1951** D. G. CATCHESIDE *Genetics of Micro-Organisms* iv. 72 Not too much reliance must be placed in the homocaryosis of a strain maintained for some time by vegetative transfers. **1955** G. M. SMITH *Cryptogamic Bot.* (ed. 2) I. xi. 414 Multinucleate mycelia of Mucorales and of other fungi may be homokaryotic..or they may be heterokaryotic. **1969** G. SERMONTI *Genetics Antibiotic-Producing Microorganisms* ii. 38 In such cases a balanced combination of two (or more) genotypes enjoys a selective advantage over either homokaryon. *Ibid.* v. 165 They often continue to segregate even after homokaryosis has been established.

homological, *a.* Add: **2.** *Philos.* = *AUTOLOGICAL *a.* Hence **homologica·lity,** the property of being homological; **homolo·gically** *adv.*, (*b*) by virtue of being homological.

1940 [see *HETEROLOGICAL *a.*]. **1952** *Mind* LXI. 85 Neither is the word *short,* simply because its meaning is predicable of its own verbal sign, homologically predicable of itself. *Ibid.* 86 This anomalous distinction between two such comparable predicates seems to be incompatible with genuine heterologicality and homologicality. *Ibid.* 88 A homological predicate, genuinely predicable of itself.

homologous, *a.* Add: **4. b.** *Cytol.* Of chromosomes: pairing at meiosis, and normally (except in the case of the sex chromosomes of some species) identical in morphology and in arrangement of genetic loci.

1903 W. S. SUTTON in *Biol. Bull.* IV. 238 The double basis of hybrid characters is to be found in the pairs of homologous chromosomes of the presynaptic germ-cells. **1920** W. E. AGAR *Cytol.* v. 125 It was found that there were in each diploid nucleus two chromosomes of each size... In the meiotic prophase the two chromosomes of each type, usually called homologous chromosomes, pair together to form the bivalents. **1970** AMBROSE & EASTY *Cell Biol.* x. 327 The nature of the forces responsible for the pairing of homologous chromosomes in the early stages of prophase I, and for their separation at the diplotene stage, is not yet understood.

c. *Med.* Derived from or involving an organism or organisms of the same species; also, involving or containing antibodies or antigens that react specifically with one another, as when an antibody has been produced by injection of an antigen.

1915 *Jrnl. Path. & Bacteriol.* XX. 76 Heterologous immunity, in which cancer cells from one species are used as antigens to immunise animals of strange species, is.. different in many ways from homologous immunity. **1928** BUCHANAN & FULMER *Physiol. & Biochem. Bacteria* I. iii. 361 By the use of ox serum and complement he could secure marked agglutination of bacteria in a dilution of the homologous antiserum by itself too weak to produce any trace of agglutination. **1933** W. W. C. TOPLEY *Outl. Immunity* vi. 91 The antiserum that is produced by the inoculation into a suitable animal of a particular bacterium is frequently referred to as a homologous serum. **1946** K. LANDSTEINER *Specificity Serol. Reactions* (rev. ed.) i. 8 Reactions of an antibody with the corresponding antigen are said to be homologous, while heterologous reactions..are those taking place with substances other than the inciting antigen. **1958** *Immunology* I. 111 Morgan (1947) injected rhesus monkeys with homologous brain and cord in water-in-oil emulsion containing killed *Mycobacterium tuberculosis.* **1961** *Lancet* 29 July 245/1 Serum-autoantibodies against, for example, thyroid or brain can be readily elicited in rabbits or guineapigs by immunisation with the relevant homologous or, indeed autologous, tissue. **1968** J. C. NORMAN et al. *Organ Perfusion & Preservation* xxvii. 375 The feasibility of heterologous or homologous intermediate hosts for human resuscitative storage is untried.

homolysis (hǒmǫ·lisis). *Chem.* [f. HOMO- + *-LYSIS.] The splitting of a molecule into two neutral atoms or radicals.

1938 [see *HETEROLYSIS 2]. **1966** W. A. PRYOR *Free Radicals* ix. 119 Molecule-induced homolysis is postulated to occur when radicals are formed at an anomalously rapid rate from the interaction of nonradical species.

Hence **homoly·tic** *a.*, of the nature of or involving homolysis; **homoly·tically** *adv.*, by homolysis.

1941 Homolytic [see *heterolytic* after *HETEROLYSIS]. **1952** *Sci. News* XXVI. 57 A covalent bond may..break by homolytic fission, each of the electrons separating with one of the atoms, giving two free atoms, e.g.: H—Cl→H— + Cl—. **1964** N. G. CLARK *Mod. Org. Chem.* xxv. 515 Heat and/or illumination first causes a molecule of chlorine to break homolytically into two chlorine atoms.

homomorphic, *a.* Add: **d.** *Zool.* Applied to a colony in which all the constituent individuals are alike.

1891 T. J. PARKER *Lessons Elem. Biol.* xii. 137 There are no special reproductive individuals, so that the colony is *homomorphic.* **1931** W. C. ALLEE *Animal Aggregations* ii. 23 Homomorphic colonies have all the individuals morphologically similar and may be found among sponges and at certain times among hydroids and bryozoans.

e. *Cytol.* Applied to homologous chromosomes that do not differ in size or form; opp. *HETEROMORPHIC *a.* 1 c.

1917 E. E. CAROTHERS in *Jrnl. Morphol.* XXVIII. 449 The unusual conditions of the chromosomes in this group have made advisable the introduction of four new terms. 1. Homomorphic—used to designate those tetrads made up of morphologically similar homologues. **1925** E. B. WILSON *Cell* (ed. 3) xii. 937 Twenty-eight male offspring have thus been examined from five matings with especial reference to three chromosome-pairs..which may be either heteromorphic or homomorphic. **1968** J. A. SERRA *Mod. Genetics* III. xxiii. 533 These bodies are homomorphic sex chromosomes..not heterochromosomes.

2. *Math.* Related or produced by a homomorphism; giving rise *to* a second set under a homomorphism; that is a homomorphism.

1935 *Proc. Nat. Acad. Sci.* XXI. 482 We define a continuous homomorphic mapping π_m of $\mathfrak{H}_p{}^{m+1}(\mathfrak{G})$ into $\mathfrak{H}_p{}^m(\mathfrak{G})$. **1939** *Amer. Jrnl. Math.* LXI. 783 Two homomorphic rings. **1941** BIRKHOFF & MACLANE *Surv. Mod. Algebra* xiii. 350 This device for getting a field as a homomorphic image of a polynomial ring is important in the discussion of algebraic numbers. **1966** *Mathematical Rev.* XXXI. 15/2 It is homomorphic to (i.e., can be contracted into, by identification of sets of connected vertices) the complete graph of order *k.* **1968** I. ADLER *Groups in New Math.* xiii. 230 If there is a homomorphism that matches the members of one group with the members of another, we say that the first group is homomorphic to the second, and that the second group is a homomorphic image of the first group.

transf. **1959** S. BEER *Cybernetics & Management* vi. 49 A black Box is homomorphic with a cybernetic system, because the latter has undergone a many–one simplifying transformation (which makes it tractable) without losing its key characteristic (of indefinability).

Hence **homomo·rphically** *adv.* *Math.*, by a homomorphism.

1941 BIRKHOFF & MACLANE *Surv. Mod. Algebra* xiii. 350 The direct sum $A+B$ of two rings A and B may be mapped homomorphically on the summand B by the correspondence $(a, b) \to b$. **1952** EILENBERG & STEENROD *Found. Algebraic Topology* i. 7 If G and H are groups, the notation ϕ: $G \to H$ means that ϕ maps G homomorphically into H. **1971** M. HERZOG in Powell & Higman *Finite Simple Groups* v. 200 G is p-solvable if and only if it can be mapped homomorphically on $N_G\ (P)/W$.

homomorphism (hǫmomǭ·ɹfiz'm). [f. HOMO- + Gr. μορφ-ή form + -ISM.] **1.** (In Dict. s.v. HOMOMORPHIC *a.*)

2. *Math.* [See *-MORPHISM.] A many-to-one (or one-to-one) transformation of one set into another that preserves in the second set the operations or relations between the elements of the first.

1935 *Duke Math. Jrnl.* I. 2 There exists an operation F defined topologically for all the chains and such that $F\{c_p\}$ is a homomorphism of $\{c_p\}$ into $\{c_{p-1}\}$, and of $\{c_0\}$ into the identity. **1941** BIRKHOFF & MACLANE *Surv. Mod. Algebra* vi. 155 Under any homomorphism $G \to G'$, the identity e of G goes into the identity of G', and inverses into inverses. **1959** E. M. PATTERSON *Topology* (ed. 2) iv. 82 In fact, there is a homomorphism between the groups (not to be confused with homeomorphism). **1965** PATTERSON & RUTHERFORD *Elem. Abstract Algebra* iii. 79 A mapping f of a ring R_1 into a ring R_2 is called a homomorphism if $f(x+y) = f(x)+f(y)$, $f(xy) = f(x)f(y)$ for all $x, y \in R_1$. **1969** F. HARARY *Graph Theory* xii. 143 If G' is the graph resulting from a homomorphism ϕ of G we can consider ϕ as a function from V onto V' such that if u and v are adjacent in G, then ϕu and ϕv are adjacent in G'.

transf. **1966** S. BEER *Decision & Control* vi. 113 A scientific model is a homomorphism on to which two different situations are mapped, and which actually defines the extent to which they are structurally identical.

homonuclear (hǫmoniū·kliăɹ), *a.* [f. HOMO- + NUCLEAR *a.*] **a.** *Physics* and *Chem.* Of a molecule: composed of atoms whose nuclei are alike, i.e. atoms of the same element or (more strictly) the same isotope.

1930 *Physical Rev.* XXXVI. 617 In the case of homonuclear molecules (molecules composed of atoms whose nuclei are identical in charge and mass), any electron state may be either 'odd' or 'even'. **1970** *Nature* 25 Apr. 354/1 Vibrational levels of N_2^+, like those of N_2, are metastable because both molecules are homonuclear.

b. *Chem.* Taking place on the same ring in a molecule.

1938 G. H. RICHTER *Textbk. Org. Chem.* xxix. 596 In discussing the reactions of naphthalene it is customary to speak of homonuclear substitution if the groups are entering the same ring, and heteronuclear substitution if the radicals are entering different rings. **1951** I. L. FINAR *Org. Chem.* xxix. 586 Substitution products of naphthalene... When OH..or NH·CO·CH_3 is in the 2-position, homonuclear substitution usually takes place in the 1-position.

homonym. Add: **1. c.** *Taxonomy.* A generic name or a binomial that duplicates a name attached to a different plant or animal.

1892 *Bull. Torrey Bot. Club* XIX. 290 Homonyms.—The publication of a generic name or a binomial invalidates the use of the same name for any subsequently published genus or species respectively. **1920** *Jrnl. Bot.* LIX. 156 Specific names should be rejected when they are homonyms. **1951** G. H. M. LAWRENCE *Taxon. Vascular Plants* ix. 213 A name of a taxon is illegitimate and must be rejected if it is a later homonym, that is, if it duplicates a name previously and validly published for a taxon of the same rank based on a different type. **1967** R. E. BLACKWELDER *Taxonomy* xxii. 463 Priority determines which homonym can be retained as an acceptable name. **1972** W. T. STEARN *A. W. Smith's Gardener's Dict.*

Plant Names (rev. ed.) 13 Similar names applied to different plants are called homonyms. The rejection of later homonyms has caused a number of unavoidable but regrettable name changes.

homonymous, *a.* **1.** Delete †*Obs.* and add later examples in *Taxonomy*.

1896 WALSINGHAM & DURRANT *Rules for Nomencl.* 9 Invalid names considered merely as words are of three classes:—(1) Homonymous (*i.e.* the same name applied to different conceptions). **1964** *Internat. Code Zool. Nomencl.* 55 Homonymy does not exist between two identical species-group names originally or subsequently placed in different genera that bear homonymous names.

2. b. Add to def.: Also applied to diplopia in which images are doubled in this way. Of hemianopia: characterized by the loss of vision in the same half (left or right) of the visual field of each eye.

1882 Homonymous hemianopia [see *HEMIANOPIA]. **1884** H. E. JULER *Handbk. Ophthalmic Sci.* v. 383 This projection of the object to o′ is on the same side as the deviating eye L, and the diplopia is therefore called homonymous. **1966** S. LERMAN *Basic Ophthalmol.* viii. 467 If the left eye deviates inward..the patient will suffer from a homonymous (uncrossed) diplopia.

homonymy. (Later examples in *Taxonomy*.)

1896 WALSINGHAM & DURRANT *Rules for Nomencl.* 9 A name homophonous with a valid name is invalid in accordance with the rule governing homonymy. **1964** [see *HOMONYMOUS *a.* 1].

homo-organic, var. *HOMORGANIC *a.*

Homoousion (hǫmo,au·ziǫn, -au·siǫn, -ū·-), *sb.* and *a.* *Theol.* [eccl. Gr. ὁμοούσιον, neut. of ὁμοούσιος: see HOMOOUSIAN *a.* and *sb.*]

A. *sb.* *The Homoousion* (τὸ ὁμοούσιον): the term ὁμοούσιος as used, e.g. in the formula promulgated by the Council of Nicæa in A.D. 325, to express the doctrine that the Son is 'of one substance' with the Father (τῷ πατρί); the doctrine itself: opposed to the term ὁμοιούσιος (see *HOMOIOUSION). The masc. form **homoousios** is also used.

[**1683:** see *HOMOIOUSION.] **1781** GIBBON *Decl. & F.* II. xxi. 251 Their [*sc.* the Arians'] patron, Eusebius of Nicomedia,..confessed, that the admission of the *Homoousion*, or Consubstantial..was incompatible with the principles of their theological system. *Ibid.* 252 The mysterious *Homoousion*, which either party was free to interpret according to their peculiar tenets. **1833** J. H. NEWMAN *Arians* iv. 333 The Novatians, as maintaining the Homoousion, were included in the persecution. **1875** *Encycl. Brit.* II. 538/2 At length the tenet of the *Homoiousion* was substituted for that of the *Homoousion* at the Council of Rimini (Ariminum) in 360. **1921** C. H. TURNER *Catholic & Apostolic* (1931) 129 The very existence of Christianity in any full sense of the term was at stake over the Homoousion. **1969** C. D. DARLINGTON *Evol. Man & Society* xiv. 311 Why not agree, he asked, to the *homoousion* or consubstantiality of the Father and Son? **1971** *Cath. Dict. Theol.* III. 39/2 What Nicaea had done with the homoousios to overcome Arianism, Trent was to do with transubstantiation to overcome other heresies.

B. *adj.* (Usu. in form *homoousios*.) Of the same essence or substance: = HOMOOUSIAN *a.* a.

1834 *Penny Cycl.* II. 317/1 In the western part of the Roman empire, all adversaries of the doctrine of Athanasius, that the Son was *homoousios*, or of the *same* essence with the Father, were called Arians; although some of these opponents taught..that the Son was *homoiousios*, or of *similar* essence. **1936** G. L. PRESTIGE *God in Patristic Thought* x. 197 According to the Valentinians..the abortive and degenerate fruit of the final aeon in the divine Absolute (pleroma), was homoousios with angelic ('spiritual') beings. *Ibid.* 198 A piece of marble closely resembling Mr. Gladstone..is made of different stuff from that of which Mr. Gladstone himself consisted: it is in the image of Mr. Gladstone, but not homoousios with him. **1969** A. RICHARDSON *Dict. Chr. Theol.* 347/2 The Lord and Lifegiver could not be Homoousios with those to whom he gives life.

homophile (hǫ·mofəil). [f. HOMO- + -PHIL, -PHILE.] A term for a homosexual (regarded as a person belonging to a particular social group rather than as someone who is sexually abnormal). Also *attrib.* or as *adj.*

1960 G. WESTWOOD *Minority* v. 71 The so-called homophile organizations on the Continent provide wider facilities. In Amsterdam the 'Cultuur-en-Ontspanningscentrum' (C.O.C.) maintains clubrooms..and regular lectures are arranged on homosexuality. **1960** *News Chron.* 13 Oct. 4/6 Nor do Danes frown much on sex abnormalities. Danish 'homophiles' have their own monthly magazine. **1961** *Encounter* May 75 The relationships between homophiles seem to approximate very closely to the relationships between adult heterosexual men and women. **1963** CORY & LE ROY *Homosexual & his Society* xx. 245 The great bulk of publicity about the existence of homophile organizations—as they are usually called, somewhat euphemistically—has been, of necessity, by word of mouth. *Ibid.* 247 The participants and sympathizers in the homophile movement. **1965** *Guardian* 23 Apr. 11/5 The Dutch Society of Homophiles, set up 18 years ago as a private club for homosexuals. **1971** *Daily Colonist* (Victoria, B.C.) 15 Oct. 20/8 Homosexuals want legal marriage for tax reasons and to foil the designs of relatives, George Hyslop, founder of a Toronto homophile organization, told the Canadian Mental Health Association.

homophonic, *a.* Add: **3.** *Philol.* = HOMOPHONOUS *a.* 2.

1942 [see *BIMORPHEMIC *a.*].

homoplastic, *a.* Add: **2.** *Med.* and *Biol.* Of transplantation: involving the transfer of tissue from one individual to another of the same species. Of transplanted tissue: obtained from another individual of the same species as the recipient.

[**1889** L. OLLIER in *Arch. de Physiol. normale et path.* I. 168 Nous divisons les greffes en trois catégories: Les greffes autoplastiques... Les greffes homoplastiques, c'est-à-dire empruntées à un autre individu, mais à un sujet de la même espèce. Les greffes hétéroplastiques.] **1909** *Jrnl. Med. Res.* XXI. 320 He [*sc.* Carrel] also distinguishes an autoplastic transplantation, when the segment is taken from the same animal; a homoplastic, when the segment is taken from another animal of the same species; and a heteroplastic, when the segment is taken from an animal of another species. **1912** *Ann. Surg.* LVI. 381 Autoplastic bony pieces are in respect to regeneration much to be preferred to homoplastic. **1935** *Jrnl. Amer. Med. Assoc.* 8 June 2076/1 These homoplastic grafts all sloughed, while autoplastic grafts were highly successful on the same patient. **1958** *Immunology* I. 1 The homoplastic transplantation of the cortex of the adrenal gland in mice.

So **homopla·stically** *adv.*, between individuals of the same species; **ho·moplasty**, homoplastic transplantation, homotransplantation.

1912 *Ann. Surg.* LVI. 378 The best material for free bony grafts is living, periosteum covered bone, if possible from the same individual himself (autoplasy [*sic*]). Or in case this is impossible, from another individual (homoplasty). **1923** H. NEUHOF *Transplantation of Tissues* ii. 31 The results have seemed to indicate that blood relationship has a bearing on the success of homoplasty. **1926** *Jrnl. Exper. Zool.* XLV. 52 Fore-limb buds of R. palustris tadpoles were transplanted homoplastically beneath the integument of the back. **1929** *Ann. Surg.* XC. 929 The lower the organism in the phylogenetic scale, the better the results obtained with homoplasty. **1942** *Univ. Calif. Publ. Zoöl.* LI. 43 Gastrular anlagen were implanted homoplastically into tadpoles.

homopolar (hǫmo,pōu·lăɹ), *a.* [f. HOMO- + POLAR *a.*] **1.** *Bot.* (In Dict. s.v. HOMO-.)

2. *Electr.* Of an electric generator or its operation: having or involving such an arrangement of magnets that the direction of the flux does not alternate with relation to the motion of the armature conductor(s), so that a direct current is generated without the use of commutators.

1896 S. P. THOMPSON *Dyn.-Electr. Machinery* (ed. 5) 475 (*heading*) Homopolar ('unipolar') dynamos. *Ibid.*, Where the motion is such that the conductor moves continuously past poles of one kind only, the inductive operation is said to be homopolar. **1938** MEARES & NEALE *Electr. Engin. Pract.* I. iv. 233 A homopolar dynamo is essentially a low voltage, heavy-current machine, but..it is generally more satisfactory to employ a motor generator driven from the ordinary supply mains. **1962** [see **Faraday('s) disc*].

3. *Chem.* [ad. G. *homöopolar* (R. Abegg 1906, in *Zeitschr. f. anorg. Chem.* L. 309); cf. *homœopolar* s.v. *HOMŒO-.] Formed by or arising out of the sharing of electrons between neutral atoms, without ionization; covalent.

1922 C. H. DESCH *Metallography* (ed. 3) xv. 341 In all probability the new theory of valency based on the distribution of electrons in the molecule, will provide a satisfactory explanation of the formulæ of compounds of electrically similar ('homopolar') elements. **1930** G. THOMSON *Atom* 219 In such compounds the two atoms are on an equal footing and the compounds are called homopolar. **1940** MOTT & GURNEY *Electronic Processes in Ionic Crystals* i. 9 The transition from polar to homopolar binding. **1972** M. H. BATTEY *Min. for Students* i. 9/1 The covalent (or homopolar) bond is formed when two atoms..share a pair of electrons, one electron being supplied by each atom.

homorganic (hǫmǫɹgæ·nik), *a.* Also occas. **homo-organic.** [f. HOMO- + ORGANIC *a.*] **1.** *Bot.* (In Dict. s.v. HOMO-.) Now *rare* or *Obs.*

2. In *Phonetics* (substitute): produced by the same vocal organ or organs; sharing a specific type of articulation.

1864, 1880 [in Dict.]. **1958** PRIEBSCH & COLLINSON *German Lang.* (ed. 4) II. i. 113 An affricate is a combination of a stop..with its homorganic spirant. **1959** M. SCHLAUCH *Eng. Lang. Mod. Times* 9 A liquid or a nasal plus a homorganic voiced stop. **1960** Z. S. HARRIS *Struct. Ling.* 532 These occur only after voiced or voiceless consonants homo-organic with their own. **1972** *Archivum Linguisticum* III. 39 A preceding alveolar is lost, and a homorganic nasal intervenes following a bilabial or velar stop.

homosexual (hōu·mo-, hǫmose·ksiuăl), *a.* and *sb.* [Irreg. f. HOMO- + SEXUAL *a.*] **A.** *adj.* Involving, related to, or characterized by a sexual propensity for one's own sex; of or involving sexual activity with a member of one's own sex, or between individuals of the same sex.

1892 C. G. CHADDOCK tr. *Krafft-Ebing's Psychopathia Sexualis* III. 255 He had been free from homo-sexual inclinations. *Ibid.* 256 The homo-sexual woman offers the same manifestations, *mutatis mutandis*. **1897** H. ELLIS *Stud. Psychol. Sex* I. i. 2 Among animals in a domesticated or confined state it is easy to find evidence of homosexual attraction, due merely to the absence of the other sex. **1914** G. B. SHAW in *New Statesman* 14 Nov. 21/2 The forty tolerated homosexual brothels of Berlin. **1921** E. J. KEMPF *Psychopath.* xiii. 645 Her social interests were decidedly homosexual. **1921** *Blackw. Mag.* Jan. 134/2 What the nature of the friendship was we cannot say; it may have been homo-sexual, a love which was common among the later Greeks. **1929** R. GRAVES *Good-Bye to all That* iii. 40 In English preparatory and public schools romance is necessarily homosexual. **1942** *Jrnl. Compar. Psychol.* XXXIII. 160 Homosexual mountings are characteristic of the male Rhesus monkey, particularly during adolescence. **1948** A. C. KINSEY et al. *Sexual Behav. Hum. Male* xxi. 610 A considerable portion of the population..has at least some homosexual experience between adolescence and old age. **1961** E. WAUGH *Unconditional Surrender* II. vii. 173 'I'm sure you aren't a pansy.' 'Pansy?' 'You're not homosexual?' Even this did not disconcert Uncle Peregrine... 'Good gracious, no. Besides the "o" is short. It comes from the Greek not the Latin.' **1963** A. HERON *Towards Quaker View of Sex* iii. 24 Not all effeminate men are homosexual, and few homosexual men can be really described as effeminate. **1965** ROSEN & GREGORY *Abnormal Psychol.* xviii. 381 Homosexual behavior in human females, also known as lesbianism or sapphism,..is less likely to arouse social censure than male homosexuality. **1973** *Daily Tel.* 5 Apr. 9/8 For the first time at a National Union of Students conference homosexual and lesbian students spoke out openly.

B. *sb.* A person who has a sexual propensity for his or her own sex; *esp.* one whose sexual desires are directed wholly or largely towards people of the same sex.

In non-technical contexts it is often taken to mean a male homosexual, a female one being termed a lesbian.

1912 E. PAUL tr. *A. Moll's Sexual Life of Child* v. 127 An adult homosexual who as a child once did some needlework for a joke. **1932** S. GIBBONS *Cold Comfort Farm* xi. 153 There were many homosexuals to be seen in Hyde Park. **1954** W. MAYER-GROSS et al. *Clin. Psychiatry* iv. 179 Male homosexuals are frequently classified into the active and the passive type; female homosexuals into the masculine and feminine. **1955** *Sci. News Let.* 21 May 334/3 The idea that homosexuals are necessarily bad security risks is debunked in a report ..before the American Psychiatric Association. **1969** A. GLYN *Dragon Variation* vii. 198 Uses quite a lot of cologne, doesn't he? Is he a homosexual? **1973** *Daily Tel.* 10 July 6/3 Homosexuals and lesbians make up a sizeable minority of the population.

Hence **homose·xualist**, a homosexual.

1931 A. EILOART tr. *Heyer's Hypnosis* xiii. 204 It should be considered that a homosexualist thus suggestively transformed for weeks or even months, marries.. within that time. **1933** H. WILLIAMSON *Gold Falcon* i. 19 His book..proving..that Hamlet should be played as a homosexualist in vain love with Horatio had just been published. **1961** —— *Innocent Moon* v. 100 Even Jesus.. according to Nordau..was a homosexualist and should have been locked up. **1971** *Southerly* XXXI. 84 He consigned me to the lavatory-cleaning brigade together with a group of homosexualists.

homosexuality (hōu:mo-, hǫ:moseksiuæ·lĭti). [f. prec. + -ITY.] The quality of being homosexual, homosexual character or nature; also, homosexual behaviour or activity.

1892 C. G. CHADDOCK tr. *Krafft-Ebing's Psychopathia Sexualis* III. 185 (*heading*) Great diminution or complete absence of sexual feeling for the opposite sex, with substitution of sexual feeling and instinct for the same sex. (Homo-sexuality, or contrary sexual instinct.) **1892** J. A. SYMONDS *Let.* 21 Oct. in P. Grosskurth *J. A. Symonds* (1964) 269 There is an inborn bias toward homosexuality. **1897** H. ELLIS *Stud. Psychol. Sex* I. iv. 101 Bourneville believes that 75 per cent. of the inmates of the Parisian venereal hospitals have practised homosexuality. **1948** A. C. KINSEY et al. *Sexual Behav. Hum. Male* xxi. 615 Among many clinicians this work has been taken to mean that the sex hormones control the heterosexuality or homosexuality of an individual's behavior. **1959** B. WOOTTON *Social Sci. & Social Path.* 15 Many citizens..prefer to look on adult homosexuality as a matter of private taste. **1965** ROSEN & GREGORY *Abnormal Psychol.* xviii. 381 All persons..have a greater or lesser tendency to homosexuality as well as heterosexuality. **1972** *Daily Tel.* 11 Mar. 3/2 'Gay Cambridge', the Cambridge branch of the Campaign for Homosexual Equality,..claimed that sex education at school did not adequately cover homosexuality.

homose·xually, *adv.* [f. as prec. + -LY[2].] In a homosexual manner; with respect to homosexual activities or homosexuality.

1921 J. C. FLÜGEL *Psycho-anal. Stud. of Family* ii. 16 Homosexually disposed parents would..tend to bring up homosexual children. **1921** E. J. KEMPF *Psychopath.* ii. 95 One of our patients..has been fighting strong cravings to become homosexually submissive. **1933** *Jrnl. Mental Sci.* LXXIX. 144 One was homosexually assaulted at the age of 12. **1948** A. C. KINSEY et al. *Sexual Behav. Hum. Male* xxi. 632 A homosexually experienced male could undoubtedly find a larger number of sexual partners among males than a heterosexually experienced male could find among females. **1963** A. HERON *Towards Quaker View of Sex* iii. 25 It is seldom that a public figure feels he can afford to disclose that he is in fact homosexually inclined. **1973** P. EVANS *Bodyguard Man* xxiii. 145, I thought you might be homosexually attracted to each other.

homotopic (hǫmotǫ·pik), *a.* [f. HOMO- + Gr. τοπικ-ός in respect to place (see TOPIC *a.* and *sb.*).] **1.** (In Dict. s.v. HOMO-.)

2. *Math.* [ad. G. *homotop* (Dehn & Heegaard *Analysis Situs* in *Encykl. d. math. Wiss.* (1907) III. I. I. 165).] Related by a homotopy *to* another complex or path, or the mapping of which it is an image; that is a homotopy.

1918, 1930 [see *HOMOTOPY]. **1956** E. M. PATTERSON *Topology* i. 11 A curve which can be deformed continuously into another is said to be homotopic to it. **1961** HOCKING & YOUNG *Topology* iv. 149 We may view homotopic mappings as being members of a one-parameter family of mappings with a continuous parameter. **1967** W. S. MASSEY *Algebraic Topology* ii. 64 Two continuous maps ϕ_0, $\phi_1 : X \to Y$ are homotopic if and only if there exists a continuous map $\phi : X \times I \to Y$ such that, for $x \in X$, $\phi(x, 0) = \phi_0(x)$, $\phi(x, 1) = \phi_1(x)$.

Hence **homoto·pically** *adv.*, by a homotopy; as regards homotopy.

1930 S. LEFSCHETZ *Topology* ii. 77 We will say that *A* and *A'* are homotopically deformable, or simply deformable, into one another, over *G*. **1952** F. BAGEMIHL et al. tr. *Pontryagin's Found. Combinatorial Topology* iii. 83 The mappings ϕ and θ are said to be homotopically inverse to one another. **1968** H. F. CULLEN *Introd. Gen. Topology* vii. 368 The usual space E^1 of real numbers is homotopically equivalent to the trivial space consisting of 0 alone, say.

homotopy (hǫ·motǫpi, hǒmǫ·tǒpi). *Math.* [ad. G. *homotopie* (Dehn & Heegaard *Analysis Situs* in *Encykl. d. math. Wiss.* (1907) III. I. I. 164): see prec. and -Y³.] **a.** A mapping that deforms one path continuously into another in such a way that all the intermediate paths lie within the topological space of which the two given paths are subspaces (see quot. 1970). **b.** The property of being homotopic.

1918 O. VEBLEN *Analysis Situs* (Cambridge Colloq. Lect., Vol. 5, Pt. 2) v. 126 The term *homotopy* will be used to designate a deformation in the general sense.. and two generalized complexes..will be said to be homotopic if one can be carried into the other by means of a homotopy. **1930** S. LEFSCHETZ *Topology* ii. 77 The singular translation of *A* into *A'* just described is called a homotopic deformation, or homotopy, or simply deformation. **1951** M. H. A. NEWMAN *Topology of Plane Sets of Points* (ed. 2) vii. 179 It is homotopies..and not identities between paths that are interesting. **1956** E. M. PATTERSON *Topology* i. 11 Homotopy plays an important part in modern topology. **1961** HOCKING & YOUNG *Topology* iv. 151 Theorems about homotopy are but special cases of more general theorems on the extension of mappings. **1970** C. R. F. MAUNDER *Algebraic Topology* ii. 25 Two continuous maps $f, g: X \to Y$ are homotopic (or 'f is homotopic to g') if there exists a continuous map $F: X \times I \to Y$, such that $F(x, 0) = f(x)$ and $F(x, 1) = g(x)$, for all $x \in X$. The map F is said to be a homotopy, and we write $f \simeq g$ for 'f is homotopic to g'.

homotransplant (hǫmotra·ns,plɑnt), *sb. Med.* and *Biol.* [f. HOMO- + TRANSPLANT *sb.*] **a.** A piece of tissue or an organ taken from one individual and transplanted (or intended for transplantation) to another individual of the same species.

1929 *Ann. Surg.* XC. 934 Eight days after operation, the homotransplant appeared well fixed. **1947** *Jrnl. Bone & Joint Surg.* I. 621 In order that homotransplants of bone may be available for use, methods of storing and preservation must be considered. **1963** R. Y. CALNE *Renal Transplantation* iii. 33 Experimental renal homotransplants initially have the appearance and behaviour of autotransplants.

b. A homotransplantation operation.

1955 *Jrnl. Clin. Invest.* XXXIV. 329/1 Dederer.. performed a homotransplant of a kidney from one puppy to another of the same litter.

homotransplant (hǫ:motrɑns,plɑ·nt), *v. Med.* and *Biol.* [f. prec. sb.] *trans.* To transplant from one individual to another of the same species.

1953 *Brit. Jrnl. Surg.* XL. 447/1 Attempts at homotransplanting kidneys in humans in France have had no more success than the animal experiments of the past fifty years. **1955** *Proc. R. Soc.* B. CXLIII. 560 When ovary and skin are homotransplanted concomitantly, the ovary may survive while the skin is destroyed. **1961** *New Scientist* 7 Sept. 593/1 The natural history of a kidney homotransplanted between genetically dissimilar people.

So **homotranspla·nted** *ppl. a.*

1939 *Proc. Soc. Exper. Biol. & Med.* XLI. 474 (*heading*) Persistence of medullary tissue in homotransplanted adrenals. **1961** *New Scientist* 7 Sept. 593/1 A homotransplanted kidney starts to function within fifteen minutes of establishing the new circulation of blood.

homotransplantable (hǫ:motrɑns,plɑ·ntǎb'l), *a. Med.* and *Biol.* [f. prec. vb., after *transplantable*.] Capable of being successfully transplanted from one individual to another of the same species.

1957 *Jrnl. Nat. Cancer Inst.* XVIII. 529 It has been suggested..that chromosomal imbalance in homotransplantable tumors produces a simplified antigenic composition of the tumor cells. **1962** FELDMAN & YAFFE in Wolstenholme & Cameron *Transplantation* (Ciba Foundation symposia) 170 Further serial transfers through 3–4 transplant generations established homotransplantable tumour lines.

Hence **ho:motransplantabi·lity.**

1957 *Jrnl. Nat. Cancer Inst.* XVIII. 529 The only nonmalignant tissue reported as showing some degree of homotransplantability is the ovary of the rat. **1967** W. ANDERSON *Boyd's Path. Surgeon* (ed. 8) ix. 107 In the past it was possible to transplant a tumor only to another member of the same species (homotransplantability).

homotransplantation (hǫ:motrɑns,plɑntēi·ʃən). *Med.* and *Biol.* [f. HOMO- + TRANSPLANTATION.] The operation of transplanting tissue from one individual to another of the same species.

1905 A. CARREL in *Jrnl. Amer. Med. Assoc.* 25 Nov. 1645/2 If the organ is replaced in the same animal from which it was removed, the operation is called an autotransplantation. If it is placed in another animal of the same species it is called a homotransplantation, while if it is placed in an animal of a different species, the operation is called a heterotransplantation. **1915** *Ibid.* 4 Dec. 1966/2 Homotransplantations between related and nonrelated rabbits. **1917** *Ann. Surg.* LXV. 702 Autotransplantation and homotransplantation of segments of veins and arteries are perfectly feasible. **1953** *Brit. Jrnl. Surgery* XL. 447/1 It is in the chronic group of cases that homotransplantation of kidneys would be necessarily first applied. **1971** *Nature* 22 Jan. 270/1 Minced skeletal muscle regenerates with autotransplantation and homotransplantation in the rat, and with heterotransplantation in the mouse.

homotype. Add: **1.** (Later example.)

1939 *Ann. Ent. Soc. Amer.* XXXII. 695 Homotype: 1. That which is constructed on the same plan or type—as metameres of the body. *Not* a nomenclatural term.

2. *Taxonomy.* A specimen identified as a type by someone other than the author of the original description, after comparison with the holotype.

1896 WALSINGHAM & DURRANT *Rules for regulating Nomencl.* 13 A specimen named by another than the author, after comparison with the type, is called a Homotype... We have added the term *Homotype* to those proposed by Mr. Oldfield Thomas. **1939** *Ann. Ent. Soc. Amer.* XXXII. 695 Homotype:... 2. Equals Homoeotype. **1967** R. E. BLACKWELDER *Taxonomy* xxix. 591 Specimens identified as to time or person of identification. Metatypes, homotypes (homoeotypes), and so on.

homotype (hǫ·motəip), *a. Cytol.* [f. HOMO- + Gr. τύπος TYPE *sb.*¹] = *homœotypic, -typical* adjs. (s.v. *HOMŒO-).

1895 [see *heterotype* s.v. *HETERO-]. **1907** C. E. WALKER *Essent. Cytol.* v. 46 The first division following the meiotic is very commonly given a special name—the 'homotype' division. **1920** L. DONCASTER *Introd. Study Cytol.* v. 67 This second division is therefore spoken of as a homotype mitosis.

homotypic, -typical (hǫmoti·pik, -ti·pikǎl), *adjs.* [f. HOMOTYP(E + -IC, -ICAL.] **1.** (In Dict. s.v. HOMOTYPE.)

2. *Cytol.* = *homœotypic, -typical* adjs. (s.v. *HOMŒO-).

1904 *Amer. Naturalist* XXXVIII. 741 This mitosis differs from that of the 'typical' mitoses of cells and is called 'homotypic'. **1916** BAINBRIDGE & MENZIES *Essent. Physiol.* (ed. 2) xv. 456 In the second division each chromosome splits longitudinally in the ordinary way (homotypical mitosis). **1931** J. E. FRAZER *Man. Embryol.* i. 3 In the second maturation division each cell with its reduced chromosome number divides into two cells containing like numbers... Hence this division is an ordinary or 'homotypical' one. **1965** J. WILKINSON tr. *Langeron's Outl. Mycol.* ix. 378 Interkinesis is very short and the two daughter-nuclei very rapidly enter the prophase for the second meiotic (homotypic) division. **1972** *Nature* 21 Apr. 375/1 He did not believe that cancer should be thought of as a disease of cells nor of homotypic collections of cells.

3. *Ecol.* Consisting of individuals of a single species.

1930 W. M. WHEELER in E. V. Cowdry *Human Biol.* 141 Many species often assemble to form aggregations on the same tree or flower, or under the same stone, and these aggregations may be either homotypic, i.e. consisting of members of the same species, or heterotypic, when individuals of more than one species assemble. **1931** W. C. ALLEE *Animal Aggregations* i. 15 Homotypical associations consist of members of the same species which have arisen either sexually or asexually, which may have remained together because they are the offspring of the same parent, or which may have become accidentally associated together although of different parentage.

homozygote (hǫmozəi·gōᵘt). *Biol.* [f. HOMO- + ZYGOTE.] A diploid individual that has identical alleles at one or more genetic loci. Also *attrib.* or as *adj.*, homozygous.

1902 BATESON & SAUNDERS *Rep. Evol. Comm. R. Soc.* I. 126 Similarly, the zygote formed by the union of gametes having similar allelomorphs, may be spoken of as a homozygote. **1902** W. BATESON *Mendel's Princ. Heredity* 23 This *Aa* is the hybrid, or 'mule' form, or as I have elsewhere called it, the heterozygote, as distinguished from *AA* or *aa* the homozygotes. **1903** —— in *Nature* 19 Mar. 463/1 The homozygotes will all have pink eyes. **1909** R. H. LOCK *Rec. Progress in Study of Variation* (ed. 2) vii. 185 Let the F_1 plants, arising from the smooth yellow heterozygote grains, be crossed with the wrinkled white parent. **1927** HALDANE & HUXLEY *Animal Biol.* ii. 67 Homozygote parents. **1930** R. A. FISHER *Genet. Theory Nat. Selection* i. 8 The heterozygote when mated to either kind of homozygote would produce both heterozygotes and homozygotes. **1949** DARLINGTON & MATHER *Elem. Genetics* xiii. 276 If we breed a homozygote, or a group of like homozygotes, the offspring will be genetically..identical both with their parents and with one another. **1965** T. DOBZHANSKY *Heredity & Nature of Man* v. 156 Persons who inherit this gene from both parents (homozygotes) die of fatal anemia.

Hence **ho:mozygo·sis**, the fusion of two genetically identical gametes; the state or condition of being homozygous; **ho:mozygo·sity,** the state or condition of being homozygous; the degree or extent to which an individual is homozygous with respect to its complement of genetic loci; **ho:mozygo·tic** *a.*, of or pertaining to homozygosis; homozygous; **ho:mozygo·tically** *adv.*; **homozy·gous** *a.*, having identical alleles at one or more genetic loci.

1902 BATESON & SAUNDERS *Rep. Evol. Comm. R. Soc.* I. 152 The various homo- and hetero-zygous combinations. **1905** W. BATESON in *Rep. Brit. Assoc. 1904* 348 The other possibility is that this phenomenon is due to simultaneous homozygosis of independent allelomorphs. **1916** *Mem. N.Y. Bot. Gard.* VI. 349 Such a condition might also arise from inbreeding in which what is called 'homozygosity' might develop, giving similarity to the hereditary complex. **1925** D. F. JONES *Genetics Plant & Animal Improvement* xv. 503 Only by bringing sexually reproducing organisms to a fairly high degree of homozygosity can there be any possibility of successfully predicting the outcome in particular matings. **1927** *Hereditas* VIII. 77 Both *V. tricolor* and *V. arvensis* are homozygotic in respect of the modifying gene. *Ibid.* 147 One gene.., when homozygotically present, turns the full yellow to a yellowish white. **1942** *Nature* 10 Jan. 54/2 Such self-mating gives immediate homozygosis. **1949** DARLINGTON & MATHER *Elem. Genetics* xiii. 279 The homozygotic potential will remain as such so long as cross-breeding is absent or at least restricted to like homozygotes. **1957** C. H. WADDINGTON *Strategy of Genes* ii. 48 Further, gene-fixation and the passage to homozygosity, will be still more delayed if the environment does not remain perfectly uniform. **1969** *Sci. Jrnl.* Dec. 86/2 Various disorders due to homozygosity for rare recessive genes..are much commoner in such inbred populations than in outbred populations. **1970** AMBROSE & EASTY *Cell Biol.* x. 335 White-eyed females would only be observed if they were homozygous for this recessive gene.

homrai (hōᵘ·mrəi). [Nepal.] A large black-and-white hornbill, *Buceros bicornis*, which is found from India to Sumatra.

1832 B. H. HODGSON in *Jrnl. Asiatic Soc. Bengal* I. 251 The Homrâi reaches its full size in four and [*sic*] five years; it is gregarious and sedate. **1882** D. G. ELLIOT *Monogr. Bucerotidæ* [s.v. *Dichoceros bicornis*] (*heading*) The Homrai. *Ibid.* 3 The Nepaulese name for this species, 'Homrai', is derived from the notes it is accustomed to utter. **1905** *Pall Mall Gaz.* 24 Apr. 6/3 This curious bird (*Dichoceros bicornis*) is also known as 'Homrai'. **1939** F. N. CHASEN *Birds of Malay Peninsula* IV. 90 (*heading*) The Great or Homrai Hornbill.

hon.¹ (ǫn), abbrev. of HONOURABLE, HONORABLE.

1721 in D. Wilkins *Leges Anglo-Saxonicæ* List of Subscribers, The Hon. Henry Booth of the Middle Temple, Esq. **1777** *Jrnls. Continental Congress* (U.S.) X. 10 The following Gentlemen were chosen, viz. Hon. John Hancock, Samuel Adams, [etc.]. **1861** T. HUGHES *Tom Brown at Oxf.* I. iii. 39 The fourth man of the breakfast-club, the Hon. Piers St. Cloud, was in his third year. **1873** 'MARK TWAIN' & WARNER *Gilded Age* (1874) xxxiii. 304 Mr. O'Riley, still bearing the legislative 'Hon.' attached to his name. **1914** W. S. CHURCHILL in *World Crisis* (1923) I. viii. 186 Why cannot the right hon. and learned Gentleman (Sir Edward Carson) say boldly, [etc.]. **1922** JOYCE *Ulysses* 379 Over against the Rt. Hon. Mr. Justice Fitzgibbon's door. **1925** T. DREISER *Amer. Trag.* III. xiv. 182 One Hon. Alvin Belknap, of Belknap and Jephson, of this same city. **1938** N. MARSH *Artists in Crime* ii. 13 He's an Hon., you know, and old Lord Pilgrim is doddering to the grave. **1945** N. MITFORD *Pursuit of Love* ii. 14, I was a Hon, since my father, like theirs, was a lord. **1962** 'M. INNES' *Connoisseur's Case* v. 54 So old Mrs. Coulson..was an Hon?

hon.² (ǫn), abbrev. of HONORARY *a.*

1840 *Wiltshire Topographical Soc. Laws & Regulations*, Members of the Wiltshire Topographical Society... Geo. Alexander, Esq. Architect, London, *Hon. Sec.* **1876** *Monthly Packet* Feb. notices p. [5] Your correspondent could obtain further information from the Hon. Sec. **1957** R. W. ZANDVOORT *Handbk. Eng. Gram.* I. ii. 34 Members wishing to resign..are requested to notify the hon. secretary before January 1st. **1966** J. BETJEMAN *High & Low* 44 (*title*) The Hon. Sec.

hon.³ (hɒn), colloq. abbrev. of HONEY *sb.* (sense 5 in Dict. and Suppl.).

1906 *Dialect Notes* III. 141 *Hon'*, sweetheart, darling, baby. 'Going to school, hon'?' Very common in addressing children of a tender age. *a* **1911** D. G. PHILLIPS *Susan Lenox* (1917) I. ix. 155 'Never mind, hon,' he said... 'My, but you're purty!' **1953** *Fortune* July 158/2 She saw I was reading. 'What you got there, hon?' she asked me. **1954** P. HIGHSMITH *Blunderer* (1956) xxviii. 201 'Let's go, hon.' Bill often proposed leaving before his wife did. **1959** [see *DARL].

Honan (hōᵘnā·n). The name of a province of N. China, used to designate: **a.** a variety

of silk manufactured there; **b.** ceramics of the Sung dynasty, probably manufactured there.

[**1878** J. J. Young *Ceramic Art* II. v. 149 The aubergine, or purple egg-plant violet, was also made under Sung, and is one of the celebrated productions of Kiun, in the province of Ho-nan.] **1923** *Daily Mail* 24 Apr. 1 Fine quality real Silk Honans, beautifully printed. **1923** Hobson & Hetherington *Art Chinese Potter* Pl. XCVIII, Bowl of conical form with rounded sides and pointed base;.. Probably Honan ware. Sung dynasty. **1960** H. Hayward *Antique Coll.* 144/2 *Honan wares*, black- and brown-glazed Chinese porcelain wares of the Sung dynasty, probably made in Honan province. **1968** J. Ironside *Fashion Alphabet* 250 *Honan.* This is a silk pongee cloth from the Honan area of China, which has a particularly uniform colour. **1972** *Times* 30 May 11/2 (Advt.), A large Honan deep bowl.

honcho (hǫ·ntʃo). *slang* (chiefly *U.S.*). Also **hancho.** [ad. Jap. *han'chō* group leader.] Originally, the leader of a small group or squad; hence, anyone in charge in any situation; the 'boss'. Hence as *v. trans.*, to oversee; to be in charge of.

1947 J. Bertram *Shadow of War* VII. i. 212 But here comes the *hancho*. This boat must be finished to-night. **1955** *Amer. Speech* XXX. 118 *Honcho.* 1. *n.* A man in charge. (This is a Japanese word translated roughly as 'Chief officer', brought back from Japan by fliers stationed there during the occupation and during the Korean fighting...) 2. *v.* To direct a detail or operation. **1964** *Sat. Rev.* (U.S.) 10 Oct. 82/2 Jack Bullock, who *honchoes* the Curaçao casino. **1967** *N.Y. Times* 4 June IV. 1 Mr. Komer expects to be able to name these 45 key provincial *honchos*, and he hopes to place civilians in at least a quarter of the posts. **1972** C. Weston *Poor, poor Ophelia* (1973) xiii. 77 It's out of our territory, but I'll call Pete Springer. He's honcho in that division. **1973** *New Yorker* 30 July 24/1, I was the first employee who was not one of the honchos.

honda (hǫ·ndă). *Western U.S.* Also **hondo, -oo, -ou, -u.** [Sp. *honda* sling.] The eye at the end of a lasso through which the rope passes to form a loop (see also quot. 1958). Also *fig.*

1887 *Scribner's Mag.* II. 508/2 The common [cowboy] terms are..*heel*, to lariat an animal by the hind leg, *hondou* (derivation unknown, though probably from the Spanish *honda*, the eye of a needle), the slip-knot of the lariat. **1894** *Dialect Notes* I. 324 *Hondoo, hondou*, the slip-knot of a reata. **1895** *Montgomery Ward Catal.* 338/1 Lariat Hondas... Hondas for lariats; firmly pressed rawhide. **1933** *Amer. Speech* Feb. 28/2 *Hondo*, a small loop made of metal or rawhide to prevent the rope from burning or cutting the hands and to hold the loop open. **1958** *Ibid.* Dec. 270 *Hondoo*, the loop plaited in the end of a rope to make a running noose. Also the metal grommet or thimble inserted in that loop. **1964** 'F. O'Rourke' *Mule for Marquesa* xi. 177 He tied the lead lines to a slip rope, dropped the loop over a rock, wedged the honda.

Honduran, Hondurean (hǫndiūə·răn, -riăn), *a.* and *sb.* [f. next: see -AN.] **A.** *adj.* Of, pertaining to, or characteristic of Honduras. **B.** *sb.* A native or inhabitant of Honduras or British Honduras. So **Hondura·nean, -a·nian** *adjs.* and *sbs.*

1895 Savage & Gunter *His Cuban Sweetheart* II. xii. 166 The Honduranean magnates. *Ibid.* III. xiii. 184 The sunburned neck of the average Honduranean. **1902** R. H. Davis *Capt. Macklin* iii. 105 The Honduranian consul. **1911** D. Folkmar *Dict. Races or Peoples* 77 Honduran (see *Spanish American*). **1918** D. G. Munro *Five Republics Central Amer.* vi. 131 It must not be supposed, however, that the Honduraneans are necessarily inferior, intellectually or physically, to the inhabitants of the other republics. **1926** *Glasgow Herald* 17 June 10 The Honduran steamer Olancho. **1927** *Blackw. Mag.* Aug. 186/1 Living under Honduranian laws..these people, once British, are gradually being forced to give up their birthright. **1934** A. Huxley *Beyond Mexique Bay* 27 They are true-born Panamanians, Nicaraguans, Hondureans, or whatever it may be. **1941** P. E. James *Latin America* xxiii. 691 From it [*sc.* the banana world] Honduras derives financial profit through taxation but it cannot be considered to form a coherent part of the Honduran state. **1950** *Caribbean Q.* II. II. 3 The poetry and painting of contemporary British Hondurans. **1959** W. S. Stokes *Latin American Politics* ix. 194 Even with such liberal land laws.. which has permitted practically all Hondurans..to own land, Honduras has not been able to achieve democratic government. **1972** *Guardian* 29 Jan. 1/1 Some major move up to the Honduran frontier.

Honduras (hǫndiūə·răs, hǫndiuræ·s). The name of a Central American republic and of the nearby British Honduras (now Belize), used *attrib.* to designate various plants native to the area, as **Honduras bark,** the dried bark of the tree *Picramnia antidesma*, also called *cascara amarga*, and formerly used to treat dysentery, syphilis, and other diseases; **Honduras cedar,** a local species of *Cedrela*, esp. *C. odorata*; **Honduras mahogany,** *Swietenia macrophylla*; **Honduras rosewood,** a species of *Dalbergia*, esp. *D. stevensonii*; **Honduras sarsaparilla,** the dried root of *Smilax ornata*, used in various medical preparations or as a flavouring.

1887 *Colonial & Indian Exhib., Rep. Col. Sect.* 256 'Majoe bitter'..has been lately introduced into medicine in the United States under the name of 'Honduras bark' or 'Casc[ar]a amarga'. **1931** M. Grieve *Mod. Herbal* I. 166 Cascara amarga... Synonyms. Mountain Damson Bark. Simaruba. Honduras Bark. **1875** T. Laslett *Timber & Timber Trees* xxxii. 266 The Cuba, Honduras, and Mexican Cedars are varieties of the *Cedrela odorata*. **1919** W. Winn *Timbers* i. 95 Cedar, *Cedrela odorata*, also known as..Honduras Cedar. **1950** C. W. Bond *Colonial Timbers* 73 Honduras cedar is of considerable value for decoration. **1962** R. J. Streets *Exotic Forest Trees Brit. Commonwealth* 221 'Honduras Cedar', 'West Indian Cedar'. A native of the continent of tropical America and several of the West Indies. **1803** T. Sheraton *Cabinet Dict.* 254 From this province [*sc.* Honduras] is imported the principal kind of mahogany in use amongst cabinet-makers, which generally bears the name of Honduras mahogany. **1851** Chaloner & Fleming *Mahogany Tree* v. 48 Honduras Mahogany is found to work as freely and bend as readily as English Oak. **1902** G. S. Boulger *Wood* II. 237 Honduras mahogany, reaching 50 ft. at its first branch and 3 ft. in diam., yields logs 25–40 ft. long and 12–24 in. square, or even larger. **1969** T. H. Everett *Living Trees of World* 212/1 The Honduras mahogany is native from southern Mexico and Central America to Peru, Bolivia and Brazil. **1904** H. Stone *Timbers of Commerce* 64 Rosewood. Dalbergia sp... Alternative Names. Honduras Rosewood. **1956** *Handbk. Hardwoods* (Forest Prod. Res. Lab.) 205 Honduras rosewood grows to a height of 50–100 ft. **1830** G. Spratt *Flora Medica* II. 212 The Honduras Sarsaparilla has a whitish or dirty brown cuticle. **1840** [see Sarsaparilla 1 b]. **1950** R. C. Wren *Potter's Cycl. Bot. Drugs* (ed. 6) 308 Honduras Sarsaparilla is generally imported in long thin bundles with few rootlets attached.

honest, *a.* Add: **1. b.** *to make an honest woman (of)*: also used colloq., without depreciatory reference, in sense 'to marry'.

1818 Scott *Hrt. Midl.* in *Tales my Landlord* 2nd Ser. IV. ix. 201 Effie was married—made, according to the common phrase, an honest woman. **1927** W. E. Collinson *Contemp. Eng.* 108 The old phrase to make an honest woman (of a girl in trouble) is often used in jest in innocent contexts. **1968** R. Harris *Nice Girl's Story* v. 38 When are you going to be made an honest woman?

3. e. *honest broker*: a sobriquet (tr. G. *ehrlicher makler*) for the German statesman Bismarck; more generally, a representative of a country attempting to mediate diplomatically between two opposing nations, states, etc.; also *transf.*, any such mediator in industrial or other disputes.

[**1878** *Times* 21 Feb. 5/1 To my [*sc.* Bismarck's] mind, it is rather the mediation of an honourable broker who really wishes to carry on business.] **1884** W. Beatty-Kingston tr. *Busch's Our Chancellor* II. ii. 130, I [*sc.* Bismarck] don't picture to myself a peace-mediator playing the part of an arbitrator..; but a more modest one [*sc.* rôle], something like that of an honest broker, who really wants to transact business. **1884** in J. R. Ware *Passing Eng.* (1909) 154/1 *Honest broker*, matrimonial agent. 'Marriages are not all made in heaven; some of them are made by marriage brokers..though the "honest broker" does not seem to find the trade very remunerative.' **1926** Fowler *Mod. Eng. Usage* 548/1 *Honest broker*, Bismarck. **1934** *S.P.E. Tract* XLII. 88 *Honest broker*, coined by Bismarck as *ehrlicher Mäkler* 1878. **1967** *Guardian* 4 Feb. 9/3 (*heading*) 'Honest broker' role still possible for Britain. *Ibid.* 9/4 An 'honest broker' must have something special to offer, Britain has..immense diplomatic experience and Anglo-Saxon commonsense. **1968** G. Jones *Hist. Vikings* IV. ii. 371 A compromise was reached whereby Edmund should have Wessex and Knut the rest of the country. Among the honest brokers was Eadric Streona. **1970** *Times* 31 Mar. (Australian Suppl.) p. ii/3 On another corner of the Asian board Australia acted the comparatively successful honest broker between the United States and the kingdom of Cambodia representing Cambodia in Saigon and the United States in Phnom Penh. **1973** *Times* 9 Feb. 1/6 As Rhodesia and Zambia were not on speaking terms an intermediary or 'honest broker' had to be found.

f. *Honest Injun*: see *Injun b.

g. *Honest John*: (*a*) *colloq.* an honest man; (*b*) an American type of missile designed to carry a nuclear warhead.

1935 *Amer. Speech* X. 20/1 Any honest citizen; a hard-working fellow...*honest John.* **1954** *Birmingham* (Ala.) *News* 7 Mar. A24/5 The Army is stockpiling the plane-killing Nike units, and semi-guided field artillery rockets designated as the 'Honest John'. **1957** P. Frank *Seven Days to Never* iii. 95 The atomic cannon and Honest John rockets..began to arrive in Europe. **1973** 'H. Howard' *Highway to Murder* v. 57 One thing for sure was that she trusted me to play Honest John. **1973** *Guardian* 7 June 1/5 Britain, West Germany and Belgium are to buy the American Lance battlefield nuclear missile—to replace the obsolescent Honest John.

4. d. *honest-to-God, honest-to-goodness*: genuine(ly, real(ly. *colloq.* (orig. *U.S.*).

1913 J. London *Valley of Moon* I. x, Honest to God, Saxon, he don't like all his horses as much as I like the last hair on the last tail of the scrubbiest of the bunch. **1916** 'B. M. Bower' *Phantom Herd* iii. 45 The real honest-to-goodness-twelve-months-in-the-year West. **1916** Joyce *Portrait of Artist* v. 212 Oh, honest to God, if the crook of it caught him that time he was done for. **1918** B. Hall *Diary* in Hall & Niles *One Man's War* (1929) xxxiv. 352 The only honest-to-God aviator the Americans have ever produced—Raoul Lufbery! **1921** Galsworthy *To Let* III. v, She was..'honest to God' indifferent to it all. **1924** W. M. Raine *Troubled Waters* xiii. 144 Few will believe it, but it's an honest-to-goodness fact. **1929** W. H. Thomson *That Terrier 'Brick'* xiii. 69 Honest-to-goodness, I didn't know that I was doing anything wrong. **1933** E. Caldwell *God's Little Acre* i. 11 'A real honest-to-God albino?' Shaw asked. 'As real as the day is long.' **1937** [see *copper-bottomed *a.*]. **1937** J. B. Priestley *Two Time Plays* p. xi, It was not until I substituted for him an honest-to-goodness exiled German professor that the play began to look right. **1945** *Tee Emm* (Air Ministry) V. 40 Plain honest-to-God engine failure. **1952** S. Kauffmann *Philanderer* (1953) iii. 50, I don't see a glimmer nowadays. Or if I do, I honest-to-goodness think it's a disappearing glimmer. *Ibid.* v. 80 The fact that we honest to God really dislike each other is thundering out loud now that the entertainment has stopped. **1959** 'J. Welcome' *Lady is Tramp* viii. 125 I'm just pure honest-to-God terrified. **1960** *Farmer & Stockbreeder* 5 Jan. (Suppl.) 4 Like all good meals, there'll be bread and butter with it—not just a substitute for butter, but the real thing, the honest-to-goodness dairy product. **1963** *Times* 4 Mar. 11/6 One recalls a very distinguished industrialist (an individualist himself) who said he preferred 'honest to God engineers and creative designers'. **1963** J. A. T. Robinson (*title*) Honest to God. **1973** J. Thomson *Death Cap* vii. 107 It's an honest-to-God mushroom and..I'd have it for tea to prove it.

5. b. Used to emphasize the truth of a statement. *colloq.* (orig. *U.S.*).

1876 'Mark Twain' *Tom Sawyer* ix. 100 Tell me, Joe,—*honest*, now, old feller—did I do it, Joe? **1901** Merwin & Webster *Calumet 'K'* viii. 160 Max..said to his sister: 'Honest, Hilda, I don't see how he does it.' **1913** A. Bennett *Regent* II. viii. 236 'But I'm not sarcastic!' he protested. 'Honest?'.. 'Honest!' he solemnly insisted. **1923** R. D. Paine *Comr. Rolling Ocean* vi. 105 He is not so bad as he sounds, honest, Jud. **1928** F. B. Young *My Brother Jonathan* II. iv, If it weren't for the life at Prince's I don't think I could stick it..honest! **1972** 'J. & E. Bonett' *No Time to Kill* viii. 103 Of course I don't know a thing, but, honest, I can't see anyone here doing these people in.

honestly, *adv.* Add: **2. b.** Used parenthetically or as an exclamation, either to emphasize the honesty of one's intentions, statements, etc., or as an expression of exasperation.

1898 G. B. Shaw *Mrs. Warren's Profession* III. 204 Honestly, dear Praddy, do you like seeing them together? **1921** —— *Back to Methuselah* III. 129 *Mrs Lutestring.* You were kind enough to say that I frighten you. *Burge-Lubin.* Honestly, you do. **1929** E. O'Neill *Dynamo* I. ii. 32 Honestly, I think you've got a nerve to ——. **1957** N. Marsh *Off with his Head* iii. 56 No, honestly, this is just *too* mummerset. **1970** 'D. Shannon' *Unexpected Death* (1971) ii. 24 Angel said, 'Honestly! *More* rain. I'll be going stir-crazy..cooped up in here.' **1973** *Courier & Advertiser* (Dundee) 21 Feb. 13/5 Honestly, some of these drivers should have their heads seen to!

honey, *sb.* (*a.*). Add: **4. b.** A colour resembling that of honey. Also *attrib.* and *Comb.* (see sense 6 c in Dict.).

1814 P. Syme *Werner's Nomencl. Colours* 34 Honey Yellow, is sulphur yellow mixed with chesnut brown. **1838** Honey-yellow [in Dict., sense 6 c]. **1888** C. T. Whitmell *Colour* XII. 183 Yellows may be distinguished as.. honey..gold, [etc.]. **1923** *Daily Mail* 8 May 14 In Reseda,..Champagne, Honey, Copper. **1958** *Times* 16 Aug. 4/7 The Leccesi were fortunate in having close by an inexhaustible supply of honey-gold limestone. **1959** A. K. Lang in H. Q. Masur *Murder Most Foul* (1973) 76 A confection of honey blonde hair. **1973** G. Beare *Snake on Grave* iv. 23 Her skin was deeply tanned, a smooth honey gold.

5. Now common in N. Amer., whence also in Britain and elsewhere.

1859 Mrs. Stowe *Minister's Wooing* xxiii. 215 Come to ole Candace!..Honey, darlin', ye a'n't right—dar's a dreffut mistake somewhar'. **1919** C. H. Darling *Jargon Bk.* 17 *Honey*, sweetheart. **1929** M. Connelly *Green Pastures* (1930) I. v. 55 Come on, honey, an' meet de folks. **1939** [see *chin *sb.*[1] 1 d]. **1952** *Manch. Guardian Weekly* 20 Mar. 3 She doesn't have a thing that you haven't got, honey, but she has it over here. **1952** S. Kauffmann *Philanderer* (1953) i. 15 'I think you know I really understand it. But, honey, I ——.' A little pause here. **1961** J. Heller *Catch-22* (1962) xviii. 178 'Be thankful you've got me,' she insisted. 'I am, honey.' **1962** J. Ludwig in R. Weaver *First Five Years* 22 'Honey,' he said to the girl, 'let your *babbe* stay out here with the baby.' **1964** L. Nkosi *Rhythm of Violence* 27 Men are monsters!..Especially black men, honey. **1968** *New Society* 29 Aug. 305/1 'Honey' as an endearment, now rediscovered by southern Englishmen via Hollywood.

b. Anyone or anything good of its kind. *slang* (orig. *U.S.*).

1888 *Missouri Republican* 24 Feb., Dave is a honey. **1933** *Amer. Speech* VIII. III. 35/1 [Pugilist slang] *Bearcat*, an excellent fighter, a *honey.* **1934** H. N. Rose *Thesaurus of Slang* ii. 3/1 Anything pleasing or attractive: *a honey.* **1935** [see *dilly *sb.*[5]]. **1939** *Evening News* 7 Nov. 4/5 A shot you are pleased with is a 'honey' or a 'peach' or an 'eagle'. **1946** G. Gibson *Enemy Coast Ahead* xiii. 185 On the controls she [*sc.* an aeroplane] was as light as could be. This ship was certainly a honey. **1949** *N.Y. Times* 2 Oct. 1 It is a honey of a taut melodrama. **1958** M. Allingham *Hide my Eyes* xvi. 160 It had been a honey of an evening. **1959** *Vogue* Nov. 119 The Mini-Minor is a honey for parking. **1968** *Globe & Mail* (Toronto) 3 Feb. 38/1 (Advt.), A real honey, automatic power steering, power brakes, radio.

c. (See quot. 1960.) *U.S. slang.*

1934 L. Hellman *Children's Hour* I. 27 *Martha*:.. has she always been like this? *Cardin*: She's always been a honey. Aunt Amelia's spoiling hasn't helped any, either. **1960** Wentworth & Flexner *Dict. Amer. Slang* 265/1 *Honey*, a person who is difficult to please; a difficult problem or task.

7. honey ant: substitute for def.: = ***HONEY-POT** 4; add earlier and later examples; **honey-baby** *colloq.* = HONEY *sb.* 5; **honey-bucket** *N. Amer. slang*, a container for excrement; **honey-bun, honey-bunch** *colloq.* = HONEY *sb.* 5; **honey-buzzard**, a buzzard-like bird, *Pernis apivorus*, native to Europe and Asia, whose chief food is the contents of bees' and wasps' nests; **honey chile** chiefly *Southern U.S.* (esp. *Black*) *colloq.*, = HONEY *sb.* 5; **honey-creeper**: substitute for def.: a South American bird of the sub-family Cœrebinæ or a Hawaiian bird of the family Drepanididæ; add earlier and later examples; **honey-flow**, the secretion of honey or nectar by flowers; **honey-gilding**, (*a*) a dull gilding made from gold-leaf and honey, and used to decorate porcelain; (*b*) the process of applying such a solution; **honey-gold**, = **honey-gilding* (*a*); **honey mouse** = **honey possum*; **honey possum**, a small West Australian marsupial, *Tarsipes spenseræ*.

1868 *Amer. Naturalist* II. 382 A species of 'Honey-ant' is also found in Texas. **1874** *Ibid.* VIII. 366 The average weight of a non-producing ant is two milligrammes, that of a full honey-ant two hundred and forty milligrammes, a contrast simply immense. **1882** H. C. McCOOK (*title*) The honey ants of the Garden of the Gods. **1910** W. M. WHEELER *Ants* xx. 362 Honey ants have been reported from North America, South Africa and Australia. **1923** *Jrnl. Proc. R. Soc. W. Austral.* IX. 47 The geographical distribution of the various honey ants seems to point to drought as one of the most important factors in their development. **1944** *Living off Land* ii. 25 The bushman who finds honey ants can consider himself in champion class. **1948** E. WAUGH *Loved One* 134 She was my honey-baby. **1959** *Times* 20 June 7/6 Most people know..what is meant by..'a honey-baby'. **1931** BROPHY & PARTRIDGE *Songs & Slang 1914–18* 318 *Honey-bucket*, latrine receptacle for excreta. *Canadian.* **1962** F. G. VALLEE *Kabloona & Eskimo in Central Keewatin* 48 And where do they get the money? From emptying honey buckets for the Whites and mostly sitting on their butts. **1963** *Observer* 22 Dec. 13/3 The plumbing is definitely un-American. We were warned that the 'honey-buckets' would be a draughty experience. **1969** *Beaver* (Winnipeg, Man.) Summer 6/2 A woman taxi driver tells me most houses have honey-buckets, and galvanized [bath] tubs filled by hand. **1911** *Dialect Notes* III. 544 Honey-bunch, honey-bun. **1913** *Maclean's Mag.* Mar. 58/2 'Come, honey-bun,' she enticed. **1949** *Horizon* XIX. 239 Now, honey-bun, let's talk it over. **1957** M. SUMMERTON *Sunset Hour* iii. 46 'You might have warned me you were coming!' 'No time, honey bun.' **1969** R. TASHKENT *Ambiguous Man* iii. 34 I'm sorry, honeybun—sorry. Guess I'm a little upset. **1904** G. H. LORIMER *Old Gorgon Graham* 150 Honey, Honey, Funny Honey-bunch. **1912** *Collier's* 5 Oct. 34/2 Why, can't you see, Honey-bunch, can't you see? **1937** A. REID in *Famous Plays* (Gollancz) 721 Jenny..control yourself! *Jenny*: Very well, honey bunch! I'll try for the present. **1942** WODEHOUSE *Money in Bank* (1946) xiv. 122 But where does that get us, honeybunch? **1949** F. SARGESON *I saw in my Dream* 144 Honeybunch..what's it like sleeping all on your lonesome? **1678** J. RAY tr. *Willughby's Ornith.* II. 72 The Honey-Buzzard. For bigness it equals or exceeds the common Buzzard. **1766** T. PENNANT *Brit. Zool.* 67 (*heading*) The Honey Buzzard. **1825** P. J. SELBY *Illustr. Brit. Ornith.* I. 23 The Honey Buzzard preys upon moles, mice, and small birds. **1971** *Country Life* 25 Mar. 705/2 Seven species breed regularly within the city limits [*sc.* West Berlin]..honey-buzzard (4–5 pairs). **1926** T. S. STRIBLING *Teeftallow* viii. 67 Stan up fo yo' baby... Thah you ah, honey chile, lookin' yo' baby in de eye. **1948** MENCKEN *Amer. Lang.* Suppl. II. vii. 125 Southern speech has suffered cruelly on the stage and in talkies, where kittenish actresses from the domain of General American think that they have imitated it sufficiently when they have thrown in a few *you-alls* and *honey-chiles*. **1957** O. NASH *You can't get there from Here* 96, I early abandoned the hopeless fight against honey-chile and you-all. **1957** TRAGER & SMITH *Outl. Eng. Struct.* 82 There are current in popular literature allusions to 'Brooklynese' or 'honey-chile' accents. **1971** J. YARDLEY *Kiss a Day* viii. 153 Honey chile may well be talking through the back of her gorgeous neck. **1973** *Listener* 5 July 21/3 They [*sc.* the speakers] [were not] supposed to be rendering Deep South 'honey-chile' drawls. [**1822** J. LATHAM *Gen. Hist. Birds* IV. 207 Some few, indeed, of the Creepers have the tongue divided at the end and such no doubt are capable of licking honey from flowers.] **1872** COUES *N. Amer. Birds* 91 The Cærebidæ, or honey-creepers of the tropics. **1912** BRABOURNE & CHUBB *Birds S. Amer.* I. 395 Turquoise Honey-Creeper. **1944** G. C. MUNRO *Birds of Hawaii* 89 (*heading*) Hawaiian Honey-creepers. Drepanididae. Hawaiian Honey-creeper Family. **1970** R. MEYER DE SCHAUENSEE *Guide Birds S. Amer.* 368 Honeycreepers form a composite family of groups of birds much unlike each other... They share the habit of feeding on the pollen and nectar of flowers, as well as on berries, small seeds and insects. **1893** S. SIMMINS *Mod. Bee-Farm* (rev. ed.) 255 Frequent rainfalls destroy all chance of a good honey flow. **1894** *Farm, Field & Fireside* 13 July 352/3 There is no reason why a swarm hived towards the end of the honey-flow should not at once have its energies directed to storing surplus. **1955** E. HILLARY *High Adventure* i. 14 All through the exciting months of the honey-flow, the dream of a bumper crop would drive us on. **1958** *Irish Beekeepers' Manual* (Stationery Office, Dublin) xvi. 53 One or more crates of sections may be removed at any time during the honey flow, after the sections in a crate have been completely sealed. **1972** *Country Life* 3 Feb. 253/1 The worker bee at the height of the honey flow, as it is called by beekeepers, works so hard that it wears itself out and dies in a short time. **1958** M. WYKES-JOYCE *7000 Yrs. Pott. & Porc.* 271/2 Honey gilding. **1960** R. G. HAGGAR *Conc. Encycl. Cont. Pott. & Porc.* 207/1 Honey-gilding was a more satisfactory process. **1960** H. HAYWARD *Antique Coll.* 129/1 Honey gilding was used at the Chelsea and Worcester porcelain factories. **1971** *Country Life* 10 June 1416/3 When heavily laid on in broad masses, honey gilding could be further enriched with light and shade patterns by chasing with a finely pointed agate. **1954** G. SAVAGE *Porcelain* viii. 220 Gilding was often lavish, but of the brassy mercuric variety, whereas, for much of the eighteenth century, honey gold was sparingly and tastefully applied. **1965** FINER & SAVAGE in *Lett. of J. Wedgwood* 8 The porcelain manufacturers used, first honey-gold..and later, mercuric gilding. **1923** *Austral. Zoologist* III. 148 The *Tarsipes* are known throughout the district as 'Honey Mice', which is such an excellent vernacular name, when one considers the habits detailed later on, that I venture to submit it for general use. **1965** Honey-mouse [see **honey possum*]. **1941** E. TROUGHTON *Furred Animals of Australia* 80 The Honey Possum is readily distinguished by having three well-marked dark brown stripes along the back. **1965** *Austral. Encycl.* VII. 234/1 Honey-possum (*Tarsipes spenserae*). Restricted to the south of Western Australia, this species (which is also known as the honey-mouse), feeds on nectar, pollen, and small insects, gathered from blossoms.

b. In names of plants and fruits: **honey agaric** = **honey fungus*; **honey banana**, a West Indian name for a diploid variety of *Musa acuminata*, bearing small, sweet, thin-skinned fruit; also ellipt. *honey*; **honey fungus**, a fungus, *Armillaria mellea*, which causes a root disease in trees and shrubs, indicated by honey-coloured toadstools around affected plants and black threads like boot-laces attached to their roots; **honey-locust** (earlier and later examples); **honey mushroom** *U.S.* = **honey fungus*; **honey-ware** = BADDERLOCKS.

1894 W. SOMERVILLE tr. *Hartig's Text-bk. Dis. Trees* I. 207 *Agaricus melleus.* The Honey Agaric. This fungus belongs to the most widely distributed and destructive of parasites. **1909** E. W. SWANTON *Fungi* II. 176 *A[rmillaria] mellea*..'Honey Agaric'. **1945** M. C. RAYNER *Trees & Toadstools* ii. 35 The Honey Agaric forms its sporophores only after the tissues in which it grows have been killed. **1938** *Jrnl. Jamaica Agric. Soc.* XLII. 460 The Red banana, Honey, Apple and Fillbasket eventually found their way here. *Ibid.* 464 (*heading*) Honey [banana]. This variety is..also known by the names Sucrier and Lady's Finger... The skin is very thin and ripens to a deep yellow. The flavour of the fruit is very sweet and gives the variety its name. **1959** N. W. SIMMONDS *Bananas* v. 76 Notes on the principal clones. AA group. (a) 'Sucrier'. Principal synonyms..'Honey'..(West Indies). **1961** [see *FIG *sb.*[1] 1 c]. **1895** W. SCHLICH *Man. Forestry* IV. iii. 382 The honey fungus (*Agaricus melleus*, L.)..causes a well-known disease amongst conifers. **1919** W. E. HILEY *Fungal Dis. Common Larch* viii. 153 (*heading*) The effects of the honey fungus on its hosts. **1962** *Amateur Gardening* 27 Jan. 25/1 The honey fungus, Armillaria mellea, produces thick black threads or rhizomorphs somewhat similar to black leather laces. **1971** *Homes & Gardens* Sept. 97/2 Honey fungus or armillaria.. sometimes attacks and kills the roots of trees and shrubs. **1743** J. F. GRONOVIUS *Flora Virginica* 194 *Gleditsia*,.. Honey-locust. **1759** P. MILLER *Gardeners Dict.* (ed. 7) I, s.v. Gleditsia. The first sort [of *Gleditsia*] is very common in most parts of North America, where it is known by the Title of Honey Locust. **1819** A. L. HILLHOUSE tr. *Michaux's N. Amer. Sylva* II. 137 In different parts of the United States, this species [sc. *Gleditsia triacanthos*] is called indifferently Sweet Locust and Honey Locust. **1838** [see *GLEDITSCHIA]. **1863** [see *sweet locust* (SWEET *a.* and *adv.* C. 1 b)]. **1869** [see LOCUST *sb.* 5]. **1968** N. TAYLOR *Guide to Garden Shrubs & Trees* 135 Honey-Locust (*Gleditsia triacanthos*). A spiny-trunked native tree [*i.e.* native to U.S.A.] with small, numerous leaflets, greenish-yellow flowers, and a twisted, persistent pod. **1938** J. S. BOYCE *Forest Pathology* vi. 110 *Armillaria mellea*..known as the honey mushroom, causes this disease. **1849** D. LANDSBOROUGH *Pop. Hist. Brit. Seaweeds* 111 In Scotland in the Lowlands, it is by some called badder-locks, and hen-ware, which may be a contraction of honey-ware, the name given to it in the Orkney Islands. **1933** J. GRAY *Lowrie* 34 He never said onything aboot tangles, hinniwirs, an' dills.

honeycomb, *sb.* Add: **5. b.** *Textiles.* Used *attrib.* of a fabric in which the warp and weft threads form ridges and indentations, producing a cell-like appearance.

1879 T. R. ASHENHURST *Weaving & designing Textile Fabrics* 250 Another cloth which may be mentioned is one known as the honeycomb cloth, which presents to the eye a series of ridges and cavities. **1913** *T. Eaton & Co. Catal.* Fall & Winter 131/3 Full Bleached English Honeycomb Quilts..fringed all round..for single beds. **1921** *Daily Colonist* (Victoria, B.C.) 5 Apr. 18/4 (Advt.), Honeycomb Towels at, each, 15c. **1929** WOODHOUSE & BRAND *Towels & Towelling* ix. 99 The unbroken diamond in the first unit..is filled in with the 8-thread honeycomb weave. **1968** 'A. GILBERT' *Night Encounter* iii. 41 High bed with a honeycomb quilt.

c. A structure consisting of numerous intersecting surfaces designed to reduce turbulence and straighten the air flow in a wind tunnel.

1912 *Sci. Amer.* 14 Sept. 220/1 The usual method of eliminating swirls and irregularities of speed is to pass the air through a sheet metal 'honeycomb' at the front end [of the tunnel]. **1918** COWLEY & LEVY *Aeronautics* I. 8 At both ends of the channel proper there are placed two metal honeycombs. **1947** A. POPE *Wind-Tunnel Testing* ii. 60 If the contraction ratio of the tunnel is large, and a good honeycomb is installed, the turbulence can be low indeed. **1966** OWER & PANKHURST *Measurem. Air Flow* (ed. 4) vii. 200 The resistance coefficient of a honeycomb or a gauze is conveniently expressed in term of the loss of pressure..suffered by the air in passing through it.

d. A material consisting of a regular network of parallel, open-ended cells formed out of many bent or moulded strips (e.g. of metal or plastic) bonded together; it is usually used faced on both sides with sheeting, forming a *honeycomb sandwich.* Freq. *attrib.*

1937 *Jrnl. Franklin Inst.* CCXXIV. 282 Barkley-Grow Aircraft Corp...has fabricated an all metal honeycomb structure of great strength and lightness. **1946** *Mod. Plastics* Sept. 130/2 Standard thicknesses of honeycomb have been selected. *Ibid.*, Fire resistance may be obtained with stainless steel or laminated asbestos paper skins on asbestos honeycomb core. **1949** *Aircraft Engin.* XXI. 12/1 This flooring material is a honeycomb sandwich of aluminium alloy. **1964** OLEESKY & MOHR *Handbk. Reinforced Plastics* IX. 492 Honeycomb sandwich flooring is currently being used in large computer room applications. **1966** *New Scientist* 26 May 523/3 Temperature-resistant honeycomb has been used in heat-sensitive areas of many aircraft.

6. honeycomb coil *Electronics*, an inductance coil in which the turns cross one another obliquely and adjacent ones are separated, giving a criss-cross pattern; **honeycomb moth** (earlier example); **honeycomb radiator**, a radiator for an internal-combustion engine that is pierced by numerous short tubes running from front to back through which the air passes, the ends of which give it a honeycombed appearance; **honeycomb wall**, a (brick) wall containing numerous small openings close together at regular intervals.

1922 *Wireless World* 30 Dec. p. xiv (Advt.), Gimbal type Honeycomb coil. **1959** K. HENNEY *Radio Engin. Handbk.* (ed. 5) iii. 9 Honeycomb coils were a type of universal winding with relatively few, widely spaced turns per layer giving a typical 'honeycomb' appearance. **1840** J. & M. LOUDON tr. *Köllar's Treat. Insects* I. 75 This enemy is the caterpillar of a moth, called the..honeycomb-moth. **1904** A. B. F. YOUNG *Compl. Motorist* iii. 55 The front of the car consists of a water-tank pierced like a honeycomb throughout its whole surface with apertures of equal dimensions; this is known as a 'honeycomb radiator'. **1919** *Jane's All the World's Aircraft* 16b A 'V' type honeycomb radiator is fitted directly behind the airscrew. **1946** A. W. JUDGE *Mod. Petrol Engines* vii. 261 The honeycomb radiator, which has been so widely used in automobile and aircraft work, consists of a series of thin brass tubes expanded at their ends and joined together at these ends by a soldering process. **1894** J. P. ALLEN *Pract. Building Constr.* (Index), Honeycomb walls. **1913** G. G. SAMSON *Every Man his own Builder* iii. 108 Some people build them [*sc.* sleeper walls] as 'honeycomb' walls. **1969** *New Yorker* 5 Apr. 99/1 A honeycomb wall turns into an entrance to whatever place they imagine.

honeycomb, *v.* Add: **4.** *Building.* To build as a honeycomb wall.

1908 C. F. MITCHELL *Brickwork & Masonry* (ed. 2) ii. 103 To facilitate the circulation of air beneath the basement floors, these walls are usually honeycombed. **1964** E. C. ADAMS *Sci. in Building* I. v. 170 This [*sc.* ventilation] can be done..by 'honeycombing' sleeper walls.

honeycombing, *vbl. sb.* Add: **2.** (See quot. 1945); also **honeycombed** *a.*, of, pertaining to, or having such a defect.

1919 S. J. RECORD *Identification Economic Woods U.S.* (ed. 2) I. 58 When the interior finally dries, the internal strains frequently become so great that large checks open up, producing a honeycombed condition. **1938** H. E. DESCH *Timber* xi. 133 When the interior dries below the fibre saturation point it..is restrained from shrinking, and interior checks may result. This condition is known as honeycombing. **1945** D. J. SCHWARTZ et al. *Fund. Shopwork* 458 *Honeycombing*, a form of defective separation in wood which usually occurs in the interior and follows the medullary rays. It is caused by improper seasoning. **1966** A. W. LEWIS *Gloss. Woodworking Terms* 14 *Check*, small seasoning cracks or shakes, invisible from the outside of the wood; also called 'honeycombing'.

honey-dew. Add: **3.** (Earlier U.S. example.)

1843 J. LUMSDEN *Let.* 15 May in *Amer. Memoranda* (1844) 14 The manufacturing of the nigger-head,..pigtail, honey-dew, and other varieties of the stimulating and soothing herb.

4. A colour resembling that of a honeydew melon.

1921 *Daily Colonist* (Victoria, B.C.) 19 Oct. 5/6 (Advt.), Combination dark tones and lighter hues, such as algonquin, honeydew, jade. **1949** *Brit. Colour Council Dict. Colours Int. Decoration* III. 13 *Honeydew*, a colour name.. adopted here as a more attractive name for B.C.C. standard Carrot.

5. honeydew melon, a cultivar of the musk melon, *Cucumis melo*, which has a smooth ivory or pale yellow skin and sweet greenish flesh.

1916 *Country Gentleman* 2 Sept. 1615/1 (*heading*) The honey dew melon. *Ibid.*, A new melon has recently been introduced... It has been christened Honey Dew... The Honey Dew is the result of crossing the Rocky Ford cantaloupe with a South African melon somewhat resembling a Casaba. It was propagated by John E. Gauger,

of Colorado. **1923** A. Ward *Encycl. Food* 314 The Honey Dew has a smooth, somewhat warted, creamy-white to greyish skin. **1959** P. Roth *Goodbye, Columbus* (1969) iii. 46 And there were melons—cantaloupes and honey dews. **1962** Whitaker & Davis *Cucurbits* ix. 189 All 'Honey Dew' melons should have an adequate ethylene treatment. *Ibid.* x. 207 The cultivars 'Hales's Best' and 'Honey Dew' were..low in soluble solids.

honey-eater. Delete clause beginning *spec.* and substitute: **b.** An Australasian bird of the family Meliphagidæ.

1822 J. Latham *Gen. Hist. Birds* IV. 208 None of them, although the tongue be cloven into two filaments, are at all fringed at the edges, as is the case with very many of the honey-eaters. **1845** J. Gilbert in J. Gould *Mammals of Australia* I. tab. 5 It [sc. *Tarsipes rostratus*] inserted its long tongue precisely in the way in which the Honey-eaters among birds do theirs into the flower-cups for honey. **1862, 1864–5** [in Dict.]. **1901** A. J. Campbell *Nests & Eggs Austral. Birds* I. 354 The range of the splendid little Black Honeyeater extends across the southern part of Australia. **1936** [see *coach-whip 1 b]. **1964** A. L. Thomson *New Dict. Birds* 375/2 The diet of the majority of honeyeaters consists of a mixture of nectar, pollen, and insects.

ho·ney-fu:ggle, -fu:gle, *v. U.S. colloq.* Also **-fackle, -fogle.** [app. f. Honey *sb.* + Fugle *v.*¹, perh. after dial. *connyfogle* (E.D.D.).]

1. *trans.* **a.** To dupe, deceive, swindle.

1829 *Virginia Literary Museum* I. 458 *Honeyfuggle*, to quiz, to cozen. **1856** *Knickerbocker* XLVIII. 286 They go cavorting out, honey-fuggling their consciences. **1888** *Century Mag.* XXXVI. 81/2 A-tryin' to honey-fugle the varmint to git 'im to come underneath. **1902** W. N. Harben *Abner Daniel* xix, He's been tryin' to honey-fuggle the old man into a trade. **1906** *Dialect Notes* III. 141 He can't honey-fuggle him.

b. To obtain by duplicity or wheedling.

1905 D. G. Phillips *Plum Tree* xxiii, Whatever terms he could honeyfugle out of my conciliation-mad candidate. **1942** Berrey & Van den Bark *Amer. Thes. Slang* § 223/7 Coax; wheedle..honeyfogle.

2. *intr.* To act in an underhand or indirect way, in order to deceive or to obtain by duplicity.

1856 *Congress. Globe* 22 July, App. 965 Pardon me for using the word, but Sharp 'honey-fuggled' around me. **1888** *Missouri Republican* 20 Jan. (Farmer), Noonan's companion objected to this honey-fugling by knocking the demonstrative stranger down. **1906** *Nation* (N.Y.) 22 Feb. 149 'Don't honey-fugle,' he advised the committee, 'but go to the bottom in any way possible.' **1941** *Time* 26 May 16/3 Things which..Baruch had to wangle by what he called 'buttering & honey-fuggling'. **1952** T. Pyles *Words & Ways Amer. Eng.* vi. 129 Even today some of these 'tall' words, words like..*to honeyfogle*..are popularly regarded as picturesque and admirably American.

honey-guide. 1. Substitute for def.: A small tropical bird of the predominantly African family Indicatoridæ, which feeds on insects, honey, and beeswax, a habit which makes some species useful as guides to bees' nests. Add earlier and later examples.

1777 A. Sparrman in *Phil. Trans. R. Soc.* LXVII. 43 The Dutch settlers thereabouts have given this bird the name of *Honig-wyzer*, or Honey-guide, from its quality of discovering wild honey to travellers. **1900** *Ibis* 7th Ser. VI. 691 Having heard the story of the Honey-guide before, I was much interested. **1955** *Bull. U.S. Nat. Mus.* CCVIII. 1 The honey-guides are a small family of picarian birds related to the barbets, the woodpeckers, and the toucans. **1966** E. Palmer *Plains of Camdeboo* xii. 215 It is not only the honey-guides..that use other birds' nests.

honeyish, *a.* Delete † *Obs.* and add later example.

1969 P. Dickinson *Pride of Heroes* 40 There is honeyish Mrs Singleton in her dottily beautiful car.

honeymoon, *sb.* Add: **1. b.** (Later examples.)

1969 *Daily Tel.* 9 Sept. 1/2 MPs fear that the honeymoon between the troops and the civilians might be over. *Ibid.* 13 Sept. 3 It is an open secret that the honeymoon between Xerox and Rank Organisation is over. **1971** *Guardian* 15 Jan. 12/1 The Government has had its honeymoon, free from captious criticism, as Mr Wilson promised.

c. *second honeymoon*, a holiday or trip, resembling a honeymoon, taken by a couple who have been married for some time.

1872 Princess of Wales *Let.* 31 Jan. in G. Battiscombe *Queen Alexandra* (1969) viii. 118 This quiet time we two have spent here together now has been the happiest days of my life... It has been our second honeymoon. **1894** G. du Maurier *Trilby* III. viii. 152 So Taffy and his wife have come for their second honeymoon, their Indian-summer honeymoon, alone. **1910** *Nat. Police Gaz.* 16 July 3/4 They acted as if they were on their second honeymoon. **1967** 'M. Hunter' *Cambridgeshire Disaster* xxi. 137 They began what he called an extended second honeymoon, driving where she liked.

2. *attrib.* (see also in Dict. sense 1) and *Comb.*, as *honeymoon couple, period*; **honeymoon suite** = **bridal suite*.

1881 E. W. Hamilton *Diary* 26 Dec. (1972) I. 205 Lord Lyons says that Gambetta has got very well through his first short (honeymoon) session, and has displayed great vigour and tact as a parliamentary leader. **1904** *Daily Chron.* 31 Mar. 6/6 The young honeymoon couple were heard of at Newport, Mon. **1970** W. J. Burley *To kill a Cat* v. 81 A honeymoon couple stood close, arms round each other. **1953** E. Simon *Past Masters* II. i. 69 The Labour Government's honeymoon period looks like having come to an end. **1970** *Guardian* 9 Dec. 11/1 This Government's honeymoon period has been significantly shorter than previous in-coming Governments'... The package of..increased charges announced by the Chancellor on October 27 was the chief single cause of a rapid deterioration in the Government's popularity. **1956** 'E. McBain' *Cop Hater* (1958) ix. 80 The cafe still served as a sort of no-man's-land between the respectable workaday world..and the sinful..brothels... Jenny's served the same purpose as the shower stall does in a honeymoon suite. **1967** C. O. Skinner *Madame Sarah* viii. 163 Bernhardt enjoyed Chicago. Her quarters at the Palmer House roused in her continual..mirth, for she occupied the 'honeymoon suite'. **1968** B. Norman *Hounds of Sparta* xxvii. 183 'The *honeymoon* suite, for God's sake.'..'I knew nothing about that, believe me.'

honeymooner. (Earlier and later examples.)

1845 W. G. S. Cavendish *Handbk. Chatsworth & Hardwick* 196 Other honeymooners here [*sc.* at Hardwick]. **1968** *Punch* 18 Sept. 398/1 Hawker-Siddeley have dramatised for us the folly of paying a man £15,000 a year to sit around in an airport lounge with a lot of delayed honeymooners.

honey-pot. Add: **2. b.** ? orig. *Austral.* Term applied to the action of jumping into a swimming-pool, etc., with one's hands clasped round one's drawn-up legs.

1941 in Baker *Dict. Austral. Slang.* **1951** J. Frame *Lagoon* 16 She would dive backwards and do a honey-pot into the water.

3. The female pudenda. *slang.*

1719 T. D'Urfey *Pills* III. 342 For when you have possession got, Of Venus Mark, or Hony-pot. **1970** G. Greer *Female Eunuch* 265 If a woman is food, her sex organ is for consumption also, in the form of *honey-pot*.

4. In full *honey-pot ant*. An ant belonging to one of several North American, Australian, or South African genera in which some of the workers become distended with surplus food, which is regurgitated when it is needed by the rest of the colony.

1880 *Jrnl. Linn. Soc. Zool.* XV. 185 Certain individuals in each nest serve as animated honey-pots. **1927** Haldane & Huxley *Animal Biol.* xii. 291 (*caption*) A store-chamber of the honey-pot ant. **1934** A. Russell *Tramp-Royal in Wild Australia* xxxviii. 253 Worker ants and honey-pot ants. *Ibid.*, The honey-pot stores the honey in its abdomen. **1968** P. P. & M. W. Larson *Lives of Social Insects* xxi. 157 Honeypots, or repletes..serve their nest mates simply as receptacles for the colony's extra food supplies. *Ibid.* (*caption*) Honeypot ants represent an adaptation of some ant species to dry and inhospitable environments. **1970** Brown & Taylor in *Insects of Australia* (C.S.I.R.O.) xxxvii. 956/1 Some formicine ants in arid areas..store regurgitated honey-dew and nectar in the enormously distended crops of special large 'honeypot' workers.

5. Something very attractive or tempting, *spec.* an attractive girl or young woman, one who invites or attracts attention. Also *attrib.*

1929 H. A. Vachell *Virgin* iii. 58 What a honeypot she was, whether in or out of breeches and boots. **1945** A. L. Rowse *West-Country Stories* 4 His honey-pot young wife. **1972** *Daily Tel.* 7 Jan. 11/2 This mother, who is a tart, decides to set the girl up as a photographer's model, and a great honey-pot she turns out to be for the local talent who come in droves to photograph her splendid features. **1972** *Guardian* 15 Aug. 16/1 The hordes of eager students that descend on London..present too tempting a honey-pot for the smart operators to stay away from. **1973** *Times* 29 May 14/5 Concentrating facilities at centres of attraction, so-called 'honeypot' areas, and discouraging motorists from heading towards 'quiet' areas.

honeypot: see *hanepoot.

‖**hongi** (hǫ·ŋi), *sb. N.Z.* [Maori.] The pressing of noses together as a form of salutation. Hence as *v. intr.*

1843 E. Dieffenbach *Trav. N.Z.* I. i. ii. 61 Leaving him to indulge his natural feeling in hongi..or nose-rubbing. **1862** *Richmond–Atkinson Papers* (1960) I. xiii. 791 A great many of them hongi'd with Parris and seemed very glad to see him. **1882** T. H. Potts *Out in Open* 23 The hongi, a method of salutation by rubbing noses together, we saw frequently performed. **1905** W. B. *Where White Man Treads* 63 Our chief..as is our custom, presented his nose for the 'hongi', which the stranger, not understanding, ignored. **1941** Baker *N.Z. Slang* ii. 21 We have to thank our original inhabitants for specifying, inaccurately as might be expected, the expression *to rub noses* as the equivalent of the Maori ceremony known as *hongi*. (The nose is pressed, not rubbed.) **1949** P. Buck *Coming of Maori* (1950) iii. vi. 418 The visiting party..pressed noses with the chief mourners. The nose pressing (*hongi*) process sometimes occupied much time. **1952** R. Finlayson *Schooner came to Atia* xvi. 83 The Maori people in New Zealand greet friends with the hongi. **1959** Tindale & Lindsay *Rangatira* xvi. 149 He greeted..Rona-Nui by gripping both her hands and pressing his nose and forehead against hers in the hongi salutation.

Hong Kong (hǫŋ kǫŋ). [Name of a British crown colony in the South China Sea.] **1.** *Croquet.* (See quot. 1863.)

1863 M. Reid *Croquet* 10 A ball croque'd beyond the boundaries is sent to 'Hong Kong', or 'up the country'. **1897** *Encycl. Sport* I. 253/2 *Hong Kong, Off to* —. The old term for the driving of an opponent's ball from the croquet to the extreme corner of the ground. **1957** V. Nabokov *Pnin* v. 131 Madam Shpolyanski insisted it was perfectly acceptable and said that when she was a child her English governess used to call it a Hong Kong.

b. Colloq. phr. *to go to Hong Kong*, to go away, to go 'to hell'.

1880 R. Jefferies *Hodge & M.* I. ii. 40 The excitement of the day was a pleasurable sensation, and as for his master he might go to Kansas or Hong-Kong. **1921** A. Brazil *Fortunate Term* xii. 160 Opal Earnshaw may go to Hong-Kong if she likes. I don't care about her and her meannesses.

2. Used *attrib.*, *spec.* to designate a strain of the influenza virus discovered in Hong Kong in 1968, and influenza caused by it.

1911 *Encycl. Brit.* XIII. 659/1 The only legal tender is the Mexican dollar, and the British and Hong-Kong dollar, or other silver dollars of equivalent value duly authorized by the governor. **1968** *Weekly Epidemiological Rec.* 16 Aug. 411 (*table*) Influenza... A2/Hong Kong/1/68. *Ibid.* 23 Aug. 421/2 Preliminary tests of paired sera..have shown very poor results against the new Hong Kong variant. *Ibid.* 30 Aug. 448/2 The Hong Kong strains should be classified as viruses A2. **1968** *Jrnl. Amer. Med. Assoc.* 16 Sept. 23/1 (*heading*) Experts attend Hong Kong flu talk in Atlanta. **1968** *Times* 23 Dec. 6/2 He was not feeling his best and had what scientists felt could be the symptoms of Hongkong influenza. **1970** *New Scientist* 8 Jan. 45/2 It made sad listening for those abed with Hongkong 'flu. **1973** J. Goodfield *Courier to Peking* viii. 101 When she finally got to the Hong Kong and Shanghai Bank, she..withdrew fifty Hong Kong dollars.

‖**honi soit qui mal y pense** (on*i* swa k*i* mal *i* pãñs). [Fr.] 'Shame on him who thinks evil of it'; a proverb, orig. used as the motto for the Order of the Garter. (See Garter *sb.* 2.)

13.. *Gaw. & Gr. Knt.* (ad fin.), Hony soyt qui mal pence. **1589** Puttenham *Eng. Poesie* ii. 116 King *Edwarde* the thirde, her Maiesties most noble progenitour, first founder of the famous order of the Garter, gaue this posie with it. *Hony soit qui mal y pense*, commonly thus Englished, Ill be to him that thinketh ill. **1716** [see Garter *sb.* 8]. **1776** H. Walpole *Let.* 22 Aug. (1857) VI. 370, I will prevent all clamour, by adopting St. George's motto,—'*Honi soit qui mal y pense*'. **1887** *Athenæum* 5 Nov. 600/1 The maxim 'Honi soit qui mal y pense' is one which needs to be frequently invoked by the friendly narrator and critic of Samoan manners. *a* **1930** D. H. Lawrence in Lawrence & Gelder *Young Lorenzo* (1931) 262 So Tolstoi says that all nude study is bad art—Honi soit qui mal y pense. **1959** *Chambers's Encycl.* III. 510/2 The reason for the adoption of the garter and the motto *Honi soit qui mal y pense* as the emblem and motto of the order is also unknown.

Honiton (hɒ·nitən, hǫ·n-). The name of a town in Devonshire used *attrib.* to designate a type of pillow lace which is made there, consisting of floral sprigs either hand-sewn on to fine net, or joined by bars of other lace-work, as *Honiton guipure, lace, sprig*. Also *absol.* = *Honiton lace*.

1831 M. Edgeworth *Let.* 11 June (1971) 548, I..made myself very comfortable finishing sewing the Honiton edge on my frill. **1840** *Observer* 16 Feb. 8/2 Her Majesty the Queen wore on her head a wreath of orange blossoms and a veil of Honiton lace. **1851** *Illustr. Catal. Gt. Exhib.* iii. iii. 559/1 Honiton guipure mantle. Bridal scarf and rich flounce in Honiton lace. *Ibid.* 560/1 Specimen of lace net..for the application of Brussels and Honiton sprigs. *Ibid.*, Tamboured lace scarf, imitation of Honiton, manufactured in London. **1858** Simmonds *Dict. Trade, Honiton lace*, a pillow, or cushion, lace made in Devonshire, remarkable for the beauty of its figures and sprigs, which are sewed on to net by the needle. **1865** F. B. Palliser *Hist. Lace* xxxii. 382 Queen Adelaide..gave the order for a dress to be made of Honiton sprigs. **1882** *Encycl. Brit.* XIV. 188/2 Honiton pillow lace resembles Brussels lace. **1895** *Army & Navy Co-op. Soc. Price List* 15 Sept. 1126 Real Lace Handkerchiefs. Honiton. **1963** *Times* 8 Mar. 14/7 Her..crinolined profusion of Honiton lace and orange blossom under a train of silver moiré.

honk, *sb.* Add: **b.** The harsh sound of a motor-horn. Also *v. intr.*, to emit such a sound (said of the horn, the motor vehicle, or the driver); also *transf.*; *trans.*, to utter with such a sound; to cause to make the sound 'honk'; to remove or drive away by the hooting of motor vehicles. Hence **ho·nking** *vbl. sb.* and *ppl. a.* orig. *U.S.*

1895 F. Remington *Pony Tracks* 256 The irrepressible Dan begins to 'honk' on his horn. **1906** 'O. Henry' *Four Million* 51 She would honk loudly the word 'Clara'. **1910** —— *Strictly Business* (1917) v. 57 The honk of the returned motor car at the door. **1911** R. W. Chambers *Common Law* x. 312 Where now the lonely taxi honks. **1911** H. S. Harrison *Queed* i. 6 Now and then a chauffeur honked by. **1914** R. & E. Shackleton *Four on Tour* 83 The [motor] horn was honked suddenly. **1915** *Literary Digest* 4 Sept. 467/1 Nearly a dozen autos may be always seen 'honking' their way through Nome's busy thoroughfares. **1924** *Glasgow Herald* 18 Aug. 8 The thundering and purring and swishing and honk-ing of the road traffic. **1926** [see *beat *v.*¹ 3 c]. **1927** *Observer* 28 Aug. 10 In the shadiest lanes we were honked and hooted out of the way. *Ibid.* 18 Sept. 8/3 The leisured stroller..is being 'honked' off the highway. **1928** *Ibid.* 22 Jan. 10/7 'Sunstar'..is feeling fit again and proposes to honk off to Doncaster to-night. **1929** *Times* 2 Jan. 15/5 The car had been honking underneath my office window for some time. **1931** G.

ATHERTON *Sophisticates* III. v. 295 The narrow thoroughfare was crowded with honking cars and taxis. **1955** *Times* 11 May 4/1 Much honking of horns from the cars round the ground. **1958** [see *BLEEP *sb.*]. **1969** *New Yorker* 29 Mar. 27/1 There was little honking; and our driver..was relaxed and cheerful. **1973** C. EGLETON *Seven Days to Killing* ix. 99 Dodging through the honking traffic.

honker. Add: **b.** The horn of a motor vehicle. **c.** One who 'honks' (in various senses). **d.** *slang.* A nose.

1891 *Outing* (U.S.) Oct. 43/1 Though a fair 'honker', I cannot successfully imitate the constantly varying note of the snow goose. **1928** *Funk's Stand. Dict.*, *Honker*, the warning horn of a motor-car. **1948** R. PARK *Harp in South* xxi. 267 It's yer own fault for having such a God-forgotten honker [*sc.* a large nose]. **1965** *New Statesman* 6 Aug. 183/3 The honker and the light-flasher drew up alongside. **1972** *Jazz & Blues* Sept. 12/1 Others in the R & B field..are just dismissed as 'honkers'.

honkers (hǫ·ŋkəɹz), *a. slang.* [Etym. unknown.] Drunk.

1957 R. LONGRIGG *Switchboard* v. 191 He stumbled out on to the lawn... 'Honkers.' 'Poor man. Pushed.' **1958** *News Chron.* 22 May 4/5 You drink wallop, sludge, or plasma (it's all ale or beer). If you get drunk you are honkers, plastered,..blotto. Or just plain paralytic. **1970** C. WOOD *Terrible Hard* xii. 167 Roll on Wednesday week and we'll all get honkers on champers.

honk-honk, reduplication of *HONK *sb.* b.

1908 H. G. WELLS *War in Air* ii. 43 A curious, amusing, wheezing sound had got into his 'honk, honk'. *Ibid.* 58 Honk-honking and emitting weird cries. **1909** S. FORD (*title*) Honk, honk!! Shorty McCabe at the wheel. **1915** T. BURKE *Nights in Town* 210 The honk-honk of motors. **1917** *Ideas* 23 Mar. 23/2 With a wild 'honk-honk!'..the motor rounded the corner. **1935** WODEHOUSE *Blandings Castle* ii. 44 'Good-bye.' 'Honk-honk!' said Freddie moodily.

honky (hǫ·ŋki, hʌ·ŋki). *U.S. Black slang.* Also **honkey, honkie.** [Etym. unknown; perh. a var. of *hunky* (see *HUNK *sb.*³).] A white man; white men collectively. Also *attrib.* or as *adj.*

Disparaging in all applications.

[**1946** MEZZROW & WOLFE *Really the Blues* xii. 216 First Cat: Hey there Poppa Mezz, is you anywhere? Me: Man I'm down with it, stickin' like a honky. *Ibid.* 374/2 *Honky*, factory hand.] **1967** *Newsweek* 24 Apr. 16/1 'Go for the honkies'... The chemistry in tranquil Nashville, Tenn., spelled riot... Stokely Carmichael..exhorted: 'You have to go for the honkies..who are keeping you in the ghettos... Victims should never, ever apologize for their use of violence.' **1967** *Guardian* 29 Aug. 7/5 'Honky' (the white man) was using weapons like the Vietnam war. **1969** 'J. MORRIS' *Fever Grass* xxv. 248, I killed for the same thing you want. You're not like the rest of these honkeys. **1970** *Peace News* 17 Apr. 8/4 It is the pacifist who must declare, out of his own values, that there are neither Panthers nor Pigs, neither Niggers nor Honkies but only human beings. **1971** *Black Scholar* 35/1 You screamed on me 'bout that honky gunsel upstairs. **1971** *Black World* Mar. 69/2 Blacks should 'beware of honkies bearing gifts'. **1971** *Guardian* 1 May 9/1 Many blacks..came to see it [*sc.* the African-American Institute] as a 'honky' (white) conservative force. **1971** *It* 9–23 Sept. 8/3 The phoniness of news, TV, rich honky pop stars, etc. **1971** B. MALAMUD *Tenants* 46 Mary forcefully shoved him away. 'Split, honky, you smell.' *Ibid.* 133 'Now you leave this honky to me,' said Bill. 'He is my guest.'

honky-tonk (hǫ·ŋkitǫŋk). *colloq.* (orig. *U.S.*). Also **honkatonk, honkey-tonk.** [Etym. unknown.] **1.** A tawdry drinking-saloon, dance-hall, or gambling-house; a cheap night-club. Also in somewhat extended uses, and *attrib.* or as *adj.*

1894 *Daily Ardmoreite* (Ardmore, Okla.) 24 Feb. 1/4 The honk-a-tonk last night was well attended by ball-heads, bachelors and leading citizens. **1924** *Étude* Sept. 595/3 These dance resorts were known as 'Honky-Tonks'—a name, which in itself suggests some of the rhythms of Jazz. **1927** C. SANDBURG *Songbag* 232 It was moaned by resonant moaners in honky tonks of the southwest. **1928** M. C. SHARPE *Chicago May* 287 *Honky-tonk*, gaudy saloon with back-room hangout. **1930** C. E. MULFORD *Deputy Sheriff* xiii. 168 'This place ain't no damn' honkatonk, stranger,' reproved the bar-tender... 'Folks get throwed outa here sometimes.' **1935** A. J. POLLOCK *Underworld Speaks* 57/1 *Honkey tonk*, an underworld dance hall in which female entertainers are employed. **1936** *Delineator* Nov. 48/2 The inner room of a honky-tonk on a back street..New Orleans. **1940** W. FAULKNER *Hamlet* IV. ii. 387 Its master whose anonymous dust lay with that of his blood and of the progenitors of saxophone players in Harlem honky-tonks. **1945** J. STEINBECK *Cannery Row* i Honky-tonks, restaurants and whore-houses. **1950** A. LOMAX *Mr. Jelly Roll* 54 These honkey-tonks ran wide open twenty-four hours a day... Their attendance was some of the lowest caliber women in the world and their intake was the revenue from the little, pitiful gambling games they operated. **1955** A. ROSS *Australia 55* 108 The town itself, a little honky-tonk in character, boasts many saloons. **1957** G. LASCELLES in S. Traill *Concerning Jazz* 77 Others of possibly less talent were doing stalwart work as accompanists to the blues singers in the honky-tonks of New Orleans and St. Louis. **1962** *Daily Tel.* 31 May 19/4 A Parliamentary Bill would have to be promoted if the Norfolk Broads were to be saved from further 'honky-tonk development of the very worst type'. **1969** I. & P. OPIE *Children's Games* 15 It is not only Battersea Park (the enchanted garden of our childhood) that has been turned into a honky-tonk.

2. Rag-time music or jazz of a type played in honky-tonks, esp. on the piano. Freq. *attrib.*, passing into *adj.*, as **honky-tonk piano,** an out-of-tune or tinny-sounding piano. Cf. *BARREL-HOUSE 2.

1933 *Fortune* Aug. 90/2 Sometimes they spent weeks in preparation for a single recording date, yet they never sacrificed the informal, honky-tonk spirit. **1936** *Swing Music* Autumn 62/2 Superficially, 'Honky Tonk' is the musical interpretation of a train journey; fundamentally it is a twelve-bar blues. **1942** BERREY & VAN DEN BARK *Amer. Thes. Slang* § 579/4 *Honkytonk*, primal 'swing' of the style played in the bordels of New Orleans, Memphis and St. Louis, in which a free rein is given to improvising. **1946** R. BLESH *Shining Trumpets* (1949) ix. 202 Among them were masters of the blues and barrel-house piano (or, as Morton calls it 'Honky Tonk music'). **1953** *Observer* 27 Dec., The barrelhouse piano, also known as the..honkytonk piano. **1964** *Amer. Folk Music Occasional* I. 45 They didn't play for no white folks, because the white folks didn't want that kind of music, they called it honky-tonk. **1972** *Drive* Spring 78/2 Happy, beery men thumping honky-tonk pianos.

‖ **honnête homme** (onętom). [Fr.] An honest, decent man; a gentleman.

1666 W. TEMPLE *Let.* 1 Apr. in *Wks.* (1720) II. 18 Confessor is honneste Homme. **1709** SWIFT *Let.* 13 Nov. in *Lett. Lit. Men* (Camden, 1843) 341, I ever thought it a mighty oversight in Courts to let the *honnete homme*, the *homme d'esprit*, and *homme de bien*, gain ground among them. **1923** OGDEN & RICHARDS *Meaning of Meaning* i. 21 The *honnête homme* may be unprepared for the lengths to which verbal ingenuity can be carried. **1931** T. S. ELIOT *Charles Whibley* 10 Whibley had this discretion, that of the *honnête homme* as critic, to select subjects suited to his own temperament. **1937** A. HUXLEY *Ends & Means* i. 2 The *honnête homme* makes his appearance as the ideal of seventeenth-century gentlemen. **1960** J. BAYLEY *Characters of Love* iii. 131 Iago..is in many ways a terrible parody of the Augustan *honnête homme*. **1970** *Times* 12 May 11/1 His opening speech on tobacco, far from being a declaration on behalf of the *honnête homme*, is a means of forcing his will.

honorand (ǫ·nərænd). [ad. L. *honōrand-us*, gerundive of *honōrāre* HONOUR *v.*]. Someone to be honoured, spec. with an academic honorary degree.

1950 A. P. HERBERT *Independent Member* lxxxiii. 478 The Honorands, the eight or nine distinguished persons who are to be voted Honorary Doctors. **1961** M. BEADLE *These Ruins are Inhabited* (1963) xii. 170 The American honorand at *this* June's Encaenia. **1966** *New Statesman* 10 June 849/1 A kind of *festschrift* without an honorand. **1971** *Oxford Times* 25 June 30/1 There was brilliant sunshine for the Encaenia... For the first time for eight years there was no woman in the procession of honorands.

honorial (ǫnōᵊ·riăl), *a.* [f. HONOUR, HONOR *sb.* + -IAL.] Of or relating to titles of honour, or persons of title or rank; of or pertaining to an honour (sense 7).

1810 EVANS & BRITTON in J. Britton *Beauties Eng. Wales* XI. Norfolk 53 (*heading*) Civil, political, and honorial history. **1828** T. ALLEN *Hist. County York* I. II. vi. 327 (*heading*) Ecclesiastical and civil government, honorial history. **1943** F. M. STENTON *Anglo-Saxon Eng.* xvii. 628 On every great honour..there appear tenants holding considerable estates... The honorial barons, as tenants of this class may conveniently be called, have received less attention..than is their due. *Ibid.*, In the honorial court..the lord's baronial tenants played a leading part. **1962** H. R. LOYN *Anglo-Saxon Eng.* viii. 329 Honorial courts dealt primarily with military feudal questions.

‖ **honoris causa** (ǫnōᵊ·ris kǭ·zēⁱ, kau·zā). [L.: lit., for the sake of honour.] In order to honour or out of respect for a person mentioned; now used chiefly as a description of such university degrees as are conferred upon persons in recognition of certain distinctions or achievements without the customary academic examination or thesis.

1611 CORYAT *Crudities* 240, I wil once more speake of our most worthy Ambassadour Sr Henry Wotton, *honoris causâ*. **1626–7** in T. Birch *Crt. & Times Chas. I* (1848) I. 193 His colleagues shall be the Earl of Salisbury, *honoris causâ*, and Sir Richard Western. **1882** *Standard* 19 Dec. 2 (Stanford), Receiving the degree of D.D., *honoris causa*, from the late Dr. Sumner, Archbishop of Canterbury in 1857. **1935** *Discovery* Nov. 325/2 Uvarov was honoured by the University of Madrid with the degree of Doctor *honoris causa*. **1955** *Times* 26 May 12/5 He was instructor to the Oxford University Air Squadron and was given the degree of M.A. *honoris causa* at the end of his term of duty. **1963** [see *ACADEMICIAN 1].

honour, *sb.* Add: **5. e.** Now, in many universities, a course of study or a series of examinations in a subject or group of subjects of a higher or more specialized character than is required for a pass or ordinary degree. (Cf. *honours degree, school* in *10.)

8. a. Also at Bridge (see quots. 1909 and 1936). Phr. *honours are even*: often used fig. to denote equality in a contest (real or imaginary).

1886 *Biritch, or Russian Whist* 4 There are five honours, viz.:—Ace, King, Queen, Knave and Ten, if trumps are declared. **1909** W. DALTON *'Saturday' Bridge* 5 Honours consist of ace, king, queen, knave, and ten of the trump suit. When there are no trumps they consist of the four aces. **1920** B. CRONIN *Timber Wolves* iii. 62, 'I don't know your name?'..'But then I don't know yours, do I? That makes the honours even, don't you think?' **1927** W. E. COLLINSON *Contemp. Eng.* 31 The card-expressions now most prevalent in a figurative application are drawn in the main from bridge, e.g. to call one's hand (or one's bluff), to finesse, Honours are even, After you, partner, etc. **1936** E. CULBERTSON *Contract Bridge Complete* xxxviii. 421 An honour-card is technically a ten or higher card. **1939** N. DE V. HART *Bridge Players' Bedside Bk.* 22, I got home by playing for split honours. **1947** S. HARRIS *Fund. Princ. Contract Bridge* II. i. 43 South should remember to lead a top honour from the hand which contains double honours in sequence. **1967** P. ANDERTON *Play Bridge* vii. 49 You drop 100 points on going down but get 100 for honours.

10. honour(s) board, a board at a school or college on which are inscribed the names of members who have gained honours; **honours degree,** an academic degree with honours or obtained in an honour school; similarly *honours examination*; **honour(s) list,** (*a*) a class list of candidates who have been successful in an examination for honours; (*b*) a list of honours conferred by the Sovereign, as at the New Year; also *fig.*; **honour-man** (earlier example); **honour-roll,** a roll of honour; **honour(s) school,** a course of study designed for those who aim at an honours (as distinguished from a pass) degree (at Oxford University, 'qui honorem ambiunt'); similarly *honour moderations*, colloq. *honour mods.*; **honour system,** a system in which examinations are completed, services paid for, etc., without, or with only a minimum of, supervision; **honour-trick** *Bridge*, a combination of cards which may be expected to win a trick.

1931 E. WAUGH *Remote People* 211 They have honour boards, on which the name of one boy is inscribed every year. **1960** C. DAY LEWIS *Buried Day* vi. 129 My name was never inscribed on the University Honours Board in the Big School. **1851** *Oxf. Univ. Cal.* 127 A reference will be made in the lists of Honours and ordinary Degrees, to the distinctions awarded by the Moderators. **1904** *Daily Chron.* 31 Oct. 4/4, I cannot deal here with the wholly false and mischievous qualification of an 'Honours Degree' that the rich women are answerable for. **1969** *Oxf. Univ. Handbk.* 159 About one third of the students at Oxford are working for honours degrees in mathematics or natural science. [**1852** *Oxf. Univ. Commission Rep.* III. 62 With regard to the Examination for Honours, the course of classical reading seems to have become more and more limited.] **1885** *Oxf. Univ. Cal.* p. iii, Honours Examinations for Women. **1927** C. E. MALLET *Hist. Univ. Oxf.* III. xxiii. 168 The Honours Examination at Oxford was established. *Ibid.* 170 In 1830, a Fourth Class in Honours was provided, and the Honours examination was separated from the examination for the ordinary Pass degree. **1972** *Univ. Oxf. Exam. Decrees* 33 No person whose name shall be placed in any Class List issued by the Moderators shall be admitted again as a candidate in the same Honours Examination. **1849** THACKERAY *Pendennis* I. xix. 179 A man may be famous in the Honours-lists and entirely unknown to the undergraduates. **1862** *Oxf. Univ. Cal.* 273 Honours Lists issued by Moderators. **1910** H. G. WELLS *New Machiavelli* (1911) III. i. 304 The New Year and Birthday honours lists are always very sagely and exhaustively considered. **1923** J. M. MURRY *Pencillings* 272 It will dawn upon me when I read my own name in capitals at the top of the Honours List, created Baron for my services to literature. **1929** *Melody Maker* Dec. 1169/1 This disc goes right into the honours list. **1964** *Granta* 2 Nov., He hoped as it was Coronation year to do rather better than usual in the New Year's honours list. **1839** J. ROMILLY *Diary* 12 Jan. (1967) 161 This year we have allowed our Lecture rooms to the Honor-men. **1911** *Rep. Brit. Assoc.* 219 It has been suggested that if students are not encouraged to come to the university younger the better men should be allowed to enter for Honour Mods. after six months. **1913** Honour mods. [see *DIVVERS]. **1922** *Rep. R. Comm. Oxf. & Camb.* 29 The marked vitality of Honour Classical Moderations bears witness to the interest still awakened by the classical languages and literatures. **1965** W. R. WARD *Victorian Oxford* x. 213 Scholarship was now examined at Honour Moderations and the final school was left unencumbered for the examination of history and philosophy. **1970** *Oxf. Univ. Cal.* 195 The prizes are awarded each year by the Moderators for Honour Moderations in English Language and Literature. **1909** *Daily Chron.* 7 Apr. 3/3 Such is the honour-roll of these sturdy spirits. **1949** Honor roll [see *BULLETIN 4]. **1902** *Encycl. Brit.* XXXIII. 603/2 At Oxford there are now the following 'Final Honour Schools'. **1923** *Granta* 2 Mar., At Oxford the Honours School of English claims that its 'first' is harder to win than a 'first' in any other School there. **1965** W. R. WARD *Victorian Oxford* x. 220 Rawlinson alleged that the standard in the non-classical honour schools would be less than the proposed mixed degree. **1970** *Oxf. Univ. Cal.* 194 Candidates must be members of the University reading for a Final Honour School. **1904** *Pittsburgh Gaz.* 3 Dec. 4 The most successful plan of combating the tendency of college students to cheat in examinations has been some form of an 'honor system' by which the pupil is implicitly trusted and his statement accepted that he used no dishonest aids. **1934** H. G. WELLS *Exper. Autobiogr.* I. vi. 323 He had in operation an honour system of discipline that was far in advance of

the times. **1936** *S.P.E. Tract* XLV. 181 *Honor system* denotes the practice, adopted at certain institutions, of conducting written examinations without supervision, the candidates being put upon their honour to use no illegitimate aids. **1958** *Sunday Times* 16 Mar. 22/5 Self-service stores must run on the honour system. **1966** *Listener* 24 Feb. 266/2 On the buses and trams an 'honour' system: you throw your money into a coin box.. and tear off your own ticket. **1969** 'E. LATHEN' *Come to Dust* xiv. 140 Two young women had been discovered.. in circumstances all too clearly proscribed by the parietal rules and Brunswick's honor system. **1931** E. CULBERTSON *Contract Bridge at Glance* 6 A defensive honour-trick is a card, or combination of cards, which may be expected to win even if the opponents play the hand at a trump. **1959** REESE & DORMER *Bridge Player's Dict.* 116 The Culbertson system, which first popularized the honor-trick method of valuation, uses the following table for counting honor-tricks.

honourable, *a.* Add: **2. b.** (The only Lord Mayors and Provosts in the United Kingdom who are entitled to be styled 'Right Honourable' are the Lord Mayors of London, York, and Belfast, and the Lord Provosts of Edinburgh and Glasgow.)

3. *honourable mention*: see MENTION *sb.* 2 e.

1866 *Lond. Gaz.* 26 June 3646/1 Grand prizes and money awards of the total value of 250,000 francs (£10,000), 100 Gold Medals,..5000 Honourable Mentions. **1869** *Bradshaw's Railway Manual* XXI. App. 99 Honourable mention.—International Exhibition, 1862.

Honved (hǫ·nvēˢd). [Hungarian, = *hon* home + *véd* defence.] The name given to the Hungarian second-line formation during the revolutionary war of 1848–9; later also used of the militia reserve. Also, a member of either force.

1854 E. O. S. *Hungary & its Revolutions* 429 The new army,..namely, the Honveds, National Guards, and Volunteers. **1875** *Encycl. Brit.* II. 604/2 The Hungarian militia, or 'honveds', as they are called. **1913** *Times* 7 May 7/3 It [*sc.* an ordnance factory] will supply the needs of the Honved troops and of the Hungarian quota of the joint army and navy. **1931** F. ECKHART *Short Hist. Hungarian People* vii. 192 At his [*sc.* Kossuth's] impassioned speeches, the *Honvéds* (Defenders of the Fatherland) assembled..round the standards of the King of Hungary. **1956** C. A. MACARTNEY *October Fifteenth* I. i. 15 The Magyars did not mind taking commissions in the Honvéd, which, however, was a body not much more serious than our own militia of the day. **1959** D. SINOR *Hist. Hungary* xxix. 267 Some 152,000 Hungarian *honvéd* (as the soldiers of this war were called)..had to face the 1,200 guns of an enemy some 370,000 strong. **1962** C. A. MACARTNEY *Hungary* vii. 163 The rank and file of the *Honvéd* were as a rule conscripted into the Imperial forces and sent to foreign stations.

honyock, honyocker, varr. *HUNYAK.

hooch (hūtʃ). *colloq.* (orig. and chiefly *N. Amer.*). Also **hootch.** [Abbrev. of *HOOCHINOO.] **a.** = *HOOCHINOO 2. **b.** In more general use, Alcoholic liquor, spirits, esp. of low quality or illegal provenance.

1897 M. H. E. HAYNE *Pioneers of Klondyke* 91 The manufacture of 'hooch', which is undertaken by the saloon-keepers themselves, is weirdly horrible. **1903** *N.Y. Even. Post* 25 Sept. 3 In this bottle was some of the native spirits called 'hooch', distilled from sugar and graham flour. **1904** E. ROBINS *Magnetic North* ix. 161 Apart from the question of drinking raised again by the 'hootch',..they were ready to eat the more. **1907** R. W. SERVICE *Songs of Sourdough* (1908) 18 A broken wreck with a craze for 'hooch', and never a cent to my name. **1922** G. C. F. PRINGLE *Tillicums of Trail* 41 I've cut out the hootch. It was getting me at White Horse. **1923** C. J. DUTTON *Shadow on Glass* 200, I thought of our modern 'hooch ships' that were doing the same thing. **1927** *Punch* 20 Apr. 428/3 He knows what the poor want in the great black city of Chicago. They want cash. He knows what the thirsty want. They want hooch. **1927** *Amer. Speech* III. 167/2 *Hootch*, bad whiskey. **1953** M. SCOTT *Breakfast at Six* xii. 99 He's sure to have lots of hootch outside, and he'll get more expansive as the evening goes on. **1960** *Times* 5 Feb. 9/5 He apparently received consignments of empty whisky bottles from Madrid, which were filled with the 'hooch'. **1964** *Globe & Mail* (Toronto) 15 Dec. 31/8 The least the authorities could do when they make a raid would be to pack the confiscated hootch and ship to some underprivileged country. **1969** *New Yorker* 5 Apr. 97/1 The people of the city were prepared to swallow any old hootch under the rule of some wild thirst. **1970** *Times* 15 Oct. 30/3 The distilled spirits industry..wages an expensive propaganda campaign against..hooch.

hooch, hootch: see *HOOCHIE.

hoochie (hū·tʃi). *Mil. slang.* Also **hooch, hoochy, hootch.** [? ad. Jap. *uchi* dwelling.] A shelter or dwelling (esp. one that is insubstantial or temporary).

1952 *San Francisco Examiner* 26 Oct. 18/4 The 'hoochie' is a GI term for a bunker or a prepared defensive position. **1954** *Britannica Bk. of Year* 637/2 In its final stages, the war in Korea yielded a number of new terms, among them the British soldier's name for a dugout—a Hoochie. **1960** *Amer. Speech* XXXV. 264 Cinderella-san lived in hootchie with sisters. **1960** (*citing an Army weekly newspaper in Korea*) in *Sat. Rev.* (1968) 26 Oct. 35/3 All through our hootch, Not a creature was stirring. **1964** *N.Y. Times* 4 Sept., *Hooches*, the huts woven from banana leaves and roofed with straw or corrugated tin that are the standard housing for Vietnamese outside the cities. Some Americans have appropriated the term for their own quonset-styled barracks. **1966** *Flying* Dec. 54/2 A hootch (a house or a hut is known as a hootch in Vietnam). **1968** *N.Y. Rev. Books* 4 Jan. 4/1 Such targets as hooch lines (rows of houses along a road or canal). **1968** *TV Times* (Austral.) 6 Mar. 11/1, I was lying in a little scrap of a tent the Australians call a hoochie. **1969** I. KEMP *Brit. G.I. in Vietnam* iv. 75 Around us were scattered the makeshift 'hooches' of the A.R.V.N. soldiers, built of bamboo, wattle and mud; rectangular in shape with sloping, thatched roofs, they were..small. **1969** *Time* 5 Dec. 18/3 Calley's men in less than 20 minutes ignited 'hootches' and chased all the villagers..into groups, and shot everyone. **1971** *Fremdsprachen* XV. 207 A stereo set was blaring in an enlisted men's hootch shortly after midnight.

Hoochinoo (hū·tʃinū), and varr. [ad. Tlingit *Hutsnuwu*, lit. 'grizzly bear fort'.] **1.** A member of a small Indian tribe found in Admiralty Island, Alaska. Also *attrib.* or as *adj.* In *pl.* the tribe.

1878 DENNIS in W. G. Morris *Rep. Customs Dist. Alaska* (1879) 122 On top of this there came a fight among the Hootzenoo Indians here. **1890** M. BALLOU *New Eldorado* (ed. 5) 321 We pass the Indian village of Kootznahoo, occupied by a tribe of the same name, a people who have always proved to be restless and aggressive. **1915** J. MUIR *Trav. Alaska* (1917) 211 They were about to set out on an expedition to the Hootsenoos to collect blankets as indemnity or blood-money for the death of a Chilcat woman from drinking whiskey furnished by one of the Hootsenoo tribe.

2. An alcoholic liquor made by Alaskan Indians, esp. the Hoochinoo tribe; also any inferior alcoholic drink (esp. whisky) in Alaska and the Canadian north-west.

1877 *Puget Sound Argus* (Pt. Townsend, Wash.) 23 Nov., I have frequently seen soldiers go to the Indian ranch for their morning drink of kootznehoo. *c* **1898** in P. Berton *Centennial Food Guide* (1966) 58/2 Whenever whisky runs short the Yukoner falls back upon a villanous decoction..known as 'hootchinoo', or 'hootch'. **1899** *Boston Jrnl.* 11 Jan. 4/5 Recently the House gave its official sanction to the word by enacting that no whisky, beer or 'hoochinoo' shall be sold in Alaska. **1937** C. L. ANDREWS *Wrangell & Gold of Cassiar* 49 A discharged soldier named Doyle..went to Hootznahoo, showed them how to distill a villainous compound from molasses, yeast, berries, sugar, or other compounds. It was first so called from the village, 'Hootznahoo' paraphrased as 'Hoochinoo'. **1958** P. BERTON *Klondike Fever* 27 Another was to collect the excise duty on all locally made hootchinoo.

b. In full *hoochinoo still.* A still for the manufacture of hoochinoo.

1879 *Chicago Tribune* 14 May 6/3 We accidentally dropped upon a hootchenoo still in full operation. **1883** J. WRIGHT *Among Alaskans* 150 Mr. Dennis had appointed the most reliable Indians as policemen, giving them authority, under United States revenue customs laws, to seize and destroy the hoochinoos or whisky-stills.

hoochy-coochy: see *HOOTCHY-KOOTCHY.

hood, *sb.* Add: **5. j.** A waterproof folding top or cover of a perambulator, motor vehicle, charabanc, etc.; the movable cover of a typewriter or other machine.

1866 *Leisure Hour* XV. 349/1 Children are likely to be exposed for longer times to the scorching sun or the piercing wind in a perambulator (if without hood or sunshade) than when carried in arms. **1895** *Army & Navy Co-op. Soc. Price List* 15 Sept. 1172 Perambulators..with ..reversible jointed hood. **1904** A. B. F. YOUNG *Compl. Motorist* (ed. 2) viii. 198 It is a fine-weather vehicle, but a hood can be supplied for use in wet weather. **1912** *Motor Man.* (ed. 14) iii. 101 Complete protection can be obtained with a hood by fitting side curtains, which can be let down. **1942** *Short Guide Gt. Brit.* (U.S. War Dept.) 26 The top of the car is the hood. **1967** R. MOLLON *Nursery Handbk.* (1968) i. 37 Be sure that the pram..has a good waterproof hood. **1969** C. CAMPBELL *Sports Car* (ed. 3) ix. 226 An open cockpit and an erect windscreen completely spoil the airflow pattern over a sports car and a higher maximum speed is always given with the hood erect. **1971** *Daily Tel.* 24 Nov. 11/4 The weather during the test was too unpleasant to try the MGB as it should really be driven, with the hood down.

k. In various animals, esp. *Nautilus macromphalus* (see quots.).

1883 *Encycl. Brit.* XVI. 674/1 This part of the external annular lobe of the fore-foot [of *Nautilus*] is called the 'hood'. **1888** ROLLESTON & JACKSON *Anim. Life* 456 In *Nautilus*..the fore-foot is divisible into an outer and inner portion. The outer portion..is thickened dorsally where it abuts against the coil of the shell and forms the hood. **1902** *Encycl. Brit.* XXV. 543/2 Movable (hinged) sclerite (so-called hood) [of *Cryptostemma karschii*] overhanging the first pair of appendages. **1932** BORRADAILE & POTTS *Invertebrata* xvi. 527 When the animal [sc. *Nautilus*] is retracted into the living chamber the hood acts as an operculum. **1967** H. W. & L. R. LEVI tr. *Kaestner's Invertebr. Zool.* I. xv. 418 The sheaths of the dorsal (anterior) tentacles are fused into a hood that is used in *Nautilus* to cover most of the aperture when the body is withdrawn.

l. A covering for the head of a horse.

a **1884** KNIGHT *Dict. Mech.* Suppl. 461/1 *Hood*, that part of a horse blanket which covers the horse's head and neck. **1963** BLOODGOOD & SANTINI *Horseman's Dict.* 105 *Hood*, horse's head covering with eyeholes (with or without ear coverings) of serge, wool or rubber.

m. *Photogr.* (See quot. 1918.) In full, *lens hood.*

1892 [see *FINDER 3 d]. **1892** *Photogr. Ann.* II. 41 Have two caps for each lens, one to fit the hood and one to fit the other end of the mount. **1918** *Photo-Miniature* Mar. 25 *Lens hood*, the detachable rim of a lens-tube somewhat larger in diameter and carrying the lens-cap. Also any separate device of tubular box- or bellows-form fitted to the lens-tube, to screen the lens from strong light. **1939–40** *Army & Navy Stores Catal.* 906/2 Voightländer cameras... Fitted with a large brilliant view finder and deep hood. **1961** G. MILLERSON *Technique Television Production* iii. 28 (*caption*) Interchangeable camera lenses with lens hoods.

n. A protecting cover, also sometimes acting as a reflector, placed over a lamp.

1907 *Yesterday's Shopping* (1969) 260/3 Candle reading lamp. Telescopic corrugated hood. **1913** J. B. BISHOP *Panama Gateway* v. vi. 382 The reflecting hood is provided with shading skirts, which prevent the glare of the lamp filament from penetrating into distance along the axis of the canal. **1939–40** *Army & Navy Stores Catal.* 277/3 The Reader. Chrome-plated with specially designed hood to shade light.

o. The bonnet of a motor vehicle. orig. and chiefly *U.S.*

1929 W. FAULKNER *Sartoris* II. vi. 145 He lifted the hood and removed the cap from the breather-pipe. **1942** *Short Guide Gt. Brit.* (U.S. War Dept.) 26 What we call the hood (of the engine) is a bonnet. **1960** *Times* 14 Sept. 12/6 You..discover that not only does the engine wear a hood instead of a bonnet but [etc.]. **1970** *Globe & Mail* (Toronto) 26 Sept. 29/5 (Advt.), A Rolls Royce whose hood was draped in white damask set with candelabra and plates.

p. A roughly shaped hat of felt, straw, or similar material for the hatter to shape by blocking or stitching.

1932 D. C. MINTER *Mod. Needlecraft* 159/1 Felt or felted hoods and hats are beaten, steamed, and moulded from the flat. **1963** P. MOYES *Murder à la Mode* vii. 122 The shapeless felt 'hoods' which would eventually be steamed and seamed into smart hats.

8. hood dryer (see quot. 1966).

1962 *Guardian* 5 Dec. 6/4 Hairdryer, brush, comb and hood dryer. **1966** J. S. COX *Illustr. Dict. Hairdressing* 80/2 *Hood dryer*, a hair dryer in the form of a hood secured to a pedestal.

hood (hud), *sb.*² Abbrev. of HOODLUM (in Dict. and Suppl.).

1930 *Amer. Mercury* Dec. 456/1 None of those St. Louie hoods are going to cut in here, see? **1934** J. T. FARRELL *Young Manhood* xiv. 218 Jim Doyle stood by the kitchen sink, a cigar pasted in his round, jolly face, and he greeted them, calling them hoods. **1959** *Manch. Guardian* 5 Aug. 1/1 The 'News' suggests 'a special committee to greet the Kremlin's No. 1 Hood at the Washington Airport'. **1966** WODEHOUSE *Plum Pie* vii. 177 The hood was beating the tar out of me.

hooded, *a.* **2.** (Further examples.)

1785 LATHAM *Gen. Syn. Birds* III. II. 426 Hooded M[erganser]...Size nearly that of a Wigeon. **1875** *Encycl. Brit.* III. 421/1 The Mitred Basilisk occurs in Guiana, the Hooded Basilisk in Amboyna. **1890** LD. LUGARD *Diary* 15 Mar. (1959) I. 144, I saw here [*sc.* in East Africa] the large hooded raven. **1938** *Brit. Jrnl. Psychol.* XXVIII. 334 Of the progeny of the hooded rats..I took at random six females. **1942** C. BARRETT *On Wallaby* iv. 78 Hooded crows were on parade long before reveille. **1954** M. K. WILSON tr. *Lorenz's Man meets Dog* x. 107 Our hooded capuchin, Gloria,..was rather larger than a cat. **1955** *Arctic Terms* 40/1 *Hooded seal*, a large seal, *Cystophora cristata*, of the North Atlantic, dark in color with a unique inflatable muscular bag on its nose. Also called 'bladder-nose'. **1961** *Coast to Coast 1959–60* 62 I've heard that there is a place hereabouts which is a haunt of the hooded robin. **1972** *Country Life* 17 Feb. 381/1 The hooded crow, or hoodie, as it is commonly called in Scotland where the grey-mantled bird is seen as often as..the ordinary..crow.

hooden, var. *HODEN.

hoodlum. Add: (Earlier and later examples.) Now in more general use outside the U.S.

1871 *Cincinnati Commercial* 6 Sept. (Suppl.) 2/5 Surely he is far enough away here in this hideous wild of swamp, to escape the bullying of the San Francisco 'hoodlums'. **1929** F. A. POTTLE *Stretchers* (1930) iv. 64 Then we were a mob of unorganized, distrustful, sick, and unshaved hoodlums, whose one burning desire was to escape from the army and go back home. **1935** A. SQUIRE *Sing Sing Doctor* iv. 43 The hoodlums of the neighbourhood.. flattered him, and he ran along with the gang. **1952** R. FINLAYSON *Schooner came to Atia* 4 He's not one of that gang of hoodlums. **1959** [see *BELSEN]. **1970** G. F. NEWMAN *Sir, You Bastard* viii. 208 The man is a vicious hoodlum.

hoodlumism (earlier and later examples).

1872 *Newton Kansan* 14 Nov. 4/1 The Rev. Dr. Cunningham in a recent sermon traced the history of 'Hoodlumism'. **1920** [see *group-behaviour* (*GROUP *sb.* 6 b)]. **1970** G. GREER *Female Eunuch* 271 A new all-time low in political scurviness, hoodlumism.

2. hoodlum wagon *U.S.* (see quot. 1920).

1908 *Sat. Even. Post* 31 Oct. 39/2 The jolting of the hoodlum-wagon now focused the herd's attention. **1919**

H. L. Wilson *Ma Pettengill* iii. 79 The hoodlum wagon going back next morning to see what could be salvaged. **1920** J. M. Hunter *Trail Drivers of Texas* 299 A second wagon for carrying the extra beds and bringing wood and water into camps..This equipage is called the hoodlum wagon. **1968** R. F. Adams *Western Words* (ed. 2) 152/1 *Hoodlum wagon*, a cowboy's name for the bed wagon.

hoodoo, *sb.* **1.** Substitute for def.: One who practises voodoo. (Earlier, later, and *attrib.* examples.)

1875 L. Hearn *Amer. Miscellany* (1924) I. 127 Supposing you fall in love with a girl and can't get her, and that you go to one of these hoodoos, he will do something awful to her with charms. *Ibid.*, She would die..unless she could get some other hoodoo doctor to take the charm away by a counter charm. **1881** *Harper's Mag.* Apr. 738/2 Suddenly she..rushed forward with an African yell and joined in the dance as wild as any Hoodoo among them. **1946** R. Tallant *Voodoo in New Orleans* 16, I heard people say hoodoos was cannibals and used to eat babies. *Ibid.* 195, I got Adele to a good hoodoo woman and she uncrossed her.

2. (Earlier and later examples.)

1882 J. H. Beadle *Western Wilds* (ed. 2) xxxiv. 558 If you can find an Indian tradition to match it, your hoodoo is complete. **1916** H. Crane *Let.* 26 Jan. (1965) 3 Examination time is on... Latin and Geometry are due tomorrow. They are my hoodoos. **1945** E. Waugh *Brideshead Revisited* vii. 177 So you see things never looked like going right. There was a hoodoo on us from the start. **1958** L. van der Post *Lost World of Kalahari* viii. 195 By nightfall everyone..seemed convinced there was a permanent hoodoo on us.

3. A fantastic rock pinnacle or column of rock formed by erosion or other natural agency; an earth-pillar. Also *attrib.* orig. *U.S.*

1879 W. Whitman *Specimen Days & Collect.* (1882) 148, I had wanted to go to the Yellowstone river region—wanted specially to see..the 'hoodoo' or goblin land of that country. **1884** H. Butterworth *Zigzag Journ. Western States* 54 There is a region there called Goblin Land, full of lofty stone monuments, the remnants of erosion, called hoodoos. **1921** *Chambers's Jrnl.* June 373/2 Strange, isolated pillars, the 'hoodoos' stood like vedettes on the heights. **1940** *Canad. Geogr. Jrnl.* Feb. 84/2 The presence in Jasper Park of..earth pillars or 'hoodoos' similar to those at Banff. **1941** C. A. Cotton *Landscape* iii. 15 The picturesque minor surface-relief forms termed hoodoo columns and earth pillars are slender residual columns of unconsolidated sediment. **1968** R. W. Fairbridge *Encycl. Geomorphol.* 46/1 Occasionally, denudation of badland slopes can produce interesting features such as earth pillars and hoodoos with an overhanging 'hat'.

B. *adj.* Unlucky, bringing bad luck.

1889 *Kansas Times & Star* 17 Sept., Joe Bracken took sick Friday, September 13, but says that hoodoo date doesn't discourage him. **1904** *New York Globe* 2 Apr. 1 It is hard to find a crew for a 'hoodoo' ship. **1909** 'O. Henry' *Roads of Destiny* vii. 110 He's the hoodoo planet of the heavens. **1922** *Blackw. Mag.* Sept. 321/1 My name is Armstrong—Hoodoo Armstrong. **1926** *Scots Observer* 30 Oct. 21/2 That particular service was hoodoo.

hoodoo *v.* (earlier and later examples).

1886 *Harper's Weekly* 25 Dec., The surest way to provide against being 'hoodooed', as American residents call it, is to open one's pillow from time to time. **1888** *Judge* (U.S.) 21 July 239/2 A Washington paper..drops into the following poetry, which is sufficient to hoodoo the organization for the balance of the season. **1902** Kipling *Traffics & Discov.* (1904) 7, I wasn't going to deadhead along o' *that* crowd... 'Twould have hoodooed my gun for all time. **1914** V. Lindsay *Congo* 5 Mumbo-Jumbo will hoo-doo you.

hoo·doism. [f. Hoodoo *sb.*] **a.** The practice of hoodoo rites. **b.** The faculty of attracting misfortune.

1881 *Harper's Mag.* Apr. 737/1 What *is* Hoodooism, anyhow? **1921** *Double Dealer* July 22/1 The white folks gaze at the negro with incredulous eye and wonder what amazing story of hoodooism will come from his lips. **1966** *Listener* 14 Apr. 542/3 Hoodoo-ism is not confined to steam locomotives. I have known a hoodoo diesel rail car.

hooer (hū·ər). *Austral.* and *N.Z.* [Representation (in various spellings) of a vulgar or colloq. pronunciation of *whore.*] **a.** = Whore 1. **b.** A strong term of abuse (of a man or woman).

1937 in Partridge *Dict. Slang* 401/2. **1969** D. Niland *Dead Men Running* iii. 86 The cheek of that hooer, I thought; a dirty-looking stranger. **1971** *N.Z. Listener* 22 Mar. 12/3 The dirty hua didn't even take a shower before he shot through.

hooey (hū·i). *slang* (orig. *U.S.*). [Orig. unknown.] Humbug, nonsense.

1924 P. Marks *Plastic Age* 100 My prof's full of hooey. He doesn't know a C theme from an A one. *Ibid.* 160 'Bunk!' he exclaimed. 'Hooey!' **1931** E. Linklater *Juan in Amer.* iii. v. 247 *We'll* be on Broadway if you don't talk hooey like that 'worth while' crack. **1932** Wodehouse *Hot Water* xiii. 223 Well, of all the hooey! **1934** *Discovery* Jan. 4/2 The United States of America, whose capacity for new words passes all belief, is responsible for hooey. **1935** *Punch* 10 Apr. 400/1 You have been misled, Hubert. I see it all. Somebody has been telling you the old, old story... Hooey, Hubert. Boloney. **1935** L. MacNeice *Poems* 21 Ireland is hooey, Ireland is A gallery of fake tapestries. **1948** V. Palmer *Golconda* xxv. 210 All this political hooey..doesn't affect me. **1952** Partridge *From Sanskrit to Brazil* 94 These charges of anachronism are, to put it courteously, sheer 'hooey'. **1966** Auden *About House* 21 Lip-smacking Imps of mawk and hooey Write with us what they will. **1970** G. Greer *Female Eunuch* 81 The horse between a girl's legs is supposed to be a gigantic penis. What hooey!

hoof, *sb.* **1.** *on the hoof*: delete (a butcher's phrase). Add examples. Also *transf.* and *fig.*

1818 H. B. Fearon *Sk. Amer.* 220 Cattle..are sold in this State, on the hoof, for about 3 dollars per hundred weight. **1902** *Encycl. Brit.* XXV. 186/1 The estimated dead weight of the sheep imported on the hoof for slaughter. *a* **1936** Kipling *Something of Myself* (1937) iii. 71 Why buy Bret Harte, I asked, when I was prepared to supply home-grown fiction on the hoof? **1957** Wodehouse *Over Seventy* iv. 53 An august figure, weighing seventeen stone or so on the hoof. **1971** *Farmers Weekly* 19 Mar. 67/3 You can't grade hoggets on the hoof.

5. *hoof-fall, -hold*; **hoof and tongue sickness** = *foot-and-mouth disease* (*s.v.* Foot *sb.* 35); **hoof-rot** = *foot-rot* (*s.v.* Foot *sb.* 35); **hoof stick**, an instrument for manicuring the nails.

1867 *Queenstown Free Press* 22 Jan. (Pettman), We have had a great deal of hoof and tongue sickness amongst our cattle. **1910** J. Farnol *Broad Highway* ii. xlvii, Nodding sleepily with every plodding hoof-fall. **1923** H. Sutcliffe *Wrack o' Doom* ii, The broken lands that gave no hoof-hold. **1863** H. S. Randall *Pract. Shepherd* ii. 25 Scab and hoof-rot, those dire scourges of the ovine race. **1893** W. B. E. Miller et al. *Dis. Live Stock* v. 355 (*heading*) Hoof rot—foot rot. **1960** *Woman* 30 Jan. 15/2 First she lifts her cuticles gently with a hoof stick. **1970** *Observer* 8 Feb. 36/7 Keep the cuticle free from the nail with a rubber hoof stick.

hoof, *v.* Add: **1.** (Later examples.)

1877 J. Habberton *Jericho Road* i. 7 If we get stuck way up the river, so's we have to lay up all summer, and you have to hoof it in deep water. **1888** 'Buffalo Bill' *Story of Wild West* 531, I finally concluded that my prospects were good for 'hoofing' the whole distance. **1910** W. M. Raine *B. O'Connor* iv. 58 He hoofed it back to the cabin. **1923** Belloc *Sonnets & Verse* 111 A score of stout fellows who..Hoofed it amain, Rain or no rain. **1958** S. Ellin *Eighth Circle* (1959) ii. xvii. 177 They hoofed it all the way down to Barrow Street. **1972** C. Weston *Poor, Poor Ophelia* (1973) xvii. 109 Man's not very sick if he's out hoofing around that early.

b. To dance. (Also with *it.*) *slang.*

1925 *Amer. Speech* I. 36/2 A 'hoofing act' is entirely made up of step dancing. **1926** C. Van Vechten *Nigger Heaven* 13 Le's hoof, Ruby urged. Le's sit down, Anatole commanded. **1928** *Daily Express* 2 July 11/5 Mr. Tommy Nolan proposed to his partner, Miss Anna King. She accepted him, and they planned their wedding and honeymoon while 'hoofing'. **1958** 'A. Gilbert' *Death against Clock* iii. 27 A pretty nifty dancer himself in his young days and still able to hoof it quite neatly. **1972** I. Hamilton *Thrill Machine* xv. 64 She sings, she hoofs a little, she does some straight narration.

2. b. To dismiss, expel, eject. Usu. with *out.*

1893 Farmer & Henley *Slang* III. 340/2 To hoof out. **1905** *Daily Chron.* 22 Apr. 9/2 Well, at least we know for certain..that he was hoofed out of the Guards. **1915** V. Woolf *Voyage Out* xxiii. 376 They've hoofed out the prostitute. **1924** Galsworthy *White Monkey* iii. viii, A packer we had, who got hoofed for snooping books. **1928** D. L. Sayers *Unpleasantness at Bellona Club* i. 8 They'd hoof me out of the Club if I raised my voice beyond a whisper. **1959** *Punch* 6 May 600/2 They hoofed the London Museum out of Lancaster House. **1973** 'B. Mather' *Snowline* v. 60 The Bengali doctor came in at that stage and hoofed Mukkerjee out of it.

So **hoo·fer** *slang* (orig. *U.S.*), a dancer.

1923 *N.Y. Times* 9 Sept. vii. 2/1 Hoofer, a dancer, also a heel-beater. **1928** [see *femme 1]. **1928** *Sunday Express* 8 Apr. 5/7 To-morrow Roy Lloyd, who was the hoofer in 'Broadway', takes up the part. **1936** 'J. Tey' *Shilling for Candles* vi. 59 The little Broadway hoofer was blossoming into the song-and-dance star. **1959** *News Chron.* 19 June 8/2 Holly..gets herself involved with a no-good hoofer in a low night club. **1969** *Daily Tel.* 17 Jan. 21/5 An orthodox tale of stage success: unknown girl hoofer becoming overnight hit by breaking all the Ziegfeld rules. **1973** *Sunday Express* 8 July 6/4 She was impressed by one of the male dancers... The one-time hoofer ended up by working for her for 40 years.

hoo-ha (hū·hā). *colloq.* Also **hoo-hah, hou-ha.** [Orig. unknown.] A commotion, a rumpus, a row.

The use in quot. 1932 seems to be without parallel.

1931 *Punch* 14 Oct. 402/1 The devil of a hoo-ha in the papers about increasing the demand for English-grown corn. **1932** T. S. Eliot *Sweeney Agonistes* 30 You've had a cream of a nightmare dream and you've got the hoo-ha's coming to you. **1937** N. Marsh *Vintage Murder* vi. 63 He came up under cover of all the hoo-hah on the stage some time after the event. **1944** 'N. Shute' *Pastoral* ix. 206 There's a bit of a hoo-hah on about your tea-party. **1954** *Times Lit. Suppl.* 24 Sept., After all the hou-ha in the *Observer* about the death of the novel, perhaps we ought to be wearing a mourning-band. **1955** E. C. R. Lorac *Ask Policeman* xvii. 187 He could cut off home after the hoo-ha died down and claim his inheritance. **1959** B. Goolden *For Richer, for Poorer* xiii. 232, I don't think Mummy will make much of a hoo-hah if she knows it's not for long. **1963** *Sunday Express* 15 Sept. 8/7 What has all the houha about the prodigious jump in productivity meant to the housewife? **1968** *Listener* 27 June 837/1 And there was a terrific hoo-ha over this because they all thought I should go and be a termination case or something. **1971** *Country Life* 27 May 1328/2 Some of these lovely irises may..be grown..successfully without much hoo-ha.

hook, *sb.*[1] Add: **1. b.** *pl. slang.* The fingers or hands. So *to get one's hooks on* or *into*: to get hold of.

1829 W. Maginn tr. *Vidocq's Mem.* IV. 261 To his clies my hooks I throw in. **1877** *Five Years' Penal Serv.* iv. 259 In a week or two a man can bring his hooks and feelers into full working trim again. **1917** E. Wallace *Just Men of Cordova* x. 169 Put your lamps over my shiners, run your hooks over me Astrakhan collar. **1926** *S.P.E. Tract* xxiv. 122 *Get one's hooks on*, get hold of. **1930** 'E. Queen' *French Powder Myst.* xxvii. 230 About these volumes... I noticed a queer hesitancy on your part when I first got my hooks into them. **1954** J. Potts *Go, Lovely Rose* viii. 41 Maybe he's eloped with that fat Lang dame. She's been trying to get her hooks into him all winter.

c. A thief, a pickpocket. *slang.* (Cf. Hook *v.* 6, Hooker[1] 1.)

1863 *Once a Week* IX. 555/1 The party who picks the pocket while the 'stiff-dropper' is attracting the victim's attention is called 'the hook'. **1885** M. Davitt *Leaves from Prison Diary* I. xi. 106 *Hooks*, these individuals, who are also known as 'guns' and 'buzzers', in prison slang, constitute the pickpocket class in its various specialities. **1901** *Westm. Gaz.* 4 Sept. 4/1 The very same 'hook' was caught..a second time red-handed at another station. **1926** N. Lucas *London & its Criminals* xviii. 246 The 'hook' is the 'whizzer' who actually picks the pocket. **1935** A. J. Pollock *Underworld Speaks* 57/2 *Hook*, the pickpocket who does the actual stealing. **1968** G. J. Barrett *Guilty, be Damned* x. 116 We've nothing on him. But then we've nothing on half the hooks in Eastport.

2. b. on the hook: in various *fig.* uses, e.g. ensnared, in the power (of someone); in one's grasp; attached to some occupation, habit, etc. Cf. *off the hook* (sense 15 f below).

a **1635, 1730** [in Dict.]. **1927** H. Crane *Let.* 12 Aug. (1965) 304, I do hope that I can count on your assistance to the extent of the monthly amount until I can get something on my hook. **1932** L. C. Douglas *Forgive our Trespasses* xii. 233 Presently Angela was again on the hook in twenty score of composing-rooms. **1958** 'J. Brogan' *Cummings Rep.* xii. 126 She had made me wretchedly conscious of my shortcomings; that is how she had me on the hook. **1963** 'D. Rutherford' *Creeping Flesh* i. 72 'He really is on the hook.' 'The hook?' 'This drug habit.' **1970** G. F. Newman *Sir, You Bastard* ii. 60 Poor bastard might as well have been fined today as kept on the hook.

4. b. A hook upon which (in early models) the receiver rested. (The expression is still used when the reference is to the cradle upon which a telephone rests.)

1885 *List of Subscribers* (United Telephone Co.) p. iii, When your bell rings..take the Telephone *off the hook*... Unless the telephone is *on* the hook, the Subscriber *cannot call* or *be called* by the Exchange. **1921** *Conquest* Jan. 126/3 On removing the receiver from the hook, the subscriber's line is connected to a selector. **1955** W. Gaddis *Recognitions* ii. v. 508 Otto hung the receiver back on its hook. **1970** G. F. Newman *Sir, You Bastard* 262 Another phone crossed Sneed's mind, the one in his own flat with its receiver off the hook.

10. d. *Logic. colloq.* A name for the sign $\supset$, used as the implication sign (cf. *horse-shoe 2 f.). Also, more commonly, a reading of the sign: thus '$p \supset q$' is read '*p*, hook, *q*'.

In colloquial use among logicians since 1955 or earlier.

1967 R. Neidorf *Deductive Forms* 65 'If...then'.. will be symbolized by a hook, $\supset$. **1971** G. Hunter *Metalogic* 54 We shall call the tilde and the hook the connectives of P.

11. (Earlier examples.)

1600 Hakluyt *Voy.* III. 743 A hooke or headland. **1832** E. C. Wines *Two Years in Navy* i, We were kept off the hook, waiting either for wind or tide.

13. (Earlier and later examples.)

1896 *Badminton Mag.* Sept. 278 Leg-hitting..has found a goodly representative in the 'hook', as invented by E. M. Grace. **1904** F. C. Holland *Cricket* 26 Short-pitched balls are best disposed of by a hook. **1948** E. W. Swanton *Denis Compton* i. 14 The hook (that is the leg-side hit off the back foot) is another and more orthodox favourite. **1972** *Observer* 23 Apr. 24/8 Two regal hooks by Cowdrey were matched in the next over by two lordly cover-drives from Dexter.

b. *Boxing.* A short swinging blow with the elbow bent. Also *transf.*

1898 *Daily News* 9 Nov. 8/5 After Smith had put a left hook on the chin the issue was not in doubt. **1910** J. Driscoll *Ringcraft* 94 It only needs practice to convince anyone that the straight blow will always get there before the swing or the hook. **1929** *Evening News* 18 Nov. 16/4 With a couple of left hooks to the head. **1945** *Diamond Track* (Army Board, N.Z.) 7/1 The Division carried out the outflanking movements, the celebrated 'left hooks' which forced the enemy out of the two great strongholds. **1961** B. Fergusson *Watery Maze* x. 251 Some of the Mediterranean landing-craft had already been promised to India, to help the British mount amphibious hooks down the coast of Arakan. **1971** *Daily Express* 17 Feb. 14/7 Salah..was pinned and punished by Clark's jabs and hooks.

c. *Golf.* The act of hooking.

1890 W. Simpson in H. G. Hutchinson *Golf* vi. 204 Press ever so little when your club is turned in and yourself over-reached, and the hook is certain.

15. e. (Earlier and later examples.)

1840 H. Cockton *Life Valentine Vox* xii. 95 No man was ever able to write his own life complete. He's certain to go off the hooks before he has finished it. **1921** Galsworthy *To Let* i. i. 9 Old Timothy; he might go off the hooks at any moment. I suppose he's made his Will.

f. *off the hook*: out of a difficult situation. Cf. *on the hook* (sense 2 b above).

1864 Trollope *Small House at Allington* II. xxix. 296 'Poor Caudle!' he said to himself; 'he's hooked, and he'll never get himself off the hook again.' **1954** J. Potts

Go, Lovely Rose xii. 77 'It's an idea,' said Dr Craig...It would get Hartley off the hook, sure enough. **1962** M. URQUHART *Frail on North Circular* xxv. 140 Let Broadbent think he's off the hook and then give it another twist. **1966** *New Yorker* 25 June 49 Then he smiled, and I knew I was off the hook. **1969** A. GLYN *Dragon Variation* vii. 199 You mean she lost the kid? Well! Well, that sure lets old Walter off the hook!

16. (Earlier and later examples.)

1812 *Boston Gaz.* 23 Nov. (Th.), They forget that Rodgers himself says that he went upon his own hook. **1836** D. CROCKETT *Exploits & Adv. Texas* (1837) 13 But now I start anew upon my own hook. **1899** J. LONDON *Let.* 30 Mar. (1966) 26 When I was just sixteen I broke loose and went off on my own hook. **1927** E. W. SPRINGS *Nocturne Militaire* vi. 178 You know a man has to be crazy to go after a balloon on his own hook. **1940** M. LOWRY *Let.* Spring (1967) 21 They objected to my going east on my own hook..because they would not trust me. **1952** F. YERBY *Woman called Fancy* xvi. 307 I'm not going out of this house with you on my own hook.

b. *to sling* or *take one's hook*: to go away, be off, decamp. *slang* or *dial.*

1874, 1897 [see SLING *v.*^{1} 3 d]. **1885** O. ALLAN *Sinbad the Sailor* 22, I 'took the office' and I took my hook. **1886** M. PEACOCK *Tales Lindsey Folk-Speech* 106 An' soa he teks his hook back agaain to steam-hoose yard. **1890** KIPLING *Barrack-Room Ballads* (1892) 34 Before you sling your 'ook, at the 'ousetops take a look. **1892** 'F. ANSTEY' *Mr. Punch's Model Music-Hall Songs* 130 Take your 'ook while you can. **1928** *Daily Express* 10 May 7 Magistrate: How is your husband cruel to you? Wife: He will not speak to me, and he tells me to sling my hook. **1955** L. P. HARTLEY *Perfect Woman* xxii. 193 Anyhow, she's gone, walked out, slung her hook. **1959** [see *BREEZE *sb.*^{2} 3 b].

16*. *hook, line, and sinker*: completely, without reservations.

1838 G. W. PATTERSON in T. W. Barnes *Mem. T. Weed* (1884) v. 60 We are gone, hook, line, and sinker. **1865** *Weekly New Mexican* 25 Aug. 1/3 Without him Chavez [*sc.* a candidate for Congress] is gone hook, line, and sinker. **1924** WODEHOUSE *Bill the Conqueror* ii. 59 The old man swallowed those references of yours, hook, line and sinker. **1936** N. COWARD *To-night at 8.30* II. 58, I fell for it hook, line and sinker. **1945** E. WAUGH *Brideshead Revisited* I. ii. 38 You, my dear Charles,.. have gone straight, hook, line and sinker, into the very worst set in the University.

17. a. *hook bolt* (examples).

1923 *Man. Seamanship* (H.M.S.O.) II. 300 It will be necessary [during salvage operations] to drill a few extra holes for hook bolts which will be used to secure the patch temporarily to the ship's side... The hook bolts are shipped in the holes ready for use. **1940** *Chambers's Techn. Dict.* 421/2 *Hook bolt*, a galvanised-iron bolt formed out of rod which is bent at one end into a hook serving as the head, and threaded at the other to take a nut; used for fixing corrugated sheeting. **1956** *Archit. Rev.* CXIX. 213/1 For fixing to metal purlins, a standard range of hook-bolts and U-bolts is available.

c. *hook-winged* adj. **d.** *hook-fishing.*

1745 ELLIS *Mod. Husb.* VI. II. 67 Those poor People.. may have the single Engines for Hook-fishing fixed within their Houses. **1841** J. JOHNSON tr. *Van der Donck's New-Netherlands* in *N.Y. Hist. Soc. Coll.* 2nd Ser. I. 177 Those the people call weak crabs, and they make excellent bait for hook fishing. **1851** *Illustr. Catal. Gt. Exhib.* IV. 926/1 Hook-fishing is within 3 fathoms, either in the river or in open sea. **1905** *Spectator* 7 Jan. 12/1 Every autumn the great coffee-coloured, hook-winged skua-gulls come down from the North and patrol the midway air. **1939** L. MACNEICE *Autumn Jrnl.* vi. 27 A vulture hung in air..His hook-winged shadow wavered. **1968** T. KINSELLA *Nightwalker* 17 Hook-winged geese or hawks.

18. hook-and-ladder *U.S.*, apparatus consisting of ladders and hooks used by firemen; often *attrib.*; **hook gauge**, an instrument for accurately determining the surface level of water and consisting of a hook and pointer attached to a fixed vernier, the hook being brought up until its tip just pierces the surface of the water; **hook-hit** = 13 b above; **hook-ladder**, a ladder with hooks at one end by which it can be suspended; **hook-pot** (see quot. *a* 1865); **hook rug** = **hooked rug*; **hook shop** *slang*, a brothel; **hook-shot** *Basketball*, a twisting shot started when the player has his back to the basket and completed as he pivots round towards the basket; **hook stroke** *Cricket*, a stroke made by hitting a short-pitched ball, after it has risen, round to leg with a horizontal swing of the bat; **hook tender** *N. Amer.* (see quot. 1905).

1821 *Minutes Boston* (Mass.) *Selectmen* XXXIX. 187 Mr. George G. Channing..declines taking command of the Fire Hook & Ladder company. **1865** *Chambers's Jrnl.* 29 July 469/2, 18 hook-and-ladder trucks. **1909** *Strand Mag.* Apr. 363 There stood the engines and the 'hook-and-ladder'. **1902** *Westm. Gaz.* 11 June 8/1 Other Americans pointed with pride to their hook-and-ladder system, which forms such an important aid to the New York fireman. **1949** *Los Angeles Times* 18 May 8/1 The Fire Department obligingly backed up a hook-and-ladder truck. **1875** *Jrnl. Franklin Inst.* XCIX. 250 The depth on the weir was observed by means of a hook-gauge. **1880** *Encycl. Brit.* XII. 477/2 The hook gauge used first by Mr. U. Boyden of Boston, in 1840. **1934** H. ADDISON *Text Bk. Appl. Hydraulics* xv. 304 Hook and point gauges. These are the simplest and most reliable gauges for measuring ranges of head not exceeding about 3 ft. (60 cms.) with a probable error of 1/1500 ft. (0·2 mm.). **1890** R. G. A. ALLANSON-WINN *Boxing* (ed. 2) ix. 43 There is another half-arm hit, called the 'hook-hit', in which the elbow is not so much bent as it is with the real 'contracted-arm'. **1919** G. B. SHAW in *Manch. Guardian* 1 Nov. 7/6 He missed that chance of a hook hit at the white chokers. **1858** SIMMONDS *Dict. Trade*, Hook-ladder. **1905** *Westm. Gaz.* 17 Oct. 7/1 The escape was rushed up, ladders extended, hook-ladders placed into position. **1972** *Times* 20 Sept. 3/3 Window cleaners..made their final assault on the upper storeys by jumping out of windows..by lowering a hook ladder from the summit. *a* **1865** SMYTH *Sailor's Word-Bk.* (1867) 388 *Hook-pots*, tin cans fitted to hang on the bars of the galley range. **1886** R. BROWN *Spunyarn & Spindrift* v. 66 A hook-pot of tea a-piece. **1896** *Idler* Mar. 173/1 There you'd see them crowding about the doors at meal-times, flourishing their hook-pots. **1913** J. MASEFIELD *Daffodil Fields* 33 Tin dishes, sailors' hookpots. **1951** T. CAPOTE *Grass Harp* (1952) i. 12 There was a hook rug on the floor. **1967** E. SHORT *Embroidery & Fabric Collage* iii. 83 The canvas [is] the one normally used for hook rugs, i.e. three holes to the inch. **1889** BARRÈRE & LELAND *Dict. Slang* I. 473/1 *Hook shop*, a brothel. **1935** A. J. POLLOCK *Underworld Speaks* 57/2 *Hook shop*, a house of ill fame. **1954** J. STEINBECK *Sweet Thursday* vi. 49 This kid could be pure murder in a hook-shop. **1957** *Encycl. Brit.* III. 181B/1 Farther out.. players use a one-hand shot from a stride, jump or standing position, and a hook shot which is overhead. **1969** Z. HOLLANDER *Mod. Encycl. Basketball* 43 Washington, led by hook-shot artist Jack Nichols, defeated Oregon State. **1969** *New Yorker* 14 June 79/1 You go through Harlem and you'll see kids less than five feet tall with pretty good jump shots and hook shots. **1897** K. S. RANJITSINHJI *Jubilee Bk. Cricket* 175 Batsmen of the old school very much disliked the hook-stroke on principle. **1908** *Daily Chron.* 15 May 8/2 He began exploiting the full drive and the hook stroke. **1911** C. B. FRY in P. F. Warner *Bk. Cricket* 226 Ranjitsinhji found almost as little difficulty in making his famous 'hook strokes'. **1945** N. CARDUS *Eng. Cricket* 38 Maclaren was the grand manner personified; with his hook-stroke he dismissed the fastest ball from his presence. **1893** *Atlantic Monthly* Feb. 196/1 Each man, being hired for a definite purpose, as chopper, hook-tender, barker, [etc.]..keeps closely to his own job. **1901** *Daily Colonist* (Victoria, B.C.) 3 Nov. 5/2 Seventy-five cents was taken off hook-tenders and other men not necessarily expert. **1905** *Terms Forestry* (U.S. Dept. Agric.) 40 *Hook tender*, the foreman of a yarding crew; specifically, one who directs the attaching of the cable to a turn of logs. **1966** *Sun* (Vancouver) 12 Jan. 25/5 Moore said the industry needs more managers, logging operators, hook-tenders..'and even chokermen'.

hook, *sb.*^{2} *local.* Variant of HUCK *sb.*^{1} Also **hook-bone.** The projecting upper part of the thigh bones of cattle near the hip-joint. Cf. HUCK *sb.*^{1} and HUCKLE-BONE.

1808 T. H. HORNE *Compl. Grazier* (ed. 3) 9 The roof [of a bull ought to be] wide, particularly over the chine and hips, or hooks. **1844** H. STEPHENS *Bk. Farm* II. 161 Between the shoulders and the hook. *Ibid.* III. 1253 The broad hook-bones, with the narrow chest, are not entirely occasioned in cows by calf-breeding. **1858** C. L. FLINT *Milch Cows* 17 The Ayrshire farmers prefer their dairy bulls..broad at the hook-bones and hips, and full in the flanks. **1900** *Westmorland Gaz.* 3 Feb., Advt. (E.D.D.), Strayed, two Herdwick ewes; marked red pop near shoulder and near hook. **1935** *Amer. Speech* X. 271/1 *Hooks*, hip bones of a cow. **1960** *Farmer & Stockbreeder* 8 Mar. 95/2 As is good breadth between the hookbones.

hook, *v.* Add: **3.** (N.Z. examples of *to hook off*, to make off.)

1938 F. S. ANTHONY in D. M. Davin *N.Z. Short Stories* (1953) 219, I hooked off on my own and rambled aimlessly about. **1940** F. SARGESON *Man & Wife* (1944) 75 If Ted saw her coming up the road he'd hook off if he could before she got near. And if he couldn't I'd hook off while they had their barney.

4. c. To make (rugs) with a hook: see *HOOKED *a.* 4. *U.S.*

1882 *Harper's Mag.* Dec. 126/1 Cynthy Ann..hooked rugs from early in the morning until late into the night. **1945** B. MACDONALD *Egg & I* 66 A time to repair machinery, hook rugs, patch quilts, mend harness and perform other leisurely tasks.

d. *intr.* To use a crochet needle.

1854 C. M. YONGE *Castle Builders* vi. 81 Miss Townsend ..hooked away with her crochet needle.

e. *to hook up:* to establish a link *with*, to make a connection *with*. Also const. *to*, and with direct object. Cf. *HOOK-UP.

1925 H. CRANE *Let.* 27 Oct. (1965) 218 They want to hook the book up with an illustrious name. **1929** WODEHOUSE *Mr. Mulliner Speaking* v. 172 What I would propose is that we take a short cut through the fields to the station, hook up with the five-fifty express at Goresby, [etc.]. **1943** E. C. WICKS et al. *Shopwork* vi. 113 Whenever electricity is needed for any purpose, the particular job must be wired or 'hooked-up' to feed the electrical current to the necessary place. **1953** P. C. BERG *Dict. New Words* 94/1 *Hook-up*, v.t., to connect two or more broadcasting systems for the time needed to broadcast a common item on their otherwise different programmes. **1971** *Ink* 12 June 12/1 David Mercer's moving and intelligent portrait of a Marxist drama critic who can't hook up his ideology with his unresolved feelings towards his impossible working-class father. **1971** M. TAK *Truck Talk* 84 *Hook up*, to couple a tractor to a trailer. **1972** *Edmonton* (Alberta) *Jrnl.* 31 Aug. 3/4 RCMP and city police forces in Alberta have begun hooking up to a national computer system.

5. b. Usu. in pa. pple. *hooked* (*on*): addicted (to), captivated (by). *slang.*

1925 *Writer's Monthly* June 486/2 *Hooked*, to become a drug addict. **1931** D. RUNYON *Guys & Dolls* (1932) vi. 115 Waldo Winchester is hooked. **1953** W. BURROUGHS *Junkie* (1972) 11, I drifted along taking shots when I could score. I ended up hooked. *Ibid.* vi. 61 When you are hooked, the effects are not dramatic. **1964** *Daily Tel.* 25 Nov. 22/6 The chances are that he is hooked on opium, morphine or heroin. **1965** *New Statesman* 16 Apr. 620/3 Other cities have admirers, even lovers, but Liverpool has only addicts: either you are hooked the very first time you step out of Lime Street Station to be confronted by the bulk of St George's Hall, or you never get the message. **1966** E. McGIRR *Funeral was in Spain* 137 She was half-way to being hooked: one of the punks she was with was a pusher. **1967** M. M. GLATT et al. *Drug Scene* ii. 21 Once you're registered, you're hooked. It's too depressing when you're hooked, besides a girl looks terrible on heroin. **1967** *New Scientist* 25 May 478 Hopes that the millions of men and women 'hooked' on tobacco may soon be able to satisfy their craving with a 'safe' cigarette are not supported by the facts. **1970** *Daily Tel.* 8 May 3/2 Hundreds of domestic pets die each year after becoming 'hooked' on slug bait.

7. c. To solicit as a prostitute. Cf. *HOOKER^1 4. *slang.*

1959 'E. McBAIN' *Killer's Wedge* (1961) vi. 57 She's been in the city for almost a year, Pete. Hooking mostly. **1965** —— *Doll* (1966) v. 66 The girl was a prostitute... The girl had been hooking in the neighborhood for little more than a week. **1969** DISCH & SLADEK *Black Alice* v. 53 Bessie's girls didn't have to go out hooking in hotel lobbies or honkytonks, no indeedy. **1971** W. HANLEY *Blue Dreams* xix. 313 A high-class hooker couldn't be entirely without redeeming social value. Especially one who..taught English and hooked on the side.

8. c. For the use in *Cricket* cf. *hook stroke* (*HOOK *sb.*^{1} 18). (Further examples.) Also *absol.*

1896 *Badminton Mag.* Oct. 482 Gregory, in attempting to hook Peel, put the ball straight into Richardson's hands. **1898** K. S. RANJITSINHJI *With Stoddart's Team* (ed. 3) iii. 50 He [*sc.* C. Hill] seemed able to 'drive', or 'hook', or 'glance'..with equal skill and success. **1904** [see *COVER *sb.*^{1} 1 d]. **1955** [see *BOUNDARY 2 b]. **1955** *Times* 9 May 15/2 Then, when he must have been looking ahead to a century, he was leg-before-wicket hooking at Heine. **1972** 'J. ROSS' *Here lies Nancy Frail* xii. 145 I'm bloody useless with a two wood... I hook like hell with it.

d. *Boxing.* To strike (one's opponent) a swinging blow with the elbow bent (cf. *HOOK *sb.*^{1} 13 b). Also *absol.*

1898 *Daily News* 24 Nov. 8/3 Corbett hooked with his right hard on Sharkey's jaw. **1910** J. DRISCOLL *Ringcraft* 86 Wild attempts to hook him on his well protected jaw. **1973** *Times* 14 Feb. 9/3 Bugner..clubs rather than hooks.

e. *Rugby Football.* To secure (the ball) with the foot, as hooker, when it is placed in the scrummage. Also *intr.*

1906 GALLAHER & STEAD *Compl. Rugby Footballer* vii. 110 In Britain it is the custom to hook the ball in the scrum with the outside feet crossing over those on the inside. **1913** *Daily Graphic* 24 Mar. 15/1 D. A. Greer..may be of use to Ireland henceforward, especially as 'hooking' is his forte. **1927** WAKEFIELD & MARSHALL *Rugger* 183 The front row tried trick hooking and foot-up tactics. **1955** *Times* 1 Aug. 2/3 Kroon's brilliant hooking has been a feature of the season's provincial matches.

13. *to hook Jack*: to play truant. *U.S. colloq.* (Cf. *HOOKEY 1.)

1877 BARTLETT *Dict. Amer.* (ed. 4) 294 *Hook Jack*, to play truant. New England. **1890** *Dialect Notes* I. 22 *Hookey*, in 'to play hookey', meaning *to play truant*, used in Maine, but not usual in Boston, where the phrase was and is to 'hook Jack'. **1892** *Ibid.* 216 In all the period from 1840 to 1850 the current phrase among the boys was *to hook Jack*. **1905** J. C. LINCOLN *Partners of Tide* iv. 70 The boy 'hooked Jack' for a whole day. **1967** *Publ. Amer. Dial. Soc.* XLVII. 7 *Hook jack*, 'play hookey'.

hook-billed, *a.* (Later examples.)

1785 J. LATHAM *Gen. Synopsis Birds* III. 495 Hook-billed Duck, *Raii Syn.* p. 150.2. **1881** *Amer. Naturalist* XV. 182 The male [of hump-back salmon] is slab-sided, hook-billed and distorted. **1911** *Encycl. Brit.* XXII. 219 Among the breeds differing in structure may be mentioned ..the hook-billed and tufted ducks.

Hooke (huk). The name of Robert *Hooke* (1635–1703), English inventor and natural philosopher, used, chiefly in the possessive, to designate his discoveries and inventions, as **Hooke('s) coupling,** a Hooke's joint; **Hooke's law,** the law, valid within the limits of elasticity, that the strain produced by a stress of any one kind is proportional to that stress; **Hooke's (universal) joint,** a kind of universal joint for transmitting rotary motion from one shaft to another.

1825 J. NICHOLSON *Oper. Mech.* 32 Hooke's universal joints are sometimes used to communicate motion obliquely. **1853** *Trans. R. Soc. Edin.* XX. 93 The fundamental assumption from which the following equations are deduced is an extension of Hooke's law. **1883** *Encycl. Brit.* XV. 762/2 Two Hooke's couplings. **1906** A. E. H. LOVE *Treat. Math. Theory Elasticity* (ed. 2) iv. 110 Many materials used in engineering structures, e.g. cast iron, building stone, cement, do not obey Hooke's Law for any strains that are large enough to be observed. **1930** *Engineering* 31 Jan. 134/1 A Hooke's joint is provided to allow for the vertical motion of the [gear] boxes. **1959** C. E. PEARSON *Theor. Elasticity* v. 83 The familiar Hooke's-law experiment in which a metal wire is stretched by a tensile load. **1968** R. H. BACON *Car* xx. 268 Most universal joints are based on the Hooke coupling.

Hence **Hookean, hookean** (hu·kiăn) *a.* [-AN], obeying Hooke's law; linearly elastic.

1956 J. C. JAEGER *Elasticity, Fracture & Flow* ii. 99 (*heading*) The perfectly elastic or 'Hookean' substance.

1960 *McGraw-Hill Encycl. Sci. & Technol.* X. 476/2 On extension of polymeric materials, both rubberlike and Hookean elasticity may be present. **1968** C. G. Kuper *Introd. Theory Superconductivity* ix. 146 The elastic vibrations of a lattice of discrete point masses, coupled by Hookean springs. **1972** *Physics Bull.* Nov. 651/3 For most practical purposes alkali silicate glasses are hookean solids exhibiting a linear stress–strain curve to fracture.

hooked, *a.* Add: **4.** *hooked mat, hooked rug,* a mat or rug made on a canvas ground with woollen yarn which is pulled through with a hook. orig. *U.S.*

1880 W. D. Howells *Undiscovered Country* 415 Hooked rugs and embroidered tidies were as worthy a place in Mrs. Ford's simple house as most of the old-fashioned things. **1917** L. M. Montgomery *Anne's House of Dreams* (1926) ii. 10 Nobody seems to want anything but hooked mats now. **1932** D. C. Minter *Mod. Needlecraft* 223 (*heading*) Hooked rugs. **1960** G. Lewis *Handbk. Crafts* 91 A hooked rug is a very satisfying thing to make. **1964** Mrs. L. B. Johnson *White House Diary* 21 May (1970) 144 After the speech Mrs. Breathitt presented me with a beautiful hooked rug—an art still practiced by the old people in the area. **1969** H. A. Horwood *Newfoundland* 7 A hooked mat is a kind of tapestry made by Newfoundland women who got the art from their mothers who had it handed down to them from the first European settlers. **1970** *Globe & Mail* (Toronto) 26 Sept. 45/6 (Advt.), Superior antiques..including..hooked and braided rugs.

hooker[1]. Add: **3.** Also simply *hooker*; and in many other technical usages.

1881 *Instr. Census Clerks* (1885) 134/2 Hooker (to special trade when stated or determinable). Hooker (Undefined)..Factory Labourer. **1900** *Westm. Gaz.* 16 May 8/1 No one received injuries, the hookers having received warning by the clashing of the cage. **1919** *Camp Worker* (Vancouver) 26 Apr. 5/2 The best hooker that ever gave signals for the high-rigger, while his short-handed crew changed the haul-back without the assistance of a grass-line. **1921** *Dict. Occup. Terms* (1927) § 043 *Onsetter;..hooker, hooker-at-shaft..;* stands at bottom of shaft in coal or shale mine to push full tubs on to cage and remove empty ones. *Ibid.* § 943 *Hooker, cloth hooker, piece hooker, hooker-and-lapper.* **1966** H. Sheppard *Dict. Railway Slang* (ed. 2) 6 *Hooker,* shunter. **1967** *Amer. Speech* XLII. 291 Hookers come and attach hooks on slings from the overhead cranes, or travelers, that move over the yard transferring loads between saws and stacks.

4. A prostitute. *slang* (chiefly *U.S.*).

1845 in N. E. Eliason *Tarheel Talk* (1956) 277 If he comes by way of Norfolk he will find any number of pretty Hookers in the Brick row not far from French's hotel. **1914** Jackson & Hellyer *Vocab. Criminal Slang* 45 *Hooker,* a prostitute. **1929** T. Wolfe *Look Homeward, Angel* (1930) xxx. 435, I hope you have sense enough now to leave those old hookers alone? **1932** J. Dos Passos *1919* 43 Ain't you got the sense to tell a good girl from a hooker? **1952** J. Steinbeck *East of Eden* xlv. 504 Joe could find any hooker in any town in a few hours. **1964** *Esquire* Nov. 85/2 They were attractive but not very imaginative, they looked like hookers on horses. **1971** [see *hook *v.* 7 c].

5. A cow or ox that 'hooks' (see Hook *v.* 11). *U.S.*

1866 *Harper's Mag.* May 816/1 He..asked 'Why that pipe [*sc.* a hookah] was like a cow?' having in mind the obvious answer that it was a hooker. **1885** 'C. E. Craddock' *Prophet Gt. Smoky Mts.* ii. 48 The red cow jes' hooked down the bars, bein' a turrible hooker. **1902** G. H. Lorimer *Lett. Merchant* vii. 84 You want to.. distinguish between a cow that's a kicker, but whose intentions are good..and a hooker, who is vicious on general principles.

6. *Rugby Football.* A player in the centre of the front row of the scrummage on either side who endeavours to obtain the ball by hooking it. Cf. *hook *v.* 8 e.

1905 *Daily Chron.* 13 Sept. 7/4 The two front men—called 'hookers'—can get the ball just as well as three. **1906** [see *back *a.* 1]. **1927** Wakefield & Marshall *Rugger* 166 Some hookers prefer to have the weight on the loose-head side. **1963** *Times* 14 Jan. 3/1 Thorne had been on the fringe of this new honour as a hooker for several years, and Davis and Owen look a sound second row. **1971** *Times* 15 Feb. 9/2 For a hooker Pullin often showed up well in the loose.

b. *Cricket.* One who uses the hook stroke.

1900 W. J. Ford *Cricketer on Cricket* 102 Like Hill he is a splendid hooker. **1911** P. F. Warner *Bk. Cricket* 208 He has a lovely shot over extra-cover's head,..and on a slow wicket is a fine puller and hooker. **1972** *Cricket World* 1. 8/2 Keith [Stackpole] has long been regarded as only a puller, hooker and cutter but, last season, developed so much that he also drove strongly.

hooker[4] (hu·kəɹ). *dial.* and *N. Amer. colloq.* [Orig. unknown.] A glass of whisky, a dram; usu. with qualifying word (e.g. *stiff*), a drink (of brandy, etc.).

1833 J. Kennedy *Geordie Chalmers* iv. 45 Ye'll be nane the waur o' a hooker after yer fricht. **1865** W. H. L. Tester *Poems* 133 Sandy liket a hooker, an' brawlie I kent, The drap creatur' wad set him a speakin'. **1887** *Grip* (Toronto) 21 May 7/2 We went in and were served out with a pretty stiff hooker each. **1906** H. Green *At Actors' Boarding House* 62 A stiff hooker of whiskey, and then another had the expected effect. **1927** *Black Mask* Feb. 37/1 It took a stiff hooker of whiskey and a lot of words to thaw her into understanding. **1930** H. Craddock *Savoy Cocktail Bk.* 1. 97 The Juice of 1 Lemon. 4 Hookers Whisky. **1939** C. Morley *Kitty Foyle* xxvii. 268 She gave me such a hooker of brandy I went right to sleep. **1955** 'T. P. Kelley' *Black Donnellys* 63 Danny was quiet enough until he got about six hookers under his belt.

Hooker[5] (hu·kəɹ). The name of William *Hooker* (1779–1832), botanical artist, used in the possessive in *Hooker's green,* a bright green colour used in water-colour painting.

1853 *Dict. Archit.* (Archit. Publ. Soc.) II. 84/2 This method of imitating the mixture of ultramarine with yellow has grown into a system, but the colour is not durable: as in the cases of Hooker's green and Varley's green. **1886** *Jrnl. Bot.* XXIV. 52 His memory is associated by artists with the colour called after him, 'Hooker's Green'. **1948** F. A. Staples *Water-Color Painting* i. 2 For paints get the following water colors in tubes: Alizarin Crimson,..Hooker's Green Dark. **1951** R. Mayer *Artist's Handbk.* ii. 51 *Hooker's green,* a mixture of Prussian blue and gamboge. Sold in two shades, yellowish and bluish.

hookey (hu·ki). Also **hooky.** [Cf. Hook *sb.* 14, *v.* 6, *v.* *13, and Hooky-crooky.] **1.** *to play hookey*: to play truant. Also *transf. colloq.* (chiefly *N. Amer.*).

1848 in Bartlett *Dict. Amer.* **1866** *Harper's Mag.* May 779/1 Kate used to..entreat him not to get feruled, nor play 'hookey'. **1867** 'Mark Twain' *Amer. Drolleries* 20 He would not play hookey, even when his sober judgment told him it was the most profitable thing he could do. **1883** E. Eggleston *Hoosier School-Boy* ix. 47 They remembered that the geography lesson was a hard one, and so they played 'hookey'. **1904** W. N. Harben *Georgians* vii. 77 'I sorter feel like playin' hookey myself,' he admitted. **1908** C. E. Mulford *Orphan* xii. 150 I'll play on them, too, when they gets home! Off playing hookey from work when we all of us aches from double shifts. **1923** Wodehouse *Inimitable Jeeves* xiv. 172 He's played hookey from the choir so often that the vicar told him..he would fire him out. **1957** W. H. Whyte *Organization Man* iii. xi. 144 Such solitary contemplation during the office day..is regarded ..as a form of hooky. **1960** I. Wallach *Absence of Cello* (1961) 98 'I like to play hooky now and then.'.. 'You can't just call it hooky.' **1965** *Globe & Mail* (Toronto) 22 Apr. 23/8 Youngsters who play hooky are..merely afraid of their classrooms.

2. blind hookey: see Blind *a.* 16. Also *fig.* or *transf.*

1852 G. C. Mundy *Our Antipodes* III. iii. 85 The process of emigration was formerly—as compared with its present gradual perfection—a very blind-hookey kind of game. **1909** J. R. Ware *Passing Eng.* 34/1 *Blind Hookey,* a leap in the dark; *e.g.,* 'Oh, it's Blind Hookey to attempt it.' **1925** *Blackw. Mag.* Aug. 286/2 It is..the common practice of politicians to play blind hookey with the great interests entrusted to them.

Hookey Walker: see Walker *int.*

hookless, *a.* Add: **b.** Of a garment: having no hooks, with its hooks missing.

1906 *Westm. Gaz.* 25 Sept. 2/1 Blouses, in various stages of hookless decrepitude.

hook-nosed, *a.* (Later examples.)

1938 [see *fawn-eyed* s.v. *fawn *sb.*[1] 4]. **1958** L. Durrell *Mountolive* ii. 55 Cherry-starred Japan, hook-nosed Lima.

hookum (hū·kŏm). *India.* Also **hookm, hukm.** [a. Hindi, a. Arab. *ḥukm,* f. *ḥakama* (cf. Hakim).] A command, order, or instruction from a person in authority. Also *transf.* (see quot. 1925).

1838 E. Eden *Let.* 17 Dec. in *Up Country* (1866) II. ii. 13 An officer came to ask his 'hookum', or orders. **1843** Lady Sale *Jrnl. Disasters Afghanistan* 39 The troops ..instead of receiving *hookm* to enter the city, the Shah almost rudely inquired why they had come! **1858** W. H. Russell *Diary in India* 7 Oct. (1860) II. xii. 226 We had no hookum from the commissioner or deputy. **1886** [see *dastoor, dastur(1)]. **1895** B. M. Croker *Village Tales* (1896) 224 His coat was restored to him, with a 'hookum', to say that he was free. **1925** Fraser & Gibbons *Soldier & Sailor Words* 120 *Hookum,* a regulation. The correct thing, *e.g.,* 'That's the hookum'. An old Army colloquial term.

hookum-snivey (hu·kəm sni·vi). *dial.* and *slang.* Also **hook and snivey (snivvy), hook 'em snivey, hookem snivey, hookem-snivvy, hook um snivey.** [app. orig. *hook and snivey,* prob. f. Hook *sb.* or *v.*] An imposture or deceit; also, a contrivance for undoing the bolt of a door from the outside. Also *attrib.* or *adj.,* deceitful, tricky.

1781 G. Parker *View Soc.* II. 81 He..would stand no Hook and Snivey, or Nix the Buffer. **1802** R. L. & M. Edgeworth *Irish Bulls* 129, I ranged them fair and even with my hook-em-snivey. **1823** 'J. Bee' *Dict. Turf* 98 Hook and Snivvy—practised by soldiers in quarters, when they obtain grub for *nix,* by connivance with the slavey, or her mistress. **1874** Hotten *Slang Dict.* 194 Sometimes used as an irrelevant answer, by street boys. As, 'who did that?'—'Hook um snivey'—actually no one. **1892** S. Hewett *Peasant Speech of Devon* 89, I tellee 'onesty is the best policy. Niver yü be up tü hookem-snivey ways. **1905** E. Phillpotts *Secret Woman* ii. xi, An' some lying an' doing all manner of hookem-snivey deeds. **1928** —— *Ring Fence* xvi. 132 I'd a lot rather put my thoughts into work, so as you should have a wedding worthy of you and no hookem-snivey marrying in a corner. **1950** L. A. G. Strong *Which I Never* vi. 184 'Tisn't like him to do any sort of hookem-snivvy tactics.

hook-up (hu·kʌp). orig. *U.S. colloq.* [f. phr. *to hook up*: Hook *v.* 4 b, *4 e, 5.] A connection or combination, esp. of radio or television broadcasting facilities.

1903 A. H. Lewis *Boss* 116 It'll put us in line for a hook-up with th' reform bunch in th' fight for th' town next year. **1911** H. Quick *Yellowstone Nights* vii. 191 The Golden Fountain..had no lawyer against us. It was a funny hook-up. **1922** L. D. Brigham *How to make Vacuum Wireless Receiving Sets* 39 The remainder of the hook-up is just like the other amplifier hook-ups. **1927** *Observer* 11 Dec. 16/5 National appeals are possible by wireless when the various American 'Radio Corporations' agree to a 'national hook-up'. **1929** *Lit. Digest* 18 May 79/1 These lines are the skeleton of a gigantic aerial hook-up that now seems destined to cover South America. **1930** P. W. Slosson *Gt. Crusade* x. 278 A radio hook-up brought the whole nation to the [prize] ring side. **1932** E. Wallace *When Gangs came to London* xxi. 186 There had to be either a hook-up or one side had to go out of business. **1944** E. J. Teichert *Ferrous Metall.* (ed. 2) II. xi. 227 The electrical hook-up..is of such a nature that the two motors act as a unit. **1950** Wodehouse *Nothing Serious* 16 He could not have been better informed regarding it if the facts had been broadcast on a nation-wide hook-up. **1957** *Times* 31 Oct. 11/4 This American precedent of appearing in person on a nation wide hook-up. **1959** *Punch* 28 Oct. 360/3 Are you now in favour of a Lab–Lib hook-up? **1967** *Electronics* 6 Mar. 80/1 How do you create a galvanometer..that doesn't require hours of delicate dial twiddling, trapdoor adjustments or experimental hook-ups? **1970** *New Yorker* 12 Sept. 25 Discussing layouts, viewing charts, and getting computer information via a Picturephone/Computer hookup are just a few of the areas being pursued.

hook-worm. *Zool.* [Cf. G. *hakenwurm,* mod.L. *Uncinaria,* f. L. *uncīnus* hook (both coined by J. A. Fröhlich 1789, in *Naturforscher* XXIV. 136).] A parasitic nematode worm of the family Ancylostomatidæ, which infests man, other mammals, or birds, using hook-like organs to attach itself to the host's intestinal lining. Hence **hook-worm disease** = *ankylostomiasis; **hookworm-ridden** *a.,* infested with hookworms.

1902 *Rep. Bur. Anim. Industry 1901* (U.S. Dept. Agric.) 183 (*title*) The significance of the recent American cases of hookworm disease (Uncinariasis, or Anchylostomiasis) in Man. **1902** C. W. Stiles in *Amer. Med.* III. 777 (*title*) A new species of hookworm..parasitic in man. **1909** *Times* 29 Oct. 5/6 A commission of eminent medical men to investigate the hook-worm disease. **1925** R. W. G. Hingston in E. F. Norton *Fight for Everest: 1924* iii. vi. 352 Porters should be vaccinated, and given suitable treatment for hook-worm. **1931** [see *ankylostomiasis]. **1932** W. Faulkner *Light in August* i. 3 Department annals would not now even be remembered by the hookworm-ridden heirs-at-large. **1950** F. A. Brown *Selected Invertebr. Types* 237 It is believed that infected African Negroes brought into the United States established the hookworm in at least part of its present range. **1964** J. E. Larsh *Outl. Med. Parasitol.* xiii. 119 Long-continued anemia, characteristic in chronic hookworm disease, is most detrimental in children. **1968** N. D. Levine *Nematode Parasites* iii. 106 Prevention of hookworm infections in dogs and cats depends upon sanitation.

hooley (hū·li). Chiefly *Irish.* Also **huly, wholee.** [Origin unknown.] A noisy party, a spree (see also quots.).

1877 Bartlett *Dict. Amer.* (ed. 4) 302 *Huly,* a noise, uproar. 'To raise *huly*.' New England. **1947** *Béaloideas* XVII. 273 *Hooley,* a dance or 'spree' in a private house, often to celebrate a wedding, etc. **1950** *Ibid.* XX. 191 *Wholee, Hooley,* a party or dance in a country house. *John gave a right wholee last night.* **1960** *News-Call Bulletin* (*San Francisco*) 4 Jan. 16/1 She can be seen at all the best hoolies in town. **1966** 'L. Lane' *ABZ of Scouse* 50 *'ooley,* a dispute, a fight or a riot. **1966** *Listener* 12 May 687/2 Sir Laurence tries to make it one of those peculiar Irish occasions, a hooley: swinging from wild hilarity to nostalgic sadness.

hooligan (hū·ligăn). [Origin unascertained.

The word first appears in print in daily newspaper police-court reports in the summer of 1898. Several accounts of the rise of the word, purporting to be based on first-hand evidence, attribute it to a misunderstanding or perversion of *Hooley* or *Hooley's gang,* but no positive confirmation of this has been discovered. The name *Hooligan* figured in a music-hall song of the eighteen-nineties, which described the doings of a rowdy Irish family, and a comic Irish character of the name appeared in a series of adventures in *Funny Folks.*]

A young street rough, a member of a street gang. Also *attrib.* and *transf.*; *spec.* **Hooligan Navy** *U.S. Naut. slang,* the U.S. Coast Guard Service.

1898 *Daily News* 26 July 5/1 It is no wonder..that Hooligan gangs are bred in these vile, miasmatic byways. *Ibid.* 8 Aug. 9/3 The constable said the prisoner belonged to a gang of young roughs, calling themselves 'Hooligans'. **1898** *Daily Tel.* 6 Aug. (Ware), William Lineker, described as a Hooligan, sets upon an inoffensive man. **1898** *Daily Graphic* 30 Aug. 4/4 Mr. White..stated that every Saturday and Sunday nights gangs like the 'Hooligan gang' came to his house, broke the windows, glass, &c., and made disturbances. **1898** *Westm. Gaz.* 15 Sept. 1/2 The Khalifa was, after all, only a sort of Soudanese Hooligan. **1901** *Pall Mall Mag.* Feb. 198 Nobody will claim honesty as a Hooligan virtue. **1922** L. Hisey *Sea Grist* 7 Haven't even been in the Hooligan Navy? Just land lubbers. **1932** H. Walpole *Fortress* iii. 439 Crowds of roughs and hooligans, urged on by the more violent

Chartists, drove their way towards the stands with shouts and threats. **1938** Auden & Isherwood *On Frontier* III. ii. 110, I always suspected that you and your gang of hooligans would rat. **1962** L. Farago *Tenth Fleet* 119 Thus was born the Coastal Picket Patrol or, as the Coast Guard called it, the Corsair Fleet. Its own personnel, mostly amateur yachtsmen, preferred to refer to it as the 'Hooligan Navy'. **1963** *Daily Tel.* 27 Dec. 1/6 Some driving he had seen amounted to 'downright hooligan behaviour'. **1971** *Guardian* 29 July 11/4 Rome's young black-shirted hooligans like to taunt the long-haired guitar-strummers by roaring around them on motor-cycles.

Hence **hoo·ligan** *v. intr.*, to act as a hooligan; also *trans.*, to treat (a person) roughly; **hoo:ligane·sque** *a.*, like a hooligan; **hooliga·nic** *a.*, resembling that of hooligans; **hoo·liganism,** the characteristic behaviour of hooligans, rough horseplay; **hoo·liganize** *v. intr.*, to act as a hooligan.

These derivatives, with the exception of *hooliganism*, are only occasional, but they are inserted here because of their additional testimony to the currency of *hooligan*.

1898 *Pall Mall Gaz.* 19 Aug. 9/3 Any unauthorized person found trespassing on the aforesaid sphere would be Hooliganed without further notice. **1899** *Ibid.* 5 Jan. 2/3 The proprietor of Lord Tennyson (in wax) says that it was a certain young man, who, with others,..when called upon to desist, Hooliganed about and threw the late Laureate's head at him. *Ibid.* 1 Feb. 2/3 Larking about in the usual hooliganesque way. **1902** *Daily Chron.* 20 Sept. 5/6 Stay then your Hooliganic lark. **1898** *Daily Tel.* 12 Aug. 5/7 'Hooliganism', or youthful ruffianism. **1898** *Daily Graphic* 22 Aug. 14/2 The avalanche of brutality which, under the name of 'Hooliganism'..has cast such a dire slur on the social records of South London. **1900** *19th Cent.* July 90 To strike at the very roots of truancy, juvenile crime, and Hooliganism. **1911** *Catholic Times* 1 Sept., The recent outbreak of hooliganism [in Liverpool]. **1955** *Times* 14 June 6/6 In a talk with journalists he denied one by one the Government's charges of hooliganism against Catholics. **1973** *Oxford Mail* 23 Jan. 8/2 The ban had been imposed on safety grounds 'following incidents on Sunday night involving hooliganism by youngsters'. **1901** *Pall Mall Mag.* Feb. 198 The Hooligan..would Hooliganise less..if in his ruffianism he risked a cut of it [*sc.* the whip].

hoon (hūn), *sb.*^{1} *India.* Also hun. [Hindi (Skr. *hūna*).] A gold coin, the pagoda.

1807 F. Buchanan *Journ. Madras* II. 310 Huns, or Pagodas. **1876** J. Grant *Hist. India* I. xxvi. 140/1 The pagoda..was called a *hoon* by the Mohammedans, and a *varaha* by the Hindoos. **1877** J. Dowson *H. M. Elliot's Hist. India* VII. 84 Part of the two *lacs* of *huns* (pagodas), which was the stipulated amount of his annual tribute. **1962** R. A. G. Carson *Coins* 508 Gold was struck in two denominations, the heavier hun or pagoda and the smaller fanam.

hoon (hūn), *sb.*^{2} *Austral. slang.* [Origin unknown.] A lout, a rough; a crazy person, a 'clot'; a ponce.

1938 X. Herbert *Capricornia* xxi. 309 'You flash hoon,' he went on. 'Kiddin' you're white, eh?' **1953** Baker *Australia Speaks* v. 124 Women whose activities are not organised by hoons..are called battlers. **1965** *Telegraph* (Brisbane) 5 July 8/4 *Hoon*, a crackpot. **1967** *Sunday Truth* (Brisbane) 9 July 32/4 Two louts..walked up behind him. The biggest hoon ruffled up his hair and tried to put his half-smoked cigarette in the young man's hair. **1969** *Courier-Mail* (Brisbane) 8 Jan. 2/4 Advertising these locations [*sc.* of radar speed traps], also advertises the locations where they are not being used, thus giving the hot-rod hoons an open go.

hoon, *v.*, var. Hone *v.*^{2}

1837 J. Hogg *Tales by Ettrick Shepherd* II. 235, I heard a kind o' hooning sound. **1955** D. Niland *Shiralee* 36 Macauley felt her scrabbling over the blanket, and then sitting beside his bulk, hooning to herself.

hoondee, hoondi, hoondy, varr. *Hundi.

hoonoomaun, var. *Hanuman.

hoop, *sb.*^{1} Add: **1. c.** A circular ring, often with paper stretched over it, through which acrobats or performing animals leap. Also *fig.*, esp. in phr. *to go* (or *jump*) *through* (*the*) *hoop*(*s*: to undergo an ordeal or trial. Similarly *to put through the hoop*(*s*.

1793 in T. Frost *Circus Life* (1875) 43 Through the Hoop on Fire, fourteen feet high, by Mr. Porter and Mr. Ducrow. **1869** B. Clarke *Crocker* 88 When a rider..has been jumping through paper hoops held up at intervals round the ring. **1875** T. Frost *Circus Life* 185 All aspirants to saw-dust honours..are required to..hold hoops, balloons, banners, &c. **1914** W. W. Gibson *Borderlands* 55 *Merry Andrew*. I missed a hoop This afternoon... I've not missed A hoop since I was six. I'm forty-two. **1917** Wodehouse *Man with Two Left Feet* 192 It was his business to make money, and, when called upon, to jump through hoops and sham dead at the bidding of his wife and daughter Mae. **1919** 'B. Cable' *Old Contempt.* 209 Then Tommy Dodd got hold of his sergeant and 'put him through the hoop'. **1925** Fraser & Gibbons *Soldier & Sailor Words* 120 *Hoop, through the*: up for punishment. **1926** Galsworthy *Silver Spoon* xi. 81 Let the papers jump through their hoops as much as they liked. **1930** M. Kennedy *Fool of Family* xxvii. 275 Disagreeable thoughts were going to assail him...If he had ever let them get hold of him he would never have got through his hoop. *Ibid.* xxx. 314 'Let's hide..upstairs..' 'No use. They'll all come up to look at Henry VIII's bed.' 'Oh, well. Then it's through the hoops.' **1938** H. Nicolson *Diary* 7 Apr. (1966) 333, I come back to find that the F.A. Committee have put Paul through the hoops also, asking whether he is 'pro-Chamberlain' or 'pro-Eden'. **1943** R. Chandler *Lady in Lake* (1944) xxxix. 205 She got the men that way, she could make them jump through hoops. **1958** *Economist* 1 Nov. 390/2 The most controversial new legislation may still be the bill which will oblige any British government to go through the parliamentary hoop when imposing certain economic controls. **1958** 'A. Gilbert' *Death against Clock* 139 He may have jumped through the hoop right away. **1969** *Times* 12 May 15/5 Their..irritations are put through nightly hoops.

2. b. A circular wooden frame in which a cheese is moulded.

[**1790** W. H. Marshall *Rural Econ. Midl. Counties* I. 349 The cheese vats of this district are merely 'hoops' of ash, with a boarden bottom.] **1857** *Trans. Ill. Agric. Soc.* II. 181 These vats warm, scald, and work the curd ready for the hoop without being removed. **1877** *Rep. Vermont Board Agric.* IV. 54 Most of the cheese made about here was bought and shipped almost as soon as it was out of the hoops. **1951** *Oxf. Jun. Encycl.* VII. 156/1 The curd ..is 'milled' or torn into small particles, mixed with salt, and packed into a hoop or mould.

7. (Later examples.)

1857 C. Kingsley *Two Years Ago* II. vi. 226 She drew off a diamond hoop, and put it quietly into his hand. **1926** J. Black *You can't Win* xv. 199, I go in her joint and drop a hoop to one of her frowsy little brums for nine dollars. **1970** C. Major *Dict. Afro-Amer. Slang* 67 *Hoop*, ring.

8. c. *U.S. Basketball.* The (rim of the) basket. Also, a goal scored by throwing the ball through the basket.

1893 in Z. Hollander *Mod. Encycl. Basketball* (1969) 8 The baskets are strong iron hoops, with braided cord netting. **1937** F. C. Allen *Better Basketball* ii. 29 (*heading*) Standardized basketball nomenclature... Baskets—not Buckets,..hoops, nets, or strings. **1967** *Boston* (Mass.) *Herald* 1 Apr. 17/1 Jim Small scored the first hoop of the game. **1969** Z. Hollander *Mod. Encycl. Basketball* xvii. 419 He drove for the hoop and tried to make contact while making the basket.

d. A band in contrasting colour on a jockey's blouse, sleeves, or cap. So **hooped** *a.*

1898 *Dorling's List Epsom Races* 27 May 1/3 Rose hoops, rose cap..black hooped sleeves. **1961** F. C. Avis *Sportsman's Gloss.* 228/2 *Hoops*, narrow bands of white or coloured silks going round the jockey's blouse; also known as Rings. **1970** *Accent* June 35/1 Wives try to get colours as close to those of their husbands... The Duchess of Devonshire's silks are straw with a brown hoop on the cap. *Ibid.* 35/2 (*caption*) Maroon hooped sleeves.

e. *Austral.* A jockey.

1941 Baker *Dict. Austral. Slang* 36 *Hoop*, a jockey. **1957** 'N. Culotta' *They're Weird Mob* (1958) v. 72 Best hoop in the country. **1963** *Sunday Mirror* (Sydney) 20 Jan. 43/1 Glamour hoop Athol Mulley in the saddle. **1967** E. McGirr *Hearse with Horses* ii. 33 Old Paddy was not a great deal more successful as a trainer than I was as a hoop.

13. b. hoop-ash (earlier examples); **hoop-back,** (a chair with) a hooped back; also *attrib.* in *hoop-back chair*; **hoop-pine** (examples); **hoop-skirt** (earlier and later examples); also *fig.*; **hoop-snake,** substitute for def.: a non-venomous American snake, *Farancia abacura*, popularly believed to roll like a hoop; = *horn-snake* (*b*) s.v. Horn *sb.* 29; (add examples); **hoop stress,** the stress in a cylinder or in a spherical shell corresponding to the hoop tension; **hoop tension,** the circumferential tension in a transverse section of a cylinder or in a spherical shell subjected to radial pressure; **hoop-wood,** add to def.: *U.S.* the black ash, *Fraxinus nigra*, or the winterberry, *Ilex lævigata*; in Jamaica, *Zygia latifolia.*

1763 [see *buck-eye 1]. **1832** D. J. Browne *Silva Amer.* 133 On the Ohio it is called Hoop Ash and in Kentucky, Hack Berry. **1905** P. Macquoid *Hist. Eng. Furnit.* II. viii. 198 Early hoop-back chairs..were slow in obtaining favour. **1924** Macquoid & Edwards *Dict. Eng. Furnit.* I. 244 The tall back is reminiscent of early eighteenth century walnut chairs... A deliberate attempt at Oriental effect may be seen in..the shaping of the hoop-back. **1934** *Burlington Mag.* Nov. 204/1 The chair.. has a splat formed of framework..the uprights continue in the top-rail so as to form a fine 'hoop-back'. **1935** [see *comb-back* s.v. *comb *sb.*^{1} 9]. **1952** J. Gloag *Short Dict. Furnit.* 506 The two main types of design in Windsor chairs are: the comb back and the hoop back... In the latter, the back is shaped like a bow, into which the spindles are socketed. **1884** A. Nilson *Timber Trees N.S.W.* xv. 33 (*heading*) Araucaria. (Natural Order Coniferae.).. A. Cunninghamii.—Moreton Bay Pine; Colonial Pine; Hoop Pine.—A noble tree with a pyramidal or somewhat flattened head. **1920** B. Cronin *Timber Wolves* i. 21 Well, what wood are they using for their matches now? I'll tell you. Their substitute is Queensland hoop pine, and I ain't heard any complaints yet. **1956** M. West *Gallows on Sand* xv. 153, I showed her the great hoop-pines, whose seeds had been carried by birds from the mainland [of Australia]. **1969** T. H. Everett *Living Trees of World* 25/1 Another Australian species is the Richmond-river-pine or hoop-pine (*A. cunninghamii*), the latter name deriving from its bark, which has horizontal cracks in encircling bands. **1857** Underhill & Thompson *Elephant Club* 193 Lady with hoop-skirt hails the driver. **1896** *Emporia* (Kan.) *Gaz.* 15 Aug., We have raked the old ash heap of failure..and found an old human hoop skirt who has failed as a business man. **1906** *Springfield Weekly Republ.* 19 July 1 Populism was a 'hoopskirt' article of statesmanship. **1916** E. Pound *Lustra* 54 You're a very depleted fashion, A hoop-skirt, a calash. **1784** J. F. D. Smyth *Tour in U.S.* I. 265 From the above circumstance, peculiar to themselves, they have also derived the appellation of hoop snakes. **1840** *Southern Lit. Messenger* VI. 380/2, I never believed in the existence of hoop-snakes neither, until I went out into the western country. **1937** A. H. Verrill *Strange Reptiles* ii. 7 Thousands of otherwise intelligent and educated persons believe in the mythical 'hoop snake' which is supposed to take its tail in its mouth and roll like a hoop with incredible speed. **1956** C. H. Pope *Reptile World* 156 Tens of thousands of country people see hoop snakes rolling about like hoops, but these snakes quickly stop rolling and crawl when a herpetologist looms in sight. **1909** Webster, Hoop stress. **1930** *Engineering* 23 May 679/2 S is the apparent hoop stress. **1966** C. C. Barnes *Power Cables* (ed. 2) xii. 179 The maximum pressure in the cable is therefore dictated by the hoop stress developed in the sheath. **1973** *Sci. Amer.* Dec. 18/1 The tensile strength must be sufficient to withstand the 'hoop stress' resulting from centrifugal forces, otherwise the [fly]wheel would fly apart. **1896** Hoop tension [see Stress *sb.* 5 c]. **1902** *Kynoch Jrnl.* Oct.–Nov. 17/1 Since the ratio of the inner to outer radius is now 1·595, the hoop tension at the inner surface = 62·8 tons. **1950** *Jrnl. R. Aeronaut. Soc.* LIV. 133 The earliest specimens of these [parachutes]..took account of 'hoop tensions', 'pressure across the fabric', etc. **1821** J. Fowler *Jrnl.* (1898) 21 We get out at our ushal time; at ten miles pased a point of Rocks and a Hoop wood tree on them. **1908** N. L. Britton *N. Amer. Trees* 622 Winterberry—*Ilex lævigata*..is also called the Smooth winterberry and Hoopwood. **1920** Fawcett & Rendle *Flora of Jamaica* IV. 150 (*heading*) Z[ygia] latifolia..Horse wood, hoop wood.

hooped, *a.* Add: **1.** (See also *hoop *sb.*^{1} 8 d.)

3. Rounded like a hoop.

1852 *Trans. Mich. Agric. Soc.* III. 137 The breeder will do well to seek in his animal a proper form, viz...good, hooped ribs. **1934** M. F. McTaggart *Handbk. Horse Owners* II. 40 The ribs should be well hooped and deep.

4. *Comb.* **hooped-back** *a.*, said of a chair with a hooped back. (Cf. **hoop-back.*)

1906 P. Macquoid *Hist. Eng. Furnit.* III. ii. 60 In the hooped-back chair..the splat begins to show signs of subdivision. **1941** *Burlington Mag.* June 187/1 Hooped-back chairs with compass seats were produced in the provinces until after Chippendale's *Director* made its appearance. **1960** H. Hayward *Antique Coll.* 145/1 Hooped-back chair.

hoop-ee, *int.* (Cf. Hoop *int.* and *whoopee.)

1846 J. J. Hooper *Adv. Simon Suggs* iii. 31 Hoop-ee! *won't* they roll over the floor.

hoop-la (hū·plā). Also **houp-la.** [f. Hoop *sb.*^{1} + La *int.*] A game in which persons throw rings on to a surface containing a number of articles, the object being to gain any of these as a prize by throwing a ring so as to encircle it completely. Also *attrib.*

[**1907** *Yesterday's Shopping* (1969) 1031/1 Hoopla!.. The players endeavour to throw balls..through circles poised on the Clown's head and hands.] **1909** *London Mag.* Sept. 26 A new game: Hoop-la! **1910** *Daily Chron.* 14 Jan. 3/5 A showman placed his 'hoopla' near the Promenade at Whitley, Northumberland, and invited the public to throw rings (at so many a penny) for prizes. **1912** A. S. M. Hutchinson *Happy Warrior* v. i. 279 All Maddox's smaller-fry—coker-nut shies, hoop-la's, Living Mermaid. **1924** *Other Lands* Jan. 68/2 Houp-la stalls are a great attraction. **1927** *Blackw. Mag.* Sept. 358/2 We..finally sought refuge from the mob in a 'hoopla' stall, where we tried our luck. **1935** *Punch* 18 Sept. 319/1 One also tried one's hand at clock-golf, Houp-là! and throwing little balls into a bucket from which they instantly sprang out again. **1959** P. H. Johnson *Humbler Creation* xlviii. 329 His wife..had the hoop-la [stall at a fête]. **1964** K. Rosewall in A. Trengove *Art of Tennis* 26 Most people do things like dealing cards, and playing table tennis and hoop-la backhanded. **1973** P. Moyes *Curious Affair of Third Dog* x. 135 You will not turn down my heartfelt appeal to you to preside over the Hoop-La stall.

hoop-la, var. *houp-la *int.*

hoopless (hū·plės), *a.* [f. Hoop *sb.*^{1} + -less.] Having no hoop.

1885 A. Munro *Siren Casket* 65 Two hoopless pails.

hoop-petticoat. 2. Substitute for def.: In full, *hoop-petticoat narcissus* or *daffodil.* A plant of the species *Narcissus bulbocodium* or *N. cantabrica*, so called from the shape of the yellow or white flowers. (Earlier and later examples.)

1731 P. Miller *Gardener's Dict.* (*s.v.* Narcissus) 35 Rush-leaf'd Daffadil, with very narrow Petals, and a large tubulous Cup, commonly call'd The Hoop-Petticoat. **1790** *Curtis's Bot. Mag.* III. tab. 88 (*heading*) Narcissus Bulbocodium. Hoop Petticoat Narcissus. **1841** J. W. Loudon *Ladies' Compan. Flower Garden* 190/1 The genus Narcissus is a very extensive one, embracing, as it does, the Jonquils, the Polyanthus Narcissus, the little Hoop Petticoat, the Poet's Narcissus, and the Daffodils, besides numerous others. **1934** E. A. Bowles *Handbk. Narcissus* xix. 211 It is hard to believe that the white Hoop Petticoat was ever found so far to the north as Cantabrica. **1952** C. E. L. Phillips *Small Garden* xiii. 164 The 'hoop-petticoat daffodil' (*N. bulbocodium*), 6 ins., like a little bugle with virtually no perianth. **1961** P. M. Synge *Collins Guide to Bulbs* 232 Bulbocodium group. These are the hoop petticoats and they are nearly all subsp., varieties or forms of *N. bulbocodium*, a very large and variable sp., the exception being the early white-flowered forms known as *monophyllus* and *foliosus* which

have now been separated under the name *N. cantabricus.* **1970** C. Lloyd *Well-Tempered Garden* 137, I dug up a congested clump of the hoop petticoat daffodil.

hooray (var. Hurrah), *int.* Used in Australia and New Zealand (in Australia also **hooroo** and other variants) in the sense 'good-bye'. Cf. *hurroo *int.* (*sb.*).

1898 *Bulletin* (Sydney) 4 June (*red page*), In many places the salutation 'good-day' or 'good-night' is simply 'Hooray!' **1937** J. A. Lee *Civilian into Soldier* vi. 255 His companion..thrust bac' 'is seat, stood erect, called 'Horray!' and was gone. **1941** Baker *Dict. Austral. Slang* 36 Hooroo. **1945** —— *Austral. Lang.* xiv. 251 Some authentic local equivalents [of *so long!*]..are *hooray! aroo!* and *see you!*.. employed for many years, especially in rural areas, to denote 'good-bye'. **1948** D. Ballantyne *Cunninghams* (1963) i. vi. 35 'Bye-bye, Mr. Cunningham.' 'Hooray,' Gil said. **1960** N. Hilliard *Maori Girl* 128 'Well, hooray.' 'Hooray.' **1963** A. Lubbock *Austral. Roundabout* 83 Be seein' yer soon in England. Hooray! Aroo! Good on yer, Pom. **1965** *N.Z. Listener* 15 Oct. 9/4 Best of luck on the lake. Hooray! **1969** *Coast to Coast 1967–68* 74 The others have, one by one, ..lurched off—'Hooroo!' 'Seeya, mate!'

hooroosh, var. Hurroosh *sb.* and *v.*

1836 *Knickerbocker* VIII. 208 When they were all free, they began to sky-lark and kick up a hooroosh in all quarters. **1839** J. D. Hooker *Jrnl.* in L. Huxley *Life* (1918) I. iv. 91 He used..to start up, take his stick, shout, hooroosh..and scare the poor little snips out of their senses. **1851** H. Melville *Moby Dick* III. xxxiv. 208 What a hooroosh aloft there! **1959** *News Chron.* 21 Oct. 6/5 Sex hormones..went off with a great hooroosh. Both breeders and butchers are now..having second thoughts.

hoose, hooze, *sb.* Delete *local.* Substitute for def.: A parasitic bronchial disease of animals; = Husk *sb.*[2] (Earlier and later examples.)

a **1722** [see Husk *sb.*[2]]. **1922** Joyce *Ulysses* 309 A hoose drench for coughing calves. **1932** Gaiger & Davis *Vet. Path. & Bact.* xxxii. 440 Parasites are a frequent cause of bronchitis in animals, particularly in cattle, sheep and swine. The condition is popularly known as 'husk' or 'hoose'. **1960** W. R. Wooldridge *Farm Animals* (ed. 2) vii. 299 Husk: Hoose: Parasitic Bronchitis. This disease is caused by a heavy infestation of lambs, up to one year of age, with the round worm, *Dictyocaulus filaria.* Adult sheep are fairly resistant to infection.

hoosegow (hū·sgau). *U.S. slang.* [ad. S. Amer. or Mex. Sp. *juzgao* = *juzgado* tribunal:—L. *jūdicātum*, pa. pple. of *jūdicāre* to Judge.] Prison.

1911 *Popular Mag.* 15 May 104/1 No thanks for th' little lady savin' th' bunch of you from th' 'hoose-gow'. **1920** *Public Opinion* 3 Dec. 560/3 Only the keeper and the kept in the hoosegow knew it. **1927** 'J. Barbican' *Confess. Rum-Runner* iv. 47, I have had one dose of the hoosegow, and I can tell you I don't want any more. **1937** J. Worby *Other Half* x. 99 We soon got to the hoose-gow and I was once again frisked for weapons. **1940** Wodehouse *Quick Service* xix. 237 This guy Weatherby is a right guy, and he doesn't go to any hoosegow, not while I have my strength. **1955** *Beaver* Autumn 4 They would cheerfully accept ten years in the hoosegow before they would again face Ole the Terror. **1963** J. Joesten *They call it Intelligence* vi. xxxiii. 293 Since he had already spent..much time in the hoosegow..he was..set free. **1973** D. Ramsay *Deadly Discretion* 163 I'm not going to answer any questions... Okay. Off we go to the hoosegow.

hoosh (hūʃ), *sb. slang.* [Origin unknown.] A kind of thick soup.

1905 R. F. Scott *Voy. 'Discovery'* I. 445 The cook.. proceeded to prepare the ingredients of the *hoosh*, by which term the hot, thick soup that constituted the sledging meal was generally known. **1911** —— *Jrnl.* 29 Nov. in *Last Exped.* (1913) I. xvi. 479 They had some of Chinaman's undercut in their hoosh yesterday. **1919** E. H. Shackleton *South* xii. 239 The hoosh-pot with our precious limpets and seaweed was kicked over in the rush. **1922** *Chambers's Jrnl.* Jan. 73/2 The thick savoury 'hoosh' of pemmican and broken plasmon biscuit.

hoosh (hūʃ), *int.* An exclamation used in driving animals, etc.

1874 Hardy *Far from Madding Crowd* I. x. 131 Saying 'Hoosh!' to the cocks and hens when they go upon your seeds. **1900** *Contemp. Rev.* Oct. 512 A loud 'hoosh' from the Kaffir roused one of the Englishmen.

hoosh (hūʃ), *v. colloq.* [f. prec. word; cf. Shoo *int.* and *v.*] *trans.* To force or turn or drive (an animal, etc.) *off* (or *out*, etc.); also *intr.*, to move (rapidly). Cf. also quot. 1943.

1908 *Athenæum* 11 Apr. 450/1, I hooshed them, hooshed them all into the shed. **1928** A. A. Milne *House at Pooh Corner* vi. 100 'Well done, Pooh...That was a good idea of ours... Hooshing you to the bank like that.' '*Hooshing* me?' said Eeyore in surprise. 'Hooshing *me*? You didn't think I was *hooshed*, did you? I dived. Pooh dropped a large stone on me, and so as not to be struck heavily on the chest, I dived and swam to the bank.' **1933** L. A. G. Strong *Sea Wall* xvii. 283 We could hoosh the whole lot of them off of the line, and the train could go by. **1934** A. Russell *Tramp-Royal in Wild Australia* iii. 27, I untied my camel, 'hooshed' it down and mounted it. **1936** A. Thirkell *August Folly* ix. 283 Oh, she's dressing, and Aunt Palmer hooshed me out. **1939** Joyce *Finnegans Wake* 112 Trust her to propagate the species and hoosh her fluffballs safe through din and danger! **1943** Hunt & Pringle *Service Slang* 39 Hooshing, purely an R.A.F. word, which means landing at great speed. **1956** 'A. Bridge' *Lighthearted Quest* ii. 37 Why do you go hooshing off to find him in this completely wild-cat way?

hooshtah (hū·ʃtā), *int.* Also **hushdar.** [Echoic.] A shout of encouragement, etc., to a camel. Hence as *vb.* Also occas. as *sb.*, a camel.

1903 R. Bedford *True Eyes & Whirlwind* xxxvi. 201 Their string of five camels..were water-swollen, so that they looked like five great footballs set up on sticks. One by one Quinn and Lawler 'hooshta'ed' them to the ground. **1906** *Daily Chron.* 8 Jan. 6/7 So the camel was hooshtahed down and strapped. **1911** C. E. W. Bean '*Dreadnought' of Darling* xxiv. 211 He made a noise, probably 'Hooshta', as he went—'Hooshta' seems to be the only noise an Afghan ever does make to a camel. **1936** F. Clune *Roaming round Darling* xxiv. 258, I remembered over in Cairo the cameliers used to shout 'Hooshta, hooshta' to their camels... Jack the Ripper..returned and wishtered and hooshtered to Galahad, who stopped, and gently genuflected himself while the sore torn-seated Poet dismounted. **1942** C. Barrett *On Wallaby* iv. 62 Many a time we've been out in the Sinai desert guarding a grazing mob of 'hooshtas'. **1964** H. M. Barker *Camels & Outback* 74 All the time the standard oriental 'hushdar' was hissed as if it were spelt with many 's's'.

Hoosier (hū·ʒiəɪ). *U.S.* Also **hoosher.** [Origin unknown.] **a.** A nickname for a native or inhabitant of the state of Indiana.

1826 in *Chicago Tribune* (1949) 2 June 20/3 The Indiana hoosiers that came out last fall is settled from 2 to 4 milds of us. **1834** *Knickerbocker* III. 441 They smiled at my inquiry, and said it was among the 'hoosiers' of Indiana. **1835** J. H. Ingraham *South-West* I. ix. 105 The primitive navies..manned..by 'real Kentucks'—'Buck eyes'—'Hooshers' and 'Snorters'. **1860** Emerson *Cond. Life* ii. 58 These Hoosiers and Suckers are really better than the snivelling opposition. **1885** *Outing* (U.S.) Nov. 152/2 Oh, say, papa. Did you notice that young Hoosier and his bride who sat opposite me at breakfast? **1947** *Harper's Mag.* Jan. 67/2 Other Hoosiers ridicule them as hillbillies. **1958** *Economist* 1 Nov. 417/2 Indiana, whose inhabitants go by the obscure name of Hoosiers, is a deeply conservative state.

b. An inexperienced, awkward, or unsophisticated person.

1846 J. Gregg *Diary & Lett.* 22 Aug. (1941) I. 212 Old King is one of the most perfect samples of a Hoosier Texan I have met with. Fat, chubby, ignorant, and loquacious as Sancho Panza..we could believe nothing he said. **1857** E. L. Godkin in R. Ogden *Life E. L. Godkin* I. 157 The mere 'cracker' or 'hoosier', as the poor [southern] whites are termed. **1874** J. W. Long *Amer. Wild-Fowl Shooting* viii. 144 'Greenhorns' and 'hoosiers', as the regular hunters call such fellows. **1926** *Amer. Mercury* Jan. 64/2 The word hoosier is applied to any one who is incompetent. **1955** *Publ. Amer. Dial. Soc.* xxiv. 174 Thus *hoosier grift* is the crowd at a country fair.

c. *attrib.* Of or belonging to Indiana. **Hoosier cake** (see quot. 1859).

1839 J. Plumbe *Sk. Iowa* 46 (Th.), The Hoosier State has reason to rejoice in the amount and value of its waters. **1845** *Knickerbocker* XXV. 374 Three hundred miles of Hoosier mud. **1859** Bartlett *Dict. Amer.*, *Hoosier cake*, a Western name for a sort of coarse gingerbread, which, say the Kentuckians, is the best bait to catch a hoosier with, the biped being fond of it. **1871** E. Eggleston *Hoosier Schoolmaster* (1872) Pref., It has been in my mind since I was a Hoosier boy. **1878** J. H. Beadle *Western Wilds* i. 18 No grammar of the 'Hoosier' language has ever been published. **1907** *Chicago Evening Post* 4 May 5 A rose festival will be given by the Indiana Society of Chicago, comprising hoosier business men of the city. **1916** *Daily Colonist* (Victoria, B.C.) 23 July 1/2 He [*sc.* James Whitcomb Riley] made a study of the 'Hoosier' dialect. **1956** H. Gold *Man who was not with It* (1965) xiv. 116 She left a print like feathers tipped with toes in the Hoosier loam. **1972** *Christian Science Monitor* 28 Sept. 16/3 Some folkway yarns about logrolling in the early Hoosier days.

Hence **Hoo·sierism,** a peculiarity of Indiana, esp. in speech.

1843 'R. Carlton' *New Purchase* 63 Thus the cabin lady kept on doing up her small stock of English into Hoosierisms and other figures. **1878** J. H. Beadle *Western Wilds* i. 18 The native of Indiana finds..that he must drop some of his 'Hoosierisms'.

hoot, *v.* Add: **1. c.** To laugh. *colloq.*

1926 T. E. Lawrence *Seven Pillars* (1935) x. cxxii. 659 At this onslaught I cackled out like a chicken, with the wild laughter of strain... I hooted out again. **1928** S. Vines *Humours Unreconciled* xv. 201 The first time I came across it, 'Shakespeare has no bloody relation with Schiller', I just hooted. **1959** N. Mailer *Advts. for Myself* (1961) 168 The others hoot, they giggle, they are weak from the combination of their own remarks and the action of the plot. **1969** *New Yorker* 28 June 37/2 She'd mention him tragically, then hoot with laughter.

4. Also, to emit the sound of a motor-horn (said of the horn, the motor vehicle, or the driver). Also *trans.*

1912 Beerbohm in *Seven Men* (1919) 129 Our car neither slackened nor hooted. **1927** [see *honk *sb.* b]. **1957** A. Clarke *Later Poems* (1961) 58 Badge and holy medal guide Your cars home, hooting through our dirtiest lanes. **1966** J. Betjeman *High & Low* 65 Who dares to come hooting at *me*? I only give way to a Jag.

hoot, *sb.*[1] Add: **1. b.** A sound produced mechanically by a motor-horn, factory whistle, or the like.

1904 A. B. F. Young *Compl. Motorist* (ed. 2) xii. 258 You should have a connection from the exhaust pipe led into a small reservoir and thence into the horn, so that on turning a tap a prolonged hoot will be emitted. **1927** *Scots Observer* 14 May 17/1 An imperative horn hoot made him turn his head. **1963** H. Garner in R. Weaver *Canad. Short Stories* (1968) 2nd Ser. 52 A long hoarse hoot of the factory whistle announced the lunch break.

c. A laugh; a cause of laughter, a joke, a very amusing situation. *colloq.*

1942 Berrey & Van den Bark *Amer. Thes. Slang* § 281/4 Something humorous,..*hoot. Ibid.* § 408/1 Humorist; amusing person,..*hoot.* **1969** *Punch* 17 Dec. 990 All the chaps chuck their clubs in a heap, and the wives have to pick a club and go off with the owner; it's going to be an absolute hoot! **1970** 'D. Halliday' *Dolly & Cookie Bird* iii. 23 Jansy can imitate anybody. So can I... We'd have the whole form in hoots. **1971** *Guardian* 27 Sept. 10/1 It's a little quaint ('a bit of a hoot,' Dews would say) to hear him mention Peter Brook first. **1973** 'D. Halliday' *Dolly & Starry Bird* xiii. 188, I started talking shop, a hoot for Jacko, if he had heard me.

hoot (hūt), *sb.*[2] *colloq.* (orig. *U.S.*). [Perhaps the same as Hoot *sb.*[1] or *int.* Cf. *hooter[2].] The smallest amount or particle; a whit or atom. Chiefly with negative and in phrases *to give* (*care, matter*) *two hoots* (*a hoot*).

1878 J. H. Beadle *Western Wilds* xxxviii. 615, I got onto my reaper and banged down every hoot of it before Monday night. **1923** R. D. Paine *Comr. Rolling Ocean* xii. 214, I am glad of that even if he did tell me that as a supercargo I wasn't worth a hoot in hades. **1925** N. Venner *Imperfect Imposter* iv, I can't see this place gives a hoot whether I'm here or not. **1925** Fraser & Gibbons *Soldier & Sailor Words* 120 I don't care two hoots in hell. **1926** A. P. Herbert *She-Shanties* 36 We did not care a hoot. **1926** T. E. Lawrence *Seven Pillars* (1935) vi. lxxx. 447 Not that my maimed will now cared a hoot about the Arab Revolt. **1927** *Observer* 9 Oct. 13 It doesn't matter two hoots how much Oxford is filmed. **1939** Joyce *Finnegans Wake* 351, I did not care three tanker's hoots..for any feelings. **1943** K. Tennant *Ride on Stranger* xix. 214, I don't see that it matters two hoots in hell if you don't function. **1947** O. Sitwell *Novels of G. Meredith* 4 The human being who is not worth a tinker's cuss,—or, in a more elegant simile, two hoots—does not exist. **1957** A. Grimble *Return to Islands* iv. 78 Not that they gave a hoot for what I might say. **1963** V. Nabokov *Gift* iv. 235 He most definitely did not give a hoot for the opinions of specialists. **1966** *Listener* 27 Oct. 613/1 Winston Churchill was idiosyncratic in that he did not care a hoot about being thought a gentleman.

hoot (hūt), *sb.*[3] *N.Z. slang.* Also 9 **hootoo, hout, hutu,** etc. [ad. Maori *utu* Utu.] Money paid as recompense; (as a generic term) money.

1820 J. Butler in Barton *Earliest N.Z.* (1927) iii. 66 He and his people went and robbed Boyle for the (hutu) payment. **1828** W. Horton *N.Z.* 1/3 He then seized one of our axes..saying that should be the *hutu* or payment for what he had done. **1830** G. L. Craik *New Zealanders* x. 242 What he now wanted, he said, was *hootoo*, or payment. **1834** E. Markham *N.Z. or Recollections of it* (MS.) 5 The Cabin boy counted 8 Teeth marks and the Hout or Compensation money was 8 Figs of Tobacco. **1842** *N.Z. Jrnl.* LXI. 117/2 Ask them [*sc.* Maoris] what is the *hute* or price. **1879** J. Barr *Old Identities* xxxvii. 333 The land that's waste they'll parcel oot..And sell't to all that's got the hoot. **1917** *Chrons. N.Z.E.F.* 5 Sept. 28/1 Pig Island N.C.O.'s only go for the extra couple of bob a day..the hoot is all they're chasing. *c* **1926** 'Mixer' *Transport Workers' Song Bk.* 5 He gets his 'hoot', forgets his dues. **1938** X. Herbert *Capricornia* xx. 274 On the construction you could make a pot of hoot in no time. **1953** *Landfall* VII. 250 Put on a quid for me, for a place—I've got the hoot. **1961** B. Crump *Hang on a Minute* 144 Reckon we ought to have something to aim at, like getting a bit of hoot together to buy a little farm or a place to live or something. **1967** K. Giles *Death & Mr Prettyman* ii. 57, I got the idea of starting a chain of those places..for blokes without much hoot and wanting a clean bed. **1970** *N.Z. Listener* 30 Jan. 12/2 'Hoot?' I said. I hadn't heard that word for money in years. I suppose in an isolated cut-off place..slang would ossify.

hootch, var. *hooch, *hoochie.

hootchy-kootchy (hū·tʃi,kū·tʃi), *sb.* and *a.* Also **hoochie(-y)-coochie, hootchie-kootchie, hootchy-kootch,** etc. [Origin unascertained.] **A.** *sb.* A kind of erotic dance. **B.** *attrib.* and *Comb.*; also as *adj.*, indecent, 'suggestive'.

[**1890** B. Hall *Turnover Club* vii. 75, I have been told that one night 'Hoochy-Coochy' Rice, the minstrel man—they always call Billy 'Hoochy-Coochy' because he invariably says that whenever he comes on stage—entered [Charlie] Hoyt's room..and stole a new song.] **1898** F. P. Dunne *Mr. Dooley in Peace & War* (1899) 18 He's seen th' hootchy-kootchy an' th' Pammer House barber shop. *Ibid.* 36 Hootchy-kootchy girls dancin' before him. **1901** *Everybody's Mag.* Oct. 437/2 The Doctor was too professional to relish the hootchie cootchie dance. **1904** [see *bark *v.*[1] 2 b]. **1925** *Manch. Guardian Weekly* Aug. 103/4 That hootchy-kootchy sort of intonation. **1931** 'D. Stiff' *Milk & Honey Route* xiv. 155 Enlivening them with the vitality of a hoochy-coochy dancer. **1934** F. Scott Fitzgerald *Tender is Night* xv. 273 There was the sound of a whining, tinkling hootchy-kootchy show. **1945** *Record Changer* (Fairfax, Virginia) Jan., The Chicago World Fair of 1893..gave the widest possible publicity to the new Negro dances..the cakewalk, the pasamala, the hoochie koochie, the bully dance and the bombershay. **1949** R. Harvey *Curtain Time* v. 38 They expected a theatre man to be brassy and leering, like a sideshow barker at a hoochie-koochie tent. **1950** Blesh & Janis *They all played Ragtime* viii. 149 A spate of exotic dances became the talk, from the hoochie-coochie to the bombashay. **1962** W. Stegner *Wolf Willow* iv. iii. 256 A travelling group of hootchie-kootchie dancers pitched a tent in the brush and sent their impressario through town

advertising 'performances'. **1973** *Parade* 24 June 12/1 I'm trying to counteract the hootchy-kootchy aura that the dance has.

hoot(e)nanny, hootananny (hū·t(ə)næni). orig. *U.S. dial.* [Origin unknown.] **1.** A 'thingumajig'. **2.** An informal session or concert of folk music and singing. Also *transf.*

1929 *Amer. Speech* V. 151 *Hootananny*, the same as gadget. **1940** *Washington* (Seattle) *New Dealer* 25 July 4 (Advt.), The New Dealer's Midsummer Hootenanny. You Might Even Be Surprised! **1959** [see *CEILIDH]. **1962** W. SCHIRRA in *Into Orbit* 31 Don't worry about it. That's just the hootenanny valve on the watchamacallit fluttering a little. **1963** *Daily Mail* 11 Sept. 8/4 Hootenanny..is to the folk singer what a jam session is to the jazzman. **1964** *Radio Times* 5 Mar. 25/1 The Hoot'nanny Show. **1964** *Punch* 2 Sept. 348/1 A report of one of the side-shows in the psychiatrists' hootenanny held in London last week. **1964** MRS. L. B. JOHNSON *White House Diary* 13 Jan. (1970) 44, I love folk music, but the name 'Hootenanny' rather repels me. **1972** *Time* 5 June 4/2 Memorial Day: a three day national hootenanny.

hooter¹. Add: **c.** The horn of a motor vehicle.

1908 *Lincoln Rutland & Stamford Merc.* 19 June 5 No hooter was sounded on the car when rounding this dangerous corner. **1972** M. IRVING *Mr Purpose* 10 Mike pulled up outside Joanna's house, beeped on the hooter and she appeared.

d. *slang.* The nose.

1958 F. NORMAN *Bang to Rights* 52 He held it [*sc.* a handkerchief] up to his face as though he was going to blow his hooter. **1972** *Times* 18 July 12/5 Derek Griffiths is a young coloured comedian with a face like crushed rubber..and a hooter to rival Cyrano de Bergerac.

hooter². *U.S. colloq.* = *HOOT *sb.*²

1839 *Havana* (N.Y.) *Republican* 21 Aug. (Th.), Now the Grampus [*sc.* a vessel] stopt, and didn't buge [= budge] one hooter. **1889** *Commercial* (Cincinnati) 17 Oct., It has not harmed the Republican cause in Ohio a hooter. **1896** *Harper's Mag.* XCII. 784/1 Now I can have all I want, I don't care a hooter! **1900** E. A. DIX *Deacon Bradbury* xii, 'Do you mean that you don't know anything about the matter at all?'..'Not a hooter.'

Hoover (hū·vəɹ). Also **hoover. 1.** (With capital initial.) The proprietary name of a make of vacuum cleaner (patented in 1927). **2.** *Loosely.* (With small initial.) Any vacuum cleaner. Hence as *v. trans.*, to clean with a Hoover (or, by extension, any vacuum cleaner). Also *intr.*

1926–7 *Army & Navy Stores Catal.* 115 (Advt.), A Hoovered room..is..free from dust. **1934** *Punch* 10 Jan. 36/1 Her bodywork's smart and strikes the eye Clean-swept as though with a Hoover. **1934** S. BECKETT *More Pricks than Kicks* 67 He waddled out of the bar..into the lowly public..like a bit of dirt into a Hoover. **1939** N. STREATFEILD *Luke* 187, I was Hoovering my passage. **1940** H. G. WELLS *All Aboard for Ararat* iii. 91, I shall feel like a man trying to sell Hoover cleaners to an Arab encampment in a dust storm. **1944** M. SHARP *Cluny Brown* x. 68 Are you the one who hoovers the east corridor? **1946** M. DICKENS *Happy Prisoner* ix. 185 I've been swept out of the kitchen, and dusted out of the dining-room, and Hoovered out of the drawing-room. **1955** P. WENTWORTH *Vanishing Point* xi. 69 It was Miss Maxwell who hoovered the carpet and dusted all those innumerable ornaments. **1960** P. MORTIMER *Saturday Lunch with Brownings* 202 Louisa was vacuuming the sitting-room..'Do you mind moving, because I want to Hoover over there?' **1960** C. WILSON *Ritual in Dark* I. v. 101 The carpeting was a plain fawn colour, and looked as if it had only just been hoovered. **1971** *Engineer* 11 Nov. 66/3 How many housewives Hoover the carpet with an Electrolux?

Hooverize (hū·vərəiz), *v. U.S.* [f. the name of Herbert C. *Hoover* (1874–1964), food commissioner 1917–19, and President of the U.S. 1929–33 + -IZE.] *intr.* To be sparing or economical, esp. in the use of food.

1917 H. B. GROSS in *N.Y. Tribune* 13 June 10/7 It is now assured that Mr. Hoover is about to become our food regulator..and since he has..exhorted the public to exercise the utmost economy in the use of foodstuffs.. I suggest that 'to Hooverize' be universally adopted as expressing the assistance every one of us..can render in that direction. **1919** W. T. GRENFELL *Labrador Doctor* (1920) ii. 20 To make sure that there were no truants, all hands were forced to 'Hooverize'. **1932** *Blue Valley Farmer* (Okla. City) 7 Jan. 5/6 Once before he made us Hooverize When Wilson had his war.

Hence **Hoo·verizing** *vbl. sb.*

1918 *Lit. Digest* 12 Jan. 14/2 Hooverizing is commonly regarded as something new. **1918** *Harper's Bazaar* Mar. 62/2 The butter-colored straw with its horn of abundance, overflowing with many colored fruits.., is doubly significant to-day with our enforced Hooverizing.

Hooverville (hū·vəɹvil). *U.S.* [f. the name of Herbert C. *Hoover* (see prec. word) + *-ville* terminal element in many place-names.] A temporary shanty town.

The reference is to the temporary accommodation provided for unemployed workers in the economic depression of the early 1930s.

1933 *New Republic* 24 May 40/1 Hoovervilles are in a separate nation, with separate codes. **1939** J. STEINBECK *Grapes of Wrath* xix. 319 There was a Hooverville on the edge of every town. **1946** V. LINCOLN in *55 Short Stories from New Yorker* (1952) 36, I found White Creek Row. It was the town's Hooverville..a tragic, shocking, sordid shanty town. **1949** *Sat. Rev.* 6 Aug. 116 They called them 'Hoovervilles'. Evicted families lived in tin-and-cardboard shacks. **1952** *Economist* 6 Sept. 554/2 A tragic island of unemployment, a new, 1952 Hooverville. **1973** J. JONES *Touch of Danger* xviii. 108 It was all like some weird..Hooverville. They were cooking their suppers over the open fires.

hop, *sb.*¹ Add: **1. b.** Usu. in *pl.* Beer. Also (as *hop*) in *Comb.* Chiefly *Austral.* and *N.Z. slang.*

1929 W. R. BURNETT *Little Caesar* VI. iv. 218 That dame's full of hop. **1930** *Bulletin* (Sydney) 1 Jan. 11/4 The proprietor provided a beer party, and the riot that arose out of the hop-drinking led to the school's first raid. **1940** F. SARGESON *Man & Wife* 24 Before Bill came back half a dozen Maoris had shouted her, and each time she had less than half a glass of beer... She was keen enough on the hops he said, but she was like that.

3*. A narcotic drug; *spec.* opium.

1887 *Lantern* (New Orleans) 14 May 4/2 As long as a smoker can obtain his 'hop'. **1903** ADE *In Babel* 110 Me settin' around on my shoulder-blades lookin' like one o' these bamboo boys full o' hop. **1911** C. B. CHRYSLER *White Slavery* xi. 89 When a 'fiend' is full of 'hop' he is cunning as the devil. **1916** [see *COOK *v.*¹ 2 d]. **1924** G. BRONSON-HOWARD *Devil's Chaplain* vi. 97 It was he who controlled the available supply of 'hop'. **1933** C. DE LENOIR *Hundredth Man* iv. 63 'Sure,' I replied, 'but what are you going to do when you can't get a card of "hop" for love or money?' **1955** *U.S. Senate Hearings* (1956) VIII. 4161 Opium in the underworld is referred to [as]..'hop'.

4. a. (sense 3*) *hop-dream, -pipe.*

1896 H. M. BLOSSOM *Checkers* viii. 169 Half the time I think that I must be asleep, and trying to 'cash a hop-dream'. **1931** E. LINKLATER *Juan in Amer.* v. 401, I listened like I was in a hop-dream. **1934** J. M. CAIN *Postman always rings Twice* xiv. 163 'That paper..was still in the files, see?'..'You mean that hop dream she called a confession?' **1887** *Lantern* (New Orleans) 21 May 4/1 The rising smoke that curls up from the bowl of the 'hop' pipe. **1926** H. CRANE *Let.* 19 Jan. (1965) 259 He might as well be in elfin land with a hop pipe in his mouth.

b. hop-back (examples); **hop-bush** (later examples); **hop fiend** *slang* = *HOPHEAD 1; **hop joint** *slang*, an opium den; **hop-pad** *slang* = **hop joint*; **hop toy** *slang*, a container used for smoking opium.

1888 F. FAULKNER *Theory & Practice Mod. Brewing* (ed. 2) ix. 145 The well-boiled wort filtered from hops and coagulated precipitate—and what this amounts to is seen under the false-bottom plates of hop-back—left on cooler floor..undergoes..evaporation. **1892** H. E. WRIGHT *Handy Bk. Brewers* i. 20 The boiling having lasted from one and a half to two hours..the copper is 'turned out' or 'struck', the boiling wort, hops and all, rushing out through an opened valve or tap into the *hop-back*, a vessel sometimes rectangular, sometimes circular in shape. **1937** 'N. BLAKE' *There's Trouble Brewing* ii. 51 'Shall I send a man to look in the hop-back?' he added. 'The hop-back?' asked Nigel mystified. 'That's right. Where the wort drains into.' **1936** F. CLUNE *Roaming round Darling* xvii. 163 Lemon-bushes, minus the lemon, and a hop-bush, not hopping; but O'Malley said the old people used this bush for making bread. **1968** K. WEATHERLY *Roo Shooter* 108 A thick patch of hop bush. **1898** L. J. BECK *N.Y. Chinatown* xviii. 165 A hop fiend went on a weary stroll, In search of a friend who a pill could roll. **1911** C. B. CHRYSLER *White Slavery* xi. 89 Opium smokers, 'hop fiends' or 'hop heads' as they are called, are the fiercest of all the White Slavers. **1887** *Lantern* (New Orleans) 4 June 5/2 The police..raided them 'hop joints'. **1905** J. LONDON *Jacket* xvi. 212 Chinatown dumps and hop-joints. **1923** E. WALLACE *Clue of New Pin* xix. 167 'Running a philanthropic hop joint?' asked the other sarcastically. **1931** D. RUNYON *Guys & Dolls* (1932) i. 25 They find they are nothing but speak-easies, although one is a hop joint. **1935** A. J. POLLOCK *Underworld Speaks* 58/2 *Hop joint*, a place where opium is bought and smoked by addicts. **1946** MEZZROW & WOLFE *Really Blues* (1957) xiv. 245 A little..coal bin.. we cleaned out and converted into our hop-pad. **1881** *N.Y. Medical Record* 5 Nov. 512/1, I procured a full outfit for smoking [opium]..: A pipe..and a buffalo-horn box (*hop toy*) for holding the opium. **1887** Hop toy [see *COOK *v.*¹ 2 d]. **1926** J. BLACK *You can't Win* xvii. 238 At last the little horn container, the 'hop toy', is empty. **1955** *U.S. Senate Hearings* (1956) VIII. 4162 Hop toy—container for smoking opium.

hop, *sb.*² Add: **1. c.** *to catch* (or *take*) *on the hop*: to take unawares, to surprise, to catch in the act.

1868 *Broadside Ballad, The Chickaleary Cove* (Farmer), For to catch me on the hop..You must wake up very early in the morning. **1872** R. D. BLACKMORE *Maid of Sker* I. xxv. 301 He caught me on the hop; at a moment of rumours and serious warnings. **1887** *Brit. Med. Jrnl.* 21 May 1103/1 The attendants taking him, as it were, 'on the hop'. **1927** R. A. FREEMAN *Certain Dr. Thorndyke* I. xi, The police..caught him fairly on the hop with all the stolen property in his possession. **1947** 'N. SHUTE' *Chequer Board* iii. 68 But when you catch them on the hop, then you got to be plenty tough. **1959** *New Statesman* 14 Nov. 654/2 Some months ago our second child caught us on the hop and Jean had him here in this two roomed house. **1973** A. BEHREND *Samarai Affair* viii. 83 Ships are wayward things, and she may have taken a sudden turn which caught Gosling on the hop.

d. That distance which can be or is traversed in an aircraft or motor vehicle at one stretch; one stage of a long-distance journey.

1909 *Flight* 3 July 398/1 M. Breguet has a biplane there and has made one or two short 'hops'. **1927** *Daily News* 7 June 7/1 By flying from New York to Eisleben..in one hop. **1931** D. RUNYON *Guys & Dolls* (1932) x. 214 Finally after an extra long hop in an automobile we come to the outskirts of a..little burg. **1954** A. HUXLEY *Let.* 9 May (1969) 707 We leave for Cairo the day after tomorrow.. then proceed to Beirut, Damascus and Istambul—short hops by air. **1958** *Observer* 10 Aug. 5/8 Companies.. operate their jets on a number of economically valuable short hops. **1968** K. WEATHERLY *Roo Shooter* 69 They had about three hundred miles to go, and because of the road conditions they decided to do it in two hops.

e. *Radio.* A transmission path from one point on the earth to another that involves a single reflection from some region of the atmosphere.

1939 *Proc. Inst. Radio Engin.* XXVII. 640/2 The great-circle multiple-hop mode of propagation usually observed during all-daylight-path periods with 18-megacycle signals. **1966** *Electronics* 17 Oct. 137 This 178-mile tropo hop will connect Flyingsdales [*sic*] Moor, a ballistic missile early warning radar site..to Martlesham Heath.

f. *to go on the hop, to play the hop*: to play truant. *slang.* (Cf. *HOP *v.*¹ 6 a.)

1959 I. & P. OPIE *Lore & Lang. Schoolch.* xvii. 372 A truant may also..be said to be..'hopping it' (in Rochdale 'going on the hop'). **1968** L. BERG *Risinghill* 15 Another boy said: I got the cane for playing the hop... Playing the hop, and fighting.

g. *long hop* (Cricket): see LONG *a.*¹ 18 d.

2. (Later examples.)

1892 KIPLING *Barrack-r. Ballads* 64 To dance with blowzy housemaids at the regimental hops. **1948** J. BETJEMAN *Sel. Poems* 115 You going to the Hanks's hop to-night? **1970** D. M. DAVIN *Not Here, Not Now* II. iii. 65 What about coming to the Arts Faculty bob hop on Saturday?

b. *on the hop*: on the go, with no chance to relax, busy, active; enjoying oneself.

1863 T. THOMPSON in E. Corvan et al. *Choice Collection Tyneside Songs* 129 Wiv some varry canny chiels, All on the hop and murry. **1892** E. J. MILLIKEN *'Arry Ballads* 22 A fierce-looking party, all elbows, was likeways A deal on the 'op. **1908** G. H. LORIMER *J. Spurlock* iv. 78 I'd been on the hop ever since morning, for being in love with Anita was a strenuous calling. **1923** J. MANCHON *Le Slang* 158 *To be on the hop*, être en bombe. **1952** A. HUXLEY *Let.* 29 Sept. (1969) 652 C is kept on the hop all the time, fetching, carrying, shopping etc.

3. a. Also *spec.*, as an athletic event. Also *hop, step, and long jump*. Hence *hop, step, and jumper*. (Further examples.)

1760 STERNE *Tr. Shandy* (ed. 3) I. xii. 48 Yorick.. would as often answer with a pshaw!—and if the subject was started in the fields—with a hop, skip, and a jump, at the end of it. **1906** *Westm. Gaz.* 30 Apr. 7/1 The preliminaries of the hurdles, standing high jump, hop-step, and long jumps will also be decided. **1908** *Times* 7 July 16/5 July 25..10 a.m.—Athletics—hop, step, and jump. *Ibid.* 25 July 10/1 The hop, step, and jump fell to the United Kingdom, when an Irishman, T. J. Ahearne, created a British record of 48 ft. 11¼ in. **1909** *Daily Chron.* 24 Sept. 9/3 The hop-step-and-long-jump handicap. **1928** *Observer* 17 June 28/4 The only hop, step, and jumper of quality. **1935** *Encycl. Sports* 349/2 *Hop-Step-and-Jump*, Athletic event, of very ancient practice in the North of the British Isles. Now included in the Olympic Games, it has become the object of much specialization. Known also as the hop, skip and jump. **1961** CHAPMAN & ABRAHAMS *Track & Field Athletics* x. 71 It is not often that a Hop, Step and Jump athlete is able to use the more efficient Hitch-kick long jump action. **1966** *Publ. Amer. Dial. Soc.* XLVI. 21 The paper had to be a *hop, skip, and jump* through the various sorts of annotations that Schele De Vere had made.

d. Used as adv. phr.

1906 *Smart Set* June 102/1 To go hop, skip and jump over the earth's surface.

Hop (hɒp), *sb.*³ *Austral. slang.* [Abbrev. of *John Hop*: see *JOHN I c.] A policeman.

1923 D. H. LAWRENCE *Kangaroo* xvi. 356 It's our boys who've got things in hand. And handed them over to the Hops. **1933** *Bulletin* (Sydney) 8 Feb. 12 The Hops were taking the shattered body out of the water. **1959** BAKER *Drum* II. 118 *Hop*, a policeman.

hop, *v.*¹ Add: **4. c.** To jump on to (a moving vehicle); to obtain (a ride, a lift) in this way; to catch (a train, etc.). *colloq.* (orig. *U.S.*).

1909 W. STEVENS *Let.* 21 Jan. (1967) 125, I used to 'hop' coal-trains and ride up the Lebanon Valley. **1918** in F. A. Pottle *Stretchers* (1930) 214 The other day, I hopped a truck and went 'to the front'. **1929** *Lit. Digest* 30 Nov. 30/2 Boys are predominantly the ones who 'hop' rides on trucks, trains and other vehicles. **1935** M. M. ATWATER *Murder in Midsummer* xiii. 117 Before midnight he intended to hop the twelve-twenty out. **1940** J. CARY *Charley is My Darling* xlii. 167, I hopped a lorry once with Su, half-way to Twyport. **1967** C. O. SKINNER *Madame Sarah* vi. 119 She and some friends hopped a train for Liverpool and drove to the Cross Zoo.

6. a. *to hop the wag*: to play truant. *slang.*

1861 MAYHEW *London Labour* III. 113, I used to hop the wag from school. **1903** J. LONDON *People of Abyss* xxiii. 280 The boy told a certain bishop, 'At ten we 'ops the wag...' Which is to say, at ten they play truant. **1959** *Guardian* 24 Oct. 4/5 Episodic truancy during the last year at school—known as 'hopping the wag'. **1964** M. TODD *Ever Such a Nice Lady* iii. 30 The two of them had 'hopped the wag' from school one afternoon.

c. *to hop it*: to be off, go away quickly.

1914 W. OWEN *Let.* 24 Aug. (1967) 279, I should hop it, immejit. **1915** *Scotsman* 13 Jan. 7/3 The Zeppelin kept

a few miles in the rear of us, and finally hopped it. **1916** 'BOYD CABLE' *Action Front* 186 'Are we going to stick it here?' said one. 'Didn't the sergeant say something about 'opping it?' **1924** M. NEWMAN *Consummation* IV. xviii. 216 J. H. hopped it for all he was worth. A perfect tornado of bombs pursued him. **1934** T. S. ELIOT *Rock* i. 12 The commission bloke on the door looks at us and says: "op it!'

d. *to hop in* (*out*): to get into (out of) a car, etc.

1914 KIPLING *Diversity of Creatures* (1917) 388 Oh, hop in and drive... We want that beer! **1933** M. DE LA ROCHE *Master of Jalna* viii. 89 Why don't you hop in,..and go with them? **1955** M. GILBERT *Sky High* xiv. 196 Hop out, Rupert. **1963** B. S. JOHNSON *Travelling People* i. 23 I'm making for Aberfyllin,..but I think I can take you about thirty miles along this road... Hop in. **1972** D. DEVINE *Three Green Bottles* 8 A car had pulled up just down the road... 'Hop in. I'll take you.'

e. With *off*. To be off, depart; *spec.*, to start on a 'hop' (*HOP *sb.*[2] 1 d) in an aircraft.

1922 C. E. MONTAGUE *Disenchantment* ii. 18 What the 'ell did you ever come to me for? 'Op off! Out of it! **1926** —— *Rough Justice* viii. 113 Molly and Auberon suddenly felt the breathless stillness of the place infringed by a low, earnest voice on the shore near them: 'It's 'im! 'Op orf!' It was the voice of an aged ferryman they knew. **1926** *Daily Colonist* (Victoria, B.C.) 7 July 5/5 The detailed story of Lieutenant Reece reveals the fact that on Friday morning..he had hopped off from Digby Island for Naden Harbor. The plane was heavily loaded, and it was not without some difficulty that he got away. **1930** *Morning Post* 5 Aug. 9/2 Given favourable weather, he will hop off for England to-morrow, his first stage to Bima..taking him across the Timor Sea. **1934** W. STEVENS *Let.* 12 Feb. (1967) 267 If all goes well, I shall hop off for Florida in a day or two.

f. Colloq. phr. *to hop into bed* (*with*): to have (casual) sexual intercourse (with). Cf. *BED *sb.* 6 c.

1951 E. COXHEAD *One Green Bottle* viii. 229 Hopping quick into bed would be all you'd think of. **1968** 'J. WELCOME' *Hell is where you find It* iii. 44 His features were quite strikingly handsome... You'd think every woman he met would have only one thought and that was to hop into bed with him. **1971** C. WHITMAN *Death Suspended* i. 22 Duncan wouldn't waste too much time on her unless she was willing to hop into bed.

7. hop-off *Aeronaut.*, the take-off of an aircraft; **hop-over** *Army slang*, an assault; hence **hop over** *v.*, to attack, to go 'over the top'.

1926 *Daily Colonist* (Victoria, B.C.) 13 Jan. 1/7 The expedition planes will be..flown..to Point Barrow, where the hop-off for the Polar flight will be made. **1927** S. BENT *Ballyhoo* i. 36 To the mere hop-off by Lindbergh the *New York Times* gave three first page eight-column streamers. **1918** H. MATTHEWS in Murdoch & Drake-Brockman *Austral. Short Stories* (1951) 243 They didn't have the dash of the Australians in the hop-over. **1929** *Papers Mich. Acad. Sci., Arts & Lett.* X. 299 *Hop over*, Australian for 'go over the top'. **1933** PARTRIDGE *Words, Words, Words!* III. 194 In the hop-over, many hoped for and some got a wound sufficiently serious to cause them to be sent 'home'.

hop-dog. Add: **1.** Also a cutting tool used in hop-gardens.

1880 [in Dict.]. **1914** BLUNDEN *Waggoner* (1920) 50 Sharpened hopdog, at whose blow The stubborn cluster drops. *Ibid.* 70 *Hopdog*, long-handled curved knife for hop-gardens.

2. (Earlier and later examples.)

1872 C. M. YONGE *P's & Q's* iv. 30 The beautiful cocoon which the hopdog was spinning—a delicate apple-green fellow, with white tooth-brush tufts down his back, black velvet slashings..and a rose-coloured feather in his tail. **1961** R. SOUTH *Moths Brit. Is.* I. 117 As it is, or was previous to the modern 'washing', common in hop gardens at picking time, it was christened the 'hop dog'. **1968** P. JENNINGS *Living Village* 100 There are still people who use expressions such as.. *hot cat* (hairy caterpillar), *hop dog* (green caterpillar).

hope, *sb.*[1] Add: **4. a.** Freq. in negative in phr. *not a hope* (*in hell*). Also used ironically for: an expectation which has little or no chance of being fulfilled; esp. in ints., usu. expressing resignation, *some hope*(*s*)*!*, *what a hope!*

1899 R. WHITEING *No. 5 John St.* xxix. 297 What a hope for a night like this! **1915** F. PALMER *My Year of War* 231 'What hopes!' was the current phrase I heard among the men in these trenches. **1923** [see *HELL *sb.* 10 b]. **1929** J. B. PRIESTLEY *Good Companions* I. iv. 115 'Well, lads, wot's it yer want?' demanded their hostess. "Cos if it's steaks and chips and feather beds, you've got a bloody hope.' *Ibid.* II. i. 249 If there was enough money behind to rent His Majesty's Theatre, it could go on better still. It amounted to *that.* 'What a hope!' she concluded bitterly. **1933** A. G. MACDONELL *England, their England* xvi. 280 Not a hope!..The dailies have gone to press ages ago. **1936** [see *EARTHLY *a.* 1 c]. **1940** 'G. ORWELL' *Diary* 20 June in *Coll. Ess.* (1968) II. lvii. 352 There is a move on foot to get our police records..at Scotland Yard destroyed. Some hope! The police are the very people who would go over to Hitler. **1948** C. DAY LEWIS *Otterbury Incident* v. 53 'Well, you'd better start giving back the money..,' jeered Tuppy. 'What a hope!' **1959** S. GIBBONS *Pink Front Door* xvii. 206 Not a hope..not a single bloody ghost of a hope in hell. **1966** 'K. NICHOLSON' *Hook, Line & Sinker* v. 63 He..wants to put on a good show for her. What a hope. **1966** F. HOYLE *Oct. First* vi. 60 I've given them the idea I might come up with some explanation... Some hopes. **1967** P. MOYES *Murder Fantastical* xv. 229 'His book is probably in the Lucky Dip.'.. Maud made a face. 'Some hope of finding it in that case,' she said. **1969** J. ASHFORD *Prisoner at Bar* iv. 33. I told Mrs. Green we hadn't a hope in hell, but she said it wasn't the money, it was the principle. **1971** C. EGLETON *Last Post for Partisan* xvii. 176 'Make sure you get the right mix of weapons and explosives.' 'You've got a hope.'

5. hope chest chiefly *U.S.*, a chest or box in which a young woman hopefully collects articles towards a home of her own in the event of her marriage. (Cf. *bottom drawer* (*BOTTOM *sb.* 19).)

1911 G. S. PORTER *Harvester* xx. 504 It was a big, burl-maple box, designed after the hope chests that he saw advertised in magazines. **1922** M. B. HOUSTON *Witch Man* vii. 80 The bedspread that three years before she had laid unfinished in Kaid's hope chest. **1959** 'J. R. MACDONALD' *Galton Case* (1960) xi. 88 A metal box about the size of a hope chest. **1960** *New Left Rev.* Nov.–Dec. 12/2 The bride..had a good six patents dealing with biochemistry in her hope chest. **1973** *Welcomat* (Philadelphia) 10 Oct. 12 Liza Minelli has just bought her third wedding dress and packed it away along with the others in her hope chest.

hope, *v.* Add: **3. d.** Phr. *to hope against hope* [after Rom. iv. 18]: to hope where there are no reasonable grounds for doing so; to hope very much. Hence **hope-against-hope** *sb.*

1813 J. MONTGOMERY *World before Flood* 90 Hope against hope, and ask till ye receive. **1915** W. S. MAUGHAM *Of Human Bondage* lxxviii. 403 He mentioned the place and time at which they were to meet, and hoping against hope kept the appointment. **1955** G. GREENE *Quiet American* II. i. 93, I had hoped against hope that he would have gone before she returned. **1963** V. NABOKOV *Gift* i. 69 Fyodor still hoped against hope that this was a metaphysical paradox and not a traitorous *lapsus.* **1968** W. SANSOM *Grand Tour Today* ix. 181 Matisse's wonderful chapel of stained light..has nothing to do with the usual hope-against-hope that modern concrete building will 'harmonise' with older surroundings.

hoped, *ppl. a.* **1. b.** (Later examples.)

1947 *Sci. News* IV. 37 The patience in collecting and sifting evidence that goes on steadily from the moment a body is found to the hoped-for sequel when a suspect is charged. **1967** *Listener* 30 Mar. 426/1 They gave the hoped-for succession of industries from 40,000 to 9,000 years ago.

hopeful. 2. b. *sb.* (Later examples.)

1860 G. H. LEWES *Let.* 26 Sept. in *Geo. Eliot's Lett.* (1954) III. 349 My hopeful and his parent will appear at the 'Bedford' on Monday morning. **1899** F. J. CROWEST *Beethoven* 41 He committed this hopeful, only now some nineteen years of age, to the care of an old lawyer friend. **1957** W. THIELENS in R. K. Merton *Student-Physician* 133 This difference is more than partially due to *anticipation* by medical school hopefuls of the more demanding entrance requirements. **1972** *Daily Tel.* (Colour Suppl.) 27 Oct. 9/2 A dozen new applications arrive each day and are filed away with all the other hopefuls anxious to establish themselves on the circuits.

hopefully, *adv.* Add: **2.** It is hoped (that); let us hope. (Cf. G. *hoffentlich* it is to be hoped.) orig. *U.S.* (Avoided by many writers.)

1932 *N.Y. Times Book Rev.* 24 Jan. 11/4 He would create an expert commission..to consist of ex-Presidents and a selected list of ex-Governors, hopefully not including Pa and Ma Ferguson. **1965** T. L. BECKER *Political Behavioralism & Mod. Jurisprudence* p. v, Hopefully, this study, generated from the friction of highly polarized viewpoints, is the first of many steps directed towards satisfying a long-standing curiosity. **1965** *New Yorker* 27 Mar. 35/1 We asked her when she expected to move into her new apartment, and she answered, 'Hopefully on Tuesday.' **1966** in N. P. Vakar *Word Count Spoken Russian* p. viii, Professor Vakar's study will prove of enormous value... It should—and, hopefully, it will—be followed by a similar analysis of..syntactic patterns. **1967** *Lebende Sprachen* XII. 5/1 Machines will hopefully enable the scientist to find quickly the information he needs. **1969** *Language* XLV. 667 Hopefully, Tucker will publish supplements to this chapter. **1970** *Daily Tel.* 12 Feb. 21 The cost of developing a new 'Dash 50' series of engines, that hopefully will power Lockheed's 'extended range' jet, is put at around £75 million. **1970** *Sci. Jrnl.* May 27/2 By the time this issue..is on the bookstalls, *Apollo 13* should have completed its own trip to the Moon, hopefully with as little incident as its two predecessors. **1971** *Guardian* 13 Apr. 9/5 Prototype wooden rocking horses... Hopefully they will be available in the autumn at prices from £120.

hopeless, *a.* Add: **2.** Also in weakened use: ineffectual, inadequate, unable to stand up for oneself; incompetent, stupid.

1854 E. TWISLETON *Let.* 23 Oct. (1928) xiii. 245 Prussia is as *fainéant* as ever, and seems quite hopeless. **1922** W. S. MAUGHAM *Writer's Notebk.* (1949) 188 'You can't do a thing for people like that,' he said. 'They're hopeless.' **1932** R. LEHMANN *Invitation to Waltz* III. xiv. 240 But of course Mum's hopeless. She thinks virgins are sacred to all men. **1963** D. CORY *Hammerhead* ii. 26 'Who's this..?' 'That's Cary Grant, you are *hopeless*, Johnny.' **1967** O. NORTON *Now lying Dead* i. 3 'I'm *hopeless*,' she went on. 'I made a teapot once. It looked dinky. Only it wouldn't *pour*, don't you see.'

hophead (hǫ·phed). **1.** [f. *HOP *sb.*[1] 3* + *HEAD *sb.* 7 e.] An opium-smoker; a drug-addict. *slang* (orig. and chiefly *U.S.*).

1911 C. B. CHRYSLER *White Slavery* xi. 89 Opium smokers, 'hop fiends' or 'hop heads', as they are called, are the fiercest of all the White Slavers. **1915** G. BRONSON-HOWARD *God's Man* ii. 130, I told Beau to hunt up a skirt before, but you know these hop-heads—always putting things off. **1931** E. WALLACE *On the Spot* ii. 21 A hop-head will spill his friends' secrets to buy more hop. **1934** D. HAMMETT *Thin Man* xi. 72 'What's a junkie?' she asked. 'Hop-head.' **1947** E. E. CUMMINGS *Let.* 21 Sept. (1969) 180 Can someone imagine what any moujik coolie or hophead of any crevice of the Orient would sense, upon receiving such a gospel? **1959** J. CHRISTOPHER *Scent of White Poppies* ix. 144 Did you ever see a hophead when he's been kept short of what he wants? **1973** H. NIELSEN *Severed Key* vii. 75 I'll mail the letter to that hophead lawyer.

2. [*HOP *sb.*[1] 1 b.] A drunkard, a tippler. *N.Z. slang.*

[**1942** *N.Z.E.F. Times* 17 Aug. 16/3 (*caption*) Private Harry Hophead seen leaving Shepheards after a brief visit (very).] **1948** D. BALLANTYNE *Cunninghams* (1963) II. ix. 166 It's Betty that can't hold the liquor... She's a real lily of a hophead. **1952** *Landfall* VI. 208 Among young people greetings like 'Hophead'..are accepted as flattery.

Hopi (hō·pi). [Native name.] The name of a group of North American Indians living chiefly in north-eastern Arizona; also, a member of this tribe; their language. Also *attrib.*

1877 *Buffalo Soc. Nat. Sci. Bull.* 170 The title of '*Moquis*' has been applied to this confederacy by its enemies, and signifies the dying race. I understand that they usually speak of themselves as '*Ho-pees*' (our people). **1893** T. DONALDSON *Moqui Pueblo Indians* 13 The name which they call theselves by is Ho-pi, or Ho-pi-tuh-lei-nyu-muh, meaning 'peaceful people'. **1927** W. CATHER *Death comes for Archbishop* VII. i. 197 Last year, in May, he had been on his way to the Hopi Indians. **1927** D. H. LAWRENCE *Mornings in Mexico* 135 The Hopi country is in Arizona, next the Navajo country. *Ibid.*, The Hopis are Pueblo Indians, village Indians, so their reservation is not large. **1933** L. BLOOMFIELD *Language* iv. 72 The Shoshonean family..including..Comanche, and Hopi. **1937** R. H. LOWIE *Hist. Ethnological Theory* vii. 82 Swanton has shown..that in North America..many higher tribes, like the Hopi, are strictly matrilineal. **1952** A. HUXLEY *Let.* 12 Oct. (1969) 657 The ways I look at the world, are determined—determined in profoundly different ways according to whether I speak Chinese, Maori, Hopi, or English. **1956** D. ABERCROMBIE *Probl. & Princ.* i. 12 Hopi is an example of a language which lacks expression..for concepts of time. **1957** C. F. & F. M. VOEGELIN in *Int. Jrnl. Amer. Linguistics Mem. No. 14* (*title*) Hopi domains, a lexical approach to the problem of selection. **1959** E. TUNIS *Indians* 25/2 Even today an elderly Hopi will jog trot twenty miles to his cornfield, work all day, and jog home again. **1969** *Observer* (Colour Suppl.) 18 May 34/1 She is a Hopi, one of the less-known tribes. **1973** HOLT & MARJORAM *Math. in a Changing World* ii. 65 The difference between a noun and a verb to a Hopi Indian, Whorf discovered, is that a noun is more permanent than a verb.

‖ **hopo** (hō·po). [From an Afr. language. A trap for game consisting of two converging hedges in the form of the letter V, with a pit at the angle, into which the game is driven.

1866 J. LEYLAND *Adv. Far Interior S. Afr.* iii. 124 Two hedges are formed (called the hopo) a mile long, and the same distance at the extremity, gradually narrowing till it comes to the sides of the pit. **1932** R. CAMPBELL *Taurine Provence* 50 That natural death-trap or hopo, where the plain treacherously converges into a triangular precipice.

hopped, *a.* Add: **2.** [f. *HOP *sb.*[1] 3* + -ED[2].] Chiefly with *up*. Stimulated by, or under the influence of, a narcotic drug. Also *to hop up* v. phr., to stimulate with a narcotic drug. *U.S. slang.*

1924 G. C. HENDERSON *Keys to Crookdom* 408 *Hopped up*, intoxicated on opium. **1927** C. F. COE *Me—Gangster* iii. 43 They do their shooting when they are all hopped up with dope. **1927** E. HEMINGWAY *Men without Women* (1928) 194 I'm not drunk. I'm hopped to the eyes. **1957** *Listener* 6 June 912/2 It is possible these men were physically hopped up, or perhaps 'mushroomed-up' would be the better word, by consuming a European fungus. **1958** J. D. MACDONALD *Executioners* (1959) vii. 108 A hopped-up kid can be bought for less, but the job would be bungled. **1968** 'J. WELCOME' *Hell is where you find It* vi. 80 Why didn't you go to his funeral? Too busy hopping yourself up in Paris? You do that for kicks, too, I suppose? **1973** *Guardian* 14 Apr. 10/3 Chuck Berry don't drink either but he gets hopped.

b. *hopped-up*. Excited, enthusiastic. *U.S. slang.*

1923 C. WITWER in *Collier's* 27 Jan. 28/4 He's especially hopped up about the piano down in the music room. **1935** WODEHOUSE *Let.* 4 Feb. in *Performing Flea* (1953) 79, I got all hopped up and felt that it wasn't possible to give 'em too much of this superb stuff. **1936** J. STEINBECK *In Dubious Battle* v. 69 You organize the stiffs and get 'em all hopped up with a bunch of bull. **1939** C. MORLEY *Kitty Foyle* xxii. 214 There were a lot of dames hopped up with culture and good grammar. **1973** 'I. DRUMMOND' *Jaws of Watchdog* viii. 107 A hopped-up son with anarchist-pacifist connections.

3. *hopped-up*. Of a motor vehicle: having its engine altered to give improved performance. Also *transf. U.S. slang.*

1945 *Amer. Speech* XX. 226/2 *Hopped up.* Applied to a plane built for speed. Taken from the 'hopped up' automobiles of the high-school set. **1946** *Sat. Even. Post* 14 Sept. 14/2 Today a hot rod is a hopped-up, stripped-down flivver. **1954** *Amer. Speech* XXIX. 98 *Hopped up*,.. 'souped up'; said of a car with any added speed equipment. **1958** *House & Garden* Mar. 62 The American

housewife..with her hopped-up central heating. **1971** *Islander* (Victoria, B.C.) 16 May 10/3 At the urge of the hopped-up motor in seconds they were tearing up Nanaimo Street.

hopper[1]. Add: **1.** (Later example.)

1943 *N.Y. Times* 9 May II. 5/4 Listen, hoppers clot the action when the Duke or the Count start to beat it out.

c. *Baseball.* A ball which having been struck rebounds from the ground. *U.S. slang.*

Quot. 1914 appears to have a different sense.

1914 'B. L. STANDISH' in *Top-Notch Mag.* 30 Sept. 138/1 Courtney missed a hopper, though he almost fancied his bat lightly touched the whistling ball as it sped past. **1943** *Amer. Speech* XVIII. 104 *Baseball jargon*... Names for a grounder are *hopper*, [etc.]. **1968** [see *BASEMAN].

2. (Further examples.)

a **1870** R. M. CHIPMAN *Notes on Bartlett* 202 *Hopper*, a grasshopper, especially the ravaging locust called grasshopper at the West. **1933** *Bulletin* (Sydney) 5 July 21/2 One man says he counted 2000 hoppers [*sc.* kangaroos] in one paddock. **1946** *E. African Ann. 1946–7* 44/1 Youths have been out in the district beating and burning locusts... Besides these commendable efforts in destroying hoppers the Samburu have made a most useful war contribution. **1966** E. PALMER *Plains of Camdeboo* xv. 247 Our locust of the Karoo, the brown locust, *Locustana pardalina*, is well-known to us as a tiny dark hopper, later becoming black and orange.

10. c. *hopper window*; **e. hopper-boy** (examples); **hopper-dredge** or **-dredger**, a vessel combining the functions of a hopper and a dredger, being fitted with hoppers that receive the material dredged up and allow it to be discharged through the bottom at the place of deposit.

1787 in *Rep. U.S. Comm. Patents* (1850) 574 The other [device], denominated an hopper-boy, so constituted as to spread the meal over the floor of a mill to cool. **1813** *Niles' Reg.* V. Add. A. 6/2 Our Hopper-boy was an upright shaft revolving round with an arm. **1896** *Engin. Index* II. 120 The hopper dredge, 'Percy Sanderson', holding 1250 tons of debris and provided both with steel buckets and a suction pump. **1967** *Shipbuilding & Shipping Rec.* 6 July 21/1 (*heading*) 'McFarland'... A fully automated hopper dredge for the U.S. Army. **1876** SIMONS & BROWN *Brit. Pat. 4382*, This Invention, which relates to improvements in hopper dredgers, has for its object..to effect the discharge of the load or contents of hopper dredgers on to the adjoining river or canal bank. **1969** R. HAMMOND *Mod. Dredging Pract.* iv. 101 Direct pumping ashore to disposal areas is another function performed by a hopper dredger. **1939** *Archit. Rev.* LXXXVI. 166 The windows have a side-hung casement and a long top-hung hopper window for night ventilation.

hopperdozer (hǫ·pəɹdōᵘzəɹ). *U.S.* [f. HOPPER[1], perh. after *bull-dozer* (1876); see also quot. 1878.] A contrivance for catching and destroying insects, consisting essentially of an elongated pen or frame which is filled or smeared with some poisonous or glutinous substance and slowly drawn or pushed over the ground.

1877 *Pioneer Press* (St. Paul & Minneapolis) 19 May 5/4 (*heading of letter by A. B. Robbins*) A hopperdozer. *Ibid.* 22 May 1/5 The grasshoppers in this vicinity have hatched out very thickly... People are beginning to destroy them in various ways, principally with sheet iron hopperdozers covered with coal tar. **1878** *Ann. Rep. U.S. Entom. Commission 1877* xiii. 390 The simple pan..known as the Robbins 'hopperdozer. [*Note*] A word that came into very general use last year among farmers..and which doubtless takes its origin from doze, in reference to the toxic effect of the coal-tar on the locusts. **1904** W. C. EDGAR *Story Grain Wheat* ii. 21 Large areas of wheat are saved by means of a machine termed in America the 'hopperdozer'. **1932** *Chieftain* (Tecumseh, Nebraska) 5 May, Mechanical 'hopperdozers' have some value in the control of grasshoppers on fairly level fields of alfalfa. **1962** METCALF & FLINT *Destructive & Useful Insects* (ed. 4) ix. 471 On the whole, hopperdozers are much more expensive to operate and less efficient than poisoning.

hoppergrass. orig. and chiefly *U.S. dial.* = GRASSHOPPER.

1829 *Virginia Lit. Museum* I. 458 *Hoppergrass.* This word is often used in the south for grasshopper. **1892** *Rep. Vermont Board Agric.* XII. 163 Alas! the 'hopper grasses' came and carried it away. **1934** R. CAMPBELL *Broken Record* viii. 200 Spectacles make men look like ridiculous hoppergrasses. **1955** E. POUND *Classic Anthol.* I. 7 'Chkk! chkk!' hopper-grass, Nothing but grasshoppers hopping past. **1970** C. MAJOR *Dict. Afro-Amer. Slang* 67 *Hopper grass*, grasshopper.

hopperings (hǫ·pəriŋz), *sb. pl.* [f. HOPPER[1] + -ING[1].] Gravel retained in the hopper in gold- or diamond-washing.

1893 *Westm. Gaz.* 29 Apr. 7/3 The yield of diamonds from the hopperings is 6½ carats per 100 loads. **1898** *Daily News* 27 Jan. 9/5 Washed 197 loads from the mine, 3,725 loads lumps and hopperings producing 126 carats.

hopping, *ppl. a.*[1] Add: **1.** (Later example.)

1916 H. G. WELLS *Mr. Britling* I. i. 24 The hopping inconsecutiveness of English conversation.

2. hopping-john (earlier, later, and W.Ind. examples); **hopping-mad**, for '*dial.* and *U.S.*' read 'orig. *dial.* and *U.S.*' (further examples); now usu. written without a hyphen.

1838 C. GILMAN *Recoll. Southern Matron* xviii. 124 Before me..was an immense field of *hopping John.* [*Note.* Bacon and rice.] **1969** *Daily Tel.* 13 May 24/6 The dinner consisted of such things as collard greens, fried chicken, water melon, cornbread and 'hopping John', a dish of black-eyed peas and rice that is supposed to bring luck. **1970** M. SLATER *Caribbean Cooking* 32 'Peas and Rice'..is cooked on every island, down from the Bahamas, where it is known as Hoppin' John, to the South American mainland. **1833** S. SMITH *Life & Writings Major J. Downing* 139, I had a long talk with the General t'other day—he was hopping mad. **1915** WODEHOUSE *Psmith, Journalist* vii. 44 Dey was hoppin'-mad, de whole bunch of dem. **1922** [see *CLAIM *v.* 2 c]. **1954** [see *EDITOR 3 b]. **1960** *Guardian* 7 July 8/5 Would-be [telephone] subscribers get hopping mad. **1973** B. GRAEME *Two & Two make Five* vii. 67 Old Sourpuss must be hopping mad.

3. = **hopping mad.*

1894 'MARK TWAIN' in *Century Mag.* Jan 338/1 Oh, my lan', ole Marse was jes a-hoppin'! **1942** I. GLEED *Arise to Conquer* vi. 57 David will be hopping. **1960** E. W. HILDICK *Boy at Window* xi. 80, I was mad, real hopping! **1973** R. HAYES *Hungarian Game* xxxi. 185 'I wonder what they're fishing for.' 'Whales... And they got everyone hopping about it.'

hoppity. Add: (Later examples.)

1895 *Montgomery Ward Catal.* 235/1 The Game of 'Hopity'..is a game of skill... The particular feature of the game is the popular jumping move, pieces being allowed to jump over friend and foe alike to reach the opposite side of the board. **1969** E. H. PINTO *Treen* 222 Halma or hoppity was introduced about 1890.

hoppity[2] (hǫ·piti). Also **-ety.** A fanciful extension of HOP *v.*[1], used adverbially or as *adj.*, often repeated or with the word *hop* to suggest a hopping or hobbling movement. Cf. *HIPPETY.

1825, 1880, 1886 [see *HIPPETY]. **1924** A. A. MILNE *When we were very Young* 60 Christopher Robin goes Hoppity, hoppity, Hoppity, hoppity, hop. **1936** W. DE LA MARE *Wind blows Over* 46 William had been even more lively and hoppity than usual. **1943** F. THOMPSON *Candleford Green* viii. 125 A tame thrush which he had found in the fields with a broken wing and brought home..would follow him round the garden, *hoppity-hop.* **1963** *Times* 10 May 5/3 Two no-balls from Greenhough, whose run up, like Christopher Robin, goes hoppity hoppity.

Hoppus (hǫ·pŏs). Also **hoppus.** The name of Edward *Hoppus*, 18th-century English surveyor, used *attrib.* and in the possessive to designate a method of measuring the cubic content of round timber used in the British Commonwealth, and tabulated in his *Practical Measuring now made Easy* (1736) (known in later editions as *Hoppus's Tables* and *Hoppus's Measurer*); it involves multiplying the length in feet by the square of the quarter-girth in inches and dividing the result by 144; **Hoppus foot**, a recent name for the 'cubic foot' as arrived at by the Hoppus method, approximately equal to 1·27 true cubic feet.

[**1820** R. MONTEATH *Forester's Guide* xxvi. 173 It will contain 2 solid inches and one-third of an inch, according to the measurement of Hoppus.] **1894** A. D. WEBSTER *Pract. Forestry* (ed. 2) xxv. 175 Timber-measuring is rather a vexed question, some following what is known as Hoppus's system, and others advocating that of Horton. **1924** A. C. DRUMMIE *Pract. Forestry* xxvii. 244 The standard usually adopted is the quarter girth Hoppus measure system, with the customary allowance for bark. **1941** S. E. WILSON *Decimal Hoppus Tables* 6 When the Hoppus system is employed to measure cylindrical bodies the solid foot amounts to $4/\pi$ or 1·273 cubic feet... To call the unit..a cubic foot is accordingly inaccurate and misleading... To avoid confusion we call the 'solid foot' of this system a 'Hoppus Foot', defining it as the unit of solid contents according to the Hoppus system of measuring round timber. **1947** H. L. EDLIN *Forestry & Woodland Life* xx. 144 The unit generally used in Britain for measuring round logs, trees, and plantations, is the customary cubic foot, or Hoppus foot. **1951** R. H. HORDERN *Woodworking Ind. Managem.* viii. 123 The 144 divisor used in the Hoppus System will show approximately 27 per cent less cubic content than the tree actually measures. **1970** *Timber Trades Jrnl.* 14 Mar. 53/3 Average volume of the trees was 25·4 Hoppus ft, and the price reached was 3s 5¼d per Hoppus ft. **1971** *Daily Tel.* 7 Jan. 12/5 The hoppus foot, a traditional measure for timber,..will be replaced next month by the cubic metre and metric tonne.

hoppy (hǫ·pi), *a.*[1] [f. HOP *sb.*[1] + -Y[1].] **1.** Tasting or smelling of hops; beery.

1893 *Harper's Mag.* Feb. 458 Jest so it don't tas'e hoppy, I ain't pertic'lar; but from hoppy bread *de*liver me! **1964** *Listener* 26 Mar. 534/3 Over cool dinner, the sour hoppy breath.

2. Of, pertaining to, or characterized by drugs or drug-taking. *U.S. slang.* (Cf. *HOP *sb.*[1] 3*.)

1942 BERREY & VAN DEN BARK *Amer. Thes. Slang* § 509/30 *Hoppy*, smelling of drugs. **1946** MEZZROW & WOLFE *Really Blues* (1957) vii. 98 Detroit is really a hoppy town—people must order their opium along with their groceries.

hoppy (hǫ·pi), *a.*[2] *colloq.* [f. HOP *sb.*[2] + -Y[1].] Characterized by, or predisposed to, hopping; lively, full of movement; limping, lame.

1902 in *Eng. Dial. Dict.* III. 232 'To go hoppy' is to walk rather lame. Among the working classes, lame persons are often nicknamed 'Oppy', as 'Oppy Smith', which denotes a certain Smith who is somewhat lame. **1914** JOYCE *Dubliners* 171 He had a game leg and for this his friends called him Hoppy Holohan. **1934** A. WOOLLCOTT *While Rome Burns* (1936) 42 Juventino Rosas.. who once wrote a pleasant and rather hoppy waltz. **1942** BERREY & VAN DEN BARK *Amer. Thes. Slang* § 53/15 *Rapid*; *quick*, hoppy. *Ibid.* § 131/11 *Crippled*; *lame*, hoppy. **1968** K. WEATHERLY *Roo Shooter* 119 It's a damned good thing these hoppy bastards [*sc.* kangaroos] can't understand me.

hoppy (hǫ·pi), *sb.*[1] *colloq.* [f. HOP *sb.*[2] + -Y[6].] A lame man.

1904 'No. 1500' *Life in Sing Sing* xiii. 249/2 *Hoppy*, a cripple. **1909** S. WATSON *Wops the Waif* iii. 5 Who-ay, Cully, here's Hoppy with the Rozin. **1962** J. FRANKLYN *Dict. Nicknames* 49 *Hoppy*, the nickname of anyone who walks with a limp.

hoppy (hǫ·pi), *sb.*[2] *U.S. slang.* [f. HOP *sb.*[1] + -Y[6].] An opium addict. (Cf. *HOP *sb.*[1] 3*.)

1922 E. F. MURPHY *Black Candle* II. i. 114 The Chinese here still furnish a large percentage of the 'hoppies'. **1924** G. C. HENDERSON *Keys to Crookdom* xxiv. 301 Even the 'hoppies' themselves look down on a user of cocaine. **1941** B. HECHT *1001 Afternoons in N.Y.* 129 A lush, a prosty, a hoppy, and a pain in the neck, say the police.

hop-sack. Add: **2.** Also *attrib.*, and in form *hopsac.*

1907 *Yesterday's Shopping* (1969) 831 Ascot Scarfs.. made from..Hopsack shot silk. **1923** *Daily Mail* 5 July 1 Hopsac suiting,..in pretty Heather Mixture grounds. **1930** *Daily Express* 8 Sept. 11/5 Hopsack Tweed. **1968** *Surfer Mag.* Jan. 27/1 Can you tell me the approximate weight of a piece of hopsack cloth secured with resin to the front third of my board?

hop-toad. *U.S.* [HOP *sb.*[2] or *v.*[1]] A toad.

1827 *Massachusetts Spy* 28 Nov. (Th.), An inhabitant of the Middle States talks of 'hop-toads',—as if all toads were not hoppers. **1830** F. TROLLOPE in *Dom. Manners* (1949) 428 Hop toads is little creatures what hop like a frog. **1844** MRS. STOWE *Mayflower* (1849) 157 I'd always find him stopping to chase hoptoads, or off after chipsquirrels. **1847** *Knickerbocker* XXIX. 183, I have so often ..a tender leaning towards little pigs and hop toads. **1913** G. STRATTON-PORTER *Laddie* xiii. I like hop-toads, owls, and shitepokes. **1966** J. DOS PASSOS *Best Times* (1968) i. 12 We studied with passionate interest the egg-laying habits of the hoptoads that shrilled so loud.

Hopton wood (hǫ·ptən wu·d). Also **Hopton-Wood, Hoptonwood.** The name of a wood and neighbouring quarries close to Wirksworth, Derbyshire, used *attrib.* and *absol.* to designate a pale brownish- or greyish-white carboniferous limestone used for building and decorative purposes.

[**1811** J. FAREY *Gen. View of Agric. & Minerals Derbyshire* I. 419 *List of..Building-Stone Quarries, or Delphs*... Hopton-Wood, in Middleton by Wirksworth.] **1888** G. H. BLAGROVE *Marble Decoration* 86 *Hopton Wood.* This stone deserves to rank as a marble, for it will take an excellent polish. **1911** J. WATSON *Brit. & Foreign Building Stones* 117 Hopton Wood Stone has been employed for constructing many important buildings, including the Guildhall (1789), and the Imperial Institute (1881), in London. **1962** *Times* 3 Aug. 7/1 Any opaque stone—sandstone, bath, hoptonwood, basalt. **1967** G. SIMS *Last Best Friend* vii. 62 A fine example of lapidary art..cut on a panel of Hopton-Wood stone. **1973** *Times* 14 May 14/8 Later he began to experiment with native stones, such as Hopton Wood and Ancaster.

‖ **hora** (hōᵊ·ră). Also **horah, horra.** [Rum. *horă*; Heb. *hōrāh.*] A Rumanian and Israeli round-dance; the music or song to which it is performed.

1878 J. W. OZANNE *Three Yrs. in Roumania* xii. 157 The *hora*, the Roumanian dance *par excellence.* **1911** *Encycl. Brit.* XXIII. 849 The popular songs of Rumania, the 'doine', the 'hora', [etc.]. **1923** *Chambers's Jrnl.* 20 Oct. 745/1 The favourite amusement of the Roumanian peasant is his dance, especially the traditional 'hora' danced in a circle. **1925** *Countries of World* V. 3431/2 Laughing girls..ready to dance the 'hora' with the men [in Rumania]. **1946** KOESTLER *Thieves in Night* viii. 61 [They] had formed the first ring of the horra, the stamping and swaying round-dance, a savage ring-polka. *Ibid.* 352 They were singing one of the popular horras, a folk-song with a passionate, almost hysterical tune. **1960** A. WESKER *I'm talking about Jerusalem* (1961) III. ii. 49 Let's do an Israeli dance..(*Starts doing a Zanny Hora on his own*). **1967** *Guardian* 15 July 6/2 Can you think of any other Army where officers and enlisted men would dance the hora together? **1967** *Observer* 8 Jan. 23/4 Catchy, minor-key *hora* strummings. **1969** *New Yorker* 6 Sept. 117/1 There is a scholarly argument over whether the Rumanian hora predates the Hebrew hora or vice versa. A diplomatic Rumanian-style answer is that both are of Mediterranean origin, the hora having been brought to Rumania by the Roman legions. **1971** *Observer* 17 Jan. 21/7 You were building, building, building. And on Friday nights I [*sc.* Mrs. Golda Meir] danced the Horah into the night.

horæ (hōᵊ·ri). [L., pl. of *hōra* HOUR.] A book of hours (HOUR 5, 6).

1875 *Quaritch's Gen. Catal.* Suppl. 51 The earlier editions of Kerver's series of Horæ. **1927** *Observer* 27 Nov. 22/4 An exquisite Flemish Horæ of about 1500. **1967** D. DIRINGER *Illum. Book* (ed. 2) vii. 406 An interesting

Horae of the Bodleian Library, at Oxford..was executed in France about 1430–40. A French Dominican *Horae* of the British Museum..was executed between 1425 and 1450.

horah, var. *HORA.

horary, *a.* Add: **4.** *horary astrology* (examples).

1835 'ZADKIEL' *Lilly's Introd. Astrol.* xxxv. 285 All these coincidences must be considered by the genuine searcher after truth as strong evidences of the truth of planetary influence, as evinced in *horary astrology.* **1911** 'SEPHARIAL' *Man. Occultism* vi. 98, I am quite convinced from experience that there is much that is both fictitious and erroneous in Horary Astrology. **1951** M. E. HONE *Mod. Text-bk. Astrol.* xv. 272 The practice of Horary Astrology was very popular in the Middle Ages, and its best known exponent was William Lilly (1602–81). *a* **1963** L. MACNEICE *Astrol.* (1964) i. 19 Casting horoscopes to answer questions is called 'horary' astrology.

horary, *sb.* Add: **2. b.** A timed programme or plan. So **hora·rium.**

1851 J. B. PAGANI *Life Rev. A. Gentili* III. ii. 151 He drew up a regular horary to promote recollection and compunction. **1921** *Ampleforth Jrnl.* Jan. 139 Adapting ourselves to the School horarium we began dinner at 5 p.m. **1922** *Westm. Gaz.* 7 Oct., His scheme of breaking the Germans in 24 hours on a meticulously timed 'horary'.

Horatian, *a.* (*sb.*) Add: (Earlier and later examples.) So **Hora·tianism.**

1750 C. SMART (*title*) The Horatian canons of friendship. Being the third satire of the first book of Horace imitated. **1850** THACKERAY *Pendennis* II. iii. 25 According to the Horatian maxim, a work of art ought to lie ripening (a maxim, the truth of which may, by the way, be questioned altogether). **1925** C. D. BROAD *Mind & its Place* xi. 492 It is wrong to live in accordance with the Horatian ethics. **1936** F. R. LEAVIS *Revaluation* iv. 137 [Matthew] Green, in his Horatianism, is a good positive Augustan. **1945** AUDEN *Coll. Poetry* 121 The bland Horatian life of friends and wine. **1964** *English Studies* XLV (Suppl.) 217 It shows a deeply felt appreciation of ethical norms, a truly English horatianism that Cobbett, for all his lack of a classical education, inherited from the eighteenth century. **1965** B. SWEET-ESCOTT *Baker Street Irreg.* 14 Others may wonder whether such a book *ought* to have been published, even after an interval which now exceeds the Horatian decade.

‖ **horchata** (ǫrtʃā·ta). Also **orchata.** [Sp.] A popular Spanish and Latin-American chufa-flavoured soft drink.

1859 in *Century Mag.* (1898) Dec. 312 *Orchata* is also a favorite drink; it is made from the juice of almonds, and is as white as milk. **1922** J. HERGESHEIMER *Bright Shawl* (1923) 63 She preferred rather than an ice, an orchata, and sipped it slowly. **1932** E. HEMINGWAY *Death in Afternoon* xx. 271 The taste of horchata, ice-cold horchata. **1968** J. M. WHITE *Nightclimber* ii. 9, I debate whether to order a *horchata* or a *zumo de limón*, and when the waiter arrives I ask for the latter. **1969** R. & D. DE SOLA *Dict. Cooking* 121/1 *Horchata*, almond-flavoured soft drink popular throughout Latin America and Spain.

horde. Add: **1. c.** *Anthropol.* A loosely-knit social group consisting of about five families.

[**1894** H. CUNOW *Verwandtschafts-Organisationen der Australneger* iii. 28 In Dr. Hodgkinson's Werk 'Australia from Port Macquarie to Moreton Bay' (London 1845).. wird überall..die Bezeichnung 'tribe' gebraucht, ich habe dafür den meines Erachtens besser passenden Ausdruck 'Horde' gewählt. Unter 'tribus' ist stets die aus mehreren verwandten Horden bestehende grössere Volksgemeinschaft, der Stamm, zu verstehen.] **1896** F. H. GIDDINGS *Princ. Sociol.* iii. 275 Practically the horde as a component of the tribe is nearly, but not quite, identical with the clan. **1918** A. A. BRILL tr. *Freud's Totem & Taboo* iv. 208 Man, too, lived originally in small hordes in which the jealousy of the oldest and strongest male prevented promiscuity. **1939** *Geogr. Jrnl.* XCIV. 89 Davidson points out that the horde, a unit of about five families, in all some thirty-five persons, was the largest political unit known to the Australians. **1948** W. McDOUGALL *Introd. Soc. Psychol.* (ed. 29) Suppl. iv. 402 That..primitive society took the form of a horde, the leader of which horde, the horde-father, actuated by his sexual jealousy, habitually treated his sons with extreme brutality.

hordeolum (hǭɪdī·ōlǝm). *Path.* Pl. **hordeola.** [Altered form of late L. *hordeolus* a sty, dim. of L. *hordeum* barley.] A sty on the eyelid.

[**1622** R. BANISTER *Treat. Dis. Eyes* (ed. 2) IV. xiii. E 6 b (*heading*) Of the wart, or barly corne on the Eyelidde, commonly called..a Stian,..in Latin, hordeum, or hordeolum.] **1806** J. BRIGGS tr. *Scarpa's Dis. Eye* ii. 75 The appearance of a white spot upon..the hordeolum should not induce the surgeon to be hasty in opening it. **1833** W. LAWRENCE *Dis. Eye* xix. 341 Some hordeola form more quickly, with greater suppuration and no slough. **1908** *Practitioner* Feb. 288 Epiphora may be due to..a hordeolum. **1966** S. LERMAN *Basic Ophthalm.* viii. 459 A hordeolum (stye) is caused by a purulent inflammation in the glands of Zeis at the base of the eyelashes.

Hori (hōᵊ·rī), *sb. N.Z.* Also with lower-case initial. [Maori form of 'George'.] A contemptuous term for a Maori.

1933 F. E. BAUME *Half-Caste* 26 'Hori', he [*sc.* the driver] said to Paul (as a negro is 'Sambo' a Maori is 'Hori' to the poor white). 'You like a drink, eh?' **1942** *National Education* (N.Z.) Mar. 59/1, I looked at the eighty husky Horis in their gum-boots, denim trousers.., tattered shirts. **1944** J. H. FULLARTON *Troop Target* xi. 87 But all you Horis are related. **1960** N. HILLIARD *Maori Girl* III. vii. 219 All *horis* come off the farm, I think. **1963** *N.Z. News* 23 July 6/2 The Maori representative on the Dominion Council..asked the R.S.A. to lead a move to eliminate racial and other discords fostering Communism and instanced the use of *Hori*, as a general term for a Maori, as distasteful and creating friction.

horizon, *sb.* Add: **5. b.** *Soil Sci.* Any of several layers in the soil which lie roughly parallel to the surface and are distinguishable by differences in physical properties, as colour, texture, or structure, or in chemical reaction.

A typical soil shows the following horizons (from the surface downwards): the A-horizon, generally the horizon of eluviation; the B-horizon, generally the horizon of illuviation; and the C-horizon, consisting of partly weathered parent material. Within the A-horizon and B-horizon further horizons may be distinguished (as B_1, B_2, B_3 horizons), though some writers refer to such horizons as zones or layers rather than as horizons.

1923 *Soil Sci.* XVI. 97 The soil assumes added importance as a factor when the chemical and physical differences of the separate horizons are studied in relation to root development. **1927** C. F. MARBUTT tr. *Glinka's Great Soil Groups* 9 Russian investigators use the word *Horizon* rather than stratum to designate the various layers in the soil profile. **1948** WHITE & RENNER *Human Geogr.* xxiv. 406 A marked zone of lime accumulation occurs at a moderate depth in the 'B' horizon. The 'C' horizon or subsoil is brown. **1968** P. BURINGH *Introd. Study Soils Trop. & Subtrop. Regions* v. 74 A much lighter reddish A_2 horizon, much lower in clay and much higher in sand, is clearly visible. **1971** E. A. FITZPATRICK *Pedology* i. 4/1 In some cases the contrast between horizons is dramatic and self-evident, while in others it is very subtle.

c. *Archæol.* A level at which a particular group of remains is found, or which is taken as representing a particular culture or cultural period.

1926 D. A. E. GARROD *Upper Palaeolithic Age* i. 34 Thanks to his journal it is possible to attempt a reconstruction of the archeological horizons which existed at the time of excavation. **1935** *Nature* 6 Apr. 550/1 Mr. Harrod was able to indicate the horizon of discovery very closely. The spear-head was found at the base of the lowest draw of peat. **1959** J. D. CLARK *Prehist. S. Afr.* iv. 90 Nitrogen tests confirm that the remains are contemporary with the horizon in which they were found. **1962** R. MASON *Prehist. Transvaal* iv. 85 The Florisbad Peat 1 horizon has a radiocarbon age of more than 35,000 B.P. and may be associated with a Middle Stone Age industry. ..Four radiocarbon age estimations for Later Stone Age horizons in Matjes River Cave give ages varying from 11,250±400 B.P. to 5,400±250 B.P. **1973** *N.Y. Times* 15 July x. 1/1 Investigations have uncovered 15 distinct *horizons* (the archeological term for strata bearing traces of human habitation).

6*. *Embryology.* One of a numbered sequence of stages in the development of the human embryo.

1942 G. L. STREETER in *Contrib. Embryol.* No. 197. 213 (*heading*) Developmental horizons in human embryos. *Ibid.* 214 In searching for a suitable expression for the age groups under consideration..it was decided to follow the practice of other sciences and make use of the word 'horizons'. **1956** G. H. BOURNE *Biochem. & Physiol. Bone* xiii. 376 Each age group or 'horizon' is characterized by a certain degree of differentiation and organization of various tissues and organs. **1968** J. B. THOMAS *Introd. Human Embryol.* vi. 55 He [*sc.* Streeter] initially proposed 25 'horizons' for the human embryonal period, but this was later revised to 23. *Ibid.* viii. 80 With the appearance of these branching villi proposed horizon VII is reached.

6.** *Mining.* In horizon mining, a system of approximately horizontal tunnels lying in the same horizontal plane; the plane containing these tunnels.

1948 *Coal* Nov. 6/3 A further upper horizon was..fixed at a depth of 115 yards in the South Pit. **1960** J. SINCLAIR *Winning Coal* iii. 51 The coal lying between a pair of horizons is worked in such a manner that the coal flows downwards to the lower level and ventilation is ascensional. **1966** VOROBJEV & DESHMUKH *Advanced Coal Mining* II. xxxvi. 871 In steep and inclined coal seams (25°–9°) level division of the mining area with main workings on each horizon is preferable.

7. horizon-blue [Fr. *bleu horizon*], a light shade of blue, the colour of the uniform of the French Army during and after the war of 1914–18; such a uniform; also as *adj.*; **horizon mining,** a method of working inclined seams from approximately horizontal tunnels driven through the various strata to intersect the seams, there being several systems or 'horizons' of tunnels, one below another, connected by vertical shafts.

1919 J. BUCHAN *Mr. Standfast* xiv. 248 There was very little khaki or horizon-blue about. **1926** 'C. BARRY' *Detective's Holiday* i. 9 'It is thus,' the man in horizon blue began..'This morning..a fisherman..discovered.. the body of a man who had been murdered.' **1942** E. PAUL *Narrow St.* xvii. 136 Monsieur Saint-Aulaire found himself over-stocked with horizon-blue material, the Chamber having agreed that French soldiers and officers should wear khaki in the future. **1954** W. FAULKNER *Fable* (1955) 14 The whole ring of..faces was stained with a faint,..reflected horizon-blue. **1972** J. WILLIAMS *Home Fronts* viii. 137 Little girls decked out in 'horizon-blue' policemen's caps and cloaks. **1947** *Coal* Nov. 16/3 Horizon mining is planned to cut out heavy dip haulages, replacing them with locomotives. **1953** *Times* 15 Aug. 2/3 The site of the second modern horizon-mining development of the west Wales coalfield. **1963** J. SINCLAIR *Planning & Mechanized Drifting at Collieries* viii. 163 Probably the most important decision in planning a horizon-mining project is the position of the horizons and the vertical interval between them.

horizontal, *a.* (*sb.*) Add: **2. a.** *horizontal equivalent*, the distance between two points or two adjacent contours measured in a horizontal plane (rather than along the ground); *horizontal rainbow*, a spectrum occasionally seen on or just above the surface of a lake, appearing as an oval or as an open curve with its arms pointing away from the observer.

1889 G. W. USILL *Pract. Surveying* x. 199 The known difference of height thereof are [*sic*] called the vertical intervals, and their distance apart upon the survey are termed the horizontal equivalents. **1906** *Nature* 26 Apr. 608/2 (*heading*) A horizontal rainbow. **1916** *Monthly Weather Rev.* (Wash.) XLIV. 66/1 In general these horizontal rainbows are confined to the early hours of the day. **1952** MONKHOUSE & WILKINSON *Maps & Diagrams* ii. 74 If two points on a hill-side are projected on to a horizontal plane, as they are on a map, the distance between them is known as the Horizontal Equivalent (H.E.). **1957** G. E. HUTCHINSON *Treat. Limnol.* I. vi. 419 The horizontal rainbow, or iris, is a relatively rare phenomenon, though it has been observed on a number of lakes in many parts of the world.

b. *horizontal bar* (earlier and later examples); † *horizontal rudder* Aeronaut., an elevator on an aircraft.

1827 G. HAMILTON *Elem. Gymnastics* 55 The performer, taking hold of the horizontal bar, swings backward and forward. **1843** *Lancet* 27 May 302/1 [I] made her exercise twice a day on a horizontal bar erected for the purpose. **1875** T. FROST *Circus Life* ix. 161 The rising school of young gymnasts..began to practise on..the horizontal bar, and the flying rings. **1875** *Aëronaut. Soc. Gt. Brit. 9th Ann. Rep. 1874* 56 This problem M. Renaud has solved by means of his automatic rudder... The idea occurred to him of placing a small horizontal rudder behind the sustaining planes. **1878** M. JEWRY *Warne's Model Cookery* Inside front cover (Advt.), Practical Instructions on the Horizontal Bar, Parallel Bars. **1884** *Punch* 8 Mar. 117/1 Let the Ladies learn gymnastics..They'll improve too pale complexions..After practice on the ladders and the horizontal bars. **1903** A. BENNETT *Truth abt. Author* ii. 16 He..taught us to fence, and to do the lesser circle on the horizontal bar. **1909** C. C. TURNER *Aerial Navig.* viii. 121 The aviator must further correct this instability by control of the horizontal rudder. **1913** A. E. BERRIMAN *Aviation* vii. 71 Originally the elevator was often called the horizontal rudder. **1964** G. C. KUNZLE *Parallel Bars* i. 36 In this case it is very similar to position 2 (c)..on the Horizontal Bar.

3. a. Uniform; producing or based on uniformity. Chiefly *U.S.*

1842 *Congress. Globe* 17 Mar. 331 Was it expected that this committee would send in a horizontal tariff? **1872** *Ibid.* 28 Mar. 2016/2 The horizontal reduction of duties would do incalculable injury. **1890** *Ibid.* 9 May 4392/2 The Democratic bill made a horizontal cut of 20 per cent. **1907** *Daily Chron.* 23 Sept. 5/3 The 'Journal of Commerce' [N.Y.] says that the North German Lloyd Company announced yesterday a practically horizontal cut of 25 dols. on the eastward and westward passages. **1963** *Times* 22 May (Margarine Suppl.) p. viii, The Council of the European Community has already issued a directive in connexion with the use of colour additives. This follows what is known as the 'horizontal' system, meaning that it is of application to all food products.

b. In Industry: (see quots. 1959 and 1968). *horizontal combination, integration, merger*, an industrial merger of firms engaged in the same stages or types of manufacture; so *h. combine*, the organization resulting from such a merger.

1927 *Observer* 27 Mar. 5 Looking with a benevolent eye on horizontal combines. **1930** M. CLARK *Home Trade* 204 There have been the combinations of one business with one or more of the same type. To this type the term 'horizontal combine' is usually applied. **1930** *Economist* 29 Mar. 710/2 Horizontal integration took place in the alcohol and solvents industry. **1959** *Listener* 9 July 46/2 The cotton industry is what is called a horizontal industry... As a rule the processing is done in stages in which the goods pass from one producer to another. **1960** NANASSY & SELDEN *Business Dict.* 96 *Horizontal combination*, formation of a business by combining two or more concerns engaged in the same kind of business. **1962** H. O. BEECHENO *Introd. Business Stud.* v. 40 When business units of the same type combine..it is called horizontal integration. **1967** *Economist* 15 Apr. 253/3 He also held that all mergers must be judged by the same standards, whether they be vertical, horizontal or conglomerate. **1968** J. IRONSIDE *Fashion Alphabet* 232 The textile and fashion industry works in two ways—horizontal or vertical... The 'horizontal' system means that in each stage of its manufacture..the textile goes through different hands. ..In the 'vertical' system, everything from weaving..to making up the garments..is done under one organisation.

c. Denoting a relationship, movement, etc., between a social group of a particular status, class, age-group, etc., and another of similar specifications, as opp. a 'vertical' relationship with a higher (or lower) authority, class, age-group, etc.

1931 H. G. WELLS *Work, Wealth & Happiness of Mankind* (1932) xi. 540 The only remaining physical differences between man and woman are becoming horizontal,

i.e., differences between individuals in the same class, and not vertical differences, in which all women are put below all men, or vice versa. **1949** KOESTLER *Promise & Fulfilment* III. i. 289 The trend of social migrations is a 'horizontal' drift from village and agriculture to town and industry, and a 'vertical' drift from working-class to middle-class occupations. **1959** *Listener* 12 Feb. 280/2 When the children's interests turn outwards, when they develop loyalties of a horizontal sort. **1959** N. MAILER *Advts. for Myself* (1961) 374 The old exploitation was vertical—the poor supported the rich. To this vertical exploitation must now be added the horizontal exploitation of the mass by the State and by Monopoly. **1967** *Listener* 13 July 62/2 This horizontal integration of Saudi-Arabian Arab with Egyptian Arab ultimately gave way to the vertical integration of Egyptian peasant with Egyptian professional man.

d. *horizontal union* = **craft union.*

1937 H. FELDMAN *Probl. Labor Relations* iv. 255 Shall the mass production industries..be organized on a 'horizontal' (craft union) basis, or in 'vertical' (industrial) unions? **1950** THEIMER & CAMPBELL *Encycl. World Politics* 425/1 Unions may be craft unions, also known as horizontal unions, or industrial unions, also known as vertical unions.

4. *Mus.* (See quots. 1955 and 1970.)

1886 G. B. SHAW *How to become Mus. Critic* (1960) 122 The fact that M. Gounod has put too much sugar in it for the palate of a British Protestant might be condoned if the music were not so very horizontal. There is nearly always a pedal flowing along, and the other parts are slipping chromatically down to merge in it. **1900** C. W. PEARCE *Composers' Counterpoint* iii. 28 Composers..have re-established the beautiful horizontal polyphony of the two-dimensional period, upon the perpendicular lines of the modern harmonic school. **1942** E. BLOM *Mus. in Eng.* ii. 21 Vertical hearing, i.e. listening to the chordal incidence of parts rather than to their separate horizontal flow. **1955** L. FEATHER *Encycl. Jazz* ii. 53 Similarly 'horizontal' or 'linear' refers to the relationship of the notes or chords as they are played one after the other, read horizontally across the manuscript. **1962** *Listener* 9 Aug. 225/3 In Webern's texture the distinction between the horizontal and vertical is in a process of complete liquidation. **1970** W. APEL *Harvard Dict. Mus.* (ed. 2) 842/1 Much like woven fabric, music consists of horizontal ('woof') and vertical ('warp') elements. The former are the successive sounds forming melodies, the latter the simultaneous sounds forming harmonies.

B. *sb.* **2.** (Later examples.)

1955 *Oxf. Jun. Encycl.* VIII. 429/1 The theodolite is also used to measure vertical angles, that is, angles above or below the horizontal. **1962** *Listener* 15 Mar. 479/2 Bonnard derived his use of horizontals and verticals within the picture from Gauguin.

3. An evergreen Tasmanian tree or, in exposed positions, a shrub, *Anodopetalum biglandulosum.* Also *attrib.*, as *horizontal scrub*, the mat of vegetation formed by interlocking branches of a group of these trees.

1888 R. M. JOHNSTON *Geol. Tasmania* p. vi (Morris), The Horizontal is a tall shrub or tree. **1891** *Australasian* 4 Apr. (Ibid.), That stuff as they calls horizontal, a mess of branches and root. **1898** MORRIS *Austral Eng.* 202/2 Horizontal scrub. **1927** *Blackw. Mag.* Oct. 471/2 These tentacles of horizontal were generally clothed with a thick velvety covering of damp green moss. **1936** *Discovery* Jan. 15/1 If he meets with a patch of 'horizontal scrub', he will clamber over the tree tops. **1949** D. WALKER *We went to Australia* xxi. 200 Arid mountain country covered with 'horizontal scrub'. This extraordinary growth shoots upward for some twenty feet, the boughs then interlocking over very large areas; and so thickly matted is it that you can walk on the scrub some twenty feet from the ground. **1957** *Forest Trees Austral.* (Commonw. Forestry & Timber Bur.) 218/1 Associated species include myrtle beech..and shrub species such as horizontal.

4. [Fr. (*grande*) *horizontale.*] A prostitute. Also *grand horizontal*; also in French form. *slang.*

1888 E. DOWSON *Let.* 13 Nov. (1967) 18, I shall let the liaison run its course—it will be very amusing & not as costly as an affair with a regular horizontale. **1909** J. R. WARE *Passing Eng.* 154/2 Horizontal. **1928** A. PHILIPS *Boy at Bank* v. i, More than ten thousand professional 'horizontals' are light o' loves. **1963** *Times* 4 Apr. 16/2 The 'grand horizontals' were merely in the argot of the day the leading fashionable cocottes. **1967** *Observer* 8 Oct. 26/2 A *grisette* is cheaper than a regular *horizontale.* **1967** C. O. SKINNER *Madame Sarah* iii. 44 La Païva, a contemporary 'grand horizontal', had attained respectability by marrying. **1970** *New Yorker* 28 Feb. 113/1 He is overshadowed throughout by Aunt Augusta, the still unretired *grande horizontale* of seventy-three.

horizontally, *adv.* Add: Later examples in senses 3 c and 4 of *HORIZONTAL *a.*

1934 *Hound & Horn* VII. 596 He [*sc.* Stravinsky] is tired of..exploiting the folk tune, horizontally, vertically, atonally, seriously or comically. **1956** M. STEARNS *Story of Jazz* (1957) xii. 126 Everybody had an interesting part, for the idea was to move horizontally rather than vertically. **1958** *Listener* 9 Oct. 547/2 Differences throughout the Arab sector run both vertically and horizontally: between religious sects, social strata, settlers and nomads. **1959** *Ibid.* 13 Aug. 245/1 A society so divided vertically as well as horizontally.

Horlick (hǭ·ɹlik). The name of the British-born American industrialist W. *Horlick* (1846–1936), used in the possessive to designate the trade-name of the malted milk-powder or the drink made from this, which was first manufactured by his firm in 1883.

1891 *Trade Marks Jrnl.* 19 Aug. 784 (*heading*) Horlick's. .. A desiccated and granulated preparation of malt extract and milk as a food for infants and invalids. James Horlick,..London, E.C.; manufacturer. **1907** *Yesterday's Shopping* (1969) 510/3 Horlick's malted milk. **1932** L. GOLDING *Magnolia St.* II. iv. 324 The Horlick's mugs danced on the trestle tables. **1936** R. LEHMANN *Weather in Streets* I. v. 152 'Hot milk?'..'No, thank you, Mum. Not even Horlick's.' **1958** J. CANNAN *And be a Villain* vii. 150 A tray of 'night-caps', hot milk for Evadne, a whisky and soda for Laura, Horlick's for herself. **1966** J. CLEARY *High Commissioner* iii. 53 A spoonful of Horlicks in a glass of Scotch and I'll be fine. **1973** J. WILSON *Truth or Dare* ii. 24 She..rinsed out the Horlicks mugs.

horme (hǭ·ɹmi). *Psychol.* Also **hormé.** [C. G. Jung's ad. Gr. ὁρμή impulse.] Vital or purposeful energy. Hence **ho·rmic** *a.*, of, pertaining to, or characterized by horme; **ho·rmism,** the theory of, or belief in, such purposeful energy; so **ho·rmist,** an adherent of hormism.

[*a* **1680** CUDWORTH *Treat. Freewill* (1838) 30 Now this love and desire of good,..is not a mere passion or *horme*, but a settled resolved principle. *Ibid.* 57 Epicurus.. conceived that brutes were not merely passive to their own fancies and *hormae*, but that they could add something of their own to them.] **1915** JUNG in *Jrnl. Abnormal Psychol.* IX. 396 The terminology—extraversion and introversion—depends upon my energic conception of mental phenomena. I assume a hypothetical energy which I designate as *hormé.* **1915** W. H. B. STODDART *New Psychiatry* 4 This word 'horme' has a wide signification, applicable to all the instincts. **1920** T. P. NUNN *Education* ii. 21 To this element of drive or urge, whether it occurs in the conscious life of men and the higher animals, or in the unconscious activities of their bodies and the (presumably) unconscious behaviour of lower animals, we propose to give a single name—*horme.* **1926** W. McDOUGALL *Outl. Abnormal Psychol.* 27 Jung says, 'I postulate a hypothetical fundamental striving which I designate *libido*'; and in a footnote..'This energy may also be designated as hormé. Hormé is a Greek word (ὁρμή)—force, attack, press, impetuosity, violence, urgency, zeal. It is related to Bergson's "élan vital". The concept hormé is an energetic expression for psychological values.' *Ibid.* 121 The vital or hormic energy of B's organism. **1927** *Contemp. Rev.* June 769 A kind of hormic determinism. **1931** R. S. WOODWORTH *Contemp. Schools Psychol.* 213 Purpose can properly be carried over into abnormal psychology, as has been done by the hormic psycho-pathologists, Freud especially. **1937** *Jrnl. Theol. Stud.* XXXVIII. 330 Miss Ikin is herself a thoroughly competent psychologist, with a Freudian training, but with a much wider interest in psychology of the hormic type than is usual in those whose concern has been with 'deep analysis' or psycho-analysis proper. **1944** L. COHN in H. Treece *Herbert Read* 58 McDougall adheres to the same 'dionysian' or hormic conception of the soul which is to-day represented by Bergson, Freud, [etc.]. **1948** *Brit. Jrnl. Psychol.* June 187 The hormic-tension theory, (which explains pleasure as connected with the lowering of tension and unpleasure with its increase). **1948** W. McDOUGALL *Introd. Soc. Psychol.* (ed. 29) Suppl. vii. 465 'Pleasure and pain are also motive forces depending upon individual experience.' ..To admit this is to combine hedonism with hormism. *Ibid.* 471 The hormist can find no clear instances that support Woodworth's thesis and can point to a multitude of instances which indicate an absence of..power. **1953** HINSIE & SCHATZKY *Psychiatric Dict.* (ed. 2) 653/1 Hormism is..opposed to hedonism. **1958** W. STARK *Sociology of Knowledge* 239 Though the sympherontic and hormic theories are commonly regarded as sociologies of knowledge.

hormogonium (hǭɹmogōᵘ·niǒm). *Bot.* Pl. **hormogonia.** [mod.L.: see HORMOGONE.] = HORMOGONE.

1880 W. G. FARLOW *Marine Algae* in *Rep. Commissioner Fish & Fisheries 1879* (U.S. Senate Misc. Document 59, 46th Cong., 2nd Session) App. A. 12 The cells intermediate between the two heterocysts escape in the form of a small chain called a hormogonium. **1948** *New Biol.* V. 13 Most filamentous blue-green algae form hormogonia. **1965** F. E. ROUND *Biol. Algae* ii. 24 The short lengths of trichomes thus released are known as hormogonia.

hormonal (hǭɹmōᵘ·năl, hǭ·ɹmonăl), *a. Physiol.* [f. *HORMON(E + -AL.] Of, involving, or effected by a hormone or hormones; that is or acts as a hormone.

1926 *Chem. Abstr.* XX. 3029 (*heading*) The hormonal-nervous regulatory system of fat metabolism. **1949** M. MEAD *Male & Female* xvi. 338 This domestic crisis.. is reinforced by the hormonal instability and emotional fears that surround the menopause. **1953** *Jrnl. R. Hort. Soc.* LXXVIII. 165 The use of hormonal regulators of plant growth. **1955** R. G. HARRY *Mod. Cosmeticol.* (ed. 4) iv. 95 The remark is often made that the mother-to-be has never 'looked so young' or 'so beautiful'. Undoubtedly this effect is due to hormonal influences. **1968** *Times* 11 Nov. 10/8 Apes and most monkeys have menstrual cycles, and in some species the pattern of sexual activity is known to be under hormonal control.

Hence **hormo·nally** *adv.*, by means of a hormone or hormones; as a hormone.

1939 B. HANSTRÖM *Hormones in Invert.* ix. 84 *Dixippus* shows a morphological and a physiological colour-change which are both hormonally regulated. **1955** R. I. DORFMAN in Pincus & Thimann *Hormones* III. xii. 593 A group of hormonally active steroids, estrogens. **1970** *Sci. Jrnl.* June 68/1 They were both able to mate normal individuals to hormonally sex reversed animals which had exactly the same chromosomes.

hormone (hǭ·ɹmōᵘn). *Physiol.* [ad. Gr. ὁρμῶν, pres. pple. of ὁρμᾶν to set in motion (f. ὁρμή onset, impulse), with assimilation to -ONE.] **1. a.** Any of numerous organic compounds that are secreted into the body fluids of an animal, particularly the bloodstream, by a specific group of cells and regulate some specific physiological activity of other cells; also, any synthetic compound having such an effect.

1905 E. H. STARLING in *Lancet* 5 Aug. 340/1 These chemical messengers, however, or 'hormones'..as we might call them. **1906** —— *Recent Adv. Physiol. Digest.* 75 The first products of digestion act on the pyloric mucous membrane, and produce in this membrane a substance which is absorbed into the blood stream, and carried to all the glands of the stomach, where it acts as a specific excitant of their secretory activity. This substance may be called the gastric secretin or gastric hormone. **1924** [see *growth-hormone* s.v. *GROWTH[1] 5]. **1930** R. A. FISHER *Genet. Theory Nat. Selection* 131 The investigation of the influence of the sex hormones has shown how genetic modifications of the whole species can be made to manifest themselves in one sex only. **1931,** etc. [see *GONADOTROPHIC, -TROPIC *a.*]. **1951** A. GROLLMAN *Pharmacol. & Therapeutics* xxvi. 581 The estrogenic hormones are responsible for certain secondary sex characteristics in the female, such as the plumage markings of some birds. **1955** *Sci. News Let.* 24 Sept. 198/3 Hormones are chemicals made by the adrenal, sex, pituitary and other body glands. **1959** A. C. GUYTON *Function Human Body* i. 11 Adrenocortical hormones secreted by the two adrenal cortices..control the passage of proteins, salts, and perhaps other substances through the cell walls. **1967** *Martindale's Extra Pharmacopoeia* (ed. 25) 1277/2 Synthetic sex hormones have usually been developed from the basic steroid structure of the naturally occurring testosterone. **1968** PASSMORE & ROBSON *Compan. Med. Stud.* I. xxv. 40/1 Insulin is a powerful hormone whose actions affect the structure and function of every organ in the body. **1969** *Times* 16 June 3/8 Testosterone..is the chief of the male sex hormones known as androgens. **1970** W. B. YAPP *Introd. Animal Physiol.* (ed. 3) ii. 59 The acid of the gastric juice is secreted under the action of gastrin, a hormone secreted and liberated into the blood by the stomach wall..when it is mechanically stimulated.

b. Restricted to those compounds that have a stimulating (rather than an inhibiting) effect (cf. *CHALONE). Now *rare.*

1914, etc. [see *CHALONE]. **1955** J. T. & O. T. LEWIS tr. *Houssay's Human Physiol.* (ed. 2) li. 561 The word 'hormone' is used also for substances that do not excite activity but rather inhibit it. According to Sharpey-Schafer, the term 'autocoid' would be appropriate for all chemical messengers; 'hormone' for chemical messengers that stimulate activity; and 'chalone' for those which inhibit it. This terminology has not been generally adopted.

2. Any of numerous organic compounds produced by plants which regulate growth and other physiological activities; also, any synthetic compound having such an effect.

1917 *Bot. Gaz.* LXIII. 50 In other plants the hypothetical geotropic substance might be associated with the shoot-forming hormone. **1927** *Biol. Abstr.* I. 244/2 Growth hormone of *Zea* coleoptile tips. **1951** *Jrnl. Chem. Education* XXVIII. 113 We now use plant hormones to propagate plants, prevent preharvest drop of apples,..and defoliate plants without killing the stems. **1952** MEYER & ANDERSON *Plant Physiol.* (ed. 2) xxviii. 555 Other terms commonly used to designate plant hormones are phytohormones, growth hormones, growth substances, and growth regulators. **1960** *Biol. Abstr.* XXXV. 4920/1 The action of synthetic plant hormones on pathogenic fungi was studied. **1966** R. M. DEVLIN *Plant Physiol.* xxii. 532 Bud dormancy in woody species may be regulated by some balance or ratio between a dormancy-inducing hormone and gibberellins. **1968** Y. VARDAR (*title*) Transport of plant hormones. **1970** [see *CYTOKININ]. **1970** WAREING & PHILLIPS *Control of Growth & Differentiation in Plants* iv. 62 Whereas the effects of most animal hormones are rather specific, a plant hormone can elicit a wide range of responses depending upon the type of organ or tissue in which it is acting.

3. *attrib.* and *Comb.*, as *hormone activity, balance, therapy, treatment, weedkiller; hormone-like* adj.; *hormone-controlled* ppl. adj.; **hormone cream,** a skin cream that contains one or more sex hormones.

1936 *Discovery* Nov. 362/1 Such complex subjects as inhibition, reflex action, hormone activity, etc. **1914** H. R. HARROWER *Pract. Hormone Therapy* iii. 45 The intricacies of the hormone balance are fully as complicated as those of the nervous system. **1950** *Sci. News* XV. 134 Rheumatoid arthritis is related to the hormone balance of the body. **1963** A. HERON *Towards Quaker View of Sex* 54 In most mammals, the oestrous cycle of the female, hormone-controlled, is an important factor. **1938** *Encycl. Brit. Bk. of Yr. 1938* 588/1 The group of hormone and vitamin creams, etc., known collectively as 'biological' preparations. **1961** 'R. M. DASHWOOD' *Provincial Daughter* 85 A very good Hormone Cream which many clients find helpful after a certain age. **1962** *Punch* 12 Dec. 845/2 The Consumers' Association finds no reason for buying oestrogenic hormone creams. **1937** *Contrib. Boyce Thompson Inst.* VIII. 338 Characteristic responses of plants to hormone-like substances have been described. **1914** H. R. HARROWER *Pract. Hormone Therapy* p. xii, At present the application of hormone therapy in general practice is the exception rather than the rule. **1921** *Endocrinology* V. 538 Convincing results of hormone therapy in gynecology. **1949** KOESTLER *Insight & Outlook* x. 138 Hormone therapy and neuro-surgery aim at restoring equilibrium by action somewhere in the middle. **1955** A. HUXLEY *Let.* 5 Feb. (1969) 731 Hormone treatment is now being given. **1972** *Lancet* 3 June 1246/2 In 1 case hormone treatment was given

for mastitis. **1950** *N.Z. Jrnl. Agric.* Apr. 328/3 There is no danger in using hormone weedkillers on pastures.

Hence **ho·rmonize** *v. trans.*, to treat with a hormone; **ho·rmonized** *ppl. a.*, treated with a hormone; containing a hormone.

1940 *Proc. Amer. Soc. Hort. Sci.* XXXVII. 1015 Hormonized Dust gave satisfactory results with many kinds of cuttings. *Ibid.* 1016 Forty-seven days after potting, plants rooted with Hormonized Dust were 7 days ahead of untreated plants in shoot production. **1947** *Biol. Abstr.* XXI. 2043/1 Field expts. with potatoes hormonized by heteroauxin. **1950** *Ibid.* XXIV. 1611/2 The germination of seeds of endive and Brussels sprouts is not improved by hormonizing the seeds or fruits with indole-acetic acid. **1959** *Times* 16 Feb. 15/5 Its carcass did not set well on cooling, and this had led to most of the butchers' complaints about hormonized beef. **1960** *Farmer & Stockbreeder* 16 Feb. 78/1 America's top authorities confirm there is absolutely no risk with hormonized meat.

hormonic (hǭɹmǫ·nik, hǭɹmōu·nik), *a. Physiol.* [f. *HORMON(E + -IC.] = *HORMONAL *a.*

1914 [see *CHALONE]. **1928** *Brit. Med. Jrnl.* 18 Feb. 255/1 The functional (hormonic) over-activity of the anterior lobe of the pituitary gland. **1933** T. C. MERRILL tr. *Voronoff & Alexandrescu's Testicular Grafting* 2 Animals which are too young and employed before the establishment of puberty and the production of free hormonic secretion, are unsuitable.

hormonology (hǭɹmonǫ·lǒdʒi). *rare.* [f. *HORMON(E + -OLOGY.] The study of hormones; endocrinology.

1918 *Endocrinology* II. 62 (*heading*) A bit of hormonology, with practical applications. **1944** KOESTLER in *Horizon* Mar. 170 The whole body of ideas had undergone a radical transformation: Relativity and Quantum mechanics, Hormonology and Psycho-analysis. **1970** *Sci. Jrnl.* June 44/1 It used to be a shibboleth of hormonology that such messenger molecules were not affected by the chemical process they influenced.

horn, *sb.* Add: **3. b.** Each of the erect and permanent bony processes, covered with hairy skin, growing on the head of a giraffe; also applied to a smaller protuberance in front of the other two.

[**1598** [implied by quot. s.v. GIRAFFE 1].] **1753** *Chambers's Cycl.* Suppl. s.v. *Zurnapa*, Its head is wholly of the make of the stag's, but differs in size, and has two little obtuse horns, which are not more than six fingers breadth long, and are hairy. **1840** tr. *Cuvier's Anim. Kingdom* 138 The Giraffe..is characterized by conical horns in both sexes, that are always covered with a hairy skin, and never fall...In the middle of the forehead, there is an eminence or third horn, broader and much shorter, but equally articulated by suture. **1879** *Encycl. Brit.* X. 619/2 In captivity it [*sc.* the giraffe] is said to make use of its skin-covered horns as weapons of defence. **1965** D. MORRIS *Mammals* 393 The Giraffe is easily the tallest of all the mammals... Both sexes have short, hair-covered horns.

5. Also jocularly, the human nose. *slang.*

1893 FARMER & HENLEY *Slang* III. 351/1 *Horn*, the nose. **1935** ERSINE *Underworld & Prison Slang* 45 *Horn*, a man's nose, *bugle.* **1945** L. SHELLY *Jive Talk Dict.* 12/2 *Horn*, the nose.

b. Also, to restrict one's expenditure, esp. of money.

1920 GALSWORTHY *In Chancery* I. i. 7 In the meantime, no more children! Even young Nicholas was drawing in his horns, and had made no addition to his six for quite three years. **1941** A. L. ROWSE *Tudor Cornwall* xiv. 363 His will was a very cautious affair: he had to draw in his horns. **1957** I. MURDOCH *Sandcastle* i. 16 If we don't get some extra money from somewhere we shall have to draw our horns in pretty sharply. No more Continental holidays, you know.

c. An erect penis; an erection. Also in phr. *to have (get) the horn*, to be sexually excited. (Not in polite use.)

1785 GROSE *Dict. Vulgar T.*, *Horn Cholick*, a temporary priapism. **1879–80** *Pearl* (1970) 257 A man with light trousers, of decency shorn, Stop and talk to young ladies while having the horn. **1889** BARRÈRE & LELAND *Dict. Slang* I. 475/2 'To have the *horn*', to be in a state of sexual desire. **1922** JOYCE *Ulysses* 263 Got the horn or what? he said. **1968** J. R. ACKERLEY *My Father & Myself* xiii. 148 He remarked to me then with a chuckle that the thing that had worried him most was that he might not be able to 'get the horn' again. **1968** L. BERG *Risinghill* 121 'Why does a boy get the "horn"?' 'The "horn" or the erection of the penis is necessary to make sure that the sperm is placed well inside the body of the woman.' **1972** *Guardian* 3 Apr. 11/3 Dirty old goat... He only bows his head to get his horn up.

6. b. *horns of consecration*: in Mycenæan art, a pictorial symbol or object, often found together with the double axe and pillar, connected with the Cretan worship of the ox.

1901 A. J. EVANS in *Jrnl. Hellenic Studies* XXI. 196 The columns of the Knossian shrine apparently approach the outer edge of the openings, leaving room, however, in front of them for the 'horns of consecration'. **1939** V. G. CHILDE *Dawn Europ. Civilization* (ed. 3) v. 73 The cult of the Mother Goddess, associated, as in Crete, with the symbols of the dove, the double-axe, the sacred pillar and horns of consecration. **1939** J. D. S. PENDLEBURY *Archæol. Crete* v. 274 The double axe itself is found as a votive offering and as a cult object between the horns of consecration. **1970** BRAY & TRUMP *Dict. Archaeol.* 149/2 Minoan religion is somewhat obscure, but includes a Mother Goddess who was worshipped in many shrines equipped with figurines..the sacred double axe and horns of consecration.

7. Delete †*Obs.* and add later example.

1942 D. POWELL *Time to be Born* (1943) i. 24 Julian was almost pathologically jealous of her, fearing the final indignity of horns.

11. b. In *Golf*, the substance of which part of the face of a wooden club is made.

1743 T. MATHISON *Goff* I. 5 Fenc'd with horn the head. **1801** J. STRUTT *Sports & Pastimes* II. iii. 81 Goff..is performed with a bat,..the curvature is affixed to the bottom, faced with horn and backed with lead. **1839** *Chambers's Jrnl.* 22 June 173/3 The curvature, made of thorn, is affixed to the bottom, faced with horn, and backed with lead. **1890** H. G. HUTCHINSON *Golf* iii. 65 There is, however, something to be said in favour of dispensing altogether with the 'horn' in the case of brass-soled clubs.

c. *by the (great) horn spoon*: used as a fanciful oath or formula of asseveration. *U.S.*

1842 *Amer. Nat. Song Bk.* II. 222 He vow'd by the great horn spoon..He'd give them a licking, and that pretty soon. **1848** LOWELL *Biglow P.* 1st Ser. v. 16 'I should like to shoot The holl gang, by the gret horn spoon!' sez he. **1853** *Knickerbocker* XLI. 115 'By the horn spoons!' repeated the skipper suddenly. **1897** *Outing* (U.S.) XXX. 380/2 'By the Great Horn Spoon!' the voice shouted, 'here's a chunk of civilization.' **1948** *Time* 22 Nov. 25/1 Operators had sworn by the Great Horn Spoon that they would not negotiate with Harry ('The Nose') Bridges.

13. b. *to blow* (U.S. *toot*) *one's own horn*: 'to blow one's own trumpet' (see TRUMPET *sb.* 3).

1859 'MARK TWAIN' *Lett.* (1917) I. 43 Permit me to 'blow my horn'. **1860** G. D. PRENTICE *Prenticeana* 63 'Blowing your own *horn* I see,' said his comrade. **1903** A. W. PATTERSON *Schumann* 167 Surely these side-lights upon the straightforwardness and integrity of the man entirely free him from the calumny of ever being guilty of 'blowing his own horn'. **1940** A. E. HERTZLER *Doctor & his Patients* (1941) ii. 47 He that tooteth not his own horn, the same shall not be tooted. **1949** E. S. GARDNER *Case of Half-Wakened Wife* ii. 9 Gregory, on the other hand, had been reticent, inarticulate, sensitive, a man who modestly refrained from tooting his own horn and didn't like to hear others talk about themselves.

c. *French horn* (earlier and later examples).

1682 *Loyal Protestant & Domestick Intelligencer* 7 Mar. [2]/2 (Advt.), Any Gentleman may be furnished with Trumpets, French horns, Speaking Trumpets. **1771** C. BURNEY *Pres. St. Mus.* 149 There were two organs, and two pair of French horns. **1961** R. M. PEGGE in A. Baines *Mus. Instruments* xii. 297 In England [*sc.* in the 18th cent.]..the French horn was chiefly used for the purposes of entertainment in the pleasure gardens and on the river, two performers playing duets being the usual thing. Rich men of family and fashion sometimes included in their retinues French horn players, often Negroes, to add *panache* to their equipages.

f. An instrument attached to motor vehicles, etc., which is sounded as a warning signal. Also *attrib.*

1901 *Graphic* LXIV. 268/3 The hideous toot-toot of its horn. **1914** R. & E. SHACKLETON *Four on Tour in Eng.* 83 The horn was honked suddenly. **1939** H. HODGE *Cab, Sir?* 19 And plenty of hornwork. The more the toots the bigger the tip. **1965** *New Statesman* 22 Oct. 594/2 The car..is taking over this enchanting city [*sc.* Rome]... The official campaign to cut down horn-maniacs appears to be a total failure. **1969** *Highway Code* 49 You must not..sound your horn at night (11.30 p.m.–7 a.m.) in a built-up area. **1973** *Sat. Rev. Soc.* (U.S.) May 42 Horn alarms: many inexpensive devices that can be hooked into the automobile horn can now be bought for less than $10.

g. A horn-shaped pastry case; an ice-cream cornet.

1908, 1960 [see *cream horn*, *CREAM *sb.*[2] 7]. **1927** 'R. CROMPTON' *William—in Trouble* viii. 202 In one hand it held a stick of rock; in the other an ice cream horn. It licked them alternately. **1933** —— *William—the Rebel* xi. 212, I c'n eat twenty ice-cream horns. **1951** *Good Housek. Home Encycl.* 426/1 For savoury horns use a mixture such as those suggested for bouchées. **1969** *Main Cookery Bk.* (ed. 14) 172 Pastry horns can only be made using a special cone-shaped pastry case.

h. *Jazz slang.* A trumpet.

1935 *Hot News* May 5/1 He just threw his horn away and went into a pawnshop and bought another. **1938** D. BAKER *Young Man with Horn* 9 And then he learned to play a horn—a trumpet, if there's anybody here who doesn't know what kind of a horn a horn is—and that was his proper medium. **1955** R. DAVIS in A. J. McCarthy *Jazzbook 1955* 40 Bunk was the subject of articles in the *New York Herald-Tribune* and the magazine *Time*, in which he was somewhat superlatively described as a 'genius of the horn'. **1959** G. AVAKIAN in M. T. Williams *Art of Jazz* (1960) 68 Each of these trio cuttings ends with Bix picking up his horn to play the coda.

i. *Jazz slang.* Any kind of wind instrument.

1937 *Metronome* Jan. 25/1 Satchmo, I was only kiddin'. I'll give you your horn back. **1938** [see prec.]. **1966** *Melody Maker* 30 July 8/3 Every instrument became a horn. When a guy said 'Can I bring my horn for a sit in,' you never knew whether he'd show up with a goofus or a glockenspiel. **1966** *Crescendo* Aug. 21/2 If I'm happy with the horn I've got, the mouthpiece, the set-up, the reed and everything.

j. The player of a horn (senses 13 c, *h and *i).

1945 L. SHELLY *Jive Talk Dict.* 35 *The Horn*, the famous trumpeter. **1947** R. DE TOLEDANO *Frontiers of Jazz* p. ix, Did you ever try to relax while some fine horns were blowing, like for instance, Maxey, Pee Wee, and Bird? **1955** KEEPNEWS & GRAUER *Pict. Hist. Jazz* i. 14 Freddie Keppard was among the very great New Orleans horns. **1955** S. WHITMORE *Solo* iv. 52 Take Buddy Bolden, if you will. A great horn. **1968** *Globe & Mail* (Toronto) 17 Feb. 26 'We've been lucky,' Harry Freedman, English horn, said. 'Ozawa has..done much to build up the orchestra.'

k. *the horn*: the telephone. *U.S. colloq.*

1945 L. SHELLY *Jive Talk Dict.* 31/1 *On the horn*, telephoning. **1962** [see *FLAT *adv.* 3 b]. **1967** D. C. COOKE *c/o American Embassy* (1968) xi. 104 I've been on the horn half the night trying to get you. **1970** C. ARMSTRONG *Protégé* vii. 89 I'll have to get on the horn tomorrow and poke up my contacts.

14*. a. A trumpet- or cone-shaped accessory of early gramophones and phonographs that collects sound to be recorded and amplifies the sound reproduced; a similar structure in some kinds of loud-speaker that contains the diaphragm in its throat and is designed to transmit its vibrations to the air. Also *attrib.*

1897 *Sears, Roebuck Catal.* 485/2 The Graphophone or Talking Machine is a most wonderful invention... By using the horn they can be distinctly heard in every part of a large hall. **1904** S. R. BOTTONE *Talking Machines* 62 The horn or trumpet which collects the sounds should be of *papier mâché*, and not of metal. **1911** *Encycl. Brit.* XXI. 468/2 The person making the record sings or plays in front of a horn or funnel. **1927** *Wireless World* 16 Nov. 664 When broadcasting first started, the only type of loudspeaker on the market was one which had.. a straight conical horn. **1931** B. BROWN *Talking Pictures* v. 121 Some of the first horns to be used in sound pictures were of the straight trumpet type. **1934** C. LAMBERT *Music Ho!* iv. 257 The old pre-electric horn recording, with its euphoniums instead of 'cellos, and its handful of Stroh violins. **1946** T. RATTIGAN *Winslow Boy* I. 12 He points to a gramophone—1912 model, with horn—lying on a table. **1956** C. FOWLER *High Fidelity* vi. 103 Most tweeters used in high-fidelity systems employ small diaphragms which work into a horn of some sort. **1957** L. DURRELL *Justine* II. 141 The same night, on the old horn gramophone..I heard some amateur's recording. **1969** *Listener* 23 Jan. 121/3 A pre-electric horn gramophone. **1970** R. D. FORD *Introd. Acoustics* v. 98 Horns are also very useful for improving the performance of loud-speakers at low frequencies.

b. *Radio.* Any hollow waveguide that increases in one or both transverse dimensions towards the open end and can consequently act as a transmitting or receiving aerial. Also *attrib.*, as *horn aerial*, *antenna.*

1936 W. L. BARROW in *Proc. Inst. Radio Engin.* XXIV. 1328 [The pipe can be flared into a horn-shaped radiator]. *Ibid.*, The application of horn radiators is not confined to the hollow tube system, for they may be fed by a coaxial or other lines... Thus, electromagnetic horns may be used as radiators in the wave band below ten meters. **1939** *Ibid.* XXVII. 51 The operation of the electromagnetic horn 'antenna'. **1949** H. E. PENROSE *Princ. & Pract. Radar* xxii. 511 In general, the longer the opening of the horn, the more directive is the resulting field pattern. **1961** H. JASIK *Antenna Engin. Handbk.* x. 7 The pyramidal horn is frequently used as a standard horn of known gain in making measurements of other antennas. **1961** MICZAIKA & SINTON *Tools of Astronomer* viii. 261 Often a parabola is fed by a wave guide that terminates in a horn aimed at the disk. **1962** [see *ANTENNA 5]. **1970** [see *DESPIN *v.*]. **1972** *Daily Tel.* 28 June 11/8 Mounted inconspicuously in its front grille were two four-inch-square radar 'horns'—one for transmitting, the other for receiving.

19. b. Also, any cornu.

1802 C. BELL *Anat. Brain* 15 The Choroid Plexus.. will be seen sinking backwards into the great inferior horn of the Ventricle. **1901** J. BERRY *Dis. Thyroid Gland* i. 6 Small portions of the larynx and pharynx are embraced by the upper horns [of the thyroid]. **1957** R. T. WOODBURNE *Essent. Human Anat.* iv. 300/1 The coccygeal horns..articulate with the horns of the sacrum and enclose the fifth sacral intervertebral foramen. **1972** *Nature* 22 Oct. 521/1 In the spinal cord..the motoneurones of the ventral horn..are subject to a variety of inhibitory influences.

21. b. (Examples.)

1849 F. PARKMAN *Calif. & Oregon Trail* iv. 41 My long heavy rifle encumbered me, and the low sound it made striking the horn of my saddle startled him. *a* **1861** T. WINTHROP *Canoe & Saddle* (1862) 212, I threw Klale's bridle over his neck, and grasping the horn, swung myself into the saddle. **1947** *Harper's Mag.* July 42/1 He took off his battered gray hat and rested it on the horn of his saddle.

g. *Electr.* Either of the pointed projections at the edge of a pole-piece of an electric motor or generator.

1886 S. P. THOMPSON *Dyn.-Electr. Machinery* (ed. 2) v. 88 The greatest amount of such eddy-currents will be generated..where the magnetic perturbations are greatest and most sudden... This should be at the leading corner or 'horn' of the pole-piece of the generating dynamo. **1923** A. S. LANGSDORF *Princ. Direct-Current Machines* (ed. 3) ii. 91 Increased area is secured by means of pole shoes bolted or dove-tailed to the core in the case of solid poles, or by means of projecting tips or horns punched integrally with the sheets composing a laminated pole.

h. *Aeronaut.* (i) A short lug or lever projecting from a control surface to which the wire for moving the surface is attached.

1920 H. WOODHOUSE *Textbk. Appl. Aeronaut. Engin.* 319/2 *Horn-control arm*, an arm at right angles to a control surface to which a control cable is attached, for example, aileron horn, rudder horn, elevator horn, etc. More commonly called a Mast. **1928** CHATFIELD & TAYLOR *Airplane* v. 75 The cables from the horns on the ailerons are led to the stick. **1952** A. Y. BRAMBLE *Air-Plane Flight* vii. 101 Notice the curved projecting pieces above and below on each aileron. These are called 'horns', and from these we see wires running forward into holes in the wing.

(ii) A part of an aileron or other control surface that extends across the axis of rotation over part of its length and serves to improve the balance of the surface; so *horn balance, -balanced* adj.

1921 *Aeronaut. Jrnl.* XXV. 539 The most common method of balancing ailerons is to have a 'horn' or projection on the aileron beyond the wing tip and forward of the aileron hinge. *Ibid.* 554 The horn method of balancing elevators. **1922** *Encycl. Brit.* XXX. 23/2 This so-called 'horn' balance proved unsatisfactory. **1939** *Jrnl. R. Aeronaut. Soc.* XLIII. 424 This effect was noticed during the war on horn-balanced rudders, and has now been used in the design of elevators. **1952** W. J. DUNCAN *Control & Stability Aircraft* vii. 195 A horn balance is a local protuberance of the control surface lying forward of the hinge axis... The horn may lie behind the main surface (shielded horn) or be exposed to the airstream. **1968** B. DICKINSON *Aircraft Stability & Control* x. 235 If the horn extends to the leading edge of the aerofoil it is referred to as an 'unshielded' horn.

25. b. *Electr.* Each of a pair of rod conductors that diverge in a vertical plane from a narrow gap at the base, designed to extinguish any arc that forms in the gap and used to protect power lines from voltage surges; so *horn arrester, gap*; also, a projecting rod conductor that protects an insulator by attracting away from it any arc that forms.

1911 *Trans. Amer. Inst. Electr. Engin.* XXIX. I. 582 The relief gaps were removed before the lightning season of 1908. The grounded horn was left in place to act as a lightning rod. *Ibid.* 600 We placed the horn gaps on the towers, about 500 feet apart. **1930** *Engineering* 7 Mar. 314/2 Insulators on high-voltage lines are protected by arcing horns. **1968** P. J. FREEMAN *Electric Power* ix. 253 The shape of the horn gap forces the arc upwards by magnetic and thermal effects and the arc is self-extinguishing. **1969** L. CSUROS in *Power Syst. Protection* (Electr. Council) III. xii. 20 The arcing horns shown on the 132 kV bushings serve the main purpose of protecting the metal fittings on..the bushing by providing a suitable anchorage for the fault arc.

27. a. *horn-call.*

1912 G. MOORE *Hail & Farewell! Salve* vi. 102 If I knew Elgar, I'd write and ask him to send me a horn-call. **1954** J. R. R. TOLKIEN *Two Towers* i. 15 Suddenly the horn-calls ceased. **1959** D. COOKE *Lang. Mus.* ii. 57 Wagner..makes a musical demonstration of the natural 'rightness' of the harmonic series, for the horn-call is preceded by the low E flat on the basses. **1971** *Country Life* 18 Feb. 358/1 Siegfried promptly announces his arrival by horn-call and wastes no time in walking into the trap.

c. *horn-like.*

1929 D. H. LAWRENCE *Pansies* 26 Honking horn-like into the twilight. **1951** S. SPENDER *World within World* 162 The syllables which she unerringly chose to emphasize changed her speech into horn-like blasts.

28. *horn-handled* adj.

1922 JOYCE *Ulysses* 619 A blunt hornhandled ordinary knife with nothing particularly Roman or antique about it. **1925** W. DE LA MARE *Connoisseur* (1926) 51 His horn-handled and gold-mounted umbrella.

29. horn aerial, antenna (see *HORN *sb.* 14* b); **horn balance** (see *HORN *sb.* 21 h (ii)); **horn-band** (examples); **horn-bug** (earlier and later examples); **horn cell** *Anat.*, any of the ganglion cells of the cornua of the spinal cord; **horn-distemper** (example); **horn-fisted** *a.*, having hands made horny by hard work; **horngarth** [GARTH[1]] (see quot. 1928); **horn gate** *Founding*, a horn-shaped gate (GATE *sb.*[4] 1 a) that curves downward from a runner and then upwards into a mould cavity, discharging through its narrow end; **horn-man** (earlier and later examples); *spec.* in Jamaica among the Maroons, a man who blew the horn, giving signals; **horn-poppy**: substitute *Glaucium flavum* for *G. luteum*; (examples); **horn-pout** (earlier and later examples); **horn-rimmed** *a.*, denoting spectacles having rims made of horn; **horn-rims**, horn-rimmed spectacles; **horn-ring** (see quot. 1928); **horn speaker**, a loud-speaker that incorporates a horn; **horn spectacles** = **horn-rims*; **horn-tip** (example); **horn-worm**: substitute for def.: *U.S.*, the larva of moths of the genus *Protoparce*, which includes *P. sexta*, a pest of tobacco, and *P. quinquemaculata*, which attacks the tomato and certain other vegetables; also, the larva of other hawkmoths of the family Sphingidæ; (add later examples).

1849 J. G. DALYELL *Musical Memories Scotland* v. 170 The Russian horn-band consists of a multitude of performers whose concert comprehends the most simple music... Each instrument emits only a single note. *Ibid.* 171, I heard the Russian horn-band in this country, in the year 1833. **1938** *Oxf. Compan. Mus.* 441/1 In Russia..in the middle of the eighteenth century, proprietors of large estates established *horn bands*, much on the principle of our present day handbell ringing, each player being provided with one instrument of the appropriate size for the easy production of one note... The horns were straight ones (not circular). **1776** J. TRUMBULL *McFingal* (Th.), Thought horn-bugs bullets, or, through fears, Muskitoes took for musqueteers. **1869** MRS. STOWE *Oldtown Folks* xxvii. 341 Youre saucy enough to physic a horn-bug. **1899** *Mem. Amer. Folklore Soc.* VII. 63 Horn-bugs, May-bees, May-flies, [etc.]. **1898** *Med. Chron.* IX. News 39 Collateral branches.. are structures of enormous importance..representing the most direct path of nerve communication between the sensory surface..and the ventral horn cells. **1969** J. H. GREEN *Basic Clin. Physiol.* xx. 114/2 When the anterior horn cell sends a nerve impulse along the motor nerve, every muscle fibre in the motor unit contracts. **1843** *Knickerbocker* XXI. 254 Hence it is as important to keep the bee-moth out of hives as the horn-distemper out of cattle. **1929** F. C. BOWEN *Sea Slang* 69 *Horn-Fisted*, a seaman with hands hardened with work. **1961** F. H. BURGESS *Dict. Sailing* 117 *Horn-fisted*, possessing tough hands, and a character to match, through hard work. **1779** L. CHARLTON *Hist. Whitby* II. 96 The Hornegarth..seems to have been a certain stake and yether hedge, made up in the beginning of summer by all those in Whitby-Strand who held land of the Abbot. **1890** *Hornes' Guide to Whitby* 18 About the year 1315,..the *Horngarth* was made at the town of Whitby, with wood from the abbot's forest. **1894** J. C. ATKINSON *Memorials Old Whitby* 50 There is no reason whatever for questioning the conclusion that the Horngarth service..must date back to pre-conquest times. **1928** *Daily Express* 24 May 3 What is the ceremony of 'planting the Horngarth'?.. Driving in a hedge of stakes near Whitby Harbour to the sound of a horn, a custom dating to feudal times, to prevent cattle from straying into the harbour. **1909** *Hawkins' Mech. Dict.* 287/1 Horn gate. **1910** E. L. RHEAD *Princ. & Pract. Ironfounding* ix. 202 Horn gates are shown in Fig. 96... The tapering form and circular sweep allow of their removal without disturbance of the sand. **1934** LAING & ROLFE *Man. Foundry Pract.* vi. 126 The semi-circular in-gates are known as 'horn-gates'. **1803** R. C. DALLAS *Hist. Maroons* I. iii. 70 One of Quao's men, a hornman,.. consented to accompany Captain Adair. **1957** J. KEROUAC *On Road* (1958) I. iv. 201 The hornman sat absolutely motionless. **1961** F. G. CASSIDY *Jamaica Talk* viii. 166 Among the Maroons an important person was the *horn-man*, who gave signals with a horn or conch. **1972** *Down Beat* 16 Mar. 26/2 Farmer and Heath are two of the best-matched hornmen at work in the idiom today. **1851** P. H. GOSSE *Nat. Sojourn Jamaica* 39 The Mexican Horn-poppy (*Argemone*), the West Indian Vervain (*Stachytarpha*),..and others. **1909** *Chambers's Jrnl.* July 445/2 The wild wallflower and horn-poppy..bloom in mid-air. **1798** *Gaz. U.S.* (Philad.) 3 Aug. (Th.), The company concluded to go, for the sake of seeing a horn pout—when at last I drew one up—and behold! what was it, but a cat fish! **1832** *Coll. New H. Hist. Soc.* III. 87 On each side of their body and close to the head is a formidable weapon called a *horn*, and hence the name *Horn-pout*. **1910** *Outlook* 9 July 529 On the other side of the pond we met Sam Noyes, who was catching horn-pouts. **1943** B. DAMON *Sense of Humus* 22 First he brought her a mess of horn pouts he had caught. **1894** *Idler* V. 452 Putting on a pair of horn-rimmed eye-glasses, he read it through very carefully. **1901** KIPLING *Kim* i. 10 The lama mounted a pair of horn-rimmed spectacles of Chinese work. **1922** Horn-rimmed [see *BEAVER[4]]. **1923** *Westm. Gaz.* 12 Apr., A long-necked youth who was talking to a horn-rimmed female. **1931** R. CAMPBELL *Georgiad* ii. 34 Women!..Who mock at horn-rimmed spectacles. **1973** *Times* 16 June 1/4 The London strip club owner..heavily disguised with..a beard and thick, horn-rimmed spectacles..was approached by three detectives. **1927** *Punch* 20 Apr. 424/3 He removed his horn-rims and began polishing them vigorously. **1959** *Encounter* July 59/1 In open-necked tennis shirt and heavy horn-rims. **1970** *New York* 16 Nov. 56/3 Junius glowers over his horn rims. **1928** *Daily Tel.* 16 Oct. 17 The horn-ring, an attachment fitted on the steering wheel so that the motorist can sound his horn without lifting his hand from the circumference of the wheel. **1962** *Which?* Apr. (Suppl.) 74/1 Horn-ring assembly came adrift from steering wheel causing horn failure. **1973** J. M. WHITE *Garden Game* 189, I..put my hand on the horn-ring, pushed it down and held it there. The noise sounded shattering. **1928** L. S. PALMER *Wireless Princ. & Pract.* xi. 428 To reproduce such extremes without distortion is quite beyond the power of any existing horn speaker. **1957** *Encycl. Brit.* XIV. 409/1 Horn speakers may be made quite efficient. **1893** M. BEERBOHM *Let.* 19 Aug. (1964) 53 An old sexton too with horn-spectacles. **1915** J. BUCHAN *Salute to Adventurers* xi. 163 Then he produced some papers, and putting on big horn spectacles, proceeded to instruct me in them. **1923** V. WOOLF in *Dial* LXXV. 21 Mrs Dalloway, remembering Kensington Gardens and the old lady in horn spectacles. **1808** T. ASHE *Travels* III. xxxiii. 89 They sell them furs and horn tips, and receive in exchange ball powder, whiskey, tobacco, beads, ornaments, and blankets. **1784** J. SMYTH *Tour U.S.* II. 132 The other [species] is the horn-worm.. of a vivid green colour, with a number of pointed excrescences or feelers, from his head like horns: these devour the [tobacco] leaf. **1850** *Rep. U.S. Comm. Patents, Agric. 1849* 459 The horn-worm is deposited on the smooth or upper surface of the leaf in an egg by the tobacco fly. **1962** METCALF & FLINT *Destructive & Useful Insects* (ed. 4) xiv. 656 The winter stage of the hornworms is very often spaded up or plowed out in the spring. *Ibid.* 657 In the tomato hornworm larvae the horn is black and there are eight stripes..; while in the tobacco hornworm the horn is red and there are seven oblique stripes. **1972** *Sci. Amer.* June 73/2 The caterpillars of *Manduca sexta*..are the hornworms that feed on tobacco and tomato plants.

horn, *v.* **2.** Delete † *Obs.* and add later examples.

1952 S. SELVON *Brighter Sun* viii. 157 Look at yuh, yuh nasty dog! Yuh suspect she horning yuh! Yuh ain't have no shame? Dat poor gul don't even look at any odder man but you. **1970** 'W. HAGGARD' *Hardliners* i. 5 She'd given him a daughter and called it a day, horning him quite shamelessly.

3. b. *fig.* To push, as an ox with its horns. *U.S.*

1851 J. J. HOOPER *Widow Rugby's Husb.* 69 You horned me off to get a chance to get gaming witnesses out of the way. **1881** *Times* (Philad.) 5 June (Th.), Mac Veagh is trying his best to horn Blaine out of the Cabinet herd, just as young buffalo bulls horn out the old ones.

c. *intr.* To push or butt *in* (*on* or *with*). *colloq.* (orig. *U.S.*).

1912 C. MATHEWSON *Pitching in a Pinch* 213 Many of them try hard to 'horn in' with the men who have made good as Big Leaguers. **1924** C. E. MULFORD *Rustlers' Valley* xviii. 201 Why did Chet horn in on Baldy's arrest? **1927** *Bulletin* 15 Apr. 12/3 'Well, your little playmate certainly queered things,' he said. Thorn shrugged. 'I'm sorry, chief; but I couldn't help it. You saw how he horned in.' **1932** D. L. SAYERS *Have his Carcase* xiv. 186 Glaisher might not like this horning in on his province. **1936** WODEHOUSE *Laughing Gas* xvi. 173, I suppose she felt she owed you something, after horning in on your big scene like that and trying to steal your publicity the way she did. **1939** *Airman's Gaz.* Dec., The lesson for today chicks is how to horn in on the radio racket. **1942** 'B. J. ELLAN' *Spitfire!* xii. 61 Hurricanes had probably been chasing this Dornier when I had come in and attacked. Perhaps after all I was horning in on them! **1970** G. F. NEWMAN *Sir, You Bastard* iv. 114 A proportion of detectives everywhere were at it; it was simply a question of finding them and horning in.

6. *trans.* and *intr.* To sound a horn; to signal to (someone) with a horn; to proclaim (something) loudly (as if) by sounding a horn.

1874 HARDY *Far from Madding Crowd* II. xii. 147 Jan meanwhile merging his..thoughts..in a song:—'To-morrow-to-mor- w!..To-mor-row, to-mor—'. 'Do hold thy horning, Jan!' said Oak. *Ibid.* II. xxvii. 335 'I am afeard your labour in keeping it close will be throwed away,' said Coggan...'Labe Tall's old woman will horn it all over parish in half an hour.' **1892** G. MEREDITH *Poems* 77 He entreats..Compassion..For his fierce bugler horning onset. **1908** R. BROUGHTON *Mamma* v. 45 Silence save of the nightly traffic roaring and ringing and horning past outside. **1923** W. DE LA MARE *Riddle* 209 The screech of its engine, horning up into the windless air. **1946** A. M. WALTERS *Moondrop to Gascony* xv. 199 We horned the small convoy to a stop as we approached Tanet.

hornbeam. 1. Substitute for def.: A tree of the genus *Carpinus* (family Betulaceæ), native to Asia, Europe, and North America, esp. *C. betulus*, the common hornbeam, which is native to Great Britain, or *C. caroliniana*, the American hornbeam; so called from its hard, close-grained wood. (Add earlier U.S. and further examples.)

1671 in *Early Rec. Providence, R.I.* (1893) III. 107 Boundeth on..the northwesterne Corner with a horne beame or peckled tree marked on too sides. **1791** W. GILPIN *Remarks on Forest Scenery* I. iv. 48 Very nearly allied to the beech..is the hornbeam. It grows like it, when it is suffered to grow; but it is generally seen only in clipped hedges. **1968** J. ARNOLD *Shell Bk. Country Crafts* xxxi. 330 When threshing was done with flails, the floors were made of hornbeam planks, and until lignum vitae came to this country hornbeam was used for bowls and still is for butchers' blocks.

hornblendite (hǭ·ɹnblendəit). *Petrogr.* Also †-yte. [f. HORNBLEND(E + -ITE[1].] A granular rock largely or entirely composed of hornblende.

1874 J. D. DANA *Man. Geol.* (ed. 2) II. i. 70 Hornblendyte.—A very tough, granular, crystalline rock, consisting of hornblende, and hardly schistose in structure. **1901** *Jrnl. Chem. Soc.* LXXX. II. 170 Hornblendite from Brandberget, consisting essentially of hornblende. **1930** PEACH & HORNE *Geol. Scotl.* 26 The ultrabasic rocks (pyroxenites, hornblendites) generally form lenticles. **1967** P. J. WYLLIE *Ultramafic & Related Rocks* i. 2/2 Hornblendites vary widely in mineralogy, and various combinations of hornblende, pyroxene, olivine, and biotite are known.

horned, *a.* Add: **1. c.** *fig.*

1889 W. B. YEATS *Wanderings of Oisin* 137 Between the hornèd hills. **1955** E. POUND *Classic Anthol.* III. 195 High spouts the water, from the hornèd spring.

2. b. horned adder, an African snake, *Bitis cornuta*, belonging to the viper family; **horned dace** *U.S.*, a small freshwater fish, *Semotilus atromaculatus*, of the family Cyprinidæ; **horned frog**, (*b*) a South American frog of the genus *Ceratophrys* which has horn-like projections on its eyelids; **horned helmet**, the gastropod mollusc, *Cassis cornuta*, or its shell, from which cameos are cut; **horned lizard** = *horned frog* (*a*) (*s.v.* HORNED *a.* 2 b); **horned poppy**, the yellow sea-poppy, *Glaucium flavum*; **horned pout**, an American catfish, *Ictalurus* (formerly *Ameiurus*) *nebulosus*, introduced into western Europe about 1880, = *horn-pout* (HORN *sb.* 29); **horned rattlesnake**, a desert snake, *Crotalus cerastes*, found in the south-western U.S. and Mexico; = SIDE-WINDER[2]; **horned screamer**, a large black and white bird, *Anhima cornuta*, distinguished by a hornlike process on its forehead and found in marshy country in the northern half of South America; **horned snake**, (*a*) = *hoop-snake* (s.v. *HOOP *sb.*[1] 13 b); (*b*) = **horned viper*; **horned toad**, (*a*) = *horned frog* (*a*)

(*s.v.* HORNED *a.* 2 b); (*b*) = **horned frog* (*b*); **horned viper,** a venomous African snake, *Cerastes cornutus,* distinguished by a horny scale above each eye.

1878 A. AYLWARD *Transvaal of To-Day* xii. 244 The horned adder—a rather rare variety—is one of the worst of these pests. **1929** W. ROSE *Veld & Vlei* 175 The Horned Adder..favours sandy localities, where, buried to the eyes, it watches for any lizards or mice that are unwary enough to approach within striking distance. **1947** J. STEVENSON-HAMILTON *Wild Life S. Afr.* xxxvi. 329 The Horned Adder... Also a dangerous viper, is usually found in sand regions. **1842** *Nat. Hist. N.Y., Zool.* IV. 199 The Horned Sucker is common in most of the fresh-water streams of this state... It is known under the various popular names of *Barbel, Dace,* and *Horned Dace.* **1896** JORDAN & EVERMANN *Fishes Amer.* I. 222 *Semotilus Atromaculatus...* Horned-dace; Creek-chub. **1963** P. A. PARSONS *Outdoor Life Compl. Bk. Fresh Water Fishing* iv. 45 They [*sc.* creek chubs] are often called horned dace, and are found in creeks and rivers from Montana and New Mexico to the Atlantic Coast and south to Florida. **1831** E. GRIFFITH et al. tr. *Cuvier's Animal Kingdom* IX. 395 It is of the horned frogs, with concealed tympanum, that Gravenhorst has made his genus Stombus, but they have teeth like the others, and should not be approximated to the toads. **1902** P. FOUNTAIN *Gt. Mountains & Forests S. Amer.* xi. 290 In all outward aspects they resemble toads... They are very revolting-looking creatures, and are mostly of the species known as South American horned frogs. The common horned frog of Brazil is among them. **1962** H. R. SMYTH *Amphibians & their Ways* xviii. 225 The Horned Frog possesses sharp teeth on his upper jaws and sharp bony processes on the lower jaw; what is more, he does not hesitate to use those teeth. **1863** Horned Helmet-shell [see HELMET *sb.* 5]. **1876** *Encycl. Brit.* IV. 740/1 The black helmet (*Cassis tuberosa*) of the West Indian seas, the horned helmet (*C. cornuta*) of Madagascar..are also employed [for cameos]. **1966** A. G. MELVIN *Sea Shells of World* 92/2 *Cassis cornuta* L. Indo-Pac[ific]. Horned Helmet. Whitish... Interior is golden brown. **1806** W. CLARK in R. G. Thwaites *Lewis & Clark Exped.* (1905) IV. 325 The Horned Lizzard is also common. **1844** J. GREGG *Commerce Prairies* II. 231 Horned frog..horned lizard, as those of earlier times more rationally called it. **1931** *Times Educ. Suppl.* 13 June p. iv/3 Among the new arrivals..some horned lizards known in America as 'horn toads' are of special interest. **1969** A. BELLAIRS *Life of Reptiles* II. xii. 498 The spiny little horned lizards (*Phrynosoma*) are able to squirt drops of blood from their eyes for several feet. **1548–1870** Horned poppy [see POPPY *sb.* I. 3]. **1909** *Daily Mail* 5 Aug. 9/3 The horned poppy is particularly plentiful in Start Bay. **1938** R. GATHORNE-HARDY *Wild Flowers in Britain* vi. 41 The Yellow Horned Poppy..is named from the long curved fruit, which, like an orange tree, it bears at the same time as its blossom. **1963** W. BLUNT *Of Flowers & Village* 140 Of course you know the horned poppy—*Glaucium flavum.* **1837** Horned pout [see POUT *sb.*[1]]. **1839** STORER & PEABODY *Rep. Fishes Mass.* 102 The Horned Pout..is highly esteemed as an article of food. **1890** K. D. WIGGIN *Timothy's Quest* 126 The baby horned-pouts rustled their whiskers drowsily. **1969** A. WHEELER *Fishes Brit. Isles & N.W. Europe* 222/1 Horned Pout... A common fish in still or slow-flowing waters, it is found in many ponds, canals and lowland rivers in western Europe. Not so far reported as feral in the British Isles. **1870** *Proc. Calif. Acad. Sci.* IV. 67 The following do not occur west of this region..Horned Rattlesnake, [etc.]. **1888** *Buck's Handbk. Med. Sci.* VI. 166/1 Crotalus cerastes Hallowell, Horned Rattlesnake, 'Sidewinder'. **1965** R. & D. MORRIS *Men & Snakes* viii. 193 This special form of locomotion..occurs in..the horned rattlesnake or 'sidewinder' of North America. **1785, 1869–73** Horned screamer [see SCREAMER 3 a]. **1970** R. MEYER DE SCHAUENSEE *Guide to Birds S. Amer.* 30/1 Horned screamer... General plumage glossy greenish black. **1775** J. ADAMS *Diary* 21 Sept. in *Wks.* (1850) II. 426 Every dip of his pen stung like a horned snake. **1784** [see *bull-snake* (*BULL *sb.*[1] II)]. **1812** A. PLUMPTRE tr. *Lichtenstein's Trav. S. Afr.* I. I. vii. 95 The heat of the day brought out a great many snakes; we killed two of very venomous kinds, one the horned snake, as it is called (*coluber cerastes*). **1851** D. B. WOODS *Sixteen Months at Gold Diggings* 134 It answers the description of the horned snake. It is said that, taking the end of its tail in its mouth, it will form a perfect hoop with its body, rolling rapidly over till it reaches the object at which it aims. **1864** T. BAINES *Explor. S.-W. Afr.* xiii. 374, I found and captured a cerastes, or horned snake, sixteen or eighteen inches long, lying in the path. **1806** *Massachusetts Spy* 16 July (Th.), A venerable Philosopher [*sc.* Thomas Jefferson] sitting in the middle of an immense Map, marked with vast prairies, huge rivers, and mountains of salt: surrounded by piles of Mammoth's bones, stuffed squirrel skins, and horned toads. **1883** [in Dict.]. **1914** E. G. BOULENGER *Reptiles & Batrachians* iv. 70 The genus *Phrynosoma,* the Horned Toads, as these small, much flattened lizards are often called, inhabit the Southern United States and Mexico. **1956** C. H. POPE *Reptile World* 282 The grotesqueness of horned toads makes their bluffing antics ludicrous in the extreme. **1901** H. GADOW in *Cambr. Nat. Hist.* VIII. vi. 218 These 'horned toads' make a squeaking noise when teazed. **1956** G. DURRELL *Drunken Forest* vii. 134 'Horned toads ..three beauties.'.. The largest..was about the circumference of a saucer, and three-quarters of his bulk seemed to consist of head. **1767** *Phil. Trans.* LVI. 287 The ..horned viper of Egypt..is very rare, and scarce to be found in any of the cabinets of natural curiosities in Europe. **1863** [see CERASTES]. **1926** T. E. LAWRENCE *Seven Pillars* (1935) IV. xlvii. 269 This year the valley seemed creeping with horned vipers. **1957** SCHMIDT & INGER *Living Reptiles of World* 162/2 The sharp-tailed worm lizard..is thought erroneously by the natives to be the very poisonous young of the horned viper, *Cerastes cornutus.* **1973** 'A. HALL' *Tango Briefing* iii. 47 'Mine was a horned viper—see that?' He showed me the fang-marks.

3. b. horned cairn, a type of long barrow peculiar to Scotland.

1877 W. GREENWELL *Brit. Barrows* 481 They are in all particulars, except in shape, like the 'horned' long cairns. **1907** T. R. HOLMES *Anc. Brit.* I. iii. 106 Intimately related to certain chambered long barrows and the famous horned cairns, which exist only in Caithness. **1954** S. PIGGOTT *Neolithic Cultures* viii. 238 These 'horned cairns' as they have been known since the nineteenth-century definition of the type.

Horner (hǭ·ɹnəɹ). The name of W. G. *Horner* (1786–1837), English mathematician, used *attrib.* and in the possessive (esp. in *Horner's method*) to designate a method for finding the real roots of a polynomial equated to zero by means of successive approximations.

It involves finding by trial the largest integer α_1 less than the root (x); transforming the equation to one with a root $x^1 = x - \alpha_1$ (or $10(x - \alpha_1)$, to avoid fractions); finding the largest one-place decimal (or integer) α_2 less than the new root; and so on, each approximation α_1, α_2, etc., providing one digit of the solution.

1842 *Penny Cycl.* XXIV. 341/1 The use of Horner's method is very much more easy than that of Newton. **1875** L. HENSLEY *Scholar's Algebra* xiii. 197 Horner's process..is applicable to find the roots of equations of all degrees. **1879** *Encycl. Brit.* VIII. 500/2 Horner's method (1819) gives the root as a decimal, figure by figure. **1913** W. P. MILNE *Higher Algebra* viii. 352 The determination of the two consecutive integers between which the required root of $f_2(x) = 0$ lies is therefore an easy matter very early in the Horner approximating process. **1957** K. S. KUNZ *Numerical Analysis* ii. 23 The Horner method was devised to reduce such pencil work. **1966** W. E. GROVE *Brief Numerical Methods* i. 1 Horner's method is not used in computing, for it is designed for hand calculation.

‖ **hornero** (ǫɹnē·ro). [Sp., baker.] A South American bird of the genus *Furnarius,* esp. *F. rufus;* also called baker-bird, OVEN-BIRD.

1880 E. GIBSON in *Ibis* IV. 16 Furnarius Rufus. (Red Oven-Bird) Native name 'Hornero'... This species is.. probably one of the best-known of our Buenos-Ayrean birds. **1911** J. A. THOMSON *Biol. Seasons* II. 163 A masterpiece along the line illustrated by swallow and martin is the nest of some of the South American oven-birds (Furnarius)—for instance, of that species (F. rufus) which is called the 'hornero' or baker. **1956** G. DURRELL *Drunken Forest* I. 21 The oven-bird appears to have more than his fair share of personality and charm...An elderly peon..solemnly told me that he would never harm an *hornero.* **1970** R. MEYER DE SCHAUENSEE *Guide to Birds S. Amer.* 201 The name 'ovenbirds' has often been applied to this family [*sc.* Furnariidæ] because of the oven-like mud nests built by horneros.

Horner's syndrome. *Med.* [Named after J. F. *Horner* (1831–86), Swiss ophthalmologist.] A condition marked by abnormalities on one side of the face (including a contracted pupil, drooping upper eyelid, sunken eye, and a local inability to sweat) and caused by damage to the sympathetic nerves on that side of the neck.

1929 *Arch. Surg.* XVIII. 2025 The symptom-complex known variously as Claude Bernard–Horner syndrome (in France),..but usually and more rightly as Horner's syndrome. **1968** PASSMORE & ROBSON *Compan. Med. Studies* I. xxiv. 89 Interruption of the cervical part of the sympathetic chain of ganglia produces a condition known as Horner's syndrome. **1971** *Brit. Med. Bull.* XXVII. 33/2 The presence of a single underlying lesion can readily be inferred from the detection of several symptoms or signs (e.g. Horner's syndrome).

hornet[1]. Add: **2.** Also, trouble, opposition. (Further examples.) Also, *to stir up a hornets' nest.*

1739–40 RICHARDSON *Pamela* (1740) I. xxvi. 78, I rais'd a Hornet's Nest about my Ears, that..may have stung to Death my Reputation. **1921** GALSWORTHY *To Let* I. i. 21 An acid humour stirred in his Forsyte blood; a subtle pain divided by hair's-breadth from pleasure. If only June did not suddenly bring her hornets about his ears! **1921** H. CRANE *Let.* 26 Nov. (1965) 71 But I also find that J stirred up a hornet's nest in me this summer with his words about getting away from current formulae. **1928** G. B. SHAW *Intell. Woman's Guide Socialism* lxxiv. 360 It is unlikely that a Proletarian House of Commons will suffer the nation's children to go on being taught Capitalist and Imperialist morality in the disguise of religion; and yet, the moment the subject is touched, what a hornet's nest is stirred up! **1966** *Listener* 4 Aug. 177/3 Judges have stirred up a hornets' nest in the sacred territory of 'the right to strike'. **1969** I. KEMP *Brit. G.I. in Vietnam* xiii. 200 On the third landing zone we ran into a hornet's nest. **1973** W. TUTE *Resident* iv. 67 The Ambassador wants you removed. You've got a hornet's nest buzzing round your head in Whitehall.

hornfels (hǭ·ɹnfels), *sb. Petrogr.* [a. G. *hornfels,* f. *horn* horn + *fels* rock.] A fine-grained, non-schistose rock composed mainly of quartz, micas, and feldspars and formed by the contact metamorphism of an argillaceous rock. Hence **hornfe·lsic** *a.,* composed of, or having the character of, hornfels.

1854 DANA *Syst. Min.* (ed. 4) II. 246 The Hornfels of the Germans is a massive compound of quartz and feldspar breaking with a smooth flinty fracture. **1888** J. J. H. TEALL *Brit. Petrogr.* xii. 374 We use the term hornfels instead of its etymological equivalent, hornstone, because in many cases the rocks termed hornfels are distinctly crystalline and not at all like what is commonly termed hornstone in this country. **1951** TURNER & VERHOOGEN *Igneous & Metamorphic Petrol.* xv. 373 Structure is typically granoblastic (hornfelsic) or maculose. **1965** G. J. WILLIAMS *Econ. Geol. N.Z.* vii. 73/2 The conglomerates are quartzose in some places, and elsewhere contain granite, greywacke and hornfelsic components.

So **ho·rnfels** *v. trans.,* to metamorphose (a rock) to hornfels; **ho·rnfelsed** (-felst, -felzd) *ppl. a.,* **ho·rnfelsing** *vbl. sb.*

1901 *Rep. Brit. Assoc.* 634 The Old Red Sandstone is indurated and often hornfelsed to a varying distance from the margin. **1922** *Nature* 12 Jan. 62/1 Hornfelsed green rocks. **1930** PEACH & HORNE *Geol. Scotl.* ii. 70 The hornfelsing of the orthogneisses. **1947** *Q. Jrnl. Geol. Soc.* CII. 395 The hornfelsed graywacke is slightly silicated. **1970** G. NEWALL et al. *Mechanism of Igneous Intrusion* iv. 49 The granite is in contact with hornfelsed pillow lavas.

hornified, *ppl. a.* Also, adorned with horns; of a horn-like texture.

1789 J. BYNG *Diary* 30 June in *Torrington Diaries* (1935) II. 113 We enter'd the old cloisters, now glazed up; and so hornified are their walls, as to give horrible presage; their being horns of all sorts of wild cattle. **1963** R. R. A. HIGHAM *Handbk. Papermaking* ii. 36 The hornified cellulose fibres are not capable of assuming their original shape because of the permanent set that has taken place in the structural walls of the fibres.

horniness. Add: **2.** A state of sexual excitement. Cf. *HORNY *a.* 2 b.

1963 T. PYNCHON *V.* i. 37 He was visited on a lunar basis by these great unspecific waves of horniness, whereby all women within a certain age group and figure envelope became immediately and impossibly desirable. **1969** P. ROTH *Portnoy's Complaint* 102 Do I really experience this restlessness, this horniness? **1971** *Esquire* July 48/4 He establishes adolescent horniness as a condition too furtive and bewildered..to admit of real caring.

hornist. (Earlier and later examples.)

1836 *Knickerbocker* VIII. 71 Some evil-disposed citizens having no taste for music went to his honor the Mayor, and lodged grievous complaints against the distinguished *hornist.* **1906** *Westm. Gaz.* 1 Mar. 12/1 Vivier was solo hornist in the orchestra of the Imperial Opera.

hornless, *a.* Add: **2.** Without a horn (*HORN *sb.* 14* a).

1909 *Talking Machine News* Oct. 337 Portable hornless machine. **1913** B. CLEMENTS-HENRY *Gramophones & Phonographs* ix. 54 Some modern disc machines are hornless. **1934** N. W. MCLACHLAN *Loud Speakers* xv. 256 A hornless speaker with baffle 4 ft. square. **1957** *Encycl. Brit.* XIV. 409/1 In the direct-radiator or hornless speakers the diaphragm is made large enough to radiate directly into unconfined air.

horn-mad, *a.* Add: **c.** Lecherous. Cf. *HORN *sb.* 5 c. *slang.*

1893 FARMER & HENLEY *Dict. Slang* III. 356 *Horn-mad,*..sexually excited; lecherous. **1937** in PARTRIDGE *Dict. Slang.* **1951** R. CAMPBELL *Light on Dark Horse* xvii. 251 The evil-minded and horn-mad levantine.

hornswoggle (hǭ·ɹnswǫg'l), *v. colloq.* (orig. *U.S.*). [Prob. fanciful.] *trans.* To get the better of; to cheat or swindle; to hoodwink, humbug, bamboozle.

1829 *Virginia Lit. Museum* I. 458 *Hornswoggle,* to embarrass irretrievably. **1834** W. A. CARRUTHERS *Kentuckian in N.Y.* I. 61, I wish I may be horn swoggled, if ever I thought [etc.]. **1860** *Oregon Argus* 12 May (Th.), P. F. is going to hornswoggle the Douglas Democrats. **1904** *Boston Herald* 27 June 6 One practical working theory in advertising circles is that the ad's chief function is to hornswoggle the consumer. **1911** H. QUICK *Yellowstone Nights* iii. 82 If you'll stand by..and see your old father hornswoggled out of his eye-teeth you'll never see a cent of my money. **1958** *Spectator* 11 Apr. 448/3, I am sure the manufacturers hornswoggle us and sell us a lot of useless trim and gadgets. **1968** *Guardian* 28 Feb. 18/8 In this wretched week we get a report from the Government Actuary which is quoted to hornswoggle us into increased insurance contributions. **1970** *Sunday Times* 28 June 11/3 The Americans look for value; you can't..hornswoggle them.

horny, *a.* (*sb.*) Add: **2. b.** Sexually excited; lecherous. (Chiefly used of a man.) *slang.* Cf. *HORN *sb.* 5 c.

1889 BARRÈRE & LELAND *Dict. Slang* I. 476/1 *Horny,* lecherous, in a state of sexual desire, in rut. **1918** *Dialect Notes* V. 25 *Horny,* amative. **1949** H. MILLER *Sexus* (1969) v. 104 Her thick, gurgling voice saying..: 'Get it in all the way...please, please do... *I'm horny.*' *Ibid.* x. 239 When I look at this thing I get horny again. **1965** J. L. HERLIHY *Midnight Cowboy* (1966) II. v. 120 You *are* a gorgeous-lookin' piece, Cass. Gets a guy all horny just *lookin'* at you. **1968** M. RICHLER *Cocksure* xi. 63 When.. he used to make a habit of watching the hockey games.. he always felt horny. **1970** T. LEWIS *Jack's Return Home* 43 The talk'd got filthier. It'd made me very horny. **1971** *Black World* Oct. 65/1 Ain't that the horny bitch that was grindin with the blind dude.

7. *horny-browed, fisted* (example); **horny-head** (in full **hornyhead chub**) *U.S.,* a North American cyprinid fish, *Nocomis biguttatus;* occasionally also used for *Campostoma anomalum,* a smaller cyprinid.

1916 JOYCE *Portrait of Artist* iii. 158 Goatish creatures with human faces, horny browed, lightly bearded and

grey as indiarubber. **1912** W. Owen *Let.* 2 July (1967) 148 A bushy-browed and horny-fisted blacksmith's assistant. **1882** Jordan & Gilbert *Synopsis Fishes N. Amer.* 212 *C[eratichthys] biguttatus*..Horny Head; River Chub; Jerker. **1933** *Amer. Speech* VIII. 50/1 Horny-head... A chub-like fish with short, horny protuberances on the scales, those on top of the head being largest. **1963** P. A. Parsons *Outdoor Life Compl. Bk. Freshwater Fishing* iv. 45 Hornyhead chubs, excellent bait for members of the pike family, are durable on the hook. **1965** A. J. McClane *Standard Fishing Encycl.* 891/2 Stoneroller. *Campostoma anomalum.* Also known as hornyhead and knottyhead, it is a brownish-olive minnow with a brassy luster.

B. *sb.* **2.** A policeman. *slang.*

1753 J. Poulter *Discoveries* (ed. 2) 39 *A Horney*,..a Constable. **1789** G. Parker *Life's Painter* xiv. 116 There's no horneys, traps, scouts, nor beak-runners amongst them. **1856** J. Strang *Glasgow & its Clubs* 187 Town officers..were then better known by the appellation of red-coat officers or *hornies.* **1922** Joyce *Ulysses* 160 Can't blame them after all with the job they have especially the young hornies.

3. A cow; a bullock. *Sc.* and *Austral. slang.*

1808 A. Scott *Poems* 81 Bedown the green the hornies rowt. **1879** G. Macdonald *Sir Gibbie* I. xiv. 194 Hornie—so named, indeed, because of her readiness to use the weapons with which Nature had provided her..was in fact a malicious cow. **1933** *Bulletin* (Sydney) 18 Jan. 25 Polled cattle graded better than the hornies. **1938** X. Herbert *Capricornia* (1939) xx. 273 Hornies, or beasts with ingrowing horns. **1943** Baker *Dict. Austral. Slang* 40 *Horney-steerer*, a bullock driver.

horoeka (hǫro,ī·ka). [Maori.] A small, round-headed New Zealand tree, *Pseudopanax crassifolium*, which has a juvenile form with long, toothed leaves; = *lancewood 2.

1831 G. Bennett in *London Med. Gaz.* 5 Nov. 150/1 (*heading*) The Horoeka Tree of New Zealand. This tree.. has not yet been observed by botanists either in flower or fructification. **1838** J. S. Polack *New Zealand* II. 399 *Horoeka*..is generally found on elevated lands, grows to the height of thirty feet. **1868** J. Buchanan in *Trans. N.Z. Inst.* I. Essays iii. 33 Horoeka (*Panax crassifolium*). A singular-looking plant in all stages of its growth. Three varieties are found at Dunedin, only distinguishable, in the young state, by the method of inflorescence. **1899** T. Kirk *Students' Flora N.Z.* 222 *P[anax] crassifolium*... A round-headed tree..20 ft.–60 ft. high... *Horoeka.* a **1939** 'R. Hyde' *Houses by Sea* (1952) 64 They cut the yellow twisted horoeka For sticks.

horomai, var. *haeremai.

horopito (hōə-, hǫropī·to). [Maori.] A small, aromatic, evergreen New Zealand tree, *Pseudowintera axillaris*; = Pepper-tree b.

1847 G. F. Angas *Savage Life* II. 17 A straggling shrub, with bright green shining leaves, resembling those of the nutmeg-tree; and a profusion of rich and delicate blossoms, looking like waxwork...The natives call this plant horopito. **1889** T. Kirk *Forest Flora N.Z.* pl. 2 (*caption*) The horopito, or pepper-tree of the settlers. **1963** Poole & Adams *Trees & Shrubs N.Z.* 40 *Pseudowintera axillaris* (J. R. & G. Forst.) Dandy. (Flowers borne in the axils of the leaves.) Horopito. Small tree reaching 8 m. **1966** *Encycl. N.Z.* II. 117/1 Horopito..is unpalatable to deer.

horra, var. *hora.

horrendous, *a.* Delete *rare* and add later examples.

1952 S. Kauffmann *Philanderer* (1953) vi. 97 The effect on the family of this drastic change in their financial status was horrendous. **1963** *Daily Tel.* 31 July 10/2 Blackmail and horrendous tales of Western avengers on their heels are probably as effective instruments as any. **1972** *Nature* 28 Apr. 434/2 Elsewhere there are horrendous accounts of how organochlorine pesticides contaminating food have killed large numbers of people.

‖**horribile dictu** (hǫrī·bĭli di·ktu). [mod.L., by analogy with *mirabile dictu.] Horrible to relate.

1854 Geo. Eliot in *Westm. Rev.* Oct. 467 In some circles the effort is, who shall make the best puns, (*horribile dictu!*) or the best charades. **1883** G. Meredith *Let.* 16 Mar. (1970) II. 691 Louis Stevenson wrote to me from Marseilles in the winter... I, *horrible* [sic] *dictu*, have not yet replied to him. **1935** Huxley & Haddon *We Europeans* ii. 64 Puffed up with pride and, *horribile dictu!*, even with wealth.

horrible, *a.* (*sb.*, *adv.*) **B.** *sb.* (Further examples.)

1851 H. Melville *Moby Dick* I. xxxviii. 273 Such a waggish leering as lurks in all you horribles! **1899** [see *penny horrible* s.v. Penny 11]. **1909** *Daily Chron.* 3 Sept. 1/6 Both boys said yesterday that they had been reading 'penny horribles' about burglaries. **1917** A. Conan Doyle *His Last Bow* i. 51 There is but one step from the grotesque to the horrible.

horrid, *adv.* (Later examples.)

1867 S. Hale *Lett.* (1919) 25 I'm horrid sorry there was such a gap in my letters then. **1899** Kipling *Stalky & Co.* 135 Fags bully each other horrid. **1932** —— *Limits & Renewals* 80 The New Armies are horrid quick on the trigger.

horrifically, *adv.* (Later examples.)

1972 *Daily Tel.* 24 Feb. 2/6 The Aldershot explosion which caused the deaths of seven people went 'horrifically wrong' as an act of IRA retaliation, said Miss Bernadette Devlin. **1972** *Oxford Times* 27 Oct. 19/1 A young doctor is promised a job..if he can discover which of four horrifically insane patients is really the head of the asylum.

horrifiedly (hǫ·rifəid,li), *adv.* [f. Horrified *ppl. a.* + -ly².] In a horrified manner.

1908 R. Broughton *Mamma* v. 49 A thought which they have been horrifiedly chasing like a rat or a scorpion out of his or her own mind. **1923** J. S. Huxley *Ess. Biologist* i. 56 It is easy enough to see items on the debit side, and indeed to be so horrifiedly fascinated by it as not to have eyes for anything else. **1951** *Theatre Arts* Dec. 78 He is fondling her white throat with his fingers and she horrifiedly realizes it is these same clutching digits that have strangled his earlier victims.

horrisonous, *a.* Delete † *Obs.* and add later examples.

1901 *Daily Chron.* 31 Dec. 5/1 Sophie oft wakes on my snorting horrisonous. **1962** L. Deighton *Ipcress File* xv. 91, I listened to the ululating wail and horrisonous mewl.

horror, *sb.* Add: **3. c.** As *int.* (usu. *pl.*). An exclamation indicating shock, surprise, fear, etc.

1879 L. Troubridge *Life amongst Troubridges* (1966) xi. 152 Went to Shepherd's Bush. Oh, horror—stinking underground. *Ibid.* 153 The train went off without us! Oh, horror, no other train to Penzance. **1893** *Ladies' Home Jrnl.* Feb. 6/4 Horrors!..You don't mean that you're going to carry it any further? **1914** E. R. Burroughs *Tarzan of Apes* (1917) xvi. 137 Horrors! The lion was bounding along in easy leaps scarce five paces behind. **1928** 'Brent of Bin Bin' *Up Country* xvi. 284 After that was Miss Oswald—horrors, supposing she proposed too! **1973** *Times Lit. Suppl.* 31 Aug. 1007/3 Lord Crouch pulls strings to get..the Yard for the murder near his stately home, but horrors!—for him, anyway—when what he gets is [Inspector] Dover.

5. (Further examples.)

1805 E. Fremantle in A. Fremantle *Wynne Diaries* (1940) 4 Mar. III. 160 He [Count Barlowsky] is a little horror. **1846** E. Hall *Diary* 11 June in O. A. Sherrard *Two Victorian Girls* (1966) xvii. 162 Took the horrors for a drive, and even in the carriage Sydney and Cornelia could not behave themselves. **1849** Thackeray *Pendennis* I. xxxvii. 362 That collection of old fogies..ought to be cast in wax, and set up at Madame Tussaud's—.. In the chamber of horrors! **1859** *Macm. Mag.* Dec. 132/2 A series of magic lantern slides from some 'chambers of horrors', which he presumes to call the *Legend of the Ages.* **1889** Barrère & Leland *Dict. Slang* I. 235 *Chamber of Horrors*, the Peeresses' gallery at the House of Lords, from its being railed round as if it contained objectionable or repulsive inmates. **1891** Farmer *Slang* II. 69 *Chamber of Horrors*, sausages. **1899** *Daily Chron.* 2 Mar. 9/1 This.. room..is one of terrible interest, for the 'flimsies' record the lost and overdue vessels, and the place bears the gruesome and apt title of 'Chamber of Horrors'. **1909** J. R. Ware *Passing Eng.* 69/2 *Chamber of Horrors*, the name of the corridor or repository in which Messrs Christie..locate the valueless pictures that are sent to them. **1922** Joyce *Ulysses* 613 He stowed the weapon in question away as before in his chamber of horrors, otherwise pocket. **1958** *Spectator* 6 June 746/2 Children adore reading about little horrors being taken down a peg. **1959** A. Huxley *Let.* 13 Feb. (1969) 866 Passages on infant damnation from St. Augustine... Passages on Jesus as a salesman from Bruce Barton. And so forth. A few pages of these wd constitute a stimulating Chamber of Horrors. **1959** *Times Lit. Suppl.* 10 July 409/2 A diary kept by an elderly horror whose name we never learn.

b. = **horror film.*

1958 *Vogue* July 47 The American horrors pour out at an average of three a month: The Man without a Body, Back from the Dead, etc. **1958** *Economist* 6 Dec. 868/2 'Horror' is a generic term covering a wide range of films whose only common link is that they all contain a monster.

6. *horror joke, -loving* (example), *magazine, -photograph, story, -struck* (earlier and later examples); **horror comic,** a children's comic (sense *B. 2) in which the principal ingredients of the pictures and stories are violence and sensationalism; **horror film, movie, picture,** a film designed to horrify, usu. by the depiction of violence and the supernatural.

1954 *Time* 8 Nov. 60/3 Public criticism of horror comics. **1959** J. Cary *Captive & Free* lvi. 244 She had been all for the Bill putting down the horror comics, though her husband had been against it. **1964** M. Argyle *Psychol. & Social Probl.* iv. 51 There has been considerable public anxiety about the possible effect of television shows, films and horror comics on children. **1973** *Guardian* 28 Mar. 10/6 It was jokey in a horror-comic way, but I don't think horror is a reasonable reaction to a horror-comic. **1936** *Variety* 1 July 1/5 Recently showed ..horror films and Sino-Japanese War cruelty shots. **1952** M. McCarthy *Groves of Academe* (1953) iii. 31 Miss Rejner and her boy-tutee..sat transfixed, as in a horror-film, watching the knob turn. **1965** *Listener* 18 Nov. 805/1 The connoisseur of the horror film knows instinctively that *Son of Dracula* will lack the blood chilling quality of *Dracula.* **1971** B. W. Aldiss *Soldier Erect* 10 My eyelids flickered like an ancient horror film, revealing acres of white-of-eye. **1963** Auden *Dyer's Hand* 372 A few years ago, there was a rage in New York for telling 'Horror Jokes'. **1909** *Westm. Gaz.* 1 May 13/2 The same horror-loving multitude flocks to its haunts of pleasure. **1939** R. Chandler *Big Sleep* x. 75 A fresh-faced kid was reading a horror magazine. **1965** Mrs. L. B. Johnson *White House Diary* 3 June (1970) 280 Tall plants called gorgonian..for all the world like those plants you see in horror movies. **1972** 'R. Crawford' *Whip Hand* i. iii. 11 A horror movie, vehicle for a Hollywood godling who had been in his grave for a decade. **1954** Koestler *Invis. Writing* xxxi. 333 He insisted on adding to the book a supplement of horror-photographs on glossy paper. **1937** *New Yorker* 9 Jan. 13/2 Mr. Arthur L. Mayer took over the..theatre, put in horror pictures (zombies and draculas), and he has made it pay every week. **1960** *Times* 14 Jan. 6/3 The world-wide success of the so-called 'horror' pictures made by Hammer Films. **1937** E. Snow *Red Star over China* i. i. 22 A torrent of horror-stories about Red atrocities. **1963** *Listener* 7 Mar. 428/1 The horror story afforded scope for the more primitive fears and desires that had gradually been squeezed out of the English novel. **1970** *Nature* 5 Dec. 900/2 Both argued that the 'horror stories' of genetic engineering are completely out of the question, at least in the foreseeable future. **1814** Jane Austen *Mansf. Park* III. vi. 134 William and Fanny were horror-struck at the idea. **1953** R. Lehmann *Echoing Grove* 23 Horror-struck, they continued to stand watching.

‖**horror vacui** (hǫrɔɹ vækiū,əi). *Art.* [mod.L., lit. 'the horror of a vacuum'.] The dislike of leaving empty spaces, e.g. in an artistic composition.

1845 W. Plate *Ptolemy's Knowl. Arabia* 5 Ptolemy had a tendency towards putting the inland towns too far east; but whether it was a mere *horror vacui*, or some misunderstanding, that induced him to do so, cannot be decided. **1937** *Burlington Mag.* Apr. 183/1 Pictures..showing looser compositions, less *horror vacui*, and a less trenchant treatment of light and drapery. **1954** M. Rickert *Painting in Britain* v. 108 True to the thirteenth century artist's *horror vacui*, he fills the lower corner of his miniature with more architecture..to balance that on the other side. **1960** R. Lister *Decorative Cast Ironwork* iv. 123 Castings were used in place of hand-carved or forged iron fittings,..loading them with detail with which to placate the current *horror vacui.* **1968** *Listener* 5 Dec. 774/2 A further tension builds up between the desire to create space and the desire to fill it. Sometimes the space-filling seems compulsive... *Horror vacui* struggles with claustrophobia. **1972** E. Lucie-Smith *Eroticism in Western Art* ix. 180 Nudes..fill the whole picture-space as if the artist suffered from *horror vacui.*

hors. Add: ‖**hors concours** (or koṅkūr), *adv.*, not competing; hence, without a rival; unequalled.

1884 *Tablet* LXIII. 804/2 A work such as..would, were it shown in the *Salon*, range him Hors Concours. **1931** *Times Lit. Suppl.* 7 May 353/3 Dickens and Wilkie Collins were regarded as *hors-concours*; Trollope, however, he despised. **1941** V. Nabokov *Real Life S. Knight* (1945) xvi. 138 Most husbands are fools, but that one was *hors concours.*

horse, *sb.* Add: **1. f.** Colloq. abbreviation of Horse-power.

1904 [see Tonneau]. **1931** *Star* 8 May 13/1 Each of them with a few 'horses' in reserve. **1932** Kipling *Limits & Renewals* 341 Sign—refill, and let me away with my horses (Seventy Thundering Horses!). **1973** R. C. Dennis *Sweat of Fear* vi. 41 The Mercedes..pointed north at high speed, but there was never any chance of its outdistancing me. I had too many horses under my foot.

3. c. (Later example.)

1930 W. Faulkner *Rose for Emily* in *Coll. Stories* (1951) ii. 121 So she vanquished them [*sc.* the city authorities] horse and foot, just as she had vanquished their fathers thirty years before.

4. (Further examples.)

1840 R. H. Dana *Bef. Mast* (1854) xxii. 125 Though 'a bit of a horse'..yet he was generally liked by the crew. **1844** *Southern Lit. Messenger* X. 489/2 'Huzzah!..went round the crowd, while Jeptha's..friends swore he was 'a horse'. **1847** W. T. Porter *Quarter Race Kentucky* 39 Good mornin', old hoss. **1925** J. Metcalfe *Smoking Leg* 26 There you are, old horse; don't say I never did you a good turn. **1930** D. L. Sayers *Strong Poison* iv. 48 It's your triumph at having secured a disagreement that gives you away, old horse. **1973** 'A. Hall' *Tango Briefing* i. 10 'It *is* a joke, isn't it?' 'As far as I know, old horse.'

6. a. (Later examples.)

1937 *Times* 13 Apr. (Brit. Motor Suppl.) p. vi/3 Good progress..is most noticeable with the mechanical horse ..and the trolley omnibus. **1963** *Amer. Speech* XXXVIII. 44 *Horse*.., a tractor or power unit.

c. (Examples.)

1785 J. Wesley *Let.* 17 July (1931) VIII. 281 Constant exercise. If you can have no other, you should daily ride a wooden horse, which is only a double plank nine or ten feet long, properly placed upon two tressels. **1875–98** [see Vaulting *vbl. sb.*² 2 b]. **1949** E. Williams *Wooden Horse* ii. 37 A vaulting horse, a box horse like we had at school. You know, one of those square things with a padded top and sides that go right down to the ground. **1962** *T.V. Times* 9 Mar. 22/3 Trampoline, pommelled horse and vaulting box. **1973** J. Burrows *Like an Evening Gone* iii. 40 Sporting equipment of a modest kind..a vaulting horse and a set of P.E. mats.

e. (Later example.)

1921 [see *broom *sb.* 6].

7. b. (Later U.S. examples.)

1846 D. Corcoran *Pickings* 83 One carried his saw slung on his arm, and the other had his 'horse' mounted on his shoulder. **1850** N. Kingsley *Diary* (1914) 103 Worked at hewing some sticks for horses to use the Pit Saw.

8. h. A groyne. *local.*

1852 J. Wiggins *Embanking* x. 232 Expensive works ..such as those called '*horses*' in Essex, and '*groins*' in Sussex and Hants.

i. In other uses (see quots.).

1904 Goodchild & Tweney *Technol. & Sci. Dict.* 290/2 *Horse*, (*Plast.*) the wood backing of a zinc mould, used by plasterers for running mouldings. (*Plumb.*) A wooden finial, etc., forming a core which is to be covered with lead. **1946** N. Wymer *Eng. Country Crafts* vi. 62 When the sticks are well 'cooked' the craftsman takes them, one by

one, from the sand and pulls them through a 'horse'.. a wooden plank with niches cut out of the side—to straighten them. **1957** R. Lister *Decorative Wrought Ironwork* 229 *Horse*, a kind of stake..with perforations for holding other tools. **1964** W. L. Goodman *Hist. Woodworking Tools* 153 Holding his work in a vertical pedal-operated vice or 'horse'.

11. (Earlier example.)

1778 W. Pryce *Mineralogia Cornubiensis* 323 *Horse*, a portion of dead ground in a Lode, which widens like a horse's back from the spine.

b. A mud or sand bank. *dial.*

1926 H. A. Tripp *Suffolk Sea Borders* vi. 109 Below Waldringfield is a 'horse' in mid-channel—'horse' being the name given to banks that crop up with rounded backs like the back of a horse. **1929** E. A. Robertson *Three came Unarmed* ix. 149 Now the shoal-water of this coast is..full of under-water mud-banks or 'horses' which come dry or are barely covered at low tide.

14. (Earlier example.) Also *live horse*: work done and not charged for.

1770 P. Luckombe *Conc. Hist. Printing* 499 If any journeyman set down in his bill on Saturday night more work than he has done, that surplus is called Horse. **1859** Bartlett *Dict. Amer.* 247 *Live horse*, in printers' parlance, work done over and above that included in the week's bill.

14*. Heroin. *slang* (orig. *U.S.*).

1950 *Time* 28 Aug. 2/2 There are the usual thrill-seekers who take goof balls..quite often ending up as confirmed addicts of..heroin (H, horse, white stuff). **1951** *N.Y. Times* 13 June 24/3 Then one day we met another fellow and he offered us some heroin. I sniffed this too. We called it 'horse' and 'H'. **1961** *John o' London's* 16 Nov. 548 'Pot' is marijuana, and 'horse' heroin. **1962** J. Baldwin *Another Country* (1963) I. i. 14 His first taste of marijuana, his first snort of horse. **1963** L. Deighton *Horse under Water* xl. 158 Diacetyl-morphine. Which is what you would call 'heroin', or 'H', or 'horse'. **1969** *Daily Tel.* 31 Jan. 24/6 He had seen the effects of an overdose of 'horse' before. The skin becomes greenish and there was frothing at the mouth.

17. *to change* (*swap*) *horses in midstream* (*while crossing a stream*): to change one's ideas, plans, etc., in the middle of a project, process, etc.; *to talk horse* (earlier U.S. example); *to play horse with* (U.S.): to treat roughly or unceremoniously; *to hold one's horses*: see *hold *v.* 11 c.

1855 T. C. Haliburton *Nat. & Hum. Nat.* II. 337 Doctor, I am a borin of you, but the fact is, when I get a goin 'talkin hoss', I never know where to stop. **1864** A. Lincoln in *Compl. Wks.* (1894) II. 531, I do not allow myself to suppose that either the Convention or the League have concluded to decide that I am either the greatest or best man in America, but rather they have concluded that it is not best to swap horses while crossing the river, and have further concluded that I am not so poor a horse that they might not make a botch of it in trying to swap. **1896** Ade *Artie* xvii. 163 Do you think I'm goin' out ridin' with her and have a lot o' cheap skates stoppin' to play horse with her everywhere we go? **1904** W. H. Smith *Promoters* x. 169 You've got to have some well-matured plan ..if they try to play horse with you again. **1911** L. J. Vance *Cynthia* x. 157 Why does Madame Savaran insist on coming along to see that he doesn't play horse with her stake in the venture? **1923** —— *Baroque* viii. 49 Remember the Wop detective that used to play horse with the Black Handers. **1940** 'H. Pentecost' *24th Horse* v. 42 Don't come if you don't want to... Change horses in midstream if you want to. **1948** A. J. Toynbee *Civilization on Trial* 195 'Herodianism'..does not really offer a solution. For one thing, it is a dangerous game...It is a form of swapping horses while crossing a stream, and the rider who fails to find his seat in the new saddle is swept..to a death. **1951** H. S. Davies *Gram. without Tears* vi. 56 From the point of view of strict old-fashioned grammar, this is obviously bad; it involves a change from the singular to the plural horse in mid-stream of the sentence. **1969** *Listener* 13 Mar. 360/1 Another play which changed horses in midstream was William Ingram's *Double Take*. The long dialogue between the nervous kidnapper and his oddly calm victim was inconsequential and tense and had one thinking hopefully of Pinter.

18. (Further examples.)

1832 E. C. Wines *Two Years in Navy* I. 73 Most of us had not 'worked out our dead horses'. *Ibid.*, Dead horses are debts due to the purser on account of advances of pay. **1863** S. Butler *First Yr. Canterbury Settlement* x. 146 Some good hands are very improvident... They will come back possibly with *a dead horse to work off*—i.e. a debt at the accommodation house. **1872** *Globe* 1 Aug. 3/1 For..twenty minutes..the Premier..might be said to have rehearsed that..lively operation known as flogging a dead horse. **1886** F. T. Elworthy *W. Somerset Word-Bk.* 186 Work done in redemption of debt is called working out the dead-horse. **1907** *Westm. Gaz.* 7 Mar. 5/2 Mr. Philip S. Head, auctioneer and house agent, stated that 'Hillside' had been on his books for three years. Some people when asking for a house had stated that they did not want 'the haunted house'... His Lordship: Do you think 'Hillside' will always be 'a dead horse'? **1927** J. Sampson *Seven Seas Shanty Bk.* 45 For the first month at sea he was working for nothing—in other words he was working out the 'dead horse'. **1935** *Yachting* Dec. 82/3 *Dead horse*. The common sailor was advanced one month's pay at time of signing the articles. This usually went to his boarding-house keeper for alleged debts. During the first month out, he was said to be 'working off the dead horse'; and at the end of this period it was the custom..to make an effigy of a horse and throw it overboard with suitable ceremonies. **1970** *New Yorker* 10 Oct. 109/1 All this critical analysis would be a flogging of a dead horse. **1971** *Cabinet Maker & Retail Furnisher* 1 Oct. 14/2 If this is the case, we are flogging a dead horse in still trying to promote the scheme.

22. b. *to mount the high horse* (earlier example); *to ride the high horse* (examples); *to come, etc., off one's high horse*, to climb down, to become less arrogant.

1782 T. Pasley *Private Sea Jrnls.* (1931) 252 Whether Sir George will mount his high Horse or be over-civil to Admiral Pigot seems even to be a doubt with himself. **1809** Malkin *Gil Blas* ii. vii. ¶ 5 Riding the high horse with all the arrogance of greatness. *Ibid.* ix. i. ¶ 2 Do not ride a higher horse than a thousand jockeys of quality whom I could name. **1843** Thackeray in *Fraser's Mag.* Apr. 469/2 It would be *his* turn to sneer and bully, and ride the high horse. **1887** G. R. Sims *Mary Jane's Mem.* 116 They were awfully civil, and let Mrs. Master John ride the high horse over them. **1920** A. Christie *Mysterious Affair at Styles* x. 224, I decided that I would descend from my high horse, and once more seek out Poirot at Leastways Cottage. **1928** W. S. Maugham *Ashenden* ix. 153 Come, come, my dear fellow, do not try to ride the high horse. You do not wish to show me your passport and I will not insist. **1928** *Sunday Express* 15 Jan. 6/4 The cable companies have come off the high horse at last in entering into negotiations with the wireless group. **1936** A. Christie *Murder in Mesopotamia* xix. 162 I'd like to see Sheila honest enough to come off her high horse and admit that she hated Mrs. Leidner for good old thorough-going personal reasons. **1950** W. Saroyan *Assyrian & Other Stories* 219 Only his mother felt that Mayo was not a rude boy, but his father frequently asked Mayo to get down off his high horse and act like everybody else. **1959** *Economist* 20 June 1079/1 Politicians..riding on high horses.

25. a. *to eat like a horse* (later examples); *to work like a horse* (examples); *a horse of another colour* (further examples).

1798 *Aurora* (Philad.) 27 Aug. (Th.), Whether any of them may be induced..to enter into the pay of King John I. [i.e. President Adams] is 'a horse of another colour'. **1829** G. Griffin *Collegians* II. xxii. 160 'I never tought o' dat,' said Danny... 'Dat's a horse of anoder colour.' **1853** [see *colonialism 1 b]. **1856** C. Reade *Never too Late* I. ii. 47 A gentleman is a horse of another colour than this Robinson. **1877** [see *hoss 1]. **1937** W. S. Maugham *Theatre* ii. 23 I'll give you a three years' contract, I'll give you eight pounds a week and you'll have to work like a horse. **1937** K. A. Porter *Noon Wine* 38 He never got married, for one thing, and he works like a horse. **1948** J. Carter *Taste & Technique in Book-Collecting* (1949) ii. 24 Buxton Forman's *A Shelley Library*, however, was a horse of a different colour: no mere handlist but a fully annotated and richly informative study of Shelley's original editions. **1952** 'N. Shute' *Far Country* 80 Going into the saloon for every meal, and eating like a horse. **1966** *Listener* 5 May 661/1 A horse of a somewhat different colour is that tycoon of the brush, pop-man Salvador Dali. **1971** J. Philips *Escape a Killer* (1972) i. ii. 18 She could now 'eat like a horse'.

c. *horses for courses*: a theory that each racehorse is suited to a particular race-course, and will do better on that course than on any other; also *fig.*; *horse and horse* (U.S.): equally matched, neck and neck; *the horse's mouth*: the original, authentic source of information, esp. in phr. *straight from the horse's mouth*; *horse-and-buggy* (U.S.): bygone, old-fashioned (app. used as quasi-*sb.* in quot. 1926).

a **1859** in Bartlett *Dict. Amer.* (1859) 204, I sot down to old sledge along with Jake Stebbins. It was horse and horse, and his deal. **1898** A. E. T. Watson *Turf* vii. 160 A familiar phrase on the turf is 'horses for courses'. **1908** G. H. Lorimer *J. Spurlock* i. 3 It was horse and horse between the professors. **1926** Maines & Grant *Wise-Crack Dict.* 9/2 *Horse and buggy*, young lady out of date—with long hair. **1927** K. Eubank (*title*) Horse and buggy days. **1928** Wodehouse in *Strand Mag.* Aug. 114/1 The prospect of getting the true facts—straight, as it were, from the horse's mouth—held him..fascinated. **1929** *Daily Express* 7 Nov. 18/4 Followers of the 'horses for courses' theory. **1929** A. Huxley *Let.* 1 Dec. (1969) 320 One or other of us may very likely be over..when there will be a chance of getting your news 'straight from the horse's mouth'. **1930** F. Yeats-Brown *Bengal Lancer* xii. 172 We discuss..what Sir Mark Sykes said, straight from the horse's mouth. **1934** C. Day Lewis *Hope for Poetry* vi. 29 A pandemonium of slogans,..tips from the horse's mouth, straight talks,..etc. **1944** J. Cary (*title*) The horse's mouth. **1949** *This Week Mag.* 9 Jan. 5/1 Wherever this horse-and-buggy court is held, your chances of going scot-free are slim. **1957** *Times Lit. Suppl.* 11 Oct. 609/1 She thinks that our docility, our patience, our contentedness or even complacency with charming, outmoded, horse-and-buggy ways of doing things are, as reflected in the public will, endangering our country's future. **1958** *Listener* 7 Aug. 207/1 Keats' letters remain the horse's mouth. **1958** *Ibid.* 2 Oct. 536/1 Mr. Butler [*sc.* a sculptor] spoke his own commentary: it was an odd mixture of naïveté and insight, a 'horse's mouth' statement vastly preferable to some smooth literary piece by an art critic. **1962** *Daily Tel.* 23 Oct. 15/3 (*headline*) End of 'horse and buggy' medicine. **1963** *Punch* 18 Sept. 430/1 People enjoy what they are capable of enjoying—horses for courses. **1972** *Daily Tel.* 12 July 10/5 Horses for courses is a sound adage in motoring as well as the turf, and few British motorists would look to Czechoslovakia for their car. **1972** J. L. Dillard *Black English* vi. 242 Such horse-and-buggy terms as *whiffletree* and *singletree*.

26. b. *horse-hide* (later examples), *-line*, *-market* (earlier U.S. example), *-marrow*, *-piss* (later examples; also *fig.*), *-sausage*, *-serum*, *-show*, *-team*.

1843 *Ainsworth's Mag.* IV. 116 There were..coracles or boats of horse-hides..to be seen. **1900** *Westm. Gaz.* 16 May 7/3 Horse-hide brawn is now being extensively made. **1959** *Sears, Roebuck Catal.* Spring & Summer 528/3 Work Gloves... Top grain horsehide or cowhide drivers. **1902** J. H. M. Abbott *Tommy Cornstalk* 27 If you have the last couple of hours' 'watch' on the horse-lines, you see it all. **1932** *Times Lit. Suppl.* 3 Mar. 146/3 In the night a boy on the horse-lines was killed and the flag was taken. **1934** Blunden *Mind's Eye* 79 We were transferred to some old horse-lines. **1817** V. Brown *Jrnl.* 11 Jan. in *Maryland Hist. Mag.* (1916) XI. 372 This day spent in the Horse Market trying to sell the two Horses. **1909** *Daily Chron.* 15 Apr. 4/6 The plum pudding and horse-marrow sauce. **1922** Joyce *Ulysses* 75 The sweet oaten reek of horsepiss. **1935** L. Durrell *Spirit of Place* (1969) 33 It cost 6 dracks—3d per bottle... In England I couldn't buy a bottle of horse-piss for 3d. **1973** H. Miller *Open City* xv. 170 Dominic looked straight at Michael. 'Horse piss... You're talking baloney.' **1900** *Westm. Gaz.* 16 May 7/3 Breakfast consisted of horse sausages. **1908** *Daily Chron.* 17 Jan. 5/3 The horse-sausage boat. **1909** *Practitioner* Dec. 867 The introduction of such large quantities (200 c.c.) of horse-serum. **1926** *Encycl. Brit.* II. 772/1 Particular reference may..be made to the recent therapeutic use of horse serum in the treatment of.. blackwater fever. **1964** M. Hynes *Med. Bacteriol.* (ed. 8) vii. 74 The illustration is that of a rabbit immunized with horse-serum. **1856** *Porter's Spirit of Times* 181/2 The performances at the horse show..were very interesting. **1865** *Once a Week* XIII. 133/1 Within the last few years there has been a mania for shows; we have had dog shows, donkey shows, baby shows, and last, not least, horse shows. **1931** Horse-show [see *astride c *adj.*]. **1973** *Country Life* 8 Mar. 652/1 Royal Windsor horse show, Home Park, Windsor. **1817** S. R. Brown *Western Gaz.* 107 [The walls] are..wide enough on the top to admit a horse team and waggon. **1866** *Rep. Indian Affairs* 294 At Leech lake and Winnepeg, eight government oxen and two horse teams were employed ploughing during the season. **1908** *Westm. Gaz.* 27 June 6/3 Hannah's husband was drowned whilst swimming his horse-team across the flooded river.

c. *horse-barn*, *-blanket*, *-feed* (examples), *-paddock* (examples), *-pen*, *-rack*, *-road* (earlier examples), *-rod* (examples), *-shed*, *-stable*, *-trough* (earlier and later examples).

1854 M. J. Holmes *Tempest & Sunshine* xix. 266 I'd as soon be married in the horsebarn as there. **1885** *Rep. Indian Affairs* 130 The horse-barn, carpenter-shop, warehouse, and some small buildings. **1818** in *Knickerbocker* XXIX. 470 But wiser Bill Van Snort the jockey,.. Spread his horse-blanket in the manger. **1884** 'Mark Twain' *Huck. Finn* vi. 40 There was an old horse-blanket nailed against the logs at the far end of the cabin. **1967** S. Beckett *No's Knife* 23 He spread a horse blanket on the ground in a corner on the straw. **1818** J. Owen *Jrnl.* 13 Dec. in *Southern Hist. Assoc. Publ.* (1897) I. 96 No provisions to be had for horse feed. **1823** Horse-feed [see Feed *sb.* 3 b]. **1894** *Country Gentlemen's Catal.* 23/2 The Metropolitan Tram and 'Bus Companies..have not gone scientifically into the question of horse feed. **1968** R. M. Patterson *Finlay's River* 91 They had no time to linger on that good horse-feed: summer was already on its way. **1873** Trollope *Harry Heathcote* (1874) ii. 33 While they were still in the horse-paddock, Harry turned from the track. **1966** G. W. Turner *Eng. Lang. Austral. & N.Z.* vii. 144 Before the school bus was common country schools used to provide a horse-paddock for children who rode to school. **1738** in L. Chalkley *Chron. Scotch-Irish Settlement Virginia* (1912–13) II. 376 One of ye corners of Col. Carter's Horsepen. **1839** J. K. Townsend *Narr. Rocky Mts.* v. 210 Most of the men were immediately put to work making horse-pens. **1846** J. W. Webb *Altowan* I. iv. 116 Pointing out a spot for a horse-pen..he was not long in disappearing. **1633** in *Country Life* (1972) 24 Feb. 470/1 In the stable a horsracke. **1887** *Harper's Mag.* Jan. 231/2 They alighted at the horse-rack nearest the law-office. **1739–40** Richardson *Pamela* (1740) I. 185 This Pasture..is about half a Mile, and then comes to a Common, and near that a private Horse-road. **1803** D. Wordsworth *Jrnl.* 1 Sept. in *Tour Scotland* (1874) 146 There was no horse-road..but a person on foot..might make his way. **1843** W. Carleton *Traits* I. p. xiii, Beaten on the..head, with a kind of stick between a horse-rod & a cudgel. **1968** D. Braithwaite *Fairground Archit.* iii. 49 The horse rods extended below the platform, passing through radial slots. **1768** *Penn. Gaz.* 28 Jan. in *N.J. Archives* (1904) 1st Ser. XXVI. 24 There are belonging to the premises..a new large horse-shed, [etc.]. **1836** W. Dunlap *Mem. Water Drinker* (1837) I. 120 He..seated himself upon a bench under..the horse-shed in front of the house. **1849** Thoreau *Week on Concord & Merrimack Rivers* 80 Driving a poor beast to some meeting-house horse-sheds among the hills. **1959** W. R. Bird *These are Maritimes* ii. 53 We remembered seeing many little country churches with ancient horse sheds still at the rear. **1803** in W. P. & J. P. Cutler *Life & Corr.* (1888) II. 125 Keep your horse-stable free from dung. **1854** R. Glisan *Jrnl. Army Life* (1874) xii. 160 All the hotels and public buildings have carriage houses and horse stables. **1904** T. Watson *Bethany* i. 8 Among corn-cribs, cow-pens, horse-stables, pig-styes..and worm-fenced cotton fields. *c* **1826** D. W. Jerrold in M. R. Booth *Eng. Plays of 19th Cent.* (1973) IV. 106 Oh dear, and I shall go off at last without knowing the secret. I'll stay in the horse-trough. **1867** 'T. Lackland' *Homespun* i. 140 There were times.. when the horse trough was tight frozen. **1973** P. Moyes *Curious Affair of Third Dog* i. 13 The village green, with its Victorian stone horse-trough and ugly but touching war memorial.

d. *horse-broom* (examples), *-bus*, *-cab*, *-cart* (later examples), *-railway* (U.S.), *-rake* (earlier and later examples).

1840 *Picayune* (New Orleans) 22 Aug. 2/5 A new thing has appeared in the streets of New York in the shape of a horse broom for street sweeping. **1908** *Daily Chron.* 11 Nov. 5/2 Last night the Bermondsey Borough Council decided to dispense with ten horse-brooms for street-sweeping and to employ fifty men to take their place. **1905** *Westm. Gaz.* 14 Dec. 6/3 This applies equally to motor-'buses as to horse-'buses. **1963** *Times* 24 May p. vi/3 One critic described the dozen passengers sitting six a side, opposite each other, in the poorly designed, inadequately ventilated, boxlike structures of the early London horsebus as 'trussed fowls in a poulterer's window'. **1973** G. Butler *Coffin for Pandora* vi. 135, I had not walked all the way back. There was a horse bus to Folly Bridge. **1906** *Westm. Gaz.* 31 May 12/1 Ordinary

horse-cab fares. **1907** *Daily Chron.* 3 July 5/2 The immediate doom of the horse cab. **1964** in S. Nowell-Smith *Edwardian England* iii. 122 Six years later, the number of motor-taxis had grown to over 6,300 and there were now fewer than 5,000 horse-cabs. **1658** *Rec. Early Hist. Boston* (1877) II. 147 Henceforth all horse-carts shall bee led by the carters with a rayne. **1821** Horse-cart [see *ASS *sb.* 4 b]. **1863** D. G. MITCHELL *My Farm* 135 An active man with a sharp scythe, a light horse-cart and a Canadian pony. **1863** W. WHITMAN *Specimen Days* (1882–3) 31 At the end of the then horse railway route on Seventh street. **1878** *Harper's Mag.* Jan. 192 He..thought some hunting grounds might be found near the terminus of the horse-railway. **1817** in *Trans. Ill. State Hist. Soc. 1910* 147 The ground has to be cleared of the Cornstock by..cutting them down and drawing them together with a horse Rake. **1913** D. H. LAWRENCE *Sons & Lovers* ix. 249 He had been on the horse-rake, and, having finished, came to help her to put the hay in cocks. **1945** 'G. ORWELL' *Animal Farm* iii. 24 Boxer and Clover would harness themselves to the cutter or the horse-rake (no bits or reins were needed in these days, of course).

e. *horse-barrack* (earlier examples).

1778 J. WESLEY *Jrnl.* 22 June (1938) 201 A new-built horse-barrack. **1783** W. DYOTT *Diary* 28 Feb. (1907) I. 10 There is a horse barracks with one troop of the 2nd horse.

f. *horse-cabby, -duffer* (Austral.), *-stealer* (later examples), *-tender, -thief, -trainer* (examples); *horse-duffing* (later example), *-eating, -hunting, -maiming, -stealing, -thieving,* sbs. and adjs.

1939 H. HODGE *Cab, Sir?* 270 The old horse-cabby. **1963** A. LUBBOCK *Austral. Roundabout* 161 Horse- and cattle-duffers. **1936** M. FRANKLIN *All that Swagger* x. 92 Cattle- and horse-duffing became staple industries in the wilds of Monaro. **1910** *Daily Chron.* 14 Jan. 1/5 Saxony is not the only horse-eating part of Germany. **1960** A. CLARKE *Later Poems* (1961) 87 Horse-eating helps this ill-fare state To Sunday plate. **1848** H. W. HAYGARTH *Recoll. Bush Life Austral.* vi. 61 Cattle-hunting in Australia is excellent sport..with less speed than in horse-hunting. **1908** *Daily Chron.* 24 Oct. 1/2 Apart from the horse-hunting we had harness to repair. **1907** *Westm. Gaz.* 6 Sept. 5/1 Another case of horse-maiming. **1908** *Daily Chron.* 14 Aug. 8/6 Three horse-maiming outrages. **1730** in *Man. Corpor. N.Y.* (1864) 677 That one Solomon Jennings hath been a notorious Horse-Stealer for many years past. **1837** W. IRVING *Capt. Bonneville* (1895) I. 41 One of the most..predatory tribes of the mountains; horse-stealers of the first order. **1737** *London Mag.* Aug. 456/1 At Norwich, 2 Men receiv'd Sentence of Death for Horse-stealing. **1837** W. IRVING *Capt. Bonneville* (1895) I. 43 This wild, horse-stealing tribe. **1858** T. VIELÉ *Following Drum* 123 Horse-stealing from the Mexicans is a..branch of their business. **1871** E. EGGLESTON *Hoosier Schoolmaster* (1872) vi. 70 The whole region..had the reputation of being infested with thieves, who practiced horse-stealing. **1937** *Discovery* Aug. 245/2 The horse-stealing scenes in *The Merry Wives*. **1898** W. J. LOCKE *Idols* xxiii. 323 Two sturdy and swarthy peasants..pausing by the horse-tender, received a voluble account of the situation. **1907** *Daily Chron.* 12 Nov. 8/1 He pushed close to the horse-tender, a Somali. **1768** *Boston Chron.* 10 Oct. 388/3 People..who have assembled..with the view of driving all horse thieves..from amongst them. **1891** M. E. RYAN *Told in Hills* II. v. 61 She intimated yesterday that he might be a horse-thief. **1893** KIPLING *Land & Sea T.* (1923) 230 Murderers, horse-thieves, and cattle-lifters. **1835** R. M. BIRD *Hawks of Hawk-Hollow* II. xiii. 137 Down you rogue, or I'll indict you for horse-thieving. **1874** R. GLISAN *Jrnl. Army Life* xxxii. 463 A band of.. horse-thieving, prairie Indians. **1945** DYLAN THOMAS *Let.* 28 Aug. (1966) 283 Mean, green, horse-thieving Wales. **1889** *Cent. Dict.*, Horse-trainer. **1906** *Daily Chron.* 4 Jan. 7/1 Only one British subject is reported to have been killed during the rising—a horse-trainer, who was accidentally shot. **1921** *Daily Colonist* (Victoria, B.C.) 9 Oct. 36/2 Mr Carley, of Epsom, England, licensed horse-trainer under the English Jockey Club.

g. *horse-drawn* (examples), *-driven* adj.

1890 O. WILDE in *19th Cent.* July 140 On foot, or in horse-drawn chariot, the warriors go forth to battle. **1969** *Times* 25 Apr. 11/3 The modern equivalent of the correspondents who no doubt wrote to you when the first steam train appeared and said that we should..travel as God intended, by horse-drawn carriage. **1900** *Daily News* 2 Oct. 7/1 To his efforts..the cities of Philadelphia and Chicago owe their emancipation from the..delay of horse-driven public conveyances. **1936** *Discovery* Mar. 75/1 An ancient horse-driven windlass. **1968** C. A. DOXIADIS *Between Dystopia & Utopia* 8 We still cross our big cities at nine miles per hour, which was the speed of a horse-driven cart at the beginning of the century. **1973** *Guardian* 18 May 10 A petition..was taken in a horse-driven carriage to Kensington Town Hall yesterday.

h. *horse-faced* (later examples), *-headed* adj.

1916 E. POUND *Lustra* 53 The horse-faced lady of just the unmentionable age. **1937** C. S. FORESTER *Happy Return* 113 One of the horsefaced mannish women whom he particularly disliked. **1910** W. J. LOCKE *Simon* xii. 146 The horse-headed Englishman cried '*banco*'.

27. a. horse-bite, (*a*) a bite given by a horse; (*b*) *colloq.*, a rough slap on the thigh with the hand (example is *N.Z.*); **horse-book** (*a*), a book about horses; (*b*), a betting-book; **horse brass** (see quot. 1963); **horse-bucket** (earlier U.S. example); **horse butcher**: add to def.: also, a man who sells horse-meat (*HORSE-MEAT 2); **horse-doctor** (later examples); **horse-doctoring** (example); **horse feathers** *U.S. slang*, nonsense, rubbish, balderdash; **horse-fiddle** *U.S.* (see quot. 1872); **horse-high** *a. U.S.*, (*a*) as high as a horse; (*b*) too high for a horse to jump over; also *fig.*; **horse-holder,** (*b*) *Mil.*, each of the mounted horse artillery gunners who take charge of the dismounted horses while the gun is in action; **horse-knacker** (example); **horse lot** *U.S.*, a piece of ground on which horses are pastured; **horse manure,** (*a*) = HORSE-DUNG; (*b*) = **horse shit*; **horse opera** *colloq.* (orig. *U.S.*), a 'Western' film or television series; **horse-ride,** (*a*) a road for horse-traffic; (*b*) a ride taken mounted on a horse; **horse shit** *U.S. slang*, nonsense; **horse-sickness**: substitute for def.: an acute virus disease of horses and related animals, marked by fever, difficulty in breathing, or swelling of the head, and endemic in Africa; add earlier and later examples; **horse's neck** *slang* (orig. *U.S.*), a beverage of ginger ale flavoured with lemon-peel, with or without the addition of whisky, brandy, or gin; **horse's tail** (see *HORSE-TAIL 1 c); **horse-tailer** [TAIL *v.*[1] 5] *Austral.*, one who 'tails' or follows horses; **horse-trade** *U.S.*, a deal in horses; also *fig.* or *transf.*; hence **horse-trader** (in quots. 1963 and 1972 = heroin-trader; cf. sense 14* above); **horse-trading** *vbl. sb.*, (*a*) *U.S.* dealing in horses; (*b*) *transf.*, hard or unfair bargaining; **horse-wrangler** (later examples).

1885 'MARK TWAIN' in *Century Mag.* Dec. 197/1 Bowers, already irritated by the pain of the horse-bite. **1949** F. SARGESON *I saw in my Dream* II. xiii. 117 He brought his hand down smartly on Len's leg, giving him a horse-bite that made him jump. **1643** in *Essex Co. Prob. Rec.* (1916) I. 30, I give to him my horse booke alsoe a pitchforke. **1909** *Times Lit. Suppl.* 21 Jan. 23/1 Colonel..Dodge..is the author of two admirable horse-books. **1962** K. ORVIS *Damned & Destroyed* xiv. 91 A guy I know runs a horse-book on University. **1911** E. LOVETT *Folk Lore Horse* 3 (*heading*) Horse brasses. It is almost impossible to walk through any of our towns without meeting with horses..bedecked with certain brass ornaments. *Ibid.* 7 We now turn to the other typical horse brass, viz., the crescent. **1945** 'G. ORWELL' *Animal Farm* iv. 34 It consisted of a brass medal (they were really some old horse-brasses which had been found in the harness-room). **1960** 'R. EAST' *Kingston Black* xiv. 135 A great glittering display of silver darts trophies and horse brasses. **1963** BLOODGOOD & SANTINI *Horseman's Dict.* 107 *Horse brasses*, decorative metal ornaments in a great variety of designs hung on draft-horse harness. Probably originating in the amulets used on camels in the East and horses in Mediterranean countries to ward off the 'evil eye'. **1827** J. F. COOPER *Red Rover* II. viii. 134 There was a horse-bucket kicking about her decks. **1905** *Daily Chron.* 26 May 5/6 Whole families have been affected by the meat, and even the horse-butcher himself who sold the meat is among the victims. **1942** E. PAUL *Narrow St.* vi. 48 A golden horse above the green and white awning..was the emblem of the horse butcher, M. Monge. **1810** M. L. WEEMS *Lett.* (1929) III. 11 A collection in which there is not a single Bible..nor Dream-book, nor Horse Doctors. **1894** *Congress. Rec.* 1 Mar. 2500/1 We found..that he was a veterinary surgeon, called in New England a 'horse doctor'. **1930** T. S. ELIOT tr. *St.J. Perse's Anabasis* 65 The vast court of the horse-doctor. **1807** W. IRVING et al. *Salmagundi* (1814) xv. 345 He is..resorted to as an oracle to resolve any question about..horse-doctoring. **1928** *Amer. Speech* IV. 98 Mr. William De Beck, the comic-strip comedian..assumes credit for the first actual use of the word horsefeathers. **1934** J. O'HARA *Appointment in Samarra* (1935) vi. 163 'And my orders is to see that you keep your knees together, baby.' 'Horse feathers,' she said. **1936** [see *BUTTON *v.* 3]. **1936** WODEHOUSE *Laughing Gas* xvi. 173 'Oh, horse-feathers!'.. The expression which she used was new to me, but one could gather its trend. Her ribald and offensive tone jarred upon me. **1966** A. A. FAIR *Widows wear Weeds* xiv. 160 'We lose our licence; Sellers gets fined and maybe you get prosecuted for perjury.' 'Horsefeathers!' Bertha snorted. **1967** J. GARDNER *Madrigal* ii. 21 Mostyn pointed out that..they could court-martial him *in camera*... On reflection, Boysie realised that this was all a load of horse feathers. **1807** J. JENNINGS *Let.* 19 Sept. in *Ind. Hist. Coll. Soc. Publ.* (1932) X. 164 The French..convened around the house of the new couple..playing on horse fiddles. **1843** *Knickerbocker* XXI. 46 The clangor of trumpets, the clattering of pans, the grinding of horse-fiddles. **1872** E. EGGLESTON *End of World* xlvi. 294 Bill Day had a gigantic watchman's rattle, a hickory spring on a cog-wheel. It is called in the West a horse-fiddle, because it is so unlike either a horse or a fiddle. **1911** H. QUICK *Yellowstone Nights* viii. 212 In addition to the horse-fiddles and bells and horns Absalom had arranged some private theatricals. **1859, 1879** Horse-high [see *hog-tight* adj. s.v. *HOG *sb.*[1] 13 a]. **1896** W. A. WHITE *Real Issue* 147 In the summer the field stood horse-high with corn. *a* **1930** D. H. LAWRENCE *Sex, Lit. & Censorship* (1955) 12 The Clean Books League, whose object was to make the law..'horse-high, pig-tight, and bull-strong'. **1972** *Christian Science Monitor* 28 Sept. 16/4 The pioneers.. tipped the stumps up with their roots in the air, and lined them along so they were, as the saying went, 'horse-high, hog-tight, and bull-strong'. **1837** A. F. OAKES *Madras Horse Artillery* 18 The rear rank are horse-holders. **1875** *Man. Field Artillery Exerc.* VIII. 285 The horse-holders do not dismount. **1902** J. H. M. ABBOTT *Tommy Cornstalk* 35 When cavalry are dismounted for skirmishing, one man of every four—the horse-holder, or number three—is out of action. **1936** C. S. FORESTER *General* 7 In a long straggling line..lay the troopers of the squadron..firing away. In a gully to the rear..were the horses and horseholders. **1937** *John o' London's* 5 Feb. 762/2 [A girl] promised to wait for me. She didn't, though. Too impatient. Married a horse-knacker. **1847** W. T. THOMPSON in *Spirit of Times* 24 July 250/2 Way he went.., down around the house, through the horse lot, and into the old field. **1850** *Rep. Comm. Patents 1849: Agric.* 144 The man..has..no time to make manure, or to haul out and spread the little that is dropped in his horse-lot. **1889** *Harper's Mag.* June 123/2 In the horse lot she found her father putting on his coat. **1966** *Publ. Amer. Dial. Soc.* XLII. 19 Horselot, the enclosure around a stockbarn. **1843** S. L. DANA *Muck Man. Farmers* (ed. 2) vi. 135 The dung of pigeons is 2-7ths stronger than horse manure. **1954** A. G. L. HELLYER *Encycl. Garden Work* 127/2 Horse manure can be used safely for all plants and crops for which animal manure is desirable. **1956** *Dict. Gardening* (R. Hort. Soc.) (ed. 2) II. 1011/1 Horse manure is especially valuable in mushroom growing. **1957** J. OSBORNE *Entertainer* viii. 67 She's not interested in all that horse manure about Canada. **1964** *New Statesman* 1 May 674/1 Imagine his furious indignation if a similar *contretemps* had arisen (as well it might) at a Washington club because one had been reported as saying on television that federal policy on racial discrimination in the South is a load of horse-manure. **1927** *Motion Picture Classic* 2 July 26/1 Horse Opera..is an opus of the West where men are cowboys. **1948** 'J. TEY' *Franchise Affair* xix. 227 That happens only in detective-stories and the last few minutes of horse-operas. **1957** E. HYAMS *Into Dream* 244 An officer who looked like a bad-man Mexican in an early horse-opera. **1958** *Times* 17 Nov. 8/6, 21 per cent. of the available time is devoted to westerns (28 of these 'horse-opera' series are being broadcast). **1903** *Daily Chron.* 6 Nov. 3/3 On one side of it there will be a horse-ride, and on the other..a gravelled walk for foot passengers. **1906** W. OWEN *Let.* 15 Aug. (1967) 31 Mr Smallpage has just been for a horse-ride. **1955** M. MCCARTHY *Charmed Life* (1956) iii. 66 Pardon me if I say that's horse shit. **1959** W. BURROUGHS *Naked Lunch* 98 Gentlemen of the jury,..are we to gulp down this tissue of horse shit? **1970** *It* 12–25 Feb. 2 'This is definitely the weekend of the big bust!' 'Horseshit! You've said the same thing for the past six weekends!' **1822** J. CAMPBELL *Trav. S. Afr. 2nd Journey* I. ii. 32 The horse sickness.. was prevailing much at that time. **1899** W. J. K. LITTLE *Sk. & Stud. S. Afr.* (ed. 2) iv. 93 Let us hope..rinderpest, horse-sickness, and the locusts will yet be conquered. **1947** J. STEVENSON-HAMILTON *Wild Life S. Afr.* vi. 50 The zebra..has..the immense advantage of being entirely immune from Horse Sickness and Nagana disease. **1963** JUBB & KENNEDY *Path. Domestic Anim.* II. 585/1 Even in districts where horsesickness recurs annually, the distribution tends to be limited to low-lying areas such as valleys, swamps, and areas with summer rain. **1903** 'C. E. MERRIMAN' *Lett. from Son* 177 Every man then visited the tool-house, where a tin wash-boiler filled with what they call here 'horse's neck', a savage compound of whiskey and hard cider, occupied the place of honor. **1925** J. METCALFE *Smoking Leg* 138 A tall young man in a grey suit whose drink was horse's neck in summer and Burton in the winter. **1936** E. AMBLER *Dark Frontier* xiii. 219, I ordered a Horse's Neck, remembered how bad the gin was ..and had a small beer instead. **1938** L. MACNEICE *I crossed Minch* II. xv. 211 If I could sit in a garden shady With a Horse's Neck or a White Lady. **1968** *Daily Tel.* (Colour Suppl.) 13 Dec. 43/3 Brandy and soda, or brandy and some soft drink like ginger ale—the Horse's Neck—have become women's drinks. **1933** *Bulletin* (Sydney) 16 Aug. 20/2 Then the horse-tailer pulled out, and an abo. was given the job. **1954** B. MILES *Stars my Blanket* xxiii. 202 The 'horse tailers', whose job it was to look after the mob of spare horses. **1968** K. WEATHERLEY *Roo Shooter* 100, I was only twenty at the time and working as horse-tailer for a cattle-drover. **1846** *Knickerbocker* XXVIII. 361 He was employed in..an action brought by a man against another for cheating him in a 'horse-trade'. **1902** A. D. MCFAUL *Ike Glidden* iii. 22 His self-confidence could not admit of a thought that he could be fooled in a horse trade. **1923** *Daily Mail* 15 June 9 [New York World] We hope that foreign Powers will not be weak enough to consent to such unprincipled horse trade. **1850** L. H. GARRARD *Wah-to-Yah* vii. 109 The unfair horsetrader might have taken my scalp. **1912** I. S. COBB *Back Home* 3 The swapping ring below the wagonyard was..clamorous with the chaffer of the horse-traders. **1932** W. FAULKNER *Light in August* xiii. 283 A room where it will be quiet when her time comes, and not every durn horsetrader or courtjury that passes through the hallway. **1963** T. TULLETT *Inside Interpol* iv. 44 There is another process ..that of turning the morphine into heroin, and the price then soars to £600 a pound. Even this gigantic profit is not enough for the 'horse-traders', as these criminals are known. **1972** H. C. RAE *Shooting Gallery* II. 67 And how many horse-traders are there in this part of the world? **1826** T. FLINT *Recoll.* 64 Horse-trading..seems to be a favorite and universal amusement. **1853** J. G. BALDWIN *Flush Times Alabama* 273 An enterprising young gentleman..engaged..in the horse-trading line. **1891** C. ROBERTS *Adrift Amer.* 190 We stayed in camp here for two days, during which time we did some horse-trading. **1902** A. D. MCFAUL *Ike Glidden* iv. 28 A horse-trading expedition. **1939** I. BAIRD *Waste Heritage* xix. 262 There is too damn much horse-trading going on around here. **1947** *Forum* 24 May 4/3 It was certain that some hard bargaining had taken place in that upstairs conference room, political horse-trading at which South Africa's politicians are adept. **1969** *Times* 25 Apr. 28/3 Employers in the Lancashire textile industry were accused..of 'horse trading'. **1971** *New Scientist* 20 May 460/1 A powerful ingredient in all this horsetrading is the continually deteriorating employment situation in the aerospace industry. **1902** O. WISTER *Virginian* x. 109 The foreman of the 76 outfit, and the horse-wrangler from the Bar Circle-L. **1968** R. M. PATTERSON *Finlay's River* 102 Various packers and horse wranglers, with their pack-trains, moved with the party or made rendezvous with them as the work demanded.

b. horse ant (later examples); **horse bot:** substitute for def.: the fly *Gasterophilus intestinalis*, esp. its larva which is a parasite of horses; also **horse bot-fly**; add examples; **horse-stinger** (later examples).

1908 *Westm. Gaz.* 16 Apr. 10/3 The 'horse-ant',..

(*Formica rufa*), the big fellow which builds the great heaps, usually of pine-needles. **1945** C. P. Haskins *Of Ants & Men* ix. 167 Typical of this group [*sc.* raiding ants] is *Formica rufa*, the 'horse ant' or 'fallow ant' of England and Europe, whose great thatched mounds form a conspicuous feature of the German forests. **1840** J. & M. Loudon tr. *Köllar's Treat. Insects* I. 53 The Horse-bot, a larva proceeding from a fly resembling a humble-bee with two wings. **1925** A. D. Imms *Gen. Textbk. Ent.* III. 652 The horse bot-flies..lay their eggs on the hair. **1928** Metcalf & Flint *Destructive & Useful Insects* xxii. 779 The common horse bot may easily be told by the faint smoky spots on the wings. **1968** *Oxf. Bk. Insects* 138/2 *Horse-bot fly* (Gasterophilus intestinalis). This belongs to a separate sub-family in Muscidae—the Gasterophilinae. **1910** *Encycl. Brit.* VIII. 468/1 Dragon-fly... In many parts of England are termed 'horse-stingers'. It is almost needless to say that (excepting to other insects..) they are perfectly innocuous. **1966** 'J. Hackston' *Father clears Out* 134 Flies, mosquitos, beetles, March flies, blowflies, and horsestingers.

c. horse-bean: substitute for def.: a leguminous plant grown as food for cattle, as *Vicia faba*, *Canavalia ensiformis*, *Parkinsonia aculeata*, or their seeds; add earlier and later examples; **horse mushroom**, a species of edible mushroom, *Agaricus arvensis*, larger and coarser than the common mushroom; **horse-nicker**, a large West Indian shrub, *Cæsalpinia bonduc*, or its seeds; **horse poison**, a West Indian plant, *Isotoma longiflora*; **horse-weed** *U.S.* (examples).

1684 I. Mather *Remark. Prov.* (1890) 216 The stone weighed about seven grains, being much in the shape of our ordinary horse-beans. **1942** Castetter & Bell *Pima & Papago Agric.* 60 Of somewhat less importance were the seeds of..Jerusalem thorn or horsebean (*Parkinsonia aculeata*). **1964** J. M. Kingsbury *Poisonous Plants of U.S.* 43 *Parkinsonia aculeata*, horsebean. *Ibid.* 362 *Vicia faba* L. Fava bean, broad bean, horse bean. **1965** E. G. B. Gooding et al. *Flora of Barbados* 198 *Canavalia ensiformis* (L.) DC. (Horse bean, Overlook bean, Sword bean, etc.) is sometimes grown as a vegetable. The young pod is sliced, and eaten like French beans. **1866** Lindley & Moore *Treas. Bot.* II. 598/1 The horse-mushroom need not be excluded on account of its supposed unwholesomeness. **1890** R. D. Blackmore *Kit & Kitty* III. iii. 39 Mingling with the true Agaric some very fine 'Horse-mushrooms'. **1966** *Times* 28 Apr. 16 Horse mushrooms are bigger and stronger flavoured than proper field mushrooms. **1750** Horse-nicker [see Nicker *sb.*[4]]. **1871** C. Kingsley *At Last* I. i. 36 The grey horse-nicker-beads of our childhood. **1965** E. G. B. Gooding et al. *Flora of Barbados* 176 *Caesalpinia bonduc*... Grey nicker, Horse-nicker... Shrub, often scrambling by means of prickles. **1851** P. H. Gosse *Nat. Sojourn Jamaica* 80 One of the most venomous of plants (*Isotoma longiflora*) commonly called Horse-poison. **1955** *W. Indian Med. Jrnl.* IV. 73 *Isotoma longiflora*..Madam Fate; Star Flower; Horse Poison. **1790** L. Castiglioni *Viaggio negli Stati Uniti* II. 333 *Collinsonia canadensis*, Lin. Horse-weed. **1874** J. W. Long *Amer. Wild-Fowl Shooting* xxiii. 239 The hunter usually selects a position..amongst the high 'horse-weeds' bordering the field. **1892** B. Torrey *Foot-path Way* 72 Acres and acres of horseweed. **1963** H. A. Gleason *Illustr. Flora North-eastern U.S.* III. 475/1 *Conyza canadensis* (L.) Cron. Horseweed. Coarse annual... A weed in waste places.

horse, *v.* Add: **13. a.** To make fun of, to 'rag', to ridicule; to indulge in horseplay; to fool *about* or *around*. orig. *U.S.*

1901 *Munsey's Mag.* XXV. 407/1 Because we chose to chew his statements and remove the bones before we swallowed them, he developed the idea that we had no interest in the work and were trying to 'horse' him. **1901** F. H. Spearman *Held for Orders* 173 'Are you horsing me?' he exclaimed, raising his voice angrily. **1928** P. Buranelli et al. *Cryptogram Bk.* p. i, Always playing jokes on each other, they began to 'horse' each other cryptographically. **1928** *Amer. Speech* III. 219 *Horse around*, to indulge in fooling or horseplay. **1940** R. Chandler *Trouble is my Business* (1950) 8 Quit horsing around. **1942** *R.A.F. Jrnl.* 2 May 15 Why must you continually horse around, Ginger? **1952** W. G. Hardy *Unfulfilled* 48 Peter horsed around and ducked Elise and she ducked him. **1954** 'W. Henry' *Death of Legend* 32 Dingus was really mad about it; he wasn't just horsing now. **1959** E. Allen *Man who chose Death* v. 49 You saw scores like him..laughing and horseing with the pretty..young Italian girls. **1959** *Punch* 10 June 776/2 The professor thought I was horsing about and came down to me. **1961** Wodehouse *Ice in Bedroom* vi. 47 When you've cleaned up pretty good, you don't want to be horsing around down in the suburbs. **1961** J. Heller *Catch-22* (1962) xxxii. 340 They were having a whale of a good time as they helped each other set up their cots. They were horsing around. **1971** *It* 2–16 June 7/1 Two black kids..were horsing around just outside the club.

b. To philander; to 'sleep *around*'.

1952 S. Kauffmann *Philanderer* (1953) ii. 32 It isn't as if I didn't love her. I'd die for her. Literally. Then why do I have to go horsing around with dames? **1956** S. Longstreet *Real Jazz* 67 'This is a respectable band,' he said, 'and there ain't goin' to be any immoral horsin' goin' on. Whoever you start sleepin' with this trip, that's how you end the tour!' **1956** C. Smith *Deadly Reaper* xxv. 201 She'd be horsing around with Nicky, giving me grounds for divorce.

horse-back. Add: **3.** (Earlier example.)

1851 J. S. Springer *Forest Life* 41 The pumpkin Pine is..found..also on abrupt ridges, called horse-backs.

5. horseback opinion *U.S.*, an opinion given (as) from horseback, without opportunity for full consideration of the question.

1879 *Congress. Rec.* 23 Apr. 728/1, I am not here as a judicial authority or oracle. I can only give a horseback opinion. **1903** A. Adams *Log of Cowboy* vi. 72 My sister gives it as a horseback opinion that she'd been engaged to this fellow nearly eight months.

horse-boat. Add: **1. b.** A type of landing-craft.

1907 *Daily Chron.* 25 Feb. 6/3 Exercises with the new form of steel horse-boat were carried out..on Saturday by an A.S.C. contingent... At the stern is a large flap which falls down to facilitate landing. **1923** *Man. Seamanship* (H.M.S.O.) II. 215 Horseboats would be excellent for landing troops except for the fact that they are unhandy.

2. For def. read: *N. Amer.* A boat whose paddle-wheels are driven by horses working a tread-mill. †*Obs.* exc. *Hist.* (Further examples.)

1823 I. Holmes *Account U.S.A.* 315 One of the horse-boats which cross the North River..is of a very peculiar construction. **1829** *Brockville* (Upper Canada) *Gaz.* 28 Aug. 2/5 In crossing the lake..the Steamboat Montreal and the horse-boat came in contact with each other. **1897** R. E. Robinson *Uncle Lisha's Outing* 257 They wended their way to the ferry just in time to see the horse boat come splashing into port, the four horses plodding their unprogressive journey on the revolving wheel. **1928** *Old-Time New Eng.* Apr. 161 Before the wreck of the *Belknap* a new type of freighter, the horse-boat, appeared on the lake. The first one of its kind was built on Long Island in 1838. It was an open scow propelled by paddle-wheels, the motive power being supplied by a pair of horses tramping a treadmill.

horse-breaker. Add: †**2.** A courtesan; a demi-mondaine; a prostitute. Freq. *pretty horsebreaker*. *Obs.*

1861 *Times* 28 June 12/4 They are, in the end, only fit for the company of 'horsebreakers'. *Ibid.* 12/5 If she thinks men prefer the society of 'pretty horsebreakers'..she never was more mistaken. **1861** *Punch* 13 July 13 (*caption*) *Stout Equestrian.* 'Dou [*sic*] you know, love, I'm rather sorry I got this hat, for suppose I should be taken for a "pretty horsebreaker"!' **1865** *Public Opinion* 30 Sept. 352/2 These *demi-monde* people,..horsebreakers, hetairæ..are by degrees pushing their way into 'society'. **1865** C. Knight *Shadows of Old Booksellers* v. 112 He..was intimate with all the high — (read 'pretty horse-breakers') in town... Some of these girls he often asked to dine with him. **1966** D. Crow *Theresa* xvi. 189 While Brewster's aim was to show her up as a pretty horse-breaker, hers was to proclaim her purity. **1970** G. Greer *Female Eunuch* 265 The vestiges of sensual innocence hung around long enough to endow us with obsolete terms like..*pretty horsebreaker*.

horse-gear. 1. (Later examples.)

1941 *Proc. Prehist. Soc.* VII. 130 The bulk of the hoard is Celtic horse-gear. **1960** G. E. Evans *Horse in Furrow* xvii. 220 An unorthodox use of a piece of horse-gear..should be recorded.

2. (Later examples.)

1904 Goodchild & Tweney *Technol. & Sci. Dict.* 291/1 *Horse gear*, the device used for yoking horses to machinery. **1940** *Chambers's Techn. Dict.* 119/2 *Horse gear*, a device for producing mechanical power by means of a lever attached to gears, which is operated by..[a] horse walking in a circle.

horse guard. 4. (Earlier and later N. Amer. examples.)

1828 A. Wetmore *Diary* 30 May in *Mo. Hist. Rev.* (1914) VIII. 185 Formed our wagons into an oblong square, and set a horse guard. **1907** J. R. Cook *Border & Buffalo* (1938) 279 The horse-guard brought in the horses. **1971** J. McDougall *Parsons on Plains* v. 40 When you reach the horse guard..tell him to catch my horse Badger for you.

horsehair. Add: **c. horsehair snake** *U.S.*, = *horsehair-worm*.

1897 *Outing* (U.S.) XXX. 434/2 The creature referred to as a mystery is what is termed the 'horsehair snake', in reality, a hairworm. **1949** *Sci. Monthly* Jan. 56/2 Another mythical serpent, confined to the rural scene, is the horse-hair snake..the worm *Paragordius varius*. **1966** *Publ. Amer. Dial. Soc.* XLII. 19 Horsehair snake. Actually a long slender worm (*Gordius*, sp.), which spends one portion of its life in the body of a large insect and the other in shallow water, as in a watering trough. Thus arose the folk belief that these worms were originally horsehairs.

horsehead. 4. (Examples.)

1884 *Bull. U.S. Nat. Museum* No. 27. 438 *Selene argentea*..Horsehead. **1905** D. S. Jordan *Guide to Study of Fishes* II. xvii. 276 *Selene vomer*, the horse-head-fish, or look-down, is similarly but even more distorted. **1966** Leim & Scott *Fishes of Atlantic Coast of Canada* 251 Atlantic lookdown... *Selene vomer* (Linnaeus) 1758. Other common names: horsehead, moonfish.

horse-hoer. (Examples.)

1744 W. Ellis *Mod. Husb.* I. 145 It will be a difficult Point for the Horse-hougher to keep his Horse and Instrument..exact. **1935** J. Joyce *Let.* 19 Feb. (1966) III. 345 If they put on *Floradora* with George Robey in the name part the horsehoers would not notice.

horse-jockey. Add: **b.** *U.S.* One who traffics in horses. Hence **ho·rse-jo:ckeying** *vbl. sb.*

1744 A. Hamilton *Itinerarium* (1907) 31 May 3, I met one Matthew Baker, a horse-jockey. **1783** in S. E. Baldwin *Simeon Baldwin* (1919) 120 The conversation was upon News—horsejockeying—& other indifferent subjects. **1784** in *Connecticut Hist. Soc. Coll.* (1930) XXIII. 204 Ship Building is carried on with Vigor in this State, & the Horse Jockey business flourishes. **1792** J. Belknap *Hist. New-Hampshire* III. ix. 144 Few [horses] live and die on the plantations where they are bred; some are exported..; but the most are continually shifted from one owner to another, by means of a set of contemptible wretches called horse-jockies. **1866** 'Mark Twain' *Lett. fr. Hawaii* (1967) 50 The Kanaka horse jockey is fertile in imagination and elastic in conscience. *Ibid.* 288 Brown bought a horse from a native at Waiohinu for twelve dollars, but happening to think of the horse-jockeying propensities of the race, he removed the saddle and found that..recent hard riding had polished most of the hide off his back.

horseless, *a.* Add: Applied *c* 1895–1910 to motor vehicles.

1895 [in Dict.]. **1900** *T. Eaton & Co. Catal.* Christmas 5/1 Horseless carriage, large size, wind with key, best spring, 50 c. **1901** *Chambers's Jrnl.* Jan. 14/2 The three great trusts that control the making and using of these horseless machines. **1905** *Ibid.* Jan. 111/1 Farmers, who now look askance at horseless vehicles. **1973** J. Wainwright *Devil you Don't* 144 An Olde Worlde coaching town which hadn't yet got round to noticing the arrival of the horseless carriage.

horse marine[2]. Add: **2.** Phr. *tell that to the horse marines*: a colloquial expression of incredulity. Cf. Marine *sb.* 4 c.

1892 [in Dict.]. **1921** W. S. Maugham *Circle* II. 65 *Elizabeth*: He's never even kissed me. *Arnold*: I'd try telling that to the horse marines if I were you.

ho·rse-ma:stership. [See -ship.] Skill in managing horses.

1904 *Westm. Gaz.* 21 Sept. 10/1 Thereupon a trumpeter, who knew something about horse-mastership, instantly sounded the forage-call. Two minutes later every animal was standing quietly in its appointed place. **1925** E. O. Shebbeare in E. F. Norton *Fight for Everest, 1924* 365 Unless any other member of the Expedition better fitted by his knowledge of horsemastership undertakes the care of the mess mules. **1927** *Daily Tel.* 26 Apr. 16/7 The Army in India polo team..has undertaken a very difficult and interesting feat of horse-mastership. The problem to be solved is that of transporting a large stable of ponies from India to America. **1937** H. Belloc *Crusade* iii. 67 The rest of the work was foot-slogging and horsemastership. **1971** *Country Life* 30 Dec. 1829/3 The present upsurge of interest in all aspects of horse-manship and horsemastership.

horse-meat. Add: **2.** = Horse-flesh 1.

1853 S. N. Carvalho *Jrnl.* 1 Feb. in J. Bigelow *Mem. J. C. Fremont* (1856) xvii. 441 He sent a Mexican..with cooked horsemeat. **1868** *All Year Round* 22 Feb. 252/2 Horse-meat is a common..article of food. **1870** *Food Jrnl.* 1 Dec. 620 The almost impossibility of obtaining beef and mutton naturally forced the use of horse-meat upon the people. **1904** *Westm. Gaz.* 23 Dec. 10/1 Every day the purveyors and the consumers of horsemeat increase in numbers. **1910** *Daily Chron.* 14 Jan. 1/5 The price of horse meat was 3½d. a lb. **1972** T. P. McMahon *Issue of Bishop's Blood* (1973) xi. 171 A very suave-type fellow then came to Hymie with a tale about..buying frozen horse meat to meet the chain's need for huge quantities of frozen beef.

horse-mill. (Later U.S. examples.)

1848 E. Bryant *California* xxi. 269 The flour consumed by Captain Sutter is ground by a very ordinary horse-mill. **1889** *Century Mag.* Feb. 520/2 A horse-mill—a long pole on which a man sits, and to which a horse or mule is hitched. **1971** *Country Life* 30 Sept. 848/1 Some of these groups of stone-built barns, byres and arcaded cartsheds, relieved on occasion by a circular horse-mill, [etc.].

horse plum. 2. *N. Amer.* Substitute for def.: Either of the two common wild plums, *Prunus americana* or *P. nigra*.

1790 S. Deane *New-Eng. Farmer* 222/2 The horse-plum, a very pleasant tasted juicy fruit, of a large size. **1827** *Western Monthly Rev.* I. 322 The fruit is of the size of a common horse plum. **1908** N. L. Britton *N. Amer. Trees* 494 Canada Plum—*Prunus nigra* Aiton. Also called Horse plum, this is a small, bushy tree, occurring in woods and neglected lands from Newfoundland to Alberta, and southward to Georgia.

horse-power. Now commonly written as one word. Add: **1. c.** With qualifying words, esp. **brake horsepower**, the power available at the shaft of an engine, measurable by means of a brake; **indicated horsepower**, the power produced within the cylinders, as shown by an indicator.

1859 W. J. M. Rankine *Man. Steam Engine* v. 479 Nominal Horse-power is a conventional mode of describing the dimensions of a steam engine, for the convenience of makers and purchasers of engines, and bears no fixed relation to indicated or to effective horse-power. **1881** [in Dict., sense 1]. **1887** *Encycl. Brit.* XXII. 493/2 The efficiency of the mechanism is the ratio of the 'effective' or 'brake' horse power to the indicated horse power. **1904** *Westm. Gaz.* 30 Mar. 10/2 The *Good Hope* and the *Drake*..are of 14,100 tons displacement and 30,000 indicated horse-power. **1943** A. P. Fraas *Aircraft Power Plants* vi. 110 The power required to turn the engine over, or friction horsepower,..increases rapidly with

rpm. **1968** R. H. Bacon *Car* ii. 17 The power developed in the cylinder..is called the indicated horsepower or i.h.p. Some of this power is absorbed by the friction of various parts of the engine. The power remaining, that is the power that can be used for work, is called the brake horsepower or b.h.p. **1972** *Daily Tel.* 15 Mar. 11/5 The latest car is almost a hundredweight heavier while the net brake horsepower is only up by six.

4. *Comb.* **horsepower-hour**, a unit representing the work performed or energy consumed in working at the rate of one horsepower for one hour.

1899 J. Perry *Steam Engine* xvi. 250 Units of Energy used Commercially. 1 horse-power hour = ..1,980,000 foot-pounds. **1906** *Westm. Gaz.* 28 June 2/1 An output of 36 cubic feet of oxygen per horse-power hour. **1949** G. P. Sutton *Rocket Propulsion Elem.* i. 18 The specific fuel consumption is based on the horsepower output, and its units are pounds of fuel per horsepower-hour. **1963** F. D. Jones & Schubert *Engin. Encycl.* (ed. 3) 662, 1 horsepower-hour = 0·746 kilowatt-hour.

horse-sense. For '*U.S. colloq.*' read '*colloq.* (orig. *U.S.*)'. (Add earlier and later examples.)

1832 J. K. Paulding *Westward Ho!* II. 60 He's a man of good strong horse sense. **1911** H. S. Harrison *Queed* xviii. 223 A rich vein of horse-sense underlay Byrd's philanthropic enthusiasms. **1920** R. Macaulay *Potterism* II. iii. 88, I am sure both parties credited them with too much idealism and too little plain horse-sense. **1930** Chesterton *Four Felons* 252 What I say is horse-sense, for all that. **1942** *Short Guide Gr. Brit.* (U.S. War Dept.) 2 We can defeat Hitler's propaganda with..plain, common horse sense; understanding of evident truths. **1960** I. Wallach *Absence of Cello* 72 Summoning up his best horse sense (and trying to forget that the horse is an uncommonly stupid animal), Andrew said, 'I agree with Mr Clifton.' **1973** E. Lemarchand *Let or Hindrance* v. 41 All horse sense on your part, old man, but I've got a tiresome hunch that it's not going to be as straightforward as all that.

horseshoe, *sb.* Add: **2. e.** A horseshoe bend. *U.S.*

1795 in *Amer. Speech* (1963) XXXVIII. 183 In the bend, or horse shoe..is a neck of land about 4 or 500 yards wide. *a* **1910** [see *fetch *v.* 9].

f. *Logic.* (See quots. 1926, 1954.) Cf. *hook *sb.*[1] 10 d.

1926 H. M. Sheffer in *Isis* VIII. 231 The authors (1)..inform us, 'unofficially', that they are privately convinced that 'either *p* is false or *q* is true' (2) *means* '*p* implies *q*'; and they henceforth regard '*p* horseshoe *q*' as *meaning* '*p* implies *q*'. **1952** F. B. Fitch *Symbolic Logic* 15 The horseshoe symbol can be read as 'implies', but a more accurate reading is the *if-then* reading. **1954** I. M. Copi *Symbolic Logic* ii. 17 We introduce the new symbol '⊃', called a horseshoe, to represent the partial meaning common to all conditional statements. **1959** *Listener* 30 Apr. 757/2 He spent another [term] worrying about the ordinary use of the words 'if-then' whereas logicians had assured us that nothing but the 'horse-shoe' was worth talking about.

5. b. *horseshoe arch* (later example), *curve, moustache, table* (earlier examples).

1770 Duchess of Northumberland *Diary* 10 June (1926) 139 In the midst of the Room were two Horse Shoe Tables the ends of which pretty near touching form'd a Kind of Oval. **1857** C. M. Yonge *Let.* 1 Oct. (1903) viii. 212 A great horse-shoe table, holding 116 people. **1875** 'Mark Twain' in *Atlantic Monthly* Aug. 192/2 The water cuts the alluvial banks of the 'lower' river into deep horseshoe curves. **1926** F. M. Ford *Man could stand Up* I. i. 17 The gentlemen with sergeant-majors' horse-shoe moustaches. **1950** G. Brenan *Face of Spain* ii. 42 The double horseshoe arches, striped buff-white and brick-rose, arrest one by their strangeness and novelty.

d. horseshoe magnet (earlier example).

1785 G. Adams *Ess. Magnetism* (ed. 2) 419 To touch horseshoe magnets.

horse-tail. Add: **1. c.** Usu. **horse's tail.** A woman's hair-style in which the hair is arranged to resemble the shape of the tail of a horse; a 'pony-tail'.

1872 Trollope *Eustace Diamonds* (1873) II. xxxiv. 100 How a man can like to kiss a face with a dirty horse's tail all whizzling about it, is what I can't at all understand. **1953** R. Fuller *Second Curtain* v. 79 Her hair done in a fringe and horse's tail. **1955** G. Freeman *Liberty Man* I. iii. 48 She had blondish hair tied into a horse's tail with a piece of black ribbon. **1960** 'J. & E. Bonett' *No Grave for Lady* ii. 27 She wore jeans and a cotton sweater, her hair was in a horse-tail.

d. (See quots.)

1880 L. Higgin *Handbk. Embroidery* i. 8 'Japanese gold thread'..must..be laid on, and stitched down with a fine yellow silk, known as 'Maltese', or 'Horse-tail'. **1960** B. Snook *Eng. Hist. Embroidery* 104 A woman's court dress (1780)... Variation is obtained by the use of floss silk and horsetail, a tightly twisted silk.

horsewhip, *sb.* (Later examples.)

1843 *Knickerbocker* XXII. 56 I'd like to have some on 'em tied to a tree, and have fair play at 'em with this horse-whip. **1856** P. Cartwright *Autobiogr.* (1858) viii. 74 They came drunk, and armed with..horse-whips. **1965** S. Hult tr. *G. de Coulteray's Sadism in Movies* 111 It is horsewhips with which Christine Nordeu and Bery Baxter are armed in *Idol of Paris.*

horsfordite (hǭ·ɹsfǭɹdəit). *Min.* [f. the name of E. N. *Horsford* (1818–1893), American chemist: see -ite[1].] A brittle, silvery white antimonide of copper, perhaps Cu_5Sb.

1888 Laist & Norton in *Amer. Chem. Jrnl.* X. 62 This new mineral is named horsfordite, in honor of Professor Horsford, formerly Rumford Professor of Chemistry at Harvard University. **1923** J. W. Mellor *Inorg. & Theoret. Chem.* III. xxi. 7 The antimonide: horsfordite, Cu_6Sb. **1970** *Min. Abstr.* XXI. 340/2 The properties of cuprostibite are compared with and differ considerably from those of horsfordite, chalcostibite, tetrahedrite, and famatinite.

horst (hǭɹst). *Geol.* [a. G. *horst* heap, mass, cluster, sandbank, etc.; introduced in its geol. sense by E. Suess (*Antlitz d. Erde* (1883) I. I. iii. 167).] A block of the earth's surface which has been raised relative to the surrounding land and is bounded by faults on some or all sides.

1893 *Q. Jrnl. Geol. Soc.* XLIX. 77 We have, therefore, sunken *massifs* both west and east of the Dürrenstein; that mountain itself remains at a higher level between the two, and may be called a 'Horst' in the sense originally applied by Suess. **1904** H. Sollas tr. *Suess's Face of Earth* I. I. iii. 126 If the outer borders of two fields of subsidence approach each other so that a ridge is left between them, on both sides of which the two areas of depression descend more or less in the form of steps, then we have what we shall distinguish, making use again of a common mining word, as a *horst.* **1910** [see *graben]. **1914** G. A. J. Cole *Growth of Europe* ii. 22 Far older masses have asserted themselves..as horsts, that is, as upstanding blocks from which material has been faulted down on all sides. **1942** M. P. Billings *Struct. Geol.* xi. 205 Horsts range in size from those that are only a few inches wide to those that are many miles wide. **1944** A. Holmes *Princ. Physical Geol.* xix. 416 Between the horsts of the Vosges and the Black Forest the Rhine flows through a rift valley. **1970** *Sci. Amer.* Feb. 37/3 The evidences of crustal movement are in plain view as wide-open fissures, horsts and grabens that form a classic graben structure of steps down the sides of a major depression.

Horst Wessel (hǭɹst ve·sěl). The name of the author (1907–1930) of the words of the official anthem of the German Nazi party, used *attrib.* in *Horst Wessel lied, song.* Also *ellipt.*

1937 V. Bartlett *This is my Life* x. 165 Hundreds of arms went out in the Hitler salute, hundreds of voices yelled the *Horst Wessel Lied.* **1968** R. Collin *Locust on Wind* xv. 137 This time it will be lounge suits instead of brownshirts, and no Horst Wessel while we're on television. **1968** J. Blackburn *Young Man from Lima* xvii. 173 The Horst Wessel song was one of the greatest hymns of hate that had ever been composed. **1969** *Guardian* 6 Oct. 10/6 In spite of the fears of churchmen, 'Lay, lady, lay' is likely to cause less damage than the 'Horst Wessel Lied'. **1970** *New York* 16 Nov. 35/2 Someone wondered when the cornball band..was going to..get down to the serious strains of the Horst Wessel Song.

hortal, *a.* Delete *Obs. rare*[−1] and add later example.

1926 G. C. Druce in J. J. Walker *Nat. Hist. Oxford Distr.* 119 Other hortal plants which have become established are several species of North-American Asters.

hortensia (hǭɹte·nsiă). [mod.L. (P. Commerson in A. L. de Jussieu *Genera Plantarum* (1789) 214), f. *Hortense*, adopted Christian name of the wife of J.-A. Lepaute (1720–*c* 1787), French clockmaker.] A variety of the common hydrangea, *Hydrangea macrophylla*, var. *hortensia*.

1799 *Curtis's Bot. Mag.* XIII. 438 Authors have entertained very different opinions as to what this plant really is; Jussieu following Commerson makes it an Hortensia,..Dr. Smith an Hydrangea. **1866** Lindley & Moore *Treas. Bot.* II. 598/2 Hortensia. (Fr.) *Hydrangea Hortensia.* **1906** *Daily Chron.* 9 Feb. 5/1 The bouquet was of artificial hortensias. **1961** *Amateur Gardening* 7 Oct. 25/1 A medium sized pure white 'hortensia'. **1969** *Dict. Gardening* (R. Hort. Soc.) Suppl. 42/1 Hydrangea. Cultivars of *H.* × *macrophylla*... (*a*) Hortensias. Globose corymbs of mostly sterile flowers.

horticultural, *a.* Add: **2.** Comb. *horticultural exhibition, fête, show.*

1847 F. A. Kemble *Let.* 23 June in *Rec. Later Life* (1882) III. 204 Some *unique* foreign flower, sent..to blossom at the Chiswick horticultural exhibition. **1840** J. Romilly *Diary* 16 July (1967) 197 We then went to the Horticultural Fete in the dining room..at Downing. **1843** *Ainsworth's Mag.* IV. 100 A dazzling conservatory that looked like a horticultural show. **1853** C. M. Yonge *Heir of Redclyffe* i. 3 This [camellia] is to go to the horticultural show. **1858** Queen Victoria *Let.* 21 Apr. in R. Fulford *Dearest Child* (1964) 93 We have just returned from a horticultural show in St. James's Hall. **1952** *Oxf. Jun. Encycl.* VI. 14 The most important horticultural show is the Chelsea Flower Show. **1973** P. Moyes *Curious Affair Third Dog* viii. 104 A sort of scroll proclaiming that Henry Heathfield had taken second prize for tomatoes at the County Horticultural Show.

horticulturally (hǭɹtikʊ·ltiŭrăli, -tʃəɹ-), *adv.* [See -ly[2].] In the way of horticulture.

1899 O. Wilde *Importance of being Earnest* II. 69, I spoke horticulturally. My metaphor was drawn from fruits. **1927** *Observer* 27 Nov. 13/3 It is not only horticulturally that the Riviera is making ready.

hortonolite (hǭɹtǫ·nǒləit, hǭ·ɹtənǒləit). *Min.* [f. the name of Silas Ryneck *Horton* (b. 1820), American amateur mineralogist + -o + -lite.] A silicate mineral, $(Fe, Mg)_2SiO_4$, yellow or greenish-yellow on fresh fracture, having a preponderance of iron over magnesium and often some substitution by manganese (see also quot. 1955).

1869 G. J. Brush in *Amer. Jrnl. Sci.* XCVIII. 19 It is proper to designate this new variety with a special name, and I propose for it the name *Hortonolite*, after Mr. Horton, who first discovered the mineral. **1939** *Amer. Mineral.* XXIV. 24 At present the names commonly accepted, in order of increasing richness [of Fe_2SiO_4] in the fayalite molecule are forsterite, chrysolite, hyalosiderite, hortonolite and fayalite. **1955** M. H. Hey *Index Min. Species* (ed. 2) 124 *Hortonolite.* 4[(Fe, Mg)$_2$SiO$_4$], with Fe·· > Mg (in Hortonolite proper, Fe_2SiO_4 50 to 70 mols. %)... The original Hortonolite contains 4% MnO. Olivine family. **1968** Embrey & Phemister tr. *Kostov's Mineralogy* 291 Titanolivine is rich in Ti; hortonolite is rich in iron.

‖ **hortus conclusus** (hǫ·ɹtŭs kǫnklū·sŭs). [Lat., = enclosed garden, in reference to *Song Sol.* iv. 12.] **a.** An enclosed, inviolate garden; in spiritual and exegetical tradition, the symbol of the soul, the Church, or the virginity of Mary. **b.** In Art, a painting of the Madonna and Child in an enclosed garden. Freq. *transf.*

1624 Donne *LXXX Sermons* (1640) xvii. 165 The University is a Paradise, Rivers of knowledge are there, Arts and Sciences flow from thence. Counsell Tables are *Horti conclusi* (as it is said in the Canticles). **1852** A. B. Jameson *Legends Madonna* p. xlviii, The Enclosed Garden (*Hortus conclusus*)... I have seen this enclosed garden very significantly placed in the background of the Annunciation, and in pictures of the Immaculate Conception. Sometimes the enclosure is formed of a treillage or hedge of roses, as in a beautiful Virgin by Francia. **1940** 'M. Innes' *There came both Mist & Snow* i. 7, I shall get more surely on the rails if I drop ancestry and the *hortus conclusus* of history and begin again with some account of the Priory itself. **1947** 'N. Blake' *Minute for Murder* ix. 208 People that would trample over her little *hortus conclusus.* **1956** M. Swan *Paradise Garden* xvii. 161 The protective hedges of his *hortus conclusus* were rotten and useless with disease. **1957** N. Frye *Anat. Criticism* 152 The symbol of the body of the Virgin as a *hortus conclusus.* **1963** *Listener* 21 Mar. 520/2 Nepal has long been the *hortus conclusus* of the fabulous Ranas.

Horus (hōə·rŭs). [late L., ad. Gr. Ὧρος, ad. Egyptian *Hor.*] The name of an Egyptian deity, represented in art as having the head of a hawk, used *attrib.* to designate an image of this deity.

1851 [see *Hathor]. **1875** *Encycl. Brit.* VII. 715/2 Hathor is associated with Horus, but her genealogical place is not clear. **1923** *Glasgow Herald* 13 Feb. 8 The horus birds. **1923** D. H. Lawrence *Birds, Beasts & Flowers* 199 The golden Great and glistening-feathered legs of the hawk of Horus. **1972** *Times* 18 May (Egypt Suppl.) p. iv/3 The falcon was sacred to Horus, the sky god who bore the sun on his head.

Hosanna. Add: **B. 2.** *attrib.* **Hosanna Sunday,** Palm Sunday.

1868 M. E. C. Walcott *Sacred Archæol.* 422 Hosanna (save us, we pray) Sunday, in the East and Southern Europe. **1899** J. Hastings *Dict. Bible* II. 418/2 In Christian usage, Palm Sunday, to which our Lord's entry has given name, has in certain periods and regions been called 'Hosanna Sunday' or 'Day of Hosannas', or simply 'Osanna'.

hose, *sb.* Add: **5. c.** *Golf.* The socket into which the shaft of an iron club is fitted.

1893 H. Hutchinson *Golfing* 21 A method of obviating the trouble of occasionally hitting the ball on the hose of these short-faced clubs. **1953** R. Harris *Sixty Yrs. Golf* iii. 37 The sand-track iron is a most formidable looking bludgeon... The hose or socket is 6½ inches.

7. *hose-carriage* (earlier example), *-cart* (earlier and later examples); also **hose company** *U.S.*, a company in charge of a fire-hose; **hose-pipe** = Hose *sb.* 3; hence as *v.*, to spray (as) with a hose.

1829 *Massachusetts Laws* XI. 237 If any person shall..damage..any Engine, Hose Carriage...he shall be convicted. **1865** *Trans. Ill. Agric. Soc.* VI. 320 A large amount of three-inch hose always ready on hose carts. **1906** *Westm. Gaz.* 27 July 6/2 Two new..fire-stations,..with a horsed-escape, a manual fire-escape, and a hose-cart. **1806** *Massachusetts Spy* 21 May (Th.), The efforts of several hose and fire companies at length prevailed. **1860** O. W. Holmes *Prof. Breakf.-t.* iv. 106 More widely known through the Movamensing Hose-Company, and the Wistar parties. **1948** *Times-Picayune Mag.* (New Orleans) 5 Dec. 21/2 The next and last contestant is Sound Point Protection Hose Company Number One! **1835** J. Martin *Gaz. Virginia* 139 The height of the reservoir, above these streets,..gives a jet of water by means of hose pipes, of some 60 to 80 feet elevation. **1872, 1884** Hose-pipe [in Dict.]. **1928** *Daily Express* 27 Sept. 8 A stream of the chief's choicest acid would be hosepiped his way. **1930** R. Campbell *Poems* 17 With your fountain-pen to spray the flowers, The hosepipe of your literary hours. **1940** *Flight* 5 Dec. 468*a*/1 A stripped Lewis gun as used on trawlers and such-like ships for 'hose-piping' dive-bombers and low-fliers. **1948** Partridge *Dict.*

Forces' Slang 96 *Hosepipe*, to spray liquid fire from a flame-thrower. **1973** J. FLEMING *You won't let me Finish* xvii. 133 Around the cage were elephantine hose pipes to be used in case of emergency to protect the people at ground level.

hose, *v.* Add: **2.** Also with *down*. Also *fig.* and *transf.* and as *sb.*

1931 E. E. CUMMINGS *Let.* 7 Jan. (1969) 119 Precisely as a cannon exploded, searchlights hozed the environs. **1936** [see *BALDY]. **1939** H. HODGE *Cab, Sir?* ii. 15 A shirt-sleeved washer..is hosing down a late-night cab. **1947** *Book Nine* (Caxton Press, N.Z.) 23 Treat him [*sc.* the patient] sweet, Floss. Hose him out and get him clean for us. **1961** W. VAUGHAN-THOMAS *Anzio* v. 86 SP guns, out on the right, hosed them with fire, but they pushed on resolutely. **1964** C. WILLOCK *Enormous Zoo* ix. 170 Roger Wheater hoses him with a blistering swathe of Swahili. **1969** *Gloss. Landscape Work* (*B.S.I.*) v. 25 *Hosing down*, the application of water by means of a hose to clean down buildings or other surfaces; or as a daily routine to control pests, dirt and humidity. **1971** *Guardian* 26 Aug. 22 Visitors to Piccadilly Circus, London, keeping out of the way of the regular hose-down.

hosier. Add to def.: Also used more generally for a men's outfitter or haberdasher.

1837 N. WHITTOCK et al. *Compl. Bk. Trades* 289 *Haberdasher and hosier.* Each of those trades merge in the other, occasionally;..our Hosiers seldom confine their dealings to the wares which clothe our legs. **1892** P. L. SIMMONDS *Comm. Dict. Trade Products* 197/2 *Hosier*, one who deals in stockings, shawls, gloves, braces, laces, and under garments, etc. **1921** *Dict. Occup. Terms* (1927) 344/3 *Hosier*,..is usually also an outfitter. **1935** WODEHOUSE *Luck of Bodkins* xvi. 192 Monty passed a finger round his collar. A perfect fit, made to measure by the finest hosier in London, it seemed to be too tight. **1936** —— *Laughing Gas* xii. 119 In the matter of pyjamas I've always been a trifle on the choosy side. I'm not one of those fellows who just charge into a hosier's and grab anything.

hospital, *sb.* Add: **6.** *hospital nurse, tent*; **hospital bed,** (*a*) a (metal) bed as used in hospitals, higher than an ordinary bed to facilitate nursing, and freq. adjustable in several ways; also *hospital bedstead*; (*b*) an available place in hospital for a bed patient; **hospital blue**(s), the blue uniform worn by wounded soldiers in the wars of 1914–18 and 1939–45; **hospital corps,** the medical corps in the U.S. Navy; so **hospital corpsman**; cf. *CORPSMAN; **hospital letter,** a letter referring a patient for free treatment in a hospital; **hospital paper** = **hospital letter*; **hospital porter** (see *PORTER *sb.*²); **hospital ship,** (*b*) a ship for conveying sick and wounded soldiers to their own country or to an area remote from the battlefield; **hospital steward** (*a*) (examples); **hospital train,** a train for conveying wounded soldiers from the front to the base hospitals.

1823 C. MATHEWS *Let.* 7 Feb. in A. Mathews *Mem. Charles Mathews* (1838) III. 365, I slept in a bed on the road without even posts for curtains—a regular hospital-bed. **1952** *Oxf. Jun. Encycl.* X. 190/2 Small sums paid weekly during health might entitle contributors to a hospital bed in time of need. **1970** *New Yorker* 29 Aug. 55/1 He lends people hospital beds, which he happened to get at a good price. **1973** C. MULLARD *Black Brit.* iv. 46 Overnight, blacks were suddenly held responsible for the unemployment figures.., lack of adequate social services, schools and hospital beds. **1860** F. NIGHTINGALE *Notes on Nursing* viii. 47 Hospital bedsteads are..very much less objectionable than private ones. **1919** 'I. HAY' *Last Million* vi. 67 Convalescent soldiers in hospital blue. **1920** J. M. BARRIE *Kiss for Cinderella* (1928) III. 445 Danny, who is slightly lame and is in hospital blue. **1920** [see *AIRER]. **1957** R. CAMPBELL *Portugal* ii. 29, I was clothed in army hospital-blues. **1973** B. TURNER *Hot-Foot* iv. 20 Some day I would be spotted as a wanted man by someone who knew me either in khaki or in hospital blues. **1899** *Statutes at Large U.S.A.* XXX. 474 June 17, 1898..Be it enacted..That a hospital corps of the United States Navy is hereby established. **1945** *Amer. Handbk.* (Office War Information) xxvi. 386 Men of the Hospital Corps include pharmacists... They may be found in the amphibious units of the Marine Corps, in the dressing stations of warships, and in submarines. **1901** E. ROOT in Bacon & Scott *Mil. & Colonial Policy U.S.* (1916) 374 An order was made fixing the enlisted strength..exclusive of hospital corps men, at 77,287. **1943** *Sci. News Let.* 29 May 343 Soon a Hospital Corpsman with a larger kit of supplies comes along and quickly ministers to the wounded man. **1890** W. BOOTH *In Darkest Eng.* I. iii. 26 He had hoped to have obtained a hospital letter at the Mansion House so as to obtain a truss for a bad rupture. **1848** THACKERAY *Van. Fair* lvii. 514 Women..who are hospital-nurses without wages. **1893** O. WILDE *Lady Windermere's Fan* IV. 120 You would like me to retire into a convent or become a hospital nurse, or something of that kind. **1936** A. THIRKELL *August Folly* ix. 265 Jessica got up and the hospital nurse left. **1962** A. CHRISTIE *Mirror Crack'd* ii. 13 In real illness you could have a proper hospital nurse, at vast expense and procured with difficulty, or you could go to hospital. **1838** C. M. YONGE *Let.* 25 Sept. in C. Coleridge *C. M. Yonge* (1903) iv. 139 Mr. Rudd, the tall man we took the hospital paper to, is dead. **1890** —— *More Bywords* 260 Jane Cox is come for a hospital paper, ma'am. **1683** Hospital ship [in Dict.]. **1899** *Westm. Gaz.* 20 Nov. 6/2 The American hospital-ship *Maine*. **1916** 'BOYD CABLE' *Action Front* 172 Swinging at top speed down the line to the base and the hospital ship and home. **1944** F. CLUNE *Red Heart* 12 I've seen my mates consigned to the deep on a hospital ship..in war-time. **1856** R. GLISAN *Jrnl. Army Life* (1874) 350 Besides the sick, hospital steward, hospital attendants, and some three others, there will be no troops. **1895** *Outing* (U.S.) Dec. 255/2 The non-commissioned staff comprises a sergeant-major, a quarter master-sergeant, a commissary-sergeant, and a hospital steward. **1812** *Niles' Reg.* II. 131/1, 300 hospital, horsemen's and common tents. **1862** G. B. MCCLELLAN *Let.* 31 July in *Own Story* (1887) 458 They are nearly all in hospital-tents and are well provided for. **1936** C. DAY LEWIS *Friendly Tree* i. 14 Holding the wound shut..until he reaches the hospital-tent. **1874** B. F. TAYLOR *World on Wheels* I. xxiv. 162 The saddest train upon which the writer ever took passage was the Hospital Train, with its maimed and mangled burden. **1916** 'BOYD CABLE' *Action Front* 172 That he might be lying warm and comfortable in the soothing ease of a bed in the hospital train. **1937** V. BARTLETT *This is my Life* iv. 51, I spent my twenty first birthday in a hospital train... The Medical Officer in charge..was an old school friend.

hospitality. Add: **1. c.** Applied in conventional phr. to the admission of correspondence, etc., to a newspaper.

1913 *Punch* 16 Apr. 298, I thank you for the hospitality of your columns.

d. *to partake of* (or *enjoy*) *His* (or *Her*) *Majesty's hospitality*: to be in prison. *jocular.*

1894 *Strand Mag.* Sept. 296/2 Partaking of Her Majesty's hospitality, in a building specially erected for gentlemen who need a compulsory holiday. **1938** F. D. SHARPE *Sharpe of Flying Squad* xiv. 157 One awful thug I know, who is now enjoying His Majesty's hospitality, beat his woman up regularly.

4. *attrib.* and *Comb.* (Further examples.) Now commonly used of a room, suite of rooms, etc., in a hotel, TV studio, etc., set aside for the entertainment of guests with drinks.

1959 *Encounter* Aug. 8/1 The eminent person is ushered into..the 'hospitality' room [at the BBC]. **1960** *News Chron.* 2 Mar. 4/4 The drinks, consumed rather dismally in the hospitality room,..conspire to make a TV appearance an ordeal. **1963** J. N. HARRIS *Weird World Wes Beattie* (1964) ii. 20 At these conventions a lot of big companies put in hospitality suites—snake rooms, they call them. **1966** M. HASTINGS *Cork on Telly* i. 10 There was no time to talk to him in the hospitality room before the programme. **1969** *Observer* 8 June 38/1 The Americans led off by introducing Shatalov and Yeliseyev to the taste of bourbon from the hospitality cupboards of the private room at the American exhibition stand. **1970** *Globe & Mail* (Toronto) 25 Sept. 40/1 Opportunities ..in the ever-growing hospitality field [in motels]. **1970** *Globe Mag.* (Toronto) 26 Sept. 6/3 There aren't many bands or hospitality suites or funny hats. **1971** *Bahamas* XXIII. III. 34/1 She moved into the hospitality industry where her personality assets were plus factors. **1972** *Guardian* 20 Mar. 11/1 She said it in the Hospitality Room ..right after the show.

hospitalize (hǫ·spitălaiz), *v.* [f. HOSPITAL *sb.* + -IZE.] *trans.* To place or accommodate in a hospital.

Freq. commented on as an unhappy formation.

1901 *Daily Chron.* 10 Sept. 6/2 The disease was spreading rapidly owing to the people refusing to hospitalise first cases. **1904** *Ibid.* 28 Oct. 8/3 The pauper who is hospitalised in an English casual ward. **1946** *Nature* 3 Aug. 170/1 Cases hospitalized in the Carmichael Hospital for Tropical Diseases, Calcutta. **1955** *Sci. News Let.* 15 Jan. 39/3 Surgery..was performed on 70% of the hospitalized children. **1961** *Observer* 19 Nov. 29/6 On the second day after the mutiny the ship's doctor insisted that the lives of a passenger and a wounded member of the crew depended on their being hospitalised. **1970** G. GREER *Female Eunuch* 239 The more the state undertakes to protect a man from illness..the more it has the right to sacrifice him..to hospitalize his children.

Hence **ho:spitaliza·tion,** confinement to, or accommodation in, a hospital.

1909 in WEBSTER. **1918** A. WOOLLCOTT *Let.* 12 Jan. (1946) 40 My present brief hospitalization is traceable to eye-strain. **1932** *Nation* 25 May 604 The activities of the Legion..began with a demand for pensions and hospitalization for those disabled in war service. **1937** R. S. MORTON *Woman Surgeon* vi. 70 The systematic hospitalization of the sick poor furnished a wealth of clinical material. **1967** *Spectator* 28 July 114/1 Private hospitalisation and medicine has been increased in price by this Government so that, while the rich people can cope, the moderately well off can no longer do so. **1971** COWDRY & STEINBERG *Care of Geriatric Patient* (ed. 4) xxvii. 352/1 Application of new scientific knowledge to clinical medicine has profoundly affected the hospitalization requirements of elderly patients.

hoss (hǫs), dial. (also U.S.) var. of HORSE *sb.* **1.** = HORSE *sb.* 1 and 25 a.

1815 D. HUMPHREYS *Yankey in Eng.* v. 77 The boys.. see a ghost in the form of a white hoss; and an Indian in every black stump. **1849** N. KINGSLEY *Diary* (1914) 88 My supper consisted of beans, old hoss, and hard bread. **1877** J. M. BAILEY *Folks in Danbury* 37 But this is a hoss of another colour. **1877** F. Ross et al. *Gloss. Holderness* 78 *Hoss*, a horse. **1887** T. DARLINGTON *Folk-Speech S. Cheshire* 225 *Hoss-wesh*, a horse-pond. **1888** F. R. STOCKTON *Dusantes* 15 'These hosses won't do much at holdin back,' he said. **1889** M. PEACOCK *Taales fra Linkisheere* 130 In cums a greät black hoss, all drippin' wi' wet. **1958** S. E. HYMAN in A. Dundes *Mother Wit* (1973) 55/1 He had him a big black hoss.

2. *U.S.* = HORSE *sb.* 4.

1843 in *Amer. Speech* (1965) XL. 130 Sez he old hoss, I'll eat you up jis like I would a cabbage. **1844** *Yale Lit. Mag.* X. 168 Well, hoss, I reckon I will. **1847** *Knickerbocker* XXIX. 204 We've sworn to give the first strange old hoss that comes along this road an up-and-down beating. **1847, 1857** [see HORSE *sb.* 4]. **1904** W. N. HARBEN *Georgians* xv. 148 'Went back on us, ole hoss,' Jim said, cordially. **1940** *Amer. Speech* XV. 216/1 Varmint might be applied to a contemptible person..but in Florida hound or hoss would as likely be used.

2*. = *HORSE *sb.* 14*. *U.S. slang.*

1968 *Sun Mag.* (Baltimore) 13 Oct. 19/3, I was square to them, one step lower because I wasn't on hoss.

3. *attrib.* and *Comb.* = HORSE *sb.* 26 and 27.

1837 R. M. BIRD *Nick of Woods* II. iv. 63, I do [know].. all the parts injacent and outjacent, circumsurrounding the hoss-stump. **1877** J. HABBERTON *Jericho Road* xv. 142 Losin' your health when you started with Sam Reeves' hoss-gang. **1909** 'O. HENRY' *Roads of Destiny* xvi. 263 Amos Colvin and me were thicker than two hoss thieves more than ten years. **1942** BERREY & VAN DEN BARK *Amer. Thes. Slang* § 608/9 *Western picture*, hoss opera, opery.

host, *sb.*² Add: **2.** *mine host* (later examples).

1909 WODEHOUSE *Mike* xii. 66 That was the supreme moment in mine host's life. **1934** —— *Right Ho, Jeeves* x. 123, I entered the saloon bar and requested mine host to start pouring. **1973** J. PORTER *It's Murder with Dover* vii. 67 Dover set about cross-questioning the landlord... Mine host stuck to his guns.

3. b. *Biol.* and *Med.* An animal or person that is the recipient of tissue, an organ, etc., that has been transplanted into it from another.

1906 *Brit. Med. Jrnl.* 22 Dec. 1796/1 Entire organs may be transplanted by anastomosis of their blood vessels to suitable points on the circulatory apparatus of the host. **1923** H. NEUHOF *Transplantation of Tissues* i. 9 Experiments..continued from six to nine months showed the transplant completely replaced by a connective tissue derived from the host. **1958** *New Biol.* XXVII. 42 The host reacts to the antigens of the graft by producing antibodies. **1961** *New Scientist* 5 Jan. 45/3 Cells of both the donor of the graft tissue, and the recipient host, played a part in the immune reaction.

5. a. *Geol.* A mineral mass containing a different mineral; a rock containing an ore deposit or foreign rock. Freq. *attrib.*

1889 *Cent. Dict.* III, *Host*, a mineral which incloses another. **1950** E. E. WAHLSTROM *Introd. Theor. Igneous Petrol.* iv. 80 Perthites are intergrowths of two feldspars. Commonly the host mineral (that is, the more abundant mineral) is potash feldspar. **1965** G. J. WILLIAMS *Econ. Geol. N.Z.* i. 1/1 These are the host-rocks of the gold mineralization west of the Alps.

b. *Physics* and *Chem.* A crystal lattice or molecular structure containing a foreign ion, atom, or molecule; *spec.* (i) a crystal or a crystalline material to which a small amount of some impurity has been added to make it luminescent; (ii) that component of a clathrate compound that encloses or surrounds the other component. Usu. *attrib.*

1939 *Trans. Faraday Soc.* XXXV. 126 It may be imagined that the function of the activating impurity is to enter the host lattice and produce therein centres of distortion. **1950** H. W. LEVERENZ *Introd. Luminescence of Solids* vi. 369 A host crystal should not be strongly absorbing in the spectral region where efficient luminescence emission is to be produced. **1956** *Nature* 22 Dec. 1410/1 Various instances are known of continuous crystalline 'host' lattices within which 'guest' molecules may be trapped... Among inorganic lattices the best known are the crystalline zeolites. **1961** L. F. & M. FIESER *Adv. Org. Chem.* xxii. 771 They are similar to the urea inclusion complexes..except that the host is a covalently bonded molecule with a hole in it. **1967** VANDERS & KERR *Mineral Recognition* v. 85/2 At high temperatures, foreign ions are dissolved in the solid host crystal. **1968** *Proc. Internat. Conf. Luminescence Budapest* (1966) I. 1289 Luminescence of crystalline phosphors is strongly connected with the structure of the host crystal.

6. *attrib.* and *Comb.* (see also sense *5), as (sense 1) *host country, government, population, society*; (sense 3) *host animal, cell, -parasite* (used appos.), *plant*; *host-specific* adj. (so *host-specificity*); *host-controlled, -induced* adjs.

1956 *Nature* 10 Mar. 453/1 It is reasonable to attribute these changes to the high dose of radiation delivered to the host-animal and so to identify the cells containing them as host cells. **1954** *Science* 16 July 110/1 (*heading*) Action of T_2r^+ bacteriophage on host-cell membranes. **1958** *Spectator* 22 Aug. 252/1 The life of the virus is so closely linked with that of the host cell that one cannot be attacked without injury to the other. **1965** *Ann. Rev. Microbiol.* XIX. 365 Host-controlled modification of viruses is a general term applied to those cases in which passage through certain host strains imparts one or more new, nonheritable properties to the virus without altering its genetic information content. **1959** *Manch. Guardian* 21 July 1/7 The technical staff of control posts..should consist of one-third host-country nationals. **1962** *Times* 18 Dec. 11/7 The 'host countries'..are [not] able economically to absorb the refugees permanently. **1969** H. MACINNES *Salzburg Connection* ix. 131 Switzerland is the host country. **1960** *Economist* 15 Oct. 263/1 Certain of the important 'host governments' of countries where the oil is actually produced chose not to come. **1953** *Cold Spring Harbor Symp. Quant. Biol.* XVIII. 237 (*heading*) Host-induced modifications of viruses. **1946** *Nature* 6 July 30/2 Host–parasite relations. **1964** V. J. CHAPMAN *Coastal Veget.* iii. 77 Plants of course may exhibit host–parasite relations. **1888, 1889** Host plant [in Dict., sense 3]. **1959** SOUTHWOOD & LESTON *Land & Water Bugs* viii. 239 This species may be found in great abundance on its host-plant. **1971** *Guardian* 24 June 7/2 The

feelings of any host population towards immigrants included suspicion, fear, and irritation. **1961** S. R. Herman in J. A. Fishman *Readings Sociol. Lang.* (1968) 509 Our analysis implies a cautionary note for the attitude of a host society to newcomers. The host society may legitimately wish to encourage the use of its language by the newcomers, but it may aggravate the problem of adjustment if it insists too strictly on the adherence to its language norms. **1969** *Listener* 13 Nov. 664/1 Just one sign of the equivocal welcome meted out by the host society. **1972** *Jrnl. Social Psychol.* LXXXVI. 159 The changers displayed more of behavioral and psychological affinities toward the host society than the nonchangers. **1969** *New Scientist* 13 Mar. 23/1 WHO workers introduced a host-specific pathogenic fungus which kills mosquito larvae. **1951** Whitby & Hynes *Med. Bacteriol.* (ed. 5) xxiv. 376 The viruses have the same wide range of host-specificity as the bacteria.

host, *sb.*[4] Add: **2.** Also applied to the wafer before consecration (quots. 1687, 1881).

host, *v.*[2] **1.** Delete † *Obs.* and add later examples. Also, to receive into one's town, country, etc.; to be the host at (a party, dinner, etc.); to compère (a television show, etc.).

1939 *John o' London's* 7 Apr. 42/3, I am not surprised that Messrs. Auden and Isherwood came away with a sense of deep and humble respect for the people and the country who had hosted them. **1957** J. Kerouac *On Road* (1958) 87 He went right out and bought a pint of whisky to host me proper. **1958** I. Asimov *Whiff of Death* (1968) vi. 55 Those comments applying to him were read at the celebration dinner hosted (invariably) by Anson himself. **1967** *Boston Sunday Herald* 26 Mar. 1. 12/2 Dorchester man has been hosting a series of unusual farewell parties. **1967** *Boston Globe* 30 Mar. 15/2 The delegation of 25 men and women..will be hosted by the Greater Boston Chamber of Commerce and Burlington town officials. **1967** *New Yorker* 1 Apr. 129 (Advt.), Bob Hope hosts the annual Academy of Motion Picture Arts and Sciences presentation. **1969** N. Cohn *A WopBopaLooBop* (1970) ix. 88 He..sold Murray the K T-shirts and hosted albums of Murray the K's Golden Gassers. **1969** *New Yorker* 29 Mar. 24/1 Let us host you at the Kahala Hilton, on one of Oahu's most beautiful beaches. **1969** *Guardian* 19 July 9/1 There will be David Frost, hosting ITV's night-long bonanza of touchdown and pop stars. **1973** *Times* 9 Feb. 8/8 The session was hosted by Mr William Fulbright.

b. Delete *nonce-use* and add later examples.

1957 *Time* 2 Sept. 34/2 Critic John Crosby, currently on leave from his TV syndicated column to polish up on his broadcast manners, will host. **1962** H. Kane *Killer's Kiss* xxviii. 216, I must do a bit more hosting—I'm expecting some special people.

hosta (hǫ·stă). [mod.L. (L. Trattinick 1812, in *Archiv der Gewächskunde* I. 55; formerly used by N. J. Jacquin *Icones Plantarum Horti Schönbrunnensis* (1797) I. 60 for a plant now included in the genus *Cornutia*), f. the name of N. T. *Host* (1761–1834), Austrian physician.] A plant of the genus so named (formerly called *funkia), native to Japan and eastern Asia and belonging to the family Liliaceæ; a plantain-lily.

[**1828** *Bot. Reg.* XIV. 1204 Willdenow proposes to unite Hosta with Cornutia. **1930** L. H. Bailey in *Gentes Herbarum* II. 119 Mostly they [*sc.* plantain lilies] are known as species of Funkia, but Hosta is now the accepted name to those who follow the International Rules of nomenclature.] **1931** W. T. Stearn in *Gardeners' Chron.* 11 July 27/1 The Hostas, or Funkias, as they are commonly called, are hardy Liliaceous perennials, well-known in gardens on account of their decorative foliage. **1961** *Amateur Gardening* 4 Nov. 23/1 For the moist but well-drained part plants that you could grow are.. hydrangeas,..hemerocallis, hostas. **1971** *Country Life* 25 Feb. 438/1 All hostas have good leaves, but there are some which we more particularly grow for foliage, than for flowers.

hostage, *sb.*[1] Add: **3.** *spec.* in phr. *to give*, etc., *a hostage to fortune*: to deliver one's future happiness, success, etc., into the hands of fate.

1607–12 [in Dict.]. **1732** T. Fuller *Gnomologia* 253 Wife and Children are Hostages given to Fortune. **1875** M. E. Braddon (*title*) Hostages to fortune. **1934** J. E. Neale *Queen Elizabeth* xiv. 235 But to enter on war was to give hostages to fortune. Her instinct was to gamble on avoiding it. **1950** W. S. Churchill *Second World War* IV. i. xi. 194 Once several good outfits are prepared, any one of which can attack a Japanese-held base or island and beat the life out of the garrison, all their islands will become hostages to fortune. **1965** *Listener* 4 Nov. 728/2 Every manufacturer who indulges in advertising is giving a hostage to fortune in that he is inviting public confidence in his goods and service, and he will rapidly go out of business if he cannot live up to his claims. **1968** *Ibid.* 28 Nov. 710/2 Denmark was almost a hostage to fortune by being in Nato at all.

5. *attrib.*

1858 F. J. Child *Eng. & Scottish Ballads* VI. 234 Fifteen lords in the hostage house Waiting Wallace for to see. **1905** *Westm. Gaz.* 26 Sept. 8/2 The hostage camps [in the Gaboon]. **1909** *Daily Chron.* 18 Nov. 1/7 The dragging of a man to the hostage house [in the Congo]. **1931** H. G. Wells *Work, Wealth & Happiness of Mankind* (1932) vii. 275 Here all over again were the murders, the mutilations..the hostage houses, and the atrocities.

hostel, *sb.*[1] Add: **2. b.** = **youth hostel*. Hence ho·steller; **ho·stelling** *vbl. sb.*

1931 *Times* 21 Jan. 11/6 The Youth Hostels Association. ..It is hoped that this summer there will be 50 hostels where..a night's lodging may be obtained. **1932** *Y.H.A. Handbk. Hostels* 19 Much of the Y.H.A. Insurance of property in Hostels is now undertaken by the National Office. *Ibid.*, Write to the Warden at the Hostel and quote your membership number. **1951** E. Coxhead *One Green Bottle* i. 26 House used to be a climbing centre, but now it's been taken for one of those youth hostels. Pity. Some of the hostellers climb, I believe. *Ibid.* x. 256, I treated myself to a few days' hostelling. **1961** *Countryman* LVIII. 434 There were always plenty of hostellers to fill the boat. **1967** *Rambling & Youth Hostelling* ('Know the Game' Series) 31 The YHA Map is useful for tour planning. It will enable you to see the network of hostels in the area you are visiting. **1970** P. Carlon *Souvenir* xii. 106 Her daughter's friends were allowed to go hostelling and hiking. **1973** *Guardian* 1 Jan. 6/3 In the most expensive..hostels, the overnight charge will go up from 35p to 40p for young hostellers.

hostess. Add: **2.** Also in archaic phr. *mine hostess*.

1832 [in Dict.]. **1962** *Listener* 19 July 113/3 *Mine Hostess*, as *La Locandiera* is called in Clifford Bax's otherwise excellent English translation, is one of the dozen or so greatest comedies.

b. A woman employed to entertain customers at a night-club, etc.; also in derogatory sense: a prostitute.

1931 Durante & Kofoed *Night Clubs* xxi. 190 Joan Sawyer—and what a girl she was!—the foremost dancer and hostess of the day, ran the shows. **1933** *New Statesman* 18 Mar. 331/2 If a young man dances with a 'hostess' he scurries back at the finish. **1937** C. R. Cooper *Here's to Crime* ix. 189 Women, reaching the dregs, become the 'hostesses' in what are known as 'jukin' joints'. **1959** *Economist* 11 Apr. 105/2 This question of hostesses is one of the most hotly debated in the night club business. It is also revealing since, broadly speaking, it is a management's policy towards hostesses that determines the standing of a night club. **1963** *Listener* 7 Feb. 260/3 American Bunny Clubs, with their Freudian fantasy-tease hostesses. **1968** *Sunday Times* 30 June 5/5 He..got Miss C. to admit ..'that the word hostess is a polite euphemism for prostitute'. **1970** G. Greer *Female Eunuch* 131 Many a prostitute, whether she calls herself a..hostess, or a common whore, imagines that she is exploiting the male sex. **1970** *Guardian* 22 Aug. 8/6 The French authorities have been able to organise a traditional Legion recreation centre, whose Somali hostesses are under regular medical supervision. **1972** P. A. Whitney *Snowfire* (1973) i. 2 Juniper Lodge in the Poconos was looking for an après-ski hostess to help with guests during the evening hours. **1973** *Times* 30 May 4/3 We were able to call it Europe's biggest hostess service and had an interesting offer of more than 200 girls.

c. = **air hostess*; also, a woman similarly employed on a train.

1936 *Jrnl. R. Aeronaut. Soc.* XL. 525 On American aeroplanes for many years now we have had, as part of the staff, 'hostesses', young women of 20 to 30 years of age, generally trained nurses, whose duties are to make passengers 'feel at home' aloft. **1940** *Amer. Speech* XV. 213/2 *Hostess*..now suggests a professional person paid for her services, as the hostess at a hotel, on an airplane, or on pullman cars. **1953** R. Lehmann *Echoing Grove* 252 She'll be a hostess on a transglobal airline. **1958** *Times Lit. Suppl.* 17 Oct. 598/4 Illuminating testimonies by hostesses of various air lines. **1970** *Times* 17 Nov. 19/7 Five years ago..she was one of the first Gatwick hostesses. They're British Rail's answer to an air hostess.

4. *hostess apron, dress, gown, pyjamas, robe, skirt, trolley*.

1968 *Wanganui* (N.Z.) *Chron.* 15 Nov. 8/3 (*winner of competition*) Hostess apron: Mrs. S. 1, Mrs. A. J. M. 2. **1970** N. Armstrong et al. *First on Moon* xiv. 352 Kate Collins, wearing her mother's pink hostess apron, was passing coffee. **1951** *Country Life* 16 Nov., The picture or hostess dress has been re-instated for informal evenings. **1963** *Times* 27 Feb. 12/5 Sleeveless hostess dresses. **1968** *Guardian* 30 Apr. 7/1 Full-length hostess dresses, long-sleeved or sleeveless. **1938** 'E. Queen' *Four of Hearts* (1939) x. 143 She looked ravishing in a silver lamé hostess-gown. **1945** E. Bowen *Demon Lover* 178 Her cretonne house-coat, the nearest thing to a hostess gown that she had. **1963** M. McCarthy *Group* v. 92 Instead of a dress, Kay was wearing a cherry-red velvet sleeveless hostess gown. **1945** F. & R. Lockridge *Payoff for Banker* (1948) vi. 58 Dorian did not have hostess pyjamas of quite this cut—quite this daring—and would hardly have worn them if she had. **1970** *Daily Progress* (Charlottesville, Va.) 21 Mar. C 2/3 It's time to turn to wearing the long 'hostess pyjamas' for seasonal glamour in entertaining. **1964** *N.Y. Times* 15 Nov. Sect. xi. 9 (Advt.), Button-front hostess robe of soft fleece. **1966** Mrs. L. B. Johnson *White House Diary* 6 Aug. (1970) 406, I put on my white hostess robe that Lyndon had bought me in Paris ten years ago and went in to see Luci. She was eating breakfast. **1966** *Daily Tel.* 19 Dec. 9/4 The kilt that grew—and grew—and grew—becomes the Christmas hostess skirt that's on view at all the cosiest fireside parties. **1963** *Guardian* 25 Nov. 6/3 The latest model of the L. G. Hawkins hostess trolley..in which you can carry four dishes and a joint from the kitchen.

hostess (hō̆u·stės), *v.* [f. the sb.] *trans.* and *intr.* To be the hostess at (a party, etc.); to act as hostess. So **ho·stessing** *vbl. sb.*

1928 *Sunday Express* 6 May 16 She observed herself think that possibly Athene felt political 'hostessing' to be her vocation. **1946** *Lincoln State Jrnl.* 24 Jan., Wednesday was the day of the party which Mrs. Herbert Folsom..hostessed..in honor of Mr. Thomas Mauck. **1951** 'J. Wyndham' *Day of Triffids* xii. 215 She had led one of those fringe careers—modelling dresses,.. hostessing for obscure clubs. **1957** J. Frame *Owls do Cry* xxviii. 123 It will be my first *real* experience of hostessing to people who really matter. **1961** *Spectator* 27 Oct. 605 The hell of hostessing is..that one can know ..what things make a good hostess and still be quite unable to achieve them. **1962** *Aeroplane* CII. 229/2 The book..details the growth of the aviation industry. This is vital for anyone interested in 'Hostessing', because a proper appreciation of the industry's background is invaluable in assessing the job as a whole and its importance in helping to 'sell' the airlines. **1968** C. Nicole *Self Lovers* ii. 22 Vanessa thought hostessing large political gatherings would grow easier with experience.

hostessy (hō̆u·stesi), *a.* [f. Hostess + -y[1].] Pertaining to, or typical of, a hostess; hospitable.

1930 J. B. Priestley *Angel Pavement* iii. 108 And then, too, all the time you were so worried and anxious about the food and the serving, you were expected to be keeping the conversation going, terribly bright and hostessy. **1939** 'N. Blake' *Smiler with Knife* 21 She would assume a gushing, hostessy manner. **1945** *Penguin New Writing* XXVI. 62 Betty Mordon began by being affably hostessy towards him. **1967** D. Francis *Blood Sport* i. 13 Idle hostessy chat. **1973** J. Burrows *Like an Evening Gone* i. 18 Greta has been making hostessy interested noises.

hostile, *a.* (*sb.*) Add: **2. b.** *to go hostile*: to become angry. *Austral.* and *N.Z. colloq.*

1941 W. D. Haydon *N.Z. Soldiers* 17 Wouldn't he go hostile if he knew who pinched his bacon. **1945** Baker *Austral. Lang.* ii. xv. 263 *To go hostile* means to become angry.

3. *Comb.* **hostile ice** (see quot. 1966); **hostile ord** *Naval slang*, an ordinary seaman who joins the Navy in wartime for the period of hostilities only.

1964 *Polar Record* XII. 197 Hostile ice. **1966** T. Armstrong et al. *Gloss. Snow & Ice* 19 *Hostile ice*, from the point of view of the submariner, an ice canopy containing no large ice skylights or other features which permit a submarine to surface. **1919** W. Lang *Sea-Lawyer's Log* iii. 37 To the active service man the 'hostile ord', as the temporary seaman is called, is a mere interloper, one who has joined the Navy to 'dodge Kitchener', as they put it, and they do not hesitate to tell him so.

B. *sb.* (Earlier and later examples.)

1838 *N.Y. Mirror* 27 Jan. 245/3 Yesterday five Delaware chiefs, who had gone from the main army to the stronghold of the hostiles, reappeared with four Indians. **1963** *Guardian* 8 Sept. 6/6 There were rumours that Naga hostiles were getting help from China. **1966** A. Firth *Tall, Balding, Thirty-Five* iv. 48 It is most unlikely that a hostile could select such a person as yourself to assist them. **1969** *Hindu* 3 Aug. 1/5 A strong contingent of security forces has been rushed to.. Ukhrul..to intercept over 400 China-trained Naga hostiles.

hostility. Add: **1. c.** *hostilities, -y only*: used in the Navy to describe a seaman enlisted only for the duration of a war, or such an enlistment.

[**1917** 'Taffrail' *Off Shore* 81 Even in our small ships we carry some of the 'hostility men'.] **1942, 1961** [see *H.O.* s.v. *H III]. **1946** J. Irving *Royal Navalese* 7 Once again the 'Hostility Only' man took his silent stand beside the slender handful of us professional seamen. **1948** *Hansard Commons* 17 Mar. 2083 Recruiting on a hostilities only engagement was not open in the branch of their choice in the Royal Navy and Royal Marines. **1973** *Times* 31 Jan. 16/7 He enrolled in the Royal Navy as a 'hostilities only' rating.

hot, *a.* Add: **1. e.** At a high voltage, 'live'. Esp. in U.S. slang phrs. *hot chair, seat, squat*, the electric chair.

1925 *Sat. Even. Post* 29 Aug. 18/3 A judge sentenced a boy fifteen years old to the electric chair... A newspaper reporter said he heard the lad announce that he was not afraid to die 'in the hot seat'. **1927** *Flynn's Weekly* 1 Jan. 819/1, I never shot nobody... Lotsa times I don't carry a gun. That's one thing I try to dodge—the hot chair. **1928** J. P. McEvoy *Showgirl* xii. 180, I ought to get something for that don't you think? The chair maybe—better known as the hot squat. **1930** *Sel. Gloss. Motion Pict. Techn.* (Acad. Motion Pict., Hollywood), *Hot*, electrically charged, particularly when dangerous. **1937** *Printers' Ink Monthly* Apr. 54/2 *Hot mike*, a microphone in which the current is flowing. A live microphone. **1940** *Chambers's Techn. Dict.* 424/1 *Hot*, said of a conductor which is charged to a dangerously high potential. Colloquial. **1944** 'P. Quentin' *Puzzle for Puppets* ix. 74 When they get me on to the hot seat, I won't even burn. **1952** R. Chandler *Let.* 11 Jan. in *R. Chandler Speaking* (1966) 128 That scene at the end where the girl visits him in the condemned cell a few hours before he gets the hot squat!

4. Delete † *Obs.* and add later examples in astrological usage.

1819 J. Wilson *Dict. Astrol.* 268 Aries..is a vernal, hot, dry, fiery, cardinal,..fortunate, hoarse, bitter sign. **1889** R. Baughan *Influence of Stars* 12 Aries..is a hot and fiery sign, and produces a lean body. **1909** Kipling *Rewards & Fairies* (1910) 257 Between Mars and Luna, the one red, t' other white, the one hot, t' other cold.., stands..a natural antipathy.

6. a. (Further examples.) Freq. const. *for* or *on* (= keen on, eager for), or with *inf.* With negative construction: unsuccessful, not good or skilful.

1862 [see *dusty *a.* 4 d]. **1865** G. Meredith *Let.* ?8 Dec. (1970) I. 320, I am very hot upon *Vittoria*. Lewes says it must be a success. *a* **1877** Swinburne *Lesbia Brandon* (1952) iii. 75 He was always rather hot upon that

song. **1924** P. MARKS *Plastic Age* xi. 112, I didn't flunk out but my record isn't so hot. **1925** T. E. LAWRENCE *Let.* 7 Sept. (1938) 485 The Squadron Leader is hot on punishment. **1932** *Blue Valley Farmer* (Okla. City) 28 Jan. 2/3 For president he's not so hot. Business won't support him. **1934** J. M. CAIN *Postman always rings Twice* vi. 57 He was all hot to show me something. **1934** N. COWARD *Play Parade* I. p. x, It..established me both as a playwright and as an actor... Until then I had not proved myself to be so hot in either capacity. **1937** 'J. BELL' *Murder in Hospital* vii. 133 They're quite hot on First-Aid at these race tracks and he had a tourniquet on. **1937** *Tablet* 23 Oct. 553/2 Reviewed long ago with hot delight. **1946** MEZZROW & WOLFE *Really Blues* 375 *Hot for*, enthusiastic about, in favor of. **1952** *Manch. Guardian Weekly* 8 May 5/4 American radio listener, hot for news and excitement, leans forward. **1960** S. KAUFFMANN *If it be Love* II. i. 121 He's very hot on the Babbage Square move. He thinks it's a good idea. **1967** R. RENDELL *New Lease of Death* ii. 22 The Victorians.. were not too hot on design. **1969** D. GRAY *Murder on Honeymoon* xix. 118 Bryce was very hot on never having a drink in the bar.

c. (Further examples.) Also of a play, book, etc.: licentious. Phr. (U.S. slang) *to have* (or *get*) *hot pants*, to be (or become) aroused with sexual desire. Also, *hot pants*, a highly sexed (young) woman. Cf. senses *10 b and *12 c.

1892 E. J. MILLIKEN *'Arry Ballads* 37 As most of our plays are now cribbed from the French, wy they're all pooty 'ot. **1898** J. D. BRAYSHAW *Slum Silhouettes* 31 She was a 'an'some gal, was Daisy..but..she wos a fair scorcher, jist abart as 'ot as they make 'em. **1908** *Daily Chron.* 22 June 6/5 Publishing firms..discovered that money was to be made out of what they called 'the hot novel'. **1927** K. NICHOLSON *Barker* II. ii. 112 When you had him all hot pants you married him. **1933** D. L. SAYERS *Murder must Advertise* viii. 148 He said to Mr. Tallboy he thought the headline was a bit hot. And Mr. Tallboy said he had a nasty mind. **1935** J. T. FARRELL *Judgement Day* xvi. 383 A burlesque show. The hottest ones were south of Van Buren. **1936** J. STEINBECK *In Dubious Battle* 64 Every time the sun shines on my back all afternoon I get hot pants. **1961** S. PRICE *Just for Record* v. 36 You've got the hot-pants for some good-looking piece. **1963** M. MCCARTHY *Group* iii. 48 I've still got hot pants for her, if you want to call that love. **1963** L. MEYNELL *Virgin Luck* ii. 30, I was just a hot little bit throwing myself at the head of the nearest presentable male. **1966** C. ROBERTSON *Judas Spies* iii. 31 His second wife, this blonde hot pants. **1968** K. AMIS *I want it Now* i. 39 It would help to hold off little hot-pants, and might distract him from the thought of what he was so very soon going to be doing to her. **1968** O. WYND *Sumatra Seven Zero* x. 159 'You ought to marry.' 'That can wait. I haven't got as hot pants as I look.' **1971** W. HANLEY *Blue Dreams* xiii. 221 'I'm hot as a firecracker is what I am,' she said demurely.

d. Of an action: exceptionally good or fine. Of a person: exceptionally smart or skilled or successful (in some action or kind of work). Of dice, cards, etc.: unusually lucky or successful.

1895 S. CRANE *Red Badge of Courage* xvii. 169 'Hot work!' cried the lieutenant deliriously. **1914** *Daily Express* 30 Nov. 5/7 The Deutsches have some pretty hot snipers. **1919** A. A. MILNE *First Plays* 44 He did the ninth [hole in golf] in three...How's that for hot? **1934** J. T. FARRELL *Young Manhood* iv. 61 I'm shakin' fair, brother. They're just hot for me this time. The dice get hot for a guy like this maybe once in his whole life. **1944** D. RUNYON *Runyon à la Carte* (1946) 101 Here is Big Nig hotter than a stove, and here I am without a bob to follow him with... Nig can make sixes all night when he is hot. **1968** *Surfer* IX. 63 Cabell is really ripping it up in Hawaii now, too, but Young and McTavish are so hot it's unbelievable. **1970** *Surf '70* (N.Z.) 17/3 Walsh is not the only hot surfer in New Plymouth.

7. c. Of a ball: hit or thrown hard, and difficult for the other side to deal with.

1867 *Ball Players' Chron.* 6 June 3/4 The hot one he sent to pitcher. **1868** H. CHADWICK *Game of Base Ball* 41 *Hot Balls.* This term is applied to balls sent very swiftly to the hands from the bat, or thrown in swiftly. **1882** *Australians in Eng.* 37 Lockwood gave Murdoch a hot chance at point. **1886** F. H. BURNETT *Little Lord Fauntleroy* (1887) vi. 122 He..gave a dramatic description of a wonderful 'hot ball' he had seen caught. **1917** C. MATHEWSON *Second Base Sloan* 125 The players..had not handled a ball since the summer before and the 'hot ones' made them wince and yell.

d. Associated with or affected by a trade-union dispute. orig. *U.S.*

1901 *Denver Republican* 19 Aug. 1/1 (*headline*) Non-union men invading 'hot' section. **1940** F. RIESENBERG *Golden Gate* 312 Docks had become dangerously congested, for the teamsters joined with the I.L.A., refusing to haul 'hot cargo'. **1947** *Seafarers Log* 25 Apr. 13/2 Officers would no longer go through a picket line to move a hot ship. **1959** *Economist* 2 May 423/2 'Hot cargo' clauses in transportation contracts, under which a lorry-owner agrees not to handle freight coming from another employer with whom the union has a dispute.

e. Of stolen property: easily identifiable and so difficult to dispose of. In extended use: stolen. Also applied to a person wanted by the police.

1925 *Collier's* 8 Aug. 30/2 Stolen bonds are 'hot paper'; stolen diamonds 'hot ice'. **1926** [see *hock-shop* s.v. *HOCK *sb.*[7] b]. **1931** *Amer. Speech* VII. 109 *Hot car hustler*, car thief. **1931** 'D. STIFF' *Milk & Honey Route* 207 A person is hot when he is wanted by the law. No hobo will travel with a man who is hot. **1942** M. SCHLAUCH *Gift of Tongues* (1943) 269 Jewels become 'ice', and stolen jewels..'hot ice'. **1943** P. CHEYNEY *You can always Duck* ix. 151 Look, I'm hot, see? The cops here are after me. **1943** R. CHANDLER *Lady in Lake* (1944) xi. 64 The best stunt would be to unload it on a hot car dealer. **1953** W. BURROUGHS *Junkie* (1972) iii. 36 Herman pulled out a silk dress he had under his coat—as I recall somebody unloaded a batch of hot dresses on us for three grains of morphine. **1958** 'A. GILBERT' *Death against Clock* 70 It [*sc.* a stolen brooch] was too hot to touch at present. **1960** H. L. LAWRENCE *Children of Light* ii. 34 You come here, in a hot car... And the police know. **1969** *Times* 4 July 3/8 Many stolen works of art have been recovered recently..which suggests that thieves are finding them too hot to handle. **1973** P. MOYES *Curious Affair of Third Dog* xv. 207 Griselda was 'hot'. Griselda had to disappear.

f. Of a motor vehicle or aircraft: fast or powerful (esp. in relation to size). *colloq.* Cf. *HOT ROD.

[**1924** T. E. LAWRENCE *Let.* 20 Feb. (1938) 456 Hot speed on a motor-bike.] **1944** *Sat. Even. Post* 24 June 80/2 PV's can outrun all but the fastest of Jap fighters, but they pay for their speed by landing hot. **1951** *N.Y. Times Mag.* 21 Oct. 59/2 Certainly, the pure jet does land a little 'hotter' than the propeller plane. **1966** T. WISDOM *High-Performance Driving* ii. 31 Small 'hot' machines like a Mini Cooper and a Renault Gordini. **1968** *Hot Car* Nov. 7 It was a 'hot little car'.

8. a. *to get* (or *be*) *hot*: in a game or pursuit, to come (or be) near the discovery of something concealed. Also *transf.*

1876 [see *COLD *a.* 12 b]. **1882** *Cassell's Bk. In-Door Amusem.* (ed. 2) 29 The progress of the player is usually announced by assuring him that he is 'very cold', 'cold', 'warmer', 'warm', 'hot', 'very hot', or 'burning', according as he is far from or near to the article to be discovered. **1899** E. W. HORNUNG *Amat. Cracksman* 252 'Not there, not there,' said Raffles; 'but you're getting hot. Try the cartridges.' **1931** *Times Lit. Suppl.* 29 Oct. 832/4 He needs it [*sc.* personality] to act quickly and effectively when an appliance fails, or when an investigator gets 'hot'.

b. Read: Of a colour: intense, vivid, glowing. Add later examples.

1933 *Burlington Mag.* Apr. 176/2 De Vos had long admired Rubens and emulated his hot tones. **1958** *Vogue* Mid-Sept. (Extra Issue) 87 Hot pink velour hat. **1962** *Harper's Bazaar* Oct. 124/3 A new hot orange lipstick. **1967** D. FRANCIS *Blood Sport* xii. 144 A..hot pink-orange tunic.

f. *Metallurgy* and *Founding.* Of metal, esp. iron: completely fluid; sufficiently above the melting point to flow readily (see also quots. 1904, 1908[1]). So *hot-metal*, in the sense 'molten iron', is used *attrib.*, as in *hot-metal process*, a steel-making process in which the charge consists wholly or chiefly of molten iron. (See also *hot metal* in sense 12 c below.)

1888 *Lockwood's Dict. Mech. Engin.* 182 *Hot metal.* Molten iron and brass are said to be hot when their temperature is higher than that required for the class of work for which they are intended. **1902** G. R. BALE *Mod. Iron Foundry Pract.* I. x. 177 In pouring..the metal should be run 'hot'.., for when the metal is poured 'dull'..it is too sluggish to expel its gases. **1904** GOODCHILD & TWENEY *Technol. & Sci. Dict.* 291/1 Metal of any kind is said to be 'hot' when it is at a temperature sufficiently high for some definite operation to be carried out. Thus a smith may say iron is hot when it is just at a welding or a forging heat. **1908** B. STOUGHTON *Metall. Iron & Steel* ii. 37 The term 'hot iron' has come to be synonymous in the minds of blast-furnace foremen with iron high in silicon and low in sulphur. *Ibid.* xiii. 361 When I say 'hot iron' here, I mean 'fluid iron', i.e., the degree of heat above the melting-point. **1929** C. R. HAYWARD *Outl. Metall. Pract.* xxii. 463 (*caption*) Hot-metal mixer at South Chicago... A ladle supported by a crane is delivering metal. **1946** *Firth Brown Gloss. Metall. Terms* 11 In the hot-metal process, iron from the blast furnace goes through the mixer to the open hearth furnace, and constitutes 75% or more of the charge. **1951** G. R. BASHFORTH *Manuf. Iron & Steel* II. xii. 356 The cupola metal replaces the molten pig iron employed in the hot-metal open-hearth process. **1966** J. D. SHARP *Elem. Steelmaking Pract.* viii. 160 Ore, if used, is normally placed directly on top of the lime, or fed to the furnace immediately after the hot metal.

g. orig. *U.S.* Applied to jazz or highly elaborated and florid dance music with a marked beat and strong emotional appeal, freq. improvised; also to the performer or to the place where played and in other uses; opp. *COOL *a.* 4 d; *hot lick* (see *LICK *sb.* 7).

1924 *Variety* 9 July 9/3 The style in vaudeville jazz bands this coming season will tend toward the 'sweet' and 'hot' dance orchestras. *Ibid.* 24 Sept. 26-c/1 Leon Beiderbecke is a 'hot' trumpet. *Ibid.* 26-c/2 The boys step on it and get 'hot' at various intervals. **1926** [see *CHORUS *sb.* 6 c]. **1927** *Dancing Times* Apr. 117 We are in the days of the '*hot*' chorus. *Ibid.* May 149 'Hot Music' is still so much in its infancy over here that I do not propose to deal very fully with it for the moment. **1927** *Melody Maker* June 531/3 A rendering from an orchestration or an extemporisation made in this way is usually termed..'hot', the word 'hot' being intended to convey lilting, dance-inspiring rhythm with the accents irregularly placed but strongly portrayed, modern, or as some call them, extreme harmonies, and phrases based on these harmonies worked round the melody. **1928** *Gramophone* VI. 300/2 It is not a question of 'hot' dance music or 'straight' dance music. **1933** *Fortune* Aug. 47/1 Continuing in the language of jazz, it may be explained that Lawrence Brown is a *hot* trombonist with Duke Ellington's famous Negro jazz orchestra. That is to say, he excels in spontaneous, highly syncopated solos. **1933** *Punch* 18 Oct. 441/3 Miss Elizabeth Welch, a coloured lady,..sings what is known as a hot jazz song about Solomon in a startling but rather fascinating way. **1934** [see *CHORUS *sb.* 6 c]. **1935** *Vanity Fair* (N.Y.) Nov. 38/3 Hot artists often escape from the routine of their commercial work to the night clubs of Harlem. *Ibid.*, These are the only truly hot bands. **1938** *Oxf. Compan. Mus.* 777/2 Louis Armstrong (claimed by one of his admirers as 'certainly the greatest of all hot musicians..'). **1946** MEZZROW & WOLFE *Really Blues* xi. 195 Hugues [Panassié]..sure kept himself busy.., launching the Hot Clubs of France. **1947** [see *BEAT *v.*[1] 30 d]. **1947** AUDEN *Age of Anxiety* (1948) ii. 40 Emble did likewise but his choice was a hot number. **1949** F. MACLEAN *Eastern Approaches* I. vi. 78 In the station buffet an extremely 'hot' band with a good sense of rhythm played fairly recent jazz from New York. **1953** J. G. MOORE *Relig. Jamaican Negroes* 126 *Hot*, said of drums at Cumina ceremony when the fast rim beat indicates the presence of zombies in the drum. **1956** H. LYTTELTON in S. Traill *Play that Music* 79 Shall it be a trumpet or a cornet? I have no strong views either way—a good 'hot' style can be achieved on either instrument. *Ibid.* 84 'Hot' tone cannot be defined on paper... It can be heard in essence in the playing of Bunk Johnson, Tommy Ladnier ..and Louis Armstrong. *Ibid.* 85 Vibrato plays an important part in hot jazz, being used as a means of expression. **1970** P. OLIVER *Savannah Syncopators* 31 The idea of 'hot rhythm' is one which Richard A. Waterman borrowed from jazz and applied to African drumming.

h. Of a Treasury bill: newly issued.

1928 *Evening News* 18 Aug. 11/6 The hot Treasuries were offered at 4 3-16 per cent., without finding buyers. **1929** *Times* 16 Nov. 18/1 The 'hot' Treasury Bills were dealt in at 5 13-32 per cent. **1929** *Observer* 17 Nov. 3/3 'Hot' bills yesterday morning changed hands in very small amounts at 5 5-16 per cent. **1959** *Times* 15 Sept. 17/5 'Hot' bills were again sold to the clearing banks.

i. Radioactive; *esp.* so radioactive as to be dangerous; so *hot laboratory*, a laboratory designed for the safe handling of highly radioactive material; also *hot atom*, an atom that has high kinetic or internal energy as a result of a nuclear process.

1942 POLLARD & DAVIDSON *Appl. Nucl. Physics* vii. 139 Almost all the 'hot' sodium was in the form of NaOH. **1945** H. D. SMYTH *Gen. Acct. Devel. Atomic Energy Mil. Purposes* viii. 84 Later a 'hot laboratory', i.e., a laboratory for remotely-controlled work on highly radioactive material, was provided. **1946** *Sci. News Let.* 10 Aug. 84/1 A large part of Bikini lagoon remained.. 'hot' with radioactivity. **1947** *Time* 10 Nov. 82/2 'Hot' (radioactive) atoms have already caused plenty of trouble in laboratories. **1950** *Sci. Amer.* Mar. 44/3 The bizarre chemical effects sometimes produced by radioactive atoms have given rise to a fascinating new branch of investigation known as hot atom chemistry. *Ibid.* 47/1 The immense recoil energy of the hot carbon atoms will effect chemical reactions that would not ordinarily occur. **1955** *Times* 12 Aug. 6/4 The elaborate precautions needed in so-called 'hot' laboratories—those in which large quantities of radioactive materials are manipulated. **1955** *Sci. News Let.* 27 Aug. 134/3 At Hanford atomically 'hot' strontium is kept in large tanks until it cools down. **1958** H. ETHERINGTON *Nuclear Engin. Handbk.* VII. 48 The building arrangement should be such that one cannot pass from a hot to a 'cold' area without going through a clothing-change facility. **1964** M. GOWING *Britain & Atomic Energy* x. 286 The new laboratories at Chalk River..included a 'hot' laboratory for remote handling. **1972** *Nature* 25 Feb. 443/1 The Mössbauer effect has been used to elucidate..hot atom effects, nuclear lifetimes, [etc.].

9. b. Of news: sensational, striking, exciting. Phr. *hot from* (or *off*) *the press*: just printed.

In quot. 1945[2] a fanciful use.

1908 [see *HEADLINE 2 d]. **1914** *Daily Express* 30 Sept. 4/5 'Hot news'..must be provided for the people, and thus we learn from the Vienna 'Abendblatt' that General French is a prisoner. **1945** KOESTLER *Twilight Bar* I. 34 News? You bet it is news... Hot? You bet it is hot. **1945** *Tee Emm* (Air Ministry) V. 52 The gen it contains is hot from the griddle. **1955** *Times* 19 Aug. 2/5 But it is for novelties, hot from the press or the copyist's desk, that discontent is calling. **1958** *New Statesman* 3 May 557/2 Television: Curran comments that to this the response of the American press (as it is to some extent that of the British press) is to leave aside all but the hottest news because radio and television can cover it with more actuality and immediacy and to concentrate instead on.. personalities. **1969** *Times* 5 July 8/6 There has just arrived hot off the..presses a new publication called The Open Secret.

10. b. *absol.* as *sb. pl.* Strong sexual desire. *slang.*

1947 in Wentworth & Flexner *Dict. Amer. Slang* (1960) 274/1 I'd never get the deep undying hots for that rah rah collitch [boy]. **1951** AUDEN *Nones* (1952) 18 Jack likes Jill who worships George Who has the hots for Jack. **1961** S. PRICE *Just for Record* vi. 49 One day Lamb was going to get the hots for some painted woman. **1968** M. RICHLER *Cocksure* vi. 44 Well, me, I've got the hots for Polly Morgan. **1973** *Times Lit. Suppl.* 10 Aug. 921/5 It is Blodgett who has the hots for Smackenfelt's mother-in-law.

11. a. *hot and cold*: short for 'hot and cold water' (in a hotel, etc.). Phr. *to go hot and cold* (*all over*), *to go all hot and cold*: to experience alternate sensations of heat and cold as from shock or embarrassment. Also used trivially.

1908 *Sears, Roebuck Catal.* 610/4 Brass nickel plated compression bath cocks. Combination hot and cold. **1910** *Bradshaw's Railway Guide* Apr. 1012/1 High-class boarding establishment... Bath (hot and cold). **1914** BARRIE *Admirable Crichton* III. 130 He's working out

that plan for laying on hot and cold. **1928** *Daily Mail* 3 Aug. 10/6 The figures given..as to my earnings..made me go all hot and cold—I wonder what I can have done with all that money! **1931** *Times* 16 Mar. 1/5 (Advt.), First-class guest house,..fitted hot and cold and gas fires. **1944** A. Thirkell *Headmistress* i. 23 'There is a basin with hot and cold,' she said. **1973** A. Price *October Men* v. 64 His wife had said..that she had gone 'all hot and cold' after nearly being run over.

d. Also, *to give it* (to a person) *hot and strong* (and similar phrases).

1880 E. W. Hamilton *Diary* 25 July (1972) I. 27 Wilfrid Blunt goes in 'hot and strong' for making the Province a sort of independence. **1881** [see *bite *v.* 1 b]. **1931** T. R. G. Lyell *Slang* 412 *To give it a person hot and strong*, to punish a person severely, either physically or verbally; to give a good scolding to. **1938** A. G. Macdonell *Autobiogr. of Cad* ii. 14 Jedediah never spent a penny on the estate unless he was legally compelled to—and then the man who legally compelled him got it hot and strong in double quick time.

g. *hot under* (or occas. *in, around*) *the collar*: feeling anger or resentment, agitated (cf. sense 6 b); *hot and bothered*: in a state of exasperated agitation; also used (with hyphens) as attrib. phr.

1895 *Horse Rev.* 31 Dec. 1840/3 He would storm erround' dat room an' git hot under de collar. **1906** J. London *Let.* 1 Nov. (1966) 217, I must confess that he got me rather hot in the collar. **1918** E. Pound *Let.* 4 June (1971) 138 After years of this sort of puling imbecility one gets hot under the collar and is perhaps carried to an extreme. **1919** *Red Cross Mag.* Dec. 3/1 He fumbles around, gets hot under the collar and falsely accuses them of being a nuisance. **1921** M. Arlen *Romantic Lady* iv. v. 161, I was getting very hot and bothered about the whole thing. **1923** Kipling *Independence* 16 It [*sc.* each generation] goes to its grave hot and bothered, because no new birth has been vouchsafed for its salvation. **1930** A. P. Herbert *Water Gipsies* 279 She was delighted, though she had been caught in that rag, and still felt hot and bothered. **1932** *N.Y. Times Bk. Rev.* 7 Feb. 18/4 We thought it must belong to the 'Hot-and-Bothered Virgin on a Gunboat', 'Hot-and-Bothered Virgin at the South Pole' series. **1941** *Q. Jrnl. Speech* Oct. 361 [speech of the Frontier] Hamilton.. spoke sharply to some of the men and Ike, with the licence allowed to an old retainer, suggested that there was no need to 'get hot under the collar'. **1941** F. Reinfeld *Keres' Best Games of Chess* 43/2, I suddenly began to go hot under the collar as I noticed the powerful move. **1958** *Listener* 23 Oct. 649/2 Then she emerged, hot and bothered, glasses half down her nose. **1961** J. Barlow *Term of Trial* i. ii. 22 Most of the teachers..urged silence in hot-and-bothered threats. **1969** *Bucks Examiner* 25 July 7/1 Very few subjects can get parents as hot under the collar as education. **1970** J. Porter *Dover strikes Again* i. 7 Twenty-five years in the police had not tarnished Superintendent Underbarrow's basic serenity... He made it a point of honour never to get hot around the collar about anything.

h. *hot dog*: see as main entry in Suppl.

i. *a bit hot*: somewhat unreasonable.

1931 T. R. G. Lyell *Slang* 410 To dismiss the lad just because he forgot to post a letter is a bit hot. **1946** K. Tennant *Lost Haven* (1947) xiii. 204 She has to be humoured although I do think it's a bit hot her boy friend calling just as if she owned the place.

k. *hot as* (in hyperbolic comparisons), esp. (*as*) *hot as hell*.

1849 N. Kingsley *Diary* (1914) 19 Hot as blazes—glad to get under awnings. **1850** W. M'Collum *California* 20 It was a delightful, salubrious spot—'hot as blazes' to be sure, but fanned by gentle breezes. **1889** Farmer *Americanisms* 293/2 Hot as the Devil's kitchen. **1896** *N.Y. Dramatic News* 4 July 7/1 This afternoon was as hot as blazes. **1912** *Dialect Notes* III. 579 Hot as hammered hell. **1922** E. O'Neill *Hairy Ape* (1923) vi. 62 I'll be fire—under de heap—fire dat never goes out—hot as hell. **1935** A. J. Pollock *Underworld Speaks* 58/2 *Hot as a 45*, wanted by the police. **1935** Dylan Thomas *Let.* July (1966) 159 He's got a..hot-as-hell conservatory with a fountain. **1953** R. Graves *Poems* 29 From every-which-a-way, hot as a two-buck pistol. **1967** *Word Study* Dec. 4/1 One of the most common comparisons in English—is probably 'as hot as hell'.

12. a. *hot-eyed, -looking, -tailed, -toned* adjs.

c. hot-ache (later example); hence **hot-aching** *a.*; **hot beef,** rhyming slang for 'Stop thief!' e.g. in phr. *to give* (a person) *hot beef*; **hot bottle,** a hot-water bottle; **hot box** *U.S.*, an overheated journal-box, esp. of a railway carriage; also *fig.* or *transf.*; **hot bricks,** chiefly in phr. *like a cat on hot bricks*, denoting a situation of extreme discomfort and restiveness, or expressing swiftness or nimbleness of movement; **hot bulb,** in a semi-Diesel engine, an uncooled chamber connected to the cylinder head which is maintained at a sufficiently high temperature to vaporize fuel oil injected into it prior to compression in the cylinder; any mass of metal that performs the same function in such an engine, usu. *attrib.*; **hot cakes** orig. *U.S.*, (*a*) griddle-cakes, flannel-cakes; (*b*) in phr. *to sell* or *go* (*off*) *like hot cakes*, to be sold or disposed of very rapidly; to be in great demand; **hot cathode,** a cathode intended to be heated, so that electrons are emitted thermionically; also *attrib.*; **hot chisel,** a short thick chisel used for cutting or nicking hot metal and having a sharper edge than a cold chisel; **hot-closet** (earlier example); **hot cross bun** (see Bun *sb.*² 1, Cross-bun); **hot cupboard,** (*a*) an airing cupboard; also *fig.*; (*b*) a cupboard in which plates, dishes, etc., may be made warm; **hot diggety (dog)** *U.S. slang*, an exclamation of joy or surprise; cf. *hot dog 3; **hot-dip** *a.*, involving, used for, or applied by hot dipping; **hot dipping,** the application of a coating to an article either by dipping it in a bath of hot liquid (e.g. molten metal), or by dipping it hot in a bath of liquid; so **hot-dipped** *a.*, said of the coating; **hot flashes, flushes** *pl.*, a menopausal symptom which manifests itself by a momentary sensation of heat, freq. accompanied by a heightening of facial colour and perspiration; **hot iron** (see sense 8 f above); **hot-iron test** *Cheesemaking*, a test to determine the acidity of the curd; **hot line,** a direct, exclusive communication channel between two points; *spec.* the direct telephone link between Washington and Moscow (and similar lines); also *attrib.* and *fig.*; **hot-making** *a. colloq.*, embarrassing; **hot-melt** *a.*, solid at normal temperatures but capable of being melted for application (e.g. as a coating); **hot metal,** (*a*) molten iron: see sense 8 f above; (*b*) used *attrib.* to designate printing machines and methods in which type made by the machine from molten metal is used; **hot money,** capital which is transferred from one country to another in order to avoid the effects of currency devaluation or to profit from high interest rates or possible revaluation; also *attrib.*; **hot pants,** brief shorts worn by girls and young women as a fashion in the early 1970s; cf. *to have* (or *get*) *hot pants* s.v. sense 6 c above; hence **hot-panted, hot-pantsed** *adjs.*; **hot-plate** (examples); also, a heating element on an electric cooker; (*b*) a plate with a cover for keeping food hot; (*c*) a low, portable heating appliance with a flat top for keeping food hot or heating vessels, food, etc., placed on it; **hot potato,** in fig. phr. (to drop something) *like a hot potato*; also, a ticklish subject, an embarrassing problem; *rhyming slang*, a waiter; **hot seat,** (*a*) (see sense 1 e above); (*b*) used as in sense 7 b in Dict.; (*c*) (see quots. 1933 and 1938); (*d*) an ejection seat in an aircraft; **hot set,** a hot chisel, esp. one with a wooden handle; **hot shift** orig. *U.S.*, a mechanism enabling a change of gear to be made while a vehicle is moving without interrupting the drive to the wheels; **hot shoe,** a socket on a camera to which a flashgun may be connected; also *attrib.*; **hot spring,** any spring whose waters issue forth at a temperature appreciably higher than that of the ground; **hot squat** (see sense 1 e above); **hot-stove** *N. Amer.*, used *attrib.* of a discussion about a particular sport (e.g. baseball or ice hockey) between periods of play or in an off-season; also applied to anyone discussing a sport in this way; **hot tear** *Metallurgy*, a rupture produced in a casting or ingot as the metal cools and contracts; so **hot tearing** *vbl. sb.*; **hot top** *Metallurgy*, a refractory container for holding a reservoir of molten metal at the top of a mould during the solidification of an ingot; **hot tube,** in some early internal combustion engines, a metal or porcelain tube, closed at the end, which projected from one end of the cylinder and was heated externally by a flame, so that it ignited the mixture forced into it during the compression stroke; usu. *attrib.* in *hot-tube ignition*; **hot war,** an open war, involving active hostilities (opp. **cold war*); hence *hot-warrior*; **hot wave,** a spell of exceptionally hot weather, a heat wave; **hot wind,** a dry, very hot wind that blows over land for large distances from the interior in Australia, the United States, and elsewhere; **hot-wire** *attrib.*, denoting electrical instruments the indications or operation of which are based on the change in the length or resistance of a wire with changing temperature; as *v. trans.* (*N. Amer. slang*), to by-pass the ignition system of a motor vehicle (as a preliminary to stealing the vehicle); hence **hot-wired** *ppl. a.*; **hot with** (earlier examples).

1917 D. H. Lawrence *Look! We have come Through!* 155 Their scent is lacerating and repellent, it smells of burning snow, of hot-ache. *Ibid.* 156 What kind of ice-rotten, hot-aching heart must they need to root in! **1879** *Macm. Mag.* XL. 506/2 He followed, giving me hot beef (calling 'Stop thief'). **1896** A. Morrison *Child of Jago* x. 95 It was now that he first experienced 'hot beef'—which is the Jago idiom denoting the plight of one harried by the cry 'Stop thief'. **1973** G. Butler *Coffin for Pandora* vii. 157 'Hot beef, hot beef,' cried the schoolboys. 'Catch him...' **1845** Mrs. Gaskell *Lett.* (1966) 824 Please let Meta's feet be warm in bed (a hot bottle she has here by Dr H' direction). **1860** F. Nightingale *Notes on Nursing* i. 11 Hot bottles, hot bricks, or warm flannels.. should be made use of until the temperature is restored. **1967** S. Knight *Window on Shanghai* xxxi. 139 The Chinese don't use hot-bottles unless they're ill. **1848** *Merchant's Mag.* XIX. 656 Such a thing as a 'hot box' to a car has not been known,..since the sprinkler has been in use. **1873** 'Mark Twain' & Warner *Gilded Age* xlvi. 419 A hot box had to be cooled at Wilmington. **1899** S. Hale *Lett.* (1919) 343 He was excellent with the horses and very careful about hot-boxes and watering. **1910** J. Hart *Vigilante Girl* x. 140 If that near hind box was to begin to talk different, I'd pull up and examine it right away. Mebbe I'd save a hot box by doin' it. **1971** D. J. Smith *Discovering Railwayana* x. 56 *Hot box*, axle box overheated through lack of lubricants or overwork. **1971** *Flying* (N.Y.) Apr. 48/3 Lovely airplane but its another hotbox. [**1678** J. Ray *Coll. Eng. Proverbs* (ed. 2) 285 To go like a cat upon a hot bake-stone.] **1862** Whyte-Melville *Inside Bar* ii. 248 A well-bred, raking-looking sort of mare... Beautiful action she had, stepped away like a cat on hot bricks. **1886** 'J. S. Winter' *Army Society* xvi, Lady Mainwaring looked..like a cat on hot bricks. **1958** 'A. Gilbert' *Death against Clock* 165 Crook also was like a cat on hot bricks. **1961** Wodehouse *Service with Smile* iii. 42 Having become accustomed to this kind of thing myself..I have lost that cat-on-hot-bricks feeling which I must have had at one time. **1911** *Motor Boat* 26 Jan. 66/3 If you are nervous of electric ignition you should choose a hot-bulb ignition engine. **1919** W. Pollock *Hot Bulb Oil Engines* i. 2 All engines of the low compression type using heavy oils, and hot surface ignition of the injected spray are included under the title of hot bulb oil engines, although some makers use plates or discs, instead of bulbs. **1922** *Encycl. Brit.* XXXI. 519/1 Prior to starting the hot-bulb is blow-lamp-heated for 10 to 15 minutes. **1958** *Van Nostrand's Sci. Encycl.* (ed. 3) 823/1 It [*sc.* the semi-Diesel engine] has a hot bulb, which is a certain mass of metal incorporated in the cylinder head in such a way that a portion of it projects slightly in the combustion space. **1683** W. Penn *Sel. Works* (1782) IV. 309 Their entertainment was..twenty bucks, with hot cakes of new corn. **1839** C. F. Briggs *Adventures H. Franco* I. xi. 74 'You had better buy 'em, Colonel,' said Mr. Lummucks, 'they will sell like hot cakes.' **1879** *Congress. Rec.* 15 May 1368/1 Four per cent bonds..go off like hot cakes. **1891** Farmer *Slang* II. 18/2 s.v. *Cake*, Buckwheat and other hot cakes form a staple dish at many American tables. **1893** P. H. Emerson *Signor Lippo* xii. 37 It went off like hot cakes. **1908** *Daily Chron.* 4 Aug. 3/4 Ice creams at 3d. a time went 'like hot cakes'. **1925** J. Gregory *Bab of Backwoods* xi. 141 So they got the blaze going, bacon sizzling, the frying-pan balanced on the fire, hot-cakes mixed and coffee set to boil. **1930** E. Waugh *Vile Bodies* x. 183 Those who were fortunate enough to own cottages or public houses at the more dangerous corners..were selling tickets like very expensive hot cakes. **1949** H. Kurath *Word Geogr. Eastern U.S.* 34 Flannel cake is..rather uncommon in..Philadelphia, where hot-cake is in common use. *Ibid.* 35 Hot-cakes for griddle cakes made of flour. **1966** *Publ. Amer. Dial. Soc.* 1964 xlii. 16 *Flapjacks*, the commonest name for pancakes. *Batter* (or *batty*) *cakes*, *flitters* (or *flitter cakes*), *fritters*, *griddle cakes*, *hot cakes* are all known. **1971** *Petticoat* 17 July 3/1 You'll find amazing hessian bags.. selling like hot cakes for only £1.50. **1913** *Physical Rev.* II. 412 The idea of using a hot cathode in a Röntgen tube was not new. **1930** *Engineering* 31 Oct. 560/2 The hot-cathode discharge tube was free from these restrictions. **1943** *Electronic Engin.* XVI. 260/3 The instrument incorporates a hot-cathode, low-voltage, cathode-ray tube. **1959** *Listener* 12 Mar. 454/1 The hot cathode, as it was called in 1930, consisted of a small rod of alkaline earth oxide held in a tungsten coil. **1889** *N. & Q.* 23 Feb. 151/1 Cold and hot chisels are used for cutting cold and hot iron (or metal) respectively. **1964** S. Crawford *Basic Engin. Processes* xiii. 274 The process used to remove surplus metal from the forging with the aid of hot chisels or hot sets. *a* **1817** Jane Austen *Northanger Abbey* (1818) II. viii. 148 The ancient kitchen..rich in the massy walls and smoke of former days, and in the stoves and hot closets of the present. **1733** Hot cross bun [see Cross-bun]. **1825** [see Bun *sb.*² 1]. **1880** A. Beardsley *Let.* 1 Apr. (1971) 12 On Good Friday we had hot cross buns for breakfast. **1908** A. Huxley *Let.* 17 Apr. (1969) 26, I am almost prostrated just now by an *Enourmous* [sic] Hot cross Bun. **1941** C. Hole *Eng. Custom & Usage* iv. 43 Hot-cross buns are eaten throughout England on Good Friday... These little cakes..seemed to be descended from the wheaten cakes eaten at the Spring Festival alike by Greeks, Romans and Saxons. **1970** Simon & Howe *Dict. Gastron.* 90/2 Hot Cross buns are heavily spiced and eaten on Good Friday. **1930** S. Beckett *Whoroscope* 2 Them were the days I sat in the hot-cupboard throwing Jesuits out of the skylight. **1931** —— *Proust* 51 The Cartesian hotcupboard of the Guermantes library. **1950** *Chambers's Encycl.* VII. 256/2 One [electric cooker] for an ordinary family..would include..a hot cupboard enclosed by a drop door between the hob and the oven, and an oven. **1953** M. Dickens *No More Meadows* i. 20 The bathroom, which housed a boiler and a monstrous hot cupboard. **1959** *Observer* 12 Apr. 14/5 The bathroom..is assumed to be on first-floor level, adjoining a bedroom with access to water-heater hot-cupboard from the passage. **1967** N. Freeling *Strike Out* i. 11 Saskia took a plate from the hot cupboard. **1924** *Dialect Notes* V. 270 Hot diggity. **1927** *Sun* (Baltimore) 3 Apr. ii. 1. 12/2 When it comes to 'hot dog', there's no more to be said, unless it is, perhaps, to add a frill and make it 'hot diggety dog'. **1939** Ryerson & Clements *June Mad* iii. 178 I'll..get

cleaned up and into my..tux!.. Hot diggity! **1947** M. LOWRY *Let.* May (1967) 142 All I wanted was..a single word or phrase like: O.K., Hot Diggety, or even We are not amused. **1952** M. R. RINEHART *Swimming Pool* xi. 104 Hot diggety dog! Ain't that something? **1923** *Foundry* (Cleveland) 1 June 454/3 It has been shown that the deterioration of malleable in the hot-dip galvanizing process is intimately connected with the phosphorus and silicon content of the iron. **1960** *Farmer & Stockbreeder* 22 Mar. 138/2 (Advt.), Rust-proofing by the Hot-dip Galvanizing process ensures complete protection against weather. **1961** *New Scientist* 13 Apr. 38/2 The industrial process for the hot dip tinning of steel has been practised successfully for many years. **1971** *Engineering* Apr. 61/2 Croda Chemicals Ltd..supply both hot-dip strippable wax coatings as well as plastics. *Ibid.* 63/1 These are hot-dip compounds and provide coats impervious to moisture. **1936** *Jrnl. Amer. Zinc Inst.* XVII. 70 We began to collect samples of hot dipped spelter coated or galvanized sheets that had been subjected to varying periods of service. **1952** KIRK & OTHMER *Encycl. Chem. Technol.* VIII. 901 The normal hot-dipped coating consists of an alloy layer covered with a layer of pure coating metal. **1931** *Amer. Machinist* 8 Jan. 59/2 In hot dipping, crevices are sealed shut and filled with metal. **1954** *Plastics Engin. Handbk.* (Soc. Plastics Industry, Inc.) x. 300 Successive hot-dipping of objects in a tank of plastisol over the course of several hours will raise the temperature of the plastisol. **1924** A. J. SMALL *Frozen Gold* 222 Hot-eyed, livid-faced men. **1936** *Times Lit. Suppl.* 3 Oct. 788/4 The Herr Doktor, who was hot-eyed, not weary-eyed. **1969** *Listener* 5 July 21/3 For some tastes, to embark on a Doris Lessing book has always meant a tough regime of entrail-inspection and hot-eyed political pamphleteering. **1910** H. S. CROSSEN *Diagn. & Treatm. Dis. Women* (ed. 2) xiv. 851 'Hot flashes'..can hardly be classed as pathological. **1933** R. G. HOSKINS *Tides of Life* xii. 282 This..phenomenon is accompanied by.. the well-known 'hot flashes'. **1959** M. F. WILLIS *Let.* in 'I. Devi' *Yoga for You* (1960) 200 These benefits have continued with the extra good fortune of getting rid of seventy-five per cent of the hot flashes. **1910** W. B. BELL *Princ. Gynaecol.* iii. 89 The 'hot flushes'..are produced by rapid changes in the condition of the vaso-motor system. **1946** P. M. F. BISHOP *Gynaecol. Endocrinol.* iii. 33 A premature menopause complete with hot flushes becomes established. **1948** L. MARTIN *Clinical Endocrinol.* viii. 185 The general symptoms of the menopause are well marked in over 50 per cent of women, but some entirely escape and others suffer only minor discomfort from 'hot flushes'. **1971** M. LEE *Dying for Fun* xxxvi. 174, I keep getting hot flushes. It's my age. **1889** *Jrnl. Brit. Dairy Farmers' Assoc.* V. II. 70, I depend entirely on the hot iron test at this stage [of cheese-making]. *Ibid.*, To determine when the curd is ready for salting the hot iron test is again resorted to. **1955** J. G. DAVIS *Dict. Dairying* (ed. 2) 209 *Hot iron test.* This test is held in great esteem by some cheesemakers, but is very crudely carried out. **1955** *N.Y. Times Mag.* 7 Aug. 10/1 To hold this breakthrough to a minimum is 'ConAd's' job. It has twelve air divisions, tied in by 'hot line' communications with one another and with the Army, Navy and Civil Defense Administration. **1962** *Flight Internat.* LXXXI. 401/1 'Hot line' communications are by radio. **1963** *Guardian* 6 Apr. 1/3 Mr Tsarapkin's acceptance of a 'hot' White House–Kremlin telephone or teleprinter line. **1963** *Daily Tel.* 21 June 16 *Hot line.* At Geneva yesterday the United States and Russia signed an agreement to set up a direct link between the Kremlin, the Pentagon and, presumably, the White House. **1963** *Ibid.* 6 Sept. 23/4 The British Overseas Airways Corporation yesterday opened its own 'hot line'. It is an instantaneous electronic reservations system between London and New York. **1965** *New Statesman* 17 Sept. 390/2 The hand [of the Pope] hesitates to reach for the hot-line to the Holy Ghost. **1966** *Maclean's Mag.* 17 Sept. 3 About 20 orators arose, one after another, to espouse everything from (predictably enough) free university tuition to local night shopping and radio hot lines. **1966** *Melody Maker* 15 Oct. 6 Is he a mystic with a direct hot-line to heaven? **1969** *Times* 9 Aug. 4/2 President Nixon and..the West German Chancellor, announced today that they had agreed to set up a 'hot line' for communication between Washington and Bonn. **1970** *Daily Tel.* 17 Mar. 13/2 'Hot lines' are becoming *de rigueur* these days—Washington–London–Moscow, to say nothing of London–Canberra. **1971** *Ibid.* 26 July 3/3 On five days during the Moon mission, ITN will have a 'hot line' over which viewers can put questions to a panel of experts. **1936** J. CURTIS *Gilt Kid* v. 50 She wasn't quite so hot-looking as Maisie... That judy certainly had passion. **1959** *Tamarack Rev.* XII. 23 How could a hot-looking girl turn out so cold? **1931** *Sunday Times* 22 Feb. 4/1 This, to use the current phrase, hot-making play. **1958** B. NICHOLS *Sweet & Twenties* i. 34 How was it that Queen Marie delivered such hot-making effusions? **1939** *Manuf. Pulp & Paper* (ed. 3) V. § 4. 84 Hot-melt coatings will probably become familiar as paper coatings in the near future. **1946** *Nature* 30 Nov. 801/1 The production of hot-melt inks for carbon paper. **1954** *Plastics Engin. Handbk.* (Soc. Plastics Industry, Inc.) viii. 234 Hot-melt compounds of ethyl cellulose have become available..as another tooling material... Worn or damaged tools..can be reclaimed by remelting and recasting. **1969** *New Scientist* 19 June 641/3 The process is based on the use of papers precoated during production with a very thin film of 'hot-melt' plastic resin. **1960** *McGraw-Hill Encycl. Sci. & Technol.* X. 601/2 If type produced on 'hot metal' machines is to be used, the type is set, proved, read, and corrected. **1964** TURNBULL & BAIRD *Graphics of Communication* v. 83 Hot-metal composition is done on various type-casting machines. **1971** *Brit. Printer* Aug. 61/1 Harris-Intertype has introduced a low-cost photo text setter, the price of which is said to be comparable to that of a modern, manual hot-metal machine. **1936** P. J. O'BRIEN *Forward with Roosevelt* xi. 191 The movements of 'refugee capital', or as President Roosevelt and other financiers..described it, 'hot money', was an important consideration in the question of currency stabilization. **1951** J. R. WINTON *Dict. Econ. Terms* (ed. 3) 45 *Hot money*, a term used to describe the movement between different countries of balances and capital assets, withdrawn from one country through a loss of confidence as a result of war scares, possibilities of currency depreciation, [etc.]. **1958** *Spectator* 24 Jan. 117/2 Anybody who can afford to pay the 'hot' money price. **1971** *Daily Tel.* 3 Feb. 15 The huge volume of 'hot money' coming from abroad to chase high interest rates in Britain. **1971** *New Scientist* 25 Feb. 428/2 Where we once had ladies in gowns and earrings to elocute the score at us, we now have hot-panted dolly-birds who can't add up. **1972** *Guardian* 29 May 8/1 The miniskirted or hotpanted lass. **1970** *Women's Wear Daily* 23 Nov. 31/2 As for hotpants, we haven't seen anything in the market...They're going to have to be styled very imaginatively. Otherwise, they're going to look like old-fashioned short shorts. **1971** *Daily Tel.* 26 Jan. 4/8 'Hot pants', the fashion craze for abbreviated shorts for day or evening wear, is becoming the dominant fashion in the children's wear field, according to designers and manufacturers in New York. *Ibid.* 8 Nov. 12/8 Hotpants have rather quickly died a fashion death. **1971** *Daily Colonist* (Victoria, B.C.) 26 May 2A/1 Bibbed hot pants in easy care cotton. Styled with back zip. **1971** W. HANLEY *Blue Dreams* xi. 178 But, she couldn't wait! Hot-pantsed little... It was all perfectly clear now! **1845** E. ACTON *Mod. Cook.* vii. 159 The hot plates, or *hearths* with which the kitchens of good homes are always furnished. **1846** S. ETIEVANT *Brit. Pat. 11,096*, In the Drawing,..the spit on to which the material to be roasted is placed is affixed to the hot plate J, which carries the pots for charcoal K. **1861** C. E. FRANCATELLI *Cook's Guide* 3 (Advt.), Smoke Jacks, Hot Plates,.., Steam Tables, and..other description of..Cooking Apparatus. **1925** G. L. HILL *Ariel Custer* vii. 99 A gas hot plate with two burners. **1925** L. STALLINGS *Plumes* vii. 175 The hot plate..was set upon a bracket next the water closet. **1936** *Catal. Chem. Apparatus* (F. E. Becker & Co.) (ed. 25) 436 Gas Heated Hot Plate, polished smooth steel top on wrought-iron stand. **1938** *Trans. Amer. Soc. Mech. Engin.* LX. 70/1 Cores, crossbands and veneers..were glued on a hydraulic hot-plate press with hide or bone glue. **1966** *Which?* Feb. 45/2 All the other cookers had spiral hotplates with continuously variable controls. **1969** Hotplate [see *CORDLESS *a.*]. **1971** *Sci. Amer.* Aug. 108/3, I use butyl phthalate..and heat it with small laboratory hot plates operated at a temperature of 350 degrees Fahrenheit. [**1840** *Picayune* (New Orleans) 11 Sept. 2/2 Let's drop Nancy Daly like a hot praytee and proceed.] **1846** *Spirit of Times* 6 June 170/1, I dropped the divine's arm 'like a hot potatoe'. **1861** H. RHYS *Theatr. Trip Canada & U.S.* xi. 96 A deep growl..made me drop the article like a hot potato. **1886** B. P. POORE *Perley's Reminisc.* I. 448 They dropped him like a hot potato when they learned that he had accepted a place on the Republican Committee of his State. **1909** J. R. WARE *Passing Eng.* 155/1 *Hot potato* (False Rhyming—Music Hall, 1880). Waiter. **1930** W. S. MAUGHAM *Cakes & Ale* xiv. 169 She dropped him, but not like a hot brick or a hot potato. **1952** M. MCCARTHY *Groves of Academe* (1953) xiii. 257 It was a very hot potato... I chose to ignore the question. **1958** *Economist* 20 Dec. 1062/2 It has..dropped the hot-potato question of future UN forces. **1961** C. MCCULLERS *Clock without Hands* x. 199 The Judge had been distressed when Johnny agreed to take the case, was amazed at first at the way he handled it—hot potato that it was. **1963** *Listener* 14 Feb. 308/1 Tories continue to treat *laissez-faire* enterprise as a political hot potato. **1969** *New Scientist* 16 Oct. 116/1 The current hot potato in the sociological field is the question of poverty in Britain today. **1933** C. E. LEACH *On Top of Underworld* xii. 185 No catalogue of the methods of con-men would be complete without an exposure of this time-honoured 'ramp' [the 'Rosary' confidence trick], and of its companion, the 'Hot Seat'. **1938** F. D. SHARPE *Sharpe of Flying Squad* xxviii. 286 You've got to hand it to the Hot Seat Boys. They're clever little devils. For the benefit of the great overworld public—Hot Seat Mob is the title bestowed by the Underworld on the gentlemen we so often read about under the heading of Confidence Tricksters. **1942** *Time* 6 Apr. 49/1 We are an entire nation of people who are trying to wage a war and everyone is trying, himself, to keep out of the hot seat. **1950** *Nat. Geogr. Mag.* Sept. 311/1 (*heading*) Jets' 'Hot Seat' saves lives. **1959** *Observer* 11 Oct. 21/4 The cosy climate of gracious-uxorious living shattered by hot-seat-phobia. **1961** *Economist* 2 Dec. 913/1 The 'hot seat' issue of Chinese representation. **1966** *Listener* 28 July 143/1 After fifteen months in this critical hot seat..between listeners and the BBC I am saying my farewell. **1969** *Times* 24 June 25/1 (*headline*) Return to the hot seat. **1888** *Lockwood's Dict. Mech. Engin.* 183 *Hot set*, a smith's set,..used for the nicking and cutting of hot metal. **1894** G. HUGHES *Construction Mod. Locomotive* III. II. 155 Upon each side of the vertical an angle of 45° is marked, that is, nicked cold and afterwards heated and removed by a hot set. **1964** S. CRAWFORD *Basic Engin. Processes* xiii. 270 The hot set is used for cutting or marking hot material, often used in conjunction with a hardie. **1971** *Power Farming* Mar. 15/4 The tractor of the late seventies would be similar in layout to present-day models ... The main differences would be in driver comfort,.. greater use of hot-shift transmission and quick-attach systems for implements. **1972** *Good Motoring* Dec. 12/1 Driver-controlled epicyclic gearboxes in which various ratios were engaged or disengaged under load ('hot shift' is the American phrase) by means of friction clutches. **1971** *Amat. Photographer* 13 Jan. 57/1 (Advt.), Center flash contact (hot shoe). **1972** *Ibid.* 12 Jan. 71/2 (Advt.), Dual flash synchronisation system accepts virtually every type of flash unit with 'hot shoe' or plug-in coupling. **1972** L. GAUNT *Praktica Way* 118 Their single flash contact is in the accessory shoe and is designed for use with flashguns with a contact in the foot (the so-called 'hot-shoe' contact). **1669** W. SIMPSON *Hydrologia Chymica* 154 Some other causes there are of hot springs, *viz.* subterraneal fires. **1780** [see GEYSER 1]. **1850** [see SPRING *sb.*[1] 2 b]. **1961** *Times* 18 Mar. 11/1 Hot springs are found throughout the island [*sc.* Iceland]. **1952** *Time* 18 Feb. 55 *Hot stove leaguer*, in the U.S., anyone who likes to talk at length..about recent developments in his favorite sport—which is usually baseball. **1959** *Ottawa Citizen* 25 June Suppl. 7/1 The auto industry has its own hot-stove league—the off-season gatherings of stylists, planners and engineers who talk of what might have been or what might yet be. **1962** *Hockey Canada* Nov. 12/2 Things we have missed may be mulled over in Hot Stove sessions which are as old and as popular as the sport of hockey itself. **1965** *Globe & Mail* (Toronto) 13 Jan. 26/4 King Clancy.. joined Bower..on the Hot Stove panel yesterday. **1680** ? BUCKHURST in Rochester *Poems* 78 Until her Hot-Tail'd Majesty..Had worne her Gems on Holy Days. **1933** *Jrnl. Iron & Steel Inst.* CXXVII. 566 The application of certain principles of casting design is important in eliminating the danger of hot-tears. **1955** HEINE & ROSENTHAL *Princ. Metal Casting* xvi. 350 A rigid mold is also a potential cause of hot tears. **1945** *Jrnl. Iron & Steel Inst.* CLI. 380P The degree of hot tearing..can be minimised or often eliminated by using steel with a lower sulphur content. **1967** A. H. COTTRELL *Introd. Metall.* xiii. 180 Another practical problem of shrinkage is hot tearing. **1961** *New Left Rev.* July–Aug. 43/1 A swinging musician with a great sense of the Blues, and 'hot-toned'. **1928** *Jrnl. Iron & Steel Inst.* CXVII. 831 Corrugated ingots of acid steel cast with hot tops to eliminate segregation and piping are used for the larger forgings. **1954** A. R. BAILEY *Text-bk. Metall.* ix. 388 A 'hot top'..acts as a reservoir for feeding the ingot, the pipe eventually occurring in this portion, which is discarded. **1890** W. ROBINSON *Gas & Petroleum Engines* iii. 35 The hot tube gives a good regular ignition. *Ibid.*, With hot-tube ignition..there is the possibility of premature and irregular explosions. **1912** ASKLING & ROESLER *Internal Combustion Engines* II. ii. 122 Ignition by hot tube is only employed for small engines. **1963** BIRD & HUTTON-STOTT *Veteran Motor Car* 67, 1899 Clément-Panhard... Engine: Transverse, inclined, rear, 1-cyl., 90 × 120 mm., A.I.V. (i.o.e.), hot-tube ignition. [**1768** J. LEES *Jrnl.* (1911) 39 The Chipawas..were at this time in a hot war with the *Sous.*] **1947** *Newsweek* 17 Nov. 25/2 The ideological war of the Communists is as ruthless and as determined..as a hot war. **1955** *Times* 5 July 11/6 It is a reasonable assumption that a hot war would be measured in months if not weeks. **1973** R. HAYES *Hungarian Game* 340 U.K. Counterintelligence..blew the cover of every *Abwehrabteilung*..agent in Britain during the hot war. **1966** *New Statesman* 22 July 116/2 It is more likely that the hot warriors..want to use rash behaviour in Hanoi to authenticate the next escalation. **1888** *Encycl. Brit.* XXIII. 805/1 The occasional occurrence of 'hot waves' which sweep over large areas of country, raising the temperature much above its normal height, is one of the most striking and most disagreeable features of the climate of the country [*sc.* the U.S.A.]. **1901** *Daily Colonist* (Victoria, B.C.) 23 Oct. 5/2 The 'hot wave', as the weather man calls it, was general along the coast and extended some way east. **1936** *Discovery* Mar. 78/2 The only periods when Buchan's spells appear to be at all true in London and the south are his cold wave of February 7th to 14th, and the hot wave from July 12th to 15th. **1968** G. R. RUMNEY *Climatol.* xi. 198 The familiar but unwelcome heat wave, or hot wave, of eastern North America. **1797** *Encycl. Brit.* VI. 402/1 A sign of the approaching *Simoom* or hot wind. **1804** WELLINGTON *Disp.* (1837) III. 180 A desire to give his troops some repose, and not to expose the Europeans to the hot winds in Hindustan. **1850** R. G. CUMMING *Five Yrs. Hunter's Life S. Afr.* I. 60 At certain seasons..northerly breezes prevail: these are termed by the colonists 'hot winds'. **1900** W. STEBBING *C. H. Pearson* 289 He revelled in the Victoria hot-wind days which shrivelled up everybody else. **1910** W. L. MOORE *Descr. Meteorol.* x. 187 The 'hot winds' of our western plains [in the U.S.A.]. **1971** J. GENTILLI *Climates of Austral. & N.Z.* v. 68 In the southern interior, especially in Victoria, these hot winds laden with dust are known as brick-fielders. **1889** *Telephone* 15 Mar. 136/1 The actual stress in the platinum silver wire in our hot-wire voltmeter was not sufficient. **1904** *Electrician* Nov. 150/1 An oscillating circuit containing..a delicate hot-wire ammeter. **1914** *Phil. Trans. R. Soc.* A. CCXIV. 404 (*heading*) On the design of portable hot-wire anemometers. *Ibid.* 405 Standard thermometer wire is the most suitable for the purpose of hot-wire anemometry. **1922** *Encycl. Brit.* XXXI. 186/2 A case of great importance from its industrial application in hot wire valves is one where all the ions are negative and are emitted from the cathode. **1923** E. W. MARCHANT *Radio Telegr.* iv. 44 Other forms of detector for wireless circuits are the electrolytic, the hot wire 'barretter' and the crystal. **1933** *Phil. Mag.* XVI. 50 The sound recording instrument was a tuned hot-wire microphone. **1957** HALTINER & MARTIN *Dynamical & Physical Meteorol.* xiv. 218 Hot-wire anemometers are..highly sensitive instruments capable of measuring mean wind velocities over very short periods (down to 0·1 sec.). **1957** E. G. RICHARDSON *Techn. Aspects Sound* II. ix. 361 The turbulence data..were measured inside the jet stream by the use of hot wire equipment. **1966** R. THOMAS *Spy in Vodka* (1967) i. 7, I was pleasantly surprised to find my car intact. The German juvenile delinquents..can hot-wire a car in a time that makes their American counterparts look sick. **1968** *Daily Colonist* (Victoria, B.C.) 5 Sept. 19/2 Newton told court he yelled his intention to 'hot-wire' the Thomas car (bypass the need for an ignition key). **1962** *Amer. Speech* XXXVII. 269 *Hot-wired*, designating a motor vehicle which has had the ignition switch short-circuited by a thief. **1843** *Ainsworth's Mag.* IV. 437 The 'hot with' set our tongues in motion. **1856** C. READE *Never too Late* III. xxx. 289 'Hot with,' demanded the waiter in a sharp mechanical tone... The landlady..poured first the brandy then the hot water into a tumbler.

d. Used before numerous vbl. sbs. and pa. pples. (ppl. adjs.) that denote an industrial or manufacturing process or its result, from which arise transitive vbs. as back-formations; so **hot drawing**, the drawing of wire, tubing, or the like with the application of heat or while hot; *hot-drawn* adj.; *hot-draw* vb.; **hot gilding** (in Dict., sense 12 c); **hot moulding**, moulding in which heat is applied either to the material to be moulded (as in injection moulding) or to the mould (as in compression moulding); *hot-moulded* adj.; *hot-mould* vb.; **hot rolling**, the rolling of metal while it is at an elevated temperature; *hot-rolled* adj.;

hot-roll vb. Also HOT-PRESS *v.*, *HOT-WORK *v.*

1899 Hot-drawn [in Dict., 12 c]. **1910** H. P. TIEMANN *Iron & Steel* 336 With hot drawing the thickness of the walls is not generally carried below ¼ in. **1952** J. DELMONTE *Plastics Molding* xiii. 409 It is much more feasible to stock a few sizes and then, when a special tubing is required, hot-draw the tubing down to the required dimension. **1963** H. R. CLAUSER *Encycl. Engin. Materials* 685/1 Typical applications for these steels are..hot-drawing dies..and die casting dies. **1938** H. I. LEWENZ tr. *Brandenburger's Processes & Machinery Plastics Industry* i. 1 Hot moulding, where the hardening process ..takes place to some extent simultaneously with the moulding of the paste by tools, which..are heated. *Ibid.* 7 Hot-moulded articles. **1962** *Times* 13 Feb. 4/6 They have offered to build a racing eight by the hot-moulded method. **1964** N. G. CLARK *Mod. Org. Chem.* xvii. 359 The product is a colourless, transparent solid which may be machined, or hot-moulded. **1878** Hot-rolled [see *cold-rolled* (*COLD *a.* 18)]. **1888** *Proc. Inst. Civil Engineers*, XCIV. 236 (*caption*) Billet [of mild steel]. Reduced by hot rolling to wire rod. **1925** Hot-roll [see *base box* (*BASE *sb.*[1] 20)]. **1928** *Jrnl. Iron & Steel Inst.* CXVII. 840 A description of the hot-rolling, cold-rolling and drawing operations in the manufacture of nickel steel. **1955** *Times* 12 July 8/3 The new Duisburg mill will be able.. to produce 180,000 tons of hot-rolled steel products a month. **1967** A. H. COTTRELL *Introd. Metall.* xxii. 439 In steel-making..the ingots are taken from their moulds while still hot and then stored in a soaking pit or furnace ready for hot-rolling at 1000–1200° C.

hot, *adv.* **2.** (Later examples.)

1884 'MARK TWAIN' *Huck. Finn* xv. 126 As soon as I got started I took out after the raft, hot and heavy, right down the tow-head. **1922** JOYCE *Ulysses* 160 If a fellow gave them trouble being lagged they let him have it hot and heavy in the bridewell. **1924** T. E. LAWRENCE *Let.* 19 Mar. (1938) 459 *A[rabia] D[eserta]* is selling hot in U.S.A. **1927** *Melody Maker* Aug. 782/2 The verse is then taken 'hot' by the trumpet. **1928** *Ibid.* Feb. 184/2 They are..played 'hot'. **1934** T. S. ELIOT *Rock* i. 12 The shareholders ain't there, and their divvies ain't 'ardly there either, 'cos they paid too 'ot for their shares.

hot, *v.* Add: **1.** With *up.* To become hot. Also *fig.*

In quot. 1909 the passive use is somewhat unusual.

1909 W. OWEN *Let.* 23 Aug. (1967) 55, I *did* take a holiday, on account of the day being so 'hotted up'. **1936** WODEHOUSE *Laughing Gas* xiii. 146 It did not need a razorlike intelligence to show me that things were hotting up, and that flight was the only course. **1958** *Daily Mail* 3 Sept. 1/2 The cold war being fought out between Britain and Iceland in the rich fishing grounds of the northern seas hotted up yesterday. **1967** M. CHANDLER *Ceramics in Mod. World* iv. 132 The higher the frequency the more the insulator will hot up. **1969** *Times* 28 July 18/6 (*heading*) Pacific air route battle hots up.

2. (Later examples.)

1903 M. CROMMELIN *Crimson Lilies* (1913) xxiv. 176 You put something on your outside, while I hot up some tea..to put in your inside. **1928** GALSWORTHY *Swan Song* II. iv. 138 Let me hot up your stew. **1952** S. SELVON *Brighter Sun* ix. 188 Urmilla went to hot the food.

3. *fig.* or *transf.* with *up. spec.* (*a*) To become 'warm' or unpleasantly excited, near the point of anger. (*b*) *pass.* Of an internal-combustion engine, a car, etc.: to be 'tuned up'; to have the power increased so as to be capable of higher speeds. Also *trans.* and in *ppl. a.*, and in extended uses.

1923 WODEHOUSE *Inimitable Jeeves* x. 108 The atmosphere was consequently more or less hotted up when Cyril..breezed down centre. **1928** *Morning Post* 20 Oct. 10/7 This car..is not in any sense a 'hotted up' Morris six-cylinder. **1939** R. LEHMANN *No More Music* 56 *Jan*: Excitable girl. *Miriam*: You seem to have hotted her up nicely. **1945** *Jrnl. R. Aeronaut. Soc.* XLIX. 205/1 The Americans have had considerable success in 'hotting up' engines once intended for airline use. **1946** A. LEE *German Air Force* 13 The special hotted-up engines flown by ace pilots. **1950** *Hansard Commons* CCCCLXXII. 2036 Our present submarines are being 'hotted-up' with fast battery drive. **1958** J. CAREW *Wild Coast* xii. 161 The drummerboys hotted up the rhythm. **1958** *Spectator* 6 June 740/2 The *Observer* complains that Mr. Allsop's style has 'the hotted-up, black-and-white, metaphor- and smart-allusion-besotted quality typical of one kind of popular journalism'. **1958** *Times* 12 Aug. 7/2 The General Assembly is the place to hot things up. **1959** *Listener* 9 Apr. 628/1 Hotting up hymn tunes was the absolute end. **1960** *Guardian* 5 Jan. 4/4 A rather hotted-up radio receiver. **1962** *Listener* 5 Apr. 595/2 The hotted-up economic and ideological conflicts of the latter part of the nineteenth century. **1968** *Hot Car* Oct. 61 If you hot up your car, don't forget to step up your braking power. **1973** 'M. INNES' *Appleby's Answer* xvii. 150 Far from cooling up, he might hot up, and simply jump the gun. **1973** *Guardian* 28 May 2 Sir Alec Douglas-Home.. was launching into..the need to avoid actions which would 'hot up this cod war'.

hot air. 1. *attrib.* or as *adj.* (See HOT *a.* 12 c.)

1813 M. EDGEWORTH *Let.* 26 Apr. (1971) 27 When first the hot air flues were opened..the hot air all escaped. **1841** C. CIST *Cincinnati* (Advt.), Manufacturers of Hot Air Furnaces, Stoves, &c. **1853** *Hunt's Merchant's Mag.* XXVIII. 282 Hot-air vessels are to take the place of steamships. **1854** [see HOT *a.* 12 c]. **1861** MRS. BEETON *Bk. Housek. Managem.* 1009 A better arrangement is to have a hot-air closet,..heated by hot-air pipes,..and clothes-horses on castors..for drying purposes. **1892** STEVENSON & OSBOURNE *Wrecker* i. 24, I designed..a hot-air grating for the offices. **1905** G. BACON *Balloons* i. 23 To this day large hot-air balloons inflated by the same methods employed a hundred years ago occasionally take passengers aloft. **1908** *Sears, Roebuck Catal.* 606/3 Standard American Plumbing. Hot Air and Hot Water Heating. **1940** *Chambers's Techn. Dict.* 424/1 *Hot-air heater*, one which supplies warm air through gratings in the floor or openings in the walls. *Ibid.*, Hot-air turbine. **1964** M. HYNES *Med. Bacteriol.* (ed. 8) iii. 27 The syringe, clean, assembled and lubricated, is packed in a glass or metal tube and subjected to a temperature of 160° C for 1 hour in the hot-air oven. **1970** *New Yorker* 3 Oct. 28/2 We can..move hot-air registers around simply by making holes in the floor. **1973** *Times* 8 Jan. 2/5 (*caption*) A hot-air airship, claimed to be the world's first, making its maiden flight yesterday from Newbury, Berkshire.

2. *colloq.* (orig. *U.S.*). Vaporous or boastful talk, pretentious or unsubstantial statements or claims; also *attrib.*, as in *hot-air artist* or *merchant*, one who indulges in talk of this kind.

1873 'MARK TWAIN' & WARNER *Gilded Age* xliv. 399 The most airy scheme inflated in the hot air of the Capital only reached in magnitude some of his lesser fancies, the by-play of his constructive imagination. **1900** ADE *Fables in Slang* 126 They strolled under the Maples, and he talked what is technically known as Hot Air. **1906** [see *BLUE SKY 2]. **1910** *Sat. Even. Post* 2 July 13/3 'Hot-air artists' was a phrase uncoined; the farmer called them 'jawsmiths'. **1911** H. B. WRIGHT *Winning of Barbara Worth* 327 The presence av sich..a hot air merchant..is a disgrace to any..company. **1914** [see *BULL *sb.*[4] 3]. **1920** 'SAPPER' *Bull-Dog Drummond* xii. 308 Author—so-called. Hot-air factory, but useful up to a point. **1922** *Daily Mail* 20 Nov. 8 Much 'hot air' from the politicians. **1932** [see *BULL *sb.*[4] 3]. **1956** A. WILSON *Anglo-Saxon Att.* II. iii. 365 Gerald in his new mood thought only he shouldn't have poll-parroted his life away in humbug and hot air. **1963** *Times* 17 May 13/7 Anti-European slogans shouted by politicians were mere hot air. **1970** T. COE *Wax Apple* (1973) xxiv. 170, I think you're just full of hot air... I don't believe you know anything.

hot bed. Add: **3*.** *U.S. slang.* A bed, usu. in a flop-house, used continuously, day and night, by different people for limited periods. Also, the flop-house in which such beds are found.

1945 L. SHELLY *Jive Talk Dict.* 26/1 *Hot bed*, cheap flop house. **1953** POHL & KORNBLUTH *Space Merchants* (1955) vii. 77 The dorm was jammed with about sixty bunks... Since production went on only during daylight hours, the hot-bed system wasn't in use. My bunk was all mine. **1968** P. OLIVER *Screening Blues* vi. 253 In city streets where hot-bed apartments and kitchenettes were the only dwelling units available to Negroes,..the automobile parked in the street became the front parlour. **1970** C. MAJOR *Dict. Afro-Amer. Slang* 67 *Hotbed*,..in a flophouse a public bed for the price of 25 cents per eight hours.

hotch, *v.* Add: **3.** *intr.* To swarm.

a **1779** in *E.D.D.* **1797** *Edin. Mag.* Dec. 458 The floor i' now is just a hotchin' thrang. **1825** *Blackw. Mag.* Mar. 369 When there's sae strong a spirit of life hotchin' ower yearth and sea in this very century. **1893–4** R. O. HESLOP *Northumb. Words* II. 387 The place is fair hotchin wi' rabbits. **1909** *Daily Chron.* 17 May 4/4 'The county,' he said, in his broad Ayrshire accent, 'is fair "hotching" ..with them.' **1961** B. FERGUSSON *Watery Maze* v. 111 They found themselves delayed in Lisbon, a city then hotching with spies. **1965** J. CAIRD *Murder Reflected* ix. 108 Tripped over a stool. The place hotches with them. **1967** 'H. CALVIN' *DNA Business* xiii. 148, I expect the office will be simply hotching with typists.

hotch, *sb. Sc.* [f. HOTCH *v.*] A jerk or jolt.

1721, 1824 in *E.D.D.* **1773** R. FERGUSSON *Poems* (1956) II. 124 Uncanny hotches Frae clumsy carts or hackney-coaches. **1914** N. MUNRO *New Road* ii. 24 *She* never mentioned it, but every time I did, I saw her give a hotch upon her chair.

hotcha (hǫ·tʃă). *slang* (chiefly *U.S.*). Also **hotcha cha, hot-cha(-cha)**, etc. [Fanciful extension of HOT *a.*] **1.** Used in combination with the traditional interjection *hey nonny nonny* (cf. HEY 2).

1932 KAUFMAN & RYSKIND *Of thee I Sing* in *Famous Plays* (1933) 694 With a hey, nonny nonny, and a ha cha cha! **1937** WODEHOUSE *Lord Emsworth & Others* ii. 99 Good morning, Phipps. What ho, what ho, with a hey nonny nonny and a hot cha-cha. **1954** *Word Study* Oct. 6/1 Many of us..find Shakespeare's *Hey nonny nonny* a bit naked without the *hotcha cha.*

2. *int.* Expressing enthusiastic approval. Also as *adj.*, attractive, desirable.

1934 J. O'HARA *Appointment in Samarra* (1935) i. 21 Did you ever see her in a bathing suit? Hot-cha! **1939** R. CHANDLER *Big Sleep* ix. 71 He run Sternwood's hotcha daughter,..off to Yuma.

3. *adj.* Of jazz: hot.

1937 S. KING-HALL *King-Hall Survey 1936* ix. 93, I seemed to notice a tendency, towards the end of 1936, for what one of my daughters calls 'Hotcha' music to be replaced by 'Swing' music. **1947** R. DE TOLEDANO *Frontiers of Jazz* ii. 13 In 1934..the number of people who had anything more than a hotcha idea of jazz could be numbered on the fingers of a hand. **1957** W. C. HANDY *Father of Blues* vii. 98 Hot-cha music was the stuff we needed, and it had to be mellow. **1960** C. RAY *Merry Eng.* 60 There are hotcha gramophone records.

hotchi witchu (hǫ·tʃi wi·tʃū). Also **hotchi witchi.** [Romany.] The gypsy name for a hedgehog.

1843 BORROW *Zincali* (ed. 2) I. I. v. 98 They [*sc.* gypsies] have been seen..to roast hotchiwitchu or hedgehog. **1928** *Sunday Dispatch* 2 Sept. 3/3 The gypsies call the animal 'Hotchi witchu', we speak of him as the hedgehog. **1935** 'X. PETULENGRO' *Romany Life* xix. 79 As we sat..eating our *hotchi-witchi*, some gentlemen.. passed near us and were curious to see what smelt so good. **1963** C. DUFF tr. *Clébert's Gipsies* v. 185 One of the dishes peculiar to Gypsies is the hedgehog..(in English Gypsy *hotchi-witchi*).

Hotchkiss (hǫ·tʃkis). The name of B. B. *Hotchkiss* (1826–85), American inventor, used *attrib.* to designate certain cannon and rifles invented by him, and a machine-gun developed by his successors.

1878 W. MORGAN-BROWN *Brit. Pat. 3017* 30 July, This Invention consists in several important improvements on the Hotchkiss revolving cannon and other machine guns. *Ibid.*, The gunner may have entire control over the laying, sighting, and firing of a Hotchkiss revolving cannon. **1880** *Encycl. Brit.* XI. 285/1 Hotchkiss Magazine Gun. **1886** *Harper's Mag.* Oct. 793/2 The types adopted by the United States navy are the Hotchkiss revolving cannon and rapid-firing single-shot guns. **1890** *Handbk. Six-Pounder Hotchkiss Quick-Firing Gun* 12 The shell is fitted with..a brass Hotchkiss band. *Ibid.*, The fuze may be either the Nordenfelt or the Hotchkiss, Mark II, pattern. **1890** G. S. CLARKE *Fortification* xiii. 191 Twelve Hotchkiss machine guns. **1899–1900** *Kynoch Jrnl.* Dec.–Jan. 31/2 The Hotchkiss Automatic Gun. **1900** [see POM-POM]. **1902** *Encycl. Brit.* XXIX. 166/1 In the Hotchkiss and also in the Skoda systems the mechanism is of the vertical breech block type. **1908** *Trade Marks Jrnl.* 3 June 906 Hotchkiss... Guns, gun mountings, gun carriages, and other appurtenances and accessories for guns. .. The Hotchkiss Ordnance Company, Limited,..London,..manufacturers. *Ibid.*, Hotchkiss... Ammunition (explosive). The Hotchkiss Ordnance Company, Limited, ..London,..manufacturers. **1926** T. E. LAWRENCE *Seven Pillars* (1935) III. xxviii. 168 The Frenchman began by presenting six Hotchkiss automatics complete with instructors. **1959** *Chambers's Encycl.* V. 676/2 The Hotchkiss light machine-gun..was adopted for cavalry use.

hot damn, *int. phr. U.S.* An intensified form of 'damn!'.

1936 J. STEINBECK *In Dubious Battle* 90 Hot-damn, listen. **1957** J. KEROUAC *On Road* (1958) IV. ii. 257 Hot damn, I could go with you? **1971** *Black World* Apr. 73 Pop pulled garbage in an old-law tenement building. Hot-damn..every night.

hot dog. [DOG *sb.*] **1. a.** *N. Amer. slang.* One who is skilled or proficient in some pursuit (see also quot. 1900). Also *attrib.* or as *adj. phr.*, good, superior.

Freq. with connotations of 'showing off'. In some sports, e.g. Skiing, applied to 'trick' or 'stunt' or spectacular variations of normal movements.

1896 W. C. GORE in *Inlander* Jan. 148 *Hot-dog*, good, superior. 'He has made some hot-dog drawings for ——.' **1900** *Dialect Notes* II. I. 42 *Hot-dog*. 1. One very proficient in certain things. 2. A hot sausage. 3. A hard student. 4. A conceited person. **1966** *Atlantic Monthly* Mar. 131 We had this one [basketball] player, Alston Mackintosh,.. who could hit nine out of ten from the foul line with his back to the basket. He was a real hot dog. **1968–70** *Current Slang* (Univ. S. Dakota) III–IV. 71 *Hot dog*, one who shows off by squealing his tires and gunning his motor as he drives around among his friends. A crowd pleaser who is actually obnoxious. A showoff. To show off. **1973** *Internat. Herald Tribune* 9 Feb. 13/1 'Hot dog', or acrobatic, skiing has become a fast-growing sport in the United States. **1973** *Times* 23 Feb. (Canada Suppl.) p. vii/8 The local 'hot dogs', mostly teenagers who probably learnt to ski almost as soon as they could stand up, skate over mounds of hard-packed snow 4 ft high like sprinters over hurdles. **1973** *Time* (Canad. ed.) 16 July 51/1 Cedeno pulls off so many flashy plays in the field that some National League players accuse him of being a 'hot dog'—baseballese for show-off. **1973** *Globe & Mail* (Toronto) 1 Sept. 35/1 This year..it was generally agreed that McQuay must change his hotdog antics or go. **1974** *Ibid.* 20 Feb. 34/5 Dan Genge..admits that it was those same little hills that made him what he is—one of Ontario's coolest hot-dog skiers. *Ibid.* 34/8 There has to be something of the mountain climber in the hot-dog skier. They must do something harder, tougher, higher each year. **1974** *Hockey News* (Montreal) 22 Feb. 35/1 Critics label him a 'hot dog' and a 'show-off' and several unprintable things.

b. *Surfing slang.* A particular kind of surfboard, somewhat smaller than a 'gun' (*GUN *sb.* 13**). Also *attrib.* or as *adj. phr.*

1963 *Observer* 13 Oct. 15/6 He always owns two boards at any one time, one 'hot dog' board and a 'big gun' (which is a foot or so longer) for riding really big waves. **1965** [see *GUN *sb.* 13**]. **1966** *New Yorker* 31 Dec. 28 He's a hot-dog surfer and he used to be real wigged on Zen. **1967** *Surfabout* III. VII. 38/1 Joey Hamasaki is an excellent surfer and she could possibly beat Joyce in small hot-dog surf. **1970** [see *GUN *sb.* 13**].

So **hot dogger**, a surfer who rides a 'hot dog'; **hot dogging**, the action of riding such a board (see also quot. 1963[2]). Hence (as a back-formation) **hot-dog** *v.*

1961 *Life* 1 Sept. 48 Almost every wave carries a 'hot dogger' doing tricks or sometimes even dressed in outlandish garb. **1962** T. MASTERS *Surfing made Easy* 64 *Hot dogging*, performance surfing, fast turns, quick movements, etc. **1963** *Pix* (Austral.) 28 Sept. 63 Looking good on a little wave is hard. If you can hot dog on two foot waves you are 'king'. **1963** *Observer* 13 Oct. 15/4 From all these movements..has developed the modern style of surfing

known as 'hot dogging': a spectacular, virtuoso style which concentrates on fast slides across the face of the waves, rapid turns, cut-backs, flick-offs and a repertoire of classic riding stances which have evolved in much the same way as the classic passes of the Spanish bullfight. **1966** Hot dogging [see *BOMBORA]. **1966** *Surfer* VII. IV. 39 There were plenty of hot-doggers—or trick riders as we called them then—in Hawaii when I was surfing there during the 1920's.

2. A hot sausage enclosed as a sandwich in a bread roll. orig. *U.S.*

1900 [see sense 1 a above]. **1908** 'O. HENRY' *Gentle Grafter* vii. 97 Sitting on a cake of ice we ate seven hot dogs. **1920** S. LEWIS *Main St.* 304 Lining one block of Main Street were the 'attractions'—two hot-dog stands, [etc.]. **1926** *Spectator* 11 Sept. 373/1 The President of the Brooklyn team asked them to his box and gave them hot dogs. **1928** S. VINES *Humours Unreconciled* ii. 35 If one trained on hot dog, pumpkin pie, graham flour, ice-cream sundaes. **1932** E. WILSON *Devil take Hindmost* i. 1 The hot-dog stands on the motor roads sell gin. **1955** *Times* 3 Aug. 10/5 Tell the miners what Yarmouth has to offer—Tommy Trinder, Charlie Chester, Ronnie Ronalde, 'hot-dogs', bathing beauties, and all. **1957** *London Mag.* Dec. 19 There is a pier with all the usual sideshows, hot dogs, hamburger and ice cream stands. **1970** *New Yorker* 12 Sept. 50/3 She came back with a hot dog... The smell.. was..persuasive.

3. *int.* Expressing delight or strong approval. Cf. *hot diggety* (*dog*) s.v. *HOT *a.* 12 c. *U.S. slang.*

1906 *Dialect Notes* III. II. 141 *Hot dog*,..bravo! **1924** [see *ATTABOY *int.*]. **1934** WODEHOUSE *Right Ho, Jeeves* x. 113 Hot dog! Tell me more. **1935** M. M. ATWATER *Murder in Midsummer* xv. 138 'Hot dog!' cried Wally, his eyes shining. 'That's the old fight!' **1944** T. RATTIGAN *While Sun Shines* I. 202 Hot dog! There's some Scotch. **1965** *Amer. Speech* XL. 85 The ubiquitous *hot dog!*

hotel, *sb.* Add: **1. b.** *Hôtel de Ville* (examples).

1744 M. W. MONTAGU *Let.* 12 June (1966) II. 331 Here [*sc.* in Avignon] are 2 Consuls chose every year..and there is as much struggling for that Dignity in the Hotel de ville as in the Senate. **1789** A. YOUNG *Jrnl.* 30 July in *Trav. France* (1792) I. 149 Two bourgeois musketeers conducted me to the hotel de ville. **1797** *Encycl. Brit.* VIII. 683/1 The *hotel de ville* is what we call a *town-house* or town-hall. **1841** C'TESS BLESSINGTON *Idler in France* I. 4 It was then given to a certain Pierre Boys, in exchange for a piece of ground to erect a new hôtel-de-ville. **1846** DICKENS *Pictures from Italy* 9 Sometimes an hotel de ville, sometimes a guard-house. **1957** J. S. BROMLEY in Wallace-Hadrill & McManners *France: Govt. & Society* 147 Louis XIV made his first formal visit to the Hôtel de Ville, in 1687, to 'forgive' the City [of Paris] for its share in the Fronde. **1973** *Times* 22 Feb. 5/1 M Louis Pradel..dominates the hôtel de ville.

d. hôtel garni, a furnished apartment; an hotel or boarding-house supplying breakfast.

1774 H. WALPOLE *Let.* 7 Sept. (1857) VI. 114, I now live in dread of my biennial gout, and should die of it in an *hôtel garni*. *Ibid.* 28 Sept. 126 Take care of your papers at Paris,.. In the *hôtels garnis* they have double keys to every lock. **1858** GEO. ELIOT *Let.* 17 Apr. (1954) II. 450 He took us to two Hôtels Garnis—places where you get lodgings and attendance and coffee and nothing else. **1896** E. DOWSON *Let.* c. 12 Jan. (1967) 339, I have just risen from a bed of sickness, incomparably uncomfortable, as in my *hotel garni*, one is reduced under such circumstances to living entirely on milk the only nourishment that one can procure. **1968** *Guardian* 28 Dec. 5/5 The cheapest alternative to *le camping*..is the *hotel garni*, providing only bed and breakfast.

e. hôtel particulier, a large privately owned town house or block of flats.

1934 JOYCE *Let.* 13 July (1966) III. 309 Right opposite is a hotel particulier of 2 storeys. **1964** *Time Off in Paris* (Observer) 16 The big Haussman-period blocks of flats (*hotels particuliers*), that are still the main form of housing in central Paris, were built each to contain different social strata, and so they still do today. **1969** N. FREELING *Tsing-Boum* xx. 144 There were still some hôtels particuliers, last bastions of privilege. **1970** *Times* 28 Nov. 12/5 Their *hotel particulier* in Paris contains countless treasures.

4. *hotel-bill, bus, clerk, garage, -keeper, -keeping, lobby, manager, omnibus, porter, prowler, register, room, tout.*

1872 GEO. ELIOT *Middlem.* IV. VII. lxx. 123 Raffles's pockets..were sure to carry..hotel-bills of the places he had stopped in. **1903** JOYCE *Let.* 26 Feb. (1966) II. 31, I was favoured with my hotel-bill on Tuesday. **1973** P. AUDEMARS *Delicate Dust of Death* xii. 175 The 10 per cent surcharge would have been added to the hotel bill. **1878** *Harper's Mag.* Jan. 194 The traveller reaches his stopping-place by hotel 'bus, carriage, or by the democratic street cars. **1923** E. F. WYATT *Invis. Gods* IV. iii. 221 He was marshalling them all toward a hotel bus. **1856** F. L. OLMSTED *Journey Slave States* (1861) V. 333 An easy and gentleman-like employment as that of hotel-clerk and bar-keeper. **1945** L. R. TRYON *Poor Man's Doctor* 185, I suppose the actor is better trained than most of us at inventing stratagems for getting past the hard and watchful eyes of hotel clerks. **1910** *Bradshaw's Railway Guide* Apr. 1101 Best Hotel Garage in London. **1829** *Virginia Lit. Museum* 336/1 The Proctor is required to make a monthly report..of any matters relating to the students or hotel-keepers which may be worthy of being noticed. **1869** W. H. H. MURRAY *Adventures in Wilderness* 35 The 'hotel guides' are paid so much per month by the hotel-keepers. **1879** *Scribner's Monthly* June 242/1 Her husband had left town suddenly on a horse belonging to the hotel-keeper. **1916** JOYCE *Portrait of Artist* (1969) i. 29 He..began to speak with the voice of the hotelkeeper. **1870** 'F. FERN' *Ginger-Snaps* 247 Having then left what, in my opinion, is the perfection of hotel-keeping. **1959** *News Chron.* 19 Aug. 6/2 French small hotel-keeping at its most terrible. **1912** M. NICHOLSON *Hoosier Chron.* 182 A number of idlers in the hotel lobby regarded him with a new interest. **1964** M. MCLUHAN *Understanding Media* (1967) II. xxxi. 341 Shoddy match-wood bars and hotel lobbies. **1910** W. J. LOCKE *Simon* xv. 199 The correctly attired hotel manager in the attitude in which he habitually surveyed the lay-out of the *table d'hôte*. **1972** I. HAMILTON *Thrill Machine* viii. 34 The hotel manager led her and her group towards the lift. **1878** R. L. STEVENSON *Inland Voyage* 37 The driver of the hotel omnibus. **1910** *Bradshaw's Railway Guide* Apr. 1049 The Hotel omnibus meets the principal London trains. **1847** F. A. KEMBLE *Let.* 31 May in *Rec. Later Life* (1882) III. 190, I..despatched one of the hotel porters thither to hunt for her. **1881** LADY C. SCHREIBER *Jrnl.* (1911) II. 343 The officious Hotel porter had told a lot of other people. **1968** *Guardian* 11 Apr. 5/2 Now we are going to set off along the A 10—the hotel porter will direct you to it. **1928** M. C. SHARPE *Chicago May* 286 Hotel Prowlers, sneak thieves. **1962** K. ORVIS *Damned & Destroyed* v. 40 Hotel-prowlers and house-prowlers. **1860** in *Abraham Lincoln Q.* (1949) Mar. 262, I found the name of Mr Bates on the hotel register. **1899** E. WHARTON *Greater Inclination* iv. 99 She must take her place in the hotel register as Mrs. Garnett. **1971** P. M. HUBBARD *High Tide* i. 10 The hotel register still lay open on the desk where I had signed it. **1946** E. O'NEILL *Iceman Cometh* (1947) IV. 202 You know how it is, traveling around. The damned hotel rooms. **1972** R. LOCKRIDGE *Something up Sleeve* i. 13 The jurors had been escorted back to their hotel rooms. **1881** Hotel tout [see TOUT *sb.*[1] 2]. **1922** S. LESLIE *Oppidan* i. 7 He had picked them up at the station like a hotel-tout.

hoteldom (hote·ldəm). [f. HOTEL *sb.* + -DOM.] The realm of hotels, hotels collectively.

1904 *Westm. Gaz.* 1 June 9/2 Then our representative turned his attention to hoteldom. **1927** *Glasgow Herald* 28 Mar. 11/1 There is to be an addition to London hoteldom. **1964** *Sat. Rev.* (U.S.) 21 Mar. 28 The biggest thing in hoteldom lately is non-eating.

hotelier (‖otəlye, (h)ote·li,ēi, hote·liəɪ). Also **hôtelier.** [Fr.] The keeper or proprietor of an hotel.

1905 *Westm. Gaz.* 10 Mar. 12/1 Some enterprising hotelier. **1907** *Ibid.* 7 Sept. 11/2 He grudges the lucky Swiss hôtelier his millions. **1930** *Observer* 20 Apr. 7 That prince of hoteliers, the late M. Ritz. **1956** R. BRADDON *Nancy Wake* i. 6 He was an immaculately dressed *hôtelier*, a director-manager of the Palm Beach Hotel. **1959** F. STARK *Riding to Tigris* 12 In all which countries hotelier schools exist. **1966** *Illustr. London News* 3 Sept. 11 He is on the board of 36 companies, and..can fairly claim to be the biggest hotelier in Europe. **1972** L. P. BACHMANN *Ultimate Act* iv. 33 One has to learn many languages to be a proper hôtelier... I attended hôtelier school in Switzerland.

hot-foot, *adv.* Add: **2.** *attrib.* or as *adj.* Acting with haste or promptitude.

1901 *Spectator* 2 Nov. 631/1 He had to make the most arduous hot-foot journeys across the country. **1904** 'O. HENRY' *Cabbages & Kings* v. 90 He was private secretary of the late hot-foot president of this grocery and fruit stand that they call a country. **1940** C. DAY LEWIS tr. *Georgics of Virgil* I. 28 If you observe the hotfoot sun and the moon's phases, To-morrow will never cheat you.

B. *sb.* **1.** Prompt or rapid action or movement; a quick escape, as in the phrases *to do a hot foot* (or *foots*), *to give* (someone) *the hot foot, to come* (or *go*) *on the hot foot*. *U.S. slang.*

1869 *Congress. Globe* 15 Jan. 389/3 The honorable Senator..admonishes us of the importance of hot-foot in this business, if I may say so, of allowing the testimony to be taken at once. **1897** *Pop. Sci. Monthly* Apr. 833 To run from a police officer is *to do a hot foot*. **1903** 'H. MCHUGH' *Back to Woods* iv. 66 Did somebody give you the hot-foot and make a quick exit? **1905** —— *You can search Me* iii. 55 If somebody ever steals his hammer he'll be doing hotfoots for the handout. **1915** H. L. WILSON *Ruggles of Red Gap* (1917) ii. 27 We'd better report to her before she does a hot-foot over here. **1926** *Flynn's* 16 Jan. 639/1, I know that th'fly was jerry because he gave me th'once over as I was comin' out and I went on th' hoot-foot... I beat it. **1929** C. F. COE *Hooch!* x. 241 You dress an' grab a cab, see? Come down here to Zuroto's on the hot foot.

2. A beating on the soles of the feet; more usually, a practical joke in which a match is put against the victim's foot and then lit. Also *fig.*

1906 A. H. LEWIS *Confessions of Detective* I. iii. 32 I'd become learned in certain mysteries, among others, the 'hot foot'... Given a man, unconscious by..rum,..you can restore him..by smartly beating the soles of his feet. **1934** D. RUNYON in *Hearst's International* Sept. 84/1 The way you give a hot foot is to sneak up behind some guy.. and stick a paper match in his shoe between the sole and the upper along about where his little toe ought to be, and then light the match. **1943** J. MITCHELL *McSorley's Wonderful Saloon* (1946) 18 Drunks reel over from the Bowery and..the kids give them hotfoots with kitchen matches. **1948** MENCKEN *Amer. Lang.* Suppl. I. v. 392 The Army also discourages the old soldiers' game of *hot-foot*, which consists in inserting matches between the soles and uppers of a sleeping comrade's shoes, and then lighting them. **1959** *Encounter* Dec. 30/2 His prose should never be quiet. It must always shock with the hot-foot.

hot-foot, *v. colloq.* (chiefly *U.S.*). [f. prec.] *intr.* To go hot-foot; to make haste. Also with *it*. Hence **hot-foo·ted** *ppl. a.*

1896 ADE *Artie* iii. 22, I hot-foots up to the dance. **1896** [see *DINKY *a.*[1]]. **1903** W. B. YEATS *In Seven Woods* 37 The hot-footed sun, And the cold sliding slippery-footed moon. **1904** *Sun* (N.Y.) 27 Aug. 10 Thousands hot footed to the corner of Broadway. **1906** *Dialect Notes* III. II. 141 *Hotfoot it*, to hasten. **1911** R. D. SAUNDERS *Col. Todhunter* ii. 34 Great Scott and Maria, you must have hot-footed it away from your vittles, young man! **1926** C. HARRIS *Flapper Anne* ii. 92 At the present nothing was further from her thoughts than marrying Sealy, but she craved the triumph of bringing him hotfooted to Milledge. **1928** *Observer* 29 Jan. 22/3 Words of such enthusiasm send one at once hot-footed to the [Crystal] palace to see for oneself. **1934** J. O'HARA *Appointment in Samarra* (1935) vii. 214 When O'Dowd did hear..he would hot-foot out to Quilty and make the sale. **1951** *Manch. Guardian Weekly* 18 Jan. 15 He short-circuits Mr. Kingley's pedestrian approach and makes a bee-line for Koestler's original like the prodigal hot-footing it home. **1970** G. GREER *Female Eunuch* 195 She hotfoots to Mexico.

hot gospeller. [GOSPELLER.] (See GOSPELLER 5 b, where defined.) Also *transf.* Hence **hot gospelling** *vbl. sb.* and *ppl. a.*; **hot-gospel** *v. trans.* and *intr.*

1562, 1874 [see GOSPELLER 5 b]. **1875** TENNYSON *Q. Mary* 271 There are Hot Gospellers even among our guards. **1899** R. WHITEING *No. 5 John St.* viii. 71 That terrible old Hot Gospeller who..screams undying hate of all institutions. **1923** W. S. CHURCHILL *World Crisis 1911–14* ii. 29 Like Henry VIII, he [*sc.* A. J. Balfour] decapitated Papists and burned hot Gospellers on the same day for their respective divergencies..from his..compromise. **1923** J. M. MURRY *Pencillings* 107, I do not think.. I can fairly be accused of advocating hot-gospelling or holy-roaring as the short road to good writing. *Ibid.* 275 He has made me bold, not to say thrasonical. I am become a hot-gospeller, a crusader. Dr. Henry Bradley himself is timid and lukewarm compared to me. **1931** R. LEHMANN *Let. to Sister* 9 Do you remember that frothing hot-gospelling temperance-man?.. He told them how he himself had found salvation when going upstairs late one night—drunk, he manfully admitted. **1933** *Times Lit. Suppl.* 19 Oct. 713/1 The hot-gospeller Spooner marries the thin-lipped Harriet. **1952** R. CAMPBELL *Lorca* i. 7 Every sub-poetaster is hot-gospelling world-messages. **1955** A. L. ROWSE *Expansion Eliz. Eng.* ix. 331 The hot-gospelling of Knox and the spread of Calvinism. **1958** *Spectator* 31 Jan. 124/3 Mr. Dulles's hot-gospelling speech. **1965** G. MCINNES *Road to Gundagai* vi. 110 In the true..hot-gospelling tradition, he ladled out the brimstone. **1968** *Times* 6 Nov. 3/4 The hot-gospeller H. H. Nininger, who preached the value and importance of meteorites. **1970** *Daily Tel.* (Colour Suppl.) 13 Mar. 47/1 He was not hot-gospelling for pop or for the American way of life. **1972** *Daily Tel.* 4 Dec. 11/3 The film..is 'Marjoe', a..deeply cynical documentary on the American weakness for hot-gospelling revivalists.

hot-house, hothouse, *sb.* Add: **3. b.** Also *attrib.*

1838 DICKENS *Nickleby* (1839) xxi. 201 Mrs. Wititterly is of a very excitable nature, very delicate, very fragile; a hothouse plant. **1840** MILL *Let.* 3 Dec. (1910) I. 119 *You* will be interested in the modern German art;..it appears to me a feeble, hot-house product. **1853** C. READE *Peg Woff.* ii. 46 She is so fresh and natural. They are all hot-house plants. **1911** G. B. SHAW *Getting Married* Pref. 156 A hothouse atmosphere of unnatural affection· **1964** *English Studies* XLV. 50 Those delicate, hot-house feelings. **1966** *Listener* 28 July 143/2 Opera will never cease to be a hothouse plant in this country until a wider public appreciates it. **1973** 'E. PETERS' *City of Gold & Shadows* ii. 31 This hot-house community of time-expired settlers and pay-happy leave-men.

6. (Earlier and *attrib.* examples.)

1707 H. SLOANE *Voy. to Jamaica* I. p. ciii, One Prince, a lusty Negro, had been ill of the Yaws..and flux'd for it in one of the Chirurgeons Hot-Houses. **1788** H. MACNEILL *Observ. Treatm. Negroes Jamaica* 8 He [*sc.* a sick slave] is put into a house particularly appropriated to the purpose, (a lazaretto or *hot-house*, as it is generally called). **1790** W. BECKFORD *Descr. Acct. Jamaica* II. 17 This building has a narrow piazza in front, at the end of which is a small apartment for the nurse or hot-house woman. **1827** *Hamel, the Obeah Man* I. xxii. 244 The hothouse-keeper indulged him with a plentiful dose of grog. **1834** R. R. MADDEN *Let.* 4 Apr. in *Twelvemonth's Residence W. Indies* (1835) I. 154 The hot-house doctor is generally a negro disqualified by age or infirmity for labour in the field. He has charge of the medicines.

hot line: see *HOT *a.* 12 c.

Hotnot (hǫ·tnǫt). *S. Afr.* An abbreviated pejorative form of Hottentot.

1913 C. PETTMAN *Africanderisms* 217 *Hotnot*, a common Dutch pronunciation of Hottentot. **1939** J. S. MARAIS *Cape Coloured People* i. 31 The 'colloquial Afrikaans' for Coloured People is not, as Professor Macmillan thinks,..'Hotnots'—at any rate in the western Cape—but 'bruin mense'. 'Hotnot' is a term of contempt. **1949** *Cape Times* 8 July 8 His uncouth remarks about 'Hotnots, Coolies and Kafirs'. **1956** A. SAMPSON *Drum* xv. 201 They joked and laughed about apartheid, and about being mistaken for white men, and being called bushmen, hotnots, coolies, with compulsory wounding laughter. **1966** A. SACHS *Jail Diary* xvi. 133 That was my Grandfather's place..before the British took it away, and he even allowed a few Hotnots to sleep in the house.

hot-pot, hot pot. Add: **2.** (Earlier example.)

1851 *London at Table* I. 21 At the bottom of the table,.. let there be a hot-pot.

3. *Racing slang.* (See quots. and cf. HOT *a.* 8 e.)

1922 *N. & Q.* 23 Sept. 206/2 *Hot pot*, a horse which has been heavily backed. **1945** BAKER *Austral. Lang.* xvii. 299 'Truth' has always devoted special attention to sporting news and, as a consequence, has developed racing jargon considerably... A favourite is a hot-pot.

hot-press, *sb.* Add: Also, a similar apparatus used in making plywood (see next). Also *attrib.* (Further examples.)

1938 *Trans. Amer. Soc. Mech. Engin.* LX. 60/1 The great scarcity of hot presses in plywood plants. *Ibid.* 60/2 In the hot-press operation with resin film, the resin film is cut to dimension and laid between the sheets of veneer. **1943** SIMONDS & ELLIS *Handbk. Plastics* xi. 433 The panels are formed in these hot presses under pressures ranging from 100 to 300 lb. per sq. in. *Ibid.*, At 220° F., hot-press panels are completely bonded in from 3 to 10 minutes' cure in a hot press. **1968** KIRK & OTHMER *Encycl. Chem. Technol.* (ed. 2) XV. 903 By far the largest production [of plywood] is in a hot press in which thermosetting resins are the adhesive basis.

hot-press, *v.* Add: (Further examples.) Also, to press (veneers, etc.) between heated platens for a period in order to bond them together to make plywood.

1932 *Trans. Amer. Soc. Mech. Engin.* LIV (sect. WDI). 1/2 The necessity for hot-pressing is the chief disadvantage [of blood-albumin glues]. **1943** SIMONDS & ELLIS *Handbk. Plastics* xi. 433 Wherever the type of plywood permits it, hot pressing offers quite a few advantages to the manufacturer over cold pressing. **1957** *Times* 23 Dec. 11/2 A decision was taken to introduce hot-pressing in the veneer mills. **1968** J. ARNOLD *Shell Bk. Country Crafts* 214 After the drying, the cloth is 'hot-pressed'.

b. *trans.* To shape under pressure in a heated die or mould.

1913 J. V. WOODWORTH *Drop Forging* viii. 254 The Burdict hot-pressed nut-machine. **1938** H. I. LEWENZ tr. *Brandenburger's Processes & Machinery Plastics Industry* i. 5 Constant improvements..have taken place in the production of paste for hot pressing. **1947** KIRK & OTHMER *Encycl. Chem. Technol.* I. 561 Alloys that can be made in no other way can be produced by compressing and sintering metal powders or by hot pressing loosely compacted slugs. **1967** M. CHANDLER *Ceramics in Mod. World* vi. 173 An alternative technique for forming silicon nitride is to hot-press it.

hot rod. orig. *U.S.* A motor vehicle specially modified to give high power and speed; the driver (also **hot rodder**) of a hot rod. Hence **hot-rod** *v. intr.*, **hot-rodding** *vbl. sb.* Also *attrib.* and *fig.*

1945 *Life* 5 Nov. 87 A 'hot rod'..is an automobile stripped for speed and pepped up for power until it can travel 90 to 125 mph. Most hot rods are roadsters. **1949** *Life* 7 Nov. 123 (*caption*) Policeman holds fistful of licenses confiscated from hot-rodders. *Ibid.*, In Los Angeles and Dallas, where 'hot-rodding' is at its peak, hundreds of youngsters spend their spare time in suicidal games on wheels. **1953** J. N. LEONARD *Flight into Space* 87 All over the United States and in many other parts of the world are groups of enthusiasts who dream of hot-rodding off the tedious earth. **1953** *Time* 21 Sept. 85/1 Every day during the show he thrilled the crowds with the airborne hot-rodding that Britain encourages at Farnborough. **1955** *Sci. News Let.* 1 Oct. 213/1 Teenagers are as accident prone with shotguns as they are with hot rods. **1957** J. KEROUAC *On Road* (1958) 15 A hotrod kid came by with his scarf flying. **1958** J. D. MACDONALD *Executioners* (1959) iv. 52, I don't want her hot-rodding around in the night, going to those drive-ins. **1958** *Woman* 9 Aug. 14/1 Hot-rod road scorchers. **1958** *Observer* 30 Nov. 10/5 Bernstein and his direct knowledge of hot-rodders and what they are after. **1959** *Observer* 25 Jan. 7/4 Mike Hawthorn, champion racing driver and the idol of hot-rods all over the world. **1959** *Sunday Times* 22 Mar. 24/8 My old two-litre hot-rod after its last disastrous tune-up. **1959** *Encounter* Dec. 30/2 Almost every popular magazine nowadays is likely to be written in a hot-rod style which bursts with energy in every sentence. **1962** *Punch* 17 Oct. 559/3 The youth of these islands.. looked on the motor-cycle as their hot rod. **1967** *Listener* 23 Nov. 682/1 The Beach Boys made their reputation.. ostensibly by taking surfing and hotrodding as their subject. **1971** *Daily Tel.* (Colour Suppl.) 3 Sept. 41/1 The first hair freaks I ever saw in California were not hippies, but surfers and hotrodders.

hot-short, *a.* Add: Hence **hot-sho·rtness**, the quality or state of being hot-short.

1890 H. M. HOWE *Metall. of Steel* I. iv. 42/1 Manganese ..by bodily removing sulphur from cast-iron and probably from steel,..prevents hot-shortness, both red and yellow. **1961** S. A. HISCOCK *Lead & Lead Alloys for Cable Sheathing* vii. 221 By subtracting 20° C. from the 'cracking-temperature'..some indication will be obtained of the extrusion temperature which must not be exceeded if 'hot-shortness'..is to be avoided.

hot-shot. Restrict †*Obs.* to senses in Dict. and add: Also **hot shot, hotshot. 1. b.** An important or exceptionally capable person. Also *attrib. colloq.* (orig. *U.S.*).

1933 *Amer. Speech* Oct. 35/2 *Hot shot*, a champion, a leading contender, an excellent fighter. **1943** 'B. HALLIDAY' *Murder wears a Mummer's Mask* xviii. 205 All the important critics were there—the hot shots from the East whose wire stories to their papers could make or break an actress. **1951** J. D. SALINGER *Catcher in Rye* iii. 23 He was telling us all about what a swell guy he was, what a hot-shot and all. **1952** S. KAUFFMANN *Philanderer* (1953) xiv. 234 The only relaxation I would have would be going out with the local hot-shots. **1961** J. HELLER *Catch-22* (1962) xxii. 230 How about getting us a hotel-room if you're such a hotshot? **1973** J. WAINWRIGHT *Pride of Pigs* 103 These hot-shot scientists. They love the limelight.

3. *U.S. slang.* (See quots.)

1925 *Writer's Monthly* May 486/2 *Hot shot*, a fast freight. **1931** 'D. STIFF' *Milk & Honey Route* 207 *Hot shot*, a fast freight or passenger train.

4. *U.S. slang.* (See quots.)

1953 W. BURROUGHS *Junkie* (1972) 157 *Hot Shot*... Poison, usually strychnine, passed to an addict as junk. The peddler sometimes slips a hot shot to an addict because the addict is giving information to the law. **1971** E. E. LANDY *Underground Dict.* 106 *Hot shot*,..1. Injection of poison that user believes to be good drugs, a method of getting rid of police informers. 2. Injection of a drug that is of higher potency than the addict is accustomed to.

5. Used *attrib.* to designate a wind tunnel in which an arc discharge in a pressurized chamber is used to produce a hypersonic pulse of gas in an evacuated test chamber, the two chambers being separated initially by a diaphragm that is ruptured by the discharge.

1959 *Engineering* 13 Feb. 219/2 A wind tunnel, which will test models at the speed of satellite rockets, is expected to be in use in the United States toward the end of this year... Known as a 'hotshot' tunnel, it makes use of a powerful electric arc to pressurise the air. **1971** *Sci. Amer.* Sept. 14/2 The heated gas in the arc chamber is the working gas of a hotshot tunnel with a working section of 2·5 meters and a Mach number of about 20.

hot spot. Also **hot-spot. I. 1.** *Physiol.* One of numerous small areas on the skin that are specially sensitive to heat.

1888 W. STIRLING tr. *Landois's Text-bk. Human Physiol.* (ed. 3) xiv. 836 The chain of the 'cold-spots' usually does not coincide with those of the 'hot-spots'. **1911** *Encycl. Brit.* XXVII. 97/1 There are points [on the skin], stimulated by addition of heat, hot spots, while others are stimulated by withdrawal of heat, cold spots. **1926** S. WRIGHT *Applied Physiol.* I. 21 If all the 'hot' and 'cold' spots are marked out, the areas of skin between them are found to be insensitive to punctate thermal stimuli.

II. A spot that is hot (*lit.* and *fig.*). **2.** [SPOT *sb.*[1] 10.] A small area in a surface or body that is at a higher temperature than its surroundings.

1919 G. KAPP *Princ. Electr. Engin.* II. vi. 143 The average internal temperature of a winding can be more accurately deduced from a resistance test, whilst for the discovery of so called 'hot spots' thermo-couples must be used. **1936** D. M. ROBINSON *Dielectric Phenomena in High Voltage Cables* ii. 16 A cable subjected to excess voltage may develop local hot spots, and..frequently fails at or near the hottest of these points. **1947** *Sci. News* IV. 150 With a metal sliding on glass with a load of a few pounds, visible hot spots (temp. 520–570° C.) can be seen when the sliding speed is as low as one or two feet per second. **1958** H. ETHERINGTON *Nuclear Engin. Handbk.* xii. 17 Hot-spot effects usually require a correction in the calculation of maximum temperature. **1959** H. F. TAYLOR et al. *Foundry Engin.* x. 277 Under normal conditions of cooling, metal at the center of the *d* region is a hot spot, the last to solidify. **1970** *Times* 30 Oct. 23/2 A small.. infra-red television camera..for detecting the 'hot spots' in overhead power lines and substations which can lead to serious breakdowns. **1972** *Physics Bull.* May 284/2 This effect has been used to detect hot spots and hence structural flaws in systems as diverse as integrated circuits and the human body.

3. [HOT *a.* 7 b, SPOT *sb.*[1] 8.] **a.** A night-club or other place of lively public entertainment.

1931 D. RUNYON *Guys & Dolls* (1932) iii. 53 There are very seldom any customers in Good Time Charley's until along about five o'clock in the morning..and then it is sometimes a very hot spot indeed. **1937** J. WEIDMAN *I can get it for you Wholesale* xxv. 227 The line in Winchell's column: Martha Mills..is doing the hot spots with what prominent young manufacturer of feminine haberdashery? **1940** *Time* 15 Apr. 98/2 Eschewing Hollywood hotspots, they prefer at-homes with the quieter younger set. **1954** G. SMITH *Flaw in Crystal* iv. 39 The Wind in the Willows [a roadhouse] had been a noted hot-spot when I was a schoolboy. **1954** *Manch. Guardian Weekly* 26 Aug. 7/1 Intellectuals..went on a kind of jazz-slumming in the Harlem hot spots.

b. A place of danger; *spec.* a place where war is being actively engaged in or experienced.

1941 *Illustr. Lond. News* CXCIX. 200 (*caption*) Miss Cowles, an American journalist, whose pre-war assignments took her to most of the 'hot-spots' of Europe [*sc.* Prague, Berlin, Warsaw, etc.]. **1966** *Economist* 19 Feb. 711/2 The Administration wanted to distinguish financially between men who had been in 'hot spots' and those who had only served in non-combat zones. **1973** G. BEARE *Snake on Grave* xii. 62 You're putting yourself on the hot-spot, Sammy.

4. Specific technical applications in the literal sense.

a. In an internal combustion engine, a portion of the manifold or combustion chamber that is heated in order to facilitate vaporization of the liquid fuel; also, a region of overheating that tends to cause pre-ignition. **b.** *Astr.* A region in the sun's corona (generally associated with a solar flare) that is temporarily at a higher temperature than normal and is emitting a characteristic spectrum of radiation. **c.** *Electronics.* In a mercury-arc rectifier with a pool cathode, that part of the pool of mercury with which the arc is in contact and from which electrons are emitted.

a. 1924 *Motor Manual* (ed. 25) ii. 32 As an additional means towards obtaining efficient carburation a 'hot spot' arrangement is provided on a number of cars. **1929** *Times* 2 Nov. 4/7 The inlet manifold is jointed to the exhaust centrally, and thus a hot-spot is provided. **1934** *Jrnl. R. Aeronaut. Soc.* XXXVIII. 960 Thus making absolutely sure of high compression without hot spots acting as sparks in the combustion chamber. **1959** *Chambers's Encycl.* VII. 639/1 [In the petrol engine] pre-ignition is usually caused by an unsuitable plug or some local hot-spot, e.g. the exhaust valve head. **1968** *Practical Motorist* Dec. 459/1 Some hot spots are fitted with a thermostatically controlled flap which diverts the mixture away from the hot spot once the engine is running at normal temperature.

b. 1936 *Harvard Coll. Observatory Circ.* No. 410. 22 This region [of the chromosphere] appears to be one of abnormal excitation, possibly caused by a 'hot spot' near the limb of the sun at the time of the eclipse. **1958** *Sci. Amer.* Aug. 41/2 When the sun is observed with a radio telescope tuned to 10 centimeters, the hot spots in its atmosphere stand out brilliantly. **1966** *McGraw-Hill Encycl. Sci. & Technol.* XIII. 282/2 Coronal hot spots, indicated by emission of the yellow line of Ca XV at 5694 A above the photosphere by some 30,000 km, have been found in all spectrographic observations of the corona over a limb flare.

c. 1937 W. G. DOW *Fund. Engin. Electronics* xix. 426 The cathode 'hot spots' of mercury-pool-type mercury vapor rectifiers dodge about erratically on the mercury surface. **1971** B. SCHARF *Engin. & its Lang.* xx. 277 Where the arc terminates on the surface of the mercury a 'hot spot' occurs which forms the source of electronic emission.

5. Technical senses representing transferred senses either of *hot* or of the phr. as a whole.

a. In an ingot or casting (see quot. 1908). **b.** A particularly active part of a forest fire; so **hot-spotting** *vbl. sb.* (see quot. 1953). **c.** *Theatr., Photogr.*, etc. An area that is markedly brighter than its surroundings. **d.** *Nuclear Sci.* An area where the radiation level is much higher than in the surroundings; a local concentration of radioactivity. **e.** *Genetics.* A part of a gene especially liable to undergo mutation.

a. 1908 B. STOUGHTON *Metall. Iron & Steel* xii. 349 These localities, where the segregation is high, and which are known, when very bad, as 'hot spots', are sometimes porous or surrounded by porous parts of the casting. **1938** ROSENHOLTZ & OESTERLE *Elem. Ferrous Metal.* ii, Hot spots are irregularities occasioned by the uneven distribution of the coarse and fine parts of the charge in such a way that the coarse parts are concentrated near the furnace walls.

b. 1938 *Fire Control Notes* Oct. 26 This work includes such jobs as..burning out material between the line and the fire edge, and reduction of hot spots. **1940** *Ibid.* July 141 It is well for the scout to carry a pulaski or light ax for blazing or hot-spotting. **1953** *Brit. Commonw. Forest Terminol.* I. 77 *Hot-spotting*, checking the spread of fire on hot spots alone or at salient points, as an emergency measure employed in advance of control-line construction.

c. 1952 GRANVILLE *Dict. Theatr. Terms* 99 *Hot spot*, a bright spot in an area of uneven lighting. **1958** *New Scientist* 25 Dec. 1569/3 Some areas on the document will be reproduced as dark grey.., while on others, known colloquially as 'hot spots', there will be such a powerful reflection of light that any markings on such areas may be completely blotted out. **1971** L. B. HAPPÉ *Basic Motion Pict. Technol.* vii. 218 A brighter central area, or hot spot, is particularly obvious when a short focal length lens is used on a camera and a long focal length on the projector.

d. 1955 *Bull. Atomic Sci.* Feb. 46/2 One would expect 'hot spots' even far downwind but since the history of the bomb cloud would already be several hours 'old' by then, there would be a corresponding drop in intensity. **1955** *Sci. Amer.* Aug. 37/1 A particularly malignant feature of some of the radioisotopes is their tendency to concentrate in 'hot spots' instead of distributing themselves evenly through the bone or other tissue they invade. **1962** *Listener* 19 July 104/2 The concentration of radioactive substances into 'hot spots' may well be exaggerated in the rapidly dividing cells of the foetus.

e. 1958 BENZER & FREESE in *Proc. Nat. Acad. Sci.* XLIV. 115 A striking feature of the map is the existence of certain 'hot spots', where mutations recur with high probability. **1964** W. HAYES *Genetics of Bacteria & their Viruses* viii. 171 Out of 1,612 spontaneous mutations ..more than 500 occur at a single site or 'hot spot' in the B cistron. **1967** E. STEINER tr. *Esser & Kuenen's Genetics of Fungi* v. 300 A hot spot probably consists of a single base pair, at least one member of which is particularly sensitive to a specific mutagen.

hot stuff. a. A person or thing out of the ordinary run, something of surpassing excellence or merit; sometimes with implication of moral censure; also, specif., a woman reputed to be highly sexed. Also *attrib.*, esp. (i) sexually explicit, (ii) extremely capable or efficient. *colloq.* (orig. *U.S.*).

1889 *Kansas City* (Missouri) *Times & Star* 14 Nov., 'Miss Middleton's Lover.' Were there room for two words in that last line, 'Hot Stuff' might be appropriate. **1900** *Dialect Notes* II. 42 Hot-stuff. 1. A person of good quality; often ironical. 2. A person having merit. **1905** WODEHOUSE *Head of Kay's* 252 Kay's are hot stuff, Jimmy. **1908** *Varsity Vices* May 5/1 Gad, though, but she's tremendously hot stuff, the little devil. Stood her a bust at the Zoo. **1909** WODEHOUSE *Mike* xvii. 101 The book was obviously the last word in hot stuff. **1911** F. SWINNERTON *Casement* i. 41, I say, Trevell..you had any dealings with Jimpton? Eh? He's hot stuff..what! **1912** C. MACKENZIE *Carnival* x. 111 I'm not going to have fellows say my sister's hot stuff. **1912** *Strand Mag.* Jan. 22/2 Clarence in goal was the nearest approach to an indiarubber acrobat.. to be seen off the music-hall stage. He was, in brief, hot stuff. **1915** H. WILSON *Diary* 9 Sept. (1927) I. 249 Here is Sarrail..to urge a plan about which he knows nothing. And all because he is a Radical-Socialist. Hot stuff. **1917** A. WAUGH *Loom of Youth* II. i. 111 This side [*sc.* a Rugby football team] was certainly 'pretty hot stuff'. **1923** H. G. WELLS *Men like Gods* I. vi. 102 'Raced us from Hounslow,' said Mr. Burleigh's driver. 'Real hot stuff.' **1928** *Punch* 21 Mar. 328/1 His father had

influence.., being a frightfully hot-stuff surgeon. **1931** *Amer. Speech* Feb. 204 *Hot stuff*, new, up-to-date material or new incidents; approved as being startling, or the 'latest'. **1931** W. Deeping *Road* viii. 86 I'm getting my new M.-B. next week. Hot stuff. She'll do eighty. **1936** E. M. Forster *Abinger Harvest* 43 During the interval we discussed, not whether the Scallies were good, but whether they were better or worse than the Wags. They were less hot stuff, that was admitted on all sides. **1940** Graves & Hodge *Long Week-End* iv. 52 Elinor Glyn was the reigning queen of popular love literature and considered 'very hot stuff'. **1944** M. Paneth *Branch Street* 64 The men say of her, 'Joan is hot stuff.' **1965** D. Lodge *Brit. Mus. is falling Down* vii. 125 A sort of novel,..the story of his affair with Mother, with just the names changed. It's hot stuff, as we used to say at school. **1965** H. Porter *Cats of Venice* 91 Singapore boy hot stuff, hot stuff!

b. *slang.* Stolen goods. Cf. Stuff *sb.*[1] 10 b.

1924 G. C. Henderson *Keys to Crookdom* ix. 117 Pawnshops and second-hand stores establish a reputation for handling 'hot stuff' and there are very few such establishments that will refuse to buy from a known thief. **1962** K. Orvis *Damned & Destroyed* vii. 51 So you're handling a bit of hot stuff as well as joy-popping?

So **hot-stuff** *v. trans.* (*Army slang*), to scrounge, steal; **hot-stuffed** *ppl. a.*; **hot-stuffer**, a scrounger.

1914 H. Rosher *In R.N.A.S.* (1916) 36, I at once hot-stuffed one of his inlet valves and set the men to work changing it. **1929** *Papers Mich. Acad. Sci., Arts & Lett.* X. 300/1 *Hot-stuffed*, stolen. *Ibid.*, *Hot-stuffer*, a thief. **1950** E. Partridge *Here, There & Everywhere* 81 *Hotstuff*, to appropriate illicitly, to steal.

hotsy-totsy (hǫ·tsi,tǫ·tsi), *a. slang* (orig. *U.S.*). ['Coined *c* 1926 by Billie De Beck, Amer. cartoonist' (Webster).] Comfortable, satisfactory, just right. Hence ho:tsy-to·tsiness.

1926 B. Reynolds *Cocktail Continentale* ii. 29 And they sure can fix up a rip-snotin', raring, tearing, hotsy-totsy time, honey boy. **1926** Dunning & Abbott *Broadway* xx. 178 They complimented each other in the language of the night clubs. 'Everything is hotsy-totsy!' whooped the loud Ruby. **1927** Wodehouse *Small Bachelor* vi. 95 It seemed to me that I was absolutely hotsy-totsy. **1935** —— *Luck of Bodkins* xxii. 282 And a fat chance..there is of any hotsy-totsiness resulting from anything Ambrose can do. **1940** N. Marsh *Surfeit of Lampreys* (1941) xviii. 281 Daddy's all hotsy-totsy now as regards money. **1944** H. Croome *You've gone Astray* xxi. 214 Now she thinks another man would be all hotsy totsy. **1952** [see *babe 3 b]. **1958** L. A. G. Strong *Treason in Egg* ix. 165 All is hotsy-totsy. **1964** W. Markfield *To Early Grave* (1965) iv. 77 He became a big-time hotsy-totsy critic. **1973** J. Mann *Only Security* xii. 162 What the law allows me, is mine... So that's all hotsy totsy.

Hottentot. 1. Substitute for def.: One of the two sub-races of the Khoisanid race (the other being the Sanids or Bushmen), characterized by short stature, yellow-brown skin colour, and tightly curled hair. They are of mixed Bushman-Hamite descent with some Bantu admixture, and are now found principally in South-West Africa. Also, a member of this race. (Add further examples.)

1924 A. C. Haddon *Races of Man* (ed. 2) 41 An early migration of Hamites mixed with this population [*sc.* Bushmen] and gave cattle and elements of their language to the mixed people who in South Africa are known as Hottentots. **1930** I. Schapera *Khoisan Peoples of S. Africa* iii. x. 239 There is little information as to the existence of food taboos among the Hottentots in more recent times. **1965** H. B. Isherwood *Racial Contours* viii. 308 Opinion seems to be gaining ground that the Bushman and the Hottentot bear so many features indicating a divergent evolutionary history that they should be classed as a separate race altogether and not grouped under the heading of Negroid. The title provisionally proposed is Khoisanoid, based on the name by which these people know themselves. **1970** P. Oliver *Savannah Syncopators* 31 Alan P. Merriam has identified as distinct musical regions those of the Hottentot-Bushman. **1974** J. R. Baker *Race* xvii. 318 The Hottentots, Korana, and Bushmen are not to be regarded as people adapted by natural selection to a desert life.

b. (This derogatory sense, which was based on a failure to understand an alien culture, appears now to be very rare.)

c. (In full *Hottentot fish*.) A South African marine food fish of the genus *Pachymetopon*, esp. *P. blochii*.

1798 S. H. Wilcocke tr. *Stavorinus' Voy. E. Indies* I. 560 The Hottentot-fish, which is like a sea-bream. **1838** J. E. Alexander *Exped. Disc. Int. Afr.* I. 88 The delicious Roman fish, Hottentot. **1921** *Ann. S. Afr. Mus.* XXI. 721 The Hottentot is one of the commonest Cape fishes. **1949** J. L. B. Smith *Sea Fishes S. Afr.* 276 The Hottentot slipped away with the next wave.

d. The Khoisan language spoken by the Hottentots.

1884 [see Click *sb.*[1] 5]. **1910** *Encycl. Brit.* IV. 871/2 Their language..has in common with Hottentot..the peculiar sounds known as 'clicks'. **1921** E. Sapir *Lang.* iii. 55 Certain languages, like the South African Hottentot and Bushman, have also a number of inspiratory sounds. **1953** J. B. Carroll *Study of Language* ii. 57 He..doubts very much the validity of certain early theories that such languages..as Bantu and Hottentot are in any way related to the Semitic-Hamitic group. **1972** *Stand. Encycl. S. Afr.* V. 605/1 Afrikaans and South African English have taken over words from Hottentot, such as *buchu, dagga, kanna*.

2. *attrib.* or as *adj.* (Further examples.)

1797 *Encycl. Brit.* VIII. 684/2 The Hottentot language is..said to be a composition of the most strange and disagreeable sounds. *Ibid.* 685/1 A general opinion has prevailed that the Hottentot women have a kind of natural vail which covers the female parts. *Ibid.* 687/2 In a craal, or Hottentot village, the huts are most commonly disposed in a circle. **1811** in W. J. Burchell *Trav. S. Afr.* (1822) I. xv. 371 The most dangerous malady is a kind of cancerous sore or ulcer, called in the colony the *Hottentots Zeer* (Hottentot Sore). **1828** J. Philip *Res. S. Afr.* I. p. xviii, The missionaries..were called 'Hottentot predicants' (ministers), by way of contempt. **1924** *Internat. Jrnl. Psycho-Anal.* V. 41 It might perhaps be not without significance that three of the five patients informed me of their own accord that they possessed 'Hottentot nymphae'. **1933** I. Schapera *Early Cape Hottentots* p. xii, In Hottentot mythology ||Gaunab figured as a malevolent chief. **1965** H. B. Isherwood *Racial Contours* viii. 308 Associated with the Naman and talking their language are the primitive Bergdama or Hankhoin people, who are virtually under Hottentot tribal rule. **1974** J. R. Baker *Race* vi. 97 When Van Riebeck and his little company of emigrants from the Netherlands landed at Table Bay in 1652, they were met by Hottentot herdsmen.

3. Hottentot apron (see *apron *sb.* 5 c); **Hottentot('s) bean (tree)** *S. Afr.*, a shrub or tree of the genus *Schotia*, esp. *S. latifolia*, or its fruit; **Hottentot fish** (see sense 1 c above); **Hottentot('s) god** *S. Afr.*, a praying mantis, formerly worshipped by the Hottentots; **Hottentot('s) tea** (examples).

1801 J. Barrow *Acct. Trav. S. Afr.* I. 189 Not so with the Hottentot bean... This plant is the African *Lignum vitae*. **1833** S. Kay *Trav. Caffraria* 106 The Hottentot's bean tree. **1921** T. R. Sim *Native Timbers S. Afr.* 192 Hottentots Bean Tree. *Schotia*, sps. **1965** F. von Breitenbach *Indigenous Trees S. Afr.* II. 327 *Schotia afra*... Hottentot's Bean... The roasted beans are eaten by some tribes. **1785** G. Forster tr. *Sparrman's Voy. Cape G. Hope* I. 211 A genus of insects (the *mantis*) called by the colonists the *Hottentot's god*. **1957** W. Tapson *Old Timer* i. 10 Flyingants and glowworms and dragonflies and hottentot-gods. **1961** L. van der Post *Heart of Hunter* xii. 161 When they noticed the reverence in which the Mantis was held by some of the aborigines of the Cape, they inaccurately called him the Hottentot's God. **1962** *Cape Times Week-end Mag.* 10/1, I like Hottentot Gods, bloodthirsty little savages as they may be. **1850** L. Pappe *Florae Capensis Medicae Prodromus* 17 *Helichrysum serpyllifolium*..goes by the name of *Hottentot's tea*,..and is much liked by the coloured people, who infuse it as tea. **1972** *Stand. Encycl. S. Afr.* V. 611/1 Hottentot tea... *Helichrysum orbiculare* = *H. serpyllifolium*... Another species, which is also called Hottentot-tea, is *H. nudifolium*.

hottie, hotty (hǫ·ti), *sb. colloq.* [f. Hot *a.* + -y[6].] A hot-water bottle.

1947 H. Walsh *Fourth Point of Star* xx. 102, I am going to..rub my feet with meth., then get into bed with a hotty. **1956** D. M. Davin *Sullen Bell* vi. 40 Get a hotty for yourself. **1960** V. Anderson *Daughters of Divinity* vi. 51 And show her where to fill her hotty? **1967** R. Harris *All my Enemies* xiii. 117 You look rotten, Jenny. At least have a hottie to clutch.

hot water. Add: **1.** *attrib.* (Further examples.)

1855 Mrs. Gaskell *Lizzie Leigh* 163 Pack up for each his portion of the dainty dish, and send it separately, in hot-water trays. **1872** *Young Englishwoman* Nov. 610/2 Cover for a hot-water tin. **1877** E. S. Dallas *Kettner's Bk. of Table* 332 Hot-water paste for raised pies. **1895** Kipling *Day's Work* (1898) 373 He turned to explore the hot-water dishes on the sideboard. **1904** Goodchild & Tweney *Technol. & Sci. Dict.* 291/1 *Hot water system*, a method of warming effected by means of hot water or steam circulating in a system of closed pipes. **1921** *Daily Colonist* (Victoria, B.C.) 24 Mar. 3/1 Attractive modern home, hot water heating, lot 90 × 180, three bedrooms, [etc.] **1926** W. de la Mare *Connoisseur* 48 In spite of the hot-water-fountain on the counter it was..cooler in here. **1926** S. T. Warner *Lolly Willowes* i. 46 The maid..laid the folded towel across the hot-water can. **1932** *Edinburgh Bk. Plain Cookery Recipes* 149 Hot-Water Crust. Used for Savoury Dishes. **1950** *N.Z. Jrnl. Agric.* Dec. 575/1 In almost all houses the hot-water cupboard was used for airing clothes. **1956** G. Taylor *Silver* ix. 191 Hot-water jugs were set on classical tripod legs with a spirit lamp between. **1970** Simon & Howe *Dict. Gastron.* 290/2 Hot-water crust is a stiff dough moulded to make a filling of meat or game.

b. Special comb.: **hot-water bottle**, a receptacle made of rubber, metal, or other material that may be filled with hot water and used for warming a bed, or for applying local heat to the body; **hot-water pipe** usu. *pl.*, the pipe(s) in a water-heating system.

1895 *Montgomery Ward Catal.* 107/1 Challenge Hot Water Bottles, pure rubber. **1897** [in Dict., sense 1 *attrib.*]. **1900** J. Vaizey *About Peggy Saville* xxv. 229 I'd have a fire and an india-rubber hot-water bottle, and I'd lie and sleep. **1926–7** *Army & Navy Stores Catal.* 151/1 Aluminium hot water bottles. Round 9 in. **1932** D. C. Minter *Mod. Needlecraft* 248/1 Hot-water bottle cover..cut to fit. **1946** G. Mikes *How to be an Alien* 25 Continental people have sex life; the English have hot-water bottles. **1972** S. Hynes *Edwardian Occasions* 169 The narrative is slacker and more trivial, begins to take note of the hot-water bottle and the nine o'clock news. **1842** *Trans. Hort. Soc.* II. 435 All the experience obtained at the Garden goes to demonstrate the great inferiority of flues to hot water pipes as a mode of heating. **1852** Dickens *Bleak Ho.* (1853) xxviii. 274 The hot-water pipes that trail themselves all over the house..fail to supply the fires' deficiencies. **1912** Beerbohm *Christmas Garland* 26 The faint yet heavy fragrance exhaled from the hot-water pipes. **1973** G. Butler *Coffin for Pandora* v. 106 The luxurious ways of Sarsen House kept all the rooms warm with hot-water pipes.

hot-work, *v.* [f. *hot *a.* 12 d + Work *v.* 12 e.] *trans.* To work (metal), e.g. by rolling, forging, etc., while it is hot and above the temperature at which recrystallization takes place. Usually in vbl. sb. **hot working.**

1896 H. H. Campbell *Manuf. Structural Steel* xiv. 192 (*heading*) Influence of hot working on steel. **1916** D. K. Bullens *Steel & its Heat Treatment* ii. 38 Steel which has been hot-worked down to the A_{r1} point will show a finer grain. **1932** E. Gregory *Metall.* ii. 59 The modification of structure which is brought about by hot-working is of greater importance. **1967** A. H. Cottrell *Introd. Metall.* xviii. 313 This is one of the reasons for hot working such metals. *Ibid.* xxi. 405 This is the basis of industrial hot working processes in which metal ingots or billets are given massive deformations by comparatively small applied stresses.

Also **hot work** *sb.*, hot working.

1905 J. W. Mellor *Crystall. Iron & Steel* 77 Hot work has no direct action upon the structure of the steel. **1928** H. M. Boylston *Introd. Metall. Iron & Steel* xiii. 369 All mechanical treatment may be divided into two classes, namely, hot work and cold work. **1961** J. N. Anderson *Appl. Dental Materials* (ed. 2) v. 44 Hot work, on the other hand, involves simultaneous deformation and recrystallization.

houbara (hubā·rā). Also **hobara, hubara, oubara, ubara.** [mod.L. (C. L. J. L. Bonaparte *Saggio d'una Distribuzione Metodica degli Animali Vertebrati* (1832) 84), f. Arab. *hubārī* bustard.] A bustard, *Chlamydotis undulata*, found in North Africa and Asia as far east as India and Persia, and formerly included in a genus *Houbara*.

1827 J. Malcolm *Sk. Persia* I. 56 The beautiful speckled Hubara, with his head erect and wings outspread. **1836** *Penny Cycl.* VI. 59/2 Arabs are accustomed to compare the eyes of their most beautiful women to those of the *Oubara*. **1876** *Encycl. Brit.* IV. 579/1 Two species, known indifferently by the name of Houbara (derived from the Arabic), frequent the more southern portions of the [Palæarctic] Region. **1883** *List Animals* (Zool. Soc.) (ed. 8) 517 *Houbara Bustard*. **1905** J. I. S. Whitaker *Birds Tunisia* II. 285 North of the Mediterranean the Houbara is of merely accidental occurrence, but it inhabits North-east Africa. **1925** *Blackw. Mag.* Mar. 339/1 The hobara, or lesser bustard. **1963** *Times* 24 May 13/7 The great Houbara bustard yielded, as evidence of its continued presence..only a single stray feather in one area and a couple of sucked eggs.

Houdan (hū·dăn). Name of a town in the department of Seine-et-Oise, France, used to designate a breed of domestic fowl characterized by black and white plumage, a heavy crest, five toes on each foot, and by its prolific laying.

1871 W. M. Lewis *People's Pract. Poultry Bk.* 23 The Brahma, Cochin, Leghorn, Poland, and Houdan stand relatively in the position here named [as egg-layers]. **1873** C. M. Yonge *Pillars of House* I. ii. 28, I am hardly prepared to say whether it is a Hamburg or a Houdan, or a more unambitious Dorking. **1883** [see *Crèvecœur]. **1902** *Encycl. Brit.* XXXI. 876/2 A race originated in France by crossing Houdans with Dorkings and Light Brahmas, and known as the Faverolles. **1925** *Glasgow Herald* 16 Jan. 6 During the war I had a houdan who ruled my hen run. **1960** *British Poultry Standards* (ed. 2) 72 Introduced into England in 1850, the Houdan is one of the oldest French breeds.

Houdini (hūdī·ni). The professional name (Harry *Houdini*) of an American escapologist, Erich Weiss (1874–1926), used to denote an ingenious escape, or a person who embodies the characteristics of Houdini. Also *attrib.* Hence (occas.) as *v. intr.*, to escape.

1923 *N.Y. Times* 9 Sept. vii. 2/1 *Houdini*, to get out of something, to escape. **1923** J. E. Baxter *Locker Room Ballads* 20 With a dozen balls in play at once And each of them doing Houdini stunts. **1930** J. Fait *Big House* 120 Don't do no Houdini, or we'll lay you out. **1946** Mezzrow & Wolfe *Really Blues* 373/1 *Do a Houdini*, disappear. **1958** [see *escapologist]. **1962** L. Deighton *Ipcress File* xxv. 164 There was no chance of a 'Houdini' through the boltwork. **1967** L. J. Brown *Cat who ate Danish Modern* xiii. 117, I have to buckle the harness good and tight or he'll wiggle free... That cat's a Houdini. **1971** *Guardian* 24 Aug. 7/4 Houdini act saved injured climber in air crash.

houghmagandy (hǫχmagæ·ndi). Chiefly *Sc.* (now *rare*). Also **hochmagandy, hough-magandie.** [Fanciful formation, perh. f. Hough *sb.* + Canty *a.*] Fornication.

a **1700** J. Maidment *New Bk. Old Ballads* (1885) 11 And well I wot he kens the gate To play at hough-magandy. **1785** Burns *Holy Fair* in *Poems & Songs* (1968) I. 137 An' monie jobs that day begin, May end in *Houghmagandie*. **1805** R. Tannahill *Poems* (1876) 44 The priest convenes his scandal court, Tae ken what houghmagandie sport Has been gaun on within the

parish. **1962** V. NABOKOV *Pale Fire* 212 She would have preferred him to have gone through a bit of wholesome houghmagandy with the wench.

houhere (hau·hīəri). *N.Z.* [Maori, f. *hou* to bind together + *here* tie.] A small tree of the native genus *Hoheria*, esp. *H. populnea*; also called lacebark or ribbonwood.

1879 J. HECTOR *Handbk. N.Z.* 93 Houhere, ribbonwood of Dunedin. **1906** T. F. CHEESEMAN *Man. N.Z. Flora* 79 The Maoris apply the names *hoihere* or *houhere* to varieties *a* and *b* indifferently; the European settlers usually call all the forms 'ribbon-wood' or 'lacebark', names which are, unfortunately, also used for *Plagianthus betulinus*. **1946** *Jrnl. Polynesian Soc.* LV. 149 *Houhere*, a tree (*Hoheria populnea*), ribbonwood, lacebark, thousand-jacket. One of the three or four deciduous Maori trees. **1968** *Landfall* XXII. 255 White edge of the sea White as the flower Of lace-bark, Te houhere, White edge of the sea Eating the land.

hound, *sb.*[1] Add: **4. e.** Used with a preceding substantive to designate a person who has a particular enthusiasm for, or interest in, the object or activity specified; esp. in ***news-hound*. *colloq.* (orig. *U.S.*).

1918 *Hatchet* 7 Apr., 'Got what all figured out,' queried the news hound eagerly. **1926** *Amer. Speech* II. 45 *Comma hound*, applied to teachers of English composition. **1928** L. NORTH *Parasites* 270 Much was made by the Zimski publicity hounds of this one hundred-per-cent Americanism of the little [film] star. **1968** *Word Study* Dec. 2/2 The enthusiast is a *bug* or a *hound*, as in *radio bug* or *hi-fi hound*. Closely related to this use of *hound* is its use as 'one who frequents', as in *tavern hound*. **1973** *Sat. Rev. Soc.* (U.S.) May 65/3 A real fun guy,..a super-duper party hound.

6. Substitute for def.: In north-eastern Canada: the old squaw or long-tailed duck, *Clangula hyemalis*. (Further examples.)

1779 G. CARTWRIGHT *Jrnl.* 19 May (1792) II. 440 There were several hounds and gulls, with some pigeons and black-divers among them. **1861** L. DE BOILIEU *Recoll. Labrador Life* 160 The bird called the Hound—a graceful fowl, rather larger than a teal—is very abundant. **1959** W. L. MCATEE *Folk-Names Canad. Birds* (ed. 2) 14 Old Squaw [is also called] hound (the Chorus of sound from a number of these birds suggests the baying of a pack of hounds).

7. a. *hound-dog, -pup.*

1649 *Early Rec. Dedham, Mass.* (1892) III. 162 That care can be taken that the young hound doges be in time taught to hunt. **1911** R. D. SAUNDERS *Col. Todhunter* ii. 24 I'm as hungry as a young hound-dog this very minute. **1949** *Chicago Daily News* 6 July 14/3 He's got about nine houn' dawgs. **1857** F. L. OLMSTED *Journey Texas* (1861) 52 The child..five miles from a neighbor;..[with] hound-pups and negroes for playmates. **1878** J. H. BEADLE *Western Wilds* xxviii. 439 What he wouldn't steal, a hound pup wouldn't pull out of a tan-yard. **1932** KIPLING *Limits & Renewals* 293 Though well-meaning as a hound-pup..her face and figure were against her.

b. hound-work, the work done by the hounds in hunting.

1928 *Isis* (Oxf.) 14 Nov., Some very pretty houndwork now ensued. **1932** *Morning Post* 19 Nov. 14/4 (*heading*) Pytchley Houndwork. **1971** *Country Life* 7 Oct. 897/2 The fascination of good hound-work.

hound, *sb.*[2] **2.** *U.S.* (Earlier examples.)

1847 *Rep. U.S. Comm. Patents 1846* 264 The placing on the rear ends of the extended hounds..the adjustable sway bar. **1854** BARTLETT *Pers. Narr. Explor. Texas* II. xl. 456 Mr. Flotte's large carriage got mired; and in the struggle to extricate, the tongue and hounds were broken.

hound, *v.* Add: **2.** Also with *out*, to drive away.

1922 JOYCE *Ulysses* 628 Spain decayed when the Inquisition hounded the jews out. **1930** G. B. SHAW *Apple Cart* I. 41 If I attempt to fight them I shall be hounded out of public life. **1945** E. WAUGH *Brideshead Revisited* ii. 50 He daren't show his great purple face anywhere. He is the last, historic, authentic case of someone being hounded out of society.

hou·ndstooth. Also hound's tooth, hound's-tooth, hounds' tooth, houndtooth. [f. HOUND *sb.*[1] + TOOTH *sb.*] A small irregular design of broken check. Also, a fabric of this design; a suit, coat, etc., of such fabric.

1936 *New Yorker* 7 Mar. 44/2 (Advt.), We carry sports jackets in checks, plaids, and hound's tooth patterns. **1951** J. D. SALINGER *Catcher in Rye* ii. 32 If you're not going out any place special, how 'bout lending me your hound's tooth jacket? *Ibid.*, No kidding, you gonna use your hound's tooth to-night, or not? **1957** *Observer* 1 Dec. 11/5 Giant houndstooth designs made day dresses with jackets: so did imitation tweeds. **1959** *Woman's Own* 6 June 11/3 Clare..put on her 'good' hounds-tooth check. **1959** *Sunday Express* 14 June 14/3 Patterns are clean and singularly chic—a bold hounds' tooth check or a variety of confetti spots. **1959** *Times* 23 Sept. 5/2 The choice of cloths is famous for its variety—ranging from subdued houndstooths to full-blooded overchecks. **1959** *Guardian* 4 Dec. 6/5 In the woollens, small houndtooth designs and overchecks are liked. **1959** G. FREEMAN *Jack would be Gent.* i. 18 Moyra glanced at James, covertly admiring his hound's-tooth check suit. **1971** *Homes & Gardens* Aug. 57/1 The dining chairs are covered in a toffee and black houndstooth check. **1972** P. CLEIFE *Slick & Dead* xix. 143 Wearing my natty houndstooth instead of uniform.

houngan (hū·ngăn). Also hougan, hungan. [Native name in Haiti.] A priest of the Voodoo cult.

1929 W. B. SEABROOK *Magic Island* 304 There are many things my father (who was one of the great *hougans* of the past generation) could do which I cannot do. He could make thunder. **1932** J. J. WILLIAMS *Voodoos & Obeahs* iii. 91 Is there a Voodoo initiation whereby a neophyte, it matters not who he is, thanks to the good will of the hougan, may be admitted to the congregation? **1937** M. J. HERSKOVITS *Life Haitian Valley* xii. 223 Persistent failure to achieve cures will lose a *hungan* his reputation and his practice. **1941** J. G. LEYBURN *Haitian People* viii. 168 While the Vodun houngan sits quietly by, a special officiant..reads or pretends to read from the Catholic prayer book. **1966** G. GREENE *Comedians* I. iii. 83 A zombie who has left his grave at the command of an *houngan*.

houp-la (hū·pˌlā), *int.* Also hoop-la. [Cf. F. *houp-là!*] An exclamation accompanying a quick or sudden movement. Also as *sb.*, commotion, ballyhoo.

1870 O. LOGAN *Before Footlights* xxiii. 280 But the tearful clown cries 'houp-la!' while his baby is lying dead at home. **1877** *N.Y. Tribune* 2 Mar. 7/1 The Stock Exchange to-day commenced its business of speculation with a grand 'hoop la'. **1917** H. GARLAND *Son of Middle Border* xxiii. 286 Hoopla! We had taken wing! **1917** *Punch* 23 May 340/2 A beam of pleasure, succeeded by a falling of the countenance, then a look of decision, ended in a 'Houp-là' as the Japanese doll descended into the basket. **1925** F. M. FORD *No More Parades* I. ii, But ..Hoopla!..He executed with his gloved right thumb in the moonlight a rapid pirouette. **1929** C. A. N. GARSTIN *Houp La!* xxiv. 308 'Houp la!' Bill sighed, letting his head fall back. **1948** *Carpenter* Mar. 16 Organized some three years ago amid a great hoopla of Communist propaganda and promotion, it has creaked along in a very erratic and unpredictable manner. **1973** *Guardian* 16 Mar. 10/3 There is sometimes so much surrounding hoop-la that you lose sight of the various tactics.

houp-la, var. *HOOP-LA.

hour. 1. b. Restrict †*Obs.* to sense in Dict. and add: In *pl.* with numerals rendered in figures (followed by those of minutes), expressing the number of hours since midnight (chiefly in the armed services and in passenger timetables). Cf. *HUNDRED *sb.* and *a.* 1 d.

1939 *Punch* 2 Aug. 124/1 It is 21.00 hours on the last day of our month's training. **1941** *Punch* 21 May 486 A lorry is leaving R.M.P. at 0915 hours. **1967** [see *HOVERING *vbl. sb.* a (ii)]. **1968** A. HAMMERSLEY *Weather & Life* iv. 49, 6 hours G.M.T., i.e. 6 a.m. **1971** R. BUCKNALL *Trains* 46 With this time scale, 6 minutes would represent six hours, or 06.00.

c. Used to denote the distance of the sun above the horizon in the morning or afternoon. *U.S.*

1637 in *Essex Inst. Hist. Coll.* (1869) IX. 66 The keeper.. [is] to take the Cattle at the pen at Sun halfe an hour highe. **1683** in *New Hampsh. Hist. Soc. Coll.* (1866) VIII. 133 At night, about sun half an hour high. **1762** in *Narragansett Hist. Reg.* (1883–4) II. 219 We..got to the Ferry the sun about two hours high at night. **1824** *New Hampsh. Hist. Soc. Coll.* I. 244 Though the sun was an hour above the horizon, it was now as dark as midnight. **1836** *Knickerbocker* VIII. 352 The sun is two hours up yet. **1907** M. H. NORRIS *Veil* i. 3 The sun was an hour high when he entered a narrow road overgrown with grass.

d. (orig. *hour-mile.*) The distance which can be traversed in an hour.

[*a* **1646** J. GREGORY *Posthuma* (1650) 318 One Hour-Mile of a Journie upon Hors, answereth to four English Miles.] **1785** G. FORSTER tr. *Sparrman's Voy. Cape G. Hope* II. 81 This place is situated at the distance of two hours (uurs) from that which we had just quitted. **1792** E. RIOU tr. *J. van Reenen's Jrnl. Journey from Cape G. Hope* p. xii, Throughout the journal the word hour is to be considered as distance, and not time. Travellers at the Cape of Good Hope reckon distance by hours: one hour being supposed equal to about a league. **1798** S. H. WILCOCKE tr. *Stavorinus' Voy. E. Indies* I. 58 A Dutch mile, which they in general call an hour, is about three miles and a half English. **1877** J. C. GEIKIE *Life & Words Christ* I. 388 Three hours from Jerusalem. **1907** in A. H. Anderson *Reading* Advts. p. xlviii a, Dulverton... 4 Hours from London, 1 Hour from Taunton and Exeter. **1970** *Country Life* 2 July 62/1 (Advt.), Radnorshire... Kington 6½ miles. Birmingham 1½ hours. An attractive period house.

e. Used as the second element, representing 'for one hour', in the names of some units of measurement, as *ampere-hour, horsepower-hour, kilowatt-hour, man-hour* (see under the first element).

f. A unit of measure of work done.

1900 *Daily News* 10 Jan. 8/3 It should be understood that the tailors' 'hour' is not one of time, but merely the word employed for an unit of calculation.

2. b. (Earlier example.)

1852 *12th Rep. Col. Land & Emigr. Comm.* in *Parl. Papers* XVIII. 151 They are not required to work 'long hours', five hours a day is what is required of them.

c. (See quot. 1955.) Cf. *children's hour* (*CHILD *sb.* 22).

1930 *Economist* 3 May 985/1 It is argued that an advertiser who broadcasts tedious over-vulgar, or over-highbrow material in his 'hour' will eventually discover that he is losing money. **1955** M. REIFER *Dict. New Words* 102/1 *Hour*, a scheduled radio or television feature, originally one hour long; the term now refers to any length program. **1972** *Daily Tel.* 20 Apr. 12/5 The star of *The Bob Monkhouse Comedy Hour* (ITV)..is almost guaranteed to turn me off.

3. c. (Further examples.)

1816 JANE AUSTEN *Emma* II. vii. 123, I am not fond of dinner-visiting... Late hours do not agree with us. **1821** BYRON *Don Juan* III. lxvi. 36 Late hours, wine, and love are able To do not much less damage than the table. **1970** *Brewer's Dict. Phr. & Fable* (rev. ed.) 550/2 *To keep good hours*, to go home early every night; to go to bed betimes; to be punctual at one's work.

d. *to* (or *till*) *all hours*: late at night; after midnight.

1931 BELLOC *Hist. Eng.* IV. I. 161 She..had had him, and one, Culpepper, in her room up to all hours. **1932** A. J. WORRALL *Eng. Idioms* viii. 58, I sat up to all hours trying to finish my work. **1934** B. DE HOLTHOIR tr. *Duhamel's News from Havre* xiii. 196 She made up for lost time by sitting up till all hours of the night. **1945** E. WAUGH *Brideshead Revisited* iv. 264 She sits up to all hours with her wireless. **1961** R. CHAPMAN *Father Faber* viii. 161 He read till all hours and undertook heavy penances.

hourage (auə·rĕdʒ). *rare.* [f. HOUR + -AGE.] The aggregate number of hours spent in working or travelling; extent or distance in hours. Also, rate of travel in hours.

1924 *Glasgow Herald* 29 Dec. 7, 52,000 individuals.. were taken for short flights, the total 'hourage' being 2400. **1968** *Times* 19 Feb. 5/2 When you've finished your optimum hourage you must stop clean and briskly.

hour-glass. Add: **d.** A marking (as on a spider) in the shape of an hour-glass.

1937 *Discovery* Dec. 368/1 Two female Black Widows, showing the 'hour-glass' markings. **1962** METCALF & FLINT *Destructive & Useful Insects* (ed. 4) xxi. 1009 (*caption*) The black widow spider, *Latrodectus mactans*. At left, the female from the underside, showing the characteristic hourglass-shaped spot.

2. Special Comb.: **hour-glass structure** *Petrol.*, a structure present in certain rocks in which the mineral crystals have the shape of an hour-glass.

1888 J. J. H. TEALL *Brit. Petrogr.* vii. 159 The hour-glass structure already mentioned as occurring in the picrites is occasionally found in the normal plagioclase-augite rocks. **1932** F. F. GROUT *Petrogr. & Petrol.* 100 'Hourglass' structure is occasionally noted in augite. **1959** W. W. MOORHOUSE *Study of Rocks in Thin Section* vi. 166 The larger grains and phenocrysts may be zoned, or they may show hourglass structure.

house, *sb.*[1] Add: **2.** *the House* (earlier and later examples).

1835 DICKENS *Sk. Boz* (1836) 1st Ser. I. 3, I suppose you must have an order into the house. **1888** MRS. H. WARD *R. Elsmere* II. III. xix. 140 If they turn us out.. there'll be nothing left but the House for us old 'uns.

b. *to bow down* (or *worship*) *in the house of Rimmon* (after 2 Kings v. 18): to pay lip-service to some principle which one does not accept; to sacrifice one's principles for the sake of conformity.

1718 DEFOE in W. Lee *Life & recently discovered Writings Defoe* (1869) I. p. xiii, Thus I bow in the House of Rimmon, and must humbly recommend myself to his Lordship's Protection. **1903** KIPLING *Five Nations* 104 Duly with knees that feign to quake—Bent head and shaded brow,—Yet once again, for my father's sake, In Rimmon's House I bow. **1956** N. ANNAN in J. Morris *From Third Programme* 150 If you bow down in the house of Rimmon you admit that its values are more important than yours.

c. *on the house*: at the expense of the tavern, saloon, etc. Also *transf.* and *fig.* orig. *U.S.*

1889 *Kansas City* (Missouri) *Times & Star* 30 Nov., The first drink Thursday was 'on the house' in the leading saloons. **1934** J. A. LEE *Children of Poor* (1949) 26 'I must have a drink.' Here, have one on the house. **1944** AUDEN *For Time Being* (1945) 77 A voice I'd heard before, I think, Cried: 'This is on the House.' **1958** M. DICKENS *Man Overboard* xiii. 214 Laundry and cleaning were on the house. **1959** N. MAILER *Advts. for Myself* (1961) 95 One night just for the hell of it he has one on the house with the society gal, and she gets pregnant. **1967** W. SOYINKA *Kongi's Harvest* 18 *Daodu*:...Naturally it's on the house. *Secretary*: No, thank you. I prefer to pay for my drinks.

4. c. (Earlier examples.) Also, in day schools, a division of the school for purposes of organization and games or other competition. Also *attrib.*

1855 J. A. SYMONDS *Let.* Oct. (1967) I. 64 Tom Parr who has just joined his regiment came down here today with an old house fellow. **1856** —— *Let.* June I. 73, I had them sent to the Head of the House who flogged two. **1857** —— *Let.* 15 Nov. I. 126 Yesterday I played in a house match. **1899** KIPLING *Stalky & Co.* 124, I thought the house-prefects might know more about it than I did. They ought to. They're giddy palladiums of public schools. **1908** A. HUXLEY *Let.* Nov. (1969) 29 M'tutor, who is also my house tutor and my division beak, is a dear man. **1922** C. E. MONTAGUE *Disenchantment* vii. 93 A boy of this kidney, while looking on at a vital house match, will give his mind ease by telling a friend what 'a lot of stinkers' the other house are. **1925** *City of Oxford Sch. Mag.* Mar. 8 Kerry House hold the new cup for the winning House for the first year. *Ibid.* July 33 In the points counting for the House Shield. **1949** W. B. GALLIE *Eng. School* ii. 31 He managed to infuse his ideas into the masters who coached the school's junior fifteens,

house fifteens, and so on. **1965** A. Nicol *Truly Married Woman* 76 An important football house-match was scheduled for that afternoon. **1966** P. Willmott *Adolescent Boys E. London* v. 93 After registration I took house prayers as House Captain.

f. Also, *spec.* (i) = *house of ill fame* (House *sb.*[1] 11).

c **1810** W. Hickey *Memoirs* (1960) iv. 63, I was informed with vast glee by these wild young men that..they had discovered two new houses of infinite merit. *a* **1922** T. S. Eliot *Waste Land Drafts* (1971) 5 I've kept a decent house for twenty years. **1931** R. Campbell *Georgiad* ii. 45 The old 'Matronas' of the Southern Race Can run their 'houses' with a smiling face, Business and pleasure to one end unite. **1954** P. Adler (*title*) A house is not a home. **1962** *John o' London's* 1 Feb. 115/1 The girls who had worked in 'houses' were unfitted, by temperament and training, for any other sort of life. **1968** L. Durrell *Tunc* ii. 47 'You see,' said Mrs. Henniker piteously 'what we are up against all the time? How to run a respectable house what I mean?'

(ii) A couture establishment.

1864 *2nd Rep. Children's Employment Comm.* 39 in *Parl. Papers* XXII. 1 At some houses all in the show-room are expected to wear black glacé silk. **1880** in L. de Vries *Victorian Advts.* (1968) *Messrs. Jay* import from the first houses in Paris Models of every style. **1931** S. Jameson *Richer Dust* v. 145, I have good taste. I could think of dresses. I should have to go round the various houses. **1938** D. Smith *Dear Octopus* III. i. 108, I can go to Raquelle's London house if I like. **1967** *Guardian* 24 July 4/6 Instead of showing their collections four weeks after the other houses, Givenchy and Balenciaga..show on August 3.

(iii) A printing or publishing house.

1683–4 J. Moxon *Mech. Exerc., Printing* (1962) 16 A Printing-House may admit of a twofold meaning; one..relative to the House or Place wherein Printing is used; the other..only the Printing Tools... Thus they say ..such a one has remov'd his Printing-House, when thereby they only mean he has remov'd the Tools us'd in his former House. **1871** G. Meredith *Let.* 3 July (1970) I. 448 The debt has been left unsettled owing to my having kept back my work to perfect it more. It was honourably incurred by me out of consideration for your house. **1935** *Times Lit. Suppl.* 4 Apr. 217/4 Already there obtained something approaching what is now called 'the style of the house'. **1959** N. Mailer *Advts. for Myself* (1961) 399 There was no one in the house who had guts enough to say that *Some Came Running* was a washer-woman at 1,200 pages, and could be fair at 400.

(iv) Used *attrib.*, in *house journal, magazine*, etc., a publication written for and circulated within a business firm, group, etc.

1907 *Electr. World* XLIX. 674/1 The subject of 'house organs' for manufacturing concerns was discussed. **1915** *Writer's Bulletin* Jan. 75/1 *The Hoggson Magazine*.. is an example of the artistic heights to which the 'house organ' may attain. **1925** *Writer's Monthly* June 466/1 These little magazines, or internal house organs, as they are called by the advertising fraternity, are usually of an inspirational character. **1959** *Times Rev. Industry* Mar. 5/2 Publications such as..house magazines. **1962** *Punch* 7 Mar. 375/2 Forty per cent of Sixth Form boys..read *Punch*, or so..their house-journal, *Sixth Form Opinion*, tells us. **1969** 'E. Lathen' *Murder to Go* xvii. 171 *Chicken Feed*, house organ of the Chicken Tonight organization, was not due for three weeks. **1970** T. Hilton *Pre-Raphaelites* ii. 49 *The Germ*..was the first house journal of a self-consciously avant-garde artistic group. **1970** *Vogue* May 48/2 They want..to make the cinema altogether a pleasant experience, with programmes, discussions, attractive usherettes..and a house magazine. **1971** *Nature* 5 Mar. 3/1 *Physical Review*, the house journal of the American Physical Society.

g. (Further examples.) Also, of stage or cinema performances closely following each other, *first, second house*. *House full*: the announcement posted outside a place of entertainment to indicate to the public that there is no room available; also *transf.*

1835 Dickens *Sk. Boz* (1836) 1st Ser. II. 202 There'll be a full house to-night—six parties in the boxes already. **1891** House full [in Dict.]. **1898** J. Hollingshead *Gaiety Chron.* ii. 115 No 'house full' boards were exhibited outside the theatre. **1906** J. M. Synge *Lett. to Molly* (1971) 49, I dreamed also that Tolstoi..came to our plays..and that there was a very bad house. **1906** *Daily Chron.* 23 Dec. 3/2 It would be natural to suppose that the book trade this Christmas has been a 'house full' affair. **1914** *Aeroplane* 2 Sept. 211/1 Both Services have practically put up the 'House Full' sign, and have a waiting list yards in length. **1921** G. B. Shaw *Let.* 27 Dec. in *To a Young Actress* (1960) 12 Until you can hit the boy at the back of the gallery in a three hundred pound house. **1924** in L. Warwick *Death of Theatre* (1960) vi. 62 The management have long felt that many first-class productions have been spoilt by the rush of two houses. **1930** J. B. Priestley *Angel Pavement* vii. 358 If I can get two seats for the first house tomorrow night, will you come with me? **1939** Joyce *Finnegans Wake* 62 It was after the show at Wednesbury that one tall man.. returning late..from the second house..had a barkiss revolver placed to his face. **1940** H. G. Wells *Babes in Darkling Wood* II. i. 137 He might go into some cinema... Or he might get in for the second house at the Holborn or Pavilion? **1968** *Blues Unlimited* Dec. 4 He played little guitar the first house but sang 'Two ways to skin a cat'.

h. Used *attrib.* of a permanent or resident band, jazz group, etc.

1934 S. R. Nelson *All about Jazz* iv. 76 There are many combinations which only record and play over the radio... These orchestras are often composed of prominent members of famous bands, in which case they are known as 'house' combinations. **1958** J. C. Holmes *Horn* (1959) 34 The drummer for the house band good-naturedly chased Wing's warm-up runs with precise rim-shots. **1966** *Crescendo* Nov. 23/1 He was part of the house rhythm section for Prestige Records. **1968** *Blues Unlimited* Nov. 26 The earlier Tampas are better—though hardly classifiable as 'house band'.

5. Also *son, daughter of the house*.

1802 C. Wilmot *Let.* 3 Jan. in *Irish Peer* (1920) 32 Lady Mount Cashal was handed out of the Room by Monsieur l'Abbé Sièyes, and I by Monsieur, the Son of the House. **1926** Wodehouse *Heart of Goof* ii. 54 The modern butler..looks like the son of the house. **1949** 'M. Innes' *Journeying Boy* xiii. 167 Mr Thewless..felt that the son of the house might turn out to be someone to rely upon. **1968** 'D. Torr' *Treason Line* 30 The daughter of the house, a slim, petite girl.

9. b. *Curling.* The space within the outermost circle drawn round the tee.

1883 J. Macnair *Channel-Stane* 1st Ser. 50 The stone draws past everything save the winner, which is knocked clear of the house. **1914** J. G. Grant *Complete Curler* II. vii. 91 The space within the 7-foot ring is colloquially known as the 'house' (*Scotice*, 'hoose'), or sometimes 'parish'. **1969** R. Welsh *Beginner's Guide Curling* xii. 89 A player will strike out the shot and his own stone will also roll out, leaving an empty house.

c. Lotto played (orig. in the Army) as a gambling game with special cards and checks. Also, the *house-caller* or *house-man* who organizes the game, the winning of the game or the call announcing this, or the prize given. See also *housey-housey.

1900 *Strand Mag.* Apr. 419/2 When they were not drilling they were playing 'House'. **1917** A. G. Empey *From Fire Step* 125 The two most popular games are 'Crown and Anchor' and 'House'. *Ibid.* 126 As soon as the *estaminet* is sufficiently crowded the proprietors of the 'House Game' get busy. **1918** R. D. Holmes *Yankee in Trenches* v. 60 If you get all your numbers covered, you call out 'house', winning the pot. **1919** [see *clickety-click* (*click *sb.*[1] 8)]. **1920** G. K. Rose *2/4th Oxf. & Bucks Lt. Infty.* 200 On the air floated the monotonous enumeration of 'House'. **1923** *Daily Mail* 9 June 7 The game of 'house', or 'box and numbers'. **1933** [see *clickety-click* (*click *sb.*[1] 8)]. **1936** F. Richards *Old-Soldier Sahib* iii. 69 It takes two men to work a game of House: one calls out the numbers, the other collects the money and issues the cards. **1945** *Gen* 30 June 27/1 The house-caller announced that the amount of the house was two and a half piastres short of ten pounds. **1951** *Amer. Speech* XXVI. 99/1 *House*, the man who runs the game is spoken of as the 'house' or the 'house man'. **1973** *Guardian* 12 June 20 They were in a crooked [Bingo] game... Certain cards were stacked for a quick House against others which were..distinct long-shots.

11. Also *house of accommodation* (cf. *accommodation 7 b), *house of assignation* (cf. *assignation 10).

1749 J. Cleland *Mem. Woman Pleasure* II. 12 This was the safest, politest, and, at the same time, the most thorough house of accommodation in town. **1834** *Sun* (N.Y.) 10 Apr. 2/2 Such men as Samuel Q. Wright, (a bank man) the keeper of a notorious house of assignation, and prostitution. **1861** B. Hemyng in H. Mayhew *London Labour* Extra vol. (1862) 255/1 Keepers of houses of assignation, where the last-mentioned class [sc. ladies of intrigue] may carry on their amours with secrecy. **1928** 'Brent of Bin Bin' *Up Country* x. 146 They started a house of accommodation in the most unlikely place for patrons. **1973** G. Butler *Coffin for Pandora* i. 26 Just as some of them could rise to an elegant house in Brompton, others could sink to a house of accommodation off the Haymarket or even worse.

13. *house-to-house*. Also *ellipt.* or as *sb.*, = a house-to-house collection, search, etc.

1936 'F. O'Connor' *Bones of Contention* 37 We'll make a house-to-house. **1969** B. Weil *Dossier IX* vi. 44 The house-to-house paid off. We got someone in the mews to talk. **1970** R. Rendell *Guilty Thing Surprised* xii. 142 Three of us have done a house-to-house in Myfleet. **1973** W. J. Burley *Death in Salubrious Place* v. 93 The house-to-house and the questionnaire both appear to have covered the ground pretty well.

16*. *to play* (*at*) *house*(*s*): to play at being a family and running a house (see also quot. 1968).

1871 J. H. Ewing *Flat Iron for Farthing* (1873) vii. 67 Polly and I had nothing to do.., which led us into the very reprehensible habit of 'playing at houses' in Uncle Ascott's gorgeously furnished pew. *Ibid.* 71 You know we *couldn't* play houses in the church where papa goes. **1918** 'K. Mansfield' *Lett. to J. M. Murry* (1951) 220 They always seem to think we were so very very young at the Villa Pauline—playing houses—going to bed under the table for a minute with the cloth pulled down for a blind. **1957** J. Kirkup *Only Child* ix. 120 If we were lucky, and the weather was fine, we would be allowed to have tea in our tent, and to play houses with the fireside things—the tongs, the little brush, the shovel and the ash-rake. **1959** H. Gardner *So what else is New?* xiv. 140 'Let's play house, Sally,' the boy said. **1968** *Sun* (Baltimore) 18 Sept. B7/8 He's tried several times to get me to go to his apartment. I've always refused... I'm not ready to play house yet. **1969** Gish & Pinchot *Lillian Gish* ii. 17 Whenever Dorothy and I were in the same company with Mother, our favorite game was to go to the theater early, dress in Mother's clothes, and play house on stage.

18. Also, *to pull a house over one's head*; *to throw the house out of the windows*: delete *Obs.* and add later example; *as safe as houses* (later examples); *to go* (*all*) *round the houses*: *fig.* to beat about the bush, to reach the point in a lengthy or roundabout way; *to put* (or *set*) *one's* (*own*) *house in order*: to arrange one's affairs properly.

1611 Bible *2 Kings* 20:1 And the Prophet Isaiah the sonne of Amos came to him, and saide vnto him, Thus saith the Lord, Set thine house in order: for thou shalt die, and not liue. **1861** Geo. Eliot *Silas Marner* iii. 53 You'll have less pleasure in pulling the house over my head, when your own skull's to be broken too. **1871** Hardy *Desp. Rem.* III. iv. 92, I shall be high-treasoned—as safe as houses. **1880** E. W. Hamilton *Diary* 25 Apr. (1972) I. 3 Layard has telegraphed from Constantinople that the Turk is becoming really alive to the necessity of 'putting his house in order'—(if that broken-down establishment will admit of repair). **1913** E. Phillpotts *Widecombe Fair* v. 36 They say things, and do things, and even think things, that you'd fear must throw the house out of windows, and wreck the home for evermore. **1923** J. S. Huxley *Ess. Biologist* vii. 292 The theologians..fail in the majority of cases to set their own house in order, to organize the inner reality to react with the outer. **1932** 'A. Bridge' *Peking Picnic* xix. 238 Kidnapping Frenchmen is simply too unremunerative for words, whereas we're a perfect gold mine, safe as houses. **1949** A. Wilson *Wrong Set* 49 You had better put your own house in order before you go listening to wicked lies. **1955** *Times* 31 Aug. 7/5 If the conservative parties did not put their houses in order, Japan would soon see a Socialist Government in power. **1958** F. Norman *Bang to Rights* 129 Alright but I wish you wouldn't go all round the houses. **1965** V. Canning *Whip Hand* iv. 43 You mean your little story..wasn't true?..You went a hell of a way round the houses about this. **1965** *New Statesman* 14 May 749/3 Such a policy of firmness would make it clear to all that we are determined to put our economic house in order.

19. a. *house-back, -bell, -front* (later examples), *-number, -paddock* (Austral.), *-pile, -site, -wiring*. **b.** *house-boot, -cloth* (examples), *-dress* (examples), *-frock, -gown* (earlier example), *-jacket, -linen, -plant* (earlier and later examples), *-slipper, -telephone* (also *-phone*). **c.** *house affairs* (later example). **d.** *house-servant* (earlier and later examples), *-slave, -steward* (later example).

1862 D. G. Rossetti *Let.* 22 Feb. (1965) II. 443 House-affairs get still further complicated. **1913** C. Mackenzie *Sinister St.* I. ii. 29 He..wished that he could disappear in such company round corner after corner of the world beyond the grey house-backs. **1948** C. Day Lewis *Otterbury Incident* 69 Between this path and the house-backs there are some small yards. *a* **1817** Jane Austen *Northanger Abbey* (1818) II. xiii. 249 The loud noise of the house-bell. **1834** *Chambers's Edin. Jrnl.* III. 414/1 He rung the teacher's house-bell. **1921** W. de la Mare *Crossings* 88 The far-away house-bell clangs into the room. **1652** R. Verney *Let.* in M. M. Verney *Mem.* (1894) III. ii. 46 Sir Ralph is much taken with some 'old men's house boots', called Scarfaroni. **1914** Joyce *Dubliners* 123 Then she took off her working skirt and her house-boots. **1597** T. Deloney *Jacke Newb.* (1630) sig. G3, [They] put an house-cloath about his necke in stead of a fine towell. **1934** H. G. Wells *Exper. Autobiogr.* I. iv. 149 Rolls of crash, house cloth, ticking and the like. **1897** *McClure's Mag.* X. 66 She looked charming in her long, soft house-dress. **1921** *Daily Colonist* (Victoria, B.C.) 2 Apr. 9/5 House Dresses in V-neck style with kimona sleeves, pockets and belt, open down the front and come in stripes, checks and plain colors. **1966** 'S. Ransome' *Hidden Hour* iv. 50 A woman wearing a house dress, evidently one of the tenants. **1925** *Sears, Roebuck Catal.* 28 A neat, trim gingham house or porch frock is an asset to every woman's wardrobe. **1952** C. W. Cunnington *Eng. Women's Clothing* iv. 135 House-frocks are now all-important as a result of the war economies. **1905** *Westm. Gaz.* 12 Dec. 9/1 The house-fronts of miles and miles of London streets are entirely carried on iron girders. **1963** *Times* 4 June 11/7 The drabness of house-fronts, that so deceive the casual visitor. **1832** *Chambers's Edin. Jrnl.* I. 121/3 Sometimes the fit takes the direction of a new gown for going out with on bad days,..at another time 'a house gown'. **1922** Joyce *Ulysses* 452 In housejacket of ripplecloth. **1926** *Daily Colonist* (Victoria, B.C.) 1 Jan. 11/1 (Advt.), Christmas Goods Now on Sale. Dressing Gowns, House Jackets, Ties, [etc.]. **1857** Mrs. Gaskell *Let.* 7 Dec. (1966) 492 Then we came home; and have been desperately busy ever since, looking over stores, and clothes, and house-linen, and preserves. **1905** *Westm. Gaz.* 8 Nov. 5/2 No arrangements had been made for her reception. There was no silver, no house-linen. **1895** *Montgomery Ward Catal.* 396/2 House numbers, 3 inch, made of brass and nicely nickel plated. **1972** C. Weston *Poor, Poor Ophelia* (1973) vi. 29 Casey began looking for house numbers. **1908** Mrs. A. Gunn *We of Never-Never* vi. 64 To the north-west are the stock-yards and house paddock—a paddock of five square miles. **1951** J. K. Ewers in Murdoch & Drake-Brockman *Austral. Short Stories* 335 The scrawny gums by the house-paddock. **1908** S. Ford *Side-Stepping with Shorty* ix. 137 There was no answer to the call on the house 'phone. **1935** *Archit. Rev.* LXXVIII. 73 Raymond McGrath designed standard signal lights, clocks, buzzer and house-phone mountings. **1970** 'W. Haggard' *Hardliners* i. 11 There was a house-phone on the impressive desk. **1930** M. Mead *Growing up in New Guinea* ii. 13 Around the stout house-piles the tides run. **1970** R. Lowell *Notebk.* 47 Where the Brook Trout dolphins by the housepiles, Grows common..as hamburger. **1873** *Young Englishwoman* Nov. 562/2 Those who have cultivated house plants for years. **1970** D. Bartrum *Exotic Plants for Home* ii. 29 All the house plants we buy from the florists are amenable to pot culture. **1743** W. Ellis *Mod. Husbandman* Oct. xxii. 238 There are two Sorts of Men Taskers, the Day Labourer, and the constant House Servant. **1882** W. D. Hay *Brighter Britain* I. 37 That's a new dairy-maid and house-servant my friend's just engaged. **1916** *Gilbert & Ellice Islands Protect. Rep. for 1914–15* 15 The Ellice boy, who is much inferior to the Gilbertese in all things that really matter, makes a better house servant. **1966** B. Kimenye *Kalasanda Revisited* 23 His house servant was away on leave, and the drawbacks of bachelorhood were making themselves acutely felt. **1913** J. London *Let.* 1 Mar. (1966) 373 The hedges around

the house-site. **1949** M. Mead *Male & Female* ii. 40 Considerations..that one would normally consider in choosing a house-site. **1738** F. Moore *Trav. Inland Afr.* 110 Some people have a good many House-Slaves..and they live so well and easy, that it is sometimes a very hard Matter to know the Slaves from their Masters. **1962** S. Wynter *Hills of Hebron* vi. 81 His master was fond of him and made his mother a house-slave so that Cato could grow up in the big house. **1972** *Village Voice* (N.Y.) 1 June 24/1 Whitey has always pitted one black against the other. The field slaves and the house slaves. **1895** *Montgomery Ward Catal.* 512/1 Ladies' toilet and house slippers. **1965** B. Sweet-Escott *Baker St. Irreg.* vi. 161 His feet encased in a pair of black velvet house-slippers embroidered in white with the letters 'A. E.' **1922** Joyce *Ulysses* 304 The house-steward of the amalgamated cats' and dogs' home was in attendance. **1889** *Telephone* I. xxiii. 534/1 The installation of a house telephone recommends itself in large hotels. **1921** [see *camouflage *v.*]. **1950** T. S. Eliot *Cocktail Party* II. 94 The house-telephone rings. **1968** J. Fleming *Hell's Belle* i. 34 The humblest hotel in Paris has a house-telephone. **1901** *Chambers's Jrnl.* Sept. 616/1 We now propose to consider installations which require, in addition to the ordinary house-wiring, the machinery necessary for the production of the electric current. **1963** *Times* 6 May p. vii/2 The traditional type of housewiring involved separate circuits for the different kinds of load.

20. *house-cat* (earlier and later examples).

1607 Topsell *Four-f. Beasts* 107 Her tayle longer then an ordinary house cats. **1963** B. Vesey-Fitzgerald *Cat Owner's Encycl.* 54 But we do not know which species it was that first became the house-cat. **1973** R. Ludlum *Matlock Paper* vii. 61 His clumsy, long-haired house cat had knocked over a stray glass.

21. *house decoration, -decorator, -hunting* (later examples), *-letting* (examples), *-move* sb., *-moving*.

1881 C. C. Harrison *Woman's Handiwork* I. 4 Industrial arts applied to house-decoration. **1914** W. Owen *Let.* 11 Aug. (1967) 276 She has an important business..selling House Decorations, Embroideries, and so on. **1911** G. S. Porter *Harvester* xv. 321 As a house decorator you surpass yourself. **1929** F. M. Ford *Let.* 14 Sept. (1965) 189 House-decorators find that books work into rooms with admirable effect. **1935** *Burlington Mag.* July 44/2 The colouring of cupboards and friezes and similar house-decorators' tasks. **1930** *Times Lit. Suppl.* 31 July 625/2 To engage playfully in house-hunting. **1960** *Guardian* 15 Feb. 4/2 Her recent house-hunting in London. **1839** Dickens *Let.* 19 Nov. (1965) I. 603, I am in the agonies of house-letting, house-taking, title-proving, [etc.]. **1909** *Westm. Gaz.* 1 Oct. 2/2 The Scotch House-Letting and Rating Bill. **1923** E. Bowen *Encounters* 92, I shouldn't have thought that a house-move was exactly the most leisurely time. **1961** *Times* 17 Aug. 11/2 Rearranging my books..after a house-move. **1926** R. Macaulay *Crewe Train* II. x. 184 I'm extraordinarily sleepy, with all this house-moving.

23. house-agent (earlier and later examples); **house appointment,** a position as a house-physician or house-surgeon in a hospital; **house arrest,** detention in one's house; also (with hyphen) as *vb.*; **house-author,** an author employed by a theatre; **house bill,** (*a*) a poster or programme describing a theatrical performance; (*b*) a bill of exchange drawn by a business house on itself; **house-bound** *a.* (examples); **house-boy** (examples); **house-burnt** *a. U.S.*, designating tobacco which in the course of being cured in a tobacco-house has been injured or spoilt by disease; so **house-burn** *v. intr.* and (rare) *trans.*, to become or render house-burnt; also **house-burning** *vbl. sb.*; **house call,** a visit made to a patient in his own home by a doctor, chiropodist, etc.; **house cap,** a school cap made of the colours adopted by a particular house, esp. one awarded for proficiency in games; **house-car** (examples); **house-carpenter** (later U.S. examples); **house church** (see quot. 1967); **house-cleaning** *sb.*, the cleaning of the inside of a house; hence (as a back-formation) **house-clean** *v.*; also *transf.*; **house-cleaner,** one who cleans the inside of a house; **house-coat,** a woman's informal coat-dress for wearing at home; **house colours** [*colour *sb.*[1] 6 c], colours representing a house (sense 4 c above) at a school; **house detective,** a private detective employed by a business firm, hotel, etc.; **house detention** = **house arrest*; **house dinner,** a dinner given to the staff or the occupants of a house at a school, etc.; **house-dweller,** one who lives in a house (opp. a nomad, etc.); so **house-dwelling; house finch,** a red-headed N. American finch of the genus *Carpodacus*, esp. *C. mexicanus*; **house-furnishing,** the furnishing of a house; also *pl.* in concrete sense; **house-girl,** a female domestic servant or, formerly, a slave; **house governor,** the head of administration in a hospital; **house guest,** a guest staying in a private house; **house-help** (examples); **house journal:** see sense 4 f (iv) above; **house lights,** lights on the audience side of the stage curtain in a theatre; **house longhorn, longicorn (beetle),** *Hylotrupes bajulus*, a wood-boring beetle of the family Cerambycidæ; **house magazine:** see sense 4 f (iv) above; **house-manager,** the manager of a theatre, club, concert-hall, etc.; **house moth,** either of two moths, *Hofmannophila pseudospretella* or *Endrosis sarcitrella*; **house mouse,** *Mus musculus*, which lives in buildings as well as in open fields; **house-mover** *N. Amer.*, (*a*) a person whose business is to move furniture; (*b*) a machine or apparatus for the physical removal of houses; **house Negro, house nigger** *U.S.* (*rare* exc. *Hist.*), a Negro household servant; **house officer,** a junior full-time member of the medical staff of a hospital, usually (but not always) resident; *esp.* one whose post is tenable by qualified doctors who are not yet fully registered; **house organ:** see sense 4 f (iv) above; **house-painting** (examples); **house-parent,** a house-mother or house-father acting singly or jointly as head of a community of (young) persons living together as a family; **house-parlourman,** a male servant who does work corresponding to that of a house-parlourmaid; **house-party** (earlier example); also = **house-rent party* (below); **house physician,** add to def.: now usually (in Great Britain) a house officer working in the field of general medicine; (later examples); **house-pride,** pride in one's house, desire to keep one's house clean and tidy; so **house-proud** *a.*, proud of one's house, desirous to see it always at its best (sometimes implying excessive preoccupation with it); **house-raising** (earlier and later examples); **house-rent party** *U.S.*, orig. a party aimed at raising money to pay the rent of a house; later, any 'jam' session in a house or apartment; also *house-rent stomp, strut*; **house seat,** a seat in a theatre, etc., reserved by the management for special guests; **house style,** the distinctive printing methods and regulations, including the preferred spellings and conventions of punctuation, of a publishing or printing business; also *transf.*; **house surgeon,** add to def.: now usually (in Great Britain) a house officer working in the field of surgery; (later examples); **house-tax** (earlier examples); **house-trap,** a portable bird-trap made of wire netting in which bait has been laid; **house-type,** a type of house; **housewares** *sb. pl.* (chiefly *N. Amer.*), kitchen utensils and other utilitarian household articles; **house-work,** the work required to keep a house clean and in order; **house-wrecker** = Housebreaker 2; **house wren,** the common N. American brown wren, *Troglodytes aedon*.

1843 *Ainsworth's Mag.* IV. 64 House-agents and auctioneers are their attendant sprites. **1922** T. S. Eliot *Waste Land* (1923) iii. 16 A small house agents' clerk. **1961** *Lancet* 26 Aug. 497/1 After house-appointments he graduated M.D. in 1900. **1963** *Ibid.* 19 Jan. 176/1 After holding house-appointments, he became an assistant bacteriologist in the Glasgow public-health laboratories. **1936** F. L. Schuman *Hitler & Nazi Dictatorship* Epilogue ii. 441 He was subjected to 'house arrest' for his protection. **1945** M. Allingham *Coroner's Pidgin* xv. 126 In the normal way when I put a person under house arrest and she breaks it, I pull her in. **1948** A. Koestler in *Partisan Rev.* XV. I. 33 All of them are..in fact, under a kind of curfew or house arrest. **1958** *Listener* 13 Nov. 762/2 Galileo lived the remaining years of his life under house arrest. **1963** *Economist* 31 Aug. 732/2 The Hodgsons, banned, house-arrested and persecuted in South Africa. **1970** *New Yorker* 17 Oct. 179/1 The Chinese continue to support Prince Sihanouk, who is said to be living under house arrest in Peking. **1971** *Rand Daily Mail* 4 Sept. 12/4 Father Desmond was banned and house arrested after the book was published, probably for daring to write it. **1864** P. Paterson *Glimpses Real Life* xxvii. 262 August, or even earlier, when the 'house-author' and the manager determine what it [*sc.* the pantomime] is to be. **1903** *Daily Chron.* 6 July 7/4 He was house-author to a theatre at Sydney. **1829** H. Foote *Compan. to Theatres* 138 The usual bills of the theatres are termed house bills. **1909** *Daily Chron.* 2 Mar. 3/2 That particular bill of exchange, the 'house bill'—a bill drawn by a firm or company on itself. **1878** *Harper's Mag.* Jan. 277/1 The rains set in furiously, and I was completely house-bound. **1960** *Sunday Express* 10 July 11/4 His ailing, house-bound wife is attended to by a home help. **1966** *New Statesman* 21 Jan. 80/3 Housebound married graduates. **1899** *Daily News* 8 June 5/7 Odd jobs as boot and knife cleaning, or where the boys are described as 'house-boys'. **1910** *Cape Times* 8 Oct. 2 House-boy; good references;..apply 6, St. Barnabas Street. **1926** S. G. Millin *S. Africans* III. i. 74 There might be black houseboys instead of white housemaids. **1944** *Living off Land* viii. 159 He [*sc.* a Papuan] may be an experienced 'house-boy' in which case he will make his own arrangements for employment. **1955** B. Manvers *Shadow of Happiness* i. 19 That's my houseboy; he has an unpronounceable name, so I call him John. **1971** *E. Afr. Jrnl.* Mar. 5/1 She is procured by the African houseboys for their employer—a white expatriate. **1640** *Archives of Maryland* (1883) I. 98 Bad Tobacco shall be judged ground leafes, Second Crops leafs, notably brused or worm eaten, or leaves house burnt, sun burnt, [etc.]. **1772** *Maryland Hist. Mag.* (1919) XIV. 363 For 3 weeks past the Weather has been very unfavourable for the tob[acc]o Cured by fier very much & I suppose has House burnt all tob[acc]o not fierd. **1850** *Rep. Comm. Patents Agric. 1849* (U.S. Dept. Agric.) 321 Splitting tobacco is admired by many who contend that it cures brighter..and [is] less likely to house-burn. *Ibid.* 324 In this crop every leaf was saved, none lost by worms nor by 'house-burning' (that is suffering, or even rotting from being hung too thick). **1897** *Bradstreet's* 25 Oct. 1/4 Some of the leading growers report several crops as 'house burnt' and inclined to rot. **1966** *Publ. Amer. Dial. Soc.* XLV. 16 Tobacco will house burn in wet weather if you don't fire it. **1960** R. H. Blum *Managem. Doctor–Patient Relationship* ix. 203 The readiness of the physician to make house calls is important to patients. **1973** R. C. Dennis *Sweat of Fear* xii. 85, I opened the door, and there she was... I said, 'Doctor, I didn't know you made house calls.' **1899** Kipling in *Windsor Mag.* Dec. 33/1 'S'pose we're collared?' said Beetle, cramming his red and black house-cap into his pocket. **1907** *Daily Chron.* 15 June 4/7 The pride of a little boy who wins his house cap at school. **1856** W. Ferguson *Amer. by River & Rail* 338, I was glad to withdraw myself and my stool within the doorway of a house-car, as the covered freight-trucks are called. **1858** *Pennsylvania Rail Road Ann. Rep.* 14 The Rolling Stock..consisted..of..Eight-wheeled House Cars. **1741** W. Stephens *Jrnl.* 1 Apr. in *Colonial Rec. Georgia* (1908) IV. Suppl. 118 The other was looked on as a Master House-Carpenter of Repute. **1758** in S. M. Hamilton *Lett. to Washington* (1899) II. 365 And all this without one farthing expence (except about nine pence per day to the best house Carpenters). **1855** *Knickerbocker* XLVI. 222 Beech timber is held in great esteem by ship-builders and house-carpenters. **1964** *New Society* 26 Mar. 5/2 Four house-churches meet regularly on week nights in people's homes in Notting Hill. They are a mixture of discussion, worship, sharing of problems and a social occasion. **1967** D. T. Kauffman *Dict. Relig. Terms* 239/1 *House Church*, church program carried out and centered in homes rather than ecclesiastical structures. **1970** *Daily Tel.* 7 Aug. 10 At the 'house church' each member is given a duplicated sheet with questions and information on the subject for discussion. **1865** Mrs. Stowe *House & Home Papers* 45 He could not come in the spring for then they were house-cleaning. **1942** Partridge *Usage & Abusage* 154/2 *House-clean* or *houseclean* 'to clean (the) house', seems to me to be a permissible—and very convenient—word. **1954** *Manch. Guardian Weekly* 1 July 2 The sub-committee should houseclean its staff. **1959** 'J. R. Macdonald' *Galton Case* (1960) xii. 93 With all the outside work I do, I don't get time to houseclean. **1959** *Time* 12 Jan. 26/3 Seldom had a government been so thoroughly housecleaned between midnight and dawn. **1905** *Daily Chron.* 16 May 5/5 A house-cleaner..who was maddened with liquor, to-day shot..his landlady. **1863** B. Taylor *Hannah Thurston* ii. 26 The first thing..was immediately to summon old Melinda..whose speciality was house-cleaning. **1928** Foy & Harlow *Clowning through Life* 294 The Chicago horror was a blessing in one respect—namely, in that it brought about a country-wide house-cleaning. **1936** *Discovery* Jan. 16/2 For one beautiful little specimen [of worked flint] the writer was indebted to the house-cleaning of a busy rabbit. **1951** H. Reichenbach *Rise Sci. Philos.* xviii. 310 A good deal of house-cleaning is necessary before a philosophy of the social sciences can be constructed. **1959** *Times* 8 June (Latin Amer. Suppl.) 1/3 The new Cuban leaders are bitter that world opinion is now outraged by their house-cleaning methods. **1965** F. Sargeson *Mem. Peon* iv. 91 A char whom she employed for house-cleaning duties. **1969** *New Yorker* 31 May 72/3 A real political house-cleaning. **1916** in *Vogue* (1966) 15 Oct. 3/1 (Advt.), Artificial Silk Sports or House Coat in pretty, quiet striped colourings. **1937** *New Yorker* 16 Jan. 48/2 The Bendel negligee department is famous for its housecoats. **1946** 'S. Russell' *To Bed with Grand Music* viii. 105 He came back..to find Deborah in a house-coat, cooking supper. **1958** 'A. Gilbert' *Death against Clock* 45 She was in a house-coat—that's what they call dressing-gowns these days. **1973** J. Wainwright *Pride of Pigs* 50 She..slipped a housecoat over her nightdress and made her way downstairs. **1914** 'I. Hay' *Lighter Side School Life* viii. 224 Have you got your House colours? **1939** 'G. Orwell' in *Crit. Ess.* (1946) 63 That mystic world of quadrangles and house-colours. **1961** D. Bates *Fly-Switch from Sultan* xix. 106 So I started a brothel... It was run on the best public-school lines, and there were prefects and houses and in a manner of speaking there were house colours as well. **1898** *McClure's Mag.* X. 525/2 A house detective [had] observed the whole transaction. **1922** F. Scott Fitzgerald *Beautiful & Damned* II. i. 135 The group was joined by the hastily summoned house-detective. **1939** M. Allingham *Mr Campion & Others* 178 [He] was quite an ornament in the City police... When he retired he received the job of house detective here. **1969** J. Wainwright *Take-Over Man* v. 75 It's your reputation. Don't blame me if the house detective finds us and boots us out of the servants' entrance. **1958** *New Statesman* 3 May 555/2, I found an old journalist friend in his second year of house detention because he had been courageous enough to buck the army. **1870** E. L. Blanchard *Diary* 7 Apr. in C. W. Scott *Life E. L. Blanchard* (1891) II. 382 Dine at 7 at Arundel [Club], being the first 'house' dinner proposed. **1909** *Westm. Gaz.* 1 Oct. 3/3 Many of them who dwell in tents during summer and autumn become house-dwellers in Wandsworth..during winter. **1954** J. R. R. Tolkien *Fellowship of Ring* I. iv. 101 Most of the inhabitants..were house-dwellers. **1941** 'R. West' *Black Lamb* II. 103 The gypsies..would not dream of going into the church while the house-dwelling Christians were still about. **1869** *Amer. Naturalist* III. 183 About the gardens [in California] is the House Finch. **1917** T. G. Pearson *Birds Amer.* III. 7 House Finch... Other names [include] Crimson-fronted Finch; Red-headed Linnet [etc.]. **1961** O. L. Austin *Birds of World* (1962) 302/2 Very similar to the Purple Finch is the slightly smaller and brighter Mexican House Finch, a common garden bird from California southward through Mexico. **1791** Cowper *Let.* 30 Aug. in *Corr.* (1904) IV. 117 Such

[chairs] as will suit may be found probably at Maurice Smith's, of house-furnishing memory. **1858** *Leslie's Illustr. Weekly* 23 Jan. 127 Goods for Winter Use in the Housefurnishing Line. **1865** Mrs. Stowe *House & Home Papers* 61 That such is not always the case in the real home comes often from the mistakes in the house-furnishing. **1904** *Sun* (N.Y.) 9 Aug. 8 The feminine preference for garments and house furnishings over locomotives and drop forgings. **1835** M. Morrison *Let.* 5 Nov. in N. E. Eliason *Tarheel Talk* (1956) 277 We have been intending for some time to buy a house girl. **1884** J. C. Harris *Mingo* 91 Jenny, the house-girl, refused to sleep at the quarters. **1906** *Dialect Notes* III. 141 *House-girl*, maid of all work. **1945** B. A. Botkin *Lay my Burden Down* 55 Part white children sold for more than black children. They used them for house girls. **1951** R. Campbell *Light on Dark Horse* xxiii. 335 We had, at that time, two fine house-girls, the sisters Eugenia and Florentina Diaz y Medina. **1971** *E. Afr. Jrnl.* Mar. 6/1 Lawino condemns the missionaries who only wanted to make her a house-girl. **1905** M. F. Reaney *Med. Profession* iii. 39 The actual daily command is vested in the secretary or house-governor. **1934** E. MacManus *Hosp. Admin. Women* I. i. 13 The Secretary or Superintendent, who may be known either as House Governor, or by some other title, may be..a member of the Medical Staff of the Hospital—with wide experience and a gift for administration. **1961** *Times* 18 July 3/2 (Advt.), Hospital..House Governor and Secretary. **1964** G. L. Cohen *What's Wrong with Hospitals?* iii. 47 Matron will hand complaints to the Catering Officer, who refers to the House Governor, who sends a memo to the management committee. **1921** *Daily Colonist* (Victoria, B.C.) 1 Apr. 8/3 Miss Helen MacDonald..invited a number of her girl friends to meet her house guest, Miss Helen Whiteside. **1961** *Times* 27 Sept. 16/5 His house-guests hunt in the day. **1970** N. Armstrong et al. *First on Moon* iii. 61 She was conscious about getting ready for houseguests—her father and stepmother. **1835** T. C. Haliburton *Clockmaker* (1837) 1st Ser. viii. 62 Well, he roared like a bull, till black Lucretia, one of the house helps, let him go. **1958** *Listener* 14 Aug. 249/1 Foreign house-helps in London, S.W. **1970** *Canadian Antiques Collector* Feb. 24/1 Presently in came two well-dressed house-helps, one with a splendid gilt lamp..and another with a tea-tray. **1920** Wodehouse *Jill the Reckless* (1922) xviii. 260 The house-lights went up. **1957** *Oxf. Compan. Theatre* (ed. 2) 465/2 After 1765 the house lights and concealed footlights on traps cover the area in front of the proscenium. **1938** *Leaflet Forest Prod. Res.* XIV. 1 The House Longhorn beetle (*Hylotrupes bajulus* L.)..confines its attack to seasoned softwood timbers. *Ibid.* 2 This leaflet has been prepared to bring the House Longhorn beetle to the notice of architects, builders and property owners. **1962** *New Scientist* 15 Mar. 614/3 Massive timber struts..were already known to harbour death-watch beetles and the house longicorn. **1964** N. E. Hickin *Househ. Insect Pests* viii. 83 The House Longhorn Beetle is a pest of softwood. **1906** *Westm. Gaz.* 7 Nov. 10/2 Lord Selborne..was once the house-manager of the club. **1924** Wodehouse *Bill the Conqueror* xviii. 269 Give it to the house-manager at the Bijou and he'll fix you up with a couple of seats any night you want. **1968** M. Culpan *Vasiliko Affair* ii. 14 The house-manager, a courteous but wary young man in a dinner jacket. [**1897** *Proc. Dorset Nat. Hist. & Antiq. Field Club* XVIII. 147, I think that this moth is one of the most universally distributed, being found, I expect, in pretty nearly every house in the kingdom.] **1932** *Entomologist's Monthly Mag.* LXVIII. 77 (*title*) *Borkhausenia pseudospretella* and other house moths. **1966** J. R. Busvine *Insects & Hygiene* (ed. 2) xiii. 354 The house moths are probably species which originated as feeders on dry vegetable matter and have become adapted to dry animal remains. **1835** L. Jenyns *Man. Brit. Vertebr. Animals* 31 *M[us] Musculus*, Linn. (House Mouse.) — Fur dusky gray above with a tinge of yellow; beneath cinereous. **1909** *Westm. Gaz.* 17 Sept. 3/1 We do not suppose that the creation of the first house mouse awaited the building of the first house. **1916** G. E. H. Barrett-Hamilton *Hist. Brit. Mammals* II. 635 In all probability the House Mouse is of Asiatic origin. **1964** H. N. Southern *Handbk. Brit. Mammals* v. 86 Break-back traps used on a large scale for catching House Mice can produce useful figures [for population studies]. **1838** D. Stevenson *Sk. Civ. Engin. N. Amer.* 316 He and his father..had followed the business of 'house-movers' for fourteen years. **1867** *Atlantic Monthly* Jan. 106/2 Jedwort had over a house-mover from the North Village. **1959** *Times* 18 June (Suppl. Queen in Canada) p. vi/3 In all, 525 homes were lifted from their old foundations and, cradled in the steel framework of the housemovers, moved to their new locations. **1711** *Boston News-Let.* 21 May 2/2 (Advt.), A Young House-Negro Wench of 19 Years of Age that speaks English to be Sold. **1771** in *Maryland Hist. Mag.* (1919) XIV. 135 You will have it that my People are not well fed, it is true they do not live so well as our House negroes, But full as well as any Plantation negroes. **1884** J. C. Harris *Mingo* 191 The house negroes stood in mortal dread of Blue Dave. **1936** M. Mitchell *Gone with Wind* iii. 49 The house-negroes..considered themselves superior to white trash. **1880** J. C. Harris *Uncle Remus* (1884) 116 Dey er mighty biggity, dem house niggers is, but I notices dat dey don't let nuthin' pass. **1970** G. Jackson *Let.* 4 Apr. in *Soledad Brother* (1971) 207 This running dog..was transmitting the credo of the slave to our youth, the mod version of the old house nigger. **1971** K. Wheeler *Epitaph for Mr. Wynn* (1972) xii. 149 Barton called him a house nigger... By Barton's lights, I suppose he was. **1973** *Black World* June 13/1 The murder of Mrs. Mann by the Black maid in the Bullins play affirms the maid's Blackness and consummates her transition from a foot-shuffling house nigger to a proud Black woman. **1934** E. MacManus *Hospital Admin. Women* II. iii. 65 When doing 'a morning round' with a House Physician or Surgeon, the Ward Sister will put him in possession of any new facts relating to each patient before they reach that patient's bed. The Sister should stand on one side of the bed, the House Officer on the other. **1966** *Lancet* 24 Dec. 1399/1 A man holds a senior house-officer post for up to eighteen months. **1969** S. G. Hill in Milne & Chaplin *Mod. Hosp. Managem.* iii. 46 In most hospitals and in most specialties, the medical team comprises the consultant who is the senior doctor, the registrar (a doctor of some four or five years' experience), and either a junior house officer (a newly qualified doctor holding a pre-registration post) or senior house officer (a doctor with rather more experience, often from overseas). **1973** *Lancet* 17 Feb. 17 (Advt.), Burton Road Hospital, Dudley... Applications are invited for the post of Senior House Officer in Geriatrics... Resident staff comprises of 1 Registrar and 2 Senior House Officers. *Ibid.* (Advt.), Chester City Hospital... Applications are invited for the post of House Officer (Geriatrics), pre- or post-registration... Accommodation will be available. **1875** E. Spon *Workshop Receipts* 105/1 House-Painting.—To produce the different tints, various colours are added to the white-lead base. *a* **1877** Knight *Dict. Mech.* II. 1597/2 In house-painting, the pigment most extensively used is white-lead. **1929** D. H. Lawrence *Phoenix II* (1968) 602 There were several brushes for house-painting. **1951** M. Buchanan *Children's Village* 18 There are almost 200 children in the Village now. Each house has in it 15 or 16 boys and girls, their house-parents,..and a teacher-help. **1964** *New Statesman* 10 Apr. 582/1 (Advt.), House-parents for African-Asian married students' hostel. **1923** *Daily Mail* 25 Jan. 5 A number of men are becoming house-parlourmen. **1931** *Morning Post* 10 Aug. 16/6 House-parlourman Required for maisonette. **1961** *Times* 17 Oct. 1/3 House-Parlourman wanted. **1876** Trollope *Amer. Senator* (1877) I. xxiv. 248 Partners were selected within the house party. **1956** M. Stearns *Story of Jazz* (1957) xiii. 145 Its ancestry was long obscured by labels such as 'house-party', 'rent-party', 'parlor social', or simply 'Harlem' piano style. **1968** *Blues Unlimited* Nov. 11 He was around here in town then playing houseparties. **1905** M. F. Reaney *Med. Profession* iii. 39 Finally, there is a junior staff of house physicians and surgeons and the like, working directly under the visiting staff, and responsible for the treatment of the patients in their absence. **1934** House physician [see *house officer* above]. **1962** D. Margerson *Med. as Career* vi. 42 Two pre-registration posts, those of house physician and house surgeon, must be held before full registration is granted. **1970** *New Yorker* 23 May 73/3 Alek Primrose plays..a house physician so nearsighted that he sometimes consults closets. **1908** *Daily Chron.* 3 Nov. 4/7 'A Quoi Tient la Superiorité des Anglo-Saxons?' It is in 'house pride'. **1909** *Ibid.* 7 Dec. 1/2 The 'instinct of house-pride' seems almost never entirely wanting in the home studied. **1936** *Punch* 19 Oct. 600/1 The joke of Felix's housepride continues a trifle too long. **1849** C. Brontë *Shirley* II. vii. 169 You are what you call house-proud; you like to have everything handsome about you. **1899** *Daily News* 17 Oct. 4/7 It is a bad thing for the mother of a family if she cannot be a little 'house-proud'. **1932** *Times Lit. Suppl.* 1 Sept. 603/2 His wife, house-proud as most North Country women are. **1960** *Times* 4 Mar. 13/7 Even under discouraging conditions.. you will see ample proof of house-proud families. **1704** in *Essex Inst. Hist. Coll.* (1866) VIII. 223, I was at my L[and-]Lords house raising. **1829** *Vindicator* (Montreal) 22 Dec. 3/2 A man..who, with some others, attended at a house-raising six miles from this town. **1843** *Amer. Pioneer* II. 451 The frequent necessity for united efforts at house-raisings, log-rollings, corn-huskings, &c. **1927** J. D. Freeman *When West was Young* 415 They would.. reach the West in time for a big house-raising which would be given them by the entire neighborhood. **1949** *Time* 2 May 22/2 It was just like an old-fashioned house-raising bee. **1925** *Inter-State Tattler* 27 Feb. 8/2, I am a tamer of wild women and bitterly against house-rent parties. **1926** Whiteman & McBride *Jazz* viii. 177 Big sessions of blues were held in the South among the colored people, the biggest of all at 'house rent stomps' when a negro found himself unable to pay his rent. **1938** [see *down *prep.* 2 e]. **1955** Shapiro & Hentoff *Hear me talkin to Ya* xii. 210 Joe..would bash at numerous functions and house-rent stomps along Carlisle and John Streets. **1956** M. Stearns *Story of Jazz* (1957) xv. 168 A house-rent party, an unstable social phenomenon that was stimulated by Prohibition and made necessary by the Depression. **1964** W. R. Dixon in J. H. Clarke *Harlem* 138 The legends of the house rent parties are legion. **1968** *Blues Unlimited* Nov. 22 There are the more 'functional' Texas and Chicago house-rent pianists. **1952** W. Granville *Dict. Theatr. Terms* 100 *House seats*, free seats given by courtesy of the house. **1810** *Irish Mag.* Feb. 67/2 The true riding housestile is distinguished in every page. **1940** Graves & Hodge *Long Week-end* xxv. 434 The publisher..has discovered..the 'house-style'. **1960** *Design* July 40/1 The present house style is by no means the first evidence of Watneys' interest in design. **1967** L. B. Archer in Wills & Yearsley *Handbk. Managem. Technol.* 128 The range of design activities which can be loosely termed 'house style' design. *Ibid.* 139 *House style*, the characteristic shapes and colours by which the products, paperwork, and property of a firm may be recognized. **1967** *Listener* 17 Aug. 220/2 It is the galleries which tend to have a 'house style'..which mount the most coherent exhibitions. **1905, 1962** House surgeon [see *house physician* above]. **1934** House surgeon [see *house officer* above]. **1787** in O. Browning *Despatches fr. Paris* (1909) I. 207 It is said that the Timbre, the House-Tax, and *le commerce des Grains* will be strongly oppos'd. **1825** Malthus *Diary* 17 June (1966) 232 Complaints of the weight of taxes—Capitation tax. House tax. **1833** J. S. Mill in *Monthly Repos.* VII. 580 A tradesman in Regent Street pays precisely as much house-tax (56l. 13s. 4d.) as the Duke of Devonshire pays for Chatsworth. **1939** *Brit. Birds* XXXIII. 32 Descriptions of some well-known methods such as the..house-trap, and bat-fowling have already been received. **1960** E. Ennion *House on Shore* iv. 37 House traps of one kind or another, aviaries to all appearances, are to be found in many enthusiastic ringers' gardens. **1936** *Discovery* Apr. 99/2 A distinctive Irish house-type. **1953** L. Kuper *Living in Towns* i. 7 A single house-type has been used in such a way as to create variety and interest, by the grouping of the units in different numbers and relationships. **1955** D. Chapman *Home & Social Status* vi. 84 The families living in different house-types have different social and economic characteristics. **1921** *Daily Colonist* (Victoria, B.C.) 1 Apr. 7/1 (Advt.), Extra values in reliable house wares today and Saturday. **1969** *Sears, Roebuck & Co. Spring Catal.* 565/3 Housewares. **1970** *Toronto Daily Star* 24 Sept. 29/2 (Advt.), 'Perma-Glo' 9-pc. Teflon Cookware Set..Housewares. **1971** *Sunday Express* (Johannesburg) 28 Mar. (Home Jrnl.) 9/3 (Advt.), Housewares..Grapefruit knife ..Bathroom Scales. **1841** A. Bache *Fire-Screen* 119 Mrs. Gibbs, a woman who sometimes came to assist in doing house-work, had followed Mrs. Brown into the parlour. **1871** *Rep. Indian Affairs* (U.S.) (1872) 378 While the boys are engaged in out-door work, the girls could be employed in sewing or house-work. **1928** D. H. Lawrence *Phoenix II* (1968) 531 No woman does her housework with real joy unless she is in love. **1896** A. Morrison *Child of Jago* xvii. 177 The old buildings were sold..to the house-wreckers. **1903** *Westm. Gaz.* 7 Sept. 8/2 The hand of the housewrecker. **1936** House-wrecker [see *demolition 3]. **1808** A. Wilson *Amer. Ornith.* I. 133 The House Wren inhabits the whole of the United States, in all of which it is migratory. **1848** [see Wren 1 b]. **1872** *Amer. Naturalist* VI. 275 Here the common 'house' wren is bleached and faded. **1904** E. Glasgow *Deliverance* v. i. 442 A half-finished nest which a house-wren had begun to build. **1961** O. L. Austin *Birds of World* (1962) 248/2 Most familiar of these [cavity-nesting species] is the common House Wren, a widespread species of 30-odd races which ranges from southern Canada south to Cape Horn and the Falkland Islands.

house, *v.*[1] Add: **7.** Also with *up*.

1873 J. H. Beadle *Undevel. West* i. 40 We can house up, you know, and keep warm on the prairie in winter, but we can't house up and keep cool in the timber in the summer.

house-break, *v.* Add: **2.** *trans.* To train (a domestic animal) to be clean in the house. Also *transf.*, to train (a person) to adopt a specified mode of behaviour within a house. Freq. in pa. pple. or ppl. a. *house-broken*. Chiefly *U.S.*

1900 *Daily Chron.* 27 Aug. 7/4 Malcourt, house-broken, runs to heel with the rest. **1905** T. Roosevelt *Let.* 14 May in *Works* (1926) XIX. 487 Skip is housebroken, but he is like a real little Indian. **1922** *Hotel World* 20 May 6/2, I am 'bawled out' by the dog owner saying that the management of such and such a hotel never objects to a house-broke dog being taken care of in a room. **1932** Wodehouse *Hot Water* xii. 207 House-broken husband though he was, he still had an eye for beauty. **1945** J. Steinbeck *Cannery Row* xx. 82 He didn't even house-break her [*sc.* a puppy]. **1948** G. Vidal *City & Pillar* II. x. 256 We weren't like all these other people here; we weren't housebroken. **1955** W. W. Denlinger *Compl. Boston* 148 Some prospective dog owners fear the ordeal of housebreaking a dog. **1961** Wodehouse *Service with Smile* (1962) ii. 36 You won't mind if I bring a friend with me?..He is house-broken and eats whatever you're having yourself.

housebreaking. Add: Formerly usu. denoting such a crime committed by day, for which *burglary* was the equivalent at night; now applied to such an act committed by day or night. (Further examples.)

1966 *8th Rep. Crim. Law Rev. Comm.* 85 in *Parl. Papers 1966–7* (Cmnd. 2977) XXXIX. 1 The present offence of housebreaking, by day at least, is not regarded as within that class, for many cases are dealt with by fine. **1966** *New Statesman* 7 Oct. 504/2 All this will be the result of abolishing a host of anomalies in the ancient law of burglary and housebreaking (a distinction which..will itself disappear). The Bill makes a bonfire of them. **1973** 'J. Patrick' *Glasgow Gang Observed* iii. 27 Under the law of Scotland 'housebreaking' covers the forced entry of 'any roofed building', i.e. shops, factories, garages, as well as private houses.

house-building. (Later examples.)

1865 Mrs. Stowe *House & Home Papers* 270 Why don't you write a paper on house-building? **1946** *Nature* 5 Oct. 462/1 The various forms of co-operative activity undertaken by the village.., such as road-making, bridge-building or house-building. **1969** *Times* 16 July 22/5 There are doubts about the growth pattern of house-building in this country.

housecraft (hau·s,kraft). [f. House *sb.*[1] + Craft *sb.* 12.] The art of managing a house; skill in domestic duties. Also *attrib.*

1906 L. H. Yates (*title*) Modern housecraft. **1910** *Daily Chron.* 1 Mar. 9/1 Ignorance of housecraft is the favourite reproach brought against the modern woman. *Ibid.*, St. Martha's College of Housecraft. **1914** J. Collings *Colon. Rural Brit.* I. vi. 116 Among the 'optional' subjects contained in the 'Regulations for the Training of Teachers for Elementary Schools' is that of 'Rural Science' (and 'Housecraft' for girls). **1930** *Birmingham Post* 10 Dec. 4/3 Housecraft classes at the Victoria Institute. **1951** *Archit. Rev.* CIX. 285/1 As housecraft activities take up more space than science, the housecraft centre is on the first floor. **1956** W. H. G. Armytage in D. L. Linton *Sheffield* 206 This was the ancestor of the present handsome College of Housecraft opened at Totley after the Second World War.

housee: see *housey-housey.

household. Add: **8. household appliance,** a piece of equipment (e.g. a vacuum cleaner) used in the house; **household book,** a book in which household accounts are noted; **household effects,** the movable contents of a house; **household linen,** linen for the bedroom, table, etc.; **household management,** the art of running a house; **household name,** a name familiar to everyone; **household science** orig. *N. Amer.*, = **domestic science*; **household snake** = *house snake 2.

1926 *Encycl. Brit.* II. 375/2 The outstanding feature in the development of household appliances..has been the greatly extended use of those operated electrically. **1935** *Discovery* Sept. 247/2 The fame of Norwich is also spread by its mustard and starch, electrical machinery and household appliances, aircraft, ironwork and other progressive industries. **1957** *Encycl. Brit.* XI. 813/2 Modern household appliances can be divided into two main headings, electrical and nonelectrical. **1599** M. Hoby *Diary* 18 Feb. (1930) 104 Then to supper: after, I looked of the Houshould book, and then went to priuat praers. **1780** S. Pegge in *Forme of Cury* p. xxxv, The present dean of Carlisle, to whom I stand indebted for his useful notes on the Northumberland-Household Book. **1866** Trollope *Belton Est.* (ed. 3) II. vi. 145 Though she could not succeed in making retrenchments, she could and did succeed in keeping the household books. **1931** S. Jameson *Richer Dust* xviii. 503 Mrs James, pen stirring the clotted ink at the bottom of the bottle, bent close over the pages of her Household Book. **1891** [see Effect *sb.* 4 b]. **1933** *Burlington Mag.* May p. xv/2 The English furniture generally is of better quality than that associated with 'household effects'. **1642** Lady Sussex *Let.* in F. P. Verney *Memoirs* (1892) I. xi. 253 She gives all her linen to to of hur grandchildren not naminge hur householde linen, but in generly hur linen. **1811** Jane Austen *Sense & Sens.* I. v. 56 Household linen, plate, china, and books. **1967** E. Short *Embroidery & Fabric Collage* iii. 72 (*caption*) A basically simple design which could be adapted to almost any article of household linen. **1742** Richardson *Pamela* (ed. 3) III. ix. 50 Let your Servants, under your Direction, do all that relates to Houshold Management. **1801** Jane Austen *Let.* 14 Jan. (1932) I. 111 It will be an amusement to Mary to superintend their Household management, and abuse them for expense. **1861** Mrs. Beeton (*title*) The book of household management. **1862** Tennyson *Idylls of King, Dedication* l. 40 A Prince indeed, Beyond all titles, and a household name, Hereafter, thro' all times, Albert the Good. **1907** W. Russell *Arterial Hypertonus* v. 34 The names of Claude Bernard, Brown-Séquard, Waller, and Schiff are 'household names' in this connection. **1958** *Times* 27 Feb. 11/2 Our first encounter with so many household names in his list which were then unknown. **1969** *New Yorker* 29 Nov. 166/2 Spiro Agnew was then a household name only in his own household. **1970** *Times* 11 Mar. 21/1 (Advt.), We produce packs for a lot of household names. **1938** *Univ. Toronto Cal. 1938–39* (verso of title-p.), In the Faculty of Household Science, the University offers courses leading to the degree of Bachelor of Household Science. **1953** *Univ. London Cal. 1953–54* 464 Queen Elizabeth College... Admitted in 1928 as a School of the University for the B.Sc. Degree in Household and Social Science and for the Degree of B.Sc. (Nutrition) and B.Sc. (Household Science) in 1953. **1963** F. F. Laidler *Gloss. Home Econ. Educ.* 46 *Household science*, a comprehensive study of the scientific, technological and sociological aspects of the household. **1894** W. Crooke *Pop. Relig. & Folk-Lore N. India* vii. 276 (*heading*) The household snake. **1921** A. Evans *Palace of Minos* I. 509 Such a household snake is known, indeed, as *domachitsa* or 'house-mother'. *Ibid.*, In its homely origin, from the religious tending of the household snake, the cult itself may be supposed to be of old indigenous tradition. **1962** R. W. Hutchinson *Prehist. Crete* viii. 208 The cult of the household snake has not entirely died out even now.

housekeep, *v.* (Later examples.)

1900 Kipling in *Daily Express* 26 June 4/5 One or other of them would housekeep for him the year round. **1947** N. Marsh *Final Curtain* ii. 26 Millamant who, since the death of her husband, has house-kept for her father-in-law. **1954** *Encounter* May 20/1 The widow whom she housekeeps for.

housekeeping, *sb.* Add: **1.** Also *transf.*

1966 *Listener* 29 Sept. 448/1, I do not wish to consider ..this..in terms of national housekeeping. **1969** *Times* 2 June (Fire Protection Suppl.) p. i, One of the most important things in industrial fire protection..is what we call good housekeeping—cleanliness, tidiness, the careful removal of rubbish.

3. Used *attrib.* of a rented holiday cabin or cottage equipped for light housekeeping; similarly, *housekeeping rooms, suite*, etc., furnished accommodation with cooking facilities. *N. Amer.*

1935 M. M. Atwater *Murder in Midsummer* xx. 190 The house in which she had her tiny suite of 'housekeeping rooms'. **1968** *Globe & Mail* (Toronto) 15 Jan. 24/3 (Advt.). In sunny warm Grand Cayman. Furnished for 4, housekeeping ocean front cottages. **1968** W. Muir *Belonging* xx. 285 We had booked 'a house-keeping suite' without knowing what that was and found a sitting-room and bedroom..with a small kitchenette and a shower. **1970** *Globe & Mail* (Toronto) 26 Sept. 47/3 (Advt.), Housekeeping cabins fully equipped. **1972** *Amer. Automobile Assoc. Tour Book 1972–73* (Southwestern states) 214 (Advt.), Kinnikinnik Motor Lodge... Featuring 1 & 2 Rm. Units... Large Housekeeping Cottage. **1972** *Prince Edward Island Tourist Accommodations* 49 (Advt.), Brudenell Resort... Housekeeping chalets: single $16 to $20, double $20 to $28, extra person $4. **1973** *Kingston* (Ont.) *Whig-Standard* 5 Mar. 28 (Advt.), Single furnished light housekeeping room, refrigerator, stove and sink. *Ibid.* 8 Mar. 37/9 (Advt.), Near Kingston General Hospital, Queen's, on Union Street. All housekeeping facilities.

4. Short for **housekeeping allowance, money*.

1946 G. Kersh *Clean, Bright & Slightly Oiled* ii. 16 He never give her no housekeeping. **1966** 'O. Mills' *Enemies o Bride* ii. 20 'Do you want some money?' 'No, it doesn't matter. I haven't got the housekeeping off the Gaffer yet, that's all.' **1970** J. Porter *Rather Common Sort of Crime* ii. 25 You'll go throwing your money around but if I ask you for a bit more housekeeping, that's a different story.

5. Those operations of a computer, organization, etc., which make its work possible but do not directly constitute its performance. Freq. *attrib.*

1956 *Jrnl. Assoc. Computing Machinery* III. 269 Most of the errors..turned up in the logical or housekeeping operations, building loops, tallying, etc. **1958** Gotlieb & Hume *High-Speed Data Processing* v. 80 In programming a problem for a data-processing machine many of the instructions are not of an arithmetic nature but fall into a class called organizational or housekeeping instructions. **1962** *IBM Systems Jrnl.* I. 72 The necessary routines such as housekeeping, timekeeping, utility routines, association of equipment, etc. **1966** *Sunday Mail Mag.* (Brisbane) 2 Jan. 12/6 The airline industry calls this process 'housekeeping'. It [*sc.* inspection of aircraft fuel tanks for traces of fungus, etc.] has to be done with painstaking thoroughness. **1967** *Oxford Computer Explained* 15 Housekeeping Suites are run on demand, usually twice a week. **1970** A. Chandor et al. *Dict. Computers* 182 Housekeeping functions include the setting of entry conditions, clearing areas of store if the program expects these to be set to some initial condition,..performing standard input/output routines. **1971** *Sci. Amer.* June 66/1 The computer provides status information on the equipment and performs many routine 'housekeeping' chores, such as adjusting currents in the spectrometer magnets and logging beam currents and other quantities of interest. **1971** *Nature* 27 Aug. 662/3 Mechanized methods of library housekeeping are also considered.

6. *attrib.* and *Comb.*, as *housekeeping book, goods, keys*; **housekeeping allowance, money**, a sum of money regularly set aside for housekeeping expenses.

1914 A. Bennett *Price of Love* xvi. 309 She had received no housekeeping allowance for more than a week. **1965** in P. Jennings *Living Village* (1968) 123 Housekeeping allowance £7. **1849** Dickens *Dav. Copp.* (1850) i. 7, I kept my housekeeping-book regularly, and balanced it with Mr. Copperfield every night. **1930** A. Bennett *Imperial Palace* xxx. 200 The figures of the housekeeping-books had..startled her. **1899** *Daily News* 26 June 10/6 There is a satisfactory trade doing in damasks, and housekeeping goods. **1900** *Ibid.* 17 Sept. 2/7 Housekeeping goods and damasks. **1852** Dickens *Bleak Ho.* (1853) vi. 48 The housekeeping keys, Miss. **1885** C. M. Yonge *Two Sides of Shield* I. i. 12 She gave him money—not father's housekeeping money, but what she got for herself by writing. **1962** E. O'Brien *Lonely Girl* ix. 107 My father forgot about housekeeping money when he drank. **1966** L. Southworth *Felon in Disguise* vi. 86 Her husband had provided her with sufficient housekeeping money for her immediate needs.

housemaid. Add: **c.** *housemaid's knee* (examples).

1831 *Lond. Med. & Physical Jrnl.* LXVII. 42 The third of the cases..was of the common description: the bursa very slightly thickened, but distended with fluid, uneasy, and painful, the most ordinary state of the housemaid's knee. **1889** J. K. Jerome *Three Men in Boat* i. 3 The only malady I could conclude I had not got was housemaid's knee. **1912** Adami & McCrae *Text-bk. Path.* xii. 678 'Housemaid's knee', 'miner's elbow', and 'weaver's bottom' are all well-known forms of bursitis. **1971** *Daily Tel.* 19 Apr. 2 Occupational rheumatism known by a variety of names like weaver's bottom, housemaid's knee, and golfer's shoulder, is costing the country ..millions of pounds a year.

d. Other collocations containing the possessive form, as *housemaid's box*, a box with a container for ashes and a tray above for brushes, dusters, etc.; *housemaid's closet, cupboard*, a cupboard or small room where brooms, cleaning materials, etc., are kept, slops emptied, etc.; *housemaid's gloves*, gloves worn for protection when cleaning grates, etc.

1861 Mrs. Beeton *Bk. Househ. Managem.* 988 Her housemaid's box, containing black-lead brushes..and all utensils necessary for cleaning a grate. **1909** H. G. Wells *Tono-Bungay* III. i. 266 Housemaid's boxes it'll be a pleasure to fall over. **1950** J. Cannan *Murder Included* viii. 146 Sylvia, carrying a housemaid's box, fled at their approach. **1857** C. M. Yonge *Dynevor Terr.* I. xiv. 229 Mrs. Martha might some day let her stand in the housemaid's closet, to behold her idol issue forth in the full glory of an evening dress. **1873** —— *Pillars of House* II. xix. 162 From a housemaid's closet half-way up, Alda was bringing to light a basin. **1906** M. H. Baillie-Scott *Houses & Gardens* x. 31 The housemaid's closet with its slop sink and spaces for pails and brooms. **1911** L. Weaver *House & its Equipment* 103 In small houses where there is not a housemaid's closet. **1950** J. Cannan *Murder Included* iii. 55 There's a sort of housemaids' closet just at the head of the main staircase, and..they had an electric heater put in there so that the housemaid could make the early morning tea for everybody. **1873** L. Troubridge *Life amongst Troubridges* (1966) vi. 52 He..spent nearly all the evening sulking and sobbing in the sink (in the housemaid's cupboard). **1952** G. Raverat *Period Piece* iv. 68 They..used to cry..in the housemaids' cupboard. **1863** Dickens *Uncomm. Trav.* (1866) xxvii. 194/2 A tall straight sallow lady..who does her household work in housemaid's gloves. **1962** G. Avery *Greatest Gresham* vii. 132 Mabel..wearing housemaid's gloves, was cleaning the brass.

houseman. Add: **4.** *U.S. slang.* A burglar.

1904 'No. 1500' *Life in Sing Sing* 255/2 *Houseman*, a burglar. **1911** G. Bronson Howard *Enemy to Society* v. 147 Say a 'house man' or a 'sneak' or a 'second-story' man or a 'peteman'—anything but a 'cracksman'. **1924** G. C. Henderson *Keys to Crookdom* App. B. 408 *Houseman* burglar, prowler.

5. A person responsible for general duties in a private house, hotel, etc.

1934 in Webster. **1960** 'N. Shute' *Trustee from Toolroom* 277 She went through to tell the house-man to clear away the tea. **1961** *Times* 20 July 3/1 Houseman-Handyman..Valet/Houseman. **1968** *Daily Tel.* (Colour Suppl.) 13 Dec. 24/4 His marvellous home..with a Spanish houseman and an Italian cook.

6. A house physician or house surgeon; now usually (in Great Britain) a junior doctor who, having passed all the qualifying examinations, is working for a time in a hospital under a certain amount of supervision prior to being fully registered as an independent medical practitioner.

1938 *Amer. Speech* XIII. 228/2 House men (residents and interns) and 'O.R.' (operating room) nurses take their turn being on call for emergency operations. **1942** M. Dickens *One Pair of Feet* vi. 83, I hate these Housemen—stuck-up little boys, they think they know everything. **1962** *Becoming a Doctor* (B.M.A.) 27 The law requires that newly qualified doctors shall be 'provisionally registered' for a year immediately after they have taken their Finals. They are qualified doctors, but full registration must wait upon the results of two obligatory six-month appointments in hospitals specially approved for the purpose. These hospital appointments are in medicine, surgery, or obstetrics—that is to say, in any two of these three. During this time the young doctor is what is called a 'houseman' or, more correctly, a junior house officer. **1962** D. Margerson *Med. as Career* ix. 57 What are the houseman's duties? The *complete* care of the patients. When they come into hospital he takes down the full story of their illnesses; examines them; arranges for the special tests which aid diagnosis; and prescribes the initial treatment. At least once a day.. the houseman visits all his patients. *Ibid.*, The houseman is the patient's *personal* doctor while he is in hospital. Other doctors—the consultants and his registrar assistants—will be involved in diagnosis and treatment, but none will be as close to the patient..as the houseman. **1965** N. Wymer *Behind Scenes Hospital* iii. 31 The registrars, in turn, are assisted by the house physicians and house surgeons, who, unlike their seniors, live in the hospital and therefore are known as 'housemen'. **1970** *Times* 25 Nov. 11/4 Either consultant or houseman may be called from the clinic for consultation.

Hence **hou·semanship**, the state or position of being a houseman (sense *6).

1969 *Guardian* 10 Mar. 5/4 After six years of concentrated study..the girl is hurled into her first housemanship. The pressure of her first hospital can terrify her. **1972** *Times* 31 Oct. 6/8 Many [doctors] will be completing their housemanship this year.

housemaster. Add: **2.** Also in some day schools, and *transf.*

1963 R. Pedley *Comprehensive School* iii. 124 The house in a day school simply has not got this basis... Take, for example, a housemaster who does quite a lot of administration. **1965** H. Davies *Culture & Grammar School* v. 85 Where senior house masters exist..they should be able to exercise an effective supervision over the boys in their care. **1966** *Listener* 10 Mar. 342/2 We continue to put some offenders..under the care of individual probation officers and Borstal housemasters.

Hence **hou·semasterly** *adj.*, like or characteristic of a housemaster.

1961 A. Wilson *Old Men at Zoo* ii. 112, I should have to hear myself speak in these housemasterly tones many times before I had done with the business. **1963** *Times Lit. Suppl.* 8 Feb. 87/2 The effect is at once toughly moral and academic, a house-masterly harangue.

house-mistress. Add: **2.** At a girls' school, a person responsible for certain aspects of the supervision of the pupils; in a boarding school, the mistress in charge of one of the boarding houses.

1912 A. Brazil *New Girl at St. Chad's* iii. 42 Her house-mistress would not have been ready to overlook any deficiency in punctuality. **1961** *Evening Standard* 26 July 25/6 (Advt.), Education Committee..Housemistress (non-teaching) required..Technical School for Girls. **1972** *Daily Tel.* 24 Nov. 6/6, I shall continue as housemistress and shall teach mathematics and religious education. **1973** *Radio Times* 8 Nov. 81/1 Miss Gee, housemistress of Guldeford House at Benenden School, recalls Princess Anne's time there.

house-mother. Add: (Earlier and later examples.) Also in extended uses.

1834 Carlyle *Sart. Res.* II. i, in *Fraser's Mag.* Feb. 177/2 The good Gretchen..hovered round him, as only a true housemother can: assiduously she cooked and sewed and scoured for him. **1936** *Variety* 8 July 46/1 The cynical college man who dominates his fair-haired pal, the prim house mother—they're all here and more. **1959** *Tablet* 7 Mar. 240/1 Resident Roman Catholic Housemother required to act as Deputy to Housemother-in-charge. **1970** *Observer* 25 Jan. 6/5 The house mother—a woman who calls daily to look after a family in their own home. **1971** 'M. Innes' *Awkward Lie* iv. 71 Calling young women house-mothers must be one of Overbury [School]'s notably few concessions to the march of time.

house snake. For entry s.v. House *sb.*[1] 23 substitute: **1.** One of several North American snakes belonging to the genera *Elaphe* and *Lampropeltis*.

1807 in *Mass. Hist. Soc. Coll.* (1815) 2nd Ser. III. 54 The milk or house snake, speckled like a rattlesnake. **1884** 'Mark Twain' *Huck. Finn* xxxix. 396 We went for

the snakes, and grabbed a couple of dozen garters and house-snakes. **1958** R. Conant *Field Guide Reptiles U.S.* 171 Sometimes called 'house snake', but 'barn snake' would be more descriptive, for it would reflect the frequency with which farm buildings are entered in search of rodents.

2. A snake kept as a household god.

[**1742** C. Owen *Ess. towards Nat. Hist. Serpents* 218 Ælian speaks of domestick Serpents, that were in the Houses of the Egyptians, and look'd upon as household Gods. *Ibid.*, The Arabians reputed Serpents sacred Beings... They take them into their Houses, feed and worship them as Genii, or Guardians of the Place. **1868** J. Fergusson *Tree & Serpent Worship* 25 There are house serpents which are accounted in the northern parts of Sweden as household gods.] **1894** W. Crooke *Pop. Relig. & Folk-Lore N. India* vii. 276 Should rain drive the house snake out of his hole, he is worshipped. **1935** A. Evans *Palace of Minos* IV. I. 153/2 When the house snakes died the master and mistress of the house died too. **1962** R. W. Hutchinson *Prehist. Crete* viii. 124 It was the house snake that was fed and revered as the genius, the guardian angel of the house. **1965** R. & D. Morris *Men & Snakes* ii. 47 A gallant housesnake..refused to desert the Macedonian village of Kalenova when the human inhabitants fled.

3. A southern African snake of the genus *Boædon.*

1907 R. L. Ditmars *Reptile Bk.* xxxii. 300 (*heading*) The Red Coluber; Corn Snake; Red Chicken Snake; Mouse Snake; Scarlet Racer; House Snake *Coluber guttatus*, (Linn.). **1911** *East London* (Cape Province) *Dispatch* 1 Sept. 7 These house snakes are more serviceable to man than cats, for they can follow rats and mice into their hiding places. **1932** *Discovery* XIII. 364/2 The brown house snake, *Boodon* [sic] *lineatus*, is far more efficient than a cat in keeping down rats and mice, as it penetrates into their holes and destroys the young. **1962** V. F. M. Fitz-Simons *Snakes S. Afr.* 123/1 In search of its prey it is often attracted to, and found in and about, human settlements, and has thus got the name of House Snake.

house-top. Add: **b.** *fig.* A public place; esp. (with allusion to Luke xii. 3) in phrase *to proclaim, declare,* or *cry on* or *from the house-top(s)*, to make public, to proclaim so that everyone knows. Also *attrib.*

1870 *Brewer's Dict. Phr. & Fable* 712/1 *Proclaim on the housetop*, to proclaim or make known to every one; to blab in public. **1895** *Ibid.* (rev. ed.) 632/1 To cry from the house-top. To proclaim (it) from the house-top. **1899** *Westm. Gaz.* 15 Nov. 3/2 The policy of house-top virtue. **1906** J. Jackson tr. *Thoughts of Marcus Aurelius* 35 A man who has done a good deed should be like a horse that has run its race..: in other words, he ought not to proclaim it from the house-tops. **1911** C. G. Robertson *Eng. under Hanoverians* II. iv. 345 To cry on the house-tops that it was merry in England before the new industry came up. **1931** L. Birch *Pyramid* xviii. 233 Someone should come forward and cry from the housetops that all friendships that are romantic are not, for that reason, immoral. **1934** 'G. Orwell' *Burmese Days* iii. 52 My friend, you do not think that. If truly you disapprove of the British Empire, you would not be talking of it privately here. You would be proclaiming from the housetops. **1955** L. P. Hartley *Perfect Woman* xxiii. 200 Don't worry; I didn't expect you to proclaim it on the house-tops, and I shan't either.

hou·se-train, *v.* [Train *v.*[1]] *trans.* To train (a domestic animal or infant) to be clean in the house. Also *transf.*, esp. = *house-break *v.* 2 *transf.*; and *fig.*

1924 W. J. Locke *Coming of Amos* vii. 89 If you hadn't been house-trained by your excellent mother I should say that you've been making a beast of a night of it. **1928** *Punch* 25 Apr. 455/1 It [*sc.* a cheque] is house-trained and was clean about the bank. **1930** Kipling *Thy Servant a Dog* 70 It are that dash-Toby-Dog! C'm with, and house-train him! **1937** A. Huxley *Ends & Means* xii. 180 The work of the late Dr. Suttie, whose book, *The Origins of Love and Hatred*, contains an interesting chapter on the effects of early house-training upon the emotional life of human beings. **1939** S. Spender tr. *Toller's Pastor Hall* I. 41 Goethe wasn't quite house-trained either, you know. First place he was a Freemason, and second too much of a cosmopolitan. **1944** N. Streatfeild *Myra Carrol* 100 Birds aren't ever house trained. **1950** B. Russell *Unpop. Ess.* vii. 127 Some boys never learn to be what, in animals, is called 'house-trained'. **1955** M. Hastings *Cork & Serpent* xvii. 243 After thirty years of marriage, I haven't been able to house-train him yet. **1956** A. Huxley *Adonis & Alphabet* 155 It is easy to house-train a cat or a dog. **1958** [see *billetee]. **1959** *Elizabethan* Apr. 22/2 Mr. Rochester has a lot of the Wild Man in him... But he is also a good deal more house-trained than Heathcliff. **1961** *Listener* 26 Oct. 645/2 We house-train puppies on a similar basis. **1969** Auden *City without Walls* 63 Rumours ran through the city That the Tsar's housedog Was not house-trained. **1969** *Times* 11 July 20/5 (Advt.), Capable girl, willing help run..Highland fishing cottage and two house trained small boys. **1973** J. Wainwright *Devil You Don't* 37 You house-trained him, when he was a kid. Trained him to use the totty. Trained him in table-manners.

housey-housey (hau·si,hau·si). Also **housie-housie, housy-housy** and abbrev. **housey, housie,** (*rare*) **housee.** [f. *house *sb.*[1] 9 c + -y[6].] A later name for the game of 'house' (see also quot. 1964).

1936 F. Richards *Old-Soldier Sahib* iii. 69 To draw a crowd they would shout: 'Housee, housee, housee!' **1937** Partridge *Dict. Slang* 410/2 Housey-housey! **1938** in Mencken *Amer. Lang.* Suppl. (1945) I. 461/1 The game so popular in army circles in Hong Kong under the name of *tombola* is now sweeping South London as a craze called *housey-housey*. It is played for the most part by housewives who are attracted to open-door booths by a glittering display of cutlery and chromium-plated clocks. **1945** *Penguin New Writing* XXVI. 30 He was shouting numbers hoarsely from the Housey-Housey stall. **1949** S. P. Llewellyn *Troopships* 3 Men playing housie-housie (tombola). **1949** E. de Mauny *Huntsman in Career* 163 Someone started up a 'housey' school. **1957** J. Frame *Owls do Cry* 42 Like the woman down the road..having parties every Saturday night with housey-housey and drink. **1960** *Times* (Canada Suppl.) 16 Mar. p. xv/5 Gala dances and housie-housie at night, bring people into contact. **1964** A. Wykes *Gambling* x. 249 The call used to assemble a group for a game of house was 'housey-housey'. **1967** *Stage* 2 Mar. 4/1 'Housey'-addicts never had it so good! **1971** B. W. Aldiss *Soldier Erect* 30 Desperate till now to get off the hated boat with its hated routines of exercise and housey-housey, I was suddenly reluctant to leave the shelter of a familiar place.

housing, *sb.*[1] Add: **1.** (Later examples.)

1848 *Rep. U.S. Comm. Patents 1847* 168 The tobacco was hardly worth the housing. **1850** *Rep. Comm. Patents: Agric. 1849* (U.S. Dept. Agric.) 321 This mode is pursued easily by simply splitting..the plant..before it is cut down for housing. **1930** A. P. Herbert *Water Gipsies* viii. 96 Honest John Raven worked hard and late at the office, and sometimes brought home papers with him, or if not he talked 'housing' or threw off little anecdotes about 'National Insurance'. **1973** *Oxford Times* 9 Nov. 9/4 One problem we both have is of course that of housing.

6. b. *spec.* A massive metal frame or pillar that supports one end of a set of rolls in a rolling mill.

1869 H. S. Osborn *Metallurgy of Iron & Steel* III. iv. 771 (*heading*) View of a housing, and section of rollers and foundation. **1938** *Extension Course Ferrous Metall.* (Penn. State Coll.) (ed. 2) II. xii. 203 The housings are very heavy cast iron or steel frames, designed to support the rolls and adjusting mechanism securely in place. **1965** M. H. T. Alford tr. *Tselikov & Smirnov's Rolling Mills* v. 135 The weight of housings is taken by their feet which bear on the foundations through girders.

d. A structure that supports and encloses the bearings at the end of an axle or shaft; a journal-box. Hence more widely, a rigid case or cover that encloses and protects an axle or any other mechanism or piece of apparatus.

1889 *Cent. Dict.*, *Housing*, a housing-box; a journal-box. **1915** V. W. Pagé *Model T Ford Car* iii. 111 The bevel pinion meshes with a large bevel gear..which is attached to the differential housing. **1916** J. E. Homans *Automobile Handbk.* xvi. 177 The housings of the oil pump, water pump, [etc.]. **1922** L. Bell *Telescope* x. 242 The housing, just big enough to take in the equatorial with the tube turned low, opens on the south side and then can be rolled northward on its track..well clear of the instrument. **1935** *Times* 2 Oct. 6/5 Helical springs working in a closed oil-filled housing. **1949** Frazee & Bedell *Automotive Fundamentals* viii. 458 In conventional automobiles and trucks, the rear-axle housing supports the rear-end load on the road wheels. In addition, the housing contains the driving mechanism and carries the rear-wheel bearings. **1958** *Times* 9 May 13/7 The safety housings on the toggle switches. **1962** *Which? Car Suppl.* Oct. 139/2 The water pump to heater hose was chafing on thermostat housing. **1968** P. H. Smith *Triumph Autobk. Two* (ed. 2) vii. 101/1 The outer ends of the axle-shafts are carried in trunnion mounted bearing housings which are attached to vertical pressed steel links. **1972** *Sci. Amer.* Jan. 68 (Advt.), A large diascopic illuminator and a set of episcopic illuminators; a 4 × 5″ bellows..; a mirror reflex housing; and a sensitive spot meter.

7. *housing association, problem, project, question, scheme, site, unit*; **housing development** [*development 3 d], the act or process of planning and building a group of houses (a **housing estate**) and associated services on a site; **housing list**, a waiting-list for council houses; **housing screw**, a screw by means of which the rollers in a rolling mill can be adjusted and the thickness of the metal controlled.

1957 *Act* 5 & 6 *Eliz. II* c. lvi. §189 'Housing association' means a society, body of trustees or company established for the purpose of..facilitating or encouraging the construction or improvement of houses. **1970** *Internat. & Compar. Law Q.* XIX. II. 205 Discussion inevitably ranged into such related topics as..housing associations and co-operatives. **1971** P. Gresswell *Environment* 131 The main object of Housing Associations is to provide houses to let for local people. **1951** *Amer. City* Sept. 104/1 The builders of Lakewood Park..envisioned the building of a community, including parks, play grounds, schools, churches, and a major shopping center. More than 30,000 people are already living in the 7,200 homes..that have been completed. There is a fact more than bigness, however, that puts this housing development among the pioneers. **1959** N. Mailer *Advts. for Myself* (1961) 153 He looks down six stories into the giant quadrangle of the Queens housing development. **1920** *Times* 18 Nov. 9/4 It will afford..much-needed means of access to the L.C.C. Housing Estate at Dagenham. **1931** *Economist* 12 Dec. 1136/2 Weaker [building] societies may become mere appanages of speculative builders, agents, and other interests concerned with 'housing-estate' exploitation. **1936** W. Holtby *South Riding* I. vi. 68 More land for housing estates. **1956** J. M. Mogey *Family & Neighbourhood* 73 The housing-estate family developed a much more critical attitude. **1964** M. Argyle *Psychol. & Social Probl.* xv. 183 The Census of 1961 showed that more people than before live in suburbs and housing estates. **1952** M. Laski *Village* xiii. 181 Roy had put his name down on the housing-list at the Town Hall. **1968** L. Berg *Risinghill* 46 The bannisters broke and she fell down the stairs and broke her leg. She's been on the housing list twenty-five years. **1899** S. A. Barnett in H. Barnett *Canon Barnett* (1918) II. xlix. 311 The housing problem..is bound up with the industrial problem, with the education problem, with the social problem, and with the religious problem. **1911** G. B. Shaw *Getting Married* Pref. 117 They were content to have the whole national housing problem treated on a basis of one room for two people. **1947** *Tribune* 24 Jan. 12/1 They began talking about the housing problem. **1973** *Guardian* 18 May 16/1 One of the reasons for Britain's housing problem is that many houses are in the wrong place. **1938** *Jrnl. Social Forces* May 528 (*title*) Some eighteenth century housing projects in France. **1967** S. Sontag *Death Kit* (1968) 10 All the housing projects are unadorned boxes built of brick. **1970** *Globe & Mail* (Toronto) 25 Sept. B7/5 A $1,644,512 loan for a 139-unit apartment house in a Hamilton low rental housing project. **1899** *Daily News* 19 July 5/5 Milner had charge of the Housing Question after the boom was launched. **1903** W. Thompson *Housing Handbk.* p. v, The past twelve years, spent in..the promotion of a number of housing schemes. **1918** Lloyd George *Slings & Arrows* (1929) 199 Your housing schemes must, in the majority of cases, be schemes outside the house. **1966** J. Betjeman *High & Low* 22 We pounded through a housing scheme. **1874** *Jrnl. Iron & Steel Inst.* I. 352 The top and bottom rolls are simultaneously raised or lowered by four housing screws. **1951** *Engineering* 5 Jan. 2/1 The housing screws are of 0·5 per cent. forged carbon steel. **1926** *Daily Chron.* 13 May 2/7 Work on a Bristol housing site has stopped owing to transport difficulties. **1972** *Country Life* 30 Nov. 1487/1 Every housing site has its own unique character. **1951** M. McLuhan *Mech. Bride* 38/2 It means an extension of housing units. **1970** G. Greer *Female Eunuch* 227 No clever orientation of clean and efficient housing units..can break down the suspicion that the Oedipal unit feels.

Hova (hōu·vă, hɒ·vă). Also **Ovah.** [Malagasy.] **a.** A member of the dominant race of the Malagasy Republic (formerly Madagascar); also, in restricted use, one of the middle class, as distinct from the nobles and the slaves. Also *collect.* **b.** The language of this race. Also *attrib.*

1839 *Penny Cycl.* XIV. 259/2 The Ovahs, who inhabit the elevated plains in the interior, are in height rather above the European standard. **1858** W. Ellis *Three Visits to Madagascar* 468 In Madagascar itself different dialects exist. The spoken language of the Hovas..differs from that on the coasts. **1883** *Encycl. Brit.* XV. 171/1 The Hòva, who occupy the central province of Imérina. *Ibid.* 172/2 The majority of Hòva houses are built of layers of the hard red clay of the country. **1887** *Fortn. Rev.* Mar. 435 Only a few months ago French politicians..called the Hovas barbarians. **1911** J. G. Frazer *Golden Bough: Magic Art* (ed. 3) I. vii. 397 The Hovas and other tribes of Madagascar. **1915** J. Sibree *Naturalist in Madagascar* xxii. 299 Their [*sc.* Sàkalàva] language presents a good deal of difference from the Hova form of Malagasy, both in vocabulary and in pronunciation, yet the groundwork and the grammar is essentially the same. **1972** A. Sillery *Africa* (ed. 2) ii. 114 The most important native people, as well as the most numerous and advanced, are the Merina or Ambaniandro, commonly called Hova, whose homeland is Imerina on the plateau near Antananarivo.

hoven, *ppl. a.* Add: Also as *sb.*

1845 S. Judd *Margaret* II. v. 284 Glad you got through with the pock so well...its worse than horn-ail, hoven or core. **1877** *Rep. Vermont Dairym. Assoc.* VIII. 107 Hoven in cattle is caused by over-feeding upon succulent food like green clover. **1878** [see *bloat *sb.* 1 b]. **1891** [see *blowing *vbl. sb.*[1] 2 d]. **1902** *Phil. Trans. R. Soc.* CXCIX. A. 400 The symptoms of 'hoven' are not unlike those of prussic acid poisoning. **1962** [see *bloat *sb.* 1 b].

hover, *sb.* Add: **1. a.** Also, a state of hovering. (Further examples.)

1961 *Hovering Craft & Hydrofoil* Oct. 32/2 Floatation and sea-keeping capability while floating and during transition from hover to high forward speed. **1962** *Air-Cushion Vehicles* July 16 The skirts have withstood the early trials well, most of the wear having occurred during tethered hovers on hard standing. **1967** B. W. McCormick *Aerodynamics of V/Stol Flight* v. 106 The helicopter rotor in hover or in vertical climb is relatively easy to analyze. **1969** I. Kemp *Brit. G.I. in Vietnam* iii. 61 Major Bracken eased back on the cyclic..and our speed dropped until we were almost in a hover. **1971** *Physics Bull.* Nov. 655/3 With careful design the tilting rotor propeller can be efficient in both hover and cruise.

3. Also, a shelter used in the brooding of chickens.

1907 *Elem. Sch. Teacher* Mar. 410 A hover which was made of felt was hung in the brooder. **1936** *Nature* 3 Oct. 583/1 The merits of the various systems of hovers and battery brooders are discussed.

3*. 'A floating island, or bed of reeds' (E.D.D.). Chiefly Norfolk *dial.*

1892 P. H. Emerson *Son of Fens* xiv. 120 'Have you got enough damming boards for another dam?' 'Yes... We shan't want many; there's a hover there.' **1893** H. Cozens-Hardy *Broad Norfolk* 77 *Hover*, a floating island. **1955** *Times* 3 Aug. 10/2 Now the lesser bulrush which grows on the 'hover' (excellent word to denote a table of floating vegetation) round the edge of the open water is all a-quiver.

hover, *v.*[1] Add: **1. c.** Of a helicopter or other aircraft: to remain stationary in the air, relative to the ground.

1892 *Railroad & Engin. Jrnl.* Nov. 508/2 With 60 turns of the rubber the apparatus would just hold its own—i.e., hover in the same spot, against a wind of

9 ft. per second. **1926** J. L. Pritchard *Bk. Aeroplane* ix. 177 It had distinct possibilities of achieving what the helicopter sets out to achieve, rising, descending vertically in still air and hovering. **1935** P. H. Sumner *Aircraft* II. 63 To be of any practical use the helicopter aircraft must be capable of forward motion in addition to rising vertically and hovering. **1972** *Daily Tel.* 3 July 2 (*caption*) A Sea King helicopter..hovering over Rockall in the Atlantic.

d. Of a hovercraft: to be supported on its air-cushion, esp. while stationary; also *transf.*, to travel in a hovercraft.

1962 *Hovering Craft & Hydrofoil* Aug.–Sept. 20/1 Hovering at speeds below 10 knots..over water, the depression in the water surface beneath the craft gives a measure of 'keel' effect. **1962** *Air-Cushion Vehicles* Oct. 81/2 The rudder, however, is ineffective at low speeds or while hovering. **1967** *Jane's Surface Skimmer Systems 1967–68* 31/2 Echo sounding transducers..will remain immersed whether the craft is 'hovering' or underway. **1968** *Nature* 10 Aug. 549/1 (*heading*) Hover over from Dover. **1970** *Motoring Which?* July 111/2 A control stick adjusted the airflow from the fan, to make the craft hover or go forwards.

6. To maintain in a hovering state.

1967 B. W. McCormick *Aerodynamics of V/Stol Flight* v. 162 The gross weight that can be hovered at the power available is found by correcting the thrust for download.. and for overlap. **1969** *Aeroplane* LXXIII. 708/2 In the case of the rescue system preferred by the USA Coast Guard..the helicopter is hovered in contact with the water and a working platform is extended from the craft.

hover- (hǫ·vəɹ), the first element of *hovercraft, prefixed to other sbs. to denote things of a similar form or serving a similar purpose to the thing denoted by the sb., but having some connection with hovercraft or their principle of operation. **a.** Used to form the names of vehicles and other things that utilize an air-cushion as a means of support, as *hoverbus, -car, -ferry, -kiln, -liner, -pallet, -ship, -train, -truck, -vehicle.*

1962 *Daily Tel.* 1 Mar. 17/1 (*heading*) Hover-buses planned for south coast. **1961** *New Scientist* 31 Aug. 503 What they have in mind is a streamlined hovercar, seating 100 or more, travelling on..an elevated concrete track at speeds of around 300 m.p.h. **1970** *Nature* 17 Jan. 214/2 In the British design, the hovercar straddles a concrete beam of box-shaped cross-section. **1961** *New Scientist* 29 June 785/2 Denny's..hope by next year to produce an actual passenger-carrying hover-ferry... They ultimately envisage a hovercraft capable of carrying 50 to 70 passengers at about 20 knots. **1970** *Ibid.* 11 June 528/2 Both the hoverferry and the general purpose version have been subjected to an engineering modification programme. **1965** *Ibid.* 2 Dec. 633/1 The hoverkiln relies upon air pads to lubricate the pallets on which pottery is slowly conveyed through the baking kilns. **1962** *Listener* 16 Aug. 258/3 Plans for atomic-powered hoverliners. **1970** *New Scientist* 11 June 528/2 The original dreams of large hoverliners seem to have been shelved. **1966** *Times* 14 Oct. 11/7 The Ulster Prince, a 4,600-ton drive-on ferry.., will be equipped with 'hoverpallets'. **1967** *Jane's Surface Skimmer Systems 1967–68* 21/2 Palletised loads can be 'floated' in on hover-pallets, supplied with air from the main compressor. **1961** *Guardian* 23 June 10 The passenger-carrying 'hovership'..is a substantial advance towards bringing these curious vessels that are neither of the sea nor of the air into practical, everyday use. **1971** *Country Life* 8 Apr. 830/2 In *The Future of Ships*..D. Phillips-Birt looks at projects for 4,000 and 5,000-ton hovership freighters. **1961** *New Statesman* 14 July 67/1 The possibility of hovertrains. **1971** *Daily Tel.* 16 Apr. 6/7 A French demonstration hovertrain has been running for 18 months on an 11-mile stretch of elevated monorail outside Orléans. **1960** *Daily Tel.* 12 Aug. 11/7 A series of Hovertrucks. **1963** *Guardian* 6 June 3/3 The 'hover truck', a development from the Hovercraft which some farmers in East Anglia regard as an essential farm implement of the future. **1962** *Daily Tel.* 6 June 22/3 What we have in mind is that hover vehicles, vehicles designed to be supported on a cushion of air, shall be considered as motor vehicles whether or not adapted for use on the roads.

b. Used to form the names of things related to the operation and requirements of hovercraft, as *hoverport, -rail, -track, -way* [after *motorway*].

1967 *Guardian* 6 Feb. 3/2 A British hoverport in the south. **1967** *Jane's Surface Skimmer Systems 1967–68* 16/2 The route will be between a new hoverport in Pegwell Bay area and a French terminal..east of Calais harbour. **1962** *Engineering* 5 Jan. 6/2 A high-speed hover-rail system..could also be cheaper than motorways. **1965** *New Scientist* 5 Aug. 318/3 The hovertrack, of concrete, would be elevated, and on it would run a 'train' probably capable of carrying several passengers at 100 miles an hour. **1973** *Daily Tel.* 7 Sept. 18/2 The strong constituency interest in the future of the hovertrack centre. **1960** *Times* 12 Aug. 6/4 They will be capable of operating over land, water, marsh or broken ice, or along rough bulldozed 'hoverways' in undeveloped areas. **1962** *Hovering Craft & Hydrofoil* May–June 15/1 It is desirable that definite 'hoverways' be established and shown on charts, especially where these traverse commercial routes where the density of shipping is high.

hovercraft (hǫ·vəɹkrɑft). Also **Hovercraft.** Pl. **-craft.** [f. Hover *v.*[1] + Craft *sb.*[1]] A vehicle or craft that can be supported by a cushion of air ejected downwards against a surface close below it, and can in principle travel over any relatively smooth surface (as a body of water, marshland, gently sloping land) while having no significant contact with it.

For some years from 1961 registered as a proprietary term but now in the public domain.

1959 [see *ground effect* s.v. *Ground *sb.* 17 d]. **1959** *Daily Mail* 6 Apr. 5/2 The sea-saucer has been officially christened the Hovercraft. **1960** A. Croome *Hover Craft* iv. 60/1 When the 455 h.p. engine is started the air-cushion quickly builds up underneath and the Hovercraft rises off the ground (or water) and hovers there very steadily. **1961** C. S. Cockerell in *Hovering Craft & Hydrofoil* Oct. 8 My wife and I tried to find a name and settled for the not altogether appropriate word 'Hovercraft'. **1962** *Daily Tel.* 12 Mar. 13 British United Airways intends..to start the first Hovercraft service in the world this summer. **1965** *Guardian* 5 Jan. 3/3 Air cushion vehicles—or hovercraft, if you prefer the term. **1967** *Jane's Surface Skimmer Systems 1967–68* 24/2 Designed initially for military logistic-support duties, the BH. 8 is a twin-engined, 80 ton, open-water hovercraft with bow and stern loading doors. **1972** *Drive* Spring 75/2 From the attractive cliff gardens there are exciting views of modern hovercraft roaring in and out of Pegwell Bay.

ho·ver-height. Also **hoverheight.** [f. Hover *v.*[1] + Height *sb.*] The distance separating the underside of a hovercraft (either stationary or in motion) from the surface below it when the vehicle is supported on its air-cushion.

1959 *Times* 2 Sept. 11/6 Even quite small Hovercraft can have a hover-height of several feet. **1961** *New Scientist* 2 Feb. 266/3 The installation of the second engine ..reduced the 'hoverheight' by 2½ inches to 8 inches. **1962** *Hovering Craft & Hydrofoil* Oct. 13/1 In rough conditions, speed can be reduced and the hover-height increased to give adequate wave clearance. **1967** *Jane's Surface Skimmer Systems 1967–68* 44/1 Its hover height can be varied to a maximum of three feet, depending on loading.

hovering, *vbl. sb.* **a.** (Further examples: see *Hover *v.*[1] 1 c, d.)

1916 M. A. S. Riach *Air-Screws* ix. 113 The value of (V) is zero, and the machine remains stationary. This is the condition already established for 'hovering' flight. **1960** Houghton & Brock *Aerodynamics* viii. 179 In steady hovering, the weight is balanced by the jet thrust and the force due to the 'cushion' of air below the craft. **1962** *Daily Tel.* 4 Sept. 17/1 Their hovering manœuvres, ..and the transformation in the air to 'normal' fast flying fighter planes, marked a new era in the development of aircraft.

(ii) Motion of a hovercraft while it is supported on an air-cushion: see *Hover *v.*[1] 1 d.

1967 *Hovercraft World* Jan.–Apr. 14/1 We waved goodbye..at 10.15 hours heading for Wexford, 75 miles away. The fog soon lifted and this leg was a straightforward piece of 'hovering'.

hove-to: see Heave *v.* 20 c.

hoving (hōu·viŋ), *vbl. sb.* Also **hooving.** [Hove *v.*[2]] Swelling (of cheese).

1743 W. Ellis *Mod. Husbandman* May vii. 93 Others to prevent the Cheese's Hoving, will mix skim and new milk together. **1811** [see Hove *v.*[2] 3]. **1858** C. L. Flint *Milch Cows* 265 Heat would make them [*sc.* cheeses] sweat..which extracts the fat, and tends to induce hooving.

Hovis (hōu·vis). The registered trade mark of a brand of flour; also, a loaf of brown bread made from this flour. Also *attrib.*

1890 *Trade Marks Jrnl.* 16 Nov. 1137/2 *Hovis.* Flour and Articles of Food, made partly or wholly of Flour, Richard Smith, Corn Flour Mills, Macclesfield, Cheshire. **1895** G. B. Shaw *Let.* 23 Dec. (1965) 584 Eat stewed fruit and hovis. **1898** *Christian World* 3 Feb. 4/5 Our representative was told that 'Hovis' was the concoction of a Cambridge undergraduate, being compounded of 'hominis' and 'vis', 'strength of man'. **1907** *Yesterday's Shopping* (1969) 510/3 Hovis Food—No. 1, for infants... No. 2, for children and invalids. **1930** S. Beckett *Whoroscope* 3 So we drink Him and eat Him And the watery Beaune and the stale cubes of Hovis. **1932** Dylan Thomas *Let.* (1966) 5 Give me a half-pint, a Hovis. **1962** L. Deighton *Ipcress File* i. 10 He had a long thin nose, a moustache like flock wallpaper, sparse, carefully combed hair, and complexion of a Hovis loaf. **1967** A. Laski *Seven Other Years* iii. 32 She liked the shapes of bread, and the different colours..some, Hovises and wholemeals, dark and interesting.

how, *adv.* (*sb.*[3]) Add: **A.** *adv.* **2. a.** *how are you?*: (in quot. 1918) used ironically in sense 'indeed!' Also, *how goes it?* = How-do-you-do 1; *how's* (or *how are*) *things* (or, orig. Austral. and N.Z., *tricks*)*?*; *how do?*: = How-do-you-do.

1598 Florio *Worlde of Wordes* 41/1 How now? how goes it? go to, it is well. **1764** [see Go *v.* 18]. **1799** [see Do *v.* 19]. **1886** H. Baumann *Londinismen* 79/2 *How-do*, how d'you do? **1892** I. Zangwill *Childr. Ghetto* I. 147 'Well, how goes it, Reb Moshé?' said Reb Shemuel with his cheery smile. **1918** Joyce *Exiles* i. 2 *Beatrice.* Did he practise the piano while I was away? *Brigid.* Practise, how are you! **1926** K. S. Prichard *Working Bullocks* viii. 86 They halloed and yelled to him: 'H'lo, Red!' 'How's things?' **1928** H. Crane *Let.* 27 Mar. (1965) 321 How goes it with your translations..? *a* **1930** D. H. Lawrence *Mod. Lover* (1934) 192 Hello, you two. How's things? **1934** *Passing Show* 27 Jan. 5/4 Hey, Morrison, old socks. How's things? **1939** C. Belton *Outside Law in N.Z.* xxv. 129 'Hallo. How are things?' I greeted him. **1940** H. G. Wells *Babes in Darkling Wood* I. iv. 90 'How do, Father?' said Gemini. **1941** *Coast to Coast 1941* 195 'G'day,' he said. 'How's tricks?' **1949** D. M. Davin *Roads from Home* I. iii. 49 How's things?..How's tricks with you? **1971** B. Malamud *Tenants* 149 'I won't be coming around to say howdo this Friday, Irene,' Bill said tonelessly. **1973** L. Meynell *Thirteen Trumpeters* xiv. 211 'How's tricks?' he enquired. 'I'm fine. I slept like a top.'

b. (Earlier and later examples.)

1833 *New Sporting Mag.* V. 325 'Well thrown by Huddleston!'—'How's that?' 'Run out!' **1927** G. A. Terrill *Out in Glare* iv. 62 The ball swerved—pitched; the inner edge of his bat grazed it. 'Rap!' it had got him on the pad. *''s that?'* cried Verlenden, unaware of the graze. **1973** A. Mann *Tiara* ii. 13 The sharp click of bat on ball, and un-Italian cries of 'Owzat!'..showed that cricket was well underway.

4. c. *how much*: used in humorous colloq. requests for the repetition of something not heard or not understood. Also, *how much?* = what? eh? (Cf. *what price* so-and-so?)

1852 F. E. Smedley *Lewis Arundel* xxxiv. 292 'Then my answer must mainly depend on the exact height of the principles.' 'On the how much?' inquired Frere, considerably mystified. **1914** C. Mackenzie *Sinister St.* II. III. i. 509 'I've got to get..a picture of Mona Lisa.' 'Mona how much?' said Alan. 'La Gioconda, you ass.' **1927** E. Bowen *Hotel* ii. 11 'She is a Hedonist.' 'A *how*-much?' 'A Hedonist.' **1928** [see *Gawd]. **1934** T. S. Eliot *Rock* i. 12 *Ethelbert*: Ain't you ever 'eard me speak o' the principles of Social Credit Reform? *Alfred*: 'Ow much? *Ethelbert*: What Major Douglas 'as to say about banks. **1938** E. Bowen *Death of Heart* II. iv. 243 'A friend of mine—could he ever come and stay here?'..'Could he how much?' said Daphne. **1949** Wodehouse *Uncle Dynamite* ii. 23 'You're like me, a gentle coffee-caddy.' 'A how much?'

d. *and how!*: excl. used to indicate that the effect of something is difficult to describe = and no mistake, very much so! orig. *U.S.*

1865 B. Taylor *Let.* 16 June in M. H. Taylor *Life & Lett. Bayard Taylor* (1884) II. xviii. 434, I finished an article for the 'Atlantic' that day. As if I were not 'a tool of the elements!' 'And how?' as the Germans say (Americanicé—'You'd better believe it!'). **1932** J. W. Drawbell *Good Time!* xvii. §3 'How's that for your orders from a typical American woman?' 'You mean it, Peggy?' 'And how!' 'Baby!' **1932** T. E. Lawrence *Lett.* (1938) 752, I want to meet Yeats and Epstein and Eliot some day and how. **1933** E. E. Cummings *eimi* 83, I have fallen, fallen And How; tumbled into exactly 180 minuteless minutes of 'materialist dialectic'. **1948** 'N. Shute' *No Highway* ii. 37 'Did Mr. Honey take it seriously?' she asked. 'And how!' I said. **1963** V. Nabokov *Gift* iii. 175 One foot is buried in rich mud, the other is about to kick—and how!—the hideous, tar-black ball. **1965** *Listener* 25 Nov. 874/1 'Alas,' wrote Harrington, 'all earthly things do fail to mortals in enjoyment.' And how.

e. *how about that?*: Isn't that good, pleasing, surprising, etc.? *colloq.* (orig. *U.S.*).

1939 *Time* 25 Sept. 8/3 How about that? **1966** *Word Study* Dec. 2/2 How bout that.

f. *how's about?* = how about? (How *adv.* 4 a). *colloq.* (chiefly *U.S.*).

1952 *Holiday* Jan. 41/1 How's about a drink? **1961** Partridge *Dict. Slang* (ed. 5) Suppl. 1184/1 How's about having a drink?

7. b. *how —— can you get?*: see *Get *v.* 33 b.

9. Also *ellipt.*, as *how to*, and often used *attrib.*, as *'how-to' discourse, 'how-to-do-it' manual*, etc. Also (in titles of books, etc.) followed by a verb.

1838 H. Martineau (*title*) How to observe: morals and manners. **1857** (*title*) How to publish: a manual for authors. **1922** Joyce *Ulysses* 634 You had to come back.. to show the understudy in the title rôle how to. **1923** A. Bennett (*title*) How to make the best of life. **1941** Beals & Brody *Lit. Adult Educ.* 453 Nearly all councils also make some provision for supplying information, such as distributing manuals of the 'how-to-do-it' variety. **1942** H. Haycraft *Murder for Pleasure* p. vii, One or two 'how-to-write-it' manuals. **1946** C. Morris *Signs, Lang. & Behavior* v. x. 143 It is 'how to' discourse: discourse informing one how to rivet, how to play the flute. **1959** *Times Lit. Suppl.* 6 Nov. p. xxxviii/4 Light fiction, popular uplift, or how-to-do-it-books. **1960** *Farmer & Stockbreeder* 19 Jan. 43/1 A how-to-cook-turkey booklet! **1968** *Sat Rev.* 27 July 26/3 Most of the how-to books at this time of year are busy with water sports. **1972** T. P. McMahon *Issue of Bishop's Blood* (1973) xii. 176 She had washed her face, and though it doesn't say so in the women's how-to-books, there are some women who look great that way.

18. *here's how!* (Later examples.)

1925 [see *bung-ho *int.*]. **1951** J. B. Priestley *Festival at Farbridge* II. i. 152 'Well,' said Mr. Hull, holding up his glass,..'here's how!' **1959** E. Burgess *Divided we Fall* xi. 132 Martin was clasping a tumbler half filled with whisky. 'Here's how,' said the fat man.

19. how come? *colloq.* (orig. *U.S.*) phr.: how did (or does) it come about (that)? Cf. Come *v.* 20.

1848 Bartlett *Dict. Amer., How-come?* rapidly pronounced huc-cum, in Virginia. Doubtless an English phrase, brought over by the original settlers, and propagated even among the negro slaves. The meaning is, How did what you tell me happen? How came it? **1897** R. M. Stuart *In Simpkinsville* 230 She heard Miss Euphemia wonderin' the other day how come the right shoulder of her black silk dress to wear out. **1930** *Sat. Even. Post* 8 Mar. 12/1 These firms assert blandly to..journalists who ring them up, wishful to know how come, they have

nothing against women. **1932** T. S. ELIOT *Sweeney Agonistes* 17 Hello Doris! Hello Dusty! How do you do! How come? how come? will you permit me —. **1938** M. K. RAWLINGS *Yearling* iv. 34 That's how come him to have appetite for a nip o' pore old Betsy. **1957** *New Yorker* 13 July 19/1 These days, the sensation of the stamp-collecting world is United Nations commemorative stamps. How come? **1958** G. MITCHELL *Spotted Hemlock* xviii. 210 How come *they* didn't spot her? **1959** H. HOBSON *Mission House Murder* xviii. 122 'How come you make it murder?' he asked. **1969** in Halpert & Story *Christmas Mumming in Newfoundland* 213 How come you ain't got Wallace with you tonight? **1971** *Black World* Oct. 62/1 So that's how come I asked My Man Bovanne to dance. **1973** T. ALLBEURY *Choice of Enemies* iv. 16 'Well, we are getting a bit like the Krauts, you know.' 'How come?'

B. *sb.*[3] **2.** (Examples of U.S. usage.)

1845 W. G. SIMMS *Wigwam & Cabin* 1st Ser. 7 You joined the army again, and come in with Greene? Was that the how? **1878** J. H. BEADLE *Western Wilds* ii. 27 Daddy went off at last, and that was the how of my first trip. **1916** 'B. M. BOWER' *Phantom Herd* xvi. 272, I calc'late that's about the how of it. **1949** *Amer. Speech* XXIV. 39 In recent years *method, explanation,* and *the how*..promise to force *modus operandi* into the archives.

how (hau), *int.*[2] [Cf. Sioux *háo*, Omaha *hau*.] An ejaculation, orig. used by Indians of north-eastern North America in a variety of applications. Also repeated.

First noticed in the early 17th century by the French missionary Jean de Brébeuf, describing Huron oratory as he had observed it in Ontario. The Hurons showed their approval of a speech by a shouted *haau* (Jesuit Relations, documents pertaining to 1636, Thwaites, Vol. X, p. 259).

1817 J. BRADBURY *Trav. Interior Amer.* 95 We were interrupted by one of the chiefs crying 'How', signifying amongst the Indians 'Come on', or 'let us begin'. **1841** G. CATLIN *Lett. on N. Amer. Indians* II. 172 'How! how!' vociferated all of them, thereby approving what was said, giving assent by the word *how*, which is their word for yes. **1868** *Harper's Mag.* Feb. 301/2 The Indians..complimented 'Little Bill' with a succession of how-how-hows! **1911** *N.Y. Even. Post* 28 Jan. (Suppl.) 3 The expression 'How', used by army men in giving a toast, is equivalent to the expression, 'Here's to your health'. Some think it is merely the Indian corruption of 'How d'ye do?' abbreviated by the Indian to 'How'. Others believe the expression is derived from the Indian language direct. **1962** *Alberta Hist. Rev.* Autumn 11/1 The Blackfoot Indians usually greet a white man with 'How, How!' sometimes, 'How wa-pe'.

how (hau), colloq. abbreviation of HOWITZER.

1915 *Times* 14 Apr. 7 The boom in the distance from one of our 'hows'. **1919** C. P. THOMPSON *Cocktails* 133 A couple of batteries of heavy Hows.

howardite (hau·ăɹdəit). [f. the name of Edward *Howard* (fl. 1802), English chemist: see -ITE[1].] **1.** *Min.* A supposed silicate of iron and magnesium found in some meteorites.

1848 C. U. SHEPARD in *Amer. Jrnl. Sci.* VI. 253 The earthy constituent of this stone, like that of the Iowa meteorite..appears to be a tersilicate of the protoxyd of iron and magnesia, a mineral which though frequent in meteoric stones, has never yet been distinctly recognized, and which in a future paper on American Meteorites, I shall more particularly describe under the name of *Howardite*, after the Hon. Mr. Howard, that celebrated chemist, who was the first British writer whose labors contributed to elucidate the history of these extra-terrestrial bodies. **1955** M. H. HEY *Index Min. Species* (ed. 2) 127 Howardite (of Shepard). A doubtful meteoritic silicate of Fe and Mg.

2. *Astr.* [ad. G. *howardit* (G. Rose 1863, in *Physikal. Abhandl. d. K. Akad. d. Wiss. zu Berlin* 29).] Any of a group of achondritic meteorites principally composed of hypersthene and anorthite.

1881 L. FLETCHER *Guide Coll. Meteorites* (Brit. Mus.) 17 Perhaps for those aerolites which contain little or no nickel-iron the division into Howardites, Eukrites, Chladnites, Chassignites, Shalkites, and Carbonaceous is the most convenient. **1915** O. C. FARRINGTON *Meteorites* iii. 35 Of a total of nine meteorites belonging to the class of howardites, five have fallen in Russia. **1916** *Mineral. Mag.* XVIII. 36 The angrites, nakhlites, howardites, eucrites, and sherghottites..are richer in lime..than chondritic stones generally. **1971** B. MASON in I. G. Gass et al. *Understanding Earth* viii. 117 (*table*) [Achondrites are] sometimes divided into calcium-poor achondrites (aubrites, diogenites, chassignite, ureilite) and calcium-rich achondrites (angrite, nakhlite, howardites, eucrites).

how-come-ye-so, *adj. phr. archaic dial.* or *slang.* Tipsy.

1816 *Monthly Mag.* 1 July 494/2 [Degrees of intoxication.] How came you so. **1824** T. HOOK *Sayings & Doings* III. (Merton) xiii. 89. She used to be—'Lord, how come ye so!' every night. **1827** J. F. COOPER *Red Rover* I. x. 258 It is quite in reason to believe your husband was..a little of what I call how-come-ye-so. **1843** *Knickerbocker* XXII. 366 We were never 'groggy', 'intoxicated',..'how-came-ye-so'..or 'tight', but once. **1904** J. C. LINCOLN *Cap'n Eri* xii. 223 Drank rum by the hogshead... Well, one evenin' Labe was comin' home pretty how-come-you-so, and he fell into Jonadab Wixon's well.

how-do-ye, how-d'ye, howdy, *phr.* and *sb.* Add: Also **how de. 1.** (Further examples.) Freq. in colloq. phr. *to tell* (a person) *howdy*.

c **1828** T. O. LARKIN in *Calif. Hist. Soc. Q.* (1937) XVI. 25 They (Southerners) often correct Yankees in their speaking... In those words they are right, but not in.. how de for how do you do. **1837** A. WETMORE *Gaz. Missouri* 287 With a smile of welcome as she gave her hand, said, 'Howdy, Joseph.' **1850** J. PRICE *Let.* 17 Apr. in *Mississippi Valley Hist. Rev.* (1924) XI. 241 Tell Mother and the doctor Howdy. **1856** A. J. HOOLE *Let.* 8 June in *Kansas Hist. Q.* (1934) III. 56 Give my love to.. all enquiring friends; tell..all the negroes howdie for me. **1917** J. M. GRIDER *War Birds* 20 Sept. (1927) 10 All the soldiers in the harbor came over to tell us howdy. **1928** L. NORTH *Parasites* i. 30 Mr. Ashton greeted Henry a trifle more warmly... 'Howdy,' he said. **1973** J. MANN *Only Security* ii. 16, I ought really to go in and say howdy to her.

3. (Further examples.)

1931 *Times* 5 Nov. 13/4 The howdy folk of Kentucky may bring forth their best. **1932** E. WALLACE *When Gangs came to London* xxiii. 224 It seems that this guy has been on howdy terms with the Big Boy ever since he came to town.

how-do-you-do. Add: Also **how d'you do. 2.** (Later examples.)

1832 J. R. UNDERWOOD *Jrnl.* in *Filson Club Hist. Q.* (1941) XV. 43 Joel Yancey..was always ready with a *how d'ye do.* **1928** D. H. LAWRENCE *Let.* 27 Mar. (1962) II. 1049 Goethe *began* millions of intimacies, and never got beyond the how-do-you-do stage. **1938** J. CARY *Castle Corner* iv. 213 When he came..to make love as carelessly as how d'you do, he felt betrayed and lost.

howdy: see *HOW-DO-YE.

howe. Now the more usual spelling of How *sb.*[2] 2.

1947 *Proc. Prehist. Soc.* XIII. 33 When we reach the 10th century there were brochs in Caithness and Orkney.. deemed eligible burial howes. **1963** *Field Archaeol.* (Ordnance Survey) (ed. 4) 45 Round burial mounds..are the commonest objects of antiquity met with in the field. They are called by different names in different parts of the country..barrow, low, howe, cairn. **1968** G. JONES *Hist. Vikings* II. iii. 117 The mightiest of all northern howes, Raknehaugen.., over a hundred metres in diameter and some eighteen metres high, is an empty cenotaph. **1971** G. M. BROWN *Fishermen with Ploughs* 7 Lust builds a howe over the burning ghost.

Howeitat (hōᵘweitā·t). Also **Haueytat, Howeïtat, Huwaitat, Huweitat.** [Arab. *(al-) Ḥuwayṭāt*, Arab tribes in north-western Saudi Arabia.] **A.** *sb.* (A member of) a Bedouin tribe of northern Saudi Arabia. **B.** *adj.* Of or pertaining to this people.

a **1817** J. L. BURCKHARDT *Notes on Bedouins* (1831) I. 29 El Haueytat..are about three hundred horsemen, but can furnish a large body of armed camel-drivers... In seasons of drought the Haueytat approach Gaza or Hebron. **1838** J. R. WELLSTED *Trav. Arabia* II. ix. 167 The Howeïtát Bedowins occupy the coast from Magnah to Jebel 'Antar. **1917** T. E. LAWRENCE *Let.* 10 July (1938) 225 Sherif Nasir stayed in Kaf to enrol Rualla, Sherarat and Huweitat for the Akaba expedition. **1926** —— *Seven Pillars* (1935) III. xxx. 173 With his [*sc.* Feisal's] northern neighbours, the coastal Howeitat, he had already made a beginning. **1957** H. ST. J. PHILBY *Forty Years in Wilderness* v. 99 The tribes mentioned were Huwaitat..and some others.

however, *adv.* Add: **6.** Used by itself, or followed by points of suspension, as an interjection, or as a formula concluding, introducing, or modifying an utterance in some contextual way.

1876 GEO. ELIOT *Dan. Der.* II. IV. xxxii. 319, I have not yet written a word... And I told the girls to leave it to me. However! **1901** BEERBOHM *Variety of Things* (1928) 217 [I] doubt whether my creative power in caricature can be quite so strong as I had supposed. However... **1936** 'N. BLAKE' *Thou Shell of Death* viii. 137 Comes of givin' a vote to every hayseed and short-weight grocer in the —— However, hrrumph, where was I? **1964** D. WARNER *Death of Dreamer* I. i. 9 We don't want to know where the stuff comes from but where it goes *to*. However!.. **1966** I. JEFFERIES *House Surgeon* i. 11, I.. said, 'However. Not to interrupt what you were asking me.' **1968** M. WOODHOUSE *Rock Baby* vii. 66 'Our component reliability was very high indeed during trials. However.' 'Go on,' I said.

howff. (Later examples.)

1950 *John o' London's* 24 Nov. 617/1 He was just seventeen.., when he began to haunt the howffs (drinking-places) of Edinburgh's underworld. **1957** CLARK & PYATT *Mountaineering in Brit.* II. xi. 196 The crags were still relatively inaccessible—in spite of the use of boat and motor-car in conjunction with tents, howffs, or bivouacs.

howgozit (haugōᵘ·zit). *Aeronaut.* orig. *U.S.* [Corruption of *how goes it?* (see *HOW *adv.* 2 a).] A graph which essentially represents the amount of fuel remaining in an aircraft in relation to that needed to complete a journey or return to the point of departure. Also *attrib.*

1941 *Jrnl. R. Aeronaut. Soc.* XLV. 308 The 'Howgozit Curve' was developed by our ocean captains... Its purpose is to present..a continuous flow of information as to the fuel reserve remaining aboard the aircraft and the fuel required for completion of the flight to destination, or back to the point of departure. **1945** H. E. BENHAM *Aerial Navigation* iv. 92 In flight the actual progress of the aircraft..is plotted on the 'howgozit' for comparison with the forecasted data. The slope of the actual progress line as compared with the forecasted line and its tendency toward destination or dry tanks provides a vivid picture of the flight's progress. **1960** *Aeroplane* XCVIII. 98/2 An auto-landing indicator..will provide 'howgozit' information about the progress of the final approach.

howk, *v.*: see *HOLK, HOWK *v.* in Suppl.

howl, *sb.* Add: **1. b.** A howling noise produced in a loud-speaker as a result of electrical or acoustic feedback; howling.

1921 *Wireless World* 10 Dec. 568/1 Ear-splitting howls associated with valve reception. **1928** L. S. PALMER *Wireless Princ. & Pract.* x. 374 The typical 'howl' to which low-frequency amplifiers are subject. **1939** H. J. HICKS *Princ. & Pract. Radio Servicing* xiii. 228 If the resistance-capacity filter in the a.v.c. line loses its effectiveness, a howl will result. **1962** E. E. ECKLUND *Repairing Home Audio Systems* xiii. 246 Rumble, feedback, and howl are caused by mechanical vibrations being transmitted to the pickup.

howler. 1. b. Substitute for def.: In full, *howler monkey*. A South American monkey of the genus *Alouatta*. (Add earlier and later examples.)

1800 G. SHAW *Gen. Zool.* I. I. 72 The Allouates, or Howlers, inhabit the moist forests, in the neighbourhood of waters and marshes. **1906** E. INGERSOLL *Life Anim.: Mammals* 43 The howlers, arguatos, or alluates are the largest and most powerful of South American apes and the dullest, and are peculiar in having no thumb or only a rudimentary one, and in having the hyoid bones in the throat (of the males only) widely enlarged and cavernous, so as to form a curious hollow organ, by which their voice is so increased as to be audible two miles. **1932** S. ZUCKERMAN *Soc. Life Monkeys* xi. 192 The well-known howler monkeys (genus *Alouatta*) of the forests of the northern half of South America are usually found in small parties. **1958** J. CAREW *Black Midas* ii. 26 A big white devil does sit on a treetop roarin' like a howler baboon. **1964** *Listener* 5 Nov. 710/2 Fighting is rare in wild gibbons and apparently absent in wild howler monkeys. **1967** S. A. ALTMANN *Social Communication among Primates* xvii. 329 Other groups of howlers avoid areas from which such calls come.

† **4.** *Telephony.* A device (used by the exchange) for producing a howling noise in a receiver in order to attract the subscriber's attention. *Obs.*

1886 *Jrnl. Soc. Telegr. Engin.* XV. 322 We supply what we call a 'howler', and whenever a subscriber leaves his tubes hanging this howler is at once put on. **1917** G. D. SHEPARDSON *Telephone Apparatus* viii. 137 For reminding careless subscribers who neglect even to hang up the receiver..the operator..may send out a strong current of comparatively high frequency from the 'howler'.

howling, *vbl. sb.* Add: **1. b.** The emission of howls (*HOWL *sb.* 1 b) by a loud-speaker; undesirable feedback at audio frequencies in an amplifier.

1920 *Radio Rev.* Apr. 356 The resistance R_3 and condenser C_3 connected to the grid of the selected valve are increased in value until maximum amplification is obtained without 'howling'. **1939** H. J. HICKS *Princ. & Pract. Radio Servicing* xiii. 228 Open by-pass condensers across any of the tube elements..will often cause howling. **1953** J. E. HAINES *Automatic Control of Heating* xiv. 340 The variation exhibits a definite rhythm—in a manner analogous to the howling of a telephone when the sound waves from the receiver are fed back to the transmitter. **1966** *McGraw-Hill Encycl. Sci. & Technol.* I. 520/2 Suppression of the low frequencies..in rooms that are excessively reverberant..increases the intelligibility of the speech and reduces the possibility of acoustic feedback (howling).

howling, *ppl. a.* Add: **1.** Spec. *howling baboon, monkey* = *HOWLER 1 b.

1769 E. BANCROFT *Ess. Nat. Hist. Guiana* ii. 133 The Howling Baboons, as they are here called, seem to be the animals which are here described by Marcgrave, and which are called by the natives of Brasil, Guereba. *Ibid.* 135 There is another Monkey, somewhat larger than the howling Monkey, which is covered with long reddish hair. **1802** [see MONKEY *sb.* 1 b]. **1863** H. W. BATES *Naturalist on River Amazons* I. ii. 72 Morning and evening the howling monkeys make a most fearful and harrowing noise. **1887** J. G. WOOD *Illustr. Nat. Hist. for Young People* 15 The Howling Monkeys are larger and not so agile as the Spider Monkeys. **1924** C. W. DOMVILLE-FIFE *Among Wild Tribes of Amazons* viii. 121 On reaching camp..in the half light it was just possible to see the huddled and impaled body of a furry guaribas, or howling monkey (*simia mycetes*). **1959** *Jrnl. Mammalogy* XL. 317 (*title*) Field observations on a howling monkey society.

3. (Further examples.) Also, extreme, great. *colloq.*

1884 'MARK TWAIN' *Huck. Finn* xliii. 437 Le's all three slide out of here, one of these nights, and get an outfit, and go for howling adventures amongst the Injuns. **1908** *Magnet* I. 1, 'You howling ass!' shouted Bulstrode. 'I tell you he's busted my two-guinea camera.' **1933** *Times Lit. Suppl.* 27 Apr. 283/4 If his book is not a big, a very big, a 'howling' success..but I need offer no 'if's'.

4. As *adv.* In the highest degree. (Cf. *screamingly.*) *colloq.*

1895 *Century Mag.* Sept. 678/2 It's howling lonesome at the Mule Deer. **1899** KIPLING *Stalky & Co.* 45 He'll be howling drunk to-night. **1928** *Sat. Even. Post* 4 Feb. 100/4 Glad! You're howling right I'm glad.

howlite (hau·ləit). *Min.* [f. the name of Henry *How* (d. 1879), mineralogist of Nova Scotia, who first described it: see -LITE.] A hydrated calcium borosilicate, $Ca_2B_5SiO_9(OH)_5$, that typically occurs as white nodules forming compact structureless masses resembling unglazed porcelain.

1868 J. D. DANA *Syst. Min.* (ed. 5) 598 *Howlite*. Silicoborocalcite *H. How*... 1868. Howlite *Dana*. In small rounded imbedded nodules. Texture compact, without cleavage; also chalk-like or earthy. **1917** *Amer. Mineralogist* II. 1 Not all fine grained, compact hydrous calcium borate is priceite; a number of such specimens from California localities..have been examined microscopically and all proved to be howlite. **1957** *Ibid.* XLII. 521 The mineral howlite, $H_5Ca_2SiB_5O_{14}$, has been recorded from a number of localities in California and elsewhere..and microscopic crystals have been described.., but in general the mineral is massive and very fine granular.

Howship (hau·ʃip). *Anat.* The name of John *Howship* (1781–1841), English surgeon, used in **Howship's lacuna** (earlier *lacuna of Howship*): one of the numerous microscopic depressions or pits, irregular in shape and usually containing osteoclasts, that are found on the surface of bones and bony tissue where resorption is occurring.

1876 C. S. TOMES *Man. Dental Anat.* v. 175 Microscopic examination of the bone at this point shows that the lacunae of Howship..abundantly cover its surface. **1911** T. W. WIDDOWSON *Notes on Dental Anat.* viii. 44 Upon any part of the roots of the temporary teeth, undergoing absorption, cup-shaped depressions, Howship's lacunae, occur. **1970** J. M. VAUGHAN *Physiol. Bone* ii. 43 They [*sc.* osteoclasts] may be found closely applied to bone in Howship's lacunae.

howsomever. **2.** (Later examples.) *U.S. colloq.*

1896 'M. RUTHERFORD' *Clara Hopgood* xxiii. 215 He allus begins to argue with me. Howsomever, arguing isn't everything. **1929** H. W. ODUM in A. Dundes *Mother Wit* (1973) 183 Howsomever, hard times in American camps whut I'm talkin' about. **1933** E. E. CUMMINGS *Let.* 26 May (1969) 123, I fear that naught will compare with domesticity, howsomeever. **1939** *Amer. Speech* XIV. 128 The great drive for 'correctness' of the later eighteenth and early nineteenth did succeed in branding as 'vulgarisms' such hitherto acceptable forms as..*howsomever, mought, sarvent,* [etc.].

howtowdie (hautau·di). *Sc.* Also **howtoudie, how-towdy.** ['Not recorded in O.Sc. but appar. O.Fr. *hétoudeau, estaudeau,* a fat young chicken for the pot' (*S.N.D.*).] A dish whose main ingredient is a chicken (see quot. 1951).

1728 A. RAMSAY *Poems* II. 230 They all, in an united Body, Declar'd it a fine fat How-towdy. **1759** E. CLELAND *New & Easy Method Cookery* (ed. 2) iv. 91 You may do Howtoudies, or any white Fowl, the same Way. **1901** *Daily Chron.* 17 Aug. 8 Howtowdie is another old Scotch dish. **1951** *Good Housek. Home Encycl.* 513/1 *Howtowdie*, a Scottish dish consisting of boiled chicken with poached eggs and spinach. **1970** SIMON & HOWE *Dict. Gastron.* 222/2 *Howtowdie*, Scots for pullet, possibly related to the old French *hutaudeau*... Eggs are poached in gravy or broth and placed around the bird on the carving dish, each on a pat of spinach.

Hoxnian (hǫ·ksˌniăn), *a.* [f. *Hoxne*, name of the village in Suffolk where the type site is situated: see -IAN.] Epithet of the second (penultimate) interglacial in Britain (identified with the Mindel-Riss interglacial of continental Europe), and of a stage of the middle Pleistocene; hence, of or contemporaneous with this interglacial or stage. Also *absol.* as *sb.*, the Hoxnian interglacial or the Hoxnian stage.

1956 WEST & DONNER in *Q. Jrnl. Geol. Soc.* (1957) CXII. 86 Hoxnian Interglacial. [*Note*] A general name suggested for this interglacial period. **1963** R. G. WEST in *Proc. Geologists' Assoc.* LXXIV. 171 Evidence for sea-levels during the Hoxnian Stage is summarized in Fig. 9. **1964** K. P. OAKLEY *Frameworks for dating Fossil Man* iii. 29 In Britain the silver fir (*Abies*) is absent from Cromerian diagrams, abundant in the Late Temperate phase of the Hoxnian. **1968** R. G. WEST *Pleistocene Geol. & Biol.* xii. 276 Often they are overlain by interglacial or Flandrian beach gravels, and..they are probably mostly Hoxnian or older. **1969** *Proc. Geol. Soc.* Aug. 152 It is recommended that for the Pleistocene and Holocene of the British Isles the following ages/stages be adopted as a regional scale... Pleistocene:.. Wolstonian, Hoxnian, Anglian, Cromerian, [etc.]. **1970** *Phil. Trans. R. Soc.* B. CCLVII. 414 *Buxus* pollen has been found in the Hoxnian deposits at Birmingham. **1970** *Times* 10 Mar. 16/6 In the closing stage of the Hoxnian, the pine became the dominant forest tree.

Hoxtonian (hǫkstōu·niăn), *sb.* [f. *Hoxton*, the name of part of the borough of Shoreditch in London + -IAN.] A native or inhabitant of Hoxton; the variety of English spoken in Hoxton.

a **1935** T. E. LAWRENCE *Mint* (1950) II. xxii. 159 Adam and Eve on a raft (Hoxtonian for fried eggs on toast). **1935** G. INGRAM *Cockney Cavalcade* xii. 197 The West End—a place entirely foreign to most Hoxtonians.

hoy, *int.* Add: **B.** *sb.* **2.** *Austral.* A gambling game, resembling lotto, in which playing-cards are used. Also *attrib.*

1965 *Courier-Mail* (Brisbane) 2 Mar. 15 A hoy evening which the Royal Society of St. George planned to hold at St. George House. **1969** *Ibid.* 25 Feb. 6/10 Juliet Jones couldn't object to a few games of hoy. **1969** *Sunday Mail* (Brisbane) 24 Aug. 3/3 Police said that bingo, or hoy, which was played in the same way, was illegal in Queensland. **1971** *Tel.* (Brisbane) 3 Nov. 4/2, I have been advised that the radio competition is above board, but have had no ruling on the game hoy.

Hoyle (hoil). The name of Edmond *Hoyle* (1672–1769), author of several works on card-games (the earliest, on whist, dated 1742): often cited typically for an authority on card-playing. Phr. *according to Hoyle,* according to the highest authority, in accordance with strict rules.

1906 'O. HENRY' *Four Million* (1916) 14 The financial loss of a dollar sixty-five, all so far fulfilled according to Hoyle. **1945** A. A. OSTROW *Compl. Card Player* p. vii, It has been the custom to call books of rules on card and board games 'Hoyles', so that 'according to Hoyle' has come to mean 'according to accepted rules'. **1962** R. BARKER *Clue for Murder* v. 38 This one [*sc.* murder]'s right out of the book—strictly according to Hoyle. **1965** J. M. CAIN *Magician's Wife* (1966) xix. 147, I want our marriage to be strictly on the beam—the way it is in the books, absolutely according to Hoyle. **1971** *Melody Maker* 21 Aug. 34/7 If everything goes according to Hoyle, I'll go into semi-retirement there.

hsien, var. *HIEN.

H-test: see *H III.

huaca (wā·kă). [ad. Sp. *huacca, guaca,* from Quechua.] **a.** The name for the all-pervading spirit thought by the Peruvian Indians to be disseminated through the whole world; also, any material object thought to be the abode of such a spirit. **b.** A prehistoric Peruvian tomb or temple, usually a truncated pyramid of stone, and often of immense size.

1847 W. H. PRESCOTT *Hist. Conquest Peru* I. I. iii. 93 The subjects of the Incas enrolled among their inferior deities many objects in nature, as the elements,..great mountains and rivers... These consecrated objects were termed *huacas,*—a word of most prolific import; since it signified a temple, a tomb, any natural object remarkable for its size or shape, in short, a cloud of meanings. **1860** W. BOLLAERT *Antiquarian, Ethnol. Res. Chile* 161 A huaca was discovered, in 1830, at the entrance of the valley of Taparapacá; it was surrounded with stones. **1862** D. WILSON *Prehist. Man* I. ix. 298 The huacas or tombs of the Incas. **1875** *Encycl. Brit.* II. 452/2 The most interesting remains in Peru are those called *Huacas*; but whether they were forts, or palaces, or tombs, is not as yet clearly ascertained. **1901** A. H. KEANE *Central & S. Amer.* I. 208 Of these ruins the largest, as well as the most characteristic, are the truncated pyramids here [*sc.* Peru] called *huacas*, or burying-places. **1902** *Encycl. Brit.* XXV. 380/1 The most prolific source of Peruvian relics is the sepulchres or huacas. **1960** M. SAVILL tr. *Leicht's Pre-Inca Art & Culture* iv. 74 The ancestral worship in the land expressed itself most vividly in the veneration of the so-called Huacas, a word which signifies not only the large temples and pyramids but a host of small and insignificant objects sacred to the Indians.

huaco (wā·ko). Also **guaco.** [See quot. 1931[1].] In Peru, Bolivia, and Chile, ancient pottery and other Indian antiquities.

1931 *Connoisseur* Feb. 95 The term *huaco* is derived from the Indian word, *huaca*, meaning 'a holy place', and refers to the cemeteries and tombs from which, with few exceptions, all the examples of pre-Incaic art are obtained. *Ibid.* 97 The linear decoration of the stirrup *huacos* tend [*sic*] to portray some form of action... In the static *huacos* the legs are almost invariably crossed. **1933** *Burlington Mag.* Aug. p. xii (Advt.), The pottery includes six rare Huacos from Paracas, with green colouring. **1959** G. WOODCOCK *Incas & Other Men* IV. iv. 229 The Mochica pots—..called *huacos* by the modern Peruvians—were made specifically as grave furniture, intended to hold food and chicha for the dead.

huarache (wară·tʃi). Also **guaracha, guarache, guarachi, huaracho.** [Mex.-Sp.] A leather-thonged sandal, orig. worn by Mexican Indians.

1887 F. C. GOOCH *Face to Face with Mexicans* xii. 433 Leathern aprons and sandals of the same, called *guarachi*. **1892** *Dialect Notes* I. 190 *Huaracho*, -*s*, a kind of sandals worn by Indians and the lower classes generally. Used generally in the plural only. **1909** *Cent. Dict.* Suppl., Guaracha. **1926** D. H. LAWRENCE *Plumed Serp.* viii. 130 The dark feet in the glare of the torch looked almost black, in huaraches that had red thongs. **1928** *Funk's Stand. Dict.*, *Guaracha*, a Mexican-Indian sandal. **1943** *N. & Q.* 24 Apr. 262/1 The Mexican Indian uses a leather-thonged sandal, which he calls guarache. **1957** J. KEROUAC *On Road* (1958) I. ii. 13 My shoes..were Mexican huaraches, plantlike sieves not fit for the rainy night of America. **1963** C. BEALS *Latin Amer.* (1964) i. 11 *Guarache* sandals shuffled like a storm of autumn leaves.

Huastec (wā·stek). Also **Huasteca, Huastek, Huaxtec, Huaxteca.** [ad. Sp. *huasteco, huaxteco.*] **a.** An Indian people inhabiting parts of Mexico; a member of this tribe. **b.** The language of the Huastecs.

1845 *Trans. Amer. Ethnol. Soc.* I. 4 A comparison of near three hundred words of the Mexican, Otomi, and Huasteca, exhibits but very few, and perhaps accidental, coincidences. **1875** H. H. BANCROFT *Native Races Pacific States* I. vi. 674 The Huastecs, Huaxtecs, Guastecs, or Cuextecas inhabit portions of the states of Vera Cruz and Tamaulipas. **1914** T. A. JOYCE *Mexican Archæol.* vii. 196 The presence of a spout distinguishes Huaxtec pottery from Mexican. **1931** T. GANN in Gann & Thompson *Hist. Maya* i. 11 The Huaxtecas..were evidently a section of the people left behind in their old home. **1946** S. G. MORLEY *Anc. Maya* iii. 39 The Maya-speaking, Maya-appearing Huasteca never shared with the Maya of the Yucatan Peninsula the latter's unique culture. **1948** D. DIRINGER *Alphabet* I. vii. 123 The Huastec..already separated from the main stock in ancient times. **1955** *Amer. Speech* XXX. 126 Huastek.

hub[1]. Add: **2.** *up to the hub* (earlier examples).

1800 *Aurora* (Philadelphia) 23 May (Th.), 'This is not a half measure—I like to do things by the lump—and this bill you will allow is up to the hub.' Those who are acquainted with the slang language of the American Caucuses will be able to explain what is meant by up to the hub. **1815** D. HUMPHREYS *Yankey in Eng.* 33 I've bin up to the hub, and didn't flinch..nor won't back out now.

5. **hub brake,** a brake that acts on the hub of a (cycle) wheel; so **hub-braking; hub-cap,** a covering for the hub of a wheel of a vehicle.

1883 H. STURMEY *Tricyclists' Indispensable Ann.* (ed. 3) 94 There are three great classes of brakes now in use, viz.:—Tyre, ground, and hub brakes. **1936** F. J. CAMM *Every Cyclist's Handbk.* xvii. 108 The cyclist should..take great care to prevent oil entering the shell of a hub brake. **1973** *Sci. Amer.* Mar. 90/2 Two other types of brake made their appearance later. One is the coaster brake, or back-pedaling brake, which is particularly popular in the U.S. The other is the hub brake, or drum brake, of the type used in automobiles and motorcycles. **1909** *Daily Chron.* 20 Mar. 8/5 It combines hand control and hub braking. **1913** *Collier's* 11 Jan. 11. 7/1 Their wheels, perhaps, have plain hub caps. **1954** A. HUXLEY *Let.* 5 Dec. (1969) 716 One would like to find out..why..so many cubists..used forms which are identical with those obtained by photographing reflections in curved surfaces. Did the suggestion actually come from hub caps and the backs of spoons? **1957** L. DURRELL *Justine* 27 The great silver Rolls with the daffodil hub-caps. **1959** *Times* 9 Jan. 12/6, I looked forward to removing the hub-cap. **1972** J. BROWN *Chancer* xiv. 188 You name it, we found it. All this and neat little packets of H. in the hub-caps.

hubara, var. *HOUBARA.

hubba-hubba (hɒ·băˌhɒ·bă), *int. U.S. slang.* Also **haba-haba.** [Origin unknown.] Used to express approval, excitement, or enthusiasm. Also as *sb.*, nonsense; ballyhoo.

1944 in *Amer. Speech* (1947) XXII. 35 The inevitable fact is that the cry 'Haba-Haba' is spreading like a scourge through the land. **1945** *Amer. Speech* XX. 261 *Hubba-hubba*, originally gibberish, now means the spirit of double-time and eagerness; it is a verb, adjective or noun, an imprecation, warning or insult. **1946** 'S. STERLING' *Where there's Smoke* iv. 36, I suppose you think that's a lot of hubba-hubba. **1970** C. MAJOR *Dict. Afro-Amer. Slang* 68 *Hubba hubba*, expression of approval.

Hubbard (hɒ·băɹd). Chiefly *N. Amer.* In full, *Hubbard squash*: a variety of *Cucurbita maxima* yielding large green or yellow fruits.

1868 *Mich. Agric. Rep.* VII. 349 Thos. Smith, Hamtramck [exhibited] 8 Hubbard squashes. **1898** E. N. WESTCOTT *David Harum* xxiii, Turnips, Hubbard squash, succotash. **1921** *Daily Colonist* (Victoria, B.C.) 20 Oct. 7/4 Hubbard Squash, today's selling per lb. 4c. **1925** *Brit. Weekly* 26 Feb. 520/5 It was truly an old-fashioned Thanksgiving dinner. We had..celery, onions, and hubbard squash. **1963** J. ORGAN *Gourds* xii. 121 *C. maxima* is best represented in commerce by such popular varieties as the Hubbards, Boston Marrow and Delicious. **1971** *Rand Daily Mail* 27 Mar. 22/2 Hubbard Squash (sugar pockets). Good demand. 140c to 200c.

Hubble (hɒb'l). *Astr.* The name of Edwin P. *Hubble* (1889–1953), U.S. astronomer, used in the possessive and *attrib.* to designate concepts arising out of his work, as **Hubble('s) constant** (or † **factor**), the ratio of the recessional speed of a galaxy to its distance, usu. expressed in km. per second per megaparsec; also, the reciprocal of this, usu. expressed in years and capable of being interpreted as the time that has elapsed since the galaxies first began to recede (at constant speeds) from a single point; **Hubble('s) law,** the red shifts of the spectra of distant galaxies (and hence their speeds of recession) are proportional, on average, to their distances.

1933 *Monthly Notices R. Astron. Soc.* XCIV. 159 We can consider a possible extension of Hubble's Law, and it will be seen that this may lead to a method for determining the cosmical constant and the sign of curvature in the generally accepted form of space-time. **1938** *Physical Rev.* LIII. 207/1 We can also derive a relation between *f* and Hubble's factor *u*... *u* is about 500 km per sec. per mega-parsec. or $1{\cdot}6 \times 10^{-17}$ sec.$^{-1}$. **1952** H. BONDI *Cosmol.* v. 39 The relation may be written $V = r/T$

where T is a constant..depending..on the average in trinsic luminosity of a nebula. On this interpretation the radial velocity of a nebula is proportional to its distance... The reciprocal of the constant T is known as Hubble's constant and may be evaluated to be about 540 km./sec./megaparsec. This value leads to $T = 1{\cdot}8 \times 10^9$ years. **1957** *Encycl. Brit.* VI. 502B/2 A better appreciation of the meaning of this number, H, which came to be called Hubble's constant, is given by its reciprocal $1/H$ = 5,400,000,000 years. **1971** D. W. SCIAMA *Mod. Cosmol.* iii. 45 (*caption*) The expansion of the Universe as seen from another galaxy. The recession velocity is still proportional to the distance. Thus Hubble's law does not favour the Milky Way. *Ibid.* 46 Hubble's constant is now believed to be about 10 million years. *Ibid.* 48 Any systematic evolution in the intrinsic properties of the galaxies would contribute to the observed deviation from the simple Hubble law. **1972** *Sci. Amer.* Feb. 41/2 The new value of the Hubble constant is 53 ± 5 kilometers per second per megaparsec, or almost exactly one-tenth of Hubble's original value. **1973** *Physics Bull.* Nov. 652/1 Present estimates of the Hubble constant yield a value of R/R in a range (1–2) × 10^{10} years.

hubless (hʊ·blės), *a.* [f. HUB[1] + -LESS.] Without a hub.

1970 *Official Jrnl.* (*Patents*) 31 Dec. 4577/1 Circumferentially loaded and snubbered hubless wheel surface locomotion apparatus. **1971** *New Scientist* 10 June 632/2 A load belt is wrapped round both the hubless rollers and the load hub in a tortuous path so as to apply any load from above as a circumferential load on the hubless wheels. **1971** *Daily Tel.* (Colour Suppl.) 8 Oct. 16 (Advt.), Hubless 5½" sport wheels. Radial-ply tyres.

‖**hubris** (hiū·bris). [a. Gr. ὕβρις (cf. *HYBRIS).] Presumption, orig. towards the gods; pride, excessive self-confidence.

1884 *Daily News* 28 Oct. (Ware), Boys of good family, who have always been toadied, and never been checked, who are full of health and high spirits, develop what Academic slang knows as *hubris*, a kind of high-flown insolence. **1923** J. M. MURRY *Pencillings* 272 So confident indeed did I become that I began to join in the scholarly chuckle at the vainglorious and foolhardy man—was ever a purer case of *hubris*? **1924** G. B. SHAW *Saint Joan* v. 60 You have stained yourself with the sin of pride. The old Greek tragedy is rising among us. It is the chastisement of hubris. **1950** A. HUXLEY *Themes & Variations* 259 The Greeks..knew very well that hubris against the essentially divine order of Nature would be followed by its appropriate nemesis. *a* **1963** C. S. LEWIS *Poems* (1964) 3 Walk carefully, do not wake the envy of the happy gods, Shun Hubris. **1965** *Listener* 23 Sept. 449/2 There they learned morality and conduct; the virtues of nobility and the golden mean and the menace of *hubris*. **1971** *Country Life* 11 Mar. 541/1 Not much in the way of punishment for *hubris* will be seen falling on the heads of the publicity-maniacs.

hubristic, *a.* Delete *rare* and add later examples. Also **hubri·stical.**

1904 *Westm. Gaz.* 6 May 2/1 These Chamberlainites are very hubristic. **1923** J. M. MURRY *Pencillings* 272, I was feeling at my ease, perhaps even a little hubristical myself. **1930** *Punch* 1 Oct. 381/2 This deleterious and delirious Dean, Who of the fount of Hippocrene Drank in a manner most hubristic. **1961** *Times* 18 May 17/2 It was hubristic of the band to play the National Anthem in an eighteenth century version.

hubristically (hiubri·stikăli), *adv.* [See -LY[2].] With hubris; in a presumptuous manner.

1907 *Athenæum* 19 Oct. 473/1 He was..rather inclined to treat cavalierly, not to say hubristically, the quiet people who [etc.].

Hubshee (hʊ·bʃi), *sb.* and *a.* Also 7 **Abbasie, Hobsy,** 8 **Hobshy, -ee, Habashi,** 9 **Haffshee, Hubshi.** [Pers. *ḥabšī*, Arab. *ḥabašī*, of or belonging to Habesh or Abyssinia.] **A.** *sb.* An Ethiopian, an Abyssinian. **B.** *adj.* Ethiopian, Abyssinian. In Anglo-Indian usage both *sb.* and *adj.* may be loosely applied to an African Negro (see quot. 1901).

1601 J. SANDERSON *Trav. Levant* (1931) 108 Abbasies of Ethiopia. **1698** J. FRYER *New Acct. E.-India & Persia* 147 They speak of his *Hobsies* after this manner, That with their Swords they are able to cut down Man and Horse. *Ibid.* 168 He being from an *Hobsy Cophir* made a free Denizen. **1757** J. H. GROSE *Voy. E.-Indies* 238 The Moors are also fond of having Abyssinian slaves known in India by the name of Hobshee Coffrees. **1789** *Seir Mutaqherin* III. 36 (Y.), In India Negroes, *Habissinians, Nobis* (*i.e.* Nubians), &c. &c. are promiscuously called Habashies or *Habissians*, although the two latter are no Negroes. **1834** J. FORBES *Oriental Mem.* (ed. 2) II. 473 The master of a family adopts a slave, frequently a Haffshee Abyssinian, of the darkest hue, for his heir. **1888** *Contemp. Rev.* Feb. 167 'Hubshees', who looked, though they were not, Negroes, have in India carved out thrones. **1901** KIPLING *Kim* vii. 179, I would not appear to her as a *hubshi* (nigger). **1932** —— *Limits & Renewals* 214 Whether he had been General or Sweeper—Sahib—Mussulman—Yahudi—Hubashi—or heathen.

huchen (hū·kən, hū·χən). Also **hucho.** [G.] A large salmonid fish, *Hucho hucho*, native to the Danube and its tributaries.

a **1829** H. DAVY *Consolations in Travel* (1830) iv. 204 The trout, salmon, hucho and others of the salmo genus. **1897** *Encycl. Sport* I. 14/1 Mahseer in India, the hucho in Bavaria, the monster trout of the Canadian lakes..are alike taken by the spinning rod. **1905** *Westm. Gaz.* 2/2 The huchen is excellent food. *Ibid.* 7/3 The Committee have proceeded with the experiment of attempting the intro, duction into the river [*sc.* the Thames] of the huchen, the non-migratory salmon. **1962** D. W. TUCKER tr. *Sterba's Freshwater Fishes of World* 56 Huchen do very well in captivity. **1971** B. J. MUUS *Freshwater Fish Brit. & Europe* 62/1 The huchen is found in the Danube and part of its tributaries, and only exceptionally in lakes.

huckleberry. Add: **b.** *huckleberry pie.*

1775 P. V. FITHIAN *Jrnl.* (1934) II. 68 We have.. boil'd potatoes & huckleberry-pie. **1869** [see **cranberry pie*]. **1947** *Mazama* Sept. 1/1 Smell that turkey, those roasting ears, and the huckleberry pies? **1972** *Punch* 1 Mar. 292/3 A sliver of freeze-dried huckleberry pie with apple pandowdy and French fries.

2. *U.S. colloq.* A small amount, degree, or extent.

1832 J. K. PAULDING *Westward Ho!* I. 182 [I once got] within a huckleberry of being smothered to death. **1920** E. BOK *Americanization of Edward Bok* 165 He always kept 'a huckleberry or two' ahead of his readers.

3. A person, *spec.* (*derog.*) a person of little consequence.

[**1835** *Gent's. Vade-Mecum* (Philadelphia) 22 Aug. 2/4 Orson, the wild man of the woods is nothing to him—not a circumstance—not a huckleberry.] **1868** *New Eng. Base Ballist* 3 Sept. 17/1 Now then, my huckleberry, look sharp! you're wrong! **1889** 'MARK TWAIN' *Connecticut Yankee* 338 The Saracen..is no huckleberry.

4. In various phrases: *to be someone's huckleberry*: to be someone's sweetheart, friend, or partner; *to be a huckleberry to* (or *over*) *someone's persimmon*: a proverbial phrase (see quots.).

1832 J. K. PAULDING *Westward Ho!* I. ix. 80 If the [broad-]horn gets broadside to the current, I wouldn't risk a huckleberry to a persimmon that we don't every soul get treed, and sink to the bottom. **1834** D. CROCKETT *Narr. Life* ix. 70 But to do this, and write the warrants too, was at least a huckleberry over my persimmon. **1856** W. G. SIMMS *Eutaw* 553 My larning ain't a huckleberry to your persimmon. **1880** A. A. HAYES *New Colorado* (1881) v. 68 The first words that we heard him speak settled his nationality, for..he sententiously remarked, 'Hi'm 'is 'uckleberry.' **1885** D. D. PORTER *Incidents Civil War* 204 'I am the fleet-surgeon of the Mississippi squadron!'..'I'm a huckleberry above that persimmon, 'cause I'm the chief cook.' **1889** [see PERSIMMON 3]. **1926** N. N. PUCKETT in A. Dundes *Mother Wit* (1973) 8/2 Sir, you is a huckleberry beyon' my persimmon. **1936** J. TULLY *Bruiser* (1946) 37 Well, I'm your huckleberry, Mr. Haney. **1951** *Publ. Amer. Dial. Soc.* xv. 56 I'll be your huckleberry.

huckster, *sb.* Add: **2. b.** An advertising agent chiefly concerned with the preparation of advertising programmes for radio broadcasting.

1946 F. WAKEMAN (*title*) The hucksters. **1947** *Britannica Bk. of Year* 840/2 *Huckster*, a radio advertising man. **1965** *English Studies* XLVI. 464 *Huckster*, broker... Also used colloquially of an advertisement copy writer.

Hence **hu·cksterism,** the theory or practice of being a huckster (usu. disparaging).

1951 *Newsweek* 27 Aug. 80 Robert Saudek, a three-time Peabody Award winner for documentaries. Saudek, a soft-spoken man without a hint of hucksterism. **1957** *N.Y. Times* 6 Jan. E 11/4 An attack on Southern schools of journalism for 'kicking the humanities around' while emphasizing 'hucksterism' and 'quick turnover' in education. **1960** *Encounter* XV. 27 One can find 'hucksterism'.. among academic people in search of reputations. **1972** *Village Voice* (N.Y.) 1 June 26/2 What particularly appeals to me about the 'Jack La Lanne Show' is its serious, heartfelt hucksterism. **1973** *Observer* 2 Dec. 7/3 This high-pressure hucksterism, backed by the multi-billion investment.., has failed to impress many scientists.

huddle, *sb.* Add: **1., 1. b.** (Later examples.)

1906 *Daily Chron.* 5 Mar. 6/6 A really fine organic city and not a mere gigantic huddle of apartment dwellings. **1924** W. M. RAINE *Troubled Waters* viii. 79 Beyond the post office a great huddle of sheep was being driven forward. **1959** *Listener* 26 Feb. 384/3 Stanley Spencer's 'Temptation of St. Anthony', with its huddle of precisely drawn nudes.

4. A close or secret conference; esp. in phr. *to go into a huddle*, to hold a secret conference, to consult specially (about something). *colloq.*

1929 E. LOOKER *White House Gang* i. 13 The Gang was recruited, and..it went into a huddle, to confound all rules of deportment in high places. **1932** *Harper's Mag.* Apr. 600 'When an agent comes,' explains René, 'we have a little *conférence*. We go into what you call a huddle, yes?' **1934** E. LINKLATER *Magnus Merriman* xi. 128 Your girl-friend'll need to go into a huddle to think up something to beat that one. **1938** F. SCOTT FITZGERALD *Let.* 5 Sept. (1964) 93 I'm going into a huddle on this script and probably won't be able to write you again at length before Vassar starts. **1947** J. BERTRAM *Shadow of War* 318 He went into a huddle with one of his minions. **1959** 'A. GILBERT' *Third Crime Lucky* iii. 49 If he writes in he wants to make some of what he never earned over to us there'll be a huddle. **1972** M. YORKE *Silent Witness* v. 121 Then she got scared when he was missing and that's why she and Roy were in a worried huddle this morning.

5. *Bridge.* A period of meditation during which a player considers his next call or play.

1934 *Amer. Speech* IX. 11/1 A *huddle* is a session of silent thought indulged in by a player either during the bidding or during play. **1964** *Official Encycl. Bridge* 248/1 If the huddle is followed by a positive action, usually no harm is done to the opponents.

huddledom (hʊ·d'ldəm). [f. HUDDLE *sb.* + -DOM.] A state or condition of confusion and disorder.

1923 *Glasgow Herald* 24 May 9 The huddledoms of haunting disease, poverty, and overcrowding. *Ibid.* 31 May 6 Into this huddledom..came a youth, David Watt Torrance.

Hudson Bay (hʊ·dsǫn bēi). The name of a body of water in northern Canada (also with the possessive form *Hudson's*, from the name of the trading company, the Hudson's Bay Company), used in numerous phraseological combinations (see esp. Avis et al. *Dict. Canadianisms*), e.g. **Hudson('s) Bay blanket, Hudson's Bay tea.**

1900 J. LONDON *Son of Wolf* 181 Prince wrapped a Hudson Bay blanket about her with a mock reverence. **1912** 'R. CONNOR' *Corporal Cameron* 438 Tall, she looked.. lithe and strong, her close-fitting Hudson Bay blanket coat revealing the swelling lines of her budding womanhood. **1920** A. STRINGER *Prairie Mother* 263, I sat there wrapped up in one of Dinky-Dunk's four-point Hudson-Bays. **1943** R. E. & D. SWANSON *Rhymes Haywire Hooker* (1953) 51 The stranger smiles and then he says: 'Why, them is four point Hudson Bays!' **1948** *Beaver* Mar. 14 A tea used to be made from Hudson's Bay tea or Labrador tea. **1955** W. G. HARDY *Alberta Golden Jubilee Anthol.* 85 In his last days, the old warrior was a familiar sight in his Hudson Bay blanket coat. **1961** E. E. RICH *Hudson's Bay Company* III. xxvi. 738 In 1849–50 the American government had bought some Hudson's Bay blankets to distribute as gifts to the Indians. **1968** L. J. BRAUN *Cat who turned on & Off* (1969) iii. 25 One man in a Hudson Bay blanket coat carried a small dog dressed to match. **1970** *Beaver* Winter 22 Labrador tea, also known as Hudson's Bay tea across much of Northern Canada, is a pretty evergreen shrub whose robustly aromatic leaves make it one of the most famous teas of the north country.

Hudsonian (hʊdsōu·niăn), *a.* [f. the name of an English navigator, Henry *Hudson* (died *c* 1611), discoverer of the North American bay, river, and strait which bear his name: see -IAN.] Of or pertaining to Hudson Bay and the surrounding land, *esp.* in the names of animals and the territory from Labrador to Alaska, as far south as the tree line, classified as the Hudsonian biogeographical zone.

1835 J. J. AUDUBON *Ornith. Biogr.* III. 727 The Hudsonian Godwit. *Limosa Hudsonica*..is scarcely ever found farther south along the coast than the State of Maryland. **1858** S. F. BAIRD in *Rep. Explor. Route to Pacific* (U.S. War Dept.) IX. 744 *Numenius Hudsonicus.* Short-billed or Hudsonian Curlew... Atlantic and Pacific Coasts of North America. **1871** *Bull. Mus. Compar. Zool. Harvard* II. 401 The Hudsonian Fauna doubtless embraces outlying islands of the Canadian Fauna, as the upper part of the White Mountains, and the summits of some of the higher peaks in the Adirondacks. **1939** *Beaver* June 48/1 The Hudsonian chickadees and Canada jays would come near, making life a bit more cheerful. **1947** R. T. PETERSON *Field Guide Birds* (ed. 2) 266 *Parus hudsonicus*: (1) Hudsonian Brown-capped Chickadee, *P. h. hudsonicus.* **1948** A. L. RAND *Mammals E. Rockies* 15 The Hudsonian zone in Alberta is poorly characterized by mammals. **1952** T. M. STANWELL-FLETCHER *Tundra World* 42, I was startled by a series of loud, wild 'tit-tit-tit-tit-tit' notes from a big brown bird which leapt into the air a few feet in front. A Hudsonian curlew of course. **1952** D. F. PUTNAM *Canad. Regions* 139/1 The Hudsonian Life Zone..extends from the timber limit to the south of James Bay, Lake Mistassini and Pointe des Monts on the North Shore. **1964** A. L. THOMSON *New Dict. Birds* 713/2 The smaller Whimbrel *N*[*umenius*] *phaeopus* is Holarctic (its American race being sometimes called 'Hudsonian Curlew'). *Ibid.* 715/1 The Hudsonian Godwit *L*[*imosa*] *haemastica* migrates from North America to South America.

Hudson seal. [f. the name of Henry *Hudson* (see *HUDSONIAN *a.*) + SEAL *sb.*[1]] Musk-rat fur that has been plucked and dyed to give the appearance of seal fur. Also **Hudson Bay seal.**

1914 J. W. JONES *Fur-Farming in Canada* (ed. 2) 7 When the furdressers and dyers produced a clipped and dyed muskrat skin that resembled sealskin almost perfectly, it was found that it would not sell under its own name..[the] high-priced fur is now sold as 'Hudson Bay seal'. **1920** *Eye Opener* (Calgary) 11 Sept. 1/4 The jackpot is to be the real thing in Hudson seal coats this coming winter. **1921** *Daily Colonist* (Victoria, B.C.) 2 Oct. 8/5 First Quality Hudson Seal Coat, fancy silk lined; extra large collar and cuffs of Alaska sable. **1936** D. McCOWAN *Animals Canad. Rockies* xv. 134 When a muskrat skin has been tanned and the coarse outer hair removed the remaining soft silky undercoat is known to furriers as Hudson seal. **1945** H. MACLENNAN *Two Solitudes* (1946) II. 219 Paul looked out the window and saw.. women in black Hudson seal coats with their hands in black muffs, men with fur caps.

hue, *sb.*[1] Add: **3. c.** That attribute of a colour by which it is recognized as a red, a purple, a green, etc., and which approximately corresponds to its dominant wavelength (or to that of its complementary colour); it constitutes, along with saturation ('tint', purity, intensity) and lightness ('shade'), one of the

three attributes required for the complete specification of any colour.

In this sense hue is the quality in which different 'hues' (as distinct from 'tints' and 'shades': see SHADE *sb.* 4) differ; cf. quot. 1835 below and quot. 1859 s.v. TINT *sb.*[1] 2 a.

[**1835** G. FIELD *Chromatography* iii. 28 By mixing his colours with white, the artist obtains..tints; by mixing colours with colours, he obtains compound colours, or hues; finally, by mixing colours or tints with black, he gets..shades.] **1855** J. C. MAXWELL in *Trans. R. Scottish Soc. Arts* IV. 395 There will be two things on which the nature of each ray will depend:—(1.) its intensity or brightness; (2.) its hue, which may be estimated by its position in the spectrum, and measured by its wave length. *Ibid.* 396 Colours differ not only in intensity and hue, but also in tint; that is, they are more or less pure. **1872** —— in *Not. Proc. R. Inst. Gt. Brit.* VI. 263 Colour may vary in hue, tint, and shade... A difference in hue may be illustrated by the difference between adjoining colours in the spectrum. **1900** G. H. HURST *Colour* i. 13 The hue of a colour is that constant which is commonly denominated by the term colour, as blue, or green, or red. **1936** A. B. KLEIN *Colour Cinematogr.* i. 89 There are about 130 steps of just distinguishable difference in hue in the spectrum. **1939** M. LUCKIESH *Colour* 39 The names of colors are often taken from the hue and usually imply it. **1955** P. D. TREVOR-ROPER *Ophthalm.* x. 137 Monochromatic light may alter its apparent hue as it becomes more unsaturated, red turning to pink, orange to yellow. **1960** G. M. WYBURN *Nervous Syst.* vi. 83 Colour or hue, which is our interpretation of variations in light wavelength is comparable to the pitch of sound. **1966** R. R. COUPE *Sci. of Printing Technol.* ix. 209 To describe completely a colour, we must take into account three different properties, namely hue, saturation and lightness.

hue (hū·e), *sb.*[3] *N.Z.* [Maori.] A local name for the bottle gourd, *Lagenaria vulgaris.*

1843 E. DIEFFENBACH *Trav. N.Z.* II. iv. 49 The calabashes (hue) were..the next addition to their stock of eatables. **1868** W. COLENSO in *Trans. N.Z. Inst.* I. III. Essay. 36 The Hue, or gourd, (a species of *Cucurbitæ*), gave useful Calabashes, and vessels of several kinds and sizes, from a gill to three gallons. **1905** W. B. *Where White Man Treads* 15 Besides being a succulent delicacy when young, the matured vegetable hue, with its strong, horny rind, could be put to the uses of many utensils, as drinking cups, bowls, etc., and, most important of all, water and oil flasks. **1921** H. GUTHRIE-SMITH *Tutira* viii. 55 The land [was] usually too poor for the cultivation on a great scale of such exotics as..the *hue* (*Lagenaria vulgaris*). **1949** P. BUCK *Coming of Maori* (1950) II. i. 91 The gourd (*hue*) was grown principally to provide containers for water and for preserved birds.

hueless, *a.* **2.** (Later examples.)

c **1865** E. DICKINSON *Poems* (1955) II. 737, I sight the Aprils—Hueless to me until thou come. **1932** CHESTERTON *Chaucer* viii. 264 The sort of harsh and hueless light that can be seen in the black engravings in the old Family Bibles.

huemul, var. *GUEMAL.

huerta (ʰwē̃ə·ɹtă). [Sp.] A piece of irrigated land in Spain or in the Spanish-speaking areas of Latin America; also, an orchard.

1838 A. GANIHL *Mexico vs. Texas* i. 13 He was resting himself, and enjoying the cool of the evening breeze, under a spreading orange tree, in his *huerta.* **1841** BORROW *Zincali* I. II. iv. 287 The justicia will compel us to restore the ass; we have, however, already removed her to our huerta out of the town. **1859** T. R. WARREN *Dust & Foam* viii. 225 In each of these huertas is a reservoir, built of masonry, through which water is constantly flowing. **1924** *Glasgow Herald* 28 July 5 The huertas merge into a delicious confusion of flower and fruit. **1934** M. R. SHACKLETON *Europe* vii. 89 From the Ebro delta to Cape de la Nao in Valencia, the irrigated districts ('huertas', from Lat. *hortus* = a garden) are practically continuous along the coast. **1958** FISHER & BOWEN-JONES *Spain* iv. 52 Originally developed by the Moslems, the 'huertas' are small, highly cultivated plots which depend on irrigation water brought by an intricate system of channels, aqueducts and lifts.

huff, *v.* Add: **1.** Survives in phr. *to huff and puff.* (In some contexts not distinguishable from sense 4.)

1890 J. JACOBS *Eng. Fairy Tales* xiv. 69 Then I'll huff, and I'll puff, and I'll blow your house in. **1959** *Times* 11 Nov. 13/6 But it would be unrealistic to think that by huffing and puffing at him..the General can be made to change his mind. **1963** *Guardian* 1 Oct. 8/6 Mr. Liukov may huff and puff..about pernicious Western influences ..but the Bulgarians..are discovering..a sense of humour. **1967** *Listener* 13 July 57/2 Sarah [Churchill] herself never mastered the techniques of politics; she huffed and she puffed but at the end of it all few houses had been blown down. **1971** *Daily Tel.* 13 Jan. 1 Ministers were undisturbed by all the huffing and puffing against the Industrial Relations Bill at the Albert Hall last night.

7. (Earlier and later examples.)

1793 M. RISHTON *Let.* 12 Aug. in F. Burney *Jrnls. & Lett.* (1972) II. 185, I am a horrid Coward and get huffed every time we drive out. **1800** *Aurora* (Philadelphia) 18 Dec. (Th.), The Philadelphia Gazette is huffed at our stating a fact. **1906** J. M. SYNGE *Lett. to Molly* (1971) 50 Dont imagine I'm huffed or anything, little heart, I'm only weary. **1969** *Listener* 17 Apr. 535/2, I don't know whether to be huffed or pleased about it.

11. *Mil. slang.* To kill.

1919 *Athenæum* 23 May 360/2 Unmitigated slang, like..'to huff' for 'to kill'. **1925** FRASER & GIBBONS *Soldier & Sailor Words* 122 *To be huffed,* to be killed. **1933** PARTRIDGE *Words, Words, Words!* III. 197 The English synonyms for death..*huffed; out of mess,* dead.

huff, *sb.* Add: **1.** Survives in phr. *huff and puff.* (In some contexts influenced by sense 2.)

1961 *John o' London's* 9 Nov. 517/3 Nor do I really fancy Papermac's huff-and-puff. **1962** *Listener* 19 July 112/2 It seems a pity that this new era in telecommunications should be accompanied by an international huff-and-puff over priorities which at its worst comes perilously near to sub-lunar soap-opera. **1966** *Listener* 26 May 772/3 Even Ernesto is essentially a pallid version of those huff-and-puff baritones of Donizettian melodrama. **1967** G. SIMS *Last Best Friend* ix. 82 '—ing old woman,' Spiegl said. 'All huff and puff.' **1973** *Times* 16 Mar. 14/4 We are going through a period of a great deal of huff and puff generated by consumer organizations.

huff-duff (hʌ·fˌdʌf). [Representing the pronunc. as a word of the initials *h. f. d. f.,* for *h*igh-*f*requency *d*irection-*f*inder.] A device for determining the direction of incoming high-frequency radio signals, enabling their source to be located when bearings are obtained by two or more such devices.

1946 *N.Y. Herald-Tribune* 16 Jan. 22/1 'Huff duff', with a range that makes it possible to detect and plot radio signals of as little as fifteen seconds' duration emitted halfway around the globe from plotting stations. **1955** C. S. FORESTER *Good Shepherd* ii. 39 Huff-Duff reports foreign transmission. **1962** L. FARAGO *Tenth Fleet* viii. 162 They used decoy subs to befuddle the Huffduff.

huffkin (hʌ·fkin). *local.* Also **uffkin.** [Origin unknown.] A kind of tea-cake made chiefly in Kent.

1790 in *Eng. Dial. Dict.* **1869** *N. & Q.* 4th Ser. IV. 76/1 Most people know what muffins and crumpets are, but in East Kent the former..are known as *uffkins.* **1887** PARISH & SHAW *Dict. Kentish Dial., Huffkin, hufkin,* a kind of bun or light cake, which is cut open, buttered, and so eaten. **1928** *Daily Express* 14 Mar. 5/4 Our merry teas after net-ball, cricket, or football, without huffkins would be very 'dry'. **1952** F. WHITE *Good Eng. Food* v. iv. 199 This quantity makes 10 huffkins weighing 2½ oz. each.

huffle, *v.* Add: **1. c.** Of the wind: to make a sound as of blowing in gusts. So **hu·ffle** *sb.,* a sudden gust of wind, or the sound made by this.

1862 W. BARNES *Poems Rural Life* 3rd Coll. 122 Where sharp-leav'd ashès' heads did twist In hufflèn wind, an' driftèn mist. **1878** HARDY *Ret. Native* I. I. iii. 70 The winds do huffle queerer to-night than ever I heard 'em afore. **1889** S. BARING-GOULD et al. *Songs of West* 9 At the huffle of the gale, Here I toss and cannot sleep. **1891** 'L. MALET' *Wages of Sin* III. VI. ii. 82 A huffle of wind, hot with the festering reek of the streets away across the river, fluttered the leaves... The wind huffled again.

huffler. Add: Still used of bargemen.

1824 *Gentl. Mag.* Aug. 111/2 We have a class of people in these parts called *Ufflers,* i.e. men in the barging line out of employ, who attend as extra help to get the craft home in our inland navigation. **1918** *Chambers's Jrnl.* Feb. 109/1 Here it is that the barge skippers and the barge mates and the river 'hufflers' congregate. **1927** *Daily News* 27 May 6/6 If it is necessary to take on a third hand, he is generally regarded as being quite an inferior person, and is known as a 'huffler'. **1948** H. BENHAM *Last Stronghold of Sail* ii. 29 There were 'hufflers' in plenty in those days to come aboard and lend a hand.

hugaboo (hʌ·găbū:). [Fanciful, prob. infl. by BUGABOO, HULLABALOO, etc.] Portentousness, pomposity.

1930 *Eng. Rev.* Feb. 140 The silly hugaboo of minutes and protocols. **1932** S. GIBBONS *Cold Comfort Farm* i. 9 Marriages..should take place in churches, with all the usual paraphernalia and hugaboo.

hügelite (hü·gĕləit). *Min.* [ad. G. *hügelit* (V. Dürrfeld 1914, in *Zeitschr. f. Kryst. u. Min.* LIII. 183), f. the Ger. family name von *Hügel*: see -ITE[1].] A yellow or brown mineral originally described as a hydrated vanadate of lead and zinc but later shown to be a hydrated arsenate of lead and uranium.

1914 *Chem. Abstr.* VIII. 310 The name hügelite is suggested for the vanadate previously described. **1916** *Mineral. Mag.* XVII. 352 Hügelite... A hydrated vanadate of lead and zinc occurring as yellow monoclinic needles on corroded galena at Reichenbach, Baden. **1962** *Amer. Mineralogist* XLVII. 418 Hügelite was described by Dürrfeld (1913) as a hydrous lead zinc vanadate... Transparent to translucent crystals are brown to orange-yellow... Microchemical tests showed Pb, U and As as main components, but no Zn, V or P... The formula is proposed as $Pb_2(UO_2)_3(AsO_4)_2(OH)_4.3H_2O$.

huggable (hʌ·găb'l), *a.* [f. HUG *v.* + -ABLE.] Such as invites hugging.

1898 D. C. MURRAY *Tales* 205 Eminently kissable little face; eminently huggable little figure. **1908** *Daily Chron.* 5 Nov. 7/5 The 'Teddy' Bear is such a huggable creature that..he almost compels a caress. **1928** L. ROSSITER *Sex Age* viii. § 5 Sorry, Jacko. But you do look so huggable tonight. **1970** *Daily Tel.* 16 Dec. 11 Huggable rag doll..with removable dress.

Hughie (hiū·i). *Austral.* and *N.Z. slang.* Also **Huey.** [Diminutive of the name *Hugh*: see -IE, -Y[6].] The 'god' of weather, especially in phr. *send her down, Hughie!*

1937 PARTRIDGE *Dict. Slang* 209/1 New Zealanders and Australians say *send her down, Hughie!* **1958** *Tararua* XII. 27 The derisive phrases, 'Send it down, Hughie' and 'Let it come down, Hughie', go back to early in this century and are variants of the British military catch-phrase 'Send it down, David'... St. Hugh has long been associated with rain. **1962** *Austral. Women's Wkly.* Suppl. 24 Oct. 3/2 Come on, Huey, send the waves up. **1967** J. CLEARY *Long Pursuit* vii. 151 'Good on you, Hughie,' he said gratefully and with true religion... Hughie was the Australian working man's vernacular for the Lord. **1971** *N.Z. Listener* 19 Apr. 57/1 Well, that night Hughie sent it down, a nor' wester followed by a southerly buster.

hug-me-tight (hʌ·gˌmiˌtəit). [f. the phr. *hug me tight.*]

1. A woman's short close-fitting jacket, usu. made of wool. orig. *U.S.*

1860 *Godey's Lady's Bk.* Dec. 544 Hug me tight. A garment to be worn under a cloak. **1869** L. M. ALCOTT *Little Women* II. v. 68 She..made him..demand fiercely the meaning of a 'hug-me-tight'. **1910** *N.Y. Even. Post* 24 Dec., Suppl. 3 Hug-me-tights and mittens, all knit at home by grandmother. **1924** *Mod. Draper* II. 94 Articles, such as spencers, hug-me-tights, etc., which are worn above the undergarment, and under the outer garment. **1934** E. BOWEN *Cat Jumps* 130 Mrs. Archworth sat propped up in bed in a hug-me-tight trimmed with marabout. **1959** *Guardian* 25 Nov. 6/4 For that extra degree of warmth..over the shoulders..this cuffed hug-me-tight of the same tweed as the dress. **1972** F. B. MAYNARD *Raisins & Almonds* 45 A variety of cozy garments called hug-me-tights.

2. A type of buggy. Also *attrib. U.S. Hist.*

1901 W. N. HARBEN *Westerfelt* i, I seed 'em takin' a ride in his new hug-me-tight buggy yesterday. **1902** —— *Abner Daniel* v, He's got a new buggy—a regular hug-me-tight. **1948** *Jrnl. Amer. Folk-Lore* Apr.–June 212 Those roads were so bad..that they kept making the buggies narrower and narrower... Some of them got so narrow they used to call them 'Hug-Me-Tights'.

Hugoesque (hiūgoe·sk), *a.* [f. the name of Victor M. *Hugo* (1802–1885), French author + -ESQUE.] Resembling the character or style of V. Hugo. Also subst. with *the.*

1893 E. SALTUS *Madam Sapphira* xiii. 164 That would be mediæval. I mean nothing so Hugoesque. **1904** *Daily Chron.* 3 Mar. 3/2 There is a touch of the Hugoesque in Rodwell. **1960** J. LODWICK *Asparagus Trench* 20 Almost Hugoesque in his unflagging pursuit of maids.

hugsome (hʌ·gsŏm), *a.* [f. HUG *v.* + -SOME[1].] Such as invites hugging, huggable (see also quot. 1893).

1893 FARMER & HENLEY *Slang* III. 375/2 *Hugsome adj.* (colloquial), carnally attractive; fuckable. **1894** *Outing* (U.S.) XXIV. 417/1 A [bear's] long, straining, hugsome hug, which breaks the dog's ribs. **1942** BERREY & VAN DEN BARK *Amer. Thes. Slang* § 427.1 Hotsy-totsy, hugsome hussy, humdinger, irresistibelle.

huh, *int.* Add: (Later examples.) Also as an expression of interrogation.

1890 'O. THANET' *Expiation* ix. 166 A loud snort of contempt from the gallery betrayed that Hizzie had heard. 'Huh!' she bawled, 'you yent gwine get killed up, not long's ye kin *run!*' **1924** *Dialect Notes* V. 270 *Huh* (surp., disg., enquiry). **1937** L. B. MURPHY *Social Behavior & Child Personality* ii. 53 Agatha said, 'Want to play in the sand box, Theodore, huh? Do you?' **1940** R. CHANDLER *Farewell, My Lovely* xxi. 169 Pretty trivial in my case, huh? **1948** F. & R. LOCKRIDGE *Pinch of Poison* xvi. 151 'Listen, Mullins,' Weigand pleaded. 'Don't think, huh?' **1953** *Manch. Guardian Weekly* 20 Aug. 7/2 'I could go back there, I mean some other time.' 'But not now, huh?' **1969** K. AMIS *Green Man* iv. 182 God's purpose. Huh. I'm no more qualified than the next man to tell you what that is. **1970** *Washington Post* 30 Sept. D 4/2 'Oh boy that's just what he needs,' he said, cheerlessly. 'Tell him to take it easy, huh?' **1971** *Black World* Apr. 59 Hell, its all my fault, huh? **1972** *Canad. Jrnl. Ling.* XVII. 94 Whatever its origin and history, *huh?* is currently in widespread use in the United States. **1972** *Southerly* XXXII. 54 Because the fun part is over. They think. Huh! **1973** A. PRICE *October Men* ix. 126 'Huh!' Macready snorted derisively.

hühnerkobelite (hünəɹkōᵘ·bĕləit). *Min.* [f. *Hühnerkobel,* name of a hill near Lam in eastern Bavaria, Germany: see -ITE[1].] An olive-green phosphate of sodium, calcium, bivalent iron, and bivalent manganese, (Na, Ca) $(Fe^{++}, Mn^{++})_2$ $(PO_4)_2$, in which iron predominates over manganese.

1950 M. L. LINDBERG in *Amer. Mineralogist* XXXV. 75 It is here proposed to give the name hühnerkobelite to the material from Hühnerkobel and from Norrö, not isostructural with true arrojadite. **1965** *Amer. Mineralogist* L. 713 (*heading*) Hühnerkobelite crystals from the Palermo No. 1 pegmatite, North Groton, New Hampshire.

huhu (hū·hū). *N.Z.* [Maori.] The beetle *Prionoplus reticularis,* or its larva (in full *huhu grub*), found in decayed timber.

1848 R. TAYLOR *Leaf from Nat. Hist. N.Z.* 5/1 Insects ..Huhu, a grub which bores into wood. **1926** R. J. TILLYARD *Insects Austral. & N.Z.* xx. 232 *Prionoplus reticu-*

laris Wh., the largest of all New Zealand beetles, measures up to two inches in length and is dark brown..; it is very common and flies to light. The larva, called 'Hu-hu' by the Maoris, is eaten as a delicacy; it bores into fallen forest timber. **1949** F. SARGESON *I saw in My Dream* I. vii. 52 The children..looked for wetas and huhus. **1956** T. SUTHERLAND *Green Kiwi* ii. 45 The timber tunnelled by the mokoroa or huhu grubs. **1960** B. CRUMP *Good Keen Man* 45 My next mate was a Maori... I once found him tearing a rotten log to pieces, scattering powdery wood all over the place as he searched for huhus. When he found one he'd pick the butter-coloured grub out with his fingers and eat it as it was. **1966** *Encycl. N.Z.* I. 187/2 Among the more conspicuous New Zealand beetles are the 'Huhu' (*Prionoplus reticularis*), a large dead-wood borer of the family Cerambycidae, [etc.].

huh-uh (*ʌ·ˌʌ*), *int. U.S.* An expression of negation. Also **uh-huh*, **uh-uh*.

1948 F. & R. LOCKRIDGE *Pinch of Poison* xvi. 152 Mullins shook his head. 'Huh-uh,' he said. 'She ain't the type.' **1962** *Amer. Speech* XXXVII. 230 Foreign visitors to the United States, who have learned the proper affirmative and negative responses of *yes* and *no*, are often bewildered by the widespread colloquial use of *uh-huh* and *huh-uh*.

hu-hu-hu (hūˌhūˌhū). Also **hoo-hoo-oo.** Representing a repetition of the sound of Hoo *int.* and *sb.*

1884 [see Hoo *int.* and *sb.*]. **1911** T. E. LAWRENCE *Home Lett.* (1954) 154 With a mighty firing of guns & pistols, and the hu-hu-hu and violent tahleel of the women [*sc.* native women in Syria].

‖ **hui** (hū·i). [Maori and Hawaiian.] In New Zealand, a large social or ceremonial gathering; in Hawaii, a formal club or association.

1858 J. MORGAN *Let.* 21 June in *Richmond–Atkinson Papers* (1960) I. 408 The *hui* at Rangiaohia to promote the Maori King movement broke up. **1898** M. H. KROUT *Hawaii* 18 Those present, with forty members of a royalist society called *Hui Kalaiaina*, marched to the palace. **1921** H. GUTHRIE-SMITH *Tutira* x. 81 The large *huis*—gatherings—of the Heretaunga people. **1948** KUYKENDALL & DAY *Hawaii* xxv. 274 The enterprise of oriental business men was strengthened by the local practice of forming a *hui*, the Hawaiian name for an informal syndicate which enables Chinese or Japanese members to take great advantage of a business opportunity. **1954** J. SHERIDAN in *Ellery Queen's Mystery Mag.* Oct. 15/2 Our fishing *hui*'s beginning to pay. **1959** M. SHADBOLT *New Zealanders* 20, I mean it's common knowledge about what happens at the pa when there's a big hui. There's always too much liquor there, and the boys and girls mix freely. **1960** N. HILLIARD *Maori Girl* III. vii. 220 We'll have fowls. Go to all the *huis*. **1973** *Parade* (Austral.) Sept. 11/1 The Maori custom of steeping the grain in water until it was half-rotten, and then serving it up as a special dish at a tribal hui.

Huichol (witʃōᵘ·l). [Sp., from the native name.] **A.** *sb.* **a.** A people of Mexican Indians; a member of this people. **b.** The language of this people. **B.** *adj.* Of or pertaining to this people or their language.

1900 *Mem. Amer. Mus. Nat. Hist.* III. I. i. 22 According to the Huichol myths, corn was once deer, the deer having been the chief source of food in earliest times. *Ibid.* vi. 154 With the Huichol, the 'eye' is the symbol of the power of seeing and understanding unknown things. *Ibid.* ix. 185 Peculiar to certain rain-making feasts are a stick and a dried armadillo, which form the paraphernalia of the clown.., called in Huichol Sikwaíki. **1903** C. LUMHOLTZ *Unknown Mexico* II. v. 91 The Huichols occasionally made comments that appeared very fair reasoning powers. **1964** E. A. NIDA *Toward Sci. Transl.* x. 228 'Glorified God' (Mark 2:12) becomes in Huichol 'said to God: You are of good heart.' **1972** *Language* XXXVIII. 847 Hockett adds Huichol which has /ɨ/ instead of /ü/.

Huk (hʌk). [Abbrev. of Tagalog *Hukbalahap*, f. initial syllables of *huk*bó army + *ba*yan people, country + *la*ban against + *hap*an Japanese (i.e. *hukbó ng bayan laban sa hapon* people's army against the Japanese).] A guerrilla movement in the Philippines, orig. against the Japanese in World War II, later popularly identified with communism. Also *attrib.*

1947 *Britannica Bk. of Year* 840/2 *Huks*, shortening of Hukbalahaps, a Tagalog word meaning 'armed peasants', 'people's army'. **1951** H. MACINNES *Neither Five nor Three* xv. 209, I read the article..about the Philippines. It seems that the Huks have nothing to do with Communism. **1966** *Economist* 22 Oct. 359/2 Killings and ambushes by Huk guerrillas..have recently been common in central Luzon. **1967** *Ibid.* 4 Feb. 414/2 The Huks, who began as anti-Japanese guerrillas, carried on an armed rural rebellion from 1950 to 1954. **1971** W. LAQUEUR *Dict. Politics* 403 Since 1965 there has been a revival of *Huk* activity. **1972** *Times* 30 Sept. 15/4 The Huks are well-educated, ideologically-motivated men.

‖ **hukilau** (hukīlau·). [Hawaiian, f. *huki* to pull + *lau* net.] An Hawaiian fishing party usually involving many people and much revelry.

1954 J. SHERIDAN in *Ellery Queen's Mystery Mag.* Oct. 20/1 Oh, we're going to a hukilau. *Ibid.* 21/2 We're about ready for the hukilau... He led us seaward, explaining to Bill that *huki* means pull and *lau* means leaf, from the *ti* leaves which are used to frighten fish into the net. **1972** *New Yorker* 8 Apr. 84/1 (Advt.), Come to a hukilau,..a sort of Polynesian fish-in.

hukm, var. *HOOKUM.

hula (hū·lă). Also † **hura**; **hula-hula.** [Hawaiian.] **a.** An Hawaiian dance, with six basic steps, which portrays through symbolic and imitative gestures natural phenomena, sports, and historical or mythological subjects. Also *attrib.* Hence as *vb.*, to dance the hula.

1825 W. ELLIS *Jrnl. Tour Hawaii* 59 At 4 p.m. the musicians from Kau again collected on the beach, and the dancers commenced a *hura*. *c* **1835** LOWELL SMITH in M. D. Frear *Lowell & Abigail* (1934) 102 [The public disturbance of] perpetual hulas, drumming and dancing accompanied by howling and intonations. **1851** F. A. BUCK *Yankee Trader in Gold Rush* (1930) 81 They also take advantage of this to have a grand Hoolah Hoolah, or native dance. **1853** *Putnam's Mag.* II. 21/1 And now the floor was cleared, and preparation made for the great feature of the evening, viz., the *Hula-hula*. **1866** 'MARK TWAIN' *Lett. fr. Hawaii* (1967) 70 The girls danced the lascivious hula-hula—a dance that is said to exhibit the very perfection of educated motion. *Ibid.* 170 The flower and evergreen trumpery worn by the hula girls. **1868** *Daily Territorial Enterprise* (Virginia City, Nevada) 29 Aug. 3/1 We have borne ourselves with calm fortitude at a Sandwich Island *hula-hula*. **1892** STEVENSON & OSBOURNE *Wrecker* xvii. 259, I was entertained to a sea-bathe, indiscriminate cocktails, a dinner, a *hula-hula*. **1898** [see *grass skirt* (*GRASS *sb.*[1] 13)]. **1899** W. C. MORROW *Bohemian Paris* 96 The hula-hula of the Hawaiian women lacks the grace, dash and abandon of the Turkish dance. **1919** F. O'BRIEN *White Shadows South Seas* 4 Kelly began 'Tome! Tome!' a Hawaiian hula. **1927** [see *EMPENNAGE]. **1928** L. NORTH *Parasites* 14 It appeared that you could buy anything from a home to a Hula-skirt on time-payment. **1954** 'N. BLAKE' *Whisper in Gloom* I. iii. 49 A dusky maiden in hula-hula skirt, brassiere, and little else. **1954** *Ellery Queen's Mystery Mag.* Oct. 30/1 Her *hula* was very good. *Ibid.* 31/1 David was the one who taught me to swim and to *hula*. **1956** 'N. SHUTE' *Beyond Black Stump* viii. 236 With straw hula skirts..for sale in one corner among the picture postcards. **1970** *Observer* (Colour Suppl.) 15 Feb. 26/2 An ability to hula well does not.. appear to be a quality inherent in every Tahitian.

b. *hula hoop*, a tubular, plastic hoop (HOOP *sb.*[1] 3) used for spinning round the body with movements akin to those of the hula; hence *hula-hoop* v. intr., *hula-hooping* vbl. sb. and ppl. a.

1958 *Economist* 11 Oct. 144/2 In a manner reminiscent of a primitive tribal ritual, the Hula Hoop..can be made to spin round the torso, or arm or leg or neck, by a broad swaying motion resembling the hip swinging of a Hawaiian hula dancer. **1958** *Observer* 9 Nov. 10/4 Hula-hooping children. **1958** *Times Lit. Suppl.* 21 Nov. p. xxix/3 Hoops, also of ancient origin, had virtually disappeared from shops and streets, until the sudden recent craze for 'hula' hoops brought them out in a new form. **1958** *Times* 19 Dec. 12/5 If she had been a little younger he would have asked her if she had been hula-hooping the previous day. **1959** *Times* 3 Jan. 10/4 As training they are advocating two hours of 'hula-hooping' every morning. **1969** *Official Gaz.* (U.S. Patent Office) 1 July TM16/2 Wham-O Mfg. Co., San Gabriel, Calif... Junior Hula Hoop... For plastic toy hoops. **1970** *Which?* Sept. 288/2 Remember hula-hoops and dislocated hips? **1973** *Daily Tel.* (Colour Suppl.) 6 Apr. 27/2 Few 'craze' toys have as long a life as the yo-yo: the hula-hoop and the late, unlamented 'clacker-balls' are examples which had success but were soon forgotten.

hule (ū·lĭ). Also **ule, ulé, ulli.** [Mexican Sp. *(h)ule*, Nahuatl *ulli* or *olli* caoutchouc.] A Central American tree of the genus *Castilloa* (formerly *Castilla*), or the crude rubber obtained from it. So **hule·ro, ule·ro,** a collector of rubber.

1846 J. LINDLEY *Veget. Kingd.* 271 The tree Ule of Papantla, from which caoutchouc is obtained in that country. **1874** T. BELT *Naturalist in Nicaragua* 33 The Mexicans played with balls made from it, and it still bears its Aztec name of *Ulli*, from which the Spaniards call the collectors of it *Ulleros*. **1880** *Encycl. Brit.* XII. 835/2 Torquemada mentions..that an oil was extracted from the 'ulli', or rubber, by heat, possessing soft and lubricous properties... Even at that early date the Spaniards used the juice of the ulé tree to waterproof their cloaks. **1894** *Outing* XXIII. 353/1 Curious tales the huleros tell of carved rocks hidden in those fastnesses. *Ibid.*, This home of the gatherer of *hule*. **1920** *Edin. Rev.* Oct. 356 The garments he wears are splashed with ulli. **1959** J. C. T. UPHOF *Dict. Economic Plants* 79/2 *Castilla costaricana* Liebm. Hule (Moraceae).—Tree. Costa Rica. Latex from stem is source of a good rubber.

hull, *sb.*[2] Add: **1.** Also of an airship, flying boat, etc.

1918 *Aviation* 15 Mar. 231/1 A hull for flying boats having its elevational aspect determined by lines rounding off rearwardly. **1923** *Gloss. Aeronaut. Terms (B.S.I.)* iv. 35 *Hull*, the main flotation body of a boat sea plane. **1923** GLAZEBROOK *Dict. Appl. Physics* V. 128/2 The curves may be taken as representing the type of distribution which had been found for models of airship hulls. **1936** [see *air stewardess* (*AIR *sb.*[1] III. 4)]. **1950** *Gloss. Aeronaut. Terms (B.S.I.)* I. 37 *Hull*, the main structural and flotation body of a flying boat or boat amphibian. **1951** *Oxf. Jun. Encycl.* IV. 396/2 The hull of a flying boat has a planing bottom like a speedboat.

2. b. *hull down*: also *attrib.* and *fig.* Used also of a tank (see quot. 1948[2]).

1883 [in Dict.]. **1899** *Westm. Gaz.* 29 Nov. 1/3 He shook his fist at the hull-down coasting schooner. **1905** J. C. LINCOLN *Partners of Tide* xiv. 264 You've got me beat, hull down. **1933** 'L. LUARD' *All Hands* 132 We was goin' to see our Mary [Pickford]. Don't alf 'old with 'er. She's got the rest of 'em 'ull down. **1944** *Return to Attack* (Army Board, N.Z.) 18/1 Using the slight undulations of the desert to get hull down and so present the smallest target, they manœuvred for position. **1948** C. DAY LEWIS *Poems 1943–47* 29 Alas, hull-down upon hope's ashen verge Hastens the vessel that our joined hands launched. **1948** PARTRIDGE *Dict. Forces' Slang* 96 *Hull down*, a position for tanks and self-propelled guns where only the turret was visible, the rest being protected by a bank or fold in the ground. **1953** C. DAY LEWIS *Italian Visit* iv. 51 A cloud vibrating In the wash of the hull-down sun. **1960** C. S. LEWIS *Studies in Words* iv. 105 But ten years later he and Cowley are leagues apart, each 'hull down' to the other.

hullabaloo, *v.* Add: Also *trans.*; **hullabaloo·ing** *ppl. a.*

1936 M. FRANKLIN *All that Swagger* x. 93 On harvest days they were hullabalooed from bed before dawn. **1952** DYLAN THOMAS *Coll. Poems* p. ix, Ho, hullaballoing clan Agape, with woe In your beaks, on the gabbing capes!

hullo, *int.* Add: Also used in response to a telephone call and (freq. repeated) to express surprise. Cf. *HALLO *int.*, *HELLO *int.* b.

1900 C. H. CHAMBERS *Tyranny of Tears* 3 [Goes to telephone.] Hullo! hullo! [Gives them a ring up.] Are you there? **1906** *Daily Chron.* 31 May 4/7 The telephone ..we both begin with the same word: 'Hullo!' **1931** D. L. SAYERS *Five Red Herrings* xix. 193 'Hullo-ullo-ullo!' he said. 'So here we are again.' **1959** *Listener* 13 Aug. 248/2 If, when you take off the receiver, you say 'Hullo!' just think how absurd that is. Why, you might be saying 'Hullo!' to a total stranger. **1972** N. MARSH *Tied up in Tinsel* viii. 198 Hullo-ullo! I thought there was something there.

hully gee (hʌ·li dʒī·), *int.* Chiefly *U.S.* Also **holly gee.** [Corruption of *Holy Jesus*.] An exclamation of delight or surprise.

1895 E. W. TOWNSEND *Chimmie Fadden Explains* 58 And holly gee! I never knowed de Duckess could do it! *Ibid.* 69 'Holly gee!' says de mug, 'don't do dat,' he says, and slips me a fiver. **1898** 'O. THANET' *Heart of Toil* 76 Hully gee, Michael, but you are just *there*, and don't you forget it. **1907** F. H. BURNETT *Shuttle* xxiii. 238 To be treated as a gentleman by a gentleman—by 'a fine old swell like this—Hully gee!' **1936** F. CLUNE *Roaming round Darling* i. 3 We picked up a pair of wire-strainers, his leather coat, and a typewriter: then hully-gee! we were off again over the hideous Pyrmont Bridge. **1945** MENCKEN *Amer. Lang.* Suppl. I. 664 *Hully gee* (for *Holy Jesus*) was introduced by Edward W. Townsend's Chimmie Fadden and Major Max (New York, 1895), but it disappeared with the decay of the Bowery boy as an American comic type.

hully gully (hʌ·li gʌ·li). [Etym. unknown.] A dance that is a modification of the frug.

1964 *Cambr. Rev.* 10 Oct. 1/2 Two or three hours of the Hully-Gully. **1966** *Amer. Speech* XLI. 143 Mee, Charles L., Jr. Discotheque Man... [Names and briefly describes current dances: the Hully-Gully, the Frug, La Bostella, the Jerk.] **1968** D. HALLIDAY *Dolly & Singing Bird* ii. 23 We danced a Hully Gully. And then..Johnson performed a frenzied Watusi. **1969** N. COHN *AWopBopaLooBop* (1970) ix. 85 Dance-crazes bossed pop right up until the Beatles broke. There was the Hully Gully, the Madison, [etc.].

hulsite (hʌ·lsəit). *Min.* [f. the name of Alfred *Hulse* Brooks (1871–1924), American geologist: see -ITE[1].] A black borate of bivalent and trivalent iron, magnesium, and calcium in which there is some substitution of tin for trivalent iron, known only from an Alaskan locality.

1908 KNOPF & SCHALLER in *Amer. Jrnl. Sci.* CLXXV. 323 Examination of this deposit showed that an unknown mineral..was present in considerable abundance. We propose for it the name *hulsite*, in honor of Mr. Alfred Hulse Brooks, geologist in charge of the Division of Alaskan Mineral Resources. **1954** *Amer. Mineralogist* XXXIX. 524 X-ray powder photographs of ludwigite, paigeite, pinakiolite, hulsite, warwickite, sussexite, and camsellite were taken.

hulwa (hʌ·lwa). Also 7 **helwa, holway.** [a. Urdu and Arab. *ḥalwā* sweetmeat.] A kind of sweetmeat in India, Persia, etc.; = *HALVA. Cf. *HALAWI.

1662 J. DAVIES tr. *Olearius's Voy. Ambass.* 311 At Tabris, they make a certain Conserve of it [*sc.* duschab], which they call Helwa. **1698** J. FRYER *New Acct. E.-India & Persia* 358 Every Friday Night, at the Sacrament of *Holwey*, (or Wafer made up in Sweetmeats). **1884** *Times* 30 May 8 Provisions ran short and the voyagers had to live on hulwa, a glutinous sweetmeat.

hum, *v.*[1] Add: **1.** (Later examples.)

1924 *Foundry* (Cleveland) 1 Apr. 63 (Advt.), The wheels surely are humming in the foundries. **1937** WODEHOUSE *Lord Emsworth & Others* ix. 299 We buzzed on through the pleasant countryside... The engine of the two-seater hummed smoothly. **1972** *Daily Tel.* 23 Mar. 21/2 Computers hummed and slide rules flashed as City analysts tried to come to grips with the new corporation tax yesterday.

3. Further examples of sense 'to be in a

condition of busy activity'. Phr. *to make things* (or something specified) *hum*: to bring to such a condition, to liven things up.

1884 'MARK TWAIN' *Huck. Finn* 224 He lit into that horse with his whip and made him fairly hum. **1887** M. ROBERTS *Western Avernus* iii. 34 The owner of the farm..came home, and, in American parlance, 'fairly made things hum'. **1898** [in Dict.]. **1902** E. BANKS *Autobiogr. Newspaper Girl* xviii. 205 We took you on this paper to help us make things hum! I understand you made things hum over in England. **1906** *Nation* (N.Y.) 18 Jan. 44 The colleges are making athletic reform hum, as if to make up for lost time. **1911** E. M. CLOWES *On Wallaby* x. 265 But still things are, as the American would express it, 'beginning to hum' in the irrigation line. **1914** G. ATHERTON *Perch of Devil* I. xxx, I want money to spend in Butte,..and make things hum. **1922** H. S. WALPOLE *Cathedral* I. vii. 135, I hardly need to tell you that he's not quite the man to make things hum. **1966** 'J. HACKSTON' *Father clears Out* 107 By gum! Wouldn't it just make things hum? **1973** *Times* 16 Jan. 17/7 Our view is that if you get the logistics right and do get concentration of the best modern equipment you can really get something humming in the 1974 period.

hum, *v.*² Add: **2.** *trans.* and *intr.* To borrow (without any intention of returning); to scrounge. *Austral. slang.*

1918 *Aussie* Sept. 4/2 Don't *shout* cigarettes, *hum* them. **1925** FRASER & GIBBONS *Soldier & Sailor Words* 122 *To hum*, to cadge. **1935** *Bulletin* (Sydney) 30 Jan. 21/4 Where other 'Bidgee whalers 'hummed' a town for booze, Mick 'hummed' it for tea, going from house to house with his plea: 'Missus, could y' spring a cup o' tea?' **1938** X. HERBERT *Capricornia* (1939) xviii. 234 Gertch—you old blowbag! You're only humming for a drink. Nick off home.

hum (hʌm), *v.*³ *slang. intr.* To smell disagreeably. Hence **hum** *sb.*³, a disagreeable smell.

1902 C. H. E. BROOKFIELD *Random Reminisc.* xi. 200 The burglar..finds a piece of Camembert cheese in the buffet, and exclaims: 'Lor'! it do 'um!' **1906** E. DYSON *Fact'ry 'Ands* xv. 197 Ther hum iv it was so fearful... Killin' cats is rotten luck. **1927** W. E. COLLINSON *Contemp. Eng.* 23 Things didn't smell, but ponged, niffed or hummed. *Ibid.*, An awful pong or hum. **1946** I. L. IDRIESS *In Crocodile Land* xvi. 111 The abos certainly did 'hum'. **1970** *Daily Tel.* 31 Oct. 1/3 When the wind drops this stuff really hums.

hum, *sb.*¹ Add: **I. 1. c.** *Med.* In full *venous hum*. A continuous humming sound sometimes heard during auscultation in the upper chest and the sides of the neck, esp. in children and in cases of anæmia, and attributed to the turbulence of the flow of venous blood.

1839 J. HOPE *Treatise Dis. Heart* (ed. 3) I. iv. 118 By the adroit management of the stethoscope..the venous murmur may often be raised, by a gradual swell, into a more or less musical hum, such as is yielded by a child's humming-top. I propose to denominate this the Venous Hum; for..this is..more intelligible than *noise of the devil*, by which term, derived from a plaything known to few, M. Bouillaud has designated the hum in question. **1876**, **1891** [see VENOUS *a.* 2]. **1907** H. S. ANDERS *Physical Diagnosis* xiv. 346 The venous hum or *bruit de diable* heard over the jugulars. **1960** J. S. BUTTERWORTH et al. *Cardiac Auscultation* (ed. 2) ix. 81 The venous hum is usually heard only in the upright position. *Ibid.*, The hum will disappear with finger compression of the jugular veins.

d. *Electronics.* (Usu. without *a* or *pl.*) Unwanted low-frequency variations in current or voltage (the cause of which is usually the alternating frequency of the mains) which will give rise in a loudspeaker to a steady humming sound; the sound so produced.

1929 K. HENNEY *Princ. Radio* xvi. 406 A hum output of 44 millivolts. **1934** J. H. REYNER *Television* viii. 90 The hum appears as a series of black bands moving slowly across the screen. **1950** A. MARCUS *Radio Servicing* xv. 714 An antenna that is too close and parallel to a power line may pick up hum by induction. **1966** R. KING *Electrical Noise* i. 3 Mains hum..may be generated from cathodes of thermionic valves heated by alternating current or by electromagnetic induction from near by mains frequency transformers and chokes.

III. hum-bucking coil *Electronics* [BUCK *v.*⁶], a coil arranged so as to cancel the hum in another coil by providing a signal of the opposite phase.

1940 *Chambers's Techn. Dict.* 425/1 Hum-bucking coil. **1950** A. MARCUS *Radio Servicing* xv. 715 Some loudspeakers, especially of the electrodynamic type, have hum-bucking coils. **1967** P. SPRING *Tape Recorders* vii. 90 The hum-bucking coil..picks up hum in opposite phase to the hum picked up by the head and of such magnitude that the two hum signals cancel.

hum, *sb.*² Add: **2.** A persistent borrower, a scrounger. *Austral. slang.*

1919 V. MARSHALL *World of Living Dead*, The 'hum', the unskilled derelict or derelict-to-be who stands upon the 'pub' corner kerb, 'bites' all and sundry, and, at regular intervals, succeeds in getting lumbered for 'vag'. **1953** CADDIE *Sydney Barmaid* xxxiii. 183 The speciality of the hum is the lone drunk.

hum, *sb.*³: see *HUM *v.*³

hum (hiūm), *sb.*⁴ *Physical Geogr.* [Serbo-Croat, = hill.] A small, usually conical, hill characteristic of karst topography.

1921 *Geogr. Rev.* XI. 602 (*caption*) General view of a polje strewn with hums. *Ibid.* 604 The former limestone mass being represented by isolated fragments which Cvijic calls 'hums'. **1937** WOOLDRIDGE & MORGAN *Physical Basis Geogr.* xix. 289 Residual limestone masses or hummocks rising above polje floors are called 'hums'. **1971** B. W. SPARKS *Rocks & Relief* v. 204 The interfluvial areas are finally reduced to little hillocks known as hums.

huma (hū·mă). Also **Huma**, **Ûma**. [Hind., a. Pers. *humā* phœnix.] A fabulous bird of the east, said to be a restless wanderer but to bring luck to any person over whom it hovers.

1841 R. C. WELLESLEY *Primitiæ et Reliquiæ* 104 (*heading*) The Ûma, or Indian Eagle, the bird of prosperous empire. *Ibid.* 105 The throne of the Sultan of Mysore.. was surmounted by a representation of the Ûma, which is now deposited at Windsor Castle. *Ibid.* 106 A bird called by the natives the Ûma and which bore the appearance of a small eagle or vulture, built its nest..in the garden of Mr. Petrie, where Lord Wellesley resided while at Madras... The natives superstitiously ascribed much of the success of the war to the influence of the Ûma. **1858** O. W. HOLMES *Autocrat of Breakfast-Table* i. 8, I am like the Huma, the bird that never lights, being always in the cars, as he is always on the wing. **1905** *Spectator* 14 Jan. 47/2 The legendary 'huma' of Eastern tradition.

human, *a.* (*sb.*). Add: **A. 3. b.** Belonging or relative to man, relating to or characteristic of activities, relationships, etc., which are observable in man, as distinguished from (*a*) the lower animals; (*b*) machinery or the mechanical element; (*c*) mere objects or events, as *human affairs, angle, chain, condition, document, element, factor, fly, interest, note, period, relations, rights, situation, story, torch, torpedo.* Also **human engineering** orig. *U.S.*, the scientific study of the interaction of man and his working environment and the exploitation of this interaction in the interests of efficiency; the application of the human sciences to the design of machines; so **human engineer; human equation**: see *EQUATION 3 b; **human-factors engineering** = **human engineering*; so **human-factors engineer.**

1741 HUME *Ess. Moral & Pol.* I. 176 Such mighty Revolutions have happened in human Affairs.. as are sufficient to beget the Suspicion of still farther Changes. **1798** Human affairs [see AFFAIR *sb.* 2 a.]. **1877** L. H. MORGAN *Anc. Society* III. i. 399 From its limited prevalence it made but little impression upon human affairs. **1949** W. L. WARNER in M. Fortes *Social Struct.* 2 Current procedures for class stratification..require too large a field staff of experts, often making it impossible for the interested student of human affairs to use a knowledge of social class to understand his particular problem. **1941** *Ann. Reg. 1940* 317 The Press mirrored the age, copying from America tabloid news, the 'human angle', and..illustrations. **1908** *Pop. Mechanics* Jan. 15/2, 50 men formed a human chain and pulled him out. **1926** B. A. MCKELVIE *Huldowget* iii. 40 Every male in the village was a link in the human chain. **1963** Human chain [see *CHAIN *sb.* 5 f]. **1814** *Edin. Rev.* XXII. 199 The means of bettering the human condition. **1957** P. COVENEY *Poor Monkey* xii. 276 Lawrence's perception of the 'human condition'. **1960** C. DAY LEWIS *Buried Day* v. 87, I could not myself opt out of the human condition, as to some degree the pacifist must do. **1892** W. H. MALLOCK (*title*) A human document. **1896** *Badminton Mag.* 195 Regarded as a human document my guide looked dog-eared, thumbed and a trifle mildewed. **1938** *Ann. Reg. 1937* 320 Dr. Roberts' book is a 'human document' of great value. **1887** *Scribner's Mag.* I. 93/2 He managed, with masterly ingenuity, so to leave out the *human* element..that he gave hardly a glimpse of what it really is. **1897** *Trans. Inst. Naval Architects* 111 It is all very well to say the men are careless, but the human element has to be reckoned with. **1907** R. HERRIOT (*title*) The human element. A novel. **1908** *Modern Business* Aug. 65/1 System and organisation may be perfect on paper..but this does not necessarily lead to.. efficiency. There is another element—the human element. **1913** *Pall Mall Mag.* July 46/2 You must remember that in regard to the human element, we are..behind Germany. The point is that they have the human element—a large body of pilots, observers, artisans, trained during the last sixteen years. **1944** *Electronic Engin.* XVI. 334 The additional errors due to the human element (observation and reaction times) can be eliminated. **1957** GOODE & MACHOL *System Engin.* xxx. 500 Selection and training of operators..come within the province of the human engineer. **1934** WEBSTER, Human engineering. **1944** *Amer. N. & Q.* June 48 Los Angeles.. has more than its quota of 'spiritual engineers'..not to mention a 'School of Human Engineering' in a college curriculum... Such an academic unit might legitimately concern itself with anything..from anatomy and physiology to sociology. **1950** *Lancet* 1 Apr. 645/2 The field which has variously been described as 'fitting the machine to the man', human engineering, that part of industrial psychology not concerned with vocational guidance, etc. **1957** GOODE & MACHOL *System Engin.* xxx. 481 The primary object of attention in human engineering is the man–machine link. **1970** *New Scientist* 23 July 199/3 Human engineering..involves a careful moulding of an educational system to nurture what is most useful and beneficial in each individual. **1921** B. S. ROWNTREE (*title*) The human factor in business. **1943** J. B. PRIESTLEY *Daylight on Saturday* x. 65 He was worried about his production figures... In the last resort it was the human factor that counted. **1967** L. B. ARCHER in Wills & Yearsley *Handbk. Managem. Technol.* 130 In the U.S.A. the subject [ergonomics] is called 'human engineering' or 'human factors engineering' and the man may be described as a human factors engineer. **1969** *New Yorker* 56/2 A group of engineers called human-factors engineers has had as much to do as anybody else with making the astronauts seem like black boxes. **1964** E. J. MCCORMICK (*title*) Human factors engineering. **1919** *Alameda* (Calif.) *Times-Star* 11 Jan. 1/3 Besides being a 'Human Fly', Williams has other unusual accomplishments. **1960** *Observer* 25 Dec. 7/6 The climber..is likely to be agile and athletic, but there is generally no need for him to be what the Press calls a cat burglar or human fly. **1824** BYRON in T. Medwin *Conversations Lord Byron* 237 There was another objection: all the human interest would have been destroyed, which I have even endeavoured to give my Angels. **1860** DICKENS in *All Year Round* 28 Jan. 321/1 Figuratively speaking, I travel for the great house of Human Interest Brothers. **1912** *Collier's* 21 Sept. 21/3 Fu, not understanding the American newspaper idea of 'human interest', elected to think I had written a eulogy of him deliberately. **1913** E. C. BENTLEY *Trent's Last Case* ii. 23 'Prostrated by the shock,' hinted the reporter, '..human interest.' **1915** W. P. LIVINGSTONE *Mary Slessor* (1916) II. vii. 46 Her simple but vivid style, the human interest of her story..made so great an impression that the ladies of Glasgow besought the Committee to retain her for a time. **1930** WODEHOUSE *Very Good, Jeeves!* x. 263 Just one of those human-interest stories, if you know what I mean. **1933** LEAVIS & THOMPSON *Culture & Environment* 141 What do you understand by the phrase 'human interest', and what..is vicious in the journalistic practice it derives from? **1970** *Times* 27 Feb. 13/4 What about that boy with blood pouring from his eye, who has now become an extra in a 'human interest' story? **1920** FAIRGRIEVE & YOUNG *Brit. Isles* p. vi, This series of elementary books is just what its name denotes—human. Everywhere the human note is predominant and the relation of man to his environment insisted upon. **1882** A. GEIKIE *Text-bk. Geol.* 901 The long succession of Pleistocene ages shaded without abrupt change of any kind into what is termed the Human or Recent Period. *Ibid.* 902 The Human Period is above all distinguished by the presence and influence of man. **1916** G. B. SHAW *Overruled* 57 Spontaneous human relations.. on the one hand and the property relation..on the other. **1926** B. WEBB *My Apprenticeship* i. 52 A poisonous cynicism about human relations. **1954** D. RIESMAN *Individualism Reconsidered* IV. xiv. 222 Men who take courses [in] human relations in order..[to] get along with their colleagues in the office. **1967** M. ARGYLE *Psychol. Interpersonal Behaviour* x. 198 Experience with management training shows that lectures on 'human relations' are often very popular. *Ibid.* 199 Follow-up studies show that lectures on human relations lead to improved scores on questionnaires. **1791** T. PAINE *Rights of Man* 110 The representatives of the people of France..considering that ignorance, neglect, or contempt of human rights, are the sole causes of public misfortunes..have resolved to set forth..these natural, imprescriptible, and unalienable rights. **1877** *Independent* (N.Y.) 18 Jan. 2/2 'What does that little rat know about human rights?' Pack said. **1941** 'G. ORWELL' in *Horizon* Aug. 134 An attempted definition of fundamental human rights. **1945** *Charter of United Nations* Art. 1 par. 3, To achieve international cooperation..in promoting and encouraging respect for human rights. **1969** *New Yorker* 14 June 78/2 More middle-class blacks will become involved in human rights. **1961** J. B. WILSON *Reason & Morals* ii. 46 The tragedy of the human situation (itself a Freudian phrase). **1872** B. JERROLD *London* iii. 28 The sad human stories that crowd the emigrant vessel. **1945** E. WAUGH *Brideshead Revisited* II. ii. 233 A woman reporter..had come..to get a 'human story' of the dangers of my journey. **1959** *Times Lit. Suppl.* 27 Mar. 173/3 The 'human story' and even the characters are but adjuncts of the whirling selling machine. **1969** *Guardian* 21 Jan. 1/1 Two more 'human torch' protests... A second Czechoslovak has tried to take his life as a political protest by setting fire to himself. **1944** *Hutchinson's Pict. Hist. War* 12 Apr.–26 Sept. 21/2 A new and devastating weapon called the 'human torpedo'. It can be likened to a miniature submarine. **1953** *Jane's Fighting Ships 1953–54* 151 Damaged in Northern waters in 1944 and repaired and reconstructed as 'Kaitan' (Human Torpedo) carrier.

c. As a subdivision of a science: that branch of the science which is concerned with the study of man, as *human ecology, geography, psychology.*

1933 Human ecology [see *ECOLOGY]. **1957** [see *bio-ecology* (*BIO-)]. **1965** *New Scientist* 28 Jan. 208/3 The tag for the necessary science is 'human ecology'—the comprehensive investigation of the effects of our environment on our well-being. **1919** FAIRGRIEVE & YOUNG (*title*) Human geographies. **1936** *Discovery* Feb. 56/2 This map is a valuable contribution to human geography. **1959** *Listener* 6 Aug. 219/3 Endless information about the human geography of England at the end of the eleventh century. **1961** L. D. STAMP *Gloss. Geogr. Terms* 242/1 Human geography, the geographical study (the complement of physical geography) of those features, objects and phenomena of the Earth's surface which relate directly, or are due, to man and his activities. **1924** R. M. OGDEN tr. *Koffka's Growth of Mind* 16 To bridge the gap between human and animal-psychology.

5. b. *human-tainted.*

1929 D. H. LAWRENCE *Pansies* 73 Communion with the Godhead, they used to say in the past. But even that is human-tainted now, Tainted with the ego and the personality.

B. *sb.* (Further examples.)

1832 F. TROLLOPE *Dom. Manners Amer.* I. 70, I expect the sun will rise and set a hundred times before I shall see another human that does not belong to the family. **1898** H. S. CANFIELD *Maid of Frontier* i. 18 A man could ride from here to forty-mile the other side of Edwardsville and never see a human. **1902** O. WISTER *Virginian* iv. 56 'They are just like humans,' the Virginian concluded. **1905** A. CONAN DOYLE *Return of Sherlock*

Holmes 27 You will see it often in humans. **1909** H. G. WELLS *Ann Veronica* ii. 43 In all the species of animals the females are more important than the males; the males have to please them. Look..at the competition there is everywhere, except among humans. **1922** JOYCE *Ulysses* 501, I always understood that the act so performed by skittish humans with glimpses of lingerie appealed to you in virtue of its exhibitionististicicity. **1971** *Physics Bull.* Jan. 49/1 A third hailed him, as a great scientist and a superb human.

2. With *the*: (*a*) the human race, humanity; (*b*) that which is human, that which relates to man or humanity.

1841 E. B. BROWNING *Let.* 28 Aug. (1897) I. 88, I may say so now—as far as the human may say 'yes' or 'no' of their futurity. **1844** —— *Poems* I. 109 While the human in the minor Makes the harmony diviner. **1919** M. K. BRADBY *Psycho-Analysis* 205 The distinctively animal gives way in order to express the distinctively human.

humane, *a.* Add: **1. d.** Applied to certain weapons or implements which inflict less pain than others of their kind, *spec.* applied to an implement for the painless slaughtering of cattle.

1904 *Daily Chron.* 24 May 5/3 The doctors style the bullets 'humane'. **1920** *Act* 10 & 11 *Geo. V* c. 43 §(8) (*h*) Any..butcher..having in his possession..any humane killer for the purpose of such business. **1927** *Daily Express* 6 Aug. 7/3 That the humane killer was a dangerous instrument to those who used it. **1973** *Times* 11 Jan. 2/6 Three veterinary surgeons..had thought he must be put down. This was done..using a humane killer.

humanics. (Later examples.)

1937 R. S. MORTON *Woman Surgeon* xxxi. 351 The business side of practice is necessary, but its art and humanics are what carry us on. **1952** *King Geo. VI & Industry: a Tribute* (Industr. Welfare Soc.) p. ii, We give ungrudging honour to these pioneer students of the new science of what has been termed 'Industrial Humanics'. **1958** *Progress* Autumn 266/2 But, to British eyes, the American method looks superficial; it seems to rest on two doubtful assumptions... The second is that what Americans have called the 'humanics' of the subject can be reduced wholly to its 'mechanics'.

humanism. Add: **5.** *Philos.* A pragmatic system of thought introduced by F. C. S. Schiller and William James which emphasizes that man can only comprehend and investigate what is with the resources of the human mind, and discounts abstract theorizing; so, more generally, implying that technological advance must be guided by awareness of widely understood human needs.

1903 F. C. S. SCHILLER *Humanism* p. xvi, I propose.. to convert to the use of philosophic terminology a word which has long been famed in history and literature, and to denominate Humanism the attitude of thought which I know to be habitual in William James and in myself. **1904** W. JAMES *Coll. Ess. & Rev.* (1920) xxxii. 450 No one can ever foresee what terms will succeed in the struggle to gain currency... 'Humanism' is perhaps too 'whole-hearted' for the use of philosophers, who are a bloodless breed; but, save for that objection, one might back it, for it expresses the essence of the new way of thought, which is, that it is impossible to strip the human element out from even our most abstract theorizing. **1907** F. C. S. SCHILLER *Studies in Humanism* 12 Humanism..is merely the perception that the philosophic problem concerns human beings striving to comprehend a world of human experience by the resources of human minds. **1945** E. A. BURTT in *Humanist* V. III. 108 It may seem presumptuous, if not paradoxical, to suggest that a movement claiming the name 'humanism', and emphasizing rational comprehension as the foundation of every good achievement, might fail lamentably in its understanding of man. **1959** P. TILLICH *Theology of Culture* II. viii. 121 He [*sc.* Sartre] calls his existentialism humanism. But if he calls it humanism, that means he has an idea of what man essentially is. **1961** O. REISER in J. S. Huxley *Humanist Frame* 240 A major objective of a scientific Humanism is the organization of human knowledge for the purpose of human progress. **1966** C. H. D. CLARK *Scientist & Supernatural* v. 174 Humanism glorifies science without telling us how the laws of science arose nor how they are to save us from our innate selfishness. **1969** K. KAUNDA *Towards Complete Independence* 43 Our philosophy of Humanism stresses above all the importance of man as an individual.

humanist. Add: **5.** *Philos.* One whose beliefs are in accordance with *HUMANISM 5. Also *attrib.*

1903 F. C. S. SCHILLER *Humanism* p. xxi, A *humanist* philosopher is sure to be keenly interested in the rich variety of human thought and sentiment, and unwilling to ignore the actual facts for the sake of bolstering up the narrow abstractions of some *a priori* theory of what 'all men must' think and feel... The humanist, accordingly, will tend to grow *humane*, and tolerant of the divergences of attitude which must inevitably spring from the divergent idiosyncrasies of men. **1904** W. JAMES in *Mind* XIII. 462 Bergson in France, and his disciples the physicists Wilbois and Leroy, are thorough-going humanists in the sense defined. **1949** J. GUTMAN in P. A. Schilpp *Philos. Ernst Cassirer* II. xiii. 464 Thus as an historian and as a humanist Cassirer once again raised the standard of self-knowledge, [and] reaffirmed the doctrine that the unexamined life is no life for man. **1961** L. ELVIN in J. S. Huxley *Humanist Frame* 272 The Humanist is content to leave it to the free play of thought, so long as thought *is* kept free. **1963** J. S. HUXLEY *Human Crisis* 19 Today, the new humanist vision is giving us the key idea of man as the agent for the whole future of evolution on this planet. **1966** C. H. D. CLARK *Scientist & Supernatural* v. 175 The humanist trust in reason alone is actually unreasonable, since logic would suggest that affluence and scientific advancement ought to be accompanied by increasing mental satisfaction. **1968** A. J. AYER *Humanist Outlook* 4 Present-day humanists are in fact the intellectual heirs of those nineteenth-century freethinkers.

humanistic, *a.* (*sb.*). Add: **A. 2.** Pertaining to or characteristic of humanism. (Cf. *HUMANISM 5.)

1904 W. JAMES *Coll. Ess. & Rev.* (1920) xxxii. 451 But humanistic empiricism will have many other steps forward to make before it conquers all antagonisms. **1923** B. RUSSELL *Prospects Industr. Civilization* II. xiii. 266 The distinction between the mechanistic and the humanistic conceptions of excellence is the most fundamental of all distinctions between rival sets of ideals. *Ibid.*, The humanistic conception..regards the good as something existing in the lives of individuals, and conceives social co-operation as only valuable in so far as it ministers to the welfare of the several citizens. **1932** C. K. OGDEN *Jeremy Bentham* 9 It was to French influences, to Fénélon, to Helvétius and to Voltaire,..that Bentham owed his first humanistic stimulus. **1961** B. WOOTTON in J. S. Huxley *Humanist Frame* 350 Plainly, what is actually happening in the world is the result of the accommodation of religions to evolving humanistic ideas and not *vice versa*. **1968** H. J. EYSENCK in A. J. Ayer *Humanist Outlook* 271 The future of humanistic thought on this subject is completely bound up with the growth of psychological knowledge—without this it must remain nothing more than an alternative superstition.

B. *sb.* Delete †*Obs.* and add later example.

1952 KOESTLER *Arrow in Blue* xxvi. 240, I would shift the emphasis in popular education from stale humanistics to a lively comprehension of the mysteries of the universe and life.

humanistically, *adv.* Add: Also in relation to *HUMANISM 5.

1904 W. JAMES *Coll. Ess. & Rev.* (1920) xxxii. 451 'Radium', for example; humanistically, both the *that* and the *what* of it are creations of yesterday. But we believe that ultra-humanistically they existed ages before their gifted discoverers were born. In what shape? There's the rub! for we have no non-humanistic categories to think in. **1909** —— *Meaning of Truth* iii. 79 The reader would conceive the knowing humanistically. **1944** *Scrutiny* XII. 111. 210 The brilliant vitality of the keyboard writing.. itself tends to render this passion more directly and humanistically dramatic than the more religious (if no less intense) keyboard style of Gibbons.

‖**humanitas** (hiumæ·nitas). [L.] = HUMANITY.

1944 *Atlantic Monthly* Nov. 73 Philosophers of the ancient world would consider these to be strange limitations..upon the spiritual jurisdiction of a school which concerns itself with *humanitas*. **1948** E. POUND *Pisan Cantos* lxxxiv. 117 Yin had these three men full of humanitas (manhood). **1964** *Economist* 4 Jan. 37/3 The fundamental *humanitas* of the author. **1964** L. HJELMSLEV in R. H. Robins *Gen. Ling.* i. 10 Linguistic theory is led by an inner necessity to recognize..man and human society behind language... At that point linguistic theory has reached its prescribed goal: *humanitas et universitas*. **1970** *Times Lit. Suppl.* 23 Apr. 442/4 The concern for a conception of society, life and *humanitas* that doesn't eliminate the depth in time.

humanization. Add: **c.** The treatment of cow's milk to render it suitable for consumption by infants.

1905 F. L. DODD *Municipal Milk* 14 The humanization adapts the milk to infants' digestive processes. **1932** V. E. M. BENNETT *Welfare Infant & Child* v. 70 When cows' milk is to be used for feeding the infant two modifications are always requisite... These two processes are known respectively as Humanization and Pasteurization.

humanize, *v.* Add: **5.** To treat (cow's milk) in order to make it more closely resemble human milk and suitable for consumption by infants.

1897 *Amer. Jrnl. Med. Sci.* CXIII. 374 Dufour.. describes a rather simple method of humanizing cow's milk. **1970** *Pharmaceutical Handbk.* (Pharm. Soc. Gt. Brit.) 379 In 'humanising' cow's milk, extra cane sugar or glucose is added because human milk contains more lactose than cow's milk.

humanized, *ppl. a.* Add: **3.** Of milk (see *HUMANIZE *v.* 5).

1888 *Baby* Dec. 15/1 This humanised cow's milk is the only natural food for artificially feeding infants, and the weakest of them thrive on it as on breast milk. **1901** *Westm. Gaz.* 19 Oct. 5/3 The Borough Council of Battersea has determined to undertake the supply of sterilised and humanised milk. **1947** A. B. MEERING *Handbk. Nursery Nurses* xxii. 202 Humanised dried milk is fresh cows' milk, dried, and the content rendered as near as possible to human milk. **1955** WOHL & GOODHART *Mod. Nutrition* xxxiv. 919 'Humanized milks'..imitate to a greater or lesser extent the caloric proportions, the mineral content or the fat of breast milk. *Ibid.*, The need for the humanized products is..questionable.

humanoid (hiū·mănoid), *a.* and *sb.* [f. HUMAN *a.* (*sb.*) + -OID.] **A.** *adj.* Of human form or character; man-like; *spec.* (*a*) distinguished from anthropoid as being more human in character (cf. *HOMINOID *a.* and *sb.*); (*b*) as a term in Science Fiction.

1918 MRS. D. G. RITCHIE *New Warden* xvi. 186 Religion ..had its origin in the funk and cunning of the humanoid ape. **1922** *Glasgow Herald* 23 Dec. 4 Then came the separating off of the larger Anthropoid Apes, leaving the main stem humanoid. **1936** C. J. WARDEN *Emergence Human Culture* iii. 87 The humanoid stock must become specialized along human lines or forever perish from the earth. **1952** V. NABOKOV *Nabokov's Dozen* (1959) 207 Inhabitants of foreign planets, 'intelligent' beings, humanoid or of various mythic makes. **1965** *Punch* 7 Apr. 525/3 Ruined machinery..leads our heroes to a planet revolving around Altair, where they meet a humanoid race. **1966** L. COHEN *Beautiful Losers* (1970) I. 96 It was just a shape of Edith: then it was just a humanoid shape: then it was just a shape.

B. *sb.* A humanoid animal or being.

1925 J. A. THOMSON *Concerning Evolution* iii. 210 The humanoids and the anthropoids parting company between a million and two million years ago. **1936** C. J. WARDEN *Emergence Human Culture* iii. 87 The humanoids that managed to survive from age to age became less ape-like and more man-like as time went on. **1958** *Manch. Guardian* 26 Sept. 4/3 The humanoids who are accidentally brought to earth by these means inevitably turn out to be superior to us. **1965** *Listener* 14 Jan. 56/2 The culmination is reached when peaceful humanoids are ruled by vicious insects or lizards.

humantin (hiumæ·ntin). *Zool.* [a. Fr. *humantin* (G. Rondelet *Histoire des Poissons* (1558) XIII. viii. 301), of uncertain origin.] A spiny shark, *Oxynotus centrina*, of the family Oxynotidæ, found in the Mediterranean Sea and off the coast of Portugal.

Gamillscheg's suggestion that it is perhaps f. Fr. *humer* 'to inhale' arbitrarily modelled on Fr. *lamantin* LAMANTIN is chronologically inconclusive. The word is also sometimes identified with L. *humus* 'humus, soil', from the habit that the humantin has of lying in the mud on the sea-bed, but the connection remains uncertain.

[**1862** T. GILL in *Ann. Lyceum Nat. Hist. N.Y.* VII. 376 Cuvier, in his Regne Animal, proposed the following division..Les Humantins (Centrina Cuv.). **1880–84** F. DAY *Fishes Gt. Brit. & Ireland* II. 319 *Centrina salviani*...Name.—La Humantin, French. Habits.—Is supposed to inhabit great depths.] **1925** J. T. JENKINS *Fishes Brit. Isles* 320 *The Humantin* (*Centrina salviani*). In this shark each dorsal fin has a strong spine. **1959** A. HARDY *Fish & Fisheries* ix. 181 The humantin, *Oxynotus centrina*, an even rarer straggler to our waters from the coasts of Portugal, is noteworthy for its peculiar spines situated within its large dorsal fins.

hum-bird. (Later U.S. examples.)

1834 C. A. DAVIS *Lett. Jack Downing* 6 They both came within a humbird's eye of it. **1872** SCHELE DE VERE *Americanisms* 377 The tiny *Mango* Hummingbird (*Trochilus colubris*)..is known familiarly..as *Humbird* or *Hummer* simply. **1891** R. T. COOKE *Huckleberries* (1896) 167, I never see a humbird fuller o' buzz than little Prudy.

humble, *a.*[1] Add: **1. c.** *your humble*: used ellipt. for 'your humble servant'.

1765 [in Dict.]. **1835** DICKENS *Let.* 2 May (1965) I. 58 The next stage, your humble, caught them before they had changed. **1926** D. H. LAWRENCE *Let.* 4 Jan. (1962) II. 875 As for your humble, he says his say in bits. **1929** KIPLING *Limits & Renewals* (1932) 359 'And where *does* he get his champagne?' 'From grateful appendices—same as your bloody 'umble,' said Scree.

3. *humble-hearted, -minded* (earlier and later examples).

1961 NEW ENG. BIBLE *Matt.* xi. 29 Bend your necks to my yoke, and learn from me, for I am gentle and humble-hearted. **1580** T. POUNDE in H. Foley *Jesuits in Conflict* (1873) 109 That might soe be amonge the humble-minded. **1905** W. JAMES *Mem. & Stud.* (1911) v. 77 It must be confessed that T. D. never was exactly humble-minded. **1961** NEW ENG. BIBLE *1 Pet.* iii. 8 Be full of brotherly affection, kindly and humble-minded.

humble-jumble. Delete †*Obs.* and add later example. Also **hu·mble-ju·mbled** *ppl. a.*

1929 H. S. WALPOLE *Hans Frost* I. ix. 98 The ironic disappointment of fixing pretty sentences together, all, humble-jumble, on the table of his mind. **1940** *Horizon* Jan. 61 It is the Big Bed of Ware combined with the Procrustean bed, in which, humble-jumbled or stretched or curtailed to fit, they all lie most curiously together.

Humboldtian (humbō^u·ltiăn), *a.* [f. name of K. Wilhelm von *Humboldt*, German philologist (1767–1835) + -IAN.] Of, pertaining to, or characteristic of Humboldt or his work.

1901 H. OERTEL *Lect. Study of Lang.* i. 45 Entirely Humboldtian in conception is James Byrne's General Principles of the Structure of Language (1885). **1907** E. SAPIR in *Mod. Philology* V. i. 141 Steinthal, himself an enthusiastic follower and developer of Humboldtian views, most emphatically denies any indebtedness on Humboldt's part to Herder. **1964** R. H. ROBINS *Gen. Ling.* viii. 335 Within typological comparison, the Humboldtian tripartite division, properly understood, may be said to be a more significant system of classification than some others. **1965** N. CHOMSKY *Aspects of Theory of Syntax* 199 It seems to me that 'deep structure' and 'surface structure', in the sense in which these terms will be used here, do correspond quite closely to Humboldtian 'inner form' and 'outer form'. **1967** R. L.

Brown tr. *W. von Humboldt's Conception Ling. Relativity* 15 Boas also came under Humboldtian influence in another way.

humbug, *sb.* **5.** Delete *dial.* and add later examples.

1936 J. L. Hodson *Our Two Englands* vii. 115 A middle-aged member of the [Bradford Wool] Exchange moved about offering a paper bag of sweets; cheeks became swollen with humbugs. **1959** I. & P. Opie *Lore & Lang. Schoolch.* ix. 166 'Lollies' is also becoming a general term, and so is 'gob-stoppers' for 'any sweet difficult to chew', as humbugs, large aniseed balls, and fruit drops.

humbug, *v.* Add: **2.** Const. *about.* To make less progress than expected, to flounder *about,* to wallow. *local U.S.*

1840 R. H. Dana *Two Yrs. before Mast* xxxiv. 433 For several days we lay 'humbugging about' in the Horse latitudes, with all sorts of wind and weather. **1879** [in Dict.]. **1908** G. S. Wasson *Home from Sea* vi. 189 We pitch-poled and humbugged about in them latitudes till the Cap'n..was sick and tired of the whole business. **1933** P. A. Eaddy *Hull Down* x. 214 For several days we were kept humbugging about with light variable breezes.

humdinger (hʌ:mdi·ŋəɹ). [Origin unknown.] **1.** *slang* (orig. *U.S.*). A remarkable or outstanding person or thing, anything of notable excellence.

1905 *Dialect Notes* III. 62 *Hum-dinger,* term of admiration. 'She's a humdinger.' **1916** 'B. M. Bower' *Phantom Herd* vi. 100 That pit'cher's a humdinger! **1926** *Brit. Weekly* 12 Aug. 399/1 They showed me a new game. I tell you Red, it's a humdinger. *Ibid.* 2 Sept. 456/3 She was a humdinger. She even puts a brand on Brangwyn, and she's no slouch. **1935** *Punch* 10 Apr. 399/2 Say, she knew her own mind, did that jane. A regular humdinger of a dame. **1937** N. Marsh *Vintage Murder* vii. 72, I reckon he's all right. Gosh, I reckon he's a humdinger. **1943** Hunt & Pringle *Service Slang* 40 *A humdinger,* any fast aircraft or vehicle; any engine which runs really well. **1958** *Times* 16 June 4/4 The last set was a humdinger, to use a transatlantic expression.

2. *Electronics.* A voltage divider connected across the heater circuit of a valve with the variable tap connected to a source of fixed potential, so that the hum introduced by the heater can be reduced by suitably biasing it with respect to the cathode.

1938 *Admiralty Handbk. Wireless Telegr.* II. Index, Humdinger. **1947** *Electronic Engin.* XIX. 82/3 It is.. suggested that the centre point on the 'humdinger' be returned to a suitable tapping on the cathode bias battery. **1967** P. Spring *Tape Recorders* vii. 90 It is customary to have a centre-tapped heater winding, or better still, a humdinger. This is adjusted until the hum level is at a minimum.

Humean, Humian, *a.* Add: Also as *sb.*

1890 W. James *Princ. Psychol.* I. x. 330 And if, with the Humians, one deny such a principle and say that the stream of passing thoughts is all, one runs against the entire common-sense of mankind. **1960** *Guardian* 2 Mar. 7/2 Most unbelievers in our society are Humeans; and one can be a Humean in this sense without ever having heard of Hume.

humect, *v.* **1.** (Later example.)

1923 E. Pound *Let.* 16 Jan. (1971) 184 Jock Hieland-man..ran Unto the river Liffey, Peeled off his breeches and jumped in, Humecting thus his hairy skin.

humectant, *a.* and *sb.* Restrict ? *Obs.* to senses in Dict., for **a, b** read **A, B,** and add: **A.** *adj.* **2.** Moisture-retaining.

1953 *Manuf. Chemist* May 202/2 The humectant action is provided by a combination of glycerin and propylene glycol. **1960** *McGraw-Hill Encycl. Sci. & Technol.* VI. 221/1 Because of its humectant properties, it is sprayed on tobacco before it is processed to prevent crumbling.

B. *sb.* **2.** A substance used to reduce the loss of moisture; *spec.* a food additive that does this.

Quot. 1854–67 in Dict. belongs here.

1951 M. B. Jacobs *Chem. & Technol. Food & Food Products* (ed. 2) III. xxxvii. 1979 Substances which retain moisture are known as humectants. They..prevent loss of moisture when incorporated into the foodstuff. **1954** *Chem. & Engin. News* 15 Feb. 685/2 The product can be used as..a humectant for cellulose and paper products, polishes, and tobacco. **1963** *Residue Rev.* II. 54 Some humectants have been used experimentally to reduce evaporation under conditions of low humidity... Rain can, of course, wash the chemical from the leaf surface. **1972** *Sci. Amer.* Mar. 19/3 Humectants, which are hygroscopic, offset changes in the humidity of the environment to which food is exposed.

humgruffin. Add: Also **humgruffian.**

1825 J. K. Paulding *John Bull in Amer.* iv. 29 Another declared she would not give a pin to save such a rude humgruffian from starvation.

humhum. *Hist.* Also 7 hammome, hummum, 8 hump-hump. [Origin obscure.] A coarse Indian cotton cloth.

1620 in W. Foster *Eng. Factories India 1618–21* (1906) 193 Of sahannes and hammomes thiere are but fewe at presant in towne. **1687** *London Gaz.* No. 2269/2, 4172 pieces of Hummums. **1695** J. F. *Merch. Wareho. laid Open* 22, I shall begin with a Callico called Hummums. **1745** in J. F. Watson *Ann. Philad.* (1830) 179 Quilted humhums, turkettees, grassetts, [etc.]. **1801** in C. Cist *Cincinnati in 1841* (1841) 179 Among other goods..hum-hums. **1809** P. Freneau *Poems* I. 31 Hum-hums are here—and muslins—what you please. **1820** *Massachusetts Spy* 5 Jan. (Th.), The bleach rotted linen..or the sleazy humhum. **1894** A. M. Earle *Costume Colonial Times* 142 *Hum-hum,* a plain coarse-meshed Indian fabric made of cotton, much advertised in the middle of the [18th] century. We read of 'blue Hum-hums' and 'Hump-humps for Sacks' for sale in various Boston newspapers, from 1750 to 1770. **1952** *Brewer's Dict. Phr. & Fable* (rev. ed.) 477/1 *Humhum* (U.S.A.), a thin cambric material.

humic, *a.* Delete *Chem.* and add to def.: present in or of the nature of humus; rich in humus; also, formed or derived from plant remains. (Further examples.)

1891 *Chem. News* 22 May 248/2 The part played by humic matters in the fixation of nitrogen. **1918** Stopes & Wheeler *Monogr. Constit. Coal* 19/2 Potonié's separation of coals into two main groups, sapropelic and humic, is now widely adopted... But the use of the phrase 'humic coals' is much in want of elucidation, as it, too, is given different meanings by different authors. As used by Potonié and most palæontologists, it means that the coal was formed from 'humic débris', or the various largely undecayed accumulations of mixed organs of plants... When the word 'humic' is applied to coals by chemists.. it may convey the implication that 'humic acid' exists in the substance of the coal. **1936** S. A. Waksman *Humus* iii. 62 One may..feel justified in abandoning without reservation the whole nomenclature of 'humic acids'. **1954** W. Francis *Coal* v. 245 Humic substances are the major constituents of all normal coals. **1957** G. E. Hutchinson *Treat. Limnol.* I. ix. 609 The peaty sediments (*dy*) of brown humic lakes. **1960** N. Polunin *Introd. Plant Geogr.* xv. 497 Humic matter in solution may result in a browning of waters coming in from leached soils. **1966** B. Simpson *Rocks & Minerals* xx. 234 The first group is the Humic Coals in which woody tissue is of paramount importance in the composition... The second group, the Sapropelic Coals, have little woody tissue in their composition. **1971** *Nature* 19 Nov. 150/2 They are usually found in moist, humic soil, often near water.

humidification (hiumi:difikē̍ⁱ·ʃən). [f. Humidify *v.*: see -fication.] The process of making moist or humid; *esp.* the process of rendering the air humid by means of special apparatus or techniques.

1890 J. Nasmith *Mod. Cotton Spinning Machinery* 10 The [spinning] rooms..should be heated to a certain temperature. Closely allied to this question is that of humidification. It is not only essential to have heat, but that must be accompanied by..moisture. **1940** A. C. Noé tr. *Stutzer's Geol. Coal* viii. 307 A peculiar case of weathering and humidification of coal is found in karst districts, producing a sooty material... The sootiness is caused by the access of karst water. **1945** *Times* 31 Aug. 2/3 Air-conditioning with humidification and cleaning by electrical filtration. **1970** D. Kut *Warm Air Heating* viii. 124 Humidification of the air prevents the build-up of static electricity.

humidify, *v.* Add: So **humi·dified** *ppl. a.*

1921 C. V. Ekroth in A. Rogers *Industr. Chem.* (ed. 3) li. 1164 Humidified air keeps the exposed surfaces of the food soft and permeable. **1956** H. Williamson *Methods Bk. Design* xxii. 358 Specially humidified paper will have to be wrapped in waterproof material. **1971** *Nature* 24 Dec. 471/2 They..are maintained at 36° C in a humidified atmosphere of 5% CO_2 in air.

humidistat (hiū̆mi·distæt). Also **humidostat.** [f. Humidi(ty (or Humid *a.* + -o) + -stat.] **1.** (See quot.) *rare.* ? *Obs.*

1909 *Cent. Dict.* Suppl., *Humidostat,* a small chest or cabinet lined with sheet-metal and fitted with some device for holding a damp sponge or piece of felt: used to keep cigars moist.

2. An automatic apparatus for regulating the humidity of the air in a room or building; also called a *hygrostat.*

1918 Allen & Walker *Heating & Ventilation* xvi. 248 In a compressed-air system of control, a diaphragm valve ..may be operated by means of a 'hygrostat' or 'humidostat', which corresponds to the thermostat of a temperature control system. **1936** *Archit. Rev.* LXXX. p. lxviii/1 The control consists of a thermostat, a humidistat and a change-over rotary switch which together control the supply of hot or cold humidified or dehumidified air as required. **1970** I. G. Walls *Greenhouse Gardening* viii. 55 Humidistats can be used..to put into operation mist nozzles in an air stream.

humidor (hiū̆·midǭɹ). [f. Humid *a.*, after *cuspidor.*] A box, cabinet, or room in which cigars or tobacco are kept moist; also, any apparatus, such as damp sponges, for keeping cigars, the atmosphere, etc., moist.

1903 *Sun* (N.Y.) 4 Mar. 6/3 (Funk), A humidor as large as a small cottage occupies most of the ground floor. **1922** *Detective Mag.* Nov. 100 The cigar was soft and fresh from the humidor. **1927** P. Marks *Lord of Himself* 198 Take a cigarette out of that humidor. **1955** Sturdevant & Brauer in J. C. Brauer *Dental Asst.* xx. 287 The impression should be stored in a humidor in order to minimize dimensional change. **1963** *Punch* 8 May 669/1 Champagne coolers and waste-paper baskets, to say nothing of door-stops and humidors. **1973** R. Hayes *Hungarian Game* viii. 61, I fumbled with the F.O.'s humidor for a Havanna.

humify (hiū̆·mifəi), *v.*[2] [f. Hum(us + -ify.] **a.** *trans.* To convert (plant remains) into humus. **b.** *intr.* To undergo humification. So **hu·mified** *ppl. a.*

1906 E. W. Hilgard *Soils* (1930) viii. 132 Excluding the unhumified while fully dissolving the humified matter. *Ibid.* viii. 139 Snyder..caused various substances to humify by mixing the pulverized material intimately with a soil poor in humus. **1926** *Technol. Rep. Tôhoku Imp. Univ.* VI. i. 10 As humification advances more and more, the cell walls are quite humified. **1936** S. A. Waksman *Humus* iv. 64 Plant material added to the soil has first to be 'humified' before the nutrient elements contained therein become available for plant growth. **1948** G. W. Leeper *Introd. Soil Sci.* xi. 136 Residues of plants are said to be humified when they lose their structure and identity in the soil.

So **humifica·tion**[2], the process by which plant remains are converted into humus; the state of being humified that results.

1897 *Minnesota Agric. Exper. Station Bull.* No. 53. 13 Analyses were made of both the soil, and the material used for humus production. After the humification process had been carried on for a year the material was weighed and analyzed. **1926** [see above]. **1958** F. E. Zeuner *Dating Past* (ed. 4) iii. 64 A change in the rate of peat-growth from a slow one (allowing humification to begin in the layers near the surface), [etc.]. **1968** R. G. West *Pleistocene Geol. & Biol.* iv. 54 The amount of humification may be measured in the field by adding a little sediment to a few ml of dilute KOH.

humilific (hiū̆mili·fik), *a.* (*sb.*). Now *rare* or ? *Obs.* [f. L. *humilis* Humble + -fic.] Humiliating, self-depreciating, that humiliates or tends to humble; also as *sb.*, a humble expression. (Opp. to *honorific.*)

1892 *Spectator* 13 Feb. 244/1 Among the Chinese and Japanese..merely honorific and humilific expressions. **1904** V. V. Banford in J. E. Hand *Ideals of Sci. & Faith* 120 The distinction between honorific and humilific occupations. **1905** D. Sladen *Playing Game* i. vii, That conversation.., so full of the 'unfortunate mistake' vein, so burdened down with Japanese 'humilifics'.

hummable (hʌ·măb'l), *a.* [f. Hum *v.*[1] + -able.] That may be hummed; apt for humming.

1941 *Time* 10 Nov. 54 Cole Porter's score, though never haunting, is often hummable. **1966** *New Statesman* 8 Apr. 512/2 Georges Delerue's music is a hummable element. **1970** *Daily Tel.* 19 Nov. 14/5 The soloist starts off with a most poetical and, what's more, hummable eleven note row. **1972** *Guardian* 11 Jan. 8/6 The hummable simplicity of Rome's melodies.

hummaul, hummaum: see Hammal, Hammam.

hummel, *a.* Add: **1. b.** Applied to a hornless stag. Also *absol.*

1907 *Spectator* 5 Jan. 11/1 The 'hummel' stag—that ungainly beast with no horns at all—is a better fighter than the 'switch-horn'. *Ibid.* 11/2 The supremacy of the 'hummels' and 'switch-horns' in battles with their own kind. **1925** J. Buchan *John Macnab* iv, A hummel, a great fellow of fully twenty stone. **1964** G. K. Whitehead *Deer Gt. Brit. & Ireland* vii. 156 Some stags never grow any antlers at all and are known as hummels. These beasts would appear to be just as capable of breeding as their antlered brethren. **1972** *Country Life* 17 Feb. 424/3 The hummel or antlerless stag is not welcome on the purely sporting estate.

hummer, *sb.*[1] Add: **3. b.** A person or thing of extraordinary excellence. *colloq.*

1907 C. E. Mulford *Bar-20* (1914) xxiv. 229 She's a hummer—stands two hands under him, and is a whole lot prettier than that picture Cowan has got over his bar. **1919** Wodehouse *Damsel in Distress* (1920) xx. 235 Well, you can't get there quicker than in my car. She's a hummer. **1920** C. E. Mulford *Johnny Nelson* (1921) xvii. 186, I claim I was justified—an' I'll leave it to you if th' joke on Wolf wasn't a hummer? **1934** N. Scanlan *Winds of Heaven* xvi. 150 When the new car was swung out on to the wharf, Mike walked round it and touched it lovingly. 'She's a hummer, Dad.' **1945** Baker *Austral. Lang.* ii. xvi. 286 A *wow* or *hummer* [to an American] is a *bonzer* or *big twist* [to an Australian].

4. b. *slang.* False or mistaken arrest (see quot. 1963).

1932 *Evening Sun* (Baltimore) 9 Dec. 31/4 *Hummer,* false arrest. **1961** Rigney & Smith *Real Bohemia* p. xv, *Hummer,* an arrest which accidentally leads to a more serious charge. **1963** Mencken *Amer. Lang.* xi. 730 *Hummer,* any kind of charge placed against a suspect so that he can be held although there is insufficient evidence to hold him on the charge for which he is really wanted.

hummer, *sb.*[2] Add: **2.** A scrounger. *Austral. colloq.*

1919 W. H. Downing *Digger Dial.* 29 *Hummer,* a cadger. **1945** Baker *Austral. Lang.* ii. v. 108 *Hummer, poler* and *bot-fly* are additional synonyms for a cadger.

humming, *ppl. a.* **1. c.** *humming-top* (earlier examples).

1819 Keats *Let.* 27 Sept. (1958) II. 216, I shall..make his little Boy a present of a humming top. **1837** *London Med. Gaz.* 1 Apr. 8/1 He compares it to the sound of a humming-top, or some such toy, called a '*diable*' in French.

hummingly (hʊ·miŋli), *adv.* [See -LY².] With a humming sound.

1908 *Daily Chron.* 21 Jan. 6/5 He..endeavours to follow the service and join hummingly in the hymns. **1923** *Daily Mail* 6 Aug. 6 However warm the sun and hummingly populous the air, they [*sc.* the swifts] will go.

hummus (hu·mŭs). Also hoummos. [ad. Turk. *humus* mashed chick-peas.] In Middle Eastern countries (and also, more recently, elsewhere) an hors d'œuvre made from ground chick-peas and sesame oil flavoured with lemon and garlic.

1955 E. DAVID *Bk. Mediterranean Food* 158 Hummus... Cook the chick peas..pound them, [etc.]. **1967** *Guardian* 8 Dec. 6/4 Order the paste of ground chick peas, oil, and lemon which is called hummus. **1969** M. J. PHILIPPOU *101 Arabian Delights* 48 Hoummos ib bandora. Chick peas in tomato sauce... Hoummos ib Taheeneh. Chick peas in Taheeneh. **1970** SIMON & HOWE *Dict. Gastron.* 223/1 *Hummus bi Tahina*, a widely known, traditional..Arab dish of cooked, puréed chick peas... It is served as a *mezze* or appetizer in Arab countries. **1973** *Nation Rev.* (Melbourne) III. 31 Aug. 1460/4 Passing up the usual *hummus* as a starter.

humoral, *a.* **1. a.** (Further examples.) Also in mod. use, contained in or involving the blood or other body fluid; involving or consisting of a chemical agent, esp. one present in the blood (such as hormones or ions).

humoral theory: (*a*) the theory that immunity is due to the presence of bactericidal substances in the blood (rather than the action of whole cells); (*b*) the theory that the transmission of nerve impulses at a synapse or a neuromuscular junction involves a chemical (rather than an electrical) agent. (See also sense 1 c in Dict.)

1898 W. S. L. BARLOW *Man. Gen. Path.* ix. 408 It was obvious..that a purely humoral theory..is insufficient, that natural immunity cannot be explained by the presence of 'alexins' in the blood. **1924** E. D. ADRIAN in *Brain* XLVII. 400 The 'inhibiting substance' theory (and the 'humoral' theory of Loewi and others) derives all its evidence from the peripheral inhibition of cardiac or plain muscle. **1935** O. LOEWI in *Proc. R. Soc.* B. CXVIII. 302 Some important investigations..suggest the possibility that the stimulation also of spinal nerves is transmitted by humoral means, namely, by liberation of acetylcholine. **1950** G. P. WRIGHT *Introd. Path.* vii. 113 The early history of immunology contains many vigorous controversies which arose from the sharp division of opinion between the so-called 'cellular' and 'humoral' schools. **1952** W. E. LE GROS CLARK *Tissues of Body* (ed. 3) xiii. 356 The conception of chemical (or humoral) transmitters [of nerve impulses] suggests an alternative explanation. **1968** PASSMORE & ROBSON *Compan. Med. Studies* I. xxvii. 2/1 The immune response can be purely humoral, mediated by circulating antibodies, or cellular, mediated by small lymphocytes, but often mixtures of both mechanisms are found. **1971** A. C. GUYTON *Textbk. Med. Physiol.* (ed. 4) xxv. 284/2 Superimposed onto the intrinsic regulations of the circulation..are two additional types of regulation: (1) nervous and (2) humoral. **1971** *Nature* 26 Feb. 593/1 Human breast cancer..may well be initiated by a virus but promoted by humoral factors, in particular sex hormones.

humorism. Add: **2. b.** A humorous saying or remark.

1897 'MARK TWAIN' *Notebook* (1935) 335 In a dream I have at last encountered a humorism that actually remained one after waking. **1902** *Sat. Rev.* 15 Nov. 620/1 The most sparkling witticisms and the most obvious humourisms have fallen flat. **1907** *Daily Chron.* 26 June 7/5 His eloquent remarks were snatched up by the people he met and mistaken for brilliant humorisms. **1920** D. H. LAWRENCE *Women in Love* (1921) ii. 34 Gerald smiled grimly at this humorism.

humorize, *v.* Add: **3.** *trans.* To make humorous.

1893 W. B. YEATS *Celtic Twilight* 195 Our tales..hopelessly humorize the creatures [*sc.* water-goblins and water-monsters].

humous (hiū·məs), *a.* [f. HUM(US + -OUS.] Present in or of the nature of humus; rich in humus. Cf. *HUMIC *a.*

1866 H. WATTS tr. *Gmelin's Hand-bk. Chem.* XVII. 473 Hermann..distinguishes eleven different humous substances. **1902** *Jrnl. Chem. Soc.* LXXXII. II. 521 Oats and soy beans..were grown in humous soil. **1909** GROOM & BALFOUR tr. *Warming's Oecol. Plants* xlvi. 195 The weightiest cause of the physiological dryness of the soil probably lies in the presence of free humous acids. **1968** R. G. WEST *Pleistocene Geol. & Biol.* iv. 55 Humous substances.

hump, *sb.* Add: **1. c.** Also, the flesh of the hump of other animals.

1805 M. LEWIS *Jrnl.* 13 June in *Orig. Jrnls. Lewis & Clark Expedition* (1904) II. 151 My fare is really sumptuous this evening; buffaloe's humps, tongues and marrowbones. **1823** J. FRANKLIN *Narr. Journey Shores Polar Sea* 115 The meat [of the buffalo] which covers the spinal processes themselves, after the wig is removed, is next in esteem for its flavour and juiciness, and is more extensively termed the hump by the hunters. **1861** C. J. ANDERSSON *Okavango River* 130 Rhinoceros hump was..a frequent and favourite dish of mine. **1863** Rhinoceros hump [see RHINOCEROS 3]. **1909** *Daily Chron.* 5 Jan. 4/7 'Humps have arrived.' So runs the legend in an old-established shop in Green-street, Leicester-square. *Ibid.*, A beef hump. **1913** C. PETTMAN *Africanderisms*, *Hump*... A favourite piece with South African housewives for salting.

d. *to live on one's hump*: to be self-sufficient, to operate from resources accumulated earlier: with reference to the camel's hump as a reserve of nourishment.

1909 *Westm. Gaz.* 11 Sept. 7/2 During nearly three weeks in this glorious place I have lived on my own hump.

2. b. A mound in a railway yard up which vehicles are pushed by an engine and down the other side of which they run by gravity and are switched to the proper track.

1901 *Railroad Gaz.* 4 Jan. 2/1 All that was necessary to take advantage of this mode of distributing cars, was to put a 'hump' in the switching track. **1911** *Encycl. Brit.* XXII. 842/1 Another method [of shunting], which was introduced into America from Europe about 1890, is that of the summit or 'hump'. **1921** *Daily Mail Yr. Bk.* 112/1 The London and South-Western Company has constructed at Feltham a new 'hump' marshalling yard. **1955** *Times* 12 July 3/4 They had approved new works at Perth, including the construction of a fully mechanized hump marshalling yard. **1958** *Times* 11 Feb. 15/3 We have carried out development on equipment..for assisting the automatic operation of hump sorting yards. **1971** D. J. SMITH *Discovering Railwayana* x. 56 *Hump yard*, goods yards or sidings worked by gravity shunting methods.

c. A mountain barrier high enough to make both land and air travel difficult. Chiefly *U.S.*

1914 *Sat. Even. Post* 4 Apr. 10/2 There ain't a kid like him this side of the Hump [*sc.* mountain range in west of N. America]—nor t'other side either. **1931** 'D. STIFF' *Milk & Honey Route* 208 'Over the hump' means to cross the mountains to the West Coast. **1936** K. MACKENZIE *Living Rough* xv. 216 We're sure a pair of nuts riding the outside over the hump this time of the year. **1944** *Time* 26 June 52/1 They're flying it over 'The Hump'—the towering Himalayas between India and China. **1970** 'B. MATHER' *Break in Line* v. 64 'I think he'll be making for Rangoon, then over the bloody hills to China.'..'You really expect me to walk over the Hump?'

d. *transf.* and *fig.* The critical point (in an undertaking, ordeal, the ascent of a seaplane, etc.), esp. in the phr. *over the hump*, over the worst, well begun. (Cf. *2 c.) Also, the high point, peak (of a graph, etc.).

1914 JACKSON & HELLYER *Vocab. Criminal Slang* 46 *Hump*,..the half-way point in a prison sentence. Example: 'How long have you got yet on your bit? I'm just over the hump.' **1914** *Techn. Rep. Advisory Comm. Aeronaut. 1912–13* 244 The floats of the flaring bow type require only about half the E.H.P. to surmount the hump. **1922** W. R. INGE *Lay Thoughts* (1926) II. i. 89 If we look at a chart of the births and deaths in Germany..each war is marked by a peak in the line showing the death rate and a ravine in the line showing the birth rate. But the ravine is followed by a hump..making good the numbers lost. **1929** D. HAMMETT *Dain Curse* (1930) xxii. 253 Today won't be like yesterday. You're over the hump, and the rest of it's downhill going. **1935** P. W. F. MILLS *Elem. Pract. Flying* v. 71 In rising from the normal semi-submerged state there is a critical point known as passing the hump, before the reaching of which point the floats are definitely water-bound. After passing the hump the floats very nearly emerge from the water and commence to hydroplane. The time taken to reach the 'hump' and the ease with which it is passed, vary greatly. **1938** *Amer. Speech* XIII. 188/2 Once a cocaine addict is *over the hump* he says he is *coasting* or *in high*. **1952** *Economist* 27 Sept. 771/1 The machine tool industry is probably 'over the hump' of its..task. **1959** *Listener* 19 Feb. 316/2 Things were very difficult with us that year, and the Americans helped *us* over the hump. **1960** *Economist* 8 Oct. 135/1 The 'hump' in imports that was desired has turned into a steady climb. **1965** *Listener* 16 Dec. 985/1 East German farming is getting over the hump.

3. Phr. *to give* (a person) *the hump* (examples).

1887 F. GALE *Game of Cricket* viii. 187 So let's alter the law, Without any more jaw, Or you'll give an old buffer the hump. **1910** E. M. FORSTER *Howards End* vi. 51 That tune fairly gives me the hump. **1939** T. S. ELIOT *Family Reunion* 18 You seem to be wanting to give us all the hump. I must say, this isn't cheerful for Amy's birthday.

b. A walk or hike with a load on one's back. (Cf. HUMP *v.* 2.) *Austral.* and *N.Z. slang.*

1863 J. G. WALKER *Jrnl.* 7 Jan. (MS.) 4 It was a precious hump [over the hill for provisions]. **1890** 'R. BOLDREWOOD' *Miner's Right* v, We get a fair share of exercise without a twenty-mile hump on Sundays.

3*. *to get a hump on*, to hurry. (Cf. *HUMP *v.* 3.) *U.S. colloq.*

1892 *Harper's Mag.* Feb. 487/2 'We went fast enough then.' 'We do seem to be gittin' a leetle less hump on oursel's than we did then.' **1940** W. E. WILSON *Wabash* 231 'Let's git a hump on, Allen,' Abe said; and the two boys dipped their oars deeper into the brown water.

3.** Sexual intercourse; hence, a woman who makes herself available for sexual intercourse. *coarse slang.*

1931 G. IRWIN *Amer. Tramp & Underworld Slang* 105 *Hump*,..sexual intercourse. **1969** E. R. JOHNSON *Mongo's back in Town* (1970) ii. 18 It might be a good idea to line up a Christmas hump for himself. **1969** P. ROTH *Portnoy's Complaint* 134 Now you want to treat me like I'm nothing but some hump. **1970** 'D. CRAIG' *Young Men may Die* vi. 48 It was hard to believe she could be more than an ad hoc hump for Lamartine.

4. *hump rib* (earlier U.S. examples); hump speed *Aeronaut.*, the speed of a seaplane or hovercraft at which the drag due to the water is a maximum (cf. quots. 1914², 1935 for sense *2 d).

1834 in *Oreg. Hist. Soc. Q.* (1916) XVII. 126 The tongue, the heart, the marrow bones and the hump ribs is all they use when meat is plenty. **1839** J. K. TOWNSEND *Narr. Rocky Mts.* iii. 164 They..appeared to be surveying, with the keenness of morning appetite, the fine 'hump ribs' which were roasting before them. **1915** *Techn. Rep. Advisory Comm. Aeronaut. 1913–14* 369 It was not practicable to fit air-holes to the second step, but it is probable that a slight reduction of power at the 'hump' speed could be obtained by this means in smooth water. **1938** *Jrnl. R. Aeronaut. Soc.* XLII. 559 The relative distance and time required to reach hump speed depend largely on the value of the accelerating force at high speeds. **1962** *New Scientist* 24 May 388/1 As a hovercraft accelerates from rest there is a so-called 'hump-speed' (about 14–18 knots) above which the drag suddenly drops.

hump, *v.* Add: **1. d.** *transf.* of inanimate things.

1901 'LINESMAN' *Words by Eyewitness* (1902) 168 With the berg humping its mighty shoulders far behind them.

2. (N.Z. and U.K. examples.) Also *to hump it*. See also *BLUEY *sb.*

Several of the examples suggest that the object is not necessarily carried *on the back*.

1863 J. GOLDIE *3rd Diary* 19 Feb. in J. H. Beattie *Pioneers explore Otago* (1947) 147 Digger custom, we humped our swag containing our house, our bed, our grub. **1863** J. G. WALKER *Jrnl.* Mar. (MS.) 4 Humping it over from the Tiviot on our backs would not do as it was too hard work. **1864** J. C. RICHMOND *Let.* 12 May in *Richmond–Atkinson Pap.* II. 111 It is very hard work humping your blankets and tucker. **1865** E. R. CHUDLEIGH *Diary* 16 July (1950) 193 Humping all their belonging with them. **1866** B. L. FARJEON *Shadows on Snow* 66 [Diggers]. The best thing we can do..is to try and hump it back again tomorrow. **1916** 'TAFFRAIL' *Pincher Martin* xii. 218 We'll have to hump the whole bloomin' lot out again, damn an' blast him! **1922** T. E. LAWRENCE *Let.* 7 Sept. (1938) 365, I went off to hump their swill to the camp pigs. **1924** —— *Let.* 20 Jan. (1938) 456 If it is the best I can do with a pen, then it's better for me to hump a rifle or spade about. **1925** FRASER & GIBBONS *Soldier & Sailor Words* 122 *To hump*, to lift, to carry. *Ibid.*, *To hump it*, to march with full kit, to tramp on foot. **1955** M. GILBERT *Sky High* viii. 112 Couldn't you hump around the heavy lectern vases. **1960** *Sunday Express* 6 Mar. 8/4 He..tugged out a suitcase containing his full-dress uniform, humped it across the pavement. **1971** B. W. ALDISS *Soldier Erect* 78, I followed behind him, humping the wireless set. **1971** *N.Z. Listener* 22 Mar. 13/1 He's humpin' a haversack. **1973** C. BONINGTON *Next Horizon* xii. 171 John and Dougal took the lead, while Layton and I followed, humping loads... I humped my big rucksack, taking the occasional photograph.

3. (Further U.S. and other examples.) Also, to hurry.

1884 'MARK TWAIN' *Huck. Finn* xxix. 307, I never hunted for no back streets, but humped it straight through the main one. **1906** D. COKE *Bending of Twig* xv. 71 'We shall have to hump ourselves for call-over,' he said..as they dashed up the hill. **1908** G. H. LORIMER *Jack Spurlock* i. 9 He..said to the cop on guard, 'One of them Ha'voids [= Harvard students],' and to me, 'Hump yourself.' **1928** 'SAPPER' *Female of Species* ii, Peter—your Sunbeam, and hump yourself. *Ibid.* xiv, That finger will connect with the trigger and the result will connect with you. So, hump yourself. **1968** M. WOODHOUSE *Rock Baby* vi. 48, I..humped myself into my coat.

b. In extended use.

1905 *Smart Set* Sept. 117/1 You'll have to get this machine to hump it all she knows. **1929** J. B. PRIESTLEY *Good Companions* I. i. 3 As you look down on Bruddersford, you feel..that it is only biding its time, that it will hump its way through somehow.

4. (Later example.)

1898 A. BEARDSLEY *Let.* 16 Jan. (1971) 427 Letter writing humps me dreadfully.

5. *trans.* and *intr.* To have sexual intercourse (with). *coarse slang.*

1785 GROSE *Dict. Vulgar T.*, *Hump*, to hump, once a fashionable word for copulation. **1931** G. IRWIN *Amer. Tramp & Underworld Slang* 105 *Hump*, to have intercourse. *Ibid.* 263 In 1914–1918..*hump* and *niggle* were used of both sexes, *screw* and *shag* were operatively male. **1961** J. HELLER *Catch-22* (1962) xiii. 131 The girls had shelter and food for as long as they wanted to stay. All they had to do in return was hump any of the men who asked them to. **1962** J. BALDWIN *Another Country* (1963) I. i. 14 A nigger..lives his whole life, lives and dies according to a beat... He humps to that beat and the baby he throws up in there..comes out nine months later like a goddamn tambourine. **1965** M. BRADBURY *Stepping Westward* vii. 345 Story is he humped the faculty wives in alphabetical order. **1971** W. HANLEY *Blue Dreams* vii. 90 Gazing at her, the hem of her skirt pushed by the attitude of her dazzling legs far back along her thighs, he thought, Jesus, what would it be like to hump her?

humpback, *sb.* (*a.*). Add: **A. 3.** Also = *humpback salmon, sucker.

1881 *Amer. Naturalist* XV. 182 The hump-back, taken in salt water about Seattle, shows the same peculiarities. **1913** *Chambers's Jrnl.* Oct. 729/1 The 'steel-head', the 'dog-salmon', and the 'humpback'. **1955** [see *CHINOOK b]. **1963** *Vancouver Sun* 13 Aug. 14/1 Humpback is the old and still popular name for the pink salmon. **1965** A. J. MCCLANE *Standard Fishing Encycl.* 411/1 The humpback [sucker] prefers the slow-moving parts of larger streams.

B. humpback salmon = *GORBUSCHA, HADDO; humpback sucker *U.S.*, *Xyrauchen*

texanus, a freshwater fish of the Colorado basin.

1869 *Mainland Guardian* (New Westminster, B.C.) 25 Sept. 2/1 The Oleys or Hones appear every alternate year; they are known as the Humpback salmon. **1881** *Amer. Naturalist* XV. 177 The fact that the hump-back salmon runs only on alternate years in Puget sound..is well attested. **1891** [see *GORBUSCHA]. **1965** A. J. MCCLANE *Standard Fishing Encycl.* 410/2 Humpback sucker *Xyrauchen texanus.* **1971** B. MUUS *Freshwater Fish Brit. & Europe* 64/2 The humpback salmon is distinguished from other Pacific salmon by its short, 2-year life-cycle.

hump-backed, *a.* Add: *Esp.* in the names of fishes; cf. *HUMPBACK *sb.* (*a.*).

1807 tr. *Garytschev's Voy.* 28 We managed..to lay in a stock for ourselves of the hump-backed salmon, and other such fish. **1884** G. B. GOODE *Fisheries U.S.: Nat. Hist. Aquatic Animals* 323 It is a frequent summer visitor all along the coast as far north as Wood's Holl, Massachusetts, where it has a peculiar name, the people there calling it the 'Hump-backed Butterfish'. **1896** JORDAN & EVERMANN *Check-List Fishes N. & Mid. Amer.* 241 *Xyrauchen cypho.* Razor-back Sucker; Hump-backed Sucker. **1902** *Encycl. Brit.* XXVI. 391/1 The dog-salmon and the humpbacked have no commercial value. **1973** *Times* 10 Jan. 7/2 He watched two fishing boats return fully laden with hump-backed salmon.

humped, *ppl. a.* Add: Also *humped-up*.

1885 T. ROOSEVELT *Hunting Trips* iv. 104 The cattle.. standing humped up in the bushes. **1906** W. S. MAUGHAM *Bishop's Apron* v. 71 The coachman..sat on his box in a slovenly, humped-up fashion. **1931** G. O. RUSSELL *Speech & Voice* xiv. 137 The high-arching and humped-up-rounding position of the tongue.

humpenscrump (hʌ·mpənskrʌmp). [*dial.* (not in *E.D.D.*), perh. f. HUMP *sb.* + (*Old Father*) *Scrump*, a freq. appellation of Big Head in traditional English folk-plays; cf. HUMSTRUM and SCRUMP.] A musical instrument of rude construction; a hurdy-gurdy (sense 1 a).

[**1923** R. J. E. TIDDY *Mummers' Play* 172, I old father scrump with a bell on my rump... A man..kicked a hump up on to my shoulder and there remains the hump now.] *Ibid.* 173 [*stage directions*] Instruments Tin whistle. Jew's Harp. Father Scrump carries the humpenscrump made with a tin with wires across and bridge and a stick with notches for a bow. **1933** E. K. CHAMBERS *Eng. Folk-Play* 70 The musical instrument is generally a fiddle, or a rustic substitute called a hurdy-gurdy or humpen-scrump. **1954** L. MACNEICE *Autumn Sequel* 142 The humpenscrump that charmed some forebear's ear Now makes the roast pigs caper in Cockayne.

humper (hʌ·mpəɹ). [f. HUMP *v.* + -ER[1].] Something or someone that humps, in the senses of the verb. (For quot. 1895 cf. *HUMP *v.* 3.)

1895 *Columbus* (Ohio) *Dispatch* 27 Mar. 1/3 We were coming along on time. Engine 586 is a humper, and Rankin, my fireman, was keeping her hot. **1897** KIPLING *Capt. Cour.* vii. 142 Hark to her [*sc.* a ship]! She's a humper! **1961** *Spectator* 7 Apr. 471 The carrying of a second man, or 'humper', on newspaper delivery vans in London. **1967** *Times Rev. Industry* Feb. 35/2 Worked in the Smithfield meat market..earning 30s. as a humper.

humpish (hʌ·mpiʃ), *a.* [f. HUMP *sb.* + -ISH[1] 2.] Somewhat like a hump, somewhat squat and dumpy.

1936 W. HOLTBY *South Riding* II. v. 130 Lydia stood up, a humpish stocky schoolgirl. **1939** R. FRY *Last Lectures* v. 68 They are squat and humpish renderings, often of seated forms.

humpty. Add: Also as *sb.*, a low padded cushion seat, a dumpty.

1924 *Drapery Sale Catal.*, Humptys and Cushions. **1926** *Brit. Weekly* 18 Mar. 600/2 The ladies of the village are busy making 'humpties', soft cushion seats to pull up on the rug before the peat fire. **1928** *Daily Express* 23 Jan. 5/2 Home-made Humpty.

humpy, *sb.* Add: Also **humpie.** In extended use: a hut (not necessarily one occupied by an Aboriginal). (Further examples.)

1911 *Chambers's Jrnl.* Sept. 591/2, I knew where this humpie was. **1927** M. TERRY *Through Land of Promise* xiii. 161 The manager's house..had been a small humpie consisting of four stone walls capped by a tin roof. **1928** 'BRENT OF BIN BIN' *Up Country* viii. 130 They are big tents or humpeys of bark, with flags on top to show if they are English or Russian or some other nation. **1942** C. BARRETT *On Wallaby* i. 14 The old fossicker was.. seated outside a bark humpy. **1953** 'N. SHUTE' *In Wet* x. 348 His camp consisted of a tent for himself and his wife, and a humpy shelter made of gum tree boughs for his white ringer, Phil Fleming. **1969** *Australian* 7 June 16/1 There's a drawing in Petty's Australia Fair that shows an Aboriginal urchin in front of his family's humpy in the carcass of a Holden. **1971** *World Archaeol.* III. 168 Structures (termed 'humpies' by Europeans) which are the year-round type of dwelling used by mission-dwelling Aborigines.

humpy (hʌ·mpi), *sb.*[2] *Austral. slang.* Also **humpie.** [f. HUMP *sb.* 1 + -Y[6].] A camel.

1934 A. RUSSELL *Tramp-Royal in Wild Australia* i. 19 There's a spare riding camel in my outfit you can have... Only you'll have to rough it..rough it hard, too..same as me. But the humpie's there if you want it. *Ibid.* iii. 29 He is the despised 'humpie', the 'filthy camel'. **1945** BAKER *Austral. Lang.* 214 A camel is an *oont* or a *humpy*.

humpy, *a.* Add: **1. b.** Out of humour; melancholy, sad. Cf. HUMP *sb.* 3.

1889 J. K. JEROME *Three Men in Boat* i. 10 Harris said he thought it would be humpy. He said he knew the sort of place I meant; where everybody went to bed at eight o'clock, and you..had to walk ten miles to get your baccy. **1911** 'IAN HAY' *Safety Match* xii. 194, I have got into the way of bringing you my little troubles, and turning to you generally if I felt dismal or humpy. **1920** *Glasgow Herald* 29 July 4, I mention these facts so that readers may be reassured if they are inclined to be 'humpy'... Many among us..are never so happy as when they are making themselves miserable by looking at the black side of things. **1941** 'R. WEST' *Black Lamb* I. 71 He had found himself tired and wounded and humpy and alone after a day's hunting.

humulene (hiū·miulīn). *Chem.* [f. mod.L. *humul-us* (in *Humulus lupulus*, taxonomic name of the hop) + -ENE.] A colourless liquid sesquiterpene, $C_{15}H_{24}$, identical with α-caryophyllene and forming the principal constituent of oil of hops.

1895 A. C. CHAPMAN in *Jrnl. Chem. Soc.* LXVII. 62 The evidence I have given as to its chemical individuality justifies me, I think, in adding to this list the sesquiterpene of the essential oil of hops, for which I venture to propose the name humulene. **1951** *Jrnl. Chem. Soc.* 22 Humulene ($C_{15}H_{24}$), the chief sesquiterpene constituent of hop oil and a minor constituent of the high-boiling terpene fraction of clove oil, has been shown to be present in the essential oil of Egyptian hashish.

humulone (hiū·miulōun). *Chem.* Also **-on** (-ǫn). [ad. G. *humulon* (I. W. Wöllmer 1916, in *Ber. d. Deut. Chem. Ges.* XLIX. 780), f. as prec. + -ONE.] A bitter, yellow, crystalline, cyclic ketone, $C_{21}H_{30}O_5$, that is an important constituent of hops and has strong antibiotic activity.

1916 *Jrnl. Chem. Soc.* CX. I. 494 A contribution to the chemistry of 'humulon' or 'α-hop bitter acid' or 'lupulic acid'. **1937** HOPKINS & KRAUSE *Biochem. appl. to Malting & Brewing* iv. 221 Both humulon and lupulon are secreted in the hop cone during growth and become more or less resinified. **1964** KIRK & OTHMER *Encycl. Chem. Technol.* (ed. 2) III. 302 By far the most important constituents of the hops are the bitter substances, humulone, lupulone, and their transition products, which give beer its characteristic taste. **1967** E. PARYSKI tr. *Korzybski's Antibiotics* II. vi. 1447 Lupulon and humulon strongly inhibit the growth of gram-positive micro-organisms and acid-fast bacilli.

Hun, *sb.* Add: **4.** *gen.* A person of brutal conduct or character; *esp.* during and since the war of 1914–18 applied, often without animus, to the Germans (or their allies); a German. Also *attrib.*

[The immediate source of the application of *Hun* to the Germans was the speech delivered by Wilhelm II to the German troops about to sail for China on 27 July 1900. See the following examples:

1900 *Times* 30 July 5/3 According to the Bremen *Weser Zeitung* the Emperor said [27 July at Bremerhaven]:—'..No quarter will be given, no prisoners will be taken. Let all who fall into your hands be at your mercy. Just as the Huns a thousand years ago, under the leadership of Etzel (Attila) gained a reputation in virtue of which they still live in historical tradition, so may the name of Germany become known in such a manner in China that no Chinaman will ever again even dare to look askance at a German.' **1900** *Daily News* 20 Nov. 5/3 Herr Bebel [in the Reichstag] dwelt..at some length on the so-called Hun letters, and stigmatized the cruel and barbarous methods of European warfare in China. **1900** *Times* 21 Nov. 5/2 A great portion of the speech of the Socialist leader [Bebel] was devoted to the so-called 'Letters from the Huns' (*Hunnenbriefe*)—epistles from German soldiers in China to their relatives at home giving an account of the cruelties which have been perpetrated by the army of occupation.]

1784–5 in *Publ. Navy Rec. Soc.* (1906) XXXI. 55 Andrew Duff, Midshipman. Dead. A drunken Hun. **1862** H. TIMROD *Poems* (1901) 143 Shout! let it reach the startled Huns! And roar with all thy festal guns! It is the answer of thy sons, Carolina!

1902 KIPLING in *Times* 22 Dec. 9/5 In sight of Peace.. With a cheated crew, to league anew With the Goth and the shameless Hun! **1914** —— in *Queen* 5 Sept. 388/2 Stand up and meet the war. The Hun is at the gate! **1915** E. CANDLER in *Daily Mail* 5 Apr. 4/3 She [*sc.* a Norfolk girl] told me how the eldest [brother 'at the front'] had held up three 'Huns' in a mill... She used the word 'Hun' quite naturally, with no hint of contempt or bitterness. **1916** 'BOYD CABLE' *Action Front* 133 Do you suppose our friend the Flighty Hun won't have a peep at us to-morrow morning? **1916** 'TAFFRAIL' *Pincher Martin* xiv. 269, I suppose you know, Peter,..that we were bang on the top of a Hun minefield. *a* **1918** [see *CRASH *v.* 6 a]. **1918** *Times* 12 Dec. 9/4 'Supposed' statements..of American 'advisers'..simply smell of Hun propaganda. **1932** [see *BIT *sb.*[2] 4 h]. **1941** [see *crash-land* v.]. **1942** *Tee Emm* (Air Ministry) II. 63 The squadron has, after those months of inaction, started to bag Huns. **1945** [see *ABROAD C *sb.*]. **1958** P. KEMP *No Colours or Crest* vi. 104 They ambushed a cartload of Huns the other day.

b. A flying cadet: see quots. *Air Force slang* (in the war of 1914–18).

1916 H. BARBER *Aeroplane Speaks* 36 The Aeroplane.. remonstrates...'See the Medical Officer, you young Hun.' **1918** E. M. ROBERTS *Flying Fighter* 233 An aeroplane.. was flying over the street, but I don't know what the couple of British Huns in it were trying to do. *Ibid.* 336 Every pilot is a Hun until he has received his wings. **1925** FRASER & GIBBONS *Soldier & Sailor Words* 123 The word 'Hun'..was used..for a newly-joined young officer qualifying for his 'wings', in consequence of the destructive effect on the instructional aeroplanes which young officers while learning to fly usually had.

Hence (sense *4) **Hu·ndom**, the state of being a 'Hun'; **Hu·nnish** *a.*, whence **Hu·nnishness**; **Hu·nless** *a.*, lacking Germans.

1916 F. LAWRENCE *Mem. & Corr.* (1961) 211, I saw you being martyred on account of my Hundom! **1918** *Punch* 27 Mar. 207/2 The Hunnish conduct of the German officer who egged on the natives. **1920** *Blackw. Mag.* Feb. 154/1 The islands were entirely Hunless. **1924** C. J. TOLLEY *Mod. Golfer* 7 The only piece of Hunnishness we ever encountered at Heidelberg was at the hands of an appalling doctor, who..thought fit to inoculate us against every known disease. **1928** *Manch. Guardian Weekly* 2 Nov. 350/2 Once give the better England clear evidence that Hunnishness is not the sole attribute of the German spirit, and [etc.].

5. *Comb.*, as *Hun-folk, -hater, -land, -talk; Hun-eating, -hunting, -pinching.*

1928 *Manch. Guardian Weekly* 2 Nov. 350/2 There were two Englands—(a) the impossible Hun-eating England and (b) the better England. **1923** KIPLING *Irish Guards in Gt. War* I. 343 The Battalion..watched about them.. the muddy-faced Hun-folk. **1920** R. MACAULAY *Potterism* II. i. 58 He would have to include among his jingoes and Hun-haters some fighting men too. **1925** FRASER & GIBBONS *Soldier & Sailor Words* 123 *Hun hunting*, an Airman's phrase for going out to look for, or chase, the enemy. **1916** *Daily Mirror* 1 Nov. 4/4 Gott strafe England.., the recognised toast throughout Hunland. **1918** [see *EGG *sb.* 3 d]. **1920** *Glasgow Herald* 20 Nov. 5 No such sentiments could be admitted in Hunland. **1925** FRASER & GIBBONS *Soldier & Sailor Words* 124 *Hunland*, a term generally used in the War by Airmen for the country behind enemy lines, wherever it might be. **1917** A. G. EMPEY *Over Top* 295 '*Hun pinching*', raiding German trenches for prisoners. **1959** P. MOYES *Dead Men don't Ski* iii. 34 You ask her, Roger... You're the expert in Hun-talk.

hun, colloq. abbrev. of *HONEY 5 b.

1896 ADE *Artie* xiv. 126 'Look at the new hat on her.'.. 'It's a hun,' remarked Artie.

hun, var. *HOON *sb.*[1]

Hunanese (hūnănī·z), *a.* and *sb.* [f. *Hunan*, name of a province of southern China + -ESE.] **A.** *adj.* Of, pertaining to, or characteristic of Hunan or of the Chinese spoken there. **B.** *sb.* **a.** An inhabitant of Hunan. **b.** The dialect of Hunan.

1937 J. R. FIRTH *Papers in Ling. 1934–51* (1957) vii. 80 It will be found convenient to regard the Hunanese monosyllable as having one, two, or perhaps three places in which the phonetic diacritica may be said to occur. **1937** E. SNOW *Red Star over China* II. iii. 65 Li Chiang-lin was a Hunanese. **1948** J. R. FIRTH *Papers in Ling. 1934–51* (1957) ix. 127 With the help of Mr. K. H. Hu, of Changsha, I studied the pronunciation and phonology of his dialect of Hunanese. **1957** *Times Lit. Suppl.* 8 Nov. 677/1 The structural analysis of an element in a Hunanese dialect. **1964** L. MITCHISON *Gillian Lo* v. 54 Ai-yang was clucking with excitement, her Hunanese accent..strong. **1967** *Everyman's Encycl.* VI. 643/2 Since the time of the Taiping rebellion..the Hunanese have been noted for their pride and obstinacy in admitting outside control. **1972** *N.Y. Times* 3 Nov. 24/6 It is probably correct to say that there are tricky but fruitful points of similarity between Hunanese food and the food of southern France. **1972** 'M. HEBDEN' *Killer for Chairman* II. iv. 162 There was a variety of dialects among the crowd from Chekiangese and Hunanese to the difficult Szechwanese.

hunch, *v.* Add: **2. b.** To nudge (a person) so as to direct attention to someone. Also *fig.* *U.S.*

a **1852** F. M. WHITCHER *Widow Bedott Papers* (1883) 76 She kept a hunchin' Miss Coon and grinnin'. **1884** 'MARK TWAIN' *Huck. Finn* xxv. 246 Then the king he hunched the duke, private. **1906** *Life* 1 Feb. 147 Soon some fellow hunched the Legislature, and then there had to be more or less investigating done.

c. *intr.* To push or lunge forward. *U.S.*

1911 S. E. WHITE *Bobby Orde* (1916) xvii. 196 Bending to his task the pusher at the rear dug his toes in, while the others hunched. **1913** G. S. PORTER *Laddie* viii. 232 She sat astride the foot log, and hunched along with her hands. **1925** C. E. MULFORD *Cottonwood Gulch* xix. 259 They hunched closer, hugging knees under chin.

3. Also without *up*.

1906 U. SINCLAIR *Jungle* xviii, Hiding his hands in his pockets and hunching his shoulders together. **1906** 'K. HOWARD' *Old Game* II. i. 54 She merely hunched her shoulders, swung on her heel, and marched off.

hunch, *sb.* Add: **1. b.** A hint, 'tip'. (Cf. prec. 2 b.)

1849 T. M. GARRETT in *Amer. Speech* (1951) XXVI. 183/1 Another piece [of writing] gave a few hunches to the inexperienced freshman. **1901** 'H. MCHUGH' *John Henry* 57 The reason it's so good is because I took my hunch from Rud. Kipling's style. **1922** Z. GREY *To Last Man* ii. 36 All shootin' arms an' such are at a premium in the Tonto... An' I was givin' you a hunch to come loaded.

4. A premonition or intuitive feeling that something will happen or may be the case; a presentiment.

1904 S. E. WHITE *Silent Places* xviii. 200 'I hope your hunch is a good one,' replied Dick. **1907** R. W. SERVICE *Songs of Sourdough* (1908) 52 Then you've a haunch [*sic*] what the music meant. **1918** E. M. ROBERTS *Flying Fighter* 62 This particular night Fritz had a hunch that somebody was going to pass the place behind the screen. **1926** G. D. H. & M. COLE *Blatchington Tangle* xiii. 97, I had an awful hunch what it was. **1938** *Brit. Jrnl. Psychol.* July 7, I relied not so much on conscious thought, as on what Americans call a 'hunch'. **1955** *Times* 9 May 5/2 A churchwarden's 'hunch' could never be a wholly satisfactory substitute for professional knowledge in regard to the care of churches. **1960** M. SPARK *Ballad of Peckham Rye* ii. 14 'Only a hunch,' said Dougal. 'I may be wrong.' **1973** 'H. HOWARD' *Highway to Murder* viii. 89 My sixth sense told me I'd got myself an extra shadow. That hunch was all I had to go on.

hunched, *a.* Add: Also with advbs.

1910 W. DE LA MARE *Three Mulla-Mulgars* x. 144 His little hunched-up friend. **1920** *Chambers's Jrnl.* 110/1 A long..sinuous beast that hopped in a series of hunched-up bounds. **1921** C. E. MULFORD *Bar-20 Three* xxi. 267 He..clawed himself into a saddle..and rode for safety, hunched over and but half conscious.

hundi (hu·ndi). *India.* Also **hoondee, hoondi, hoondy.** [Hind. *hundī* (Skr. *huṇḍikā* bill of exchange).] A negotiable instrument, such as a bill of exchange or promissory note, used by native bankers in India and worded in the vernacular; also, money remitted by such an instrument.

1619 in W. Foster *Eng. Factories India 1618–21* (1906) 85 [They advise the dispatch of bills of exchange for rupees] hundies [17,100]. **1620** *Ibid.* 182 The exchange of rup[ees] secaus for hundies. **1810** T. WILLIAMSON *East India Vade Mecum* II. 330 Hoondies (i.e. bankers' drafts) would be of no use whatever to them. **1913** J. M. KEYNES *Indian Currency & Finance* vi. 197 The *hoondees* they buy and sell to each other..are chiefly the traders' *hoondees* bearing the shroffs' own endorsements. **1930** *Economist* 12 Apr. 820/1 Bills (hundis) of the native type. **1963** *Times* 18 May 8/4 It is thought that gold smuggling gangs obtain funds by operating the 'Hundi' system among Pakistani immigrants in Britain. **1969** *Commerce* (Bombay) 26 July 150/2 Apprehensions..may push up the rate of interest in the free market from 15–18 per cent to 20–24 per cent against the hundies, promissory notes and short loans.

hundred, *sb.* and *a.* Add: **1. b.** (*b*) *the Hundred Days*: the immediate source of the phrase is the speech delivered by Louis de Chabrol de Volvic, prefect of Paris, to Louis XVIII in 1815 ('Cent jours se sont écoulés depuis le moment fatal où votre majesté quitta sa capitale'). Add examples; also *transf.*

1827 SCOTT *Life Napoleon Buonaparte* IX. i. 33 Here, therefore, ended that short space..that period of an Hundred Days, in which the events of a century seem to be contained. **1862** C. KNIGHT *Popular Hist. Eng.* VIII. ii. 21 This landing in the Gulf of St. Juan on the 1st of March was the introductory scene to the great drama called 'The Hundred Days'. **1887** O. W. HOLMES (*title*) Our hundred days in Europe. **1956** J. M. BURNS *Roosevelt* ix. 169 The President asked for quick authorization of a civilian conservation corps...This bill interested Roosevelt himself as much as any single measure of the Hundred Days. **1965** T. C. SORENSEN *Kennedy* ix. 242 'I'm sick of reading how we're planning another "hundred days" of miracles,' he [*sc.* J. F. Kennedy] said, 'and I'd like to know who on the staff is talking that up. Let's put in that this won't all be finished in a hundred days or a thousand.' **1965** MRS. L. B. JOHNSON *White House Diary* 10 Apr. (1970) 257 Lyndon talked of the harvest of legislation. He said that never has there been such a hundred days. **1966** H. WILSON *Purpose in Power* I. 1 (*heading*) The first hundred days.

(*c*) *Hundred Years War,* the intermittent war between England and France from 1337 to 1453, arising out of the claim of the English kings to the French crown.

1874 J. R. GREEN *Short Hist. Eng. People* 275 The Hundred Years' War had ended. **1959** M. MCKISACK *14th Cent.* 127 Like the second world war of the twentieth century, the Hundred Years War gathered momentum slowly. Gascony was declared confiscate in May 1337 and in October Edward laid his claim to the French Crown; but there was no organized campaigning for another two years. **1961** E. F. JACOB *15th Cent.* 505 In the spring of 1453 Charles VII opened the last campaign of the Hundred Years War in overwhelming force.

(*d*) Phr., the *Hundred Flowers*: name given to a period of approximately six weeks in the summer of 1957 when certain elements of the Chinese population were invited to criticize the political system then obtaining in Communist China. (See quot. 1958².)

1958 L. F. EDWARDS tr. *Fauré's Serpent & Tortoise* xiv. 121 In the intellectual China of the Hundred Flowers, no one has the right to be a counter-revolutionary, but one has, to a certain extent, the right to be an idealist. **1958** *Listener* 6 Nov. 718/1 The campaign for free speech [in China] that followed the encouraging words of Mao Tse-tung—'let a hundred flowers bloom'—was evidently designed as an operation to find out what precisely were the prevailing criticisms of policy. **1959** *Ibid.* 5 Feb. 255/1 The intellectuals [in China] who blossomed with criticism during the brief Hundred Flowers Movement. **1973** *Ibid.* 2 Aug. 147/3 The humiliations which the Party had suffered during the so-called Hundred Flowers period.

d. After a numeral, used to express the two noughts in the figure representing the number of hours since midnight. Cf. *HOUR 1 b.

1953 P. C. BERG *Dict. New Words* 95/1 *Hundred,* the two noughts in the numerical symbols of full hours; e.g. we will meet at nine hundred hours [= 9.00 a.m.]. **1967** B. KNOX *Blacklight* vi. 135 'What's the time?'..'Coming up for seven-forty-five sir.' 'Let's be formal and say near enough to twenty hundred hours... Wait till twenty-two hundred, mister.' **1973** A. HUNTER *Gently French* i. 13, I got back to Elphinstone Road at about oh-one hundred hours.

2. b. Phrases: *not a hundred miles from*; *within a hundred miles of*: near, close to, in or at; also *fig.*; (*all the same in*) *a hundred years* (*hence*) (and similar expressions): gnomic formulas of consolation for present adversity; *a hundred of bricks*: see *BRICK *sb.*¹ 5; *a hundred to one*: a hundred chances to one; hence, an expression indicating very *slight* probability (implying 'a hundred to one against') or very *strong* probability ('a hundred to one in favour of').

1647 M. VERNEY in F. P. Verney *Mem.* (1892) II. xiv. 370 Tis a hundred to one pegg's husband turns them out of his house again within a fortnight. **1675** T. JORDAN *Triumphs of London* 21 Though now she be pleasant and sweet to the sense, Will be damnably mouldy a hundred year hence. **1760** STERNE *Tristram Shandy* II. IV. ix. 72 What a chapter of chances, said my father... 'Twas a hundred to one—cried my uncle *Toby.* **1783** in J. Ritson *Select Coll. Eng. Songs* II. 14 We shall be nothing An hundred years hence. **1821** *Kaleidoscope* 27 Feb. 277/3 A sporting gentleman passing by a house, not a hundred miles from —— street. **1827** P. EGAN *Anecdotes of Turf* 270 Within one hundred miles of the great Chancery shop of the kingdom. **1838** DICKENS *Nickleby* (1839) ix. 76 As she frequently remarked when she made any such mistake, it would be all the same a hundred years hence. **1852** *Leisure Hour* I. 52/2 Scandalous transactions said to have transpired between two 'well-known' individuals 'not a hundred miles off'. **1874** L. TROUBRIDGE *Life amongst Troubridges* (1966) ix. 75 Let's look cheerful—it will be all the same a hundred years hence. **1888** 'R. BOLDREWOOD' *Robbery under Arms* III. iv. 50 If he gets clear off.. you're right. But it's a hundred to one against it. **1891** KIPLING *Life's Handicap* 171 Did you ever know old Hummy behave like that before or within a hundred miles of it? **1895** A. W. PINERO *Benefit of Doubt* II. 109 Don't fret; it'll be all the same a hundred years hence. **1903** J. M'GOVAN *Brought to Bay* 74 This retreat, he admitted, was not a hundred miles from the spot where they were at that moment seated. **1914** C. MACKENZIE *Sinister St.* II. IV. ix. 1105 'Oh, well, it'll be all the same in a hundred years.' She picked up her white gloves, and swaggered across the crowded beerhall. **1925** W. S. MAUGHAM *Painted Veil* i. II, I say, you must pull yourself together. It's a hundred to one it wasn't Walter. **1955** D. GARNETT *Aspects of Love* I. 27 Of course it is a hundred to one that the girl is just a tart he has picked up in Montpellier. **1968** C. WATSON *Charity ends at Home* vi. 69 Certain information has reached me privately concerning the disposal of funds raised not a hundred miles from here in the name of so-called 'charity'. **1971** G. HOUSEHOLD *Doom's Caravan* iv. 174 All the same a hundred years hence, as my Nanny used to say. **1973** M. WOODHOUSE *Blue Bone* xvi. 174, I don't want you, Rodway, or you, Quickie, within a hundred miles of me, ever.

c. orig. *U.S.* *a* or *one hundred per cent*: used adjectivally or adverbially with the meaning 'entire(ly), complete(ly)'. Hence *hundred-per-center, hundred-per-centism.*

1911 H. S. HARRISON *Queed* vii. 90 You do more work in twenty-four hours than you're doing now, besides feelin' one hundred per cent. better all the time. **1918** T. ROOSEVELT in *N.Y. Times* 19 July 6/6 There can be no fifty-fifty Americanism in this country. There is room here for only 100 per cent. Americanism... No man who is not 100 per cent. American is entitled to the support of any party. **1923** *Westm. Gaz.* 1 Jan., An administrator is 100 per cent. successful only when he gets every individual in the factory..working as enthusiastically as if he were working for himself on his own job. *Ibid.* 9 Feb., Under a hundred per cent. disability. **1923** *Smart Set* Feb. 30 (*title*) Diary of a 100% American. **1926** W. R. INGE *Lay Thoughts* 135 Such detachment would not be possible to a 'hundred per cent. American'. *a* **1927** W. W. WOOLLCOTT (*title of poem*) I am a one hundred percent. American. **1928** *Publishers' Weekly* 26 May 2164/2, I have frequently encountered excellent accounting systems which were 100 per cent. useless. **1928** *Observer* 4 Mar. 13/2 Perhaps New York is not the place for the Hundred-per-centers. I certainly never met any. *Ibid.* 8 Apr. 8/2 He is really another victim of hundred-per-centism. **1931** G. B. SHAW *Platform & Pulpit* (1962) 232 The first thing that would occur to a real hundred per cent. American in Russia is that..it must be a splendid country to make money in. **1931** *Times Lit. Suppl.* 29 Jan. 76/3 The inevitable 'honest-to-God' hundred-per-cent. American young man..besieges and wins Valerie's heart. **1931** G. D. H. COLE in W. Rose *Outl. Mod. Knowl.* 666, I see no sign of the actual approach of this hundred per cent. American paradise. **1946** *Amer. Speech* XXI. 34/1 *Hundred per center,*..one who observes all customs and traditions without demur. **1946** *R.A.F. Jrnl.* May 169 The bomber crews had to make 100 per cent. certain of putting their H.E. loads right on the objective. **1968** M. WOODHOUSE *Rock Baby* xxiv. 233 You're one hundred per cent sure they'll never make any sort of bang, then?

d. *a hundred per cent*: fit, well, recovered. Freq. in negative contexts.

1960 N. MITFORD *Don't tell Alfred* xiv. 155, I don't feel a hundred per cent. **1965** V. CANNING *Whip Hand* xi. 131 'How's the arm?' 'It wasn't broken... It's almost a hundred per cent now.' **1965** N. FREELING *Criminal Conversation* I. viii. 52, I wasn't quite well, not ill but not quite a hundred per cent, and he did make me better. **1967** I. HAMILTON *Man with Brown Paper Face* xv. 214 Actually, I'm not completely one hundred per cent. **1973** 'D. CRAIG' *Bolthole* ii. 30 He's been, well, off colour, yes. Not ill, but not a hundred per cent.

4. a. (Later U.S. examples.)

1838 *Knickerbocker* XI. 15 When requested..to say how much flour she should make into bread, at their first baking, she answered..'I suppose about a quarter of a hundred.' **1852** *Trans. Mich. Agric. Soc.* III. 332 To dispose of the compound of acorns, ground nuts and carrion for $2 per hundred. **1861** *Trans. Ill. Agric. Soc.* IV. 373 We want a horse sixteen hands high, that will weigh fifteen hundred.

7. (Later examples.)

1922 G. K. CHESTERTON in *Illustr. London News* 12 Aug. 234/1 There ought not to be anything but a plural for.. the sweets called hundreds and thousands. **1932** A. CHRISTIE *Thirteen Problems* i. 22 'Cooks nearly always put hundreds and thousands on trifle, dear,' she said. 'Those little pink and white sugar things.' **1953** DYLAN THOMAS *Under Milk Wood* (1954) 60 Brandyballs, winegums, hundreds and thousands, liquorice sweet as sick. **1967** N. FREELING *Strike Out* 87 Little sugary pellets like hundreds and thousands.

hundredth, *a.* and *sb.* Add: **B.** *sb.* **2.** *Old Hundredth,* a hymn tune which first appeared in the Geneva psalter of 1551 and was later set to Psalm 100 in the 'old' metrical version of the Geneva Psalter (hymn 166 in 'Hymns Ancient and Modern'); the psalm itself. Also *attrib.*

[**1790** BRADY & TATE *New Version Psalms* 240 The Psalms in this Version of four Lines in a single Stanza.. may properly be sung as the old 100 Psalm.] **1837** T. BACON *First Impr. Hindostan* I. vi. 153, I have often.. heard the organ pealing forth the solemn notes of the old hundredth psalm. **1837** DICKENS *Pickw.* xxxii. 349 Brother Mordlin had adapted the beautiful words of 'Who hasn't heard of a Jolly Young Waterman?' to the tune of the Old Hundredth. **1840** —— *Old C. Shop* xviii. 192 The dog..ground hard at the organ..and applied himself..to the Old Hundredth. **1853** MRS. GASKELL *Cranford* xv. 298, I found out from the words, far more than from the attempt at the tune, that it was the Old Hundredth she was crooning to herself. **1934** R. FERGUSON *Celebrated Sequels* 25 Our vicar's wife says that on the whole we had better stick to the Old Hundredth. **1955** M. GILBERT *Sky High* i. 7 'What's the last hymn next Sunday..?' 'Hundred and Sixty-six. Old Hundredth. You all know *that.*'

hung, *ppl. a.* Add: **3.** *U.S.* Of a jury: unable to agree. Cf. *HANG *v.* 6 b, 17 c.

1848 E. BRYANT *California* (1849) xxvi. 291 The jury.. were what is called 'hung'; they could not agree, and the matters in issue, therefore, remained exactly where they were. **1962** *Listener* 10 May 799/1 No one would deny that a deadlocked jury—what the Americans call a hung jury—is a bad thing. **1965** J. PORTER *Dover Two* v. 63 What with hung juries, appeals and pleas for mercy, they'd had it [*sc.* the story] on ice for a long time.

4. *slang.* Suffering from excess of liquor (or drugs). Also **hung-over** (cf. *HANG-OVER 2), having or affected by a hang-over.

1950 R. STARNES *And when she was Bad* (1953) xvi. 76 Brafferton just came in, looking as hung over as you can get. **1952** J. VAN DRUTEN *I am a Camera* (1954) 90 Enters ..wearing a dressing gown and looks hung-over. 'I say, you don't look too well this morning.' 'I've got a terrible hangover.' **1958** *Amer. Speech* XXXIII. 225 Drunks are *hung,* too. **1960** *Homes & Gardens* Aug. 70/2 It is said to have therapeutic qualities on hungover mornings. **1960** I. SHAW *Two Weeks in another Town* x. 125 He awoke late, feeling headachy and hung-over from the liquor of the night before. **1962** K. ORVIS *Damned & Destroyed* vii. 48 A score or more of addicts—all hungover. **1963** H. SLESAR *Bridge of Lions* i. 7, I know you're hung, Mr. Drew. **1968** J. HUDSON *Case of Need* vi. 126, I was hung over from a party after the game. Really hung. Too hung. **1972** C. DRUMMOND *Death at Bar* v. 139 Christ! You look hung over!.. What about drinks all round?

hungal, var. *HANGUL¹.

Hungarian. Add: **A.** *adj.* **1.** *Hungarian bonnet* or *cap,* the shell of a marine gastropod mollusc, *Capulus ungaricus*; *Hungarian grass U.S.* (*obs.*), the forage grass, foxtail millet, *Setaria italica.*

1845 *Encycl. Metrop.* VII. 288/2 In the Hungarian Bonnet, *Pileopsis Ungarica,* the tip of the shell seems to drop backwards and downwards. **1854** P. H. GOSSE *Nat. Hist. Mollusca* 212 The only British species [of *Pileopsis*] is commonly known by the appellation of Torbay Bonnet..; it also bears the names of Fools-cap Limpet, Cap of Liberty, and Hungarian Bonnet. **1859** *Guide Illinois Central Railroad Lands* 34 *Hungarian Grass.* This cereal, first introduced by the Hungarian exiles, is becoming a favorite with the farmers. **1883** *Rep. Indian Affairs* 23 About 12 acres were planted with Hungarian grass. **1901** E. STEP *Shell Life* 220 The Hungarian Cap or Cap of Liberty (*Capulus hungaricus*) is shaped much like the cap of Liberty, the beak or apex being spirally curved back. **1971** S. P. DANCE *Seashells* 103/2 A thick periostracum is a characteristic feature of some cap shells and is well seen in the Hungarian Cap.

b. Pertaining to Hungary, as *Hungarian band,* a band specializing in the performance of Hungarian music; *Hungarian point, stitch* (see quot. 1934).

1882 B. POTTER *Jrnl.* 2 July (1966) 19 Mr. Edwin Lawrence had the Hungarian Band last week... They are mostly string instruments. **1894** G. DU MAURIER *Trilby* III. VIII. 133 A large photograph..of Svengali, in

the military uniform of his own Hungarian band. **1907** *Yesterday's Shopping* (1969) 1055 Blue Hungarian Band... Handsome National Uniforms... Any number from 4 to 30 may be engaged. **1921** A. G. I. Christie *Samplers & Stitches* vii. 90 *Hungarian stitch*... The stitch illustrated in the diagram is often seen in canvas embroidery, used for filling in a background whilst, perhaps, Tent or Cross stitch works out the intricacies of the pattern. **1932** D. C. Minter *Mod. Needlecraft* 60/1 Some geometric all-over pattern, such as Hungarian stitch. **1934** M. Thomas *Dict. Embroidery Stitches* 125 *Hungarian stitch*, a Canvas Stitch which produces a most attractive pattern, and may be worked either all in one colour or in contrasting shades. **1972** *Country Life* 8 June (Suppl.) 50 Queen Anne walnut wing-chair..covered in its original Hungarian point needlework.

hunger, *sb.* Add: **4. e. hunger-march,** a march, undertaken usually by the unemployed, in order to call attention to their needs and claims; so **hunger-marcher; hunger-pain,** pain due to hunger; also *Path.* (see quot. 1905); **hunger strike,** the action of a person, esp. a prisoner, who refuses food in order to induce someone to yield to his demands; so **hunger-strike** *v. intr.*, to go on hunger-strike; **hunger-striker, hunger-striking** *vbl. sb.*; **hunger swarm,** the swarming of bees caused by lack of food.

1908 *Westm. Gaz.* 16 July 10/3 A statement of the purpose of the 'Hunger March'. **1939** N. Monsarrat *This is Schoolroom* I. 33 Hunger-marches, May Day processions.. they were all new. **1972** M. Jones *Life on Dole* I. i. 11 Among the older people, there was grave talk of the days of mass unemployment and the Hunger Marches. **1908** *Westm. Gaz.* 16 July 10/3 He had no knowledge the 'Hunger Marchers' were coming there that day. **1922** *Ibid.* 29 Dec., Unemployed hunger marchers are persisting in their determination to see the Prime Minister. **1950** Koestler *God that Failed* I. 28 Europe trembled under the torn boots of hunger-marchers. **1820** Hunger-pain [see Hunger *sb.* 4 a]. **1905** B. G. A. Moynihan in *Lancet* 11 Feb. 341/1 If the pain does not come on for from two to four hours after a meal..the patient will often complain of what I have been accustomed to call 'hunger pain'. **1943** E. Bowen *Seven Winters* 25 The vacuum, the hunger-pain, set up in me from being unable to read. **1889** *Century Mag.* Nov. 107/2 Here I heard..the narrative of the hunger-strike of the four women in the prison of Irkutsk. **1903** H. Chisholm tr. *L. Deutsch's Sixteen Yrs. in Siberia* 78 Upon these conditions I consented not to prolong my 'hunger-strike'. **1908** *Westm. Gaz.* 18 Mar. 5/1 The Central Prisons Administration has circularised the provincial Governors regarding the so-called 'hunger strikes', which are a characteristic feature of Russian prison life. **1914** E. Pankhurst *My Own Story* III. v. 292 She has hunger-struck in prison. She submitted herself for more than five weeks to the horrible ordeal of feeding by force. **1916** W. J. Locke *Wonderful Year* xvii. 247 'I've been to prison.' Martin..asked if she hunger-struck. **1937** Koestler *Spanish Testament* II. 333, I had intended to stop my hunger strike as soon as my letter to the Consul had been sent off. **1970** *Times* 11 May 8/4 In February Feron went on hunger strike in protest but was taken ill and for a month existed only on drugs. **1973** *Jewish Chron.* 19 Jan. 44/5 He will stage a 48-hour hunger strike outside the Soviet Embassy. **1922** *Blackw. Mag.* Aug. 146/1 He gave his orders for the release of the hunger-strikers. **1972** *Guardian* 1 Dec. 12/1 Already the names of McSwiney and MacCaughey, hunger-strikers of an earlier era, are being conjured up. **1916** W. J. Locke *Wonderful Year* xxiii. 329 Her duties involved incendiarism, imprisonment, and hunger-striking. **1870** A. Pettigrew *Handy Bk. Bees* 150 We have known swarms starved out of their hives. Having made a few pieces of comb, and being without food, no eggs were set in them and the bees, through sheer want, cast themselves on the wide world. These are called 'hunger-swarms'. **1886** F. R. Cheshire *Bees* II. iv. 168 Bees sometimes abscond because their stores have run out, and circumstances are desperate. Such have usually been called 'hunger' or 'vagabond' swarms. **1928** C. Williams *Story of Hive* iii. 22 Bees on the point of starvation will, in a spirit of desperation, leave their hive in a body. This exodus is known as 'a hunger swarm'. **1954** C. G. Butler *World of Honeybee* xiii. 154 Another type of honeybee swarm is sometimes recognisable, the type which in Europe is usually known as a 'hunger' swarm, and which occurs when a colony is starving.

hung-over: see *hung *ppl. a.* 4.

hungry, *a.* **2. a.** Delete ?*Obs.* and add: *the hungry forties*, the decade beginning in 1840, characterized in the British Isles by much poverty and unemployment.

1905 Mrs. C. Unwin (*title*) The hungry forties. **1910** A. Baker *Poor against Rich* 34, I mention the Hungry Forties, because a lot of poor people have allowed themselves to be misled during the last election, by the fear of dear food. **1920** J. Collings in J. L. Green *Life Jesse Collings* I. iv. 29 During the 'hungry forties' eggs were sold twenty for a shilling. **1958** *Spectator* 20 June 792/1 During the famine in Ireland at the end of the Hungry Forties, it was not uncommon [etc.].

hung up (hʌ·ŋ,ʌp), *a.* and *adj. phr.* Also **hung-up.** [f. *hang up* (Hang *v.* 28 d).] **1.** Put into abeyance, delayed.

1878 [see Hang *v.* 28 d].

2. *slang.* Confused, bewildered, mixed-up. Also *hung-up on*, obsessed with, preoccupied with (cf. also quot. 1961).

[**1909** J. R. Ware *Passing Eng.* 156/1 *Hung up*, from the American—where personal catastrophe is referred to by this phrase.] **1945** L. Shelly *Jive Talk Dict.* 21/1 *All hung up*, completely bewildered. **1957** [see *daddy 3]. **1958** *New Statesman* 6 Sept. 294/2 Helping each other in those phases in which they are 'hung up'. **1961** Rigney & Smith *Real Bohemia* p. xv, *Hung up, to be*, one's behavior is 'stuck' in one pattern. **1966** *Sunday Times* (Colour Suppl.) 13 Feb. 35/4 *Hung up*, obsessed, cf. 'he is hung up on that girl'. **1966** *New Statesman* 1 Apr. 458/3 The U.S. is 'hung up', paralysed into inaction because it cannot reconcile the political goal of uniting Germany with the ideological necessity of maintaining Western Europe as an anti-communist fortress. **1968** *Word Study* Feb. 5/2 American students of poetry have been hung up on the lines ever since. **1969** *It* 11–24 Apr. 13/4 How we manage to generate so many good things on this hung-up, repressed little island I simply don't know. **1970** *Daily Tel.* 26 Nov. 9/2 You get so hung-up with the place you feel like going out and smashing something. **1971** *New Scientist* 4 Mar. 485/2 Roszak is very hung up on the power that science grants. **1971** B. Malamud *Tenants* 54 He was more than a little hung up, stupid from lack of sleep, worried about his work.

hunh (hʌ(n)). *U.S. dial.* (esp. in *Black English*). Used as an intensifier after a question.

1935 in Z. N. Hurston *Mules & Men* (1970) I. x. 206 You got mo' poison in yuh than dat snake dat wuz so poison tell he bit de railroad track and killed de train, hunh? **1955** W. Gaddis *Recognitions* I. iv. 155 Hunh? What do you think of that, hunh? **1970** D. L. Lee in S. Henderson *Understanding New Black Poetry* (1973) III. 341 Can u do it, hunh? i say hunh, can u stop moving like a drunk gorilla? **1973** *Black World* Apr. 60 How about one more..for ol' times, hunh?

hunk, *sb.*[1] Add: **1. b.** A large man or woman.

[**1823** in *Dialect Notes* (1913) IV. 47 *Hunk*, bulk. A large body.] **1941** Baker *Dict. Austral. Slang* 37 *Hunk*, a large man. **1945** L. Shelly *Jive Talk Dict.* 13/1 *Hunk*, stalwart male. **1946** B. Treadwell *Big Book of Swing* 124/2 *Hunk*, very masculine male. **1957** J. Kerouac *On Road* (1958) 62, I looked at Lee Ann. She was a fetching hunk, a honey-colored creature.

hunk, *sb.*[2] and *a.* Add: **B.** *adj.* **b.** Colloq. phr. *to get hunk* (*with*): to get even (with). Also const. *on*.

1845 *Spirit of Times* 24 May 146 Those who lost their money on Fashion had two or three chances to 'get hunk', especially on the last day. **1903** A. H. Lewis *Boss* vii. 93 No, I don't blame Sheeny Joe... Still, while I don't blame him, it's up to us to get hunk an' even on th' play. **1949** *Boston Globe* (Fiction Mag.) 12 June 2/4 Suppose I show you how to get hunk with the cheapskates? **1950** in H. E. Goldin *Dict. Amer. Underworld Lingo* 79/1 That fink (informer) tried to get hunk on me for glomming (stealing) his broad (girl) by belching (informing) on me.

hunk (hʌŋk), *sb.*[3] *N. Amer. slang.* Also **hunkey, hunkie, hunky.** [Cf. *bohunk.] A nickname applied, usually disparagingly, to immigrants to the U.S.A. from east-central Europe. Also *attrib.* Cf. *honky.

1896 *N.Y. Herald* 13 Jan. 3/4 The average Pennsylvanian contemptuously refers to these immigrants as 'Hikes' and 'Hunks'. The 'Hikes' are Italians and Sicilians. 'Hunks' is a corruption for Huns, but under this title the Pennsylvanian includes Hungarians, Lithuanians, Slavs, Poles, Magyars and Tyroleans. **1910** *Sat. Even. Post* 3 Sept. 18/1 Almost every..Hunky or Dutchman who lands in New York has in his 'kick' or wallet, the written address of some boarding house. **1914** Jackson & Hellyer *Vocab. Criminal Slang* 47 *Hunkie*, current in localities where North European laborers abound. A corruption of Hungarian, but employed to signify a Continental European who is unwashed and unnaturalized. **1928** S. Lewis *Man who knew Coolidge* I. 53 Too many foreigners—fellows with Wop names and Hunky names. **1929** *Amer. Speech* June 372 *Hunkey*, same as Bohunk. **1932** [see *goof *v.* 1 a]. **1934** J. O'Hara *Appointment in Samarra* (1935) I. v. 83 The hunkeys, the schwackies..—regional names for non-Latin foreigners—probably were inside getting drunk. **1936** *Scrutiny* V. 1/5 The twelve-hour day kept the myriads of 'hunkies' who toiled in Mellon mills out of brawls and brothels. **1939** *Archit. Rev.* LXXXV. 219/2 It has to be close to the town because most of the workmen are foreign-born hunkies and do not readily adapt themselves to living conditions in Lyndora. **1962** C. L. Barnhart in Householder & Saporta *Probl. Lexicogr.* 178 Greaser, guinea, hunky, Jap, kike. **1971** *Maclean's Mag.* Oct. 78/1, I don't know if I should get mad if someone insults the Irish, or makes cracks about Polacks or Hunkies.

hunker, *v.* For *Sc.* read 'orig. *Sc.*' Add earlier and later examples.

1720 A. Pennecuik *Streams from Helicon* I. 80 And hunk'ring down upon the cald Grass. **1902** *Dialect Notes* II. 237 (Pioneer dialect of S. Illinois.) *Hunker down.* 1. To crouch in sitting. 2. To kneel. **1907** Kipling *Actions & Reactions* (1909) 187 We heard Imam Din hunker down on the floor. One gets little out of the East at attention. **1928** Barrie *Peter Pan* II, in *Plays* 39 Hunkering on the ground..the six are not unlike village gossips gathered round the pump. **1945** J. Steinbeck *Cannery Row* vii. 26 Mack and the boys sat on the floor, played cards hunkered down. **1946** K. Tennant *Lost Haven* (1947) ix. 129 Kelly got up, came out, and hunkered down by the sunny office wall. George hunkered down beside him. **1962** *Coast to Coast 1961–62* 85 The old woman had hunkered down, poking intently at an *hibachi*, some embers glowing darkly beneath. **1973** *N.Y. Times* 14 Aug. 34/3 One 14-year-old boy sat on a hornet when he hunkered down to get a better view of the green.

hunkerish (hʌ·ŋkəriʃ), *a. U.S. colloq.* [f. Hunker *sb.* + -ish[1].] Conservative, old-fashioned.

1857 *Lawrence* (Kansas) *Republ.* 2 July 3 This has in times past, been considered rather a hunkerish neighbourhood. **1888** W. Lawrence *Life Amos A. Lawrence* 139 His Kansas experience did not move Mr. Lawrence from his hunkerish sympathies in politics. **1905** *Springfield* (Mass.) *Weekly Republ.* 8 Sept. 1 The hunkerish conservatism which Mr. Cannon and the Senate stand for.

hunkerism (see under Hunker *sb.*). (Earlier and later examples.)

1845 R. Tyler *Let.* 19 Apr. in L. G. Tyler *Lett. & Times Tylers* (1896) III. 161 Every appointment made for New York or Pennsylvania or Maryland is a restoration of *Hunkerism.* **1848** C. A. Loomis *Let.* 23 Jan. in *Mich. Hist. Mag.* (1926) X. 216 Old Hunkerism is predominant, but it is hunkerism without brains. **1906** *Springfield* (Mass.) *Weekly Republ.* 6 Dec. 8 The old republican hunkerism.

hunkers, *sb. pl.* For *Sc.* read 'orig. *Sc.*' Add earlier and later examples.

1756 M. Calderwood *Journey in Eng. & Low Countries* (1842) 164 It goes down with a step, which makes the door so low, that if any body from without speaks to you, they must sit down on their hungkers. **1831** S. Lover *Legends & Stories of Ireland* 200 Up sits the fox on his hunkers. **1888** in W. B. Yeats *Fairy & Folk Tales* 109, I seen an ould woman sittin' on her hunkers. **1896** *Dialect Notes* I. 419, I had to sit on my *hunkers*. Myersville, Md., and Tannersville, Pa. **1935** A. J. Cronin *Stars look Down* I. ii. 17 Some colliers..squatted upon their hunkers against the wall. **1947** T. H. White *Elephant & Kangaroo* (1948) xx. 160 Mr. White seized Brownie by the tail—she had been sitting on her hunkers beside him.

hunkey, hunkie, hunky, varr. *hunk *sb.*[3]

hunky (hʌ·ŋki), *a.*[1] *U.S. slang.* [f. Hunk *sb.*[2] and *a.* + -y[1].] In good condition; safe and sound; all right: = Hunk *a.*

1861 'A. Ward' in *Vanity Fair* (N.Y.) 15 June 273/1 He (Moses) folded her to his hart, with the remark that he was 'a hunkey boy'. **1878** B. Harte *Man on Beach* 47 She's all hunky, and has an appetite. **1889** K. Munroe *Golden Days* xii. 125 If I'd took good care of that map.. we'd been all hunky at this minute. **1907** C. E. Mulford *Bar-20* ix. 105 That was all hunky for a while. **1926** *Bulletin* 21 Oct. 4/2 I'll be all hunky. Nurse Dainton tends me like I was made of glass.

So **hu:nky-do·ry, -do·rey** [second element of unknown origin] *a.*, satisfactory, fine.

1866 *Galaxy* 1 Oct. 275, I cannot conceive on any theory of etymology..why anything that is 'hunkee doree'..should be so admirable. **1868** in G. C. D. Odell *Ann. N.Y. Stage* (1936) VIII. 390 [Even Samuel Slater admitted that Tostee, when and if she sang, was] hunky-dory. **1907** N. Munro *Daft Days* xxi, Before one marries it's hunky-dory—it's fairy all the time. **1907** M. C. Harris *Tents of Wickedness* iv. ii. 341 I've had my luncheon, and I feel better already. Oh, it's all hunky-dory. **1943** N. Balchin *Small Back Room* 172 Well, unless the electricity they taught me is all wrong, that ought to be hunky-dory. **1956** D. M. Davin *Sullen Bell* III. iv. 233, I thought everything was hunkydory and you were well on the way to being a big executive. **1969** J. Gardner *Founder Member* ii. 17 Everythink's 'unkey dorey 'ere. No problem.

hunky (hʌ·ŋki), *a.*[2] [f. Hunk *sb.*[1] + -y[1].] Thick-set, solidly built.

1911 E. Ferber *Dawn O'Hara* vii. 89 Rather be hunky and healthy than skinny and sick. **1959** *Listener* 23 Apr. 733/1 A vast, hunky, surly man.

hunt, *sb.*[2] Add: **3*.** A hunting or oscillatory motion (see *hunt *v.* 7 b, *hunting *vbl. sb.* 1 f).

1920 *Nature* 11 Mar. 46/1 It moves backwards and forwards very slightly, and this motion we term the 'hunt'. **1934** *Brit. Jrnl. Psychol.* XXIV. 399 The 'angle of hunt', i.e. the angle of oscillation about the mean radial velocity, cannot exceed 360/*N* degrees, where *N* is the number of segments in the armature. **1937** *Jrnl. R. Aeronaut. Soc.* XLI. 410 The well behaved short period oscillation develops into an irritating hunt. **1952** A. Tustin *Automatic & Manual Control* 280 If the amplitude is not too large, and..we know how to reduce the amplitude by increasing the hunt frequency, it is possible to check a mean position of the system.

3.** *Telephony.* An operation of hunting by a selector or switch (see *hunting *vbl. sb.* 1 g).

1927 W. E. Hudson *Director Syst. Autom. Telephony* ii. 42 Relay C..is used to determine when the impulse train is finished so as to allow the automatic hunt to start. **1966** Rubin & Haller *Communication Switching Syst.* i. 31 The hunt motion is a vertical move of the wipers along the contact bank.

4. *hunt-breakfast* (earlier and later examples); **hunt ball,** a ball given by members of a hunt.

1807 *Sporting Mag.* XXXI. 40/1 The annual Hunt Ball took place at Chepstow. **1853** Mrs. Gaskell *Ruth* I. i. 13 The annual hunt-ball was to take place. **1933** A. Powell *From View to Death* iv. 113 Ungainly young men who had had a glass too much of champagne at hunt-ball suppers. **1968** A. Diment *Bang Bang Birds* x. 193 Penny told us about a hunt ball she had attended recently. **1973** K. Giles *File on Death* iv. 90 'E provides the catering for the 'unt ball at seven guineas the ticket. **1877** Trollope *Amer. Senator* II. xxiv. 254 That old farmer at the hunt breakfast. **1973** K. Giles *File on Death* v. 133 The other

one..kept pawing the ladies..and falling off his horse after the Hunt Breakfast.

hunt, *v.* Add: **3. b.** (U.S. examples.)

1818 E. P. Fordham *Pers. Narr. Trav.* (1906) 221 The next day I shall cross the Little Wabash to 'hunt land'. **1834** *Visit to Texas* i. 10 An old Tennessean and his wife with their sons were going 'to hunt land'. *Ibid.* xiii. 122 He sometimes sends out three or four men to collect and mark them. This is called hunting cattle. **1891** M. E. Ryan *Told in Hills* iv. iii. 309 All were sleepy enough to hunt beds early. **1903** A. Adams *Log of Cowboy* iii. 38 Flood..suggested that all hands hunt their blankets and turn in for the night.

4. (See *huntaway *sb.*)

7. b. *intr.* Of a governor, a synchronous electric motor or generator, etc.: to run alternately faster and more slowly than the desired speed. Hence more widely of other machines, systems, etc.: to oscillate *about* a desired speed, position, or state to an undesirable extent, to jump backwards and forwards.

1877 *Proc. Inst. Mech. Engin.* 273 Siemens' interesting governor..had..a great tendency to 'hunt',..if it was first left a little behind, and then got an excess of force, it would be constantly 'hunting' or oscillating about a mean position. **1894** *Rep. Brit. Assoc. Adv. Sci.* 759 A Watt governor..does not hunt if designed for stability. **1902** *Trans. Amer. Inst. Electr. Engin.* XVIII. 374/2 The motors attempt to follow the generator exactly. If the latter pulsates, the motors pulsate also; they vibrate about a mean position, 'hunting' or pumping. **1921** M. Walker *Diagn. Troubles Electr. Machines* vi. 239 In the case of steam turbines and steam engines, it is possible for the governor to hunt in a perfectly periodic manner. **1951** S. Deutsch *Theory & Design Television Receivers* xiii. 431 If the feedback loop is underdamped, the oscillator frequency will swing below 15,750 cycles per second, whereupon the correcting voltage causes a swing above 15,750 cycles per second, etc. In other words, the oscillator will 'hunt' about the correct frequency. **1953** *Electronic Engin.* XXV. 156/1 Since the torque balance has an on-off action..it has a tendency to hunt. **1969** *Daily Tel.* 10 Jan. 26/4 The British train will be able to use existing railway tracks because of a new type of suspension...This will stop the train 'hunting' sideways. **1969** J. Argenti *Managem. Techniques* 99 If the action is too late or too weak, control will be inadequate, if too early or too strong the system will 'hunt'—i.e. swing violently above and below the standard. **1970** 'J. Earl' *Tuners & Amplifiers* iii. 74 On weak stereo signals this circuit can 'hunt' over mono and stereo in a very disconcerting manner, switching to stereo as the signal rises and back to mono as it falls.

8*. *Telephony.* Of a selector or switch: to carry out the operation of hunting (*hunting *vbl. sb.* 1 g). Const. *for, over.*

1924 W. Aitken *Autom. Telephone Syst.* III. lvi. 275 Dialling O..results in the starting of a free-trunk finder, which automatically hunts for the calling line. **1924** H. H. Harrison *Introd. Strowger Syst. Autom. Telephony* i. 26 The preselector or line switch..hunts to find one of ten or more idle group selectors. **1933** K. B. Miller *Telephone Theory & Pract.* III. v. 250 It is usual to adjust the speed to permit the selector to hunt over a group of 30 trunks in 1 second. **1961** *Proc. Inst. Electr. Engin.* CVII. b. Suppl. 161/2 A maximum of 1·8 millisec is required to select a channel,..and a further period of 900 microsec to hunt for a free channel.

9. b. *N.Z.* (See quot. 1933.)

1933 L. G. D. Acland in *Press* (Christchurch, N.Z.) 28 Oct. 17/7 *Hunt down,* to hunt the sheep off the higher parts of their winter country on to lower, safer spurs when snow is expected; e.g., 'We hunted down every day for a week, but no snow came.' **1961** B. Crump *Hang on a Minute* 85, I want you blokes to go round to the Snow Hut and hunt the sheep down into the valley from the open spur.

huntaway (hʌ·ntăwēɪ), *sb.* **a.** *Austral.* and *N.Z.* [f. vbl. phr. *to hunt away* (Hunt *v.* 4), which is further illustrated below.] (See quot. 1933.) Also (written either as *huntaway* or as *hunt away*) as *vb.*

1913 [see *heading *vbl. sb.* 4 b]. **1933** L. G. D. Acland in *Press* (Christchurch, N.Z.) 28 Oct. 17/7 *Huntaway,* a dog whose work is to drive sheep forward when mustering. As a verb the word is used in two senses, illustrated in the sentences: 'That dog hunts away well' and 'I hunt away with that dog'. **1934** *Bulletin* (Sydney) 16 May 38/3 Rock, the kelpie leading-dog, and Bruce, the nondescript little hunt-away, had never possessed any aspirations towards leadership. **1931** T. A. Harper *Windy Island* (1934) iii. iii. 217 Vixen had turned her mob neatly over to Rough, who was hunting them away down the mountainside. **1934** J. Lilico *Sheep Dog Mem.* 27 The dogs would head, lead, huntaway, force and back. **1954** *Landfall* VIII. 221 Couple of times someone offered him big money for two good huntaways. **1961** B. Crump *Hang on a Minute* 74 They sold..two huntaway pups. **1966** Baker *Austral. Lang.* (ed. 2) iii. 73 A huntaway is sometimes known as a forcing dog. **1968** *N.Z. News* 28 Aug. 16/1 The huntaway barks loudly to shift sheep.

b. Nelson huntaway (see quots.). *N.Z.*

1941 Baker *N.Z. Slang* vi. 59 *Nelson huntaway,* a stone rolled down a hillside to move stock below instead of sending a dog out. **1949** P. Newton *High Country Days* 29 Brownie sent a boulder hurtling down the face—a 'Nelson huntaway'.

hunter. Add: **3. b.** The Jamaican cuckoo, *Hyetornis pluvialis.*

1847 Gosse & Hill *Birds Jamaica* 277 *Hunter.* Old Man.—Rainbird... The appellation of Rainbird is indiscriminately applied to both this and the preceding [sc. *Saurothera vetula*], as is, in a lesser degree, that of Old Man. I use a term by which I have heard it distinguished, ..perhaps derived from the perseverance with which it hunts..for its prey. **1960** J. Bond *Birds W. Indies* 116 Chestnut-bellied cuckoo. *Hyetornis pluvialis.* Local names: Old Man Bird; Hunter; Rain Bird.

5. c. hunter-spider = sense 3 a.

1867 *Amer. Naturalist* I. 409 This very large hunter-spider [*sc.* the tarantula] makes its appearance in Texas some years as early as the twenty-fifth of May.

d. hunter's green (see quot. 1957).

1872 *Young Englishwoman* Nov. 599/1 Sombre greens,..*chasseur,* or hunter's-green, myrtle, cypress. **1957** M. B. Picken *Fashion Dict.* 181/2 *Hunter's green,* dark, slightly yellowish green.

e. hunter-killer *a.,* designating a naval vessel or group of vessels equipped to locate and destroy enemy vessels, esp. submarines. Also as *sb.*

1948 *U.S. Naval Inst. Proc.* LXXIV. 505/2 The other two will be classified as 'hunter-killers'—destroyers with the prime purpose of tracking down submarines, instead of operating on convoy duty. **1950** *Jane's Fighting Ships 1950–51* 7 A new anti-submarine type of light cruiser, known as a hunter-killer ship, will be completed in 1951. **1957** *Times Lit. Suppl.* 20 Dec. 771/3 The escort carrier Guadalcanal and her 'hunter-killer' group of four escort destroyers. **1962** *Daily Tel.* 10 Dec. 18/4 Britain's first nuclear hunter-killer submarine, is expected to leave the ..yard of her builders,..on Wednesday or Thursday for sea-trials. **1972** *Sci. Amer.* July 16/3 A hunter-killer submarine is large enough to carry an array of hydrophones to produce a narrow listening beam for long-range detection.

hunterman (hʌ·ntəɹmæ̃n). [f. Hunter + Man *sb.*[1]] Used widely outside the British Isles as a local term for 'hunter, huntsman'.

1891 'Mark Twain' tr. *Hoffmann's Slovenly Peter* (1935), Behold the dreadful hunterman In all his fateful glory stand. **1907** W. Jekyll *Jamaican Song & Story* 137 Dory Dunn is a hunterman. **1913** *Chambers's Jrnl.* 22 Feb. 184/1 Nearly every village has its professional 'hunterman', whose duty it is to kill the larger game which do damage to the crops. **1922** H. B. Hermon-Hodge *Up against it in Nigeria* iv. 55 Huntermen are for the most part undependable. **1930** 'Greenhorn' *Tinker, Tailor* xi. 272 His hunterman came back to look for him and shot the python. **1933** *Amer. Speech* VIII. i. 50/1 *Hunterman,* hunter. One often sees this in country newspapers [of Ozarks]. **1954** G. Durrell *Bafut Beagles* vi. 116, I tink dis hunter man be best for all.

hunting, *vbl. sb.* Add: **1. d.** With *adv.*: also *hunting-down.*

1901 *Westm. Gaz.* 7 Sept. 5/1 Sweeping movements will give place to hunting-down tactics where the country favours the latter. **1945** *Tribune* 9 Nov. 11/1 The hunting-down of war criminals.

f. The action of a machine, instrument, system, etc., that is hunting (see *hunt *v.* 7 b); an undesirable oscillation about an equilibrium speed, position, or state.

1880 R. E. Crompton *Electr. Light for Industr. Use* 21 This causes a swinging or, as it is called by engine men, a 'hunting' action of the governor. **1894** *Rep. Brit. Assoc. Adv. Sci.* 759 If the isochronous governor works a slow-acting relay the hunting may be so serious that the steam supply alternates between complete cut-off and full supply. **1920** *Whittaker's Electr. Engineer's Pocket-bk.* (ed. 4) 223 If the damping is very small, oscillations or hunting may go on for a considerable time before the machine finally rotates steadily. **1932** *Discovery* Oct. 331/1 There was no suggestion of 'hunting' and the image remained exactly central in the [television] screen for the whole half hour. **1942** *Rev. Sci. Instruments* XIII. 218 The recording is easily accomplished at pen speeds of 12·7 cm per second across 25 cm of chart without 'hunting' taking place. **1943** *Electronic Engin.* XV. 438/2 A method for the determination of the power angle oscillations of a synchronous motor during hunting is described. **1950** *Gloss. Aeronaut. Terms* (*B.S.I.*) 8 *Hunting,* an uncontrolled oscillation about the flight path, the amplitude of which remains approximately constant. *Ibid.* 45 *Hunting,* angular oscillation of a [rotor] blade about the drag hinge. **1951** *Engineering* 6 Apr. 401/3 The train was derailed..because of a slight but periodic variation in the cant of the track which synchronised with the hunting periodicity of the engine. **1951** S. Deutsch *Theory & Design Television Receivers* xiii. 431 Hunting is revealed by a horizontal weaving or vibration of the picture. **1959** *Times* 27 Apr. (Rubber Industry Suppl.) p. vi/5 The control of the side-to-side swaying known to railway engineers as 'hunting'. **1968** *Practical Motorist* Dec. 459/1 *Hunting,* a rhythmical increase and decrease in the idling speed of an engine, caused by an over-rich mixture. **1971** *Nature* 2 Apr. 283/1 Society, regarded as a non-linear feedback system, is showing the signs of oscillation ('hunting') which one expects.

g. *Telephony.* An operation in which a selector or switch automatically goes through a group of lines until it reaches a free one and makes connection with it; now used esp. of the connection of a calling line with one of a group of outgoing lines.

1912 J. Poole *Pract. Telephone Handbk.* (ed. 5) xxxii. 528 There is no 'hunting' for disengaged lines as in the case of selectors. **1933** K. B. Miller *Telephone Theory & Pract.* III. v. 263 Automatic trunk hunting may be necessary to find an idle line. **1966** Rubin & Haller *Communication Switching Syst.* i. 31 In the Ericsson 500-line switch..the select motion is a rotation and the hunting action is radially outward to a free trunk.

3. a. *hunting boat, boot* (examples), *bridle, cap* (examples), *carpet, coat* (examples), *country* (later example), *excursion* (examples), *knife* (earlier and later examples), *path, pony, print, rifle, tie.*

1828 *Western Monthly Rev.* I. 577 The passengers of the hunting boats..saw him. **1894** Hunting boat [see *bidarka]. **1895** *Montgomery Ward Catal.* 521/1 Men's black English grain leather 'hunting boots', double sole, laced leg and instep. **1928** S. Sassoon *Mem. Fox-Hunting Man* 143, I was going to try on my new hunting clothes and my new hunting boots. **1957** M. B. Picken *Fashion Dict.* 181/2 *Hunting boot,* high, laced boot with waterproof sole. **1939–40** *Army & Navy Stores Catal.* p. xxxix, Hunting bridles. **1963** Bloodgood & Santini *Horseman's Dict.* 111 *Hunting bridle,* any bridle suitable for hunting. **1963** E. H. Edwards *Saddlery* iii. 32 Hunting bridles should be made of leather having plenty of substance and the width of the cheek will probably be ⅝ in. with the rein. **1814** J. Mayne *Jrnl.* (1909) 184 The postilions..do not, like our royal drivers, wear hunting-caps. **1946** M. C. Self *Horseman's Encycl.* 219 *Hunting cap,* the velvet cap worn by farmers, Masters and Servants of the hunt. **1931** A. U. Dilley *Oriental Rugs & Carpets* Pl. 9 (*caption*), Finest Extant Hunting Carpet, Middle Sixteenth Century. **1960** H. Hayward *Antique Coll.* 146/1 *Hunting carpets,* Persian carpets with elaborate hunting scenes, realistically depicted. **1789** R. F. Greville *Diary* 16 Jan. (1930) 171 Asked Me if I had my hunting Coat with Me. **1909** *Westm. Gaz.* 9 Oct. 15/1 Ladies..may always choose a little, short coat, known to French tailors as a hunting coat. **1921** *Daily Colonist* (Victoria, B.C.) 15 Oct. 10/1 (Advt.), Pheasant Shooting Begins..Hunting Coats, with front and rear game pockets, $8.75. **1928** S. Sassoon *Mem. Fox-Hunting Man.* 136 Stephen, who was wearing a pink silk cap and a long-skirted black hunting-coat, silently received from the groom the saddle and weight-cloth. **1946** M. C. Self *Horseman's Encycl.* 219 Nothing even faintly resembling the English hunting country exists in North America. **1801** A. Mackenzie *Voy. from Montreal* 113 The Indians went on an hunting excursion. **1856** M. J. Holmes *'Lena Rivers* xxvi. 282 He had gone off on a hunting excursion. **1803** in *Minnesota Hist.* (1940) XXI. 126 When the defendant came to pierce his tent with his hunting knife..the larger part of the goods had already been moved to the spot agreed upon. **1933** B. Willoughby *Alaskans All* 3 His flannel shirt, high laced boots, the hunting-knife in his belt..made it difficult for me to realize he was a priest. **1949** *Chicago Tribune* 22 June II. 1/4 A policeman took a 6 inch hunting knife from the waist of one of the white boys. **1820** in *Minnesota Hist.* (1942) XXIII. 249 We found a hunting path which..led directly to Sandy Lake. **1821** T. Nuttall *Jrnl. Trav. Arkansa 1819* 167 We here crossed by a hunting path. **1886** *Outing* Apr. 7/1, I was riding a well-trained hunting pony. **1967** N. Freeling *Strike Out* 72 He makes these series of kind of huntin' prints. **1973** M. Mackintosh *King & Two Queens* v. 76 Eighteenth-century English hunting prints hung on the pine-panelled walls. **1856** in *Kansas State Hist. Soc. Trans.* (1890) IV. 504 The marauders were well armed with muskets,..hunting rifles,..bowie-knives, etc. **1886** *Outing* Mar. 615 No hunting-rifles in the world possess greater accuracy. **1956** 'E. McBain' *Cop Hater* (1963) xix. 143 He said he'd shot himself while cleaning his hunting rifle. *c* **1840** Lady Wilton *Art of Needlework* xiii. 189 The Hibernian Tie: The Eastern Tie: The Hunting Tie: The Yankee Tie. **1907** *Yesterday's Shopping* (1969) p. xxxix, Hunting ties, ladies'.

b. hunting-box (earlier examples); **hunting tartan** (see quot. 1959); so **hunting Stewart tartan,** etc.

1799 *Times* 1 June 4/3 A Family Cottage, or Hunting Box, pleasantly situate in a sporting part of the country. **1814** Jane Austen *Mansf. Park* III. x. 208 Some small hunting-box in the vicinity of every thing so dear. **1855** A. Stanley *Let.* 8 Sept. (1927) iii. 74 The carpets are Royal Stewart Tartan and green Hunting Stewart. **1864** Queen Victoria *Let.* 26 Mar. in R. Fulford *Dearest Mama* (1968) 312 What is Anna's dress made of? I am going to send her a Hunting Stewart velvet. **1871** *Monthly Packet* Oct. 396 Their new winter frocks of Hunting Stewart tartan. **1959** Bain & MacDougall *Clans & Tartans* (ed. 4) 28 Hunting tartans are worn for sport and outdoor activities. Brown or some other dark hue is the predominant colour. When a Clan possessed a brightly coloured tartan it was unsuitable for hunting purposes, and hunting setts [patterns] were devised to make the wearer less conspicuous. The colours were arranged so that, when concealed in the heather, the tartan blended with the surroundings. **1969** O. Hesky *Sequin Syndicate* x. 102 A kimono in the colours of the Royal Stuart hunting tartan.

hunting, *ppl. a.* Add: **b. hunting spider** (later examples); **hunting wasp,** a wasp that preys upon other insects.

1916 A. T. de Mattos tr. J. H. Fabre (*title*) The hunting wasp. **1925** R. W. G. Hingston in E. F. Norton *Fight for Everest, 1924* 287 Beetles and hunting-spiders found a shelter on it [*sc.* a moraine]. **1928** —— *Problems of Instinct* 100 Hunting wasps..sting their victims with surgical precision. **1941** W. S. Bristowe *Comity of Spiders* II. v. 230 Some of these hunting spiders seek their prey by day and others by night. **1948** 'J. Crompton' *Hunting Wasp* i. 17 A large number of the hunting wasps sing at their work. **1964** V. B. Wigglesworth *Life of Insects* xiii. 227 The hunting wasp *Philanthus* stocks its solitary nest solely with honey-bees. **1966** E. Palmer *Plains of Camdeboo* xiv. 233 On the farm we know most of the diurnal species as jagspinnekoppe or hunting spiders.

Huntingdon (hʌ·ntɪŋdən). The title of Selina, Countess of *Huntingdon* (1707–91), used in (*Lady* or *Countess of*) *Huntingdon('s) Connection* to designate a Calvinistic Methodist sect founded by her. So **Huntingdo·nian** *a.* and *sb.*

[**1773** J. Wesley *Let.* 22 Oct. (1931) VI. 51, I am afraid

Lady Huntingdon's preachers will do little good wherever they go. They are wholly swallowed up in that detestable doctrine of Predestination, and can talk of nothing else.] *a* **1800** M. Robinson *Mem.* (1803) I. 90 Though Mr Harris was not a disciple of the Huntingdonian School, he was a constant church visitor on every Sunday. **1874** J. H. Blunt *Dict. Sects* 205/1 *Huntingdon Connexion*, a sect of Calvinistic Methodists... Its history dates from the year 1748. **1884** *Encycl. Dict.* IV. 241/2 The denomination which rose out of his zealous labours was generally called ..the Countess of Huntingdon's Connexion... Called also Lady Huntingdon's Connexion and Huntingdonians. **1970** *Brewer's Dict. Phr. & Fable* (rev. ed.) 556/2 *Huntingdonians*, members of 'the Countess of Huntingdon's Connexion', a sect of Calvinistic Methodists founded in 1748... The churches founded by the countess..are mostly affiliated with the Congregational Union.

hunting-ground. Add: **b.** (Earlier example.)

1877 Lady C. Schreiber *Jrnl.* 22 Mar. (1911) II. 6 Our favourite hunting-ground, Holland, appeared particularly fruitful.

c. (Earlier and later examples.)

1826 J. F. Cooper *Last of Mohicans* (1831) 400 A young man has gone to the happy hunting grounds. **1938** D. du Maurier *Rebecca* ii. 13 My faithful Jasper has gone to the happy hunting grounds. **1972** *Nature* 17 Mar. 98/1 The effect of liquid sodium on other metals has been a particularly happy hunting ground for chemists.

Huntingtonian (hʌntiŋtōᵘ·niăn). [f. the name of William *Huntington* (1745–1813), an Antinomian preacher.] An adherent of the teachings of William Huntington.

1815 J. Blackner *Hist. Nottingham* iv. 114 Bethel chapel is now called Providence chapel; and is occupied by an inconsiderable party of Huntingtonians, without a regular preacher, they being adherents to the tenets of the late William Huntington, of coal-heaving celebriety [*sic*]. **1921** M. A. Canney *Encycl. Relig.* 184/2 *Huntingtonians*, the followers of William Huntington (1745–1813).

Huntington's chorea. *Med.* [f. the name of George *Huntington* (1851–1916), American neurologist, who described it in 1872 + Chorea.] A rare hereditary disease of the brain manifested in middle age and characterized by irregular body movements, disturbance of speech, and progressive dementia. Also *Huntington's disease.*

1889 *Jrnl. Nerv. & Mental Dis.* XVI. 69 To Huntington has generally been accorded the credit of first describing hereditary chorea, and writers even speak of the affection as 'Huntington's chorea'. **1892** *Jrnl. Mental Sci.* XXXVIII. 560 Cases of hereditary chorea (Huntington's disease). **1969** *New Scientist* 10 July 80/2 The onset of Huntington's chorea usually occurs rather late in reproductive life, at around 40 years of age. **1972** *New Yorker* 29 Jan. 30/3 Woody Guthrie..died, in 1967, after a fifteen-year battle with Huntington's disease.

huntite (hʌ·ntəit). *Min.* [f. the name of Walter Frederick *Hunt* (b. 1882), American mineralogist + -ite¹.] A white carbonate of magnesium and calcium, $CaMg_3(CO_3)_4$.

1953 G. T. Faust in *Amer. Mineralogist* XXXVIII. 4 (*heading*) Huntite, $Mg_3Ca(CO_3)_4$, a new mineral. **1968** *Nature* 28 Dec. 1309/2 Investigations of sediments from the hypersaline environment of the Tuz Gölü, a seasonal salt lake in Central Anatolia, Turkey.., showed that huntite, $CaMg_3(CO_3)_4$, dolomite and magnesite are often present in the playa muds. **1973** *Nature* 5 Jan. 17/2 In next Monday's *Nature Physical Science* (January 8), Veen and Arndt describe for the first time the occurrence in soils of the mineral huntite, $CaMg_3(CO_3)_4$. *Ibid.* 17/3 Alias pahn-jahn, huntite powder is a white pigment which the Aborigines prefer to kaolin-based paint for personal and other decorative purposes.

huntsman. Add: **3. huntsman's cup, huntsman's horn** (examples); **huntsman spider**, a spider of the family Sparassidæ, which is widely distributed in warm regions.

1848 A. Gray *Man. Bot.* 25 S[arracenia] purpurea, L. (Sidesaddle-flower. Huntsman's Cup.) **1864** E. W. Paige *Catal. Flowering Plants Schenectady County* 7 Sarracenia Purpurea. Common Huntsman's Horn. **1936** K. C. McKeown *Spider Wonders Austral.* v. 79 The Huntsman Spiders, or, as they are more popularly known, Triantelopes, do not seem to fear man. **1945** C. H. Curran *Insects of Pacific World* xi. 293 The huntsman-spiders of the tropics include as one of their best known members the domestic *Heteropoda venatoria.* **1954** C. J. Hylander *Macmillan Wild Flower Bk.* 149 Common Pitcher-plant. *Sarracenia purpurea.* This species is also known in various parts of its range as Sidesaddle Flower and Huntsman's Cup. *Ibid.*, Trumpets. *Sarracenia flava.* The tubular insect-catching leaves of this species are longer and more slender, looking more like horns than pitchers. (In fact, another common name is Huntsman's Horn.) **1967** *Sunday Mail Mag.* (Brisbane) 9 Apr. 2/5 There was the Huntsman spider who adopted us and took up residence behind a painting in the living-room.

hunyak (hʌ·nyæk). *U.S.* Also honyock, -er. [f. Hungarian *a.* and *sb.* after Polack.] = *hunk *sb.*³ (See also quot. 1941.)

Only in disparaging use.

1911 W. P. Dillingham *Dict. Races* 92 *Magyar*, Hungarian Hun, or Hunyak in popular language. **1919** S. Lewis *Free Air* (1924) ix. 94, I could buy out half these Honyockers! **1938** 'E. Queen' *Four of Hearts* (1939) 17 Tossing away the stockholders' dough like a hunyak on Saturday night. **1941** *Sat. Even. Post* 7 June 29/1 'Honyocks', the Yankee neighbors called them [*sc.* immigrants from Central Europe]. 'Honyocker' came to be..generally applied to any farmer who tries to raise grain and livestock in the high prairies of the Northwest. **1943** H. A. Smith *Life in Putty Knife Factory* xii. 185 Speaking as a pure-bred honyock out of the Middle West. **1957** P. Frank *Seven Days to Never* vii. 201 She cooked a Hungarian goulash better than any he'd tasted at a hunyak table. **1958** H. B. Allen in *Publ. Amer. Dial. Soc.* xxx. 8 *Honyock*.. a boorish and uncouth farmer of foreign background. *Honyocker* (rarely *honyock*) was applied, on the contrary, to anyone who fenced in the open range. **1965** P. De Vries *Let me count the Ways* xii. 160 It was a kind of protest—the passionate outcry of honyocks everywhere.

Hupa (hū·pă, hū·pǭ). Also 9 Hoopah, Hoopa. [Yurok *hupǭ* Hupa (i.e. from the name for this tribe in the language of their neighbours, the Yurok). The *-p-* is a glottalized consonant (Dr. Sturtevant).] A tribe of Athapascan Indians in California; a member of this tribe; also their language. Also *attrib.* or as *adj.*

1853 H. R. Schoolcraft *Hist. & Stat. Information Indian Tribes* III. 139 The lower Trinity tribe is, as well as the river itself, known to the Klamaths by the name of Hoopah. **1872** *Overland Monthly* Aug. 157/1 The Hoopas closely resemble the Cahrocs in *physique.* **1885** *Rep. Indian Affairs* (U.S.) 6 It would be a benefit not only to the Government but to the Hoopa Indians, if their reservation were abandoned. **1903** G. W. James *Indian Basketry* (ed. 3) 53 On the lower Trinity River are the Hupas, the main reservation being in the Hoopa valley. **1921** [see *Apache 1]. **1936** J. Kantor *Objective Psychol. Gram.* xvii. 244 In Athapascan (Hupa) the prefix *neen* denotes past time in both substantives and verbs. **1965** *Canad. Jrnl. Ling.* Spring 132 The Wailaki and Hupa correspondent forms.

hurdle, *sb.* Add: **1. b.** Also *pl.*, an athletic event consisting of a hurdle-race.

1887 T. B. Reed *Fifth Form St. Dominic's* i. 8 He is certain..to win the mile and the 'hurdles' at the Athletic Sports. **1897** *Isis* (Oxf.) 13 Nov. 63/1 Three events..: hundred yards, broad jump, and hurdles. **1905** *Athlete* Aug. 80/1 R. S. Stromach retained his title in the hurdles. **1930** *Daily Express* 8 Sept. 9/5 In the 80 metres hurdles. **1948** [see *clock *v.*¹ 1 b]. **1973** *Country Life* 13 Sept. 693/2 The first peak for the British crowd was the 400 metres hurdles.

e. *fig.* An obstacle or difficulty.

1924 R. Campbell *Flaming Terrapin* ii. 34 Their slim keels like horses bounded free To leap the foamy hurdles of the sea. **1928** —— *Wayzgoose* i. 28 O'er lingual hurdles coax your tongues to prance. **1966** *Listener* 6 Jan. 13/2 Family planning has some major..hurdles to overcome. **1969** *Radio Times* 24 July 23/5 Andrew Cooper describes the hurdles to be cleared by business men eager to win the prize of a seat on the Board of Directors. **1971** *Nature* 11 June 346/2 The shuttle's hardest hurdle, however, is in the Senate.

3. hurdle-race (earlier example).

1836 W. Dyott *Diary* 23 Mar. (1907) II. 228 Lichfield March races;..a hurdle race, a new-fashioned sport much in vogue with the fox-hunters.

hurdle, *v.* Add: **4.** *intr.* To run a hurdle-race; to jump over an obstacle, as in a hurdle-race. Also *fig.* Hence **hu·rdling** *vbl. sb.*; also *attrib.*

1896 Ade *Artie* vii. 60 Artie did not know the tune or the words, so he merely whistled it on speculation, and when he came to the doubtful parts he hurdled. **1897** *Encycl. Sport* I. 52/2 Few good sprinters will take to hurdling, as there is little doubt that the mechanical and artificial action necessary in hurdling interferes with speed on the flat. *Ibid.* 53/1 Hurdling and long jumping ability often go together. **1912** [see *field events* (*field *sb.* 21)]. **1923** R. D. Paine *Comrades of Rolling Ocean* xv. 256 He hurdled aboard this True American steamer as soon as he hit New York. **1928** *Daily Mail* 31 July 11/5 When Lord Burghley hurdled easily to victory. **1955** *Times* 13 Aug. 4/2 Higham hurdled with great élan.

hurdy-gurdy. Add: **2.** (Earlier example.)

1868 *Rep. J. Ross Brown on Min. Resources west of Rocky Mts.* (U.S. Treasury Dept.) 101 In 1866 they struck into pay and erected a 10-stamp mill, which is driven by a hurdy-gurdy wheel.

4. hurdy-gurdy girl *N. Amer. Hist.*, a dance hostess in a hurdy-gurdy house; **hurdy-gurdy house** *N. Amer. Hist.*, a disreputable type of cheap dance-hall.

[**1860** C. E. De Long in *Calif. Hist. Soc. Q.* (1931) X. 256 Rode over to young Hill's to see Tom Smith married to a hurdy gurdy.] **1865** *Harper's Mag.* June 4/1 Hurdy-gurdy girls are singing bacchanalian songs. **1958** P. Berton *Klondike* 6 A circus parade of camp-followers crowded in upon them, saloon-keepers, and hurdy-gurdy girls. **1973** *Islander* (Victoria, B.C.) 18 Nov. 12/3 A dance with a 'hurdy-gurdy' girl cost $10 a whirl! **1866** *Beadle's Monthly* Oct. 280/1 Hurdy-gurdy houses, with dancing-girls, music, and long bars. **1874** T. B. Aldrich *Prudence Palfrey* vii. 115 At sundown the dance-house would open, —the Hurdy-Gurdy House, as it was called. **1955** P. F. Sharp *Whoop-up Country* 192 The saloons and hurdy-gurdy houses of Benton, Macleod, and Calgary.

hu·rdy-gu·rdyish, *a.* Resembling the sound of a hurdy-gurdy; also *fig.*

1923 *Daily Mail* 22 June 6 The concertina or harmonium music is too hurdy-gurdyish. **1931** *Observer* 27 Sept. 10 A cheap, hurdy-gurdyish fellow.

hurlbutite (hɒ̄·ɹlbʌtəit). *Min.* [f. the name of Cornelius Searle *Hurlbut* (b. 1906), American mineralogist + -ite¹.] A colourless or greenish-white phosphate of calcium and beryllium, $Be_2Ca(PO_4)_2$.

1952 M. E. Mrose in *Amer. Mineralogist* XXXVII. 931 The mineral here described as hurlbutite was first found as a large broken crystal on the dump at the pegmatite known as the Smith mine. **1961** *Soviet Physics—Doklady* V. 1143 The structures of danburite $CaB_2Si_2O_8$ and hurlbutite are similar to the structure of the feldspars, in particular to anorthite $CaAl_2Si_2O_8$. **1968** I. Kostov *Mineral.* 449 Faheyite is hexagonal, occurring in acicular crystals, babefphite tetragonal.., hurlbutite orthorhombic.

hurler. Add: **5.** A pitcher at baseball. *N. Amer. slang.*

1926 *Daily Colonist* (Victoria, B.C.) 22 July 12/3 Fifty-six runs were scored in a Three-I League baseball game yesterday in which Springfield defeated Peoria... Thirteen hurlers appeared. **1965** O. Nash in *Times Lit. Suppl.* 25 Nov. 1036/5 When I am told that the hurler kicks, rocks, and either deals or delivers. **1968** *Globe & Mail* (Toronto) 10 July 26/5 But in a season dominated by pitchers, the hurlers once again reigned supreme.

Hurler² (hɒ̄·ɹləɹ). The name of Gertrud *Hurler*, German pædiatrician (qualified 1894), used in the possessive (and also *attrib.*) in *Hurler('s) disease, syndrome* = *gargoylism 2.

1937 W. R. Ashby et al. in *Brain* LX. 175 We share the dislike of many workers for eponymous titles, but since the other four diseases in this group have..been designated by the names of those writers who have contributed largely to their elucidation, we consider that at this juncture it would be inadvisable to depart from this practice. We suggest, therefore, in place of the title 'Gargoylism' the title 'Hurler's disease'. **1938** *Jrnl. Pediatrics* XII. 579 (*heading*) Hurler's syndrome (gargoylism). **1970** Cohen & Cathcart in Keefer & Wilkins *Medicine* xxxv. 687 (*heading*) Hurler syndrome (gargoylism). *Ibid.*, The two clinical forms of Hurler's disease (one an autosomal recessive and the other a sex-linked recessive) are currently being related more specifically to these mucopolysaccharide abnormalities.

Huron (hiūᵊ·rǫn). Also 7 Hiroon. [Fr., f. earlier *hure*, rough hair of the head.] A confederation of five Iroquoian tribes formerly inhabiting a region adjacent to Lake Huron; a member of one of these tribes; also their language. Also *attrib.* or as *adj.*

1658 F. Gorges in *Maine Hist. Soc. Coll.* (1847) II. 67 The Hiroons, who being neuters are friends both to the one [*sc.* the Iroquois] and the other [*sc.* the French]. **1756** A. Butler *Lives Saints* II. 650 The saint wrote earnestly to the general of the Society, desiring to be employed on a mission to the barbarous Hurons and Iroquois in Canada. **1782** 'J. H. St. John de Crèvecœur' *Lett. from Amer. Farmer* (1783) iv. 90 The Nattic, like the Huron, in the north-western parts of this continent, must have been the most prevailing one [*sc.* language] in this region. **1786** *Mem. Amer. Acad. Arts & Sci.* II. i. 125 The Huron, or Wyandot language having no affinity to the Shawanese, Delawares, and other nations. **1789** [see *Five Nations*]. **1823** J. S. Mill *Autobiogr.* (1924) 267 No one, I apprehend, would insult the understanding of this Society..by maintaining..that the Hurons and the Iroquois are the happiest and the most enlightened of mankind. **1832** 'M. Doyle' *Hints on Emigration to Upper Canada* (ed. 2) 17 The soil in the Huron territory is a rich sandy loam. **1845** [see *buckle *sb.* 1 e]. **1880** A. H. Sayce *Introd. Sci. of Lang.* II. ix. 291 The Hurons of North America believe that the souls of the departed turn into turtle-doves. **1933** L. Bloomfield *Lang.* iv. 72 The Iroquoian family..includes, among others, the Huron (or Wyandot) language. **1959** *Listener* 9 July 75/2 He [*sc.* the American writer] can always feel himself to be a noble savage, a Huron, confronted by the degenerate, corrupt, or over-sophisticated stock from which he sprang. **1973** *Ibid.* 25 Oct. 549/1 The Jesuits..negotiated with the Hurons and Iroquois, as they treated with the *daimyos.*

hurrah. Add: **4.** *attrib.* or *adj.* in various *slang* or *colloq.* uses = shouting hurrah, uproarious, blindly enthusiastic; joyous, 'glad'.

1835 *Franklin Repos.* (Chambersburg, Pa.) 2 June 2/3 The New York delegation cared nothing for principles! To them..the men who could secure for the ticket and for *Martin Van Buren* the *hurra boys* was every thing! **1836** *Congress. Globe* 17 Feb., App. 115 [Some have declared] that his election had been brought about by the 'hurrah boys', and those who knew just enough to shout 'hurrah for Jackson!' **1903** *N.Y. Even. Post* 30 Oct. 16 Added to this solid element is the hurrah crowd whose enthusiasm has a venal tone. **1907** N. Munro *Daft Days* xii. 102 'And what are you doing with your hurrah clothes on?' 'I like to put on my Sunday clothes when I'm writing Charles.' **1909** *Daily Chron.* 20 July 1/2 'Hurrah-boats', as the bluejacket aptly calls excursion steamers. **1925** Fraser & Gibbons *Soldier & Sailor Words* 124 *Hurrah boats*, a Navy term for the pleasure steamers of touring trippers that go round the Fleet at Naval Reviews, usually cheering as they pass ships. **1926** *Flynn's* 16 Jan. 640/1, I had many a pal among th' touts and hurrah boys. **1928** *Daily Express* 4 Dec. 10/3 'Hurrah boys' are college students. **1964** N. Freeling *Double-Barrel* v. 176 We seem to have got quite a hurrah letter from the burgomaster. And there was a hint that I may be promoted.

Hurrian (hu·riăn), *sb.* and *a.* Also Harrian; (less freq.) Harri, Hurri; Kharri, Khurri, -ian. [f. Hittite and Assyrian *Ḫar·ri*, *Ḫur·ri* + -an.] **A.** *sb.* **a.** Name of a widespread non-

Semitic people in the Middle East during the second and third millennia B.C., sometimes identified with the Horites. Also, a member of this people. **b.** The language (written in cuneiform) of this people, not known to be related to any other language. **B.** *adj.* Of or pertaining to the Hurrians or their language. Hence **Hu·rrianize** *v. trans.*, to make Hurrian in form or character.

1911 *Encycl. Brit.* XVIII. 182/2 It is clear that Mesopotamia had now a further new element in its population, bearing apparently the name Kharri. **1928** C. DAWSON *Age of Gods* 302 Harrian is practically identical with the language of the people of Mitanni. *Ibid.*, The dominant element in Mitanni was..Indo-Iranian, in origin, but there is no trace of this in the Harrian language. **1929** J. GARSTANG *Hittite Empire* ii. 34 North of it [*sc.* Assyria].. was Alshe, a Harrian dependency; while..eastern Taurus was apparently wholly in possession of the Harrians, whose seat must probably be sought in Armenia itself, possibly in the neighbourhood of Lake Van. **1930** *Dublin Rev.* Jan. 9 Hurrian was one of the languages of the eastern part of the Hittite Empire. *Ibid.* 11 Nahmaulel..may be either Hurrianized Semitic, or wholly 'foreign'—*i.e.*, presumably Caucasian or Hurrian. **1939** L. H. GRAY *Foundations of Lang.* 380 Khurrian (or Kharrian). **1944** I. J. GELB *Hurrians & Subarians* i. 1 Both Hurrians and Subarians, their lands and their languages, are mentioned frequently in the cuneiform inscriptions discovered in the early 19th century during the British excavations at Kuyunjik. **1948** A. L. KROEBER *Anthropol.* (rev. ed.) xvii. 713 Soon after 1500 the Harri established themselves for a few brief centuries in Mitanni on the upper Euphrates. **1949** W. F. ALBRIGHT *Archaeol. of Palestine* viii. 183 The Hurrian language was a complex agglutinative tongue, resembling Sumerian or Turkish more closely in structure than either Semitic or Indo-European, but not related to any of them. **1952** O. R. GURNEY *Hittites* i. 26 In 1457 B.C. the Hurrian domination was brought to an end by the victories of Tuthmosis III in his eighth campaign. **1957** *Chambers's Encycl.* VII. 156/1 The foundation of strong Amorite kingdoms..was followed by the establishment of Hurrian states on the upper Euphrates. *Ibid.*, The Hittites..took little part at first in the struggle in Syria between Egypt and the Hurrians. **1960** K. M. KENYON *Archaeol. in Holy Land* vii. 182 There are the Ḫurri, who seem to have established themselves on the middle Euphrates at the beginning of the millennium. **1972** *Times* 31 Aug. 12/6 David Willstar..succeeded in deciphering the musical notation of Hurrian hymns found on pieces of clay in the French dig at Rash-ash-shamra, dating from 1300 B.C.

hurricane. Add: **2. c.** A space from which trees, etc., have been cleared by the force of a hurricane. (Earlier *hurricane ground*: see 3 in Dict.) *U.S.*

1735 J. HEMPSTEAD *Diary* (1901) 291 The Stack..was made in the Hurrycane this Side the Swamp. **1833** [see *DRIVE *sb.* 1 c]. **1891** W. F. SWASEY *Early Days & Men Calif.* 15 In Missouri, cause and effect had been blended in the common designation of 'hurricane'.

3. *hurricane season* (earlier Amer. example); **hurricane-deck** (earlier U.S. example); **hurricane-lantern** = *hurricane-lamp*; **hurricane roof** = *hurricane-deck*; **hurricane wind**, a very strong wind associated with a tropical cyclone or hurricane; also, any wind of hurricane force.

1833 *Niles' Reg.* XLIV. 261/1 The hull of the boat sunk, leaving a part of the hurricane deck..floating on the surface. **1903** *Motoring Ann.* 306 A hurricane-lantern, the highly inflammable vapour of petrol, and a 'flash-back', resulted in the total destruction of the car. **1954** G. DURRELL *Bafut Beagles* ix. 166 In among the twinkling hurricane lanterns they were all dancing the polka. **1839** *Picayune* (New Orleans) 29 Mar. 2/2 The snag went through the guards, cabin and hurricane roofs. **1883** *Century Mag.* June 222/1 The..steamers..hidden to their hurricane roofs in cargoes of cotton bales. **1740** W. STEPHENS *Jrnl.* 26 Oct. in *Colonial Rec. Georgia* (1908) IV. Suppl. 18 The two Frigates..being apprehensive of the hurricane Season, retired into a safe Harbour at Charles-Town. **1921** J. W. REDWAY *Handbk. Meteorol.* xiii. 156 Hurricane winds at Galveston were estimated to have a velocity of 125 miles per hour. **1923** [see *GALE *sb.*³ 1 a]. **1954** G. T. TREWARTHA *Introd. Climate* (ed. 3) v. 209 In large storms in the western North Atlantic, the diameter of the hurricane winds may exceed 100 miles.

hurroo, *int.* (*sb.*). Add: **2.** *Austral.* = *hooroo* (s.v. *HOORAY *int.*).

1913 J. STEPHENS *Here are Ladies* 102 [He] called hurroo to the boys, and sauntered out of the place with a great deal of dignity and one week's wages in cash. **1942** E. LANGLEY *Pea Pickers* II. viii. 171 'Hurrooo!' Off he went, through the dead gums, to catch the boat to Bairnsdale.

hurry, *sb.* Add: **5. b.** (Earlier examples.)

1778 F. BURNEY *Evelina* II. xiii. 102 He won't put his tricks upon me again, in a hurry. **1812** LADY LYTTELTON *Let.* 28 Apr. in *Corr.* (1912) 132 That, you see, is very neat, and sounds as if it would not be forgotten in a hurry.

8. hurry call (orig. *U.S.*), a call for immediate help in an emergency; a request for immediate action.

1901 *Munsey's Mag.* XXIV. 798/1 If it was a hurry call, she would send them to Gilchrist. **1908** G. H. LORIMER *Jack Spurlock* i. 11 In answer to a hurry-call from his wife to get rich. **1915** WODEHOUSE *Something Fresh* iii. 73 His friends..send in a hurry-call to police headquarters. **1938** F. D. SHARPE *Sharpe of Flying Squad* v. 63 A wireless 'hurry call' was flashed out from the Yard and a Flying Squad car raced to the house. **1964** WODEHOUSE *Frozen Assets* ix. 160 Percy would be sending out hurry calls for the police.

hurrygraph (hʌ·rigrɑf). *U.S.* [f. HURRY *sb.* + -GRAPH after PHOTOGRAPH *sb.*] Something done, produced, or experienced in a hurry, esp. a hasty glance or fleeting impression.

1851 *Oquawka* (Ill.) *Spectator* 3 June 1/1 Just as we are 'putting up' this hurry graph a flat boat is passing up First street laden with several hundred sacks of grain. **1886** *Cassell's Family Mag.* June 417/1 Idyllic countryside stations,..the town-tired traveller catches 'hurry-graphs' of them sufficiently tempting for him to wish that the 'limited mail' were a City omnibus. **1887** J. J. HISSEY *Holiday on Road* 331 The traveller by rail..notices only its beauty [i.e. of the country] from the 'hurrygraphs' he gets. **1918** *Hist. Amer. Lit.* I. iii. 242 Fleeting impressions, 'dashes at life', ephemera, 'hurrygraphs' were his forte.

hu·rry-up. *colloq.* [f. vbl. phr. *to hurry up*, HURRY *v.* 2.] **1.** Used *attrib.*: involving or requiring haste; completed in a hurry. **hurry-up wagon**, one equipped to act in an emergency; a police van. *U.S.*

1893 W. K. POST *Harvard Stories* 118 The manager.. told him to send for a hurry-up wagon, and run us all in. **1902** H. L. WILSON *Spenders* 466 He would not be compelled to seek one of those 'hurry-up' lunch places with its clamour and crowd. **1907** *Putnam's Monthly* July 487/1 A hurry-up telegram. **1916** B. HALL *Diary* 23 Sept. in Hall & Niles *One Man's War* (1929) xxiv. 191 He had to..wait for some hurry-up repairs. **1930** *Dixon* (Ill.) *Evening Telegraph* 24 Sept. 2/2 It is hoped there will be a large attendance at the 'hurry-up' meeting this evening. **1943** *Copper Camp* 191 A frantic bartender called the police and Callahan was once more looking out of the hurry-up wagon on his way to the City Hall. **1949** *Sunday World-Herald Mag.* (Omaha) 13 Feb. 5/2 It is often necessary to make a hurry-up call to a registered donor who is known to have the right type of blood.

2. Used as simple *sb.*: an encouragement or demand to hurry up.

1944 J. H. FULLARTON *Troop Target* I. vii. 61 Let's give 'em a bit of a hurry up, Jock. **1952** S. KAUFFMANN *Philanderer* (1953) xi. 186 Ordinarily he would have been irritated to learn that Benjamin (and therefore Tappan) had not yet looked at his material—especially after the big hurry-up they'd given him. **1956** H. GOLD *Man who was not with It* (1965) iv. 32 The hurry-up which the sight of death gives us. **1966** BAKER *Austral. Lang.* (ed. 2) x. 218 *Give* (someone) *a bit of hurry up*, to demand or encourage prompt action.

hurt, *v.* Add: **3. c.** Of an injured limb, etc.: to be the source of pain to (one). (Cf. the corresponding intr. sense 8.)

1850 F. E. SMEDLEY *Frank Fairleigh* xxxiv. 280, I gave that [*sc.* the ankle] a twist somehow, and it hurts me dreadfully. **1871** *Two Little Bruces* viii. 76 My arm hurts me most. **1911** G. B. SHAW *Doctor's Dilemma* I. 12 Sometimes I think it's my heart: sometimes I suspect my spine. It doesnt exactly hurt me; but it unsettles me completely.

8. (Later examples.)

1902 *Dialect Notes* II. 237 *Hurt*, v. i., to ache; to pain. **1970** J. HANSEN *Fadeout* (1972) x. 83 I'm sorry you're hurting... But I'm glad I found you. **1972** *N.Y. Times* 4 June 4/5 When I heard that first lap time..I thought I'd be hurting.

hurt, *ppl. a.* Add: **c.** Of an inanimate thing: injured, damaged. *U.S. colloq.*

1930 *Publishers' Weekly* 15 Feb. 863 The annual 'hurt book' sales.

hurtness (hʌ̆·ɹtnės). [f. HURT *ppl. a.* + -NESS.] The state of being hurt.

1909 *Daily Chron.* 12 Oct. 7/3 Her voice conveyed the gentlest intimation of hurtness. **1922** JOYCE *Ulysses* 341 She kissed away the hurtness.

husband, *sb.* Add: **6. a.** (*b*) *husband-catching, -hunter, -seeking.*

1899 *Daily News* 26 Sept. 7/5 One of the greatest reasons of my contempt for them is their husband-catching propensities. **1949** M. MEAD *Male & Female* i. 7 In some societies it is girls for whom parents must collect a dowry or make husband-catching magic. **1905** *To-Day* 8 Mar. 173/1 She will demand a better article than the mere husband-hunter has been able to stand out for. **1932** *Times Lit. Suppl.* 21 Jan. 40/4 Arabella Trefoil is a husband-hunter of shameless duplicity and greed. **1899** *Daily News* 26 Sept. 7/5 Their object in life is..plain—husband seeking.

c. Combinations with *husbands'*, in specialized senses: as **husbands' boat, train,** etc., in former times a means of transport run chiefly for the convenience of men wishing to join their wives on holiday, esp. applied to ships, etc., run on Saturday; **husband's tea** *colloq.*, very weak tea.

1869 *Porcupine* XI. 172/2 Passengers by the 'husbands' boat' are more heavily laden with provisions. **1870** *London Soc.* XVIII. 170 The Husbands' boat can carry lovers too! **1909** *Daily Chron.* 24 July 8/6 The New Palace Steamers announce that their p.s. Koh-i-noor will be making the 'husband's boat' trip to-day as usual. **1874** HOTTEN *Slang Dict.* s.v. *Water-bewitched*, Sometimes very weak tea is called 'husband's tea'. **1886** A. HORNBLOW tr. *Normand's Splashes from Parisian Ink-Pot* 163 A special train, the husband's train, would permit him to arrive at Tréport the same night.

d. husband–wife *a.*, pertaining to or involving a husband and his wife.

1956 J. M. MOGEY *Family & Neighbourhood* 61 'My wife trusts me' indicates excellent husband–wife adjustment. **1959** *Encounter* July 73/1 [This book] is by a husband–wife duet of French journalists. **1960** *Guardian* 14 Apr. 8/6 The quintessential husband–wife relationship. **1965** *Language* XLI. 124 The husband–wife team of Pavle and Milka Ivić.

husbandom (hʌ·zbăndəm). *rare.* [f. HUSBAND *sb.* + -DOM.] The position or condition of a husband, married state (of a man).

1895 HARDY *Jude* III. ix. 236 'Wifedom has not yet annihilated you.'..'Nor has husbandom you, so far as I can see!' **1926** *New Republic* 12 May 358 If husbandom and fatherhood are still being practiced when he comes to maturity.

hush, *sb.*² Add: **1. b.** (Later examples.) Also *attrib.* and *Comb.*

1917 T. E. LAWRENCE *Home Lett.* (1954) 336, I wonder what the censor will make of this letter?.. There is a 'Hush' policy over the Red Sea and Arabia. **1917** H. G. WELLS *Let.* Nov. in *Exper. Autobiogr.* (1934) II. ix. 711 In Britain and France 'hush' in the interests of diplomacy is being organized with increasing violence. **1919** H. F. B. WHEELER *War in Underseas* 317 Mighty 'hush' ships which lived and moved..on the surface of great waters. **1920** *Argus* (Melbourne) 29 May 6 Time seems to have left..no surviving link between the frigate of Trafalgar and the 'hush-boat' of to-day. **1930** *Publishers' Weekly* 31 May 2735/2 Youngsters that are reared on the 'hush plan'. **1968** *Guardian* 31 July 6/6 It's still a source of Labour amazement that the Harry Nicholas scheme didn't leak in advance of the coup. Nicholas ringleaders maintained unique hush, and may do so again.

3. *Phonetics.* The sibilant [ʃ] or [ʒ]. Also *attrib.* and *Comb.*

1933 L. BLOOMFIELD *Lang.* vi. 100 These hushes or abnormal sibilants are separate phonemes [š, ž], as in *shin* [šin], *vision* [ˈvižn̩]. **1953** *Archivum Linguisticum* V. II. 68 The distinction between hiss- (Fr. *sifflantes*) and hush-sibilants (Fr. *chuintantes*) emerges..between the 'complementary' Indo-European types Latvian and Lithuanian. **1964** E. PALMER tr. *Martinet's Elem. Gen. Ling.* iii. 64 We obtain the following classes:..'apical' t d n; 'hiss' s z; 'hush' š ž.

hush, *a.* Add: **b.** Secret. Cf. *HUSH-HUSH.

This use merges with *HUSH *sb.*² 1 b *attrib.*

1944 H. CROOME *You've gone Astray* xxii. 218 A tremendous journalistic job..something important and hush. **1945** N. STREATFEILD *Saplings* i. 10 'I've got some new gadgets to make...' 'What sort of things?' 'It's all a bit hush.' **1957** 'J. WYNDHAM' *Midwich Cuckoos* vi. 50, I don't know what goes on at The Grange, but I do know that it is very hush. **1966** *Economist* 9 July p. xxvi/1 Volkswagen..is keeping very hush about its solution to the pollution problem.

hush, *v.*¹ Add: **1. c.** *to hush one's mouth*: to be quiet, stop talking; so *hush my mouth!*, used as an exclamation of surprise. *U.S. dial.*

1903 *Dialect Notes* II. 317 'Hesh your mouth,' i.e. stop talking. **1931** *Amer. Speech* VII. 29 Hush mah mouf. **1972** G. BAXT *Burning Sappho* ii. 42 Pat..glared at him. 'You hush your mouth Malcolm.'

hushaby, *v.* Add: Also, to speak softly. (*Nonce-use.*)

1934 S. BECKETT *More Pricks than Kicks* 85 'Too good of you to come' she hushabied.

hush-hush. Reduplicated form of HUSH *int.*, used *attrib.* or as *adj.* to denote any object of manufacture, process, plan, or policy, the details or existence of which are kept secret; *occas.* a person engaged in such matters; also, secrecy.

1916 H. YOXALL *Let.* 22 Sept. in *Fashion of Life* (1966) iv. 32 The hush-hush Tanks were splendid. **1919** C. P. THOMPSON *Cocktails* 133 The Flying Tank fixed the job without calling on that elaborate organisation for anything more hush-hush than a couple of batteries of heavy Hows. **1920** *Glasgow Herald* 3 May 8 The dramatic arrival at Baku in July, 1918, of General Dunsterville's 'hush-hush' force after its splendidly adventurous march through Persia. *Ibid.* 12 Aug. 4 Minute accounts of the hush-hush birth of this new monster of war. **1922** *Ibid.* 30 Aug. 9 A 'hush-hush' Bristol monoplane. **1927** A. E. W. MASON *No Other Tiger* i. 11 He had never been able to take the hush-hush men seriously. **1927** LLOYD GEORGE *Slings & Arrows* (1929) 184 That 'hush, hush' policy which prevailed before the war. **1931** *Morning Post* 5 June 12/4 Italian 'hush hush' car in Irish race. **1937** A. CHRISTIE *Murder in Mews* vi. 127 'A burglary? What was taken?' 'Oh, I don't know. It's all very hush-hush.' **1942** [see *CAKE *sb.* 7 c]. **1955** [see *closed door]. **1955** *Times* 26 May 4/3 In each party the idea of a broadsheet was the secret of a few. It was intended to be the 'hush-hush' weapon. **1970** *Private Eye* 22 May 20 A hush hush top-level inquiry. **1973** A. CHRISTIE *Postern of Fate* III. xvii. 249 The present trend of political thinking is that hush-hush, necessary as it is at certain times, should not be preserved indefinitely.

hush-hush, *v.* [Reduplicated form of HUSH *v.*¹] *trans.* To say 'hush, hush' to; to quiet, silence.

1861 *New Monthly Mag.* Feb. 151, I don't feel the zest now that I used to feel cutting through the water with.. that merry, wicked little dog, Phil Hervey, for coxswain;

he's a bishop now, and hush-hushes you. **1883** G. Meredith *Poems & Lyrics* 49 Not the pines with the faint airs afloat, Hush-hushing the nested dove. **1928** *Daily Express* 12 June 10/4 She might have done it long ago if she had not been firmly hush-hushed by men.

hush-money. (Later examples.)
1953 H. Miller *Plexus* (1963) x. 352 The cops will be sitting on our necks...The natural thing, under the circumstances, would be to put something aside for hush money. **1957** *Economist* 9 Nov. Suppl. 11/2 She would write her memoirs and include in them faithful records of her association with every noble lord who failed to pay hush money to the tune of two hundred pounds.

hush puppy, hush-puppy (hʌ·ʃ pʌ·pi). [f. Hush *v.*[1] + Puppy *sb.*] **1.** *U.S.* (See quots.)
1918 *Dialect Notes* V. 18 *Hushpuppy*, a sort of bread prepared very quickly and without salt. **1942** M. K. Rawlings *Cross Creek Cookery* 28 Fresh-caught fried fish without hush puppies are as men without women. **1947** *This Week Mag.* (U.S.) 4 Oct. 27/1 What's a hush puppy? You mean you don't know that Southern fried bread like a miniature corn pone—but glorified? It's made of the white cornmeal of the South, smooth and fine as face powder. **1960** *Harper's Bazaar* July 48 Crisp, brown 'hush puppies', crunchy morsels of deep-fried cornmeal batter. **1964** *Cookbk.* (Amer. Heritage) (1967) 220 Hush Puppies are usually served with fried fish. **1967** *Daily News* (N.Y.) 5 Mar. II. 4 I'm going to eat hush-puppies, wear a snuffler and every night sing 'Silent Night'.
2. The proprietary name (*Hush Puppy*) of a lightweight soft shoe. Also *attrib.*
1961 *Trade Marks Jrnl.* 15 Nov. 1616/1 Hush Puppies. Shoes. Wolverine Shoe and Tanning Corporation. **1963** *Observer* 13 Oct. 9/1 Abbott makes 'Hush Puppies', the lightweight..shoes. **1965** *Amer. Speech* XL. 249 Hush puppies, a brand of nationally advertised shoes for men and women. **1966** 'O. Mills' *Enemies of Bride* xxiii. 196 An intelligent..woman in..Hush-puppy shoes. **1969** P. Dickinson *Pride of Heroes* 38 Mr Singleton wore rubber-soled Hush-Puppies which went squeak-squeak on the shiny surface.

husi, var. *jusi.

husk, *sb.*[1] Add: **4. d.** A figure or ornament somewhat resembling a husk.
1934 *Burlington Mag.* Oct. p. xv/2 The tablet is carved with festoons, and the frieze and jambs inlaid with festoons and pendants of husks and coloured marble. **1955** R. Fastnedge *Eng. Furnit. Styles* 285 *Husk*, with 'honeysuckle' and 'wheat-ear' a favourite ornament on furniture of the Adam and Hepplewhite periods. **1971** *Country Life* 3 June 1356/3 The ground paint was decorated with motifs such as festoons of drapery and husks, interlacing hearts, urn patterns, and so on.
5. (sense *4 d) *husk design, festoon, ornament, pattern.*
1904 P. Macquoid *Hist. Eng. Furnit.* vii. 191 The sides are inlaid with the..husk design so popular at this time. **1973** *Country Life* 31 May 1567 Chestnut wood window seats..the..legs..faced by well carved husk design. **1770** J. Wedgwood *Let.* 20 Aug. (1965) 94 First, his Majesty approved of the husk festoons in particular, and I think more so than the desert pattern. **1934** *Burlington Mag.* Oct. 165/1 The back shows the honeysuckle, husk or catkin ornament. **1960** H. Hayward *Antique Coll.* 146/2 *Husk ornament*, an ornamental motif resembling the husk of a wheat ear used continually by architects and craftsmen during the Adam period. **1876** C. Schreiber *Jrnl.* 14 Nov. (1911) I. 485 A good set of Wedgwood, husk pattern.

husk, *v.*[1] Add: Also *transf.* and *fig.*
1878 B. F. Taylor *Between Gates* 182 The rough dresses of the men..out of which they husk themselves. **1892** Kipling *Barrack-Room Ballads* 199 Go husk this whimpering thief..: Winnow him out 'twixt star and star. **1910** C. E. Mulford *Hopalong Cassidy* xviii. 110 He determined to husk Meeker's body from its immortal soul.

husk, *v.*[2] Add: **2.** *intr.* Of the voice: to be or to become husky.
1922 H. Titus *Timber* xxix. 254 Her voice husked for the first time. **1958** *Sunday Times* 29 June 11/1 The birds sing louder than the crooner husking from the loudspeaker.

husker. (Earlier example.)
1780 E. Parkman *Diary* (1899) 279 Breck was very generous in treating ye huskers with Liquor.

husky, *sb.*[1] Add: **a.** (Earlier and *attrib.* examples.)
[**1743** J. Isham *Obs. Hudson's Bay* (1949) 155 Among'st the Northward Indians, and Ehuskemay's they have neither of these beasts.] **1830** in K. G. Davies *N. Quebec & Labrador Jrnl. & Corr.* (1963) 115 There was a cry that the river was full of *Hoskies* (Esquimaux). **1922** *19th Cent.* Feb. 274 As a seamstress the 'husky' woman has no equal.
c. In full *husky dog.* (Earlier and later examples.)
1852 R. Collinson *Jrnl. H.M.S. Enterprise 1850–55* (1889) 218 On his way to the ship [the dog] was kidnapped by the natives, and not being of a pure huski breed, would most likely be prized by them. **1872** *Canadian Monthly* Oct. 307/1 The 'huskie', or Esquimaux dogs..are only fed once a day. **1878** *Sask. Herald* (Battleford, N.W.T.) 18 Nov. 3/1, I had with me a 'Huskie' dog. **1886** *Colonial & Indian Exhib. Rep. Col. Sect.* 75 The original Husky has always been an animal requiring firm treatment. **1947** *New Biol.* III. 152 The most widely used type of sleigh dog is the huskie, employed mainly by Eskimos. **1970** *Islander* (Victoria, B.C.) 22 Feb. 5/1 We now had about 30 husky dogs on deck, and the noise they made when they all howled together was blood-curdling.

husky (hʌ·ski), *sb.*[2] *U.S.* [f. *husky *a.* 1 b.] A strong, stoutly-built person; one whose appearance suggests strength and force.
1864 *Old Piute* (Virginia, Nev.) 17 May, He demanded to see the Charter of the concern, which was read by the Rev. Geo. Birdsall, in his usual impressive manner, and the 'husky' accepted the apology. **1884** 'Mark Twain' *Huck. Finn* xxix. 305 It was a beautiful time to give the crowd the slip; but that big husky had me by the wrist. **1916** C. Sandburg *Chicago Poems* 60 The real huskies that are doing the work of the world. **1929** W. Heyliger *Builder of Dam* v. 46 You're going to need muscle, and he's a husky. **1945** *Jefferson Co. Republican* (Golden, Colo.) 26 Sept. 1/3 One faculty member who strayed too close to the Washington Avenue bridge was picked up bodily by ten huskies and tossed in the murky waters below.

husky, *a.* Add: **1.** (Later example.)
1905 *Daily Chron.* 14 Sept. 3/6, I have always understood that brown bread is far superior to white bread in muscle-making power and (unless very husky) in digestibility.
b. Tough and strong (like a corn-husk); big, strong, and vigorous. Also *transf. N. Amer.*
1869 Mrs. Stowe *Oldtown Folks* xvii. 191 Them wild Injuns..they're so kind o' wild, and birchy, and husky as a body may say. **1889** *Kansas City* (Missouri) *Times & Star* 1 Apr., Mike Burnett, the husky ex-fire chief. **1894** *Outing* XXIV. 447/1 He lit out of the country soon as he got husky enough to travel. **1897** *Ibid.* XXX. 364/2 A husky run down old Ontario in a gale from the West brought *Nox* into Charlotte harbor. **1906** *Eye Opener* (Calgary) Aug. 1/6 Watty himself is a husky all-round athlete. **1909** S. E. White *Rules of Game* I. ix. 51 Good food and leisure and heredity gave me a husky build. **1932** J. Dos Passos *1919* 263 Husky looking young men in khaki. **1958** *Times* 29 Nov. 9/3 If something more husky is preferred, one can camp or stay in one of the small uninhabited cabins which are to be found throughout Lapland.

huss, *sb.* Delete '*Obs.*' and add to def.: the lesser or greater spotted dogfish, *Scyliorhinus caniculus* or *S. stellaris.* (Later examples.)
1963 *Newnes Encycl. Angling* 232/2 Until recently, dogfish have been sold in the shops under the more glamorous name of rock salmon... Today, the recommended names in the retail shops are huss, flake and rig. **1965** S. Norton-Bracy in *Newnes Compl. Guide Sea Angling* 117/2 The lesser spotted dogfish (*Scyliorhinus canicula*), a smaller edition of the greater spotted, is also known by many names, probably the best known of them being robin huss. .. Many anglers seem to think it should have been 'robbing' huss, due to its habit of nipping off the bait. **1967** R. Arnold *Anglers' Handbk.* xv. 161 The most popular dogfish, from the angler's standpoint, is the bull huss, or large spotted dog, or nurse hound. **1972** A. Wrangles *Inshore Sport Fishing* v. 117 Lesser spotted dogfish... Local names. Sandy dog, dogger, rough hound, blind Jimmy, huss, etc. *Ibid.* 118 Greater spotted dogfish. .. Local names. Bull huss, nurse hound, etc.

hussar, *sb.* Add: **3.** *hussar cap.*
1846 *Knickerbocker* XXVII. 287 [He had] a smart hussar cap of green chestnut burrs. **1854** B. F. Taylor *Jan. & June* 85 Hens with hussar caps.

Husserlian (husə̄·ɹliăn), *a.* [f. name of Edmund *Husserl*, German philosopher (1859–1938) + -ian.] Of, pertaining to, or characteristic of Husserl or his work.
1932 *Mind* XLI. 247 Coming from the same Husserlian school. **1939** E. Welch *Edmund Husserl's Phenomenology* II. ii. 78 All of these theories, on Husserlian grounds, are based on nothing but pure prejudice. **1950** *Mind* LIX. 127 As it is we have Hegelian and Husserlian phenomenology on one hand and Kierkegaardian preaching on the other. **1965** *Language* XLI. 492 It is therefore a transcendental English, an English idealized out of controllable experience, an English known only to Husserlian pure egos.

hustle, *v.* Add: **2. d.** *U.S. colloq.* To obtain, produce, or serve by hustle or pushing activity. Also with *up.*
In some contexts spec. = 'to steal' (cf. sense 2 a in Dict.).
1840 *Southern Lit. Messenger* VI. 414/2 Can't you go out to the woodpile and hustle me up a few chips to start this fire? **1908** *Grand* Dec. 614 Anita was really hungry and hustled up the luncheon in..an unromantic, business-like sort of way. **1914** R. Grau *Theatre of Science* 80 He had to write his own scenarios, direct the productions and 'hustle props'. **1926** J. Black *You can't Win* vi. 65 Don't think because you couldn't hustle a can that you ain't entitled to your coffee. **1940** S. Lewis *Bethel Merriday* iii. 35 When you grow up..you try to squirm into prison, or get a nice job hustling hash..anything to avoid going on the stage. **1950** [see *fix *sb.* 5]. **1953** W. Burroughs *Junkie* (1972) ix. 86 'Do you want to score?' he asked. 'I'm due to score in a few minutes. I've been trying to hustle the dough.' **1957** P. Mansfield *Final Exposure* ix. 134 Perhaps they can hustle up some coffee. **1967** M. M. Glatt et al. *Drug Scene* iii. 34 Hustling is a generic term which usually refers to any number of strategies addicts may use to obtain drugs. **1970** H. E. Roberts *Third Ear* 8/2 *Hustle, hustling*, to be aggressively, actively engaged in the acquisition of goods and money.
e. To sell or serve (goods, etc.), esp. in an aggressive, pushing manner. *N. Amer. slang.*
1887 *Grip* (Toronto) 5 Mar. 6/2 She hustled the hash at Gilhooley's on Blank St. **1894** T. R. Dewar *Ramble round Globe* 84 Almost every second man you meet..is now either 'hustling lumber' or farming at four or five dollars a week. **1973** *Black World* Aug. 56/2 He hustled the watch to a barber for 35 bills.

4. (Later examples.)
1903 *Westm. Gaz.* 25 Feb. 5/2 The 'Decapod' will 'hustle' in true American fashion. **1906** 'O. Henry' *Four Million* 62 Do you think I'm going to let you hustle for wages while I philander in the regions of high art? **1908** G. H. Lorimer *Jack Spurlock* v. 87, I decided that..I'd hustle over to the nearest trust company.
5. *intr.* To engage in prostitution. *slang.*
In quot. 1954 used transitively in sense 'to "work" an area, soliciting as a prostitute'.
1930 J. Dos Passos *42nd Parallel* v. 411 She showed him a snapshot of her steady...I don't hustle when he's in town. **1954** J. Steinbeck *Sweet Thursday* i. 4 If you were hustling a state you should do honour to that state. **1957** C. MacInnes *City of Spades* II. ii. 117 'You're positive she's not hustling?' 'Muriel..is no harlot.' *Ibid.* 120 Hustling with Jumble queers. **1959** *Listener* 10 Dec. 1048/1 She.. revolted in revenge against her family, 'hustled' in Piccadilly, hated men as clients, took a ponce. **1960** *Guardian* 23 Sept. 26/7 Several clubs have been threatened with proceedings for keeping a brothel if they allow prostitutes to hustle on the premises. **1970** *Daily Colonist* (Victoria, B.C.) 8 Feb. 11/1 To put it bluntly, she was hustling, and liked the rewards in the shape of cash and jewelry.

hustle, *sb.* Add: **3.** (Further examples.) Also with *a.* (Cf. *move *sb.* 6.)
1902 W. N. Harben *Abner Daniel* ii. 19, I..told 'em to git a hustle on the'rse'ves. **1908** [see *drive *sb.* 1 i]. **1968** *Globe & Mail* (Toronto) 15 Jan. 21/1 Earl Balfour is a veteran hockey player who well remembers the secret to success—hustle.
4. A swindle, racket; a means of deception or fraud; a source of income; a paid job. *slang* (orig. *U.S.*).
1963 R. I. McDavid *Mencken's Amer. Lang.* 729 *Hustle*, a racket which one pushes to get his bread. **1965** 'Malcolm X' *Autobiogr.* vi. 87 Each of the military services had their civilian-dress eyes and ears picking up anything of interest to them, such as hustles being used to avoid the draft..or hustles that were being worked on servicemen. **1969** R. Pharr in A. Chapman *New Black Voices* (1972) 63, I got me a good hustle. I write over $200 worth of numbers a day, which gives me a cool 40 bucks. **1972** *Observer* 20 Aug. 7/4, I was stark broke.. from the horses..and the cards. It didn't really matter because I was on a hustle.

hustler. Add: **1.** (Further examples.) Also, a thief, a criminal; one who makes his living dishonestly or by begging; a pimp. *slang.*
1914 Jackson & Hellyer *Vocab. Criminal Slang* 47 *Hustler*,..a grafter; a pimp who steals betimes. The genteel thief is designated a 'hustler'. **1926** *Clues* Nov. 161/2 *Hustler*, members of the underworld in general. **1953** W. Burroughs *Junkie* (1972) 158 *Pop corn*, someone with a legitimate job, as opposed to a 'hustler' or thief. **1957** C. MacInnes *City of Spades* II. ix. 164 They's wreckage of jazz musicians.., ponces, and other hustlers like myself... I pimp around the town, picking the pounds up where I can. **1972** *Observer* 20 Aug. 7/4 Once, the hustler was the odd man out.
2. a. For *U.S.* read 'orig. *U.S.*', and add further examples. Also, a salesman, esp. one who is energetic or aggressive.
1886 *Publishers' Weekly* 18 Dec. 965/1 Young man, a 'hustler' in every respect, wants a strictly first-class position with a 'live' book house. **1891** *Grip* (Toronto) 18 Mar. 254/1 An enterprising down East Hustler lately conceived the idea of crowding the 'Best Fifty Books' into one volume, and selling the same by subscription. **1907** F. H. Burnett *Shuttle* xxiii. 235 I'm not passing myself off as anything but an ordinary business hustler..—just under salesman to a typewriter concern. **1907** *Westm. Gaz.* 6 Sept. 4/1 His proper title is The Hustler, and his real business is to hustle from morning till night every man and woman..connected with the business. **1926** *Daily Colonist* (Victoria, B.C.) 10 Jan. 32/3 (Advt.), Hustler wanted, 25 years or older, to sell a high-grade appliance. **1954** A. M. Bezanson *Sodbusters invade Peace* 194 Chris was a hustler, and brought to our partnership a type of aggressiveness I lacked. **1971** *Black World* Apr. 38/1 He pulls in $1,500 some weeks, and he's a *small-time* hustler.
c. A prostitute. *slang.*
1924 G. C. Henderson *Keys to Crookdom* 408 *Hustler*, prostitute. **1929** D. Hammett *Red Harvest* iii. 27 'Who is this Dinah Brand?'..'A soiled dove..a de luxe hustler, a big-league gold-digger.' **1952** J. Steinbeck *East of Eden* 436 They would think she was just a buzzed old hustler. **1960** P. Goodman *Growing up Absurd* (1961) ix. 194 The juvenile delinquents, like the hustlers (male prostitutes), fancy themselves as movie heroes in sports cars. **1970** *Women Speaking* Apr. 4/2 Man keeps her on the defensive by a constant barrage of insulting words that describe her in sexual terms:..hustler, slut.

hustling, *vbl. sb.*[1] Add: **b.** Robbery, esp. with violence.
1823 'J. Bee' *Slang* 102 *Hustling*, forcible robbery, by two or more thieves seizing their victim round the body, or at the collar. **1826** *New Newgate Calendar* V. 337 Transported for hustling. **1972** *Observer* 20 Aug. 7/4 'Hustling' has been growing steadily for years... By 1968,..of 150 cases of bag-snatching, 87 were alleged to have been committed by black youths.
c. Prostitution, soliciting as a prostitute.
1924 G. C. Henderson *Keys to Crookdom* 408 *Hustling*, streetwalking. **1938** 'M. Benney' *Scapegoat Dances* vi. 77 Bond Street might be better. There's good 'ustling there. **1959** Anon. *Streetwalker* iv. 85, I had to use the flat for hustling. **1969** *Jeremy* I. iii. 22/2 *Hustling*, working as a male prostitute.

hut, *sb.* Add: **4.** *hut-door, -tax* (earlier and later examples); **hut circle** *Archæol.*, a circle

of earth or stones indicating the circumference of a previously existing hut; **hut-keeper** (earlier and later examples).

1865 Hut-circle [in Dict.]. **1913** *Rep. Brit. Assoc. Adv. Sci.* 205 The district is rich in prehistoric remains, including some hut circles. **1963** W. F. GRIMES in Foster & Alcock *Culture & Environment* v. 105 There is the likelihood of confusion with hut-circles or barrow-rings, or even with small defensive earthworks. **1906** *Macmillan's Mag.* Nov. 13 He went back to the fire, drawing the hut-door close. **1794** G. THOMPSON *Slavery & Famine* (1947) 37 The women [convicts] have a more comfortable life than the men; those who are not fortunate enough to be selected for wives..are made hut-keepers. **1911** C. E. W. BEAN *'Dreadnought' of Darling* xi. 98 In the early days in Australia..they used to have shepherds..men living out in lonely huts twenty miles back on the run, generally with a hutkeeper to mind their little log 'humpy'. **1855** J. W. COLENSO *Ten Weeks in Natal* p. xxviii, This hut-tax was first sanctioned by Earl Grey in 1848. **1935** G. GREENE *Basement Room* 120 Chief say no white man been here long time..since he pay hut tax. **1969** *Tanzania Notes & Records* July 10 Every adult male native not liable to hut-tax..had to pay 1–3 rupees a year.

hut (hɒt), *int.* A call to a horse (see quots.).

1856 *N. & Q.* 2nd Ser. I. 395 When a horse forgets what he is doing, and becomes careless, he is reminded of his duty by a sharp *hut.* **1899** *Pall Mall Mag.* Feb. 262 'Hut, you beast!' he added, as Englishmen do, when the mare nuzzled into his neck.

hutch, *sb.* Add: **4. hutch table** *N. Amer.* (see quot. 1961).

1928 W. NUTTING *Furnit. Treas.* Illustration 1770 (*caption*) Pine Chair Table. More Properly Hutch Table on Shoes..18th Century. **1961** WEBSTER, *Hutch table,* a combination table and chest whose top can be tilted back to convert the unit into a chair or settee. **1970** *Globe & Mail* (Toronto) 25 Sept. 37/3 (Advt.), Genuine antique Canadiana pine turn-over hutch table, oval 72″.

hutch, *v.* Add: **1. b.** *intr.* To crouch or squat. Also *trans.*, with *body* (or the like) as object. Freq. as *pa. pple.* or *ppl. a.*

In restricted regional use.

1874 E. WAUGH *Chimney Corner* (1879) 151, I wonder how thou can for shame..sit keawerin' theer, hutch't of a lump, like garden-twod. **1892** MRS. H. WARD *Hist. David Grieve* vi. 139 Hutched thegither like an owd man o' seventy. **1894** J. T. CLEGG *David's Loom* v. 58 Fortin' hutches at mi feet! **1898** —— *Works* II. 302 So poor Ab were as ill off as afore, an' hutcht into his corner in a face as long as a bass fiddle. **1905** W. B. *Where White Man Treads* 76 He will..hutch on his heels and watch, and comment. *Ibid.* 161 When we arrived, Taupoki hutched down on his heels without greeting, and fixed his eyes on George's boot-trees. **1918** D. H. LAWRENCE *New Poems* 35 Sleep-suave limbs of a youth with long smooth thighs Hutched-up for warmth. **1956** W. GOLDING *Pincher Martin* 7 He hutched his body towards the place where air had been but now it was gone. **1959** —— *Free Fall* ix. 170 Busily I hutched along the walls, knees down, hands against concrete.

Hutchinson (hɒ·tʃinsən). The name of Sir Jonathan *Hutchinson* (1828–1913), English surgeon, used in the possessive (and also *attrib.*) to designate various diseases, diagnostic signs, etc., as **Hutchinson('s) tooth** (the condition of having) a permanent incisor tooth, often in the middle of the upper set, with a narrow, notched biting edge, found chiefly in children with congenital syphilis; usu. *pl.*; **Hutchinson('s) triad**, a rare triad comprising Hutchinson's teeth, interstitial keratitis, and eighth-nerve deafness, diagnostic of congenital syphilis.

1890 BILLINGS *Med. Dict.* I. 656/1 Hutchinson's teeth. **1906** *Dental Rev.* Jan. 12, I have seen several cases of typical Hutchinson teeth that were certainly in no way connected with a syphilitic taint. **1908** *Practitioner* Jan. 5 He had well-marked Hutchinson's teeth. **1908** E. L. KEYES *Syphilis* xxxvi. 533 Hutchinson's triad, consisting of dental, ocular, and auditory stigmata. **1949** H. T. KARSNER *Human Path.* (ed. 7) xvi. 547/2 The Hutchinson tooth has normal width at the gum line with sides tapering to an incisal edge of diminished mesiodistal dimensions. **1968** A. J. ROOK *Textbk. Dermatol.* I. xxii. 704/2 Interstitial keratitis, Hutchinson's teeth and eighth-nerve deafness form 'Hutchinson's triad'.

Hutchinsonian, *a.* and *sb.* Add: **A.** *adj.* **2.** (Also *hutchinsonian.*) *Med.* Of an incisor tooth: having the characteristic appearance described s.v. **Hutchinson('s) tooth* (see prec.).

1900 C. H. MAY *Man. Dis. Eye* viii. 126 These changes are especially marked in the upper central incisor teeth (Hutchinsonian teeth). **1930** JEANS & COOKE *Prepubescent Syphilis* x. 220 The typical hutchinsonian teeth may be associated with a syphilitic lesion in the premaxillae. **1957** S. L. ROBBINS *Textbk. Path.* xx. 698/2 The following may occur singly or together in congenital syphilis: the Hutchinsonian incisor..and the 'mulberry molar'.

hutchinsonite (hɒ·tʃinsənəit). *Min.* [f. the name of Arthur *Hutchinson* (1866–1937), English mineralogist + -ITE[1].] A sulpharsenite of lead and thallium $(Tl, Pb)_2As_5S_9$, often with some copper and silver, that occurs as small red orthorhombic crystals.

1905 R. H. SOLLY in *Mineral. Mag.* XIV. 72 Hutchinsonite usually occurs as very small crystals in the white dolomite, or is closely associated with sartorite and rathite. **1954** *Mineral. Abstr.* XII. 452 Hutchinsonite..is now described from the Segen Gottes Pb-Zn mine at Wiesloch, where it occurs as minute (usually 1μ) needles embedded in calcite, blende, pyrite, &c., with associated Pb sulpharsenites.

hutia (hutī·ă). Also **houtia, jutia, utia.** [a. Sp. *hutía,* f. Taino *huti, cuti.*] Any of several rodents of the family Capromyidæ, including *Capromys* and closely related genera, native to Cuba, the West Indies, and northern South America.

[**1793** B. EDWARDS *Hist. Brit. Colonies W. Indies* I. I. 90 The *agouti* is sometimes called *couti,* and *coati.* It was corrupted into *uti* and *utia,* by the Spaniards.] **1834** H. MCMURTRIE tr. *Cuvier's Animal Kingdom* 84 The Houtias have four molars. **1839** *Penny Cycl.* XV. 509/2 According to Bomare, the Utias is a species of rabbit of the size of a rat, which inhabits the West Indies. **1851** P. H. GOSSE *Naturalist's Sojourn Jamaica* 468 (*heading*) The Utia, or Indian Cony. *Ibid.* 469 A few years ago M. Fournier brought to Europe specimens of the animal which still bears in Cuba the name of Utia. **1877** *Encycl. Brit.* VI. 680/2 The only peculiar quadruped known in the island [of Cuba] is the *jutia* or *hutia.* **1939** *Geogr. Jrnl.* XCIII. 275 There exists on this island [*sc.* Swan Island] the hutia or capromys, a curious guinea-pig-like rodent of which only some four species are known. **1971** L. MATTHEWS *Life of Mammals* II. vii. 213 The family Capromyidae contains the coypu and the hutias, the latter name spelt 'jutia' in Spanish. *Ibid.* 214 Hutias are stout bodied, short limbed, rat-like rodents.

hutted, *a.* (Further examples.)

1948 *Sci. News* VII. 45 A hutted laboratory has been established, as a centre for field studies at Rossdhu, Loch Lomond. **1955** *Times* 3 June 2/6 The transfer, from a hutted class-room overshadowed by the science block, has been entirely a matter of self-help. **1973** *Times* 11 Jan. 15/3 Charing Cross Hospital is certainly not a hutted structure.

Hutterite (hɒ·tĕrəit), *sb.* (*a.*). [f. the name of Jacob *Hutter* (d. 1536), a Moravian Anabaptist + -ITE[1].] A member of an Anabaptist sect established by Jacob Hutter in Moravia, or of immigrant communities in North America having similar beliefs. Also **Hu·tite, Huttite. b.** *attrib.* or as *adj.* Of, pertaining to, or holding the doctrines of, the Hutterites. Also **Hut(t)e·rian** *a.*, esp. *Hutterian Brethren.*

1645 E. PAGITT *Heresiography* (ed. 2) 33 Hutites, who boast themselves to be the only children of God, and heires of heaven. **1897** J. L. & E. G. MULLIKEN tr. *Kautsky's Communism in Cent. Europe* v. 214 The community of the Huterites in Moravia has the greatest significance in the history of socialism. **1924** *Jrnl. Pol. Econ.* XXXII. 472 Huterian communities were established all over Moravia. **1931** J. HORSCH *Hutterian Brethren* i. 10 In the matter of the toleration of the Hutterian brethren there was a great principle at stake. *Ibid.* iii. 65 He warned the nobility who still had Hutterites in their service of the consequences, threatening them with imperial disfavor. **1935** R. J. SMITHSON *Anabaptists* xi. 205 The Anabaptists of the Reformation period survive to the present day not only in the Hutterites but also in the Mennonites. **1953** R. MOON *This is Saskatchewan* 75 To the northwest of Shaunavon are Hutterite communities. **1957** *Encycl. Brit.* IX. 90/2 The Hutterite Brethren, about 300 of whom settled in South Dakota in 1875–77 in three [farm] colonies, grew in size to 93 colonies in 1951. *Ibid.*, The Hutterites support themselves through diversified farming and stock raising. **1959** *Listener* 11 June 1039/1 The bizarre setting of a Hutterite community in Alberta. **1969** *Times* 9 Jan. 4/4 Today's 15,000 Hutterites, a Protestant sect descended from 440 pioneers who emigrated to North America in the 1870s, are expected to number more than 55 million by A.D. 2168 if the present rate of growth continues.

hutting, *vbl. sb.* (s.v. HUT *v.*). (Later examples.)

1937 *Discovery* Mar. 70/1 The irregularities of the hutting area. **1945** W. S. CHURCHILL *Victory* (1946) 108 Full hutting..is nearing completion.

huttonite (hɒ·tŏnəit). *Min.* [f. the name of Colin Osborne *Hutton* (b. 1910), American mineralogist born in New Zealand + -ITE[1].] A silicate of thorium, $ThSiO_4$, that occurs as colourless or very pale cream monoclinic crystals.

1950 A. PABST in *Nature* 22 July 157/2 The name 'huttonite' is proposed for a newly recognized monoclinic mineral of the composition $ThSiO_4$. **1957** *Amer. Mineralogist* XLII. 764 We also have synthesized huttonite hydrothermally. **1968** I. KOSTOV *Mineral.* 294 Huttonite is monoclinic.., isostructural with monazite $CePO_4$, and is dimorphous with thorite.

Hutu (hū·tu). Also **BaHutu, Bahutu.** [Bantu name. *Ba* is a plural prefix.] The name of a Bantu people which forms the majority of the population of Rwanda and of Burundi; one of these people. Also *attrib.* or as *adj.*

1959 *Times* 9 Nov. 8/6 The Bahutu were reported to be attacking houses and villages. **1964** H. J. DE BLIJ *Geogr. Subsaharan Afr.* xiv. 280/1 The BaHutu comprise perhaps 84 per cent of the total population of the combined countries, but they have been the serfs of the WaTusi. **1965** *Observer* 17 Jan. 2/1 As a Hutu, the Prime Minister tried to discourage the extremist Tutsis who..try to overthrow the Hutu Government of Rwanda. **1973** 'S. HARVESTER' *Corner of Playground* II. v. 109 Tutsi, known to Whitey as Watutsi, once overlords of Rwanda, whose ancestors..enslaved the Hutu people.

‖ **hutung** (hu·tuŋ). [Chin.] In northern Chinese cities: a narrow side-street, an alley.

1922 *Blackw. Mag.* Dec. 730/2 Old Sung, the curio-dealer of the Soochow *hutung.* **1923** *Ibid.* Dec. 726/2, I sat and listened to Pang the Soochow *hutung* dealer. **1960** *Times* 17 May 9/4 These hutungs—the lanes off Peking's still unkept main streets—are scarcely changed either. **1972** *Times* 6 Dec. 18/1 Modern buildings..provide a front for the old hutungs (side streets). *Ibid.* 18/2 In places the hutungs are only just wide enough for a man to pass.

Huxham (hɒ·ksăm). The name of John *Huxham* (1692–1768), English physician, used in the possessive in **Huxham's tincture (of bark)**, compound tincture of cinchona bark, first described in Huxham's *Essay on Fevers* (1750) and formerly used as a bitter tonic and febrifuge; also *ellipt.* as **Huxham.**

1788 T. HEALDE tr. *New Pharmacopoeia R. Coll. Physicians London* 192 Tinctura corticis Peruviani compositа... This medicine has been celebrated under the name of Huxham's Tincture. It is given as a corroborant and stomachic..to convalescents after long fevers; and sometimes, in larger doses, for the cure of agues in persons averse to taking Bark in substance. **1808** JANE AUSTEN *Let.* 15 June (1952) 190, I hope Huxham is a comfort to you; I am glad you are taking it. **1901** S. O. L. POTTER *Handbk. Materia Medica* (ed. 8) 271 Huxham's Tincture of Bark, 1788 (Unofficial), is still used. **1952** *Martindale's Extra Pharmacopœia* (ed. 23) I. 364 Tinctura Cinchonæ Composita (B.P.C.). *Syn.* Huxham's Tincture of Bark.

Huxley (hɒ·ksli). The name of T. H. *Huxley* (1825–95), English biologist, used in the possessive in **Huxley's layer**, a layer, one or more cells thick, of horny flattened nucleated cells lying inside Henle's layer in the inner root-sheath of the hair follicle, described by him in 1845.

1853 BUSK & HUXLEY tr. *Kölliker's Man. Human Histol.* I. 187 These [cells] which form a simple or a double layer (*Huxley's* layer) are constantly situated internal to the common, and as far as I have seen, always single, fenestrated layer of cells. **1890** *Gray's Anat.* (ed. 12) 61 The inner root-sheath consists of a delicate cuticle next the hair; then of one or two layers of horny, flattened, nucleated cells, known as Huxley's layer, and finally of a single layer of non-nucleated, horny, cubical cells, called Henle's layer. **1954** *Physiol. Rev.* XXXIV. 115 Above the lower bulb region [of the hair follicle], immediately central to the external sheath, is Henle's layer of the internal sheath. Huxley's layer and the cuticle are next in order.

Huxleyan, Huxleian (hɒ·ksliăn), *a.* [f. the name *Huxley* (see below) + -AN.] **a.** Of, pertaining to, or characteristic of T. H. Huxley (see prec.), or his work. Also as *sb.*

1889 E. DOWSON *Let.* 26 May (1967) 81 A reasonable Huxleian agnosticism is logical & consistent. **1901** *Science* 22 Mar. 453/2 Yet it is worth while, now and then, to take stock of advances subsequent to, and largely consequent on, the Huxleian declaration. **1907** W. JAMES *Meaning of Truth* (1909) vi. 154 Your genuine truth-lover must discourse in huxleyan heroics, and feel as if truth, to be real truth, ought to bring eventual messages of death to all our satisfactions. **1909** —— *Mem. & Stud.* (1911) viii. 186 The major premise is: 'Any spirit-revelation must be romantic.' The minor of the spiritist is: 'This *is* romantic'; that of the Huxleyan is: 'this is dingy twaddle.' **1939** *Jrnl. R. Anthrop. Inst.* LXIX. 148, I have descanted long enough on my Huxleian text, and hardly know whether I have vindicated or contravened its essential purport. **1973** *Nature* 22 June 436/1 The result is a true Huxleian tragedy—a beautiful and virtuous hypothesis butchered by a gang of ugly facts.

b. Of, pertaining to, or characteristic of Aldous Huxley, English novelist (1894–1963), or his work.

1934 *Punch* 9 May 531/1 It [*sc.* the travel book] opens.. on a cruising liner, with some acid and Huxleyan comments on the people who frequent these modern portents. **1961** *Times* 11 Dec. 13/6 An Orwellian or Huxleian world, isolated, stream-lined, packaged. **1971** *Daily Tel.* (Colour Suppl.) 19 Mar. 39 His first 'serious' book, a futurist, slightly Huxleyan novel about life in 1980.

Huygens (həi·gĕnz). Also (erron.) **Huyghens.** The name of Christiaan *Huygens* (see HUYGHENIAN *a.*), used, chiefly in the possessive, to designate inventions, principles, etc., devised or enunciated by him, as **Huygens' construction**, the geometrical construction for finding the position of a wave front by using Huygens' principle; **Huygens' eyepiece**, a Huygenian eyepiece (see HUYGHENIAN *a.*); **Huygens' principle**, a principle of wave propagation, according to which each point on a wave front may be regarded as a source of new secondary waves, and the resultant effect of all these waves constitutes the propagation

of the wave front, their envelope at a later time representing a new position of it.

[**1835** *Rep. Brit. Assoc. Adv. Sci. 1834* 308 The composition of the grand, or primary wave, by the union of the several secondary or partial waves, in this demonstration, has been denominated the principle of Huygens.] **1840** *Phil. Mag.* XVII. 243 (*heading*) On the application of Huyghens's principle in physical optics. **1899** W. WATSON *Text-bk. Physics* III. i. 353 The construction for finding the position..of the wave-front, at a time *t* by means of the tangent to a series of circles, the radius of each of which is equal to the space passed over by the wave in a time *t*, is due to Huyghens, and is known as Huyghens's construction for the wave-front. **1900** J. C. P. ALDOUS *Elem. Course Physics* x. 577 The chief negative eye-piece is Huyghens' eye-piece. **1957** *Encycl. Brit.* XV. 439/1 The Huygens eyepiece..is the most common type used with the microscope. **1959** BORN & WOLF *Princ. Optics* viii. 370 Fresnel was able to account for diffraction by supplementing Huygens' construction with the postulate that the secondary wavelets mutually interfere. **1970** M. V. KLEIN *Optics* i. 20 To follow the propagation of the optical disturbance..we have, in theory, only to make repeated applications of Huygens' principle. *Ibid.* 21 The Huygens construction.

huzoor (hŭzuᵊ·ɹ). Also 8 huzzoor, huzur. [a. Arab. *ḥuḍūr* (pronounced in India as *ḥuzūr*) presence (employed as a title), f. *ḥaḍara* to be present.] An Indian potentate; often used as a title of respect.

1776 *Trial of Joseph Fowke* Depositions 17/2 [They] endeavour to lay their complaints before the Huzzoor. **1843** C. J. C. DAVIDSON *Diary Trav. Upper India* I. 77 The huzoor's countenance..is as immovably tranquil as that of Boodh. **1898** *Longman's Mag.* May 80 What pleasure hath this slave in life, save to do the Huzoor's will? **1899** KIPLING *Land & Sea Tales* (1923) 229 'Huzoor! (Your Highness!)' said Imam Din, stooping low. **1957** M. M. KAYE *Shadow of Moon* xxx. 438 'Be swift, my father,' said Niaz pleasantly. 'Do not keep the Huzoor waiting.'

hwyl (hū·il). Also (erron.) hwyll. [W.] An emotional quality which inspires and sustains impassioned eloquence; also, the fervour of emotion characteristic of gatherings of Welsh people.

1899 *Daily News* 1 Mar. 7/5 What is termed the Welsh 'hwyl', a form of eloquence which seems to exert remarkable influence on the hearers. **1928** *Observer* 15 July 11/3 The National Eisteddfod is a microcosm of Wales. There you may see preacher and ploughman, collier and clerk, all rubbing shoulders and all under the influence of the intangible and untranslatable 'hwyl' of the Eisteddfod. **1959** W. GOLDING *Free Fall* ii. 57 Father Anselm..was not emotional, no Welsh hwyll for him. **1970** *Daily Tel.* 16 June 7 Plaid Cymru, full of 'hwyl' and hope, are making an all out effort to repeat in Cardigan the success they achieved..in Carmarthen. **1973** *Ibid.* 13 Jan. 16 There should be a considerable degree of hwyl on board HMS Glamorgan today when 20 members of the London Glamorgan Society are entertained to lunch.

hyacinth. Add: **2. b.** (Further examples.) **Cape H.**, a plant of the genus *Galtonia*, esp. *G. candicans*; **Peruvian H.**, *Scilla peruviana*; **Roman H.**, an early-flowering variety, bred from *Hyacinthus orientalis* var. *albulus*.

[**1629** J. PARKINSON *Parad.* xi. 126 The Starry Iacinth of Peru, being thought to have growne in Peru, a Province of the West Indies, but he that gave that name first unto it, eyther knew not his naturall place, or willingly imposed that name, to conceale it, or to make it the better esteemed.] **1659** T. HANMER *Garden Bk.* (1933) 36 The Branch'd Hyacinths of Peru,..very rare here. **1673** J. RAY *Observations Journey Low-Countries* 250 In the ditches by the wayside, I observed growing wild..the lesser Grape Hyacinth, and Hepatica. **1731** P. MILLER *Gardeners Dict.* s.v. *Hyacinthus*, The Hyacinth of Peru may also be rais'd from Seeds in the same manner as the common Hyacinths. *Ibid.*, Another Hyacinth..is now preserved in curious Collections of Exotick Plants; it was originally brought from the Cape of Good Hope. **1877** [see ROMAN *a.*[1] 14 b]. **1911** J. WEATHERS *Bulb Bk.* 282/1 There is a blue Roman Hyacinth that flowers somewhat later than the white form. **1917** L. H. BAILEY *Stand. Cycl. Hort.* VI. 3117/2 [*Scilla*] *Peruviana*... Cuban Lily. Peruvian Jacinth. Hyacinth of Peru. *Ibid.* 3118/1 The Hyacinth of Peru is not hardy in Mass[achusetts]. **1924** J. WEATHERS *My Garden Bk.* xx. 348/1 Galtonia (after the S. African explorer, Francis Galton). Cape Hyacinth. **1936** T. S. ELIOT *Coll. Poems* 127 Lord, the Roman hyacinths are blooming in bowls. **1956** A. M. COATS *Flowers & their Histories* I. 122 The Spire Lily or Cape Hyacinth..is on the other hand not a true hyacinth, although closely related to the family; it has therefore been renamed *Galtonia candicans*. **1961** P. M. SYNGE *Collins Guide to Bulbs* 162 The Roman Hyacinths tend to flower among the earliest and the spikes are rather looser and more delicate.

3. b. A variety of pigeon, characterized by its blue-black colour and white markings.

1855 *Poultry Chron.* III. 9/1 Those pretty spangled Toys..known by various names, as Porcelains, Hyacinths, Ermines, &c. **1879** L. WRIGHT *Pract. Pigeon Keeper* 208 Victorias are simply Hyacinths of a lighter shade. **1935** R. MANNERING *Lyell's Pigeon-Keeping for Amateurs* (ed. 4) 107 The Hyacinth is among those breeds which do not reveal their true colouration and markings until after the first moult. **1965** W. M. LEVI *Encycl. Pigeon Breeds* 189 The Hyacinth appears to have much in common with the Suabian, and they are probably related.

hyaline, *a.* and *sb.* Add: **A.** *adj. hyaline cast*, a more or less transparent urinary cast composed mainly of precipitated protein; *hyaline cell*, (*a*) *Bot.*, a cell without chlorophyll, found in the leaves and stem of certain mosses; † (*b*) *Med.* (also *hyaline leucocyte*), a type of white blood-cell; = *MONOCYTE (*Obs.*); *hyaline membrane disease* (or *syndrome*), a condition in some newborn (esp. premature) babies in which the lung spaces are lined with a hyaline membrane, causing severe dyspnœa and often early death.

1870 *Jrnl. Bot.* VIII. 229 In neither [species of *Dicranum*] do I find the beautiful chlorophyllose contents observable in the Finland specimens..nor are the longitudinal rows of hyaline cells, in the centre of the basal wing, so well defined. **1881** *Practitioner* Oct. 243 The urine contained red corpuscles, albumin, and hyaline casts. **1894** KANTHACK & HARDY in *Jrnl. Physiol.* XVII. 96 The hyaline cell occurs both in blood and in the extra-vascular spaces. **1896** H. N. DIXON *Student's Handbk. Brit. Mosses* 9 The pores in the hyaline cells of the branch leaves [of *Sphagnum* species] are..occasionally found on the face of the hyaline cells. **1906** *Jrnl. Pathol. & Bacteriol.* XI. 67 The immature hyaline cell is an evenly round or oval cell. *Ibid.* 79 Others consider that the lymphocytes are the young forms of hyaline leucocytes. **1929** *Encycl. Brit.* III. 742/1 The large hyaline cell may really include two quite different cells of similar appearance. **1931** A. PINEY *Recent Adv. Hæmatol.* (ed. 3) ii. 18 The large hyaline leucocyte or monocyte is not easy to place with complete certainty in either the group of granulocytes or of lymphocytes. **1938** G. M. SMITH *Cryptogamic Bot.* II. iv. 87 The hyaline cells of leaves and similar cells in the cortex of a stem play an important role in the absorption and retention of water. **1953** *Adv. Pediatrics* VI. 173 If an infant does not exhibit respiratory difficulty within the first 12 hours of life I do not believe it will die of hyaline membrane disease. **1955** *Jrnl. Pediatrics* XLVII. 40/1 The triad of pathologic changes in the lungs of infants who die with the pulmonary hyaline membrane syndrome consists of atelectasis, vascular engorgement, and an eosinophilic hyaline-like membrane which lines alveolar ducts and alveoli. **1958** *New Biol.* XXVI. 102 The leaves [of *Sphagnum*] are composed of large empty 'hyaline' cells, with narrow green cells between them. **1966** *Lancet* 24 Dec. 1384/2 Mid-stream urine showed small numbers of hyaline and granular casts. **1973** *Sci. Amer.* Apr. 75/1 In the past some infants with hyaline membrane disease recovered spontaneously. Many became exhausted and died.

hyalinization (həi:ălinəizēⁱ·ʃən). *Med.* [f. HYALIN(E *a.* and *sb.* + -IZATION.] A change of tissue into a homogeneous, translucent, often firm, mass somewhat resembling glass under the microscope; hyaline degeneration.

1919 *Amer. Jrnl. Med. Sci.* CLVII. 673 Undoubtedly there are other factors [affecting malignancy and benignancy] such as lymphocytic infiltration, fibrosis, hyalinization, [etc.]. **1926** *Arch. Path.* II. 338 The muscle lesion usually consists of hyaline degeneration of the contractile substance of the fibers... The hyalinization of the muscle may result in rupture with subsequent hemorrhage. **1961** *Lancet* 22 July 182/2 Histologically the aneurysmal sac was composed of dense fibrous tissue showing hyalinisation. **1963** WALTER & ISRAEL *Gen. Path.* v. 71 Hyalinisation of the walls of many small arterioles may occur as part of the aging process.

So **hy·alinized** *ppl. a.*, having the appearance that results from hyalinization.

1929 *Arch. Path.* VIII. 906 The corpus fibrosum..consists of irregularly outlined and more or less thoroughly hyalinized fibrous tissue. **1962** *Lancet* 27 Jan. 191/1 This exudate becomes hyalinised to form membranes, lining the sacs, and dense plugs in the alveolar ducts.

hyalo-. Add: **hy·alomere** *Cytol.* [*-MERE], the lightly staining ground-substance of a blood platelet; **hy:alo-ophi·tic** *a. Petrol.* [ad. G. *hyaloophitisch* (B. Polenov 1899, in *Trav. de la Soc. Impér. des Naturalistes, St. Pétersbourg* XXVII. 473)] (see quot. 1920); **hy:alopilitic** (-pəili·tik) *a. Petrol.* [ad. G. *hyalopilitisch* (H. Rosenbusch *Mikrosk. Physiogr. d. Min. u. Gesteine* (ed. 2, 1887) II. 466), f. Gr. πῖλ-ος felt + *-itic* (see -ITE[1])], characterized by or having needle-like microlites embedded in a glassy ground-mass; **hy·alosome** *Cytol.* [ad. G. *hyalosom* (S. M. Lukjanow 1887, in *Arch. f. mikrosk. Anat.* XXX. 551): see *-SOME[4]], a lightly staining cell structure resembling the nucleolus.

1936 P. E. SMITH et al. *Bailey's Text-bk. Histol.* (ed. 9) vi. 150 Structurally they [*sc.* blood platelets] consist of a central granular mass (chromomere)..and a peripheral hyaline zone (hyalomere). **1969** A. W. HAM *Histol.* (ed. 6) xiv. 303/1 Most of a platelet appears to consist of a fairly clear ground substance which is colored only a very pale blue with a blood stain and is called its hyalomere. **1920** A. HOLMES *Nomencl. Petrol.* 120 *Hyalo-ophitic texture*, Polenov, 1899, a texture resembling ophitic texture, in which the spaces of an open network of felspar laths are occupied by glass; a limiting case of intersertal texture. **1954** H. WILLIAMS et al. *Petrogr.* ii. 20 Where glass takes the place of pyroxene, the texture is called hyaloophitic. **1888** J. J. H. TEALL *Brit. Petrogr.* 443 The normal structure of the andesites is the hyalopilitic. **1959** W. W. MOORHOUSE *Study of Rocks in Thin Section* v. 159 Hyalopilitic lavas are glassy with felted microlites. **1889** *Q. Jrnl. Microsc. Sci.* XXX. 168 They are therefore distinguished..as (a) 'karyosomes'..; (b) 'plasmasomes'..; (c) 'hyalosomes', which are not stained (vide Lukjanow).

hyaluronic (həi:ăliurǫ·nik), *a. Biochem.* [f. HYAL(OID *a.* (from its first being isolated from the hyaloid or vitreous humour of the eye) + *URONIC *a.*] *hyaluronic acid*: a viscous mucopolysaccharide composed of acetylglucosamine and glucuronic acid units, widely found in animal tissues (e.g. in synovial fluid, in the ground-substance of connective tissue, and in the vitreous humour of the eye) as well as in bacterial capsules.

1934 MEYER & PALMER in *Jrnl. Biol. Chem.* CVII. 631 Data on the preparations of this acid for which we propose ..the name 'hyaluronic acid', from hyaloid (vitreous) + uronic acid. **1957** *Sci. News* XLV. 85 *In vivo*, hyaluronic acid has the important function of offering resistance to penetration by foreign matter, including agents of infectious disease. **1969** *New Scientist* 24 Apr. 167/2 Dr W. C. McCutchen..was adamant that if the hyaluronic acid is removed from synovial fluid, it still lubricates efficiently.

Hence **hyalu·ronate**, a salt of hyaluronic acid.

1946 *Biochem. Jrnl.* XL. 583 (*heading*) The influence of hydrolysates of hyaluronate upon hyaluronidase production by micro-organisms. **1970** R. W. MCGILVERY *Biochem.* xxiv. 585 Solutions of hyaluronate have a high viscosity, and it is especially concentrated in the synovial fluid of the joints.

hyaluronidase (həi:ăliurǫ·nidēⁱz, -ēⁱs). *Biochem.* [f. *hyaluronid-* (f. *HYALURON(IC *a.* + *-ASE.] Any of the enzymes which catalyse the depolymerization of hyaluronic acid, thereby reducing its viscosity and rendering tissue containing it more permeable.

1940 CHAIN & DUTHIE in *Brit. Jrnl. Exper. Path.* XXI. 325 Hyaluronic acid is the substrate for the 'mucolytic' enzyme in spreading factor solution which accordingly is termed 'hyaluronidase'. **1951** A. GROLLMAN *Pharmacol. & Therapeutics* xxix. 652 To accelerate the rate of absorption from the skin and subcutaneous tissues, hyaluronidase may be added to the infusion. **1967** *Martindale's Extra Pharmacopoeia* (ed. 25) 886/1 The diffusion of local anaesthetics is accelerated by the addition of 1000 units of hyaluronidase to each 20 ml. of the anaesthetic solution. **1970** AMBROSE & EASTY *Cell Biol.* xii. 391 The sperm acrosome secretes enzymes (including hyaluronidase) which assist penetration [of the ovum].

hyan (həi·ăn). *local.* Also **hyant, hyen, hyon.** [Origin unknown.] An acute, usually fatal, infectious disease of cattle or, occasionally, sheep, caused by the bacterium *Clostridium chauvœi*; = *black quarter* (s.v. BLACK *a.* 19), BLACKLEG 1, SPEED *sb.* 10 a.

1789 *Trans. Soc. Arts* VII. 73, I..should annually have attempted to rear one hundred [calves], were it not for the disorder called here [*sc.* Scarisbrook] the *Hyon*. **1795** J. AIKIN *Descr. Country round Manchester* 325 Great numbers of calves having been taken off by a disease here called the *hyon*. **1801** *Sporting Mag.* XVII. 153 Drinks to be given to young calves for striking of the *Hyen*. **1881** [see SPEED *sb.* 10 a].

hyawa (həi·ăwă). Also **haiowa, hayawa, hiawa, hyawai.** [Arawak (Makuchi) *haijawa*. In Du. *hajawa* (1770).] One of several balsam-bearing trees or shrubs of Guyana, esp. *Protium heptaphyllum*. Also *attrib.*

1825 C. WATERTON *Wanderings S. Amer.* 190 They paint themselves with the Roucou, sweetly perfumed with Hayawa. **1840** R. SCHOMBURGK *Descr. Brit. Guiana* 98 The latter tree [sc. *Amyris ambrosiaca*], called *Haiowa* or *Sepou* by the Indians, is most abundant. **1851** *Illustr. Catal. Gt. Exhib.* IV. 980/1 Hyawai gum or incense, from the River Demerara. **1887** *Colonial & Indian Exhib. Rep. Col. Sect.* 295 Hyawa gum..is very fragrant when burnt. **1899** J. RODWAY *In Guiana Wilds* 208 Then it struck him that a torch would be useful, as he saw a hyawa bush growing near. **1924** RECORD & MELL *Timbers Trop. Amer.* 335 The bastard cedar, incense tree, or 'hiawá' of British Guiana is *P*[*rotium*] *heptaphyllum* March.

hyawaballi (həi:ăwăbæ·li). Also **haiariballi, hiawaballi, haiowaballi.** [Arawak (Makuchi) *hyawaballi*, f. *HYAWA + *-balli* resembling.] A timber tree of Guyana, *Tetragastris panamensis*.

1851 *Illustr. Catal. Gt. Exhib.* IV. 985/1 Transverse and vertical sections of the hyawaballi tree, from the River Demerara. **1887** *Colonial & Indian Exhib. Rep. Col. Sect.* 451 Hiawa-Balli. **1917** *Timehri* IV. 260 Hiowa-balli... Hard, heavy, compact, fine grain. **1943** RECORD & HESS *Timbers of New World* 109/2 The Haiowaballi of British Guiana is *T*[*etragastris*] *panamensis*. **1952** D. B. FANSHAWE *Vegetation Brit. Guiana* 60 *Tetragastris* sp. (Haiawaballi) community. **1956** *Handbk. Hardwoods* (Forest Prod. Res. Lab.) 107 Haiariballi is a timber of British Guiana. Material received at the Laboratory showed the timber to be worthless for commercial sawing.

Hy Brasil, Hy-Brazil (həi bră̆zi·l). Also 9 **Brasil Rock, O'Brazil.** [Cf. BRAZIL[1].] Name originally applied to one of the larger islands of the Azores; subsequently and chiefly to a legendary island located off the west coast of Ireland.

[**1436** A. BIANCO *Atlas* (1869) (*caption*) Y de borzil.] **1812** J. PURDY *Mem. N. Atlantic Ocean* IV. i. 128 *Brasil Rock*, in lat. 51° 10′, and long. 15° 58′..although its existence has been doubted..it was, however, seen in the year 1791. **1843** G. GRIFFIN *Works* VIII. 210 On the ocean that hollows the rocks where ye dwell, A shadowy land has appeared as they tell; Men thought it a region of sun-

shine and rest, And they called it O'Brazil—the isle of the blest. **1899** Kipling *Stalky & Co.* p. vii, Far and sure our bands have gone—Hy-Brasil or Babylon. **1906** —— *Puck of Pook's Hill* 14 Sir Huon..setting off from Tintagel Castle for Hy-Brasil. **1948** L. MacNeice *Holes in Sky* 30 Both myth and seismic history have been long suppressed Which made and unmade Hy Brazil. **1967** V. Gielgud *Conduct of Member* xviii. 139 Want to go a long way.. Cipangu—or better, Hy-Brazil. The world was more fun when its countries had names like these.

hybrid, *sb.* and *a.* Add: **A.** *sb.* **2. b.** *Petrol.* A hybrid rock (see sense B. 2 b below).

1918 *Q. Jrnl. Geol. Soc.* LXXIV. 129 Compared with the Potter-Fell type..they would be hybrids, the former are transitional varieties. **1934** *Ibid.* XC. 599 The hybrid or its parent magma rose along the bedding-planes of the sediments. **1950** E. E. Wahlstrom *Introd. Theor. Igneous Petrol.* x. 234 The products of intermingling of these magmas originally were called hybrids, a term which..has come to have a broader meaning and now includes all rocks resulting from the assimilation or melting of solid igneous rocks by later intrusions from the same source.

c. *Physical Chem.* A hybrid orbital (see sense B. 2 d below).

1932 *Physical Rev.* XL. 62 A hybrid of 3 *d*, 4 *s*, and 4 *p* electrons. **1962** P. J. & B. Durrant *Introd. Adv. Inorg. Chem.* v. 144 The bond angles, at a given atom, are determined by the angles between its *σ* hybrids. **1968** K. F. Reid *Prop. & React. Bonds in Org. Molecules* iii. 43 The second kind of hybridized orbital, termed the trigonal hybrid, arises through the hybridization of one *s* and two *p* A[tomic] O[rbital]s.

B. *adj.* **1. b.** As the first element in the names of varieties of rose, esp. **hybrid China,** a variety produced by crossing *Rosa chinensis* and *R. semperflorens,* characterized by a long flowering period; **hybrid perpetual,** a cross between *Rosa damascena* and a hybrid China rose; **hybrid polyantha** = *floribunda; **hybrid tea,** a cross between a hybrid perpetual and a tea-scented rose (*Rosa odorata*).

1837 T. Rivers *Rose Amateur's Guide* I. 20 Perhaps no plant presents such a mass of beauty as a finely grown hybrid China rose in full bloom. **1848** W. Paul *Rose Garden* II. 121 The Bourbon Perpetual..is a division embracing the varieties of Hybrid Perpetual, in which the characters of the Bourbon Rose are strikingly developed. **1859, 1890** [see Perpetual *sb.* 1 b]. **1890** *Gardeners' Chron.* 1 Feb. 132/1 Primrose Dame and Vicomtesse Folkestone are also included with hybrid Teas. **1931** M. Grieve *Mod. Herbal* II. 688/1 The most suitable are the so-called Hybrid Perpetuals, flowering from June to October. **1945, 1956** [see *floribunda]. **1951** *Dict. Gardening* (R. Hort. Soc.) IV. 1824/1 Hybrid Perpetual Roses.. originated in the crossing of the Damask Rose with the Hybrid China varieties. **1968** A. Christie *By Pricking of Thumbs* vi. 82 Got some old-fashioned roses here... Better than them new-fashioned Hybrid Teas. **1970** [see *floribunda]. **1973** *Rose Ann.* 37 The first of the new race to bear the characteristics of the hybrid tea was 'Victor Verdier' (1859), although some may claim that 'La France' (1867) was the first true hybrid tea rose.

2. b. *Petrol.* Of rock: formed by the mixing of two different magmas or by the incorporation into an intruding magma of adjacent solid rock (esp. rock of the same origin as the magma).

1904 A. Harker *Tertiary Igneous Rocks Skye* xi. 183 The processes..were of a less simple kind, mere admixture being supplemented by diffusion. The resulting hybrid rocks..are thus only in a general sense intermediate in composition between the two parent rocks, and may be abnormal in comparison with any ordinary igneous rocks formed from a single magma. **1954** H. Williams et al. *Petrogr.* vi. 110 Most diorites..are probably hybrid rocks, and many contain xenoliths that exhibit various stages of magmatic reaction.

c. *Computers.* Utilizing or involving both analogue and digital methods.

1959 E. M. Grabbe et al. *Handbk. Automation, Computation, & Control* II. xxix. 4 The purpose of the hybrid system..is to combine the advantages noted above for each of the two types of conventional computer, while at the same time obviating the disadvantages. **1964** *Ann. N.Y. Acad. Sci.* CXV. 573 More complex operations such as multiplication are not as critical to most hybrid operations and can be slower. **1968** *Brit. Med. Bull.* XXIV. 193/1 The limited accuracy of analogue computers..can be overcome by using 'hybrid' computers in which certain elements..are digitally designed to preserve accuracy.

d. *Physical Chem.* Applied to a bond or valence orbital obtained by the linear combination of two or more different atomic orbitals.

1939 L. Pauling *Nature Chem. Bond* iii. 82 The strength of the best *s*–*p* hybrid bond orbital. **1960** J. W. Linnett *Wave Mech. & Valency* viii. 128 The appropriate hybrid orbitals are the most successful for indicating the spatial distribution of the electrons. **1968** K. F. Reid *Prop. & React. Bonds in Org. Molecules* iii. 42 The 2*s* and the three 2*p* orbitals of the excited atom are treated in such a way that..they combine to produce four equivalent orbitals, each termed a tetrahedral or sp^3-hybrid orbital, which have their axes directed towards the four corners of a regular tetrahedron.

3. Special Combs.: **hybrid coil** *Electr.,* a type of transformer used in two-wire telephone circuits when amplification in both directions is required, having four pairs of terminals so arranged that if the impedances connected to two pairs balance, a voltage applied to a third pair divides equally between them without inducing a voltage in the fourth pair; also called a *hybrid transformer*; **hybrid swarm** *Ecol.,* a variable population caused by the hybridization of neighbouring species; **hybrid vigour** = *heterosis 3.

1925 C. A. Wright *Telephone Communication* x. 244 Conjugate alternating-current bridges or hybrid coils.. are generally used in repeater and multiplex telephone lines. **1959** K. Henney *Radio Engin. Handbk.* (ed. 5) xxviii. 33 Instead of connecting the respective input of one amplifier and output of the other amplifier directly to a line circuit, there is introduced a balancing coil or so-called hybrid coil. **1926** *Nature* 30 Oct. 623/2 (*heading*) The naming of wild hybrid swarms. *Ibid.* 624 Nor do the 'Rules' have in view the existence of the highly polymorphic hybrid swarms—in no few cases hundreds or probably thousands of distinct individuals—that are known to exist. **1947** *New Phytologist* XLVI. 229 The Oxlip is confined in Britain to a small area in East Anglia, and at the edges of this area Oxlip-Primrose hybrid populations are found; such well-defined hybrid swarms are not common amongst British plants. **1963** E. Mayr *Animal Species & Evol.* vi. 118 The barrier between two sympatric species sometimes breaks down so completely, locally or over wide areas, that the two parental species are replaced by a hybrid swarm that serves as a continuous bridge between the two parental extremes. **1969** Briggs & Walters *Plant Variation & Evol.* xi. 186 Hybrid swarms are found in which there is a remarkable range of variation. **1941** *Stand. Handbk. Electr. Engin.* (ed. 7) xxii. 2055 (*caption*) Principle of hybrid transformer. **1962** *Newnes Conc. Encycl. Electr. Engin.* 379/1 A separating device consisting of a pair of matched 'hybrid' transformers is a common method of securing two-way amplification. [**1909** E. M. East in *Amer. Naturalist* XLIII. 179 In every case an increase in vigor over the parents [*sc.* maize plants] was shown by the crosses.] **1918** Babcock & Clausen *Genetics Rel. Agric.* xii. 230 Not all species hybrids, however, display hybrid vigor. **1949** C. C. Lindegren *Yeast Cell* xxvii. 27/2 The degeneration or 'running out' of hybrids showing heterosis has been one of the principal problems of hybrid vigor. **1970** *Watsonia* VIII. 131 Its robust growth, vigorous vegetative spread and large fronds..suggest hybrid vigour.

hybridization. Add: **1. b.** *Petrol.* The formation of a hybrid rock.

1926 G. W. Tyrrell *Princ. Petrol.* ii. 31 There is a good deal of commingling of the magmas, with enclosure of fragments and hybridisation, along the interior contacts. **1968** B. Bayly *Introd. Petrol.* ix. 100 At the interface between a magma and a solid rock, the possibility of interpenetration exists... Where the environment is solidified magma from an earlier stage of the same magmatic event, the process is called hybridization; when, as is more common, the environment is some independent solid, the process is contamination.

c. *Physical Chem.* The mathematical combination of atomic orbitals to form a hybrid orbital.

1932 *Physical Rev.* XL. 1037, sp^3 hybridization is encountered only when the repulsions between the four electrons of the H atoms are included. **1962** P. J. & B. Durrant *Introd. Adv. Inorg. Chem.* v. 145 Table 5.1 shows some of the valence states of atoms which can be produced by the hybridisation of atomic orbitals. **1968** [see *hybrid *sb.* and *a.* A. 2 c].

d. *Biochem.* The formation of a hybrid macromolecule by artificially recombining complementary subunits (single polynucleotide strands in the case of nucleic acids and individual polypeptide chains in the case of proteins) obtained from slightly different varieties of the same molecular species or (in the case of RNA–DNA hybrids) of similar molecular species.

1959 Wolstenholme & O'Connor *Biochem. Human Genetics* (Ciba Found. Symp.) 123 Vinograd, Schroeder and Hutchinson (1959) have shown by an ingenious 'hybridization' experiment involving haemoglobin labelled with ^{14}C that the *α* chains of haemoglobins A and S are interchangeable and therefore similar. **1962** *Science* 21 Dec. 1329/1 It is perhaps not surprising that s-RNA is resistant to hybridization since x-ray analysis..suggests that s-RNA is a hairpin structure kept together by a highly regular system of hydrogen bonding. Until this secondary structure is disrupted there is no opportunity for pairing between s-RNA molecules and complementary sequences in the DNA. **1965** *Jrnl. Molecular Biol.* XII. 830 Hybridization in solution has one obvious disadvantage, stemming from the fact that RNA-DNA formation must compete with the re-formation of the DNA-DNA complexes. **1966** Lehmann & Huntsman *Man's Haemoglobins* xxi. 224 (*heading*) Hybridisation of abnormal human haemoglobin variants. **1968** W. A. Schroeder *Primary Struct. Proteins* 206/1 (*index*) Hybridization of ribonuclease. **1972** *Arch. Biochem. & Biophysics* CL. 407 (*title*) Hybridization of rabbit muscle and liver phosphofructokinases. **1972** W. V. Brown *Textbk. Cytogenetics* ii. 13/1 The biochemical techniques of nucleic acid hybridization, either DNA-DNA or RNA-DNA.., have recently been providing new and unexpected understanding about the DNA sequences in the nucleus.

e. *Cytology.* The fusion, by artificial means or in artificial cultures, of two somatic cells of different karyotypes to form a hybrid cell containing the nuclear material of both.

1961 *Nature* 13 May 653/2 (*heading*) Karyological demonstration of hybridization of mammalian cells *in vitro*. **1965** *Proc. Nat. Acad. Sci.* LIII. 1040 Hybridization of somatic cells *in vitro*..has since been shown to occur in mixed cultures of many different pairs of cultured mouse cells. **1970** *Nature* 18 Apr. 280/2 Somatic cell hybridization is a potentially useful technique for the introduction of genetic variability into plant species. **1970** *McGraw-Hill Yearbk. Sci. & Technol.* 214/2 Whereas these first experiments involved two closely related transformed mouse cell lines,..somatic hybridization can occur between cells derived from different species, such as mouse and man.

2. *fig.*

1960 E. R. Goodman in J. A. Fishman *Readings Sociol. of Lang.* (1968) 733 One should add that the idea of 'hybridization' or fusion of languages, which Stalin continued to use, was Marrist in origin. **1964** M. McLuhan *Understanding Media* v. 48 The crossings or hybridizations of the media release great new force and energy as by fission or fusion. **1971** *Farmer & Stockbreeder* 23 Feb. 3/1 We shall be the old Stockbreeder Redivivus: not dead, not reborn, just rejuvenated. Or, if you prefer it, reinvigorated by hybridization; for we join forces with the *British Farmer*, the journal of the NFU.

hybridize, *v.* Add: **1. c.** *Physical Chem.* To combine (atomic orbitals) mathematically so as to obtain hybrid orbitals.

1933 [implied in *hybridized *ppl. a.*]. **1939** L. Pauling *Nature Chem. Bond* iii. 96 It is found on hybridizing these orbitals that four strong bonds directed to the corners of a square can be formed. **1962** Cotton & Wilkinson *Adv. Inorg. Chem.* iii. 67 The *s* and the three *p* orbitals are hybridized to produce four sp^3 hybrids.

d. *Biochem.* To cause (a subunit of a macromolecule) to combine *with*, or become attached *to*, a complementary subunit of the same or a very similar molecular species from a different source; to cause (two such subunits) to combine together.

1959 *Jrnl. Amer. Chem. Soc.* LXXXI. 3169/1 When labelled and unlabelled hemoglobins are hybridized, the hybrids contain both labelled and unlabelled chains. **1965** *Jrnl. Molecular Biol.* XII. 829 The procedure involves immobilizing denatured DNA on nitrocellulose membrane filters, hybridizing complementary RNA to the membrane-fixed DNA, and eliminating RNA 'noise'. **1966** Lehmann & Huntsman *Man's Haemoglobins* xxi. 226 When canine haemoglobin and human haemoglobin are hybridised together, the new hybrids that result differ considerably in their mobility. **1969** *Nature* 10 May 573/1, 100 *μg* of RNA was hybridized with 50 *μg* of DNA. **1972** *Arch. Biochem. & Biophysics* CL. 407 Phosphofructokinases from rabbit muscle and rabbit liver were hybridized by dissociation at low pH followed by recombination at neutrality. **1972** S. L. Wolfe *Biol. Cell* ix. 199/1 The best evidence that transcription is asymmetric comes from experiments in which RNA is hybridized with its DNA template... The RNA will form hybrid double helices with no more than 50 percent of its template DNA... Thus the RNA is complementary to only one of the two DNA strands, and only one..serves as a template for RNA transcription.

2. c. *Biochem.* Of a protein or nucleic acid: to exchange complementary subunits in hybridization (sense *1 d). Const. *with* (or *to*).

1962 *Science* 21 Dec. 1331/2 Their sequences are unique, since they hybridize readily only to homologous DNA. **1965** *Jrnl. Molecular Biol.* XII. 830 RNA molecules possessing an extensive secondary structure will not hybridize until their own melting temperature is approached. **1969** *Times* 16 May 14/7 Each kind of RNA chemically recombines or hybridizes with the DNA segment off which it was copied. **1971** *Biochemistry* (Easton, Pa.) X. 3509/2 Hexokinases A and B can hybridize in 0·1 M sodium phosphate solution at pH values near 8. **1972** S. L. Wolfe *Biol. Cell* ix. 206/2 For example, rRNA from *Drosophila* will hybridize to some degree with chick DNA or vice versa, even though there are wide differences in base composition of the total DNA complement from the two species.

3. *fig.* (*trans.*).

1964 M. McLuhan *Understanding Media* v. 50 With literacy now about to hybridize the cultures of the Chinese, the Indians, and the Africans. **1971** *Nature* 24 Sept. 241/2 In the more remote future it may well be, when further improvements in the combustion intensity of low grade fuel mixtures are required, that they will be achieved by hybridizing the high and low temperature branches.

hybridized (həi·bridəizd), *ppl. a.* [f. prec. + -ed[1].] Obtained by hybridization; hybrid (in various senses).

1859 [see Hybridize *v.* 1]. **1926** G. W. Tyrrell *Princ. Petrol.* viii. 165 Wholesale enclosure of Dalradian quartzites and mica-schists within a large mass of norite..has led to the formation of a zone of hybridised or contaminated rocks, full of xenoliths in all stages of digestion. **1933** *Jrnl. Chem. Physics* I. 502 The valence orbital.. could be of the strongly hybridized type. **1955** [see *fine art 2]. **1959** G. E. W. Wolstenholme et al. *Significant Trends Med. Res.* (Ciba Found. Symp.) 7 The N-terminal residues of the hybridized hemoglobin S were labelled with Sanger's reagent. **1968** [see *hybrid *sb.* and *a.* A. 2 c]. **1969** *Nature* 10 May 573/2 The rat from which the hybridized RNA was obtained.

hybris (həi·bris). [ad. Gr. ὕβρις.] = *hubris.

1920 *Public Opinion* 27 Aug. 195/2 During one of these the oppressor, possessed of place and power, imagined in his hybris, that he might extend his arm across the ocean. **1929** *Encycl. Brit.* XXII. 53/1 Themis is the servant or companion of Zeus... Her opposite is Hybris (ὕβρις), insolent encroachment upon the rights of others. **1949** *Horizon* Aug. 87 Hybris means believing that you *are* a god, i.e., that you cannot suffer; pride means a defiant attempt to *become* a god. **1969** *Commonweal* 22 Aug. 524 America, like all earlier empires, is going to march to the brink of *hybris* and plunge in.

hydathode (həi·dăþōud). *Bot.* [a. G. *hydathode* (G. Haberlandt 1894, in *Sitzungsber. Akad. Wiss. Wien* CIII. I. 494), f. Gr. ὑδατ-, ὕδωρ water + ὁδός way, path.] A pore or gland which discharges water from the leaf of a plant.

1895 *Jrnl. R. Microsc. Soc.* 333 Under the name *hydathode*, Prof. G. Haberlandt designates those organs, which are frequently found in the leaves of tropical and other plants, especially designed for the storing up or excretion of water. *Ibid.*, A very simple type of hydathode occurs in the leaves of grasses. **1897** J. C. Willis *Man. Flowering Plants* I. 116 Water-pores or hydathodes are openings, resembling stomata, upon leaves or elsewhere, through which the plant excretes water. **1914** M. Drummond tr. *Haberlandt's Physiol. Plant Anat.* x. 487 Many of our native plants are provided with organs which secrete water in the liquid form. Such hydathodes are even more widely distributed among plants inhabiting the humid tropics. **1931** E. C. Miller *Plant Physiol.* vii. 390 The physiological significance of the hydathodes and of the loss of water by guttation is not definitely known. **1953** K. Esau *Plant Anat.* xvi. 433 Hydathodes are structures that discharge water from the interior of the leaf to its surface. **1967** C. D. Sculthorpe *Biol. Aquatic Vasc. Plants* iv. 90 The possibility remains that the hydathodes [of water plants] are functionless relict structures.

hydatidiform, *a.* (s.v. Hydatid *sb.* (*a.*)). Add: *hydatidiform mole*, a uterine mole (Mole *sb.*[5]) formed by the proliferation and distension of the chorionic villi; also, the condition of having such a mole in the uterus.

1859 *Lancet* 15 Oct. 397/2 A case in which a specimen of the hydatidiform mole was expelled from the uterus seven months after the birth of a first child. **1971** T. J. Deeley *Gynaecol. Cancer* xv. 228 The incidence of hydatidiform mole is about 1:700–1:3,000 known pregnancies.

hydatidosis (həidătidōu·sis). *Path.* [f. Hydatid *sb.* (*a.*) + -osis.] A pathological condition resulting from infestation with tapeworm hydatids.

1925 *Med. Jrnl. Austral.* 24 Oct. 502/1 The whole abdominal cavity may be packed with cysts of all sizes—a condition which has been called hydatidosis. **1966** *Lancet* 24 Dec. 1422/1 Subjects with pulmonary hydatidosis.. were tested.

Hyde (həid). Name of the evil personality assumed by Dr. Jekyll in R. L. Stevenson's story, 'Strange Case of Dr. Jekyll and Mr. Hyde' (1886): used allusively in reference to the evil side of a person's character. (Cf. *Jekyll.)

1887 *Puck* (U.S.) XXII. 188 Is that you, Livingston?.. No, m'dearsh, it'sh Doct' Hyde. **1915** 'I. Hay' *First Hundred Thousand* xiv. 192 But we encountered surprisingly few Hydes. Nearly all were Jekylls. **1960** *Encounter* Sept. 9/1 Normally we let Hyde loose only when for some reason he is socially acceptable. The Saturnalia existed to satisfy his demands. **1967** V. Nabokov *Speak, Memory* (ed. 2) viii. 165 One ribald and agile boy (could it be I after all—the Hyde of my Jekyll?) managed to silhouette his foot.

Hyde Park (həi·d pā·ɹk). The name of a park in central London, of which a part (known as Speakers' Corner) is traditionally the scene of 'soap-box' oratory, used allusively (freq. *attrib.*) of the type of speaker, oratory, etc., found there. So **Hyde Pa·rkian** *a.*, having the quality (of voice) of a Hyde Park orator.

1892 G. B. Shaw *Let.* 21 Apr. (1965) 337 Her voice has become much more powerful—quite Hyde Parkian in its pedal notes. **1897** *London Handbk.* 143/1 They [*sc.* 'contentious Jews'] pose as martyrs in the cause of liberty, and certainly any man well deserves such an honourable title who will listen unflinchingly to two hours of Hyde Park oratory. **1912** C. Mackenzie *Carnival* xii. 132 Love..was as incredible to her as..to a Hyde Park materialist. **1914** 'I. Hay' *Knight on Wheels* (ed. 2) xix. 186 This is a peculiarity of the Hyde Park orator. Set him on his legs, and in ten minutes he has wandered..from the point. **1934** 'G. Orwell' *Burmese Days* xvii. 245 He told Flory 'not to start talking like a damned Hyde Park agitator', and then read him a snappish little sermon. **1937** *Discovery* Aug. 254/1 Each having something to say like so many Hyde Park orators. **1965** C. Fremlin *Jealous One* xi. 85 Everyone..competing, like Hyde Park orators, for an audience for their particular problem. **1966** *Listener* 24 Feb. 287/2 A few jibes against the Christian Church more reminiscent of Hyde Park oratory than of Voltaire and Gibbon. **1972** 'E. Lathen' *The Longer the Thread* xi. 106 A small Hyde Park seemed to have sprung up on the green. A whole medley of impassioned orators was in full voice.

hydnocarpic (hidno,kā·ɹpik), *a. Chem.* [f. next + -ic.] *hydnocarpic acid*: a crystalline alicyclic acid, $C_5H_7{\cdot}(CH_2)_{10}{\cdot}COOH$, which in the form of its glycerides is one of the chief constituents of chaulmoogra oil and hydnocarpus oil.

1905 Power & Barrowcliff in *Jrnl. Chem. Soc.* LXXXVII. I. 885 The acids obtained from the respective Hydnocarpus oils consist chiefly of chaulmoogric acid and a lower homologue of the same series, the latter having been isolated..also from chaulmoogra oil. This new acid has the formula $C_{16}H_{28}O_2$, and is designated hydnocarpic acid. **1960** K. S. Markley *Fatty Acids* (ed. 2) I. ii. 215 All these oils contain one or more fatty acids having a terminal cyclopentenyl ring, especially chaulmoogric, hydnocarpic, and gorlic acid, which account for 80 to 90% or more of the total fatty acids of these oils. *Ibid.* 217 *dl*-Hydnocarpic acid has been synthesized.

Hence **hydnoca·rpate**, a salt or ester of hydnocarpic acid.

1905 *Jrnl. Chem. Soc.* LXXVII. I. 890 Ethyl Hydnocarpate, $C_{15}H_{27}{\cdot}CO_2Et$. **1927** *Proc. R. Soc. Med.* XX. 999 The veins become blocked by sodium hydnocarpate in some cases. **1953** R. A. Raphael in E. H. Rodd *Chem. Carbon Compounds* IIa. iv. 119 When ethyl hydnocarpate is reduced by the Bouveault–Blanc process, an alcohol is obtained which can be converted..to chaulmoogric acid.

hydnocarpus (hidnokā·ɹpŏs). *Bot.* [mod.L. (J. Gaertner *De Fructibus et Seminibus Plantarum* (1788) I. 288), f. Gr. ὕδνον truffle + καρπός fruit, from the resemblance of the fruit to a truffle.] **a.** A tree of the genus so called, belonging to the family Flacourtiaceæ and native to tropical Asia.

1928 *Daily Express* 20 Feb. 2/1 Hydnocarpus oil is obtained from the dried fruit of the hydnocarpus tree. **1953** N. L. Bor *Man. Indian Forest Bot.* 145 In *Hydnocarpus* the fruits are produced on the branches.

b. *attrib.*, as *hydnocarpus therapy*; **hydnocarpus oil,** a yellowish oil or soft cream-coloured fat obtained from the seeds of trees of the genus *Hydnocarpus*, esp. *H. wightiana* and *H. anthelminthica*, and used, formerly extensively, in the treatment of leprosy.

1905 Hydnocarpus oils [see *hydnocarpic *a.*]. **1927** *Proc. R. Soc. Med.* XX. 1011 Since early in 1921 we have used the preparations of chaulmoogra and hydnocarpus oils in our Hospital for Lepers, at Dichpalli, Hyderabad State. **1967** *Martindale's Extra Pharmacopoeia* (ed. 25) 494/2 Although largely replaced by the sulphones, hydnocarpus oil is still employed in the treatment of leprosy, especially in endemic areas in the East where it is cheap and readily available. **1964** R. G. Cochrane *Leprosy* (ed. 2) xxi. 377, I do not hold with many workers that the day of hydnocarpus therapy has disappeared.

hydra. 7. b. *hydra-headed* adj. (later examples).

1842 *Ainsworth's Mag.* II. 43 The Puff Literary is hydra-headed. **1899** *Daily News* 8 Feb. 7/5 The hydra-headed leadership of the Irish party. **1963** *Daily Tel.* 20 Nov. 14/2 The hydra-headed challenge of London's mounting traffic congestion.

hydralazine (həidræ·lăzīn). *Pharm.* Also **hydrallazine.** [f. hydr*azino*ph*thal*azine, f. *hydrazino- + *phthalazine.] A sympatholytic drug, $C_8H_5N_2{\cdot}NH{\cdot}NH_2$, used in the form of the hydrochloride, a white crystalline powder, in the treatment of hypertension.

1952 *Jrnl. Amer. Med. Assoc.* 1 Nov. 861/2 Hydrallazine Hydrochloride for 1-hydrazinophthalazine hydrochloride. **1953** *Jrnl. Pharmacol. & Exper. Therap.* CIX. 182 Hydrallazine..stimulates the heart and increases cardiac output. **1963** *Brit. Pharmacopœia* p. xxviii, British Pharmacopœia... Hydrallazine hydrochloride. International Pharmacopoeia... Hydralazine hydrochloride. **1970** A. Goth *Med. Pharmacol.* (ed. 5) xiv. 157 Hydralazine (1-hydrazinophthalazine; Apresoline) is a potent antihypertensive drug, but it can produce serious toxic reactions.

hydramnios (həidræ·mniŏs). *Path.* Also **hydramnion.** [f. Hydr- + Amnios, Amnion.] Excessive accumulation of amniotic fluid during pregnancy.

1838 F. Churchill *Outl. Princ. Dis. Females* 145 'Hydramnios', or excess of liquor amnii.., is said to result from a general serous diathesis. **1885** W. T. Lusk *Sci. & Art Midwifery* (ed. 3) xv. 288 The causes of hydramnion are hardly to be found in a single morbid condition. **1961** *Lancet* 30 Sept. 742/2 She came into hospital three times during her eighth pregnancy with..mild hydramnios.

hydrapulper (həi·drăpʌlpəɹ). *Paper-making.* Also **Hydrapulper.** [Irreg. f. Gr. ὑδρ(ο-, combining form of ὕδωρ water + Pulper.] A large vessel with a set of motor-driven rotating vanes at the bottom, designed to break up the fibres of wood pulp or other paper stock in water.

1941 *Techn. Pap. Addr. Techn. Assoc. Pulp Pap. Ind.* XXIV. 384/2 The hydrapulper is simply a cylindrical open-top tank with a dished bottom at the center of which is a heavy impeller. **1951** J. N. Stephenson *Pulp & Paper Manuf.* II. i. 67 Straw bales..are fed as rapidly as possible into a Hydrapulper..containing the required amount of chemical in hot water. **1966** *Paper Technology* VII. ii. 135 These rejects are in a suspension and could possibly be extracted from the bottom of the hydrapulper tub. **1967** E. Chambers *Photolitho-Offset* xvi. 244 This acidity in uncoated paper can be traced to aluminium sulphate, which is added in the beater or hydrapulper during paper manufacture.

hydrarch (həi·drāɹk), *a. Ecol.* [f. Gr. ὕδωρ, ὑδρ- water + ἀρχή beginning.] Of a succession of plant communities: having its origin in a watery habitat.

1913 W. S. Cooper in *Bot. Gaz.* LV. 11 The terms xerarch and hydrarch are here used for the first time, for the purpose of indicating a natural and important classification of plant successions. The former is applied to those successions which, having their origin in xerophytic habitats, such as rock shores, beaches, and cliffs, become more and more mesophytic in their successive stages; the latter to those which, originating in hydrophytic habitats such as lakes and ponds, also progress towards mesophytism. **1929** Weaver & Clements *Plant Ecol.* iv. 55 Successions beginning in ponds, lakes, marshes, or elsewhere in water are termed hydrarch. **1960** N. Polunin *Introd. Plant Geogr.* xi. 324 They [*sc.* the seres] are distinguished as 'hydrarch', 'mesarch', or 'xerarch', according to whether their initiation is under damp, median, or dry conditions.

hydrase (həi·drēiz, -ēis). *Biochem.* [f. Hydr- + *-ase.] Any enzyme which catalyses an addition reaction between water and a substrate or the reverse process.

1943 Sumner & Somers *Chem. & Methods of Enzymes* iv. xvii. 296 The hydrases add water to organic compounds without causing a splitting. **1961** P. D. Boyer et al. *Enzymes* (ed. 2) V. xxviii. 455 Among enzymes catalyzing the addition of groups to double bonds (and the reverse reaction), the hydrases (or dehydrases) form the largest group.

hydrastinine (həidræ·stinīn). *Chem.* [ad. G. *hydrastinin* (Freund & Will 1887, in *Ber. d. Deut. Chem. Ges.* XX. 88), f. Hydrastin(e + -ine[5].] A synthetic alkaloid, $C_{11}H_{13}NO_3$, derived from hydrastine and sometimes employed in the form of the hydrochloride to control uterine bleeding.

1887 *Jrnl. Chem. Soc.* LII. I. 383 [Freund and Will] have examined the base hydrastinine, $C_{11}H_{11}NO_2+H_2O$, obtained together with opianic acid where hydrastine is treated with oxidising agents. **1929** *Encycl. Brit.* XI. 961/1 The hydrolytic product, hydrastinine, is an important drug, being used as an internal styptic. **1970** S. W. Pelletier *Chem. Alkaloids* iii. 65 Oxidative hydrolysis of hydrastine with dilute nitric acid results in the formation of two fragments, opianic acid and hydrastinine.

hydrastis (həidræ·stis). [mod.L. (J. Ellis in Linnæus *Systema Naturæ* (ed. 10, 1759) II. 1088): etym. unkn.] The dried rhizome and roots of the herb golden seal or yellow root (*Hydrastis canadensis*), or an extract or tincture of them, formerly used medicinally as a bitter stomachic and to control uterine bleeding.

1865 Wood & Bache *Dispensatory U.S.A.* (ed. 12) 459 Hydrastis might probably be advantageously prepared in the form of a fluid extract. **1882** R. Bentley *Man. Bot.* (ed. 4) 425 Hydrastis is..used by the Indians of the Western States of North America to dye various shades of yellow. **1908** *Practitioner* Jan. 96 Styptol and hydrastis.. are recommended for arresting haemorrhage from the non-pregnant organ. **1951** A. Grollman *Pharmacol. & Therapeutics* 757 Color may also be imparted by the addition of..Hydrastis Tincture (N.F.) which..is soluble in alcohol and hydro-alcoholic preparations giving a yellow color. **1967** *Martindale's Extra Pharmacopoeia* (ed. 25) 592 Hydrastis..in the treatment of post-partum haemorrhage..is much inferior to ergot.

hydratable (həidrēi·tăb'l), *a.* [f. Hydrat(e *v.* + -able.] Capable of becoming hydrated.

1953 J. Davidsohn et al. *Soap Manuf.* I. xiii. 220 Animal fats..are for the most part substantially free of phosphatides or other hydratable substances. **1956** *Soil Sci.* LXXXII. 198 Hydratable products may be formed as the clay minerals decompose.

hydratase (həi·drătēiz, -ēis). *Biochem.* [f. Hydrat(e *v.* + *-ase.] = *hydrase.

1922 *Chem. Abstr.* XVI. 936 The enzymes can be divided into hydratases, hydrolases and oxido-reductases. **1953** *Adv. Enzymol.* XIV. 237 Hence the enzyme hitherto called 'fumarase' should be renamed fumaric hydratase.

hydrate, *v.* Add: **b.** *intr.* To undergo hydration, to become combined with water.

1909 in Webster. **1921** J. R. Partington *Text-bk. Inorg. Chem.* xl. 846 The residue of anhydrous $CaSO_4$ rapidly takes up water, but if the heating has been more intense the residue hydrates only very slowly. **1947** R. H. Bogue *Chem. Portland Cement* xxv. 435 Complete hydration..was obtained by mixing the compounds with water to form a plastic paste, allowing the pastes to hydrate in sealed containers for a month, [etc.]. **1962** Harris & Gruber in A. Pirie *Lens Metabolism Rel. Cataract* 382 If the block is sufficient, more sodium is gained than potassium lost and the lens hydrates in a predictable manner.

hydratuba (həi:drătiū·bă). [f. Hydra II. 6 + Tuba[1], formerly *Hydra tuba*, when the organism was thought to be a species of *Hydra*; in reference to the shape of the larva.] The polyp-like larval stage of a jellyfish of the class Scyphozoa; a scyphistoma.

1847 J. G. Dalyell *Rare & Remarkable Animals Scotl.* I. iii. 76 (*heading*) Hydra tuba, the Trumpet Polypus. *Ibid.* 77 The body of the *hydra tuba* is a hollow cone five lines in length, thick and fleshy. **1898** A. Sedgwick *Student's Text-bk. Zool.* I. iv. 159 In the *Ephyroninæ* the development is generally accompanied by an alternation

of generations; the asexual generations being represented by the *Scyphistoma* (*Hydra tuba*) and *Strobila*; but in exceptional cases it is direct (*Pelagia*). **1901** SHIPLEY & MACBRIDE *Zool.* iii. 64 Each [planula] fixes itself and develops into a little polyp, called a Hydratuba, not unlike a *Hydra* in appearance. **1927** *Glasgow Herald* 5 Nov. 6/2 This [*sc.* the larva] settles as a polyp-like form, the hydratuba, and this, by a kind of budding, gives origin to little saucer-like discs which grow into medusæ. **1932** BORRADAILE & POTTS *Invertebrata* v. 155 At certain seasons the whole hydratuba is segmented by transverse horizontal furrows. **1951** *Microscope* VIII. 193 (*title*) Planula, hydratuba and ephyra stages of the common jellyfish.

hydraulic, *a.* and *sb.* Add: **A.** *adj.* **1.** Further special collocations.

hydraulic engineering (see quots.); so *hydraulic engineer*; *hydraulic gradient*: (a line representing) the variation along a pipe or channel of the head due to elevation and pressure in a liquid flowing along it; *hydraulic jump*: an abrupt change from a fast, shallow flow to a slower, deeper flow at some point in a liquid flowing in an open channel; *hydraulic radius* or *mean depth*: a length equal to the cross-sectional area of the liquid in a channel or pipe divided by the length of the wetted perimeter.

1838 *Penny Cycl.* XII. 382/1 Besides the construction of harbours for ships, the formation of the aqueducts which supplied the cities with water must have constituted an important part of the duties of the hydraulic engineer among the antients. **1916** J. PARK *Textbk. Pract. Hydraulics* p. x, A valuable work of reference for all hydraulic engineers. **1835** *Rep. Brit. Assoc. Adv. Sci. 1834* 473 Practical works in hydraulic engineering of great magnitude and extent have been carried on in England. **1858** G. R. BURNELL *Rudiments Hydraulic Engin.* I. i. 1 Hydraulic Engineering will be considered to include.. questions connected with building in water. *Ibid.* 2 Hydraulic engineering is principally confined to the operations in which water acts as an incompressible fluid. **1940** *Chambers's Techn. Dict.* 427/1 *Hydraulic engineering*, that branch of engineering chiefly concerned in the design and production of hydraulic machinery, pumping plants, pipelines, etc. **1956** A. H. COMPTON *Atomic Quest* II. 106 His.. degree in hydraulic engineering at the University of Iowa. **1881** *Encycl. Brit.* XII. 484/2 Hence [the line] CD is termed the virtual slope or hydraulic gradient of the pipe. **1935** A. J. MARTIN *Work of Sanitary Engin.* viii. 92 If a series of open-ended vertical pipes were carried up from the main at intervals, the water would rise in each of them up to the line of the hydraulic gradient. **1951** W. L. RUSSELL *Princ. Petroleum Geol.* xii. 212 By using..high hydraulic gradients, oil globules and gas bubbles may be forced through these sandstones. **1922** H. E. BABBITT *Sewerage* iv. 74 The hydraulic jump will occur when a high velocity of flow is interrupted by an obstruction in the channel, by a change in grade of the invert, or the approach of the velocity to the 'critical' velocity. **1969** CHIA-SHUN YIH *Fluid Mech.* v. 226 Tidal bores observed in estuaries are hydraulic jumps propagating against flowing water. **1797** *Encycl. Brit.* XVIII. 891/1 Column I..contains the hydraulic mean depths of any conduit in inches...The column is continued to 100 inches, which is fully equal to the hydraulic mean depth of any canal. **1829** *Nat. Philos.* (Libr. Useful Knowl.) I. vi. 5/2 Suppose the whole quantity of water to be spread on a horizontal surface, equal in extent to the bottom and sides of the river, when the height at which the water would so stand is called the hydraulic mean depth. **1930** *Engineering* 7 Feb. 180/1 By means of the following table, maximum scour can be calculated from calculated values of the hydraulic mean depth. **1876** L. D'A. JACKSON tr. *Kutter's Mean Velocity of Discharge of Rivers* i. 2, *r* is the mean hydraulic radius, or the quotient of the water section by the wetted perimeter. **1948** D. W. TAYLOR *Fund. Soil Mech.* vi. 109 The ratio of volume to surface area of flow channel may be used as an alternative definition of hydraulic radius.

2. (The term is used in connection with liquids other than water.)

hydraulic buffer, a device for checking the recoil of a mounted gun, consisting of a piston in a cylinder filled with liquid; *hydraulic intensifier*, a device for obtaining an increase in pressure in a hydraulic system, usu. comprising two cylinders of different diameters containing pistons that are joined to one another.

1871 G. E. VOYLE *Dict. Artillery Terms* (ed. 2) 45/1 The Hydraulic Buffer. **1876** VOYLE & STEVENSON *Mil. Dict.* (ed. 3) 54/2 Where guns are mounted on carriages and platforms fitted for hydraulic buffers, the buffer will invariably be kept on the platform filled with the proper quantity of oil. **1899** G. D. HISCOX *Mech. Movements* VII. 153 Hydraulic intensifier.—High pressure obtained from low pressure by differential pistons. **1959** *Chambers's Encycl.* VI. 646/1 A hydraulic buffer or brake consists of a cylinder filled with liquid, a piston and a piston rod. **1962** WALSHAW & JOBSON *Mech. Fluids* ii. 32 A 100 ton press with a 12 in. stroke is to be operated from a main in which the pressure is 40 lbf/in² gauge, via a hydraulic intensifier with a 4 ft stroke.

b. *hydraulic brake*: (*a*) a brake that utilizes the resistance to motion experienced by a piston or rotor in a chamber full of liquid; also, a hydraulic buffer; (*b*) a brake that operates by means of friction but is actuated hydraulically; (*c*) a dynamometer that works on the principle of the hydraulic brake (sense (*a*)).

(*a*) **1874** *Engineering* 11 Sept. 194/3 (*heading*) Hydraulic brakes. **1894** J. A. EWING *Steam-Engine* ix. 269 Many governors are furnished with a dash-pot, which is a hydraulic or pneumatic brake, consisting of a piston connected to the governor, working loosely in a cylinder which is filled with oil or with water. **1902** *Encycl. Brit.* XXXI. 897/1 The buffer-stop to be seen in terminal railway stations, and the hydraulic brakes of quick-firing guns, are examples. **1959** [see sense 2 above]. **1962** D. J. MYATT *Machine Design* i. 151 Because braking torque is a function of speed of rotation of the brake rotor, electric and hydraulic brakes should not be depended upon to hold a load stationary.

(*b*) **1875** *Engineering* 8 Jan. 29/1 The hydraulic brake comprises a pump, a cistern, and an accumulator for collecting and storing the power, a regulator, and apparatus for applying that power in retarding the speed of the train. **1876** J. W. BARRY *Railway Appliances* vii. 286 In the hydraulic break the pressure on the pistons is derived from the pressure of a small hydraulic accumulator. **1924** WRIGHT & SMITH *Automotive Construction & Operation* xiv. 331 Several cars have adopted the hydraulic-brake system for all four wheels. **1963** D. V. W. FRANCIS *Morris Minor* i. 11/1 Lockheed hydraulic brakes operate on 7-in. brake drums.

(*c*) **1890** *Min. Proc. Inst. Civil Engin.* XCIX. 169 At the same meeting, Mr. William Froude gave an account of his hydraulic brake, for measuring the power of large engines. **1925** A. W. JUDGE *Automobile Engines* I. vi. 170 The Froude hydraulic brake..is now largely employed for automobile engine tests. In this case the power is absorbed by hydraulic resistance.

c. Of a liquid: used, or suitable for use, in hydraulic brakes or other hydraulic equipment. (Not used predicatively.)

1941 E. MOLLOY *Hydraulic Equipment* 86 A valve on the master-brake cylinder..allows the hydraulic fluid to escape, under pressure, to the brake cylinder in the wheel. **1951** *Adv. Chem. Ser.* V. 241 Hydraulic fluids..include those made from petroleum, synthetic oils, and aqueous solutions containing antifreeze and rust inhibitors. **1967** E. R. BRAITHWAITE *Lubrication* iii. 161 Fire-resistant hydraulic oils represent a class of lubricants in which there is increasing interest. **1971** *Drive* New Year 33/2 It is advisable to change hydraulic fluid every eighteen months or 24,000 miles.

3. (Earlier examples.)

1829 *Arcana of Sci. & Art* 246 When the bridge of Louis XVI was constructed, much advantage was derived from mixing with the hydraulic mortar which was used, a portion of the clinkers..which had passed through the grates of the glass bottle furnace, at Meudon. **1843** *Civil Engin. & Arch. Jrnl.* VI. 157/2 Hydraulic lime will harden in a very short time. *Ibid.*, Roman cement, the most hydraulic of all mortars.

hydraulic (həidrǭ·lik), *v. U.S.* [f. *hydraulic* in *hydraulic mining*.] *trans.* To work or obtain by the methods of hydraulic mining. Hence **hydrau·lic(k)ing** *vbl. sb.*

1868 *Rep. J. Ross Browne Mineral Resources* (U.S. Treas. Dept.) 94 They can hydraulic away about 300 feet along the face of their Claim, but beyond that the hill is too deep to pay for piping. **1880** G. T. INGHAM *Digging Gold* ix. 243 Two steam pumps have been..forcing water from French Creek up to these dry diggings for hydraulicing. **1892** C. F. LUMMIS *Tramp across Continent* viii. 122 To run a fifteen-mile pipe-line from the Sandias to Golden, and thus bring water to hydraulic the enormous areas of gold-bearing gravel. **1904** J. LYNCH *Three Yrs. Klondike* (1967) ix. 127 Those grounds can only be dredged or hydraulicked. **1908** W. R. CRANE *Gold & Silver* v. 379 In 1903 the Crown Mountain Mining Company..hydrauliced the material in sluices to a 60-stamp mill. **1928** W. A. CHALFANT *Outposts Civilization* 42 From which it was said the owner hydraulicked $90,000 worth of gold. **1965** *Mineral Facts & Problems* (U.S. Bureau of Mines) 231 Some kaolin deposits are mined by hydraulicking.

hydraulicity. (Examples.)

1843 *Civil Engin. & Arch. Jrnl.* VI. 157/2 In constructions of this kind..the lime should possess some degree of hydraulicity, in order that it may harden before the injurious action of frost comes upon it. **1902** J. BLACK *Illustr. Carpenter & Builder Ser.: Plastering* iii. 46 The hydraulicity is greatest when the limestone contains thirty per cent. of clay. **1959** *Chambers's Encycl.* III. 320/2 The calcium oxide..retains all these impurities and the proportion in which they are present greatly affects the properties of the lime, notably its hydraulicity.

hydraulus (həidrǭ·lɒs). *Mus.* Also **hydraulis.** [L., f. Gr. ὕδραυλος hydraulic organ (cf. αὐλός pipe).] A type of water organ popular in classical times; = *hydraulic organ* (HYDRAULIC *a.* 2).

1874 W. CHAPPELL *Hist. Mus.* I. xiii. 328 Philōn defines..a kind of 'syrinx played by the hands, which we call hydraulis'. **1903** C. F. A. WILLIAMS *Story of Organ* ii. 35 Sylvester made an organ that was played by 'warm water'; this was..the hydraulus. **1934** *Times Educ. Suppl.* 27 Jan. p. iv/2 [The Albert Hall organ] has..been heard as an accompaniment to choral singing, and, like the hydraulus in the Roman amphitheatres of old, to gladiatorial spectacles. **1970** *Oxf. Compan. Mus.* (ed. 10) 496/2 Hydraulus, hydraulis, or water organ. This is the most ancient form of organ known. *Ibid.*, In general appearance the hydraulus is like any small organ of today.

hydrazide (həi·drăzəid). *Chem.* [f. HYDRAZ(INE + -IDE.] Any compound which may be represented as R·CO·NH·NH_2; also, any derivative of such a compound in which univalent radicals replace one or more of the hydrogen atoms.

1888 *Jrnl. Chem. Soc.* LIV. 686 Malonyl hydrazide, $CH_2(CO \cdot NH \cdot NHPh)_2$..crystallises..in white leaflets. **1955** Z. E. JOLLES in E. H. Rodd *Chem. Carbon Compounds* IIIA. vi. 320 Hydrazo compounds and hydrazides yield the corresponding azo derivatives by oxidation.

hydrazine. Add: Now used as a rocket propellant.

1950 *Sci. News* XV. 77 One class [of propellants], called hypergols, react as soon as they come together... Such pairs are..hydrazine hydrate and hydrogen peroxide. **1955** *Sci. News Let.* 1 Oct. 212/1 Monopropellants, whose chemical structures carry both fuel and oxidizer, were listed by him as ethylene oxide, hydrazine, hydrogen peroxide and nitromethane. **1960** *Aeroplane* XCIX. 638/2 Achieving a lunar orbit would depend largely on the hydrazine engine which has yet to be tested in flight. **1969** *Times* 3 June (Suppl.) p. iii/7 Aerozine 50—an equal blend of hydrazine and unsymmetrical dimethyl hydrazine.

hydrazinium (həidrăzi·niɒm). *Chem.* [f. HYDRAZIN(E + *-IUM b.] **a.** The ion H_2N—NH_3^+ derived from hydrazine (or a substituted ion derived from this in which univalent radicals replace one or more of the hydrogen atoms). Usu. *attrib.* **b.** The less common ion H_3N^+—NH_3^+ (or a substituted ion derived from this in which univalent radicals replace one or more of the hydrogen atoms). Usu. *attrib.*

The application of the terms *hydrazinium* and *hydrazonium* has been inconsistent. Some authors have favoured using one or other of them (with or without a distinguishing numeral) for both ions, whilst some prefer *hydrazinium* for $N_2H_6^{++}$ and *hydrazonium* for $N_2H_5^+$; others would abandon the names entirely. The International Union of Pure and Applied Chemistry recommends *hydrazinium*(1+), *hydrazinium*(2+), respectively, for the two ions (*Nomencl. Inorg. Chem.* (ed. 2, 1971), Rule 3.17).

1927 *Chem. Abstr.* XXI. 2672 These 'acid products' really contain hydrazinium salts. **1936** *Jrnl. Amer. Chem. Soc.* LVIII. 1606/2 The ionization constants for the hydrazinium ion as an acid and hydrazinium hydroxide as a base have been determined. **1949, 1954** [see *HYDRAZONIUM a, b]. **1955** *Chem. & Engin. News* 3 Jan. 70/3 A. C. Nixon..suggests that 'hydrazonium' be retained for $H_2NONH_3^+$ [*sic*] and 'hydrazinium' be applied to $^+H_3N \cdot NH_3^+$. **1957, 1966** [see *HYDRAZONIUM c]. **1964** J. W. LINNETT *Electronic Struct. Molecules* iv. 64 The NN bond-length in hydrazine, H_2N—NH_2, is 1·47 Å whereas that in the hydrazinium ion, $H_3\overset{+}{N}$—$\overset{+}{N}H_3$, is 1·40 Å. **1966** COTTON & WILKINSON *Adv. Inorg. Chem.* (ed. 2) xii. 335 Two series of hydrazinium salts are obtainable, those of $N_2H_5^+$ and those of $N_2H_6^{2+}$.

hydrazino(-) (həidrăzī·no). *Chem.* A combining form of HYDRAZINE, denoting the univalent radical —NH·NH_2 (or a substituted radical derived from this in which univalent radicals replace one or more of the hydrogen atoms); also used *attrib.* as an independent word.

1907 *Jrnl. Chem. Soc.* XCII. I. 880 The present work was undertaken to determine the conditions under which the hydroxyls of phenols can be displaced similarly by the hydrazino-group ·NH·NH_2. **1919** *Chem. Abstr.* XIII. 1304 (*heading*) Hydrazino acids. *Ibid.*, Dihydrazine hydrazinodimalonic acid. **1952** E. H. RODD *Chem. Carbon Compounds* I. xii. 841 Hydrazinoacetic acid, $NH_2NHCH_2CO_2H$. **1953** C. C. CLARK *Hydrazine* iii. 35 Hydrogenation of hydrazones and azines to hydrazino compounds is possible in many cases. *Ibid.* 36 (*heading*) Hydrazino acids and esters.

hydrazo(-) (həi·drăzo). *Chem.* A combining form of HYDRAZINE, denoting the bivalent radical —NH·NH— (not linked to the same atom) or a substituted radical derived from this in which univalent radicals replace one or both of the hydrogen atoms; also used *attrib.* as an independent word.

1872 *Jrnl. Chem. Soc.* XXV. 694 It also unites with hydrogen, giving rise to hydrazophenylene, $C_{12}H_{10}N_2$. **1877** *Ibid.* I. 307 On boiling the hydrazo-compound with hydrochloric acid, the isomeric dibromobenzidine..is obtained. **1907** *Chem. Abstr.* I. 498 (*heading*) Hydrazo derivatives. **1955** [see *HYDRAZIDE]. **1958** PACKER & VAUGHAN *Mod. Approach Org. Chem.* xviii. 608 Azoxybenzene gives hydrazobenzene but not azobenzene with alkaline reducing agents.

hydrazoate (həidrăzōᵘ·ēit). *Chem.* [f. HYDRAZO(IC *a.* + -ATE⁴.] = *AZIDE.

1910 [see *AZIDE]. **1938** *Van Nostrand's Sci. Encycl.* 583/2 Hydrazoic acid reacts..with metals..to form azides or hydrazoates (or trinitrides).

hydrazone (həi·drăzōᵘn). *Chem.* [ad. G. *hydrazon* (E. Fischer 1888, in *Ber. d. Deut. Chem. Ges.* XXI. 984), f. HYDRAZ(INE + -ONE.] Any compound which contains the group =N·NH_2 (attached to a single carbon atom) and which is thus a condensation product of an aldehyde or ketone with hydrazine; also, any substituted derivative, =N·NHR or =N·NRR′, of such a compound.

1888 *Jrnl. Chem. Soc.* LIV. 590 The name hydrazone is proposed for the compounds of hydrazine with aldehydes and ketones. **1938** ALLEN & BLATT in H. Gilman *Org. Chem.* I. vi. 569 Oximes, hydrazones, and phenylhydrazones are utilized primarily for isolating and identifying carbonyl compounds. **1970** *Nature* 5 Sept. 1048/1 Experiments..suggested that the hydrazone side-chain of rifampicin was essential for its antiviral activity.

hydrazonium (həidrăzōᵘ·niɒm). *Chem.* [f. HYDRAZ(INE + *-ONIUM.] **a.** = *HYDRAZINIUM a. **b.** = *HYDRAZINIUM b.

See the note s.v. *HYDRAZINIUM.

[**1876** *Jrnl. Chem. Soc.* II. 528 The author [*sc.* E. Fischer]

has isolated a body of the formula $C_6H_5.N_2H_2(C_2H_5)(C_2H_5Br)$, which he names phenyldiethylhydrazoniumbromide.] **1949** *Chem. & Industry* 26 Feb. 134/2 The ions derived from hydrazine are also troublesome. The one most commonly encountered, $N_2H_5^+$, is called hydrazinium in the 1940 Rules but hydrazonium in Chemical Abstracts (1945). Since the ion is essentially a substituted ammonium, the latter is strictly the more correct, but neither affords a means of distinguishing $N_2H_5^+$ from $N_2H_6^{++}$, which occurs in a few compounds. The two names could be used in fact for this purpose, but the distinction is best achieved, without confusion, by writing

$N_2H_5^+$ Hydrazonium (I) or (+1)
$N_2H_6^{++}$ Hydrazonium (II) or (+2).

1953 C. C. CLARK *Hydrazine* iii. 36 The asymmetric dialkyl hydrazines are also strong bases. They react quantitatively with active alkyl chlorides to form water soluble hydrazonium salts: $R_2NNH_2 + R'X \rightarrow R_2NNH_2.R'X$. **1954** *Chem. & Engin. News* 6 Sept. 3548/3 As a name for the ion $H_2N.NH_3^+$ there has been some division of usage between 'hydrazonium' and 'hydrazinium'; and some have applied one or other of these names to the ion $^+H_3N.NH_3^+$ as well as to the ion of single charge. The newly revised inorganic rules propose to settle the question by naming $N_2H_5^+$ 'hydrazinium (1+)' and $N_2H_6^{2+}$ 'hydrazinium (2+)'. This does not seem to us an ideal solution, to give two different ions (which are not isomers) the same name except for an affixed numeral. Might not the name 'hydrazinium' be retained for $N_2H_5^+$ and some such name as 'hydrazidiinium' coined for $N_2H_6^{2+}$? **1955** [see *HYDRAZINIUM]. **1957** [see sense c].

c. [Cf. *HYDRAZONE.] The ion $R{=}N{\cdot}NH_3^+$ that results from the addition of a proton to a hydrazone; also, any substituted ion derived from this in which univalent radicals replace one or more of the hydrogen atoms.

1957 *Chem. Rev.* LVII. 1022 The cation having the formula $R_3\overset{+}{N}NR_2$ has been given many names. Emil Fischer called the first known representative of this type a 'hydrazonium bromide' but later referred to the same compound as an 'azonium bromide'. *Chemical Abstracts* has used the names 'azinium', 'azonium', 'hydrazinium', and, most commonly of late, 'hydrazonium' for the same type. As a logical extension of the recommendations recently made for naming $[H_3NNH_2]^+$, it is suggested that the name 'hydrazinium' be adopted... It is suggested here that the name 'hydrazonium' be restricted to salts of hydrazones (including quaternary salts). **1966** P. A. S. SMITH *Chem. Open-Chain Org. Nitrogen Compounds* II. ix. 149 Quaternary hydrazinium salts can also be obtained by the hydrolysis of quaternary hydrazonium salts ($R_3\overset{+}{N}{-}N{=}CR_2X^-$).

hydric (həi·drik), *a.*[2] *Ecol.* [f. Gr. ὕδωρ, ὑδρ- water + -IC.] Of a habitat: having a plentiful supply of water.

1926 COOPER & WEESE in *Ecology* VII. 390 In order..to provide terms which shall be applicable to both plants and animals, we suggest that the adjectives 'xerophytic', 'hydrophytic' and 'mesophytic' be entirely abandoned as useless and misleading. In their place we offer the terms 'xeric', 'hydric' and 'mesic', to be defined as follows: Xeric (hydric, mesic): characterized by or pertaining to conditions of scanty (abundant, medium) moisture supply. **1947** R. F. DAUBENMIRE *Plants & Environment* iii. 148 Hydric, xeric, and mesic are commonly encountered in ecologic literature...These adjectives, if used, should be applied only to habitats. **1960** N. POLUNIN *Introd. Plant Geogr.* xi. 328 Typically this mean [between two seres] is inhabited by mesophytes and is said to be 'mesic', though relatively xeric (dry) and hydric (damp) exceptions exist. **1968** R. F. DAUBENMIRE *Plant Communities* iii. 116 Bare areas may be classified according to their characteristic water relations: wet or hydric, as a pond bottom; dry or xeric, as a rock surface exposed to the sun; or intermediate mesic, as a glacial moraine.

hydridic (həidrəi·dik), *a. Chem.* [f. HYDRID(E + -IC.] Of an atom of hydrogen: having a negative charge (like the hydrogen in ionic hydrides).

1966 PHILLIPS & WILLIAMS *Inorg. Chem.* II. xxxiii. 565 Boron-hydrogen bonds generally react with Grignard reagents as if they contained hydridic hydrogen. **1966** K. M. MACKAY *Hydrogen Compounds Metallic Elem.* v. 155 The behaviour of hydrogen in the hydride complexes reflects a change from acidic hydrogen in the carbonyl hydrides to basic, hydridic, hydrogen in the other compounds. **1968** *Inorg. Chem.* VII. 1952/2 The nature of the hydrogens in boron hydrides varies from hydridic (or negative) in diborane(6) to protonic (or positive) in the moderately strong acid decaborane(14).

hydrion (həi·drəiˌən, həi·driˌǫn). *Chem.* [Contraction of *hydr(ogen) ion*: see *-ION[3].] The hydrogen ion or proton.

1901 J. WALKER in *Chem. News* 4 Oct. 162 The proposals which I make for naming the positive and negative radicals of salts, acids, and bases considered as ions are as follows:—...If we use with Ostwald a dot to express unit positive charge, we have for some typical kations:—Hydrion..H·. Sodion..Na·. **1921** *Phil. Mag.* XLII. 455 There are only two elements, Sir Ernest Rutherford's proton (hydrion) and electron. **1930** *Nature* 20 Sept. 434/2 The hydrion concentration (*p*H) of the rain has been recorded. **1943** *Thorpe's Dict. Appl. Chem.* (ed. 4) VI. 381/2 There is a great excess of hydroxyl ions over hydrions. **1968** PASSMORE & ROBSON *Compan. Med. Stud.* I. p. xxxii (Index), Hydrion excretion, by kidney.

hydro[2] (həi·drou). Short for HYDRO-ELECTRIC (*power, plant*). Also *attrib.* In Canada also = *hydro-electric power supply*. Cf. *HYDRO-POWER.

1916 A. BRIDLE *Sons of Canada* 185 The product of Niagara..is Hydro-Electric—familiarly abbreviated to Hydro. **1925** *Rep. Brit. Assoc. Adv. Sci. 1924* 43 Various hydro systems were formed as circumstances dictated. **1938** 'R. HYDE' *Nor Years Condemn* x. 200 Did I ever tell you about that hydro I was on, a bit South? **1939** F. P. GROVE *Two Generations* 230 The telephone and hydro wires are down. **1947** E. A. MCCOURT *Music at Close* 71 There was talk of water works, a hydro plant, a newspaper, paved streets. **1949** L. PETERSON *Chipmunk* 149 Claude wrote out the address..on the envelope of the hydro bill he'd forgotten to pay. **1952** D. F. PUTNAM *Canad. Regions* xvii. 387/2 The cities of Alberta, also, have good sources of power including coal, natural gas and hydro. **1958** *New Statesman* 11 Oct. 480/1 Geological reserves of coal are estimated to constitute about four-fifths of all Russia's coal deposits, and much of this coal lies on the surface and this favours the development of thermal-power stations to supplement the hydro-stations of the River Angara. **1962** R. F. LEGGET *Geol. & Engin.* (ed. 2) x. 354 Across the Niagara River is the..Niagara power project of the Power Authority of the State of New York, constructed a few years after the Ontario hydro project. **1963** *B.S.I. News* Feb. 14/2 The hydro developments in Scotland really got under way in the early 1950s. **1970** *Globe & Mail* (Toronto) 26 Sept. 47/2 (Advt.), T.V. outlets in each room, drapes and hydro included.

hydro-. Add: **hy:dro-alcoho·lic** *a.*, in or consisting of a mixture of an alcohol and water; **hy:dro-aroma·tic** *a. Chem.*, having one or more benzene rings which are partially or completely hydrogenated (reduced); also as *sb.*, a hydro-aromatic compound; **hy:dro-bio·logy**, the biology of aquatic plants and animals; hence **hydrobiolo·gical** *a.*, **hydro-bio·logist,** one engaged in the study of hydrobiology; **hydrobi·otite** *Min.*, (*a*) a hydrated variety of biotite; (*b*) any clay composed of an intimate mixture of biotite and vermiculite; **hydroca·lumite** *Min.* [f. blend of CAL(CIUM + ALUM(INATE], a transparent, colourless to light green hydrated hydroxide of calcium and aluminium, $Ca_2Al(OH)_7.3H_2O$; **hy·drocast** *Oceanography* [contraction of *hydrographic cast* (CAST *sb.* 5)], a long cable having sampling bottles attached at intervals along it; also, a sampling operation in which this is used; **hydroce·llulose** *Chem.* [a. F. *hydrocellulose* (A. Giraud 1875, in *Compt. Rend.* LXXXI. 1106)], any of the chemically heterogeneous substances produced by the partial hydrolysis of cellulosic material; **hydro-cera·mic** *a.*, designating porous, unglazed pottery used for cooling or filtering; **hy·dro-chore** [Gr. χωρεῖν to spread], a plant whose seeds are dispersed by water; hence **hydro-cho·ric, -ous** *adjs.*, **hy·drochory,** the dissemination of seeds by water; **hy·droclone** [CY)CLONE] = **hydrocyclone*; **hy·drocœl(e)** (-sīl) *Zool.* [Gr. κοιλία cavity of the body], the water-vascular system of an echinoderm; also **-cele**; **hydro-cy·clone,** a device in which centrifugation in a conical vessel is employed to remove or separate particles in suspension in a flow of liquid; **hy·drodrill,** a device for injecting water or fertilizers near the roots of plants; also as *v. trans.*; **hy·dro-extract** *v. trans.* [back-formation from *hydro-extractor*], to dry by means of a hydro-extractor; so *hy·dro-extracting* vbl. sb.; also **hy·dro-extraction**; **hy:droformyla·tion** *Chem.*, the catalytic addition of both carbon monoxide and hydrogen to an olefin to produce an aldehyde; **hydroga·rnet** *Min.*, any mineral whose formula is that of a garnet in which water molecules replace some or all of the silicate groups; **hy·droglider,** a form of craft designed to glide on the surface of water (see also quot. 1961); **hydrogro·ssular** *Min.*, a calcium aluminosilicate with a composition varying between that of hibschite and that of grossular (see quot. 1966); **hydrohalite** (-hæ·ləit) *Min.* [ad. G. *hydrohalit* (J. F. L. Hausmann *Handbuch d. Mineralogie* (ed. 2, 1847) II. 1458)], a hydrated chloride of sodium, $NaCl.2H_2O$; **hy:drohetærolite** (-hetīə·roləit) *Min.*, a hydrous oxide of zinc and manganese similar to hetærolite; **hydroki·neter** (also -kine·ter) [Gr. κινητής, -ήρ one that sets going], a device for heating water at the bottom of large boilers by injecting surplus steam; **hydrola·ccolith** *Physical Geogr.* [from its resemblance to a LACCOLITH], an underground mass of ice in a region of permafrost which tends to increase in size and thrust up the overlying soil forming a mound; a mound so formed, esp. a pingo; so **hy:drolaccoli·thic** *a.*; **hy:drometallu·rgical** *a.*, of or pertaining to hydrometallurgy; **hydromo·rphic, -mo·rphous** *adjs. Soil Sci.*, (of a soil) developed and maintained in contact with a high water-table; (of a soil-forming process) acting in conjunction with a high water-table; **hydro-mu·scovite** *Min.*, a variety of muscovite containing more water and less potassium than that mineral; **hydro·philid,** a water-beetle of the family Hydrophilidæ; also as *adj.*, of or pertaining to an insect of this type; **hy·dro-plant,** plant for generating hydro-electric power; a hydro-electric generating station; **hydrosere** *Ecol.*, a plant succession having its origin in a wet habitat; **hy·dro-ski** *Aeronaut.*, a hydrofoil on a seaplane or amphibious aircraft that skims the surface of the water and provides hydrodynamic lift; **hy·drospace,** the underwater realms; **hydrospire** (earlier examples); **hydrotroilite** (-trōu·iləit, -troi·ləit) *Min.* [ad. Russ. *gidrotroilit* (M. Sidorenko 1901, in *Mém. Soc. Naturalistes Nouv.-Russie* XXIV. I. 119)], a black hydrated ferrous sulphide, $FeS.nH_2O$, occurring in the mud of lakes and inland seas; **hydrotu·ngstite** *Min.*, a hydrated tungstic acid, $H_2WO_4.H_2O$, occurring as minute green tabular crystals; **hy·drowire** *Oceanography* [contraction of *hydrographic wire*], a cable used for hydrocasts.

1887 A. M. BROWN *Contrib. Animal Alkaloids* 46 The hydro-alcoholic solution of the alkaloid was injected hypodermically into a dog of medium size. **1951** Hydro-alcoholic [see *HYDRASTIS]. **1969** *Biochim. & Biophys. Acta* CXCIV. 265 (*heading*) Optical rotatory dispersion of polyglutamic and polyuridylic acids at low temperatures in fluid hydro-alcoholic solvents. **1900** E. F. SMITH tr. *V. von Richter's Org. Chem.* (ed. 3) II. 290 Hexahydrobenzene is the parent hydrocarbon of the hydroaromatic substances. **1940** *Industr. & Engin. Chem.* Apr. 528/2 The cyclization of paraffins to hydroaromatics is preceded by dehydrogenation. **1951** I. L. FINAR *Org. Chem.* xix. 390 Many benzene derivatives may be reduced to the corresponding cyclohexane compounds, and because of this, cyclohexane and its derivatives are known as the hydroaromatic compounds. The cyclic terpenes are hydroaromatic compounds. **1933** *Geogr. Jrnl.* LXXXI. 533 It [*sc.* the Arctic Institute of the U.S.S.R.]..carries on geological, geomorphological, hydrological and hydrobiological investigations. **1932** *Ecology* XIII. 110 The fresh water hydrobiologists, especially the limnologists, have developed a third type of nomenclature based more upon the habitat than on the biotic communities. **1938** Hydrobiologist [see *HYDROLOGIST]. **1964** *Oceanogr. & Marine Biol.* II. 379 The three large brackish water lagoons on the continental coast of the Baltic..have long attracted the interest of hydrobiologists. **1972** *Nature* 28 July 194/1 It is hoped that the committee will be able to produce a register of hydrobiologists working in Britain. **1928** K. E. CARPENTER *Life Inland Waters* p. viii, The life of the ocean [has]..engrossed the energies even of followers of the new tradition in Hydrobiology. **1941** J. G. NEEDHAM in *Symposium Hydrobiol.* 3 Hydrobiology is an offshoot from the old maternal rootstock of natural history. **1965** *Math. in Biol. & Med.* (Med. Res. Council) 309 His [*sc.* Antonio Moroni's] main interests are human population genetics and hydrobiology. **1880** H. C. LEWIS in *Proc. Acad. Nat. Sci. Philadelphia* 319 Such mica exfoliates slightly when heated, is uniaxial, fusible with difficulty, and might be called Hydrobiotite for convenience. **1892** E. S. DANA *Dana's Syst. Min.* (ed. 6) 632 Hydrobiotite *H. C. Lewis.* A hydrated biotite. The name has been similarly but more definitely used by Schrauf. **1934** J. W. GRUNER in *Amer. Mineralogist* XIX. 558 Specimens 9 and 10 belong to a species for which the name *hydrobiotite* is proposed. This name was used long ago by Schrauf and others to designate biotite-like material high in water. *Ibid.* 575 X-ray diagrams are necessary to distinguish vermiculite from hydrobiotite. **1962** W. A. DEER et al. *Rock-Forming Min.* III. 251 Mixed layer clays with vermiculite as a constituent are not uncommon, the most well known being 'hydrobiotite', a random mixture of vermiculite and biotite. **1934** C. E. TILLEY in *Mineral. Mag.* XXIII. 607 In allusion to its composition as an hydrated calcium aluminate ($4CaO.Al_2O_3.12H_2O$) the name hydrocalumite is proposed. **1968** I. KOSTOV *Mineral.* 215 Apart from hydrocalumite, which is rather soft.., the other minerals are hard. **1960** *McGraw-Hill Encycl. Sci. & Technol.* IX. 267/1 Such a laboratory is located near the winches used for running out and retrieving a long string of water-sample bottles (hydrocasts). **1968** D. F. MARTIN *Marine Chem.* I. i. 8 The vessel must be stationary for the time needed to complete the hydrocast. **1971** *Nature* 7 May 37/1 In 1966, one hydrocast in this narrow and steep-sided deep revealed a temperature of 29·07° C and a salinity of 74·2‰. Attempts to place a hydrocast in the Chain deep on this cruise failed because of high winds and consequent ship drift. **1876** *Jrnl. Chem. Soc.* I. 696 Hydrocellulose is also formed when cellulose is impregnated with dilute acid and submitted to a temperature of about 100°. **1920** E. SUTERMEISTER *Chem. Pulp & Paper Making* i. 9 The formation of friable hydrocelluloses by acids is of great importance industrially for upon it is based the carbonization process for separating cotton from wool. **1956** *Nature* 18 Feb. 319/2 The hydrocelluloses produced by the action of mineral acids on cotton and wood. **1883** J. W. MOLLETT *Illustr. Dict. Art & Archæol.* 174/1 *Hydroceramic* (vessels), Gr., vessels made of a porous clay, in which liquids were put for the purpose of cooling them; they were a kind of *alcarazas*. **1940** *Chambers's Techn. Dict.* 428/2 *Hydroceramic*, porous unglazed pottery, used for filters and for cooling vessels. **1905** F. E. CLEMENTS *Res. Methods Ecol.* iv. 216 Hydrochores..comprise all plants distributed exclusively by water, whether the latter

acts as ocean currents, tides, streams, or surface run-off. *Ibid.* 218 Most hydrophytes are hydrochorous. **1940** *Chambers's Techn. Dict.* 428/2 *Hydrochoric*, dispersed by water. **1969** L. van der Pijl *Princ. Dispersal Higher Plants* v. 61 It is difficult to describe concisely the structural modifications of hydrochory. *Ibid.*, Many hydrochores bend their fruit stalks down..whereas in *Nuphar* (not purely hydrochorous) the seeds mature above water. **1965** D. Bradley *Hydrocyclone* i. 1 'Hydraulic cyclone' has been abbreviated to 'hydrocyclone' and even 'hydroclone'. **1967** Whistler & Paschall *Starch* II. i. 46 The starch stream..must be further purified by passing..through hydroclones to reduce the protein content. **1888** *Phil. Trans. R. Soc.* B. CLXXIX. 266 After separating from the hydrocele the anterior body-cavity grows towards the ectoderm on the right side. **1900** E. R. Lankester *Treat. Zool.* III. viii. 23 Whatever may be the homologies of the hydrocoel, there is..no nephridial or other excretory system in Echinoderma. **1962** D. Nichols *Echinoderms* x. 121 This [sac] is called the left axohydrocoel, the anterior part being the axocoel..and the posterior the hydrocoel. **1952** *Chem. Abstr.* XLVI. 1668 Data are presented on hydrocyclones used as thickeners in starch processing, as classifiers for highly viscous and non-Newtonian liquids and as washers in ore prepn. **1962** *Engineering* 3 Aug. 146/1 The cone-shaped nozzle at the bottom of the hydrocyclones used by the National Coal Board..(for the separation and thickening of coal and shale fines from water). **1962** *New Scientist* 4 Oct. 31/3 They are using a specially-designed 'hydrodrill' to inject relatively small amounts of water into the soil, placing it directly in the plant's root zone. *Ibid.*, The vine cuttings are simply dropped into holes which have been hydrodrilled. **1928** C. E. Mullin *Acetate Silk* xxxviii. 437 Yarns or loosely knit fabrics which are not liable to crease may be hydroextracted in the ordinary rotating cage or drum machine. **1952** E. Kornreich *Introd. Fibres & Fabrics* viii. 143 Fabrics can also be hydroextracted by winding them on a perforated beam which is then inserted in a suitable whizzer. **1882** *Spon's Encycl. Industr. Arts* v. 1839 Centrifugal hydro-extracting machines..have been tried for separating beet-juice from the pulp. **1895** *Trans. Soc. Engin. 1894* 227 (*heading*) The principles and practice of hydro-extraction. **1912** H. H. Hodgson tr. *Masselon's Celluloid* v. 71, 100 kilogrammes of bleached pulp after hydro-extraction should weigh 60 kilogrammes. **1963** A. J. Hall *Textile Sci.* ii. 53 The water in wet viscose rayon materials is best removed by hydro-extraction. **1949** *Jrnl. Amer. Chem. Soc.* LXXI. 3051 (*heading*) Hydroformylation of unsaturated compounds with a cobalt carbonyl catalyst. **1969** S. A. Miller *Ethylene* xiv. 1169 The *OXO* reaction or 'hydroformylation' is now an important industrial process. **1941** E. P. Flint et al. in *Jrnl. Res. Nat. Bureau of Standards* (U.S.) XXVI. 14 An extension of the study revealed that silica could replace water in both $3CaO.Al_2O_3.6H_2O$ and $3CaO.Fe_2O_3.6H_2O$, and that the end products of these substitutions are grossularite garnet, $3CaO.Al_2O_3.3SiO_2$, and andradite garnet, $3CaO.Fe_2O_3.3SiO_2$, respectively... The hydrous members of the series may be termed 'hydrogarnets' to indicate their relationship to the naturally occurring garnets. **1966** W. A. Deer et al. *Introd. Rock-Forming Min.* 23 In the hydrogarnets there is replacement of SiO_2 by $2H_2O$, with vacant Si spaces in the structure. **1921** *Glasgow Herald* 23 July 7/2 The idea of using hydrogliders for passengers and for mail purposes on the lochs in the outlying districts of Scotland. **1927** *Ibid.* 26 July 9 The hydroglider which has been constructed..to accomplish the crossing of the Atlantic from Cherbourg to New York. **1961** F. H. Burgess *Dict. Sailing* 119 *Hydroglider*, a type of boat that is designed with air-screws as its main means of propulsion. **1943** C. O. Hutton in *Trans. & Proc. R. Soc. N.Z.* LXXIII. 174 (*heading*) Hydrogrossular, a new mineral of the garnet–hydrogarnet series. *Ibid.*, All of the isomorphous mixtures between plazolite and grossularite are termed by the writer, hydrogrossular. **1966** W. A. Deer et al. *Introd. Rock-Forming Min.* 26 Hydrogrossular has been taken as the name for members of the series $3CaO.Al_2O_3.3SiO_2$—$3CaO.Al_2O_3.6H_2O$ with a composition between grossular and hibschite (plazolite), $3CaO.Al_2O_3.2SiO_2.2H_2O$. **1861** H. W. Bristow *Gloss. Mineral.* 185/1 *Hydrohalite*... A hydrous chloride of sodium. **1949** *Mineral. Abstr.* X. 459 A drop of sea-water..evaporated at a low temperature..yields hexagonal flakes (¼ mm.) of hydrohalite, NaCl. $2H_2O$. **1928** C. Palache in *Amer. Mineralogist* XIII. 308 The following data establish the characters of unaltered hetaerolite. For the partly hydrated mineral hitherto described, the name hydrohetaerolite may well be employed. **1942** [see *hetærolite]. **1955** *Amer. Mineralogist* XL. 350 Hydrohetaerolite has the same structure as hausmannite, except that one sixth of the trivalent manganese occupying the octahedral sites are randomly absent, and the balance of charge is supplied by hydrogen bonds. **1883** A. E. Seaton *Man. Marine Engin.* xx. 376 (*heading*) Weir's hydrokineter. *Ibid.* 377 There are many other ways of promoting the circulation when steam is up, but none do this so efficiently during the time of raising steam as the hydrokineter. **1951** *Engineering* 20 Apr. 483/3 Surplus steam from the waste-heat boiler will be used..to keep the Scotch boilers warm and ready for service, Weir hydrokineters being fitted to the Scotch boilers to maintain a circulation. **1955** M. Hollander tr. *Kuenen's Realms of Water* v. 220 (*caption*) Hydrolaccolith or hummock caused when ground-water under artesian pressure is checked by formation of layers of ice. **1961** L. D. Stamp *Gloss. Geogr. Terms* 244/2 The pingos in East Greenland but not those in the Mackenzie delta are hydrolaccoliths. **1968** R. W. Fairbridge *Encycl. Geomorphol.* 845/2 The genetic term *hydrolaccolith*, which applies to all ice-intrusions, is not just synonymous with pingo. **1970** E. Watson tr. *Tricart's Geomorphol. Cold Environments* II. i. 78 These ice masses and the hills which they raise are called hydrolaccoliths. **1963** D. W. & E. E. Humphries tr. *Termier's Erosion & Sedimentation* 412 An arctic soil phenomenon..formed in the permafrost by a hydrolaccolithic process. **1890** Webster, Hydrometallurgical. **1929** *Encycl. Brit.* VI. 406/1 Hydro-metallurgical treatment..is eminently suited for low grade ores. **1959** J. Newton *Extractive Metall.* vii. 436 Hydrometallurgical methods are widely employed today in the treatment of low-grade oxidized uranium ores. **1938** M. Baldwin et al. in *U.S. Dept. Agric. Yearbk.* 991 The terms 'halomorphic', 'hydromorphic', and 'calomorphic' are not entirely satisfactory, since soil genetics rather than soil characteristics are implied. **1970** E. M. Bridges *World Soils* iii. 25/1 These poorly drained or hydromorphic soils frequently occur in the lower parts of the landscape. **1927** *Russian Pedol. Investigations* v. 26 Recently a single group has been formed which is..known by the name..of 'hydromorphous' soils (Neustruev). **1932** G. W. Robinson *Soils* xv. 301 Hydromorphous processes are those which take place under the influence of ground-water. **1889** A. Johnstone in *Q. Jrnl. Geol. Soc.* XLV. 364 Margarodite, gilbertite, damourite, and sericite are mineralogists' names for varieties possessing the same composition as muscovite, differing from the latter mineral merely in containing at least about 5 per cent. of water. All of these varieties..ought to be known under one term. The common name proposed for them by the Author is hydromuscovite. **1966** W. A. Deer et al. *Introd. Rock-Forming Min.* 202 Hydromuscovites have high H_2O and low K_2O content. **1899** D. Sharp in *Cambr. Nat. Hist.* VI. v. 219 The pupae of Hydrophilides repose on the dorsal surface. **1958** F. Balfour-Browne *Brit. Water Beetles* III. 3 The mandibles of *Hydrophilus* also differ from..those of all our other Hydrophilids. **1964** R. M. & J. W. Fox *Introd. Compar. Ent.* iii. 73 The hindleg of the hydrophilid beetle is provided with a fringe of hairs. **1927** J. G. Tarboux *Electr. Power Equipm.* ii. 31 High-voltage transmission lines must be used to connect the hydro plant to the load center. **1966** *McGraw-Hill Encycl. Sci. & Technol.* XIV. 399/2 Installed capacity of hydroplants cannot be counted upon for perpetuity because of the gradual filling of reservoirs with sediment. **1926** Tansley & Chipp *Study of Vegetation* ii. 19 The earlier stages of a prisere are altogether different, according to whether the succession begins on a wet or a dry habitat... Such successions may be conveniently called *hydroseres* and *xeroseres* respectively. **1952** P. W. Richards *Tropical Rain Forest* xiii. 283 During the course of the hydrosere there is a gradual change from open water to relatively dry conditions. **1967** C. D. Sculthorpe *Biol. Aquatic Vasc. Plants* xii. 417 In the ultimate stages of the hydroseres plant debris is less and less completely decomposed. **1952** *Jrnl. R. Aeronaut. Soc.* LVI. 334/2 Somewhat allied to the hydrofoil is the hydro-ski. These obtain their lift from the water pressure on their lower surface in a similar manner to the planing lift of the [flying] boat planing bottom. **1954** *Flight* 17 Sept. 433 The Sea Dart hydro-ski fighter..which is land-based, but which uses water (or snow or ice) for take-off and landing. **1960** K. C. Barnaby *Basic Naval Archit.* (ed. 3) 448 Modifications of the submerged type consist in replacing the forward hydrofoils by partly submerged planing surfaces or 'hydroskis'. **1964** *Adv. Hydroscience* I. 2 The use of acoustic energy to perform all those functions in hydrospace for which electromagnetic energy is employed in aerospace. **1966** *New Scientist* 22 Dec. 691/1 Other categories of plot [in science fiction] include a growing preoccupation with 'inner space' or 'hydrospace'. **1869** E. Billings in *Amer. Jrnl. Sci.* XCVIII. 76 In order to avoid the use of double terms, I propose to call them 'hydrospires'. *Ibid.* 77 In *Caryocrinus ornatus* there are thirty hydrospires. **1913** *Mineral. Mag.* XVI. 362 Hydrotroilite. **1957** G. E. Hutchinson *Treat. Limnol.* I. xi. 723 The rather poorly characterized ferrous sulfide of lake sediments, supposedly FeS, has received the name hydrotroilite. **1940** Kerr & Young in *Program & Abstr. 21st Ann. Meeting Min. Soc. Amer.* 9 Since this mineral appears to be an intermediate product in the alteration of ferberite to tungstite and since it resembles tungstite in many of its physical properties, the name hydrotungstite is suggested. **1963** *Amer. Mineralogist* XLVIII. 935 A similarity between the *x*-ray patterns for hydrotungstite (tungstic acid, $H_2WO_4.H_2O$) and molybdic acid ($H_2MoO_4.H_2O$). **1955** *Deep-Sea Research* III. (Suppl.) 170 A jelly bottle..will remain uncongealed long enough to permit slope determinations to be made of hydrowires. **1969** R. Lange *Chem. Oceanogr.* v. 80 The sampler is attached to the hydrowire with a screw clamp and a snap clamp.

† **hydro-aeroplane** (həi:dro,ēə·rŏplēin). *Obs.* Also (*U.S.*) **hydro-airplane.** [f. Hydro- + *aeroplane *sb.*, *airplane.] An aircraft designed to land on and take off from the water; a seaplane.

1909 *Westm. Gaz.* 7 Jan. 4/2 Before the present year expires the hydro-aeroplane will be an accomplished fact. **1914** *Scotsman* 21 Dec. 8/2 A German hydro-aeroplane threw two bombs on Calais this afternoon. **1922** *Encycl. Brit.* XXX. 49/2 Its performance as a hydro-aeroplane suffered from the extra weight and resistance of the floats. **1930** *Flight* 25 July 837/1 You [*sc.* G. H. Curtiss] invented the hydroaeroplane and the flying-boat and thus opened the way for trans-Atlantic flight. **1932** Chatfield & Taylor *Airplane & its Engine* (ed. 2) xiv. 316 The term *seaplane*..is synonymous with *hydroairplane*, a word too clumsy ever to have come into common use.

hydroborane (həidro,bōə·rēin). *Chem.* Also **-boran.** [ad. G. *hydroboran* (A. Stock 1926, in *Ber. d. Deut. Chem. Ges.* LIX. 2229): cf. *borane.] The name used by A. Stock for any of the hydrides of boron that are richer in hydrogen than others with the same number of boron atoms.

1927 *Chem. Abstr.* XXI. 541 When all of the B atoms are tervalent..the names should be 'diboran', 'triboran', 'decaboran', etc., for B_2H_4, B_3H_5, $B_{10}H_{12}$, etc. The names for the hydroborans [*printed* hydroborons] are illustrated by the following: B_2H_6 = dihydro-diboran, B_5H_9 = dihydro-pentaboran, B_5H_{11} = tetrahydro-pentaboran, etc. **1933** A. Stock *Hydrides of Boron & Silicon* i. 18 The less stable hydrides, which are richer in hydrogen, should be called 'hydroboranes', e.g. dihydrotetraborane (B_4H_{10}).

hydroborate (həidro,bōə·rēit), *sb. Chem.* [f. Hydro- + Borate.] = *borohydride.

1950 *Chem. Abstr.* XLIV. 12392/1 (Index), *Hydroborates.* See such headings as *Aluminium borohydride* and *Lithium borohydride.* **1963** *Jrnl. Amer. Chem. Soc.* LXXXV. 2725/1 Among the numerous derivatives of boranes and hydroborate ions known there are no compounds reported to date containing an NO group directly attached to one of the boron atoms. **1964** R. M. Adams *Boron* vi. 373 While the latter name [*sc.* borohydride] belongs to the ferrocyanide type which has long been disapproved by the IUPAC, it has become so firmly established in American usage that it will be used interchangeably with hydroborate in this chapter.

hydroborate (həidro,bōə·rēit), *v. Chem.* [Back-formation from next.] *trans.* To add a borane or other boron compound to (another compound) by hydroboration.

1961 *Jrnl. Amer. Chem. Soc.* LXXXIII. 2550/1 β-Pinene..was hydroborated internally in diglyme with sodium borohydride and boron trifluoride etherate. **1964** Kirk & Othmer *Encycl. Chem. Technol.* (ed. 2) III. 709 Dienes can be hydroborated utilizing diisoamylborane and diphenyldiborane.

Hence **hy:drobora·ting** *vbl. sb.*

1962 H. C. Brown *Hydroboration* i. 28 The treatment of internal acetylenes, such as 3-hexyne, with the theoretical quantity of hydroborating agent results in the formation of the corresponding trivinylborane.

hydroboration (həi:dro,bōərēi·ʃən). *Chem.* [f. Hydro- + Bor(on + -ation.] The addition of a linked boron–hydrogen pair of atoms in a molecule across a double or triple bond between a carbon atom and another atom; for example,

$$=\!B\!-\!H + \overset{|}{\underset{|}{C}}\!=\!\overset{|}{\underset{|}{C}} \rightarrow =\!B\!-\!\overset{|}{\underset{|}{C}}\!-\!\overset{|}{\underset{|}{C}}H.$$

1957 Brown & Rao in *Jrnl. Org. Chem.* XXII. 1136/2 (*heading*) Hydroboration of olefins. A remarkably fast room-temperature addition reaction of diborane to olefins. *Ibid.* 1138/2 The hydroboration reaction should provide a useful and convenient synthetic route for the transformation of olefins into organoboranes, alcohols, and other functional derivatives. **1966** Steinberg & Brotherton *Organoboron Chem.* II. viii. 225 The reaction sequence can be formulated to involve hydroboration of the carbon–nitrogen triple bond followed by a hydrogen shift and final cyclization. **1971** *Nature* 20 Aug. 536/2 Many related organic syntheses depend on the hydroboration of acetylenes or dienes as the first step.

hydrocarbon. Add: **b. hydrocarbon oil,** any oil consisting chiefly of hydrocarbons.

1864 *Mechanics' Mag.* 22 Jan. 55/3 (*heading*) Petroleum and hydro-carbon oils for generating steam. **1904** G. H. Hurst *Textile Soaps & Oils* iv. 115 The cheapest oils are the so-called mineral or hydrocarbon oils. **1942** *Progress Appl. Chem.* XXVII. 82 The analysis of hydrocarbon oils is a valuable aid in the control of refinery processes such as cracking.

hydrocele, var. *hydrocœl(e)* (s.v. *hydro-).

hydrocephalic, *a.* Add: **B.** *sb.* A person affected with hydrocephalus.

1908 A. F. Tredgold *Mental Deficiency* (*caption* to Plate xix), Male hydrocephalic. **1930** D. Paterson *Sick Children* xii. 331 Fifty per cent. of all hydrocephalics suffer from convulsions. **1971** *Nature* 17 Sept. 171/1 Medicine is keeping alive idiots, hydrocephalics and cases of spina bifida.

hydrocephalus. Delete the last sentence of the definition.

hydrochlorothiazide (həi:dro,klōəro,þəi·ăzəid). *Pharm.* [f. Hydro- + *chlorothiazide.] A white crystalline powder which is a diuretic and saluretic sulphonamide drug, $C_7H_8ClN_3O_4S_2$, analogous to chlorothiazide, and which is given orally in the treatment of œdema and as an adjuvant in the treatment of hypertension.

1958 *Experientia* XIV. 458/1 Hydrochlorothiazide is the generic name of a new diuretic agent manufactured by CIBA. **1959** *Lancet* 13 June 1221/2 Hydrochlorothiazide promotes less bicarbonate excretion than chlorothiazide, but the loss of potassium after the two drugs is not significantly different. **1965** J. Pollitt *Depression & its Treatment* v. 72 In mild cases [of premenstrual depression]..Hydrochlorothiazide with potassium chloride (Hydrosaluric K) 25–75 mg. daily or on alternate days from 7–10 days premenstrually is effective. **1968** J. H. Burn *Lect. Notes Pharmacol.* (ed. 9) 105 Hydrochlorothiazide and hydroflumethiazide are ten times stronger than chlorothiazide.

hydrocolloid (həidro,kǫ·loid). Also (with hyphen) **hydro-colloid.** [f. Hydro- + Colloid *a.* and *sb.*] Any substance that will form a gel on the addition of water; a gel so produced. Also *attrib.* or as *adj.*

1926 *Brit. Pat.* 271,306, The subject matter of the present invention is a reversible hydro-colloid mass which may serve for..enabling castings to be taken from the oral cavity for dental purposes. **1946** C. K. Tseng in J. Alexander *Colloid Chem., Theoret. & Appl.* VI. xxxi. 717 Agar is a reversible hydrocolloid and materials made with it must be warmed to a solution and cooled to a gel. **1954** *Adv. Chem. Ser.* XI. 92 Irish moss extractive, also known as carrageenin,..is a hydrocolloid gum. **1955**

STURDEVANT & BRAUER in J. C. Brauer *Dental Asst.* xx. 287 The reversible hydrocolloids are used for tray impressions to form casts of the teeth and jaws.

Hence **hy:drocolloi·dal** *a.*

1928 *Chem. Abstr.* XXII. 1659 A mixt. of rubber, fatty substances and resins is incorporated, in fine distribution, in a hydrocolloidal mucilaginous basic substance such as sea weeds or algaceous plants. **1947** J. C. RICH *Materials & Methods Sculpture* v. 96 Commercial hydrocolloidal compositions. **1956** J. N. ANDERSON *Appl. Dental Materials* xx. 240 All hydrocolloidal gels consist largely of water enclosed rather loosely within the gel fibrils.

hy·dro-coo:ler. orig. *U.S.* [See next and -ER[1].] An apparatus for hydro-cooling, usually consisting of a water tank with cooling equipment and a conveyer.

1947 *Ice & Refrigeration* Nov. 33/2 Hydro-coolers are used commercially today to pre-cool celery, asparagus, peas,..and carrots. **1958** *Agriculture* LXV. 133 Small-scale tests were made with a small and simple hydrocooler consisting of two tanks, one containing blocks of ice and water and the other for submersion of the watercress. **1964** A. E. CANHAM *Electr. Hort.* xiii. 137 The capacity of hydro-coolers varies from the large 2 000 crate-per-day unit down to the 200 crate-per-day packaged unit.

hy·dro-coo:ling, *vbl. sb.* orig. *U.S.* [HYDRO- a.] A method of preserving the freshness of vegetables or fruit after harvesting and packing by immersing them for a time in chilled water (or, sometimes, by spraying them).

1942 *Ice & Refrigeration* Nov. 302/2 The hydro-cooling machine takes 130 boxes of asparagus at a time. *Ibid.*, After this hydro-cooling the produce is loaded into trucks. **1955** WORK & CAREW *Veg. Prod. & Marketing* (ed. 2) iv. 62 Dipping in very cold water (hydrocooling) is much more rapid. **1964** A. E. CANHAM *Electr. Hort.* xiii. 135 Hydro-cooling provides an excellent simple, effective and rapid method of cooling produce which is not seriously affected by the presence of moisture.

Hence (as a back-formation) **hy·drocool** *v. trans.*, to chill by this method; **hy·drocooled** *ppl. a.*

1945 *Refrig. Engin.* Apr. 275/3 Test boxes of..Bing cherries were handled in the following manner:..(3) hydrocooled for 7 min. in a water bath of melting ice at 32°. **1945** *Proc. Amer. Soc. Hort. Sci.* XLVI. 196 As far as cracking and decay in storage are concerned, it apparently made little difference whether the hydrocooled fruit was packaged wet or dry. **1958** *Agriculture* LXV. 133 Comparison was made between the behaviour of samples hydrocooled to 34–35°F and control samples which had received no cooling.

hydrocortisone (həidro,kǭ·ɹtizōun). *Biochem.* and *Pharm.* [f. HYDRO- + *CORTISONE.] A steroid hormone, $C_{21}H_{30}O_5$, which is produced by the adrenal cortex and involved in the regulation of carbohydrate metabolism, and which is prepared synthetically for use as an anti-inflammatory and anti-allergic agent.

1951 *Jrnl. Amer. Med. Assoc.* 22 Dec. 1631 Hydrocortisone acetate had a constant anti-inflammatory effect on the rheumatoid arthritic joint when administered locally. **1952** *Ibid.* 27 Dec. 1664/2 One eye was treated with cortisone while the more severely involved eye was treated with hydrocortisone. **1953** *Jrnl. Amer. Chem. Soc.* LXXV. 5369/1 We have isolated a fungus..which converts Compound S directly to the biologically active steroid, 17α-hydroxycorticosterone (Kendall's Compound F, hydrocortisone, Reichstein's Compound M). **1963** *Lancet* 19 Jan. 142/1 Hydrocortisone has revolutionised the treatment of itching skin diseases. **1965** *New Scientist* 1 July 32/3 The glucocorticoids, of which cortisone and hydrocortisone (cortisol) are the principal members, are.. mainly concerned with carbohydrate metabolism. **1967** *Martindale's Extra Pharmacopoeia* (ed. 25) 448 Hydrocortisone is administered by mouth and by intramuscular injection and it is applied externally in ointments, creams, and lotions. **1970** R. W. MCGILVERY *Biochem.* xxiii. 565 The most active of the glucocorticoids in humans is cortisol, or hydrocortisone.

hydrocracking (həi·dro,krækiŋ), *vbl. sb.* [f. HYDRO- + *cracking* vbl. sb. (see *CRACK *v.* 23).] The catalytic cracking of crude petroleum or a heavy distillate by subjecting it to the action of gaseous hydrogen at a high temperature and pressure, so that long-chain paraffins and other hydrocarbons undergo hydrogenolysis; also called *hydrogenation cracking*.

1940 *Jrnl. Soc. Chem. Industry Japan* (Suppl. binding) XLIII. 363/1 The 'Hydro-Cracking' is a method of cracking in which mineral oil is decomposed in the presence of high pressure hydrogen. **1955** V. HAENSEL in B. T. Brooks et al. *Chem. Petroleum Hydrocarbons* II. xxix. 205 Hydrocracking produces lower boiling hydrocarbons which have higher octane numbers and lower densities than the parent hydrocarbons. **1970** *Adv. Chem. Ser.* CIII. vi. 113 When the modern version of hydrocracking was announced in 1959, capacity was 1000 barrels per day. As the decade ended capacity..was approaching 1,000,000 barrels per day.

Hence (as a back-formation) **hy·drocrack** *v. trans.*, to subject to, or convert by means of, hydrocracking; **hy·drocracked** *ppl. a.*, obtained by hydrocracking. Also **hy·drocracker**, an apparatus or plant where hydrocracking is carried out.

1940 *Jrnl. Soc. Chem. Industry Japan* (Suppl. binding) XLIII. 363/1 The hydro-cracked gasoline is reputed to be of superior quality. **1959** R. J. HENGSTEBECK *Petroleum Processing* xii. 274 Any heavy petroleum stock can be hydrocracked. **1965** *Chem. & Engin. News* 29 Mar. 32/2 (*heading*) Gulf adds hydrocracker at Port Arthur refinery. **1970** *Adv. Chem. Ser.* CIII. vi. 119 The feed is hydrocracked efficiently to jet fuel with minimum formation of lighter products. *Ibid.* 120 The hydrocracker should be operated to give maximum liquid yields.

hy:drodesu:lphuriza·tion. Also (*U.S.*) **-sulfur-.** [f. HYDRO- + DE- II. 1 + SULPHUR + -IZATION.] The removal (as hydrogen sulphide) of sulphur from crude petroleum or a petroleum product by the action of a catalyst and gaseous hydrogen at a moderately high temperature and pressure.

1950 *Industr. & Engin. Chem.* Sept. 1882/2 Several high sulfur gas oils were reduced in sulfur contents to those of gas oils from sweet crudes by hydrodesulfurization..at 750° F., 300 pounds per square inch pressure,.. and 1000 cubic feet of hydrogen per barrel of charge. **1967** *Proc. 7th World Petroleum Congr.* IV. 167/2 Hydrodesulphurization has long been recognized as a means of removing sulfur [from] residual oils and asphalts.

Hence (as a back-formation) **hy:drodesu·lphurize** *v. trans.*, to subject to hydrodesulphurization; **hy:drodesu·lphurized** *ppl. a.*, **-desu·lphurizing** *vbl. sb.* Also **hy:drodesu·lphurizer**, an apparatus in which this process is carried out.

1950 *Industr. & Engin. Chem.* Sept. 1881/1 Instead of processing the gas oil, it is possible to hydrodesulfurize the entire crude. **1955** *Industr. Chemist* XXXI. 351/1 The first commercial hydrodesulphurizer applying the Shell trickle technique was recently started up. **1960** *Times Rev. Industry* Jan. 31/1 The regeneration of hydrodesulphurising catalysts for further use. **1967** *Proc. 7th World Petroleum Congr.* IV. 168/2 The hydrodesulfurized product tends to be relatively rich in nickel.

hydrodictyon (həi:dro,di·kti,ǫ̆n). *Bot.* [mod.L. (A. W. Roth *Catalecta Botanica* (1800) II. 237), f. HYDRO- + Gr. δίκτυον net.] A green freshwater alga of the genus so called; = *water-net* (WATER *sb.* 31).

1841 W. H. HARVEY *Man. Brit. Algæ* p. viii, Among British Algæ, the only structure analogous to these exists in *Hydrodictyon*, which grows in the form of a perfect net, with regular meshes. **1872** H. C. WOOD *Contrib. Hist. Fresh-Water Algæ N. Amer.* 94 When the hydrodictyon disappear in the fall it is months before they reappear in the spring. **1927** WEST & FRITSCH *Treat. Brit. Freshwater Algae* 101 A new *Hydrodictyon*-net or *Pediastrum*-plate is formed..by the asexual method. **1967** I. MORRIS *Introd. Algae* iv. 50 *Hydrodictyon* colonies consist of large numbers of cylindrical cells joined terminally with two others to form an open net-like structure.

hy:drodyna·mically, *adv.* [f. HYDRODYNAMIC, -DYNAMICAL *adjs.*: see -ICALLY.] From the point of view of hydrodynamics.

1957 G. E. HUTCHINSON *Treat. Limnol.* I. i. 156 Schriever (1955) concludes that Croke's final theory is hydro-dynamically impossible. **1971** *Nature* 11 June 383/2 The turbulent boundary layer found near the sediment water interface may be described hydrodynamically in one of three ways.

hydrodynamicist (həi:dro,dəinæ·misist). [f. HYDRODYNAMIC(S + -IST.] An expert in or a student of hydrodynamics.

1961 *Aeroplane* CI. 553/2 Hydrodynamicists..were less interested in ships travelling in shallow water at a particular speed..than in sea-going ships or river-going ships at any speed. **1970** N. DE NEVERS *Fluid Mech.* x. 324 By 1900 the two schools had gone their separate ways, the hydrodynamicists publishing learned mathematical papers with little bearing on engineering problems and the hydraulicians solving engineering problems by trial and error.

hydro-electric, *a.* Add: Also **hydroelectric. 1.** (Earlier example.)

1827 J. CUMMING *Man. Electro Dynamics* IV. 115 Retaining the name *Hydro-electric*, for current produced by the intervention of fluids.

2. (Earlier example.)

1844 *Rep. Brit. Assoc. Adv. Sci. 1843* 39 (*heading*) On the electricity of high-pressure steam, and a description of a hydro-electric machine.

3. Generating electricity by utilizing the motive power of water; generated by, or relating to generation by, such means.

1884 *Engineering* 11 Jan. 38/3 A Hydro-Electric Syphon... A most ingenious scheme for draining the valley of the city of Mexico by means of electrical power generated by the fall of water raised by electrically driven pumps. **1899** *Min. Proc. Inst. Civil Engin.* CXXXVI. 433 (heading) Hydro-electric installation at Mont-Dore. **1904** *Electrical Mag.* I. 592/1 On the river Ain..near Lake Geneva, a hydro-electric plant has recently been completed. **1905** *Daily Chron.* 18 Sept. 4/5 Abundant hydro-electric power. **1927** CREAGER & JUSTIN *Hydro-Electric Handbk.* xxxv. 874 Hydro-electric plants are much more reliable than steam plants. **1951** T. H. CARR *Electric Power Stations* (ed. 3) II. xxiv. 579 Hydro-electric stations are usually located in wild, mountainous districts. **1955** *Bull. Atomic Sci.* Oct. 281/2 Hydroelectric power is never likely to contribute more than a small fraction of the total energy consumption of the world, since the total potential capacity is relatively limited. **1963** W. E. BALLARD *Metal Spraying* (ed. 4) xiv. 479 In hydro-electric schemes, metal spraying has often been used for the protection of the large pipes bringing the water down from a high altitude to the turbines. **1972** *Daily Tel.* 11 Apr. 13/6 Brazil wants to build a huge hydro-electric dam on the upper reaches of the River Parana.

hy:dro-ele·ctrical, *a.* [f. prec. + -AL.] = *HYDRO-ELECTRIC *a.* 3.

1925 *Trans. Soc. Engin.* 127 In New Zealand the largest hydro-electrical power scheme..is controlled by the Christchurch County Council. **1930** BAKER & CONKLING *Water Supply & Utilization* i. 17 (*heading*) Recent growth of hydroelectrical development in the United States.

hy:dro-electri·city. [f. HYDRO- + ELECTRICITY.] **1.** (In Dict. s.v. HYDRO-ELECTRIC *a.*: earlier example.)

1828 F. WATKINS *Pop. Sk. Electro-Magnetism* 61 The term hydro-electricity, applied to that which emanates from a voltaic combination.

2. Electricity generated by utilizing the motive power of water.

1904 *Electrical Mag.* I. 378/1 (*heading*) Hydro-electricity in California. *Ibid.* 592/1 (*heading*) Hydro electricity for small French factories. **1959** *Petroleum Handbk.* (Shell Internat. Petroleum Co.) (ed. 4) 19 There are..limitations to the future growth of hydro-electricity. **1972** *Sci. Amer.* Dec. 13/2 With ample supplies of coal and hydroelectricity China should be able to devote much of the oil..to a petrochemical industry.

hydrofining (həi·drofəiniŋ), *vbl. sb.* [f. HYDRO- + RE)FINING *vbl. sb.*] A catalytic process in which a petroleum product is stabilized and its sulphur content reduced by treatment with gaseous hydrogen under relatively mild conditions, so that unsaturated hydrocarbons and sulphur compounds undergo selective hydrogenation.

1931 C. ELLIS *Hydrogenation Org. Subst.* xlviii. 578 The term *hydrofining* is best applied to those treatments by hydrogen which are carried out at temperatures in the lower ranges,..where no extensive alteration of the carbon-containing molecule occurs. On the other hand, where great disturbance of carbon structure results the process is better denominated *hydroforming*. **1955** *Petroleum Refiner* May 154/1 Hydrofining was found to.. improve the burning quality of West Texas No. 1 fuel oil. **1970** J. R. HUGHES *Storage & Handling Petroleum Liquids* (ed. 2) 5 Hydrofining and autofining aim to remove or reduce the content of unwanted sulphur compounds.

So **hy·drofined** *ppl. a.*, obtained by hydrofining.

1931 C. ELLIS *Hydrogenation Org. Subst.* xlviii. 577 The hydrofined lubricating oils are not as readily oxidized as the untreated oils. **1955** *Petroleum Refiner* May 153/2 The quality of the raw and hydrofined distillates was determined by inspection tests, measurement of hydrogen content, and burning-quality tests.

hydroflumethiazide (həi:droflūmeþəi·ăzəid). *Pharm.* [f. HYDRO- + *flumeth-* (f. FLU(ORO- + METH(YL + *CHLOROTH)IAZIDE.] A white crystalline compound, $C_8H_8F_3N_3O_4S_2$, analogous to hydrochlorothiazide and having similar effects and uses.

1959 *Lancet* 12 Sept. 303/2 Two substances related to chlorothiazide—hydroflumethiazide and hydrochlorothiazide—have recently been produced, and are effective in much smaller quantity. **1964** A. GOTH *Med. Pharmacol.* (ed. 2) xxix. 358 Hydroflumethiazide (Saluron) has the same structural formula as hydrochlorothiazide, except that F_3C replaces Cl. **1968** [see *HYDROCHLOROTHIAZIDE].

hydrofoil (həi·drŏfoil). [f. HYDRO- + FOIL *sb.*[1], after *aerofoil.*] **1.** A plane designed to give rise to a force (other than drag) when moving through a liquid; *spec.* (*a*) a plane (usually one of two or more) attached to a vessel by means of which the hull is lifted clear of the water at speed; (*b*) one attached to a seaplane to facilitate take-off by increasing the hydrodynamic lift; (*c*) one attached at the side of a ship to act as a stabilizer.

1920 *Chambers's Jrnl.* 28 Feb. 207/2 [A boat.] Under each wing at its forward end is a series of narrow steel planes known as hydrofoils. **1933** *Aeroplane* 24 May 945/1 The possibility of using hydrofoils to cure porpoising and to revolutionise the design of flying-boats. **1939** *Jrnl. R. Aeronaut. Soc.* XLIII. 552 A special landing and take-off gear in the form of hydrofoils which will be retracted in flight. **1958** *New Scientist* 27 Feb. 15/3 The aerofoils of the sails and the hydrofoil of the keel are separated by the hull of the yacht. **1966** *McGraw-Hill Encycl. Sci. & Technol.* XIII. 212/1 Diving planes [on a submarine] are pairs of hydrofoils which extend from the sides of the ship. **1968** J. E. PLAPP *Engin. Fluid Mech.* xii. 486 The hydrofoil..is a wing designed to operate in water instead of air. **1972** *Daily Tel.* 28 Sept. 6/5 The mono hull has surface-piercing hydrofoils which lift the craft out of the water. **1973** *Nature* 12 Jan. 114/2 The use of hydrofoils for a wide variety of purposes such as propeller blades on boats, as sailboat keels, ship rudders, submarine and torpedo fins, lifting surfaces of hydrofoil boats, and shroud ring stabilizers for missiles, has prompted efforts to increase the lift-to-drag ratio.

2. A vessel fitted with hydrofoils for raising it clear of the water.

1959 *Times Rev. Industry* Nov. 41/1 This speed..will

be valuable for work on high speed motor boats or hydrofoils. **1962** *Daily Tel.* 12 Feb. 16/8 The United States Maritime Administration..believes there is a big future for hydrofoils as passenger vessels. **1968** [see *FOIL-BORNE *a.*]. **1969** *N.Z. Listener* 12 Dec. 19/1 Jaunting up Auckland Harbour on the hydrofoil. **1970** R. C. DORF *Mod. Control Syst.* x. 351 The Denison is an 80-ton hydrofoil capable of operating in seas ranging to 9 ft in amplitude at a speed of 60 knots. **1972** *Guardian* 27 May 5/3 The Thames's first modern commuter service—by Italian hydrofoil—opened yesterday.

3. *attrib.*, as *hydrofoil boat, craft, service, ship.*

1950 *Electronic Engin.* XXII. 205 A hydrofoil boat—one which has wings extending into the water to support it in motion so that the hull is out of the water—has speed and stability advantages. **1960** *Times* 19 Jan. 10/7 The United States Government has awarded a contract for the construction of a hydrofoil ship capable of carrying 100 passengers at speeds up to 90 miles an hour. **1960** *New Scientist* 15 Sept. 703/2 The hydrofoil craft is particularly suited for river work. **1964** *Weekly News* (Auckland) 8 July 30 The beginning of the hydrofoil service to Waiheke Island ..means that island residents..can now make the trip between Auckland and Matiatia in 20 minutes. **1973** *Cook's Continental Timetable* June 456 Hydrofoil Services. Journey 35 minutes [from Naples] to Capri.

hydroformate (həi·dro,fǭ·ɹmēⁱt). [f. as next + *-ate*, after *filtrate, precipitate*, etc.] A product obtained by hydroforming.

1953 A. A. DRAEGER et al. in *Sci. Petroleum* V. II. 266/2 For the production of high purity aromatic chemicals, however, additional processing of the hydroformate is required. **1969** KIRK & OTHMER *Encycl. Chem. Technol.* (ed. 2) XX. 538 Then the..light hydrocarbons are removed by distillation in a 'product stabilizer'; the undistilled portion constitutes the product or 'stabilized hydroformate'.

hydroformer (həi·dro,fǭ·ɹməɹ). [f. next + -ER[1].] In an oil refinery, an apparatus or plant where hydroforming is carried out.

1941 *Refiner & Natural Gas Manuf.* May 66/2 The potential toluene production of the hydroformer amounts to about 5,000,000 gallons per year. **1959** *Times Rev. Industry* Nov. 72/3 To achieve petrol of a higher octane number a powerformer in place of the traditional hydroformer is to be employed.

hydroforming (həi·dro,fǭɹmiŋ), *vbl. sb.* [f. HYDRO- + *-forming*, after REFORMING *vbl. sb.*] In the petroleum industry, a catalytic reforming process that converts the paraffins and alicyclic compounds in low-octane petroleum naphtha to aromatic compounds by dehydrogenation at a high temperature and moderate pressure in the presence of gaseous hydrogen. Freq. *attrib.*

1931 [see *HYDROFINING *vbl. sb.*]. **1941** *Oil & Gas Jrnl.* 27 Mar. 87/1 The first commercial hydroforming plant was placed in operation recently. **1953** A. A. DRAEGER et al. in *Sci. Petroleum* V. II. 266/2 The hydroforming process is employed by the petroleum refining industry both to elevate the anti-knock quality of petroleum naphthas.. for inclusion in premium quality gasolines and to produce aromatic compounds of high purity for specialized uses. **1959** *Times Rev. Industry* Aug. 112/2 Examples of.. new knowledge include the technique of making high octane gasoline by hydroforming and fluid catalytic cracking. **1969** KIRK & OTHMER *Encycl. Chem. Technol.* (ed. 2) XX. 534 Toluene is produced principally from petroleum by the hydroforming of selected petroleum naphthas..which are rich in naphthenic hydrocarbons.

Hence (as a back-formation) **hy·droform** *v. trans.*, to subject to hydroforming; **hy·dro-formed** *ppl. a.*, produced by hydroforming.

1941 *Nat. Petroleum News* 2 Apr. R-102/1 The anti-knock quality of hydroformed gasoline has not yet been thoroughly evaluated. **1949** P. C. CARMAN *Chem. Constitution & Properties Engin. Materials* xxvii. 824 A low octane feed boiling 90°–200° C. can be hydro-formed at 480°–540° C. and 100–300 p.s.i. to given an aromatised motor fuel with an octane rating of 80. **1953** A. A. DRAEGER et al. in *Sci. Petroleum* V. II. 274/1 These factors..make it a desirable procedure to hydroform cracked naphthas in admixture with virgin naphthas.

hydrogasification (həi:drogæsifikēⁱ·ʃən). [f. HYDRO- + GASIFICATION.] The production of methane directly from coal by treatment with hydrogen (or hydrogen and steam) at a high temperature and pressure.

1954 *Proc. Amer. Gas Assoc.* 644/2 Pressure hydrogasification produces high-Btu oil gases with satisfactory combustion characteristics. **1963** H. H. LOWRY *Chem. Coal Utilization* Suppl. xx. 996/1 The hydrogasification of coal to produce methane has an inherent thermochemical advantage. **1967** *McGraw-Hill Yearbk. Sci. & Technol.* 139/2 Up to 70% of the hydrogen needed for hydrogasification is made in place by reaction of steam with carbon. **1968** *Chem. & Engin. News* 29 July 12/3 Coal hydrogasification has reached the pilot-plant stage.

So **hydroga·sifier**, an apparatus in which hydrogasification is carried out.

1966 *Chem. & Engin. News* 18 Apr. 70/1 There is a net heat of reaction and this serves to supply the necessary heat for the hydrogasifier..to operate adiabatically.

hydrogel (həi·drǒdʒel). [f. HYDRO- + GEL(ATIN.] A gel or gelatinous precipitate in which the liquid constituent is water.

1864 [see *ALCOSOL]. **1895** THOMSON & BLOXAM *Bloxam's Chem.* (ed. 8) 123 Colloids..can generally exist in solution (the hydrosol form), but are apt to separate as a jelly (the hydrogel form) from such solutions. **1938** R. G. TORRENS *Dental Dis.* vi. 90 Gelatine is a hydrosol when warm and a hydrogel when cold. **1972** *Physics Bull.* June 336/1 Probably a wide range of factors can precipitate the clotting process including..surface texture and surface wettability as relating to hydrogel formation.

hydrogen. Add: **1. b.** An atom of hydrogen.

1920 *Jrnl. Amer. Chem. Soc.* XLII. 1431 A free pair of electrons on one water molecule might be able to exert sufficient force on a hydrogen held by a pair of electrons on another water molecule to bind the two molecules together. **1957** G. E. HUTCHINSON *Treat. Limnol.* I. iii. 196 The hydrogens, owing to their capacity to form hydrogen bonds.., will act as if they had unsatisfied single valencies.

2. a. *hydrogen* (*sc.* hydrogen bomb) *warhead*; **hydrogen bomb**, an immensely powerful bomb in which the energy released is derived from the fusion of hydrogen nuclei in an uncontrolled self-sustaining reaction initiated by a fission bomb; **hydrogen bond**, a weak bond between a strongly electronegative atom with a lone pair of electrons in one molecule and a hydrogen atom covalently bonded to another strongly electronegative atom or group in the same or a different molecule; hence *hydrogen-bonded* pa. pple. and ppl. adj., *-bonding* vbl. sb.; **hydrogen (gas) electrode**, an electrode (usu. of platinum coated with platinum black) partially immersed in a solution that contains hydrogen ions and hydrogen gas, so that an equilibrium between the ions and the molecules is established on the surface of the electrode enabling it to be used as a standard of zero potential (e.g. in measurements of other electrode potentials and of *p*H); **hydrogen ion**, the positive ion H^+ (the proton) derived from a hydrogen atom by the loss of its electron; a solvated form of this in a solution, esp. the hydrated form H_3O^+ (cf. *HYDRONIUM).

1947 *N.Y. Times* 13 Apr. IV. 9/5 Hydrogen bomb. New and improved atomic bombs were discussed at the recently held forum of the Northern California Association of Scientists. **1948** *Sci. News Let.* 17 July 35/1 This is the 'hydrogen bomb' that certain high officials in past months have vaguely..hinted may be made. **1951** C. ROBERTS *Terrace in Sun* i. 12 Would the hydrogen bomb that could reduce New York to a tangled skeleton penetrate thus far? **1954** W. S. CHURCHILL in *Hansard Commons* 30 Mar. 1840 The development of the hydrogen bomb raises strategic and political issues. **1972** *Sci. Amer.* Dec. 13/3 China exploded a fission device in 1964 and a fusion device in 1967, and it has tested several hydrogen bombs since that date. **1923** G. N. LEWIS *Valence* ix. 109 The hydrogen atom can form a loose attachment to another pair of electrons, thus forming the hydrogen bond. **1939** L. PAULING *Nature Chem. Bond* ix. 264 Although the hydrogen bond is not a strong bond..it has great significance in determining the properties of substances. **1966** *McGraw-Hill Encycl. Sci. & Technol.* XIV. 387/2 Ordinary ice consists of water molecules joined together by hydrogen bonds in a regular arrangement. **1970** AMBROSE & EASTY *Cell Biol.* iii. 110 When double-stranded DNA is heated to near 100°C, the hydrogen bonds between the two chains break and the strands separate. **1950** *Jrnl. Amer. Chem. Soc.* LXXII. 5349/2 Each residue is hydrogen-bonded to the third residue from it in each direction along the chain. *Ibid.*, The second hydrogen-bonded spiral is the five-residue spiral. **1936** *Ibid.* LVIII. 1903/2 One isomer should show complete hydrogen bonding detectable by appropriate physical methods. **1898** *Jrnl. Chem. Soc.* LXXIV. II. 89 A similar method may be used in the titration of acids and bases, if a hydrogen electrode be employed..being made of gold electrolytically coated with palladium. **1942** GLASSTONE *Introd. Electrochem.* x. 352 The hydrogen gas electrode cannot be employed in solutions containing oxidizing agents. **1964** R. G. BATES *Determination of pH* ix. 230 The hydrogen electrode is the ultimate standard for the determination of pH values, but..other electrodes reversible to hydrogen ion are commonly employed for routine pH measurements. **1896** *Jrnl. Chem. Soc.* LXX. II. 638 Etherification occurring, with or without the addition of a catalysing acid, is primarily caused by the activity of the hydrogen ions present. **1935** *Discovery* Nov. 322/1 Every process of manufacture is subject to constant scientific control, regulating temperature, humidity,..hydrogen-ion concentration. **1939** L. PAULING *Nature Chem. Bond* ix. 266 The positive hydrogen ion is a bare proton. **1942** GLASSTONE *Introd. Electrochem.* ix. 308 The hydrogen ion in solution is not to be regarded as a bare proton, but as a combination of a proton with, at least, one molecule of solvent. **1968** M. S. LIVINGSTON *Particle Physics* vi. 120 Experiments on the deflection of hydrogen-ion beams in electric and magnetic fields. **1954** in *Amer. Speech* (1957) XXXII. 137 That missile, or I.B.M. as the experts call it, will be an accurately guided rocket..capable of carrying a hydrogen warhead over a range of 4000 to 5000 miles.

b. *hydrogen cyanide*, the more usual term in modern usage for hydrocyanic acid; *hydrogen peroxide*, a colourless, viscous, somewhat unstable liquid, H_2O_2, which can act as an oxidizing and a reducing agent, is usu. prepared as an aqueous solution, and is used esp. as an oxidizing and bleaching agent, in the manufacture of peroxides and organic compounds, as a weak antiseptic, and (in concentrated form) as a rocket propellant.

1882 *Jrnl. Chem. Soc. Index of Subjects 1873–1882* 215/2 Hydrogen cyanide. **1948** *New Biol.* IV. 71 The most common fumigants in use in this country are hydrogen cyanide;..methyl bromide; [etc.]. **1872** *Jrnl. Chem. Soc.* XXV. 922 (*heading*) Determination of nitrates, nitrites, and hydrogen peroxide by solution of indigo. **1907** G. S. NEWTH *Text-bk. Inorg. Chem.* (ed. 12) II. iii. 226 When such a discoloured picture [in oils] is washed over with dilute hydrogen peroxide, the black sulphide is oxidised into the white lead sulphate. **1951** A. GROLLMAN *Pharmacol. & Therapeutics* xxv. 514 Hydrogen peroxide solution differs from most other disinfectants in the short duration of the action, which passes off as soon as all the oxygen is liberated. **1962** J. GLENN in *Into Orbit* 192 The hydrogen peroxide jets began to turn the capsule round to orbital attitude.

c. In journalistic and colloquial use: of the age, era, etc., marked by the advent of the hydrogen bomb.

1953 *Ann. Reg. 1952* 403 [Pres. Truman's] references to the bomb..firmly dated the beginning of the 'hydrogen era' as occurring in the period of the Truman Administration. **1954** *Commonweal* 10 Dec. 279/2 An unexpected wind shift and fallout of radioactive ashes made some unfortunate Japanese fishermen..the first public victims of the hydrogen age. **1959** *Times Lit. Suppl.* 29 May 315/1 His naval reforms..seem unimportant..in the hydrogen age.

3. *Comb.* **hydrogen-like** *a. Physics*, consisting (like the hydrogen atom) of a nucleus to which is bound a single negatively charged particle; characteristic of such an atom.

1927 E. N. DA C. ANDRADE *Struct. Atom* (ed. 3) ix. 190 An atom of helium from which one electron has been altogether removed, and an atom of lithium from which two electrons have been altogether removed, constitute similar systems, and may be called hydrogen-like. **1927** J. FISHER tr. *Born's Mech. Atom* iii. 155 The orbit of the radiating electron was hydrogen-like for large values of *k*, since it is situated in an approximately Coulomb field of force. **1951** S. DUSHMAN *Fund. Atomic Physics* ix. 131 A hydrogenlike atom, having a nucleus of charge *Ze* and one electron revolving about this nucleus in a circular orbit. **1969** K. ZIOCK *Basic Quantum Mech.* v. 89 Muonic atoms have hydrogen-like spectra.

hydrogenase (həidrǫ·dʒĕnēⁱz, -ēⁱs). *Biochem.* [ad. F. *hydrogénase* (J. de Rey-Pailhade 1900, in *Bull. de la Soc. chim. de Paris* XXIII. 668), f. HYDROGEN + *-ASE.] Any enzyme which catalyses the addition of hydrogen to an organic substrate.

1900 *Jrnl. Chem. Soc.* LXXVIII. II. 678 The evolution of gas [from the yeast] is almost immediately arrested by the addition of sulphur, a fact which suggests that the ferments in question are closely related to philothion or hydrogenase. **1943** *Jrnl. Biol. Chem.* CLI. 384 Hydrogenase is closely related to the nitrogen-fixing system in *Azotobacter.* **1965** A. H. ROSE *Chem. Microbiol.* vii. 142 There exists a close relationship between the ability of organisms..to fix nitrogen, and the presence in the organisms of the enzyme hydrogenase. **1966** FRENKEL & COST in Florkin & Stotz *Comprehensive Biochem.* XIV. viii. 417 Hydrogenase activity can also be observed in certain algae which can carry out photoreduction of CO_2 with molecular hydrogen.

hydrogenator (həidrǫ·dʒĕnēⁱtəɹ). [f. HYDROGENAT(E *v.* + -OR.] A vessel or apparatus in which hydrogenation is carried out.

1914 C. ELLIS *Hydrogenation of Oils* xi. 192 The contents are thoroughly agitated and transferred to the hydrogenator where the actual hydrogenation takes place. **1963** *Times* 17 Jan. 7/1 The revolutionary feature of the gas recycle hydrogenator..is that it can produce high quality town gas solely from light petroleum distillate.

hydrogenic, *a.* Restrict *rare* to sense in Dict. and add: **b.** *Physics.* = *hydrogen-like* adj.

1935 CONDON & SHORTLEY *Theory Atomic Spectra* v. 137 Energy levels in hydrogenic atoms. **1960** J. C. SLATER *Quantum Theory of Atomic Struct.* I. viii. 190 The wave function of an electron in such a spherical field is very similar to the hydrogenic function given in Eq. (7–31). **1970** G. K. WOODGATE *Elem. Atomic Struct.* ii. 20 The equation therefore applies to all the hydrogenic atoms hydrogen, deuterium, tritium, muonium, positronium, etc.

hydrogenite (həidrǫ·dʒĕnəit). [ad. F. *hydrogénite* (P. Mauricheau-Beaupré 1908, in *Compt. Rend.* CXLVII. 310), f. HYDROGEN + -ITE[1] 4 a.] Either of two powders formulated to provide a convenient and portable means of generating hydrogen: (*a*) a mixture of aluminium filings, mercuric chloride, and potassium cyanide; (*b*) a mixture of ferrosilicon, sodium hydroxide, and usually also calcium hydroxide.

1908 *Jrnl. Chem. Soc.* XCIV. II. 829 Aluminium filings are mixed with a small quantity of mercuric chloride and potassium cyanide in powder. The product, to which the name 'hydrogenite' is given, has D = 1·42. **1911** *Chem. Abstr.* V. 1499 'Hydrogenite' is a compressible powder consisting of an alloy of Si and a base of soda lime, and when ignited by a suitable 'match' it reacts spontaneously..with the evolution of H. **1922** J. W. MELLOR *Comprehensive Treat. Inorg. & Theoret. Chem.* I. vii. 285 A mixture, devised by G. F. Jaubert (1910), containing 25

parts of 90–95 per cent. ferrosilicon or manganosilicon, 60 of sodium hydroxide, and 20 slaked lime, is commercially known as hydrogenite. **1963** G. S. Brady *Materials Handbk.* (ed. 9) 678 A mixture of ferrosilicon and sodium hydroxide, called hydrogenite, which yields hydrogen gas when water is added, is used for filling balloons.

hydrogenolysis (həiːdrǒdʒěnǫ·lĭsis). *Chem.* [f. Hydrogen + -o + Lysis, after *hydrolysis*.] The splitting of a bond accompanied by the addition of an atom of hydrogen to the atoms originally bonded (one or both of these being carbon atoms).

1931 C. Ellis *Hydrogenation Org. Subst.* xlv. 522 For reasons of convenience we shall use 'hydrogenolysis' for all processes in which fuel material is treated with hydrogen at high pressures and high temperatures... Another general term frequently used..is 'destructive hydrogenation'. **1932** *Jrnl. Amer. Chem. Soc.* LIV. 4685 The hydrogenolysis of carbon–carbon linkages. **1971** Anderson & Baker in J. R. Anderson *Chemisorption & Reactions Metallic Films* II. viii. 189 The overall hydrogenolysis and disproportionation reactions may be represented by $CH_3NH_2 + H_2 \rightarrow CH_4 + NH_3$; $2CH_3NH_2 \rightarrow (CH_3)_2NH + NH_3$.

hydrogeologist (həiːdro͵dʒi͵ǫ·lǒdʒist). [f. Hydrogeolog(y + -ist.] An expert in, or student of, hydrogeology.

1935 *Geogr. Jrnl.* LXXXV. 551, I might indicate a few lines of research which..require the services of hydrogeologists. **1964** *Discovery* Oct. 7/3 An FAO hydrogeologist..has put the importance of groundwater very high.

hydrograph (həi·drǒgrɑf). [f. Hydro- + -graph.] † **1.** An instrument for transmitting sound under water and recording messages so received. *Obs. rare.*

1893 *Westm. Gaz.* 19 Oct. 7/3 (*heading*) Talking through the water. The wonders of the hydrograph.

2. A graph showing the variation of level, speed of flow, or another quantity at some point on a river. orig. *U.S.*

1897 *Monthly Weather Rev.* (U.S.) XXV. 129/1 Hydrographs for typical points on seven principal rivers are shown on Chart VI. **1936** *Water-Supply Paper U.S. Geol. Survey* No. 771. 71 Among the graphic devices that have been widely used in the study of stream-flow data is the hydrograph of discharge, which depicts the average flows by days,..years, or other time intervals. **1969** *Stud. & Rep. Hydrol.* I. 125 A linear distributed-system model..predicts a flood hydrograph from rainfall information and catchment characteristics.

hydroid, *sb.* Add: **2.** *Bot.* [a. G. *hydroid* (H. Potonié 1883, in *Jahrb. K. Bot. Gartens Berlin* II. 243).] An element forming part of the *hydrome tissue of a plant.

1887 W. Hillhouse tr. *Strasburger's Handbk. Pract. Bot.* v. 58 The perfect wood-cells..consist only of dead cell-walls, and, as..they simulate the tracheæ, i.e. vessels, they are known as tracheïdes, more recently as hydroïdes. **1968** Bell & Woodcock *Diversity Green Plants* iv. 126 Surrounding a core of tracheid-like cells (sclereids), containing scattered thin-walled cells (hydroids), is a zone of cells conspicuously large in transverse section. **1971** E. V. Watson *Struct. & Life Bryophytes* (ed. 3) ix. 126 Collectively these tissues are known as hadrom and leptom (analogues respectively of xylem and phloem) but the constituent elements are conveniently termed hydroids and leptoids.

hydrol (həi·drǫl). [f. Hydr- + -ol.] **1.** *Chem.* [f. Benz)hydrol.] Any substituted derivative of benzhydrol (diphenylcarbinol), $(C_6H_5)_2CHOH$; *esp.* Michler's hydrol (see *Michler).

1897 *Jrnl. Chem. Soc.* LXXII. i. 353 (*heading*) Condensation of hydrols with aromatic amines in presence of sulphuric acid. **1937** F. C. Whitmore *Org. Chem.* 833 The dye intermediate, Michler's hydrol, is *pp'*-$(Me_2N)_2$-benzhydrol. **1956** E. H. Rodd *Chem. Carbon Compounds* IIIb. xvii. 106 They are too unstable and reactive to be used as dyes but some of the hydrols are intermediates for the synthesis of triarylmethane dyes. **1971** R. L. M. Allen *Colour Chem.* viii. 111 The formaldehyde then condenses with two molecules of unchanged dimethylaniline, giving 4,4'bis(dimethylamino)diphenylmethane, and this is oxidised to the corresponding hydrol.

2. *Chem.* A name suggested for the simple water molecule, H_2O, as a basis for the systematic nomenclature of its polymers, $(H_2O)n$.

1900 W. Sutherland in *Phil. Mag.* L. 460, I propose for international convenience to call H_2O hydrol, $(H_2O)_2$ dihydrol, and $(H_2O)_3$ trihydrol. Steam is hydrol, ice is trihydrol, and water a mixture of dihydrol and trihydrol. **1915** W. M. Bayliss *Princ. Gen. Physiol.* viii. 234 It is to be supposed that the molecular forces, which permit the molecules of hydrol to press unusually closely together [in water], disappear when the new group constituting ice is formed, so that the latter occupies the greater volume. **1957** G. E. Hutchinson *Treat. Limnol.* I. iii. 196 Sutherland (1900)..supposed liquid water to consist of dihydrol H_4O_2 with trihydrol H_6O_3 in solution... Other workers believed that hydrol H_2O was also present, at least near the boiling point.

3. [perh. f. Hydrol(ysis.] A dark viscous liquid of unpleasant taste left as a mother liquor when starch is subjected to acid hydrolysis and dextrose is allowed to crystallize out.

1926 *Jrnl. Amer. Chem. Soc.* XLVIII. 2627 The fermentable part of 'hydrol' is chiefly *d*-glucose. **1953** *Jrnl. Assoc. Official Agric. Chemists* XXXVI. 457 Hydrol, or corn sugar molasses, is obtained as a by-product in the manufacture of dextrose from starch. **1954** I. A. Preece *Biochem. Brewing* xi. 327 In badly attenuated beers there may be a notable amount of maltotriose present.., whilst if such material as hydrol is used as a sugar adjunct it may be expected to find some gentiobiose.

hydrolase (həi·drǒlēⁱz, -ēⁱs). *Biochem.* [a. F. *hydrolase* (Battelli & Stern 1921, in *Arch. internat. de Physiol.* XVIII. 413), f. Hydrol(ysis + *-ase.] Any enzyme which catalyses the hydrolysis of a substrate.

1922 *Jrnl. Chem. Soc.* CXXII. i. 1077 Ferments are divided into three groups..namely hydratases..; hydrolases producing esterification or hydrolysis; and oxydoreductases. **1955** Neilands & Stumpf *Outl. Enzyme Chem.* xvi. 188 Lipases and phosphatases, being hydrolytic enzymes, logically fall into the group of hydrolases. **1970** W. H. Fishman *Metabolic Conjugation & Metabolic Hydrolysis* 373 The demonstration of the existence of latent hydrolases in the tadpole tail.

hydrolith (həi·droliþ). [ad. F. *hydrolithe* (G. F. Jaubert), f. Hydro- + Gr. λίθος stone.] A commercial name for calcium hydride as used as a convenient source of hydrogen (evolved when water is added).

1906 *Chambers's Jrnl.* 28 July 558/1 A new chemical compound somewhat akin to the calcium carbide familiar as a generator of acetylene gas has been placed on the market recently under the name of hydrolithe. **1967** G. D. Parkes *Mellor's Mod. Inorg. Chem.* xxx. 697 Calcium hydride..is a colourless, crystalline compound which has been used under the name of hydrolith for making hydrogen.

hydrological, *a.* (Further examples: cf. *hydrology 2.)

1913 R. F. Fox *Princ. & Pract. Med. Hydrol.* p. xi, Several chapters are devoted to a discussion of the *indications* for hydrological treatment in different chronic ailments and diseases. *Ibid.* x. 106 A cardinal fact in hydrological medicine. **1921** *Oxf. Index Therap.* 452 It is convenient to consider hydrological treatment from two points of view. **1957** G. E. Hutchinson *Treat. Limnol.* I. iv. 221 (*heading*) The hydrological cycle and the water balance of lakes.

hydrologist. (Examples.)

1938 *Times* 19 Feb. 13/2 With Papanin..on Franz Josef Land..were P. P. Shirshoff, a hydrologist and hydrobiologist, E. K. Federoff, [etc.]. **1971** *Nature* 30 July 301/1 Flood, erosion, drought and pollution..are also the chief problems facing the hydrologist.

hydrology. Add: **2.** *Med.* The branch of medicine concerned with treatment by baths and waters. *rare.*

[Cf. quots. 1670, 1716 s.v. Hydrological *a.*] **1850** J. Bell (*title*) Dietetical and medical hydrology. A treatise on baths;..with a description of bathing in ancient and modern times. **1913** R. F. Fox (*title*) The principles and practice of medical hydrology being the science of treatment by waters and baths.

hydrolube (həi·drolⁱūb). [f. Hydro- + *lube*, repr. first syllable of *lubricant*.] Any of various non-flammable hydraulic fluids having water and a glycol as the principal constituents.

1944 *U.S. Naval Res. Lab. Rep.* P-2273. 23 Sprays of 'Hydrolube' fluids made from a polymer thickened mixture of ethylene glycol and water required over 80% oxygen to propagate a flame. **1947** *Ibid.* P-3020. 3 The name 'Hydrolube' was selected by this laboratory early in the war..for any hydraulic fluid consisting of a polymer-thickened, corrosion-inhibited, aqueous solution having one or more glycols as major organic components. **1956** *Chem. & Engin. News* 3 Sept. 4245/3 The Navy..uses 'hydrolubes' in aircraft carrier catapult systems.

hydrolysable (həi·droləizăb'l). *Chem.* Also (chiefly *U.S.*) **-lyzable.** [f. *hydrolys(e *v.* + -able.] Capable of being hydrolysed.

1908 *Jrnl. Chem. Soc.* XCIV. i. 199 (*heading*) Cacao butter, especially its non-hydrolysable constituents. **1913** *Jrnl. Amer. Chem. Soc.* XXXV. 629 Those esters which are most easily hydrolyzable with excess of alkali. **1946** L. E. Wise *Wood Chem.* vi. 150 The disaccharide..must be hydrolyzable by alkali. **1965** Phillips & Williams *Inorg. Chem.* I. xiv. 522 The metals with basic oxides do not give readily hydrolysable salts.

hydrolysate (həidrǫ·lĭsēⁱt). *Chem.* Also (chiefly *U.S.*) **-lyzate.** [f. *hydrolys(e *v.* + *-ate*, after *filtrate, precipitate*, etc.] A product of, or preparation obtained by, hydrolysis.

1915 *Jrnl. Amer. Chem. Soc.* XXXVII. 1634 The hydrolysate in this instance was jet-black. **1944** L. F. & M. Fieser *Org. Chem.* xvi. 408 The determination of the proportion of the different amino acids present in a given protein hydrolyzate. **1964** *Oceanogr. & Marine Biol.* II. 149 Paper chromatography is a useful tool to establish the presence or absence of amino acids and other substances in hydrolysates and tissue extracts.

hydrolyse (həi·droləiz), *v. Chem.* Also (chiefly *U.S.*) **-lyze.** [f. Hydrolysis, after *analyse, analysis*.] **1.** *trans.* To subject to hydrolysis; to decompose by hydrolysis.

1880 [see Hydrolysis]. **1902** *Westm. Gaz.* 6 Jan. 2/1 Grape sugar is formed by hydrolysing cellulose with acids. **1944** L. F. & M. Fieser *Org. Chem.* xvi. 404 Proteins are hydrolyzed by acid or alkali and by enzymes, and in the case of the simple, nonconjugated proteins, the products consist of mixtures of amino acids. **1955** *Sci. Amer.* May 37/1 When a peptide or protein is hydrolyzed—treated chemically so that the elements of water are introduced at the peptide bonds—it breaks down into amino acids. **1968** C. A. Hampel *Encycl. Chem. Elem.* 567/1 The trivalent praseodymium ion occurs as $[Pr(H_2O)n]^{3+}$ and is only weakly hydrolyzed in aqueous solutions. **1971** *Nature* 17 Sept. 209/1 Crude starfish extracts were hydrolysed with hydrochloric acid.

2. *intr.* To undergo hydrolysis.

1920 *Jrnl. Biol. Chem.* XLIII. 173 The gum hydrolyzes quantitatively into levulose. **1931** Levene & Bass *Nucleic Acids* vii. 195 Embden and Schmidt..compared the rates of hydrolysis of the three substances and found that the muscle adenylic and inosinic acids hydrolyze at about the same rate, whereas the other adenylic acid hydrolyzes much faster. **1951** C. R. Noller *Textbk. Org. Chem.* v. 79 Although highly toxic to animals, it hydrolyzes rapidly to harmless phosphoric acid and ethyl alcohol when exposed to moist air. **1964** N. G. Clark *Mod. Org. Chem.* viii. 131 Tertiary halides hydrolyse most easily and primary halides are most resistant.

Hence **hy·drolysed** *ppl. a.*, **hy·drolysing** *vbl. sb.* and *ppl. a.*

1900 Perkin & Kipping *Org. Chem.* (rev. ed.) x. 188 The rapidity with which hydrolysis takes place depends.. on the nature of the ethereal salt and of the hydrolysing agent. **1912** *Jrnl. Biol. Chem.* XII. 297 Osborne and Guest ..obtained 59·2 per cent nitrogen in amino form in completely hydrolyzed gliadin. **1935** R. H. A. Plimmer in Harrow & Sherwin *Textbk. Biochem.* v. 157 Arginine may be directly precipitated from the hydrolyzed solution of the protein. **1943** *Thorpe's Dict. Appl. Chem.* (ed. 4) VI. 388/2 An alcoholic solution of potassium hydroxide is sometimes used for hydrolysing purposes. **1973** *Daily Tel.* 16 Feb. 17/3 In a world of monosodium glutamate and hydrolised protein, her work is a living testimonial of a fine palate.

hydrolysis. Substitute for def.: Any reaction in which a bond is broken by the agency of water and the hydrogen and hydroxyl of the water become independently attached to the two atoms previously linked; the decomposition or splitting of a compound in this way. Also applied to the analogous decomposition of an organic compound by the action of an acid or alkali, and to any reaction between a water molecule and an ion that produces a hydrogen or hydroxyl ion. (Add further examples.)

1900 Perkin & Kipping *Org. Chem.* (rev. ed.) x. 188 All ethereal salts are decomposed by water, mineral acids, and alkalies, the change..being spoken of as hydrolysis... $CH_3 \cdot COOC_3H_7 + KOH = CH_3 \cdot COOK + C_3H_7 \cdot OH$. **1935** R. H. A. Plimmer in Harrow & Sherwin *Textbk. Biochem.* v. 155 Hydrolysis of proteins to the amino acids is effected by boiling with acids, or alkalis, or by the action of the enzyme trypsin. **1938** C. D. Hurd in H. Gilman *Org. Chem.* I. vii. 617 In reactions in which the C—N bond is severed by hydrolysis, it is universally characteristic for the nitrogen to attract the hydrogen of water, and carbon the oxygen or hydroxyl. **1948** Glasstone *Textbk. Physical Chem.* (ed. 2) xii. 986 The hydrolysis must then be represented by $M(H_2O)n^+ + H_2O \rightleftharpoons H_3O^+ + M(H_2O)_{n-1}OH$. **1950** P. J. Durrant *Org. Chem.* xxix. 447 Many of the chemical reactions occurring in fermentation and in the metabolism of living organisms are hydrolyses. **1951** Kirk & Othmer *Encycl. Chem. Technol.* VII. 741 The reaction of a nitrile with water to form an amide $CH_3CN + H_2O \rightarrow CH_3CONH_2$ is thought of as a hydrolysis, although it is also a hydration. **1964** N. G. Clark *Mod. Inorg. Chem.* xi. 201 Hydrolysis [of nitriles] may be effected either by hot mineral acids..or by hot alkali...$CH_3 \cdot CN + 2H_2O + HCl \rightarrow CH_3 \cdot COOH + NH_4Cl$... $CH_3 \cdot CN + H_2O + NaOH \rightarrow CH_3 \cdot COONa + NH_3$.

hydroly·tically, *adv. Chem.* [f. Hydrolytic *a.*: see -ically.] By means of hydrolysis; as regards hydrolysis.

1928 *Chem. Abstr.* XXII. 200 (*heading*) Ion exchange of zeolitic silicates with hydrolytically dissociated salts. **1963** F. M. Dean *Naturally Occurring Oxygen Ring Compounds* v. 135 The furan ring can sometimes be opened hydrolytically. **1969** *Jrnl. Materials Sci.* IV. 432/2 These groups must be bonded to the silicon in a hydrolytically and thermally stable manner.

hydromagnetic (həiːdro͵mægne·tik), *a.* [f. Hydro- (in *hydrodynamic*) + Magnetic *a.* (in *electromagnetic*).] Of, relating to, or involving an electrically conducting fluid (as a plasma or molten metal) acted on by a magnetic field.

1943 H. Alfvén in *Ark. f. Matem., Astr. och Fysik* XXIXb. ii. 7 As the term 'electromagnetic-hydrodynamic waves' is somewhat complicated, it may be convenient to call the phenomenon 'magneto-hydrodynamic' waves. (The term 'hydromagnetic' is still shorter but not quite adequate.) **1955** *Proc. R. Soc.* A. CCXXXIII. 310 Hydromagnetic waves in rare ionized gases are of interest in connexion with galactic magnetic fields, the heating of the corona and other astrophysical problems. **1963** Alfvén & Fälthammar *Cosmical Electrodynamics* (ed. 2) iii. 73 In the sun all phenomena which are large enough to be observed visually from the earth are hydromagnetic, and the same holds for interstellar clouds. **1966** Ferraro & Plumpton *Introd. Magneto-Fluid Mech.* (ed. 2) i. 13 It is this coupling between the electromagnetic and mechanical

forces which characterizes hydromagnetic phenomena. **1973** *Nature* 9 Nov. 58/2 Nobody can yet give a hydromagnetic description of the process by which the neutron star captures the plasma.

Hence **hy:dromagne·tically** *adv.*, from the point of view of hydromagnetics.

1970 *Nature* 4 Apr. 48/1 Warm plasmas are considered hydromagnetically.

hydromagnetics (həi:droˌmægne·tiks), *sb. pl.* (const. as *sing.*). [f. prec.: see -IC 2.] The branch of physics concerned with hydromagnetic phenomena; = *MAGNETOHYDRODYNAMICS.

1953 T. G. COWLING in G. P. Kuiper *Sun* viii. 532 The subject of hydromagnetics is a new one. **1958** *New Scientist* 27 Feb. 12 The theory of an interaction like this, between a fluid and a magnetic field, is a central problem of the new science of hydromagnetics.

hydrome, hydrom (həi·drōᵘm). *Bot.* [ad. G. *hydrom* (H. Potonié 1883, in *Jahrb. K. Bot. Gartens Berlin* II. 243), f. HYDRO- + *-ome* as in *rhizome*, etc.] The water-conducting section of a vascular bundle.

1900 B. D. JACKSON *Gloss. Bot. Terms* 273/1 Tracheome, stated by Potonié not to be the tracheal, but the hydral system of the bundle, he therefore names it Hydrome. **1911** J. M. COULTER et al. *Textbk. Bot.* II. iii. 682 The conductive portion of the xylem is known as *hadrome* (or *hydrome*). **1929** *Encycl. Brit.* XVII. 6/1 The hydrom strand is either slightly developed or altogether absent. **1969** K. ESAU *Phloem* viii. 268 The corresponding conducting cells are hydroids (from hydrom, part of hadrom consisting of conducting cells only).

hydronium (həidrōᵘ·niə̆m). *Chem.* [a. G. *hydronium* (A. Hantzsch 1907, in *Zeitschr. f. phys. Chemie* LXI. 306), contraction of *HYDR(OX)ONIUM.] A name for the hydrated hydrogen ion (usu. represented as H_3O^+).

1908 *Jrnl. Chem. Soc.* XCIV. II. 15 Just as a molecule of ammonia may attach itself to a hydrogen ion, forming the ammonium ion $NH_4^{\cdot}$, so it is supposed that a molecule of water may similarly attach itself, forming the 'hydronium' ion $H_3O^{\cdot}$, so that a solution of a little water in sulphuric acid is a dissociated solution of hydronium sulphate. **1937** F. C. WHITMORE *Org. Chem.* 341 The effective catalyst is the hydronium ion, $(H_3O)^+$. **1940** *Jrnl. Chem. Soc.* 1410 When the hydrogen ion is considered to occur (in aqueous solution or in a compound) in the form $[H_3O]^+$, it is advisable to call it the hydronium ion (not hydroxonium ion). **1956** *Jrnl. Amer. Chem. Soc.* LXXVIII. 5999 (*heading*) The vibrational spectrum of the hydronium ion in hydronium perchlorate. **1959** *Nomencl. Inorg. Chem.* (*I.U.P.A.C.*) 26 The ion H_3O^+..is to be known as the oxonium ion when it is believed to have this constitution, as for example in $H_3O^+ClO_4^-$, oxonium perchlorate. The widely used term hydronium should be kept for the cases where it is wished to denote an indefinite degree of hydration of the proton, as, for example, in aqueous solution. [*The latter sentence is dropped in ed. 2 (1971).*] **1966** *Mineral. Mag.* XXXV. 1071 The existence of the individual H_3O^+ pyramidal complex, called the hydronium ion, or sometimes the hydroxonium or oxonium ion, in crystalline substances is a well-established fact.

hydrophil (həi·drŏfil), **-phile** (-fəil), *a.* [f. HYDRO- + -PHIL.] = *HYDROPHILIC *a.*

1903 *Electrician* 30 Oct. 42/1 He applied two electrodes.., contact being made by means of hydrophil cotton impregnated with a 1 per cent solution of zinc chloride. **1915** W. W. TAYLOR *Chem. Colloids* i. 7 The term lyophile has been applied to those systems in which there is marked affinity between the phases, and lyophobe to the others. When water is the dispersion medium the terms hydrophile and hydrophobe are commonly used. **1930** J. ALEXANDER *Colloid Chem., an Introd.* (ed. 3) iii. 39 Colloids of the reversible type are..said to be hydrophile or lyophile, while the irreversible colloids are hydrophobe or lyophobe. **1963** A. J. HALL *Textile Sci.* i. 10 Synthetic fibres are made from organic hydrophobic (water-repellent) polymers—the natural fibres are hydrophile (water-attractive). *Ibid.* 13 The hydrophile fibre wool..contains about 18% of moisture in its ordinary air-dry state. **1971** *Nature* 12 Feb. 489/2 The outer walls of the respiratory trumpets of mosquito pupae are hydrophil while the inner lining is hydrophuge.

hydrophilia (həidrŏfi·liă). *rare.* [f. HYDRO- + Gr. φιλία fondness.] A love of being near water.

1904 G. S. HALL *Adolescence* II. xii. 195 Others..can sit by the hour, seeing and hearing the movements of water in sea or stream. The best demonstration of the fact of this hydrophilia is the amount of cold..that it will overcome. **1959** *Times Lit. Suppl.* 31 July 450/4 A symptom of the derangement of sober, law-abiding citizens succumbing to hydrophilia is public confession... These very readable confessions can infect hardened land-lubbers with sea fever.

hydrophilic (həidrŏfi·lik), *a.* [f. HYDRO- + Gr. φίλ-ος loving + -IC.] **a.** Having an affinity for water, readily absorbing water; relating to such an affinity.

1901 *Buck's Handbk. Med. Sci.* (ed. 2) III. 694/1 The ear should be very carefully dried out, as of course the effectiveness of this solution depends upon the hydrophilic properties of the materials employed. **1954** KIRK & OTHMER *Encycl. Chem. Technol.* XIII. 919 The hydrophilic fibers can absorb and transfer water, and as such they are not naturally water-repellent. **1963** R. R. A. HIGHAM *Handbk. Papermaking* ii. 37 Because of the natural affinity of cellulose for water, paper is termed hydrophilic (water-receptive). **1971** *Nature* 19 Nov. 126/3 Attached to their hydrocarbon tails phospholipid molecules also..have hydrophilic head groups.

b. *spec.* in *Physical Chem.* [after Fr. *hydrophile* (J. Perrin 1905, in *Jrnl. de Chim. phys.* III. 85)]: applied to a hydrosol that does not readily form a precipitate, and to a gel that readily forms a sol on the addition of water or on being warmed.

1915 M. H. FISCHER tr. *Ostwald's Handbk. Colloid-Chem.* ii. 50 Different names are employed in the literature for these two sets of colloids... J. Perrin [calls them] 'hydrophilic' and 'hydrophobic' colloids. **1936** J. H. PARSONS *Dis. Eye* (ed. 8) xvi. 322 It has all the properties of a hydrophilic gel, undergoing turgescence in an alkaline, deturgescence in an acid aqueous medium. **1948** GLASSTONE *Textbk. Physical Chem.* (ed. 2) xiv. 1235 Sols of gums, starches, proteins and soaps, provide instances of hydrophilic systems. **1967** M. E. HALE *Biol. Lichens* iv. 53 The imbibition of water by a hydrophilic gel.

Hence **hydrophili·city**, hydrophilic quality.

1953 *Chem. Abstr.* XLVII. 9035 'Hydrophil[ic]ity' is defined as the ratio, by wt. of the hydrophilic to hydrophobic groups in the same mol. **1970** R. D. SWISHER *Surfactant Biodegradation* ii. 32 The nonionic hydrophilic groups have a multiplicity of elements..which have a cumulative effect; increasing their numbers in the group increases the hydrophilicity of the aggregate.

hydrophilous, *a.* Add: **c.** *Bot.* Of plants, dependent upon water as the agency of pollination or dissemination of seeds; formerly = **hydrophytic* (see quot. 1898).

1883 D. W. THOMPSON tr. *Müller's Fertilisation of Flowers* III. 567 The plants of this order [*sc.* Naiadaceæ] are anemophilous or hydrophilous. **1898** POUND & CLEMENTS *Phytogeogr. Nebraska* I. iii. 67 Hydrophilous fungi..are algæ-like aquatic fungi. **1902** *Encycl. Brit.* XXV. 437/1 Dissemination is effected by the agency of water, of air, of animals—and fruits and seeds are therefore grouped in respect of this as hydrophilous, anemophilous, and zooidophilous. **1920** A. ARBER *Water Plants* xviii. 235 Certain plants, however, present transitional methods of pollination, which without being actually hydrophilous, show approaches to this state. **1967** C. D. SCULTHORPE *Biol. Aquatic Vasc. Plants* ix. 248 The ultimate adaptation to aquatic life is the formation of wholly submerged hydrophilous flowers. **1973** PROCTOR & YEO *Pollination of Flowers* viii. 283 Among the most specialised of all hydrophilous species are the Eelgrasses (*Zostera*).

hydrophily (həidrǫ·fīli). *Bot.* [f. HYDRO- + Gr. φιλία friendship.] Pollination by the agency of water.

1920 A. ARBER *Water Plants* xviii. 236 The family Hydrocharitaceae..includes within itself all stages in the transition from entomophily to hydrophily. **1967** C. D. SCULTHORPE *Biol. Aquatic Vasc. Plants* ix. 249 The probable affinities of these few specialised plants support the belief that hydrophily and marine life are both recently acquired habits. **1973** PROCTOR & YEO *Pollination of Flowers* viii. 277 The adaptations to pollination by water (*hydrophily*) are diverse, so that it is hardly possible to speak of a syndrome of hydrophily.

hydrophobe. Add: **2.** A hydrophobic substance.

1924 H. FREUNDLICH in R. H. Bogue *Theory & Applic. Colloidal Behavior* I. xii. 320 The dyestuff sols..are so little affected by alkali salts that they cannot be classed as true hydrophobes. **1970** R. D. SWISHER *Surfactant Biodegradation* ii. 31 As an example of hydrophobes which are not derived from hydrocarbons we can cite the polyoxypropylenes.

B. *adj.* = *HYDROPHOBIC *a.* 2.

1915, 1930 [see *HYDROPHIL, -PHILE *a.*]. **1970** R. D. SWISHER *Surfactant Biodegradation* vi. 207 Increased distance between the sulfonate group and the far end of the hydrophobe group increases the speed of primary biodegradation of ABS and possibly of other surfactant types.

hydrophobia. Add: **3.** The property of a substance of being hydrophobic.

1956 *Soil Sci.* LXXXII. 163 All treated powdered clays had to overcome an initial hydrophobia which took place during the first few minutes of contact with water. **1958** J. J. BIKERMAN *Surface Chem.* (ed. 2) iii. 239 At a first approximation, hydrophoby may mean good miscibility with benzene and poor miscibility with water.

hydrophobic, *a.* (*sb.*) Add: **2. a.** Tending to repel, or not to absorb, water; pertaining to such a lack of affinity.

1938 A. D. WHITEHEAD tr. *Jordan's Technol. Solvents* i. 13 This group have a pronounced solvent power for non-polar or weakly polar, that is hydrophobic, materials. **1947** *Jrnl. Res. Nat. Bureau of Standards* (U.S.) XXXVIII. 106/1 It is common practice..to treat fabrics intended to be water repellent with various hydrophobic compounds. **1954** KIRK & OTHMER *Encycl. Chem. Technol.* XIII. 919 With hydrophobic fibers, fabric structure to a large degree will control water repellency. **1963** [see *HYDROPHIL, -PHILE *a.*]. **1967** E. CHAMBERS *Photolitho-Offset* xiv. 205 The image is oleophilic (ink-accepting) and hydrophobic (water-rejecting), making an excellent imaging material for an offset lithographic plate.

b. *spec.* in *Physical Chem.*: applied to a hydrosol that readily forms a precipitate and on evaporation or cooling gives a solid that cannot readily be converted back into a sol.

1915 [see *HYDROPHILIC *a.* b]. **1948** GLASSTONE *Textbk. Physical Chem.* (ed. 2) xiv. 1235 Typical examples of hydrophobic sols are those of metals, sulfur, sulfides and sulfur halides.

Hence **hydrophobi·city**, hydrophobic quality.

1947 *Jrnl. Res. Nat. Bureau of Standards* (U.S.) XXXVIII. 105/1 The difference between these two energies will depend upon the relative humidity, the hydrophobicity of the surface,..etc. **1963** A. J. HALL *Textile Sci.* ii. 63 These newer fibres have several different and useful properties which are associated with their increased hydrophobicity. **1969** *Nature* 15 Feb. 637/2 A quantitative treatment for comparing the average hydrophobicities of proteins.

hydrophyte. Substitute for entry: [ad. Da. *hydrophyt*, mod.L. *hydrophyta* (J. F. Schouw *Grundtræk til en almindelig Plantegeographie* (1822) 132), f. Gr. ὑδρο- water + φυτόν plant.] An aquatic plant, or one needing a water-logged environment for its growth. (Further examples.) Hence **hydrophy·tic** *a.*

1858 A. GRAY *Introd. Struct. & Syst. Bot.* 536 *Hydrophyte*: a water-plant. **1894** F. W. OLIVER et al. tr. *Kerner's Nat. Hist. Plants* I. 75 It is usual to designate all plants that grow in water as hydrophytes or water-plants. **1905** F. E. CLEMENTS *Res. Methods Ecol.* iv. 209 The effect of these conditions is to produce a plant xerophytic as to its aerial parts, and mesophytic or even hydrophytic as to subterranean parts. **1920** A. ARBER *Water Plants* i. 3 The ultimate term in the acceptance of aquatic conditions is reached in certain hydrophytes with submerged flowers, in which even the pollination is aquatic. **1934** *Discovery* XV. 11/1 Suitable protection [for mosquitoes] may be furnished by grass or other hydrophytic vegetation. **1955** G. M. SMITH *Cryptogamic Bot.* (ed. 2) II. v. 97 As the mat [of vegetation] becomes drier..the *Sphagnum* eventually disappears and the hydrophytic angiosperms are replaced by those of a more mesophytic type. **1967** C. D. SCULTHORPE *Biol. Aquatic Vasc. Plants* v. 147 Experimental data on the water relations of submerged hydrophytes do not lend themselves to generalisation. **1973** *Nature* 12 Jan. 88/2 A halophytic vegetation covered the basin during the past century with a hydrophytic woodland forming in the first quarter of the present century.

hydroplane (həi·drŏplēⁱn), *sb.* [f. HYDRO- + PLANE *sb.*³ (in sense 2, after *aeroplane*).] **1.** A movable horizontal plane (usually one of several) projecting from the side of a submarine and used to control movement in a vertical plane and to provide stability during motion under water.

1901 *Submarine Torpedo Boats* (Lake Torpedo Boat Company) 19 The depth of submergence beneath the surface is maintained nearly constant by hydroplanes, one or more on each side of the vessel. **1902** *Sci. Amer.* 22 Nov. 346/2 While submerged..the boat has a reserve buoyancy, and in order to totally submerge it is necessary to employ the hydroplanes. **1907** S. LAKE in *Trans. Inst. Naval Archit.* XLIX. 39 The practicability of navigating on the bottom and of opening a door for the purpose of conducting mining operations, &c, together with the hydroplanes, were the features most questioned in connection with my plans for a submarine torpedo-boat submitted to the U.S. Government in 1893. **1911** *Encycl. Brit.* XXIV. 921/1 Another technical point in the design of submarines..is the desirability or otherwise of 'bow-rudders' or 'hydroplanes'. **1919** *Jane's Fighting Ships* 118 They..have large rudder and hydroplane areas and small reserve of buoyancy for quick diving and rapid handling. **1954** K. C. BARNABY *Basic Naval Archit.* (ed. 2) vi. 93 In the submerged condition, there usually remains a small excess of buoyancy...This is overcome by means of the horizontal diving rudders or 'hydroplanes'.

2. A motor boat designed to skim the surface of the water by means of a bottom that consists in part of one or more flat surfaces sloping upwards towards the bow. Also *hydroplane boat.*

1904 *Sci. Amer.* 8 Oct. 250/3 Hydroplanes—new forms of gliding boats. This name, formed on the analogy of aeroplane, is suggested for vessels which, instead of floating in water, glide over its surface as sleighs glide over ice. **1907** *Engineering* 4 Oct. 457/2 (*heading*) The Crocco and Ricaldoni hydroplane boat. **1909** *Westm. Gaz.* 5 Jan. 4/2 We have exhibited marked enterprise in regard to the hydroplane. **1909** *Ibid.* 9 Mar. 4/1 The Alla-Va, a hydroplane boat having more than ordinary pretensions to speed, has been placed in the unrestricted racer class. **1913** W. OWEN *Let.* 28 Sept. (1967) 199 Hydroplanes are in the habit of planing over the [River] Garonne. **1936** E. G. BARRILLON in W. F. Durand *Aerodynamic Theory* VI. 137 In a hydroplane in motion, the water does not act by static pressure alone, but also by a..dynamic force analogous to that on the wings of an airplane. **1957** *Times* 8 Nov. 10/3 [Mr. Donald Campbell's] hydroplane Bluebird, which is powered by a Metropolitan-Vickers jet engine, was timed over the measured kilometre at 260·107 m.p.h. **1965** R. SHECKLEY *Game of X* (1966) xviii. 127 The hydroplane climbed out of the water, balancing on her two sponsons.

†**3.** = *HYDRO-AEROPLANE, *SEAPLANE. *Obs.* exc. *Hist.*

1911 *Daily Colonist* (Victoria, B.C.) 9 Apr. 1/1 Glenn Curtiss, the aviator, gave a successful exhibition of his new hydroplane on the surface of Salt Lake this afternoon, ascending from and descending upon the water. **1913** W. S. CHURCHILL in *Hansard Commons* 17 July 1501 We have decided to call the naval hydroplane a seaplane, and the ordinary aeroplane or school machine, which we use in the Navy, simply a plane. **1913** *Q. Rev.* Apr. 471 For reconnaissance, the work is better done by hydroplanes costing a few hundreds apiece. **1914** *Daily Express* 19 Sept. 3/4 His flights in a hydroplane attracted the attention of the King at Weymouth a couple of years ago. **1969**

K. Munson *Pioneer Aircraft 1903–14* 161/2 Two other intermediate designs of 1907 were another airship, the No. 16, and a wingless hydroplane, the No. 18, which underwent taxying tests on the Seine.

hydroplane (həi·drŏplēⁱn), *v.* [f. prec. sb.] *intr.* **1. a.** To travel in a hydroplane boat.

1909, 1918 [see *hydroplaning* vbl. sb. below].

b. To skim the surface of the water by the use of hydroplanes.

1914 *Techn. Rep. Advisory Comm. Aeronaut. 1912–13* 237 The machine at once hydroplaned on leaving its shed. **1928** C. F. S. Gamble *Story N. Sea Air Station* i. 32 Having succeeded in making his machine hydroplane on her floats. **1936** J. Grierson *High Failure* v. 91 Once one is hydroplaning it is much easier to go on accelerating until flying-speed is gained. **1938** C. Winchester *Wonders World Aviation* I. 39 When the seaplane has gathered sufficient speed it climbs over its own wave and so hydroplanes or skims along the surface.

2. Of a motor vehicle, etc.: to aquaplane. Chiefly *U.S.*

1962 *Daily Tel.* 17 May 17/5 Flooding on the Kingston by-pass caused a car travelling at speed to 'hydroplane' and..turn completely round. **1969** C. Campbell *Sports Car* (ed. 3) vii. 179 Aquaplaning (hydroplaning in America)..is in effect a high-speed skating of the tyre on a film of water when travelling on wet roads. **1973** R. Hayes *Hungarian Game* xxviii. 164 The 707 skipped once as its wheels hydroplaned on the wet runway.

So **hy·droplaning** *vbl. sb.*

1909 *Westm. Gaz.* 5 Jan. 4/3 It is due entirely to its performance at Southampton that hydroplaning has gained recognition in this country. **1918** *Chambers's Jrnl.* 20 July 541/1 The water..provides the finest possible field for motor-boating in small craft, and, I should imagine, for hydroplaning. **1922** *Encycl. Brit.* XXX. 50/2 Hydroplaning efficiency..could be sacrificed for sea-worthiness. **1938** C. Winchester *Wonders World Aviation* I. 37 Running on the step is the expression used to describe the hydroplaning of a seaplane on the surface of the water. **1969** [see sense 2 above].

hydroponics (həi:drǫpǫ·niks). [f. Hydro- + Gr. πόνος work: see -ic 2.] The process of growing plants without soil, in beds of sand, gravel, or similar supporting material flooded with nutrient solutions. Hence **hydropo·nic** *a.*, **hydropo·nically** *adv.*; **hydropo·nicist**, one who practises hydroponics; **hydropo·nicum**, the building or garden in which hydroponics is practised.

1937 W. F. Gericke in *Science* 12 Feb. 178/1 'Hydroponics', which was suggested by Dr. W. A. Setchell, of the University of California, appears to convey the desired meaning better than any of a number of words considered. **1938** *California Monthly* Feb. 13/2 My first planting..was set in the hydroponicum on September 18, 1936. *Ibid.* 40/3 The important factors..must be understood by the hydroponicist, as they must be understood by the successful gardener. **1940** *Times* 20 Apr. 1 (Advt.), Hydroponics (crops without soil)..easy if you use Gromost hydroponic mixture. **1940** *Manch. Guardian Weekly* 17 May 394/4 Hydroponics received a great impetus in the United States shortly after the trans-Pacific air line was established. **1951** A. C. Clarke *Sands of Mars* viii. 94 The local brew..was completely synthetic—the joint offspring of hydroponic farm and chemical laboratory. **1951** J. S. Douglas *Hydroponics* iii. 30 A farm or garden devoted to soilless cultivation is usually called a hydroponicum. **1955** *Sci. News Let.* 30 Apr. 282/3 Chemical gardening or hydroponics makes a favorite exhibit. **1956** *Jrnl. Brit. Interplanetary Soc.* XV. 20 As hydroponicists have pointed out, soil is in no way a perfect medium. **1961** *Astronautica Acta* VII. 134 Men have survived over extended periods on hydroponically produced plant food. **1967** *Technology Week* 23 Jan. 48/1 Water and minerals from the Moon can be used to grow food hydroponically. **1970** *New Scientist* 5 Feb. 259/3 The potential of hydroponics..is only just beginning to be tapped. **1971** *Daily Colonist* (Victoria, B.C.) 13 May 1/4 Hydroponic grass has produced encouraging results with dairy herds, increasing their milk yield. **1973** *Listener* 13 Sept. 338/2 Growing vegetables like aubergines and sweet corn and green peppers hydroponically—that is, without soil.

hydropower (həi·droˌpauᵊɹ). Also **hydro-power** (with hyphen) and as two words. [f. Hydro- (in *hydro-electric*) + Power *sb.*[1]] Hydro-electric power.

1933 F. F. Fowle *Stand. Handbk. Electr. Engineers* (ed. 6) xiii. 1295 (*heading*) Steam power and its relation to hydro power. **1946** *Nature* 3 Aug. 160/1 The inexhaustible nature of hydro-power. **1969** *New Scientist* 18 Sept. 565/1 In the north western states..fossil fuel is expensive and nearly all potential hydropower sites have already been exploited. **1971** *Sci. Amer.* Sept. 157/3 Tidal energy and other forms of hydropower.

hydroskimmer (həidroˌski·məɹ). [f. Hydro- + Skimmer *sb.* 7.] An amphibious air-cushion vehicle, supported by peripheral jet-generated air. Orig., the name assigned by the Bureau of Ships to an experimental craft of the U.S. Navy.

1960 *Bureau of Ships Jrnl.* Feb. 22 Hydro-skimmer Model A David Taylor Model Basin. **1962** *Ibid.* Apr. 27/2 The Bureau of Ships has awarded a contract..for the design and construction of a 22-ton hydroskimmer research craft, designated SKMR-1...The craft will have four cushion fans..which will provide the lift needed. **1965** *Naval Engineers Jrnl.* June 364/1 Ground effect machines are very much in the picture of the Amphibious Force of the future. One such machine is the hydroskimmer which rides free of the surface on an air cushion... They will skim over land, sand bars, marshes, mud flats and open water with equal ease. **1970** M. W. Cagle *Flying Ships* i. 1 One of our first tasks..is to straighten out the varied and confusing terminology which surrounds words like 'hovercraft', 'PAK-V' and 'hydroskimmer', and cryptic initials like ACV, GEM, TAC, CAB, SEV, and SES.

hydrosol (həi·drŏsǫl). [f. Hydro- + Sol(ution.] A sol in which the liquid constituent is water.

1864 [see *alcosol]. **1895, 1938** [see *hydrogel]. **1937** *Industr. & Engin. Chem.* (News Ed.) 10 Mar. 104/2 Gold hydrosols nearly always contain unreduced gold compounds, which are fully reduced to metal hydrosols under suitable conditions. **1954** R. L. Parker tr. *Niggli's Rocks & Min. Deposits* xi. 463 In mineralogy the hydrosols—i.e., the colloidal solutions with water as the dispersing medium—are almost the only sols of any importance.

hydrothermally (həidropþə̄·ɹmăli), *adv.* [f. Hydrothermal *a.* + -ly[2].] By hydrothermal action.

1941 *Ecology* Oct. 448/2 The hydrothermally altered andesites and basalts of parts of the Great Basin. **1957** [see *huttonite]. **1962** W. A. Deer et al. *Rock-Forming Min.* V. 329 Pure hydroxyapatite crystals up to 0·3 mm. in length have been synthesized hydrothermally by the hydrolysis of monetite..at 300°C. and 1250 lb./in.^{2} saturated steam pressure. **1965** G. J. Williams *Econ. Geol. N.Z.* vi. 61/1 All writers presumed the gold to have been derived hydrothermally from granitic sources.

hydrotropic, *a.* Add: **2.** *Physical Chem.* [f. *hydrotropy.] Of, pertaining to, or produced by hydrotropy; causing a substance that is otherwise only slightly soluble in water to dissolve readily.

1916 *Jrnl. Chem. Soc.* CX. II. 555 (*heading*) Hydrotropic phenomena. **1946** *Industr. & Engin. Chem.* Apr. 382/2 Most hydrotropic solutions precipitate the solute on dilution with water. **1954** P. A. Winsor *Solvent Properties Amphiphilic Compounds* v. 123 The reduction in solvent action on dilution..is very great with hydrotropic salts of lower molecular weight.

hydrotropically (həidroˌtrǫ·pikăli), *adv.* [f. prec.: see -ically.] **1.** *Bot.* In a manner that results in a movement towards water.

1915 *Ann. Bot.* XXIX. 281 A disturbance of the equilibrium within the cells would thus be effected in exactly the same way as by the difference of osmotic pressure in hydrotropically stimulated roots.

2. *Physical Chem.* As regards hydrotropy.

1928 *Chem. Abstr.* XXII. 770 Hydrotropically active salts. **1951** E. Hägglund *Chem. Wood* iv. 261 The extracted lignin can be precipitated from the solution by diluting the latter to a lower concentration of the hydrotropically active salt.

hydrotropy (həidrǫ·trǫpi). *Physical Chem.* [ad. G. *hydrotropie* (C. Neuberg 1916, in *Biochem. Zeitschr.* LXXVI. 107), f. Hydro- + Gk. τροπή turn, turning.] The phenomenon whereby a substance that is only slightly soluble in water will readily dissolve in certain aqueous solutions.

1928 *Chem. Abstr.* XXII. 770 (*heading*) The applicability of Traube's rule to the phenomenon of hydrotropy. **1950** J. W. McBain *Colloid Sci.* xvii. 268 Hydrotropy occurs in concentrated solutions of salts or of colloidal electrolytes. **1954** P. A. Winsor *Solvent Properties Amphiphilic Compounds* i. 5 With the amphiphilic salts of short chain length (e.g. C_3—C_8) the 'solubilization' effect becomes marked only with their rather concentrated aqueous solutions and has, in this case, been termed 'hydrotropy'.

hydrovane (həi·drŏvēⁱn). [f. Hydro- + Vane.] **a.** = *hydroplane *sb.* 1.

1919 *Times* 22 Mar. 8/1 The submarine commander.. could do a 'crash dive', that is, go under with full weight on, hydrovanes set hard down, and taking in water ballast. **1940** 'N. Shute' *Landfall* ii. 49 British submarines carried identification marks upon the hydrovanes.

b. = *hydrofoil 1.

1920 *Glasgow Herald* 27 Apr. 7 The possibilities of the large flying boat are very great...Hydrovanes may be found..to give good results for reducing landing shocks and increasing the 'getting off' efficiency. **1936** *Jrnl. R. Aeronaut. Soc.* XL. 476 A combination of ship and hydrovane can only reduce the overall resistance to propulsion. **1939** *Ibid.* XLIII. 402 It is proposed to provide flying boats with hydrovanes. **1967** *New Scientist* 9 Mar. 460/3 The special type of hydrofoil anchor designed by Kingston..has hydro-vanes rigged in such a way as to be self-reversing in tidal currents.

hydroxamic (həidrǫksæ·mik), *a. Chem.* [tr. G. *hydroxamsäure* hydroxamic acid (H. Lossen 1869, in *Ann. d. Chem. u. Pharm.* CL. 315), f. *hydrox(ylamin* Hydroxylamine + *am(id* Amide: see -ic.] *hydroxamic acid*: any of the acyl derivatives, R·CO·NHOH or $(R\cdot CO)_2$-NHOH, of hydroxylamine (see quot. 1966).

1875 *Jrnl. Chem. Soc.* XXVIII. 751 (*heading*) Distillation of hydroxamic acids. *Ibid.* 766 The ethers of aromatic hydroxamic acids. **1926** *Biochem. Jrnl.* XX. 1362 The hydroxy-acids present in rape oil give hydroxamic acids whose sodium salts are soluble in alcohol. **1966** Millar & Springall *Sidgwick's Org. Chem. Nitrogen* (ed. 3) ix. 333 The mono N-acyl derivatives of hydroxylamine are usually referred to as hydroxamic acids, a name which strictly refers to structure (I). They can clearly have the alternative structure (II) which should be called a hydroximic acid. In no case are the two isomers known as separate compounds: (I) R·C=O (II) R·COH and a com-

|
NHOH ‖
NOH

pound of this class..can react as if it had either structure. Commonly the term hydroxamic is used to imply either of these structures.

hydroxide. Add: **2.** *attrib.*, as *hydroxide ion.*

1955 *Chem. & Engin. News* 1 Aug. 3190/3 The name 'hydroxyl' has long denoted the group OH. In organic contexts it is undoubtedly correct; but the expression 'hydroxyl ion' is very frequently used, although possibly less logical than 'hydroxide ion'. **1959** *Nomencl. Inorg. Chem.* (I.U.P.A.C.) 30 Certain polyatomic anions have names ending in -ide. These are: OH^- hydroxide ion [etc.]... The OH^- ion should not be called the hydroxyl ion. The name hydroxyl is reserved for the OH group when neutral or positively charged.

hydroxo- (həidrǫ·kso). *Chem.* A combining form of Hydroxyl, denoting a coordinated hydroxyl group; also used *attrib.* as an independent word.

1907 *Jrnl. Chem. Soc.* XCII. II. 560 This salt and others of the same series are classified by the author [*sc.* A. Werner] as hydroxonitrosotetra-ammineruthenium salts. *Ibid.*, Precipitates of the neutral hydroxo-salts. **1940** *Jrnl. Chem. Soc.* 1411 When the hydroxyl group is bound in a complex, Werner's system of notation should be used, according to which the hydroxyl groups are designated *hydroxo-* or *ol-* groups. **1965** Phillips & Williams *Inorg. Chem.* I. xiv. 532 Examples include..the formation in alkaline solution of the polynuclear cationic hydroxo-complexes of the cobalt(III) ion, e.g. $[Co(en)_2(OH)]_2^{4+}$ where en is ethylenediamine.

hydroxocobalamin (həidrǫ:ksokobǫ·lămin). *Biochem.* [f. *hydroxo- + *cobalamin.] An analogue of cyanocobalamin (vitamin B_{12}) in which the cyanide ion is replaced by a hydroxide (OH^-) ion.

1950 [see *cobalamin]. **1961** *Lancet* 26 Aug. 483/1 For the treatment of pernicious anæmia hydroxocobalamin appears to be equal in activity to cyanocobalamin and is better retained. **1970** *Times* 24 Jan. 7/3 The condition can be successfully treated by injection of hydroxocobalamin, a special form of vitamin B_{12}.

hydroxonium (həi:drǫksōᵘ·niəm). *Chem.* [a. G. *hydroxonium* (A. Hantzsch 1907, in *Zeitschr. f. phys. Chemie* LXI. 306), f. Hydr- + *oxonium.] = *hydronium.

1925 *Chem. Abstr.* XIX. 2309 (*heading*) Action of ammonium chloride vapor on metals and similarity of ammonium salts and hydroxonium salts as acids. *Ibid.* 2310 This expt. provides an important confirmation of Hantzsch's hydroxonium theory. **1940, 1966** [see *hydronium]. **1956** *Jrnl. Chem. Soc.* 2913 (*heading*) Raman spectra and constitution of solid hydrates. Hydroxonium perchlorate, nitrate, hydrogen sulphate, and sulphate. **1957** G. E. Hutchinson *Treat. Limnol.* I. iii. 197 Three of the hydrogen atoms could be at 0·99 A. and one at 1·77 A., corresponding to the hydroxonium ion H_3O^+.

hydroxy-. Add: **3.** Special Combs.: **hydro:xyamphe·tamine** *Pharm.*, a sympathomimetic amine that is a hydroxy derivative of amphetamine but lacks its stimulant effect on the central nervous system, and is used (as a solution of the hydrobromide) as a nasal decongestant and a mydriatic; methyl tyramine, $HO\cdot C_6H_4\cdot CH_2CH(NH_2)CH_3$; **hydro:xybenzo·ic** *a.*, in *hydroxybenzoic acid*, any of three derivatives, $HO\cdot C_6H_4\cdot COOH$, of benzoic acid having a ring-substituted hydroxyl group; *spec.* the *ortho* isomer, salicylic acid; **hydro:xybuty·ric** *a.*, in *hydroxybutyric acid*, any monohydroxy derivative of a butyric acid; *spec.* the acid $CH_3CHOHCH_2$-COOH, one of the 'ketone bodies'; **hydro:xycitrone·llal**, a monohydroxy derivative, $C_{10}H_{20}O_2$, of citronellal, prepared synthetically and used extensively in perfumery to give the odour of lily of the valley; **17-hydro:xycorticoste·roid** *Biochem.*, any corticosteroid that has a hydroxyl group attached at position 17 of the steroid nucleus; **hydro:xycorticoste·rone** *Biochem.* = *hydrocortisone; **hydro:xyly·sine**, an amino-acid, $H_2N\cdot CH_2CHOH(CH_2)_2CH(NH_2)COOH$, found principally in collagen; **hydro:xyme·thyl**, the univalent radical —CH_2OH, in which a hydroxyl group replaces one of the hydrogen atoms of a methyl group; **hydro:xymethyla·tion**, the introduction of a hydroxymethyl group into a compound; **hydro:xymethylcy·tosine**, a pyrimidine base, $C_4H_4N_3O$·CH_2OH, that is present in place of cytosine in the DNA of certain bacteriophages; **hydro:xypro·line**, any of the monohydroxy

derivatives, $C_5H_9NO_3$, of proline; *esp.* 4-hydroxyproline, the lævorotatory form of which is a non-essential amino-acid (strictly, an imino-acid) that is an important constituent of collagen and elastin; **hydro:xytry·ptamine,** any of the ring-substituted monohydroxy derivatives, $C_{10}H_{16}N_2O$, of tryptamine, esp. *SEROTONIN (5-hydroxytryptamine).

1948 *Arch. Otolaryngol.* XLVIII. 659 The product used ..provides..800 units of penicillin per cubic centimeter in a 1 per cent solution of hydroxyamphetamine hydrobromide (paredrine hydrobromide). **1876** *Jrnl. Chem. Soc.* II. 85 (*heading*) A new hydroxybenzoic acid. **1888** BLOXAM *Chem.* (ed. 6) 524 Salicylic or hydroxybenzoic acid, $C_6H_4.HO.CO_2H$, is prepared artificially by combining phenol with soda, and heating the product in carbonic acid gas. **1958** PACKER & VAUGHAN *Mod. Approach Org. Chem.* xxiv. 796 The most important hydroxy-benzoic acid is salicylic acid (*o*-hydroxybenzoic acid). **1879** *Jrnl. Chem. Soc.* XXXVI. 615 (*heading*) Hydroxybutyric acid, $C_4H_8O_3$. **1970** W. S. HOFFMAN *Biochem. Clin. Med.* (ed. 4) iv. 149 The so-called ketone bodies, namely, acetoacetic acid, β-hydroxybutyric acid, and acetone..are formed during the oxidation of fatty acids. **1929** *Chem. Abstr.* XXIII. 95 Pure rhodinal..was prepd. by vacuum distn. of hydroxycitronellal. **1951** P. Z. BEDOUKIAN *Perfumery Synthetics & Isolates* 231 Hydroxycitronellal has not been found in nature and is entirely a development of the laboratory. **1951** *Jrnl. Clin. Endocrinol. & Metabolism* XI. 1029 Treatment with adrenocorticotropic hormone led to an increase in concentration of the 17-hydroxycorticosteroids. **1968** *Brit. Med. Bull.* XXIV. 225/2 Simple steroid screening tests such as single determinations of 17-hydroxycorticosteroid in plasma or in collections of urine. **1943** REICHSTEIN & SHOPPEE in *Vitamins & Hormones* I. 356 17-Hydroxycorticosterone... Isolated and described as 'Substance M' by Reichstein (55) and by Kendall et al. (54), who called it 'Compound F'. **1961** *Lancet* 7 Oct. 796/1 Further reports on the urinary levels of 17-hydroxycorticosterone.. of such patients will be awaited with interest. **1925** *Chem. Abstr.* XIX. 2347 Hydroxylysine does not occur in casein or ovalbumin. **1969** *New Scientist* 3 July 11/1 One [family] excreted excessive quantities of hydroxylysine. **1937** *Chem. Abstr.* XXXI. 9888/3 (Index), Hydroxymethyl group, detn. in resol. **1964** G. H. HAGGIS et al. *Introd. Molecular Biol.* ix. 218 In 5-hydroxy-methylcytosine, a hydroxy-methyl (—CH_2OH) group replaces the hydrogen at position 5. **1948** H. WYNBERG tr. *Theilheimer's Synthetic Methods Org. Chem.* I. 147 (*heading*) Hydroxymethylation of phenols with formaldehyde. **1968** H. V. APOSHIAN in H. Fraenkel-Conrat *Molecular Basis Virol.* v. 504 Shortly after infection with a T-even phage, a new enzyme is produced which catalyzes the hydroxymethylation of dCMP at the 5 carbon atom. **1952** WYATT & COHEN in *Nature* 20 Dec. 1072/1 We have now resolved this discrepancy by isolation from *T*-even bacteriophages of a new pyrimidine base, identified as 5-hydroxymethylcytosine. **1968** H. V. APOSHIAN in H. Fraenkel-Conrat *Molecular Basis Virol.* v. 499 The unusual base, 5-hydroxymethylcytosine, is not found in uninfected *E. coli.* **1905** *Jrnl. Chem. Soc.* LXXXVIII. I. 545 (*heading*) Synthesis of hydroxypyrrolidinecarboxylic acids (hydroxyprolines). **1965** A. MEISTER *Biochem. Amino Acids* (ed. 2) I. i. 87 3-Hydroxyproline was first obtained from cattle Achilles' tendon collagen. **1967** *New Scientist* 24 Aug. 375/1 In fish from cold water the precise proportion of the imino-acid hydroxyproline in the important protein collagen..was lower than that in fish from warm water. **1949** *Jrnl. Biol. Chem.* CLXXX. 968 Tentatively, then, the constitutional formula of 5-hydroxytryptamine.. may be assigned to this vasoconstrictor principle. **1956** *Nature* 18 Feb. 332/2 The pharmacologically active substance 5-hydroxytryptamine is known to be liberated from platelets during clotting. **1956** *Chem. Abstr.* L. 5630 (*heading*) A new synthesis of bufotenine and related hydroxytryptamines. *Ibid.* 5631 6-Hydroxytryptamine.

hydroxyapatite (həidrǫ:ksi,æ·pătəit). [f. HYDROXY- + APATITE.] Calcium phosphate hydroxide, ideally $[Ca_3(PO_4)_2]_3.Ca(OH)_2$, which occurs as a rare mineral of the apatite group (in which hydroxyl replaces all or most of the fluorine of the commoner fluorapatite), and which is the principal inorganic constituent of tooth enamel and bone.

1912 *Bull. U.S. Geol. Surv.* No. 509. 100 The three formulas developed are repeated here... To the list are added those of apatite, both the fluorapatite and the hypothetical hydroxyapatite... Hydroxyapatite, $9CaO.3P_2O_5.CaO.H_2O$. **1917** *Jrnl. Chem. Soc.* CXI. 638 The mineral constituents of bone consist in the main of hydroxyapatite, $(Ca_3P_2O_8)_3Ca(OH)_2$, mixed with a certain amount of calcium carbonate. **1962** W. A. DEER et al. *Rock-Forming Min.* V. 333 The hydroxyapatite..in talc schist and the fluor-hydroxyapatite in chlorite schist, both from a serpentinite near Holly Springs, Georgia, are considered to be metamorphic in origin. **1964** A. WHITE et al. *Princ. Biochem.* (ed. 3) xli. 781 It seems likely that in bone, divalent cations other than Ca^{++} can replace Ca^{++} in the hydroxyapatite crystal lattice, whereas anions other than phosphate and hydroxyl may be adsorbed on the vast areas of surface offered by the minute crystals. **1971** *Physics Bull.* July 411/1 The enamel of a tooth is composed of hydroxyapatite crystals in prismatic form.

hydroxylapatite (həidrǫ:ksil,æ·pătəit). [f. HYDROXYL + APATITE.] = *HYDROXYAPATITE.

1927 N. H. & A. N. WINCHELL *Elem. Optical Mineral.* (ed. 2) II. viii. 128 The following formulas and names are tentatively assigned to minerals closely related to apatite. ..Hydroxylapatite (unknown alone) $3Ca_3P_2O_8.Ca(OH)_2$. **1946** *Nature* 6 Apr. 453/1 It is generally believed that bone salts are constituted either of hydroxylapatite which has absorbed calcium carbonate or of carbonato-apatite. **1951** C. PALACHE et al. *Dana's Syst. Min.* (ed. 7) II. 882 Fluorapatite, chlorapatite, and hydroxylapatite conform to the formula $Ca_5(PO_4)_3(F,Cl,OH)$. **1962** WALEY & VAN HEYNINGEN in A. Pirie *Lens Metabolism Rel. Cataract* 343 Chromatography on a column of calcium phosphate (hydroxylapatite).

hydroxylase (həidrǫ·ksilēiz, -ēis). *Biochem.* [f. HYDROXYL + *-ASE.] Any enzyme which catalyses the hydroxylation of a compound.

1953 *Jrnl. Biol. Chem.* CCI. 187 The authors propose.. the term 11β-hydroxylase..for the enzyme whose function and properties have been described here. **1970** E. HEFTMANN *Steroid Biochem.* vii. 64 Animal tissues contain hydroxylases that mediate the introduction of oxygen into specific positions of steroids to produce α- or β-oriented hydroxyl groups.

hydroxylate (həidrǫ·ksilēit), *v.* *Chem.* [f. HYDROXYL + -ATE[3].] **a.** *trans.* To introduce a hydroxyl group into (a molecule or compound). **b.** *intr.* To accept a hydroxyl group.

1951 P. Z. BEDOUKIAN *Perfumery Synthetics & Isolates* 232 The tertiary carbon atom hydroxylates with greater ease than the secondary carbon atom. **1954** G. M. BADGER *Struct. & Reactions Aromatic Compounds* vii. 308 Such a reaction mixture also hydroxylates aromatic compounds. **1970** E. HEFTMANN *Steroid Biochem.* x. 97 Either pregnenolone or progesterone may be hydroxylated at C-17 by an enzyme.

So **hydro·xylated, hydro·xylating** *ppl. adjs.*

1900 *Rep. Brit. Assoc. Adv. Sci.* 298 The hydroxylated nucleus of the tribromonaphthol. **1930** *Chem. Abstr.* XXIV. 2988 $H_2S_2O_8$ may be used as a hydroxylating agent. **1954** G. M. BADGER *Struct. & Reactions Aromatic Compounds* vii. 308 Hydrogen peroxide becomes a very effective hydroxylating agent in the presence of mineral acid. **1961** *Engineering* 31 Mar. 462/2 Hydroxylated carboxylic acids.

hydroxylation (həidrǫksilēi·ʃən). *Chem.* [f. HYDROXYL + -ATION.] The introduction of a hydroxyl group into a molecule or compound.

1879 *Jrnl. Chem. Soc.* XXXVI. 139 (*heading*) Hydroxylation by direct oxidation. **1962** H. HEATH in A. Pirie *Lens Metabolism Rel. Cataract* 364 Ascorbic acid is an essential cofactor for the hydroxylation of tryptophan to 5-hydroxytryptophan.

hydroxylic (həidrǫksi·lik), *a.* *Chem.* [f. HYDROXYL + -IC.] Of or containing a hydroxyl group.

1898 *Jrnl. Chem. Soc.* LXXIII. 997 The substance is therefore an anhydride of nitrocamphor,..but it must necessarily be derived from a hydroxylic modification. **1948** GLASSTONE *Textbk. Physical Chem.* (ed. 2) ix. 680 Hydroxylic solvents, e.g., water and alcohols. **1950** *Symposium Hydrogen Bond 1949* (R. Inst. Chem.) 4 The oxygen atom of one molecule coordinates with the hydroxylic hydrogen atom of another, thus forming the weak intermolecular bond responsible for molecular association. **1963** C. N. R. RAO *Chem. Applications Infrared Spectroscopy* iii. 175 The important bond in hydroxylic compounds arises from the O–H stretching vibration.

hydroxyprogesterone (həidrǫ:ksi,prōudʒe·-stĕrōun). *Biochem.* and *Pharm.* [f. HYDROXY- + *PROGESTERONE.] Any of several synthetic derivatives of progesterone that have a hydroxyl group in place of one of the hydrogen atoms of the steroid nucleus; *esp.* the derivative in which the hydroxyl group is at position 17, used (chiefly as the caproate ester) as a long-acting progestational compound in cases of *corpus luteum* deficiency.

1941 *Jrnl. Biol. Chem.* CXXXIX. 855 It was found to be the hitherto unknown steroid..17-hydroxyprogesterone.., a position isomer of desoxycorticosterone. **1948** W. H. PEARLMAN in Pincus & Thimann *Hormones* I. xi. 441 Erhart and co-workers..described the preparation of 12(α)-hydroxyprogesterone..from desoxycholic acid..; the substance was found to be lacking in physiological activity. **1954** *Nature* 30 Oct. 839/2 Various derivatives of progesterone by oxidation at C_{11} such as..11-α-hydroxyprogesterone and 11-β-hydroxyprogesterone..have been found to be only about 3–10 per cent as progestational as progesterone. **1962** N. APPLEZWEIG *Steroid Drugs* v. 100 When administered to pregnant women for the prevention of habitual abortion, Norlutin and 17α-hydroxyprogesterone caproate have been shown on occasion to cause masculinization of the female fetus. **1968** J. H. BURN *Lect. Notes Pharmacol.* (ed. 9) 93 The progestogen [in contraceptive pills] is either a 19–norsteroid derivative.. or a 17–hydroxy-progesterone derivative.

hydroxyquinoline (həidrǫ:ksi,kwi·nŏlīn). *Chem.* [f. HYDROXY- + QUINOLINE.] Any of the seven monohydroxy derivatives, C_9H_7NO, of quinoline, esp. *OXINE (8-hydroxyquinoline).

1881 *Jrnl. Chem. Soc.* XL. 613 An excellent yield of hydroxyquinoline is obtained by fusing the sulphonic acid with three times its weight of soda. **1925** *Chem. Abstr.* XIX. 1572 The formation of 4-hydroxyquinoline is suspected. **1937** A. W. GROVES *Silicate Analysis* vi. 131 The perfection of the separation of aluminium, iron, titanium, and zirconium from beryllium by means of 8-hydroxyquinoline now affords the improved method for the determination of beryllia which is adopted here. **1947** *Biochem. Jrnl.* XLI. 544/2 It was found that oxine alone of the seven isomeric hydroxyquinolines had chelating ability. **1970** *Watsonia* VIII. 23 Root tips..were given a pretreatment in a 0·002M solution of 8-hydroxyquinoline.

hydroxyzine (həidrǫ·ksizīn). *Pharm.* [f. HYDROXY- + PIPERA)ZINE.] A tranquillizing drug which is usu. administered as the hydrochloride, a white bitter-tasting powder, and is a complex derivative of piperazine.

1956 *Jrnl. Amer. Med. Assoc.* 16 June 604/1 Hydroxyzine (Atarax) hydrochloride is a new tranquilizing drug that is currently under clinical investigation. **1968** J. H. BURN *Lect. Notes Pharmacol.* (ed. 9) 59 Hydroxyzine appears to relieve anxiety without impairing critical faculties.

hyena. Add: **hyenoid** *a.* (example).

1945 G. G. SIMPSON *Princ. Class. & Class. Mammals* III. 224/1 The genera here set aside..are large, later Tertiary canids with heavy jaws, rather distantly convergent toward the hyenas, and so sometimes called 'hyænoid dogs'.

hygeen, hajeen (hidʒī·n, hădʒī·n). Also 6 **hugiun,** 8 **hajan,** etc., **hyghgeen,** 9 **hadjeen, hejeen, hejin.** [Arab. *hajīn* dromedary, pronounced in Egypt *hagīn* (cf. Syriac *hagīnā*, *huġānā*, Talmudic *hōgnā*). Origin uncertain.] A riding dromedary.

1600 J. PORY tr. *Leo's Geographical Hist. Afr.* IX. 338 Of camels there are three kinds; whereof the first being called Hugiun [orig. *quarum primi Hugiun nuncupati*] are grosse, and of a tall stature. **1713** *Guardian* No. 124 There has not been a Tyger, Leopard, Elephant or Hyghgeen, for some Years past, in this Nation, but I have taken their particular Dimensions. **1790** J. BRUCE *Trav.* IV. 332 If.. there was danger, [he] should return..mount a hajan or dromedary, and [etc.]. **1803** W. WITTMAN *Trav. in Turkey* 216 A smaller and more slender species of the camel, called *hedgin*, is mounted by the natives and others, and is capable of making a greater progress, on a journey, than a horse. **1830** [see *DELOUL]. **1864** J. A. GRANT *Walk across Afr.* 419 A 'Hadjeen', or riding camel, is indispensable to comfort. **1865** W. G. PALGRAVE *Narr. Journey through Arabia* I. 325 The dromedary is the race-horse of his species, thin, elegant,..light of step, easy of pace,.. though yet more often the dromedary enjoys his special title of 'hejeen' or 'dolool'. **1875** [see *DELOUL]. **1890** S. W. BAKER *Wild Beasts* II. 374 As a general rule, the hygeens are not so powerfully proportioned as those which carry baggage. **1908** *Animal Managem.* 276 The riding camel (..Hagheen, Egypt).

hygric (həi·grik), *a.* *rare.* [f. Gr. ὑγρός moist, wet + -IC.] Relating to water or moisture.

1902 *Jrnl. Nerv. & Mental Dis.* XXIX. 751 Various deviations from the normal in the hippocampal convolution contribute..support to the hypothesis that hygric illusions may be referred to that area. **1907** *Trans. Med. Soc. London* XXX. 371 The patient has complained of.. 'hygric sensibility', that is to say..whatever she touches with her hands..feels wet to her.

hygro-. Add: **hygrothe·rmograph,** an instrument that records the temperature and humidity of the air on a single chart.

1929 WEAVER & CLEMENTS *Plant Ecol.* xi. 264 It is convenient for comparison to record both humidity and air temperature upon the same record sheet... Such an instrument is called a hygrothermograph. **1969** *Ecology* L. 742/1 Hygrothermograph readings were taken..at three elevations above ground and four exposures.

hygrophilous (həigrǫ·filəs), *a.* *Ecol.* [ad. Fr. *hygrophile* (J. Thurmann *Essai de Phytostatique* (1849) I. 268), f. HYGRO- + Gr. φίλος loving.] Of plants: growing in a moist environment. Also **hy·grophile** *sb.*, a plant of this type.

1863 [in Dict. s.v. HYGRO-]. **1878** A. HENFREY *Elem. Bot.* (ed. 3) IV. i. 661 Plants are divided into *Xerophiles*, or those capable of existing in very dry climates; *Hygrophiles*, or those which can only exist in the presence of abundant moisture. **1883** [in Dict. s.v. HYGRO-]. **1903** W. R. FISHER tr. *Schimper's Plant-Geogr.* I. iii. 260 The Rain-forest is evergreen, hygrophilous in character, at least thirty meters high. **1914** M. DRUMMOND tr. *Haberlandt's Physiol. Plant Anat.* viii. 439 The degree of development of this tissue..at once shows whether any given plant is distinctly hygrophilous or xerophilous in character. **1934** H. GILBERT-CARTER tr. *Raunkiaer's Life Forms of Plants* viii. 321 More or less hygrophilous communities are succeeded by mesophilous woods of oak and beech. **1957** P. DANSEREAU *Biogeogr.* iv. 206 Hygrophilous plants are 'moisture-loving'.

hygrophyte (həi·grofəit). *Bot.* [f. HYGRO- + Gr. φυτόν plant.] A plant that grows in a moist habitat. Hence **hygrophy·tic** *a.*

1903 W. R. FISHER tr. *Schimper's Plant-Geogr.* i. 17 Typical hygrophytes have weakly developed roots, elongated axes, and large thin leaf-blades. **1932** FULLER & CONARD tr. *Braun-Blanquet's Plant Sociol.* v. 126 Hygrophytes, moisture-loving species with favourable water economy,..have morphological devices that permit the free loss of water. **1936** M. I. NEWBIGIN *Plant & Animal Geogr.* vii. 126 The actual appearance of the forests in any area depends on the competition between the hygrophytic species proper and those adapted to withstand seasonal drought. **1952** J. CLEGG *Freshwater Life* 50 The plants in the marshy area surrounding the pond are..not truly aquatic...They are usually referred to as hygrophytes.., in contrast to the true water-plants, which are called

hydrophytes. **1960** N. Polunin *Introd. Plant Geogr.* xi. 325 With further rising in level of the soil surface and relative depression of the water-table, shrubs and ultimately trees enter and in time give rise to a hygrophytic woodland. **1965** Bell & Coombe tr. *Strasburger's Textbk. Bot.* 177 In the hygrophytes we find large, thin, delicate laminae, rich in sap.

hygrostat (həi·grostæt). [f. Hygro- + -stat.] = *humidistat 2.

1915 R. C. Carpenter *Heating & Ventilating Buildings* (ed. 6) xx. 525 Some form of differential hygrostat.. controls the wet bulb temperature with respect to the dry bulb temperature so as to maintain a constant relative humidity. **1918** [see *humidistat 2]. **1937** *Archit. Rev.* LXXXI. p. lxxii/1 Heating and humidifying equipment are incorporated in each unit, the desired temperature and humidity being automatically controlled by thermostats and hygrostats. **1965** *Bull. Entomol. Res.* LVI. 265 Kitchen & Gall (1953) describe a modified Friez hair hygrostat which they used to control a humidifier for an insect breeding room.

Hyksos (hi·ksōus), *sb. pl.* Also 7–8 **Hicsos, Hycsos.** [ad. Gr. Ὑκσώς interpreted by Manetho either as 'shepherd kings' or as 'captive shepherds', ad. Egyptian *heqa khoswe* chief of foreign lands.] A people of mixed Semitic-Asiatic stock, probably including a proportion of Habiru, who gave their name to the fifteenth Egyptian Dynasty (1650–1558 B.C.) which ruled the eastern delta. Also *attrib.* or as *adj.*

1602 T. Lodge tr. *Josephus' Works* 769 This nation was called Hicsos, which signifieth Kings shepheards,..but in other coppies I find that *Hicsos*, is not interpreted kings shepheards, but shepheards that were captiues. **1743** W. Stukeley *Abury* xiii. 78 The shepherds who quitted Egypt, under the conduct of our Hercules, call'd themselves Hycsi, as Manethon informs us in Josephus & Eusebius in chronol. The word imports royal shepherds, valiant, freemen, heroes. **1788** Gibbon *Decl. & F.* V. l. 184 Under the name of Hycsos, the shepherd kings, they had formerly subdued Egypt. **1877** *Encycl. Brit.* VII. 735/1 The invasion and conquest, at least in part, of Egypt by the Hyksos..is undoubtedly the chief cause of the obscurity of this age. **1899** A. H. Sayce *Early Israel* Introd. p. xxv, A Hyksos Pharaoh and his Hebrew vizier. **1931** J. G. Duncan *Digging up Biblical Hist.* II. 163 Hyksos pottery. **1931** M. M. Green tr. *Schneider's Hist. World Civilization* I. ii. 42 Aahmes took the capital of the Hyksos in the Delta about 1580 B.C. **1955** E. Pound *Section: Rock-Drill* xciii. 83 Where the spirit is clear in the stone as against Filth of the Hyksos, butchers of lesser cattle. **1957** [see *dark ages]. **1960** K. M. Kenyon *Archaeol. in Holy Land* vii. 184 At the period at which the Hyksos appear in Palestine and Egypt, we have on the move groups of Hurrians and Habiru, and the most probable explanation of the Hyksos is that they were recruited from such bands. **1971** *Encycl. Judaica* VIII. 1142 The Hyksos..attempted to Egyptianize and assimilate Egyptian culture. This synthesis is attested by the Hyksos religion.

hymenectomy (həimĕne·ktŏmi). *Surg.* [f. Hymen[2] + *-ectomy.] Excision of the hymen.

1931 in R. J. E. Scott *Gould's Med. Dict.* (ed. 3). **1962** *Lancet* 26 May 1117/2 After consulting a gynæcologist she underwent an operation for a hymenectomy 8 days before the hearing of the petition.

Hymettian (həime·tiăn), *a.* [f. L. *Hymettius* (f. *Hymettus*, Gr. Ὑμηττός) + -ian.] Of or belonging to Mount Hymettus in Attica, famous in antiquity for its honey and marble; hence *poet.* honeyed, sweet (cf. Hyblæan).

1601 Holland tr. *Pliny's Nat. Hist.* xvii. i. 499 Foure goodly pillars of Hymettian Marble. **1658** J. Rowland tr. *Moufet's Theater of Insects* 908 He that will make a good mixture of wine and honey, must mingle with new Hymettian Honey, old Falernian Wine. **1795** Coleridge *To R. B. Sheridan* in *Poetical Works* (1912) I. 88 Thy temples with Hymettian flow'rets wreath'd.

hymn, *sb.* Add: **2. b. hymn of hate,** the *Hassgesang* of the German poet Ernst Lissauer (1882–1937), an anti-British song; freq. *transf.*

1914 [see *hate *sb.*[1] 1 c]. **1915** A. Huxley *Let.* 26 Apr. (1969) 70 We're losing our heads and our senses of humour—and soon we shall be reduced to writing Hymns of Hate—then we're lost. **1916** *Anzac Book* 44 No 'Hymn of Hate' has yet been composed which would give expression to the hatred which has possessed me. **1918** G. B. Shaw *Pen Portraits* (1932) 40 Mr Chesterton, in his wildest hymns of hate, will break into a joke on his top note. **1945** H. G. Wells *Happy Turning* viii. 31 (*heading*) A hymn of hate against sycamores. **1963** E. Hyams *New Statesmanship* 8 This must not also entail blinking the facts about the Germans even if one did not join in the hymn of hate. **1966** B. Kimenye *Kalasanda Revisited* 67 She boarded the bus whilst still employed on her hymn of hate.

hymnarium (himnē^ə·riŭm). Pl. **-ia.** [med.L.] = Hymnary.

1924 *Glasgow Herald* 7 June 4 The extensive hymnaria attributed to the famous Bishop of Milan [St. Ambrose].

hyp, var. *hype *sb.*[1]

hypabyssal (həipăbi·săl), *a.* *Petrol.* [ad. G. *hypabyssisch* (attributed by H. Rosenbusch 1891, in *Tschermak's min. u. petrogr. Mittheil.* XII. 386, and by W. C. Brögger *Die Eruptivgesteine des Kristianiagebietes* (1894) iii. 123, to Brögger, 1886): see Hypo- 4.] Of igneous rock: formed from magma which has intruded into and solidified among other rocks; intermediate between plutonic and volcanic.

1895 *Mineral. Mag.* XI. 115 It [*sc.* sölvsbergite] is a true dyke-rock ('hypabyssal' rock). **1896** *Science Progress* IV. 476 Brögger has insisted on the necessity of a division intermediate between the plutonic and the volcanic, which he terms 'hypabyssal'. **1896** *Q. Jrnl. Geol. Soc.* LII. 613 The laccolitic rocks..would seem to belong to what Prof. Brögger calls hypabyssal. **1926** G. W. Tyrrell *Princ. Petrol.* vi. 106 The hypabyssal group includes the rocks of dykes, sills, and small laccoliths, etc., which occupy an intermediate position in the crust between the deepseated plutonic bodies, and the surficial lava flows. **1951** Turner & Verhoogen *Ign. & Metamorphic Petrol.* iii. 51 Some writers recognize an intermediate (hypabyssal) class to include rocks that have crystallized at moderate depth. **1969** Bennison & Wright *Geol. Hist. Brit. Isles* x. 251 The Great Whin Sill is the largest hypabyssal intrusion in Britain.

hypacusis (həipăkiū·sis). *Med.* Also **-acousis, -acusia, -akusis.** [mod.L., f. Hyp- + Gr. ἄκουσις hearing (ἀκούειν to hear).] Diminished acuteness of hearing. Cf. *hyperacusis.

1886 *Syd. Soc. Lex.*, Hypacusia. *Ibid.*, Hypacusis. *Ibid.*, Hypakusis. **1895** T. B. Hyslop *Mental Physiol.* ix. 273 Hypakusis—diminution of sense of hearing, seen in various forms of insanity. **1967** A. B. Graham *Sensorineural Hearing Processes* xii. 143 Some patients with hypacusis as against normal-hearing patients.

hypalgesia, -ic: see *hypo-.

hypanthium (həipæ·nþiŭm). *Bot.* = *hypanthodium.

1866 Lindley & Moore *Treas. Bot.* II. 611/2 Hypanthium. The fleshy enlarged hollow of the end of a flower-stalk, such as occurs in the rose, apple, or myrtle. **1887** W. Hillhouse tr. *Strasburger's Handbk. Pract. Bot.* xxx. 349 The five-celled ovary is here [*sc.* in the apple] immersed in a hollowed flower-stalk, a so-called hypanthium. **1912** H. H. Rusby *Man. Struct. Bot.* iii. 46 The enclosed portion of the calyx really is adherent, but it is not visible, since it is enclosed and concealed by the hollow torus, which is known as a Hypanthium. **1968** A. Cronquist *Evol. & Class. Flowering Plants* iii. 87 It is customary and convenient to define the hypanthium in terms of external descriptive morphology rather than on evolutionary homologies.

hypanthodium (həipænþōu·diŭm). *Bot.* [mod.L. (H. F. Link *Elementa Philosophiae Botanicae* (1824) ix. 265), f. Hypo- + Anthodium.] In certain plants, an enlargement of the receptacle, sometimes becoming fleshy and surrounding the ovary.

1832 J. Lindley *Introd. Bot.* ii. 108 If the receptacle is fleshy, and is not enclosed within an involucrum, as in Dorstenia and Ficus, it is then called by Link Hypanthodium. **1861** R. Bentley *Man. Bot.* 204 The Hypanthodium..is formed by a receptacle which is usually of a fleshy nature becoming more or less incurved.

hyparterial, *a.* Substitute for def.: Situated below the pulmonary artery. (Add examples.)

1882 *Quain's Elem. Anat.* (ed. 9) II. 511 From the continuation of the bronchus four dorsal and as many ventral hyparterial branches are given off in succession in each lung. **1921, 1962** [see *eparterial *a.*].

hype (həip), *sb.*[1] *slang* (orig. *U.S.*). Also **hyp.** [Abbrev. of Hypodermic.] **a.** A drug-addict. **b.** A hypodermic needle or syringe. **c.** A hypodermic injection. Cf. *hypo *sb.*[3]

1924 G. C. Henderson *Keys to Crookdom* xxiv. 306 Next down on the list is the 'hype' or morphine-user. Morphine is taken by hypodermic injections. **1929** [see *bang *sb.*[3]]. **1936** *Amer. Speech* XI. 122/2 *Hype*, the hypodermic needle used to inject narcotics. **1952** D. E. Hulburd *H is for Heroin* ii. 52 They smoked two marijuana cigarettes apiece that an old addict—'an old hype'—had sold Hortense. **1955** *U.S. Senate Hearings* (1956) VIII. 4164 Terms for morphine addicts: 'Hype', 'Hygelo', 'Head', 'Fiend', 'Needle man', 'Junky', 'Junker'. **1963** *New Society* 7 Nov. 9/1 'Once a hype, always a hype,' the American narcotics addict says. **1972** J. Wambaugh *Blue Knight* (1973) i. 11 They were dumb strung-out hypes. *Ibid.*, The tall one is wearing a long-sleeved shirt buttoned at the cuff. To hide his hype marks.

hype (həip), *sb.*[2] *slang* (orig. *U.S.*). [Origin unknown.] **a.** An instance of short-changing; a person who does not give the correct amount of change. **b.** (The usual current sense.) Deception, cheating; a confidence trick, a racket, a swindle, a publicity stunt.

1926 *Clues* Nov. 161/2 *Hype*, short change artist. **1926** [see *hype *v.*[1]]. **1935** A. J. Pollock *Underworld Speaks* 60/2 *Hype*, a short change artist. A person who does not give the correct amount of change to a customer. **1955** D. W. Maurer in *Publ. Amer. Dial. Soc.* xxiv. 85 Sometimes he has auxiliary *rackets*, such as the *hype* or some form of the *short con.* **1962** J. Baldwin *Another Country* (1963) ii. iv. 336 Life is a *bitch*, baby. It's the biggest hype going. **1966** C. Himes *Heat's On* xxii. 173 That was how Gus got the money...That shocked her; she had believed Gus's hype about his wife leaving him a farm. **1967** N. Mailer *Cannibals & Christians* i. 29 The hype had made fifty million musical-comedy minds; now the hype could do anything. **1968** *Sunday Times* 11 Aug. 5/1 Hype is an American word for the gentle art of getting a tune into the pop charts without actually selling any records. Its methods are various: from the crudest bribery to devious techniques for upsetting the..calculations of chart-compilers. **1969** *Listener* 25 Sept. 420/3 All the 'hype' and conning that goes into the establishing of every star. **1970** L. Sanders *Anderson Tapes* li. 135 He's been on the con or hustling his ass or pulling paper hypes. **1972** *Publishers Weekly* 6 Mar. 2/2 They carried off the biggest money-making hype in sports history.

hype (həip), *v.*[1] *slang* (orig. *U.S.*). Also **hipe.** [Origin unknown.] To short-change, to cheat; to deceive, to con, esp. by false publicity. So **hy·ping** *vbl. sb.* and *ppl. a.*

1926 Maines & Grant *Wise-Crack Dict.* 9/2 *Hype*, to overcharge. As, 'That place has a hype on this week.' **1931** G. Irwin *Amer. Tramp & Underworld Slang* 99 *Hipe*, to cheat or short change...Perhaps connected with the North-England 'hipe', to find fault with, to slander; perhaps from 'high pressure'. **1945** L. Shelly *Jive Talk Dict.* 13/1 *Hype* (v.), to try a trick. **1946** Mezzrow & Wolfe *Really Blues* 375 *Hype* v., to deliver a phony but convincing line. **1962** J. Baldwin *Another Country* (1963) iii. i. 402 He doesn't seem to be trying to hype me, not even when he talked about his wife and kids. **1968** *Sunday Times* 11 Aug. 5/1 The dominance of the charts over the pop music industry is such that many thousands of pounds may depend on these hyping operations. **1969** N. Cohn *A WopBopaLooBop* (1970) v. 51 Hype is a crucial word. In theory it is short for hyperbole. In practice, though, it means to promote by hustle, pressure, even honest effort if necessary, and the idea is that you leave nothing to chance. Simply, you do everything possible. Hype has become such an integral part of pop that one hardly notices it any more. **1969** *Sat. Rev.* (U.S.) 27 Sept. 25/1 You can't hype kids into buying things they don't want...They hate hype. **1970** *It* 27 Feb.–13 Mar. 15/1 Paying..lip-service to furiously hyping publicists. *Ibid.*, A lunchtime hyping session. **1971** *Listener* 15 Apr. 467/1 Bogus alternatives are hyped into prominence and fortune with appalling ease. **1971** *Bookseller* 23 Oct. 2053/2 In America a practice exists (known as 'hyping' in the record business) whereby a film company which has acquired the rights in a title forces it on to the bestseller list by sending young publicity men around armed with hundred-dollar bills and instructions to buy twenty or more copies from selected book shops.

hype (həip), *v.*[2] *U.S. slang.* [f. *hype *sb.*[1]] Usu. as **hyped** *pa. pple.* or *ppl. a.* (const. *up*): stimulated, worked up (as if from the effects of a hypodermic injection).

1938 D. Castle *Do Your Own Time* xxi. 200 Y' gotta lay off the wimmin, an' don't hype y'rself up till y' goes out t' heist a joint. **1946** Mezzrow & Wolfe *Really Blues* iv. 54, I was so hyped-up I couldn't sit still. **1950** in Wentworth & Flexner *Dict. Amer. Slang* 278/2 No fireworks [in this movie], no fake suspense, no hyped-up glamour. **1970** V. Johnston *Phantom Cottage* (1971) xxi. 165 If some hyped-up character goes past at seventy miles an hour, we'll take out after him. **1973** *Publishers Weekly* 12 Feb. 64/3 Witty, intellectual fun that keeps his readers hyped up and on their mettle. **1973** *Time* 25 June 16/2 As he works, Mitchell has at times been so hyped up that Martha once asked his doctor to prescribe medication to slow him down.

hyper[2] (həi·pəɹ). *U.S. slang.* [Cf. *hype *v.*[1]] (See quot. 1914.)

1914 Jackson & Hellyer *Vocab. Criminal Slang* 47 *Hyper*, current amongst money-changers. A flim-flammer. **1931** G. Irwin *Amer. Tramp & Underworld Slang* 106 *Hyper*, a 'short change' artist...The logical explanation.. is that the word came from 'hyp', a contraction of hypochondria.

hyper-. Add: **I. 1. b.** *hyper-analysis.*

1942 C. S. Lewis in *Essays & Stud.* XXVII. 18 This brings us to..the psycho-analysis of psycho-analysis itself. Such a hyper-analysis..would not refer to 'really scientific people', but to the great mass of ordinary people who read psycho-analytic books with avidity and undergo their influence.

2. *hyperphrygian* (examples).

1761 Stiles in *Phil. Trans. R. Soc.* 1760 LI. 713 The modes being thus augmented to fifteen..their meses will be found to stand..in the following order. Hyperlydian, Hyperæolian, Hyperphrygian or Hypermixolydian. **1922** Joyce *Ulysses* 493 It is susceptible of nodes or modes as far apart as hyperphrygian and mixolydian.

3. b. In substantives in which *hyper-* has the sense 'the analogue in a space of four or more dimensions of (what is denoted by the second element) in ordinary three-dimensional space'; as *hypercube, -cylinder, -plane, -sphere, -surface.*

1895 *Proc. R. Soc.* LVIII. p. xxxi, The manifoldness in this space..is the quadri-quadric two-dimensional amplitude common to thirteen quadric hyper-cylinders. **1903** C. M. Jessop *Treat. Line Complex* xiii. 244 Any linear equation of the form $\sum_{1}^{5} a_i X_i = 0$ singles out ∞^3 points from S_4, which will then form a space of three dimensions; the locus of these ∞^3 points will be called a hyperplane. *Ibid.* 251 In four-dimensional space, the three-dimensional quadric spaces through the intersection of S_3^2 and $X_5 = 0$ ..may be termed 'hyperspheres'. **1909** *Sci. Amer.* 3 July 6/2 Just as portions of our space are bounded by surfaces,..so portions of hyperspace are bounded by hypersurfaces (three-dimensional), i.e., flat or curved 3-spaces. *Ibid.* 6/3 Of these [regular hyper-solids], C_8 (or the hypercube) is the simplest, because, though with more bounding solids than C_5, it is right-angled throughout. **1955** O. Klein in W. Pauli *Niels Bohr* 100 Let..x^1, x^2, x^3, x^4 be

the four space-time coordinates regarded as *c*-numbers, x^1, x^2, x^3 forming a space-like hypersurface for any given value of the general time coordinate x^4. **1966** A. BATTERSBY *Math. in Managem.* v. 122 When the number of variables exceeds three..we could represent the process of solution by a series of three-dimensional solid bodies showing successive cross-sections of the solution space when cut by the 'hyper-plane' of P. **1968** ROSENBERG & JOHNSON *Geom.* xiii. 520/2 If the solid cube moves in a direction 'perpendicular' to its original space, it may trace a solid hypercube. **1969** R. J. BUMCROT *Mod. Projective Geom.* ii. 30 Subspaces of dimensions 1, 2, $n-1$ are called, respectively, lines, planes, and hyperplanes. **1970** E. E. KRAMER *Nature & Growth Mod. Math.* vii. 160 To say that a relation like $x^2+y^2+z^2+w^2 = 9$ is a hypersphere with radius 3 is so much easier than to state that the relation is the set of all ordered quadruples of real numbers such that the sum of the squares of these four numbers is always 9. **1972** *Computer Jrnl.* XV. 214/1 The problem of optimising a function globally over the vertices of a hypercube is encountered, for example, in hierarchical classification.

II. 4. (Further examples of the unlimited extension of this use.) **a.** *hyperarchaic, -civilized, -colloquial, -educated, -excitable, -pure* adjs. **b.** *hyperarchaism, -characterization, -determination, -dialecticism, -dialectism.* **c.** *hypercharacterize* vb.

1956 K. CLARK *Nude* 380 Considering that they were spoken of as 'hyper-archaic', his restorations were remarkably self-effacing. **1956** *Archivum Linguisticum* VIII. 124 Attributable to assimilation and hyperarchaism. **1957** *Ibid.* IX. 79 If a given linguistic formation develops in such a way as to allow..one of its distinctive features to stand out more sharply than at the immediately preceding stage, one may speak of hypercharacterization (or hyperdetermination) of that feature, in the diachronic perspective. *Ibid.* 80 One may analyse Sp. dial. *Jesuso* and *Raquela* as hypercharacterized, with respect to gender, in comparison with standard *Jesús* and *Raquel.* **1915** *Times Lit. Suppl.* 13 May 160/3 Only in a hyper-civilized and introspective society such themes would be possible. **1940** O. JESPERSEN *Mod. Eng. Gram.* V. xxiii. 437 It sounds hyper-colloquial..when too many *don't, isn't* are substituted for *do not, is not,* etc. in reading serious prose aloud. **1960** T. B. W. REID *Historical Philol. & Ling. Sci.* 6 Reactions such as those known as hyperurbanism and hyperdialecticism. **1925** P. RADIN tr. *Vendryès's Lang.* I. ii. 50 There are many hyper-dialectisms, for instance, in the Doric of the Pythagorean authors. **1914** J. JOYCE *Dubliners* 238 The generation which is now on the wane..had certain qualities of hospitality, of humour, of humanity, which the new and very serious and hypereducated generation..seems to me to lack. **1886** *Lancet* 13 Mar. 485/2 Even normal mental impulses may cause undue motorial demonstrations if the spinal centres are hyper-excitable, as is seen in strychnine poisoning, hysteria, &c. **1972** *Nature* 10 Mar. 74/1 The animal became hyperexcitable with exaggerated startle response. **1958** *Times Rev. Industry* June 26/2 Production of hyper-pure silicon entails purifying the selected chemical to a very high degree.

IV. (In the following words *e* often replaces *æ, œ,* esp. in U.S. usage; the alternative spelling is not given for each word individually.)

hyperabdu·ction, extreme abduction (sense 3); so **hyperabdu·ct** *v. trans.*, **-abdu·cted** *ppl. a.*; **hype:raldoste·ronism** *Med.*, any condition characterized by excessive secretion of aldosterone; aldosteronism; **hyperalgic** (-æ·ldʒik) *a. Path.*, of, pertaining to, or affected with hyperalgia (hyperalgesia); **hy:perbilirubinæ·mia** *Physiol.* [Gr. αἷμα blood], an abnormally high concentration of bilirubin in the blood; **hypercalcæmia** (-kælsī·miă) *Physiol.* [CALC(IUM + Gr. αἷμα blood], an abnormally high concentration of calcium in the blood; so **hypercalcæ·mic** *a.*; **hypercalcuria** (-kælsiūᵊ·riă), **-calciuria** (-kælsi,yūᵊ·riă) *Physiol.* [-URIA], an abnormally high concentration of calcium in the urine; **hyperca·pnia** *Physiol.* [Gr. καπνός smoke], an abnormally high concentration of carbon dioxide in the blood; so **hyperca·pnial** (*rare*), **-ca·pnic** *adjs.*; **hypercathe·xis** (pl. **-exes**) *Psychol.*, an excessive degree of cathexis; **hy:percellula·rity** *Path.*, an excess of cells at a site in the body; so **hyperce·llular** *a.*, containing more than the normal number of cells; **hy:perchloræ·mia** *Physiol.*, an abnormally high concentration of chlorides in the blood; **hy:perchlorhy·dria** *Physiol.* [CHLORHYDR(IC *a.*], an abnormally high concentration of hydrochloric acid in the gastric juice; so **hy:perchlorhy·dric** *a.*; **hy:percholesteræ·mia, -cholesterolæ·mia** *Physiol.* [Gr. αἷμα blood], an abnormally high concentration of cholesterol in the blood; so **hy:percholesterolæ·mic** *a.*; **hy:percoagulabi·lity** *Med.*, an excessive tendency (of the blood) to coagulate; so **hypercoa·gulable** *a.*; **hyperda·ctyly** *Zool.* [Gr. δάκτυλ-ος finger] = POLYDACTYLY; **hyperemo·tional** *a.*, affected by or displaying an abnormal degree of emotion; hence **hy:peremotiona·lity,** hyperemotional behaviour; **hypereute·ctic** *a.*, (of an alloy of iron) containing a higher proportion of carbon than the eutectic composition (i.e. more than about 4·3%); (in quot. 1902 = **hypereutectoid, eutectoid* itself not having been coined at that date); **hypereute·ctoid** *a.* (of steel) containing a higher proportion of carbon than the eutectoid composition (i.e. more than about 0·8%); **hy·perform** *Linguistics* [contraction of *hypercorrect form*], a hypercorrect spelling or pronunciation; **hy·perfragment** *Nuclear Physics* [*HYPER(ON], a hypernucleus, esp. one produced by the breaking up of a heavier one (see quot. 1964); **hyperfu·nction** *Med.*, over-activity or over-production (in a gland or other part of the body); so **hyperfu·nctional** *a.*, **hyperfu·nctioning** *vbl. sb.* and *ppl. a.*; **hy:pergammaglo:bulinæ·mia** *Physiol.* [Gr. αἷμα blood], an abnormally high concentration of gamma globulins in the blood; hence **hy:pergammaglo:bulinæ·mic** *a.*; **hypergeusia** (-giū·ziă) *Med.* [Gr. γεῦσις taste], excessive acuteness of the sense of taste; **hy:perglobulinæ·mia** *Physiol.* [Gr. αἷμα blood], an abnormally high concentration of globulins in the blood; hence **hy:perglobulinæ·mic** *a.*; **hyperglycæ·mia** *Physiol.*, an abnormally high concentration of sugar in the blood; so **hyperglycæ·mic** *a.*; **hyperimmu·ne** *a. Med.*, subjected to, resulting from, or produced by hyperimmunization; having a high concentration of antibody; **hy:perimmuniza·tion** *Med.*, the production of a high concentration of antibody in the serum of an animal, esp. by the repeated injection of the same antigen; so **hyperi·mmunize** *v. trans.*, to produce such a condition in (an animal); **hyperi·mmunized** *ppl. a.*; **hyperinfe·ction** *Med.*, continued infection with parasitic worms owing to their larvæ developing into adult worms without leaving the body; so **hyperinfe·ctive** *a.*, causing or characterized by hyperinfection; **hyperinflation** (also hyphened), an acute form of economic inflation; **hy:perinsulinæ·mia** *Physiol.* [Gr. αἷμα blood], an abnormally high concentration of insulin in the blood; **hyperi·nsulinism** *Med.*, a condition in which the body produces excessive insulin, usu. as a result of a tumour of the islets of Langerhans in the pancreas; the presence of an excessive amount of insulin in the body; **hy:perirritabi·lity** *Med.*, increased irritability; abnormally high responsiveness to stimuli; so **hyperi·rritable** *a.*; **hyperkalæmia** (-kălī·miă), **-kaliæmia** (-kæli,ī·miă) *Physiol.* [mod.L. *kalium* potassium (see KALI) + Gr. αἷμα blood] = **hyperpotassæmia* below; hence **hyperkalæ·mic** *a.*; **hy:perkerato·sis** *Path.*, (*a*) (see quot. 1848); now *rare* or *Obs.*; (*b*) excessive development of the horny layer of the skin; **hyperkine·sia** *Path.* = *hyperkinesis* (s.v. HYPER- IV); **hyperkinetic** *a.* (examples); **hy:perleucocyto·sis, -leukocyto·sis** *Path.* = LEUCOCYTOSIS; **hyperlipæ·mia** *Physiol.*, an abnormally high concentration of fats (or lipids) in the blood; any condition characterized by this; **hy:permagnesæ·mia** *Physiol.* [Gr. αἷμα blood], an abnormally high concentration of magnesium in the blood; **hyperma·nia** *Psychiatry*, (*a*) *sometimes used to mean* a severe degree of mania with partial or complete disorientation, often accompanied by violent behaviour and forming a stage in manic-depressive illness; (*b*) used *erron.* for *HYPOMANIA (quot. 1928: see also quot. 1956 for **hypermanic*); hence **hyperma·nic** *a.*; **hypermatu·re** *a. Ophthalm.*, applied to a cataract in its final stage (see quots.); so **hypermatu·rity;** **hypermeta·bolism** *Physiol.*, metabolism at a high rate; so **hy:permetabo·lic** *a.*, of hypermetabolism; **hypermobi·lity** *Med.*, abnormally great freedom of movement or flexibility in a joint; so **hypermo·bile** *a.*, characterized by or exhibiting hypermobility; **hy·permorph** *Genetics* [Gr. μορφ-ή form], any allele which is functionally more effective that the corresponding wild-type allele; so **hypermo·rphic** *a.*; **hypermoti·lity** *Med.*, excessive movement, esp. of the stomach and intestines; **hypernatræ·mia** *Physiol.* [NATR(IUM + Gr. αἷμα blood], an abnormally high concentration of sodium in the blood; hence **hypernatræ·mic** *a.*; **hypernephro·ma** *Path.* [NEPHR(O- + *-OMA], a malignant tumour of the cortical parenchyma of the kidney; orig. such tumours were believed to derive from misplaced tissue of the suprarenal gland (whence the name) and were described in other tissues besides that of the kidney; so **hy:pernephro·matous** *a.*; **hypernu·cleus** *Nuclear Physics* [*HYPER(ON], a nucleus in which a hyperon replaces one of the nucleons; a composite particle in which a hyperon is bound to one or more nucleons; hence **hypernu·clear** *a.*; **hyperosmo·tic** *a. Physiol.* = *HYPERTONIC *a.* 2; const. *to*; **hyperphagia** (-fēⁱ·dʒⁱă) *Med.* [Gr. -φαγία -PHAGY], an abnormally great desire for food; excessive eating; hence **hyperphagic** (-fæ·dʒik) *a.*, of or exhibiting hyperphagia; **hyperphalangia** (-fălæ·ndʒiă), **-phalangism** (-fălæ·ndʒiz'm), **-phalangy** (-fæ·lăndʒi) *Med.* and *Zool.* [L. *phalang-*: see PHALANX], the condition of having more digital phalanges than normal, esp. in cases where polydactyly is absent; **hyperpho·ria** *Ophthalm.*, latent strabismus in which there is a tendency for one eye to be directed above (or below) the line of sight of the other; so **hyperpho·ric** *a.*; **hy:perphosphatæ·mia** *Physiol.* [Gr. αἷμα blood], an abnormally high concentration of phosphates (or other phosphorus compounds) in the blood; so **hy:perphosphatæ·mic** *a.*; **hyperpiesia** (-pəi,ī·ziă), **-piesis** (-pəi,ī·sis, -pəi·ėsis) *Med.* [Gr. πίεσις pressure], high blood pressure, hypertension, esp. when without evident cause (the two words were distinguished in meaning by Allbutt: see quots.); hence **hyperpie·tic** *a.*; **hy:perpigmenta·tion** *Med.*, excessive pigmentation; so **hy:perpigme·nted** *ppl. a.*, exhibiting hyperpigmentation; **hyperpitu·itarism** *Path.* [PITUITAR(Y *a.* + -ISM], increased hormone secretion by the pituitary body; hence **hyperpitu·itary** *a.*, of, pertaining to, or affected with hyperpituitarism; **hy·perploid** *a. Genetics* [*-PLOID], having one or a few extra chromosomes (orig. also chromosome fragments) in addition to a haploid, diploid, triploid, etc., set; containing such cells; also as *sb.*, a hyperploid cell or individual; so **hy·perploidy,** the condition of being hyperploid; **hyperpnœa** (həipəɹnī·ă, -pnī·ă) *Physiol.* [Gr. πνοή breath, breathing], deep and rapid breathing; panting; so **hyperpnœ·ic** *a.*; **hy:perpotassæ·mia** *Physiol.* [Gr. αἷμα blood], an abnormally high concentration of potassium in the blood; so **hy:perpotassæ·mic** *a.*; **hyperprose·xia** *Psychol.* [Gr. προσέχ-ειν to turn (one's attention) (ἔχειν to hold, possess mentally)], the concentration of attention on one stimulus to the exclusion of all others; **hy:perproteinæ·mia** *Physiol.* [Gr. αἷμα blood], an abnormally high concentration of protein in the blood; **hyperrea·ctive** *a. Med.*, reacting unusually strongly to certain stimuli; of or pertaining to this tendency; so **hy:perreacti·vity;** **hyperrhythmical** *a.* (earlier example); **hypersa·line** *a. Biol.*, (of naturally occurring water) more salty than typical sea water; hence **hypersali·nity,** the condition of being hypersaline; **hy:persexua·lity,** a condition in which the sexual instinct is abnormally strong; **hyperso·mnia** *Med.* [L. *somnus* sleep], a condition characterized by abnormally long or frequent periods, or abnormal depth, of sleep; hence **hyperso·mnic** *a.*, of, exhibiting, or producing hypersomnia; **hyperspace,** also, any non-Euclidean space; (further examples, illustrating its currency in *Science Fiction*); **hyperspa·tial** *a.*, of or in hyperspace; **hypersplenism** (-sple·niz'm) *Path.* [SPLEN-], overactivity of the spleen; *spec.* a condition characterized by a general destruction of blood cells, often associated with enlargement of the spleen but in which direct involvement of the spleen is now considered doubtful; so **hypersple·nic** *a.*; **hypersta·tic** *a. Engin.*, statically indeterminate, i.e. having more members or supports than the minimum required to render it stable (and therefore requiring more than considerations of equilibrium alone for the calculation of all the internal forces and moments); of or pertaining to such a structure; **hyperste·reograph** *Photogr.*, a picture or pair of photographs taken by hyperstereoscopy; **hy:perstereo·scopy**

Photogr., stereoscopic photography in which the separation of the two viewpoints is greater than the distance between the eyes, resulting in a greater stereoscopic effect or exaggerated perspective; hence **hy:perstereosco·pic** *a.*; **hypersusce·ptible** *a. Med.* = *HYPERSENSITIVE *a.* 2; so **hy:persusceptibi·lity; hyperte·lorism** *Med.* [Gr. τῆλ-ε at a distance + ὁρίζειν to separate from: see -ISM], a condition in which the eyes are abnormally far apart, freq. found accompanying other congenital malformations of the face; **hypertro·pia** *Ophthalm.*, strabismus in which one eye is directed above the line of sight of the other; **hy:peruricæmia** (-yūᵊrisī·miă) *Physiol.*, an abnormally high concentration of uric acid in the blood; = LITHÆMIA, URICÆMIA; hence **hy:peruricæ·mic** *a.*; **hypervelo·city,** a speed that is (relatively) very high; usu. *attrib.*; **hy:pervitamino·sis** *Path.* [-OSIS], any condition caused by excessive intake of a vitamin, esp. over a prolonged period; **hypervolæ·mia** *Physiol.* [VOL(UME *sb.* + Gr. αἷμα blood], an increased volume of circulating blood in the body; hence **hypervolæ·mic** *a.*

1945 *Amer. Heart Jrnl.* XXIX. 7 The pulse in the left arm could be obliterated only by having the patient hyperabduct his arm above a 150-degree angle. *Ibid.* 6 The habit of sleeping with the arms in the hyperabducted position. **1905** GOULD *Dict. New Med. Terms* 299/2 Hyperabduction. **1945** *Amer. Heart Jrnl.* XXIX. 4 The term 'hyperabduction' is used in this paper to mean that phase of circumduction which brings the arms together above the head... Actually, the term hyperabduction, although accepted in anatomic terminology, is not..an entirely logical term, for abduction is movement away from the median plane of the body, and beyond the 90° angle; the arm in so-called hyperabduction actually again approaches the median plane. **1966** J. E. FLYNN *Hand Surg.* xiv. 696/1 Hyperabduction of the arm alone could stretch the subclavian artery sufficiently to produce occlusion in certain persons. **1955** CONN & LOUIS in *Trans. Assoc. Amer. Physicians* LXVIII. 229 What is the relationship of hyperaldosteronism to the production of renal arteriosclerosis? **1966** R. B. SCOTT *Price's Textbk. Pract. Med.* (ed. 10) vii. 436/2 Patients with hyperaldosteronism usually present in one of two ways, either with manifestations of hypertension or with muscular weakness and hyporeflexia sometimes sufficiently severe to cause episodic paralysis. *Ibid.* 437/1 Without treatment hyperaldosteronism is fatal, the patient usually dying of the hypertensive vascular complications. **1946** *Nature* 10 Aug. 202/1 We obtained successful results with this substance in other hyperalgic conditions, namely, cervical neuritis and trigeminal neuralgia. **1968** CAHN & HEROLD in A. Soulairac et al. *Pain* IV. 367 We have defined these changes as a hyperalgic state. **1923** *Q. Jrnl. Med.* XVI. 409 These latter cases are on the border line between 'physiological hyperbilirubinaemia' and the actual disease known as haemolytic (acholuric) jaundice. **1965** W. TAYLOR *Biliary Syst.* 647 (*heading*) Bilirubin excretion in congenital hyperbilirubinaemia. **1925** *Jrnl. Biol. Chem.* LXIII. 444 Dog 51 showed typical symptoms of hypercalcemia. **1970** C. N. GRAYMORE *Biochem. Eye* viii. 551 Hypercalcaemia results from vitamin D poisoning, hyperthyroidism and severe renal damage. **1932** *Physiol. Rev.* XII. 605 The occurrence of..hypercalcemic symptoms. **1930** *Jrnl. Biol. Chem.* LXXXVII. p. xv (*heading*), Calcium and phosphorus metabolism in relation to certain bone diseases. I. Hypercalcuria. **1961** *Lancet* 26 Aug. 455/2, 10 of the 28 patients with hypercalciuria had no evidence of renal calcification. **1964** D. M. DUNLOP *Textbk. Med. Treatm.* (ed. 9) 757 A variety of disorders which are associated with hypercalciuria tend to cause stone formation. **1908** *Amer. Jrnl. Physiol.* XXI. 140 Hypo- and hyper-capnia are abnormal conditions. **1962** *Lancet* 2 June 1183/2 The combination of hypoxia and hypercapnia is often lethal. **1908** *Amer. Jrnl. Physiol.* XXI. 141 An asphyxial (or hyper-capnial) condition of the blood supply to the spinal bulb. **1955** *Jrnl. Physiol.* CXXIX. 405 The achievement of a steady state of hypercapnic ventilation. **1962** *Lancet* 8 Dec. 1224/2 When pH was kept normal by the infusion of this organic buffer..circulation was unaltered in the hypercapnic dog. **1923** FREUD in *Internat. Jrnl. Psycho-Anal.* IV. 6 Our consideration of the first case, the jealousy paranoia, led to a similar estimate of the importance of the quantitative factor, by showing that there also the abnormality essentially consisted in the hyper-cathexis (over-investment) of the interpretations of another's unconscious behaviour. **1950** J. STRACHEY tr. *Freud's Totem & Taboo* iii. 89 The psychological results must be the same in both cases, whether the libidinal hypercathexis of thinking is an original one or has been produced by regression. **1968** D. RAPAPORT et al. *Diagn. Psychol. Testing* (rev. ed.) iii. 108 The drive cathexes are kept in balance and control, harmonizing with and not encroaching upon the ego's functions, nor demanding that it employ its hypercathexes to curb them. **1955** *Bull. N.Y. Acad. Med.* XXXI. 135 Under such circumstances the marrow is hypercellular but the blood is cytopenic. **1967** J. METCOFF *Acute Glomerulonephritis* vi. 110 Some lobules may be quite hypercellular. **1908** *Lancet* 23 May 1467/2 In the older or quiescent stages [of carcinoma of the tongue] the hypercellularity disappears. **1967** J. METCOFF *Acute Glomerulonephritis* vi. 110 Mitotic figures..are easy to find in areas of hypercellularity. **1921** *Endocrinology* V. 802 One or two days before the onset of menstruation.. there is generally an absolute and relative hyperchloremia. **1969** R. L. SEARCY *Diagn. Biochem.* i. 14/1 Treatment with ammonium chloride can lead to..hyperchloremia. **1891** F. P. FOSTER *Med. Dict.* III. 1938/2 Hyperchlorhydria. **1893** *Med. Ann.* 169 Hyperchlorhydria and hypochlorhydria are not identical with hyperacidity and hypoacidity. **1957** I. AIRD *Compan. Surg. Stud.* (ed. 2) xxxiii. 710 *Hyperchlorhydria* is present in 90 per cent of duodenal ulcers. **1903** *Med. Rec.* 7 Feb. 229/2 In the last year the pain increased, and the disturbance was always of the hyperchlorhydric type. On entrance to the hospital, a small, painless tumor was clearly felt in the region of the pylorus. **1926** J. A. RYLE *Gastric Function* 119 The fractional test-meal gives hyperchlorhydric curves. **1894** GOULD *Dict. Med.* 589/1 Hypercholesteremia. **1916** *Physiol. Abstr.* I. 327 (*heading*) Experimental hypercholesteræmia. **1969** R. L. SEARCY *Diagn. Biochem.* xviii. 170/2 Hypercholesteremia usually..accompanies hypothyroidism. **1916** *Arch. Internal Med.* XVII. 768 In pregnancy hypercholesterolemia occurs physiologically. **1970** *Nature* 31 Oct. 465/1 Growth hormone is as efficacious as thyroid hormone in preventing hypercholesterolaemia. **1916** *Arch. Internal Med.* XVII. 784 Cells which have been bathed in and irritated by hypercholesterolemic blood. **1961** *Lancet* 7 Oct. 802/2 Cases of familial hypercholesterolæmic xanthomatosis. **1934** WEBSTER, Hypercoagulability, -coagulable. **1962** *Lancet* 8 Dec. 1230/2 This permits one to anticipate the periods of blood hypercoagulability and thus to prevent thromboembolism successfully. **1972** *Nature* 28 Apr. 452/1 All showed adverse changes which might lead to a hypercoagulable or hyperthrombotic state compared with the non-smoker. **1902** WEBSTER Suppl., Hyperdactyly. **1929** R. S. LULL *Org. Evol.* (ed. 2) xx. 297 As though extra toes over the normal five had been added (hyperdactyly). **1965** W. B. YAPP *Vertebrates* v. 93 The paired limbs show both more digits and more joints than usual—hyperdactyly and hyperphalangy. **1946** O. FENICHEL *Psychoanal. Theory of Neurosis* xx. 478 A 'generally frigid' person has forgotten childhood emotions; the hyperemotional person is still a child. **1971** *Jrnl. Gen. Psychol.* LXXXIV. 245 Loud vocalization..is a prominent characteristic of vigorous fighting among rats and has been labelled..an index of hyperemotional behavior among normally silent species. **1958** *Science* 19 Sept. 655/2 These animals did show a gradual, but only partial, development of hyperemotionality. **1972** *Nature* 25 Aug. 454/1 According to some reports, bulbectomy also induces irritability and hyperemotionality resembling the classic septal 'rage' syndrome. **1902** *Encycl. Brit.* XXIX. 573/2 The undisturbed slow cooling from the molten state of a hyper-eutectic steel containing 1·00 per cent. of carbon. **1912** W. H. HATFIELD *Cast Iron* i. 13 Hypereutectic alloys deposit primary iron-carbide along the line B′C. **1959** A. G. GUY *Elem. Physical Metall.* (ed. 2) vi. 186 As the composition changes from hypoeutectic (less than eutectic) to hypereutectic (more than eutectic) in terms of metal *B*, the primary crystals change from alpha phase to beta phase. **1911** *Encycl. Brit.* XIV. 805/2 The large massive plates of cementite which form the network or skeleton in hyper-eutectoid steels. **1966** A. PRINCE *Alloy Phase Equilibria* vi. 107 Hyper-eutectoid alloys on cooling from the austenite phase region deposit cementite over a range of temperature until *A*1 is reached. As before, the remaining austenite then transforms to pearlite. **1933** L. BLOOMFIELD *Lang.* xxvii. 479 This may be disclosed by isolated relic forms, or by the characteristic phenomenon of hyper-forms. **1937** *Amer. Speech* XII. iii. 168 Hyperforms are by no means always attempts to imitate city pronunciation. **1964** H. KÖKERITZ in D. Abercrombie et al. *Daniel Jones* 141, I have heard the hyperform [həˌrɑs] from a colleague now deceased. **1955** W. F. FRY et al. in *Physical Rev.* XCIX. 1561 Following a suggestion of M. Goldhaber, we propose to call a nuclear fragment containing a bound hyperon or some other unstable particle, a hyperfragment. **1963** K. NISHIJIMA *Fund. Particles* vi. 290 The study of hyperfragments offers almost the only source of getting information about the Λ-nucleon force. **1964** *Progress Nuclear Physics* IX. 172 The nucleus in which the capture occurs is usually broken up and the Λ^0-hyperon may be bound in one of the fragments that are emitted...Fragments such as these are referred to as hyperfragments. **1909** *Jrnl. Amer. Med. Assoc.* 24 July 252/2 Massalongo's supposition that the disease represents a condition of hyperfunction—hyperpituitarism—has been widely discredited. **1961** *Lancet* 16 Sept. 655/1 There was general agreement that the diagnosis of adrenocortical hyperfunction should be made preoperatively. **1962** *Circulation Res.* X. 250 (*heading*) Compensatory hyperfunction of the heart and cardiac insufficiency. **1934** WEBSTER, Hyperfunctional. **1961** *Jrnl. Amer. Med. Ass.* 29 July 232/1 One hyperfunctional nodule proved to contain a papillary carcinoma in an adenoma. **1970** N. SIMIONESCU *Histogenesis Thyroid Cancer* iv. 28 (*heading*) The hyperfunctional cell. **1918** *Endocrinology* II. 46 A hyperfunctioning thyroid may be poor in colloids. **1926** Hyperfunctioning [see *hypofunctioning* s.v. *HYPO- II]. **1954** A. WHITE et al. *Princ. Biochem.* xliii. 946 Hyperfunctioning of the adrenal cortex in man is seen as a result of tumors composed of cortical cells. **1961** *Lancet* 16 Sept. 655/2 There was disagreement..about whether adrenalectomy for patients with hyperplastic or hyperfunctioning glands should be total or subtotal. **1947** DORLAND & MILLER *Med. Dict.* (ed. 21), Hypergammaglobulinemia. **1958** *Immunology* I. iii. 245 Hypergammaglobulinaemia was a feature of the acute phase when complement levels were very low. **1971** *Nature* 31 Dec. 558/2 We have obtained evidence in support of the idea that hypergammaglobulinaemia represents an immunological host response to tumour-associated antigen(s). *Ibid.* 559/1 A hundred instances of individual immunoglobulin increases occurred in the fifty hypergammaglobulinaemic mice. **1855** R. G. MAYNE *Expos. Lex. Med. Sci.* (1860) 480/1 Hypergeusia. **1888** *Encycl. Brit.* XXIII. 80/2 Increase in the sense of taste is called hypergeusia, diminution of it hypogeusia, and entire loss ageusia. **1936** *Jrnl. Clin. Invest.* XV. 475 (*heading*) Acid-base equivalence of the blood in diseases associated with hyperglobulinemia. **1966** *McGraw-Hill Encycl. Sci. & Technol.* VIII. 256/2 The diseases usually associated with hyperglobulinemia are multiple myeloma, kala-azar, Hodgkin's disease, [etc.]. **1958** DAMESHEK & GUNZ *Leukemia* viii. 187 Hyperglobulinemic purpura. **1894** GOULD *Dict. Med.* 590/1 Hyperglycemia. **1966** WRIGHT & SYMMERS *Systemic Path.* I. xxiii. 693/2 It has become obvious that diabetes mellitus is a syndrome and not a disease, and that a number of diverse factors may produce prolonged hyperglycaemia. **1903** *Med. Rec.* 24 Jan. 123/1 In coma diabeticum..it is likely that the hyperglycæmic condition stands at the foundation of a diminished electrical conductivity of the serum. **1969** R. L. SEARCY *Diagn. Biochem.* liii. 461/2 This theory.. could account for the hyperglycemic tendency. **1927** *Lancet* 15 Jan. 117/2 Fluids from ten different hyperimmune..rats. **1940** *Jrnl. Bacteriol.* XXXIX. 66 Mice born of hyperimmune mothers are themselves immune to intranasally administered virus. **1957** CUSHING & CAMPBELL *Princ. Immunol.* i. 24 For many laboratory procedures, or for the production of potent therapeutic serums, animals are injected for many weeks or even months. Such animals are often referred to as being hyperimmune. **1958** *Immunology* I. 82 Titres of hyperimmune sera. **1913** DORLAND *Med. Dict.* (ed. 7) 445/2 Hyperimmunization. **1968** F. HAUROWITZ *Immunochem. & Biosynthesis Antibodies* x. 209 Hyperimmunization is the routine method used in the production of high antibody titers. **1905** *Rep. Brit. Assoc. Adv. Sci.* 553 Spreuill ..by hyper-immunising sheep with virulent blood has succeeded in producing a serum efficacious in cases of Blaauw tongue. **1968** GELL & COOMBS *Clin. Aspects Immunol.* (ed. 2) xlviii. 1278 It is even possible to hyperimmunize a horse with more than one major antigen at the same time. **1927** *Lancet* 15 Jan. 117/2 A hyperimmunised rat. **1962** *Ibid.* 27 Jan. 208/2 They seem a likely source of the plasma cells which accumulate in the lung in hyperimmunised animals. **1931** E. C. FAUST in *Amer. Jrnl. Hygiene* XIV. 209 In addition to the direct and indirect types of Strongyloides..there is a distinct hyperinfective type..which is responsible for the so-called 'auto-infection' (i.e. 'hyperinfection') of individuals who have once become parasitized. **1943** CRAIG & FAUST *Clin. Parasitol.* (ed. 3) xiv. 249 In cases of hyperinfection, all or some of the rhabditoid larvæ in the lumen of the bowel metamorphose into dwarfed filariform larvæ *en transit* down the bowel, and..may produce reinfection. **1960** J. M. WATSON *Med. Helminthol.* xii. 116/2 The belief formerly held that the parasitic forms had a life-span of as much as fifteen years, based on the continuance of the infection in individuals removed from all possibility of external re-infection, did not take account of the possibility of auto-infection and hyper-infection. **1931** Hyperinfective [see *hyperinfection* above]. **1936** A. C. CHANDLER *Introd. Human Parasitol.* (ed. 5) xvii. 359 The course of development of these larvae may follow any of three different lines..indirect, direct, and hyperinfective. **1930** F. D. GRAHAM (*title*) Exchange, prices and production in hyper-inflation. **1952** P. EINZIG *Inflation* i. 23 When inflation has reached an extreme stage it may be described as 'hyper-inflation'. **1970** *Daily Tel.* 21 Dec. 3/7 The bulletin suggests a prices and incomes policy and a wealth tax, to deal with the emerging problem of hyper-inflation [in Australia]. **1924** *Jrnl. Amer. Med. Assoc.* 6 Sept. 729/2 Hypoglycemia is the result of hyperinsulinemia. **1962** *Lancet* 12 May 1003/2 Either hyperplasia or tumour of the islet-cells of the pancreas, without evidence of hyperinsulinæmia. **1924** S. HARRIS in *Jrnl. Amer. Med. Assoc.* 6 Sept. 729/2 It was this line of reasoning that caused me to think that there may be such a condition as hyperinsulinism. **1962** *Lancet* 13 Jan. 73/2 It seems reasonable to suppose that the characteristic hyperinsulinism immediately after these babies are born is the result of abnormal stimulation of the fœtal pancreas in utero by maternal hyperglycæmia and/or by some other factor. **1969** R. L. SEARCY *Diagn. Biochem.* xxxv. 322/1 Hyperinsulinism is now a well-characterized condition known to be caused by a functioning tumor termed an insulinoma or nesidioblastoma. **1913** L. FORSTER tr. *Biedl's Internal Secretory Organs* II. 61 Rudinger's contention that the condition of hyperirritability arises in the ganglion cells of the anterior cornua..did not survive the test of experiment. **1935** D. H. SHELLING *Parathyroids* vi. 115 In 1876, the older Chvostek described hyperirritability of the facial nerve as a sign of tetany. **1960** *Adv. Pediatrics* XI. 107 Symptoms of acute hypernatremia are hyperirritability to stimuli despite extreme lethargy, coma, [etc.]. **1922** L. F. BARKER et al. *Endocrinol. & Metabolism* I. I. 165 If the sympathetic nerve cells are hyperirritable, sympathetic action predominates in the individual. **1954** *Pediatric Clinics N. Amer.* May 347 The infant was markedly dehydrated and alternately hyperirritable and drowsy. **1949** *New Gould Med. Dict.* 483 Hyperkalemia. **1955** ELKINTON & DANOWSKI *Body Fluids* xxii. 483 Hyperkalemia is characteristic of adrenocortical insufficiency. **1961** *Lancet* 19 Aug. 399/2 Respiratory failure and hyperkalæmia are the main lethal factors. **1969** J. H. GREEN *Basic Clin. Physiol.* xvi. 89/1 This combination of a high blood potassium, with a high blood acid content, is termed hyperkalaemic metabolic acidosis. **1972** *Lancet* 1 July 36/2 If..the patient still tends to be hyperkalæmic, exchange resins can be given ollray once or twice a day. **1841** W. LAWRENCE *Treat. Dis. Eye* (ed. 2) xiv. 368 Conical Cornea. Synonymes:— Sugar-loaf cornea; *staphyloma conicum*..hyperceratosis. **1848** DUNGLISON *Dict. Med. Sci.* (ed. 7) 442/2 *Hyperceratosis*, staphyloma of the cornea. **1907** W. A. PUSEY *Princ. & Pract. Dermatol.* 88 The term hyperkeratosis is applied to those conditions of the stratum corneum in which there is an increased thickness of the horny layer with complete cornification of the cells. **1970** JUBB & KENNEDY *Path. Domestic Animals* (ed. 2) II. x. 568/2 Hyperkeratosis may be..diffuse as in cattle poisoned with chlorinated naphthalenes. **1971** *Brit. Med. Bull.* XXVII. 29/2 The hyperkeratoses and pigmentation that accompanied the arsenical cancers of the hand. **1848** DUNGLISON *Dict. Med. Sci.* (ed. 7) 442/2 Hypercinesia. **1875** R. FOWLER *Med. Vocab.* (ed. 2) 245/1 Hyperkinesia. **1935** *Jrnl. Mental Sci.* LXXXI. 835 Articulatory and respiratory hyperkinesias were the pathological basis of the coprolalia. **1961** *Lancet* 23 Sept. 683/2 He was re-admitted..with an acute choreiform illness, consisting of hyperkinesia and constant writhing movements. **1888** *Med. Chron.* VII. 391 (*heading*) The treatment of chorea and other hyperkinetic diseases with physostigmine. **1935** *Jrnl. Mental Sci.* LXXXI. 834 The onset of a hyperkinetic encephalitis was associated with tics. **1966** *Med. Ann.* 308 The hyperkinetic syndrome in children is characterized by hyperactivity, short attention span, impulsivity..and poor social adjustment. **1972** *Village Voice* (N.Y.) 1 June 36/2 Court suits can also be of help in discovering the full extent of the drugging of so-called hyperactive or hyperkinetic children. **1897** *Lippincott's Med. Dict.* 493/2 Hyperleucocytosis. **1898** *Allbutt's Syst. Med.* V. 420 In the

second stage..a hyperleucocytosis occurs. **1951** *Jrnl. Clin. Endocrinol. & Metabolism* XI. 1027 Although her pneumonia was clearing..hyperleucocytosis, hypokaliemia, and the picture of metabolic alkalosis developed. **1894** Gould *Dict. Med.* 590/2 Hyperlipemia. **1936** *Physiol. Abstr.* XX. 818 In the rabbit hyperlipæmia was obtained with olive oil. **1955** H. J. Deuel *Lipids* II. v. 349 A moderate hyperlipemia (increased blood fat level) may occur. **1966** *Lancet* 24 Dec. 1379/2 The recognition that some hyperlipæmias are 'carbohydrate-induced'..further suggests that dietary carbohydrate influences serum-triglyceride. **1933** Hyper-magnesaemia [see *hypomagnesæmia* s.v. *hypo- II]. **1955** Elkington & Danowski *Body Fluids* xxii. 482 Hypermagnesemia is present. **1928** *Daily Express* 10 May 7 'He is suffering from hyper-mania, a state of unnatural excitement,' said Dr. Mould. **1945** W. S. Sadler *Mod. Psychiatry* xxxvii. 439 While three stages of mania are recognized—hypomania, acute mania, and hypermania—there is a fourth classification which has been denominated delirious mania. **1963** H. H. Kendler *Basic Psychol.* v. xiv. 510/1 A patient with hypermania, the more intense form, behaves like a raving maniac. **1956** W. H. Whyte *Organization Man* (1957) 408 A few mild neuroses conceded here and there won't give you too bad a score, and..you have the best margin for error if you err on the side of being 'hypermanic'—that is, too energetic and active. **1963** H. H. Kendler *Basic Psychol.* v. xiv. 510/1 A young soldier who exhibited at different times both hypomanic and hypermanic reactions. *Ibid.* 510/2 This hypermanic episode lasted about two weeks. **1897** *Lippincott's Med. Dict.* 494/1 *Hypermature cataract*, the final stage of progressive cataract, in which the lens substance breaks down, shrinking into a hard mass or becoming liquefied. **1962** D. G. Cogan in A. Pirie *Lens Metabolism Rel. Cataract* 294 When the entire cortex becomes liquefied the cataract is said to have become hypermature. **1904** L. W. Fox *Dis. Eye* xii. 309 The last stage is that of hypermaturity or overripeness. **1964** S. Duke-Elder *Parsons' Dis. Eye* (ed. 14) xix. 271 If the process is allowed to go on uninterruptedly the stage of hypermaturity sets in when the cortex becomes disintegrated and transformed into a pultaceous mass. **1962** *Lancet* 22 Dec. 1317/2 There is no hint of an environmental factor which could have caused this very persistent hypermetabolic state. **1971** N. R. Alpert *Cardiac Hypertrophy* 55 The particular factor that stimulates the growth of the heart acts upon the heart continuously during the hypermetabolic period. **1937** *Physiol. Abstr.* XXII. 528 It [*sc.* rectal temperature] may remain low during intense hypermetabolism. **1958** Dameshek & Gunz *Leukemia* viii. 185 Occasional cases of chronic lymphocytic leukemia are associated with extraordinary degrees of hypermetabolism (+60–+80 per cent). **1941** *Jrnl. Heredity* XXXII. 232 (*heading*) Hypermobile joints in all descendants for two generations. **1967** *Ann. Rheumatic Dis.* XXVI. 423/2 Her mother had generalized osteo-arthritis and..was probably hypermobile. **1927** *Jrnl. Amer. Med. Assoc.* 28 May 1711/2 The father's feet were normal, except for the hypermobility of the joints. **1941** *Jrnl. Heredity* XXXII. 232/2 All members of this generation show hypermobility, in varying degrees, of the joints of the fingers, thumbs, knees and elbows. **1967** *Ann. Rheumatic Dis.* XXVI. 423/2 The isolated joint hypermobility..is considered to be the result of generalized familial ligamentous laxity. **1949** Darlington & Mather *Elem. Genetics* vii. 152 The hypermorph is more efficient than the wild-type gene...The wild-type gene is hypomorphic to its hypermorphic mutant and amorphic to its neomorphic mutant. **1932** H. J. Muller in *Proc. 6th Internat. Congr. Genetics* I. 242 Since it has been found that there are reverse mutations of hypomorphic genes.., we must regard the allelomorphs thereby resulting not as hypomorphic but as hypermorphic to their immediate progenitor genes. **1966** E. A. Carlson *Gene* xiii. 112 Another type of activity exaggerated or increased the normal activity of genes; most reverse mutations would be examples of such hypermorphic activity. **1894** Gould *Dict. Med.* 590/2 Hypermotility. **1926** J. A. Ryle *Gastric Function* 83 Abnormally rapid emptying or hypermotility [of the stomach]. **1949** Koestler *Insight & Outlook* vii. 107 Pathological laughter may thus be classed among other forms of hypermotility—epileptic attacks, tantrums, tics—caused by similar release phenomena. **1932** Dorland & Miller *Med. Dict.* (ed. 16) 605/2 Hypernatremia. **1969** L. G. Wesson *Physiol. Human Kidney* xxvii. 552/1 Hypernatremia (plasma sodium concentration in excess of 150 mM/L) is observed in a variety of clinical situations. **1955** *Arch. Internal Med.* XCV. 21/1 A severe hyponatremic rather than hypernatremic acidosis. **1900** Dorland *Med. Dict.* 310/2 Hypernephroma. **1912** *Q. Jrnl. Med.* V. 157 The objects of this paper are:—(1) To classify and describe the commoner adrenal tumours... (3) To present new reasons against the hypothesis that renal hypernephromata are derived from adrenal rests. **1916** E. H. Kettle *Path. Tumours* 132 The term hypernephroma is applied to a particular group of tumours, in the belief that they are derived from suprarenal tissue. **1921** *Jrnl. Obstetr. & Gynæcol.* XXVIII. 23 (*heading*) A comparison between ovarian 'hypernephroma' and luteoma and suprarenal hypernephroma. **1923** *Guy's Hosp. Rep.* LXXIII. 193 The hypernephromata of the kidneys arise in the renal epithelium. **1967** J. S. King *Renal Neoplasia* ii. 24 The patient..had a large renal tumor..which proved to be a hypernephroma when examined microscopically. **1946** *Jrnl. Urol.* LV. 18 (*heading*) Renal adenomas in hypernephromatous kidneys: a study of their incidence, nature and relationship. **1962** *Sci. Amer.* Jan. 53/2 The discovery of hyperfragments led to a rapid development of a new field: hypernuclear physics. **1971** *Nature* 28 May 226/2 Subjects of special interest in Poland include hypernuclear physics and strong interactions. **1957** *Ann. Rev. Nuclear Sci.* VII. 473 Nuclear matter can bind Λ to form systems stable for a time comparable with the Λ mean life. Such systems are well known and are called hypernuclei or hyperfragments. **1965** R. H. Dalitz *Nuclear Interactions of Hyperons* ii. 5 The lightest Λ-hypernucleus known is $_{\Lambda}H^3$. *Ibid.* 14 Λ-Hypernuclei will generally have excited states, whose spectra will be of interest for hypernuclear physics. **1892** *Jrnl. Chem. Soc.* LXII. i 557 This flow may be counterbalanced by subjecting the hyperosmotic solution to external pressure. **1903** *Med. Rec.* 24 Jan. 121/2 The crystalloid substances rapidly accumulate in the serum, causing it to be hyperosmotic. **1905** W. H. Howell *Text-bk. Physiol.* 885 A hypertonic or hyperosmotic solution in one whose osmotic pressure exceeds that of serum. **1964** *Oceanogr. & Marine Biol.* II. 307 Their body fluids are hyperosmotic to the surrounding water. **1941** T. C. Ruch et al. in *Amer. Jrnl. Physiol.* CXXXIII. 434 Both monkeys exhibited some type of disturbance of the chewing mechanism and a striking hyperphagia and adiposity. **1946** *Physiol. Rev.* XXVI. 549 The word hyperphagia was chosen because it does not have the subjective, psychological connotations of the terms 'hunger', 'appetite', 'satiety' and 'bulimia', and because the word 'polyphagia'..implies 'omnivorousness'... Hyperphagia is taken to mean simply, increased eating. **1969** W. Haymaker et al. *Hypothalamus* xv. 529/2 Hyperphagia and obesity have now been produced by bilateral destruction within or near the midregion of the hypothalamus in the monkey, dog, cat, rabbit, rat and mouse. **1943** *Yale Jrnl. Biol. & Med.* XV. 839 After 6 obese animals..had been completely fasted to return their weight to normal, they were again hyperphagic and became obese a second time on re-feeding. **1972** *Science* 9 June 1124/1 A hyperphagic response occurs when calcium in excess of its normal concentration is perfused..in the ventromedial region. **1899** *Jrnl. Anat. & Physiol.* XXXIII. 213 Prof. Pfitzner..read papers on brachyphalangia, hyperphalangia and on the inferior tibio-fibular joint. **1969** W. T. Mustard et al. *Pediatric Surgery* (ed. 2) II. lxxxiii. 1423 Hyperphalangia refers to an excessive number of phalanges in the longitudinal axis. **1891** Flower & Lydekker *Introd. Study Mammals* viii. 234 The Ichthyopterygia have been shown..to have gradually acquired their hyperphalangism as an adaptive character. **1959** J. J. Byrne *Hand* xv. 273 Hyperphalangism consists of an excessive number of phalanges, the thumb being most commonly involved with three phalanges. **1898** *Jrnl. Anat. & Physiol.* XXXII. p. ii (*heading*) The ossification of the terminal phalanges of mammalian fingers, in relation to hyperphalangy. **1946** R. R. Gates *Human Genetics* I. xi. 404 The fingers show considerable variation, including hyperphalangy (four joints instead of three). **1951** C. K. Weichert *Anat. Chordates* x. 485 The paddlelike limbs of plesiosaurs and ic[h]thyosaurs have a very large number of phalanges (hyperphalangy). **1886** Hyperphoria [see *exophoria* s.v. *exo-]. **1964** S. Duke-Elder *Parsons' Dis. Eye* (ed. 14) xxx. 472 It is impossible to be sure whether there is absolute hyperphoria of one eye or hypophoria of the other, the condition being relative. **1887** *Arch. Ophthalm.* XVI. 163 Only a comparatively small proportion of hyperphoric persons experience in marked degree this inability to see small objects well. **1970** *Jrnl. Gen. Psychol.* LXXXII. 111 The average period of perceived sweep..was not significantly affected by the hyperphoric condition. **1926** *Amer. Jrnl. Physiol.* LXXVI. 472 Hypercalcemia, hyperphosphatemia, cessation of kidney function and acidosis. **1969** R. L. Searcy *Diagn. Biochem.* xlvii. 418/1 Hyperphosphatemia has long been regarded as an early sign of kidney failure. **1955** H. J. Deuel *Lipids* II. iv. 324 A hyperphosphatemic reaction does not occur in dogs whose bile ducts have been ligated and transected. **1915** C. Allbutt *Dis. Arteries* I. i. 10 Lately I have preferred the etymology of hyperpiesia for the malady, and hyperpiesis for the hæmodynamic aspect of it. **1923** J. F. H. Dally *High Blood Pressure* v. 64 Hyperpiesia is the term applied by Sir Clifford Allbutt to a clinical morbid series characterised by persistently raised blood pressure (hyperpiesis) in association with hypertrophy of the heart and changes in the vessels. **1927** *Physiol. Rev.* VII. 474 (*heading*) Hyperpiesia or essential hypertension. **1951** R. Hargreaves *This Happy Breed* vii. 77 He must 'wangle' an extra half bag of coal from the Q.M. stores without provoking in the presiding demi-god an advanced condition of hyperpiesia. **1895** C. Allbutt in *Abstr. Trans. Hunterian Soc.* (1896) LXXVII. 47 The symptoms of arterial hyperpiesis are often of a functional nervous character. **1961** G. Pickering *Nature Essential Hypertension* ii. 5 His [*sc.* Allbutt's] term hyperpiesis, however, never became widely used. **1968** —— *High Blood Pressure* (ed. 2) i. 3 There remains a large residue in which no specific lesion can be found—hyperpiesis, primary hypertension, essential hypertension, high blood pressure without evident cause. **1915** C. Allbutt *Dis. Arteries* I. ix. 60 The following seemed to be a case of mixed senile and hyperpietic disease. **1920** L. M. Warfield *Arteriosclerosis* (ed. 3) viii. 187 In the hyperpietic cases the arteries undergo a transient thickening. **1890** Billings *Med. Dict.* 669/2 Hyperpigmentation. **1899** G. T. Jackson *Dis. Skin* (ed. 3) 394 Nævus Pigmentosus... A congenital, circumscribed hyper-pigmentation of the skin. **1956** D. M. Pillsbury et al. *Dermatol.* xxxviii. 868 Endocrine disturbances are..commonly associated with hyperpigmentation such as is seen..during pregnancy, and with exophthalmic goiter. *Ibid.* 873 These areas [of the skin] are whitish and often present a well defined hyperpigmented border. **1970** Jubb & Kennedy *Path. Domestic Animals* (ed. 2) II. x. 568/2 The production of pigment in the basal cells is..a common response to injury so that acanthotic areas may also be hyperpigmented. **1909** H. Cushing in *Jrnl. Amer. Med. Assoc.* 24 July 249/1 (*heading*) The hypophysis cerebri. Clinical aspects of hyperpituitarism and of hypopituitarism. [*Note*] From an etymological point of view the terms *hyper-*, *hypo-*, *dys-*, and *a-pituitarism* are doubtless of badly mixed parentage, but there are certain obvious objections to such a combination as *hypohypophysism*. **1939** M. A. Goldzieher *Endocrine Glands* lvii. 341 The only condition to be distinguished from true gigantism, i.e. primary eosinophile hyperpituitarism, is the secondary hyperpituitarism attendant on primary insufficiency of the gonads. **1924** G. B. Shaw *St. Joan* p. xix, St Teresa's hormones had gone astray and left her incurably hyperpituitary or hyperadrenal or hysteroid or epileptoid or anything but asteroid. **1954** K. E. Paschkis et al. *Clin. Endocrinol.* iii. 31 Hyperpituitary giants may develop acromegalic features in later life. **1930** *Jrnl. Genetics* XXII. 306 In generations subsequent to the breakage it is possible for some individuals—'hyperploids'—to inherit the chromosome fragment (attached or unattached) in addition to two otherwise normal sets of chromosomes. *Ibid.* 329 Hypoploid and hyperploid individuals. **1957** C. P. Swanson *Cytol. & Cytogenetics* vi. 177 Individuals having irregular chromosome numbers are called aneuploids...The terms hyperploid and hypoploid have also been used, but less frequently. **1930** *Jrnl. Genetics* XXII. 309 Text-fig. 11 illustrates hyperploidy of parts of the *X*-chromosome. **1969** N. S. Cohn *Elem. Cytol.* (ed. 2) xvi. 373 An addition or loss of less than an entire set of chromosomes..is called aneuploidy, and it subsumes two classes, hypoploidy and hyperploidy. **1860** R. Fowler *Med. Vocab.* 157/2 *Hyperpnœa*, excessive respiration—e.g. panting. **1877** M. Foster *Textbk. Physiol.* 260 Respiratory movements become deeper..and the rate of the rhythm is hurried... In this respect, dyspnœa, or hyperpnœa as this first stage has been called, contrasts very strongly with the peculiar respiratory condition caused by section of the vagi. **1904** *Jrnl. Physiol.* XXXI. p. xlv, The hyperpnœa of healthy men during exercise. **1962** *Lancet* 27 Jan. 172/1 Usually this significant hyperpnœa is coupled with a red suffusion of the face. **1909** *Jrnl. Physiol.* XXXVIII. 401 Where the subject had been made hyperpnœic by want of oxygen, apnœa followed after a few breaths of normal air. **1961** *Lancet* 29 July 249/2 The blood-pressure rises in the hyperpnœic phase [of breathing]. **1932** Dorland & Miller *Med. Dict.* (ed. 16) 606/2 Hyperpotassemia. **1963** J. H. Bland *Clin. Metabolism Body Water* xxi. 574/1 Muscle weakness and paralysis are commonly observed in both hypopotassemia and hyperpotassemia. **1953** *Lancet* 11 July 60/1 (*heading*) Hyperpotassæmic paralysis. **1902** A. R. Defendorf *Clin. Psychiatry* 17 Distractibility is not to be confused with 'hyperprosexia', which consists in the total absorption of the attention by a single process. **1940** Henderson & Gillespie *Text-bk. Psychiatry* (ed. 5) v. 107 Increase of attention (hyperprosexia) is less common, and is sometimes associated with a sensory hyperaesthesia. **1948** Hyperprosexia [see *aprosexia]. **1922** *Physiol. Abstr.* VII. 493 The hyperproteinæmia does not run parallel with precipitin formation. **1969** R. L. Searcy *Diagn. Biochem.* xvii. 154/1 Extreme degrees of hyperlipemia or hyperproteinemia may falsely lower serum electrolyte measurements. **1940** *Amer. Heart Jrnl.* XIX. 408 The majority of individuals with essential hypertension..manifest..marked reactions of blood pressure to various internal and external stimuli. This suggests that the mechanism for regulating blood pressure..is hyperreactive. **1955** *Sci. Amer.* Apr. 44/3 In this hyperreactive state the body responds with rapid formation of antibody to a second invasion, either by live or by killed virus. **1940** *Amer. Heart Jrnl.* XIX. 412 The vascular hyperreactivity of some patients with essential hypertension is extreme. **1970** *Clin. Sci.* XXXIX. 793 (*heading*) Vascular hyper-reactivity with sodium loading and with desoxycorticosterone induced hypertension in the rat. **1611** J. Hoskins in *Coryat's Crudities* sig. e6 Encomiological Antispasticks..rythmicall and hyper-rythmicall. **1953** *Publ. Inst. Marine Sci.* III. 175 Hypersaline lagoons..occur in several parts of the world. **1964** *Oceanogr. & Marine Biol.* II. 283 Natural water containing dissolved solids in concentrations equivalent to salinities of 40 to 80‰ is referred to [in this review] as hypersaline water. **1971** D. S. McLusky *Ecol. of Estuaries* vi. 97 Hypersaline seas should not be confused with inland brines or salterns, such as the Utah Salt Lakes of America. **1957** *Publ. Inst. Marine Sci.* IV. 198 Fish have been killed by..hypersalinity. **1970** B. H. McConnaughey *Introd. Marine Biol.* i. 24 Unusually high salinities (hypersalinity) are rare in marine environments. **1915** *Amer. Jrnl. Obstetr. & Dis. Women* LXXII. 279 In many cases where dementia precox develops, a previous attack of mental disturbance has existed and the patient is to a certain extent forced by the family into the marital state on account of hypersexuality. **1964** C. W. Lloyd *Human Reprod.* xxv. 456 Temporal lobe lesions generally cause humans and monkeys to have decreased sexual responsiveness, but occasionally hypersexuality may develop. **1876** Dunglison *Dict. Med. Sci.* (rev. ed.) 523/1 Hypersomnia. **1910** *Lancet* 8 Oct. 1093/1 Dr. Albert Salmon..differentiates hypersomnia, which is an increase in normal sleep, from somnolence, apathy, and torpor,..and from the drowsiness which occurs in old people. **1939** N. Kleitman *Sleep & Wakefulness* xxv. 361 Cerebral neoplasms have been known to produce interference with the sleep–wakefulness rhythm mainly in the direction of hypersomnia. **1966** *McGraw-Hill Encycl. Sci. & Technol.* XII. 376/1 The best known cause of hypersomnia is epidemic or lethargic encephalitis. **1929** *Jrnl. Nerv. & Mental Dis.* LXIX. 5 It is unquestionably in infundibular tumors that one encounters..the hypersomnic form of brain tumors. **1955** A. B. Baker *Clin. Neurol.* II. xxi. 1203 The hypersomnic patient closely resembles a normally sleeping individual. **1892** W. W. R. Ball *Math. Recreations & Problems* x. 191 The term hyper-space was used originally of space of more than three dimensions but now it is often employed to denote any non-Euclidean space. *Ibid.* 201 Riemann has shown that there are three kinds of hyper-space of three dimensions. **1947** I. Asimov in *Astounding Science Fiction* Mar. 117/2 Fooling around with hyper-space isn't fun... We run the risk continually of blowing a hole in normal space–time fabric. **1956** E. H. Hutten *Lang. Mod. Physics* v. 171 The propagation of the wave must be described as taking place, in most instances, in a multi-dimensional hyper-space, and not in ordinary space. **1961** *Times Lit. Suppl.* 1 Sept. 577/3 Time Travel, like hyperspace, is one of the classical Science-Fiction presumptions. **1973** *Publishers Weekly* 17 Sept. 58/3 The crew of the first interstellar voyage through hyperspace comes back as monsters. **1909** Webster, Hyperspatial. **1919** R. T. Browne *Mystery of Space* viii. 263 This is undoubtedly the weakest point in the structure of the hyperspatial geometries. **1943** C. L. Hull *Princ. Behavior* xi. 181 It seems unlikely that the Fisher-design type of experiment will yield dependable indications of the complex hyperspatial curvatures which will almost certainly be found. **1946** *Blood* I. 28 Five cases of thrombocytopenia associated with well defined splenomegaly of nonleukemic and non-neoplastic origin ('symptomatic hypersplenic thrombopenia'). **1949** Britton & Neumark tr. *Leitner's Bone Marrow Biopsy* viii. 151 Hypersplenic anæmias. **1963** Basu & Aikat *Trop. Splenomegaly* iii. 20 The clinical recognition of the hypersplenic state. **1914** *Arch. Internal Med.* XIV. 145 There may exist for the spleen conditions associated with a hyperactivity of some of its functions, let us say the function of influencing hemolysis. To such a condition the term 'hypersplenism' may be applied. **1955** W. Dameshek in *Bull. N.Y. Acad.*

Med. XXXI. 114 Who first used the term 'hypersplenism' is not accurately known, but it began to appear in Chauffard's writings from 1907 on and subsequently, and in those of Morawitz and Eppinger at a late date. **1963** BASU & AIKAT *Trop. Splenomegaly* iii. 20 Hypersplenism..is a clinical term indicating non-specific overactive function of the spleen in a variety of clinical disorders. **1930** *Engineering* 3 Oct. 421/3 The method is used to solve problems arising in the design of hyperstatic systems, such as arches and portal openings, with sufficient precision. **1959** J. A. L. MATHESON et al. *Hyperstatic Struct.* I. vi. 320 The behaviour of multi-storey buildings..in terms of the composite action of the floors and walls with the frame..is essentially a very complicated hyperstatic problem. **1966** J. S. C. BROWNE *Basic Theory of Struct.* v. 100 Extra or redundant bars will produce a truss that is hyperstatic. **1952** E. F. LINSSEN *Stereo-Photography* x. 147 If we take a hyperstereograph..of a mountain formation..which starts a kilometre away from us, we must beware not to include any trees or houses which are in our immediate neighbourhood. **1971** C. R. ARNOLD *Appl. Photogr.* xiii. 373 This tendency to produce a model effect is a well-known feature of hyperstereographs. **1939** HENNEY & DUDLEY *Handbk. Photogr.* xx. 588 The hyperstereoscopic effect..can add greatly to a stereograph's effectiveness by its strong emphasis of the depth quality. **1956** *Focal Encycl. Photogr.* 570/2 Consecutive photographs from an aerial survey series form hyperstereoscopic pairs. **1911** *Cassell's Cycl. Photogr.* 298/2 Hyperstereoscopy. **1926** A. W. JUDGE *Stereoscopic Photogr.* iii. 32 Hyper-stereoscopy is of much assistance in obtaining a true impression of distant hill or mountain scenery. **1958** *Newnes' Compl. Amat. Photogr.* xxvi. 231 If..we wish to take pictures of scenes such as distant mountains then, providing there are no objects in the foreground nearer than about 300 ft., we can use the long base separation method known as hyperstereoscopy. **1906** Hypersusceptibility [see 'HYPERSENSITIVE *a.* 2]. **1924** *Jrnl. Immunol.* IX. 86 The production of skin hypersusceptibility without infection. **1914** *Q. Jrnl. Med.* VII. 273 The so-called anaphylactic or hypersusceptible state. **1971** *Brit. Med. Bull.* XXVII. 57/1 Hypersusceptible individuals may still develop the disease despite the reduction of dust concentrations to a very low level. **1924** D. M. GREIG in *Edin. Med. Jrnl.* XXXI. 560 The outstanding peculiarity of the cranial deformity for which I propose the name ocular hypertelorism, or briefly, hypertelorism, is the great breadth between the eyes. **1957** *Arch. Ophthalm.* LVII. 607/2 This is an instance of hypertelorism associated with mental retardation. **1972** *Daily Tel.* (Colour Suppl.) 22 Sept. 21/4 Jeanine..was born 28 years ago with the fish eyes, one on each side of the face, and the monstrously deformed nose characteristic of hypertelorism (Grieg's Disease). **1897** Hypertropia [see *exotropia* s.v. *EXO-]. **1950** F. H. ADLER *Physiol. Eye* x. 406 In a case of right hypertropia..if the right superior oblique is at fault, the head will be strongly tilted toward the left shoulder. **1894** GOULD *Dict. Med.* 592/1 Hyperuricemia. **1924** *Arch. Internal Med.* XXXIV. 504 Blood uric acid values of 3·5 mg. per hundred cubic centimeters..were considered as presenting a hyperuricemia. **1970** W. S. HOFFMAN *Biochem. Clin. Med.* (ed. 4) xv. 756 Hyperuricemia may be due either to overproduction of uric acid or to undersecretion. **1962** *Lancet* 15 Dec. 1273/1 My own experience with three hyperuricæmic patients, two with a history of gout and one without,..lends support to Dr. Eidlitz's letter. **1955** A. E. EGGERS et al. *Compar. Anal. Performance Long-Range Hypervelocity Vehicles* 24 Mar. (N.A.C.A. Rep. RM A54L10) 2 On the basis of equal ratios of mass at take-off to mass at the end of powered flight, the hypervelocity vehicle compares favourably with the supersonic airplane. **1960** *Nature* 29 Oct. 353/2 If the fused earth were hurled in the manner that ejectamenta from hypervelocity impact[s] in stone are hurled, then the maximum entry velocity [etc.]. **1962** J. L. POTTER et al. in F. R. Riddell *Hypersonic Flow Res.* 599 A small, low density, hypervelocity, continuous wind tunnel. **1964** *Bull. Amer. Physical Soc.* IX. 308/2 (*heading*) Attainability of fusion temperatures under high densities by impact shock waves of microscopic solid particles accelerated to hypervelocities. **1972** *Science* 2 June 979/2 Hypervelocity impact craters on the moon. **1928** *Biochem. Jrnl.* XXII. 1461 In the case of the fat-soluble vitamins..several instances of supposed hypervitaminosis have been recorded. **1963** *Lancet* 5 Jan. 34/2 As in hypervitaminosis D, the increased intestinal absorption of calcium is probably responsible for the high urinary calcium. **1971** J. Z. YOUNG *Introd. Study Man* xl. 582 A European would produce up to 800 000 I.U. [of vitamin D] per day in the tropics and might therefore suffer from hypervitaminosis, for the body has no way of detoxicating any excess. **1925** BROWN & ROWNTREE in *Arch. Internal Med.* XXXV. 132 In view of..confusion,..terms as follows are suggested: (1) normovolemia for normal blood volume, (2) hypervolemia for increased blood volume, and (3) hypovolemia for decreased blood volumes. These terms are self-explanatory and apply only to volume states. **1964** I. N. KUGELMASS *Biochem. Clinics* IV. 270 Hypervolemia in acute and subacute glomerulonephritis with pulmonary edema increases with the duration of anuria. **1948** *Amer. Jrnl. Physiol.* CLV. 338 Table 1A shows the bilateral rises in auricular pressure of 4 hypervolemic cats.

hyperacusis (-ăkiū·sis). *Med.* Also -acousis, -acusia, -akusis. [mod.L., f. HYPER- 5 + Gr. ἄκουσις hearing (ἀκούειν to hear), after F. *hypercousie* (J. M. G. Itard *Traité des Maladies de l'Oreille et de l'Audition* (1821) II. 4).] Abnormally acute hearing, often resulting in pain on hearing only moderately loud sounds.

1825 J. M. GOOD *Study of Med.* (ed. 2) IV. 245 Hearing painfully acute and intolerant of the lowest sounds...It is the hypercousis, or, as it should rather be, the hyperacusis of M. Itard. **1894** T. M. HOVELL *Treat. Dis. Ear* xlv. 656 Hyperacusia, of a pathological kind, may be associated with increased power of other special senses. **1927** LAKE & PETERS *Handbk. Dis. Ear* (ed. 5) xiv. 267 Hyperacousis is usually found (as otalgia) in females. **1971** D. E. ROSE *Audiol. Assessment* iii. 44 Other symptoms of disorders of the ear are..increased aural sensitivity to sound (recruitment and hyperacusis).

hyperbaric (həipəɹbæ·rik), *a.* *Med.* [f. HYPER- 5 + Gr. βαρύς heavy + -IC.] **a.** Of a solution for spinal anæsthesia: having a greater density than the cerebro-spinal fluid.

1930 W. H. JONES in *Brit. Jrnl. Anæsthesia* VII. 110, I shall use the terms hyper-, iso- and hypo-baric, to describe solutions which have specific gravities greater than, equal to, or less than that of the cerebro-spinal fluid. **1946** J. L. SOUTHWORTH et al. *Pitkin's Conduction Anesthesia* xvii. 761/2 The anesthetist should know in advance whether the anesthetic solution is hypobaric, hyperbaric, or isobaric, so that the posture of the patient can be regulated accordingly. **1962** J. ADRIANI *Chem. & Phys. Anaesthesia* (ed. 2) xxxi. 652/2 Hyperbaric solutions gravitate caudad if the body is inclined in the head-up, supine position after injection, while hypobaric solutions migrate cephalad.

b. At a pressure greater than normal (often, greater than the partial pressure of the gas in the atmosphere); employing or pertaining to such gas.

1963 *Lancet* 16 Nov. 1022/1 It is our firm impression that hyperbaric oxygen is the most effective method of resuscitation yet devised for the severely asphyxiated newborn infant. **1965** *Economist* 20 Feb. 780/2 Hyperbaric oxygen chambers have been used increasingly in the treatment of diseases involving oxygen deficiency. **1966** *Lancet* 24 Dec. 1394/2 A hyperbaric chamber was made from a large domestic pressure cooker. **1968** *Sci. Jrnl.* Nov. 64/2 Some kidneys survived when hyperbaric nitrogen was employed. **1972** *Lancet* 22 Sept. 639/1 Patients with advanced growths are being given hyperbaric oxygen (3–4 atmospheres absolute) for a period immediately before and during irradiating. **1973** C. BONINGTON *Next Horizon* xiv. 199 The following six weeks passed..in hospital, recovering from frost-bite. I spent much of the time as a guinea-pig for a new method of treatment called hyperbaric oxygen, which entailed hours spent lying in a cylinder filled with two atmospheres of oxygen. You had to wear a special anti-static tunic..apparently, in oxygen so pure and concentrated, even the slightest static electricity could have caused a fire.

hyperbolic, *a.* Add: **2. b.** *hyperbolic navigation*: navigation that utilizes the difference in the times of arrival or the phases of signals transmitted in synchronism by two radio stations to determine a hyperbola on which the receiver must lie, two intersecting hyperbolas from two pairs of stations determining its position; so *hyperbolic system*, etc.

1945 *Electronics* Nov. 94/1 Loran..is one of a family of systems known as 'hyperbolic navigation systems', which measure the relative time of arrival of two or more radio signals sent synchronously from known points. **1959** [see *DECCA]. **1972** *Jrnl. Inst. Navigation* XXV. 308 The navigator has three main aids—d.f. using the world-wide chain of shore-based transmitter beacons, the short-range hyperbolic systems, mainly Decca, and his own radar.

hypercatalectic, *a.* Add: Used of Old English verse.

1813 J. J. CONYBEARE in *Archæologia* (1814) XVII. 265 Of the Trochaic species, with the Hypercatalectic syllable, as, Ahte ic, ealdor, stol. **1894** *Trans. Philol. Soc. 1891–4* 386 Expanded lines, called by German scholars *Schwell-verse* or *Streck-verse*, are hypercatalectic.

hypercharge (həi·pəɹtʃɑːɹdʒ). *Nuclear Physics.* [f. *hyper(onic) charge*: see quot. 1956.] A property of hadrons that is conserved in strong interactions and is represented by a quantum number *Y* that is the same for all the particles of a charge multiplet (isospin multiplet), being equal to twice their average charge quantum number.

The hypercharge Y of a particle is related to its charge Q and the third component, I_3, of isospin by $Y = 2(Q - I_3)$; and to its strangeness S and baryon number B by $Y = S + B$.

1956 J. SCHWINGER in *Physical Rev.* CIV. 1164/2 It is now natural to suppose that the K meson, with isotopic spin $\frac{1}{2}$, possesses a similar physical property [to the nucleonic charge] in the nature of a charge, which is also dynamically realized by a coupling with the π field. We shall term this new property hyper(onic) charge Y, with $Y = +1$ characterizing the K^+K^0 multiplet, and $Y = -1$ describing the antiparticles $\bar{K}^0K^-$. As the agent for the dynamical exhibition of nucleonic and hypercharge, the π field does not itself bear these charges. **1964** *New Scientist* 20 Feb. 460/3 According to the conservation of baryons and hypercharge, the omega-minus should be produced in collisions between K-minus mesons and protons and should decay (weakly, with a change of hypercharge) to a xi-particle and pion, or to a lambda-particle and K-minus. **1972** G. L. WICK *Elem. Particles* v. 92 All of the strongly interacting particles fall into families which are specified by three quantum numbers—hypercharge, isotopic spin and baryon number. *Ibid.*, In the final analysis, either strangeness or hypercharge will suffice as a quantum number. In practice experimenters prefer to use strangeness—largely for historical reasons... On the other hand, some theoreticians have adopted the new terminology as it is easier to manipulate in the equations.

hyperchromasia (həi:pəɹkromēi·ziă). Also in anglicized form **hyperchromasy** (-krōu·măsi) (*rare*). [mod.L., f. HYPER- 5 + Gr. χρῶμα, χρώματ- colour (in sense 2 repr. CHROMATIN): see -IA[1].] **1.** *Med.* **a.** Excessive coloration or pigmentation of the skin.

1889 *Cent. Dict.*, *Hyperchromasia*, a pathological condition marked by excess of pigment. **1908** *Practitioner* Aug. 349 A condition known as hyperchromasia, in contradistinction to achromasia, or leucodermia.

b. = *HYPERCHROMIA.

1929 R. B. H. GRADWOHL tr. *Schilling's Blood Picture* II. 107 Special, generally designated erythrocytic blood pictures... Hyperchromasia: generally increased pigmentation. **1966** J. W. LINMAN *Princ. Hematol.* iii. 60 Large or excessively thick cells that stain more darkly than normal are described as being hyperchromatic or as displaying hyperchromasia.

2. *Cytology.* The condition, in a cell or nucleus, of having an abnormally large amount of chromatin.

1930 *Med. Jrnl. Austral.* 22 Feb. 244/1 A detailed examination of carcinoma cells shows that hyperchromasy is the dominant cytological feature of these components. **1948** *Amer. Jrnl. Path.* XXIV. 1200 Cytologic descriptions of tumors are limited to generalities such as..hyperchromasia of nucleus. **1971** *Nature* 31 Dec. 547/2 The individual tumour cells were more rounded with nuclear hyperchromasia.

hyperchromatic (həipəɹkromæ·tik), *a.* [f. HYPER- 5 + CHROMATIC *a.* (in sense 2, CHROMAT(IN + -IC).] **1.** *Med.* **a.** Of the skin: excessively pigmented.

1894 in GOULD *Dict. Med.* 589/2.

b. = *HYPERCHROMIC *a.* 1.

1929 R. B. H. GRADWOHL tr. *Schilling's Blood Picture* II. 113 Single or many large hyperchromatic cells (megalocytes, occasional megaloblasts). **1966** [see *HYPERCHROMASIA 1 b].

2. *Cytology.* Of a cell or nucleus: having an abnormally large amount of chromatin.

1896 E. B. WILSON *Cell* ii. 68 In many cancer-cells many of the nuclei are especially rich in chromatin (hyperchromatic cells). **1930** *Med. Jrnl. Austral.* 22 Feb. 244/1 Highly differentiated, hyperchromatic sarcoma cells. **1966** WRIGHT & SYMMERS *Systemic Path.* II. xxxii. 1128/1 Not infrequently the nucleus of the tumour cells varies considerably in size; it may be large and hyperchromatic ..or it may appear as a small, irregular, pyknotic structure.

hyperchromatosis (həi:pəɹkrōumătōu·sis). [mod.L., f. HYPER- 5 + CHROMAT(O-, CHROMAT(IN + -OSIS.] **1.** *Med.* Excessive colouring or pigmentation, esp. of the skin.

1886 *Syd. Soc. Lex.*, *Hyperchromatosis*, Auspitz's term for an excessive deposit of pigment in the epidermis. **1919** *Encycl. Medica* (ed. 2) VI. 272 *Hyperchromatosis*, excessive pigmentation, especially in certain skin diseases.

2. *Cytology.* [ad. G. *hyperchromatose* (R. Woltereck 1898, in *Zeitschr. f. wiss. Zool.* LXIV. 604).] An abnormally large number of chromosomes or amount of chromatin in a cell or nucleus.

1898 *Jrnl. R. Microsc. Soc.* 628 They are remarkable for their excess of chromosomes (hyperchromatosis), and for the tendency these have to group themselves in dyads and tetrads. **1913** J. RITCHIE in Pembrey & Ritchie *Text-bk. Gen. Path.* viii. 240 In malignant tumours the division of the chromosomes between the poles is often unequal... This can be recognized by the existence of differences in size and staining qualities of the nuclei, and the two phenomena are sometimes referred to as hyperchromatosis and hypochromatosis. **1946** *Nature* 31 Aug. 304/1 A hyperchromatosis and pyknosis of the nucleus which has hitherto been wrongly interpreted as a degeneration.

hyperchromia (həipəɹkrōu·miă). *Med.* [f. as next + -IA[1].] A hyperchromic condition of the blood or of an erythrocyte (see *HYPERCHROMIC *a.* 1).

1931 *Amer. Jrnl. Med. Sci.* CLXXXII. 521 There might be two types of pernicious anemia—the megaloblastic, associated with macrocytosis and hyperchromia, and the erythroblastic, associated with microcytosis and hypochromia. **1935** WHITBY & BRITTON *Disorders of Blood* iii. 49 Hyperchromia is inevitably associated with macrocytosis. **1958** G. C. DE GRUCHY *Clin. Haematol.* ii. 43 Because it is now customary to describe the haemoglobin content of cells in terms of concentration rather than absolute amount, the term hyperchromia is best avoided.

hyperchromic (həipəɹkrōu·mik), *a.* [f. HYPER- 5 + Gr. χρῶμ-α colour + -IC.] **1.** *Med.* Characterized by or designating a colour index greater than one, or red blood cells that contain more hæmoglobin than normal and show little or no central pallor.

1924 T. R. WAUGH in *Canad. Med. Assoc. Jrnl.* XLVII. 114/2 The color index is high, though total cell volume may be considerably reduced. Such a condition may be termed, therefore, hyperchromic. We find this type of anaemia..especially in pernicious anaemia. **1935** WHITBY & BRITTON *Disorders of Blood* vi. 116 The anæmia produced by a deficiency of the hæmopoietic principle is invariably macrocytic and almost always markedly hyperchromic. **1942** M. M. WINTROBE *Clin. Hematol.* vi. 225 It has been assumed that the red corpuscles in this condition [*sc.* pernicious anæmia] are 'hyperchromic' or supersaturated with hemoglobin. This is not true...The darker appearance of these corpuscles..is due to their increased thickness. **1960** C. H. SMITH *Blood Dis. Infancy & Childhood* v. 62 Hyperchromic anemias identify conditions in which macrocytes prevail and in which the color index is greater than unity.

2. Characterized by or exhibiting an increase in the extent to which light (usually,

ultra-violet radiation) is absorbed; chiefly in *hyperchromic effect*.

1939 W. R. BRODE *Chem. Spectroscopy* vii. 128 Ethylene..has an absorption band at 1545 f (1950 A) in the extreme ultraviolet, but the conjugated coupling of two or more ethylene radicals together results in both hyperchromic and bathochromic effects. **1955** G. SCHMIDT in Chargaff & Davidson *Nucleic Acids* I. xv. 569 The quantitative degradation of PNA to mononucleotides by alkali is accompanied by an increase of approximately 20% in the absorption at 260 mμ (hyperchromic effect). **1958** *Nature* 29 Nov. 1503/2 The hyperchromic degradation of polymers. **1968** M. W. STRICKBERGER *Genetics* v. 73 The double-stranded form [of DNA] is called hypochromic, and the loose, single-stranded form is called hyperchromic.

Hence **hy:perchromi·city**, the property of absorbing more (ultra-violet) light.

1958 *Nature* 29 Nov. 1502/1 In view of the profound importance of the anomalous ultra-violet absorption characteristics of nucleic acids in relationship to the fine structure of the macromolecule, the hyperchromicity of a number of relatively simple polynucleotide derivatives was studied. **1968** M. W. STRICKBERGER *Genetics* v. 73 Hyperchromicity [of DNA] can be induced by heating.

hy:perconjuga·tion. *Physical Chem.* [f. HYPER- 1 b + CONJUGATION.] A direct interaction between the electrons of a methyl or substituted methyl group in a molecule and the electrons of an adjacent conjugated system, the former being attracted towards the latter.

1939 R. S. MULLIKEN in *Jrnl. Chem. Physics* VII. 340/2 In the cyclic dienes..there is interaction between this [pair of electrons] and the unsaturation orbitals, resulting in what may be called 'cyclic conjugation'. This phenomenon has been..discussed by Hückel, except for the case where A is CH_2. For this case we may introduce the term 'hyperconjugation', meaning an additional conjugation beyond that ordinarily recognized. [*Note*] The term..was suggested by Professor W. G. Brown, as an improvement on the term 'superconjugation' at first used by the writer. **1949** *Q. Rev.* III. 229 Delocalisation of this type is known as σ-hyperconjugation, and since σ electrons are relatively tightly bound, the resulting energy of delocalisation is likely to be very small. Consequently, σ-hyperconjugation is generally ignored. **1952** *Chem. & Engin. News* 17 Nov. 4881/2 Hyperconjugation denotes resonance interaction by alkyl, and particularly methyl, substituents in systems exemplified by

$$H_3{\equiv}C{-}C{=}C \leftarrow\!\!\rightarrow H^+H_2C{=}C{-}C^-.$$

1962 M. J. S. DEWAR *Hyperconjugation* i. 13 The evidence..for the importance of hyperconjugation is much less conclusive than has been commonly supposed. **1965** PHILLIPS & WILLIAMS *Inorg. Chem.* I. xi. 400 Hydrogen is also unable to act as a π-donor, except possibly to a small extent in groups of hydrogen atoms as in CH_3, the so-called hyperconjugation effect.

Hence **hyperco·njugated** *ppl. a.*, exhibiting hyperconjugation.

1949 *Q. Rev.* III. 233 The carbon–carbon distance in acetaldehyde is approximately 0·04 A. less than the normal value, and..the shortening has been attributed to hyperconjugated structures. **1959** E. S. GOULD *Mechanism & Struct. Org. Chem.* ii. 49 Hyperconjugated structures in which a shift of electron density..has left the C—H bonds with partial no-bond character.

hypercorre·ct, *a. Linguistics.* Also **hyper-correct** (with hyphen). [f. HYPER- 4 a. + CORRECT *a.*] Of a spelling, pronunciation, or construction: erroneous through being falsely modelled on an apparent analogy. Also of a speaker using such a form.

1922 O. JESPERSEN *Lang.* xv. 294 Such hypercorrect forms are closely related to those 'spelling pronunciations' which become frequent when there is much reading of a language whose spelling is not accurately phonetic. **1937** *Amer. Speech* XII. 167 When James the footman says *chicking* for 'chicken' he is being hypercorrect, leaning over backward to be correct. **1972** *Archivum Linguisticum* III. 4 Modern authors have focussed on the [French] imperfect subjunctive as a hypercorrect grammatical form and have used it to characterize or satirize the pedantic and the pretentious.

Hence **hypercorre·ction, -corre·ctness.**

1934 WEBSTER, Hypercorrection, -ness. **1935** *Language* XI. 143 It is only by unceasing vigilance that hypercorrection can be avoided by one whose native dialect has this phonological feature and who wishes to correct it. **1955** *Archivum Linguisticum* VII. 142 Phonemic interference may be due to..phone substitution and hypercorrectness. **1959** M. SCHLAUCH *Eng. Lang. in Mod. Times* vi. 167 The zeal of social inferiors for hypercorrectness. **1964** H. KÖKERITZ in D. Abercrombie et al. *Daniel Jones* 141 Salmon..tends to become ['sɑmən] by hypercorrection. **1972** *Language* XLVIII. 484 Hypercorrections like *tesk, mast* (for 'mask') seem to establish that *tes, mas* are full forms in NNE and not stylistic reductions.

hyperdrive (həi·pəɹdrəiv). *Science Fiction.* Also **hyper-drive.** [f. HYPER- + DRIVE *sb.*; perh. suggested by *hyperspace, overdrive.*] A fictitious device by which a spaceship is enabled to travel from one point to another in a shorter time than light would take (usually by passing out of ordinary space into 'hyperspace' for the journey); also, the state of so travelling.

1955 B. DAVENPORT *Inquiry into Sci. Fiction* 11 A 'hyperdrive'..may be defined simply as something that *does* enable ships to travel faster than the speed of light, no matter what Einstein says. **1959** P. ANDERSON *Virgin Planet* (1966) iii. 20 The ship went into hyperdrive and outpaced light. **1960** K. AMIS *New Maps of Hell* (1961) i. 20 The author will fabricate a way of getting around Einstein..[by] a device known typically as the space-warp or the hyper-drive. **1965** D. MORGAN in J. Carnell *New Writings in S-F* III. 144 The jolt as he came out of hyper-drive..had confirmed what he had suspected for some months. **1968** M. S. LIVINGSTON *Particle Physics* i. 7 No responsible scientist would attempt to justify support for research in this field with prediction of an 'anti-matter engine'..or a 'hyper-drive' for spaceships.

hyperemia, var. HYPERÆMIA.

hyperesthesia, var. HYPERÆSTHESIA.

hyperextend (həipəɹ,ekste·nd), *v.* [f. HYPER- 4 c + EXTEND *v.*] *trans.* To extend, in the sense opp. to FLEX *v.*, (a joint, or a part of the body moving about a joint) so as to attain an abnormally great angle. So **hyperexte·nded** *ppl. a.*

1883 *Brain* V. 348 The toes are spread out and hyperextended. **1886** *Ibid.* IX. 169 Between this ridge and the toes there is a deep hollow, to which the hyperextended first phalanges form an almost perpendicular boundary. **1903** TUBBY & JONES *Mod. Methods Surg. Paralyses* II. 218 Treatment should consist in rendering the forearm supine and hyperextending the wrist. **1927** *Jrnl. Amer. Med. Assoc.* 28 May 1711/1 The fingers could be hyperextended until they touched the dorsum of the wrist. **1963** *Lancet* 5 Jan. 6/1 An injury in which the neck has been forcibly hyperextended or flexed.

Also **hyperexte·nsion,** the state of being hyperextended.

1883 *Brain* V. 480 There is a slight hyper-extension at the torso-phalangeal, and flexion at the phalangeal joints. **1905** A. B. JACKSON *Influence Growth on Deformities* iv. 85 The best result after this affection is a knee ankylosed in extension or hyperextension. **1961** *Lancet* 5 Aug. 297/1 The common pattern of deformity was flexion..and dislocation of the hip, with extension or hyperextension of the knee. **1968** J. WINEARLS *Mod. Dance* (ed. 2) ii. 48 In the case of the backwards contraction, the spine is really in hyper-extension.

hyperextensible (həi:pəɹ,ekste·nsib'l), *a.* [f. prec., after *extensible.*] Capable of being hyperextended. So **hy:perextensibi·lity.**

1946 R. R. GATES *Human Genetics* I. xi. 449 All the finger joints are hyperextensible. *Ibid.* 448 Hyperextensibility or doublejointedness of the thumbs may occur in the first joint or the second. **1961** *Lancet* 2 Sept. 526/2 There were obvious transverse palmar folds and hyperextensibility of the joints.

hyperfine (həi·pəɹfəin), *a. Physics.* [tr. G. *hyperfeinstruktur* hyperfine structure (W. Pauli 1924, in *Naturwiss.* 12 Sept. 741/1), f. HYPER- + *feinstruktur* *FINE STRUCTURE.] *hyperfine structure*: (the presence of) multiplets of closely spaced lines in a spectrum that are closer together than those of fine structure; *esp.* multiplets that result from the further splitting of lines by the coupling between the magnetic moment (and higher multipole moments) of the atomic nucleus and the electromagnetic field of the electrons. Also (with ellipsis of *structure*), of or pertaining to this phenomenon.

1927 *Proc. Nat. Acad. Sci.* XIII. 430 The hyper-fine structure of λ 2537 of mercury has been shown..to consist of five lines of very nearly equal intensity. *Ibid.* 431 Each of the five hyper-fine structure lines has a triplet Zeeman pattern. **1942** J. D. STRANATHAN *Particles of Mod. Physics* x. 400 Other details of characteristic line spectra, known as hyperfine structure, have made it necessary to assign also to the nuclei of atoms certain magnetic moments. **1950** D. HALLIDAY *Introd. Nucl. Physics* xiii. 479 Hyperfine studies of optical spectral lines. **1953** N. F. RAMSEY in E. Segrè *Exper. Nucl. Physics* I. III. i. 358 If this fine structure is examined more closely, it is often found that each line of the fine structure can in turn be resolved into further lines or 'hyperfine structure' with a separation of the order of 1 cm^{-1}. **1954** H. SEMAT *Introd. Atomic & Nucl. Physics* (ed. 3) viii. 273 Two distinct types of hyperfine structure have been observed. One type..has been explained as due to the presence of two or more isotopes of the element. **1958** CONDON & ODISHAW *Handbk. Physics* VII. vi. 88/1 Nuclear electric quadrupole hyperfine structure in molecular spectra has yielded a number of nuclear spins and quadrupole moments. **1962** [see *FINE STRUCTURE 1 a]. **1965** C. M. H. SMITH *Textbk. Nucl. Physics* viii. 229 If the number of hyperfine components can be counted, the nuclear spin *I* is obtained.

hyperfocal (həipəɹfōu·kăl), *a.* [f. HYPER- 1 + FOCAL *a.*] Applied to the distance on which a camera must be focused to give the maximum depth of field (see quot. 1957), and to the object plane at this distance.

1905 WASTELL & BAYLEY *Hand Camera* viii. 96 The best position for the lens..is sometimes called the 'hyperfocal distance'...By dividing the hyperfocal distance by two we get the distance beyond which everything is in focus. **1957** AMOS & BIRKINSHAW *Television Engin.* I. ix. 178 If a lens system is focused on infinity, the images are in focus..for all objects lying between infinity and the hyperfocal distance. If, however, the lens system is focused on the hyperfocal distance, images are in focus for all objects lying between infinity and half the hyperfocal distance. **1961** G. MILLERSON *Technique Television Production* iii. 34 We can adjust any camera lens system so that it is focused on its hyperfocal plane.

hypergamy (həipə̄·ɹgămi). *Anthrop.* [f. HYPER- + *-GAMY.] A term first used by W. Coldstream, to denote the custom which forbids the marriage of a woman into a group of lower standing than her own; also *transf.*, of any marriage with a partner of higher social standing. Hence **hype·rgamous** *a.*, pertaining or relating to hypergamy.

1883 D. C. J. IBBETSON *Rep. Census Panjáb 17 Feb. 1881* I. 356 They [*sc.* the social rules]..may be referred to two laws, which I shall call the laws of isogamy and hypergamy... Mr. Coldstream writes from Hushyárpur:...For 12 years past certain classes of Khatris..have been agitating to extend the principle of isogamy, and to free themselves from the rule of contracting hypergamous alliances for their daughters. **1903** RISLEY & GAIT *Rep. Census India 1901* § 701 *Hypergamy*, or 'marrying up' is the custom which..compels [a woman] to marry in a group equal or superior in rank. A hypergamous division, therefore, is a group forming part of a series governed by the foregoing rule. **1909** E. S. HARTLAND *Primitive Paternity* I. 266 The Brahmans everywhere follow a custom known as *hypergamy*, by which a man may marry or have sexual relations with a woman of lower rank, but no man of lower rank may marry into a caste above his own. **1921** *Nature* 13 Jan. 646/1 Dr. Rivers said that the term 'hypergamy' had been used loosely by both Sir Herbert Risley and Dr. W. Crooke to denote marriage between groups which differ in rank, but for the sake of clearness the term should be confined to those instances in which there was a characteristic difference between the marriage rules for the two sexes. **1929** *Encycl. Brit.* IV. 979/2 The ancient hypergamous rule which allowed a woman to be married to a man of higher class. **1951** *N. & Q. Anthropol.* (ed. 6) II. iii. 94 Sometimes there is a hypergamous system in which a socially inferior sub-caste can obtain wives from another and higher sub-caste on payment. **1957** *New Statesman* 4 May 566/2 The curse which is ruining, in fantasy if not in their own lives, these brilliant young men of working-class origin and welfare-state opportunity is what anthropologists have dubbed male hypergamy. **1966** *Ibid.* 15 Apr. 548/2 Hypergamous young men claim that the district [*sc.* Chelsea] offers more available classy girls than other art-school areas. *Ibid.* 2 Dec. 832/1 English women have long been able to go in for hypergamy.

hypergelast (həipə̄·ɹdʒilæst). [f. HYPER- 4 + Gr. γελαστής a laugher, f. γελᾶν to laugh; cf. GELASTIC *a.*] (See quot. 1877.)

1877 G. MEREDITH *Ess. Comedy* in *New Q. Mag.* VIII. 2 We have another class of men..whom we may term hypergelasts; the excessive laughers. **1902** *Times Weekly Educ. Suppl.* 19 Dec. p. ii/2 As to the savage, he is a great laugher—a hypergelast, in fact. **1933** *Scrutiny* I. 356 Meredith's hypergelasts are enemies of the Comic spirit, but his ideal audience all laugh, in their polite drawing-room way. **1947** N. CARDUS *Autobiogr.* I. 47 The word 'hypergelast'..denoting the loud vacant laughers.

hypergol (həi·pəɹgǫl). *Astronaut.* [a. G. *hypergol* (one of a series of terms ending in *-ergol*), app. f. HYPER- + Gr. ἔργ-ον work + -OL 3.] A hypergolic rocket propellant.

1947 *Jrnl. Brit. Interplanetary Soc.* VI. 104 Fuels are broadly classified in three groups, monergols, hypergols and non-hypergols. *Ibid.* 105 The distinct property of hypergols is that the reaction is self-starting. **1950** [see *HYDRAZINE]. **1969** R. T. HOLZMANN *Chemical Rockets* ii. 140 The use of hypergols is both simple and safe.

So **hypergo·lic** *a.*, igniting spontaneously on contact with the oxidant or another propellant; also as *sb.*, a hypergol.

1947 *Jrnl. Brit. Interplanetary Soc.* VI. 106 A third method is to inject auxiliary fuels, hypergolic or self-igniting monergolic, into the chamber before the main fuels. **1965** *Ibid.* XX. 154/2 Ignition does not pose problems as the propellent is hypergolic. **1970** N. ARMSTRONG et al. *First on Moon* i. 28 During the second week of June it was time to start putting hypergolic propellants into the fuel tanks. *Ibid.* iv. 75 The self-igniting..hypergolics which went into the separate control systems of the command and service module and the lunar module.

hypermarket (həi·pəɹmāɹkėt). [f. HYPER- + MARKET *sb.*, translating F. *hypermarché* (f. *marché* market, after *supermarché* *SUPERMARKET).] A very large self-service store, usually situated outside a town, having an extensive car park and selling a wide range of goods.

1970 *Guardian* 1 Oct. 7/1 A proposed new 'hypermarket', a gigantic supermarket which could be the precursor of complete shops as big as whole villages. **1971** *Times* 14 July 19/4 The catalyst has been the imminent arrival in the United Kingdom of Carrefour hypermarkets. **1971** *Observer* 3 Oct. 15/2 Hypermarkets are like retail factories, vast warehouse-type buildings. **1972** *New Statesman* 28 Jan. 101/1 By 1966 four hypermarkets (i.e. units of over 25,000 sq. ft. of floor space) had been set up. These huge self-service stores have caught on in France more than in Britain—today there are 144 of them. **1972** *Daily Tel.* 23 May 22/7 Although only a quarter the size of the typical hypermarket, it has all the other ingredients—one-level parking, discount prices, a substantial non-food sector, and late opening.

hypermetric, *a.* Add: **1.** Used of Old English verse.

1892 F. J. MATHER in *Mod. Lang. Notes* VII. 200 It will be well to note the occurrences of hypermetric lines in the different poems. **1906** G. P. KRAPP *Andreas* p. xlvii, *Beowulf* (which contains twelve hypermetric lines). **1958** A. J. BLISS *Metre of Beowulf* 96 The distribution of hypermetric verses varies from poem to poem. **1970** M. SWANTON *Dream of Rood* 61 Blocks of hypermetric verse used contrapuntally to accommodate significantly more complex thematic material.

hypermetrical, *a.* Add: Used of Old English verse.

1891 J. W. BRIGHT *Anglo-Saxon Reader* 238 These hypermetrical half-lines occur either singly or in groups, and usually add dignity to the sense and movement of the passage. **1922** F. KLAEBER *Beowulf* p. lxxi, Groups of emphatic hypermetrical types are introduced three times. **1935** A. C. BARTLETT *Larger Rhet. Patterns Anglo-Saxon Poetry* 70 The hypermetrical irregularities of the other Anglo-Saxon poems. **1958** A. J. BLISS *Metre of Beowulf* 88 It is common ground that the vast majority of hypermetrical verses end with a group of syllables which is exactly equivalent to an ordinary verse.

hypermodern (həipəɹmǫ·dəɹn), *a.* [f. HYPER- 4 a. + MODERN *a.*] Excessively modern; *spec.* in Chess, of or pertaining to the strategy, first used in the early 20th cent., of controlling the centre of the board with pieces at a distance.

1923 *Brit. Chess Mag.* Sept. 338 What is claimed as hyper-modern turns out to be..respectably medieval. **1945** KOESTLER *Yogi & Commissar* III. i. 127 His flair for hyper-modern avant-garde methods in Economy,..and Warfare. **1951** 'ASSIAC' *Adventure in Chess* II. v. 75 This 'hypermodern' move has been all the rage during the last few years. **1966** G. N. LEECH *Eng. in Advertising* xxii. 196 These extra features..add animation to the language, imparting a racy, hyper-modern image of the product. **1970** A. SUNNUCKS *Encycl. Chess* 41 An exponent of the ideas of the hypermodern school of chess.

Hence **hypermo·dern, hypermo·dernist** *sbs.*; **hypermode·rnity.**

1923 J. HART tr. *Reti's Mod. Ideas in Chess* v. 122 The Hyper-moderns are the greatest opponents of routine play. **1925** *Brit. Chess Mag.* May 219 *Humpeldinck's opening*..may be fairly described as the *dernier cri* of hypermodernity, the most up-to-date of the 'hyper-modern' openings. **1959** B. J. HORTON *Dict. Mod. Chess* 89/2 The long-term plan of the hypermodernist was to allow the enemy to occupy the center and then to demolish him later.

hypernic (həi·pəɹnik, həipə̄·ɹnik). [f. HYPER- + *Nic(aragua.*] A wood from one of several tropical American trees, esp. *Hæmatoxylon brasiletto*, or the red dye extracted from it. Also *attrib.*

1897 C. T. DAVIS *Manuf. Leather* (ed. 2) xlii. 567 Take 10 lbs. hypernic chips... Add the hypernic solution by degrees. **1924** RECORD & MELL *Timbers Tropical Amer.* 247 The wood [of *Haematoxylon brasiletto*] from Nicaragua is known..in the trade as Nicaragua wood or 'hypernic', the latter term coined to indicate a superlative quality of the wood from that country, but subsequently applied rather indiscriminately to any red dyewood or dyewood extract. **1971** R. J. ADROSKO *Nat. Dyes & Home Dyeing* 26 Besides being called by the other common names for brazilwood, braziletto was also known as Nicaragua wood and hypernick.

hyperon (həi·pĕrǫn). *Nuclear Physics.* [app. f. HYPER- + *-ON[1].] Any of a group of unstable sub-atomic particles that includes all the baryons apart from the proton and neutron; any strongly interacting particle with half-integral spin and a mass greater than that of the nucleons.

1953 *Compt. Rend. du 3me Congrès Internat. sur le Rayonnement Cosmique* 269 Nomenclature more frequently used during the conference... Groups of particles... H-particles (hyperons): symbol H: particles with mass intermediate between those of the neutron and the deuteron (this definition to be revised if 'fundamental' particles heavier than the deuteron are found). **1963** S. TOLANSKY *Introd. Atomic Physics* (ed. 5) xxiii. 391 The baryons..can best be subdivided into two groups namely (a) the familiar nucleons,..(b) the extremely unstable somewhat heavier particles, now called hyperons. **1965** *New Scientist* 18 Mar. 738/3 The SU(3) symmetry relates not just the proton and the neutron one to another, but includes also in one multiplet the six particles known as hyperons.

Hence **hypero·nic** *a.*

1956 [see *HYPERCHARGE]. **1969** *Physical Rev. Lett.* XXII. 1238/1 Σ^- hyperons are formed in the targets through the reactions $K^- + p \to \Sigma^- + \pi^+$ and $K^- + n \to \Sigma^- + \pi^0$, and upon capture by target nuclei make hyperonic atoms. **1970** *Physics Lett.* XXXIII. B. 230/2 The capture of the Σ^- hyperons takes place in atomic levels with high main quantum number *n*...The typical pattern of the Σ hyperonic X-rays is determined by the fact that the Σ^- hyperon..is a strongly interacting particle.

hyperosmolality (həi:pəɹ,ǫzmolæ·liti). *Med.* [f. HYPER- + *OSMOLALITY.] = *HYPEROSMOLARITY.

1959 *Pediatric Clinics N. Amer.* VI. 259 In severe hyperosmolality there may be a striking reduction of cerebro-spinal fluid pressure. **1963** *Amer. Jrnl. Cardiol.* XII. 654/2 Hypernatremia and hyperosmolality of serum result from loss of water without sodium. **1972** [see **hyperosmolar* adj.].

hyperosmolarity (həi:pəɹ,ǫzmolæ·riti). *Med.* [f. HYPER- + *OSMOLARITY.] The condition (in a bodily fluid, esp. serum) of having abnormally high osmotic pressure; also, the condition (in an individual) of having such serum.

1947 *Amer. Jrnl. Dis. Child.* LXXIV. 684 The less the ability of the kidney to excrete urine of high solute content, the more readily hyperosmolarity of the body fluid develops. **1958** *Jrnl. Chronic Dis.* VII. 1 The ultimate effect of hyperosmolarity of serum is dehydration of cells. **1963** *Lancet* 20 Apr. 891/1 We saw a patient with marked hyperosmolarity, due to an unusually high plasma-sodium, dehydration, and moderate ketonuria, but no loss of consciousness. **1965** *Neurology* XV. 205/1 Hyperosmolarity secondary to hypernatremia in various clinical states is known to be associated with severe neurological disturbances.

So **hyperosmo·lar** *a.*, of, exhibiting, or associated with hyperosmolarity.

1953 *Amer. Jrnl. Med.* XV. 185/1 After discontinuance of pitressin the hyperosmolar state promptly recurred. **1966** *Lancet* 26 Mar. 679/2 Eight patients with hyperosmolar non-ketoacidotic diabetic coma were new diabetics with an average age of 63 years. **1972** *Science* 19 May 815 Malone et al. stated that severe hyperosmolar dehydration could be responsible for the entire galactose toxicity syndrome. However, we have concluded..that hyperosmolality per se is not the major factor responsible.

hyperparasite. (Earlier and later examples of the various forms.)

1833 A. H. HALIDAY in *Entomol. Mag.* I. 482, I am not aware that any of them [*sc.* a group of ichneumons] are hyperparasitic. **1889** *Cent. Dict.*, Hyperparasite, hyperparasitism. **1897** L. O. HOWARD *Study in Insect Parasitism* 14 Many parasites suffer..from the attacks of hyperparasites. **1906** J. W. FOLSOM *Entomol.* x. 312 (*heading*) Hyperparasitism. **1914** *Entomologist* XLVII. 77 C. W. Colthrup sent me..two females which he had captured with three specimens of the hyperparasite *Hemiteles areator*. **1932** E. STEP *Bees, Wasps, Ants* 185 These parasites [*sc.* Braconidæ]..are in turn attacked by still smaller species—hyperparasites. **1951** G. LAPAGE *Parasitic Animals* ix. 264 Many species of Hymenoptera implant their eggs inside the bodies of other parasitic insects, so that they provide good examples of hyperparasitism. **1952** A. LYSAGHT tr. *Caullery's Parasitism & Symbiosis* vi. 108 Sometimes, too, under new conditions, a parasite changes into a hyperparasite. **1964** T. C. CHENG *Biol. Animal Parasites* 143/1 Various species of *Nosema* and *Glugea* are capable of hyperparasitism in larval and adult helminths. *Ibid.*, One species of *Nosema*..is hyperparasitic in tapeworms.

hy:perparathy·roidism. *Med.* [f. HYPER- 5 + PARATHYROID + -ISM.] A condition in which there is an abnormally high level of parathyroid hormone in the blood, resulting in the loss of calcium from the bones, which become brittle.

1917 C. VOEGTLIN in *Surg., Gynecol. & Obstetr.* XXV. 249 A condition which might justly be termed hyperparathyroidism is unknown at the present time. **1948** ALBRIGHT & REIFENSTEIN *Parathyroid Glands* iii. 67 It is a fact, however, that one may have severe hyperparathyroidism and show no clinical, roentgenological, or histological evidence of bone disease... For all practical purposes, it usually comes down to whether or not the patient drinks milk. **1966** WRIGHT & SYMMERS *Systemic Path.* II. xxxii. 1127/1 Secondary hyperparathyroidism occurs when more parathyroid hormone is required by the body than under normal circumstances. **1971** RIMOIN & SCHIMKE *Genetic Disorders Endocrine Glands* iv. 87 The symptoms of primary hyperparathyroidism are essentially those of hypercalcemia.

Hence **hy:perparathy·roid** *a.*, of or having hyperparathyroidism.

1961 *Lancet* 16 Sept. 641/1 Hyperparathyroid bone disease was the first form of the disorder to be recognised. **1966** WRIGHT & SYMMERS *Systemic Path.* II. xxxii. 1130/1 'Parathyroid poisoning' is a term that has been applied to the sudden increase in the extent of metastatic calcification of organs..when a high calcium diet is forced on the hyperparathyroid patient.

hyperphoric, *a.* Add: **2.** *Ophthalm.* (See s.v. *HYPER- IV.)

hy:perpolariza·tion. *Physiol.* [f. HYPER- + POLARIZATION.] An increase in the potential difference across the membrane of a nerve fibre above the normal resting potential, so that the inside of the fibre becomes (or is) even more negative with respect to the outside.

1946 LORENTE DE NÓ & FENG in *Jrnl. Cellular & Compar. Physiol.* XXVIII. 412 This overshooting is analogous to the temporary hyperpolarization of the membrane (positive after-potential) which occurs after the end of tetani. **1955** *Acta Physiol. Scand.* XXXV. 12 The hyperpolarization usually amounts to 25–35 mV. *Ibid.*, The rate of hyperpolarization is about 150 mV/sec. **1966** C. F. STEVENS *Neurophysiol.* ii. 13 Any change which decreases the inside–outside potential difference is known as a depolarization, whereas an increase in the membrane potential is called a hyperpolarization. **1971** *Nature* 9 July 123/1 Lundberg inserted intracellular electrodes in secretory cells of this gland and observed a hyperpolarization of 5–20 mV with a latency of 200–400 ms after applying single shocks to the chorda tympani nerve.

So **hyperpo·larize** *v. trans.*, to produce such a change in (a nerve fibre); *intr.*, to undergo such a change; **hyperpo·larizing** *vbl. sb.*

1950 *Jrnl. Cellular & Compar. Physiol.* XXXV. Suppl. II. 105 It appears that presynaptic impulses may exert upon the ganglion cells a catelectrotonic (depolarizing) action as well as an anelectrotonic (hyperpolarizing) action. **1955** *Jrnl. Physiol.* CXXX. 394 On hyperpolarizing the motoneurone..the amplitude of the e.p.s.p. was only slightly affected. **1971** *Nature* 23 July 269/2 In one pair of touch cells..a depolarizing or a hyperpolarizing synaptic potential was observed when the anterior or the posterior cell was stimulated. **1973** *Ibid.* 9 Mar. 102/1 Most of these cells only hyperpolarize in response to light.

hypersensitive (həipəɹse·nsitiv), *a.* [f. HYPER- 4 a + SENSITIVE *a.*] **1.** Sensitive to an abnormal or excessive degree; over-sensitive.

1871, 1897 [in Dict. s.v. HYPER- IV]. **1892** *Jrnl. Mental Sci.* XXXVIII. 525 Charcot and his pupils..believe in the influence of the magnet in hysteria, where the nervous system is hyper-sensitive. **1912** D. H. LAWRENCE *Phoenix II* (1968) 269 This soldier poet is so straight, so free from the modern artist's hyper-sensitive self-consciousness, that we would have more of him. **1939** E. & C. PAUL tr. *Stekel's Technique Analytical Psychotherapy* xx. 283 A woman brought up on religious lines, morally hypersensitive, who pursues ideal aims. **1972** *Oxford Times* 19 May 7/1 Mr Francis Barnes, defending, described Jeffries as a 'retiring and hypersensitive' man who had lived as a semi-recluse for 17 years.

2. *spec.* in *Med.*: characterized by the fact that a marked adverse bodily response may be evoked by some specific substance or agent which (in similar amounts) has no such effect on most individuals. Const. *to*.

1899 E. O. JORDAN tr. *Hueppe's Princ. Bacteriol.* vi. 337 Behring has found that it is possible..to immunize animals so highly..that they..become hyper-sensitive to the toxin. **1906** *Jrnl. Amer. Med. Assoc.* 29 Sept. 1007/2 At first glance it would appear much more important for an organism to be hyposensitive than hypersensitive to infectious processes, but a closer study of the complex problems of immunity develops the curious fact that resistance to disease may be largely gained through a process of hypersusceptibility. **1922** *Jrnl. Immunol.* VII. 128 The similarity of symptoms of drug reactions with those of foreign proteins in specifically hypersensitive persons. **1935** N. P. SHERWOOD *Immunol.* xxiii. 465 One injection of a nontoxic dose of horse serum will render guinea pigs hypersensitive to a second injection of the antigen provided an interval of almost ten days is allowed to intervene. **1951** WHITBY & HYNES *Med. Bacteriol.* (ed. 5) vii. 95 Human idiosyncrasy..differs in some important respects from anaphylaxis. The exciting agent is not necessarily an antigen; patients may become hypersensitive, for example, to drugs with a very simple chemical structure. **1964** W. G. SMITH *Allergy & Tissue Metabolism* i. 7 In patients who are specifically hypersensitive to a single allergen, it is very likely that sensitisation has been brought about by a previous contact with the allergen. *Ibid.* 13 A vast literature exists on histamine..and leaves no doubt about its involvement in the hypersensitive state.

3. *Photogr.* Of a film or plate, or its emulsion: hypersensitized (see *HYPERSENSITIZE *v.* b).

1937 *Discovery* May p. xliv (Advt.), Hypersensitive panchromatic roll film. **1965** M. J. LANGFORD *Basic Photogr.* x. 179 Red-pan or hypersensitive pan materials are..sensitive to red and respond up to 6,800 Å.

hyperse·nsitiveness. [f. prec., after *sensitive, sensitiveness.*] = next. **a.** *gen.* **b.** *Med.* (See *HYPERSENSITIVE *a.* 2.)

In medical use *hypersensitiveness* was at first commoner than *hypersensitivity*, but the latter is now more usual.

a. 1876 [in Dict. s.v. HYPER- IV]. **1898** W. SCHEPPEGRELL *Electr. in Dis. Nose, Throat & Ear* xxi. 218 In hyperesthetic rhinitis, Sajous recommends that each point of hypersensitiveness be destroyed by means of the electrocautery. **1917** GLUECK & LIND tr. *Adler's Neurotic Constitution* (1921) 164 Every one who has become acquainted with the hypersensitiveness of neurotic subjects knows with what slight cause they feel themselves to be undervalued. **1939** E. & C. PAUL tr. *Stekel's Technique Analytical Psychotherapy* xxi. 327 A persistent illusion of a bad smell, disturbances of taste,..may all be indications of an uneasy conscience; so may hypersensitiveness of certain areas of skin. **1951** I. COMPTON-BURNETT *Darkness & Day* 21 One feels that being alive to all the troubles about one is a sign of sensitiveness and feeling, when it may be hypersensitiveness and trying for other people.

b. 1906 *Jrnl. Amer. Med. Assoc.* 29 Sept. 1009/1 As far as we know, this is the first recorded instance in which hypersensitiveness, or anaphylaxis, has been experimentally shown to be transmitted from a mother to her young. **1922** *Jrnl. Immunol.* VII. 128 The condition now known as human hypersensitiveness or allergy. **1940** BECKER & OBERMAYER *Mod. Dermatol. & Syphilol.* vii. 75/2 The resulting inflammation is of the vesicular type, but a condition of hypersensitiveness does not have to be considered, since everyone's skin reacts to this solution. **1953** F. K. HANSEL *Clin. Allergy* iii. 58 The existence of an inherited predisposition is certainly not a prerequisite to the development of hypersensitiveness.

hy:persensiti·vity. [f. as prec., after *sensitivity.*] The state or fact of being hypersensitive. **a.** *Med.* (See *HYPERSENSITIVE *a.* 2.) **b.** *gen.*

a. 1914 *Q. Jrnl. Med.* VII. 273 Richet, in 1902, introduced the term 'anaphylaxis' to explain certain phenomena of hypersensitivity. *Ibid.* 275 Before hypersensitivity can manifest itself a period of time must be allowed

to elapse between the first and second injection. **1929** H. G. WELLS *Chem. Aspects Immunity* (ed. 2) ix. 225 One of the most spectacular phenomena discovered in immunity is that of hypersensitivity to foreign proteins. **1946** *Nature* 19 Oct. 554/2 Most human beings appear to give very similar results when subjected to the same degree of exposure [to insect bites], though special cases of hypersensitivity and severe allergy also occur. **1947** L. SCHWARTZ et al. *Occup. Dis. Skin* (ed. 2) iv. 43 The tendency to hypersensitivity may be inherited; it may be due to..a pigment deficiency causing hypersensitivity to light; or there may be a true allergy caused by exposure to an allergen. **1964** M. HYNES *Med. Bacteriol.* (ed. 8) viii. 104 Dermal hypersensitivity [ed. 5–7 (1951–61): hypersensitiveness] to dyes, solvents, etc., is most conveniently demonstrated by a patch test. **1970** PASSMORE & ROBSON *Compan. Med. Stud.* II. xxii. 19/1 It was soon found that hypersensitivity could be evoked also by intrinsically harmless substances such as..simple chemicals.

b. 1954 J. A. HADFIELD *Dreams & Nightmares* xi. 221 If that were so, hypersensitivity of hearing would be ruled out. **1956** I. MURDOCH *Flight from Enchanter* x. 140 It was as if Mischa were deliberately reducing him to a state of hypersensitivity and confusion. **1970** D. W. SWANSON et al. *Paranoid* iii. 61 The patient's hypersensitivity to others' feelings and failings can be disconcerting when focused on the interviewer. **1972** *Daily Colonist* (Victoria, B.C.) 27 Feb. 4/5 A hypersensitivity to criticism hangs them all up in time.

hy:persensitiza·tion. [f. next + -ATION.] The action or process of hypersensitizing, or the state of being hypersensitized. **a.** *Med.* **b.** *Photogr.*

a. 1908 *Jrnl. Amer. Med. Assoc.* 15 Feb. 528/1 The remarkable phenomenon of hypersensitization or anaphylaxis. **1947** L. SCHWARTZ et al. *Occup. Dis. Skin* (ed. 2) iv. 39 If such a worker is able to keep on working, the dermatitis clears up... In other words exposure first causes a hypersensitization, then further exposure causes a dermatitis, and still further exposure causes hyposensitization. **1959** *New England Jrnl. Med.* CCLX. 170/2 The use of human gamma globulin rather than that derived from animal plasma significantly diminishes the risk of hypersensitization to a foreign protein.

b. 1933 CARROLL & HUBBARD in *Bureau of Standards Jrnl. Res.* X. 212 We shall use the term 'hypersensitization' to cover any case in which increase in sensitization by a dye is produced by treatment with a material itself colorless or absorbing a spectral region different from that of the dye. *Ibid.* 213 In our experiments hypersensitization always involved an increase in relative sensitivity to the longer wave lengths. **1956** *Electronic Engin.* Feb. 78/1 The processes of hyper-sensitization (treatment before exposure) and latensification (treatment after exposure) may give an increase in relative speed of up to two or three times with normal development. **1964** J. ROUBIER *Odham's Pract. Photogr. & Film-Making* ii. 34 The effective speed of an emulsion can be raised by 100% or even 150% by hypersensitisation.

hypersensitize (həipəɹse·nsitəiz), *v.* [f. HYPER- 4 c + SENSITIZE *v.*] *trans.* To render hypersensitive. *spec.* **a.** *Med.* (See *HYPERSENSITIVE *a.* 2.) **b.** *Photogr.* To increase the speed of (a photographic film or plate, or its emulsion) by immersion in a special solution, exposure to light, or other means, usually before it is exposed in the taking of a photograph (cf. *LATENSIFICATION). So **hyperse·nsitized** *ppl. a.*, **hyperse·nsitizing** *vbl. sb.*

1897 G. B. SHAW *Let.* 16 Apr. (1965) 746 Teddy, though hypersensitized..and petulated by more luxury than was good for him in the way of a mammy seems highly and nervously intelligent. **1914** *Q. Jrnl. Med.* VII. 277 In anaphylaxis the degree of specificity is difficult to determine, as a hypersensitized animal has an increased susceptibility to any toxin. *Ibid.* 280 A serum may have strong hypersensitizing power for passive anaphylaxis and yet have no precipitating power. **1917** E. POUND *Let.* 10 Nov. (1971) 123 Still, what the hell else are you? I mean apart from being a citizen, a good fellow.., a grouch, a slightly hypersensitized animal, etc.?? **1920** *Jrnl. Franklin Inst.* CLXXXIX. 25 (*heading*) Hypersensitizing commercial panchromatic plates. **1929** E. J. WALL *Pract. Color Photogr.* (ed. 2) xiii. 173 The exposure with these hypersensitized plates and the aesculin filter is about one-tenth of that required for the normal plate. **1954** tr. *L. P. Clerc's Photogr.* (ed. 3) viii. 178/2 The first exposure 'hypersensitizes' the material towards the second. **1969** M. J. LANGFORD *Adv. Photogr.* viii. 171 'Hypersensitizing' or increasing the speed of an emulsion *before* camera exposure can be carried out chemically or by means of light.

hypersonic (həipəɹsǫ·nik), *a.* [f. HYPER- + *SONIC *a.*, after *supersonic*, *ultrasonic*.] **1.** Of, pertaining to, or designating sound waves or vibrations with a frequency greater than about 1000 million Hz. (Cf. *ULTRASONIC *a.*)

1937 B. V. R. RAO in *Nature* 22 May 885/1 Spontaneously existing sound-waves of thermal origin of very high frequencies ('hyper-sonic waves'). **1938** —— in *Proc. Indian Acad. Sci.* A. VII. 163 It appears desirable to designate the portion of the acoustic spectrum having a frequency higher than a thousand mega-cycles per second as the 'hyper-sonic' region, while the 'ultra-sonic' region may be taken to extend from one to a thousand megacycles per second. **1948** *Rep. Progress Physics* XI. 205 Workers in India particularly have used *hypersonic* to denote ultrasonic phenomena (of thermal origin) at frequencies of the order of 1000 Mc/sec. or higher. **1960** *Physical Rev.* CXVII. 1248 The hypersonic absorption was studied for longitudinal and transverse waves at various frequencies up to 4000 Mc/s. **1963** J. BLITZ *Fund. Ultrasonics* vi. 167 Bömmel and Dransfeld measured the attenuation of both longitudinal and shear waves in quartz at frequencies ranging from 1,000 to 4,000 Mc/s using a hypersonic technique. **1971** *Nature* 24 Sept. 238/2 Mechanical surface waves can now be generated up to 10 GHz. Mechanical waves of these frequencies (up to 100 GHz) are often termed hypersonic.

2. Involving, pertaining to, capable of, or designating speeds greater than about five times the speed of sound. (Cf. *SUPERSONIC *a.*)

1946 *Jrnl. Math. & Physics* XXV. 247 Hypersonic flows are flow fields where the fluid velocity is much larger than the velocity of propagation of small disturbances, the velocity of sound. **1958** *Engineering* 14 Mar. 347/2 Flow about bodies at subsonic, supersonic, and hypersonic speeds. **1958** *Times* 19 Dec. 11/7 Hypersonic travel is just possible in the foreseeable future. **1960** *New Scientist* 14 July 88/2 The hypersonic wind tunnel is almost more necessary than the supersonic... A tunnel capable of producing..air speeds between Mach 10 and Mach 27 (something near 18,000 m.p.h.) is now in daily use. **1960** *Nature* 6 Feb. 346/2 The transition from the supersonic to the hypersonic régime occurs at a Mach number of about 5, but all the characteristic features of the latter régime may only become well developed at a much higher Mach number of, say, 15. **1969** *Courier Mail* (Brisbane) 17 Apr. 2 The construction of a 500-seat hypersonic aircraft could cost as much as £4000 million.

hypertely (həipə̄·ɹtĭli, həi·pəɹte:li). *Zool.* [ad. G. *hypertelie* (C. Brunner 1873, in *Verh. Zool.-Bot. Ges. Wien* XXIII. 133), f. Gr. ὑπερτέλειος beyond completeness, f. τέλος end.] Extreme development of size, patterns of behaviour, mimetic coloration, etc. beyond the degree to which these characteristics are apparently useful. Also *fig.* Hence **hyperte·lic** *a.*

1895 D. SHARP in *Cambr. Nat. Hist.* V. xiii. 323 Brunner..came to the conclusion that they [*sc.* close resemblances] cannot be accounted for on the ground of mere utility, and proposed the term Hypertely to express the idea that in these cases the bounds of the useful are transcended. **1920** G. D. H. CARPENTER *Naturalist on Lake Victoria* x. 196 Special procryptic colouring never fails to arouse wonder from its extreme perfection... This complimentary [*sic*] doctrine has been termed Hypertely. **1936** *Nature* 10 Oct. 603/2 We find that intraspecific selection frequently leads to results which are mainly.. useless to the species as a whole, including 'hypertelic' characters. **1937** A. HUXLEY *Ends & Means* xiv. 262 We are doing our best to develop a militaristic 'hypertely', to become, in other words, dangerously specialized in the art of killing our fellows. **1953** G. G. SIMPSON *Major Features of Evolution* ix. 282 Almost any case in which size, structure, or habit..is carried to extremes may be cited as hypertely. *Ibid.* 287 Many of the characters commonly designated as hypertelic are striking secondary sexual characters. **1965** B. E. FREEMAN tr. *Vandel's Biospeleol.* xi. 168 Hypertely represents the end of a long orthogenetic evolution.

hypertensin (həipəɹte·nsin). *Biochem.* [f. *HYPERTENS(ION, -IVE *a.* + -IN[1].] Either of two polypeptides, of which one (*hypertensin I*) is formed in the blood by the action of renin on a protein (hypertensinogen), and the other (*hypertensin II*) is derived from it by the loss of two amino-acid residues, causes a rise in blood pressure, and stimulates the secretion of aldosterone; also, analogous polypeptides in animals. Now usually called *angiotensin*.

1939 J. M. MUÑOZ et al. in *Nature* 9 Dec. 980/1 This substance, which we name hypertensin, is different from adrenalin, tyramin, pitressin and urohypertensin. **1954** *Jrnl. Exper. Med.* XCIX. 282 Two types of hypertensin have been demonstrated... The first type..has been designated hypertensin I. It can be rapidly converted to a second, approximately equally pressor compound, hypertensin II. **1956** *Nature* 17 Mar. 527/2 The isolation and purification of a hypertensin peptide, resulting from the action of rabbit renin on ox serum. **1959** A. WHITE et al. *Princ. Biochem.* (ed. 2) xxx. 750 Hypertensin I preparations of slightly different composition have been described, depending on the sources of the renin and the substrate used. *Ibid.*, Hypertensin has also been called angiotonin. A uniform nomenclature has been proposed which would designate this compound as angiotensin.

Hence **hy:pertensi·nogen** [ad. F. *hypertensinogène* (E. Braun-Menendez 1940, in *Compt. Rend. de la Soc. de Biol.* CXXXIV. 489): see *-OGEN], a globulin produced by the liver and present in blood, from which hypertensin I may be liberated by renin.

1941 *Amer. Jrnl. Physiol.* CXXXV. 214 Braun-Menendez has preferred the term hypertensinogen, which implies that it is the substrate on which renin acts. **1965** *New Scientist* 25 Nov. 561/3 Kidney cells, in the presence of a poor blood flow.., secreted an enzyme called renin which converted a normal constituent of plasma (hypertensinogen) into a new substance (hypertensin).

hypertension (həipəɹte·nʃən). [f. HYPER- 5 + TENSION *sb.*] **1.** *Med.* Abnormally or excessively high 'tension' or pressure of a bodily fluid. **a.** Of arterial blood; *essential hypertension*, hypertension that has no apparent cause and cannot be explained as a consequence or symptom of some other lesion.

1893 *Brit. Med. Jrnl.* 4 Nov. 997/1 'Hypertension' and 'hypotension' are regarded not as indications, but as *mala in se.* **1927** *Physiol. Rev.* VII. 464 More recent writers have coined the name 'essential hypertension'. **1955** G. W. PICKERING *High Blood Pressure* vi. 130 By current practice which takes not a very high figure, such as 150/100, as the lower limit of hypertension, essential hypertension becomes by far the commonest form of hypertension. **1957** *New Scientist* 9 May 23/1 Hypertension causes one in every four deaths in the United States. **1966** WRIGHT & SYMMERS *Systemic Path.* I. iii. 106/1 The hypertension sometimes found in patients with hyperthyroidism is usually limited to elevation of the systolic pressure (systolic hypertension).

b. Of the intra-ocular fluid.

1918 R. H. ELLIOT *Glaucoma: Textbk. for Student* v. 303 The treatment of established glaucoma. In these cases the hypertension is commonly associated with evidence of ocular congestion. **1969** DUKE-ELDER & JAY in S. Duke-Elder *Syst. Ophthalm.* XI. ix. 630 In some cases the rise in the intra-ocular pressure has been slight and transient, to some extent possibly because the formation of aqueous may have been inhibited by the hypertension itself in a physiological compensatory mechanism.

2. A state of great (nervous or emotional) tension.

1936 *Times Educ. Suppl.* 28 Nov. 429/3 In every such case the nervous instability and hypertension should be treated by relaxation and psychological readjustment. **1947** *Year Bk. Arts in N.Z.* III. 152 Mind burst out... Man's understanding tangled, ripped. Extremes are too much with us and the hypertensions. **1953** J. MASTERS *Lotus & Wind* vii. 101 The opportunity for which she had been tensely waiting was upon her. In a few minutes, as this hypertension and ruthlessness faded in her, it would be gone. **1972** D. HASTON *In High Places* xii. 140 Flying out of Katmandu, I felt really pleased at having a chance to come back so quickly...There was friendliness all around; urgency to do things didn't seem to exist. None of the hypertensions of the West. A relaxing atmosphere.

hypertensive (həipəɹte·nsiv), *a.* and *sb. Med.* [f. prec. + -IVE.] **A.** *adj.* Of, exhibiting, or associated with hypertension, esp. of the blood; tending to raise the blood pressure.

1904 T. C. JANEWAY *Clin. Study Blood-Pressure* vii. 221 The bath-treatment of typhoid fever seems to have as distinct an effect on the blood-pressure curve... I cannot but feel that this hypertensive effect is evidence of an action on the vaso-motor system. **1918** *Endocrinology* II. 94 In case of the more strongly hypertensive extracts, kidney dilation and diuresis, together with augmented blood pressure, occur as the primary reaction. **1939** D. M. DUNLOP *Textbk. Med. Treatm.* 654 Digitalis..does not raise blood pressure in the hypertensive patient. **1954** S. DUKE-ELDER *Parsons' Dis. Eye* (ed. 12) xiv. 212 This involves a rise determined..by the difficulty experienced by the sticky albuminous aqueous in escaping through the filtration channels at the angle of the anterior chamber (hypertensive iridocyclitis). **1956** *Nature* 17 Mar. 523/2 These [compounds] are highly effective in lowering blood pressure and relieving certain hypertensive symptoms. **1971** *Brit. Med. Bull.* XXVII. 39/1 Hypertensive heart disease, diagnosed on electrocardiographic and radiographic criteria, is also more common among negroes.

B. *ellipt.* as *sb.* A person with arterial hypertension.

1939 D. M. DUNLOP *Textbk. Med. Treatm.* 652 Many hypertensives tend to over-eat. **1961** *Lancet* 2 Sept. 510/2 The systolic and diastolic blood-pressures were slightly higher in the hypertensives' sons. **1972** *Daily Tel.* 22 Nov. 13/8 In hypertensives, prostaglandins can lower the blood pressure.

hyperthermia (həipəɹþə̄·ɹmiă). *Med.* Also in anglicized form **hyperthermy** (həi·pəɹþəɹmi) (*rare*). [f. HYPER- 5 + Gr. θέρμη heat + -IA[1].] The condition of having a body temperature substantially above the normal either as a result of natural causes or artificially induced (e.g. for therapeutic purposes).

1886 *Syd. Soc. Lex.*, Hyperthermy. **1887** A. M. BROWN *Contrib. Animal Alkaloids* 143 Intoxication by the extractive matters is accompanied by hyperthermia. **1898** *Nature* 24 Nov. 95 Researches on lesions of the nervous centres produced by hyperthermy. **1921** F. A. WELBY tr. *Luciani's Human Physiol.* V. ii. 82 Billroth..found that the temperature rose to 42·2° after fracture of the sixth cervical vertebra; in a similar case Simon observed a hyperthermia of 44°. **1935** *Jrnl. Amer. Med. Assoc.* 18 May 1788/2 As with all other forms of treatment for chronic infectious arthritis, the results of hyperthermia depend to a marked extent on the duration and activity of the disease. **1941** *Virginia Med. Monthly* Mar. 158/1 It was decided to give the patient another period of hyperthermy, but in view of the attack of substernal pain a medical check-up was requested. **1971** *New Scientist* 15 July 133/2 The gazelles..cannot withstand desiccation to the extent that camels do, and do not show the same degree of hyperthermia. **1971** L. B. ROWELL in E. Simonson *Physiol. Work Capacity & Fatigue* vii. 149 Hyperthermia will be accompanied by high rates of sweat loss and dehydration.

So **hyperthe·rmic** *a.* [cf. Gr. ὑπέρθερμος over-warm], of, or exhibiting hyperthermia.

1896 [in Dict. s.v. HYPER- IV]. **1898** W. S. L. BARLOW *Man. Gen. Path.* x. 434 The symptoms presented by a hyperthermic animal when its temperature is reaching a dangerous height are those of severe distress, respiration and pulse are accelerated, and the animal lies outstretched. **1948** [see *HYPOTHERMIC *a.*].

hyperthy·roidism. *Med.* [f. HYPER- 5 + THYROID *a.* (*sb.*) + -ISM.] A condition in

which the thyroid gland produces more hormone than normal, resulting in an increased rate of metabolism, often with wasting of muscle and loss of weight together with restlessness and emotional instability.

1900 DORLAND *Med. Dict.* 311/1 Hyperthyroidism. **1909** G. DOCK in Osler & McCrae *Syst. Med.* VI. xvii. 431 Hyperthyroidism..seems to be the cause of the exophthalmos. **1912** *Med. Ann.* 3 Sleeplessness following..fevers, hyperthyroidism, and hysteria. **1961** L. MARTIN *Clinical Endocrinol.* (ed. 3) i. 22 A goitre and signs of mild hyperthyroidism are not uncommon [in gigantism]. **1970** S. GROLLMAN *Human Body* (ed. 2) xvi. 507 The most common form of hyperthyroidism, resulting from a diffuse increase in thyroid tissue, is known as exophthalmic goiter, Graves' disease, or Basedow's disease.

Hence **hyperthy·roid, -thyroi·dic** *adjs.*

1916 *Internat. Jrnl. Surg.* XXIX. 312 (*heading*) The etiology of the exophthalmos in hyperthyroid goitre. **1916** *Med. Times* (N.Y.) 7 July 207/1 An impression is given by the hypothyroidic eye which is just the reverse of that made by the typical hyperthyroidic, or exophthalmic organ. **1968** *Listener* 18 July 70/1, I had recently been diagnosed as hyperthyroidic. **1971** N. R. ALPERT *Cardiac Hypertrophy* 55 The pumping function of the hyperthyroid heart.

hypertonia (həipəɹtōu·niă). *Med.* Also in anglicized form **hypertony** (həipə̄·ɹtŏni) (*rare*). [mod.L., f. HYPER- 5 + Gr. τόν-ος TONE *sb.* + -IA¹.] The condition (in muscle or muscular tissue) of being hypertonic.

1842 DUNGLISON *Dict. Med. Sci.* (ed. 3) 368/1 Hypertonia. **1881** J. ROSS *Treat. Dis. Nervous Syst.* I. I. v. 178 The condition of motor excess, or of increased tonus, may be called hypertony. **1905** *Med.-Chir. Trans.* LXXXVIII. 212 The arterial hypertonia is to be regarded as a result of the greater strain thrown on the circulatory mechanism. **1914** A. MORISON *Sensory & Motor Disorders Heart* v. 203 Exaggerated tonic cardiac action tends to be succeeded by..a minus quantity. Hypertonia necessarily yields to hypotonia. **1933** W. R. BRAIN *Dis. Nervous Syst.* i. 8 Not all muscle-groups exhibit hypertonia in equal degree in hemiplegia. **1962** *Lancet* 27 Jan. 222/1 She was re-examined..and found to have variable and bizarre hypertonia of the jaw, tongue, and neck muscles.

hypertonic (həipəɹtǫ·nik), *a.* [f. HYPER- 5 + TONIC *a.*] **1.** *Med.* Exhibiting or characterized by excessive tone or tension (in muscle or muscular tissue).

1855 R. G. MAYNE *Expos. Lex. Med. Sci.* (1860) 484/1 *Hypertonicus*, of or belonging to hypertonia: hypertonic. **1886** *Lancet* 13 Mar. 486/2 For convenience I describe the group of symptoms under the term 'hyper-tonic paresis', a symptomatic nomenclature which commits to no theory. **1907** W. RUSSELL *Arterial Hypertonus* i. 3 The degree of contraction may exceed the limits of normal variation, and when it does the term hypertonic contraction, or merely arterial contraction, will be used here. **1933** W. R. BRAIN *Dis. Nervous Syst.* i. 8 Immediately following a capsular haemorrhage the paralysed limbs are completely flaccid... After a variable interval..tone gradually returns to the affected muscles and they ultimately become hypertonic or 'spastic'. **1966** *McGraw-Hill Encycl. Sci. & Technol.* X. 528/1 When the stretch reflex is absent, the muscle is hypotonic or flaccid; when stretch reflexes are exaggerated..the muscles are hypertonic or spastic.

2. *Physiol.* Of a solution: having a higher osmotic pressure than some particular solution (usually that in a cell, or a bodily fluid). Const. *to*.

1895 *Jrnl. Physiol.* XVIII. 107 None of the water is taken up from hypertonic or isotonic solutions. **1936** A. P. MATHEWS *Princ. Biochem.* xxxiv. 364 If the solution have an osmotic pressure greater than that of the blood, it is said to be hypertonic to the blood. **1951** WHITBY & HYNES *Med. Bacteriol.* (ed. 5) vi. 73 The optimum salt concentration is usually near the range of isotonicity to body cells; markedly hypertonic saline diminishes the reaction. **1970** A. F. BRADING in E. Bülbring et al. *Smooth Muscle* vi. 172 Tissues will swell in hypotonic solutions, and shrink in hypertonic ones.

hypertonicity (həi:pəɹtǫ̆ni·siti). [f. prec. + -ITY.] The condition of being hypertonic.

a. *Med.* Of muscle or muscular tissue (see *HYPERTONIC *a.* 1); = *HYPERTONIA.

1886 *Brain* IX. 231 A condition of extreme functional over-activity of the ganglion cells of the anterior cornua of the cord and medulla, causing hyper-tonicity of the entire muscular system. **1923** J. F. H. DALLY *High Blood Pressure* v. 64 Arterial hypertonicity, in larger or smaller areas, is met with in a host of disorders. **1949** *Jrnl. Neurophysiol.* XII. 371 Hypertonicity of muscles with hyperactive deep reflexes or clonus.

b. *Physiol.* Of a solution (see *HYPERTONIC *a.* 2); the extent to which a solution has higher osmotic pressure than some other.

1896 T. L. STEDMAN *20th Cent. Pract.* VII. 284 The hypertonicity of the plasma is easily calculated. **1906** *Amer. Jrnl. Physiol.* XV. 359 When the hypertonicity is slight, the degree of recovery is relatively greater than in the case of the more concentrated solutions. **1963** E. ERNST *Biophysics Striated Muscle* (ed. 2) 131 The next experiments were planned in such a way that the loss of water [from the muscle] due to the hypertonicity of the medium should be balanced by water taken up by the swelling elicited by lactic acid.

hypertonus (həipəɹtōu·nǒs). [f. HYPER- 5 + TONUS.] **1.** *Ophthalm.* A state of increased pressure of the intra-ocular fluid; = *HYPERTENSION 1 b. Now *rare*.

1891 F. P. FOSTER *Med. Dict.* III. 1944/1 *Hypertonus*, that condition of the eye in which the intra-ocular tension is increased, sometimes without any organic disease being present. **1918** R. H. ELLIOT *Glaucoma: Textbk. for Student* v. 300 It would appear, then, that the thrombotic type of glaucoma possesses a very distinct inflammatory element; it thus comes into line with the hypertonus which we find secondary..to intra-ocular tumours.

2. *Med.* = *HYPERTONIA.

1904 *Rev. Neurol. & Psychiatry* II. 775 The arms showed the typical muscular rigidity (hypertonus) of paralysis agitans, while the legs were markedly hypotonic. **1923** J. F. H. DALLY *High Blood Pressure* v. 65 To some extent raised blood pressure may be differentiated from arterial hypertonus by instrumental methods. **1924** *Brain* XLVII. 333 General hypertonus may, however, be inferred from a slight increase of the tendon reflexes. **1950** *Physiol. Rev.* XXX. 466 After the somnolence and plastic hypertonus had passed, marked poverty of movement still persisted. **1971** RASCH & BURKE *Kinesiology* (ed. 4) iv. 83 The limb is then said to be spastic. In man such hypertonus occurs only in the antigravity muscles.

hyperu·rbanism. [f. HYPER- 5 + URBANISM.] Extreme urbanism; *spec.* in *Philol.*, the manner of speech arising from an effort to avoid provincialism; a hypercorrect form of speech or phrase resulting from this. So **hyperu·rban** *a.*, exhibiting hyperurbanism; **hyperu:rbaniza·tion** *sb.*

1925 P. RADIN tr. *Vendryès's Lang.* ii. 49 Hyper-urbanism consists in those excesses brought about by consideration for correct speech. *Ibid.*, *Plaustrum* for *plostrum*, *cauda* for *coda*... These are hyper-urbanisms. **1928** L. BLOOMFIELD in *Language* IV. iv. 286 Hyper-urban forms occur, e.g., *foot* pronounced as [fy:t] instead of [fu:t]. **1933** —— *Lang.* xviii. 309 We may take *cōda* to be the older of the two Latin forms, and *cauda* to be a hyper-urban (over-elegant) variant. *Ibid.* xix. 330 This flavor of the [y:]-variants appears strikingly in the shape of hyper-urbanisms: in using the elegant [y:], the speaker sometimes substitutes it where it is entirely out of place. **1935** *Language* XI. ii. 106 Social climbers betray themselves by hyper-urbanisms, such as [a] in *bass* or *lass*. **1937** *Amer. Speech* XII. 175 The women who wear gloves on the most informal occasions have probably acquired the habit of never forgetting them, and so-called hyper-urbanization in speech as well as in dress, often springs from..a sense of social insecurity. **1940** C. C. FRIES *Amer. Eng. Grammar* vi. 94 There appeared in the Standard English materials some uses of *whom* which should probably be looked upon as hyperurbanisms. **1951** TRAGER & SMITH *Outl. Eng. Struct.* iii. 85 The hyperurbanism *Between you and I* for the standard *Between you and me*.

hyperventilate (həipəɹve·ntilēit), *v.* *Physiol.* [f. HYPER- 5 + VENTILATE *v.*, or back-formation from next.] **a.** *intr.* To breathe deeply or rapidly.

1931 *Jrnl. Neurol. & Psychopath.* XII. 14 It is..of much interest to ascertain to which changes the epileptic organism reacts with a seizure when the patient hyperventilates. **1961** *Flight* LXXX. 760/1 An experienced pilot who had..been told..that he hyperventilated and should regulate his breathing. **1968** *Everybody's* (Austral.) 12 June 31/4 Ron Taylor, perhaps Australia's greatest underwater expert, advises: Don't hyperventilate to the stage where you become dizzy. **1970** *Sci. Amer.* Feb. 56/1 They do not need to hyperventilate as much as lowlanders do when the latter go to high altitudes.

b. *trans.* To produce hyperventilation in.

1931 *Jrnl. Neurol. & Psychopath.* XII. 15 Our method has been..to hyperventilate the person in question with two or three of the methods. **1953** *Physiol. Rev.* XXXIII. 447 Brown et al...hyperventilated subjects for 24 hours in a body respirator at rates just under those producing tetany. **1968** C. OSBORNE tr. *Stenuit's Dolphin* vii. 119 When a..skin-diver hyperventilates his lungs by deep breathing.., he loads the haemoglobin of his blood with a reserve of oxygen.

hy:perventila·tion. *Physiol.* [f. HYPER- 5 + VENTILATION.] An increased or excessive exposure of the lungs to oxygen, resulting in a more rapid loss of carbon dioxide from the blood; the action of bringing this about (in oneself, by deep or rapid breathing, or in another individual).

1928 *Canad. Med. Assoc. Jrnl.* LVIII. 210/2 Such a 'hyperventilation' tetany occurring under clinical conditions has been but seldom reported. **1932** *Arch. Neurol. & Psychiatry* XXVIII. 574 We injected into each animal 0·1 mg. of strychnine sulphate per kilogram of body weight and started hyperventilation after..twenty to thirty minutes. **1951** H. DAVSON *Textbk. Gen. Physiol.* vi. 124 Special mechanisms for heat dissipation such as sweating or hyperventilation of the lungs. **1961** *Lancet* 26 Aug. 474/2 Another cause of fainting, more often related to emotional than to physical states, is hyperventilation. **1965** *Handbk. Physiol.: Circulation* (Amer. Physiol. Soc.) III. liii. 1889/2 It is not at all difficult by hyperventilation to cause a severe gaseous alkalosis with dizziness, blurred vision, mental confusion, numbness of extremities,..and muscle spasm, rarely going on to..convulsions and unconsciousness. **1970** *Sci. Jrnl.* June 84/1 The noticeable hyperventilation (heavy breathing) which occurs at orgasm shows up clearly on the tracing.

hy·phenate, *sb.* [f. *HYPHENATED *a.* 2.] A hyphenated person.

1916 *Yorks. Post* 4 Mar. 6/7 The Hyphenates throughout the country are greatly excited. **1920** *Glasgow Herald* 27 Nov. 6 This political hyphenate or composite is desirous of running a Home Rule for Scotland campaign. **1922** *Contemp. Rev.* Dec. 693 The 'hyphenates'—Irish and Germans, Poles and Russians and Italians—..joined in the condemnation of Wilsonism.

hyphenated, *a.* Add: **2.** Applied to persons (or, by extension, their activities) born in one country but naturalized citizens of another, their nationality being designated by a hyphenated form, e.g. *Anglo-American, Irish-American*; hence, to a person whose patriotic allegiance is assumed to be divided. Also in extended use. orig. *U.S.*

1893 FARMER & HENLEY *Slang* III. 386/2 *Hyphenated American*, a naturalised citizen, as German-Americans, Irish-Americans, and the like. **1900** *Daily News* 15 Aug. 3/1 My opponents were of the hyphenated variety—Dutch-Americans and Irish-Americans predominating. **1904** *Westm. Gaz.* 3 Jan. 3/2 American politics, where men who call themselves Irish-Americans, German-Americans, Dutch-Americans, and so on, are contemptuously referred to as 'hyphenated Americans'. **1907** *Nation* (N.Y.) 7 Nov. 410 Some of these hyphenated American journals. **1915** *Lit. Digest* 4 Sept. 462/1 Hyphenated residents will continue to insist that American newspapers should be strictly neutral. **1948** *Manch. Guardian Weekly* 3 June 7/1 'Hyphenated Americans'—undigested immigrant stock. **1965** B. SWEET-ESCOTT *Baker St. Irreg.* i. 37 It was thought that, with the whole of western Europe under Nazi domination, hyphenated Americans might provide recruits for work in occupied territory. **1973** *Times* 17 Oct. 6/8 This did not go down well with the Greek community here [*sc.* in the U.S.], or with other groups of 'hyphenated Americans'.

hyphening (həi·fəniŋ), *vbl. sb.* [f. HYPHEN *v.* + -ING¹.] The action of the vb. HYPHEN.

1929 *Conc. Oxf. Dict.* p. ix, A consequence of this reformed hyphening is that the presence of a hyphen in such a compound [as *tipsy cake*] assures the reader that the word-stress falls on the first part.

hyphenism (həi·fəniz'm). *U.S.* [f. HYPHEN + -ISM; cf. *HYPHENATED *a.* 2.] The state of being a hyphenated American; the attitude or conduct involved or implied by this.

1930 P. W. SLOSSON *Great Crusade* (1931) xi. 288 The years..so marked by hyphenism and the echoes of Old World feuds.

hyphomycetes (həi:foməisī·tīz, -ts), *sb. pl.* Also in *sing.* form **hyphomycete.** *Bot.* [mod.L. (E. M. Fries *Systema Mycologicum* (1821) I. p. xxx), f. Gr. ὑφή web + μύκητες fungi.] Imperfect fungi of the group Hyphomycetes; filamentous moulds bearing naked, asexual spores.

1836 M. J. BERKELEY in J. E. Smith *Eng. Flora* V. II. 328 Hyphomycetes... Sporidiferous flocci naked (not included in a uterus or seated on a proper receptacle). **1857** —— *Introd. Cryptogamic Bot.* 297 The species contained in the division *Hyphomycetes*, consist of Fungi which, like *Mucorini*, are known under the common name of moulds. **1887** H. E. F. GARNSEY tr. *A. de Bary's Compar. Morphol. & Biol. Fungi* i. 1 In the more simple Fungi the branched hypha alone constitutes the thallus; such forms are termed Hyphomycetes, Filamentous Fungi (Fadenpilze), or Haplomycetes. **1930** C. THOM *Penicillia* iv. 24 A hyphomycete genus such as Penicillium..is an aggregation of species with a common type of asexual fruiting. *Ibid.* xi. 147 Penicillium is characterized and discussed here as a 'form-genus' in the great aggregate of form genera commonly known as the Hyphomycetes. **1971** M. B. ELLIS *Dematiaceous Hyphomycetes* 7 About 50 per cent of the specimens sent to the Commonwealth Mycological Institute are hyphomycetes.

hypnago·gically, *adv.* [f. HYPNAGOGIC *a.*: see -ICALLY.] In a hypnagogic manner.

1957 P. MCKELLAR *Imagination & Thinking* iii. 40 Confusion of hypnagogically imaged music with the noises of reality also occurred, and more than one of our subjects descended the stairs believing that the wireless had been left on.

hypnoanalysis (hipnoˌănæ·lisis). Also **hypno-analysis.** [f. HYPNO- (taken as combining form of *hypnosis*) + ANALYSIS.] Psychoanalysis performed while the subject is under hypnosis; psychotherapy that combines psychoanalysis with hypnosis.

1920 J. A. HADFIELD in H. C. Miller *Functional Nerve Dis.* v. 71 The method which I venture to name 'Hypno-analysis' consists simply in hypnotizing the patient and inducing him to speak of his troubles. **1949** KOESTLER *Insight & Outlook* x. 146 The less drastic forms of psychotherapy like psycho-, narco-, and hypnoanalysis..are all primarily means of releasing functional components of the psychoneural apparatus which had been repressed by faulty integration. **1963** W. S. KROGER *Clin. & Exper. Hypnosis* xlvii. 323/1 Hypnoanalysis is particularly indicated for psychoneurotics who do not respond to brief hypnotherapeutic procedures.

Hence **hypnoa·nalyst**, one who uses hypnoanalysis; **hy:pnoanaly·tic** *a.*, of or involving hypnoanalysis.

1922 *Jrnl. Abnormal Psychol.* XVI. 344 (*heading*) A hypnoanalytic study of two cases of war neurosis. **1945** *Diseases Nervous Syst.* VI. 374/1 The hypnoanalyst..is thrust into a form of relationship with his patient that transcends even the transference situation obtaining in routine psychoanalysis. **1947** LECRON & BORDEAUX

Hypnotism Today xiii. 229 Basically, hypnoanalytic treatment is modified psychoanalysis with inclusion of hypnotism for brevity. **1960** I. BENNETT *Delinquent & Neurotic Children* iv. 124 Lindner (1944) undertook the hypno-analytic treatment of a criminal psychopath. **1963** W. S. KROGER *Clin. & Exper. Hypnosis* xlvii. 323/2 The process utilizes free associations, dreams, analyses and re-collections, all of which are interpreted by the hypno-analyst.

hypnogogic, var. HYPNAGOGIC *a.*

1906 E. SALTUS *Vanity Square* II. i. 154 The hypnogogic hallucinations continue. **1933** *Scrutiny* I. 380 In this hypnogogic state the mind makes no selection. **1962** *New Scientist* 2 Aug. 267/3 The next section contains a quantity of fascinating material on such topics as..'night jerks', which occur in the hypnogogic state (his spelling 'hypnagogic' is not a useful innovation). **1972** [see *HYPNOPOMPIC *a.*].

hypnoid (hi·pnoid), *a.*² *Psychol.* [a. G. *hypnoid* (Breuer & Freud 1893, in *Neurol. Centralblatt* XII. II. 43), f. Gr. ὕπν-ος sleep + -OID.] Applied to a state of consciousness characterized by heightened suggestibility or dissociation, such as occurs in hysterical conditions.

1898 B. SIDIS *Psychol. of Suggestion* xxiii. 234 By the term 'hypnoid' I indicate the coexistence of two or more fully independent functioning constellations of moments-consciousness, such as is presented in the phenomena of automatic writing and of hysteria. **1902** W. JAMES *Var. Relig. Exper.* xvi. 413 To the medical mind these ecstasies signify nothing but suggested and imitated hypnoid states. **1924** J. RIVIERE et al. tr. *Freud's Coll. Papers* I. 34 Splitting of consciousness..exists in a rudimentary fashion in every hysteria and..the tendency to this dissociation—and therewith to the production of abnormal states of consciousness, which may be included under the term 'hypnoid'—is a fundamental manifestation of this neurosis. **1951** R. BRUN *Gen. Theory Neuroses* III. 333 Fantasies in hypnoid conditions, such as constantly occur in hysteria, will even more readily produce regressive excitations in the most disparate organs.

Also **hypnoi·dal** *a.*, in the same sense.

1898 B. SIDIS *Psychol. of Suggestion* xxiii. 239 In hypnoidal states past, outlived experiences heave up into the upper consciousness. **1921** *Discovery* Nov. 294/1 A similar [half-waking] state can be produced artificially and is called light hypnosis or the hypnoidal state. **1970** R. R. MONROE *Episodic Behavioral Disorders* ii. 45 Abrupt alteration in awareness, such as [is] seen in petit mal or hypnoidal states.

hypnopædia (hipnopī·diă). Also **-pedia.** [f. HYPNO- + Gr. παιδεία education.] The exposure of a sleeping subject to lessons played on a radio, tape recorder, etc.; teaching or learning by this method, 'sleep-learning'.

1932 A. HUXLEY *Brave New World* ii. 27 The principle of sleep-teaching, or hypnopædia, had been discovered. **1959** *Listener* 26 Feb. 385/1 Subliminal persuasion, hypnopaedia, brain-washing. **1969** *New Scientist* 30 Jan. 216/1 Sleep learning or hypnopedia, as its practitioners prefer to call it, is now acquiring a new status among Soviet teaching circles. **1971** *Nature* 24 Sept. 290/1 The opening chapters dispel misconceptions many people have about hypnopaedia.

Hence **hypnopæ·dic** *a.*, of or involving hypnopædia; **hypnopæ·dically** *adv.*

1932 A. HUXLEY *Brave New World* iv. 82 The sort of words that suddenly make you jump..they seem so new and exciting even though they're about something hypnopædically obvious. *Ibid.* x. 173 Listening unconsciously to hypnopædic lessons in hygiene and sociability. **1970** *Globe & Mail* (Toronto) 26 Sept. 7/1 The Russians are also learning..how to avoid the fatigue brought on by repeated hypnopedic sessions.

hypnopompic (hipnopǫ·mpik), *a.* [f. HYPNO- + Gr. πομπ-ή sending away (f. πέμπειν to send) + -IC.] That accompanies the process of awakening from sleep.

a **1901** F. W. H. MYERS *Human Personality* (1903) I. p. xvii, To similar illusions accompanying the *departure* of sleep, as when a dream-figure persists for a few moments into waking life, I have given the name *hypnopompic*. *Ibid.* iv. 125 Equally remarkable are the hypnopompic pictures. **1925** *Proc. Soc. Psychical Res.* XXXV. 331 Of these four examples only the first is hypnagogic; Herschel's was a day-vision (at the breakfast-table), and the other two are hypnopompic. **1972** *Science* 16 June 1203/3 The ASC's [*sc.* altered states of consciousness] experienced by almost all ordinary people are dreaming states and the hypnogogic and hypnopompic states, the transitional states between sleeping and waking.

Hypnos (hi·pnǫs). [Gr. Ὕπνος (ὕπνος sleep) (see below).] Name of the god of sleep in Greek mythology.

1906 T. E. LAWRENCE *Home Lett.* (1954) 40 It is eleven o'clock now and I ought to have thoughts on Hypnos. **1938** W. DE LA MARE *Memory* 38 What of the strange world that teems—Where brooding Hypnos reigns—with dreams? **1970** *Oxf. Classical Dict.* (ed. 2) 535/2 Throughout antiquity Hypnos was usually thought of as a winged youth who touches the foreheads of the tired with a branch..or pours sleep-inducing liquid from a horn.

hypnotherapy (hipnoþe·răpi). [f. HYPNO- (taken as combining form of *hypnosis*) + THERAPY.] Psychotherapy that involves the use of hypnotism.

1897 *Lippincott's Med. Dict.* 496/1 *Hypnotherapy*, the therapeutic use of hypnotism. **1907** *Alienist & Neurologist* XXVIII. 447 Constant current..cephalic galvanization..is a valuable addition to hypnotherapy, medical or otherwise, in psychiatry. **1931** A. EILOART tr. *Heyer's Hypnosis & Hypnotherapy* xiii. 204 Occasionally impotence or spasm of the vagina..are suitable subjects for hypnotherapy. **1947** LECRON & BORDEAUX *Hypnotism Today* xii. 196 Direct persuasive suggestion under hypnosis was the type of hypnotherapy used by the old medical practitioners of hypnotism. **1958** *Sunday Times* 17 Aug. 15/5 Hypnotherapy has a rightful place in medical treatment. **1960** *Spectator* 25 Nov. 838 Scientific training is attempted in the..two-year Hypnotherapy Centre course.

Hence **hypnothe·rapist,** one who employs hypnotherapy. Also **hy:pnotherapeu·tic** *a.*, of or involving hypnotherapy; **hy:pnotherapeu·tically** *adv.*

1892 *Jrnl. Mental Sci.* XXXVIII. 522 (*heading*) Hypno-therapeutic treatment. **1944** BRENMAN & GILL *Hypnotherapy* (1947) iv. 79 Erickson..who frequently collaborates with psychoanalysts in his hypnotherapeutic work, often utilizes the insights of psychoanalysis. **1958** *Spectator* 15 Aug. 236/1 Hypnotherapist and hypnoanalyst. **1963** Hypnotherapeutic [see *HYPNOANALYSIS]. **1963** W. S. KROGER *Clin. & Exper. Hypnosis* xlvii. 323/2 Age-regression was hypnotherapeutically induced in several patients as an emergency measure to prevent suicide. **1970** *Daily Tel.* 8 June 11/4 Hypnotherapists have found that migraine has psychological causes.

hypo, *sb.*² (Earlier example.)

1855 [see PRINT *sb.* 13].

hypo (həi·po), *sb.*³ *slang.* [Abbrev. of HYPODERMIC.] A hypodermic needle or injection; a drug-addict.

1904 *San Francisco Chron. Suppl.* 30 Oct. 4 (caption to picture showing a morphine addict) The 'Hypo'. **1925** *Writer's Monthly* June 486/2 Hypo, a hypodermic syringe or a hypodermic needle. **1926** J. BLACK *You can't Win* xii. 159 'Vag these two hypos', said the cop to the desk man. **1936** G. K. ZIPF *Psycho-Biol. of Lang.* ii. 31 *Hypo* may be a truncation of a *hypodermic injection*..or it may be an abbreviation of '*hyposulfite of soda*'. **1942** *R.A.F. Jrnl.* 3 Oct. 30 Horrible rumours about the ease with which a hypo. needle will break. **1953** W. BURROUGHS *Junkie* (1972) ii. 21 An eyedropper is easier to use than a regular hypo, especially for giving yourself vein shots. **1956** H. GOLD *Man who was not with It* (1965) ii. 18 He..dragged his fingers along the little scabs from the hypo. **1973** J. WAINWRIGHT *Devil you Don't* 89 The night medic ..held the loaded hypo.

hypo (həi·po), *v. slang.* [f. *HYPO *sb.*³] To administer a hypodermic injection (to). Also *fig.* Hence **hy·poing** *vbl. sb.*

1925 *Flynn's* 7 Feb. 489/2 *Hypo*, to use a hypodermic syringe. **1945** *Variety* 24 Oct. 4/4 (*heading*) Many new pix to hypo bond preems [i.e. new pictures offered as inducements for bond premieres]. **1956** C. D. SIMAK *Strangers in Universe* (1958) 14 Apparently not too dangerous. Not with every single soul hypoed and immunized and hormoned to his eyebrows. **1960** *Time* (Dom. ed.) 25 Jan. 90/3 Because of continuing hypo-ing, his arms and legs become abscessed. **1968** *Listener* 31 Oct. 567/3 This impulse is very much hypo'd up during an election year.

hypo-. Add: **II.** (In the following words *e* often replaces *æ*, *œ*, esp. in U.S. usage; the alternative spelling is not given for each word individually.) **hypalgesia** (-dʒī·siă) *Med.* [Gr. ἄλγησις sense of pain], diminished sensitivity to pain, hypalgia; so **hypalge·sic** *a.*, exhibiting or tending to produce hypalgesia; **hypoaci·dity** *Physiol.*, a deficiency of acid constituents, esp. in the gastric juice; **hypoacti·vity** *Physiol.*, diminished activity, *esp.* diminished secretory activity of a gland; **hypoæsthesia** (həi:po,esþī·ziă) *Path.* = HYPÆSTHESIA; hence **hypoæsthe·tic** *a.*; **hy:poalbuminæ·mia** *Physiol.* [Gr. αἷμα blood], an abnormally low concentration of albumins in the blood; **hypoalge·sia** *Med.*, = **hypalgesia*; **hypocalcæmia** (-kælsī·miă) *Physiol.* [CALC(IUM + Gr. αἷμα blood], an abnormally low concentration of calcium in the blood; hence **hypocalcæ·mic** *a.*; **hypoca·pnia** *Physiol.* [Gr. καπνός smoke], an abnormally low concentration of carbon dioxide in the blood; **hy:pochloræ·mia** *Physiol.*, an abnormally low concentration of chlorides in the blood; **hy:pochlorhy·dria** *Physiol.* [CHLORHYDR(IC *a.*], an abnormally low concentration of hydrochloric acid in the gastric juice; so **hy:pochlorhy·dric** *a.*; **hypocho·rdal** *a. Zool.* [CHORD *sb.*¹], ventral to the notochord or spinal cord; **hypoesthesia,** var. *hypoæsthesia* above; **hypoeute·ctic** *a.*, (of an alloy of iron) containing a lower proportion of carbon than the eutectic composition (i.e. less than about 4·3%); (in quot. 1902 = **hypoeutectoid*, *eutectoid* itself not having been coined at that date); **hypoeute·ctoid** *a.*, (of steel) containing a lower proportion of carbon than the eutectoid composition (i.e. less than about 0·8%); **hypofu·nction** *Med.*, diminished or insufficient activity or production (in a gland or other part of the body); so **hypofu·nctional** *a.*, **hypofu·nctioning** *vbl. sb.*; **hy:pogammaglo:bulinæ·mia** *Path.* [Gr. αἷμα blood], an abnormally low concentration of gamma globulins in the blood; also, a disorder of which this condition is characteristic; **hypoge·nitalism** *Path.*, hypogonadism; also, underdevelopment of the genitalia; **hypogeusia** (-giū·ziă) *Med.* [Gr. γεῦσις taste], diminished acuteness of the sense of taste; **hypoglycæ·mia** *Physiol.*, an abnormally low concentration of sugar in the blood; so **hypoglycæ·mic** *a.*, of or exhibiting hypoglycæmia; tending to reduce the blood-sugar level; **hypogo·nadism** *Path.*, the reduction or absence of gonadal activity, esp. of hormone secretion; so **hypogo·nadal** *a.*; **hypoischium** (-i·skiŏm) *Zool.* [ISCHIUM], a small cartilaginous or bony process that projects backwards from the ischial symphysis in the pelvic arch of many reptiles and some other vertebrates, supporting the ventral wall of the cloaca; hence **hypoi·schiac, -i·schial, -ischia·tic** *adjs.*; **hypokalæmia** (-kălī·miă), **-kaliæmia** (-kæli,ī·miă) *Physiol.* [mod.L. *kalium* potassium (see KALI) + Gr. αἷμα blood], = *hypopotassæmia* below; hence **hypokalæ·mic** *a.*; **hypokine·sia, -kine·sis** *Path.*, abnormally decreased muscular movement; **hy:poleucocyto·sis, -leukocyto·sis** *Path.* = *leucopenia* (s.v. LEUCO-); **hy:pomagnesæ·mia** *Physiol.* and *Vet. Sci.* [Gr. αἷμα blood], an abnormally low concentration of magnesium in the blood, important in cattle as the cause of grass tetany; hence **hy:pomagnesæ·mic** *a.*; **hypometa·bolism** *Physiol.*, metabolism at a low rate; **hy·pomorph** *Genetics* [Gr. μορφ-ή form], any allele which is functionally less effective than the corresponding wild-type allele; so **hypomo·rphic** *a.*; **hypomoti·lity** *Med.*, diminished movement, esp. of the stomach and intestines; **hyponatræ·mia** *Physiol.* [NATR(IUM + Gr. αἷμα blood], a lower than normal concentration of sodium in the blood; hence **hyponatræ·mic** *a.*; **hy:po-osmo·tic, hyposmo·tic** *adjs. Physiol.* = *HYPOTONIC *a.* 1; const. *to*; **hypophalangia** (-fălæ·ndʒiă), **-phalangism** (-fălæ·ndʒiz'm), **-phalangy** (-fæ·lăndʒi) *Med.* [L. *phalang-*: see PHALANX], the congenital absence of one or more digital phalanges; **hypopho·neme** [*PHONEME] *Linguistics*, in the terminology of stratificational grammar, a phonological unit (see quots.); so **hypophone·mic** *a.*, **hypophone·mically** *adv.*; **hypopho·ria** *Ophthalm.*, latent strabismus in which there is a tendency for one eye to be directed below the line of sight of the other; **hy:pophosphatæ·mia** *Physiol.* [Gr. αἷμα blood], an abnormally low concentration of phosphates in the blood; so **hy:pophosphatæ·mic** *a.*; **hy:pophosphata·sia** *Path.*, a familial congenital disease associated with an abnormally low level of alkaline phosphatase in the body and defective bone development; **hypopitu·itarism** *Path.* [PITUITAR(Y *a.* + -ISM], diminished hormone secretion by the pituitary body; hence **hypopitu·itary** *a.*, of, pertaining to, or affected with hypopituitarism; **hypopla·nkton,** plankton found in the layer of water directly above the bottom of the ocean; **hypopleu·ra, -pleu·ron** *Ent.* (pl. **-pleura**), the region on the thorax of Diptera underneath the metapleuron and above the middle and posterior coxæ; so **hypopleu·ral** *a.*; **hy·poploid** *a. Genetics* [*-PLOID], having one or a few chromosomes (orig. also chromosome fragments) missing from a haploid, diploid, triploid, etc., set; containing such cells; also as *sb.*, a hypoploid cell or individual; so **hy·poploidy,** the condition of being hypoploid; **hy:popotassæ·mia** *Physiol.* [Gr. αἷμα blood], an abnormally low concentration of potassium in the blood; so **hy:popotassæ·mic** *a.*; **hy:poproteinæ·mia** *Physiol.* [Gr. αἷμα blood], an abnormally low concentration of protein in the blood; so **hy:poproteinæ·mic** *a.*; **hy:poprothrombinæ·mia** *Med.* [Gr. αἷμα blood], an abnormally low concentration of prothrombin in the blood; a disorder so characterized; so **hy:poprothrombinæ·mic** *a.*; **hy·poscope** *Mil.* [-SCOPE, after *periscope*], a form of periscope for attachment to a rifle or

for use as a hand instrument; **hyposecre·tion,** diminished secretion; **hyposmotic:** see *hypo-osmotic* above; **hy:posthenu·ria** *Med.* [Gr. *σθέν-ος* strength + -URIA], the secretion of urine of abnormally low specific gravity; **hypotaurine** (-tǭ·rīn) *Chem.* [a. F. *hypotaurine* (Chatagner & Bergeret 1951, in *Compt. Rend.* CCXXXII. 450)], a pale yellow crystalline amino-acid, $NH_2(CH_2)_2SO_2H$, found in some higher organisms; 2-aminoethanesulphinic acid; **hypothermal,** (*c*) *Petrol.*, of, pertaining to, or designating mineral and ore deposits formed by hydrothermal action at relatively high temperature and pressure; **hypotrichosis** (-trikōu·sis) *Path.* [ad. G. *hypotrichose* (R. Bonnet 1892, in *Anat. Hefte* I. I. viii. 235), f. Gr. *τρίχωσις* growth of hair, f. *τριχοῦν* to cover with hair (*θρίξ, τριχ-* hair)], partial or complete absence of hair; hence **hypotricho·tic** *a.*; **hy:povitamino·sis** *Path.* [-OSIS], any condition caused by vitamin deficiency; **hypovolæ·mia** *Physiol.* [VOL(UME *sb.* + Gr. *αἷμα* blood], a decreased volume of circulating blood in the body; hence **hypovolæ·mic** *a.*; **hypoxæmia** (həipǫksī·miă) *Med.* [ad. F. *hypoxémie* (P. A. Piorry *Traité de Méd. pratique* (1847) III. 123), f. *ox-ygène* + *-émie* (Gr. *αἷμα* blood)] = *ANOXÆMIA; **hypoxia** (həipǫ·ksiă) *Med.* [OX(YGEN + -IA[1]] = *ANOXIA; hence **hypo·xic** *a.*, of or pertaining to hypoxia; deficient in oxygen.

1881 J. Ross *Treat. Dis. Nervous Syst.* I. iii. 84 Eulenberg has proposed the term hypalgesia or hypalgia, to indicate diminution of painful reaction, while limiting analgesia to its abolition. **1906** *Jrnl. Nerv. & Mental Dis.* XXXIII. 324 (*heading*) Hypesthesia and hypalgesia and their significance in functional nervous disturbances. **1971** P. C. Lund *Spinal Anesthesia* vii. 318 Sharp needles are..utilized to determine the level of hypalgesia which precedes the development of analgesia. **1911** Stedman *Med. Dict.* 405/2 Hypalgesic. **1916** L. F. Barker *Monographic Med.* IV. 137 The effect of summation of stimuli should..be noticed, by drawing a sharp needle lengthwise over an analgesic or hypalgesic area. **1935** *Discovery* Aug. 226/2 One very fortunate property which such a generator appears to possess is its pain-relieving virtue, or hypalgesic action, a very useful condition when treating post-operative cases. **1900** Dorland *Med. Dict.* 311/2 Hypoacidity. **1902** *Encycl. Brit.* XXXI. 551/2 Hyperacidity from lactic may obscure hypoacidity of hydrochloric acid. **1943** E. Urbach *Allergy* (1944) ii. 67 Gastric hypo- or anacidity is often observed. **1910** *Bull. Johns Hopkins Hosp.* XXI. 127/2 Conditions therefore simulating grades of hypoactivity. **1914** *Arch. Internal Med.* XIV. 145 Hypo-activity of the thyroid and pituitary. **1965** B. E. Freeman tr. *Vandel's Biospeleol.* xxi. 351 The majority of the follicles of the thyroid..show signs of hypoactivity. **1906** *Jrnl. Nerv. & Mental Dis.* XXXIII. 324 Hypoesthesia is the term heretofore employed to express this condition, but its awkward form at least excuses the employment of hypesthesia as a more euphonious and therefore more satisfactory expression. **1967** D. Sinclair *Cutaneous Sensation* viii. 148 'Hyperaesthesia' and 'hypoaesthesia' are similarly misused. **1940** *Lancet* 17 Feb. 303/2 Complete recovery [from frostbite] may apparently take place, but after a variable interval neuralgic pains may begin. The skin is usually hypoæsthetic. **1937** *Acta Med. Scand.* XCI. 336 A simple method for the determination of hypoalbuminemia and hypoproteinemia..is afforded by the determination of the specific gravity of serum. **1962** *Lancet* 6 Jan. 52/1 This loss of protein may be significant in the pathogenesis of the hypoalbuminæmia of kwashiorkor. **1929** Dorland & Miller *Med. Dict.* (ed. 15) 584/1 Hypo-algesia. **1945** *Jrnl. Clin. Invest.* XXIV. 505 A patient had 'hypoalgesia' to pin prick on parts of his left hand. **1968** A. Soulairac et al. *Pain* 36 The marked hypoalgesia recorded in this animal was associated with a double right lesion. **1925** *Jrnl. Biol. Chem.* LXVI. 345 Hypocalcemia was produced..by thyroparathyroidectomy. **1960** *Farmer & Stockbreeder* 22 Mar. 135/2 What is the glucose dosage for young pigs with hypocalcæmia? **1962** A. Sorsby in A. Pirie *Lens Metabolism Rel. Cataract* 298 Congenital cataract..can be caused by such frankly environmental disturbances as..maternal hypocalcæmia. **1935** D. H. Shelling *Parathyroids* vi. 148 Other means of demonstrating hypocalcemic tetany are now available. **1908** Hypocapnia [see *hypercapnia* s.v. *HYPER- IV]. **1961** *Lancet* 26 Aug. 475/1 The combination of extreme hypoxia with hypocapnia may well be fatal. **1927** *Amer. Jrnl. Med. Sci.* CLXXIII. 649 (*heading*) Acute intestinal obstruction: mechanism and significance of hypochloremia and other blood chemical changes. **1963** H. L. Bockus et al. *Gastroenterology* (ed. 2) I. xxviii. 646/2 If hypochloremia and alkalosis are present, gastric retention and vomiting have probably preceded the bout of bleeding. **1893** Hypochlorhydria [see *hyperchlorhydria* s.v. *HYPER- IV]. **1971** J. Song *Path. Sickle Cell Dis.* xviii. 355 The usual hypochlorhydria present in this disease may account for some of the gastric manifestations. **1921** *Chem. Abstr.* XV. 894 When the concn. varies between 0.010 and 0.012 sp. gr. the indications are that it [*sc.* the stomach] contains dissolved alimentary residues and tends to be hypochlorhydric. **1971** J. Song *Path. Sickle Cell Dis.* xviii. 356 Many individuals present hypochlorhydric states of a like degree. **1901** *Gray's Anat.* (ed. 15) II. 96 The future vertibræ..are soon joined across the middle line on the ventral aspect of the notochord by a hypochordal cartilaginous bar. **1962** M. Jollie *Chordate Morphol.* vi. 153 This splint is the ventral, perichondral ossification of the hypochordal cartilage. **1902** *Encycl. Brit.* XXIX. 572/2 They are called hyper-eutectic or hypo-eutectic according as this excess is cementite or ferrite, i.e., according as their carbon-content is above or below the 0·90 per cent. which the eutectic itself contains. **1926** W. E. Woodward *Metallogr. Steel & Cast Iron* i. 27 In a 2·0% C steel 0·3% C (=4·5% Fe_3C) will have been required to form the eutectic portion of the hypo-eutectic alloy. **1959** Hypoeutectic [see *hypereutectic* adj. s.v. *HYPER- IV]. **1911** *Encycl. Brit.* XIV. 805/2 This ferrite flows around and immediately heals over any cracks which form in the small quantity of cementite interstratified with it in the pearlite of hypo-eutectoid steels. **1966** A. Prince *Alloy Phase Equilibria* vi. 107 The structure of a hypo-eutectoid Fe—Fe_3C alloy is one of ferrite with pearlite, the latter appearing in characteristic form. **1905** Gould *Dict. New Med. Terms* 303/2 Hypofunction. **1913** L. Forster tr. *A. Biedl's Internal Secretory Organs* 53 Vassale thinks that the new formation of tissue points to a hyper-function of the gland, the wasting of the colloid to a hypo-function. **1920** *Endocrinology* IV. 344 Hypofunction of the thyroid. **1972** *Lancet* 12 Aug. 299/2 There was a high frequency of sexual hypofunction and testicular atrophy among male patients. **1933** A. W. Rowe *Differential Diagn. Endocrine Disorders* viii. 116 'Hyperfunction' indicates a condition..in direct antithesis to..the known hypofunctional state. **1961** *Jrnl. Amer. Med. Assoc.* 29 July 232/2 Of 43 hypofunctional nodules, only 2 proved to be due to carcinoma. **1926** J. S. Huxley *Ess. Pop. Sci.* 291 Whenever we can trace the effect of a hypo- or hyper-functioning of one of these [ductless] glands, we find that it affects..a complex of characters..related to the performance of a single function. **1954** A. White et al. *Princ. Biochem.* xliii. 936 In circumstances of adrenal cortical hypofunctioning..there is a failure of normal renal tubular reabsorption of sodium. **1955** *Jrnl. Amer. Med. Assoc.* 13 Aug. 1344 (*heading*) Hypogammaglobulinemia associated with a severe wound infection. **1970** Passmore & Robson *Compan. Med. Stud.* II. xviii. 103/1 Individuals with hypogammaglobulinaemia..produce little or no detectable circulating antibody and are vulnerable to bacterial invasion, but are not so susceptible to viral infection. **1972** *Lancet* 27 May 1151/2 Patients with the common variable type of severe hypogammaglobulinæmia exhibit lymphocytes with surface immunoglobulins. **1917** Stedman *Med. Dict.* (ed. 4) 458/2 Hypogenitalism. **1922** L. F. Barker *Endocrinol. & Metabolism* I. 157 Obesity is a frequent manifestation of hypogenitalism, either the physiological hypogenitalism of the menopause or the acquired form due to disease or to the surgical removal of the ovaries. **1964** L. Martin *Clinical Endocrinol.* (ed. 4) vii. 222 Hypogenitalism [in males] means abnormally small size or underdevelopment of the male external genitalia which need not necessarily include testicular failure. **1888** Hypogeusia [see *hypergeusia* s.v. *HYPER- IV]. **1969** C. Pfaffmann *Olfaction & Taste* 578 Treatment with D-penicillamine had produced hypogeusia (a decrease in taste acuity). **1894** Gould *Dict. Med.* 594/2 Hypoglycemia. **1911** *Jrnl. Biol. Chem.* X. 160 Recent investigations on the production of hypoglycaemia. **1960** *Farmer & Stockbreeder* 9 Feb. 102/1 Hypoglycæmia is a symptom rather than a disease on its own. **1923** *Jrnl. Physiol.* LVII. 318 The blood became hypoglycæmic. **1965** J. Pollitt *Depression & its Treatment* vi. 78, 20–80 units of soluble insulin before breakfast may be necessary to produce a mild hypoglycæmic reaction. **1970** Passmore & Robson *Compan. Med. Stud.* II. vi. 18/1 Today, approximately one-third of the total diabetic population is being treated with an oral hypoglycaemic agent. **1933** *Med. Jrnl. & Rec.* CXXXVII. 457/2 The vast majority of hypogonadal patients were within normal weights. **1944** R. S. Hotchkiss *Fertility in Men* iv. 90 Disproportional height span of legs and torso suggest the hypogonadal state. **1961** W. C. Young *Sex & Internal Secretions* (ed. 3) I. v. 348 Hypogonadal disorders of man. **1918** Stedman *Med. Dict.* (ed. 5) 469/1 Hypogonadism. **1933** *Jrnl. Amer. Med. Assoc.* 7 Jan. 70/2 A method for the assay of blood and urine for testicular hormone..has been used as a laboratory test for hypogonadism. **1966** R. B. Scott *Price's Textbk. Pract. Med.* (ed. 10) vii. 450/1 The term female hypogonadism implies a deficiency of both the ovulatory and hormone secretory functions of the ovary. **1970** Passmore & Robson *Compan. Med. Stud.* II. xii. 11/2 In children hypogonadism leads to delayed puberty. **1951** C. K. Weichert *Anat. Chordates* x. 485 A posterior prolongation from the ischial symphysis in *Sphenodon* and in many lizards and turtles is called the hypoischiac process, or cloacal bone. **1910** Parker & Haswell *Text-bk. Zool.* (ed. 2) II. 354 In the Chelonia..both pubes and ischia meet in ventral symphyses, and epipubic and hypoischial cartilages may be present. **1959** W. Montagna *Compar. Anat.* v. 116 In lizards an epipubic cartilage projects anteriorly and an hypoischial cartilage projects posteriorly from the symphysis. **1897** W. N. Parker tr. *Wiedersheim's Compar. Anat. Vertebr.* (ed. 2) 117 In Hatteria there is a marked epipubis and a hypoischiatic process continuous with the epipubic cartilage. *Ibid.* 118 A longitudinal fibro-cartilaginous ligament, continuous anteriorly with the plug-like epipubic cartilage and posteriorly with the hypoischium. **1925** J. S. Kingsley *Vertebr. Skeleton* 265 Squamata... The hypoischium, usually movable, is well developed and may be cartilage or bone in the adult. **1949** *Jrnl. Clin. Invest.* XXVIII. 409 (*heading*) Some observations on the development of hypokaliemia during therapy of diabetic acidosis. **1951** *Dorland's Med. Dict.* (ed. 22) 713/2 Hypokalemia, hypokaliemia. **1972** *Lancet* 1 July 36/2 Hypokalæmia may be seen in any stage of renal failure. **1953** *Jrnl. Clin. Invest.* XXXII. 538 (*heading*) The effect of potassium in nephrectomized rats with hypokalemic alkalosis. **1962** *Lancet* 1 Dec. 1145/1 During this period the patient became hypokalæmic. **1886** *Syd. Soc. Lex.*, Hypokinesia. *Ibid.*, Hypokinesis. **1927** I. S. Wechsler *Clin. Neurol.* IV. 391 Instead of hypokinesis there may be hyperkinetic phenomena. **1970** *Nature* 4 Apr. 21/1 Parkinsonism is..characterized by tremor, rigidity of the limbs and poverty of movement (hypokinesia). **1897** *Lippincott's Med. Dict.* 498/1 Hypoleucocytosis. **1898** [see *leucopenia* s.v. Leuco-]. **1930** H. Downey in E. T. Bell *Text-bk. Path.* xxviii. 599 In pernicious anemia we see an example of neutrophile hypoleukocytosis. **1933** *Jrnl. Clin. Invest.* XII. 982 (*heading*) Clinical manifestations of hypo- and hyper-magnesaemia. **1971** *Arable Farmer* Feb. 70/2 A high level of potash in the soil..can lead to hypomagnesaemia (grass staggers) in dairy cows. **1960** *Times* 28 Nov. 16/5 Hypomagnesaemic tetany was common on sheep that were rapidly transferred back from good pasture to poorer hill grazing. **1932** Dorland & Miller *Med. Dict.* (ed. 16) 6111/2 Hypometabolism. **1962** T. L. Sourkes *Biochem. Mental Dis.* xxiv. 302 This syndrome has been variously termed metabolic insufficiency, non-myxedematous hypometabolism, and euthyroid hypometabolism. **1932** H. J. Muller in *Proc. 6th Internat. Congr. Genetics* I. 235 Scute-1 is therefore a hypomorph. **1946** *Nature* 12 Oct. 520/1 This mutant allele is therefore a hypomorph to the normal allele. **1962** I. H. Herskowitz *Genetics* xxiv. 210/1 Mutants having a similar but lesser effect than the normal gene are called hypomorphs. **1932** H. J. Muller in *Proc. 6th Internat. Congr. Genetics* I. 235 Apricot, like eosin, is a mutant gene which produces an effect similar to that of the normal allelomorph, but a lesser effect...It is..like a lesser-normal. I therefore call it a 'hypomorphic' mutant. **1962** I. H. Herskowitz *Genetics* xxiv. 210/1 We can represent the relationship between the normal gene and its hypomorphic mutants diagrammatically. **1900** Dorland *Med. Dict.* 312/2 Hypomotility. **1914** C. G. Stockton *Dis. Stomach* ix. 183 (*heading*) Diminished gastric motion, hypomotility, gastric atony. **1970** *Radiology* XCIV. 303/2 An upper gastro-intestinal examination..failed to show any abnormality, except for generalized hypomotility of the stomach and small intestine. **1935** Dorland & Miller *Med. Dict.* (ed. 17) 649/1 Hyponatremia. **1969** L. G. Wesson *Physiol. Human Kidney* xxvii. 554/1 Hyponatremia may be defined somewhat arbitrarily as a plasma sodium concentration less than 130 mM/L in man. **1955** *Arch. Internal Med.* XCV. 21/1 Infants who present hyponatremic acidosis. **1905** W. H. Howell *Text-bk. Physiol.* 885 A hypotonic or hyposmotic solution is one whose osmotic pressure is less than that of serum. **1957** B. T. Scheer et al. *Rec. Adv. Invertebr. Physiol.* 237 The antennal secretion of *P. crassipes* is slightly hypo-osmotic to the blood in 50% sea water. **1963** R. P. Dales *Annelids* v. 104 The ability to form a hyposmotic urine. **1971** W. J. McCauley *Vertebr. Physiol.* i. 9 If it has a lower osmotic pressure, it is said to be a hypoosmotic solution. **1916** *Genetics* I. 90 Various types of developmental malformation of the hands and feet have been described under such terms as..hypophalangia. **1911** Stedman *Med. Dict.* 411/2 Hypophalangism. **1965** *Arch. Internal Med.* CXV. 581/2 The present family is unique in that hypophalangism is limited to the fourth digits and associated with symphalangism. **1929** R. R. Gates *Heredity in Man* viii. 154 Brachyphalangy combined with hypophalangy (less than five fingers) was transmitted for six generations. **1966** S. M. Lamb *Outl. Stratif. Gram.* 18 Such cases have particularly attracted the attention of linguists in hypophonemic systems... The hypophonemic and hypersememic strata might be called the phonetic and semantic, respectively. *Ibid.* 19 The hypophonemic system appears not to have a sign pattern. *Ibid.* 28 The tactics of the hypophonemic stratum of a language specifies how hypophonemes (i.e. phonological components) are arranged in segments and clusters. **1968** J. Algeo in *South Atlantic Bull.* XXXIII. ii. 2 The distinctive features of sound, the hypophonemes in Lamb's terminology, are relatively easy to study because there are so few of them—only about twelve to fifteen in most languages. Sample hypophonemes are *plosion, spirancy, nasality, labiality,* and *unvoicing.* **1969** *Language* XLV. 303 Such alternations would be treated as alternate realizations of these phonons in terms of the units of the lower phonological stratum, the hypophonemes. *Ibid.* 307 In Figure 6 the first vowels of /gləsə́/ and /dəbə́/ would be treated as the same, as /Vo/ hypophonemically. ..They would be the same only when viewed as hypophonemic signs, which include non-distinctive as well as phonemic elements. **1932** L. C. Martin *Introd. Appl. Optics* II. iv. 143 In Hypophoria one eye turns downwards. **1964** [see *hyperphoria* s.v. *HYPER- IV]. **1935** D. H. Shelling *Parathyroids* vi. 138 Fish has found hypophosphatemia as well as hypocalcemia. **1962** *Lancet* 2 June 1169/1 The other forms of rickets and osteomalacia are of the vitamin-D-resistant type, and are characterised by persistent hypophosphatæmia. **1946** M. R. Everett *Med. Biochem.* (ed. 2) viii. 628 The Fanconi syndrome (intractable hypophosphatemic rachitis accompanied by acidosis and renal glycosuria). **1968** R. F. Pitts *Physiol. Kidney & Body Fluids* (ed. 2) xiii. 237/2 One or the other parent is hypophosphatemic. **1948** J. C. Rathbun in *Amer. Jrnl. Dis. Children* LXXV. 831 It was therefore decided to call this disease 'hypophosphatasia' to single out the remarkably low alkaline phosphatase levels. **1957** *Amer. Jrnl. Med.* XXII. 730/1 There is now good evidence that hypophosphatasia is a specific genetically determined metabolic disease characterized by three salient features: (1) abnormal mineralization of bone, (2) diminished alkaline phosphatase activity, and (3) increased urinary excretion of phosphorylethanolamine. **1909** Hypopituitarism [see *hyperpituitarism* s.v. *HYPER- IV]. **1921** *Glasgow Herald* 10 Sept. 4/5 There were several causes of dwarfism; sometimes disorders of the thyroid gland were the cause, but other varieties were produced by hypo-pituitarism. **1961** *Lancet* 30 Sept. 760/2 Prof. H. L. Sheehan showed that, in severe postpartum hypopituitarism, patients who had occasional uterine bleeding had just as great a destruction of the anterior pituitary as those who had permanent amenorrhœa. **1921** *Endocrinology* V. 800 A presentation of five cases of preadolescent hypopituitary infantilism. **1955** R. H. Williams *Textbk. Endocrinol.* (ed. 2) ix. 604 The hypopituitary dwarfs usually show marked retardation of their epiphysial development. **1902** *Encycl. Brit.* XXXIII. 933/2 It is possible that the plankton immediately over the bottom [of the ocean] may prove to be sufficiently distinct to be separately classed as hypoplankton. **1903** *Nature* 5 Nov. 23/2 There is evidence that certain forms [of Copepoda] are confined to the bottom, and form part of a true hypoplankton. **1942** H. U. Sverdrup et al. *Oceans* xvii. 814 The swimming powers of many animals put them midway between the plankton and the nekton, and many forms..live both on or near the bottom and are sometimes called hypoplankton. **1955** C. C. Davis *Marine & Fresh-Water Plankton* i. 28 The hypoplankton consists of plankters living near the bottom. **1884** *Trans. Entomol. Soc. Lond.* 503 *Hypopleura*, a distinct piece above the two last pairs of coxæ, and behind the sternopleura, from which it is separated by a suture. **1951** Colyer & Hammond *Flies*

Brit. Isles 24 Spiracles or apertures of the tracheae (breathing-tubes) are located before the mesopleuron and behind the hypopleuron respectively. **1951** L. S. West *Housefly* ii. 28 The hypopleura lies behind the middle coxa, the sternopleura just in front. **1884** *Trans. Entomol. Soc. Lond.* 511 Hypopleural bristles. **1930** *Jrnl. Genetics* XXII. 306 Other individuals—'hypoploids'—may fail to inherit the fragment. *Ibid.* 313 Viable heteroploid or hypoploid zygotes. **1957** Hypoploid [see *hyperploid* s.v. *Hyper- IV]. **1930** *Jrnl. Genetics* XXII. 329 The phaenotypic effects of hypoploidy and hyperploidy of every portion of the chromatin. **1969** Hypoploidy [see *hyperploidy* s.v. *Hyper- IV]. **1932** Dorland & Miller *Med. Dict.* (ed. 16) 612/2 Hypopotassemia. **1949** *Jrnl. Clin. Invest.* XXVIII. 409/1 Hypopotassemia may appear during therapy of diabetic acidosis or coma. **1963** Hypopotassemia [see *hyperpotassæmia* s.v. *Hyper- IV]. **1950** *Jrnl. Amer. Med. Assoc.* 16 Dec. 1328 A resultant hypopotassemic, hypochloremic alkalosis. **1953** *Lancet* 11 July 60/1 The more familiar hypopotassæmic paralysis. **1934** *Jrnl. Biol. Chem.* CV. 327 (*heading*) The effect of nutritional hypoproteinemia on the electrolyte pattern and calcium concentration of serum. **1961** *Lancet* 5 Aug. 299/1 Hypoproteinæmia may be due to impaired synthesis of protein (especially albumin) in malnutrition or liver disease, or..to abnormal loss of protein in starvation, after injury, and from discharges. **1935** *Clin. Sci.* II. 60 Hypoproteinæmic. **1942** *Jrnl. Amer. Med. Assoc.* 3 Jan. 22 The disturbed osmotic relations in the hypoproteinemic dog. **1966** J. W. Linman *Princ. Hematol.* v. 156 Hypoproteinemic dogs or rats. **1936** *Jrnl. Exper. Med.* LXIII. 798 Titration of prothrombin, however, revealed a very marked hypoprothrombinemia. **1961** *Lancet* 19 Aug. 390/1 Subacute intestinal obstruction associated with excessive hypoprothrombinæmia due to oral anticoagulant therapy. **1962** *Ibid.* 27 Jan. 177/1 Two types of hereditary hypoprothrombinæmia are known to exist. **1942** *Chem. Abstr.* 20 Nov. 7087 The danger of the hypoprothrombinemic hemorrhage was very slight. **1955** *Arch. Internal. Med.* XCV. 2/2 The opportunity to study various types of congenital hypothrombinemic states repeatedly over a period ..has furnished data on their clinical course. **1902** *Daily Chron.* 16 July 9/1 The 'Hyposcope' competition..the peculiarity of which is that, by an optical contrivance, the marksman, completely under cover, may fire round a corner, so to speak, at an enemy. **1915** *Illustr. London News* 20 Feb. 236/1 A trench-periscope (or, to give it its correct name, a hyposcope)... The Hyposcope is on the principle of the camera-obscura. **1909** *Jrnl. Amer. Med. Assoc.* 24 July 251/2 A condition of hyposecretion of this part of the gland. **1939** B. J. E. Ihre *Human Gastric Secretion* vii. 95 A reduced rate of secretion (hyposecretion). **1900** Dorland *Med. Dict.* 313/2 Hyposthenuria. **1909** J. B. Herrick in Osler & McCrae *Syst. Med.* VI. vi. 126 Unless hyposthenuria be counteracted by polyuria, renal insufficiency must result. **1971** J. Song *Path. Sickle Cell Dis.* xv. 284 Hyposthenuria in sickle cell anemia was considered a reversible renal defect by Keitel et al. **1951** *Chem. Abstr.* XLV. 6232, $H_2N(CH_2)_2SO_2H$, tentatively named hypotaurine. **1965** A. Meister *Biochem. Amino Acids* (ed. 2) I. i. 75 This amino acid [*sc.* L-cysteinesulfinic acid], and the product of its decarboxylation, hypotaurine,..have been found in the free state in rat brain. **1966** *Biochim. et Biophys. Acta* CXVII. 495 (*heading*) The occurrence of hypotaurine and other sulfur-containing amino acids in seminal plasma and spermatozoa of boar, bull and dog. **1922** W. Lindgren in *Econ. Geol.* XVII. 293 The terminology proposed..would be as follows:..A. Hydrothermal deposits. *a.* Epithermal. Formed by ascending hot waters near the surface in or near effusive rocks at relatively low temperature and pressure. *b.* Mesothermal. Formed by ascending hot waters in or near intrusive rocks at intermediate temperature and pressure. *c.* Hypothermal. Formed by ascending hot water in or near intrusive rocks at high temperature and pressure. ..The prefix 'hypo' has been substituted for 'kata' to correspond with Ransome's now generally accepted terms of 'hypogene waters', the suggestion implied being that the hypogene waters are principally derived from the region of the hypothermal deposits. **1969** Bennison & Wright *Geol. Hist. Brit. Isles* x. 247 The latter [mineral veins] are of two phases, hypothermal and mesothermal, usually of different and characteristic trend. **1970** Park & MacDiarmid *Ore Deposits* (ed. 2) xii. 294 Many minerals of the igneous metamorphic zone continue without interruption into the hypothermal zone. **1896** T. L. Stedman *20th Cent. Practice* V. 575 Bonnet..suggests designating any lack of hair through error of development, hypotrichosis. **1968** A. J. Rook et al. *Textbk. Dermatol.* II. xlvi. 1377 Congenital hypotrichosis of sufficient degree to cause social embarrassment..is not uncommon. **1937** *Jrnl. Biol. Chem.* CXVIII. 627 The administration of cystine stimulated hair growth in the hypotrichotic rat. **1923** Stedman *Med. Dict.* (ed. 7), Hypovitaminosis. **1946** *Nature* 7 Sept. 342/2 The excretion of aneurin was decreased on account of deficient renal function, a fact not signifying hypovitaminosis in this case. **1925** Hypovolemia [see *hypervolæmia* s.v. *Hyper- IV]. **1935** Harrow & Sherwin *Textbk. Biochem.* xv. 413 Simple hypovolemia occurs in obesity and in certain types of renal edema. Polycythemic hypovolemia occurs in conditions of.. water deprivation. **1965** R. P. Morehead *Human Path.* xxi. 501/2 Deficient water absorption leads to hypovolemia, dehydration, or both. **1952** *Jrnl. Amer. Med. Assoc.* 6 Sept. 11 The question of whether the normovolemic or the hypovolemic patient or animal should be used in evaluation of plasma expanders. **1961** A. C. Guyton *Textbk. Med. Physiol.* (ed. 2) xxxvii. 482/2 One of the most common types of shock..is that caused by hemorrhage; this is called hemorrhagic shock and is a type of hypovolemic shock. **1886** *Syd. Soc. Lex.*, Hypoxæmia. **1936** *Brain* LIX. 115 The hypoxaemia of arterial and of arm vein blood encountered in a large proportion of epileptics is an expression of the stagnant physical and mental state which so often accompanies epilepsy. **1971** Porter & Knight *High Altitude Physiol.* 36, 25 per cent of the reported cases of chronic mountain sickness have some type of pathology which *per se* produces hyperventilation and hypoxaemia. **1941** *Ann. Internal Med.* XIV. 1245 During hypoxia..blood flow is increased. **1967** *New Scientist* 26 Jan. 195/1 Today, the single most important cause of perinatal deaths is intrauterine hypoxia, in which the foetus becomes starved of oxygen because of impaired metabolism in the placenta. **1970** *Sci. Amer.* Feb. 53/2 Life on the mountains is made rigorous not only by hypoxia but also by cold. **1958** C. C. Adams et al. *Space Flight* 243 The hypoxic zone, less than three miles up, where the decreased oxygen pressure brings human psychological and physiological discomfort. **1966** *Lancet* 24 Dec. 1381/2 Polycythæmia secondary to hypoxic lung disease. **1970** *Sci. Amer.* Feb. 56/1 The mountain dwellers' metabolism also appears to be affected by the hypoxic conditions.

hypoacusis (həi:po͵ăki̯ū·sis). Also **-acousia, -acousis.** [f. Hypo- 4: see *hypacusis.] = *hypacusis.

1947 Ackerman & del Regato *Cancer* vii. 336 A unilateral diminution in the sense of hearing, hypoacousia, is very commonly found accompanying tumors of the nasopharynx. **1961** Stedman *Med. Dict.* (ed. 20) 740/2 Hypoacusis. **1969** *New Scientist* 10 July 53/2 Their ears have been done in by discotheques and it's not expressions of dumb insolence they're displaying but the symptoms of hypoacousis.

hypo-allergenic (həi:po͵ælədʒe·nik), *a.* orig. *U.S.* Also **hypoallergenic.** [f. Hypo- 4 + *allergenic *a.*] Having little tendency to cause an allergic reaction; specially prepared or treated so as to cause no reaction in persons allergic to the normal product.

1953 *Jrnl. Soc. Cosmetic Chemists* Aug. p. x (Advt.), Investigations indicate that Modulan is hypo-allergenic. **1953** *Arch. Otolaryngol.* Nov. 541 The cosmetic-sensitive patient must mingle in society with persons who are not wearing hypoallergenic powder. **1957** S. Kramer in E. Sagarin *Cosmetics* xxxviii. 879 Hypo-allergenic cosmetics are an important contribution to the allergic woman in that they enable her to continue the use of cosmetics. **1962** L. H. Crisp *Clin. Immunol. & Allergy* 187 Hypo-allergenic milk..is milk denatured by heating. **1972** *Times* 22 Aug. 6/5 Ashley clothes fit in with hypo-allergenic cosmetics,..ethnic dress, conservation and home grown food.

hypobaric (həipobæ·rik), *a.* *Med.* [f. Hypo- 4 + Gr. βαρ-ύς heavy + -ic.] Of a solution for spinal anæsthesia: having a lower density than the cerebro-spinal fluid.

1930, etc. [see *hyperbaric *a.* a]. **1971** P. C. Lund *Princ. & Pract. Spinal Anesthesia* vii. 300 When administering hypobaric local anesthetic solutions in large volumes..the rate of injection is relatively unimportant but the positioning very important.

hypocentre (həi·posentəɹ). Also (*U.S.*) **-center.** [f. Hypo- 2 + Centre *sb.*] **1.** The focus of an earthquake, the point within the earth where it originates.

1905 C. Davison *Study Rec. Earthquakes* i. 3 The region within which the displacement occurs is sometimes called the hypocentre, but more frequently the seismic focus, or simply the focus. **1938** [see *centrum 2]. **1972** *Sci. Amer.* May 58 The first seismic waves to leave the region of the break (the hypocenter) are waves of alternate compression and rarefaction.

2. = *ground zero* (*ground *sb.* 18).

1960 *Observer* 29 May 26/1 The Hiroshima survivors are unusual in having experienced a single whole-body exposure, the dose varying according to distance from the hypocentre (point directly beneath centre) of the explosion. **1962** J. F. Loutit *Irradiation* ii. 75 The incidence of leukemia..is high for those who were exposed near to the hypocenter.

hypochondria. 2. Add to def.: Now identical in meaning with Hypochondriasis (q.v. in Dict. and Suppl.); it remains the commoner term among laymen. (Further examples.)

1839 F. Winslow *Physic & Physicians* II. 155 Cowper's madness, most undoubtedly, originated from some bodily ailment... All through his disorder, the digestive organs were impaired... Such, indeed, was the true source of his hypochondria. **1899** J. Macpherson *Mental Affections* viii. 147 The two affections [*sc.* melancholia and hypochondria] are different in so far as the emotional depression, combined with the intellectual disturbance of melancholia, is not present in hypochondria. **1928** R. D. Gillespie in *Guy's Hosp. Rep.* LXXXVIII. 409 The term hypochondria appears always to have referred to preoccupation with complaints of illness, and usually of bodily illness. **1955** *Times* 4 Nov. 5/4 The fantastic array of purges, nerve sedatives, tonics,..processed this, irradiated that, and impregnated the other shows that hypochondria is widespread.

hypochondriac, *a.* and *sb.* **A.** *adj.* **1.** Delete ?*Obs.* and add earlier and later examples.

1599 R. Surflet tr. *A. Du Laurens' Discourse Preservation of Sight* 125 The Hypochondriake disease..[is] a drie and hote distemperature of Mesenterium, the liver and spleene. **1965** W. G. Klopfer in B. B. Wolman *Handbk. Clin. Psychol.* 830/2 Hypochondriac symptoms commonly occur and may, if no discernible cause for the symptom is found, be due to exaggerated needs for attention and other psychological desires.

b. (Earlier example.)

1599 R. Surflet tr. *A. Du Laurens' Discourse Preservation of Sight* 131, I have seene two Hypochondriake persons..raging mad.

B. *sb.* **1.** (Further examples.)

1888 R. Roose *Nerve Prostration* I. xv. 348 The hypochondriac is always dwelling upon his symptoms, and constantly talks about his health. **1916** M. H. Fussell *Monographic Med.* V. xii. 781 Hypochondria is more likely to be confounded with neurasthenia [than with hysteria], but as the hypochondriac believes he is ill and constantly talks about his symptoms, and hysteriacs also..complain of various symptoms there may be confusion. **1932** H. S. Walpole *Fortress* IV. v. 693 She was no hypochondriac, but from a kind of outside consideration she summoned her forces. Had she a headache? Did her eyes smart? How was her throat? **1955** *Sci. Amer.* Apr. 104/3 He was a hypochondriac and a crank, chronically dyspeptic and unamiable. **1973** *Times* 27 Sept. 15/1 George S. Kaufman..was..an obsessive card player, compulsive womanizer, necrophobe, hypochondriac.

2. (Earlier example.)

1599 R. Surflet tr. *A. Du Laurens' Discourse Preservation of Sight* 126 The other part where the Hypochondriake breedeth, is the liver.

hypochondriasis. Add to def.: Now regarded as a condition characterized by a morbid preoccupation with one's bodily health together with unfounded beliefs and exaggerated anxieties about real or imagined ailments, usually the symptom of a neurotic disorder. (Further examples.)

1798 A. Crichton *Inquiry Mental Derangement* II. 339 Hypochondriasis, therefore, is chiefly characterized by erroneous notions relating to the patient's own frame, and by painful corporeal feeling. **1855** *Asylum Jrnl.* I. 214/1 Hypochondriasis and melancholia monomania were not clearly distinguished by physicians until recent years. **1905** M. Craig *Psychol. Med.* vii. 114 Though hypochondriasis is usually found in patients in whom no known bodily disease can be diagnosed, it may be associated with organic disease, the hypochondriacal symptoms being.. the patient's misinterpretation of true physical signs. **1956** H. P. Laughlin *Neuroses Clin. Pract.* x. 451 Sigmund Freud very early included Neurasthenia, along with Anxiety Neurosis and Hypochondriasis, as the so-called 'actual neuroses'. *Ibid.* xi. 500 In some psychiatric quarters today Hypochondriasis is regarded simply as a symptom complex, or merely as a manifestation which is present as a part of many other emotional reactions, rather than as a separate diagnostic entity.

hypochoristic (həi:pokŏri·stik), *a.* Erroneous (but increasingly used) form of Hypocoristic *a.*

1931 G. Stern *Meaning & Change of Meaning* 262 *Bob* has been considered a hypochoristic shortening of *Robert.* **1933** L. Bloomfield *Lang.* xxiii. 424 It seems..that forms like *Bob, Dick* existed as common nouns, perhaps with symbolic connotation, before they were specialized as hypochoristic forms of *Robert, Richard.* **1958** A. S. C. Ross *Etymology* 167 The hypochoristic form..of a name.. is the 'familiar' form, as MnE *Liz* for *Elizabeth.*

hypochromasia (həi:pokrōᵘmē̆·ziă). *Med.* [mod.L., f. Hypo- 4 + Gr. χρῶμα, χρώματ- colour: see -ia¹.] = *hypochromia b.

1929 R. B. H. Gradwohl tr. *Schilling's Blood Picture* III. 258 Regarding the color index, marked decrease is called hypochromasia. **1930** H. Downey in E. T. Bell *Text-bk. Path.* xxviii. 586 In addition to hypochromasia, poikilocytosis may develop. **1942** M. M. Wintrobe *Clin. Hematol.* ii. 68 Hypochromia, hypochromasia or 'achromia' are terms used to describe cells in which this normal pallor is increased.

hypochromatic (həipokrōᵘmæ·tik), *a.* *Med.* [f. Hypo- 4 + Chromatic *a.*] **a.** Of the skin: deficient in pigment.

1894 in Gould *Dict. Med.* 593/2.

b. = *hypochromic *a.* 1.

1929 R. B. H. Gradwohl tr. *Schilling's Blood Picture* II. 112 Remissions, often very extensive, are striking... The blood picture may appear normal again and may become temporarily hypochromatic. **1930** H. Downey in E. T. Bell *Text-bk. Path.* xxviii. 585 In this type of anemia one may find all gradations from cases showing abundant signs of regeneration to the simple hypochromatic types. **1971** V. F. Fairbanks et al. *Clin. Dis. Iron Metabolism* (ed. 2) iii. 129 Hypochromatic changes in the erythrocyte ..may occur in a variety of unrelated disorders including iron-deficiency anemia.

hypochromatosis (həi:pokrōᵘmătōᵘ·sis). *Cytology.* [mod.L., f. Hypo- 4 + Chromat(o-, Chromat(in + -osis.] An abnormally small amount of chromatin or number of chromosomes in a cell or nucleus.

1913 [see *hyperchromatosis 2]. **1919** *Encycl. Medica* (ed. 2) VI. 311 Hypochromatosis is a deficiency in chromatin—thus nuclear hypochromatosis is the condition of the nucleus of a cell in which there is a reduction in the number of chromosomes.

hypochromia (həipŏkrōᵘ·miă). *Med.* [f. as next + -ia¹.] **a.** (See quot. 1890.)

1890 Gould *New Med. Dict.* 201/2 *Hypochromia*, abnormal pallor or transparency of the skin, occurring in certain skin diseases. **1968** A. J. Rook et al. *Textbk. Dermatol.* I. xxii. 724 The lesions always retain their tendency to merge together producing progressive atrophy of the skin with tendency to hypochromia and achromia.

b. A hypochromic condition of the blood or of a red blood cell (see *hypochromic *a.* 1).

1931 [see *hyperchromia]. **1966** J. W. Linman *Princ. Hematol.* v. 177 Because of the clear-cut relationship between iron deficiency and hypochromia, it has often been assumed erroneously that this morphologic abnormality must be the result of iron lack or a block in iron incorporation. **1972** *Nature* 10 Mar. 71/2 Lead seems to affect red

cells chiefly by..interfering with haemoglobin synthesis, as judged by..hypochromia of the red cells.

hypochromic (həipokrōᵘ·mik), *a.* [f. Hypo- 4 + Gr. χρῶμ-α colour + -ic.] **1.** *Med.* Characterized by or designating a colour index less than one, or red blood cells that contain less hæmoglobin than normal and show an increased central pallor; esp. in *hypochromic anæmia.*

1924 T. R. Waugh in *Can. Med. Assoc. Jrnl.* XLVII. 114/1 Such anaemias consequently show considerable variation in their blood pictures. If the response is slight ..the red cells are small, and stain poorly,..and the color index is low. This type is therefore hypochromic. **1935** Whitby & Britton *Disorders of Blood* vi. 126 Hypochromic anæmia, especially, is more often a symptom than a disease. **1958** G. C. de Gruchy *Clin. Haematol.* ii. 42 In the tail of the film the cells are often distorted and flattened, and hypochromic cells may actually appear normochromic. **1966** J. W. Linman *Princ. Hematol.* v. 157 Most hypochromic anemias are caused by iron lack.

2. Characterized by or exhibiting a decrease in the extent to which light (usually, ultra-violet radiation) is absorbed; chiefly in *hypochromic effect.*

1946 *Ann. Rep. Progr. Chem.* XLII. 118 For substituents attached to the carbonyl group, the effects are quite different, both $\lambda_{max.}$ and $\epsilon_{max.}$ being usually decreased (hypso- and hypochromic effects). **1959** *Jrnl. Amer. Chem. Soc.* LXXXI. 6003/1 In general the oxidation of a methylthio group to a methyl sulfone involves a hypsochromic shift of from 10 to 40 mμ... This hypsochromic shift usually is accompanied by a definite hypochromic effect. **1968** [see *hyperchromic *a.* 2].

Hence **hy:pochromi·city**, the property of absorbing less (ultra-violet) light.

1958 *Nature* 29 Nov. 1502/1 In view of the zero hyperchromicity of polyguanylic acids at alkaline *p*H's, the variation of hypochromicity with *p*H was examined for a number of derivatives. **1960** D. Shugar in Chargaff & Davidson *Nucleic Acids* III. xxx. 59 When the extinction of a given oligonucleotide is lower than that of its constituent mononucleotides, it is 'hypochromic' or exhibits 'hypochromicity'.

hypocone (həi·pokōᵘn). *Zool.* [f. Hypo- + Cone *sb.*[1]] An external cusp on the inner back corner of a mammalian upper molar tooth.

1888 H. F. Osborn in *Amer. Naturalist* XXII. 1072 The first 'secondary' cusps (hypocone—hypoconid), added to the upper and lower molars of the primitive triangle, modify the crown from a triangular to a quadrangular shape. **1891** [in Dict. s.v. Hypo-]. **1933** A. S. Romer *Vertebr. Paleontol.* xii. 248 In the upper molars the tooth tends to square itself up usually by the addition of a fourth cusp, the hypocone, at the inner back corner. **1968** R. Zangerl tr. *Peyer's Compar. Odontol.* 187 In the upper jaw a talon formed in that a second lingual cusp developed next to the protocone, a so-called hypocone.

hypoconid (həipokōᵘ·nid). *Zool.* [f. *hypocon(e + *-id[5].] A cusp on a mammalian lower molar tooth corresponding to the hypocone on an upper molar.

1888 H. F. Osborn in *Amer. Naturalist* XXII. 1075 There is no evidence as to the origin of the hypoconid, which as a rule preceded the hypocone. **1919** J. H. Mummery *Microsc. Anat. Teeth* i. 36 In man the trigonid is represented by the protoconid and metaconid only,.. and the five cusps are made up of these and three cusps of the talonid—the hypoconid, entoconid, and hypoconulid. **1968** R. Zangerl tr. *Peyer's Compar. Odontol.* 187 In the lower jaw three cusps developed on the talonid: counting labio-lingually, hypoconid, hypoconulid, and entoconid. **1970** *Nature* 25 July 356/1 The crest connecting the entoconid and the hypoconid was continuous.

hypoconulid (həipokōᵘ·niulid). *Zool.* [f. *hypocon(e + *-ul-* + *-id[5].] An intermediate cusp between the principal ones on the heel of a mammalian lower molar tooth.

1897 H. F. Osborn in *Amer. Naturalist* XXXI. 1002 The talonid widened into a basin-like shelf supporting an outer cusp, the 'hypoconid'; an intermediate cusp, the 'hypoconulid', and an inner cusp, the 'entoconid'. *Ibid.* 1003 Why notice such a detail as the posterior intermediate cusp or hypoconulid? **1933** A. S. Romer *Vertebr. Paleontol.* xii. 248 A hypoconulid may also appear in the heel. **1972** *Nature* 24 Mar. 180/1 *Oligopithecus* as well as the other Fayum catarrhines share the distinct lingually placed and somewhat prominent hypoconulid.

hypocoristic, *a.* Add: Also as *sb.*

1889 in *Cent. Dict.* **1930** *Times Lit. Suppl.* 1 May 361/2 Mere riddles..where there is no question of..stop-voicing of hypocoristics. **1953** K. Jackson *Lang. & Hist. Early Brit.* II. 555 The AS. personal names *Cata, Ceatta*..are from Pr[imitive] W[elsh] hypocoristics. **1957** R. W. Zandvoort *Handbk. Eng. Gram.* ix. ii. 303 The technical term or attributive 'pet' is 'hypocoristic' (adj. and noun).

hypodermic, *a.* Add: **1.** (Earlier example.)

1863 *Lancet* 17 Oct. 444/1 Many..speedily furnished the journals with their experience of the 'hypodermic treatment'.

b. Also, a hypodermic injection or syringe.

1893 *Funk's Stand. Dict., Hypodermic,* a hypodermic syringe or injection. **1907** I. McIsaac *Primary Nursing Technique* vii. 104 Hypodermics are given in the chest or fleshy part of the arm or thigh. **1969** *Daily Tel.* 11 Apr. 28/5 He..preferred a hypodermic of nicotine to a cigarette inhaled. **1970** *Ibid.* (Colour Suppl.) 18 Sept. 18 Divers.. began to use large hypodermics designed to inject a 10 c.c. dose of formalin, enough to kill a starfish within hours.

c. *fig.* (adj. and sb.).

1901 *Harper's Mag.* CII. 786/1 Novelty is at a ruinous premium, and amusement a hypodermic to be taken in large doses, ever increased. **1903** *Monthly Rev.* Jan. 44 The admission of clergymen to the schools at certain hours for the purpose of administering a sort of hypodermic injection of religion is futile. **1936** W. Plomer *Visiting Caves* 46 The hypodermic steeple Ever ready to inject The opium of the people. **1959** *Listener* 12 Feb. 300/3 Admirers may find his appreciation of Waugh's more hypodermic humour respectful rather than hilarious. *Ibid.* 5 Nov. 796/1 The professional intimate, the confidential heart-worm with the hypodermic technique, is one of the horrors of television.

hypodermically, *adv.* (Earlier example.)

1863 C. Hunter in *Lancet* 17 Oct. 444/1 The alkaloids of belladonna, aconite, and other medicines were first employed hypodermically by myself.

hypodigm (həi·podəim, -dim). *Taxonomy.* [ad. Gr. ὑπόδειγμα example.] The material on which the description of a species is based.

1940 G. G. Simpson in *Amer. Jrnl. Sci.* CCXXXVIII. 418, I therefore propose the term 'hypodigm' (pronounced hy'-podim, from the Greek ὑπόδειγμα, 'token, example'). All the specimens used by the author of a species as his basis for inference, and this should mean all the specimens that he referred to the species, constitute his hypodigm of that species. *Ibid.*, The hypodigm, whether it include one specimen or a thousand, is a sample from which the characters of a population are to be inferred. **1953** E. Mayr et al. *Methods & Princ. Syst. Zool.* xii. 237 A hypodigm is all the available material of a species. This term is mentioned here because it is occasionally used in the paleontological literature. **1963** Davis & Heywood *Princ. Angiosperm Taxon.* i. 11 The hypodigm changes with our knowledge of the species. **1972** *Nature* 24 Mar. 180/1 The sixteen teeth which make up the hypodigm of this taxon [sc. *Purgatorius unio*] have, however, been correctly allocated.

hypogamy (həipǫ·gămi). *Anthrop.* [f. Hypo- + *-gamy.] The marriage of a woman into a lower caste or into a tribe of lower standing than her own. Hence **hypo·gamous** *a.*, pertaining or relating to hypogamy. Cf. *hypergamy.

1946 J. H. Hutton *Caste in India* v. 48 Hypogamy, on the other hand, is associated with a bride-price. *Ibid.*, Hypogamous marriages..are *pratiloma*, against the grain, that is, against what is natural or proper, since the status of the bride is in this case higher than that of the bridegroom. **1949** R. K. Merton *Social Theory* (1951) i. 60 This pattern, which we may call caste hypogamy, is not institutionalized, but it is persistent. **1956** R. Pieris *Sinhalese Social Organization* v. i. 177 A very rare case of *hypogamy*, that is, women marrying *below* their caste. **1957** *New Statesman* 4 May 566/3 The fictions of D. H. Lawrence have several examples of the lady marrying downwards (hypogamy, in anthropological vocabulary).

hypoid (həi·poid), *a.* and *sb. Mech.* [Said to be a contraction of *hyperboloid* or of *hyperbolic paraboloid* (in reference to the shape of the teeth on the wheel).] **A.** *adj.* **a.** Applied to a kind of gear similar to a spiral bevel gear but having the pinion offset from the centre-line of the wheel, so that it can be used to connect shafts whose axes do not intersect; it is commonly employed in motor vehicles to transmit the power from the propeller shaft to the axle.

1926 *Jrnl. Soc. Automotive Engin.* June 575/1 Hypoid-gears are tapered gears having offset axes. **1935** *Times* 2 Oct. 6/5 The rear axle is fully-floating, and final drive is by hypoid spiral bevel gears. **1937** *Jrnl. Applied Mech.* IV. A-31 The behavior of lubricants in the region of boundary lubrication has become of added importance due to the recent adoption of hypoid gears in automobiles. **1941** F. D. Jones *Engin. Encycl.* I. 676 The chief advantages of hypoid gears are noiseless operation, increased load-carrying capacity, the possibility of high reduction and low numbers of teeth, long life, and high efficiency. **1969** K. Ball *Rover 2000 1963–1969 Autobook* vii. 64/1 The unit contains a hypoid crownwheel and pinion for the final drive from the power input shaft to the half shafts.

b. Suitable for or employing a hypoid gear.

1937 *S.A.E. Jrnl.* (*Transactions*) XLI. 557/2 Six or seven months ago the lubrication of hypoid axles in the field was a much more serious problem than it is today. *Ibid.* 563/1 One lubricant submitted by a manufacturer as an extreme-pressure hypoid lubricant was found to be a 'straight' mineral oil when analyzed. **1963** *Times* 3 May 10/6 A four-speed, all synchromesh gearbox..incorporates the hypoid final drive. **1969** G. M. Mitchell *Jowett Javelin, Jupiter 1947–1953 Autobook* vi. 65/1 For lubrication of this axle, hypoid lubricant only should be used.

B. *sb.* A hypoid gear.

1935 R. Trautschold *Stand. Gear Bk.* ix. 144 Hypoids are machined in practically the same manner as spiral gears. **1962** D. W. Dudley *Gear Handbk.* ii. 12 Sufficient offset of the hypoid permits straddle mounting of the pinion and the gear.

hypolimnion (həipoli·mniǫn). Pl. **hypolimnia.** [f. Hypo- 2 + Gr. λιμνίον, dim. of λίμνη lake.] The lower, cooler layer of water below the thermocline in a stratified lake.

1910, 1936 [see *epilimnion]. **1957** G. E. Hutchinson *Treat. Limnol.* I. v. 341 The hypolimnia of all lakes. **1960** *New Scientist* 31 Mar. 773/3 The hypolimnion.. has become deoxygenated as the vegetation decomposes and provides ideal living conditions for sulphate-reducing bacteria. **1971** *Nature* 26 Feb. 596/1 In summer months.. the upper layers warm up more quickly than the lower regions and a sharp division in temperature—a thermocline—is formed...The reservoir or lake becomes divided into a lower, anaerobic cool layer or hypolimnion and an upper, warm aerobic epilimnion.

Hence **hypolimne·tic** [cf. Gr. λιμνήτης living in marshes], **hypoli·mnial** *adjs.*, of or within the hypolimnion.

1928 *Proc. Linn. Soc.* CXL. 101 On account of the depth the hypolimnetic body of water is great compared with the epilimnetic. **1940** Hypolimnial [see *epilimnion]. **1964** *Oceanogr. & Marine Biol.* II. 126 Alsterberg (1927) suggests that hypolimnetic (upper) water movements are confined to thin horizontal laminae, with currents in alternate directions.

hypomania (həipomē·niă). *Psychiatry.* [mod.L., ad. G. *hypomanie* (E. Mendel *Die Manie* (1881) ii. 38): see Hypo- 4.] A minor form of mania, often part of the manic-depressive cycle, characterized by elation and a feeling of well-being together with quickness of thought.

1882 *Jrnl. Nerv. & Mental Dis.* IX. 432 This description ..belongs not to acute mania properly so-called, but to the hypomania of Mendel,..or the so-called subacute mania of asylum reports. **1892** D. H. Tuke *Dict. Psychol. Med.* I. 618/2 *Hypomania,* a name given to subacute attacks of mania, which are marked by an initial melancholia, retardation of the flow of ideas, and consequently as incoherence, restlessness, increased self-consciousness with delusions of a grandiose character and perversion of sexual instincts. **1904** T. Johnstone tr. *Kraepelin's Lect. Clinical Psychiatry* vii. 60 This combination of symptoms..we designate by the name of Mania, or, if the individual disturbances are only slightly developed,.. by that of Hypomania. **1912** B. Hollander *First Signs of Insanity* xviii. 225 The chief mental characteristic of this disease, known as hypomania, is a loss of mental inhibition and consequently a rapid, ill-regulated, and easily disconnected train of thought. **1927** Henderson & Gillespie *Text-bk. Psychiatry* vii. 121 While such conditions as hypomania, acute mania, and delirious mania can readily be recognised,..the differentiation of these states is not by any means clean cut. **1963** N. H. Pronko *Textbk. Abnormal Psychol.* x. 367 The mildest degree of manic excitement is termed hypomania, and concerns essentially speed and direction of thought rather than thought content. **1971** *Brit. Med. Bull.* XXVII. 77/2 Is a mild hypomania, with some euphoria and flight of ideas, but no delusions or gross behavioural disturbance, to be called psychotic or not?

hypomaniac (həipomē·niæk). [f. prec., after Maniac *a.* and *sb.*] = *hypomanic *sb.*

1910 B. Hollander *Mental Symptoms Brain Dis.* iii. 25 The good spirits of the hypomaniac seem, excepting for occasional slight abatement, to be inexhaustible. **1965** Rosen & Gregory *Abnormal Psychol.* xiv. 291/2 Like simple depressives, many hypomaniacs receive no treatment.

hypomanic (həipomæ·nik), *a.* and *sb.* [f. as prec., after *manic *a.* and *sb.*] **A.** *adj.* Of or affected with hypomania.

1927 Henderson & Gillespie *Text-bk. Psychiatry* vii. 126 The hypomanic elation showed the usual characteristics—overactivity (with erotic tendencies coming to the fore), an infectious and excessive gaiety, over-talkativeness..and lack of sustained attention. **1941** S. H. Kraines *Therapy Neuroses & Psychoses* xv. 359 Early in the attack she appeared to the casual observer to be merely an active, vivacious girl;..she was hypomanic only in relation to her accustomed and usual behavior. **1965** [see *cyclothymic* s.v. *cyclo-].

B. *sb.* A person affected with hypomania.

1932 *Brit. Jrnl. Psychol.* XXIII. 155 The expansive hypomanic greets us with the sunny smile of happiness. **1938** S. Beckett *Murphy* ix. 168 A hypomanic teaching slosh to a Korsakow's syndrome. **1954** W. Mayer-Gross et al. *Clin. Psychiatry* v. 196 Hypomanics are realistic, quick to grasp opportunities, versatile and often rather superficial.

Hence **hypoma·nically** *adv.*

1958 M. Argyle *Relig. Behaviour* ix. 107 Hysterics tend to become hypomanically excited at revival meetings.

hyponym (həi·ponim). [f. Hypo- + Gr. ὄνομα name.] **1.** *Taxonomy.* A name made invalid by the lack of adequate contemporary description of the taxon it was intended to designate.

1904 *Bull. Torrey Bot. Club* XXXI. 258 A specific or subspecific name is a hyponym when it has not been connected with a description identifiable by diagnostic characters or by reference to a type specimen, figure or locality. **1904** *Science* 25 Mar. 509/2 Some are hyponyms, never having been associated with a recognizable binomial species. **1946** D. B. Swingle *Textbk. Syst. Bot.* (ed. 3) ix. 225 A name not so described or identified is a hyponym and nonvalid for the group for which it was intended. *Ibid.* 226 Homonyms and hyponyms result in the formation of synonyms, for these names must be replaced by usable terms, leaving them as synonyms.

2. *Linguistics.* One of two or more words related by hyponymy.

1963 J. Lyons *Structural Semantics* iv. 69, I say that *scarlet* is a hyponym of, or is included in, *red.* **1965**

Language XLI. 509 Hyponyms are placed under the head word.

hyponymy (həipǫ·nimi). *Linguistics.* [f. HYPO- + Gr. ὄνομα after SYNONYMY, etc.] (See quot. 1963.)

1955 C. E. BAZELL in *Litera* II. 34 There is a relation of hyponymy when one word may invariably be replaced by a second word, but not vice-versa, without change of meaning. **1962** F. W. HOUSEHOLDER in Householder & Saporta *Probl. in Lexicogr.* 280 Thorough investigation of semantic structure is desirable, and where we have already sufficient knowledge to indicate relationships of incompatibility, hyponymy..etc., this should be done in the most economical way possible. **1963** J. LYONS *Structural Semantics* iv. 69 Hyponymy is the relation that holds, for instance, between *scarlet* and *red*, or between *tulip* and *flower*, in English...It may be defined in terms of unilateral implication. Thus, *X is scarlet* will be understood (generally) to imply *X is red*; but not conversely. **1970** A. CAMERON et al. *Computers & O.E. Concordances* 92, I would draw your attention to the sketchy attempt to state the sense-relations of Old English words in terms of ..hyponymy (or inclusion of sense: ⊂ sign).

hy:poparathy·roidism. *Med.* [f. HYPO- + PARATHYROID + -ISM.] A condition in which there is an abnormally low level of parathyroid hormone in the blood, resulting in hypocalcæmia and hyperphosphatæmia with consequent tetany and other signs of neuro-muscular excitability.

1910 OCHSNER & THOMPSON *Surg. & Path. Thyroid & Parathyroid Glands* xx. 345 In a patient suffering greatly from subtetanic hypoparathyroidism..tetany has for two years been averted. **1938** SMITH & GAULT *Ess. Path.* lx. 746/1 The relationship of tetany to hypoparathyroidism is dependent primarily upon a drop in blood calcium. **1966** WRIGHT & SYMMERS *Systemic Path.* II. xxxii. 1126/1 The commonest cause of hypoparathyroidism is, of course, accidental removal of the glands during thyroidectomy. **1970** *Med. Ann.* 199 The tragedy of hypoparathyroidism lies in the lifelong burden of its control.

Hence **hy:poparathy·roid** *a.*, of, resulting from, or having hypoparathyroidism.

1910 OCHSNER & THOMPSON *Surg. & Path. Thyroid & Parathyroid Glands* xii. 205 To the internist the question of a hypoparathyroid etiology in the various tetanies became of interest. **1950** COPE & HAMLIN in S. Soskin *Progr. Clin. Endocrinol.* ii. 110 Following operative correction of hyperparathyroidism, patients may have chronic tetany of continued hypoparathyroid origin. **1970** C. N. GRAYMORE *Biochem. Eye* iv. 309 Lens lesions indistinguishable from hypoparathyroid cataract.

hypopharynx. Add: **2.** *Anat.* The lower, laryngeal part of the pharynx (into which the larynx opens), extending from the epiglottis to the top of the œsophagus.

1907 *Lancet* 25 May 1421/1, I propose to give a description of a new and excellent method of inspecting the laryngeal part of the pharynx, the hypopharynx as it is also called. **1954** W. H. HOLLINSHEAD *Anat. for Surgeons* I. viii. 405/2 The laryngeal pharynx or hypopharynx extends from just above the level of the hyoid bone superiorly to the cricoid cartilage inferiorly, narrowing rapidly to become continuous with the esophagus. **1962** *Lancet* 28 Apr. 901/2 The patients were placed in the lateral head-down position owing to bleeding from the hypopharynx.

†**hypo·physal,** *a. Obs.* [f. HYPOPHYS(IS + -AL.] = *HYPOPHYSIAL *a.*

1877 *Gray's Anat.* (ed. 8) p. cxxx, Others refer the hypophysal part of the pituitary body to epiblastic elements derived from the buccal part of the epiblast only. **1892** C. S. MINOT *Human Embryol.* (1897) xxvi. 574 The hypophysal diverticulum now elongates and its upper end expands to a considerable vesicle.

hypophyseal, var. *HYPOPHYSIAL *a.*

hypophysectomy (həi:pofise·ktŏmi). *Surg.* [f. HYPOPHYS(IS + *-ECTOMY.] Excision of the hypophysis.

1909 REFORD & CUSHING in *Bull. Johns Hopkins Hosp.* XX. 106/1 The effects of total canine hypophysectomy. **1939** M. A. GOLDZIEHER *Endocrine Glands* I. 270 Adult amphibia show atrophy of both ovaries and testes after hypophysectomy. **1962** *Lancet* 15 Dec. 1235/1 Women with advanced breast cancer who subsequently fail to respond to adrenalectomy or hypophysectomy excrete significantly smaller amounts of urinary 11-deoxy 17-oxosteroids than do women who respond. **1967** S. TAYLOR et al. *Short Textbk. Surg.* xv. 189 Adrenalectomy and hypophysectomy are being performed much less often now than a few years ago, because remissions are unpredictable and often short-lived.

Hence **hy:pophyse·ctomize** *v. trans.*, to deprive of the hypophysis, perform hypophysectomy on; usu. as **hy:pophyse·ctomized** *ppl. a.*

1910 *Bull. Johns Hopkins Hosp.* XXI. 131/1 Two of the partially hypophysectomized animals survived for 5 months. **1912** H. CUSHING *Pituitary Body & its Disorders* I. 11 Of a litter of three puppies..one, the largest, was partially hypophysectomized, one was fed daily..with powdered extract of the whole gland..: the third and smallest was kept as a control. **1934** C. J. WIGGERS *Physiol. Health & Dis.* (1935) lxvii. 1055 Hypophysectomized tadpoles neither grow nor metamorphose. **1936** *Jrnl. Path. & Bacteriol.* XLII. 403 A tendency to maintenance of body weight after grafting of pituitary cultures into hypophysectomised rats has been taken as evidence of replacement of pituitary function. **1966** W. S. HOAR in Harris & Donovan *Pituitary Gland* I. vi. 246 The Amphibians are relatively easy to hypophysectomize. **1970** *Nature* 31 Oct. 464/2 Administration of growth hormone to hypophysectomized rats essentially prevented the appearance of any hypercholesterolaemia.

hypophysial (həipofi·ziăl), *a.* Also **hypophyseal** (həipofi·ziăl, həi:pofisī·ăl). [f. HYPOPHYSI(S + -AL; *hypophyseal* by alteration of *hypophysial*.] Of or pertaining to the hypophysis.

1882 *Jrnl. Linn. Soc.* (*Zool.*) XVI. 133 In the Mammalian series I have to observe that, in the lower and smaller members, as the brain loses in relative size and complexity, the pineal or conarial and pituitary or hypophysial bodies and connections show a relatively larger size. **1893** *Jrnl. Path. & Bacteriol.* I. 360 In the dog there is a more or less symmetrical lateral arrangement of the hypophyseal fissures. **1909** H. CUSHING in *Jrnl. Amer. Med. Assoc.* 24 July 254/1 Symptoms of hypophyseal origin doubtless occur in association with many diseases in which they are overlooked. **1912** —— *Pituitary Body & its Disorders* III. 233 In clinical conditions of hypophyseal deficiency somnolence is a conspicuous feature. **1943** G. W. CORNER in *Science* 15 Jan. 68 In the 1864 revision of Webster..epiphyseal appears before epiphysial; in the revision of 1909 apophyseal enters the lists; in the current (1934) revision hypophyseal appears, and the spelling with -eal is preferred in all three cases...Possibly 'epiphyseal' goes back to the days when the noun was often written 'epiphyse', or possibly some writers thought it was advisable to make the adjectives from the genitives of the Greek nouns (e.g., *epiphyseos, hypophyseos*). Much more likely, however, the spelling has been influenced by an American trend in the pronunciation... At the present time (and as far as my observation goes, for decades past) American speakers almost universally place the primary accent on the fourth syllable, e.g., hypophysḗal... In spite of the fact that '-eal' is philologically irregular, I make bold to suggest that it be adopted as standard in American scientific writing,..in conformity with our well-nigh general pronunciation of the three words in question. **1955** G. W. HARRIS *Neural Control Pituitary Gland* v. 124 The pathway by which a stimulus passes from the hypothalamus to the anterior pituitary appears to be by means of the hypophysial portal vessels. **1962** *Gray's Anat.* (ed. 33) 1038 The hypophysis receives its blood supply from the internal carotid artery through a superior and an inferior hypophyseal artery on each side.

hypophysiotrophic (həi:pofiziotrōᵘ·fik), **-tropic** (-trōᵘ·pik, -trǫ·pik), *a. Physiol.* [f. HYPOPHYSI(S + -O + *-TROPHIC, *-TROPIC.] Regulating the activity of the hypophysis.

1962 B. HALÁSZ et al. in *Jrnl. Endocrinol.* XXV. 147 Histological and functional evidence has been obtained which defines what may be called the 'hypophysiotrophic' region of the hypothalamus. **1968** C. B. JØRGENSEN in Barrington & Jørgensen *Perspectives in Endocrinol.* viii. 489 The existence of more diffuse 'hypophysiotropic' regions within the hypothalamus has been supported by the results of recent studies. **1970** *Nature* 25 Apr. 322/2 These results allow us to claim the preparation, for the first time, of a hypothalamic hypophysiotropic releasing factor.

hypophysis. Add: Pl. **hypophyses** (həipǫ·fisīz). **3.** [First used by S. T. Soemmerring (*De Corporis Humani Fabrica* (rev. ed., 1798) IV. 70).] Add to def.: A small endocrine organ that is attached or adjacent to the hypothalamus in the brain of vertebrates, has two lobes distinct in origin, nature, and function (cf. *ADENO- and *NEUROHYPOPHYSIS), and produces a number of hormones, some of which regulate the activity of other endocrine organs; in man it lies within a cavity of the sphenoid bone under a covering of *dura mater* and is attached by the infundibulum to the undersurface of the brain. (Examples.)

The application of the term has varied. Some writers have restricted it to the anterior or the posterior lobe only (differentiating the hypophysis from the pituitary body); others have taken it to include not only the two lobes but also the infundibulum.

1825 A. MONRO *Elem. Anat. Human Body* II. VI. ii. 371 The Pituitary Gland, or Hypophysis, is a small oblong-shaped body, which is inclosed by the dura mater, and situated in the tela sphenoidalis. **1877** W. TURNER *Introd. Human Anat.* I. v. 213 This ventricle is prolonged downwards into a funnel-shaped process, the infundibulum, which is connected with the pituitary body, or hypophysis cerebri. **1898** W. H. HOWELL in *Jrnl. Exper. Med.* III. 246 The hypophysis cerebri is usually described as consisting of two lobes. One, the large anterior lobe, is distinctly a glandular structure... Properly speaking the term hypophysis cerebri should be restricted to this lobe, and this significance is now given to it by morphological writers, although in human anatomy it is still commonly employed to include the so-called posterior lobe as well. *Ibid.* 247 Extracts were made of both the hypophysis cerebri, or anterior lobe, and the infundibular body. **1899** F. H. GERRISH *Text-bk. Anat.* 534 The hypophysis has been found greatly enlarged in cases of giantism, and hence has been supposed to sustain a relation to the stature of the individual. **1906** J. P. McMURRICH *Devel. Human Body* (ed. 2) xiv. 428 At its extremity the hypophysis comes in contact during the fifth week with the enlarged extremity of Rathke's pouch..and applies itself closely to the posterior surface of this..to form with it the pituitary body. **1915** A. M. PATERSON *Man. Embryol.* II. i. 110 The pituitary body has a double origin... The tuber cinereum, infundibulum, and posterior lobe (hypophysis cerebri) are outgrowths from the ventral aspect of the diencephalon. The anterior lobe of the pituitary body is derived from Rathke's pouch. **1919** W. B. BELL *Pituitary* 2 The word 'hypophysis', strictly speaking, refers to the epithelial portions of the Pituitary—the pars anterior and the pars intermedia—and should only be used in this connexion. **1926** G. R. DE BEER *Compar. Anat. Pituitary Body* ii. 26 The term *pituitary body* should be used to denote the well-defined anatomical unit consisting of four parts—anterior, intermedia, nervosa, and tuberalis. Other structures, such as the infundibulum and the tuber cinereum, may be grouped with the pituitary body to form a functional unit, the pituitary complex. The term *hypophysis* is often loosely used as synonymous with pituitary body, but wrongly, since it definitely refers only to the epithelial constituent of the body. **1936** *Jrnl. Morphol.* LX. 127 A cytological study of the hypophyses of more than 100 female bats. **1940** *Res. Publ. Assoc. Res. Nerv. & Mental Dis.* XX. 22 The mammalian hypophysis consists of three major divisions: lobus glandularis, lobus nervosus and the infundibulum or neural stalk. This classification has been recommended by the International Commission on Anatomical Nomenclature (1935). **1944** E. T. BELL *Text-bk. Path.* (ed. 5) xxviii. 755 The hypophysis exercises a certain amount of control over the other glands of internal secretion and the growth and activity of various organs by means of specific hormones which it elaborates. **1954** A. WHITE et al. *Princ. Biochem.* xlv. 957 The hypophysis is one of the most important endocrine glands in the body, exerting a profound influence over other endocrine structures and thereby regulating a large portion of the endocrine activity of the organism. **1960** B. I. BALINSKY *Introd. Embryol.* xviii. 452 The agent necessary for activating the thyroid gland is produced in the anterior (epidermal) lobe of the hypophysis.

hypoplastic (həipoplæ·stik), *a. Med.* [f. *hypoplasia* (s.v. HYPO- II) + *-PLASTIC.] Of an organ or tissue: undersized at maturity owing to insufficient growth; *hypoplastic anæmia*, anæmia that is due to an insufficient production of red blood cells by the bone-marrow.

1877 tr. *H. von Ziemssen's Cycl. Pract. Med.* XVI. 543 The sexual organs will remain relatively hypoplastic, or will be late in arriving at functional maturity. **1906** C. P. EMERSON *Clin. Diagn.* v. 515 By hypoplastic anæmia is meant one due to insufficient blood formation. **1915** *Brit. Dental Jrnl.* XXXVI. 174 In studying the etiology of hypoplastic teeth, development and calcification may be divided into three distinct periods. **1918** *Amer. Jrnl. Med. Sci.* CLVI. 49 The aorta was described as hypoplastic in 101 cases...In 71 of these cases hypoplasia was determined by actual measurement of the relative width of the pulmonary artery and the aorta. **1938** DIAMOND & BLACKFAN in *Amer. Jrnl. Dis. Children* LVI. 464 In the past seven years we have had the opportunity to see an intermediate type of anemia—hypoplastic rather than completely aplastic. This condition has been characterized by slowly progressive anemia.. with the production of a small and inadequate number of reticulocytes from bone marrow which shows moderate hypoplasia. **1961** L. MARTIN *Clinical Endocrinol.* (ed. 3) vii. 199 The breasts were large but the nipples hypoplastic. **1963** M. C. G. ISRAËLS *Diagn. & Treatm. Blood Dis.* viii. 59 Senile hypoplastic anæmia is really a premature diminution of bone-marrow activity.

hyposensitization (həi:posensitəizēⁱ·ʃən). *Med.* [f. HYPO- 4 + SENSITIZATION, after *hypersensitization*.] The process of diminishing the sensitivity of a hypersensitive individual (as by the introduction of the allergen in a series of gradually increasing doses); a state of diminished sensitivity so produced.

1922 R. A. COOKE in *Jrnl. Immunol.* VII. 241 On account of the confusion that must result from the use of the well defined term 'desensitization' to designate clinically lessened sensitiveness in allergy it is suggested that the latter be referred to as a 'hyposensitization'. **1941** J. W. THOMAS *Allergy in Clin. Pract.* i. 11 When complete avoidance is impossible or impractical, hyposensitization with inhalants..should be considered. **1953** F. K. HANSEL *Clin. Allergy* xxxix. 750 The terms desensitization and hyposensitization are used interchangeably to designate a lessening of sensitization or an increase of tolerance. **1971** O. SWINEFORD *Asthma* ix. 148 Treatment of allergic asthma by injecting extracts of allergens is called hyposensitization.

Hence **hypose·nsitize** *v. trans.*, to subject (an individual) to such a process; also *absol.*; **hypose·nsitized** *ppl. a.*

1931 W. T. VAUGHAN *Allergy & Appl. Immunol.* xx. 249 If contact with the allergen then produces no symptoms, he is..desensitized. If his symptoms are improved but not entirely relieved, he is hyposensitized. **1939** —— *Primer of Allergy* vii. 67 We can hyposensitize with practically any of the allergens which are inhaled (except chemicals). **1944** E. URBACH *Allergy* x. 249 Coca has succeeded in hyposensitizing a patient with turpentine allergy..by injecting turpentine dissolved in sterile almond oil every seven days. **1971** O. SWINEFORD *Asthma* ix. 148 How does one hyposensitize a patient?

Hypospray (həi·posprēⁱ). Also **hypospray.** [f. HYPO(DERMIC *a.* + SPRAY *sb.*[2]] The proprietary name of a kind of jet injector (see *JET *sb.*[3] 9).

1947 *Life* 24 Nov. 65/1 Known as the Hypospray, this new device 'blasts' a microscopically small jet of medicinal fluid into the body tissues. **1948** *U.S. Pat. Off. Gaz.* 7 Sept. 69/1 *Hypospray*. R. P. Scherer Corporation, Detroit, Mich... For Hypodermic Injection Devices. **1948** *Amer. Practitioner* III. 206/1 The Hypospray may be used to

give either intramuscular or subcutaneous injections. **1956** *Ann. Rheumatic Dis.* XV. 231/2 A practical feature of the hypospray injection is the simplicity of the technique. The physician can inject several joints in a short time without the preliminary preparation required for needle injection. **1969** *Ibid.* XXVIII. 61/2 The Hypospray was considerably less painful and more acceptable to patients.

hypostasis. Add: **7.** *Genetics.* [Back-formation from *HYPOSTATIC *a.* 3] The inhibition of the expression of one gene by the action of another non-allelic (epistatic) gene.

1917 *Genetics* II. 615/1 (Index), Hypostasis. **1962** I. H. HERSKOWITZ *Genetics* vii. 53/1 Genes whose detection is hampered by nonallelic genes are said to be hypostatic, i.e., to exhibit hypostasis. As dominance implies recessiveness, so epistasis implies hypostasis.

8. *Linguistics.* The citing of a word, word-element, etc., as an example, a model, etc. Also, a linguistic element thus referred to.

1933 L. BLOOMFIELD *Lang.* ix. 148 Hypostasis, the mention of a phonetically normal speech-form, as when we say, 'That is only an *if*', or 'There is always a *but*', or when we talk about 'the word *normalcy*' or 'the name *Smith*'. One may even speak of parts of words, as..'the suffix *-ish* in *boyish*'. **1940** *Language* XVI. 238 When the sign is combined with a morpheme or is used in another grammatical category (hypostasis)..it is said to be characterized or positivized. **1961** *Lingua* X. 175 All I want to say is that the subject of this paper is..how to analyse linguistic signs occurring in *suppositio materialis* or (as I shall henceforth say) in hypostasis. **1963** *Ibid.* XII. 211 Sometimes hypostasis forms are used in other syntactical functions than subject, object or part of an adverbial adjunct, but at least those three functions are the most frequent in English. **1967** K. L. PIKE *Lang. in Rel. Human Behavior* (ed. 2) 108 Spelling words aloud is a form of hypostasis. *Ibid.* 484 This is treating sentences in hypostasis.

hypostatic, *a.* Add: **3.** *Genetics.* Of, causing, or affected by hypostasis (sense *7). Const. *to*.

1907 [see *EPISTATIC *a.*]. **1961** A. MÜNTZING *Genetic Res.* vi. 58/2 We may also say that B is hypostatic to A. **1965** J. A. SERRA *Mod. Genetics* I. iii. 62 The effect of one gene, the epistatic gene, is superimposed on the effect of another, the hypostatic gene, either by obscuring the phenotypic effect of the hypostatic gene, or by inhibiting its effect.

hypotension (həipote·nʃən). *Med.* [f. HYPO- 4 + TENSION *sb.*] Abnormally low 'tension' or pressure of a bodily fluid. **a.** Of arterial blood.

1893 [see *HYPERTENSION 1 a]. **1938** *Lancet* 31 Dec. 1510/2 Hypotension is sometimes accompanied by.. postural giddiness. **1966** WRIGHT & SYMMERS *Systemic Path.* I. iii. 110/1 Moderate degrees of hypotension may.. occur in patients with chronic wasting diseases, especially when they are confined to bed for long periods.

b. Of the intra-ocular fluid.

1909 A. M. RAMSAY *Diathesis & Ocular Dis.* v. 46 The easiest..method..is to puncture the sclerotic with a broad needle... This causes immediate hypotension. **1969** DUKE-ELDER & JAY in S. Duke-Elder *Syst. Ophthalm.* XI. x. 724 The subject of ocular hypotension has excited much less interest and speculation than that of hypertension.

hypotensive (həipote·nsiv), *a.* *Med.* [f. prec. + -IVE.] Of, exhibiting, or associated with hypotension, esp. of the blood; tending to lower the blood pressure.

1904 T. C. JANEWAY *Clin. Study Blood-Pressure* vi. 153 Typhoid fever is more frequently hypotensive in the average case than the other acute diseases, pneumonia least. **1927** *Medicine* VI. 147 It is also true that many hypotensive subjects possess great bodily vigor. **1951** A. GROLLMAN *Pharmacol. & Therapeutics* xi. 213 It is also used..to combat a drop in blood-pressure occurring during spinal anesthesia and in other acute hypotensive states due to vasomotor failure. **1961** *Lancet* 29 July 222/2 Patients with severe arterial hypertension were given hypotensive drugs only if they had been so treated previously. **1966** *Ibid.* 26 Mar. 677/1 A few hours after admission the patient became hypotensive and vasopressor drugs had to be used. **1973** *Times* 2 Oct. 15/2 One of the most common fatal side-effects is that it becomes hypotensive (low blood pressure).

hypothalamo-hypophysial (həipoþæ:lămo,-həipofi·ziăl), *a.* Also **-eal.** [f. *HYPOTHALAM(US + -O + *HYPOPHYSIAL *a.*] Of, pertaining to, or connecting the hypothalamus and the hypophysis; applied *spec.* to a tract of nerve fibres that runs from the hypothalamus to the neurohypophysis.

1934 *Arch. Neurol. & Psychiatry* (Chicago) XXXII. 217 The entity of the fibers traversing the infundibulum and entering the posterior lobe of the hypophysis is called the hypothalamo-hypophyseal fasciculus ('faisceau hypothalamo-hypophysaire'). **1950** G. W. HARRIS in *Jrnl. Physiol.* CXI. 347 The hypophysial stalk has two main component parts, the hypothalamo-hypophysial tract of nerve fibres associated with the neurohypophysis, and the hypophysial portal vessels associated with the adenohypophysis. **1971** N. G. SUTTON *Anat. Brain & Spinal Medulla* v. 78 A series of hypothalamohypophyseal portal vessels descend in the form of numerous blood sinusoids to end among the cells of the adenohypophysis. **1972** *Nature* 5 May 15/1 These connexions..may prove to be an important component of the pathways which subserve the marked effect of light on the hypothalamo-hypophysial activity.

Also **hypothala:mico-hypophy·sial, -eal** *a.*, in the same sense.

1934 *Trans. Coll. Phys. Philadelphia* II. 223 Diabetes insipidus and Fröhlich's syndrome are due to disturbances of this hypothalamico-hypophyseal mechanism. **1944** J. HOFFMAN *Female Endocrinol.* xv. 226 A neuro-endocrine unit which has recently attracted much attention is the so-called hypothalamico-hypophyseal system. **1961** *Lancet* 2 Sept. 522/2 Lesions have been found in the hypothalamicohypophyseal system in only a few cases of primary diabetes insipidus.

hypothalamus (həipoþæ·lămɒs). *Anat.* [mod.L. (W. His (at Waldeyer's suggestion) 1893, in *Arch. f. Anat. u. Physiol.* (*Anat. Abth.*) 159), f. HYPO- + THALAMUS.] The lower part of the diencephalon of the brain in vertebrates, lying below and in front of the thalamus and forming the floor and part of the wall of the third ventricle; in mammals it acts as the chief co-ordinating region of the autonomic nervous system and helps to regulate the hormonal activity of the adenohypophysis.

Writers vary in counting as part of the hypothalamus (*a*) the infundibulum and neurohypophysis, and (*b*) the subthalamic tegmental region.

1896 *Jrnl. Compar. Neurol.* VI. 309 (*in list of anatomical names*) Hypothalamus. **1899** L. F. BARKER *Nervous Syst.* xlvi. 666 These various fibres..pass through the pedunculus cerebri..to reach the diencephalon, where most of them in all probability terminate in the hypothalamus, in the thalamencephalon, or in the nucleus lentiformis. **1909** *Gray's Anat.* (ed. 17) 849 The hypothalamus..includes the subthalamic tegmental region and the structures which form the greater part of the floor of the third ventricle, viz. the corpora mamillaria, tuber cinereum, infundibulum, pituitary body, and optic commissure. **1942** L. H. HYMAN *Compar. Vertebr. Anat.* (ed. 2) xiv. 434 The hypothalamus reaches its greatest development in fishes, where it is an important correlation center for olfactory, gustatory, and other sensory impulses. **1944** J. HOFFMAN *Female Endocrinol.* xv. 231 Proof that the hypothalamus regulates the gonadotropic function of the anterior hypophysis is still lacking. **1956** A. C. GUYTON *Textbk. Med. Physiol.* l. 633/1 When a surgeon operates in the region of the hypothalamus, simply tugging on the tissues is likely to cause such intense changes in heart rate, blood pressure, blood glucose level, body temperature, etc., that the operative mortality is approximately 40 per cent from these factors alone. **1962** T. W. TORREY *Morphogenesis Vertebr.* xviii. 510 In all vertebrates it is the hypothalamus which exercises control over such truly involuntary actions as temperature regulation, sexual reactions, breathing rate, emotional responses, and the rhythm of sleep. **1964** PARKER & HASWELL *Text-bk. Zool.* (ed. 7) II. 245 [In the dogfish, *Scyliorhinus*] the hypothalamus in the floor of the diencephalon is well-developed and may, as in 'higher' vertebrates, be concerned with the regulation of various unconditioned reflexes and visceral functions. **1968** A. VAN TIENHOVEN *Reprod. Physiol. Vertebr.* viii. 207/1 The hypothalamus thus performs the task of being an intermediary between the nervous system, of which it is part, and the endocrine system, to which it can send 'hormonal' information. **1968** *Times* 10 Oct. 8/5 One part of the brain which contains noradrenaline is the hypothalamus, which has the function of controlling body temperature by monitoring the temperature of the blood and directing the body systems to lose or conserve heat. **1972** *Sci. Amer.* Nov. 24/1 The pituitary gland is attached by a stalk to the region in the base of the brain known as the hypothalamus.

Hence **hypotha·lamic** *a.*, of or pertaining to the hypothalamus.

1899 L. F. BARKER *Nervous Syst.* xlvi. 683 In man the fibres of the main mass of white matter in the hypothalamic region..do not pass through the hilus into the thalamus. **1938** J. BEATTIE in W. E. Le Gros Clark et al. *Hypothalamus* 100 Sleep..is due to a damping-down of hypothalamic activity. **1942** O. LARSELL *Anat. Nerv. Syst.* iii. 28 The thalamus and hypothalamus are bounded from each other by the hypothalamic sulcus. **1954** T. L. PEELE *Neuroanat. Basis Clin. Neurol.* xiv. 310/2 Hypothalamic lesions..have resulted in a loss of cyclical sexual activities and genital atrophy. **1968** A. VAN TIENHOVEN *Reprod. Physiol. Vertebr.* viii. 249/1 Some of the hypothalamic hormones, e.g. oxytocin and vasopressin, are stored in the neurohypophysis.

hypothecate, *v.* Add: **2.** *trans.* = HYPOTHESIZE *v.* 2.

1906 *Nature* 7 June 136/1 Mr. Cowell hypothecated a resisting medium through which the earth travels. **1912** R. FRY in *Gt. State* ix. 271 Mr. Wells's Modern Utopia ..hypothecates a vast superstructure of private trading. **1915** E. B. HOLT *Freudian Wish* i. 4 One will best..not hypothecate to this end any such thing as 'psychic energy'. **1920** E. POUND *Let.* 12 Sept. (1971) 161 You are talking through your hat when you suggest that I..was ever ass enough to have picked 'La Figlia' for the fantastic occasion you hypothecate. **1952** *Pediatrics* IX. 724 One had to hypothecate the existence of a mutation of organisms.

hypothermia (həipoþɜ̄·ɹmiă). *Med.* Also in anglicized form **hypothermy** (həi·poþɜ̄ɹmi) (*rare*). [f. HYPO- 4 + Gr. θέρμ-η heat + -IA[1].] The condition of having a body temperature substantially below the normal, either as a result of natural causes or artificially induced (e.g. for cardiac surgery).

1886 in *Syd. Soc. Lex.* **1887** A. M. BROWN *Contrib. Animal Alkaloids* 143 Intoxication by animal alkaloids is accompanied by hypothermia. **1898** W. S. BARLOW *Man. Gen. Path.* x. 441 Emphysema and some other forms of pulmonary disease..are associated with a slight degree of hypothermia. **1903** *Jrnl. Nerv. & Mental Dis.* XXX. 574 The same toxic agent which acts on the nervous system producing the condition of epilepsy may be the cause of the hypothermy in these cases. **1937** *Brit. Encycl. Med. Pract.* III. 499 The reduction of the metabolic processes in cretinism is shown, as in myxoedema, by hypothermia. **1955** *Sci. News Let.* 18 June 389/2 When patients are given 'frozen sleep', or hypothermia, for operations inside the heart, they can be quickly warmed to normal by diathermy. **1964** *Courier-Mail* (Brisbane) 18 July 2 His problem probably had been 'hypothermia'—low body temperature—quite common in cold weather in elderly people who do not keep themselves sufficiently warm. **1966** *New Statesman* 11 Nov. 697/1 The experts concluded that 'hypothermia is a serious though unspectacular condition with a very high mortality rate'.

So **hypothe·rmic** *a.* [cf. Gr. ὑπόθερμος somewhat hot], of or exhibiting hypothermia.

1898 W. S. L. BARLOW *Man. Gen. Path.* x. 440 A general sluggishness of nerve and of muscle in hypothermic persons and animals is always noticeable. **1948** A. R. MORITZ in W. A. D. Anderson *Path.* vi. 143 The severity of injury caused at any given temperature tends to be proportional to the duration of the hypo- or hyperthermic episode. **1961** *Lancet* 2 Dec. 1216/2 The complete absence of residual signs of cerebral dysfunction was particularly noteworthy in one patient who remained hypothermic and unconscious for seven days.

hypothetic. B. *sb.* **2.** Restrict *obs.* to senses in Dict. and add: *sb. pl.* The making of hypotheses; hypothesizing.

1890 A. LANG *Life Sir Stafford Northcote* (ed. 2) II. xiii. 89 That belongs to the science of hypothetics, and anyone may sincerely believe that matters might have been kept quiet by a sagacious and well-informed policy. **1958** *New Biol.* XXV. 15 Perhaps we shall be helped to estimate its importance by an exercise in hypothetics.

hypothe:tico-dedu·ctive, *a.* *Philos.* [f. HYPOTHETIC(AL *a.* + -O + DEDUCTIVE *a.*, prob. as ad. It. *ipotetico-deduttivo* hypothetical-deductive (M. Pieri 1900, in *Mem. d. R. Accad. d. Sci. di Torino* XLIX. 173).] Making use of or consisting in the testing of the consequences of hypotheses (i.e. seeing whether the consequences are consistent with observation) as a means of determining whether the hypotheses themselves are false or can be accepted.

1912 *Philos. Rev.* XXI. 642 The type of reasoning that takes place in the hypothetico-deductive fields of thought. **1929** H. A. WOLFSON *Crescas' Critique of Aristotle* i. 25 The Talmudic hypothetico-deductive method of text interpretation. **1949** tr. *H. Weyl's Philos. Math. & Nat. Sci.* I. i. 27 Pure mathematics, in the modern view, amounts to a general hypothetico-deductive theory of relations; it develops the theory of logical 'molds' without binding itself to one or the other among the possible concrete interpretations. **1952** J. O. WISDOM *Found. Inference Nat. Sci.* xxiv. 223 Many difficulties in the nature of the causal relation and inductive inference are obviated by using the scheme of explanation provided by the hypothetico-deductive system, according to which a hypothesis is accepted when it has been 'tempered' by severe testing and has not been falsified. **1953** R. B. BRAITHWAITE *Scientific Explanation* i. 9 It is this hypothetico-deductive method applied to empirical material which is the essential feature of a science. **1957** G. H. VON WRIGHT *Logical Probl. Induction* (ed. 2) 208 The theory of induction cannot, in the name of the hypothetico-deductive method, be banished from holding a prominent place within the methodology of science. **1963** *Listener* 12 Sept. 378/1 This alternative interpretation of the nature of the scientific process..is sometimes called the 'hypothetico-deductive' interpretation, and this is the view which Professor Karl Popper..has persuaded us is the correct one. **1971** J. Z. YOUNG *Introd. Study Man* xxi. 283 It is by adopting the 'hypothetico-deductive' system that men have been able to make forecasts much more far-reaching and reliable than those of any animal.

Hence **hypothe:tico-dedu·ctively** *adv.*, by the hypothetico-deductive method.

1953 R. B. BRAITHWAITE *Scientific Explanation* ix. 299 The latter of these propositions is establishable hypothetico-deductively without reference to the establishment of the former.

hypothy·roidism. *Med.* [f. HYPO- 4 + THYROID *a.* (*sb.*) + -ISM.] A condition in which the level of thyroxine in the blood is abnormally low resulting in a decreased metabolic rate and which when severe causes cretinism (if the condition was congenital) and myxœdema (if acquired).

1905 GOULD *Dict. New Med. Terms* 304/1 Hypothyroidism. **1909** G. DOCK in Osler & McCrae *Syst. Med.* VI. xviii. 447 The known results of hypothyroidism or athyroidism are: 1. Congenital myxœdema... 2. Infantile myxœdema... 3. Spontaneous myxœdema of adults. **1955** *Sci. News Let.* 24 Sept. 207/3 The tragic effects of hypothyroidism in babies, such as dwarfing and mental retardation, may be prevented by early diagnosis and adequate treatment. **1961** L. MARTIN *Clin. Endocrinol.* (ed. 3) iii. 111 Transient neonatal hypothyroidism may also result from maternal overdosage with antithyroid drugs during pregnancy. **1966** WRIGHT & SYMMERS

Systemic Path. II. xxxi. 1103/2 It is customary to refer to the milder forms as hypothyroidism and to reserve the term myxœdema for the severer clinical varieties.

Hence **hypothy·roid, -thyroi·dic** *adjs.*

1909 G. Dock in Osler & McCrae *Syst. Med.* VI. xviii. 448 Many other conditions, especially certain forms of infantilism and obesity, are classed by some writers as hypothyroid states. *Ibid.* 455 Hypothyroid infants. **1916** *Med. Times* (N.Y.) 7 July 207/1 The hypothyroidic eye is *dull*, seemingly small, apparently sunken, expressionless, in short, featurally insignificant. **1968** Passmore & Robson *Compan. Med. Stud.* I. xxv. 18/2 The hypothyroid person is characteristically cold, sluggish and constipated and often has mild anaemia.

hypotonia (həipotōu·niă). Freq. in anglicized form **hypotony** (həipǫ·tǒni). [mod.L., f. Hypo- 4 + Gr. *τόν-ος* Tone *sb.* + -ia[1].]

1. *Ophthalm.* A state of reduced pressure of the intra-ocular fluid.

1886 *Syd. Soc. Lex., Hypotony*.. Applied by Nagel to the globe of the eye when less resistant than normal. **1892** A. Duane tr. *Fuchs's Text-bk. Ophthalm.* ii. vii. 360 Diminution of the intra-ocular pressure (hypotonia) is found in very diverse affections of the eyeball. **1951** H. S. Sugar *Glaucomas* xxiv. 371 Hypotony, particularly after the trephining operation, may result from too rapid drainage into the conjunctiva. **1966** S. Lerman *Basic Ophthalm.* iv. 246 Another major cause of postoperative hypotony..is a serous detachment of the ciliary body.

2. *Med.* The condition (in muscle or muscular tissue) of being hypotonic.

1886 *Syd. Soc. Lex., Hypotony,* defective tone of a part, or an organ, or a structure. **1907** *Practitioner* Oct. 547 Undue muscular strain on the ankle, knee, hip, and spine, which, together with hypotonia, tends to break down the long arch. **1914** [see *hypertonia]. **1933** W. R. Brain *Dis. Nervous Syst.* i. 12 A lesion of this path causes hypotonia, which is manifested in flaccidity and a diminished resistance to stretching of the affected muscles. **1962** *Lancet* 6 Jan. 22/1 Her growth was stunted and the muscles showed a marked hypotonia with genu recurvatum.

hypotonic (həipǒtǫ·nik), *a.* [f. Hypo- 4 + Tonic *a.*] **1. a.** *Physiol.* Of a solution: having a lower osmotic pressure than some particular solution (usually that in a cell, or a bodily fluid). Const. *to.*

1895 *Jrnl. Physiol.* XVIII. 114 The passage of a salt from a hypotonic fluid into the blood-plasma. **1946** *Nature* 9 Nov. 665/2 The fluid obtained in this way was hypotonic to the cœlomic fluid. **1951** H. Davson *Textbk. Gen. Physiol.* vii. 163 If the plasma surrounding the cells is steadily diluted (i.e., made hypotonic), the latter increase in volume until they finally burst. **1970** [see *hypertonic *a.* 2].

b. *Ophthalm.* Of the eye: having a reduced intra-ocular pressure.

1918 R. H. Elliot *Glaucoma: Textbk. for Student* ii. 19 The case of a hypotonic eye (with a Schiötz reading corresponding to a tension of 8 to 15 mm. of Hg.) such as may be met with after a trephining or other sclerectomy operation. **1966** S. Lerman *Basic Ophthalm.* iv. 246 A hypotonic eye indicates that a leaking wound may be present.

2. *Med.* Exhibiting or characterized by diminished tone or tension (in muscle or muscular tissue).

1904 [see *hypertonus 2]. **1908** *Practitioner* Oct. 560 The lower extremities have been thin, powerless, and extraordinarily hypotonic. **1966** [see *hypertonic *a.* 1].

hypotonicity (həi:potǫ̆ni·siti). [f. prec. + -ity.] The condition of being hypotonic.

a. *Physiol.* Of a solution (see *hypotonic *a.* 1 a): the extent to which a solution has a lower osmotic pressure than some other.

1906 *Amer. Jrnl. Physiol.* XV. 367 Osmotic changes in the direction of hypotonicity. **1939** A. Krogh *Osmotic Regulation Aquatic Animals* 66 Enid Edmonds..found a slight but definite hypotonicity, viz. ocean water 622 mM., blood of the crab 577 mM. **1972** *Lancet* 2 Dec. 1160/2 Hypotonicity of the plasma was observed only on the 3rd and 4th postoperative days, when the daily intake of isotonic dextrose exceeded 1500 ml.

b. *Med.* Of muscle or muscular tissue (see *hypotonic *a.* 2); = *hypotonia 2.

1910 A. Abrams *Diagn. Therapeutics* v. 711 This hypotonicity of the muscles..may also be noted in executing other unaccustomed movements of the muscles of the hand. **1934** C. J. Wiggers *Physiol. Health & Dis.* (1935) xlix. 765 Gastric hypotonicity does not necessarily interfere with emptying the stomach, because the tone of the pyloric sphincter is also reduced, and consequently less intragastric pressure is required to expel the chyme. **1959** E. B. Smith et al. *Princ. Human Path.* lv. 912/1 The hypercalcemia causes interesting clinical findings incident to..hypotonicity of muscle.

hypotonus (həipǒtōu·nǒs). [f. Hypo- 4 + Tonus.] **1.** *Ophthalm.* = *hypotonia 1. Now *rare.*

1891 F. P. Foster *Med. Dict.* III. 1955/2 *Hypotonus,* that condition of the eye in which the intra-ocular tension is below normal, without being of necessity accompanied by any organic disease of the eyeball. **1918** R. H. Elliot *Glaucoma* ii. 22 If too large and too free a channel is cut in the ocular tunic, the escape of fluid is so rapid that a condition of hypotonus results.

2. *Med.* = *hypotonia 2.

1904 *Rev. Neurol. & Psychiatry* II. 776 The legs showed very marked hypotonus. **1928** J. F. H. Dally *Low Blood Pressure* ii. 22 Hypotonia (vascular hypotonus) represents a dynamic and physical state of diminished tonus of the smooth muscle in the walls of arteries and veins. **1939** W. Haymaker tr. *Bing's Textbk. Nervous Dis.* xi. 318 Hypotonus of the quadriceps is sometimes so marked in tabes that the heel can be brought up to the buttock.

hy:poventila·tion. *Physiol.* [f. Hypo- 4 + Ventilation.] A diminished or insufficient exposure of the lungs to oxygen, resulting in a reduced oxygen content of the blood or an increased carbon dioxide content (or both).

1932 *Arch. Neurol. & Psychiatry* XXVIII. 580 To combat this physiologic hypoventilation, the animals were subjected to artificial respiration of normal frequency and depth. **1954** A. White et al. *Princ. Biochem.* xxvii. 715 Hypoventilation of whatever origin (morphine poisoning, pneumonia, pulmonary edema, etc.) has the opposite effect and lowers extracellular pH. **1961** L. Martin *Clinical Endocrinol.* (ed. 3) ii. 55 A cardio-respiratory syndrome has been described by Berlyne (1958) in cases of extreme obesity, of which alveolar hypoventilation is the basic defect.

hypsi-. Add: **hy·psiconch** (-kǫŋk), **hypsi-conchic** (-kǫ·ŋkik), **-conchous** (-kǫ·ŋkəs) *adjs. Anthropol.* [Gr. *κόγχ-ος* eye-socket], having orbits that are high in relation to their width, with an orbital index of 89 (formerly, 85) or more; so **hy·psiconchy,** the condition of being hypsiconchic; **hypsithe·rmal** *a. Geol.* [ad. It. *ipsotermico* (A. Chiarugi 1936, in *Nuovo giorn. bot. ital.* XLIII. 55)], designating that period of the geologically recent past (*c* 7000 to *c* 600 b.c.) when relatively warm conditions prevailed in the northern hemisphere; also *absol.*

1920 H. H. Wilder *Lab. Man. Anthropometry* 67 Hypsiconch..[Orbital index of] 85+. **1960** M. F. A. Montagu *Introd. Physical Anthropol.* (ed. 3) 606 Hypsiconch..[Orbital index of] 85·0 – ×. **1902** Hypsiconchic [see *chamæcephalic* adj. s.v. *chamæ-]. **1960** J. Comas *Man. Physical Anthropol.* vii. 409 Hypsiconchic..[an orbital index of] 89·0 and over. **1885** *Jrnl. R. Anthropol. Inst.* XIV. 71 Hypsikonchous..[Orbital index of] 85·1 and over. **1965** *Dorland's Med. Dict.* (ed. 24) 717/2 *Hypsiconchous,* having an orbital index over 85. **1902** *Biometrika* I. 460 In both sexes there is sensible correlation between the palate and orbital indices, hypsiconchy being associated with brachystaphyline characters. **1957** Deevey & Flint in *Science* 1 Feb. 182/2 The long, warm interval spanned by Danish pollen zones V through VIII, which has been dated from approximately 7000 b.c. to approximately 600 b.c., we propose to call the *hypsithermal* interval. We have changed the spelling of Chiarugi's *ipsotermico* to conform with the English style of Greek adjectives and to express the customary distinction between *hypsi-*, high, and *hypso-*, a height. **1957** *Bull. Geol. Soc. Amer.* LXVIII. 1895 The period from 7000 b.c. to 600 b.c. is now known as the hypsithermal interval, rather than by its former but less suitable designations (postglacial climatic optimum, thermal maximum). **1967** Martin & Wright *Pleistocene Extinctions* 135 The onset of widespread aridity [in Australia], which Gill (1955) equates with the Climatic Optimum or Hypsithermal of the Northern Hemisphere. **1968** R. W. Fairbridge *Encycl. Geomorphol.* 1051/2 Modern deposits may have obtained their maximum growth during the hypsithermal phase of postglacial time.

hypsochrome (hi·psokrōum), *a.* and *sb.* [f. as next.] **A.** *adj.* = next.

1892 *Jrnl. Soc. Chem. Industry* 31 Oct. 807/2 Groups causing deepening are distinguished as 'bathochrome', whilst those to which heightening of the colour is due are termed 'hypsochrome'. **1908** *Jrnl. Chem. Soc.* XCIV. i. 477 (*heading*) Measurement of the effect of certain hypsochrome and bathochrome groups on the colour of azobenzene. **1917** Fort & Lloyd *Chem. Dyestuffs* xiv. 130 Acylation..always gives hypsochrome properties, whether acting upon amines or hydroxy groups.

B. *sb.* A hypsochromic atom or group.

1917 Fort & Lloyd *Chem. Dyestuffs* xiv. 130 Groups or atoms that cause an intensification of colour when introduced into compounds have been called Bathochromes, and those that decrease the colour of a compound Hypsochromes.

hypsochromic (hipsokrōu·mik), *a.* [ad. G. *hypsochrom* (M. Schütze 1892, in *Zeitschr. f. physik. Chem.* IX. 136), f. Hypso- + Gr. *χρῶμ-α* colour: see -ic.] Causing or characterized by a lightening of colour, or a shift of the absorption spectrum towards shorter wavelengths.

1892 *Jrnl. Chem. Soc.* LXII. i. 562 Definite atoms or groups of atoms on entering a molecule cause..a characteristic rise [*read* fall] ('bathochromic groups'), or fall [*read* rise] ('hypsochromic groups'), of the tint. **1932** S. J. Gregg tr. *Eggert's Physical Chem.* 559 The hydrogen atom itself is hypsochromic in nature, for on removing the unsaturated character of a chromophoric group by adding hydrogen to it the absorption band migrates toward the ultra-violet. **1946** [see *hypochromic *a.* 2]. **1957** *Jrnl. Biol. Chem.* CCXXIX. 716 In addition to the reduction in extinction there is a hypsochromic shift of 2 to 3 mμ accompanying the formation of the polymers. **1972** Rys & Zollinger *Fund. Chem. & Applic. Dyes* x. 153 As a rule, the vatting of indigo derivatives..produces a hypsochromic shift.

hypsograph (hi·psograf). [f. Hypso- + -graph.] = *hypsographic curve.*

1937 *Geogr. Jrnl.* XC. 60 The verticality in all the hypsographs at low elevations is explained by the high coastal cliffs and deep V-shaped valleys which prevail.

hypsography. Add: Hence **hypsogra·phic** *a.*, hypsographical; *hypsographic curve*, a curve showing the area or proportion of the earth's (solid) surface, or of a part of it, above any given elevation or depth.

1895 *Geogr. Jrnl.* V. 577 The author points out how the generalized hypsographic curve of the Earth's surface defines the continental plateau. **1937** [see *clinographic *a.*]. **1971** *Nature* 16 July 181/2 Kuenen was able to show from the world hypsographic curve that under present conditions a eustatic rise of 100 m would flood about ⅙ to ⅕ of the continents.

hypsometric, *a.* Add: *hypsometric curve* = *hypsographic curve.*

1924 J. G. A. Skerl tr. *Wegener's Orig. Continents & Oceans* ii. 28 If the whole earth be divided into square kilometres and these are arranged in a series according to their height above sea-level, the well-known..hypsometric curve of the earth's surface is obtained. **1954** W. D. Thornbury *Princ. Geomorphol.* xxi. 531 A hypsometric curve obtained in this way permits comparison of forms of drainage basins of different sizes and altitudes.

hyraceum (həiərēi·siŏm). Also **hyracium.** [f. mod.L. Hyrax, once used as the name of a genus including these animals.] A secretion produced by the African rock hyrax, *Procavia capensis*, formerly used as a fixative for perfume.

1866 Brande & Cox *Dict. Sci., Lit. & Art* II. 182/1 Hyracium. An article imported, as a substitute for castor, from the Cape of Good Hope, and derived from one of the species of *Hyrax.* **1892** P. L. Simmonds *Commercial Dict. Trade Products* (rev. ed.) Suppl. 462/2 Hyraceum, a secretion of the Cape badger, at one time considered to have medicinal properties. **1923** W. A. Poucher *Perfumes & Cosmetics* i. 3 Hyraceum is a secretion having a most disagreeable odour of excreta and urine, and is obtained from a species of monkey [*sic*]. It is occasionally used as a substitute for Castor... This material is not recommended. **1966** C. Sweeney *Scurrying Bush* ii. 34 The faeces of the rock rabbit..contains a substance called hyraceum, which is..incorporated in various perfumes. **1971** D. J. Potgieter et al. *Animal Life S. Afr.* 394/1 These deposits [of the dried urine of the dassie] contain hyraceum, a valuable material used in perfumery.

hyracotherium (həiə:răkopīə·riŏm). Also H-. [mod.L., f. Hyraco- + Gr. *θηρίον* wild beast.] An extinct mammal of the genus so called; a primitive type of horse.

1840 R. Owen in *Proc. Geol. Soc.* III. 163 The resemblance of the molar division..in the new genus, for which the name of Hyracotherium is proposed, and the Chæropotamus, is sufficiently close. *Ibid.,* The incisor teeth with the ossa intermaxillaria are wanting in the specimen of the Hyracotherium. **1851** [in Dict. s.v. Hyraci-, hyraco-]. **1904** *Daily Chron.* 4 Jan. 9/1 Illustrations were given of a four and a five-toed horse, the extinct hyracotherium, no bigger than a Newfoundland dog. **1931** *Discovery* XII. 32/1 The evolution of the horse from the little hyracotherium of the Eocene period—a creature not much larger than a cat—is admirably shown. **1955** *Sci. News Let.* 12 Feb. 104/1 The ancient horse, *Hyracotherium,* was not very much of a horse by modern standards. It was about the size of a shepherd dog and, unlike modern horses, it had four functional toes.

Hyrcan (hə̄·ɹkăn), *sb.* and *a.* Also 6–7 **Hircan,** 6 **Hyrcane.** [ad. L. *Hyrcānus,* a. Gr. *Ὑρκανός*.] = next.

Hyrcan tiger, after L. *Hyrcanæ tigres* (Virgil *Æn.* iv. 367).

1567 W. Barker tr. *Xenophon's Discipline of Cyrus* iv. sig. O2ᵛ, Cyrus beholding the feates of the Medes and Hyrcanes, did as it were, rebuke him selfe. **1584** B. Rich *Second Tome Simonides* sig. C1, These Souldiers, like to Hircan Tigers, reuenge them selues on their owne bowelles. **1592** Daniel *Delia* xviii, But yet restore thy fearce and cruell minde, To Hyrcan tygers, and to ruthles Beares. **1602** T. Lodge tr. *Josephus' Workes* 755 Conspiring with the king of the Hyrcans to passe into Media. **1605** Shakes. *Macb.* iii. iv. 101 The arm'd Rhinoceros, or th'Hircan Tiger. **1911** in W. James *Mem. & Stud.* xv. 395, I took the Hyrcan tiger by the scruff And tore him piecemeal.

Hyrcanian (həɹkēi·niăn), *sb.* and *a.* [f. L. *Hyrcānia* (Gr. *Ὑρκανία*) + -an. Cf. prec.] **A.** *sb.* A native or inhabitant of Hyrcania, an ancient region on the Caspian Sea. **B.** *adj.* Of or pertaining to this region.

Hyrcania was the wild region *par excellence* to the ancients.

1567 W. Barker tr. *Xenophon's Discipline of Cyrus* viii. sig. C8, Of the Hyrcanians, the Colonells son. **1596** Shakes. *Merch. V.* ii. vii. 41 The Hircanion deserts. **1602** —— *Ham.* ii. ii. 472 The rugged Pyrrhus like th'Hyrcanian Beast. **1607** [see *Cimbrian *a.* and *sb.*]. **1671** Milton *P.R.* iii. 317 The Hyrcanian cliffs Of Caucasus. **1777** J. Richardson *Dict. Persian, Arabic & Eng.* I. 1172/2 The red Hyrcanian or Tabristan willow. **1820** Shelley *Ode to Liberty* viii, in *Prometh. Unb.* 213 From what Hyrcanian glen or frozen hill,..Didst thou lament

the ruin of thy reign? **1824** CARLYLE *Let.* 4 Dec. (1909) II. 44 Frightful as the Hyrcanian Tiger. **1838** *Penny Cycl.* XII. 419/2 Josephus..mentions a king of the Hyrcanians in the time of Vespasian. **1885** *Encycl. Brit.* XVIII. 603/1 In [A.D.] 59 the Hyrcanian ambassadors were able to return home. *Ibid.*, The Hyrcanians were still independent *c.* 155. **1973** R. L. FOX *Alexander the Great* ix. 141 In the Caicus valley..the colonists from distant Hyrcania..lived on in the land called the Hyrcanian Plain, where Cyrus had settled them two centuries earlier. *Ibid.* xi. 160 Medes, Armenians, Hyrcanians, North Africans and Persians themselves..fled through the stockade.

Hy-spy. (Later examples of the form 'I spy'.)

1890 W. JAMES *Princ. Psychol.* II. xxiv. 421 It is the same instinct which leads a boy playing 'I spy' to hold his breath when the seeker is near. **1906** *Folk-Lore* XVII. 97 *Key Hoy.* Possibly a modification of 'I Spy'. **1963** *Times* 13 May 15/7, I lament the passing of our daily games of catch-as-catch-can in the cupboards, hide-and-seek behind the wardrobe and I-spy under the piano!

hyssop. Add: **4.** *hyssop-heavy, -laden* adjs.

1899 W. B. YEATS *Wind among Reeds* 52 The hyssop-heavy sponge, the flowers by Kidron stream. **1881** O. WILDE *Poems* 229 No need have we of hyssop-laden rod.

hysteresis. Delete '*Electr.*' and substitute for def.: A phenomenon observed in some physical systems, by which changes in a property (e.g. magnetization, or length) lag behind changes in an agent on which they depend (e.g. magnetizing force, or stress), so that the value of the former at any moment depends on the manner of the previous variation of the latter (e.g. whether it was increasing or decreasing in value); any dependence of the value of a property on the past history of the system to which it pertains. (Further examples.)

1882 J. A. EWING in *Proc. R. Soc.* XXXIV. 40 All changes of magnetisation produced by slow or fast, continuous or discontinuous, changes of the magnetising force exhibit hysteresis. **1903** *Nature* 17 Dec. 160/2 In the relationship of stress to strain, or twisting couple to twist produced, rocks exhibit a marked hysteresis. **1906** *Biochem. Jrnl.* II. 72 The slow change in osmotic pressure observed in colloidal solutions, such as that back to normal conditions in gelatine after a short period at a higher temperature,..indicates a kind of hysteresis in such solutions, or a very slow return to equilibrium after the state of aggregation has been disturbed. **1931** E. S. HEDGES *Colloids* xv. 197 The hysteresis in the case of agar is..far more striking, gelation occurring at about 40° and melting at about 85°. **1939** L. F. BATES *Mod. Magnetism* ix. 279 Temperature hysteresis, i.e. the ferromagnetic loses its ferromagnetism at θ_f on heating and regains it at a temperature below θ_f on cooling. **1950** J. W. MCBAIN *Colloid Sci.* xi. 166 There is a good deal of hysteresis, that is, a time lag between the cooling and the setting to be expected of the jelly. **1956** J. F. D. SMITH in McPherson & Klemin *Engin. Uses of Rubber* v. 130 An inspection of load-deflection diagrams reveals that the loading line may not be the same as the unloading line, for hysteresis plays an important part in flexometers. **1965** A. P. BORESI *Elasticity Engin. Mech.* iv. 103 Whenever a body exhibits the phenomenon of hysteresis—that is, of returning to its original size and shape only slowly or not at all—its behavior is not perfectly elastic.

b. = **hysteresis loss*.

1896 *Min. Proc. Inst. Civil Engin.* CXXVI. 216 If B = 2,500 were taken as the limit of the cycle the hysteresis of this 'record' specimen would be only 0·16 watt per lb.

2. *Comb.*, as **hysteresis curve** = **hysteresis loop*; **hysteresis loop**, a graph showing how the value of some property of a hysteretic system varies as the agent causing it is varied from one value to another and back again, having the form of a closed curve whose area is a measure of the loss of energy in the cycle; **hysteresis loss**, the energy dissipated as heat in a system as a result of hysteresis.

1894 *Rep. Brit. Assoc. Adv. Sci.* 577 The three stages of magnetic displacement each have a sharply defined position on the hysteresis curve. **1954** C. ZWIKKER *Physical Prop. Solid Materials* xii. 208 Permanent magnet materials are chosen for having a large area of loop on the *B–H* hysteresis curve. **1896** F. BEDELL *Princ. Transformer* iii. 32 Curves of magnetization for a complete cycle, or 'hysteresis loops', as they are called, are shown in Fig. 33. **1897** A. G. WEBSTER *Theory Electr. & Magn.* ix. 394 The hysteresis-loop..has an important physical significance. **1946** *Rubber in Engin.* (H.M.S.O.) iv. 69 The stress–strain curve for rubber on retraction does not follow the same course as during extension, but forms a hysteresis loop. **1966** MCCLINTOCK & ARGON *Mech. Behavior Materials* i. 6 Under cyclic straining, any kind of inelastic strain leads to a hysteresis loop on a stress–strain plot. **1893** *Proc. R. Soc.* LIV. 76 Great permeability does not necessarily imply small hysteresis losses. **1927** T. F. WALL *Applied Magnetism* xv. 233 A simple and rapid means for measuring the hysteresis loss in a transformer. **1962** A. EDWARDS in D. Hadfield *Permanent Magnets* vi. 294 If the flux density in a magnet continually increases and decreases in use, there is hysteresis loss at every cycle and some eddy-current loss.

hysteresial *a.* (earlier and later examples).

1887 *Rep. Brit. Assoc. Adv. Sci. 1886* 551 The hysteresial dissipation of energy per unit volume of iron is the same whether the magnetic circuit be open or closed. **1971** J. A. C. HARWOOD in C. M. Blow *Rubber Technol. & Manuf.* iii. 69 Stress softening, a hysteresial phenomenon observed at moderate and high extensions, is probably also viscoelastic in origin.

hysteretic (histəre·tik), *a.* [Prob. f. HYSTERESIS after such pairs as *synthesis, synthetic* and *prosthesis, prosthetic*; but cf. Gr. ὑστερητικός 'which comes on later'.] Of, pertaining to, or exhibiting hysteresis.

1892 *Trans. Amer. Inst. Electr. Engin.* XI. 25 Two other sets of determinations of the hysteretic loss of energy, for the frequency of 170 complete periods per second, were made on two laminated horse shoe magnets. *Ibid.* 43 This figure shows well the three characteristic forms of hysteretic curves. **1931** S. R. WILLIAMS *Magnetic Phenomena* i. 60, η is called the hysteretic constant or coefficient of hysteresis loss, which varies from one ferromagnetic body to another. **1958** C. L. MANTELL *Engin. Materials Handbk.* XXXII. 10 Hysteretic properties of elastomers also affect their utility in applications where resilience is important. **1971** *Nature* 15 Jan. 155/3 A slow change in the concentration of a metabolite may still be rapid compared with the hysteretic adjustment of the activity of an enzyme that it controls.

Hence **hystere·tically** *adv.*, by means of or as a result of hysteresis.

1904 *Electr. World & Engin.* 30 July 163/2 The actual condenser dissipates energy hysteretically in the dielectric. **1956** *Aeronaut Q.* VII. 60 A general theory of small hysteretically damped vibration.

hysterical, *a.* and *sb.* Add: **B.** *sb.* **3.** = HYSTERIC *a.* and *sb.* B. 2.

1892 A. W. PINERO *Magistrate* III. i. 136 (The sound of a shriek from Agatha and Charlotte.) *Lugg...* Don't notice them. They're hystericals. They're mild now to what they have been. **1922** M. SADLEIR *Excursions in Victorian Bibliogr.* 2 This is a book about first editions, and will be read only by the initiate. If we be hystericals, we have at least our weakness in common. **1950** E. HEMINGWAY *Across River* xxxix. 229 'I've stopped [crying],' she said. 'I'm not an hysterical.'

‖ **hysterica passio** (histe·rikă pæ·sio). [L., = 'hysteric passion'. See HYSTERIC.] = HYSTERIA I.

1603 S. HARSNET *Declaration Popish Impostures* vi. 25 Maynie had a spice of the Hysterica passio, as seems from his youth. **1605** [see MOTHER *sb.* 12]. **1934** W. B. YEATS *King of Gt. Clock Tower* 22 But popular rage *Hysterica passio* dragged this quarry down. **1963** *Listener* 17 Oct. 626/2 Before watching 'The Mersey Sound'..I took tranquillizers to forestall a fit of *hysterica passio.*

hystericky, *a.* (Earlier U.S. example.)

1823 J. F. COOPER *Pilot* II. xiv. 239 In order that the women need not be 'stericky in squalls.

hysteriform, *a.*[2] (Examples.)

1887 W. PHILLIPS *Man. Brit. Discomycetes* 384 *Stictis hysterioides.* Desm. Immersed, closed, hysteriform, then erumpent. **1957** SNELL & DICK *Gloss. Mycol.* 79/1 Hysteriform... Elongated, boat-shaped and cleft, resembling the sporocarps of the genus *Hysterium.*

hystero-[1]. Add: **hystero·rrhaphy** *Surg.* [*-RRHAPHY] = *hysteropexy* (s.v. HYSTERO-[1]).

1887 H. A. KELLY in *Amer. Jrnl. Obstetr.* XX. 34 It is my purpose here formally to propose, and to formulate rules for the adoption of a new operative procedure in the treatment of..intractable cases of retroflexion, and of prolapsus uteri... In accordance with the principles here laid down, the term 'Hysterorrhaphy' is used to define the suspension by suture of a viciously posed uterus. **1953** R. W. TE LINDE *Oper. Gynecol.* (ed. 2) vi. 107 Ventrofixation, hysterorrhaphy and hysteropexy were terms applied to the earliest operation in which an attempt was made to suspend the retroplaced uterus. The chief interest of this operation is now historical.

hystrichosphere (hi·striko,sfīəɹ). *Palæont.* [ad. mod.L. *hystrichosphæra* (O. Wetzel 1933, in *Palaeontographica* A. LXXVIII. 32), f. Gr. ὕστριξ, ὑστριχ- porcupine + σφαῖρα ball.] Any of numerous kinds of microscopic planktonic fossil organisms characterized by a spherical or oval shape with numerous short thin projections.

1957 *Q. Jrnl. Geol. Soc.* CXII. 416 In the clays, dinoflagellates and hystrichospheres were abundant and formed a considerable proportion of the combustible organic matter. **1963** *Palaeontology* VI. 83 The hystrichospheres having spines closed distally exhibit an overall range in shell diameters from 5 μ to 240 μ.

hyther (həi·þəɹ). [See quot. 1907.] A quantity determined from temperature and humidity and intended to represent the discomfort attributable to their combined effect; also, a unit on a scale of 0 to 10 expressing this.

1904 W. F. TYLER in *Jrnl. Balneology* VIII. 25 A number of persons..were requested to estimate daily at noon the degree of 'hyther' on a scale of 0 to 10. This word hyther was introduced to indicate the sensation caused by a warm climate, and supposed to be due to the combined effect of heat and humidity. **1907** —— in *Monthly Weather Rev.* June 268/1, I consider the term 'sensible temperature' to be rather misleading, temperature being only one factor in the subjective effect. It was for this reason that..I coined the word *hyther* from *hydro* and *thermos.* **1931** A. CASTELLANI *Climate & Acclimatization* ii. 39 It was observations like these that caused Tyler to attempt to correlate personal sensations with meteorological data, and to formulate his 'hyther' degrees, by which he meant the degree of discomfort caused by high air temperatures associated with high relative humidity. **1937** *Nature* 9 Jan. 79/1 Their sensations [of temperature] were recorded on an arbitrary scale extending from 1 to 10; the numbers on the scale have been called hythers, hyther 10 being taken to represent an 'unbearable condition'.

hythergraph (həi·þəɹgrɑf). *Climatology.* [f. Gr. ὑ-ετός rain + θέρ-μη heat + -GRAPH.] A climograph having temperature and either humidity or precipitation as coordinates; usu., one in which the mean monthly values of these coordinates are plotted for each month of the year, the plotted points for each successive month then being joined by straight lines.

1918 T. G. TAYLOR *Austral. Environment* viii. 30 The two chief controls..are temperature and rainfall... To the graph representing these controls I have given the name *hythergraph*—from the Greek words for rain and heat. [*Note*] Tyler has used the word 'hyther' to express the joint effect of humidity and temperature. **1940** *Ecology* XXI. 189/1 Though shown..as being an area of tall grass, the hythergraphs of stations in the area depart somewhat from the typical grassland figure and approach diagrams of the deciduous forest. **1950** CONRAD & POLLAK *Methods in Climatol.* (ed. 2) vii. 221 The annual variation of the combined rainfall–temperature element is represented by the graphs shown in Fig. 58. These curves are called hythergraphs.

I

I. Add: **I. 2. b. i-mutation, i-umlaut** (also *i/j-mutation*, etc.) *Philology*, the fronting influence of an **i* or **j* on the vowel of a preceding syllable in one and the same word; also, the result of this. So **i-mutated, i-umlauted** ppl. adjs.

1870 F. A. March *Compar. Gram. Anglo-Saxon Lang.* 13 i-umlaut of *ô*: *fôt*, *fêt*(*e*). **1891** A. L. Mayhew *Synopsis Old Eng. Phonol.* 41 In North. and Mercian *oe* = *e*, the *i*-umlaut of *o*. **1906** H. C. Wyld *Hist. Study Mother Tongue* i. 10 This particular kind of change, known as *i*-mutation, occurs in hundreds of words in O.E., though, as a rule, the *i* or *j* which caused the fronting, disappeared. **1908** J. & E. M. Wright *Old Eng. Gram.* iii. 28, *a* was the only vowel which underwent *i*-umlaut in OS. and OHG. **1927** *Englische Studien* 10 Nov. 81 There was, by the side of OE. *scēat*..an i-mutated variant *sciete* or *scyte* with the same sense. **1927** E. V. Gordon *Introd. Old Norse* 246, $ø_2$ was the *w*-mutation of *ę* or (rarely) a late *i*-mutation of *ǫ*. **1945** S. Einarsson *Icelandic* i. v. 30 The I-Shift (..i-umlaut, i-mutation) is so called because it was caused by an *i* or a *j*—now often lost—in the ending of a word. **1953** L. F. Brosnahan *Some Old Eng. Sound Changes* 63 The phenomenon of *i*- or *j*- mutation.

II. 7. a. In *Physics I* (rarely *i*) is the symbol of the quantum number of nuclear spin. [Adopted by Back and Goudsmit 1928, in *Zeitschr. f. Physik* XLVII. 175.]

1930 Pauling & Goudsmit *Struct. Line Spectra* xi. 203, i is a new quantum number, the nuclear spin quantum number. **1932** Bacher & Goudsmit *Atomic Energy States* 20 The spectrum of bismuth, for which the nuclear moment *I* is $4\frac{1}{2}$, is an interesting example of this type of hyperfine structure. **1966** D. H. Whiffen *Spectroscopy* iii. 22 Intrinsic nuclear angular momenta are quantised and may be expressed as $I\hbar$ where *I*..is called the spin quantum number. **1967** [see *F III. 1 k].

b. Occas. used as the symbol of the quantum number of isospin (more commonly **T*).

1953 *Progress Theoret. Physics* IX. 420 In general, selection rules are intimately connected with the conservative quantities which we shall inquire for a system involving Fermions. Those are the total angular momentum *J* and the total isotopic spin *I* of the system. **1962** A. Ramakrishnan *Elem. Particles & Cosmic Rays* i. 31 We use the symbol *t* for the isotopic spin operator of a system of particles and *τ* for a single particle, their eigenvalues being denoted by *T* and *I* respectively.

III. I., Intelligence (see also I.Q. below); I.A.A., indoleacetic acid (indolylacetic acid); I.A.E.A., International Atomic Energy Agency; I.A.T.A., International Air Traffic (or Transport) Association; I.B.A., Independent Broadcasting Authority; I.B.M., intercontinental ballistic missile; International Business Machines (used to denote the computers made by this firm); I.C., in charge, in command; integrated circuit; (*Linguistics*) immediate constituent; I.C.A., Institute of Contemporary Arts; I.C.A.O., International Civil Aviation Organization; I.C.B.M., intercontinental ballistic missile; I.C.E., internal combustion engine; I.C.F.T.U., International Confederation of Free Trade Unions; I.C.I., Imperial Chemical Industries; I.C.S., Indian Civil Service; I.D., identification, identity (card); I.D.A., International Development Association; I.D.B., illicit diamond buyer, buying; I.E., Indo-European; I.F., i.f., intermediate frequency (see *intermediate *a.* and *sb.* A. 3); I.F.F., Identification, Friend or Foe; I.F.R., Instrument Flight Rules; I.G.Y., International Geophysical Year; I.L.O., International Labour Organization; I.L.P., Independent Labour Party; I.L.S., Instrument Landing System; I.M.C.O., Intergovernmental Maritime Consultative Organization; I.M.F., International Monetary Fund; I.P.A., International Phonetic Alphabet (or Association); i.p.s., inches per second; I.Q., intelligence quotient (see *intelligence *sb.* 8); I.R., infra-red; I.R.A., Irish Republican Army; I.R.B.M., intermediate range ballistic missile; I.R.O., International Refugee Organization; I.R.S., Internal Revenue Service (*U.S.*); I.S.O., Imperial Service Order; International Organization for Standardization; I.T.A., Independent Television Authority; I.T.A., i.t.a., initial teaching alphabet; I.T.U., International Telecommunication Union; I.T.V., Independent Television; I.U., i.u., international unit; I.U.(C.)D., intra-uterine (contraceptive) device; I.V., i.v., intravenous(ly); also as *sb.*, an intravenous drip, injection, etc.; I.W.W., Industrial Worker(s) of the World.

1917 'Contact' *Airman's Outings* iv. 87 An air reconnaissance is essentially the observer's show; its main object being to supply the 'I' people at headquarters with private bulletins from the back of the German front. **1925** Fraser & Gibbons *Soldier & Sailor Words* 125, *I*, the Service abbreviation for 'Intelligence', *i.e.* information of military value. **1972** G. Lyall *Blame the Dead* xiii. 86 'What were you in?' '"I" Corps.' **1947** *Jrnl. Biol. Chem.* CLXIX. 465 Indoleacetic acid (IAA) tends to stimulate growth in the light. **1969** *New Scientist* 7 Aug. 272/1 Isolated bacteria were cultured and shown to form IAA from the amino acid tryptophan. **1958** *Times* 20 Jan. 6/4 Mr. Robert McKinney, United States member of the I.A.E.A. board of governors. *Ibid.*, The United States last year already declared its intention to match all contributions of materials to the I.A.E.A. made by other countries up to June, 1960. **1958** P. Noel-Baker *Arms Race* p. xvii, IAEA, International Atomic Energy Agency (established in Vienna, October 1957). **1963** *Times* 28 Sept. 6/7 Sir Roger Makins, chairman of the British Atomic Energy Authority and chief delegate to I.A.E.A. **1931** *Flight* 20 Mar. 255/1, I..submitted therefore to the International Air Traffic Association, IATA, a suggestion for organising, at the earliest possible moment, a general European air mail net. **1962** *Daily Tel.* 11 Sept. 12/3 The continuance of rate-cutting could not be tolerated if IATA was to continue its work. **1970** *Internat. & Compar. Law Q.* 4th Ser. XIX. i. 125 It is something of a surprise that the United States Government and the International Air Transport Association (IATA)..should be proposing a system of absolute liability. **1971** *Guardian* 12 Nov. 1/8 The Sound Broadcasting Bill..authorises the new stations under the control of the Independent Television Authority—renamed the Independent Broadcasting Authority...The IBA could be advanced up to £2 millions to set up the services. **1971** *Times* 12 Nov. 8/5 The IBA would have the same obligation in radio to devote sufficient time to accurate and impartial news. **1954** I.B.M. [see *ballistic *a.* d]. **1955** *Ann. Reg. 1954* 402 Reports from the United States referred to a rocket called I.B.M. (intercontinental ballistic missile), a wingless rocket-shaped device already perfected to travel 2,500 miles and expected to have a range of 5,000 miles in due course. **1955** R. J. Schwartz *Compl. Dict. Abbrev.* 89 *I.B.M.*, International Business Machines. **1956** S. Bellow *Seize the Day* (1957) ii. 42 When he saw the two sums punched out so neatly on the cards he cursed the company and its IBM equipment. **1956** A. Huxley *Adonis & Alphabet* 109 Thanks to finger-printing, punched cards and IBM machines, they know practically everything about practically everyone. **1963** I. Fleming *On H.M. Secret Service* i. 16 Bond's mind ticked and whirred, selecting cards like an IBM machine. **1970** *Amer. Jrnl. Physics* XXXVIII. 1294/2 Computations on the *j*th particle velocity..have been carried out on the Oberlin College IBM 360/44. **1928** T. E. Lawrence *Let.* 19 July (1938) iv. 615 No, I am not adjutant, to this camp. Just typist, and i/c files, and duty rolls. **1947** R. S. Wells in *Language* XXIII. ii. 81 We aim in this paper to replace by a unified, systematic theory the heterogeneous and incomplete methods hitherto offered for determining immediate constituents (hereafter abbreviated IC, plural ICs). **1953** *Language* XXIX. 88 Shannon has conducted experiments in ordinary English orthography, and the reviewer has conducted similar ones, with the proper audiences, in terms of phonemic notation, the results of which bear on the stated correlation between IC-analysis and information theory. **1958** *Spectator* 15 Aug. 219/1 If you were i/c security, it was obviously necessary to flush the lavatories of spies. **1962** L. Deighton *Ipcress File* viii. 51 The above named article of War Department property..should be returned to officer i.c. special issue room. **1962** B. M. H. Strang *Mod. Eng. Struct.* vi. 79 They are immediate constituents (ICs), i.e. the forms that directly go to make up that which is under analysis. They themselves have ICs. **1965** *Canad. Jrnl. Ling.* Fall 45 Chomsky develops.. IC analysis by his grammatical model of 'phrase structure + transforms'. **1965** *Listener* 11 Nov. 763/2 The commanding officer; the 2 I.C.; the adjutant. **1966** *Electronics* 17 Oct. 87 The major problems in using IC's. **1969** *New Scientist* 18 Dec. 601/3 The IC memory is three times faster than the conventional memory. **1970** 'J. Earl' *Tuners & Amplifiers* ii. 28 In a few years' time the majority of radio tuners will carry ICs as well as a few transistors and junction diodes. **1971** D. Crystal *Linguistics* iv. 212 In IC analysis, however, such disambiguation was impossible. **1958** *Listener* 20 Nov. 842/1 At the I.C.A. there is an exhibition of three collagists. **1969** *Ibid.* 27 Mar. 436/3 The ICA has taken us aback by giving some public performances of a radio work, reproducing it stereophonically in a darkened theatre. **1947** *Times* 17 May 3/5 (*headline*) Italy nominated for I.C.A.O. **1955** *Sci. Amer.* Jan. 94/3 The specialized agencies of the United Nations..ICAO (International Civil Aviation Organization). **1963** *Thorn Electr. Industr. Group Profile* 25 The system has been approved.. by the ICAO. **1955** *Newsweek* 30 May 13 The Air Force is now calling the Intercontinental Ballistic Missile the ICBM. **1956** *Spaceflight* Oct. 24/1 The relatively small margin in performance between the I.C.B.M. and a satellite vehicle suggests that great use will be made of it in the future. **1965** I. Fleming *Man with Golden Gun* ii. 28 Their U-boat fleet and their ICBMs. **1950** *Chambers's Encycl.* XV. 586/2 I.C.E.: *see* Internal Combustion Engine. **1958** *Listener* 20 Nov. 835/2 The present advanced state of the internal combustion engine, or 'I.C.E.' as my log-book calls it. **1968** *Economist* 25 May 45/3 But now a modern version of the steam engine has appeared as the major threat to the ICE. **1955** *Times* 30 May 4/4 First, the I.C.F.T.U. will continue its fight to ensure that all workers' rights are respected. **1968** *Telegraph* (Brisbane) 18 Apr. 10/2 Mr Mick Jordan..represents the International Confederation of Free Trade Unions (ICFTU)—a world-wide anti-Communist union body. **1934** H. G. Wells *Exper. Autobiogr.* II. viii. 638 Brunner Mond & Co. was only the embryo of I.C.I. **1964** M. Gowing *Britain & Atomic Energy 1939–1945* ii. 75 I.C.I. offered to take over..the Halban and Kowarski research. **1931** *Times Lit. Suppl.* 14 May 390/3 The late Ross Scott, I.C.S. **1957** J. Masters *Far, Far the Mountain Peak* iii. 27 If Peter has really made up his mind to go to the I.C.S.—it will be wonderful. **1971** *Shankar's Weekly* (Delhi) 18 Apr. 22/4 The Prime Minister called the ICS Secretaries of the Central Departments some weeks ago and admonished them. **1955** R. J. Schwartz *Compl. Dict. Abbrev.* 90 *Id*, identification. **1963** T. Pynchon *V.* xiii. 373 Pig was understandably nervous, trying simultaneously to salute, produce ID and liberty cards. **1965** *New Statesman* 3 Dec. 880/3 'ID's'..are pretty obscure to English readers as translations..of..*papiers* (identity documents). **1968** A. Diment *Bang Bang Birds* v. 75, I had the usual range of forged driver's licences, ID cards, credit chits. **1970** *Globe & Mail* (Toronto) 28 Sept. 7/1 Once inside I was forced to produce my driver's licence, draft card, student I.D. **1971** *Leader* (Durban) 7 May 1/1 The loss of the money was not important. I am more concerned about my ID card, as I am presently applying for a house in Unit 10. **1972** J. Ball *Five Pieces Jade* ii. 21 Tibbs was politely asked for his ID. He produced his police credentials. **1961** *Ann. Reg. 1960* 472 The major development among international agencies was the establishment of the International Development Association (I.D.A.). **1965** *Economist* 26 June 1512/2 The World Bank's 'soft-loan' subsidiary, the International Development Association (IDA), already lends for up to fifty years. **1884** M. A. Carey-Hobson *At Home in Transvaal* II. xli. 520 'The fellow had money there, with which he turned I.D.B.' 'What's that?'..'Illicit diamond buyer.' **1886** W. M. Kerr *Far Interior* I. i. 15 In spite of the vigilance of the detective department a great deal of illicit diamond buying is successfully carried on; hence the well-known 'IDB', which refers to the illegal trade. **1909** H. G. Wells *Tono-Bungay* ii. i. 122 Barmentrude.. used to be an I.D.B.—an illicit diamond buyer. **1917** *New Statesman* 17 Nov. 150/1 To represent the typical Bolshevik as a German agent..is just as clever and fair as to try to make out that an I.D.B. from the Rand..is the type of a British Imperialist. **1972** P. Driscoll *Wilby Conspiracy* (1973) xiii. 163 He does a bit of IDB on the side. So what? He's a jeweller. **1894** V. Henry *Compar. Gram. Eng. & Ger.* v. 113 The greater part of such roots as began with the group in question exhibited already in the I.-E. period a peculiar alternation. **1964** R. H. Robins *Gen. Ling.* viii. 307 The I-E language family is represented all over the world today. **1927** H. J. Round *Shielded Four-Electrode Valve* viii. 77 It should be possible to do with only one stage of intermediate frequency on account of the gain per stage in H.F. and I.F. **1956** Tibbs & Johnstone *Frequency Modulation Engin.* (ed. 2) ix. 387 Second channel interference can be avoided by choosing the i.f. to be greater than half the band of frequencies to be covered. **1963** J. A. Walston *Transistor Circuit Design* xxiii. 321 The difference frequency (IF frequency) ..must be such that the transistor will function as an amplifier. **1945** *Electronic Engin.* XVII. 686 An I.F.F. unit can be briefly described as being a transmitter-receiver device installed in friendly aircraft whose purpose is to reply to the interrogation of the friendly Radar station. **1961** *Listener* 30 Nov. 909/1 The I.F.F. radar identification sets in our bombers. **1948** *Jrnl. R. Aeronaut. Soc.* LII. 90/1 The biggest factor affecting reliable running is the time difference between operations under clear and low visibility conditions, C.F.R. (Contact Flight Rules) and I.F.R. (Instrument Flight Rules) as they are called. **1964** *Times Rev. Industry* Apr. 40/3 Under IFR, electronic navigation equipment defines the position, and facilitates landing in bad weather or at night. **1955** *Sci. News Let.* 15 Jan. 42/1 Scientists from at least 39 countries, including Russia, are now making plans for coordinated research efforts during 1957–58 in a world-wide investigation of the earth, its seas and air. The many-pronged attack, aimed at a better understanding of the planet we live on, is known as the International Geophysical Year, or IGY. **1964** *Economist* 11 Jan. 128/3 The IGY lasted 30 months. **1924** B. Webb *Diary* 8 Jan. (1956) i. 2 The P.M. to meet Thomas, the French head of the I.L.O. at Geneva. **1969** *Listener* 1 May 614/3 We're going to give legislative backing to the ILO conventions on the right to join trade unions. **1893** G. B. Shaw *Let.* 24 Apr. (1965) 390 My remarks..were not levelled at the I.L.P. **1917** A. Huxley *Let.* 12 Nov. (1969) 136, I suppose it would pain the poor Duke too much if he sat in Parliament as a member of the I.L.P. **1932** Auden *Orators* iii. 104 The Simonites, the Mosleyites and the I.L.P. **1946** Koestler *Thieves in Night* ii. 91 Max, who has an enormous, sniffing tapir-nose and an unkempt I.L.P.-mane. **1959** *Listener* 22 Jan. 179/3 A number of intellectuals and I.L.P.-ers. **1947** *Shell Aviation News* No. 108. 3/1 I.L.S. (Instrument Landing System), G.C.A. (Ground Control Approach), ground radar and flight radar are all proven, available, and should be installed. **1966** *New Scientist* 13 Jan. 65/1 The special Trident has been trying the ILS of other airports, ..and has actually made 'hands-off' landings at them. **1954** *Chambers's Encycl. World Survey* 42/2 The Intergovernmental Maritime Consultative Organization (IMCO). **1970** *Globe & Mail* (Toronto) 28 Sept. 6/2 After the Torrey Canyon disaster the Intergovernmental Maritime Consultative Organization (IMCO) turned to the machinery of the international convention on safety of life at sea to try to establish rules that would ease the threat of pollution. **1948** G. Crowther *Outl. Money* (rev. ed.) ix. 330 The main purpose of the I.M.F...is to provide countries that have deficits with the foreign currencies they

require to cover those deficits. **1965** *New Statesman* 23 Apr. 632/2 A determination to invoke the scarce currency clause in the IMF agreement to legalise discrimination against chronically surplus countries. **1933** L. Bloomfield *Lang.* vi. 103 There has arisen a convention of transcribing British English, not by the symbols..in accord with the principles of the IPA alphabet. **1954** Pei & Gaynor *Dict. Ling.* 105 *I.P.A.*, The International Phonetic Alphabet. **1961** *Amer. Speech* XXXVI. 201 The modified IPA symbols used in the [linguistic] Atlas. **1970** *Publ. Amer. Dial. Soc. 1968* L. 5 The phonetic notation used in transcribing the responses of the informants is.. a finely graded phonetic alphabet based on that of the IPA. **1959** W. S. Sharps *Dict. Cinematogr.* 104/2 *I.P.S.*, abbreviation for inches per second. **1968** *Times* 29 Nov. p. ii/1 The rise of the tape recorder was attested by the publication of commercial tapes at 7½ i.p.s. **1922** R. S. Woodworth *Psychol.* xii. 274 Brightness or dullness can also be measured by the intelligence quotient, which is employed so frequently that it is customarily abbreviated to 'I.Q.' **1948** A. Huxley *Let.* 3 June (1969) 582 Cecil Burt sees a drop in the average intelligence of the British population..of 5 IQ points before the end of the present century. **1959** N. Mailer *Advts. for Myself* (1961) 150 Any man in the infantry or cavalry who has a good I.Q. is sure to have his name turned up..whenever a new typist is needed. **1968** *Scottish Daily Mail* 16 July 2/1 The questionnaire is a tongue-in-cheek parody of the IQ tests which the U.S. Government gives would-be employees. **1972** *Science* 20 Oct. 232/2 The IQ tests ignore much in us that is artistic, contemplative, and nonverbal. **1957** *Which?* Autumn 7/2 An investigation into the effects, on bottle-makers, of the infra-red and ultra-violet (often referred to as I.R. and U.V.) radiations. **1967** *Electronics* XL. 127/1 A scope tracing that shows i-r energy as a curve derived from the video signal, with the amount of energy determining vertical deflection. **1921** G. B. Shaw *Matter with Ireland* (1962) 245 The I.R.A. is flushed with success. **1932** *Morning Post* 23 Aug. 10/3 A force of 200 men of the I.R.A. have seized Donamon Castle. **1939** J. B. Priestley *Let People Sing* ii. 24 So they thought he was the I.R.A., eh? That explained the bomb, of course. **1959** *New Statesman* 7 Nov. 615/2 The IRA is now really discredited; young men in the dreary pubs which offer the only way out of the drearier provincial towns of Ireland must find other amusements than plotting. **1971** *Guardian* 11 Aug. 10/2 The IRA and the Provisionals use the South as a sanctuary. **1957** *Economist* 30 Nov. 774/2 IRBMs are to begin flowing to Europe by late 1958. **1960** *Ibid.* 30 July 460/3 In April the official defence policy was laid in ruins with the abandonment of Britain's IRBM, Blue Streak. **1947** *Times* 15 May 5/7 Resettlement will still remain one of the main features of the I.R.O. **1948** *Hansard Commons* 11 Mar. 1531/1 I.R.O. consented to act as our agents. **1955** *Sci. Amer.* Jan. 95/1 IRO (International Refugee Organization). **1963** *Listener* 7 Mar. 412/1 The I.R.S. takes good care that the United States citizen abroad knows just where he stands, taxwise. **1964** *Financial Times* 12 Mar. 24/3 The attitude of the I.R.S. in 1958, after they had caught up with Mr. Wilson, was to say: 'We're not concerned with your troubles.' **1972** *New York Law Jrnl.* 22 Aug. 4/4 (*heading*) IRS issues rulings on political dinners. **1902** *Encycl. Brit.* XXXI. 340/1 The members of the order have the distinction of adding the letters I.S.O. after their names. **1909** *Whitaker's Almanack* 118 Thos. H. Sanderson Sanderson, G.C.B., K.C.M.G., I.S.O. **1946** *N.Y. Times* 2 Nov. 22/6 Howard Coonley..has been elected president of the new International Organization for Standardization, formation of which has been completed by delegates from twenty-five nations meeting in London... Gustave L. Gerard..has been chosen vice president of the new organization which will be known informally as ISO. **1969** *Jane's Freight Containers 1968–69* 400/1 The equipment covered by this plan is standard ISO 20 ft steel containers with fork-lift pockets, and standard 40 ft ISO aluminium containers. **1955** *Ann. Reg. 1954* 385 While viewing through I.T.A. stations would not be possible for some time, competitive bidding for 'stars' went on actively. **1962** *Rep. Comm. Broadcasting 1960* 1 in *Parl. Papers 1961–2* (Cmnd. 1753) IX. 259 There is a distinction to be drawn..between the ITA and independent television (ITV). The ITA is the Authority, the public corporation set up by the Television Act, 1954: independent television comprises not only the ITA but also the programme companies. **1965** *Guardian* 2 Feb. 3/8 Mr Gordon Walker .., adviser to the ITA foundation,..would have to learn more about the initial teaching alphabet. **1967** *New Statesman* 6 Oct., All the mothers know everything about O- and A-levels, have taken the measure of the 11-plus.., and some have heard of i.t.a. **1950** *Chambers's Encycl.* XI. 470/1 The International Telecommunications Union (I.T.U.). **1962** *B.B.C. Handbk.* 113 The BBC also participates in the work of the International Telecommunication Union (ITU), a specialized agency of the United Nations with its headquarters in Geneva. **1958** 'A. Gilbert' *Death against Clock* 93 All they talk about is what they saw on ITV last night. **1958** *Spectator* 27 June 827/3 As the General Election approaches, both BBC and ITV must know where they stand. **1969** *Listener* 24 Apr. 559/3 While shepherds washed their socks by night And turned on ITV, The Angel of the Lord came down And switched on BBC. **1950** *Chambers's Encycl.* XIV. 347/2 The League of Nations standard of requirement for vitamin B_1 is 300 I.U. per day. **1951** *Good Housek. Home Encycl.* 339/1 The chief food value of apricots lies in their roughage and in their vitamin A content—approximately 1,000 i.u. per serving. **1962** *Lancet* 6 Jan. 12/1 A small bottle..of some 60 ml. capacity, filled to the top with normal saline and containing 1000 I.U. of heparin. **1963** *New Scientist* 19 Dec. 716/3 A simple, cheap, safe and effective method of birth control..known as IUCDs (intrauterine contraceptive devices). **1966** *New Statesman* 18 Mar. 370/1 The IUCD consists of a small loop or coil of plastic material which is inserted into the uterus. **1965** *New Scientist* 27 May 606/3 When as occasionally happens, conception occurs and gestation proceeds with the IUD *in situ*, [etc.]. **1967** *Time* 7 Apr. 73 The IUD's underlying principle traces back to an old practice of Arab cameleers: putting a round, smooth stone in the womb of a female camel at the start of a long trade journey, to avoid the economic loss of having the animal get pregnant. **1973** *Guardian* 29 June 13/3 With the nationalisation of birth control virtually every GP in the country will be inserting IUDs. **1951** *Dorland's Med. Dict.* (ed. 22) 766/2 *I.V.*, abbreviation for intravenously (by intravenous injection). **1961** *Amer. Speech* XXXVI. 145 *I.V.*,..an intravenous infusion. **1970** *New Yorker* 21 Nov. 64/2 One of the doctors from Surgery will be coming down soon to put in your I.V. and a stomach tube. **1971** *Guardian Weekly* 24 Apr. 5/1 The bedside IV feeding bottle. **1972** *Nature* 8 Dec. 351/1, 3 African green monkeys were inoculated i.c. (0·2 ml.) and i.v. (0·3 ml.). **1917** B. Hall *Diary* 25 July in Hall & Niles *One Man's War* (1929) 278 The Government had some trouble in Los Angeles with the I.W.W. **1919** H. L. Wilson *Ma Pettengill* vii. 212 Even the youngest [girl]..had tenaciously held out for a grown man's pay, which made her something even worse than a Bolshevik; it made her an I.W.W. **1920** M. Beer *Hist. Brit. Socialism* II. iv. xviii. 356 Similar views..led in 1905 to the formation of the Industrial Workers of the World (I.W.W.). **1957** *Encounter* Apr. 65/1 That strange and unique contribution of America to anarcho-syndicalism, the 'Wobblies' (officially the Industrial Workers of the World, or IWW..) organised great masses of unskilled workers and led strikes..that were as much social rebellions as economic conflicts. **1969** Taft & Ross in Graham & Gurr *Violence in Amer.* viii. 285 Unlike the other national federations.., the IWW advocated direct action and sabotage.

I, *pers. pron.* Add: **I. 2.** (Further examples.)

1744 J. Steuart *Letter-Bk.* (1915) 449 The postscript to your letter..gave my wife and I unexpressable joy. **1866** *Harper's Mag.* Jan. 162/2, I have heard him..make a bet that 'between you and I' is correct, and refuse to be convinced of his error. **1959** *N.Z. Listener* 25 Sept. 11/2, I have heard 'between you and I, old man', and 'people like you and I', from graduates in some arts other than the art of speech. **1971** *Guardian* 20 Aug. 24/4 'There were two grilles between Eugene and I, and we must have been about six feet apart,' she said. **1972** J. Rossiter *Rope for General Dietz* ii. 24, I was sure they were looking for Michael and I. **1973** *Oxford Mail* 27 Aug. 4/4 After showing photographer Bill Radford and I her stitching skill she went back to the tea table.

II. 6. The narrator of a work of fiction, appearing on his own account. Also *attrib.* or as *adj.*

1946 'G. Orwell' in *Observer* 10 Feb. 3/3 The 'I' of the story describes himself as a Democrat. **1962** *John o' London's* 19 Apr. 372/1 The tendency for novelists to move away from the 'I' kind of storytelling. **1965** *English Studies* XLVI. 390 The point of view of the 'I' narrator is perfectly maintained throughout the tale. **1969** *Listener* 30 Jan. 151/3 The 'I' of David Martin's tense and elusive story.

III. I AM, I am (later examples). Also in weakened colloq. use: a (self-)important person.

1915 D. H. Lawrence in *Signature* 18 Oct. 8 David dancing naked before the Ark, asserting the oneness, his own oneness, the one infinity, *himself*, the one God, I AM. **1926** S. T. Warner *Lolly Willowes* III. 184 Jim thought himself quite a Great I AM. **1928** D. H. Lawrence *Lady Chatterley* x. 131, I am a cypher. You are the great I-am! as far as life goes. *a* **1940** F. Scott Fitzgerald *Last Tycoon* (1949) vi. 138 'Get one that can talk—tell him to bring one of his books along.' He spoke as if he wanted to meet a member of the 'I am' cult. **1954** W. Faulkner *Fable* 57 Lifting its voice against the Absolute, the ultimate I-Am. **1965** N. Gulbenkian *Pantaraxia* xi. 227 Cyril Radcliffe..did not take the short-cut favoured by so many of his colleagues who say..: 'I am the great I am, Queen's Counsel.' **1970** D. Francis *Rat Race* i. 13 He had none of the 'I am' aura which often clings around the notably successful.

Also *I and Thou, I-and-Thou.* In the theology of M. Buber: describing a relationship between two people, as opposed to that between a person and an object. Also *attrib.*

1937 R. Smith tr. *Buber's Ich–Du* (*title*) I and Thou. **1958** D. M. Baillie *Out of Nazareth* xxii. 157 Divine realities can only be known in a personal 'I-and-Thou' relationship. **1968** L. Berg *Risinghill* 64 Such teachers had never seen their pupils as fellow human beings before, as Martin Buber's 'I' and 'Thou'.

-i, *suffix*, a termination used in the names of certain Near-Eastern and Eastern peoples, as *Iraqi, Israeli, Pakistani.*

-ian, *suffix.* Add: **2.** *Min.* [Abstracted from the adjs. *magnesian, manganesian.*] Used to form, from the (Eng. or L.) names of the elements, adjectives having the sense 'having a (small) proportion of a constituent element replaced by (the element concerned)' (see quot.).

1930 W. T. Schaller in *Amer. Mineralogist* XV. 568 Can a uniform, clearly understandable scheme of nomenclature be adopted to express a minor and variable isomorphous replacement of an essential chemical element of a mineral by another analogous element?.. The writer has concluded that the ending *ian*, or *oan* if it is desired to indicate a lower valency, is the most satisfactory, and its consistent use is here advocated... If the chemical element has only one valency or the author does not wish to bring up the question of valency, *ian* should be used.

-iana, *suffix.* See Ana *suff.* and add examples. Cf. also *Australiana, *Canadiana, etc.

1679 [see *bibliographical *a.*]. **1718** [see Shakesperiana]. **1728** J. Smedley (*title*) Gulliveriana: or, a fourth volume of Miscellanies, being a sequel to the three volumes published by Pope and Swift. To which is added, Alexanderiana, etc. **1776** [see *Johnsoniana]. **1800** (*title*) Walpoliana. **1838** (*title*) Railroadiana. A New History of England, or Picturesque..Sketches.. Descriptive of the Vicinity of the Railroads. **1879** G. J. Finch-Hatton *Voices through Many Years* III. 85 Gladstoniana. *Ibid.* 118 Grevilliana. **1890** *Century Mag.* Aug. 515/2 A number of these 'whaleiana' hang in the 'Captains' Room'. **1898** W. Graham *Last Links with Byron* 120 Several writers of Keatsiana follow that most inaccurate of writers,..Leigh Hunt. **1902,** etc. [see *Edwardiana *sb. pl.*]. **1929** *Daily Tel.* 22 Jan. 6/5 The personal papers of James Boswell..are being published... Sixteen or eighteen volumes will eventually be needed to hold all the new Boswelliana. **1952** J. Carter *ABC for Bk.-Collectors* 19 Boswelliana, Railroadiana, Etoniana... Harveiana and Dickensiana..Wiseiana. **1972** *Country Life* 27 Jan. 223/2 In his..biography *William Butterfield* ..Dr Paul Thompson has hauled in Butterfieldiana in shoals..churches, colleges, schools, hospitals, cottages.

ianthinite (*i*,æ·-, əi,æ·nþĭnəit). *Min.* [ad. Du. *janthiniet* (A. Schoep 1926, in *Natuurwetenschappelijk Tijdschrift* VII. 97), f. Gr. ἰάνθιν-ος violet-coloured: see -ite[1].] A hydrated oxide of uranium found as orthorhombic crystals of a dark violet colour.

1927 *Mineral. Abstr.* III. 232 Small (to 2 mm.) black crystals with a violet tinge and semi-metallic lustre were found in veinlets in pitchblende from the Kasolo mine in Katanga, and are named ianthinite. **1954** *Amer. Mineralogist* XXXIX. 1018 Ianthinite reportedly contains only quadrivalent uranium and has a formula of $2UO_2.7H_2O$.

Iapygian (əi,ăpi·dʒiăn), *a.* and *sb.* [f. L. *Iāpygius*, f. *Iāpyx, -ygem*, a son of Dædalus said to have ruled over southern Italy: see -ian.] **A.** *adj.* Of or pertaining to the ancient natives and district of Iapygia, the name given by the Greeks to the peninsula of Apulia in southern Italy. **B.** *sb.* **a.** A native of Iapygia. **b.** The language of the Iapygians; = *Messapian *sb.* b.

1773 J. Langhorne tr. *Denina's Diss. Anc. Republics Italy* 26 The Iapygyans and Messapians [lost] fifty thousand infantry. **1864** P. Smith *Hist. World* II. 138 It is here..that we find traces of the Iapygian race, in the peninsula called by the Greeks Messapia. **1880** *Encycl. Brit.* XIII. 443/2 The peninsula which stretches eastward towards Greece was inhabited by a people termed by the Greeks Messapians or Iapygians. **1882** *Ibid.* XIV. 327/1 Inscriptions have been found in considerable numbers, written in a language known as Iapygian or Messapian. **1888** King & Cookson *Princ. Sound & Inflexion Gr. & Latin* 30 Of the Iapygian in the extreme south and the Ligurian in the north, very little is known. **1959** *Chambers's Encycl.* VII. 778/1 In Apulia..the Iapygian tribes of Messapii, Daunii and Peucetii established themselves.

iarfine (ī·aɹfinĭ). *Irish Hist.* [Ir., f. *iar* after + Fine *sb.*[2]] One of the four branches of the Irish clan structure comprising the men in the third grade of relationship to the chief. Cf. *geilfine, *indfine.

1875 H. S. Maine *Lect. Early Hist. Inst.* 209 The eldest member of the Iarfine moved into the Indfine. **1879** *Anc. Laws Ireland* IV. p. xlix, In all the Brehon Law Tracts there are references to an existing organization, generally known as the Geilfine system, and to the four classes designated as the Geilfine, Deirbfhine, Iarfine, and Indfine. **1921** E. MacNeill *Celtic Ireland* x. 162 If the *Iarfine* and the *Indfhine* existed as communal family groups,..the explanation is to be found in the reluctance to disturb the family holdings when the *Derbfhine* had run its course. **1967** F. J. Byrne in Moody & Martin *Course Irish Hist.* iii. 49 The brehon lawyers drew up a very elaborate scheme of the different degrees of relationship. The *geilfhine*..was the normal family group... And the *iarfine* and *indfhine* the second and third cousins respectively.

-iasis, *suffix*, the form in which -asis *suff.* always occurs as a living mod.L. suffix.

Iatmul (yæ·tmul). [Native name.] A people of New Guinea, living near the Great Sepik River; their language. Also *attrib.* or as *adj.*

1932 G. Bateson in *Oceania* II. 245 (*title*) Social structure of the Iatmül people of the Sepik River. *Ibid.* 248 In the Iatmül language as in English, adjectival words precede the nouns which they qualify. In Iatmül there is no equivalent of the English conjunction 'and'. *Ibid.* 249, I have thought it most convenient to use the simple word Iatmül to denote that part of the linguistic group which lives on the banks and close to the Sepik river. **1943** S. W. Reed *Making of Mod. New Guinea* i. 22 The Iatmul of the Middle Sepik River, who number approximately 10,000 persons, live in twenty-odd villages on either side of the river. *Ibid.* 23 In an isolated mountain enclave west of the Iatmul area and north of the Sepik River dwell the Kwoma. **1949** G. Bateson in M. Fortes *Social Struct.* 35 The sayings, actions, and organization of the Iatmul had certain characteristics. **1949** M. Mead *Male & Female* iii. 52 A Iatmul head-hunter, calling in his age-grade to rape his recalcitrant wife into submission. *Ibid.* App. 403 We had to analyze the language..and this was true also..of Mr. Bateson's original work in Iatmul. **1951** R. Firth *Elem. Social Organiz.* i. 22 The chronic state of the Iatmül culture.

iatrochemist. (Earlier example.)
1668 E. Maynwaring *Medicus Absolutus* ix. 78 The Compleat Chymical Physitian. This Iatro-chymist and Hermetick Philosopher, is educated from his Youth in all necessary learning..that he may be introduced into the Medical Art legitimately.

iatrochemistry (əiˌætroˌke·mistri). [f. Iatro- + Chemistry, after the family of mod.L. words beginning *iatrochem-*, *iatrochym-* (cf. Chemic *a.* and *sb.*).
These words appear to have originated in the (translated) work of Paracelsus (d. 1541): **1573** I. Dalhemius tr. *Paracelsus' Chirurgia Magna* I. ii. xiii. 21 Verum quia Iatrochymista [*so in* Opera Omnia (1658), *but here printed* latrochymista] sum: vtrumq3 enim scio & Medicinam & chemiam. They afterwards occur in medical works in L. by other writers, e.g. G. Phædro *Opuscula iatro-chemica quatuor* (1611); D. Burnet *Iatrochymicus, siue de præparatione et compositione medicamentorum chymicorum artificiosa* (1616).]
The theory or school of thought that existed in the 16th and 17th centuries and regarded medicine and physiology as subjects to be understood in terms of the chemistry of the time (see Chemiatric *a.*).
1830 T. Thomson *Hist. Chem.* I. v. 201 The most eminent of all the English supporters of iatro-chemistry was Thomas Willis, who was a contemporary of Sylvius. **1881** Roscoe & Schorlemmer *Treat. Chem.* III. i. 4 Towards the sixteenth century, the cultivators of this science [*sc.* alchemy]..exhibited activity mainly in two directions, in the first place in the prosecution of the branch science of metallurgy, and secondly, in the development of iatrochemistry. **1909** P. J. Hartog in *Dict. Nat. Biogr.* XIII. 176/2 Mayow stands immeasurably above such men as Willis and Sylvius, with their medley of half-digested Cartesianism and iatrochemistry. **1958** L. Thorndike *Hist. Magic & Exper. Sci.* VIII. xxvii. 117 The alchemy and iatrochemistry and medicine of the late seventeenth century differed little from that of the early seventeenth century, especially in Germany.

iatrogenic (əiˌæ:trodʒe·nik), *a. Med.* [f. Iatro- + *-genic.] Induced unintentionally by a physician through his diagnosis, manner, or treatment; of or pertaining to the induction of (mental or bodily) disorders, symptoms, etc., in this way.
1924 E. Bleuler tr. *Brill's Textbk. Psychiatry* xiii. 502 Not entirely unimportant, unfortunately, is the iatrogenic origin of neurotic manifestations. **1948** L. Kanner *Child Psychiatry* (ed. 2) ix. 143 Difficulties, arising from medical clumsiness in the handling of patients, are common enough to have originated the diagnosis of iatrogenic, or physician-determined, conditions of health. **1952** A. Huxley *Devils of Loudun* vii. 219 Like the sulpha poisoning and serum-fevers of the present, the Loudun epidemic was an 'iatrogenic disease', produced and fostered by the very physicians who were supposed to be restoring the patients to health. **1970** *Brit. Med. Bull.* XXVII. 13/2 The epidemic of iatrogenic deaths in asthmatic children shows the need for continuous monitoring of vital statistics. **1971** *Sci. Amer.* June 99/1 Although it is not common in this country, iatrogenic goiter—goiter caused by medical treatment—is becoming a more significant factor. Sulfonamides prescribed for urinary-tract infections..and many iodine-containing compounds administered as expectorants in the treatment of asthma are potentially goitrogenic. **1973** *Guardian* 18 Jan. 12 Drug induced (iatrogenic) conditions are on the increase.
So **iatro·geny**, the iatrogenic induction of a disorder.
1927 Henderson & Gillespie *Text-bk. Psychiatry* xiv. 416 Too often we find that in the causation of a psychoneurotic illness there has entered a very large element of 'iatrogeny'. **1940** Hinsie & Shatzky *Psychiatric Dict.* 275/1 When the physician..gives any diagnosis that serves as the nucleus around which the patient builds a neurosis or psychosis, the condition is known as iatrogeny. **1973** *Interfaces* May 45 The biographers of Alfred Nobel have not dealt satisfactorily with the question of his full grasp of the powers of iatrogeny (prize in physiology and medicine).

iatromathematically, *adv.* (Later example.)
1889 H. E. Handerson tr. *Baas's Outl. Hist. Med.* 503 Edward Barry thought that the age of a man could be calculated Iatro-mathematically from the frequency of the pulse.

iatromathematics. Restrict † to sense in Dict. (s.v. Iatromathematical *a.*) and add: **b.** The iatromathematical theory or school of thought.
1830 T. Thomson *Hist. Chem.* I. v. 209 He was a zealous supporter of iatro-mathematics, and as such a professed antagonist of the iatro-chemists. **1889** H. E. Handerson tr. *Baas's Outl. Hist. Med.* 504 This was accomplished.. at a time when within its borders Iatro-chemistry and Iatro-mathematics were still in the perfection of their bloom. **1961** J. R. Partington *Hist. Chem.* II. xii. 442 Some steps in the direction of Iatromathematics (probably influenced by Galileo) were taken by Santorio Santorio (Sanctorius Sanctorius, 1561–1636),..who discovered insensible perspiration..by living on the platform of a large balance, on which he worked and took his meals.

iatromechanical, *a.* (Earlier and later examples.)
[**1801** K. Sprengel *Versuch einer pragm. Geschichte d. Arzneikunde* (ed. 2) IV. xiv. 500 Die Schule..heisst die iatromathematische oder iatromechanische.] **1856** C. G. Comegys tr. *Renouard's Hist. Med.* viii. x. 533 After the death of the celebrated professor of Leyden [*sc.* Boerhaave], the iatro-mechanical doctrine fell apart. **1971** *Nature* 30 July 351/1 Long established Aristotelian doctrines began to crumble before the assault of Baconian empiricism and atomism modified by Descartes, Gassendi and Boyle: the emergence of the iatrochemical and iatromechanical 'schools' of medicine completed the rout.

iatromechanics (əiˌætroˌmĭkæ·niks), *sb. pl.* (const. as *sing.*). [f. Iatro- + Mechanics.] = *iatromathematics b.
1886 *Syd. Soc. Lex.*, *Iatromechanics*, the same as Iatromathematics. **1889** H. E. Handerson tr. *Baas's Outl. Hist. Med.* 496 Subsequently an effort was made to bring Iatro-chemistry into accord with Iatro-mechanics. **1926** C. G. Cumston *Introd. Hist. Med.* xvii. 274 Specificity..was to end in a sort of Kabbalism or in union with chemistry or physics.., and, from the latter, were soon to develop the new systems of Iatro-chemistry and Iatro-mechanics. **1953** M. H. Fisch in E. A. Underwood *Sci., Med. & Hist.* I. iv. 546 It was perhaps on the strength of the Neapolitan edition of this his major work, a contribution to iatromechanics along Cartesian lines, that Santanelli became professor of medicine at Naples in 1708.
So **iatromecha·nic, -mechani·cian, -me·chanist,** one belonging to the iatromathematical school.
1856 C. G. Comegys tr. *Renouard's Hist. Med.* viii. x. 548 The Iatro-chemists and the Iatro-mechanics had attempted in vain to explain the functions of organized bodies by the general laws of matter. *Ibid.* xi. 576 The essence of inflammation consists..with the Iatro-mechanician, in the obstruction of the vessels. **1899** F. S. Lee tr. *Verworn's Gen. Physiol.* i. 18 The hopes of the iatromechanics and iatrochemists of being able completely to resolve vital phenomena into physics and chemistry were not fulfilled. **1926** C. G. Cumston *Introd. Hist. Med.* xix. 320 Lancisi, Hecquet and Baglivi.—These three names are those of the leaders of organicism at the beginning of the XVIIIth century. They were supposed to be Iatro-mechanicians with a smattering of Hippocraticism and Galenism. **1943** Garrison & Morton *Med. Bibliogr.* 6 Hoffmann of Halle was the most important of the Iatromechanists. He believed an ether-like 'vital fluid' to be present in the nervous system and to act upon the muscular system, giving them 'tonus'. **1955** E. H. Ackerknecht *Short Hist. Med.* x. 111 The iatrochemists were never accepted to the extent that the iatromechanists were.

iatromechanism (əiˌætroˌme·kăniz'm). [f. Iatro- + Mechanism.] = *iatromathematics b.
1885 *Index-Catal. Library Surg.-General's Office, U.S. Army* VI. 769 (*subject heading*) Iatro-mechanism. **1886** *Syd. Soc. Lex.*, *Iatromechanism*, the doctrine of the Iatromechanics. **1926** C. G. Cumston *Introd. Hist. Med.* xxi. 351 Towards the end of the XVIIth century Iatromechanism so completely counterbalanced Iatrochemistry that the mechanics of the living being rather than the composition of the humours became the object of study.

iatrophysical, *a.* Substitute for def.: = Iatromathematical *a.* b. (Earlier and later examples.)
1883 *Encycl. Brit.* XV. 810/2 The iatro-physical school of medicine grew out of physiological theories. **1954** R. H. Major *Hist. Med.* I. 506 Borelli was unquestionably the perhaps unwitting founder of a new school of medicine—the Iatro-physical School, whose most extreme advocates sought the explanation of all medicine in physics or in mechanics, just as the Iatro-chemists found the ultimate explanation in fermentation.

iatrophysicist (əiˌætroˌfi·zisist). [f. next, after *physics, physicist.*] = Iatromathematician.
1889 H. E. Handerson tr. *Baas's Outl. Hist. Med.* 497 In therapeutics the Iatro-physicists..managed in accordance with the principles of genuine (Hippocratic) experience. **1917** A. H. Buck *Growth of Med.* xxviii. 366 It became customary to employ the terms, 'iatrochemists' and 'iatrophysicists' in speaking of the partisans of the two schools of medicine (the iatrochemical and the iatrophysical or iatromechanical). **1957** *Encycl. Brit.* XV. 201/1 The language and the theories of the iatrophysicists, the iatrochemists and the vitalists..have long been discarded.

iatrophysics (əiˌætroˌfi·ziks), *sb. pl.* (const. as *sing.*). [f. Iatro- + Physics.] = *iatromathematics b.
1886 in *Syd. Soc. Lex.* **1889** H. E. Handerson tr. *Baas's Outl. Hist. Med.* 501 William Cockburn (about 1696) too embraced Iatro-physics eclectically. **1928** C. Singer *Short Hist. Med.* iv. 127 Numerous fresh theories arose, of which the more important can be classed under the three headings Iatrophysics, Iatrochemistry, and Vitalism. **1945** D. Guthrie *Hist. Med.* xi. 204 Sydenham..rejected entirely the ideas of iatrophysics or iatro-chemistry. **1961** J. R. Partington *Hist. Chem.* II. viii. 297 Domenico Sanguinetti and Joseph del Papa..were practically the only Italian physicians of the time to oppose the chemical theory and prefer Iatrophysics.

Iban (ī·bæn, ībæ·n), *sb.* and *a.* [Native name.] **A.** *sb.* A people of Sarawak, also known as the Sea Dyaks; a member of this people, and the name of their language. **B.** *adj.* Of or pertaining to this people.
1911 F. W. Page-Turner in *Sarawak Mus. Jrnl.* I. 133 A child which they adopted and named Diang Idah who is the origin of the tribe called Iban. *Ibid.*, Tiang Laju is thus the origin of the Iban race as the grand-parents of Diang Idah came from there. **1960** *Guardian* 9 Nov. 10/3 The population includes Ibans (also known as Sea Dayaks). **1962** B. Harrisson *Orang-Utan* ii. 53 An Iban Dayak from the Sebuyan area in the Second Division of Sarawak. **1967** B. Sandin *Sea Dayaks of Borneo* p. xix, 'Iban' is a term of Kayan origin which did not come into general use until quite late in the nineteenth century, while the term 'Sea Dayak' was imposed by the Brookes... The Ibans originally had no term which recognised their indisputable ethnic unity. **1969** *Franciscan Missionary Herald* XXXIV. 35 Mother St. Robert and Sister Otteran speak Iban. *Ibid.* 36 The interior of an Iban Long-house.

Ibanag (ī·bănāg), *sb.* and *a.* [Native name.] **A.** *sb.* The name of one of the peoples inhabiting northern Luzon in the Republic of the Philippines, of a member of this people, and of their language. **B.** *adj.* Of or pertaining to this people.
1885 *Encycl. Brit.* XVIII. 753/1 The other tribes of the Philippines—the Ilocanes, Pampangos, Pangasinanes, Ibanags or Cagayans,..&c. **1900** F. H. Sawyer *Inhabitants Philippines* 252 The Ibanags inhabit the Babuyanes and Batanes Islands. **1901** *Rep. Philippine Comm.* III. 405 In order to state very briefly how the remaining Philippine languages or dialects are related we select from among them some of the principal ones... These are the Ibanag and Ilocano, of North Luzon. **1924** D. P. Barrows *Hist. Philippines* (rev. ed.) 11 The valley of the Cagayan [is inhabited] by a people commonly called Cagayanes, but whose dialect is Ibanag. **1937** *Publ. Inst. Nat. Lang.* (Manila) I. 3 The Institute..has taken unto itself the task of studying as many..languages as it could possibly manage, and has included..Ibanag and Ivatan. **1942** J. R. Hayden *Philippines* 864 Ranging in number from between 700,000 and 800,000 to about 60,000 are the Bikol,..Ibanag, and Sambal groups. **1958** G. F. Zaide *Hist. Filipino People* ii. 11 The Malayan Filipinos..comprise the..Ilokanos, Bikols, Kagayans (Ibanags), Pampangans.

Iberian, *a.* and *sb.* Add: **A.** *adj.* **3.** Pertaining to the Iberians of Britain (cf. *B. *sb.* 3).
1880 *Encycl. Brit.* XII. 605/2 Extreme exponents of the theory do not hesitate to speak of the Iberian ancestors of the people of England. **1907** T. R. Holmes *Anc. Brit.* 65 The race to which they [*sc.* neolithic inhabitants of Britain] belonged is often called the Iberian, though there is no reason to believe that its British representatives belonged to the Iberian rather than to some other branch of the Mediterranean stock.
B. *sb.* **3.** A neolithic inhabitant of Britain, considered as one of a branch of the continental Iberians.
1880 W. B. Dawkins *Early Man in Brit.* 322 The Silures, identified by Tacitus with the Iberians, were left only in those fastnesses which were subsequently a refuge for the Welsh against the English invaders. **1900** W. A. Dutt *Norfolk* 7 The Iceni..were probably mentally as well as physically superior to the Iberians. **1920** H. F. Henderson *Relig. in Scotl.* i. 11 The Iberians absorbed the Celts without serious dilution of their original characteristics. **1957** G. Ashe *King Arthur's Avalon* i. 15 Throughout a long stretch of years the inhabitants of Britain were dark little Iberians.

iberis (əibīᵊ·rĭs). [mod.L. (J. J. Dillenius in Linnæus *Systema Naturæ* (1735)), prob. f. Gr. Ἴβηρες Iberians, as several species come from Spain, but cf. Gr. ἰβηρίς, L. *iberis* a kind of cress.] A low-growing herb or sub-shrub of the genus so called, native to southern Europe and western Asia, and bearing flattened heads of small white, pink, or purple flowers; = Candytuft.
1768 P. Miller *Gardeners Dict.* (ed. 8) s.v. Iberis 7, Iberis with roundish crenated leaves. **1788** Mawe & Abercrombie *Every Man his Own Gardener* (ed. 12) 582/2 Round leaved alpine Iberis, Evergreen linear-leaved Cretan Iberis. **1871** W. Robinson *Hardy Flowers* viii. 25 How pretty and useful even as tiny evergreen shrubs, are the Iberisis! **1931** M. E. Stebbing *Hardy Flower Gardening* x. 170 Catmint, *Iberis*, and similar half-shrubby plants should have each shoot pulled off with a downward jerk. **1971** A. Scott-James *Down to Earth* xi. 128 Iberis (both annual and perennial), valerian,..polyanthus and sedum have all grown contentedly in my garden.

Ibero- (əibīᵊ·ro), combining form of Iberian *a.* and *sb.*, with the meaning 'Iberian and'.
1891 Rhys in *Academy* 26 Sept. 268/2, I believe Picts and Iberians to have belonged to one and the same family, which I have ventured to call Ibero-Pictish. **1896** A. H. Keane *Ethnology* 378 *margin*, The Ibero-Berber problem. **1900** tr. *J. Deniker's Races of Man* 285 Tawny white skin, black hair. Short stature, dolichocephalic Ibero-insular. **1920** *Glasgow Herald* 24 Sept. 6 The Ibero-American Republics. **1927** [see *Getulian A. *adj.* b]. **1955** *Proc. Prehist. Soc.* XXI. 50 As for the micro-burins of the Capsian and Iberomauretanian, it seems possible to relate them to ours. **1955** *Archivum Linguisticum* VII. 68 The immense resources of Ibero-Romance have rarely been tapped. **1963** *Economist* 7 Dec. 985/3 The new Ibero-French relationship. **1964** C. F. & F. M. Voegelin in *Anthropol. Ling.* Nov. VI. viii. 1 (*title*) Languages of the world: Ibero-Caucasian and Pidgin-Creole. **1971** *Language* XLVII. 232 Klimov rejects the migrational theory for the Ibero-Caucasian languages, regarding them as autochthonous.

Ibibio (ibĭbī·o), *sb.* and *a.* [Native name.] **A.** *sb.* A people of Southern Nigeria; a member of this people; their language. **B.** *adj.* Of or pertaining to this people.

1822 J. ADAMS *Sk. Voy. Afr.* v. 77 Three-fourths of all the negroes sold at Bonny were Heebos, the remaining fourth was composed of..the Ibbiby. **1862** H. GOLDIE *Dict. Efik Lang.* v. p. xlix, A few Ibibio words are inserted. **1890** —— *Calabar & its Mission* i. 13 By far the greater part of the oil exported is produced by the tribes behind, especially by Ibibio. **1905** C. PARTRIDGE *Cross River Natives* ii. 33 The district of Calabar is peopled by..the Efiks, the Ibibios, and the Ekois. *Ibid.* ii. 43 Most of the native labour is drawn from the Ibibio country. **1915** D. A. TALBOT *Woman's Mysteries of Primitive People* xv. 213 Among the Ibibios different funeral rites are prescribed according to age, position, and manner of death. **1919** H. H. JOHNSTON *Compar. Study Bantu & Semi-Bantu Lang.* I. 814 My information regarding..*Ibibiω*, and the allied *Kwō* dialect..has been chiefly obtained from the Rev. Hugh Goldie's *Dictionary of the Efik Language.* **1925** J. A. MACCULLOCH *Mythol. All Races* VII. 111 The head-pad..figures in some curious magical ceremonies of the Ibibio. **1932** *Africa* V. 503 One West African language, viz. Ibibio, spoken by about three-quarters of a million people in the Calabar province of Southern Nigeria. **1936** J. G. FRAZER *Aftermath: Suppl. Golden Bough* i. 18 Among the Ibibios of Southern Nigeria, 'old women may not touch soup made in deep pots, lest they receive too much nourishment therefrom, which will cause them to live beyond the allotted span'. **1958** J. S. COLEMAN *Nigeria* i. 31 The Ibo and Ibibio languages belong to different branches of the large Niger–Congo linguistic family. **1960** *Times* 5 Oct. 18/7 Astonishing..naturalism in the very large Ibibio mask in wood.

Ibicencan (ibiþe·ŋkăn), *sb.* and *a.* Also **Ibicenco, Ibizenco.** [f. Sp. *ibicenca* native or inhabitant of Ibiza, *ibicenco* pertaining to Ibiza + -AN.] **A.** *sb.* A native or inhabitant of Ibiza, an island off the Mediterranean coast of Spain. **B.** *adj.* Of or pertaining to Ibiza, esp. in *Ibicencan hound* (= *IVICENE *sb.*).

1911 J. E. C. FLITCH *Mediterranean Moods* ix. 188 The Ibicencos have never naturalised the guitar. *Ibid.* 199 They sang chiefly in Catalan, and the song had a different character from that of the Ibicenco peasants. **1952** E. WHELPTON *Balearics* xv. 189 The Ibicencans..were for centuries considered to be savage barbarians. **1959** *Encounter* Oct. 39 The Ibicencan hounds—pale rib-thin beasts. **1969** C. IRVING *Fake!* (1970) xii. 139 He liked the Ibizencos, too, a friendly and dignified island people. **1970** *Globe Mag.* (Toronto) 26 Sept. 12/1 There is a native strain of dogs on the island, the Ibicencan hounds, said to be descended from the hunting hounds of the ancient Egyptians. **1972** *Times* 3 Feb. 25/6 One of the most attractive apartment developments..in typical Ibicenco style.

-ibility [F. *-ibilité*, L. *-ibilitātem*, *-tās*], termination of abstract sbs. from adjs. in -IBLE.

ibis. Add: **2.** *Angling.* The name of a type of artificial fly; now more usu. applied to a sort of red-dyed feather used in making this type of fly.

1863 *Harper's Mag.* Oct. 691/2 He trailed his 'ibis' lightly across the dark eddy at the edge of the foam. **1931** *Hardy's Anglers' Guide* (ed. 53) 75 Wet flies for brook trout... Ibis. **1961** A. C. WILLIAMS *Dict. Trout Flies* (ed. 3) 294 Tail: Red ibis feather. *Ibid.* 299 Tag: Bright red wool, or scarlet ibis. **1973** *Country Life* 7 June 1585/3 The butcher is a well-tried trout fly... It is made from what is known as dyed ibis (a hen's feather, dyed bright red), silver tinsel, [etc.].

3. A fashion colour (see quot.).

1927 *Daily News* 9 May 2/3 A skirt of satin..in the new pale apricot known as 'ibis'.

4. *attrib.* and *Comb.*, as *ibis-headed*, *-red* adjs.

1910 *Daily Chron.* 19 Feb. 6/2 Thoth, god of wisdom, was ibis-headed. **1907** *Westm. Gaz.* 29 Oct. 4/3 A pretty blouse of white lace, so arranged with ibis-red velvet as to have the effect of a smart little bolero. **1909** *Ibid.* 21 June 5/2 An ibis-red coat and skirt.

Ibiza (ibī·þă, ivī·þă). The name of one of the Balearic Islands, used esp. *attrib.* to denote a local breed of dog, the *IVICENE.

1935 *Hutchinson's Dog Encycl.* II. 924/1 (*caption*) The Ibiza hound..is reputed to refuse to interbreed with any other type of dog. **1948** B. VESEY-FITZGERALD *Bk. Dog* I. 73 An Ibiza hound, one of the rarest breeds I know and found..only in the Balearics. *Ibid.*, The Ibiza is not, at first sight, prepossessing.

Ibizan (ibī·þăn, ivī·þăn), *a.* [f. *IBIZ(A + -AN.] = *IBICENCAN *a.* **Ibizan hound** = *IVICENE *sb.* Also as *sb.*, the language of Ibiza; an Ibizan hound.

1911 J. E. C. FLITCH *Mediterranean Moods* viii. 169 An Ibizan oasis. **1936** M. K. SHEPPARD *Cottage in Majorca* iii. 51 Their gold ornaments were similar to those of the Ibizan women. **1952** E. WHELPTON *Balearics* xv. 199 See the local dances and hear the strange Ibizan music. *Ibid.* xvi. 201 Ibizan, like Mallorquin, is based on Catalan. **1971** F. HAMILTON *World Encycl. Dogs* 371 As a hunter the Ibizan Hound is unequalled. **1972** *Country Life* 10 Feb. 329/2 When the sporting varieties were exhibited the classes were almost entirely filled with pharaoh hounds and Ibizan hounds. *Ibid.* Suppl. 17 Ibizans..Irish Terriers..Jack Russell Terriers. **1972** *Listener* 13 July 55/2 Irving, with help from another Ibizan writer, put together the book.

Ibo (ī·bo), *a.* and *sb.* Also **Ebo, Igbo.** [Native name.] **A.** *adj.* Of or pertaining to the Ibos (see below). Cf. EBOE in Dict. and Suppl.

Some of the examples refer to Ibos in the U.S.A. and the West Indies.

1732 *South Carolina Gaz.* 20/1 Stolen..an old Ebo Negro Man;..had on a blue Negro Cloth Frock. **1774** E. LONG *Hist. Jamaica* II. III. ii. 403 The Ebo men are lazy, and averse to every laborious employment; the women performing almost all the work in their own country. **1799** [see NEGRO 3 a]. **1822** J. ADAMS *Sk. Voy. Afr.* iii. 41 Breeché, in the Heebo language, signifies gentleman. **1834** [see EBOE]. **1884** *Encycl. Brit.* XVII. 319/1 Soudan and Guinea...Ibo group. **1899** E. A. WISE in *Niger & Yoruba Notes* Nov. 37/1 We are morally pledged to do this by having a Mission in the Ibo country for over 40 years. **1950** D. JONES *Phoneme* 21 The Igbo language of Nigeria. **1951** R. FIRTH *Elem. Social Organiz.* v. 165 Some of the Ibo people of South-Eastern Nigeria construct elaborate series of clay figures. **1960** *Spectator* 21 Oct. 616 The squalor and nobility of life in an Ibo tribe. **1968** *Listener* 19 Sept. 353/1 The Ibo officer who had just murdered the Premier of the Northern Region. *Ibid.*, The Ibo leader, Ojukwu, and his five or six million Ibo are now concentrated within a narrowing portion of their former region.

B. *sb.* **1. a.** A Negro people of the lower Niger in Africa; also, a member of this people.

1757 *St Jago Intelligencer* 14 May, 1 Ebo, 1 Angola, 1 Mundingo. [**1789** O. EQUIANO *Life* I. i. 18 Mahogany-coloured men from the south west of us: we call them *Oye-Eboe*, which term signifies red men living at a distance.] **1822** J. ADAMS *Sk. Voy. Afr.* iii. 40 To this nation the Heebos express a strong aversion. *Ibid.* 41 The Heebos, in their persons, are tall and well-formed. **1822** *Amer. Beacon* (Norfolk, Va.) 3 Sept. 2/1 (Th. Suppl.), Monday Gell is an Ebo, and now in the prime of life. **1836** F. H. RANKIN *White Man's Grave* I. v. 106 Shortly after arriving, when Settlers and Maroons were to me as equally black and undistinguishable as Soosoos and Ibbos, I innocently inflicted deep injury on the sensitive mind of the laundress by inquiring why she had omitted to bring home some particular article of dress. **1911** *Encycl. Brit.* XIV. 223/2 The Ibo are a strong well-built Negro race. **1954** M. GLUCKMAN in *Institutions Primitive Soc.* vi. 70 In the past, an Ibo in Nigeria could only travel safely in distant parts to trade by following chains of relationship from place to place. **1960** *Guardian* 15 July 15/3 The Ibos (or better, the Igbos) live mainly in the Eastern Region [of Nigeria]. **1961** *Listener* 30 Nov. 901/2 The intensely individualistic and vital Ibo in the south-east [of Nigeria]. **1973** *Black World* Jan. 9/1 Another example is the figure of Ikenga—god of fortune among the Igbos—in whose left hand is a skull.

b. The language of this people, which constitutes one of the major language groups of Nigeria.

1880 MRS. G. STURGE tr. *Burdo's Niger & Benueh* viii. 141 'The King, our master,' one of them said to me in the language of Ebo. **1883** R. N. CUST *Sk. Mod. Lang. Afr.* I. xi. 223 Ibo or eboe: commences at the apex of the Delta of the Niger...There appear to be four dialects. **1950** FORDE & JONES *Ibo & Ibibio Speaking Peoples* 11 *Igbo* is one of the Kwa languages. **1955** [see *FANTI *sb.* and *a.* a]. **1958** J. S. COLEMAN *Nigeria* i. 18 Before the British occupation..the present Eastern region consisted of small semiautonomous communities of Ibo- and Ibibio-speaking peoples. **1962** *Amer. Speech* XXXVII. 227 A case of disagreement taken from Ibo, a tone language. **1968** CHOMSKY & HALLE *Sound Pattern Eng.* 378 In a language such as Turkish there are four classes of harmonizing words, rather than two as in Nez Perce or Igbo.

ibogaine (ibōᵘ·gă,īn). *Chem.* [a. F. *ibogaïne* (Dybowski & Landrin 1901, in *Compt. Rend.* CXXXIII. 749), f. *iboga*, Congolese name and specific epithet (E. H. Baillon 1889, in *Bull. de la Soc. linn. de Paris* I. 782) of the shrub (see def.): see -INE⁵.] The principal alkaloid, $C_{20}H_{26}N_2O$, of the shrub *Tabernanthe iboga* of equatorial Africa, a colourless crystalline compound that is a pentacyclic indole derivative and acts as a stimulant of the central nervous system when ingested, producing intoxication.

1902 *Jrnl. Chem. Soc.* LXXXII. I. 114 The active principle, ibogaine,..is present in the bark and wood and particularly in the roots of the plant. **1955** *Amer. Jrnl. Psychiatry* CXII. 467 Concerning ibogaine, the natives of French West Africa do not ascribe to it any hallucinogenic property. 'When questioned they insist that it has an action identical with that of alcohol without impairing the reason.' **1960** *Acta Crystallogr.* XIII. 553 Ibogaine, $C_{20}H_{26}N_2O$, is an alkaloid in which an indole ring system is attached to a seven-membered nitrogen containing ring, two sides of which form part of an adjoining tricyclic *iso*-quinuclidine ring system.

Ibsenism (i·bsəniz'm). [f. the name of Henrik *Ibsen* (1828–1906), Norwegian dramatist and poet + -ISM.] The dramatic principles and aims characteristic of the writings of Ibsen and the Ibsenites, which examined and criticized social conventions. So **Ibs(c)e·ne, Ibs(c)e·nity** *nonce-wds.* (with play on *obscene, obscenity*); **Ibsene·sque, Ibse·nian, I·bsenish** *adjs.*, of, pertaining to, or resembling the style or views of Ibsen; **I·bsenist, I·bsenite,** an admirer or imitator of Ibsen; also as *adjs.* = *Ibsenian adj.

1889 E. DOWSON in *Lett.* (1967) 432 The brave little band of Ibsenites. **1890** G. B. SHAW *London Music 1888–89* (1937) 283 A reprobate who greatly prefers Ibsenism to Walter Besantism. **1891** —— (*title*) The quintessence of Ibsenism. *Ibid.* 141 When one of the more specifically Ibsenian parts has to be filled, it is actually safer to entrust it to a novice than to a competent and experienced actor. *Ibid.* App. 158 Without being necessarily an Ibsenist, a critic may see at a glance that abuse of the sort quoted..is worthless. *Ibid.* 159 Mr William Archer expressly guards himself against being taken as an Ibsenist doctrinaire. **1892** *National Observer* 17 Dec. 107/1 When the din of political factions is silent, and Ibscenity has faded into a literary curiosity. **1893** *Ibid.* 7 Jan. 190/2 Her story is amateurish, sentimental, Ibsene. But Ibsenity is in the air. **1893** *Athenæum* 16 Dec. 857/3 The suicide of the woman..is nothing if not Ibsenish. It is unheroic, unromantic, ineffective, insignificant. **1895** G. B. SHAW in *Sat. Rev.* 9 Nov. 618/1 The material is what we now call Ibsenite: the technique is that of Scribe. **1902** CHESTERTON *Lunacy & Lett.* (1958) 39 The resistance of the conventional mind to Ibsenism..is fundamentally right. **1902** M. BEERBOHM in *Sat. Rev.* 24 May 644/2 Ellida..is the usual Ibsenist heroine, propounder of the regular Ibsenist ideas. **1902** W. B. YEATS *Let.* 4 Dec. (1954) 386 He [*sc.* Joyce]..did not knock at the gate with his old Ibsenite fury. **1905** *Daily Chron.* 7 July 8/4 She takes what might be called an Ibsenian view of humanity. **1906** M. BEERBOHM in *Sat. Rev.* 5 May 552/2 A strong-minded, Ibsenesque heroine, with a contempt for social conventions. **1906** W. STEVENS *Let.* 27 Apr. (1967) 91 You always were an Ibsenist, without knowing it. **1912** R. MACAULAY *Views & Vagabonds* vi. 112 She thinks they're Ibsenesque, but really they're like Miss Yonge in a fit of religious doubt. **1916** *Everyman* 5 May 54/2 Their passion for the erotic and Ibsene. **1916** T. MACDONAGH *Lit. in Ireland* 18 The drama of modern Ireland, in English, is..not free from the faults of impressionism, of quasi-scientific Ibsenism, of unreal gloom and of shallow cynicism. **1928** *Radio Times* 16 Mar. 564/2 Two distinguished Ibsenites..will be heard from London to-night. **1957** A. MILLER *Coll. Plays* (1958) Introd. 12 When *All My Sons* opened on Broadway it was called an Ibsenesque play. **1966** *Punch* 9 Feb. 206/1 The first love—for all her professed Ibsenist rationalism—won't let him go. **1970** *Daily Tel.* 30 Oct. 12/2 The play..remained Scandinavian in..its Ibsenite thesis that the truth is dangerous to man's precarious happiness. **1972** *Listener* 7 Sept. 310/1 The formation of the 'new woman' of the Ibsenite and Shavian period. **1973** *Times* 8 June 11/6 This meeting between Dr Miller and Charles Darwin, for example, had something unmistakably Ibsenish about it.

icaco (ikā·ko). [a. Sp. *icaco*, *hicaco*, f. Taino *hikako*.] A small tree, *Chrysobalanus icaco*, of the family Rosaceæ, native to tropical America and the West Indies; the fruit of this tree. Also called COCO-PLUM.

1752 P. MILLER *Gardeners Dict.* (ed. 6) s.v. Chrysobalanus. This Genus of Plants is titled by Father Plumier *Icaco* which is the Indian name of this Fruit. **1756** P. BROWNE *Civil & Nat. Hist. Jamaica* 250 (*heading*) Chrysobalanus... Icaco... The Cocco Plumb Tree. **1852** T. ROSS tr. *A. von Humboldt's Personal Narr. Trav. Amer.* II. xvii. 136 Hedges of bead-trees encircled groups of icacoes laden with fruit. **1887** C. A. MOLONEY *Sk. Forestry W. Africa* 347 Icaco or Cocoa Plum of the West Indies. **1943** RECORD & HESS *Timbers of New World* 454/2 The best known species [of *Chrysobalanus*] is the Coco Plum or *Icaco*, *C. icaco* L., which has a large edible fruit so wrinkled as to suggest the face of a monkey.

Icarian, *a.*¹ (Later examples.)

1936 E. SITWELL *Sel. Poems* 249 Eagle-winged Icarian flights. **1972** *Daily Tel.* (Colour Suppl.) 1 Dec. 16/1 In the view of some social philosophers and historians, space flight is an Icarian venture at its best—and an extravagance at its worst.

Icarus (i·kărŏs). *Gr. Myth.* The name of the son of Dædalus, who attempted to fly by means of artificial wings fastened with wax (see ICARIAN *a.*¹): used allusively.

[**1589** GREENE *Menaphon* (Arb.) 53, I feare..in the height of my thoughts soaring too high, to fall with wofull repenting Icarus.] **1591** SHAKES. *1 Hen. VI*, IV. vi. 56 Then follow thou thy desp'rate Syre of Creet, Thou Icarus, thy Life to me is sweet. *Ibid.* vii. 16 There di'de My Icarus, my Blossome, in his pride. **1594** NASHE *Unfort. Trav.* I3ᵛ, These insolent fancies are but Icarus feathers, whose wanton waxe melted against the sun. **1694** D'URFEY *Don Quix.* II. Ep. Ded. sig. A1ᵛ, The roving Icarus in Poetry, By you is levell'd, when he soars too high. **1924** B. RUSSELL (*title*) Icarus, or, The future of science. **1931** *Times Lit. Suppl.* 24 Sept. 714/2 Much that he [*sc.* D'Annunzio] has given is not pure gold, but decorative lumber comparable to the ill-assorted trophies of the Vittoriale from which, an Icarus who has ceased to fly, he makes well-calculated sallies.

ice, *sb.* Add: **2. c.** Phrases. *on ice*: (*a*) kept out of the way until wanted, in reserve; in custody, in prison; (*b*) of a venture, game, etc.: sure of being achieved or won, a certainty; *to cut no ice*: to carry no weight, to fail to impress; hence *to cut ice*: to impress, to make an effect.

1890 A. C. GUNTER *Miss Nobody* xx. 231 For Election. Gussie de P. Van Beekman... On ice! **1894** P. L. FORD *Hon. Peter Stirling* 328 They say she's never been able to find a man good enough for her, and so she's keeping herself on ice. **1895** J. S. WOOD *Yale Yarns* 12 Such speeches! Eloquence cut no ice at *that* dinner. **1897** *Scribner's Mag.* Sept. 305/1 And it don't cut no ice with

you whether folks call you inconsistent or not. 1916 J. BUCHAN *Greenmantle* ix. 117 Because the German mercantile marine was laid on ice till the end of the war, they had turned him on to this show. 1917 A. CONAN DOYLE *His Last Bow* 291 It cuts no ice with a British copper to tell him you're an American citizen. 1924 A. HUXLEY *Let.* 28 Oct. (1969) 235, I was very glad..to hear that you liked *Those Barren Leaves.* It cuts more ice, I think, than the others and is more explicit and to the point. 1930 W. S. MAUGHAM *Cakes & Ale* iv. 48 There was a softness in Roy's voice such as I imagined he would use if he were telling a prospective father that his wife was about to gratify his wishes. It cut no ice with me. 1930 G. B. SHAW *Apple Cart* I. 7 Oh, sit down, man, sit down. Youre in your own house: ceremony cuts no ice with me. 1931 *Sat. Rev. Lit.* (U.S.) 18 July 978/2 Among the words and phrases common among racketeers, not yet in general use..there are the following:..*on ice*, in the penitentiary. 1932 E. BOWEN *To North* xxiii. 247 Sheer man-to-man envy of Markie for cutting so much ice. 1933 D. L. SAYERS *Murder must Advertise* xix. 322 Their idea is to put you on ice quietly till they've had time to settle up their affairs. 1936 E. S. GARDNER *Case of Sleepwalker's Niece* xiv. 131, I figured that and the record of the telephone call would be enough to put the case on ice. 1936 WODEHOUSE *Laughing Gas* xviii. 195 Take him back to his room and keep him there on ice till it's time to go to the studio. 1944 W. S. MAUGHAM *Razor's Edge* vii. 276, I haven't signed on the dotted line yet, but it's on ice. The fella I'm going in with was a roommate of mine at college..and I'm dead sure he wouldn't hand me a lemon. 1945 *Chicago Daily News* 4 Oct. 12/1 They ..accumulated enough runs in the first inning to put the game on ice. 1953 W. BURROUGHS *Junkie* (1972) x. 103 'I sent for the wagon,' said the guy with the pipe. 'We'll take them over to the third precinct and put them on ice.' 1954 KOESTLER *Invis. Writing* xxxiv. 369 He will for a considerable time be 'put on ice'—isolated from any contact with other members. 1955 *Times* 12 May 14/5 Burns demanded that the purse be handed over before he entered the ring. He ended a bitter argument by declaring: 'That cuts no ice with me. I want the referee to hold the money.' 1957 A. GRIMBLE *Return to Islands* 75 The problem that his resignation had left on ice, for whomever it might concern. 1965 *New Statesman* 14 May 771/2 Presumably the book, finished in 1957, was put on ice, for Mr Wood can hardly have hoped to get away in Beaverbrook's lifetime with much of the discussion of his 'brash brutality'. 1973 'I. DRUMMOND' *Jaws of Watchdog* xii. 154 Scotland Yard could not keep him on ice that long. He would have to be brought to a court to be charged. 1973 J. PORTER *It's Murder with Dover* vii. 63 MacGregor remembered..that logical argument didn't cut much ice with Dover and he abandoned it.

d. A piece or pieces of ice placed in a drink, or into which a bottle, etc., is placed to cool the contents.

1833 C. REDDING *Hist. Mod. Wines* xiv. 316 Before drinking, the wine should be kept an hour in ice. 1846 A. SOYER *Gastronomic Regenerator* 701 When the syrup is a little cool, taste if palatable, place a little upon some ice, and if strong enough fill your mould, which place in ice. *a* 1922 T. S. ELIOT *Waste Land Drafts* (1971) 61 Where's a cocktail shaker, Ben, here's plenty of cracked ice. 1927 E. GLYN *'It'* xii. 110 A perfect dinner had been ordered—the champagne was on ice.

3. (Further examples.)

1884 'MARK TWAIN' *Huck. Finn* xxxii. 333 'How'd you get your breakfast so early on the boat?' It was kinder thin ice, but I says: 'The captain see me standing around.' 1904 [see *COIN *sb.* 6]. 1938 E. BOWEN *Death of Heart* III. ii. 343 The *idea* of her never leaves me quiet, and by coming into this room she drives me on to the ice. 1962 J. G. BENNETT *Witness* xxii. 287 Thus, without knowing it, I was treading on very thin ice.

4. b. = **ice pigeon.*

1881 J. C. LYELL *Fancy Pigeons* 81 The smooth-legged chequered or spangled ones are known in this country as Ural ice, while the rough-legged spangled birds are called Siberian ice.

c. Diamonds; jewellery. *slang* (orig. *U.S.*).

1906 H. GREEN *At Actors' Boarding House* 26 Her in evenin' clothes and a bunch of ice on her hands. 1915 G. BRONSON-HOWARD *God's Man* IV. iv. 281 Along comes a guy..a piece of ice in his tie that made Tiffany's front window look like a hardware exhibit. 1924 WODEHOUSE *Leave it to Psmith* ix. 184 Diamonds, Eddie. A necklace. ..Some of the best ice I've saw in years. 1925, 1942 [see *HOT *a.* 7 e]. 1936 J. G. BRANDON *Pawnshop Murder* i. 2 The glitter of stolen 'ice' or other jewels spread out upon the table. 1942 M. SCHLAUCH *Gift of Tongues* (1943) 269 Jewels become 'ice'. 1959 *Listener* 23 Apr. 706/2 'Shiners' and 'ice' to the light-fingered boys, the diamond is known to the gemmologist as the hardest..of all minerals. 1961 WODEHOUSE *Ice in Bedroom* i. 11 Yes, someone got away with her bit of ice all right. 1972 'H. HOWARD' *Nice Day for Funeral* i. 30 Prager caught sight of five hundred grand in cracked ice.

d. Profit from the illegal sale of theatre, cinema, etc., tickets. *U.S. slang.*

1927 *Theatre Mag.* Sept. 30/2 Thousands of tickets for special attractions in the large movie houses are sold over the box-office counter to speculators by the treasurers of the houses, their charge, or 'ice', running to as much as $1 a ticket on the 'sell-outs'. 1960 *Observer* 30 Oct. 1/17 'Ice'..is the money from the sale of hot tickets..and enables..box office clerks to buy themselves Cadillacs. 1964 *Economist* 25 Jan. 313/2 Kick-backs—'ice' as it is called on Broadway—on theatre tickets whose prices are marked up illegally.

e. Protection money. *slang.*

1948 E. L. JOHNSON in E. L. Irey *Tax Dodgers* (1949) xiii. 229 Willie..said, 'The extra hundred sixty is ice.' 'Ice' is argot for graft or protection fees. 1951 *Economist* 29 Sept. 747 Gross..who had confessed to paying this sum in 'ice' for the protection that made it possible for him to earn $100,000 a year. 1951 E. KEFAUVER *Crime in Amer.* (1952) xvii. 186 When the combine's books finally were seized, examination disclosed recorded payments totalling $108,000 for the service known as 'juice', which is the California gambling profession's euphemism (in Florida the term is 'ice') for 'protection' money.

5. b. (Earlier and later examples.)

1723 J. NOTT *Cook's & Confectioner's Dict.* sig. B4 Make Ice with the White of an Egg, powder'd Sugar, Orange or Lemon Flowers. 1885 C. M. YONGE *Nuttie's Father* II. v. 61 How dreadfully hard the ice on the wedding cake was, so that when Annaple tried to cut it the knife slipped.

7. a. *ice-dancer* (so *ice-dancing* vbl. sb.), *-merchant, -show, -wagon; ice-cutter* (examples). Also *ice-clear* adj.

1946 S. SPENDER *European Witness* II. iii. 146 The ice-clear light of that part of Germany. 1948 C. DAY LEWIS *Poems 1943–1947* 87 Toward my expectation's bed They move in a hushed, ice-clear trance. 1970 R. LOWELL *Notebk.* 204 Once or twice, blurt your ice-clear sentence. 1791 J. LONG *Voy. & Trav. Indian Trader* 120 The fishing party consisted of..natives of Canada, who, being provided with axes, ice-cutters..set off. 1969 *New Scientist* 13 Mar. 574/2 A new type of ice-breaker is needed for breaking up solid ice. We have devised one and christened it an ice-cutter. 1925 E. LAW *Dancing on Ice* iii. 24 To the question what should ice-dancers do to acquit themselves properly, the obvious answer is, that they should first learn exactly what the valse-figure is. 1969 *Times* 15 Nov. 10/8 Only one skater now remains of that team of six brilliant ice dancers. 1925 E. LAW *Dancing on Ice* v. 46 Invite the independent judgment of..some one who knows and understands the whole theory and practice of ice-dancing. 1969 *Times* 15 Nov. 10/8 The world ice dancing champions..will not be competing. 1864 *Chambers's Jrnl.* 99/1 The men take the ice to ice-merchants, who are ready to buy it in any quantity. 1973 *Post Office Telephone Directory Section 471, London Yellow Pages Classified (North)* 177/2 (*heading*) Ice and cold storage companies and ice merchants. 1950 *Oxf. Jun. Encycl.* IX. 432/2 Of recent years 'ice shows' have been made popular in the U.S.A. and Canada. 1966 *Listener* 29 Dec. 959/1 Original plays..and an ice-show. 1865 J. D. BURN *Three Years among Working-Classes U.S.* 304 The ice-waggons may be seen with their crystal loads flying about the towns in all directions from May to the end of September. 1898 J. LONDON *Let.* 30 Nov. (1966) 6 Saturday I worked on an ice wagon. 1905 *Sketch* LI. 38/1 The earliest on his rounds was the man with the ice-waggon, who put down on the door-step of each house a block of ice. 1971 M. TAK *Truck Talk* 88 *Ice wagon*, a refrigerated trailer. 1972 *News & Observer* Raleigh, N. Carolina) 30 Dec. 4/2 We don't hear much (nowadays] about..ice wagons, branch-lines.

b. *ice-barrier* (examples), *-blockade, -bridge, -cake* (examples), *-cover, -crystal, -edge, -face, -flake, -fringe, -hump, -lake* (examples), *-margin, -ridge* (examples), *-spicule, -waste* (examples).

1874 G. CAMPBELL *Let.* 14 Feb. in *Log Lett. from 'Challenger'* (1876) ii. 99 We had hoped to see the great ice-barrier, that endless wall of ice two hundred feet in height which fringes the southern continent. 1934 I. W. HUTCHISON *North to Rime-Ringed Sun* x. 106 The ice-barrier was thickening fast, and as it seemed impenetrable under the westerly gale..we cast the *Trader*'s anchor. 1939 L. MACNEICE *Autumn Jrnl.* xxiv. 95 The waters of life are free of the ice-blockade of hunger. 1969 in Halpert & Story *Christmas Mumming in Newfoundland* 32 The winter ice-blockade which made the inshore fishery a limited seasonal operation. 1792 E. P. SIMCOE *Diary* 15 Feb. (1911) vii. 77 Coll. Simcoe and I were going to walk on the ice bridge. 1880 'MARK TWAIN' *Tramp Abroad* II. xl. 115 A young porter..started across an ice-bridge which spanned a crevasse. 1909 *Westm. Gaz.* 2 Sept. 9/2 After twenty days we found an ice-bridge over the water between the continental ice and the Polar ice. 1870 *Canad. Illustr. News* 26 Mar. 334/1 One ice-cake after another struck her boat. 1923 R. FROST *New Hampshire* (1924) 65 The seal yelp On an ice cake. 1953 *Canad. Geogr. Jrnl.* July 150/1 A strip of open water stretched between shore and ice-cake which filled most of the bay. 1960 S. PLATH *Colossus* (1967) 44 Farther out, the waves will be mouthing icecakes. 1966 T. ARMSTRONG et al. *Illustr. Gloss. Snow & Ice* 21 *Ice cake*, a floe smaller than 10 m across. 1882 A. GEIKIE *Text-bk. Geol.* III. ii. 416 On the ice-worn surface of Norway singular cavities..known as 'giants' kettles'..have had an origin under the massive ice-cover which once spread over that peninsula. 1958 PRIEBSCH & COLLINSON *German Lang.* (ed. 4) ii. 22 The ice-cover made the whole of Scandinavia and Northern Germany uninhabitable. 1849 THOREAU *Week Concord Riv.* 394 It matters not through what ice-crystals it is seen. 1919 D. H. LAWRENCE in *Eng. Rev.* June 485 Some, blonde, blue-eyed, northern, are evidently water-born, born along with the ice-crystals and blue, cold deeps. 1956 *Nature* 18 Feb. 321/2 Collisions occurring between ice crystals and small hailstones. 1947 G. RAWSON *Arctic Adventures* ix. 187 The cutter reached the ice edge, and a man sprang out of it. 1966 T. ARMSTRONG et al. *Illustr. Gloss. Snow & Ice* 22 *Ice edge*, the boundary at any given time between open water and sea, river or lake ice of any kind, whether drifting or fast. 1856 E. K. KANE *Arctic Explorations* I. xvi. 187, I had to walk through the broken ice, which rose in toppling spires over my head, for nearly fifty yards, before I found an opening to the ice-face, by which I was able to climb down to them. 1898 J. O. MAUND in W. A. Morgan *'House' on Sport* 276 Above the ice face snow slopes lying at a much less rapid angle led to the final rock peak. 1915 E. POUND *Cathay* 23 Hung with hard ice-flakes, where hail-scur flew. 1937 *Discovery* July 220/1 Two of them..were the first to land on the ice-flake. 1902 *Spectator* 25 Oct. 604/1 Persecuted until they were practically driven off the seas, they took refuge furthest north along the ice-fringe. 1966 T. ARMSTRONG et al. *Illustr. Gloss. Snow & Ice* 23 *Ice fringe*, a very narrow ice piedmont, extending less than about 1 km inland from the sea. 1910 W. DE LA MARE *Three Mulla-Mulgars* 67 Floating like a cork among the ice-humps. 1961 *Times* 24 Apr. 14/7, I cannot tell whether an icehump is two inches high or a dangerous two feet. 1934 Ice-lake [see *GEOCHRONOLOGICAL *a.*]. 1957 G. E. HUTCHINSON *Treat. Limnol.* I. i. 8 The earliest postglacial Baltic was an ice lake. 1889 G. F. WRIGHT *Ice Age N. Amer.* xx. 482 The buried vegetable deposits under consideration do not mark a warm climate, but a climate much colder than the present—such a vegetation, in fact, as would naturally flourish near the ice-margin. 1958 F. E. ZEUNER *Dating Past* (ed. 4) 22 As the ice-margin retreated the varves followed it. 1892 C. T. DENT et al. *Mountaineering* vi. 223 Nothing tends more to weary and render him [*sc.* a mountaineer] careless than some hours of step-cutting on an ice-ridge. 1929 F. SMYTHE *Climbs & Ski Runs* xv. 288 We gained the foot of the rock pitch separating the third ice-ridge from the fourth. 1957 J. BLISH *Fallen Star* vii. 104 The ice-ridge on our left screamed, broke free and reared skyward. 1881 *Nature* 10 Feb. 338/2 The ice-spicules are built up 'in the teeth' of this current. 1962 F. I. ORDWAY et al. *Basic Astronautics* iii. 90 Three in number, they [*sc.* the rings of Saturn] are very thin in comparison to their width, and are made up of millions upon millions of..particles, pebbles, grains of dust, and perhaps ice spicules. 1905 *Westm. Gaz.* 9 Dec. 16/1 There is neither the sport nor the game that cheers the Northern ice-wastes. 1964 F. WARNER *Early Poems* 80 Lonely ice-wastes.

c. *ice-coated, -covered* (later example), *-locked* (examples) adjs.

1880 'MARK TWAIN' *Tramp Abroad* II. xxxiv. 32 They came to an ice-coated ridge. 1928 *Observer* 15 July 22 Ice-coated ships. 1956 *Nature* 17 Mar. 508/1 The lofty ice-covered interior of Antarctica. 1866 J. G. WHITTIER *Snow-Bound* 50 Wide swung again our ice-locked door. 1907 *Westm. Gaz.* 21 Oct. 2/3 Ice-locked Polar snows. 1972 S. BURNFORD *One Woman's Arctic* i. 13 Now the strait was ice-locked.

d. *ice-dammed* (see sense 8 below), *-hearted* (later example) adjs.

1950 G. BARKER *News of World* 49 Just as the ice-hearted stars Stand around like avatars. 1960 S. PLATH *Colossus* (1967) 23 At the source Of your ice-hearted calling—Drunkenness of the great depths.

e. *ice-breaking* (earlier and later examples), *-cutting* (examples), *-making* (earlier example).

1824 *Canad. Mag.* III. Dec. 541 He accosted us all gaily, without any of that long ice-breaking conversation about the weather, which generally occupies the first half-hour of our stage-coach journeys. 1956 *Nature* 31 Mar. 600/2 The two expeditions will share a large ice-breaking sealer. 1970 *Daily Tel.* 21 Mar. 15 Canadian seal-hunting ships with ice-breaking capacity. 1854 THOREAU *Walden* 229 The only obvious employment, except wood-chopping, ice-cutting, or the like business. 1908 *Westm. Gaz.* 29 May 2/1 The ice-cutting looks so like harvesting or hay-making. 1960 J. J. ROWLANDS *Spindrift* 75 Few remember the days of ice-cutting. 1864 *Chambers's Jrnl.* 13 Feb. 101/1 The attention of some millions of persons was attracted, in the International Exhibition of 1862, to two ice-making machines of a very remarkable character.

8. ice-age, also *fig.* and *Comb.*; **ice-apron** (earlier example); (*b*) (see quot. 1958); **ice-arm,** an arm or projecting portion of ice; **ice-ax** (usu. **ice-axe**), (*b*) an implement for cutting ice for domestic purposes; = **ice-pick* (*a*); **ice-block,** (*a*) a block of ice; also *fig.*; (*b*) Austral. = **ice-lolly*; **ice-blue,** a very pale blue; **ice-box** (further examples); also (*U.S.*), a refrigerator (see also quot. 1971); also *transf.*; **ice-bucket** = *ice-pail*; **ice-capade** [jocular blend of ICE *sb.* + ESCAPADE], an event, show, etc., that takes place on ice; **ice-car,** a refrigerating van adapted for the transport of perishable goods; **ice-cart,** a cart in which ice is conveyed for delivery; **ice-cave** (examples); (*b*) a hollow in the ice at the lower end of a glacier; (*c*) a kind of small domestic refrigerator (*disused*); (*d*) a cave hollowed out of ice as a shelter; **ice-cellar** *N. Amer.*, a cellar kept cool by blocks of ice and used to preserve food; **ice-chest** (earlier and later examples); **ice-chimney,** a chimney (CHIMNEY *sb.* 8) formed in ice; **ice-claw** = CRAMPON *sb.* 3; **ice-cloud,** a cloud consisting of ice crystals; **ice colour,** any of a class of azo dyes which are insoluble in water, being formed directly on the fibre by impregnating it with one component of the dye (naphthol or a naphthol derivative) and then immersing it in a solution of the other (a diazo compound); so called because the solutions originally used needed to be kept ice-cold; **ice contact** *Physical Geogr.*, a surface or deposit that was originally formed in contact with a body of ice; usu. *attrib.*, esp. in *ice-contact slope*, a (usually steep) slope so formed; **ice-craft** (later examples); **ice-crop,** the yield of ice in a single winter or from a certain place; **ice cube,** a small block of ice formed in a mould in a refrigerator and used to chill drinks; **ice-dam,** a dam across a river formed by a glacier; so **ice-dammed** *a.*; **ice-dyke,** a narrow crevasse filled with ice columns; **ice-farm,** (*a*) a place where ice is formed by allowing water to freeze in specially hollowed-out beds, or in shallow earthenware pans; (*b*) a place where

naturally frozen ice is stored; **ice-fishing** (examples; see also quot. 1907); hence [as a back-formation] *ice-fish* v. intr.; *ice-fisherman*; **ice-flowers,** delete †*Obs.* and add later examples; (*b*) (see quot. 1955), also in *sing.*; **ice-front,** the margin of a glacier, ice-shelf, or ice-sheet; **ice-gorge** (earlier example); **ice-green,** a very pale green; **ice guard,** (*a*) (see quot. 1905) *U.S.*; (*b*) *Aeronaut.*, a wire grid that may be fitted in the intake of an aero-engine, so that any ice forms on it rather than in the engine; **ice-hammer,** (*a*) a hammer for breaking ice to be used in drinks; (*b*) a hammer used in mountaineering (see quot. 1932); **ice-harvest,** the ice-crop; the period during which the ice-crop is gathered; **ice hockey,** a game developed from field hockey but played on ice; also *attrib.*; **ice-jam,** the blocking of a channel with broken ice; the jam so formed; also *fig.*; **ice-lane** (see quot.); **ice line,** in a phase diagram of water, a line representing the conditions of temperature and pressure at which ice and water will be in equilibrium in the absence of water vapour; **ice-lobe,** a portion of a continental ice-sheet that projects from the main area; **ice-lolly,** a water ice on a stick; **ice-machine** (examples); **ice-maiden** *colloq.*, a 'cold' or unresponsive woman; **ice-maker** (later example); (*b*) = *ice-machine*; **ice-mould,** a hollow utensil used in shaping ice; **ice-needle,** (*a*) a strong needle used to break up a lump of ice; (*b*) any elongated, needle-like ice crystal; **ice-pack** (later examples); (*b*) a pack (PACK *sb.*[1] 11) prepared with ice; **ice-pan,** a small slab of floating ice; **ice-pick,** (*a*) a small domestic tool with a sharp spike designed for breaking up ice (e.g. for drinks); (*b*) in Mountaineering, a pick (PICK *sb.*[1]); **ice pigeon,** a breed of domestic pigeon whose prevailing colour is a pale bluish lavender; **ice-pitcher** (examples); **ice-piton,** a piton used to assist climbing on ice; **ice-plate,** a small, usu. glass, plate on which ice-cream is served; **ice-point,** a temperature at which ice and water are in equilibrium; *spec.* the temperature (0°C.) at which ice is in equilibrium with water saturated with air and under standard atmospheric pressure, formerly taken as a primary fixed point but now replaced for this purpose by the triple point; **ice-pole** *Canad.*, a long pole used by seamen for levering against ice-floes, etc.; **ice-push,** lateral pressure exerted on a shore as a sheet of floating ice expands following changes in temperature; also, an ice-rampart formed as a result; **ice-rampart,** a ridge of beach material along a shore-line which has been forced up by the lateral movement of floating ice; **ice-rink** (see RINK *sb.*[2] 3); **ice-run,** a stretch of ice prepared for tobogganing; also *fig.*; **Ice Saints** (see quot. 1922); **ice-scape** [after LANDSCAPE], (a picture of) ice scenery; **ice-scour, -scouring,** the action of an ice-sheet or glacier in eroding the land and modifying and producing landforms; so **ice-scoured** *a.*; **ice-screw,** also, an ice-piton (q.v.) which is screwed, rather than hammered, into the ice; **ice-shed,** a divide between two expanses of moving ice; **ice-shelf,** a floating sheet of ice permanently attached to a land mass; **ice-skate** = SKATE *sb.*[2] 1; also as *vb.*; so *ice-skater*, *ice-skating* vbl. sb.; **ice-spirit,** frost as a nature-spirit; **ice sport,** a sport taking place on ice; **ice step,** a step cut into ice; **ice-storm,** a storm of freezing rain that leaves a deposit of ice on trees, etc.; **ice-tongue,** any body of ice that projects from a glacier, iceberg, or ice-sheet, esp. one that is relatively long and narrow (see also quot. 1893); **ice-tray,** a tray used in a refrigerator for making ice cubes; **ice-wedge,** a vertical wedge-shaped mass of ice in the soil of a permafrost region; **ice-white** *a.*, having a whiteness like that of ice; **ice wool** = *EIS WOOL.

1957 C. DAY LEWIS *Pegasus* 24 Cold chisels of wind, ice-age-edged. **1966** *Listener* 10 Mar. 338/2 With..the certainty by 1950 that America and Russia both possessed atomic weapons, the world entered the new ice-age of the cold war between the big two. **1973** A. PRICE *October Men* ix. 122 The temperature was perhaps slightly less arctic now he had said his piece, but that was no sure sign that a second..ice age was not about to set in. **1871** *Scribner's Monthly* II. 170 It [has been] necessary to construct enormous breakwaters, having ice-aprons of strong oak timber. **1958** ARMSTRONG & ROBERTS in *Polar Record* IX. LIX. 93 *Ice apron*, a thin mass of snow and ice adhering to a mountain side. **1928** *Daily Tel.* 4 Sept. 11/5 He..had mistaken the Frederikshaab ice arm for the Sukkertoppen ice arm. **1960** J. J. ROWLANDS *Spindrift* 69 It was the magic of his [*sc.* an ice-vendor's] skill in using an ice-axe that enthralled me. **1963** I. DEUTSCHER *Prophet Outcast: Trotsky* v. 504 He [*sc.* Trotsky] grappled with the murderer, bit his hand, and wrenched the ice-axe from him. **1853** Ice-block [in Dict., sense 7 b]. **1864** G. M. HOPKINS *Notebks. & Papers* (1937) 27 Those wastes where the ice-blocks tilt and fret. **1957** J. BLISH *Falling Star* ix. 120 We built Wentz's igloo with..the one Keystone ice-block at the summit. **1958** *Church Times* 3 Jan. 3/1 Hopes of some thaw in the international ice-block rose with the publication of warm greetings of peace and goodwill sent by the Russian leaders. **1962** J. R. BERNARD in *Southerly* XXII. 97 Without loss we add to..the meaning of..ice-block that of frozen confection. **1966** BAKER *Austral. Lang.* (ed. 2) xiii. 290 *Ice-block*, a small block of coloured and sweet-tasting ice on a stick. **1935** *N. & Q.* 5 Jan. 7/2 From a draper's catalogue for the coming winter sales, I cull a few names of colours to me at least new: Ice-blue, [etc.]. **1952** 'J. ROSS' *Yellow Drawing-Room* ix. 138 An ice-blue satin skirt. **1958** A. WILSON *Middle Age of Mrs Eliot* II. 219 The walls [were] distempered ice blue. **1970** W. SMITH *Gold Mine* xxv. 57 His office was in white and ice-blue. **1846** *St. Louis Reveille* 9 Sept. 4/5 Everything requisite for funerals, such as Hearse, Carriages,..Ice, Ice-boxes. **1877** [see *BAVAROISE]. **1908** WODEHOUSE & WESTBROOK *Globe by the Way Bk.* 13/2 His brain worked like a buzz-saw in an ice-box. **1927** *Rev. Eng. Stud.* Oct. 435 This healthy linguistic instinct is seen in *e.g.* the substitution of *raincoat* for *mackintosh*, *ice-box* for *refrigerator*. **1938** D. CASTLE *Do Your Own Time* v. 45 Scavengers..cut down the hanged men, place them in cheap coffins, and cart them to the 'ice box', as the morgue is known in prison. **1943** WYNDHAM LEWIS *Let.* 31 Mar. (1963) 352 We are freezing out here [*sc.* in Canada] slowly, in this icebox of a country. **1963** *Amer. Speech* XXXVIII. 173 *Icebox*, a co-ed engaged to a young man in a distant college who refuses to date at all while at college. **1971** M. TAK *Truck Talk* 87 *Ice box.* (1) A refrigerated trailer used for hauling produce and perishables. (2) The bunker for ice in a bunk-and-blower type cooling system in an insulated trailer. **1919** BARRIE *Alice Sit-by-the-Fire* II. 61 Supper for two, champagne in an ice-bucket. **1929** E. HEMINGWAY *Farewell to Arms* xxv. 276 The champagne in the ice-bucket and our glasses on the table. **1939** N. MONSARRAT *This is Schoolroom* II. vii. 176 A magnum of GH Mumm ready to hand in an ice-bucket. **1959** N. MARSH *False Scent* (1960) iv. 94 Gantry tipped some [water] out of the ice bucket. **1941** *Time* 10 Feb. 67/1 Another touring frostbite fiesta called *Ice-Capades of 1941*. **1963** *Times* 7 Mar. 3/6 Football.. finally broke out of the strangling cocoon of snow, ice and mud to be rediscovered as a thing of excitement and calculated skill almost forgotten during the recent ice-capades. **1909** *Chambers's Jrnl.* Aug. 560/2 In Canada there is also a special ice-car service for the carriage of butter to Montreal. **1842** *Knickerbocker* XX. 205 Before an omnibus or hotel or restaurant or ice-cart had assumed its popular cognomen. **1864** T. L. NICHOLS *40 Yrs. Amer. Life* I. 247 Every morning the ice-cart comes round. **1873** *Young Englishwoman* July 334/1 Ice-carts call as regularly as does the baker. **1889** A. B. MARSHALL *Cookery Bk.* p. xx (Advt.), Marshall's patent ice cave.. will freeze a quantity of water placed in the inner cave into a solid mass. **1897** *Geogr. Jrnl.* June 670 The term 'ice-cave'..should especially apply to the hollows in the ice at the lower end of glaciers, whence the glacier waters make their exit. **1911** *Madame* 20 May 318/1 Various forms of iced pudding, which, even if you do not happen to possess one of A. B. Marshall's ice caves, are still quite possible to prepare with very little trouble. **1926–7** *Army & Navy Stores Catal.* 167/3 Ice caves with loose shelves. Japanned iron. **1930** F. SMYTHE *Kangchenjunga Adventure* ii. 45 In lieu of tents, ice caves were carved in the solid ice at Camps Eight and Nine, large enough to hold six to eight persons. **1933** J. BUCHAN *Prince of Captivity* I. iii. 95 He would draw terrible pictures of an ice-cave at Gundbjorns Fjord, and two dead men. **1950** *Chambers's Encycl.* VII. 359/1 The so-called ice caves (not to be confused with caves in glacier ice) are caves in solid rock which, although situated below the line of perpetual snow, nevertheless contain large deposits of ice. **1961** R. M. PATTERSON *Buffalo Head* iv. 136 We explored..finding..mountain sheep, ice caves, the fairest of alpine rock gardens, [etc.]. **1771** J. R. FORSTER tr. *Kalm's Trav. N. Amer.* III. 232 Some of the people of quality make use of ice-cellars, to keep beer cool. *Ibid.*, These ice-cellars are commonly built of stone, under the house. **1865** MILTON & CHEADLE *N.W. Passage by Land* vi. 82 They even went down into the ice-cellar, where the meat is kept. **1883** *Harper's Mag.* July 261, I visited one of the..largest beer factories, and took copious notes about..the ice cellars colder than Siberia ever dared to be. **1921** *Chambers's Jrnl.* 21 May 395/2 Seeds of maple and wheat have been observed growing into blocks of ice in an ice-cellar. **1841** C. CIST *Cincinnati in 1841* (Advt.), Manufacturer of packing-boxes, ice-chests, trunk and segar boxes, &c. **1935** 'J. GUTHRIE' *Little Country* xxiv. 359 Young Merryweather..thought the place like an ice chest. **1972** *Even. Telegram* (St. John's, Newfoundland) (Advt. Suppl.) 27 June 1 Foam plastic ice chest 99¢. **1929** F. SMYTHE *Climbs & Ski Runs* xv. 293 The ice-chimney continued for some distance with great difficulty. **1934** *Discovery* Mar. 60/2 We were obliged to negotiate some ugly ice-chimneys. **1955** J. E. B. WRIGHT *Technique Mountaineering* v. 97 Ice chimneys may be pitches in couloirs and icefalls. **1920** G. W. YOUNG *Mountain Craft* vii. 286 Any man who wishes to make big ascents is well advised if he begins early to learn how to use ice-claws (or crampons). **1954** W. NOYCE *South Col* v. 79 Crampons or ice-claws are sets of metal spikes on frames tied to the feet to assist walking up ice. **1955** G. BAND *Road to Rakaposhi* xii. 141 Climbers have managed for so long without these useful 'ice-claws' in the Himalayas. **1883** R. H. SCOTT *Elem. Meteorol.* 403 (Index), Ice clouds. **1900** W. ALLINGHAM *Man. Marine Meteorol.* xvi. 154 Halos and other refraction phenomena afford proof that cirro-stratus is an ice cloud. **1963** D. IRVING *Destruction of Dresden* III. i. 106 Ice clouds were blanketing Europe. **1903** C. SALTER tr. *G von Georgievics's Chem. Dye-Stuffs* 82 This method is employed to produce dyeings of considerable beauty and fastness, which now play a great part in dyeing cotton piece goods and in calico printing (Ice colours). **1968** E. N. ABRAHART *Dyes* vi. 161 A small range of Ice Colours, so called because the preparation of the diazo solutions by the dyer needed ice, was built up. **1896** *Amer. Geologist* XVIII. 152 The tracing on the ground of the ice-contacts shows that other morainal belts come into the region about Wickford from the southeast. *Ibid.*, The accompanying map..exhibits by special designations the position of the ice-contact slopes or moraine terraces. **1968** R. W. FAIRBRIDGE *Encycl. Geomorphol.* 438/2 Ice contact deposits outline the holes and tunnels in the last wasting of the basal ice. **1970** C. A. LEWIS *Glaciations Wales* ii. 29 The fresh ice-contact slopes (15°–20°) and re-entrant features noted on the inner flanks of the Cors Geirch terraces are present also on their eastern side. **1923** G. D. ABRAHAM *First Steps to Climbing* iv. 45 We find the Mount Everest Expedition largely composed of rock-climbing specialists whose knowledge of snow and ice-craft is almost negligible. **1955** E. HILLARY *High Adventure* 16 Harry was New Zealand's outstanding climber, with a tremendous reputation for brilliant ice-craft. **1853** A. BUNN *Old Eng. & New Eng.* I. ii. 31 Content ourselves by observing that the ice-crop (as it is drolly called).. proved to be a fair average one. **1864** *Chambers's Jrnl.* 100/1 Producing an ice-crop which will pay all expenses and leave a profit. **1929** M. LIEF *Hangover* vii. 128 She dashed into the kitchen and came back with a bowl of ice-cubes and some more bottles. **1939** *Vogue's Cookery Book* 122 Ice cubes for summer drinks can be made decorative by freezing cherries..inside them. **1949** *Consumer Reports* June 250/1 Four medium-size ice-cube trays. **1962** J. BRAINE *Life at Top* iv. 71 She took out the ice cube tray. **1883** *Proc. Amer. Assoc. Adv. Sci.* XXXII. 207 Among the most interesting results of the author's survey in Ohio, was the demonstration of the existence of an ice-dam across the river at Cincinnati. **1935** W. J. MILLER *Introd. Physical Geol.* (ed. 3) xiv. 396 Existing ice-dam lakes are not common, and few, if any of them, are large. During the Ice Age, however, thousands of them formed and lasted only as long as the ice dams existed. **1914** W. B. WRIGHT *Quaternary Ice Age* iii. 71 Two main chains of ice-dammed lakes in the Cleveland valleys to the north of Pickering are described by Professor Kendall. **1965** G. DE BOER in A. Small *Fourth Viking Congress* 207 The whole flat floored, hill girt hollow, is readily seen for what it is, the bed of a former ice-dammed lake. **1905** W. H. SHERZER in *Smithsonian Misc. Coll.* XLVII. 468 Ice dykes. These consist of narrow crevasses, two to fifteen inches across, completely filled with columnar ice. **1889** *Pall Mall Gaz.* 6 Feb. 3/1 When the winter fairly sets in the scene on an ice-farm is a busy one. **1908** *Sci. Amer.* 25 Jan. 58/2 Natural ice making in the tropics—the peculiar 'ice farms' of hot Bengal. **1963** *Brit. Columbia Digest* Nov.–Dec. 31 It'll be nothing less than wonderful if I manage to make one good steelhead trip and icefish in three lakes all winter. **1960** M. SHARCOTT *Place of Many Winds* vii. 123 The ice-fisherman..earns a few extra cents a pound. **1963** *Times* 12 Mar. 9/6 In most cases, the ice fisherman will avail himself (at a modest fee) of the services of a resort owner who ploughs roads across the ice and clears sites for the ice houses. **1890** T. H. BEAN in *Forest & Stream* XXXV. 417 (*title*) Ice fishing in arctic Alaska. **1907** J. G. MILLAIS *Newfoundland* i. 9 Twenty years at the 'ice fishing' (seal hunting)..will try the strongest man. **1970** *Globe & Mail* (Toronto) 25 Sept. 35/6 (Advt.), Sand beach, floating dock, very private, ice fishing. **1909** E. SHACKLETON *Heart of Antarctic* II. 341 Ice-flowers occurred on freshwater ice at Clear Lake. **1911** J. MASEFIELD *Jim Davis* iii. 26 The frost had covered the window with ice-flowers, so that we could not see through the glass. **1955** *Arctic Terms* 42/1 *Ice flower*, a delicate tuft of frost or rime, resembling a fern or flower, that occasionally forms on surface sea ice around a salt crystal nucleus. **1965** P. WAYRE *Wind in Reeds* vi. 79 All along the tide mark the frost had formed delicate ice-flowers. **1890** *Bull. Geol. Soc. Amer.* I. 201 Further inland, where plains are found up to altitudes of a thousand or more feet above sea level, I think the water in which they accumulated was fresh water, temporarily ponded by the ice front. **1957** G. E. HUTCHINSON *Treat. Limnol.* I. xv. 833 The receding ice front passed Hertford about 19,500 years ago. **1966** B. B. BAKER et al. *Gloss. Oceanogr. Terms* (ed. 2) 83/1 *Ice front* (also called *front*, *ice cliff*, *ice face*, *ice wall*), (1) the seaward facing, cliff-like edge of an ice shelf (so called by the British Antarctic Place-names Committee), (2) any vertical wall of ice. **1862** *Congress. Globe* 2896/1 The island is..below the bend in the Delaware, and hence mainly out of danger from ice gorges. **1925** E. SITWELL *Troy Park* 40 Leaves like a starry crown Are clear as the splintered star ice-green That is a crown for a negro queen. **1934** L. B. LYON *White Hare* 16 The washed sky opened like an arctic rose, ice-green. **1938** W. DE LA MARE *Memory* 62 Skies ice-green. **1905** *Forestry Bureau Bull.* (U.S.) No. 61, 40 *Ice guards*, heavy timbers fastened fan shaped about a cluster of boom piles at an angle of approximately 30 degrees to the surface of the water. They prevent the destruction of the boom by ice, through forcing it to mount the guards and be broken up. **1947** *Jrnl. R. Aeronaut. Soc.* LI. 298/2 In the early stages of the war some Mosquitos had flown home from Sweden through bad icing weather. The machines had reached home, but there was a complaint that they had lost 2 lb. of boost because the ice guards had iced up completely. **1907** *Yesterday's Shopping* (1969) 599/4 Electro-plated ice tongs and ice hammer. **1932** *Mountaineering Jrnl.* Dec. 100 The ice-hammer is used for chiselling steps and handholds as well as for driving in pitons. **1933** G. D. ABRAHAM *Mod. Mountaineering* ix. 175 Young Continental experts..have evolved the ice hammer which is used for driving in the pitons. **1953** J. HUNT *Ascent Everest* I. iv. 38 The more familiar gear..rope and line, pitons, snaplinks, icehammers and axes. **1864** *Chambers's Jrnl.* 100/2 The season of the ice-harvest being short and uncertain. **1884** [in Dict., sense 6]. **1904** *Westm. Gaz.* 17 Mar. 2/1 Men with horses were ploughing the ice-harvest of the river. **1883** *Boy's Own Paper* 13 Oct. 30/1 For ice hockey the ball is from six to seven inches in circumference. **1898**

Daily News 28 Nov. 8/7 The first ice hockey match at Niagara took place on Saturday. **1907** *Westm. Gaz.* 4 Dec. 7/2 An ice-hockey match at Prince's last night. **1909** *Ibid.* 18 Jan. 12/4 The great ice carnivals, skating championships, and ice-hockey matches. **1940** Auden *Another Time* 26 Superb at ice-hockey, a prince at the dance, He's fierce as the tigers, secretive as plants. **1970** *Guardian* 5 Jan. 14/5 Canada yesterday withdrew from this year's world ice hockey championships after losing their battle to allow professionals to take part. **1846** R. H. Bonnycastle *Canada & Canadians in 1846* II. 3, I have mentioned that, in the spring of 1845, an ice-jam, as it is called here, occurred, which suddenly raised the level of the Niagara thirty and forty feet above its ordinary floods. **1863** [in Dict., sense 7 a, s.v. *ice-jam*]. **1909** *Westm. Gaz.* 23 Apr. 8/2 The great ice-jam at Niagara. **1924** M. H. Mason *Arctic Forests* 246 In the depth of winter they travelled by dog-sled over the rough ice jams of Bear River. **1959** *Washington Post* 3 Feb. A.16/1 A willingness to explore new ideas could help break the East–West ice-jam. **1962** R. B. Fuller *Epic Poem on Industrialization* 158 The inevitable Social-economic ice jam. **1893** Kipling *Seven Seas* (1896) 29 Down a cruel ice-lane, That opened as he sped, We saw dead Henry Hudson Steer, North by West, his dead. **1879** *Encycl. Brit.* VIII. 731/2 At this point the steam line, ice line, and hoar-frost line intersect, and it has therefore been called the triple point. **1937** M. W. Zemansky *Heat & Thermodynamics* xi. 177 In investigating the ice line of water at very high temperatures, Bridgman and Tammann discovered four new modifications of ice. **1893** *Jrnl. Geol.* I. 131 Moraines formed by the Great Miami ice lobe. **1954** W. D. Thornbury *Princ. Geomorphol.* xvi. 384 The edges of the ice caps were probably never straight for any great distance, but in addition to many minor reentrants and projections along their margins there were numerous larger protrusions or ice lobes down lowlands. **1949** *Ice Cream Topics* June 12 Ice lollies or iced lollies..sell at 1d. or 2d. and capture the kiddy trade, being cheaper than cones and wafers filled with ice cream. **1957** *Times* 22 Aug. 8/6 They..drip ice-lollies on the desk. **1970** *Daily Tel.* (Colour Suppl.) 2 Jan. 24/4 Ishmahil licked at a spoon of caviar as if it were an ice-lolly. **1850** T. Masters *Short Treat. Production Ice* iii. 19 The patent ice machine and its various modifications. Before giving a detailed description of the ice machine,..it will be as well to mention a few of the prominent advantages it possesses. **1873** C. M. Yonge *Pillars of House* II. xvii. 129 Is he awake? I have brought some more ice... I have a little ice-machine for Indian use. **1897** 'Mark Twain' *Following Equator* iii. 62 The ice-machine has traveled all over the world. **1973** *Country Life* 8 Feb. 345/1 There are enough hotels..to suit any pocket. And swimming pools, air-conditioning and ice-machines are usually included. **1953** Dylan Thomas *Under Milk Wood* (1954) 61 The butcher's unmelting icemaiden daughter veiled for ever from the hungry hug of his eyes. **1968** V. Canning *Melting Man* v. 134 Now stop doing an ice-maiden act on me. Write it off to experience. **1970** B. Turner *Another Little Death* xx. 118 Her ice-maiden act was a cover for frustrated lust. **1927** *Daily Tel.* 11 May 18/3 New patent non-chemical refrigerator and ice-maker. **1969** K. Amis *Green Man* i. 12 The ice-maker had broken down. **1970** *Cape Times* 28 Oct. (S.A. Fishing Rev.) 6/6 (Advt.), South African Agents for Skokie international seawater ice makers. **1846** R. Ford *Gatherings from Spain* vii. 74 The leading animal is furnished with a copper bell with a wooden clapper..which is shaped like an ice-mould. **1864** *Chambers's Jrnl.* 101/1 A continuous current through the cistern containing the ice-moulds. **1873** *Young Englishwoman* July 334/1 We put in a block as large as the tin will hold, and then with an ice-needle, price one shilling, break up the rest of the ice. **1928** *Funk's Stand. Dict.*, *Ice-needles*, n.pl., a deposit of ice, especially in gravelly soil, in the form of vertical needles. **1937** *Jrnl. R. Aeronaut. Soc.* XLI. 598 A further very rare case occurs when at a high altitude in the 'ice needle clouds'..a light accretion of hoar frost..forms on the aeroplane. **1965** H. Riehl *Introd. Atmosphere* v. 100 Ice needles are long thin crystals forming on very cold winter days through sublimation... Floating leisurely in the air, they provide a magnificent spectacle when the sun is shining on them. **1970** R. J. Small *Study of Landforms* x. 323 Another process which leads to the upheaval of material in the active layer [of the soil] is the development of small localised ice-masses and ice-needles ('pipkraker'). **1900** *Daily Chron.* 12 Nov. 5/6 The condition of Lord Roberts's daughter is somewhat serious. Ice-packs have been applied. **1926** *Daily Colonist* (Victoria, B.C.) 3 Jan. 3/3 The letter informed the President [Coolidge] that the [Detroit Aviation] society was about to join in an attempt to explore the ice pack between Point Barrow and the Ice Pole. **1930** *Times Educ. Suppl.* 25 Jan. p. iv/1 Rocky outcrops and ice-packs. **1955** *Sci. Amer.* Apr. 52/3 The Atka saw very little of the drifting ice pack that surrounds the continent. **1973** R. Ludlam *Matlock Paper* xiv. 129 There's a nurse in there with ice packs and stuff if localized pain bothers her. **1901** *Geogr. Jrnl.* July 40 The ice-pans appear to drift capriciously backward and forward, and, without any apparent cause, they will select some unexpected course. **1926** *Blackw. Mag.* July 67/1 An awful journey through a country devoid of human beings, across treacherous moving ice-pans. **1934** I. W. Hutchison *North to Rime-Ringed Sun* xii. 120 Suddenly out of the mist, upon an ice-pan, stood the little shrivelled figure of an old Eskimo hunter of seals. **1963** *Calgary Herald* 20 Sept., Turquoise ice pans (last year's ice) cluttered the water just off shore. *a* **1877** Knight *Dict. Mech.* II. 1169/1 *Ice-pick* (Domestic), an awl-shaped tool to break ice into fragments. **1879** F. R. Stockton *Rudder Grange* i, It is not probable that I can sell that ice-pick after you have used it for ten years. **1883** [in Dict. sense 7 a, s.v. *ice-crusher*]. **1937** E. A. M. Wedderburn *Alpine Climbing* ii. 29 A Hammer for driving in ring-spikes may be combined with an ice-pick; this weapon is..useful for cutting steps..in very steep ice. **1953** E. S. Gardner *Case of Green-Eyed Sister* (1959) viii. 97 J. J. Fritch was killed by repeated stabs with an ice-pick. **1960** *News Chron.* 11 June 2/8 Jacques Mornard, ice-pick assassin of Leon Trotsky. **1881** J. C. Lyell *Fancy Pigeons* 81 The Ice Pigeon. This variety derives its name from its beautiful lavender blue colour, considered by the German fanciers to resemble blue ice. **1969** C. R. Hill *Pet Library's Pigeon Guide* viii. 151 (*caption*) White barred blue Ice Pigeon, young cock. A German exhibition breed. *Ibid.* 152 Ice pigeon, blue spangled, old hen. **1865** *Nation* (N.Y.) 3 Aug. 159/3 (Advt.), At this season of the year nothing adds more to one's comfort than to drink freely of the contents of our new pattern richly double-plated ice pitchers. **1883** 'Mark Twain' *Life on Mississippi* xviii. 221 Take that ice-pitcher down to the texas-tender. **1932** *Mountaineering Jrnl.* Dec. 100 Ice-pitons are made of wrought iron not too soft and not too brittle, 7 to 10 inches long and saw-toothed along both edges. **1954** W. Noyce *South Col* vi. 110 We then fixed the bridge and tied it down with ice pitons. **1956** C. Evans *On Climbing* vii. 114, I should be reluctant to trust a piton for this, since ice-pitons are less certain in their hold than rock-pitons. **1876** Lady C. Schreiber *Jrnl.* (1911) I. 443 Small ice-plates have now become the object of our pursuit. **1902** H. James *Wings of Dove* v. x. 178 The very servant who came to receive Milly's empty ice-plate. **1907** *Yesterday's Shopping* (1969) 944 (*caption*) Ice plates. **1903** *Phil. Trans. R. Soc.* A. CC. 108 The Comité International adopted as the normal scale of temperature the scale of a constant-volume hydrogen thermometer, in which the pressure at the ice-point was 1000 millims. of mercury. *Ibid.*, The coefficient for hydrogen, at a pressure of 100 millims. of mercury at the ice-point, is given..as 0·00366254. **1941** *Temperature* (Amer. Inst. Physics) i. 10 A limitation of this scale *sc.* Kelvin's [thermodynamic scale] is that if we make the fundamental interval from the ice point to the steam point 100 degrees, the actual temperature of the ice point is subject to experimental determination. **1966** *Units & Standards of Measurement: Temperature* (Nat. Physical Lab.) (ed. 2) 18 Changes made in 1960 to the text of the International Temperature Scale of 1948... The triple-point of water was given formal status as one of the defining fixed points of the scale... Its value was given as 0·01°C (Int. 1948) and the ice point appeared among the secondary fixed points with the value 0·000°C. **1851** W. P. Snow *Voy. 'Prince Albert'* 154 The slackest and thinnest part of the floe, or fragment, was cut into with the axes and chisels until some fortunate blow or prise of the ice-pole rent and loosened it. **1906** J. Lumsden *Skipper Parson* 107 This useful instrument also serves as an ice pole, enabling the daring sealer..to leap from 'pan to pan'. **1970** *Globe & Mail* (Toronto) 28 Sept. 4/4 Men working on the ice..should hold a boat-hook or small ice-pole in their hands. **1911** *Jrnl. Geol.* XIX. 157 He has never detected any evidence of ice push against shores as a result of expansion. **1939** P. G. Worcester *Textbk. Geomorphol.* xii. 383 Although unimportant on most sea shores, the shores of many lakes that freeze over in winter are profoundly affected by ice push. **1957** G. E. Hutchinson *Treat. Limnol.* I. vii. 532 This sheet may then exert pressure on the shore, forcing gravel and stones landward and building an ice push or ice rampart. **1969** J. L. Davies *Landforms Cold Climates* iv. 63 Seasonally frozen lakes in the tundra and elsewhere may form ice-push ramparts around their edges. **1901** E. R. Buckley in *Trans. Wisc. Acad. Sci., Arts & Lett.* XIII. 142 The diurnal and weekly changes of temperature during the winter months cause a sufficient expansion and contraction of the ice covering the inland lakes of Wisconsin to shove up the sand, gravel, boulders, and sod along the shores into peculiar ridges, known as ice ramparts. **1968** R. W. Fairbridge *Encycl. Geomorphol.* 546/1 Along the margins of ice-covered lakes and seas and the shores of the Arctic Ocean the effects of floating ice pressure (under wind stress) may be observed, leading to the building of large pressure-ridges in the beach gravels and other littoral deposits... The terms ice-shore ridges and ice ramparts are also sometimes used. **1886** *Field* 13 Mar. 310/1 Nor is it less strange that so few ice rinks are found in England. **1930** *Daily Express* 16 Aug. 3/1 By the middle of October there will be at least nine ice-rinks in London alone. **1953** X. Fielding *Stronghold* 277 The surface of this winding watercourse was like that of a shattered ice-rink. **1900** *Daily News* 30 Nov. 5/2 The new ice-run for tobogganers..is almost ready for use. **1910** H. G. Wells *Hist. Mr. Polly* vi, Mr. Polly swerved a little from the conversational ice-run upon which he had embarked. **1895** *Brewer's Dict. Phrase & Fable* (new ed.) 643/2 *Ice Saints*, those saints whose days fall in..'the black-thorn winter'. **1922** *Meteorol. Mag.* LVII. 177 The quasi-periodic occurrence of a cold spell lasting for a few days early in May is a well-known popular belief... On the Continent three 'Saint Days', those of St. Mamertius, St. Pancras and St. Gervais, falling on May 11th, 12th and 13th..are popularly known as the *Eisheiligen*, or 'Ice Saints'. **1936** *Times* 13 Feb. 14/1 May will be remembered mainly on account of the severe frost during the period 12th to 19th, an impressive vindication of the firmly rooted tradition of the 'Ice Saints'. **1969** *Guardian* 7 June 7/5 There was the normal cold iceburst in mid-May, but it came a week later than the proverbial 'Ice Saints' days on the Continent. **1904** J. D. Hooker *Let.* 3 Dec. in L. Huxley *Life J. D. Hooker* (1918) II. 457 His landscapes, seascapes and ice-scapes are most interesting. **1936** J. Grierson *High Failure* ix. 208, I had never before experienced the hypnotic splendour of the ice-scape. It seemed as though I were flying in a dream. **1969** *Sunday Times* 9 Feb. 6 The whole icescape was awash with light. **1936** Finch & Trewartha *Elem. Geogr.* xvii. 364 The surface configuration of plains where ice scour was predominant is characterized by rounded rock hills and broad open valleys with comparatively low local relief. **1968** R. W. Fairbridge *Encycl. Geomorphol.* 502/2 The basins of the Great Lakes..were formed by a combination of stream erosion during Mesozoic to Pleistocene times and glacial ice scour in the Pleistocene. **1936** Finch & Trewartha *Elem. Geogr.* xvii. 364 The drift of ice-scoured plains commonly is neither deep enough nor continuous enough to be tillable except in patches. **1954** W. D. Thornbury *Princ. Geomorphol.* xvi. 385 In areas where the surface over which the ice caps moved was mountainous..the result was not an ice-scoured plain, but a general smoothing off..of the topography. **1901** *Science* 5 Apr. 552/1 Ice-scouring during maximum glaciation reached far up the mountain slopes above the trough walls. **1957** G. E. Hutchinson *Treat. Limnol.* I. i. 57 The Saint Gotthard lakes..are noted..as having been formed by ice-scouring. **1965** D. Bathgate in *Scottish Mountaineering Club Jrnl.* XXVIII. 109 At the shortest point I surmounted the steep part, fixed an ice screw, and then traversed back across the centre of the ice to about twenty feet above the belay. **1968** P. Crew *Encycl. Dict. Mountaineering* 71/1 Ice-screws are very effective as they can be used on most types of ice..with a reasonable degree of security and they are very easy to remove after use. **1971** C. Bonington *Annapurna South Face* x. 116 It's difficult to get an ice-screw started, rather like an ordinary screw in hard wood—you first have to tap out a little hole to allow the thread to get a purchase **1894** J. Geikie *Gt. Ice Age* (ed. 3) 830 The ice-shed in Sandinavia did not coincide with the water-parting.. **1932** E. G. Woods *Baltic Region* 159 When the ice-shed lay east of the watershed..a considerable amount of ice and also water flowed along the originally eastward-sloping valleys towards the west. **1957** J. K. Charlesworth *Quaternary Era* I. iv. 77 The iceshed, more than 1000 miles (1600 km) long, seems to lie behind South Victoria Land and Dronning Maud Mountains. **1914** T. W. E. David in *Geogr. Jrnl.* XLIII. 606 If the meaning of the term 'shelf' can be extended to include old pack ice, old bay ice, 'schollen-eis', piedmonts aground or afloat, glacier tongues, etc., it may be termed the ice shelf coast, or, as it is hardly a true coast at all, simply ice shelf. **1940** *Beaver* June 22/1 The men worked with feverish energy to repair the damage caused by the treacherous ice shelf. **1958** *Times* 13 Jan. 9/6 We..made our very laborious way..on to the flat going of the Ross ice shelf itself. **1958** J. H. Zumberge *Elem. Geol.* x. 180 Masses of ice that break off from the edge of the various ice shelves form the huge tabular icebergs unique to the Antarctic region. **1897** *Sears, Roebuck Catal.* 97/2 Ice skates. **1912** T. Dreiser *Financier* 36 He was an adept at turning all sorts of practical tricks, such as..taking the agency for the sale of a new kind of ice-skate from an ice-skate company. **1948** *Evening News* 2 Jan. 2/6 Two nephews are down on the creek ice-skating. **1950** *Oxf. Jun. Encycl.* IX. 432 There are three principal kinds of ice skates: those for figure-skating, for hockey, and for racing. **1937** Ice-skater [see *audition *v.* 2]. **1957** *Encycl. Brit.* XX. 730/1 An additional valuable impetus in bringing figure skating before the public was the ice-skating carnival. **1973** E.-J. Bahr *Nice Neighbourhood* vi. 61 We told him about the museums, free exhibits, outdoor concerts, ice-skating, bicycling. **1897** E. L. Voynich *Gadfly* iii. viii. 353 He might have recalled some splendid and fearful ice-spirit of the mountains. **1900** *Month* Jan. 85, I took you for that evil thing, the ice-spirit, who freezes the limbs of our people. **1901** (*title*) Ice sports. **1908** *Daily Chron.* 27 July 4/4 Boating in summer and ice sports in winter. **1898** J. O. Maund in W. A. Morgan *'House' on Sport* 276 It took but a moment before our ice steps were filled with these hailstones. **1908** *Westm. Gaz.* 25 Jan. 14/1 We stood in the ice-steps. **1931** *Discovery* Feb. 41/1 To cut ice-steps all along so great a ridge will be an affair not of hours but of a day or two. **1876** 'Mark Twain' *Punch, Brothers, Punch!* (1878) 17 We have to credit the weather with..the ice-storm. **1886** J. Geikie *Outl. Geol.* 50 By repeated thawings and regelations the branches and boughs are gradually loaded with ice and snow, and becoming top-heavy, the trees are liable to fall, even when no wind is blowing. Should one be overthrown, it collides against its neighbour, and this in turn falls upon another, until shortly the trees are seen crashing to the ground in all directions. This is what is known in North America as an ice-storm. **1899** *Daily News* 20 An 'ice storm' in Somerset..reminded me of a sudden hailstorm. **1921** R. Frost *Mountain Interval* 29 But swinging doesn't bend them down to stay. Ice-storms do that. **1965** *Kingston* (Ontario) *Whig-Standard* 13 Dec. 19/1 Nearly every cloud has a silver lining and Sunday's ice-storm was no exception. **1968** Ice storm [see *freezing *ppl. a.* 1]. **1893** *Funk's Stand. Dict.*, *Ice-tongue*, a steep, narrow cliff of ice, rising high above glacial névé, and extending upward toward the higher mountain-peaks. **1896** *Amer. Geologist* XVIII. 155 Between the ice-tongue which filled the cove and the hills on the west, coarse gravels were deposited. **1919** E. Shackleton *South* viii. 129 At the head of an ice-tongue that nearly closed the gap through which we might enter the open space was a wave-worn berg. **1968** R. W. Fairbridge *Encycl. Geomorphol.* 673/1 Where the borders of these ice sheets roughly coincide with the coastal mountain ranges, the ice spills through them in the form of ice rivers called outlet glaciers or ice tongues. **1936** *New Yorker* 29 Feb 37/2 (Advt.), Then think of ice-trays—stacks of them. **1962** *Which?* June 176/2 We filled the ice trays with cold water..and set the thermostats to coldest. **1965** M. Spark *Mandelbaum Gate* iv. 109 A scarred, lop-sided oil refrigerator..stood in the passage outside, from which anyone who wanted beer took it, depositing the money in the ice-tray. **1915** *Jrnl. Geol.* XXIII. 642 The constant association of ice wedges with definite loci of frost cracks. **1970** C. A. Lewis *Glaciations Wales* ii. 29 Near Traian (328365) a large fossil ice-wedge..cuts the deposits in a small quarry. **1928** *Daily Express* 10 Oct. 3/3 Where an ice-white salmon stream flows through a gorge. **1931** *Daily Tel.* 21 May 6/3 A gown of very heavy ice white satin. **1882** Ice wool [see *eis wool]. **1926** *Daily Colonist* (Victoria, B.C.) 10 Jan. 18/1 Ice Wool Scarves in a good assortment of colors, stripes or plain shades, with contrasting stripe borders.

ice, *v.* Add: **1. a.** *to ice up.* Also, to hold fast with ice.

1899 C. J. C. Hyne *Further Adventures Capt. Kettle* xii, The boats are frozen on to the chocks... Did you never see a boat iced up before?

4. b. To kill. *U.S. slang.*

1969 *New Yorker* 15 Feb. 51 A friend of his had come to his apartment..in clothes that were spattered with blood, and announced, 'I just iced two girls.' **1973** *Guardian* 6 Mar. 14/3 A would-be assassin who considers it his mission to 'ice the fascist pig police'.

5. b. Esp. of aircraft: to become covered with ice (and thus rendered ineffective). Const. *up.* Chiefly in *pass.*

1928 *Aviation* 16 Apr. 1032/2 Once a plane has become iced-up, two alternatives for clearing away the accumulation of glazing may be available. **1940** *Times* (Weekly ed.) 10 Jan. p. ii/4 During the operations a snowstorm was encountered and the aircraft became badly iced-up, in addition to being subjected to anti-aircraft fire. **1943** *Aeronautics* Mar. 60/1 The wings and controls may be iced up. **1947** *Sci. News* IV. 72 A ship has often been thoroughly de-greased by wind-swept rain and spray before it becomes iced-up. **1950** T. LONGSTAFF *This my Voyage* ii. 24 By now we were all looking like Arctic travellers, well iced-up.

-ice, -icè (isi), *suffix*², in med.L. forming adverbs from adjs., as *ANGLICE, *GALLICE, *ironice*, SCOTTICÈ, SCOTICÈ, and hence used occas. to form jocular nonce adverbs on English stems, as *golficè*.

1743 POPE *Dunciad* I (*footnote to l. 23*), *Ironicè*, alluding to Gulliver's representations of both. **1886** *Golficè* [see *DIVOT *sb.* 2].

iceberg. Add: **2.** Delete 'Arctic'. (Further examples.)

1830 *Edin. Encycl.* XVII. 12/1 The floating iceberg remains to be considered...In many parts of the Antarctic regions, they are met with in vast numbers, and of a prodigious size. **1961** A. DEFANT *Physical Oceanogr.* viii. 274 The flat-topped Antarctic icebergs immerse to greater depths.

b. *transf.* Used allusively with reference to the larger portion of an iceberg being unseen (and hence a largely unknown quantity, problem, etc.).

1961 in WEBSTER. **1964** *Observer* 26 July 10/4 This.. situation is illustrated by what is..called the iceberg of disease. Above the surface is the illness we know about. **1965** *Listener* 21 Oct. 614/2 These were only the visible part of the iceberg. Most of the organs of the left..were greatly influenced. **1969** M. GILBERT *Etruscan Net* II. ii. 109, I believe that Broke's been made the victim of an elaborate frame-up. I think, to employ a well-known metaphor, that all we can see at the moment is the tip of the iceberg, and that there is depth beyond depth below it. **1973** *Daily Tel.* 19 Feb. 2/1 They believe the number of prosecutions for such offences represent only 'the tip of the iceberg', and that many undischarged bankrupts..are violating the law undetected.

4. iceberg lettuce *U.S.*, a crisp light-green lettuce.

1893 *Burpee's Farm Annual* 28 As long as our supply lasts we will send a sample packet of the iceberg lettuce free for trial. **1904** W. W. TRACY *Amer. Varieties Lettuce* 56 *Iceberg* [*lettuce*], a decidedly crisp variety, strictly cabbage-heading, large, late, slow to shoot to seed. **1933** F. M. FARMER *Boston Cooking-School Cook Bk.* (rev. ed.) xxviii. 420 Iceberg or California Lettuce. Cut in halves or quarters. Remove hard center. **1960** 'I. DEVI' *Yoga for You* (1965) 189 One head romaine or any other green salad, except iceberg lettuce, which contains almost no chlorophyll. **1966** *McGraw-Hill Encycl. Sci. & Technol.* VII. 478/2 Crisphead or iceberg lettuce is the most widely grown type. **1970** 'J. MORRIS' *Candywine Devel.* xx. 223 He took a loaf of French bread, an iceberg lettuce and three onions from the refrigerator.

ice-boat. Add: **3.** A fishing-vessel equipped with facilities for the refrigeration of fish. *N. Amer.*

1878 *Saskatchewan Herald* (Battleford) 29 July 4/1 The crew of the Lady Ellen are building an ice-boat for the fishing trade this winter. **1941** E. J. KAMMER *Socio-Econ. Survey Marshdwellers Louisiana* viii. 118 Ice boats are larger than the ordinary trawl boat and are used only for transporting shrimp. **1970** *National Fisherman* Sept. 18-A/4 They were ice boats, designed for a 10-ton capacity.

ice-breaker. Add: **1.** (Earlier example.)

1819 D. THOMAS *Trav. Western Country* 247 Notwithstanding these precautions, and that of placing ice-breakers to the south, [the bridge] was only saved from destruction the ensuing winter by the intrepidity of.. one of the proprietors.

2. b. *transf.* Cf. *to break the ice* (ICE *sb.* 2 b).

1883 'MARK TWAIN' *Life on Mississippi* xxxix. 365 They closed up the inundation with a few words—having used it, evidently, as a mere ice-breaker and acquaintance-ship-breeder—then they dropped into business. **1904** *Daily Chron.* 27 Feb. 4/6 If you must use an ice-breaker, the pianola is decidedly effective..as a cure for shyness. **1961** BOWMAN & BALL *Theatre Lang.* 178 *Icebreaker*, a fast song for chorus girls—Musical comedy. **1963** BARNARD & LAUWERYS *Handbk. Brit. Educ. Terms* 110 *Ice-breaker*, a term used to describe a preliminary to a series of tests. It is designed to accustom the candidate to the experience which he is about to undergo, but its results are not counted in the ultimate assessment of the tests. **1963** M. MCCARTHY *Group* i. 19 The recipe was an ice-breaker..everyone tasted it and agreed that it was the maple syrup that made all the difference. **1968** *Daily Tel.* 15 Nov. 16/7 Swearing, in addition to its cathartic effect and as a means of non-violent assault.., is also an ice-breaker. **1973** *Sun-Herald* (Sydney) 26 Aug. 80/3 Then they went on to 'icebreakers'—short talks about themselves, reading a message they'd selected from a book.

ice-cream. Add: (Earlier and later examples.)

1744 in *Pennsylvania Mag. Hist. & Biogr.* (1877) I. 126 Among the rarities..was some fine ice cream, which, with the strawberries and milk, eat most deliciously. **1751** H. GLASSE *Art of Cookery* (ed. 4) 333 (*heading*) To make Ice Cream..set it [*sc.* the cream] into the larger Bason. Fill it with Ice, and a Handful of Salt. **1957** *Min. Agric. Food Standards Comm. Rep. Ice Cream* (H.M.S.O.) 4 The bulk of ice cream now produced in this country is made from margarine and other non-milk fats... We recommend that special provision should be made to reserve the description 'dairy ice cream'..for ice cream in which the fat content is wholly milk fat.

attrib. (Further examples.)

1821 *National Advocate* (New York) 3 Aug. 2/2 Among the number of ice cream gardens in this city, there was none in which the sable race could find admission and refreshment. **1844** J. COWELL *30 Yrs. among Players* II. iii. 64/2 With the ice-cream profits, he purchased bricks and mortar, and built the *Chatham Theatre*. **1851** A. O. HALL *Manhattaner* 46 How the ice cream saloons resound with clattering spoons. **1854** *Rep. Trans. Pennsylvania State Agric. Soc.* 363 Three ice cream freezers. **1873** J. H. BEADLE *Undevel. West* xxviii. 623 Two months vigorous courting will cost more than that—particularly in the ice-cream season. **1878** N. A. DONNELLEY *Lakeside Cook Bk.* 30/2 Ice Cream Cake. **1880** E. W. WILCOX *Buckeye Cookery & Pract. Housek.* 83 Ice-cream cake... Make good sponge-cake... Fill with ice-cream just before serving. **1881** C. C. HARRISON *Woman's Handiwork* III. 223 Finger-bowls and ice-cream plates were ruby Bohemian glass. **1884** *Milnor* (Dakota) *Teller* 27 June, An ice cream parlor where the dudes and dudines sip.. congealed milk and sugar. **1886** *Mobile* (Alabama) *Daily Reg.* 23 Apr. 2/3 (Advt.), Drink Ice Cream Soda. **1904** *Proc. R. Soc.* LXXIII. 504 Using the modified ice-cream mixer described by Moody. **1905** Ice-cream cake [see *angel-cake*]. **1909** *Sat. Even. Post* 15 May 11/2 The remainder is about equally divided among popcorn, ice cream cones, and candy. **1934** *Archit. Rev.* LXXVI. 159/1 (*caption*) 40-gallon ice-cream fountain. **1947** *Ibid.* CI. 212/1 Across the road, though, competition has set in, not only from the tricycle ice-vendors but from the Ice Cream Parlours. **1950** G. GREENE *Third Man* ii. 16 The American zone, which you couldn't mistake because of the ice-cream parlours in every street. **1961** E. WILSON in R. Weaver *Canad. Short Stories* (1968) 2nd Ser. 14 How about an ice-cream cone? **1961** C. WILLOCK *Death in Covert* iii. 73 The liveried servants held flambeaux like ice-cream cornets. **1966** J. CLEARY *High Commissioner* i. 19 An ice-cream van went slowly by, its bell tinkling. *a* **1966** M. ALLINGHAM *Cargo of Eagles* (1968) xv. 162 An ice cream tricycle was already doing good business. **1968** P. JENNINGS *Living Village* 204 The dreadful hoarse tintinnabulations, as though a giant were banging a dulcimer, which herald the urban ice cream van. **1972** *Guardian* 2 Sept. 9/2 He fetched his mother an ice-cream cornet.

Hence **ice-crea·mer**, an (Italian) ice-cream vendor; so (*derogatory*) an Italian.

1901 E. W. HORNUNG *Black Mask* 110 He had every low-down Neapolitan ice-creamer on my tracks. **1940** N. MITFORD *Pigeon Pie* iii. 41, I remembered that there are Chinks and Japs and Fuzzy Wuzzies and Ice Creamers and Dagos, and so on. **1949** L. P. HARTLEY *Boat* i. 3 Italians are not people according to our ideas... Ice-creamers, some call them, but it's too polite for them.

iced, *ppl. a.* Add: (Further examples.)

1673 J. RAY *Observations Journey Low-Countries* 267 Many..with a barrel at their backs and glasses in their hands, crying *Acqua ghiacciata*, or *Acqua nevata. i.e.* Snowed water or iced water. **1777** P. THICKNESSE *Year's Journey* I. xxviii. 240 Their chocolate, lemonade, iced water, fruits, &c. are their chief luxuries. **1831** B. H. SMART *Outl. Sematology* iii. 237 The thirsty wight who, in a state of profuse perspiration, calls for a glass of iced-water, may know there is danger in the draught. **1848** Iced champagne [see *ball supper* s.v. *BALL *sb.*² 4]. **1877** *Forest & Stream* VIII. 411/1 Courtney..became very sick immediately after taking a glass of iced tea after his dinner, and was unable to row. **1879** M. E. BRADDON *Vixen* III. vii. 187 Afternoon tea at Ashbourne included iced coffee. **1880** *Amer. Punch* Jan. 4/1 Some were talking of.. the cooling and invigorating influences of 'iced tea'. **1902** H. JAMES *Wings of Dove* v. x. 172 The small cup of iced coffee she had vaguely accepted from somebody. **1913** W. STEVENS *Let.* 7 July (1967) 179 A spread of chicken salad, ..watermelon, iced-tea etc. **1930** A. BENNETT *Imperial Palace* xvii. 109 The cocktail jugs, the iced-water jugs. **1952** W. M. MILLER *View from Stars* (1965) 42 She..drank a glass of iced tea. **1954** *Good Housek. Cookery Bk.* (rev. ed.) 453 (*heading*) Iced coffee. **1958** *Listener* 14 Aug. 229/1 Fifteen of the family hang over the back and laugh at you through their iced lollies. **1960** *News Chron.* 6 Aug. 1/1 Prince Charles bought an iced-lolly. **1972** H. OSBORNE *Pay-Day* IV. i. 163 Every year..another hotel with an iced-water tap rises out of the mud.

2. Of a cake, bun, etc.: covered with icing. Of preserved fruit: = GLACÉ *a.* 2.

1858 P. L. SIMMONDS *Dict. Trade Products, Iced*, cakes frosted with sugar. **1866** MRS. BEETON *Preserves & Confectionery* 5 Iced Apples, or Apple Hedgehog... Cover the apples very smoothly all over with the icing. *Ibid.* 89 Iced currants... Lay them to dry on paper, when the sugar will crystallize round each currant. **1892** *Encycl. Pract. Cookery* I. 240/1 Iced cake. **1973** *Fortnum & Mason Christmas Catal.* 4/2 Iced and decorated Christmas cake.

b. (See quots.) Cf. FROSTED *ppl. a.* 3 b.

1829 J. C. LOUDON *Encycl. Plants* 1100/1 Iced..covered with particles like icicles. **1900** B. D. JACKSON *Gloss. Bot. Terms, Iced*, having a glittering papillose surface, as *Mesembryanthemum crystallinum*.

ice-house. Add: **2.** A hut made of ice or snow.

1857 G. F. MCDOUGALL *Eventful Voy. 'Resolute'* 426 The remains of two ice houses yet existed, but were rapidly thawing away, under the influence of the heat of the sun. **1958** *Listener* 25 Sept. 482/2 They sat marooned for four days in an icehouse 14,000 feet up.

Iceland. Add: **Iceland falcon**, *Falco rusticolus islandicus*, a variety of gyr-falcon native to Iceland; **Iceland gull**, *Larus glaucoides*, a grey and white Arctic gull.

1771 *Gentl. Mag.* XLVI. 297/1 The Iceland Falcon..is a noble and stately bird. **1822** *Mem. Wernerian Nat. Hist. Soc.* IV. 181 They [*sc.* the Shetland fishermen] have distinguished this bird by the name of Iceland *Scorie*, (or the Young Iceland Gull); *Scorie* being the general Shetlandic appellation for the young of several species of the gull family. **1843** W. YARRELL *Hist. Brit. Birds* I. 27 Those specimens obtained from Iceland were called exclusively Iceland Falcons. *Ibid.* III. 461 The Iceland Gull sometimes makes its appearance in winter at the mouth of the Elbe. **1901** H. H. SLATER *Man. Birds Iceland* 31 The Iceland Falcon is a remarkably handsome bird. **1927** M. U. HACHISUKA *Handbk. Birds Iceland* 40 The Iceland Falcon is a national emblem. **1930** *Ibis* 415 The Iceland Gull apparently fills the same 'niche' in Godthaab Fiord as the Herring-Gull..in the British Isles. **1956** D. A. BANNERMAN *Birds Brit. Isles* V. 21 In Ireland the Iceland gyr-falcon has been recorded five times. *Ibid.* 22 The Iceland falcon was not nearly as uncommon as had been supposed. **1962** *Ibid.* XI. 334 In flight the Iceland gull looks more graceful and has more rapid wing-beats.

iceman. Add: **1.** (Earlier example.)

1851 W. P. SNOW *Voy. 'Prince Albert'* 302 Ten men formed the number of the working seamen; there were no 'icemasters', nor regular 'ice-men': but most of the sailors were long accustomed to the ice.

2. (Earlier example.)

1845 *Times* 10 Feb. 5/4 The ice in the Serpentine yesterday was not above an inch thick, and through the exertions of the icemen of the Royal Humane Society, no persons ventured on except a few boys.

3. (Earlier example.) Also, one who delivers ice for domestic use.

1844 *Maysville* (Kentucky) *Eagle* 7 Sept. 1/3, I do wish an ice man would come this morning. **1870** 'F. FERN' *Ginger-Snaps* 179 Let no grocer boy or ice-man fondly hope to retain the celestial spark, while he briefly deposits his wares in my kitchen. **1959** N. MAILER *Advts. for Myself* (1961) 230 We played our games. I was the iceman and she was the housewife.

ice-master. **1.** (Earlier example.)

1851 [see *ICEMAN 1].

Icenian (əisī·niăn), *sb.* and *a.* Also **Icenæan** (əisinī·ăn). [See -IAN.] **A.** *sb.* A member of the Iceni, an ancient British tribe inhabiting the district roughly corresponding to modern Norfolk and Suffolk.

1598 R. GRENEWEY tr. *Tacitus' Annales* XIV. x. 209 The chiefest of the Icenians..were dispossessed of al their ancient inheritance. **1670** MILTON *Hist. Britain* II. 55 The Icenians, a stout people untouch'd yet by these Warrs. **1864** TENNYSON *'Boädicea'* in *Enoch Arden* 169 Hear Icenian, Catieuchlanian, hear Coritanian, Trinobant!

B. *adj.* **1.** Of or pertaining to the Iceni or the district they inhabited. Also **Ice·nic** *a.*

1757 J. DYER *Fleece* III. 72 This method still Norvicum favours, and the Icenian towns. **1830** *Forby's Vocab. E. Anglia, Mem.* p. xxxix, With only one more extract I will close what remains to be said respecting the Icenian Glossary. *c* **1873** A. D. BAYNE *Royal Illustr. Hist. E. Eng.* I. 393 Some Icenic names are supposed to remain in several towns of Norfolk and Suffolk. *Ibid.* 395 There are thousands of pits in many places, and these are supposed to have been the foundations of Icenian huts. **1900** W. A. DUTT *Norfolk* 39 Some authorities have suggested that that important Icenic settlement was at Caistor. **1921** R. A. S. MACALISTER *Text-bk. Europ. Archæol.* I. 158 To this type of flint, or to the supposed industry which it represents, has been given the name *Icenian*. **1962** T. C. LETHBRIDGE *Witches* vii. 95 Hiccafrith becomes the Sun husband of the Icenaean moon and horse goddess, Ma Gog.

2. *Geol.* Applied to the Norwich Crag, Chillesford Beds, and Weybourne Crag of Norfolk and Suffolk (sometimes, to the Norwich Crag alone) and to the period when they were deposited, formerly regarded as late Pliocene but now held to be early Pleistocene; occas. used as the epithet of a stratigraphical stage in Britain. Also *absol.*

1896 *Q. Jrnl. Geol. Soc.* LII. 782 He [*sc.* H. B. Woodward] was..glad that Mr. Harmer now agreed that the beds belonged to one formation; and if it were desirable to use a term that should correspond with the other group-names used by the Author, he would suggest that the old term 'Icenian' be used for this Norwich Crag Series. **1900** F. W. HARMER in *Ibid.* LVI. 721 For the deposits hitherto known as Norwich Crag.., which extend..from Aldeburgh in Suffolk to Horstead and Burgh in Norfolk, a distance of more than 40 miles in one direction, and 20 miles, from Hoxne to Southwold, in another, I adopt the name Icenian, originally proposed for the Crag-formation generally by S. P. [*sic*] Woodward. *Ibid.*, The Icenian Period. **1931** GREGORY & BARRETT *Gen. Stratigr.* xvi. 228 The Sicilian Series is represented in England by the Norwich Crag, Chillesford Beds, and Weybourne Crags, which were grouped by Harmer as the Icenian. **1957** J. K. CHARLESWORTH *Quaternary Era* II. xxxii. 697 The impoverished state of many Icenian shells may (doubtfully) have been due to a freshened North Sea which resulted when the Scandinavian ice..blocked the northern outlet of that sea. **1968** R. G. WEST *Pleistocene Geol. & Biol.* xiii. 337 A major time of extinction [of species of mollusc] was after Icenian Crag times, and before the Hoxnian temperate stage.

ice-plant. Add: Also used in Tasmania to refer to two species of *Tetragonia.*

1889 J. H. MAIDEN *Useful Native Plants Austral.* 63 *Tetragonia implixicona*...Called 'Ice Plant' in Tasmania. Baron Mueller suggests that this plant be cultivated for spinach. **1898** E. E. MORRIS *Austral Eng.* 429/1 Spinach, New Zealand, *n. Tetragonia expansa* Murr...called also *Iceplant*, in Tasmania. **1944** *Mod. Jun. Dict.* (Whitcombe & Tombs) 204 Ice plant...The Tasmanian name for a plant allied to 'New Zealand spinach', and to the mesembryanthemum or 'pig-face'.

icer (əi·səɹ). [f. ICE *v.* + -ER[1].] One who ices; *spec.* a worker who prepares icing and applies it to the surface of cakes, pastry, etc.

1909 WEBSTER, *Icer*, one who ices. **1921** *Dict. Occup. Terms* (1927) §433.

ice-water. (Later examples.)

1803 C. WILMOT *Let.* 6 Mar. in *Irish Peer* (1920) 160 Ice water is their [*sc.* the Neapolitans'] greatest luxury. **1846** *Knickerbocker* XXVIII. 187 They may pour in a large spoonful of that [*sc.* brandy], and then fill it up with ice-water. **1889** *Harper's Mag.* Sept. 560/1 Here were found..the huge brown hogsheads for ice-water. **1906** *N.Y. Even. Post* 25 July 4 A glass of ice-water placed before us the moment we sit down to breakfast;..a pitcher of ice-water sent to our bed-rooms. **1910** W. DE LA MARE *Three Mulla-Mulgars* xxi. 280 Colder than ice-water. **1969** *New Yorker* 6 Sept. 35/1 She will..arrange them, filling the Chinese bowl with ice water, carefully clipping the stems. **1972** *Straits Times* 25 Nov. 10/6 They were sitting at an ice water stall when they saw four men approaching them from the direction of Sembawang Circus.

ice-work. Add: **3.** *Mountaineering.* Climbing on icy surfaces; the techniques of such climbing.

1856 A. WILLS *Wanderings High Alps* xiv. 288 Our ice hatchet..was..better adapted to the mere ice-work we had then to perform. **1892** C. T. DENT et al. *Mountaineering* iv. 125 For a snow expedition—that is, one in which snow and ice work will probably form the chief difficulties—the numbers of a party may be largely increased even to eight or ten. **1940** F. S. CHAPMAN *Helvellyn to Himalaya* iv. 89, I was not much good on really difficult rock, my experience of step-cutting and ice-work was small. *Ibid.* v. 98 At last, in early September, by developing an entirely new technique of ice-work, the ridge was reached.

ice-worm (əi·s'wɒ̄ɹm). [f. ICE *sb.* + WORM *sb.*] **a.** A small oligochaete worm, *Mesenchytræus solifugus*, found in North American glaciers and ice fields; also called glacier-worm and snow-worm. **b.** *Canada.* An imaginary creature that first 'appeared' during the Klondike gold rush.

a. [**1885** J. LEIDY in *Proc. Acad. Nat. Sci. Philadelphia* 408 The little worms of the ice appear to be an undescribed species. **1886** *Bull. Washburn Coll. Lab. Nat. Hist.* I. 186 What was popularly supposed to be an Ice Worm was found in the ice used in Salina, Kansas, toward the latter part of the summer of 1885.] **1904** G. EISEN in C. H. Merriam *Harriman Alaska Exped.* XII. 61 It is not impossible that the various glaciers of Alaska contain several species of black ice worms. **1949** *Nature* 24 Dec. 1098/1, I found a considerable number of the oligochaetous annelids known as ice-worms. **1970** *Nature* 14 Feb. 587/1 During the day, ice worms, which are black and about three quarters of an inch long, were found clumped together 6–12 inches deep under the drainage furrows of the névé.

b. 1901 *Klondike Nugget* 10 Apr. 2/2 In a country where ice worms abound there is no telling but that deadly serpents may also be found. **1964** *Edmonton Jrnl.* 11 July 27/1 The Klondike ice worm, immortalized in Robert Service's The Ice Worm Cocktail, has been imported to Edmonton.

Ichabod (i·kăbǫd). Name given by Eli's daughter-in-law to her son, used as an exclamation of regret, in allusion to 1 Sam. iv. 21 (she named the child Ichabod, saying, 'The glory is departed from Israel').

1702 I. MATHER (*title*). Ichabod, or A discourse, shewing what cause there is to fear that the glory of the Lord, is departing from New-England. **1812** BOGUE & BENNETT *Hist. Dissenters* IV. vi. 383 The orthodox dissenter would inscribe, 'Ichabod, the glory is departed'. **1901** 'A. HOPE' *Tristram of Blent* xxi, 'Bring me some cold beef,' he commanded, and the waiter brought it with an air that said 'Ichabod' for the Imperium. **1904** 'H. S. MERRIMAN' *Last Hope* xxi, 'Ichabod,' he said, with a short laugh. **1915** *N. & Q.* 6 Feb. 110/1 At one time the Scriptural name Ichabod was used, presumably with a knowledge of its derivation, with the sense of alas! regretting the good old times. **1941** J. GORE *King George V* xi. 125 An income-tax, still adjusted from time to time in pennies below a shilling, left to the newly rich and the owners of ancient wealth, newly recruited, plenty over for luxurious living and only a scintilla of justification for crying *Ichabod.* **1957** A. MACNAB *Bulls of Iberia* xiii. 139 Belmonte—the first torero ever to wear a bowler hat, ichabod!

Hence **Ichabo·dian** *a.*, regretful, lamenting.

1887 *Daily News* 1 Dec. 2/1 Dirges were sung with an Ichabodian refrain.

Ich dien (iχʸ dī·n). [a. G. *ich dien* = I serve.] Used as the motto of the Prince of Wales, adopted with the crest of ostrich feathers after the battle of Crécy (1346), from John of Luxembourg, King of Bohemia, who was killed in the battle. So *concr.* for the Prince of Wales himself, and allusively.

Spelt *ich diene* on the tomb of the Black Prince, Edward Prince of Wales, at the time of his burial at Canterbury in 1376.

a **1529** SKELTON *Sp. Parrot* in *Poetical Works* (1843) II. 5 *Ic dien* serueth for erstrych fether. **1545** in *Catal. Seals Dept. MSS. Brit. Mus.* (1892) II. 232 Henry VIII. Ich Dien. **1677** F. SANDFORD *Geneal. Hist. Kings Eng.* III. iv. 182 Prince Edward..deplumed his Casque of those Ostrich Feathers, which..became his Cognizance,.. with Scroles containing this Motto, ICH DIEN, that is, *I serve.* **1780** H. WALPOLE *Let.* 23 Sept. (1858) VII. 441 If *Ich Dien* does not wear one, he at last, ..boudes those who voted against the Admiral. **1923** D. H. LAWRENCE *Birds, Beasts & Flowers* 170 That pale fragment of a Prince up there, whose motto is *Ich dien.* *a* **1930** —— *Phoenix* (1936) 588 The whole world screams *Ich dien.*

ichebo, -u, ichibo, -u, varr. ITZEBU.

I Ching (ī·ˌtʃiŋ). [Chin., lit. = Book of Changes.] The name of an ancient Chinese divination manual, based on symbols known as the eight trigrams and sixty-four hexagrams.

1876 T. MCCLATCHIE tr. *Classic of Change* p. v, The mere translating of the Yih King is not without difficulties; but to decipher the *system* taught therein, is impossible without some knowledge of other pagan systems. **1952** *Musical Q.* XXXVIII. 128 Cage has often used the I-Ching, an old Chinese method of throwing coins or marked sticks for chance numbers, like our use of dice. **1957** *Encycl. Brit.* V. 519/2 Wên Wang..is said to have produced the *I Ching*, or *Canon of Changes*, a volume based upon the trigrams and later viewed with great veneration and incorporated into the Confucian canon. **1965** L. T. CULLING *Incredible I Ching* 8 There was no language attached to the I Ching of Fu Hsi—only eight figures, or Trigrams. **1968** *Listener* 19 Sept. 377/1 By means of chance operations—the use of the I-Ching, filling in imperfections in the manuscript paper, tossing coins—the parameters of pitch (and therefore form) were removed from the domains of the composer's will and taste. **1970** FENG & KIRK *Tai-Chi* 7/2 Although it was an ancient document when Confucius first encountered it, I Ching is traditionally awarded the status of a 'Confucian' classic. **1971** R. VAN OVER *I Ching* I. ii, The text of the *I Ching* was an early valuable reference for ministers and leaders in ancient China as well as the average citizen. **1972** *Last Whole Earth Catalog* (Portola Inst.) 433/3 And then, way back under the bed, face down on the floor, opened at the hexagram called Youthful Folly, D.R. found their *I Ching.* **1973** *Listener* 15 Feb. 209/1 Margaret is 'into' astrology, and consults the *I-Ching* each morning.

ichneumoned (ikniū·mənd), *a.* [f. ICHNEUMON 2 + -ED[2].] Infested with parasitic ichneumon flies.

1897 W. F. KIRBY in R. Lydekker et al. *Conc. Knowledge Nat. Hist.* 576 Ichneumoned larvæ generally attain their full growth, and then die. **1944** W. J. STOKOE *Caterpillars Brit. Butterflies* 99 A very large proportion of any [Large Tortoiseshell caterpillars] collected are almost certain to be found 'ichneumoned'.

ichor. Add: **2.** (Further examples.) Now chiefly *poet.*

1930 BLUNDEN *Poems* 128 Meanwhile the woods with ichor in their limbs Wake in a dance of slow religious love. **1960** S. PLATH *Colossus* (1967) 77 The ichor of the spring Proceeds clear as it ever did From the broken throat, the marshy lip. **1970** R. P. WARREN *Incarnations* 15 The great-gashed navel's cup Pours forth the ichor that had filled it up.

4. *Geol.* A fluid or 'emanation' from a magma which is held to cause granitization of rock.

1926 J. J. SEDERHOLM in *Bull. de la Comm. Géol. de Finlande* XII. LXXVII. 89 The writer proposes to introduce, instead of the word granitic juices, the term granitic ichor, preliminarily with no more strictly defined signification than that possessed by the word juice. It will soon be possible..to give to the term a stricter definition. **1934** *N.Z. Jrnl. Sci. & Technol.* XV. 354 The minerals described..constitute an assemblage typical of an area mineralized by granitic ichor. **1965** A. HOLMES *Princ. Physical Geol.* (ed. 2) viii. 183 When he [*sc.* Sederholm] was urged to define his 'ichor' in more material terms, as he often was, he suggested 'a magma containing much water in a gaseous state'.

ichthammol (i·kþæ̆mǫl). *Pharm.* Also † **ichthamol.** [f. ICHTH(Y)OL with insertion of AMM(ONIA.] Ichthyol (as defined in Suppl.).

1907 *Brit. Pharm. Codex* 89 Ammonii Ichthosulphonas. Ammonium Ichthosulphonate. Synonyms.—Ichthamol; Ammonium Sulpho-ichthyolate. Ammonium ichthosulphonate consists of the ammonium salts of the sulphonic acids prepared from ichthyol—the oily product of the destructive distillation of a greyish bituminous schist.. found in the Karwendel Mountains. **1950** [see *ICHTHYOL]. **1956** D. M. PILLSBURY et al. *Dermatol.* xxvi. 388 In a patient with atopic dermatitis..our own single preference for an initial ointment is one containing 2 to 3 per cent ichthammol in zinc oxide ointment USP. **1967** *Martindale's Extra Pharmacopoeia* (ed. 25) 1406/2 Ichthammol has occasionally been administered by mouth..as an expectorant and intestinal antiseptic but it is irritant to the gastric mucosa.

ichthyo-. Add: **ichthyoacanthoto·xism** (i:kþioˌăkæ:nþo-) [Gr. ἄκανθο- thorn (f. ἀκή point) + TOX-[1]], poisoning resulting from a venomous sting or bite by a fish; **i:chthyosa:rcoto·xism** [SARCO- + TOX-[1]], poisoning resulting from the ingestion of a fish whose flesh is poisonous; **ichthyoto·xism** [TOX-[1]], poisoning resulting from the natural poison or venom of a fish.

1953 B. W. HALSTEAD in *Copeia* I. 32/2 The following nomenclature and classification is proposed: Ichthyotoxism is the general term which would be used to include the forms of intoxication resulting from contact with both 'poisonous' and 'venomous' fishes... Ichthyotoxism may be of two types: (a) Ichthyosarcotoxism... (b) Ichthyoacanthotoxism. **1962** K. F. LAGLER et al. *Ichthyol.* iv. 131 The field of ichthyotoxism includes the various forms of intoxication resulting from eating poisonous fishes (ichthyosarcotoxism) or being stung by venomous fishes (ichthyoacanthotoxism). **1953** Ichthyosarcotoxism [see *ichthyoacanthotoxism* above]. **1960** Ichthyosarcotoxism [see *CIGUATERA]. **1962** K. F. LAGLER et al. *Ichthyol.* v. 160 The strongest evidence as to the origin of ichthyosarcotoxism now points to the feeding habits of fishes. [**1898** V. C. VAUGHAN in T. L. Stedman *20th Cent. Pract.* XIII. 33 (*heading*) Fish poisoning (ichthyotoxismus).] **1900** DORLAND *Med. Dict.* 315/2 Ichthyotoxism. **1922** *U.S. Naval Med. Bull.* XVII. 201 Poisoning by inherent fish poisons is called 'ichthyotoxism'. **1953** Ichthyotoxism [see above].

ichthyol. Add: Also, the dark, viscous liquid obtained by sulphonating the distillate and neutralizing the product with ammonia, in which form the substance has been most commonly employed (see quot. 1950). (Earlier and later examples.)

Ichthyol has been registered as a proprietary name.

1884 *Trade Marks Jrnl.* 1 Oct. 908 Ichthyol... Ichthyol Gesellschaft Cordes, Hermanni & Co., Hamburg; merchants... Chemical substances prepared for use in medicine and pharmacy. **1900** A. R. CUSHNY *Text-bk. Pharmacol. & Therapeutics* II. 379 Ichthyol is the ammonia salt of a sulphonic acid derived from the tar of a bituminous shale which is found in the Tyrol. **1907** [see *ICHTHAMMOL]. **1932** C. J. MILLER *Clin. Gynecol.* v. 105 Eroded and inflamed services are often temporarily improved by local applications of tincture of iodine..or some similar agent, after which tampons saturated with ichthyol and glycerine are inserted into the vagina. **1950** *Jrnl. Soc. Chem. Industry* LXIX. 107/1 There is confusion in the nomenclature: the British Pharmacopoeia defines ichthammol as 'the ammonium salts of sulphonic acids of an oily substance, prepared from a bituminous schist, together with ammonium sulphate and water'. The oily substance..is commonly known as ichthyol. The B.P.C. however, states that ichthyol is a proprietary name for a brand of ichthammol. Unna..urged the use of the unsulphonated oil and the restriction of the name ichthyol to this material... When [sulphonated and] neutralized with ammonia, the product was variously known as ammonium ichthyosulphonate, the original name of ichthyol, and finally as ichthammol: this is the ichthammol of the B.P. **1962** *Brit. Jrnl. Plastic Surg.* XV. 278 All burns have had the same basic treatment—exposure and regular painting of the burned areas and surrounding skin with glycerin and ichthyol.

ichu (ī·tʃū). Also **icho, ychu.** [Quechua.] An alpine grass, *Stipa ichu*, growing on the uplands of the Andes, where it is used for fodder and thatching.

[**1781** H. RUIZ *Relación del Viaje* (1931) 137 Se mantiene porción de ganado bacuno y carneros de Castilla con el Icho y con el corto, pero abundante pasto.] **1891** E. B. CLARK *Twelve Months Peru* 136 The coarse *ychu* grass, growing in tufts upon the mountain slopes. **1921** *Glasgow Herald* 23 Apr. 10/1 The great ichu-covered steppes of the plateau. **1950** T. H. GOODSPEED *Plant Hunters in Andes* iv. 119 Herds of llamas and alpacas graze the ichu. **1964** A. R. STEELE *Flowers for King* ii. 42 Other desired specimens rating special mention [in 1776] were cinchona, the source of quinine; *icho* grass from the high mountain plateaus, useful for matting and cordage. *Ibid.* vii. 99 The scientists..swung perilously upon a raw-hide rope bridge one cold midnight by the light of *icho* grass flares.

icing, *vbl. sb.* Add: **1.** Also *fig.* in phr. *the icing on the cake*, the 'trimmings'.

1969 *Listener* 3 Apr. 468/3 All this theology is icing on the cake... '*Pas sérieuse*'..is an epithet I would apply to the whole book. **1970** *Globe & Mail* (Toronto) 26 Sept. 12/1 The missionaries have a dubious legacy, says Father Gallagher. 'We had been giving them the icing and not the cake, the Christian tools with which they need to meet the circumstances in life they face.' **1973** R. PERRY *Nowhere Man* v. 100 It was quite a neat ploy, the icing on the cake.

2. b. Preservation by means of ice; refrigeration with ice.

1883 R. F. WALSH *Irish Fisheries* (Fish. Exhib. Publ.) 17 A rate for fish carrying is then struck; this includes icing.

3. Also *Aeronaut.* (esp. with *up*), the formation of ice on an aircraft. (Further examples.)

1929 R. DUNCAN *Air Navigation & Meteorol.* (ed. 3) xii. 124 What goes on during the action known as icing-up, or the accumulating of ice-coats on the plane's surfaces. **1937** *Evening News* 29 Jan. 8/3 The latest theory connects the very fine rain with one of the most dangerous phenomena in flying: icing-up of the wings. **1945** *Tee Emm* (Air Ministry) V. 48 Icing-up caused him to lose

control of the aircraft. *Ibid.* 53 Icing may occur, which requires hot air and..reduces available engine power. **1955** *Times* 12 Aug. 5/1 The Hull Trawler Officers' Guild are meeting soon to discuss the icing up of trawlers, and it is expected that they will make recommendations to the trawler owners. **1957** *Economist* 21 Sept. 965/1 This warns pilots to fly no higher than 16,000 feet whenever they meet conditions likely to bring on the Britannia's particular form of icing trouble. **1958** 'N. SHUTE' *Rainbow & Rose* viii. 295 There was no icing on the aircraft. **1966** T. ARMSTRONG et al. *Illustr. Gloss. Snow & Ice* 27 *Icing*, the accumulation of a deposit of ice on exposed objects, e.g. aircraft, ships, aerials, instruments. Icing may be produced by the deposition of water vapour or by the freezing on impact of droplets in the air.

4. *icing sugar*: finely powdered sugar.

1889 A. B. MARSHALL *Cookery Bk.* iii. 41 *Royal Icing.*—To two and a half pounds of icing sugar put seven or eight whites of fresh eggs and half a tablespoonful of lemon juice strained. **1896** J. T. LAW *Grocer's Manual* 232/1 Icing sugar is that [sugar] which is ground to a very fine, impalpable powder, resembling flour, and should consist of pure cane sugar; for beet sugar..is not capable of high crystallisation. **1907** *Yesterday's Shopping* (1969) 42 Sugars... Loaf..Granulated..Icing. *c* **1938** *Fortnum & Mason Price List* 58/2 Icing sugar..per tin 1/2. **1970** SIMON & HOWE *Dict. Gastron.* 365/1 Icing sugar..is used to make icing..and meringues. **1972** J. WILSON *Hide & Seek* i. 19 Where's the icing sugar?..There's only the gran and castor there.

ickle (i·k'l), *a.* A hypocoristic form of LITTLE *a.*: in childish use. Also **i·ckly.**

1846 DICKENS *Dombey* (1848) i. 5, I came down from seeing dear Fanny, and that tiddy ickle sing. **1905** E. M. FORSTER *Where Angels fear to Tread* viii. 278 Good ickle quiet boysey, then. **1906** E. DYSON *Fact'ry 'Ands* xiv. 184 Oo's mummy's ickle sly-boots, oo is—*oo is!* Baby's a baddy baddy 'icky bubb-bubb. **1936** 'G. ORWELL' *Keep Aspidistra Flying* i. 26 A Peke, the ickle angel pet, wiv his great big Soulful eyes and his ickle black nosie—oh so ducky-duck! **1937** R. MACAULAY *I would be Private* I. i. 19 Was it a nice ickly boy, then? **1968** 'P. HOBSON' *Titty's Dead* xi. 121 She changed her role. Now she was Daddy's ickle girl.

icky, ikky (i·ki), *a.* and *sb. colloq.* [Origin uncertain.] **A.** *adj.* **a.** *Jazz.* Ignorant (of true swinging jazz and liking the 'sweet' kind). *U.S.* **b.** Sweet, sickly, sentimental; hence a general term of disapproval: nasty, repulsive, sticky, etc.; also, ill, sick.

1935 *Vanity Fair* (N.Y.) Nov. 71/2 If the straight music is also oversweet, the term *icky* (a pseudo-baby-patter word, meaning 'little') is frequently employed to denote this. **1938** D. BAKER *Young Man with Horn* IV. vii. 277 Smoke Jordan tried hard to get him to..maybe take a vacation, Florida's nice. 'Get yourself wheeled up and down like an icky banker?' **1939** JOYCE *Finnegans Wake* 555 His wrinkly waste of methylated spirits.. and pulverised rhubarbarorum, icky. **1942** D. POWELL *Time to be Born* (1943) x. 229 'A pet-shop on the first floor? But Miss Haven! Really!' gasped Miss Finkelstein. 'How *icky*!' **1945** L. SHELLY *Jive Talk Dict.* 26/2 *Icky vicki*, stupid gal. **1952** S. KAUFFMANN *Philanderer* (1953) 13 'It's just that—oh, I don't know—now everything's so icky.'..Another of her dubious charms. The high-school words. **1959** S. BELLOW *Henderson Rain King* xiv. 200 Under the thickened rain clouds, a heated, darkened breeze sprang up..choky, sultry, icky. **1964** C. CHAPLIN *Autobiogr.* xxi. 352 He must hide his blindness... His stumblings and bumpings into things make the little girl laugh joyously. But that was too 'icky'. **1964** *Harper's Bazaar* Nov. 110/2 Roast chestnuts or icky home-made fudge. **1967** H. HUNTER *Case for Punishment* vi. 108 She wears the most *fright*-ful cardigans. Always some sort of *ikky* colour—to go with everything, I suppose. **1968** J. HUDSON *Case of Need* IV. iii. 239 I'm not hungry... The food tastes icky. **1970** *New Yorker* 28 Nov. 122/2 We pick out the icky things in men and call them male, and then we say that the woman who has them..we say she's a male-identifier. **1972** R. QUILTY *Tenth Session* 21 A group of ton-up boys dipped their icky fingers in the sugar bowls. **1972** M. WOODHOUSE *Mama Doll* ix. 117, *I* showed *him*..lots of gore, you know, and he went all green and icky and dashed off.

B. *sb.* **1.** A person who is ignorant of true swinging jazz and likes the 'sweet' kind. *U.S.*

1937 *Amer. Speech* XII. 180 Musicians unable to swing, and who therefore can only play corn are called 'long hairs' and those who enjoy listening to their music are 'Ickies'. This term implies definite bovine qualities. **1938** *Better English* Nov. 51/2 *Icky*, one who is not hip but thinks he is. **1939** *Words* Oct. 108/1 *Ickies*..are hicks who'll never be able to tell a sweet from a swing arrangement. **1955** L. FEATHER *Encycl. Jazz* x. 346 *Icky* (*Obsolete*), person with poor musical taste.

2. Something which is sickly, disagreeable; sickness.

1969 D. FRANCIS *Enquiry* vii. 88 Poppy's got the morning ickies again. I'll be glad when this lousy pregnancy's over.

Also in extended (and possibly unconnected) expressions, as **icky-boo** *a.*, ill (in quot. 1970[2] written *icky-poo*); **ickylickysticky** *a.* (nonce-wd.), unpleasantly sticky.

1920 'SAPPER' *Bull-Dog Drummond* ix. 234 Can it be that my little pet is feeling icky-boo? Face going green—slight perspiration—collar tight. **1922** JOYCE *Ulysses* 570 They blow ickylickysticky yumyum kisses. **1930** 'SAPPER' *Finger of Fate* 188 The jolly old tum-tum is not icky-boo or anything like that. **1970** 'B. MATHER' *Break in Line* v. 57 Call the airline office..and tell 'em you're feeling an icksy bit icky-boo and want a stopover. **1970** *New Yorker* 14 Nov. 55 (*caption*) If any..engine conkouts, or fires make you feel icky-poo, you just come and tell.

icon. Add: **3. b.** *Philos.* (See quot. 1934.) Also *transf.*

a **1914** C. S. PEIRCE *Coll. Papers* (1931) I. III. iii. 195 It has been found that there are three kinds of signs which are all indispensable in all reasoning; the first is the diagrammatic sign or *icon*, which exhibits a similarity or analogy to the subject of discourse. *Ibid.* 196 There may be a mere relation of reason between the sign and the thing signified; in that case, the sign is an *icon.* **1934** *Mind* XLIII. 497 An *icon* is a sign which represents its object by virtue of having some character in common with the object: the colour of a colour-card as representing the colour of the object which it resembles is an icon, and a map as representing spatial relations is an icon. **1949** *Poetry* (Chicago) Jan. 234 *Icons*, images, which are the aesthetic signs of the poem, analogous to the symbolic signs of scientific discourses; they have, as signs, semantic objects, or refer to objects, and, in addition, as iconic signs, resemble those objects. **1954** W. K. WIMSATT *Verbal Icon* (1967) p. x, The term *icon* is used to-day by semeiotic writers to refer to a verbal sign which *somehow* shares the properties of, or resembles, the objects which it denotes.

Iconian (əikōu·niăn), *a.* and *sb.* [-AN.] **A.** *adj.* Of or pertaining to Iconium (mod. Konya), a town in southern Asia Minor where St. Paul preached, or to the church established there (Acts xiii. 5, xiv. 1–7). **B.** *sb.* A native or inhabitant of Iconium.

1899 W. M. RAMSAY in *Expositor* Aug. 112 There were strife and wrangling and jealousy between the Antiochean Church and the Iconian Church about precedence and comparative dignity. **1911** —— *First Christ. Cent.* xxv. 168 St. Paul addressed the Iconian audiences in Greek. *Ibid.* 171 The Iconians clung to their Phrygian character as opposed to the Lycaonian.

iconic, *a.* Add: **c.** *Semiotics.* Pertaining to or resembling an icon (sense *3 b). Also *transf.*

1939 C. W. MORRIS in *Kenyon Rev.* I. IV. 415 The aesthetic sign..is an iconic sign (an 'image') in that it embodies these values in some medium where they may be directly inspected (in short, the aesthetic sign is an iconic sign whose designatum is a value). **1949** [see *ICON 3 b]. **1956** E. H. HUTTEN *Lang. Mod. Physics* ii. 15 Sometimes, the sign is similar to the thing it stands for, in the manner in which a picture represents, and we have iconic signs. **1964** T. W. MCRAE *Impact of Computers on Accounting* v. 132 There are many kinds of model. The one described above is an *iconic* model, that is a physical representation of the original item. **1965** C. H. SPRINGER et al. *Adv. Methods and Models* i. 6 He might use..an *iconic* model, which doesn't *act* like the real thing (as the analog model does) but only *looks* like it. **1966** M. PEI *Gloss. Ling. Terminol.* 118 *Iconic*, characterized by a symbolism which purports to present an image of the object described (Chinese pictographs). **1970** *English Studies* LI. 279 Non-roman notations are generally 'iconic', i.e. 'the symbols are not arbitrary signs, but in some way resemble what they stand for'. **1971** *Language* XLVII. 416 There is..growing evidence that language contains many elements which are iconic—that is, imitative of non-linguistic reality.

ico·nically, *adv.* [f. ICONIC *a.*: see -ICALLY.] In an iconic manner.

1946 C. MORRIS *Signs, Lang. & Behavior* 193 Such conflict is presented iconically in the music itself. **1973** *Times Lit. Suppl.* 5 Oct. 1188/4 The rhythm..depicts the distance iconically, since the farther away the goal, the fewer cycles of the dance occur in a given period.

iconicity (əikŏni·siti). [f. ICONIC *a.* + -ITY.] The quality or fact of being iconic (in various senses).

1946 C. MORRIS *Signs, Lang. & Behavior* 191 Spoken language contains some sounds which are clearly iconic ('onomatopoetic'); the extent of its iconicity is a difficult matter to determine. **1971** *Language* XLVII. 425 In some cases, there is iconicity between language and a non-human communication system. **1972** *Sci. Amer.* Sept. 91/2 The only element of genuine representation (also called iconicity) in such a case is the actual shape of the geographical features, although even these are normalized according to given rules of transformation to allow a part of the globe to be shown on a flat map.

iconism. Add: Revived in *Semiotics* in sense 'the quality or fact of being an icon or intentional sign'.

1971 *Language* XLVII. 417 Among homotherms—that is, warm-blooded vertebrates, such as birds and mammals—iconism is less salient. Yet it seems to be present, at least latently, in the 'intention movements' exhibited..by herring gulls who are about to take flight and who seem, by spreading their wings, not only to be preparing for flight themselves but also to be inviting neighboring gulls to fly with them.

icono-. Add: **i:conodu·le** = ICONODULIST; **iconopho·bia,** hatred of images; also **i·conophobe, iconopho·bic** *adjs.*, of or pertaining to one who hates images.

1893 *Funk's Stand. Dict.*, *Iconodule, iconodulist*, one who serves images; an image-worshipper; iconolater. **1900** 'ODYSSEUS' *Turkey in Europe* 230 The division of Asia representing Iconoclasts and Europe Iconodules is almost without exception. **1901** E. GOSSE in *Daily Chron.* 22 Nov. 3/3 The sentiment of the author is vehemently on the side of the Iconodules. **1939** A. TOYNBEE *Study of Hist.* IV. 595 The indomitable Iconodule Patriarch Germanus found a worthy successor in the reigning Patriarch Nicêphorus. **1967** H. CHADWICK *Early Church* xviii. 283 The iconodules replied: (*a*) we venerate not the icons but those whom they depict [etc.]. **1958** *Times Lit. Suppl.* 23 May 278/3 Saxl himself believed that such an approach to history was natural, and indeed inevitable, in an age of illustrated papers and the film and television; but the English are notoriously iconophobe, and it may still be necessary to insist on this point. **1926** H. READ *Eng. Stained Glass* ii. 16/1 Free from the iconophobia which infested Southern Christianity, the Romanesque builders freely developed the art of sculpture. **1963** AUDEN *Dyer's Hand* 359 The *Mayflower* carried iconophobic dissenters.

iconographical, *a.* Add: (Further examples.)

1958 *Times Lit. Suppl.* 12 Dec. 716/3 The book is a *tour de force* in iconographical method. **1962** *Daily Tel.* 20 Nov. 17/4 The space between is filled entirely by Nicolas Untersteller's superb, sparkling glass, dark red and blue in patterns that are both good abstracts and also tell an iconographical story. **1962** *Listener* 27 Dec. 1087/1 Parallel with the abundance and high quality of abstract art is a great deal of what one may call iconographical art. Let me remind you of a few names: Bacon, Balthus, Giacometti, Dubuffet, Asger Jorn, de Kooning.

So **iconogra·phically** *adv.*

1959 *Times* 17 Jan. 9/1 Iconographically they [paintings] are of great interest in relation to the usages of the Eastern Church.

iconography. Add: **2.** (Further examples.) Also *transf.*

1939 E. PANOFSKY *Stud. Iconology* i. 3 Iconography is that branch of the history of art which concerns itself with the subject matter or meaning of works of art, as opposed to their form. **1957** *Times Lit. Suppl.* 8 Nov. 680/1 The iconography of the watermark is a new aspect of the study of the migration of symbols at present so popular among art historians. **1960** *Listener* 8 Dec. 1041/2 The fashion of so-called 'iconography' at this moment has produced many cumbersome interpretations. **1962** *Ibid.* 27 Sept. 473/2 The iconography of a work of art is its dramatic structure seen in terms of characters, situations, and images that are related to a specific religious, social, or historical context. **1969** *Ibid.* 17 Apr. 533/2 Now people are interested in iconography, in saying what the subject represents, and offering infinitely ingenious interpretations of every picture. **1970** *Oxf. Compan. Art* 555/1 *Iconography*, a term in art history..extended in the 20th c. to cover the whole descriptive investigation of the subject matter of the figurative arts... Iconography..studies the development of the themes which artists use, for instance the transformation of the images of planets in astrological manuscripts, the rise of genre painting, the origins of still life, and the use of political satire.

iconological, *a.* (Further examples.)

1938 E. PANOFSKY in *Jrnl. Warburg Inst.* I. 23 From the purely iconological point of view the Ottawa picture may be compared to the two Cassone panels. **1958** *Times Lit. Suppl.* 23 May 278/3 On the contrary, the uniquely valuable and fruitful idea embodied in the Warburgian programme is the iconological idea; it is of universal application, and thus of service to all the special historical disciplines mentioned.

iconology. 1. (Further examples.)

1939 M. PRAZ *Stud. 17th-Cent. Imagery* I. iv. 184 Iconology during the period of enlightenment in philosophy and in literature, takes the place held by emblematics during the age of the Jesuits and the Baroque. **1949** WELLEK & WARREN *Theory of Lit.* xi. 125 The conceptual and symbolic meanings of works of art ('Iconology'). **1956** E. PANOFSKY *Meaning in Visual Arts* 31 The discovery and interpretation of these 'symbolical' values (which are often unknown to the artist himself and may even emphatically differ from what he consciously intended to express) is the object of what we may call 'iconology' as opposed to 'iconography'. **1958** *Times Lit. Suppl.* 23 May 278/3 If the Institute were not called after its founder, *tout court*, and had to find a compendious title to describe its activities, it might surely best be called an Institute of Iconology, as being a body dedicated to the study and interpretation of historical processes through visual images.

iconometer (əikŏnǫ·mĭtəɪ). *Photogr.* [f. ICONO- + -METER.] (See quots.)

1894 E. L. WILSON *Cycl. Photogr.* 194/1 *Iconometer*, view-meter; a pocket instrument which quickly indicates what kind of objective to use..from a given standpoint, or..the standpoint suitable for a view with a given objective. **1918** *Photo-Miniature* Mar. 25 *Iconometer*, a view-meter of 'direct-vision' pattern, i.e., consisting of an open frame with an eyehole or lens fixed behind it. **1919** *Brit. Jrnl. Photogr. Alm.* 244 A view-meter, or iconometer, is a separate accessory for ascertaining the picture produced by any given lens and size of plate.

iconometry (əikŏnǫ·mĭtri). [ad. F. *iconométrie* (A. Laussedat 1892, in *Ann. du Conservatoire d. Arts et Métiers* IV. 374), f. Gr. εἰκονο- ICONO-: see -METRY.] The process of taking measurements from photographs of an area and using them to make a map or survey of it.

1898 *Ann. Rep. U.S. Coast & Geodetic Survey 1897* II. 628 Iconometry means the measuring of dimensions of objects from their perspectives ('Bildmesskunst'), and this term could well be applied to those graphic constructions which serve to convert perspectives into horizontal projections; iconometry is the reverse of perspective drawing. **1923** D. CLARK *Plane & Geodetic Surveying* II. vi. 244 In plotting the map, the distances and elevations

required must be obtained from the perspective dimensions on the photographs. The process—termed iconometry—is therefore the reverse of perspective drawing. **1934** R. E. DAVIS et al. *Surveying* (ed. 2) xxvii. 787 The iconometry of aerial photographic surveying is much less accurate than that of terrestrial work.

Hence **iconome·tric, -me·trical** *adjs.*, employing or forming part of this process; **iconome·trically** *adv.*, in or by means of iconometry.

1898 *Ann. Rep. U.S. Coast & Geodetic Surv. 1897* II. 631 The correct orientation of the picture traces forms the most important part of iconometric plotting. *Ibid.* 630 If..two different perspectives..of the same object..are given, the dimensions and the position of the object with reference to the two stations may be determined iconometrically. **1906** J. A. FLEMER *Elem. Treat. Phototopogr. Methods* i. 6 It is not easy to make free-hand sketches of landscapes geometrically accurate enough to be used iconometrically in place of the landscapes. *Ibid.* vi. 121 (*heading*) Graphical iconometrical plotting methods. **1934** R. E. DAVIS et al. *Surveying* (ed. 2) xxvii. 775 (*heading*) Iconometric interpretation of the stereoscopic view. **1944** A. L. HIGGINS *Higher Surveying* iii. 219 [Photogrammetry.] Office Work. Apart from the preparation of negatives and prints, this consists of (1) plotting the triangulation, (2) iconometrical plotting, and (3) topographical mapping.

iconoscope (əikǭ·nŏskōup). [f. ICONO- + -SCOPE.] †**1.** [a. F. *iconoscope* (E. Javal 1866, in *Compt. Rend.* LXIII. 927).] (See quot. 1890.) *Obs.*

1866 *Chem. News* 7 Dec. 273/2 (*heading*) On a new instrument, the iconoscope, intended to give relief to plain images examined with the two eyes. **1890** BILLINGS *Med. Dict.* 678/2 *Iconoscope*, an instrument for suppressing binocular parallax. It makes real objects appear flat like pictures, but..gives to flat pictures a relief like that obtained by a monocular view, by removing those binocular sensations that keep the observer reminded of the flatness of the picture. It may be described briefly as a small telestereoscope reversed. **1900** C. WEILAND tr. *Tscherning's Physiol. Optics* xxiii. 321 The iconoscope of Javal resembles somewhat an inverted telestereoscope. *Ibid.*, Looking through the iconoscope the relief is more marked than when simply closing one eye.

2. A kind of television camera tube (now little used) in which the target plate that receives the image consists of a mosaic of photoemissive material on an insulating sheet that is backed with a conducting sheet, the video signal being obtained from the variation in the current flowing to or from this latter sheet as the mosaic is scanned with an electron beam.

The term was registered in the U.S.A. as a trade name in 1935 but it is now a generic term in the public domain.

1933 V. K. ZWORYKIN in *Jrnl. Inst. Electr. Engin.* LXXIII. 437/1 The device has been named the 'iconoscope', and it consists of a vacuum tube containing an electron-emitting gun and a photo-sensitive surface of a unique type. This photo-sensitive surface is scanned by an electron beam from the gun, which serves as a type of inertialess commutator. **1935** [see *DEFINITION 5 c]. **1953** AMOS & BIRKINSHAW *Television Engin.* I. iv. 68 Iconoscope camera tubes have given satisfactory results in television services over a number of years. **1961** G. MILLERSON *Technique Television Production* 50 A familiar effect with the iconoscope camera-tube, shading appears as gradual darkening or lightening over parts of the picture. **1966** *McGraw-Hill Encycl. Sci. & Technol.* XIII. 464/1 The iconoscope was used in early live television broadcasting but is now used only in motion picture reproduction... The vidicon is replacing the iconoscope as a film reproducer.

b. Applied to a modified form of the instrument intended as an infra-red telescope or detector.

1946 *Electronic Engin.* XVIII. 317 Another instrument used by the Germans was an infra-red iconoscope. It does not differ in general principle from the iconoscope used in television, the only difference being in the photosensitive layer. Whereas in television, a mosaic layer..is used, the infra-red instrument uses a semiconducting layer, the resistance of which changes on irradiation. **1949** A. R. WEYL *Guided Missiles* 97 The final installation would have been the 'Electric Eye' iconoscope target-finding device of Rambauske which was, however, not operationally developed when the War came to an end.

iconotropy (əikǒnǭ·trŏpi). [f. Gr. εἰκών, εἰκον- ICON + τροπή a turn, turning: cf. TROPE.] The misinterpretation by one cult of the icons, etc., of another (earlier) cult, so as to bring the beliefs and myths depicted into accord with those of the later cult. Hence **iconotro·pic** *a.*, of a myth, tradition, etc., suggestive of an origin in such a misinterpretation.

1946 R. GRAVES *King Jesus* 355 A similar technique of misinterpretation—let us call it iconotropy—was adopted in ancient Greece as a means of confirming Olympian religious myths at the expense of the Minoan ones which they superseded... In iconotropy the icons are not defaced or altered, but merely interpreted in a sense hostile to the original cult. *Ibid.* 356 The story of Lot and the Sodomites suggests the same ancient icon from which Herodotus derived his iconotropic account of the sacking of the Temple of the Love-goddess Astarte at Ascalon by the Scythians. **1955** —— *Greek Myths* I. 21 If some myths are baffling at first sight, this is often because the mythographer has accidentally or deliberately misinterpreted a sacred picture or dramatic rite. I have called such a process 'iconotropy'... Greek myth teems with iconotropic instances. **1958** *Observer* 7 Sept. 18/8 Professor Webster appears to subscribe to Mr. Robert Graves's theory of iconotropy, or the misinterpretation of myths from visual sources.

icos-, icosa-, icosi-. Add: **b.** In *Chem.* (usu. spelt **eicos-**) denoting the presence in a molecule of twenty atoms of some element (usu. carbon). [App. first so used in G. *eikosylen* (Lippmann and Hawliczek 1879, in *Ber. d. Deut. Chem. Ges.* XII. 72).] So **ei·cosane** [-ANE 2 b], a hydrocarbon, $C_{20}H_{42}$, of the paraffin (alkane) series, esp. the normal isomer; **eicosa·nic** *a.*, in *eicosanic acid*, = **eicosanoic* adj.; **eicosano·ic** *a.*, in *eicosanoic acid*, a saturated fatty acid, $C_{19}H_{39}COOH$, of which the normal isomer (also called arachidic acid) is a waxy solid present in small amounts in many natural oils and fats; **eicosenic** (-ī·nik) *a.*, in *eicosenic acid* [tr. G. *eikosensäure* (M. Bodenstein 1894, in *Ber. d. Deut. Chem. Ges.* XXVIII. 3403)], = **eicosenoic* adj.; **eicoseno·ic** *a.*, in *eicosenoic acid*, an unsaturated fatty acid, $C_{19}H_{37}COOH$, of which one isomer, 9-eicosenic acid (gadoleic acid), is a minor constituent of many fish oils and another, 11-eicosenic acid, occurs in the wax of certain plant seeds; **eicoso·ic** *a.*, in *eicosoic acid*, = **eicosanoic* adj.

1889 G. McGOWAN tr. *Bernthsen's Text-bk. Org. Chem.* 34 (*table*) $C_{20}H_{42}$. Eicosane. **1948** A. W. RALSTON *Fatty Acids* xi. 882 The following are the melting and boiling points which have been reported for the higher normal saturated hydrocarbons: nonadecane, $C_{19}H_{40}$, 32°, —; eicosane, $C_{20}H_{42}$, 38°, $b_{0.5}$ 148°; [etc.]. **1966** *Nomencl. Org. Chem.* (I.U.P.A.C.) (ed. 2) A. 6 The first four saturated unbranched acyclic hydrocarbons are called methane, ethane, propane and butane. Names of the higher members of this series consist of a numerical prefix and the termination '-ane'... Examples:..6 Hexane. 7 Heptane... 20 Eicosane. **1923** *Chem. Abstr.* XVII. 2560 Normal eicosanic acid is found in nature in the oil of *Nephelium lappaceum* J. as a glyceride. **1953** HEILBRON & BUNBURY *Dict. Org. Compounds* (rev. ed.) II. 464, *n*-Eicosanic Acid (Arachidic acid, *n*-nonadecane-1-carboxylic acid, eicosoic acid, eicosanoic acid). **1924** *Chem. Abstr.* XVIII. 4318/2 (Index), Eicosanoic acid. *See* Arachidic acid. **1948** A. W. RALSTON *Fatty Acids* i. 44 The vegetable oils generally contain less than 1% of eicosanoic acid. *Ibid.*, Coffee bean oil contains 2·11% of eicosanoic acid..and peanut oils from 3 to 4%. **1895** *Jrnl. Chem. Soc.* LXVIII. I. 127 Icosenic acid, $C_{20}H_{38}O_2$, is formed when behenolic acid is heated with fused caustic potash at 250–270°. **1953** HEILBRON & BUNBURY *Dict. Org. Compounds* (rev. ed.) II. 464 Δ^{10}-Eicosenic Acid (Eicosenoic acid). **1936** *Jrnl. Chem. Soc.* 1755 The fatty matter present in the seeds of *Simmondsia californica* Nutt. ..is a mixture of wax-esters, and not glycerides... The chief acid is $\Delta^{11:12}$-eicosenoic. **1951** A. W. JOHNSON et al. in E. H. Rodd *Chem. Carbon Compounds* IA. ix. 640, 9-Eicosenoic acid, gadoleic acid, $CH_3(CH_2)_9CH{:}CH(CH_2)_7COOH$ is a common component of fish and marine animal oils such as herring and shark liver oil. **1954** E. W. ECKEY *Vegetable Fats & Oils* xiv. 435 Investigations made after eicosenoic acid had been isolated from rapeseed oil and shown to exist in substantial proportion in hare's ear mustard oil confirmed the presence of this C_{20} monoethenoic acid in rapeseed oil and indicated that it occurs generally in oils of the Cruciferae. **1923** *Chem. Abstr.* XVII. 4447/2 (Index), Eicosoic acid (eicosanic acid), *n*-. **1951** I. L. FINAR *Org. Chem.* ix. 144 Some still higher acids are found in waxes: arachidic (eicosoic), $C_{20}H_{40}O_2$ (m.p. 77°), behenic (docosoic), $C_{22}H_{44}O_2$ (m.p. 82°), [etc.].

icosidodecahedron. (Examples.)

1911 *Encycl. Brit.* XXII. 28/2 The icosidodecahedron..is a 32-faced solid, formed by truncating the vertices of an icosahedron so that the original faces become triangles. **1939** H. S. M. COXETER *Ball's Math. Recreations & Ess.* (ed. 11) v. 136 The compound of five cubes has the 30 facial planes of a triacontahedron. Reciprocally, the compound of five octahedra has the 30 vertices of an icosidodecahedron. **1972** *Science* 12 May 654 (*caption*) Icosidodecahedron, its first two stellations, and its final stellation.

ictal (i·ktăl), *a. Med.* [f. ICT(US + -AL.] Of, pertaining to, or caused by an ictus (sense *2 c).

1950 PENFIELD & RASMUSSEN *Cerebral Cortex of Man* ix. 161 The ictal paralysis of normal function passes over into postictal paralysis. **1968** SCHMIDT & WILDER *Epilepsy* ii. 35 Ictal emotional experience is frequent among patients with temporal lobe epilepsy.

ictas, ictus, varr. *IKTAS *sb. pl.*

ictero- (i·ktĕro), combining form of Gr. ἴκτερος jaundice, as in **i:cterogene·tic** (*rare*), **icteroge·nic** *adjs.*, causing jaundice.

1897 *Allbutt's Syst. Med.* IV. 38 This drug is the most notable of all icterogenetic poisons. **1903** DORLAND *Med. Dict.* (ed. 3) 331/1 Icterogenic. **1944** *Lancet* 16 Sept. 365/1 Icterogenic yellow fever vaccine. **1962** *Lancet* 19 May 1057/2 'The pill' should not be overlooked when the medicine-chest is scrutinised for potentially icterogenic drugs.

ictus. Add: **1.** Used of Old English verse.

1823 J. BOSWORTH *Elem. Anglo-Saxon Gram.* 246 [quoting J. J. Conybeare] The ear is satisfied, not by the number of syllables, but by the recurrence of the accent, or ictus, if one may call it so. **1888** A. H. TOLMAN in *Publ. Mod. Lang. Assoc.* III. 21 March..declares that 'the time from each ictus to the next is the same in any section'. **1953** F. P. MAGOUN in *Speculum* XXVIII. 458 The first down-beat or ictus in the off-verse does not here alliterate with the preceding on-verse.

2. c. A stroke, seizure, or fit. Also in some mod.L. phrases.

1890 GOULD *New Med. Dict.* 204/1 *Ictus*, a stroke or attack of disease coming without premonition. **1890** BILLINGS *Med. Dict.* I. 679/1 *Ictus sanguinis*, apoplexy. **1908** A. CHURCH *Dis. Nervous Syst.* 487 Especially severe attacks of tickling in the throat, arrest of respiration, unconsciousness, and epileptic attacks have been described as *ictus laryngeus*. **1931** I. S. WECHSLER *Textbk. Clin. Neurol.* (ed. 2) IV. 345 The clinical course [of apoplexy] may be conveniently divided into (1) the acute apoplectic stroke or ictus, and (2) the stage of paralysis. **1939** W. HAYMAKER tr. *Bing's Textbk. Nervous Dis.* xvii. 444 The most striking symptom of apoplectic stroke (*ictus apoplecticus*) is sudden loss of consciousness. **1961** *Lancet* 29 July 223/1 The conscious level chosen for stratification of patients in the trial was that at twenty-four hours after the ictus.

icy, *a.* Add: **4.** *icy-clear.*

1922 W. DE LA MARE *Down-adown-Derry* 93 Fleet-foot deer Lap of its waters icy-clear. **1925** BLUNDEN *Masks of Time* 41 Icy-clear The air of a mortal day shocks sense.

id² (id). *Psycho-analysis.* [A use of L. *id* it, as a rendering of G. *es* it, which was adopted by Freud (*Das Ich und das Es* (1923)) following its use in a similar sense by G. Groddeck (*Das Buch vom Es* (1923)).] The inherited instinctive impulses of the individual, forming part of the unconscious and, in Freudian theory, interacting in the psyche with the ego and the super-ego. Also *attrib.*

[**1917** FREUD *Briefe* 5 June (1960) 316 [*To Georg Groddeck*] Ich muß Anspruch auf Sie erheben, muß behaupten, daß Sie ein prächtiger Analytiker sind, der das Wesen der Sache unverlierbar erfaßt hat. Wer erkennt, daß Übertragung und Widerstand die Drehpunkte der Behandlung sind, der gehört nun einmal rettungslos zum wilden Heer. Ob er das 'Ubw' [*sc.* Unbewußte, 'unconscious'] auch 'Es' nennt, das macht keinen Unterschied.] **1924** J. RIVIERE et al. tr. *Freud's Coll. Papers* II. xxi. 250 The essay..describes the various allegiances the ego owes, its mediate position between the outer world and the id, and its struggles to serve all its masters at one and the same time. [*Translators' note.*] To translate the German '*es*', which means 'it' and thus implies the impersonality of the mind apart from its ego, the Latin '*id*' has been selected. *Ibid.* 254 Keep in mind this dissection of the mental apparatus that I have proposed, namely, into ego, super-ego and id. **1927** J. RIVIERE tr. *Freud's Ego & Id* ii. 27 We need feel no hesitation in finding a place for Groddeck's discovery in the fabric of science. I propose to take it into account..by following Groddeck in giving to the other part of the mind, into which this entity [*sc.* the ego] extends and which behaves as though it were Ucs [*sc.* unconscious], the name of Id (Es). [*Note*] Groddeck himself no doubt followed the example of Nietzsche, who habitually used this grammatical term for whatever in our nature is impersonal and, so to speak, subject to natural law. **1942** *Essays & Stud.* XXVII. 12 Dreams..that fulfil the much darker wishes of the Id. **1943** H. READ *Educ. through Art* vi. 176 The super-ego is the direct representative of the unconscious, of the id, and hence the possibility, indeed, the inevitability, of a conflict with the ego. **1952** SHAFFER & LAZARUS *Fund. Concepts Clin. Psychol.* vi. 188 The forces which keep the id impulses in check as an adaptation to the pressures of the outside world comprise the ego. **1957** J. BRAINE *Room at Top* xxvi. 208 Roy, a quiet type normally, seemed to become, as Charles said, all Id when he'd had one over the eight. **1961** R. W. LUNDIN *Personality* i. 21 The id is entirely unconscious, having no contact with reality except through the ego. One may liken the id to the primitive or animal nature of man. **1962** R. FINE *Freud* xi. 156 The id is the source of all drives, the reservoir of instincts. **1965** C. M. & S. GROSSMAN *Wild Analyst* xii. 109 It became clear, when the two books [*sc.* Groddeck's *Das Buch vom Es* and Freud's *Das Ich und das Es*] were translated, that it had been wise to distinguish between the 'Id' and the 'It', because Freud's concept of the Id, broadened as it was, was still not as broad as Groddeck's concept of the It. *Ibid.* 110 He [*sc.* Groddeck] gave Freud the Id as a gift—he, too, had borrowed it, from Nietzsche. **1967** R. R. GREENSON *Technique & Pract. Psychoanal.* I. i. 20 The combing of her hair stirred up repressed id impulses which brought her into conflict with her ego and super-ego... There were indications that her ego already was relatively depleted and her id lacked adequate discharge possibilities... As a consequence the fantasies mobilized by the hair combing increased the id tensions to a point where they flooded the infantile defenses of the ego and involuntary discharges took place, eventuating in acute symptom formation.

-id². Add: **b.** *Astr.* Added to the name of a constellation to form the name of a meteor in a shower having its radiant point in that constellation, as *Andromedid, Leonid, Lyraid, Perseid*; also more widely used (cf. *BIELID).

c. Used as a terminal element in the names of epic poems, as ÆNEID, *HERACLEID, THEBAÏD.

-id, *suffix*[5], in the nomenclature of mammalian teeth, used to indicate a structure forming part of a tooth in the lower jaw. Cf. *HYPOCONID, *HYPOCONULID.

1897 H. F. OSBORN in *Amer. Naturalist* XXXI. 1006 The suffix *-id* is employed arbitrarily to distinguish the elements of the lower molars from those of the upper. **1949** A. S. ROMER *Vertebr. Body* x. 304 The names of specific cones are formed by adding..prefixes..and, where necessary, by suffixes: -ul(e) indicates a minor cusp, and -id a lower jaw element.

Idæan (əidī·ăn), *a.* Also **Idaian.** [f. L. *Īdæus*, Gr. Ἰδαῖος (f. *Īdā*, *Īdē*, Ἴδη) + -AN.] Of, belonging to, or dwelling on Mount Ida, either (*a*) a mountain in Asia Minor near the ancient Troy; or (*b*) the chief mountain in Crete, the birthplace of Zeus.

1590 SPENSER *F.Q.* II. vii. 55 Here eke that famous golden Apple grew,..For which th'Idæan Ladies disagreed. *Ibid.* II. viii. 6 Like as Cupido on Idæan hill. *a* **1649** DRUMMOND OF HAWTHORNDEN *Works* (1711) 7/1 Trembling Roofs of Trees..Which make Idæan Woods in every Crook. **1810** SCOTT *Lady of Lake* I. xxvi. 32 Where Ellen's hand had taught to twine The ivy and Idæan vine. **1820** SHELLEY *Prometh. Unb.* III. i. 97 Pour forth heaven's wine, Idæan Ganymede, And let it fill the Dædal cups like fire. **1876** GLADSTONE *Homeric Synchr.* 123 Teucer, son of Scamander and of an Idaian Nymph. **1921** *Public Opinion* 17 June 568/3 The sad dwellers on the Idaean plain. **1970** *Oxf. Classical Dict.* (ed. 2) 540/1 *Idaean dactyls*, literally the Fingers of Ida, but whether the Phrygian or the Cretan Ida and whether their name refers to craftsmanship, dwarfish size, or something else, the ancients were in doubt.

id al-fitr: see *ID-UL-FITR.

Idalian (əidē·liăn), *a.* [f. L. *Idalius*: see -AN.] Of or belonging to the ancient town of Idalium in Cyprus, where Aphrodite was worshipped.

1599 NASHE *Lenten Stuffe* 34 Those debonaire Idalian nimphs and their spangled trappings. **1697** DRYDEN tr. *Virgil's Æneis* I. 955, I mean to plunge the Boy in pleasing Sleep, and, ravish'd, in Idalian Bow'rs to keep. **1799** T. CAMPBELL *Pleasures of Hope* II. 55 Some cottage-home.. With peace embosom'd in Idalian bow'rs! **1832** TENNYSON *Œnone* in *Poems* 60 Idalian Aphroditè oceanborn. **1928** J. H. MOZLEY tr. *Statius* I. 187 Golden Venus..on her way from the height of Eryx to the Idalian groves.

iddingsite (i·diŋzəit). *Min.* [f. the name of Joseph P. *Iddings* (1857–1920), American geologist + -ITE[1].] A red-brown to orange-brown silicate of calcium, magnesium, and trivalent iron having an indefinite composition and formed as an alteration product of olivine.

1893 A. C. LAWSON in *Bull. Dept. Geol. Univ. Calif.* I. 30 The common characteristic of all facies of these eruptive rocks is the presence, as a phenocryst of a mineral which..has received but little attention... The most extended and satisfactory note that has yet appeared regarding it is by Prof. J. P. Iddings... For this reason and also in recognition of Professor Iddings' eminent services to the science of petrography, it is proposed to name the mineral iddingsite. **1900** H. E. GREGORY in *Bull. U.S. Geol. Survey* No. 165. 181 This alteration product appears somewhat like the iddingsite found in the Californian teschenite. **1961** *Amer. Mineralogist* XLVI. 96 The optical homogeneity of many 'iddingsites' suggests that, even if the material is not to be regarded as a definite compound with relatively fixed chemical constitution, there is some structural control over the alteration process. **1966** W. A. DEER et al. *Introd. Rock-Forming Min.* 5 The compositions of both iddingsite and bowlingite show considerable variation.

iddy-umpty (idi,ɒ·mpti). Also **iddy-iddy-umpty.** Conventional verbal representation of the dots and dashes of the Morse code.

1906 *Punch* 24 Jan. 60/3 An 'Iddy Umpty' Idyll. **1914** *Daily Express* 15 Dec. 4/5 To see men practising the 'iddy-umpty', as they call it, with the back of a sheath-knife on the top of an empty tobacco-tin in lieu of a regulation 'dummy-key'. **1924** *Glasgow Herald* 23 June 10 For my sins of commission and of omission—as far as the worship of that fetish 'Iddy-Umpty' was concerned—I became for a time an inmate of the great signalling camp at Swanage. **1925** FRASER & GIBBONS *Soldier & Sailor Words* 126 *Iddy* (or *Itty*) *Umpty*, an expression first used in India in teaching the dot-and-dash Morse system to native troops. An 'Iddy Umpty' in that way came to be used as a term for a signaller.

-ide. Add: The use of this suffix has been greatly extended in organic chemistry, notably in the generic names of various kinds of naturally occurring compounds, as *GLYCOSIDE, *PEPTIDE, SACCHARIDE (qq.v.); it is used *spec.* to form the names of glycosides from those of the corresponding sugars (as *galactoside* from *galactose*, *furanoside* from *furanose*).

2. *Chem.* Used to form *LANTHANIDE and later (by analogy) *ACTINIDE, signifying a similarity in properties to lanthanum and actinium, respectively.

idea, *sb.* Add: **4.** *big idea*: the purpose, intent. Freq. in ironic phr. *What's* (or *what is*) *the big idea?* orig. *U.S.*

1908 G. H. LORIMER *Jack Spurlock* vii. 151 That's not the Big Idea, I know; it's the idiotic one, but the market for idiocy is unlimited. **1917** R. W. LARDNER *Gullible's Travels* (1926) iii. 83 Then we done a little spoonin' and then I ast her what was the big idear. **1927** A. P. HERBERT *Plain Jane* 52 But now I'm not wanted no more Unless it's for scrubbing a floor, And if that's what a person is for—Well, what's the Big Idea? **1933** M. LOWRY *Ultramarine* v. 220 What's the big idea not telling me before? **1937** A. CHRISTIE *Death on Nile* I. i. 35 You're crazy! What's the big idea? **1951** M. MCLUHAN *Mech. Bride* 43/1 Latch onto our big idea index for deep consolation? **1962** P. GREGORY *Like Tigress at Bay* vii. 76 Jill entered, her face pale. 'What was the big idea?'

9. b. *to have no idea*: (*a*) not to anticipate or expect (a situation or occurrence); (*b*) to be unable to comprehend; usu. in phr. *you have no idea.*

1852 E. RUSKIN *Let.* 17 Apr. in M. Lutyens *Effie in Venice* (1965) II. 298 In two days he got it done and they are grateful you have no idea. **1866** [in Dict.]. **1916** 'TAFFRAIL' *Pincher Martin* vii. 114 He's that conceited, you've no idea.

c. Colloq. phr. *to get* (or *have*) *ideas* (*into one's head*): to conceive notions of a particular kind, usu. undesirable or harmful; *spec.* to entertain a notion or intention of being rebellious, violent, etc.

c **1848** F. A. KEMBLE *Let.* in *Rec. Later Life* (1882) III. 322 A young boy..brought up in a girl's convent, and taken out for a week, during which he..sups and gets tipsy at the mess, and, in short, 'gets ideas' of all sorts. **1932** H. C. WYLD *Universal Dict. Eng. Lang.*, *To get ideas into one's head*, to cherish illusions. **1935** J. C. SQUIRE *Reflections & Memories* 10 Babus would get ideas into their heads, but the Mutiny had taught its lesson and the redcoat had the situation well in hand. **1941** I. BAIRD *He rides Sky* 146 That's the second happy couple I've seen busted up in a month and it's cured me if I ever had ideas. I'd no more marry with a war on than jump over the moon. **1955** W. C. GAULT *Ring around Rosa* vii. 82 Don't get any ideas, Brock Callahan. There are times when I simply—I mean, there's a definite therapeutical need for some form of release in a society as hectic as ——. *Ibid.* xiii. 156 Don't get any ideas, Callahan. This is an easy trigger.

d. Used after a possessive to denote a person's conception of an ideal, typical, or adequate example of the person or thing specified.

1903 G. B. SHAW *Man & Superman* III. 111 Is that your idea of a woman's mind? I call it cynical and disgusting materialism. **1907** —— *John Bull's Other Island* I. 7 Now thats my poor English idea of a whisky and soda. **1919** E. O'NEILL *In Zone* in *Moon of Caribbees* (1923) 22 If this is your idea of a joke I'll have to confess it's a bit too thick for me to enjoy. **1933** —— *Ah, Wilderness!* (1934) I. 21 Gosh, he's always reading now. It's not my idea of having a good time in vacation. **1969** *Listener* 10 July 39/3 He would not be everyone's idea of a military dictator.

e. An idea worthy of consideration or capable of realization; a possibility; usu. in phr. *it's* (or *that's*) *an idea. colloq.*

1914 G. B. SHAW *Misalliance* 27 Thats an idea. Thats a new idea. I believe I ought to have made Johnny an author. **1919** —— *Inca of Perusalem* in *Heartbreak House* 197 Thats an idea. I will. **1942** A. CHRISTIE *Body in Library* i. 19 It *might* be. It's an idea, Jane. **1973** K. GILES *File on Death* i. 16 'I suppose I can take my Sergeant.'..'It might be an idea...Your Sergeant might wheedle his way where Chief Inspectors fear to tread.'

12. *idea-monger*; **idea(s) man,** a creative, inventive, or ingenious man.

1840 H. REEVE tr. *A. de Tocqueville's Democracy in Amer.* III. I. xiv. 123 For some few great authors..you may reckon thousands of idea-mongers. **1909** *Englishwoman* Apr. 305 Ibsen..was not merely an ideamonger, but a dramatist. **1923** *Glasgow Herald* 25 Jan. 4/2 Mr. Wells is a prolific idea-monger. **1938** 'E. QUEEN' *Four of Hearts* (1939) i. 10 You're an idea man, and that's what they pay off on in Hollywood. **1940** *Ann. Reg. 1939* 363 Bryan Wallace was appointed Ideas Man to the Government. **1954** KOESTLER *Invis. Writing* xxxi. 333 He looked like the nonchalant impresario and idea-man of the great Comintern variety show. **1958** [see **copywriter*]. **1960** *Guardian* 16 Nov. 7/3 David Bean, the ideas man, has specialized in exposing traps laid for consumers. **1967** *Ibid.* 17 Feb. 8/5 Dilettante ideas-men like Teilhard de Chardin.

ideal, *a.* and *sb.* Add: **A.** *adj.* **1. c.** *Sociol.* **ideal type** [ad. G. *idealtypus* (M. Weber 1922, in *Grundriss d. Sozialökonomik* I. i. 3), f. IDEAL *a.* + *typus* TYPE *sb.*[1]], a hypothetical construct made up of the salient features or elements of a social phenomenon, or generalized concept, in order to facilitate comparison and classification of what is found in operation. Also (with hyphen) *attrib.* Hence **ideal-typical** *a.*, of or pertaining to an ideal type; **ideal typology,** the concept of ideal types.

1928 P. A. SOROKIN *Contemp. Sociol. Theories* xii. 677 The outlined 'spirit of modern capitalism' is an example of one of the 'ideal types' of Max Weber. **1936** WIRTH & SHILS tr. *Mannheim's Ideology & Utopia* iv. 189 The pure types..of the utopian mind are constructions only in so far as they are conceived of as *ideal-types*. *Ibid.* 204 Max Weber always insisted that his general typology was created in order to characterize ideal-typical tendencies, and not immediately perceivable unique constellations. **1947** HENDERSON & PARSONS tr. *Weber's Theory Social & Econ. Organiz.* I. i. 84 As a type ('ideal type') which has the merit of clear understandability and lack of ambiguity. **1949** R. K. MERTON *Social Theory* xiv. 329 The Puritan ethic, as an ideal-typical expression of the value-attitudes basic to ascetic Protestantism generally, so canalized the interests of seventeenth-century Englishmen. **1962** T. B. BOTTOMORE *Sociol.* ii. 33 Weber's exposition of his 'ideal type' method. **1964** GOULD & KOLB *Dict. Social Sci.* 311/2 *Ideal-type analysis* denotes a method of sociological analysis associated with the name of M. Weber. **1964** I. L. HOROWITZ *New Sociol.* 42 Accounts of history that..were at best 'ideal-typologies' with strong subjective biases. *Ibid.* 456 The idealized or ideal-typical individual entrepreneur as against the political collectivity.

2. b. *ideal language* (Philos.): a supposed language which would mirror the world perfectly (cf. **logically perfect language*).

1922 B. RUSSELL in tr. *Wittgenstein's Tractatus* Introd. 8 The whole function of language is to have meaning, and it only fulfils this function in proportion as it approaches to the ideal language which we postulate. **1944** M. BLACK in P. A. Schilpp *Philos. B. Russell* 251 The 'ideal language' is, by definition, the symbolism which would be entirely free from the philosophical defects which Russell claims to find in ordinary language. **1953** G. E. M. ANSCOMBE tr. *Wittgenstein's Philos. Investigations* I. § 81 It may look as if what we were talking about were an *ideal* language. **1963** R. CARNAP in P. A. Schilpp *Philos. R. Carnap* 29 When we found in Wittgenstein's book statements about 'the language', we interpreted them as referring to an ideal language; and this meant for us a formalized symbolic language. **1964** M. BLACK *Compan. to Wittgenstein's Tractatus* xx. 133 In this section W. seems to be subscribing to the ideal of an 'ideal language'. But cf. 5.5563*a* (ordinary language is perfectly in order). **1967** *Encycl. Philos.* VII. 361 The frequently recurring project of an ideal language is to be found for the first time in the very first extant treatise on language. **1973** A. KENNY *Wittgenstein* iv. 70 In an ideal language,..to each element of the propositional sign would correspond a single object in the world.

4. b. *ideal construction* (Philos.): a mental conception formed by abstracting properties found in experience and recombining or developing them; the process of forming such a conception.

1874 G. H. LEWES *Foundation of Creed* I. 288 Hume did not clearly understand that Science is essentially an ideal construction very far removed from a real transcript of facts. **1877** —— *Physical Basis of Mind* I. i. 8 This unity is only recognised in an *ideal construction* which lets drop all concrete differences. *Ibid.* III. i. 314 Science.. is the systematisation of Experience under the forms of ideal constructions. **1883** F. H. BRADLEY *Princ. Logic* I. ii. 75 Ideal constructions connected, by an inference through identity of quality, with the real that appears in present perception. **1890** W. JAMES *Princ. Psychol.* I. xiii. 533 We have a *conception* of absolute sameness,.. but this..is an ideal construction got by following a certain direction of serial increase to its maximum supposable extreme. **1901** G. F. STOUT *Man. Psychol.* (ed. 2) IV. vi. § 7. 531 The external world as an ideal construction is a social product. **1917** J. GIBSON *Locke's Theory of Knowledge* iv. 78 The nature of ideal construction as the discovery of possible alternatives admitted by the nature of some universal. **1946** *Mind* LV. 153 Suppose, however, that Euclidean points are ideal constructions.

6. b. *Geom.* [ad. F. *idéal*, introduced in this sense by J. V. Poncelet (*Traité des Propriétés proj. des Figures* (1822) I. ii. §§ 50 ff.).] Having no proper existence in real Euclidean geometry as the thing so designated, but introduced into projective or complex geometry in order to do away with what would otherwise be exceptions to generalizations; chiefly in *ideal point*, the single point (at infinity) at which two parallel lines are regarded as intersecting; similarly *ideal line*, *plane*, the single line (or plane) at infinity that is regarded as containing all the ideal points (or lines) of a plane (or of space).

1879 *Encycl. Brit.* X. 389/1 We may say that all points at infinity in a line *appear* to us as one, and may be replaced by a single 'ideal' point. **1885** C. LEUDESDORF tr. *Cremona's Elem. Projective Geom.* xxi. 226 The segment *HH'* has been called an ideal chord of the conic... Accepting this definition we may say that a diameter contains the middle points of all chords, real and ideal, which are parallel to the conjugate diameter. **1937** B. C. PATTERSON *Projective Geom.* i. 4 Such considerations lead us to assume the existence, in each plane, of one and only one ideal line. It is the locus of all the ideal points of the plane, and it is also the line of intersection of the plane with all parallel planes. *Ibid.* 5 We assume..the existence of an ideal plane of space, the locus of all ideal points and ideal lines of space. **1962** W. T. FISHBACK *Projective & Euclidean Geom.* iv. 32 We created the projective plane by adding ideal points and an ideal line to the Euclidean plane.

7. ideal case, one perfect or supremely excellent of its kind; **ideal copy** *Bibliogr.*, the most complete and perfect copy possible of an issue of a printed book, as properly described in a descriptive bibliography from the examination and analysis of multiple particular copies; **ideal fluid,** a hypothetical fluid that has no viscosity (no internal friction) and is incompressible; **ideal gas,** a hypothetical gas

(which actual gases approach more or less closely in their behaviour) for which the product of the pressure and the volume (of a given mass) is proportional to its absolute temperature; **ideal home,** used, esp. in titles as *Ideal Home Exhibition, Ideal Home Magazine,* in the sense 'a well-designed functional house (and its contents)'; **ideal observer** *Philos.* (see quot. 1957); **ideal state,** an imaginary perfectly constituted political community, harmonious and stable; **ideal utilitarianism,** in ethics, any form of utilitarianism which takes other intrinsic goods besides pleasure as ultimate ends, together constituting an ideal end; so **ideal utilitarian,** an adherent of ideal utilitarianism; also as *attrib. phr.*, of or pertaining to such a theory.

1847 W. WHEWELL *Philos. Inductive Sci.* (ed. 2) XI. v. 49 A body left to itself will move on with unaltered velocity;..(taking this as our Ideal Case) we find that all actual cases are intelligible. **1961** E. NAGEL *Struct. of Sci.* xiii. 463 A..device commonly employed in the natural sciences is to formulate a law for a so-called 'ideal case'... For example, Galileo's law for freely falling bodies is formulated for bodies moving in a vacuum. **1949** F. BOWERS *Princ. Bibliogr. Descr.* ii. 113 An *ideal copy* is a book which is complete in all its leaves as it ultimately left the printer's shop in perfect condition and in the complete state that he considered to represent the final and most perfect state of the book...[*Footnote*] Nothing is invented in the description of an ideal copy. Instead, all the evidence to be gained from the examination of numbers of copies is analyzed..in order to discover what was the actual most perfect form of the book achieved by the printer within an issue. **1952** J. CARTER *ABC for Bk.-Collectors* 102 Though it is possible for an individual example of the book in question to conform to it, the 'ideal copy' is a sort of Platonic archetype, exhibiting the final intention of the author, publisher and printer at the completion of printing, in so far as this is capable of being established. **1969** E. W. PADWICK *Bibliogr. Method* iii. 29 Partly because each library is mainly concerned with its own collection, and partly because of the extreme rarity of many incunabula, bibliographical descriptions of these works are based more often than not on the examination of works in a single collection and not on the characteristics of an ideal copy. **1972** P. GASKELL *New Introd. Bibliogr.* 321 A bibliography based on analytical techniques is not the same thing as a catalogue of particular books... Indeed it does not describe particular books but ideal copies of its subjects, following the examination of as many actual copies as possible of each one. **1857** THOMSON & JOULE in *Proc. R. Soc.* VIII. 556 If a solid..be carried uniformly through a perfect liquid. [*Note*] That is, as we shall call it for brevity, an ideal fluid, perfectly incompressible and perfectly free from mutual friction among its parts. **1948** V. L. STREETER *Fluid Dynamics* i. 6 Many conclusions concerning the motion of a solid through an ideal fluid are applicable with slight modification to the motion of an airship through the air or to the motion of a submarine through the ocean. **1891** G. KAMENSKY tr. *Mendeléeff's Princ. Chem.* I. ii. 139 For a so-called perfect (ideal) gas, or for considerable variations of density, the elementary expression $pv = Ra(t+\alpha t)$, or $pv = R(273+t)$ should be accepted. **1948** GLASSTONE *Textbk. Physical Chem.* (ed. 2) iii. 192 For a given mass of an ideal gas at constant pressure, therefore,..the volume is proportional to the absolute temperature. This relationship..is the basis of an ideal gas scale of temperature. *Ibid.*, Instead of defining an ideal gas as one obeying the laws of Boyle and Gay-Lussac, it may be described as one to which Boyle's law is applicable, and whose internal energy is independent of its volume at all temperatures; it can be shown.. that these two postulates include Gay-Lussac's law. **1913** R. FRY *Lett.* (1972) II. 371 You left a letter here from the Ideal Home Exhibition people asking Lewis to do decorations. *Ibid.* 373 I've not heard a word about the Ideal Home. Has it been a success..? **1925** A. HUXLEY *Those Barren Leaves* I. iv. 41 Agreeing..was a labour-saving device..a necessity in this Ideal Home. **1935** *Burlington Mag.* Jan. 3/2 The plans rather suggest an Ideal Home Exhibition. **1967** K. GILES *Death in Diamonds* vi. 105 A big room furnished with a modernity which might be next year's Ideal Home. **1967** 'M. HUNTER' *Cambridgeshire Disaster* vi. 40 A baby grand piano..which gave a slightly Mayfairish touch of sophistication to the otherwise Ideal Homes format. **1969** *New Yorker* 29 Nov. 56/3 What d'you bet he considers it the Ideal Home? **1972** R. PERRY *Fall Guy* v. 86 The furniture wasn't out of Ideal Home..affording me no aesthetic pleasure whatsoever. **1952** R. FIRTH in *Philos. & Phenomenol. Research* XII. 317 (*title*) Ethical absolutism and the ideal observer. **1957** P. EDWARDS in Edwards & Pap *Mod. Introd. Philos.* 390 The..'ideal observer' theory of Adam Smith and others..maintains that 'X is good' can be translated into some such statement as 'If there were an omniscient, disinterested and dispassionate observer he would approve of X'. **1959** R. B. BRANDT *Ethical Theory* vii. 174 We must explain further the properties of the 'ideal observer'. **1971** T. D. CAMPBELL *Adam Smith's Sci. of Morals* vi. 128, I shall argue..that to present Smith's theory as a form of Ideal Observer theory is a mistake. **1972** J. RAWLS *Theory of Justice* § 30. 185 Suppose that the ideal observer is thought of as a perfectly sympathetic being. **1874** W. WALLACE tr. *Hegel's Logic* Prolegomena xix. p. cxlvi, The measure dominates the conception of Plato's ideal state. **1892** B. JOWETT tr. *Plato's Dialogues* (ed. 3) V. Index 442 Ideal state, the, difficulty of. **1901** R. L. NETTLESHIP *Lect. Republic of Plato* (ed. 2) vi. 131 An outline is given of the institutions of the ideal state. **1931** L. R. PALMER tr. *Zeller's Outl. Hist. Greek Philos.* II. iii. 126 The Syracusan Hermocrates was to describe the degeneration from the original ideal state to the present. **1946** A. GRAY *Socialist Tradition* iii. 63 The actual description of life in the ideal state—the social gadgets—may appear trivial and puerile. **1952** K. R. POPPER *Open Soc.* (ed. 2) I. iii. 21 In believing in such an ideal state which does not change, Plato deviates radically from the tenets of historicism. **1967** *Encycl. Philos.* VI. 330/2 In the *Republic*,..Plato delineates his famous Ideal State, or 'Callipolis'. **1970** J. PASSMORE *Perfectibility of Man* xii. 258 Kant looked forward..to an ideal State, or, in his later writings, to an 'ethical Commonwealth'. **1907** H. RASHDALL *Theory of Good & Evil* I. vii. 184 This view of ethics, which combines the utilitarian principle that Ethics must be teleological with a non-hedonistic view of the ethical end, I propose to call Ideal Utilitarianism. According to this view actions are right or wrong according as they tend to produce for all mankind an ideal end or good, which includes, but is not limited to, pleasure. **1930** W. D. ROSS *Right & Good* ii. 19 The theory of 'ideal utilitarianism', if I may for brevity refer so to the theory of Professor Moore. *Ibid.* 23 The 'ideal utilitarian' theory can only fall back on an opinion..that one of the goods is the greater. **1959** R. B. BRANDT *Ethical Theory* xiv. 355 Universal personal pluralism (often called 'ideal utilitarianism'). *Ibid.* xv. 385 Some ideal utilitarians (for example, Hastings Rashdall) think that qualities of character like veracity, sexual purity, and temperance have great intrinsic value. **1970** J. N. FINDLAY *Axiological Ethics* iii. 46 There is no reason why an ideal utilitarianism may not sometimes place so high a value on certain actions..as to let them outweigh all consequences.

B. *sb.* **1.** (Earlier example.)

1796 F. A. NITSCH *Gen. View Kant's Princ. concerning Man* 52 Materialism, Idealism, Spiritualism, and Scepticism, are merely Ideals, which can only be approached, but never reached.

3. *Math.* [a. G. *ideal* sb., introduced in this sense by R. Dedekind (in P. G. L. Dirichlet *Vorles. über Zahlentheorie* (ed. 2, 1871) Suppl. x. 452) after the adjectival use in *ideale zahl* ideal number (E. E. Kummer 1846, in *Ber. über die zur Bekanntmachung geeigneten Verh. d. K. Preuss. Akad. d. Wiss. zu Berlin* 87).] A subring that contains all products of the form *rx* and *xr*, where *r* and *x* are elements of the ring and of the subring, respectively; also called a *two-sided ideal*; *left* (or *right*) *ideal*, a subring that contains all products of the form *rx* (or *xr*).

1898 *Bull. Amer. Math. Soc.* IV. 228 The relation between Dedekind's ideals and Kronecker's forms is discussed. **1911** *Encycl. Brit.* XIX. 856/1 It is a fundamental theorem that every ideal can be resolved into the product of a finite number of prime ideals, and that this resolution is unique. **1937** A. A. ALBERT *Mod. Higher Algebra* (1938) xi. 253 Right ideals (right invariant subrings) are defined analogously, and we call $\mathfrak{M}$ an ideal (invariant subring) if it is both a right and a left ideal. When $\mathfrak{A}$ is commutative every right ideal is a left ideal so that every right or left ideal is an ideal. **1952** E. T. BELL *Math.* v. 80 The particular subvarieties of a ring called ideals have proved of great significance in the general theory of rings, particularly with regard to the structure or morphology of rings. Ideals entered modern algebra through the theory of algebraic numbers..in the 1870s, but it was only in the 1920s and 1930s that their deeper relevance for much of algebra and algebraic geometry was recognized. **1969** F. M. HALL *Introd. Abstr. Algebra* II. vii. 181 An important example of an ideal is the subring of multiples of *n* in the ring of integers. *Ibid.*, Even when *R* is commutative not all subrings are ideals.

idealistic, *a.* Add: **2.** *Sociol.* In the theory of P. A. Sorokin, a type of culture which is a synthesis of spiritual and material values. Cf. *IDEATIONAL *a.* 2 and *SENSATE *a.*

1937 [see *IDEATIONAL *a.* 2]. **1952** A. L. KROEBER *Nature of Culture* I. xviii. 165/2 These 'sensate', 'ideational', and 'idealistic' supersystems are not segments of cultures at all... They are essentially polar *qualities*. **1965** C. P. & Z. K. LOOMIS *Mod. Social Theories* vii. 446 European culture is classified as idealistic during the 12th to 14th centuries. **1967** T. PARSONS *Sociol. Theory & Mod. Soc.* IV. xii. 388 The idealistic pattern is conceived as intermediate between the two, not in the sense of a simple 'compromise', but rather of a synthesis which can achieve a harmonious balance between the two principal components.

ideate, *a.* **2.** Concerned with ideas as opp. to reality (cf. IDEA *sb.* 8).

1966 *New Statesman* 23 Sept. 434/3 A bad best-seller, its characters mere contrivances and its talk vacuously ideate. **1968** *Listener* 1 Aug. 149/1 It is not the absence of ideas but the absence of things..which most diminishes Williams's poems. He preached upon 'things' till it argued him ideate.

ideational, *a.* Add: **1.** (Later examples.)

1894 CREIGHTON & TITCHENER tr. *Wundt's Lect. Hum. & Animal Psychol.* xiii. 204 In both cases we are only dealing with a particular consequence of the principle of *ideational unity*. **1916** *Proc. Nat. Acad. Sci.* II. 631 Despite widespread interest in the evolution of reasoning, the comparative study of ideational behaviour has been neglected. **1958** *Times Lit. Suppl.* 12 Sept. 515/1 These regulators..are apprehended by, for instance, consciousness as 'archaic images' or 'ideational instincts'. **1970** *Jrnl. Gen. Psychol.* Oct. 144 The technique might differentiate more clearly for response style than for ideational content. **1971** J. Z. YOUNG *Introd. Study Man* xxxv. 489 It has also been called the 'area of ideational speech' or indeed 'word store'.

2. *Sociol.* A term used orig. by P. A. Sorokin (see quot. 1937) to describe a type of culture based on spiritual values and ideals, whose material needs are the minimum necessary to forward those ideals. (See also *IDEALISTIC *a.* 2 and *SENSATE *a.*)

1937 P. A. SOROKIN *Social & Cultural Dynamics* I. I. ii. 67 Of these two systems one may be termed *Ideational* culture, the other *Sensate*. *Ibid.* 68 Some [cultures] have contained a balanced synthesis of both pure types. This last I term the *Idealistic* type of culture. (It should not be confused with the Ideational.) **1944** H. P. FAIRCHILD *Dict. Sociol.* 148 *Ideational*,..a type of culture which exalts the spiritual above the material values. **1964** *Economist* 8 Aug. 563/1 Conservatism is not, like socialism, liberalism or democracy, an 'ideational' ideology but 'situational'. **1966** P. A. SOROKIN *Sociol. Theories Today* xi. 381 The phase of growth or 'spring' of Danilevsky–Spengler–Toynbee's civilizations is similar in several traits with Sorokin's ideational. **1970** G. A. & A. G. THEODORSON *Mod. Dict. Sociol.* 194 Rather than stressing the manipulation of the empirical world to improve the quality of life..the ideational culture emphasizes adjustment to the existing world.

ideationally (əidi,ēⁱ·ʃənăli), *adv.* [f. IDEATIONAL *a.* + -LY[2].] By means of ideation.

1890 W. JAMES *Princ. Psychol.* II. xix. 127 Under ordinary circumstances, the entire brain probably plays a part in draining any centre which may be ideationally active. **1910** R. R. RUSK in *Brit. Jrnl. Psychol.* III. 379 The dissociation of the perceptually excited elements of consciousness from the ideationally excited factors. **1952** *Mind* LXI. 350 The interpretation..relates it [*sc.* the sensation] ideationally to other items.

ideatum (əidi,ēⁱ·tə̆m). *Philos.* [mod.L., neut. of *ideātus*: see IDEATE *a.* and *sb.*] = IDEATE *sb.*

1708 BERKELEY *Works* (1948) I. 100 The distinction between Idea and Ideatum I cannot otherwise conceive than by making one the effect or consequence of Dream, rêverie, Imagination, the other of sense & the Constant laws of Nature. **1889** 'SCOTUS NOVANTICUS' *Metaphysica Nova et Vetusta* (ed. 2) 81 We are entitled to start with.. perfect equivalence between the idea and the ideatum. **1920** S. ALEXANDER *Space, Time & Deity* II. 84 The object ..of which we are conscious as an idea or ideatum. **1933** *Mind* XLII. 303 Here the relation between a mode-factor in one attribute and its correlate in the other attribute is the absolutely unique relation of an idea to its ideatum.

‖ **idée** (*ide*). The French word for 'idea' used in certain French phrases, as:

idée fixe (*ide fiks*): a fixed idea (see FIXED *ppl. a.* 2), an obsession.

1836 H. GREVILLE *Diary* 20 Feb. (1883) 88 The King.. has some *idée fixe* about marrying the Duke of Orleans. **1877** L. W. M. LOCKHART *Mine is Thine* (1878) I. vii, At all events, the attraction of the heart would require to be something out of the common run if it were to subdue this *idée fixe*. **1922** JOYCE *Ulysses* 245, I am sure he has an *idée fixe*, Haines said. **1941** AUDEN *New Year Let.* II. 29 Prefer our idées fixes to be True of a fixed Reality. **1953** C. DAY LEWIS *Italian Visit* ii. 28 Then fast, faster Drawn by the magnet of his *idée fixe*, Head down, tail up, he's charging the horizon. **1965** D. LODGE *Brit. Mus. is falling Down* viii. 133 'What's wrong?' Adam complained. 'Isn't everyone entitled to his *idée fixe?*' **1973** 'M. INNES' *Appleby's Answer* vi. 60 Not an *idée fixe* of mine... Jack of all trades, you might say. **1974** *Times Lit. Suppl.* 15 Feb. 162/1 Impatience in the search makes it fatally easy to freeze a hypothesis into a rigid system of *idées fixes*.

idée maîtresse (*ide mẹ̄trẹ̄s*): a leading idea (cf. *master-idea* s.v. MASTER *sb.*[1] 25 b).

1939 *Times Lit. Suppl.* 16 Dec. 729/1 Mystified by M. Romains's apparent reluctance to confide his *idée maîtresse*, one could not always avoid an injured and carping note of appreciation. **1958** *Listener* 7 Aug. 193/2 The *idée maîtresse* of his outlook. **1966** *Ibid.* 6 Oct. 500/2 The leading idea, the *idée maîtresse*, of the Enlightenment.

idée mère (*ide mẹ̄r*): = *mother idea* (s.v. MOTHER *sb.*[1] 16 a).

1841 MILL *Let.* Aug. in *Works* (1963) XIII. 483, I think you should dwell much more..on the *idée mère* of..the article. **1863** —— *Utilitarianism* v. 69 The *idée mère*, the primitive element, in the formation of the notion of justice, was conformity to law. **1908** H. JAMES *Awkward Age* Preface p. viii, They especially emphasise that truth of the vanity of the *a priori* test of what an *idée-mère* may have to give. **1916** G. SAINTSBURY *Peace of Augustans* i. 5 Dryden..had too much of the divine freedom and variety of poetry in him to follow up the *idées mères* of this couplet. **1931** R. FRY *Lett.* (1972) II. 653 It's a remarkable book even if it's hypothetical and he may have got an *idée mère*.

idée reçue (*ide rəsü*): a generally accepted notion or opinion (cf. RECEIVED *ppl. a.* 1).

1937 E. BOWEN in *New Statesman* 13 Mar. 418/1 He, too, lines up *idées reçues*. **1957** E. WILSON *Piece of my Mind* vii. 105 The foolish old *idée reçue* that Greek literature is the real thing and Latin a second-rate imitation. **1964** *Listener* 9 Jan. 92/2, I sympathized with his dismay that he should be considered right wing, because he did not accept left wing *idées reçues*. **1970** *Times* 23 Feb. 12/1 Your sort of pianist is always..unwilling to accept *idées reçues*, even when they come with most authoritative credentials. **1974** *Times Lit. Suppl.* 22 Mar. 303/2 It sweeps the *idées reçues* of sociologists, town planners and other rationalists into the dustbin.

idempotent, *a.* Also pronounced (əi:dĕmpōᵘ-tĕnt). Add def.: Of a quantity or element *a*: having the property that $a \times a = a$, where $\times$ represents multiplication or some other (specified) binary operation. Also applied to

an operator or set for which this is true for any element *a* and to statements expressing this fact. (Further examples.)

1937 A. A. ALBERT *Mod. Higher Algebra* (1938) iii. 88 A matrix *E* is called idempotent if $E^2 = E$. **1937** *Duke Math. Jrnl.* III. 629 We recall that $A \supset B$ if and only if $A = (A, B)$ and $B = [A, B]$, and that union and cross-cut are associative, commutative, and idempotent operations. **1940** W. V. QUINE *Math. Logic* 56 A binary mode of statement composition..is said to be..idempotent if ⌜$\phi \equiv .\phi\kappa\phi$⌝ is true for all statements ϕ. **1941** BIRKHOFF & MACLANE *Surv. Mod. Algebra* xi. 313 All of these except for the idempotent laws and the second distributive law correspond to familiar laws of arithmetic. **1941** *Mind* L. 274 The element is only idempotent with respect to the combining relation defined as the combining relation of the group. **1950** W. V. QUINE *Methods of Logic* (1952) § 1. 3 '*pp*' reduces to '*p*'. Conjunction is idempotent, to persist in the jargon. **1959** E. M. MCCORMICK *Digital Computer Primer* 181 It is further apparent..that $A + A = A$ and..that $A \times A = A$. These are sometimes referred to as the idempotent laws. **1967** A. GEDDES tr. *Dubreil & Dubreil-Jacotin's Lect. Mod. Algebra* i. 22 If every element of *E* is idempotent, the composition law is called idempotent and *E* is called an idempotent set.

B. *sb.* An idempotent element; also in more restricted use (see quot. 1958).

1941 BIRKHOFF & MACLANE *Surv. Mod. Algebra* i. 6 Prove that the following rules hold in any integral domain:..(h) the only 'idempotents' (that is, elements *x* satisfying $xx = x$) are 0 and 1. **1958** S. KRAVETZ tr. *Zassenhaus's Theory of Groups* (ed. 2) 182 The element *e* is called an idempotent if $ee = e$ and if *e* is not a zero element. **1960** C. E. RICKART *Gen. Theory Banach Algebras* i. 35 Let $\mathfrak{A}$ be a Banach algebra and let *e* be a proper idempotent in $\mathfrak{A}$ (that is, $e \neq 0$, 1 and $e^2 = e$).

Hence **idempotence** (stress variable), **idempo·tency**, the property of being idempotent.

1940 *Mind* XLIX. 461 The truth is that Eddington, in spite of all that he says about getting all the mathematics he wants out of the idempotency of the *J* symbols, employs them in accordance with the laws of ordinary algebra whenever he thinks fit. **1940** W. V. QUINE *Math. Logic* 60 In the case of conjunction and alternation, repetition of components has..been seen to be immaterial (idempotence). **1957** P. SUPPES *Introd. Logic* ix. 205 Equations (9) and (10) express what is usually called the idempotency of union and intersection. **1959** K. R. POPPER *Logic Sci. Discovery* 351 $p\ (aa, b) = p\ (a, b)$...This is the law of idempotence, sometimes also called the 'law of tautology'. **1960** P. SUPPES *Axiomatic Set Theory* ii. 27 The next three theorems assert the commutativity, associativity, and idempotence of union. **1968** *New Scientist* 16 May 339/1 Idempotency..occurs if an operation produces no change in the number or set on which it operates.

idem sonans (əi·dem sōᵘ·nænz). *Law.* [L., lit. = sounding the same.] Identity of sound in pronunciation; the occurrence in a document of a material word or name misspelt but having the sound of the word or name intended. Also *adj.*, homophonous *with*.

1848 WHARTON *Law Lexicon* 304/2 The courts will not interfere in setting aside proceedings on account of the misspelling of names, provided..there is an *idem sonans* between the pronunciation of the right name and that which is inserted in the proceedings; as Lawrance, instead of Lawrence, Reynell for Reynolds, Beniditto for Benedetto. **1856** *Newsp. & Gen. Reader's Compan.* II. § 1749 The verb was unluckily *idem sonans* with another word. **1919** H. L. MENCKEN *Amer. Lang.* viii. 273 In America, with a language of peculiar vowel sounds and even consonant-sounds struggling against a foreign invasion unmatched for strength or variety..the legal rule of *idem sonans* is of much wider utility than anywhere else in the world.

-idene, *suffix. Chem.* [Prob. taken from *ETHYLIDENE (ad. F. *éthylydène* (A. Lieben 1858, in *Compt. Rend.* XLVI. 663), f. *éthylène* with insertion of the *-yd-* of *aldehyde*).] Forming the names of bivalent organic radicals in which both valencies derive from the same atom. Cf. *-YLIDENE.

1927 *Chem. Abstr.* XXI. 4576/1 *-idene* added to any radical usually means a double bond at point of attachment. **1966** *Nomencl. Org. Chem.* (I.U.P.A.C.) (ed. 2) A. 16 Bivalent and trivalent radicals derived from univalent acyclic hydrocarbon radicals whose authorized names end in '-yl' by removal of one or two hydrogen atoms from the carbon atom with the free valences are named by adding '-idene' or '-idyne', respectively, to the name of the corresponding univalent radical.

ident. Colloq. abbrev. of IDENTIFICATION (or **identification bracelet*), IDENTIFY *v.* orig. *U.S.*

1952 *Jewelers' Circular–Keystone* Sept. 65 (Advt.), Popular 'Idents' that build profitable sales. **1955** R. J. SCHWARTZ *Compl. Dict. Abbrev.* 90 *Ident*, identification (US Army). **1965** 'D. SHANNON' *Death-Bringers* (1966) i. 12 The group being showed thousands of mug shots at Records, hoping for a possible ident. **1966** M. & G. GORDON *Undercover Cat prowls Again* (1967) xiv. 95 It was so dark he couldn't make a positive ident until the girl was halfway along. **1967** R. J. SERLING *President's Plane is Missing* iii. 55 'Washington Center, Air Force One. Squawk ident.' 'Roger, identing.' **1970** P. LAURIE *Scotland Yard* ix. 196 A searcher..ploughs through the four thousand or so forms..in the slim hope that one will match, giving him an 'ident'.

identical, *a.* Add: **2. c.** *identical points* = *corresponding points* (*CORRESPONDING *ppl. a.* 1 b).

1841 W. MACKENZIE *Physiol. Vision* xvi. 253 (*heading*) Corresponding or identical points of the retina. **1880** L. OWEN tr. *Giraud-Teulon's Elem. Treat. Function of Vision* I. ii. 16 The same object being depicted upon the two retinae, at homologous points, must give rise to a single sensation.... This..has been called the doctrine of identical points. **1932** S. DUKE-ELDER *Text-bk. Ophthalm.* I. xxvii. 1028 Points on the two retinæ from which images are projected to the same place in the common visual field are called corresponding (or identical) points.

d. *identical twin*, one of a pair of twins who, as a result of being monozygotic, are of the same sex and very similar to one another in appearance; usu. *pl.* Opp. **fraternal twin*. Similarly *identical triplet*.

1889 S. SCHÖNLAND tr. *Weismann's Ess. Heredity* vi. 381 Under conditions of nutriment which are as identical as possible, *two* egg-cells develope into unlike twins, *one* into identical twins; although we cannot yet affirm that the latter result invariably follows. **1938, 1941** [see * FRATERNAL *a.* c]. **1964** M. ARGYLE *Psychol. & Social Probl.* vi. 77 The best method of studying the extent of genetic factors is by means of identical and fraternal twins. **1972** A. CHRISTIE *Elephants can Remember* xiv. 190 There was a project on hand..to follow up the general lives of selected pairs of identical twins. **1973** *Oxford Times* 6 Apr. 8 On Monday the first LP by the only identical triplet sisters act in British show business was released.

B. *sb.* **1.** *pl.* Identical things.

1696 J. SERGEANT *Method to Sci.* 264 We can as easily define their Abstract Notions as we can the other, (or rather much more easily) and consequently Reduce them to their Identicals. **1903** J. GOTT *Lett.* (1918) 195 Most of the books..worry me with endless and subtle refinements and hair-splitting distinctions between identicals. **1943** W. V. QUINE in *Jrnl. Philos.* 4 Mar. 113 One of the fundamental principles governing identity is that of *substitutivity*—or, as it might well be called, that of *indiscernibility of identicals*.

2. An identical twin.

[**1932** A. HUXLEY *Brave New World* i. 8 'Can you tell us the record for a single ovary..?'..'Sixteen thousand and twelve; in one hundred and eighty-nine batches of identicals.'] **1938** [see * FRATERNAL *a.* c]. **1964** M. ARGYLE *Psychol. & Social Probl.* vi. 77 If it is found that identicals are more alike in some respect than fraternals, this suggests that the condition [*sc.* a mental disorder] is to some extent inherited.

identifiability (əide:ntifəiˌăbi·liti). [f. IDENTIFIABLE *a.* + -ITY.] The property of being identifiable.

1898 W. JAMES in R. B. Perry *Tht. & Char. W. James* (1935) II. 369 The identifiability of these objects in different fields. **1959** P. F. STRAWSON *Individuals* i. 17 The possibility that the identifiability of particulars of some sorts may be in some *general* way dependent on the identifiability of particulars of other sorts.

identification. Add: **1. b.** Esp. in *Psychol.*, the (freq. unconscious) adaptation of one's ideas and behaviour to fit in with those of a person or group seen as a model. (Further examples.)

1913 A. A. BRILL tr. *Freud's Interpr. of Dreams* iv. 126 Identification is a highly important factor in the mechanism of hysterical symptoms; by this means patients are enabled in their symptoms to represent not merely their own experiences, but the experiences of a great number of other persons. **1930** W. HEALY et al. *Struct. & Meaning Psychoanal.* v. 240 Identification is the unconscious molding of a person's own Ego after the fashion of one that has been taken as a model. **1950** *Brit. Jrnl. Psychol.* XLI. 176 It was..clear from her stories and her behaviour at school that J. W. succeeded in making a 'good identification'. **1964** *Listener* 21 May 825/2 The participatory emotions...are mediated by processes variously known as empathy, *rapport*, projection, and identification. **1972** *Sci. Amer.* Jan. 36/3 Girls often are socialized in early childhood to satisfy their achievement needs passively by identification with the accomplishments of their father or their brothers.

4. A document such as a passport, driving licence, health card, or a disc or mark that serves to identify a person, or indicates his nationality, military unit, etc. Also *collect.*

1947 *Amer. College Dict.* 599/1 *Identification*, something that identifies one: *have you any identification?* **1958** P. KEMP *No Colours or Crest* vi. 100 We got good identifications—all from the 1st Alpine Division. **1964** MRS. L. B. JOHNSON *White House Diary* 10 June (1970) 164 What we should have done was to ask them all to wear some identification. **1965** M. BRADBURY *Stepping Westward* v. 272 Got any identification? **1970** *Globe & Mail* (Toronto) 28 Sept. 7/1 Once inside I was forced to produce my driver's licence, draft card, student I.D., and all other identification I had on me.

5. *attrib.* and *Comb.* [cf. * IDENTITY 10], as *identification badge, bracelet, card, mark, papers*; **identification beacon** *Aeronaut.* (see quot.); **identification disc,** a disc carried or worn by a person (usu. one in the armed forces), giving his name, etc., as a means of identification; **identification lamp, light,** a light (e.g. on an aircraft) that provides a means of identification; **identification panel,** a sign used to indicate the position of ground troops to friendly aircraft; **identification parade,** a parade of persons from among whom a suspect is to be identified; **identification patch** (see quot.); **identification plate,** the registered number plate of a motor vehicle; **identification signal** (see quot. 1918); **identification tag** *N. Amer.* = * *identification disc*; also *transf.*

1945 Identification badge [see *film badge* (* FILM *sb.* 7 b)]. **1951** *Gloss. Aeronaut. Terms* (*B.S.I.*) III. 24 *Identification beacon*, a beacon displaying a coded light and identifying a geographical point. **1969** *New Yorker* 30 Aug. 57/2 (Advt.), The 17-jewel movement attaches to a rich gold..identification bracelet. **1970** *Ibid.* 24 Oct. 48/2 He gave her his identification bracelet, from which he had had eight links removed. **1908** *Westm. Gaz.* 13 Feb. 5/2 An identification-card with his photograph on it. **1969** *New Yorker* 10 May 29/1 Residents will show identification cards to gain admittance. **1915** R. BROOKE *Let.* Mar. (1968) 665 Round my neck with my identification-disk. **1915** *Sphere* 11 Dec. p. iv/3 Copies of the soldiers' identification discs in gold. **1930** T. B. BRUCE *Missing* 13, I burnt all letters and papers..keeping only my identification disc. **1935** H. G. WELLS *Things to Come* 15 An identification disk—his introduction card so to speak—will be carried. **1932** *Gloss. Aeronaut. Terms* (*B.S.I.*) (proofs) IX. 7 *Identification lamp*, a lamp mounted on an aircraft for purposes of recognition. **1933** *Gloss. Aeronaut. Terms* (*B.S.I.*) XIII. 78 *Identification light*, a light on or near a beacon having a character differing from, but serving to identify, it. **1946** R. A. MCFARLAND *Human Factors Air Transport Design* xii. 608 Accidents may arise from misinterpretation of identification lights on other aircraft. **1897** E. L. VOYNICH *Gadfly* III. i. 253 For you to go there just now, with all your identification marks, would be to walk into a trap with your eyes open. **1901** *Westm. Gaz.* 24 Apr. 3/2 He found fifteen other bodies, searched them for their identification marks. **1904** *Ibid.* 30 Aug. 4/3 The identification marks of the cartridges of all the known armies of the world. **1942** B. A. SHIELDS *Princ. Flight* vii. 231 When an aircraft is licensed, it is assigned an identification mark. *Ibid.*, The identification mark signifies the type of flying in which the airplane is permitted to engage. **1944** *Ann. Reg. 1943* 251 The Germans also resented the wearing..of..colours of the R.A.F. aircraft identification marks. **1918** E. S. FARROW *Dict. Mil. Terms* 305 *Identification panels*, in aëroplane balloon signalling, panels which are displayed at the sound signal of the aircraft or upon the initiative of the command post. **1957** P. KEMP *Mine were of Trouble* viii. 139 We had white identification panels spread on the crest in front of us, to indicate our forward positions. **1903** *Westm. Gaz.* 28 Dec. 7/2, 300 men who had no workmen's identification papers. **1918** Identification papers [see *GOODS *sb. pl.* 1 b]. **1927** W. E. COLLINSON *Contemp. Eng.* 78 The shortcomings of the identification parades at the police-station. **1965** W. SOYINKA *Road* 54 Perhaps ..if you promised not to look in his face..so that you could not recognise him at an identification parade. **1966** A. SACHS *Jail Diary* xi. 109 Perhaps they are taking me to another cell, or they are going to put me on an identification parade. **1972** *Police Rev.* 10 Nov. 1472/3 You think it is necessary to hold identification parades in this case. **1918** E. S. FARROW *Dict. Mil. Terms* 305 *Identification patch*, tags placed upon the backs of the men's coats when advancing behind a barrage. **1901** *Motor-Car World* II. 74/1 Identification-plate. **1906** *Westm. Gaz.* 26 Aug. 8/2 The Commission recommends that identification plates should 'be rigidly fixed in an upright position'. **1909** *Ibid.* 24 June 4/1 Five marks for identification plates. **1918** E. S. FARROW *Dict. Mil. Terms* 305 *Identification signals*..which will identify the authority sending the communication..are assigned from division headquarters and each consists of one letter and one numeral. **1946** *Happy Landings* July 9/1 The identification signal could still be heard. **1918** Identification tag [see *dog tag* (*DOG *sb.* 18 a)]. **1918** E. S. FARROW *Dict. Mil. Terms* 305 An identification tag by which he can be identified if killed or wounded. **1960** J. J. ROWLANDS *Spindrift* 146 A small boy with an identification tag tied to his lapel walked silently beside the stewardess. **1964** GOULD & KOLB *Dict. Social Sci.* 244/2 Some students suggest that there is a great concern among those desirous of upward mobility to discard their ethnic identification tags.

identificational (əidentifikēⁱ·ʃənăl), *a. Linguistics.* [f. IDENTIFICATION + -AL.] Relating to being identified or not; involving identification.

1933 L. BLOOMFIELD *Lang.* xii. 203 The class-meaning is, roughly, 'identificational character of specimens'. **1964** E. A. NIDA *Toward Sci. Transl.* iii. 44 A communication..can be called identificational, for the source.. exhibits a high degree of identification with the receptor.

identificatory (əidentifikēⁱ·təri), *a.* [f. IDENTIFICAT(ION + -ORY².] Serving to bring about identification (in various senses).

1943 *Internat. Jrnl. Psycho-Anal.* XXIV. 97/1 Thus identificatory thinking is employed for the purpose of avoiding what is unpleasurable and obtaining what is pleasurable. **1949** KOESTLER *Insight & Outlook* xii. 175 This identificatory rite survives with great vigour to our day in the ceremony of the eucharistic meal. **1959** P. F. STRAWSON *Individuals* ii. 82 Kant was very careful to empty this 'I' of referential, identificatory force. **1965** *Philos.* XL. 336 The relevant rules of difference are of course those of space-time and its trustworthiness as an identificatory medium. **1972** *Computers & Humanities* VII. 121 Each line includes identificatory information such as page number, abbreviated poem title, line number, and whether the line is a variant or not.

identifier. Add: **1.** (Later example.)

1959 E. FENWICK *Long Way Down* ii. 15 Where the hell's your identifier?

b. One who identifies himself with a cause, group, etc.

1966 *New Statesman* 8 July 56/3 He [*sc.* Mark Twain]

lacked the moral or imaginative resources of other identifiers, like Dickens or Balzac.

2. a. That which identifies.

1894 'MARK TWAIN' in *Century Mag.* June 237/2 There was never a twin..that did not carry from birth to death a sure identifier. **1907** *Yesterday's Shopping* (1969) 633/2 Gamekeepers' identifiers... will burn for a period of 3 to 4 minutes. **1973** A. QUINTON *Nature of Things* iii. 61 The view that the identity of things through time is due to the presence in them of an identifying component or substance, an identifier, as I shall call it.

b. *Linguistics.* A linguistic element that has the function of identifying.

1946 [see *DESCRIPTOR]. **1965** *Language* XLI. 73 The noun phrase..may be regarded as a string consisting of identifier tagmeme, manifested here by *a.*; [etc.].

c. *Computers.* A sequence of characters arbitrarily devised to identify or refer to a set of data, a location in a store, or a point in a program.

1958 *Communications Assoc. Computing Machinery* Dec. 11 Strings of letters and figures enclosed by delimiters represent new entities. However, only two types of such strings are admissible: 1. Strings consisting of figures ζ only represent the (positive) integers G (including 0) with the conventional meaning. 2. Strings beginning with a letter λ followed by arbitrary letters λ and/or figures ζ are called identifiers. They have no inherent meaning, but serve for identifying purposes only. **1960** *Computer Jrnl.* III. 67/2 An identifier may be used in an ALGOL 60 program as a simple variable. This means that the program, when ultimately translated and run on a computer, will associate a particular storage location with that identifier. The number held in this store at any stage in the calculation is called the current value of the variable. **1962** R. V. OAKFORD *Introd. Electronic Data Processing Equipment* vii. 245 An INPUT declaration defines one or more input-data sets, each of which is given a name in the form of an identifier. **1967** COX & GROSE *Organiz. Bibliogr. Rec. by Computer* II. 19 Such a file sequence carried an 8-character identifier and a sequence-number. **1968** CORLETT & TINSLEY *Pract. Programming* ii. 14 Reference is made to the memory of a computer by giving names or identifiers to variables... Identifiers are also used to denote labels which mark particular points in a program. **1973** *Computers & Humanities* VII. 144 The first ten columns contain identifiers for manuscript, book, question, and line number.

identify, *v.* Add: **1. b.** *to identify oneself with*: also, to model oneself on, esp. unconsciously; to feel oneself to be associated with or part of; freq. *absol.* with ellipsis of the refl. pron. Also occas. *intr.*, to perform or undergo such a process with regard to something unspecified. (Further examples.)

1913 A. A. BRILL tr. *Freud's Interpr. of Dreams* iv. 126 If she has put herself in the place of her friend, or, as we may say, has identified herself with her friend. *Ibid.* 127 An hysterical woman identifies herself most readily..with persons with whom she has had sexual relations. **1940** 'G. ORWELL' *Inside Whale* 51 Sam Weller, Mark Tapley, Clara Peggotty..identify with their master's family. **1955** *Publ. Amer. Dial. Soc.* XXIV. 5 The teen-agers who almost compulsively identify with this semicriminal subculture. **1958** *Observer* 2 Feb. 14/3 Readers can immediately identify with her nice puzzled hero. **1958** M. ARGYLE *Relig. Behaviour* v. 40 Other investigators have studied the beliefs of children who.. 'identify' themselves with their parents—i.e. wish to be liked by them, wish to resemble them. **1959** *Listener* 31 Dec. 1174/2 An engaging series of attempts and failures to 'identify', as cricket-master at a prep school, or as a journalist on a go-getting daily. **1967** G. STEINER *Lang. & Silence* 81 Because we are trained to give psychological and moral credence to the imaginary..we may find it more difficult to identify with the real world. **1968** *Blues Unlimited* Sept. 8 Finally Tina came on and tore the joint up. She signified, the women identified and the men just drooled. **1969** *Times* 17 Oct. 18/5 Everyone identified madly and Biba's knew no failure. **1972** *Where* Jan. 18/2 Thus the parents, in conversation at home, are able to identify themselves with the place and people under discussion.

3. To discover, perceive; to localize. *colloq.*

1922 D. H. LAWRENCE *England, my England* 45 After a lapse and a new effort, he identified a pain in his head.

identikit (əide·ntikit). Also **identi-kit.** [Blend of IDENTI(TY + KIT *sb.*[1]] A composite picture of a person whom the police wish to interview assembled from features described by witnesses. Also *transf.*

1961 *Observer* 12 Mar. 5/7 About forty police forces in this country are now testing an American device called an 'Identi-Kit', which is used to translate witnesses' descriptions of a person into visual terms. **1961** *Spectator* 1 Sept. 277 The identi-kit must depend..on the memory of the witness being questioned. **1962** *Times* 19 Apr. 13/2 The identi-kit method of political detection is not really very plausible here. **1963** *Listener* 19 Sept. 416/2 At their worst the genres of contemporary fiction provide no more than a kind of 'identikit' novel, prefabricated from ready-made elements. **1967** *Spectator* 29 Sept. 359/1 One at least managed to build up an identikit description of the soul: 'A most wonderful, delicate, small thing'. **1969** G. GREENE *Trav. with my Aunt* II. iii. 245, I don't resemble whatever identikit portrait you have of me. **1969** *Times* 13 Mar. 13/1 If one were looking at that time for an Identikit of an England side to defend the World Cup in Mexico in 1970 one would scarcely have recognized the person we were looking for. **1971** 'J. ASHFORD' *Bent Copper* vi. 43 He'd called in the D.C. from H.Q. who specialised in Identikit and..the D.C. had built up several faces. **1973** *Times Lit. Suppl.* 9 Mar. 255/1 The identikit of this regime [in Greece] is predictably unpleasant.

‖ **Identitätsphilosophie** (ide·ntitēits,filǫ·sǒfi). Also **i-.** [G., identity-philosophy.] The term used for a system, propounded by, among others, F. W. Schelling (1775–1854), that assumes the fundamental identity of spirit and nature.

1866 H. SIDGWICK in A. & E. M. Sidgwick *Henry Sidgwick* iii. 151, I am coming more and more to the opinion that the whole 'Identitäts-philosophie' (Fichte, Schelling, and Hegel) is a monstrous mistake. **1905** W. JAMES *Meaning of Truth* (1909) v. 128 Humanism, here, is only a more comminuted *identitätsphilosophie.* **1905** —— *Ess. Radical Empiricism* (1912) iv. 134 This the post-Kantian idealists..acknowledged by calling their doctrine an *Identitätsphilosophie.* **1938** *Mind* XLVII. 281 Spinoza's doctrine is not an Identitätsphilosophie; that is to say, the one and only substance has no underlying identical nature, which is only manifested in different ways in the attributes.

identity. Add: **6.** Also *attrib.*, as *identity formula, relation, sentence.*

1940 W. V. QUINE *Math. Logic* 232 *I* is..the identity relation $\hat{x}\hat{y}$ $(x=y)$. **1965** B. MATES *Elem. Logic* ix. 146 It will be useful to introduce a couple of obvious conventions for writing identity-formulas. *Ibid.* 149 The identity relation among the elements of one domain will be different from that among the elements of another. *Ibid.*, Thus every identity-sentence would be either trivial or absurd. **1967** *Encycl. Philos.* IV. 123/1 When we utter an identity sentence such as 'Venus is the morning star', what we wish to express..is that the terms 'Venus' and 'the morning star' both mean the same thing. **1970** J. D. CARNEY *Introd. Symbolic Logic* vii. 160 The identity relation has some rather special properties.

7. (*old*) *identity*: a person long resident or well known in a place. *N.Z.* and *Austral.*

1862 *Otago, Its Goldfields & Resources* 9 The exclusive spirit of the 'old identity'. **1874** A. BATHGATE *Colonial Experiences* iii. 26 The term 'old identities' took its origin from an expression in a speech made by one of the members of the Provincial Council, Mr E. B. Cargill, who, in speaking of the new arrivals, said that the early settlers should endeavour to preserve their old identity... A comic singer [R. Thatcher] helped to perpetuate the name by writing a song. **1879** W. J. BARRY *Up & Down* xx. 197 The 'old identities' were beginning to be alive to the situation. **1889** *Bulletin* (Sydney) 28 Sept. 8/1 Many of the old identities of '52 and '53 will remember the license-hunting and shanty-raiding days. **1893** *Auckland Weekly News* 9 Dec. 7 Both these old identities are in possession of all their faculties to a wonderful degree. *Ibid.* 28 Another old identity passed away on Dec. 1 in the person of Mr. Thomas Hunt. **1929** 'M. BARNARD ELDERSHAW' *House Is Built* (1945) v. 111 He was the sort of man who becomes an old identity almost at once, so that the residents of the Parramatta Road..soon thought they had been seeing him drive past in his indescribably sailorly fashion all their lives. **1942** 'M. INNES' *Daffodil Affair* II. ii. 46 Ron's dad was a well-known identity Cobdogla-way. **1944** *Mod. Jun. Dict.* (Whitcombe & Tombs) 205 In Australia and New Zealand a very old resident in a place is called an 'old identity'. **1962** J. R. BERNARD in *Southerly* XXII. II. 97 We [Australians] add to..identity that of outstanding local citizen. **1970** *N.Z. Woman's Weekly* 9 Nov. 19/1 Havelock North identity Mrs C. E. Turner-Williams..at 98 stitches happily on.

8. *Math.* **a.** An element of a set which, if combined with any element by a (specified) binary operation, leaves the latter element unchanged.

1894 *Bull. Amer. Math. Soc.* I. 61 Given an (abstract) group G_n..with elements s_1 = identity, s_2, s_n. **1937** R. D. CARMICHAEL *Introd. Theory Groups of Finite Order* xiii. 395 For every *a* we have $ai = a = ia$. Then we call *i* an identity with respect to the rule of combination of the group. *Ibid.* i. 17 Since the identity plays the role of unity in multiplication, it is often denoted by the symbol 1. **1941** BIRKHOFF & MACLANE *Surv. Mod. Algebra* i. 2 The number zero has the characteristic property that it leaves unaltered any number to which it is added; hence we say that zero is an 'identity element' for addition. By formal analogy, the 'unity' 1 is an identity for multiplication. **1966** MEYER & HANLON *Fun with New Math* i. 12 The number one is the multiplicative identity, for the product of it and any other number leaves the second number unchanged. **1971** E. C. DADE in Powell & Higman *Finite Simple Groups* viii. 254 The associativity in *G* easily implies that of multiplication in *FG*, and the identity 1_G of *G* is also the identity for *FG*.

b. A transformation that gives rise to the same elements as those to which it is applied.

1910 VEBLEN & YOUNG *Projective Geom.* I. iii. 65 The correspondence which makes every element of the system correspond to itself is called the identical correspondence or simply the identity, and is denoted by the symbol 1. **1959** E. M. PATTERSON *Topology* (ed. 2) ii. 20 If $A \subset B$, the transformation $i: A \to B$ defined by $i(a) = a$ is a one-one transformation called an inclusion; in particular, if $A = B$, the inclusion $i: A \to A$ is called the identity. **1961** H. S. M. COXETER *Introd. Geom.* ii. 29 If the product of two transformations is the identity, each is called the inverse of the other, and their product in the reverse order is again the identity.

9. *S. Afr.* (See quot. 1924.)

1924 E. H. BROOKES *Hist. Native Policy S. Afr.* iii. 62 Most modern thinkers on the Native question argue as if there were no *via media* between the principle which refuses to acknowledge any real difference between Europeans and Natives, the policy of identity as we may call it,..and the principle which insists on the subordinate position of the Native in the body politic, the policy of subordination. **1961** *Listener* 30 Nov. 898/2 These influences..led in South Africa to the policy sometimes known as 'identity', of regarding all men as much the same. *Ibid.*, The earlier British policy of identity broke down.

10. *attrib.* and *Comb.* with the meaning 'that serves to identify the holder or wearer', as *identity bracelet, card, certificate, disc, papers, patch*; also **identity element** *Math.* = *IDENTITY 8 a; **identity matrix** *Math.*, a matrix in which all the elements of the principal diagonal are one and the remainder zero, so that its product with another matrix gives that matrix; **identity parade** = **identification parade.*

1968 J. IRONSIDE *Fashion Alphabet* 167 *Identity bracelet*, a gold or silver chain with a flat space for the owner's name. **1973** G. SIMS *Hunters Point* xiii. 124 On his wrists a gold watch and a gold identity bracelet. **1900** *Westm. Gaz.* 2 Jan. 3/1 When troops are going on service each man has issued to him what is known as a field dressing and an identity card. **1931** *Times Lit. Suppl.* 1 Jan. 2/2 He..forged an identity card, and procured a pistol. **1940** *Ann. Reg. 1939* 101 Some 65,000 enumerators, who.. issued identity cards for all the persons mentioned in the forms. **1953** C. DAY LEWIS *Italian Visit* i. 14 The identity cards that inform us Not who we are or might be, but how we are interchangeable. **1961** *Daily Mail* 20 July 9/3 Millions of people may soon have to carry special medical identity cards... A card..would contain information about their illnesses..any special drugs they were taking. **1972** *Daily Tel.* 23 Nov. 6 The BBC is to tighten up security at its London studios and offices by issuing identity cards to staff. **1918** *Act* 8 *Geo. V* c. 6 § 11 Every person who receives, detains or has in his possession any identity certificate, life certificate, or other certificate. **1909** *Daily Chron.* 15 June 5/5 Rations for three days, ammunition, field bandages, and identity discs were issued to the men. **1911** *Punch* 15 Mar. 181/1 By the March Army Orders the identity discs issued to officers and men in war time are in future to be issued to the former in peace time. **1915** 'I. HAY' *First Hundred Thousand* vi, Its called an Identity Disc. Every soldier on active service wears one. **1919** J. B. MORTON *Barber of Putney* i, In due course came vaccination and inoculation, and identity discs. **1956** R. ST. B. BAKER *Dance of Trees* vi. 79 When the top soil of Tel Fara was excavated we found modern spurs, identity discs, even a copy of the *Tatler*..reminders of the days of Allenby. **1902** *Trans. Amer. Math. Soc.* III. 486 There exists a left-hand identity element, that is, an element i_l such that, for every element a, $i_l a = a$. **1966** MAY & MOSS *New Math for Adults Only* vi. 33/2 Zero is the identity element in addition and one is the identity element in multiplication. **1941** BIRKHOFF & MACLANE *Surv. Mod. Algebra* viii. 197 Corresponding to the identity transformation $y_i = x_i$ is the $n \times n$ identity matrix *I*, which has entries 1 along the principal diagonal (upper left to lower right) and zeros elsewhere. **1908** *Daily Chron.* 21 Feb. 4/6 The 'identity papers', which every man and woman in Prussia must carry about with them. **1955** 'A. GILBERT' *Is she Dead Too?* viii. 141 Put a gorilla in a set of ginger reach-me-downs and you could put up the pair of 'em in an identity parade and no one could tell the difference. **1973** E. LEMARCHAND *Let or Hindrance* vii. 69 We may ask you to come along to an identity parade. **1959** M. LEVIN *Eva* 37 The Ukrainians didn't have to wear identity patches, since the Germans considered them allies.

b. *Philos. attrib.* and *Comb.* as *identity doctrine, sign, thesis*; **identity theory,** the materialist theory that physiological and mental perceptions are identical; hence *identity theorist*, a person professing belief in the identity theory.

1920 S. ALEXANDER *Space, Time & Deity* II. 9 The statement..is a species of the identity doctrine of mind and body, maintaining that there are not two processes, one neural, the other mental, but one. **1950** W. V. QUINE *Methods of Logic* (1952) 211 It is the use of the identity sign between variables, rather than between singular terms, that is fundamental. **1965** HUGHES & LONDEY *Elem. Formal Logic* xxxvii. 258 We need one further symbol, which is written '=' and is known as the identity sign. **1951** G. HUMPHREY *Thinking* viii. 245 Inspired by the behaviourists one group of advocates of what may be called the 'identity theory' has stressed the importance of the so-called implicit speech movements which occur during thinking. **1966** *Amer. Philos. Q.* III. 227/2 Some philosophers..infer that the Identity Theory is an empirical theory. *Ibid.* 233/2 Some Identity Theorists are anxious to eliminate mental properties. **1967** *Encycl. Philos.* V. 339/1 The identity theorist uses the familiar philosophical distinction between significance and reference..to make the claim that mentalistic and physicalistic expressions..will turn out as a matter of empirical fact to refer to or denote one and the same thing, namely physical phenomena. **1954** H. FEIGL in P. A. Schilpp *Philos. R. Carnap* (1963) 259 The prima facie implausibility of the identity thesis arises..mainly from the psychological incompatibility of images such as of nervous tissue..with the qualities of some data of consciousness. **1967** *Philos. Rev.* LXXVI. 201 In recent years, a number of philosophers have argued in favor of materialism in the form of an identity thesis—that is, a thesis to the effect that mental events are identical with certain physiological events.

c. Belonging or relating to identity (sense 2), as in **identity crisis,** a phase of varying severity undergone by an individual in his need to establish his identity in relation to his associates and society as part of the process of maturing. Also *transf.*

1954 *Jrnl. Amer. Psychoanal. Assoc.* II. Apr. 327 George Bernard Shaw arranged for himself a psychosocial moratorium at the age of twenty when his identity crisis led him to leave..his family, friends and familiar work. **1959** *Listener* 29 Oct. 746/2 The prolonged identity crisis of this great young man. **1965** *Times Lit. Suppl.* 25 Nov. 1078/4 A sympathetic study of 'identity crisis'

might appear peculiarly relevant to many Americans. **1968** *Internat. Encycl. Social Sci.* VII. 63/2 An era's identity crisis is least severe in that segment of youth which is able to invest its fidelity in an expanding technology. **1971** R. A. CARTER *Manhattan Primitive* (1972) xv. 137 Girl is on the verge of a breakdown, in deep identity crisis. **1971** M. MCCARTHY *Birds of America* 110 His college tutor, a stupid Freudian, had advised his mother that Peter had an 'identity problem'. **1974** *Times Lit. Suppl.* 19 Apr. 409/1 A middle-aged cuckold with piles and an identity crisis.

ideo-. Add: i:deogene·tic *a.*, producing ideas or images; i:deokine·tic *a. Path.*, denoting that form of apraxia in which the sufferer retains the motor ability to perform an action or movement and understands a request to perform it, but cannot perform it on request; **ideophone** (later example); (b) a term used principally in Bantu linguistics to refer to particular classes of onomatopœic and sound-symbolic words found in these languages; hence **ideopho·nic** *a.*

1904 *Jrnl. Philos.* 21 July 412 In the ideogenetic thinking of artists, the word-symbols are not used. **1908** *Jrnl. Nervous & Mental Dis.* XXXV. 636 There is a great variety of abnormal manipulations..of objects, which are described under the head of apraxia. These may be divided into (1) manifestations of ideomotor apraxia (ideokinetic, of Liepmann, formerly motor apraxia). **1914** H. LIEPMANN in *17th Internat. Congr. Med.* XI. ii. 100 Both limb-kinetic, and particularly ideokinetic apraxia, generally have ideational defective reactions admixed with them. **1933** W. R. BRAIN *Dis. Nervous Syst.* i. 95 Apraxia has been analysed by Liepmann into limb-kinetic apraxia.., ideo-kinetic apraxia, due to a dissociation between ideational and kinaesthetic processes, and ideational apraxia. **1947** F. B. WALSH *Clin. Neuro-Ophthalm.* i. 75/1 In ideokinetic apraxia there is a transferring of movement to other parts of the body, omission of movements, and the production of amorphous movements. **1909** *Cent. Dict.* Suppl., *Ideophone.* In *phonetics*, the auditory symbol of a word or phrase that is perceived as a whole and thus constitutes a single idea. Ideophones are distinguished as *sensory* or *motor*, according as the sound or group of sounds corresponding to the word or phrase is heard or spoken. **1935** C. M. DOKE *Bantu Ling. Terminol.* 118 *Ideophone*, a vivid representation of an idea in sound. A word, often onomatopoeic, which describes a predicate, qualificative or adverb in respect to manner, colour, sound, smell, action, state or intensity. The ideophone is in Bantu a special part of speech, resembling to a certain extent in function the adverb. **1953** W. J. ENTWISTLE *Aspects of Lang.* xi. 360 The use of ideophones by Zulus and other Bantus shows that the quality of an action is of more interest to them than its specific nature. **1954** G. V. SMITHERS in *Archivum Linguisticum* VI. 73 Some English Ideophones. *Ibid.* 82 The term *ideophone* may as fittingly be applied to the English words of both groups [onomatopœic and imitative] as to those in other languages. **1955** L. W. LANHAM *Study of Gitonga of Inhambane* ix. 220 Certain irregular usages of the tenses given above are observable when ideophones are incorporated as predicative stems. **1964** *Afr. Lang. Stud.* V. 87 Examination..brought to light, both in Swahili and in kindred languages of the Coastal area, a number of what have been..called ideophones. **1954** *Archivum Linguisticum* VI. 83 It seems that certain types, at least, of ideophonic root can be struck out in various languages at various periods. **1962** G. FORTUNE *Ideophones in Shona* 37 Ideophonic forms, ideophonic constructions as well as ideophonic phonemes..are peculiar to 'free expression' as contrasted with 'formal speech'. **1964** *N. & Q.* Oct. 372/2 An infallible sign that the word is an ideophonic formation.

ideogram. (Further examples.) Also used in *transf.* senses, esp. of figurative diction.

1940 E. POUND *Let.* 16 Jan. (1971) 333 Early characters were pictures, squared for aesthetic reasons. But I think in a well-brushed ideogram the sun is seen to be rising. **1951** H. KENNER *Poetry E. Pound* 89 The Anglo-Saxon scholar's term for just such a vivid figure is 'kenning': the particulars by which the person or object in question is known. 'Whale-road', 'soul-bearer', are both ideogram and metaphor. **1959** N. G. L. HAMMOND *Hist. Greece* i. 34 The ideograms (signs which portray objects) and the symbols for numbers narrow the field of its interpretation somewhat, but much is left open to doubt. **1962** W. NOWOTTNY *Lang. Poets Use* iv. 78 The particulars which inhabit these schemes, though extraordinarily difficult to summate, permit themselves to be assimilated to a common ideogram of decline (of the year, of the day, of a fire). **1964** E. PALMER tr. *Martinet's Elem. Gen. Ling.* v. 152 The members of an American board of examiners showed that they agreed neither on the position of the accent in *ideogram* nor on the quality of the first two vowels of the word. **1972** *Times* 29 June 16/3 Traditional graphic symbols and ideograms..were used extensively by the Manding.

ideogrammic (idi̯o̹græ·mik), *a.* [f. IDEOGRAM + -IC.] Of the nature of an ideogram; expressed by means of symbols. Also **ideogramma·tic** *a.*

1929 W. J. LOCKE *Ancestor Jorico* i. 15 The swift ideogrammic air-speed which Toby and Jones have invented between themselves is a mystery. **1951** H. KENNER *Poetry E. Pound* 84 Joyce's catalogue of Bloom's books in *Ulysses* is the simplest possible application of the ideogrammic method. **1962** Y. MALKIEL in Householder & Saporta *Probl. Lexicogr.* 22 Special features worthy of mention include: the use of abbreviations or peculiar ideogrammatic classifiers to mark for a given word its grammatical or semantic category. **1962** M. MCLUHAN *Gutenberg Galaxy* 22 No pictographic or ideogrammic

or hieroglyphic mode of writing has the detribalizing power of the phonetic alphabet. **1967** *Punch* 18 Jan. 80 To others, the 'No Entry' sign (a highly ideogrammatic white bar on a red disc) variously indicated a pedestrian crossing, a level crossing, a Belisha beacon, the end of a speed limit, a first aid post, and a major road ahead.

ideograph. (Further examples.)

1911 *Encycl. Brit.* XV. 172 The usual charge for advertisement is from 7d. to one shilling per line of 22 ideographs (about nine words). **1951** H. KENNER *Poetry E. Pound* 89 The Chinese ideograph, like the metaphor, deals in exceedingly condensed juxtapositions. **1972** *Computers & Humanities* VI. 259 There is a basic corpus of 2,444 morphemes, each corresponding to a single Chinese logograph (ideograph).

ideographic, *a.* (Further examples.) Of ideographs: representing ideas pictorially or figuratively.

1948 D. DIRINGER *Alphabet* 174 An outside initiative has suggested the replacing of the Japanese ideographic-syllabic script by the Latin alphabet. **1955** P. HERON *Changing Forms of Art* 109 This long picture..was new: it represented, as far as Picasso is concerned, the defeat of the plastic by the ideographic. **1964** M. A. K. HALLIDAY et al. *Linguistic Sciences* 49 The Chinese script is not ideographic: the symbols do not represent ideas, they represent formal items of the language. **1972** *Computers & Humanities* VI. 260 Because of an ideographic writing system extending back for 3,500+ years and still shared by all the Chinese languages, cognates can be visually identified.

ideological, *a.* Add: **2. b.** Of or relating to an ideology (sense *4).

1914 *Atlantic Monthly* June 775/1 If Mr. Mencken's earnest seekers after truth wish to evolve ideological schemes of municipal taxation..then, indeed, the newspaper discussions of these questions would be bewildering to these visionary workers in the realms of pure reason. **1925** M. EASTMAN *Since Lenin Died* iv. 32 Without realising this, you cannot penetrate beneath the ideological surface of the dispute which followed. **1937** *Times* 2 Nov. 17/2 Japan will be an absentee at Brussels... So will Germany... The inconvenience, to say no more, of ideological attitudes has been very swiftly illustrated. **1939** *Times* 2 Nov. 8/2 The attacks on Great Britain and France for waging ideological warfare (is not Communist warfare ideological?) and at the same time being actuated by imperialistic motives are an obvious contradiction in terms. **1940** E. POUND *Cantos* lv. 56 But his brat was run by his missus And they had an ideological war. **1952** *Ann. Reg.* 1951 4 The rulers of Russia inherited imperialism and added to it an ideological imperialism. **1963** *Daily Tel.* 14 Oct. 12/2 Though it has been left this year to Albania to sponsor Communist China's membership, it will still be supported by her newly declared ideological foe, the Soviet Union, and by the victim of her aggression, India. **1969** *Guardian* 11 Sept. 7/2 Nor was he ever 'ideological', in the sense required by New Left dogmatists.

Hence **ideologically** *adv.* (later examples.)

1957 P. WORSLEY *Trumpet shall Sound* iii. 67 It.. represents a conscious step towards the establishment of forms of organization, which..were independent both organizationally and ideologically. **1970** *Daily Tel.* 10 Jan. 12 As China's strength and numbers grow she becomes less prepared..to play second fiddle to Russia ideologically. **1971** *Ibid.* 3 Apr. 10/5 The Soviet system remains ideologically and politically committed to the destruction of our way of life.

ideologist. Add: **3.** A proponent or adherent of an ideology (sense *4).

1888 MARX & ENGELS *Manifesto of Communist Party* 14 Just as..the nobility went over to the bourgeoisie, so now a portion of the bourgeoisie goes over to the proletariat, and in particular a portion of the bourgeois ideologists, who have raised themselves to the level of comprehending..the historical movement. **1937** *Daily Herald* 20 Jan. 1/7 We are not content to see Europe arming feverishly under the contending standards of rival ideologists.

ideologue. (Later examples.)

1955 *Times* 6 June 7/7 From outside it is so easy to think of the Russians as a nation of ideologues. **1961** *Spectator* 9 June 826 When the plotters and ideologues come up for trial. **1972** *Sat. Rev.* (U.S.) 20 May 34/2 Women's Liberation ideologues and strategists have advanced some fine, socially refined arguments. **1972** *Observer* 10 Dec. 36/2 One of the stated principles of this outfit's chief ideologues is to steer clear of the politicos.

ideology. Add: **4.** A systematic scheme of ideas, usu. relating to politics or society, or to the conduct of a class or group, and regarded as justifying actions, esp. one that is held implicitly or adopted as a whole and maintained regardless of the course of events. Also *Comb.*

1909 *Westm. Gaz.* 4 May 10/2 It may be worth while giving some account of the ideology behind the German proposal, and of the details as worked out in the Conservative programme, bearing in mind that it is the scheme of a reactionary Agrarian party. **1936** WIRTH & SHILS tr. K. Mannheim (*title*) Ideology and Utopia. **1939** AUDEN in *I Believe* (1940) 22 It is despair at finding a solution to this problem which is responsible for much of the success of Fascist blood-and-soil ideology. **1955** E. SHILS in *Encounter* V. 52 (*title*) The end of ideology? **1966** D. JENKINS *Educated Society* iv. 177 The processes of ideology-formation can go on even in the most high-

minded of circles. **1970** D. D. RAPHAEL *Probl. Pol. Philos.* i. 17 Ideology..is usually taken to mean, a prescriptive doctrine that is not supported by rational argument.

ideoplasm (i·di̯o̹plæz'm). *Spiritualism.* [f. IDEO- + -*plasm* after *ECTOPLASM.] = *ECTOPLASM. So i:deopla·smic *a.*; i·deoplasmy (see quot. 1961).

1926 A. CONAN DOYLE *Hist. Spiritualism* I. i. 7 Ectoplasm..has also been called 'ideoplasm', because it takes on in an instant any shape with which it is impressed by the spirit. **1961** W. H. SALTER *Zoar* vi. 63 The hypothesis of 'ideoplasmy', that is to say, the view that materialisations are produced from the medium's energy and a substance ('ectoplasm') supplied by him with the assistance perhaps of the sitters, and that they take form in accordance with the thoughts of those present. *Ibid.* vi. 69 A clumsy attempt, whether ideoplasmic or fraudulent, to imitate the established conception of a spirit?

ideoplastic (idi̯o̹pla·stik), *a.* [ad. F. *idéoplastie* (J. P. Philips *Cours théorique et pratique de Braidisme* (1860) ii. 44), adj. *idéoplastique*, f. IDEO- + PLASTIC *a.* 5.] Denoting those physiological or artistic processes which are supposed to be moulded or modified by mental impressions or suggestions; also, pertaining to the suggestive function of the imagination; so **ideopla·stically** *adv.*, in a manner influenced by mental or imaginative impressions; **ideopla·sty**, **ideopla·sy**, imagination in its suggestive capacity, esp. as modifying certain physiological functions or processes.

Somewhat specialized uses in spiritualistic writings are not clearly distinguishable from the above. Durand de Gros (see quot. 1901) and J. P. Philips (see etym.) are names of the same person.

1901 BALDWIN *Dict. Philos. & Psychol.* I. 507/2 *Ideoplastic*, applied to the physiological functions considered as liable to modification from suggested ideas (used originally by Durand de Gros). *Ibid.*, *Ideoplasy*, suggestions operative in the production of physiological changes. **1919** A. CONAN DOYLE *Vital Message* App. 209 We accept Dr. Geley's statement that they are 'ideoplastic'. **1929** *Encycl. Brit.* I. 51/1 For half a century no perceptible progress was made on the idea thrown out by Durand (1855, 1860) that a clear distinction should be effected between the 'ideoplastic' and hypotaxic phenomena. **1935** *Burlington Mag.* Mar. 110/1 As regards the ideoplastic character of pre-Greek art..it is called ideoplastic because the artist renders what he *knows* about the object rather than what he sees. *Ibid.* 121/2 He built up his works ideoplastically. **1943** H. READ *Educ. through Art* v. 136 Later writers..relate this two-fold distinction to Verworn's classification of primitive art as physioplastic and ideoplastic. **1960** *Times Lit. Suppl.* 12 Aug. 576/2 The 'ideoplasty' presumed to cause the body of a medium to extrude and model ectoplasm into the image, telepathically received, of old Aunt Kate. **1961** R. CROOKALL *Supreme Adventure* II. i. 60 The substance composing their environment resembles ectoplasm in being ideo-plastic and responding automatically to their thoughts, feelings, expectations, hopes and fears.

-idin, *suffix. Chem.* [f. -ID(E + -IN[1].] Used to form the names of the anthocyanidins, as in *cyanidin, delphinidin, pelargonidin, peonidin*.

-idine, *suffix. Chem.* [f. -ID(E + -INE[5].] Used to form the names of many organic compounds containing nitrogen which, with few exceptions (as *guanidine*), contain one or more rings; esp.: **a.** Certain amino derivatives (*a*) of simple monocyclic aromatic hydrocarbons, as *cumidine, cymidine, mesidine, toluidine, xylidine*, or of derivatives of such hydrocarbons, as *cresidine*; (*b*) of symmetrical bicyclic aromatic hydrocarbons, as *benzidine, naphthidine, tolidine*. **b.** Certain aminophenol ethers, as *anisidine, phenetidine*. **c.** Certain heterocyclic compounds with nitrogen in the ring (the use of the suffix in some cases implying that the ring is saturated), as *piperidine, pteridine, pyridine, pyrrolidine*. (Hence, in mod. systematic nomenclature, forming the suffixes *-iridine, -etidine* and *-olidine*, as in *aziridine*.) **d.** Pyrimidine nucleosides, as *cytidine, thymidine, uridine*. **e.** Certain alkaloids, as *anhalidine, pilocarpidine, quinidine*.

idio-. Add: **idiochro·mosome** *Cytology* = *sex chromosome*; **idioglo·ssia** [Gr. ἰδιόγλωσσος of distinct tongue], a form of dyslalia in which the person affected consistently makes substitutions in his speech sounds to such an extent that he seems to speak a language of his own; **idiographic** *a.*, (*b*) concerned with the individual, pertaining to or descriptive of single and unique facts and processes (opp. NOMOTHETIC *a.*); **idiolalia** (-lē̆i·li̯ă) [*-LALIA] = *idioglossia* above; **idiophone**, a percussion

instrument that consists simply of elastic material (as metal, wood, etc.) capable of producing sound (as opp. to a *MEMBRANOPHONE in which stretched skin is used as the agent of sound); **idiopho·neme** *Linguistics*, a phoneme in individual speech; hence **idiophone·mic** *a.*; **idiore·tinal** *a.*, applied to what is seen when the eyes are shut and there is no external stimulation of the retina; **idio(r)rhy·thmic** *a.* (later example); also as *sb.*; **i:dioventri·cular** *a. Med.*, proper to the ventricle alone; used of the rhythm of contraction set up within the ventricle when the normal auricular stimulus to ventricular contraction is blocked.

1905 *Science* 20 Oct. 500/2 In type *B* all of the spermatozoa contain the same number of chromosomes.., but they are..of two classes, one of which contains a large and one a small 'idiochromosome'. **1920** L. DONCASTER *Introd. Study Cytol.* xi. 159 Most frequently the idio-chromosomes lag behind the autosomes in the spermatocyte anaphases, and the presence of such a lagging pair has sometimes been the first observed indication of the existence of a pair of idio-chromosomes. **1891** WHITE & BIRD in *Proc. R. Med. Chirurg. Soc. Lond.* III. 92 The two children..express themselves in..sounds..unlike those of any known language, but the same sound is always used by the same child to express the same word. Each child has thus a language of its own, and the authors have named the defect to which this peculiarity is due 'Idioglossia'. **1940** *Nature* 6 July 33/1 A child may develop idioglossia, that is, a language of its own; this is not a gibberish but is found on study to be subject to certain laws of sound-changes. **1961** W. R. BRAIN *Speech Disorders* xii. 137 For a number of years the child may not speak at all. Sooner or later, however, most patients acquire a vocabulary of their own which is comprehensible only to those who have been closely associated with them. This defective form of speech is called 'idioglossia' and 'lalling', and constitutes one form of dyslalia. [**1894** W. WINDELBAND *Geschichte & Naturwissenschaft* (1904) 12 Das wissenschaftliche Denken ist — wenn man neue Kunstausdrücke bilden darf — in dem einen Falle nomothetisch, in dem andern idiographisch.] **1909** *Cent. Dict.* Suppl., Idiographic. **1931** A. WOLF in W. Rose *Outl. Mod. Knowl.* 570 History..is idiographic, that is to say, it is concerned with individuals and individual events in all their particularity. *a* **1943** R. G. COLLINGWOOD (1946) *Idea of Hist.* 166 Idiographic science, which is history. **1971** *Jrnl. Gen. Psychol.* Apr. 320 The findings imply that it is possible to study both normative and idiographic data about the emotional response to sound. **1931** ROBBINS & STINCHFIELD *Dict. Terms Disorders Speech* (Amer. Speech & Healing Assoc.) 15 *Idiolalia*, a form of dyslalia characterized by so extreme vowel and consonant substitution that a child's speech may be made unintelligible and appear to be another language to one who has not the key to the literal changes; but the same word is always used to express the same idea. **1933** S. M. STINCHFIELD *Speech Disorders* iii. 51 Idiolalia. This is a form of dyslalia characterized by the substitution of unusual and inaccurate sounds for vowels and consonants..; the same sound..is always used to express the same idea, however. Many refer to it as idioglossia. [**1913** C. SACHS *Real-Lexikon der Musikinstrumente* 195/1 Wir schlagen deshalb vor, dieser Klasse die Bezeichnung 'Idiophone', also 'ihrer Natur nach klingende' Instrumente zu geben.] **1940** C. SACHS *Hist. Mus. Instrum.* (1942) 455 The first of the five main classes is called *idiophones*. **1954** [see * AUTOPHONE 2]. **1970** W. APEL *Harvard Dict. Mus.* (ed. 2) 414/1 Idiophones. Struck: triangle, gong, bell [etc.]. Shaken: rattle, sistrum, crescent. Plucked: Jew's harp, music box. Rubbed: glass harmonica, nail violin. **1971** *Sci. Amer.* Dec. 92/1 The instrument used to send messages in the Upper Congo is made solely of wood, and the entire instrument vibrates when it is struck. It is thus an idiophone, like metal gongs and the wood and metal bars of the xylophone and the glockenspiel. **1955** A. A. HILL in *Q. Jrnl. Speech* XLI. 255 The old concept of the phoneme turned on individual speech, the idiolect. Individual phonemic structures are therefore structures of idiophonemes. **1958** —— *Introd. Ling. Struct.* iv. 58 Phonemes in individual speech can be called 'idiophonemes'. *Ibid.* iv. 60 Irregularities can characterize the over-all pattern as well as the idiophonemic patterns. **1959** *Amer. Speech* XXXIV. 265 The diaphonemic inventory is a composite of all the idiophonemic inventories. **1890** BILLINGS *Med. Dict.* 679/2 Idioretinal light. **1929** C. MURCHISON *Found. Exper. Psychol.* iv. 183 If the intensity of the stimulus is zero over the entire area of the retina, the accompanying experience is not typically a black, but is, instead, a dark gray, which is sometimes known as the 'idioretinal light' and is attributed to retinal self-excitation. **1938** R. S. WOODWORTH *Exper. Psychol.* xxii. 540 The readiest way of experiencing expanse color is to close the eyes and observe the gray field of idioretinal light. **1934** *Downside Rev.* LII. 483 But Mount Athos in 1928 still had nearly 5,000 monks, including the 'idiorrhythmics' with their very special kind of life. **1957** *Oxf. Dict. Chr. Ch.* 676/2 *Idiorrhythmic*, a term applied to certain monasteries on Mount Athos. **1960** D. ATHILL tr. *Valentin's Monks of Mt. Athos* 45 But the idiorhythmics keep their property? Indeed they do, and they have to look after it as well as possible because on their death everything they own goes to the monastery. **1909** *Heart* I. 70 The continuous ventricular rhythm, at about 30 per minute, met with in complete heart-block (idioventricular rhythm). **1961** *Lancet* 9 Sept. 575/2 During this interval electrocardiographic monitoring should clarify the diagnosis of..idioventricular rhythm with inadequate cardiac output.

idioblast (i·dioblast). [f. IDIO- + -BLAST.] **1.** *Bot.* (In Dict. s.v. IDIO-.)

2. *Cytology.* [a. G. *idioblast* (O. Hertwig *Zelle und Gewebe* (1893) I. ix. 272).] A hypo-

thetical structural unit of living protoplasm. *Obs. exc. Hist.*

1893 *Nature* 2 Feb. 315 He [*sc.* O. Hertwig]..suggests the employment of the term 'Idioblasts' for the minute elementary particles, which Darwin called 'gemmules' in his hypothesis of pangenesis. **1925** E. B. WILSON *Cell* (ed. 3) 1134 *Idiosome*, the same as *idioblast, plasome, pangen* etc.

3. *Petrol.* [a. G. *idioblast* (F. Becke 1904, in *Compt. Rend. IX Sess. Congr. Géol. Internat.* II. 564)], a mineral crystal within a metamorphic rock which has developed its own characteristic crystal faces.

1920 A. HOLMES *Nomencl. Petrol.* 122 *Idioblast*, Becke, 1903, a term applied to pseudoidiomorphic crystals, such as garnet, occurring in metamorphic rocks. **1962** T. F. W. BARTH *Theoret. Petrol.* (ed. 2) 288 The majority of the minerals in metamorphic rocks are irregular in outline, xenoblasts; but some minerals are frequently bounded by their own crystal faces, idioblasts.

So **idiobla·stic** *a. Petrol.*, (of a mineral crystal within a metamorphic rock) having its own characteristic crystal faces; (of a crystal face) having its own characteristic form; **idioblastic order, series**, a ranking of minerals expressing their relative ability to develop idioblastic crystals when competing with each other.

1908 *Q. Jrnl. Geol. Soc.* LXIV. 482 Most of the hornblende existing in the amphibolite..is clearly secondary, and from its idiomorphic forms would be called 'recrystallized'.. For such cases Prof. F. Becke has proposed the term idioblastic. **1954** H. WILLIAMS et al. *Petrogr.* ix. 166 It is possible to list metamorphic minerals in a generalized sequence—the crystalloblastic series (idioblastic order)—such that each tends to develop idioblastic surfaces against any other mineral placed lower in the series.

idiogram (i·diogræm). *Cytology* and *Med.* [ad. Russ. *idiogramma* (S. Navashin: in *Zhurn. Russk. Bot. Obshch.* (1921) VI. 171 he is reported as having used the term in his lectures for many years): see IDIO- and -GRAM.] = *KARYOTYPE *sb.* 1b: usually, a diagrammatic or systematized representation of a chromosome complement (of one cell or of many) indicating the number of chromosomes, their relative lengths, the position of the centromeres, etc.

1927 *Genetics* XII. 64 The relative size of the chromosomes, peculiar shape, and especially the presence of satellites (S. Nawaschin, 1912) and constrictions (Sakamura 1915, 1920) furnish criteria for distinguishing the members of a given complement, or using the terminology of S. Nawaschin, they characterize the idiogram or the specific arrangement of the diploid nuclear plates. **1934** L. W. SHARP *Introd. Cytol.* (ed. 3) ix. 128 The diagrammatic representation of a karyotype, as in Fig. 70, is called an idiogram (S. Nawaschin, 1921). **1957** C. P. SWANSON *Cytol. & Cytogenetics* (1958) v. 118 The shape and size of chromosomes are his guideposts, and their constancy has enabled him to determine for purposes of comparison the karyotypes or idiograms (haploid complements) of many plants and animals. *Ibid.* xiii. 448 When represented in diagrammatic fashion..the karyotype is usually referred to as an idiogram. **1966** D. M. KRAMSCH tr. *Grundmann's Gen. Cytol.* ii. 108 All the chromosomes of one set form the karyotype specific for each species and with such a chromosomal idiogram it is possible in certain cases to demonstrate relationships between the species. **1969** R. R. EGGEN in Davidsohn & Henry *Todd-Sanford Clin. Diagn.* (ed. 14) xxxii. 1224 (*caption*) Idiogram of a normal human cell... The male karyotype differs from the female in that male cells normally have a single X chromosome and therefore have only 15 group C chromosomes. **1971** *Nature* 11 June 887/1 The average forms of all chromosomes of a complement are defined by an idiogram, based on a large number of karyotypes. **1973** *Lancet* 24 Feb. 420/1 Strictly speaking the actual pictures [of chromosomes] are karyotypes, and an idiogram is a diagram of the chromosome state of an individual.

idiolect (i·diolekt). *Linguistics.* [f. IDIO- after DIALECT.] The linguistic system of one person, differing in some details from that of all other speakers of the same dialect or language.

1948 B. BLOCH in *Language* XXIV. 7 The totality of the possible utterances of one speaker at one time in using a language to interact with one other speaker is an *idiolect*. **1948** R. A. HALL Jr. in *Studies in Linguistics* VI. ii. 31 Language exists in individuals, as a set of habits which each individual possesses (an *idiolect*). **1953** C. E. BAZELL *Ling. Form* 96 It must not be supposed that such [linguistic] systems are necessarily less determinate than for instance that of a single idiolect as recorded over a short space of time. **1953** J. B. CARROLL *Study of Lang.* ii. 10 Indeed each member of a speech community may be said to possess his own *idiolect*, his own personal variety of the language system. **1953** *Internat. Jrnl. Amer. Ling.* XIX. ii. Suppl. 40 Hockett defined 'idiolect' as the individual's total repertory of speech habits over a short period of time. **1958** A. A. HILL *Introd. Ling. Struct.* ii. 13 The English which is described in the personal dialect of a single speaker or, to use the technical term, a single idiolect. **1964** M. A. K. HALLIDAY et al. in J. A. Fishman *Readings Sociol. of Lang.* (1968) 158 A person's idiolect may be identified, through the lens of the various registers, by its grammatical and lexical characteristics. **1964** R. H. ROBINS *Gen. Ling.* ii. 51 The lower limit of dialect division comes down to the individual speaker, and for this limiting case

of dialect the term *idiolect* (the speech habits of a single person) has been coined. **1970** W. LABOV in *Rep. 20th Round Table Meeting on Ling. & Lang. Stud.* 89 So we are dealing not with the idiolect of the investigator, but the idiolect of one isolated boy whose position in the community is quite uncertain.

Hence **idiole·ctal** *a.*, of or pertaining to an idiolect; **idiole·ctally** *adv.*

1953 *Internat. Jrnl. Amer. Ling.* XIX. ii. Suppl. 37 Utterances are swiftly and with assurance identified despite idiolectal differences. **1958** *Archivum Linguisticum* X. ii. 146 Who..pronounces *cow* and *bough* with different diphthongs, unless idiolectally and idiosyncratically? **1965** *Language* XLI. 502 Idiolectal diversity is an inevitable result of the..productivity inherent in every single individual's linguistic habits. **1972** *Ibid.* XLVIII. 314 We believe these variations to be idiolectal rather than dialectal.

idiom. Add: **3. b.** A characteristic mode of expression in music, art, or writing; an instance of this.

1921 J. B. McEwen *First Steps Mus. Comp.* 5 To put it in somewhat colloquial terms, the composer of ancient music wrote melody, the composer of modern music writes tunes. It is no part of my purpose to make comparisons between these two idioms. *Ibid.*, An intentional reversion to the contrapuntal idiom. **1923** H. CRANE *Let.* 9 Feb. (1965) 121 Tate has a whole lot to offer when he finds his way out of the Eliot idiom. **1927** *Grove's Dict. Mus.* (ed. 3) II. 537/2 The folk-songs of all nations have been cultivated..for the sake, mainly, of their undoubted freshness and spontaneity of idiom as compared with pseudo-classical models. *Ibid.* 538/1 The study of this melodic music has suggested many harmonic idioms of notable freshness and beauty. **1939** *Burlington Mag.* Aug. 90/1 Buildings and industrial products which are now the accepted 'idiom' of design throughout the modern world. **1955** *Times* 9 May 3/1 We in this country have had experience of Anglo-American cooperation in film-making, and, whatever may be said in its favour from the practical, economic point of view, it certainly tends to blur and weaken the natural idiom and character of the countries involved. **1957** S. DANCE in S. Traill *Concerning Jazz* 43 The three great names in the presentation of jazz in the pure New Orleans idiom..were King Oliver, Jelly Roll Morton and Louis Armstrong. **1958** B. JAMES in P. Gammond *Duke Ellington* ii. 145 Ellington's music had its origins in the New Orleans style, as has so much else worthwhile in the jazz idiom.

4. (Further examples.)

1866 GEO. ELIOT *Let.* 15 Aug. (1955) IV. 301, I took unspeakable pains in preparing to write Romola—neglecting nothing I could find that would help me to what I may call the 'Idiom' of Florence, in the largest sense one could stretch the word to. **1870** G. M. HOPKINS *Jrnls. & Papers* (1959) 195, I noticed it [*sc.* snow]..sketched in intersecting edges bearing 'idiom'..I have no other word yet for that which takes the eye or mind in a bold hand.. not being beauty nor true inscape yet gives interest. **1936** R. CAMPBELL *Mithraic Emblems* 46 To form the idiom of her flesh I faceted in clearest thought An arctic crystal in whose mesh Of frosty rays the sun is caught.

5. *Comb.* **Idiom Neutral**, an international language based on Volapük, devised chiefly by W. Rosenberger, and first published in English in 1903.

1903 W. ROSENBERGER (*title*) Idiom neutral. **1907** W. J. CLARK *Internat. Lang.* ii. v. 99 The famous linguistic club of Nuremberg is remarkable for having gone through the evolution from Volapük to Idiom Neutral *via* Esperanto. **1922** A. L. GUÉRARD *Short Hist. Internat. Lang. Movement* ii. vi. 137 Idiom Neutral is entirely based on the principle of greatest internationality, at least so far as root-words are concerned. **1949** M. PEI *Story of Lang.* (1952) vi. iii. 443 In 1902 an academy of Volapük experts devised a radical simplification of their tongue, which they rechristened Idiom Neutral.

idiomaticity (idiomǎti·siti). [f. IDIOMATIC *a.*: see -ICITY.] The quality or state of being idiomatic.

1965 *Language* XLI. 504 Mrs Palmer's translation is.. accurate, without sacrificing freedom or idiomaticity. **1971** T. F. MITCHELL in *Archivum Linguisticum* II. 57 Although such correspondences [as *make up to* = *flatter, make it up to* = *compensate*, etc.] are usually suggestive, they are apparently not a necessary condition of idiomaticity.

idiomorphism (idiomọ̄·ɪfiz'm). *Min.* [f. IDIOMORPH(IC *a.* + -ISM.] The condition of being idiomorphic.

1908 *Q. Jrnl. Geol. Soc.* LXIV. 482 Professor F. Becke.. points out that, in the formation of the crystalline schists, the relative idiomorphism is not to be considered as denoting the order in which they have formed. **1951** TURNER & VERHOOGEN *Ign. & Metamorphic Petrol.* iii. 56 Idiomorphism seems..a doubtful criterion of early crystallization in the case of certain consistently idiomorphic accessories, such as apatite.

idiosome (i·diosōum). [f. IDIO- + *-SOME[4].]
†**1.** *Biol.* A supposed ultimate unit of living matter. *Obs.*

1894 C. O. WHITMAN in *Biol. Lectures 1893* (Wood's Hole, Mass., Marine Biol. Lab.) 123 It will find the secret of organization, growth, development, not in cell-formation, but in those ultimate elements of living matter, for which *idiosomes* seems to me an appropriate name. **1899** [see PANGENE].

2. *Cytology.* [Proposed (as F. *idiosome*) by C. Regaud (*Arch. d'Anat. microsc.* (1910) XI. 343) as a better word than *idiozome*.] = *IDIOZOME.

1918 *Amer. Jrnl. Anat.* XXIV. 37 (*heading*) The development of the idiosome in the germ-cells of the male guinea-pig. **1934** L. W. Sharp *Introd. Cytol.* (ed. 3) xiv. 216 In another series of forms (mollusks, amphibia, other vertebrates) the Golgi bodies are closely aggregated about the centrioles where their lightly staining substance flows together to form the idiosome. **1953** O. E. Nelsen *Compar. Embryol. Vertebr.* iii. 126 The idiosome (idiozome) is a rounded body of cytoplasm which, in many animal species, takes the cytoplasmic stain more intensely than the surrounding cytoplasm.

idiosyncrasy. Add: **1.** *spec.* An individual's hypersensitivity *to* a drug or other substance which is ingested or inhaled or which otherwise comes into contact with the body. (Further examples.)

1887 *Brit. Med. Jrnl.* 20 Aug. 431/1 Dr Daniel Bernouilli, of Basle, reports an instance of idiosyncrasy with respect to antipyrin. **1893** *Edin. Med. Jrnl.* XXXVIII. 627 No very tenable theory has been put forward to explain the reason of idiosyncrasy to drugs. **1912** *Jrnl. Amer. Med. Assoc.* 13 Apr. 1088 The view that the peculiar idiosyncrasies, so-called, with respect to certain articles of diet—strawberries, cheese..cow's milk, etc.—are forms of anaphylactic reactions is steadily growing. **1922** *Jrnl. Immunol.* VII. 128 Peculiar drug reactions, known as idiosyncrasies, were well recognized, but they were not identified as allergies until 1916. **1932** *Jrnl. Soc. Chem. Industry* 13 May 440/2 Mention was made..of the frequent lack of adequate proof of the supposed irritant action of certain dyes and of the difficulties due to idiosyncrasy. **1971** *Lancet* 25 Sept. 698/2 Idiosyncrasy to CS has not been reported, and the old and young do not seem to be at exceptional risk.

idiot, *sb.* Add: **4. idiot asylum,** a term formerly used for a hospital for the mentally ill; **idiot board** *colloq.*, a prompting board held before a television speaker but not projected on the film; **idiot box** *colloq.*, a television set; also *transf.*; **idiot card** *colloq.*, = **idiot board*; **idiot fringe,** (*a*) a fringe of hair in a style once worn (see quots.); (*b*) (*occas.*) = **lunatic fringe*; **idiot light** *colloq.*, a warning light, usu. red, that goes on when a fault occurs in a mechanical or electrical device; **idiot sheet** *colloq.*, = **idiot board*; **idiot stick** *U.S. slang*, a shovel; **idiot stitch,** tricot-stitch, the easiest stitch in crochet work.

1866 J. MacGregor *Thousand Miles in Rob Roy Canoe* (ed. 2) vi. 104 Close to the inn was the idiot asylum, an old castle with poor demented women in it. **1880** 'Mark Twain' *Tramp Abroad* I. xxv. 250 They meant an asylum—an *idiot* asylum. **1952** *Newsweek* 4 Aug. 51/2 The Republicans and the Democrats got their 'idiot boards' free. **1961** G. Millerson *Technique Television Production* x. 194 (*caption*) Held-up cue card, idiot board, goof sheet. **1971** *Radio Times* 4 Nov. 6/4, I can never work with an auto-cue or idiot board. I learn my lines before the show. **1959** P. Bull *I know Face* xi. 193 The rationing period, when my very existence depended on the magic idiot-box. **1965** *Lancet* 2 Jan. 46/2 Often they may be found, in semi-hypnotic state, watching the 'idiot box' with its endless stream of images and fullness of sound, all signifying nothing. **1972** P. Flower *Cobweb* ii. 72, I thought you spent all your time with the idiot box. **1973** *Ann. N.Y. Acad. Sci.* CCXI. 282 We assume that the modern general purpose computer is an idiot-box capable of performing only the simplest of routines. **1959** *Globe & Mail* (Toronto) 18 Sept. 1/7 No one held up an 'idiot card'—a prompter's card for actors who have forgotten their lines. **1960** B. Keaton *Wonderful World of Slapstick* (1967) 238 They had worked out an interesting technique for these foreign-language remakes. They used 'idiot cards'. On these the foreign words are spelled out in phonetic English and held up beyond camera range. **1969** *New Yorker* 27 Sept. 86/3 We had all the written questions put on idiot cards, and then the people read them before the camera. **1886** H. Baumann *Londinismen* 81/1 *Idiot-fringe*, fransenartig auf die Stirn herabgekämmtes Haar der Fabrikmädchen, Hökerweiber u.s.w. **1923** J. Manchon *Le Slang* 130 *Fringe*, le devant des cheveux dans la coiffure à la chien (habituelle chez les femmes de la basse classe). On dit aussi idiot-fringe. **1965** *Spectator* 5 Mar. 286/1 An article on a small and dying idiot-fringe sect of nationalists in North Germany. **1968** E. McGirr *Lead-Lined Coffin* iii. 173 He watched the idiot lights in the dashboard..for the warning red which would betoken he had lost the oil. **1971** M. Tak *Truck Talk* 88 *Idiot light*, a small light sometimes found on the front end of a tractor, the light turns on when the ignition is started. **1961** A. Berkman *Singers' Gloss. Show Business* 29 *Idiot sheet*, a large placard or paper roll, on which is [*sic*] printed the actual lines to be spoken by an announcer or performer. The printed characters are large enough to be seen from quite a distance from the camera. **1962** R. Bretz *Techniques Television Production* 487 When cue cards first came into use for full script purposes, they were known derisively as 'idiot sheets'. **1942** Berrey & Van den Bark *Amer. Thes. Slang* § 75/32 *Shovel*, idiot stick. **1968** R. F. Adams *Western Words* (rev. ed.) 158/1 *Idiot stick*, what the miner calls his shovel; sometimes shortened to *idiot*. **1882** Caulfeild & Saward *Dict. Needlework*, *Idiot stitch*, one of the names given to Tricot Stitch.

idiozome (i·diozōᵘm). *Cytology.* Also **idiosome** (q.v. above). [ad. G. *idiozom* (F. Meves 1896, in *Anat. Hefte* (Abt. 2) VI. 315), f. Idio- + Gr. ζῶμ-α loin-cloth, band, girdle.] A rounded structure present in the cytoplasm of developing germ cells in members of most animal groups, in certain of which it forms part of (or is associated with) the Golgi apparatus in spermatids and spermatocytes and develops into the acrosome of the spermatozoon.

1899 *Zool. Jahrbücher* (*Abt. für Anat.*) XII. 14 At the pointed end of the cell lies a spherical or oval body, homogeneous in appearance, which is stained more deeply by the action of Hermann's fixative than the enveloping cytoplasm... Meves..proposes for it the name 'Idiozom', which I shall adopt in the present paper... In the idiozome of the resting spermatogonium I have been unable to detect any granules which could be regarded as centrosomes. **1920** L. Doncaster *Introd. Study Cytol.* vii. 102 The acrosome is described in some forms as arising from a mass of denser protoplasm known as the idiozome. **1928** C. W. Metz in E. V. Cowdry *Special Cytol.* II. xxxvi. 1282 The Golgi bodies..usually appear first in the form of small granules or rods, which during the growth stages typically collect about the idiozome. **1952** G. H. Bourne *Cytol. & Cell Physiol.* (ed. 2) vi. 254 The Golgi apparatus in developing male germ and other cells is frequently associated with a differentiated area of cytoplasm near the nucleus, called the idiozome.

idle, *a.* (*sb.*). Add: **3. b.** (See quot. 1956.)

1956 J. Masters *Bugles & Tiger* ii. 46 The word 'idle' meant anything the staff considered unsoldierly. We *were* idle; we had idle haircuts, idle rifles, idle bicycles; we *did* idle salutes, idle jumps. **1959** *News Chron.* 4 Aug. 1/4 'Idle' is a Brigade [of Guards] adjective that describes everything that is not perfection in execution. A bootlace undone is an idle bootlace. **1963** D. Walder *Bags of Swank* vi. 65 Ransome looked at the lecturer's hip pocket now revealed as undone. 'Idle and naked,' he said loudly to Lilburne.

4. (Further examples.) Freq. in phr. *the idle rich.*

1865 Mill *Auguste Comte* 160 He allows of no idle rich. **1900** B. Matthews *Confident To-Morrow* 178 Mr. Dircks wishes to shift the burdens of the worthy poor upon the shoulders of the idle rich. **1926** *Encycl. Brit.* I. 527/1 We must remember as a rule the 'idle rich' do not represent idle riches. **1938** *Times Lit. Suppl.* 11 June 403/3 The crew, Reds of various shades, mutiny and drive ashore the idle-rich passengers. **1960** C. Day Lewis *Buried Day* viii. 171 The idle rich, the boss class, fleeing..from the wrath to come. **1964** M. Argyle *Psychol. & Social Probl.* xv. 185 There has been a decline of the old 'idle rich' upper middle class, living partly on unearned income and passing on wealth and advantages to its children. **1971** *Daily Tel.* 20 Oct. 10/4 More than 25,000 Coventry workers were idle yesterday as a result of the dispute.

5. c. *Electr.* Of a wire on an armature: having no electromotive force induced in it. Of a component of an alternating current: 90° out of phase with respect to the voltage; wattless, reactive.

1884 S. P. Thompson *Dynamo-Electr. Machinery* iii. 33 Where the coils are working in series, it has been considered advantageous to arrange the commutator to cut out the coil that is in the position of least action, as the circuit is thereby relieved of the resistance of an idle coil. *Ibid.* vii. 126 The advantage originally claimed for this construction, namely, that it allows less of the total length of wire to remain 'idle' on the inner side of the ring, is rather imaginary than real. **1904** R. M. Walmsley *Electr. in Service of Man* II. vi. 1069 This current.. contributes nothing to the power, and is therefore often referred to as the idle current. **1908** Slingo & Brooker *Electr. Engin.* (new ed.) ix. 354 The portions connecting the horizontal limbs are always idle, inasmuch as they do not cut, but only slide through, the lines of force.

d. Of money: out of circulation.

1931 *Times Lit. Suppl.* 19 Feb. 124/2 It may be thought that saving cannot exceed investment because idle money automatically becomes the basis of bank credit. **1965** Seldon & Pennance *Everyman's Dict. Econ.* s.v. Dishoarding. A distinction is made between 'active' money in circulation and financing current transactions and 'inactive' money held in idle balances.

8. a. *idle-handed* (later example), *-minded* (so *-mindedness*).

1899 *Westm. Gaz.* 21 Aug. 2/3 The empty-headed and idle-minded exist in both sexes. **1899** *Leisure Hour* Dec. 153 Hence the dull lives of many children of the poor, their occasional trend towards mischief from sheer idle-mindedness. **1917** Kipling *Years Between* (1919) 47 But the idle-minded overlings who quibbled while they died. **1927** T. Wilder *Bridge San Luis Rey* 100 Even the busiest mother stands for a moment idle-handed. **1928** *Oxford Poetry* 39 Because this place is full of moneyed young men And indolent phallophil idleminded girls.

b. idle Dick, Jack *S. Afr.*, formerly used as a local name for the grass-bird, *Sphenœacus afer*; **idle-fellow,** formerly, a fellow of a college who had no formal duties; so **idle fellowship.**

1901 A. C. Stark *Birds S. Afr.* II. 168 *Sphenœacus natalensis.* Natal Grass-Bird... 'Idle Dick' and 'Lazy Dick' of English Colonists. **1919** R. Frost *Let.* 8 Aug. (1964) 132, I am going..to Ann Arbor to become an idle-fellow of the University of Michigan for one year. **1884** in J. R. Ware *Passing Eng.* (1909) 157/1 Much has been said against what are called idle Fellowships. **1909** J. R. Ware *Ibid.* 156/2 *Idle fellowships* (*Oxford and Cambridge*), the old as distinct from the new fellowships. Parliamentary action swept away towards the end of the 19th century most of these fatal sinecures. **1884** R. B. Sharpe *Layard's Birds S. Afr.* (rev. ed.) 281 It..will suffer itself to be taken with the hand rather than rise again; for this reason it has acquired the name of *Idle Jack* or *Lazy Dick.* **1893** A. Newton *Dict. Birds* 458 Idle Jack, a local name in the Cape Colony for *Sphenœacus africanus* (Grass-bird).

B. *sb.* **4.** [f. the vb.] Idling (of an engine); idling speed.

1939 C. H. Fisher *Carburation & Carburettors* iv. 96 If the throttle is closed completely the adjustment of the idling mixture is rendered too sensitive, hence it is usual to give a very small opening of the throttle when adjusting the idle. **1943** A. P. Fraas *Aircraft Power Plants* vii. 134 As the throttle is opened farther..the idle needle is withdrawn very rapidly and so has no effect on fuel flow at powers above an idle. **1966** *McGraw-Hill Encycl. Sci. & Technol.* II. 478/2 Because of increased piston and other friction with a cold engine, greater throttle opening as well as more fuel is required for idle at that time. **1972** *Practical Motorist* Oct. 160/3 Start the engine and set the tick-over to 650 rpm, using the air screw. Now turn the jet adjusting screw one way or the other until the smoothest idle is achieved.

5. *attrib.* (in sense *B. 4: cf. *idling *vbl. sb.* 2), as *idle jet, needle, nozzle, power, range, stroke.*

1943 A. P. Fraas *Aircraft Power Plants* vii. 119 A high metering head..is used to induce a flow of fuel through an idle jet. **1943** Idle needle [see sense *B. 4]. **1968** C. F. Taylor *Internal-Combustion Engine* II. vi. 200 Further opening of the throttle gradually exposes the idle nozzle to the full manifold depression, which may be as much as 10 psi..below atmospheric pressure in a normal idling engine. **1946** R. H. Thorner *Aircraft Carburetion* ii. 65 The richest mixture is required at the carburetor during the lowest idle power. **1939** C. H. Fisher *Carburation & Carburettors* iv. 95 Since most engines idle with a manifold depression of about 16″ of mercury,..any good carburettor can be made to deliver a wide band of mixture strengths covering the idle range. **1896** W. Norris *'Otto' Cycle Gas Engine* ii. 6 The idle strokes of the 'Otto' cycle are far from theoretically correct.

idle, *v.* Add: **1.** (Later example.)

1938 M. K. Rawlings *Yearling* ix. 75 The woodbox was low and Jody idled outside to fill it.

3. (Earlier and later examples.)

1788 E. Sheridan *Jrnl.* (1960) 138 And to compleat all, they beg'd him to see another person who idled him two hours more. **1968** *Globe & Mail* (Toronto) 5 Feb. 21/7 Gilchrist was..idled with a leg injury. **1972** *Nat. Geographic* Sept. 322 (*caption*) *Idled by war*, workers await the call to return to the Karnaphuli Rayon and Chemicals plant in Chandraghona.

4. a. *intr.* Of an engine: to run while disconnected from a load or out of gear, so that it performs no external or useful work; also, to run very slowly.

1916 [implied in * idling *vbl. sb.* 1]. **1920** V. W. Pagé *Useful Hints Motorists* iii. 78 Turn petrol adjustment to the right..until motor idles smoothly. **1925** A. W. Judge *Carburettors & Carburation* iii. 37 The ideal carburettor should:..(4) Enable the engine to run very slowly when 'idling', without undue waste of fuel. **1932** Chatfield & Taylor *Airplane & its Engine* (ed. 2) viii. 169 Airplane engines must be able to idle, that is run very slowly, in order to keep the landing speed as low as possible. **1934** *Boys' Mag.* XLVII. 23/2 One after another the four engines were started, 'revved' with a deafening roar singly and all together, and then left quietly 'idling'. **1953** G. E. M. Anscombe tr. *Wittgenstein's Philos. Investigations* I. § 132 The confusions which occupy us arise when language is like an engine idling, not when it is doing work. **1965** P. H. Smith *High-Speed Two-Stroke Petrol Engine* x. 212 The engine is..idling at tick-over speed. **1970** *Commercial Motor* 25 Sept. 64/2 Neither vehicle had much mileage on the clock which was probably the reason why the engines idled badly.

b. *trans.* To cause (an engine) to idle; *to idle down*, to slow down and idle (an engine).

1925 E. W. Knott *Carburettor Handbk.* i. 41 It is surprising what a small degree of throttle opening is necessary to pass the requisite amount of mixture to 'idle' an engine. **1938** J. Steinbeck *Long Valley* 17 She heard him drive to the gate and idle down his motor. **1938** *Amer. Speech* XIII. 131/2 In case of some delay, the engineer may idle down or slow down the tractor. **1972** H. Buckmaster *Walking Trip* 163 David slowed the car and idled it by the side of the road.

idler. Add: **3. b.** A wheel or roller that when in contact with a moving belt, tape, or the like transmits no power but serves to support it, guide it, or make it taut. Freq. *attrib.*

1899 G. D. Hiscox *Mech. Movements* II. 37 A single belt, with two idlers, for tightening and directing the half twist of the belt. **1908** [see *belt conveyor* (*belt *sb.*[1] 6)]. **1951** *Wire Ropes in Mines* (Inst. Mining & Metall.) 290 Supporting idlers are necessary to prevent severe whipping and vibration, if the distance is great between the drum and head sheave. However, if it is at all possible, the installation of idler sheaves should be avoided. **1962** A. Nisbett *Technique Sound Studio* 256 On a tape deck, the idler presses the tape against the capstan when the drive is switched on. **1969** *Times* 2 May (Suppl.) p. viii/7 This means that idler rolls made to this design will operate on conveyors at speeds up to and in excess of 1,000 ft. a minute. **1970** *Jrnl. Soc. Dyers & Colourists* LXXXVI. 87/1 The web follows an up-and-down zigzag path over idler rollers. **1972** *Reader's Digest Repair Manual* 551/4 Incorrect speed is generally due to a worn idler wheel.

4. *Railways.* (See quots.)

1909 *Cent. Dict.* Suppl., *Idler*, in *railroading*, an empty car; an empty. **1962** *Amer. Speech* XXXVII. 133 *Idler*, an empty car which is coupled to another car having a load of logs longer than the car, thus permitting the load to be coupled into a train.

‖ **idli** (i·dli). [Tamil.] A steamed cake of rice and black gram, popular in southern India.

1958 R. K. Narayan *Guide* i. 16 Give me coffee and *idli*, please, first thing in the day. **1961** K. Nagarajan

Chron. Kedaram iii. 64 There was no lack of mirth or old-fashioned cheer; plenty of *pongal* and *idlis* were consumed. **1971** *Hindustan Times Weekly* (New Delhi) (Suppl.) 4 Apr. p. iv/3, I learnt Tamil..even got initiated into the mysteries of *idlis*. **1971** *Illustr. Weekly India* 25 Apr. 49/1 Dev closes the generation gap between Hema and him by the handsome device of welcoming this *idli*-white 'It Girl' with open arms. **1972** *New Yorker* 26 Aug. 28/1 Sell this poor child two *idlies*. Give him freshly made ones, not yesterday's. *Ibid.*, The *idlies*—so soft and pungent, with green chutney spread on top.

idling, *vbl. sb.* (s.v. Idle *v.*). Add: (Further examples, corresponding to *idle *v.* 4.)

1916 R. T. Nicholson *Bk. of Ford* 151 You will run very economically, but you will find starting and 'idling' very difficult. **1925** A. W. Judge *Carburettors & Carburation* iv. 57 For slow running, or 'idling', two adjustments are provided. **1949** I. Katz *Princ. Aircraft Propulsion Machinery* xx. 216 Idling is desirable from the standpoint of warm-up prior to flight. **1966** *McGraw-Hill Encycl. Sci. & Technol.* II. 478/1 Slight intake or exhaust valve leaks can make smooth idling impossible.

2. *attrib.* (esp. designating parts of an engine concerned with idling), as *idling adjustment, condition, jet, mixture, passage, screw, speed.*

1924 B. G. Elliott *Automobile Repairing* x. 133 Carburettors which have idling adjustments may be adjusted to overcome loading. **1940** *Chambers's Techn. Dict.* 437/1 *Idling adjustment*, a setting of the slow-running jet and throttle position of a carburettor, so as to give regular idling. **1943** A. P. Fraas *Aircraft Power Plants* vii. 131 The model *H* idle system depends on a small hole in the tip of the metering pin to restrict the fuel flow under idling conditions. **1929** *Motor World* 11 Jan. 23/2 In the new Zenith a special idling jet, fed by its own independent compensating jet, is employed. **1942** B. A. Shields *Air Pilot Training* xiii. 216 The engine is supplied with fuel for starting and idling by a special arrangement called an idling jet. **1959** *Motor Manual* (ed. 36) iii. 55 Here the idling mixture is adjusted manually. **1925** A. W. Judge *Carburettors & Carburation* iv. 100 There is a slow running, or idling passage, of the usual pilot jet type. **1972** *Drive* New Year 99/2 The throttle-stop, or idling screw, will be found where the accelerator cable meets the carburettor; the mixture screw is at the base of the carburettor. **1932** Chatfield & Taylor *Airplane & its Engine* (ed. 2) viii. 139 The idling speed is generally about 200 r.p.m. when the airplane is at rest on the ground. **1973** M. Woodhouse *Blue Bone* xii. 128, I..opened the hood, screwing up the throttle control rod a couple of turns to raise the idling speed.

idling, *ppl. a.* (s.v. Idle *v.*). (Further examples, corresponding to *idle *v.* 4.)

1936 E. S. Gardner *Case of Stuttering Bishop* (1937) iii. 41 The ever-present throbbing undertone of sound.. from idling motors. **1968** [see *idle nozzle* s.v. *idle *sb.* 5].

Ido (ī·do). [In this language, = offspring.] An artificial language, based on * Esperanto, selected by the 'Delegation for the Adoption of an Auxiliary International Language' (founded at Paris in 1901), and made public in 1907. Hence **I·dist, I·doist,** a student or speaker of Ido; also *attrib.*

The official name is 'Linguo Internaciona di la Delegitaro (Sistema Ido)'.

1908 *Daily Chron.* 7 Sept. 7/2 The new language has been named 'Ido', and its inventor [M. de Beaufront, of Geneva] claims that it is easier to learn and is more methodical than Esperanto, its parent. **1916** H. G. Wells *Mr. Britling* I. v. § 10 'There would be no English, no Germans, no Russians. Just Esperantists.'..'Or Idoists,' said Herr Heinrich. **1922** O. Jespersen *Lang.* xviii. 347 Anyone who has written much in Ido [etc.]. **1926** *Encycl. Brit.* III. 906/1 In 1907 two Frenchmen, Messrs. Couturat and de Beaufront, produced a modification of Esperanto which they named simplified Esperanto. Owing to Esperantist protests, the 'linguo internaciona' was renamed Ido...The Idists claim that Ido is Esperanto rendered more scientific and natural. *Ibid.*, The chief Idist grammarian, Dr. Max Talmey, advocates what he calls 'Improved Ido' or 'Ilo' or 'Arulo'. **1928** O. Jespersen *Internat. Lang.* I. 24 The practical experiences of Volapükists, Esperantists and Idists..have shown that the fears of sceptics are groundless with regard to pronunciation. **1946** H. Jacob *On Choice of Common Lang.* 79 The British section of the Ido-union. **1947** —— *Planned Auxiliary Lang.* 57 Idists practising the language for many years.

idolize, *v.* Add: **1.** Also *absol.*

1919 M. K. Bradby *Psycho-Anal.* 65 For instance, one person may be prone to jealousy, another to idolise.

Idomenian, -enean (əidomī·niăn, əidomenī·ăn), *a.* and *sb.* [f. *Idomeneus*, f. Gr. Ἰδομενεύς, a king of Crete + -an.] **A.** *adj.* Of or belonging to a race imagined by Thomas Reid, an 18th-c. metaphysician, to have no sense but sight, and to believe that space has only two dimensions. **B.** *sb.* A member of this race.

1764 T. Reid *Inquiry Human Mind* vi. 252 'The Idomenians,' saith he, 'are many of them very ingenious, and much given to contemplation.' *Ibid.* 255 The geometry of the Idomenians agrees in every thing with the geometry of visibles. *Ibid.* 257 A person of great genius, who is looked upon as having had something in him above Idomenian nature. *Ibid.*, The Idomenian faculties were certainly intended for contemplation. *Ibid.* 258 Every Idomenian firmly believes, that two or more bodies may exist in the same place. **1871** A. C. Fraser *Life Berkeley* x. 400 The invisibility of that sort of distance can thus be proved even to the Idomenian. **1890** W. James *Princ. Psychol.* II. xx. 214 One of Reid's Idomenians would frame precisely the same conception of the external world that we do, if he had our intellectual powers.

idryl (i·dril, əil). *Chem. Obs.* exc. *Hist.* [a. G. *idryl* (C. Bödeker 1844, in *Ann. d. Chem. u. Pharm.* LII. 102), f. Idr(ialin 2 + -yl.] **a.** A mixture of fluoranthene and other hydrocarbons (see quot. 1952) orig. obtained from the mercury ores of Idrija, in north-west Yugoslavia, and thought to be a single compound. **b.** = *fluoranthene.

1845 C. Bödeker in *Chem. Gaz.* 15 Feb. 73 One of the products obtained in the working of the bituminous mercurial ores in Idria is the so-called *Stupp*, a soft black mass mixed with globules of mercury. It was supposed to contain idrialine, but in its stead another hydrocarbon was found, idryle C^3H, and a more accurate examination has proved that idrialine..is an oxide of idryle. **1866** H. Watts tr. *Gmelin's Hand-bk. Chem.* XVII. 477 Idryl. $C^{42}H^{14}$... The crystals are nearly colourless, with a tinge of yellowish-green...Idryl assumes a golden-yellow colour in cold oil of vitriol. **1877** *Chem. News* 16 Nov. 222/2 G. Goldschmidt, 'Idryl'. This body, found by Bödeker in Idria, is ascertained to consist of several hydrocarbons... Besides chrysen, pyren, anthracen, phenanthren, a new hydrocarbon, $C_{15}H_{10}$, was isolated, and receives the name originally applied to the mixture. **1892** Roscoe & Schorlemmer *Treat. Chem.* (new ed.) III. vi. 523 Fluoranthene, $C_{15}H_{10}$, is found in coal-tar, and is also identical with idryl, one of the constituents of 'stuppfett'. **1926** H. G. Rule tr. *Schmidt's Text-bk. Org. Chem.* II. xvii. 513 Fluoranthene or Idryl, m.p. 110°, b.p. 250° (at 60 mm.). **1952** *Chem. Rev.* L. 483 In 1844 Boedeker..distilled these ores, with production of a similar hydrocarbon which he named idryl. Much later Goldschmiedt..showed..that idryl consisted of anthracene, phenanthrene, chrysene, pyrene, and a hitherto unknown hydrocarbon, $C_{15}H_{10}$, to which he gave the name idryl. Simultaneously with Goldschmiedt's discovery, Fittig and Gebhard..isolated..a hydrocarbon which was named fluoranthene and was claimed to be identical with Goldschmiedt's idryl.

‖ **id-ul-fitr** (i·d,ul,fit'r). Also (a better form) **id al-fitr.** [Arab. *'īd al-fiṭr*.] The Feast of breaking the Ramadan Fast, or Lesser Bairam, celebrated on the 1st of the month of Shawwāl: one of the two major festivals in Islam.

1734 G. Sale tr. *Koran* Prelim. Disc. vii. 150 The first of them is called, in Arabic, *Id al fetr*, i.e. The feast of breaking the fast, and begins the first of Shawâl, immediately succeeding the fast of Ramadân. **1832** G. A. Herklots tr. *Shurreef's Qanoon-e-Islam* xxiv. 261 The *Eed-ool-fitr* (or feast of alms), called also the feast of *Rumzan*, is observed on the first day of the month *Shuwal*. **1836** E. W. Lane *Acct. Manners & Customs Mod. Egyptians* II. 238 It is also called '*Eed el-Fitr* (or the Festival of the Breaking of the fast). **1896** E. Sell *Faith of Islám* (ed. 2) vi. 319 A very usual form of the Khuṭbah of the 'Ídu'l-Fiṭr which is preached in Arabic is as follows...We praise and thank him for the 'Ídu'l-Fiṭr, that great blessing, and we testify that beside him there is no God. **1909** *Daily Chron.* 18 Oct. 6/4 Undisturbed by the hum of the traffic in Holborn, the Imam lifted up his voice, and..droned out the Idul-Fitr prayer. **1970** *Cambr. Hist. Islam* II. 907 *'Id al-Fiṭr*, 'the Feast of the Breaking of the Fast' or *al-'Id al-Ṣaghīr* (the Small Feast), held after the end of Ramaḍān, the month of fasting. **1972** *Mainichi* (Japan) *Daily News* 6 Nov. 11/4 (Advt.), Kobe Muslim Mosque. Idul-Fitr prayers will be held at 9.00 a.m. on Tuesday, November 7th.

Idumæan (əidiumī·ăn, id-), *sb.* and *a.* Also **-ean.** [f. L. *Idūmæa*, a. Gr. Ἰδουμαία, f. Heb. *Edōm* Edom + -an.] **A.** *sb.* A member of the race inhabiting Idumæa. **B.** *adj.* Of or belonging to Idumæa or Edom, an ancient kingdom situated between Egypt and Palestine.

c **897** Ælfred tr. *Gregory's Pastoral Care* (1871) 387 Ezechiel...cwæð ðæt hie wolden weorðan forlorene & oferwunnene mid orsorgnesse, swa swa Idumeas wæron. **1382** Wyclif *3 Kings* xi. 1 Forsothe kyng Salomon to brennyngly louede many hethen wymmen, the douȝter forsothe of Pharao, and Moabitis, and Amonytis, and Ydumees, and Cidonees, and Ethees. **1537** tr. *Original & Sprynge of Sectes* 55 Idumeans. **1602** Lodge tr. *Josephus' Workes* 679 Simon the sonne of Cathla,..spake vnto the Idumæans from a tower, and commanded them to cast down their armes. **1737** W. Whiston tr. *Josephus' Works* 381 He fell upon the Idumeans, the posterity of Esau, at Acrabattene. **1838** *Penny Cycl.* XII. 437/1 The Idumæans marched to the assistance of Jerusalem when it was besieged by Titus. **1863** *Chambers's Encycl.* V. 343/1 The family was of Idumean descent. *Ibid.* 499/2 The Idumæan, Antipater. **1880** *Encycl. Brit.* XI. 754/1 Herod was the name of a family of Idumæan origin. **1936** C. Roth *Short Hist. Jewish People* viii. 78 The age-long enmity between the Jews and Idumaeans (Edomites), which had found its expression in the raids of Judah the Maccabee, culminated in the final subjection of the country. **1968** P. Needham tr. *Gelzer's Caesar* v. 251 The Idumaean Antipater, the minister of the Jewish High Priest Hyrcanus.

idyll, idyl (and derivs.). Now also commonly with pronunc. (id-). (See Fowler *Mod. Eng. Usage* (1926) 253, R. Bridges in *S.P.E. Tract* (1929) xxxii. 403, and A. C. Gimson *Everyman's Eng. Pronouncing Dict.* (1969) 241.)

idyllic, *a.* Add: Hence **idy·llicism.**

1941 L. MacNeice *Poetry of Yeats* v. 86 This snob idyllicism. **1964** *Economist* 25 Jan. 294/1 There is little idyllicism left.

Idzo, var. *Ijo *sb.* and *a.*

ieie (ī·e,ī:e). Also **ie.** [Hawaiian.] A climbing screw-pine of the genus *Freycinetia*, esp. *F. arborea*, whose prop-roots yield a fibre. Cf. Kie-kie.

1883 C. F. G. Cumming *Fire Fountains* I. vii. 128 Vines without number, the most notable being one called the *ié*. **1903** R. C. L. Perkins in *Fauna Hawaiiensis* I. 400 All those [birds] that were utilised could readily be caught by a bait of flowers, excepting perhaps the Ou, and this bird probably not less easily on account of its fondness for the ripe Ieie. **1915** W. A. Bryan *Nat. Hist. Hawaii* xvi. 211 Another plant peculiar to the lower woods..is the ieie, a climbing shrub. **1970** S. Carlquist *Hawaii* xvii. 337 *(caption)* The flowers of the ieie are surrounded by short leaves bright orange in color.

if, *conj.* (*sb.*). Add: **3. a.** *if I were you*: (examples).

1814 Jane Austen *Mansf. Park* I. vi. 109 If I were you, I should not think of the expense. *Ibid.* 112 'Mr Rushworth,' said Lady Bertram, 'if I were you, I would have a very pretty shrubbery. One likes to get out into a shrubbery in fine weather.' **1869** Trollope *Phineas Finn* II. xli. 30 'Of course you'll go,' said Phineas. 'I should, if I were you.' **1974** D. Gray *Dead Give Away* vi. 65 I'd lay off stirring up trouble for a bit if I were you.

4. a. (Later examples.)

1848 [see Twitch *v.*[1] 8 a]. **1965** *New Statesman* 16 Apr. 598/3 If Mr Stewart is top of the Tory pops, other ministers are also high up in the charts. **1967** *Listener* 17 Aug. 205/1 If my father's people were mill-workers.., my mother's people were agricultural workers. **1969** *Ibid.* 24 Apr. 585/1 If Mozart was a life-long admirer of J. C. Bach, his views on Clementi were disparaging, to put it mildly.

6. Also *if any* (see Any *a.* 2); *if anything*, if in any degree, perhaps even; *if not, why not* (see Why *adv.* 4 b).

1711 If any [see Any *a.* 2]. **1836** G. C. Lewis *Let.* 15 July (1870) 54 The writer says that the wages are nearly equal; if anything, the King's wages are rather the lowest. **1851** H. Spencer *Social Statics* xxviii. 392 If anything, we were comparatively deficient in these respects. **1873** Lytton *Kenelm Chillingly* II. iv. vi. 257 Shall I ever be in love? and if not, why not? **1909** P. A. Vaile *Mod. Golf* v. 92 If anything, touch the grass first. **1921** *Wireless World* IX. 187/1 L. M. T...asks..(3) If a diagram he sends is correct and, if not, why not. **1931** Belloc *Hist. Eng.* IV. ii. i. 260 If anything the ritual of King-worship was even more exaggerated in her case than in the case of Henry or of Edward. **1944** K. A. Esdaile *St. Martin in the Fields* ii. 50 If anything, the destruction was greater than in 1547. **1967** *Listener* 23 Feb. 261/1 At the start of every month I have to send him an account..of my earnings, if any.

7. (Later examples.)

1846 *Swell's Night Guide* 49 And, so help me never! if his nibs didn't go and dossed with her the same night. **1914** *Sat. Even. Post* 4 Apr. 10/1 'If it ain't Frisco Red!' exclaimed one prone figure. **1925** T. Dreiser *Amer. Trag.* I. xvii. 145 'Oh, Gee, well, ain't that the limit?'..'If you aren't the grouch.' *Ibid.* II. iii. 184 Well, by jing, if it ain't Tom.

8. c. as if: also followed by a clause containing the present tense.

Further examples in Fowler *King's Eng.* (ed. 3) pp. 165–6.

1693 Dryden tr. *Persius' Satires* I. 61 As if 'tis nothing worth that lies conceal'd. **1751** H. Fielding *Amelia* II. v. iii. 110 They seem indeed to be over-burthened with Limbs, which they know not how to use, as if when Nature hath finished her Work, the Dancing-Master still is necessary to put it in Motion. **1862** Thackeray *Philip* II. viii. 173 As if a coarse woman..has a right to lead a guileless nature into wrong! **1963** D. Storey *Radcliffe* xxxvi. 367 As if everything that appears to live ..is simply imitating some distant and incoherent ideal.

g. *if and when*, in reference to a future time but with a strong element of doubt.

1926 Fowler *Mod. Eng. Usage* 254/1 *If & when.* Any writer who uses this formula lays himself open to entirely reasonable suspicions on the part of his readers...There is the suspicion that he is a timid swordsman who thinks he will be safer with a second sword in his left hand. **1940** G. B. Shaw *Matter with Ireland* (1962) 283 If and when the situation becomes grave enough to convince America that I have no alternative, I will reoccupy your ports. **1963** *Amer. Speech* XXXVIII. 255 If and when a study of local words in Missouri appears, we will be able to trace the same patterns in that state too.

10. *Comb.* **if-clause,** a clause of condition or supposition introduced by the word *if*; **if-shot, if-stroke** *Cricket*, 'a stroke considered to be unsound and likely to cause the batsman's dismissal if the ball is hit' (Lewis).

1893 Turner & Hallidie *Primary Eng. Gram.* 113 The *if*-clause tells us *when*, or *under what circumstances* the desert would be a paradise. **1904** C. T. Onions *Adv. Eng. Syntax* 57 A Complex Sentence consisting of an Adverb Clause of Condition (the If-Clause, sometimes called the Protasis) and a Principal Clause (sometimes called the Apodosis) is called a Conditional Sentence. **1926** Fowler *Mod. Eng. Usage* 576/2 It [*sc.* the word

were] is entirely out of place in an *if*-clause concerned with past actualities & not answered by a *were* or *would be* in the apodosis. **1964** *English Studies* XLV. 85 The meaningful weight of the complete sentence may move from the *if*-clause to the headclause. **1966** G. N. Leech *Eng. in Advertising* vi. 61 Favourite openings are..*if* clauses. **1897** K. S. Ranjitsinhji *Jubilee Bk. Cricket* iv. 165 In its worst form this [slipping the ball] is commonly known nowadays as the 'if-stroke'. Originally it was called the 'but-stroke', after its great exponent, the Sussex wicket-keeper [Butt]; but some wag suggested that it should be called in preference the 'if-stroke', because if you hit the ball you are nearly sure to be out. **1920** D. J. Knight in P. F. Warner *Cricket* 36 It is essentially an 'if' shot, and must, to a certain extent, be unsound. **1922** *Cricketer Ann. 1922–23* 62 We will not indulge in 'cowshots' or 'ifshots'.

ifé (ī·fe). Also **ife.** [Native name.] A tropical African plant, *Sansevieria cylindrica*, of the family Liliaceæ, which yields a fibre formerly used as a substitute for hemp.

1859 *Curtis's Bot. Mag.* LXXXV. 5093 About three years since there were received at the Foreign Office, and transferred to the Admiralty, samples of a peculiar fibre and cordage under the name of Ifé, said to be derived from a new plant at the Portuguese settlement, Angola. **1866** Lindley & Moore *Treas. Bot.* II. 617/2 Ife. An Indian name for *Sanseviera* [sic] *cylindrica*. **1892** P. L. Simmonds *Commercial Dict. Trade Products* (rev. ed.) 462/1 Ife, a name in India for the *Sansievera* [sic] *cylindrica*, a plant useful for its fibre.

Ife (ī·fe). The name of a town in Western Nigeria, the religious centre of the Yoruba people, used *attrib.* to designate the art of the Yoruba people, *spec.* the bronzes and terracottas of which the first examples were found there in 1912.

[**1913** R. Blind tr. *Frobenius' Voice Afr.* I. xiv. 293 Various comparatively coarse stone monuments are raised above the earth in Ifé. Below it we found old sculptured stonework..bronze work far exceeding that of Benin in its perfection and representative skill, and at last some terra-cottas amazing to those who inspect them.] **1939** *Burlington Mag.* LXXV. 152/2 The Ife terra-cottas and bronzes show the most diverse racial characteristics, from the Semitic..running through all the ranges to the Negroid. **1949** Fagg & Underwood in *Man* XLIX. 2 (*caption*) The exhibition of Ife bronzes at the British Museum, July–September 1948. **1959** *Chambers's Encycl.* II. 609/2 All the Ife heads are technically and artistically on the highest level. The portrait-like treatment, with absolutely correct proportions, is extremely realistic and the modelling is of a beautiful sensitiveness and vitality. As works of art they rank even higher than the more impersonal and conventional Benin heads. **1960** *Times* 5 Oct. 18/7 The features of the Ife heads suddenly appear again.

iff. A written form of abbreviation of the phrase 'if and only if', always read as 'if and only if', used in *Math.* and *Logic* to introduce a condition that is necessary as well as sufficient, or a statement that is implied by and implies the preceding one.

1955 J. L. Kelley *Gen. Topology* vii. 232 *F* is equicontinuous at *x* iff there is a neighborhood of *x* whose image under every member of *F* is small. **1961** R. R. Stoll *Sets, Logic, & Axiomatic Theories* i. 5 Two sets are equal iff (if and only if) they have the same members. **1964** T. O. Moore *Elem. Gen. Topol.* i. 2 We use 'iff' as an abbreviation for 'if and only if'. **1965** B. Mates *Elem. Logic* viii. 137 $\phi \in \Delta$ iff ϕ is derivable from Δ. **1971** G. Hunter *Metalogic* 16 Hereafter we abbreviate 'if and only if' to 'iff'. **1972** *R. Inst. Philos. Lect.* V. 34 An integer *n* is prime iff the only integers which divide it without remainder are itself and one.

iffy (i·fi), *a.* orig. *U.S.* [f. If *conj.* + -*f*- + -y[1].] Of a question, proposal, prospect, etc.: full of 'ifs', contingent, doubtful.

1937 *World this Week* 9 May, Very 'iffy', Mr. Roosevelt might characterize such talk. **1941** *Chicago Daily News* 17 Jan., The President had been asked the status of some proposal, or of some event..whether this event was likely to happen... The president replied that the whole thing was 'iffy'. **1941** Baker *Dict. Austral. Slang* 37 *Iffey*, uncertain, unsound, 'chancey'. **1941** *Time* 14 July 15/3 His chances of pulling out a plum were rather iffy. **1963** *Weekly News* (Auckland) 5 June 39/1 This gamble..is far too 'iffy' to be classed as a prudent business procedure. **1963** *Times* 12 June 12/7, I have no comment to make on it. As Mr. Roosevelt said, this would be giving hypothetical answers to 'if-y' questions. **1971** E. Fenwick *Impeccable People* xiii. 72 We knew this was rather an iffy tenant, morally speaking, before we rented. *Ibid.* 73 Now..she looks a little iffier. **1973** *Listener* 20 Sept. 364/2 If the Police do their job, if the new law is effectively enforced, these are very 'iffy' points indeed.

Ifugao (i·fugau), *sb.* and *a.* [Native name.] **A.** *sb.* The name of a people of northern Luzon in the Republic of the Philippines, of a member of this people, and of their Malayo-Polynesian dialect. **B.** *a.* Of or pertaining to the Ifugao people. Also **I·fugaon.**

1859 J. Bowring *Visit to Philippine Islands* viii. 171 This race [*sc.* Itaneg] has a mixture of Chinese blood, the Ifugaos of that of the Japanese. **1875** F. Jagor *Trav. Philippines* v. 55 [Dialects of] Nueva Vízcáya: Gaddan, Ifugao, Ibilao, Ilongote. **1900** F. H. Sawyer *Inhabitants Philippines* I. xxviii. 271 The Ifugaos, who bear a strong resemblance to the Japanese, inhabit a territory in central Nueva Vizcaya. *Ibid.* 272 The Spaniards built and garrisoned a chain of forts in the Ifugao territory to keep them in order. **1901** A. G. Robinson *Philippines* x. 166 Following these tongues [*sc.* Visayan, Ilocano]..are the Pampangan..Ibanag, Ifugao, Ibilao [etc.]... Most of them are dialects, though sufficiently different to be practically unintelligible to those of other groups. **1914** D. C. Worcester *Philippines Past & Present* xx. 535, I assured him that we were friends who had come to get acquainted with the Ifugaos. *Ibid.* 536 An Ifugao climbed down from above. *Ibid.* 537 My mission to the Ifugao country was to establish kindly relations with the people. **1944** W. E. Harney *Taboo* (ed. 3) 21 The Melville Island native shield..may have come from the shields of the 'Ifugao' of the Philippine Islands. **1964** E. A. Nida *Toward Sci. Transl.* iii. 50 In Ifugao in the Philippines and in Moré, a language of the Haute Volta, 'hair' and 'feathers' are included under the same term. **1968** R. Nelson *Philippines* 131 (*caption*) The Ifugaos are talented and artistic woodcarvers. *Ibid.* 133 (*caption*) An Ifugaon peasant..leaving his tobacco field.

igarape (igarapē·). Also **-apé, -ipe.** [Pg.] In South America, a tributary or other water-channel wide enough for a canoe.

1853 A. R. Wallace *Trav. Amazon* ii. 41 Sometimes we would start down the igaripé in the montaria, not returning till late in the afternoon. *Ibid.* vii. 168 The word *igaripé*, applied to all small streams, means 'path of the canoe'. **1860** Mayne Reid *Odd People* 38 Travelling can only be done by water, either upon the great rivers, or by the narrow creeks (igaripes) or lagoons. **1866** L. Agassiz in *Atlantic Monthly* July 58/1 We turned..into a narrow stream, which has the character of an Igarapé in its lower course. **1933** *Discovery* Jan. 24/2 It is intersected by innumerable water-ways, the igarapés, along which the tide ebbs and flows. **1944** S. Putnam tr. *E. da Cunha's Rebellion in Backlands* ii. §1. 59 The filling of the river [*sc.* Amazon] brings a stoppage of life. Caught in the meshes of the *igarapés*, man displays a rare stoicism.

Igbirra (i·gbirǎ). Also **Igbira.** [Name of an area in Kabba province, Northern Nigeria.] The name of a tribe in Northern Nigeria; a member of this tribe; also, their language.

1863 J. Thomas *Jrnl.* 24 July in *Jrnls. & Notices Native Missionaries River Niger* (1864) 88 He went to our school-room and offered a prayer in Igbira. **1880** Mrs. G. Sturge tr. *Burdo's Niger & Benueh* xv. 265 (*heading*) Attack by the Igbiras. **1883** R. N. Cust *Sk. Mod. Lang. Afr.* I. xi. 226 Williams, a Negro Catechist..has lately made Translations into Igbira, some of which are used in Divine Service. **1925** C. K. Meek *Northern Tribes Nigeria* II. vii. 114 The Igbira mummify the body by pouring in gin or beer. **1958** J. S. Coleman *Nigeria* i. 24 Some of these [pagan tribes] were organized into unconsolidated village groups..others (for example, Igbirra, Bede, Bachama, and Igala) had achieved a certain measure of tribal unity. **1967** *Encycl. Brit.* XIII. 233/1 The native authority for Igbirra division, inhabited mainly by a tribe of the same name, consists of an elected council representative of the five Igbirra clans.

Igbo: see *Ibo *a.* and *sb.*

iggerant: see *ignorant *a.* 5.

‖ **iggri, iggry** (i·gri), *int.* Also **iggoree** *adv.* [Representing Egyptian colloq. Arab. pronunc. of *ijri*, imper. of *jarā* to run.] Hurry up! Also as *sb.* in phr. *to get an iggri on.*

1919 W. H. Downing *Digger Dial.* 29 *Iggoree*, quickly. **1925** Fraser & Gibbons *Soldier & Sailor Words* 127 *Iggry* (*iggri*),..a phrase in use in the Egyptian Expeditionary Force. 'Iggry Corner' at Bullecourt was so named by Australian troops who had been stationed in Egypt, as being an exceptionally dangerous locality from shell fire, where it was necessary to move rapidly. **1946** *Penguin New Writing* XXVIII. 173 'Come on, Chalky,' he pleaded, 'get an iggri on!'

igloo. Add: **3.** *transf.* A small dome-shaped building or construction (see quots.).

1956 W. A. Heflin *U.S. Air Force Dict.* 262/2 *Igloo*.., a dome-shaped or rounded structure, usually made of reinforced concrete and earth, normally used for storage of explosives. **1969** *Jane's Freight Containers 1968–69* 438 (*caption*) A moulded fibreglass igloo unit as used by Delta Airlines. **1970** *Observer* 19 Apr. 6/8 The nerve gas is to be stored in 100 concrete igloos. **1970** *New Scientist* 21 May 382/2 The main advantage is that the igloos, unlike most other emergency shelters, can be made on the site; hence there are no major transport problems. **1972** *Evening Telegram* (St. John's, Newfoundland) 28 June 12/7 Igloos are spun-glass shells shaped to fit the bellies of jet-liners or the fuselages of all-cargo DC-8s. The use of the system is one of the main reasons for the rapid growth in air cargo operations.

ignimbrite (i·gnimbrəit). *Geol.* [f. L. *ign-is* fire + *imbr-is, imber* shower of rain, storm-cloud + -ite[1].] Any pyroclastic rock, typically a welded tuff, deposited from or formed by the settling of a *nuée ardente.

1932 P. Marshall in *N.Z. Jrnl. Sci. & Technol.* XIII. 200 The type of rocks formed in this way varies greatly, but it is suggested that they should all be included in a separate group, for which the name 'Ignimbrite' seems satisfactory. **1959** A. McLintock *Descr. Atlas N.Z.* 11 Early in the Pleistocene Period, huge eruptions there formed a plateau of rhyolitic rock known as 'ignimbrite', some 10,000 square miles in extent. **1962** E. A. Vincent tr. *Rittmann's Volcanoes* ii. 80 Ignimbrites, or welded tuffs, are formed in enormous quantities from overflowing glowing clouds in fissure eruptions of very acid magmas. The incandescent ash particles are intimately fused to one another and attain a largely pseudo-liquid state, especially in the deeper portions of the deposit, so that the massive rock which results often shows columnar jointing and is easily confused with a rhyolitic lava. **1969** C. Ollier *Volcanoes* vii. 73 Ignimbrite will be used here in the sense of Cook (1966). This is a rock unit term, and should not be used as a petrological term: several petrological types can give rise to ignimbrites though rhyolite and andesite predominate. Neither does the term imply any post-depositional alteration such as welding, though this may be present. **1970** *Nature* 12 Sept. 1125/1 This..is matched in volume only by the large welded tuff sheets of the central North Island of New Zealand, the type locality for ignimbrite.

ignitability, -ibility. (Later examples.)

1925 Coward & Wheeler *Ignition of Firedamp* 20 The ignitibility of any mixture by an electric spark is inversely proportional to the rate of movement of flame in that mixture. *Ibid.* 21 The relative ignitibilities of a wide range of inflammable methane-air mixtures. **1953** Kirk & Othmer *Encycl. Chem. Technol.* XI. 326 Ignition temperature, ignitibility, stability, and hygroscopicity are important in determining the certainty of functioning [of pyrotechnic compositions]. **1966** *Lancet* 24 Dec. 1404/1 Comparing circumstances in pure oxygen at 1 atmosphere with those in air at the same pressure one finds that there is a thousandfold increase in the ignitability of most substances.

ignite, *v.* Add: **4.** *trans.* and *intr.* To strike (an arc).

1917 *Proc. IRE* V. 298 It is assumed that the arc ignites every third time on the edges. **1919** E. W. Stone *Elem. Radiotelegr.* (1920) viii. 152 The arc is now 'struck' or ignited by this potential. **1933** [see *ignitron].

igniter. Add: **b.** (Further examples.)

1886 D. Clerk *Gas Engine* viii. 205 The first few explosions cause a condensation of water upon the points and the spark then fails... The igniters then require to be uncoupled. **1902** *Min. Proc. Inst. Civil Eng.* CXLIX. 453 The hydrocarbon vapour sucked in from the carburettor ..causes the igniter to glow brightly. **1905** H. J. Spooner *Motors & Motoring* 46 The principal features of the sparking plug or igniter. **1907** *Westm. Gaz.* 18 Nov. 10/2 The low-tension plugs and igniters are neatly placed in the sides of the cylinder heads. **1950** J. V. Casamassa *Jet Aircraft Power Syst.* xiv. 206 When the engine reaches a predetermined speed, the starter, ignition coils, and the flame igniters are automatically cut out. **1950** *Sci. News* XV. 78 One class [of propellants], called hypergols, react as soon as they come together, a property which eliminates the need for an igniter of some sort. **1954** J. W. T. Walsh *Textbk. Illuminating Engin.* (ed. 2) xii. 172 A special form of distance controller..switches on the igniter just before the gas is admitted to the burner. **1962** F. I. Ordway et al. *Basic Astronautics* x. 417 The solid rocket motor is composed of a cylindrical combustion chamber, a nozzle, a solid propellant grain, and an igniter.

2. *Electronics.* Also **ignitor.** A small rod of some refractory material that dips into the pool of mercury in an ignitron and serves as an auxiliary anode for restriking the arc in each cycle.

1933 *Electronics* VI. 166/1 At the present stage of development [of the ignitron] the instantaneous current required by the igniter to start the arc reliably is from 5 to 30 amperes. **1937** A. V. Eastman *Fund. Vacuum Tubes* iv. 107 One of the major problems in the design of Ignitrons is to make certain that the anode will pick up the discharge as soon as the igniter strikes. **1952** Young & Bueche *Fund. Electronics & Control* vi. 253 Because the ignitor can be controlled to cause initiation of the arc at any point in the positive half cycle, the average anode current flow can be controlled as in the case of thyratrons. **1962** C. Susskind *Encycl. Electronics* 361/1 In pulse-type circuits where capacitors are discharged, the ignitor can be made to start the discharge in less than 1 μsec.

ignition. Add: **2. b.** *spec.* A means of producing the spark in an internal-combustion engine; an ignition system, or the device that activates it. (Further examples.)

1906 *Daily Chron.* 12 May 3/5 All good cars nowadays have the two independent ignitions, the accumulator and coil, and the magneto driven by a cog-wheel on the engine shaft. **1961** W. Hartley *Motorist's Home Repair Bk.* v. 70 There is no need to do more than insert the starting handle and have the engine turned over slowly (with the ignition switched off, of course!) while a petrol-moistened piece of silk is held against the commutator. **1972** J. Gores *Dead Skip* (1973) xiv. 97 A..Mustang with the driver's window open and the key in the ignition.

3. *Electronics.* The striking or initiation of an arc.

1919 E. W. Stone *Elem. Radiotelegr.* (1920) viii. 152 The potential existing across the arc at this instant is termed the extinction voltage as distinguished from that at ignition. It is less than the ignition voltage. **1927** J. G. Tarboux *Electr. Power Equipm.* iv. 128 The ignition anode is now drawn up by the spring..and at the point of rupture with the mercury an arc is started. **1945** '*Electr. Engineer*' *Ref. Bk.* x. 3 The action of the mercury-arc rectifier requires the cathode spot to be produced first by some auxiliary device before the arc can be established. This is generally effected by drawing an arc between the cathode and a small auxiliary anode, a process termed ignition. **1962** *Newnes Conc. Encycl. Electr. Engin.* 380/1 The ignitron differs from the other mercury-arc rectifiers..in the method used for ignition of the arc.

4. *attrib.* and *Comb.* (esp. in terms relating to internal-combustion engines and motor

vehicles), as †*ignition box*, †*chamber*, *circuit*, *system*; **ignition advance,** the extent to which the moment when the spark occurs precedes the moment of greatest compression of the mixture in a cylinder of an internal-combustion engine, usu. expressed in terms of the angle between the two corresponding positions of the crank-shaft; **ignition coil,** an induction coil in an internal-combustion engine for converting a low-voltage current into one whose voltage is sufficient to produce the spark; **ignition key,** a key for operating an ignition switch in the form of a lock; **ignition lag,** the delay following the occurrence of the spark (in a spark-ignition engine) or the injection of the fuel (in a compression-ignition engine) before the pressure first begins to rise as a result of combustion; **ignition plug** = * *sparking plug*; **ignition point** = * *ignition temperature*; **ignition rating** (see quot. 1940); **ignition switch,** the switch by means of which the ignition circuit of a motor vehicle may be closed or opened (thereby allowing the engine to be started, or stopping it); **ignition temperature,** the lowest temperature at which a combustible substance in air will ignite and continue to burn; **ignition tube,** (*a*) *Chem.*, a small cylindrical vessel of heat-resistant glass in which a substance may be heated for purposes of analysis; †(*b*) a *hot tube* (*HOT *a.* 12 c) in some early internal-combustion engines.

1908 H. E. WIMPERIS *Internal Combustion Engine* viii. 282 It is permissible to set the ignition to take place.. slightly before the dead centre... This reduces the arc of ignition advance throughout which the magneto is called upon to generate an effective spark. **1946** A. W. JUDGE *Mod. Petrol Engines* ii. 32 For weaker mixtures the flame rates are lower so that a greater ignition advance is necessary than for correct or slightly rich mixtures. **1900** G. D. HISCOX *Horseless Vehicles* xi. 184 The ignition of the charge is effected by heating the nickel tubes projecting about 2½ inches from the rear ends of the cylinders into the ignition box. **1894** B. DONKIN *Text-bk. Gas, Oil, & Air Engines* I. xi. 140 At a given moment, a zig-zag passage in the slide valve is brought opposite the ignition chamber, and opens communication between it and the admission port into the cylinder. **1907** R. B. WHITMAN *Motor-Car Princ.* vi. 74 While wire is sometimes used on ignition circuits for the return as well as the lead, the most usual method is to utilise the metal of the engine to return the current to its source. **1900** G. D. HISCOX *Horseless Vehicles* vii. 127 (*heading*) Electric ignition coils. **1953** I. FRAZEE et al. *Automotive Fuel & Ignition Syst.* vii. 247 The ignition coil must produce sufficient voltage and current to ignite the fuel mixture at the various engine speeds encountered. **1933** D. L. SAYERS *Murder must Advertise* ix. 155, I have the ignition keys of both cars. **1934** *Punch* 3 Oct. 388/3 Stepping into Humbottle's car am surprised to hear burst of gruff laughter...This probably explained by absence of ignition-key. **1962** J. BRAINE *Life at Top* xix. 190 She turned the ignition key; the car jerked forward convulsively, then stopped. 'Put it in neutral first,' I said. **1972** *Police Rev.* 1 Dec. 1577/3 They removed the ignition keys and sent a message by radio for an officer to attend with the breath test equipment. **1932** *Fuel* XI. 187/1 At a definite temperature the ignition lag becomes infinitely great and ignition no longer takes place. **1900** G. D. HISCOX *Horseless Vehicles* vii. 130 (*heading*) Electric ignition plug. **1902** A. C. HARMSWORTH et al. *Motors* viii. 161 The ignition plugs may be examined to see that they are not coated with oil. **1933** I-B. O. SNEEDEN *Introd. Internal Combustion Engineering* ix. 164 The number of ignition plugs per cylinder is not limited to one. Two are often used. **1887** *Proc. Amer. Acad. Arts & Sci.* XXII. 483 In..trials, which I made with sound pine wood, I soon found that the ignition point was greatly affected by the way in which the sample was heated. *Ibid.* 486 The ignition point of the pine wood varied from 330°..to 218°. **1922** GLAZEBROOK *Dict. Appl. Physics* I. 338/2 The ignition points of oils are frequently required in connection with internal combustion engine problems. **1922** *Wireless World* IX. 727/1 Extensive use was made of portable accumulators..on motor cycles. The intermittent discharge through a trembler contact gave an apparent duration of double the hours at..a certain current. This led to the ignition rating of portable cells which is..misleading..for wireless work. **1940** *Chambers's Techn. Dict.* 437/2 *Ignition rating*, a special rating (in ampere-hours, q.v.) employed for accumulators used for supplying ignition systems; it is generally twice the continuous rating at a low discharge rate. **1952** *Ellery Queen's Mystery Mag.* XIX. 31/2 There was a car parked in front of the entrance, a Ford coupe, 1937...The key was in the ignition switch. **1902** A. C. HARMSWORTH et al. *Motors* viii. 159 The magneto ignition system..consists of a magneto-electric rotary machine, combined with a series of mechanical contact-breakers. **1943** A. P. FRAAS *Aircraft Power Plants* viii. 140 The so-called battery ignition system has been used almost universally in automobiles... All the larger and many of the smaller aircraft engines make use of magneto ignition systems. **1956** H. E. MILBURN *Motor-Cars To-Day* vi. 115 A normal ignition system consists of an induction coil, a condenser, a contact breaker, a distributor, a sparking plug for each cylinder of the engine, a switch, and the necessary connecting wires. **1881** *Jrnl. Iron & Steel Inst.* II. 679 (*heading*) Ignition temperature of mixed gases. **1897** F. GROVER *Pract. Treat. Mod. Gas & Oil Engines* xix. 196 (*heading*) Ignition temperatures of explosive gaseous mixtures. **1968** *Fuel* XLVII. 119 According to D. W. van Krevelin the ignition temperature of coal depends on experimental conditions such as furnace design, way of heating, particle size, oxygen concentration and coal rank. **1874** F. CLOWES *Elem. Treat. Pract. Chem.* II. 30 (*heading*) Small ignition tubes. **1890** W. ROBINSON *Gas & Petroleum Engines* vii. 229 The average life of ignition tubes in the Differential was 180 hours, and in the Cycle engine 120 hours. **1962** A. ATKINSON *Compl. Pract. Chem.* xii. 272 Heat a little of the substance in an ignition tube or in a small dry test-tube until no further change occurs.

ignitor, var. *IGNITER 2.

ignitron (ignəi·trɒn). *Electronics.* [f. IGNIT(E *v.*, IGNIT(ION + *-T)RON.] A kind of mercury-arc rectifier capable of handling large currents and having a pool cathode, a single anode, and an igniter to initiate the arc afresh in each cycle (the timing of this being used to control the output).

1933 D. D. KNOWLES in *Electronics* VI. 164/1 The Ignitron* is the latest arrival in the rapidly growing family of industrial electronic tubes. It is a tube in which conductivity is established by igniting the arc. [**Note*] Pronounced like the word 'ignite'. **1951** *Engineering* 14 Sept. 323/3 The ignitrons, which are water-cooled,.. act as an electronic contactor which controls the current in the primary of the welding transformer. **1962** *Newnes Conc. Encycl. Electr. Engin.* 380/2 The larger ratings of ignitron are constructed with a double-walled stainless steel envelope, water being circulated in the jacket so formed for cooling. **1967** H. COTTON *Adv. Electr. Technol.* xv. 726 Typical applications of the ignitron are (*a*) small-power spot welding, (*b*) large-power control of variable-speed d.c. motors, such as certain types of colliery winder.

ignorance. Add: **3.** (In full *the time* or *days of ignorance*; tr. Arab. *jāhilīyah* state of ignorance, f. *jāhil* ignorant.) The period of Arabian history previous to the teaching of Muhammad.

1788 GIBBON *Decl. & F.* V. l. 185 Of the time of ignorance which preceded Mahomet, seventeen hundred battles are recorded by tradition. **1895** A. MENZIES *Hist. Relig.* 213 The Arabs called the period before Islam the 'time of ignorance'; in that period they considered their race had no history. **1904** W. P. KER *Dark Ages* 14 The student of heroic poetry may admire the temper of the Arabian Dark Ages—'the Ignorance'. **1937** P. H. HITTI *Hist. Arabs* vii. 87 The term *jāhilīyah*, usually rendered 'time of ignorance' or 'barbarism', in reality means the period in which Arabia had no dispensation, no inspired prophet, no revealed book.

ignorant, *a.* Add: **1. b.** (Later examples.)

1875 'MARK TWAIN' in *Atlantic Monthly* Jan. 71/1 This fellow had..an ignorant silver watch and a showy brass watch chain. **1892** —— *Amer. Claimant* Pref., It ought to be the ablest weather that can be had, not ignorant, poor-quality, amateur weather.

5. *dial.* and *colloq.* Ill-mannered, uncouth.

¶ Sometimes written as *iggerant* in imitation of vulgar speech.

1886 R. E. G. COLE *Gloss. Words S.W. Lincs.* 71 *Ignorant*, ill-mannered. **1886** F. T. ELWORTHY *West Somerset Word-Bk.* 363 *Ignorant*, wanting in manners. The usual description of a rough, uncouth lout. **1946** K. TENNANT *Lost Haven* (1947) xvii. 273 He used the word 'ignorant' in the country sense of knowing nothing of good manners. **1965** *Listener* 22 July 137/3 He writes what he *thinks* 'a Puerto Rican' is thinking (very elemental, Latin, iggerant, dumb, baffled, passionate). **1966** 'L. LANE' *ABZ of Scouse* 49, I jes' can't stan' that feller, 'e's plain bloody 'iggerant. **1968** *New Society* 22 Aug. 266/1 Ignorant, meaning 'bad-mannered', is non-U.

‖ **ignotum per ignotius** (ignōu·tʊ̆m pɔː ignōu·ʃiʊ̆s or ignōu·tiʊ̆s). [late L., lit. the unknown by means of the more unknown.] An attempt to explain what is obscure by something which is more obscure, leading to 'confusion worse confounded'.

c **1386** CHAUCER *Canon's Yeoman's Tale* 1457 And Plato answerde vnto hym anoon, 'Take the stoon that Titanos men name.' 'Which is that?' quod he. 'Magnasia is the same,' Seyde Plato. 'Ye, sire, and is it thus? This [is] *ignotum per ignocius* [v.r. *ignotius*]. What is Magnasia, good sire, I yow preye?' *c* **1450** LYDGATE *Secrees* (1894) 588 With goldeyn Resouns in taast moost lykerous, Thyng per ignotum prevyd per ignocius. **1584** R. SCOT *Discov. Witchcr.* III. xvii. 67 Confuteth that opinion by a notable reason, called *Petitio principij*, or rather, *Ignotum per ignotius.* *a* **1734** R. NORTH *Examen* (1740) II. i. 28 When he drops his own Authority, and brings Fact to confirm all, the vouching that Fact by his own pure Parole, is a Cheat termed *Ignotum per ignotius.* **1888** *Athenæum* 22 Dec. 843/2 When Arabic names are twisted and mis-copied..the identification of sites resolves itself into a case of 'ignotum per ignotius'. **1931** *Times Lit. Suppl.* 30 July 590/3 [He] even goes so far on one occasion as to explain an Egyptian *chiaoush* as being analogous to an Indian *chobdav*, which to some readers may be a case of *ignotum per ignotius.* **1935** *Ibid.* 2 May 289/1 A distinct failure to escape the imputation of *ignotum per ignotius.*

Igorot (ī·gǒrōut). Also **Igolot(e)**, **Igorrot(e)**, **Ygorrote.** [ad. Sp. *Ygolote* (A. de Morga, 1609), f. the native name.] Name of a people inhabiting northern Luzon in the Republic of the Philippines. Also as *collect. sing.* and *attrib.*

1821 W. WALTON tr. *T. de Comyn's State of Philippine Islands* p. xli, An expedition was also sent against the Igorrots, inhabiting the mountains of the interior, where gold is obtained. *Ibid.* ii. 32 The Igorrot Indians, who occasionally come down from the mountains to barter with the Christians, use certain coarse jars or vessels of copper. **1840** *Penny Cycl.* XVIII. 88/2 The Ygorrotes, who inhabit the mountains east of the Gulf of Lingayen, are distinguished by a peculiar physiognomy and a lighter colour. **1875** F. JAGOR *Trav. Philippines* 131 The Ygorrotes are not Christians. **1885** *Encycl. Brit.* XVIII. 753/1 The Igorrotes or Igolotes proper (for the name is by many writers very loosely applied to all the pagan mountain tribes of Luzon) inhabit the districts of Bangued, Lepanto, Tiagan, Bontoc. **1898** D. C. WORCESTER *Philippine Islands* 438 One of the Igorrote peoples is believed to be descended from the followers of the Chinese invader Limahong. **1903** BARROWS in *Philippine Jrnl. Sci.* Oct. 796 The powerful and numerous Igorot of northern Luzon. **1914** D. C. WORCESTER *Philippines Past & Present* I. 343 This once prosperous little Igorot hamlet had been burned by the Spaniards. **1925** K. MAYO *Isles of Fear* 256 The Igorots proper, however, number only about 70,000. **1957** *Encycl. Brit.* XII. 75/1 There are.. two broad groupings of the Igorot as a whole. **1967** WERNSTEDT & SPENCER *Philippine Island World* III. ix. 349 The peoples and cultures of the North Luzon Highlands... Popular reference adopted the term 'Igorot' for the whole population,..although the term properly is only the Tagalog word for 'mountain-dwelling' or 'mountaineer'.

iguana. 2. A name used in Africa for a large monitor lizard of the genus *Varanus*, esp. *V. niloticus*, the aquatic Nile monitor.

1753 N. OWEN *Jrnl. Slave-Dealer* (1930) 32 They [*sc.* the Bulums] eat alegators, guanas and long worms. **1801** J. BARROW *Acct. Trav. S. Afr.* I. v. 346 None of the people with me could testify to have seen any other species of that genus [*sc.* crocodile] frequenting the water, except Iguanas, from six to ten feet in length. **1803** T. WINTERBOTTOM *Acct. Native Africans Sierra Leone* I. iv. 69 Although they have several species of lizards, they use only one as an article of diet, the *guana*, lacerta iguana, which they esteem delicate food. **1834** T. PRINGLE *Afr. Sk.* II. vi. 210 One of the deep lagoons formed by the river, and which the [Moravian] brethren have named the Leguan's Tank, from its being frequented by numbers of the large amphibious lizard called the leguan or guana. **1875** J. J. BISSET *Sport & War* xx. 179 Hence [*sc.* from under water] the 'Iguana', a small kind of crocodile, proceed on shore at night and take chickens from the hen-roosts. **1900** H. A. BRYDEN *Animals Afr.* xv. 174 In South Africa this reptile [*sc.* the Nile Monitor] is often miscalled an 'iguana'. **1947** J. STEVENSON-HAMILTON *Wild Life S. Afr.* xxxv. 315 There are two large monitor lizards or leguaans of the genus *Varanus* found in South Africa. These are sometimes called 'iguanas', though the true iguanas are almost all confined to the New World, and the popular term may be merely a corruption of this name. **1964** J. P. CLARK *Three Plays* 30 They struggled like Two iguanas till outspent, they stopped.

iiwi (ī,ī·wi). [Hawaiian.] A Hawaiian bird, the honeycreeper *Vestiaria coccinea*, whose red feathers were formerly used to make the cloaks of native chiefs.

1779 J. KING *Jrnl.* Mar. in Cook *Voy. Pacific Ocean* (1784) III. vi. 119 The birds of these islands are as beautiful as any we have seen... Another is of an exceeding bright scarlet colour;..its native name is *eeeeve.* **1890** WILSON & EVANS *Aves Hawaiienses* I. 1 Vestiaria Coccinea. Olokele or Iiwi. *Ibid.* 3 The call-note of the 'Iiwi' is peculiar. **1899** A. H. EVANS in *Cambr. Nat. Hist.* IX. vii. 564 The splendid feather-cloaks of the Hawaiian kings.. were of old chiefly composed of the plumage of the 'Mamo' (*Drepanis pacifica*) and the 'Iiwi' (*Vestiaria coccinea*). **1915** W. A. BRYAN *Nat. Hist. Hawaii* xxxi. 430 The beautiful red iiwi..is infested with three genera [of bird-lice]. **1944** G. C. MUNRO *Birds Hawaii* 93 With bright scarlet body, black wings and tail, and rose colored, inch long, curved bill, the iiwi is one of the most beautiful of the Hawaiian native birds. **1970** S. CARLQUIST *Hawaii* xi. 198 Iiwis are still relatively common in a number of forest areas of the Islands.

Ijo (ī·dʒo), *sb.* and *a.* Also **Ejo, Idzo, Ijaw. A.** *sb.* The name of a tribe inhabiting the Niger delta, on the coast of Nigeria; a member of this tribe; the language of this tribe. **B.** *adj.* Of or pertaining to the Ijo tribe.

1856 W. B. BAIKIE *Narr. Voy. Niger* iii. 40 The people are of the same tribe as those who inhabit the tract of country up to the Rio Formoso, where however they are called Ejo or Ojo, by which name also they are known at Abó, at Brass, and even at Bonny. By English palm-oil traders they are often termed Jo-men. **1883** R. N. CUST *Sk. Mod. Lang. Afr.* I. 220 Within the Idzo Language-Field many of the Ibo-speaking Races reside. **1906** A. G. LEONARD *Lower Niger* II. i. 52 So extremely touchy and sensitive are these people—the Ijo particularly so,—so easily piqued and disturbed, even by the mildest of chaff, that they have no hesitation in taking their own lives or the lives of others, on the spur of the moment. *Ibid.* I. iv. 42 An examination of the six or more dialects of Ijo and the five of Bini..shows that they are dissimilar not only to each other, but to the other neighbouring tongues. **1926** P. A. TALBOT *Peoples S. Nigeria* IV. iii. 82 Ijaw is a very primitive negro tongue, perhaps the most ancient in West Africa, and..has not the smallest affinity with any other. **1958** J. S. COLEMAN *Nigeria* xviii. 390 Demands for a separate state were made by minority groups in the Middle Belt in the Northern Region, by the Ijaw peoples of the Delta area, and elsewhere. **1966** M. CROWDER *Story Nigeria* v. 80 The Ijo exported dried fish and salt, which they panned in the salt water creeks, to the peoples of the hinterland in exchange for vegetables and tools. **1971** P. YOUNG in J. Spencer *Eng. Lang. W. Afr.* 180 The Nigerian poet and novelist,

Gabriel Okara. His novel *The Voice* exhibits a highly idiosyncratic syntax obtained, according to Okara, by a direct substitution of the syntax of his native Ijaw for normal English syntax.

ijolite (ī·yolǝit). *Petrogr.* [ad. G. *ijolith* (Ramsay & Berghell 1891, in *Geol. Fören. i Stockholm Förh.* XIII. 304), f. *Ijo*, Sw. rendering of Finnish *Ii*, the name of a village and district on the Finnish coast near Oulu and also the initial element in the names of local geographic features, as *Iijärvi, Iijoki, Iivaara*: see -LITE.] A plutonic igneous rock consisting essentially of nepheline and pyroxene and containing no felspar.

1897 A. HARKER *Petrol.* (ed. 2) 52 The 'ijolite' of Ramsay and Berghell from Finland, a nepheline-pyroxene-rock free from felspar but sometimes rich in garnet. **1962** W. T. HUANG *Petrol.* iv. 139 Much of the ijolite on Alnö Island, Sweden, and Magnet Cove, Arkansas, contains abundant melanite garnet.

Hence **ijoli·tic** *a.*, resembling or of the nature of ijolite.

1938 *Mineral. Abstr.* VII. 36 Masses of limestone and ijolitic intrusives. **1954** H. WILLIAMS et al. *Petrogr.* iv. 72 Most of these ijolitic rocks..owe their characteristics largely to contamination of magma by assimilation of limestone. **1966** R. L. JOHNSON in Tuttle & Gittins *Carbonatites* I. 221 Here there are a number of carbonatite complexes, which include granites, syenites, nepheline syenites and small amounts of ijolitic rocks within their limits.

‖**ikat** (ī·kat). [Mal., lit. 'to tie, fasten'. A technique of fabric decoration common in Indonesia and Malaysia, in which warp or weft threads, or both, are tied at intervals and dyed before weaving; also, a fabric of this kind.

1931 C. F. IKLÉ (*title*) Ikat technique and Dutch East Indian ikats. **1942** *Ciba Rev.* Aug. 1586 The ikat process can be applied to the warp, the weft, or to both systems of the threads of a fabric. **1953** C. A. GIBSON-HILL *Malay Arts & Crafts*, § Hand-woven cloths. A variant form (of cloth) is sometimes introduced by a tie-and-dye technique (*ikat chuai*), in which short lengths of the woof are tied round with dye-proof strips of banana leaf and the skein then immersed in the dye. **1959** *Chambers's Encycl.* IV. 703/1 A..technique known as *ikat* is practically limited to Indonesia. In this method the warp threads of a cloth are set out before weaving and tied at intervals before dyeing. **1968** *Encycl. Brit.* XII. 180/1 In the textiles in *batik* (wax-resist) and *ikat* (pre-dyed thread)..Indonesian art has shown a continuing vigour.

‖ **ikbal** (i·kbal). [Turkish.] A member of the harem of an Ottoman Sultan.

1910 *Encycl. Brit.* XII. 950/2 The so-called Odalisks.. are subdivided according to the degree of favour.., into *Ikbals* ('Favourites') and *Geuzdés* (literally the 'Eyed' ones), those whom the sultan has favourably noticed. **1937** *Times Lit. Suppl.* 16 Jan. 36/3 The Sultan selected his favourites, or *ikbals*. **1956** A. D. ALDERSON *Struct. Ottoman Dynasty* ix. 80 If the relationship showed any signs of permanence, she was promoted to the rank of 'Ikbal' (Fortunate). **1962** J. FLEMING *When I grow Rich* iii. 40 She had ceased to be an *ikbal* (the name given to those members of the harem who actually slept with the Shadow of God upon Earth).

ike (ǝik), colloq. abbrev. of *ICONOSCOPE 2.

1937 *Amer. Speech* XII. 101 As the microphone is a *mike* so the television iconoscope is an *ike*. **1947** L. A. SPOSA *Television Primer* 224 *Iconoscope* (*Ike*), a cathode-ray camera pickup tube developed by RCA.

ike: see *IKEY *sb.* and *a.*

‖ **ikebana** (ikibā·nă). [Jap., lit. 'living flowers'.] The art of Japanese flower arrangement in which flowers are displayed according to strict rules, sometimes in conjunction with other natural objects, in formal arrangements.

1901 F. BRINKLEY *Oriental Series: Japan* III. i. 9 Another remarkable outcome of the Military epoch was the art of flower arrangement. The name applied to it, *ike-bana*, or 'living flower', explains at once the fundamental principle..that the flowers must be so arranged as to suggest the idea of actual life. **1934** A. KOEHN *Art Jap. Flower Arrangement* 2 The word 'ikebana' is used for all forms of Japanese Flower Arrangement. **1960** KOESTLER *Lotus & Robot* II. vii. 191 It has its charm; and so has ikebana, the Art of Flower Arrangement. **1965** W. SWAAN *Jap. Lantern* xix. 227 Chrysanthemums are particularly popular for *ikebana*. **1966** *New Statesman* 3 June 809/1 On a pole in the street..I saw a signboard that advertised a local *ikebana* school. **1967** 'G. BLACK' *Wind of Death* x. 197 There was no *ikebana* flower arrangement.

ikey (ǝi·ki), *sb.* and *a.* *slang* and *dial.* Also **ike, iky, I-.** Familiar abbreviated form of the Jewish name *Isaac* (also **ikeymo**, f. *Isaac* and *Moses*), used typically for: a Jew or someone taken to be or resembling a Jew; also, a (Jewish) receiver, moneylender, etc.; *transf.*, a loafer; a tip, information; (*Austral.*) a bookmaker. As *adj.*, (*a*) artful, crafty, knowing, 'fly'; (*b*) having a good opinion of oneself, 'stuck-up'.

Derogatory and offensive in all uses as applied to persons.

1835 DICKENS *Sk. Boz* (1836) 1st Ser. II. ii. 44 'Let me alone,' replied Ikey, 'and I'll ha' vound up..in five seconds.' **1864** HOTTEN *Slang Dict.*, *Ikey*, a Jew 'fence'. **1870** LEYBOURNE in Farmer & Henley *Slang* (1896) IV. 2 My name it is ikey Bill, A Whitechapel Covey am I. **1881** *Punch* 10 Sept. 110/1 'Arf ikey of course, put-up bizness. **1887** PARISH & SHAW *Dict. Kentish Dial.* 83 *Ikey*, proud. **1889** BARRÈRE & LELAND *Dict. Slang*, *Ikey* (popular), a Jew;..Also said of any one who thinks himself knowing, smart, and has a great opinion of himself. **1892** CHEVALIER in Farmer & Henley *Slang* (1896) IV. 2 Artful little ikey little ways. **1897** I. SCOTT *How I stole 10,000 Sheep in Austral. & N.Z.* 33 Jim now hit on a rather 'Iky' way to do the ride to Wellington. **1906** RUSSELL & RIGBY *Making of Criminal* i. 7 His clothes are so very poor that he does not like..'to show himself up' by appearing in them, especially if they are of a kind only affected by the professional loafer or 'ike'. **1913** D. H. LAWRENCE *Sons & Lovers* ix. 241, I want people to think we're awful swells. So look ikey. **1922** JOYCE *Ulysses* 458 Three cheers for Ikey Mo! **1927** T. PRENTIS *Music-Hall Memories* 16 Sez as I'm as ikey as the Dook of Boocle-oo. **1934** *Bulletin* (Sydney) 18 Apr. 11/1 She laid the odds, as smartly and acutely, I'll bet, as any trousered Ikey Mo. **1936** J. G. BRANDON *Dragnet* xiii. 132 'E passed the ike, that there was somethink on there. **1941** *Penguin New Writing* III. 69 Go indoors an' 'elp yer sister with the washing-up, you lazy young ike. **1942** P. ABRAHAMS *Dark Testament* I. xiii. 72 Any guy his pal. Chink, ike. **1954** J. SYMONS *Narrowing Circle* xxx. 135 I'm a Hackney Jew, Dave. At school they called us Ikeymoes and Jewboys. **1966** F. SHAW et al. *Lern Yerself Scouse* 36 *Yer very ikey*, you are very dandified. **1969** *Private Eye* 6 June 14 (*caption*) Pull your head in, ikey mo! **1972** R. PLAYER *Oh! Where are Bloody Mary's Earrings* vi. 168 The Ikeys will win—you can stake your life on that.

Hence **ike, i·ky** *v.* (see quot. 1932); **i·keyness**, the quality of, or an act of, being ikey.

1911 D. H. LAWRENCE *White Peacock* vii. 484, I haven't been to see them lately—can't stand Meg's ikeyness. **1932** *Amer. Speech* VII. 401 *Iky*, to jew down the price; to cheat. 'He ikied me out of my turn.' **1960** WENTWORTH & FLEXNER *Dict. Amer. Slang*, *Ike v.*, to cheat; to lower the price by haggling; to 'Jew down'.

iktas (i·ktăs), *sb. pl.* *N. Amer. colloq.* Also **ectas, ictas, ictus, iktics, iktus.** [Chinook.] Goods; belongings; things.

1856 *Democratic State Jrnl.* (Sacramento, Calif.) 4 Oct. 3/1 They are getting short of blankets and other *ictas*. *a* **1861** T. WINTHROP *Canoe & Saddle* (1863) iv. 53 My motley retinue followed me humbly, bearing 'ikta', my traps, and their own plunder. **1892** in *Brit. Columbia Hist. Q.* (1941) Oct. 302 They chiefly took their pay in blankets and provisions and other ectas—the balance in coin. **1951** R. P. HOBSON *Grass beyond Mountains* 101 We got eighteen horses, a summer's grub and all the ictus we need for the time being. **1965** S. G. LAWRENCE *Forty Yrs. on Yukon Telegraph* vi. 34, I must get some iktics together and hide.

ikunolite (iki*ū*·nolǝit). *Min.* [Named after the *Ikuno* mine in Hyōgo prefecture, Japan, where it was first found: see -LITE.] A bismuth sulphide, Bi_4S_3, that contains some selenium in place of sulphur and occurs as grey foliated masses.

1959 A. KATO in *Mineral. Jrnl.* II. 398 The chemical properties and X-ray studies clarified this mineral to be a new species of the composition $Bi_4(S, Se)_3$ with rhombohedral symmetry. The writer has called this mineral ikunolite after the locality name. **1961** *Mineral. Abstr.* XV. 43/2 Ikunolite resembles joseite-A (Bi_4TeS_2) in structure, crystallography, and optical properties. **1962** *Amer. Mineralogist* XLVII. 1431 The bismuth sulfide mineral ikunolite (Bi_4S_3) was first described by Kato (1959). ..A second occurrence of this mineral has recently been found in specimens from the bismuth-molybdenite pipes at Kingsgate in the New England district of New South Wales.

-il, -ile, *suffixes.* Add: **2.** Following cl.L. and med.L. ordinal numerals of the type *quartīlis, quintīlis, sextīlis* (Eng. QUARTILE, etc.), *-ile* (-ǝil) is used in *Statistics* to form substantives denoting (*a*) those values of a variate that divide a population into the indicated number of groups, equal in size, and (*b*) the groups themselves; so *octile* and *quartile* (1879), *decile* (1882), *percentile* (1885).

Ila (ī·lă), *sb.* and *a.* Also **Ba-ila.** [Native name.] **A.** *sb.* **1.** An African of a Bantu people in Zambia (formerly Northern Rhodesia); also used as collect. sing. = this people. **2.** The Bantu language of this people. **B.** *adj.* Of or pertaining to this people or their language.

1907 E. W. SMITH *Handbk. Ila Lang.* i. 1 The Ila language is spoken by the Baila,..a people living in North-West Rhodesia. *Ibid.* i. 3 In Ila, as in all Bantu languages, alliteration..is not an accident of style, it is the very essence of the language. **1911** *Encycl. Brit.* III. 359/2 Next is a group which might be styled the Subiya-Tonga-Ila, though some authorities think that Tonga and Ila deserve to be ranked as an independent group. **1920** SMITH & DALE (*title*) Ila-speaking peoples of Northern Rhodesia. *Ibid.* p. xxvii, They are very mixed, but now the language of them all is Ila. **1956** W. V. BRELSFORD *Tribes N. Rhodesia* viii. 55 The Ila have a great and deserved reputation as fighting men, but their comparative paucity in numbers and the possession of great herds of cattle made them a constant prey to the bigger tribes of Barotseland. **1959** *Chambers's Encycl.* I. (*caption*, facing p. 140) A chief of the Ila peoples, photographed wearing ivory bracelets and *impande*, the insignia of office. *Ibid.* II. 109/2 The Ba-ila live in independent communities. **1960** R. C. BELL *Board & Table Games* I. 121 *Chisolo*. This is played by the Ba-ila speaking peoples of Northern Rhodesia. **1970** P. OLIVER *Savannah Syncopators* 26 The Ila and Tonga people are neither of them West African,..being of the Middle Zambesi 2,300 miles away.

‖ **Ilag** (ī·lag). [Ger. abbrev. form of *Internierungslager*.] A prison-camp for civilian internees in Nazi Germany.

1941 WODEHOUSE *Berlin Broadcasts* in *Performing Flea* (1961) i. 261 An Oflag is where captured officers go. Stalags are reserved for N.C.O.s and privates. The civil internee gets the Ilag.

ilala (ilā·la). *S. Afr.* Also **lala.** [Zulu.] A fan palm, *Hyphæne natalensis*, native to the coastal region of Natal.

1868 J. CHAPMAN *Trav. S. Afr.* II. 464 *Ilala*, Hyphæne. **1884** E. P. MATHERS *Trip to Moodie's* 29 There is a natural drink..which..goes by the name of kaffir beer.. it is the exudation of a native palm tree (*ilala*). **1911** *Encycl. Brit.* XIX. 253/2 Of palms there are two varieties [in Natal], the ilala (*Hyphaene crinita*), found only by the sea shore and a mile or two inland, and the isundu (*Phoenix reclinata*). **1954** T. V. BULPIN *Ivory Trail* iv. 44 He..passed the hot hours in plaiting a hat from lala palm leaves. *Ibid.* xi. 114 The elephants..also had a liking for this potent lala palm wine. **1966** D. VARADAY *Gara-Yaka's Domain* viii. 89 He ruled the troop like a despot from his rocky keep above a growth of ilala palms.

Ilamba, var. *LAMBA *sb.* and *a.*

ilb (ilb). Also **ailb, elb.** [Arab.] A spiny tree of the genus *Zizyphus*, esp. *Z. spina-Christi*, found in North Africa and the Middle East.

1894 *Kew Bull.* 330 *Zizyphus Lotus* Linn. A tree 20–30 feet high. Very common in Hadramaut. Native name, 'Ailb'. Extends through North Africa and South Europe. **1914–16** E. BLATTER *Flora of Aden* 158 *Zizyphus spina Christi*... Arabic name: Elb. **1940** F. STARK *Winter in Arabia* 118 It is only because of the English peace that he can count on the safe and quiet possession of his own waterless strip of 'ilb trees and plough. **1963** *Times* 12 Mar. 12/6 One looks out over fields of millet and barley, waving date palms and sturdy *ilb* trees.

Ilchester (i·ltʃestǝɹ). The name of a town in Somerset, used *attrib.* or *ellipt.* as *sb.* to designate a cheese mixed with beer, chives, and spices.

1963 *Guardian* 11 Jan. 7/7 Mr Ken Seaton, landlord of the Ilchester hotel, Ilchester, has developed a new cheese, made with beer and chives and spices. He calls it Ilchester. **1965** T. FITZGIBBON *Art Brit. Cooking* 132 Ilchester cheese is a recent commercially blended cheese made in Ilchester, Somerset, from Cheddar cheese, Worthington beer, spices and chives. **1965** *Harrods Food News* May, Ilchester is Cheddar with Beer and Spices. **1967** T. A. LAYTON *Wine & Food Soc. Guide Cheese & Cheese Cookery* ii. 68 Ilchester cheese is the creation of a Yorkshireman, Ken Seaton, who hit upon the recipe almost by accident only six years ago. **1971** *Selfridge Christmas Food Catal.* 10/2 Ilchester cheese with Beer and Chives. 4 oz. pot, each 17½ p.

ileal (i·liăl), *a.* [f. ILE(UM + -AL.] Of, within, or supplying the ileum.

1893 in *Funk's Stand. Dict.* **1895** R. T. MORRIS *Lect. Appendicitis* v. 100 (*heading*) The experimental production of ileal intussusception with carbonate of sodium. **1902** D. J. CUNNINGHAM *Text-bk. Anat.* 802 The ileal branch [of the superior mesenteric artery]..turns upwards and to the left in the lowest part of the mesentery. **1934** LAKE & MARSHALL *Surg. Anat. & Physiol.* xxxiii. 521 An appreciable degree of obstruction of the small gut ('ileal stasis'). **1971** *Brit. Med. Bull.* XXVII. 26/2 Epidemics of ileal obstruction were first recognized in 1964.

ileo-. Add: **i:leocolo·stomy** *Surg.* [*-STOMY], the operation of joining, and creating a passage between, a part of the ileum and a part of the colon so that the intervening part of the intestines is bypassed; the connection so formed; **i:leo-ileo·stomy** *Surg.* [*-STOMY], the operation of joining, and creating a passage between, two parts of the ileum so that the intervening part is bypassed; the connection so formed; **i:leo-si·gmoid** *a.*, between or connecting the ileum and the sigmoid flexure of the colon; **i:leosigmoido·stomy** *Surg.* [*-STOMY], the operation of joining, and creating a passage between, the sigmoid flexure of the colon and a part of the ileum so that the intervening part of the intestines is bypassed; the connection so formed; **ileostomy,** substitute for def.: the operation of attaching the ileum to the abdominal wall and constructing an artificial anus so that the

intestinal contents are evacuated directly from the ileum; also, the opening or artificial anus thus made; (examples).

1887 *Trans. Internat. Med. Congr. 9th Session* I. 485 An ileo-colostomy or ileo-rectostomy..should be done in all cases of irreducible ileo-cæcal invagination. *Ibid.* 475 Intestinal anastomosis, by making an ileo-colostomy by lateral apposition of the ileum to colon below the invagination. **1967** J. H. Garlock *Surg. Alimentary Tract* ix. 427 In the same category, one may include the bypassing operation of ileocolostomy. **1887** *Trans. Internat. Med. Congr. 9th Session* I. 479 Two adjacent coils of the ileum were united by making an ileo-ileostomy. **1889** [in Dict.]. **1901** N. Senn *Pract. Surg.* xxiii. 833 Jejuno-ileostomy and ileo-ileostomy by apposition with decalcified bone-plates..is an operation almost devoid of danger. **1903** Ileo-sigmoid [see **colo-colic* adj.]. **1968** J. C. Goligher et al. *Ulcerative Colitis* xiii. 237 The first such operation involving an ileo-sigmoid anastomosis was recorded by Lilienthal as early as 1901. **1892** *Lancet* 16 Apr. 864/2 (*heading*) Ileo-sigmoidostomy (Senn's method) for intestinal obstruction due to malignant disease of the hepatic flexure of the colon. **1964** H. E. Bacon *Cancer Colon, Rectum & Anal Canal* xv. 806/1 Ileosigmoidostomy..shortcuts the entire colon and renders it more or less functionless. **1890** Billings *Med. Dict.* I. 682/1 Ileostomy. **1891** T. Bryant in *Lancet* 3 Jan. 1/1 The operation I am about to describe may well be called 'ileostomy'. **1926** *Brit. Jrnl. Surg.* XIII. 711 Against ileostomy, however, we urge the loss of an important sphincter and portion of the digestive tract. **1968** J. C. Goligher et al. *Ulcerative Colitis* xiii. 236 The creation of a terminal ileostomy. **1968** Colcock & Braasch *Surg. Small Intestine in Adult* xiii. 179 The great majority of patients with ulcerative colitis who need surgery will require a complete removal of the colon and rectum and an ileostomy. *Ibid.* 181 A temporary ileostomy appliance is cemented to the skin over the ileostomy. **1971** M. Sparsberg (*title*) Ileostomy care.

Iliac (i·liæk), *a.*[2] [ad. L. *Iliacus*, a. Gr. Ἰλιακός: see Iliad.] Pertaining or relating to ancient Ilium; Ilian.

1878 Gladstone *Homer* 37 The other epics of the Iliac Cycle differ in their narrative from the Iliad.

iliacus (iləi·ăkŏs). *Anat.* [late L.: see Iliac *a.* (*sb.*).] = *iliac muscle* (s.v. Iliac *a.* 2). Also † *iliacus internus, iliacus muscle.*

1615 H. Crooke *Descr. Body Man* x. vi. 744 The thighes are each of them bent by two [muscles] called Psoas and Iliacus. *Ibid.* xxxviii. 811 The second Bender is called Iliacus internus the inward haunch-Muscle. **1726** W. Cheselden *Anat. Humane Body* (ed. 3) ii. ii. 123 Iliacus internus, arises from the concave part of the ilium, and from its lower edge, and passing over the ilium near the os pubis, joins the former muscle [*sc.* psoas magnus], and is inserted with it, to be employed in the same action. **1733** G. Douglas tr. *Winslow's Anat. Expos. Struct. Human Body* I. iii. x. 53 The Iliacus and Psoas thus united pass under the Ligamentum Falloppii. **1875** *Encycl. Brit.* I. 840/2 The thigh can be bent on the abdomen by the action of the psoas, iliacus, and pectineus, which lie in front of the joint. **1967** G. M. Wyburn et al. *Conc. Anat.* vi. 158 The iliacus and psoas muscles pass behind the inguinal ligament and the iliacus joins the tendon of the psoas.

iliahi (īli,ā·hi). [Hawaiian.] One of several trees of the genus *Santalum*, esp. *S. freycinetianum*, which grow in Hawaii and yield an aromatic wood.

1825 W. Ellis *Jrnl. Tour Hawaii* 247 *Iliahi*, sandal-wood. **1888** W. Hillebrand *Flora Hawaiian Islands* 389 *Santalum*...The following species are weakly defined, and all furnish an equally fragrant wood..while the name of the tree is 'Iliahi'. **1915** W. A. Bryan *Nat. Hist. Hawaii* xv. 219 The iliahi furnished the first article of export which attracted commerce to the islands. **1970** S. Carlquist *Hawaii* xiv. 269 Typical of this low stature is the coastal iliahi, or sandalwood (*Santalum ellipticum* var. *littorale*), which is a low, rounded shrub with succulent leaves, gray-green in color. Inland sandalwoods are all trees.

Ilian (i·liăn, əi·liăn), *a.* (*sb.*). [f. *Ili*(*um* + -an.] Of or pertaining to any of the successive towns of Ilium in the Trojan Plain; also as *sb.*, an inhabitant of Ilium.

1582 R. Stanyhurst tr. *Virgil's Æneis* i. (Arb.) 26 Whilst stood the great Ilian empyre. **1626** G. Sandys tr. *Ovid's Met.* xiii. 222 To th'Ilian Court I went. **1847** J. Leitch tr. *Müller's Anc. Art* 483 Coins of the Ilians. **1869** Tozer *Highl. Turkey* I. 44 The site of the ancient Village of the Ilians. **1876** Gladstone *Homeric Synchronism* 34 He appears as the representation of the Dardanian Branch, with a sidelong jealous eye towards the predominating Ilian House of Priam. **1881** *Jrnl. Hellenic Stud.* II. 18 After the victory, he [*sc.* Alexander] gave substantial proof of gratitude to the Ilian gods and heroes. **1888** *Encycl. Brit.* XXIII. 579/2 The temple of the Ilian Athene. *Ibid.*, It was politic to recall the legend of Roman descent from Æneas. Lucius Scipio and the Ilians were alike eager to do so. **1927** W. W. Tarn *Hellenistic Civilisation* ii. 70 Antigonus I..created three sectional Leagues: the Ionian..the Ilian..and the Islanders. **1941** M. Rostovtzeff *Social & Econ. Hist. Hellenic World* I. iii. 154 Some of the leagues had existed before, such as the Ionian, Aeolian, Ilian (?), Lycian, and Carian leagues in Asia Minor. **1957** *Encycl. Brit.* XXII. 505/1 In their temple of Athena the Ilians showed him arms which had served in the Trojan war.

Iliat (i·liāt). Also **Eylat, Ilat, Iliaut, Iliyat, Illyat.** [Turkish *īlāt*, pl. of *īl* country, wandering pastoral tribe (cf. *rūm-eyli* 'country of the Romans', Rumelia).] One of several tribes of nomads scattered throughout Persia.

1840 *Penny Cycl.* XVII. 472/1 The wandering tribes of Persia are comprehended under the general term of *Iliyats* or *Ilat*, and are found in every part of Persia. **1865** *Chambers's Encycl.* VII. 420/2 The nomad or pastoral tribes, or eylats (*eyl*, a clan), often spelt *illyats*, are of four distinct races—Turkomans, Kurds, Lûurs, and Arabs. **1888** *Encycl. Brit.* XXIII. 661/1 They are known by the name of Ilāt or Iliyāt. **1902** D. G. Hogarth *Nearer East* 160 The nomad 'Iliats' who wander here and there.

iligant (i·ligănt), *a.* ¶ Used, chiefly as an Irishism, for Elegant *a.* (sense ¶ 8). See also *illigant.

1822 M. Edgeworth *Let.* 4 Mar. (1971) 361 We have an excellent job landau..and quite *iligant* coachman horses and *all*—for one pound per day. **1833** [see *elegant *a.* 8]. **1846** *Punch* XI. 79 A large assortment of most iligant blunderbuss's. **1888** [see Elegant *a.* 8].

ilima (ilī·mă). [Hawaiian.] A shrub of the genus *Sida*, esp. *S. fallax*, bearing yellow or orange flowers.

1888 W. Hillebrand *Flora Hawaiian Islands* 43 *Sida*... A large genus, distributed over the warmer regions of the entire globe.—Nat[ive] name of all species: 'Ilima'. **1915** W. A. Bryan *Nat. Hist. Hawaii* xv. 209 Two species of ilima occur in the lower zone throughout the group. Their bright yellow flowers, so much used in leis, are well known. **1920** *Glasgow Herald* 16 Apr. 8 Three magnificent wreaths of ilima, the Hawaiian royal flowers. **1970** S. Carlquist *Hawaii* xiv. 269 *Sida fallax*, the ilima, is a mat with yellow-orange flowers and finely hairy white leaves, common near the shores of all the islands.

ilk, *a.*[1] Add: **3.** ¶Also, by further extension, = kind, sort.

1790 J. Fisher *Poems* 155 Ilk ane a cap an' cloak o' silk Has got, as if she was a lady, An' that indeed, o' nae sma' ilk. **1881** J. A. Morgan *Shakes. Myth.* i. 36 Milton was the enemy of all the ilk. **1897** *Evesham Jrnl.* 23 June (E.D.D.), The horses most famous for marvellous exploits must have blood as well as bone, but only certain districts of the Green Isle can produce this ilk. **1899** *Westm. Gaz.* 29 June 3/2 Two very new hats of quite another 'ilk'. *Ibid.* 6 July 3/2 A coat of this 'ilk' is quite another matter from the coat of the tailor costume. **1969** *Times* 8 May 8/6 This habit is confined to Tory backbenchers like..Rear-Admiral Morgan Giles and others of that ilk. **1973** E. McGirr *Bardel's Murder* ii. 42 One doesn't like or dislike a fellow of that ilk... He was a kind of barrow boy in a shop.

ill, *a.* and *sb.* Add: **A.** *adj.* **8. b.** = Sick *a.* 2.

1928 C. F. S. Gamble *Story N. Sea Air Station* 244 Before they could be attended they were given too much food and were violently ill as a result. **1929** A. Conan Doyle *Maracot Deep* 153 The sight was so horrifying that we were all ill.

ill-. Add: **A. III. 4. ill-favour** *v. trans.*, to treat badly, to be inimical to or hostile towards.

1899 F. J. Crowest *Beethoven* 128 His environment generally throughout his early life ill-favoured the contemplative mood. **1908** *Westm. Gaz.* 21 Aug. 2/1 Fortune ill-favoured them in many skirmishes.

7. a. *ill-acquired* (example); **b.** *ill-constructed, -pleased*; **c.** *ill-adapted* (example), *-adjusted, -armed* (examples), *-assorted* (earlier and later examples), *-balanced* (examples), *-concealed* (examples), *-conducted* (example), *-considered* (examples), *-directed* (examples), *-equipped, -governed* (examples), *-informed* (examples), *-lit* (example), *-performed, -qualified, -supported* (example).

1848 Mill *Pol. Econ.* II. v. § 1. 293 The same reckless prodigality with which they squandered any other part of their ill-acquired possessions. **1878** W. James *Coll. Ess. & Rev.* (1920) 53 If his powers correspond to the wants of this social environment, he may survive, even though he be ill-adapted to the natural or 'outer' environment. *Ibid.*, Individuals who, by their special powers, satisfy these desires are protected by their fellows and enabled to survive, though their mental constitution should in other respects be lamentably ill-'adjusted' to the outward world. **1903** *Daily Chron.* 25 June 4/1 In this ill-adjusted world men have to take what they can get. **1807** J. Barlow *Columb.* vi. 225 Ridgefield and Compo saw his valorous might, With ill armed swains put veteran troops to flight. **1942** W. S. Churchill *End of Beginning* (1943) 32 China, ill-armed or half-armed, has ..withstood the main fury of Japan. **1814** Ill-assorted [see Assorted *ppl. a.*]. **1938** W. S. Churchill *Into Battle* (1941) 29 Three..Ministers of the Crown have been ..prejudiced by being given..ill-assorted tasks. **1864** G. M. Hopkins *Poems* (1948) 119 The clouds come like ill-balanced crags. **1956** K. Clark *Nude* vii. 284 Could fill an ill-balanced nature with destructive envy. **1895** B. M. Croker *Village Tales* 38 As time wore on, there actually arose an ill-concealed jealousy of their old corps. **1960** *Farmer & Stockbreeder* 8 Mar. 63/3 The report of the Cook Committee was awaited with 'ill-concealed impatience'. **1839** Mill in *Westm. Rev.* Apr. 497 There is a notion abroad that they are the ill-conditioned and ill-conducted portion. **1835** —— in *London Rev.* II. iii. 116 In the English aristocracy there has surely been.. crude and ill-considered legislation enough. **1956** E. E. Evans-Pritchard *Nuer Relig.* iii. 96 It was because this was not appreciated by British administrators that the role..of the prophets was very largely misunderstood and their treatment of them ill-considered. **1847** Mill *Let.* 19 June in *Works* (1963) XIII. 721 The long paper.. is full of unfinished & ill constructed..sentences. **1944** R. Chandler *Let.* 26 Jan. in *R. Chandler Speaking* (1966) 42 A column and a half of respectful attention will be given to any fourth-rate, ill-constructed, mock-serious account of the life of a bunch of cotton pickers in the deep south. *a*1849 Poe *Works* (1865) I. 418 Some feeble and ill-directed efforts resulted in complete failure on their part, and, of course, in total triumph on mine. **1947** *Mind* LVI. 132 They have thus been led to offer facile, but ill-directed, rebutments of the refutation. **1956** *Nature* 10 Mar. 446/2 At present we are ill-equipped to do so. **1962** W. Nowottny *Lang. Poets Use* i. 5 The exhausted and ill-equipped army. **1685** tr. *Arnauld & Nicole's Logic* I. iii. 68 Such a Presumption and Rashness is a sign of an ill-govern'd and ill-qualified mind. **1860** Ruskin *Unto this Last* in *Cornh. Mag.* Sept. 281 In the inactive or ill-governed nation, the gradations of decay and the victories of treason work out also their own rugged system of subjection and success. **1824** Ill informed [see Informed *ppl. a.* 2 b]. **1961** New Eng. Bible *Rom.* x. 2 To their zeal for God I can testify, but it is an ill-informed zeal. **1905** W. Holman Hunt *Pre-Raphaelitism* I. iii. 46 With small and ill-lit studios, and without means to pay models, he [*sc.* Haydon] could never do justice to his intellectual conceptions. **1890** W. James *Princ. Psychol.* I. x. 369 The only service that transcendental egoism has done to psychology has been by protests against Hume's 'bundle'-theory of mind. But this service has been ill-performed. **1946** A. L. Bacharach *Brit. Mus.* i. 12 The Churches, who never seemed to realise the paralysing effect their badly written, ill-performed music was having on their congregations. **1861** Trollope *Orley F.* (1862) I. xxi. 161 An angry ill-pleased wife is no pleasant companion for a gentleman on a long evening. **1685** Ill-qualified [see **ill-governed*]. **1733** A. Baxter *Inquiry Human Soul* ii. xxvi. 81 The Atheist's ill-supported, tottering world.

IV. 8. *ill-visaged* adj.

1865 G. M. Hopkins *Poems* (1948) 142 And John shall lie, where winds are dead, And hate the ill-visaged cursing tars. **1894** Ill visaged [see Visaged *a.*].

B. **ill assurance**, want of assurance; **ill-formed** *a.* (earlier example and context in Locke); so **ill-formedness**.

1905 *Macm. Mag.* Dec. 151 As they grew out of the restive sensitiveness of youthful ill-assurance,..they turned with gratitude towards their parent. *c* **1909** D. H. Lawrence *Collier's Friday Night* (1934) ii. 51 Ernest (flushing up at the sound of her ill-assurance). *a* **1672** A. Bradstreet *Several Poems* (1678) 236 Thou ill-form'd offspring of my feeble brain. **1690** Locke *Hum. Und.* IV. iv. §16 They..make bold..to destroy ill-formed and mis-shaped Productions. **1972** *Language* XLVIII. i. 82 These have to do with (1) dialect variations and (2) degree of ill-formedness. **1972** A. Makkai *Idiom Struct. Eng.* 84 Let us now examine a few cases of lexemic illformedness.

Illano (*ilyā·no*). Also **I(l)lanon, I(l)lanum.** [Native name.] A member of a Moro people of Mindanao in the Republic of the Philippines; also, the language of this people. (Cf. Moro[2].) Hence **Illano·an** *a.*

1779 T. Forrest *Voy. New Guinea* xii. 302 They possess an island in the very heart of the Philippines, called Burias, where has been a colony of Illanos, for many years. **1821** W. Walton tr. *T. de Comyn's State of Philippine Islands* viii. 231 Long have the inhabitants of the Philippines deplored..the ravages committed on their coasts and settlements by..the Malanos, Ilanos and Tirones Moors and others. **1840** *Penny Cycl.* XVIII. 87/1 He was informed that the Illanos from that island [*sc.* Magindanao] had formed a settlement on Burias. **1848** F. S. Marryat *Borneo* 21 Pirate's Bay, so called from its being a favourite resort of the Illanoan pirates. **1898** F. T. Bullen in *National Rev.* Aug. 857 There is yet another small section of the inhabitants of this Archipelago, who were once the terror of the surrounding seas... These have long been known as 'Illanons'. **1900** F. H. Sawyer *Inhabitants Philippines* 364 The Moros Illanos..inhabit the country between the Bay of Iligan and Illana Bay, also round Lake Lanao, the Rio Grande and Lake Liguan. **1957** *Encycl. Americana* XIX. 472a/1 Some of the best-known Moro groups are the..Lanao Filipinos (divided into the Maranaos and Ilanums or Iranums). *Ibid.* XXI. 751/1 The principal languages and dialects with the number of persons speaking each were divided into the following groups:..Ilanon-Lanao-Lanao..109. Ilanon-Lanao-Maranoy..170,195.

illatinate (ilæ·tinĕt), *a.* (*sb.*). *rare.* [f. Il-[2] + Latin *a.* and *sb.* + -ate[2], after Illiterate *a.*] Having no knowledge of Latin; ignorant of Latin. Also as *sb.*

1922 S. Leslie *Oppidan* xxv. 345 They appeal even to the illatinate. **1941** E. Marsh tr. *Horace's Odes* Preface p. vii, Unless the version can give the illatinate reader some notion of Horace's quality as a poet, it is a superfluity.

illative, *a.* and *sb.* Add: **A.** *adj.* **4.** *Gram.* Denoting the case expressing motion into.

1890 A. S. Gatschet *Klamath Indians* 483 The suffix marks as well (1) a motion or direction toward an object or into a place or country, as (2) a stay or rest at or in a place, region, country. It is more frequently used in the former sense, and hence I have called the case the illative case. **1958** A. S. C. Ross *Etym.* 167 *Illative case*, the case of 'motion towards', as in Finnish *Helsinkiin* 'to Helsinki'. **1959** [see *elative *a.*]. **1968** C. J. Fillmore in Bach & Harms *Universals in Linguistic Theory* 9 Redden..finds five case indices in Walapai..and identifies each of these with terms taken from the tradition of case studies:..*-l* is illative/inessive, [etc.].

B. *sb.* **1.** Delete † *Obs.* and add examples.

a **1868** C. Byington *Gram. Choctaw Lang.* (1870) viii. 54 Conjunctions are divided into the following classes:.. Illatives; therefore, wherefore, on account of, yomohmi hokvt, yomahmi hokah. **1870** F. A. March *Compar. Gram. Anglo-Saxon Lang.* §481 Causals and illatives are very often omitted.

Illawarra (ilăwǫ·ră). The name of a district in New South Wales, used *attrib.* to designate certain trees native to the region.

1884 A. Nilson *Timber Trees N.S.W.* 39 *C[argillia] australis*.—Black Plum; Illawarra Plum. *Ibid.* 82 *F[renela] rhomboidea*.—Illawarra Mountain Pine. **1889** J. H. Maiden *Useful Native Plants Austral.* 422 *Elæocarpus reticulata* var. *Kirtoni*, is known as 'Illawarra Ash', or 'Mountain Ash'. **1904** —— *Forest Flora N.S.W.* I. 9 *Ficus rubiginosa*... Vernacular Names.—'Port Jackson Fig', 'Illawarra Fig', from the best known localities. **1907** *Ibid.* II. 53 This tree [sc. *Callitris Muelleri*] is usually known as Cypress Pine. The names 'Port Jackson Pine' and 'Illawarra Mountain Pine' should be received with caution, as *C. cupressiformis* may be included. **1965** *Austral. Encycl.* IV. 58/2 The Port Jackson, Illawarra, or rusty fig (*F. rubiginosa*) is confined in its native state to New South Wales, but is extensively planted as a shade and ornamental tree throughout Australia.

b. In full *Illawarra* (*dairy, milking*) *shorthorn*: see quot. 1911.

1911 *N.Z. Jrnl. Agric.* May 274 The breed..known as the Illawara Milking Shorthorn, a dairy type of Shorthorn evolved on the south coast districts of the State from a Shorthorn–Ayrshire foundation, but now bred for about thirty years to a Shorthorn dairy type. *Ibid.*, One very good point of the Illawara is that while it is a heavy producer, the milk is generally of a very satisfactory butterfat standard. **1912** M. A. O'Callaghan *Dairying in Australasia* vii. 111 The Scotch type of Ayrshire is nearly as different from the Australian type, as is the English shorthorn dairy cow from what we know as the Illawarra dairy Shorthorn. **1934** *Bulletin* (Sydney) 25 July 41/1 Southern India is to try Australia's own dairy cattle—the Illawarra shorthorn from the N.S.W. South Coast. **1965** *Austral. Encycl.* V. 64/1 During the nineteenth century a special breed of dairy cattle, the Australian Illawarra Shorthorn, was developed.

ill effect, ill-effect. [Ill *a.* 5, Effect *sb.* 1.] (Usually in *pl.*) A harmful or deleterious effect, an unpleasant consequence.

1675 in McHutchin & Quirk *Isle of Man Charities* (1831) 6 The mean provision of the Clergy in that Isle, and the ill effects which necessarily attend upon the same. **1704** *Hist. Man* xlvii. 195 Envy, and the ill Effects of it. **1767** [see Ill *a.* 3 a]. **1845** *Douglas Jerrold's Shilling Mag.* I. 174 Equal ill effect, either from his liking the Princess too much, or too little. **1884** W. Pye *Surg. Handicraft* 531 One year after the accident he..could go to a ball and dance every dance without any ill effects. **1923** R. Lynd *Blue Lion* xxi. 162 It would be mere perversity to quarrel with these [dishes] because there are no ill-effects from eating them. **1971** J. Z. Young *Introd. Study Man* xxii. 294 Any genes that confer reproductive advantage early in life will be selected, even if they are pleiotropic and have ill-effects later.

illegal, *a.* Add: **2.** Special Comb.: **illegal immigrant,** orig. a Jew who entered or attempted to enter Palestine without official permission during the later years of the British mandate; now used more generally; so *illegal immigration*; **illegal operation,** an abortion procured illegally.

1939 *Times* 31 May 11/1 These illegal immigrants come practically penniless, and have no documents to indicate their origin. **1946** *Times* 23 Sept. 4/3 The British 'clamp down' on illegal immigrants. **1949** Koestler *Promise & Fulfilment* vi. 59 The hunting down of 'illegal immigrants' became gradually an obsession with the Palestine authorities. **1963** J. Joesten *They call it Intelligence* ii. viii. 73 Once in this country, Abel headed straight for New York, a good place for an illegal immigrant. **1970** [see B. *sb.* 1]. **1970** *Times* 2 July 1/4 Police..took away 40 men who had come from the Punjab... All the men had been established as illegal immigrants. **1939** *Times* 31 May 11/1 Illegal immigration into Palestine probably dates back to Turkish times, but it is now assuming alarming proportions. **1969** *New Yorker* 29 Nov. 151/1 Moshe Pearlman.. an organiser of illegal immigration to Palestine..for all his wit and sophistication, still takes his Zionism very seriously. **1910** Chesterton *G. B. Shaw* 145 Mr. Granville Barker's play of *Waste*, in which the woman dies from an illegal operation. **1927** *Rev. Eng. Stud.* Oct. 433 There is a very interesting misuse of words..due..to a yet older human failing: taboo. As instances may serve *lavatory, illegal operation, social evil, a certain disease.* **1938** 'M. Benney' *Scapegoat Dances* iv. 46 He had given his knowledge, time, and money to relieving the distresses of the street-walkers..when necessary, performing illegal operations on them. **1943** G. Greene *Ministry of Fear* i. ii. 24 A man who deals in something disreputable—pornographic books or illegal operations. **1958** *New Statesman* 7 June 722/1 Estimates suggest that something like 200,000 illegal operations are performed every year in this country.

B. *sb.* **1.** = **illegal immigrant.*

1939 *Times* 31 May 11/1 Placing the illegals in concentration camps is no solution. **1946** Koestler *Thieves in Night* 328 The old tramper was lost—but there were two others on their way with eight hundred illegals this time. **1960** H. Agar *Saving Remnant* viii. 208 The British announced that all future 'illegals' would be taken to Cyprus. **1970** *Sunday Times* (Colour Suppl.) 1 Feb. 29/4 In the year 1968 alone 142,000 illegal immigrants were caught... There is no onus upon an employer not to take on illegals.

2. A Soviet secret agent working in a foreign country.

1968 W. Garner *Deep, Deep Freeze* xii. 133 An Illegal's first job was to pass vital information with the minimum of delay. **1969** —— *Us or Them War* xxxiii. 251 What if he'd come over as an 'illegal', with a long-term programme? **1969** H. MacInnes *Salzburg Connection* xx. 281 We'd like to catch that colonel and the rest of his illegals.

illegit, illegit. (ilĭdʒi·t), colloq. abbrev. of Illegitimate *a.* (*sb.*).

1913 A. Lunn *Harrovians* viii. 152 'Was he a blooming illegit?' asked Kendal. **1952** 'C. Brand' *London Particular* xiii. 166 She was supposed to be having this illegit. **1955** J. Cannan *Long Shadows* v. 86 Perhaps Mousie's illegit was a boy. **1958** 'C. Carnac' *Long Shadows* xv. 200 Somerset House..registers the illegits. as carefully as the rest. **1962** C. Watson *Hopjoy was Here* iii. 33 The mother is *Miss* Cork. Miriam's illegit. **1967** E. Coxhead *Thankless Muse* iii. 61 She's a year younger than me and it's only a matter of minutes before she'll bring home the illegit. **1973** *Nation Rev.* (Melbourne) 111. 31 Aug. 1463/1 If it was an illegit, why no mention in the womens lib chapter?

illegitimate, *a.* Add: **A. 2. d.** *Racing.* Formerly applied to steeplechasing and hurdle racing as distinguished from flat-racing.

So called from the fact that before the formation of the Grand National Hunt Committee these forms of racing were not under any rules and were not recognized by any racing tribunal.

1888 *Daily Chron.* 31 Oct. (Farmer), A much smarter performer at the illegitimate game than she was on the flat. **1889** Barrère & Leland *Dict. Slang* I. 481/2 *Illegitimate* season, also called the dead season. **1898** A. E. T. Watson *Turf* viii. 171 The Jockey Club gave no countenance to 'illegitimate' sport.

e. Of drama: more concerned with spectacle than with literary quality. Cf. Legitimate *a.* 2 b.

1812 *Dramatic Censor 1811* 158 We are grieved to behold that hunger for spectacle, and the illegitimate Drama, which so glaringly prevails with the more numerous and coarser part of an English Public. **1842** *Times* 28 Jan., A magnificent Barbary lion, trained for performing in the illegitimate drama, 105 guineas. **1949** *Archit. Rev.* CV. 122/1 The popular tradition, which cared little about lines of demarcation between the 'legitimate' and 'illegitimate' stage.

B. *sb.* **b.** *spec.* An illegal immigrant in Australia. *Obs.* exc. *Hist.*

1827 [= ed. 1 of quot. 1828 in Dict.; for II. 108 read II. 116]. **1941** Baker *Dict. Austral. Slang* 37 *Illegitimates,* free settlers (obs.). **1945** —— *Austral. Lang.* ii. 42 These were the type of people who styled themselves the *aristocracy, sterling*..and, since they had no 'legal' reasons for coming to Australia..also bore the title *illegitimates.* **1966** G. W. Turner *Eng. Lang. Austral. & N.Z.* i. 9 Historians..may draw on *illegitimates* or *pure merinos* as the Australian equivalent of a donnish joke, but they are not current in general Australian speech.

illfare. Add: Used more or less *joc.* in phr. *the Illfare State* (opp. *Welfare State*).

1952 C. Palmer (*title*) The British Socialist Ill-fare State; an examination of the Welfare State. **1962** *Punch* 28 Feb. 352/1 What is the Illfare State?

ill health, ill-health. [Ill *a.* 7, Health *sb.* 2 a.] An unsound, disordered condition of health; that state of health which is characterized by the presence of some disease or by the imperfect functioning of the physical processes.

1698 J. Locke *Let.* 6 Apr. in H. R. F. Bourne *Life J. Locke* (1876) II. 464 As for writing, my ill-health gives me little heart or opportunity for it. **1717** [see Philosophical *a.* 3]. **1732** [see Ill *a.* 8]. **1782** [see Health *sb.* 2 a]. **1783** Johnson *Let.* 22 Sept. (1892) II. 336 That I have not written sooner, you may impute to absence, to ill-health, to any thing rather than want of regard. **1814** Jane Austen *Mansf. Park* I. ii. 38 Lady Bertram, in consequence of a little ill-health, and a great deal of indolence, gave up the house in town. **1855** Macaulay *Hist. Eng.* III. xi. 63 Danby..under the plea of ill health.. withdrew from court. **1911** A. C. Benson *Diary* 31 Aug. (1926) 220 The pictures of her [*sc.* Mrs. Carlyle] in 1854.. are hauntingly terrible—the mixture of ill-health and unhappiness very conspicuous. **1931** J. S. Huxley *What dare I Think?* ii. 61 They have..rescued many people from ill-health.

illigant, ¶ var. *Iligant *a.*

1819 M. Wilmot *Let.* 3 Sept. (1935) 16 An *ill*igant black silk dress. **1898** J. D. Brayshaw *Slum Silhouettes* 21 It was agreed on all hands that he was 'an illigant corpse, and as foine a bhoy as ever was stretched'. **1939** Joyce *Finnegans Wake* i. 14 She found hersell sackvulle of.. small illigant brogues, so rich in sweat.

illinium (ili·niǒm). *Chem.* [Named after the University of *Illinois*, where the work reported in quot. 1926 was carried out: see -ium.] A disused name for the element now called *promethium.

1926 J. A. Harris et al. in *Nature* 5 June 792/2 X-ray analysis confirmed the theory and showed the presence of element number 61 in those fractions... The name assigned to the element is Illinium (Il). **1939** [see *florentium]. **1947** *Nature* 4 Jan. 8/2 The names 'masurium' and 'illinium' are so firmly rooted in text-books and tables that recent work on artificial isotopes of the elements 43 and 61 is sometimes referred to as the production of species of masurium and illinium. **1951** J. R. Partington *Gen. & Inorg. Chem.* (ed. 2) xvi. 436I Promethium, an artificial element, fills the place of atomic number 61 missing in the natural rare-earth series, the supposed natural 'illinium' not having been confirmed. **1962** [see *florentium].

Illinoian (ilinoi·ăn), *sb.* and *a.* [f. *Illinoi(s + -an.] **A.** *sb.* A native or inhabitant of the state of Illinois.

The more usual form is *Illinoisan.

1835 C. F. Hoffman *Winter in West* II. 246 The Yankees..call us old Illinoians 'Suckers'. **1867** A. D. Richardson *Beyond Mississippi* xi. 132 Most readers have heard Ohioans spoken of as 'Buckeyes',..Illinoians as 'Suckers'.

B. *adj. Geol.* Of, pertaining to, or designating the third Pleistocene glaciation in North America, now generally identified with the Riss glaciation in the Alps. Also *absol.*, the Illinoian glaciation or the deposits it produced.

1896 T. C. Chamberlin in *Jrnl. Geol.* IV. 875 While returning from my last visit to the field in which the Kansan, Illinoian, Iowan, and Wisconsin formations were seen in close succession, I made a memorandum of impressions respecting their relative ages. **1899** *Bull. Geol. Soc. Amer.* X. 116 The color of the Illinoian till, where fresh and unweathered, is quite like that of the Iowan, and the boulders are somewhat similar... Judging by the changes that had been wrought in the surface of the Illinoian before the loess was laid down on it, this sheet of till is at least 5 or 6 times as old as the Iowan. **1934** R. A. Daly *Changing World of Ice Age* i. 29 In the Middle West of North America, five Glacial stages have been proved, and named, from oldest to youngest, the Nebraskan, Kansan, Illinoian, Iowan, and Wisconsin stages... However, the Iowan glaciation may have been merely a phase of the Wisconsin. **1957** J. K. Charlesworth *Quaternary Era* I. xxiii. 466 Lakes were impounded by Illinoian ice in Pennsylvania and Illinois on the older drift and for a short time in Iowa..on the Illinoian drift by the displacement of the Mississippi. *Ibid.* II. l. 1528 F. Leverett..estimates post Early Wisconsin time as 70,000 years and obtains *c.* 200,000 years since the Illinoian, more than 500,000 years since the Kansan, and probably one million years since the Nebraskan. **1970** B. Mears *Changing Earth* xv. 384/1 A eustatic fall of 500 feet, more or less, seems likely for the Illinoian stage.

Illinois (ilinoi·). Also 8 Il(l)inese. Pl. **Illinois.** [Amer. Indian.] **1.** *pl.* The members of a confederation of Algonquian Indian tribes formerly inhabiting an area in and around the state of Illinois.

[**1670** *Relations des Jésuites* (1858) 86 Les Ilinois peuples tirans au Sud, ont cinq grands Bourgs.] **1703** tr. *Lahontan's New Voy. N.-Amer.* I. 231 Some Ilinese at Chegakou. **1722** D. Coxe *Descr. Carolana* 16 The River of the *Alinouecks*, corruptly by the French call'd *Illinois.* **1766** R. Rogers *Ponteach* ii. ii, This same Chekitan a Captive led The fair Donanta from the Illinois. **1834** J. M. Peck *Gazetteer Illinois* 102 The Illinois, a numerous nation of Indians who were destitute of the cruelty of savages. **1907** F. W. Hodge *Handbk. Amer. Indians* I. 598/2 Seemingly belonging to the Illinois. **1949** *Chicago Tribune* 20 Feb. (Grafic Mag.) 14/4 These Indians called themselves *Illini* (the native word for men) but the French called them *Illinois.*

2. The language of this people.

1703 tr. *Lahontan's New Voy. N. Amer.* I. xvi. 130 About two a clock in the Morning two Men approach'd to our little Camp, and call'd in *Illinese*, that they wanted an Interview. **1933** L. Bloomfield *Lang.* iv. 72 The languages..of the Great Lakes region (..Illinois, Miami, and so on).

3. *attrib.* or quasi-*adj.* Of or pertaining to the Illinois Indians or to the state of Illinois.

1703 tr. *Lahontan's New Voy. N. Amer.* I. 231 Upon the Ilinese Lake, and the adjacent Country. **1764** J. Grant *Let.* Dec. in *Amer. Hist. Rev.* (1915) XX. 827, I find Your Lordships' have included the Illinois Indians in the Northern District. **1785** T. Jefferson *Notes Virginia* (1787) 37 Paccan, or Illinois nut..grows on the Illinois. **1785** H. Marshall *Arbustrum Amer.* 69 *Juglans pecan.* The Pecan or Illinois Hickery. This tree is said to grow plenty in the neighborhood of the Illinois river. **1818** M. Birkbeck *Lett. from Illinois* 104, I am an Illinois farmer. **1857** [see *combine *sb.* c]. **1861** *Daily Dispatch* (Richmond, Va.) 1 Aug. 2/3 The consternation in Washington, upon the arrival there of the Illinois Xerxes [*sc.* Abraham Lincoln], was indescribable. **1865** *Trans. Illinois Agric. Soc.* V. 865 The Chick-pea has again been heralded as a valuable acquisition upon the prairies under the name of Illinois coffee. **1948** *Chicago Tribune* 26 June 1. 7/8 Starved Rock obtained its name from a legend which says that a band of Illinois Indians perished there in 1769.

Illinoisan (ilinoi·ăn, -oi·zăn). Also **Illinoisian.** [f. *Illinois + -an.] A native or inhabitant of the state of Illinois. Cf. *Illinoian *sb.*

1836 *Public Ledger* (Philadelphia) 14 Oct. (Th. 447), The Illinoisans are called Suckers. *c* **1848** W. Whitman in *Amer. Speech* (1961) XXXVI. 297 Illinoisians [are called] *Suckers.* **1855** *N.Y. Tribune* 31 Dec. 6/1, I had told him I was an Illinoisian, and an editor. **1890** W. Whitman *Compl. Prose Works* (1892) 504 Abraham Lincoln, familiar, our own, an Illinoisian. **1947** *Illinois: Descriptive & Hist. Guide* 3 He who would describe a typical Illinoisan may well find..that his only valid generalization is that an Illinoisan is one who resides in Illinois. **1948** *Aurora* (Illinois) *Beacon-News* 7 Nov. 3/1 The Illinoisan..boarded the Truman victory special at Union station here to welcome the President home.

1972 *Jrnl. Illinois State Hist. Soc.* LXV. 245 Nor should Illinoisans be surprised that politics is ever present.

illipe(e, var. Illupi (in Dict. and Suppl.).

illiquid, *a.* Add: **b.** Of an asset, investment, etc.: not easily or readily realizable. Hence **illiqui·dity,** the character of being illiquid.

1913 *Globe* 24 Oct. 6/4 Is cottage property a safe investment for the Reserve Fund? It is an illiquid asset, and a sudden drain on a fund thus locked up might be very inconvenient. **1927** *Glasgow Herald* 18 Apr. 9 The illiquidity of credit in Japan. **1930** *Times* 26 Mar. 26/7 Slow and illiquid loans and investments. **1948** G. Crowther *Outl. Money* (rev. ed.) ii. 80 There is some difference between having a variety of small loans in different degrees illiquid, and being closely associated..with one or two large concerns that are known to be doing badly. **1971** *Nature* 5 Feb. 363/2 Some of the officers of the British Association seem to be hoping that they can solve their chronic problem of what is called illiquidity by merging either with the Royal Society of Arts or with the Royal Institution. **1972** *Real Estate Rev.* Winter 27/2 Illiquidity is generally valued at about 1·5 percent to 2·0 percent in most analyses of the capitalization rate, so the equity trust shareholder holds his own quite nicely in the return contest upon closer inspection. **1973** M. Woodhouse *Blue Bone* xv. 167 One is liquid or illiquid at awkward times, just as with any other business.

illite (i·ləit). *Min.* [Named after the state of *Ill(inois: see -ite[1].] Any of a group of clay minerals that belong to the mica group and are characterized by a lattice that does not expand through the absorption of water; *esp.* a mineral structurally and chemically similar to muscovite but differing in having more water and silicon and less potassium. Also used as a generic term for these minerals.

1937 R. E. Grim et al. in *Amer. Mineralogist* XXII. 816 There remains only the alternative of giving a new name to the mica occurring in argillaceous sediments, and the term *illite*, taken from the State of Illinois, is here proposed. It is not proposed as a specific mineral name, but as a general term for the clay mineral constituent of argillaceous sediments belonging to the mica group. **1944** *Mineral. Mag.* XXVII. 60 Illite is not a stable mineral under humid temperate conditions. *Ibid.* 61 According to Fleischer, bravaisite may be the specific mineral species in illites. **1953** R. E. Grim *Clay Mineral.* iii. 36 Grim, Bray, and Bradley gave the general formula for illites as $(OH)_4K_y(Si_{8-y}{\cdot}Al_y)$ $(Al_4{\cdot}Fe_4{\cdot}Mg_4{\cdot}Mg_6)O_{20}$. In muscovite *y* is equal to 2, whereas in illite *y* is less than 2 and frequently equal to 1 to 1·5. According to the formula, illites would include both trioctahedral and dioctahedral types, and no attempt was made to differentiate between biotite and muscovite types of crystallization. At the present time the name illite is generally used, and will be used herein, for clay-mineral micas of both dioctahedral and trioctahedral types and of muscovite and biotite crystallizations. **1957** R. C. Mackenzie *Differential Thermal Investigation of Clays* x. 260 Studies by Jackson et al. (1952) and Barshad (1954) suggest that illite itself should be considered as an interstratified mineral with mica and montmorillonite layers. **1959** C. S. Hurlbut *Dana's Man. Min.* (ed. 17) v. 463 Illite is the chief constituent in many shales. **1962** W. A. Deer et al. *Rock-Forming Min.* III. 213 The structure of illite is essentially that of a mica in that it contains layers with a plane of octahedrally coordinated cations sandwiched between two inward pointing sheets of linked (Si, Al)O_4 tetrahedra. *Ibid.* 214 A less common illite in which sodium is the inter-layer cation is called brammallite (Bannister, 1943). **1972** *Nature* 28 Jan. 220/1 The essential point about the quickclays is that they contain non-swelling clay minerals such as illite, chlorite and vermiculite, but not montmorillonite.

Hence **illi·tic** *a.*, containing, composed of, or characteristic of illite.

1949 Kirk & Othmer *Encycl. Chem. Technol.* IV. 31 The illite group of minerals occurs abundantly in marine shales and in many soils, particularly in soils derived from illitic shales. **1963** D. W. & E. E. Humphries tr. *Termier's Erosion & Sedimentation* vi. 153 On the recent volcanic rocks of the northwest coast of Sumatra, H. Erhart (1954) has observed illitic soils between sea level and a height of 4,000 feet. **1972** *Nature* 28 Jan. 220/1 There are also, however, quickclays containing more than 80% particles finer than 2 μm, mainly of illitic nature.

illiteracy. Add: Also used more generally in sense: ignorance, lack of understanding (of any pursuit, activity, etc.). Cf. next.

1965 W. Lamb *Posture & Gesture* x. 128 Our 'illiteracy' in physical behaviour communications is related to our puppet-like proclivities. **1970** *Nature* 11 Apr. 96/1 The responsibility for carrying out the act was left to local authorities, many of which are apparently more alarmed at being thought to provide 'sex on the rates' than by the widespread sexual illiteracy in the British population. **1973** *Times Lit. Suppl.* 15 June 660/5 Combating what was not yet called physical illiteracy and teaching girls and women ease and freedom of carriage and movement.

illiterate, *a.* Add: Also used more generally in sense: characterized by ignorance or lack of learning or subtlety (in any sphere of activity). Cf. prec.

1953 *Ann. Reg. 1952* 397 The pre-war type of speculative builder's house, which by its illiterate design.. had been largely responsible for the poor reputation of English suburban architecture. **1956** C. S. Lewis *Let.* (1966) 268 One must first distinguish the effect which music has on..people like me who are musically illiterate and get only the emotional effect. **1962** *Sunday Times* (Colour Suppl.) 10 June 4 The 'traditionalists', who are in the main musically illiterate.

‖ **illiterati** (ilitĕrā·ti, -ē·təi), *sb. pl.* [ad. L. *illitterātī*, pl. of *illitterātus.*] Illiterate, unlearned, or uneducated people. Cf. Illiterate *sb.*

1788 H. Walpole *Let.* 4 July (1905) XIV. 51 A lower species, indeed, is that of the scribes..who every night compose a journal for the satisfaction of such *illiterati.* **1822** *Blackw. Mag.* XI. 608 Ye're the most tinkler-tongued pack of illiterati. **1962** *Listener* 22 Nov. 877/1 Weekly periodicals for the younger *illiterati.*

illocution (ilokiū·ʃən). *Philos.* [f. Il-[1] + Locution.] An act such as ordering, warning, undertaking, performed in saying something. Hence **illocu·tionary** *a.*

1955 J. L. Austin *How to do Things with Words* (1962) viii. 99, I shall refer to the doctrine of the different types of function of language..as the doctrine of 'illocutionary forces'. *Ibid.* 101 Act (B) or Illocution: He urged (or advised, ordered, &c.) me to shoot her. *Ibid.* ix. 109 It is the distinction between illocutions and perlocutions which seems likeliest to give trouble. *Ibid.* 113 We must avoid the idea..that the illocutionary act is a *consequence* of the locutionary act. **1955** [see *eo ipso *advb. phr.*]. **1963** M. Furberg *(title)* Locutionary and illocutionary acts. **1964** *Philos. Rev.* LXXIII. 58 Describing and evaluating ..are only two among hundreds of kinds of illocutionary force. **1972** J. Rawls *Theory of Justice* §62. 406 Nor do I oppose the view that a certain illocutionary force is central to 'good'. **1973** *Times Lit. Suppl.* 5 Oct. 1161/5 The illocutionary act was the act performed by a speaker *in* saying something, such as the act of asking or answering a question.

illogic. (Later examples.)

1955 *Bull. Atomic Sci.* Apr. 131/1 So there was no illogic or softheadedness in the Commission's concern about the dangers inherent in the investigative process or in clearance determinations. **1965** *Sunday Times* (Colour Suppl.) 23 May 21/1 There's no room for illogic in an Ellery Queen mystery. **1972** *Nature* 1 Sept. 54/2 With the same illogic with which the Englishman will eat cow but not dog, will hang game but not chicken.

ill treatment, ill-treatment. [Ill *a.* 2, Treatment 1. Cf. Ill-treat *v.*] Bad or unfavourable treatment; rough handling; harsh or unsympathetic dealings.

1667 T. Sprat *Hist. R. Soc.* 401 A just occasion of lamenting the ill Treatment which has bin most commonly given to Inventors. **1676** Locke *Jrnl.* 23 Aug. in *Ess. Law Nature* (1954) 275 Making yourself an enemy to all by ill-treatment. **1677** —— tr. *Nicole's Ess.* (1828) 112 Ill treatment and persecutions would certainly fall to their lot. **1713** [see Ill *a.* 2 a]. **1811** A. Graydon *Mem.* 292 In revenge for some real or supposed ill-treatment. **1818** *Public Ledger* 8 Apr. 3/2 Alledged ill-treatment during a short confinement in that prison. **1864** E. B. Pusey *Daniel* i. 21 Who revenge on man their illtreatment at the hand of man. **1879** G. Meredith *Egoist* II. v. 94 He contemplated her with an air of stiff-backed ill-treatment. **1905** Chesterton *Heretics* 79 A permanent possibility of selfishness arises from the mere fact of having a self, and not from any accidents of education or ill-treatment.

illuk (i·luk). [Sinhala.] The name used in Sri Lanka (Ceylon) for a coarse grass, *Imperata cylindrica*; = *lalang.

1864 G. H. K. Thwaites *Enumeratio Plantarum Zeylaniæ* v. 369 *I[mperata] arundinacea*... Common in the hotter parts of the island. Nom. vulg. 'Illook'. The leaves make an excellent thatch. **1931** E. K. Cooke *Geogr. Ceylon* ii. x. 164 The grass of Talawa is usually long and coarse, very different from the average patana grass; it usually reaches about three or four feet in height. The best known species are mahna and illuk. **1950** [see *chena]. **1956** R. W. Szechowycz in S. Haden-Guest et al. *World Geogr. Forest Resources* xxii. 485 There is a total absence of undergrowth [in the savanna forest zone of Ceylon], and the herb layer consists of grasses, of which *Imperata cylindrica* (illuk) is the most prominent.

illume, *sb.* (Later *poet.* example.)

c **1882** E. Dickinson *Poems* (1955) III. 1069 Better an ignis fatuus Than no illume at all.

illuminance (iliū·minăns). *Optics.* [f. L. *illūmin-āntem* (see Illuminant *a.* and *sb.*) + -ance.] The amount of luminous flux per unit area; = Illumination 1 b.

1943 D. H. Jacobs *Fund. Optical Engin.* iv. 66 We have derived equations that give the illumination (or illuminance) only at points on the axis of the system. **1949** H. Margenau et al. *Physics Princ. & Applications* xliv. 621 Illuminance is expressed in lumens/ft^2 (foot candles) or lumens/m^2 (luxes). **1955** R. C. Brown *Textbk. Physics* IV. l. 902 The illumination (sometimes called 'intensity of illumination' and also illuminance) of a surface is defined as the luminous flux incident per unit area on the surface. **1961** F. W. Weymouth in Hirsch & Wick *Vision Aging Patient* iv. 41 Since the extent of dark adaptation is..curtailed with age, the performance at low levels of illuminance begins to decline even before the age of 40 years. **1970** *Nature* 24 Jan. 347/2 Each pattern..was projected..at an average screen illuminance of 3 millilamberts.

illuminate, *ppl. a.* and *sb.* **A.** *adj.* **2.** Delete †*Obs.* and add later example.

1909 *Westm. Gaz.* 19 May 4/2, I once knew a follower of the Rosy Cross, an illuminate member.

B. *sb.* (Later example.) Also *spec. pl.* = Illuminati b.

1906 *Edin. Rev.* July 49 The influence of the German 'illuminates' on the French lodges. **1946** G. G. Scholem *Major Trends Jewish Mysticism* (rev. ed.) iv. 121 The outspoken illuminates and ecstatics.

illuminate, *v.* Add: **1. c.** To direct a beam of any kind of radiation at (an object or region): used esp. of radio waves and microwaves in connection with radar and telecommunication.

1942 [implied in *illuminated *ppl. a.* 1 b]. **1947** Crowther & Whiddington *Science at War* i. 6 The power radiated proved ample to detect aircraft, flying at a height..sufficient to bring them within the space 'illuminated', at the range of 75 miles. **1948** Pollard & Sturtevant *Microwaves & Radar Electronics* iv. 126 The..antenna pattern from a 30-inch-diameter dish illuminated at 3·2 centimeters..is shown. **1957** R. Watson-Watt *Three Steps to Victory* 470 Of the secondary radiations, excited by 'illuminating' the craft by ground installations emitting light, heat, sound or radio-waves, the first two are excluded by atmospheric absorption. **1973** *Physics Bull.* Mar. 149/1 A cold cathode discharge source..provided a beam of electrons which could illuminate an object such as an aperture or a wire grid.

7. b. (For Dict. entry read:) *intr.* To take fire, to light up; of a town, etc.: to be decorated with lights as a sign of festivity or celebration. Also, to become excited (see also quot. 1926).

1706 Defoe *Review* 2 Mar. 108 The other Gentleman and his Man coming, and holding a real Candle up to Decide it, Affirm'd the Doctors Candle was Lighted; the Grave Gentleman went on, with an *Ay, I think it does begin to Illuminate.* **1801** [in Dict.]. **1843** *Punch* IV. 256 If Stockport and Paisley do not..illuminate when they shall hear the glad tidings, then is the spirit of manufacture dead to gratitude. **1871** 'Mark Twain' *Sk. New & Old* (1875) 176 For eight-and-forty hours no soul in all the barony but did dance and sing, carouse and illuminate, to celebrate the great event. **1926** Wood & Goddard *Dict. Amer. Slang* 24 *Illuminated*, lit, drunk. **1927** E. H. C. Moberly Bell *Life & Lett. C. F. Moberly Bell* 96 The people illuminate, and go mad with frenzy for Gordon, and curse the Mahdi. **1972** *Jrnl. Social Psychol.* LXXXVII. 90 Subjects were asked to estimate the probability that an alleged peer..would shock them when a light illuminated.

illuminated, *ppl. a.* Add: **1. b.** Made, or being, the target of (non-visible) radiation of some kind.

1942 J. C. Slater *Microwave Transmission* vi. 275 The illuminated region can be considerably greater than the distance between poles. **1950** J. D. Kraus *Antennas* xii. 345 An antenna with a uniformly illuminated circular aperture 10 wavelengths in diameter has a gain of 600 or nearly 28 db with respect to a ½-wavelength dipole antenna. **1966** Tolstoy & Clay *Ocean Acoustics* vi. 198 The dimensions of the illuminated area are much larger than the acoustic wavelength.

5. a. Also as *sb. rare.*

1923 E. Pound *Let.* 12 May (1971) 187 Price 25 dollars per copy, and 50 and 100 bones for Vellum and illuminateds.

illuminating, *vbl. sb.* (s.v. Illuminate *v.*). Add: Also *attrib.*, as **illuminating engineering,** the branch of engineering and applied science concerned with the design, installation, and modification of artificial lighting; so **illuminating engineer.**

1906 *(title)* Transactions of the Illuminating Engineering Society. **1907** *Installation News* Nov. 3 That latest addition to the ever-growing family of specialists—the Illuminating Engineer—is providing the electrical industry and press with a good deal to think about. **1930** *Engineering* 31 Jan. 143/2 The development of the science of illuminating engineering has been continuous during the past few decades.

illuminatingly, *adv.* (Later examples.)

1965 *Language* XLI. 216 The adjective structures illuminatingly discussed by Lees. **1972** *Nature* 28 Jan. 204/2 Another examination scheme has also proved illuminatingly effective.

illumination. Add: **1.** (Further examples, corresponding to *illuminate *v.* 1 c.)

1942 J. C. Slater *Microwave Transmission* vi. 275 Vertically the illumination falls off gradually in intensity as the poles are approached. **1948** Pollard & Sturtevant *Microwaves & Radar Electronics* iv. 127 A horn feed illumination is the most widely favored. **1966** Tolstoy & Clay *Ocean Acoustics* vi. 199 It is convenient to measure the scattered signal relative to the signal reflected by a mirror-like surface when the illumination factor, source position, receiver position, etc., are the same.

b. For 'reflected from' read 'incident on'. (Further examples.)

1943, 1955 [see *illuminance].

illu·minatively, *adv. rare.* [f. Illuminative *a.* + -ly[2].] In an illuminative way.

1925 T. Dreiser *Amer. Trag.* (1926) II. iii. xxviii. 349 These hard, white-painted walls brightly lighted..by incandescent lamps in the hall without at night—yet all so different from Bridgeburg,—so much more bright or harsh illuminatively.

‖ **Illuminé** (ilümine). Also with lower-case initial. [Fr.: see ILLUMINEE.] One of the Illuminati.

1794 A. PAGET *Let.* in *Paget Papers* (1896) I. 20 It would be highly interesting to Your Lordship to get some information relative to the people called *Illuminés.* **1799** [see ILLUMINEE]. **1816** SCOTT *Antiq.* I. xiii. 289 A simple youth whispered me that he was an *Illuminé,* and carried on an intercourse with the invisible world. **1927** R. FRY *Let.* 19 Aug. (1972) II. 605 Simon Bussy..said..that I was an *illuminé* who imagined such things and then got excited about them.

illuminized (ili̇ū·minəizd), *ppl. a. rare.* [f. ILLUMINIZE *v.* + -ED¹.] Initiated (see ILLUMINIZE *v.* 2).

1920 *19th Cent.* July 104 A great Masonic meeting which was held in 1786 at Frankfurt—whither the headquarters of illuminised Freemasonry were removed after the famous Congress.

illuminometer (ili̇ūminǫ·mĭtəɹ). [f. ILLUMIN(ATION + -O + -METER.] A photometer, *esp.* one for measuring the illumination of surfaces (rather than the intensity of light sources).

1895 HOUSTON & KENNELLY in *Operator & Electr. World* 9 Mar. 309/2 The question at issue is..the degree of illumination actually produced, and this question cannot be decided by the photometer, but requires the use of an illumination measurer or illuminometer. *Ibid.* 310/2 We call our instrument an illuminometer and have filed applications for a patent on the same. **1908** *Illuminating Engineer* (London) I. 714/2 It was proposed to use it [*sc.* Houston and Kennelly's photometer] for candlepower photometry as well as for the measurement of illumination. The unfortunate name 'illuminometer' was given to the instrument, and..this mongrel word is sometimes used at the present day. **1953** KIRK & OTHMER *Encycl. Chem. Technol.* XI. 326 The luminous intensity of the flame..can be measured by an illuminometer consisting of a barrier-layer photocell connected to a micro-ammeter. **1971** *Jrnl. Gen. Psychol.* LXXXIV. 125 Exposure times of 40, 150, and 3500 msec and luminances of three and 30 fc, as read with a Macbeth Illuminometer, were employed.

illupi. Add: So *illipe butter,* any of various vegetable fats.

1904 J. LEWKOWITSCH *Oils, Fats, & Waxes* (ed. 3) II. xiv. 702 The commercial fat is a mixture of Mowrah seed oil with Mahua butter or illipe butter, the fat from *Bassia latifolia.* **1911** *Encycl. Brit.* XX. 47 Mahua butter, Illipé butter. **1951** A. E. BAILEY *Industr. Oil & Fat Products* (ed. 2) vi. 141 Mowrah fat, or illipé butter, which is obtained from the Indian plant *Bassia longifolia,* resembles shea butter in being relatively unsaturated, and correspondingly soft.

illusion. Add: **4. b.** *the argument from illusion* (Philos.): the argument that the objects of sense-experience, usually called ideas, appearances, or sense-data, cannot be objects in a physical world independent of the perceiver, since they vary according to his condition and environment.

1932 H. H. PRICE *Perception* ii. 27 It is commonly held that the *Argument from Illusion* (as it is called) is sufficient to refute Naïve Realism. **1936** A. J. AYER *Lang., Truth & Logic* viii. 228 The so-called argument from illusion. **1940** —— *Found. Empirical Knowl.* i. 3 The answer is provided by what is known as the argument from illusion. **1959** J. L. AUSTIN *Sense & Sensibilia* (1962) iii. 20 The primary purpose of the argument from illusion is to induce people to accept 'sense-data'. **1971** A. FLEW *Introd. Western Philos.* 353 We can characterize the Argument from Illusion as the attempt to show that..what we actually see is never things but only the appearances of things.

5. (Earlier and later examples.)

1857 *Lawrence* (Kansas) *Republican* 28 May 3 Lace, Gimp, Straw, Silk, Blend, Hair and Illusion Bonnets. **1865** F. B. PALLISER *Hist. Lace* xxxv. 423 M. Doguin, who afterwards used the fine silks, and invented that popular material first called 'zephyr', since 'illusion'. **1869** L. M. ALCOTT *Little Women* II. xiv. 207 She put on Flo's old white silk ball dress, and covered it with a cloud of fresh illusion. **1873** *Young Englishwoman* Jan. 50/1 White muslin, trimmed with white lace, illusion veil. **1902** *Daily Chron.* 13 Dec. 8/4 It was trimmed with ruches of black tulle illusion. **1967** *Boston Sunday Herald* 30 Apr. v. 2/3 The headpiece was a lace mantilla with an illusion veil.

6. *attrib.* and *Comb.,* as *illusion effect; illusion-disturbing, -proof* adjs.

1909 W. M. URBAN *Valuation* ix. 275 The elimination of illusion-disturbing moments is a conscious process. **1971** *Jrnl. Gen. Psychol.* LXXXV. 77 Differences in the magnitude of the illusion-effect were introduced. **1924** G. B. SHAW *Saint Joan* p. xvi, Napoleon or any other illusionproof genius.

Hence **illu·sionless** *a.,* not characterized by illusions.

1897 G. B. SHAW in *Academy* 16 Jan. 67/2 Illusionless conversation..when the old people in Ibsen..tell each other the frozen truth. **1964** S. BELLOW *Herzog* 229 His face was illusionless, without need of hypocrisy.

illusional (ili̇ū·ʒənăl), *a.* [f. ILLUSION + -AL.] Pertaining to, characterized by, or subject to illusions.

1900 DORLAND *Med. Dict.* 317/1. **1923** *Daily Mail* 1 Mar. 4 On reception into prison he was suspicious, illusional, and confused. **1942** *Art Digest* 15 Jan. 30 She also goes in for illusional effects, such as an interwoven lost-and-found sensation in *Malaga Cathedral* and the vaporous beach scene *Le Bar.*

illusioned (ili̇ū·ʒənd), *ppl. a.* [f. as prec. + -ED².] Full of illusions.

1920 *Glasgow Herald* 6 July 6 A fervent but illusioned admirer. **1921** GALSWORTHY *To Let* III. vi. 267 Even his love felt tainted, less illusioned, more of the earth. **1971** *Guardian* 11 Oct. 10 We remain totally illusioned..about the general good intentions of those who practise the art of government.

illusionism. Add: **2.** The use of illusionary effects in art or sculpture.

1951 M. L. WOLF *Dict. Arts* 345/2 *Illusionism,* the effort in painting or sculpture to create as nearly as possible an illusion of visual reality. **1960** [see *FANTASIST]. **1961** M. LEVY *Studio Dict. Art Terms* 62 *Illusionism,* the practice of Trompe L'Oeil painting. **1962** *Times* 6 Apr. 17/3 It [*sc.* the attitude and style of pop-art] is a gaudy glamorization of its subject which deliberately crashes its visual gears from abstract pattern right through to *trompe-l'oeil* illusionism.

illusionist. Add: **2.** (Earlier example.)

1850 *Punch* XIX. 215/2 The novel trick of shifting the lectern, will be introduced by that celebrated illusionist, the Rev. Mr. Cozens.

Hence **illusioni·stic** *a.,* pertaining to illusionism or the illusionists.

1911 *Encycl. Brit.* XXIII. 482/1 The lighting is carefully calculated with a view to illusionistic effect under the local conditions. **1938** *Mod. Lang. Rev.* Oct. 549 The tendency..to employ an illusionistic realism for the purpose of sensationalism..is what lies behind Wölfflin's conception of 'baroque'. **1944** *Burlington Mag.* Aug. 199/1 Compared with this the Byzantine solution may still be called illusionistic. **1958** *Times* 24 Sept. 3/1 They [*sc.* Dali's pictures] are irritatingly artificial concoctions with passages..quite amazingly inept for a specialist in illusionistic devices. **1968** *Times* 21 Dec. 19/1 There was an upsurge of decorative architecture in Bavaria, Franconia and Swabia. It was illusionistic and what the writer calls 'a-tactonic'.

illustrate, *v.* **3.** Delete † *Obs.* and add examples.

1843 DICKENS *Mart. Chuz.* (1844) ii. 10 Charity..did so well set off and illustrate her sister! **1917** *Mod. Lang. Rev.* XII. 205, I do not desire to illustrate my version of 'the Fause Knight', but merely to claim that it throws new light on the subject matter of the original ballad.

4. (Later examples.) Still *rare.*

1858 J. H. NEWMAN *Mission of Benedictine Order* in *Sel. Ess.* (1902) 191 The famous Congregation of Cluni, illustrated by St. Majolus, St. Odilo, Peter the Venerable. **1931** [see *DITHER *sb.* b]. **1952** G. SARTON *Hist. Sci.* I. xi. 277 We now come to the greatest mathematician of the century, the first man to illustrate the name of Hippocrates.

6. Also *absol.*

1863 O. M. MITCHELL *Astron. Bible* 168 The subject is difficult. Permit me to illustrate.

illustrating, *ppl. a.* (Later example.)

1840 M. EDGEWORTH *Let.* 30 Dec. (1971) 574 The *illustrating* speech of the Irishman to the waiter of 'I'd wish to have the ham and the butter separate'.

illustrational, *a.* Delete *rare* and add examples. Also as *sb.*

1926 R. FRY *Transformations* 147 Rodin's concern is with the expression of character and situation, it is essentially dramatic and illustrational. **1955** P. HERON *Changing Forms of Art* III. xi. 168, I believe Sutherland's phantasy is essentially illustrational, poetic, non-plastic. **1959** *Listener* 6 Aug. 206/1 Everything in fiction as in life had to satisfy his [H. James's] 'appetite for the illustrational'.

illustrious, *a.* Add: **3. c.** *most illustrious*: the special epithet of the Order of St. Patrick.

[**1783** *London Gaz.* 4–8 Feb. 1/1 The King has been pleased to order Letters Patent to be passed under the Great Seal of the Kingdom of Ireland, for creating a Society, or Brotherhood, to be called Knights of the Illustrious Order of St. Patrick.] **1858** B. BURKE *Bk. Orders Knighth.* 102 (*heading*) The Most Illustrious Order of Saint Patrick. **1971** *Whitaker's Almanack* 259 The Most Illustrious Order of Saint Patrick... *Ribbon,* Sky Blue. *Motto,* Quis separabit?.. (No conferments since 1934).

illustriousness. Add: **2.** [tr. G. *durchlaucht.*] With possessive adjective as a title of dignity or honour given to German princes.

1929 'S. N. D.' *Sir W. Howard Visct. Stafford* iv. 48 His Electoral Illustriousness, the Prince Palatine of the Rhine.

illuvial (ili̇ū·viăl), *a. Soil Sci.* [f. IL-¹ + *-luvial,* as in ALLUVIAL, ELUVIAL *adjs.*] = *ILLUVIATED *ppl. a.*; also, resulting from illuviation.

1924 *Geol. Mag.* LXI. 451 Three main horizons are generally recognized,..the A or eluvial horizon, the B or illuvial horizon, and the C horizon, which consists of the parent material. **1932** G. W. ROBINSON *Soils* iv. 92 We may also distinguish a type of clay which has been enriched by illuvial accumulation. **1952, 1963** [see *ELUVIAL *a.* 2].

illuviation (ili̇ūviē̆i·ʃən). *Soil Sci.* [f. prec. + -ATION.] The deposition of salts or colloids in a soil horizon from percolating water which has removed them from another, generally superior, horizon, So **illu·viated** *ppl. a.,* having received material by illuviation.

1928 *Bull. Amer. Soil Survey Assoc.* IX. 31 Illuviation. *Ibid.* 37 The illuviated horizons of the solum. **1932** *Forestry* VI. 28 The different horizons are designated by capital letters...'B' the horizon of illuviation or deposition. **1949** W. W. WEIR *Soil Sci.* (ed. 2) vi. 116 Horizons, commonly topsoil layers, that have lost materials through eluviation are described as eluvial or eluviated; and horizons, commonly subsoil layers, that have received the materials, illuvial or illuviated. **1955** F. E. BEAR *Chem. of Soil* i. 37 In pedology, the term eluviation has been applied to the loss of material from the surface horizon, and the term illuviation, to the gain of material by the subsoil horizon.

ill-wish, *v.* Add: Also *absol.* Hence **ill-wish** *sb.,* the evil or misfortune wished.

1853 T. Q. COUCH in J. Brand *Observations Pop. Antiq.* (1870) III. 101 The witch's malice, or, as it is termed, 'the ill-wish'. **1899** S. BARING-GOULD *Bk. of West* II. 16 A bard, and after him a saint, might not ill-wish unless he had been refused a just request. *Ibid.,* If he ill-wished unjustly, then it was held that the ill-wish returned on the head of him who had launched it.

illy, *adv.* For '*dial.*' read 'chiefly *U.S.*', and add later examples.

1903 *Atlantic Monthly* July 116 Which is far better than if it had rushed into illy considered legislation. **1904** CLAIBORNE *Old Virginia* 268 (Th.), I dropped one of my gauntlets,..which I could illy afford to lose. **1925** T. DREISER *Amer. Trag.* (1926) II. xlvi. 57 By contrast with Sondra, how illy-dressed in the blue traveling suit..she had equipped herself for this occasion. **1927** C. A. & M. R. BEARD *Rise Amer. Civilization* II. 213 To meet a crisis of this kind labor was illy prepared. **1965** *Sat. Rev.* (U.S.) 5 June 28/1 *The Blue Hen's Chick* is no graceful memoir of a life well or illy spent.

Illyrian (ili·riăn), *a.* and *sb.* [f. L. *Illyrius,* a. Gr. Ἰλλυριός.]

A. *adj.* **1.** Of or pertaining to the Illyrians or to ancient Illyria (or Illyricum), a country lying east of the Adriatic and at an early period extending northwards to the Danube.

1553 N. GRIMALDE tr. *Cicero's Bookes of Dueties* (1558) II. f. 88ᵛ Bargulus, the Illirian robber, of whom mention is made in Theopompus. **1593** SHAKES. *2 Hen. VI,* IV. i. 108 Bargulus the strong Illyrian Pyrate. **1678** J. DAVIES tr. Appian (*title*) The History of Appian, of Alexandria. In Two Parts. The First consisting of the Punick, Syrian, Parthian, Mithridatick, Illyrian, Spanish, and Hannibalick, Wars. **1776** GIBBON *Decl. & F.* I. i. 27 The provinces of the Danube soon acquired the general appellation of Illyricum, or the Illyrian frontier. **1797** *Encycl. Brit.* II. 714/2 The Heneti, an Illyrian people. **1880** *Ibid.* XII. 709/1 The Danube..was the limit of the Illyrian tribes towards the north. **1935** HUXLEY & HADDON *We Europeans* vi. 179 The Dinaric (Illyrian) type [of people] is found on both sides of the northern Adriatic, the Illyrian mountain system with extensions to the north and south. **1953** [see *BANDKERAMIK].

b. Of or belonging to Illyria, a former division of Austria-Hungary, since 30 October 1918 forming part of Yugoslavia.

Illyrian Provinces, a division, made by Napoleon Bonaparte in 1809, of various Austrian territories lying north and east of the Adriatic, and abolished in 1814–15, after which it was made a nominal kingdom of the Austrian Empire.

1820 C. KELLY *Hist. French Revolution* I. xiii. 614 The treaty of Vienna has given to France a great extent of territory on the Adriatic sea: this territory is formed into the Illyrian republic. **1838** *Penny Cycl.* XII. 445/2 Napoleon,..in 1809, gave to several tracts of territory ceded by Austria..the name of the Illyrian Provinces. **1845** *Encycl. Metrop.* XIII. 1084/2 Meanwhile the war in the Illyrian provinces..received a fresh complication from the secession of Bavaria from the French alliance. *Ibid.* XX. 559/1 The Emperor of Austria rules the Illyrian Kingdom with uncontrolled authority. **1921** *19th Cent.* May 856 The Illyrian provinces..provided a strong bulwark against Austria. **1965** *New Cambr. Mod. Hist.* IX. xi. 331 The Illyrian provinces taken from Austria in 1809 remained directly under the control of Napoleon through a governor-general.

c. In literary use, pertaining to the regions lying along the east coast of the Adriatic.

This corresponds to the literary use of *Illyria,* which was retained even when the name had no political significance.

1852 M. ARNOLD *Empedocles on Etna* I. ii. 41 The Adriatic breaks in a warm bay Among the green Illyrian hills... There those two live, far in the Illyrian brakes. **1853** TENNYSON *To E. L.* in *Poems* 352 Illyrian woodlands, echoing falls Of water. **1950** J. C. FENNESSY *Way to Sea* xvii. 131 Lapis lazuli blue as the Illyrian sea.

d. Used in the names of breeds of dog that originated in this part of Yugoslavia, as *Illyrian hound, Illyrian sheepdog.*

1935 *Discovery* Oct. 310/2 The fierce dogs of the Yugoslav South..are now officially called Illyrian Sheepdogs **1948** A. LOKAR in B. Vesey-Fitzgerald *Bk. Dog* II. 519 The Illyrian Sheepdog is..the best-known Yugoslav sheep-herding dog and is in big demand in the hills in summer, and in the valleys when the sheep and goats come down for winter feeding. **1964** E. F. DAGLISH tr. *Schneider-Leyer's Dogs of World* 198 The Illyrian Hound is not directly descended from the oft-mentioned Celtic Hound. **1971** F. HAMILTON *World Encycl. Dogs* 376 Illyrian Hound. This medium-sized hound is named for

Illyria, that ill-defined region of present-day Yugoslavia which borders the Adriatic.

2. Pertaining to the group of ancient dialects represented by the modern Albanian; also, to a division of the eastern branch of the Slavonic languages.

1607 TOPSELL *Four-f. Beasts* 10 Cynocephales, are a kinde of Apes... In the French, Germain, and Illyrian tongues, they are called of some Babian. **1824** J. JOHNSON *Typographia* II. 444 The names to the above letters are in the Illyrian and Servian tongues. **1833** *Penny Cycl.* I. 256/2 The hypothesis of the Albanians being descended from the Illyrians, cannot receive confirmation from comparing it with the old Illyrian tongue. **1928** C. DAWSON *Age of Gods* xvi. 375 Our knowledge of the Illyrian languages is so slight.

B. *sb.* **1.** One of an Indo-European people who inhabited ancient Illyria, and who were conquered by the Romans in the third and second centuries B.C.

1584 B. RICH tr. *Herodotus' Famous Hystory* f. 62ᵛ, The people Eneti comming of the Illyrians. **1788** LEMPRIÈRE *Classical Dict.* s.v. *Pausanias*, He accompanied the prince in an expedition against the Illyrians. **1880** *Encycl. Brit.* XII. 709/1 It would not be easy to draw any line of demarcation at this early time between the Illyrians and their neighbours on the west, south, and east. **1928** C. DAWSON *Age of Gods* xiv. 325 The Bronze Age in Eastern Europe. The Thracians and the Illyrians. **1935** HUXLEY & HADDON *We Europeans* vii. 213 The Albanians are in part the descendants of the old Illyrians and are noteworthy for the preservation of many archaic customs and of a primitive form of Aryan language. **1949** *Oxf. Classical Dict.* 966/1 Zeus..is found as 'Father', which attribute is very common in Greek too, among the Romans, Indians, and Illyrians.

2. An inhabitant of the former Austrian kingdom of Illyria.

1836 N. WISEMAN *Lect. Doctr. Cath. Ch.* I. vii. 256 M. Boraga, an Illyrian, obtained permission of the Bishop to open a new mission among the Indians on the Grand River.

3. A member of the Slavonic race now living in the territory of ancient Illyria; also applied loosely to any people inhabiting this region, without reference to the various political meanings of the name.

1845 *Encycl. Metrop.* XIII. 533/2 Fortunately at this crisis he [*sc.* Leopold II] obtained the support of the Illyrians.

4. The language of Illyria, or the group of ancient dialects represented by the modern Albanian; also, a division of the eastern branch of the Slavonic languages, spoken in the same or adjacent districts.

1888 J. WRIGHT tr. *Brugmann's Elem. Compar. Gram. Indo-Gmc. Lang.* I. 12 Russian..Bulgarian and Illyrian. **1904** [see *ETEOCRETAN *a.* and *sb.*]. **1912** W. W. SKEAT *Sci. Etym.* 127 There is, however, sufficient evidence to show that the Old Illyrian was an independent descendant from the original Indo-germanic stock. **1958** P. KEMP *No Colours or Crest* v. 76 Indeed Albanian, which is supposed to be derived from ancient Illyrian, must be one of the most difficult of European languages to learn.

So **Illy·ric** *a.* [ad. L. *Illyricus*, Gr. *'Ιλλυρικός*], **Illy·rican** *sb.* = *ILLYRIAN *sb.* 4. Hence **I·llyrism,** (*a*) advocacy of Slovene, Croatian, and Serb nationalism; (*b*) see quot. 1957; so **I·llyrist** *a.* and *sb.*

1753 R. CLAYTON *Jrnl. from Cairo to Sinai* 34 We had in our company persons who were acquainted with Arabic, Greek,..Illyrican, German [etc.]. **1838** *Penny Cycl.* XII. 447/2 Antient Illyria..was inhabited by a people called by the general name of the Illyric nations. **1854** E. O. S. *Hungary & its Revolutions* 236 Louis Gay, a young man of literary attainments,..took the lead in a movement which obtained the name of Illyrism. **1877** *Encycl. Brit.* VI. 783/2 The so-called Morlacks, or Dalmatians proper, who..speak a Slavonic dialect usually distinguished as the Illyric. **1910** *Ibid.* VII. 475/2 A nationalist or 'Illyrist' party was formed..to combat Hungarian influences. *Ibid.*, Conflicts between Illyrists and Magyarists. *Ibid.*, The Hungarians had obtained a royal manifesto hostile to Illyrism. **1957** *Ibid.* XX. 789/2 Between the Slovenes and the Croats there are transition dialects, and about 1840 there was an attempt (Illyrism) to establish a common literary language.

ilmenorutile (iːlmĕnorū·təil, -il). *Min.* [ad. G. *ilmenorutil* (N. von Kokscharow *Materialen zur Mineralogie Russlands* (1854–7) II. 352): see ILMENITE and RUTILE.] A black variety of rutile containing iron, niobium, and tantalum.

1861 H. W. BRISTOW *Gloss. Mineral.* 189/2 *Ilmenorutile*, Von Kokscharow. A variety of Rutile occurring in the form of the fundamental pyramid, without any prismatic planes. **1929** *Encycl. Brit.* XIX. 774/1 The colour [of rutile] is usually reddish-brown, though..black in the ferruginous varieties ('nigrine' and 'ilmenorutile'). **1962** W. A. DEER et al. *Rock-Forming Min.* V. 35 Apart from the ferroan and ferrian varieties of rutile, there is also the niobian variety, or ilmenorutile, with up to 60 per cent. of $Fe(Nb,Ta)_2O_6$ with Nb > Ta. **1968** *Daily Tel.* 12 Nov. 14/4 The ilmenite mines are in the Jeseniky mountain range near the Polish border, and in Pisek, south of Pilsen, where the mines contain ilmeno-rutile, a more complex mineral suitable for the production of thorium as a trigger for H-bombs, as well as titanium.

Ilocano (*i*lokā·no). [Philippine Sp., f. *Ilocos*, the name of two provinces, lit. 'river men', f. Tagogal *ilog* river.] **a.** A member of a people inhabiting the north-western part of Luzon in the Republic of the Philippines. **b.** The language of this people. Also *attrib.* So **Ilo·can** *a.* and *sb.*; **Ilo·ko, Ylo·co.**

1840 *Penny Cycl.* XVIII. 88/2 The other tribes that are numerous, the Pampanga, Zambales, Pangasinan, Ylocos, and Cagayan, inhabit the other plains and lower country. **1885** *Encycl. Brit.* XVIII. 753/1 Other tribes of the Philippines—the Ilocanes, Pampangos, Pangasinanes,..Vicols, &c. **1898** D. C. WORCESTER *Philippine Islands* 438 Of these [tribes] the Tagalogs and Ilocanos are the most important. **1900** F. H. SAWYER *Inhabitants Philippines* 250 Many converted Tinguianes and Igorrotes who speak the Ilocan dialect. **1901** *Rep. Philippine Comm.* III. 400 The first booklets in Ilocano are in Tagalog characters. **1905** F. W. ATKINSON *Philippine Isl.* 238 The Ilocanos, who inhabit the northern province of Ilocos Norte, Ilocos Sur, and Unión, in Luzón. **1914** D. C. WORCESTER *Philippines Past & Present* I. 21 The Ilocanos are one of the eight civilized peoples who collectively make up the Filipinos. **1925** K. MAYO *Isles of Fear* 50 Families..of the energetic Ilocano tribe. **1958** G. MIKES *East is East* 88 The twenty million inhabitants of the islands [*sc.* Philippines] have about seventy native tongues... Sugbuanon, Iloko, Bikol and Samarnon are not among the major forces of civilisation, nor is even Tagalog, the most widespread and most cultivated of the native tongues. **1962** H. C. CONKLIN in Householder & Saporta *Probl. Lexicogr.* 135 In passing, it may be noted that pronoun systems in Tagalog, Ilocano..and some other Philippine languages exhibit very similar..semantic relationships. **1964** E. A. NIDA *Toward Sci. Transl.* ix. 195 On the other hand some languages, e.g. Quechua, Aymara, Ilocano and Eskimo, include much more in the verb than is included in a Greek verb.

ilsemannite (i·lsəmănəit). *Min.* [ad. G. *ilsemannit* (H. Höfer 1871, in *Neues Jahrb. f. Mineral., Geol. u. Palaeont.* 567), f. the name of J. C. *Ilsemann* (1727–1822), German chemist: see -ITE¹.] A black or dark blue secondary molybdenum mineral, perhaps a hydrated oxide of molybdenum, $Mo_3O_8.nH_2O$, which occurs as earthy masses or crusts and as a blue stain and dissolves in water to give a blue solution.

1871 *Jrnl. Chem. Soc.* XXIV. 1173 Ilsemannite...The author gives this name to native molybdic molybdate, $MoO_2.4MoO_3$, occurring at Bleiberg in Carinthia, as a bluish-black to black, mostly earthy or cryptocrystalline deposit, between groups of crystals of barium sulphate. **1923** *Bull. U.S. Geol. Survey* No. 750. 16 Ilsemannite, like wulfenite, is probably formed from some unknown mineral, perhaps a sulphide. **1951** *Amer. Mineralogist* XXXVI. 611 In general, most mineralogists seem to have applied the name 'ilsemannite' to any molybdenum compound or mixture which is water soluble and turns the solution a typical molybdenum-blue color. **1959** *Econ. Geol.* LIV. 257 Ilsemannite is forming rapidly on the walls of the older mine workings.

image, *sb.* Add: **1. d.** (*c*) In pregnant use, a person attracting amused or contemptuous glances, a 'sight'. *colloq.*

1851 H. MAYHEW *London Labour* I. 193/1 One boy, whose young woman made faces at it, got quite vexed and said, 'Wot a image you're a-making on yourself!' **1880** *Punch* 25 Dec. 298/2 Uncle Bowpot, the florist, lives here. Sech a rummy old image he is. **1898** CONRAD *Tales of Unrest* 138 How goes it, you old image? **1937** PARTRIDGE *Dict. Slang* 420/2 *You little image*, a term of affectionate reproach.

4. a. living image, a person with a striking resemblance to another; similarly **spit and image**: see SPIT *sb.*² 3 b and **spitting image.*

1829 G. GRIFFIN *Collegians* (ed. 2) I. ix. 187 Sure I'd know that face all over the world,—your own liven' image, ma'am. **1884** in *N. & Q.* (1963) Mar. 106/1 (*title*) Her living image. **1889** KIPLING *Life's Handicap* (1891) 28 At the end..stood the livin' spit an' image o' mysilf worked on the linin'. **1895** Spit and image [see SPIT *sb.*² 3 b]. **1931** R. CAMPBELL *Georgiad* i. 15 Here's the first number—see, upon the cover, The living image of a country lover. **1961** L. WOOLF *Growing* iv. 232 When I saw the priest—I have seen his spit and image in many cathedrals,..—I had no doubt that he was God's financial adviser.

5. Also, with qualifying adj.: a mental representation due to any of the senses (not only sight) and to organic sensations.

1890 W. JAMES *Princ. Psychol.* I. ix. 266 A deaf and dumb man can weave his tactile and visual images into a system of thought quite as effective and rational as that of a word-user. *Ibid.* xiv. 592 We then saw no need of optical and auditory images to interpret optical and auditory sensations by. **1897** tr. *Ribot's Psychol. of Emotions* xi. 145 In the two following cases the 'olfactory image' only exists in a single instance. **1899** *Amer. Jrnl. Psychol.* Oct. 25 Haptical images, beside being vague and ill defined, offer peculiar difficulties. **1904** E. B. TITCHENER in *Jrnl. Philos., Psychol. & Sci. Methods* 21 Jan. 38, I have no doubt, in my own case, of the existence of visual and auditory images...I have no doubt, from the reports of others, of the existence of free kinaesthetic images, verbal or other. **1923** H. G. BAYNES tr. *Jung's Psychol. Types* xi. 554 When I speak of image in this book, I do not mean the psychic reflection of the external object, but a concept essentially derived from a poetic figure of speech; namely, the *phantasy-image*, a presentation which is only indirectly related to the perception of the external object...Although, as a rule, no reality-value belongs to the image, its significance for the psychic life is often thereby enhanced, *i.e.* a greater *psychological* value clings to it.

b. A concept or impression, created in the minds of the public, of a particular person, institution, product, etc.; *spec.* a favourable impression; esp. in phr. *public image.* Cf. **brand-image.* Also *attrib.* and *Comb.*, as *image-builder, -building.* Cf. *IMAGE-MAKER.

Quots. 1908 are isolated uses. This sense developed from advertising parlance in the late 1950s.

1908 CHESTERTON *All Things Considered* 179 When courtiers sang the praises of a King they attributed to him things that were entirely improbable...Between the King and his public image there was really no relation. **1908** G. WALLAS *Human Nature in Politics* ii. 84 The origin of any particular party may be due to a deliberate intellectual process... But when a party has once come into existence its fortunes depend upon facts of human nature of which deliberate thought is only one. It is primarily a name, which, like other names, calls up when it is heard or seen an 'image' that shades imperceptibly into the voluntary realisation of its meaning...Emotional reactions can be set up by the name and its automatic mental associations. **1958** J. K. GALBRAITH *Affluent Soc.* xiii. 152 The first task of the public relations man, on taking over a business client, is to 're-engineer' his image to include something besides the production of goods. **1959** I. ROSS *Image Merchants* (1960) i. 17 The whole breed may be called the Image Merchants—the men who endlessly 'create', 'delineate', 'adumbrate' and 'project' the most flattering 'images' of their clients. 'Image' is perhaps the favorite noun in public relations..whether the image be that of a corporation, an industry, a product. **1960** *Punch* 16 Mar. 379/2 What..is the *image* of chemical warfare which you are projecting to the public at the moment? **1961** *Listener* 2 Nov. 732/2 He [*sc.* John Reith] created what in modern jargon would be called a public image of the B.B.C. Programmes moved with smooth efficiency..behind a screen of anonymity. **1962** *Ibid.* 27 Sept. 460/2 Mr Gaitskell has improved his image by his determination at Scarborough and after. **1964** *Economist* 3 Oct. 49/1 Mr Goldwater's professional image-builders. **1965** *New Society* 22 Apr. 7/1 An image is a surface presentation intended to elicit favourable responses, whether..justified by the actual reality or not; a reputation was related to the actual and enduring characteristics. **1966** G. N. LEECH *Eng. in Advertising* xx. 182 The relation between metaphor and image-building can be seen in extracts from a campaign for Kellogg's Corn Flakes. **1966** 'C. E. MAINE' *B.E.A.S.T.* v. 61 'Are you warning me off or telling me to join the queue?' 'Neither, I'm just image building.' **1967** M. ARGYLE *Psychol. Interpersonal Behaviour* vii. 125 Butlers, Lord Mayors, and film stars, as well as teachers, psychotherapists, and salesmen, all need to project a certain image of professional competence. **1967** *Economist* 28 Jan. 347/2 In these soft, image-conscious days (in Britain anyway) not many of the big ones would care to abuse this position. **1967** *Daily Tel.* 21 Feb. 16/4 This master-stroke of image-building, the climax of a long campaign, can mean one of two things. **1969** *New Yorker* 27 Sept. 86/3 About the only piece of image advertising I did at Bates was for the Chase Manhattan Bank. **1971** *Physics Bull.* Jan. 12/3 The ivory tower image dies hard even though few academic physicists can succeed these days in research without establishing wide contacts outside their own departments. **1973** *Listener* 15 Nov. 662/3 [*Princess*] *Anne*:..The trouble with horses—this is why one has such a terrible image, horsey image—is that if you have anything to do with them they do take up an awful lot of time.

7*. *Math.* The element or set into which a given element or set is mapped by a particular function or transformation; const. *of* the element *by* or *under* the function. *Inverse image*, the set of all elements that are mapped into a given element or set by the function or transformation.

1889 *Cent. Dict.*, s.v. *Image.* When imaginary quantities are represented by points on a plane, a point representing any given function of a quantity represented by another point, the former point is said to be the image of the latter. **1905** J. PIERPONT *Lect. Theory Functions Real Variables* I. iv. 146 Let $u_1 = f_1(x_1 \ldots x_n) \ldots u_m = f_m(x_1 \ldots x_n)$ be defined over a domain X... When x ranges over X, u..runs over the domain U. It is convenient for brevity to call U the image of X. **1959** E. M. PATTERSON *Topology* (ed. 2) ii. 19 Any correspondence which associates with each element of a set A a unique element of a set B is called a function or transformation from A to B, and is denoted by $f: A \to B$... If $a \in A$, the element of B corresponding to a is called the image of a by or under f, and is denoted by $f(a)$. If $C \subset A$, the elements of B related to elements of C by f form a set $f(C)$ called the image of C by f. If $b \in f(A)$, the set of all elements $a \in A$ such that $b = f(a)$ is called the inverse image of b by f. **1965** J. J. ROTMAN *Theory of Groups* ii. 17 Let $f: G \to H$ be a homomorphism. Prove that the image of $f = \{h \in H: h = f(x)$ for some $x \in G\}$ is a sub-group of H. **1972** E. HILLE *Methods Classical & Functional Analysis* ii. 56 A mapping T from $\mathfrak{X}$ into $\mathfrak{Y}$ is a collection of ordered pairs (x, y), $x \in \mathfrak{X}$, $y \in \mathfrak{Y}$, such that every x of $\mathfrak{X}$ belongs to one and only one pair (x, y). Here $y = T(x)$ is called the image of x induced by T... Note that y may be the image of several points x and it is not excluded that all of $\mathfrak{X}$ may be mapped on a single point y.

7.** *Radio.* An undesired signal whose frequency is as much above that of the local oscillator of a superheterodyne receiver as the signal sought is below it, so that if allowed to reach the frequency converter it too will give rise to the intermediate frequency (and consequently be heard as interference). Freq. *attrib.*, as *image frequency, interference.*

1932 F. E. TERMAN *Radio Engin.* xiii. 467 One of the

chief functions of the tuned radio-frequency input amplifier is to prevent simultaneous reception of two stations in this way. By tuning this amplifier to the desired signal, the undesired or 'image' frequency is discriminated against. **1940** *Amat. Radio Handbk.* (ed. 2) 24/2 Interference is still likely to result from an incoming signal of such a frequency as to produce the correct intermediate frequency. This is known as 'image' or 'second channel interference'. **1950** K. HENNEY *Radio Engin. Handbk.* (ed. 4) xvii. 802 Since the function of the converter is to produce the difference between applied frequencies, it cannot distinguish between the signal and the image and produces i-f output from each. **1962** *B.B.C. Handbk.* 130 The selectivity of the receiver is improved and this reduces 'second channel', alternatively called 'image', interference. This is generally characterized by an irritating whistle of constantly changing pitch, sometimes accompanied by unwanted morse signals and programme modulation. Much of the interference experienced in the short-wave broadcast bands is due to such image effects. **1967** R. L. SHRADER *Electronic Communication* (ed. 2) xviii. 392/1 A second RF amplifier will reject the image very well. However, at frequencies in the 30-MHz range, for example, even the two RF amplifiers may not reject images satisfactorily.

8. *image-apprehension, -association, -brilliance, -complex, -field, -formation, -motif, -pattern, -sound, -substitute, -type, -world*; *image-crowded, -laden, -ridden, -seeing* adjs.; **image cluster** (see CLUSTER *sb.* 3 b); **image converter,** an image tube, *esp.* one for converting an invisible image formed by infra-red or other invisible radiation into a visible one; **image dissector,** a kind of television camera tube in which a photo-emissive surface receives the image and the corresponding pattern of emitted electrons is deflected in a scanning pattern to and fro across a point anode, producing the video signal; **image frequency:** see sense 7** above; **image iconoscope,** a kind of television camera tube combining the iconoscope and the image dissector, the target plate receiving not the optical image (as in the former) but a pattern of emitted electrons produced by the image at a photo-emissive surface (as in the latter); **image intensifier,** an image tube or other device in which an image is formed by light or other radiation on a photo-emissive or photoconductive surface and the resulting flow of electrons utilized to produce a corresponding visible image of increased brightness; **image interference:** see sense 7** above; **image orthicon,** a kind of television camera tube in which a flow of electrons, produced as in an image tube, strikes a thin glass sheet and forms on it a pattern of positive charges corresponding to the picture, the video signal being derived from the variation this produces in a scanning electron beam that strikes the other side of the sheet (neutralizing the charge at that point) and returns to the electron gun and associated electron multipliers with an intensity reduced in accordance with the magnitude of the neutralized charge; **image toy,** a small decorative figure in earthenware, esp. one made in the 18th century by John Astbury (see *ASTBURY) or Thomas Whieldon; **image tube,** an electron tube in which an image, formed by light or other electromagnetic radiation on a photo-emissive surface, causes it to emit a corresponding flow of electrons which may be used to reproduce the image in a different form (as in an image converter or an image intensifier).

1962 I. M. CROMBIE *Exam. Plato's Doctrines* I. iii. 120 The criteria employed in calling things ducks do not constitute more than an image-apprehension of duckdom. *a* **1930** D. H. LAWRENCE *Apocalypse* (1932) 97 The curious image-association. The oriental loved that. **1950** *Essays & Stud.* III. 39 The striking image-associations of this passage were noted by W. Clemen in *Shakespeares Bilder.* **1946** *Nature* 19 Oct. 533/2 Under the title 'geometrical properties of visual instruments' are discussed such questions as field-size..and image-brilliance in different parts of the field. **1946** E. A. ARMSTRONG *Shakespeare's Imagination* 184 As no two poets employ the same image clusters, therefore works of doubtful provenance can be assigned to a poet with certainty if it contains clusters..characteristic of writings known to be authentic. **1961** *N. & Q.* Apr. 156/2 Particular stress is put on imagery and image-clusters in the cases of *Edward III* and *The Two Noble Kinsmen.* **1963** *Ibid.* Sept. 332/1 One's faith in image-clusters as evidence for authorship tends..to be diminished by such a coincidence. **1966** *English Studies* XLVII. 302 A Bible-inspired image-complex in Vaughan's poems. **1946** *Electronic Engin.* XVIII. 157/1 The principle of the infra-red image convertor is fairly well known. **1950** P. PARKER *Electronics* xvii. 843 An image converter is a device which converts an image formed by light-rays on a photo-cathode into one formed by electron beams...The name image converter is generally kept, however, for tubes in which the electron image is formed on a fluorescent screen. **1952** *Electronic Engin.* XXIV. 307/1 The case of an image convertor of the ME1200 type will enable infra-red photographs to be taken using normal high-speed emulsions. **1959** *Proc. IRE* XLVII. 905/1 A group of American astronomers have undertaken the development of an image-converter tube which permits the electron image to emerge through a thin membrane or foil to expose an external photographic plate. **1968** L. LEVI *Appl. Optics* vi. 266 Image converters greatly enhance night vision..and have in this capacity served in both military and zoological applications. **1911** W. B. YEATS *Plays for an Irish Theatre* p. ix, We feel our minds expand convulsively or spread out slowly like some moon-brightened image-crowded sea. **1934** P. T. FARNSWORTH in *Jrnl. Franklin Inst.* CCXVIII. 411 Means for producing these saw-tooth currents and means for synchronizing them between the 'Image Dissector', or transmitting tube, and the..receiving tube, are discussed. **1968** *Brit. Med. Bull.* XXIV. 261/2 A non-storage camera tube of the type known as an 'image dissector' also possesses some very favourable properties, particularly in so far as resolution is concerned. *Ibid.* 261/1 The only instruments of real interest at the moment seem to be those capable of automatic measurement of optical density at many different points of an image field. **1923** J. S. HUXLEY *Ess. Biologist* ii. 81 Even in the most 'intelligent' of birds or mammals, the power of image-formation is very probably absent, and the power of concept-formation..certainly so. **1972** *Jrnl. Social Psychol.* LXXXVII. 37 Mental imagery and image formation have recently become a topic of concern again. **1939** *Proc. IRE* XXVII. 547/1 These image iconoscopes are practical working tools, advanced well beyond the laboratory stage. **1957** AMOS & BIRKINSHAW *Television Engin.* (rev.) I. iv. 75 Image iconoscopes, in common with all high velocity tubes, have tended to be superseded by image orthicons in nearly all television services. **1939** L. M. MYERS *Electron. Optics* viii. 449 We might term the device an image intensifier. *Ibid.* 450 An image intensifier was indeed the unrealised and unrealisable dream of the mechanical optical television engineer. **1954** *Radiology* LXIII. 870 An ideal image intensifier would receive only information-bearing X-ray signals from the subject and construct therefrom an image of arbitrary size and brightness. **1959** *Proc. IRE* XLVII. 909/1 An entirely different principle of image amplification is used in the solid-state image intensifier... In the simplest form of this device, a phosphor layer is placed between two conducting plates to which an electric field of about 100 v is applied. If an ultraviolet image is focused on the screen thus formed, a marked increase in light emission is produced. **1967** *New Scientist* 25 May 485/2 At Herstmonceux experiments are in progress on a number of different types of image intensifier to find the most suitable system to be used in conjunction with the 100-in. Newton telescope. **1904** *Westm. Gaz.* 27 Aug. 6/2 This heavily-scented, image-laden atmosphere. **1943** D. GASCOYNE *Poems 1937–1942* 33 Blows back With long-held burning breath through eyeholes bored By image-laden rays. **1937** U. ELLIS-FERMOR *Some Recent Res. Shakes. Imagery* 25 This [*sc.* Kolbe's *Shakespeare's Way*]..has some illuminating suggestions about the underlying image-motifs in the plays. **1945** *Birmingham* (Alabama) *News* 29 Oct. 9/1 The product of RCA engineers..the device is known as an 'image orthicon'. **1946** *Proc. IRE* XXXIV. 428/2 The image orthicon derives its increased sensitivity over the iconoscope and orthicon from (1) the higher photosensitivity of a conducting photocathode relative to that of an insulating mosaic; (2) the multiplication by secondary emission of the electron image at the target; and (3) the use of an electron multiplier for the signal current. **1953** AMOS & BIRKINSHAW *Television Engin.* I. v. 101 The image orthicon tube may be regarded as a combination of an orthicon tube with an image stage similar to that used in the image iconoscope. **1971** H. E. ENNES *Television Broadcasting* i. 20 There are three basic types of pickup tubes used in television cameras: the image orthicon, the vidicon, and the lead oxide. The image orthicon is used primarily in monochrome studio and field cameras for live pickups. **1947** C. DAY LEWIS *Poetic Image* 84 Its image-pattern is so skilfully composed from certain theme-images. **1949** A. M. FARRER *Rebirth of Images* i. 22 The evidence for the unity of the Johannine writings.. lies in the identity of image-pattern in the Gospel and the Apocalypse. **1935** AUDEN & ISHERWOOD *Dog beneath Skin* I. 33 Our impulses are unseasonal and image-ridden. **1929** A. HUXLEY *Holy Face* 21 Image-seeing and poetical. **1929** D. H. LAWRENCE *Pornogr. & So On* (1936) 73 It is, for him, complete for he is void of image-seeing imagination. **1925** I. A. RICHARDS *Princ. Lit. Crit.* 119 But the degree of correspondence between the image-sounds, and the actual sounds that the reader would produce, varies enormously. *Ibid.* 120 *Something* takes the place of vivid images in these people and.. provided the image-substitute is efficacious, their lack of mimetic imagery is of no consequence. **1957** MANKOWITZ & HAGGAR *Conc. Encycl. Eng. Pottery & Porcelain* 115/1 *Image toys,* earthenware, stoneware or porcelain figures. **1960** H. HAYWARD *Antique Coll.* 147/1 *Image toys,* contemporary designation of mid-18th cent. Staffordshire pottery figures. **1971** *Country Life* 2 Dec. 1505/1 Pioneer maker of image toys in Staffordshire was John Astbury (1688–1742), his colours restricted to the browns and whites of his burnt clay. **1936** *Jrnl. Optical Soc. Amer.* XXVI. 187/2 The construction of the photosensitive cathode to be used in any given image tube will, of course, depend upon the spectral region in which maximum sensitivity is desired. **1940** ZWORYKIN & MORTON *Television* iv. 91 The image tube is of importance because it can be combined with the Iconoscope to make a television pick-up tube which is many times more sensitive than the normal Iconoscope. **1969** *New Scientist* 10 July (Optics Suppl.) 21/1 Objects illuminated with non-visible radiation..can be seen with the aid of these devices. The image tube can also intensify very faint images..so that they become visible. **1971** *Nature* 3 Sept. 37/1 The difficulties associated with studying very faint [celestial] objects are very great, because of the increasing difficulty in detecting photons against the natural and man-made noise, even with the use of image-tube techniques. **1925** I. A. RICHARDS *Princ. Lit. Crit.* 123 If this were not the case the absence of glaring differences between people of different image-types would be astonishing. **1904** *Daily Chron.* 8/2 Immersed in this innocent, harmless, image-world. **1953** R. MANHEIM tr. *Cassirer's Philos. Symbolic Forms* I. 78 All live in particular image-worlds, which do not reflect the empirically given, but which rather produce it in accordance with an independent principle.

image, *v.* Add: **1.** (Later examples.)

1957 A. C. CLARKE *Deep Range* xv. 129 The familiar rocky terrain was imaged on TV and sonar screen. **1970** *Physics Bull.* Nov. 490/2 Figure 1*a* shows the simplest possible optical system which includes both a parallel beam in which the working space can be placed (*B*) and a lens which can image it on to a receptor.

4. a. (Later examples.)

1860 J. MCCOSH *Intuitions* I. i. 11 The mind of man has the power of imaging or representing in old forms by the memory, and in new forms by the imagination, whatever it has at any time known or experienced. **1924** T. H. Y. TROTTER *Music & Mind* v. 56 Whether or not it is necessary for the listener to image in his mind the scene to be represented is a moot point. **1972** *Science* 16 June 1208/1 Some recall past events by imaging the scene.

imaged, *a.* **1.** (Later examples.)

1889 W. B. YEATS *Wanderings of Oisin* II. 23 Between the lids of one The imaged meteors had shone and run. **1935** W. EMPSON *Poems* 13 Drink deep the imaged solid of the bone.

imageless, *a.* Add: (Later example.)

a **1930** D. H. LAWRENCE *Last Poems* (1932) 214 The gods are nameless and imageless.

b. Special Comb.: *imageless thought* (see quot. 1934); so *imageless thinking.*

1896 G. F. STOUT *Analytic Psychol.* I. I. iv. 85 An imageless thought is no absurdity, however opposed such a conception may be to..those who..regard consciousness as a kind of picture gallery. **1909** E. B. TITCHENER *Lect. Exper. Psychol. Thought-Processes* iii. 113 Binet..gives illustrations of imageless thought that must undoubtedly be classed with the conscious attitudes. **1920** S. ALEXANDER *Space, Time & Deity* I. 213 Observation..has convinced us of the existence of 'imageless thinking', which seemed so inconceivable to some earlier psychologists. **1921** B. RUSSELL *Analysis of Mind* xi. 226 Similar remarks apply to the general idea of 'imageless thinking', concerning which there has been much controversy. **1934** H. C. WARREN *Dict. Psychol.* 131/2 *Imageless thought,* an idea, thought, or train of thinking which is wholly lacking in sensory contents. **1948** R. S. WOODWORTH *Contemp. Schools Psychol.* (ed. 2) iv. 74 Watson pointed an accusing finger at the 'imageless thought' controversy. **1953** J. B. CARROLL *Study of Lang.* iii. 74 One outcome of Wundt's work..was the discovery, around 1900, of 'imageless thought'—a kind of subjective behaviour, noted in the process of thinking, which could not be described as..sensation and perception. **1972** *Science* 12 May 630/2 This casual attitude toward definition means that he need never ask whether..there are 'imageless' concepts or thoughts.

image-maker. Add: **b.** *fig.* (in sense *5 b of image). So **i·mage-ma:king** *sb.* and *adj.* (various senses).

a **1930** D. H. LAWRENCE *Last Poems* (1932) 83 The gibe of image-making love. **1953** S. SPENDER *Creative Element* 50 For Yeats, spiritualism put him in touch, as he thought, with the image-making collective unconscious of all civilizations. **1960** *Guardian* 7 Oct. 17/4 [Owing] to the failure of the image-makers..neither candidate seems to have put across a strong or provocative personality. **1967** *Listener* 3 Aug. 140/3 Darwin and Einstein..must have been endowed with an extraordinary capacity of image-making to be able to see the world in a startlingly new shape. **1969** *Times* 1 Aug. 6/7 The image-makers said that he was the family's best politician. **1971** *Daily Tel.* 23 Mar. 13/1 The population at large are as inwardly proud of their political rough-houses as they are of such image-makers as Ned Kelly, the waterless outback and Aussie-rules football. **1972** E. LUCIE-SMITH *Eroticism in Western Art* xv. 262 Since erotic art obeys the necessity to be specific, photography..offered powerful competition to more traditional kinds of image-making in this field.

imager. Add: **2.** (Later example.) Also, one who forms a mental image or images; something that reproduces an image (e.g. in radar).

1960 A. HUXLEY *Let.* 17 July (1969) 893 Your work with imagers sounds very interesting. Have you any idea why some people visualize and others don't? **1963** *Listener* 28 Mar. 547/2 One regular hypnagogic imager has amusing images that would form excellent subject matter for a Walt Disney cartoon. **1967** C. L. WRENN *Word & Symbol* 10 Poets have always regarded themselves as..the bearers of truth and imagers of reality. **1971** *Daily Tel.* (Colour Suppl.) 10 Dec. 34/1 The Army regards radar as an integral part of the night-vision family; just as important as image intensifiers or thermal imagers.

imagic (i·mėdʒik), *a.* [f. IMAGE *sb.* + -IC.] Image-like.

1937 'C. CAUDWELL' *Illusion & Reality* 237 The manifest content is imagic phantasy. **1953** *Essays in Crit.* III. 431 'Soundlessly' shares with 'Spawning' the imagic honours. **1957** N. FRYE *Sound & Poetry* 136 The 'New Criticism', chiefly concerned with the imagic and referential meaning (semantic) levels.

imaginability. Delete *rare*$^{-1}$ and add later example.

1953 G. E. M. ANSCOMBE tr. *Wittgenstein's Philos. Investigations* I. 120 There is a lack of clarity about the role of *imaginability* in our investigation.

imaginal, *a.*[1] Restrict † *Obs. rare* to sense b and add later examples. Also, of or pertaining to a mental image.

Quot. *a* 1901 is perh. a transferred use of IMAGINAL *a.*[2] *a* 1901 F. W. H. MYERS *Human Personality* (1903) I. Gloss. p. xviii, *Imaginal*,..metaphorically applied to transcendental faculties shown in rudiment in ordinary life. 1925 [see *ATTITUDE 5]. 1925 J. E. TURNER *Theory Direct Realism* iv. 42 The imaginal and ideal elements, although of course they are undoubtedly present in the percipient's mind, never reveal themselves to him in their proper nature. 1935 *Brit. Jrnl. Psychol.* Apr. 445 The imaginal retention of a previously perceived common element. 1951 G. HUMPHREY *Thinking* ii. 32 Pure intellection as contrasted with thinking on imaginal terms. *Ibid.* iv. 129 Sensory aspects of experience which we may call imaginal, affective and cognitive.

Hence ima·ginally *adv.*

1925 I. A. RICHARDS *Princ. Lit. Crit.* xviii. 157 As the eye wanders imaginally from point to point the relations between the parts of the picture-space change.

imaginary, *a.* Add. **1. a.** *imaginary museum* = *musée imaginaire* (see *MUSEE 2).

1963 *Times Lit. Suppl.* 23 Aug. 642/5 Mr. Skelton's readers are given hardly any notion of the imaginary museums in which poets roam and of which they too must be habitués if they are to appreciate poems more than superficially. 1967 *Listener* 25 May 679/2 Marino's *Galeria*, the 'imaginary museum' where one assembles one's favourite works of art from a number of different locations.

imagination. Add: **6.** *imagination-consciousness, -game, -image, -mill, -process, -world; imagination-liberating, -manufactured, -stunning* adjs.

1901 E. B. TITCHENER *Exper. Psychol.* I. I. 1 An imagination-consciousness, our mind as it is when we are imagining something. 1926 E. BOWEN *Ann Lee's, & Other Stories* 53 But the imagination-game palled upon him. 1890 W. JAMES *Princ. Psychol.* II. xviii. 50 Imagination-images..feel subject to our spontaneity [etc.]. 1933 R. TUVE *Seasons & Months* i. 28 It was not the imagination-liberating concept of Nature. 1902 *North Amer. Rev.* Dec. 768 The [Christian] Science..secures to him life-long immunity from imagination-manufactured disease. 1899 *Harper's Mag.* Dec. 40/1 His imagination-mill was hard at work in a minute. 1890 W. JAMES *Princ. Psychol.* II. xviii. 72 The imagination-process *can* then pass over into the sensation-process. In other words, genuine sensations *can* be centrally originated. 1892 'MARK TWAIN' *Amer. Claimant* x. 88 The imagination-stunning material development of this century. 1904 *Daily Chron.* 19 Oct. 8/1 This glimpse into the imagination-world of London.

imagine, *v.* Add: **5. c.** *colloq.* To believe or suppose. Also used with aposiopesis in phr. *can you imagine?*

1947 N. MARSH *Final Curtain* x. 150 We all opened our letters yesterday morning, at breakfast. Can you imagine? I got down first and really—such a shock! 1952 E. GRIERSON *Reputation for Song* iii. 20 'Is your mother coming down?' 'I imagine so.' 1961 *Guardian* 25 May 10/4 Naïvely imagining that MI 5 was only blood-hounding those with suspected Cliveden or Mosley ideas. 1968 D. DEVINE *Sleeping Tiger* i. 12 Peter borrowed the Jag to bring her here and he scraped it on the gate! Can you *imagine*? 1971 C. BONINGTON *Annapurna South Face* iii. 28 At times, though, in these hectic weeks of organization, as I imagine happens with any expedition, it seemed we should never make our deadline for packing all our gear ready to go to India. 1973 *Listener* 20 Dec. 841/2 This prospect must bring a lot of cheer to the Speaker... I imagine that after Mr Ford's swearing-in he slept the sleep of the just.

imaging, *vbl. sb.* (see under IMAGE *v.*). (Later examples.)

1920 S. ALEXANDER *Space, Time & Deity* I. 25 In imaging the act of mind is provoked from within. 1920 J. LAIRD *Study in Realism* iv. 67 Imaging has a different bodily margin from perceiving. 1943 *Mind* LII. 333 'Imagination' sometimes means the forming and contemplating of mental images, visual, auditory or other; this is more appropriately called 'imaging'. 1953 H. H. PRICE *Thinking & Experience* viii. 236 All these people, whose thoughts are concerned with the spatial relations of things..would be completely at a loss if the power of visual imaging suddenly deserted them. 1971 *Sci. Amer.* Aug. 83/1 'Imaging' is a control process in which verbal information is remembered through visual images; for example, Cicero suggested learning long lists (or speeches) by placing each member of the list in a visual representation of successive rooms of a well-known building.

Imagism (i·mĕdʒiz'm). Also imagism. [f. IMAGE *sb.* + -ISM.] **1.** Name given to a movement in poetry, originating in 1912 and represented by Ezra Pound, Amy Lowell, and others, aiming at clarity of expression through the use of precise visual images.

In the early period often written in the Fr. form *Imagisme*.

1912 E. POUND *Let.* 1 Aug. (1971) 38 I should like the name 'Imagisme' to retain some sort of a meaning. It stands, or I should like it to stand for hard light, clear edges. *Ibid.* 12 Aug. (1971) 39 If you want to drag in the word Imagisme you can use a subtitle 'an anthology devoted to Imagisme, vers libre and modern movements in verse' or something of that sort. 1913 *Poetry* (Chicago) Mar. 198 (*title*) Imagisme. Some curiosity has been aroused concerning *Imagisme*... Editor's Note—In response to many requests for information regarding *Imagism* and the *Imagistes*, we publish this note by Mr. Flint... *Imagism* is not necessarily associated with Hellenic subjects, or with *vers libre* as a prescribed form. 1915 E. POUND *Let.* Jan. (1971) 48 If I had acceded to A. L.'s [*sc.* Amy Lowell's] proposal to turn 'Imagism' into a democratic beer-garden, I should have undone what little good I had managed to do by setting up a critical standard. 1917 *North Amer. Rev.* CCV. 106 The third characteristic of The New Poetry, and particularly of Imagism, is what might be metaphorically described as faithfulness to the architectural line. 1924 T. MAYNARD *Our Best Poets* 198 Imagism brings together, with an indulgent catholicism, those who use metre with a brilliant exactness, and those who use only cadence. 1929 A. NOYES *Return of Scare-Crow* iv. 52 The sharp-edged imagism with which our younger writers are experimenting today. 1931 G. HUGHES (*title*) Imagism and the Imagists. 1967 *Listener* 2 Mar. 297/2 Pound may have believed that his imagism ..was an alternative to symbolism, but there is no reason now for us to agree with him.

2. *Philos.* (See quot. 1953.)

1952 R. I. AARON *Theory of Universals* ii. 20 It might be argued that what Hobbes was attacking..was imagism rather than conceptualism, the notion [*i.e.* imagism] that there must be an image before us whenever we universalize. 1953 H. H. PRICE *Thinking & Experience* viii. 234 The theory that thinking consists in operating with mental images..has no generally accepted name. I am going to call it 'Imagism'.

Imagist (i·mĕdʒist). Also imagist and in Fr. form **Imagiste.** [f. as prec. + -IST.] **1.** An adherent of Imagism (sense 1). Also *attrib.* or as *adj.*

1912 E. POUND *Let.* Aug. (1971) 10 I send you all that I have on my desk—an over-elaborate post-Browning 'Imagiste' affair and a note on the Whistler exhibit. *Ibid.* Oct. (1971) 11 I've had luck again, and am sending you some *modern* stuff by an American, I say modern, for it is in the laconic speech of the Imagistes, even if the subject is classic. 1913 [see *IMAGISM 1]. 1914 R. ALDINGTON in *Egoist* 1 June 201/1 (*title*) Modern poetry and the Imagists. *Ibid.* 202/1 Why do we call ourselves 'Imagists'? .. I think it is a very good and descriptive title... Let me say from memory what I, as an Imagist, consider the fundamental doctrines of the group... We do not say 'O how I admire that exquisite, that beautiful..woman'.. but we present that woman, we make an 'Image' of her, we make the scene convey the emotion. 1915 *Egoist* 1 May 70/2 One of the first 'Imagist' poems by T. E. Hulme. 1919 *Hist. Amer. Lit.* II. 266 *Isle of la Belle Rivière*..was written in what is now called imagist verse, at the age of thirty. 1922 *Edin. Rev.* July 101 In much of the work of the imagists..we find a more or less conscious, and more or less effective yielding to that influence. 1931 [see *GROUND *sb.* 11 b]. 1931 [see *IMAGISM 1]. 1960 AUDEN *Homage to Clio* 42 No 'imagist' poem can be more than a few words long. 1970 *English Studies* LI. 269 This period also saw the birth and death of other more obviously revolutionary groups such as the Vorticists, Imagists, [etc.].

transf. 1962 *Times* 3 May 18/4 Two of the most rip-roaring imagists of European action-painting. 1962 *Listener* 27 Sept. 484/2 The Pirandellists, the Symbolists, the Kafkarians, the Imagists.

2. *Philos.* An adherent of imagism (sense 2). Also *attrib.* or as *adj.*

1948 *Mind* LVII. 481 He [*sc.* Ewing] backs it up with his criticisms of Behaviourist accounts of Belief and Verbalist and Imagist accounts of Thinking. 1953 H. H. PRICE *Thinking & Experience* viii. 239 The Imagist does not deny that words have meaning, but he holds that they have it only indirectly, as substitutes for images. *Ibid.* 241 The starting point of the Imagist theory..is private thinking, and private thinking of the 'free' symbol-using kind. 1972 *Science* 12 May 630/2 Thus he can adopt an imagist theory of meaning after carefully listing several objections to it which are never answered.

Hence **imagi·stic** *a.*, of or pertaining to Imagism (both senses); **imagi·stically** *adv.*

1916 E. POUND *Let.* 17 Apr. (1971) 76 Some of the things [*sc.* poems] seem to me 'just imagistic', neither better nor worse than a lot of other imagistic stuff that gets into print. 1921 H. CRANE *Let.* 22 July (1965) 63 In an imagistic way [this] singularly seems to agree with the substance of your opinion. 1940 *Kenyon Rev.* 277 The words 'fog' and 'bloody' .. must be taken not only.. imagistically but symbolically. 1944 *Mind* LIII. 216 Imagistic, literary, associative, or other kinds of meaning. 1963 *Listener* 14 Feb. 300/3 This imagistic language is carried to its logical conclusion in the controversial ending to the film. 1969 *Jrnl. Eng. & Gmc. Philol.* LXVIII. 219 The reason is imagistically indicated in the immediately preceding lines. 1973 *Times Lit. Suppl.* 2 Nov. 1348/3 He works for the most part imagistically, spacing small, autonomous chunks of perception around a page, resolutely subduing 'theme' to the eye-stopping images which compose it.

imago. Add: **c.** *fig.*

1921 *19th Cent.* Feb. 214 Since 1914 every constituent element that has been supposed to go to the making of great men—spacious times, tension, supreme effort, turmoil, battle, revolution—has abounded, but the imago has not emerged.

2. *Psycho-analysis.* A subjective image of someone (esp. a parent) which a person has subconsciously formed and which continues to influence his attitudes and behaviour. So *father-imago, mother-imago.*

1916 B. M. HINKLE tr. *Jung's Psychol. of Unconscious* (1918) 492 Here I purposely give preference to the term 'Imago' rather than to the expression 'Complex', in order ..to invest this psychological condition, which I include under 'Imago', with living independence in the psychical hierarchy... 'Imago' has a significance similar on the one hand to the psychologically conceived creation in Spitteler's novel..and on the other hand to the ancient religious conception of 'imagines et lares'. 1919 M. K. BRADBY *Psycho-Anal.* 59 That web of ideas and emotions which is woven in the course of the child's life round the image of the parent or 'parent imago'. 1924 J. RIVIERE et al tr. *Freud's Coll. Papers* II. xxviii. 313 If the physician should be specially connected in this way with the father-imago (as Jung has happily named it) it is quite in accordance with his actual relationship to the patient. 1927 W. E. COLLINSON *Contemp. Eng.* 107 Most educated people will by now have heard of the Oedipus complex and will have a nodding acquaintance with libido and imago and may have, with distressing results, tried on themselves the method of free-association. 1948 M. KLEIN in S. Lorand *Psycho-Analysis Today* 65 The super-ego of the child does not coincide with the picture presented by its real parents, but is created out of imaginary pictures or *imagos* of them which it has taken up into itself. 1956 R. F. C. HULL tr. *Jung's Coll. Wks.* V. iv. 57 In most of the existing religions it seems that the formative factor..is the father-imago, while in the older religions it was the mother-imago. 1967 BRUSSEL & CANTZLAAR *Chambers's Dict. Psychiatry* 121 *Imago*, in Jung's *analytical psychology*, a conception of another person that one acquires in infancy or childhood and carries through to adulthood in the unconscious.

imagy (i·mĕdʒi), *a.* [f. IMAGE *sb.*: see -Y[1].] Of the nature of an image.

1937 *Aristotelian Soc. Suppl. Vol.* XVI. 213 We could suggest that an event has two sorts of constituents, *sensible* ones and *imagy* ones. 1953 H. H. PRICE *Thinking & Experience* vii. 201 The type-word 'cat' has *imagy* tokens as well as overtly perceptible ones.

imambara (imā·mbără, imāmbā·ră). Also **imambarah, -barra, -bra, imaum-.** [Hind., f. Arab. IMAM + Hind. *bāṛā* enclosure.] In India, a building in which Shiite Muslims assemble at the time of Muharram; the gardens, courtyards, etc., surrounding such a building; also, any large tomb.

1837 E. EDEN *Jrnl.* 28 Dec. in *Up Country* (1866) I. ix. 87 In the afternoon we went to see the Emaumberra and Rooma Durwanee, two of the most magnificent native buildings I have seen yet. 1867 J. FERGUSSON *Hist. Archit.* II. v. viii. 702 In Lucknow there..is..one building especially, the Imambara, which..is not unfit to be spoken of in the same chapter as the earlier buildings. 1883 *Encycl. Brit.* XV. 49/2 The immense Imámbára, or mausoleum of Asaf-ud-daulá [at Lucknow]. 1886 YULE & BURNELL *Hobson-Jobson*, Imaumbarra. 1907 *Westm. Gaz.* 4 Apr. 10/2 The imambra connected with the Mohammedan morgue at Lucknow. 1955 J. TERRY *Charm Indo-Islamic Archit.* 40 (*heading*) Imambara, Lucknow, 18th century. A large hall built by a king of Oudh for famine-relief work. 1964 A. A. A. FYZEE *Outl. Muhammadan Law* (ed. 3) 319 An imāmbāra is a private apartment set apart by a member of the Ithnā ʿAsharī Shiite faith for the performance of certain ceremonies at Muḥarram and other times; it is not a public place of worship like a mosque.

Imam Bayildi (imā·m ba·yildi). Also Imam Baildi. [Turk., lit. = the priest fainted (supposedly from pleasure at, or because of the cost of, the dish).] A dish consisting of aubergines stuffed with an onion-and-tomato mixture and cooked in oil.

1935 M. MORPHY *Recipes of all Nations* 767 This vegetable [*sc.* the aubergine] is extremely popular in Turkey, and one of the commonest ways of preparing it is called *Imam Baïldi*..'the Swooning Imam'—the Imam having fainted with delight when he first partook of this wondrous dish. 1952 HOWE & ESPIR *Sultan's Pleasure & other Turkish Recipes* 75 *The fainting imam* (Patlican Imam Bayildi). There is an amusing story connected with this traditional dish. 1958 I. ORGA *Turkish Cooking* 114 *Aubergine Imam Bayildi*... Take the onion mixture and fill the aubergines with this then lay them side by side in a wide-bottomed saucepan. 1969 R. STOUT *Death of Dude* (1970) xii. 176 Eggplant stuffed with a purée which the Turks call *Imam Baïldi*—'Swooning Imam'. Onions browned in oil, tomatoes, garlic, salt and pepper. 1972 J. RATHBONE *Trip Trap* x. 111 'Some more Imam Bayildi?' He motioned to the aubergine stew. 1973 *Guardian* 26 Jan. 11/1 A dish of aubergine..named Imam Bayildi or The Imam Fainted.

Imari (imā·ri). The name of a town in the north-west of the Japanese island of Kyushu, used *attrib.* and *ellipt.* to denote a type of Hizen porcelain.

1875–80 AUDSLEY & BOWES *Keramic Art Japan* I. 5 The productions of these numerous factories are usually exported from the seaport of Imari, and are therefore commonly known as Imari ware. 1878 J. J. YOUNG *Ceramic Art* vi. 175 The chief kinds of [Japanese] porcelain are the Hizen (also called Imari and Arita), [etc.]. 1890 B. H. CHAMBERLAIN *Things Japanese* 284 The second variety of Kutani ware may often be mistaken for 'old Japan' (i.e., Imari porcelain). 1902 *Encycl. Brit.* XXIX. 725/1 In the term 'Hizen porcelains' are included not merely the richly decorated Imari ware—the 'Old Japan' of Western collectors [etc.]. 1954 H. GARNER *Oriental Blue & White* 63 The so-called 'Old Imari' wares. 1954 G. SAVAGE *Porcelain* 43 The *Imari* style is also Japanese, and was based on native textiles and brocades. 1969 *Guardian* 16 July 18/2 Japanese Kakiemon and Imari patterns were copied at Canton for shipment to Europe. 1970 *Ashmolean Mus. Rep. Visitors 1969* 47 Oil jug, Japanese export Imari porcelain, overglazed in red and gold. 1971 *Times* 5 Apr. 14/5 Delicate [chamber] pots in Imari porcelain and Wedgwood.

imbalance (imbæ·lăns). [f. IM-[2] + BALANCE *sb.*] An unbalanced condition; a lack of

proper proportion or relation between corresponding things.

Orig. a technical term in Ophthalmology but now used generally in many subjects and contexts.

1898 *Ophthalmic Rec.* VII. 87 Some advocates of operative interference for ocular imbalance in the functional neuroses fail to recognize the fact that heterophoria, or even squint, may be only a symptom. **1930** G. Hamilton *Med. Social Terminol.* 25 *Intellectual imbalance*, the state of an individual with special abilities or disabilities, markedly competent in some respects and deficient in others, but not well integrated or compensated. **1934** *Scrutiny* III. III. 230 It is a matter of common observation that a high degree of artistic discrimination can go along with an extreme paucity or imbalance of general emotional life. **1937** *Nature* 16 Jan. 90/2 The operating mechanism [of the human constitution] is the autonomic nervous system, which, especially in sensitive subjects is liable to ..pass into imbalance or dysfunction, and eventually permanent disease. **1949** S. Duke-Elder *Text-bk. Ophthalm.* IV. xlvi. 3964 Operative treatment is the alternative measure to correct a heterophoria, and is particularly applicable in essential imbalance when the cause is anatomical. **1949** Janis & Fadner in H. D. Lasswell et al. *Lang. Pol.* II. viii, This Coefficient of Imbalance is intended to be applicable to all types of communications..except those in which the communication is arbitrarily restricted to specified symbols. **1952** *N.Y. Times* 6 May 28/2 The trade imbalance and the drain of gold and hard currency reserves have lessened. **1953** *Manch. Guardian Weekly* 7 May 3/3 Which will prevent their own budgets from remaining in disastrous imbalance. **1954** *New Biol.* XVI. 80 While the maintenance of an adult organism is achieved by the exact balance of synthetic and degradative processes, growth is realized by a degree of imbalance in which synthetic processes predominate. **1957** *Economist* 7 Sept. 780/1 Increasing the existing imbalance between male and female employment. **1957** *English Studies* XXXVIII. 97 A remarkable corrective to this imbalance appeared in the writings of Henry Sweet. **1957** *Listener* 26 Dec. 1080/3 Shows clearly the imbalance created by an exodus of young persons (predominantly females) from the rural areas. **1961** *Lancet* 22 July 211/1 Imbalance in the mental diet results in greed. **1962** *Ibid.* 2 June 1167/2 Though the mammalian body has striking powers of recovery from the effects of long-maintained hormonal imbalance, there must be limits to the stresses which can safely be imposed. **1967** *Boston Sunday Globe* 21 May H 3/1 The imbalance problem [proportion of black and of white people] could be solved in such a setup... The 20 or so schools in a park would be able to share many facilities and personnel. **1969** *Times* 5 Aug. 9/5 The imbalance in the world's financial system has become grotesque. **1970** *New Society* 5 Feb. 222/1 Imbalances between homes and people emerge. **1973** *Sci. Amer.* Sept. 133/3 The marked increase in the average salary reflects both the imbalance of supply and demand for health workers and, more important, the highly desirable increased value placed on such workers.

imbauba (imbǭ·bă, imbă,*ū*·bă). [a. Pg. *imbaúba, umbaúba*, f. Tupi *ambauba, umbauba*.] A Brazilian tree of the genus *Cecropia*, esp. *C. peltata*, which has a hollow stem and yields a softwood timber; also called *trumpet-tree, trumpet-wood.* Cf. *cecropia 1.

1849 R. Spruce *Notes of Botanist on Amazon & Andes* (1908) I. i. 39 Many leaves are grey or hoary beneath, as in the Cecropias (or Imba-úbas, as they are called by the Indians). **1924** Record & Mell *Timbers Trop. Amer.* 145 There are various species of *Cecropia* in Brazil, at least twelve in the Amazon region, and they are generally known by the name of 'imbaúba' or 'embaúba'. **1927** R. R. Gates *Botanist in Amazon Valley* iv. 83 Another characteristic tree fringing the bank..in front of the main forest, is imbauba. **1931** B. Miall tr. *Guenther's Naturalist in Brazil* xvii. 319 Another kind of Aztec ant inhabits the interior of the trunk of the Imbauba-tree.

imbecilic (imbĭsi·lik), *a.* [f. Imbecile *sb.* + -ic.] Characteristic of an imbecile; idiotic.

1918 D. Flatau *Yellow English* xxxv, Looking round with an imbecilic grin. **1927** *Daily Express* 3 Dec. 4 Courteline..collected..the most hideous and imbecilic portraits he could find. **1960** 'A. Burgess' *Right to Answer* ii. 18 There was a kind of imbecilic helper in the public bar. **1968** *Punch* 7 Feb. 194/1 Extrovert delegates prance about singing, blowing horns and shouting imbecilic slogans.

Hence **imbeci·lically** *adv.*, in an imbecile manner.

1946 B. Marshall *George Brown's Schooldays* 28 Pretended not to pray or looked imbecilically heathen.

imbed, *v.*, **imbedded,** *ppl. a.*, varr. Embed *v.*, Embedded *ppl. a.* (Later examples.)

1950 C. R. Hine *Machine Tools for Engineers* xii. 240 The fine, sharp abrasive particles become imbedded in the lap and it is ready for use. **1969** *N.Y. Rev. Bks.* 16 Jan. 4/4 Some of the divergences between Freud and Jung are, however, better attributed to the fact that they chose opposed solutions to the problem of how to imbed the idea of the unconscious into already existing traditions of Western thought. **1971** *Nature* 18 June 437/2 It will be noted that the regions of the three brightest sources are further imbedded in very dense areas; in fact, they are close to the centroids of the Coma cluster. **1971** Powell & Higman *Finite Simple Groups* iii. 174 The process simply imbeds one Chevalley group in another. **1972** *Physics Bull.* May 284/3 Indeed, the liquid crystalline properties inherent in this bilayer structure are almost certainly important for the organization of molecules imbedded in the membrane as well as for controlling transport through it.

Also **imbe·ddedness.**

1952 T. Parsons *Social System* 361 Philosophical investigation, as distinguished from the general imbeddedness of philosophical problems..in any system of action.

imberb (imbə̄·ɹb), *a. rare.* [ad. F. *imberbe*, f. L. *imberbis* (see Imberbic *a.*).] Beardless.

1923 A. Huxley *Antic Hay* iii. 42 A face of such childish contour and so imberb that he looked like a little boy playing at grown-ups.

imbibitional (imbibi·ʃənăl), *a.* [f. Imbibition + -al.] Of, pertaining to, or resulting from imbibition.

1916 *Science* 6 Oct. 502/2 (*heading*) Imbibitional swelling of plants and colloidal mixtures. **1924** *Jrnl. Agric. Sci.* XIV. 204 (*heading*) Remarks and observations on imbibitional soil moisture. **1931** E. C. Miller *Plant Physiol.* iv. 166 Very strong imbibitional forces may be developed within the plant even when the cell walls and protoplasm contain considerable water. **1959** *Chambers's Encycl.* VI. 331/2 In the early stages of water absorption by the barley grain,..the imbibitional pressure may reach 900 atm.

imbonga, imbongo, varr. *mbongo.

imbruement. (Earlier example.)

1859 J. S. Blackie *Let.* 20 Sept. (1909) 143 To the gratification of the old Adam, but with no imbrument [*sic*] to the new.

imbuya (imbwī·ă). Also **imbuia, embuia.** [ad. Pg. *imbuia*, f. the local name for the tree.] A Brazilian timber tree, *Phoebe porosa*, or the wood obtained from it.

1919 *Jrnl. Forestry* XVII. 156 Embuia is the timber de luxe of the four southern Brazil States. **1929** *Tropical Woods* XVIII. 17 Imbuia, or Embuia, one of the best known hardwood timbers of southern Brazil, is used in the United States to a limited extent as a substitute for Walnut, and is sometimes sold as Brazilian Walnut. *Ibid.* 19 The wood of Imbuia varies from yellowish or olive to chocolate-brown, either plain or beautifully variegated and figured. **1947** J. C. Rich *Materials & Methods Sculpture* x. 289 *Imbuya* is a brown wood imported from Central and South America. It is occasionally called Brazilian walnut because of the similarity of its color to walnut. It is softer than black walnut and is usually available in logs and thin planks. **1956** *Handbk. Hardwoods* (Forest Prod. Res. Lab.) 115 Imbuya is also known as 'Brazilian walnut' or embuia (Brazil). **1969** B. J. Rendle *World Timbers* II. 100 Imbuya is variable in colour, from yellowish-brown to chocolate-brown, and may be plain or variegated. **1971** *Cape Times* 13 Feb. 14/6 (Advt.), Solid imbuia kist with brass trims: excellent condition.

imerinite (imərī·nəit). *Min.* [a. F. *imerinite* (A. Lacroix *Minéral. de la France* (1910) IV. 787), f. *Imerina* (F. *Imérina*), name of a region in central Madagascar: see -ite¹.] A colourless or pale blue hydrated silicate of sodium, magnesium, and iron, $Na_2(Mg,Fe^{II},Fe^{III})_6Si_8O_{22}(O,OH)_2$, related to richterite.

1913 *Mineral. Mag.* XVI. 363 Imerinite... A soda-amphibole containing only a small amount of sesquioxides and so allied to soda-richterite. **1963** W. A. Deer et al. *Rock-Forming Min.* II. 353 The names imerinite (Lacroix, 1921) and szechenyite (Krenner, 1900), used for members of the richterite series from Madagascar and Burma respectively, serve no useful purpose and should be abandoned.

imhofite (i·mhǫfəit). *Min.* [ad. G. *imhofit* (G. Burri et al.: see quot. 1965), f. the name of Josef *Imhof*, 20th-c. Swiss mineral collector: see -ite¹.] A soft, white sulphide of thallium and arsenic occurring as tiny monoclinic plates.

1965 G. Burri et al. in *Chimia* XIX. 409 [*English summary of an article in German.*] The description of a new thallium arsenosulfosalt, imhofite, found in the Lengenbach quarry, is given. **1969** *Mineral. Abstr.* XX. 15/2 The structures of the following complex sulphides are summarized:..imhofite, proustite, [etc.]... The greater part of these minerals are from Lengenbach, Binn valley, Switzerland.

imidazole (imi·dăzōᵘl). *Chem.* [ad. G. *imidazol* (Hantzsch & Weber 1887, in *Ber. d. Deut. Chem. Ges.* XX. 3119), f. *imid* Imide + Az(o- + *-ol* *-ole.] **a.** A colourless, crystalline, heterocyclic compound consisting of the five-membered ring NH—CH=N—CH=CH. Also called *glyoxaline. **b.** Any of the derivatives of this compound.

1892 *Jrnl. Chem. Soc.* LXII. 313 Derivatives obtained by displacing a CH group in these by N are designated imidazole = $C_3H_3(NH)N$, oxazole = $C_3H_3(O)N$, and thiazole = $C_3H_3(S)N$ respectively. **1900** E. F. Smith tr. *V. von Richter's Org. Chem.* (ed. 3) II. 480 The glyoxalines or imidazoles. **1936** L. J. Desha *Org. Chem.* xxiv. 493 Pyrazole and imidazole, $C_3H_4N_2$, are isomers differing in the relative positions of the nitrogen atoms. **1946** [see *glyoxaline]. **1951** A. Grollman *Pharmacol. & Therapeutics* xi. 216 Certain imidazole derivatives also exert actions similar in some respects to the sympathetic amines. **1953** R. H. Wiley in H. Gilman *Org. Chem.* IV. viii. 787 The imidazole nucleus is found naturally in the amino acid histidine..; in the purines..; in biotin..; and in histamine. **1968** [see *glyoxaline]. **1968** L. A. Paquette *Princ. Mod. Heterocyclic Chem.* vi. 185 Imidazole and pyrazole..readily form salts with metal ions.

imide. Add: [First formed as F. *imide* (A. Laurent 1835, in *Ann. de Chim. et de Phys.* LIX. 400).] Substitute for def.: Any compound containing the group —NH— (or the substituted form —NR—) attached either to two atoms of a metal or to one or two carbon atoms (which strictly should form part of an acidic group or groups). (Further examples.)

1857 W. A. Miller *Elem. Chem.* III. 231 The imides are bodies formed from the amidated acids by depriving these compounds of two equivalents of water. **1892** E. F. Smith tr. *V. von Richter's Chem. Carbon Compounds* (ed. 2) 365 The imides result by substituting the divalent acid radicals for two of the hydrogen atoms of ammonia. **1950** N. V. Sidgwick *Chem. Elements & their Compounds* I. 666 Imides proper $R{\cdot}C{<}^{OH}_{NH}$ (cyclic imides like phthalimide are of course of a different type) are scarcely known except as possible tautomeric forms of amides; their alkyl derivatives, the imino-ethers $R{\cdot}C{<}^{O\cdot R}_{N\cdot R}$, change easily and irreversibly into the disubstituted amides $R{\cdot}C{<}^{O}_{NR_2}$. **1951** C. R. Noller *Textbk. Org. Chem.* xiii. 195 The monoacyl derivatives of ammonia, primary amines and secondary amines, having the general formula $RCONH_2$, RCONHR, or $RCONR_2$, are known as amides. Diacyl derivatives of ammonia, $(RCO)_2NH$, and of primary amines, $(RCO)_2NR$, also are known and are called imides. Except for the cyclic imides..their preparation usually is more difficult. **1962** P. J. & B. Durrant *Introd. Adv. Inorg. Chem.* xix. 695 The imides, for example lithium imide Li_2NH, contain the group >NH. Lithium, calcium, germanium, tin, and lead form imides.

imidic (imi·dik), *a. Chem.* [In first quot. ad. F. *imidique* (A. Haller 1895, in *Compt. Rend.* CXX. 1194), but in later use prob. independently formed: see Imide and -ic.] Of the nature of an imide; in mod. use applied to organic acids of the type R·C(NH)OH and their derivatives.

1895 *Jrnl. Chem. Soc.* LXVIII. I. 648 Compounds containing the group $NH\bar{R}\bar{R}'$ might be called imidic acids. **1919** *Decennial Index Chem. Abstr. 1907–1916* 3325/1 Imidic acids. **1951** I. L. Finar *Org. Chem.* ix. 161 Imidic esters, which are also known as imino-ethers, are best prepared by passing dry hydrogen chloride into a solution of an alkyl cyanide in anhydrous alcohol. **1965** C. R. Noller *Chem. Org. Compounds* (ed. 3) xiv. 272 The tautomeric form of an amide, $R\overset{\overset{NH}{\|}}{C}{-}OH$, is a nitrogen analog of a carboxylic acid and is known as an imidic acid. Although the imidic acids cannot be isolated because of the greater stability of the amide form, their derivatives are easily prepared.

iminazole (imi·năzōᵘl). *Chem.* [f. *imin(e + Az(o- + *-ole.] = *imidazole.

1901 *Jrnl. Chem. Soc.* LXXX. I (*heading*) Preparation of substituted iminazoles. **1926** H. G. Rule tr. *Schmidt's Text-bk. Org. Chem.* III. iii. 578 The ring system of the iminazoles, like that of the pyrazoles, consists of three carbon and two nitrogen atoms... Iminazole, the parent compound of the series, is formed..by the action of ammonia on glyoxal, and hence is also known as glyoxaline. **1968** [see *glyoxaline].

imine (i·mīn). *Chem.* [ad. G. *imin* (A. Ladenburg 1883, in *Ber. d. Deut. Chem. Ges.* XVI. 1150), formed by altering *amin* Amine (cf. Imide, Amide).] Any compound containing the group =NH (or the substituted form =NR) attached to one carbon atom that forms part of a non-acidic organic group, or containing it in symmetrical compounds of the type R·NH·R; also applied (unsystematically) to other compounds in which it is attached to two carbon atoms (strictly, atoms forming part of non-acidic groups), esp. when they are part of a ring (as in ethylene imine, $(CH_2)_2NH$).

1883 *Jrnl. Chem. Soc.* XLIV. 910 (*heading*) Imines. **1889** G. M'Gowan tr. *A. Bernthsen's Text-bk. Org. Chem.* 194 If two hydrogen atoms in a molecule of ammonia are replaced by a divalent alcohol radicle, 'Imines', e.g. ethylene imine, $(C_2H_4)NH''$, result. **1909** *Proc. Chem. Soc.* XXV. 309 Some confusion exists owing to the present system of nomenclature adopted for the imino-compounds. These substances, which possess the group C:NH, are obviously just as different from the secondary amines having the group ${}^{C}_{C}{>}NH$ as the ketones with the group C:O are different from the ethers with the group ${}^{C}_{C}{>}O$, yet the general name of imine is applied to both these classes. **1935** *Jrnl. Amer. Chem. Soc.* LVII. 2328/1 (*heading*) The preparation of ethylene imine from mono-

ethanolamine. **1950** N. V. SIDGWICK *Chem. Elements* I. 666 Imines of the type (C)(C)>C=N·H rarely occur and are always unstable. **1967** I. L. FINAR *Org. Chem.* (ed. 5) I. viii. 181 Aldehydes react with primary amines to form imines (Schiff bases)... R·CHO + R′NH$_2$ → R·CH=NR′ + H_2O. **1970** AMBROSE & EASTY *Cell Biol.* viii. 267 The sugar molecules form imine linkages (=NH) with the partially dissociated protein complexes.

imino(-) (imī·no). *Chem.* Comb. form of *IMINE; also used *attrib.* as quasi-*adj.* So *imino-chloride, -compound*; *iminosulphonic acid*; **imino-acid,** any organic acid that contains an imino-group; also (now *rare*), an imidic acid; **imino-ester** or **-ether,** any compound that contains —C(NH)OR and is consequently an ester of an imidic acid; more correctly called an *imido-ester*; **imino-group,** the group =NH as it occurs in imines (in quot. 1906 it denotes what is more correctly called an *imido-group*).

1903 *Jrnl. Chem. Soc.* LXXXIV. I. 692 The formation and properties of some iminoacid anhydrides of the type of the hypothetical iminoformic anhydride, NH:CH·O·CH:O. **1937** Imino-acid [see *imino-ether* below]. **1953** FRUTON & SIMMONDS *Gen. Biochem.* iii. 49 The hydrolysis of a protein leads to the formation of a variety of amino acids... The compounds having the general formula shown are termed α-amino acids, whereas proline and hydroxyproline are more correctly designated α-imino acids; for convenience, however, these two cyclic compounds are also called amino acids. **1961** *Jrnl. Clin. Invest.* XL. I. 843/1 Since nearly all of the hydroxyproline of the body is found in collagen, it has been suggested.. that the urinary excretion of the imino acid may be an important index of collagen metabolism. **1967** *New Scientist* 24 Aug. 375/1 The precise proportion of the imino-acid hydroxyproline in the important protein collagen. **1900** *Jrnl. Chem. Soc.* LXXVIII. I. 295 The authors think it probable that aliphatic substituted imino-chlorides of aromatic acids are readily decomposed into alkyl chlorides and aromatic nitriles or their polymerides. **1904** *Ibid.* LXXXV. 1726 (*heading*) The formation and reactions of imino-compounds. **1924** C. HOLLINS *Synthesis Nitrogen Ring Compounds* vii. 203 The yield of imino-compound.. was very small. **1908** *Jrnl. Chem. Soc.* XCIV. I. 419 The catalysis of imino-esters. **1935** H. J. LUCAS *Org. Chem.* xxi. 314 In the presence of anhydrous hydrogen chloride, nitriles add alcohols to form imino esters: $CH_3C{\equiv}N$ + $HOC_2H_5 \rightarrow CH_3C(OC_2H_5){=}NH$. **1951** C. R. NOLLER *Chem. Org. Compounds* xiii. 242 The corresponding *O*-alkyl derivatives, RC(=NH)—OR, are known and are called imido esters (less correctly imino esters or imido ethers). **1897** *Jrnl. Chem. Soc.* LXII. II. 804/2 (Index), Imino-ethers. **1937** TAYLOR & BAKER *Sidgwick's Org. Chem. Nitrogen* (rev. ed.) v. 154 The imino-ethers, which can also be regarded as esters of imino-acids and are sometimes called imino-esters have the general formula R·C(OR′): NH. **1906** *Jrnl. Chem. Soc.* LXXXIX. II. 1837 The members of the former class contain the grouping CO<(NH·CO·)(NH·CO·), whereas in no member of the latter class is this grouping present... Each of the imino-groups contained in the above-mentioned grouping, being connected with two carbonyl groups, will be possessed of acidic properties. **1966** NOWAKOWSKI & CLARKE tr. *Kretovich's Princ. Plant Biochem.* i. 16 Proline, strictly speaking, is not an amino acid, as it contains an imino group (=NH). **1896** *Jrnl. Chem. Soc.* LXX. II. 911/1 (Index), Iminosulphonic acid.

Examples of the general use (without hyphen) as quasi-*adj.*

1901 *Proc. Chem. Soc.* XVII. 61 A liquid base of 'imino' odour. **1937** F. C. WHITMORE *Org. Chem.* I. 226 This product loses water to form the imino analog of formaldehyde, $H_2C{=}NH$.

imipramine (imi·prămīn). *Pharm.* [Rearrangement of some elements of *dimethyl*-amino*propyl*-*imin*o*dibenzyl*, a systematic name for this compound: see -INE[5].] A tricyclic tertiary amine, $C_{19}H_{24}N_2$, given orally as the hydrochloride, a white crystalline compound, in the treatment of endogenous depression.

1958 *Amer. Jrnl. Psychiatry* CXV. 459 (*heading*) The treatment of depressive states with G 22355 (imipramine hydrochloride). **1960** *Brit. Med. Jrnl.* 30 Jan. 348/2 We have..noted the development of jaundice and also hypomania in patients receiving therapeutic doses of imipramine. **1963** *Lancet* 23 Mar. 638/2 The administration to pregnant rabbits of imipramine ('Tofranil') led to the development of fœtal abnormalities. **1964** HAFLIGER & BURCKHARDT in M. Gordon *Psychopharmacol. Agents* I. iii. 77 Imipramine has no influence upon monoamine oxidase. *Ibid.* 89 The most frequent side effects of imipramine..include dryness of the mouth, sweating, disturbance of accommodation, constipation, insomnia, and giddiness. **1965** *Nursing Times* 5 Feb. 187/1 Either electro-convulsive therapy or one of the antidepressant drugs (such as imipramine—Tofranil) will probably be used. **1965** J. POLLIT *Depression & its Treatment* iv. 58 Imipramine is effective mainly in Type S classical (retarded) depressions, and in depressed patients of middle age and over. It is less valuable in atypical depression, and in sensitive or hysterical personalities the ordinary mild side effects may cause bitter complaint. **1972** *Brit. Med. Jrnl.* 1 Apr. 45/2 These fairly substantial figures do not support the view that imipramine is liable to cause fetal abnormalities if given to pregnant women.

imitation. Add: **1. c.** *Psychol.* The adoption, whether conscious or not, during a learning process, of the behaviour or attitudes of some specific person or model.

[**1807** WORDSWORTH *Poems* II. 153 The little Actor cons another part..As if his whole vocation Were endless imitation.] **1895** J. M. BALDWIN *Mental Development* xii. 351 First..biological or organic imitation... Second: we pass to psychological, conscious, or cortical imitations. *Ibid.* 352 *Plastic Imitation.* This phrase is used to cover all cases of reaction or attitude, toward the doings, customs, opinions of others, which once represented more or less conscious adaptations..but which have become what is ordinarily called 'secondary automatic' and subconscious. **1899** H. C. WARREN tr. *Tarde's Social Laws* 42 Giving the word imitation the very wide meaning accorded to it..by Mr. Baldwin..one might regard imitation as the fundamental fact, not only of social and psychological life, but of organic life as well, where it would appear as the necessary condition of habit and heredity. **1903** E. C. PARSONS tr. *Tarde's Laws of Imitation* p. xiv, By imitation, I mean every impression of an inter-psychical photography..willed or not willed, passive or active. **1924** F. H. ALLPORT *Social Psychol.* x. 239 Before the rise of a really critical science of behavior the term 'imitation' enjoyed wide repute in social theory... Our treatment of imitation must therefore be mainly negative. **1946** D. MCCARTHY in L. Carmichael *Manual of Child Psychol.* 497/1 An interesting controversy..on the problem of the relationship between imitation and comprehension of language. **1968** *Internat. Encycl. Social Sci.* VII. 96/1 Learning by vicarious experience has historically been referred to as 'imitation'.

5. (Further examples.)

1840 H. REEVE tr. *A. de Tocqueville's Democracy in Amer.* III. I. xi. 100 Imitation-diamonds are now made which may be easily mistaken for real ones. **1871** *Post Office Directory Leather Trades* 66 (*heading*) Imitation leather makers... Kid leather dressers... Kid reviver makers. **1902** *Encycl. Brit.* XXVIII. 611/1 This is a very different thing from the imitation diamond so common in shop windows. Here the chemist has only succeeded in making a paste or glass..wanting the hardness and 'fire' of the real stone. **1904** GOODCHILD & TWENEY *Technol. & Sci. Dict.* 303/1 *Imitation parchment*, ordinary paper passed through a bath of sulphuric acid, which has the peculiar effect of 'toughening' the fibres. **1904** *Westm. Gaz.* 6 Oct. 4/2 Contempt of imitation jewels, imitation furs, imitation lace. *Ibid.*, A lovely coat of..imitation sealskin. **1916** E. POUND *Lustra* 53 The small child in the soiled-white imitation fur coat. **1929** D. H. LAWRENCE *Pansies* 124 Will the Proustian lot go next? And then our English imitation intelligentsia? **1937** E. J. LABARRE *Dict. Paper* 159/1 Imitation art paper is a highly finished printing [paper] prepared by the addition of a heavy percentage of china clay to the pulp and a water-finish. **1940** *Chambers's Techn. Dict.* 552/1 *Mock leno*, a fabric in which openwork effect is produced by a grouping of threads, which, however, do not cross, as they do in leno and gauze fabrics. Also called imitation gauze. **1954** *Paper Terminol.* (Spalding & Hodge) 32 *Imitation kraft*, a quality of wrapping paper made from unbleached sulphite, mechanical pulp and waste papers and coloured brown to give the appearance of Kraft. **1957** *Encycl. Brit.* IV. 775/2 Imitation gauze weaves.. are..largely utilized in the production of..embroidery cloths. *Ibid.* XIII. 850 A/2 The first feasible imitation leathers were based on patents issued in the United Kingdom in 1851. *Ibid.* XIX. 635/1 Imitation rum is produced by flavouring a neutral spirit..with high-ester Jamaican rum or with artificial essences. **1963** R. R. A. HIGHAM *Handbk. Papermaking* 282 *Imitation art*, paper which is highly finished by the action of super-calendering and water finishing and which contains a high percentage of china clay in the furnish.

imitativeness. (Later example.)

1973 *Daily Tel.* (Colour Suppl.) 9 Feb. 7/2 The imitativeness in these films is even more striking than their lack of artistry.

imma, var. *IMMY.

immanence. Add: (Further examples.) Also *attrib.*, as **immanence philosophy,** a theory evolved in Germany at the end of the nineteenth century that reality exists only through being immanent in conscious minds.

1901 BALDWIN *Dict. Philos. & Psychol.* I. 520/2 The immanence-philosophy (philosophy of the immediately given or science of pure experience) is the doctrine of a group of recent German thinkers. **1931** W. R. B. GIBSON tr. *Husserl's Ideas* II. ii. 133 Apart from perception, we find a variety of intentional experiences which essentially exclude the real immanence of their intentional objects. **1953** D. H. FREEMAN tr. *Dooyeweerd's New Critique Theoret. Thought* I. I. i. 112 It appears, that also modern phenomenology and Humanistic existentialism move in the paths of immanence-philosophy. **1970** D. M. LEVIN *Reason & Evidence in Husserl's Phenomenology* i. 16 If we suppose that the absence of spatial profiles could be a sufficient condition for immanence, then it would seem that we should have to consider mathematical entities and axioms as immanent objects.

immanental (imăne·ntăl), *a.* Delete *rare* and add later examples. Also, of or pertaining to philosophical immanence.

1897 W. M. URBAN *Hist. Princ. Suff. Reason* i. 8 The postulate of an immanental logic..becomes a permanent element. **1909** —— *Valuation* i. 9 The immanental reference..is a present state, referring, not beyond the present state, but to something more deeply implicit. **1920** A. S. PRINGLE-PATTISON *Idea of God* (ed. 2) 219 This lower pantheism..is common in the popular cults of the East, where the immanental unity of the divine is little more than the idea of a teeming nature. **1930** C. J. WRIGHT *Miracle in Hist.* 214 Theism can only abide with the recognition of the immanental activity of God in His universe. **1955** *Scottish Jrnl. Theol.* VIII. 88 This process is illustrated in religious which tend towards cosmic pantheism, impersonal fatalism, Platonic idealism, immanental piety, rigorous legalism, and ego-centric eudaemonism.

immanentism (i·mănĕntiz'm). [f. IMMANENT *a.* + -ISM.] Belief in immanence, esp. the immanence of the Deity. So **i·mmanentist** *a.*, holding or characterized by this belief; also as *sb.*, one who believes in the immanence of the Deity.

1907 *Hibbert Jrnl.* July 919 Immanentism..explains away rather than explains that irrational fact of experience which we call evil. **1916** C. C. MARTINDALE *Life Mgr. R. H. Benson* II. 392 To this Immanentist school would thus belong St. Teresa, Dame Juliana of Norwich, ..and Francis de Sales. **1918** M. D. PETRE *Modernism* x. 207 He has been charged with immanentism. **1930** *Times Lit. Suppl.* 14 Aug. 648/2 Mr. Wright stands for a modern, liberalizing and immanentist theology. **1931** *Ibid.* 22 Oct. 812/2 The pure phenomenology which resolves Being into Becoming by a sheer immanentism. **1945** *Mind* LIV. 275 Immanence and transcendence are logical complementaries, and..few thinkers can long afford to remain mere immanentists or mere transcendentists. **1952** *Mind* LXI. 102 Aristotle criticised Platonic doctrine, attacking the theory of Ideas from the 'immanentist' standpoint. **1965** *Rev. Eng. Stud.* XVI. 94 Mr. Miller speaks of the feeling that God is near at hand as God's 'immanence'... The Victorian age was notoriously a period in which immanentist theologies were fashionable.

immature, *a.* Add: **2. d.** *Ophthalm.* Of a progressive cataract: characterized by a marked but incomplete opacity, with the lens usually swollen and its superficial layers still largely transparent.

1850 B. E. BRODHURST *Of Crystalline Lens & Cataract* 57 The terms mature, and immature,..are well adapted to express the stage of progress at which any particular cataract may have arrived. **1904** L. W. FOX *Dis. Eye* xii. 311 The special difficulties..in removing a cataract before maturity are that parts of the cortex, clear at the time of operation, will remain adherent to the capsule of the lens, and later undergo the process of opacification... Some operators, however, operate on immature cataracts, washing out the tenacious material with a syringe. **1970** A. H. KEENEY *Ocular Exam.* ix. 143/2 Early (incipient or immature) cataracts cause changes in refraction..marked by increasing myopia at an age when refraction should either be stable or show increasing hyperopia.

e. Of a soil: not having a fully developed profile. Of a soil profile or its parts: not fully developed.

1926 C. F. MARBUT in Tansley & Chipp *Study of Vegetation* vii. 139 In every region there are hillside soils as well as alluvial and colluvial deposits in which the texture profile will not be well developed because of the short time during which the material has been subjected to the forces of soil development. Such soils are immature or have imperfectly developed profiles. **1927** N. M. COMBER *Introd. Sci. Study Soil* xiii. 139 Glinka divides all soils in the first instance into two groups:—(1) Immature or endodynamomorphic soils, in which the processes of formation have not had full play..(2) Mature or ektodynamomorphic soils, in which the processes of formation have had full play. **1963** D. W. & E. E. HUMPHRIES tr. *Termier's Erosion & Sedimentation* vi. 138 When erosion is greater than the rate of formation, the soil is immature. **1968** R. W. FAIRBRIDGE *Encycl. Geomorphol.* 273 These soils (lithosols) are immature and without soil profiles.

immediacy. Add: **4.** *pl.* Immediate needs.

1923 H. G. WELLS *Men Like Gods* III. iv. 288 The old things and the foul things, customs, delusions, habits,.. base immediacies, triumph over us!

immediate, *a.* Add: **3. b.** *immediate constituent* (Linguistics): a grammatical subdivision of a sentence, phrase, or word, which can sometimes be analysed into further such constituents; in the case of a word, so as to reveal its morphological structure. (Opp. **ultimate constituent*.)

1933 L. BLOOMFIELD *Lang.* xiii. 210 The principle of immediate constituents will lead us..to class a form like *gentlemanly* not as a compound word, but as a derived secondary word, since the immediate constituents are the bound form *-ly* and the underlying word *gentleman*. **1943** *Language* XIX. 79 In separating immediate constituents, one attempts to disturb as little as possible the relationship between the meaning of the parts of the combination and the meaning of the combination as a whole. **1958** A. A. HILL *Introd. Ling. Struct.* viii. 127 Immediate constituent analysis is the process of segmenting a complex construction by successive single cuts. **1961** R. B. LONG *Sentence & its Parts* 491 Immediate Constituents. This term is often used of what are here called simply components. **1963** F. G. LOUNSBURY in J. A. Fishman *Readings Sociol. of Lang.* (1968) 45 Linguistic analysis proceeds by the method of 'immediate constituents', i.e., by division of a larger unit into two immediate constituents... In the end, a systematic pursuit of a different set of policies in immediate-constituent division would, in fact, produce a different grammar of the same language. **1963** J. LYONS *Structural Semantics* ii. 14 It has sometimes been assumed that all the sentences of a particular language can be analysed syntactically in terms of the immediate-constituent, or phrase-structure model. **1964** R. H. ROBINS *Gen. Ling.* vi. 240 The processes of immediate constituent analysis.. by which the longest and most complex sentences can be reduced by analysis to successive expansions of one of a few simple basic sentence structures. **1967** F. P. DINNEEN *Introd. Gen. Ling.* ix. 263 In analyzing the sentence

Poor John ran away, Bloomfield found that it contains five morphemes: *poor, John, ran, a-*, and *way*. They are also the ultimate constituents of the sentence, but the immediate constituents are *Poor John* and *ran away*. **1971** P. GAENG *Introd. Princ. Lang.* v. 91 The sentence *The rebellious students walked to the dean's office* consists of two main parts—two immediate constituents—namely, *the rebellious students* and *walked to the dean's office.* Each part, in turn, consists of two parts, and each of these consists of two parts, until by cutting the sentence into smaller and smaller groupings, we reach the level of single words or morphemes, the ultimate constituents.

4. c. *immediate access store*: in a computer, a store whose access time is negligible compared with the time required for other operations.

1960 G. N. LANCE *Numerical Methods for High Speed Computers* i. 5 The memory..can usually be separated into distinct parts. Firstly, there is the high-speed or immediate access store. **1964** F. L. WESTWATER *Electronic Computers* iv. 79 Magnetic core stores are often referred to as immediate access stores (I.A.S.).

Immelmann (i·məlmæn). Also erron. **Immelman.** The name of F. *Immelmann* (1890–1916), a German fighter pilot, used alone or *attrib.* in *Immelmann turn*, to designate an evasive manœuvre in the air. Also as *v. intr.*, to execute this manœuvre.

1917 B. K. ADAMS *Amer. Spirit* (1918) 27 Next I tried the so-called Immelman turn. **1918** J. M. GRIDER *War Birds* (1927) 206 As I half rolled on top of him, he half rolled too and when I did an Immelman, he turned to the right and forced me on the outside arc and gave his observer a good shot at me. **1919** *Conquest* Dec. 68/1 One of the most useful stunts employed during the war was the 'Immelman turn', its name being that of the aviator who introduced it. In this manœuvre the machine rears up suddenly, turns sideways over the vertical, and emerges in the opposite direction. **1923** W. T. BLAKE *Flying* 43 *Immelmann turn.* This manœuvre is more commonly termed a 'half-roll' in England. **1934** V. M. YEATES *Winged Victory* III. viii. 254 He could turn better than the Pfalz, and felt he was winning the duel. After its tail, round and round. It straightened and he fired but it immelmanned away. He went after it, but it dived away all out. **1942** *R.A.F. Jrnl.* 27 June 18 Three outside snap rolls, a flick at 110 m.p.h., a stall off an Immelman and a power inverted spin. **1952** J. STEINBECK *East of Eden* xiv. 131 It..made Immelmann turns..and flew over the field upside down. **1967** *Boston Sunday Herald* 14 May (Comic Section), Wow! A loop th' loop! How about a Immelmann turn?

immensikoff (ime·nsikɒf). ? *Obs.* [See quot. 1896.] Jocular name for a heavy overcoat.

1870 D. J. KIRWAN *Palace & Hovel* xxxiv. 504 The chorus..of a popular street and music-hall song, which every one is now humming in London..as follows: '..I fancy I'm a Toff; From top to toe I really think I looks—Immensekoff.' **1889** *Pall Mall Gaz.* 25 Sept. 6/1 Heavy swells clad in Immensikoffs, which is the slang term, I believe, for those very fine and large fur robes affected by men about town. **1896** FARMER & HENLEY *Slang* IV. 3/1 *Immensikoff*, a fur-lined overcoat. From the burden of a song, 'The Shoreditch Toff', sung (*c* 1868) by the late Arthur Lloyd, who described himself as Immensikoff, and wore an upper garment heavily trimmed with fur. **1911** A. BENNETT *Hilda Lessways* I. vii. 70 His white muffler and large overcoat (which Dayson called an 'immensikoff').

immersal (imɜ·ɪsăl). *rare.* [f. IMMERSE *v.* + -AL.] = IMMERSION 2.

1901 GREENOUGH & KITTREDGE *Words* 98 Theological and philosophical studies are also pursued with vigor, and this means an immersal in Latin.

immersement. (Later example.)

1903 W. JAMES *Let.* 29 Dec. in R. B. Perry *Tht. & Char. W. James* (1935) II. 331 Your letter finds me in my nineteenth day of immersement, with grippe, still weak as a 'cat'.

immersion. Add: **3.** (Later example.)

1971 *Nature* 17 Dec. 406/1 None of the light curves showed any signs of an atmosphere on Io: in all cases the curves were flat just before and after occultation with abrupt changes in intensity at immersion and emersion.

5. (sense 1) **immersion foot**, a condition similar to trench foot caused by prolonged exposure of the feet to wet and usually cold conditions; **immersion heater**, a heater (usually electric) whose element may be immersed in the liquid to be heated; *esp.* one having a thermostatic control and designed to be fixed inside a domestic hot-water cylinder; **immersion suit**, a garment designed to give the wearer buoyancy when in the water and to provide insulation from the cold.

1941 *Lancet* 6 Dec. 690/1, I have never seen a case of immersion-foot, and for its adequate description we must await the reports of those whose war experience has brought them greater opportunities of observing it. **1967** *New Scientist* 25 May 449/3 In the Pacific during the second World War a warm water variety of immersion foot was common. **1969** J. McM. MENNELL *Foot Pain* v. 104 Immersion foot is similar to trench foot, but the wet environment seems to be more important than the cold; it may occur with relatively warm immersion. **1914** M. LANCASTER *Electr. Cooking, Heating, Cleaning* 208 The water in cylinder A..is heated by the immersion heater B. *Ibid.* 209 An additional immersion heater could be fitted, current for which would pass through the meter,..to be switched on if at any time the demand for hot water were much beyond the ordinary requirements. This auxiliary immersion heater could be controlled automatically by a thermostat..switch. **1935** *Jrnl. R. Aeronaut. Soc.* XXXIX. 455 The lubricating oil being kept at a temperature by immersion heaters in the oil tanks. **1936** *Archit. Rev.* LXXX. p. lxii/3 In many parts of the country..automatically controlled immersion heaters are being fitted as auxiliary heaters to fuel fired boilers. **1944** T. A. LONGMORE *Med. Photogr.* 140 The immersion heater is an electrically heated poker or element which is placed in the developer to raise its temperature and is withdrawn before the solution is put to its normal use. **1951** *Good Housek. Home Encycl.* (1956) 76/1 Portable immersion heaters and boiling rings. **1958** *House & Garden* Mar. 70/2 The Agamatic also provides hot water—in the summer an immersion heater takes over. **1963** *Times* 8 Jan. 5/5 Mrs. Henderson told him that she decided not to have a bath, left the immersion heater on, and went to bed. **1951** R. H. DAVIS *Deep Diving & Submarine Operations* (ed. 5) I. xiv. 275 Immersion suits can be worn..to protect the escaper from the cold, and..to keep him afloat. **1968** *New Scientist* 15 Feb. 348/1 The immersion suit consists essentially of a double-layer rubber suit which can be inflated... Not only does this provide flotation but also excellent insulation.

immigrant, *sb.* (Later *attrib.* examples.)

1969 *Times* 18 July 4/8 Wolverhampton's Grove School..was described as the '90 per cent immigrant school'. *Ibid.*, There was some criticism..at this high proportion of immigrant children. **1971** *Economist* 12 June 31/2 Those [*sc.* children] born in England to immigrant parents cease to be classified as immigrant schoolchildren after their parents have been here 10 years, while those born overseas remain within the category no matter how long they have been in England. **1973** *Times* 9 Nov. 2/4 Allowance must be made for immigrant children to adjust to a new social and educational environment.

immigration. Add: Also *attrib.*

1872 *Atlantic Monthly* Apr. 456/1 Natives of Europe.. not included in the immigration reports [etc.]. **1879** *Bradstreet's* 10 Dec. 2/3 It is our idea that immigration societies are doing us no good. **1880** D. M. GORDON *Mountain & Prairie* 298 Such companies, spurred into activity by the prospect of profitable land sales, will probably be more zealous than Government immigration agents. **1890** *Stock Grower & Farmer* 25 Jan. 7/2 Col. Edward Haren, of the immigration department of the Santa Fe, is in the city on his return from Albuquerque. *Ibid.* 22 Feb. 3/2 This territory has never had an immigration 'boom'. **1904** F. BRADSHAW *Alien Immigration* 121 When the alien has passed the Immigration Department his troubles are not yet over. **1905** *Act* 5 *Edw. VII* c. 13 § 1 An immigrant shall not be landed in the United Kingdom from an immigrant ship except at a port at which there is an immigration officer appointed under this Act. **1906** *Daily Chron.* 21 May 1/7 Mr. Seddon, Premier of New Zealand, has challenged the right of the British Government to interfere with Australasian immigration legislation. **1907** *Westm. Gaz.* 30 Jan. 8/2 The Premier [of Australia] has..liberalised the immigration regulations. **1922** *Encycl. Brit.* XXXII. 854/1 By the Immigration Act passed in 1921 the number of immigrants admitted from any one country in the year July 1 1921 to June 20 1922, was restricted to 3% of the persons of that nationality resident in the United States in 1910. **1926** *Ibid.* III. 21/1 Since the opening of immigration [into Palestine] with the promulgation of the Immigration Ordinance (1920) [etc.]. **1949** KOESTLER *Promise & Fulfilment* iv. 40 It is conceivable that they could have achieved sufficient pressure at least to mitigate the immigration bar of 1939. *Ibid.* vi. 56 Except the small number of those who already held pre-war immigration certificates. *Ibid.* 60 The majority..were Zionists..who at the eve of the war had been waiting for their turn on the immigration quota. **1969** *Times* 19 July 8/3 The controversy over Britain's immigration policy. **1971** 'D. HALLIDAY' *Dolly & Doctor Bird* ii. 25 He carried a Turkish passport through Immigration Controls. **1973** P. GEDDES *Ottawa Allegation* v. 63 The immigration officer..took his time over Fender's passport.

absol., the immigration checks or authorities. *colloq.*

1966 F. HOYLE *Oct. First* i. 5 We got into London airport more or less on time. Quickly we were into the reception hall and through immigration. **1972** J. POTTER *Going West* 17 He produced his passport and transit card for immigration.

2. *collect.* The body of immigrants. *U.S.*

1852 H. STANSBURY *Exped. Valley Gt. Salt Lake* 126 In the autumn, another large immigration arrived under the president, Brigham Young, which materially added to the strength of the colony. **1857** *Trans. Illinois Agric. Soc.* II. 365 The immigration was generally a moral, correct people. **1948** *Sat. Rev.* (U.S.) 17 July 20/1 A far vaster immigration..began pouring through the city portals.

immiscible, *a.* Add: Usu. *spec.* of a liquid: incapable of forming a true solution *with* or *in* another liquid. (Later examples.)

1934 A. J. MEE *Physical Chem.* x. 436 (*heading*) Vapour pressure of a mixture of immiscible liquids. **1964** D. F. EGGERS et al. *Physical Chem.* viii. 276 Steam distillation is frequently used to carry over organic substances immiscible in water.

immiserization (imi:zərəizēⁱ·ʃən). Also (slightly earlier) **immiseration.** [f. IM-[1] + MISER(ABLE *a.* + -IZATION; tr. G. *verelendung.*] The act of making or becoming progressively more miserable; pauperization, impoverishment. So **immi:serifica·tion**, in the same sense; **immi·serize** *v. trans.*, to impoverish.

1942 J. A. SCHUMPETER *Capitalism, Socialism & Democracy* (1943) iii. 22 The glowing indictment of 'exploitation' and 'immiserization'. **1948** R. STRAUSZ-HUPÉ in *Philos. of Sci.* X. 270 Fifty years ago the Revisionists pointed out the fallacies of Marx's theory of the immiseration of the proletariat. **1971** J. VAIZEY *Social Democracy* 37 The general trend of real wages, after 1850, was upwards, and the general immiserisation of the proletariat was not brought about. *Ibid.* 48 The international industrial system had been created; the proletariat was not immiserised; and the modern nation-state had been created. **1975** D. MCLELLAN *Marx* iii. 44 Marx was thinking in terms of trends and projected into the future tendencies that he saw in contemporary society. One of the most important of these trends was the immiserization of the proletariat. Marx was usually chary of claiming that the proletariat would become immiserized in any absolute sense.

immittance (imi·tăns). *Electr.* [f. IM(PEDANCE + (AD)MITTANCE.] Admittance or its reciprocal, impedance: used when it is desired to refer to both quantities without making a distinction between them.

1957 D. WOODS in *Proc. Inst. Electr. Engin.* CIV. C. 507/2 Immittance is the basic parameter of any a.c. measuring system for electrical quantities. [*Note*] Immittance is used to convey the general idea of impedance or admittance. **1960** CLEMENT & JOHNSON *Electr. Engin. Sci.* xi. 341 Each element *R*, *L*, and *C* of a network has an immittance to sinusoidal current. **1969** P. M. CHIRLIAN *Basic Network Theory* viii. 496 We can eventually calculate the input current $\mathbf{I}_1(s)$. This will be expressed as $\mathbf{V}_2(s)$ times some function of the immittances of the ladder network.

immobilism (imōᵘ·biliz'm). [ad. F. *immobilisme* (also used).] A policy or attitude of extreme conservatism or opposition to progress.

1949 *Time* 17 Oct. 34 Successful 'immobilism' (patient compromise, appeasement, moderation). **1955** *Times* 5 May 10/7 The Radicals..wished to remain a party of the left; social and political *immobilisme* (opposition to progress) was the best ally of Communism. *Ibid.* 24 Aug. 6/1 There could be no question of allowing themselves to be swayed by a question of superstition or of fetishism, which would be contrary to national dignity. But in any case, M. Faure added, it had been clearly agreed that they would not adopt a policy of immobilism. **1959** *Economist* 21 Feb. 662/2 This outright *immobilisme* [among farmers] condemns itself. **1961** *Encounter* XVII. II. 21 The notorious *immobilisme* of French society. **1967** *Economist* 8 Apr. 110/2 Mr Callaghan will have made a sad present to industrial immobilism if he throws any such opportunity for reducing surtax away.

immobilize, *v.* Add: **2.** *Soil Sci.* and *Bot.* To convert (a plant nutrient) from a form in which it can be utilized by a plant to one in which it cannot; to assimilate and thereby render unavailable to (other) plants. Also *absol.*

1951 *Proc. Soil Sci. Soc. Amer.* XV. 168/2 Fertilizer and nonfertilizer nitrogen must have been absorbed and immobilized in proportion to their relative available concentrations in the soil. **1952** L. M. THOMPSON *Soils & Soil Fertility* ix. 135 If there is a deficit of nitrogen in the added organic matter, the microbes will immobilize ammonia and nitrates from the soil. **1958** *U.S. Dept. Agric. Yearbk.* 1957 760/1 The addition of fresh straw or sawdust to the soil may greatly increase the number of bacteria. These remove available nitrogen and phosphorus from the soil and immobilize them within their cells. **1967** FRIED & BROESHART *Soil–Plant Syst.* vii. 240 Soluble phosphates that are applied to the soil are generally immobilized. **1971** *Nature* 9 Apr. 403/1 *Becium homblei*..grows on soils rich in copper, and it has been shown to accumulate heavy metals. Other plants also have this characteristic, and their ability to immobilize in insoluble form..has been noted.

immobilization (further examples, corresponding to the foregoing sense of the vb.).

1951 *Proc. Soil Sci. Soc. Amer.* XV. 166/2 Immobilization is here used to denote the process of conversion of inorganic nitrogen to organic combinations either through plant uptake or through microbial absorption. **1952** L. M. THOMPSON *Soils & Soil Fertility* ix. 132 Either plants or microorganisms may convert NH_4^+ or NO_3^- to organic form (chiefly protein). The conversion of inorganic compounds to organic form is called immobilization. **1956** *Proc. Soil Sci. Soc. Amer.* XX. 217/2 The tie-up (immobilization) or release (mineralization) of soil nitrogen depends very much on the chemical composition of the material undergoing decomposition. **1970** *Analytical Biochem.* XXXIII. 341 The physical entrapment of enzymes in insoluble matrices seems to provide a general method of immobilization.

immobilized (imōᵘ·biləizd), *ppl. a.* [f. IMMOBILIZE *v.* + -ED[1].] Rendered immobile or stationary.

1923 *Edin. Rev.* Jan. 179 The left and centre of the enemy was held... It was now possible to attempt a decisive attack on an immobilised enemy.

immoralism (imɒ·răliz'm). [ad. G. *immoralismus* (Nietzsche), f. IMMORAL *a.* + -ISM.] The reverse or negation of moralism; a system of thought or practice which rejects moral law.

1907 *Athenæum* 23 Mar. 348/1 The system..of Nietzsche, with all its blasphemy and immoralism. **1918** *Hibbert Jrnl.* Apr. 378 The sickly social idealism.. which treated the most healthy immorality so much more harshly than it treated the most unhealthy immoralism. **1929** B. H. STREETER *Primitive Church* v. 179 The theoretic basis of Gnostic immoralism was a distinction between the ultimate Good God and the more or less evil Creator of the material universe. **1973** E. R. DODDS *Anc. Concept*

of Progress 105 Nietzsche himself recognized the affiliation of his immoralism to the sophistic movement.

immortable (imǭ·ɹtăb'l), *a.* [f. IMMORT(AL *a.* + -ABLE.] Having the capacity to live after death. So **immortabi·lity.**

1922 J. Y. SIMPSON *Man & Attainment of Immortality* xiii. 275 The contention that eternal life..is morally conditioned, that man, in short, is immortable rather than immortal. **1930** S. D. MCCONNELL (*title*) Immortability. An Old Man's Conclusions. **1950** S. EDDY *You will survive after Death* 3 We may have at least..'immortability'—a fitness in the quality of human personality for survival.

immortal, *a.* **2. b.** (Later examples.)

1928 E. C. WEBSTER *Pot Holes* 3, I am as fond of Burns as any, and have read a good deal of his poetry,..but I am not one of those who believe that the Immortal Memory can only be preserved by a yearly pickling in alcohol. **1959** *Times* 17 Apr. 15/3 His record of devotion to the 'Immortal Memory'—a toast which he had proposed all over Scotland and England—was typical of this special cult which the wandering Scot has carried all over the globe. **1973** *Listener* 15 Mar. 344/2 The Johnson celebration..the toast to 'the immortal memory'.

immortelle. Add: (Further examples.) Also *attrib.* and *Comb.*, *transf.*, and *fig.*

1883 'MARK TWAIN' *Life on Mississippi* xlii. 431 A milder form of sorrow finds its inexpensive and lasting remembrancer in the coarse and ugly but indestructible 'immortelle'—which is a wreath or cross or some such emblem, made of rosettes of black linen, with sometimes a yellow rosette at the conjunction of the cross's bars,—kind of sorrowful breastpin, so to say. **1890** A. MARTIN *Home Life Ostrich Farm* i. 21 Pink and white *immortelles*, gladioli, ixias, and irises of all kinds abound. **1929** D. H. LAWRENCE *Pansies* 6 Anyhow I offer a bunch of pansies, not a wreath of *immortelles*. I don't want everlasting flowers. **1936** *Times Lit. Suppl.* 21 Nov. 935/1 Poor little immortelles surviving from that old gorgeous efflorescence of linguistic misuse. **1960** R. G. HAGGAR *Conc. Encycl. Cont. Pott. & Porc.* 67/2 *Blaublümchenmuster*, (German) blue flower pattern: 'aster' or 'immortelle' pattern. *Ibid.* 239/2 Early [Klösterle] wares were decorated in blue with popular Meissen 'Immortelle' and 'bird on rock' designs. **1963** V. NABOKOV *Gift* iii. 153 Even if he had put on the light the immortelle-like yellowness of daytime electricity would have been no help at all. **1968** E. LOVELACE *Schoolmaster* i. 7 The immortelle holds its scarlet blossoms still. **1970** *New Yorker* 22 Aug. 38/3 The old man was himself like a trophy of immortelles. **1971** E. M. ROACH in J. Figueroa *Caribbean Voices* I. 22 The giant immortelles Splash fire on the hills.

immram (i·mram). Also **imram.** Pl. **im(m)rama.** [ad. O.Ir. *imram* (mod.Ir. *iomramh*), f. *imm-rá* to row around.] Any of the stories of fabulous sea voyages written in Ireland in the seventh and eighth centuries. Also *attrib.*

1895 A. NUTT in K. Meyer *Voy. of Bran* iv. 161 The *imrama* literature has been investigated by Professor Zimmer with all his wonted acuteness. **1917** *Mod. Philology* XV. 450 The *imram* is a sea-voyage tale in which a hero, accompanied by a few companions, wanders about from island to island, meets Otherworld wonders everywhere, and finally returns to his native land. **1948** M. DILLON *Early Irish Lit.* vi. 124 Of the seven immrama mentioned in the two lists of sagas, only three have come down to us. **1951** G. TURVILLE-PETRE *Heroic Age of Scandinavia* ix. 94 It is by no means improbable that the *Immrama* contain distorted descriptions of scenes, which the hermits had witnessed on their travels. **1962** *Guardian* 14 Dec. 7/4 The suggested relation between 'Gulliver's Travels' and the Early Irish *immram.* **1964** G. JONES *Norse Atlantic Saga* i. 7 The best known of the Irish *Imrama*..records the travels of St. Brendan. **1967** DILLON & CHADWICK *Celtic Realms* viii. 200 The briefer account of Brendan's voyage is included in the *Vita*,..and we thus possess two apparently independent accounts of the saint's *immram.*

immune, *a.* (*sb.*). Add: **2. a.** Also *transf.* and *fig.*, wholly protected *from* something injurious or distasteful; not susceptible or responsive *to* something.

1898 MERCIER in *Brit. Med. Jrnl.* 3 Sept. 586/1 There is for every insane person a certain sphere of conduct for which he ought to be entirely immune from punishment. **1900** *Daily News* 5 July 3/2 A man whose achievements should render him immune from all mud throwing. **1922** D. H. LAWRENCE *England, my England* 235 Among the graves, she felt immune from the world. **1944** A. HOLMES *Princ. Physical Geol.* xvii. 367 No place can be regarded as permanently immune from shocks. **1947** *Jrnl. R. Aeronaut. Soc.* LI. 293 Ice guards..proved of considerable value during the war when used on aircraft which themselves were not completely immune from icing. **1955** *Sci. Amer.* June 96/3 The magnetic-core memory..is relatively immune to unwanted electrical disturbances. **1973** *Human World* Feb. 8 The vision of the future that is to carry them through is the high-rise block of flats, the motorway... And if the 'underprivileged' prove immune to sense and prosperity? Well, thinks Mr Maddox, they can't. **1973** *Sci. Amer.* Feb. 83/1 The system is extremely complicated and therefore would be rather expensive and not as reliable or immune to functional failure as one would like. **1973** *Daily Tel.* 7 Mar. 18 Orwell was a bad poet and immune to the arts (though a most likeable man). **1974** *Ibid.* 16 Feb. 9/1 The white pawns are immune from Black's bishop.

b. as *sb.* Substitute for def.: An immune individual. (Further examples.)

1909 *Rep. Brit. Assoc. Adv. Sci.* 764 All extracted immunes [*sc.* wheat plants immune to yellow rust] should breed true to this feature. **1951** WHITBY & HYNES *Med. Bacteriol.* (ed. 5) viii. 105 After an epidemic the community remains free from that disease until the proportion of immunes declines and the density of susceptibles is once more raised to pre-epidemic level.

3. *Med.* (Only in *attrib.* use.) Relating to immunity or its development; serving to bring immunity about.

1907 MUIR & RITCHIE *Man. Bacteriol.* (ed. 4) xix. 484 Various substances..remove the opsonic property from a normal serum, while they have no effect on an immune-opsonin. **1928** L. E. H. WHITBY *Med. Bacteriol.* ii. 19 The immune substances produced by the animal are termed antibodies. **1946** K. LANDSTEINER *Specificity Serological Reactions* (rev. ed.) i. 4 The immune antibodies ..react as a rule only with the antigens that were used for immunizing and with closely similar ones. **1953** S. RAFFEL *Immunity* iv. 40 (*heading*) Mechanisms of acquired immunity. Antibody as a specific immune mechanism. **1969** *Times* 24 Mar. 4/7 Antilymphocytic serum.. combats the particular immune defence mechanism responsible for rejecting tissue grafts.

b. Specific collocations: *immune body* = *ANTIBODY; *immune globulin,* (*a*) a preparation containing antibodies obtained from normal individuals or from ones immunized against a specific disease, and suitable for use as an antiserum; (*b*) = *IMMUNOGLOBULIN; *immune response,* the reaction of the body to the introduction into it of an antigen; *immune serum,* serum which contains antibodies, esp. one which can confer immunity to the corresponding antigen on a recipient; = *ANTI-SERUM b.

1899 MUIR & RITCHIE *Man. Bacteriol.* (ed. 2) xix. 485 Ehrlich has recently applied his theory of antitoxines to the lysogenic action of sera towards bacteria and red corpuscles... His observations show that the body specially developed in the blood of the animal treated—the 'immune-body', enters into firm combination with the red corpuscles. **1900** P. EHRLICH in *Proc. R. Soc.* LXVI. 443, I have sought..to make clear the mechanism concerned in the action of these two components—the stable, which may be designated 'immune body', and the unstable, which may be designated 'complement'—which, acting together, effect the solution of the red blood corpuscles. **1937** Immune body [see *AMBOCEPTOR]. **1971** HERBERT & WILKINSON *Dict. Immunol.* 91 *Immune body*, obsolete synonym for antibody. **1935** *Jrnl. Amer. Med. Assoc.* 17 Aug. 493/1 The use of Immune Globulin (Human) in the modification of measles has been known for a considerable period. **1948** H. J. PARISH *Bacterial & Virus Dis.* ix. 67 Placental extract or 'human immune globulin' is an extract of placental globulins and has approximately the same potency as adult serum. **1958** —— *Antisera, Toxoids, Vaccines & Tuberculins* (ed. 4) ix. 78 Large pools of adult plasma normally contain a variety of protective antibodies..located mainly in the gamma fraction of the globulin or, as it is sometimes called, the immune globulin. **1966** *Lancet* 24 Dec. 1403/2 A technique of immunodiffusion of serum through agar gave a sensitive and fairly accurate measure of the concentrations of the three main classes of immune globulins—γ G, γ M, and γ A. **1953** *Jrnl. Nat. Cancer Inst.* XIV. 755 The over-all pattern presented is one of interference with an immune response of the host. **1963** GELL & COOMBS *Clin. Aspects Immunol.* i. 5 Before we can understand much about 'immune' responses and their results, protective or damaging, on the host, we need to know more about the separation of antibody responses from the 'cellular' responses which result in delayed (non-antibody dependent) sensitivity. **1964** *New Scientist* 1 Oct. 10/2 The 'immune response' is an important feature of a vertebrate animal's defence mechanism. **1902** R. T. HEWLETT *Man. Bacteriol.* (ed. 2) v. 140 For the lysis of a given quantity of bacteria a certain amount of immune serum is necessary. **1946** K. LANDSTEINER *Specificity Serological Reactions* (rev. ed.) i. 7 Sera that contain antibodies as the result of the injection of antigens are called 'immune sera' (antisera). **1955** *Sci. Amer.* Mar. 65/2 In experimental work, antibody, or what is known as immune serum, is produced by injecting virus into an animal. **1970** GOLD & PEACOCK *Basic Immunol.* vii. 247 Chiefly noted in man in connexion with immune serum therapy, serum sickness has also been widely studied as an experimental disease in laboratory animals.

immu·ne, *v. rare.* [f. the adj.] *trans.* To render immune.

1849 G. S. FABER *Let.* 16 May in R. Chapman *Father Faber* (1961) xi. 220, I think if a little experience does not immune me to the row..I *must* go to the back. **1928** HARDY *Coll. Poems* 431 The vision That immuned me from the chillings of misprision.

immunize, *v.* Add: **2.** *intr.* Of an organism or substance, regarded as an antigen: to produce immunity in an individual into which it is introduced.

1942 *Jrnl. Bacteriol.* XLIII. 405 Strains we have classified as weakly antigenic (in so far as they fail to immunize significantly against homologous virus injected intracerebrally). **1951** WHITBY & HYNES *Med. Bacteriol.* (ed. 5) viii. 108 It is possible to kill bacteria without so altering their antigenic structure that they no longer immunize against living bacteria. **1973** *Nature* 30 Mar. 330/1 The ability of lactating mammary gland to immunize against D1 and D2 mammary tumour growth.

immunizer (i·miunəizəɹ). [f. IMMUNIZE *v.* + -ER[1].] That which renders immune; *occas.*, one who uses or advocates immunization.

1927 *Daily Express* 18 June 9/2 'Immuniser' for Cancer. ..It may well be that chemical and medical research will discover this natural immuniser, which will strengthen resistance to cancer in all individuals. **1931** *Amer. Jrnl. Cancer* XV. 627 Formalin..is a less potent immuniser than antiserum. *Ibid.*, No single mode of treatment is entirely satisfactory both as a 'destroyer' and as an 'immuniser'. **1950** G. B. SHAW *Farfetched Fables* 90 Lying advertisements of panaceas, prophylactics, elixirs, immunizers, vaccines, antitoxins, vitamins, and professedly hygienic foods. *Ibid.*, They are in fact exalting every laboratory vivisector and quack immunizer above Jesus and St James.

immuno- (imiŭ·no, i·miuno), used as comb. form of IMMUNE *a.*, IMMUNITY, *IMMUNOLOGY, and related words. (In the following words secondary stresses are in general left unmarked, since they vary in the manner indicated above.)

immuno-assay (imiŭnoˌæ·se), a bio-assay performed by means of immunological methods; **immunobio·logy** = *IMMUNOLOGY (see quot. 1970); so **immunobiolo·gic, -biolo·gical** *adjs.*; **immunoche·mistry,** chemistry as applied to immunology; the chemistry of immunological phenomena; so **immunoche·mical** *a.*, of or pertaining to immunochemistry; using the methods of immunochemistry; **immunoche·mically** *adv.*; **immunoche·mist,** a student of or expert in immunochemistry; **immunodiffu·sion,** diffusion of immunologically active substances; a technique for investigating antigens and antibodies by observing any precipitates that may form when initially separate portions of them are allowed to intermingle by diffusion through a gelatinous or other medium; **immuno-ele:ctrophore·sis,** a technique for characterizing the proteins in a mixture (such as serum) by first separating them by electrophoresis and then subjecting them to immunodiffusion (in the same or a different medium); so **immuno-ele:ctrophore·tic** *a.*, **-phore·tically** *adv.*; **immunofluore·scence,** a method of demonstrating antibodies (or antigens) in microscopic preparations by introducing corresponding antigens (or antibodies) labelled with a fluorescent dye; fluorescence emitted by such preparations; so **immunofluore·scent** *a.*, of, pertaining to, or involving this method; **immunogene·tic** *a.*, of or pertaining to immunogenetics; so **immunogene·tically** *adv.*; **immunogene·tics,** the related study of immunology and genetics, either as a branch of genetics in which immunological methods and knowledge are employed, or as the study of the genetic aspects of immunological phenomena and substances; **immunohæmato·logy** (*U.S.* **-hematology**), the immunology of the blood; so **immunohæmatolo·gic, -lo·gical** *adjs.*; **immunopatho·logist,** a student of or expert in immunopathology; **immunopatho·logy,** the pathology of the immune response; the study of immunological phenomena and substances in relation to pathology; hence **immunopatholo·gic, -lo·gical** *adjs.*; **immunoprophyla·xis,** the prevention of disease by immunization; so **immunoprophyla·ctic** *a.*, of or pertaining to immunoprophylaxis; *sb.*, an agent that prevents (a) disease by producing immunity; **immunosuppre·ssant,** an agent which has an immunosuppressive effect; also *attrib.*; **immunosuppre·ssed** *a.*, (of an individual) rendered unable to react immunologically to an antigen; **immunosuppre·ssion,** the suppression of the immune response of an organism; **immunosuppre·ssive** *a.*, suppressing the immune response of an organism; **immunosympathe·ctomy** [*-ECTOMY, used *loosely*], the destruction of many of the sympathetic ganglia of a new-born animal by injection of an antiserum for the appropriate nerve growth-factor; so **immunosympathe·ctomized** *ppl. a.*, treated in this way; **immunothe·rapy,** treatment of disease by the production of immunity (whether by the introduction into the individual of appropriate antibodies, etc., or by the stimulation in it of an immune response); **immunotransfu·sion,** the transfusion of blood which has been previously immunized against the recipient's infection.

1959 *Nature* 21 Nov. 1648/2 We have previously reported on the immuno-assay of beef insulin. **1969** R. HALL et al. *Fund. Clin. Endocrinol.* xiv. 258/1 The hormone that reacts with anti-insulin serum in the immunoassay technique for insulin accounts for only a

small part of the total ILA in plasma. **1930** *Jrnl. Amer. Med. Assoc.* 12 Apr. 1188/2 [*tr. a Finnish title*] Immunobiologic conditions in tuberculosis. **1959** *Biol. Abstr.* XXXIII. 1822/1 A few statements on the reflex mechanism of immunobiological processes. **1966** E. D. Day *Found. Immunochem.* vii. 87 One definition [of *hapten*] is immunobiological. **1957** (*title*) Journal of microbiology, epidemiology and immunobiology. **1970** Alexander & Good *Immunobiol. for Surgeons* i. 1 In its older and classical meaning, it [*sc.* immunology] was the study of immunity, the processes by which organisms defend themselves against infection... More recently, cellular immunity has been recognized as being important in processes which have to do with recognition phenomena, self-characterization, growth and development, heredity, aging, cancer, and transplantation. With this expansion, immunology has exceeded the limits of its original meaning, and immunobiology has become a preferable term for this expanding field. **1925** C. H. Browning *Immunochem. Stud.* 15 The immunochemical properties of serum. **1948** Kabat & Mayer *Exper. Immunochem.* i. 5 The application of immunochemical methods has extended far beyond the study of immunity to disease and has become a valuable tool in the characterization of proteins and polysaccharides. **1960** *Jrnl. Immunol.* LXXXV. 37 (*heading*) Immunochemical studies of human serum Rh agglutinins. **1961** Webster, Immunochemically. **1966** *Lancet* 31 Dec. 1435/1 In certain human antiserums, dog insulin is immunochemically distinguishable from pork insulin although both have the same aminoacid sequence. **1948** M. Heidelberger in Kabat & Mayer *Exper. Immunochem.* p. vi, The immunochemist is in possession of a store of marked molecules, antigens and antibodies, each as distinctively marked with respect to the other as if it contained a radioactive tracer element. **1970** *Nature* 18 July 229/2 Immunochemists from ten laboratories cross matched almost seventy antibodies to the proteins of the vertebrate eye lens when an international working party on crystallin immunochemistry met in..Edinburgh University. **1971** Nossal & Ada *Antigens, Lymphoid Cells, & Immune Response* i. 2 The key discoveries about lymphocytes and antibody-producing cells..have been less fully digested by immunochemists. **1907** S. Arrhenius *Immunochem.* p. vii, I have given to these lectures the title 'Immuno-chemistry', and wish with this word to indicate that the chemical reactions of the substances that are produced by the injection of foreign substances into the blood of animals, *i.e.* by immunisation, are under discussion in these pages. **1956** *Nature* 3 Mar. 426/2 Virulent and protective avirulent strains have been studied comparatively by the methods of immunology, immunochemistry and biochemistry. **1970** Immunochemistry [see *immunochemist* above]. **1959** *Nature* 30 May 1512 (*heading*) Cellulose acetate as a medium for immunodiffusion. **1966** *Lancet* 24 Dec. 1403/2 A technique of immunodiffusion of serum through agar gave a sensitive and fairly accurate measure of the concentrations of the three main classes of immune globulins. **1971** *Nature* 8 Jan. 119/2 Antibody studies were made using immunodiffusion techniques set up with cerumen suspensions and with IgA and IgG antibody. The IgA or IgG antibody was then placed in the centre well; diffusion was allowed to take place..and precipitin lines were recorded. **1958** *Federation Proc.* XVII. 530/2 (*heading*) Starch gel immunoelectrophoresis. **1964** G. H. Haggis et al. *Introd. Molecular Biol.* ii. 25 (*caption*) The identification of protein fractions present in human plasma using immunoelectrophoresis. **1968** H. Harris *Nucleus & Cytoplasm* v. 104 The antigens..were isolated as antigen-antibody complexes by immuno-electrophoresis. **1955** Williams & Grabar in *Jrnl. Immunol.* LXXIV. 158 (*heading*) Immunoelectrophoretic studies on serum proteins. **1970** J. T. Barrett *Textbk. Immunol.* v. 114 A valuable modification of gel precipitation tests is the immunoelectrophoretic procedure of Grabar and Williams. **1961** A. J. Crowle *Immunodiffusion* iv. 101 According to Ryback (1959), plasmin exists immunoelectrophoretically as two zones in the beta region. **1960** *Jrnl. Biophysical & Biochem. Cytol.* VII. 43 (*heading*) Observations of measles virus infection of cultured human cells. I. A study of development and spread of virus antigen by means of immunofluorescence. **1961** *Lancet* 16 Sept. 663/2 The nuclear immunofluorescence obtained with heated and unheated sera was compared. **1971** tr. *K. Federlin's Immunopath. Insulin* 32 In direct immunofluorescence, the tissue is first covered with a layer of labelled antibody or antigen, then freed from the uncombined agent by several washings, and finally mounted with a coverslip. **1959** *Proc. Soc. Exper. Biol. & Med.* CI. 289 (*heading*) Quantitative determination of infectious units of measles virus by counts of immunofluorescent foci. *Ibid.* 290/2 The cells were..prepared for immunofluorescent microscopy. **1970** Harris & Sinkovics *Immunol. Malignant Dis.* i. 37 Other immunofluorescent studies by Morton have demonstrated antibodies to osteosarcoma in the serum of patients with this tumor. **1936** Irwin & Cole in *Jrnl. Exper. Zool.* LXXIII. 85 (*heading*) Immunogenetic studies of species and of species hybrids in doves. **1970** W. H. Hildemann *Immunogenetics* iii. 86 The newest area in which immunogenetic characterization of microorganisms has provided substantial insights involves the many viruses capable of inducing cancer. *Ibid.* vii. 224 (*heading*) Immunogenetic concepts of cancer and aging. **1971** *Nature* 12 Nov. 103/1 The paternal strains, A/J and A2G respectively, are immunogenetically identical at the major H-2 histocompatibility locus. **1947** M. R. Irwin in *Adv. Genetics* I. 133 The term 'immunogenetics' was proposed by the author some years ago to designate studies in which the technics of both genetics and immunology were employed jointly... The term indicates the study of genetic characters as yet only detectable by immunological reactions. **1965** P. L. Carpenter *Immunol. & Serol.* (ed. 2) ix. 265 The use of serologic techniques in genetics is expanding. Genes control the formation of antigenic substances, so detection of antigens provides an objective and useful tool for study of genes. The term immunogenetics is applied to this field of research. **1971** J. A. Bellanti *Immunol.* iii. 60 Immunogenetics includes all those processes concerned in the immune response which may have a genetic basis. In the past, the term has been largely restricted to mean genetic markers on immunoglobulin polypeptide chains. **1954** *Amer. Jrnl. Clin. Path.* XXIV. 1333 It is just 50 years ago that the first immunohematologic test was introduced by Donath and Landsteiner. **1959** H. S. Lawrence *Cellular & Humoral Aspects Hypersensitive States* v. 133 (*heading*) Immunohematologic disease. **1967** *Biol. Abstr.* XLVIII. 172/2 (*heading*) Significance of immunohematological methods of investigation. **1950** *Brit. Med. Jrnl.* 16 Sept. 673/1 (*heading*) Immuno-haematology. **1954** *Amer. Jrnl. Clin. Path.* XXIV. 1334 Serologic technics applied to the study of diseases of blood added up to what is called immunohematology, a separate and distinct subdivision of hematology... Immunohematology encompasses diseases of blood of which the causes, the pathogenesis, or the clinical manifestations have been shown to be determined by an antigen–antibody reaction. **1972** Immunohematology [see *isoagglutinogen* s.v. *iso-]. **1960** *Federation Proc.* XIX. 208/2 (*heading*) An immunopathologic study of avian nephrotoxic nephritis in the rabbit. **1959** Grabar & Miescher *Immunopath.* 17 Attention has been focussed on the immunopathological consequences of leucocyte isoantigens. *Ibid.* 41 Much data of interest to immunopathologists. **1970** *Nature* 19 Sept. 1196/2 Studies on the amino-terminal sequences of a number of myeloma and pathological immunoglobulin chains also evoked much interest among the immunopathologists. **1959** Grabar & Miescher *Immunopath.* 13 Immunopathology presumably covers all immune phenomena associated with general pathology—the majority of the reactions of course being physiogenic and beneficial to the host—others again being inconsequential or even harmful. **1971** K. Federlin (*title*) Immunopathology of insulin. **1960** *Biol. Abstr.* XXXV. 168/2 (*heading*) Poliomyelitis: the present status of some epidemiological and immunoprophylactic problems. **1964** D. F. Gray *Immunol.* x. 95 Immuno-prophylactic procedures include not only the long-term protection afforded by active immunization against a number of the epidemic and endemic diseases to which urban man is prone, but also short-term passive protection against immediately anticipated infection. **1972** *Lancet* 21 Oct. 876/1 Administration of B.C.G. to mice who no longer have palpable disease does not prolong their life... This is true whether or not B.C.G. had been given as an immunoprophylactic. **1964** *Canad. Jrnl. Public Health* LIII. 346 (*heading*) Advances in the immunoprophylaxis of smallpox. *Ibid.*, In the last twenty years progress in this field [*sc.* smallpox] has been less dramatic than in other fields of immunoprophylaxis of virus diseases, such as poliomyelitis or measles. **1972** *Lancet* 21 Oct. 875/2 (*heading*) Immunoprophylaxis and immunotherapy of leukæmia with B.C.G. **1965** *Jrnl. Immunol.* XCV. 1019/1 Immunosuppressant compounds such as chloramphenicol.., actinomycin D.., 6-mercaptopurine..and corticosteroids. **1970** M. C. Vale tr. *Nezlin's Biochem. Antibodies* v. 282 One of the most active immunosuppressants is cyclophosphamide. **1967** *Jrnl. Nat. Cancer Inst.* XXXVIII. 754/1 Pretreatment..with this alkylating agent resulted in..increased growth and earlier tumor deaths in the immunosuppressed animals. **1965** *Jrnl. Immunol.* XCV. 1019/1 The mechanism of acriflavine-induced immunosuppression remains unknown. **1968** *New Scientist* 13 June 557/1 Reports of increasing success in combating graft rejection, following improvements in tissue typing and immunosuppression. **1963** *New England Jrnl. Med.* CCLXVIII. 1315 (*heading*) Prolonged survival of human-kidney homografts by immunosuppressive drug therapy. **1968** *Observer* 5 May 3/3 To stem any rejection of the new heart, Mr West is now receiving immuno suppressive treatment with a drug. **1970** Balner & Beveridge *Infections & Immunosuppression Subhuman Primates* 194/2 Most of the immunosuppressive agents currently in use are entirely non-specific, that is to say they depress all aspects of immune reactivity and thereby the immunological defences against infectious microorganisms as well. **1961** Levi-Montalcini & Angeletti in Kety & Elkes *Regional Neurochem.* vii. 369 The injected and untreated animals did not differ from each other. Immunosympathectomized mice became pregnant, nursed and took care of the litter as controls. **1964** *Nature* 26 Dec. 1315/1 'Immunosympathectomized' rats, in which extensive irreversible atrophy of the peripheral sympathetic system is produced by injecting, during the first few days of life, an antiserum to nerve growth factor.., appear healthy, grow, reproduce and have normal gastro-intestinal function. **1962** *Internat. Jrnl. Neuropharmacol.* I. 163 Immunosympathectomy performed in newborn mice, results in a striking depletion of NA in the heart of the same adult animals. **1972** J. B. Martin in Steiner & Schönbaum *Immunosympathectomy* xii. 196 The use of immunosympathectomy in analyzing the importance of adrenergic innervation of individual glands is limited to some degree by the incomplete effect produced by the antisera to nerve growth factor. Thus, immunosympathectomy should be valuable in investigations of the role of sympathetic innervation of those glands (pineal, pituitary, thyroid) in which denervation is nearly complete. It is of limited use in studies of the abdominal glands or genital tract. **1913** R. L. Crockett in *N.Y. State Jrnl. Med.* XIII. 213/2 For some time I have been trying to discover what place (if any) vaccine therapy or, as I prefer to call it—immuno-therapy—had in the branches to which I limit my practice. **1937** *Jrnl. Amer. Med. Assoc.* 19 June 2171 Further investigations on active immunotherapy of whooping cough. **1969** *Daily Colonist* (Victoria, B.C.) 9 Oct. 40/4 He said immunotherapy—injection of materials into the body to stimulate development of tumor-resistant anti-bodies—had been successful with eight of his patients. **1971** J. A. Bellanti *Immunol.* xix. 510 Immunotherapy is passive immunization through the use of serum or gamma globulin which confers temporary protection to one host by the introduction of antibodies actively produced in another. **1919** A. E. Wright in *Lancet* 29 Mar. 500/2 The therapeutic method here employed is..a combined method of serum therapy and transfusion. We may perhaps call it 'immuno-transfusion'. **1941** Kolmer & Tuft *Clin. Immunol.* x. 256 To increase the amount of protective antibody in the donor's blood, the donor may be injected with vaccine prior to the withdrawal of his blood. This type of transfusion is referred to as immunotransfusion.

immunogen (imiū·nodʒĕn). *Biol.* and *Med.* [f. *immuno- + -gen.] **1.** An antigenic substance, or a preparation of it, believed to reside in the ectoplasm of the bacterial cell and to be removed by washing.

Immunogen has been registered as a proprietary name in Great Britain and the U.S.A.

1923 *Trade Marks Jrnl.* 31 Jan. 181 Immunogen... Parke Davis & Company. **1923** *Official Gaz.* (U.S. Patent Office) 18 Dec. 550/1 Immunogen... Immunizing Agents Used for the Prophylaxis and Treatment of Diseases of Bacterial Origin. **1926** Horder & Ferry in *Brit. Med. Jrnl.* 31 July 179/2 As it would appear from these results ..that the antigenic or immunizing portion of the bacterial cell is more ectoplasmic than endoplasmic in origin, it is proposed to call this type of antigen an 'ecto-antigen', and for products prepared in such a manner as to contain only this ectoantigen the designation 'immunogens' is suggested, to distinguish them from other antigenic products already in use. **1928** *Jrnl. Amer. Med. Assoc.* 15 Dec. 1914/2 There is no difference between vaccines and immunogens. Their sphere of action is the same. Generally speaking it would be best to prepare vaccines or immunogens from 'autogenous material', but when that is not practicable commercial preparations may be used. **1929** J. W. Bigger *Handbk. Bacteriol.* (ed. 2) vi. 88 'Immunogens' (Horder & Ferry) are the washings of bacteria. They are stated to contain the immunizing substances of bacteria without the toxins. **1934** *Jrnl. Amer. Med. Assoc.* 22 Sept. 939/2 A little girl..was given..doses of catarrhal immunogen (Parke-Davis) on biweekly visits. *Ibid.*, Immunogen (Parke, Davis & Co.) may be a mixture of antigenic substances. It is not on the accepted list of New and Nonofficial Remedies.

2. Any substance that elicits an immune response or produces immunity in the recipient (see quots.).

1959 A. D. Bussard in *Ann. Rev. Microbiol.* XIII. 280 The following terms will be used..in the course of this review: immunogenicity: ability of a substance to direct the formation of a specific antibody; antigenicity: ability of a substance to react with an antibody under a given set of conditions. An immunogen is a substance exhibiting immunogenicity and an antigen, a substance exhibiting antigenicity. **1971** S. O. Freedman et al. *Clin. Immunol.* i. 3 Although the terms immunogen and antigen are frequently used interchangeably, they are not necessarily synonymous. Immunogenicity may be defined as the capacity of a substance to initiate a humoral or cell-mediated immune response, whereas antigenicity may be defined as the capacity of a substance to bind specifically with the antibody molecules whose formation it has elicited... Employed correctly, the term immunogen specifies that a substance acts at the afferent limb of the immune response... Most conventional antigens possess both immunogenic and antigenic capacities. **1972** *Science* 2 June 1028/3 Pneumococcal polysaccharides are generally considered weak immunogens since they elicit poor primary antibody responses.

immunogenic (imiūnodʒe·nik), *a.* *Biol.* and *Med.* [f. *immuno- + *-genic.] Of, pertaining to, or possessing the ability to elicit an immune response.

1933 *Jrnl. Amer. Med. Assoc.* 24 June 2013/2 (*heading*) An immunogenic paradox. **1934** *Index Medicus* XV. 637/2 Appearance of impedin in production of specific opsonin by local application of immunogenic salves to skin. **1942** *Jrnl. Bacteriol.* XLIII. 397 There is ample evidence in the literature to suggest that fixed virus strains differ in their immunogenic properties. **1962** *Lancet* 5 May 965/1 This incidence had been reduced by early vaccines, but more recent batches had not been sufficiently immunogenic. **1971** *Nature* 4 June 286/3 Why cells become more immunogenic after neuraminidase treatment is not yet clear.

Hence **immunogeni·city**, immunogenic property. Also **immunoge·nesis**, the formation or production of antibodies; bodily processes, collectively, that constitute an immune response.

1944 *Science* 16 June 496 Minute amounts..exhibited marked antityphoid immunogenicity. **1948** Biester & Schwarte *Dis. Poultry* (ed. 2) 567 The criteria of immunogenesis and pathogenesis. **1950** *Jrnl. Bacteriol.* LIX. 263 Textbooks..commonly state that a high degree of encapsulation is responsible for the reportedly poor immunogenicity of this fungus. **1956** *Jrnl. Immunol.* LXXVI. 217/1 It is demonstrated that the immunogenicity of immune globulin is suppressed by the simultaneous injection of other serum components. **1960** A. Hofman et al. tr. A. N. Gordienko (*title*) Control of immunogenesis by the nervous system. **1968** D. Osoba in B. Cinader *Regulation Antibody Response* xii. 232 (*heading*) The regulatory role of the thymus in immunogenesis. **1970** *New Scientist* 19 Mar. 543/1 Irradiation with gamma rays, which render it non-infective without.. loss of mobility or immunogenicity.

immunoglobulin (imiū:no-, i:miuno,glǫ·biŭlin). *Biochem.* and *Med.* [f. *immuno- + globulin.] Any of the group of proteins present in the serum of vertebrates which are characterized by their structure, in being a mixture of larger ('heavy') and smaller ('light') polypeptide chains, linked usu. by disulphide bonds, and by their function in that all known antibodies are immunoglobulins.

1959 J. F. Heremans in *Clin. Chim. Acta* IV. 643 The data..seem to point to the existence of a system of closely related, though not identical, proteins which are

capable of acting as antibodies. These are: (a) γ-globulin (7S, low carbohydrate content, heterogeneous mobility)..; (b) β_{2A}-globulin (also 7S, high carbohydrate content, high mobility)..; and (c) β_{2M}-globulin (19S, high carbohydrate content, high mobility). The outlined similarities in nature and function clearly call for the adoption of a common name for all these substances. A word such as 'immunoglobulins' would seem to be suitable. **1965** *New Scientist* 11 Mar. 626/1 The body's 'immune' defence mechanism against bacteria, viruses and other foreign materials depends largely on the presence in the blood serum of a family of proteins known as immunoglobulins. **1970** GOLD & PEACOCK *Basic Immunol.* iii. 93 A new nomenclature was proposed in which the prefix γ or Ig stood for immunoglobulin and a suffix denoted the particular class of immunoglobulin. Thus the 7S, 160,000 M.W., gamma-globulins became IgG or γG, the macroglobulins became IgM or γM, and the third class of immunoglobulins, IgA or γA... Two other classes of human immunoglobulin, IgD..and IgE.., are now known. **1970** ROTHSCHILD & WALDMANN *Plasma Protein Metabolism* xvi. 259 The immunoglobulins are a group of structurally related proteins produced by plasma cells and lymphocytes. **1970** *Nature* 12 Dec. 1040/1 These studies have shown that immunoglobulins are composed of light chains (molecular weight 23,000) and heavy chains (55,000) which are linked through disulphide bonds. **1971** *Ann. N.Y. Acad. Sci.* CXC. 8 The lamprey has 6·6S and 14S immunoglobulins which have similar light and heavy chains.

immunology (imiunǫ·lŏdʒi). [f. IMMUN(ITY + -OLOGY.] The science which treats of the phenomena and causes of immunity (sense 5).

1910 *Jrnl. Amer. Med. Assoc.* 5 Mar. 828/1 Relations between pharmacology, immunology and experimental therapy. **1911** *Ibid.* 25 Feb. 578/2 The science of immunity, or immunology, would explain the mechanism by which the animal body is enabled to resist disease. **1947** *Nature* 4 Jan. 15/2 The hope that they [*sc.* incipient cancers] may elaborate specific antigenic substances, and thus provide serological tests, goes back to the first years of immunology. **1963** GELL & COOMBS *Clin. Aspects Immunol.* p. xvii, Immunology has two aspects, its use as a tool and its investigation as a biological phenomenon.

Hence **immunolo·gic** (chiefly *U.S.*), **-lo·gical** *adjs.*, of or pertaining to immunity or immunology; **immunolo·gically** *adv.*, from the point of view of immunology; as regards the phenomena, properties, etc., of immunity; **immuno·logist**, an expert in or student of immunology.

1912 *Jrnl. Exper. Med.* XVI. 635 Hemolysins, precipitins, or other bodies included in the province of the immunologist. **1914** BILLINGS & IRONS *Forchheimer's Therapeusis Internal Dis.* V. iii. 121 (*heading*) Immunological reactions in diagnosis. **1919** Immunologic [see *ALLERGY a.]. **1929** R. T. HEWLETT in *Syst. Bacteriol.* (Med. Res. Council) III. 375 Dickson had previously observed that the Nevin cheese strain differed immunologically from other strains with which he was working. **1955** *Sci. News Let.* 12 Mar. 168/1 Because of his lack of gamma globulin, the Minnesota boy has what his doctors term almost complete 'immunologic paralysis', meaning the mechanism in his body that should help him develop immunity, or resistance, to disease has been paralyzed. **1960** *New Biol.* XXXI. 103 It seems..that any potentially antigenic material which comes into contact with the cells during the stage of immunological immaturity fails subsequently to cause antibody formation. **1963** *Times* 25 Jan. 7/7 In such a case the twins are immunologically tolerant of each other's tissues. **1967** W. O. WEIGLE *Natural & Acquired Immunologic Unresponsiveness* i. 1 The evidence available suggests that the acquisition of an immunologic unresponsive state to self is not genetically determined, but is acquired early in life before maturation of the immune mechanisms. **1968** *Sunday Tel.* 28 Jan. 4/4 Dr. M. C. Botha, the immunologist who conducted the tests. **1973** J. GOODFIELD *Courier to Peking* x. 120 You hear the voice of the true immunologist. *Ibid.* 126 The question was a highly technical one and understanding it demanded a thorough background in immunological theory.

immuration (imiurē·ʃən). [f. IMMUR(E *v.* + -ATION.] = IMMUREMENT.

1895 POLLOCK & MAITLAND *Hist. Eng. Law* I. II. ii. 427 Stephen Langton seems to have condemned two of the laity to that close imprisonment which was known as immuration. **1959** J. L. M. TRIM in Quirk & Smith *Teaching of Eng.* iii. 77 [Speech training] may easily lead to..an increasing immuration of the individual instead of the liberation which education should bring. **1963** *Yale Rev.* Winter 291 The first, the cloistered family, guarded the purity of the flesh and preserved the ideal of chastity through the Dark Ages by immuration.

immy (i·mi). Also **imma, immie.** [perh. f. IMITATION.] **a.** (See quot. 1928.) **b.** A type of marble as used by children.

1928 *Funk's Stand. Dict., Immy*, a choice marble made in imitation, as of a cornelian or an agate. **1936** *Fortune* June 36/2 Like glass for stained-glass windows and water tumblers, marble glass has a soft lime base, which makes an immie so resilient. **1941** BAKER *Dict. Austral. Slang* 37 *Imma*, a type of marble. **1952** [see *AGATE *sb.* 1 b]. **1972** *Sat. Rev.* (U.S.) 29 Jan. 8 Shooting marbles was played by four or five boys kneeling around a circle... In the center there were a lot of marbles—'immies', as they were called.

imp. Abbreviation of *imperative, imperator, imperatrix, imperfect, imperial, impersonal, important, imprimatur, imprint, improvement.*

impact, *sb.* Add: **b.** Now commonly the effective action of one thing or person upon another; the effect of such action; influence; impression. Esp. in phr. *to make an impact* (*on*).

1946 *Sat. Rev. Lit.* (U.S.) 28 Dec. 15/1 The impact of the images, their skilful juxtaposition, and the bold page layouts make words superfluous. **1952** B. RUSSELL (*title*) The impact of science upon society. **1958** *Church Times* 8 Aug. 7/1 The story..is presented by means of narrative and dramatic episodes in a manner familiar to all radio-listeners, but it is the lighting which makes the great impact. **1965** *Listener* 26 Aug. 297/1 However much you give them, you are not going to make a significant impact on growth, though you may make an impact in the charitable sense. **1966** *Economist* 10 Dec. 1144/3 What has had an impact on food distributors, apparently, is the opening of an investigation by the Federal Trade Commission into supermarket games and stamps. **1967** E. SHORT *Embroidery & Fabric Collage* i. 18 The most dynamic colour combination if used too often loses its impact. **1969** LD. MOUNTBATTEN in *Times* (India Suppl.) 13 Oct. p. i/1 He [*sc.* Gandhi] made such an impact on me that his memory will forever remain fresh in my mind. **1973** *Daily Tel.* 5 Mar. 6/2 The main impact of the campaign will be made by full-page newspaper advertisements.

2. Special Comb.: **impact crater**, a crater or a hollow in the ground believed to have been produced by the impact of a meteorite; **impact extrusion**, a process for producing tubular objects in which metal in a die is struck by a punch that fits into it and forces the metal between their two surfaces and out of the die; **impact head** = **impact pressure*; **impact load**, a load imposed suddenly and for a short time, as when one body strikes another; **impact loading**, (the application of) an impact load; **impact pressure**, the total pressure in a moving fluid in the direction of flow, being equal (in the case of a fluid of negligible viscosity) to the sum of the dynamic pressure and the static pressure; **impact resistance** = **impact strength*; **impact strength**, the ability of a solid to withstand an impact or shock; strength as measured by an impact test; **impact test**, any of various tests for measuring the resistance of a body to suddenly applied stress in which it is broken, usually by a blow, under standard conditions; **impact tube**, a thin tube (usu. rigid with a right-angled bend) which may be placed in a flow of fluid with an open end facing upstream, so that the impact pressure in the fluid may be found by measuring the pressure in the tube; cf. **Pitot tube*.

1895 G. K. GILBERT in *Bull. Philos. Soc. Washington* XII. 265 The inquiry has followed three lines. First, an investigation of the ellipticity of lunar craters; second, an experimental investigation of the relation between incidence angle and ellipticity of impact craters; third, a more refined investigation of the orbital relations affecting the incidence angles of moonlets. *Ibid.* 291 Does the earth exhibit impact craters? If not, then erosion and sedimentation have destroyed them. **1965** R. B. BALDWIN *Fund. Survey Moon* vii. 66 If it can be shown that the impact craters on earth are..similar to lunar craters.. we will be on firm ground in considering that the lunar craters..were formed by the impacts..of meteorites. **1967** *Listener* 20 Apr. 521/2 Another impact crater is that at Wolf Creek in Australia, where the diameter is half a mile. **1935** *Metal Industry* 11 Oct. 373/1 A new..heavy duty press..for the cold impact extrusion of aluminium tubes and shells in one operation. **1963** H. R. CLAUSER *Encycl. Engin. Materials* 340/1 Parts produced by impact extrusion are essentially longitudinally oriented, e.g., collapsible tubes, cans, etc. **1928** G. MARTIN *Treat. Chem. Engin.* xvi. 3 A connection between the density of a fluid W and the power required to move it through a pipe of area A when the impact head is l_1 in. of water and the dynamic head is l in. of water. **1924** E. E. MANN *Introd. Pract. Civil Engin.* x. 166 Wind pressure on roofs is of the nature of an impact load. **1928** C. F. S. GAMBLE *Story N. Sea Air Station* 10 Her two stream-lined gondolas..were designed to be capable of sustaining severe impact loads when alighting on water. **1963** D. A. FIRMAGE *Fund. Theory of Struct.* iii. 56 Impact load is only a minor portion of the total load on any bridge. **1948** COURANT & FRIEDRICHS *Supersonic Flow & Shock Waves* iii. 240 The basic problem of wave propagation in a bar of elastic-plastic material is concerned with the motion resulting from impact-loading, i.e., from a velocity being suddenly imparted to one end of the bar and then maintained there. **1973** *Sci. Amer.* Feb. 85/1 It has been equipped with a grille structure that distributes the impact loading more uniformly. **1919** A. B. EASON *Flow & Measurem. Air & Gases* xiv. 237 The increase in the value of the impact pressure in the case of wind blowing directly on an opening will be due to the fact that more of the momentum of the air is destroyed than when air blows on the small area of the Pitot tube mouthpiece. **1966** DAILY & HARLEMAN *Fluid Dynamics* vi. 128 For liquids of small viscosity, Eq. (6–71) can be used to compute the velocity from the stagnation or impact pressure measured on the blunt nose of a probe in a steady flow. **1934** B. STOUGHTON *Metall. Iron & Steel* (ed. 4) xiii. 404 Impact Resistance of Steel.—The resistance of steel to shock decreases very much with lowered temperature. **1958** C. L. MANTELL *Engin. Materials Handbk.* III. 12 The impact resistance of standard malleable iron, measured by the Charpy test using a notch, 0·394-in. square bar, and 0·079-in. depth of notch is about 16·5 ft-lb. **1904** *Proc. Inst. Mech. Engin.* IV. 1227 The more or less consistent relation that appeared to exist in Messrs. Sankey and Kent-Smith's tests between impact strength and reduction of area. **1939** *Proc. Amer. Soc. Testing Materials* XXXVIII. II. 39 There are..8,000,000 molded phenol plastic telephones in use... The extent to which..breakage occurs..is determined largely by the impact strength of the molding material. **1952** WOOD & VON LUDWIG *Investment Castings for Engineers* x. 209 Both beryllium copper and aluminum bronze will develop higher tensile strength and hardness when heat treated, but they will not have good impact strength, whereas manganese bronze is one of the toughest cast metals available. **1967** M. CHANDLER *Ceramics in Mod. World* iv. 118 The impact strength of all ceramic materials..is rather low. **1899** W. C. UNWIN *Testing Materials of Construction* (ed. 2) 239 (*heading*) Example of an impact test. **1915** [see *CHARPY]. **1918** *Machinery* 31 Jan. 477/1 Tensile impact tests, in which a sudden tensile stress is applied to a specimen by means of a falling weight, have also been practised..in recent years. **1943** F. D. JONES *Engin. Encycl.* (ed. 2) II. 680 The torsion impact test breaks the specimen by twisting. **1971** B. SCHARF *Engin. & its Lang.* iv. 24 The most common impact test in this country [*sc.* Great Britain] is the Izod test, in which a notched test piece fixed at one end is broken by a blow from a pendulum hammer, the energy absorbed in fracturing the specimen being recorded... Another method widely used in other countries and increasingly also in this country is the Charpy impact test, in which a notched test piece supported at both ends is broken by a blow from a striker, on the face opposite to and immediately behind the notch, the energy absorbed in fracturing the specimen being recorded. **1916** *Trans. Amer. Soc. Mech. Engin.* XXXVII. 1410 For high pressures, the manometer attached to the impact tube can be replaced by a mercury column or steam gage attached to a receiver in the main where velocity is largely reduced. **1934** J. H. PERRY *Chem. Engineers' Handbk.* 689 The length and shape of the tip, so long as the opening faces upstream, usually have little effect upon the head indicated by an impact tube. **1966** DAILY & HARLEMAN *Fluid Dynamics* ix. 178 The actual readings from impact tubes will depend both on the viscous effect and on the size of the pressure-sensing hole in the probe tip.

impact, *v.* Add: **3.** *intr.* **a.** To come forcibly into contact with a (larger) body or surface. Const. various preps.

1916 [see IMPACTING *ppl. a.* below]. **1929** 'SEAMARK' *Down River* vi. 172 Something impacted with a soft thud against Lingard's temple. **1945** *Jrnl. Sci. Instrum.* XXII. 191 A jet of air issuing from a slot and impacting on a plane surface. **1962** F. I. ORDWAY et al. *Basic Astronautics* v. 201 The Soviet Lunnaya Raketa was launched early in the afternoon of September 12, 1959 and impacted onto the Moon's surface just after midnight on September 14, Moscow time.

b. *fig.* To have a (pronounced) effect *on*.

1935 W. G. HARDY *Father Abraham* 370 For there was about them an air of eagerness and of shuddering expectation which impacted on his consciousness and fascinated even while it repelled him. **1956** *Oxf. Mag.* 8 Nov. 81/1 The Magazine..is not the place for consideration of national and international events except in so far as they impact on Oxford.

4. *trans.* To cause to impinge or impact *on, against*, etc.

1945 *Jrnl. Sci. Instrum.* XXII. 187 Experimental results for the efficiency of jets in impacting particles are correlated. **1964** K. STEWART in White & Smith *High-Efficiency Air Filtration* ii. 57 All impactors make use of the inertia effect which particles exhibit when the gas stream in which they are suspended is constrained to turn abruptly. The particle under suitable conditions cannot follow the stream lines and is impacted against a collecting plate. **1972** J. O. LEDBETTER *Air Pollution* A. v. 187 An aerosol moving toward an obstacle may impact particles on the obstacle.

Hence **impacting** *ppl. a.*, impinging, colliding.

1916 'BOYD CABLE' *Action Front* 95 No ping and smack of impacting lead hailed about them. **1961** *Sci. Amer.* Nov. 58/2 The impacting bodies may have been asteroids or comets. **1972** *Daily Tel.* 17 Apr. 6/8 These particles.. cannot be measured or analysed from the Earth's surface. On the Moon, however, the impacting particles leave trails in the detector. **1973** *Nature* 13 July 68/2 Craters of the size of St Magnus Bay and The Firth would be formed by impacting meteorites of masses about 1 million tons.

impacted, *ppl. a.* Add: **b.** Applied *spec.* to fæces lodged in the intestine (cf. *IMPACTION 2); also *transf.*, applied to (a part of) the intestine when so blocked.

1844 *Boston Med. & Surg. Jrnl.* XXX. 309 (*heading*) History of a case of impacted colon. **1850** *Lancet* 19 Jan. 80/2 The bowel is found in a state of great distention from an impacted mass closely adhering to its walls. **1875** *Cincinnati Med. News* VIII. 353 (*heading*) Remarkable case of impacted colon, with suppression of urine. **1902** J. P. TUTTLE *Treat. Dis. Anus* (1903) xiv. 545 Distressing symptoms are relieved either by the loosening up of an impacted fæcal mass, or possibly by the undoing of a volvulus or intussusception. **1972** F. A. JONES in Jones & Godding *Managem. Constipation* iv. 128 In some patients, impaction may have already led to severe symptoms, with acute distress, and it is then necessary to organize the immediate removal of the impacted faeces.

c. Applied to a bone fracture in which the broken parts are driven together so as to become locked.

1850 J. A. ORR *Princ. Surg.* II. xi. 153 Impacted fracture is when one broken extremity of the bone is driven into and lodged in the other. **1921** BAETJER & WATERS *Injuries & Dis. Bones & Joints* v. 102 When the fracture is just behind the head [of the femur] or in the middle of the neck, impaction is relatively rare. Fracture at the base is generally impacted. **1967** E. L. RALSTON et al.

Handbk. Fractures vii. 116 Impacted fractures [of the humeral neck] even with angulation of 25 to 30 degrees are best treated with the use of a sling and swathe and early active exercises.

d. Applied to a tooth which, owing to obstruction by another tooth or by bone, fails to erupt properly and remains partly or wholly within the jaw-bone.

1876 H. Moon in T. Bryant *Pract. Surg.* (ed. 2) I. xiii. 546 In all cases where the impaction of a lower wisdom tooth is a source of irritation, the impaction should be at once got rid of... The serious results which may attend purulent inflammation about an impacted wisdom tooth, will receive notice later. **1928** H. Prinz *Dis. Soft Struct. Teeth* i. 29 Impacted teeth usually do not cause painful symptoms unless they meet on their path of retarded eruption an obstruction or they exert pressure upon nerve fibers. **1971** Costich & White *Fund. Oral Surg.* viii. 93/2 The maxillary third molars frequently fail to erupt but may not necessarily be regarded as impacted teeth.

2. That has impinged upon or struck something.

1952 *A.M.A. Arch. Industr. Hygiene & Occup. Med.* V. 464 Although the size of impacted particles can be measured under a microscope, the impaction principle.. is used more as a method of sampling than as a method of determining the particle-size distribution.

b. That has been struck by an impacting body; also *fig.* (*U.S.*) of an area: affected by a larger demand than usual on public services, esp. schools.

1924 in *Sci. Amer.* (1974) July 12/1 One need only study a large raindrop falling into a still pool of water. There is first a surging outward of the impacted water. **1963** *Economist* 25 May 777/2 The..scheme for aid to 'impacted' areas (where schools are over-loaded). **1967** *Compton Yearbk.* 232/1 Funds were also earmarked for.. federally 'impacted' areas, that is, areas where the families of federal workers had swollen school enrollments. **1970** *Time* 6 Apr. 12 Nixon..proposed that $1.5 billion in federal funds be made available to 'racially impacted areas'..to help desegregating school districts meet their special needs. **1971** *Nature* 16 July 162/2 The shape of a newly formed impact crater is caused by the sudden release of the kinetic energy of the impacting mass within a small volume somewhat below the original impacted surface.

impacter, var. *impactor.

impaction. Add: **I. 1.** (Further examples, corresponding to *impacted *ppl. a.* 1 c, d.)

1876 [see *impacted *ppl. a.* 1 d]. **1921** [see *impacted *ppl. a.* 1 c]. **1957** J. G. Bonnin *Textbk. Fractures* i. 8 Impaction is important in aiding fixation and indicates, as a rule, that little displacement has occurred. **1972** D. E. Waite *Textbk. Pract. Oral Surg.* xi. 141 They also vary widely in degree of impaction; some are partially erupted, while others are completely encased in bone.

2. *spec.* in *Med.* **a.** The lodging of a mass of (usu. hardened) fæces in the intestine so that defecation is prevented or impeded; hence, the obstruction of (a part of) the intestine in this way.

1853 *Assoc. Med. Jrnl.* I. 606 (*heading*) Impaction of the rectum from unground wheat. **1866** *Clin. Lect. & Rep.* (London Hospital) III. 193 Three cases of obstruction of the bowels..produced by the impaction of hardened fæces in the rectum, and colon. **1902** J. P. Tuttle *Treat. Dis. Anus* xiv. 543 In simple constipation and in impaction there is always a channel for the escape of gases from the bowels. **1943** Niles & Martin in E. J. Stieglitz *Geriatric Med.* xxxv. 599 Rectal impaction is much more common in the aged. *Ibid.*, Colonic impaction (scybala) is seen occasionally in old people, especially among those who are bedridden. **1972** [see *impacted *ppl. a.* 1 b].

b. *concr.* A mass of (usu. hardened) fæces lodged in the intestine so as to impede defecation.

1902 J. P. Tuttle *Treat. Dis. Anus* xiv. 542 The author has known a patient to suffer from a continuous diarrhœa for six weeks..apparently from no other cause than an impaction of fæces in the sigmoid flexure. **1931** M. C. Pruitt *Mod. Proctology* xviii. 350 It is important to determine..whether the impaction is hard or soft. **1958** A. F. R. Andresen *Office Gastroenterol.* 442 Small impactions can usually be induced to pass by means of a cleansing enema.

II. 3. The process of causing something to impinge or impact on something else (cf. *impact *v.* 4); also, the action of so impinging (cf. *impact *v.* 3).

1945 [see *impactor 2]. **1952** *A.M.A. Arch. Industr. Hygiene & Occup. Med.* V. 476 Larger and heavier particles are thrown onto a collecting surface in front of the jet, while smaller and lighter particles escape impaction. **1956** P. L. Magill et al. *Air Pollution Handbk.* xiii. 32 The impaction of aerosol particles on cylinders has been given considerable attention since it provides an insight into the functioning of fibrous filters. **1972** J. O. Ledbetter *Air Pollution* A. vi. 230 Impaction devices.. that depend upon the wind to carry out the impaction.

impactite (impæ·ktəit). *Geol.* [f. Impact *sb.* + -ite[1], after *tektite.] Any piece of glassy material formed in or around a meteorite crater by the heat of impact.

1940 V. E. Barnes *N. Amer. Tektites* in *Univ. Texas Publ.* no. 3945, p. 558 Spencer's meteorite splash origin.. is valid for the formation of certain glasses. Glasses of this type will be distinguished in general from most of those now included under tektites. These meteorite splashes should be given a distinctive name such as 'impactites'. This name was suggested by Dr. H. B. Stenzel. **1960** I. Vidziunas tr. *Krinov's Princ. Meteoritics* vii. 435 This presence of numerous fragments of impactites in the area of meteoritic craters served as a basis for considering these objects to be fragments of fused terrestrial quartz sand. **1964** *New Scientist* 16 Jan. 160/1 The expert can easily distinguish tektites from..impactites (silica glass found around some meteorite craters).

impactive (i·mpæktiv, impæ·ktiv), *a.* [f. Impact *sb.* + -ive.] Of, pertaining to, or characterized by impact; having an impact.

1934 F. Scott Fitzgerald *Tender is Night* 5 Feeling the impactive scrutiny of strange faces, she took off her bath-robe and followed. **1942** W. Faulkner *Go down, Moses* 197 They faced one another, not close yet at slightly less than foils' distance, erect, their voices not raised, not impactive, just succinct. **1955** *Financial Times* 17 Jan. (Packaging Suppl.) 6/4 Mechanical tests have been devised for studying vibration, impactive shocks and compression loads in stacking. **1969** *Esquire* Feb. 20 Even more impactive, maybe, is The Spot, where the waitresses wear what they please.

impactor (impæ·ktəɪ). Also **impacter.** [f. Impact *v.*: see -or, -er[1].] **1.** A device or machine that delivers impacts or blows.

1916 *Chambers's Jrnl.* Dec. 830/2 The impactor golf-machine is a new invention. **1950** J. H. Perry *Chem. Engineers' Handbk.* (ed. 3) 1129/2 The Impactor..is a reversible hammer crusher without a discharge grating or cage. **1966** *McGraw-Hill Encycl. Sci. & Technol.* V. 471/1 To increase the effectiveness of the forging blows, the impacter forging machine was developed.

2. An impinger, esp. one in which the particles are deposited on a dry surface rather than in a liquid.

The distinction between impactors and impingers explained in quot. 1945 is rarely made.

1945 K. R. May in *Jrnl. Sci. Instrum.* XXII. 187 (*heading*) The cascade impactor: an instrument for sampling coarse aerosols. *Ibid.* 188 The method which has been adopted for depositing the sample is direct impaction of the particles on to glass slides which may be coated with a suitable medium...The terms 'impactor' and 'impaction' were suggested by Prof. J. H. Gaddum to avoid confusion with 'impinger' instruments... In 'impingers' a fine jet of air is directed at very high speed on to a flat surface to obtain the maximum efficiency of deposition of small particles. In the case of 'impactors' jet speeds are lower and larger particles are dealt with. **1956** P. L. Magill et al. *Air Pollution Handbk.* x. 30 Most cascade impactors are now operated using high air velocities. *Ibid.* 29 A single-stage impactor..is often useful because of its simplicity of operation. **1964** [see *impact *v.* 4]. **1971** *Nature* 12 Feb. 501/1 Partition of single uredospores between the first and second stage of a cascade impactor indicated a terminal velocity of 0·6 cm s^{-1}.

impair, *sb.*[2] Add: In roulette (with pronunc. ɑ̃pɛ̄r), an odd number, or a number marked 'impair'.

1850 *Bohn's Hand-bk. Games* 348 (Roulette) The impair wins, when the ball enters a hole numbered impair. **1891** 'L. Hoffmann' *Cycl. Card & Table Games* 626 If he places his money on Impair, he bets that the ball will drop into an odd number. **1902** *Encycl. Brit.* XXXII. 304/1 Pair indicates even numbers, impair odd numbers. **1966** 'W. Haggard' *Power House* xii. 125 The croupier was paying out. Mortimer was on the *Impair* side. **1973** L. Meynell *Thirteen Trumpeters* iv. 66 His right hand was.. stretching out to place his stake on the next throw (a green on *pair*)... '*Impair*' was called.

impaired, *ppl. a.* Add: **2.** Of a driver or his driving: adversely affected by the influence of alcohol or narcotics. *Canad.*

1951 *Act* (Canada) 15 *Geo. VI* c. 47 §14 Driving while ability to drive is impaired. **1957** (*title*) Report on impaired driving tests (Crime Detection Laboratories of the Royal Canadian Mounted Police). **1967** W. S. Avis et al. *Dict. Canad. Eng., Senior Dict.* 573/2 *Impaired driver*, one whose driving ability has been impaired by alcohol or narcotics. **1970** *Toronto Daily Star* 24 Sept. 37/1 Ange Gardien..was charged with impaired driving. **1972** *Evening Telegram* (St. John's, Newfoundland) 24 June 1/1 A police spokesman said the car received only slight damage. The driver was arrested and charged with impaired driving. **1973** *Kingston* (Ontario) *Whig-Standard* 18 Apr. 15/2 Another motorist..was fined $175 and prohibited from driving for four months on a charge of impaired driving. **1973** *Daily Colonist* (Victoria, B.C.) 26 Apr. 41/3 Georg Edward Haines..was fined $350 following his plea of guilty to a charge of being impaired early Wednesday in Victoria while in care or control of a vehicle. *Ibid.*, Edward Weiland..pleaded guilty to a two-count Victoria charge of impaired driving and refusing to take a breath-analysis test. **1974** *Kingston* (Ontario) *Whig-Standard* 16 Jan. 5/4 A snowmobile operator was one of five persons assessed penalties ranging from $175 to $200 each in county court Tuesday on impaired driving charges.

impala (impā·lă, -pæ·lă). Also **impalla, mpala.** = Pallah.

1875 W. H. Drummond *Large Game & Nat. Hist. S. & S.-E. Afr.* vii. 330 The roibok or impalla..is about the size of a small reed-buck doe, though more slenderly made. *Ibid.*, These impalla..could easily distance any dog I possessed. **1886** W. M. Kerr *Far Interior* I. ii. 29 It was here [*sc.* Boatlanama] that I shot my first antelope —a fine impala (*Æpyceros Melampus*), with a good head. **1888** P. Gillmore *Days & Nights by Desert* xvii. 136 (*caption*) The Mpala Antelope (*Æpyceros Melampus*). **1896** [see Pallah]. **1907** P. Fitzpatrick *Jock of Bushveld* 302 We sat like statues as the impala walked out from its stall between Teddy's knees. **1931** *Times Lit. Suppl.* 3 Dec. 983/4 Graceful photographs of impalla, eland, and other antelope. **1947** J. Stevenson-Hamilton *Wild Life S. Afr.* xiii. 87 The impala (*Æpyceros melampus*) —Discovered by..Lichtenstein more than a hundred years ago, and variously termed impala, pallah, and rooibok, this antelope may claim to be one of the most beautiful and graceful members of the existing African fauna. **1965** A. Nicol *Truly Married Woman* 44 It was, after all, only a red-buck, an impalla, that they were afraid of. **1971** L. H. Matthews *Life of Mammals* II. xiv. 394 Impala in East Africa do not move far from their restricted home range.

impale, *v.* Add: **4. c.** *fig.* To transfix (a person) with one's gaze. Hence **impa·ling** *ppl. a.*

1877 *My Mother-in-Law* vi. 60 Mrs. Pinkerton devoted herself to impaling me with her eyes once in a while. **1903** *Critic* XLIII. 349/2 There was an impaling fierceness in his eyes.

impalement. Add: **4. b.** The act or fact of being impaled upon rocks, the spikes of a gate, or the like.

1874 *Belgravia* Aug. 175 There was..one tall church-steeple which by the celerity of its approach appeared.. anxious that I should be impaled on its apex... I declare that the grotesqueness of the position of impalement— all legs and wings, like a cockchafer—..visibly occurred to me. **1885** *Austral. Med. Jrnl.* New Ser. vii. 436 A case of laceration of the rectum and jejunum by accidental impalement. **1887** *Graphic* 19 Mar. 307/2 His ship was rescued after impalement on a rock. **1921** *Contemp. Rev.* Aug. 272 Do you remember climbing the gate and just avoiding impalement? **1971** *Brit. Med. Jrnl.* 26 June 748/1 Perforation of the bladder following rectal impalement is extremely rare.

impaler. (Later example.)

1969 *New Yorker* 6 Sept. 106/2 Ceauçescu..probably the most popular Rumanian national leader since Vlad IV, called the Impaler, who successfully fought the Turks in the mid-fifteenth century.

impalla, var. *impala.

imparting, *vbl. sb.* (in Dict. s.v. Impart *v.*). (Later example.)

1952 *Mind* LXI. 309 Lying..is the deliberate imparting of false information in order to deceive.

impasto. Add: **2.** *Ceramics.* (See quots.)

1903 M. L. Solon *Hist. Old French Faïence* 188 *Impasto*, clay or enamel colours laid so thickly on to the ware as to stand up in relief from its surface. **1960** R. G. Haggar *Conc. Encycl. Cont. Pott. & Porc.* 233/1 '*Impasto blue*', inky blue pigment which is applied thickly and stands up in slight but palpable relief on early 'oak-leaf' pots made at Florence.

impastoed (impɑ·stoud), *ppl. a.* Encrusted with paste.

1923 *Blackw. Mag.* May 641/2 [He] thrust the point of his palette-knife under an impasto'd mass of paper.

impaternate (impǎtə̄·ɹnět), *a. Biol.* [f. Im-[2] + Patern(al *a.* + -ate[2].] Produced parthenogenetically by a female without fecundation by a male.

1934 in Webster. **1936** *Nature* 11 July 78/1 If the queen bee is diploid and heterozygous for a recessive factor, she..would be expected to produce impaternate haploid drones, equal numbers of which would show the dominant or the recessive character. **1965** [see *deuterotoky* s.v. *deutero-].

impayable, *a.* **3.** (Later examples.)

1906 G. Meredith *Let.* 23 Nov. (1970) III. 1579 His [*sc.* Whistler's] tales of his student life in Paris..were *impayable*. **1954** P. Bottome *Against Whom?* xxiii. 177 As a patient, she is unsatisfactory..as a girl she is *impayable*!

impeccableness (impe·kǎb'lnės). [f. Impeccable *a.* + -ness.] The character or condition of being impeccable.

1696 J. Sergeant *Method to Sci.* i. vi. 64 Original Sin, Impeccableness in the Saints in Heaven, Obdurateness in Sin in the Divels. **1901** F. H. Burnett *Making of Marchioness* ii. xiv. 233 With her ruby and her coronets and her lodging-house street, she is of an impeccableness —she does not even know she could be doubted. **1952** *New Yorker* 15 Nov. 166/2 They are inclined to be seduced by pieces whose chief charm rests in a thin, careful impeccableness.

impedance. Substitute for def.: The overall opposition to an electric current, arising from the combined effect of resistance R and reactance X and measured by the ratio of the e.m.f. to the resulting current (peak or r.m.s. values); it may be represented as a scalar quantity whose value is $\sqrt{(R^2+X^2)}$ or as a complex number $R+jX$. (Further examples.)

1923 E. W. Marchant *Radio Telegr.* ii. 15 If the conductor is a long straight wire it offers comparatively little obstruction or 'impedance' to the passage of a current; while, if it is wound up into a coil it will offer a very high 'impedance' to the passage of the high-frequency current. **1926** A. T. Dover *Theory & Pract. Alternating Currents*

iii. 49 The sides *OC*, *CE*, *OE* of triangle *OCE* are proportional to the resistance, reactance, and impedance respectively. On account of this feature the triangle *OCE*, when drawn to an ohm scale, is called the impedance triangle of the circuit. Impedance is therefore a complex quantity, i.e. it is only completely specified when its magnitude and inclination, or alternatively its two perpendicular components with respect to the current, are given. **1930** M. G. MALTI *Electr. Circuit Analysis* vii. 87 A sine voltage $E_{12} = 70 - j50$ is impressed on a series circuit of impedance $Z_L = 15$ cis $30°$ ohms. What is the complex expression for the current? **1931** MOYER & WOSTREL *Radio Handbk.* ii. 76 The term $\sqrt{(R^2 + X^2)}$, known as the impedance of the circuit, takes the place in alternating-current calculations of the resistance in direct-current work. **1948** A. L. ALBERT *Radio Fund.* v. 128 If the impressed voltage is divided by the input current of *any* line, a value of impedance is obtained, and for *any* line this is called the input impedance. *Ibid.* 129 The characteristic impedance, usually designated by Z_0, is the input impedance of a line infinite in length. **1961** H. JASIK *Antenna Engin. Handbk.* xxxi. 2 A variable load impedance connected to a source will receive the maximum possible power from the source when it is adjusted to equal the complex conjugate of the impedance of the source. **1962** C. SUSSKIND *Encycl. Electronics* 422/2 The impedance of dynamic, ribbon, carbon, and magnetic microphones is nearly always less than 40,000 ohms and is essentially resistive.

b. Something that has impedance and may be made part of a circuit.

1935 CAMPBELL & CHILDS *Measurement of Inductance, Capacitance, & Frequency* xiii. 260 The unknown impedance Z is put in series with the known resistance R, and across them is connected a potential divider with slider Q. **1966** *McGraw-Hill Encycl. Sci. & Technol.* VII. 39/1 Standard resistors, capacitors, and inductors are often used as comparisons for unknown impedances.

2. *Mech.* and *Acoustics.* Any of several analogous properties of oscillatory mechanical systems that represent the force, pressure, etc., necessary to produce a given speed, rate of flow, etc., esp. *mechanical impedance*, the ratio of the force on an oscillating body or particle to the resulting velocity; *specific acoustic impedance*, in a wave, the ratio of the (excess) pressure at any point to the resulting particle velocity (i.e. the mechanical impedance per unit area of the wave-front); *acoustic* (or *acoustical*) *impedance*, the ratio of the average (excess) pressure over an imaginary surface in a wave to the resulting rate of volume flow across it (i.e. the specific acoustic impedance, averaged over the surface, divided by the area of the surface).

The qualifying adjs. are often omitted in contexts where there is no danger of ambiguity.
1919 A. G. WEBSTER in *Proc. Nat. Acad. Sci.* V. 275 (*heading*) Acoustical impedance, and the theory of horns and of the phonograph. *Ibid.*, The term 'impedance'..has been productive of very great convenience in the theory of alternating currents of electricity. Unfortunately, engineers have not seemed to notice that the idea may be made as useful in mechanics and acoustics as in electricity. In fact, in such apparatus as the telephone one may combine the notions of electrical and mechanical impedance with great advantage. *Ibid.*, If we have any oscillating system into which a volume of air X periodically enters under an excess pressure p, I propose to define the impedance by the *complex* ratio $Z = p/X$. **1927** I. B. CRANDALL *Theory Vibrating Syst.* ii. 71 In most parts of the text it is convenient to take the mechanical impedance as the ratio of maximum force to maximum velocity. Strictly, the velocity is analogous to current density rather than to total current...The *acoustic* impedance per unit area, *divided by the area*, is what corresponds most closely to the electrical impedance. **1934** N. W. MCLACHLAN *Loud Speakers* i. 4 The difference between acoustical and mechanical impedance must not be confused. In the one case waves travel in some form of conduit or channel which impedes their progress. The greater the area the smaller the impedance. In the mechanical form something is being driven, so the greater the area driving the medium the greater the impedance opposing motion. **1936** P. M. MORSE *Vibration & Sound* vi. 192 A consideration of the behavior of the specific acoustic impedance of a plane wave will enable us to work out the details of its interaction with various mechanical systems. **1953** *Sci. News* XXIX. 11 Whenever in the layers lying below the bed of the sea there is a sudden change in the acoustic impedance (that is in the product of the density of the material and the velocity of sound waves in it), there is a reflecting boundary. **1955** HUETER & BOLT *Sonics* ii. 33 The concept of acoustic impedance is useful in the analysis of lumped systems, such as cavity resonators, sirens, jets, etc. **1960** R. B. LINDSAY *Mech. Radiation* ix. 218 The excess pressure in a sound wave is taken to correspond with the electromotive force, and the volume current (the product of the particle velocity ξ and the area of the wavefront S) is assumed to be analogous to the electric current. Hence it is natural to define the acoustic impedance of a wave as $Z = Pe/X$, where X = volume current = $S\xi$. With the use of the complex notation for wave quantities the impedance will usually be complex. We first examine..the case of a plane harmonic wave of angular frequency w...The impedance of such a wave is then $Z = \rho_0 V/S$, a real quantity. The numerator is called the specific acoustic impedance of a plane wave and denoted by Z_s. It is the impedance for a unit area of wavefront. **1961** BICKLEY & TALBOT *Introd. Theory Vibrating Syst.* xi. 139 The example is that of torsional waves on a shaft...The [angular] velocity is proportional to the transmitted torque... Now in the electrical analogy the ratio of force to velocity is that of e.m.f. to current, a ratio which the electrical engineer calls impedance. It is

therefore convenient to call the ratio of transmitted torque to angular velocity (and the analogous quantity in other cases) the transmission impedance. **1963** C. T. MORROW *Shock & Vibration Engin.* I. vi. 127 A high impedance indicates that even a large force results in little motion; it suggests massiveness and rigidity. A low impedance indicates that motion is easy to produce; it suggests lightness and flexibility. A resistive impedance indicates that the energy supplied at the point is absorbed, as in a dashpot... A reactive impedance indicates that energy supplied is stored, as in..a compressed spring.

3. Special Comb.: **impedance bond,** a kind of rail bond used to connect electrified rails in adjoining signalling sections, having a low resistance (so that the direct traction current can pass unhindered) and a high inductance (so that the alternating signalling currents are confined to their respective sections); **impedance-matching,** the adjustment of impedances in such a way as to minimize the power reflected or the reduction in the power transferred that occurs when an oscillatory current or other wave meets a change in impedance; also *attrib.*

1926 HARDING & EWING *Electr. Railway Engineering* (ed. 3) xix. 258 The development of the two-rail signal system making use of impedance bonds..marked the beginning of a new era in the development of the new railway signal systems. Practically all of the automatic block signals which are being installed on both alternating- and direct-current railways at present are of this general type. **1967** G. F. FIENNES *I tried to run Railway* v. 49 Installing impedance bonds in the track. **1929** E. MALLETT *Telegr. & Telephony* vii. 160 Impedance matching is necessary in order that the maximum available power may be absorbed where it is required. **1934** *Jrnl. Inst. Electr. Engin.* LXXV. 803/2 Impedance-matching transformers have to be used at both ends of the screened lead-in feeder. **1968** *Listener* 22 Feb. 235/3 The bony levers [of the middle ear] reduce the amplitude of vibration and so serve as what an engineer would call an 'impedance-matching transformer'. This gives efficient transfer of energy from the air to the denser fluid in the cochlea of the inner ear.

impeller. Add: **b.** Also occas. **impellor.** A part of a machine or apparatus designed to impart motion to a fluid by rotation, esp. in a restricted space (as in a centrifugal pump or compressor).

1890 P. R. BJÖRLING *Pumps* 190 The pump being charged with water, the impeller or fan is set in motion at a great speed, imparting centrifugal motion to the water contained in the impeller, and so driven into the casing or body of the pump. **1923** *Daily Mail* 13 July 12 Cooling is by the thermo-syphon system assisted by a water impellor. **1934** *Archit. Rev.* LXXV. 203 Fresh air..is drawn into the eyes of the fans—the largest of which has a capacity of 641,000 cu. ft. of air a minute and an impellor diameter of 28 ft. **1942** R. A. BEAUMONT *Aeronaut. Engin.* 100/1 The mixture, thrown outwards at high velocity by the rapidly revolving impellor, passes through diffuser vanes into a chamber, from which it is delivered to the induction pipes. **1947** A. W. JUDGE *Mod. Gas Turbines* viii. 206 The compressor has a double-sided impeller with twenty-nine vanes on each side which enables the maximum air intake area to be obtained for a given tip diameter. **1956** MCCABE & SMITH *Unit Operations Chem. Engin.* vi. 282 In these machines mixing is done by a mechanically driven impeller, which creates a flow pattern in the liquid. *Ibid.* 283 The three main types of mixing impellers are paddles, turbines, and propellers. **1966** *McGraw-Hill Encycl. Sci. & Technol.* V. 334/2 A fluid coupling consists of an impeller on the input or driving shaft and a runner on the output or driven shaft... Impeller and runner are bladed rotors, the impeller acting as a pump and the runner reacting as a turbine.

impellingness (impe·liŋnės). *rare.* [f. IMPELLING *ppl. a.* + -NESS.] The quality of being impelling.

1922 F. H. BURNETT *Robin* i. 1 A certain impellingness of mood suggested that exercise would be a good thing.

impellor, var. *IMPELLER.

imperative, *a.* and *sb.* Add: **A.** *adj.* **1. b.** *imperative logic* (Philos.): the theory of logical reasoning based on the commands and obligations contained in the imperative mood.

[**1839** MILL *Let.* 4 Nov. in *Works* (1963) XIII. 412 Above all mine is a logic of the indicative mood alone—the logic of the imperative, in which the major premiss says not *is* but *ought*—I do not meddle with.] **1939** *Philos. of Sci.* VI. 453 (*heading*) A logic of the doubtful. On optative and imperative logic. **1952** R. M. HARE *Lang. Morals* I. ii. 27 It is important to realize that *modal* imperative logic is as distinct from the logic of simple imperatives as in the case of the indicative mood. **1958** *Analysis* XVIII. 50 A thoroughgoing reduction of deontic logic to imperative logic would require Procrustean amputations.

B. *sb.* **2. b.** (Earlier example.)
1796 F. A. NITSCH *Gen. View Kant's Princ. concerning Man* 195 An Imperative..which is founded upon reason itself..is a Categorical Imperative which represents an action as necessary in itself.

imperativism (impe·rătiviz'm). *Philos.* [f. IMPERATIV(E *a.* and *sb.* + -ISM 2.] Reasoning based on the concept of obligation contained in the imperative mood (see IMPERATIVE *a.* 1

and *1 b). Hence **impe·rativist,** one who bases his reasoning on a concept of obligation; as *adj.*, of or pertaining to reasoning based on such a concept.

1926 R. B. PERRY *Gen. Theory of Value* iii. 79 They have been driven to adopt a metaphysical 'voluntarism' or 'imperativism'. **1950** S. E. TOULMIN *Exam. Place of Reason in Ethics* iv. xiii. 189 The 'imperativist' is prepared to consider the present account because it represents for him a sophisticated imperative theory. **1952** *Mind* LXI. 96 The imperativist analysis of moral indicatives cannot be correct. **1960** *Philos. of Sci.* XXVII. 374 This exposure tells against the 'imperativist' interpretation of law-sentences. **1963** W. SELLARS in Castañeda & Nakhnikian *Morality & Lang. of Conduct* 163 A rough approximation to more sophisticated analyses of the imperativist type. **1965** *Philos. Rev.* LXXIV. 108 It is Zink, and not the regiment of imperativists, emotivists,.. and noncognitivists, who is faithful to the insights of Moore and Wittgenstein.

imperception. (Later examples.)
1961 W. R. BRAIN *Speech Disorders* xiii. 143 Hughlings Jackson..first recognized both agnosia and apraxia. He called the former 'imperception'. **1968** P. MCKELLAR *Experience & Behaviour* x. 260 The selective imperception of the virtuous actions or motivation of people we dislike.

impercipience. (Later examples.)
1905 *Westm. Gaz.* 30 Sept. 4/1 It is only our physical or mental impercipience that leaves the sluggish..mind an easy prey to the promptings of vulgarity. **1925** A. QUILLER-COUCH *Charles Dickens* 71 A lost child, mooning incuriously along the hedgerows with an impercipience rivalling that of a famous Master of Trinity. **1971** *Country Life* 1 Apr. 785/2 H. G. Wells making one of his terrifying comments (terrifying for impercipience).

imperfect, *a.* (*sb.*). Add: **A.** *adj.* **8. b.** Of a stage in the life cycle of a fungus: not producing or not known to produce sexual organs. Of a fungus, having (apparently) no sexual stage: belonging to the group designated *imperfect fungi* (or formally, in mod.L., *Fungi Imperfecti*), in which are included all those fungi which, because a sexual stage is missing or unknown, cannot be assigned to other taxa.

1895 M. C. COOKE *Introd. Study Fungi* xxii. 259 The group now under consideration is analogous, in external features, to the *Pyrenomycetes*, but wholly deficient of asci. The perithecia, or pseudoperithecia, include only stylospores, and have been assumed to be imperfect representatives, or imperfect stages or conditions, of the *Pyrenomyceteae*, and hence called 'imperfect capsular fungi'. **1898** *Jrnl. R. Microsc. Soc.* 660 (*heading*) Rabenhorst's cryptogamic flora of Germany (Fungi Imperfecti). **1908** *Ibid.* 626 Similar cultures were successfully carried through with *Gnomoniella tubiformis* on alder leaves, of which the 'imperfect' form was proved to be *Leptothyrium alneum*. **1952** C. J. ALEXOPOULOS *Introd. Mycol.* xiii. 312 A great many fungi are known which have septate mycelium and which, so far as anyone has been able to discover, reproduce only by means of conidia. Since these fungi apparently lack a sexual stage (perfect stage), we call them, commonly, 'imperfect fungi', and technically, Fungi Imperfecti. **1971** P. H. B. TALBOT *Princ. Fungal Taxon.* v. 77 The phase associated with asexual spores or sterile mycelia is known as the imperfect state of the fungus, while that associated with production of zygotes or of spores resulting from any type of sexual process is the perfect state.

10. *imperfect induction* (Philos.): a term signifying induction (see INDUCTION 7) from an incomplete set of instances, usu. used in contrast to the notion of perfect induction.

[**1843** MILL *Logic* I. iii. ii. § 1. 352 The induction is asserted not to be perfect, unless every single individual of the class A is included in the antecedent.] *a***1856** W. HAMILTON *Lect. Metaphysics & Logic* (1860) III. 325 This Imperfect Induction they [sc. logicians] held in contingent matter to be contingent. **1870** W. S. JEVONS *Elem. Lessons Logic* xxv. 213 The assertion that all the planets move in one direction round the sun..is derived from Imperfect Induction; for it is possible that there exist planets more distant than the most distant-known planet Neptune. **1914** C. READ *Logic* (ed. 4) xv. 197 Imperfect Induction..is..the method of showing the credibility of an universal real proposition by an examination of *some* of the instances it includes. **1957** J. PASSMORE *100 Yrs. Philos.* i. 22 Conventionally, two sorts of induction had been distinguished: perfect and imperfect... We are driven back upon 'imperfect' induction, as..the only sort of inductive inference.

11. *imperfect competition* (Econ.): competition diluted by elements of monopoly so that individual producers or consumers are able to exercise some control over the market price.

1881 F. Y. EDGEWORTH *Math. Psychics* ii. 48 This condition, though not spontaneously generated by imperfect as by perfect competition, should be introduced *ab extra.* **1933** J. ROBINSON (*title*) The economics of imperfect competition. **1937** *Q. Jrnl. Econ.* LII. 529 'Imperfect competition' is a more familiar expression in England, while the term 'monopolistic competition' is more familiar in the United States. **1948** E. H. CHAMBERLIN *Monopolistic Competition* (ed. 6) p. ix, Monopolistic Competition is a fusion of the..theories of monopoly and competition, whereas Imperfect Competition contains no monopoly. **1961** *Rev. Econ. Stud.* XXVIII. 182 Writers on imperfect competition in the product and factor markets have paid little attention to this question. **1969** D. C. HAGUE *Managerial Econ.* iv. 87 Imperfect

competition, that is to say..markets where there is not either pure competition or monopoly.

B. *sb.* **3.** *pl.* Goods of which the quality is not high enough for them to be sold to the public, except at a reduced price.

1952 *Amer. Speech* XXVII. 264 Textile products which ..do not come up to standard quality are referred to as *imperfects, seconds,* and *run-of-the-mill.* **1962** E. Godfrey *Retail Selling & Organization* II. x. 95 The retail buyers.. buy up manufacturers' and wholesalers'..factory imperfects. **1962** S. Strand *Marketing Dict.* 358 *Imperfect,* merchandise below standard... In many cases imperfects are useful products, but because of a manufacturer's flaw..they are removed from prime merchandise. **1969** *Observer* 9 Nov. 1/8 (Advt.), 'Imperfects' offered at a much reduced price.

imperfectibility. (Later example.)

1971 *Nature* 31 Dec. 523/1 The same principle of imperfectibility applies to all sex chromosome mechanisms.

imperfection. Add: **4. a.** *Printing. pl.* Letters that are wanting in a fount; types cast to make up a deficiency in a fount.

1681–5 Fell *Let. to Marshall* 24 Oct. (MS.), The compositor upon Mr. Junius his lexicon wants several imperfections, that we cannot supply without his Matrices. **1683–4** J. Moxon *Mech. Exerc. Printing* (1962) 344 When the Founder has not Cast a proportionable number of each sort of Letter, the wanting Letters are called Imperfections, as making the rest of the Fount unperfect. **1771** P. Luckombe *Hist. & Art of Printing* 243 Less occasion to cast imperfections, which often prove very hurtful to a new fount of letter; as they are seldom exact to the prior sorts..: so that, was it not for the eagerness of the Compositor,..many a sort, cast for perfecting, would be returned. **1808** C. Stower *Printer's Gram.* 56 It should be an invariable rule with master printers to examine imperfections before they go into the hands of the compositor. **1888** C. T. Jacobi *Printers' Vocab.* 61 *Imperfections,* short sorts required to perfect a typefounder's bill for a fount of a certain weight. **1924** *Southward's Mod. Printing* (ed. 5) I. xx. 124 The fount should be carefully examined with a view of ascertaining whether there are any imperfections—the founder's storekeepers sometimes making mistakes in the apportionment of particular letters. **1962** Davis & Carter in J. Moxon *Mech. Exerc. Printing* 344 (*footnote*) Typefounders charge for sorts at a higher rate than for founts; but sorts to supplement a fount, if ordered within three months of delivery of the fount, are called 'imperfections' and charged at fount-price.

b. *Bookbinding.* A surplus or missing sheet of a work.

1683–4 J. Moxon *Mech. Exerc. Printing* (1962) 315 He Doubles or Quires up all the other Heaps and..writes upon them Imperfections of (the Title of the Book), and Writes on it the Signature of the Sheet that is Wanting. **1790** A. Smith *Let.* 25 May in *Sotheby Catal.* (19 July 1937) lot 74, The bookbinder informed me..that one of the copies is imperfect, wanting the sheet E. I will beg the favour of you to send down the imperfection by the first parcel you send to Scotland. **1835** J. Hannett *Bibliopegia* I. 13 If any sheet is wanting or belongs to another volume, or is a duplicate, the further progress of the work must be suspended, till the imperfection is procured or exchanged. **1888** C. T. Jacobi *Printers' Vocab.* 61 *Imperfections,* sheets required by a binder to make good books imperfect through bad gathering, collating, or spoiled sheets. **1963** Kenneison & Spilman *Dict. Printing* 95 *Imperfections,* sheets rejected by the binder and returned to the printer to be replaced.

imperfective, *a.* (*sb.*). Add: **A.** *adj.* **2.** (Further examples.) Also, by extension, of a similar form or aspect in some non-Slavonic languages.

1912 [see *durative *a.*]. **1924** [see *aspect *sb.* 9 b]. **1955** *Word* XI. 546 In general it shows the action as completed (perfective) or incomplete (imperfective) relative to the time of the action of the main verb. **1957** R. W. Zandvoort *Handbk. Eng. Gram.* I. ii. 33 The aspect expressed by the present participle..is called *imperfective* or *durative.* **1958** H. G. Lunt *Fund. Russian* 59 The imperfective aspect does not say anything about the end of the action. **1972** *Language* XLVIII. 169 By accident, some presents with imperfective meaning contained an *e,* e.g. *bher-e-* 'carry'.

B. *sb.* **2.** An imperfective verb, case, or aspect.

1939 *Language* XV. 230 In a space of ten lines..there are four present imperfectives. *Ibid.,* The imperfectives, whether present or past, definitely indicate a repeated or a continuing action. **1949** *Ibid.* XXV. 403 There is only one present tense, namely an imperfective. **1949** *Archivum Linguisticum* I. II. 176 Imperfectives, if not iterative, become perfective by prefixing a preposition. **1962** K. Katzner *Russian Review Text* 183 The Imperfectives are called the *Determinati* and the *Indeterminati.* **1962** *Word* XVIII. 17 These 'secondary' imperfectives enter, in turn, into a derivational relation with the 'primary' imperfectives. **1965** *Canad. Jrnl. Linguistics* Spring 117 Agentives are apparently built upon future duratives, not upon imperfectives. **1966** *Jrnl. Linguistics* II. ii. 249 The distribution 52% perfectives, 48% imperfectives, confirms that the relative frequency..of the Russian marked and unmarked members differs sharply. **1972** Hartmann & Stork *Dict. Lang. & Ling.* 20 Ancient Greek, for example, had perfective, imperfective, and aorist.

Hence **imperfectiviza·tion** *Gram.,* the making of a verbal form or tense 'imperfective'; the condition of being 'imperfective'.

1943 *Language* XIX. 273 The statement of 'means of imperfectivization' is a list of suffixes. **1962** *Word* XVIII. 15 Its function is basically grammatical, i.e. that of imperfectivization. **1966** *Jrnl. Linguistics* II. ii. 249 A formal distinction, as regards morphological potentiality, secondary imperfectivization, is made.

imperial, *a.* and *sb.* Add: **A.** *adj.* **2. c.** Designating certain decorations or orders.

1878 *London Gaz.* (Suppl.) 4 Jan. 113/1 The Queen has been graciously pleased..to institute and create an Order of Distinction, to be styled and designated 'The Imperial Order of the Crown of India'. **1902** *Encycl. Brit.* XXXI. 340/1 The Imperial Service Order was..instituted on 26th June 1902, to commemorate King Edward's coronation. *Ibid.,* The Imperial Order of the Crown of India is conferred for like purposes as the order of the Indian Empire. **1971** *Whitaker's Almanack* 261 The Imperial Service Order..consists of the Sovereign and Companions (not exclusively male) to a number not exceeding 1325 of whom 750 may belong to the Home Civil Services and 575 to Overseas Civil Services.

d. *Imperial Defence*: defence of Great Britain and of its dependent territories.

1897 G. S. Clarke (*title*) Imperial defence. **1902** *Encycl. Brit.* XXVI. 401/1 The appointment in 1879 of a royal commission to consider the question of Imperial defence, which presented its report in 1882, led to a considerable development and reorganization of the system of Imperial fortifications. **1910** *Ibid.* III. 254/1 His [*sc.* A. J. Balfour's] institution of the permanent Committee of Imperial Defence, and of the new Army Council (1904), were reforms of the highest importance. **1938** *Ann. Reg. 1937* 67 The national defence was being quite adequately organised by the Committee of Imperial Defence.

e. Designating a policy or an institution concerned with the development of commerce between the constituent parts of the British Commonwealth (formerly the British Empire); esp. in *imperial preference,* a system of tariff concessions granted by members of the British Empire or Commonwealth to one another.

1902 *Encycl. Brit.* XXVI. 397/2 The foundation of the Imperial Federation League—in 1884. *Ibid.* XXXIII. 393/1 The British Empire League, and the Imperial Trade Defence League endeavour to promote inter-Imperial trade. *Ibid.* 681/2 On 4th July she laid the foundation stone of the Imperial Institute. **1912** J. S. Huxley *Individual in Animal Kingdom* ii. 54 All the wheat in Canada, with Imperial Preference to help, would not keep her [*sc.* the English nation] from starvation. **1922** *Encycl. Brit.* XXX. 1016/2 At the end of April [1917] Mr. Bonar Law announced..that the Imperial War Cabinet had accepted the principle of Imperial Preference. *Ibid.* 1025/2 The main feature of the budget [1919] was the establishment at last of imperial preference. **1927** *Daily Tel.* 5 Mar. 8/7 Appreciation of the work of the Imperial Economic Committee and the Empire Marketing Board for the development of the market for Dominion produce in Great Britain. **1931** G. C. Tryon (*title*) Short history of imperial preference. **1958** *Listener* 18 Sept. 407/2 Both [*sc.* Australia and New Zealand] have sought to give foreign suppliers a better competitive position in their own markets by reducing imperial preferences to oil the wheels of reciprocity. **1971** A. Shonfield in A. Bullock *20th Cent.* xiv. 331/2 The Imperial Preference system was successful in helping the British industrial recovery in the 1930s.

8. b. or **B. 5. b.** (The old measurements have been replaced: see quots.)

1952 E. J. Labarre *Dict. Paper* (ed. 2) 130/1 *Imperial.* Now standardized for writings and printings at 30″ × 22″ and for wrappings at 29″ × 22½″, for boards at 30″ × 22½″ and their multiples. **1968** *Specification Sizes Papers & Boards (B.S.I.)* 14 (*heading*) Table 2. Writing and printing papers and offset cartridges... Imperial..22 × 30. *Ibid.* 15 Table 3. Ledger papers... Imperial..22 × 30. *Ibid.* 17 Table 7. Paste boards; and duplex, triplex and ivory boards... Paste imperial..22½ × 30. *Ibid.,* Table 8. Drawing cartridges... Imperial..22 × 30.

10. *imperial elephant, mammoth* [tr. of *Elephas imperator* (J. Leidy 1858, in *Proc. Acad. Nat. Sci. Philadelphia* 10), which was later included in the genus *Mammuthus*]: a fossil mammal, *Mammuthus imperator,* found in Pleistocene remains in south-western North America; *imperial pigeon,* a large fruit-eating pigeon, esp. one of the genus *Ducula,* found in south-eastern Asia, including India, and the Pacific region.

1913 W. B. Scott *Hist. Land Mammals W. Hemisphere* xii. 485 The largest of American proboscideans was the Imperial Elephant. **1910** H. F. Osborn *Age of Mammals* vi. 442 The Columbian and imperial mammoths were for a time at least contemporaneous with the mastodon. **1945** A. S. Romer *Vertebr. Paleont.* (ed. 2) xxi. 416 *M[ammuthus] imperator,* the imperial mammoth of southern North America, was more advanced in size and dental development. **1966** Imperial mammoth [see *baluchitherium]. **1864** T. C. Jerdon *Birds India* III. 455 *Carpophaga sylvatica...* Imperial Pigeon of Europeans in the South of India. **1895** *Jrnl. Bombay Nat. Hist. Soc.* X. 360 The green Imperial Pigeon..may be frequently met with nearly all over North Cachar. **1913** E. C. S. Baker *Indian Pigeons & Doves* 103 Hodgson's Imperial Pigeon is less quarrelsome than most of the family. **1934** 'G. Orwell' *Burmese Days* xiv. 211 Flo [*sc.* a dog]..came running excitedly up..with the big imperial pigeon in her mouth. **1967** D. Goodwin *Pigeons & Doves of World* 384 The large species of fruit pigeons are often termed the imperial pigeons because of their impressive and majestic-looking if somewhat ponderous appearance.

B. *sb.* **8.** (Earlier examples.)

The earlier examples confute the attribution of the style to the Emperor Napoleon III (who became Emperor in 1852).

[**1829** Balzac *La Maison du Chat-qui-Pelote* in *Œuvres* (1938) I. 64 Sa figure..était encore animée par de petites moustaches relevées en pointe et noires comme du jais, par une impériale bien fournie,..et par une forêt de cheveux noirs assez en désordre.] **1835** S. Horsley *Let.* in R. B. Gotch *Mendelssohn & his Friends in Kensington* (1934) 192 What with his black hair longer than ever, a *beard* which he is now cultivating to a great length, mustachios and an imperial,..made you suspect the fact of his having escaped across the country from some wandering menagerie. **1838** H. Mozley *Let.* 2 Nov. in D. Mozley *Newman Family Lett.* (1962) 77 Mr. Sidney Herbert..is..a silly looking coxcomb, with a most disfiguring imperial. **1839** *Blackw. Mag.* Oct. 507/2 An imperial—*i.e.* a dirt-coloured tuft of hair.

imperialism. Add: **2.** (Earlier and U.S. examples.)

1878 J. Chamberlain *Let.* 15 Oct. in J. L. Garvin *Life J. Chamberlain* (1932) I. 267 This infernal Afghan business is the natural consequence of Jingoism, Imperialism, 'British interests', [etc.]. **1899** H. H. Bancroft *New Pacific* viii. 145 The word imperialism is used in this connection in a modern, American sense, as applicable to the empire of industry as well as to domain... It [implies].. the extension of political and commercial influence, particularly in the Pacific. **1899** Carnegie in *North Amer. Rev.* Jan. 5 Imperialism implies naval and military force behind; moral force, education, civilization are not the backbone of Imperialism. **1914** *Cycl. Amer. Govt.* II. 152/1 As used in American politics, imperialism is employed to designate the policy on which the United States has embarked of acquiring territory not a part of the United States proper, nor contiguous to it.

3. Used disparagingly. In Communist writings: the imperial system or policy of the Western powers. Used conversely in some Western writings: the imperial system or policy of the Communist powers.

1918 *Manch. Guardian* 13 Dec. 7/4 The Menshevik and the small bourgeois parties have published a declaration calling on workers all over the world to rally to the support of the Russian Revolution against the Imperialism attacking it. **1939** Varga & Mendelsohn (*title*) New data for V. I. Lenin's 'Imperialism, the highest stage of capitalism'. **1957** C. Hunt *Guide to Communist Jargon* xxiv. 82 The term imperialism has largely replaced Capitalism in the Communist vocabulary. *Ibid.* 83 The essential features of imperialism are the concentration of capital, the merging of industrial and banking capital into 'finance capital' and the division of the world between national and international monopolies. **1957** *Encycl. Brit.* VI. 135/2 They [*sc.* the Communists] regarded the cause of World War II to be not German aggression but British and French imperialism. **1964** Gould & Kolb *Dict. Social Sci.* 319/2 It is sometimes said that Russian control of East European countries is 'Russian imperialism'.

imperialist. Add: **1.** (Later example.)

1900 *Westm. Gaz.* 14 Sept. 2/2 It is interesting to note a new use of the word Imperialist in to-day's *Daily News*: 'A troop of American cavalry surprised 300 Imperialists at Shaho...' This is from Pekin—clearly Imperialist is to be the way of distinguishing the Chinese Imperial troops from rebel Boxers.

3. (Later U.S. example.)

1900 *Congress. Rec.* 11 Jan. 766/2 The trouble with these imperialists is that they confound the Government of the United States with their puny President.

3*. An advocate of 'imperialism' (sense *3).

1963 [see *capitulationism]. **1969** *Times* 8 Aug. 1/2 'We all know,' Mr. Katushev said, 'how violently the imperialists are fighting on all fronts..to give support to anti-socialist forces.'

4. (Later examples.) Also *Comb.*

1937 [see *capitalist]. **1957** C. Hunt *Guide to Communist Jargon* xxiv. 83 Lenin does not seem to have regarded the actual possession of an empire as essential to it [*sc.* imperialism], so that, according to his theory, the United States is an imperialist Power, as communist propaganda daily represents it. **1967** H. Arendt *Origins Totalitarianism* (new ed.) v. 130 The imperialist-minded businessmen were followed by civil servants who wanted 'the African to be left an African'. *Ibid.* viii. 257 The imperialist-inspired 'parties above parties' had never known how to profit from popular hatred of the party system as such. **1969** *Times* 8 Aug. 1/2 President Ceausescu [of Rumania] argued that the socialist world was strong enough to safeguard itself against imperialist tactics. *Ibid.* 21 Aug. 7/3 The Soviet Union stood revealed for what it now is—an imperialist power. **1973** D. Miller *Chinese Jade Affair* xviii. 174 The K.M.T. group.. would probably suggest that K. Lawson was engaged in a typical Western imperialist plot.

imperialistic, *a.* (Later examples.)

1933 N. Waln *House of Exile* III. iii. 223 His remarks were a stirring appeal to the citizens of China to unite against the 'Imperialistic Foreign Devil'. **1958** [see *colonial *a.* 1 a]. **1969** *Listener* 24 Apr. 568/3 They show the unwavering will of the people to make up for all the damage done by these imperialistic traitors in the shortest possible time.

imperishable. Add: Also as *sb.*

a **1910** 'Mark Twain' *Mysterious Stranger* (1916) iii. 27, I am of the aristocracy of the Imperishables. **1964** *New Statesman* 3 Apr. 514/2, I have seen *Oliver Twist,*..and a number of Jules Verne's imperishables.

impersistent, *a.* (Earlier and later examples.)

a **1866** J. Grote *Exam. Utilitarian Philos.* (1870) xix. 324 We ought..to know whether some races are strong and persistent,..others weak and impersistent, so as to yield to others and die out. **1965** G. J. Williams *Econ. Geol. N.Z.* iii. 27/2 Various impersistent shoots were worked in the Pandora and South Keep-it-Dark mines.

impersonalism (impə̄·ɹsənăliz'm). [f. IMPERSONAL *a.* + -ISM.] The character of being impersonal; the absence of personal contacts. So **impe·rsonalist**, one who is, or aims at being, impersonal; **impersonali·stic** *a.*

1899 *Speaker* 9 Dec. 263/1 The weak point in the armour of the impersonalist is the dedication. **1908** *Daily Chron.* 26 May 3/4 The workmen are getting the impersonalism of Socialism without its humanity. **1920** F. M. FORD *Let.* 30 June (1965) 109 There is the whole open question of Impersonalism to discuss. **1932** J. C. POWYS *Glastonbury Romance* xxvi. 907 It was the appearance of Dave Spear's figure now—for the impersonalist had decided to disobey Zookey—that drove the tipsy giant to his next move. **1968** *Austral. Jrnl. Philos.* XLVI. 257 The existence of such principles, principles which are perfectly consistent as 'impersonalistic' principles are actually used but which would be inconsistent if 'impersonalistic' principles were used in the way being supposed, does not, however, give impersonalism any sort of advantage over nonimpersonalism.

impersonally, *adv.* **2.** (Earlier example.)

1854 A. G. HENDERSON tr. *Cousin's Philos. of Kant* vii. 178 There is a state..where the reason manifests itself almost entirely impersonally.

impersonalness (impə̄·ɹsənălnes). [f. IMPERSONAL *a.* + -NESS.] Impersonal quality; absence of personality.

1871 P. BROOKS *Let.* 11 Jan. in A. V. G. Allen *Phillips Brooks* (1908) 247 When I see a small audience I lose the impersonalness of the thing. I think of individuals and that always puts me out. **1955** P. HERON *Changing Forms of Art* 233 In his painting it never matters one jot when his beautiful girl has a distinctly anonymous air. Her impersonalness is part of her charm. **1956** A. TOYNBEE *Historian's Approach to Relig.* iv. 44 The impersonalness of an oecumenical empire as an institution makes itself felt in the remoteness of its metropolis from the daily life of the great majority of its subjects.

imphee. (Earlier examples.)

1857 *Country Gentleman* 11 June 379/2 A plant bearing the name of *Imphee*, or *Imphey*, or *Imphye*..which it is alleged is identical with the Chinese Sugar Cane, has been introduced by Mr. Leonard Wray, from Southern Africa. **1862** T. BAINES *Jrnl.* 5 Apr. in *Explor. S.-W. Afr.* (1864) xiv. 438, I..spent the intervening time with a circle of old fellows, who gave me imphi (holcus saccharatus) stalks to chew.

impi. (Earlier and later examples.)

1862 G. H. MASON *Zululand* xv. 200 There is always an 'Impi', (or army,) preparing for an attack on some neighbouring district. **1970** *Cape Times* 28 Oct. 2/9 Lands rich in grass and game and savage impis. **1971** *Rand Daily Mail* 4 Dec. 3/4 Dressed in full tribal regalia of leopard skin and feathers he led the dancing and singing impis who paid homage to their king.

impinge, *v.* **3.** Delete *Obs.* and add example.

1910 *Practitioner* July 109 The striker's thumb..impinges the skull of his opponent.

impinger (impi·ndʒəɹ). [f. IMPING(E *v.* + -ER[1].] Any of various instruments for collecting samples of the particles suspended in air (or another gas), this being either drawn into a liquid or directed in a jet against a flat surface so that some particles are deposited.

1922 *Rep. Investigations U.S. Bureau of Mines* No. 2392. 3 The analytical procedure necessary when using this new impinger-bubbler apparatus is almost identical with that employed with the Palmer apparatus. **1932** *Jrnl. Industr. Hygiene & Toxicol.* XIV. 301/1 The Greenburg-Smith impinger was introduced in 1922. **1936** DRINKER & HATCH *Industr. Dust* vii. 116 The impinger flasks, stoppers, etc., should be washed..in..the sampling fluid. **1945** [see *IMPACTOR 2]. **1972** BLAKESLEE & RECKNER in R. D. ROSS *Air Pollution & Industry* v. 270 Dry impingers are capable of depositing particles in distinct size ranges on surfaces such as microscope slides. Several units are connected in series, each containing an orifice which is aimed at the surface.

impinging, *ppl. a.* (Later example.)

1955 *Sci. News Let.* 14 May 308/1 Mercury vapor inside the vacuum tube gives the glow as its atoms are excited by impinging electrons.

implant, *v.* Add: **1. b.** *Med.* Surgically to place or insert (tissue, or something inorganic) in the body: used esp. when what is inserted does not correspond with what is naturally found at the site that receives it.

1886 W. D. YOUNGER *Implantation of Teeth* 8, I have since tried implanting teeth which have been extracted for weeks and months. **1887** *Lancet* 12 Feb. 334/2 In his early attempts he used fresh teeth, which he obtained from other dentists..and endeavoured to keep alive by implanting them in cocks' combs. **1919** *Jrnl. Amer. Med. Assoc.* 26 July 301/1 On the other hand, the pathologic opaque [corneal] graft, implanted in sound tissue, grows normal and in time becomes transparent. **1927** *Lancet* 15 Jan. 120/2 Animals not infrequently recover from tumours implanted into them. **1941** *Jrnl. Amer. Med. Assoc.* 27 Sept. 1070/1 In January 1940 a 200 mg. tablet of testosterone was implanted. After another month, hair appeared on the upper lip..and the penis further increased in size. **1952** *Brit. Jrnl. Radiol.* XXV. 423/2 A method of implanting radioactive Ta^{182} wire for the treatment of patients with carcinoma of the bladder is described. **1963** *Lancet* 12 Jan. 78/1 The amnion was prepared and implanted by the method of Troensegaard-Hansen (1956). In 8 cases where symptoms were unilateral the implant was placed in the affected leg. **1964** *Ann. N.Y. Acad. Sci.* CXI. 1063 During the past 3 years the pacemaker has been implanted in 43 patients ranging in age from 39 to 85 years.

3. b. Delete *rare* and add to def.: to furnish *with* by insertion or implantation. (Further examples.)

1919 *Lancet* 29 Mar. 490/2 We are dealing with serum implanted with gas-gangrene bacilli. *Ibid.* 493/2 An agar surface implanted with a serophytic organism. **1956** *Brit. Jrnl. Radiol.* XXIX. 509/1 When the whole area.. has been 'implanted' with the introducing needles, their stilettes are removed and tantalum wires..are passed down their lumina. **1968** *Canad. Jrnl. Physics* XLVI. 671/1 A silicon sample implanted at room temperature with As ions. **1971** *Nature* 18 June 454/2 Sprague-Dawley male albino rats were stereotaxically implanted..with stainless steel cannula systems for the injection of.. various amines.

4. *intr. Embryol.* To be or become implanted; to undergo implantation (sense *6).

1954 *Contrib. Embryol.* XXXV. 219/1 It appears.. that the human blastocyst in the same stage of development implants earlier than that of the macaque. **1963** C. G. HARTMAN *Mechanisms Conception* vii. 349 After transfer to pseudopregnant hosts, the blastocysts implanted..with about the same frequency of success as blastocysts transferred without cultivation. **1967** STRONG & CORNEY *Placenta in Twin Pregnancy* ii. 16 They may implant at adjacent sites so that the placentae in growing would fuse to form a dichorionic, but single placenta. **1970** *Sci. Jrnl.* June 48/1 Fertilization takes place in the Fallopian tube and some days later the fertilized egg implants into the lining of the uterus.

implant (i·mplɑnt), *sb.* [f. IMPLANT *v.*] **a.** Anything implanted, esp. within the body.

1890 *Sat. Rev.* 15 Nov. 551/2 It seemed to tell of an ineradicable implant of commercial hypocrisy. **1911** *Chem. Abstr.* V. 2499 However, since after extirpation of these implants the hypersensitiveness persisted, it would seem that sessile receptors are not essential. **1919** *Jrnl. Amer. Med. Assoc.* 26 July 301/1 A disk is cut from the opaque cornea and another from the transparent periphery, and the disks are transposed. The transparent implant being impermeable, like all autografts, becomes invaded by the abnormal elements surrounding it. **1952** *Brit. Jrnl. Radiol.* XXV. 421/1 A radon-seed implant has proved to be a useful method of treatment for early carcinoma of the bladder. **1961** J. N. ANDERSON *Appl. Dental Materials* (ed. 2) viii. 79 They [*sc.* chrome-cobalt alloys] can..be used as an 'implant' beneath the gum to which a denture may be fastened. **1963** [see *IMPLANT *v.* 1 b]. **1968** *New Scientist* 11 Jan. 80/1 In recent years surgeons have been fitting an increasing number of implants to fix and repair damaged bones. **1968** *Brit. Med. Bull.* XXIV. 242/1 Radium implants for radiation therapy. **1968** *Canad. Jrnl. Physics* XLVI. 667/1 Since the implanted atoms are confined to a surface region less than 0·1 μ thick, a well-defined 'impurity' peak is observed in the scattering spectra. [*Note*] In the case of phosphorus implants..the mass difference between P and Si is too small for the 'impurity' peak to be resolved.

b. An act or operation of implanting something; an implantation.

1941 *Jrnl. Amer. Med. Assoc.* 27 Sept. 1069/1 Our more recent multiple 50 mg. pellet implants were performed with a trocar. **1970** *Times* 28 Apr. 5/4 French doctors today made the world's first implant of an atomic powered heart simulator into a human being.

implantable (implɑ·ntăb'l), *a.* [f. IMPLANT *v.* + -ABLE.] Capable of being implanted (in the body).

1960 C. N. SMYTH *Med. Electronics* 253 (*heading*) An implantable pacemaker for the heart. **1965** *Adv. Biol. & Med. Physics* X. 367 It is conservatively estimated that over 4000 implantable cardiac pacemakers have been used to date with gratifying results. **1972** *Physics Bull.* June 336/2 Since there is no sign of complex implantable functioning organs at the present stage of medical engineering technology, devices which replace heart, lung, kidney or liver remain outside the body.

implantation. 5. b. Add def.: The (or an) operation of implanting something in the body (see *IMPLANT *v.* 1 b). (Earlier and later examples.)

1885 M. HAY tr. *H. von Ziemssen's Handbk. Gen. Therapeutics* II. 399 The method described by Bruns, and characterised by him as dry injection or implantation... In this, the drugs are likewise applied in thin cylinders or plugs, for the introduction of which..a special form of implantation needle is used. **1886** W. D. YOUNGER (*title*) Implantation of teeth and pericemental life. **1887** *Lancet* 12 Feb. 334/1 Implantation is the ingrafting of a natural tooth into an artificial socket. **1929** *Jrnl. Amer. Med. Assoc.* 1 June 1900/2 In cases..in which it is not possible to remove the oviducts without removing the ovaries, Michel cuts off a piece of one of the resected ovaries..and sutures it to the uterus... He obtained good results in six out of seven cases in which he used his method of autoplastic implantation of a portion of an ovary. **1938** *Lancet* 10 Sept. 606/2 A very prolonged effect of certain androgens and œstrogens could be obtained by a single implantation, under the skin, of pure dry hormone in the form of crystals or compressed tablets. **1963** *Ibid.* 12 Jan. 77/2 Troensegaard-Hansen (1956) described the treatment of intermittent claudication by implantation of human amnion into the thigh. **1969** H. A. SALHANICK et al. *Metabolic Effects Gonadal Hormones* 723 The most direct experimental approach to this problem is by the intracranial implantation of small amounts of crystalline steroids.

6. *Embryol.* The attachment of the fertilized ovum (blastocyst) to the wall of the uterus.

1902 A. KEITH *Human Embryol.* viii. 96 The implantation of the ovum in the decidua is in the posterior wall of the uterus in over 60% of cases. **1936** F. J. TAUSSIG *Abortion* iv. 70 In about ten days from fertilization, the ovum is ready for implantation. **1969** KLOPPER & DICZFALUSY *Foetus & Placenta* iii. 62 Implantation begins on the 20th day of the cycle, and probably takes several days to complete...The great majority of implantations in the case of the human take place in the fundus of the uterus and in the posterior wall.

7. *Physics.* The introduction of ions into a crystalline structure by bombardment with an ion beam.

1965 *Nuclear Instruments & Methods* XXXVIII. 169/2 Implantations reported in this paper were made in a 24 inch radius calutron. **1967** *Canad. Jrnl. Physics* XLV. 4053 Because of the nonequilibrium nature of the implantation process, the relative number of impurities on substitutional and interstitial sites may differ from that observed following conventional thermal diffusion. **1973** *Sci. Amer.* Apr. 65/3 The accelerated-ion technique offers fairly precise control of both the number of ions implanted and the depth of implantation.

implanted, *ppl. a.* (In Dict. after IMPLANT *v.*) Add: **2.** In sense corresponding to IMPLANT *v.* 3 b (in Dict. and Suppl.): having something implanted or inserted into it; *spec.* containing implanted ions.

1965 *Nuclear Instruments & Methods* XXXVIII. 172/1 Fig. 7 shows variation in the sheet resistance of an implanted area with temperature. **1970** *New Scientist* 15 Oct. Suppl. 17/2 The Japanese..have already announced an implanted microwave transistor. **1973** WILSON & BREWER *Ion Beams* iv. 300 The oxide serves..to protect against compensation of the implanted region during a subsequent diffusion.

implausibility (implǭzĭbi·lĭti). Delete † *Obs. rare* and add later examples.

1926 B. FREEMAN *Towards Answer* 7 Perhaps the thing is an impossibility or an implausibility. **1966** G. N. LEECH *Eng. in Advertising* ii. 17 The other two examples are also freakish..because of their contextual implausibility.

implausible, *a.* **2.** (Later examples.)

1971 *Nature* 5 Feb. 408/1 It is implausible that such animals should have preceded in time the small and structurally different species *Hipparion nagriensis* Hussain. **1974** *Daily Tel.* 20 Feb. 13/2 The play was..a highly stagey and implausible piece.

implausibly, *adv.* (Later examples.)

1928 *Music & Lett.* July 234 Men..able to..write categorically though implausibly. **1965** *Chicago Tribune* 10 Aug., The principal river..was variously named Konomick, Killamick, Calamick and sundry other versions which some claim, implausibly, meant 'white beaver'.

implead, *v.* **1.** Delete 'Now only *arch.* or *Hist.*', and add later examples.

1957 *Listener* 19 Dec. 1020/1 Can one implead the State concerned? *Ibid.*, At present you cannot implead a State in United Kingdom Courts except under the Warsaw Convention. **1964** *Welsh Hist. Rev.* II. 47 It was further stipulated that a similar arrangement would be adopted if Owain or Llywelyn or their heirs wished to implead any of the King's subjects. **1973** *N.Y. Law Jrnl.* 1 Aug. 1/7 The plaintiff sued the appellant for damages for fraudulent acts under the contract. The appellant impleaded the plaintiff's president on his guarantee.

implement, *v.* Delete 'Chiefly *Sc.*' and add examples of sense 1 a.

1909 *Westm. Gaz.* 30 Aug. 4/3 [The] council has been prepared to implement that agreement. **1950** C. MORRIS *Social Case-Work Gt. Brit.* 7 With the post-war flood of social legislation, social workers are required..to help to implement the laws. **1964** *Ann. Reg. 1963* 102 Henceforward the bargaining..continued until late in the year, with some decisions being announced and implemented piecemeal. **1969** *Times* 3 Sept. 11/6 Three years later Armageddon found him [*sc.* Churchill] ready at the Admiralty with plans and authority to implement that policy. **1972** *Daily Tel.* 27 June 2/7 The provision of the Act of which they are most apprehensive..has yet to be implemented by the Government.

implementation (i:mplĭmĕntē̆i·ʃən). [f. IMPLEMENT *v.* + -ATION.] The action of implementing; fulfilment.

1926 *Spectator* 16 Oct. 627/1 The Irish delegation will seek the implementation of co-equality with the States of the British Commonwealth. **1944** *Mind* LIII. 184 Professor Collingwood's *Principles of Art* attempted an implementation and restatement on the epistemological side. **1951** R. FIRTH *Elem. Social Organiz.* ii. 45 In a democratic society consent of the individual is ultimately necessary for the implementation of programmes. **1955** *Bull. Atomic Sci.* June 223/3 As a possible mode of implementation, I suggest that a civilian-directed Scientists Corps (SC) be set up within the Defense Department for an emergency. **1965** *Listener* 27 May 775/2 Such plans..were fundamentally sound in the practical potential of implementation. **1973** *Daily Tel.* 16 Mar. 6/4 The successful implementation of this policy is vital. The cost of failure is incalculable.

implicans (implikæ·nz). *Logic.* The pl. form used is **implicants.** [L., pres. pple. of *implicāre* (see IMPLICATE *v.*).] In implication (see *IMPLICATION 2 c), the active proposition; the proposition that implies. Cf. also IMPLICATE *sb.* 2. in Dict. and Suppl.

1921 W. E. JOHNSON *Logic* I. ii. 30 In the implicative function 'If *p* then *q*', *p* is the implicans and *q* the implicate. **1922** *Ibid.* II. x. 211 We shall take..the implicants and disjuncts to stand for particular propositions. **1930** L. S. STEBBING *Mod. Introd. Logic* v. 70 It is clear that the order of the implicans and the implicate is not indifferent. **1937** D. J. B. HAWKINS *Causality & Implication* 61 This factor consists in the implicans being given in reality, as opposed to merely given in thought. **1953** I. M. COPI *Introd. Logic* viii. 229 The constituent statement between the 'if' and the 'then' is called the *antecedent* (or the implicans). **1963** J. LYONS *Structural Semantics* vii. 189 Sentences of the form Np [etc.]..with their transforms and implicants..are well integrated in the field.

implicate. B. *sb.* **2.** (Later examples.)

1900 [see *extraconscious* (*EXTRA- 1)]. **1921** W. E. JOHNSON *Logic* I. iii. 35 From an implicative, combined with the affirmation of its implications, we may infer the affirmation of its implicate. **1937** D. J. B. HAWKINS *Causality & Implication* 61 What factor..must be present in order that the implicate should be dependent in being on the implicans. **1946** C. MORRIS *Signs, Lang. & Behavior* i. 22 A sign which is more general than another sign,..is an analytic implicate of the other sign. **1971** *Jrnl. Gen. Psychol.* Apr. 222 A theorem deducible only from the conjunction of axioms as their only implicate is, therefore, most probative of the theory that contains them.

implication. Add: **2. c.** *Logic.* A relationship between propositions such that the one implies the other; also, a proposition asserting such a relationship. Also *attrib.*

1906 B. RUSSELL in *Amer. Jrnl. Math.* XXVIII. 202 The subject which comes next in logical order is the theory of *formal* implication. **1922** W. E. JOHNSON *Logic* II. vi. 152 When a formula of implication is used as a premiss in the process of deduction, its implicans must first be formally certified in order that its implicate may be formally certified. **1932** LEWIS & LANGFORD *Symbolic Logic* v. 93 The dot preceding the implication-sign. **1947** H. REICHENBACH *Elem. Symbolic Logic* § 6.24 The expression to the left of the implication sign is called implicans. **1952** P. F. STRAWSON *Introd. Logical Theory* iii. 85 The futility of identifying conditional statements with material implications is obvious. **1954** I. M. COPI *Symbolic Logic* ix. 286 The proposition..may have its implication sign deleted. **1957** A. N. PRIOR *Time & Modality* i. 1 Moh Shaw-Kwei has attempted to lay down the conditions which entitle an operator to be considered as an implication-operator. **1963** W. SELLARS in Castañeda & Nakhnikian *Morality & Lang. of Conduct* 178 In other words, shall-statements, unlike implication statements, are in the object-language. **1968** J. LYONS *Introd. Theoretical Ling.* x. 446 Implication, in the sense in which it has been defined here, is in principle objectively testable.

implicational (implikēi·ʃənăl), *a. Logic.* [f. IMPLICATION + -AL.] Of, concerned with, or using implication.

1881 H. MACCOLL in *Phil. Mag.* XI. 40 (*title*) Implicational and equational logic. **1881** J. VENN *Symbolic Logic* xviii. 377 In this case the implicational mode of expression certainly tells its tale more simply and obviously. **1906** B. RUSSELL in *Amer. Jrnl. Math.* XXVIII. 198 Thus both *p* and not-*p* may be replaced, in implicational formulae, by equivalences. *a* **1943** R. G. COLLINGWOOD *Idea of Hist.* (1946) 262 This implicational relation is a compulsive one. **1951** J. ŁUKASIEWICZ *Aristotle's Syllogistic* 22 It is always easy to deduce from an implicational thesis the corresponding rule of inference. **1955** A. N. PRIOR *Formal Logic* 49 Łukasiewicz has shown that a single axiom for the 'implicational calculus' must contain at least 13 letters. **1964** *Language* XL. 264 Most of his universals are 'implicational', of the type 'if a language has a category of gender, it always has a category of number'. **1970** *Ibid.* XLVI. 551 These studies reveal that socially significant linguistic features occur in an implicational series such that the presence of some feature A in the speech of a certain individual means that the speaker will also be found to use features B, C, and D. *Ibid.* 552 Since implicational analysis requires binary decisions.. how can such..decisions be made? **1971** *Newslet. Amer. Dial. Soc.* Feb. 16 Implicational analysis..'attempts not to describe a set of speech acts but to model the idealized competence of the persons involved in those speech acts'. **1972** *Computer Jrnl.* XV. 292/2 One can define the set of all strings which are proofs in implicational calculus.

Hence **implica·tionally** *adv.*, in an implicational manner.

1922 W. E. JOHNSON *Logic* II. v. 108 Such a trio of equations are taken to be implicationally independent of one another. **1964** *Current Res. & Devel. Sci. Documentation* XIII. 220 Extensive investigations are also being carried out on procedures of proof in implicationally ordered formal systems.

implicative. Add: **A.** *adj.* (Later examples.) Also, containing at least implications or implications only.

1910 WHITEHEAD & RUSSELL *Principia* I. i. 7 The Implicative Function is a propositional function with two arguments *p* and *q*. **1930** L. S. STEBBING *Mod. Introd. Logic* v. 71 The implicative proposition cannot be simply converted. **1955** A. N. PRIOR *Formal Logic* 61 A purely implicative formula. **1967** *Listener* 5 Oct. 422/3 Substitution of implicative features for defining features—that is, the use of emotive language—is the trade-mark of propaganda. **1971** *Language* XLVII. 341 For reasons that will soon become apparent, I suggest the terms 'implicative' and 'non-implicative' verbs.

Hence **impli·cativeness,** the quality of being implicative.

1932 *Times Lit. Suppl.* 2 June 411/3 Professor Trout's chapters on the systolic and diastolic implicativeness of 'religious rapport' and 'religious dominance'. **1951** J. MILES *Primary Lang. Poetry* 493 Richards allies emotion..to order, and so supports its implicativeness in shape and form and connotation.

implicatively, *adv.* Delete ? *obs.* and add later example.

1953 PARTRIDGE *Shaggy Dog Story* iii. 84 Many years ago *Collier's Weekly* published, implicatively as reminiscence, a 'shaggy dog' that must..rank very high.

implicit, *a.* Add: **2.** *implicit definition* = **contextual definition.*

1959 K. R. POPPER *Logic Sci. Discovery* iii. 72 Sometimes the axioms are described as '*implicit definitions*' of the ideas which they introduce. **1961** E. NAGEL *Struct. of Sci.* v. 95 The fundamental assumptions of the theory provide only implicit definitions for the theoretical notions employed in them. **1973** A. QUINTON *Nature of Things* ix. 279 We can thus define a logical term as one whose meaning is wholly specified by implicit definitions.

impliedly, *adv.* (Later examples.)

1964 *Mod. Law Rev.* XXVII. III. 266 Furthermore, it must be noted that union officials could equally be drawn into a 'conspiracy to intimidate impliedly'. **1970** [see *CORPS 2 b].

implode, *v.* Add: **1.** Also *trans.* and *fig.* Hence **implo·ded, implo·ding** *ppl. adjs.*

1913 J. MURRAY *Ocean* v. 97 Only those parts of the structure would be burst inwards ('imploded') into which water could not enter rapidly enough to equalise the pressure on the two sides, say, of an iron plate. **1963** *Observer* 17 Mar. 3/3 The 'jet' could be in the outer part of the galaxy, and might represent part of the imploding star which has broken away. **1964** M. MCLUHAN *Understanding Media* I. iii. 35 In our present electric age the imploding or contracting energies of our world now clash with the old expansionist and traditional patterns of organization. *Ibid.* v. 51 Individualism is not possible in an electrically patterned and imploded society. **1973** *Sci. Amer.* Mar. 46/2 Applied evenly around the surface, these forces would suddenly implode the pellet to a density 100 times higher than that of lead.

implore, *v.* **1. c.** Delete *rare* and add further examples.

1850 F. E. SMEDLEY *Frank Fairlegh* xv. 136 'Gentlemen, don't ring the bells, pray,' implored the old man. **1887** M. CORELLI *Thelma* III. III. ii. 251 'Let me go with thee!' he implored, in broken accents. **1891** HARDY *Group Noble Dames* 101 'Oh, take it away—please take it away!' she implored.

2. Later examples; const. *for* (a thing), *of* (a person).

1870 H. SMART *Race for Wife* x, She flopped down on her knees, and implored for mercy. **1904** L. T. MEADE *Love Triumphant* ii. 15, I implored of Granny to let us leave the cottage.

implosion. Add: **3.** *fig.* (as the opposite of *explosion*).

1960 J. G. BALLARD in D. Knight *100 Yrs. Sci. Fiction* (1969) 350 The population of Sumatra, for example, has declined by over fifteen per cent in the last twenty years...Do you realize that only two or three decades ago the Neo-Malthusians were talking about a 'world population explosion'? In fact, it's an implosion. **1964** M. MCLUHAN *Understanding Media* I. vii. 71 The rush of students into our universities is not explosion but implosion. *Ibid.* II. x. 92 Our speed-up today is not a slow explosion outward from center to margins but an instant implosion and an interfusion of space and functions.

implosive, *a.* Add: **2.** *fig.* (Cf. prec. word.)

1964 M. MCLUHAN *Understanding Media* II. xi. 111 The implosive (compressional) character of the electric technology. *Ibid.* xix. 185 The implosive speed of the airplane. **1967** *Listener* 8 June 744/1 Television has an implosive effect on a culture.

Hence **implo·siveness.**

1953 C. E. BAZELL *Ling. Form* 42 If all initial occlusives are explosive and all final occlusives are implosive, it is obvious that two distinct conventions (explosiveness of initials and implosiveness of finals) need not be postulated.

impolder (impōu·ldəɹ), *v.* [ad. Du. *inpolderen*: see IM-[1] and POLDER[1].] *trans.* = *EMPOLDER *v.* Hence **impo·ldering** *vbl. sb.*

1898 D. S. MELDRUM *Holland & Hollanders* 209 Into the sea that it is proposed to impolder, there falls, at Kampen, the river Ysel. **1899** *Pall Mall Gaz.* 13 Apr. 4/2 This impoldering and pumping, the raising and keeping of dykes and dams. **1901** *Speaker* 9 Mar. 633/2 It was about this time that Haarlem Mere was impoldered. **1929** *Encycl. Brit.* XI. 648/1 A great part of the Netherlands has now been impoldered. *Ibid.* 648/2 The largest impoldering scheme on record has now been commenced.

‖ **imponderabilia** (impǫ:ndĕrăbi·liă), *sb. pl.* [neut. pl. of mod.L. *imponderābilis*, things that cannot be weighed.] Imponderables, imponderable factors.

1925 W. J. LOCKE *Great Pandolfo* xxiv. 300 A man beaten not by Fortune, not by the hostility of material influences, but by spiritual imponderabilia almost on the borderland of sanity and unreason. **1933** *Times Lit. Suppl.* 27 Apr. 283/2 The *imponderabilia* that constitute 'Toryism'. **1938** E. POUND *Let.* 12 May (1971) 316, I think Eliot would prefer your emendation. At any rate we are on ground of imponderabilia. **1942** E. WAUGH *Put out More Flags* ii. 111 Every week we have chamber music. There are certain *imponderabilia* at the Old Mill which, to be crude, have their market value. **1957** *Times* 17 Dec. 9/7 Tactically, the chiefs are in a weak position: but nobody can say what psychological *imponderabilia* may not be raked up if the attack is carried further.

imponderable, *a.* and *sb.* Add: **A.** *adj.* **a.** *fig.* (Later example.)

1959 *Manch. Guardian* 29 Jan. 5/5 It is not so much the calculable cost but the possible, imponderable one if things go wrong.

b. (Later example.)

1963 D. W. & E. E. HUMPHRIES tr. *Termier's Erosion & Sedimentation* x. 194 They [*sc.* stratification joints] seem to result from those 'imponderable' particles..which remain in suspension.

B. *sb.* (Later examples.) Now chiefly in sense 'something that cannot be estimated'.

1927 *Sunday Express* 22 May 12/4 It is not always possible to show gratitude by a gift...If we wish to keep ourselves free from the dreadful disease of ingratitude we should strive to remember these imponderables of life. **1938** S. BECKETT *Murphy* 20 Murphy's respect for the imponderables of personality was profound. **1952** M. MCCARTHY *Groves of Academe* (1953) vi. 110 'Fitness to teach' was an imponderable which he had no intention of pretending to weigh. **1960** *Times* 24 Oct. (Financial Rev.) p. xvii/5 Here the largest imponderable is first whether sufficient wool can be produced to meet the demand and secondly the challenge of synthetics. **1963** D. W. & E. E. HUMPHRIES tr. *Termier's Erosion & Sedimentation* xviii. 355 He [*sc.* A. Lombard] distinguishes between the 'imponderables' which are the salts in process of precipitation, ..and the 'ponderables' which sink rather quickly. **1964** M. GOWING *Britain & Atomic Energy* ix. 267 The British contribution was largely made up of imponderables. **1969** *Times* 17 Oct. 10/4 (*heading*) Farm imponderables in calculating cost of entry to Europe.

impoof (impū·f). Also **empofo, impofo, impoofo, impophoo.** [Zulu *i-mpofu*, f. *mpofu* tawny.] The common African eland, *Taurotragus oryx.*

1785 G. FORSTER tr. *Sparrman's Voy. Cape Good Hope* II. xiv. 205 In one of the places above referred to, I have mentioned that it [*sc.* the eland] is called by the Caffres *empofos*; I have since found..that it is likewise called by the same nation *poffo.* **1834** *Penny Cycl.* II. 89/1 The Canna,..improperly called *eland* or elk by the Dutch colonists of South Africa, and *impoof* by the Caffres. **1839** W. C. HARRIS *Wild Sports S. Afr.* x. 83 During the day I killed another impoofo, which actually measured nineteen hands two inches at the shoulder. **1875** *Encycl. Brit.* II. 101/2 The eland or impophoo (*Boselaphus Oreas*) is one of the largest of the antelopes. **1884** *Cassell's Nat. Hist.* III. 21 Writing on the hunting of these creatures, known in South Africa as the *Impoofo*, the same author [*sc.* W. Cornwallis Harris] remarks that, 'notwithstanding the unwieldy shape of these animals, they had at first greatly exceeded the speed of our jaded horses'. **1900** SCLATER & THOMAS *Bk. Antelopes* IV. 198 *Eland* of the Dutch at the Cape... *Impofo* of the Amandabele, Zulu, and Kafirs... *Mpofu* (Swaheli). **1964** E. P. WALKER et al. *Mammals of World* II. 1419 (*heading*) Elands; Elande, Eland Antilope, Impofo, Pofu, Siruwa (native names).

impoon (impū·n). [Zulu *i-mpunzi.*] The grey duiker, *Sylvicapra grimmia*, a common small antelope of southern Africa.

1839 W. C. HARRIS *Wild Sports S. Afr.* 386 The Duiker. Duikerbok of the Cape Colonists. Impoon of the Matabili. **1868** *Chambers's Encycl.* X. 570/1 *Impoon* (*Antilope* or *Cephalopus mergens*),..a small species of antelope, very plentiful in South Africa, in wooded districts. **1895** SCLATER & THOMAS *Bk. Antelopes* I. 205 *Duiker* and *Duiker-bok* of Dutch and English colonists... *Impunzi* or *Impuzi* of Matabili (also of Zulus and Swazis).

import, *sb.* Add: **3. b.** (Later examples.)

1963 A. MAIZELS *Industr. Growth & World Trade* vi. 150 An analysis has been made of the magnitude of the import-substitution that has in fact taken place in the industrial and semi-industrial countries since 1913. **1969** *Times* 13 Jan. 11/2 What many people wanted to know was how much £100 m. of import substitution was worth to the balance of payments. **1971** D. E. WESTLAKE *I gave at the Office* (1972) 121 The import duty you pay now... The export duty you pay on the way out.

4. b. import–export: *a.*, of a business: engaged in both importing and exporting goods.

1955 G. GREENE *Quiet American* I. iii. 49 'Really? What kind of business?'..'Import, export.' **1965** 'W. HAGGARD' *Hard Sell* ii. 11 He had an import-export business, mostly import.

importance. Add: **2. b.** One who is important; an important person.

1896 A. MORRISON *Child of Jago* ii. 26 The Importances from the platform came to find the tea. **1907** 'MARK TWAIN' *Christian Sci.* II. v. 147 To place the Virgin first, the Saviour second, and Mrs. Eddy third, seems to.. make it an ascending scale of Importances, with Mrs. Eddy ranking the other two and holding first place.

c. An important thing.

1938 R. GRAVES *Coll. Poems* 129 And old importances came swimming back—Wine, meat, log-fires, a roof over the head.

important, *a.* Add: **1. b.** *spec.* Of antiques or the like: very valuable.

1904 H. JAMES *Golden Bowl* II. xlii. 368 She had passed her arm into his, and the other objects in the room, the other pictures, the sofas, the chairs, the tables, the cabinets, the 'important' pieces, supreme in their way, stood out, round them. **1969** *Times* 18 Mar. 18/1 (Advt.), A highly important jewelled binding. **1973** *Country Life* 15 Nov. 76 An important tortoise shell and ormolu English Bracket Clock..by Robert Hodgkin, London, *c.* 1720.

4. Preceded by *more* or *most*: used as a kind of sentence adjective. Cf. *IMPORTANTLY *adv.* 1.

This construction is discussed in R. Quirk et al. *Gram. Contemp. Eng.* (1972) § 5.26 (p. 255).

1964 N. SPINRAD in D. Knight *100 Yrs. Sci. Fiction* (1969) 270 What were these quasi-stellar objects and, perhaps even more important, how were they giving off so much energy? **1965** J. C. DAVIS *Adv. Physical Chem.* x. 449 The carbon atom in its ground state is not completely described by hydrogen-like orbitals. More important, a carbon atom in a molecular configuration hardly resembles a free carbon atom. **1968** R. H. W. BROWN *Gardening Complete* vii. 192 It is a mistake to follow this advice too rigidly. One must wait until the soil is damp enough and, more important, warm enough. **1972** *Physics Bull.* Oct. 577/1 The participants must be fed with a stream of information at the crucial times... Most important of all, the foreign guests must be assured that the hosts will ease all problems of entry into their country. **1972** *Sunday Times* 22 Oct. 15/6 But, most important of all, it is now clear that reproducing a document which has been leaked in an unauthorised manner means [etc.]. **1973** *Sci. Amer.* Jan. 7 (Advt.), But most important of all, we begin by giving you the training you need to [etc.]. *Ibid.* 13/3 It can be readily synthesized from coal, oil or natural gas. More important, it can be produced simply by splitting molecules of water. **1973** *Daily Tel.* 13 Jan. 25/8 But, more important, a linked policy can be encashed—surrendered—before maturity date and the saver gets a high proportion of his savings returned to him.

5. *Comb.*, as *important-looking* adj.

1925 F. SCOTT FITZGERALD *Great Gatsby* iii. 45 On a chance we tried an important-looking door. **1926** 'C. BARRY' *Detective's Holiday* 42 Another important-looking person.

importantly, *adv.* **1.** (Later examples.)

Now esp. common as a kind of sentence adverb preceded by *more* or *most*; in some contexts it is interchangeable with *important* and so has the function of a quasi-*adj.* Cf. *IMPORTANT *a.* 4.

1938 C. WILLIAMS *He came down from Heaven* ii. 22 The main point is..the first outrage against *pietas*, and (more importantly) the first imagined proclamation of *pietas* from the heavens. **1941** *Jrnl. R. Aeronaut. Soc.* XLV. 309 Just as importantly, the chart is of extreme value in forming any decisions as to the desirability of modifying..the track. **1962** H. R. WILLIAMSON *Day Shakespeare Died* viii. 88 More importantly, Shakespeare, though using Holinshed as his main source, occasionally used Hall as the direct source of various passages. **1965** M. SPARK *Mandelbaum Gate* vii. 287 It appeared that Ruth assumed Barbara to be someone importantly on her side. **1965** *Listener* 27 May 791/1 Edward Dahlberg's mother is a sizeable part of his literary capital. He dealt with her importantly in two novels. **1969** *Nature* 1 Nov. 477/1 Most importantly, when the particles of the pair are brought together, they annihilate. **1972** *Ibid.* 31 Mar. 200/2 And, most importantly with an internal lipid bilayer, a membrane. **1972** *Times* 12 Apr. 16/5 Perhaps more importantly, income not applied to exclusively charitable purposes is not exempt from taxation. **1972** *Daily Tel.* 31 Oct. 14/6 But, importantly in this case, there is a well-built girl attendant who is chased about the stage by someone bearing a striking resemblance to the wild-eyed non-speaking member of the Marx Brothers team. **1972** *Times Higher Educ. Suppl.* 17 Nov., It will of course be recognized as a great modern dictionary, as we shall see presently; but more importantly,..for all the indications it gives of having registered the full impact of our so-called permissive age, is the way it preserves certain antique myths.

importation. Add: **3.** *Logic.* The inference that if a proposition implies that a second proposition implies a third, then the first and second together imply the third; the converse of *EXPORTATION 4.

1903 B. RUSSELL *Princ. Math.* ii. 16 If *p* implies that *q* implies *r*, then *pq* implies *r*. This is the principle of importation. **1918** C. I. LEWIS *Survey Symbolic Logic* iv. 231 This theorem contains Peano's..Principle of Importation. **1957** P. SUPPES *Introd. Logic* ii. 34 Law of Importation $[P \rightarrow (Q \rightarrow R)] \rightarrow [P \ \& \ Q \rightarrow R]$. **1965** HUGHES & LONDEY *Elem. Formal Logic* xv. 113 T 20 is known as the Law of Importation.., since its effect is to 'import' the antecedent of the consequent into the antecedent of the whole wff.

Hence **importa·tional** *a.*, of or relating to importation.

1935 *Mind* XLIV. 154 Importational logograms (analogous to definitions) are introduced by fiat.

importee (impɔɹtī·). [f. IMPORT *v.* + -EE[1].] A person imported from abroad.

1858 CARLYLE *Fredk. Gt.* I. IV. vi. 445 Painter Pesne, a French Immigrant, or Importee,..was sent for. **1888** *Scottish Leader* 19 Sept. 5 It was amongst the 'importees' that the row took place. **1955** *Caribbean Q.* IV. 1. 50 The most recent census, taken in 1946, counted..3,500 East Indians, descendants of indentured importees.

importune, *v.* Add: **5. b.** To solicit for purposes of prostitution.

1847 *Act* 10 & 11 *Vict.* c. 89 § 28 Every Person who.. commits any of the following Offences..may be committed to Prison... Every common Prostitute or Nightwalker loitering and importuning Passengers for the Purpose of Prostitution. **1943** C. E. VULLIAMY *Polderoy Papers* 79 Even the prostitutes no longer 'importune', but hand you politely their cards. **1958** *Times* 17 Dec. 11/4 A severe national law already punishes any man who persistently solicits or importunes for immoral purposes.

importuning, *vbl. sb.* and *ppl. a.* (Later examples.)

1958 *Times* 17 Dec. 11/4 The bill ignores the graver offence of importuning. This is mainly an activity of men. **1969** *Daily Tel.* (Colour Suppl.) 10 Jan. 7 Advertisements from importuning homosexuals.

impos., colloq. abbreviation of IMPOSSIBLE *a.*

1924 GALSWORTHY *White Monkey* I. ix, 'If you're tired we could cut that.' 'My dear! Impos.!'

imposer. Add: **b.** *Printing.* One who imposes (see IMPOSE *v.* 1 d).

1921 *Dict. Occup. Terms* (1927) § 522 *Stone hand*, imposer; imposes type, which has been set up in page form, in correct position in chase or iron frame, for printing in sheets.

impossibilism (impǫ·sĭbiliz'm). [f. IMPOSSIBLE *a.* + -ISM.] Belief in ideas, especially on social reform, which cannot reasonably be put into practice. So **impossibilist** (impǫ·sĭbilist, -pǫsi·b-) *a.*, of or pertaining to such views; also as *sb.*, one who holds such impracticable views.

1885 G. B. SHAW *Let.* 14 Dec. (1965) 146 We detect.. the..anarchical impossibilism to which your proposition of private property in ideas..must lead in practice. **1892** —— *Let.* 22 Aug. (1965) 362 They had better circulate it among the Impossibilists. **1900** *Speaker* 3 Mar. 592/1 Even amongst those who were but recently impossibilist politicians saner views are prevailing. **1906** *Westm. Gaz.* 8 Feb. 7/2 We are predicting no impossibilist policy. **1909** *Ibid.* 17 Apr. 16/3 Impossibilists in Labour Politics. **1910** *Daily News* 3 Feb. 4/2 There is no fixed hostility, and no impossibilism of attitude. **1917** CHESTERTON *Short Hist. Eng.* 76 An idealism akin to impossibilism. **1921** *Public Opinion* 29 July 107/1 In a world largely controlled by fanatics, dreamers, and impossibilists, the one thoroughly practical policy is that of the League of Nations Union. **1939** *New Statesman* 18 Nov. 712/2 An exposure of Nazi impossibilism.

impossibility. Add: **4.** *Comb.* **impossibility theorem** (see quots.). (Earlier known as the **possibility theorem*.)

[**1950** K. J. ARROW in *Jrnl. Pol. Econ.* LVIII. 342 The Possibility Theorem shows that, if no prior assumptions are made about the nature of individual orderings, there is no method of voting which will remove the paradox of voting discussed in Part I, neither plurality voting nor any scheme of proportional representation, no matter how complicated.] **1957** LUCE & RAIFFA *Games & Decisions* xiv. 333 (*heading*) Conditions on the social welfare function and Arrow's impossibility theorem. **1960** *Q. Jrnl. Econ.* LXXIV. 509 (*heading*) Proof of the Arrow impossibility theorem. **1967** K. J. ARROW in Laslett & Runciman *Philos., Politics & Society* 3rd Ser. 228 The following general theorem may be stated: There can be no constitution simultaneously satisfying the conditions of Collective Rationality, the Pareto Principle, the Independence of Irrelevant Alternatives, and Non-Dictatorship. The proof falls into two parts. It is first shown that if an individual is decisive for some pair of alternatives, then he is a dictator, contrary to the condition of Non-Dictatorship. Hence, no individual is decisive for any pair of alternatives, and the Impossibility Theorem itself then follows easily with the aid of the Pareto Principle. **1969** D. BLACK in *Jrnl. Law & Econ.* XII. ii. 227 The Impossibility Theorem shows that in the general case and apart from restrictions on the members' preferences, no committee procedure will be able to satisfy certain conditions which, Arrow suggests, a procedure might reasonably be required to meet, and that whichever committee procedure we may choose will, for certain sets of schedules, infringe one or more of the apparently reasonable conditions he specifies. **1971** W. LEE *Decision Theory & Human Behavior* iv. 103 Unhappily..reasonable conditions for deriving a social preference ranking from individual rankings are inconsistent with one another, i.e., in general there may be no social ranking conforming to the desired conditions, a conclusion known as Arrow's impossibility theorem.

impossible, *a.* and *sb.* Add: **B.** *sb.* **2.** With def. article: that which is or seems impossible.

1839 BAILEY *Festus* 266 He only holds Perfections, which are but the impossible To other beings. **1895** C'TESS MARTINENGO-CESARESCO *Liberation of Italy* xix. 394 Garibaldi..had always demanded the impossible of his men. **1904** *Daily Chron.* 6 May 7/5 The history of Christianity.. had been a triumph of the impossible. **1916** HUNEKER *Ivory, Apes & Peacocks* 34 All three were consumptives..; all three suffered from the nostalgia of the impossible. *a* **1930** F. NANSEN in *Penguin Dict. Mod. Quots.* (1971) 166/2 The difficult is what takes a little time; the impossible is what takes a little longer. **1972** *Pacifist* Nov. 3/1 Remember the Festival motto:—be realistic—demand the impossible.

impost, *sb.*[2] **1.** Add *attrib.* examples.

1850 J. H. PARKER *Gloss. Terms Grecian, Roman, Italian, & Gothic Archit.* (ed. 5) I. 258 It is better..to designate the mouldings as impost mouldings. *c* **1863** *Dict. Archit.* (Archit. Publ. Soc.) III. 15/1 The decorative impost, or point at which the ornamental impost moldings are placed, is frequently below the springing... In some archways the impost point is ornamental with horizontal moldings. **1901** R. STURGIS *Dict. Archit.* II. 464 *Impost block*, a member which gives direct support to one side of an arch, or to the adjoining parts of two arches.

impotency. 2. b. (Later examples.)

1972 *Oxford Times* 28 July 7/1 An Oxford doctor is holding special surgeries for male undergraduates suffering from impotency. *Ibid.* 7/2 Male impotency is very common.

impo·tentizing, *ppl. a. rare*[−1]. [f. IMPOTENT *a.*: see -IZE,-ING[2].] That renders one impotent.

1920 JOYCE *Let.* 24 Oct. (1957) I. 149 Moly could also be absinthe the cerebral impotentising (!!) drink of chastity.

impound, *v.* Add: **2. b.** *spec.* To confine and store (water) in a reservoir; to confine water so as to form (a reservoir).

1861 [in Dict., sense 2]. **1893** TURNER & BRIGHTMORE *Princ. Waterworks Engin.* iv. 183 The entire site should be closely contoured at every foot of elevation, in order to determine the extent of the works required to impound the desired quantity of water. **1937** *Discovery* June 186/2 It [*sc.* the dam] impounds 1,400,000,000 gallons of water. **1959** *Chambers's Encycl.* IV. 355/2 The lake impounded by the Grand Coulee is 150 mls long. **1966** G. M. FAIR et al. *Water & Wastewater Engin.* I. ii. 6 Necessary reservoirs are impounded by throwing dams across the stream valley.

Also **impounding reservoir,** a reservoir whose function is to store sufficient water to ensure an uninterrupted supply in times of relative drought; **impoundage, impoundment**: delete † and add later examples.

1875 *Encycl. Brit.* II. 225/1 With but little artificial addition, Loch Katrine, Loch Venachar, and Loch Drunkie were converted into impounding reservoirs, the first for the supply of the city, and the two latter for compensation. **1889** [in Dict.]. **1893** TURNER & BRIGHTMORE *Princ. Waterworks Engin.* iv. 172 The first-mentioned requirement is satisfied by the formation of 'impounding-reservoirs', the office of which is to gather the irregular natural yield of surface-water, in order that it may be supplied at a uniform rate; the second is met by the construction of 'service-reservoirs', tanks and cisterns, from which water is distributed as required by the hourly demands of consumers. **1954** FAIR & GEYER *Water Supply & Waste-Water Disposal* viii. 188 In the absence of adequate natural storage, engineers resort to the construction of impounding reservoirs or, more rarely, to the excavation of storage basins. *Ibid.* 192 Allowances for evaporation from the water surface that is created by the impoundage. *Ibid.* 195 When more than one reservoir is developed on a stream, the overflow from each impoundage becomes available to the reservoir next below. **1957** *Encycl. Brit.* XXIII. 432/2 Virtually all public regulatory authorities require that the impoundment be sufficiently great to provide for the release of compensation waters for downstream users. **1973** *New Yorker* 28 Apr. 29/3 There is some room for impoundment, but not to the tune of twelve billion dollars.

impracticably, *adv.* (Later examples.)

1966 *McGraw-Hill Encycl. Sci. & Technol.* X. 234/2 The tube would have to be made impracticably long to avoid cooling of the plasma by the ends. **1974** *Daily Tel.* 11 Mar. 9/2 These [proposals] are now generally recognised as impracticably complicated.

impractical, *a.* Delete *rare* and add further examples. Also = IMPRACTICABLE *a.*

1925 T. DREISER *Amer. Trag.* (1926) I. i. ii. 11 For Clyde's parents had proved impractical in the matter of the future of their children. **1929** *Amer. Speech* IV. 331 'Impractical'..is more commonly used than either 'unpractical', or 'impracticable', as it seems to squint and have both meanings. **1931** J. T. ADAMS *Epic of Amer.* iv. 112 So impractical was American cotton culture considered that..England seized eight bales. **1947** E. W. F. FELLER *Instrument & Control Manual* p. vii, The number of units to be controlled in a single plant all tend to render hand control impractical if not impossible. **1962** E. GODFREY *Retail Selling & Organiz.* ii. 21 On a busy ground floor, carpeting would be impractical. **1964** R. H. ROBINS *Gen. Ling.* i. 2 As an impractical ideal he [*sc.* the general linguist] would know something about every language. **1970** *Daily Tel.* 4 May 2/7 The scheme was reckoned to be the next best to transferable pensions, which the Government believes to be impractical at the moment. **1973** *Sci. Amer.* Mar. 113/2 The second calculating method..is too complicated and impractical to explain here.

impracticality (impræktikæ·lĭti). [f. IMPRACTICAL *a.* + -ITY.] The character of being impractical; impracticableness.

1916 H. S. WALPOLE *Dark Forest* I. iv, The Russian character..with its lack of restraint, its idealism, its impracticality. **1926** J. BUCHAN *Dancing Floor* II. x. 187 The impracticality of an entrance..at that point.

So **impra·cticalness.**

1905 *Macm. Mag.* Nov. 55 He was accused of vagueness, impracticalness, generality.

impractically (impræ·ktikăli), *adv.* [f. IMPRACTICAL *a.* + -LY[2].] In an impractical manner; to an impractical or impracticable degree; not practicably.

1947 *Math. Tables & Other Aids to Computation* II. 359 Long sequences of accurate computations which would be impractically lengthy by any other slower means. **1959** E. M. MCCORMICK *Digital Computer Primer* viii. 115 It is generally impractically expensive to obtain the very large storage. **1974** *Sci. Amer.* Jan. 93/1 The forces toward the left between these lines are impractically high; normal playing is confined to the area toward the right.

imprecise, *a.* Add: So **impreci·seness.**
1907 *Athenæum* 9 Mar. 282/3 He [*sc.* Henry James] must..deck it with the most elaborated precisions of impreciseness. **1943** A. L. Rowse *Spirit Eng. Hist.* i. 11 An impreciseness which characterises the English mind.

imprecision. Delete *rare* and add later examples.
1954 W. Stevens *Coll. Poems* 353 The romance of the precise is not the elision Of the tired romance of imprecision. **1971** *Nature* 4 June 274/1 For one thing, it pointed to strictly legal imprecisions in the legislation which at present regulates the use of transplants in Britain.

impredicable, *a.* Add: (Later examples.) Hence **impre:dicabi·lity,** the condition of being impredicable.
1906 P. Lowell *Mars & its Canals* viii. 95 Even on Mars nothing in the way of weather is absolutely predicable but impredicability. **1937** A. Smeaton tr. *Carnap's Logical Syntax of Lang.* iii. § 38. 138 Russell showed that this antinomy can also be so formulated as to apply not only to classes but to properties as well (the antinomy of 'impredicable'..). *Ibid.* iv. § 60a. 212 Hence a definition of the form given for 'impredicable' is obviously impossible. **1965** F. Sommers in M. Black *Philos. in Amer.* 272 For example, the term *clean* is *im*predicable of the equator. *Ibid.* 273 It becomes unnecessary to introduce special 'type' restrictions to account for impredicability.

impredicative (impre·dikătiv), *a.* [f. Im-[2] + Predicative *a.*] Of a proposition, thing, etc.: not definable except in terms of a totality of which it is itself a part. Hence **impre·dicatively** *adv.*; **impredicati·vity,** the state or quality of being impredicative.
1937 A. Smeaton tr. *Carnap's Logical Syntax of Lang.* iv. § 44. 162 A thing is usually called impredicative (in the material mode of speech) when it is defined (or can only be defined) with the help of a totality to which it itself belongs. **1944** K. Gödel in P. A. Schilpp *Philos. B. Russell* ii. iii. 138 What an impredicative definition would require is to construct a notion by a combination of a set of notions to which the notion to be formed itself belongs. **1963** W. V. Quine *Set Theory* § 34. 242 He [*sc.* Poincaré] called the suspect procedure impredicative. **1965** C. D. Parsons in M. Black *Philos. in Amer.* 196 Such extensions..allow impredicatively defined classes. *Ibid.* 197 This can only be because the mathematics itself involves impredicativity.

impreg (i·mpreg). Also **Impreg.** [Abbrev. of *impreg(nated *ppl. a.* 2.] A type of wood impregnated with a synthetic resin to improve its dimensional stability and resistance to distortion or decay.
1942 *Fortune* Oct. 180/2 F[orest] P[roducts] L[aboratory] makes a special 'impreg' by treating wood with raw resin so that the resin actually penetrates the wood cells. **1953** Hunt & Garratt *Wood Preservation* (ed. 2) xi. 365 The shrinkage and swelling of wood..can be reduced..by first impregnating the wood (in thin sheets) with a solution of unpolymerized phenol-formaldehyde resin, then drying the wood at moderate temperatures, and finally heating the dry wood at about 300°C to polymerize the resin in place; the product formed is called Impreg. **1953** Stamm & Harris *Chem. Processing of Wood* (1954) viii. 226 Impreg was manufactured during World War II only for military users. **1967** R. H. Farmer *Chem. in Utilization of Wood* viii. 119 Uncompressed resin-impregnated wood was first made in the United States, where it is called Impreg.

impregnability. (Earlier example.)
1847 W. Smith tr. *Fichte's Characteristics Present Age* 30 The supposed impregnability of the mode of thought which we have now described arises precisely in this way.

impregnant, *a.*[1] (*sb.*). Restrict 'Now *rare*' to senses in Dict. and add: **B.** *sb.* A substance used for the impregnation of something else. (Cf. sense 2 in Dict.)
1933 H. Bennett *Chem. Formulary* I. 441/1 Leather Soles, Impregnant for. **1948** Kirk & Othmer *Encycl. Chem. Technol.* II. 546 The bitumens employed as felt impregnants are usually soft, low-melting materials of high fluidity in the molten condition. **1955** Seymour & Steiner *Plastics for Corrosion-Resistant Applications* xii. 191 The sealing effect of the impregnant..is dependent upon an increase in molecular size of the resin used. **1959** *New Scientist* 30 July 127/3 Inside present day automotive storage battery cells..a waffle-shaped network of lead holds the impregnant that keeps the battery alive.

impregnated, *ppl. a.* Add: **2.** *spec.* **impregnated wood,** (*a*) wood saturated with a preservative; (*b*) = *impreg.
1942 *Amer. Jrnl. Bot.* XXIX. 552/1 A brown mold has been observed..on small pieces of impregnated wood. [**1942** *Fortune* Oct. 180/2 It [*sc.* 'compreg'] consists of layers of resin-impregnated wood that have been compressed together.] **1944** *Amer. Speech* XIX. 92 Plywood manufacturers..developed a technique by which the glue..is forced through the entire texture of all the plies in a laminated sheet, and 'impregnated wood' is the specific name of the resultant product. **1951** Mactaggart & Chambers *Plastics & Building* x. 114 This phenomenon [*sc.* impregnation of wood with synthetic resin] has resulted in the development of two types of impregnated wood called generally Impreg and Compreg. **1963** A. D. Wood *Plywoods of World* iv. 141 Improved and impregnated wood is more difficult to work than solid timber.

impregnation. Add: **2.** *spec.* The saturation of wood with a preservative.
1872 *Jrnl. Chem. Soc.* XXV. 186 It may be stated that the impregnation of wood with sulphate of copper, or with creosote oils, or their vapours, is of service in rendering the wood three or four times as lasting as unprepared material of the same quality. **1924** E. G. Blake *Seasoning & Preservation of Timber* iii. 24 If the principle of impregnation was to be universally adopted, the danger of the exhaustion of the world's supply would be deferred. **1946** Cartwright & Findlay *Decay of Timber* xiii. 258 Impregnation treatments are necessary whenever the timber is liable to be exposed to persistently damp conditions. **1968** *Gloss. Terms Timber Preservation (B.S.I.)* 18 *Impregnation,* strictly the saturation of wood with a preservative. Generally used to describe treatments giving a high loading of preservative in the wood, e.g. pressure treatments.

impresa. Restrict † *Obs.* to sense 2 in Dict. and add later examples of sense 1.
1865 F. B. Palliser *Hist. Lace* 435 Then follow three pages in terzette, and p. 3. dorso, the impresa of the printer, a lion rampant, holding a sword in his fore paws. **1971** *English Studies* LII. 122 The last *impresa* in the supplementary chapter is almost certainly a personal device of Daniel's dedicatee, Sir Edward Dymoke.

impress, *v.*[1] Add: **2. c.** *Electr.* To apply or establish (an e.m.f. or a potential difference) by some external means.
1881 [implied in next]. **1918** *Wireless World* VI. 145 A certain steady voltage is impressed on the grids. **1930** [see *impedance 1 a]. **1948** A. L. Albert *Radio Fund.* v. 128 If a voltage is impressed across the input terminals.. the voltage will force a current into the line.

impressed, *ppl. a.*[1] Add: **2.** *Electr.* Of an e.m.f. or potential difference: applied by some external means.
1881 *Jrnl. Soc. Telegr. Engin.* X. 271 Let M be the induction through the coil when its plane is at right angles to the lines of force of the external field, ωt the angle turned through from this plane at time t..; then $M\omega \sin \omega t$ is the impressed e.m.f. in the coil. **1929** *Encycl. Brit.* XXII. 408/1 A small current flows into the excited winding sufficient to produce a counter voltage equal to the impressed voltage. **1948** [see *impedance 1 a]. **1973** *Sci. Amer.* Oct. 125/1 Leakage through the capacitor should not exceed 10^{-10} ampere at an impressed potential of 10 volts.

impression, *sb.* Add: **2. e.** *Dentistry.* A negative copy of the teeth or oral cavity (from which a positive cast or model may be made) formed by bringing them into intimate contact with some substance that will take their shape.
1839 C. A. Harris *Dental Art* xxi. 350 Models of this kind are obtained by taking a wax impression of both jaws at the same time. **1878** C. Hunter *Mech. Dentistry* i. 7 When the composition has become sufficiently hard, the impression is withdrawn from the mouth, and cold water should be allowed to flow over it. **1940** J. Osborne *Dental Mech.* i. 1 The introduction..to the subject is the technique necessary for the accurate construction of a model, or positive likeness of the patient's mouth, from an impression or negative likeness.

3. d. *Bibliogr.* In bibliographical classification and description, a subdivision of an edition, denoting all the copies printed at one time; chiefly applicable to books of the nineteenth and twentieth centuries.
1927 R. B. McKerrow *Introd. Bibliogr.* ii. iii. 175 When dealing with early books, 'edition' and 'impression' as a rule are the same thing, for the early printer normally distributed his type immediately it had been printed from, though there were..exceptions to this. **1949** F. Bowers *Princ. Bibliogr. Descr.* xi. 379 In its purest sense an *edition* of a book consists of all copies printed at any time or times from one setting of type, or its equivalent in the form of plates or monotype rolls; i.e., it is the sum of all impressions from one setting... All the copies of any single edition are not necessarily printed at any one time but may accumulate from a series of separate *impressions* removed from each other in date... Copies of each impression compose a part of an edition. **1972** P. Gaskell *New Introd. Bibliogr.* 315 It was not unusual in the nineteenth century for stereos to be used for ten successive impressions, and for electros to be used for as many as thirty; while, if a set of plates was kept as a 'mother' from which further sets could be made, the number of successive impressions of an edition that could be printed from plates was virtually unlimited.

6. b. Esp. in phr. *first impression(s).*
1700 Congreve *Way of World* iv. i. 52 How shall I receive him? In what figure shall I give his Heart the first Impression? There is a great deal in the first Impression. *c* **1755** in R. Jackson *Hist. Rev. Pennsylvania* (1759) 270 It must have been while he was under the first Impressions given him by the Governor to our Disadvantage. **1843** Dickens *Mart. Chuz.* (1944) v. 57 First impressions, you know, often go a long way, and last a long time. **1847** [in Dict.]. **1924** E. O'Neill *Welded* i. 90 The first impression of her whole personality is one of charm, partly innate, partly imposed by years of self-discipline.

d. An imitation or impersonation of a person or thing, done by a comedian as a form of entertainment.
1953 J. Laurie *Vaudeville* 99 Some [beginners] just stuck to the regular 'impressions' and went through show biz getting by. **1969** *Times* 7 Nov. 13/3 An American entertainer..joked, sang, went on singing, and did impressions. **1971** D. Nathan *Laughtermakers* ii. 46 Peter would come in and do a few impressions of Kenneth Horne and others. *Ibid.* xiii. 227 Later on I'm going to do one or two impressions—I've got some good bird impressions, I eat worms.

7. In modern use, often implying that the belief or idea is mistaken, esp. in *under the impression.*
1860 Ruskin *Unto this Last* (1862) iv. 131, I believe that many of our merchants are seriously under the impression that it is possible for everybody, somehow, to make a profit in this manner. **1865** —— *Sesame* ii. § 86 Generally, we are under an impression that a man's duties are public, and a woman's private. **1867** W. F. Hook *Lives Abps.* V. xxi. 356 Under the impression that they had been specially assisted by the saint.

9. *Comb.*: **impression compound,** any impression material manufactured from a number of different ingredients, esp. one that is a non-elastic thermoplastic solid; **impression material,** any substance used for taking dental impressions.
1903 *Dental Rec.* XXIII. 415 Do not think a good impression of a full denture cannot be taken in impression compound. **1904** J. H. Prothero *Prosthetic Dentistry* iii. 22 Other impression materials..are furnished by the dental supply houses and are called impression compounds. The usual claim made is that they are composed of materials that can be dried after the impression is taken. **1934** F. W. Frahm *Princ. & Technics Full Denture Construction* vii. 84 A new impression compound has been added to our list of materials and is listed under the trade name of 'Dentocoll'. It is a hydro-colloidal, possessing unusual plasticity, some elasticity and a slight compressibility. **1965** Phillips & Skinner *Elem. Dental Materials* v. 37 As the formulas of the modern impression compounds are 'trade secrets', any discussion of composition cannot be very specific. In general, compounds are a mixture of waxes, thermoplastic resins, a filler, and a coloring agent. **1878** C. Hunter *Mech. Dentistry* i. 2 Wax as an impression material is now seldom used, composition (Godiva, or Stent) or plaster of Paris being now almost invariably employed. **1965** Phillips & Skinner *Elem. Dental Materials* iv. 33 If a rigid impression material has been used (i.e., plaster, compound, etc.), the mix of dental stone is poured into the impression carefully, preferably under vibration.

impressional, *a.* Delete *rare* and add later examples.
1920 S. Alexander *Space, Time & Deity* II. 138 Impressional intensity, as Mr. Stout calls what Hume described as vivacity. **1969** *R. & E. Coordinator* (Res. & Engin. Council Graphic Arts Industry) Apr. 10/2 Principal advantages of the Mailander flatbeds are stated to be..the excellent control of plate inking and dampening and impressional squeeze in order to obtain the highest quality image with little..stock waste.

impressionism. Add: **4.** *Mus.* A style of composition, originating in the late 1880s with Debussy, characterized by its harmonic system, esp. in the use by Debussy of the whole-tone scale, and departing from the strong and direct structure and themes of the Romantic composers. Also used for a type of jazz with similar 'atmospheric' characteristics.
1889 G. B. Shaw *London Music 1888–89* (1937) 128 There is a great deal in Mefistofele that is mere impressionism; and like impressionism in painting it is enchanting when it is successful. **1908** W. H. Daly *Debussy* 31 So far as one can classify Debussy's use of a 'programme' at all, it is necessary to return to the comparison with painting, and style it impressionism. **1922** *Musical Opinion* May 698/1 Let it be thoroughly understood that impressionism is no more a matter of technique, of using dots, blobs and squares..any more than musical impressionism means the use of the whole-tone scale with its implied harmonies. **1934** C. Lambert *Music Ho!* i. 25 Impressionism, as I have said, is a term easily misused, and one may doubt the logic of its use as a musical term at all; but its association with the work of Debussy and his followers is so widespread that one may conveniently use it as a generic label for that period of disruption in music of which Debussy was the dominating figure. **1947** A. Einstein *Music Romantic Era* xi. 149 His first symphonic poem *Les Éolides* (1876), inspired by Leconte de Lisle's poem, is rather a precursor of Impressionism. **1952** B. Ulanov *Hist. Jazz in Amer.* (1958) xii. 133 It was another sixteen years before the impact of Impressionism was again so directly felt in jazz. **1956** M. Stearns *Story of Jazz* (1957) xiii. 146 The Debussyesque impressionism of Smith's 'Morning Air'. **1970** *Times* 27 Feb. 13/1 Mr. Fon..was keenly aware that impressionism for Debussy was not just a vague wash.

impressionist. Add: (Earlier and later examples.) Also, an impressionist painting. Also *transf.*
1876 H. James *Parisian Sk.* (1958) 131 An exhibition for which I may at least claim that it can give rise..to no dangerous perversities of taste is that of the little group of the Irreconcilables—otherwise known as the 'Impressionists' in painting. **1933** *Burlington Mag.* Dec. 276/2 The Impressionist movement in England will never count for much. **1958** L. Durrell *Mountolive* xi. 208 They would take a slow turn up and down the picture-gallery, with its splendid collection of Impressionists.
attrib. and as *adj.* **1876** H. James *Parisian Sk.* (1958) 132 The 'Impressionist' doctrines strike me as incompatible, in an artist's mind, with the existence of first-rate talent. **1893** R. Fry *Let.* 20 Sept. (1972) I. 154, I don't quite

make out whether Elsie Howard is Impressionist; I suppose so, but I thought she was Ruskinian. **1894** G. Meredith *Let.* 5 July (1970) III. 1163 Beware of a hurried habit of mind that comes of addiction to Impressionist effects. **1969** *Listener* 28 Aug. 274/3 A letter from the aged Earl Attlee in his own impressionist typewriting, full of splendidly sinister words like 'Ghsmberlian' and 'recollȝftian'.

2. *Mus.* A composer of impressionistic music. Also *attrib.*

1908 W. H. Daly *Debussy* 10 It is convenient, even if it is an incomplete definition of his altogether novel attitude towards music, to describe Debussy as an impressionist. He is something more than an impressionist as the term is commonly understood, although in his work there is not a little which recalls the methods and the points of view of the masters of impressionist painting. **1927** [see *bitonality]. **1947** C. Gray *Contingencies & Other Ess.* iii. 91 The so-called impressionists were anticipated by him [*sc.* Liszt] in many of their most characteristic effects and procedures, sometimes by as much as half a century. **1948** *Penguin Music Mag.* Oct. 46 The half-Tristanesque, half-impressionist Nocturne. **1952** B. Ulanov *Hist. Jazz in Amer.* (1958) xii. 132 The French Impressionist composers and their American disciples and imitators made a great impression upon Bix's generation of jazz musicians. **1955** R. Blesh *Shining Trumpets* (ed. 3) xii. 281 His borrowed effects from jazz, the Impressionists, and the French Romantics. **1959** D. Cooke *Lang. Mus.* i. 2 Medieval music was largely architectural in conception: the romantics were much concerned with the literary; the impressionists with the pictorial; modern music has swung back again to the architectural.

impressionistic, *a.* Add: (Further examples.) Also, in a general sense: subjective, unsystematic (formed directly from Impression *sb.* 7 and only indirectly influenced by senses of *impressionism, -ist*).

1891 G. Meredith *Let.* 15 Apr. (1970) II. 1025 You have at times..insisted on your impressions. That is, you have put on your cap, sharpened your pencil, and gone afield as the Impressionistic poet. **1900** *Atlantic Monthly* LXXXVI. 78 As for the impressionistic writer about literature—he is apt to concern himself very little with this historical origin of a work of art. **1908** W. H. Daly *Debussy* 32 Debussy's music..deals..in suggestions... There is something swift, vague, and elusive, but strangely vivid and satisfying... But the broad, impressionistic methods are not taken to avoid difficulties of definition. **1909** W. James *Pluralistic Universe* ii. 52 Impressionistic philosophizing, like impressionistic watch-making or land-surveying, is intolerable to experts. **1915** J. Huneker *Ivory, Apes & Peacocks* 38 Laforgue..was an ardent advocate of the Impressionistic painters. **1921** *Times Lit. Suppl.* 24 Feb. 114/1 The impressionistic reporter who asked Mr. Edison what he considered the chief mark of a truly valuable invention. **1933** *PMLA* XLVIII. 598 Such rather impressionistic terminology has been found suggestive and helpful in teaching. **1934** S. R. Nelson *All about Jazz* v. 101 All these are impressionistic music of the programme type. **1947** A. Einstein *Music Romantic Era* vii. 69 Berlioz..made the two middle movements nothing but picturesque scenes—most finely impressionistic, most genuinely akin to French *plein air* painting. **1955** R. Blesh *Shining Trumpets* (ed. 3) xii. 268 An impressionistic montage of solo moods. **1958** R. A. Bone *Negro Novel in Amer.* ii. 68 The style is appropriately impressionistic, full of hyphenated adjectives aimed at vivid impressions of Harlem life. **1962** *Listener* 25 Jan. 195/3 Delius's impressionistic elusiveness. *Ibid.* 196/1 Its impressionistic string, harp and horn texture. **1973** *College English* XXXIV. 1103 Prosodic studies have tended toward tentative, impressionistic assertions and *ad hoc* methodology.

2. *Phonetics.* Non-systematic, subjective, non-structured; determined by the recorder's impressions of speech sounds, not by the sound-system of the language, dialect, etc., being recorded.

1939 H. Kurath *Handbk. Ling. Geogr. New England* iv. 122 The field workers' phonetic notations..are not phonemic, but on the contrary intentionally phonic, that is *impressionistic.* **1940** *Amer. Speech* XV. 145 This paper makes no claim to presenting a detailed impressionistic analysis of PM [i.e. Piedmont, U.S.] phonetics; it attempts merely to indicate a relative phonemic distribution. **1948** R. A. Hall *Leave Your Lang. Alone!* ii. vi. 41 Trying to describe sounds in auditory, impressionistic terms is likely to give about as accurate results as would, say, describing chemical elements in terms of their smells. The impressions we get through our senses of hearing and smell just can't be stated in clear and analyzable enough terms to be of any use in scientific work. **1960** D. Jones *Outl. Eng. Phonetics* (ed. 9) 349 Systematic transcriptions have to be distinguished from transcriptions made on a general phonetic basis without reference to the needs of any particular language. The latter may be described as 'non-systematic' or 'impressionistic'. **1962** H. Orton *Survey Eng. Dial., Introd.* i. 18 The merits and demerits of the impressionistic method need not be re-stated here. **1963** *Amer. Speech* XXXVIII. 127 The recording of the speech sounds is phonic (impressionistic) in intent. All premature phonemicization is strictly avoided.

impressionistically (impreʃəni·stikăli), *adv.* [f. Impressionistic *a.*: see -ically.] In an impressionistic manner (in various senses); from the point of view of an impressionist.

1909 W. James *Pluralistic Universe* iii. 92, I make no claim to understanding it, I treat it merely impressionistically. **1924** Galsworthy *White Monkey* ii. ii, When you smile, Miss Collins, I see you impressionistically. **1924** J. A. Hammerton *Countries of World* III. 1507/1 Their flowers..painted (impressionistically but with unerring truth of impression) in their frescoes. **1926** W. J. Locke *Old Bridge* i. i, I try to express myself..impressionistically. **1960** H. Orton in *Orbis* IX. 337 The fieldworkers transcribed the informants' responses phonetically, and impressionistically, in the phonetic alphabet of the International Phonetic Association. **1964** F. Bowers *Bibliogr. & Textual Crit.* ii. iii. 51 The hypothesis is factually, not impressionistically, based.

impressionize (impre·ʃənəiz), *v. rare.* [f. Impression *sb.* + -ize.] **a.** *trans.* To make an impression on; to introduce impressions into, to portray as an impression or set of impressions. **b.** *intr.* To gather impressions.

1894 F. M. Elliot *Roman Gossip* i. 15 He had.. imagined this *mise en scène* to impressionise his fellow-citizens. **1894** H. James *Notebks.* (1947) 160, I must picture it [*sc.* a story to be written], summarize it, impressionize it, in a word—compress and confine it by making it the picture of what I see. **1905** D. Sladen *Playing Game* i. i. 16 Instead of thinking Japan a God-forsaken country..he was impressionizing in an indolent æsthetic way.

impressive, *a.* Add: **4.** *Comb.*, as *impressive-looking* adj.

1904 *Daily Chron.* 21 July 4/5 Even in these impressive-looking statistical tables little bits of cheerfulness obstinately obtrude themselves. **1925** T. Dreiser *Amer. Trag.* (1926) ii. xl. 10 Arabella Stark..in a large and impressive-looking car, was waiting.

imprest, *sb.*[1] **1. b.** Delete †*Obs.* and add later examples.

1957 F. King *Man on Rock* iii. 81 He drew up a log-book for the car, checked the postage imprest. **1958** E. A. Robertson *Justice of Heart* iv. 48 Off you go, see the foreign editor, get an imprest—don't imagine you can squander money on this trip, though!

‖ **imprévu** (æ̃nprevü). Also **imprevu.** [Fr., f. Im-[2] + *prévu*, pa. pple. of *prévoir* to foresee.] The unexpected, the unforeseen.

1854 *Punch* 9 Sept. 106/2 Had he well read the people.., their love of *l'imprévu*? **1858** Geo. Eliot *Let.* 2 Mar. in J. W. Cross *George Eliot's Life* (1885) II. viii. 13 Perhaps we may go to Dresden, perhaps not: we leave room for the *imprévu.* **1925** G. B. Shaw *Let.* 15 Dec. in *To a Young Actress* (1960) 88, I am prudent and foresee everything. My life lacks the imprevu. **1969** R. Harper *World of Thriller* ii. 65 Stendhal..understood that without the '*imprévu*' there is no charm in human existence.

imprimatur. Add: **2.** (Later examples.)

1955 *Bull. Atomic Sci.* June 209/2 His calculations and conclusions bear no imprimatur of the Atomic Energy Commission. **1973** *N.Y. Law Jrnl.* 31 Aug. 3/1 It is well-settled contract law that courts do not give their imprimatur to such arrangements.

¶ Used confusedly = Imprint *sb.* 3. (Quot. 1971 is *fig.*)

1970 *Daily Tel.* 7 May 13/2 The agent, not the candidate, is the one liable to fines..if he..issues one word of election literature without his own and the printer's imprimatur on it. **1971** *Nature* 7 May 40/2 The site near Kültepe has been identified as the Assyrian karum Kanis and most of the tablets can thus be considered to bear the implicit imprimatur 'found at Kanis'.

‖ **imprimatura** (imprīmatū·ra). Also **imprimitura.** [ad. It. *imprimitura.*] A thin priming or ground, frequently coloured, applied to an artist's canvas or panel.

1951 R. Mayer *Artist's Handbk.* 434 *Imprimatura*, a veil or thin glaze of colour applied to a ground as a preliminary coating. Term not in very wide use. **1958** M. L. Wolf *Dict. Painting* 137 *Imprimatura*, in painting, a type of glaze applied as a toner to the canvas or other ground..an underpainting, intended to relieve the monotony of a white or gray background. **1967** J. N. Barron *Lang. of Painting* 99 *Imprimatura*, a thin glaze or veil of color brushed or rubbed over the white of a ground... It may also be used at the same time to reduce, if necessary, the absorbency of the ground.

imprint, *sb.* **3. b.** (Further examples of extended uses.)

1972 *Times Lit. Suppl.* 27 Oct. 1276/5 (Advt.), Kahn & Averill (imprint of Stanmore Press Ltd.). **1973** *Ibid.* 2 Feb. 121/4 (Advt.), Diana Burfield who, before her resignation last summer after seventeen years with the imprint, was editorial director of Tavistock [Publications].

4. (With capital initial.) An old-style type face, named after the periodical for which it was designed.

1913 *Imprint* Jan. p. vi, The newly designed type in which our pages are presented to the reader was cut by the Lanston Monotype Company at our instance... The type has been christened Imprint Old Face. **1934** A. F. Johnson *Type Designs* iv. 120 The first acceptable book type to be cut after the Old Style of 1860 was the 'Monotype' Imprint of 1913. **1966** P. M. Handover in K. Day *Bk. Typogr. 1815–1965* 160 Imprint was a reformed Caslon, regularised on the principles that had inspired old style which now resulted in another more distinguished face.

imprint, *v.* Add: **5.** *Animal Behaviour.* To bring about in (a social animal, usu. a young one) a state of habitual recognition of or trust in another animal or an object, which may thus come to be regarded as a parent; const. *to* or *on* the object of recognition. Also, of an animal or thing: to become established as an object of recognition or trust in the behaviour pattern of (a young animal) (quot. 1967): see *imprinting *vbl. sb.* 2. Usu. as *pa. pple.* **imprinted.**

1951 *Ibis* XCIII. 259 Young Partridges which had been caught after the fields had been mowed but were still only a few hours old had nevertheless already become definitely imprinted to their normal parents. **1956** W. H. Thorpe *Learning & Instinct in Animals* vi. 116 The parent Cichlid fish may become imprinted to the young as well as the young to the parent. **1963** *Ibid.* (ed. 2) xv. 414 If young birds are kept together in groups they are harder to imprint than if they are kept singly. **1966** R. & D. Morris *Men & Apes* iii. 57 Monkeys imprinted on human beings as babies will readily accept them as sexual partners on reaching maturity. **1967** M. Argyle *Psychol. Interpersonal Behaviour* i. 23 Dogs raised by humans, may be imprinted by them, and human babies who are reared by wolves may fail to be imprinted by humans. **1972** *Nature* 2 June 287/2 Many hand-reared birds become imprinted on their human handlers if isolated from their parents at an early age. **1972** *Sci. Amer.* Aug. 25/3 We also took wild ducklings from their natural mother 16 hours after hatching and tried to imprint them to humans.

i·mprinted, *ppl. a.*[2] [f. Imprint *sb.* + -ed[2].] Bearing a bookseller's own imprint (Imprint *sb.* 3).

1926 *Publishers' Weekly* 17 July 181/2 A month before publication 300,000 imprinted postcards had been asked for. **1927** *Ibid.* 25 June 2371 Imprinted brochures are now ready for distribution.

imprinting, *vbl. sb.* Add: **2.** *Animal Behaviour.* The establishment of a behaviour pattern of recognition and trust, usu. directed at its own species, during a critical period of susceptibility in a (young) social animal, esp. in birds.

1937 K. Lorenz in *Auk* LIV. 262 This process of acquiring the biologically 'right' object of social reactions by conditioning them, not to one individual fellow-member of the species, but to the species as such, is so very peculiar that I have thought it necessary to use a particular word to describe it. I have called it 'Prägung' in German, which I propose to translate into English by the term 'imprinting'. **1953** J. S. Huxley *Evolution in Action* iv. 102 Young geese which have been hatched in an incubator will attach themselves to birds of other species or even to human beings and follow them about as if they were their real parents. This so-called 'imprinting' has to take place during a critical period soon after hatching, only takes a minute or so, and is then irreversible. **1967** M. Argyle *Psychol. Interpersonal Behaviour* i. 17 There may be 'imprinting' during the first year of life: the infant becomes attached to the dominant moving object in its environment, and does its best to follow that object. **1970** *Primate Behavior* I. 130 Imprinting data suggest that in birds early experiences before or during a critical period can influence social attachment in a relatively permanent fashion.

imprisonable, *a.* Add: Of an offence, etc.: for which a person can be imprisoned.

1971 *Daily Tel.* 31 July 11/2 Before a court recommends deportation of a Commonwealth citizen who has been convicted of an imprisonable offence, the offender must be given at least seven days clear notice.

improbable, *a.* Add: **2.** Also, that does not 'look the part'.

1958 *Times* 18 Apr. 11/7 An immense arched building of blue painted woods decorated with an improbable metal dove. *Ibid.* 14 May 15/1 As if it were miraculous that this gentle and improbable individual should exist at all.

improperium (imprǒpiə·riǒm). Pl. **-ia.** *R.C. Liturg.* [late L., = reproach.] *pl.* A series of antiphons with responses forming part of the liturgical service of Good Friday, expressing the reproach or sorrowful remonstrance of Christ with the Jewish people; *sing.* one of these antiphons with its response.

1880 Grove *Dict. Mus.* II. 1/1 The *Improperia* are sung, very softly, and without any accompaniment whatever, by two Antiphonal Choirs. **1884** Addis & Arnold *Cath. Dict.* 405/1 During the adoration the 'Improperia' are sung, each improperium being followed by the Trisagion in Greek and Latin. **1959** *Collins Mus. Encycl.* 331/2 *Improperia*, part of the Roman liturgy for Good Friday.

improve, *v.*[2] **2. b.** (Later example.)

1906 L. L. Bell *Carolina Lee* 293, I could refuse an offer to improve my land, denuded and mortgaged as it is.

improved, *ppl. a.* Add: **5.** *improved wood*, thin sheets of wood attached to each other by films of synthetic resin, thus improving its resistance to distortion, shrinkage, etc.

1940 *Jrnl. R. Aeronaut. Soc.* XLIV. 673 It..could be expected that..composite wood plastics, like..'improved' wood, such as commonly used in the modern aeroplane manufacture, would be suitable for the construction of petrol containers. **1957** *N.Z. Timber Jrnl.* Aug. 59/2 Certain commercial treatments to prevent movement owing to moisture variation in wood, have resulted in what is termed 'improved wood'. **1963** A. D. Wood *Plywoods of World* iv. 138 Improved wood is the product of a combination of veneers..interleaved with a synthetic resin glue film.

improvement. **2. a.** and **b.** Restrict †*Obs.* (exc. in *U.S. dial.*) to senses in Dict. Add

further N. Amer. and N.Z. examples in sense: the turning of farmland to better account by the erection of buildings, fences, etc.; also *concr.*, the buildings, fences, etc., themselves.

1769 *Quebec Gaz.* 16 Feb. 3/1 The Possessors of such Concessions shall be entitled to such Part of them as shall be proportioned to the Improvements they have made thereon. **1841** W. Deans *Let.* 25 Mar. in J. Deans *Pioneers of Canterbury* (1937) 33 Mr Molesworth let a town acre of his for £240..for 14 years, buildings and improvements to remain at the end of the lease. **1856** 'J. Phoenix' *Phoenixiana* (1859) xxxiii. 202 Three other small buildings, unoccupied, a fence, and a grave-yard, constitute all the 'improvements' that have been made at the 'Playa'. **1891** R. Wallace *Rural Econ. Australia & N.Z.* xv. 225 Many [N.Z.] settlers naturally prefer the lease, as a perpetual leasehold is practically as good as a freehold, while it leaves a settler free to invest his capital in improvements. **1908** *Indian Laws & Treaties* (U.S.) III. 382 Any person who..shall be an actual resident upon any one such lot and the owner of substantial and actual improvements thereon. **1927** *Amer. Speech* May 358 *Improvements and land* (noun phrase), a farm with its buildings and cleared land. **1930** L. G. D. Acland *Early Canterbury Runs* viii. 180 The Studholmes had the Terrace Station... When they sold it about 1862..the only improvements on it were a shepherd's hut and a set of sheep yards. **1949** *Lubbock* (Texas) *Morning Avalanche* 23 Feb. II. 3 Good 8 inch irrigation well, large loan, good improvements, possession. **1958** *New Yorker* 6 Sept. 37, I remember it as it originally was, for my brother and I, aged eight and six, accompanied my father when he went out to make the first 'improvements'.

7. *attrib.* and *Comb.*; **improvement lease**, in the United States and Australia, a lease granted with conditions of improvement to be made by the lessee.

1840 W. Sewall *Diary* 15 Aug. (1930) 218/1 Henry and myself repairing fence west side of improvement ditch. **1849** E. Chamberlain *Indiana Gazetteer* (ed. 3) 34 They rented land on improvement leases, by which they were to have the use of from ten to twenty acres from seven to ten years, and often at the end of that time they were able to buy land for themselves. **1895** *Act* (New South Wales) 58 *Vict.* no. 18. § 26 (*heading*) Improvement leases. **1900** *Daily News* 16 May 5/3 The new improvement undertakings of the Council. **1909** *Commonwealth Law Rep., High Court Australia* VII. 1, Sec. 26 of the *Crown Lands Act* 1895..authorizes the Governor to grant 'improvement' leases of Crown lands which by reason of inferior quality, heavy timber, or other cause are not suitable for settlement until improved. **1909** *Daily Chron.* 30 Apr. 6/4 The improvement values added by enterprise. *Ibid.* 7/7 Housing and improvement schemes. **1909** *Westm. Gaz.* 19 May 2/2 The sale of sites in improvement areas. *Ibid.* 4/1 The trifling amount of improvement-sites which their predecessors have acquired. **1964** *Ann. Reg. 1963* 128 Then..the Court decided that the Council of Ministers could not transfer municipal powers to improvement boards. **1972** *Guardian* 15 June 14 Improvement grants..are overwhelmingly taken up by better-off owner-occupiers and speculative property developers.

improver[1]. Add: **2. c.** (Earlier example = *dress-improver* s.v. Dress *sb.* 4 a.)

1872 *Young Englishwoman* Oct. 554/1 The improver consists of a thick calico foundation stiffened with whalebone ..furnished with strings to tie round the waist.

(ii) Any substance or preparation added to a foodstuff by a manufacturer or processor in order to improve it in some respect (e.g. in texture or keeping quality).

1902 Leffmann & Beam *Food Analysis* 364 Improvers and Preservatives.—Mixtures of potassium nitrate, sodium chlorid, and other mineral preservatives with a little coloring-matter..are sold for improving the appearance of meat. **1925** Mojonnier & Troy *Technical Control Dairy Products* (ed. 2) xiii. 300 Several commercial products commonly known by the general term 'ice cream improvers' are in common use. These consist of rennet or pepsin mixed with certain powders such as milk sugar. These products react upon the casein in the mix, causing an increase in the viscosity. **1927** *Manch. Guardian Weekly* 11 Mar. 183/2 Indiscreet and provocative references in the press to 'improvers' and bleaching agents used in the preparation of flour for bread-making. **1960** W. J. France *Breadmaking & Flour Confectionary* xi. 109 Barbadoes and Demarara.—These sugars because of their colour, are useful brown bread improvers, adding a characteristic flavour to brown breads. **1970** Fox & Cameron *Food Sci.* viii. 165 This ageing period can be dispensed with if the flour is treated with a minute quantity of one of a number of oxidizing agents which are called flour improvers. *Ibid.*, The first four of the improvers listed increase the whiteness of the flour by bleaching the carotene and xanthophyll, which..give the flour a slight yellow tinge.

improvisation. Add: **1.** *spec.* of Old English verse.

1928 W. W. Lawrence *Beowulf & Epic Trad.* 3 We must agree to judge *Beowulf*,..not as the improvisation of an untutored minstrel, but as a well-considered work of art. **1960** *English Studies* XLI. 5 The use of traditional diction is one thing; improvisation is something else again. The two need not go together and in *Beowulf* they most emphatically do not.

improvisa·tional, *a.* [f. Improvisation + -al.] Of or relating to improvisation, impromptu.

1923 *Theatre Arts Mag.* Oct. 328 He is always true to the great school of acting of the Italian improvisational comedy. **1958** *Times* 15 Dec. 3/4 His playing of Schubert's great B flat major sonata..was far too improvisational and dreamy. **1970** P. Oliver *Savannah Syncopators* 19 Jazz, at least in its early phases, was primarily a group music, using brass and wind instruments with rhythm background, employing improvisational techniques both collectively and in solo. **1972** *Jazz & Blues* Nov. 6 Orchestral textures, improvisational complexity, harmonic innovation. **1973** *Black World* Mar. 26 A stock feature of chanted sermons: the highly rhythmic, imaginative and improvisational rendering of the Word of God.

Hence **improvisa·tionally** *adv.*

1946 R. Blesh *Shining Trumpets* (1949) ii. 33 The leader chants, often improvisationally, in strong declamatory phrases. **1963** *Times* 30 Apr. 15/4 Prokofiev's Seventh Sonata was also somewhat improvisationally showy instead of stable and strong.

improvisator. Add: *spec.* of Old English verse.

1915 W. W. Lawrence in *PMLA* XXX. 400 A direct quotation of the lay sung by the improvisator. **1928** —— *Beowulf & Epic Trad.* 261 Each individual poet..adapting, with the adroitness of the improvisator, bygone legends to the demands of special occasions.

improvise, *v.* Add: **1, 3.** *spec.* of Old English verse.

1892 J. Earle *Deeds of Beowulf* 136 The minstrel did not merely narrate, but improvised in alliterative verse. **1915** W. W. Lawrence in *PMLA* XXX. 400 A thane of the king, skilled in story..entertains the company, improvising a song in honor of Beowulf. **1948** P. F. Baum in *Mod. Philology* XLVI. 76 The minstrel..begins by improvising in verse an account of Beowulf's adventures which he had just learned about and had had little opportunity to work up beforehand. This..presupposes something different from the *Beowulf*, which certainly does not give the impression of improvising. **1961** W. Whallon in *PMLA* LXXVI. 310 The oral poet cannot pause; he must improvise continuously with no apparent effort.

improviser. Add: *spec.* of Old English verse.

1948 P. F. Baum in *Mod. Philology* XLVI. 76 Its meter and the variations exhibit by turns both the ease and freedom of the improviser and the careful workmanship of the artist.

impsonite (i·mpsǝ̆nait). *Min.* [f. *Impson*, the name of a valley in Pushmataha Co., Oklahoma + -ite[1].] An asphaltic mineral similar to albertite.

1901 G. H. Eldridge in *Ann. Rep. U.S. Geol. Survey* XXII. i. 265 This differs from albertite, however, sufficiently, it is thought, to warrant a distinctive name, and for this, impsonite is suggested, after the valley in which it is chiefly found. **1951** E. N. Tiratsoo *Petroleum Geol.* xi. 292 Impsonite..seems to be a kind of end-product in the process of bitumen formation, having a very high proportion of fixed carbon and being infusible. **1965** E. T. Degens *Geochem. Sediments* v. 263 One may distinguish between the asphaltic, e.g. wurtzilite, elaterite, albertite, and impsonite, and the nonasphaltic pyrobitumens.

impulse, *sb.* Add: **2. c.** Aeronaut. *specific impulse*: the ratio of the thrust produced in a rocket engine to the rate of consumption of propellant (expressed as mass, or weight, per second).

Equivalent to the impulse (sense 2 b) obtained per unit mass, or weight, of propellant.

1947 *Jrnl. Brit. Interplanetary Soc.* Mar. 101 The most important requirement is a low consumption, or to use a term more commonly employed in rocketry, a high 'specific impulse'; the specific impulse being the thrust obtained from the consumption of one unit of propellant mixture per second. **1950** *Sci. News* XV. 76 The most useful measure of the efficiency of a rocket is called 'specific impulse'. **1962** F. I. Ordway et al. *Basic Astronautics* x. 422 In the liquid fuel reactor hydrogen is bubbled through liquid uranium compounds. With this method specific impulses on the order of 1500 lb-sec/lb may be attained. **1971** P. J. McMahon *Aircraft Propulsion* iii. 116 In the foot-pound-second system, specific impulse has the units lbf-sec/lb. For many years it was the practice to define the specific impulse as the thrust divided by the *weight* flow rate of propellants. Using this definition the units of specific impulse became 'seconds'. *Ibid.* x. 298 The specific impulse of a cordite type propellant will be of the order of 2 000 N-s/kg when operating with a chamber pressure of 6 000 kN/m^2 and exhausting to 100 kN/m^2.

4. c. *Dancing.* (See quot. 1949.)

1949 Shurr & Yocom *Mod. Dance* 190 *Impulse*, the impetus or impelling force used to initiate a movement sequence, such as a hip contraction or a hip release. **1968** J. Winearls *Mod. Dance* (ed. 2) ii. 64 Thus with continued forward impulses the pelvis moves in a backwards –downwards–forwards–upwards–circle with an accent at the bottom of the circle.

4*. *Electr.* A sudden, momentary change in voltage or current from an otherwise steady (or slowly varying) value. (More commonly *pulse*.)

1883 E. Atkinson tr. *Ganot's Elem. Treat. Physics* (ed. 11) x. vi. 850 As they are all connected together we get, not so much a series of separate impulses, as a continuous series of currents. **1904** *Daily Chron.* 10 Dec. 7/2 It [*sc.* a tape] is inserted in the aperture of the transmitting instrument, and by the perforations the electrical impulses are created and recorded at the receiving station. **1943** A. L. Albert *Fund. Telephony* ix. 206 The vertical movement of the selector switch is controlled by the electric impulses received from the subscriber's dial. **1971** H. E. Ennes *Television Broadcasting* vii. 347 The circuit works by virtue of the fact that spurious noise impulses normally are much narrower than the desired sync pulses.

5. *attrib.* and *Comb.* **a.** Simple *attrib.*

1901 *Daily Chron.* 3 Sept. 3/7 A genuine chivalrous impulse-desire—that natural desire for companionship. **1929** D. H. Lawrence *Let.* 1 Oct. (1962) II. 1204 You are working all the time from wrong impulse-sources. **1949** M. Mead *Male & Female* xvii. 355 Modern psychology and modern literature emphasize the importance of impulse gratification.

b. Special Comb.: **impulse clock, dial,** a secondary clock operated by electrical impulses transmitted at regular intervals by a master clock; **impulse coupling** = **impulse starter*; **impulse-reaction turbine,** a turbine comprising two (or more) stages, one working on the principle of the impulse turbine and the other on that of the reaction turbine; **impulse starter,** a mechanical device which may be fitted to the magneto of an ignition system to cause its rotor to turn in a series of jerks instead of continuously, resulting in an increased voltage that facilitates the production of a spark at low speeds or when starting; **impulse tube,** a tube serving to expel a torpedo; **impulse turbine,** a turbine in which the working fluid undergoes no drop in pressure in the rotor, this being driven solely by the change it causes in the direction of flow.

1923 Langman & Ball *Electr. Horology* v. 82 Clocks coming under this section are generally..designated as dials, impulse clocks, secondary clocks, journeyman clocks, sympathetic clocks, or step by step movements. **1951** S. J. Wise *Electr. Clocks* (ed. 2) iv. 67 An impulse or repeater clock is a device which receives the timed electrical impulses transmitted by a master clock, and translates them, through its wheelwork, into seconds, minutes and hours. **1916** Impulse coupling [see *impulse starter* below]. **1943** A. P. Fraas *Aircraft Power Plants* viii. 147 To ensure a good spark at cranking speeds the magnetos for many of the smaller engines are fitted with an impulse coupling. **1931** F. Hope-Jones *Electr. Clocks* ii. 6 Circuits of electrical impulse dials, in which a master clock transmits impulses every minute or half-minute to propel the hands. **1940** —— *Electr. Timekeeping* i. 6 After many years of futile attempts to apply electricity to horology, inventors turned their attention to systems of electrical impulse dials, an obviously sane and effective method of indicating uniform time throughout a large building. **1929** T. M. Naylor *Steam Turbines* i. 4 Combination turbines or disc and drum turbines, as they are often called, are a combination of impulse and reaction types of turbine. The first part of the turbine is impulse, and the remainder of the turbine is reaction, so that this type of turbine might be called impulse-reaction. **1951** *Engineering* 5 Oct. 438/3 The high-pressure turbine is of the impulse-reaction type. **1916** V. W. Pagé *Automobile Starting* iii. 224 The device..is known as the Eisemann impulse starter coupling. This may be attached to any model of Eisemann magneto and is said to have no effect upon its regular operation except at slow speeds, when it causes the armature to rotate in a series of jumps instead of at a uniform speed. **1940** W. E. Crook *Electr. in Aircraft* vii. 93 The impulse starter..enables the engine to start on its own magnetos. It is a purely mechanical piece of apparatus, consisting essentially of a spring-loaded pawl and ratchet gear. **1877** *Illustr. London News* 14 Apr. 339/3 It is fired by what is called an 'impulse-tube', which..discharges the torpedo into the water. **1878** *Cassell's Family Mag.* 312/2 Direction is given to the torpedo by means of an iron impulse-tube built into the vessel. **1885** *Marine Engineer* 1 Sept. 144/2 The fish torpedoes lie side by side. Immediately behind them..are a couple of 'impulse tubes'. **1881** *Encycl. Brit.* XII. 524/1 In some turbines the whole available energy of the water is converted into kinetic energy before the water acts on the moving part of the turbine. Such turbines are termed Impulse Turbines, and they are distinguished by this that the wheel passages are never entirely filled by the water. **1906** W. H. S. Garnett *Turbines* iv. 42 Impulse turbines..are unsuited for the development of high speed motion from low falls. ..For running, on the other hand, at low speeds under a high fall, the impulse turbine cannot be surpassed. **1971** P. J. McMahon *Aircraft Propulsion* v. 163 The extreme case of a zero reaction stage wherein all the pressure drop occurs in the nozzle blades is known as an 'impulse turbine' in accordance with steam turbine practice. A pure impulse turbine would rarely be used for an aero-turbine engine.

c. Of or pertaining to a purchase or purchases made on impulse, usu. at the point of sale of displayed goods, as *impulse buyer, buying,* etc.

1959 *Times Lit. Suppl.* 29 May (Children's Books) 5 [Children's books] snarl 'impulse buyers' in the supermarket. **1959** *Sunday Express* 26 July 10/4 The Opposition Leader's Lady and Judy O'Grady are *'impulse buyers'* under the skin. **1959** *News Chron.* 18 Nov. 4/2 What the traders call 'impulse buying' is increasingly popular. **1962** *Sunday Express* 8 July 15/2 Top dressers.. plunge with the odd *'impulse buy'*. **1963** *Punch* 27 Nov. 772 New Prime Minister..impulse-buys sixty Phantom IIs. **1964** *Punch* 6 May 655/3 Trolleys full of impulse-bought bargains. **1965** *Mod. Law Rev.* XXVIII. v. 557 None of the reasons given for minimising the importance of 'impulse sales' apply with special force to the book trade. **1967** L. J. Braun *Cat who ate Danish Modern* x. 88 These are little boutique items for the impulse buyer. **1968** 'S. Jay' *Sleepers can Kill* vi. 66 He goes into a shop.. and buys a boat... An impulse buy, if ever there was one. **1972** *New Statesman* 26 May 709/3, I impulse-bought some crumpets the other day, because they were on the counter at the dairy.

impulse, *v.* Delete 'now *rare*' and add later examples. Also *intr.*

1931 *Times* 27 June 11/5 The interference is due..to.. sparks in stays of masts, and to loose metallic contacts, which impulse the receiver in the same way as heavy atmospherics would do. **1936** *Nature* 12 Sept. 445/2 The law and governmental forms..clearly lag behind even economic developments as impulsed by scientific discovery. **1943** *Gloss. Terms Telecomm.* (*B.S.I.*) 62 *Impulsing signal*, a signal carrying the selective information to steer the call in the desired direction. **1949** E. C. BERKELEY *Giant Brains* iii. 41 This type of relay has the property of staying..in either position until the opposite coil is impulsed. **1960** *Lang. & Speech* III. 140 (*title*) Recurrently impulsed resonators in speech and psychophysical studies. **1972** J. QUARTERMAIN *Rock of Diamond* xiii. 72 Her small voice..impulsed through the network of cables.

impulsive, *a.* Add: **4.** *Electr.* Consisting of, or of the nature of, an impulse or impulses.

1920 *Whittaker's Electr. Engineer's Pocket-Bk.* (ed. 4) 136 The passage of the spark in such a case appears to involve an impulsive rush of electricity, and the setting up of electric pulses in the neighbourhood of the spark gap can be demonstrated. **1940** *Chambers's Techn. Dict.* 440/2 *Impulsive current*, a current which comprises one or more impulses in one direction round a circuit, as in dialling. **1947** D. G. FINK *Radar Engin.* xi. 127 The impulsive type of noise (ignition interference and static) so commonly encountered on lower frequencies is generally absent in radar. **1962** *Newnes Conc. Encycl. Electr. Engin.* 466/2 Although the secondary winding [of a magneto] may have 10,000 turns, its voltage is not sufficiently impulsive, however. The contact-breaker is therefore arranged to short-circuit the primary.

impulsivity (impʌlsi·vĭti). [f. IMPULSIVE *a.* + -ITY.] The character of being impulsive or acting on impulse, without reflection or forethought; impulsiveness. Hence **impu·lsivist,** one who acts on impulse.

1891 tr. *C. Lombroso's Man of Genius* 348 The psychology peculiar to the epileptic—impulsivity, double personality, childishness. **1895** tr. *M. Nordau's Degeneration* 120 Moral insanity, however, is not present in Verlaine. He sins through irresistible impulse. He is an Impulsivist. **1925** *Public Opinion* 24 Apr. 391/2 A man of exceptional ability and yet of a febrile impulsivity. **1969** D. A. WINN in Caplan & Lebovici *Adolescence* 256 Impulsivity was prominently a part of the suicidal behavior of most of the 60 adolescents in this study. **1971** *Jrnl. Gen. Psychol.* Oct. 273 This relationship would seem to indicate an underlying impulsivity as being a modest contributor.

impunitive (impiū·nitiv), *a. Psychol.* [f. IM-[2] + PUNITIVE *a.*] Adopting an attitude of resignation towards frustration; characterized by blaming neither oneself nor others unreasonably. Contrasted with *INTROPUNITIVE *a.* and *EXTRAPUNITIVE *a.*

1938 S. ROSENZWEIG in H. A. Murray *Explorations in Personality* vi. 587 He may experience emotions of embarrassment and shame, making little of blame and emphasizing instead the conciliation of others and himself to the disagreeable situation. In this case he will be more interested in condoning than in condemning and will pass off the frustration as lightly as possible by making references, even at the price of self-deception, to unavoidable circumstances. This type of reaction may be termed 'impunitive'. **1954** G. W. ALLPORT *Nature of Prejudice* xxi. 349 Some frustrated people..are so detached and philosophical about life's frustrations that they blame no one; they are impunitive. **1958** M. ARGYLE *Relig. Behaviour* viii. 90 A related personality variable is that of punitiveness: people are said to be extrapunitive if they react to frustration by aggression directed outwards, intropunitive if the aggression is directed inwards, and impunitive if they do not react aggressively at all.

Hence **impu·nitively** *adv.*, in a way characteristic of an impunitive individual.

1958 M. ARGYLE *Relig. Behaviour* viii. 91 The humanitarians on the other hand responded impunitively. **1969** M. D. VERNON *Human Motivation* ix. 148 Unacceptable motivational tendencies..may be treated impunitively and denied entry to consciousness.

impure, *a.* (*sb.*) Add: Hence **impu·rist,** one who is not a purist.

1937 V. WOOLF *Writer's Diary* 3 Apr. (1953) 280 The purists and the impurists. **1959** 'F. NEWTON' *Jazz Scene* vi. 113 The jazz public has always been divided, but before the modernist revolution normally only into 'purists' and 'impurists'.

impurify, *v.* Delete † *Obs.* and add later examples.

1904 *Daily Chron.* 19 July 3/7 Impure aeration that.. takes place in dirty, fœtid cowsheds impurifies it [*sc.* milk]. **1928** D. H. LAWRENCE *Let.* 18 Feb. (1962) II. 1040, I am having to impurify and dilute it [sc. *Lady Chatterley's Lover*] for the market.

impurity. Add: **3. b.** An impurity atom; *esp.* an atom of dopant present at a normal lattice site in an impurity semiconductor.

1931 A. H. WILSON in *Proc. R. Soc.* A. CXXXIV. 279 Electrons on a foreign atom [in a semiconductor] do not take part directly in conduction. They must first be transferred by the effect of the lattice vibrations to an atom of the pure substance. In this case the main function of the impurities is to provide electrons for the upper unoccupied energy bands of the crystal, while acting as scatterers is only a secondary function. **1950** W. SHOCKLEY *Electrons & Holes in Semiconductors* i. 12 The conductivity [of the silicon] arises from the presence of arsenic atoms which are termed 'impurities', even though added deliberately in the otherwise pure silicon. *Ibid.* 14 Impurities with a valence of five are called 'donor impurities' because they donate an excess electron to the crystal; those with a valence of three are called 'acceptor impurities', since they accept an electron from somewhere else in the crystal.., thus leaving a hole to conduct. **1952** J. S. KOEHLER in W. Shockley et al. *Imperfections in nearly Perfect Crystals* vii. 206 The maximum value..of this force occurs when the impurity is two or three atomic distances from the dislocation. **1959** R. A. SMITH *Semiconductors* iii. 45 We must distinguish two types of impurity, substitutional impurities, which replace atoms of the host crystal on their lattice sites, and interstitial impurities which occupy positions in between the lattice sites. **1972** F. J. BAILEY *Introd. Semiconductor Devices* i. 21 By the addition of donor impurities to the silicon, large numbers of free electrons become available as current carriers.

4. Special Comb.: **impurity atom,** an atom that differs from the bulk of those present in a substance in being of a different element; **impurity level,** an energy level in a semiconductor that is due to an impurity atom and generally lies either just above the highest filled (valence) energy band (in the case of an acceptor) or just below the lowest empty (conduction) band (in the case of a donor); **impurity scattering,** scattering of current carriers by impurity atoms in a crystalline solid; **impurity semiconductor,** a semiconductor in which most of the carriers of electric current are electrons and holes from impurity atoms.

1939 A. H. WILSON *Semi-Conductors & Metals* i. 3 The [electrical] resistance in a metal is caused by the scattering of the electrons by irregularities in the crystal; these irregularities may be due to the presence of impurity atoms and strains or to the temperature motion of the atoms. **1949** *Physical Rev.* LXXV. 866/1 A substitutional impurity atom from the fifth group has one more valence electron than is required to fill the four valence bonds with neighboring silicon atoms. **1970** W. BOLLMANN *Crystal Defects* iv. 37 The elementary point defects are vacancies and interstitial atoms, and also impurity atoms. **1972** F. J. BAILEY *Introd. Semiconductor Devices* i. 21 The doping level refers to the ratio of impurity atoms to silicon atoms. For a transistor this may typically be $1:10^8$, i.e. one impurity atom for every hundred million silicon atoms. **1973** *Sci. Amer.* Feb. 93/2 If other atoms, which can be referred to as impurity atoms if their concentration is relatively small, are introduced into a helium discharge, the random collisions in the discharge will mix the impurity atoms with the helium atoms. **1933** R. H. FOWLER in *Proc. R. Soc.* A. CXL. 507 Semi-conductors with impurity levels full of electrons at low temperatures owe their conductivity to the excitation of electrons to band 1 both from the impurity levels and from band 2, the former predominating at ordinary temperatures. **1964** J. M. ZIMAN *Princ. Theory Solids* vi. 169 In a semiconductor there may also be scattering from a neutral impurity—where, for example, an electron has settled in a donor impurity level, or a hole is resident on an acceptor level. **1946** *Physical Rev.* LXIX. 258/2 (*heading*) Theory of impurity scattering in semiconductors. **1965** LINDMAYER & WRIGLEY *Fund. Semiconductor Devices* vii. 259 In crystals used for devices, thermal scattering and impurity scattering dominate the collision processes. **1946** *Trans. Amer. Inst. Electr. Engin.* Nov. 713/3 At low temperatures the conductivity of different samples varies by large factors. In this region silicon is said to be an impurity semiconductor. **1950** W. SHOCKLEY *Electrons & Holes in Semiconductors* i. 12 (*heading*) Impurity semiconductors; donors and acceptors.

imputation. Add: **4.** An economic theory of value (see quot. 1965); also (freq. *attrib.*) a form of taxation levied on company profits, usu. in phr. *imputation system, tax.* Cf. *IMPUTE *v.* 6.

1893 C. A. MALLOCH tr. *F. von Wieser's Natural Value* III. ii. 77 So far as this method succeeds in founding, upon the imputation of the return, a valuation of goods and a plan of production..it is the height of practical wisdom. To show that imputation in this sense is both allowable and practicable take one single case. **1931** A. GRAY *Devel. Econ. Doctrine* xii. 354 The most characteristic part of Wieser's contribution to the school lies in his doctrine of *Zurechnung*, which has been acclimatized in this country as 'imputation' or 'attribution'... In a sense the higher goods have no value until a value is 'imputed'..to them. **1934** F. A. VON HAYEK in C. Menger *Coll. Works* I. p. xv, He answers the problem of imputation..by saying that such quantities of the different factors as can be substituted for each other..must have equal value. **1938** E. ROLL *Hist. Econ. Thought* viii. 388 In the theory of distribution Menger is responsible for posing what is known as the problem of imputation; that is the problem of the value of goods of a higher order. **1965** SELDON & PENNANCE *Everyman's Dict. Econ.* 210 *Imputation*, the process of attributing value to productive resources in accordance with their contribution to the value of their products... The theory of imputation argued that the value of factors ('higher-order' goods) was *in all cases* determined by (imputed from) the value of the final ('lower-order') goods to whose production they contributed. **1971** *Daily Tel.* 17 Nov. 19/2 The Government.. preferred to replace it not with the French *imputation* or tax credit method but with a two-rate system... The *imputation* system..would mean that all company profits..would be taxed at the rate of 50 p.c. **1972** *Accountant* 23 Mar. 366/1 The Chancellor..would introduce a new tax based upon the imputation system. *Ibid.*, Under the imputation system, the company will pay tax on its total profits. **1972** S. MARCUS *Finance Act 1972* i. 2 Under the new 1973 method, known as the 'imputation system', all profits (except capital gains) will be taxed at the same rate, whether they are distributed or not. **1973** *Daily Tel.* 31 Mar. 19/5 Dividend covers..have been adjusted to take into account the new corporation 'imputation' tax system. *Ibid.* 2 Apr. 20 The 'imputation' method of taxing company profits..becomes the technical core of investment.

impute, *v.* Add: **6.** *Econ.* To attribute or assign (value) to a product or process by inference from the value of the products or processes to which it contributes.

1893 C. A. MALLOCH tr. *F. von Wieser's Natural Value* III. viii. 96 To each single item or quantity is imputed the smallest contribution which..can be economically aimed at by the employment of this particular item or quantity. **1893** W. SMART in C. A. Malloch tr. *F. von Wieser's Natural Value* p. xv, This determination of imputation by equations of return tells us nothing more than that certain shares *are* imputed to certain elements. **1945** E. HEIMANN *Hist. Econ. Doctrines* VIII. ii. 197 A problem..had greatly concerned the Austrians from Menger on, namely how separate shares in the product can be imputed to the cost factors when they invariably co-operate in production. **1950** DINGWALL & HOSELITZ tr. *Menger's Princ. Econ.* III. ii. 139 We logically impute this importance to the goods on whose availability we are conscious of being dependent. **1965** SELDON & PENNANCE *Everyman's Dict. Econ.* 210 The value of factors..was *in all cases* determined by (imputed from) the value of the final..goods to whose production they contributed. **1973** *N.Y. Law Jrnl.* 2 Aug. 4/4 If interest is not provided for, the Internal Revenue Service may impute interest to any deferred payments.

imputed, *ppl. a.* Add: **3.** *Econ.* Estimated, valued in relation to something else. Spec. *imputed price, value* (see quots.).

1909 WEBSTER, *Imputed value*, Econ., the value that a thing has merely for its utility in the production of something else;—called also *derived value*. **1929** *Encycl. Brit.* XXII. 960/2 Imputed price..is an estimate of the amount of money for which a given article or a given quantum of goods could be sold or bought. **1973** *Daily Tel.* 27 Mar. 23 (Advt.), With imputed tax credits this is equivalent to a franked payment of 6·5625 p per share.

imputrescibility. (Later example.)

1972 C. LÉVI-STRAUSS in P. Maranda *Mythology* xiii. 275 They are operators, which make it possible..to express..a set of equivalences connecting life and death, vegetable foods and cannibalism, putrefaction and imputrescibility, [etc.].

imram, var. *IMMRAM.

imshi (i·mʃi). *Services' slang.* Also **imshee, imshy.** [Local Arabic (Berggren).] Be off, go away. Also as *vb.*

1916 *Anzac Book* 135/2 And the King-of-all-the-Huns said, 'It is enough, Imshee!' *Note*, Imshee is the Arabic for 'go away'. The Australasian Corps, which had so far employed it only to street hawkers in Cairo, used this warcry on April 25. *Ibid.* 136/1 So they imsheed. **1919** *Athenæum* 28 July 664/2 'Imshy', go away (generally corrupted into something like 'hampshire'). **1942** *Word Study* Dec. 6/2 '*Imshi*,' said the drogo; 'you're *shikkered*!' **1965** G. MCINNES *Road to Gundagai* iv. 70 Now, imshee-allah!

‖ **imu** (ī·mū). [Hawaiian.] 'In the Hawaiian islands, a pit used for baking meat or vegetables by means of heated stones' (*Cent. Dict.* Suppl., 1909).

1928 J. C. ANDERSEN *Myths & Legends Polynesians* 296 When he reached Makila, on the confines of Lahaina, he saw a number of people heating an *imu*, or ground oven. **1954** *Ellery Queen's Mystery Mag.* Oct. 43/2 Next came the ritual of putting the pigs into the *imu*. *Ibid.* 47/1 *Imu* pork, white and succulent inside crackling brown skin.

i-mutation: see *I I. 2 b.

in, *prep.* Add: **1.** Examples of *in a ship, vessel.* Also (U.S.) *in school*, attending a school, receiving education at a school = (U.K.) *at school* (cf. SCHOOL *sb.*[1] 1 b).

In former times *in school* was also used in Britain in the sense 'attending a school': see quot. *c* 1205 s.v. SCHOOL *sb.*[1] 1 b. Also *c* 900 *Bæda's Eccl. Hist.* (1890) 190/12 Sum leornungmon in scole Scotta cynnes; *a* 1350 *Harley Lyrics* (1948) 63 Whil y wer a clerc in scole.

1848 J. F. COOPER *Jack Tier* I. iii. 80 *In* a vessel is as correct as *in* a coach, and *on* a vessel, as wrong as can be; but you can say *on board* a vessel, though not 'on the boards of a vessel'. **1916** 'TAFFRAIL' *Pincher Martin* xiv. 248 'When I was in the old *Somerset*, in nineteen-nine,' somebody would start the ball rolling, 'we had a fellow who'——. **1942** *Short Guide Gt. Brit.* (U.S. War Dept.) 8 The tales of Scott and Robert Louis Stevenson which many of you read in school. **1972** R. QUIRK et al. *Gram. Contemp. Eng.* 310 He's {at school (BrE) / in school (AmE)} (= 'He attends/is attending school'). He's in school (= (in BrE) 'He's actually inside the building—not, *eg* on the playing fields').

4. Esp. of a gradient.

1726 [in Dict.]. **1830,** etc. [see *ONE 5 b]. **1840** [see GRADE *sb.* 10]. **1861, 1868** [see GRADIENT *sb.* 1]. **1869** *Bradshaw's Railway Manual* XXI. 318 The gradients and curves are generally favourable, the steepest gradient being 1 in 82½. **1923** *Michelin Guide Gt. Brit.* (ed. 7) facing p. 277, Gradients on roads are shown thus:..1 in 20 to 1 in 14.

1 in 14 to 1 in 10. 1 in 10 and over. **1973** E. COURSE *Railways S. Eng.: Main Lines* i. 29 Over the nineteen and a half miles from Redhill to Tonbridge the maximum gradient was 1 in 250.

5. b. In phrases implying incidental distribution, e.g. *in parts, in places*.

1905 [see *CURATE 2 b]. **1922** D. H. LAWRENCE *England, my England* 132 And I sensed I was a prisoner, for the snow was everywhere deep, and drifted in places. **1924** A. D. SEDGWICK *Little French Girl* II. v, The long iron staircase down the face of the cliff was almost as steep as a fire escape in places. **1973** *Listener* 8 Feb. 167/2 The Appeal Court..found the [Warhol] film dull, dreary, and offensive in parts.

10. *in-work* (nonce-wd.), one who has work.

1924 GALSWORTHY *White Monkey* I. xii, The out-of-works and the in-works.

b. (Further examples.) Cf. also BUD *sb.*[1] 4, FLOWER *sb.* 10, FOAL *sb.* 1 b, IN-CALF *a.*, *IN-FOAL *a.*, *IN-PIG *a.*, LEAF *sb.* 3.

1813 M. EDGEWORTH *Let.* 6 Apr. (1971) 10 The coffee tree in *red berry*...The palm tree in *fruit and flower*...The banana in *fruit*. **1882** [see POD *sb.*[2] 1]. **1972** *Hilliers' Man. Trees & Shrubs* 83 Corylus avellana 'Contorta'.. A winter feature when in catkin.

12. d. Often dependent upon a superlative or a commendatory epithet: within the sphere of (a particular class or order of things). *colloq.*

1866 RUSKIN *Crown Wild Olive* ii. § 53 The newest and sweetest thing in pinnacles. **1879** [see THING *sb.*[1] 7]. **1911** W. J. LOCKE *Glory of Clementina Wing* ii, I may not be the latest thing in dandyism. **1966** G. N. LEECH *Eng. in Advertising* ix. 92 ABC: the first name in entertainment. **1974** *Radio Times* 3 Jan. 58/1 The most dazzling cruises in holiday history.

17*. With a following sb. forming attrib. phrases: *in-car*, within a car; *in-career*, of training, etc., received while in employment; *in-churn*, of a method of machine-milking direct into a churn; *in-company*, of training, etc., received while in the employment of a company; *in-depth* (see *DEPTH I. 3 c); *in-person* (cf. PERSON *sb.* 11); *in-pile*, within a nuclear reactor; *in-plant*, within a 'plant' or factory; *in-process* (cf. PROCESS *sb.* 1), of any activity, etc., that is in process; *in-process gauging* (see quot. 1968); *in-sack*, within a sack; *in-service* (cf. SERVICE[1] 1), of training, etc.: received by a person while engaged on some activity; of an object: relating to its reliability, maintenance, etc., while in use. Cf. *IN-COLLEGE *a.* (Cf. analogous uses mentioned near end of IN- *pref.*[1])

1968 *N.Y. Times* 7 Apr. 1/4 The sound problem was eventually solved with in-car speakers. **1971** *Daily Tel.* (Colour Suppl.) 4 June 39/1 These damp cloths are part of something the manufacturers..don't seem to have heard of; in-car luggage. They seem to think you can put everything in the boot. **1973** *Times* 13 Feb. 24/1 A Lucas spokesman said yesterday: 'I can confirm that we shall be entering the in-car entertainment market this year.' **1968** *New Scientist* 3 Oct. 31/2 Whether in-career re-education will be best inside or outside universities is a matter for debate. **1970** *Physics Bull.* June 242/2 The engineers' survey..includes unemployment and in-career training as well as remuneration figures. **1970** *Nature* 28 Nov. 814/2 In-career retraining may become very important in the future. **1955** J. G. DAVIS *Dict. Dairying* (ed. 2) 745 Probably the most important development has been the introduction of the 'In-Churn System'. In-churn milking passes the milk direct from the cow to the churn. *Ibid.*, In-churn recording..is carried out by means of weighing scales. *Ibid.*, In-churn cooling. **1960** *Farmer & Stockbreeder* 16 Feb. 39/3 This new..unit..provides you with modern in-churn milking. **1966** *Ann. Rep. Travelers Insurance Co. (Hartford, Conn.) 1966* 26/2 Our in-company training programs. **1969** *Timber Trades Jrnl.* 13 Dec. 35/2 There were twin pillars to training—in-company training and, for young people in particular, further education. **1970** *Times* 28 Apr. 26/7 Having already completed most of the in-company training for the introduction of decimalization. **1955** L. FEATHER *Encycl. Jazz* i. 21 Although the white jazzmen rarely found opportunities for expressing themselves freely on 'in-person' jobs, the work.. on..recording sessions compensated. **1957** S. DANCE in S. Traill *Concerning Jazz* 37 No experience of jazz can be so exciting or so illuminating as the in-person performance. **1959** *Spectator* 9 Oct. 469/1 On any one TV appearance Macmillan and Gaitskell must have been seen by more people than the sum total audience of their in-person tours. **1972** *Jazz & Blues* Nov. 18/1 Her recordings and in-person work illustrate that she is an artist who is always willing to experiment. **1960** *Times Rev. Industry* Dec. 16/2 Zirconium..is useful for 'in-pile' equipment, such as fuel element supports, tubes for control equipment, flexible hose and packing pieces. **1961** *Times* 10 May 2 The work includes:—out-of-pile and in-pile testing. **1963** B. FOZARD *Instrumentation Nucl. Reactors* iii. 33 The second type of measurement is made with in-pile detectors. **1943** *Atlantic Monthly* Sept. 55 Few of them participate in in-plant training and upgrading programs. **1958** *Technology* Feb. 414/2 The proportion of in-plant to total training is..low. **1959** *Times* 5 Feb. 2/5 They involve an application of this industry in in-plant technical scale studies. **1967** *Jane's Surface Skimmer Systems 1967–68* 62/2 The power source can be an in-plant air supply system or [etc.]. **1971** *Timber Trades Jrnl.* 21 Aug. 26/3 In-plant treatment will now be extended to other '1800' components. **1925** *Nat. Assoc. Cost Accountants Yearbk.* 24 Divide the average 'in process' inventories into the amount of transfers to finished stores. **1967** *New Scientist* 20 Apr. 140/1 In-process gauging, on the machine tool itself, could halt..appalling waste. **1968** *Gloss. Terms Air Gauging (B.S.I.)* 13 *In-process gauging*, gauging carried out during processing, e.g. measurement of a workpiece whilst it is being machined. **1971** *Computers & Humanities* VI. 41 In-process corrections, however, are very difficult to make since holes cannot be erased. **1971** *Gloss. Terms Quality Assurance (B.S.I.)* 6 *In-process inspection*, product inspection carried out at various discrete stages in manufacture. **1958** *Times* 24 Nov. 15/4 For drying grass seed.., the in-sack drier had many advantages. **1960** *Farmer & Stockbreeder* 23 Feb. 100/1 (Advt.), Heat for..in-sack grain drying. **1928** *Rep. Comm. Educ., U.S. Dept. Interior* 30 June 6 The movement for improving preservice and inservice training of teachers for rural schools. **1960** *Guardian* 13 July 5/4 Development of in-service training..for staff nurses. **1963** F. F. LAIDLER *Gloss. Home Econ. Educ.* 48 *In-service training*, the continuing education and training given to a person after he/she has begun to work in a particular occupation. **1964** M. A. K. HALLIDAY et al. *Ling. Sci.* 264 He [*sc.* the primary school teacher] needs an appropriate training in his new task, either during his initial period of training as a teacher or by means of in-service training. **1967** *Technology Week* 23 Jan. 43/2 (Advt.), Such data may well reveal over-design or design deficiencies, thus providing opportunities for improvement of safety characteristics, in-service reliability. **1972** *Lebende Sprachen* XVII. 72/2 The in-service performance of the trio is likely to dictate the specification for production models which are due to appear before the end of 1971.

21. d. (Further examples.) Not restricted to explicitly negative sentences.

1924 C. MACKENZIE *Heavenly Ladder* xvi. 223 Mark had never been near his house in a year. **1957** R. A. HEINLEIN *Door into Summer* (1960) ix. 143 The place smelled like a vault that has not been opened in years. **1971** *Daily Tel.* 1 June 4/8 The first bridge across the Bosphorus in 2,300 years..is now being built. **1972** 'E. MCBAIN' *Sadie when she Died* xiii. 42 Arlene said that she had not played tennis in three years. **1973** *Sci. Amer.* Jan. 53/1 When Mariner 9 reached Mars on November 13, 1971, the greatest dust storm in more than a century was raging.

25. (Further examples.)

1810 *Q. Rev.* Feb. 193 If a man has it in him, he can do anything any where. **1841** LYTTON *Night & Morning* (ed. 2) I. I. v. 103, I will work for you day and night. I have it in me. **1846** G. E. JEWSBURY *Sel. Lett. to Mrs. Carlyle* (1892) 224, I did care for him once, long and well—better than I have it in me to care for any man now. **1892** I. ZANGWILL *Childr. Ghetto* III. 52 That girl's got it in her, I can tell you. She'll take the shine out of some of our West-Enders. **1895** H. JAMES *Notebks.* (1947) 408, I didn't know I had it in me. **1919** BEERBOHM *Seven Men* 119 He looked to me to 'do something big, one of these days', and that he was sure I had it 'in' me. **1924** *Isis* (Oxf.) 30 Jan. 16/2 He may become a fine actor—he has it in him. **1928** FOY & HARLOW *Clowning through Life* 297, I didn't believe he had it in him. **1938** R. FINLAYSON *Brown Man's Burden* 79 They didn't think Kay had it in him to do it. **1958** *Listener* 13 Nov. 786/2 As between draughts and chess this is outweighed by the fact that there is more 'in' chess. **1960** M. SPARK *Bachelors* i. 2 'You must have it in you,' said Ronald, 'going all the way to Piccadilly for herbs.' **1973** 'E. MCBAIN' *Hail to Chief* ii. 30 If you could find it in yourself to go over to the hospital and identify your brother.

b. *nothing, not much, little*, etc., *in it*: little or no difference between competitors or any persons or things that are compared. orig. *Racing slang*.

1914 in *Concise Oxf. Dict.* **1927** *Observer* 18 Dec. 19/3 The first round there was nothing much in it. In the second round Angus..punched Mansfield round the ring. **1929** S. E. THOMAS *Elem. Econ.* (ed. 4) xxix. 523 While in the course of a year Britain imports considerable quantities of gold, she also exports almost equally large quantities, and on balance there is usually very little in it.

c. *in it*: an advantage (to be received from something). Usu. in phr. *what was* (or *is*, etc.) *in it for* (someone).

1963 T. PARKER *Unknown Citizen* v. 140 He seemed to have an inbred suspicion of any kind of offered help, he wanted to know why people were giving it, what was in it for them. **1968** *Guardian* 2 Apr. 11/1 The 'Washingtonologists' in Moscow must be getting their files out to see what is in it for the Soviet Union—and for the world. **1971** 'A. GILBERT' *Tenant for Tomb* ii. 39, I can't see what there was in it for Mrs Plum.

27. (Later examples.)

1902 H. JAMES *Wings of Dove* VI. xx. 298 'You scarcely call him, I suppose, one of the dukes.' 'Mercy, no—far from it. He's not, compared with other possibilities, "in" it.' **1907** F. H. BURNETT *Shuttle* xxxviii. 381 'Hope you had a fine time, Mr. Selden?' 'Fine! I should smile. Fine wasn't in it.' **1912** A. BENNETT *Matador* 272 We were completely outshone. I tell you, we were not *in* it, not anywhere near being in it! **1913** F. L. BARCLAY *Broken Halo* vi. 69 In fact, the Egyptian dynasties weren't in it! She was positively antediluvian! **1915** A. HUXLEY *Let.* Oct. (1969) 82 At present I share Balliol with one..man.. who rather repels me at meals by his..habit of shewing satisfaction with the food: Sir Toby Belch was not in it. **1960** L. COOPER *Accomplices* IV. ii. 224, I thought the Party knew all the technique there is about handling people, but they're not in it with the Church. **1964** H. E. F. DONOHUE *Conversations with Nelson Algren* ii. 74 All people are killers, potentially. Tigers aren't in it with people. **1966** 'J. HACKSTON' *Father clears Out* 140 A fight in the snow is a tame affair and not in it with a hot summer contest. **1968** *Globe & Mail* (Toronto) 15 Jan. 9/4 We just weren't in this one... Nobody was going to beat them today.

38. in so far: still conventionally written thus (*Hart's Rules for Compositors*, ed. 37, 1967, p. 75) but also freq. as a single word or with hyphens. Cf. IN SO FAR (as main entry).

1940 *Economist* 6 July 13/2 Insofar as it ensures that trade between the two participating countries shall be reciprocal, it is an extension of compensation trade. **1948** J. STEINBECK *Russ. Jrnl.* (1949) 10 The C-47's are a little run down insofar as upholstery and carpeting go. **1959** B. WOOTTON *Social Sci. & Social Path.* viii. 267 Differentiation between the one and the other will be called for only insofar as it affects the kind of treatment that is likely to be helpful. **1969** *Times* 31 Oct. 29/5 Enforcement, insofar as salaries are concerned, is costing nothing. **1971** *Watsonia* VIII. 205 The results of it will be used here in-so-far as they affect the classification of the group.

in, *adv.* **6. b.** Delete † *Obs.* and add later examples. Cf. *COUNT *v.* 2 b.

1884 'MARK TWAIN' *Huck. Finn* xxxi. 321 As long as I was in, and in for good, I might as well go the whole hog. **1893** —— in *Century Mag.* Jan. 342/1, I could n't venture it now; I was in too deep.

d. (Earlier example.) Also of a batsman given 'not out' by the umpire.

1744 *Laws* [of Cricket] in *New Dict. Arts & Sci.* (1755) IV. 3459/1 Laws for the strikers, or those that are in. **1844** *Blackburn Standard* 17 July, The bowler asked 'in or out?' **1871** 'THOMSONBY' *Cricketers in Council* 32 Men who run with their bats in the air are constantly run out in cases where they would have been safely 'in' if they had adopted the contrary practice. **1898** K. S. RANJITSINHJI *With Stoddart's Team* (ed. 3) iv. 70 He was given 'in' by the umpire when appealed to.

i. (Later examples of sense 'in fashion'.)

1923 *Ladies' Home Jrnl.* Sept. 50 Her hostess, in black silk crêpe, rejoices that trains are once more 'in', knowing the value of long lines and loose draperies. **1954** L. MACNEICE *Autumn Sequel* 131 Accomplishments were in, enthusiasm out. **1959** *Encounter* Sept. 60/2 Beckett is a fashionable reputation which is still 'in'. **1965** M. MORSE *Unattached* i. 24 Perhaps 'being at a party' is a qualification for being 'in'?

j. Of a school: in session, in progress. *Sc.* and *N.Z.*

1812 P. FORBES *Poems, chiefly in Sc. Dial.* 95 On Saturday, nae school being in. **1895** W. C. FRASER *Whaups of Durley* iii. 27 We would be stopped by a shout, 'The schule's in'. **1949** F. SARGESON *I saw in my Dream* I. vi. 40 But I don't remember nothing about when school was in.

k. well in. (*a*) *Racing.* Applied to a horse which has been treated leniently by the handicapper. (*b*) In comfortable or easy circumstances. *colloq.* orig. *Austral.* Also, profitably engaged in speculation.

(*a*) **1854** J. MILLS *Life Race-Horse* xvii. 111 The handicapper..considerately classed me among the middle ones, and awarded 6 st. 12 lb. as my burthen. 'He's vell in,' said my owner,..'very vell in.' **1894** G. MOORE *Esther Waters* xxx. 247 Are the 'orses he backs what you'd call well in? **1898** A. E. T. WATSON *Turf* i. 16 A horse which is well in in a little handicap.

(*b*) **1891** [see WELL-IN *adj. phr.*]. **1902** WEBSTER Suppl., *Well in*, engaged in a profitable speculation in stocks; said of a speculator whose purchases have risen considerably in value on his hands. Hence, in a general sense, prosperous; well off; well to do. (*Colloq., Australia.*) **1913** M. ROBERTS *Salt of Sea* 158 If you ain't lucky you're bound to be dishonest,..if you means to be well in all the time.

l. Of fortune or luck: favourable. (Cf. OUT *adv.* 23.)

1901 A. E. W. MASON *Clementina* i, His luck for the moment was altogether in. **1912** 'SAKI' *Chron. Clovis* 187 Her fellow-gamblers were always ready to entertain her.. when their luck was in.

9. in with. a. (Later examples.)

1925 'R. CROMPTON' *Still—William* vi. 112 So far County had persistently resisted the attempts of Mrs. Bott to 'get in' with it. **1942** E. PAUL *Narrow St.* xxiv. 213 Naturally, the Prime Minister was in with Stavisky, too. **1964** P. M. HUBBARD *Picture of Millie* ii. 15 We..go along to the Carrack for a drink..occasionally, but we're not really in with the people staying there.

12. a. in-maintenance, maintenance for a person living in a workhouse or the like; **in-patient**: now freq. used *attrib.*

1860 in C. S. DAVIES *Hist. Macclesfield* (1961) v. 267 In-Maintenance of paupers £1027 s.5 d.9. **1885** *Encycl. Brit.* XIX. 475/2 Relief given in a workhouse is termed 'in (or indoor) maintenance' relief. **1905** *Daily Chron.* 1 Sept. 2/5 For every £1 spent on out-relief in 1902–3 no less than £7 12s. 4d. was expended on in-maintenance. **1959** *Times* 13 Jan. 3/2 Inpatient therapy. **1965** *Mod. Law Rev.* XXVIII. v. 580 Persons who..are receiving in-patient treatment for mental disorder.

b. in-side *Cricket*, the side which is batting.

1837 D. WALKER *Games & Sports* 224 Batters, belonging to the In-side. **1882** *Australians in Eng.* 16 Matters are going wrong with the in-side.

15. *in on* (cf. *ON *adv.* 13): participating in; being (one of a group) in possession of knowledge concerning (something).

1923 A. CHRISTIE *Murder on Links* viii. 101 You don't mean—that you're in on *that*? **1928** E. WALLACE *Gunner* xxiii. 189 As you're in on this, Gunner, you'd better see what I've said. **1935** M. M. ATWATER *Murder in Midsummer* xxv. 235 He'll want to be in on this. **1946** [see *GROUND FLOOR b]. **1953** W. BURROUGHS *Junkie* (1972) ix. 83 They are in on narcotics, and they are connected with Communism. *Ibid.* xii. 121 If any one makes a good score, she puts out a grapevine to find out who was in on the job. **1958** B. NICHOLS *Sweet & Twenties* 197, I was very much 'in' on the birth of this song. **1959** *Listener* 12 Feb. 283/1 It does not work for the American reader, who s not in on the secret. **1970** R. LOWELL *Notebk.* 221 Anyway you should be in on it. Only In imagination can we lose the battle. **1973** 'M. INNES' *Appleby's Answer* xv. 128 Don't imagine I have the slightest wish to be in on your muckraking.

in, *a.* Add: **2. a.** Fashionable, sophisticated;

esoteric. Cf. *IN *adv.* 6 i, *IN-GROUP, *IN-JOKE, *IN-REFERENCE.

1960 *Spectator* 14 Oct. 555 A personable young *strip-peuse* at Vegas (as we 'in' people call Las Vegas). **1961** *Harper's Bazaar* Apr. 138/2 The *dahlings* of the profession —beloved by 'in' audiences who adore a coterie joke. **1965** *Melody Maker* 13 Feb. 10 Record companies release more discs in the belief that folk is the new 'in thing'. **1969** C. F. BURKE *God is Beautiful, Man* (1970) 107 He's got all the in stuff on and a big stick pin. **1969** *Daily Tel.* 2 July 19/6 The audience—totally committed to the 'pop' ideal and fully conversant with its idiomatic 'in' vocabulary—reacted suitably. **1970** O. NORTON *Dead on Prediction* ii. 41 It *is* the in place. You'd be surprised who you meet there.

b. With hyphen and so passing into IN- *pref.*[1]

1961 *Guardian* 29 Apr. 12/7 You will quickly find in N.Y. that the in-thing to do is to pronounce..Broad*way*. **1965** *Punch* 17 Nov. 721/1 Gnomes, it judged, are now in-people—possibly even top people. **1968** *Daily Tel.* 15 Nov. 16/7 The pace-setters here are upper-class girls who treat swearing as a snobbish in-thing to do. **1969** J. BRAIDWOOD *Ulster Dialect Lexicon* 17, I am informed that it has become the in-word in all Northern Ireland Ministry of Agriculture pamphlets. **1969** *New Scientist* 9 Oct. 74/1 The words 'computer' and 'education' must be two of the most overworked in-words of the decade. **1969** *Word* Feb. 38/1 Change is a contemporary theme; change is one of those in-words at the moment. **1969** *Time* 11 Apr. 55 The magazine's critics still point to its smug, In-crowd perspective. **1970** *Times* Suppl. 9 May 26/4 The in-crowd calls it [*sc.* Casablanca] 'Casa', and I offer the information here for anyone who can use it to advantage.

in, *sb.* Add: **2. ins and outs. b.** Those who are constantly entering and leaving the workhouse. Cf. *in-and-out class*, etc. (s.v. IN AND OUT, IN-AND-OUT *adv.* 4 in Dict. and Suppl.).

1884 *Daily News* 10 Dec. (Ware), There are considerable numbers of paupers..who find the workhouse a convenient retreat on emergency... They are known familiarly as 'the ins-and-outs'. **1896** *Rep. Poor Law Schools Comm.* xi. 71 The fluctuating class of children whose parents frequently discharge themselves from the workhouse and in a few days seek readmission. These cases are known among Poor Law officials as 'ins and outs'. **1905** *Rep. Brit. Assoc. Adv. Sci.* 467 The 'ins and outs' of Great Britain have characteristics which may be described as nomadic.

3. a. An introduction to someone of power, fame, or authority; influence with such a person. *colloq.* (orig. *U.S.*).

1929 E. D. SULLIVAN *Look at Chicago* (1930) ii. 21 His strong 'in' with police, built largely at the outset, with their organization's money. **1930** *Amer. Mercury* Dec. 454/1 *An in*, an introduction; to place in a position to bribe. 'Get me an in with the skipper of that precinct.' **1940** R. CHANDLER *Farewell, my Lovely* xxxvi. 276 It stands to reason that he had an in with the city government, but that don't mean they knew everything he did or that every cop on the force knew he had an in. **1947** J. STEINBECK *Wayward Bus* iv. 44 If her cousin was Clark Gable, why, that was an 'in' you couldn't beat. **1950** 'J. TEY' *To love & be Wise* xix. 248 A girl has a more difficult time getting an 'in' in a racket. **1958** N. F. LEOPOLD *Life plus 99 Yrs.* iii. 58 He had some sort of special 'in' with Warden Westbrook of the jail and was allowed more privileges than the other reporters. **1961** J. HELLER *Catch-22* (1962) xxi. 210 The only colonel he trusted was Colonel Moodus, and even he had an in with his father-in-law. **1962** J. WAIN *Strike Father Dead* v. 210 He had always been meaning to base himself in Paris for a while; all he had been waiting for was what he called 'an in'. Well, now he had got the ideal in. **1966** J. B. PRIESTLEY *Salt is Leaving* xiii. 177, I have an *in* with a couple of the directors. **1973** E. MCGIRR *Bardel's Murder* i. 18 He wondered if she had an 'in' with some manufacturer.

b. *to be on the in*: to have inside information. *U.S. colloq.*

1936 J. STEINBECK *In Dubious Battle* vi. 78 'You a big guy?' 'I'm on the in,' said the boy. **1942** BERREY & VAN DEN BARK *Amer. Thes. Slang* § 480/4 *On the in*, smarted up, wise (to), wised (up).

in. Latin preposition. Add: **in abse·ntia,** in (his, her, or their) absence.

1886 *Edin. Univ. Cal. 1885/6* 141 Conferred *in absentia*. **1938** *Times Lit. Suppl.* 5 Feb. 88/3 The clergy in general are likewise condemned, though *in absentia*. **1955** *Times* 11 July 9/3 A Goa military court has sentenced *in absentia* Peter Alvarez, former president of the Goa National Congress. **1961** L. MUMFORD *City in History* xiii. 386 Residences of royal power *in absentia*, like Londonderry, Philippeville, and Christiansand. **1965** *Listener* 7 Oct. 544/2 The *Occult Diary*..goes on principally to describe his relationship, both actual and telepathically *in absentia*, with his third wife. **1972** D. BLOODWORTH *Any Number can Play* xi. 92 The renegade..has been condemned to death *in absentia*.

in a·ctu, in practice (as opp. to theory or potentiality).

[*a* **1680** S. CHARNOCK *Works* (1684) II. 171 Some say.. we are active *in actu exercito*, but not *in actu signato*. **1749** CHESTERFIELD *Let.* 5 Dec. (1932) IV. 1453, I can only allow him *in actu primo* (to talk logic) and seldom *in actu secundo*.] **1902** W. JAMES *Varieties Relig. Experience* xviii. 451 Whatever we may be *in posse*, the very best of us *in actu* falls very short of being absolutely divine. **1905** —— *Ess. Radical Empiricism* ix. 239 Radical empiricism, unable to close its eyes to the transitions caught *in actu*, accounts for the self-transcendency or the pointing..as a process that occurs within experience. **1907** —— *Pragmatism* vi. 222 Health *in actu* means, among other things, good sleeping and digesting.

in a·ntis *Class. Arch.* [see ANTA], denoting a building in which the side walls are prolonged beyond the front and the pilasters terminating them are in line with the columns of the façade.

1848 W. SMITH *Dict. Greek & Roman Antiquities* (ed. 2) 1105/2 There were never more than ten columns in the end portico of a temple; and when there were only two, they were always arranged in that peculiar form called *in antis*. **1875** *Encycl. Brit.* II. 388/2 Temples in Antis, with a portico of two or four columns in front. **1955** L. WOOLLEY *Alalakh* ii. 71 It is tempting to restore this as a temple *in antis*, with two columns between the projecting walls (or between reveals from those walls) on the analogy of Niqme-pa's palace front. **1973** *Country Life* 20 Sept. 763/3 Its original first-floor portico, with Ionic columns *in antis*, survives.

in contuma·ciam, applied to sentences given against persons in contempt.

1892 in *Stanford Dict. Anglicised Words* 460/2. **1918** *Wireless World* VI. 156 It was only because they were for the moment beyond reach of the Italian Courts that they were condemned *in contumaciam*. **1923** *Westm. Gaz.* 28 Dec., Several of these verdicts were passed in contumaciam.

in co·rpore = **in vivo*.

1906 *Rep. Brit. Assoc. Adv. Sci. 1905* 552 The nature of the substance contained in the serum was discussed. *In vitro* it has little power. *In corpore*,..the amount.. necessary..is of no consequence. **1969** *Nature* 12 July 189/1 This is the first reported case of *in corpore* fertilization and development in the sea urchin, *Arbacia punctulata*.

in di·stans, at a distance (see *ACTIO IN DISTANS).

1890 W. JAMES *Princ. Psychol.* I. ii. 47 This blindness was probably due to inhibitions exerted *in distans*. **1909** —— *Pluralistic Universe* viii. 311 Remote professorial minds operating *in distans* upon conceptual substitutes for him [*sc.* God] alone.

in extenso (later examples).

1906 *Rep. Brit. Assoc. Adv. Sci. 1905* 257 Star Streaming. By Professor J. C. Kapteyn. (Ordered by the General Committee to be printed *in extenso*.) **1965** *Mod. Law Rev.* XXVIII. v. 618 Nearly every section is quoted *in extenso*.

in loco, (*b*) in a (*or* the) place; locally.

1671 LOCKE *Essay Draft B* (1931) § 94 p. 200 If it be said that it [*sc.* the soul] cannot change place, because it has none, for spirits are not *in loco* but *ubi*, I desire that distinction may be put into English or any other language and made intelligible. **1908** *Practitioner* Jan. 22 Some toxin either generated in loco..or reaching the skin from some distant focus of disease.

in no·mine, in the name (of): applied to (*a*) a motet or antiphon in fugal style, probably so called because originally used of a composition set to a text in which these words occurred, e.g., the Introit 'In nomine Jesu', the Psalm 'Deus, in nomine tuo'; (*b*) a free fugue in which the answer does not exactly correspond with the subject.

1636 C. BUTLER *Princ. Musick* 91 The *In-nomine's* of Parsons, Taverner, D. Ty, etc. **1876** STAINER & BARRETT *Dict. Mus. Terms* s.v., The *in nomines* which exist are chiefly the production of composers of the 16th century. **1970** W. APEL *Harvard Dict. Mus.* (ed. 2) 412/2 Purcell's two 'In nomine' compositions represent a late attempt at revival of the form.

in nu·ce, in a nutshell, in a condensed form.

1854 GEO. ELIOT tr. *Feuerbach's Essence Christianity* II. xxii. 214 The religious man is happy in his imagination; he has all things *in nuce*; his possessions are always portable. **1948** L. SPITZER *Linguistics & Lit. Hist.* iii. 100 A reduction *in nuce* of the general aesthetics of Racine. **1972** *Times Lit. Suppl.* 7 Apr. 382/1 A grand summation and cosmology *in nuce*. **1973** *Times Lit. Suppl.* 26 Oct. 1307/1 The idea of the modern family as social democracy *in nuce*.

in pe·ctore = *in petto* (see PETTO).

1858 N. WISEMAN *Recoll. Last Four Popes* vii. 333 The Pope made this speech..in this form: 'Moreover, *we create* a cardinal of the Holy Roman Church,..whom, however, we reserve *in pectore*.' **1876** *Encycl. Brit.* V. 98/1 The change which Paul III. introduced consisted in confining the secret of the unpublished nominations [of cardinals] to his own breast, keeping it '*in pectore*'. **1963** *Times* 29 May 10/2 One suggestion about the current affairs discussed with Cardinal Cicognani is that the Pope is preparing to reveal the identities of the three Cardinals whom he created *in pectore* in 1960—a device by which the Pope may keep to himself the names of certain new appointments if he feels that the moment is inopportune to publish them.

in propria persona (later examples).

1851 GEO. ELIOT *Let.* 28 Jan. (1954) I. 344 When am I to have Mr. Bray's promised letter? or to see him in propria persona. **1958** *Times* 19 Aug. 11/2 *Così fan tutte* was performed in the great hall of the Residenz, where Leopold and Wolfgang Mozart themselves had often been *in propriis personis*. **1967** *Listener* 23 Mar. 408/3 In Figaro he [*sc.* Rossini] has created the ideal character from which he can speak *in propria persona*.

in re, (*a*) in reality (see sense 21 in Dict.); (*b*) *Logic*, = *EXTRA DICTIONEM (opp. *in voce*); (*c*) *Metaph.*, (of universals) dependent for their existence on the existence of the particulars that instantiate them, as Aristotle held; having real or objective, not merely mental, existence, but not separately from particulars (cf. *ANTE REM); also **in re·bus**; (probably taken by modern writers from Duns Scotus (*c.* 1264–1308)); (*d*) in the matter of, referring to, = RE *sb.*[2]

(*a*) **1602** W. WATSON *Decacordon* 145 Wherein the Iesuits..had any speciall commoditie or gaine *in re* or *in spe* thereby. *a* **1680** S. CHARNOCK *Works* (1684) II. 853 Their Sacraments and ours were the same *in re*, though diverse in signs.

(*b*) **1847** [see *IN DICTIONE]. **1906** [see *EXTRA DICTIONEM].

(*c*) **1879** W. JAMES *Coll. Ess. & Rev.* (1920) 112 If they begin with a clear nominalistic note, they are sure to end with a grating rattle which sounds very like *universalia in re*, if not *ante rem*. **1904** [see *ANTE REM]. **1907** W. JAMES *Pragmatism* vi. 221 Like wealth, health also lives *in rebus*. **1927** [see *ANTE REM]. **1952** R. I. AARON *Theory of Universals* ii. 26 Locke here denies the *In Re* theory... The white itself is not *in re* but 'in the mind'. **1953** H. H. PRICE *Thinking & Experience* i. 10 The traditional Aristotelian doctrine of *universalia in rebus*. *Ibid.* ii. 56 There *are* universals, existing and subsisting *in rebus*.

(*d*) **1877** *Times* 18 Jan. 11/4 Court of Bankruptcy... In re B. and L. Harris. This was an adjourned sitting for public examination. The bankrupts, Messrs. Benjamin and Lawrence Harris, were merchants. **1886** *Athenæum* 20 Nov. 671/2 The alleged 'misrepresentation' *in re* Squeers *v.* Bentley. **1896** E. TERRY *Let.* 7 Dec. in *Ellen Terry & Bernard Shaw* (1931) 136 What do you mean by saying (in re The Philanderer) it is dull and bestial? **1955** *Times* 29 June 3/7 *In re* Hillier ([1954] 1 W.L.R. 700), but it did not occur to counsel in that case. **1972** *Times* 22 Feb. 14/5 In *In re Scarisbrick* ([1951] Ch 622) the Court of Appeal held that the distinction between a public or charitable trust and a private trust depended on [etc.].

in se *Philos.*, in itself. So **inseity** (in͵sī·ĭti), in-itselfness.

1868 W. JAMES *Let.* 5 Apr. in R. B. Perry *Tht. & Char. W. James* (1935) I. xv. 269 To the Greeks a thing was evil only transiently and accidentally... Bystanders could remain careless and untouched—no after-brooding, no disinterested hatred of it *in se*, and questioning of its right to darken the world. **1879** —— *Coll. Ess. & Rev.* (1920) 94 Substance *in se* cannot be directly imaged by feeling. **1909** —— *Meaning of Truth* vii. 167 Useful to test truth by, the matrix of circumstance, he thinks, cannot found the truth-relation *in se*. **1899** A. E. GARVIE *Ritschlian Theol.* ii. 48 The thing which we represent for ourselves is an existence in itself (inseity). **1940** *Mind* XLIX. 177 The *otherness* of 'self' and 'other' need in no wise conceal the inseity of the 'other' from the 'self'.

in situ (earlier example). Also *attrib.*

1740 W. STUKELEY *Stonehenge* iv. 21 Eleven of them are standing *in situ*. **1912** *Proc. Amer. Philos. Soc.* LI. 490 *In situ* forests occur frequently in shale beds. **1940** *Archit. Rev.* LXXXVII. 102/2 The foundations to receive the superstructure are formed of concrete in-situ posts. **1968** *Daily Tel.* 4 Nov. 9/6 Constructed entirely in in-situ concrete..it resembles a fortified gateway to the main hospital buildings. **1971** *Nature* 24 Dec. 432/1 The Department of the Environment, which has responsibility for *in situ* historical monuments in England.

in sta·tu nasce·ndi, in the process of creation, formation, or construction.

1890 W. JAMES *Princ. Psychol.* II. xvii. 11 Black can only be felt in contrast to white..and in like manner a smell, a taste, a touch, only, so to speak, *in statu nascendi*, whilst, when the stimulus continues, all sensation disappears. **1927** B. MALINOWSKI *Sex & Repression in Savage Society* IV. i. 180 And let us clearly and explicitly recognize that we can never observe it [*sc.* culture] *in statu nascendi*. **1948** *Sci. News* VII. 112 The ENIAC has been in use for some time, the other machines are still *in statu nascendi*.

in sta·tu pupilla·ri, as a pupil or ward; under scholastic discipline; at the universities, designating all who have not the degree of Master.

1855 *Newsp. & Gen. Reader's Compan.* § 571 A young Englishman..while still in statu pupillari. **1860** *Once a Week* 21 July 95/2, I fully admit that in later years we are all of us apt to grow sentimental about the traditions of our respective schools—I merely deny that we do so whilst we remain *in statu pupillari*. **1862** THACKERAY *Philip* III. x. 214 Other young women who are kept by over-watchful mothers too much *in statu pupillari*. **1882** *Standard* 25 Dec. 5 (Stanford), Academic and urban magnates, fellows, and tutors have predominated over guests who are *in statu pupillari*. **1903** 'SIGMA' *Personalia* 172 One of those dusky potentates *in statu pupillari*, who were nearly always represented at the Master's dinners. **1930** *Sunday Times* 12 Oct. 26/2 The possession of a motor-car makes it easy for a person *in statu pupillari* to spend a large part of his existence elsewhere than in the University. **1965** *Rep. Comm. Disciplinary Powers Vice-Chancellor & Proctors* (Univ. Oxf.) 8 Difficulties might arise if graduates *in statu pupillari* who, very often, do the same sorts of things as undergraduates, such as running university clubs, are not bound by the same regulations as their undergraduate colleagues.

in terrorem (later examples).

1960 *Times* 12 Apr. 13/7 They operate mainly *in terrorem*; the potential tax avoider will not incur the cost and complication of a transaction unless he can be reasonably sure of its result. **1970** *Internat. & Compar. Law Q.* XIX. II. 214 Perhaps no more would be necessary than a criminal sanction against rent usury operating *in terrorem*, as exists in German law. **1971** *Daily Tel.* 1 July 4/6 This idea that the Treaty of Rome, like diamonds, is forever, is held *in terrorem* over people.

in toto (further examples).

1811 G. CONSTABLE *Let.* 31 Dec. in J. Constable *Corr.* (1962) I. 73 If my opinion was requested it would not be to give up your female acquaintance in toto. **1954** M. BERESFORD *Lost Villages* vi. 186 In fact we cannot be all that certain that it was all that much less *in toto*. **1955** *Times* 4 May 22/6 These amounts, *in toto*, fall short of our requirements if the business is to continue to expand as it is doing. **1965** *Mod. Law Rev.* XXVIII. 595 Lord Cameron's reasoning is applicable *in toto* to the situation in *The Acrux*.

in u·tero, in the uterus or womb, unborn.

1713 W. CHESELDEN *Anat. Humane Body* IV. iii. 170 It seems highly necessary, that the Ducts thro' which the Body receives Nourishment after the Birth, shou'd be kept open by a Fluid passing that way whilst it is in *Utero*. **1728** CHAMBERS *Cycl.* s.v. *Generation*, For that Dr. Harvey could never discover any thing of it *in utero*. **1795** W. TURNBULL in *Mem. Med. Soc. London* IV. 364 (*title*) A case where small-pox was communicated from the mother to the child in utero. **1871** A. MEADOWS *Manual of Midwifery* (ed. 2) III. ii. 156 The placenta, which..still remains for awhile in utero. **1901** [see STOMATITIC *a.*]. **1964** M. CRITCHLEY *Developmental Dyslexia* xiii. 75 Any theory of minimal brain damage—whether or not sustained *in utero*—is also unconvincing. **1966** *Lancet* 24 Dec. 1403/2 Stiehm et al. conclude that raised levels of γM or γA globulins at birth are presumptive of in-utero infection.

in vacuo (later examples).

1937 [see *ELECTRONIC *a.* 1]. **1942** *Tee Emm* (Air Ministry) II. 140 It is more correct to regard a running fix as a means of approximating the position 'in vacuo' so to speak, when more precise methods are unobtainable. **1955** *Times* 25 May 15/3 Whatever meaning people might ascribe to the word 'tramp' *in vacuo*.

in vi·no ve·ritas, truth comes out under the influence of alcohol; a drunken person tells the truth.

1594 LYLY *Mother Bombie* in *Wks.* (1902) III. III. iii. 199, I perceiue sober men tel most lies, for *in vino veritas*. **1616** T. ADAMS *Divine Herball* 27 And though the Prouerbe be, *In vino veritas*; yet as drunke as he is, you shall neuer haue truth break out of his lips. **1831** DISRAELI *Young Duke* III. IV. vi. 50 There was Cogit, who, when he was drunk, swore that he had had a father; but this was deemed the only exception to *in vino veritas*. **1927** D. H. LAWRENCE *Mornings in Mexico* 174 They say: *in vino veritas*. Bah! They say so much! **1936** N. MARSH *Death in Ecstasy* xii. 145 We had a clear case of *in vino veritas*. *a* **1953** E. O'NEILL *Long Day's Journey* (1956) IV. 145 Got to tell you now. Something I ought to have told you long ago... Not drunken bull, but 'in vino veritas' stuff.

in vitro (vī·tro). *Biol.* [lit. 'in glass'.] In a test tube, culture dish, etc.; hence, outside a living body, under artificial conditions; also *attrib.*, performed, obtained, or occurring *in vitro*.

1894 GOULD *Dict. Med.* 623/2 *In vitro*, in the glass; applied to phenomena that are observed in experiments carried out in the laboratory with microörganisms, digestive ferments, and other agents, but that may not necessarily occur within the living body. **1901** *Jrnl. Exper. Med.* V. 355 Serum obtained by immunising with one race did not necessarily give more than a trace of reaction in vitro and none whatever in vivo when tested with another race. **1912** BROQUET & SCOTT tr. *Burnet's Microbes & Toxins* x. 193 The neutralisation in an ordinary test-tube of a toxin by an antitoxin was one of the first and most brilliant '*in vitro*' experiments in immunity. **1925** C. H. BROWNING *Immunochem. Stud.* 14 These alcoholic extracts possess the property of reacting with heterophile antibody *in vitro*. **1955** *Sci. Amer.* June 88/3 Streptomycin has little or no activity against fungi *in vitro*, but it..controls blue mold of tobacco..and rot of sugar beets—all fungus diseases. **1962** *Lancet* 5 May 936/2 The in-vitro results show that fucidin is very active ..in sterilising cultures of staphylococcus at higher concentrations. **1974** *Nature* 22 Nov. 302/1 Onset of rapid haemoglobin formation in the blood islands of the developing chick blastodisc, both *in ovo* and *in vitro*, commences at the stage of the 6- to 7-somite embryo.

in vivo (vī·vo). *Biol.* Within the living organism; also *attrib.*, performed, obtained, or occurring *in vivo*.

1901 [see *in vitro]. **1947** *Sci. News* V. 78 Some chemical interchange between the plant and the bacteria must take place *in vivo* and be largely responsible for nitrogen fixation. **1962** VAN HEYNINGEN & WALEY in A. Pirie *Lens Metabolism Rel. Cataract* 336 Proteolytic enzymes are often characterized by their action on substrates which are not known to be the natural substrates of the enzyme *in vivo*. **1973** *Nature* 16 Feb. 457/2 The *in vivo* experiments were also carried out using mice bearing a 14 day old tumour.

21. Other phrases: *in abstracto* (examples); *in articulo mortis* (later examples); *in camera* (examples); *in concreto* (examples); *in excelsis* (examples); *in flagrante delicto* (examples); also (colloq.) *in flagrante*; *in pa·ri mate·ria*, in a like case or position; *in puris naturalibus* (earlier and later examples); *in sæcula sæculorum* (later examples).

1602 W. WATSON *Decacordon* ix. 310 Which if he can bring to passe..then shall the French be so fleeced in *abstracto*..to be distracted out of their wits. **1630** [see *in concreto* below]. **1884** W. JAMES *Ess. Radical Empiricism* (1912) xii. 269 Let us fall back from all concrete attempts and see what we can do with his notion of through-and-throughness, avowedly taken *in abstracto*. **1920** D. H. LAWRENCE *Lost Girl* vii. 127 She existed *in abstracto* as far as he was concerned. **1928** O. JESPERSEN *Internat. Lang.* I. 22 Those who have spoken in favour of the idea *in abstracto*. **1933** *Times Lit. Suppl.* 13 Apr. 256/2 Towards the religious life of India Dr. Söderblom is kinder than many critics, but he, of course, is dealing with it *in abstracto* and not in its cruder manifestations. **1951** PARSONS & SHILS *Toward Gen. Theory Action* i. 99 The actor *in abstracto* is simply a set of properties by which he can be classified; in action he is involved in a system of relationships. **1967** *Word* XXIII. 385 We remember that the verb expresses nothing but the verbal idea in abstracto without containing any actualizing elements such as tense, mode, or voice. **1617** J. CHAMBERLAIN in T. Birch *Cour & Times James I* (1848) II. 1 The late lord chancellor left this world, being visited *in articulo mortis*, or not full half an hour before. **1825** SCOTT *Talisman* in *Tales Crusaders* IV. xv. 344 Nor did I mention it, save *in articulo mortis*,..to yonder reverend hermit. **1929** *Encycl. Brit.* VI. 231/1 Those under discipline were allowed to receive the eucharist when *in articulo mortis*. **1872** E. BROWNING *Exposition Laws Marriage & Divorce* 5 The Judge may, and usually does sit *in camerâ* to hear suits for nullity of marriage, where the matters to be disclosed are unfit for the public ear. **1882** *Standard* 26 Dec. 5/7 The case is one that in England would be heard *in camera*. **1955** *Times* 25 June 11/7 All documents filed in the Court be confidential and kept secret, and that every application for an adoption order should be heard and determined *in camera*. *Ibid.* 14 July 5/1 A naval court martial held *in camera* to-day in H.M.S. Victory at Portsmouth. **1966** P. MOLONEY *Plea for Mersey* 34 Fearing that the evidence might be a bit lurid the judge ordered 'Clear the court! The evidence will be heard in camera.' The accused immediately asked 'What the Hell's "in camera"..?' **1970** *Guardian* 8 Aug. 9/2 The expurgated version of the in-camera sessions. **1602** W. WATSON *Decacordon* ix. 310 Though by the law Salique the Lady Infanta may be..put from her..lawfull claime to the whole kingdome of France, in *concreto*. **1630** T. ADAMS *Workes* 633 And the Popes haue so wrought it and brought it about now, that they will not onely *in abstracto* bee had in reuerence; but *in concreto* be feared with obseruation. **1798** A. F. M. WILLICH *Elem. Critical Philos.* 39 A bare idea of a possible science, which is no where given *in concreto*. **1885** W. JAMES in *Mind* X. 41, I may satisfy him that the words mean for me just what they mean for him, by showing him *in concreto* the very animals and their arrangements, of which the pages treat. **1902** —— *Varieties Relig. Experience* ii. 31 Not a deity *in concreto*, not a superhuman person, but the immanent divinity in things..is the object of the transcendentalist cult. **1936** C. S. LEWIS *Allegory of Love* vi. 289 The symbol ..fits all, and gives *in concreto* a characteristic of our life. **1602** W. WATSON *Decacordon* i. 21 Though to vs vnknowne to be of the same church triumphant *in excelsis*. **1882** *Athenæum* 23 Dec. 854 It is an uncritical guide-book *in excelsis*. **1927** *Melody Maker* Sept. 923/3 By all means strive to become a Frankie Trumbauer, or a Jimmy Dorsey, for that is musicianship and style *in excelsis*. **1965** *New Statesman* 30 Apr. 690/1 Tchaikovsky is the Victorian Artist *in excelsis*, grand, noble, compassionate. **1612** T. SHELTON tr. *Cervantes's Hist. Don Quixote* III. viii. 190 All was done in *Flagrante*, there was no leisure to giue me torment, the cause was concluded. **1772** 'JUNIUS' *Lett.* II. lxviii. 314 A person positively charged with feloniously stealing, and taken *in flagrante delicto*, with the stolen goods upon him, is not bailable. **1876** tr. *P. J. van Beneden's Animal Parasites* 2 The sharper passes for an honest man as long as he has not been taken *in flagrante delicto*. *a* **1930** D. H. LAWRENCE *Phoenix* (1936) 17 But at last she caught him *in flagrante*. **1942** E. PAUL *Narrow St.* ii. 16 He saw, not his cringing wife and the imaginary lover he had always sworn to catch *in flagrante delicto*, but his swarthy waiter and a strange girl. **1972** D. BLOODWORTH *Any Number can Play* i. 2 A shocked Font-le-Baume caught them *in flagrante*. **1867** WHARTON *Law Lexicon* (ed. 4) 485/2 *In pari materiâ*, dealing with the same subject-matter. **1932** *Times Lit. Suppl.* 16 June 436/3 The comparison..on page 106 is not quite *in pari materia*: the three and a half million Churchfolk are adults, the thirty-five the whole population. **1955** J. L. AUSTIN *How to do Things with Words* (1962) ix. 112 Even the minimum physical action..is, being a bodily movement, *in pari materia* with at least many of its immediate and natural consequences. **1602** W. WATSON *Decacordon* vii. 204 As inclined to seeke for good to eschewe euill, and wishing after *summum bonum*, if in *puris naturalibus* they could haue obtained it. **1859** *Harper's Mag.* June 46/2 The natives..may be found not only in their primitive state, but even *in puris naturalibus*. **1930** D. H. LAWRENCE *Nettles* 18, I thought it was a commonplace That a man or a woman in a state of grace In puris naturalibus, don't you see, Had normal pudenda, like you and me. **1716** POPE *Let.* 9 July (1956) I. 347 We begin to wish you had the singing of our Poets..to yourselves, in *Sæcula Sæculorum*. **1841** THACKERAY *Misc. Ess.* (1885) 219 So Pride and Hatred continue *in sæcula sæculorum*. **1890** [see *atom-like]. **1940** *Penguin New Writing* I. 10, I thought of the British Raj as an unbreakable tyranny, as something clamped down, in saecula saeculorum, upon the will of prostrate peoples.

in-, *pref.*[1] Add: **b.** *Geom.* Representing INSCRIBED *ppl. a.* 3, as in *in-centre*, *in-circle*, *in-sphere*.

-in, *suffix*[1]. Add: Also used systematically to form the names of certain unsaturated six-membered heterocyclic monocyclic compounds having no nitrogen atom in the ring, as *dioxin*. Cf. *-INE[5].

1928 [see *-INE[5]]. **1940** in PATTERSON & CAPELL *Ring Index* 21. **1957** E. H. RODD *Chem. Carbon Compounds* IVA. 4 Six membered rings in their least hydrogenated forms have names ending in '-in' when non-nitrogenous and '-ine' when nitrogenous.

-in, *suffix*[3]. The adverb IN used as a suffix originally designating a communal act of protest by Negroes in the United States against racial segregation (cf. *SIT-IN); subsequently indicating any group protest or large gathering for some common purpose. Examples are very numerous: e.g. *apply-in*, *BE-IN, *bury-in*, *chain-in*, *cook-in*, *drive-in*, *eat-in*, *FISH-IN, *hate-in*, *join-in*, *kiss-in*, *kneel-in*, *lie-in*, *LOVE-IN, *marry-in*, *mill-in*, *pedal-in*, *play-in*, *pray-in*, *read-in*, *scrub-in*, *sew-in*, *shout-in*, *sit-in*, *sleep-in*, *solve-in*, *stall-in*, *stand-in*, *study-in*, *sweep-in*, *swim-in*, *teach-in*, *wade-in*, *walk-in*. Chiefly attached to verb stem, but also to adjectives, e.g. *fat-in*, *nude-in*, and to substantives designating a participant in the protest or gathering, e.g. *kneeler-in*, *sitter-in*, *wader-in*.

1960 *Newsweek* 16 May 34/1 Into the already-roiled waters of the South, Negroes will wade this summer in a campaign to break down segregation at public beaches—a wade-in counterpart to the widespread lunch-counter sit-ins of recent weeks. **1960** in *Amer. Speech* (1961) XXXVI. 282 Negro college students have initiated a new 'kneel-in' campaign..by attending services at white protestant Atlanta churches. **1961** in *Ibid.*, He called for *walk-ins* in art galleries and museums, *drive-ins* at segregated motels and roadside ice cream stands, *sit-ins* in court rooms, *study-ins* at segregated schools, and *bury-ins* to integrate cemeteries. *Ibid.*, Negro teen-aged boys in an impromptu swim-in at an undesignated beach drew a crowd of 300 shoving, shouting Memorial Day bathers and boaters yesterday. *Ibid.* 284 A Chattanooga, Tenn., Negro stand-in demonstrator says his son's life has been threatened. **1961** *Guardian* 26 May 11/1 The United Presbyterian Church of America...recommended a 'kneel-in' campaign as a manifestation of the belief in the right of all people to worship regardless of race. **1961** *N.Y. Times* 9 Nov. 37 Last night, twenty-four students gathered in the campus library for an all-night 'read-in' demonstration. **1963** *Time* 30 Aug. 12 Demonstrators.. prostrate themselves before bull-dozers at construction-site 'lie-ins'. *Ibid.*, The 'pray-in' at churches. **1964** *Economist* 25 Apr. 376/1 The threatened 'stall-in' of thousands of motor cars [by Negroes]. **1965** *N.Y. Times* 28 Mar. 2E/8 There have been sit-ins, lie-ins, stand-ins, eat-ins, shop-ins, sleep-ins, swim-ins, and sing-ins. **1965** *Economist* 19 June 1401/2 This week Mr Johnson countered the university 'teach-ins', protesting against his foreign policy, with a cultural 'play-in' demonstrating his respect for the arts. **1966** *Daily Tel.* 12 Aug. 11/3 William Bryden-Smith, aged 10, who wrote to us, wants to take part in the cook-in. **1967** *Ibid.* 3 Mar. 23/7 A 'kiss-in' to protest against Michigan University's stern regulations on 'public displays of affection' was described by students last night as the most enjoyable form of demonstration yet devised. **1967** *New Statesman* 17 Mar. 356/3 Last week police arrested scores of teenagers at a rave-in, and left-wing Catholics staged a pray-in. **1967** *Times* 28 Mar. 4/7 It took the police three hours to clear a 'mill-in' at the intersection of Haight and Ashbury streets, celebrated as the chief resort of the bearded and sandalled 'hippies' who travel to San Francisco from all over the United States to signify their dissent from modern society. **1967** *Observer* 11 June 10 If everyone was fat there'd be no war. No one would pass the physical.—A speaker at the New York Central Park 'Fat-in'. **1967** *Listener* 10 Aug. 188/3 This is a very exciting inversion of psychedelic soulfulness, a hate-in. **1967** *World Study* Dec. 7/1 *Chain-in*, demonstrators locking themselves to a city hall pillar,..until the mayor listened to their grievances. *Ibid.* 7/2 *Stand-in*, demonstrators lining up at a theater ticket booth until given admission to the theater, not simply to a segregated section in the rear of the house but to any area where a white patron—or a member of any race—may sit. **1968** *Lebende Sprachen* XIII. 68/1 Their action fits into a wave of unofficial, unconnected *nude-ins* so far this year in Golden Gate Park, starting with freebeachers dancing nude at the great be-in. **1968** *Listener* 26 Dec. 849/1 Charge of the Light Brigade, 20th-century style: a lie-in at Porton Microbiological Research Establishment. **1969** *New Yorker* 3 May 31/1 Another rally was held at the Campus Center, followed by what was termed a 'mill-in' at the Army, Air Force, and Marine recruiting site. **1969** *Daily Tel.* 29 Jan. 1/6 About 20 of the militants..ended their vigil yesterday with a 3 a.m. 'swim-in' in the basement pool. *Ibid.* 2 July 18/3 Practical tests in revolutionary rhetoric ('shout-ins'), wall-defacement and anti-Establishment violence. **1970** *Ibid.* 2 Mar. 16 To teach-in ..and sit-in..have now been added walk-in and work-in. The first means the occupation of premises outside undergraduates' recognised territory, the second a teach-in during vacation. **1971** *Guardian* 28 Sept. 15/3 A student sleep-in began last night. **1973** *Daily Tel.* 3 Dec. 13/8 College catering would be disrupted by students alternately boycotting canteens and then holding mass eat-ins.

in absentia: see *IN *Lat. prep.*

inacceptable, *a.* Delete *rare* and add later examples.

1908 *Westm. Gaz.* 22 Oct. 7/1 The Turkish Foreign Minister replied that the proposal was inacceptable. **1934** A. S. C. Ross in *Neuphilol. Mitt.* XXXV. 129 The perpetuation of a Victorian prudishness (inacceptable in philology beyond all other subjects). **1938** E. BEVAN *Symbolism & Belief* v. 108, I am in the company of others who find Professor Alexander's philosophy in this respect inacceptable. **1970** H. BRAUN *Parish Churches* xii. 160 Such dreariness being inacceptable to the parish churchman..Gothic forms began..to represent the appropriate Anglican architecture.

Hence **i:nacceptabi·lity**, the quality or condition of being inacceptable.

1922 *Glasgow Herald* 13 May 8 Whatever..France's attitude..might be, the inacceptability of the memorandum as a whole appears to render equally null in her eyes this detail. **1957** J. S. HUXLEY *Relig. without Revelation* (rev. ed.) iv. 75 The inacceptability, to my growing intellectual interest, of any Christian theology proffered to me.

inactivate (inæ·ktivēⁱt), *v.* [f. INACTIV(E *a.* + -ATE[3].] *trans.* To render inactive. So **ina·ctivated** *ppl. a.*

1906 *Jrnl. Physiol.* XXXIV. p. xxxvi, If only the decomposition of the substrate is considered, heat inactivates enzymes completely. *Ibid.*, The presence of inactivated enzyme has a marked influence on the reaction

between active enzyme and substrate. **1927** HALDANE & HUXLEY *Animal Biol.* ix. 189 When unaccustomed proteins enter their system, they [*sc.* higher animals] can.. destroy or inactivate them. **1949** *Jane's Fighting Ships 1949–50* 358 She has been 'inactivated', and is laid up in a state of preservation as a potential fighting ship. **1955** *Times* 11 June 6/4 It said that the vaccine is composed of three types of viruses, mixed together after they had been inactivated or killed, but in some cases live viruses were found in the final mixture after tests. **1962** *Lancet* 5 May 941/1 The pattern of serological response to inactivated poliovirus vaccines has been..well documented. **1971** J. PHILIPS *Escape a Killer* (1972) II. ii. 136 The moment we inactivate the fence, we sound an alarm.

Also **inactiva·tion**, the process of inactivating.

1906 DORLAND *Med. Dict.* (ed. 4) 353/2 *Inactivation*, the destruction of the activity of a serum by the action of heat or other means. **1936** *Brit. Jrnl. Psychol.* XXVI. 394 We shall employ the term 'impulse' in describing our experiments as implying the conscious activation and inactivation of the motor apparatus. **1946** *Nature* 27 July 121/1 The primary factor in heat damage seems to be an inactivation of the cell. **1968** *Economist* 6 July 16/3 Does the splendid nonsense word coined by the Americans, the 'inactivation' of Khe Sanh, signal another step in de-escalation?

inactivator (inæ·ktivēⁱtǫɹ). [f. prec. + -OR.] That which inactivates; also, an individual considered in respect of his or her speed of metabolizing and so inactivating a drug in the body.

1944 *Biol. Abstr.* XVIII. 2662/3 (Index), Inactivator of vit. B_1 in diets of foxes. **1946** *Nature* 10 Aug. 201/1 The inactivator or inactivators involved are susceptible to heat and do not pass through a Seitz filter. **1960** *Times* 11 Nov. 17/2 Individuals could be divided into two categories: rapid and slow inactivators of the drug. **1970** PASSMORE & ROBSON *Compan. Med. Stud.* II. ii. 14/1 Patients who are 'slow inactivators' of isoniazid are more likely to develop peripheral neuritis if given the usual dose.

inactive, *a.* Add: **2.** *Chem.* [tr. F. (*moléculairement*) *inactif* (J. B. Biot 1840, in *Ann. de Chim. et de Physique* LXXIV. 403).] Not rotating the plane of polarization of polarized light. Often qualified by *optically*.

Pasteur adopted the term from Biot (*Jrnl. de Pharm. et de Chim.* (1848) XIII. 449).

1853 L. PASTEUR in *Chem. Gaz.* 1 Sept. 323 The latter [body]..resists isomeric transformation, and remaining without alteration in the quinicine, gives this its feeble deviation to the right. The other group, which..is very active, becomes inactive when the quinine is heated so as to become converted into quinicine; so that quinicine is nothing but quinine in which one of the active constituent groups has become inactive. **1857** W. A. MILLER *Elem. Chem.* III. v. 334 It [*sc.* another modification of tartaric acid] has been termed by Pasteur, inactive tartaric acid, in allusion to its want of action upon polarized light. **1905** *Jrnl. Physiol.* XXXII. p. xxxix (*heading*) The formation of inactive arginine by enzymes from proteids which yield optically active arginine on hydrolysis with acids. **1961** L. F. & M. FIESER *Adv. Org. Chem.* iii. 83 Properties of the two active and two inactive forms of tartaric acid are given in Table 3.2. A noteworthy point is that the *dl*-form, racemic acid, melts at a higher temperature than the optically active components.

in actu: see *IN *Lat. prep.*

inadequate, *a.* Add: Also as *sb.*, an inadequate person; one whose personality is in some way insufficient to meet the expectations of society.

1962 *Guardian* 7 Nov. 8/4 How can prison help a social inadequate through his troubles? **1963** T. PARKER *Unknown Citizen* 166 The majority of them are in fact the inadequates of whom Charlie Smith is typical. **1966** *Listener* 18 Aug. 226/1 The people that we are accustomed to call inadequates or weak characters. **1971** *Guardian* 26 Mar. 14/1 So-called 'inadequates' are the victims of society which is inadequate.

in-a-door, *adv.* = INDOORS *adv.* (App. only in Blunden.)

1932 BLUNDEN *Face of England* 14 We keep in-a-door unless compelled forth. **1937** —— *Elegy* 28 Hasten here in-a-door. **1949** —— *After Bombing* 36 And dog and cat run in-a-door.

inadvisable, *a.* Delete *rare* and add later examples.

1953 *Times Lit. Suppl.* 25 Sept. 613/2 The idea..is that it would be inadvisable for Germany to annex parts of Austria. **1953** *Times* 3 Oct. 3/4 Coventry isolation hospital is now receiving only cases which it would be inadvisable to send..to the isolation hospital at..Birmingham.

inagglu·tinable, *a.* [f. IN-³ + *AGGLUTINABLE *a.*] Incapable of being agglutinated (*by*).

1919 *Lancet* 4 Oct. 607/2 This inagglutinable strain was isolated from a case a few weeks before..experiments commenced. **1934** *Jrnl. R. Anthrop. Inst.* LXIV. 34 Every individual whose corpuscles were inagglutinable by the A and B sera. **1951** WHITBY & HYNES *Med. Bacteriol.* (ed. 5) xii. 203 It [*sc.* the Vi antigen] is not affected when the organisms are killed with 75 per cent alcohol, although they may then become inagglutinable by a Vi antiserum.

Also **i:nagglutinabi·lity**, the property of being inagglutinable.

1925 C. H. BROWNING *Bacteriol.* viii. 169 Occasionally typhoid bacilli when they have been recently obtained from the living body are not susceptible to agglutination by antiserum, but such inagglutinability usually soon disappears. **1948** *Biol. Abstr.* XXII. 897 Inagglutinability of red cells occurs.

inajá (inădʒā·). [Tupi.] In full **inajá palm.** A palm tree, *Maximiliana martiana* (*regia*), native to the Amazon region.

1849 R. SPRUCE *Notes of Botanist on Amazon & Andes* (1908) I. i. 45 The pinnate fronds of the..Inajá (*Maximiliana regia*) reach sometimes 40 feet in length. **1853** A. R. WALLACE *Trav. Amazon* ii. 33 Here also grew the Inajá, a fine thick-stemmed species, with a very large dense head of foliage. **1860** MAYNE REID *Odd People* 82 These nuts [*sc.* palm-nuts] are the fruit of several kinds of palms, but the best are those afforded by two magnificent species,—the 'Inaja' (*Maximilliana* [sic] *regia*), and the 'Urucuri' (*Attalea excelsa*). **1866** LINDLEY & MOORE *Treas. Bot.* II. 726/1 *M*[*aximiliana*] *regia*, the Inajá Palm of the Amazon, has a trunk a hundred or more feet high. **1927** R. R. GATES *Botanist in Amazon Valley* viii. 174 The Inajá..is one of the common palms of the Amazon. It produces enormous masses of ovoid fruits the size of a lemon. **1966** E. J. H. CORNER *Nat. Hist. Palms* xii. 283 As a major feature of vegetation, they [*sc.* South American palms] call for botanical investigation in every respect. For example, the babaçu.., cohune.., piassava.., and inajá.

inaka, var. *INANGA.

inamorato. (Later examples.)

1941 E. R. EDDISON *Fish Dinner* (1968) xiii. 221 How would you like Shelley for your *inamorato*? **1973** 'M. INNES' *Appleby's Answer* iii. 29 You must invite him to luncheon here. And invite me as well. I'd love to meet the *inamorato*.

in and in, in-and-in, *adv.* and *sb.* Add: **A.** *adv.* **b.** Entirely in, sharing fully.

1926 J. BLACK *You can't Win* x. 131 We know you are 'right'...That's why you are declared 'in and in' with the works.

2. (See quot.)

1926 *Paper Terminol.* (Spalding & Hodge) 14 *In and in*, a method of packing reams too large conveniently to travel flat. The ream is divided in half, and the two portions clasped in and in to each other.

B. *sb.* **3.** *slang.* (See quot.)

1935 *Evening News* 29 June 3/2 The '*in-and-in*' is simply the point at which the swindler apparently risks his own money with that of the dupe.

in and out, in-and-out, *adv.* Add: **4.** *attrib.* (quasi-*adj.*). (Further examples.) Also, *in-and-out bolt* (earlier example); *in-and-out boy, man*, someone in and out of prison; a burglar; *in and out family*, formerly, a family constantly entering and leaving a workhouse; *in-and-out running* (earlier example); *in and out work*, work which is not continuous; also, irregular or unlawful practice.

1841 R. H. DANA *Seaman's Manual* 111 *In-and-out*, a term sometimes used for the scantline of the timbers, the moulding way, and particularly for those bolts that are driven into the hanging and lodging knees, through the sides, which are called *in-and-out bolts*. **1855** GEO. ELIOT in *Fraser's Mag.* June 699/2 Heavy-looking in-and-out corridors, such as one found only in German inns. **1885** *Referee* 26 Apr. 1/2 Now and again in-and-out running on the part of a horse subjects his owner to considerable annoyance. **1888** 'R. BOLDREWOOD' *Robbery under Arms* III. xviii. 277, I began to hear that there was a deal of in-and-out sort of work about my getting my freedom. **1903** *Westm. Gaz.* 29 Sept. 10/1 His engagements are only for particular plays—'in and out' work. **1904** *Daily Chron.* 14 June 9/1 One notable 'In and Out' family entered and discharged itself sixty-two times from a London workhouse in one year. **1906** E. DYSON *Fact'ry 'Ands* viii. 97 It was in 'n' out sorter work. **1910** E. M. FORSTER *Howards End* v. 38 Oh, heavens! I've knocked the In and Out card down. **1936** H. G. WELLS *Anat. Frustration* xv. 178 That does not close the Jewish problem for you. It merely brings you back to the fundamental age-long problem of this nation among the nations, this in-and-out mentality, the essential parasitism of the Jewish mycelium upon the social and cultural organisms in which it lives. **1937** C. PRIOR *So I wrote It* xvi. 191 Among the boys I knew, very few had either the courage or skill to tackle 'live gaffs' by night. Most of them were in-and-out boys. They did their eighteen months in Wandsworth or Pentonville, had a run of a month or so and went back to do a twenty-one or even a lagging. **1939** H. HODGE *Cab, Sir?* 221 An 'in and out job' is a passenger who comes back to his starting point. **1959** *Times* 31 Dec. 11/3 The discovery was announced in 1925 and met with a very in-and-out reception. **1960** *Encounter* Mar. 77/1 The *In-and-Out* Game is played...'Everyone' knows that Hemingway is not so *In* as Faulkner. **1961** PARTRIDGE *Dict. Slang* (ed. 5) II. 1143/2 *In-and-out man*, an opportunist thief. **1961** *Times* 14 Apr. 5/4 Two clubs who have had an in-and-out season meet at Old Deer Park. **1970** *Guardian* 12 Sept. 11/2 Israeli casualties were..high...The alternative ..would be a quick 'in and out' operation. **1972** *Times* 15 Dec. 14/3 'In and out' records through lapsing..are not uncommon.

B. *sb. The 'In' and 'Out'*, the name of the Naval and Military Club in London.

1925 FRASER & GIBBONS *Soldier & Sailor Words* 127 *The In and Out*, the Naval and Military Club, 94, Piccadilly. So called familiarly from the words 'In' and 'Out', painted on the pillars of the approach to the courtyard in front. **1967** *Guardian* 21 Feb. 3/6 Two London clubs, the 105-year-old Naval and Military, better known as the 'In and Out', and the 92-year-old Devonshire, may merge.

So **in-and-outer**, one who is only moderately skilled or is erratic in performance; one who holds office intermittently.

1905 *Outing* (U.S.) Feb. 572/2 Whippets run in more consistent form than horses, and there are few 'in-and-outers'. **1934** E. B. MARKS *They all Sang* 210 He was an in-and-outer..and this was one of his 'out' periods. **1952** *Assoc. Press* 8 Oct., Reynolds has 30 knockouts among his 52 victories but he has been an in-and-outer. **1960** *Farmer & Stockbreeder* 29 Mar. 53/3 There are a great many 'in-and-outers' who know mighty little of the art of breeding. **1967** *Economist* 5 Aug. 496/1 The British unfamiliarity with the American concept of 'ins and outers' —men who alternate between private careers and public service.

inanga (ī·naŋă). Also **inaka** (the South Island form). [Maori.] **1.** The New Zealand name for a small fish, *Galaxias attenuatus*, the young form of which is called whitebait.

1845 E. J. WAKEFIELD *Adventure N.Z.* II. 100 This fish is called *hinanga*, and resembles Blackwall whitebait in size and flavour. **1896** *Australasian* 28 Aug. 407/3 About the same size as this fish is the 'inaka' much used for bait. *a* **1939** 'R. HYDE' *Houses by Sea* (1952) 64 Brown women drying out inanga. **1944** *Mod. Jun. Dict.* (Whitcombe & Tombs) 209 *Inanga, Inaka*, the Maori name of the small fish called 'whitebait' in New Zealand; inanga in the north, inaka in the south. **1959** TINDALE & LINDSAY *Rangatira* x. 93 Every year shoals of the tiny, delicious inanga fish came up the creeks from the sea. **1962** *Post-Primary School Bull.* (N.Z.) XV. I. 26 Whitebait belongs to the species *Galaxias attenuatus*... The adult fish, called Inanga, reach a length of about four inches.

2. An evergreen shrub or small tree, *Dracophyllum longifolium*, belonging to the family Epacridaceæ and native to New Zealand.

1889 T. KIRK *Forest Flora N.Z.* 215 Mr. Charles Traill informs me that it [sc. *Dracophyllum longifolium*] is termed 'inaka' by the Maoris on Stewart Island. **1910** L. COCKAYNE *N.Z. Plants* 76 In similar situations [*sc.* along the coastline] the inuka (*Dracophyllum longifolium*) and the smaller New Zealand flax (*Phormium Cookianum*) are common. **1929** W. MARTIN *N.Z. Nature Bk.* viii. 126 The Inanga ranges in size from a small shrub..to a tree 15 to 30 ft. high. **1961** H. H. ALLAN *Flora N.Z.* I. 532 *D. longifolium*... Inanga... The Forsterian specimens I have seen are scrappy. **1968** *N.Z. Listener* 15 Mar. 6/5 Lying in its sheltered cove..complete with its own rata tree, inaka bushes, and great cushy heaps of golden-green moss.

ina·ngulated, *ppl. a. Ent.* [f. IN-² + ANGULATED *ppl. a.*] Angled inwardly.

1898 *Proc. Zool. Soc.* 441 The inner stripe more or less strongly inangulated below median vein, the outer stripe zigzag.

in antis: see *IN *Lat. prep.*

inapparent, *a.* Delete † *Obs.* and add later examples.

1898 J. CAIRD *Univ. Sermons* 371 These are the invisible realities, inapparent, impenetrable to sense. **1960** *New Scientist* 16 June 1521/3 This vaccine is then fed to the individual and produces an inapparent or mild infection which leads to immunity. **1970** *Ibid.* 15 Jan. 101/1 One of the most difficult variables in biological research—namely, inapparent infections, which can cause differing and misleading responses to experimental treatments.

inappositeness (inæ·pǫzitnės). [f. INAPPOSITE *a.* + -NESS.] The character or quality of being inapposite.

1893 E. SALTUS *Madam Sapphira* iii. 50 With an inappositeness which afterward was to occur to Nevius as curious. **1894** W. J. LOCKE *At Gate of Samaria* (1895) xii. 134 The words estranged them still further. They were pathetic in their ludicrous inappositeness.

inarticulacy (inaɹti·kiŭlăsi). [f. INARTICULA(TE *a.* + -CY.] Inarticulateness.

1921 *Observer* 11 Sept. 10/2 That it has not done so..we must ascribe..to the inarticulacy of the scientist himself. **1927** M. SADLEIR *Trollope: a Comm.* 41 He has virtually entreated her forgiveness for his inarticulacy. **1951** A. BARON *Rosie Hogarth* 81 Perhaps it was this, more than his inarticulacy,..that had held him back. **1970** *Listener* 30 July 157/2 Prone to miscarriages, inarticulacy, and general indecision. **1971** *Daily Tel.* 9 Oct. 9/6 'Y'know' and 'I mean' and other apologies for inarticulacy.

inaugural. B. *sb.* Add: (Earlier U.S. example.) Also, an inaugural lecture at a university.

1832 *Reg. Deb. Congress U.S.* 5 May 2778, I turn now to the other points in the inaugural. **1958** *Listener* 18 Sept. 429/3 That well-known story about Seeley's inaugural. **1965** J. A. W. BENNETT in J. Gibb *Light on C. S. Lewis* 44 The mere quotability of his Cambridge Inaugural may lead us to forget his positive achievement. **1967** *Listener* 26 Jan. 139/2 Enright's famous inaugural at the University of Singapore.

inauguration. Add: **4.** (Later U.S. examples of *Inauguration Day*.)

1893 K. D. WIGGIN *Polly Oliver's Problem* (1894) xvii. 185 As it chances to be a presidential year, we will celebrate Inauguration Day. **1948** *Denison* (Texas) *Herald* 1 July 4/3 That was when Inauguration Day was changed from March 4 to January 20, for Roosevelt's second term.

inauthentic, *a.* Delete *rare* and add later example. **inauthenticity** (later examples).

1964 S. BELLOW *Herzog* (1965) 81 The cant and rant of pipsqueaks about Inauthenticity and Forlornness. **1970** G. GREER *Female Eunuch* 152 The altruism of women is merely the inauthenticity of the feminine person carried over into behaviour. **1972** *Times Lit. Suppl.* 24 Mar. 342/2 This does not prevent the two schools of Zen from attacking each other as being inauthentic.

Hence **inauthe·ntically** *adv.*

1965 *Philos. Rev.* LXXIV. 215 The philosophers he is attacking..have written inauthentically.

i·n-basket. [Cf. IN *adv.* 12 a.] In an office, etc.: a basket or tray for incoming correspondence and other documents. Cf. *IN-TRAY.

Sometimes written as two separate words with *in* regarded adjectivally.

1940 *Amer. Speech* XV. 247 His *incoming* mail is put in an *in-basket.* **1948** 'N. SHUTE' *No Highway* v. 130, I sighed and pulled my IN basket towards me, full of the arrears of work. **1957** J. BRAINE *Room at Top* xxviii. 217 My in-basket was full. **1970** *New Yorker* 26 Sept. 40/3 She sat down beside him with pencil and paper and let him churn up the contents of his 'in' and 'out' baskets.

inbe (inbī·), *v. poet. nonce-wd.* [f. IN- *pref.*[1] + BE *v.* A. 1 ¶ (centre column p. 716). Cf. L. *inesse*.] To be within.

1921 HARDY *Late Lyrics* (1922) 70 Where such inbe, A dwelling's character Takes theirs.

in-between. Add: Hence **in-betwee·ner, inbetwee·ner**, a person who takes up an intermediate position (chiefly *fig.*).

1924 *Contemp. Rev.* Apr. 459 The undeserving and the in-betweeners far outnumber the deserving. **1927** C. SHAW *Let.* 17 May in Knightley & Simpson *Secret Lives Lawrence of Arabia* (1969) xvii. 256 In Ireland...We had The Gentry and The People: nothing else. You will say 'but the in-betweeners?' They belonged to the people. **1939** C. E. SMITH in Ramsey & Smith *Jazzmen* 247 The inbetweeners are still there but the musician has become an individual. **1942** O. NASH *Good Intentions* (1943) 162 He was a born in-betweener... He always thought that there was much to be said on both sides. **1970** *S.A. Panorama* Feb. 25/1 He joined the London Polytechnic Studios. He started as an 'in-betweener'—the name given to the most junior apprentice.

inbind (inbəi·nd), *v.* [f. IN-[1] + BIND *v.*] To bind within (usu. in *pass.* and *fig.*); to bind within a book or manuscript (cf. *INBOUND *a.*[2]).

1888 RUSKIN *Praeterita* (1889) III. i. 32 The most stern practical precept of that doctrine still holding me,—it is curiously inbound with all the rest,—was the Sabbath keeping. **1913** D. H. LAWRENCE *Sons & Lovers* x. 316 He had never been very closely inbound into the family. **1932** *Ampleforth Jrnl.* Spring 133 A transcription of the fragment inbound in the Sarum Missal in the monastery library.

inboard, *adv.*, *prep.*, and *adj.* Add: **A.** *adv.* (Earlier and later examples.)

1830 J. F. COOPER *Water Witch* III. vii. 216 Assured of the position of his enemy, he returned in-board. **1851** H. MELVILLE *Moby Dick* III. xlix. 306 Two of them clutched the gunwale..and..hurled themselves bodily inboard. **1912** BELLOC *This & That* xxxviii. 284 We picked up the little buoy..and we got it in-board. **1958** *Engineering* 28 Mar. 393/1 Movable projectors are housed in the two cylindrical frameworks of the dumb-bell assembly inboard of the star globes. **1962** S. CARPENTER in *Into Orbit* 161 You make sure the abort handle is *inboard and locked*. **1963** *Times* 12 Feb. 15/6 Inboard-mounted disc brakes. **1967** *Autocar* 5 Oct. 7/2 The Triumph 2000 port face is 'inboard' of the holding-down studs. **1971** *Times* 16 Feb. 8/6 The unsprung weight has been reduced by mounting the front and rear suspension units inboard.

C. *adj.* (Earlier and later examples.) Also, applied to parts of vehicles, aircraft, etc.

1847 WEBSTER, Inboard cargo. **1886** *Forest & Stream* 13 May 316/3 The Hampton flattie is best described as a beamy sharpie with an 'inboard jib'. **1893** *Funk's Stand. Dict.*, Inboard stroke of the piston. **1909** *Cent. Dict. Suppl.*, In *mech.*, toward the inside; toward the main center or center-line: as, an inboard stroke of the piston; an inboard bearing. *Ibid.* s.v. *Profile*. *Inboard profile*, in ship-building, a plan which shows the internal arrangements of a vessel by a longitudinal vertical section at the centerline. **1921** *Rudder* July 5 Even in large sailing boats the use of an inboard engine is sometimes not advisable. **1936** *Discovery* Dec. 380/1 We were five boats in all, some inboard launches, others with outboard motors, which passed the inspection of the river police. **1945** *Times* 30 June 4/5 A new type of drive couples the engines to contra-rotating airscrews, 16 ft. in diameter. Those driving the inboard engines can be reversed on landing to act as brakes. **1948** 'N. SHUTE' *No Highway* iii. 66 Stop the inboard engines [of the aircraft] and turn back. **1951** *Yachting Monthly* Oct. 202 Her modest inboard-cutter sail plan is easily handled by two. **1956** LOOMIS *Hotspur Story* 183 With her new inboard rig *Hotspur* is now a single-headsail cutter. **1957** M. SWAN *Brit. Guiana* 202 In the old days when the mining men, the pork-knockers, went up the river they would paddle against currents which an inboard engine can now only just fight. **1959** E. K. WENLOCK *Kitchin's Road Transport Law* (ed. 12) 19/2 Inboard brakes, that is to say brakes acting on the axle shafts. **1971** *Power Farming* Mar. 57/3 A unique feature is the individual shaft bottom drive to each cutting disc, relieving the strain on the inboard drive components compared with other designs where the cutters are powered in train. **1972** *National Observer* (U.S.) 27 May 9/3 The inboard portions of the belts are short to prevent the lap belt from slipping over the hip bone onto the stomach, where the belt might cause serious injury in an accident.

inborn, *ppl. a.* Add: **2.** *inborn error of metabolism*: any disorder or abnormality that is due to a hereditary fault in the metabolic processes of the body, generally attributable to the lack or alteration of some enzyme.

1908 A. E. GARROD in *Lancet* 4 July 3/1 Quite unlike that of the above metabolic diseases is the course of the anomalies of which I propose to treat in these lectures and which may be classed together as inborn errors of metabolism. **1909** —— (*title*) Inborn errors of metabolism. **1935** HARROW & SHERWIN *Textbk. Biochem.* xxviii. 716 The disease [*sc.* cystinuria], frequently referred to as an 'inborn error of metabolism' is rare. **1968** PASSMORE & ROBSON *Compan. Med. Stud.* I. xi. 24/2 Hereditary lack of the necessary enzyme, phenylalanine hydroxylase, leads to an inborn error of metabolism, phenylketonuria, in which phenylalanine..is transaminated extensively to phenylpyruvic acid... Presence of phenylpyruvic acid in the blood and central nervous system leads to mental retardation.

inbound, *a.*[1] (Further examples.)

1967 *Jane's Surface Skimmer Systems 1967–68* 63/1 Inbound freight is sorted on arrival at terminal. **1971** D. POTTER *Brit. Eliz. Stamps* xiii. 144 Clever collectors with new issues of stamps purchased at the all-night post office in London, would rush to stations within 50 miles or so of London to post their covers on inbound services. **1973** D. WESTHEIMER *Going Public* ix. 127 Drivers on the inbound lanes slowed to a crawl.

i·nbound, *a.*[2] [f. *INBIND *v.*; cf. BOUND *ppl. a.*[2]] Of a leaf, gathering, etc., in a manuscript or book: bound within.

1953 D. C. C. YOUNG in *Scriptorium* VIII. 15 There is an inbound quaternion of blanks.

inbreath (i·nbreþ). [f. IN *adv.* + BREATH.] A drawing in of the breath.

1921 R. GRAVES *Pier-Glass* 26 The deep in-breath, The breath roaring out. **1936** J. G. BRANDON *Dragnet* iv. 37 It was accompanied by a hissing inbreath from Ferradi. **1956** J. LOTZ in L. T. White *Frontiers of Knowledge in Study of Man* xiv. 212 In Swedish..the word *ja*, 'yes', is very often spoken on the in-breath.

in-build (inbi·ld), *v.* Also **inbuild.** [f. IN-[1] + BUILD *v.*] *trans.* To build in (see BUILD *v.* 2 b in Dict. and Suppl.). Chiefly as **i·n-bui:lt** *ppl. a.* = *built-in* (*BUILT *ppl. a.* 1 b).

1920 C. C. MARTINDALE in C. Hess *God & Supernatural* x. 342 Christ speaks of His faithful as pillars in-builded into that Temple which is Himself. **1923** *Daily Mail* 12 June 5 (Advt.), The difference between good and bad waterproofs being inbuilt, therefore invisible. **1961** *Times* 27 Mar. 5/3 The triphenyl tin compounds possess an inbuilt safety factor. **1961** *John o' London's* 7 Dec. 636/3 An in-built sense of humour. **1961** B. R. WILSON *Sects & Society* 7 The sect often in-builds a hard core of suspicion. **1965** *Catholic Herald* 5 Mar. 5/4 Any nation has an inbuilt resistance to immigrants. **1969** *Jane's Freight Containers 1968–69* 582/1 Basically it is a bi-directional roller beam with an inbuilt hydraulic jacking arrangement. **1971** *Daily Tel.* 15 Mar. 17/5 They are ten times brighter than the present traffic lights but contain an in-built device to ensure that no dazzle occurs.

in-by(e, *adv.* Add: **b.** *attrib.* (Examples.) Also used *absol.* or as *sb.*

1824 J. HOGG *Private Mem. Justified Sinner* 227 Gie up your crooning, or I'll pit you to an in-by place. **1894** J. CUNNINGHAM *Broomieburn* vi. 88 The inbye hand, Jock, would emerge from his bed in the stable-loft. **1918** *Border Standard* 18 May 2 Louping-ill or trembling is proving very destructive amongst in-by or park lambs. **1940** *Geogr. Jrnl.* XCVI. 108 Parallel galleries also served as inbye and outbye roads. **1958** *Rep. R. Comm. Common Land 1955–58* (Cmnd. 462) 274 *In-by land.* The term is widely used in the North of England and derives from the Scandinavian word (*by*) for a farm. Hence it means the fenced-in land nearest the homestead. **1960** *Farmer & Stockbreeder* 26 Jan. 56/1 Glanilyn Farm,..which has some 140 acres of in-bye... It was wasteful to use in-bye land. **1961** *Guardian* 18 Dec. 6/4 A large part of the 84 acres will be able to support pasture and contribute to the in-bye in the valley. **1971** *Country Life* 20 May 1259/1 Ewes and lambs on in-bye land at Lartington in Yorkshire.

Inc. U.S. abbreviation of INCORPORATED *ppl. a.*

1906 *Country Life in Amer.* May 16/1 (Advt.), The Engleside Company, Inc., Owners. **1928** *Publishers' Weekly* 16 June 2451/1 The retail business will be known as 'Dutton's, Inc.' **1936** MENCKEN *Amer. Lang.* (ed. 4) 244 An Englishman writes *Ltd.* after the name of a limited liability (what we would call *incorporated*) bank or trading company, as we write *Inc.* **1973** R. T. ELSON (*title*) The world of Time Inc.: the intimate history of a publishing enterprise.

Incaic (iŋkē·ik), *a.* = INCAN *a.* Also **Incaean** (iŋkă,ī·ăn), **Incarian** (iŋkēə·riăn) *adjs.*

1880 G. W. CABLE *Grandissimes* iv. 23 Possibly between the two sides of the occipital profile there may have been an Incaean tendency to inequality. **1909** *Cent. Dict. Suppl.*, Incaic, Incarian. **1926** *Glasgow Herald* 30 Jan. 8 The ruins of an ancient Incaic village. **1937** *Jrnl. R. Anthrop. Inst.* 321 The resemblance to possibly pre-Incaic pottery from the vicinity. **1963** *Times* 9 Feb. 9/7 An intact group of thousands of Incaic and pre-Incaic tombs, some dating from about 1200 B.C., was found only a few weeks ago.

incandescent, *a.* Add: Also *sb.* An incandescent lamp or burner.

1908 S. FORD *Side-Stepping with Shorty* 38 It was dark, and about half a million incandescents had been turned on. **1925** C. R. COOPER *Lions 'n' Tigers* v. 143 The great, empty building, where only a few incandescents gleamed dully. **1971** *General Electric Investor* II. II. 5 Lucalox is giving Washington double the light output of its former mercury lighting and six times the levels of its original incandescents.

incant, *v.* Restrict † *Obs.* to senses a and b in Dict. and add: **c.** *trans.* To raise by incantation. **d.** To chant, intone.

1926 *Chambers's Jrnl.* June 359/1 A little sorceress, talking to some spirit which she had incanted. **1959** *Times* 23 Sept. 3/7 The umpire incanting the score. **1961** M. SPARK *Prime of Miss Jean Brodie* ii. 22 They sat in the twilight eating toffees and incanting witches' spells.

incapacitant (inkăpæ·sitănt). [f. INCAPACIT(ATE *v.* + -ANT[1].] A substance that can be used to incapacitate a person for a time without wounding or killing him.

1961 *Today's Health* Mar. 76 If the Chemical Corps succeeds in standardizing effective incapacitants, it will represent a significant advance. **1963** *Listener* 7 Feb. 238/2 The nature of the military 'incapacitants'..includes such 'psychic poisons' as lysergic acid diethylamide, LSD-25, which produces extreme mental confusion. **1968** *New Scientist* 29 Feb. 465/1 BZ, one of the standard US incapacitants produces dizziness, heart palpitation, urinary retention and constipation. **1970** *Daily Tel.* (Colour Suppl.) 20 Feb. 19 Incapacitants are also intended for 'humane' use; their idea is to render an enemy temporarily helpless and to put him out of action for short periods.

Incaparina (inkăpărī·nă). [f. the initials of *I*nstitute of *N*utrition of *C*entral *A*merica and *P*anama + Amer. Sp. *f)ariña* powdered manioc f. L. *farina* flour, meal.] A preparation of vegetable protein, used as a dietary supplement.

1960 N. S. SCRIMSHAW in *Proc. Conf. Cottonseed Protein for Animals & Man* 18/1 The name Incaparina has now been adopted as a generic name to refer to any vegetable mixture developed by INCAP suitable for feeding to young children and containing at least 25% protein of a quality comparable to that of milk and other products of animal origin. **1964** *Listener* 28 May 866/2 'Incaparina', a mixture of cottonseed meal, maize, and several other ingredients, has been used widely in Guatemala. **1965** S. M. CANTOR in J. M. Leitch *Food Sci. & Technol.* III. 460 One of the most successful protein mixtures, Incaparina, a food product of plant origin, was developed by the Institute of Nutrition of Central America and Panama... Incaparina is an uncooked, dry powder which may be heated, flavoured, and consumed alone as a liquid, or it may be added to other foods. **1970** M. PYKE *Food Sci. & Technol.* (ed. 3) xi. 212 The nutritional value of this preparation, which is marketed under the name of 'Incaparina', is sufficiently high to allow its being fed to young children as a substitute for milk.

incapsulate, *v.* Add: Also *fig.* (see *ENCAPSULATE *v.*).

1939 R. G. COLLINGWOOD *Autobiogr.* x. 113 But this secondary life is prevented from overflowing into my primary life by being what I call incapsulated, that is, existing in a context of primary or surface knowledge which keeps it in its place and prevents it from thus overflowing. *Ibid.* 114 Historical knowledge is the re-enactment of a past thought incapsulated in a context of present thoughts. **1954** D. RIESMAN in *Amer. Jrnl. Sociol.* Jan. 382/2 Institutions incapsulate them or awaken them or destroy them. **1955** M. BELOFF *Foreign Policy & Democratic Process* 50 It may simply be that the older nations of Europe have retained, incapsulated within them, sufficient relics of their predemocratic leadership to provide the necessary ballast for the democratic sails. **1962** W. NOWOTTNY *Lang. Poets Use* vii. 146 To offer such a definition is to attempt to incapsulate a number of critical trends. **1972** *Country Life* 6 Jan. 56/3 For his ministers the problem was often to incapsulate him [*sc.* William IV] or walk round him.

incapsulation. (Later *fig.* examples.)

1934 PRIEBSCH & COLLINSON *German Lang.* viii. 344 Though German has recently turned away from such *Einschachtelung* or 'incapsulation', it still retains as a regular feature the relegation of the finite verb to the end-position of the subordinate clause. **1959** *Times Lit. Suppl.* 27 Feb. 110/3 This comes perilously near to incapsulation.

in-car *attrib.*: see *IN *prep.* 17*.

in-career *attrib.*: see *IN *prep.* 17*.

incarn, *v.* **2.** (Later examples.)

1904 HARDY *Dynasts* I. I. iii. 17 Did I incarn in moulds of all mankind. **1907** *Westm. Gaz.* 7 Feb. 8/2 Incarned as 'Superman' by G. B. S.

incarnational (inkaɹnēi·ʃənăl), *a.* [f. INCARNATION + -AL.] Of or relating to the theological doctrine of incarnation.

1912 F. VON HÜGEL *Eternal Life* viii. 166 Even the most general incarnational doctrine..must, then, be Superstition or Fanaticism for him. **1942** D. JENKINS *Nature of Catholicity* i. 12 This..widely influential tendency, with its affinities with historical Romanticism and the so-called 'Incarnational' theology, is a development of the Anglican doctrine of catholicity in the direction of Liberalism. **1954** D. L. SAYERS *Introd. Papers on Dante* 122 This Way, though it is perhaps more typically Western and might appear to be more typically Catholic and Incarnational than the other, has, I believe, never been fully mapped by any mystical theologian—unless we count Dante. **1971** *Daily Tel.* 29 July 6/3 His Christian faith is essentially this-worldly, 'incarnational', to use one of his favourite words.

incarnationist. Add: Also *attrib.* or as *adj.* So also **incarna·tionalist.**

1903 *Q. Rev.* Apr. 519 Wherever the Incarnationist idea originated, it did not originate in Hellenism. **1939** A. TOYNBEE *Study of Hist.* IV. 625 The Christology which Dr. Conybeare calls 'Incarnationist' ought properly to be called 'Conceptionist'. **1962** *Listener* 11 Jan. 68/2 This 'incarnationalist' type of doctrine—to be culled from almost every page of so very orthodox a teacher as our own Henry Scott Holland, for example—urges that the divine for us must mean the vision of a new humanity.

incendiary, *a.* and *sb.* Add: **A.** *adj.* **1. b.** (Further examples.) Used esp. of a type of aerial bomb that ignites on impact.

1885 E. S. FARROW *Mil. Encycl.* I. 666/1 (*heading*) Incendiary fire-works.—The incendiary preparations are ..incendiary-match, and hot-shot. *Ibid.* 666/2 Incendiary-match is made by boiling slow-match in a saturated solution of niter, drying it, cutting it into pieces, and plunging it into melted fire-stone. It is principally used in loaded shells. **1911** *Aero* May 37/1 The following are reckoned..to be the principal offensive uses of the war-aeroplane: (1.) Attacking supply stores and setting them on fire with incendiary bombs. **1915** *Lancet* 12 June 1249/2 The incendiary bomb may cause a serious outbreak of fire. **1917** H. WOODHOUSE *Textbk. Naval Aeronaut.* (1918) xix. 120/2 The Zeppelins also dropped incendiary bombs intended to set places on fire. **1918** E. S. FARROW *Dict. Mil. Terms* 307 *Incendiary grenade*, a form of grenade designed to scatter molten metal upon bursting. **1935** *Jrnl. R. Aeronaut. Soc.* XXXIX. 164 Reference is made to incendiary bombs with magnesium alloy case and thermit filling. **1940** *Illustr. London News* 5 Oct. 435/2 The oil bomb, which may be of various sizes, is filled in some cases with petrol, thus becoming a tremendously powerful incendiary bomb. **1941** *Ann. Reg. 1940* 69 Though large numbers of incendiary bombs were dropped the damage done by fire was kept within fairly narrow limits.

B. *sb.* **1. c.** Short for *incendiary bomb.*

1940 *Flight* 19 Dec. 522/2 The pilot found his objective at once and his incendiaries started four large fires. **1942** *R.A.F. Jrnl.* 13 June 24 You may have tried to put out an incendiary bomb by heaping..sand on it...No amount of sand will smother an incendiary. **1958** *Times Lit. Suppl.* 28 Mar. 176/1 In 1941 Lambeth Palace Library was heavily bombed. Incendiaries fell in the middle of the seventeenth-century Great Hall which was its centre.

incendiate, *v.* Add: So **ince·ndiated** *ppl. a.*, set on fire. *rare*$^{-1}$.

1922 JOYCE *Ulysses* 702 The carbonised remains of an incendiated edifice.

incendijel (inse·ndidʒel). orig. *U.S.* Also (*corruptly*) **incenderjel, incinderjell.** [f. INCENDI(ARY *a.* + JEL(LY *sb.*] An inflammable jelly used in incendiary weapons, composed of polystyrene, petrol, and benzene.

1966 *Air Force/Space Digest* (U.S.) Mar. 45/2 Nearly 700 day and night sorties were flown by B-57, A-1E, F-100, and F-8 aircraft, which dropped more than 450,000 pounds of incendijel. **1966** *New Statesman* 8 Apr. 496/1 The new jelly—or what US pilots refer to as 'incendijel'—is replacing the old soap-jelled gasoline napalm as used in Korea. **1967** (*title*) Modification kit for the MXY 377/E 32 incendijel mixing and transfer unit (U.S. Air Force Armament Lab.) (AD 830 504). **1967** *N.Y. Rev. Bks.* 20 Apr. 5/1 The Americans do not dissemble what they are up to. They do not seem to feel the need, except through verbiage: e.g., napalm has become 'Incinder-jell'. **1968** *Listener* 22 Feb. 244/2 The issues and living horror of the war disappear in a deadened, bureaucratic language—'incinderjell', 'the other side', 'body counts'. **1968** V. W. SIDEL in S. Rose *Chem. & Biol. Warfare* iii. 44 The name napalm has been retained as a generic one for weapons of this type. Recently the term has also been applied to a gel consisting of petrol, benzene, and polystyrene which is also called 'incenderjell' or Napalm-B.

incendivity (insendi·vĭti). [f. the stem of L. *incend-ere* (see INCEND *v.*) + -IVITY.] The ability to effect ignition or set on fire.

1919 *Jrnl. Chem. Soc.* CXV. 103 These results clearly establish the fact that the incendivity of a spark does not depend on the total energy of the spark. **1972** *Physics Bull.* Aug. 454/3 Later laboratory measurements..of the incendivity of spark discharges showed that if the uniform field strength in a tank roof space away from any protrusions was 500 kV m^{-1}, then brush discharges having sufficient energy to ignite an inflammable hydrocarbon-air mixture could occur at metal protrusions.

Hence (as a back-formation) **ince·ndive** *a.*, of or pertaining to incendivity; capable of effecting ignition.

1959 *Rep. Investigations U.S. Bureau of Mines* No. 5463. 19 Chemical composition alone is not sufficient to define the incendive character of an explosive. **1972** *Physics Bull.* Aug. 456/1 Differences between the incendive properties of metal to metal sparks and liquid to metal sparks. **1973** *Ibid.* Mar. 145/3 It draws attention to the risks of incendive sparks at or near deck openings resulting from static electricity.

incentive, *a.* and *sb.* Add: **A.** *adj.* **3.** Of or pertaining to a system of payments, concessions, etc., to encourage harder work or a particular choice of work.

1943 *Reader's Digest* Aug. 11/1 Mr. Charles E. Wilson.. is urging war industries to adopt 'incentive pay'—that is, to pay workers more if they *produce* more. **1948** *Ann. Reg. 1947* 283 In an effort to increase foreign trading various incentives were offered to exporters..a proportion of the foreign exchange..for the purchase of raw materials,..and 'incentive' goods for their workers. **1951** *Engineering* 2 Mar. 245/2 The body of the book is concerned with a description of the ['Armstrong Merit Sharing'] scheme...A series of 'requirements' is laid down to which it is considered that any incentive scheme should conform. **1952** 'VIGILANS' *Chamber of Horrors* 72 *Incentive bonus*, a bonus *in advance* as an encouragement, for workers, to work. **1957** *Encycl. Brit.* XXIII. 272/1 For a substantial number of wage earners compensation is defined in terms not of time units but of output, under various types of incentive systems. *Ibid.* 272/2 The essential characteristic of an incentive wage rate structure is that payment depends on output rather than work time. **1967** G. F. FIENNES *I tried to run Railway* iv. 31 Work Study became synonymous with incentive payments. **1970** T. LUPTON *Managem. & Social Sci.* (ed. 2) ii. 53 These controls were turned mainly to the manipulation of the incentive payment system.

B. *sb.* **2.** An incentive payment, scheme, etc.

1948 [see adj. sense 3 above]. **1956** HICKMAN & KUHN *Individuals, Groups & Econ. Behavior* ii. 50 Debate about this central question has hinged in large part on the issue of incentives. *Ibid.* 60 Gordon enumerates several nonfinancial incentives of some apparent importance, including power, prestige, and security. **1960** H. C. WALLICH *Cost of Freedom* iii. 81 This leaves us with incentives in the narrower sense as the third element in the triad of forces upon which we rely to call forth initiative and effort. *Ibid.* 89 Labor and management performance is not the only place where we must look for the effects of incentives.

incentre, in-centre (i·nsentəɹ). *Geom.* Also (*U.S.*) **-center.** [f. *IN-^{1} b + CENTRE, CENTER *sb.*] The centre of an inscribed circle.

1903 E. H. ASKWITH *Course Pure Geom.* i. 12 The pedal triangle has for its incentre the orthocentre of the original triangle. **1904** HALL & STEVENS *School Geom.* III. 204 Given the base and vertical angle of a triangle, find the locus of the in-centre. **1963** R. A. ROSENBAUM *Introd. Projective Geom. & Mod. Algebra* i. 3 Prove that the bisectors of the angles of a triangle are concurrent. (The point of concurrency is the center of the inscribed circle, abbreviated 'incenter'.)

incest. 3. *attrib.* and *Comb.* (Further examples.)

1819 SHELLEY *Let.* 16 Nov. (1964) II. 531 The incest scene of Amon & Tamar is tremendous. **1921** D. H. LAWRENCE *Psychoanal. & Unconscious* i. 20 At the root of almost every neurosis lies some incest-craving. *Ibid.* ii. 31 And this brings us finally to incest, even incest-worship. **1933** LD. RAGLAN *Jocasta's Crime* i. 6 Having eliminated reason, instinct, and religion as bases of the incest taboo, what have we left? The answer is magic. *Ibid.* ii. 15 There are no stronger upholders of the incest taboo than those very Australian tribes who believe that the child has no physical connexion with the father. **1946** KOESTLER *Thieves in Night* 162 The intimacy of life in the smaller Communes acts as a gradually materialising incest-barrier. **1949** —— *Insight & Outlook* xxiii. 323 Examples of such archetypes or primordial experiences are..the incest-motif. **1949** M. MEAD *Male & Female* ix. 199 Usually the primary incest-taboos are extended in various ways. **1963** A. HERON *Towards Quaker View of Sex* 56 Incest thoughts appear in human dreams. *Ibid.* 59 The sexual nature of this relationship is reinforced and with it feelings of incest-guilt, especially in the child. This situation may cause the boy or girl later to shirk contact with the opposite sex for fear of violating the incest barrier.

incestuous, *a.* Add: **2. c.** *Fig.* use of sense 2 a.

1869 D. G. ROSSETTI *Let.* 27 Aug. (1965) II. 727 'Solemn poetry' belongs to the class of phrases absolutely forbidden I think *in* poetry. It is intellectually incestuous,—poetry seeking to beget its emotional offspring on its own identity. **1971** *Listener* 2 Sept. 307/3 Systematising.. the old-boy network..would almost undoubtedly exacerbate the incestuous intolerance of the present scene.

inch, *sb.*^{1} Add: **2. a.** Esp. in phr. *within an inch of one's life* (or † *skin*): almost to the point of death; so as to be nearly killed; freq. hyperbolically and *fig.*

1726, 1839 [in Dict.]. **1854** B. P. SHILLABER *Life & Sayings Mrs. Partington* 81 I'll be tempered to whip you within an inch of your skin. **1896** W. D. HOWELLS *Impressions & Experiences* 74 The defendant..had invited her to come down the street to a certain point, and be beaten within an inch of her life. **1909** L. M. MONTGOMERY *Anne of Avonlea* xii. 126 The grammar class were parsed and analysed within an inch of their lives. **1932** 'E. M. DELAFIELD' *Thank Heaven Fasting* III. i. 250 She's always bullied Cecily within an inch of her life. **1939** L. M. MONTGOMERY *Anne of Ingleside* i. 12 He said that..everybody else would be dressed within an inch of her life. *Ibid.* iv. 30 If I had talked to my parents like that..I would have been whipped within an inch of my life.

3. e. *to give him* (or *them*, etc.) *an inch..*: example of extended use.

1973 *Times* 21 Feb. 3/1 If you turn your back for an instant or give them an inch they will park their cars on it.

4. a. *inch-wide* (earlier and later examples).

1873 *Young Englishwoman* Apr. 194/2 Inch-wide lace. **1950** W. DE LA MARE *Inward Compan.* 89 From inch-wide eyes I scan their..flames. **1964** C. DENT *Quantity Surveying by Computer* iii. 31 The new 1-inch-wide eight-channel paper tape now in use on some computers.

d. inch-rule (earlier example); **inch-taped** *a.* (nonce-wd.), covered with inch-tape; **inch-worm** (examples); also *fig.*

1850 DICKENS *Dav. Copp.* lx. 595 Neither will you find him measuring all human interests..with his one poor little inch-rule now. **1939** DYLAN THOMAS *Map of Love* 6 'His mother's womb had a tongue that lapped up mud,' Cried the topless, inchtaped lips. *a* **1861** T. WINTHROP *Life in Open Air* (1863) 123 All the green inch-worms vanish on the tenth of every June. **1881** *Harper's Mag.* Oct. 656/1 A wriggling inch-worm,..awaiting..an opportunity to measure the length of your nose. **1949** *Sat. Even. Post* 12 Mar. 33/1 One evening the Main Line local hunched its cars together like an inchworm and skidded to a halt. **1954** BORROR & DELONG *Introd. Study Insects* xxvi. 522 The larvae of geometers are the familiar caterpillars commonly called inchworms or measuring-worms. **1959** G. MATTINGLY *Defeat of Spanish Armada* xx. 218 There was only one offset to the exasperation of this inchworm progress. **1970** R. LOWELL *Notebk.* 235 Have you ever seen an inchworm crawl on a leaf,..Feeling for something to reach something?

inchastity. (Isolated later example.)

1972 *Times Lit. Suppl.* 25 Aug. 1000/4 It is difficult..to imagine how sanctions against inchastity could be re-imposed.

Inche (i·ntʃə'). Also **Enche, Enc(h)ik, Inchi.** [Mal. *enche', enchek, enchik* master, mistress.] In Malaysia, a prefixed title signifying respect, used for persons with no other special distinction; equivalent to 'Mr.'

The current official spelling (since 1972) is *Encik.*

1834 P. J. BEGBIE *Malayan Peninsula* ii. 83 It now only remains to mention the fate of Inchi Oowan Saban. **1897** *Jrnl. Straits Branch R. Asiatic Soc.* July 85 The following account of the method of rice cultivation..was written..by Inche Muhammad Ja'far. **1913** RANEE OF SARAWAK *My Life in Sarawak* xviii. 160 Inchi Sawal was a great stickler for grammar. **1937** *Jrnl. Malayan Branch R. Asiatic Soc.* XV. i. 63 Inche Abdul Raffar, Collector and Deputy Registrar, Ulu Selangor. **1951** *Proc. Legis. Council Fedn. Malaya* B159 Enche Abdullah: Sir, I beg to second the motion. **1972** *Straits Times* 4 May 1/5 Inche Ghafar clarified today that he had not made any offer for the formation of a coalition government.

in-churn *attrib.*: see *IN *prep.* 17*.

incidence. Add: **4.** *angle of incidence*, (*b*) the angle which the chord of an aircraft wing makes with the direction of the undisturbed air current.

1908, etc. [see *ANGLE *sb.*^{2} 1 ¶]. **1948** *Sci. News* VII. 28 The pilot is able to increase or decrease the lift by altering the angle of incidence. *Ibid.*, As the angle of incidence increases, the lift also increases and the aircraft is able to climb, but if the tilt is made too large the flow on the upper surface separates and eddies are formed.

8. Special Comb.: **incidence wire** *Aeronaut.*, on a biplane (see quot. 1916).

1916 H. BARBER *Aeroplane Speaks* 143 *Incidence wire*, a wire running from the top of an interplane strut to the bottom of the interplane strut in front of or behind it. It maintains the 'stagger' and assists in maintaining the angle of incidence. **1928** V. W. PAGÉ *Mod. Aircraft* v. 175 These wires are called 'incidence wires', as they keep the planes in the proper angular relation to each other.

incident, *sb.*^{1} Add: **1. b.** An occurrence or event, sometimes comparatively trivial in itself, which precipitates or could precipitate political unrest, open warfare, etc. Also, a particular episode (air-raid, skirmish, etc.) in war; an unpleasant or violent argument, a fracas.

1913 *Ann. Reg. 1912* I. 441 He had invariably done everything France wanted him to do and, especially at the time of the Agadir incident, had rejected German.. advances. **1920** W. S. BLUNT *My Diaries* II. v. 138 Bramley..had reported the incident in a serious light, and Cromer had taken it up seriously, seeing in it..a danger to the British occupation. **1920** T. E. LAWRENCE *Let.* 8 Aug. (1938) 313 Our communications are very bad, our defence positions all have both flanks in the air, and there seem to have been two incidents lately. **1930** *Economist* 30 Aug. 392/1 When some special 'incident' has occurred, a Mandatory Power frequently furnishes the Commission with additional information. **1937** V. BARTLETT *This is my Life* xiv. 245 There were very few 'incidents'. I visited almost every district of Berlin,..and I saw no man beaten..but I came back..overwhelmed with shame that people could be proud of so much bullying. **1937** L. BROMFIELD *Rains Came* I. iv. 32 One impotent little man

from Clapham, who was insolent to the Maharani, received for his pains a dismissal from the Civil Service for having made an 'incident'. *Ibid.* lv. 242 It was threatening to become an 'incident' which might unsettle the peace of India. **1938** *Encycl. Brit. Bk. of Yr. 1938* 296/1 Such incidents are bound to form an integral part of large-scale warfare under modern conditions. **1943** HUNT & PRINGLE *Service Slang* 40 There are no occasions, occurrences, or events in an airman's life. Anything that happens to him is an 'incident'..why, nobody knows. **1945** *Ann. Reg. 1944* 113 They [*sc.* the Home Guard] had given valuable aid to the Civil Defence Services in dealing with air-raid incidents. **1955** *Ann. Reg. 1954* 15 The number of 'incidents' in the Canal Zone increased. **1959** R. COLLIER *City that wouldn't Die* xi. 211 A warden doesn't write off an incident until he has personally made certain there is no one else on the premises. **1960** PARTRIDGE *Charm of Words* i. 23 If a business man speaks of incidents when he means quarrels, he has been influenced by journalism. **1973** G. GREENE *Honorary Consul* I. i. 23 The Governor didn't want any incidents.

5. *attrib.* and *Comb.* (also *incidents*). **incident book**, a book in which all relevant information is kept at an incident room; **incident office, post, room**, names for a centre set up by the police close to the scene of a crime, accident, or disaster, from which all operations are controlled and monitored.

1967 BAKER & WILKIE *Police Promotion Handbk.* IV. xxiii. 302 It will be clear from the list of duties that the manning of an Incident Post at the scene of a major disaster will call for a sufficiency of staff. **1971** 'J. FRASER' *Death in Pheasant's Eye* xxiii. 132 Three night men on duty in the Incidents Room. *Ibid.*, The Incidents Book was on Inspector Coates' table...The Incidents Book was the Bible of any murder investigation; every action was telephoned to the man who looked after the book. **1972** L. LAMB *Picture Frame* xviii. 154 Mr Glover's incident office is in a red corrugated-iron hut. **1973** *Times* 12 Mar. 1/5 The murder hunt is being led by Detective Superintendent Brian Weight, who set up an incident room at Aylesbury police station.

incident, *a.*[1] Add: **7. a.** Of light: further examples in photographic contexts.

1951 G. H. SEWELL *Amateur Film-Making* (ed. 2) ii. 21 The makers of other meters have adopted the Incident-light principle and have provided modifying attachments for their instruments. **1952** J. F. DUNN *Exposure Meters* i. 22 The term 'incident light' is used instead of 'illumination' when we wish to consider only the strength of the light being received *from* the source irrespective of the angle of inclination of the surface receiving it. **1956** *Nature* 4 Feb. 231/1 Blocks of soil were..directly examined with the aid of the incident-light equipment of a Leitz 'Ortholux' microscope. **1962** M. L. HASELGROVE *Photographer's Dict.* 130 Light falling on a surface is said to be incident on the surface. In most photographic writing this term used without qualification refers to the light incident on the subject to be photographed.

incidental, *a.* Add: **5.** Special collocations: *incidental advertisement* (see quot.); *incidental music*, music played as an accompaniment or 'background' to a play or film, or to a radio or other performance or entertainment; *incidental number*, a piece of incidental music; also *transf.*

1931 *Times Lit. Suppl.* 20 Aug. 636/3 'Incidental' advertisements, advertisements..which are printed in a separate gathering from the body of the book and sewn in at either the end or the beginning. **1864** in H. J. Byron *Orpheus & Eurydice* 2 (*heading*) The incidental music selected and arranged by Mr. Frank Musgrave. **1928** *Melody Maker* Feb. 214 (Advt.), Liber's incidental music. **1938** *Oxf. Compan. Music* 464/1 Incidental music to plays has always been an important side-line of the art and business of the composer. **1904** W. D. ADAMS *Dict. Drama* I. p. vi, Musical Composers, the latter ranging from the writers of operas and operettas to the providers of 'incidental numbers' for plays. **1912** E. WYLIE (*title*) Incidental numbers.

incidentalist (insidĕ·ntălist). [f. INCIDENTAL *a.* + -IST.] One who describes or insists on what is merely incidental and not essential.

1904 *Daily Chron.* 19 Nov. 3/1 Mr. Palmer may be described as an 'incidentalist'. **1924** H. E. FOSDICK *Mod. Use Bible* 163 Folk who insist on that kind of literal inerrancy in ancient documents are not Fundamentalists at all; they are incidentalists.

incidentality (i:nsidentæ·lĭti). *rare.* [f. INCIDENTAL *a.* + -ITY.] The quality of being incidental.

1791 *Deb. Congress U.S.* (1834) II. 1942 Hence the incidentality of this authority to the mere existence of Government is inferred.

incidentally, *adv.* Add: **2.** In point of fact: used to accompany a not immediately pertinent statement.

1925 T. DREISER *Amer. Trag.* (1926) I. I. ii. 15 Incidentally by that time the sex lure or appeal had begun to manifest itself. **1926** FOWLER *Mod. Eng. Usage* 264/2 *Incidentally* is now very common as a writer's apology for an irrelevance. **1961** A. HUXLEY *Let.* 8 Jan. (1969) 902 Pure perceptual receptivity is the basis, incidentally, of many Tantrik exercises. **1972** R. QUIRK et al. *Gram. Contemp. Eng.* 667 *Incidentally* adds explicitly that what is being said is a digression, if only slight, and an afterthought: The airlines charge half-price for students. Incidentally, I have already bought my ticket to New York.

incinderjell, var. *INCENDIJEL.

incipient, *a.* Add: **2.** *Comb.* **incipient species,** a group of plants or animals in the process of becoming sufficiently distinct to be described as a full species.

1859 DARWIN *Origin of Species* ii. 52 A well-marked variety may be called an incipient species... It need not be supposed that all varieties or incipient species necessarily attain the rank of species. **1942** E. MAYR *Systematics & Origin of Species* vii. 156 Some subspecies are incipient species, or subspecies are potentially incipient species. **1963** DAVIS & HEYWOOD *Princ. Angiosperm Taxon.* iii. 100 There is a tendency to regard subspecies as incipient species. **1971** *Nature* 2 Apr. 275/2 In *D[rosophila] paulistorum* there are a number of incipient species (usually called 'semispecies').

incipit. (Further examples.)

1963 [see *EXPLICIT b]. **1973** *Times* 2 Nov. 6/1 The *incipits*, or titular opening phrases, of more than 200 literary works current in Sumer in the early second millennium B.C.

incisal (insəi·zăl), *a. Dentistry.* [f. *incis-* stem of INCISOR, etc. + -AL.] Of, pertaining to, or designating the cutting edge or surface of an incisor or a canine tooth.

1916 M. DEWEY *Dental Anat.* ii. 44 The incisal edge of the central incisor is formed by the junction of the lingual and labial surfaces of the tooth. **1924** J. F. HOVESTAD *Pract. Dental Porcelains* xiv. 121 Frequent accidents to anterior teeth..causing loss of incisal corners or edges, have given the dentist great trouble. **1956** J. N. ANDERSON *Appl. Dental Materials* xxii. 300 The incisal edge of an anterior tooth is mainly enamel. **1969** *Gloss. Terms Dentistry* (*B.S.I.*) 80 *Incisal guidance*, the influence on mandibular movements exerted by the contacting surfaces of the mandibular and maxillary anterior teeth.

incise, *v.* Add: **1. c.** *trans. Geol.* Of a river: to cut (a channel or valley) in an underlying landform. Also *absol.* Usu. as **incised** *pa. pple.* (cf. next).

1893 *Science* 17 Nov. 278/1 The process by which the present ravines are forming is not a direct continuation of the process by which the gentler slopes of the upland were formed. The former are incised in the latter. **1896** *Nat. Geogr. Mag.* VII. 190 With the uplift of the region the meandering river would proceed to incise its channel beneath the uplifted surface. **1926** *Jrnl. Geol.* XXXIV. 31 Green River has a highly meandering course which is deeply incised in the rocks of the plateau. **1954** W. D. THORNBURY *Princ. Geomorphol.* vi. 147 Heavily loaded streams are more likely to cut laterally as they incise their valleys than those with lesser loads. **1972** *Science* 27 Oct. 409/2 Meandering rivers that have incised in bedrock and yet have maintained a sinuous pattern may be of two basic types.

incised, *ppl. a.* Add: **3.** *Geol.* Of the channel of a stream, esp. a meander: cut abnormally deeply into underlying deposits or bedrock. Also, of a landform: cut by channels.

1899 W. M. DAVIS *Physical Geogr.* ix. 254 Incised meanders and cut-off spurs occur on the Allegheny river above Pittsburg. **1906** *Bull. Geogr. Soc. Philadelphia* IV. IV. 1 (*heading*) Incised meandering valleys. *Ibid.* 9 The Potomac river..exhibits some well-defined incised meanders in a valley of monoclinal strata. **1944** A. HOLMES *Princ. Physical Geol.* xi. 198 In Utah, where recent uplift has made possible the development of many deeply incised meanders.., there are several examples of such arches. **1968** R. W. FAIRBRIDGE *Encycl. Geomorphol.* 332/2 (*caption*) Incised etchplain. *Ibid.* 548/2 A meandering river valley that has cut down its bed into the bedrock, because of uplift or lowered base level, is called incised, intrenched, entrenched, inclosed or ingrown.

incision. Add: **5*.** *Geol.* The cutting down and deepening of its channel by a river; a channel so made.

1906 *Bull. N.Y. State Mus.* No. 92. 333 So relatively inconspicuous are the incisions in this upland, that..the sky line will appear a nearly level one. **1914** *Jrnl. Geol.* XXII. 473 Lack of flats along the stream indicates that incision is still in progress. **1970** R. J. SMALL *Study of Landforms* ii. 65 A change of climate, leading to..a condition of stream underloading, will be accompanied by incision of the rivers into these deposits.

incitory (insəi·tŏri), *a. rare.* [f. *incit-* stem of INCITE *v.*, etc.: see -ORY[2].] Having the quality of inciting; stimulative, provoking.

1941 A. WARREN in N. Foerster et al. *Lit. Scholarship* iv. 147 The second [group] holds art to be incitory, an invitation to action. **1949** WELLEK & WARREN *Theory of Lit.* iii. 27 Is some literature incitory and some cathartic? **1950** *N.Y. Times* 20 Apr. 1/8 He had used his employes for espionage and to gather material for 'fictitious reports of incitory character' for the voice of America.

inclinometer. 2. (Earlier and later examples.)

1852 *Mechanics' Mag.* LVII. 416/2 An improved apparatus, instrument, or means for ascertaining or setting off the slope or level of drains, banks, inclines, or works of any description..which the patentee calls an 'inclinometer'. **1913** *Captain* Sept. 1069/2 An inclinometer, to show the angle of ascent or descent. **1919** H. SHAW *Text-bk. Aeronaut.* xiii. 169 Inclinometers of the spirit-level type, or constructed on the principle of the pendulum,.. are inaccurate when the machine is subjected to an acceleration as in turning. **1960** [see *GRADIOMETER a].

include, *v.* Add: **3. b.** Const. *out*: to exclude (oneself or someone). Hence, pleonastically, *to include* (someone) *in*.

This colloquial expression, which freq. indicates strong feelings of cynicism or disillusion, is attributed to the American film producer Sam Goldwyn.

1937 A. JOHNSTON in *Sat. Even. Post* 8 May 6/1 An ordinary man, on deciding to quit the Hays organization, might have turned to his fellow producers and said, 'Gentlemen, I prefer to stand aloof,' or, 'Gentlemen, I have decided to go my own way.' Sam [Goldwyn] said, 'Gentlemen, include me out.' **1938** *Hansard Commons* 8 Nov. 18/1 It may be that the First Commissioner of Works ..will now label the 'Aye' Lobby the 'Sez you' Lobby, and the other the 'Include me out' Lobby. **1946** WODEHOUSE *Joy in Morning* xvi. 140 Include me out...Nothing doing. **1958** G. MITCHELL *Spotted Hemlock* x. 101, I shall suggest giving you lunch and include him in. **1958** *Times Lit. Suppl.* 1 Aug. 435/1 He sees that our young men are angry; they do not see visions or dream dreams; they want neither to go back nor move forward: they only ask to be included-out of the social and historical process. **1959** M. STEEN *Woman in Back Seat* I. vii. 128 Oh, darling, please include me out! I can't bear affairs of that kind. **1967** WODEHOUSE *Company for Henry* ii. 39 You surprise me. A free meal, and he made no attempt to include himself in? **1969** V. GIELGUD *Necessary End* III. xv. 120 I'd like nothing better—in the immortal words—than to include myself out. **1971** *Daily Tel.* 13 Oct. 11/5 Half the in-jokes included me out, but I revelled in the way the actors caricatured famous folk. **1972** G. BROMLEY *In Absence of Body* iii. 33 Looking for clues? If so, include me in.

included, *ppl. a.* Add: **d.** *Linguistics.* (See quot. 1933.)

1933 L. BLOOMFIELD *Lang.* xi. 170 When a linguistic form occurs as part of a larger form, it is said to be in included position; otherwise it is said to be in absolute position and to constitute a sentence. **1949** E. A. NIDA *Morphol.* (ed. 2) 76 Some morphemes occur in included position, either partial or complete. **1952** C. C. FRIES *Struct. of Eng.* xi. 253 These are the signals of 'included' sentences... In some sentences there are devices that signal the inclusion of two or more separate sentences within the structural pattern of a single free sentence unit. **1954** PEI & GAYNOR *Dict. Ling.* 98 *Included position*, the position had by a word, phrase or other linguistic form when it is part of a larger form and does not constitute a sentence in itself. **1962** B. M. H. STRANG *Mod. Eng. Struct.* v. 82 Linguistic structures may always be either ..absolute or included.

e. Bot. *included phloem, sapwood* (see quots.).

1933 *Tropical Woods* XXXVI. 2 Included Phloem.—Phloem strands or layers included in the secondary xylem of certain dicotyledonous woods. (To replace *Interxylary Phloem.*) **1937** *Ibid.* L. 11 Strands of included phloem usually isolated, but occasionally linked by parenchyma. **1969** K. ESAU *Phloem* 3 In some genera a third category of phloem is found, *included phloem*, which consists of strands or layers embedded in the secondary xylem. **1933** *Tropical Woods* XXXVI. 3 Included Sapwood.—Masses or concentric zones included in the heartwood, which retain appearance and technical properties of sapwood. **1956** F. W. JANE *Struct. Wood* x. 212 Sometimes, heartwood is formed irregularly and patches of pale coloured wood are enclosed within the heartwood, a feature referred to as included sapwood.

inclusion. Add: **2.** More generally in technical use (e.g. *Cytology, Metallurgy*): any discrete body or particle which is recognizably different or distinct from the groundmass or relatively solid and homogeneous substance in which it is embedded. (Further examples.)

1896 E. B. WILSON *Cell* i. 15 The lifeless inclusions in the protoplasm have been collectively designated as *metaplasm* (Hanstein) in contradistinction to the living *protoplasm*. **1897** *Jrnl. Morphol.* XII. Suppl. 14 (*heading*) Discontinuous elements or inclusions. **1904** *20th Rep. Bureau Animal Industry, U.S. Dept. Agric.* 149 Borrel considers that his researches show that the microbe of sheep pox is ultramicroscopic and that the cellular inclusions described as parasites of vaccinia..cannot be the true cause of the disease. **1913** *Jrnl. Iron & Steel Inst.* LXXXVII. 655 The various kinds of slag inclusions occurring in steel..may be classified as follows: 1. Those.. dispersed throughout the metal, but mostly near the surface. 2. Those..dispersed throughout the whole mass of the metal. 3. Small inclusions..occurring between the crystals of the metal. **1939** A. JOHANNSEN *Descr. Petrogr. Igneous Rocks* (ed. 2) I. iii. 39 Von Leonhard used the term *Porphyr-Struktur* for that texture in which crystals, crystal fragments, grains, or flakes lie in a dense, unbroken groundmass. The inclusions, he said, are usually different from the groundmass and do not touch each other. **1960** F. C. STEWARD *Plant Physiol.* IA. i. 11 The metabolically active inclusions are the mitochondria, the microsomes, and the chloroplasts. **1966** *Nature* 28 May 879/2 Ice specimens..prepared with inclusions of fine air bubbles. **1967** A. H. COTTRELL *Introd. Metall.* xxi. 39[illegible] There may additionally be local groupings of dislocations created round large foreign inclusions by thermal shrinkage strains.

3. *Math.* Usu. *inclusion map*(*ping*), *function.* A mapping of a set A into a set B con-

taining A which maps each element of A on to itself.

1949 *Ann. Math.* L. 956 The symbolism $f:(X', A') \subset (X, A)$ is read: f is the inclusion map of (X', A') into (X, A). **1956** E. M. PATTERSON *Topology* ii. 20 If $A \subset B$, the transformation $i:A \to B$ defined by $i(a) = a$ is a one-one transformation called an inclusion. **1962** B. MENDELSON *Introd. Topology* (1963) i. 30 Let $A \subset X$. The function $i:A \to X$..is called an inclusion mapping or function. *Ibid.* iii. 111 Let the topological space Y be a subspace of the topological space X. Then the inclusion mapping $i: Y \to X$ is continuous. **1964** SZE-TSEN HU *Elem. Gen. Topology* i. 8 Consider the case $X \subset Y$. Then, the function $i:X \to Y$ defined by $i(x) = x \in Y$ for every $x \in X$ is called the inclusion function of X into Y... We write $i:X \subset Y$.

inclusive, *a.* Add: **1. b.** (Further examples.)

1910 *Bradshaw's Railway Guide* Apr. 1061 Bath Hotel ..Inclusive Terms from 7/6 per day. *Ibid.* 1067 Specimen Menus and very moderate Inclusive Rates per return. **1970** *Times* 21 Nov. 22/2 The first British inclusive holidaymakers are going out to the new summer resorts. **1972** *Times* 30 Sept. 11/4 Inclusive holidays offered by various tour operators.

inclusivity (inklusi·viti). *rare.* [INCLUSIVE *a.* + -ITY.] The quality of being inclusive.

1939 E. POUND *Let.* 2 Sept. (1971) 326 Re yr. extension of contents: The *real* work of a time is never done by more than four or five people with a fringe of occasional compositions. I suspect inclusivity. **1955** H. READ *Icon & Idea* ii. 36 But 'actuality' does not imply inclusivity.

incoagulable, *a.* Add: (Later example.) Hence i:ncoagulabi·lity, the property or state of being incoagulable.

1915 *Jrnl. Med. Res.* XXXII. 452 The leech extract incoagulable blood in vivo differs markedly from blood made incoagulable by receiving it into leech extract in vitro. *Ibid.* 454 In anaphylactic blood and in leech extract blood the probable explanation of a part at least of the incoagulability of the blood consists in a definite effect of these conditions on the blood platelets. **1964** W. G. SMITH *Allergy & Tissue Metabolism* ii. 17 Other workers demonstrated a deficiency in fibrinogen, platelets, and prothrombin as a cause of the incoagulability.

incoherence. Add: **4.** *Physics.* The property (of waves, or of phenomena involving them) of being incoherent (sense *5); lack of a definite or stable phase relationship between waves at different points (in space or in time).

1938 *Physica* V. 785 In the usual treatment of interference and diffraction phenomena, there is nothing intermediate between coherence and incoherence...The first term is understood to mean complete dependence of phases, the second complete independence. **1958** *Physical Rev.* CI. 7/2 This is a classical type of incoherence, such as would result if we had an assembly of classical oscillators with random initial phase. **1971** K. R. BARNES *Optical Transfer Function* ii. 7 Spatial incoherence implies that the phases of the monochromatic components of the light from all points of the object are changing at random.

incoherent, *a.* Add: **5.** *Physics.* Producing, involving, or consisting of waves that have no definite or stable phase relationship with one another.

1929 A. SOMMERFELD *Lect. Wave Mech.* vi. 91 In addition to secondary radiations of the same frequency as the incident light, we have also radiations of altered frequency... These modified radiations bear obviously no phase relationship with the exciting radiation, and might therefore be described as 'incoherent radiations'. **1953** C. E. HALL *Introd. Electron Microsc.* vii. 155 If two incoherent sources are observed with a microscope, the intensity at the image plane is the sum of the intensities from each one taken separately. **1959** BORN & WOLF *Princ. Optics* vii. 255 In beams from different sources, the fluctuations are completely uncorrelated, and the beams are said to be mutually incoherent. *Ibid.* x. 506 The light vibrations arising from different elements of the source may be assumed to be statistically independent (mutually incoherent), and of zero mean value. **1966** *McGraw-Hill Encycl. Sci. & Technol.* XII. 57/2 It is also useful to distinguish between coherent and incoherent scattering; the distinction is made on the basis of the ability of the scattered wave to interfere with the incident one. Inelastic scattering is always incoherent.

incoherently, *adv.* (Further examples, corresponding to *INCOHERENT *a.* 5.)

1938 *Physica* V. 795 For equal illuminating and observing apertures the result will be that two points just separable by the objectives are incoherently illuminated. **1961** *Encycl. Dict. Physics* I. 723/1 Incoherently radiating oscillators may very quickly become coherent through their interaction with their common radiation field.

incohesion (inkohī·ʒən). [f. IN-³ + COHESION.] Want of cohesion.

1882 H. SPENCER *Princ. Sociol.* II. v. iii. 278 Our own Indian Empire..held together by force in a state of artificial equilibrium, threatens some day to illustrate by its fall the incohesion arising from lack of congruity in components. **1922** *Public Opinion* 17 Mar. 244/2 The interminable vacillation, procrastination and incohesion of the Government at home. **1924** *These Eventful Years* I. 157 All these regimes are dependent on British support as against the incohesion of tribes and sects.

i·n-co:llege, *a.* [*IN *prep.* 17*.] Residing within the buildings of a college; of or pertaining to teaching or administration within the precincts of a college. Cf. OUT-COLLEGE *a.*

1845 J. PYCROFT *Collegian's Guide* vi. 131 There is a list of the eleven in-collegemen. **1899** in Dict. s.v. IN- *pref.*[1] ad fin., In-college residents. **1945** G. B. GRUNDY *55 Yrs. at Oxf.* 108 An in-college Bursar. **1966** *Rep. Comm. Inquiry Univ. Oxf.* II. 122 In-college teaching. *Ibid.* 143 In-college teacher.

income, *sb.*[1] Add: **6. a.** *national income*: the income of a nation as a whole, *spec.* the aggregate amount available for distribution among the agents of production.

1878 *Encycl. Brit.* VIII. 258/1 The income tax returns given in the preceding tables furnish important materials for ascertaining, if only approximately, the national income of England. **1925** S. E. THOMAS *Elem. Econ.* xvi. 214 The total of the national income represents not only the reward which flows to land, capital, labour and enterprise: it is also the total available in the hands of all members of the community for purchasing goods and services. **1931** *Times Lit. Suppl.* 19 Feb. 124/2 The national income may be divided into the income (wages, salaries and interest) of the producers of capital and consumable goods respectively. **1964** GOULD & KOLB *Dict. Social Sci.* 452/2 The term national income is used in a generic sense to refer to the net value of all economic goods and services produced by a nation during a particular time, usually a calendar year... In a more specific sense...it denotes the aggregate of all income payments accruing to the factors of production. **1971** A. SHONFIELD in A. Bullock *20th Cent.* 327/1 Many of the European nations were used to earning up to one-quarter of their national income through sales abroad.

b. (Later examples.)

a **1902** S. BUTLER *Notebks.* (1912) i. 12 All progress is based upon a universal innate desire on the part of every organism to live beyond its income. **1939** T. S. ELIOT *Family Reunion* II. ii. 105 It is as if I had been living all these years upon my capital, Instead of earning my spiritual income daily. **1953** A. HUXLEY *Let.* 16 Nov. (1969) 688 He was a retired business man, living beyond his intellectual income.

7. *income account, bracket, level*; *income-earning* adj. Also, **income funds, investment, share, stock,** investments regarded primarily as a source of income; **income group,** a section of the population graded according to income; **incomes policy,** a policy introduced in the U.K. by the Labour Government of 1964–70 for the control of inflation by attempting to restrict increases in wages, salaries, dividends, etc.; any similar programme.

1869 *Bradshaw's Railway Manual* XXI. 419 Add balance to credit of income account. **1940** Income bracket [see *BRACKET *sb.* 5 c]. **1947** *Partisan Rev.* XIV. 482 The hard core of the stratum that lives off ideas..are the graduates of the fashionable Eastern colleges whose social origin is in the upper income-bracket groups. **1969** *Times* 30 Sept. 11/8 Good citizenship is not decided by income brackets. **1972** *Listener* 6 Apr. 467/1 A poor cabbie loses his girl because her family don't like his income bracket. **1909** *Daily Chron.* 22 Feb. 1/4 No doubt many an 'old alibi' has won the pension for some young wage-earning or income-earning person. **1946** KOESTLER *Thieves in Night* 88 Of these, 6,624 Work Days were spent on income-earning labour. **1969** *Times* 15 Nov. 16/1 The neglected income funds are..coming back into favour. **1934** B. J. NEWMAN in *Encycl. Social Sci.* XIV. 93 s.v. *Slum*, The worst structural and sanitary conditions and the most degraded occupancy, usually by the lowest income groups, of any given period. **1936** *Discovery* Apr. 98/2 For the income-groups below the adequacy level an increased consumption of milk, butter, eggs, fruit, vegetables, and meat is desirable. **1957** J. BRAINE *Room at Top* vii. 62 She possessed the necessary face and figure and the right income group. **1970** *Listener* 21 May 687/1 The boom in Swiss industry after the war led to..a flood of foreign workers, mostly Italians and Spaniards of the lowest income-groups. **1900** *Westm. Gaz.* 22 Oct. 9/3 This would give a good prospect of dividend for the ordinary shares, and so make those shares not a bad 'income' investment. **1928** M. DOBB *Wages* vi. 113 The potential supply of lawyers or doctors..will be almost entirely confined..to children of parents above the income-level which makes possible a somewhat costly public school and university career. **1951** M. MCLUHAN *Mech. Bride* (1967) 117/2 What would you say was the income level of this family group? **1955** T. H. PEAR *Eng. Social Differences* 136 According to occupation or income-level. **1900** *Westm. Gaz.* 22 Oct. 9/3 Looking upon their shares as 'income shares' only. **1958** *Spectator* 27 June 849/3 A number of so-called 'income' shares in the consumer goods trades. *Ibid.*, The yields on 'income' stocks. **1965** *New Statesman* 19 Mar. 434/1 When he first goes into battle over a wage claim or a price increase—when an incomes policy is first translated into action. **1966** *Listener* 17 Mar. 391/1 The kind of incomes policy they advocate requires unemployment and short-time working to make it effective. **1969** H. PERKIN *Key Profession* v. 181 In terms of an incomes policy a long-term change in relativities was desirable in the national interest in order to restore the universities to a position from which they could compete. **1972** *Listener* 24 Aug. 239/2 The publicly and privately expressed views of the Bank of England that a formal incomes policy of some kind was needed.

income-tax. Add: Also *attrib.*

1844 A. W. KINGLAKE *Eothen* viii. 111 The fear that my party might be a company of Income-tax commissioners. **1844** *Punch* VII. 206 Infernal things. The Income-Tax papers. **1862** TROLLOPE *Small House at Allington* (1864) I. iv. 36 Mrs. Cradell..who had also succeeded in getting her son into the Income-tax Office, had placed him in charge of Mrs. Roper. **1878** [see *INCOME *sb.*[1] 6 a]. **1879** GEO. ELIOT *Let.* 23 July (1956) VII. 185, I have filled up one income-taxpaper for this district. **1902** *Encycl. Brit.* XXXIII. 194/2 An Income Tax Code. **1909** *Westm. Gaz.* 24 Sept. 5/3 Returns may be demanded in every income-tax district in which a person may reside. **1916** *Act* 6 & 7 *Geo. V* c. 24 § 37 Income tax relief on war insurance premiums. **1920** A. E. HOUSMAN *Let.* 3 Sept. (1971) 178 The additional trouble in filling up my Income Tax return. **1927** BOWLEY & STAMP *Nat. Income 1924* 17 'Income-Tax' income exceeds ordinary income under certain heads, since it includes *inter alia* various losses which do not come out in the assessment. **1941** *Time* 1 Dec. 84/2 Now appealing a three-year sentence for income-tax evasion. **1950** T. S. ELIOT *Cocktail Party* II. 105 I'd like to see *you* filling up an income-tax form. **1959** *Listener* 2 July 23/2 These customers are known in agriculture as 'income-tax farmers'. **1966** *Ibid.* 5 May 663/1 A composer worth his salt should be able to set..an income-tax demand to viable music.

incoming, *ppl. a.* Add: **e.** Of game: approaching the sportsman.

1892 W. W. GREENER *Breech-Loader* 211 It often happens that incoming and motionless ground game is shot over.

incommunicado (i:nkǫmiūnikā·do), *a.* (or *adv.*). Also ‖ **incomunicado.** [Sp. *incomunicado*, pa. pple. of *incomunicar* to deprive of communication.] Having no means of communication with other persons; isolated; in solitary confinement.

1844 G. W. KENDALL *Narr. Santa Fé Exped.* II. 255 Now that I was incomunicado—now that all intercourse with my friends was cut off,..my situation became irksome in the extreme. **1911** R. H. DAVIS *Once upon a Time* 57, I asked the official concerning Judge Rojas. 'Oh, yes,' he said readily. 'He is still *incomunicado*.' **1934** J. M. CAIN *Postman always rings Twice* x. 109 They can hold you forty-eight hours incommunicado. **1941** 'R. WEST' *Black Lamb* II. 310 This was an island: parts of it were even now *incommunicado*. **1952** M. MCCARTHY *Groves of Academe* (1953) v. 96 The defendant or victim in such cases as mine ought to be held incommunicado till his well-wishers have concluded their efforts. **1955** *Times* 4 May 10/6 The Dutch prisoners were arrested at the beginning of 1954 and held *incomunicado* for a considerable time. **1956** 'A. BRIDGE' *Lighthearted Quest* 42 Liners' captains, in her experience, kept themselves *incommunicado* except when on the high seas. **1962** I. MURDOCH *Unofficial Rose* vi. 57 Randall had been practically incommunicado for ten days. **1970** *Observer* 13 Sept. 4/7 The prisoners will be..detained again under the Terrorism Act by the Special Branch, permitted..to hold any person *incommunicado* for any length of time.

in-company *attrib.*: see *IN *prep.* 17*.

incompatibility. Add: **3.** *Pharm.* The condition (of drugs) of being incompatible (sense *5); an instance of this.

1825 R. BEST *Tables Chem. Equivalents* 29 This table refers only to chemical incompatibility. The physician must decide for himself, on the propriety of combining those substances which it designates as incompatible with each other. **1877** R. FARQUHARSON *Guide Therapeutics* 14 Incompatibility may be of different sorts, and is generally divided into chemical and physiological. **1948** GROSS & GREENBERG *Salicylates* ii. 16 Incompatibility of salicylic acid has been reported with compounds of bismuth. **1969** J. A. BEVAN *Essent. Pharmacol.* lxv. 628 The whole problem of drug incompatibility is changing as our knowledge of drug metabolism enlarges. *Ibid.* 629 In Table 65-2 some common therapeutic drug incompatibilities are listed. **1970** A. & E. F. GROLLMAN *Pharmacol. & Therapeutics* (ed. 7) i. 20 Incompatibilities between drugs may also occur when they are mixed, as a result of physical or chemical changes.

4. *Biol.* **a.** The incapacity of cells or tissue from one individual to tolerate those of some other individual when an organic union of some kind is formed between them, esp. in grafting and transplantation, in the transfusion of blood, and in parasitism.

1904 *Mass. Agric. Exper. Station Techn. Bull.* No. 2. 15 After a close study of a large number of these defective unions, the writer has reached the opinion that they are almost always due to the incompatibility of stock and cion. **1916** J. LOEB *Organism as a Whole* iii. 46 A lesser though still marked degree of incompatibility exists also in lower animals for grafts from a different species. **1916** *Mem. N.Y. Bot. Garden* VI. 429 Between bloods of members of any one class there is no incompatibility in the form of agglutination. **1927** *Jrnl. Agric. Res.* XXXIV. 675 Reciprocal grafts between the pigmented and the nonpigmented varieties showed no incompatibility whatever, as they produced well-established unions. **1935** N. P. SHERWOOD *Immunol.* xii. 270 In discussing the incompatibility of species not closely related, Loeb mentions the rigid specificity requirements for successful skin grafting or organ transplantation. **1957** MAHLSTEDE & HABER *Plant Propagation* xvi. 277 Many theories have been proposed relative to the causes of incompatibility in grafted plants. **1970** *Woman's Own* 3 Jan. 26/3 Expectant mothers will be immunized against the development of the Rhesus incompatibility which can affect their babies. **1971** *Canad. Jrnl. Bot.* XLIX. 304/2 Parasite/host combinations are referred to by the corresponding genotypes under study which specify compatibility or incompatibility of the relationship.

b. Inability to succeed in sexual reproduction under circumstances where fertile gametes are produced and brought together; *orig.* used mainly of failure of crossing between different species, but now usu. *spec.* such inability (occurring in many species of

fungi and angiosperms) between individuals belonging to the same species, which is genetically controlled and which usually acts to promote outbreeding.

1905 *Biol. Bull.* VIII. 320 The incompatibility was less marked.. In general.. the eggs crossed much more readily than did the California form. **1913** W. Bateson *Probl. Genetics* xi. 240 Whether the incompatibility between species is to be associated with that of the self-steriles also cannot be positively asserted. **1916** A. B. Stout in *Mem. N.Y. Bot. Garden* VI. 335 The term incompatibility has been, of course, used to characterize a wide range of causes of failure in reproduction, but it can well be limited in its application to those causes existing in the plants themselves which prevent fertilization in and between plants with normal reproductive organs and gametes. *Ibid.* 336 We may distinguish two quite distinct types of incompatibility: 1. Anatomical incompatibility... 2. Physiological incompatibility. **1954** *Adv. Genetics* VI. 236 The widespread distribution and high frequency of incompatibility in the higher plants and fungi indicate that it is one of the most important outbreeding mechanisms in plants. **1966** J. R. Raper *Genetics of Sexuality in Higher Fungi* iv. 52 The terms 'incompatibility' and 'incompatibility factors' as applied to this and other systems of self-sterility in the fungi are of more recent origin. **1970** *Bot. Gaz.* CXXXI. 139 (*heading*) Self- and interspecific incompatibility in the Convolvulaceae.

incompatible, *a.* Add: **5.** *Pharm.* Of a drug: reacting or interfering *with* another (specified) substance in such a way that the two should not be mixed or prescribed together; unsuited to simultaneous administration to a patient.

1812 J. A. Paris *Pharmacologia* p. vii, The incompatible substances, i.e. all those which are capable of destroying its properties, or rendering its flavour, or aspect, unpleasant, or disgusting. **1855** R. G. Mayne *Expos. Lex. Med. Sci.* (1860) 519/1 *Incompatible*, applied to substances which act chemically on each other, and which therefore cannot with propriety be prescribed together. **1881** R. Farquharson *Guide to Therapeutics* (ed. 2) 24 Infusions containing tannic acid are incompatible with metallic salts generally. **1898** E. W. Lucas *Pract. Pharmacy* xliv. 299 Incompatible substances cannot exist together in solution without mutual decomposition. *Ibid.* 301 Sodium bicarbonate is incompatible with solution of strychnia. **1917** E. A. Ruddiman *Incompatibilities in Prescriptions* (ed. 4) p. iii, The second object of the writer is to furnish the student of pharmacy with a list of incompatible prescriptions in such form that he may find out for himself what the trouble is. **1970** Goodman & Gilman *Pharmacol. Basis Therapeutics* (ed. 4) 1716/1 Cationic substances and anionic substances.. are often incompatible with each other.

6. *Biol.* **a.** Exhibiting or causing incompatibility (sense *4 a). Const. *with*.

1904 *Mass. Agric. Exper. Station Techn. Bull.* No. 2. 14 When the two members are unlike in nature and in some way physiologically incompatible (whatever that may mean), the wound does not heal readily, owing to some sort of irritation which continues to be felt at this point. **1918** *Jrnl. Immunol.* III. 99 A patient of group I, for example, requires a donor of group I, the blood of all other groups being incompatible. **1936** *Jrnl. Pomol.* XIV. 360 Later, the sour orange also proved to be incompatible as a stock with imported varieties of this species. **1962** J. D. Smyth *Introd. Animal Parasitol.* xxxii. 371 Physiological resistance. This type of resistance is due to some aspect of the host physiology being incompatible with that of the invading parasite at some stage in its life history. **1966** Wright & Symmers *Systemic Path.* I. iv. 151/2 For transfusions.. under no circumstances should the donor's red cells be incompatible with the recipient's plasma. **1971** *Canad. Jrnl. Bot.* XLIX. 303 (*heading*) Transfer of ^{35}S from wheat to the powdery mildew fungus with compatible and incompatible parasite/host genotypes.

b. Having or exhibiting incompatibility (sense *4 b); unable to cross.

1905 *Biol. Bull.* VIII. 323 No eggs segmented, but neither did the eggs in the check experiment in sea water, showing that the eggs or the sperm were poor, or else incompatible. **1913** W. Bateson *Probl. Genetics* xi. 239, I first tried Cinerarias, which are usually self-sterile, but I found no incompatible pairs of plants. **1916** *Mem. N.Y. Bot. Garden* VI. 419 The parent species were cross-incompatible. **1937** Gwynne-Vaughan & Barnes *Struct. & Devel. Fungi* (ed. 2) 5 Often, in these self-incompatible fungi, the sexual apparatus has partially or wholly disappeared. **1967** Briggs & Knowles *Introd. Plant Breeding* xv. 187 In *Gasteria*, pollen germination and tube development were not affected in incompatible pollinations.

incompetence. Add: **2. b.** *Med.* Inability to function correctly; *esp.* inadequacy of a valve or sphincter properly to regulate the passage of liquid or solid matter.

1876 [in Dict., sense 2]. **1890** F. Taylor *Man. Pract. Med.* 458 Incompetence of the aortic valves gives rise to a murmur during the dilatation of the ventricle. **1900** Dorland *Med. Dict.* s.v., *Pyloric i[ncompetence]*, passage of food undigested into the intestine. **1939** Dible & Davie *Path.* xxxii. 535 If there has been much necrosis, contraction, or deformity of the valve curtain, a definite degree of incompetence will be left. **1950** *Amer. Jrnl. Obstetr. & Gynecol.* LIX. 69 The symptoms of the incompetence of the internal os are chiefly those of habitual abortion. **1970** *Med. Jrnl. Austral.* 25 July 179/1 The incidence of round ligament vein incompetence in women greatly exceeds that of short saphenous vein incompetence. **1971** *Gut* XII. 102 Of 19 patients.., 17 (89%) exhibited duodenogastric reflux of barium indicating pyloric incompetence. **1971** *Biol. Abstr.* LII. 8355/1 Gonadotropic hormones, the prostate and an experimental model of its incompetence.

incompetency. Add: **1. b.** *Med.* = *incompetence 2 b.

1865 J. H. Bennett *Clin. Lect. Princ. & Pract. Med.* (ed. 4) vi. 577 (*heading*) Incompetency of aortic valves. **1892** W. Osler *Princ. & Pract. Med.* v. 611 An acute dilatation of the left ventricle with relative incompetency of the mitral segments. **1950** *Amer. Jrnl. Obstetr. & Gynecol.* LIX. 69 The degree of incompetency [of the internal os of the cervix] may vary.

incompetent, *a.* Add: **2. b.** *Med.* Unable to function correctly: used esp. of a valve or sphincter. (Cf. *incompetence 2 b.)

1863 W. Braithwaite in *Retrospect Med.* XLVII. 69 If.. the aortic valvular segments are rendered incompetent, we have the aortic regurgitant current. **1879** [in Dict., sense 2]. **1939** Dible & Davie *Path.* xxxii. 537 The aortic valves are incompetent and allow a certain quantity of blood to flow back into the left ventricle during diastole. **1950** *Amer. Jrnl. Obstetr. & Gynecol.* LIX. 69 An abortion due to an incompetent internal os. **1971** *Amer. Jrnl. Digestive Dis.* XVI. 307 Eight patients had free gastroesophageal reflux through a weak, incompetent sphincter. **1971** *Amer. Jrnl. Dis. Children* CXXI. 481/2 The immunologic system may be incompetent or contribute to the etiology of the disease.

5. *Geol.* Of rock or a stratum: apt to flow or to be crushed when laterally compressed; incapable of forming a simple fold and supporting any overlying strata without being distorted by plastic flow. Also applied to structures and processes dominated by such strata.

1891–92 B. Willis in *Ann. Rep. U.S. Geol. Survey* (1893) XIII. ii. 250 If the thrust be not powerful enough to raise the load there will be no uplift; or if the layers be so plastic that they yield to the thrust by swelling, then the principal result of deformation is change of form other than by simple flexure, and it assumes some phase of flowing. This is incompetent structure. **1923** *Jrnl. Geol.* XXXI. 506 Several attempts were made to reproduce the overfolds.. of the Alps by applying rotational stresses to models in which competent layers were placed between incompetent layers. **1949** C. M. Nevin *Princ. Struct. Geol.* (ed. 4) iii. 54 Folding has been divided into two groups: competent folding, where the dominantly horizontal pressures are transmitted by the competent beds acting as a strut; and incompetent folding where the forces are mostly vertical and the incompetent beds react passively. *Ibid.* 55 Immediately beneath the arch formed by a folded relatively competent bed a formation as incompetent as shale may rise as a broad simple arch, even at a considerable depth. **1967** A. I. Levorsen *Geol. Petroleum* (ed. 2) viii. 358 In these cases the salt mass acts as an incompetent formation, rising as a result of the deformation of the enclosing rocks. *Ibid.* 378 Folds in the relatively incompetent salt.

incompletability. Add: **b.** *Logic* and *Math.* The property, inherent in certain kinds of logical or mathematical system, of being incapable of providing a proof of every true proposition that can be formulated within the language of the system, no matter how many of these propositions be taken as extra axioms of the system. Cf. *incomplete *a.* 2 b.

1940 W. V. Quine *Math. Logic* Pref. p. vii, Gödel's theorem regarding the incompletability of logic and arithmetic is derived along novel lines. **1950** —— *Methods of Logic* (1952) § 42. 248 Church's argument makes essential use of Gödel's theorem of the incompletability of number theory. **1962** [see *Gödel].

incomplete, *a.* Add: **2.** Philos. *incomplete symbol* (see quot. 1910).

1910 Whitehead & Russell *Principia Math.* I. iii. 69 By an 'incomplete' symbol we mean a symbol which is not supposed to have any meaning in isolation, but is only defined in certain contexts. **1919** B. Russell *Introd. Math. Philos.* xvii. 182 Classes are in fact, like descriptions, logical fictions, or (as we say) 'incomplete symbols'. **1930** L. S. Stebbing *Mod. Introd. Logic* ix. 156 The notion of an incomplete symbol is required in order to define what is meant by a 'logical construction'. **1956** J. O. Urmson *Philos. Analysis* iii. 30 Russell is now writing as though to show that 'X' is an incomplete symbol is tantamount to showing that there are no X's. **1967** R. A. George tr. *Carnap's Logical Struct. World* ii. § 27. 48 These other signs we call, after Frege, incomplete symbols. *Ibid.* 49 An incomplete symbol designates.. a quasi object.

b. *Logic* and *Math.* Of a formal logical or mathematical system: containing true propositions for which no proof of validity is possible using only the formal rules of the system. Cf. *incompletability b.

1932 Lewis & Langford *Symbolic Logic* xi. 365 It is to be observed that there is an important respect in which each of these sets is incomplete and therefore open to further determination. **1937** A. Smeaton tr. *Carnap's Logical Syntax of Lang.* iii. 100 Now, however, Gödel has shown that not only all former systems, but all systems of this kind in general, are incomplete. **1958** Nagel & Newman *Gödel's Proof* vi. 58 Gödel showed that *Principia [Mathematica]*, or any other system within which arithmetic can be developed, is essentially incomplete. **1970** J. van Heijenoort tr. *Gödel's Completeness & Consistency in Frege & Gödel* 107 If *S* contains *Z*, *S* is incomplete, that is, there are in *S* propositions.. that are undecidable on the basis of the axioms of *S*, provided that *S* is *w*-consistent.

incompleteness. Add: **b.** (Further examples, in *Logic* and *Math.*, corresponding to *incomplete *a.* 2 b.) Also *attrib.* in **incompleteness theorem,** the mathematical proof of incompleteness (cf. *Gödel).

1932 Lewis & Langford *Symbolic Logic* xi. 365 This point of incompleteness can be brought out by contrasting examples. **1937** A. Smeaton tr. *Carnap's Logical Syntax of Lang.* iii. § 34a. 100 In spite of this necessary incompleteness of the method of derivation.., the method retains its fundamental significance. **1955** K. R. Popper in P. A. Schilpp *Philos. of R. Carnap* (1963) 200 Gödel, by his two famous incompleteness theorems, had proved that one unified language would not be sufficiently universal for even the purposes of elementary number theory. **1957** P. Suppes *Introd. Logic* iv. 70 Gödel's theorem on the incompleteness of elementary number theory is probably the most important theorem in the literature of modern logic. **1962** B. Meltzer tr. *Gödel's On Formally Undecidable Propositions* 62 The true source of the incompleteness attaching to all formal systems of mathematics, is to be found.. in the fact that the formation of ever higher types can be continued into the transfinite. **1971** G. Hunter *Metalogic* 257 This is Gödel's second incompleteness theorem.

incompletive (inkǫmplī·tiv), *a.* (*sb.*) *Gram.* [f. Incomplet(e *a.* + -ive.] An aspect of the verb indicating incompletion of an action or process; = Imperfective *a.* (*sb.*) 2.

1944 E. A. Nida *Morphol.* II. ix. 130 This imperfective aspect, which may also be called 'atelic' or 'incompletive', is often associated with the future time, with the negative or with the potential. **1964** —— *Toward Sci. Transl.* ix. 200 In the Old Testament, however, the differences between the Hebrew completive and incompletive forms are essentially contrasts between kinds of action. **1964** *Language* XL. 77 Two aspect classes of the active voice are also marked by simulfixation: the incompletive, marked by the structural absence of a simulfix, and the completive, marked by the simulfix for active voice. **1968** *Ibid.* XLIV. 293 There are four aspects in Huixtec: timeless, incompletive, completive, and perfective.

incomunicado, var. *incommunicado.

inconclusible. Delete †*Obs.* and add later example.

1930 T. S. Eliot *Ash-Wednesday* ii. 18 Conclusion of all that Is inconclusible.

Inconel (i·nkǫnel). A proprietary name of various alloys which contain nickel (70–80%), chromium (12–19%), and iron (usually between 5% and 8%), and are useful for their strength and their resistance to corrosion and oxidation at high temperatures.

1933 *Official Gaz.* (U.S. Patent Office) 12 Sept. 263/2 International Nickel Company, Inc... *Inconel.* For Nickel Alloys and Alloys of Nickel, Chromium, and Iron. Claims use since Nov. 25, 1932. **1935** *Chem. Abstr.* XXIX. 7257 (*heading*) Corrosion resistance of nickel, of copper-nickel alloys, of nickel silver and of Inconel. **1938** *Jrnl. R. Aeronaut. Soc.* XLII. 962 A further development is the alloy 'Inconel' containing about 80 per cent. Ni., 13 per cent. Cr., 7 per cent. Fe., which can be hardened by work, but not by heat-treatment... Its resistance to heat-oxidation at very high temperatures finds application in silencers and exhaust manifolds. **1966** *McGraw-Hill Encycl. Sci. & Technol.* VII. 265/2 The Inconels (Nimonics in England) are advantageous in cyclic heating and cooling service where large temperature gradients exist. **1967** D. Fishlock *New Materials* ii. 23 Inconel X-750 (75 per cent nickel) is today used extensively for the structure of the 4104 m.p.h. X-15 rocket aircraft.. whose skin.. is designed to withstand 650°C.

incongruent, *a.* (Later examples.)

1940 *Mind* XLIX. 349 Evident empirical facts (*i.e.*, rotational motion and incongruent counterparts) which Newton and Kant designated as rendering the relational theory untenable. **1951** A. Gardiner *Theory of Speech & Lang.* (ed. 2) 232 Grammar is, in the main, concerned with linguistic form in congruent function, and treats of incongruent function only in so far as this is building up new forms in which such function will be congruent. **1966** *Amer. Philos. Q.* III. 179/1 Kant made use of incongruent counterparts to establish a theory of space. **1972** *Jrnl. Social Psychol.* LXXXVI. 121 When a man's life style is incongruent with the demands of a task he must perform he will experience stress.

incongruently, *adv.* (Later examples.)

1933 *Amer. Jrnl. Sci.* XXV. 277 Fayalite melts incongruently with separation of iron. **1970** *Nature* 19 Dec. 1144/1 The ruby laser permits fairly fast deposition rates even of 'difficult' materials and, in particular, allows preparation of thin films of compounds that normally evaporate incongruently.

inconnu (i·ŋkǫniu, æṅkonü). [Fr., unknown.] **1.** A game fish, *Stenodus leucichthys*, belonging to the family Salmonidæ and found in Alaska and north-west Canada.

[**1806** S. Fraser *Lett. & Jrnls.* (1960) 231 The Indians also state that there are plenty white fish unconu some trout carp Jub, &c. in the fall of the year.] **1833** G. Back *Jrnl.* 14 Aug. in *Narr. Arctic Land Expedition* (1836) iii. 101 La Prise set a net, which.. produced a few white fish, a trout, and, what surprised the Indians, an inconnu. **1844** J. H. Lefroy *In Search Magnetic North* (1955) 99, I tried the Inconnu there, but it is far inferior to the Trout. **1905** D. S. Jordan *Guide to Study of Fishes* II. iv. 67 The In-

connu, or Mackenzie River salmon, known on the Yukon as 'charr'..belongs to this genus [sc. *Stenodus*]. **1943** *Beaver* Mar. 28 Inconnu (*Stenodus Mackenzii*), generally called 'conny', is a fish peculiar to the Mackenzie River. **1965** A. J. McClane *Standard Fishing Encycl.* 424/1 Inconnu have fair food value and are utilized to a large extent by the Eskimos.

2. (æ̃nkonü.) An unknown person; a stranger. Also fem. **-e.**

1807 *Salmagundi* 4 Apr. 142 When we toast a frenchman, we merely mean one of those *inconnus*, who swarmed to this country, from the kitchens and barber's shops of Nantz, Bourdeaux, and Marseilles. **1829** G. Griffin *Collegians* (ed. 2) I. xiii. 266 The lovely inconnue..felt her heart beat somewhat quickly. **1865** 'Ouida' *Strathmore* I. v. 76 The jewels that sparkled on the hands of the fair inconnue. **1920** F. S. Fitzgerald in *Smart Set* July 15/2 Edith murmured a conventional 'Thanks loads—cut in later,' to the *inconnu*.

inconquerable, *a.* Delete †*Obs.* and add later examples.

1905 *Daily Chron.* 4 Oct. 5/1 An inconquerable penchant to conspiracy. **1921** *Edin. Rev.* July 134 That rather ticklish matter, the government and command of the British Empire Navy,..does not present inconquerable obstacles to be overcome. **1946** W. S. Churchill *Secret Session Speeches* 29 The inconquerable, the inexhaustible adaptiveness and ingenuity of the British mind.

inconsciently (inkǫ·nʃiəntli), *adv.* [f. In-conscient *a.* + -ly².] Unknowingly.

1913 *Glasgow Herald* 18 Oct. 11/1 They stood, inconsciently perhaps, for some of the priceless intangible things without which the millennium would be a sterile and bitter anti-climax. **1929** R. Bridges *Testament of Beauty* iv. 126 Held by the inborn love of Beauty inconsciently Of preference to imitate the more beautiful things.

inconsequential, *a.* Add: Also as *sb.*

1936 L. C. Douglas *White Banners* xiii. 277 Exchanging inconsequentials and blandly taking each other's measure. **1936** *Mind* XLV. 334 The three protagonists may actually hold a few inconsequentials in common. **1957** *Economist* 2 Nov. 436 (Advt.), News never buried under frothy inconsequentials.

inconseque·ntialness. [f. Inconsequential *a.* + -ness.] Inconsequentiality.

1931 *Daily Express* 22 Sept. 10/6 The fact is, the profligacy of war expenditure, the high pay, the inconsequentialness of it all, led every one into bad, extravagant habits. **1956** *Essays in Crit.* VI. 117 Her English..having a quality of inconsequentialness.

incontinent, *a.* **3.** (Further examples.)

1901 G. B. Shaw *Admirable Bashville* II. i. 309 To begin my life a speechless babe, hairless, incontinent, Hobbling upon all fours, a nurse's nuisance. **1973** *Times* 11 June 14/2 Mrs Jones is doubly incontinent and vomits several times a day.

in contumaciam: see *in *Lat. prep.*

inconvertible, *a.* Add: **2. b.** (Earlier examples.)

1847 A. De Morgan *Formal Logic* iv. 58 The universal affirmative..and the particular negative..are not necessarily convertible, and are generally called *inconvertible*. **1849** W. Thomson *Outl. Laws of Thought* (ed. 2) liii. 216 The judgment O is usually considered inconvertible by the ordinary method. **1857** W. Spalding in *Encycl. Brit.* XIII. 606/1 They hold O to be inconvertible.

Hence as *sb.*, a proposition which cannot be converted.

1847 A. De Morgan *Formal Logic* iv. 62 As to inconvertibles, contranominal and converse are terms of the same meaning.

incoordinated, *a.* (Examples.)

1885 F. Warner *Physical Expression* 71 Co-ordinated movements and inco-ordinated movements. **1911** W. James *Mem. & Stud.* ix. 218 There was no appearance of general dismay and little of chatter or of inco-ordinated excitement.

incorporate, *v.* Add: **3. b.** *spec.* To admit a graduate of another university *ad eundem*.

incorporation. Add: **2. c.** The action of incorporating (cf. *incorporate *v.* 3 b) into another university.

1966 *Rep. Comm. Inquiry Univ. Oxf.* I. 404 Degrees in absence and by incorporation.

incorporatorship (inkǭ·ɹpŏrēⁱtəɹʃip). [Incorporator 2.] The position of an incorporator.

1873 'Mark Twain' & Warner *Gilded Age* xlii, It would be more money in my pocket, in the end, than my brother-in-law will get out of that incorporatorship, fat as it is.

in corpore: see *in *Lat. prep.*

incorrectitude (inkǒre·ktitiūd). *rare.* [f. In-³ + *correctitude.] The state of being in the wrong in one's conduct or opinions; incorrectness.

1898 *Westm. Gaz.* 4 Oct. 2/2 We are certain that it is not wise to adopt this position of positive incorrectitude. *Ibid.* 10 Nov. 2/3 He is brought round to own the incorrectitude of calling Mr. Gladstone a spider. **1947** *New Biol.* III. 163 It furnishes an everyday illustration of the incorrectitude of regarding different species as being necessarily intersterile.

incorrigibility. b. Delete † (*obs.*) and add: of not being open to proof or disproof. So **inco·rrigibilist,** one who adheres to an incorrigible theory.

1956 E. H. Hutten *Lang. Mod. Physics* vi. 226 To ascribe absolute incorrigibility to them [*sc.* sentences] is misleading since it suggests that they are never questioned within any context. **1966** *Amer. Philos. Q.* III. 101/2 The supposed incorrigibility of first person pain reports. *Ibid.*, Part of the guile of the incorrigibilist is not to disclose which reasons..he is prepared to take into account as relevant.

incorrigible, *a.* (*sb.*) **A.** *adj.* **3.** Delete †*Obs.*, and add: not verifiable; that cannot be proved false.

1946 A. J. Ayer *Lang., Truth & Logic* (ed. 2) 10 What may be said to verify them [*sc.* basic propositions] conclusively is the occurrence of the experience to which they uniquely refer...Propositions of this kind are 'incorrigible'..it is impossible to be mistaken about them except in a verbal sense. **1956** —— *Probl. Knowl.* 54 These experiential statements..are taken as basic because they are held to be 'incorrigible'. *Ibid.* 55 Experiential statements are not incorrigible in the sense that once they have been discovered to be true they cannot subsequently be denied.

B. *sb.* **2.** Something not open to verification.

1936 H. H. Price *Truth & Corrigibility* 28 Innumerable judgements..will have to be admitted as incorrigibles.

incorrigibly, *adv.* Add: Also in sense of *incorrigible *a.* 3.

1956 A. J. Ayer *Probl. Knowl.* 56 Such conditions as make it reasonable for me to claim that the statement is incorrigibly known.

in-country. Restrict *Sc.* to sense in Dict. and add: **2.** Used *attrib.*: in the country; in a contextually specified country. Cf. *in *prep.* 17*.

a **1953** Dylan Thomas *Prospect of Sea* (1955) 9 Between the incountry fields and the incoming sea. **1963** *Times* 6 Feb. 6/7 Cornwall..has agreed to give all technical assistance that is needed on payment by the Scillies of travelling and subsistence expenses, and to charge for the use of its educational and welfare institutions at the 'in-country' instead of the 'out-country' rate. **1966** *N.Y. Times* 1 May iv. 3 In South Vietnam, in what is called in Saigon the 'in-country' war, development efforts have been concentrated upon types of weapons best utilized in jungles and rice paddies. **1969** *Daily Tel.* 20 Nov. 5/3, 2,500 American Marines are to leave South Vietnam.. over a five-day period starting from today. This will reduce America's 'in-country' military strength to 484,000 troops. **1973** *Ibid.* 13 Mar. 5/2 American in-country troop strength [in Vietnam] stands at 7,170 men.

increase, *v.* Add: **6. b.** (See quot. 1957.)

1840 J. Gaugain *Lady's Assistant* 96 Increase a stitch on each wire, by knitting the last stitch in the common way; knit it again from the back part of the loop (this is the way to increase without making a hole). **1872** *Young Englishwoman* Nov. 607/1 The increasing and decreasing may..take place at the ends or in the middle of the work. In increasing in the middle, the increase is effected by taking up stitches. **1944** A. Thirkell *Headmistress* iii. 60 They..had to take off all the stitches and unravel back to where they ought to have begun increasing and pick up all the stitches again. **1957** M. B. Picken *Fashion Dict.* 182/2 *Increase*, in knitting, crocheting, tatting, etc., to add to number of stitches in row, pattern, or round so as to enlarge the piece. **1971** *Vogue's Guide to Crochet* 14 Increasing a stitch means adding a stitch, and decreasing a stitch means losing it. *Ibid.*, Care must be taken not to decrease or increase in such a way as to leave an uneven edge.

increase, *sb.* Add: **5. b.** (See *increase *v.* 6 b.)

1872 [see *increase *v.* 6 b]. **1971** M. Hamilton-Hunt tr. *Mon Tricot Knitting Dict.* 20 An increase is the method of making an extra or supplementary stitch in the course of the work... The single increases are known as simple increases... Double increases are used for darts, etc.

increasing, *vbl. sb.* (Later examples.)

1872 [see *increase *v.* 6 b]. **1932** D. C. Minter *Mod. Needlecraft* 70/1 *Increasing*... After knitting a stitch.. knit again into back of same loop. **1972** *Where* May/June 133/1 There has been a 78 per cent increasing in the principal venereal diseases, that is to say gonorrhoea, syphilis and chancroid.

increasing, *ppl. a.* Add: Esp. in *law of increasing return(s)*: the observed fact that in certain manufactures and industries the expenditure of labour or capital up to a certain point produces a more than proportionate corresponding return. Cf. *diminishing *ppl. a.* 1 b.

1890 A. Marshall *Princ. Econ.* I. iv. xiii. 379 While the part which Nature plays in production conforms to the Law of Diminishing Return, the part which man plays conforms to the Law of Increasing Return. **1925** S. E. Thomas *Elem. Econ.* x. 114 The Law of Increasing Returns..states that the expansion of an industry, in which there is no dearth of the necessary agents of production, tends to be accompanied by increasing returns.

increment. Add: **4. c.** *Forestry.* The increase in the quantity of wood produced by a tree or group of trees during a limited period; the value of this increase. Also *attrib.*, as **increment borer** [tr. G. *zuwachsbohrer* (M. R. Pressler *Zur Forstzuwachskunde* (1868) 19], a kind of auger with a hollow bit, used to measure the magnitude of this increase in individual trees, by removing a piece of wood in which annual rings can be examined; **increment boring,** the cylinder of wood removed from a tree by an increment borer.

1889 W. Schlich *Man. Forestry* I. ii. 167 The increment laid on by an individual tree does not by itself govern the increment produced per acre, because the latter is represented by the increment per tree, multiplied by the number of trees per acre. **1895** *Ibid.* III. i. 13 In the case of standing trees, the measurements are made with Pressler's Increment Borer. **1905** *Terms Forestry & Logging* (U.S. Dept. Agric. Bureau Forestry) 14 *Increment*, the volume or value of wood produced during a given period by the growth of a tree or of a stand. **1938** Weaver & Clements *Plant Ecol.* (ed. 2) ii. 34 The increment borer..removes a small core of wood from circumference to center, without injuring the tree. **1942** *Amer. Jrnl. Bot.* XXIX. 553/2 (*caption*) An increment boring from a butt treated western red cedar pole. **1967** T. E. Avery *Forest Measurements* xii. 210 In climates where tree growth is characterized by annual rings, ages of standing trees are usually determined by extracting a radial core of wood with an increment borer. **1972** N. D. G. James *Arboriculturalist's Compan.* xiv. 159 In forestry the measurement and calculation of increment can be of considerable economic importance.

6. *attrib.* and *Comb.*

1909 [see *budget *v.* c]. **1909–10** *Act* 10 *Edw. VII* c. 8 § 2 (1) The increment value of any land shall be deemed to be the amount (if any) by which the site value of the land, on the occasion on which increment value duty is to be collected.., exceeds the original site value of the land as ascertained in accordance with the general provisions of this Part of this Act as to valuation. **1971** *Jrnl. Gen. Psychol.* Jan. 68 At a 30-msec interval the difference threshold for a *decrease* in pulse interval would be 30 msec, while the difference threshold for an *increase* in pulse interval would be five msec. These two types of difference thresholds will be referred to as decrement and increment thresholds, respectively.

incrispated, *ppl. a.* For *Obs. rare*$^{-1}$ read *rare* and add later example.

1922 Joyce *Ulysses* 695 Incrispated black hairs.

in-crowd: see *in *a.* 2 b.

incubate, *v.* **3. b.** Add to def.: To maintain at a constant degree of warmth that will favour growth or continued survival (e.g. of micro-organisms); more widely, to maintain under given conditions in a controlled or artificial environment. (Further examples.)

1912 *Jrnl. Exper. Med.* XVI. 171 One volume of a 5 per cent. suspension of erythrocytes in isotonic salt solution was mixed with two volumes of serum in capillary pipettes. The pipettes were incubated at 38°C for two hours and then put in an ice box for twenty-four hours. **1938** [see *incubation 4*]. **1947** *Growth* XI. 232 The ability to ferment galactose occurs exclusively in cells that have been grown on galactose, or have been incubated in a galactose solution for a few hours. **1948** *Biochem. Jrnl.* XLIII. 538/2 The requisite amount of homogenate..is then added and incubated at 37° for 1 hr. **1962** Harris & Gruber in A. Pirie *Lens Metabolism Rel. Cataract* 373 The second method of study has been that of incubating the lens under various conditions at 37°C for a period of time prior to analysis. **1969** *Clin. Sci.* XXXVII. 99 The diffusion of glucose and potassium between erythrocytes and their medium was impaired when the red cells were packed by centrifugation and incubated for 48 hr without agitation. *Ibid.* 409 Rat liver slices were incubated in serum obtained from normal volunteers and from uraemic patients. **1970** *Sci. Jrnl.* May 19/3 The inoculated samples were incubated for up to 27 days at various temperatures—0°, 5°, 10° and 20°C. **1970** *Biol. Abstr.* LI. 11404/2 By incubating the seeds for 8 days at 15 C and then for 3 days at 25 C in a non-sterilized soil coming from a rice field..seed resistance to rotting may be estimated. **1971** *Nature* 19 Nov. 154/1 Because uterine secretions are slightly alkaline, a copper strip was incubated for 18 h in *p*H 8 carbonate buffer.

incubate (i·nkiubēⁱt), *sb.* [f. the vb. + -ate³, after *filtrate, precipitate*, etc.] A preparation, or material, that has been incubated.

1959 *Jrnl. Amer. Chem. Soc.* LXXXI. 4109/2 Aldosterone was the most abundant steroid found in incubates of adrenals from the American bullfrog, *Rana catesbeiana*. **1972** *Nature* 22 Dec. 470/2 Biosynthesized ^{14}C-labelled 11 KT was detectable in the control but not in the Cd-damaged tissue incubate. **1973** *Biochem. Jrnl.* CXXXI. 406/2 The incubates were extracted with equal volumes of ethyl acetate.

incubation. Add: **1.** More widely, the protection of its eggs by an animal, or the provision of conditions that favour their development. Also, the embryonic development of an animal within an egg.

1835–6 R. B. Todd *Cycl. Anat. & Physiol.* I. 785/2 When the process of incubation begins [in the crayfish] the surface of the yolk is first seen to become covered with star-like or serrated spots. **1905** J. Wyman in D. S. Jordan *Guide to Study of Fishes* I. xi. 170 Among the Siluroid fishes of Guiana there are several species which, at certain seasons of the year, have their mouths and bronchial cavities filled either with eggs or young, and, as is believed, for the purpose of incubation. **1931** J. R. Norman *Hist. Fishes* xvi. 320 The period of incubation [of ray eggs] lasts from four and a half to nearly fifteen months. **1960** T. H. Waterman *Physiol. Crustacea* I. xiii. 440 As in female vertebrates, the ovary of the crustaceans..secretes a hormone which prepares the mother for incubation. **1962** K. F. Lagler et al. *Ichthyol.* x. 299 To carry egg protection to its highest degree, some fishes have evolved various types of internal incubation or gestation. *Ibid.*, In a Brazilian catfish..the male parent develops an enlarged lower lip to form a pouch in which labial incubation of the eggs takes place.

4*. The process, or an instance, of incubating anything in a controlled or artificial environment (see *incubate *v.* 3 b).

1928 *Jrnl. Amer. Med. Assoc.* 3 Nov. 1338/1 The maturity-provoking hormone is definitely somewhat more stable to incubation in the presence of acid. **1938** *Biochem. Jrnl.* XXXII. 450 Batches of 100 flasks of Czapek-Dox solution..were sown with..*Helminthosporium leersii*.. and incubated in the dark at 24°. The rate of growth was slow and incubation was continued for 90 days... The mycelium was separated by filtration. **1969** *Clin. Sci.* XXXVII. 409 Incubation of slices in uraemic serum had no effect upon glycogenolysis or on glycogen synthesis, but utilisation of glucose was inhibited. *Ibid.* 410 Slices from the same animal served for incubations both with uraemic and with control sera. **1971** *Nature* 19 Nov. 154/1 An 18 h incubation of a copper strip in 2·5 ml. of saline solution alone yielded a Cu^{2+} concentration of 4×10^{-6} M.

5. *attrib.* and *Comb.* Also *incubation drive, fever, -period* (further examples); **incubation-patch**, an area of the ventral surface of a bird's body that swells and loses its feathers during the incubation of eggs, as a way of providing them with the necessary warmth; usu. called a *brood-patch*.

1953 N. Tinbergen *Herring Gull's World* xvii. 155 It is likely that his birds, by being robbed so often, had on the average a lower incubation-drive than our birds. **1954** D. A. Bannerman *Birds Brit. Isles* III. 133 Colonel Meiklejohn suggests that this cock may have been suffering from incubation fever and built the nest to satisfy its craving. **1952** J. Fisher *Fulmar* iv. 95 Fulmars have only a single incubation-patch, into which two eggs could probably not fit. **1926** H. M. Kyle *Biol. Fishes* 392/1 (*index*) Incubation period. **1940** *Jrnl. Biol. Chem.* CXXXIV. 250 In a prolonged incubation period there was observed nearly complete hydrolysis. **1943** *Biol. Abstr.* XVII. 2253/2 Av. incubation period was 380 hrs. at about 15·5°C [for the tide-pool cottid]. **1961** E. Cameron *Cockroach* ii. 24 The incubation period [of *Periplaneta americana*] is a fairly long one, and varies a good deal according to the temperature, and the relative humidity of the environment. **1969** A. Bellairs *Life of Reptiles* II. x. 444 The incubation period of eggs, from the time of fertilisation to that of hatching, is exceedingly variable. **1973** *Nature* 30 Mar. 329/2 Following a 24 h incubation period, the medium and cells which had not stuck to the well surface were decanted.

incubator. Add: **1. a.** Also, any of certain other animals having particular patterns of behaviour to keep their eggs at a higher temperature than the surrounding environment.

1969 A. Bellairs *Life of Reptiles* II. ix. 430 Of the six or more species which have acquired the brooding habit, only the Indian python is now known on good evidence to be a true incubator.

5. *Comb.* **incubator-bird** *Austral.* = Megapode, megapod.

[**1896** F. G. Aflalo *Sk. Nat. Hist. Austral.* 152 These most interesting birds do not incubate their eggs...for instead..we find them deposited in a perfectly planned, thoroughly heated incubator.] **1943** C. Barrett *Austral. Animal Bk.* xvii. 148 There are numerous species of Megapodes... All are 'incubator-birds', burying their large eggs in huge nest-mounds, to be incubated by the heat generated by decaying vegetation, or by solar heat. **1963** *Times* 12 Mar. (Austral. Suppl.) p. x/7 There are several kinds of megapode or incubator-birds in Australia, of which the best-known is the lowan or mallee-hen.

incudal (i·nkiŭdăl, inkiū·dăl), *a.* [f. L. *incus, incudem* anvil + -al.] Of or pertaining to the incus.

1890 in Billings *Med. Dict.*

incudate (i·nkiŭdēit, inkiū·dĕt), *a.* [f. as prec. + -ate².] In rotifers, designating a type of mastax in which the mallei are reduced or absent and the rami enlarged and curved.

1886 Hudson & Gosse *Rotifera* I. iii. 29 The typical trophi may, then, be named as follows:...Incudate. Mallei evanescent; rami highly developed into a curved forceps. **1896** M. Hartog in *Cambr. Nat. Hist.* II. viii. 211 In Asplanchnidæ the rami are large and hooked, constituting the 'incudate' mastax. **1967** P. A. Meglitsch *Invertebr. Zool.* viii. 263 (*caption*) Lateral and dorsal views of incudate trophi.

incudo- (inkiū·do), before a vowel **incud-**, combining form of Incus 1, in terms denoting the association of the incus with another part, as *incu:do-ma·lleal, incu:do-stape·dial, incu:do-tympa·nic* adjs.

1884 P. McBride *Guide to Study of Ear Dis.* Plate I (*heading*) Long process of the Incus, incudo-stapedial joint and posterior ramus of the stapes. **1894** Gould *Dict. Med.* 608/1 Incudo-... In composition, signifying relationship to the incus. I.-malleal... I.-orbicular... I.-stapedial... I.-tympanic. **1908** *Practitioner* Jan. 123 The lax membrane resting upon the inner tympanic wall and incudo-stapedial articulation. **1943** Fischer & Wolfson *Inner Ear* v. 191 The capsule of the incudomalleolar joint is divided [in the operation described]. **1967** *Coll. Papers Surg. Mayo Clinic* LVIII. 373 The most common ossicular injury sustained during stapedectomy is dislocation of the incudomalleal joint.

incumbent, *sb.* **2.** Delete 'Now *rare*', and add later examples.

1904 W. Osler *Aequanimitas* v. 82 His son..held the chair for nearly the same length of time, and the remainder of the period has been covered by the occupancy of John Goodsir, and his successor..the present incumbent. **1940** W. Faulkner *Hamlet* I. iii. 61 They had waited about the store to see what would happen when he arrived who.. must have still believed himself the incumbent. *Ibid.* II. i. 95 The incumbent, the Professor at that time, was an old man. **1966** P. Green tr. *Escarpit's Novel Computer* vii. 92 The training division of A.I.M.R. was still at Brive, and boasted a general manager's office; but the incumbent was in fact a low-ranking deputy-manager. **1971** *Nature* 17 Sept. p. x (Advt.), Applications are invited for the Harry Bolus Chair of Botany... It is required that the incumbent should promote work in both experimental and field botany. **1972** *Daily Tel.* 29 Nov. 8 The victory by Mr James Conway..in a ballot for general secretary of the Engineering Union is being challenged... Mr Conway, the incumbent, received 169,806 votes.

incumbent, *a.* Add: **7. b.** Occupying or having the tenure of any post or position.

1972 *Nature* 28 Apr. 417/2 The incumbent head of the Institute of Theoretical Astronomy would..expect to have more than an equal say in the appointment of his partner. **1972** *Science* 22 Sept. 1087/3 The MSU trustees ..appointed the Pontiac school's incumbent dean..to be dean of the College of Osteopathic Medicine at MSU. **1973** *Sci. Amer.* Mar. 43 (Advt.), Well beyond buffhood is the incumbent partisan of astronomy's cause at the Kodak Research Laboratories.

incunabulist (inkiunæ·biŭlist). [f. Incunabula *sb. pl.* 2 + -ist.] One who collects or is interested in incunabula.

1921 S. Gaselee in *Library* Sept. 135 To all incunabulists it [*sc.* the letter *H*] is almost indissociably the abbreviation for Hain's *Repertorium*. **1928** *Ibid.* Sept. 162 The incunabulist has to stop at the threshold of the year 1501. **1949** F. Bowers *Princ. Bibliogr. Descr.* ix. 339 Incunabulists view the information in colophons with suspicion until it is checked by other evidence. **1970** *Times Lit. Suppl.* 14 Aug. 906/2 It is well known from the work of the incunabulists that the typographical equipment of a fifteenth-century printer was identifiably unique.

in-curl (i·nkɒ̄ɪl). *Curling.* [f. In *adv.* + Curl *sb.*] = *inturn *sb.* 4.

1903 *Westm. Gaz.* 31 Jan. 3/1 The secret of the game is to be able to play the 'out-curl or in-curl' as the skip may direct.

incurve (i·nkɒ̄ɪv), *sb.* [f. Incurve *v.*] In baseball and softball, the bending or curving of a ball inwards (i.e. across the front of the batter); the course of such a ball; a ball pitched so as to curve to the right.

1886 H. Chadwick *Art of Pitching & Fielding* 14 It is essential to change the direction of the curve from an 'out-curve' to an 'in-curve'. **1906** *Spalding's Base Ball Guide* 112 An In-curve..is a ball which curves in towards the batsman as he stands in his position. **1949** M. Waddow in Smalley & Dennis *Official Softball—Track & Field Guide* 17 To throw an incurve, the ball is held in the same manner as for the fast ball.

incut, *ppl. a.* (Later example.)

1973 C. Bonington *Next Horizon* viii. 114 All the climbing [on the Avon Gorge] is similar: balancing up on sloping holds, using small, incut ledges for hand-holds, [etc.].

indamine (i·ndămīn). *Chem.* [f. Ind(o-² + Amine.] A blue dye, $NH_2{\cdot}C_6H_4{\cdot}N{:}C_6H_4{:}NH$ (also called *phenylene blue*); also, any of the derivatives of this compound, which form a group of blue and green dyes now important only as intermediates for safranine dyes.

1888 *Jrnl. Chem. Soc.* LIV. 949 (*heading*) Indamines and indophenols. **1903** C. Salter tr. *G. von Georgievics's Chem. Dye-Stuffs* 265 When di-p.-amidodiphenylamine is oxidised with potassium bichromate, there is formed a blue dye-stuff, known as Indamine or Phenylene Blue... From this are derived a whole group of dye-stuffs, which are, therefore, named 'Indamines'. **1961** L. F. & M. Fieser *Adv. Org. Chem.* xxvi. 852 The highly pigmented N-phenyl derivatives of quinonimine and quinonediimine, indophenol and indamine, are relatively stable, crystallizable substances.

indanthrene (i·ndănþrīn). Also **Indanthren(e.** [f. Indo-² + Anthr(a- + -ene.] **a.** (With lower-case initial.) Indanthrone, $C_{28}H_{14}N_2O_4$ (in quot. 1921 used for the oxygen-free parent compound, $C_{28}H_{18}N_2$: cf. quot. 1920 s.v. *indanthrone). **b.** (Usu. with capital initial.) Any of a large and important class of vat dyes derived from or containing indanthrone or other compounds based on the anthraquinone nucleus.

Indanthren(e) has been registered as a proprietary term in Great Britain.

1901 *Trade Marks Jrnl.* 23 Oct. 1063 Indanthrene. **1901** *Jrnl. Soc. Dyers & Colourists* XVII. *facing* p. 302 Indanthrene X is a blue paste insoluble in water. *Ibid.*, Indanthrene S is a coppery coloured paste which is soluble in hot water. **1903** *Jrnl. Chem. Soc.* LXXXIV. I. 446 The substance 'A', of the German Patent 135407,..can be purified by dissolving it in concentrated sulphuric acid and allowing the solution to gradually absorb water; well-formed, blue needles separate which, in the case of 'Indanthrene C', have the composition $C_{28}H_{10}O_4N_2Br_2$, and, in the case of indanthrene itself, the composition $C_{28}H_{12}O_4N_2$. **1920** [see *flavanthrone]. **1920** [see *indanthrone]. **1921** E. de B. Barnett *Anthracene & Anthraquinone* xvi. 342 The first cyclic azine of the anthraquinone series to be prepared was *trans. bisang.*-anthraquinonedihydro azine. This was placed on the market under the name Indanthrene Blue, and the name 'indanthrene' has come into general use in the literature. The word 'indanthrene', however, is a registered trade name (B.A.S.F.) and is applied to many vat dyes which are not azines. Indanthrene Blue is an anthraquinone derivative and ketonic in structure, and in order to denote its ketonic nature the name should terminate in -one. In the following pages, therefore, the word 'indanthrone' is used to denote the ketonic hydroazine, indanthrene (without a capital) being used for the parent, oxygen free hydroazine (*trans. bisang.*-dihydroanthrazine). Where 'Indanthrene' is used as a registered trade name it is spelt with a capital. **1922** *Trade Marks Jrnl.* 8 Nov. 2019 Indanthren. **1952** K. Venkataraman *Chem. Synthetic Dyes* II. xxx. 861 With the amalgamation of the German dyemakers into the IG in 1924, Indanthrene was adopted as the group name for vat dyes with the maximum all-round fastness. **1961** [see *flavanthrone]. **1971** R. L. M. Allen *Colour Chem.* x. 163 If hydroxyl groups are introduced into the molecule of Indanthren Yellow GK in positions 4 and 8 the shade becomes violet; this product is manufactured as Indanthren Brilliant Violet BBK.

indanthrone (i·ndănþrōun). *Chem.* [f. *Indanthr(ene + -one.] **a.** A blue compound, $C_{28}H_{14}N_2O_4$, which is composed of two anthraquinone nuclei linked by two imino-groups and is the parent compound of an important group of vat dyes. **b.** Any of the derivatives of this compound.

1920 F. A. Mason tr. *G. von Georgievics's Text-bk. Dye Chem.* (ed. 2) 449 Indanthrene (or more correctly *Indanthrone*, which expresses the quinoid character of the compound, whereas the name generally used would correspond to an oxygen-free compound) is a dianthraquinone-dihydroazine. **1921** [see *indanthrene]. **1921** E. de B. Barnett *Anthracene & Anthraquinone* xvi. 343 By far the most important method of obtaining the indanthrones is by fusing the β-aminoanthraquinones with caustic alkali. **1954** I. L. Finar *Org. Chem.* (ed. 2) I. xxxi. 689 Indanthrone (Indanthrene Blue R; Bohn, 1901) is prepared by fusing 2-amino-anthraquinone with potassium hydroxide in the presence of potassium chlorate or nitrate at 250°. **1959** *Jrnl. Amer. Chem. Soc.* LXXXI. 3762/2 Strong amide resonance contributes greatly to the resonance hybrid of the indanthrones.

indazole (i·ndăzōul). *Chem.* [ad. G. *indazol* (Fischer & Kuzel 1883, in *Ann. d. Chem.* CCXXI. 264), f. *indol* Indole *sb.*: see Azo- and *-ole.] **a.** A colourless crystalline compound, $C_7H_6N_2$, in which a benzene ring is fused to a pyrazole ring. **b.** Any of the derivatives of this compound.

1884 *Jrnl. Chem. Soc.* XLVI. 441 Indazole crystallises in colourless needles. **1967** Katritzky & Lagowski *Princ. Heterocyclic Chem.* 138 Indazole is the trivial name for the benzopyrazole nucleus. *Ibid.* 140 Certain *o*-toluenediazonium salts cyclize spontaneously to indazoles.

indecent, *a.* Add: **3.** (Later example.)

1965 *Times* 17 Feb. 17/2 After verdict and before sentence, while the jury were still in court, they had come to the conclusion that neither the films nor the brochure were obscene, but had concluded that they were indecent.

4. Special collocations: *indecent assault*: an assault (sense 3) of a sexual nature, but not involving rape or attempted rape. Used *colloq.* as a euphemism for rape (Webster, 1934); *indecent exposure* (see *exposure 1 f).

1861 *Act* 24 & 25 *Vict.* c. 100 § 52 Whosoever shall be convicted of any indecent Assault upon any Female.. shall be liable..to be imprisoned for any Term not exceeding Two Years, with or without Hard Labour. *Ibid.* § 62 Whosoever..shall be guilty..of any indecent Assault upon any Male Person, shall be guilty of a Misdemeanor. **1938** J. Curtis *They drive by Night* xvii. 190 You want to get pinched for indecent assault, do you? **1956** *Act* 4 & 5 *Eliz. II* c. 69 § 14 It is an offence, subject to the exception mentioned in subsection (3) of this section, for a person to make an indecent assault on a woman. *Ibid.* § 15 It is an offence for a person to make an indecent assault on a man. **1969** C. Allen *Textbk. Psychosexual Disorders* (ed. 2) xxii. 458 The Act does not provide a definition of 'indecent assault'... In the majority of cases a man..has, without invitation, put his hand

up the clothing of an unsuspecting female. **1974** *Guardian* 24 Jan. 7/3 Mr Breredon, at present serving four years for two cases of indecent assault.

indecently, *adv.* (Later examples.)

1961 New Eng. Bible *Rom.* i. 27 Males behave indecently with males. **1970** *Times* 8 Jan. 2/8 As she walked along a lonely path..a boy threw her to the ground, indecently assaulted her and stabbed her.

indecomposable, *a.* Add: (Earlier and later examples.)

1807 R. Kirwan *Logick* I. iii. v. 212 It has been laid down..that water was an element, and that elements were indecomposable. **1968** P. A. P. Moran *Introd. Probability Theory* ix. 406 A distribution containing all its probability concentrated at two points is indecomposable. **1971** Powell & Higman *Finite Simple Groups* iii. 140 A root system Δ with base Π is *indecomposable* if it is impossible to split up Π into two non-empty subsets which are orthogonal to each other.

Hence **i:ndecomposabi·lity.**

1950 *Mathematical Rev.* May 377/1 (*title*) Proof of the indecomposability of a certain graph. **1968** P. A. P. Moran *Introd. Probability Theory* ix. 409 We now consider an example of the indecomposability of absolutely continuous distributions.

indeedy (indī·di, indi·di), *adv. colloq.* (orig. *U.S.*). [f. Indeed *adv. phr.* + -y *suffix*[6].] Used as an emphatic affirmative (or negative), esp. after *yes* (or *no*): indeed, certainly.

1856 *Knickerbocker* XLVIII. 620 'Is thy eye not opened?' 'Yes, indeedy,' says I. **1872** 'Mark Twain' *Roughing It* 336 He never shook his mother... No indeedy..he looked after her and took care of her. **1932** W. Cather *Obscure Destinies* 165 I'd like to, powerful well, Mrs. Harris. I would, indeedy. **1961** *Sunday Times* 26 Mar. 13/1 He's also got two episcopal rings—'One's a spare I can use for the washing-up.' Yes, indeedy. **1965** N. Freeling *Criminal Conversation* i. ix. 62 'People always lie to policemen.' 'Yes indeedy.' **1966** 'D. Shannon' *With a Vengeance* xi. 147 'A little lower than the angels,' he said. 'Yes indeedy.' **1967** J. Porter *Chinks in Curtain* xii. 124 Yes, indeedy! That was a good question. **1970** L. Sanders *Anderson Tapes* xxviii. 73 No, indeedy.

indefinability (indĭfəinăbi·lĭti). *Logic.* [f. Indefinable *a.* (*sb.*) + -ity.] The quality of being indefinable; incapability of definition in simpler or more fundamental terms.

1903 B. Russell *Princ. Math.* § 80 The point which is chiefly important..is the indefinability of propositional functions. **1908** W. R. B. Gibson *Probl. Logic* 82 The indefinability of the proper name. **1936** *Mind* XLV. 101 He proceeds to consider the nature of such good, criticising Dr. Moore's theory of indefinability.

indefinable. B. *sb.* Delete *rare* and add later examples.

1904 *Mind* XIII. 132 On the indefinables of philosophy, especially, much new light is thrown by M. Couturat's labours. **1927** F. A. Lindemann in R. J. S. McDowall *The Mind* 137 Though the so-called physical laws will be in general consistent with reality, there is no certainty that the indefinables employed in their statement..have any fundamental significance beyond their appeal to the mental preferences..of the physicist. *Ibid.* 139 The commonest indefinables used in physics are space and time. **1932** —— *Physical Significance of Quantum Theory* 12 The indefinables upon which all our thought processes depend. *Ibid.* 14 The three indefinables commonly used in physics are length, time, and mass. **1948** *Mind* LVII. 409 What we ignored was the less exact and less elegant work of insuring that the defining but undefined general terms upon which our explanations finally depended were themselves understood. The application of these indefinables we knew could be explained only by examples but the work of providing and arranging those examples and surrounding them with comment bringing out their interconnexions we could not bring ourselves to do. **1963** *Times* 26 Jan. 4/7 Halewyn declares his allegiance to evil and gallops away to his destruction; his talk is a series of verbal conjuring tricks with indefinables.

indefinition (indefini·ʃən). [f. In-[3] + Definition.] A condition of being indefinite, of lacking definition.

1888 *Pall Mall Gaz.* 14 Nov. 5/1 This negative quality of indefinition leaves a sense of uncertainty. **1940** Blunden *Poems 1930–40* 57 About the stern defining phrase A gay indefinition plays. **1958** C. Rabin in *Aspects of Translation* 128 Turkish or Arabic with marking 'individuation + indefinition' rather than definition.

indelible, *a.* Add: **a.** Also *indelible pencil.*

1885 *Encycl. Brit.* XVIII. 490/2 In the indelible and copying pencils which have come into use in recent years, the colouring matter is an aniline preparation mixed with clay and gum. **1916** *Daily Colonist* (Victoria, B.C.) 23 July 9/1 All the newspaper offices in San Francisco yesterday received a communication written in Roman scrip [*sic*] with an indelible pencil, many of the words being heavily underscored. **1961** *Lebende Sprachen* VI. 69/2 Indelible pencil, der Tintenstift.

indemn (inde·m), *v. rare*[−1]. [See Indemn *a.*] *absol.* To indemnify.

1906 Hardy *Dynasts* II. i. viii. 177 To your ally, the Tsar, I must refer you... He can indemn.

indene (i·ndīn). *Chem.* [f. Ind(o-[2] + -ene, or as a contraction of Indonaphthene.] **1. a.** = Indonaphthene (which name *indene* has completely superseded). **b.** Any of the derivatives of this compound.

1888 *Jrnl. Chem. Soc.* LIV. 1303 (*heading*) Indene-derivatives. **1892** E. F. Smith tr. *V. von Richter's Chem. Carbon Compounds* (ed. 2) 903 The formation of the carboxyl derivatives of indene..proceeds in a manner analogous to the formation of alkyl indenes. **1956** Rodd & Van Alphen in E. H. Rodd *Chem. Carbon Compounds* IIIb. xx. 1260 (*heading*) Substituted indenes. **1968** L. K. Arnold *Introd. Plastics* ix. 111 Coumarone and indene, found in certain coal tar fractions, are polymerized to produce resins which range from those liquid at room temperature to others melting at 300° F.

2. Special Comb.: **indene resin,** any thermoplastic resin made from indene; usually = **coumarone-indene resin.*

1900 *Jrnl. Chem. Soc.* LXXVIII. i. 657 The indene resin decomposes at 290–340°. **1947** [see *Coumarone b].

indentation. Add: **5.** Special Comb.: **indentation hardness,** hardness as determined by one of the indentation tests; **indentation test,** any of various tests for determining the hardness of a solid by making an indentation in a sample under standard conditions and measuring either its size or the distance travelled by the indenter.

1918 *Proc. Inst. Mech. Engin.* Oct.–Dec. 487 Researches on indentation hardness. **1956** B. W. Mott *Micro-Indentation Hardness Testing* i. 9 The general definition of indentation hardness..is the ratio of the load applied to the surface area of the indentation. **1968** D. A. Smith *Addition Polymers* x. 447 The testing of fabricated polymer components..may include evaluation of tensile stress-strain and flexural properties.., indentation hardness, and the examination of the effects of temperature on rigidity. **1897** *Min. Proc. Inst. Civil Engin.* CXXIX. 334 (*heading*) A new indentation test for determining the hardness of metals. **1956** B. W. Mott *Micro-Indentation Hardness Testing* i. 2, (1) Static indentation test: A steady load is applied to an indenter..and the hardness is calculated from the area or depth of indentation produced. (2) Dynamic indentation test: A ball, cone or a number of small spheres is allowed to fall from a definite height and the hardness number is obtained from the dimensions of the indentation and the energy of the impact.

indenter[2] (inde·ntəɹ). Also **-or.** [f. Indent *v.*[2] + -er[1], -or.] Something that produces indentations; *spec.* a small hard sphere, pyramid, or similar object used for producing an indentation in a solid (as in an indentation test).

1929 *Proc. Inst. Mech. Engin.* i. 384 If only a fraction of the attention..had been devoted to the economical production of high quality cones or pyramids as indenters, they would now be in a more satisfactory position with regard to hardness testing. **1948** Spielmann & Elford *Road Making & Administration* (ed. 2) vii. 265 Indenters, Crimpers, and Key Cutters are no longer manufactured. **1950** *Engineering* 4 Aug. 102/3 Mechanical testing..includes..measurement of the shape of impressions made by Knoop hardness indenters. **1966** *Nature* 28 May 879/1 A hard steel indenter (sphere, cone, or pyramid) was pressed with a known load for a specified time on to the surface of a smooth block of ice. **1971** B. Scharf *Engin. & its Lang.* iv. 23 All three are indentation tests in which a weighted steel ball or other 'indentor' is applied to the test piece. The hardness is assessed according to the size of the impression (Brinell and Vickers) or the travel of the indentor (Rockwell).

indentor[2], var. *Indenter[2].

indentured, *ppl. a.* **1.** (Further examples.)

1952 S. Selvon *Brighter Sun* v. 72 He had come from India to work as an indentured labourer on the white man's plantations. **1961** [see *East Indian *sb.* 2]. **1969** S. M. Sadeek *Windswept & Other Stories* 29 My grand parents were indentured immigrants, never-the-less pioneers.

independable (indĕpe·ndăb'l), *a.* [f. In-[3] + Dependable *a.*] Not dependable; untrustworthy; not to be depended *upon.*

1802 Bentham *Let.* 27–30 June in *Works* (1843) X. 388/1 All Frenchmen are independable upon. **1897** *Geogr. Jrnl.* Feb. 122 This lady is..capricious, independable, and exacting. **1921** S. Graham *Europe* xvii. 210 English action is so sluggish and so independable.

independence. Add: **1. c.** Corresp. to *Independent *a.* 3 d.

1902 *Bull. Amer. Math. Soc.* VIII. 296 No attempt seems to have been made to prove the independence of the postulates employed to define a group. **1941** O. Helmer tr. *Tarski's Introd. Logic* § 56. 194 (*heading*) Independence of the axioms of the simplified system. **1954** I. M. Copi *Symbolic Logic* vi. 179 The axioms of a deductive system are said to be independent (or to exhibit independence) if no one of them can be derived as a theorem from the others. **1955** A. N. Prior *Formal Logic* 233 This is the method regularly used for establishing the 'independence' of the axioms in a given set, i.e. for showing that no axiom in the set is superfluous, in the sense of being derivable from the others as a theorem. **1956** J. H. Woodger tr. *Tarski's Logic, Semantics, Metamath.* 390 On account of the non-ramifiability the independence proof for such sentences cannot be carried out..by an interpretation in logic. **1962** W. & M. Kneale *Devel. of Logic* xii. 692 Bernays..turned to investigate the independence of the axioms of the calculus of propositions in *Principia Mathematica.*

3. *Independence Day* (earlier and later examples); also *transf.*

1791 J. Hiltzheimer *Diary* 4 July (1893) 170 This being Independence Day, the Governor invited several of the neighbors to dine with him. **1967** R. Lowell *Near Ocean* 17 Another summer! Our Independence Day Parade, all innocence Of children's costumes, helps resist The communist and socialist. **1970** M. Slater *Caribbean Cooking* 45 Strangers to the islands may well be taken by surprise on..Independence Day. **1972** *Times* 9 Oct. (Nigeria Suppl.) p. i/6 In his Independence Day speech last week General Gowon disclosed that the census would take place..next year.

independent, *a.* and *sb.* Add: **A.** *adj.* **3. b.** *independent suspension.*

1930 *Engineering* 7 Feb. 162/3 A special chapter on independent suspension systems. **1963** R. F. Webb *Motorists' Dict.* 135 *Independent suspension,* a form of suspension where each wheel is completely independent of the others and no connecting axle beams are used. **1973** *Country Life* 15 Dec. 1581/2 For absolute comfort and stability at very high speeds there is all round independent suspension.

d. Of one of a set of equations, axioms, or quantities in respect of the others: incapable of being expressed in terms of, or of being derived or deduced from, the others; hence applied to a set of axioms, etc., all of which have this property; *linearly independent,* (of each of a set of equations or quantities) incapable of being expressed as a linear combination of the others, i.e. satisfying no relation of the form $a_1x_1+a_2x_2+\ldots+a_nx_n = 0$ (where x_i are the quantities and a_i arbitrary constants) unless $a_1 = a_2 = \ldots = a_n = 0$.

1740 N. Sanderson *Elem. Algebra* I. ii. 105 If a problem be justly proposed, it ought to have as many independent conditions..as there are unknown quantities to be discovered by them. **1798** J. Wood *Elem. Algebra* (ed. 2) 73 These equations must also be independent, that is, not deducible one from another. **1875** *Encycl. Brit.* I. 541/1 A problem is limited when the conditions furnish just as many independent equations as there are unknown quantities to be determined: if there be fewer, the problem is indeterminate; but if there be more, the problem in general admits of no solution. **1885** [see *Legendre]. **1902** *Trans. Amer. Math. Soc.* III. 142 Hilbert states..that his body of axioms consists of independent axioms, that is, that no one of the axioms is logically deducible from the remaining axioms. **1931** L. J. Rouse *College Algebra* v. 69 The equations $2x + y = 5$ and $x - y = 4$ cannot be reduced to the same form and are therefore independent. **1941** O. Helmer tr. *Tarski's Introd. Logic* §39. 131 We strive to arrive at an axiom system which does not contain a single superfluous statement..which can be derived from the remaining axioms... An axiom system of this kind is called independent (or a system of mutually independent axioms). **1944** A. Church *Introd. Math. Logic* I. i. 25 An axiom of a logistic system is said to be independent if, in the system whose axioms and rules consist of all axioms and rules of the original system except that one, the suppressed axiom is not a theorem. **1959** G. & R. C. James *Math. Dict.* 107/1 The numbers 3 and π are linearly independent with respect to rational numbers, since $a_1\cdot3+a_2\cdot\pi$ can not be zero if a_1 and a_2 are rational numbers, not both zero. Since $-1\cdot3+(3/\pi)\pi =$ 0, 3 and π are linearly dependent with respect to real numbers. **1961** Powell & Crasemann *Quantum Mech.* v. 117 Two solutions of Eq. (5–47) (or, more generally, any two functions of x) are linearly independent if the equation $C_1\psi_1+C_2\psi_2 = 0$ cannot be satisfied identically in x for any choice of the constants C_1 and C_2 except $C_1 = C_2 = 0$. *Ibid.* 118 Two linearly independent solutions, ψ_1 and ψ_2, are a complete set in the sense that every solution of Eq. (5–47) can be expressed as a linear combination of ψ_1 and ψ_2. **1965** Hughes & Londey *Elem. Formal Logic* xviii. 132 Since A4 is non-independent, the axiom set for PM could be reduced by one. But no further reduction of this sort is possible; neither A1 nor A2 nor A3 nor A5 is a consequence of the other three under Substitution and Detachment, and these four are therefore said to be independent axioms.

5. b. *Independent Labour Party* (abbrev. I.L.P.: see *I. III): the title of the political organization founded at Bradford in January 1893 by James Keir Hardie as an offshoot of the Social Democratic Federation, for the support of parliamentary candidates of approved socialistic views; orig. as opp. the Conservative and Liberal parties, later distinct from the Labour Party.

c **1888** *Scottish Labour Party Manifesto* in M. Beer *Hist. Brit. Socialism* (1920) II. xv. 300 The formation of a distinct, separate, and *Independent Labour Party.* **1902** *Encycl. Brit.* XXXII. 668/2 Attempts had been made to influence politics directly by means of an Independent Labour Party..which bound itself to support only candidates of sound socialist views. **1922** *Ibid.* XXXII. 507/1 The Labour party..included the Independent Labour party and the Fabian Society and one or two smaller Socialist bodies. **1953** D. E. Butler *Electoral Syst. in Brit.* ii. v. 154 The total of 5 [members of parliament from outside the three major parties] for 1935 is made up of 4 Independent Labour Party members from Glasgow—where a substantial part of the Labour party had split away—and 1 Communist. **1955** *Times* 24 May 14/3 An election manifesto issued last night by the Independent Labour Party reaffirms the party's belief

that workers' control 'is an essential part of Socialism'. **1971** BUTLER & PINTO-DUSCHINSKY *Brit. Gen. Election 1970* v. 112 The failure of those other traditional spokesmen of the left, the Independent Labour party and the Socialist Party of Great Britain, was still more complete.

d. Of schools: receiving no grant from the government and not subject to the control of a local authority.

1944 *Act 7 & 8 Geo. VI* c. 31 § 70 The Minister shall appoint one of his officers to be Registrar of Independent (i.e. private) Schools. **1957** *Encycl. Brit.* VII. 989/1 The Independent Schools association..; its official publication is the *Independent School.* **1966** *Rep. Comm. Inquiry Univ. Oxf.* II. 45 Independent schools are subdivided into independent boarding and independent day schools according to whether the majority of pupils were boarders or day pupils.

e. *Independent Television (Authority)* (abbrev. I.T.A., I.T.V.: see *I. III): a corporation, independent of direct government control, engaged in commercial television broadcasting in Great Britain; also, the channel carrying their programmes; renamed in 1972 the *Independent Broadcasting Authority* (abbrev. I.B.A.: see *I. III), and widened to include commercial radio broad casting.

1954 *Act 2 & 3 Eliz. II* c. 55 §1 There shall be an authority, to be called the Independent Television Authority.. whose function shall be to provide, in accordance with the provisions of this Act, and for the period of ten years from the passing of this Act, television broadcasting services, additional to those of the British Broadcasting Corporation. **1958** *Times Lit. Suppl.* 15 Aug. p. xl/1, This brings sharply into the picture the B.B.C.'s rival, Independent Television. **1959** *Chambers's Encycl.* XI. 349/2 (*heading*) Independent Television Authority. *Ibid.*, This corporation is controlled by directors appointed by the government and leases facilities to privately financed companies, which draw their revenues from advertisements. **1960** *B.B.C. Handbk.* 165 The Postmaster General issued a broadcasting licence, for television only, at a later stage to the Independent Television Authority, which was set up under the Television Act of 1954. **1971** [see *I.B.A.* s.v. *I. III]. **1973** *Times* 13 Dec. 4/5 The Independent Broadcasting Authority will hold meetings today.. about advertising which will be lost as a result of the shorter hours of transmission announced yesterday. *Ibid.* 15 Dec. 2 BBC and independent television agreed last night to spread their closing hours.

6. b. *independent float*: in Critical Path Analysis, the amount of 'float' or leeway in any one activity which can occur without affecting the timing of the whole operation.

1963 R. E. MCGARRAH *Production & Logistics Managem.* viii. 211 'Independent float' pertains to those non-critical activities whose leeway is not affected by the starting or completion time of its preceding or succeeding activities. **1964** K. G. LOCKYER *Introd. Critical Path Analysis* v. 48 *Independent float,* the time by which an activity can expand without affecting any other activity either previous or subsequent. **1967** A. BATTERSBY *Network Analysis* (ed. 2) App. 4. 335 *Independent float* is so called because it is what remains if all preceding jobs finish as late as possible and all succeeding jobs begin as early as possible. **1967** S. WOODGATE in Wills & Yearsley *Handbk. Managem. Technol.* 80 Independent float is the minimum spare time available under any condition, i.e. either early or late. **1968** *Gloss. Terms Project Network Analysis (B.S.I.)* 8 *Independent float,* earliest date of succeeding event minus latest date of preceding event minus activity duration. (If negative, the independent float is taken as zero.)

7. *independent seconds (watch)*: see quots.

a **1877** KNIGHT *Dict. Mech.* II. 1179/1 *Independent seconds-watch,* a watch in which the action of the center seconds-hand is independent of the regular going works of the watch... For great nicety in timing, quarter and fifth second watches are now made. **1962** E. BRUTON *Dict. Clocks & Watches* 93 *Independent seconds,* clock or watch with seconds hand..which jumps from one second to the next, i.e. it is dead beat.

in-depth *attrib.*: see *DEPTH I. 3 c.

inderborite (indəɪbōᵊ·rəit). *Min.* [f. *Inder,* the name of a lake in Kazakhstan + BOR(ON + -ITE¹.] A colourless to white hydrated borate of calcium and magnesium, $CaMgB_6O_{11}.11H_2O$.

1941 G. S. GORSHKOV in *Compt. Rend. (Doklady) de l'Acad. des Sci. de l'URSS* XXXIII. 255 The new mineral is an analogon of hydroboracite and has been named inderborite after the place of finding. **1967** E. L. MUETTERTIES *Chem. Boron & its Compounds* iii. 188 The binary salt minerals, in the system $CaO.MgO.B_2O_3.H_2O$ (hydroboracite and inderborite) are probable derivatives of the colemanite-meyerhofferite trimer.

inderite (i·ndərəit). *Min.* [f. as prec. + -ITE¹.] A colourless hydrated magnesium borate, $Mg_2B_6O_{11}.15H_2O$.

1937 BOLDYREVA & YEGOROVA in *Mat. Central Sci. Investig. Geol. Prospecting Inst.* (U.S.S.R.) Gen. Ser. No. 2. 52 Inderite, a new hydrated magnesium borate—$Mg_2B_6O_{11}.15H_2O$ has been found in the Kzyl-Tau deposit (Western Kasakhstan, Inder Mountains) in the form of fine white, sometimes slightly pinkish kidney-shaped nodules. **1946** *Amer. Mineralogist* XXXI. 71 A second occurrence of inderite ($Mg_2B_6O_{11}.15H_2O$)..has been discovered. **1967** E. L. MUETTERTIES *Chem. Boron & its Compounds* iii. 161 NMR analyses have been performed on the minerals inderite, $Mg_2B_6O_{11}.15H_2O$.. borax..and tincalconite.

indestructible, *a.* Add: Used *subst.* An indestructible thing.

a **1861** T. WINTHROP *Life in Open Air* (1863) 17 My pair of these indestructibles [*sc.* socks] will outlast my last legs. **1880** J. ROSS *Hist. Corea* x. 332 The things used in the evening sacrifice are to be removed,..but spirits and indestructibles may remain. **1898** G. MEREDITH *Odes French Hist.* 76 Refreshful chatter, laughter, gailiard songs. So like Earth's indestructible they were.

indetectable, *a.* Delete *rare* and add later examples.

1930 W. DE LA MARE *On the Edge* 207 In hope of detecting that shadow's indetectible motion! **1961** D. G. JAMES *Matthew Arnold* i. 27 There always remained in him something evasive and indetectable.

indeterminacy. Delete *rare* and add later examples.

1919 J. M. KEYNES *Econ. Consequences Peace* v. 208 The Allies recognised the inconvenience of the indeterminacy of the burden laid upon Germany. **1947** P. A. M. DIRAC *Princ. Quantum Mech.* (ed. 3) i. 4 There is an unavoidable indeterminacy in the calculation of observational results, the theory enabling us to calculate in general only the probability of our obtaining a particular result when we make an observation. **1953** C. F. HOCKETT in Saporta & Bastian *Psycholinguistics* (1961) 46/1 Thus, if there is no indeterminacy, no element of choice, there can be no transmission of information. **1962** *Listener* 15 Feb. 290/1 Most murderers are now subject to a higher degree of indeterminacy in their sentence than would be the case with those who were given the maximum sentence which I am canvassing. *Ibid.* 27 Sept. 472/2 Contemporary composers such as Stockhausen are often attacked for their deliberate indeterminacy—a word which has become a technical term. **1963** D. A. FIRMAGE *Fund. Theory of Struct.* v. 118 To determine the degree of indeterminacy..remove reaction components one at a time and see if the structure is stable against all possible forces. **1971** *Archivum Linguisticum* II. 50 It will be seen that the inclusion of a single additional item serves to reduce in some measure the indeterminacy we have noted as attending the parts and the whole of words.

b. Physics. *principle of indeterminacy* (or *indeterminacy principle*) = **uncertainty principle.*

1928 A. S. EDDINGTON *Nature Physical World* x. 220 It was Heisenberg again who set in motion the new development in the summer of 1927, and the consequences were further elucidated by Bohr. The outcome of it is a fundamental general principle which seems to rank in importance with the principle of relativity. I shall here call it the 'principle of indeterminacy'. The gist of it can be stated as follows: a particle may have position or it may have velocity but it cannot in any exact sense have both. **1938** W. S. MAUGHAM *Summing Up* 289 Of late the Principle of Indeterminacy, by bringing to view certain events to which apparently no causes can be assigned, has cast a doubt on the universal efficacy of those laws upon which science has hitherto been based. **1964** D. ROSENTHAL *Introd. Properties Metals* iv. 68 There is the unavoidable lack of resolution caused by the interaction between waves and particles and deriving from the fundamental behavior of matter and energy (the indeterminacy principle). **1959** *Listener* 1 Oct. 519/1 Heisenberg's principle of indeterminacy showed that the process of observing could affect the observation. **1971** *Physics Bull.* June 329/2 It led Heisenberg to formulate his principle of indeterminacy, postulating that a measurement of one property of an entity, such as its momentum, involved an inevitable uncertainty in our knowledge of the conju gate property, such as its position.

indeterminate, *a.* (*sb.*) Add: **2. c.** Also (in *Engin.*), of a structure or its stresses, = *hyperstatic* adj. (s.v. *HYPER- IV): usu. qualified by *statically.*

1905 I. HIROI (*title*) The statically-indeterminate stresses in frames commonly used for bridges. **1919** PIPPARD & PRITCHARD *Aeroplane Struct.* xxii. 280 The principle of Least Work..enables the engineer to find the stresses in structures which are statically indeterminate, i.e. in structures with too many members. **1926** PARCEL & MANEY *Elem. Treat. Statically Indeterminate Stresses* p. v, This book has grown out of the authors' needs in teaching the subject of Indeterminate Structures during the past fifteen years. **1963** D. A. FIRMAGE *Fund. Theory of Struct.* v. 118 A truss can..be determinate, indeterminate, or unstable with respect to the system of bars. **1964** J. H. FAUPEL *Engin. Design* ii. 130 In a statically indeterminate system the basic equations of statics (ΣF and $\Sigma M = 0$) are insufficient for obtaining a solution.

e. *indeterminate sentence,* a sentence in a criminal case which leaves the prisoner's release dependent on his conduct and on the probability of his amendment; *indeterminate vowel,* the 'obscure' vowel (ə), mid-mixed-wide; = SHEVA 2.

1873 E. C. WINES *Rep. Internat. Penitentiary Congr. 1872* xxxviii. 273 It is extremely doubtful whether society will, or could, ever become reconciled to so great a change on the sudden as that from determinate to wholly indeterminate sentences. **1888** KING & COOKSON *Princ. Sound & Inflexion Gr. & Latin* 70 The same indeterminate vowel appears in Sk., where it is called a *svarabhakti* vowel. **1894** W. M. LINDSAY *Latin Lang.* 257 The obscure or indeterminate vowel (like the Hebrew shᵉva). **1962** *Listener* 15 Feb. 290/1 Indeterminate sentences have been common in western Europe and the United States for some time. **1972** *N.Y. Law Jrnl.* 14 Nov. 6/5 People, &c., v. Manuel Santos—Indeterminate sentence.

indeterminism. Add: **2.** = INDETERMINACY.

1928 *Chem. Rev.* V. 472 Because of the ambiguity resulting from the Heisenberg indeterminism principle, the future of a dynamical system can never be predicted with certainty. **1957** *Encycl. Brit.* XV. 680/1 Because *h* is so small, the indeterminism caused by the uncertainty principle is of no consequence in ordinary experience. **1969** R. B. FULLER *Operating Man. Spaceship Earth* v. 65 Heisenberg's principle of 'indeterminism' which recognized the experimental discovery that the act of measuring always alters that which was being measured turns experience into a continuous and never-repeatable evolutionary scenario.

indeterminist. Add: Also *attrib.* = **indetermini·stic** *a.*, of or pertaining to the doctrine of indeterminism.

1902 W. R. B. GIBSON in H. Sturt *Personal Idealism* III. 160 The Indeterminist, like the Britisher, is king of his own castle, and woe to the combatant who fights the battles of Freedom within that..enclosure. Of such a kind is the indeterministic challenge of Professor James. **1903** A. E. TAYLOR *Elem. Metaphysics* IV. iv. 376 The essence of the indeterminist position is the denial of the principle affirmed alike by the doctrine of self-determination and, in an unintelligent travesty, by the determinist theory that conduct results from the reaction of 'character' upon circumstances. **1907** W. JAMES *Pragmatism* 117 The chaplet of my days tumbles into a cast of disconnected beads as soon as the thread of inner necessity is drawn out by the preposterous indeterminist doctrine. **1925** A. G. HOGG *Redemption from this World* 243 Bushnell, accepting a very indeterministic type of libertarianism, postulates an unresolved plurality of 'powers' or uncaused causes. **1936** *Times Lit. Suppl.* 11 Jan. 38/4 A very lucid exposition of the indeterminist philosophy. **1940** *Mind* XLIX. 465 An erroneous belief that acceptance of the new 'indeterministic' view of physical law would make it less likely that the sun would rise tomorrow. **1969** *Adv. Hydroscience* V. 102 Indeterministic models would exclude those possessing deterministic and probabilistic properties.

index, *sb.* Add: **2.** (Further examples: cf. *INDEX *v.* 5.)

1863 J. WATSON *Theory & Pract. Art of Weaving* vi. 209 After the wheel is turned, the next process is to divide its circumference into as many divisions as will make up the number of teeth required; this is done by an index which is fixed on the spindle of the lathe. **1879** J. J. HOLTZAPFFEL *Turning & Mech. Manipulation* IV. v. 118 The index, is a steel spring or rod terminating in a point, which is inserted in any required series of holes, in any of the circles of the division plate, to retain the mandrel for the time, at rest, in certain relative positions. For example, to divide the work into 12 parts; the point of the index is placed successively in the holes 8. 16. 24. 32. etc. of the 96 circle.. and while the mandrel is arrested at these points, the work is marked.

5. d. *Computers.* A set of items each of which specifies one of the records of a file and contains information about its address.

1962 *Gloss. Terms Automatic Data Processing (B.S.I.)* 27 *Index,* a sequence or array of items with keys, used to identify or locate records. **1970** O. DOPPING *Computers & Data Processing* xvi. 261 The index can contain the addresses of all individual records, but if the file is ordered, it is usually more economic to make the index cruder. **1971** R. L. BOYES et al. *Introd. Electronic Computing* viii. 201 An index is simply a shorthand substitute for the original information and is used to assist in the location of a given record... The general form of an index..will contain these two items: 1. The index term. This is the shorthand description of a stored record... 2. Record identification or location. This may be a document number or the physical address of the record described by the index term.

8. d. *Computers.* A quantity which is fixed in relation to the set of operations laid down by a program but which assumes a prescribed sequence of values as the program is run; *spec.* (*a*) one held in an index register and used to modify the addresses of instructions; (*b*) one in a DO statement (in Fortran) or a FOR statement (in Algol) that is used to control the number of repetitions of a sequence of instructions. Freq. *attrib.*, esp. denoting the portion of an instruction specifying the appropriate index register (see also *index register* in 10 below).

1957 D. D. MCCRACKEN *Digital Computer Programming* viii. 99 Instructions which call for an index to be added are written with the one or two following the address. **1959** J. W. CARR in E. M. Grabbe et al. *Handbk. Automation, Computation & Control* II. ii. 51 When the values of the bound variables (usually indices) that assume a sequence of different values during the course of a problem solution change..such variables are changed in actual, although not notational value. By a change in such an index, therefore, no change is made in the flow diagram notation, although the actual value of free or floating variables will change. *Ibid.* 55 Many artificial instruction codes..use such index registers to speed up hand programming. A certain portion of every instruction word is used to designate just how that particular instruction is to be modified with respect to one or more such special locations, which have been filled with specified values of an index. **1961** LEEDS & WEINBERG *Computer Programming Fund.* vi. 177 Flow diagrams will be generally easier to follow if we can represent our control logic in enumerative terminology. To do this we make use of an index rather than an actual computed quantity on the flow diagram to show the count. **1962** Y. CHU *Digital Computer Design Fund.* xii. 454 The amount of change of an address, called the index value, is stored in an index register. *Ibid.*, The number in the

index field [of an instruction] designates the index register selected. **1962** HUSKEY & KORN *Computer Handbk.* xx. 29 The index is not always added, so there is an address modifier..which determines whether the index is to be added to the address or not. **1966** B. A. M. MOON *Computer Programming* vii. 117 Within the range of the DO no statement is permitted which alters the value of the index. **1969** V. J. CALDERBANK *Course on Programming in FORTRAN IV* iv. 36 The DO statement automatically causes execution of all the statements following it up to and including the statement labelled *n* for values of *i* from m_1 in steps of m_3... The counter *i* is sometimes referred to as the index of the loop. **1969** Index bit [see *INDEX *v.* 6]. **1969** C. W. GEAR *Computer Organization & Programming* ii. 53 There are four items of information to be specified—the start of the loop in memory (X), the initial value of the index (0), the increment (1), and the end condition on the index (999). **1970** O. DOPPING *Computers & Data Processing* vi. 101 The character..in the last position means that the content of the corresponding index register is to be added to the address... The last position of the instruction can be called the 'index tag'.

e. *Computers.* One of a continuous sequence of numbers each of which specifies one of an ordered set of items.

1962 R. V. OAKFORD *Introd. Electronic Data Processing Equipment* iv. 101 Assume that 15 independent quantities are stored in memory registers 0016 through 0030 and that another 15 independent quantities are stored in registers 0031 through 0045. The location of the *i*th register in the first set may be designated as A_i, while that of the second set may be designated as B_i; then *i* can be considered as an index that assumes the values 1, 2, 3,..., 14, 15. Thus A_i is equal to 0016. **1972** H. S. STONE *Introd. Computer Organization* vi. 120 The FORTRAN statement DIMENSION X(100) creates an array named X with 100 elements such that the first has index 1 and the last has index 100.

9. e. *Econ.* A number showing the variation (increase or decrease) in the prices or value of some specified set of goods, shares, etc., since a chosen 'base' period (often represented by the number 100), as a retail price index, a cost-of-living index, etc. Cf. *DOW-JONES.

1886 *Rep. Brit. Assoc. Adv. Sci. 1885* 872 The index for quantity is the same as that for value in the standard year (1883); that for 1884 is arrived at by dividing the value index by the price index, and is shown in the last column. **1922** *Encycl. Brit.* XXX. 759/1 Suppose that the modification of diet (margarine instead of butter, decrease of sugar and eggs and increase of other foods) reduces the food index to 260,..and the index is 200 instead of 305. **1927** [see *COST *sb.*² 1 e]. **1942** J. R. HICKS *Social Framework* xv. 160 The most famous of all British index-numbers is the cost-of-living index published by the Ministry of Labour. The basket of goods on which this index is based is supposed to be that consumed in a week by a representative working-class family. It is thus an index of very fundamental importance... It covers a large part of the field which would be covered by the ideal index which we should desire to have for measuring the national income in real terms. **1955** *Times* 31 Aug. 9/3 Their members have expressed lack of confidence in the index as a measurement of their living costs. **1958** *Spectator* 22 Aug. 261/2 Industrial equity shares touched bottom—161·5 for the index. **1969** *Daily Tel.* 13 June 3 The index would have dropped say 12 points, War Loan would have continued its downhill march. **1972** *Accountant* 28 Sept. 398/1 When the heaviest Index fall in a day is accompanied by a reduction in the number of Stock Exchange recorded bargains to under 8,000, it can only be assumed that the vast bulk of the 8,000 deals was the same selling way. **1973** *Daily Tel.* 12 Apr. 21/3 The provisional price index of goods manufactured for the home market rose by just over 0·25 p.c., compared with 0·5 p.c. in both January and February.

9*. [f. *INDEX *v.* 5.] A movement from one predetermined position to another during the indexing of a work-piece.

1962 G. H. DEGROAT *Metalworking Automation* v. 120 (*caption*) Another 'homemade' automated machine is this eight-spindle Borematic with two banks of four spindles each. This one bores, chamfers, and grooves servo valve bodies, finishing two parts per index at 100 pieces per hour. **1964** *Automobile Engineer* LIV. 200/2 After each index, the table is positively locked.

10. *index arm, crank, pin, spindle* (all parts of an index head or used in indexing (sense *2)); **index board,** a type of heavy paper as used for index cards; **index card,** a card for a card-index file; **index centre** *Engin.*, each of the centres (sense 5) that support work for indexing; **index circle** *Engin.*, one of the circles of holes on an index plate; **index figure** *Econ.* = sense 9 e above; **index fossil** = *guide fossil* (*GUIDE *sb.* 13); **index head** *Engin.*, an attachment used with a milling machine or gear-cutting machine that holds the work and enables it to be readily and accurately indexed between successive operations; **index horizon** *Geol.*, a horizon distinguished by certain groups of fossils found within it, or other characteristics which make it an indicator of a particular stratigraphic position; **index map,** a relatively small-scale map which is so marked as to act as an index to a series of more detailed maps; **index number,** (*a*) = sense 9 e above; (*b*) a number in an index; *spec.* the registration number of a motor vehicle; **index plate,** (*a*) in Dict.; (*b*) *Engin.*, a disc that contains regularly spaced holes arranged in concentric circles, which represent different divisions of a circle and determine the possible angular positions of work being indexed; (*c*) a plate bearing the registration number of a motor vehicle; **index register** *Computers*, a register whose contents may be added to or subtracted from the address portion of an instruction before the instruction is executed and then (by means of a second instruction) increased or decreased by a prescribed amount, so enabling the first instruction to be used for a series of identical operations on a series of different operands.

1919 H. THOMPSON *Mod. Engin. Workshop Pract.* xi. 173 By turning this index arm and spindle, motion is given to the worm and worm-wheel. **1937** E. J. LABARRE *Dict. Paper* 160/1 *Index board* or *Bristol* also termed Fourdrinier Bristol is (1) (card-) board resembling a heavy ledger specially adapted for this purpose ...(2) also a size of board $30\frac{1}{2}'' \times 25\frac{1}{2}''$. **1962** F. T. DAY *Introd. to Paper* 116/2 Index boards are made in white and tints with an even and well-finished surface...Stock size is $20\frac{1}{2}$ in. × $35\frac{1}{2}$ in., also cut sizes. **1928** *Funk's Stand. Dict.*, Index card. **1947** *Partisan Rev.* XIV. 469 He placed the books down on the main desk, stuck the envelope of index cards and cross-references under his arm and walked out. **1971** *Jrnl. Gen. Psychol.* LXXXV. 52 Ss were supplied with 3 × 5 inch white unlined index cards. *a* **1884** KNIGHT *Dict. Mech.* Suppl. 434/1 The tool-post can be removed from the sliding table, and index centers, milling vise, or any milling fixture put on, required for milling. **1913** *Lockwood's Dict. Mech. Engin.* (ed. 4) 439 *Index centres*, the head, and the tail stock between which work is carried to be pitched or indexed. **1953** L. E. DOYLE *Metal Machining* ix. 214 Index centers provide means for spacing cuts accurately around a workpiece. **1902** *Internat. Library of Technol.* II. § 15. 23 For convenience of measuring fractional parts of a turn of different values, as $\frac{3}{5}$ of a turn, $\frac{5}{17}$ of a turn,..etc., the index plate is provided with several concentric index circles, each circle having a different number of holes. **1950** J. MARTIN in A. W. Judge *Machine Tools & Operations* III. iii. 142 In ordinary plain indexing, the use of 30 holes in a 42-hole index circle would give 42/30 × 40 = 56 divisions in work. **1905** T. R. SHAW *Machine Tools* vi. 415 Forty revolutions of the index crank are required to make one complete revolution of the spindle. **1964** S. CRAWFORD *Basic Engin. Processes* vi. 172 Indirect Indexing... When using this method of indexing the worm is permanently engaged with the worm wheel, and the workpiece is rotated by means of the index-crank. **1927** Index figure [see *COSTING *vbl. sb.*]. **1930** *Engineering* 3 Jan. 23/3 The index figure of 100 being given to Great Britain in both cases. **1900** C. R. EASTMAN tr. *Zittel's Text-bk. Palaeontol.* I. 4 Having determined the chronological succession of the clastic rocks by means of their superimposition and their characteristic or index-fossils, they may be divided up into still smaller series. **1933** R. C. MOORE *Historical Geol.* xiv. 186 In precise correlation of fossil-bearing strata it is important to recognize and differentiate species that appear only in a given bed, or a short succession of beds, for the occurrence of the same species elsewhere points to equivalence in age of the containing strata. Such fossils may be termed *index fossils*. **1968** J. R. BEERBOWER *Search for Past* (ed. 2) viii. 207 Relatively few groups of organisms provide most of the index fossils. **1902** Index head [see *INDEXING *vbl. sb.* 2]. **1923** R. C. H. HECK *Mechanics of Machinery: Mechanism* v. 234 Indexing is done mostly on the milling machine and on gear cutting machines. For general service a distinct appliance called the index head is used. **1961** L. E. DOYLE et al. *Manuf. Processes* xxiv. 586 A dividing or index head is a mechanical device for dividing a circle accurately into equal parts. **1956** W. EDWARDS in D. L. Linton *Sheffield* 13 No marine horizons are known, but a widespread index-horizon with *Euestheria*, the Low '*Estheria*' Band, overlies a split-off lower leaf of the Silkstone Coal. **1969** BENNISON & WRIGHT *Geol. Hist. Brit. Isles* ix. 224 The marine horizons (called marine bands) are sometimes of great lateral extent and act as vitally important index horizons. **1869** Index-map [in Dict.]. **1932** *Discovery* May 153/1 As large a selection of the recorded information as the smaller scales will carry is issued on the standard scale of one inch, and with further selection and reduction, on the $\frac{1}{4}$ inch scale of the 'index map'. **1875** W. S. JEVONS *Money & Mechanism of Exchange* xxv. 332 A table containing the Total Index Number of prices, or the arithmetical sum of the numbers expressing the ratios of the prices of many commodities to the average prices of the same commodities in the years 1845–50. **1886** *Rep. Brit. Assoc. Adv. Sci. 1885* 871 The index number for the price of each article in 1883 is 1 or 100, according to the use or otherwise of the decimal point. **1887** *Encycl. Brit.* XXII. 466/1 The only matter connected with price which it is necessary to refer to here is the theory of the index number. **1893** *Jrnl. Soc. Arts* 3 Feb. 211/2 This total index number..merged all prices high and low in a single figure. **1900** A. L. BOWLEY *Wages in U.K. in 19th Cent.* xii. 95 (*caption*) Index numbers, showing rate of Change of Wages in the London Building Trades. **1928** J. W. F. ROWE *Wages in Pract. & Theory* 14 Index numbers based on changes in the nominal weekly rates in these industries afford a general guide to the character of wage fluctuations. **1942** [see sense 9 e above]. **1966** *McGraw-Hill Encycl. Sci. & Technol.* III. 233/1 The distribution of coal by rank, geologic age, and district is indicated in Fig. 4. The index numbers, which refer to coal districts, are grouped by continent and country in the accompanying list. **1973** *Daily Tel.* 11 July 6/6 He admitted owning a car which had an index number identical to one Miss Mallalieu had noted. **1905** T. R. SHAW *Machine Tools* vi. 413 If the index pin does not come exactly opposite a hole, there is an adjustment by means of two screws. **1879** *Jrnl. Franklin Inst.* CVIII. 106 The making of practically perfect index plates for gear cutting machines is a different matter from graduating circles for astronomical instruments. **1902** Index plate [see **index circle*]. **1923** R. C. H. HECK *Mechanics of Machinery: Mechanism* v. 235 At the other end of the worm shaft [of the index head] is the index crank C, with handle H and plunger pin Q which can be let into any hole in index plate P. **1950** J. MARTIN in A. W. Judge *Machine Tools & Operations* III. iii. 131 By the use of worm-gearing, the indirect dividing head can space work up to 360 divisions, using standard index plates. **1973** *Daily Tel.* 15 Sept. 2/5 He noticed that the index plates..had been hurriedly removed from another vehicle. **1955** R. K. RICHARDS *Arithmetic Operations in Digital Computers* xi. 348 In these machines..each instruction specifies an index register as well as an operation and an address. For each operation, the number stored in the indicated index register is automatically added to the address, and the sum is then the actual address which is used. **1957, 1970** Index register [see *INDEXING *vbl. sb.* 3]. **1970** O. DOPPING *Computers & Data Processing* vi. 101 In most modern computers address modification and counting is facilitated by index registers. *a* **1884** KNIGHT *Dict. Mech.* Suppl. 494/2 The centers are shown..attached to the index-spindle.

index, *v.* Add: **1.** Also *transf.* (cf. *INDEX *sb.* 5 d). (Further examples.)

1969 C. W. GEAR *Computer Organization & Programming* vi. 242 Each time that a file was completed, the system would index it; that is, its name would be placed in a table of file names..with an indication of where it was physically located. **1969** P. B. JORDAIN *Condensed Computer Encycl.* 242 If the cylinder index becomes too long, a master index may be created to index it.

5. *Engin.* **a.** *trans.* (Cf. quot. 1879 s.v. *INDEX *sb.* 2.) To rotate (work to be machined, or a machine part) through a given aliquot part of a complete turn; to position in accordance with intermittent motion of this kind; hence, to transfer or move from one predetermined position to another in order that different locations may be machined or different operations performed. (Cf. *INDEXING *vbl. sb.* 2.)

1902 [implied in *INDEXING *vbl. sb.* 2]. **1913** [see *index centre* s.v. *INDEX *sb.* 10]. **1936** COLVIN & STANLEY *Drilling & Surfacing Pract.* xxii. 242 Turning the indexing crank without this geared connection indexes the spindle in any desired number of graduations, or parts of a circle. **1951** H. C. TOWN in *Gen. Engin. Workshop Pract.* (ed. 2) iii. 112/2 A spring-loaded plunger..locates the turret in any one of four positions... To index the turret, the ball handle is revolved and the screw lifts the turret clear of the locating plunger, so that it can be rotated to the next..position, and then locked in position. **1953** L. E. DOYLE *Metal Machining* ix. 214 The workpiece is turned by means of the worm and wheel and is indexed by the pin that registers in holes in the face of the worm wheel. *Ibid.* xiii. 298 On a dividing head with a 40 to 1 ratio, one full turn of the crank is needed to index a 40 tooth gear from one tooth space to the next. **1959** *Machinery* XCIV. 511/2 Spacing of the holes axially along the length of the rod is accomplished by indexing the rod vertically in 0·026-in. steps by means of an accurate lead-screw. **1966** *McGraw-Hill Encycl. Sci. & Technol.* VII. 407/2 When the turret [of the lathe] is indexed for successive operations, the saddle acts as a guide for the ram in its strokes to and from the work.

b. *trans.* To produce or obtain (a desired number of divisions or operations) by indexing.

1900 *Machinery* (N.Y.) Nov. 88/2 For indexing prime numbers we must use other than the one-hole basis. **1923** R. C. H. HECK *Mechanics of Machinery: Mechanism* v. 237 The test or criterion of ability to index any number *n* is expressed by putting Eq. (89) into the form $c = 40 \times h/n$. **1936** COLVIN & STANLEY *Drilling & Surfacing Pract.* xxii. 242 The index sector is a great convenience in counting holes to index the required number of divisions. **1961** L. E. DOYLE et al. *Manuf. Processes* xxiv. 587 Several means are available for indexing numbers not obtainable with standard plain indexing, especially large numbers.

c. *intr.* To move or travel during indexing.

1901 *Machinery* (N.Y.) Jan. 147/1 To divide into 91 parts, index forward, on the front side of the plate, six spaces on the 39 circle; then index forward on the back of the plate, 14 spaces on the 49 circle. **1953** L. E. DOYLE *Metal Machining* xiii. 298 The crank must be turned $40 \div 36 = 1\frac{4}{36} = 1\frac{1}{9}$ turns to index from one space to another on the gear. **1966** *McGraw-Hill Encycl. Sci. & Technol.* VII. 409/1 A horizontal, circular table holding the rotating chucks indexes under the vertical spindles with a different operation being performed at each station. **1968** BOOTHROYD & REDFORD *Mechanized Assembly* ii. 8 With continuous transfer the work carriers are moving at constant speed whilst the workheads index backwards and forwards. *Ibid.* 13 Reciprocation of the transfer bar over a distance equal to the spacing of the workheads will cause the work carriers to index between the workheads.

6. *Computers.* To modify (an instruction or its address) by causing the contents of a specified index register to be added to the address before the instruction is executed; to provide with a number that brings about such modification; also, to carry out (a repetitive sequence of operations) by this means.

1962 Y. CHU *Digital Computer Design Fund.* xii. 454 Its contents are used to modify the address of the instruction to be indexed. **1962** R. V. OAKFORD *Introd. Electronic Data Processing Equipment* iii. 89 The counter may be added to the operand address of an instruction to index the repeated performance of an operation on a sequence of registers. **1969** C. W. GEAR *Computer Organization & Programming* ii. 52 We can indicate this in our program writing by using Y to mean the unindexed address Y (that is, the index bits are 0) and by using Y,I to mean

the address Y indexed by index register I. **1972** Bergman & Bruckner *Introd. Computers & Computer Programming* vii. 204 Since this instruction is indexed, its effective operand is 000 (operand) + 251 (contents of index register) = 251 (effective operand and address of XI).

indexation (indeksēi·ʃən). *Econ.* [f. Index *v.* + -ation.] An adjustment in rates of payment in money (e.g. wage-rates, bond prices, etc.) to reflect changes in the value of money by means of an index of such changes. Cf. *index *sb.* 9 e.

1960 *Spectator* 29 Apr. 602 The system of 'indexation' by which wages and prices rose in an officially sponsored spiral. **1972** *Times* 22 July 16/3 If the current rate of inflation continues it will be essential to introduce some form of indexation into the capital gains tax system. **1973** *Daily Tel.* 10 Feb. 31/1 The most likely form of control is by 'indexation' of business leases, which would mean that business rents would be able to rise no faster than the wholesale price index, the cost of living index or such index as the Government cares to regard as a fair indicator of the trend of inflation.

indexed, *ppl. a.* Add: **3.** *Computers.* Modified by or executed by means of an index (sense *8 d).

1957 D. D. McCracken *Digital Computer Programming* viii. 98 Examples are presented which compare an indexed loop with the nonindexed form. **1972** M. D. Freedman *Princ. Digital Computer Operation* ii. 23 An indirect address can be indexed. We will illustrate the concept of an indexed indirect address by an example.

indexible (inde·ksĭb'l, i·ndeks-), *a.* Also **-able.** [f. Index *v.* + -ible, -able.] Capable of being indexed.

1951 *Industrial Equipment News* Dec. 100 (*caption*) Indexable Kennametal tip has 4 cutting edges. **1959** C. V. L. Smith *Electronic Digital Computers* ii. 45 Most type B instructions are 'indexable'. This means that, when any such instruction is executed, the address actually referred to is the address given decreased by the contents of the index register specified by the tag bits. **1966** C. J. Sippl *Computer Dict. & Handbk.* 145/2 *Index register*... Used with indexible instruction addresses during execution. **1971** *Computers & Humanities* VI. 68 By 'indexible' we mean [to denote] a character string that..is likely to be used as a criterion for selective retrieval and/or sorting.

indexical, *a.* **c.** (Later examples.)

a **1914** C. S. Peirce *Coll. Papers* (1932) II. ii. iii. 164 Some indices are more or less detailed directions for what the hearer is to do in order to place himself in direct..connection with the thing meant...Along with such indexical directions of what to do to find the object meant, ought to be classed..*selective* pronouns. *Ibid.*, Other indexical words are prepositions, and prepositional phrases. **1957** *Lingua* VII. i. 27 Within the same vowel system, diaphonic differences are considerable, and appear to be highly indexical, both socially and regionally, in differentiating accents within England. **1970** *English Studies* LI. 276 Beside these indexical features a medium also has aesthetic properties.

indexing, *vbl. sb.* (in Dict. s.v. Index *v.*). Add: **2.** *Engin.* The intermittent rotation of work through aliquot parts of a complete turn in order that some operation may be performed on it at equal angular intervals; also, the movement of work or of a machine part or tool from one predetermined position to another during machining operations.

1902 *Internat. Library of Technol.* II. § 15. 21 Direct indexing is done by the aid of an index plate fastened direct to the index-head spindle; that is, the index plate is moved to obtain the divisions. In indirect indexing, the index plate is normally stationary, and the index-head spindle is rotated by the use of suitable gearing. Indirect indexing is divided into..simple and compound indexing. **1930** *Engineering* 30 May 693/3 During the return stroke, indexing of the worm takes place. **1936** Colvin & Stanley *Drilling & Surfacing Pract.* xxii. 243 The essential thing to remember in all indexing is that the worm wheel on the spindle has 40 teeth and that the worm is a single thread. This means that for every turn of the crank the spindle is rotated $\frac{1}{40}$ of a revolution. **1957** S. E. Rusinoff *Manuf. Processes* (ed. 2) xii. 489 In straight in-line indexing, the work piece moves intermittently from one machining station to the next in a straight line; a group of machine tools is assembled into one machine. **1961** L. E. Doyle et al. *Manuf. Processes* xxiv. 587 Linear indexing may be done on a general-purpose milling machine for such jobs as cutting rack teeth. **1964** S. Crawford *Basic Engin. Processes* vi. 172 When using this method of indexing the number of possible divisions is limited to the three-hole circles available on the front index plate. **1966** *McGraw-Hill Encycl. Sci. & Technol.* VII. 408/1 Turret indexing, actuation of the collet, feeding of stock, and spindle clutch operations are automatic.

3. *Computers.* The automatic increasing or decreasing of the address portion of an instruction, following each execution, by means of an index register, so that a succession of operands is operated on.

1957 D. D. McCracken *Digital Computer Programming* viii. 106 All we really want from the indexing is the sum of the index register contents and the indicated address. *Ibid.* 109 Locations 1200, 1208, 1216, etc., up to 1272 contain ten numbers...Write a program, using indexing, to compute the sum of the squares of these numbers and store it in 1307. **1961** Leeds & Weinberg *Computer Programming Fund.* iv. 101 Many machines have special circuitry designed to facilitate common operations associated with repetition...In mathematics, indexes, or subscripts, are used to keep track of such processes. As an outgrowth of these terms, the words *indexing* and *index arithmetic* have been given to the type of computer instruction which does this job, although indexing may be thought of as a special type of control which also takes over certain tasks of counting from the regular arithmetic instructions. **1970** Hull & Day *Computers & Probl. Solving* 197/2 Index registers have a second important use in what is called automatic address modification or indexing. This occurs when the address of an instruction is modified, just before the instruction is executed, by having the content of an index register added to it.

4. *attrib.* and *Comb.*, as *indexing pin*; **indexing head** = *index head* (*index *sb.* 10).

1901 *Machinery* (N.Y.) Jan. 145/1 A dividing or indexing head...With the tailstock shown..comprises what is commonly known as a pair of index centers. **1944** *Model Engineer* 17 Aug. 157/1 The method..is a modification of the indexing head of a milling machine. **1960** H. W. Porter et al. *Machine Shop* (ed. 2) viii. 294 The indexing head..comes equipped with three index plates. **1964** S. Crawford *Basic Engin. Processes* v. 117 A spring-loaded indexing-pin in the face of the compound-slide accurately locates the post in any one of the four positions.

indfine (i·ndfinĭ). *Irish Hist.* Also **indfhine, innfine.** [O.Ir. (mod.Ir. *innfhine*) f. *ind* end + *fine* family, Fine *sb.*[2]] One of the four branches of the Irish clan structure comprising the men most distantly related to the chief. Cf. *geilfine, *iarfine.

The fourth branch is the *derbfine* (not in Dict.).

1875 H. S. Maine *Lect. Early Hist. Inst.* 209 The eldest member of the Iarfine moved into the Indfine; and the eldest member of the Indfine passed out of the organisation altogether. **1893** P. W. Joyce *Short Hist. Ireland* i. ix. 70 A *Gelfine* organisation when complete consisted of seventeen men all related to each other:..the *gelfine* group..consisting of five; the *derfine*, the *iarfine*, and the *innfine*, of four each. **1921, 1967** [see *iarfine].

India. Add: **6.** *India calico, carpet, cotton* (example), *muslin* (examples), *shawl, silk* (examples); **India Office** (earlier examples); **India tag,** a type of tag which is used to fasten papers together and consists of a cord with a small metal bar at either end.

1805 *Times* 7 Nov. 1/1 Stout India calico, full ell-wide. *c* **1702** C. Fiennes *Journeys* (1947) 346 A pladd bed lined with Indian callicoe and an India carpet on the bed. **1931** A. U. Dilley *Oriental Rugs & Carpets* Pl. 32 (*caption*) India Carpets of Seventeenth Century from the Palace of the Maharaja at Jaipur. **1881** C. C. Harrison *Woman's Handiwork* iii. 176 Scarves of India cotton worked in tarnished gold. **1796** M. Edgeworth *Parent's Assistant* (ed. 2) II. 167 Oh, Miss Eden, your beautiful India muslin!—take care of the chimney sweeper. **1852** E. Twisleton *Let.* 10 July (1928) ii. 27, I intend to appear in my India muslin. **1929** D. H. Lawrence *Pansies* 39 A yard of India muslin is alive with Hindu life. **1869** *Bradshaw's Railway Manual* XXI. 394 Government Director of the Indian Railway Companies, India Office, Whitehall, S.W. **1880** E. W. Hamilton *Diary* 24 Apr. (1972) I. 2 Cabinet-making has been going on all day... Lord Hartington [is to go] to the India Office. **1822** D. Wordsworth *Jrnl.* 23 Sept. (1941) II. 374 The ladies.. wore gorgeously embroidered India shawls. **1837** Dickens *Mudfog Papers* (1880) 159 His view of the ladies within being obstructed by the India shawls. **1756** B. Franklin *Writings* (1905) III. 294 When you incline to buy.. India silks. **1816** Scott *Antiq.* III. vii. 142 His India silk handkerchief. **1881** C. C. Harrison *Woman's Handiwork* i. 48 The India silks manufactured for Mr. Louis Tiffany, by a well-known firm in Connecticut, from cocoons imported by themselves. **1912** *List Articles Authorised to be Supplied by H.M.S.O.*, Tags, Treasury (Insertion), Tags, India (cross-bar). **1963** R. L. Collison *Mod. Business Filing & Archives* ii. 47 The documents are then secured to the file by what is known as a Treasury or India tag— i.e. a cord with a metal tag at each end.

indialite (i·ndiălait). *Min.* [f. India + -lite.] The hexagonal dimorph of cordierite.

1954 Miyashiro & Iiyama in *Proc. Japan Acad.* XXX. 746 The present paper is concerned with the finding of a new hexagonal mineral from Bokaro coalfield, India, $(Mg, Fe^{+2})_2Al_4Si_5O_{18}$ in composition, polymorphic with cordierite. This mineral has hitherto been identified as cordierite; but..it is a distinct species, to which the name 'indialite' is proposed. **1972** M. H. Battey *Mineral. for Students* 254/1 Indialite, a dimorph of cordierite, is isostructural with beryl.

Indian, *a.* and *sb.* Add: **A.** *adj.* **1. b.** (Further examples.)

c **1702** Indian calico [see *India carpet*]. **1718** J. Steuart *Letter-Bk.* (1915) 64, I do not mean you should goe to the expense of bying Indian chints. *c* **1793** Jane Austen *Volume First* (1933) 9 Your sentiments so nobly expressed on the different excellencies of Indian & English Muslins. **1794** A. Young *Trav. France* (ed. 2) I. xix. 548 They print a great quantity of Indian callicoes. **1798** Indian shawl [see Shawl *sb.* 2]. **1830** M. Edgeworth *Let.* 13 Dec. (1971) 449, I have..laid out fifteen guineas on— an Indian shawl. **1851** J. F. Royle *On Culture & Commerce of Cotton in India* i. 22 Indian cotton is well known to have certain good qualities of its own. **1863** A. J. Munby *Diary* 12 May in D. Hudson *Munby* (1972) 160 Curtains of old Indian chintz. **1873** C. M. Yonge *Pillars of House* IV. xlii. 218 Cherry cleared her large sofa, and covered him up with her Indian silk quilt. **1879** *Queen* 1 Mar. (Advt.), An entirely new under garment successfully introduced in Silk, Merino, Gauze Merino, and Indian Gauze. **1898** A. Bennett *Man From North* xxviii. 241 Its square of Indian carpet over Indian matting. **1910** *Encycl. Brit.* VII. 258/1 The Indian cottons are usually of short staple. **1937** J. Laver *Taste & Fashion* xii. 178 A combination chemise and knickers of Indian gauze. **1938** *Decorative Art* 83 A modern Indian rug in green. **1971** *Habitat Catal.* 76/2 Indian cotton durries..simple tough cotton rugs. **1974** 'G. Black' *Golden Cockatrice* xi. 190 Blood had reached an Indian rug.

2. (Further examples.) *spec.* In reference to the endurance of tortures and hardship by North American Indians.

1737 J. Wesley *Let.* 22 July (1931) I. 225 When..He shall have chosen one or more to magnify Him,..not with a stoical or Indian indifference, but blessing and praying for their murderers. **1817** Coleridge *Biogr. Lit.* I. x. 185 Three week's truly Indian perseverance in tracking us. **1822** Wordsworth *Eccl. Sk.* 67 The shrouded Body, to the Soul's command, Answering with more than Indian fortitude. **1916** C. A. Eastman *From Deep Woods to Civilization* iii. 32 He took out his Bible and hymn-book printed in the Indian tongue. **1931** F. J. Stimson *My United States* i. 4 Indian camps were not unusual in the vacant lots outlying Dubuque. **1934** *Beaver* June 9 When word came that they had landed, I left the living room for the Indian shop. **1940** W. Faulkner *Hamlet* ii. 98 A man who was not thin so much as actually gaunt, with straight black hair..and high Indian cheekbones. **1942** *Chicago Tribune* 24 Nov. 12/3 This stone marks the site of an ancient Indian village and chipping station. **1966** *Oxf. Compan. Amer. Hist.* 405/2 Since Indian tribes acted as buffer states between French and British colonies and were invaluable allies in time of war, colonial governors always sought to make treaties of friendship with the Indians. **1969** *Islander* (Victoria, B.C.) 5 Oct. 10/3 An Indian express was sent ahead to Fort Colville. **1970** D. Brown *Bury my Heart at Wounded Knee* ii. 15 Many of the Mexicans had Indian blood. **1971** *Times* 30 Sept. 12/3 There has been a resurgence of interest in the Indians.. partly (among the young) to embrace aspects of Indian life on behalf of the counter-culture. **1971** *Times* 15 Oct. 14/4 Dr. Robert Euler..has directed salvage archeology at prehistoric Indian sites in the area to be mined. **1973** *Freedomways* XIII. 81 The book is rich with examples of Indian culture and social life as practiced by the Oglala.

4. a. Indian antelope = *black-buck* (*black *a.* 19); **Indian elephant,** the smaller of the two existing species of elephant, *Elephas maximus*; **Indian English,** the form of English used by inhabitants of India for whom English is not a native language; cf. *babu; **Indian hay** *U.S. slang*, marijuana; **Indian head** (see quot. 1957[2]); **Indian lotus,** an aquatic plant, *Nelumbo nucifera*, native to Asia, and bearing fragrant white or pink flowers; also called Egyptian or sacred lotus; **Indian tea,** tea grown in India or Sri Lanka, especially in Assam and the Darjeeling district; cf. sense 4 b below; **Indian work,** Indian handicraft, *spec.* drawn-thread work on muslin.

1888 Indian Antilope [see *black-buck* (*black *a.* 19)]. **1964** E. P. Walker et al. *Mammals of World* II. 1457/1 Blackbucks, Indian Antelopes... This animal occasionally lives in herds of several hundred members. **1607** Topsell *Four-f. Beasts* 192 The Indian Elephants are greatest, strongest, and tallest. **1965** D. Morris *Mammals* 338 Smaller than the African Elephant, the bull Indian Elephant rarely reaches 10 feet high at the shoulder. **1907** G. C. Whitworth (*title*) Indian English: an examination of the errors of idiom made by Indians in writing English. **1934** R. C. Goffin in *S.P.E. Tract* xli. 31 We have touched on the preference of Indian English for the archaic in vocabulary and phrase. **1971** *Shankar's Weekly* (Delhi) 4 Apr. 22/3 The best of Indian English et al you gave. **1939** *Jrnl. Amer. Med. Assoc.* 1 July 4/1 In America the name marihuana..is used. It has numerous picturesque names, such as muggles, reefers, Mary Warner, Indian hay, the weed and tea. **1969** *Sci. Amer.* Dec. 17 In the U.S. it [*sc.* marijuana is variously called the weed, stuff, Indian hay,..and other names. **1911** *Daily Colonist* (Victoria, B.C.) 9 Apr. 24/2 New Wash Dress Materials in Muslins..Indian head and Linen Suitings. **1957** M. McCarthy *Memories Catholic Girlhood* vi. 117 Blue Indianhead 20 yds. **1957** M. B. Picken *Fashion Dict.* 183/1 *Indian head*, trade name for sturdy, firm, cotton material of linen-weave, made in many lovely colors. Used for work, play, and sports clothing and for home furnishings. **1901** L. H. Bailey *Cycl. Amer. Hort.* III. 1065/1 (*caption*) The Indian Lotus, Nelumbium speciosum of the trade, but properly Nelumbo nucifera. **1963** W. Blunt *Of Flowers & Village* 104 The seeds of the Indian Lotus 'rattle in their sockets like teeth in the jawbone of a skull'. **1884** E. Money *Tea Controversy* (ed. 2) 10 A pound of Indian Tea of any grade will give considerably more infusions of a like strength than a similar pound of Chinese. **1893** *Illustr. London News* 11 Nov. 618/2 Indian tea shipping warehouses. *c* **1938** *Fortnum & Mason Price List* 6 State whether China or Indian Tea is preferred. **1960** *Good Housek. Cookery Bk.* 451/2 Household teas,.. are usually full-flavoured blended Indian teas. **1969** *Times* 13 Oct. (Indian Suppl.) p. x (Advt.), Darjeeling, Assam, Nilgiris. Three of the greatest names in Indian Teas. **1865** F. B. Palliser *Hist. Lace* xxi. 250 There is also a good specimen of that description of drawn muslin lace, commonly known under the name of 'Indian work', but which appears to have been made in various manners. **1882** Caulfeild & Saward *Dict. Needlework* 157/2 Fig. 299 is of a later description of Drawn Work, and would be known as Indian Work, as its foundation is muslin. **1900** E. Jackson *Hist. Hand-Made Lace* 150 Drawn-work.. was known all over Europe as Hamburg Point, Indian work (when executed in muslin). **1920** A. K. Arthur *Embroidery Bk.* ix. 90 Some of the elaborately worked pieces of Indian and Persian work, where tinsel braids are freely employed, are things to marvel at.

b. Indian agent (see *agent *sb.* 4 b); **In-**

dian apple (examples); **Indian awl** (see quot. 1941); **Indian bean** (examples); **Indian blanket,** orig. a blanket made by or for N. Amer. Indians, often used as a cloak; now also a blanket made in imitation of this; **Indian bureau** (or **Bureau**), in N. and S. America, a bureau concerned with the affairs of American Indians; *spec.* in the U.S., the Bureau of Indian Affairs; **Indian currant** = *coral-berry* (CORAL *sb.*[1] 9); **Indian devil,** a N. American name for either the wolverine or the cougar; **Indian file** (earlier and later examples); **Indian gift, giver** (later examples); so **Indian giving; Indian mound** [MOUND *sb.*[3] 4 e], in N. America, a mound or earthwork erected in former times by Indians as a burial place, fortification, etc.; **Indian paint,** a N. American perennial herb with reddish sap and thick red-tinted roots; **Indian paint-brush,** a herbaceous plant of the genus *Castilleja*; **Indian path** (earlier and later examples); **Indian pear** *N. Amer.*, a tree or shrub of the genus *Amelanchier,* or its edible fruit, a fleshy red or purple berry; **Indian pipe** (examples); also **Indian pipe-stem; Indian pony,** a type of pony descended from horses originally brought to America by Spanish colonists; **Indian reservation, reserve** (see RESERVATION 3 b, RESERVE *sb.* 5 b); **Indian rice:** substitute for def.: a North American aquatic grass, *Zizania aquatica,* or one of several similar plants resembling rice; add examples; **Indian sign(s),** a (usually faint) track or trail, etc., that reveals the presence of Indians; also a smoke-signal or other signal used by Indians; phr. *to put* (or *have*) *the Indian sign on* (someone) (see quot. 1944); **Indian tea,** any one of several N. American plants whose leaves are used to make a drink resembling tea; = *Labrador tea*; **Indian tobacco** (earlier and later examples); also applied to other plants; **Indian turnip** (earlier and later examples).

1766 W. JOHNSON *Let.* 23 Jan. in R. Rogers *Jrnls.* (1883) 216 As Commandant and Indian Agent, it will be extremely difficult to check him. **1816, 1901** [see *AGENT *sb.* 4 b]. **1974** A. MACLEAN *Breakheart Pass* iii. 44, I asked the Governor here to appoint me Indian agent for the territory; I settle differences..allocate reservations, try and stop the traffic in guns and whisky. **1847** F. PARKMAN in *Knickerbocker* XXIX. 310 The rich flowers of the Indian-apple were there in profusion. **1931** W. N. CLUTE *Common Names of Plants* 35 The May-apple (*Podophyllum peltatum*) was known to the settlers as Indian apple, but it is really a berry. **1821** G. SIMPSON *Jrnl. Occurrences in Athabasca Dept.* (1938) 142 Awls, Indian, doz. **1922** *Beaver* July 10/2 It requires but three tools to build a canoe: an axe, a 'crooked knife', and a square or Indian awl. **1941** *Beaver* Sept. 38 *Indian awl,* a square two-ended awl for bark, leather or wood. **1843** J. TORREY *Flora N.Y.* II. 25 Catalpa. Indian Bean...About habitations...The Catalpa is more esteemed for ornament than for use. **1933** [see *cigar-tree*]. **1969** T. H. EVERETT *Living Trees of World* 298/2 The Indian-bean has many more flowers in each cluster than the Western catalpa. **1764** in *New Jersey Archives* (1902) 1st Ser. XXIV. 350 There are a blue Great Coat, and an Indian Blanket missing. **1782** *Quebec Gaz.* 19 Dec. 4/1 For Sale..A Large assortment..Indian blanket Rugs. **1807** *Salmagundi* 13 Feb. 49 The shawl..thrown over one shoulder, like an Indian blanket. **1927** W. CATHER *Death comes for Archbishop* I. iii. 31 The earth floor was covered with thick Indian blankets; two blankets, very old, and beautiful in design and colour, were hung on the walls like tapestries. **1962** J. BRAINE *Life at Top* xxvi. 278 There's a cigarette burn in my Indian blanket. **1966** *Islander* (Victoria, B.C.) 27 Feb. 7/1 We smelled perfume and talcum from many Indian blankets. **1831** C. ATWATER *Remarks Tour to Prairie du Chien* 142 Taking advantage of frauds committed on the Indians, by persons connected with the Indian bureau, the Factory system gave place to the present system. **1922** D. H. LAWRENCE *Phoenix II* (1968) 239 The Indian Bureau is supposed to do the cherishing. **1972** *Buenos Aires Herald* 2 Feb. 7/1 Officials of Brazil's Indian Bureau here believe that numerous small tribes of Indians living along the projected new highway have never seen an outsider. **1785** H. MARSHALL *Arbustrum Amer.* 82 Lonicera Symphoricarpos. Indian Currants, or St. Peter's Wort. This hath a shrubby stalk, which rises from four to five feet high. **1806** LEWIS & CLARK *Orig. Jrnls. Lewis & Clark Expedition* (1905) V. 327 Deep purple berry or the large Cherry of the Current Species which is common... The engagees call it the Indian Current. **1866** [see CURRANT 3]. **1948** *South Sierran* Feb. 2/2 'Indian currant' was also in bloom. **1851** J. S. SPRINGER *Forest Life & Forest Trees* 66 A dangerous specimen of the feline species, known by woodsmen as the 'Indian devil', had prowled from time immemorial. **1901** W. M. THOMPSON *In Maine Woods* 60 The cougar, or 'Indian devil', is sometimes seen. **1937** H. H. LANGTON in P. Campbell *Trav. Interior Parts N. Amer.* 71 The Wolverine..has long been extinct in the province [*sc.* Nova Scotia], where it is remembered as the 'Injun devil'. **1965** *Wildlife Rev.* (Victoria, B.C.) Mar. 19 Cougars, also known as panthers, pumas, catamounts, mountain lions, and Indian devils, are large unspotted cats. **1758** in *Essex Inst. Hist. Coll.* (1881) XVIII. 179 They march'd in Indian file. **1873** G. M. GRANT *Ocean to Ocean* 189 As the line of march had to be in Indian file, we soon exchanged the undemonstrative 'good-bye' with him. **1922** *Beaver* Sept. 6/2 The long camp fire gave sufficient light to see the dancers, who followed one another in Indian file. **1971** *Ceylon Times Weekender* (Colombo) 3 Oct. 5/5 As the family came trotting along towards the crocodile in Indian file, the lean, rangy patriach was in the lead. **1879** B. F. TAYLOR *Summer-Savory* xxvi. 207 She is glad it [*sc.* the check] is an 'Indian gift', that the conductor did not present it to her outright. **1892** H. C. BOLTON in *Jrnl. Amer. Folk-Lore* V. 68 If an American child, who has made a small gift to a playmate is indiscreet enough to ask that the gift be returned, he (or she) is immediately accused of being an Indian-giver, or, as it is commonly pronounced Injun-giver. **1904** *N.Y. Herald* 10 Sept. 5 Later he took the position of the 'Indian giver' and wanted the money back. **1939** *Time* 23 Oct. 4/1 Call us Indian-giver. **1965** R. MANHEIM tr. *Grass's Dog Yrs.* I. 12 'You threw my knife.' 'It was my knife. Don't be an Indian giver.' **1971** M. MCCARTHY *Birds of America* 29 He wanted the little violin which Hans, an Indian giver, took back to the store. **1837** W. IRVING *Capt. Bonneville* II. vi. 71 His experience in what is proverbially called 'Indian giving' made him aware that a parting pledge was necessary on his own part. **1962** B. SPOCK *Problems of Parents* (1968) II. 50 The one-year-old who has yelled bloody murder during his physical examination may, ten minutes later..sweetly hand him a toy and then take it back. This latter trick may look like Indian giving. **1791** in *Mass. Hist. Soc. Coll.* (1794) 1st Ser. III. 24 There is an Indian mound, the base of which is about three hundred paces round, and rises in a conic form about one hundred feet. **1869** B. HARTE *Luck of Roaring Camp* 186 Cattle and sheep are gathered on Indian Mounds waiting the fate of their companions whose carcases drift by us. **1949** *Illinois State Archaeol. Soc. Jrnl.* Jan. 7/2 When the term, 'Indian Mound', is mentioned, one naturally thinks of a large ceremonial Mound which covers one to three acres of ground and is perhaps five or ten or even 20 feet in height. **1950** *Caribbean Q.* II. II. 24 Scientific excavation of the so-called Indian Mounds has brought to light masses of..pottery ware, celts. **1803** A. F. M. WILLICH *Domestic Encycl.* (Amer. ed.) IV. 442/1 Sanguinaria Canadensis, called commonly *Puccoon,* blood-wort, red-root, Indian paint, turmeric. **1931** W. N. CLUTE *Common Names of Plants* 26 The bloodroot..is also called puccoon-root, Indian paint. **1892** *Jrnl. Amer. Folk-Lore* V. 101 *Castilleia coccinea*..Indian paint-brush. **1923** 'B. M. BOWER' *Parowan Bonanza* ii. 21 He plucked a bright red 'Indian paint brush' from beside a rock. **1959** *Calgary Herald* 31 July 10/1 There is no finer feature of the autumn landscape in Alberta..than the roadside aster,..Indian paint brush and wild geranium. **1969** *Islander* (Victoria, B.C.) 5 Oct. 7/1 Sometimes the red-orange of the Indian paintbrush was like a blanket spread beneath the pines. **1634** W. WOOD *New Englands Prospect* II. vii. 71 An Indian path (which seldome is broader than a Cart's rutte). **1793** W. BENTLEY *Diary* 26 Aug. (1907) II. 51 An Indian path was visible through the town from the N.W. corner. **1794** A. THOMAS *Newfoundland Jrnl.* (1968) iv. 63, I shall resume my journey..endeavouring as well as I can to give you an idea of an Indian Path in Newfoundland. **1939** G. H. EVANS *Pigwacket* 3 To the consideration of this important gateway, through which the old Indian path entered Pigwacket, further attention will be directed. **1796** *Descr. Prince Edward Island* 5 A fruit in this Island, called the Indian Pear, is very delicious. **1856** W. E. CORMACK *Narr. Journey across Newfoundland* (1874) 19 On the skirts of the forest, and of the marshes, are found.. Indian pear [etc.]. **1873** G. M. GRANT *Ocean to Ocean* 156 The sasketoon are simply what are known in Nova Scotia as 'Indian pears'. **1956** T. H. RADDALL *Wings of Night* 12 Then came the long reach of scrub woods, wire birch and poplar mostly, with blossoming clumps of Indian pear, like patches of snow on the slopes. **1822** A. EATON *Man. Bot.* (ed. 3) 357 *Monotropa uniflora,* birds nest, indian-pipe. **1884** 'C. E. CRADDOCK' *In Tennessee Mts.* I. 60 The ashy Indian pipes silvered the roots of the trees. **1962** *Maclean's Mag.* 10 Mar. 17/1 It was a palely sprouting parasite called Indian pipe, or corpse plant, which extrudes almost overnight from rotting compost and lives only briefly. **1870** *Amer. Naturalist* III. 6 The Indian Pipestem will be found rarely in low woods. **1758** P. STEVENS *Jrnl.* 13 July in N. D. Mereness *Trav. Amer. Colonies* (1916) 314 He is given us for an Indian pony in his place. **1865** *Nor'Wester* (Red River Settlement) 21 Sept. 2/3 Our hardy Indian ponies found many purchasers at good prices. **1869** [see *BRONCO a]. **1965** D. M. GOODALL *Horses of World* 211 The descendants of these [Spanish] horses, known as Mustangs, migrated through Mexico to the United States, scattering far west and north-west. Some were captured by the Indians and subsequently became Indian ponies. **1819** D. THOMAS *Trav. Western Country* 12 This tract is an Indian reservation. **1949** *Kansas Hist. Q.* Feb. 2 They learned that Council Grove was situated on an Indian reservation and was not available for settlement. **1954** H. EVANS *Mist on River* 43 She said that this fall or next..she would try to get him into an Indian reservation school. **1792** in *Rep. Bureau Arch. Ontario* (1905) III. 215 Every farm of good land, in that part of the Country, is comprehended within the Indian reserve. **1818** F. HALL *Trav. Canada & U.S.* 131 The river Credit is an Indian reserve, well stocked with salmon. *a* **1843** [see RESERVE *sb.* 5 b *attrib.*]. **1958** *Edmonton* (Alberta) *Jrnl.* 18 June 31/7 Conditions on the two Indian reserves have improved greatly. **1822** *Minutes of Council, N. Dept. of Rupert's Land,* in *Publ. Hudson's Bay Rec. Soc.* (1940) III. 22 All the Indian rice and corn he may collect. **1872** SCHELE DE VERE *Americanisms* 409 The Indians of the Northern regions ..depend largely upon..this perennial plant, from whence it is also known as Indian rice. **1933** E. C. JAEGER *California Deserts* xiii. 165 Indian rice (*Oryzopsis hymenoides*) is frequent in porous soils, particularly on blown sand. **1805** P. GASS *Jrnl.* 30 May (1807) 93 We see a great many fresh Indian tracks or signs as we pass along. **1854** J. R. BARTLETT *Pers. Narr. Explor. Texas* I. iv. 95 They had seen 'Indian sign', and pointed out..the well-known Indian signal of a puff of smoke suddenly rising from the earth. **1866** *Rep. Indian Affairs* (U.S.) 188 On the 19th, proceeding again to the Malheur river, but found no fresh Indian signs. **1873** J. H. BEADLE *Undevel. West* xxxiv. 738, I rode around our camp, a circle of about six miles, looking for Indian signs. **1910** R. GRAU *Business Man in Amusement World* 97 He has also been careful to protect himself against 'the Indian Sign'. **1912** *McClure's Mag.* XXXIX. 235/1 He sure put the Indian sign on Tommy Ryan that time. **1916** *Boy Scouts' Year Bk.* (N.Y.) 93/2 He had proved that the Indian sign wasn't infallible... After all, then, the Indian sign was a kind of superstition. *a* **1918** G. STUART *40 Yrs. on Frontier* (1925) I. 115 Plenty of Indian signs, saw signal fires on the mountains to westward. **1929** *Bookman* Sept. 62/2 Owen Johnson always has had what is known as the 'Indian Sign' on me. I never won a bet from him and never will. **1944** R. F. ADAMS *Western Words* (1945) 83/1 To put the Indian sign on someone meant to hex or curse him with some kind of witchcraft, also to get him where you want him. **1948** V. PALMER *Golconda* x. 79 What silly notions about ourselves we can coddle! I believe the old boy's put the Indian sign on you, Neda. **1973** *Listener* 5 June 6/3 We were riding very high in terms of our legislative programme. We had the Indian sign on the Congress, so to speak. **1709** J. LAWSON *New Voy. Carolina* 91 This plant [*sc.* Yaupon] is the Indian Tea, us'd and approv'd by all the Savages on the Coast of Carolina. **1771** G. CARTWRIGHT *Jrnl.* 6 Mar. (1792) I. 100 As I judged, that Indian tea was of the same nature with the herbs which are recommended by that author [*sc.* Dr. Brookes], I had some gathered from under the snow in the woods, and gave her a pint of the strong infusion of that plant sweetened with sugar. **1794** A. THOMAS *Newfoundland Jrnl.* (1968) iv. 71, I breakfasted with Mrs Harty on Indian Tea, the growth of Newfoundland. **1925** A. HEMING *Living Forest* 131 The old woodsman infused some of the Indian tea he had gathered. **1938** *Beaver* June 23/1 Light springing feet of youths and maidens would make little impression on the tough bushes of Indian Tea. *a* **1618** Indian tobacco [in Dict., sense 2]. **1872** SCHELE DE VERE *Americanisms* 415 Indian Tobacco (*Lobelia inflata*), occasionally used instead of tobacco by virtue of its acrid leaves. **1950** C. P. LYONS *Milestones on Mighty Fraser* 89 Indian tobacco..was used by the Thompson Indians from time immemorial. **1806** *Deb. Congress U.S.* 19 Feb. 1142 Indian turnip, wild carrot, wild onion. **1856** [see TURNIP *sb.* 2 b]. **1873** J. MILLER *Life amongst Modocs* x. 128 He [*sc.* winter] cut down the banners of the spring that night, lamb-tongue, Indian turnip and catella. **1894** [see TURNIP *sb.* 2 b]. **1911** G. S. PORTER *Harvester* xix. 459 He..brought her samples of ginger leaves, Indian hemp, queen-of-the-meadow, cone-flower, burdock, baneberry, Indian turnip, [etc.]. **1949** *Nature Mag.* Apr. 178 A few of these, like Indian turnip or jack-in-the-pulpit, cowslip and milkweed, may be considered mildly inedible.

c. Chess. (i) *Indian problem* (see quots. 1878). Also *ellipt.*

1846 *Chess Player's Chron.* 96 We now publish the names of those amateurs who have sent us the correct solution of our Indian problem. **1878** S. LOYD *Chess Strategy* 96 Its entire difficulty consists in the skill with which the fact of its being an *Indian* is concealed. *Ibid.* 97 The theme of the Indian problem culminates in a stale-mating position, which has been anticipated by preparing an ambush for allowing the defence a move that may expose him to a discovered mate. *Ibid.* 100 The old Indian problem... The leading feature of the problem does not consist in the discovered check, but in the unexpected and apparently useless withdrawal of the two pieces to a remote quarter of the board, the one intersecting the protection of the other so as to allow the adverse King a move. **1913** A. C. WHITE *Sam Loyd* 287 Two of Loyd's best Indians are shown in Nos. 402 and 403.

(ii) Used to denote openings in which a player seeks to control the centre of the board with knights, fianchettoed bishops, etc., rather than by advancing his centre pawns. Now esp. *Indian defence,* where Black plays thus; also *ellipt.*

King's (or *Queen's*) *Indian defence*: an Indian defence in which Black's king's (or queen's) bishop is fianchettoed. See also *NIMZO-INDIAN *a.*

1896 H. F. CHESHIRE *Hastings Chess Tournament 1895* 369 Openings,..Hungarian,..Indian,..King's Gambits. **1899** E. E. CUNNINGTON *Mod. Chess Primer* ix. 181 Or Black may play the 'Indian Defence'. **1925** *Chess Budget* I. 117/2 A third case was in a small club tournament with the new form of Indian defence. **1929** *Chess Amateur* XXIII. 202/1 Indian Defence. Played recently in the semi-final of the Three Counties' Championship Tournament. **1942** H. GOLOMBEK *50 Great Games Mod. Chess* 67/1 (*heading*) Queen's Pawn, Queen's Indian Defence. **1950** *Hoyle's Games Modernized* (ed. 20) IV. 410 The Indian Defences (those in which Black does not play P–Q4 at an early stage). *Ibid.* 411 The *Catalan system*—a modern combination of the King's Indian and Queen's gambit. **1958** *Listener* 13 Nov. 803/3 If you favour complications, you are most likely to be suited by the queen's pawn opening and by the Sicilian and King's Indian Defences. **1964** I. A. HOROWITZ *Chess Openings* 638 King's Indian Defense... Introduced in the Leipzig tournament of 1879.

B. *sb.* **1.** Delete 'Now *rare*' and add examples in the sense of (before 1947) a native or inhabitant of the Indian sub-continent and (after 1947) of the Republic of India.

1885 H. J. S. COTTON *New India* ii. 11 The attitude of Englishmen to Indians is not of a character to inspire confidence. **1896** in *Macm. Mag.* Sept. (1906) 820 Purely Indian-raised troops. **1912** E. M. FORSTER *Let.* 25 Dec. in *Hill of Devi* (1953) 17 In the evening we went to the Tennis Club—all Indians—and drove back through the tidy little town. **1923** *Glasgow Herald* 20 Feb. 6 The possible future absorption by Indians of the bulk of Indian Army commissions and military appointments. **1946** J. H. HUTTON *Caste in India* iii. 27 It is the cultivated and educated Bengali who has been probably more than any other Indian the interpreter of the Englishman to the Indian. **1954** *Chambers's Encycl. World Survey* 210/1 Indians have long shown a genuine flair for the parliamentary system of government. **1965** N. C. CHAUDHURI

Continent of Circe iv. 89 No sensible Indian will have a moment's hesitation in saying which is preferable. **1971** M. EDWARDES *Nehru* xx. 328 The machinery that was to move Lal Bahadur Shastri, a very different sort of Indian, into the office of Prime Minister had already been put in gear.

c. One of the indigenous inhabitants of the Philippine Islands; applied esp. to one who has been converted to Christianity.

1697 W. DAMPIER *New Voy. round World* xi. 307 He fell in with these Philippine Islands, and anchored at Luconia; where he warr'd with the native Indians, to bring them in obedience to his master the king of Spain. **1817** J. MCLEOD *Narr. Voy. H.M.S. Alceste Yellow Sea* 171 The religion of the Indians under the immediate control of the Spaniards is Christianity; but at Mindanao and the other islands..it is said to be a mixture of Mahomedanism with ..Pagan rites. **1885** *Encycl. Brit.* XVIII. 752/1 Cigars they [*sc.* the Negritos of the Philippines] often smoke with the burning end between the teeth—a practice occasionally observed among the civilized Indians. **1905** F. W. ATKINSON *Philippine Islands* x. 264 The Spaniards used the term Indian in speaking collectively of these seven Christian tribes and the word Filipino in speaking of any one born in the Islands without distinction as to religious belief. **1967** D. MANNIX *Sporting Chance* ii. 35 This outfit was made by the Zubanoan Indians who live in the mountains of Mindanao. **1968** R. NELSON *Philippines* ii. 31 The majority of the people, called Indians by the Spanish, had an olive complexion.

† **d.** A member of one of the indigenous peoples of Australia and New Zealand. *Obs.*

1769 J. BANKS *Jrnl.* 21 Oct. (1896) 191 We applied to our friends the Indians [*sc.* Maoris] for a passage in one of their canoes. **1770** *Ibid.* 28 Apr. 264 During this time, a few of the Indians [*sc.* Australian Aboriginals]..remained on the rocks opposite the ship, threatening and menacing with their pikes and swords. **1825** B. FIELD *Geogr. Mem. New South Wales* 437 Some of the Indians have also seriously applied to be allowed convict-labourers..till the maize and cabbage that have been planted to their hands are fit to gather. **1830** A. F. GARDINER *Friend of Australia* xiii. 244 It is the observation of some writers, that the system pursued in Australia for educating the children of the Indians, is not attended with success.

2. (Later examples.) Also, examples of *American Indian.* Cf. *AMERIND, AMERINDIAN *sbs.*

1846 J. HALL *Wilderness & War Path* 1 The life of the American Indian is not so destitute of the interest created by variety of incident, as might be supposed by a casual observation of the habits of this singular race. **1926** S. G. INMAN *Probl. in Pan Americanism* ii. 68 The visitor to South America will see nothing more pitiful than the Indians of Peru and Bolivia, descendants of great civilizations now forgotten. **1931** F. J. STIMSON *My United States* xviii. 187 Harvard College was founded in 1636 to teach the Puritans to be preachers and to teach the Indians to be Christians. **1933** *Recent Social Trends in U.S.* (President's Res. Comm. Social Trends) I. xi. 590 Doubts as to the educability of the Indian have been dispelled by the increasing number of those creditably completing college courses and by the measures of mental tests which indicate intelligence of a high rank. **1962** *Canada Month* May 29 North American Indians number more than 500,000: 180,000 in Canada, more than half of whom live in B.C., Saskatchewan, and Ontario, and 350,000 in the U.S. **1963** *Amer. Speech* XXXVIII. 271 The military-like terms might have been introduced by American Indians who went to Haskell after completing their compulsory military service. **1965** J. BALDWIN in *Penguin Dict. Mod. Quots.* (1971) 10/2 It is a great shock at the age of five or six to find that in a world of Gary Coopers you are the Indian. **1965** *Globe & Mail* (Toronto) 26 May 3/4 Those whose names are in a register kept by the federal Indian Affairs Branch are officially Indians; others are not... The Indians have special rights. **1971** D. HEFFRON *Nice Fire & Some Moonpennies* i. 10 Hey ya know, you look like a real Indian with that head-band, you know that? **1971** *Times* 23 Aug. 10/3 In every measurable way Indians are at the bottom of the great American pile. *Ibid.* 10/6 The modern plight of the American Indian is almost entirely traceable to treachery of the white man.

b. *Red Indian* (later examples).

Still used commonly outside N. Amer. but rarely in the U.S.A. and Canada. The *Dict. of Canadianisms* (1967) labels the use 'erroneous' exc. in respect of the extinct Beothuk people in Newfoundland. The usual term in N. Amer. is 'Indian'.

1891 *Trans. R. Soc. Canada* IX. II. 124 The name Red Indians..is the translation of the Micmac name for them, Maquajik, which means redmen or red people. **1897** E. R. YOUNG *On Indian Trail* 11 Romantic missionary work among the red Indians will soon be a thing of the past. **1903** G. B. SHAW *Revolutionist's Handbk.* viii, in *Man & Superman* 212 Museums are set up throughout the country to encourage little children and elderly gentlemen to make collections of corpses preserved in alcohol, and to steal birds' eggs and keep them as the red Indian used to keep scalps. **1922** JOYCE *Ulysses* 760, I hope he hasnt long greasy hair hanging into his eyes or standing up like a red Indian. **1957** *Chronicle-Herald* (Halifax, Nova Scotia) 16 Aug. 29/8 Since then I have always liked the Red Indians. **1964** *Newfoundland Q.* Summer 12/3 The Journal takes us back to pioneer days in Labrador and Newfoundland to a day when the wigwams of the Red Indians could be seen on the shores of Exploits Bay. **1973** *Times* 5 June 8/7 There he is—a voluminously white-clad figure with headdress..and a face..which might be that of a Red Indian Chief.

c. One of the 'Indians' in a child's game. Cf. *COW-BOY 3 d.

1883 W. W. NEWELL *Games & Songs Amer. Children* i. 26 The players were divided into Indians and hunters, the former uttering their war-cry...The game ended with the extermination of one party or the other. **1941** in R. D. Abrahams *Jump-Rope Rhymes* (1969) 148 One little, two little, three little Indians. Four little, five little, six little Indians, etc. **1969** I. & P. OPIE *Children's Games* v. 181 The attraction of 'Stalking' ('Gang Stalking', 'Shadowing', 'Indians') is that the hunters can become the hunted.

4. For def. read: Any one of the languages spoken by American Indians. (Add later examples.)

1894 M. EELLS *Father Eells* 91 A school was also kept in Indian, the lessons being prepared on paper, hung up on the side of the house and read and recited. **1946** T. M. STANWELL-FLETCHER *Driftwood Valley* 114 Be that as it may, I have pronounced and spelled it, just as we do all the various other localities, as it sounds to us in Indian. **1958** *Camsell Arrow* (Edmonton, Alberta) Jan.–Feb. 1 Although [the sisters] are French and the children speak Indian, English is the language of the school.

7. Short for *Indian tea* (see sense 4 a above).

1748 M. W. MONTAGU *Let.* 17 July (1966) II. 407, I have planted a great deal [of tea] in my Garden, which.. has succeeded very well. I cannot say it is as strong as the Indian, but has the advantage of being Fresher and at least unmix'd. **1907** *Yesterday's Shopping* (1969) 1 Tea ..[Blend] Congou and Indian. **1933** E. A. ROBERTSON *Ordinary Families* xiii. 278, I ordered fresh tea..and pressed the visitor to make up her mind..whether she preferred Indian or China. **1938** [see *CHINA[1] 6]. **1958** J. CANNAN *And be a Villain* i. 39 'Couldn't you find the Earl Grey?'.. Primrose said, 'Indian 's better for pulling you together.' **1968** G. BUTLER *Coffin Following* ix. 198 You will take tea? Will you have Indian or China?

Indiana (indiˌæ·nă). The name of a state in the U.S.A., used esp. *attrib.* to designate objects, etc., from or connected with that state; esp. *Indiana limestone*, an oölitic limestone sometimes known as Bedford limestone.

1858 O. H. SMITH (*title*) Early Indiana trials; and sketches. **1894** *Country Gentlemen's Catal.* 113 Shirts.. in our special Indiana Gauze Oxford. **1934** WEBSTER, Indiana limestone. **1947** J. C. RICH *Materials & Methods Sculpture* viii. 219 Indiana limestone can be secured in buff to gray colors and is an attractive, fairly soft, and easily worked stone. **1948** MENCKEN *Amer. Lang.* Suppl. II. 616 An aged Indiana poetaster named John Finley. **1965** *Harper's Bazaar* Feb. 41 Mean black blazer in rubber-proofed Indiana, 7 gns. **1969** R. MAYER *Dict. Art Terms* 193/2 *Indiana limestone*, the limestone most widely used by American sculptors... Bedford Stone is another Indiana limestone.

Indianan: see *INDIANIAN.

Indian corn. Add: Also *attrib.*

1642 in *Essex Inst. Hist. Coll.* (1863) V. 219/2 Other poore people shalbe repayed..at the next Indian corne harvest. *a* **1738** W. BYRD *Hist. Dividing Line* (1929) 209 We encampt near one of these Indian Corn Fields, where was excellent Food for our Horses. **1751** J. BARTRAM *Observations Pensilvania to Ontario* 60 This repast consisted of 3 great kettles of Indian corn soop, or thin homony, with dry'd eels and other fish boiled in it. **1778** in *Pennsylvania Mag. Hist. & Biogr.* (1902) XXVI. 32 Went into winter quarters in Newport, in old empty houses.. and the food worse,—little bread and that made of rice and Indian corn meal. **1818** F. HALL *Trav. Canada & U.S.* xxviii. 324 The traveller..suddenly mounting a little rise, close to a poor cottage with its Indian corn patch..finds himself opposite to the Capitol of the Federal city. **1888** W. WHITMAN *November Boughs* 412 On the floor of the big kitchen, toward sundown, would be squatting a circle of twelve or fourteen 'pickaninnies', eating their supper of pudding (Indian corn mush) and milk. **1964** *Cookbk.* (Amer. Heritage) (1967) 163 Indian corn stew.

Indianesque (indiănė·sk), *a.* [f. INDIAN *a.* 2.] Of an Indian type.

a **1861** T. WINTHROP *John Brent* (1883) iv. 36 This was the Indianesque Saxon who greeted me. *a* **1861** —— *Canoe & Saddle* (1883) ii. 12 Indianesque, not fully Indian, was her countenance. **1882** J. W. STEELE *Frontier Army Sk.* (1883) 84 In all that is peculiarly Indianesque, she excels her master. **1896** *Month* Jan. 113 Most elaborate and beautiful examples of Indianesque architecture. **1942** *Chicago Tribune* 15 Nov. (Pict. Sect.) 6/2 (*caption*) Indianesque.

Indianian (indiˌæ·niăn). Also **Indianan**. [f. *INDIANA + -IAN.] A native or inhabitant of Indiana.

1784 T. JEFFERSON *Writings* (1894) III. 401 Should.. the Indianians and Kentuckians take themselves off. **1835** C. F. HOFFMAN *Winter in West* I. 226 The term 'Hooshier', ..has now become a *soubriquet*, that bears nothing invidious with it to the ear even of an Indianian. **1863** W. WHITMAN *Specimen Days* (1882–3) 48 Some unconscious Indianian, or from Ohio or Tennessee. **1877** J. HABBERTON *Jericho Road* x. 97 Small parties of discharged Illinoisans and Indianians had frequently passed through. **1900** *Congress. Rec.* 5 Feb. 1508/2 The nation..mourns the death of this distinguished soldier, and Indianians feel it as a personal loss. **1944** *Amer. N. & Q.* Mar. 188 Its advertisements..were answered by a number of Indianans. **1947** *Amer. Speech* XXII. 250 Indianan is now used officially in the State. **1948** MENCKEN *Amer. Lang.* (Suppl.) II. 620 *Hoosier*, at the start, did not signify an Indianan particularly, but any rough fellow of what was then the wild West.

Indianism (i·ndiăniz'm). [-ISM.] Action or policy devoted to the interests of Indians; advocacy of (North American) Indians.

1651 W. FRENCH in *Strength out of Weakness* (1652) 37 All the while I went on in Indianisme I was going from God. **1871** *Rep. Indian Affairs* (1872) 181 We were in our original Indianism. **1887** W. TIREBUCK in Longfellow *Hyperion, Kavanagh and Trouvères* Introd. p. xiii, Those who stood between the culture of *Hyperion* and *Kavanagh*, and the wild Indianism of Aimard and Cooper. **1923** *Spectator* 29 Sept. 422/1 In India it works out in unrest.. an exaggerated sense of Indianism—the nationalistic idea. **1950** *Caribbean Q.* II. III. 14 It is in the Antilles, in Cuba and Santo Domingo that one finds the most abundant, and some of the best manifestations of literary Indianism. **1969** *Indo-Asian Culture* Oct. 25 It was after the coming of the Buddha that Indianism travelled fast.

Indianist. Add: **2.** *attrib.* or as *adj.* Of or pertaining to American Indians.

1950 *Caribbean Q.* II. III. 14 Perhaps the finest *Indianis*, writing was produced in Brazil by Goncalves Dias and José de Alencar. **1960** *Guardian* 22 Nov. 9/6 The new generation of [Mexican] artists and architects were obsessed and inspired by..their own Indianist past.

Indianization (i:ndiănəizē·ʃən). [f. INDIANIZE *v.* 2 + -ATION.] The process of making Indian in character or composition; *spec.* the replacement of Europeans or other foreigners by native-born Indians in positions of authority.

1918 *Pall Mall Gaz.* 29 June 5/2, I do not expect as large an Indianisation of the central Cabinet as of the provincial Cabinets. **1922** *Q. Rev.* July 142 The more rapid Indianisation of the public services. **1924** J. F. BRYANT (*title*) Gandhi and the Indianisation of the Empire. **1928** *Manch. Guardian Weekly* 29 June 513/1 The Indianisation of the Indian army. **1930** *Times Educ. Suppl.* 1 Mar. 92/4 Quicken the process of 'Indianization' by recruiting the superior services..in India. **1930** *Economist* 14 June 1322/1 The rapid progress of Indianisation in the 'transferred' fields. **1969** *Eve's Weekly* (Bombay) 20 Dec. 51/1 The Indianisation of the Roman Catholic Church has come to stay in India. **1973** *Black Panther* 5 May 6/1 (*heading*) 'Indianization' at Wounded Knee.

Indianize, *v.* Add: **2.** (Earlier and later examples.) So **I·ndianized** *ppl. a.*

1702 C. MATHER *Magnalia Christi Americana* VII. 68/2 On March 18. the French with Indians, being half one, half t'other, half Indianized French, and half Frenchified Indians..fell suddenly upon Salmon Falls. **1782** 'J. H. ST. JOHN DE CRÈVECŒUR' *Lett. from Amer. Farmer* xii. 293 Many an anxious parent..went to the Indian villages where..their children had been carried in captivity... They found them so perfectly Indianised, that many knew them no longer. **1924** E. M. FORSTER *Passage to India* xxiv. 225 The invocation of Mrs. Moore continued... The syllables..became Indianized into Esmiss Esmoor. **1935** *Times* 19 June 7/4 If they really meant to Indianize the Army, did they mean to do it because they thought the Indian Army would be more efficient when it had got rid of British officers, or because they thought it would please the Indian sepoy? **1936** *Discovery* Nov. 337/1 The capital of a great Indianised empire extending over the Malay Peninsula and the islands of Java and Sumatra from the 8th to the 12th century A.D. **1963** *Times* 2 May 15/2 The house party, so to speak, includes an English doctor, an Austrian musician who has become Indianized, and an American sociologist and his wife. **1969** *Eve's Weekly* (Bombay) 20 Dec. 51/4 Their Indianised service is generally well-attended, and very little opposition has been met with.

Indianness (i·ndiănnės). [f. INDIAN *a.* + -NESS.] The quality or state of being Indian, or of displaying Indian characteristics.

1934 A. HUXLEY *Beyond Mexique Bay* 192 He had had ..enough..education to make him aware of his own Indianness. **1967** *Evening Standard* 20 Sept. 10/1 The Indianness of our summer was largely, I think, the creation of the flower children. **1969** *Guardian* 5 Mar. 7/1 She exploits her Indian-ness where she has met most disapproval. **1970** *New Yorker* 18 Apr. 103 After mastering the meaning of Negritude and *machismo* they would have to grapple with the meaning of Indianness. **1971** *Illustr. Weekly India* 11 Apr. 6/2 That non-Hindu Indians abroad tend to shake off their Indianness.

Indianologist (indiănǫ·lŏdʒist). [f. INDIAN *sb.* 2.] A student of, or authority on, the American Indian.

1894 *Nation* (N.Y.) 31 May 417/3 His ears, in the view of Indianologists, were a sure mark of aboriginal origin. **1947** *Time* 3 Mar. 37/1 The R.D.C. preferred the route that followed the old telegraph line strung diagonally across the great Brazilian plateau by General Candido Nariano Rondon, a famed Indianologist.

Indian rubber: see INDIA-RUBBER.

Indian summer. Add: **a.** (Earlier and later examples.) Also *transf.* in other countries.

1778 'J. H. ST. JOHN DE CRÈVECŒUR' *Sk. 18th-Cent. Amer.* (1925) 41 It [*sc.* snow] is often preceded by a short interval of smoke and mildness, called the Indian Summer. **1878** G. MEREDITH *Let.* 9 Oct. (1970) II. 563 Perhaps you and Mrs. Carr will do us the honour to come and see the Indian summer here. **1906** W. MARRIOTT *Hints to Meteorol. Observers* (ed. 6) 66/2 *Indian Summer*, fine weather for a few days about September 30, in North America. **1939** [see *GUPTA *a.* and *sb.*]. **1958** HAYWARD & HARARI tr. *Pasternak's Dr. Zhivago* I. iv. 110 The end of a hot golden autumn had turned into an Indian summer. **1960** J. RAE *Custard Boys* I. vi. 69 Meanwhile the Indian summer continued warm and dusty on the trodden earth of the farmyard. **1962** *Sunday Times* 16 Sept. 1/3 An Indian summer in the West Country brought peak holiday traffic jams in Devon yesterday.

fig. (Later examples.)

1918 GALSWORTHY in *Five Tales* (*title*) The Indian summer of a Forsyte. **1930** V. SACKVILLE-WEST *Edwardians* iii. 100 Meanwhile she was quite content that Sebastian should become tanned in the rays of Sylvia's Indian summer. **1962** N. DEL MAR *Richard Strauss* I. ix. 418 The works of his Indian Summer when, in the last five years of his life, inspiration came to him once more.

b. (Further examples.)

1856 MRS. STOWE *Dred* II. 221 It is a calm, still, Indian summer afternoon. **1927** M. DE LA ROCHE *Jalna* xvii. 190 The drowsy Indian-summer heat still continued, but the air had become heavier. **1961** M. BEADLE *These Ruins are Inhabited* (1963) vii. 97 Homeward bound in a lackadaisical Indian-summer mood.

India-rubber, India rubber. Add: **2*.** = RUBBER *sb.*¹ 11.

1794 EARL HOWE *Let. to Capt. Sir R. Curtis* 20 Feb. (MS. in Henry E. Huntington Library) f. 1ᵛ, If India Rubbers means pieces of the elastic Gum for rubbing out pencil lines &c., I have enough of that. **1857** M. J. HOLMES *Meadow-Brook* v, Taking my India-rubber, I erased it [*sc.* the writing]. **1910** 'I. HAY' in *Granta* 11 June, He concluded by imploring me as a personal favour to purchase an india-rubber and erase the lot. **1939–40** *Army & Navy Stores Catal.* 376/2 Artists' india-rubber... Kneaded rubber for Pastel, Chalk and Pencil.

3. *india-rubber ring.*

[**1852** MRS. GASKELL *Cranford* (1853) v. 82 Indian-rubber rings, which are a sort of deification of string.] **1939–40** *Army & Navy Stores Catal.* 812/3 Indiarubber rings. For use on hockey sticks.

b. (Further examples.)

1900 *Daily News* 23 July 3/3 (*heading*) An indiarubber enemy. **1929** E. WALLACE (*title*) The india-rubber men. **1929** F. BOWEN *Sea Slang* 72 *India rubber man*, the physical training instructor. **1949** 'M. INNES' *Journeying Boy* vii. 78 Mr. Wambus..is known as the Great Elasto, the India-rubber Man.

Indic, *a.*¹ Delete *rare* and add further examples. Also, designating the Indian branch of the Indo-Iranian languages, including the dead languages Sanskrit, Prakrit, and Pali and the living languages Hindi, Bengali, Marathi, etc.

1877 A. H. KEANE tr. *Hovelacque's Sci. of Lang.* 320 Hindui..Aryan-Indic. **1893** in *Funk's Stand. Dict.* **1909** *Indogerman. Forsch.* XXV. 177 Although the rule is not without exception even in the older Indic and Hellenic documents, it nevertheless holds true in general for the languages claimed. **1911** L. BLOOMFIELD in C. F. Hockett *Leonard Bloomfield Anthol.* (1970) 7 The Indic and the Iranian languages differ greatly in their treatment of the IE. stopped consonants. **1935** A. TOYNBEE *Study of Hist.* (ed. 2) I. 87 And so we have identified the society 'apparented' to the Hindu Society. Let us call it 'Indic'. **1937** *Discovery* Sept. 286 The American School of Indic and Iranian Studies. **1973** *Amer. N. & Q.* 83/1 Eliot began Ph.D. studies at Harvard, majoring jointly in the Indic and Philosophy Departments.

indicate, *v.* Add: **1.** *pass.* Of a course of action, treatment, etc.: to be pointed out or suggested as desirable or necessary. Also *transf.*

1880 [in Dict.]. **1886** *Brit. Med. Jrnl.* 17 Apr. 750/1 Recourse to this method is more particularly indicated when the teeth to be replaced are front teeth. **1907** *Lancet* 25 May 1462/1 Considering the great analogy which is presented between syphilis and leprosy..it seemed indicated to try on this patient the treatment by large doses of atoxyl. **1919** WODEHOUSE *Damsel in Distress* xv. 184 Strategy, rather than force, seemed to the curate to be indicated. **1922** W. R. INGE *Lay Thoughts* (1926) 235 Whenever a patient consults a doctor, the latter should always order some drug, even if drugs are not really indicated. **1946** M. PEAKE *Titus Groan* 353 My dear ladies,..I feel that some hot coffee is indicated, but what do *you* feel? **1971** *Nature* 31 Dec. 557/1 Further investigations of the directions of propagation and the presence of pacemaker function are certainly indicated. **1972** *Sci. Amer.* May 80/2 Periodic measurement of arterial and central venous pressure, blood acidity and dissolved gases may be indicated in the management of patients with heart, kidney, lung or metabolic disorders.

indication. Add: **2. b.** *Mining.* Something which indicates the presence of valuable ore, oil, etc. *U.S.*

1855 *Southern Californian* (Los Angeles) 28 Mar. 1/7 Mineral indications in Southern California..differ in many respects with the mineral indications of the earth's surface in Central, or Northern California. **1862** 'MARK TWAIN' *Lett.* (1917) I. 80 We went and looked at the ledges, and both of them acknowledged that there was nothing in them but good 'indications'. **1873** J. H. BEADLE *Undevel. West* xviii. 326 My comrades are off down the mountain side picking at 'indications', and mapping out the 'run of the country rock'. **1877** B. HARTE *Story of a Mine* 394 Luckily the fertile alluvium of these valleys..offered no 'indications' to attract the gold-seekers. **1948** *Duncan* (Oklahoma) *Daily Banner* 2 July 1/3 The location was one of three staked by the Ohio Oil Co. on indications given by the Palmer No. 1 Leard-Amerada.

indicator. Add: **1. a.** (Earlier and later examples.)

1819 (*title*) The indicator. **1907** *New Pictorial & Descr. Guide to Malvern* 56 Many of the more prominent objects and principal sites may be identified by..the help afforded by the Indicator, or Toposcope, erected on the summit of the hill. **1927** *Glasgow Herald* 4 June 9 (*headline*) Mountain Indicator. *Ibid.*, The indicator..points out over ninety places famous in Border song and story. **1967** *Listener* 10 Aug. 167/2 There's a recent book which displays, at a glance, what's distinctive about the scientific analysis of international affairs. It's the *World Handbook of Political and Social Indicators*.

d. *Philos.* = **token-reflexive word*; see quots. Also *indicator-word*.

1951 N. GOODMAN *Struct. Appearance* xi. 290 Roughly speaking, a word is an indicator if..it names something not named by some replica of the word... Among the commonest indicators are the personal indicators, the spatial indicators, and the temporal indicators. Of the personal indicators, an 'I' or 'me' normally refers to its own utterer. **1952** A. J. AYER in *Mind* LXI. 444, I shall refer to predicates instead of properties and to individual signs, to which I shall give the name of indicators, instead of individuals. **1954** *Mind* LXIII. 380 Like Professor Ayer I shall..speak of indicators and predicates rather than of individuals and properties. **1960** W. V. QUINE *Word & Object* § 21. 101 The indicator words: 'this', 'that', 'I', 'you', 'he', 'now', 'here', 'then', 'there', 'today', 'tomorrow'.

2. b. Delete *'esp.* a chemical re-agent' and add: *spec.* a substance which may be added to a solution to indicate whether the concentration of hydrogen ions or of some other ion in the solution is above or below a particular value, esp. by giving different colours for the two conditions. (Further examples.)

1874 *Jrnl. Chem. Soc.* XXVII. 191 (*heading*) Alizarin as an indicator in volumetric analysis. **1902** *Encycl. Brit.* XXVIII. 12/2 Para-nitro-phenol has colourless molecules, but an intensely yellow negative ion. In neutral, and still more in acid solutions, the dissociation of the indicator is practically nothing, and the liquid is colourless. **1930** *Jrnl. Amer. Chem. Soc.* LII. 2347 The use of various organic substances..as irreversible oxidation-reduction indicators in the titration of trivalent antimony with ceric sulfate was proposed by Rathsberg. **1938** R. E. OESPER tr. *Böttger's Newer Methods Volumetric Chem. Analysis* i. 19 The fluorescent indicators are related to the ordinary acidimetric color indicators. However, a change of the pH value of the solution produces in them no color change, but a fluorescence appears or disappears. **1939** P. J. DURRANT *Gen. & Inorg. Chem.* ix. 214 An indicator may be used for determining the *p*H value of a solution, or for deciding at what stage during an acid-alkali titration the *p*H value of a solution has reached a certain value. **1966** *Ward Lock's Compl. Gardening* v. 78 Certain chemical indicators are available for testing a soil in the field as to its approximate pH. **1970** R. U. BRUMBLAY *First Course Quant. Analysis* vi. 83 Adsorption indicators are organic compounds with rather complex molecules which undergo a change in color due to a slight structural change which occurs when they are adsorbed on the surfaces of colloidal particles.

(ii) An isotope (usually a radioactive one) used as a tracer (see *TRACER¹).

1919 [see *ISOTOPIC *a.* a]. **1926** R. W. LAWSON tr. *Hevesy & Paneth's Man. Radioactivity* xv. 122 In problems of this kind, where the radio-element is not the object but the agent of the investigation, we say that the radio-elements serve as 'indicators'. **1938** *Ibid.* (ed. 2) xviii. 168 In those rare cases in which inactive isotopes are readily accessible they can be used as indicators in fundamentally the same manner, though other methods of measurement must be used... Such experiments have been carried out with deuterium ²D and the oxygen and nitrogen isotopes ¹⁷O, and ¹⁵N. **1943** *Thorpe's Dict. Appl. Chem.* (ed. 4) VI. 432/1 The hydride of bismuth was discovered by using thorium-C as indicator and causing hydrogen to be generated in an apparatus in which this radioactive indicator had been placed. The gas which escaped was found ..to have radioactive properties. **1956** E. DE B. BARNETT *Mechanism Org. Chem. Reactions* i. 13 The use of an isotopic indicator or tracer often gives useful information as regards mechanism.

c. A geological clue to the presence of gold.

1894 R. A. F. MURRAY in A. W. Howitt *Miners' Handbk.* 5 Where the gold ceases is usually near and above the line of reef or vein whence it was derived...'Indicators' or small veins of pyrites, ironstone, and often thin bands of peculiar slate, intersected by small quartz veins, should..be carefully looked for. **1943** VON BERNEWITZ & CHELLSON *Handbk. Prospectors* (ed. 4) xvii. 200 A lead-bismuth mineral is an indicator in the Quartzburg district of Idaho. The gold is intimately associated with it, yet free.

d. *Ecology.* A group of plants or animals whose presence acts as a sign of particular environmental conditions. Also *attrib.*

1906 E. W. HILGARD *Soils* 545 Its [*sc.* alkali-heath's] perennial, deep-rooting habit of growth, and flexible, somewhat wiry rootstock, which enables it to persist even in cultivated ground, render it a valuable plant as an alkali indicator. **1920** F. E. CLEMENTS *Plant Indicators* iv. 112 These [areas of disturbance] furnish an enormous amount of indicator material. **1949** W. C. ALLEE et al. *Princ. Animal Ecol.* IV. xxix. 567/2 Typical or characteristic organisms..are biotic indicators. **1964** J. M. MACLENNAN tr. *Viktorov's Short Guide Geo-Bot. Surveying* vi. 122 The composition, structure, and other features of the plant cover may often serve as indicators of various environmental conditions. **1970** *Nature* 25 July 381/1 They [*sc.* chaetognaths] have also frequently been used as 'indicator species' for water masses.

e. A board or device in a railway station used to indicate the times and platform numbers of arriving and departing trains.

1913 LD. MONKSWELL *Railways Gt. Brit.* iii. 163 A large indicator showing the platform at which each train will depart, is displayed high up on the side of one of the buildings flanking the concourse. **1914** H. M. HALLSWORTH *Elem. Railway Operating* iii. 46 Since there are trains for different destinations frequently departing from the same platform at or about the same time passengers are liable to board the wrong train. This is a danger which must be provided for by suitable indicators. **1961** *Trains Illustr.* Jan. 22/2 (*caption*) The new train indicator board for the Cambridge main line departure platforms. **1972** *Travelling* Winter 43/3 New automatic departure and arrival indicators will be installed. **1973** *Railway Mag.* Mar. 151/2 A new form of train departure indicator is replacing the printed sheets at many stations on BR.

f. In *Cryptography* (see quot.).

1961 SHULMAN & WEINTRAUB *Gloss. Cryptogr.*, *Indicator*, a means of showing a change of key or encipherment, usually with a letter of the alphabet agreed upon in advance.

3. g. A device fitted to a motor vehicle to indicate an intended change in direction. Cf. **direction indicator*.

Now usu. consisting of two pairs of lights, one pair placed at the front and the other at the rear of a vehicle, that flash on one side or the other when operated by the driver.

1932 [see *FLASHING *ppl. a.* 1 c]. **1958** *Observer* 17 Aug. 15/6 Triggers under the steering-wheel work the self-cancelling indicators and the headlamp flasher. **1962** *Which? Car Suppl.* Oct. 133/1 All the indicators' flasher times fell within the legal limits. *Ibid.* 133/2 The rear indicators could be seen from the side. **1973** R. LEWIS *Blood Money* vi. 69 A police car..turned into the gateway, indicator flashing.

4*. *Math.* [tr. F. *indicateur* (E. Prouhet 1846, in *Nouv. Ann. de Math.* V. 176).] = TOTIENT.

1919 *Amer. Math. Monthly* XXVI. 290 E. Prouhet.. defined the term indicator of *n* as the number $\phi(n)$ of the positive integers less than *n* and prime to *n*. **1939** H. N. WRIGHT *First Course in Theory of Numbers* i. 11 Other names for $\phi(m)$ are the totient of *m* and the indicator of *m*. **1948** O. ORE *Number Theory* v. 110 We shall consider the problem of finding how many of the numbers 1, 2, 3, ..., *m*—1, *m* are relatively prime to *m*. This number is usually denoted by $\phi(m)$, and it is known as Euler's ϕ-function of *m* because Euler around 1760 for the first time proposed the question and gave its solution. Other names, for instance, indicator or totient have occasionally been used.

5. indicator lamp, light, a luminous signal indicating operating conditions (see quots. and sense 3 g above); **indicator switch,** a switch for an indicator light.

1961 *Which?* Dec. 313/2 For most cookers, we found that the indicator light going out gave a satisfactory indication that the oven was nearly at its steady temperature... The *Falco Royalty* had no indicator lamp. **1962** *Ibid. Car Suppl.* Oct. 133/2 Both front and rear indicator lights were visible from the side in the VW 1500. **1959** *Motor Manual* (ed. 36) vi. 183 When the indicator switch is moved, either for a right- or left-hand turn, current is fed to the lamps [etc.].

in dictione (in diktĭōᵘ·ni), *phr. Logic.* [L. tr. of Gr. παρὰ τὴν λέξιν (Aristotle, *Sophistical Refutations*, ch. 4).] Of fallacies: resulting from the linguistic expression used; due to ambiguity, division, etc. (Opp. *EXTRA DICTIONEM *phr.*)

1826 R. WHATELY *Elem. Logic* iii. § 1. 135 The division of Fallacies into those in the words *in dictione*, and those in the matter *extra dictionem*, has not been, by any writers hitherto, grounded on any distinct principle. **1847** A. DE MORGAN *Formal Logic* xiii. 241 The Aristotelian system of fallacies contains two subdivisions. In the first, which are *in dictione*, or *in voce*, the mistake is said to consist in the use of words: in the second, which are *extra dictionem*, or *in re*, it is said to be in the matter. **1852** [see *EXTRA DICTIONEM *phr.*]. **1870** J. MCCOSH *Laws Discursive Thought* III. § 82. 172 Fallacies from the days of Aristotle have been logically divided into those *In Dictione* and those *Extra Dictionem*, or, to use a better mode of expression, into those in Form and those in Matter. **1916** H. W. B. JOSEPH *Introd. Logic* (ed. 2) xxvii. 578 The fallacies *in dictione* are so many different forms of error that may arise through the double meanings of language. **1970** [see *EXTRA DICTIONEM *phr.*].

indie (i·ndi), colloq. abbrev. of INDEPENDENT *a.* and *sb.* (used esp. in the film industry in the United States).

1942 BERREY & VAN DEN BARK *Amer. Thes. Slang* § 217/5 *Indie*, independent. *Ibid.* § 587/4 *Indie*, an independently owned theater. *Ibid.* § 605/23 *Indie*, an independent exhibitor. **1961** A. BERKMAN *Singers' Gloss. Show Business* 29 *Indie*, independent movie producer. **1962** *Amer. Speech* XXXVII. 149 On names for 'indies'—independent motion picture companies. **1970** *New Yorker* 15 Aug. 65/1 An indie producer met a dope in a bar. An indie producer is an independent producer.

indifference. Add: **3. b.** *Psychol.* **indifference point** [tr. G. *indifferenzpunkt*], a position or value between two continua of experience, such as a temperature that is experienced as neither warm nor cold, or a feeling-value that is neither pleasant nor unpleasant.

1887 A. SETH *Hegelianism* ii. 57 Schelling proceeds to define the Absolute as the indifference-point of subject and object. **1890** W. JAMES *Princ. Psychol.* I. xv. 616 An 'Indifference-point'; that is to say..a time which we tend to estimate as neither longer or shorter than it really is, and away from which, in both directions, errors increase their size. **1901** BALDWIN *Dict. Philos. & Psychol.* I. 533 *Indifference point*,..the theoretical point at which neither of two contrasted sense or other qualities, which are supposed to depend on the same sort of stimulation, is experienced. **1938** R. S. WOODWORTH *Exper. Psychol.* xviii. 445 The 'indifference point', a phenomenon observed for many years in judgments of magnitude.

8. indifference curve (occas. **line of indifference**) *Econ.*, a graph, the co-ordinates of which are the quantities of alternative goods and services that would leave the consumer indifferent in choosing between them because he judges them of equal value. Also **indifference map** (see quot. 1972).

1881 F. Y. EDGEWORTH *Math. Psychics* I. 21 It is evident that X will step only on one side of a certain line, the *line of indifference*, as it might be called. **1894** —— in *Economic Jrnl.* IV. 426 A curve of constant advantage, or 'indifference-curve'..representing states for which the advantage to England is no greater than if there had been no trade. **1934** J. R. HICKS in *Economica* I. 53 If there are only two sorts of goods, this scale of preferences can be represented by a diagram of indifference curves... We can take as an 'index' of utility any variable which has the same value all along an indifference curve, and which increases as we proceed from one indifference curve to a higher one. *Ibid.* 61 Take any point *P* on a given indifference-map, and draw the tangent at *P* to the indifference-curve that passes through *P*. **1949** *Mind* LVIII. 197 On a graph, the line which connects these collections is the contour line, or indifference-curve, on which all collections are iso-satisfactory. **1965** *Economist* 7 Aug. 533/1 The analysis deals with indifference curves, contract curves, equi-product curves, and so on. **1969** R. BLACKBURN in Cockburn & Blackburn *Student Power* 169 The economic assumption of profit maximization is validated by the theory that business decisions only reflect the needs ('utility curve' or 'indifference curve') of the sovereign consumer. **1971** A. S. SCHWIER tr. *Pareto's Man. Pol. Econ.* iii. 119 Professor F. Y. Edgeworth.. assumed the existence of *utility*..and deduced the indifference curves from it... I consider the indifference curves as given, and deduce from them all that is necessary for the theory of equilibrium. **1972** C. GILES et al. *Understanding Econ.* viii. 97 An alternative analysis of consumer behaviour is known as indifference curve analysis. *Ibid.* 99 An indifference map represents a series of indifference curves.

indigency. Restrict †*Obs.* to senses 1 and 3, and add later examples of sense 2.

1906 *Daily Chron.* 25 Sept. 6/7 The Government has set up an Indigency Inquiry Commission. **1924** *Glasgow Herald* 7 Feb. 7 Unemployment and indigency..existed on a scale that was entirely disproportionate to the size of the white population.

indigenization (indi:dʒĭnəizēⁱ·ʃən). [f. INDIGENOUS *a.* + -IZATION.] The act or process of rendering indigenous or making predominantly native; adaptation or subjection to the influence or dominance of the indigenous inhabitants of a country; *spec.* the increased use of indigenous people in government, employment, etc. Also **indi·genist**, an advocate or supporter of indigenization; also *attrib.* or as *adj.*; **indi·genize** *v. trans.*; **indi·genized** *ppl. a.*

1942 D. FITTS *Anthol. Contemp. Latin-Amer. Poetry* 639 Vasquez is a member of the Puno indigenist school. He scatters Indian words throughout his writing and celebrates the charms of Indian girls. **1944** *Hispania* May 245 In the last twenty years Protestantism in Latin America has gained mainly in the Indian communities where latifundism is strongest... A number of *indigenists* are Protestants. **1949** *Internat. Jrnl. Amer. Ling.* XV. III, Guatemala is to be congratulated on the activities of its Indigenist Institute. **1951** *Missionary Research Library Occas. Bull.* 14 Feb. 7 It is the fascinating story of an indigenous Church in what is otherwise a 'missionary' land; and its development contains many lessons as to the proper principles of indigenization. **1951** L. THOMPSON *Personality & Govt.* 58 Navaho administration should aim primarily to guide, teach and influence the Navaho by means of indigenized methods to improve their own pattern of living. *Ibid.* 61 It is recommended..that the Navaho Agency and its services be completely reorganized, decentralized, and indigenized. **1954** *Theology* LVII. 249 Making the Church really indigenous with greater indigenization of leadership as well as support. **1962** *Economist* 21 Apr. 227/1 The process of 'indigenisation', which has narrowed managerial opportunities, is now being steadily extended to technical posts also. **1968** *Listener* 26 Dec. 859/3 The 'indigenist' movement in Haiti and the 'negrist' movement in Cuba. The indigenists, who relied mainly on a European form, the novel, turned back to the study of Voodoo. **1971** G. ANSRE in J. Spencer *Eng. Lang. W. Afr.* 163 The general tendency in word structure seems to have been in the direction of indigenisation, but more knowledge of English and sophistication in its use seems to be reversing things. *Ibid.*, The phonologically indigenised form of the English plural. **1971** *Guardian* 29 Sept. 17/4 The indigenisation policy..is unlikely to be fully pursued..because of the shortage of capital needed for Nigerians to take over from foreign concerns. **1971** *Jrnl. Educ. Thought* V. II. 75 An ethnic-sensitive planner would have substituted the legends of their hogan house, their maize-grinding mano (millstone), and other indigenizations. **1973** *Nation Rev.* (Melbourne) III. 31 Aug. 1459/6 She will help to indigenise music education in the schools.

indigent, *a.* (*sb.*) **B.** *sb.* Delete †*Obs.* and add later examples.

1903 *Westm. Gaz.* 15 Jan. 6/2 Mr. Chamberlain..gratefully accepted the offer to provide accommodation for the indigents. **1905** *Daily Chron.* 23 Sept. 5/1 The farmers submitted a lengthy list of subjects for redress, including ..settlements for indigents, &c. **1922** W. S. MAUGHAM *On Chinese Screen* VIII. 37 He was a man whose purse was always open to the indigent. **1972** *N.Y. Law Jrnl.* 31 Oct. 1/5 The Legal Defense Panel administers the program of assistance to indigents who are criminal defendants.

indigest, *v. trans.* Add: (Later example.)

1938 S. BECKETT *Murphy* 81 On this part of himself that I am about to indigest may the Lord have mercy.

b. *intr.* Also, to fail to digest.

1857 MRS. GASKELL *Let.* Dec. (1966) 489, I don't see exactly what you do in America. You indigest, all of you, and some of you make money at a great rate. **1954** W. FAULKNER *Fable* 337 'Then we will starve,' the first said. 'Or indigest,' the third said.

indigo. Add: **C. 1.** and **2.** *indigo-planter* (earlier example); **indigo weed** (earlier examples).

1772 J. HABERSHAM *Let.* 12 Aug. in *Coll. Georgia Hist. Soc.* (1904) VI. 202 We have had a great Quantity of Rain fall, which must hurt the Indigoe Planters. **1785** *Mem. Amer. Acad. Arts & Sci.* I. 473 *Indigofera*... Indigoweed. .. A durable pale blue may be obtained from the leaves and small branches. **1852** *Trans. Mich. Agric. Soc.* III. 197 My timber is generally oak, with some hickory, indigo weed, tea weed.

indigoid (i·ndigoid), *a.* (*sb.*) [a. G. *indigoid* (P. Friedländer 1908, in *Ber. d. Deut. Chem. Ges.* XLI. 773): see INDIGO *sb.* (*a.*) and -OID.] Of a dye: similar to indigotin in chemical structure, *spec.* in having another atom or atoms, esp. of sulphur, in place of one or both of the imino-groups. Hence as *sb.*, an indigoid dye.

1908 *Jrnl. Chem. Soc.* XCIV. I. 371 (*heading*) Indigoid dyes. *Ibid.*, The author applies the term 'indigoid' to dyes which are related to indigotin in that the imino-groups of the latter are substituted by a sulphur or other bivalent atom or group. **1939** J. B. CONANT *Chem. Org. Compounds* (rev. ed.) xxx. 560 Indigo, its halogenated derivatives, and certain related compounds of analogous structure are sometimes referred to as the indigoids. **1946** *Biochem. Jrnl.* XL. 669/1 This communication describes the isolation and identification of the indigoid pigments indirubin and indigotin from the acid-treated urine of a case of sprue. **1952** K. VENKATARAMAN *Chem. Synthetic Dyes* II. xxxiii. 1004 Apart from indigo itself, the thioindigoids constitute a much more important series than the indigoids. **1963** A. J. HALL *Textile Sci.* iv. 178 All these new synthetic dyes related in chemical composition to indigo are classed as indigoid dyes. **1966** KIRK & OTHMER *Encycl. Chem. Technol.* (ed. 2) XI. 562 The nomenclature of the indigoids is based on the indole.., or thionaphthene, part of the molecule.

Indio (i·ndio). [Sp. and Pg.] A member of one of various indigenous peoples of America and E. Asia in those areas formerly subject to Spain or Portugal; *spec.* (*a*) in Brazil and Mexico, an Indian, distinguished as an *Indio bravo*, if he had retained his independence, and *Indio manso* or *Indio fidele*, if he had come under European domination; (*b*) = *INDIAN *sb.* 1 c. Also **Indiano.**

1836 *Penny Cycl.* V. 365/1 All the aborigines, who lead an independent and roving life, are called in Brazil Indianos bravos, or Gentios, in contradistinction to the Indianos mansos (domesticated Indians), who have settled among, or in the neighbourhood of the Europeans. **1839** *Ibid.* XV. 158/1 The Indios Bravos generally live on the produce of the chase. **1840** *Ibid.* XVIII. 88/1 The mountains [of the Philippines] were occupied by a black race, which..was called by the Spaniards, Negritos or Aetas, while the Malays were called Indios. **1860** MAYNE REID *Odd People* 43 The 'Indios bravos',..a phrase used throughout all Spanish America to distinguish those tribes..who refused obedience to Spanish tyranny, and who preserve..their native independence and freedom. In contradistinction to the 'Indios bravos' are the 'Indios mansos', or 'tame Indians'. *Ibid.* 44 The true son of the forest—the 'Indio bravo'. **1883** *Encycl. Brit.* XVI. 218/2 The great majority of the *Indios fideles*, mestizoes, and creoles still adhere at least outwardly to the Roman Church. **1901** [see MORO[2]]. **1969** J. MANDER *Static Society* i. 28 The apparent orthodoxy of the Guatemalan *indio* may conceal the most bizarre Christian-pagan syncretism. **1970** OJEDA & CASTRO tr. *Marche's Luzon & Palawan* v. 60 The *indios* are far from giving up the plow of their fathers.

indirect, *a.* Add: **1. d.** *indirect lighting* (see quot. 1925).

1925 *Gloss. Terms Illum. & Photom.* (*B.S.I.*) 8 *Indirect lighting*, a system of lighting in which the greater part of the luminous flux reaches the area to be illuminated only after reflection from a ceiling or other object external to the fitting. **1933** *Archit. Rev.* LXXIV. 214 Indirect lighting is housed in a specially designed reflector abutting against a mirror which reflects and doubles it. **1969** *Bodl. Libr. Rec.* VIII. 117 This lighting is not only sufficient for reading, but is diffused to give adequate indirect lighting to the immediate surroundings.

2. a. spec. *indirect aggression*, aggression by one nation by other than military means; so *indirect aggressor*; *indirect evidence* = *circumstantial evidence* (CIRCUMSTANTIAL *a.* 1); *indirect rule*, a system of government in which the governed people retain certain administrative and legal, etc., powers.

1824 T. STARKIE *Pract. Treat. Law of Evidence* I. III. 478 These positions lead immediately to an inquiry into the nature and force of indirect or circumstantial evidence. **1865** Indirect evidence [in Dict.]. **1922** F. D. LUGARD *Dual Mandate Brit. Trop. Afr.* x. 199 The Governor of the Gold Coast..observed: 'The chiefs are keenly appreciative of our policy of indirect rule, and of the full powers they retain under their native institutions.' **1928** —— (*title*) Representative forms of government and 'indirect rule' in British Africa. *Ibid.* 19, I propose in this chapter to discuss..'Indirect Rule'—though 'Dependent Rule' would seem a more suitable term,—more especially in..the conditions of tropical Africa. **1931** *Economist* 28 Mar. 667/2 He [*sc.* Sir Donald Cameron]..submitted that this dream would be shattered if the policy, inaugurated in Tanganyika in 1925, of developing that territory on the lines of indirect rule by the mandatory and direct economic production by the natives were allowed to develop. **1939** H. NICOLSON *Diary* 20 July (1966) 406 The Ambassador is.. so interested in convincing them how right is the Soviet definition of 'indirect aggression' that he forgets to offer them any tea. **1940** B. WARD *Russian Foreign Policy* 28 Mutual guarantees, the definition of indirect aggression—all these were trivial points compared with the principal obstacle, the Polish guarantee. **1957** P. WORSLEY *Trumpet shall Sound* 261 This became particularly urgent, when..the growing inadequacy of direct methods of rule ..brought about the introduction of Indirect Rule in many territories. **1958** *Hansard Commons* 16 July 1245 The question is one of perverting nationalist feelings and perverting those who wish to overthrow the established order of society so that they serve to further indirect aggression. **1958** *Listener* 7 Aug. 185/1 Much has been said about President Nasser's propaganda machine, which has given rise to a new term, 'indirect aggression', which in Western eyes, it seems, may now be held as justification for military intervention. **1958** *Spectator* 8 Aug. 184/3 Nor was this member of the Baghdad Pact the only indirect aggressor against France. **1959** JOWITT *Dict. Eng. Law* II. 960/1 *Indirect evidence*, proof of collateral circumstances from which a fact in controversy, not directly attested by witnesses or documents, may be inferred. **1959** *Spectator* 21 Aug. 236/2 The invention of 'indirect rule', the system of governing a territory by allowing the existing tribal authorities to continue to administer tribal law under the restraint of a British Resident. **1962** *Listener* 18 Oct. 593/2 The legacy of Britain's policy of indirect rule in this Region of Nigeria is clearly visible in the comparatively static nature of these societies.

d. *Metallurgy.* Designating a process by which wrought iron or steel is obtained from the ore through the intermediate stage of pig iron (the usual method).

1869 H. S. OSBORN *Metall. Iron & Steel* II. ii. 274 In ancient times iron was extracted from the ore as malleable iron. This is called the direct, in contra-distinction to the present method of producing cast iron and afterward malleable, which latter is called the indirect method. **1967** W. H. DENNIS *Found. Iron & Steel Metall.* i. 13 Gradually a technique was developed of removing the derived impurities... This process was designated fining..and resulted in wrought iron... The method involved a two-stage process: (a) Reduction of iron ore to make pig iron, and (b) remelting and purifying the pig iron to make wrought iron and hence was an indirect process in contrast to the former direct process of producing iron blooms from the ore in one stage.

4. b. *Biol.* Of nuclear or cell division: mitotic.

[**1879** W. FLEMMING in *Arch. f. path. Anat. u. Physiol.* LXXVII. 3 Bei anderen..Fällen..lassen sich Bilder, die anscheinend einer directen Kerntheilung entsprachen, einer indirecten (s.u.) zudeuten.] **1880** *Jrnl. R. Microsc. Soc.* III. 51 In discussing the changes undergone by the nucleus in cell-division, Professor W. Flemming distinguishes two methods of division which have been described by various observers, the direct and the indirect. **1888** [see *AMITOTIC *a.*]. **1909** J. R. GREEN *Hist. Bot.* II. i. 181 The terms indirect, and direct, nuclear division were introduced by Flemming in 1879, and were long in favour. **1925** E. B. WILSON *Cell* (ed. 3) ii. 116 Mitosis (indirect division).

5. Of or pertaining to the work and expenses which cannot be apportioned to any particular job or undertaking, pertaining to overhead charges and subsidiary work. (Cf. *DIRECT *a.* 6 f.)

1903, 1922 [see *DIRECT *a.* 6 f]. **1925** R. J. H. RYALL *Primer of Costing* 49 Labour may be employed in..repairing machinery..or in supervising the direct workers. ..Such labour is classified as Indirect Labour. **1966** *New Statesman* 19 Aug. 256/1 The Americans..are more inclined to lay down precise standards for the number of indirect workers who ought to be employed in a particular location. **1974** *Times* 4 Feb. 15/4 Its first offer..covers.. some 4,300 'indirect' workers—men who service the production areas—in the body plant.

6. *indirect fire*, gunfire aimed at a target which cannot be seen (see quot. 1918).

1879 *Man. Siege & Garrison Artill. Exerc.* I. 23 Indirect or curved fire from guns or howitzers. *Ibid.* 24 Breaching by indirect fire would, as a rule, be by demolition and not by the formation of regular cuts. **1918** E. S. FARROW *Dict. Mil. Terms* 309 *Indirect Fire*, when the target cannot be seen, and guns are aimed by means of calculations, from map, or by bearings. *Indirect Laying Fire*, when the gun is laid for direction on an aiming point or on aiming points and elevation adjusted by sight clinometer. **1962** *Ordnance Technical Terminol.* (U.S. Army Ordnance School) (AD 660 112) 162/2 *Indirect fire*, gunfire delivered at a target that cannot be seen from the gun position or firing ship.

indiscernibi·lity. [f. INDISCERNIBLE *a.*: see -ITY.] The quality or condition of being indiscernible.

1878 S. H. HODGSON *Philos. of Reflection* II. 140 Indiscernibility in point of content is therefore the final test of truth in concrete reasoning. **1892** W. WALLACE tr. *Hegel's Logic* (ed. 2) 417 The principle of individuation or indiscernibility is: 'If two individuals were perfectly alike

[etc.]'. **1936** *Mind* XLV. 245 This latter kind of immediacy is unmediatedness, or indiscernibility of any mediation. **1953** W. V. QUINE *From Logical Point of View* viii. 139 One of the fundamental principles governing identity is that of *substitutivity*—or, as it might well be called, that of *indiscernibility of identicals*. **1955** A. N. PRIOR *Formal Logic* 264 Even if we do not admit..the 'identity of indiscernibles', we must admit the indiscernibility of identicals. **1962** W. & M. KNEALE *Devel. of Logic* x. 604, $x=y \supset (fx \supset fy)$ may perhaps be called the principle of the indiscernibility of identicals. **1973** A. QUINTON *Nature of Things* vi. 153 The indiscernibility of dreams..does not cast doubt on necessary truths.

indiscretion. Add: **2.** (Further examples.) Also, an accidental or ('calculated indiscretion') a supposedly accidental revelation of an official secret, etc.

1929 T. S. ELIOT *Dante* 63 The *Vita Nuova* is neither a 'confession' nor an 'indiscretion' in the modern sense. **1930** [see *CALCULATED *ppl. a.* 1]. **1931** *Economist* 5 Dec. 1066/1 Socialist 'indiscretions'..took the form of the publication of certain alleged confidential information as to advances to French banks and foreign Governments from the French Treasury. **1955** *Bull. Atomic Sci.* Mar. 84/2 We have useful men denied the opportunity to contribute to our scientific efforts because of their youthful indiscretions. **1961** *Spectator* 26 May 742/1 He is psychologically indiscretion-prone.

indiscutable (indiskiū·tăb'l), *a.* [f. IN-³: see DISCUTABLE *a.* Cf. F. *indiscutable* indisputable.] = INDISCUSSIBLE *a.*

1933 *Proc. Brit. Acad.* XVIII. 171 In every field, a writer may without injustice give plain warning to the world that he regards certain questions as ultimate and indiscutable. **1959** *Encounter* XII. iv. 53 The book is *indiscutable.*

indispensable, *a.* (*sb.*) Add: **B.** *sb.* (Later examples.)

1901 *Westm. Gaz.* 12 Dec. 3/1 An indispensable to the complete success of the lace blouse is a chiffon lining. **1965** *Austral. Women's Weekly* 20 Jan. 25 Inevitably in a life of constant moving one picks up indispensables.

c. (Earlier example.)

a **1828** J. BERNARD *Retrospections Stage* (1830) II. iv. 116 Black silk indispensables, and stockings.

indisseverable, *a.* Delete †*Obs.* and add later example.

1950 A. L. ROWSE *England of Elizabeth* p. viii, We next have to tackle the Church, not as a system of belief, but as a social institution—indeed as the whole of society regarded from one aspect, inextricably entwined with secular life at every level, indisseverable from it.

indisseverably, *adv.* Delete † and add later examples.

1935 W. DE LA MARE *Early One Morning* 5 The fresh and virgin waters are so rapidly and indisseverably involved with the rest. **1952** *Scottish Jrnl. Theol.* V. 307 For [Bouyer] as for Preiss eschatology and Christology are woven indisseverably together as the background of ethics.

in distans: see *IN *Lat. prep.*

indistinguishable, *a.* Add: **1.** Also as *sb.*

1903 *Daily Chron.* 24 Nov. 4/5 All this contention and uncertainty might be avoided if we abolished..the artificial distinction between two indistinguishables. **1949** H. W. B. JOSEPH *Lect. Philos. Leibniz* ii. 23 There will be a perpetual substitution of indistinguishables.

individ. Add later U.S. example. (Still *Obs.*)

1843 [see *BURG 2].

individual, *a.* and *sb.* Add: **A.** *adj.* **5. c.** Intended to serve one person; designed to contain one portion.

1889 *Cent. Dict.* s.v., An individual salt-cellar [colloq.]. **1895** *Montgomery Ward Catal.* 531/2 Individual Butter Plates. **1911** *Daily Colonist* (Victoria, B.C.) 22 Apr. 2/1 (Advt.), Table Necessities..Cut Glass Individual Salts, up from 35¢. **1948** *Good Housek. Cookery Bk.* 454 Use small individual moulds if you want jellies in a hurry. **1951** *Catal. of Exhibits, South Bank Exhib., Festival of Britain* 52/2 Individual casserole in heat-resisting glassware. **1965** T. FITZGIBBON *Art Brit. Cooking* 203 If made in individual small moulds they [*sc.* canary puddings] are called 'Castle Puddings'. **1970** K. GILES *Death in Church* i. 20 Node..dug his fork into the individual pudding.

d. *Psychol.* Relating or pertaining to the study of individuals, as opposed to that of a group or society. Also used to denote A. Adler's method of analytical psychology.

1898 *Amer. Jrnl. Psychol.* X. 329 The systematic consideration of the problems grouped under the name of 'Individual Psychology' is of but recent date. Indeed, the only treatment of the whole subject for its own sake is that contained in a paper published in 1895, by Mm. Binet and Henri. *Ibid.* 330 Individual Psychology, on the contrary, studies those psychical processes which vary from one individual to another. **1917** GLUECK & LIND tr. *Adler's Neurotic Constitution* (1921) p. v, An empiric basis is made use of in comparative individual-psychology for the purpose of establishing a fictive standard of normality in order to enable one to measure and compare with it grades of deviation from it. **1933** T. S. ELIOT *Use of Poetry* 17, I cannot accept any such theory which is erected upon purely individual-psychological foundations. **1933** W. J. H. SPROTT tr. *Freud's New Introd. Lect. Psycho-Anal.* xxxiv. 180 In reality Individual Psychology has very little to do with analysis, but..lives a sort of parasitic existence at its expense..; we cannot assent to any interference with its correct application as meaning the opposite of Group Psychology. **1951** E. E. EVANS-PRITCHARD *Social Anthropol.* iii. 45 There are various and particular objections to each of these successive attempts to explain social facts by individual psychology. **1959** L. RADL in Adler & Deutsch *Ess. Individual Psychol.* 162 At this point the close similarity between the Existentialist doctrine and Individual Psychology once again becomes strikingly apparent.

e. individual variable *Logic*, a variable that ranges over individuals. Cf. sense B. *sb.* 2 b in Dict.

1937 A. SMEATON tr. *Carnap's Logical Syntax of Lang.* 195 A ⁰v is called an individual variable. **1952** P. F. STRAWSON *Introd. Logical Theory* v. 130 To the variable '*x*' and other variables of the same type..we give the name 'individual variables'. **1954** I. M. COPI *Symbolic Logic* iv. 67 The small letter '*x*'—called an 'individual variable'—is a mere *place marker* which serves to indicate where an individual constant may be written for a singular proposition to result. **1965** HUGHES & LONDEY *Elem. Formal Logic* xxiii. 169 We shall call such variables individual-variables (meaning thereby, of course, not that the variables are themselves individuals—whatever that might mean—but that they stand indifferently for the names of individual things).

individualism. Add: **1.** (Earlier example.)

1827 L. T. REDE *Road to Stage* 59, I beg to disclaim, in these observations, any individualism; several talented persons may be found connected with such establishments.

2. (Earlier example.)

1851 MILL in *Westm. Rev.* LVI. 87 Socialism as long as it attacks the existing individualism, is easily triumphant.

6. *Bot.* [ad. G. *individualismus* (K. von Tubeuf *Pflanzenkrankheiten* (1895) I. ii. 102).] A type of symbiosis in which the product of the relationship differs from either of the component organisms. Now *rare.*

1897 A. SCHNEIDER in *Minnesota Bot. Stud.* I. 944 The best known and perhaps the most typical form of complete individualism is represented by the higher lichens. **1913** *Mycologia* V. 102 It is supposed that the relationship is becoming closer and closer, and that finally it will be so intimate that neither symbiont will be able to live independently. Then will the individualism be perfect. **1967** P. GRAY *Dict. Biol. Sci.* 268/1 *Individualism*, a type of symbiosis, in which the aggregate differs from any of its components. A lichen is a case in point.

individualistically (i:ndividiu,ăli·stikăli), *adv.* [f. INDIVIDUALISTIC *a.*: see -ICALLY.] In an individualistic manner; from the individualistic standpoint.

1894 *Internat. Jrnl. Ethics* Oct. 42 The trumpery decorations of the present-day individualistically arrayed establishment. **1922** A. G. HOGG *Redemption from this World* 245 In India the problem has been conceived individualistically, while by the Hebrews it was..conceived socially. **1925** *Contemp. Rev.* Aug. 234 They find themselves at variance of purpose with other [*sic*] less individualistically inclined. **1938** R. G. COLLINGWOOD *Princ. Art* xiv. 324 This activity..is performed not only by the man whom we individualistically call the artist, but partly by all the other artists..'influencing' him.

individuated, *ppl. a.* Add: **1. b.** Denoting a person who has been through the process of individuation (see *INDIVIDUATION 1 b).

1959 *Times Lit. Suppl.* 6 Feb. 73/1 The 'Individuated' man of Jungian analytical psychology, released from the destructive contradictions within humanity, bears a startling resemblance to the 'new man' of the Pauline Epistles, released from the bondage of sin. **1973** J. SINGER *Boundaries of Soul* xiii. 330 The wresting of consciousness, of self-awareness, from the tendency to become submerged in the mass, is the task of the individuated person.

individuating, *vbl. sb.* (Later example.)

1954 A. J. AYER *Philos. Ess.* i. 22 In ordinary speech, expressions which I have classified as indicators do the work of individuating.

individuation. Add: **1. b.** *Psychol.* In the analytical psychology of Jung, the process by which consciousness and the collective unconscious of the psyche are integrated and wholeness of the individual self is established; also *attrib.*, as *individuation process.*

1909 W. A. HAUSSMANN tr. *Nietzsche's Birth of Tragedy* 121 Apollo stands before me as the transfiguring genius of the *principium individuationis* through which alone the redemption in appearance is to be truly attained, while by the mystical cheer of Dionysius the spell of the individuation is broken, and the way lies open to the Mothers of Being. **1923** H. G. BAYNES tr. *Jung's Psychol. Types* xi. 561 Individuation, therefore, is a process of differentiation, having for its goal the development of the individual personality. **1948** G. ADLER *Stud. Analytical Psychol.* i. 3 The process of psychic growth and maturation, that is the process of integration and individuation, presents the individual with widely different situations and tasks according to the particular point he has reached in life. **1955** I. FLETCHER in J. Wain *Interpretations* 156 In its detail, the poem resembles what might be described in Jungian terms as an attempt at 'individuation', a harmonious relation between the components of the self. **1959** D. COX *Jung & St. Paul* xii. 341 Justification by Faith precedes all advance towards a full life whereas Individuation crowns an advance which has already taken place. **1973** J. SINGER *Boundaries of Soul* i. 8, I sat before the examiner and the two experts for my oral examination on The Individuation Process, which is the essence of analysis.

5. c. *Bot.* [tr. G. *individualismus* (K. von Tubeuf *Pflanzenkrankheiten* (1895) I. ii. 102).] = *INDIVIDUALISM 6.

1897 W. G. SMITH tr. *Tubeuf's Dis. Plants* viii. 87 This unification of two living beings into an individual whole, I have designated 'Individuation'.

Indo-¹. Add: *Indo-Arabian, -Arabic, -Austral;* **Indo-Abyssinian** *a.*, of or pertaining to both the Dravidians of India and the Hamites of north-east Africa; also as *sb.*, one of these peoples; **Indo-African** *a.*, of or pertaining to India and Africa, *spec.* applied to a supposed former continent now covered by the Indian Ocean; relating to Indians and Africans in South Africa; **Indo-Anglian** *a.*, of or pertaining to literature in English written by Indian authors; also as *sb.*, a writer of such literature; **Indo-British** *a.* (example); **Indo-Chinese** *a.* (later example); **Indo-Hittite** (see quot. 1930); **Indo-Malayan** *a.*, pertaining to India and Malaya; *spec.*, denoting an ethnological region comprising Sri Lanka, the Malay peninsula, and Malayan islands; **Indo-Oceanic** *a.*, pertaining to the East Indian islands and the islands of the Pacific Ocean; **Indo-Pacific** *a.*, relating to the Indian Ocean and the adjacent parts of the Pacific Ocean; also, relating to the group of languages, usually called Malayo-Polynesian, spoken in the islands of these waters; **Indo-Pakistan, -Pakistani** *adjs.*, pertaining to India and Pakistan or to their inhabitants; also **Indo-Pak** colloq. abbrev.; **Indo-Saracenic** *a.*, pertaining to the products of mixed Indian and Saracenic origin; **Indo-Scythian, -Scythic** *adjs.*, pertaining to India and Scythia; also as *sb.*; also **Indo-Scyth**, a person from these regions; **Indo-Teutonic** (earlier and later examples: still *rare*).

1896 A. H. KEANE *Ethnol.* viii. 170 Again, what is to be made of the expression 'Indo-Abyssinian', or even 'Abyssinian' at all as an ethnical term. *Ibid.* x. 229 Considerable sections of the Indo-African Continent..must have persisted far into the tertiary epoch. *Ibid.* xii. 295 It is admitted by all ethnologists that Asia is the original home of the Mongolic division, a fact which harmonises with the view that the vanished Indo-African Continent was the cradle of mankind. **1971** *Illustr. Weekly India* 18 Apr. 24/3 Dr Naicker and Dr Dadoo forged an Indo-African political alliance. **1883** in K. R. Srinivasa Iyengar *Indian Writing in English* (1962) i. 3 Indo-Anglian. **1935** A. R. CHIDA (*title*) Anthology of Indo-Anglian Verse. **1943** K. R. SRINIVASA IYENGAR (*title*) Indo-Anglian literature. **1962** *Times Lit. Suppl.* 10 Aug. 596/3 Authors such as R. K. Narayan, Dom Moraes, Balachandra Rajan (now called 'Indo-Anglians') find their public in the West, rather than inside India itself. **1969** *Sunday Standard* (Bombay) 3 Aug. (Mag. Sect.) p. vii/7 Anita Desai is one of the most competent amongst the small band of Indo-Anglian novelists who have successfully established that a branch of English literature can grow and flourish as well in India as..in Australia or Canada. **1933** BLOOMFIELD *Language* 69 The great Indo-Chinese (or Sino-Tibetan) family consists of three branches. **1884** *Encycl. Brit.* XVII. 627/1 In Europe, before the introduction of the algorithm or full Indo-Arabic system with the zero. **1896** A. H. KEANE *Ethnol.* x. 226 The..possible fusion of Melanochroid Caucasic (South Indian) and Austral Negro blood at a remote epoch in some now perhaps submerged Indo-Austral region. **1954** G. S. RAO (*title*) Indian words in English: a study in Indo-British cultural and linguistic relations. **1951** 'J. WYNDHAM' *Day of Triffids* ii. 42 Its first occurrence..took place in Indo-China... But..the Indo-Chinese specimen can have had no great lead. **1953** M. POWYS *Lace & Lace-Making* iv. 18 Indo-Chinese Venise, 20th century. The Indo-Chinese industry shows more originality in design. **1969** N. FREELING *Tsing-Boum* xiii. 90 Our Indochinese adventure finished shortly afterwards. **1930** E. H. STURTEVANT in J. T. Hatfield et al. *Curme Vol. Ling. Stud.* 142 We now know that Hittite broke away from the parent stock long before the other historic languages did and that we must thus consider Hittite and primitive IE as parallel offshoots of an earlier language, which we may call Indo-Hittite. **1964** S. K. CHATTERJI in D. Abercrombie et al. *Daniel Jones* 407 Primitive Indo-European, as it had evolved out of the earlier primitive Indo-Hittite. **1964** R. H. ROBINS *Gen. Ling.* 305 Scholars differ as to whether it [*sc.* Hittite] is an I-E language or a representative of a collateral branch forming with I-E a yet more inclusive Indo-hittite family. **1869** Indo-Malayan [see *AUSTRO-²]. **1875** *Encycl. Brit.* II. 696/2 The Indo-Malayan peninsula and Archipelago. **1936** *Discovery* Jan. 21/2 Of Indo-Malayan origin. **1896** A. H. KEANE *Ethnol.* xii. 326 *margin*, Indo-Oceanic linguistic relations. **1877** *Encycl. Brit.* VII. 280/2 The Oriental or Indo-Pacific marine region. **1880** *Ibid.* XII. 680/2 The eastward extension of the Indo-Pacific fauna. **1885** *Ibid.* XIX. 422/2 Indo-Pacific Races of Men. **1965** *Punch* 27 Jan. 116/1 Fearing that Indo-Pak hostilities would break out along the border of the North End road. **1967** L. DEIGHTON *London Dossier* 44 Most Indo-Pak restaurants have Pakistani owners, red velvet wallpaper, stars on the ceiling and undrinkable coffee. **1971** *Illustr. Weekly India* 18 Apr. 20/2 Subcontinental peace and prosperity would appear to be prime requisites for discouraging Chinese intention [*sic*] being diverted from South-East Asia to the Indo-Pak

sub-continent. **1955** *Times* 2 Aug. 5/5 Calcutta business men have generally welcomed devaluation of the Pakistan rupee as removing a main obstacle to Indo-Pakistan trade. **1968** *Times* (Pakistan Suppl.) 6 Apr. p. viii/3 The tiger population in the Indo-Pakistan subcontinent in the 1920s was 40,000; by 1966 it had fallen to 2,800. **1958** *Oxf. Univ. Gaz.* 23 Apr. 893 The taxonomy and zoo-geography of some groups of Indo-Pakistani birds. **1969** *Capital* (Calcutta) 27 Feb. 353/2 In contrast, 1967–68 was the year which came immediately after the two worst years of drought in living memory coupled with the Indo-Pakistani war. **1970** P. OLIVER *Savannah Syncopators* 14 [Gunther Schuller] considers it 'worth mentioning that Indo-Pakistani music is divided into six principal modes, three of which—afternoon modes—are nothing but the blues scale'. **1887** KIPLING *From Sea to Sea* (1899) I. iv. 31 A wonder of carven white stone of the Indo-Saracenic style. **1908** H. CRAIK *Impressions India* ii. 16 Our great grand-fathers..attempting no flimsy imitations in the Indo-Saracenic style. **1959** *Chambers's Encycl.* VII. 464/2 The Indo-Saracenic style which may be seen in centres of Mohammedan culture throughout northern India. **1841** M. ELPHINSTONE *Hist. India* I. 474 Coins of the latter nation [*sc.* the Hindus] have been found, bearing nearly the same relation to those of the Indo-Scythians that theirs did to the coins of the Greeks. **1884** *Encycl. Brit.* XVII. 660/2 The Indo-Scythian class..is fixed approximately to periods by finds in which aurei occur ranging from the earlier Roman emperors to the Antonines. **1961** H. W. BAILEY (*title*) Indo-Scythian studies: being Khotanese texts, volume IV. *Ibid.* 18 It will be possible for the historian of India to speak with more intimate knowledge of the Sakas, whom we call also the Indo-Scyths, the rulers of north India for some four hundred years. **1853** H. N. HUMPHREYS *Coin Collector's Manual* II. 706/2 Indo-Scythic kings. **1850** H. L. MANSEL *Lett., Lect. & Rev.* (1873) 11 A more extensive examination of the Indo-Teutonic languages. **1938** *Burlington Mag.* Nov. 231/1 The primeval ways of the 'Indo-Teutonic North'.

Indo-[3] (i·ndo), combining form of *Indus*, a river of the northern part of the Indian sub-continent, as in **Indo-Gange·tic** *a.*, of or pertaining to the Indus and the Ganges.

1880 *Encycl. Brit.* XII. 735/2 The Indo-Gangetic Plain covers an area of about 300,000 square miles. **1925** J. JOLY *Surface-Hist. Earth* vii. 126 The vast sedimentary collections of the Indo-Gangetic plain. **1969** *Pioneer* (Lucknow) 13 Aug. 6/4 The IIT is located on the Indo-Gangetic plain, ten kilometres west of Kanpur.

indoaniline (indo,æ·nĭlīn). *Chem.* [f. INDO-[2] + ANILINE.] **a.** A violet dye, $O{:}C_6H_4{:}N{\cdot}C_6H_4{\cdot}NH_2$. **b.** Any of the derivatives of this compound.

1886 *Jrnl. Chem. Soc.* L. 146 (*heading*) Indophenol and indoaniline. **1952** K. VENKATARAMAN *Chem. Synthetic Dyes* II. xxv. 763 Alkaline hydrolysis leads to the indophenols, sometimes called indoaniline to distinguish them from the 'true indophenols'. **1958** PACKER & VAUGHAN *Mod. Approach Org. Chem.* xix. 645 Thus aniline gives..dyestuffs such as indoaniline and the aniline blacks.

indochinite (indotʃəi·nəit). *Geol.* [f. *Indo-China* (s.v. INDO-[1]) + -ITE[1].] Any tektite from the tektite field of Indo-China.

1940 *Pop. Astron.* XLVIII. 44 The most typical indochinite specimens occur in South China and northern and central Indo-China. **1961, 1964** [see *JAVAITE]. **1969** *New Scientist* 30 Oct. 237/1 We obtain an age of the order of 0·7 m.y. for an indochinite.

indoctrinate, *v.* **1. c.** *spec.* To imbue with Communist ideas, etc. (cf. *INDOCTRINATION).

1945 MENCKEN *Amer. Lang.* Suppl. I. 306 The *reds* who emerged from hiding on the establishment of the *entente* cordiale with Russia in 1940..have revived and propagated..*to indoctrinate*, [etc.]. **1958** *Times* 22 May 6/4 It was his duty to indoctrinate leading coders who were proceeding abroad. **1958** *Oxford Mail* 5 June 6/8 Robert Ford, the English wireless operator 'indoctrinated' by the Chinese in Tibet.

indoctrination. Add: (Further examples.) Also *spec.*, the 'instruction' of prisoners of war, etc., in Communist doctrines, ideas, etc.; = *BRAINWASHING.

1935 *Nature* 11 May 801/1 Freedom or indoctrination: an enduring dilemma of Education. **1950** *Ann. Reg. 1949* 188 Communist underground activities..'subversion' and indoctrination. **1955** *Treatm. Brit. P.O.W.'s in Korea* (H.M.S.O.) 8 The political education of prisoners in the North Korean camps was not, however, confined to oral indoctrination. **1956** W. H. WHYTE *Organization Man* (1957) i. 9, I will then pick up the organization man in college, follow him through his initial indoctrination in organization life, and explore the impact of the group way upon him. **1958** *Times* 22 May 6/4 Men on the course would attend an indoctrination meeting.

indoctrinator. Delete *rare* and add examples.

1889 in *Cent. Dict.* **1952** [see *BRAINWASHING]. **1973** *Listener* 20 Dec. 845 The Armed Forces in the Soviet Union..act as the indoctrinators of the young.

indoctrinatory (indǫ·ktrinēɪ:təri), *a.* [f. INDOCTRINAT(E *v.* + -ORY[2].] That indoctrinates; relating or pertaining to indoctrination.

1953 E. E. CUMMINGS *Let.* 27 Mar. (1969) 223 Having kept my ears & eyes open, I am unaware that 'tis thanks to the indoctrinatory efforts of this gruesome gang of do-gooders that Russia is a worldpower. **1965** J. B. WILSON *Logic & Sexual Morality* 137 The simpler method..is indoctrinatory.

Indo-European, *a.* and *sb.* Add: Hence **I:ndo-Europe·anist**, a person who studies the Indo-European family of languages.

1927 *Mod. Philology* Nov. 217 This fallacy was possible because most Indo-Europeanists spoke a Germanic language and knew Latin and Greek from school and Sanskrit from grammars ultimately based on Panini. **1951** *Archivum Linguisticum* III. 114 Both Sapir and Bloomfield —who are at present usually identified with work in exotic languages—began as Indo-Europeanists. **1969** *Language* XLV. 249 The weight of this evidence seems to have persuaded a majority of Indo-Europeanists that Sievers-Edgerton's Law is a valid hypothesis.

I:ndo-Ira·nian, *a.* and *sb.* [f. INDO-[1] + IRANIAN *a.* and *sb.*] **A.** *adj.* Of or pertaining to both India and Iran; *spec.* designating a division of the Indo-European languages comprising the Indian and Iranian branches. **B.** *sb.* **a.** The Indo-Iranian languages collectively. **b.** A member of the Indo-Iranian people.

1876 T. L. PAPILLON *Man. Compar. Philol. Gr. & Latin Inflections* ii. 10 The term *Aryan*..employed..by some in the more restricted sense of *Indo-Iranian*, i.e. to denote the Asiatic sub-division of the Indo-European family. **1885** *Encycl. Brit.* XVIII. 606/1 Indo-Iranian frontier. **1888** KING & COOKSON *Princ. Sound & Inflexion Gr. & Lat.* 26 The term 'Aryan' or better 'Arian' is also applied in a more restricted sense to the Indo-Iranian group. **1895** A. MENZIES *Hist. Relig.* xxi. 380 How the Indo-Iranian religion was developed in India. **1921** E. SAPIR *Lang.* ix. 212 The peculiar, dull vowel..is entirely wanting in Germanic, Greek, Armenian, and Indo-Iranian, the nearest Indo-European congeners of Slavic. **1959** *Chambers's Encycl.* VII. 699/2 Iranian languages have developed from Indo-Iranian, one of the eastern descendants of the Indo-European parent language. The first appearance of Indo-Iranians is traced to the middle of the 2nd millennium B.C.

indole, *sb.* Add: **b.** Comb.: *indoleacetic acid*, any of the seven isomeric acetic acid derivatives, $C_8H_6N{\cdot}CH_2COOH$, of indole; *esp.* the one having the acetic acid side-chain substituted in the 3- (or β-) position, which is an important natural growth hormone in plants.

1886 *Jrnl. Chem. Soc.* L. 806 Methylindoleacetic acid, $NH\langle^{C_6H_4}_{CMe}\rangle C.CH_2.COOH$, is prepared by heating phenylhydrazinelevulinic acid..with zinc chloride. **1957** *New Biol.* XXIII. 17 Among the naturally occurring auxins, β-indoleacetic acid is widely, if not perhaps universally, distributed in the higher plants. **1958** *Plant Physiol.* XXXIII. 317 (*table*) Relative activity of indole-4-acetic acid (I-4-AA) on Avena coleoptile sections, and test for interaction with indole-3-acetic acid.

indolic (indōᵘ·lik), *a.* [f. INDOL(E *sb.* + -IC.] †**1.** *Med.* Designating a type of chronic excessive intestinal putrefaction. *Obs. rare.*

1907 C. A. HERTER *Common Bacterial Infections Digestive Tract* 279 The proposed classification recognizes three types of putrefaction which are common: the first may be called the Indolic Type,..the second..may be designated the Saccharo-butyric Type... In the third group..we find associated the characters of the indolic and the saccharo-butyric types of decomposition. **1909** *Practitioner* Feb. 227 They remark that there are three types of chronic excessive intestinal putrefaction:—(1) The indolic type, occurring in the small as well as the large intestine. In this type large quantities of indol are produced, and the stool is usually alkaline.

2. *Chem.* Containing, composed of, or characteristic of indole.

1949 *Jrnl. Biol. Chem.* CLXXX. 966 There is, then, little doubt that the empirical formula of the indolic base portion of the complex..is $C_{19}H_{14}O_2N_2$. **1958** *Jrnl. Amer. Chem. Soc.* LXXX. 126/1 The ultraviolet absorption spectrum..was recognized to be indolic. **1971** *Nature* 7 May 25/1 Indolic substances have been clearly implicated in some conditions..which are often accompanied by mental disturbances.

Indological (indolǫ·dʒikăl), *a.* [f. INDOLOG(Y + -ICAL.] Of or pertaining to Indology.

1950 *Austral. Outlook* Mar. 46 They formed the so-called 'ethical group' mainly centred at the Indological Faculty of the University of Leyden. **1957** *Contrib. Indian Sociol.* I. 14 The difficulty in Indological studies in general is that of discovering..the 'whole'. **1958** *Oxf. Mag.* 13 Mar. 368/1 Studies aspiring to be called 'indological', however, demand some knowledge of Sanskrit. **1964** *Language* XL. 114 His interests covered a broad..range of Indological subjects. **1971** *Illustr. Weekly India* 11 Apr. 35/1 The University of Kiel..had been a centre of Indological studies for over a century and a half.

Indologist (indǫ·lŏdʒist). [f. INDOLOG(Y + -IST.] A student of Indology.

1904 M. DE Z. WICKREMASINGHE in *Epigraphia Zeylanica* I. 1. p. vi, The thanks of all Indologists are due to the Ceylon Government. **1928** *Spectator* 7 Apr. 535/1 Indologists at once recognized the importance of this ample..collection of material for their studies. **1929** A. STEIN *On Alexander's Track to Indus* xii. 89 M. Sylvain Lévi, the eminent French Indologist. **1957** P. WORSLEY *Trumpet shall Sound* 224 The explanation of this absence of millenarism from Hindu India..can only be attempted by an Indologist. **1971** *Illustr. Weekly India* 11 Apr. 35/1 Hermann Jacobi (1850–1937) is remembered with great reverence by indologists as a pioneer in the field of Jain and Prakrit studies.

indolyl (i·ndŏləil, -il). *Chem.* [f. INDOL(E *sb.* + -YL.] Any of the seven isomeric univalent radicals derived from indole by removal of a hydrogen atom; freq. as a word-forming element.

1907 *Jrnl. Chem. Soc.* XCII. I. 737 Acidification of the solution precipitates α-benzoylaminoindolylacrylic acid. **1926**, etc. [see *INDOLYLACETIC *a.*]. **1937** *Chem. Abstr.* XXXI. 9489/1 Indolyl C_8H_6N— (from indole, 7 isomers). **1949** *Jrnl. Biol. Chem.* CLXXX. 966 If we subtract the formula for the indolyl group (C_8H_6N), the number of atoms which must still be put into place is very few, $C_2H_8O_2N$. **1972** W. J. HOULIHAN *Indoles* II. iv. 87, 4-Indolylisoprene has been prepared by the use of the Wittig reaction.

indolylacetic (indŏləil-, indŏlilăsī·tik), *a.* *Chem.* [f. prec. + ACETIC *a.*] *indolylacetic acid* = *indoleacetic acid.

1926 *Chem. Abstr.* XX. 759 Boiled 6 hrs. with 20% KOH it [*sc.* β-indolylacetonitrile] gives 84% β-indolylacetic acid. **1937** *Discovery* June 174/1 It [*sc.* hetero-auxin] is an acid, β-indolyl-acetic acid, and can now be bought as crystals and used for growth hormone experiments. **1972** L. J. AUDUS *Plant Growth Substances* (ed. 3) I. iii. 74 IAA (indol-3yl-acetic) is the most active, indol-1yl-acetic ..and indol-2yl-acetic..are less active but indol-4yl-acetic ..has very low activity indeed.

indomethacin (indome·þăsin). *Pharm.* [f. INDO(LE *sb.* + METH(YL + AC(ETIC *a.* (words which occur in the systematic name: see quot. 1963[1]) + -IN[1].] A yellowish-white powdery indole derivative, $C_{19}H_{16}NO_4Cl$, which has anti-inflammatory, anti-pyretic, and analgesic properties and has been given orally in the treatment of rheumatoid arthritis, gout, and similar conditions.

1963 T. Y. SHEN et al. in *Jrnl. Amer. Chem. Soc.* LXXXV. 488/2 We wish to report a new class of anti-inflammatory and antipyretic agents, substituted indole acetic and propionic acids... One member of the series, 1-(*p*-chlorobenzoyl)-5-methoxy-2-methylindole-3-acetic acid.., designated as indomethacin, has demonstrated a high degree of anti-inflammatory activity. **1963** *New Scientist* 10 Oct. 103/2 One patient, aged 73, had had arthritis for 30 years and was bed-ridden with inflamed joints and a temperature. Within three days of being given indomethacin the temperature fell to normal and pain was relieved. **1968** *Clin. Pharmacol. & Therapeutics* IX. 94 Indomethacin may be useful in treating other.. rheumatic diseases, but as yet few comparisons with other standard therapies have been made. The drug has severe side effects and should be used with caution. **1971** *New Scientist* 24 June 745/2 This..might well eliminate the gastrointestinal side-effects of drugs such as indomethacin used to treat rheumatoid diseases.

Indonesian, *a.* and *sb.* Add: (Earlier examples.) **a.** *adj.* (*b*) (Also as *sb.*) (Of, relating to, or designating) the western branch of the Malayo-Polynesian family of languages; (*c*) Of or pertaining to the federal republic of Indonesia. Also as *sb.*, a native or inhabitant of Indonesia.

The national language of Indonesia is now called *Bahasa Indonesia*.

1850 J. R. LOGAN in *Jrnl. Indian Archipelago* IV. 254, I prefer the purely geographical term Indonesia..for the Indian Islands or the Indian Archipelago. We thus get Indonesian for Indian Archipelagian or Archipelagic, and Indonesians for Indian Archipelagians or Indian Islanders. *Ibid.* 441 The partially negro character which the Polynesian or Indonesian community has acquired. *Ibid.* 446 In the Indonesian languages everything beyond the mere surface resolved itself into their phonology. **1851** *Ibid.* V. 214 In W. Indonesian the final vowels and consonants are in general in about equal proportions. **1932** W. L. GRAFF *Lang.* iii. 151 In Indonesian the infix *-um-* gives the radical a verbal active meaning. **1933** L. BLOOMFIELD *Lang.* iv. 71 The Malayan (or Indonesian) branch includes Malay... Further, it embraces the languages of the great islands of the East, such as Formosan, Javanese, [etc.]. **1948** D. WEHL *Birth of Indonesia* xii. 177 The Netherlands Government..could not but feel that they had been interrupted in the very act of bringing to birth the Indonesian Commonwealth. *Ibid.*, Two years of conflict between the Netherlands and the Indonesian Republic had ended. **1950** THEIMER & CAMPBELL *Encycl. World Politics* 228/1 Sovereignty was transferred to the Indonesian government on 27 December 1949. **1958** *Listener* 4 Dec. 914/1 The Indonesians..write their common language, Bahasa Malay, in Roman letters. **1968** M. CALDWELL *Indonesia* i. 23 The decision to promote a national language—*Bahasa Indonesia*—was taken at an All-Indonesia Youth Congress in 1928, and thereafter enthusiastically forwarded by Indonesian intellectuals and leaders. **1973** 'I. DRUMMOND' *Jaws of Watchdog* iii. 35 He found himself dancing with the little wife of an Indonesian diplomat... [He] stayed with his Indonesian unit ten. **1973** D. MAY *Laughter in Djakarta* i. 13 He had worked furiously.. learning Indonesian.

indoona, var. INDUNA (in Dict. and Suppl.).

indoor, in-door, *a.* Add: **1.** *spec.* Of amusements, games, etc., occurring or played in-doors.

1847 C. BRONTË *Jane Eyre* II. iii. 61 In-door amusements..became more lively and varied, in consequence of the stop put to out-door gaiety. **1863** THACKERAY *Virginians* xxvi. 178, I don't care for indoor games much

..but I..long to see a good English hunting-field. **1865** C. M. YONGE *Clever Woman* II. vii. 135 'How is Conrade?' 'Quite himself. Up to a prodigious amount of indoor croquet.' **1873** *Young Englishwoman* Mar. 154/2 Can you recommend me..any indoor games suitable for young children, and the words used. **1890** *Harper's Weekly* 8 Mar. 179/4 In-door baseball has not the slightest resemblance to parlor croquet. **1897** *Illustr. London News* 13 Nov. 710/3 (Advt.), Puff billiards. The latest and most amusing indoor game yet produced. **1921** *Daily Colonist* (Victoria, B.C.) 22 Oct. 10/1 Several upsets featured the play in the Canadian indoor tennis championships here yesterday. **1925** A. HUXLEY *Those Barren Leaves* I. vii. 70 'When all is said, is there a better indoor sport [than philosophy]?..' 'Possibly not... But the point is, aren't there better occupations for a man of sense than indoor sports, even the best of indoor sports?' **1926** R. MACAULAY *Crewe Train* II. iv. 88 Have you always hated indoor games? **1948** J. BETJEMAN *Sel. Poems* 35 (*title*) Indoor games near Newbury. **1949** *Daily Ardmoreite* (Ardmore, Okla.) 23 Feb. 18/2 The explosive charge..occupies a sphere of three or four inches—about the size of an indoor baseball. **1951** E. COXHEAD *One Green Bottle* ii. 54 Baiting Harry was..one of Johnny Hollinger's favourite indoor sports. **1965** J. SYMONS *Belting Inheritance* iii. 51 The sort of indoor cricket that you play on paper by picking words out of a book. **1972** *Country Life* 23 Nov. 1424/2 Miniature Croquet Sets... Great indoor game for family and friends. **1972** R. PERRY *Fall Guy* iv. 71 We once again indulged in the oldest of indoor sports.

So (*nonce-wds.*) indoo·rness, the essence of being indoors; indoo·ry *a.*, preferring to remain indoors.

1934 G. B. SHAW *Village Wooing* 120 My mother was that indoory that she grudged having to go out and do her marketing. **1949** E. BOWEN *Heat of Day* vi. 103 The concentrated indoorness of the lounge was made..greater rather than less by the number of exits.

indraw (indrǭ·), *v.* [f. IN-¹ + DRAW *v.*] *trans.* To draw in.

See also M.E.D. *indrauen.*

1883 R. JEFFERIES *Story of my Heart* vii. 116 It is lying beside the immortals, in-drawing the life of the ocean, the earth, and the sun. **1887** G. MEREDITH *Ballads & Poems* 62 Fearful..All their breath indrew. **1905** J. THORNTON in T. Stephens *Child & Religion* ix. 316 He [*sc.* Christ] 'indraws', and stores up in the interiors of the child's spirit all the good affections of innocence. **1911** W. OWEN *Let.* 17 Sept. (1967) 82 Depend upon it, whichever Fire indraws me, I shall..come out unscathed.

i·ndraw, *sb. rare.* [f. IN *adv.* 11 d + DRAW *sb.*] The act of drawing in.

1899 A. C. LYALL *Asiatic Stud.* 2nd Ser. vii. 380 There has always been an indraw from the cool uplands..into the low-lying fertile regions.

indrawing, *vbl. sb.* (Later examples.)

1904 R. J. FARRER *Garden of Asia* xvi. 147 The frock-coated officials..bow with ceremonious reverence and indrawings of the breath. **1904** F. LYNDE *Grafters* xxii. 280 His smile was a mere indrawing of the lips.

indrawn, *ppl. a.* Add: **a.** Also *fig.*

1751 [in Dict.]. **1959** *Times* 10 Dec. 15/2 The father, quiet and indrawn. **1965** *New Statesman* 27 Aug. 298/2 His [*sc.* P. Maxwell Davies's] early, very Viennese *Piano Pieces*..have an indrawn intensity which we can accept as characteristic only in the light of later events.

indubitable, *a.* Add: Also **indubitabi·lity** = INDUBITABLENESS.

1933 *Mind* XLII. 531 Even if Husserl's argument concerning the indubitability of transcendental selves be granted, it does not follow [etc.]. **1946** *Nature* 10 Aug. 185/2 There remains a residuum of indubitability consisting of our sensations themselves and the ultimate elements of rational necessity.

induce, *v.* **4.** (Further examples, illustrating the widespread occurrence of this use in technical contexts, freq. with a concrete or material obj. rather than an abstract one.)

1928 *Biol. Abstr.* II. 686/2 In the early gastrula stage the whole quadrant lying above the blastopore is capable of inducing formation of a new embryonic axis. **1931** J. NEEDHAM *Chem. Embryol.* I. 579 A piece of the brain of a free-swimming larva would still induce a medullary plate in the early embryo. **1941** *Jrnl. Nat. Cancer Inst.* (U.S.) II. 199/2 Whether carbon tetrachloride is the active agent in inducing hepatomas in mice or whether these tumors are merely the result of hepatic damage caused by carbon tetrachloride awaits further study. **1947** *Growth* XI. 228 Fifty-two compounds..were tested for their activity in inducing pectinase production. **1953** *Cold Spring Harbor Symp. Quant. Biol.* XVIII. 101/2 The transition from the prophage to the vegetative state can therefore be induced with a probability of nearly 1. **1968** *Ann. Rev. Nuclear Sci.* XVIII. 343 (*heading*) Compound nuclear reactions induced by heavy ions. **1969** *Times* 9 June 2/1 How then do D.N.A. viruses induce interferon in the cell? **1971** tr. *S. E. Bresler's Introd. Molecular Biol.* v. 487 The existence of compounds that repress and induce the formation of enzymes provides direct evidence that regulatory mechanisms are present. **1973** *Nature* 12 Jan. 132/1 Bachem..induced cataracts in guinea-pigs and rabbits with ultraviolet light. **1973** *Ibid.* 9 Feb. 367/1 Whereas ^{224}Ra with a short 3·8 day half life induces in man chiefly osteosarcomas, ^{226}Ra with a half life of 1,620 years induces both osteo and fibrosarcomas.

b. (Earlier example.)

1777 T. CAVALLO *Compl. Treat. Electr.* IV. iv. 384 The action of these plates depends upon a principle long ago discovered, viz. the power that an excited electric has to induce a contrary Electricity in a body brought within its sphere of action.

d. To initiate (labour) artificially. Cf. *INDUCTION 9.

1852 *Lancet* 2 Oct. 297/2 Under these circumstances, a new method of inducing premature labour..cannot fail of being recognised by obstetricians as a great boon. **1916** G. P. SHEARS *Obstetrics* xxvi. 573 Manual dilatation is not in itself a method of inducing labor, but it is sometimes most valuable in accelerating the progress of labor. **1968** D. C. BETHEA *Introd. Maternity Nursing* ix. 121 The mother who is to have labor induced may feel uneasy... She is likely to want to know if her labor will be longer, harder, or more painful because it is induced.

e. *Biol.* To cause (a bacterium containing a prophage) to begin the lytic cycle.

Quots. 1950, 1951 illustrate the origin of this use in sense 4 a (*induce* = produce, cause).

[**1950** A. LWOFF et al. in *Ann. de l'Inst. Pasteur* LXXIX. 833 Nous avons induit la lyse de la totalité des bactéries d'une culture de *B. megatherium.* **1951** *Jrnl. Bacteriol.* LXII. 317 Maturation from prophage into phage can be induced in every bacterium of a culture of K12 by irradiation with small doses of ultraviolet rays (Lwoff effect).] **1953** *Cold Spring Harbor Symp. Quant. Biol.* XVIII. 104/1 In order to be induced to the same extent, cultures of *B. megatherium* in minimal medium require a dose of ultraviolet light 20 times greater than cultures in yeast extract. **1959** JACOB & WOLLMAN in Burnet & Stanley *Viruses* II. ix. 332 When..inducible lysogenic bacteria are first induced and then infected with an adequate multiplicity of a mutant of the homologous phage, each bacterium releases particles of the prophage as well as of the mutant type. **1962** *Nature* 24 Nov. 783/2 Certain antitumour agents are capable of inducing lysogenic bacteria. **1970** *Jrnl. Virol.* V. 240/2 When an intermediate amount of mitomycin C (1 μg/ml) was also used to induce the culture in addition to thymine deprivation, the production of PBLB was almost doubled.

induced, *ppl. a.* Add: More widely (in sense 4 of the vb.), caused or brought into being artificially or by some extraneous agent or process; not spontaneous (cf. INDUCTION 9 in Dict. and Suppl.). (Further examples.)

1922 C. C. VAN BLARCOM *Obstetr. Nursing* xiii. 309 Induced abortion applies to the termination of pregnancy before the child is viable,..and is performed solely in the interests of the mother, as the fetus is always lost. **1929** *Biol. Abstr.* III. 1495/2 The distal skeleton of the induced limbs might be normal. **1941** *Jrnl. Nat. Cancer Inst.* II. 198/2 The incidence of spontaneous hepatomas..is decidedly below that of the induced tumors in our experimental animals. **1947** *Growth* XI. 225 (*heading*) The occurrence of substrate-induced enzyme formation. **1960** B. I. BALINSKY *Introd. Embryol.* vi. 168 In other experiments the whole of the induced neural tube was developed exclusively from host tissue. **1962** H. D. BUSH *Atomic & Nucl. Physics* v. 105 (*heading*) Induced nuclear transmutations. **1970** G. K. WOODGATE *Elem. Atomic Struct.* iii. 32 Three radiation processes are postulated: spontaneous emission,..absorption,..and induced emission.

b. *induced* (*radio*)*activity*, radioactivity brought about in otherwise non-radioactive material by its transformation under bombardment or irradiation or by the proximity of radioactive material.

[**1899** P. & M. CURIE in *Compt. Rend.* CXXIX. 714 Nous avons constaté que les rayons émis par ces matières, en agissant sur des substances inactives, peuvent leur communiquer la radioactivité, et que cette radioactivité induite persiste pendant un temps assez long.] **1900** RUTHERFORD in *Phil. Mag.* XLIX. 169 Two or three layers of ordinary foolscap-paper completely cut off the ordinary radiation given out by thorium compounds, but do not much diminish the amount of induced radio-activity. **1904** F. SODDY *Radio-Activity* ii. 33 With the power of a radio-active element to produce a radio-active emanation is bound up its power to impart radio-activity to objects in the neighbourhood. Rutherford discovered this property for the thorium emanation, and designated it the excited activity. M. and Mme. Curie..called it the induced activity. **1913** [see *EXCITED *ppl. a.* 2 d]. **1926** R. W. LAWSON tr. *Hevesy & Paneth's Man. Radioactivity* viii. 90 Before the material nature of the active deposit had been recognised, it was customary to call the activity acquired by bodies that had been in contact with emanation by the name of 'induced activity'. **1963** B. FOZARD *Instrumentation Nucl. Reactors* i. 7 When the irradiated material is removed from the neutron flux the induced activity is measured. **1966** *McGraw-Hill Encycl. Sci. & Technol.* XI. 277/2 The yield of any induced radioactivity is the initial rate of production of the activity under the particular conditions of nuclear bombardment.

2. *Biol.* Of a bacterium: that has been induced (see *INDUCE *v.* 4 e).

1951 *Jrnl. Bacteriol.* LXII. 305 The induced bacteria double in length and thickness..between irradiation and lysis. **1963** G. S. STENT *Molecular Biol. Bacterial Viruses* xii. 312 There is little doubt..that the phages are liberated by lysis of the induced lysogenic cells. **1970** *Jrnl. Virol.* V. 244/2 After mitomycin C treatment, DNA continues to be synthesized by the induced bacterium.

3. Special comb.: *induced drag*, that part of the drag on an aircraft or aerofoil which arises from the development of lift; *induced draught*, a draught towards a fan or other device that draws air through a furnace, up a chimney, etc.; *induced reaction*, a chemical reaction that is accelerated by the presence of an inductor (see *INDUCTOR 4) that reacts with one of the reactants.

1926 H. GLAUERT *Elem. Aerofoil & Airscrew Theory* x. 132 The lift force is..inclined backwards at the small angle ..and therefore gives a component in the direction of the drag force. This component is called the induced drag, since it is caused by the induced velocity of the trailing vortices. **1931, 1948** [see *DRAG *sb.* 7 e]. **1962** F. I. ORDWAY et al. *Basic Astronautics* viii. 340 There are three basic types of aerodynamics drag: skin-friction drag, form drag, and induced drag. **1887** W. A. MARTIN in *Trans. Soc. Engin. 1886* 117 In comparing the three systems, of ordinary draught, forced draught, and the author's induced draught,..it is necessary to say [etc.]. **1894** [in Dict.]. **1971** *Sci. Amer.* May 73/3 In a forced-draft [cooling] tower the fan is at the bottom and pushes the air up through the tower; in an induced-draft tower the fan is at the top and pulls the air up. **1903** *Jrnl. Chem. Soc.* LXXXIV. II. 277 The reaction between bromic and sulphurous acids is the primary spontaneous reaction; and that between bromic and arsenious acids is the secondary induced reaction. **1917** *Ibid.* CXI. I. 702 In all the experiments on induced reactions recorded above, the oxidising agents take part and are themselves reduced during the chemical change. **1964** J. R. PARTINGTON *Hist. Chem.* IV. vi. 194 Closely related to the subject of autoxidation is that of induced reactions.

inducer. Add: **2.** For '*rare*' read '*rare* except in scientific contexts'. (Further examples.)

1970 *Sci. Jrnl.* June 70/1 Corticine favours the development of the cortex and inhibits the medulla while medullarine has the opposite effect. These inducers, as they are called, also impose ovogonial or spermatogonial development upon the germ cells. **1971** *New Scientist* 24 June 745/2 Consistency is maintained by several indications.. that prostaglandins are potent inducers of fever. **1971** *Sci. Amer.* July 27/3 The search for inducers..turned up many different kinds of substances that stimulated interferon production in animals. These included bacteria, parasites, viruses, polysaccharides,..and other substances.

b. *Biochem.* Any substance (freq. the substrate of the enzyme concerned) whose presence results in (increased) production of an enzyme. (Cf. *INDUCTION 9 c.)

1953 [see *INDUCTION 9 c]. **1959** *Jrnl. Molecular Biol.* I. 175 When inducer is added at this stage, enzyme synthesis is resumed. **1971** J. Z. YOUNG *Introd. Study Man* iii. 54 The action of the inducer (lactose) is to inactivate the repressor.

inducibility (indiūsibi·lĭti). [f. INDUCIBLE *a.*: see *-IBILITY.] The property or state of being inducible; *spec.* in *Biochem.* (see *INDUCIBLE *a.* 1 c).

1953 COHN, MONOD, et al. in *Nature* 12 Dec. 1096/2 Thus 'constitutivity' and 'inducibility' are properties of enzyme-forming systems, not of enzymes *per se*, and can be used as significant expressions only in a biological frame of reference, not in a chemical one. It should be stressed that the notions of constitutivity and inducibility are relative, not absolute; in any given biological system, a certain fraction of a particular enzyme-forming capacity may be constitutive, the remaining fraction inducible. For the sake of convenience, one may wish to refer to 'an induced enzyme' or to 'a constitutive enzyme'; but it should always be kept in mind that these are shorthand expressions for 'an enzyme the formation of which is largely or entirely inducible (or constitutive) in the particular organism concerned'. **1959** *Jrnl. Molecular Biol.* I. 165 (*heading*) The genetic control and cytoplasmic expression of 'inducibility' in the synthesis of β-galactosidase by *E. coli.* **1965** M. DEUTSCH in B. B. Wolman *Scientific Psychol.* 513 Inducibility provides the basis for normative control of individual behavior in the cooperative situation. **1972** *Science* 20 Oct. 315/2 The inducibility of [the enzyme system] AHH shows genetic variation in the mouse.

inducible, *a.* Restrict *rare* to sense 2 and add: **1.** (Later examples.)

1958 *Times* 7 Nov. 7/7 This [*sc.* 'vigour tolerance'] is attributed to factors such as increased weight or improved biochemical conditions, inducible as a strain characteristic to be found in extremes of environmental conditions. **1973** *Nature* 6 July 6/1 In the case of adjuvant arthritis—inducible in rats by remote injection of water-in-oil emulsion incorporating killed mycobacteria.

b. *Biol.* Of a bacterium: capable of being induced (*INDUCE *v.* 4 e).

1953 *Cold Spring Harbor Symp. Quant. Biol.* XVIII. 102/1 A growing culture of inducible lysogenic bacteria. **1959** JACOB & WOLLMAN in Burnet & Stanley *Viruses* II. ix. 328 Within the same bacterial species, both inducible and non-inducible strains can be isolated.

c. *Biochem.* Of an enzyme or enzyme system: produced in response to the presence of an appropriate inducer.

1953 [see *INDUCTION 9 c]. **1966** E. R. M. KAY *Biochem.* xxvii. 353 Some enzymes appear only when a special, but nevertheless necessary energy source is provided, as in the case of β-galactosidase formation. Such enzymes are called 'inducible' enzymes. **1971** *Nature* 19 Nov. 135/1 In the inducible regulatory system of mammals, hormones rather than substrates..serve as inducers.

inducing, *ppl. a.* Add: **4.** That induces or brings about; causing induction (see *INDUCTION 9).

1931 J. NEEDHAM *Chem. Embryol.* I. 579 Regeneration of the adult amphibian lens takes place under the inducing influence of the retina. **1947** *Growth* XI. 237 Each of these two closely related compounds induced within the same cells the formation of different enzyme systems, each completely specific towards the inducing agent. **1950** L. G. BARTH tr. *Brachet's Chem. Embryol.* x. 345 (*heading*) Metabolism of the organization center and chemical

nature of the inducing substance. **1966** E. R. M. Kay *Biochem.* xxvii. 354 One form [of repressor] is active as a repressor, but combines with an inducer if present in the form of an inducing substrate, thereby becoming an inactive form so that the structural gene may form 'messenger' RNA normally. **1968** M. W. Strickberger *Genetics* xix. 401 The 'inducing' trigger that produces lysis in lysogenic strains..involves a change in the activity of the phage from a quiescent prophage state to a proliferative vegetative state.

induct, *v.* Add: **3. b.** *U.S.* To bring into military service.

1934 Webster, *Induct*, to enroll for military service in compliance with a draft law, as the selective service act of 1917. **1940** *Congress. Rec.* 6 Sept. 11675/2 Men..who are voluntarily inducted pursuant to this act. *Ibid.* 11676/1 The word 'inducted' I maintain means any of them [service men] because they are taken in... They are inducted either after they volunteer or after they are conscripted. **1967** *Boston Sunday Herald* 26 Mar. II. 7/7 Muhammad (Clay) was to be inducted—supposed to be inducted—into the Army April 11.

inductance. Substitute for def.: That property of a circuit or device by virtue of which any variation in the current flowing through it induces an e.m.f. in the circuit itself (self-inductance) or in another conductor (mutual inductance): without qualification usu. the former. Also, the magnitude of this, as measured by the ratio of an induced e.m.f. to the rate of change of the inducing current. (Earlier and later examples.)

1886 O. Heaviside in *Electrician* 12 Feb. 271 Conductivity and conductance are mathematically related in the same manner (except as regards 4π) as inductivity and what it is naturally suggested to call Inductance. The Inductance of a circuit is what is now called its coefficient of self-induction... When the mutual coefficient of induction of two circuits is to be referred to, it will of course be the mutual inductance. **1889** J. A. Fleming *Alternate Current Transformer* I. ii. 42 The..inductance of a circuit is, speaking generally, a quality of it in virtue of which a finite and steady electromotive force applied to it cannot at once generate in it the full current.., and when the electromotive force is withdrawn time is required for the current strength to fall to zero. **1928** Sterling & Kruse *Radio Manual* i. 20 The inductance of a circuit conductor, coil or of any apparatus is a property of that thing just as resistance is one of its properties. **1943** C. L. Boltz *Basic Radio* v. 88 In most radio work the only inductance anywhere worth considering is certainly that in coils. Nevertheless we must not forget that any conductor whatever has some inductance. *Ibid.* 90 Two coils have inductances of 2H and 4H. If they are coupled together so that only 50 per cent. of the flux is linked with all the turns, what is the value of the mutual inductance? **1957** *Encycl. Brit.* VIII. 293/2 When direct current is used, the inductance has no effect while the current is steady, but it delays the establishment of current when the circuit is first completed. **1962** Corson & Lorrain *Introd. Electromagn. Fields* vi. 232 In rationalized m.k.s. units, inductance is measured in webers/ampere, or in henrys. *Ibid.* 233 We shall now..calculate the self-inductance of a long solenoid ..and the mutual inductance between two coaxial solenoids. **1964** Goodier & Meynell *Electr.* iv. 49 A circuit will have an inductance of 1 henry if a current in it changing at the rate of 1 ampere per second induces an e.m.f. of 1 volt.

b. = *inductor 3 d.

1908 J. A. Fleming *Elem. Man. Radiotelegr.* ii. 66 One form which the inductance may take is that of a loop of one or a few turns of insulated wire. **1928** Sterling & Kruse *Radio Manual* i. 20 The most commonly employed inductance at radio frequencies consists of a single layer coil wound as an air core solenoid. **1962** D. F. Shaw *Introd. Electronics* i. 9 The coupling between inductances may reach a value close to unity if they share a ferromagnetic core.

2. Special Comb.: **inductance coil,** an inductor (sense *3 d) in the form of a loop or coil.

1902 *Encycl. Brit.* XXXIII. 232/1 The Slaby-Arco arrangement consists at the transmitting end of an inductance coil elevated above the ground; one end of this coil is connected to the earth..and the other end to a condenser, the opposite terminal of which is connected to one secondary terminal of an induction coil. **1923** E. W. Marchant *Radio Telegr.* iv. 38 The coherer may, in a simple circuit, be conveniently placed across the inductance coil.

inductee (indʊktī·). *U.S.* [-ee¹.] A person inducted into military service. Also *transf.*

1941 *Ann. Reg. 1940* 278 The Act provides that no 'inductee' may be required to serve outside the Western Hemisphere. **1956** W. H. Whyte *Organization Man* (1957) v. 58 Universal organization training..so effectively emphasises the group spirit that there is little danger that inductees will be subverted into rebelliousness. **1958** S. Ellin *Eighth Circle* (1959) II. xii. 137 You sound like an army doctor asking an inductee about his sex life.

induction. 2. Delete *rare* and add *attrib.* examples.

1962 *B.B.C. Handbk.* 162 Induction courses were also continued during the year for all senior members of staff joining the Corporation to acquaint them with its purpose, organization, and basic procedures. **1962** E. Godfrey *Retail Selling & Organization* xi. 121 It may be very useful to provide a special week or fortnight of induction training for them [*sc.* juniors]. **1965** *New Statesman* 30 Apr. 678/3 The organisation of refresher or induction courses. **1966** *Ibid.* 14 Jan. 49/1 Many firms run so-called 'induction' classes for new entrants, teaching them something about the company and its welfare provisions, perhaps giving them a brief run-down on the reasons for deductions from their wage packets, and even occasionally dealing with safety and hygiene.

4. d. *U.S.* Introduction into military service (cf. *induct *v.* 3 b). Also *attrib.*

1934 in Webster. **1940** *Congress. Rec.* 6 Sept. 11676/1 Any person..shall be afforded an opportunity to volunteer for induction. **1951** *N.Y. Herald-Tribune* 26 Dec. 11/3 You label this procedure of impressing R.O.K. Army members into your army as voluntary induction... It is nothing more than forced induction, impressment. **1967** *Boston Sunday Herald* 26 Mar. II. 7/7 Clay has been ordered to appear for induction in the Army on April 11. **1973** C. Himes *Black on Black* 209 Here is your induction papers... I hope the army likes you bettern I does. **1973** *Times Lit. Suppl.* 19 Oct. 1269/1 One summer the dreaded Induction Notice comes and he goes to war.

9. *spec.* Induction of labour.

1840 *Lancet* 7 Nov. 225/1 (*heading*) Induction of premature labour. **1916** G. P. Shears *Obstetrics* xxvi. 567 By the induction of abortion is meant the artificial interruption of pregnancy during the first twenty-eight weeks; i.e., before the fœtus becomes viable. The artificial interruption of pregnancy at any subsequent period is known as the induction of labor. **1962** *Lancet* 6 Jan. 6/2 The failure-rate was decidedly high when induction of labour was started after the calculated date for confinement had passed. **1968** D. C. Bethea *Introd. Maternity Nursing* ix. 120 Inductions may also be done for the convenience of the mother and/or the doctor.

b. *Embryol.* The determination of the development or differentiation of an embryonic region into a particular morphogenetic pattern by the influence or activity of another embryonic region; an instance of this.

1928 *Biol. Abstr.* II. 686/2 In the small yolk-plug stage both the median and paramedian parts of the posterior ⅔ of the gut roof are capable of induction. **1935** *Discovery* May 136/2 If..an organisation centre is grafted out of its usual place in an egg into new surroundings it will cause those new surroundings to develop into a complete embryo or complete organ. This 'induction' of a new embryo involves both sorts of embryological change; the production of new sorts of tissues..and the arrangement of those tissues. **1950** L. G. Barth tr. *Brachet's Chem. Embryol.* x. 397 The middle layer..gave good inductions in 16 per cent of the cases. **1958** B. M. Patten *Found. Embryol.* vi. 134 Experimental studies..have yielded extraordinarily interesting information as to the way one part of a developing embryo may influence the differentiation of other parts. When this occurs it is spoken of as induction. **1960** B. I. Balinsky *Introd. Embryol.* vi. 169 The result may be expressed as a percentage of successful inductions. **1962** T. W. Torrey *Morphogenesis Vertebr.* xviii. 481 Neural induction has been shown to occur in vertebrates other than amphibians.

c. *Biochem.* An increase in the rate at which an enzyme is synthesized by a cell (esp. in a micro-organism), or the initiation of its synthesis, as a result of the exposure of the cell to some specific substance (the inducer).

1947 *Growth* XI. 242 Where the enzymes have not been obtained in pure crystalline state.., the evidence must come mainly from a study of the specificity of the phenomenon of induction. **1951** *Biochim. & Biophys. Acta* VII. 599 These observations are incompatible with all hypotheses which imply that the induction is connected..with the activity of the enzyme. **1953** Cohn, Monod et al. in *Nature* 12 Dec. 1096/1 It might prove unpractical to abandon the use of the term 'enzyme adaptation' altogether at this stage; but we should like to suggest that.. a more accurate and significant terminology be employed. We therefore propose the following terms and designations; previously used terms are placed in parenthesis. A relative increase in the rate of synthesis of a specific apoenzyme resulting from exposure to a chemical substance is an 'enzyme induction' (enzyme adaptation). Any substance thus inducing enzyme synthesis is an enzyme 'inducer'. An enzyme-forming system which can be so activated by an exogenous inducer is 'inducible', and the enzyme so formed is 'induced' (adaptive). Although many compounds can act both as inducer and substrate, the terms are not equivalent. Certain substrates for induced enzymes are not inducers, while some inducers cannot function as substrates of the enzymes the formation of which they elicit. **1966** E. R. M. Kay *Biochem.* xxvii. 357 By many mechanisms of feedback control, repression, and induction, enzyme levels can be regulated in accord with the metabolic demands of the cell. **1971** *Nature* 26 Nov. 177/2 Substrate induction of enzymes (that is, their synthesis in response to the presence of their substrates) is now commonplace in microorganisms and not infrequent in higher animals.

d. *Biol.* The initiation of the lytic cycle in a bacterium carrying a prophage; the process of inducing a bacterium that contains a prophage.

[**1950** A. Lwoff et al. in *Ann. de l'Inst. Pasteur* LXXIX. 817 Entre l'induction et la libération du bactériophage, il s'écoule de quarante-cinq à quatre-vingts minutes. **1951** *Jrnl. Bacteriol.* LXII. 302 High titer stocks of this phage were obtained from K12 by induction of phage production with UV (the Lwoff effect).] *Ibid.* 304 The plaque count rises..to a number equal to the colony count before induction. **1953** *Cold Spring Harbor Symp. Quant. Biol.* XVIII. 101/2 In 1950, Lwoff, Siminovitch and Kjeldgaard showed that..irradiation of cultures of lysogenic *Bacillus megatherium* with ultraviolet light greatly increased the proportion of bacteria producing phage... This phenomenon is called induction. **1959** Jacob & Wollman in Burnet & Stanley *Viruses* II. ix. 326 It makes it possible to compare phage development in the same phage-bacterium system, whether after infection of sensitive bacteria, or after induction of lysogenic bacteria. **1959** *Jrnl. Molecular Biol.* I. 177 When the reverse mating (♂ non-lysogenic × ♀ λ-lysogenic) is performed, zygotic induction does not occur. **1968** Echols & Joyner in H. Fraenkel-Conrat *Molecular Basis Virol.* vi. 557 The treatments which produce induction of wild-type prophages are rather diverse (e.g., UV irradiation, growth in mitomycin C, thymine deprivation of a thymine requiring bacterium).

10. (Earlier example.)

1801 *Encycl. Brit.* Suppl. I. 572/2 (*marginal note*) A neutral body attracted, because rendered electrical by induction.

b. (Also *magnetic induction.*) Magnetic flux or (more commonly) flux density, by virtue of which an electric current experiences a magnetic force; as flux density, it is a vector quantity whose magnitude at any point is the magnetic force exerted per unit length on a conductor carrying unit current in the direction that gives rise to the maximum force, and whose direction is normal to those of the current and the force. Also (*electric induction*), electric flux or flux density, = Displacement 2 d (now somewhat *rare*). *Line of induction*, one of the imaginary lines conceived as representing, by their direction and number, the induction at each point throughout a region.

The C.G.S. unit of magnetic induction (flux density) is the gauss; in the International System of Units the tesla (= 10,000 gauss) is used.

1855 J. C. Maxwell in *Trans. Cambr. Philos. Soc.* (1864) X. 49 The unit cells in this case are portions of space in which unit of magnetic quantity is produced by unity [*sic*] of magnetizing force. The length of a cell is therefore inversely as the intensity of the magnetizing force, and its section is inversely as the quantity of magnetic induction at that point. *Ibid.* 50 If a closed conductor move transversely to the lines of magnetic induction.. there will be no current. **1861** —— in *Phil. Mag.* XXI. 168 The total amount of magnetic induction through a closed surface surrounding the pole of a magnet, depends entirely on the strength of that pole. **1873** —— *Treat. Electr. & Magn.* I. I. ii. 77 If dS is the element of the surface, the electric displacement through dS will be..$KR\cos\epsilon\, dS/4\pi$. Since we do not at present consider any dielectric except air, $K=1$. We may..avoid introducing at this stage the theory of electric displacement, by calling $R\cos\epsilon\, dS$ the Induction through the element dS. *Ibid.* 85 We have used the phrase Lines of Force because it has been used by Faraday and others. In strictness, however, these lines should be called Lines of Electric Induction. *Ibid.* II. III. ii. 24 The three vectors, the magnetization $\mathfrak{I}$, the magnetic force $\mathfrak{H}$, and the magnetic induction $\mathfrak{B}$ are connected by the vector equation $\mathfrak{B}=\mathfrak{H}+4\pi\mathfrak{I}$. **1879** *Encycl. Brit.* VIII. 75/2 For 'number of lines of force' may of course be substituted the equivalent expressions, 'induction through the circuit', or 'surface integral of magnetic induction'. **1885** O. Heaviside in *Electrician* 4 Sept. 311/1 There is a definite magnitude called by Maxwell 'the magnetic induction', which may well be called simply 'the induction'. *Ibid.* 311/2 We pass to electric displacement, the analogue of magnetic induction (noting by the way that it had better not be called the electric induction..but be called the displacement). **1922** Glazebrook *Dict. Appl. Physics* II. 449/2 *Magnetic flux*, the total amount of magnetic induction through a circuit, measured by the number of lines of induction which are linked with the circuit. **1925** F. B. Pidduck *Treat. Electr.* (ed. 2) iii. 96 It is of some importance..to inquire what happens when the polarisation is not proportional to the electric force. We now require two vectors, P, E, not in general parallel to each other, to express the state of the medium at any point... If we define a vector $D=E+4\pi P$, $\operatorname{div} D=0$. The vector D is called the electric induction. **1938** G. P. Harnwell *Princ. Electr. & Electromagn.* ix. 278 By analogy with the introduction of the electric field E in electrostatics it is convenient to introduce a vector B, known as the magnetic induction, which determines the force on a current element. The element of induction is defined by the equation $dF_1=i_1\,dl_1\times B_2$. **1957** B. I. & B. Bleaney *Electr. & Magn.* v. 116 Both a magnet and a current-carrying coil are said to produce a magnetic induction B, which exerts forces on other coils or magnets. *Ibid.* 128 With a magnetic pole, H is the force vector, while the introduction of a uniform magnetic medium throughout the whole of space leaves the magnetic induction B due to a pole unchanged. In the case of a current, B is the force vector and introduction of a magnetic medium leaves H unchanged. If the magnetizable matter does not fill the whole of space, then it is the surface integral of B, the total normal induction, which remains unchanged in magnetostatics. **1962** Corson & Lorrain *Introd. Electromagn. Fields* v. 179 If the current I is distributed in space with a current density J amperes/meter², then I becomes $J\,da$ and must be put under the integral sign...Thus, in the general case, the magnetic induction B at a point in space is given by $B=(\mu_0/4\pi)\int_\tau (J\times r_1)/r^2 d\tau$, where the integration is carried out over any volume τ which includes all the currents.

12. (Earlier example.)

1857 Bunsen & Roscoe in *Phil. Trans. R. Soc.* CXLVII. 381 The act by which the resistance to combination is diminished, and the combining power thus brought into greater activity, we call Chemical Induction.

13. (sense 10) **induction accelerator** = *betatron; **induction coil,** add to def.: a coil in which an electric current is induced; an inductance coil; *Teleph.*, a transformer in a telephone comprising two coils with a common core; (earlier and additional examples); **induction compass** = *inductor compass*; **induction furnace,** a furnace for melting metal by means of induction heating; **induction generator,** an induction motor driven at

a greater speed than its synchronous speed, so that it acts as a generator; **induction hardening,** hardening of ferrous metal by means of induction heating followed by quenching; **induction heater,** an apparatus for the induction heating of objects; **induction heating,** in which an alternating current is made to induce heating currents in the substance or object to be heated or (less commonly) in its container; **induction motor,** an a.c. electric motor in which the torque or force is due to the interaction between a moving magnetic field produced by stationary primary windings and currents induced by this field in moving secondary conductors; (sense 12) **induction period** *Chem.*, the time elapsing between the initiation of a chemical reaction and the production of detectable amounts of the product or products; **induction valve** (earlier U.S. example).

1940 D. W. KERST in *Physical Rev.* LVIII. 841/2 Of several suggestions which have been made for naming the apparatus, induction accelerator seems to be the shortest descriptive one. **1958** CONDON & ODISHAW *Handbk. Physics* IX. ix. 154/2 To make this device practical, it is necessary only to restrain the beam to a closed path around the flux and to maintain it in a stable orbit over some thousands of revolutions. Credit for the solution of the latter problem goes to D. W. Kerst, who built the first successful induction accelerator or 'betatron' in 1940. **1837** *Mag. Pop. Sci.* III. 110 A lever has also been applied to move..the induction-coil up and down along two magnetic bars. **1885** R. S. CULLEY *Handbk. Pract. Telegr.* (ed. 8) IX. 328 The current from the battery does not itself pass out to line, but through a local circuit formed by the primary wire of an induction coil. This coil has a core made of soft iron wires,..and is wound with two wires one over the other...Every variation of the battery current in the primary, produces a corresponding current in the secondary, but of a much higher potential; this last goes out to line, and acts on the distant receiver. *Ibid.* 329 The microphone, induction coil and battery, form the sending portion of the telephone. **1891** J. W. URQUHART *Dynamo Construction* 9 (*caption*) The induction coils combined with the field magnet. **1943** A. L. ALBERT *Fund. Telephony* vii. 142 When the receiver is removed..the battery causes direct current to flow through the transmitter and the primary of the transformer, often called in telephony an induction coil. **1966** *McGraw-Hill Encycl. Sci. & Technol.* VII. 72/2 Still another type of induction coil, called a reactor, is really a one-winding transformer designed to produce a definite voltage drop for a given current. **1925** *Mech. Engin.* XLVII. 796/2 Since to keep on the correct course it is only necessary to keep the pointer of the induction compass indicator on zero, it is easier to read than the magnetic compass. **1931** B. JONES *Avigation* ii. 18 The induction compass is a distant-reading magnetic compass, the part indicating the heading to the pilot being at a considerable distance from the part affected by the earth's magnetism. **1906** A. HIORTH *Brit. Pat.* 28,960 (*heading*) Improved electrical induction furnace with electrodes. **1951** G. R. BASHFORTH *Manuf. Iron & Steel* II. ix. 251 When..it was decided to dispense with the iron core of the early induction furnaces, it was necessary to increase the frequency of the current in the primary coil. **1904** G. T. HANCHETT *Alternating Currents* xiv. 173 The induction generator cannot generate its own magnetizing current, but must receive a reaction from the line which will permit the magnetizing current of displaced phase to flow in its fields. **1952** G. V. MUELLER *Alternating Current Machines* viii. 284 In an induction generator driven above synchronous speed with a negative slip..the rotor conductors are moving faster than the magnetic field of the stator. **1941** *Metals & Alloys* Nov. 687/1 Induction hardening has been applied to the surface of certain steel parts for modern tractor and road-building machinery. **1968** E. N. SIMONS *Outl. Metall.* III. ii. 142 The three main forms of surface hardening steel parts are carburizing, cyaniding, and nitriding...There are also the processes of flame hardening and induction hardening. **1919** *Electr. World* 29 Mar. 634/1 (*heading*) High-power-factor induction heaters. **1930** *Engineering* 9 May 611/2 The electric resistance [heaters]..heated the chilled surface of the roll and were not so good as the induction heaters, which generated heat within the body of the roll. **1919** H. P. TIEMANN *Iron & Steel* (ed. 2) 153 Induction furnace (induction heating). **1937** *Metals & Alloys* May 149/1 Applications of induction heating..now being installed.. include..hardening of metal surfaces by quenching after induction heating. **1954** J. W. CABLE *Induction & Dielectric Heating* xii. 319 Many types of furnaces use induction heating as an indirect source of heat...Installations using graphite crucibles, which extract energy from the magnetic field and transfer it to the charge, fall in this general classification. **1959** *Engineering* 13 Feb. 210/1 Plastics to plastics welding is most easily performed by high frequency induction heating. **1962** G. R. BASHFORTH *Manuf. Iron & Steel* (ed. 2) IV. ii. 58 Induction heating differs from the conventional methods of heating metallic components by virtue of the fact that the heat is generated within the material itself without the surface of the material coming into contact with the heating media. **1897** *Electrician* 17 Sept. 688/1 (*heading*) A 400 H.P. induction motor. **1918** P. KEMP *Alternating Current Electr. Engin.* xxvi. 394 On account of the fact that it must run at a speed rather less than that of synchronism, the induction motor is sometimes termed an asynchronous motor. **1962** *Newnes Conc. Encycl. Electr. Engin.* 492/1 In its basic form the induction motor is essentially a constant-speed motor: the variation in speed from no load to full load when running normally near synchronous speed is only a few per cent. **1971** E. R. LAITHWAITE *Linear Electr. Motors* i. 7 (*caption*) Imaginary process of unrolling a conventional motor to obtain a linear induction motor. **1973** *Nature* 9 Feb. 359/2 It is now feasible both to levitate and to propel a hovertrain using only a linear induction motor. **1902** *Proc. R. Soc.* LXX. 74 The induction and deduction periods follow as a necessity from the same general thermodynamic conceptions. **1924** H. S. TAYLOR *Treat. Physical Chem.* II. xviii. 1219 The induction period was not a function of the oxygen content of the gas—this only retarded the reaction velocity. **1953** FROST & PEARSON *Kinetics & Mechanism* viii. 156 The duration of the induction period, arbitrarily taken as the time to reach the point of inflection on the C [*sc.* concentration of product] versus *t* [*sc.* time] curve..is easily seen to be equal to the time for B [*sc.* concentration of intermediate] to reach its maximum value. **1970** [see *INHIBITION 3 b]. **1847** *Rep. Comm. Patents 1846* (U.S.) 87 The induction valve is then closed, and an expansion valve simultaneously opened.

inductionist (indʊ·kʃənist). [f. INDUCTION + -IST.] An adherent of inductive methods in philosophy or science. Cf. *INDUCTIVISM.

1893 in *Funk's Stand. Dict.* a **1915** J. C. WILSON *Statement & Inference* (1926) II. IV. i. 589 Now clearly the argument is demonstrative, and the inductionists in their opposition of induction to deduction would be obliged to call it deduction.

inductionless (indʊ·kʃənlės), *a.* *Electr.* [f. INDUCTION + -LESS.] Possessing no inductance.

1902 *Encycl. Brit.* XXX. 600/1 The wattmeter can best be standardized by employing it to measure the known power taken up in an inductionless circuit, such as a bank of incandescent lamps. **1908** J. SKELTON tr. *Kolbe's Introd. Electr.* II. vi. 347 The self-induction is thus almost entirely stopped (inductionless winding).

inductive, *sb.* Restrict † *Obs.* to sense in Dict. and add: **2.** = *INDUCTIONIST. *rare.*

1877 F. H. LAING *Ld. Bacon's 'Philosophy' Examined* xii. 110 The inductives themselves are forced..to employ ..all these words, which perpetually occur in their writings.

inductive, *a.* Add: **4.** (Further examples.)

1828 MILL in *Westm. Rev.* IX. 140 They talk in high-flown language, not always conveying very precise ideas, of a supposed system of *inductive* logic, which is to supersede the syllogistic, and really to accomplish still more than the other even attempts. *Ibid.* 150 An inductive logic would be highly useful as a supplement to the syllogistic logic, not to supersede it. **1865** —— *Auguste Comte* 58 Comte's determined abstinence from the word and the idea of Cause, had much to do with his inability to conceive an Inductive Logic. **1934** A. C. EWING *Idealism* iv. 170 An inductive logic which dispenses with such arguments. **1964** F. BOWERS *Bibliogr. & Textual Crit.* II. i. 36, I am aware that *inductive* and *deductive* as applied to reasoning have acquired philosophical half-lights that may in the end cause a subtle mind to deny that there is any difference between them. **1964** E. MENDELSON *Introd. Math. Logic* 9 In the course of this deduction, $P(n, y_1, .., y_k)$ is called the inductive hypothesis.

5. (Earlier example.) Also *inductive coupling,* coupling between two electric circuits or devices that is due to their mutual inductance; so *inductive-coupled* adj., coupled in this way; *inductive reactance,* reactance due to inductance.

1832 FARADAY in *Phil. Trans. R. Soc.* CXXII. 137 The inductive force was of course greater. **1907** Inductive coupling [see *direct coupling* s.v. *DIRECT *a.* 6 i]. **1911** *Whittaker's Electr. Engineer's Pocket-Bk.* (ed. 3) 124 The two may be added algebraically, the capacity reactance being considered as opposite in sign to the inductive reactance. **1913** A. F. COLLINS *Man. Wireless Telegr.* (ed. 3) vii. 126 (*heading*) Diagram of an inductive-coupled resonator. **1954** E. MOLLOY *Radio & Television Engineer's Ref. Bk.* vii. 7 Figs. 7 and 8, with closely-coupled inductive or direct coupling, give no harmonic voltage reduction in the aerial circuit other than that afforded by the aerial loading coil. **1960** E. HUGHES *Electr. Technol.* xi. 339 The inductive reactance is proportional to the frequency. **1966** *McGraw-Hill Encycl. Sci. & Technol.* III. 521/1 Inductive-coupled circuits have a common magnetic flux linking the two circuits.

b. Possessing inductance.

1902 *Encycl. Brit.* XXX. 599/2 In series with the inductive circuit another non-inductive circuit is joined. **1920** *Whittaker's Electr. Engineer's Pocket-Bk.* (ed. 4) 129 The current through an inductive circuit of negligible resistance lags 90° behind the impressed e.m.f. **1962** [see *CAPACITIVE *a.*]

7. *Embryol.* Of, pertaining to, or producing induction (sense *9 b).

1931 J. NEEDHAM *Chem. Embryol.* I. 578 The inductive power of the cells of the dorsal lip is not abolished by drying them. **1962** SAXÉN & TOIVONEN *Primary Embryonic Induction* i. 7 The blastoporal lip of an early gastrula, and that part of an older one, have qualitatively different inductive properties. *Ibid.*, Until 1932, the real nature of the inductive action presented an enigma. **1967** T. W. TORREY *Morphogenesis Vertebr.* (ed. 2) xviii. 359/1 When extracts are treated with proteolytic enzymes, inductive ability is destroyed.

8. Comb. *inductive-minded* adj.

1905 W. JAMES in *Mind* XIV. 191 The one condition of understanding humanism is to become inductive-minded oneself, to drop vigorous definitions, and follow lines of least resistance 'on the whole'.

inductively, *adv.* **2.** (Earlier example.)

1848 W. S. HARRIS *Rudimentary Electr.* iii. 52 The cover, being insulated, does not take up the electricity of the plate, but is acted upon inductively.

inductivism (indʊ·ktiviz'm). [f. INDUCTIVE *a.* + -ISM.] The preference for, use of, or belief in the superiority of, inductive as opposed to deductive methods; the belief that scientific laws can be inferred from observational evidence. Opp. *DEDUCTIVISM.

a **1866** J. GROTE *Treat. Moral Ideals* (1876) xviii. 425 The matter is complex..on account of the exceeding inappropriateness of the assumption of inductivism for anything in its way so idealist as Utilitarianism is. **1951** *Mind* LX. 43 Professor Popper..attacks frequently what he calls 'observationalism' or 'inductivism'. **1956** E. H. HUTTEN *Lang. Mod. Physics* vi. 229 If we take induction as a psychological process of discovery and, at the same time, as a logical method of proof, we end up with an insoluble problem...Neither Hume's scepticism nor Mill's belief in the uniformity of nature are solutions of the inductive problem, but rather they are attempts to banish a riddle. There is, to-day, an ever-increasing number of philosophers as well as of scientists who reject this inductivism, and they advise us to drop the term 'induction' altogether when describing scientific method. **1959** K. R. POPPER *Logic Sci. Discovery* I. i. 30 The view that a hypothesis can only be empirically *tested*..might be called 'deductivism', in contrast to 'inductivism'. **1962** [see *DEDUCTIVISM]. **1965** J. W. N. WATKINS *Hobbes's Syst. Ideas* ii. 34 (*heading*) Repudiation of inductivism. **1972** A. J. AYER *Probability & Evidence* iii. 74 Popper.. explicitly rejects what he calls inductivism. **1972** *Nature* 10 Nov. 110/1 The author then delineates in turn three theories of the logical structure of science—inductivism, Popperian falsificationism and positivism.

inductivist (indʊ·ktivist), *sb.* and *a.* [f. INDUCTIVE *a.* + -IST.]

A. *sb.* One who follows or upholds inductivism or inductive methods; one who holds that the method of science is inductive. Cf. prec. word.

1940 K. R. POPPER in *Mind* XLIX. 421 Jeans was.. originally an inductivist, that is, he thought that theories are obtained from experience by some more or less simple procedure. **1962** *Listener* 22 Mar. 513/2 The kind of sociologist whom Sartre despises, the cautious inductivist, collects facts but has no theoretical equipment to understand them. **1968** A. J. AYER *Origins Pragmatism* 99 The inductivist was having a run of failures. **1968** J. J. C. SMART *Between Sci. & Philos.* vi. 196 The inductivists, who wish to justify inductive procedures.

B. *adj.* Of, pertaining to, or employing inductivism or inductive methods; implying that the method of science is inductive.

1945 *Mind* LIV. 3 Certain 'inductivist' accounts of scientific procedure seem to assume that relevant evidence, or relevant data, can be collected in the context of an inquiry prior to the formulation of any hypothesis. **1956** E. H. HUTTEN *Lang. Mod. Physics* vi. 268 To believe that we learn by induction is part of the inductivist myth which identifies a psychological process with a logical method. **1960** E. H. GOMBRICH *Art & Illusion* ix. 321 This inductivist ideal of pure observation has proved a mirage in science no less than in art. **1968** J. J. C. SMART *Between Sci. & Philos.* vii. 247 It is doubtful.. whether such an inductivist account of geometry will do.

inductomeric (indʊːktǒme·rik), *a.* *Chem.* [f. INDUCTO- + *-meric* as in *ELECTROMERIC *a.*] Of, pertaining to, or designating the ability of an atom or group to become polarized along a saturated bond by an external electric field (e.g. that of another molecule).

1933 C. K. INGOLD in *Jrnl. Chem. Soc.* 1124 It cannot be doubted that a counterpart of two coexisting polarisations obtains also for polarisability effects, and that an inductive polarisability or inductomeric effect completes the scheme annexed. **1943** A. E. REMICK *Electronic Interpretations Org. Chem.* v. 61 The extent to which the inductomeric effect is called into play..will depend on the strength of the polarizing field and on the polarizability of the bond in question. **1953** C. K. INGOLD *Struct. & Mech. Org. Chem.* ii. 72 By inductomeric polarisability is understood the polarisability which atoms and groups in saturated combination exhibit along the lines of their bonds...For isoelectronic atoms with completed valency shells, inductomeric polarisability thus depends on electronegativity. **1956** E. DE B. BARNETT *Mechanism Org. Chem. Reactions* i. 4 If a powerful electron-repelling group such as a hydroxyl ion approaches a hydrogen atom of a nitromethane molecule..the resulting inductomeric effect is so great that a hydrogen atom is completely protonized. **1959** E. S. GOULD *Mechanism & Struct. Org. Chem.* vii. 208 A number of workers..prefer to differentiate inductive influences in reactants and products from those electronic shifts that occur in the activated complex as a result of the electrical demands of one reagent on another. The former are termed inductive effects, the latter inductomeric effects.

inductor. Add: **3.** (Earlier and later examples.) *Esp.* one which induces an e.m.f. or current in another part (as in an inductor alternator).

Delete quot. 1871, which appears (with corrected date) under sense c below.

1867 W. THOMSON in *Proc. R. Soc.* XVI. 67 To stems connected with the inside coatings of two Leyden phials are connected [cylindrical] metal pieces, which..I shall call inductors and receivers. *Ibid.* 68 Suppose now a small positive charge of electricity be given to the first jar. Its inductor electrifies negatively each drop of water breaking away in its centre from the continuous uninsulated water above. **1892** *Electrician* 13 May 37/2 Electric currents are produced by revolving the magnetic inductors in proximity to the magnet. **1909** R. B. WHITMAN

Motor-Car Princ. (rev. ed.) 320 The Remy magneto is of this type, and Fig. 17 is a diagram of the revolving core, or inductor, with the coil surrounding it. **1915** W. H. ECCLES *Wireless Telegr.* 204 This alternator is of the inductor type... The inductor or rotor is a chrome-nickel steel disc about a foot diameter with 300 slots cut ⅛ in. apart near its edge. **1941** A. W. JUDGE *Aircraft Engines* II. ix. 338 The polar inductor magneto has stationary magnets as well as coils, and the changes of magnetic flux are obtained by rotating soft-iron inductors between the poles of the magnets. **1956** D. WARBURTON-BROWN *Induction Heating Pract.* i. 8 In any induction heating arrangement there are three main components, namely: (a) a high-frequency generator; (b) a work-coil or inductor; (c) a work-piece.

b. A conductor or device in which an e.m.f. or current is induced; **earth inductor,** a device for investigating the earth's magnetic field, consisting essentially of a coil of wire that can be rapidly turned about an axis in its own plane so that a current is induced in it proportional to the component of the field normal to the axis of rotation.

1837 tr. Gauss in *Mag. Pop. Sci.* III. 109 A few weeks ago I had my inductor increased again, (from 3527 to about 6800 convolutions,) and now its effects are much stronger. The sensations it produces by the current being transmitted through the body..are not only very perceptible, but, when the inductor is rapidly moved, painful almost beyond endurance. **1883** E. ATKINSON tr. *Ganot's Elem. Treat. Physics* (ed. 11) x. vi. 852 The inductor itself..consists of a drum-shaped frame of soft iron wire covered with a layer of insulating material, and fixed to an axle which..is rotated...Machines of this class give continuous currents, but alternators..are also constructed. **1883** *Encycl. Brit.* XV. 240/2 This is the principle of Weber's 'earth inductor', by means of which the horizontal and vertical components of the earth's force can be measured, and in consequence the declination and inclination determined. **1901** SHELDON & MASON *Dynamo Electr. Machinery* iii. 45 By inductor is meant that part of the winding conductor which lies on the face of the armature that sweeps past the pole pieces, and.. in which E.M.F. is induced. **1940** R. R. LAWRENCE *Princ. Alternating-Current Machinery* (ed. 3) i. 1 Any direct-current generator, with the exception of the unipolar generator, is in fact an alternator in which the alternating voltage set up in the armature inductors is rectified by means of a commutator. **1966** *McGraw-Hill Encycl. Sci. & Technol.* IV. 338/2 The earth inductor has almost completely supplanted the dip circle throughout the world for precise measurement of magnetic inclination. **1973** *Sci. Amer.* Feb. 101/2 A unipolar inductor is a magnetized metal sphere. One terminal of an external circuit is attached to one of the sphere's poles of rotation and the other terminal is a stationary brush in contact with the sphere's equator. When the sphere is spun, a galvanometer in the circuit registers the passage of an electric current.

c. An induction coil (Ruhmkorff coil).

1872 J. & C. LASSELL tr. *Schellen's Spectrum Analysis* xxx. 157 By connecting the binding screws 1, 2 on one side with the inductor, and on the other side..with the platinum wire *b* of the first vessel, and a_2 of the last vessel, ..the electric current may be made to pass through all the liquids. **1904** *Electr. World & Engin.* XLIV. 513/2 A very imposing view..is given by the seven induction coils arranged upon steps in the centre of the cabinet, beginning at the bottom, with an inductor giving a 40-inch spark and ending at the top with one of 10-inch spark.

d. A device (commonly a coil) possessing inductance or used on account of its inductance.

1928 STERLING & KRUSE *Radio Manual* i. 20 Iron Core Inductance.—This form of inductor is made by winding many turns of wire on an iron core. **1950** K. HENNEY *Radio Engin. Handbk.* (ed. 4) iii. 124 Straight wires are used as inductors in h-f applications where the inductance must be very low. **1963** WILLIAMS & PRIGMORE *Electr. Engin.* v. 129 A standard mutual inductor.. can be made by winding coil No. 1 on a long straight core and winding No. 2 round the mid-portion of No. 1.

4. *Chem.* Any substance which while reacting with one substance (the 'actor') increases the rate at which this reacts with a second substance (the 'acceptor'); a substance that has an accelerating effect on a reaction but differs from a catalyst in being consumed.

1903 *Jrnl. Chem. Soc.* LXXXIV. II. 277 The substance taking part in both these reactions..is termed the 'actor'; the substance taking part only in the primary reaction.. is the 'inductor'; the substance taking part only in the secondary reaction is the 'acceptor'. **1918** *Chem. Abstr.* XII. 111 A number of reduction reactions which take place at ordinary temps. in sunlight, fail to proceed even at more elevated temps. in the dark. The reactions may be induced to take place in the dark by the addition of small amts. of certain oxidizing agents ('inductors'). **1937** *Thorpe's Dict. Appl. Chem.* (ed. 4) I. 12/2 *Acceptor*, a substance..which normally is not oxidised by oxygen (or reduced by hydrogen) but is oxidised (or reduced) when in presence of another substance termed the inductor.. which itself is undergoing oxidation (or reduction) by a third substance the actor. **1966** A. G. SYKES *Kinetics Inorg. Reactions* ix. 205 Arsenite ions are..effective in inducing the reaction between Cr^{VI} and iodide, and, at high iodide concentrations, a ratio of two equivalents of iodide to one of the inductor are likewise involved.

5. *Embryol.* A region of an embryo, or a substance produced by such a region, capable of causing induction (sense *9 b).

1929 *Biol. Abstr.* III. 1495/2 The action of the inductor, whatever it be, manifests itself in the activation of a supernumerary embryonic field. **1946** L. B. AREY *Developmental Anat.* (ed. 5) ix. 163 The specific, morphogenetic effect brought about by a chemical stimulus transmitted from one embryonic part to another is known as an induction or evocation. The part exerting this influence is an inductor or organizer, and the chemical substance emitted is an evocator. **1963** E. J. W. BARRINGTON *Introd. Gen. & Compar. Endocrinol.* vi. 152 Germ cells that enter the cortex become female, those that enter the medulla become male, and in embryological terminology these two regions are said to act respectively as female and male inductors. **1967** T. W. TORREY *Morphogenesis Vertebr.* (ed. 2) xviii. 359/1 An inherent difficulty in the identification of the 'natural' inductor lies in the minute amount available for analysis.

6. Special Comb.: **inductor alternator,** an alternator in which both armature and field windings are stationary, the current being produced by the periodic variation in the magnetic flux through the armature windings as successive teeth of a rotating inductor pass by; **(earth-)inductor compass,** any of various kinds of compass in which the earth's magnetic field is made to induce in a coil an electric current whose strength depends on the relative orientation of the coil to the field; **inductor generator** = **inductor alternator*.

1893 W. P. MAYCOCK *Electr. Lighting* II. viii. 239 Kingdon's Inductor Alternator. **1940** R. R. LAWRENCE *Princ. Alternating-Current Machinery* (ed. 3) 3 An inductor alternator is usually characterized by large armature reaction, relatively high magnetic density, small air gap and greater weight than alternators of the other types. The difficulties in the design of a satisfactory inductor alternator have caused this type of alternator to go out of use. **1965** J. HINDMARSH *Electr. Machines* viii. 482 Another special case of single-phase generator is the inductor alternator used to provide high-frequency supplies in the range 1000 to 10,000 cycles/sec for use in induction furnaces. Here, all the windings are on the stator. **1922** *Rep. U.S. Nat. Advisory Comm. Aeronaut.* No. 128. 44 The earth inductor compass..was developed by Dr. Paul R. Heyl and Dr. Lyman J. Briggs of the Bureau of Standards. **1926** *Encycl. Brit.* Suppl. I. 19/2 The earth inductor compass, developed in America, depends upon the measurement of the electromotive force induced by the earth's magnetic field in a coil rotating about a vertical axis. **1927** LINDBERGH in *Sci. Monthly* XXV. 91/1, I also had a magnetic compass; but it was the inductor compass which guided me so faithfully that I hit the Irish coast...The inductor compass was so accurate that I really needed no other guide. **1931** M. F. SCHOEFFEL in P. V. H. Weems *Air Navigation* vii. 93 Although the armature of an inductor compass is gyroscopic, yet, since it is also pendulous, it tends to..bank with the plane. **1943** REDPATH & COBURN *Air Transport Navigation* iv. 80 The principle of the inductor compass is to generate electric currents utilizing the earth's magnetic field to operate suitable indicating instruments in the cockpit. **1958** *Van Nostrand's Sci. Encycl.* (ed. 3) 386/2 The earth-inductor compass was designed..for use on aircraft, but has been rendered obsolete by the aperiodic and gyro-flux-gate instruments. **1940** *Chambers's Techn. Dict.* 446/1 Inductor generator. **1957** *Encycl. Brit.* VIII. 148/1 For a given number of poles and a given speed of rotation, an inductor generator delivers twice the frequency of the present common types of A.C. generators. In the early years of radio telegraphy the inductor generator was the best source of the frequencies required.

indulge, *v.* Add: **1. d.** (Later example.)

1951 AUDEN *Nones* (1952) 39 How jocular the bells as They Indulge the peccant shore.

8. *intr.* (Without preposition.) To gratify a desire, appetite, etc.; to take one's pleasure; *spec.* to 'partake', i.e. (too) freely of intoxicants (*colloq.*).

a **1718** T. PARNELL *Poems on Several Occasions* (1722) 125 Wretch that I was! I might have warn'd the Dame, Yet sat indulging as the Danger came. **1953** P. C. BERG *Dict. New Words* 96/2 *Indulge*, to take alcoholic liquors without restraint. **1973** P. O'DONNELL *Silver Mistress* xv. 250 Tarrant..took out his cigar case. He had not indulged all night.

indumentum (indiume·ntŏm). *Bot.* Pl. **-ta.** [a. L. *indumentum*; see INDUMENT.] The covering of hairs on part of a plant, esp. when dense, e.g. the covering of the lower surface of the leaves of many species of rhododendron. Cf. INDUMENT 2.

1847 J. LINDLEY *Elem. Bot.* (ed. 5) p. xlix, Indumentum: The hairy covering of plants, of whatever kind. **1858** A. GRAY *Introd. Struct. & Syst. Bot.* (ed. 5) 537/1 Indumentum: any hairiness or downy covering. **1930** J. B. STEVENSON *Species of Rhododendron* 364 Under surface [of leaves of *R. eriogynum*] at first clad with a thin white flaking stellate indumentum easily rubbed off and quickly falling away. **1950** J. M. COWAN *Rhododendron Leaf* i. 1 On looking at the leaves of Rhododendrons, it will be seen that the under surface is often clothed with a hairy or scale-like covering, now loose and of a fine texture like a spider's web, now dense and compact like a thick felt or wool, now a mere sprinkling of brownish dots on a green background. This leaf covering, which is very variable, is known as the indumentum. **1963** DAVIS & HEYWOOD *Princ. Angiosperm Taxon.* v. 155 To be of use for critical discrimination, indumentum must, of course, be described in detail, each type of hair present (and its disposition) being separately recorded. **1970** *Watsonia* VIII. 104 *H[ieracium] termifrons* occurs in two well-marked forms differing in shape of head and indumentum of the phyllaries. **1972** *Biol. Abstr.* LIV. 68/1 *X[imenia] caffra* differs from *X. americana* in that a dense or sparse indumentum is often present.

induna. Add: Also 9 tuna, 9– **indoona.** (Earlier and later examples.)

1835 A. SMITH *Diary* 19 June (1940) II. 79 Masalacatzie has two grades among his chiefs, viz.: *numzan* and *tuna*, the former the highest. **1837** F. OWEN *Diary* (1926) 28 A regiment is stationed at each town under several Indoonas or Captains. *Ibid.* 60 The King..was seated in his hut on a chair: his Indoonas were also present. **1955** E. A. RITTER *Shaka Zulu* xiii, These [soldiers] were now harangued for a considerable time by their fighting *indunas* or officers and given a discourse on new tactics. **1971** *Daily Dispatch* (S. Afr.) 24 May 1 In the Libode district unoccupied huts were set on fire by tribesmen. Recently a headman and his induna in the district were murdered.

b. *transf.* A person, especially a black person, in authority; a pundit.

1953 P. LANHAM *Blanket Boy's Moon* II. iv. 116 A big factory, where he had obtained the job of *Induna* or head-boy. **1953** F. ROBB *Sea Hunters* iv. 28 On deck.. Ndwe, the Induna or bossboy, heaved on the vang and centred the boom over the gaping hatchway. **1970** *News/Check* (S. Afr.) 4 Sept. 9 This followed the attack on the Press by rugby induna Dr. Danie Craven for blowing up the incidents of rough play in the second Test. **1970** W. SMITH *Gold Mine* xxix. 72 The Old One, the Shangaan Induna, lived in a Company house. **1971** in *Towards Dict. S. Afr. Eng.* 42 They have an induna there to hold you down while they X-ray you.

Hence **indu·naship,** the office or dignity of an induna.

1955 in M. Gluckman *Judicial Process among Barotse* iii. 87 This is indunaship—this is ruling.

Indus (i·ndŏs). *Astron.* [L.] = INDIAN *sb.* 5.

1838 *Penny Cycl.* XII. 467/1. **1910** *Encycl. Brit.* VII. 13/1 Johann Bayer, a German astronomer..published a *Uranometria* in 1603, in which twelve constellations, all in the southern hemisphere, were added to Ptolemy's forty-eight, viz. Apis (or Musca) (Bee),..Indus (Indian), [etc.]. **1964** D. H. MENZEL *Field Guide Stars & Planets* iv. 113 Indus (the Indian). Although the name is masculine, Flamsteed drew a female figure.

indusium. Add: **1. b.** Also *erron.* **induseum.** The thin layer of grey matter covering the upper surface of the corpus callosum. In full *indusium* (or *induseum*) *griseum*.

1890 BILLINGS *Med. Dict.* I. 693/2 Indusium griseum. **1908** *Quain's Elem. Anat.* (ed. 11) III. I. 401 The lateral striæ are similar, but their corresponding grey matter is even more rudimentary than the indusium. **1948** A. BRODAL *Neurol. Anat.* x. 330 Smaller contingents [of fibres] appear to reach it from the induseum griseum. **1963** ZEMAN & INNES *Craigie's Neuroanat. Rat* (ed. 2) vii. 147 The rest [of the hippocampal formation] curves around it and becomes continuous with the indusium. **1966** HASSLER & STEPHAN *Evolution of Forebrain* 104 The supracallosal gyrus (or induseum griseum).

industrial, *a.* and *sb.* Add: **A.** *adj.* **c.** Of a quality suitable for industrial use.

1904 GOODCHILD & TWENEY *Technol. & Sci. Dict.*, *Industrial soaps*, a term used to describe that class of soap used for special purposes, such as ox gall soap, which is useful for scouring woollen goods and cleaning carpets, soap for silk dyers, fulling soap, etc. **1904** *Chemist & Druggist* LXV. 852/2 Industrial Alcohol Committee.. appointed to inquire into the use of duty-free alcohol for industrial purposes. **1905** *Ibid.* LXVI. 630/2 There is only one way in which the influence of the spirit-duties can be satisfactorily counteracted in favour of industrial alcohol. **1906** *Act 6 Edw. VII* c. 20 § 4 The expression 'industrial methylated spirits' means any methylated spirits (other than mineralized methylated spirits) which are intended for use in any art or manufacture within the United Kingdom. **1968** J. IRONSIDE *Fashion Alphabet* 89 *Industrial*, applied to special fabrics or garments specially designed for use in particular industries.

d. Characterized by highly developed industries.

1911 C. G. ROBERTSON *Eng. under Hanoverians* II. iv. 346 Napoleon..failed to see that he fought not with a nation of shopkeepers—a commercial State—but with a nation of capitalists and artisans—an industrial State. **1948** S. LILLEY *Men, Machines & Hist.* vi. 72 England was transformed from one of the most backward to one of the most rapidly advancing commercial and industrial countries of Europe. **1953** J. D. BERNAL *Sci. & Industry in 19th Cent.* vi. 171 Only the industrial countries of Europe and the newly industrialized parts of America contributed to modern science.

e. In specific uses.

industrial accident, an accident occurring in the course of one's employment, esp. in a factory; *industrial action*, action such as a strike, a go-slow, working to rule, etc., taken by industrial or other workers; *industrial archæology*, the study of the equipment and workings of industry of former times; so *industrial archæologist*; *industrial art*, art applied to the design of industrial products; so *industrial artist*; *industrial assurance*, a form of life assurance for industrial workers, mainly to cover funeral costs, with premiums payable in small regular instalments; *industrial court*, a court for the settlement of industrial disputes; *industrial design*, design as applied to industrial products; so *industrial designer*; *industrial disease*, a disease con-

tracted in the course of one's employment, esp. in a factory; *industrial dispute*, a dispute between employers and employees; *industrial espionage*, spying directed towards discovering the secrets of a rival industrial company, manufacturer, etc.; *industrial estate*, an area of land devoted to factories and other industrial enterprises; *industrial fatigue*, fatigue in industrial workers; *industrial frequency* (see quot. 1940); *industrial injury*, an injury occurring in the course of one's employment, esp. in a factory; *industrial insurance*, (*a*) = **industrial assurance*; (*b*) insurance for industrial workers against injury or absence from work; *industrial park* (chiefly N. Amer.) = **industrial estate*; *industrial proletariat*, the section of the proletariat that is employed in industrial work; *industrial property*, the collective name applied to commercial rights derived from patents, designs, trade marks, etc.; *industrial psychology*, psychology as applied to all aspects of human involvement in industry; so *industrial psychologist*; *industrial relations*, relationships between employers and employees; *industrial revolution*, a rapid development in industry; *spec.* (freq. with capital initials) the development which took place in England in the late eighteenth and early nineteenth centuries, chiefly owing to the introduction of new or improved machinery and large-scale production methods; *industrial spy*, a person engaged in industrial espionage; *industrial union*, a union of all workers in an industry irrespective of their craft or occupation; so *industrial unionism, unionist*; *Industrial Workers of the World*, a labour organization advocating syndicalism which enjoyed its greatest support in the western United States during the early twentieth century.

1910 *Encycl. Brit.* IX. 361/1 By a law of..1910, *Sweden* adopted the principle of the personal liability of the employer for industrial accidents. **1922** *Ibid.* XXXI. 698/1 The former has legalized deductions for hospital benefits on approval of the Industrial Accident Commission. **1968** *Brit. Med. Bull.* XXIV. 256/1 A 40-year-old man with a history of several industrial accidents..presented after a fall at work. **1971** *Times* 17 Mar. 1/8 The Times regrets that, in common with other national newspapers, it will probably be unable to publish tomorrow because of industrial action. **1972** *Guardian* 15 June 26/1, I fear..that if you imprison individual dockers we are going to get full scale industrial action. **1954** M. RIX in *Country Life* 28 Oct. 1501/1 This canal..has a special interest for industrial archæologists. **1951** *History Today* July 59/2 The most fascinating subject of all is what might be called the industrial archaeology of the area. **1971** K. HUDSON (*title*) A guide to the industrial archaeology of Europe. **1850** *Punch* 29 June 10 Mind where you fix your show... Where Fashion rides and drives House not industrial Art, But 'mid the busy hives Right in the City's heart. **1851** *Illustr. Lond. News* 21 June 605/3 Premiums for works of industrial art were offered. **1863** J. B. WARING (*title*) Masterpieces of industrial art and sculpture at the International Exhibition, 1862. **1902** *Encycl. Brit.* XXV. 687/1 The awakening of interest in industrial art—sharply separated by pedantic classification from fine art—which began about the middle of the 19th century. **1930** *Times* 7 May 11/4 Industrial Artists. An Association is to be formed of artists engaged in industry. **1896** *Act* 59 & 60 *Vict.* c. 26 (*title*) Collecting Societies and Industrial Assurance Companies Act. **1920** *Rep. Industr. Assurance Comp.* (Cmd. 614) 2 The business of Industrial Assurance consists in the assurance of small sums, payable for the most part on the death of the life assured, in consideration of the payment of weekly premiums. **1935** *Economist* 2 Mar. 497/2 Following the terrible disaster at the Gresford Colliery, a sum of £10,000 was paid to some 200 families under industrial assurance policies. **1919** *Act* 9 & 10 *Geo. V* c. 69 § 14 This Act may be cited as the Industrial Courts Act, 1919. **1973** *Listener* 15 Nov. 660/1 The leaders of the AUEW see their own refusal to recognise the Industrial Court as part of the historic struggle of trade-unionists for the rights of the working man. **1934** H. READ (*title*) Art and industry, the principles of industrial design. **1967** L. B. ARCHER in Wills & Yearsley *Handbk. Managem. Technol.* 122 There is a range of products in which aesthetic appearance and convenience in use are very important, such as in furniture, domestic appliances, and office machinery. Design of this kind is called 'industrial design'. **1940** H. VAN DOREN *Industr. Design* 27 Industrial designers who take their work seriously cannot afford to play the prima donna. **1972** F. MACCARTHY *All Things Bright & Beautiful* 147 The hero of the piece was the industrial designer. **1906** *Act* 6 *Edw. VII* c. 58 § 8 (*heading*) Application of act to industrial diseases. **1974** *Guardian* 20 Mar. 1/8 A working class Yorkshire family, whose father contracts cancer through an industrial disease. **1907** *Times* 1 Feb. 4/5 The Minister of Labour [in Canada] has brought in an Industrial Disputes Investigation Act, which provides for the constitution of conciliation boards. **1973** *Times* 13 Dec. 18/8 Men for whom wage claims and industrial disputes are tools to be used in..the destruction of the existing political order. **1962** L. DEIGHTON *Ipcress File* viii. 52 His reports concern industrial espionage. **1972** K. BENTON *Spy in Chancery* ii. 22 He runs an industrial espionage service. **1953** P. C. BERG *Dict. New Words* 96/2 *Industrial estate*, a trading estate. **1972** M. JONES *Life on Dole* ix. 68 The Council declared this property to be an industrial estate. **1974** *Times* 14 Jan. 2/5 A secondary modern school on an industrial estate. **1914** *Rep. Brit. Assoc. Adv. Sci.* 176 What increase..has occurred in general morbidity in recent years, and to what extent this can be ascribed to industrial fatigue. **1950** *Chambers's Encycl.* VII. 543/1 In 1918 the Industrial Fatigue Research Board was formed. **1940** *Chambers's Techn. Dict.* 446/1 *Industrial frequency*, a term used to denote the frequency of the alternating current used for ordinary industrial purposes, usually 50 or 60 cycles. **1958** *Engineering* 14 Mar. 341/1 Two [railway] systems..which are able to utilise widely spaced substations and light overhead conductors, are the Swedish system at $16\frac{2}{3}$ cycles, and the French (and now British) system at industrial frequency (50 cycles) and 25 kV. **1933** M. CORRELL in *U.S. Women's Bureau Bull.* No. 102 (*title*) Industrial injuries to women in 1928 and 1929. **1940** *Bull. U.S. Bureau of Labor Statistics* No. 667. p. ix, Efficient accident prevention can be promoted by administrators of workmen's compensation laws by prescribing types of reports to be submitted in cases of industrial injuries which can be used in analyzing accident causes. **1946** *Industr. Welfare & Personnel Managem.* XXVIII. 214 Important changes in Industrial Law have taken place recently as a result of such measures as the Industrial Injuries Act (which supersedes the Workmen's Compensation Acts). **1971** *Morning Star* 8 Apr. 3 Industrial injuries, on average, had been halved. **1911** *Encycl. Brit.* XIV. 671/2 The system of industrial insurance was introduced into the United States in 1876. **1920** S. & B. WEBB *Hist. Trade Unionism* (rev. ed.) ix. 507 The life assurance agents—principally those employed in 'industrial' : surance—number 100,000. **1920** *Rep. Industr. Assurance Comp.* (Cmd. 614) 3 There is little thought for the development of industrial insurance upon the sound economic lines by which it might become a valuable instrument. **1955** *Barron's Nat. Business & Financial Weekly* 10 Oct. 13 (*title*) Industrial parks; planned factory districts are attracting more customers. *Ibid.* 15/3 The combined shopping center and industrial park. **1957** *Urban Land* Apr. 5/2 Several questions indicated a strong local interest in the development of industrial parks as a means of stimulating development. The Panel stated that such parks are becoming increasingly popular and effective in attracting the smaller manufacturing plants and distribution warehouses. **1963** *Amer. City* July 95/2 The new industrial park..offers the prospective industry a tract of graded land located on a wide, paved and landscaped boulevard. The attractive 'price of admission' also includes curbs, gutters and storm drains, water and sewer mains, gas, electric and telephone lines and access to railroad sidings. **1972** *Evening Telegram* (St. John's, Newfoundland) 5 Aug. 10/1 Murray and Davis Properties Ltd. has announced the opening of their new..building.. in the industrial park area. **1887** F. K. WISCHNEWETZKY tr. *Engels's Condition of Working-Class in Eng.* i. 15 (*heading*) The Industrial Proletariat. **1930** G. B. SHAW *John Bull's Other Island* Pref., in *Wks.* XI. 71 The growing political power of the industrial proletariat organized in trade unions. **1972** G. WIGG *George Wigg* i. 23 The tiny red brick houses, typical of the growth of an industrial proletariat. **1884** in Hertslet *Treaties* (1890) XVII. 408 The International Convention for the Protection of Industrial Property, concluded at Paris on the 20th March, 1883. **1952** LAUTERPACHT & OPPENHEIM *Internat. Law* (ed. 7) II. II. ii. 330 Enemy assets..are to be returned—with the important exception of industrial property (*i.e.*, patents, designs, trade marks and trade names, etc.). **1921** J. DREVER *Psychol. of Industry* iv. 46 Even when the factors affecting industrial efficiency and success are physical, the work of the industrial psychologist may still be valuable in tracing out the physiological and psychological results of physical conditions. **1936** *Discovery* Sept. 279 There are too many salients in the front line of social progress and it is the duty of the industrial psychologist to smooth these away. **1964** M. ARGYLE *Psychol. & Social Probl.* viii. 114 It is one of the major tasks confronting industrial psychologists today to discover ways of organizing such work that will make it an acceptable human activity. **1971** A. K. KORMAN *Industr. & Organizational Psychol.* i. 12 The industrial psychologist..continues to be actively concerned with the..techniques and methods which will increase the effectiveness of manpower utilization in the modern organization both from the company's and from the individual's point of view. [**1913** H. MÜNSTERBERG (*title*) Psychology and industrial efficiency.] **1917** B. MUSCIO (*title*) Lectures on industrial psychology. **1932** *Discovery* Nov. 374/1 Industrial psychology is an awkward term for the improvement of the human factor in industry, but its value is unquestionable. **1970** D. P. SCHULTZ *Psychol. & Industry* i. 1 The field of industrial psychology includes a complex of activities covering all facets of the relationship between man and his work. **1904** S. A. BARNETT et al. in H. Barnett *Canon Barnett* (1918) II. xli. 258 Luxury..leads to cruelty in our industrial relations. **1972** *Times* 4 May 4/1 Members of Parliament are likely to be given greater latitude by the Speaker in discussing..matters that have been brought before the Industrial Relations Court. **1973** *Listener* 25 Oct. 553/3 There were no shop-stewards, solicitors or industrial relations managers present. *Ibid.* 15 Nov. 660/2 The Labour Party is committed to the repeal of the Industrial Relations Act. **1848** MILL *Pol. Econ.* II. III. xvii. 119 The opening of a foreign trade..sometimes works a complete industrial revolution in a country whose resources were previously undeveloped. **1884** A. TOYNBEE (*title*) Lectures on the Industrial Revolution in England. **1911** C. G. ROBERTSON *Eng. under Hanoverians* II. iv. 341 The manufacturer of the Industrial Revolution is the modern master who provides capital, owns his mill or factory,..and creates and maintains a market. **1938** H. GRANVILLE-BARKER *Quality* 3 We sometimes refer to the Industrial Revolution as if it were a thing of the past. **1957** G. E. WRIGHT *Biblical Archaeol.* viii. 120/2 The Philistine defeat..meant *an industrial revolution.* Philistine power was broken and the secret of the iron smelting process became common property. **1973** *Guardian* 4 June 9/6 It is no good being nostalgic for society before the Industrial Revolution. **1959** K. VONNEGUT *Sirens of Titan* (1962) iii. 73 He..had a superb system of industrial spies. **1972** G. LYALL *Blame the Dead* xii. 77 This letter..would be a useful guide to any industrial spy trying to penetrate your organisation. **1923** J. D. HACKETT in *Managem. Engin.* May 344/1 *Industrial union*, a union of all workers within a plant or within an industry, irrespective of occupation or craft, and outside the control of the employer. **1928** *Britain's Industr. Future* (Liberal Industr. Inquiry) III. xiv. § 3. 155 The Industrial Unions are a modern development, inspired by the idea of enabling all the workers in an industry..to present a united front against their employers. **1937, 1950** Industrial union [see *HORIZONTAL *a.* 3 d]. **1905** *Socialist* Oct. 4/3 Industrial Unionism is the name applied to that form of trades unionism which has sprung into existence as a direct outgrowth of modern industrial conditions under which whole industries are practically owned and controlled by capitalists through the medium of a trust or combine. **1912** [see SYNDICALISM]. **1920** S. & B. WEBB *Hist. Trade Unionism* (rev. ed.) ix. 659 The revolutionary Industrial Unionism and Syndicalism preached by James Connolly and Tom Mann..between 1905 and 1912 did not commend itself to the officials of the Trade Unions. **1905** *Socialist* Oct. 4/3 The Industrial Unionist calls upon the workers to organise in a manner consistent with the economic conditions with which they are surrounded... The plan of the industrial unionist..calls for the joining of all in the one national body of the industry. **1917** G. HARVEY *Industr. Unionism & Mining Industry* v. 148 Analysis of the Arrangement of Industries (based on Industrial Unionist literature). **1905** *Industrial Workers of the World: Constitution & By-Laws* 4 This Organization shall be known as 'The Industrial Workers of the World'... And shall be composed of thirteen International Departments, subdivided in industrial unions of closely kindred industries..for representation in the departmental administration. **1912** *Century Mag.* July 473/1 Counsels of violence were emphatically rejected, despite the opposition of the ideas of the Industrial Workers of the World. **1920, 1957** [see *I.W.W.* (*I. III)]. **1962** G. WOODCOCK *Anarchism* xiv. 466 After 1905 the anarchists who were interested in labor organization tended to join the Industrial Workers of the World.

B. *sb.* **3.** A joint-stock industrial enterprise.

1908 *Westm. Gaz.* 20 Jan. 11/1 A Colonial Industrial. The prospectus of the Vryheid (Natal) Railway, Coal, and Iron Company, Limited, has now made its appearance. **1909** *Ibid.* 3 June 13/4 A large falling off is shown in the earnings of that well-known industrial, Wm. Cory and Son.

industrialization (indʊ:striăləizē^i^·ʃən). [f. INDUSTRIALIZE *v.* + -ATION.] The process of industrializing or fact of being industrialized; also, the conversion of an organization into an industry.

1906 *Westm. Gaz.* 26 Oct. 2/1 A creed..that commends itself to all whom the 'industrialisation' of American politics has revolted. **1911** G. H. MAIR *Eng. Lit.: Mod.* ix. 225 If we want a picture of the great fact of modern Scotland, its industrialisation, it is to Galt we must go. **1923** *19th Cent.* Jan. 47 It is easy to obtain an exaggerated idea of the pace at which the industrialisation of the country by means of indigenous agency is taking place. **1928** *Daily Tel.* 20 Mar. 12/6 The present rulers of Russia have staked everything upon the policy of industrialisation under State auspices. **1953** *Encounter* Oct. 78/2 The process of industrialisation produces certain social types. **1963** P. TRENCH in *Industrialized Building Syst. & Components* Oct. 10/1 It must be some ten years ago that Roger Watters..and I first talked industrialisation. I can't remember who coined the word—it may well have been neither of us... It is now the U word. *Ibid.* 10/2 Industrialisation as a process must cover everything from the use of ready mixed concrete through modular co-ordination to the closed proprietary building system. It is in fact too wide a term to be of real use but since we have no other to describe the change in the nature of building which is going on we must accept it. **1969** *Observer* 12 Jan. 9/2 Art education is a safeguard against over-organisation, industrialisation, bureaucratisation and dehumanisation. **1969** H. A. FREY tr. *Schmidt & Testa's Syst. Building* 34/2 *Industrialization of building* in the proper sense, and in contrast to building rationalization, has to do not only with selected operations, but comprises the entire construction process from the planning stage to execution. **1973** *Listener* 20 Dec. 857 Industrialisation played a big part in the drive to paint the map pink.

industrialize, *v.* Add: **b.** *intr.* To become industrial.

1965 D. E. C. EVERSLEY in Glass & Eversley *Population in Hist.* ii. 60 Countries which did not industrialize shared in this process because they began to act as granaries for areas not self-sufficient in food. **1971** *Daily Tel.* 16 Oct. 10/4 The pace at which it [*sc.* Australia] is being forced to industrialize is turning large sections of the wide brown land into a polluted wasteland.

Hence **indu·strializing** *vbl. sb.* and *ppl. a.*

1925 *Glasgow Herald* 16 Nov. 9 It appears to be the general conclusion that any industrialising schemes apart from the water-power projects cannot succeed. **1959** *Daily Tel.* 10 Mar. 13/1 Fairly good industrial production increases occurred in new industrialising countries like Pakistan, the Philippines, Formosa and South Korea. **1967** *Economist* 10 June 1105/3 Rapidly mounting food deficits are one sign of an industrialising society. **1971** A. SHONFIELD in A. Bullock *20th Cent.* 326/1 The end of colonial empires would start a race with the newly industrializing nations in which the Old World would soon be overtaken.

industrialized, *ppl. a.* (in Dict. s.v. INDUSTRIALIZE *v.*). Add: *industrialized building*, building in which industrial methods are employed, esp. prefabrication, mechanization, and standardization. Hence applied to buildings built in accordance with such methods.

1963 *Daily Tel.* 4 Feb. 18 Prefabricated units developed under 'industrialised building' methods will be made

available to small as well as big builders. **1963** *Ibid.* 2 May 14 The suggestion is that spare shipbuilding capacity should be turned over to the manufacture of component parts for industrialised housing. **1963** *Industrialised Building Syst. & Components* Oct. 5 Industrialised building is not the mere substitution of prefabrication for traditional methods or the adoption of 'systems'. We see it as the application of modern industrial methods to the planning and execution of construction projects. **1965** R. B. WHITE *Prefabrication* III. vi. 302 'Industrialized' building, or 'system' building, ..is usually taken to mean a considerable degree of prefabrication. **1967** *Times Rev. Industry* Feb. 23/2 The National Building Agency.. suggests that the number of industrialized houses in the public sector should be increased to at least 165,000. **1968** *New Scientist* 23 May 388 Industrialized buildings by their nature are less continuous than traditional structures. The degree of continuity depends on the techniques adopted to join together the prefabricated units.

industry. Add: **5. b.** *Archæol.* A collection of prehistoric implements of the same age found at an archæological site and used as evidence of the original technique of working; also, the technique so revealed.

1911 *Jrnl. R. Anthrop. Inst.* 458 (*title*) On the classification of British Stone-Age industries. **1952** [see *GRAVETTIAN *a.* and *sb.*]. **1959** J. D. CLARK *Prehist. S. Afr.* ii. 39 A single living or workshop site where a number of specimens all of the same age are associated is called an 'industry', while the term 'culture' is usually employed to describe a number of 'industries' all of the same type, and of which the distribution is more than purely local.

c. Preceded by a personal name or the like: scholarly or diligent work devoted to the study of a particular author or subject; also, the practice of a profitable occupation.

1965 *New Statesman* 9 Apr. 575/1 The Pindar industry began fairly early in antiquity, as we can still see in the surviving scholia. **1966** *Listener* 10 Nov. 685/1 The Shakespeare industry..is a very old one; I have an eighteenth-century snuffbox made from Shakespeare's mulberry tree. **1969** *Daily Tel.* 24 Apr. 22/3 The way to tackle 'Ulysses' is to plunge into it headfirst,..which is what we all had to do before the Joyce industry began. *Ibid.* 5 Aug. 14/2 The brisk pick-up of business in the abortion industry has greatly alarmed many people.

7. Comb. *industry-wide* adj.

1946 *Nature* 30 Nov. 797/1 Research should mainly be on an industry-wide basis, and for the benefit of the industry as a whole. **1958** *Listener* 24 July 116/2 It is possible to preserve industry-wide bargaining. **1971** *Publishers' Weekly* 2 Aug. 43/3 The American National Standards, Inc., the official agency for certifying industry-wide standards in the United States.

indwelling, *ppl. a.* Add: **b.** *Med.* Of a catheter, electrode, or other device: more or less permanently fixed in position either within the body or leading from the interior to the exterior of the body.

1932 DORLAND & MILLER *Med. Dict.* (ed. 16) 252/1 Indwelling catheter. **1962** *Lancet* 5 May 950/1 Infection nearly always followed on drainage by indwelling catheter. **1964** *Ibid.* 26 Dec. 1349/1 All the very immature babies..were fed from birth by indwelling tubes. **1968** *Jrnl. Thoracic & Cardiovasc. Surg.* LV. 555 (*heading*) Thoracic duct cannulation in the dog: a study of thrombotic occlusion of indwelling cannulas. **1972** *Amer. Jrnl. Physical Med.* LI. 113 (*title*) Electromyographic study of the anterolateral abdominal musculature utilizing indwelling electrodes.

-ine, *suffix*[5]. Add: also used systematically to form the names of certain six-membered monocyclic compounds having a nitrogen atom in the ring, as *azine*. Cf. *-IN[1].

1928 *Jrnl. Amer. Chem. Soc.* L. 3078 In the field of six-membered [heterocyclic] rings are found names corresponding to the above systematic names for five-membered [heterocyclic] rings, but with the suffix *-ine* or *-in* replacing -ole (or -ol), as: triazine, oxazine, thiodiazine, dioxin (the latter being non-nitrogenous). Thus the ending -ine (or -in), although regarded as properly the ending for bases, has a specific sense in which it indicates a six-membered ring. **1940** in PATTERSON & CAPELL *Ring Index* 21. **1957** [see *-IN[1]].

in-earnestness (inə̄·ɹnéstnės). *rare*⁻¹. [f. IN *prep.* + EARNESTNESS; cf. EARNEST *sb.*[1] 2 a.] Seriousness, serious intention.

1879 G. M. HOPKINS *Lett. to R. Bridges* (1955) 89, I do avoid them [*sc.* inversions], because they weaken..the earnestness or in-earnestness of the utterance.

‖ **inédit** (*inedi*). [Fr.; cf. *INEDITA.] An unpublished work. Also *fig.*, something secret or unrevealed.

1910 *Encycl. Brit.* XII. 231/1 The inner, undiscovered, minute truths of contemporary existence, the *inédit* of life. **1922** A. E. HOUSMAN *Let.* 25 Oct. (1971) 206, I know you bibliophiles and your passion for *l'inédit* regardless of merit. **1958** *Times Lit. Suppl.* 18 Apr. 212/4 Harmon is not an unknown figure, nor his journal strictly an 'inédit'. *Ibid.* 17 Oct. 592/2 There are magazines anxious for *inédits*.

inedita (ine·ditǎ). [mod.L., neuter pl. of L. *ineditus*, f. *in-* IN-[3] + *editus*, pa. pple. of *edĕre* to give out, EDIT *v.*] Unpublished writings.

1886 *Encycl. Brit.* XXI. 141/1 The luminous exposition of the grammar and the happy choice of the pieces in the chrestomathy..all inedita. **1948** *Mind* LVII. 522 Scholars ..brought to light a number of *inedita* and checked..his writings.

ineducability (ine:diŭkăbi·lĭti). [f. INEDUCABLE *a.* + -ITY.] The condition of being ineducable.

1918 *Dial* (Chicago) 23 May 492 Carlyle in despair over the ineducability of nineteenth-century minds. **1927** CARR-SAUNDERS & JONES *Survey Social Struct. Eng. & Wales* 214 The criterion of mental deficiency for adults..is social inefficiency, while for children..it is ineducability. **1964** M. CRITCHLEY *Developmental Dyslexia* xiii. 77 Perhaps the patient and his parents have resigned themselves to a state of hopeless ineducability, and no longer importune doctors and teachers.

inée (īnēi·). Also **onage, onaye.** [Fr., ad. Fang *ene*, Mpongwe *onai*.] An arrow-poison made from the seed of *Strophanthus hispidus*.

1874 LINDLEY & MOORE *Treas. Bot.* II. Suppl. 1323/1 *Onaye* or *onage*..also called Inée and Kombé. **1887** *Encycl. Brit.* XXII. 608/1 The inée or onaye poison of the Gaboon, the kombé poison of equatorial North Africa, ..are..derived from members of this genus.

ineffability. (Later examples.)

1902 W. JAMES *Var. Relig. Exper.* xvi. 381 *Ineffability. .. Noetic quality...* These two characters will entitle any state to be called mystical, in the sense in which I use the word. **1922** JOYCE *Ulysses* 709 The supernatural character of Judaic scripture: the ineffability of the tetragrammaton: the sanctity of the sabbath. **1961** M. LASKI *Ecstasy* xxii. 243 When *ineffable*, etc. is attached to a noun, 'supreme of its kind'..seems always to be implied. The *ineffability* device is particularly common among religious writers.

ineffable, *a.* Add: **1. b.** Applied to a person.

1832 [in Dict., sense 1]. **1961** WEBSTER, Ineffable bungler. **1969** *Spectator* 14 Mar. 325/3 The ineffable Mr George Thomson.

ineffectual, *a.* Add: **c.** Also as *sb.*

1925 G. GREENE *Babbling April* 4 You snobbish intellectual, Suburban ineffectual, Can't you feel that shimmy in the air?

inegalitarian (inĭgælitēə·riăn), *a.* and *sb.* [f. IN-[3] + *EGALITARIAN *a.* (and *sb.*).] **A.** *adj.* Favouring, pertaining to, or marked by inequality. **B.** *sb.* One who denies or opposes equality between persons, = INEQUALITARIAN.

1955 T. H. PEAR *Eng. Social Differences* x. 211 The views of fervent English egalitarians and inegalitarians. **1961** *Guardian* 1 May 6/7 Madame Lefauchaux is dealing with their inegalitarian deficiencies. **1971** P. WORSTHORNE *Socialist Myth* ix. 219 The forces of democracy, *in practice*, compel society towards a shape that is highly inegalitarian. **1972** *Guardian* 15 June 14/5 The present distribution of financial aid [for housing]..is highly inegalitarian in its effects. **1972** *Daily Tel.* (Colour Suppl.) 24 Nov. 20/1 Paradoxically, Australia has a most remarkably inegalitarian educational system.

Hence **inegalita·rianism.**

1966 *Economist* 15 Oct. p. xxviii/1 This increased the inegalitarianism of what rapidly became a very inegalitarian German tax system. **1971** P. WORSTHORNE *Socialist Myth* v. 70 The Labour party has come to terms with the economic purpose of inegalitarianism.

inelastic, *a.* Add: **1. b.** Of a collision (esp. between sub-atomic particles), or the scattering of one particle by another: involving a reduction in the total kinetic energy of the particles or bodies that come together, or a change in their internal energies.

1847 L. D. B. GORDON tr. *Weisbach's Princ. Mech. Machinery & Engin.* I. IV. iv. 302 The vis viva lost by inelastic impacts is equivalent to the sum of the products of the masses and the squares of their loss or gain in velocity. *Ibid.* 310 These two general formula [*sic*] also embrace the laws of perfectly elastic and perfectly inelastic impact. **1907** J. H. JEANS *Theoret. Mech.* ix. 238 When the contact between the surfaces of two bodies is of such a nature that they do not rebound at all after impact, it is said to be perfectly inelastic. **1938** *Physical Rev.* LIII. 795/1 The results of experiments on the inelastic scattering of such fast neutrons are especially suitable for theoretical investigation because the number of excited states in which the nucleus may be left when the neutron is reemitted will be large enough to make statistical considerations valid. **1942** *Ibid.* LXI. 129/1 The scattering of fast neutrons by nuclei is at least partly inelastic in the case of medium and heavy masses like Fe, Ag, and Pb. **1958** W. K. MANSFIELD *Elem. Nucl. Physics* iv. 30 The compound nucleus formed in inelastic collisions disposes of its surplus energy, the kinetic energy and binding energy of the incident neutron, by several different processes involving the ejection of particles or radiation from the nucleus. *Ibid.* 33 For inelastic scattering to occur the neutron must have sufficient energy to leave the target nucleus in an excited state. **1962** *Gloss. Terms Nucl. Sci.* (*B.S.I.*) 103 In inelastic scattering the scattered particle or photon loses energy by exciting the struck nucleus. **1966** J. HARWOOD *Introd. Mech.* xi. 138 A collision between two balls of lead or putty would be inelastic.

2. b. *Econ.* Varying less than in proportion to changes in price; (more loosely) unresponsive to changes in price: applied either to demand (for commodities, money, labour, etc.) or to supply. So **i:nelasti·city.**

1890 A. MARSHALL *Princ. Econ.* III. iii. 167 There may be..violent changes..in the price of a thing which is not necessary, if it is perishable and the demand for it is inelastic. **1913** *Q. Rev.* Oct. 520 The demand for gas is comparatively inelastic. **1925** S. E. THOMAS *Elem. Econ.* iv. 37 Demand is said to be elastic when a rise or fall in the price causes a more than proportionate rise in the amount demanded. On the other hand, demand is said to be inelastic when a fall or rise in price causes relatively little rise or fall in the amount demanded. *Ibid.*, The Elasticity and Inelasticity of Demand. **1929** *Ibid.* (ed. 4) 51 Even in the case of necessaries, the degree of inelasticity may vary considerably. **1969** D. C. HAGUE *Managerial Econ.* II. iii. 57 Demand at all of these numerical elasticities less than one is often described as being inelastic. **1973** *Lancet* 14 Apr. 815/1 Russell found that the demand for cigarettes is inelastic... This means that if prices rise by 1% demand falls, but by an amount less than 1%; total revenue from taxation would then increase just as long as demand remained inelastic.

inelastically (inĭlæ·stikăli), *adv.* [f. prec.: see -ICALLY.] In a manner characteristic of inelastic bodies; with a reduction in the total kinetic energy.

1938 *Physical Rev.* LIII. 796/1 Inelastically scattered neutrons. **1942** J. D. STRANATHAN *'Particles' of Mod. Physics* vi. 229 It is possible that a few atoms..may occasionally collide inelastically, that one atom may spend a part of its kinetic energy in raising the electron of another atom to a higher energy level. **1966** D. G. BRANDON *Mod. Techniques Metallogr.* 112 It introduces a proportion of inelastically scattered electrons into the transmitted beam. **1969** *Physics Bull.* Mar. 86/2 The primary electron transfers an amount of energy V_0 to the atom and then leaves again, being observed externally as an inelastically reflected electron of energy $V_P - V_0$.

ineluctably, *adv.* (Later examples.)

1922 JOYCE *Ulysses* 214 That lies in space which I in time must come to, ineluctably. **1939** —— *Finnegans Wake* I. 120 Those throne open doubleyous..reminding uus ineluctably of nature at her naturalest.

Also **ineluctabi·lity,** the condition of being ineluctable.

1943 *Mind* LII. 11 The limitation of the ability of a man to achieve salvation..may be, and often is, hypostasized to seeming ineluctability.

inemotivity (i:nėmōᵘti·viti). [f. IN-[3] + EMOTIVITY.] Lack of emotional sensibility.

1894 W. JAMES in *Psychol. Rev.* I. 529 M. Sollier thinks ..that in complete *inemotivity* the visceral reactions themselves do not take place. **1902** —— in *Encycl. Brit.* XXXII. 66/1 We must remember that the patient's inemotivity may have been a co-ordinate result with the anæsthesia of his neural lesions, and not the anæsthesia's mere effect.

inenarrable, *a.* Delete '† *Obs.*' and add later examples.

1914 R. BROOKE *Coll. Poems* (1918) 18 The inenarrable godhead of delight. **1923** A. HUXLEY *Antic Hay* xv. 213 Those Mohammedan ecstasies that last..six hundred inenarrable years apiece. **1936** —— *Eyeless in Gaza* xlvii. 525 The scent of the flowers was like the brief and inenarrable revelation of something more than earthly. **1967** *Listener* 5 Jan. 37/3 The music has an inenarrable greatness which quite transcends the occasion of its composition.

inenu·bilable, *a.* *rare.* [f. IN-[3] + L. *ēnūbil-āre* to make clear (see ENUBILATE *v.*) + -ABLE.] That cannot be cleared of clouds or mist, or (*fig.*) of obscurity; indistinct; inexplicable.

1903 *Sat. Rev.* 7 Feb. 169/1 This business of the avalanche is treated by the critics as something quite inenubilable. **1911** BEERBOHM *Zuleika D.* xii. 191 There is nothing in England to be matched with what lurks in the vapours of these meadows, and in the shadows of these spires—that mysterious, inenubilable spirit, spirit of Oxford.

inepticality (ineptikæ·lĭti). *rare.* [f. INEPT *a.* + -ICAL + -ITY.] = INEPTITUDE.

1923 E. E. CUMMINGS *Let.* 15 Sept. (1969) 102 A friend of mine called 'Slater' 'Brown', looks not too much like J. Christ and has attacks of total inepticality and is a very pleasant person.

inequable, *a.* Delete *rare* and add later examples.

1924 *Glasgow Herald* 21 Nov. 11 The inequable incidence of the regulations. **1926** A. E. ELLIS *Brit. Snails* 31 An important obstacle in the way of fresh-water colonization is the inequable temperature of rivers and lakes.

inequalitarian. Add: Also as *adj.*

1949 *Mind* LVIII. 207 Consider an inequalitarian society in which there are rich people who buy 'luxuries' and poor people who buy only 'necessities'. **1966** *Punch* 13 Apr. 521/2 The ritualistically observed Sunday is inequalitarian... While the rich can enjoy their private swimming-pools..and so on, the poorer elements are denied access even to the inadequate public amenities.

inequi·valence. [f. IN-[3] + EQUIVALENCE *sb.*] Lack of equivalence.

1879 A. MACFARLANE *Princ. Algebra of Logic* 53 (*heading*) The signs of inequivalence > and <.

inequivalent, *a.* Delete † *Obs.* and add later example.

1954 I. M. Copi *Symbolic Logic* v. 127 A similar pair of inequivalent propositions may be written as [etc.].

inerasable, *a.* (Earlier example.)

1811 Shelley *Let.* 17 May (1964) I. 90 Nor do I think her Xtianity of the most inerasible nature.

inert, *a.* Add: **1. c.** *inert gas*: (*a*) As an ordinary use of the adj. with *gas*: any gas that is (relatively) inert. (*b*) Usu. as (*the*) *inert gases* (now apprehended as a special collocation, analogous to the terms *alkaline earths* and *rare earths*): any of the elements of group 0 of the periodic table, viz. helium, neon, argon, krypton, xenon, and radon, all of which are colourless, odourless, and tasteless gases which were formerly thought to be completely unreactive chemically, forming no compounds (though compounds of some of the gases are now known). Cf. **noble gas*.

(*a*) **1885** W. Macgregor *Gas Engines* v. 127 Nitrogen retards the combustion of hydrogen and that of carbonic oxide... The inert gas at the same time lowers the temperature of combustion. **1911** *Encycl. Brit.* XIX. 715/1 Nitrogen is a very inert gas: it will neither burn nor support the combustion of ordinary combustibles. **1966** *McGraw-Hill Encycl. Sci. & Technol.* V. 553/2 The gas contains about 27% carbon monoxide and over 70% of inert gases (CO_2 and N_2), giving it the lowest heating value..of any of the commercially used fuel gases. **1973** *Sci. Amer.* Dec. 22/3 The flywheel and the generator-motor would operate in an atmosphere of inert gas (hydrogen or helium).

(*b*) [**1898** W. Crookes in *Proc. R. Soc.* LXIII. 411 Professor Ramsay and Mr. Travers have discovered two other inert gases accompanying argon in the atmosphere. These are called Neon and Metargon.] **1902** G. S. Newth *Text-bk. Inorg. Chem.* (ed. 9) II. iv. 232 This property of nitrogen of uniting directly with magnesium was utilised in effecting the separation of the nitrogen of the air from the small quantities of argon and other 'inert gases' contained in the atmosphere. **1927** J. W. Mellor *Comprehensive Treat. Inorg. & Theoret. Chem.* VII. xlviii. 906 The five gases—helium, neon, argon, krypton, and xenon—are colourless, and without odour. They are chemically indifferent and are hence called the inert gases or the rare gases, or the noble gases of the atm. **1939** H. J. Reich *Theory & Applications Electron Tubes* xi. 396 An external electrode may also be used to initiate breakdown of a mercury pool tube containing a small amount of inert gas. **1950** N. V. Sidgwick *Chem. Elements* I. 10 Apart from the molecular ions occurring in the gas, there is in no case satisfactory evidence of the existence of chemical compounds of any of the inert gases. **1961** G. A. Cook *Argon, Helium & Rare Gases* I. i. 1 Unlike the atoms of oxygen, nitrogen, and some of the common gaseous elements, the atoms of the inert gases do not combine to form stable diatomic molecules. **1962** *Proc. Chem. Soc.* 218/2 Although inert-gas clathrates have been described, this compound [*sc.* xenon hexafluoroplatinate (v), $Xe^+[PtF_6]^-$] is believed to be the first xenon charge-transfer compound which is stable at room temperatures.

inertia. Add: **1. c.** *Photogr.* The exposure corresponding to the inertia point, from which the Hurter and Driffield speed of an emulsion may be calculated.

c **1886** F. Hurter in W. B. Ferguson *Photogr. Res. Hurter & Driffield* (1920) 12 Supposing that a source of diffuse white light of intensity one acting directly upon a plate needed a time *t* to so far alter a bromide of silver gelatine film on that plate that an impenetrable black deposit of silver was caused upon it on development... That time *t*..measures the inertia of the plate. **1888** Hurter & Driffield *Brit. Pat.* 5545, Upon one of the fixed pair of scales..we mark what we call and hereinafter define as the 'inertia' or slowness of the plate. **1899** C. F. Townsend *Chem. for Photographers* (ed. 2) iv. 73 Several of the dots are in a straight line; this is the period of correct exposure. The straight line is prolonged to meet the base line, and the number read off, which gives the 'inertia' of the plate. **1927** C. B. Neblette *Photogr.* ix. 238 The inertia is an inverse measure of the speed of the plate: that is to say, a slow plate has a high inertia while a rapid plate has a low inertia. *Ibid.*, The precise significance of the inertia as a measure of speed is somewhat difficult to define. The exposure which it represents is not the 'threshold exposure' (the minimum exposure necessary to produce a measurable density) nor does it indicate the maximum [? *read* minimum] exposure which will give proper rendering of the gradations of the subject, but an exposure somewhere between these extremes. **1955** E. F. Teal tr. *Lobel & Dubois's Sensitometry* 96 Characteristic curves are drawn for a range of development times using a developer containing no restraining bromide. The straight line portions of the curves intersect on the log exposure axis at *E*, called the inertia point. Distance *OE* is the inertia *i* and the H. & D. speed is defined as 34/*i*, *i* being measured in log candle-metre-seconds.

3. Special Comb.: **inertia governor** *Engin.*, a governor which operates by virtue of both centrifugal force and inertia (1934 in Webster); **inertia point** *Photogr.*, the point in which the straight-line portion of the characteristic curve cuts the horizontal (log exposure) axis when produced; **inertia reel** *Motoring*, a reel which enables a safety belt looped around it to be self-adjusting, esp. in *inertia reel* (*safety*) *belt*; also the belt served by the reel; **inertia selling,** the supply of goods to persons who have not requested them, in the hope that the recipients will not take the necessary action to refuse them; **inertia starter** *Aeronaut.*, a starter (Starter 6) which utilizes the energy stored in a flywheel.

1907 Sheppard & Mees *Investigations Theory Photogr. Process* II. vi. 221 The reciprocity failure may be considered to start at much the same point relatively to the inertia points in the two plates. **1955** [see sense 1 c above]. **1957** K. M. Hornsby *Sensitometry in Pract.* ii. 9 Hurter and Driffield regarded the inertia point as a fixed characteristic of the emulsion, and they used it as a criterion by which to specify the sensitivity of emulsions. This criterion is not now recognised as an unchangeable characteristic of the emulsion since..fog will shift it to the left..and a developer containing bromide does not give a constant inertia point for all development times. **1962** *Daily Tel.* 14 Aug. 16/6 The webbing runs off a small inertia reel mounted at the foot of the door pillar. **1962** *B.S.I. News* Dec. 10/1 With the exception of inertia-reel models..all the belts on display seemed to bear a Kite-mark label. **1968** *Economist* 6 July 49/2 Not so usual are inertia reel belts, the sort that are always held at the correct tension (many injuries to wearers of seat belts may arise because they were too loose). **1970** *Motoring Which?* Apr. 43/2 Daimler V-8 250..radio (with power operated aerial), automatic (inertia reel) safety belts; two years old. **1971** *Guardian* 25 Jan. 7/7 Spaghetti belts are replaced by inertia reels. **1968** *Times* 25 Apr. 14/3 Mrs. Butler..asked if the President of the Board of Trade would take powers to control inertia selling campaigns... She deplores this exploitation of inertia sales promotion... It will be difficult for people who are subjected to inertia selling. **1970** *Times* 13 Jan. 4/6 The Daily Mail reported on the banning..of inertia selling advertisements... Inertia selling was the practice by which companies sent unsolicited goods, then pestered people for payment if they were not returned. **1970** *New Statesman* 13 Feb. 217/1 Now the Consumer Council is urging another dairy monopolist to abandon the practice of slipping homogenised milk, at 1d extra on to doorsteps .., and billing for it if it is accepted. The company denies that this is inertia selling, but does it matter what you call it? **1972** *Guardian* 14 Oct. 1/4 Disreputable trading practices which victimize the housewife. Among these are 'inertia selling' and 'pyramid selling'. **1929** *Flight* 7 Mar. 181 (*title*) Inertia starters for aero engines. **1931** D. Garnett *Grasshoppers Come* 89 He..got the engine to fire with the inertia starter. **1958** *Times* 1 July p. iv/5 Simms Motor Units Ltd. have entered a Tensec inertia starter which enables Diesel engines to be started by hand with the minimum effort.

inertial, *a.* Add: **b.** Applied to a frame of reference in which Newton's first law of motion holds, i.e. a frame in which a body continues in a state of rest or of uniform motion in a straight line unless that state is altered by an external force.

1887 [in Dict.]. **1914** L. Silberstein *Theory of Relativity* i. 5 The 'fixed-stars' system of reference... We will call [this]..following the modern habit, the inertial system, or sometimes, also, the Newtonian system of reference. **1918** A. S. Eddington *Rep. Relativity Theory Gravitation* viii. 83 The measurement of the rotation of the earth detects something of the nature of a fundamental frame of reference—at least in the part of space accessible to observation. We shall call this the 'inertial frame'. **1924** *Physical Rev.* XXIII. 543 Lange and Mach have done much to spread a relative conception of motion. Lange introduced the name 'inertial system'. **1952** C. Møller *Theory of Relativity* ii. 36 The concept of simultaneity between two events in different space points consequently has an exact meaning only in relation to a given inertial system. **1953** E. T. Whittaker *Hist. Theories Aether & Electr.* II. v. 159 In Einstein's general theory, the velocity of light at any place has always the value *c* with respect to any inertial frame of reference for this neighbourhood. **1959** J. Aharoni *Special Theory Relativity* i. 3 Let *K* be an inertial frame of reference, then, according to the principle of relativity, in every set of axes *x'*, *y'*, *z'* which moves along a straight line and with constant velocity relative to *K* it is equally possible to adjust the clocks as in *K*, and all the frames of reference so obtained are inertial and are completely equivalent to each other not only with respect to the law of inertia, but also with respect to any other law or physical relation. **1970** *Nature* 17 Oct. 273/1 The experimental observation, by Michelson and Morley and others, of the isotropic constant velocity of light in inertial frames.

2. Special collocations: *inertial guidance*, (automatic) control of the course of a vehicle or vessel by a system employing the principle of inertial navigation; *inertial mass*, mass as measured by the ratio of the force on a body to the resulting rate of change of its momentum; cf. **gravitational mass*; *inertial navigation*, navigation in which the course of a vehicle or vessel is calculated automatically by a computer, without the need for external observations or equipment, from its acceleration at each successive moment, this being measured by accelerometers whose orientation is gyroscopically controlled; *inertial system*, (*a*) (see sense b above); (*b*) a system for carrying out inertial guidance.

1955 *Aviation Age* Jan. 28 (*heading*) Dependable inertial guidance systems can be found. **1956** *Time* 30 Jan. 40/1 One [guiding system]..is 'inertial guidance'. Its heart is a subtle instrument that senses every force that acts on the flying missile...This information goes to a computer. **1958** *Economist* 16 Aug. 521/1 Navigation under the ice requires a further modern development—inertial guidance to replace conventional types of navigational aid which become unreliable near the pole or under water. **1962** F. I. Ordway et al. *Basic Astronautics* ix. 383 The heart of the inertial guidance system is the stabilized platform with its gyroscopes and accelerometers. **1920** R. W. Lawson tr. *Einstein's Relativity* xix. 65 If now, as we find from experience, the acceleration is to be independent of the nature and condition of the body and always the same for a given gravitational field, then the ratio of the gravitational to the inertial mass must likewise be the same for all bodies. **1955** Inertial mass [see **gravitational mass*]. **1954** *Aviation Age* Sept. 34/2 The idea of 'absolute' guidance—which evolves rather naturally from advanced work in inertial navigation—is startlingly promising. **1957** *Sci. News Let.* 27 Apr. 259/1 Inertial navigation is of particular importance to the military because it is jam-proof. **1969** *New Scientist* 28 Aug. 418/2 Inertial navigation systems ..depend..on the fact that an acceleration integrated twice, gives distance run and therefore position. **1952** K. W. Gatland *Development of Guided Missile* iii. 56 Attempts are being made to develop the inertial system, e.g., the technique used in the A-4 rocket. **1962** F. I. Ordway et al. *Basic Astronautics* ix. 385 A possible solution to the problem of overcoming accumulated error over long flight times is an inertial system supervised by a continuous series of fixes on celestial bodies. **1970** *New Scientist* 1 Jan. 22/2 The inertial system, already tested by BOAC during some 500 hours of flying, has been working *en route* with an average error of only one nautical mile an hour.

inertialess (inə̄·ɪʃiălės), *a.* [f. Inertia + -less.] Having no inertia; responding instantaneously to any change in the forces acting on it.

1927 *Jrnl. Franklin Inst.* CCIV. 592 This correction.. causes the servo-mechanism to deliver the position which an ideal inertialess watthour meter would have. **1933** [see *iconoscope 2]. **1937** *Discovery* Nov. 329/1 These beams of inertialess particles are regulated in large vacuum tubes. **1961** G. Millerson *Technique Television Production* ii. 19 A small gun in the camera-tube generates a continuous beam of electrical particles (electrons). This fine inertialess 'pointer' explores the charge pattern on the camera-tube screen. **1971** *Physics Bull.* July 402/1 Amongst potential advantages of laser machining are the following: (1) Light is inertialess; hence high 'tool' velocities with very rapid stopping and starting becomes [*sic*] possible.

inertially (inə̄·ɪʃiăli), *adv.* [f. Inertial *a.* + -ly[2].] By means of or as a result of inertia or inertial forces.

1957 *Astronautics* Dec. 27/1 (*title*) Servo considerations in an inertially stabilized reference system utilizing air-bearing gyros. **1971** *Sci. Amer.* June 21/1 Energy-releasing fusion reactions..can be initiated and to some extent controlled within an 'inertially confined' plasma. **1971** *Ibid.* Dec. 57/1 The catalyst is inertially removed from the product vapors in a cyclone separator.

inescapably (inėskēi·păbli), *adv.* [f. Inescapable *a.* + -ly[2].] Inevitably; undeniably. Also **inescapabi·lity**, inevitability, undeniableness.

1881 *Academy* 24 Dec. 468/2 The single word 'inescapably' (i.e., inevitably)..has crept in we know not how. **1945** *Mind* LIV. 210 Thus the inescapability of some sort of realism is proved once again! **1963** *Times* 24 May 13/7 The very clarity and inescapability of the story which the landscape tells has helped to create the beginnings of a will to remedy these evils.

inessential, *a.* (*sb.*) **B.** *sb.* (Later examples.)

1902 *Daily Chron.* 22 Apr. 3/3 If we ignore the inessentials of place, costume, speech and employment, friendship is the same to-day as it has been for a myriad of yesterdays. **1927** *Observer* 22 May 8 Stripped of its inessentials (which are too roughly handled) his story comes down to this [etc.]. **1960** J. Betjeman *Summoned by Bells* 96 All the inessentials of the Faith.

ineuphonious (inyufōu·niəs), *a.* [f. In-[3] + Euphonious *a.*] Not euphonious.

1887 *Lancaster* (Pennsylvania) *Daily Examiner* 7 Apr., The name is too remote, too foreign and too ineuphonious. **1921** *Public Opinion* 15 July 62/3 Their own ineuphonious patois..communicates its harshness to the voice itself. **1927** *Brit. Weekly* 14 July 337/3 In spite of the..drawback of a somewhat formless, ineuphonious style.

inevictable (inĭvi·ktăb'l), *a. rare.* [In-[3].] That cannot be evicted. Hence **inevi·ctably** *adv.*

1895 W. Stevens *Let.* 23 July (1967) 6 Some unnameable smathering of greasy fritters,..and of course the inevictable applesauce. **1954** W. Faulkner *Fable* (1955) 155 The scarlet-spurting stump inevictably aloft. *Ibid.* 166 The inevictable establishment in coeval space of the sum of his past.

inevitable, *a.* Add: In extended use: that cannot fail or is bound to occur, appear, be used, etc.; that is inherent (in) or naturally belongs *to* (see also quot. 1893). Hence *sb.* (with *an* or *pl.*), an inevitable fact, event, truth, etc.; a person who, or thing which, is necessarily chosen or employed.

1879 F. W. Farrar *Life St. Paul* Pref., The English version..only requires the removal of errors which were inevitable to the age in which it was executed. **1888** W. Whitman in *Century Mag.* (1911) Dec. 255/1 Grant was one of the inevitables: he always arrived; he was as

invincible as a law. **1893** *Funk's Stand. Dict., Inevitable..* jocularly, customary; usual; as, the *inevitable* row with the cabman; the *inevitable* hash for breakfast. **1901** *Westm. Gaz.* 24 Apr. 4/2 Here at length are some true inevitables. **1903** *Ibid.* 28 Aug. 3/2 After the Canadian Arch it was only an 'inevitable' that there should be a rush to the Dominion. **1927** *Observer* 17 July 9/4 A further twenty volumes of Everyman's Library... The 'Areopagitica' was another of the inevitables. **1932** *N. & Q.* 6 Feb. 107/1 Illustrations of French wit;..of the 'inevitable' phrase, that gift to the world past all praise. **1932** H. READ in H. J. & H. Massingham *Great Victorians* 400 Patmore, at this stage of his inspiration, was no inevitable poet. **1936** L. C. DOUGLAS *White Banners* viii. 167 Paul greeted them amiably, exchanged the inevitables with the comely Mrs. Edmunds [etc.]. **1965** *Listener* 22 July 112/2 It seemed that it was only a matter of time before..the United States would bow gracefully to the inevitable. **1974** *Daily Tel.* (Colour Suppl.) 4 Jan. 19/3 Walter Harris was awarded a light diet of prunes, apricots, grapefruit, broth, and the inevitable yoghurt.

inexpectation. (Later example.)
1946 M. PEAKE *Titus Groan* 390 He had made so rapid and nimble a detour of the stone table that he surprised Steerpike, appearing with such inexpectation beneath the boy's nose.

inexpellable (inekspe·lăb'l), *a. rare.* [f. IN-³ + EXPELLABLE *a.*] Incapable of being expelled.
1911 BEERBOHM *Zuleika D.* iii. 33 He loved her, and he could not help seeing her... Inexpellable was her image.

inexpertise (inekspəɹtī·z). [f. IN-³ + *EXPERTISE.] Lack of expertise.
1926 *Chicago Even. Post* 12 Nov., It results in part from ignorance of foreign politics and international relations, and from inexpertise in discussing them. **1961** J. SHERWOOD *Half Hunter* vi. 74 The élite were performing their loops and spins in an atmosphere of solemnity and calm, oblivious of the revolving mass of inexpertise around them. **1963** *Times* 9 Mar. 11/3 If one grows impatient in performance, it is more often with vocal than compositorial inexpertise.

inexplicably, *adv.* (Later examples.)
1865 G. M. HOPKINS *Poems* (1967) 162 Meadows to them inexplicably dear. **1903** G. B. SHAW *Man & Superman* p. x, Inexplicably forcing you to range the hero with his enemy the statue on a transcendent plane. **1922** JOYCE *Ulysses* 680 Was the proposal of asylum accepted? Promptly, inexplicably, with amicability, gratefully it was declined.

inexquisite (inekskwi·zit), *a. rare.* [f. IN-³ + EXQUISITE *a.*] Not exquisite.
1922 JOYCE *Ulysses* 264 The bar where bald stood by sister gold, inexquisite contrast.

in extenso: see also *IN *Lat. prep.*

inface (i·nfēⁱs). *Geomorphol.* Also **in-face.** [See quot. 1896.] The steep scarp-face of a cuesta.
1896 W. M. DAVIS in *Science* 15 May 732/2 The surrounding rims of harder stratified rocks offer interesting examples of outer slope and inface, with inner subsequent valleys, all in concentric circular arrangement. [*Note*] The invention of this excellent term, the abbreviation of 'inward facing escarpment', should be credited to Mr. L. C. Glenn, of Darlington, S.C. **1939** A. K. LOBECK *Geomorphol.* xiii. 451 Each cuesta has a steep inface and a gentle back slope, down the dip of the beds. **1954** W. D. THORNBURY *Princ. Geomorphol.* v. 133 One of the common regional expressions of gently or moderately dipping rock is the cuesta. This has an abrupt escarpment or inface on the up-dip side and a more gentle backslope or dip slope extending in the direction of the regional dip.

infall. Add: **4.** (A) falling upon or into (esp. a planet) from an outside source.
1899 *Edin. Rev.* Oct. 328 The waning atmospheric stock of carbon is reinforced by meteoric infalls. **1961** *New Scientist* 23 Feb. 465/3 Cosmic infall dust..would also provide a source of very finely divided ferrous material [on the moon]. **1969** *Nature* 20 Dec. 1160/1 Relative to the galactic gas the average velocity of infall would be about 500 km s⁻¹. **1971** I. G. GASS et al. *Understanding Earth* iii. 67/2 At present the energy of infall of a meteorite or a space rocket is very large.
b. Material that falls or has fallen.
1960 *New Scientist* 18 Feb. 387/2 There is..some evidence of it in the spectra of comets, and fragments from these continue to form part of the meteoroidal infall. **1962** F. I. ORDWAY et al. *Basic Astronautics* v. 188 On airless worlds surface materials may be..mixed with cosmic infall, including meteoritic debris.

infalling (i·nˌfǭ:liŋ), *a.* Also **in-falling.** [IN *adv.* 11 a.] Falling into or towards something (specified or understood).
1954 J. R. R. TOLKIEN *Two Towers* IV. iv. 259 They washed themselves and drank their fill at the in-falling freshet. **1969** *Nature* 20 Dec. 1160/1 The gravitational field of the galaxy, as well as the infalling gas from the universe, will sweep the halo clouds back into the galactic layer. **1971** I. G. GASS et al. *Understanding Earth* iii. 67/2 As the Earth grew and its gravitational attraction became greater so the energy released by an infalling body increased.

infant, *sb.*¹ Add: **5. a.** *infant prodigy.*
1831 [see PRODIGY 3 c]. **1924** R. M. OGDEN tr. *Koffka's Growth of Mind* ii. § 4. 49 Infant-prodigies who fail to live up to their early promise. **1939** F. PRATT *Secret & Urgent* i. 25 He was Jean François Champollion, an infant prodigy.

b. *infant industry* (see quot. 1914).
1870 *Congress. Globe* App. 29 Mar. 240/3 But, argue our defenders of monopoly, let us protect our infant industries, and when they have grown to manhood..they will need no further protection. **1906** *Daily Chron.* 17 Oct. 6/5 The argument for Protection there is not at all the infant-industry argument. **1914** *Cycl. Amer. Govt.* II. 176 *Infant Industry.* This term is applied to the need of protecting new industries in order to give them opportunity to compete with older foreign establishments.

6. *infant mistress,* a woman teacher of infants at an elementary school; *infant mortality,* the death of infants, *spec.* of those less than a year old; *infant welfare.*
1877 W. R. ALGER *Life Edwin Forrest* I. 147 The rate of infant mortality may be reduced to one per cent of its present murderous average. **1918** *79th Ann. Rep. Registrar-General 1916* (Cd. 8869) 35 Infant welfare organisations might well devote special attention to the first days of the life of illegitimate children. **1921** *N.Z. Educ. Gaz.* 1 Nov. 12/2 (Advt.), *Infant-mistress*—South Wellington (Grade VII G): £310–£320. **1922** *Encycl. Brit.* XXX. 650/2 *Infant Welfare Centres.*—The first task has been to coördinate the work at the Infant Centre and the visitation of the mothers in their own homes. *a* **1930** D. H. LAWRENCE *Phoenix II* (1968) 18 Last week the infant mistress did not come up, so I was alone. **1939** M. SPRING RICE *Working-Class Wives* p. vii, The high rates of infant mortality..in the early years of the present century. *Ibid.*, Better methods of mothercraft through the influence of the Infant Welfare Centre. **1962** *Guardian* 9 Mar. 8/2 The orders might contain..infant welfare foods (distributed as a voluntary service). **1963** B. PEARSON *Coal Flat* iii. 48 'The first infant mistress's job that's going,' she thought.

infanteer (infăntīᵊ·ɹ). *slang.* [f. INFANT(RY + -EER.] An infantryman.
1944 J. H. FULLARTON *Troop Target* xxiii. 174 A lone infanteer..watched it all from a slit trench. **1961** *Guardian* 14 Nov. 8/3 Did he and his fellow-Gunners never talk of Guardees or Infanteers?

infanticipate (infănti·sipēⁱt), *v.* Chiefly *U.S.* [f. INFANT *sb.*¹ 1 + ANT)ICIPATE *v.*] *intr.* To be in the state of expecting a child. Hence **infanti·cipating** *ppl. a.* and *vbl. sb.*
1934 W. WINCHELL in *News & Post* (Baltimore) 28 May 10/1 The J. Clark Baldwin, 3ds,..are infanticipating. **1941** in *Amer. Speech* (1942) XVII. 271/2 'Storkettes' for 'infanticipating' friends of yours. **1961** *N.Z. Listener* 8 Sept. 34/4 Although I agree that 'infanticipating' will be very hard to rival. **1963** *New Musical Express* 10 May 12/1 Frank Sinatra jnr. dating actress Jana Taylor... Infanticipating—singer Gene McDaniels' wife.
Hence **infanticipa·tion,** the state of expecting a child; the child that is *in utero.*
1934 W. WINCHELL in *News & Post* (Baltimore) 2 July 8/2 The Alan Mowbray infanticipation is due in late October. **1939** in *Amer. Speech* (1940) XV. 218/1 Cameraman Leonard Smith shot Miss O'Sullivan behind fern fronds, through leafy screens, at respectful distances, permitted his camera to drop no hint of her..infanticipation.

infantile, *a.* Add: **2.** *Geol.* Of a landscape: in the earliest stage of the cycle of erosion. Of a land form or feature: characteristic of such a landscape.
1885 *Proc. Amer. Assoc. Adv. Sci.* XXXIII. 429 Just as the surface of the deposit rises above its base-level of erosion..a smooth, unbroken plain is revealed... The smoothness of the surface and the shallow lakes are indeed truly infantile features, retained only during the earliest life of the plain, and soon lost in its further development. **1941** C. A. COTTON *Landscape* xvii. 191 The theoretical distinction between 'infantile' forms developing on a peneplain as it is slowly uplifted and the 'senile' forms it exhibited before uplift was first made by Walther Penck. **1968** R. W. FAIRBRIDGE *Encycl. Geomorphol.* 1110/2 Initial or infantile (i.e., uneroded) forms of mountains composed of such materials have indeed had no real existence, because they have been destroyed while relatively slow or intermittent upheaval has been in progress.
3. Special collocations: *infantile mortality* = **infant mortality*; *infantile paralysis,* poliomyelitis (which affects chiefly the young).
1859 W. MOORE (*title*) On infantile mortality, and the establishment of hospitals for sick children. **1901** *Daily Chron.* 14 Nov. 5/5 In England the term 'infantile' mortality applies only to the deaths of children under one year of age. **1911** G. B. SHAW *Getting Married* 135 The high birth-rate of the very poor is counterbalanced by a huge infantile-mortality in the slums. **1843** *Lancet* 27 May 301/1 There is a disease of very considerable frequency—I mean infantile paralysis—to which, I think, so much attention has not been given as its importance merits. **1916** *Daily Colonist* (Victoria, B.C.) 5 July 1/2 Twenty-five children died from the epidemic of infantile paralysis..during the 24 hours ending at 6 o'clock to-night. **1955** *Sci. News Let.* 16 Apr. 242/2 No matter how it is called, poliomyelitis, infantile paralysis, or polio for short, it is a scourge that has long been a crippler and killer. **1957** *Economist* 7 Sept. 847/1 Experience with the Salk vaccine during the past two years has convinced the National Foundation for Infantile Paralysis that the enemy is in full retreat.

infantilism (infæ·ntiliz'm). *Path.* [prob. ad. F. *infantilisme*: see INFANTILE *a.* and -ISM.] Infantile or childish condition; *spec.* **a.** The state or condition of being physically undeveloped. **b.** *Psychol.* A condition in which infantile behaviour patterns persist, owing to some emotional repression in early life, and are dominant over more appropriate reactions.
[**1871** F. V. FANEAU DE LA COUR (*title*) Du féminisme et de l'infantilisme chez les tuberculeux.] **1895** W. D. MORRISON in Lombroso & Ferrero *Female Offender* Introd. p. xvi, Sexual peculiarities, such as feminism in men, mascul[in]ism in women, and infantilism in both. **1897** tr. *T. Ribot's Psychol. of Emotions* 422 The formula which..sums up and explains the unstable is this: psychological infantilism. *Ibid.*, The term infantilism is equally applicable to the congenital and the acquired forms. The former have never left their childhood behind, the latter return to it. **1903** *Lancet* 30 May 1526/1 A case of Infantilism in a child, aged ten years, who had not grown since four years old. Her weight was 26 pounds and her height was three feet. **1909** ROBERTSON & MACKENZIE tr. *Tanzi's Text-bk. Mental Dis.* xxii. 670 There is then an arrest of the genetic instinct at the infantile stage—an erotic infantilism. **1924** J. RIVIERE et al. tr. *Freud's Coll. Papers* I. xiv. 277 The 'infantile sexual traumas' were in a sense supplanted by the 'infantilism' of the sexuality in these cases. **1924** W. B. SELBIE *Psychol. Relig.* xv. 297 The worship of God is a form of infantilism, and survives because it meets a certain elementary need and satisfies the sense of dependence which man never altogether loses. **1943** S. R. SLAVSON *Introd. Group Therapy* vii. 224 Children whose parents are in conflict with each other are not only fixed in their infantilism as a result, but use it to exploit the two parents. **1950** R. H. WILLIAMS *Textbk. Endocrinol.* ii. 49 Gonadal hypoplasia with dwarfism..is sometimes referred to as infantilism or the Lorain–Lévi syndrome. **1953** A. W. SPENCE *Clin. Endocrinol.* xli. 495 The word 'infantilism' was first used in medical literature by Lorain (1871) when he wrote the preface of the thesis of one of his pupils, Faneau de la Cour, on feminism and infantilism in tuberculous patients. **1962** R. H. WILLIAMS *Textbk. Endocrinol.* (ed. 3) xv. 933 The differentiation of persistent sexual infantilism from constitutionally delayed adolescence.

infantilistic (infæ:ntĭli·stik), *a.* [f. INFANTILE *a.* + -ISTIC.] Pertaining to, exhibiting or characterized by infantilism; abnormally immature.
1930 C. G. SELIGMAN *Races Afr.* ii. 51 Rather should they be considered to represent an early human type 'infantilistic' both physically and mentally. **1936** *Discovery* June 167/2 Negritos, a pygmy, infantilistic, dark-skinned type.

infantility. Delete † *Obs. rare*⁻¹ and add examples. Also, an instance of infantile behaviour.
1919 M. K. BRADBY *Psycho-Anal.* iii. 31 In these [*sc.* unreasoned convictions] we shall find his kinship with the primitive and with his own infantility. **1921** *Discovery* May 133/2 Its chief characteristics [*sc.* of the 'Personal Unconscious'] are its infantility and its compensatory character. **1928** *Daily Tel.* 28 Aug. 5/2 With amazing veracity and power, Tolstoy portrays all that infantility of the Russian race. **1930** A. HUXLEY *Brief Candles* 66 He laughed at every naïveté or impertinence she uttered.. and..led her on into fresh infantilities.

infantilization (infæ:ntiləizēⁱ·ʃən). [f. INFANTIL(E *a.* + -IZATION.] The action of prolonging or perpetuating a state of infancy.
1939 *Nature* 25 Feb. 325/2 Following Bolk's thesis of infantilization he would regard man as the permanent baby amongst mammals. **1943** D. M. LEVY *Maternal Overprotection* iv. 53 Infantilization consists in the performance of activities in the care of a child beyond the time when such activities usually occur. **1970** G. GREER *Female Eunuch* 98 In pushing the masochistic role as the proper role for woman, psychology reinforces the infantilization which has gone on ever since she was born. **1971** JONAS & KLEIN (*title*) Man-child: a study of the infantilization of man.
Hence **infa·ntilized** *ppl. a.*, made the object of infantilization; **infa·ntilizing** *vbl. sb.* and *ppl. adj.*
1943 S. R. SLAVSON *Introd. Group Therapy* i. 8 The period of forbearance on the part of the group therapists is much shorter with pampered and infantilized children. **1943** D. LEVY *Maternal Overprotection* v. 73 Maternal overprotection becomes largely an infantilizing process. **1965** *Listener* 29 Apr. 626/2 In this context, the infantilizing mother, who holds herself ever indispensable, is a kind of murderer.

infantinely, *adv.* Change example reference to: **1833** MILL *Lett.* (1910) I. 77.

infant-school. Add: (Earlier and further examples.) Also *infants* (or *infants'*) *school.*
The usual form is now *infant school.*
1824 S. WILDERSPIN *Importance Educating Infant Poor* 33 Rules to be observed by the Parents of Children admitted into the Spitalfields Infant School. *Ibid.* 50 An infant school may be regarded..as a combination of the school and nursery. **1839** [see *COLERIDGIAN *a.* and *sb.*]. **1921** MENCKEN *Amer. Lang.* (rev. ed.) 120 An English boy whose father is unable to pay for his education goes first into a *babies' class*..in a *primary* or *infants'* school. **1945** *Guide Educ. Syst. Eng. & Wales* (Min. Educ.) 59 *Infants School* (*Infants Department*), primary school for children of about 5 to 7 years, including in some cases classes for children of 3 and 4. **1969** I. & P. OPIE *Children's Games* xii. 331 Even beyond Infant School the girls sometimes play 'Mothers and Fathers'.

infare, *sb.* **2.** (Delete *western,* and insert earlier U.S. examples.) Also *transf.*
1744 J. MACSPARRAN *Diary* (1899) 18 Dr. Hazard and Betty Gardiner went to..Billy Hazard's weding. They

are both gone again..to the Infair. **1794** in *Amer. Pioneer* II. 223 An Infair was given to-day by Mason, to a fellow named Kuykendall, who had..run off with Mason's daughter..a few weeks ago. **1872** SCHELE DE VERE *Americanisms* 236 The minister is said to settle,..a ceremony which..in many churches is made the occasion of much ceremony, called an installation or infare, because resembling an old-fashioned wedding festival.

infatuate, *ppl. a.* Add: Hence as *sb.*, an infatuated person.

1934 in WEBSTER. **1949** *Scrutiny* XVI. 210 The earlier criticism of *Antony and Cleopatra* tended to stress the downfall of the soldier in the middle-aged infatuate.

infauna (i·nfǭnă). [ad. Da. *ifauna* (C. G. J. Petersen 1913, in *Beretn. f. d. Danske biol. Station* XXI (in *Fiskeri-Beretn.* 1912). 15), f. IN-² + FAUNA.] A collective term for animals that live just beneath the surface of the sea bed.

1914, 1964 [see *EPIFAUNA]. **1969** G. VEVERS tr. *Friedrich's Marine Biol.* v. 254 The infauna, that is the animals living in the substrate, is either liberosessile, semisessile, or more or less motile.

infeasibility. (Later examples.)

1955 *Bull. Atomic Sci.* Mar. 78/2 That such a development is not now in sight does not offer conclusive proof of technical infeasibility. **1965** H. I. ANSOFF *Corporate Strategy* (1968) viii. 130 This example is based on an actual diversification history in which the infeasibility was not recognized.

infectious, *a.* Add: **2. c.** In the names of various diseases, as *infectious hepatitis*, an acute infectious virus disease characterized by hepatitis and jaundice; *infectious mononucleosis*, an acute disease (also called glandular fever) chiefly affecting young adults, characterized by fever, swelling of the lymph nodes, and leucocytosis.

1920 SPRUNT & EVANS in *Bull. Johns Hopkins Hosp.* XXXI. 410 (*heading*) Mononuclear leucocytosis in reaction to acute infections ('infectious mononucleosis'). **1945** *Amer. Jrnl. Med. Sci.* CCX. 561 (*heading*) Homologous serum hepatitis and infectious (epidemic) hepatitis. **1970** PASSMORE & ROBSON *Compan. Med. Stud.* II. xviii. 117/1 Infectious hepatitis is usually spread by faecal contamination from a patient or convalescent carrier of the disease. **1970** A. J. ZUCKERMAN *Virus Dis. Liver* xiii. 149 Infectious mononucleosis is an endemic disease affecting principally adolescents and young adults.

infective, *a.* Add: **2. b.** *infective hepatitis* = **infectious hepatitis*.

1939 G. M. FINDLAY et al. in *Trans. R. Soc. Trop. Med. & Hygiene* XXXII. 578 To those cases where the jaundice is associated with sensitivity phenomena the term 'allergic jaundice' might be applied, while for those in which hepatitis is the primary lesion 'epidemic' or possibly 'infective hepatitis' is probably preferable to the name 'common infective hepatic jaundice' used by Rolleston and McNee (1929). **1959** [see *HEPATITIS]. **1971** *New Scientist* 25 Mar. 676/1 Infective hepatitis..results from liver cell damage caused by a virus (or viruses) usually taken in with food or drink, and picked up from the faeces of an already infected person.

‖ **infectum** (infe·ktŏm). [L. (Varro *De Lingua Latina* IX. xcvii).] (See quot. 1954².)

1954 L. R. PALMER *Latin Lang.* II. ix. 266 In Latin the three aspects of the IE. verb were reduced to two, for the verbal system shows a contrast only between the *infectum* and the *perfectum*. **1954** PEI & GAYNOR *Dict. Ling.* 100 *Infectum*, the aspectual category introduced by the Roman grammarian Varro (1st century B.C.), including the present, preterit and simple future tenses. **1965** *Amer. Speech* XL. 113 The infectum verbal form.

in-feed (i·nfīd). Also **infeed.** [IN *adv.* 11 d.] **a.** The action or process of supplying a machine; *spec.* in centreless grinding, movement of the work-piece part-way into the space between the two wheels followed by its withdrawal, in contrast to its passage right through. **b.** A mechanism that carries out this process. Freq. *attrib.*

1901 *Manning, Maxwell & Moore Catal.* 636 The upper in-feed tool is fluted. **1926** *Automotive Industries* 2 Sept. 385 The back carriage has only a straight in-feed and no longitudinal motion except for setting tools. **1937** COLVIN & STANLEY *Grinding Pract.* v. 80 Work having shoulders or heads..is ground by the infeed method. **1960** *Times Rev. Industry* Sept. 39/3 Two independently variable rates of in-feed are provided. **1964** S. CRAWFORD *Basic Engin. Processes* vii. 190 At the end of each traverse the wheel is fed in towards the work..; this movement is referred to as in-feed, and it controls reduction of work diameter. **1968** *Gloss. Terms Offset Lithogr. Printing* (*B.S.I.*) 35 *In-feed roller*, a roller aiding or controlling the forward movement of a sheet to the printing or other processing units. **1971** *Timber Trades Jrnl.* 14 Aug. 57/2 On model KDK 36, with an electric infeed, the speeds are 36 and 72 ft/min.

infer, *v.* Add: **4.** (Further examples.)

This use is widely considered to be incorrect, esp. with a person as the subject.

1813 J. S. STANHOPE in A. M. W. Pickering *Mem.* (1902) II. 377 He said nothing that could in any way infer the necessity of a retreat of the allies. **1814** SCOTT *Waverley* II. xviii. 284 They are..more benign in demeanour than their physiognomy or aspect might infer. **1946** M. PEAKE *Titus Groan* 373 That he had fulfilled his intention of inveigling his enemy to the place of his own choosing must surely infer that the initiative once again lay with him. **1969** BENNISON & WRIGHT *Geol. Hist. Brit. Isles* i. 5 A. Holmes deprecated the use of the term 'Absolute' age as inferring an accuracy which is unwarranted. **1970** *Private Eye* 2 Jan. 12, I can't stand fellers who infer things about good clean-living Australian sheilahs. **1973** *Daily Tel.* 30 June 14, I have seen references..to the watering of Ascot racecourse, inferring that the water has been taken from public mains at a time when economy is being urged on all consumers.

inferably (i·nfərăbli), *adv.* [f. INFERABLE *a.* + -LY².] By inference; = *INFERRIBLY *adv.*

1903 *Harvard Psychol. Stud.* I. 340 The extent of this differentiation—and inferably the definition of rhythmical synthesis—corresponds to the reported musical aptitudes of the subjects.

inference. Add: **1. b.** *inference rule*, in a system of logic: any rule permitting inferences of a specified form.

1962 CLARK & WELSH *Introd. Logic* ii. 93 We lay down the following cluster of inference rules. **1964** KALISH & MONTAGUE *Logic* 14 From the second and third lines of the derivation we may infer 'Q' by means of an inference rule. **1965** B. MATES *Elem. Logic* vi. 93 We need a reasonably small group of simple inference-rules.

2. (Further examples.) Also, an implication; the conclusion that one is intended to draw. Cf. *INFER *v.* 4.

1933 D. L. SAYERS *Hangman's Holiday* 147 'I don't know if you realise, Mr. Egg,' observed the inspector, 'the bearing, or, as I might say, the inference of what you said just now.' **1972** P. H. KOCHER *Master of Middle-Earth* (1973) v. 82 These four are named 'first', with the inference that they deserve priority. **1973** *Daily Tel.* (Colour Suppl.) 5 Oct. 7/2 The main inference of the propaganda is that unless we adopt the metric system Britain will lose export orders.

inferiority. Add: **2.** *attrib.* and *Comb.* **inferiority complex,** generalized and unrealistic feelings of inadequacy caused by a person's reactions to actual or supposed inferiority in one sphere, sometimes compensated for by aggressive self-assertion; *colloq.*, exaggerated feelings of personal inadequacy; also *inferiority feeling*.

1922 A. G. TANSLEY *New Psychol.* (rev. ed.) xix. 214 Thus the 'inferiority complex' may account for a whole series of well-known human traits. **1924** C. MACKENZIE *Heavenly Ladder* xxiii. 288, I could psycho-analyse all Bloomsbury now. They all suffer from an inferiority complex. Either they feel themselves intellectually inferior to Newton or physically inferior to Sandow or morally inferior to Christ. **1925** *N.Y. Times* 20 Sept. IX. 12/2 Those psychic disturbances which Freudians attribute to repressed sex impulse Adler attributes to a deficiency in the mechanism of self-assertion—to the 'inferiority complex', which today is on the tongue of thousands who have no idea of what they are talking about. *Ibid.* 12/3 Dr. Adler replied: 'Individual psychology holds that the most important key to the understanding of both personal and mass problems is the so-called sense of inferiority, or inferiority complex, and its consequences.' **1926** W. MCDOUGALL *Outl. Abnormal Psychol.* xxvii. 433 The inferiority complex is an important factor in some neurotics. **1933** W. J. H. SPROTT tr. *Freud's New Introd. Lect. Psycho-Anal.* 88 A writer who brings in the expression 'inferiority-complex' thinks he has satisfied all the demands of psycho-analysis... As a matter of fact the phrase 'inferiority-complex' is hardly ever used in psycho-analysis. **1947** N. L. MUNN *Psychol.* xi. 224/2 Alfred Adler..popularized the terms 'inferiority and superiority complex' which are regarded as outcomes of, respectively, unsuccessful and successful exploitation of the 'will to power'. **1954** L. CARMICHAEL *Manual of Child. Psychol.* (ed. 2) xviii. 1118/2 Such a child..will develop an inferiority complex and will soon slow down in his attempts to cope with his environment. **1974** *Daily Tel.* 9 Mar. 15/3 Mrs Thompson seemed to have an inferiority complex. Strangers were made to feel unwelcome. **1934** H. C. WARREN *Dict. Psychol.* 137/2 Inferiority feeling. **1937** C. DAY LEWIS *Starting Point* I. ii. 32 I'd not be sure that I wasn't doing it from false motives—from envy..or inferiority-feeling. **1961** J. A. C. BROWN *Freud & Post-Freudians* iii. 39 In order to compensate for inferiority feelings, each child develops..his own particular strategy.

inferrability (infərăbi·lity). Also **inferability.** [f. INFERRABLE *a.* + -ITY: see INFERRIBLE *a.*] = INFERRIBILITY.

1914 C. D. BROAD *Perception* ii. 128 This inferrability of one attribute from another. **1924** W. E. JOHNSON *Logic* III. viii. 104 The term 'one-one correspondence' is understood as equivalent to reciprocal inferability.

inferribly (infə̄·rĭbli), *adv. rare.* [f. INFERRIBLE *a.* + -LY².] By inference. (Cf. *INFERABLY *adv.*)

1905 J. M. ROBERTSON *Did Shakes. write Titus Andron.?* 198 It would inferribly be his latest play, as it has 69 double-endings to 461 lines of blank verse. **1913** —— *Baconian Heresy* 18 When they were written we know not ..but it was inferribly before 1623.

infestation. Add to def.: Also, the state or condition of being infested.

infield, in-field, *sb.* Add: **3.** (Examples.)

1867 H. CHADWICK *Base Ball Player's Bk. Reference* 138 The In-Field.—That portion of the field within the base lines. **1897** *Encycl. Sport* I. 76/1 Short Stop..is also called upon to back up all the positions of the in-field. **1906** *Spalding's Base Ball Guide* 15 The 'infield' team comprising the three base players and short stop. **1912** C. MATHEWSON *Pitching in a Pinch* ii. 23 Devoe beat out an infield hit. **1970** *New Yorker* 3 Oct. 32/1 Soon there will be nobody around who remembers muddy infields.

4. *Cricket.* The part of the playing area near the wicket; *collect.*, the fieldsmen stationed there (as opposed to the OUTFIELD). **b.** = *IN-FIELDSMAN.

1898 G. GIFFEN *With Bat & Ball* vii. 99 In the in-field the soil had been well watered and was fairly hard... But what of the out-field? *Ibid.* xi. 188 He is a brilliant infield. **1954** A. G. MOYES *Austral. Batsmen* iii. 46 Few bowlers..relish seeing the ball flying back over their heads, forcing them to weaken the in-field to stop the fours. **1960** E. W. SWANTON *W. Indies Revisited* vii. 167 May's in-field was spread so deep for Sobers as to invite him to take a single almost anywhere.

5. *U.S.* The area enclosed by a race-track. Also *attrib.*

1923 E. HEMINGWAY *Three Stories & Ten Poems* 36 You could see them [*sc.* horses] way off across the infield all in a bunch starting on the first swing like a lot of little toy horses. **1929** —— *Farewell to Arms* xx. 138 We..walked across the infield and then across the smooth thick turf of the course to the paddock. **1934** in B. A. Botkin *Treas. S. Folklore* (1949) II. iv. 404 His cry is echoed by a mighty 'They're off' from the packed stands and the infield crowd. *Ibid.* 407 They buried Black Gold there in the infield of the track. **1966** *Publ. Amer. Dial. Soc.* 1964 XLII. 6 *Infield*, area inside the racing course.

B. *adv.* In or towards the centre of a playing-field.

1959 *Times* 18 Feb. 5/1 Evans..came infield and burst through the centre. **1960** V. JENKINS *Lions Down Under* viii. 116 A brilliant try by Malcolm Thomas, who ran down the touch-line..before cutting in-field to touch down under the posts.

infielder, in-fielder (i·n͵fīːldəɹ). [f. INFIELD *sb.* + -ER¹.] **1.** *Baseball.* One of the players on the in-field.

1867 H. CHADWICK *Base Ball Player's Bk. of Ref.* 138 The in-fielders include the first six players of a nine. **1897** *Encycl. Sport* I. 76/2 Third Baseman..must be more on the alert..than the other in-fielders. **1905** *McClure's Mag.* June 123/2 Hutchinson, an in-fielder, had played in the same league with Johnson. **1967** *Boston Sunday Herald* (TV Mag.) 7–13 May 12/1 He hit a line drive right at the pile of baseballs, causing them to scatter in all directions. Every infielder came up with a different ball.

2. *Cricket.* = next.

1927 M. A. NOBLE *Those 'Ashes'* 193 Macartney..was going very quickly, picking out the gaps in the field or lofting the ball over the heads of the in-fielders. **1930** C. V. GRIMMETT *Getting Wickets* ii. 49 When a new batsman comes in, have your in-fielders close enough to save the singles.

in-fieldsman (i·n͵fīːldzmæ̆n). *Cricket.* [f. IN *adv.* + FIELDSMAN.] A fieldsman placed close to the wicket.

1910 *Westm. Gaz.* 19 Mar. 18/1 If the ball got past the in-fieldsmen there were men on the boundary to save the four. **1928** *Daily Tel.* 17 July 17/5 Nor was Freeman the only bowler who had his infieldsman too far away.

infight, *v.* Restrict † *Obs. rare* to sense in Dict. and add: **2.** To fight or box at close quarters; also *fig.* and *transf.* (cf. next).

1916 J. B. COOPER *Coo-oo-ee* xi. 156 Jack glued his chin to his chest and 'smothered', watching his opportunity to in-fight. **1966** T. PYNCHON *Crying of Lot 49* vi. 164 We face this anarchy of jealous German princes, hundreds of them scheming, counter-scheming, infighting.

in-fighting, *vbl. sb.*, **in-fighter.** Add: Also *fig.* and *transf.*

1907 J. LONDON *Iron Heel* ii. 38 He was unused to this fierce 'infighting', as Ernest called it. **1928** L. WOOLLEY *Sumerians* ii. 52 Two [spears] have plain butts and are intended for in-fighting. **1930** H. G. WELLS *Autocracy of Mr. Parham* IV. i. 274 The temperament and tradition of both navies disposed them for attack and in-fighting. **1936** G. B. SHAW *Millionairess* IV. 193 *Epifania.* You are two stone heavier than I; and I cannot keep my head at infighting as you can. **1960** AUDEN *Homage to Clio* 79 Untrained in a ruthless Verbal in-fighting. **1970** W. SMITH *Gold Mine* xxxi. 78 She would use even the dirtiest in-fighting to see that Rod was not overlooked. **1972** *Listener* 24 Aug. 241/1 The cheerful in-fighting that characterizes intellectual exchange between clinician and medical scientist. **1973** *Time* 25 June 38/2 Inside the Politburo, he is known as a tough infighter.

infill, *v.* Delete *rare* and add later examples. Also *intr.*

1958 *Antiquity* XXXII. 110 This had been infilled with weathered flints. **1971** *Farmer & Stockbreeder* 23 Feb. 39/1 He is renovating the drainage system, in-filling and levelling, so 230 acres can be ploughed. **1971** P. GRESSWELL *Environment* 133 It is possible to 'infill' between two distant houses. **1972** *Daily Tel.* 23 May 15/4 Get the outline first, with basic shrubs...Then 'infill' with smaller shrubs and roses. **1973** *Nature* 23 Mar. 227/1 Channels, cut by streams rejuvenated during regression of the sea, have been infilled by alluvial and terrestrial clastics.

infill (i·nfil), *sb.* = INFILLING *vbl. sb.* (various senses).

1939 *Geogr. Jrnl.* Jan. 56 While it is not theoretically impossible for great stretches of the present flood-plain to have been formerly aggraded..followed by removal of the infil [*sic*]..such an explanation involves difficulties. **1958** *Antiquity* XXXII. 110 The basis of the infill of the enclosure. **1958** *Archit. Rev.* CXXIII. 10/2 Infill panels of brick, precast concrete or coloured glass. **1966** J. S. Cox *Illustr. Dict. Hairdressing* 83/1 *Infill*, (1) The dressed hair enclosed within a specified area. (2) Knotting hair within a specified area. **1969** *New Scientist* 15 May 352/3 Sound absorbing infill is there primarily for heat and fire resistance. **1970** *Observer* 15 Mar. 7/6 Local landowners.. stand to make small fortunes out of selling their acres to the infill excavators. *Ibid.*, Welsh infill could not be used on the M4. **1971** *New Scientist* 6 May 317/1 The full four-runway airport will undoubtedly need more infill than could be provided from..dredging.

infilling, *vbl. sb.* Add: (Later examples.) Also *fig.*

1895 J. MACNEIL *Spirit-Filled Life* xiv. 100 The Lord Jesus is prepared to grant us a fresh Infilling, a 'refilling' of The Holy Ghost. **1958** *Times Rev. Industry* May 46/1 Aluminium curtain walling in conjunction with a steel framed building..reduces labour charges..incurred by the use of the normal masonry infilling. **1961** *Guardian* 27 May 5/5 In its earliest forms, watercolour was little more than an infilling for sketches in ink and bistre. **1962** *Listener* 1 Feb. 228/3 Those coloured earths which in French gardens so often provide the infilling for *broderies*. **1970** *Cabinet Maker & Retail Furnisher* 30 Oct. 201/2 Infillings of horse hair..and hand-springing are used exclusively. **1972** L. ALCOCK *By South Cadbury* viii. 178 A plausible reconstruction of the building would suggest an infilling of wattle and daub for the walls.

spec. in *Town Planning*.

1943 FORSHAW & ABERCROMBIE *County of London Plan* 35 Five types of units of dispersed industrial population: i. Infilling of gaps in incomplete schemes within the County. **1944** P. ABERCROMBIE *Greater London Plan 1944* 35 A rounding off of the communities by infilling on the backlands and vacant frontages. **1964** *Daily Tel.* 17 Mar. 23/2 No part of his plan could possibly be regarded as infilling. By which they meant one or at most two houses pushed into existing gaps. **1971** P. GRESSWELL *Environment* 134 Infilling in villages is in many cases both inevitable and desirable. **1974** *Times* 5 Feb. 10 New building, other than infilling, was more extensive on the mainland.

infiltrate, *v.* Add: (Now usu. pron. with stress on initial syllable.) **4.** *Mil. trans.* and *intr.* To penetrate (enemy lines) by the gradual or surreptitious movement of small numbers of troops; to move (one's own troops) surreptitiously into the enemy's lines. Also *fig.*, esp. for the purpose of political subversion.

1934 in WEBSTER. **1944** *Times* 1 Apr. 8/1 Skilfully infiltrating through the chain of Japanese outposts and garrisons, the force penetrated hostile territory as far as the Shan States. **1956** A. H. COMPTON *Atomic Quest* 125 Some of its branches had been infiltrated by Communists. **1958** [see *FIFTH COLUMN]. **1972** *Daily Tel.* (Colour Suppl.) 21 Jan. 27/1 There CIA agents succeeded in infiltrating several of its groups. **1972** *Daily Tel.* 30 Mar. 4/6 Terrorist groups started infiltrating from neighbouring African States. **1972** *Sunday Express* 21 May 17/5 Security men fear that Moscow would take the chance to infiltrate agents into Britain. **1972** *Daily Tel.* 19 June 2/1, I was paid..about £500 for infiltrating the IRA network in London. **1974** *Ibid.* (Colour Suppl.) 1 Mar. 7/2 Equally insidious is the way in which Communists..are infiltrated into the sphere of education.

infiltration. Add: **1. d.** The gradual penetration of one people into another.

1904 *Westm. Gaz.* 14 Nov. 5/1 In the interior of the Empire the French work of gradual 'infiltration' will proceed by not less efficacious means. **1927** PEAKE & FLEURE *Priests & Kings* 54 As time went on there seems to have been an ever-increasing infiltration of Southern Steppe-folk from the desert. **1930** J. L. MYRES *Who were the Greeks?* ii. 55 The southward infiltration of Albanian and Slav into districts formerly Romanized.

e. *Mil.* The gradual or surreptitious penetration of enemy lines by small numbers of troops.

1930 *Economist* 16 Aug. 313/1 They thus succeeded..in reaching the outlying quarters of Peshawar, albeit in small numbers, by a process of nocturnal 'infiltration'. **1933** B. H. L. HART *Future of Infantry* 27 We profited from the lesson taught us by the remarkable success, at our expense, of the new infiltration or soft spot tactics in.. 1918. **1967** *N.Y. Times* (Internat. Ed.) 11–12 Feb. 1/6 At a background briefing early in November, the American command made available infiltration figures covering the year through Sept. 30.

fig. (Cf. *INFILTRATE *v.* 4.)

1940 *Economist* 15 June 1036/1 The Nazis have developed the technique of infiltration to such a pitch that [etc.]. **1941** *Ann. Reg. 1940* 209 Great uneasiness was caused in the country by the infiltration..of thousands of able-bodied young Germans in the guise of tourists. **1949** KOESTLER *Promise & Fulfilment* II. v. 281, I wonder whether an American don is the right match for the propaganda and infiltration experts of the Soviet Union. **1958** *Times* 20 Jan. 5/7 Alleged Communist infiltration into the Oxford branch of the National Union of Railwaymen. **1973** P. EVANS *Bodyguard Man* v. 44 You're an ex-Special Branch man, supposedly a professional at infiltration techniques.

4. infiltration anæsthesia, anæsthetization of an area by the injection into it of a local anæsthetic; **infiltration capacity,** the maximum rate at which soil in a given condition can absorb water; **infiltration rate,** the rate at which soil absorbs water; infiltration capacity.

1897 *Med. Rec.* LI. 44/1 (*heading*) The method of infiltration anæsthesia: its technique and..advantages. *Ibid.* 45/2 Cocaine anæsthesia lasting from two to five minutes, infiltration anæsthesia from fifteen to twenty minutes. **1958** J. H. BURN *Lect. Notes Pharmacol.* (ed. 5) 56 Lignocaine..is a useful anaesthetic for producing nerve block and for infiltration anaesthesia. **1933** R. E. HORTON in *Trans. Amer. Geophysical Union* XIV. 446 'Infiltration-capacity' will be used to describe the maximum rate at which rain can be absorbed by a given soil when in a given condition. **1952** *Proc. Soil Sci. Soc. Amer.* XVI. 85/2 The term 'infiltration capacity'..has been an object of some controversy because it implies that an extensity is involved, whereas an intensity such as *infiltration rate* would be more apt. **1940** *Ibid.* V. 400/2 It is unfortunate that the terms 'infiltration-capacity' and 'infiltration rates' have sometimes been confused... There may be an infinite variety of rates but there is only one capacity at a particular time for a particular soil. **1952** *Ibid.* XVI. 88/1 Infiltration rate (soil). The maximum rate at which soil, in a given condition at a given time, can absorb rain. **1957** *Soil Sci.* LXXXVII. 338 After infiltration begins, increasing the initial moisture content reduces the infiltration rate.

infiltrator (i·nfiltrē^i^təɹ). [f. INFILTRATE *v.* + -OR.] One who infiltrates (esp. in sense *4 of the vb.).

1944 *Infantry Jrnl.* (U.S.) May 28 Our men had orders not to leave the lines in case of any infiltration, because our rear elements would take care of the infiltrators. **1949** KOESTLER *Promise & Fulfilment* I. xv. 165 Arab infiltrators from neighbouring countries were exercising 'considerable administrative control' in Samaria. **1953** *Wall St. Jrnl.* 1 Sept. 1/3 Police already have arrested nearly 4,000 infiltrators from the Soviet zone. **1957** L. F. R. WILLIAMS *State of Israel* x. 200 The 'economic infiltrators' who slip across [the frontier] to harvest crops on fields once their own. **1959** *Economist* 27 June 1154/1 The much greater confidence existing at Standard between union officials, shop stewards and the rank and file..is always the first target of communist infiltrators on the spot. **1970** *Guardian* 2 May 11/5 The Mekong..seldom poses problems to Communist infiltrators. They cross by raft or skiff at night.

infiltrometer (infiltrǫ·mĭtəɹ). [f. INFILTR(ATION + -OMETER.] An apparatus for measuring the rate at which soil can absorb water.

1940 P. B. ROWE *Construction, Operation & Use of North Fork Infiltrometer* (U.S. Dept. Agric.) 1 Laboratory tests of the infiltrometer and the infiltration studies in which it has been employed since it was first developed in 1934 indicate that it affords a practical and reliable means of measuring the infiltration capacity of soils under natural field conditions. **1955** R. K. FREVERT et al. *Soil & Water Conservation Engin.* iii. 47 Infiltrometers using simulated rainfall cover areas varying from less than 2 to nearly 500 square feet. **1971** *Agronomy Jrnl.* LXIII. 306/2 Ring infiltrometer tests were made in the spring and fall.

‖ **infima species** (i·nfimă spī·ʃīz). Pl. **infimæ species.** [f. L. *infima* nom. fem. of *infimus* lowest (see INFIMOUS *a.*) + SPECIES *sb.*] The lowest species of a classification or division; *concr.*, an 'infimous' person (?*obs.*).

1645 J. HOWELL *Lett.* I. xii. 23 Being contented to be the *infima species*, the lowest in the predicament of your frends. **1843** MILL *Logic* II. III. xxii. 134 Such generalizations..ought to be grounded upon an examination of all the *infimæ species* comprehended in them. **1961** T. LANDAU *Encycl. Librarianship* (ed. 2) 283/1 Any one species may, in its turn, be capable of further division into species, when for that purpose it becomes a genus—and so on down to the most minute species required, the *infima species*.

infimum (infəi·mɒm). *Math.* [L., = lowest part, neut. of *infimus* lowest (see prec.).] The largest number that is less than or equal to each of a given set of real numbers; an analogous quantity for a subset of any other ordered set.

1940 G. BIRKHOFF *Lattice Theory* ii. 16 We shall use the words 'supremum' and 'sup' synonymously with l.u.b.; similarly, we shall use 'infimum', and 'inf', and 'common part' synonymously with gr.l.b. **1949** S. LEFSCHETZ *Introd. Topology* i. 27 We shall also use on occasion the supremum and infimum of a nonvoid set *A* of real numbers, written sup *A*, inf *A*. **1964** W. J. PERVIN *Found. Gen. Topology* i. 15 In the natural ordering for the set of natural numbers, 2 is the infimum of the set of even numbers. In the case of the ordering <1, 3, 5,...; ..., 6, 4, 2>, there is no infimum to the set of even numbers even though they are bounded below. *Ibid.*, The rational numbers ordered by size are not order-complete, since the subset consisting of all rationals which are positive and have squares greater than 2 does not have an infimum, even though it is bounded below by 0. **1968** E. T. COPSON *Metric Spaces* i. 14 The infimum of a subset *A* is its greatest lower bound, and is denoted by inf *A*.

infinite, *a.* Add: **1. d.** *infinite regress* (see quots.).

1836–7 [see REGRESS *sb.* 1 *fig.*]. **1934** A. C. EWING *Idealism* iv. 149 If we once view relations as terms we are involved in Bradley's infinite regress. **1946** P. HARRISON *Oxf. Marmalade* I. iii. 27 George's criterion of niceness, however, might be described as an infinite regress. Every girl he met was nice, until he met another, and she was nicer. **1968** E. H. GOMBRICH *Art & Illusion* (ed. 3) ix. 268 Are we not led into what philosophers call an infinite regress, the explanation of one thing in terms of an earlier which again needs the same type of explanation? **1973** A. QUINTON *Nature of Things* 109 The concept of an axiom..solves the problem of the infinite regress of justification.

5. Read: *Mus.* Applied to a form of musical structure which can be repeated infinitely.

1869 [in Dict.]. **1876** STAINER & BARRETT *Dict. Mus. Terms* s.v. *Canon*, The above is also an *infinite* canon, because, anyone having such a remarkable desire as to play it for ever, could do so. **1880** GROVE *Dict. Mus.* s.v. *Canon*, Many canons lead back to the beginning and thus become 'circular' or 'infinite'. **1959** *Collins Mus. Encycl.* s.v. *Canon*, If..each part, on coming to the end of the melody, goes back to the beginning again and repeats, the result is a 'perpetual' or 'infinite' canon.

infinitesimal, *sb.* and *a.* Add: Hence **infinite·simalist,** one who supports the method of infinitesimals (sense A. 2).

1863 [see MOMENTARIAN]. **1937** *Mind* XLVI. 227 Berkeley's penetrating criticism of the postulates of the fluxionists and infinitesimalists of his day.

infinitism (infi·nitiz'm). [f. INFINITE *a.* + -ISM.] The belief that God, or the world, is infinite; or that there is an actual infinite. So **infi·nitist,** an exponent or adherent of infinitism; also *attrib.* or as *adj.*

1897, 1900 Infinitist [see *FINITIST *sb.*]. **1902** W. JAMES *Var. Relig. Exper.* 525 He [*sc.* God] is assumed..to be 'infinite'... Nevertheless..religious experience..cannot be cited as unequivocally supporting the infinitist belief. **1922** Infinitism [see *FINITISM].

infinitive, *a.* and *sb.* Add: **B.** *sb.* **3.** *attrib.* and *Comb.*, as *infinitive-adjunct, -splitter, -splitting*.

1957 R. W. ZANDVOORT *Handbk. Eng. Gram.* I. i. 9 In the fourth example the infinitive stands in apposition to the noun; in the fifth the infinitive adjunct is semi-adverbial. **1927** *Glasgow Herald* 1 Nov. 8/7 A competition..to discover the most distinguished infinitive-splitters. **1926** FOWLER *Mod. Eng. Usage* 447/1 They were obsessed by fear of infinitive-splitting.

infinitize (i·nfinitəiz), *v.* [f. INFINITE *a.* + -IZE.] *trans.* To render infinite. Also as *vbl. sb.*

1913 E. UNDERHILL *Mystic Way* 62 They aspire to infinitise life and to define infinity. **1930** [see *FINITIZE *v.*].

infinity. Add: **4. b.** In *Photogr.* also used of any distance, or the range of distances, at which an object is effectively in focus when the lens is set for the greatest possible distance. (Earlier and further examples.)

1867 SUTTON & DAWSON *Dict. Photogr.* 122 In every lens there is..a certain distance of a near object from it, between which and infinity all objects are in equally good focus. **1910** *Photogr. for Beginners* (Country Life Ltd.) ii. 13 These are called 'fixed focus' cameras, and the lens is 'set at Infinity', which means that, provided the object to be photographed is not *nearer* the camera than, say, twenty feet, everything in the picture will appear sharp. **1929** R. H. GOODSALL *Beginner's Guide Photogr.* v. 22 The next thing is to adjust the lens to correct focus... All subjects over 100 feet away will be at 'infinity', smaller distances are marked on the scale. **1939** J. M. BLAIR *Pract. & Theoret. Photogr.* ix. 89 The hyperfocal distance is the least distance at which a lens may be focussed when objects at infinity are still in focus. **1950** G. L. WAKEFIELD *Your Camera Lens & Shutter* ii. 27 In photography, an object at 100 feet away from the lens would be normally considered as being at infinity. Infinity cannot be rigidly defined in the photographic sense, but it becomes a greater distance as the focal length of the lens increases. **1974** *Trafford Catal.* Spring & Summer 890/1 Kodak 100 pocket camera outfit. Fine 3-element lens gives sharp colourful prints or slides from 4 ft. to infinity.

infirm, *a.* **1. b.** (Later example.)

1952 *Mind* LXI. 83 Clearly the argument is infirm.

infirmation. (Later example.)

1953 W. V. QUINE *From Logical Point of View* ii. 37 Method of empirical confirmation or infirmation.

infixation (infiksē^i^·ʃən). *Gram.* [f. INFIX *v.* + -ATION.] The action of infixing; the state of being infixed.

1921 E. SAPIR *Lang.* iv. 76 A peculiarly interesting type of infixation is found in the Siouan languages, in which certain verbs insert the pronominal elements into the very body of the radical element. **1964** E. BACH *Introd. Transformational Gram.* iii. 48 And the infixation of the object marker..should be brought about by a low-level rule in the grammar.

inflammability. (Further examples: see next and cf. *FLAMMABILITY.)

1966 WALLACE & WILKINSON *Res. Burns* 634 Standards of non-inflammability to which textile fabrics must conform. **1968** E. MILLER *Textiles* vi. 133 The necessity for some form of treatment which would reduce inflammability risk in fabrics has been on record since the seventeenth century at least.

inflammable, *a.* (*sb.*) (Further examples, illustrating the continued currency of the word alongside *FLAMMABLE *a.*, q.v.)

1962 MUIR & BARCLAY *Burns & their Treatm.* Foreword, It is unfortunate that children and the elderly should bear the brunt of our apparent unwillingness to.. elaborate methods of rendering clothing less inflammable. **1968** *Which?* Mar. 92 Recently..the Toilet Preparations Federation recommended to their members that inflammable hair preparations should carry a warning. **1968** E. GALE *From Fibres to Fabrics* xiv. 151 To render fabrics non-inflammable, they may be treated with mineral salts. **1972** *Sci. Amer.* Mar. 54/3 If a resulting spark has enough energy inflammables are ignited and explosions are set off.

inflammably, *adv.* (Later example.)

1922 JOYCE *Ulysses* 716 The same concupiscence, inflammably transmitted first with alarm, then with understanding.

inflammatorily, *adv.* (Earlier example.)

1840 DICKENS *Let.* 2 Oct. (1969) II. 131 Yours inflammatorily and despondingly Charles Dickens.

inflatable, *a.* Add: **B.** *sb.* An object, e.g. a dinghy, a toy, etc., which is capable of being inflated.

1954 *Official Directory—American Toy Fair* 46 Phonographs, inflatables, swimming accessories, [etc.]. **1962** *Engineering* 3 Aug. 151 No less than 17,000 Allied aircrew lives were saved by inflatables. **1970** *Guardian* 30 July 9/6 Mark Fisher..and Simon Connolly..are now preparing a DIY inflatable dome kit to order... It makes up into an inflatable 12 ft in diameter by 8 ft high. **1971** A. BULLOCK *20th Cent.* 245/1 The sculptor has a variety of ..plastics with which to make inflatables or multiples. **1971** *New Scientist* 27 Apr. 284/3 Inflatables help children move without fear. **1971** *Ink* 12 June 11/4 Children's Rights Day: Action Space with inflatables and events. **1973** *New Society* 11 Jan. 70/2 A huge plastic inflatable for people to jump around on.

inflate, *v.* Add: **4.** Also *intr.*, to resort to, exhibit, or produce (monetary) inflation.

1940 *Economist* 27 Jan. 136/1 The most direct..method of inflating, if it cannot be avoided, would..be the deliberate creation of additional credit. **1965** *New Statesman* 31 Dec. 1021/1 Even if *all* countries inflated at the same rate, some problems would remain. **1971** *Sunday Times* 24 Oct. 44/6 More recently..all types of Southern property have been inflating faster than anywhere in the country. **1973** *Time* 25 June 23/2 In the supermarket.. prices have been inflating at an annual rate of 25% or more.

inflation. Add: **6.** *spec.* An undue increase in the quantity of money in relation to the goods available for purchase; (in lay use) an inordinate rise in prices. (Earlier, later, and *attrib.* examples.)

1838 D. D. BARNARD *Speeches & Rep.* 195 The property pledge can have no tendency whatever to prevent an inflation of the currency. **1841** in X. D. MacLeod *Biogr. F. Wood* (1856) 75 We have been periodically visited by panics, revulsions, and distresses, inflations and reäctions. **1863** W. S. JEVONS *Serious Fall in Value of Gold* i. 13 The inflation of credit must be checked by the well defined boundary of available capital. *Ibid.* 14 A revulsion occasioned by a failure of the national capital must cause.. a collapse of credit, and of any inflation of prices due to credit. *Ibid.* 25 It is impossible to account for this permanent change [in prices] by any excessive speculation, inflation of currency, or credit. **1870** W. W. FOWLER *Ten Yrs. Wall St.* 315 Used ten thousand shares of the new stock to load up the bulls at these inflation prices. **1874** *N.Y. Tribune* 26 Nov. 5 An Inflation Party [has been organized] reaffirming, in effect, the financial plank of the Indiana Independents. **1922** *Encycl. Brit.* XXX. 984/1 Inflation had the effect of reducing the pre-war unit of value. **1949** *Times* 10 Sept. 5/6 Inflation is used to describe the situation in any country where there is an excess of currency and credit in relation to the work to be done, an excess of purchasing power and effective demand in relation to its goods available, with prices and wages, and prices again, rising in consequence. **1967** *Economist* 16 Dec. 1143/3 That fearsome thing called 'inflation physco. logs' is taking hold. **1972** *Accountant* 5 Oct. 434/3 He made a plea for a Dutch recommendation on inflation accounting in external reporting. **1973** *Sun* 18 Jan. 16 The Premier named inflation as public enemy No. 1.

8. inflation-proof, *v. trans.*, to protect from the effects of monetary inflation; so *inflation-proofing*; **inflation-rubber,** a removable rubber sleeve inside each teat cup of a milking machine which, as it is rhythmically inflated and deflated, squeezes the cow's teats; also ellipt. *inflation.*

1973 *Times* 26 Nov. 14/6 The Chancellor could profitably devote the budget..to inflation-proofing those of our laws and institutions which have been created on the false assumption that monetary values are constant. *Ibid.* 27 Nov. 18/6 Neither of them enjoys any automatic inflation-proofing beyond the moment of their retirement. **1974** *Guardian* 23 Jan. 10/1 The cuts affect universities in three ways: delayed building, a loss of inflation-proofing in current spending, and doubt about student grants. **1950** *N.Z. Jrnl. Agric.* Feb. 114/2 Old rubberware such as used inflations must never be allowed to accumulate..close to the dairy. *Ibid.* Oct. 301/3 Inflation rubbers give quicker milking if they retain their tension. **1960** B. CRUMP *Good Keen Man* 102 His bellowing discourse on the good and bad brands of inflation-rubbers for milking machines.

inflationary (inflē^i·ʃənări), *a.* [f. INFLATION + -ARY^1.] Of, pertaining to, characterized by, or involving (monetary) inflation.

1920 *Glasgow Herald* 21 Aug. 7 The transition from an inflationary to a deflationary period in prices. **1921** *Spectator* 28 May 677/1 The enormous Government loans, with their inflationary influence. **1930** *Time & Tide* 1 Nov. 1356 France is uneasy about the inflationary effects of the gold she has collected. **1931** *Economist* 12 Dec. 1118/1 Progressive depreciation of sterling..would..make the beginning of an all-round inflationary spiral a certainty. **1943** *Ann. Reg. 1942* 31 Increases in basic wages had not been of a kind calculated to produce the inflationary spiral. **1945** WEBSTER Add., *Inflationary gap*, the gap between an increasing purchasing power, that is, money available for spending, and a shrinking or static supply of civilian goods available for purchase, which as it widens sets in motion an inflationary spiral. **1970** T. LUPTON *Managem. & Social Sci.* (ed. 2) ii. 46 The inflationary pressure generated by collective bargaining at the workplace in conditions of full employment.

inflationism (inflē^i·ʃəniz'm). [f. as prec. + -ISM.] The condition or fact of being inflated; the policy of inflating the currency. Also *transf.* and *fig.*

1919 J. M. KEYNES *Econ. Consequences Peace* 223 The inflationism of the currency systems of Europe has proceeded to extraordinary lengths. **1930** *New Statesman* 9 Aug. 572/2 The book is a tract against inflationism. **1938** C. CONNOLLY *Enemies of Promise* ix. 93 The deflationary activities of the Cambridge critics..have replaced the inflationism of Bloomsbury. **1973** *Spectator* 3 Mar. 280/3 His real enemy is not the dialectical materialism of the Marxist militants but the dialectical inflationism of the Tories' own monetary policy.

inflectable (infle·ktăb'l), *a.* *Gram.* [f. INFLECT *v.* 3 + -ABLE.] Capable of being inflected.

1958 W. N. FRANCIS *Struct. Amer. Eng.* 594 *Noun*,..a lexical word which..is inflectable with the plural and possessive inflections (*-es*) and (*'s*). **1963** F. G. LOUNSBURY in S. Koch *Psychol.* VI. 563 The determination of the particular form of an inflectable word. **1965** *English Studies* XLVI. 30 An inflectable possessive pronoun.

inflexional, inflectional, *a.* Add: **2.** *Geom.* Of or pertaining to a point of inflexion.

1862 G. SALMON *Treat. Analytic Geom. Three Dimensions* x. 182 We shall call the two lines which meet the surface in three coincident points, the inflexional tangents at the point. **1926** S. GANGULI *Theory Plane Curves* (ed. 2) II. i. 32 Through each point there pass four lines, each of which passes through two..points of inflexion. These lines are called inflexional lines. **1966** J. H. CADWELL *Topics in Recreational Math.* x. 100 Still more special is an inflectional tangent which both touches and crosses a curve.

inflight (i·nflait), *a.* Also **in-flight.** [f. *IN *prep.* 17* + FLIGHT *sb.*^{1}] Within or during a flight.

1945 *This Week Mag.* 25 Mar. 20/3 The Air Transport Command furnished quarters..and provided another 2,000,000 'inflight' meals. **1952** *N.Y. Times* 21 Dec. X27/3 Thousands of in-flight refueling operations have been completed without a single accident. **1964** *Punch* 11 Nov. 712/2 World airlines..are offering..in-flight movies and TV. **1969** *Sunday Times* (Colour Suppl.) 17 Aug. 18/3 There are six big screens for the inflight movies which no American airline can now do without. **1972** *Lebende Sprachen* XVII. 72/1 By the spring of 1970 inflight results should be available for comparison with wind-tunnel predictions.

influence, *sb.* Add: **4. c.** *under the influence*: affected by alcoholic liquor; intoxicated, drunk.

[**1866** MAYNE REID *Headless Horseman* xix. 110 If not absolutely intoxicated, it could be seen that the ex-officer of volunteers was under the influence of drink.] **1879** 'MARK TWAIN' *Lett.* (1917) I. 367 Nobody got in the least degree 'under the influence', and we had a pleasant time. **1922** JOYCE *Ulysses* 297 Lowest blackguard in Dublin when he's under the influence. **1925** WODEHOUSE *Carry on, Jeeves!* vii. 159 Boat-Race Night. Then, if ever, you will see Bertram under the influence. **1940** L. A. G. STRONG *Sun on Water* 77 If a man under the influence tries to give you too much, sure, you slip it back into his pocket when he isn't looking. **1960** H. & M. WILLIAMS *Double Yolk* in *Plays of Year* XXI. 47 The police sergeant..asked if I'd been drinking...I'd had a drink—and then he said I must go to the station with him, as he'd have to charge me with driving under the influence.

8. influence line *Engin.*, a graph showing how the resultant moment, stress, or other quantity at a given point of a structure varies with the position of the applied (constant) load producing it; **influence pedlar** (or **peddler**) *U.S.* (see quot. 1968); hence *influence peddling.*

1902 *Encycl. Brit.* XXVI. 377/1 In dealing with the action of travelling loads much assistance may be obtained by using a line termed an influence line. Such a line has for abscissa the distance of a load from one end of a girder, and for ordinate the bending moment or shear at any given section, or on any member, due to that load. **1936** PIPPARD & BAKER *Analysis Engin. Struct.* xiv. 319 We shall consider the truss shown in Fig. 14.18 and find the influence line for the force in a diagonal bracing member as a load rolls along the bottom chord. **1972** R. C. COATES et al. *Structural Analysis* ii. 51 A bending moment diagram (shear force diagram) shows graphically the value of the bending moment (shear force) at *all* sections of a beam under a force whose position is *fixed*; an influence line for bending moment (shear force) shows graphically the value of the bending moment (shear force) at a *single* section for *all* possible positions of a movable force. **1949** *N.Y. Times* 14 Aug. E7/5 The Investigations subcommittee of the Senate Committee on Expenditures in the Executive Departments which is inquiring into the activities of the 'five percenters' and the 'influence peddlers' has discovered that selling influence may be unethical, but it is not always illegal. **1968** W. SAFIRE *New Lang. Politics* 204/2 *Influence pedlar*, one who has, or claims to have, the contacts and 'pull' supposedly necessary to get government contracts and favors from public officials, for a fee. **1971** *Wall St. Jrnl.* 20 July W1/3 The acknowledged dealer in stolen securities said part of the $100,000 he paid went to Nathan Voloshen, a convicted Washington influence peddler. **1972** *N.Y. Times* 22 Sept. 43 In 1956 a Senate investigation showed that Mr. Chotiner was engaged in influence peddling.

influenceable, *a.* (Later example.)

1970 G. GREER *Female Eunuch* 94 Deutsch..drew an extraordinary picture of woman as the ideal life-companion... 'They seem to be easily influenceable.'

influent, *a.* (*sb.*) **2.** Delete † *Obs.*, insert *arch.*, and add later example.

1922 T. HARDY *Late Lyrics* 93 No influent star endeared me, Unknown, unrecked, unproved!

B. *sb.* **2.** *Ecology.* An organism which affects the ecological balance of a plant or animal community.

1926 V. E. SHELFORD in *Ecology* VII. 389 Professor [F. E.] Clements kindly suggested the term influent to cover those organisms which have important relations in the biotic balance and interaction. **1935** [see *BIOME]. **1938** WEAVER & CLEMENTS *Plant Ecol.* (ed. 2) xviii. 478 It is more convenient to employ a distinct term and call them [*sc.* animals] influents in reference to their abundance and corresponding importance.

influential, *a.* (*sb.*) **B.** *sb.* Delete *rare* and add later examples.

1837 W. DYOTT *Diary* 16 July (1907) II. 257 And was there strongly entreated by the influentials in the South Division of the county to allow himself to be put in nomination with Lord Ingestre for the south. **1899** 'MARK TWAIN' in *Forum* (N.Y.) Mar. 29 It was their official duty to entertain the influentials after some sort of fashion. **1957** R. K. MERTON *Social Theory* (rev. ed.) 128 Two types of influentials—the local and the cosmopolitan. **1965** D. V. GLASS in Glass & Eversley *Population in Hist.* i. 19 Manuals of domestic medicine, intended not only..for the practitioner but also for the clergy and for other local 'influentials'.

influenzal, *a.* (Later examples.)

1955 *Sci. News Let.* 19 Mar. 190/2 Meningitis may also be caused by a germ called Hemophilus influenzae. This form is called influenzal meningitis, but has nothing to do with influenza. **1969** *Daily Tel.* 18 Dec. 15/3 There had been a sharp increase this month in influenzal-type illness in South-East England. **1972** *Ibid.* 20 Jan. 7 A total of 180 people died during the week ending Jan. 7 from influenza and influenzal pneumonia.

info (i·nfō^u), colloq. abbrev. of INFORMATION.

1913 *Sat. Even. Post* 15 Feb. 8/2, I can slip you the info. **1925** WODEHOUSE *Sam the Sudden* xiii. 93 So you've only to pool your info' to bring home the bacon? **1954** 'N. BLAKE' *Whisper in Gloom* ii. 29 Then we pass the info. to the police, and they raid the joint. **1968** J. C. HOLMES *Nothing More to Declare* 28 Legman..the walking dossier of scandalous info about the sex habits of politicians. **1971** *New Scientist* 9 Sept. 582 (*heading*) Generating info for schools.

in-foal (i·n,fō^{u}l), *a.* [attrib. use of phrase *in foal*: see IN *prep.* 10 b.] That is in foal.

1929 *Chilean Rev.* No. 31. 59/1 To prevent joint-ill in foals, these stations feed a teaspoonful of potassium iodide crystals twice per month to each in-foal mare. **1948** *Vet. Rec.* 25 Dec. 679/1 The in-foal mares were run out during the day until near to foaling.

infolio. Add: Also *attrib.*

1897 W. J. LOCKE *Derelicts* xx. 346 She..took up a great in-folio black-letter.

inform, *v.* Add: **5.** Const. *about, on.*

1775 SHERIDAN *Rivals* Pref. p. viii, For on subjects on which the mind has been much informed, invention is slow of exerting itself. **1863** G. MACDONALD *D. Elginbrod* III. III. x. 170 Do not hesitate to inform us on all possible subjects. **1880** DISRAELI *Endymion* II. lxi. 255 It must be a mind..fairly informed on the questions involved in the wealth of nations. **1888** MRS. H. WARD *R. Elsmere* III. xliii. 254 The Frenchman..had been informed about him. **1944** P. CHEYNEY *They never say When* xi. 172 It seems an amazing thing that you didn't inform someone about this. **1963** S. BRORSTRÖM *Increasing Frequency Preposition 'About'* VIII. 323 'Inform *about*' is an accepted construction in sentences like 'Did he *inform* you *about* it?', 'I wasn't *informed about* it', i.e. in sentences where the preposition is followed by *it.*

c. With quoted words as object.

1877 *My Mother-in-Law* xii. 112 'Baby is not very well, Charlie,' Bessie informed me. **1881** MRS. J. H. RIDDELL *Senior Partner* I. xiv. 290 'Ye're out of your mind, Janet,' Mr. McCullagh informed her.

informal, *a.* Add: **1. c.** *N.Z.* and *Austral.* Of a vote or voting-paper: not in due form, spoilt, invalid.

1957 *Wanganui Herald* 2 Dec. 5/2 (*table*) Cotterill 6121 *Mrs MacLean* 4626 *Marks* 3167. There were 39 informal votes on the preliminary count. **1965** *Parliamentary*

Handbk. Austral. 359 Victoria, 1951. No. on Rolls, 1,388,116. No. who Voted, 1,332,339. No. of Informal Ballot-papers, 90,887. **1966** *Official Year Bk. Western Austral.* 105 Number of Informal Ballot Papers, 922.

d. Pertaining to or in respect of the non-compulsory admission of a patient to a mental hospital, esp. by his or her own volition.

1959 *Act* 7 & 8 *Eliz. II* c. 72 § 5 (*heading*) Informal admission of patients. *Ibid.*, Whenever possible admission and treatment should be on an informal basis and.. compulsion should only be resorted to where it is absolutely essential in the interests of the patient and for his safety or that of the public. **1964** B. ACKNER *Handbk. Psychiatric Nurses* (ed. 9) 3 The Mental Health Act of 1959..permitted mentally ill patients to be admitted on an 'informal' basis without any documentation. **1968** K. O'HARA *Bird-Cage* vii. 65 'I don't understand this about informal patients.' 'It should have been explained to you. We don't call it certification now, but we do still need powers to protect patients from themselves.' **1970** *Times* 9 Sept. 16/6 (Advt.), Is there a Christian community who would accept a maladjusted 29-year-old girl? She is an informal patient in a mental hospital. **1972** *Guardian* 11 Aug. 11/3 An informal patient can sign for himself; the next of kin of a detained patient must give his permission.

informant. Add: **B.** *sb.* **2. c.** A person from whom a linguist, anthropologist, etc., elicits information about language, dialect, culture, etc. Used esp. in *Dialect Geography*. Also *attrib.*

1889 A. J. ELLIS *On Early Eng. Pronunc.* V. 2 Where I was unable to obtain vivâ voce or palaeotypic information, I had the same difficulty as before in interpreting the informants' orthography. **1902** *Amer. Anthropologist* IV. 732 To quote the words of my Indian informant, 'the ceremonies of the other shrines were like branches of this shrine'. **1917** *Internat. Jrnl. Amer. Ling.* I. i. 1 They were obtained by dictation from a few informants. **1933** L. BLOOMFIELD *Lang.* xix. 324 The forms were collected in each case from a single informant by means of a questionnaire of some two-thousand words and phrases. **1936** *West Virginia Univ. Stud.* I. 51 The first requirement is that both potential informants be natives. **1943** *Language* XIX. i. 42 The language must be learned from the lips of a native informant, whose sole function is to talk in his own language. **1944** *Amer. Speech* Apr. 135 The danger inherent in partial reporting, especially when based on.. inadequate informant work. **1953** J. B. CARROLL *Study of Lang.* vi. 173 A linguistic scientist..directed the classroom teaching process and used native informants as models for drill purposes. **1963** J. LYONS *Structural Semantics* iv. 76 The linguist can satisfy himself..by going around and exasperating several tobacconists with his 'informant-technique'. **1964** R. H. ROBINS *Gen. Ling.* ix. 355 The informant is not a teacher, nor a linguist; he is simply a native speaker of the language willing to help the linguist in his work. **1971** D. CRYSTAL *Ling.* Interlude 137 These characteristics of the informant sample would have to be made..explicit.

informatics (infǫɹmæ·tiks). [tr. Russ. *informátika* (A. I. Mikhailov et al. 1966, in *Nauchno-tekhnicheskaya Informatsiya* XII. 35), f. INFORMATION: see -ICS.] (See quot. 1967.) Cf. *information science* (*INFORMATION 8). Hence **informa·tical** *a.*, **informati·cian.**

1967 *FID News Bull.* XVII. 73/2 *Informatics* is the discipline of science which investigates the structure and properties (not specific content) of scientific information, as well as the regularities of scientific information activity, its theory, history, methodology and organization. **1970** *Times* 2 Sept. 9 It was agreed..that an introduction to Informatics should form an integral part of general education. **1972** *Jrnl. Librarianship* IV. 177 The name Informatics satisfies several criteria for the designation of a new discipline. *Ibid.*, Other terms can be derived from it, such as Informatician for a person who is engaged in activities in this field..and the adjective informatical, to describe the attributes of the field. **1973** *Times Lit. Suppl.* 28 Sept. 1133/1 The problem falls into two parts: the preparation of decisions, which is a matter of informatics, and the making of the decisions themselves, which is a matter of 'politics'.

information. Add: **3.** (Further examples, illustrating a contrast with *data.*)

1970 [see *DATUM 1 d]. **1970** O. DOPPING *Computers & Data Processing* i. 14 In administrative data processing, a distinction is sometimes made between data and information by calling raw facts in great quantity 'data', and using the word 'information' for highly concentrated and improved data derived from the raw facts.

c. Separated from, or without the implication of, reference to a person informed: that which inheres in one of two or more alternative sequences, arrangements, etc., that produce different responses in something, and which is capable of being stored in, transferred by, and communicated to inanimate things.

Information in this sense may at the same time be, or be regarded as, information in the following sense.

1937 *Discovery* Nov. 329/1 The whole difficulty resides in the amount of definition in the [television] picture, or, as the engineers put it, the amount of information to be transmitted in a given time. **1944** *Jrnl. Sci. Instrum.* XXI. 133/2 Information is conveyed to the machine by means of punched cards. **1953** J. C. ECCLES *Neurophysiol. Basis Mind* i. 1 We may say that all 'information' is conveyed in the nervous system in the form of coded arrangements of nerve impulses. **1953** WATSON & CRICK in *Nature* 30 May 965/2 In a long molecule many different permutations are possible, and it therefore seems likely that the precise sequence of the bases is the code which carries the genetical information. **1958** *Spectator* 4 July 22/3 The complex molecules carrying genetic information from one generation to the next. **1961** *New Scientist* 26 Jan. 201/2 The colour information is added to a conventional black-and-white signal on an amplitude and phase modulated sub-carrier located in the vision band. **1962** *Listener* 10 May 817/2 The fertilized ovum of a particular animal is not, in any obvious way, like that animal; yet its development will proceed along certain lines only. It contains the information characteristic of that particular kind of animal. **1962** *Times* 5 July 15/7 A disc is apt to give slightly inferior quality towards the centre, where the information is more crowded. **1971** R. M. DOWBEN *Cell Biol.* v. 97 Genetically transmitted information precisely determines the amino acid composition of all proteins synthesized by each cell.

d. As a mathematically defined quantity (see quots.); now *esp.* one which represents the degree of choice exercised in the selection or formation of one particular symbol, sequence, message, etc., out of a number of possible ones, and which is defined logarithmically in terms of the statistical probabilities of occurrence of the symbol or the elements of the message.

The latter sense (introduced by Shannon, quot. 1948[2], though foreshadowed earlier) is that used in information theory, where information is usually regarded as synonymous with entropy.

1925 R. A. FISHER in *Proc. Cambr. Philos. Soc.* XXII. 709 What we have spoken of as the intrinsic accuracy of an error curve may equally be conceived as the amount of information in a single observation belonging to such a distribution. *Ibid.* 710 If p is the probability of an observation falling into any one class, the amount of information in the sample is $S\{(\partial m/\partial\theta)^2/m\}$ where $m = np$, is the expectation in any one class [and θ is the parameter]. **1928** R. V. L. HARTLEY in *Bell Syst. Techn. Jrnl.* VII. 540 What we have done then is to take as our practical measure of information the logarithm of the number of possible symbol sequences. *Ibid.* 541 The information associated with 100 characters will be 500 log 2. **1935** R. A. FISHER in *Jrnl. R. Statistical Soc.* XCVIII. 47 One could, therefore, develop a mathematical theory of quantity of information from these properties as postulates, and this would be a normal mathematical procedure. *Ibid.*, As a mathematical quantity information is strikingly similar to entropy in the mathematical theory of thermo-dynamics. **1948** N. WIENER *Cybernetics* iii. 76 Thus a reasonable measure of the amount of information associated with the curve $f_1(x)$ is: $\int_{-\infty}^{\infty} (\log_2 f_1(x)) f_1(x)\, dx.$ The quantity we here define as amount of information is the negative of the quantity usually defined as entropy in similar situations. The definition..is not the one given by R. A. Fisher for statistical problems, although it is a statistical definition. **1948** C. E. SHANNON in *Bell Syst. Techn. Jrnl.* XXVII. 392 We have represented a discrete information source as a Markoff process. Can we define a quantity which will measure, in some sense, how much information is 'produced' by such a process, or better, at what rate information is produced? Suppose we have a set of possible events whose probabilities of occurrence are $p_1, p_2, \ldots, p_n$. These probabilities are known but that is all we know concerning which event will occur. Can we find a measure of how much 'choice' is involved in the selection of the event or of how uncertain we are of the outcome? If there is such a measure, say $H(p_1, p_2, \ldots, p_n)$, it is reasonable to require of it the following properties: [etc.]. *Ibid.* 394 We shall call $H = -\Sigma p_i \log p_i$ the entropy of the set of probabilities $p_1, \ldots, p_n$... The quantity H has a number of interesting properties which further substantiate it as a reasonable measure of choice or information. **1949** W. WEAVER in Shannon & Weaver *Math. Theory Communication* 99 The word *information*, in this theory, is used in a special sense that must not be confused with its ordinary usage. In particular, information must not be confused with meaning. In fact, two messages, one of which is heavily loaded with meaning and the other of which is pure nonsense, can be exactly equivalent, from the present viewpoint, as regards information. *Ibid.* 100 Information in communication theory relates not so much to what you *do* say, as to what you *could* say. That is, information is a measure of one's freedom of choice when one selects a message. **1953** D. GABOR in W. Jackson *Communication Theory* i. 2 'Information' in the exact sense of communication theory is far more restricted than the vague concept which goes by this name in everyday life. It may also be mentioned that this definition has nothing to do with the value of information. It is a measure of the minimum effort or cost by which the message can be transmitted, not of its importance or consequences. **1953** J. B. CARROLL *Study of Lang.* vii. 200 Information (in the special sense required in communication theory) may be measured in bits. **1953** C. F. HOCKETT in Saporta & Bastian *Psycholinguistics* (1961) 45/2 The keynote of the quantification of information is the matter of choice of any message, for actual transmission at a given time, from a fixed repertory of possible messages. **1956** L. BRILLOUIN *Sci. & Information Theory* p. x, Information is a function of the ratio of the number of possible answers before and after, and we choose a logarithmic law in order to insure additivity of the information contained in independent situations... This definition cannot distinguish between information of great importance and a piece of news of no great value for the person who receives it. **1957** KENDALL & BUCKLAND *Dict. Statistical Terms* 138 In a specialised sense in the theory of estimation, the amount of information about a parameter θ from a sample of n independent observations drawn at random from a population with a frequency function $f(x, \theta)$ is defined as $nE(\partial \log f/\partial\theta)^2 \equiv$

$$n \int_{-\infty}^{\infty} (\partial \log f(x, \theta)/\partial\theta)^2 f(x, \theta)\, dx.$$

1968 J. LYONS *Introd. Theoret. Ling.* ii. 84 Another important statistical notion has to do with the amount of *information* carried by a linguistic unit in a given context; and this also is determined by (or is generally held to be determined by) its frequency of occurrence in that context. **1968** P. A. P. MORAN *Introd. Probability Theory* i. 53 In statistical theory 'information' is usually 'information about a particular parameter' of a probability distribution, and is measured by the reciprocal of the square of the standard deviation of some estimator of that parameter. **1970** O. DOPPING *Computers & Data Processing* i. 19 Any language with different frequency of occurrence of different symbols has less information per symbol than another (hypothetical) language with the same number of symbol values but with equal probability of occurrence of them all.

8. *attrib.* and *Comb.*, as *information content, desk, explosion* [*EXPLOSION 4 b], *flow, gap* [*GAP *sb.*[1] 6 a], *office, service, storage, system, transfer, work*; *information-carrying, -gathering* (so *-gatherer*), *-giving, -seeking* vbl. sbs. and ppl. adjs.; **information bureau,** an office where information is given and questions are answered; also *fig.*; **information officer,** a person engaged in the provision of specialized information; **information processing,** the processing of information so as to yield new or more useful information; data processing; **information retrieval,** the tracing of information stored in books, computers, or other collections of reference material; **information room** (see quot. 1958); **information science,** (that branch of knowledge which is concerned with) the procedures by which information, esp. that relating to technical or scientific subjects, is stored, retrieved, and disseminated; hence **information scientist,** a person employed in providing an information service, or one who studies the methods used to do so. Also *INFORMATION THEORY.

1922 E. WALLACE *Flying Fifty-Five* vii. 44 Well, Jebson...You're a pretty fine information bureau! You told me that Patience hadn't a ghost of a chance. **1926** *Aslib Prospectus*, The objects of the Association are..to develop the usefulness and efficiency of special libraries and information bureaux under whatever title they may function. **1968** *Listener* 4 July 31/3 The information bureau of the Disabled Living Activities Group. **1962** *Science Survey* IV. 68 The information-carrying capacity of a wave depends directly on the frequency. **1971** J. Z. YOUNG *Introd. Study Man* p. v, The spectacular recent information that biochemistry has provided about the large molecules in the body, and especially about the information-carrying properties of the nucleic acids. **1928** *Bell Syst. Techn. Jrnl.* VII. 541 For example, in the Baudot System..the number s of primary symbols is.. 2 and the information content of one selection is log 2. **1937** J. C. WILSON *Television Engin.* xii. 426 The information-content of a television image has been evaluated solely from the point of view of what is transmitted. **1965** *Language* XLI. 385 This decomposition, or normal form, is of special interest because of various correlations with vocabulary, information-content, etc. **1967** *Economist* 11 Nov. 627/3 A national Referral Centre for Science and Technology is trying to build up a world-wide 'information desk' for advice on where and how to obtain information. **1973** D. MACKENZIE *Postscript to Dead Let.* 23, I..put the key in an envelope marked *to be called for* and left it at the Information Desk. **1964** *New Statesman* 13 Mar. 396/2 The 'population explosion' has collided with the 'information explosion'. Vastly more people and more kinds of people are chasing vastly more information about more kinds of things. **1972** *Jrnl. Librarianship* IV. 161 The advent of ISR roughly coincided with the first commercial applications of computers and it was then thought that very rapid handling of coded data was all that was needed to cope with the 'information explosion'. **1953** C. F. HOCKETT in Saporta & Bastian *Psycholinguistics* (1961) 64/1 Energy flow is power; information-flow is entropy; money-flow (at least in one direction) is income. **1965** H. I. ANSOFF *Corporate Strategy* (1968) i. 19 Product-market characteristics create operating needs, and these, in turn, determine the structure of authority, responsibility, work flows, and information flows within the firm. **1969** *Daily Tel.* 11 Jan. 12/8 Bold human causes..will not be served by ignoring the new technologies which space research is encouraging; and Britain would be well advised to close the information gap which seems to be developing. **1971** K. HOPKINS *Hong Kong* iii. 95 Mr. Woo's speech was an example of the many and repeated expressions of concern by members of the public and of Government about a so-called 'information gap' between Government and the people. **1964** M. MCLUHAN *Understanding Media* (1967) II. xxviii. 302 Man the food-gatherer reappears incongruously as information-gatherer. **1971** J. Z. YOUNG *Introd. Study Man* xxiv. 317 One of man's many paradoxes is that although with him each individual organism is more important than in other animals as an information-gatherer for the species, yet his manner of life is largely controlled by his fellows. **1964** M. MCLUHAN *Understanding Media* (1967) II. xiv. 149 In the age of instant information man..assumes the role of information-gathering. **1967** COX & GROSE *Organiz. Bibliogr. Rec. by Computer* 70 A subject-specialist studies the information needs and information-gathering habits of a group of teachers. **1908** *Westm. Gaz.* 1 July 6/3 The fish products of Canada, states one of the numerous information-giving tablets, are worth thirty million dollars a year. **1927** J. ADAMS *Errors in School* iv. 122 Instruction must be distinguished from mere information-giving. **1890** W. BOOTH *In Darkest Eng.* App. p. xiv, We shall also be glad, through the information office of Labour Department, to give you..further information. **1918** E. S. FARROW *Dict. Mil. Terms* 310 Information officers..send to their own commanders all information of military importance to them. **1935** *Aslib Rep. Proc. 12th Conf.* 38 (*heading*)

B. Fullman... (Information Officer, British Non-Ferrous Metals Research Association). **1947** *Jrnl. Documentation* II. 240, I am not a librarian at all; I am not even a trained information officer. **1970** *Aslib Proc.* XXII. IX. p. ii (Advt.), Vacancy for Scientific Information Officer at the Commonwealth Forestry Bureau. **1958** *Automation* Mar. 65 (*heading*) Information processing. **1959** *Unesco Bull. Libr.* XIII. 226 Nearly 2,000 electronic computer experts took part in the International Conference on Information Processing organized by Unesco in Paris from 15 to 20 June. **1964** T. W. McRae *Impact of Computers on Accounting* vii. 190 Even today few companies segregate 'information processing' or even 'data processing' under a separate cost head. **1970** O. Dopping *Computers & Data Processing* i. 11 Many speak of the advent of mechanized information processing as the second industrial revolution. *Ibid.* 15 When both input and output are data, that is, digital information consisting of a great number of records in standardized layout, the information processing is usually called data processing. **1950** C. N. Mooers *Theory Digital Handling Non-Numerical Information* (*Zator Techn. Bull.* No. 48) 5 The requirements of information retrieval, of finding information whose location or very existence is a-priori unknown, now requires that it be possible by some efficient technique to specify a selection of complexes Cj by means of *any* set or combination of descriptors chosen in *any* way from the vocabulary ((aj)). **1958** *Listener* 11 Dec. 983/1 Only a week or two ago there was a conference on information retrieval in Washington. **1963** *Publishers' Weekly* 23 Sept. 34/2 At the Oxford store, the feature which so far has attracted the most attention is the free bibliographical information retrieval service. **1963** *Cambr. Rev.* 12 Oct. 24/1 A book miscatalogued..is a book lost: and they [*sc.* librarians] thereby justify greater and greater expenditure on more and more elaborate systems of 'information retrieval'. **1972** *Computers & Humanities* VII. 61 Prof. D. Raj Reddy offers a set of exercises in statistics, natural language processing, language translation, poetry concordance, and information retrieval to interested readers. **1934** J. Moylan *Scotland Yard* (ed. 2) v. 132 At Scotland Yard there are Information and Operation Rooms from which the wireless cars are directed. **1940** R. Morrish *Police & Crime-Detection* ii. 28 Every Force has its 'Information Room', to which members of the public should report by telephone anything suspicious. **1958** A. Garfitt *Bk. for Police* I. iii. 77 An Information Room is established at some [police] headquarters and is the centre through which information, particularly as to crime and suspected crime, can be disseminated by wireless, teleprinter or telephone. **1970** P. Laurie *Scotland Yard* i. 16 The first floor carries the electronic complexities of the Information Room. **1960** *Computers & Automation* IX. 39/2 Moore School of Electrical Engineering, University of Pennsylvania... Prof. Saul Gorn, Chairman, Computer and Information Sciences Curriculum. **1962** *Conf. on Training Science Information Specialists 1961–62* (Georgia Inst. Technol.) 115 Information science..investigates the properties and behavior of information, the forces governing the flow of information, and the means of processing information for optimum accessibility and usability. **1963** *Library Jrnl.* LXXXVIII. 4161/1 The information sciences are conceived as: 1) the study of the properties, structure, and transmission of specialized knowledge; and 2) the development of methods for its useful organization and dissemination. **1971** C. W. Hanson *Introd. Science-Information Work* 2 'Information science' can be used to imply..the exploitation of scientific and technical information of all kinds...On the other hand, it is often used to imply the application of science and technology.. to handling information generally. **1958** *Nature* 4 Jan. 20/1 A meeting will be held on January 23..to discuss terms of inauguration of an Institute of Information Scientists. The aims of the proposed Institute would include the promotion of high standards in scientific and technical information work, the promotion of educational courses, and the establishment of qualifications for those engaged in such information work. **1963** *Aslib Proc.* XV. 100 These are post-graduate courses for those about to become information scientists. **1972** *Jrnl. Librarianship* IV. 169 The American protagonists of IS generally say that people involved in this science should be called information scientists. **1956** J. Klein *Study of Groups* x. 140 The whole elaborate process of information-seeking, evaluation and decision. **1935** E. S. Hedges in *Aslib Rep. Proc. 12th Conf.* 35 An information service which distributes in-coming information to interested quarters can be more effective than one which merely renders the information available on request. **1950** *N.Y. Times* 20 Apr. 1/8 Mr. Kolarek..has been in Czechoslovakia since September, 1945, serving first as assistant and later as chief press attache and information service director. **1968** B. E. Holm *How to manage your Information* iii. 55 The Dow Chemical Company is one of the many organizations which provides information services to its engineers. **1950** Information storage [see *information transfer* below]. **1972** *Jrnl. Librarianship* IV. 161 Somewhat later, it was realized that, to 'retrieve' information from a place, it obviously had to be stored prior to the retrieval, so the term was augmented to 'Information storage and retrieval' (ISR). **1953** C. F. Hockett in Saporta & Bastian *Psycholinguistics* (1961) 64/2 If it is necessary to maintain some analogy between an information-system and a power-system, then entropy can better be compared to voltage. **1964** T. W. McRae *Impact of Computers on Accounting* iii. 82 The objective of an information system..is to note all of the events happening within the organization being controlled, to extract those events which require to be reported and to report them to the controlling authority fast enough for compensating action to be possible. **1969** D. C. Hague *Managerial Econ.* i. 18 The information system [of a firm]..will be partly a rather mechanical system for providing routine reports about things like production, costs, sales or profits. It will also be partly a much less formal arrangement whereby those within the firm pass on information..to those who need it. **1950** *Amer. Scientist* XXXVIII. 278/2 A consideration of the effects of information storage and information transfer on physical, chemical, biological, psychological, and sociological systems..may help in understanding and predicting many of the aspects of our universe. **1964** G. H. Haggis et al. *Introd. Molecular Biol.* x. 279 Each operator with its associated structural genes forms a coordinated unit of information-transfer to which Jacob and Monod have given the name *operon.* **1935** B. Fullman in *Aslib Rep. Proc. 12th Conf.* 38 Organised information work is at present only in its infancy. **1959** *Aslib Proc.* XI. 290 The role of the textbook in technical information work is usually a fundamental one. **1972** *Jrnl. Librarianship* IV. III (inside front cover), The *Journal of Librarianship* is an independent quarterly journal dealing with all aspects of library and information work.

informational, *a.* (Later examples.)

1967 M. McLuhan *Medium is Massage* 138 Subtle electric informational media. **1971** *Nature* 2 July 66/2 The 'monogenomic' viroplast consists of viral genome, informational RNA, a complex of specific viral enzymes and structural proteins. **1971** *Jrnl. Gen. Psychol.* LXXXV. 207 Innovative substitutions of informational types of thinking in psychology. **1972** *Jrnl. Social Psychol.* LXXXVI. 111 The influence of interpersonal evaluations may result from their informational value for the individual.

informationally (infǫɹmēi·ʃənăli), *adv.* [f. Informational *a.* + -ly[2].] As regards information.

1964 Y. R. Chao in D. Abercrombie et al. *Daniel Jones* 41 Those aspects of speech which are informationally important but often acoustically weak. **1965** *Math. in Biol. & Med.* (*Med. Res. Council*) IV. 133 Here is a system [*sc.* the nervous system of higher animals] that reacts more reliably and predictably to informationally rich stimuli than to 'simple' ones. **1973** *Physics Bull.* May 281/1 Informationally, the incident speech signal requires about 50 000 bit/s to specify it.

informationless (infǫɹmēi·ʃənlės), *a.* [f. Information + -less.] Without information; carrying or conveying no information.

1965 [see *droppable *a.*].

information theory. [See *Information 3 d.] The quantitative theory, based on a precise definition of information and on the theory of probability, of the coding and transmission of signals and information.

1950 D. M. MacKay in *Phil. Mag.* Mar. 290 (*heading*) The formalisation of information theory. **1950** W. G. Tuller in *Trans. Amer. Inst. Electr. Engin.* LXIX. 1612/1 The statistical theory of communications, developed over the past few years and often called information theory, can be of real assistance in the design of communication systems. **1950** L. Brillouin in *Amer. Scientist* XXXVIII. 594 (*heading*) Thermodynamics and information theory. **1955** H. Quastler *Information Theory in Psychol.* I. 8 It is basic to information theory that any event is evaluated against the background of the whole class of events which could have happened. Information theory proposes to measure the effect of operations by which a particular selection is made out of a range of possibilities. Choice, specification, discrimination, recognition, are examples of such operations. **1960** E. Delavenay *Introd. Machine Transl.* 131 The statistical study of language in so-called information theory bears mainly on the frequency of reference of graphemes and phonemes. **1961** *New Scientist* 26 Jan. 200/2 Normal television amplitude modulation of a carrier takes no advantage of the fact that the rate of change of picture content is relatively slow, and that because of this much redundant information is continuously transmitted at the cost of considerable bandwidth. Unfortunately no system of television picture transmission has yet been devised which is more logical from an information theory point of view and does not also require a complex computing apparatus in the receiver. **1962** J. R. Pierce *Symbols, Signals & Noise* vi. 107 The two great triumphs of information theory are establishing the channel capacity and, in particular, the number of binary digits required to transmit information from a particular source and showing that a noisy communication channel has an information rate in bits per character or bits per second up to which errorless transmission is possible despite the noise. **1964** M. A. K. Halliday et al. *Ling. Sci.* I. iv. 104 Information theory, which has a place in the quantitative description of a language, implies nothing about the relative efficiency of languages or the effectiveness of language activity. **1968** *Unesco Bull. Libr.* XXII. 62 When Shannon and Weaver evolved their information theory, they..were guilty of an unfortunate use of terminology. They were concerned, of course, not with a theory of information but a theory of signals, the message-carrying capacity of a symbol, a telephone wire, or any other medium or channel of communication. **1970** O. Dopping *Computers & Data Processing* i. 21 Information theory deals largely with what happens when a random interference ('noise') is superimposed on the desired signal. **1972** *Jrnl. Librarianship* IV. 164 It is worth noting that Shannon never referred to his theory as an 'Information theory'.

Hence **information theorist.**

1953 C. F. Hockett in Saporta & Bastian *Psycholinguistics* (1961) 57/1 Neither the information theorist nor the linguist would claim that codes (*d*) and (*d'*) are identifiable with code (*a*) in quite the same way as codes (*b*) and (*c*). **1972** J. L. Dillard *Black English* i. 25 Research on the degree of intelligibility between the white man's English and Black English would be an expensive proposition... Ideally,..not only linguists but also anthropologists, psychologists, and an information theorist should be involved.

informative, *a.* Add: **2. b.** *Bridge.* = *Informatory *a.* b. So **informatively** *adv.*

1921 A. E. M. Foster *Auction Bridge made Clear* 105 There is an 'informative' double which some English players adopt... It is the double of a bid of one of a suit. **1925** —— *Auction Bridge Play & Probl.* 53 Thus Z bids 'one No Trumps' and A doubles informatively... The Informative Re-double is never left in. **1931** —— *Auction Bridge made Clear* (rev.) 103 It is no longer an 'informative' double, but a 'business' double.

informativeness (infǭ·ɹmătivnės). [f. Informative *a.* + -ness.] The quality or condition of being informative.

1924 C. Mackenzie *Old Men of Sea* v. 68 With the words Mr. Harper managed to assume an air of such bland informativeness that..his attitude reminded me of a conjurer who entreats a member of the audience to mount the stage. **1942** *Mind* LI. 60 It has been shown that the informativeness of memory plays a double part in the process of proof. **1955** *Essays in Crit.* V. 369 One of their number would write with such moral informativeness that he would catch up with Shakespeare.

informatorily (infǭ·ɹmătərili), *adv. Bridge.* [f. Informatory *a.* + -ly[2].] Informatively; in order to give information. Cf. next.

1928 *Observer* 29 Apr. 25 We should be placed in the ridiculous position that a player could not double informatorily, just because he happened to hold the suit that has been called against him. **1928** *Daily Express* 23 July 4 Unless you are prepared for any answer partner may make, do not double informatorily. **1929** W. Buller *Reflections Bridge Player* 178 Do you double two of a suit informatorily?

informatory, *a.* Add: **b.** Bridge: *informatory double*, a double which is intended to give information to one's partner, as distinct from a 'business double' which is for the purpose of scoring penalty points. So *informatory pass.*

1926 Foster & Hervey *Auction Bridge Informatory Doubles* 82 This Informatory Pass would be made against (say) a Spade bid on such a hand as [etc.]. **1927** [see *business 21 d]. **1929** W. Buller *Reflections Bridge Player* 176 'The Informatory Double' is not strictly *set* convention. **1950** *Hoyle's Games Modernised* (ed. 20) 55 If a player holds a good hand against a call of 1 or a suit, but is without sufficient strength or length in any other suit to justify him in overbidding, he doubles the original call. This is known as the *informatory double* (or *informatory raise*). **1964** G. F. Hervey *Handbk. Card Games* 161 When a player has bid one of a suit, it is usually better for the opponent to make an informatory or take-out double rather than a weak overbid. An informatory double is a request to partner to bid his best suit.

informedly, *adv.*[2] (Later examples.)

1922 *Times Lit. Suppl.* 10 Aug. 516/3 He deals briefly, but informedly, with the innumerable West African tribes. **1938** *Ibid.* 3 Sept. 573/2 There is in existence no other book dealing so thoroughly and so informedly with the problems of deafness.

info·rmedness. [f. Informed *ppl. a.* + -ness.] The fact or quality of being informed; knowledgeableness.

1946 *Scrutiny* XIII. IV. 268 The sheer informedness about society..impresses us with its range. **1960** C. Day Lewis *Buried Day* x. 221, I came to rely more and more ..upon the good sense, the informedness and seriousness of Charles Fenby. **1971** D. Crystal *Ling.* i. 11 Topics such as these are..discussed..with varying degrees of informedness.

informosome (infǭ·ɹmosōum). *Biol.* [f. Inform(ation + -o + *-some[4].] A cellular particle composed of messenger RNA and associated protein, the latter being thought to protect the messenger RNA from ribonucleases.

1964 A. S. Spirin et al. in *Zhurnal Obshcheĭ Biologii* (U.S.S.R.) XXV. 338 mRNA is transferred into the cytoplasm..in the form of specific complexes with protein; these ribonucleoprotein particles, named 'informosomes', were isolated and proved to exist as real complexes. **1971** *Nature* 15 Oct. 448/2 Over the past several years evidence has been accumulated which suggests that messenger RNAs occur in cell nuclei in the form of ribonucleoprotein particles—so-called informosomes.

infra (i·nfră), *adv.* [L.] Below, underneath, further on.

1740 J. Grassineau *Mus. Dict.* 107 Hypo, *infra, below*; this word when joined to the name of any interval or mode, &c. shews that it is lower than it was without, as *Hypo diapason* an octave lower. **1888** *Encycl. Brit.* XXVIII. 702/1 See *infra* in regard to rotary printing. **1888** Rolleston & Jackson *Forms Animal Life* (ed. 2) 459 The cell has been..supposed by various authorities to be muscular, nervous, or composed of connective tissue. See the original authorities, *infra.* **1955** A. G. Dickens *Robert Holgate* i. 3 Cf. *infra*, p. 24.

infra-. Add: **i:nfra-ato·mic** *a.*, subatomic; **infraba·sal** *Zool.*, any of a series of plates forming a ring beneath the basals in crinoids; also as *adj.*; **infra-ba·ss** *Mus.*, = *sub-bass* (1909 in *Cent. Dict.* Suppl.); also *transf.*; **infra-Chri·stian** *a.*, somewhat less than Christian; **infracortical** *a.* (examples); **infracostal** *a.* (examples); **infragla·cial** *a.*, subglacial; **infrahuman** *a.* (earlier and later examples); **i:nfra-mole·cular** *a.*, at a level of organization below that of a molecule; **infra-ra·tional** *a.*, below what is rational;

infra-speci·fic *a.*, (applied to a category) at a lower taxonomic level than a species; **i:nfra-umbi·lical** *a. Anat.*, situated below the umbilicus.

1923 J. S. HUXLEY *Ess. Biologist* i. 55 The infra-atomic world of electrons. **1966** I. ASIMOV *Fantastic Voyage* viii. 90 It was not merely radioactivity that had to be sensed, but radioactive particles that had themselves been miniaturized; and that, because of their incredibly tiny, infra-atomic size could pass through any ordinary sensor without affecting it. **1890** *Ann. & Mag. Nat. Hist.* V. 318 The atrophy of infrabasals is we see a very gradual process. *Ibid.*, The distinction between an infrabasal ring of 5 plates and one of 3, is of far inferior importance. **1962** D. NICHOLS *Echinoderms* ii. 22 In some forms an additional whorl, the infrabasals, is intercalated between the basals and the centro-dorsal. **1958** J. BLISH *Case of Conscience* (1959) II. x. 104 The infrabass of the buried city's thunder shook the glass in front of him. **1906** W. R. INGE *Truth & Falsehood in Relig.* ii. 63 It is not justifiable to take examples of infra-Christian survivals in Christianity, and use them to discredit the religion of Christ. **1917** J. DENNEY *Christian Doctrine of Reconciliation* ii. 51 As an infra-Christian mode of thinking, it sometimes curiously flawed what was otherwise pure Christian truth. **1890** *Cent. Dict.*, Infracortical. **1895** *Psychol. Rev.* Mar. 117 In man the consciousness attached to infra-cortical centres is altogether subliminal, if it exist. **1925** *Lancet* 8 Aug. 274/2 Tremor is an involuntary movement belonging to the old motor system (infra-cortical, subpallial). **1858** GRAY *Anat.* 732/2 (Index), Infra-costal muscles. **1867** *Quain's Elem. Anat.* (ed. 7) I. 243 The subcostal or infracostal muscles are small bundles lying on the inner aspect of the thoracic wall. **1922** JOYCE *Ulysses* 695 A cicatrice in the left infracostal region below the diaphragm. **1894** J. GEIKIE *Gt. Ice Age* (ed. 3) vii. 91 All such infra- or intra-glacial deposits..occur somewhat partially. **1957** J. K. CHARLESWORTH *Quaternary Era* II. xliv. 1253 The British infraglacial beach, though much narrower than the Norwegian strandflat, marks a steady level of the sea over a considerable time. **1847** J. WILSON *Lands of Bible* I. iv. 105 The gods of the Egyptian pantheon, human, superhuman, and infrahuman. **1970** *Jrnl. Gen. Psychol.* July 42 Motor responses at infrahuman level. **1972** *Science* 5 May 541/2 Microelectrode recording has shown that tilt detectors in the infrahuman visual system are each turned 20 deg or so on either side of a preferred orientation. **1899** *Phil. Mag.* XLVIII. 462 All her [*sc.* Nature's] activities at infra-molecular degrees of proximity. **1919** A. N. WHITEHEAD *Enquiry Princ. Nat. Knowledge* ii. 18 We may penetrate below the molecule to the electrons and the core which compose it, and thus obtain infra-molecular equations. **1933** *Mind* XLII. 265 In the concept of life, one may stress either its unconscious, infra-rational, chaotic fecundity or the conscious order..of its historic manifestations. **1935** *Downside Rev.* LIII. 451 Thus the indefinable element would be irrational in the sense of infra-rational. **1939** *Entomol. News* L. 198 In practice they propose infra-specific names—polynomials as well as trinomials—in proper Latin form. **1970** *Watsonia* VIII. 42 The geographical significance of this variation should not be lost sight of and may eventually receive taxonomic recognition at some infra-specific level. **1900** DORLAND *Med. Dict.* 322/1 Infra-umbilical. **1906** *Practitioner* Dec. 781 A supra-umbilical and infra-umbilical zone. **1967** *Gray's Anat.* (ed. 34) 641 In its infra-umbilical portion the linea alba is narrow.

infract, *a.*[1] Substitute *arch.* for † *Obs.* and add later example.

1901 *North Amer. Rev.* Feb. 314 The illusion renews itself in the great moments, but I wish it could be kept infract in the small.

infra-red, *a.* Substitute for entry (in Dict. s.v. INFRA-):

infra-red (infrăˌre·d), *a.* and *sb.* Also as one word (without hyphen). [f. INFRA- + RED *a.* and *sb.*] **A.** *adj.* **1.** Lying beyond the red end of the visible spectrum: the epithet of electromagnetic radiation (and of the part of the spectrum containing it) which has a wavelength greater than that of red light (about 0·7–0·8 microns) and (in modern use) less than that of the shortest microwaves (of the order of 1000 microns, i.e. 1 mm.); it is invisible, and most of the radiation from bodies below red heat is emitted in this form.

1881, 1896 [in Dict.]. **1926** *Encycl. Brit.* I. 946/2 Extending beyond the red end of the visible spectrum there are 9 octaves of infra-red radiation overlapping with very short Hertzian waves... A. Glacolewa-Arkadiewa.. has created Hertzian waves of only 0·082 mm. in wave length. **1929** *Punch's Almanack for 1930* 4 Nov. p. xxxvii (Advt.), These are like the health-giving rays of heat emitted by the sun—those short infra-red rays that.. enfold you with their beneficial warmth. **1932** HARDY & PERRIN *Princ. Optics* xi. 234 Photographs of landscapes taken by infrared light have the general appearance of night scenes because the sky appears dark and the high reflectance of chlorophyl gives foliage the appearance of intense local lighting...Photographs of extremely distant objects are made possible by infrared light because of its greater penetration through atmospheric haze. **1935** *Practitioners Libr. Med. & Surg.* VIII. I. viii. 168 Infra-red radiation..produces the sensation of heat when it comes in contact with the body. This form of radiant energy is produced..by any heated body. **1939** *Jrnl. R. Aeronaut. Soc.* XLIII. 1012 Heating elements such as the steam radiator, which does not glow, emit infra-red energy of long wave-lengths (far infra-red). The filament lamp, like the sun, is a source of near infra-red energy. This is the portion of the spectrum which lies chiefly in the wavelengths slightly longer than the red visible radiation. **1957** *House & Garden* Dec. 99 An electric Rotary Spit that automatically turns joints, steaks, chops, or poultry under penetrating infra-red heat.

2. a. Involving, producing, or pertaining to infra-red radiation or its use.

1910 *Photogr. Jrnl.* Oct. 320 The idea of photographing landscapes through the infra-red screen. *Ibid.* 330 In the infra-red photograph the shadows are practically black and the sky is very dark. **1929** *Brit. Jrnl. Photogr.* 29 Mar. 183/2 By comparing the results of ordinary photography..with those of infra-red photography. **1935** *Practitioners Libr. Med. & Surg.* VIII. I. viii. 169 The wavelength used in infra-red therapy is not of particular importance. It is mainly a determining factor in the penetration or the depth which the heat reaches. **1951** MRAK & MACKINNEY in M. B. Jacobs *Chem. & Technol. Food & Food Products* (ed. 2) III. xxxiii. 1787 Infrared lamps have been installed in a plant for natural dried cod to reduce the moisture from about 60 to 43%. **1954** 'J. CHRISTOPHER' *22nd Century* 197 He went through to the kitchen, switched the infra-red heater off and collected his breakfast. **1963** F. C. WEBB *Biochem. Engin.* xvii. 482 Small catering-size infra-red heaters are in limited use for grilling. **1968** *Times* 9 Dec. 7/2 Infra-red galaxies.. are just one of several types of cosmic objects being studied in the booming new science of infra-red astronomy.

b. Sensitive to infra-red radiation.

1932 *Discovery* Sept. 292/1 These infra-red plates are not as a rule made sensitive to the green and orange, although they retain their sensitivity to blue. **1938** *Encycl. Brit. Bk. Yr. 1938* 500/1 New films for aerial photography included a fast infra-red film. **1961** *Daily Mail* 20 July 6/3 Midas picks up a rocket by detecting the intense heat of its exhaust flame with an infra-red eye. **1973** *Daily Tel.* (Colour Suppl.) 11 May 44/3 Another student..wants the astronauts to photograph volcanoes with infra-red film which records temperature differences on the Earth rather than grades of light.

B. *ellipt.* as *sb.* The infra-red part of the spectrum; *near, far infra-red*, the part close to, or far from, the visible spectrum.

1881 *Phil. Mag.* XI. 167 Experiments supposed to prove the existence of lines in the infra-red. **1887** *Encycl. Brit.* XXII. 376/1 Becquerel finds lines in the infra-red at 11,420. **1923** GLAZEBROOK *Dict. Appl. Physics* IV. 533/2 Such solids as rock-salt have a very strong absorption band for light in the far infra-red. **1937** JENKINS & WHITE *Fund. Optics* i. 13 On the long-wavelength side of the visible lies the infrared, which may be said to merge into the radio waves at about 4×10^{-2} cm. **1960** CONN & AVERY *Infrared Methods* p. v, By restricting attention to the range from 1 to 25μ we have limited the interest to the 'near infrared' but even this embraces a range of some four to five octaves. **1966** HOUGHTON & SMITH *Infra-Red Physics* i. 1 The infra-red is that region of the electromagnetic spectrum which lies between the visible and microwave regions, i.e. between wavelengths of about 8000 Å (= 0·8 μ) and 1 mm. **1973** *Sci. Amer.* Feb. 89/2 The laser's output was in the infrared.

infrasonic (infrăsǫ·nik), *a.* Also **infra-sonic.** [f. INFRA- + *SONIC *a.*, after *supersonic, ultrasonic*, as tr. F. *infra-sonore* (E. Esclangon 1925, in *Mém. de l'Artillerie Française* IV. 647).] **A.** *adj.* **1.** Of, pertaining to, or designating sound waves or vibrations having a frequency below the audible range (i.e. less than 15–30 Hz).

1927 E. G. RICHARDSON *Sound* x. 236 The lower pitch limit is about 16 vibrations per second. Slow vibrations.. remain unperceived as tones if their rate of pulsation falls below this limit... Such 'infra-sonic' waves have been extensively studied by Esclangon. **1945** *Electronic Engin.* XVII. 328/3 These will not run well..at infra-sonic frequencies. **1960** *McGraw-Hill Encycl. Sci. & Technol.* XII. 506/1 Many problems in vibration, oceanography, seismology, and the dynamic behavior of elastic materials are analyzed by treating the phenomenon being studied as sound waves of infrasonic frequency. **1965** *Aerospace Med.* XXXVI. 817/2 It has been estimated that the very large super boosters of the future..will produce their maximum noise energy in the infrasonic range (below 20 cps). **1965** T. N. DAVIS in W. N. Hess *Space Sci.* v. 227 Infrasonic waves with periods ranging from 10–110 seconds are observed at auroral and middle latitudes. These appear only on nights of moderate or strong auroral activity.

2. Designating speeds below that of sound; subsonic. *rare*$^{-1}$.

1942 *Jrnl. R. Aeronaut. Soc.* XLVI. 85 Equations of general application are derived, proving that both for infrasonic and for ultrasonic (supersonic) velocities, an extremum of the cross-section is possible.

infrasound (i·nfrăsaund). [f. INFRA- + SOUND *sb.*[3], tr. F. *infra-son* (1906 in Robert).] Sound, or a sound, of infrasonic frequency.

1930 A. B. WOOD *Textbk. Sound* II. 213 The 'ondes de bouche' (from the mouth of the gun) consists principally of waves of very low frequency (of the order 1 p.p.s.), described by Esclangon as Infra-Sounds. **1965** *Aerospace Med.* XXXVI. 824/1 Very low sonic frequency noise and moderate levels of infrasound are commonly encountered in conventional aerospace operations. **1970** B. W. ALDISS *Moment of Eclipse* 66 This was infrasound. The plant was emitting slow air vibrations at less than ten hertz. **1971** *Observer* 28 Nov. 3/1 Many cars and lorries travelling at sustained high speeds produce such intense levels of low-frequency noise or 'infrasound' inside them that drivers can experience symptoms very similar to those produced by heavy drinking. *Ibid.*, In a wide range of passenger cars travelling at motorway speeds the sound energy is largely concentrated as intense infrasounds—most of which can be felt rather than heard.

infrastructure (i·nfrăstrʌktiŭɹ). [Fr. (1875 in Robert), f. INFRA- + STRUCTURE *sb.*] A collective term for the subordinate parts of an undertaking; substructure, foundation; *spec.* the permanent installations forming a basis for military operations, as airfields, naval bases, training establishments, etc.

1927 *Chambers's Jrnl.* 14 May 374/2 The tunnels, bridges, culverts, and 'infrastructure' work generally of the Ax to Bourg-Madame line have been completed. **1950** W. S. CHURCHILL in *Hansard Commons* CDLXXVI. 2145 In this Debate we have had the usual jargon about 'the infrastructure of a supra-national authority'. **1951** *European Rev.* Oct. 2/1 This new term 'infrastructure'.. denotes fixed military facilities such as airfields, base installations and transport systems. **1956** D. NOAKES tr. *Hodeir's Jazz* 197 What I call the infrastructure is the regularly produced two- or four-beat meter (2/2 or 4/4 measure) that characterizes any jazz performance. **1957** T. KILMARTIN tr. *Aron's Opium of Intellectuals* iv. 133 Thirty years ago, the dominant school of thought in the Soviet Union undertook..the task of analysing the infrastructure of society. **1960** *Times* 9 Dec. 14/2 Part of the Nato infrastructure programme. **1971** *Inside Kenya Today* Mar. 15/1 A.I.D. assistance will be focused on Vihiga Division and will..upgrade the infrastructure of roads and other social services. **1971** J. SPENCER *Eng. Lang. W. Afr.* 31 A very complex infrastructure of scores of vernacular languages.

So **i:nfrastru·ctural** *a.*

1963 *Economist* 13 Apr. 130/2 Very low interest rates.. for various forms of infrastructural development. **1967** *Ibid.* 23 Sept. 1104/2 Big, infrastructural programmes—the building of dams, power stations, roads, railways, harbours and airports.

infu·riant, *sb.* [f. pr. ppl. stem of med.L. *infuriāre*: see INFURIATE *v.*] Something that infuriates; an object, fact, condition, etc., which excites to anger or passion.

1953 K. AMIS *Lucky Jim* viii. 87 The sight of Welch's 'bag' and fishing-hat on a nearby chair, normally a certain infuriant, only made him hum his Welch tune. **1960** *Guardian* 7 Dec. 8/3 There would be a reasonable chance of the races working happily together if only the infuriant of Federation were removed.

infuse, *v.* Add: **1.** (Later examples.)

1908 *Amer. Jrnl. Physiol.* XXI. 144 Saline was infused into a vein. **1972** *Sci. Amer.* May 75/1 Intravenous feeding had its beginning in 1843, when the French physiologist Claude Bernard infused sugar solutions into the veins of animals.

5. Delete † *Obs.* and add: In wider use, to impregnate, pervade, imbue (*with* some quality, opinion, etc.).

1900 *Westm. Gaz.* 29 Jan. 1/3 The cant with which the political history of the war is infused and suffused. **1928** *Observer* 5 Feb. 11/4 The splendid camaraderie and corporate spirit which infuse a newspaper staff.

infusoriform, *a.* Add: [repr. G. *infusorienartig* infusorian-like (A. Kölliker 1849, in *Ber. von der k. zootomischen Anstalt zu Würzburg* II. 61).] Usu. *spec.* designating or pertaining to a stage in the life-cycle of species of the order Dicyemida (phylum Mesozoa), which comprises parasites of certain cephalopods. (Further examples.)

1877 *Q. Jrnl. Microsc. Sci.* XVII. 143 The infusoriform embryo probably distributes the species by transmitting the parasite from one cephalopod to another. **1883** *Mitt. Zool. Station zu Neapel* IV. 41 The infusoriform embryos desert the parent before the development of vermiform embryos begins. **1940** L. H. HYMAN *Invertebrates* I. iv. 236 The infusoriform stage is an asexual larva. **1964** T. C. CHENG *Biol. Animal Parasites* vii. 179/1 The infusoriform larvae escape from the parent rhombogen and leave the host. **1967** H. W. & L. R. LEVI tr. *Kaestner's Invertebr. Zool.* I. ii. 21 Only after fertilization do the ova detach, each developing into a short, egg-shaped dispersing infusoriform dicyemid.

infusorigen (infiŭsō̆ᵊ·ridʒĕn). *Zool.* [f. *infusori-* (repr. INFUSORIFORM *a.*) + -GEN.] A hermaphroditic group of cells formed within a rhombogen during the life-cycle of species of the order Dicyemida (phylum Mesozoa) and giving rise to infusoriform larvæ.

1883 C. O. WHITMAN in *Mitt. Zool. Station zu Neapel* IV. 38 The entire cell-group may be called the Infusorigen, a term used by Van Beneden as a synonym for Rhomb gen. *Ibid.* 39 There arise in the course of the history of every Infusorigen two nuclei. **1940** L. H. HYMAN *Invertebrates* I. iv. 239 After having given off a succession of pseudo-eggs, the infusorigens degenerate. **1964** T. C. CHENG *Biol. Animal Parasites* vii. 179/1 Most authorities on the Mesozoa now agree that infusorigens are hermaphrodites. **1972** *Sci. Amer.* Dec. 95/3 Some of the axoblasts, instead of developing into vermiform embryos, develop into a structure that remains within the axial cell of the adult vermiform and may be thought of as a hermaphroditic gonad. The term infusorigen has been applied to this structure, which in a sense is the only organ the Mesozoa possess.

infusorioid (infiŭsōᵊ·riˌoid), *a.* [f. INFUSORI(A *sb. pl.* + -OID.] Resembling an infusorian.

1853 A. HENFREY tr. *Braun's Phenomenon of Rejuvenescence in Nature* 281 Active, Infusorioid structures.. occur not unfrequently in the interior of decaying cells of green fresh-water Algæ.

ingathering, *vbl. sb.* Add: Applied *spec.* to the congregating of the Jews in Israel.

1952 S. SPENDER *Learning Laughter* iii. 36 But to-day there is another kind of paradox... This might be called the paradox of the Ingathering. **1964** *Economist* 16 May 703/1 The other chief fact of Israel, politically as well as economically, is the determination to make the in-gathering of Jews..viable and safe. **1971** *Listener* 14 Jan. 36/3 When Israel became a state on 15 May 1948 the first principle written into its proclamation of independence affirmed that 'the state of Israel will be open to Jewish immigration and the in-gathering of the exiles'. **1973** *Guardian* 12 Mar. 10/3 Young Israelis..feel no mission to the Jews of the Diaspora. The ingathering of the exiles is a remote slogan.

ingenium (indʒī·niʊ̆m). [L., = mind, intellect.] Turn of mind; genius; talent.

1879 W. JAMES *Let.* 10 Oct. in R. B. Perry *Tht. & Char. W. J.* (1935) II. 17 Wundt..certainly is *not* a first-class *ingenium.* **1886** G. MACDONALD *What's Mine's Mine* I. xiii. 225 It [*sc.* a poem] will serve to show something of Ian's youthful *ingenium.* **1920** T. P. NUNN *Education* 205 To school a boy in the tradition of one of these ancient occupations is to ensure (if it suits his *ingenium*) that he will throw himself into his work with spirit. **1921** *Glasgow Herald* 28 Nov. 5 His scientific ingenium was as keen as ever.

ingénue (æ̃nʒenü). [Fr., fem. of *ingénu* INGENUOUS *a.*] An artless, innocent girl or young woman; also, the representation of such a character on the stage, or the actress who plays the part. Also as *adj.* = INGENUOUS *a.* Hence **ingénueism.**

1848 THACKERAY *Van. Fair* li. 454 When attacked sometimes, Becky had a knack of adopting a demure *ingénue* air, under which she was most dangerous. **1857** G. A. LAWRENCE *Guy Liv.* xxv. 239 Mars herself could hardly play the *ingénues*, when in mature age. **1883** J. HAWTHORNE *Dust* I. viii. 134 Was this lady more or less of a woman of the world than he had imagined? Was there not, after all, something of the *ingénue* about her? **1923** C. MACKENZIE *Seven Ages of Woman* iii. 112 My dear, innocence is a charming and attractive quality; but do not be too *ingénue.* **1930** *Daily Express* 6 Oct. 5/3 French actresses grow in popularity and ingénueism the older they become. **1931** *Times Lit. Suppl.* 5 Mar. 161/4 Her French audiences, still demanding the ingénue, find her enigmatical and disquieting. **1958** *Times* 12 Nov. 3/5 The Nanetta..brings a vibrant line to music more *ingénue* than she suggests. **1967** C. O. SKINNER *Madame Sarah* viii. 171 Every one of them, with the exception of an eighteen-year-old ingénue..declared to stay. **1973** *Daily Tel.* 16 May 15/2 And we were willing to put up with the quaint tale of the philandering husband and the sweet little ingénue Nanette.

ingerence (i·ndʒĕrĕns). *rare.* [f. L. *ingerĕre* (see INGEST *v.*) + -ENCE. Cf. F. *ingérence.*] Bearing in upon; intrusion; interference.

[**1879** MARQ. SALISBURY in G. Cecil *Life Marq. Salisbury* (1921) II. 356 This is a considerable advance in the direction of 'ingérence' over anything we did either in the case of Rivers Wilson or Romaine.] **1886** *Spectator* 16 Jan. 79 The status of a protected State excludes, of course, all ingerence in the foreign or domestic affairs of the protecting State. **1920** *Edin. Rev.* July 43 It is astonishing to what extent the ingerence of Belgrade is already tolerated.

†Ingersollian (iŋgəsǭ·liăn), *a. Obs.* [f. the name of the American agnostic, Robert Green *Ingersoll* (1833–99) + -IAN.] Imbued with the tenets of R. G. Ingersoll. So **I·ngersollism,** the doctrines or tenets of Ingersoll.

1883 G. R. WENDLING (*title*) Ingersollism; from a secular point of view. **1892** STEVENSON & OSBOURNE *Wrecker* xi. 179, I don't know if you quite believe in prayer, I'm a bit Ingersollian myself.

Ingin. A U.S. colloq. spelling of INDIAN. (Cf. *INJUN.)

1683 *Early Rec. Groton, Mass.* (1880) 82 If any Ingins can proue a lagiall [=legal] titall. **1869** B. HARTE *Luck of Roaring Camp* 15 They're mighty rough on strangers, and they worship an Ingin baby. **1870** J. C. DUVAL *Adventures Big-Foot Wallace* xlvi. 303 Whenever he can get to where there's liquor, either the liquor gives out, or he gets 'Ingin drunk'.

ingle, *sb.*[2] Delete † *Obs.* and add later examples.

1926 T. E. LAWRENCE *Seven Pillars* (1935) lxxxi. 448 Abd el Kader called them whoresons, ingle's accidents, sons of a bitch,..jetting his insults broadcast to the roomfull. **1962** H. NICOLSON *Monarchy* v. 94 The Romans were startled by the arrival of this Asian ingle as their Emperor.

ingliding (i·ngləidiŋ), *ppl. a. Phonology.* [f. IN *adv.* + GLIDING *ppl. a.*] Gliding towards the central vowel sound /ə/, as in words like *air, here,* and *poor,* and in U.S. regional pronunciations like *wood* (wuᵊd), *bell* (beᵊl), *stem* (steᵊm), *pal* (pæᵊl); = *CENTRING *ppl. a.* Also **i·nglide** *sb.*

1948 R. I. McDAVID in *Amer. Speech* XXIII. 203 An apparent tendency to replace the low-country ingliding diphthongs in *date, boat* [de·ᵊt, bo·ᵊt] with the up-country upgliding type [de·ɪt, bo·ʊt] also suggests a reversal of the trend in prestige values. **1956** D. W. REED in A. A. Hill *First Texas Conference on Problems of Linguistic Analysis in English* (1962) 3 According to the Trager and Smith analysis there are nine pure vowels—/V/—and nine combinations of vowel and length or inglide. *Ibid.* 93, I think in-glide is a better name than central glide, since in-glide names a direction, central names only an area. **1959** T. H. WETMORE in *Publ. Amer. Dial. Soc.* XXXII. 76 In central Virginia Piedmont..approximately half of the informants have an inglide in the vowel of *pot. Ibid.* 112 *Off* with an ingliding diphthong is heard with equal frequency. **1961** KURATH & McDAVID *Pronunc. Eng. in Atlantic States* iii. 101/2 Before voiceless stops, inglides are less common and briefer, and in words of more than one syllable they are infrequent. **1962** *Amer. Speech* XXXVII. 70 Stressed free vowels are upgliding, and all stressed checked vowels are ingliding. **1963** *Ibid.* XXXVIII. 129 An ingliding diphthong [iə]. **1965** *Canad. Jrnl. Linguistics* Fall 64 The free segments are predominantly monophthongal or ingliding. **1972** H. KURATH *Studies in Area Linguistics* vi. 73 Elsewhere ingliding [oə ~ uə] or monophthongal [o ~ ɔ] are current.

in-goal (i·nˌgōᵘl). *Rugby Football.* [f. IN *prep.* + GOAL *sb.* 3.] (See quot. 1897.)

1897 *Encycl. Sport* I. 430/2 Those portions of the ground immediately at the ends of the field of play and between the touch-lines, produced to the dead-ball lines, are called in-goal. The goal-lines are in-goal. **1935** [see *FAIR *a.* 10 d]. **1960** V. JENKINS *Lions Down Under* xiv. 207 The penalty-try awarded when E. J. Faire obstructed A. J. F. O'Reilly in the in-goal area.

in-Go·d, *v.* [cf. *engod* (EN- *pref.*[1] B. 2).] *trans.* To deify, make divine; to take into God or into the godhead. So **in-Go·dding** *vbl. sb.*

1891 *Church Times* 20 Nov. 1128/1 The Humanity already in-Godded in the Person of the Second Person of the Holy Trinity. **1957** D. L. SAYERS *Further Papers on Dante* 187 Every creature..possesses a true self which, however much perfected or (in Dante's words) 'in-godded', is never swallowed up or lost in God. **1959** *N. & Q.* July–Aug. 301/2 Dante expounded in the *Comedy* a mystic Way of Affirmation for the 'in-Godding' of man based on the vision of the beloved.

ingoing, *vbl. sb.* Add: **2.** The sum paid by a tenant or purchaser for fixtures, etc., on taking over business or other premises.

1905 *Daily Chron.* 4 May, Furniture Business..for Sale;..ingoing about £200. **1925** *Daily Tel.* 13 May 19/3 The principal Fully-Licensed Family and Commercial Hotel... Ingoing £1,300.

ingoing, *ppl. a.* Add: **2.** Penetrating, thorough.

1928 *Blackw. Mag.* May 645/1 Whether he was quite so ingoing as this would have been is far from sure. **1928** E. C. BUTLER tr. *Grou's Meditations Love of God* p. v, He is very ingoing, and, like every spiritual writer worth his salt, very exacting. **1930** —— *Vatican Council* II. xxviii. 244 To this, the most ingoing question in regard to the Council, a sure answer may be given.

ingot. Add: **3. ingot iron,** iron which contains too little carbon to temper and is nearly pure by industrial standards, differing from wrought iron in containing no slag; **ingot stripper,** a machine for separating an ingot from the mould containing it; **ingot structure,** the arrangement of crystals in an ingot.

1877 *Trans. Amer. Inst. Mining Engin.* V. 20 Mr. A. L. Holley, Chairman of the International Committee, appointed by the Institute to consider the nomenclature of iron and steel, offered the following report:... That all compounds of iron with its ordinary ingredients, which have been cast from a fluid state into malleable masses, and which will not sensibly harden by being quenched in water, while at a red heat, shall be called ingot iron. **1938** J. NEWTON *Introd. Metall.* vii. 178 Ingot iron and wrought iron are both very low in carbon, and their physical properties approach those of pure iron. *Ibid.* xvi. 499 Ingot iron is commercially pure iron, with total impurities <0·10 per cent, which is made by a special basic open-hearth process. **1962** A. G. GUY *Physical Metall. for Engineers* v. 138 Ingot iron in the form of galvanized or enameled sheets is used for such purposes as roofing and siding. **1904** J. W. HALL in Harbord & Hall *Metall. Steel* i. 41 The 'Ingot Stripper' is a most efficient machine.. saving..all damage to the moulds from sledging to remove the ingots. **1957** CAMP & FRANCIS *Making, Shaping & Treating of Steel* (ed. 7) xv. 295 (*caption*) Schematic representation of the action of an ingot stripper in removing the molds from (left) big-end-down ingots and (right) big-end-up ingots. **1932** E. GREGORY *Metall.* ii. 49 The original ingot structure exerts a profound influence on the behaviour of the material during forging, rolling, etc. **1952** J. WULFF et al. *Metall. for Engineers* xvii. 316 Some knowledge of how steels are melted is useful for interpreting ingot structure.

ingotism (i·ŋgǒtiz'm). [f. INGOT + -ISM.] The presence of many large dendritic crystals in an ingot or casting.

1908 H. M. HOWE et al. in *Proc. Amer. Soc. Testing Materials* VIII. 185 By ingotism we mean that extremely coarse structure which exists in unannealed ingots and steel castings. **1925** *Jrnl. Iron & Steel Inst.* CXI. 525 In killed steels the ill effect, if any, of a too high casting heat is pronounced ingotism. **1957** CAMP & FRANCIS *Making, Shaping & Treating of Steel* (ed. 7) xx. 395/2 Ingots exhibiting ingotism tend to crack excessively during rolling unless light drafts are employed for the first few passes in the rolls.

ingrain, *a.* (*sb.*[2]) Add: **B.** *sb.* **2.** That which is ingrain or inherent.

1899 J. MILNE *Romance of Pro-Consul* vi. 49 The natives of the Australian North-West were a fine race physically, and, he judged, had an ingrain of Malay blood. **1918** P. T. FORSYTH *This Life & the Next* v. 55 It is the holy as what might be called the ingrain, the tissue, the physiognomy of eternal love.

ingrateful, *a.* **3.** (Later example.)

1913 F. THOMPSON *Works* II. 163 We take ingrateful, for a blinded while, Thine ignorant, sweet smile.

ingredience, *sb.* Restrict †*Obs.* to sense 1 and add later examples of sense 2.

1925 A. N. WHITEHEAD *Sci. & Mod. World* (1926) x. 237 This complete ingredience in an occasion, so as to yield the most complete fusion of individual essence with other eternal objects in the formation of the individual emergent occasion, is evidently of its own kind and cannot be defined in terms of anything else. **1955** *Scottish Jrnl. Theol.* VIII. 426 Nor can it [*sc.* history] be seen as a total process given meaning by the ingredience of non-historical reality.

ingredient, *a.* and *sb.* **A.** *adj.* **b.** (Later examples.)

1933 *Theology* XXVI. 331 The distinction between the realm of possibility and that of actuality, between 'eternal objects' and the 'actual occasions' into which the eternal objects are ingredient. **1957** G. RYLE in C. A. Mace *Brit. Philos. in Mid-Cent.* 241 He has to declare that his subject-matter consist [*sic*] not of the sentences and their ingredient words in which arguments are expressed [etc.].

Ingres (æ̃ŋgr). The name of J. A. D. *Ingres* (1780–1867), French painter, used *attrib.* in **Ingres paper** [tr. F. *papier Ingres*], a French mould-made drawing-paper; also used to describe thick mottled paper.

1910 *Winsor & Newton Catal.* in H. Macbeth-Raeburn *Sketchers' Oil Colour Manual* 37 Drawing papers..Ingres paper (imitation Michallet). **1925** V. BLAKE *Way to Sketch* ix. 79 Ingres or Michelet, either white or tinted—say the blue-grey note—is useful for making rather large sketches in Conté or carbon pencil. **1941** [see *CONTÉ]. **1968** P. NUTTALL *Picture Framing* ii. 24 There are a wide variety of papers suitable for this purpose [*sc.* mounting], such as ..Ingres paper, textured papers, silk wallpaper, marbled papers, and so on.

ingress, *v.* **1.** Revived in the U.S.

1963 V. NABOKOV *Gift* iii. 178 Boris Ivanovich, horribly smiling, squeezed sideways into the room..then, ingressing entirely, he would shut the door tightly behind him and sit by Fyodor's feet. **1970** N. ARMSTRONG et al. *First on Moon* Gloss. p. xii, *Ingress,* to enter the spacecraft.

ingressant (ingre·sănt), *a. nonce-wd.* [f. ppl. stem of L. *ingredī* to enter + -ANT[1].] Entering, in-going.

1947 AUDEN *Age of Anxiety* (1948) vi. 126 His [*sc.* God's] Good ingressant on our gross occasions Envisages our advance.

ingressive, *a.* Add: (Later examples.) **c.** *Phonetics.* Of or pertaining to utterances made while breathing in. Also as *sb.*, an ingressive verb or sound.

1931 G. O. CURME *Syntax* xix. 377 The ingressive aspect is often expressed by *begin, commence,* or *start* in connection with an infinitive or gerund or object. *Ibid.* 378 The ingressive idea is often expressed by the ingressives *get, grow, fall, turn, wax,* [etc.]. **1932** *Jrnl. Eng. & Gmc. Philol.* XXXI. 251 The former is called the ingressive aspect: '*He woke up* (i.e., entered upon the waking state) early.' **1935** [see *EFFECTIVE *sb.* 3]. **1943** K. L. PIKE *Phonetics* vi. 88 Sounds thus made are *ingressives* (or *rarefactives*). *Ibid.*, Ingressive lung-air sounds, and clicks, are produced in this way. **1961** [see *CONCEPTUALISTICALLY *adv.*]. **1963** *Amer. Speech* XXXVIII. 52 Phonemes..can be produced with an ingressive as well as an egressive air stream. **1969** M. M. FIRESTONE in Halpert & Story *Christmas Mumming in Newfoundland* 66 Some are able to 'talk like a janney'—ingressive utterances at a high pitch. **1972** R. WARDHAUGH *Introd. Ling.* iii. 32 Sometimes ingressive air, that is, air going to the lungs, may also be used. *Ibid.* 36 Ingressives are rare indeed, in English confined perhaps to certain kinds of exclamatory sounds.

ingre·ssively, *adv.* [f. INGRESSIVE *a.* + -LY[2].] In an ingressive manner.

1921 H. POUTSMA *Characters of Eng. Verb* i. 2 The actions expressed by verbs..may be..(1) indefinitely durative,..(2) ingressively durative, i.e. with the initial stage of the action more distinctly thought of than the rest. **1928** —— *Gram. Late Mod. Eng.* (ed. 2) I. 2 The combinations into which they [*sc.* copulas] enter are *a*) indefinitely durative, *b*) continuatively durative, or *c*) ingressively durative. **1969** M. M. FIRESTONE in Halpert & Story *Christmas Mumming in Newfoundland* 66 'Yes' and sometimes 'no' are indeed normally uttered ingressively in this area.

i·n-group. [Cf. *IN *a.* 2.] A small group of people, within a wider context, whose common interest tends to exclude others; also *attrib.* Hence *ingroupiness, ingroupness;* **i·n-grouper,** a member of an in-group. Cf. *OUT-GROUP.

1907 W. G. SUMNER *Folkways* i. 12 Thus a differentiation arises between ourselves, the we-group, or in-group, and everybody else, or the others-groups, out-groups.

1932 H. Becker *Syst. Sociol.* II. xi. 182 Members of such groups may indeed manifest a certain loyalty and consideration for all fellow-members, i.e., for the 'in-group'. **1939** *American Imago* Nov. 24 In-groupers must learn to tolerate..anxiety. **1942** *New Statesman* 11 July 26/3 The very progress of civilisation has laid the foundation for a vast extension of in-group mutual dependency and mutual support. **1947** *Partisan Rev.* XIV. 478 The sense of in-groupness of the bohemian intellectual provides a source of psychological security. **1950** B. Wootton *Testament Social Sci.* vi. 127 For many primitive peoples..what the sociologist calls the 'in-group' consists of a relatively small tribal community, whereas the Christian is taught..to treat all men as brothers. **1964** M. Argyle *Psychol. & Social Probl.* x. 134 It is well known that residential courses are the scene of violent in-group feelings and wild enthusiasm. **1964** *Rev. Eng. Stud.* Aug. 338 Two masterly impersonations: of the shy poet hauled before dons, and of the puzzled philistine, ready with cautious, deflationary, in-group jokes. **1965** *Listener* 4 Mar. 345/2 Mr. Gelber's mixture of sentimentality, in-groupiness, and Village dourness, can be more than a little grating. **1967** J. Gardner *Madrigal* iii. 65 Cheery as an in-grouper at party time. **1970** *Jrnl. Gen. Psychol.* Oct. 259 An error was considered..ingroup intrusion if the response was a word paired with a similar stimulus. **1971** *Listener* 18 Nov. 674/3 Their closed or in-group speech made me feel out of it. **1972** J. L. Dillard *Black English* vi. 230 American Blacks are quick to perceive pronunciation differences on the part of West Indians who migrate to cities like New York and are somewhat slow to accept them into the in-group.

ingrown, *ppl. a.* Add: **c.** *Geol.* Applied to an incised meander having a characteristic asymmetrical cross-section (see quot. 1954) as a result of lateral erosion and movement of the bed as it was being cut.

1914 J. L. Rich in *Jrnl. Geol.* XXII. 470 The In-grown Meander Valley is one whose stream, which may or may not have inherited a meandering course from a previous cycle, has developed such a course or expended its inherited one. Thus, as the stream sunk its channel lower and lower into the bed-rock, the meanders were continually growing or expanding. The term 'in-grown' has been chosen to express this idea. **1954** W. D. Thornbury *Princ. Geomorphol.* vi. 145 Two types of incised or inclosed meanders are generally recognized: (1) entrenched or intrenched meanders.., which show little or no contrast between the slopes of the two valley sides of a meander curve, and (2) ingrown meanders.., which exhibit pronounced asymmetry of cross profile with undercut slopes on the outside of the meander curves and slipoff slopes on the inside. **1960** B. W. Sparks *Geomorphol.* ix. 225 Ingrown meanders are more slowly incised, due to less rapid downcutting or to more resistant rocks.

ingubu (iŋgū·bo). *S. Afr.* Also 9 **ingoobu, ingouboo, ingubo.** [Nguni; cf. Fanagalo *ngubo*, Bantu-Botatwe *ingubo*, blanket, clothes.] Applied to articles of dress offered for sale to the native inhabitants of Natal.

1833 S. Kay *Trav. Caffraria* i. 37 He maintained that every thing around him, mountains, rivers, grass, cattle, and even his *ingubu*, 'beast-skin garment', proved the truth of what had been said respecting the being of a God. **1837** F. Owen *Diary* (1926) 25 They [*sc.* the natives] asked in exchange for their fowls, Indian corn and pumpkins, either handkerchiefs, blankets or 'ingubo' i.e. a mantle or carosse. *Ibid.* 77 He..abruptly asked me what was the use of giving all that ingoobu to the children, alluding to the Kilts of Dingareen with which I have clothed the boys. **1860** W. Shaw *Story of Mission in S.-E. Afr.* 406 A Kaffir wears this ingubu, or 'kaross', with the hairy side next to his skin, throwing it over his shoulders, from whence it hangs down to his ancles. **1899** G. Russell *Hist. Old Durban* ix. 187 Cast-off articles of European attire, known to the Natives as 'Ingouboos'.

inguinally (i·ŋgwinăli), *adv.* [f. Inguinal *a.* + -ly².] By or in the groin.

1908 *Practitioner* Aug. 255 There are also certain other disadvantages to which the inguinally retained testis is liable. **1966** C. A. W. Guggisberg *S.O.S. Rhino* iii. 68 The mammae, two in number, are situated inguinally.

Ingush (i·nguʃ, ingu·ʃ). Also **Ingoush.** Pl. **Ingoushee, Ingush, Ingushes.** [a. Russ. *Ingúsh*, the name of the former autonomous area of Ingush.] **a.** One of a North Caucasian people, forming the minor part of the population of Checheno-Ingushetia. Also *attrib.* or as *adj.* **b.** The North Caucasic language of this people.

1902 *Encycl. Brit.* XXX. 1/2 The Kabardian aristocracy, who were possessed of feudal rights over the Ossets, the Ingushes, the Abhazes, and the mountain Tatars. **1908** J. F. Baddeley *Russian Conquest Caucasus* v. 86 The Ingoush elders..[were] summoned to Mozdók. *Ibid.* xxviii. 468 The Russians..decided to gather the Ingoushee..into a few large settlements. **1910** *Encycl. Brit.* V. 548/1 Although the Ingushes speak a Chechen dialect, they have recently been proved to be, anthropologically, quite a distinct race. **1954** Pei & Gaynor *Dict. Ling.* 101 *Ingush*, a Chechen dialect (Eastern Caucasian group of the North Caucasian family of languages). **1957** [see *Chechen]. **1958** *Everyman's Encycl.* III. 189/2 A number of peoples (Chechens, Ingushes, Balkars, Karachays, and Kalmyks) were deported from N[orth] C[aucasus] to Central Asia in 1943 for alleged collaboration with the Germans, and only rehabilitated in 1957.

Ingvaeonic (iŋvi,ǫ·nik), *sb.* Also **Inguaeonic** (-gw-), **Ingweonic.** [f. L. *Ingaeuones* (Tacitus), a Germanic tribe.] From Tacitus's division of the Germanic people into Ingaeuones, Istaeuones and Hermiones, the name applied to the hypothetical language from which the earliest recorded dialects of West Germanic except Old High German descended. Sometimes used synonymously with *Anglo-Frisian. Also *attrib.*

[**1907** H. M. Chadwick *Orig. Eng. Nation* ix. 222 The identification of the Inguaeones with the Anglo-Frisian group rests on the assumption that languages of this type were once spoken in the western Baltic, a hypothesis for which no solid evidence has been produced.] **1933** L. Bloomfield *Lang.* iv. 58 We conclude that English is an offshoot of an *Anglo-Frisian* (or *Ingweonic*) dialect area, which must have been fairly extensive before the migration to Britain. **1939** *Trans. Philol. Soc.* 87 Sporadic cases of ō for 'Ingvaeonic' ā occur in OSax. **1948** *Neophilologus* XXXII. 176 The pronounced Inguaeonic characteristics of early Low German sources. *Ibid.* 181 The oldest Germanic language of the Dutch area is thus understood to have been primitive Inguaeonic. **1948** *Trans. Philol. Soc.* *1947* 14 The original Germanic language of the Low German area was not in any essential matter distinguished from Frisian... In that original state it formed with English a loose unity..having in a common articulation potentialities for common developments... This loose unity we may call Ingvaeonic. **1959** A. Campbell *Old Eng. Gram.* § 4 This West Germanic without Old High German is often called 'Ingvaeonic', because in Tacitus' threefold division of the Germans the Ingvaeones lie near the sea.

inhabited, *ppl. a.* Add: **b.** Historiated, e.g. *inhabited scroll*, an arabesque pattern of foliage in which figures, birds, etc., appear.

1952 D. T. Rice *Eng. Art 871–1100* v. 149 On [a font] at Alphington in Devon there is an inhabited scroll border which suggests the influence of a manuscript of late-eleventh-century type. **1954** M. Rickert *Painting in Brit.: Middle Ages* ii. 36 This motif..is worked into running scroll patterns enclosing at intervals lively figures of birds and animals—the so-called inhabited scroll. **1959** *Listener* 1 Oct. 538/3 The exuberance of a St. Alban's inhabited scroll. **1970** M. Swanton *Dream of Rood* 12 The narrower sides of the shaft are more purely decorative, carved with the so-called 'inhabited vine-scroll'. This is a Middle Eastern motif deriving from models like the Ravenna throne.

inhalant, *a.* Add: Also, concerned with inhalation.

1875 Huxley & Martin *Course Elem. Biol.* 105 These 'inhalent' and 'exhalent' currents go on, so long as the animal is alive and the valves are open. **1935** Twenhofel & Shrock *Invertebr. Paleontol.* ix. 314 In the earliest and most primitive pelecypods..the edges of the mantle are entirely free, but posteriorly they are folded in such a way as to produce an upper exhalant channel separated from a lower inhalant one. **1968** R. D. Purchon *Biol. Mollusca* iv. 164 S[olen] *delesserti* can also perform a swimming escape reaction by expulsion of a series of jets of water from the inhalant siphon.

inhalator (i·nhălēⁱtəɹ). orig. *U.S.* [f. Inhale *v.* + *-ator.] = Inhaler 2.

1929 *Lit. Digest* 30 Mar. 79/2 The most effective arrangement of all is to see that the city fire or police department and the hospital ambulances have inhalators. **1947** *Chicago Tribune* 17 July 32/2 Inside the ambulance is an inhalator. **1949** *Chicago Daily News* 4 May 1/4 (*caption*) [He] is administered oxygen by members of Inhalator Squad 2. **1956** *New Gould Med. Dict.* (ed. 2) 600/2 *Inhalator..*, a device for facilitating the inhalation of a gas or spray. Used for providing oxygen or oxygen–carbon dioxide mixtures for respiration in resuscitation. **1974** J. Wainwright *Evidence I shall Give* xvi. 61 It was a nasal inhalator..made of white plastic and about the size of a lipstick tube..with a tiny hole at its pointed end.

inhalatorium (inhēⁱlătōə·riŭm). *Med.* Pl. **inhalatoria.** [f. Inhale *v.* after Sanatorium.] A building or room used for the treatment of respiratory complaints by vaporized medicaments.

1906 *Chambers's Jrnl.* 347/2 In the medical institute called the Inhalatorium special rooms are set apart for the use of patients, who sit for half-an-hour at a time breathing an atmosphere charged with the vapour suited to their special complaints. **1912** *World* 7 May 697/1 The inhalatoria and gurgling-rooms. **1966** *Punch* 2 Feb. 161/2 So heigh-ho for the tap-room, the ambulatory, the graduated walks, the grandiose inhalatorium.

inhale, *v.* Add: **1.** Also *spec.* of tobacco smoke, and *absol.*, as in *do you inhale?*

1933 E. O'Neill *Ah, Wilderness!* (1934) III. i. 85 Say, you oughtn't to inhale like that! Smoking's awful bad for girls, anyway. **1970** *New Yorker* 17 Oct. 36/3 He reached for a package of Celtique cigarettes, took one, lit it, and inhaled deeply.

i·nhale, *sb. U.S.* [f. the vb.] The action of inhaling (tobacco smoke).

1934 J. O'Hara *Appointment in Samarra* (1935) v. 133 Not holding the cigarette very expertly, but taking appalling inhales. **1954** W. Faulkner *Fable* 179 Drawing the cigar to life in one slow inhale-exhale. **1959** N. Mailer *Advts. for Myself* (1961) 45 He lit a cigarette, and then after the first couple of inhales, he felt the anger coming back in him.

i·nheld, *ppl. a. rare.* [f. In *adv.* + Held *ppl. a.*] Held within.

1903 T. Hardy *Dynasts* I. I. vi. 53 His lips with inheld laughter grow deformed.

inheritance. Add: **5.** *inheritance tax* (or *taxation*) (later examples); *spec.*, orig. *U.S.*, a tax on inherited property levied on individual beneficiaries, varying according to their degrees of relationship to the testator, rather than on the estate before its distribution.

1895 E. R. A. Seligman *Ess. Taxation* v. 133 The inheritance tax to-day scarcely needs defence. It is found in almost every country...In the United States..there is now a decided movement toward the progressive inheritance tax. **1903** S. F. Weston *Princ. Justice in Taxation* viii. 289 We shall not attempt..to discuss the various theories of the inheritance tax. **1911** *Encycl. Brit.* IX. 465/2 The really vital change was the extension in 1894 of the old Probate Duty into a comprehensive impost... This 'Inheritance Tax'—to give it its scientific title—operates as a complementary property tax. **1929** A. Comstock *Taxation in Mod. State* xi. 154 Examples of inheritance taxation may be found in antiquity and in the Middle Ages... Since 1914 inheritance taxes have had a less spectacular rôle than income taxes and sales taxes. **1937** M. Newcomer in C. Shoup *Stud. Current Tax Probl.* 16 The annual burden of the estate and inheritance taxes has been taken to be the amount of the premium for life insurance sufficient to cover these taxes at death. **1965** *Listener* 2 Dec. 881/2 The positive case for inheritance taxation has become stronger. **1972** *Daily Tel.* 22 Mar. 32/6 This looks a pretty good start towards the possible inheritance tax, in substitution for estate duty.

inhibit, *v.* Add: **4.** *Psychol.* (See *inhibition 4.) Extended from sense 3.

1876 W. James *Coll. Ess. & Rev.* (1920) 30 A representation arises in a mind, but..it is inhibited by another which confronts it. **1943** C. R. Griffith *Princ. Syst. Psychol.* xvi. 596 A strong connection between two elements *a* and *b* inhibits the formation of connections between *a* and some other element *c* or *d*. **1957** Partridge *English gone Wrong* i. 22 *Inhibition* and the adjective *inhibited* and the verb *inhibit* properly denote the restraint that one psychical activity (for instance, thought) imposes upon another (as it might be fear) and also, derivatively, any psychical impediment to the free workings of body or mind or of both; it is this latter sense which has become debased to mean—as if that were a deplorable thing—the dictates of a decent self-restraint and the promptings of a natural modesty.

Hence in *Psychol.*, **inhibited, inhibiting** *ppl. adjs.*, **inhi·bitedness.**

1942 A. L. Rowse *Cornish Childhood* ii. 44 Because of his reserve, his essential inhibitedness. **1961** J. A. Brussel *Layman's Guide Psychiatry* viii. 80 This is best accomplished by removing or modifying the inhibiting factors which have blocked the individual's personality development. **1963** A. Heron *Towards Quaker View of Sex* i. 7 This still repressive and inhibited outlook towards sex. **1967** Hilgard & Atkinson *Introd. Psychol.* (ed. 4) xxii. 556/1 With neurotics who are too inhibited to discuss their feelings spontaneously, more directive methods are usually necessary. **1969** E. Mirel in P. Solomon *Handbk. Psychiatry* xxxii. 389 The 'pathologically shy' children who manifest passivity, inhibited initiative and motor action.

inhi·bitingly, *adv.* [f. Inhibiting *ppl. a.* + -ly².] In an inhibiting manner.

1941 *Scrutiny* X. 178 The nature and circumstance of the rescue leave each exquisitely and inhibitingly scrupulous about taking advantage of the other's helplessness or chivalry. **1965** *Sat. Rev.* (U.S.) 30 Oct. 91 He has also fought—rigidly, inhibitingly—with his sense of humor.

inhibition. Add: **3.** (Later examples.)

1906 C. S. Sherrington *Integrative Action Nervous Syst.* iii. 84 Classical examples of inhibition are those of the vagus nerve on the heart, and of the *corda tympani* on the blood-vessels of the submaxillary region. **1927** G. V. Anrep tr. *Pavlov's Conditioned Reflexes* iii. 43, I consider it advisable to give a brief description of inhibition of centres as observed in the field of unconditioned reflexes. **1967** R. F. Thompson *Found. Physiol. Psychol.* vii. 168 These more limited hypotheses still imply that inhibition tends to act near the region of the cell body where the spike discharge is initiated.

b. *Chem.* (See quot. 1902².)

1902 S. W. Young in *Jrnl. Amer. Chem. Soc.* XXIV. 299, I will..use the word 'inhibition' to cover the phenomena in point. *Ibid.* 302 Inhibition, *i.e.* a marked reduction of the reaction rate under the influence of minute quantities of foreign substances. **1923** [see *inhibitory *a.* 2]. **1956** *Nature* 3 Mar. 432/2 Anti-competitive (uncompetitive) inhibition, in which the inhibitor combines with the enzyme-substrate complex but not with the enzyme, has been considered theoretically. **1970** G. Odian *Princ. Polymerization* iii. 221 Polymerization is completely stopped by benzoquinone, a typical inhibitor, during an induction or inhibition period.

4. *Psychol.* A voluntary or involuntary restraint or check that prevents the direct expression of an instinctive impulse; also *colloq.*, in looser use, an inner hindrance to conduct or activity.

1876 W. James *Coll. Ess. & Rev.* (1920) 32 Doubt itself is an active state, one of voluntary inhibition or suspense. **1897** J. Adams *Herbartian Psychol.* 257 It is this work of inhibition that causes the peculiar feeling of effort that marks all voluntary attention as opposed to involuntary. **1916** A. A. Brill tr. *Freud's Wit & its Relation to Unconscious* iv. 206 One cannot possibly consider the amount of the pleasure so great as to believe that it has the power to annul deep-rooted inhibitions and repressions. **1932** E. Bowen *To North* xiv. 141 Blurred by the inhibitions of Pauline, upon which his sister dwelt with such gusto. **1936** *Discovery* Aug. 254/1 To guard against auto-suggestions and personal inhibitions of various kinds. **1965** A. L.

Fisher tr. *Merleau-Ponty's Struct. Behaviour* i. 18 That the brain possesses a general power of inhibition would be accepted. **1973** W. J. Burley *Death in Salubrious Place* iii. 56 It was light enough to see the boy's embarrassed shrug. Georgie had no such inhibitions. 'She had a thing about Vince.'

inhibi·tionism. *Psychol.* [f. Inhibition + -ism.] (See quot. 1934.) Also *gen.* A tendency towards inhibition.

1934 H. C. Warren *Dict. Psychol.* 138/2 *Inhibitionism*, the view that character is a function of the inhibition of instinctive tendencies. **1952** *Archit. Rev.* CXII. 195/2 For men of his type *fin de siècle* sensitivity and twentieth century inhibitionism are equally abhorrent.

inhibitive, *a.* (*sb.*). Delete *rare* and add later examples of the adj.

1899 W. James *Talks to Teachers* xv. 181 A familiar example of the paralyzing power of scruples is the inhibitive effect of conscientiousness upon conversation. **1902** *Jrnl. Amer. Chem. Soc.* XXIV. 299 An 'inhibitive agent' is then a substance producing an 'inhibition', or having an 'inhibitive effect'. **1944** G. B. Shaw *Everybody's Pol. What's What?* xxiii. 207 He [*sc.* Pavlov] thought he had discovered that reflexes have negative phases as well as positive ones, and can be classed as Excitatory or Inhibitive. **1952** Kirk & Othmer *Encycl. Chem. Technol.* IX. 4 Colloids apparently owe their inhibitive action to their colloidal nature. **1963** A. Heron *Towards Quaker View of Sex* i. 10 The emphasis on morality has so often gone with a cold and inhibitive attitude. **1970** G. F. Newman *Sir, You Bastard* i. 22 Permission was given to live at home provided the distance wasn't inhibitive. **1971** *Mod. Law Rev.* XXXIV. vi. 655 The principal purpose of the Act is inhibitive.

inhibitor. Restrict *rare* to sense in Dict. and add: **2.** That which inhibits.

1902 W. James *Varieties Relig. Experience* xi. 265 Danger is for most men the great inhibitor of action. **1908** W. McDougall *Introd. Social Psychol.* iii. 55 [Fear] is thus the great inhibitor of action. **1955** *Sci. Amer.* Apr. 72/2 Many seeds have water-soluble germination inhibitors in their covering. **1973** *Nature* 12 Jan. 140/1 The hydroid may contain a substance which inhibits its nematocysts from discharging and stinging other members of the colony. An occasional hydroid may provide *Pagurus* with such an inhibitor.

b. *Genetics.* A gene whose presence prevents the expression of some other non-allelic gene.

1911 *Jrnl. Genetics* I. 190 The Brown Leghorn..never produces pigmented birds and we..regard it as entirely without the factor *P*. But it possesses the inhibitor factor *I*. **1911** R. C. Punnett *Mendelism* (ed. 3) vii. 70 Probably we ought to regard the beardless as a bearded wheat in which there is an inhibitor that stops the beard from growing. **1925** D. F. Jones *Genetics in Plant & Animal Improvement* iv. 75 A fifth factor, *I*, when present, prevents any color from appearing, no matter what other factors are there. It is called an inhibitor. **1949** F. B. Hutt *Genetics Fowl* vi. 154 The first evidence that the inhibitor of dermal melanin is sex linked was found by Davenport (1906). **1965** J. A. Serra *Mod. Genetics* I. iii. 60 Inhibitors..completely hinder the manifestation of the gene with which they interact.

c. Any substance which (often in small quantities) slows down or effectively prevents a particular chemical or biochemical process or diminishes the activity of some reactant or catalyst (e.g. in corrosion, the formation of gum in petrol, or enzymic reactants).

1914 S. E. Sheppard *Photo-Chem.* vii. 289 The actual inhibitor in the case of ammonia is probably NCl_3. **1924** F. O. Rice in H. S. Taylor *Treat. Physical Chem.* II. xiv. 923 A type of negative catalysis in which the inhibitor combines with one of the reactants to form a molecular compound... The rôle of the inhibitor in all these reactions would therefore be that of a competitor for one of the molecular species undergoing change. **1925** *Jrnl. Soc. Chem. Industry* XLIV. 163 T/1 (*heading*) Water-line corrosion of iron and steel, with special reference to the action of the so-called 'inhibitors' of corrosion. **1935** *Jrnl. R. Aeronaut. Soc.* XXXIX. 791 An attractive method of preventing ice formation..is the use of some form of inhibitor which may be added to the fuel. **1938** W. V. Thorpe *Biochem. for Med. Students* x. 130 In many instances the inhibition of an enzyme can be regarded as the result of chemical combination between the enzyme and the inhibitor. **1951** I. L. Finar *Org. Chem.* I. iii. 44 Gum formation in cracked gasolines is prevented by the addition of inhibitors, which are mainly phenols or aromatic amines. **1962** H. L. Kern et al. in A. Pirie *Lens Metabolism Rel. Cataract* 385 Ouabain is a relatively specific inhibitor of cationic transport. **1962** *Lancet* 27 Jan. 192/1 It seems likely that the tissue activator may be 'unavailable' because an inhibitor is present, but this conclusion must be tentative until more is known about the nature and precise measurement of the inhibitors of fibrinolysis. **1968** R. O. C. Norman *Princ. Org. Synthesis* xv. 480 It is advisable to add a small quantity of an inhibitor to the more readily polymerized olefins..to prevent polymerization during storage. **1971** P. J. McMahon *Aircraft Propulsion* x. 298 Small quantities of various inhibitors may be used to restrict the rates of reaction in certain places. An inhibitor could for example prevent case temperatures from becoming excessive by cutting down the burning rate of propellants immediately adjacent to the case surface. **1972** *Nature* 18 Feb. 398/2 A generalized metabolic inhibitor..elicited 0% drug response by itself.

inhibitory, *a.* **2.** Delete *Physiol.* and add: More widely, that inhibits or checks anything; producing inhibition. (Further examples.)

1879 W. James *Coll. Ess. & Rev.* (1920) 129 Positivism takes a middle ground, and with a certain consciousness of the beyond, abruptly refuses by an inhibitory action of the will to think any further. **1901** B. Hollander *Revival of Phrenol.* i. 36 The frontal lobe, as the seat of the reasoning faculty, is an inhibitory apparatus against the lower and more instinctive natural impulses. **1902** *Jrnl. Amer. Chem. Soc.* XXIV. 306 The inhibitory actions in question are quite closely confined to reactions in which free oxygen is involved. **1923** *Jrnl. Physical Chem.* XXVII. 325 The inhibitory power of water in the esterification of acids in alcoholic solutions..represents a complex case of the Titoff type of inhibition. **1944** G. B. Shaw *Everybody's Pol. What's What?* xxiii. 205 Some [*sc.* conditioned reflexes] are too cruel for civilized people to tolerate, and from being what Pavlov calls excitatory have become inhibitory. **1959** *Metabolism* VIII. 101 Calcium gluconate exerted a significant inhibitory effect on insulin degradation.

inhistoricity (i:nhistǒri·sĭti). *rare.* [In-[3].] Lack of historicity.

1930 C. J. Wright *Miracle in Hist.* 8 The main fact that emerges for our study is that all of these hypotheses postulate a large amount of inhistoricity in the narratives.

inhomogeneity (inhǫ:modʒĭnī·ĭti). [In-[3].] **1.** Something that is not homogeneous with its surroundings; a local irregularity or departure from uniformity.

1899 J. Ward *Naturalism & Agnosticism* I. iv. 117 The former consists of smallest inhomogeneities,—a finely grained structure, as we say in English. **1936** *Jrnl. R. Aeronaut. Soc.* XL. 595 A local slip occurred (owing to a stress-concentration effect at a local inhomogeneity or flaw) in the zone separating the part of the crystal which had slipped from that which had not. **1955** *Jrnl. Brit. Interplanetary Soc.* XIV. 20 Just as the visual twinkling of stars gives information about atmospheric irregularities.. so the 'twinkling' of radio stars in radio wave-lengths can show up 'inhomogeneities' in the ionosphere, especially at the top. **1956** *Nature* 10 Mar. 487/1 Crystallographic cracking can be found in such an alloy, although its analysis is complicated by the presence of gross inhomogeneities and intermetallics. **1959** *New Scientist* 22 Jan. 167/1 The solidified ribbon of glass has a certain amount of distortion which cannot be avoided arising from small differences in viscosity due to chemical and thermal inhomogeneities. **1959** *Wiltshire Archaeol. & Nat. Hist. Mag.* LVII. 176 The sensitivity of the [electrical resistivity] method depends on..the size and depth below the surface of the inhomogeneity. **1971** I. G. Gass et al. *Understanding Earth* i. 36/1 Gneissose banding is also developed from original inhomogeneities in the rock such as bedding.

2. The property of being inhomogeneous; lack of homogeneity.

1916 *Sci. Abstr.* A. XIX. 154 The inhomogeneity of the field in the canal-ray tube. **1921** [see *graininess]. **1930** *Proc. R. Soc.* A. CXXIX. 221 All the evidence..tends to show that this tail is due, not to initial inhomogeneity of velocity, but to scattering or absorption. **1938** R. W. Lawson tr. *Hevesy & Paneth's Man. Radioactivity* (ed. 2) xx. 189 The condition of initially complete uniformity in distribution is not satisfied, and it is just this inhomogeneity that is utilized..for the concentration of the isotopes. **1942** *Jrnl. Biol. Chem.* CXLVI. 459 Further evidence for the inhomogeneity of ferritin is the variability of the iron, phosphorus, and nitrogen content of different crystallized ferritin samples. **1962** *Listener* 12 July 62/3 Information on fundamental crystal size and crystal shape, on lattice strain, on inhomogeneity.

inhomogeneous (i:nhǫmodʒī·niəs), *a.* [In-[3].] Not homogeneous. **a.** Not of uniform nature throughout; composed of diverse constituents; heterogeneous.

1904 *Jrnl. Physical Chem.* VIII. 425 The 58·5 percent alloy is homogeneous when annealed at 720° and quenched. It becomes inhomogeneous..if annealed at 685° and quenched. **1938** R. W. Lawson tr. *Hevesy & Paneth's Man. Radioactivity* (ed. 2) ii. 34 At the moment of their emission the α-rays from a single radioactive substance all possess the same velocity... As soon as they have traversed a sheet of an absorbing substance, however,..the pencil of rays begins to be inhomogeneous. **1956** *Nature* 25 Feb. 380/2 The relatively great variations are due partly to the inhomogeneous microstructure of the muscular tissue. **1962** Corson & Lorrain *Introd. Electromagn. Fields* xi. 400 We shall not attempt here a rigorous discussion of wave propagation in such inhomogeneous media.

b. *Math.* Consisting of terms that are not all of the same degree or dimensions.

1943 Margenau & Murphy *Math. Physics & Chem.* vii. 237 One remarkable feature of an inhomogeneous equation..is that it may not possess solutions for every value of *k* even though the homogeneous equation, with the same boundary condition, has solutions. **1946** L. Brillouin *Wave Propagation* vi. 109 This is an inhomogeneous differential equation as it stands. **1957** L. Fox *Numerical Solution Two-Point Boundary Probl.* viii. 266 In § 5 we solved the approximate finite-difference form of this problem by considering two trial solutions, $y^{(1)}$ and $y^{(2)}$, of which the former satisfied the inhomogeneous finite-difference equations and the correct initial condition, and $y^{(2)}$ satisfied the homogeneous forms..and had initial value zero. **1962** W. B. Thompson *Introd. Plasma Physics* iv. 57 Of the two possible choices for pressure, the first leads to slightly simpler results, although it does make eq. (4.5.8) inhomogeneous.

Hence **i:nhomoge·neously** *adv.*, in an inhomogeneous manner; unevenly, irregularly.

1909 in Webster. **1937** *Q. Jrnl. Geol. Soc.* XCIII. 582 A monomict, inhomogeneously, orientated, heteroaxial quartz-B-tectonite with partial recrystallization. **1966** D. G. Brandon *Mod. Techniques Metallogr.* i. 4 The difficulty comes when the features of interest are too small to be resolved at a low magnification and too widely or inhomogeneously dispersed to include a representative area..at a high magnification. **1973** *Sci. Amer.* Dec. 70/3 Owing to the random distribution of impurity ions..the energy levels are inhomogeneously broadened over the volume of the medium.

inhour (i·nˌauəɹ). *Nuclear Science.* [f. *in*(*verse*) *hour*: so named because if the reactivity is small it is inversely proportional to the corresponding reactor period (to a first approximation).] A unit for expressing the reactivity of a nuclear reactor, being the reactivity of one having a reactor period of one hour (i.e. in which the neutron flux increases by a factor *e* in one hour).

1947 H. L. Anderson et al. in *Physical Rev.* LXXII. 17/1 The unit of [control] rod position was given the name inhour (from 'inverse hour', symbol: ih), with the significance that when the control rod is displaced from the critical position by 1 inhour, the pile will have a period of (very nearly) 1 hour. *Ibid.* 21/2 The inhour is useful as a measure of rod displacement because it is a measure of pile reactivity which is independent of the position of the control rod. **1954** R. Stephenson *Introd. Nucl. Engin.* vii. 269 There is no simple relationship between inhours of reactivity and pile period observed. Thus 2 inhours of reactivity do not make the pile period equal to 2 hr, nor do they make the pile period exactly one-half an hour, although for small reactivities the number of inhours is about directly proportional to the reactivity. **1966** D. Jakeman *Physics Nucl. Reactors* ix. 340 Equation 9.69 is referred to as the inhour equation and is used to define a unit of reactivity called the inhour. This is the amount of reactivity to give a reactor period of 1 hour and for a U^{235} system is equal to a reactivity of $2{\cdot}62 \times 10^{-5}$.

in-house (i·nhaus), *a.* and *adv.* [In *adv.* 12 a.] **A.** *adj.* Of or pertaining to the internal affairs of a business or institution, etc., as distinguished from its relations with groups or persons external to itself. **B.** *adv.* Internally; without outside assistance.

1956 W. A. Heflin *U.S.A.F. Dict.* 268/1 *In-house research*, research done within the Air Force, not by contract. **1966** *Electronics* 14 Nov. 25 Under the new arrangement it's expected that more of the work will be done in-house at the Marshall Space Flight Center. **1967** *Ibid.* 6 Mar. 8/3 Although some electronic equipment makers do produce their own integrated circuits—or at least maintain an in-house capability—most still buy on the open market. **1967** Karch & Buber *Offset Processes* iii. 47 The type may be set 'in-house' or obtained from a composition house. **1968** *Lebende Sprachen* XIII. 4/1 A relatively small number of stock microcircuits..made by outside suppliers or by his own in-house facilities. **1971** *Meta* XVI. 141 The translation assignment came from a large pharmaceutical company with an in-house staff of translators. **1971** *New Scientist* 27 Apr. 251/2 More R and D should be put out to firms, thus further reducing the highly expensive 'in house' staff. **1971** E. F. Schoeters in B. de Ferranti *Living with Computer* viii. 67 This does not mean that the day of the in-house computer is coming to an end. **1972** *Science* 5 May 500/3 Postdoctoral fellows, who will be recruited to come to the academy as in-house resident scholars. **1973** R. W. Burchfield in McDavid & Duckert *Lexicogr. in English* 100 Making full use..of in-house photocopying apparatus.

inhu·manism. [In-[3].] Lack of humanism; inhumanity.

1907 W. James *Pragmatism* i. 20 You find empiricism with inhumanism and irreligion. **1933** *Archit. Rev.* LXXIII. 207/2 The dogged enthusiasm of Eric Gill.. undermined the hard-headed business-man's equally dogged belief in the sacrosanct inhumanism of graphic *laissez-faire*. **1960** H. Read *Forms of Things Unknown* xi. 178 The problem is mass-suffering, mute and absurd: in one word—inhumanism.

inhumanita·rian, *sb.* and *a.* [In-[3].] **A.** *sb.* One who does not accept the views and practices of humanitarianism. **B.** *adj.* Not accepting, or disregarding, the views and practices of humanitarianism.

1936 R. Frost *Let.* 25 July (1964) 282, I hate to be done out of it by a hard-boiled inhumanitarian. **1947** *Mind* LVI. 170 The ideals..which had inspired the French Revolution, have been dexterously transformed into justification of absolute monarchy and inhumanitarian nationalism.

inhumorous (inhiū·mǒrəs), *a.* [f. In-[3] + Humorous *a.*] Not humorous; lacking in humour. So **inhu·morously** *adv.*

1898 *Contemp. Rev.* Aug. 194 Burne Jones was sincere in his art, not fanatically or inhumorously, but quietly and subtly. **1920** *Blackw. Mag.* Aug. 138/1 Many Englishmen ..allow themselves to be convinced by hearsay that Scotsmen are inhumorously inclined. **1926** W. J. Locke *Old Bridge* ii. vi. 78 'Life is real and life is earnest'—but so is the drivelling existence of the inhumorous ant.

inio- (i·nio), also before a vowel **ini-**, combining form of Gr. ἰνίον occipital bone, occiput, and of Inion[1], used in a few medical terms, as **i:nience·phalus** [Gr. ἐγκέφαλος brain] = next; also, a monster exhibiting iniencephaly; **i:nience·phaly,** an abnormality in which part of the brain protrudes through an opening

in the occiput and which is generally accompanied by spina bifida and retroflexion of the spine; so **i:niencepha·lic** *a.*; **i:nio-glabe·llar** *a.*, extending from the inion to the glabella.

1893 *Trans. Edin. Obstetr. Soc.* XVIII. 227 A sagittal section of an iniencephalic female fœtus. **1958** R. A. Willis *Borderland Embryol. & Path.* iv. 158 (*caption*) Paramedian section of the 2-cm. iniencephalic embryo described in the text. [**1836** I. G. Saint-Hilaire *Hist. Gén. et Particulière des Anomalies* II. 308 (*heading*) Iniencéphale, *Iniencephalus*.] **1857** Dunglison *Dict. Med. Sci.* (rev. ed.) 499/2 *Iniencephalus*, a monster whose encephalon is in great part in the cranium, and in part out of it, behind, and a little beneath the cranium, which is open in its occipital portion. **1905** *Jrnl. Obstetr. & Gynaecol.* VIII. 236 (*heading*) Iniencephalus. **1925** *Surg., Gynecol. & Obstetr.* XLI. 182/2 My own specimen is a large full term female fetus, apparently perfectly developed in every way with the exception of the craniovertebral axis, which shows the characteristic features of iniencephalus. **1951** *Jrnl. Obstetr. & Gynaecol.* LVIII. 463/2 Iniencephalus is a rare condition. [**1836** I. G. Saint-Hilaire *Hist. Gén. et Particulière des Anomalies* II. 311 Les trois observations d'iniencéphalie que possède la science suffisent en effet pour fournir les élémens d'une caractéristique exacte.] **1902** *Encycl. Medica* XII. 139 This retroflexion of the foetus is often combined with defective development of the lower part of the occipital bone, when the name iniencephaly is sometimes given to it. **1968** H. Kalter *Teratology Cent. Nervous Syst.* vi. 165 Animals with craniorachischisis sometimes also had iniencephaly. **1803** J. Barclay *New Anat. Nomencl.* 146 If lines be drawn between every two of the different aspects, they will constitute the four following diameters: The Dextro-sinistral, the Corono-basilar, the Inio-glabellar, and the Inantinial. **1903** *Science* 30 Oct. 554/2 An inio-glabellar line can be drawn which will correspond very closely to the lower boundary of the cerebrum.

initial, *a.* and *sb.* Add: **A.** *adj.* **1. d.** Math. *initial condition*, each of a set of conditions giving the values (*initial values*) of dependent variables or their derivatives for a single set of values of the independent variables.

1834 W. Hamilton in *Phil. Trans. R. Soc.* CXXIV. [250 No general solution has been obtained assigning (as a complete solution ought to do) $3n$ relations between the n masses.., the $3n$ varying coordinates.., the varying time t, and the $6n$ initial data of the problem, namely, the initial coordinates.., and their initial rates of increase..; the quantities called here initial being those which correspond to the arbitrary origin of time.] 273 The problem of integrating these [differential] equations consists in proposing to assign, by their means, six relations between the time t, the masses m_1 m_2, the six varying coordinates ..and their initial values and initial rates of increase. **1890** A. R. Forsyth *Theory Differential Equations* I. iii. 82 He [*sc.* Jacobi] shewed that the introduction of 'initial values' of the variables..renders it possible to take the integrals of the first subsidiary system in a form, which leads immediately to the transformation of the equation. **1902** *Ibid.* IV. i. 4 The conditions, as to the arbitrarily assigned values to be acquired at ζ by w and its derivatives, are called the initial conditions; the values are called the initial values. **1920** H. T. H. Piaggio *Elem. Treat. Differential Equations* iv. 53 As t usually denotes time and x and y rectangular coordinates, a condition such as $z=0$ when $t=0$ is called an initial condition, while one such as $z=0$ if $x=0$, or if $x=l$, or if $y=x$, is called a boundary condition. **1957** L. Fox *Numerical Solution Two-Point Boundary Probl.* i. 5 Boundary-value problems can always be solved in theory, and often in practice, by a combination of initial-value problems, the extra initial conditions being chosen more or less arbitrarily but finally adjusted to satisfy the prescribed boundary conditions. **1968** Fox & Mayers *Computing Methods for Scientists & Engineers* iii. 30 We need two conditions, and here there are two main possibilities. In the first, giving the so-called initial-value problem, we are provided with two adjacent values y_s and y_{s+1} for some s, or possibly y_s and some linear combination of y_{s-1}, y_s, and y_{s+1}... The second possibility, giving the so-called boundary-value problem, is the specification say of y_0 and y_n, the values at the two ends of some range.

2. b. *initial teaching alphabet*, a 44-letter phonetic alphabet, originally known as the 'Augmented Roman' alphabet, devised by Sir James Pitman (b. 1901) to assist the teaching of reading and writing.

1962 J. A. Downing *I.T.A. Reading Exper.* (1964) 14 Sir James Pitman's new Initial Teaching Alphabet..has been evolved from his grandfather's 'Phonotypy' and from the 'Nue Spelling' of the Simplified Spelling Society. **1964** *Daily Tel.* 20 Mar. 19/1 The initial teaching alphabet scheme, in use experimentally for three years to make children read more easily, is to get a Government grant.

B. *sb.* **2. c.** *initial-word*, an acronym.

1939 *Jrnl. Inst. Journalists* Jan. 19/3 For one man who says 'London County Council' a thousand say 'Ellceecee', and euphony demands..that this curious initial-word, and L.M.S. and F.J.I., should all be preceded by 'an'.

4. *Bot.* An initial cell (cf. A. *adj.* 1 c).

1914 M. Drummond tr. *Haberlandt's Physiol. Plant Anat.* ii. 84 A stratification of the meristem due to the vertical seriation of the initials is sometimes evident. **1938** *Nature* 10 Dec. 1042/2 Douin..has now shown that *P. asplenioides* develops axillary branch initials, the upper developing into normal branches. **1955** *Jrnl. Ecol.* XLIII. 51 Two small..trees, bearing catkin initials, were transplanted. **1970** Raven & Curtis *Biol. Plants* ii. 129/2 These initials, or growth-initiating cells, appear to surround a group of cells in which no cell division takes place.

initialese (iniʃălī·z). [f. Initial *sb.* 2 + -ese.] Abbreviation by using the initial letters of the words to be shortened.

1955 *Amer. Speech* XXX. 110 In a dinner speech to the National Institute of Social Sciences given in New York in November, 1952..Mr Lovett frankly advocated the convenience of what he called *initialese*, a system of using initials and contractions, in order to save time. **1961** *Engineering* 17 Nov. 654 ASLE is initialese for American Society of Lubrication Engineers. **1962** *Guardian* 31 Jan. 8/2, 2,000-odd abbreviations listed in 'International Initialese'.

initialization (iniʃăləizēi·ʃən). *Computers.* [f. next + -ation.] The action or process of initializing; the computer operations involved in this.

1957 D. D. McCracken *Digital Computer Programming* xiii. 166 The programmer sitting at his desk with no more information than the trace may wish to know what happened in an early section of the program which set up the initialization. **1961** Leeds & Weinberg *Computer Programming Fund.* iii. 75 By initialization we mean the program steps which prepare the program to carry out its function. In this instance the initialization would probably correspond to rewinding a magnetic tape to its starting point. **1969** G. B. Davis *Computer Data Processing* xii. 271 The general steps for programming a loop are the following: 1. Initialization. 2. Execution. 3. Modification. 4. Test for termination.

initialize, *v.* Restrict *rare* to senses in Dict. and add: **2.** *trans.* (*Computers.*) To set to the value, or put in the condition, appropriate to the start of an operation. Const. *to*.

1957 D. D. McCracken *Digital Computer Programming* xi. 146 [Instructions] 18 and 19 initialize the address of the instruction with which numbers are brought in from temporary storage. **1961** N. Chapin *Programming Computers for Business Applic.* vii. 188 The failure..to initialize the switch would produce errors. **1963** P. M. Sherman *Programming & Coding Digital Computers* vii. 124 Another data instruction..is used to 'initialize' the ADD instruction to its initial value. **1972** *Computer Jrnl.* XV. 205/2 To trace from a base point *P*, the trace routine initialises *A* to the address of and *M* to the mode of the object pointed to by *P* and executes the following code.

Hence **ini·tialized** *ppl. a.*, **ini·tializing** *vbl. sb.* and *ppl. a.*

1957 D. D. McCracken *Digital Computer Programming* vi. 75 The preliminary steps which set up the loop and are not repeated constitute the initializing section of the loop. **1968** P. Wegner *Programming Lang.* iv. 234 Algol contains a small subset of..initialized identifiers. **1969** Maisel & Wright *Introd. Electronic Digital Computers* v. 74 Initializing procedures may also provide for such things as changes in the withholding tax rates or the Social Security laws. **1971** K. R. Britting *Inertial Navigation Syst. Analysis* i. 1 An appropriately initialized inertial navigation system is capable of continuous determination of vehicle position and velocity without use of external radiation or optical information.

initiand (ini·ʃiˌænd). [ad. L. *initiandus*, gerundive of *initiāre* Initiate *v.*: see *-and[2].] One who is about to be initiated (in quot. 1969, one who initiates).

1915 *Edin. Rev.* Jan. 127 The initiands are taken away from human society, often to a mountain, sometimes to a forest. **1931** K. E. Kirk *Vision of God* 473 A prayer of the initiand follows, in which he addresses the gods. **1969** R. Manheim tr. *Corbin's Creative Imagination in Ṣūfism* Introd. 60 To have him as a master and initiand is to be obliged to *be* what he himself *is*.

initiate, *v.* **1. b.** Delete ? *Obs.* and add later examples.

1963 S. Tolansky *Introd. Atomic Physics* (ed. 5) xxv. 423 If pure deuterium gas can be raised to a temperature of the order of 500 million degrees C., then a thermonuclear reaction should initiate. **1971** *Nature* 8 Jan. 111/2 Neutrons with incident wave vectors initiating within the cross-hatched area of the example shown satisfy the conditions for diffraction.

initiation. Add: **2. b.** *initiation ceremony, rite.*

1899 Spencer & Gillen *Native Tribes Cent. Austral.* vii. 212 All Australian natives, with rare exceptions, have to pass through some initiation ceremony before being admitted to the secrets of the tribe. **1935** B. Malinowski *Coral Gardens* II. vi. 234 The instruction may take place in the course of initiation ceremonies. **1951** R. Firth *Elem. Social Organiz.* ii. 47 Economic, ritual, and recreational affairs..are often difficult to disentangle within a complex institutional sequence of events, such as an initiation ceremony. **1916** H. B. Alexander *N. Amer. Mythol.* xi. 243 A myth which seems clearly reminiscent of initiation rites. **1937** R. H. Lowie *Hist. Ethnol. Theory* (1938) xi. 180 Boys' initiation rites probably involve circumcision. **1974** 'S. Woods' *Done to Death* 186 Tribal initiation rites in one of the Indian reservations in the United States.

initiator. Add: (Later examples.)

1943 [see *articulator 4]. **1971** I. F. Hancock in J. Spencer *Eng. Lang. W. Afr.* 117 The process of creolising in the direction of a language other than the initiator language of the pidgin form has been rather misleadingly called *relexification*.

b. An explosive or device used to detonate the main charge.

1915 A. Marshall *Explosives* xxix. 417 Of all these explosives silver azide, mercury fulminate, and the aldehyde are the only ones that have a sufficiently high acceleration to be of any use as initiators of detonation. **1944** *Compt. Rend. (Doklady) de l'Acad. des Sci. de l'URSS* XLIV. 18 One might naturally expect that the flash-point ..would be lower for the initiators than for secondary explosives. **1962** *Ordnance Technical Terminol.* (U.S. Army Ordnance School) (AD 660112) 164/1 *Initiator*, a device used as the first element of an explosive train, such as a detonator or squib... It generally contains a small quantity of a sensitive explosive. **1964** M. Gowing *Britain & Atomic Energy* ix. 264 His criticism enlivened discussions on bomb assembly, and he participated very actively in the design of the initiator.

c. *Chem.* Any substance which starts a polymerization reaction.

1940 in *Chambers's Techn. Dict.* **1951** Frith & Tuckett *Linear Polymers* ii. 50 In any large-scale production of a polymer, catalytic initiation is nearly always used...The word 'catalyst' in this connection is rather a misnomer, as it is almost always destroyed in starting off polymerisation; 'initiator' is less open to objection, but has never really established itself. **1959** Cram & Hammond *Org. Chem.* xxv. 573 There are three principal classes of free-radical initiators: 1. Compounds..which undergo thermal decomposition... 2. Photosensitizers... 3. Redox systems. **1972** Billingham & Jenkins in A. D. Jenkins *Polymer Sci.* I. i. 19 Azo-bis-isobutyronitrile is very frequently used as an initiator for research studies on radical polymerization.

in-itse·lfness. [f. phr. *in itself* (In *prep.* 22) + -ness.] The quality or state of being independent of any relation to other entities.

1906 S. S. Laurie *Synthetica* I. ix. 136 Mere sentience admits of the in-itselfness (which is the for-itselfness) of the object being revealed. **1917** A. S. Pringle-Pattison *Idea of God* xx. 399 It was the aloofness—the in-itselfness, as we might call it—of his [*sc.* Mr. Bradley's] Absolute, which made the stronger impression on contemporary thought.

inject, *v.* Add: **1. c.** *transf.* in scientific contexts: *spec.* (*a*) to introduce or feed (an alternating current or voltage) *into* a circuit or device; (*b*) to introduce (charged atomic or subatomic particles) *into* an accelerator; (*c*) to introduce (charge carriers) *into* a region of a semiconductor device.

1939 *Amat. Radio Handbk.* iii. 43/1 The triode is arranged as an oscillator injecting its oscillations into the common cathode lead of the R.F. pentode. **1945** *Jrnl. Appl. Physics* XVI. 583/1 The electrons are injected with a voltage ranging from 30 to 70 kv and, if allowed to remain in the 66-inch diameter circular orbit for the entire quarter cycle, they circle the magnetic flux about 250,000 times. **1949** Ryder & Shockley in *Physical Rev.* LXXV. 310/2 When terminal 1 is negative, no holes enter from it and holes injected from terminal 2 are spread over a wide area where their concentration is so small as to produce an inappreciable lowering of resistance. **1950** D. Halliday *Introd. Nucl. Physics* ix. 342 Protons are injected into the cavity at 4-mev energy, from a pressure-type electrostatic generator which serves as an ion source. **1956** L. P. Hunter *Handbk. Semiconductor Electronics* iii. 10 When such a junction is biased in the forward direction..electrons (*A*) are injected into the P-type region and holes (*B*) are injected into the N-type region. **1962** *Proc. IRE* L. 1784/2 At any voltage..there will be excess charge injected into the insulator. **1966** *McGraw-Hill Encycl. Sci. & Technol.* IX. 583/1 Ions are injected into the accelerator by an electrostatic machine. **1968** Marton & El-Kareh *Electron Beam & Laser Beam Technol.* 64 The beam formed by the gun is injected into a cylindrical drift tube immersed in a uniform axial magnetic field. **1970** J. Earl *Tuners & Amplifiers* vi. 139 Hum currents can be easily injected into the system with a resulting very loud 'roar' from the loudspeaker. **1972** *Physics Bull.* Mar. 175/2 A high energy electron beam is injected into a CO_2/N_2 mixture to produce uniform volume ionization of the gas [in the laser]. **1973** *Nature* 16 Feb. 444/1 Plutonium isotopes..have been injected into the stratosphere as a result of atmospheric nuclear weapons tests.

d. *Astronautics.* To put *into* (an) orbit.

1961 C. T. Morrow *Symposium Ballistic Missile & Aerospace Technol.* I. 207 Methods by which a satellite can be injected into the 24-hour equatorial or stationary orbit. **1964** Mueller & Spangler *Communication Satellites* xii. 242 Launch operations..will probably entail..a 99 per cent probability for each satellite that it will be injected into orbit, following successful launch of a single booster. **1970** *Sci. Jrnl.* Aug. 10/4 The extra load prevented it from injecting the 260 kilogramme Satellite Test Vehicle (STV) into orbit. **1970** *Nature* 10 Oct. 154/2 Energy considerations make it difficult to consider seriously proposals to inject unwanted material into orbit.

2. Delete 'Now *rare*'. Also (esp. from sense 1 b of Injection), to insert, introduce.

1950 *N.Y. Times* 20 Apr. 1/6 Senator Harry P. Cain.. sought to inject a note of caution into the debate. **1956** *Britannica Bk. of Year* 493/1 *Inject*, used in the sense of to insert, to interpolate. **1958** *Ann. Reg.* 1957 443 Films of events in the news could be 'injected' directly into the national (London) news bulletin. **1965** *New Statesman* 30 Apr. 696/1 It would inject some urgency into the lives of those..teams who plod through the season without any real hope of promotion or fear of relegation. **1969** *Listener* 2 Jan. 4/2 The raid injects new factors. **1970** *Nature* 12 Dec. 1019/1 The British government's decision to tighten the purse strings by refusing to inject a large sum of money into either the European Airbus or its rival, the BAC 3-11. **1972** *N.Y. Law Jrnl.* 31 Oct. 15/5 Issues would be injected in the consolidated proceedings which would prejudice the rights of one of the claimants.

injectable, *a.* Add: **2.** Suitable for injection into the body. Hence as *sb.*, a substance suitable for injection; *spec.* a drug or medicine that may be injected directly into the bloodstream.

1960 *Antibiotics Ann. 1959–60* 462 Thirty-three gonococcal infections in 31 unselected men have been treated with injectable tetracycline at St. Luke's Clinic. **1967** *N.Y. Times* 1 Aug. 27 The injectables are most often used by persons who formerly took amphetamines orally. **1969** *Daily Tel.* 3 July 23/3 An injectable form of the pill might be more acceptable in developing countries and help to damp down the population explosion. **1970** *Sci. Jrnl.* Aug. 8/3 Pharmacists have voluntarily restricted the supply of injectable amphetamines to hospitals. **1973** *Austral. Humanist* XXVI. 2/1 'Bad news' (he did not explain further) was 'coming up' about Copper 7 and injectables.

injected, *ppl. a.* Add: **1. b.** In sense corresponding to *INJECT *v.* 1 c.

1949 W. SHOCKLEY et al. in *Bell Syst. Techn. Jrnl.* XXVIII. 346 The electronic structure of the germanium is modified in the neighborhood of the emitter point by the presence of the injected holes. **1971** *Solid-State Electronics* XIV. 268/1 The current changes from ohmic to space charge limited when the density of the injected majority carriers exceeds that of the thermally generated ones.

injection. Add: **1. b.** (Further examples, relating to internal-combustion engines: see *fuel injection* s.v. *FUEL *sb.* 3 b.)

1894 B. DONKIN tr. *Diesel's Rational Heat Motor* ii. 60 The injection of the combustible powder–dust coal takes place gradually and continuously, during part of the stroke of the piston. **1921** W. H. BERRY *Mod. Motor Car Pract.* i. 32 Mechanical injection would permit of greater power development. **1933** A. W. JUDGE *High Speed Diesel Engines* iii. 25 Advancing..the moment of injection is equivalent to..advancing the ignition in petrol engines. **1966** *McGraw-Hill Encycl. Sci. & Technol.* V. 556/1 In a diesel engine, a fuel pump starts injection at the proper engine crank angle and meters the required quantity of fuel through the nozzle.

c. *transf.* in scientific contexts (see *INJECT *v.* 1 c).

1945 *Jrnl. Appl. Physics* XVI. 593/2 The electron injection and orbit shift circuits were instantaneous in their action. **1949** RYDER & SHOCKLEY in *Physical Rev.* LXXV. 310/1 Pronounced lowering of resistance can result from transistor action, i.e. the injection of holes into the *N*-type material from a metal contact. **1949** W. SHOCKLEY et al. in *Bell Syst. Techn. Jrnl.* XXVIII. 345 We shall discuss..evidence that holes are actually introduced into *n*-type germanium by the forward current of an emitter point... We shall refer to this important process as 'hole injection'. **1950** D. HALLIDAY *Introd. Nucl. Physics* ix. 360 Injection may be done by taking advantage of the necessary radial stability of the betatron orbit. **1952** *Adv. Electronics* IV. 225 A method for the phase control of microwave tubes..utilizes the injection of power via the output circuit of the oscillator to be controlled. **1958** W. EHRENBERG *Electr. Conduction Semiconductors & Metals* xii. 322 The injection of minority carriers is the basic effect in junction rectifiers and transistors. **1962** *Proc. IRE* L. 1781/1 Under double injection, that is, the simultaneous injection into the insulator of electrons from a cathode and holes from an anode, space-charge limitations are..partially overcome. **1971** *Nature* 9 July 77/1 Cyclotrons have an inherent advantage over tandem Van de Graaffs—there is no need to produce a negative ion for injection. **1971** *Physics Bull.* Aug. 461/1 Such [acoustic] waves are obtained either by deliberate injection from a transducer or by amplifying some of the thermally generated waves already present.

d. *Astronautics.* The placing of a spacecraft in, or its entry into, a particular orbit or trajectory; the time when this occurs; freq. *attrib.*, as **injection point**, the point at which a spacecraft enters a new orbit or trajectory.

1959 *IRE Trans. Military Electronics* III. 150/1 We will assume the vehicle's orbit consists of three phases..: first, escape hyperbola..; second, the sun-centered ellipse controlled only by sun's gravity and using injection conditions taken from the escape hyperbola leaving earth; and third,..the approach hyperbola. *Ibid.* 151/1 The properties of the trajectory after injection. **1960** *Ibid.* IV. 152/1 In order to have zero relative inclination, the injection point must be exactly in the plane of the moon's orbit. **1961** C. T. MORROW *Symposium Ballistic Missile & Aerospace Technol.* I. 208 An initial powered flight phase leads to injection of the vehicle into a coast trajectory. **1963** S. LEES *Air, Space, & Instruments* 100 For each.. location there is a readily computable impulsive velocity change (termed the 'injection velocity')..which will place the vehicle in a hyperbolic path with the desired terminal velocity. *Ibid.*, Geographical restrictions tend to limit the choice of injection points. **1966** E. BURGESS *Assault on Moon* iii. 73 A 1 mile error in position at injection can cause a miss of 650 miles.

e. *fig.*

1968 *Listener* 7 Nov. 601/1 Colonel Ojukwu has had sizable injections of capital from European sympathisers. **1970** *Daily Tel.* 7 Oct. 7 An immediate financial injection into the hard-pressed agricultural industry, worth..£54 million, is to be made by the Government. **1972** *Guardian* 22 July 1/8 The report will ask for a massive injection of Government money into the docks industry.

4*. *Math.* Also *injection map(ping)*. A one-to-one transformation, esp. (formerly) an inclusion.

1950 S. MACLANE in *Bull. Amer. Math. Soc.* LVI. 488 If S is a subgroup of G (notation $S \subset G$), then the injection κ..of S into G is that homomorphism of S into G with $\kappa(s) = s$ for every $s \in S$. **1963** D. BUSHAW *Elem. Gen. Topology* 147 If X is a subset of Y, the function $j: X \to Y$ defined by $j(x) = x$ is called the injection map from X to Y. The injection map from X to X is called the identity map on X. **1968** E. T. COPSON *Metric Spaces* vii. 86 If the inverse image of each point of E_2 is either empty or consists of a single point of E_1, the mapping $f: E_1 \to E_2$ is said to be an injection or a one-to-one mapping. If $f: E_1 \to E_2$ is an injection, $f(x_1) = f(x_2)$ implies $x_1 = x_2$; and $x_1 \neq x_2$ implies $f(x_1) \neq f(x_2)$.

5. Also freq. in terms relating to the injection of fuel into the combustion chamber of an internal-combustion engine, as *injection nozzle, period, pressure, system, time*; *injection valve* (further example). Also **injection laser,** a laser in which radiation is produced in a suitably shaped semiconductor crystal by the recombination of electrons and holes at a *p–n* junction as a result of the injection of a large enough number of electrons to produce a population inversion; **injection moulding,** a process for making moulded articles from plastics or other materials by forcing the heat-softened substance through an orifice into a cold, closed mould; hence **injection mould, injection-moulded** *ppl. a.*; **injection point** *Astronautics*: see sense 1 d above.

1963 *Proc. IEEE* LI. 602/1 (*heading*) Doping of semiconductors for injection lasers. **1966** SMITH & SOROKIN *Laser* i. 14 In contrast with the other types of lasers, the injection laser is almost two-dimensional, all the light originating from a region within a few microns of the junction plane. **1970** *New Scientist* 16 July (Telecommunications Suppl.) 16/1 The light emitted from the injection laser depends on the current passed through it. **1945** H. BARRON *Mod. Plastics* xvi. 343 Flash is not formed in a well-made injection mould. **1947** JOHNSON & DANIELS in P. I. Smith *Pract. Plastics* xiii. 187/1 The second moulding is in thermoplastic resin, injection moulded. **1969** T. C. THORSTENSEN *Pract. Leather Technol.* xv. 250 The expansion of the direct-molded sole and injection molded sole shoe is already placing requirements on the leather with regard to oil content and adhesion. **1932** *Chem. Abstr.* XXVI. 4419 (*heading*) Working plastic substances by the injection molding process. **1945** H. BARRON *Mod. Plastics* xvi. 344 The essential feature in injection moulding is to force the plastic into the mould at a sufficient speed that the mould is completely filled before the material sets by contact with the cold metal. *Ibid.*, Materials which are nowadays universally fabricated by injection moulding include cellulose acetate, ..polystyrene; methyl methacrylate resins, etc. **1967** M. CHANDLER *Ceramics in Mod. World* 10 He [*sc.* the ceramist] now employs shaping methods such as dry-pressing and injection molding, which are not traditional to his craft. **1973** A. PARRISH *Mech. Engineer's Ref. Bk.* xvi. 5 Injection moulding is a particularly important process for producing complex mouldings, primarily from thermoplastic powders or granules but also from thermosetting powders. **1900** B. DONKIN *Text-bk. Gas, Oil, & Air Engines* (ed. 3) xxiii. 416 Connected to the injection nozzle are two valves, the admission and an overflow. **1946** A. W. JUDGE *Mod. Petrol Engines* viii. 326 For larger cylinders two injection nozzles located on opposite sides of the cylinder would be used to give a better admixture of fuel and air. **1971** B. SCHARF *Engin. & its Lang.* xv. 221 The injection nozzle is normally a spring-loaded needle valve. **1916** A. GARRARD *Gas, Oil, & Petrol Engines* vii. 140 A strong spring tends to keep the valve closed, and a cam on the cam shaft operates..to hold it open during the injection period. **1934** *Engineering* 3 Aug. 111/2 The fuel pumps..differ from those fitted on most direct-injection engines in that the termination of the injection period is kept constant, the effective stroke of the pump being varied so as to alter the commencement of the injection period. **1930** *Engineering* 11 Apr. 472/1 It was therefore decided to determine the injection pressure which would give a short injection time, in conjunction with good atomisation. **1941** *Nature* 26 July 105/2 The injection system, as compared with many present carburettors, has some slight but definite advantages. **1968** C. F. TAYLOR *Internal-Combustion Engine* II. xii. 566 A few Diesel-engine builders design and manufacture their own injection systems. **1930** Injection time [see *injection pressure* above]. **1916** A. GARRARD *Gas, Oil, & Petrol Engines* vii. 139 Fig. 65 shows the form of injection valve and pulverizer adopted by the majority of makers for all kinds of fuel except the very heaviest crude oils.

injective (indʒe·ktiv), *a. Math.* [f. INJECT *v.* (or L. *inject-* ppl. stem) + -IVE.] Of the nature of or pertaining to an injection (sense 4*).

1952 EILENBERG & STEENROD *Found. Algebraic Topology* i. 8 A set of homomorphisms i_α: $G_\alpha \to G$, $\alpha = 1, \ldots, n$, determine a homomorphism $i: \Sigma_{\alpha=1}^n G_\alpha \to G$. ..If i is an isomorphism of ΣG_α onto G, then the set $\{i_\alpha\}$ is called an injective representation of G as a direct sum. **1965** J. J. ROTMAN *Theory of Groups* ix. 184 (*heading*) The injective property. **1966** SZE-TSEN HU *Introd. Gen. Topology* i. 8 A function f: $X \to Y$ is said to be one-to-one or injective iff, for every point $y \in Y$, the inverse image $f^{-1}(y)$ is either empty or a singleton.

injector. Add: **1.** Also, a device for injecting fuel into the combustion chamber or its intakes in an internal-combustion engine (or into the furnace of a steam engine, quot. 1890). (Further examples.)

1890 W. ROBINSON *Gas & Petroleum Engines* iv. 96 This oil is used to produce steam in stationary boilers. The oil is forced into the furnace in the form of fine spray by steam or compressed air, through injectors, and mixed with the air required for the combustion. **1912** R. B. WHITMAN *Gas-Engine Princ.* v. 72 This pressure vaporizer, or injector, is used on 2-cycle engines, the pressure being obtained from the crank case... An injector of this kind permits the use of kerosene. **1914, 1962** [see *fuel injector* (*FUEL *sb.* 3 b)]. **1932** *Compression Ignition Engines* ix. 115 In some buses run by a big city in the North only three cases of choked injectors have occurred in a year's running. **1947** *Jrnl. Brit. Interplanetary Soc.* VI. 107 The rocket motor can be divided into..the propellant injectors, combustion chamber and expansion nozzle. **1963** *Adv. Space Sci. & Technol.* Suppl. I. 173 In a liquid bipropellant rocket engine the injector serves the same function as the carburetor of a gasoline engine. In addition to atomizing and mixing the liquids, it meters the flow to the combustion chamber.

b. Something that injects (in sense *1 c), e.g. particles into an accelerator, or charge carriers into a semiconductor device.

1945 *Jrnl. Appl. Physics* XVI. 593/2 The polarity of the charge on the capacitors was made so as to make the second..half-cycle the period of electron acceleration thereby allowing charging of the capacitors in the injector and orbit shift circuits during the first half-cycle. **1953** *Proc. IRE* XLI. 1715/1 The efficiency of the diodes as hole injectors is lower than that usually considered desirable. **1962** [see *EMITTER 2]. **1972** *Physics Bull.* Mar. 144/2 The Linac injector is designed to accelerate protons ..along its drift tube structure to energies of 19·2 MeV.

in-joke (i·n,dʒōuk). [cf. *IN *a.* 2.] A joke enjoyed or appreciated by only a limited group of people. Cf. *IN-REFERENCE.

1964 *Economist* 31 Oct. 518/2 Professor Yamey..has published the first independent assessment of the Resale Prices Act..for those who like in-jokes. **1966** *Punch* 4 May 657/1 The dialogue peppered with British upper-class in-joke slang of the most blatant appeal to Lancashire slum-dwellers and Turkish primary schools. **1968** M. ALLINGHAM *Cargo of Eagles* vi. 82 Those who can read between the lines will find some amusement at what are called 'in-jokes' today. **1971** M. BABSON *Cover-up Story* ii. 24 They were laughing at me... It was in-joke laughter, and I was on the outside looking in.

Injun (i·ndʒən). Also **Injin. a.** Colloq. and U.S. dial. form of INDIAN *sb.* 2; also *attrib.* (Cf. *INGIN.)

1812 COL. J. COCKE in *Salem Gaz.* 28 Aug. 1/2 The people of Tenessee is antious to have orders commanded out for us to march against the injuns on the Wabash. **1850** MAYNE REID *Rifle Rangers* I. i. 5 Four till one! Injuns!—murder!—help, hyeer! **1853** *Ibid.* (ed. 2) I. iii. 24 Thur's a mighty grist o' venturin', I heern; beats Injun fightin' all holler. **1868** M. I. CARRINGTON *Ab-Sa-Ra-Ka* 83 Better not go *fur.* There is *Injuns* enough lying under wolf skins, or skulking on them cliffs. **1872** [see *HEAP *sb.* 4 d]. **1889** K. MUNROE *Golden Days* 118 No more attention was paid to the shooting of an 'Injun' than if he were a coyote. **1911** R. D. SAUNDERS *Col. Todhunter* vii. 104 But you're sure about it, too, ain't you? She ain't doin' no Injun-givin' in your case? **1937** [see *Indian devil* s.v. *INDIAN *a.* 4 b]. **1959** I. & P. OPIE *Lore & Lang. Schoolch.* viii. 134 In the United States such a child, who succumbs to the temptation of wanting back, is termed an 'Injun-giver'. **1973** *Nature* 13 Apr. 485/2 The alternative to receipt of a reprint is a slog through hundreds of miles of Injun territory. **1973** R. THOMAS *If you can't be Good* (1974) iii. 30 She had..long hair..glossy blue-black in color. Injun hair, she called it.

b. In various allusive uses and phrases: *honest Injun*, honour bright: perh. orig. an assurance of good faith extracted from Indians; *to play Injun*: to act like an Indian; to avoid being seen or captured; of children playing, to pretend to be Indians.

[**1676** J. TALCOTT *Let.* 8 June in S. Judd *Hist. Hadley* (1905) xv. 169 We sent 27 women and children to Norwich under conduct of some of those we call honest Indians.] **1876** 'MARK TWAIN' *Tom Sawyer* ii, Ben, I'd like to, honest Injun; but [etc.]. **1887** F. ANSTEY *Paleface & Redskin* in *Graphic* 31 Dec. 728/3 'Are you sure..on your honour?' he asked eagerly. 'Honest Injun!' said Lambert. **1887** H. FREDERIC *Seth's Brother's Wife* II. 160 'Is what you've be'n tellin' me here honest? Don't lie to me.' 'Honest Injun,..every word.' **1891** H. C. BUNNER *Short Sixes* 90 'Hope to die—Honest Injun—cross my breast!' said the boy. **1896** G. B. SHAW *Let.* 8 Sept. in *Ellen Terry & Bernard Shaw* (1931) 54 A thing she would never have done if she had not forgiven him quite thoroughly—honest Injun. **1902** S. E. WHITE *Blazed Trail* xix. 140 'Our compact holds now, honest Injin, doesn't it?' asked the boy anxiously. **1904** 'A. DALE' *Wanted: a Cook* 98 But, Archie, this is all true. It is, honest Injun. **1918** C. E. MULFORD *Man from Bar-20* xiv. 140 So they're combin' th' country an' patrollin'. Hereafter an' henceforth I've got to play Injun for all I'm worth. **1922** F. HAMILTON *P.J.: Secret Service Boy* ii. 85 Bar rot, Mr. Ambrose. Real honest Injun? **1922** JOYCE *Ulysses* 295 'Are you codding?' says I. 'Honest injun,' says Alf. **1950** L. A. G. STRONG *Which I Never* i. 12 'You've invented him.' 'Which I never, sir,..' 'Honest Injun?'

injunct, *v.* Add: Now in somewhat more general use. (Earlier U.S. example and later U.K. examples.)

1872 SCHELE DE VERE *Americanisms* 653 Violent contractions, derived from well-known and well-formed words, like burgled, injuncted, and excurted. **1900** *Westm. Gaz.* 12 Sept. 2/2 Sir Edward Clarke is very likely right in thinking that the Court would hesitate to injunct a man for pirating his own speech. **1957** *Times* 23 Nov. 3/2 Counsel said that Mr. Fielding wanted the Court to say that as he had first claim on Steele's services he should be injuncted from entering a contract with anyone else. But Steele could not be injuncted from going to South Africa.

injunctive, *a.* Add: **2.** *Gram.* Applied to the form of a verb (in Vedic, Hittite, etc.) having secondary personal endings and expressing injunction. Also as *sb.*

1910 A. A. MACDONELL *Vedic Gram.* VII. 316 The unaugmented forms of past tenses used modally, are sometimes called improper subjunctives, but they are more suitably termed injunctives, as they appear to have originally expressed an injunction. **1927** E. A. SONNENSCHEIN *Soul of Grammar* § 73 What a pity that no one thought of calling the [subjunctive] mood ἐπιτακτική—a term which would have been translatable by the Latin *iniunctivus*, 'injunctive', i.e. 'enjoining'. **1965** *Language* XLI. 1, *-si* imperatives derive from root injunctives, to which could be suffixed *-i* or *-u* to form imperatives. **1971** F. R. ADRADOS in *Archivum Linguisticum* II. 97 Ambrosini believes that *s* [in Indo-European] was the marker of intransitivity; Pariente calls it an injunctive characteristic. *Ibid.* 99, I think we can ascribe to older Indo-European, verbal forms of a type similar to the injunctive, well attested in Vedic and Hittite.

injured, *ppl. a.* Add: **1.** Esp. in phr. *injured innocence*, the offended attitude of one who is undeservedly accused of something; freq. with the implication that the accusation is in fact just; also occas. used to designate a person adopting such an attitude.

1713 ADDISON *Cato* III. 36 Lucia, thou injur'd Innocence! **1827** M. WILMOT *Jrnl.* 3 July in *More Lett.* (1935) 268 She next told us of an act of her benevolence towards a poacher caught in the fact, and perhaps too severely punished... Our Chezy dreadnought..speaks of him as injured Innocence. **1869** TROLLOPE *Phineas Finn* I. xvi. 132 Phineas assumed a look of injured innocence, as though his father was driving him too hard. *c* **1900** H. A. JONES in M. R. Booth *Eng. Plays of 19th Cent.* (1969) II. 364, I decline to give a certificate of injured innocence to any young person who misses her last train. **1971** J. D. MACDONALD *Seven* (1974) v. 101, I have watched the same game a lot of other times... Just don't give me injured innocence.

injuria (indʒūᵊ·riă). *Law.* [L.] An invasion of another's rights; an actionable wrong. Cf. *DAMNUM.

1876 *Wharton's Law Lexicon* (ed. 6) 477/1 *Injuria*, injury; a wrongful act done. **1898** *Encycl. Laws Eng.* VI. 485 *Injuria* can only be defined as an infringement of a legal right. **1972** *Times* 23 Feb. 27/8 The jury should be neither encouraged nor allowed to look beyond as generous a solatium as was required for the injuria simply to give effect to feelings of indignation.

injurious, *a.* Add: **4.** *injurious affection* (Law): a term used of a situation in which part of a person's land is acquired compulsorily under statutory powers and the remaining part is reduced in value, either because it is a smaller piece or because of what has been done on the land compulsorily acquired; also, of other situations in which an owner seeks compensation for the deleterious effect on his property of the exercise of statutory powers; *injurious falsehood* (Law): an actionable falsehood, a false statement claimed to have caused damage to the plaintiff in respect of his office, profession, trade or business, etc.

[**1845** *Act* 8 & 9 *Vict.* c. 18 The damage, if any, to be sustained by the owner of the lands by reason of the severing of the lands from the other lands of such owner, or otherwise injuriously affecting such lands.] **1867** *Law Rep.* (Queen's Bench) II. 239 The injurious affection of the house by the vibration, smoke, and noise. **1889** *Law Rep.* (Appeal Cases) XIV. 159 The acts complained of as an injurious affection were not done on the land taken. **1909** HALSBURY *Laws Eng.* III. 41 In assessing compensation for..injurious affection all damage that can be reasonably foreseen should be taken into account. **1932** *Act* 22 & 23 *Geo. V* c. 48 Account shall be taken of any additional injurious affection of the property. **1947** *Act* 10 & 11 *Geo. VI* c. 48 The compensation (if any) to which that person would be entitled for such injurious affection if the..land were compulsorily acquired. **1965** *Act Eliz. II* c. 56 § 10 This section shall be construed as affording in all cases a right to compensation for injurious affection to land. **1971** *Country Life* 6 May 1109/2 A claim for compensation on account of injurious affection is now made under the provisions of sections 7 and 10 of the Compulsory Purchase Act. **1972** *Daily Colonist* (Victoria, B.C.) 10 Feb. 38/3 The report also suggests that the basic formula for compensation [in case of expropriation] be based on the market value of the property expropriated plus damages for 'injurious affection'. **1907** J. W. SALMOND *Law of Torts* xv. 426 The second form of actionable misrepresentation, namely that which we have termed Injurious Falsehood. **1928** *Ibid.* (ed. 7) xv. 582 The most important example of the wrong of injurious falsehood is the use of fraudulent or misleading trade names. **1933** *Law Jrnl. Rep.* CII. 191 A false statement detrimental to the plaintiff's business, but not defamatory, carelessly made in the belief it was true, will not support an action for injurious falsehood. **1955** *Rep. Patent, Design & Trade Mark Cases* (Patent Office) LXXII. 160 The amendment of the writ has been such as to raise the cause of action known as 'injurious falsehood'. **1967** J. G. FLEMING *Introd. Law of Torts* xi. 218 The tort of injurious falsehood, partaking of elements familiar to defamation and deceit. **1973** J. D. HEYDON *Economic Torts* IV. 66 Injurious falsehood. This tort is committed where the defendant maliciously publishes to a third party written or oral falsehoods about the plaintiff in his trade which are calculated to produce and do produce actual damage. **1974** *Trans. Philol. Soc. 1973* 19 The only possibility of action would appear to be in the tort of injurious falsehood, but for a trade-mark proprietor to succeed he would have to show malice on the part of the publishers or editor of the dictionary.

injury, *sb.* Add: **4.** *attrib.* and *Comb.* *injury-feigning* vbl. sb. and ppl. a.; **injury time,** the extra time allowed in a game of football or the like to make up for time spent in attending to injuries.

1925 J. S. HUXLEY in *Brit. Birds* XIX. 93 The Purple Sandpiper which nests on the..tundra has an 'injury-feigning' performance which must be hard to beat for elaboration. *Ibid.* 94 In regard to 'injury-feigning' the Avocet is one of the most spectacular of birds. **1932** D. LACK in *Ibis* 282 Injury-feigning is, therefore, assumed to be primarily a partial paralysis due to anxiety. **1948** *Brit. Birds* XLI. 237 The cock several times gave 'lure displays' of the 'injury-feigning' type, creeping away from the dummy with wings dragging and depressed and tail fanned. **1960** *Sunday Times* 18 Dec. 20/1 The winning score..did not come until the 43rd minute of the second half in what, in the absence of any official designation, is termed 'injury time'. **1971** *New Society* 1 July 24/3 One of the better ideas in the competition is their tie-breaker. If there is a tie the teams play off to an instant death by goals scored from penalties kicked immediately after extra injury-time.

ink, *sb.*¹ Add: **2. a.** *ink fever* (nonce-word); **d.** *ink-blue, -like* (later example), *-purple; ink-shine* v. (nonce-word). Also **e.** (in Chinese calligraphy, etc.) *ink-brush, -painting, -sketch, -squeeze, -stick, -study.*

1963 *Times* 16 Feb. 11/6 Baby ink-blue mussel shells arranged in flower-like clusters with sprays of dried seaweeds in between. **1971** *Guardian* 14 Dec. 9/2 In black, tan, bottle green, honey, and ink blue. **1951** R. FIRTH *Elem. Social Organiz.* v. 164 A traditional Chinese painter works with a definite theory about the use of the ink-brush. **1922** T. E. LAWRENCE *Home Lett.* (1954) 355 This long-drawn-out battle over my narrative of the campaigns of Feisal has put an ink fever into me. I find myself always going about trying to fit words to the sights & sounds in the world outside me. **1933** W. DE LA MARE *Fleeting* 49 Whose waters..ink-like, ebon,..flow. **1925** R. FRY *Chinese Art* 9 Many ink-paintings ascribed to him [*sc.* Li Lung-mien] are extant, and a few may be originals. *Ibid.* Plate 9 (*caption*) Ink painting on silk. **1954** *Oxf. Jun. Encycl.* XII. 225/1 The greatest master of ink-painting [in Japan] was Sesshū (1420–1506). **1935** E. BOWEN *House in Paris* II. vii. 159 Toppling ink-purple clouds. **1922** JOYCE *Ulysses* 216 The jet beads of her mantilla inkshining in the sun. **1906** S. W. BUSHELL *Chinese Art* II. xiii. 136 She [*sc.* the Lady Kuan] was a clever painter of flowers and her rapid ink sketches of peonies, prunus-flowers and orchids were admirable. **1910** *Brit. Mus. Guide Exhib. Chinese & Japanese Paintings..in Print & Drawing Gallery* 32 But the typical painting of the [Ashikaga] period was the ink-sketch of landscape, bird or flower. **1935** *Burlington Mag.* Oct. 185/2 The illustrations are all line-blocks made from 'rubbings' (or, more correctly, 'ink squeezes'). **1926** F. B. WIBORG *Printing Ink* ii. 50 The Chinese never keep liquid ink... Many ink-sticks are provided with a rounded notch at the lower end to secure a firmer hold for the finger, while the upper part to be rubbed is rounded. **1935** CHIANG YEE *Chinese Eye* viii. 199 A certain Li T'ing-Kuei of the 'Five dynasties' period supplied all the leading calligraphists with ink-sticks, and he compounded them from ten parts of pine-smoke to three of powdered jade and one of gum. **1939** *Burlington Mag.* Jan. 47/1 Inksticks and experience in making inks. **1936** *Ibid.* Nov. 236/1 Chinese ink-studies.

4. ink-blot, a blot of ink; also *fig.*, and *attrib.*, esp. in **ink-blot test** *Psychol.*, a projective test in which the subject's imaginative reactions to a random ink-blot shape are analysed and used as a guide to his personality; also *ellipt.* as *ink-blot*; **ink-cap**: substitute for def.: a fungus of the genus *Coprinus*; add further examples; **ink disease,** a fungal disease caused by species of *Phytophthora*, esp. *P. cambivora*, affecting chestnut and occasionally other trees, making the surface of their roots and sometimes trunks a darker colour; **ink-feed,** the duct which carries the ink to the nib of a fountain pen; also, the feeding of ink through this duct; **ink-jerker** *U.S.*, **-spiller** = *ink-slinger*; **ink-mirror,** a surface of ink used in clairvoyance in place of a crystal; **ink-slab** (examples); (*b*) a container for ink; *spec.* in the Far East, a slab on which ink is mixed ready for writing; **ink-wash** *Japanese Painting* (see WASH *sb.* 4 b); **ink weed** *Austral.* and *N.Z.*, a perennial herb of the genus *Phytolacca*, which bears black berries containing a reddish juice (= POKE *sb.*⁴ 2 a).

[*a* **1500** ? LYDGATE *Lavenders* 18 Wasshe withe wyne the fervente ynkes blote.] **1928** J. J. B. MORGAN *Psychol. Abnormal People* iv. 145 The Rorschach test is a special development of the ink-blot test. The ordinary ink-blot test has not yielded very significant results heretofore. Rorschach, some years ago, developed a series of ink-blots which have been more successful than those used previously. **1931** *Psychol. Abstr.* V. 268 An explanation of the use of the Rorschach ink-blot test as a measure of intelligence. **1940** R. S. WOODWORTH *Psychol.* (ed. 12) v. 151 A class of tests sometimes called the 'fantasy tests'... Most used is the inkblot...A variety of things can be seen in such a blot. **1955** *Publ. Amer. Dial. Soc.* XXIV. 13 The interpretation given ink-blots by criminals reveals their unconscious motivations. **1965** *Sun* 20 May 2/2 American military planners are weighing up an 'inkblot' strategy to clear South Vietnam of Communist guerillas. **1967** E. SHORT *Embroidery & Fabric Collage* i. 28 *Ink Blots and Dribbled Paint.* These methods are not as haphazard as they would at first seem as the hand is guided to a great extent by one's intuitive sense of design. **1968** D. RAPAPORT et al. *Diagn. Psychol. Testing* (rev. ed.) ix. 272 From the perceptual point of view it *appears* that the Rorschach inkblots are 'unstructured' perceptual raw material. **1972** *Jrnl. Social Psychol.* Dec. 303 Human movement responses..may be interpreted as an index of social approach during the administration of an inkblot test. **1927** GWYNNE-VAUGHAN & BARNES *Struct. & Devel. Fungi* 301 The genus *Coprinus*, the ink cap, is one of the commonest forms with black spores. **1963** LANGE & HORA *Collins Guide Mushrooms & Toadstools* 136 *Coprinus*—'Ink caps'. Characterised in almost all species by the gradual 'auto-digestion' of the gills, and sometimes the cap, into a black ink-like fluid. **1923** *Rev. Appl. Mycol.* II. 188 The so-called 'ink' disease of chestnuts constitutes a serious damper to French sylviculture. **1932** *Forestry* VI. 182 The fungus causing the ink disease of chestnut, has a very wide distribution. **1968** F. G. BROWNE *Pests & Dis. Forest Plantation Trees* II. 915 It [*sc.* *Phytophthora cambivora*] is one of the pathogens..associated with ink disease, a severe malady of *Castanea*. **1907** *Westm. Gaz.* 23 Oct. 11/1 The Patent Spoon-Feed has successfully overcome the ink-feed difficulty. **1935** *Discovery* Jan. 15/2 He must decide whether to alter the colour of the ink, its consistency, the rate of ink-feed. **1865** *Harper's Mag.* 683/2 This rattle-brained scribbler, this miserable ink-jerker. **1905** E. F. BENSON *Image in Sand* ii, Abdul had..tried him with the simple experiment of the ink-mirror, and found him extraordinarily sensitive. **1890** C. T. JACOBI *Printing* 288/2 *Ink slab*, the table on which ink is distributed, either at press or machine. **1895** *Montgomery Ward Catal.* 210/2 Slate ink slabs... 5 inch square with heavy glass cover. **1911** *Encycl. Brit.* XXII. 354/2 A second..roller conveys the ink from this drum to the distributing table or ink slab. **1938** *Burlington Mag.* Aug. 90/2 The inkslabs and inkstones, so sought after by collectors. **1963** KENNEISON & SPILMAN *Dict. Printing* 100 *Ink slab*, that part of certain printing presses, consisting of a large, flat, steel bed, from which the distributing rollers..take ink. **1969** *Korean Folklore & Classics* I. 23 He..picked up his teacher's ink-slab. **1881** *Punch* 10 Sept. 110/2 To think people ain't got more savvy than what these inkspillers enjoy. **1936** *Burlington Mag.* Oct. 162/2 The spirited ink-wash technique. [**1906** T. F. CHEESEMAN *Man. N.Z. Flora* 1085 *Phytolacca octandra*... Ink-plant; Poke-weed.] **1913** *N.Z. Dept. Agric. Jrnl. Agric.* VII. 369 Inkweed, or pokeweed (*Phytolacca octandra*), is a poisonous plant. **1933** *Bulletin* (Sydney) 15 Nov. 28/4 Inkweed is hard to burn or eradicate if it gets a hold. **1962** N. C. W. BEADLE et al. *Handbk. Vasc. Plants Sydney Distr.* 160 Weed of waste ground. Introd. from Trop. Amer. Ink Weed. *P*[*hytolacca*] *octandra*.

ink (iŋk), *sb.*⁴ *Sc.* [var. of ING.] *pl.* Low-lying grassland subject to flooding by spring tides. Also (in *sing.*) *attrib.*

a **1692** A. SYMSON *Large Descr. Galloway* (1823) 138 Down the river, about a mile from the Church..a large plott of fine fir-planting, over-looking a rich ink ground. **1802** *Farmer's Mag.* Aug. 331 Eighty acres..consisted of a rich sea marsh, or *inks*, as we call them here, almost a true level,..about 4 or 5 acres,..16 inches lower, being a younger marsh, and nothing but what we call ink grass growing upon it. **1824** J. MACTAGGART *Gallovid. Encycl.* 280 *Inks.* On muddy, level shores,..pieces of land overflowed with spring tides, and not touched by common ones..; on these grow a coarse kind of grass. **1848** *Scottish Jrnl. Topogr.* II. 234/1 *Spurlings* to net in the inks of the Cree. **1899** *Galloway Advertiser* 27 July 1/3 Extent, 240 acres or thereby of Carse Land of excellent quality, together with a very large extent of 'Inks' or Shore Pasture. **1974** *Scottish Field* Apr. 15/4 Some of the sunsets especially, behind the Inks and Wigtown Sands, are as fine as you can see anywhere.

ink, *v.* Add: **2.** Also *fig.*; *ink over* (earlier example).

1803 *Lett. Miss Riversdale* I. 319 The Prince took down the notes in pencil..and promised to ink them over for Lady Belfont. **1929** A. C. & C. EDINGTON *Studio Murder Myst.* iii. 23 It was inked into his mind's eye, so that even when he shut his eyes..he could not shut out that awful picture. **1952** C. DAY LEWIS tr. *Virgil's Aeneid* III. 59 A streaming night inked out The sky. **1959** *Times* 26 Jan. 6/1 The Yeames is a picture surely so inked into the national memory that it would need more than condemnation of its taste to eradicate it.

inkily (i·ŋkili), *adv.* [f. INKY *a.* + -LY².] In an inky manner; like ink.

1894 STEVENSON & OSBOURNE *Ebb-Tide* I. vi. 111 The sea.., inkily blue.

inkle, *v.* **1.** Delete † *Obs.* and add examples. (In these uses a back-formation from INKLING 2.)

1901 S. BUTLER *Erewhon Revisited* 42 People like being deceived, but they also like to have an inkling of their own deception, and you never inkle them. **1904** HARDY *Dynasts* I. I. vi. 57 Thou art young, and dost not heed the Cause of things Which some of us have inkled to thee here.

inkosi (iŋkō̆ᵘ·si). *S. Afr.* Also **enkosi, inkhasi, inkos, inkose**(**e**), and with capital initial. [Zulu. Cognate forms are found in other Bantu langs. (see quot. 1937); also Bondei, Zegua, Nguru *m-gosi*, Karanga *a-hosi* man, Gogo *mugosi* chief.] **a.** The royal title of a Zulu ruler. **b.** A chief, lord; in which sense also used as a title of respect.

[**1824** W. J. BURCHELL *Trav. S. Afr.* II. xiv. 364 The different members of his family, and the *kōsies* or

subordinate chieftains, formed round us a circle two or three deep. **1827** G. THOMPSON *Trav. S. Afr.* x. 118 Calling the king, Kousie, which is not his name, but his title, *kousi* signifying king or principal chief in their language.] **1835** A. STEEDMAN *Wanderings S. Afr.* I. x. 256 Among the Zoolahs the title of *Inkose* is solely confined to the principal Chief. **1836** N. ISAACS *Trav. E. Afr.* (1937) II. 245 When the monarch is firmly seated on his throne..he becomes an absolute king, or 'Inquose'. **1846** J. C. BROWN tr. *Arbousset & Daumas's Narr. Tour N.-E. of Cape Good Hope* (1852) xxvii. 423 As if a Zulu Inkhosi could show clemency! **1899** B. MITFORD *John Ames* x. 96 Policeman he want to see Inkose. **1905** *Westm. Gaz.* 8 June 2/1 All the members of the kraals concerned will..form,..with the 'inkosi', his several wives and their brothers and sisters and children and dependent relatives, a formidable audience. **1910** J. BUCHAN *Prester John* xii. 215 Courage, Inkoos; in an hour's time you will be free. **1937** I. SCHAPERA *Bantu-Speaking Tribes S. Afr.* viii. 174 At the head of the whole tribe is the Chief (Nguni, *inkosi*; Shangana-Tonga, *hosi*; Venda, *khosi*; Sotho, *morêna*, *kxosi*). **1948** A. PATON *Cry Beloved Country* III. ii. 220, I have thought, inkosi, that we should try to keep some of them in this valley.

Hence **inkosikazi** (9 inquosegose, etc.), (*a*) the wife of a chief; (*b*) native name for a white married woman.

1835 A. STEEDMAN *Wanderings S. Afr.* I. x. 256 The Chief having many wives..the sovereignty devolves on the offspring of the *Inkose kosi*, female chieftain, or queen. **1836** N. ISAACS *Trav. E. Afr.* (1937) II. 63 All the inquosegoses were present. **1866** H. ROBERTSON *Mission Life among Zulu-Kafirs* 103 Look, Inkosikazi, here is Mary putting this in my best trowsers. **1878** H. A. ROCHE *On Trek in Transvaal* 246 He [*sc.* the washing Kaffir] acquits himself at his task better than the *Inkosigas* who bungles hers so sadly. **1948** A. PATON *Cry Beloved Country* II. viii. 175 My heart holds a deep sorrow for you, and for the inkosikazi, and for the young inkosikazi, and for the children. **1969** I. VAUGHAN *Last of Sunlit Yrs.* iii. 25 'Nkosikaas,' Moses had asked, 'what sort of a table is this?'

inky, *a.* Add: **6.** inky cap = *ink-cap* (*INK *sb.*[1] 4).

[**1891** M. C. COOKE *Brit. Edible Fungi* vi. 47 The 'Inky Mushroom' (*Coprinus atramentarius*) received that name because, when it becomes old, the gills melt away into a thick, black, inky fluid, which may be used as ink.] **1923** J. RAMSBOTTOM *Handbk. Larger Brit. Fungi* 81 One of the chief characteristics of *Coprinus* is the so-called 'deliquescence', which gives the popular name 'inky cap' to these fungi. **1967** W. P. K. FINDLAY *Wayside & Woodland Fungi* 149 (*heading*) *Coprinus:* Inky Caps.

inky (i·ŋki), *sb.* Colloq. abbrev. of *incandescent lamp.* Also **i·nkie.**

1929 *Photoplay* (Chicago) Apr. 31/2 *Inkys*, incandescent lights, the silent lights used for talking pictures in contrast to the old noisy arc lights. **1936** C. B. DEMILLE in *Words* Oct. 6/2 An incandescent lamp is an 'inkie'. **1959** W. S. SHARPS *Dict. Cinematogr.* 103/2 *Inkie* or *Inkie-Dinkie*, a small incandescent lighting unit used for local lighting. **1970** *T.V. Times* (Austral.) 1 Apr. 8/3 Put a Ted Lewis on the Inky Dinky—insert a little, dented, pipe-like piece of tin in front of the small incandescent spot light to diffuse the beam.

‖ **inkyo** (i·ŋkyo). Also **inkiyo.** [Jap., f. *in* (in the) shade, retired + *kyo* to dwell.] In Japan, the act of resigning or renouncing one's office or position; one who has thus abdicated or resigned. Also as *adj.*

1871 A. B. MITFORD *Tales Old Japan* II. 122 *Inkiyô*; abdication. The custom of abdication is common among all classes, from the Emperor down. **1896** L. HEARN *Kokoro* iii. 40 Old men and women likewise—the *inkyō* of the vicinity. *Ibid.* xii. 224 The aged *inkyō*, whose sight and hearing begin to fail, talks cheerily of the impending change that is to provide him with a fresh young body. **1911** B. H. CHAMBERLAIN *Jap. Poetry* 178 Little wonder that heads of families became *inkyo*..that is, retired from active life as early as possible. **1958** G. B. SANSOM *Hist. Japan to 1334* x. 199 It was common for the head of a great institution or a great house to retire at an early age... This custom, known as Inkyo (which means a sheltered or passive life) has not entirely disappeared.

inky-pinky (i·ŋki,pi·ŋki). *Sc.* Also **inkie-pinkie, inker-pinker,** etc. [Etym. obscure; see *Sc. Nat. Dict.*] Small beer.

The word occurs in versions of the Hallowe'en play *Galatians*; see E. K. Chambers, *English Folk-Play* (1933), 55. There are other senses and forms, on which see the *Sc. Nat. Dict.*

1835 J. MAIDMENT *Galatians* 4 Inky Pinky about seventy or eighty years since was used by the brewers in Stirlingshire to designate the smallest kind of beer. **1842** R. CHAMBERS *Pop. Rhymes Scotl.* 69/2, I have a little bottle of *inker-pinker* in my pocket.

inlaid, *ppl. a.* Add: **2. b.** Of linoleum or the like: decorated with a design that is set into the surface.

1908 *Westm. Gaz.* 30 May 7/2 The floors will be covered with Greenwich inlaid linoleum. **1959** *Sears, Roebuck Catal.* Spring & Summer 780 Easy-care inlaid vinyl... Toughest plastic used in floorcoverings. *Ibid.* 731 Inlaid linoleum.

in-lamb, *a.* (Later examples.)

1968 J. ARNOLD *Shell Bk. Country Crafts* 90 In-lamb ewes can be accommodated and cared for. **1972** *Country Life* 15 June 1580/1 When grazing is finished the in-lamb ewes are brought indoors.

inland, *sb.*, *a.*, and *adv.* Add: **A.** *sb.* **2.** (Later examples.)

1913 L. V. KELLY *Range Men* 71 Canny men and good traders, built posts in the great inland. **1934** A. RUSSELL *Tramp-Royal in Wild Austral.* iii. 29 The camel..will long continue to be in many parts, the great utility animal of the Inland. **1941** I. L. IDRIESS *Great Boomerang* xxxi. 235 New cities, new industries, and a great, far-spread population in our inland, where population is needed so urgently. **1969** 'A. GARVE' *Boomerang* ii. 39 Our inland is still very empty country, and a lot of it isn't easily accessible. **1973** *Nation Rev.* (Melbourne) 31 Aug. (Suppl.) 1/1 He enjoys studying the unique wildlife of the inland, and..the people who live and work there.

B. *adj.* **1. a.** *inland ice* (*sheet*), the ice which forms a permanent cover or ice-cap over most of Greenland; the region over which this ice extends. Hence, more widely, any mass of ice of comparable extent and thickness underlain by rock; *Inland Sea*, (*b*) (see quot. 1891).

1853 H. RINK in *Jrnl. R. Geogr. Soc.* XXIII. [149 Let us call the group of peninsulas and islands..the *outskirts* of the land [*sc.* Greenland], and the compact continent to the E. the *inland*.] 151 The exclusive origin of the icebergs from the inland ice, through the icy friths, has been mentioned. **1871** A. B. MITFORD *Tales Old Japan* I. 173 *Shikoku*, one of the southern islands separated from the chief island of Japan by the beautiful 'Inland Sea'. **1876** W. E. GRIFFIS *Mikado's Empire* I. v. 55 The 'Inland Sea' (Séto Uchi) is a name which has been given by foreigners, and adopted by the Japanese, who until modern times had no special name for it as a whole. **1880** *Encycl. Brit.* XI. 166/2 The Danes divide Greenland into two physical divisions—the 'outskirts' and the 'inland ice'. The first comprises the coast-lying land, the latter the interior. **1891** CHAMBERLAIN & MASON *Handbk. Travellers Japan* (ed. 3) 357/2 The Inland Sea is the name given to the water space lying between the Main Island on the North and the islands of Shikoku and Kyūshū on the South. **1895** *Jrnl. Geol.* III. 244 During the climax of the glacial period, when the Scandinavian 'inland-ice' invaded the low grounds of middle Europe, those low grounds supported an Arctic-alpine flora. **1898** *Q. Jrnl. Geol. Soc.* LIV. 200 In addition to these 'inland ice-sheets' there are in Spitsbergen glaciers of the ordinary Alpine type. **1943** G. WILLIAMSON *Changing Greenland* xiv. 167 Six-sevenths of Greenland's 840,000 square miles is locked in the implacable embrace of the Inland Ice. *Ibid.* xx. 254 Before leaving Disko Bay, tourists may..make an excursion to the fringe of the Inland Ice. **1958** G. B. SANSOM *Hist. Japan to 1334* xiv. 300 Before him lay the Inland Sea route to the Straits of Shimonoseki. **1966** T. ARMSTRONG et al. *Illustr. Gloss. Snow & Ice* 27 *Inland ice sheet*, an ice sheet of considerable thickness and more than about 50,000 square km in area, resting on rock. **1969** M. SMEETON *Misty Islands* ii. 19 We entered the Inland Sea through the Hayasui Seto. **1973** *Nature* 5 Oct. 251/2 Although the strong echo from the upper surface of the ice [in Antarctica] shows little variation in strength, the normal bottom echo from inland ice..shows strong fading along the flight line.

inlander. Add: (Canadian and Australian examples.)

1843 *Standing Rules* (Hudson's Bay Co.) Index, Rations and regales to Inlanders, Scale of. **1933** [see *BINGHI, BINGHI]. **1934** A. RUSSELL *Tramp-Royal in Wild Austral.* iii. 33 The amazing feat accomplished by a young inlander. **1935** A. R. EVANS *Reindeer Trek* 179 He had rushed terrified from the spot to tell a tribe of passing Inlanders. **1944** F. CLUNE *Red Heart* 61 Andrew Hume begged his parents to allow him to accompany the famous German inlander. *Ibid.* 72 Several inlanders and explorers had a go. **1968** *Globe & Mail* (Toronto) 13 Feb. 3/3 Hannah Bearskin's parents are Inlanders.

inlaut (i·nlaut). *Philol.* [G.] A medial or internal sound; a sound which occurs in the middle of a word.

1892 G. DUNN in *Classical Rev.* Feb. 1/2 Latin d as inlaut and auslaut frequently represents Indo-Germanic dh. **1950** E. M. UHLENBECK in E. P. Hamp et al. *Readings in Ling. II* (1966) 251 For the different positions (anlaut, inlaut, auslaut) it must be ascertained separately what phonemes are permissible.

inlaw (i·nlǭ), *sb.*[2] *nonce-wd.* (See quot.)

1880 G. M. HOPKINS *Note-bks. & Papers* (1937) 314 His [*sc.* the universal being's] *inlaw*, the law of his being is unlike mine.

-in-law. Add: (Further examples of *in-law* in more general use; also *attrib.*) Hence **i·n-lawship**, the state of being an in-law.

1912 D. CANFIELD *Squirrel Cage* I. i. 10 Her mother felt the usual in-law conclusion about her daughter's life. **1926** C. SIDGWICK *Sack & Sugar* i. 9 Eva had invited her future in-laws, male and female, to five o'clock a day or two before her wedding. *Ibid.* vii. 77 He is lost to every-one but his wife and his in-laws. **1939** N. S. COLBY *Remembering* i. 19 Robert's sister Catherine has to mix in-law amenities with adoring love. **1952** A. GRIMBLE *Pattern of Islands* 205 A retired..policeman, married to a local woman and on a visit to his in-laws. **1954** M. GLUCKMAN in E. E. Evans-Pritchard *Inst. Primitive Society* vi. 69 This immediately established links of in-lawship with people who were, by standards of blood-ties, his enemies. **1957** V. W. TURNER *Schism & Continuity in Afr. Soc.* ix. 258 Links of in-lawship between villages. **1964** GOULD & KOLB *Dict. Social Sci.* 368/1 An indefinite number of affinal relatives or 'in-laws'. **1965** G. MELLY *Owning-Up* xv. 190 He was living with his wife and baby daughter in his in-laws' semi out at Mill Hill. **1970** *Daily Tel.* 8 May 17 How difficult and unnatural are in-law relationships! **1970** G. F. NEWMAN *Sir, You Bastard* iii. 91 His in-laws bought the furniture for the new house. **1972** R. MILNER in W. King *Black Short Story Anthol.* 374 The small salary added to his wife's keeping his in-law landlords quiet as he sweated through his first year of accounting.

inlay, *sb.* Add: **2. b.** *Dentistry.* A filling of gold, porcelain, or other suitable material which is pre-formed to the required shape and then cemented into a cavity.

1888 *Dental Cosmos* XXX. 542 One of the chief obstacles to success..has been the difficulty of exactly fitting the inlay to the tooth. **1921** J. B. PARFITT *Operative Dental Surg.* xix. 175 An 'inlay' is a filling which is constructed outside the patient's mouth and then cemented into place in the tooth cavity. **1963** C. R. COWELL et al. *Inlays, Crowns, & Bridges* ii. 3 Originally gold inlays were prepared by a technique similar to that used for porcelain inlays. **1973** *Which?* Mar. 78/2 Your dentist would not be allowed to fill your mouth with gold inlays when ordinary amalgam fillings would do.

inlaying, *vbl. sb.* Add: **3.** *attrib.* **inlaying machine**, a machine used in the manufacture of inlaid linoleum; **inlaying-saw** (see quot.).

1908 *Westm. Gaz.* 30 May 7/2 A scheme for increasing the speed at which our inlaying machines are worked. *a* **1877** KNIGHT *Dict. Mech.* II. 1189/2 *Inlaying-saw*, a saw used in piercing stuff for buhl-work.

inleak (i·nlīk). [f. IN *adv.* 11 d + LEAK *sb.*] Leakage into the inside of something.

1909 *Cent. Dict.* Suppl., *Inleak*, the leaking of a gas or liquid into an enclosed space or pipe. **1970** *Sci. Jrnl.* Mar. 40/3 Boiloff rate of about 0·2 per cent per day is several times as high as for most above ground insulated tanks, and some frozen earth tanks have failed as a result of excessive heat inleak. **1971** *Physics Bull.* Dec. 722/3 Techniques of constructing large vacuum insulated vessels are well established, but even so the heat inleak (typically a few tens of watts) is such that large closed cycle refrigerators are needed.

i·n-leakage. [f. IN *adv.* 11 d + LEAKAGE.] = prec.

1905 *Trans. Inst. Naval Archit.* XLVII. II. 410 It was merely a race between the hand-pump and the in-leakage of water whether she was ever raised to the surface or not. **1963** B. FOZARD *Instrumentation Nucl. Reactors* iv. 40 Thereafter a steady flow of gas sufficient to prevent in-leakage of air is maintained.

inlet, *sb.* Add: **4*.** *Anat.* The upper opening into a cavity of the body; used orig. of the pelvis and later of the thorax (both as cavities of the skeleton) and of the larynx.

1828 J. QUAIN *Elem. Anat.* ii. 69 The central line or axis of the inlet, differs very decidedly from that of the outlet;..both therefore decussate towards the centre of the pelvic cavity. **1906** A. M. BUCHANAN *Manual of Anat.* I. 210 The true pelvis..presents a brim or inlet, a cavity, and an outlet. **1960** E. GARDNER et al. *Anat.* xxix. 339/1 The thoracic cavity communicates with the front of the neck by the superior thoracic aperture, or thoracic inlet. *Ibid.* lxxxii. 938/2 The inlet or auditus of the larynx.. leads from the laryngopharynx into the cavity of the larynx.

5. *inlet-cam, -chamber, -nipple, -pipe.*

1901 L. M. WATERHOUSE *Conduit Wiring* 56 Metal inlet and outlet nipples. **1903** *Architect* (Suppl.) 24 Apr. 23/2 A 5-inch pipe is carried from the inlet-chamber to the reservoir. **1907** *Westm. Gaz.* 1 Oct. 7/1 Connecting the nozzle to the inlet-pipe of the balloon, the further supply of gas was added to that already within the envelope. **1908** *Ibid.* 9 Jan. 4/1 The inlet-cam being drawn out of position..the inlet-valves become completely closed.

inlet, *ppl. a.* Add: **2.** *Needlework.* Ornamented *with* lace, etc., let in or inserted. So **i·nletting** *vbl. sb.*

1901 *Daily Chron.* 31 Aug. 8/3 Flowing skirts inlet with lace. **1904** *Ibid.* 3 May 8/5 The inletting and trimming of a serge or cloth gown with Irish lace is quite usual.

i·n-letter, *sb.*[2] [f. IN *adv.* 12 a + LETTER *sb.*[1] 4.] An incoming letter. Cf. *IN-BASKET, *IN-TRAY.

1955 C. E. CARRINGTON *Rudyard Kipling* p. vi, Every in-letter was destroyed as soon as it was answered. **1973** *Times Lit. Suppl.* 9 Nov. 1359/1 In-letters, in particular, have been sacrificed: there is only one from Margaret Gillett..as against more than 200 from Smuts to her.

i·n-line, *sb.* and *a.* Also **inline.** [f. phr. *in line* (cf. *IN *prep.* 17*).] **A.** *sb. Printing.* (See quot. 1958.) Also *attrib.* or as *adj.* orig. *U.S.*

1923 *Amer. Type Founders Co. Specimen Bk.*, Cheltenham Inline. **1931** BASTIEN & FRESHWATER *Printing Types* 133 Erbar Inline...The inline..is a masterpiece of balance and design. **1953** BERRY & JOHNSON *Encycl. Type Faces* 263 Inline fat face capitals and figures. The white line occupies only a small portion of the main strokes. **1958** *Ibid.* (ed. 2) 269 Outline or open letters should be those in which the whole interior of the stroke has been removed, shaded letters those which have a white line running down one side or the other, and Inline letters those with a white line running through the centre of the strokes. **1973** *Publishers Weekly* 1 Jan. 47/1 The third release is Neuland [type-face], which comes in a standard, two outlines, an inline and a black.

B. *adj.* **1.** (Composed of parts) arranged or situated in a line. **a.** Applied to internal-combustion engines in which the cylinders are

arranged in one or more rows (in contrast to radial engines); usu. restricted to those in which the cylinders are vertical (so excluding V engines). Also *ellipt.* or as *sb.*

1929 V. W. Pagé *Mod. Aviation Engines* II. xlvi. 1886 Engines of the in-line type and both static and rotary radial two cycle forms continue to receive attention. **1934** *Discovery* Dec. 353/1 The tendency..is to develop..the large in-line engine..composed of four banks of cylinders forming an H, and the corresponding radial engines with two circles of cylinders one immediately behind the other. **1949** I. Katz *Princ. Aircraft Propulsion Machinery* i. 13 The principal cylinder arrangements are: 1. Inline—Single crankshaft, one cylinder bank, one piston per crankpin. 2. Inline-inverted—Inverted version of inline to ease problems of installation and facilitate larger propeller swing in small aircraft. 3. Opposed-cylinder.. 4. V... 5. V-inverted [etc.]. **1958** R. D. Blacker *Basic Aeronaut. Sci.* ix. 145/2 In-line engines consist of one or more lines of cylinders placed one behind the other. The rows of cylinders may be arranged in an 'X' or 'V', as well as in a single line. **1961** J. Mackerle *Air-Cooled Motor Engines* x. 200 Twin cylinder engines are arranged in in-line parallel twins, V engines or horizontally opposed. **1969** K. Munson *Pioneer Aircraft 1903–14* 22 Wright Flyer III, *ca.* summer/autumn 1905. *Engine*: one 20 h.p. (approx.) Wright 4-cylinder water-cooled in-line. **1970** *Commercial Motor* 25 Sept. 56/2 A 370 bhp version of the Cummins 335/350 bhp six-cylinder in-line was in production. **1971** P. J. McMahon *Aircraft Propulsion* xi. 312 By the early 1930s..the inline vee..was beginning to offer strong opposition. *Ibid.*, Even though the radial made a comeback..the inline always had this fundamental advantage of a lower frontal area.

b. *gen.*

1965 A. D. & K. H. V. Booth *Automatic Digital Calculators* (ed. 3) x. 134 (*caption*) (*a*) Crossed film cryotron; (*b*) in-line cryotron. **1968** *Sci. Jrnl.* Oct. 29/3 Aerial elevation and azimuth are..shown together with range on in-line digital indicators on the control unit.

2. Taking place or situated as an integral part of a continuous, usu. linear, sequence of operations or machines (as in an assembly line); involving or employing such a sequence.

1958 S. E. Rusinoff *Automation in Pract.* xi. 167 In straight in-line indexing, the work piece moves intermittently from one machining station to the next in a straight line. **1967** *Electronics* 6 Mar. 47/1 Production volume of monolithic integrated circuits has reached a point where automatic in-line testing and sorting will pay off in reliability. **1967** *Times Rev. Industry* May 60/2 The accommodation is designed for all the latest production techniques, including automatic inspection, bulk palletisation, in-line decoration and mechanical packing. **1968** Boothroyd & Redford *Mechanized Assembly* ii. 8 An in-line assembly machine is one where the work carriers are transferred in line along a straight slideway. **1971** *Engineering* Apr. 73/1 From the point where the operator selects the proper conductor wires, a portable electro-hydraulic in-line jointing machine..completes the cycle in under 18 seconds. **1971** *Physics Bull.* July 401/2 A typical problem in a steel mill is the in-line measurement of the roundness and diameter of steel rods, which are both hot and vibrating as a consequence of the production process.

3. *Computers.* **a.** Applied to a subroutine that is written, in full, directly into a program wherever it occurs. Now *rare.*

1958 Gotlieb & Hume *High-Speed Data Processing* vi. 107 A subroutine may be incorporated into a routine in either of two ways. If the instruction sequence is of reasonable length it may be inserted directly into place in the routine of which it forms part...A subroutine used in this manner is called an open or in-line subroutine. If a subroutine consists of a long sequence of instructions, or if it must be used in several different places in the routine, it is desirable to store it separately..and enter it by means of a jump.

b. Applied to data processing in which input data are processed in the order in which they are produced or obtained, without being first sorted into batches.

1959 J. Jeenel *Programming for Digital Computers* ix. 419 Random-access storage would permit input data to be processed efficiently in the chronological order in which they arise. This type of processing, which lends itself particularly well to certain commercial applications, is frequently referred to as 'in-line processing', as opposed to 'batch processing'. **1964** T. W. McRae *Impact of Computers on Accounting* i. 17 An in-line processing system updates all of the records on the same run, and the input data do not require sorting.

c. = *on-line *a.* 1.

1959 E. M. McCormick *Digital Computer Primer* ix. 135 The input–output equipment of a computer is sometimes referred to as peripheral. If operated and controlled by the computer itself, it is in-line or on-line; if operated independently of the computer, it is off-line. **1971** N. Chapin *Computers* viii. 152 On-line peripheral equipment (or in-line, as it is sometimes called) operates under the direction of the control unit of the automatic computer.

in loco: see *in *Lat. prep.*

in-lot. 2. (Examples.)

1779 in J. R. Robertson *Petitions Early Inhabitants Kentucky* (1914) 51 [We] pray that every Actual settler.. may be entituled to Draw a free lott;..the lotts to consist of half acre in lott and five acre out lott. **1790** in *Amer. Pioneer* (1842) I. 72 Nathaniel Massie doth bind and oblige himself his heirs, &c., to make over and convey..one in-lot in said town. **1819** E. Dana *Geogr. Sk. Western Country* 74 The in-lots 62½ by 87½ feet each, were sold at public auction. **1837** W. Jenkins *Ohio Gazetteer* 109 The regular in-lots are ninety nine feet in front, extending back one hundred and ninety eight feet. **1948** E. N. Dick *Dixie Frontier* 148 The area in and around one of these stations was plotted and each settler could hold one or more 'in lots' or building plots on the townsite and one or more 'out lots' or farming areas.

in-maintenance: see *in *adv.* 12 a.

in-migrant (i·nmaigrănt), *sb.* and *a.* orig. *U.S.* [In *adv.* 11 e.] **A.** *sb.* One who migrates from one place to another in the same country. **B.** *adj.* Migrating from one place to another in the same country.

1942 *Fortune* Oct. 194 About two-thirds of the 120,000 in-migrants will be without new housing. **1943** *New England Electr. News* Aug. 32 If a demand for the houses exists among the eligible in-migrant workers in a community. **1962** *Amer. Speech* XXXVII. 16 After 1900, the largest number of in-migrants came [to New York] from the Mid-Atlantic states. *Ibid.* 22 The in-migrant Negroes from the South concentrated in their neighborhoods too.., the largest concentration being the Harlem section in uptown Manhattan. **1963** *New Society* 10 Oct. 26/1 In-migrants to Aberdeen contained a much higher proportion of..university trained women than the native population. **1966** *Publ. Amer. Dial. Soc. 1964* xlii. 29 Poor in-migrant Southerners.

in-migration (i·nmaigrēi·ʃən). orig. *U.S.* [In *adv.* 12 a.] The action of moving from one place to another within the same country, e.g. from one state to another in the United States.

1942 *N.Y. Herald Tribune* 17 May N1 An immigration of approximately 3,000 new workers. **1957** *Economist* 28 Sept. 1031/1 Nowadays, with the tide of immigration from Europe a fading memory, American cities are growing by grace of what sociologists call 'in-migration'—movements of people from other parts of the United States. **1971** *Sci. Amer.* July 18/3 Of the 12 states in this region only three ..showed an excess of in-migration over out-migration. **1972** *Real Estate Rev.* Winter 21/1 The heavy in-migration of people from the mainland following the attainment of statehood made the demand for apartment-type housing acute. **1973** *Daily Colonist* (Victoria, B.C.) 11 Oct. 5/1 Land use—controls on highrise development and limits to 'in-migration', the influx of outsiders to the Victoria area.

i·n-milk, *a.* [attrib. use of phr. *in milk*: cf. Milk *sb.* 1 c.] Of a cow: in a condition to yield milk.

1958 *Times* 11 Dec. 12/7 If an in-milk cow laid down on the grass she was likely to be milked by a hedgehog. **1960** *Farmer & Stockbreeder* 12 Jan. 13/2 Best bid of 108 gs. was made..for The Pynes Herds' in-milk Jersey heifer, Eastington June.

inmix (inmi·ks), *v.* [f. In *adv.* + Mix *v.*] *trans.* and *intr.* = Immix *v.*

1892 G. Meredith *Sage Enamoured* in *Mod. Love* 99 Then shall those noblest of the earth and sun Inmix unlike to waves on savage sea. *a* **1909** —— *Celt & Saxon* xvi. 237 Celt and Saxon are much inmixed with us. **1931** Belloc *Ess. Catholic* xvi. 318 It was badly inmixed with motives in no way Catholic.

innards (i·nǎɹdz), *sb. pl.* Dial. and vulgar alteration of *inwards* (see Inward *a.* and *sb.* B. 1 b) 'entrails'. Now in common *colloq.* use. (Marshall, 1787 (see *E.D.D.*) has only *inwards.*) Also *transf.* and *fig.*, the inside (of anything).

1825 J. Britton *Beauties Wiltshire* III. 375 *Innerds*, the entrails of a hog. **1874** 'S. Beauchamp' *Grantley Grange* I. ii. 29 It's summut i' his innards, or his yud. **1878** Trollope *Is he Popenjoy?* III. i. 7 The Marquis was still in bed. His 'in'ards' had not ceased to be matter of anxiety to Mrs. Walker. **1896** S. Baring-Gould *Dartmoor Idylls* viii. 193 I'm terrible holler in my in'erds. **1903** Kipling *Traffics & Discov.* (1904) 58 There was the cutter's innards spread out like a Fratton pawnbroker's shop. **1921** *Wireless World* 15 Oct. 439/1 The instrument is assembled from a Mk. III ebonite top,..the parts of an aeroplane 'remote control', etc... Its 'innards' were collected from many different firms at all sorts of prices. **1929** G. Mitchell *Mystery of Butcher's Shop* iv. 47 Damned nuisance about the head... He's left us everything else, including the innards. **1932** J. T. Farrell *Young Lonigan* i. 29 His innards made slight noises, as they diligently furthered the process of digesting a juicy beefsteak. **1934** *Mind* XLIII. 234 The music is so bound up with the feelings and impressions of their minds, so spun out of the composers' 'innards', that it..is inseparable from the feelings and impressions themselves. **1935** *Discovery* May 132/1 The 'innards' of the atom. **1937** *Evening News* 5 Feb. 8/2 The best larder for a good kill was his innards, and the savage's sound logic in over-eating passed down the Middle Ages as Feast Days. **1941** Wyndham Lewis *Let.* 22 Nov. (1963) 310 Next, the true innards of Fascism are uncovered. **1961** *Listener* 16 Nov. 822/3 Here is Hogarth at thirty-five, exploring the dark innards of the town. **1962** *Ibid.* 8 Mar. 405/2 The whole thing [*sc.* the jury system] can only live so long as we are not allowed to see its innards. **1971** *Physics Bull.* Jan. 27/3 Theoreticians who could not care less about planetary atmospheres but deal purely with the innards of the CO_2 molecule. **1974** *Observer* (Colour Suppl.) 13 Jan. 27/1 The next time I slid the clamp up it wouldn't grip, the sheath of the nylon rope came down with it, and the white innards stretched thin over the lip of rock.

innatism (i·nē¹tiz'm). [f. Innate *a.* + -ism.] Innate ideas, or belief in them.

1909 in Webster. **1953** *Scottish Jrnl. Theol.* VI. 441 There are discussions on innatism and ontologism.

innelite (i·nəlait). *Min.* [ad. Russ. *innelit* (S. M. Kravchenko), f. *Inneli*, Yakut name for the Inagli river: see -ite[1].] A yellow-brown complex silicate of barium, near $Ba_4Ti_{3\frac{1}{2}}Si_4O_{18}(OH)_{1\frac{1}{2}}.Na_2SO_4$, found as tabular crystals in pegmatites in the Inagli massif, South Yakutsk, U.S.S.R.

1960 *Geochem.* 741 Innelite—new barium silicate (after S. M. Kravchenko's data). *Ibid.* 745 The RE [*sc.* rare-earth] ratios in the strontium mineral lamprophyllite and the barium mineral innelite are characterized by a high relative content of La (37–64% of the total RE). **1963** *Doklady Earth Sci.* CXLI. 1297/1 Innelite..was discovered in 1957 in aegirite-akermanite-microcline pegmatites of the Inagli massif which occur in dunites. *Ibid.* 1298/1 In comparison with all other known barium silicates, innelite contains the greatest quantity of barium.

inner, *a.* (*sb.*[2]) Add: **1. b.** (Further examples.)

1875 Geo. Eliot *Let.* ?2 Feb. (1956) VI. 121 Because we seclude ourselves from acquaintance that makes us only the more glad to have friends, and you are one of the *inner circle.* **1926** H. Crane *Let.* 20 June (1965) 262 An 'inner circle' of literary initiates. *a* **1930** D. H. Lawrence *Etruscan Places* (1932) iii. 78 Here in the tombs everything is in its sacred or inner-significant aspect. **1973** *Times* 28 May 9/1 It smacks too much of the confidential procedures of an inner circle for many churchmen to feel at ease with it.

e. *Printing.* In sheet work, designating the forme containing the type pages from which the inner side of the sheet is printed and including the type page for the second page of the printed sheet.

1755 J. Smith *Printer's Gram.* 229 (*caption*) The Inner Form of a Sheet in Quarto. **1841** W. Savage *Dict. Art of Printing* 422 *Inner form*, the form that has the second page in it; it is always worked before the outer form, except there be some particular reason to the contrary. **1888** C. T. Jacobi *Printers' Vocab.* 65 *Inner forme*, the pages of type which fall on the inside of a printed sheet in 'sheet' work—the reverse of 'outer' forme. **1892** A. Powell *Southward's Pract. Printing* (ed. 4) xx. 159 The forme containing the first page is always called by printers the *outside* or *outer* forme, and that containing the second page the *inside* or *inner* forme. **1946** A. Monkman in H. Whetton *Pract. Printing & Binding* v. 61/2 So far as the four-page [imposition] schemes are concerned, therefore, it is only necessary to remember that if the job is to be worked as sheet work, pages 1 and 4 will be the outer forme and pages 2 and 3 the inner forme. **1965** *Library* XX. 14 In Table I..the data on choice of forme are abstracted from the list of books, showing for each the number of inner and outer formes printed first... Here is a grand total of 5,338 sheets [printed 1600–1800], of which 3,902, or 73 per cent were printed inner forme first.

f. *inner light*: in Quaker use (see Light *sb.* 7 b and quot. 1957).

1856 [see Inner *a.* 2]. **1909** Chesterton *Orthodoxy* v. 135 The Quaker doctrine of the Inner Light. **1957** *Oxf. Dict. Chr. Ch.* 692/1 *Inner light*, the principle of Christian certitude, consisting of inward knowledge or experience of salvation, which is upheld by the Society of Friends.

g. *Phonetics.* Denoting a sound articulated in a part of the mouth nearer the throat than that designated by the unqualified term.

1867 A. M. Bell *Visible Speech* 62 If the breath within the mouth be compressed behind the articulating organs while an *inner closure* is held, a distinct, and in some cases, a powerfully percussive effect will be produced on the abrupt separation of the organs. **1888** H. Sweet *Hist. Eng. Sounds* 5 Most of these [point and blade consonants] admit also of 'inner' and 'outer' varieties.

h. *Inner Circle*: name of one of the lines of the London (underground) railway system.

1869 *Bradshaw's Railway Manual* XXI. 217 Metropolitan District. Incorporated..(29th July, 1864), to construct a series of lines to complete an inner circle of railway north of the Thames. **1882** *Times* 24 July 10/4 The Inner Circle would connect..with the railways south of the Thames. **1884** *Times* 22 Feb. 11/3 As to the Inner Circle line, by the 1st of June, or certainly by the beginning of the second half of the current year, that great work would be finished. **1911** *Encycl. Brit.* XVI. 944/1 This company combines with the Metropolitan District to form the Inner Circle line, which has stations close to all the great railway termini north of the Thames. **1938** G. Greene *Brighton Rock* iv. iii. 177 He could feel his blood pumped from the heart and moving indifferently back along the arteries like trains on the inner circle. **1966** J. Chamier *Cannonball* i. 11 Planes whizzing around a damn sight quicker than the Inner Circle.

i. *inner tube*: in a pneumatic tyre, a separate tube, inside the cover, which is inflated with air.

1895 *Montgomery Ward Catal.* 556/3 Pneumatic Tires.. Inner Tubes complete with valve stem and valve. **1902** *Encycl. Brit.* XXXIII. 535/1 In most tyres for cycles and motor-cars, an inner tube of indiarubber is made separate from the outer cover. **1902** A. C. Harmsworth et al. *Motors* x. 223 Half the number of spare covers and inner tubes are required as compared with the requirements when the wheels are of different sizes. **1904** A. B. F. Young *Compl. Motorist* (ed. 2) ix. 250 The piercing of the outer cover and inner tube by a nail or other puncturing agent. **1912** *Motor Manual* (ed. 14) iii. 106 The inner tube has become nipped between one of the security bolts and the cover. **1923** *Michelin Guide Gt. Brit.* (ed. 7) 883 Covers, inner tubes or pneumatic tyres.

1967 N. Freeling *Strike Out* 42 He had done two hundred kilometres a day, on rough country roads with spare inner tubes slung round the neck.

j. *inner Cabinet* (or *cabinet*): an informal term for a group of decision-making people within a ministerial Cabinet or similar group.

1900 *Westm. Gaz.* 13 Nov. 2/2 No one imagines that this Committee of twenty really decides critical matters of high policy. Those are deputed to the 'inner Cabinet'. **1936** H. Nicolson *Diary* 24 Feb. (1966) 245 J. H. Thomas..says that our group is not consulted; that there is an inner Cabinet which discuss things between themselves. **1970** *Times* 3 Mar. 2 The meeting was also told that Hebdomadal council, the university's 'inner cabinet', had appointed a committee to listen to the views of the students' elected representatives. **1972** *Guardian* 11 Jan. 20/1 The TUC 'inner cabinet'—the finance and general purposes committee.

k. *inner product* (Math.) [tr. G. *inneres produkt* (H. Grassmann *Die lineale Ausdehnungslehre* (1844) p. XI): so named because an inner product of two vectors is zero unless one has a component 'within' the other, i.e. in its direction]: the sum of the products of corresponding components of two real vectors ($a_1, a_2, \ldots, a_n$) and ($b_1, b_2, \ldots, b_n$), i.e. the number $a_1b_1+a_2b_2+\ldots+a_nb_n$; in a complex vector space, the number $a_1\bar{b}_1+a_2\bar{b}_2+\ldots+a_n\bar{b}_n$, where $\bar{b}_i$ is the complex conjugate number of b_i; (see also quot. 1966).

1920 T. Muir *Theory of Determinants* III. i. 7 The theorem on the inner product of two magnitudes each of the mth 'Stufe' and consisting of m simple factors. **1922** E. H. Neville *Prolegomena Analytical Geom.* IV. i. 192 Let an ordered set of three numbers be called a triplet, and let the number $fp+gq+hr$ be called the inner product of the triplets (f, g, h), (p, q, r). **1941** Birkhoff & MacLane *Survey Mod. Algebra* vii. 181 Physicists often speak of our inner product as a 'scalar product' of two vectors. **1966** A. L. Rabenstein *Introd. Ordinary Differential Equations* vi. 156 The inner product of $f(x)$ and $g(x)$ with respect to the weight function $w(x)$ on the interval (a, b) is defined to be $(f, g) = \int_a^b w(x)f(x)g(x)dx$. *Ibid.* 157 If the inner product of $f(x)$ and $g(x)$ is zero,.. then $f(x)$ and $g(x)$ are said to be orthogonal with respect to the weight function $w(x)$ on the interval $a<x<b$. **1968** E. T. Copson *Metric Spaces* ix. 139 In order to avoid confusion between multiplication of a vector by a scalar and the scalar product of two vectors, the scalar product of two vectors is often called their inner product. *Ibid.* 140 A vector space on which an inner product is defined is called an inner product space.

l. *inner quantum number* (Physics) [tr. G. *innere quantenzahl* (A. Sommerfeld 1920, in *Ann. d. Physik* LXIII. 231)]: a quantum number now identified with that of the total angular momentum of an electron, j (*J II. 6 c).

1923 H. L. Brose tr. *Sommerfeld's Atomic Struct. & Spectral Lines* vi. 364 If we wish to exclude the forbidden lines by a principle of selection, we must..introduce a new quantum number; we call it the inner quantum number and designate it by n_i. **1926** *Proc. R. Soc.* A. CXI. 84 Each term..in general will be a multiple term consisting of several members with different values of the 'inner quantum number' j. **1967** W. R. Hindmarsh *Atomic Spectra* ii. 18 The regularities of the multiplet structure of spectra were considered in some detail by Sommerfeld... He introduced an 'inner' quantum number to distinguish the various states of a multiplet, and suggested that it may be connected with a property of the electrons in inner shells (the core electrons). The true explanation of the doublet structure of the terms of alkali metal atoms is provided by the concept of electron spin.

m. *inner reserve* (Finance): a secret reserve not disclosed in a balance-sheet and due to an understatement of certain capital assets.

1930 *Daily Express* 16 Aug. 10/1 Former Inner Reserves are now brought from the Assets in which they were hidden and are grouped in an exposed Reserve on the Liability side of the Sheet. **1955** *Times* 10 May 18/5 Your directors have now decided to transfer a part of these inner reserves in order to increase the contingencies reserve.

n. *inner-directed* adj. (Sociol.): a term coined by D. Riesman to designate persons whose behaviour and goals are directed by the standards and ideals which they formed early in life; also postulated as a cultural stage in a society. (See quot. 1950.) Cf. **other-directed* and **tradition-directed* adjs. Hence *inner direction.*

1950 D. Riesman et al. *Lonely Crowd* i. 9 The society of transitional population growth develops in its typical members a social character whose conformity is insured by their tendency to acquire early in life an internalized set of goals. These I shall term inner-directed people and the society in which they live a society dependent on inner-direction. *Ibid.* 16 The inner-directed person becomes capable of maintaining a delicate balance between the demands upon him of his life goal and the buffetings of his external environment. **1959** *Spectator* 4 Sept. 307/2 A criticism renewed by sociology—he [*sc.* C. Wilson in *The Age of Defeat*] seems to imply—can help to renew literature by restoring 'the hero', and 'the hero' will re-accredit in real life the image of the 'inner-directed' man. **1959** *Listener* 3 Sept. 363/2 Mr. Wilson discerns a similar awareness of the difference between 'inner-direction' and 'other-direction' in the existentialist writings of Camus and Sartre. **1961** M. Singer in B. Kaplan *Studying Personality* 51 The influence of parents and teachers, so vital in the formation of 'inner-direction', is being superseded by the influence of 'peer-groups' and the mass media. **1964** M. Argyle *Psychol. & Social Probl.* xv. 186 The life of managers is also changing: as in America the inner-directed individualist is being replaced by the other-directed organization man, who fits in easily with the ideas of others, and subordinates his interests to those of the concern. **1968** P. McKellar *Experience & Behaviour* xi. 288 The capacity to 'go it alone' is characteristic of the inner-directed personality. **1972** *Jrnl. Social Psychol.* LXXXVI. 224 Low authoritarian subjects are more inner-directed.

o. *inner space* [after **outer space*]: (*a*) the regions between the surface of the earth and outer space; (*b*) the regions below the surface of the sea; (*c*) [cf. sense 2] the part of one's mind or personality that is not normally experienced or within one's consciousness.

(*a*) **1958** *Times* 29 Mar. 7/4 We seem to need..names for the parts where the atmosphere is still a drag, where the Earth's gravitation is dominant... Tentatively it might be suggested that these be called..inner space. **1966** I. Asimov *Fantastic Voyage* i. 10 We would pile him into an X-52 and rocket him through inner space.

(*b*) **1958** *Times* 7 Oct. 10/3 The Seawolf's [*sc.* a submarine's] captain..had radioed in advance that he considered 'this voyage has proved the feasibility of protracted flights in "inner" space'. **1969** *Sci. Jrnl.* Apr. 64/2 There is a remarkable similarity between many of the problems faced by the astronaut in 'outer space' and those of the aquanaut in 'inner space'.

(*c*) **1958** *Sat. Rev.* (U.S.) 13 Sept. 28/2 Must this inner space continue to be peopled with imaginative dragons of strange color and dropping off places that confine the moral venture to the shallow water of one's own mainland or adjacent islands of narrow self-interest? **1961** 'J. Dunlap' (*title*) Exploring inner space: personal experiences under LSD-25. **1968** A. Diment *Bang Bang Birds* viii. 143 The Indian and Chinese prophets..knew a thing or two about inner space and the turned-on mind. They did it on contemplation though and not mushroom juice. **1969** *Daily Tel.* 20 Feb. 16/7 It is they..who are the investigators of what J. G. Ballard terms 'inner space'—the remoter recesses of man's mind under strange stresses.

p. *inner city*: the central area of a city, esp. regarded as having particular problems of overcrowding, poverty, etc. Also *attrib.* (see sense 6 below). orig. *U.S.*

1968 *Sat. Rev.* (U.S.) 16 Nov. 95 The twin concepts of decentralization and community control of the schools developed in response to the failure of schools in the inner city. **1973** *Black Panther* 17 Mar. 11/1 I'm..interested in getting a little more practical and down to present social policies in the cities, in the inner-cities; the continuing and ever occurring crisis in the inner-cities, where large numbers of people are trapped in a cycle of poverty. **1974** *Times* 19 Jan. 10/2 The problems of the inner city—a work area where almost everyone has gone home.

2. (Further examples.)

1854 Geo. Eliot tr. *Feuerbach's Essence Christianity* i. 2 The inner life of man is the life which has relation to his species. **1860** J. W. Palmer tr. *Michelet's Love* 118 A feeling that the woman's inner self will not be reached, her soul not attained. **1880** W. James *Coll. Ess. & Rev.* (1920) 217 The point of application of the volitional effort always lies within the inner world, being an idea or representation. **1886** Inner self [see *climate *sb.* 3 b]. **1899** W. James *Talks to Teachers* ii. 15 There is a stream, a succession of states, or waves, or fields (or of whatever you please to call them), of knowledge, of feeling, of desire, of deliberation, etc., that constantly pass and repass, and that constitute our inner life. **1902** —— *Varieties Relig. Experience* i. 7 Often they [*sc.* religious leaders] have led a discordant inner life, and had melancholy during a part of their career. **1905** A. Lang *Adv. among Books* 122 She [*sc.* Mrs. Radcliffe] delighted in descriptions of scenery, the more romantic the better, and usually drawn entirely from her inner consciousness. **1915** V. W. Brooks *World of H. G. Wells* v. 106 The force of a work of art does not reside in its 'inner meanings'. **1927** B. Russell *Outl. Philos.* ii. 20 We all have an inner life, open to our own inspection but to no one else's. **1930** *Amer. Jrnl. Psychiatry* 1019 The former is derived from *persona* meaning the essential or inner self. **1944** Auden *For Time Being* (1945) 35 The manifestations of the inner life should always remain so easy and habitual. **1952** Gerth & Martindale tr. *Weber's Anc. Judaism* p. xi, He displayed an inner-worldly, stoic attitude in the face of death. **1953** R. G. Davis *Ten Mod. Masters* p. xiv, Even a fairy-tale or fantasy must have its inner logic. **1971** *Daily Tel.* 6 Aug. 9/7 This is a girl with an intense inner life. **1974** *Listener* 17 Jan. 76/1 Each [Buddhist monk].. inhabits his private inner world, and yet they're in harmony with each other.

b. *inner speech* (*form*): see quots. Also *inner linguistic* (or *language*) *form, inner form.*

[**1885** D. G. Brinton in *Proc. Amer. Philos. Soc.* XXII. iv. 319 Besides the grammatical form of a language, Humboldt recognized another which he called its *internal form.*] **1888** H. A. Strong tr. *Paul's Princ. Hist. Lang.* xx. 460 The influencing force extends merely to what Humboldt and Steinthal have described as the *inner language form* ('innere Sprachform'). *Ibid.* 471 A language suffers influence in its *inner linguistic form* principally in the mouths of those who speak it as a foreign tongue. **1901** H. Oertel *Lect. Study Lang.* i. 64 This is the 'outer speech form', the external, phonetic aspect of the speech symbols. The 'inner speech form' is the definite arrangement of the prelinguistic psychical material into definite groups, the coherence of each group being secured by labelling each with one definite sound-tag. **1930** J. R. Firth *Speech* v. 44 The early discussions on inner speech did not touch the bigger question of the extensive motor accompaniment of thought. **1934** Webster, *Inner speech, Psychol.*, use of words or word images in thinking, without audible or visible speaking. *Ibid.*, *Inner speech form* (trans. of G. *innere Sprachform*, used by Humboldt and Steinthal), the mental concept or image associated with a word prior to its use or upon hearing or reading it, as the concept of a quadruped associated with the word 'animal'; abstractly, the quality by which a word evokes such a mental picture. **1970** H. C. Shands *Semiotic Approaches to Psychiatry* 10 Inner speech systems are constructed throughout the developmental period in human beings.

3. Also, *the inner woman.*

1857 Trollope *Barchester T.* III. x. 184 She ate and drank, and as the inner woman was recruited she felt a little more charitable. **1858** Hawthorne *Passages from Fr. & It. Note-Bks.* (1871) I. 190 To behave as her inner woman prompts. **1892** *Gentlewoman's Bk. Sports* I. 44 After refreshing the inner woman, I was all for trying the Sandhills again.

6. Various phrases used *attrib.*

1908 *Daily Chron.* 22 Jan. 3/3 You may browse at will among the epistles or the notes, feeling that you are always with informed, inner-circle folk. **1909** *Westm. Gaz.* 14 Apr. 10/2 What colour of glass must be used for the front door and inner-court doors? **1927** J. Adams *Errors in School* 32 An idea does not merely mean the inner-world equivalent of an outside object. **1953** C. E. Bazell *Ling. Form* 57 The rare cases of inner-verbal sequence-relevance may be dealt with analogously. **1957** C. Hunt *Guide to Communist Jargon* xxv. 88 According to the *Political Dictionary*, inner-party democracy is the consistent application of the principles of 'democratic centralism', though, to be more accurate, it stands for its democratic as opposed to its dominant centralized aspect. **1960** H. Edwards *Spirit Healing* vii. 63 Spiritual healers have long known that the origin of organic diseases most often lay in inner-self disharmonies. **1961** *Observer* 8 Oct. 10/3 It is doubtful if Mr. Gaitskell himself had thought through the problem of inner-party democracy. **1964** F. Bowers *Bibliogr. & Textual Crit.* iv. ii. 112 Any separate small pile of inner-forme sheets. **1968** *Sun* (Baltimore) 4 July A.16/3 A possible explanation of the inner-city language superiority (which had disappeared by the third grade) was, Mrs. Entwisle thought, the unrestricted time which small inner-city children spend in front of television sets. **1970** *New York* 16 Nov. 42/2 From here the city spreads in a wheel-spoke design through seven inner-city black neighborhoods. **1971** *Guardian* 26 Feb. 6/8 Camden's housing problems have often been in the spotlight for revealing inner-city trends. **1972** *Ibid.* 5 Jan. 5/2 The solution to the problem of the inner city child eludes us.

innerly, *adv.* Add: **1.** (Examples from D. H. Lawrence.)

1917 D. H. Lawrence *Look! We have come Through!* 50, I have been so innerly proud, and so long alone, Do not leave me, or I shall break. **1923** —— *Ladybird* 81 If you are true to me, innerly, innerly true, he will not hurt us.

innervation. Add: Also, the supply of nerve fibres to, or disposition of nerve fibres within, an organ or part. (Further examples.)

1879 *Jrnl. Physiol.* II. 342 More recently Severini, in his able monograph on the innervation of the blood-vessels, has laid great weight on the contractility of the capillaries. **1908** *Westm. Gaz.* 8 July 2/1 It has been found that the density of the cutaneous innervation—i.e., the number of sensitive nerve terminations in the unit of surface—is greater in small animals than in large. **1910** *Jrnl. R. Microsc. Soc.* 154 Innervation of tympanum.—Agostino Gemelli describes..the tympanal ramifications (1) of the auriculo-temporal branch of the trigeminal, and (2) of the nerve of Jacobson. **1945** *Amer. Jrnl. Physiol.* CXLIV. 477 It is tacitly assumed that if part of the innervation of a muscle is permanently destroyed, the remaining motor units..continue their normal function. **1967** Gardner & Osburn *Struct. Human Body* iv. 121/2 The nerve supply to a muscle is referred to as its innervation.

2. *Psychol.* = Kinæsthesis.

1880 W. James in *Anniversary Mem. Boston Soc. Nat. Hist.* 4 Wundt..adopts the term *Innervationsgefühl* to designate the former [*sc.* the feeling of force exerted] in relation to its supposed cause, the efferent discharge. Feelings of innervation have since then become household words in psychological literature. **1898** G. F. Stout *Man. Psychol.* I. ii. vi. 192 According to Bain, there is a direct sense of energy put forth which is independent of any results the putting forth of energy may produce. This peculiar modification of sensory consciousness has been called the sense of effort, or the innervation-sense. **1904** E. B. Titchener tr. *Wundt's Princ. Physiol. Psychol.* iii. 57 (*heading*) General principles and problems of a mechanics of innervation. **1924** J. Riviere et al. tr. *Freud's Coll. Papers* I. 63 The conversion may be either total or partial, and it proceeds along the line of the motor or sensory innervation that is more or less intimately related to the traumatic experience. **1953** Hinsie & Shatzky *Psychiatric Dict.* (ed. 2) 667/1 The expressive innervations are involuntary, even though they can be influenced, up to a point, by volition.

inning, *vbl. sb.* Add: **4.** (Earlier and later examples in Cricket and Baseball.)

1735 in H. T. Waghorn *Cricket Scores* (1899) 10 London ..got 67 notches the first innings. **1856** *Spirit of Times* 6 Dec. 229/1 After the first inning is played, the turn commences at the player who stands next to the one on the list who lost the third hand. **1955** *Times* 9 May 15/2 Afterwards he played the sort of innings that not surprisingly drives some spectators to distraction. **1968** *Washington Post* 4 July C1/7 The righthanded sinkerballer faced his greatest challenge in the sixth inning.

b. (Earlier example.)

1836 Dickens *Pickw.* (1837) xxiii. 238 It's my innings now, gov'rnor, and as soon as I catches hold o' this here Trotter, I'll have a good 'un.

Inniskilling (iniski·liŋ). Also **Enniskillen, Enniskilling, Inniskellen, Inniskillen.** The

name of the county town of Fermanagh in Northern Ireland, used *attrib.* or *absol.* to designate a regiment originally raised for the defence of that town in 1689. So **Inniski·lliner,** a member of this regiment.

[**1690** A. HAMILTON (*title*) A true relation of the actions of the Inniskillingmen, from their first taking up of arms in December, 1688 for the defence of the Protestant religion, and their lives and liberties.] **1715** in E. S. Jackson *Inniskilling Dragoons* (1909) ii. 35 A detachment of Greys and Inniskillings arrived in Edinburgh from Stirling. **1797** *Encycl. Brit.* IX. 243/2 Its [*sc.* Inniskilling's] inhabitants distinguished themselves..in the wars of Ireland at the revolution, out of which a regiment of dragoons, bearing the title of the *Inniskilleners*, was mostly formed. They form the 6th regiment of dragoons in the British Army. **1817** G. JONES *Battle of Waterloo* II. 55 The second heavy brigade of cavalry..consisted of.. the 6th, or Inniskillings. **1822** M. EDGEWORTH *Let.* 11 Feb. (1971) 347 Will you inquire for Wilkie what is put on the caps of the Inniskellen 6th Dragoons... If you know of any Dragoon that would be better than the Inniskillen tell me. **1853** J. H. STOCQUELER *Mil. Encycl.* 141/1 *Inniskilliners*, the officers and soldiers of the 6th dragoons and the 27th foot are so called, from the two regiments having been originally raised at Inniskilling, a town of Ulster. **1893** J. C. ROPES *Campaign of Waterloo* xvi. 300 In rear of the left wing..stood the Union brigade..composed of the Royal Dragoons, the Scots Greys, and the Inniskilling Dragoons. **1968** *Encycl. Brit.* IX. 185/1 At Newtownbutler, in 1689, the Protestant Enniskillen men severely defeated a superior Roman Catholic army of James II and began the victorious tradition of the 'Inniskillings', now represented in the British Army by the Royal Inniskilling Fusiliers and the 5th Royal Inniskilling Dragoon Guards. **1971** G. BLAXLAND *Regiments Depart* vi. 204 The previous December..the Inniskilling Dragoon Guards were relieved by the 1st Royal Tank Regiment.

innit, vulg. form of *isn't it.*

1959 M. GILBERT *Blood & Judgment* i. 17 That's right, innit? **1962** N. MARSH *Hand in Glove* iv. 105 Dead right, innit? **1965** *Guardian* 3 Apr. 6/3 It's some place to go innit? **1973** J. WAINWRIGHT *Touch of Malice* 56 That's a bloody good reason, innit?

innocence. 6. (Examples.)

1821 W. P. C. BARTON *Flora N. Amer.* I. 119 Fairy-flax-Bluett. Innocence. Venus' Pride. **1863** *Rep. Comm. Agric. 1862* (U.S. Dept. Agric.) 159 The 'Bluets', 'Innocence', 'Dwarf Pink', with, perhaps, some other common name, is one of the prettiest ornaments of our spring meadows. **1892** *Jrnl. Amer. Folk-Lore* V. 97 *Houstonia cærulea*, innocence. Boston, Mass. **1954** C. J. HYLANDER *Macmillan Wild Flower Bk.* 389 This familiar wild flower, also known as Innocence and Quaker-ladies, is a tufted or matted plant.

innocent, *a.* Add: **2.** *innocent party* [PARTY *sb.* 11], in matrimonial proceedings, the person adjudged to be innocent.

Since the Divorce Reform Act 1969 the usage has been legally obsolete in England, since that Act abolished the concept of a matrimonial offence as a ground for divorce and substituted for it the concept of irretrievable breakdown of the marriage.

1729 G. JACOB *New Law-Dict., Divorce*: In Divorces for Adultery, several Acts of Parliament have allowed the Innocent Party to marry again. **1835** *Tomlins's Law Dict.* (ed. 4) I. (s.v. Divorce), The commissioners appointed by Henry VIII. and Edward VI...recommend divorces *à mensa et thoro* to be abolished, and complete divorces to be allowed for adultery, desertion, bad treatment, &c., the innocent party to be allowed to marry again. **1948** J. H. S. BOSSARD *Sociol. of Child Devel.* xvi. 369 One principle usually observed is that custody goes to the so-called innocent party. **1958** *Daily Mail* 3 July 4/8 When are we going to hear the last of that time-worn phrase so beloved of newspaper columnists and the legal profession—'innocent party'? **1959** JOWITT *Dict. Eng. Law* I. 67/2 The Matrimonial Causes Act, 1857..created a Court for Divorce and Matrimonial Causes..which would grant to the innocent party a divorce *a mensa et thoro* on the ground of the other's adultery.

5. b. *innocent conveyance*, a conveyance which does not have any tortious operation, one which does not create a discontinuance or result in forfeiture.

All conveyances are now innocent by statute in England and in the United States.

1811 E. B. SUGDEN *Gilbert's Law of Uses & Trusts* (ed. 3) 232 A conveyance by lease and release is like a bargain and sale, and covenant to stand seised what is termed an innocent conveyance. **1841** H. J. STEPHEN *New Comm. Laws Eng.* I. 508 The other conveyances can, in their nature, pass no more than the grantor might lawfully transfer. For this reason, they have received, by way of distinction from a feoffment, (and others now abolished of the like nature,) the appellation of *innocent* conveyances. **1848** WHARTON *Law Lexicon* 322/2 *Innocent conveyances*, a covenant to stand seised, a bargain and sale, and release, so called, because since they convey the actual possession by construction of law only, they do not confer a larger estate in property than the person conveying possesses. **1937** W. S. HOLDSWORTH *Hist. Eng. Law* VII. 357 Both a bargain and sale and a covenant to stand seised were, unlike a feoffment, 'innocent' conveyances.

6. (Further examples.)

1799 MALTHUS *Diary* 30 June (1966) 108 He was a remarkably meek & innocent looking man. **1860** F. & J. GREENWOOD *Under Cloud* III. xiv. 307 The jovial, innocent-hearted actor. **1895** A. W. PINERO *Second Mrs. Tanqueray* I. 42 Paula..is..beautiful, fresh, innocent-looking. **1925** BLUNDEN *Eng. Poems* 19 So innocent-gay was her look. **1955** E. BOWEN *World of Love* xi. 212 Banks were innocent-blue with scabious. **1959** J. L. AUSTIN *Sense & Sensibilia* (1962) i. 4 In philosophy it is often good policy, where one member of a putative pair falls under suspicion, to view the more innocent-seeming party suspiciously as well. **1962** Y. OLSSON in F. Behre *Contrib. Eng. Syntax* 87 Like innocent-looking people, even the most innocent-looking personal pronouns are deeper than one would be led to believe.

in nomine: see *IN *Lat. prep.*

innovate, *v.* **2.** Delete † *Obs.* and add later *Comm.* examples.

1967 *Times Rev. Industry* Oct. 86/2 Nylon..was first invented in 1928, but not innovated until 1939. **1972** *Physics Bull.* Feb. 67/1 (Advt.), We've been innovating electrometer values like these for over 20 years.

3. *spec.* in *Comm.* (Later examples.)

1965 *New Statesman* 9 Apr. 561/1 There is a willing market to offset a more reluctant British industry, whose failure to innovate fast enough has certainly made the British computer industry less competitive. **1971** *Physics Bull.* Dec. 707/2 The view has been put forward that the very large firms, the dinosaurs of the 20th century, do not truly innovate and, indeed, may hinder innovation because they are so inflexible.

innovating *ppl. a.* (later examples).

1972 C. LAYTON *Ten Innovations* I. i. 7 Study is needed of other possible tax incentives for small innovating enterprises. *Ibid.* 12 The small innovating firm crosses a whole series of thresholds as it grows in size.

innovation. Add: **5.** *Comm.* The action of introducing a new product into the market; a product newly brought on to the market.

1939 J. A. SCHUMPETER *Business Cycles* I. iii. 84 Innovation is possible without anything we should identify as invention, and invention does not necessarily induce innovation. **1958** J. JEWKES et al. *Sources Invention* ix. 249 It seems impossible to establish scientifically any final conclusion concerning the relation between monopoly and innovation. **1962** E. M. ROGERS *Diffusion of Innovations* v. 124 It matters little whether or not an innovation has a great degree of advantage over the idea it is replacing. What does matter is whether the individual perceives the relative advantage of the innovation. **1967** J. A. ALLEN *Sci. Innovation & Industr. Prosperity* ii. 8 Innovation is the bringing of an invention into widespread, practical use...Invention may thus be construed as the first stage of the much more extensive and complex total process of innovation.

6. Innovation trunk, a kind of wardrobe trunk.

1912 *Bag, Portmanteau & Umbrella Trader* 20 Nov. 18/1 The Innovation Trunk Company..makes a striking show of wardrobe trunks. They also specialise in the refitting of ordinary wardrobes according to their principle. **1913** A. BENNETT *Regent* iii. 83 Many parcels and boxes, comprising diverse items in the equipment of a man-about-town, such as tie-clips and Innovation trunks. **1915** E. PHILLPOTTS *Angel in House* I. 17 Robert and Manservant enter through the main entrance carrying Innovation trunk.

innovational *a.*, also in *Comm.*

1959 J. P. LEWIS *Business Conditions Analysis* v. xxiv. 534 The insights of economics do not illuminate the process of innovation very much... On the optimistic side of the innovational outlook, it can be argued, [etc.]. **1960** L. S. SILK *Research Revolution* iii. 50 In the past, the United States has had three great innovational pushes.

innovative, *a.* Add: (Later examples.) *spec.* in *Comm.* in sense of *INNOVATION 5.

1970 N. ARMSTRONG et al. *First on Moon* i. 20 The Air Force..sounded more exciting and more innovative. **1971** *Sci. Amer.* Mar. 14 His division is now involved with ..innovative building processes and systems. **1971** *Times* 6 Sept. 12 (Advt.), Well-known American company is introducing an innovative line of electro-optical measurement systems into the European Machine Tool and Metal Working industries. **1972** *Lebende Sprachen* XVII. 72/2 In order to release scarce manpower for the later phases of the innovative process, including marketing.

Hence **i·nnovatively** *adv.*, in an innovative manner; involving innovation; **i·nnovativeness.**

1962 E. M. ROGERS *Diffusion of Innovations* vii. 195 The innovativeness continuum may be divided into adopter categories. *Ibid.* x. 285 The present chapter is an attempt to demonstrate two means of predicting innovativeness. **1971** *Bull. Amer. Assoc. Univ. Professors* Sept. 337 My other two innovatively run courses..are seemingly as successful as courses could be. **1973** *Black World* Mar. 23 The conventions of folk music might be employed in the traditional manner..or innovatively, as is Miss Brooks' 'The Sermon on the Warpland'.

innovatory, *a.* (Later examples.)

1965 *Listener* 23 Sept. 464/1 In these with-it days of innovatory cinematic trends. **1967** J. A. ALLEN *Sci. Innovation & Industr. Prosperity* ii. 25 There has been little deliberate innovatory effort over a long period. **1971** *Nature* 2 Apr. 301/3 Historians have been so impressed by the innovatory nature of modern science. **1972** *Physics Bull.* Mar. 151/2 Remembering that the major innovatory phase took place before 1939, most of this gain has resulted from sustained research and development by physicists.

in nuce: see *IN *Lat. prep.*

Innuit (i·nuit). Also **Inuit.** [ad. Inupik Eskimo *inuit* people, pl. of *inuk* man.] An Eskimo; the Eskimos collectively. Also *attrib.* or as *adj.*

1765 C. DRACHARD in *Ethnohistory* (1972) XIX. 136 They [*sc.* the Labrador Eskimos] also by way of eminence in contra-distinction to the Europeans call themselves Innuit (the Men). **1774** B. LA TROBE *Brief Acct. Mission Esquimaux Indians Labrador* 10 Formerly, they..looked upon the Europeans as upon dogs, giving them the appellation, Kablunets, that is, Barbarians, but called themselves Innuit, which signifies men. **1850** [see *ESKIMO *sb.* 1]. **1860** MAYNE REID *Odd People* 88 They [*sc.* the Esquimaux] generally call themselves 'Inuit' (pronounced enn-oo-eet), a word which signifies 'men'. **1864** *Spectator* 31 Dec. 1506 The Innuits believe in a supreme Being called Anguta, whose daughter Sidne is the creator and the tutelary deity of the Innuit people. **1864** C. F. HALL *Life with Esquimaux* I. 122 A highly-intelligent Innuit.. was boat-steerer. **1895** [see *ESKIMO *sb.* 1]. **1903** J. LONDON *People of Abyss* xxvii. 313 In Alaska, along the banks of the Yukon River, near its mouth, live the Innuit folk. **1919** W. T. GRENFELL *Labrador Doctor* (1920) vii. 140 With the influx of white settlers from Devon and Dorset, Scotland and France the 'Innuits' were driven farther and farther north. **1963** *North* (Ottawa) May–June 34 Without us the Innuit go hungry. **1973** *Sci. Amer.* Sept. 196/3 Nearly 400 sculptors of quality are represented here from the *inuit.*

innumeracy (iniū·mĕrăsi). [f. IN-[3] + *NUMERACY.] The quality or state of being innumerate.

1959 *15 to 18: Rep. Cent. Advisory Council for Educ. (Eng.)* (Ministry of Educ.) I. xxv. 271 If his numeracy has stopped short at the usual Fifth Form level, he is in danger of relapsing into innumeracy. **1960** *Times Rev. Industry* June 59/3 Handicap on British business was the 'innumeracy' of the population. **1965** *New Scientist* 5 Aug. 348/1 The word 'innumeracy', to describe an intellectual disability in regard to mathematics (and, by reference, to science) has become one of the vogue words of our time. **1970** *Daily Tel.* 22 Dec. 8 Lord Snow was complaining a decade ago about the vice of innumeracy.

innumerate (iniū·mĕrĕt), *a.* and *sb.* [f. IN-[3] + *NUMERATE *a.*] **A.** *adj.* Unacquainted with the basic principles and ideas of mathematics and science.

1959 *15 to 18: Rep. Cent. Advisory Council for Educ (Eng.)* (Ministry of Educ.) I. xxv. 270 When we say that a historian or a linguist is 'innumerate' we mean that he cannot even begin to understand what scientists and mathematicians are talking about. **1967** *Times Rev. Industry* June 108/3 'Why are so many of us innumerate?' asked Lord Annan... The answer..was quite simple. For years, girls and boys have given up maths at 15 or 16, thus maiming themselves intellectually. **1969** *Physics Bull.* Sept. 383/2 In this short book, intended for the general reader (though not for the innumerate one), a distinguished engineer describes how computers work. **1971** *Daily Tel.* 13 Oct. 2/7 It alleges that one student in every four entering colleges has had no sixth form experience, and that up to one-fifth are 'practically innumerate'.

B. *sb.* One who is innumerate; freq. (with *the*) in *pl.* sense.

1971 *Daily Tel.* 1 Feb. 15 The old gibe that 'you can prove anything with figures' is perhaps not heard so frequently now. It was the classic defence of the innumerate. **1971** *Nature* 2 Apr. 306/1 The conflict is between the technological and the humane, and derives from various related sources: first, the fable that educational research can be a science as pure as classical physics..and finally the innumerate's fascination with statistics. **1972** *Ibid.* 10 Mar. 55/1 At the other extreme stand the recalcitrant innumerate, proclaiming themselves the last defenders of humanism.

innutritious, *a.* Add: Also *transf.*

1905 *Sydney Morning Herald* 15 Feb. 4/6 The..teacher is offered for his mental food these innutritious products as the bread of life. **1916** E. V. LUCAS *Vermilion Box* cxxv. 141 As a rule I have found that the soldier who sits opposite one on railway journeys is an innutritious person, whether he has been to the front or not.

inoculant (inǫ·kiŭlănt). [f. INOCUL(ATE *v.* + -ANT[1].] A substance suitable for use in inoculation; *spec.* in *Metallurgy*, a substance with which molten metal is inoculated.

1911 *Experiment Station Rec.* XLVII. III. 234 State laws concerning the sale of seeds and legume inoculants. **1944** *Jrnl. Iron & Steel Inst.* CL. 144A The second purpose was to measure the effect of increasing-percentages of steel and varying amounts of inoculants. **1960** *Ibid.* CXCV. 222/1 The use of graphitizing inoculants, usually based on silicides, is described. **1962** A. G. GUY *Physical Metall. for Engineers* v. 149 Typical inoculants are ferrosilicon and calcium-silicon, very small amounts of which are effective in reducing flake size.

inoculate, *v.* Add: **3.** For 'a person' read 'an individual' and add to def.: To introduce (cells or organisms to be cultured) *into* a culture medium or its container. (Further examples.)

1928 L. E. H. WHITBY *Med. Bacteriol.* iii. 46 The loop or needle must be sterilized in the flame before being charged with the material to be inoculated. **1939** K. L. BURDON *Med. Microbiol.* xx. 273 At this temperature it [*sc.* agar] is still liquid and yet cool enough so that the organisms to be inoculated will not be killed by its heat. **1964** WHEELER & VOLK *Basic Microbiol.* viii. 89/1 The pour-plate method consists of inoculating the mixed culture into a test tube containing melted agar. **1970** PASSMORE & ROBSON *Compan. Med. Stud.* II. xviii. 50/1 When bacteria are

inoculated into a fresh fluid medium there is little or no increase in their number for a period.

b. Add to def.: To introduce infective material into (a plant) or cells or organisms for culture into (a culture medium or a vessel containing one). (Further examples.)

1886 H. M. Biggs tr. *Hueppe's Methods Bacteriol. Investigation* iv. 171 It [*sc.* the nutrient solution] is then inoculated with a few drops of the mixture of bacteria to be tested. **1920** E. F. Smith *Introd. Bacterial Dis. Plants* II. 112 In studying a particular disease, the student will.. seek to inoculate those parts of the plant which naturally develop the disease. **1925** [see *INOCULUM]. **1933** K. M. Smith *Rec. Adv. Study Plant Viruses* viii. 196 The plant tissue is macerated..and then rubbed over the foliage to be inoculated by means of the swab. **1956** *Nature* 18 Feb. 302/2 When White Burley tobacco seedlings in a glass-house are inoculated with the virus from cowpea..they become systemically infected. **1962** F. J. Baker *Handbk. Bacteriol. Technique* v. 56 When inoculating broth tubes, care must be taken not to spill the contents.

4. *Metallurgy.* To add a small quantity of some substance to (metal, esp. iron, about to be poured) in order to produce a smaller grain size or otherwise to modify the micro-structure of the cast metal.

1931 *Proc. Inst. Brit. Foundrymen* XXIII. 96 Small grain-size and high density can be..achieved by 'dosing' or inoculating the alloy so that prior to the main solidification taking place the alloy contains numerous evenly and finely-dispersed nuclei to form centres of crystallisation. **1933** *Jrnl. Iron & Steel Inst.* CXXXVIII. 640 A bath of iron which would normally cast white is prepared and is 'inoculated', by the addition of suitable proportions of nickel and silicon, to cause graphitisation. **1963** C. H. Samans *Metallic Materials Engin.* vi. 316 When it is desired to improve the structure of the cast iron and, consequently, its mechanical properties, the metal often is inoculated just before pouring. **1971** *Daily Tel.* 4 Nov. 5 (Advt.), Semi-continuous casting is standard practice in the [aluminium] industry and, unless the melt is inoculated or grain-refined to produce a fine-grained equiaxed structure, the process has an inherent tendency to grow massive columnar crystals.

inoculated, *ppl. a.* Add: **3.** *Metallurgy.* Applied to cast iron whose properties have been improved by inoculation.

1932 *Proc. Inst. Brit. Foundrymen* XXIV. 137 What the author says about the germ theory and inoculated irons is exceedingly interesting. **1956** *Jrnl. Iron & Steel Inst.* CLXXXIV. 89/2 The inoculated cast irons are more elastic, they have smaller damping capacities, and their electrical and magnetic properties are close to those of steels.

inoculation. Add: **2. b.** Also, the (usually intended) introduction of infective material into a plant or of cells or organisms to be cultured into a culture medium. (Further examples.)

1886 H. M. Biggs tr. *Hueppe's Methods Bacteriol. Investigation* iv. 160 Inoculations are made by picking out, with a platinum needle..a particle from a pure culture.. and introducing it quickly into the solution. **1910** Hiss & Zinsser *Text-bk. Bacteriol.* viii. 141 For the inoculation of solid media and the making of stab cultures, a straight 'needle' or wire should be used. **1920** E. F. Smith *Introd. Bacterial Dis. Plants* III. iii. 165 The inoculations may be made by spraying or by touching the leaf-tip with an infected platinum needle. **1933** K. M. Smith *Rec. Adv. Study Plant Viruses* viii. 194 The second method of artificial virus transmission is that of inoculation, using this term in its restricted sense of actual application of the virus-containing sap to the plant tissue. **1958** Pelczar & Reid *Microbiol.* viii. 81/1 After inoculation of the media.. and following a suitable period of incubation, it is possible to determine the cultural characteristics of the organism being studied.

2*. *Metallurgy.* The addition of an inoculant to molten metal, esp. iron (see *INOCULATE *v.* 4).

1932 *Proc. Inst. Brit. Foundrymen* XXIV. 122 After remelting the graphite particles were restored artificially, when the metal solidified pearlite-flake graphite. The process of putting graphite back into the melt is conveniently referred to as 'inoculation'. **1950** *Jrnl. Iron & Steel Inst.* CLXVI. 260/1 D. J. Reese gave some details of the production and properties of nodular cast iron produced in the U.S.A., using the technique of magnesium inoculation. **1963** B. Harocopos *Princ. Struct. Metall.* viii. 104 The graphite may also be made to appear as spheroids in a ferritic matrix by inoculation with an alloy of silicon, magnesium and zirconium..and the resulting iron has a U.T.S. of 32 t.s.i., elongation 15%, in the annealed state. **1968** E. N. Simons *Outl. Metall.* iv. 88 In the inoculation of cast iron in Britain calcium silicide is added to the ladle or the cupola spout at the rate of about 120 oz./ton.

inoculist. (Earlier U.S. example.)

1776 in *Narragansett Hist. Reg.* (1886–7) V. 352 Practitioners and Inoculists may be served with them [*sc.* medicines], if applied for soon.

inoculum (inǫ·kiŭlǒm). Pl. **inocula.** [mod.L., f. L. *inoculāre* to Inoculate *v.*] (A quantity of) infective material used for or capable of inoculating an organism or culture medium.

1902 J. W. H. Eyre *Elem. Bacteriol. Technique* xv. 267 (*heading*) The preparation of the inoculum. **1925** C. H. Browning *Bacteriol.* iii. 47 The needle, charged with the inoculum, is introduced into the tube and..the broth..is now said to have been 'inoculated'. **1949** N. G. Heatley in H. W. Florey et al. *Antibiotics* I. iv. 212 The reason why small inocula (down to single cells) do not normally grow out was thought to be due to the inhibitory power of a number of substances. **1950** J. C. Walker *Plant Path.* viii. 347 Since the fungi overwinter on debris, sanitary measures are helpful in reducing spring inoculum. **1970** W. H. Smith *Tree Path.* xxiii. 243 Early in an epidemic.. the absolute rate of increase of disease is small,..as only a limited quantity of inoculum is available. **1973** *Nature* 16 Feb. 456/1 It is highly tumorigenic (inocula of 10^2 cells produce fatal tumours in the animals).

inodorous, *a.* Add: **b.** [In-³.] Malodorous; having an unpleasant smell. Also *fig.* or *transf.*

1823 *Reading Mercury* in *Spirit of Public Jrnls. M.DCCC.XXIII* (1825) 206 The smell at this time was certainly somewhat inodorous, and was like almost any thing but a nosegay. **1858** *Sat. Rev.* 27 Mar. 308/1 Cerements in inodorous fallacies, he has gone to corrupt amid old arithmetical dross and the rotting refuse of deceased paradoxes. **1861** C. M. Yonge *Young Step-Mother* viii. 98 Brown, inodorous materials for petticoats, blouses, and trowsers.

inoperancy (inǫ·pərănsi). *rare*⁻¹. [f. In-³ + Operancy.] Failure to operate or function.

1936 T. S. Eliot *Coll. Poems 1909–1935* 189 Evacuation of the world of fancy, Inoperancy of the world of spirit.

inoperculate, *a.* **2.** *Bot.* Of an ascus or sporangium: lacking an operculum and therefore opening by splitting. Also as *sb.*, a fungus having this characteristic.

1879 W. Phillips tr. E. Boudier in *Trans. Woolhope Naturalists' Field Club* (1887) 202 The second [section of the family] I would call *Inoperculate Discomycetes*, or simply *Inoperculæ*, because the exit of the sporidia takes place by a small hole, formed at the extreme summit of the asci, with its margin more or less elevated, but without any appearance of an operculum. **1913** *Trans. Brit. Mycol. Soc.* IV. 402 In the inoperculate species, the spores have a tendency to septation. **1929** *Trans. Brit. Mycol. Soc.* XIV. 267 The epithecium, overlying the hymenium ..occurs in several inoperculate genera. **1943** *Mycologia* XXXV. 585 The outstanding characters of this Panamanian discomycete are unlike those of any of the stromatic inoperculates. **1950** E. A. Bessey *Morphol. & Taxon. Fungi* iii. 45 In this order [*sc.* Chytridiales] the zoospores or motile gametes escape through an exit papilla or tube whose apex softens and permits the motile cells to push out (the inoperculate series), or they escape through a sort of cap that opens like a trap door, the so-called operculum (the operculate series). **1970** J. Webster *Introd. Fungi* i. 25 In the inoperculate chytrids..the sporangium forms a discharge tube which penetrates to the exterior of the host cell.

inordinacy. (Later example.)

1943 C. Brogan *Who are 'The People'?* xi. 119 It is merely another instance of inordinacy.

inordinancy. For † *Obs.* read *rare.* Add earlier and later examples.

a **1617** P. Baynes *Christian Lett.* (1620) sig. N7ᵛ, No such inordinancy of griefe. **1955** R. Niebuhr *Self & Dramas of Hist.* (1956) 29 Hobbes..could regard the..reason ..as the cause of the inordinancy of human ambitions.

inordination. Delete † *Obs.* and add later example.

1883 G. M. Hopkins *Sermons & Devotional Writings* (1959) 133 The inordination, ugliness of sin in the frame and world of Creator and creature.

inorganic, *a.* Add: **B.** *sb.* An inorganic chemical.

1945 *Chem. & Engin. News* 10 Jan. 103 We offer: inorganics—gallium, germanium, indium metals & salts in quantity. **1968** *New Scientist* 23 May 391/1 The production of inorganics was complemented by the equally distinct manufacture of organic chemicals. **1971** *Nature* 31 Dec. 515/1 Plastics increased in volume by 16·8 per cent a year; basic organics by 13·7 per cent and inorganics by 6·1 per cent.

inositol (inōᵘ·sitǫl). *Biochem.* [f. Inosit(e + -ol.] Modern name of Inosite: any of the nine stereoisomers of hexahydroxycyclohexane, $(CHOH)_6$; *spec.* that isomer (also called *meso-inositol* or *myoinositol*) which is a member of the vitamin B complex, occurs in many animal organs esp. muscle and (often as its hexaphosphate) in plant leaves and seeds, and promotes the growth of bacteria and yeasts.

1891 Roscoe & Schorlemmer *Treat. Chem.* (new ed.) III. 214 Inositol forms large transparent monosymmetric crystals, which possess a sweet taste and are soluble..in about 6 parts of water, yielding an optically inactive solution. **1936** A. P. Mathews *Princ. Biochem.* v. 69 Inositol is found in wheat bran and in many vegetables, where it occurs often in the form of 'phytin', which is the hexa-phosphoric acid-ester of inositol. **1941** *Jrnl. Biol. Chem.* CXL. 465 The ability of substances related to mesoinositol to replace this compound in the nutrition of the mouse and of yeast has been examined. It was found that *d*-inositol, *l*-inositol..[etc.] were inactive for both species. **1948** *Adv. Carbohydrate Chem.* iii. 45 The comparative rarity of the other inositols has justified the general retention of the name inositol to denote *meso*-inositol. **1954** Cantarow & Schepartz *Biochem.* vi. 214 No manifestations attributable to inositol deficiency have been recognized in man. This may be due, in part at least, to its synthesis by intestinal bacteria. **1970** R. W. McGilvery *Biochem.* xxiv. 599 Phosphatidylinositides are compounds containing residues of inositol, a structural isomer of glucose that can be made from glucose-6-phosphate as inositol-1-phosphate.

inotropic (əin-, inotrōᵘ·pik, -trǫ·pik), *a.* *Physiol.* [ad. G. *inotrop* (T. W. Engelmann 1896, in *Arch. f. ges. Physiol.* LXII. 555): see Ino- and *-tropic.] Modifying the contractility of muscle.

1903 *Sci. Amer. Suppl.* 4 July 22992/3 The author describes..as inotropic such [influences] as lessen or destroy contractibility. **1971** *Nature* 25 June 531/1 An automated system for monitoring both the chronotropic and inotropic effects of chemical and physical agents.

So **ino·tropism,** modification of the contractility of muscle.

1902 [see *dromotropic *a.*]. **1971** *Nature* 25 June 531/1 Although inotropism is defined as a change in force, by measuring changes in optical density, we can measure indirectly the relative elongation and contraction of the cells during each contraction cycle.

in pari materia: see *in *Lat. prep.* 21.

in pectore: see *in *Lat. prep.*

in-people: see *in *a.* 2.

in-person *attrib.*: see *in *prep.* 17*.

in petto: see Petto.

in-phase (stress variable), *attrib. phr. Electr.* [f. phr. *in phase* (phase *sb.* 3).] That is in phase; of or pertaining to signals that are in phase.

1914 H. Pender *Amer. Handbk. Electr. Engineers* 1297 The active or in-phase component of the current in a circuit is that component which is in phase with the voltage across the circuit. **1940** *Amat. Radio Handbk.* (ed. 2) xii. 186/1 Besides the desired equal and opposite currents in the two wires, there are two more in-phase currents flowing in the parallel circuit. **1962** A. Nisbett *Technique Sound Studio* 264 If a monophonic signal is fed to an in-phase pair [of loudspeakers] the sound will appear to come from between and behind them. **1968** *Brit. Med. Bull.* XXIV. 253/2 Special techniques, such as in-phase rejection,..were adopted in its design to overcome interference from extraneous voltages.

in-pig (in,pi·g), *a.* [attrib. use of phrase *in pig:* see In *prep.* 10 b.] Of a sow: that is in pig; pregnant. Cf. In-calf *a.*, *in-foal *a.*

1950 *Farming* June 179 In-pig sows can of course receive a proportion of their ration as bulky food. **1959** *Times* 31 Aug. 5/3 For the first time since the..national in-pig and litter tests began..the three major awards.. have been won by the same sow. **1969** *Times* 6 Jan. 7/7 The December sample figures for England and Wales indicate a slight cutback south of the Border since September in in-pig gilts, but the number of sows in pig is still rising. **1974** *Listener* 21 Mar. 334/2 Philip had just lost all his pigs from swine vesicular disease, and was meditating buying in-pig gilts and starting again.

in-pile, in-plant, in-process *attrib.*: see *in *prep.* 17*.

in potentia: see Potentia (in Dict. and Suppl.).

in propria persona: see *in *Lat. prep.*

input, *sb.* Restrict *Sc.* to sense in Dict. and add: **2. a.** That which is put in or taken in, or which is operated on or utilized by any process or system (either material or abstract).

1893 *Phil. Trans. R. Soc.* B. CLXXXIII. 228 The pressure in the large systemic veins becomes raised during vagus action, because the quantity of blood which passes from them into the right ventricle (which we may refer to as the 'input' of the heart), in a given time, is diminished. **1929** *Prosp. Mona Copper Co.* 6 With Copper at £70 per ton on the basis of an input of 600 tons daily..a gross annual profit of about £100,000 could be expected. **1966** T. Lupton *Managem. & Social Sci.* iv. 88 To Rice..an organization is an 'open system'. It takes in inputs from the environment, converts them, and sends outputs back into the environment. **1971** *Sci. Amer.* Sept. 111/1 These carcasses are retrieved in the spring, and the meat is considered one of the more flavorsome food inputs. **1971** J. B. Carroll et al. *Word Frequency Bk.* p. vi, The Corpus is drawn from written, and edited, published materials. There is no direct oral input.

b. Energy supplied to a device or system; *spec.* an electrical signal that enters an electronic device.

1902 *Encycl. Brit.* XXVII. 574/2 The useful return or 'output' at the terminals of a large machine may amount to as much as 95 per cent. of the mechanical energy which forms the 'input'. **1931** *Daily Express* 21 Sept. 7/4 An advanced form of band-pass tuning, providing a special selector circuit between the input from the aerial and the first valve of the set. **1933** E. T. A. Rapson *Electr. Transmission & Distrib.* xiv. 163 Accurate metering of the power input to and output from the Grid is essential. **1943** C. L. Boltz *Basic Radio* xiv. 216 The input is applied between control grid and cathode. **1970** J. Earl *Tuners & Amplifiers* vi. 142 This same switch also receives an input from the a.m. section.

c. *Econ.* The total of resources necessary to production, including raw materials, use of

machinery, and manpower, which are deducted from output in calculating assets and profits. (Cf. *OUTPUT.) Also *attrib.*

1926 J. D. BLACK *Production Economics* III. xi. 277 The term *input*..will be used..to refer to the amounts of the production elements that are used in turning out any product... In the present illustration, as the inputs of seed increase,..the outputs of grain increase. **1947** *Bull. U.S. Bureau of Labor Statistics* No. 913. 11 Most persons, in using the term 'productivity', have meant the physical output obtained for a given physical input. **1953** STEINER & GOLDNER *Productivity* ii. 5 What do we mean by input? A typical product is a combination of raw materials, machinery, workers' time, power, and many other factors. Each of these is called an input. Input items are combined in the manufacturing process into products or output. Should the unit of input be one worker, or one hour of labor time, or one machine, or a ton of raw materials or a kilowatt hour of electricity? Any of these could be an input although each is different. **1958** *Economist* 15 Nov. 592/3 When the effect of other variables has been allowed for, the farmer is found to be using, even at low inputs, 4s. worth of concentrates to produce a gallon of milk which he sells for 3s. 1½d... Concentrate inputs beyond £45 per cow per year..have no additional effect..upon milk yield. **1959** *Oxf. Univ. Gaz.* 16 Mar. 796/1 The farmer also uses up large quantities of 'industrial inputs' (equipment, motor fuel, fertilizers, &c.), representing goods and services which could, directly or indirectly, have been exported if the British farmer had not used them, or which, in some cases, have to be imported. **1971** [see *input price* (5 a below)]. **1972** *VAT: Gen. Guide* (H.M. Customs) 16 Those goods and services are called his inputs, and the tax on them is his input tax. **1972** *Accountant* 13 Apr. 471/1 Historically, Britain's indirect taxes had been collectible at a single point and from a restricted clientele; VAT, on the other hand, would be all pervasive. For any person receiving taxable 'inputs', zero-rating would be found preferable, 'if at all possible' to exemption. *Ibid.* 28 Sept. 402/3 Companies with only internal transactions should ensure that they did not lose relief for VAT suffered (input tax).

d. *Computers.* Data or program instructions that are fed into or processed by a computer; also, the physical medium on which these are represented.

1948 *Math. Tables & Other Aids to Computation* III. 7 The 'input' for a computational problem (i.e., the information available before the start of the computation) consists of two kinds of elements: numbers, and 'orders'. *Ibid.* 9 The tapes which contain the input for any problem are classified into three groups. **1949** D. R. HARTREE *Calculating Instruments & Machines* (1950) vii. 80 Input and output for this machine are expressed in standard teletype code, with a coded symbol for the operation required. **1964** A. LYTEL *Fund. Data Processing* viii. 165 Punched paper tape can be read and used as a computer input. **1967** D. WILSON in Wills & Yearsley *Handbk. Management Technol.* iii. 45 It is sometimes necessary to obtain a detailed listing of all the input to determine where the error has occurred. **1973** *Time* 13 Aug. 20/2 Business gave its own donation at the office, with the computer talk of 'inputs'..and 'print-outs'.

e. *Psychol.* The resources of mental and sensory stimuli available to an individual.

1954 *Canad. Jrnl. Psychol.* VIII. 70 The maintenance of normal, intelligent, adaptive behaviour probably requires a continually varied sensory input. **1959** *Amer. Jrnl. Psychiatry* CXV. 1110/1 These studies suggest that maintaining adequate sensory input during space missions will be less of a problem than providing adequate information input. **1972** *Jrnl. Social Psychol.* LXXXVI. 220 Individuals who can tolerate diverse inputs from the environment may not be markedly affected by success or failure.

f. *Linguistics.* (See quot. 1966.) Freq. as *input string.*

1961 H. A. GLEASON *Introd. Descr. Ling.* (rev. ed.) xii. 173 It is normally stated in the form of rules which may be applied to one of the pair—an *input*—altering it to produce the other—an *output.* **1966** M. PEI *Gloss. Ling. Terminol.* 126 *Input,* in transformational grammar, the term applied to a construction that is transformed into another..which is called the *output* (input: 'he goes'; output: 'he does go', 'he does not go', etc.). **1969** W. A. COOK *Introd. Tagmemic Analysis* ii. 42 The transformational rule is simply a rule of change. This rule has an input string, a rule of change, and an output string. With kernel sentences as input, it is possible to set up a series of optional rules that will produce the output, the derived sentences. **1971** R. FOWLER in *Archivum Linguisticum* II. 136 These rules..are typical of the local transformations which follow base constituent-structure rules on the present grammatical model. Their inputs and outputs are concatenated sets of syntactic..features, and their effect is to replace or add one feature in one set.

3. A place where, or device through which, an input enters a system, esp. an electronic device.

1929 J. H. MORECROFT *Elem. Radio Communication* vii. 228 Either of these..would give a beat frequency of 50 kc., which is then 'detected' and supplied to the 'input' of the I.F. amplifier. **1933** *Boys' Mag.* XLVII. 108/2 Connect pick-up to 'input' and loud speaker to 'output'. **1946** *Math. Tables & Other Aids to Computation* II. 100 A flip-flop has two inputs and two outputs. **1963** GOULD & ELLIS *Digital Computer Technol.* iv. 33 Data passing from the input to the computer proper, or from this to the output, can be marshalled, sorted and coded..to a large extent independently of the rest of the equipment. **1971** *Hi-Fi Sound* Feb. 105/1 This recorder has inputs for microphone, radio and magnetic and/or ceramic pickup cartridges.

4. The action or process of putting in or feeding in.

1947 *Math. Tables & Other Aids to Computation* II. 356 No means of numerical input or output other than the keyboard and the display panel are provided. **1948** *Ibid.* III. 7 The speed of input is well in balance with the computing speed. **1955** *Sci. Amer.* Jan. 69/3 If a block of iron were magnetized as a single large domain..it..would require the input of a considerable amount of energy. **1964** T. W. MCRAE *Impact of Computers on Accounting* i. 15 The basic idea behind this method of input is to print the characters on the original document in a special type of magnetic ink. **1973** *Nature* 13 Apr. 440/1 What is lacking ..is a steady input of information on research and development on other fuels.

5. *attrib.* and *Comb.* **a.** simple attributive, as *input circuit, device, impedance, price, routine, tape, terminal, transformer, unit.* **b.** constituting input, as *input current, data, information, signal, voltage.*

1921 *Wireless World* 25 June 214/2 The input circuit varies according to the receiver circuit to which the connection is made. **1940** *Amat. Radio Handbk.* (ed. 2) iv. 69/1 The first general axiom is to arrange matters so that the output stages are as far as possible from the aerial or input circuits. **1930** FIELD & WEILL *Electro-Plating* 38 Fig. 11. showing the form of the input and output currents. **1948** *Math. Tables & Other Aids to Computation* III. 7 The Harvard machines use punched cards for most input data. **1948** *Ann. Computation Lab. Harvard Univ.* XVI. 248 The design of input and output devices for electronic digital computers poses a specialized problem in electrical communications. **1968** *Brit. Med. Bull.* XXIV. 191/1 The basic configuration of any computer consists of a store, a suitable input and output device, and a control mechanism. **1928** *Times* 23 Mar. 20/1 A certain input impedance which had the effect of increasing or decreasing the resistance of the tuned circuit. **1949** E. C. BERKELEY *Giant Brains* x. 175 Since the input information must be carefully verified, we shall need a second magnetic-tape device. **1956** Input information [see *BUFFER² 1 d]. **1971** *Daily Tel.* 19 May 17/2 Input prices—the price of basic materials and fuel—have risen by more than 3 p.c. since the start of the year. **1954** *Math. Tables & Other Aids to Computation* VIII. 32 The function of the Ferut Input Routine is to read information from tape, perform certain alterations on routines or numerical data and store the routines or data in assigned locations in the machine. **1962** *Gloss. Terms Automatic Data Processing* (*B.S.I.*) 42 *Input routine,* a routine, sometimes stored permanently in the computer, to control the readings of programs and data. **1950** *Mind* LIX. 440 It will seem that given the initial state of the machine and the input signals it is always possible to predict all future states. **1949** E. C. BERKELEY *Giant Brains* iii. 27 We shall need one register to read the input tape and to store the number or operation recorded on it. **1919** *Wireless World* Dec. 505/1 It will ..be convenient to provide two 'input' terminals, two terminals to which the..accumulator may be connected, and two for..an external plate battery. **1946** Input terminal [see *CONTROL *sb.* 3 f]. **1919** *Wireless World* Dec. 506/1 The leaky grid condenser..is brought into use, the input transformer..being isolated. **1962** *Gloss. Terms Automatic Data Processing* (*B.S.I.*) 81 *Input unit,* that portion of an a.d.p. system used only for input. **1966** B. A. M. MOON *Computer Programming* i. 6 Typical input units are punched card, paper tape and magnetic tape units. **1940** *Amat. Radio Handbk.* (ed. 2) ii. 28/2 When an A.C. input voltage is applied to the grid of a valve an amplified A.C. voltage appears across the output load in the anode circuit.

c. Also **input–output** (*input-output, input/output*), usu. *attrib.*

1914 H. PENDER *Amer. Handbk. Electr. Engineers* 961 With large motors it is desirable to use a generator as a load in making an input-output test. **1947** *Math. Tables & Other Aids to Computation* II. 363 Another important element of the automatic computer which affects the compromise is the input-output mechanism. **1953** *Economist* 26 Sept. 870/1 An input-output analysis of the British economic structure..will be ready by 1956. *Ibid.* 870/2 Mr. Roger Keyes..recently ordered the suspension of work on American input-output data; the colleagues he left behind..used to share his mistrust of input-output. **1964** GOULD & KOLB *Dict. Social Sci.* 452/2 Input–output tables show the interrelations among the major industry groups of the economy... Tables or matrices are constructed which show the goods-and-services inputs and outputs of each on a 'from-whom to whom' basis. **1964** T. W. MCRAE *Impact of Computers on Accounting* ii. 38 The introduction of magnetic tapes..facilitates the compact storage and fast input–output of large files. **1967** *Technology Week* 23 Jan. 11/1 (Advt.), Sigma 5..does foreground real-time control..and high-speed input/output. **1970** *Sci. Amer.* Oct. 94/2 Ordinarily it is difficult to measure the input-output relations of an ecosystem, particularly those involving nutrients. **1970** *Sunday Times* 29 Nov. 68/6 Input-output tables are brought into play to help estimate that trading profits per vehicle exceed manual pay for the men who make it.

input, *v.* Restrict † *Obs.* to senses in Dict. and add: **3.** (Stressed *i·nput.*) *Computers.* To supply or feed in (data, a program, etc.) *to*; to feed *into.* Pa. pple. **i·nput,** (less commonly) **i·nputted.**

1946 *Nature* 12 Oct. 503/2 These switches are connected up so that for any two-figure argument *x* from 00 to 99, input to the function table, the value of the function for that argument is output in the form of pulse groups on the appropriate digit lines. **1953** A. D. & K. H. V. BOOTH *Automatic Digital Calculators* viii. 62 It is possible to input up to 300 decimal digits per second. *Ibid.* 74 Working instructions do not have to be input after each shut-down. **1964** F. L. WESTWATER *Electronic Computers* vi. 104 Magnetic tape provides a fast means of inputting information. **1965** K. NICOL *Elem. Programming* iii. 14 When all your program has been input and compiled control is transferred from the compiler program to the machine code instructions of your program. **1967** W. F. BAUER in W. J. Karplus *On-Line Computing* iv. 81 He inputs the data directly into the console by electronically filling out a form which the computer provides on the cathode-ray tube. *Ibid.* 80 Data verification is done by the computer's reflecting back to the user on the cathode-ray-tube scope exactly what has been inputted. **1968** *Brit. Med. Bull.* XXIV. 222/1 At convenient intervals, the day lists are input to the computer. **1970** O. DOPPING *Computers & Data Processing* xv. 230 A series of records which are to be input to a computer or have been output from it is called a file.

inquest, *sb.* Add: **2. b.** *grand inquest*: also *transf.*

1903 *Daily Chron.* 3 July 7/1 The First Lord of the Admiralty..described it as a grand inquest of the nation.

3. c. Delete 'Now *rare*'. Now used *colloq.*, a discussion or investigation of a game, event, etc., after it has taken place.

1932 *News Chron.* 29 Feb. 8/5 She never in any case holds inquests. You can't make the next shot [in Golf] good by worrying over the last. **1934** *Punch* 3 Jan. 22/3 My intention was to wait for the inevitable inquest and then say..'I don't play much bridge you know.' **1967** J. SYMONS *Man who killed Himself* i. i. 12 'What made you double that heart call?' Clare asked... Mr. Payne wagged a finger. 'Now now. No inquests.' **1970** *Times* 20 Apr. 1/5 The Apollo 13 astronauts..tonight left Hawaii to return to Houston where they will soon begin the long inquest into the spacecraft failure.

inquiline, *sb.* (*a.*) **1. a.** Delete † *Obs.* and add later example.

1914 C. MACKENZIE *Sinister St.* II. IV. iv. 926 Half the inquilines of a night and even some of the less transient lodgers ultimately escaped owing her money.

3. *attrib.* or as *adj.* (Later example.)

1958 *Times Lit. Suppl.* 30 May 299/2 The inquiline figures painted so vigorously by Sir Osbert come to life with extraordinary clarity.

inquinate, *v.* Delete † *Obs.* and add example. Hence **i·nquinating** *ppl. a.*

1914 C. MACKENZIE *Sinister St.* II. IV. iv. 914 Street followed street, each one..being a little less able to resist the corrosion of a persistently inquinating migration. **1918** H. W. STEED in *19th Cent.* Dec. 987 It is surely enough that some of these stipulations should..have needlessly protracted the War, without their being allowed to inquinate the peace.

inquiration (inkwəiᵊrē̆i·ʃən). *dial.* [f. IN-QUIRE *v.* + -ATION.] Inquiry.

1789 C. SMITH *Ethelinde* III. 136 If so be you would acquaint me where I may make enquiration after your frinds or hern, it would come to the same thing. **1839** C. CLARK *John Noakes* v, If they their inquirations make In winter time, some will Condemn that place as no great shakes. **1850** DICKENS *Dav. Copp.* li. 516 A decent woman as spoke to her about..making secret inquiration concerning of me and all at home. **1886** HARDY *Mayor Casterbr.* II. xiv. 196 'Suppose we make inquiration into it, Christopher,' continued Longways; 'and if we find there's really anything in it, drop a letter to them most concerned.'

inquirendo. Add: **2.** An investigation.

a **1846** G. DARLEY in B. W. Procter *Procter* (1877) 286 Confound your prose lunatics who leave you no time for inquirendos upon poetic ones! **1897** L. I. GUINEY (*title*) Patrins, to which is added an Inquirendo into the Wit and Other Good Parts of His Late Majesty King Charles the Second.

inquiry, enquiry. Add: **4.** (Earlier and later examples of *inquiry room.*) Also *inquiry agency, agent.*

1850 J. GALLAHER *Western Sk.-Bk.* 243 He came into the inquiry room, and told me..that he had been living in sin. **1892** KIPLING & BALESTIER *Naulakha* xvii. 204 See here, young woman, do you run a private inquiry agency? **1901** *Daily News* 5 Feb. 4/4 The Rev. F. B. Meyer..hoped that each church would continue its..band of inquiry-room workers. **1922** *Kelly's Directory Liverpool* 1181/3 Ramage & Kelly private inquiry agents. **1971** K. GOTTSCHALK in B. de Ferranti *Living with Computer* iv. 31 Society is being confronted with..ultraviolet photography practised by inquiry agents.

in re: see *IN *Lat. prep.*

i·n-re:ference. [cf. *IN *a.* 2.] A reference understood by only a limited group of people. Cf. *IN-JOKE.

1967 *Punch* 15 Feb. 243/2 The pieces..have clearly journeyed from a lost civilisation, although..in-references to..period West End lions, have been omitted. **1968** *Listener* 26 Sept. 421/2 Peel's linking comments are liberally sprinkled with in-references to musicians and to long-playing records destined, one suspects, for infinitesimal sales.

in-rigger (i·nri:gəɹ). [f. IN *adv.* + RIGGER¹ 4.] A boat having the rowlocks formed in the gunwale.

1893 J. H. CLASPER in *Westm. Gaz.* 9 Oct. 7/3 The Düsseldorf boat was an in-rigger—for which orders are very seldom given nowadays.

‖ **inro** (i·nro). [Jap., f. Chin. *yin* seal + *lung* basket.] An ornamental nest of boxes, connected by a thin cord, made of lacquer, ivory, or the like, in which seals, medicines, and other necessaries can be carried, formerly worn by the Japanese at the girdle.

1617 W. Adams *Let.* 10 Nov. in *Trans. Asiatic Soc. Japan* (1898) XXVI. 207 Your Inro or metsin boxe Skinro told me he would sent it me from Meaco. **1882** *Century Mag.* Dec. 228/2 Gilded pictures of wave, sky, cloud, field, and house, seen on box and tray, *inro* and scroll. **1911** *Connoisseur* Mar. 209/2 Among the *objets d'art* most associated with old Japan are the *inro*, or little medicine cases which the Japanese used invariably to carry about with them. **1960** *Times* 2 Jan. 9/4 Since these garments [*sc.* kimonos] were without pockets, the Japanese carried such belongings as ink, seals, and medicines in lacquer boxes called inros. **1971** *Times Lit. Suppl.* 20 Aug. 998/5 The variety and wit of the subjects used in *inrō* decoration defy description. **1972** *Country Life* 30 Nov. 1500/1 Carved netsuke—the Japanese toggles by which the inro was prevented from falling from the belt.

inrun, *sb.* Add: **2.** [tr. G. *anlauf.*] In ski-jumping, the distance from the start to the point of taking off; an approach trestle.

1949 F. Elkins in Elkins & Harper *World Ski Bk.* 103 A group of skiers were preparing their jumping hill for a meet when a small figure was seen leaving the top of the wooden inrun. **1963** *Amer. Speech* XXXVIII. 203 Some of the English terms are literal equivalents of terms used by German-speaking skiers and might be called loan translations...inrun Anlauf.

in-running, *ppl. a.* Add to def.: That runs into a river or the sea.

1931 *Times Lit. Suppl.* 1 Oct. 738/2 'Australian Literature'..must contribute to the great stream of English literature a new in-running river.

in-sack *attrib.*: see *in *prep.* 17*.

inscape (i·nskēip), *sb.* [Origin unknown; perh. f. In *adv.* 12 + Scape *sb.*³, or ad. Inshape.] The individual or essential quality of a thing; the uniqueness of an observed object, scene, event, etc. (see quots.). Hence **i·nscape** *v. trans.*; **i·nscaped** *ppl. a.*

1868 G. M. Hopkins *Jrnls. & Papers* (1959) 127 His [*sc.* Parmenides'] feeling for instress, for the flush and foredrawn, and for inscape is most striking. *Ibid.* 129 The way men judge in particular is determined for each by his own inscape. *Ibid.* 174 Two plants especially with strongly inscaped leaves cover the mountain pastures. *Ibid.* 177 The whole cascade is inscaped in fretted falling vandykes. **1879** —— *Lett. to R. Bridges* (1955) 66 Design, pattern, or what I am in the habit of calling 'inscape' is what I above all aim at in poetry. Now it is the virtue of design, pattern, or inscape to be distinctive and it is the vice of distinctiveness to become queer. **1886** —— *Let.* 7 Nov. (1956) 373 The essential and only lasting thing left out—what I call *inscape*, that is species or individually-distinctive beauty of style. **1919** R. Fry *Let.* 29 Apr. (1972) II. 450 His [*sc.* G. M. Hopkins's] aesthetic—his 'inscape'; that's what we are after, however much we miss it. **1938** D. Gascoyne *Hölderlin's Madness* 35 All is an inscape And yet separates Thus shelters the Poet. **1944** *Downside Rev.* LXII. 185 The prefix 'in-' of 'inscape' is the operative part. 'Inscape' is the perception that comes only with contraction to a point. The inscape of a scene is not its correspondence with an externally conceived pattern; it is that scene experienced as absolutely unique, knit together in that oneness which is nameable only by relation. **1944** [see *instress *sb.*]. **1945** C. Williams *All Hallows' Eve* vii. 113 He forgot Simon..he forgot Lester... The inscape of the painting became central. **1948** W. A. M. Peters *G. M. Hopkins* i. 1 'Inscape' is the unified complex of those sensible qualities of the object of perception that strikes us as inseparably belonging to and most typical of it, so that through the knowledge of this unified complex of sense-data we may gain an insight into the individual essence of the object. **1953** W. H. Gardner in G. M. Hopkins *Poems & Prose* 229 *Twindles*..a portmanteau word inscaping 'twists' and 'dwindles'. **1970** *Country Life* 26 Feb. 484/2 In Manchester there is the fabric of buildings and structures which contribute by their reality to the inscape of the place.

inscenation (insīnēi·ʃən). [prob. after G. *inszenierung.*] Theatrical representation, *mise en scène.*

1897 G. B. Shaw in *Sat. Rev.* 13 Nov. 514/2 Maeterlinck's plays, requiring a mystical inscenation in the style of Fernand Knopf, would be nearly as much spoiled by Elizabethan treatment as by Drury Lane treatment. **1900** W. A. Ellis *Life Wagner* I. i. iii. 69 Geyer took an active part in the inscenation of his piece, in which he himself played Painter Klaus. **1963** *Times* 1 Mar. 13/1 A new inscenation of *Trovatore.* **1971** *Times* 8 June 8/2 Britten's setting of the Chester miracle play, and Mr Graham's inscenation of it, strive to recover the rough-and-tumble primitive gusto.

i·nscientist. *nonce-wd.* [cf. Inscience.] A non-scientist.

1909 W. Tuckwell *Pre-Tractarian Oxford* vi. 150 He knew nothing of Science or of Microscopes...So he came to all our Meetings, the one avowed Inscientist amongst us.

inscribable, *a.* (Example.)

1879 A. Macfarlane *Princ. Algebra of Logic* 14 The characters 'regular' and 'inscribable in a circle'.

inscript (inskri·pt), *v. rare.* [f. L. *inscript-*, ppl. stem of *inscrībĕre* to Inscribe *v.*; or back-formation from Inscription.] *trans.* To inscribe. Hence **inscri·pted** *ppl. a.*

1923 *Public Opinion* 16 Feb. 155/3 The statement at the head of this article might usefully be inscripted in all Theological Halls. **1923** *Blackw. Mag.* Feb. 151/1 It does not require inscripted monuments to perpetuate the memory of British deeds.

inscription. Add: **9.** *inscription maritime* [Fr.], the French naval system of recruiting; a list of men who may be called to serve in the French navy.

1902 *Encycl. Brit.* XXVII. 499/1 This arrangement is purely for the embodiment of the men of the Inscription Maritime. *Ibid.* XXXI. 103/1 For the purpose of the Inscription Maritime the Newfoundland fisheries were kept up at considerable expense to the nations. **1905** *Westm. Gaz.* 3 Aug. 10/1 A system called 'maritime inscription', which..furnishes a contingent of about 4,700 naval recruits every year.

in se: see *in *Lat. prep.*

insect, *sb.* Add: **4. a.** *insect-drone, -repellent.* **b.** *insect control, -eater* (later examples); *insect-borne, -feeding, -pollinated, -proof* adjs.; *insect-like* adj. or adv. (examples).

1909 R. W. Boyce *Mosquito or Man?* iv. 23 It is Dr. Beauperthuy whom we must regard as the father of the doctrine of insect-borne disease. **1946** *Nature* 21 Dec. 913/1 Analogy with filariasis elsewhere would suggest that the infection is insect-borne. **1972** *Ibid.* 21 Jan. 135/2 To prevent the spread of insect-borne diseases. **1936** *Discovery* Feb. 44/1 The legal insistence on insect control is lax or non-existent until there is an actual outbreak of some pest causing serious financial loss. **1951** A. W. A. Brown (*title*) Insect control by chemicals. **1902** W. de la Mare *Songs of Childhood* 30 Is it for fear the birds are flown, And shrills the insect-drone? **1939** 'N. Blake' *Smiler with Knife* xi. 168 The insect-drone of a lawnmower. **1908** *Westm. Gaz.* 22 Feb. 16/1 There is a class of small mammals, mostly of nocturnal habits, that come under the order of Insectivora, or insect-eaters. **1936** *Discovery* July 212/2 Bee-eaters, swallows, swifts, and other insect-eaters. **1909** *Westm. Gaz.* 23 Apr. 4/2 The migratory, insect-feeding birds from the South..begin their nesting work. **1772** G. White *Let.* 9 Mar. in *Selborne* (1789) II. xii. 147, I..believe that many of the swallow kind..do, insect-like and bat-like, come forth at mild times. **1929** D. H. Lawrence *Pansies* 118 Working men Pale and mean and insect-like, scuttling along And living like lice. **1930** R. Campbell *Adamastor* 55 Faint, insect-like and thin it came, The wistful sound those heroes made. **1911** F. O. Bower *Plant-Life* 96 In a family (Ranunculaceae) as a rule insect-pollinated. **1953** J. S. Huxley *Evolution in Action* i. 34 Insect-pollinated flowers. **1908** *Japan Chron.* 1 July 4/6 It [*sc.* a kind of paper] is said to be capable of being worked into all sorts of patterns, to be insect-proof and damp-proof. **1946** *Nature* 21 Sept. 417/2 Two insect-proof cubicles in the glasshouse were filled with healthy young turnip and Chinese cabbage plants. **1953** Scott & Fisher *Thousand Geese* v. 50 We had brought effective insect-repellents, so we were not much troubled by the biting elements of the insect population. **1971** L. Payne *Even my Foot's Asleep* xvi. 214 A musky, incense-type perfume..probably an insect repellent.

insectual (inse·ktiuăl), *a.* [f. Insect *sb.* + *-ual* as in *conceptual.*] Like an insect, small.

1912 Beerbohm *Christmas Garland* 61 That swarm of things insectual. **1965** *New Statesman* 26 Nov. 838/3 To him the attacks..are mere 'insectual backbiting'.

insecure, *a.* **1.** Delete †*Obs.* and add: *esp.* in *Psychol.*

1935 F. B. Holmes *Exper. Study Fears of Young Children* xiii. 278 Karl is very insecure and clings to adults. *Ibid.* 284 The fearful children were more frequently described as being dependent upon adults for help..and as appearing generally insecure. **1941** Pritchard & Ojemann in *Jrnl. Exper. Educ.* X. 114/1 The term 'insecurity' and its correlative 'desire for security' appear extensively in child development literature... We need methods by which we can discriminate between the relatively secure and the relatively insecure children. **1947** A. T. Jersild *Child Psychol.* (ed. 3) vii. 271 In a study..of children who were rated by their teachers as being 'insecure', it was found that such children..exhibited a greater tendency to be apprehensive. **1954** A.H. Maslow *Motivation & Personality* iii. 38 He would not have taken this attitude unless he felt rejected and disliked (insecure). **1960** R. D. Laing *Divided Self* iii. 44 The ontologically insecure person is preoccupied with preserving rather than gratifying himself. *Ibid.* 45 Three forms of anxiety encountered by the ontologically insecure person. **1967** M. Argyle *Psychol. Interpersonal Behaviour* i. 29 Individuals who are 'insecure', i.e. uncertain about how to evaluate themselves, are particularly anxious to receive approval from others. *Ibid.* vii. 126 Adolescents, who have only just formed a tentative self-image, are particularly sensitive to the reactions of others, and are 'insecure' in this sense. **1969** W. Mayer-Gross et al. *Clin. Psychiatry* (ed. 3) xi. 640 Any sudden change..may produce an emotional crisis, especially in the insecure or over-sensitive child.

insecurity. 1. Delete † and add: *esp.* in *Psychol.*

1917 Glueck & Lind tr. *Adler's Neurotic Constitution* (1921) p. x, A sickly girl..in her consciousness of an unusual insecurity leans upon her father and in so doing strives to become superior to her mother. **1932** W. H. Burnham *Wholesome Personality* ix. 329 The one outstanding condition menacing the mental health of..every youth, is some form of the emotion of fear, if not acute fear, at least a sense of insecurity. **1937** K. Horney *Neurotic Personality* ii. 36 The inner insecurity expressed in this dependence on others is the second feature that strikes us in neurotics on surface observation. **1942** E. Fromm *Fear of Freedom* v. 178 The automatization of the individual in modern society has increased the helplessness and insecurity of the average individual. **1942** B. Klopfer *Rorschach Technique* iii. x. 240 Rorschach signs of insecurity and anxiety, as opposed to signs of a balanced personality structure. *Ibid.* 241 Often the language used by the subject..reveals to some extent open insecurity or anxiety. **1969** R. C. Carson *Interaction Concepts of Personality* ii. 32 Beyond infancy the experience of anxiety..has the character of a drop in self-esteem or an increase in felt insecurity. **1969** I. Stevenson *Psychiatric Exam.* iv. 62 Insecurity accompanied by a need to impress the examiner..may also lead the patient to bring forth unnecessary details. **1971** G. E. Gardner *Emerging Personality* iii. vi. 132 First of all, a higher level of anxiety, a greater feeling of insecurity, often appears to beset the nonlearning boy.

inseity: see *in se* s.v. *in *Lat. prep.*

inselberg (i·ns-, i·nzəlbəɹg). *Geomorphol.* Also **Inselberg.** Pl. **-bergs, -berge.** [G., lit. 'island mountain'.] An isolated hill or mountain which rises abruptly from its surroundings, typically a plain in a hot, dry region.

[**1898** W. Bornhardt in *Zeitschr. der deutschen geol. Ges. (Verhandl.)* L. 71 Näher und ferner in ganz unregelmässiger Vertheilung erheben sich aus ihr die merkwürdigen Inselberge.] **1907** *Q. Jrnl. Geol. Soc.* LXIII. 166 Except around a few clustered 'island-hills' (Insel-bergen) the drainage-gradients throughout this great basin are peculiarly low. **1913** *Rep. Brit. Assoc. Adv. Sci. 1912* 476 A striking feature of these kopjes and inselberge is that they rise at intervals from an apparently level or undulating plain. **1918** *Q. Jrnl. Geol. Soc.* LXXIV. 34 The bare rounded inselberg of gneiss stands alone, like an island in an undulating sea of vegetation. **1937** Wooldridge & Morgan *Physical Basis Geogr.* xx. 310 The association of Inselberge and flat rock-plains, with or without a thin veneer of sand or gravel, is..an established fact of observation. **1954** W. D. Thornbury *Princ. Geomorphol.* xi. 295 Others have applied inselberge rather indiscriminately to any island-like hill which stands conspicuously above its surrounding, such as the so-called sugarloafs of tropical rainy climates. **1960** B. W. Sparks *Geomorphol.* xi. 257 Many African landscapes..consist of a series of isolated steep-sided inselbergs rising from an almost flat plain. **1969** Bennison & Wright *Geol. Hist. Brit. Isles* xi. 272 Two important features of Triassic geography were the hills of Charnwood and the Mendips. These were inselbergs rising above the general level of the Triassic landscape but gradually buried as the deposits accumulated.

inseminate, *v.* Add: **2.** To impregnate with semen, by natural or artificial means.

1923 *Vet. Jrnl.* LXXIX. 172 The application of artificial insemination on fox-farms could give a new impetus to the development of this industry... One male could easily inseminate twenty and more females. **1943** *Lancet* 7 Aug. 176/2 To avoid the dangers of in-breeding..the Jockey Club allowed no thorough-bred to be inseminated except by the covering stallion. **1958** *Times* 17 Nov. 15/6 They will now go to A.I. centres and will be used to inseminate a number of Friesian..cows.

insemination. Add: **c.** = **artificial insemination.*

1923 *Vet. Jrnl.* LXXIX. 171 Apart from this kind of artificial insemination of females with 'natural sperm'.. it is also necessary to indicate the possibility of insemination with the so-called 'artificial sperm'. **1944** *Jrnl. Obstetr. & Gynaecol.* LI. 527/1 One donor was usually used for 4 to 8 inseminations carried out within short intervals from each other. *Ibid.* 528/1 One single insemination with spermatozoa from a donor was followed by pregnancy. **1959** *Chambers's Encycl.* I. 652/1 When the husband is sterile and the wife fertile, insemination with semen obtained from another donor has been used with success. **1974** *Times* 21 Jan. 14/5 Increased beef inseminations may be connected with the subsidized switch out of dairying.

insensitive, *a.* Add: **2. c.** Of a mathematical or physical quantity: (relatively) unaffected in value by variations in some related quantity. Const. *to.*

1968 Fox & Mayers *Computing Methods for Scientists & Engineers* iii. 31 As r decreases, the results become increasingly insensitive to small changes in the given condition. **1970** *Nature* 25 July 334/2 The energy of interaction turns out to be rather insensitive to $\epsilon(\omega)$ at these frequencies if the layer materials are of similar density.

insentience. (Later examples.)

1924 J. M. Murry *Voyage* xii. 224 All was as it must be: happiness for one, pain for another, and for yet another insentience like his own. **1936** D. H. Lawrence *Phoenix* 344 The *insentience* of armed, bullying men, in face of living, sentient things. **1951** M. McLuhan *Mech. Bride* 13/1 It would be hard to know where to begin to peel back the layers of insentience..in such an ad. **1972** *Sci. Amer.* May 33/1 Whereas the insentience of the viscera has long been received as physiological dogma with a status comparable to the circulation of the blood, the insentience of muscle has often been called in question and probably cannot be regarded as universally accepted even today.

insequent (i·nsĭkwĕnt, insī·kwĕnt), *a.*² *Geomorphol.* [f. In-³ + *-sequent* in Consequent, Subsequent *adjs.*] Of a stream, stream valley, or drainage pattern: having a course or form that appears haphazard and exhibits no apparent relation to the form or structure of the land.

1897 W. M. Davis in *Science* 2 July 24/1 Then the side streams, growing headwards, are accidentally located; and streams of this class have been called *autogenetic* by McGee. *Insequent* may prove to be a more satisfactory name for such streams, as it is of the same etymological family as *consequent, subsequent* and *obsequent*.. As *insequent* has proved servicable [*sic*] in my lectures during the past winter, it is now submitted for trial by others. **1939** P. G. Worcester *Textbk. Geomorphol.* viii. 155 Streams that develop their valleys on flat-lying sediments or on massive rocks, such as granites, without strong structural control are called insequent streams. **1954** W. D. Thornbury *Princ. Geomorphol.* v. 114 Insequent valleys are those whose courses are controlled by factors which are not determinable. **1968** R. W. Fairbridge *Encycl. Geomorphol.* 1075/2 Such a condition, one of literally no structural control, is manifested by an insequent drainage pattern.

insert, *sb.* Add: **a.** and **b.** (Examples.)

1893 in *Funk's Stand. Dict.* **1907** *Installation News* Dec. 1/2 There are three of these loose inserts. One is a pamphlet..; the second is an advance price sheet [etc.]. **1928** R. B. H. Bell *Life Abundant* 142 This little book would not be complete without an insert on the Art of Prayer.

c. An object of one material around which another material (as concrete, plastic, or metal) sets or solidifies, or which is forced into it after it has set.

1913 G. A. Hool *Reinforced Concrete Construction* II. iv. 152 These castings are made in convenient lengths and the slot in the bottom makes it possible to place hangers or bolts at any desired location along the length of the insert. The casting can be anchored as securely in the concrete as may be necessary. **1933** L. F. Rahm *Plastic Molding* i. 10 Where the production of work is large enough to justify it, special machines may be developed for the simultaneous staking-in of multiple inserts, instead of molding these in the article. **1934** H. Chase *Die Castings* iv. 145 Inserts are usually knurled on the surface in contact with metal cast around them. **1967** B. Harocopos tr. *Technol. Gravity Die-Casting* ix. 121 In die-casting, it is possible to produce articles comprising cast-in-place inserts of ferrous metals, bronze, brass or, less frequently, of aluminium. **1968** *Gloss. Formwork Terms* (*B.S.I.*) 16 *Insert*, a piece of timber or other material cast into the concrete surface usually to provide a fixing.

d. A shot inserted into a cinema film, taken after the filming of a particular sequence.

1916 'B. M. Bower' *Phantom Herd* xvi. 269 He made all of his 'close-ups', his inserts and sub-titles. **1949** A. Huxley *Let.* 6 Mar. (1969) 593 Hitchcock..now shoots continuously a whole reel at a time, doing everything without cutting, getting the necessary close-ups and inserts..by camera movements and movements of the actors. **1957** *B.B.C. Handbk.* 119 Items presented from a central studio may be combined with 'live' or filmed inserts originating from anywhere in Britain. **1965** *Movie* Spring 26 The insert shots representing Hamp's mental images (these recall the joke insert of the mother dropping dead in *Shoot the Pianist*). **1970** *New Yorker* 26 Sept. 123/1 Keaton doesn't care much for inserts. 'I like long takes, in long-shot,' he says. 'Close ups hurt comedy.'

e. Misc. uses.

1922 M. B. Houston *Witch Man* xiv. 180 She glanced quickly through the sheets of paper lying there, even at the insert in the typewriter. **1950** *Jrnl. Acoustical Soc. Amer.* XXII. 655/1 (*heading*) Magnetic insert earphone insertable in the ear of the user... This small telephone receiver is of the earphone type such as is used with hearing aids. **1955** *Gloss. Acoustical Terms* (*B.S.I.*) 24 *Insert earphone*, an earphone of small dimensions associated with a fitting for insertion into the auditory meatus. **1961** *Times* 29 Aug. 13/7 Special inserts telling the story behind this new cigarette are contained in each packet. **1962** *B.B.C. Handbk.* 51 The BBC contributed 116 programmes and received a total of 199 complete programmes or inserts from the network. **1968** *Bodl. Libr. Rec.* VIII. 62 The printing of book-form catalogues is the principal aim of the project; these catalogues are to be maintained up to date by insert sheets. **1970** *Globe & Mail* (Toronto) 26 Sept. 52/1 (Advt.), Men's Leather Palm Wool Gloves. Expertly fashioned of a bulky knit wool with slip-resistant leather palm inserts. **1971** D. Potter *Brit. Eliz. Stamps* 11 The latest area to have taken up Queen Elizabeth British issues is Western Europe, and the Post Office has responded with overseas agencies and translation inserts in their packaged sets. **1972** *N.Y. Law Jrnl.* 31 Oct. 4/8 Such warranties can be found in many places: in the advertisements of the product, in the circulars or package inserts accompanying it.

insertable, *a.* (Later example.)

1971 *Timber Trades Jrnl.* 14 Aug. 58/1 DCE..will exhibit their Dalmatic insertable filters in a new 'knocked down' kit form on stand 21.

inserting, *vbl. sb.* (in Dict. s.v. Insert *v.*). Add: *spec.* = Insertion 2 b. ? *Obs.*

1847 Webster *Inserting*, something set in, as lace, etc., into garments. **1879** *N.Y. Fashion Bazar* 22 Nov. 10/2 The latest is a ruff of fine plaitings of Breton lace, sometimes four rows upon a narrow inserting, again put on a shell shape. **1886** *Harper's Mag.* Nov. 836/1 An elaborate trousseau made chiefly of tucks and insertings and edgings.

insertion. Add: **1. b.** *Astronautics.* = *Injection 1 d; also **insertion point** = **injection point*.

1962 J. Glenn in *Into Orbit* 192 The computers..had indicated that the insertion of the capsule was good for a minimum of seven orbits. A. Shepard *Ibid.* 174 During the first four and a half minutes of launch, before we reach the insertion point and the 'Go' or 'No Go' decision as to orbit. **1963** C. McLaughlin *Space Age Dict.* (ed. 2) 86 Insertion point. That point where a spacecraft acquires a centrifugal force equal to the gravitational field force and goes into orbit.

2. b. (Earlier example.)

c **1840** Lady Wilton *Art of Needlework* xvi. 267 Patterns, without any edging, were seemingly designed for what we should now call 'insertion' work or lace.

4. *insertion stitch*; **insertion loss** *Electr.*, the decrease in the power delivered to a load (or in the voltage across it or the current through it) as a result of the insertion of a four-terminal device or network between it and the source, expressed (usu. logarithmically, in decibels or nepers) in terms of the ratio of the power, etc., without the network in place to that with it; similarly **insertion gain**, the negative of the insertion loss when expressed in logarithmic units.

1930 T. E. Shea *Transmission Networks & Wave Filters* ii. 49 A negative insertion loss is an insertion gain, and corresponds to an increase in load current amplitude as the result of inserting a network in a circuit. **1964** V. Uzunoglu *Semiconductor Network Analysis & Design* v. 69 The insertion gain of an amplifier connected between a source and load impedance (both being specified) is defined as $P_{\text{ins}} = 10 \log P_{\text{OUT}}/P_R$, where P_R is the power which would be delivered to the load if the amplifier were removed. **1930** T. E. Shea *Transmission Networks & Wave Filters* ii. 49 Insertion loss measures the actual change in load current caused by the insertion of a network. **1971** Kim & Meadows *Mod. Network Analysis* vi. 241 The behavior of a two-port coupling network such as a filter or equalizer..for use in a communication, signal-processing, or control system is frequently studied or specified in terms of an insertion loss defined in terms of voltage or power ratios. **1932** D. C. Minter *Mod. Needlecraft* 51/2 Various..insertion stitches may be formed by working an edging stitch, as braid edging or Antwerp edging. **1934** M. Thomas *Dict. Embroidery Stitches* 128 This simple insertion stitch consists of a row of braid edging stitch worked along both edges of the material to be joined. **1967** *100 Embroidery Stitches* (J. & P. Coats Ltd.) 35 Buttonhole insertion stitch.. consists of groups of four buttonhole stitches worked alternately on each piece of fabric to be joined.

in-service *attrib.*: see *In *prep.* 17*.

insetter² (i·nse:təɹ). [f. Inset *v.* + -er¹.] A person who, or device which, insets sheets.

1891 *Pall Mall Gaz.* 27 Oct. 7/2 Compositors, printers, ..stereotypers, insetters. **1960** *Economist* 16 Apr. 275/1 An electronic bulwark called the insetter, which will enable national newspapers to carry full colour pictures—and advertisements—this autumn. *Ibid.*, It is the insetter device that has the job of correcting paper tension and high-speed 'wobble'.

‖ **inshallah** (inʃā·lā), *int.* Representing Arab. *in šā' Allah* if Allah wills (it), a very frequent pious ejaculation among Muslims.

1857 J. Bowring *Kingdom & People of Siam* II. xvi. 304 Inshallah! Such promptitude was, I believe, never before exhibited in an Asiatic Court. **1867** 'Ouida' *Under Two Flags* II. iii. 74 But,—Inshallah! we endure only for a while... Allah is great! we can wait. **1909** M. Diver *Candles in Wind* xviii. 183 Guns—*Inshallah!* The guns of the Maharajah. **1911** T. E. Lawrence *Let.* 21 May (1938) 104, I have been photographing this last week—and will more next. Developing too inshallah. **1922** *Ibid.* 20 Nov. 384 I'm hoping to find a regular means of dodging up to London... In a few days, insh'allah. **1959** W. Burroughs *Naked Lunch* 40 We aren't a matriarchy here, *Insh'allah*. **1971** *Shankar's Weekly* (Delhi) 11 Apr. 4/2 Nadir Shah Yahya Khan may fancy himself as the Scourge of Dacca. But people's voices wild with pain, Inshallah! surely they will rise again.

inshoot (i·nʃūt). *Baseball.* [f. In *adv.* + Shoot *sb.*¹] The act of causing the ball to move rapidly inward, as a ball that is pitched with a curve; a ball which moves thus.

1892 *Outing* (U.S.) Jan. 302/1 An old ball player.. taught Harry to pitch and to try some curves and 'in shoots' of his own device. **1897** *Encycl. Sport* I. 74/2 A movement of the hand, an elevation of the head by the latter [*sc.* the catcher], lets the pitcher know that this ball is to be an in-shoot, the other an out-curve. **1904** *Sci. Amer.* 16 July 42/3 The right-handed pitcher delivers his 'outshoot' with much greater effect of incurve at the plate than he can accomplish with his 'inshoot'... The speed of the ball for 'outshoot' and 'inshoot' is the same. **1940** H. L. Mencken *Happy Days* 230 When I ventured on an inshoot it was apt to be recovered, not by the catcher, but by the third baseman.

inside, *sb., a.,* etc. Add: **A.** *sb.* **2. a.** (Further examples.)

1808 Jane Austen *Let.* 20 Nov. (1952) 233 We mean.. to go one night to the play. Martha ought to see the inside of the Theatre once while she lives in Southampton. **1819** R. Woodhouse *Let.* 20 Sept. in Keats *Lett.* (1958) II. 165 He parted with me at the Coach door—I had the inside all to myself. **1969** *Times* 12 Nov. 10/7 It took one war to get a foothold in the treaty ports. That still left the 'inside'.

e. The inner history, the real facts; also, a person in possession of such information. Phr. *to be on the inside*, to have knowledge that is not generally available.

1904 W. H. Smith *Promoters* v. 101 I'll give it to you straight, for I happen to know the inside. **1926** *Flynn's* 16 Jan. 637/1 Also he spills th' info as to how many insides they is; that is, how many bargain counters has one of our gang behind it. **1932** *Daily Express* 28 Jan. 15/5, I have chatted with men who are believed to be on the inside, and they have informed me that there will certainly be changes at forward and in the three-quarter line. **1959** *Economist* 18 Apr. 252/3 This desire to be 'on the inside' is no doubt personal as well as nationalist.

4. Also, *to know* (something) *inside out*: to know (it) extremely well.

1921 A. Huxley *Let.* 24 Aug. (1969) 201 Maria and I have just come back from..Rome... What a place! It inspires one at once with a kind of passion to know it utterly and inside out. **1967** N. Freeling *Strike Out* 31 A restaurant—that's a simpler affair, and Marguerite knows it inside out.

5. In various games, a position on the field; a player in that position.

1886 W. Arnott in B. James *England v Scotland* (1969) ii. 39 The Corinthians..have perfected the tactics of the three insides. **1901** W. H. Pickering *Hockey for Ladies* ix. 33 Left inside should be able to shoot for she gets as many chances as any other forward. **1905** E. E. White *How to play Hockey* vii. 47 Touch line tactics make it imperative that the two insides should get out of position. **1935** *Encycl. Sports* 289/1 (*Association Football*) The game is begun by one of the centre-forwards, who usually taps the ball gently to either of his insides. *Ibid.* 517/2 (*Rugby*) One common fault with three-quarters..is running on a slant; it is a pathetic sight to see a fine wing man so bottled by his own 'insides' that he is forced into touch almost as soon as he has the ball. **1967** J. Potter *Foul Play* vi. 79 George and Boozy moved up on the German insides like a pair of avenging demons.

6. (See quot. 1927.) *U.S.*

1899 B. Tarkington *Gentleman from Indiana* i. 11 Presently the 'Herald' announced a news connection with Rouen, and with that, and the aid of 'patent insides', began an era of three issues a week. *Ibid.* xiv. 249 We must buy 'plate matter' instead of 'patent insides'. **1927** *Amer. Speech* II. 242/1 Only in small country papers does one find 'patent insides'. The country editor frequently buys four pages of his paper already printed, filled with 'features', fiction, and advertising. He has only to fill the four remaining pages with local news and advertising.

B. *adj.* (Further examples.)

1824 E. Weeton *Let.* 31 May–2 June in *Jrnl. of Governess* (1969) II. 276 No consideration could have induced me to travel inside the coach; the guard offered me an inside seat in the night, but I declined it. **1849** Thackeray *Pendennis* I. xxii. 206 He would not take an inside place in the coach, but sate up behind with his friend the Guard. **1855** D. K. Clark *Railway Machinery* I. 93/1, ⅝ inch lap in Sharp's inside-cylinder engines exhausts as well as the 1¼ and 1½ inch of lap, which Mr. Sinclair has found necessary in his outside-cylinder engines on the Caledonian Railway. **1857** Mrs. Gaskell *Let.* 13 Sept. (1966) 471 We..found to our dismay that there was no inside places. However we got tilted up to the top of the coach behind. **1907** F. H. Burnett *Shuttle* xxiii. 226 We didn't come over on one of the big liners.. Took a cheap one, inside cabin, second class. **1959** B. J. Farmer *Murder Next Year* ii. 7 A modern bathroom and an inside w.c. **1963** *Guardian* 7 Mar. 7/2 There are 1,045 berths on this ship, and 16 of them will be available at £35—in four-berth 'inside' cabins on C deck. 'Outside' four-berth cabins cost £55 a berth. **1971** *Ibid.* 1 Dec. 12/5 Some 200,000 families with severely disabled people need improved accommodation because they lack an inside lavatory.

b. (Earlier U.S. and later *fig.* examples.) Also of a person travelling inside a coach (cf. *sb.* 3 in Dict.).

1807 Southey *Lett. from Eng.* II. xxxvii. 125 These coaches..carry four inside passengers, two outside. **1841** E. Hall *Diary* 17 Dec. in O. A. Sherrard *Two Victorian Girls* (1966) iv. 48, I did feel very lonely and miserable as the coach drove off with the solitary inside passenger. **1886** W. D. Howells *Minister's Charge* xxv. 368 Look at the Blue-book,..it's the apotheosis of farm-boys, mechanics, insidemen, and I don't know what. **1946** K. Tennant *Lost Haven* (1947) viii. 119 The 'inside men', who fished the lakes..also appropriated any convenient grassy slope. **1948** 'N. Shute' *No Highway* vi. 165 He's an inside man... He's deeply interested in research, and he doesn't concern himself very much with user problems.

c. (Examples of *inside track* in fig. use.)

1857 *Richmond* (Virginia) *Whig* 5 Sept. 2/1 In a word, 'Gizzard-Foot' has the inside track for the Senatorship. **1882** W. James *Let.* 23 Apr. in R. B. Perry *Tht. & Char. W. James* (1935) I. 794 Whoever does it gets the inside track for promotion here on Bowen's withdrawal. **1931** L. Steffens *Autobiogr.* iv. xvii. 782 We cannot any more govern them or exploit or have the inside track in them. **1967** *Times Rev. Industry* Mar. 90/3 The real strength of the Labour Party does not lie in Transport House but on the inside track possessed by trade union officials, shop stewards and others,..all particularly important in influencing the male vote. **1972** *Accountant* 21 Sept. 359/1 At this stage in the contest, President Richard M. Nixon, as the incumbent, clearly enjoys the advantages of the inside track.

d. *fig.* Coming from 'the inside'; inner; not generally available.

1888 *Daily Inter-Ocean* 20 Feb. (Farmer), A secret service officer..claims to have inside information as to the facts in the case. **1896** S. Leavitt *Our Money Wars* ii. 11 Sometimes a few lines of inside history are worth whole books of that usually printed. **1912** C. Mathewson *Pitching in a Pinch* ix. 184 Behind this game is some 'inside' history that has never been written. *c* **1919** H. C. Witwer *Smile a Minute* i. 32 He wanted some inside dope for his paper. **1923** D. L. Sayers *Whose Body?* xiii, 'Peruvian Oil..hasn't paid a dividend for umpteen years.' 'No..but it's going to. I've got inside information.' **1924** H. Croy *R.F.D. No. 3* 157, I knew a fellow on the inside

and we used to pal around together and I got a lot of inside dope. **1932** H. Walpole *Fortress* III. 447 John.. had been most entertaining. If not of Parliament he was near it enough to have plenty of inside information. **1936** *Discovery* Apr. 129/2 His biography..gives the inside story of Coué in his years of fame. **1938** Wodehouse *Code of Woosters* vi. 139, I would be able to get together with Gussie..and learn the inside dope. **1950** D. Riesman et al. *Lonely Crowd* ix. 199 Some inside-dopesters actually crave to *be* on the inside, to join an inner circle or invent one; others aim no higher than to *know* the inside. **1959** *Encounter* Dec. 16/1 The influence of the..gossip-columnists and 'inside dopesters' has steadily risen. **1970** *Daily Tel.* 20 Apr. 17 The newest 'inside' book on the monarchy. **1972** 'H. Carmichael' *Naked to Grave* v. 59, I can get all the credit for an inside story... The way you described it to me is just tailor-made for my column. **1972** P. D. James *Unsuitable Job* iii. 90 If you want the inside dope on Garforth House, you should ask him. **1973** D. Lees *Rape of Quiet Town* i. 10 As soon as they hear I'm from the *Pictorial* they'll fall over themselves to give me the inside gen.

e. Special collocations: **inside centre** *Rugby Football,* the centre playing immediately outside the half-backs; **inside clinch** (see quot.) and cf. Clinch *sb.*[1]); **inside country** *Austral.* (see quot. 1959); **inside forward,** in association football and hockey, either of the two players, called the inside left or right (see below), of the forward line; the position of such a player; **inside half** = **scrum-half*; **inside job** *slang,* a crime committed in a house, etc., by, or with the help of, a resident or servant, etc., in the building; **inside left, right,** in association football and hockey, a player playing between the outside left or right and the centre forward; the position of such a player; **inside lining** *slang* (see quots.); **inside man** *U.S. slang,* one involved in any of various special roles in a confidence trick or robbery; **inside right** (see *inside left,* above); **inside squatter** *Austral.,* one who lives within the margin of the settlements; **inside stand** *slang* (see quot. 1935).

1936 H. B. T. Wakelam *Rugby Football* ix. 171 Returning again to outside lines-up, Now and again..we come across a side which, really imitating the five-eighth game, plays two outside-halves, or even an 'inside' and an 'outside' centre. **1960** E. S. & W. J. Higham *High Speed Rugby* ix. 111 When the inside centre receives the ball, he proceeds..to straighten his run. **1969** *Sun-Herald* (Sydney) 13 July 45/5 Barry Honan's play at inside centre was rich encouragement for the side. **1886** *Encycl. Brit.* XXI. 591/2 Inside Clinch. The end [of a rope] is bent close round the standing part till it forms a circle, when it is securely seized..thus making a running eye. **1911** C. E. W. Bean '*Dreadnought' of Darling* xxxv. 317 But, be the 'inside' country never so tame..there will always be a huge stretch of country 'outside' which cannot by any known means be closely settled. **1959** Baker *Drum* 119 *Inside country,* well-populated country near or in coastal areas, specifically in contrast to inland or outback. **1897** *Windsor Mag.* Dec. 25/2 Each of the two inside-forward positions. **1897** *Encycl. Sport* I. 418/1 Try to feed the centre and inside forwards when in your opponent's territory. **1965** *Men's Hockey* (Know the Game) (rev. ed.) 30/1 If the inside forwards are close to the centre, the opposing centre half can cover all three. **1921** E. H. D. Sewell *Rugby Football* iii. 69 In our view *all* backs should look at the inside half when the ball is being put in the scrum. **1949** *Rugby League Football* ('Know the Game' Series) 8 Scrum half back or inside half. **1969** *Programme* (Llanelli v. Swansea 1 Apr.) 6 Jim Lamb. Mewnwr. Inside-half. **1973** *Sunday Tel.* 18 Mar. 38/2 Smith, for England, was forceful at inside half. **1908** 'O. Henry' *Gentle Grafter* xi. 142 The police are calling it an inside job. **1924** G. S. Dougherty *Criminal as Human Being* 187 One of my assistants..made an investigation that convinced him an 'inside job' had been committed by the servants. **1925** A. Christie *Secret of Chimneys* xi. 121 How long have you had the idea that it might be an inside job? **1926** J. Black *You can't Win* xxi. 334 It was an inside job..done by the storekeeper to beat his creditors. **1933** D. L. Sayers *Murder must Advertise* xv. 249 You seem convinced that the murder of Victor Dean was an inside job. **1972** 'M. Innes' *Open House* ii. x. 94 Wasn't there something factitious about the whole affair? Didn't it match the hoary old formula of the inside job disguised as an outside job? **1897** *Encycl. Sport* I. 517/1 This is a comparatively easy task for inside right, but by no means so for inside left, who cannot reach out to hit the ball as it is rolled in. **1969** B. James *England v Scotland* ii. 51 Scottish inside-left J. Macpherson..collapsed in a heap. **1851** H. Mayhew *London Labour* I. 20/1 He was 'going to get an inside-lining' (dinner). **1935** A. J. Pollock *Underworld Speaks* 61/2 *Inside lining,* an exceptionally good meal. **1935** *Amer. Speech* X. 21/1 (s.v. *Steerer*), *Steerer,* an *inside man* or tipster who locates prospects for robbers or safeblowers. **1937** *N.Y. Times* 22 Dec. 22 *Inside man,* a spy placed in a plant as an employé. **1938** F. D. Sharpe *Sharpe of Flying Squad* xxviii. 288 The 'mug finder' books a room and spots a likely name in the register... When the 'mug's' name is announced in the restaurant by the page, he is followed to the telephone by the 'inside man' and identified. **1940** *Amer. Speech* XV. 119/1 Inside-men are highly specialized workers; they must have a superb knowledge of psychology to keep the mark under perfect control during the days or weeks while he is being fleeced. **1906** *Westm. Gaz.* 16 Mar. 5/1 Bloomer developed into a forward of exceptional skill in the inside-right position. **1969** B. James *England v Scotland* iii. 64 Chadwick provided an opening for inside-right Goodall to score England's second goal. **1881** A. C. Grant *Bush-Life in Queensland* II. xxxii. 171 Stations were formed for nearly a hundred and fifty miles outside John's run, and he began to regard himself as quite an inside squatter. **1959** Baker *Drum* 119 *Inside squatter,* a farmer or large land-owner in a fairly well-populated district. **1932** Wodehouse *Hot Water* xiii. 227 Oily's got himself into the house, and he's planning to let Soup in when he's good and ready... It's what's known as the inside stand. **1935** *Punch* 4 Dec. 637/3 The 'inside stand', as the business of insinuating a member of a gang into the doomed house is called. **1960** Wodehouse *Jeeves in Offing* v. 54 The butler turned out to be one of a gang of crooks, planted in the house to make it easy for them to break in. The inside stand, it's called.

C. *adv.* **1. b.** *fig.* In a position to have private information. *rare.*

1870 *Congress. Globe* 3 Feb. 1022/1, I ask the gentleman from Ohio to name the ships which he says have been sold for a song. The gentleman is inside on all these matters.

c. *slang.* In prison.

1888 *Referee* 14 Oct. 1/4 There dashes past a once member of the dangerous classes, who has been 'inside' many a time and oft, but who, having run into a bit of ready, will now go straight. **1925** E. Wallace *King by Night* xxvi. 116 You've been 'inside', and you're going in again unless you can explain..what you're doing here. **1958** *Listener* 6 Nov. 743/2 Only a very insensitive reader could reach the end of the book without feeling that he had shared the author's daily, even hourly, existence 'inside' —..the effect comprising a powerful, and frequently nauseating, picture of what life in prison, and in a Borstal, is like. **1959** 'L. Bruce' *Our Jubilee is Death* xvi. 149 She was afraid of me going inside again. **1972** C. Drummond *Death at Bar* ii. 54 Over the years she had been convicted three times, spending in all four years 'inside'.

2. (Earlier and later examples.)

1824 E. Weeton *Jrnl.* 21 July (1969) II. 309 The Liverpool fares..were all 4£ inside and 2£ out. **1847** *Punch* XII. 14 Has he [*sc.* the bus conductor] directions to say..'Full inside'? **1905** *19th Cent.* 817 To adopt an elusive bush idiom, the railways bring the country 'inside'. **1930** L. Munday *Mounty's Wife* xvii. 209 After twenty years, almost all of which we had spent 'inside', as the North is always called. **1945** Baker *Austral. Lang.* 59 When a man from the far interior comes to the city he says he is coming inside. **1957** *Arctic Spotter* (Edmonton, Alberta) Oct. 9 Not once did I meet anyone who was sorry to be 'inside'. **1970** 'D. Halliday' *Dolly & Cookie Bird* v. 66 You didn't know Daddy like I did. He was an awful old softie inside.

3. *inside of.* (Earlier example.)

1839 *Spirit of Times* 27 July 246/1 There are dozens of horses..that can trot their mile in harness inside of three minutes.

D. *prep.* (Later examples.) Now esp. in titles and headlines to indicate special or intimate knowledge.

1924 A. J. Small *Frozen Gold* i. 39, I hear all about it inside twenty-four hours. **1936** J. Gunther (*title*) Inside Europe. **1942** R. Benchley (*title*) Inside Benchley. **1972** Everson & Fitzgerald (*title*) Inside the city.

in-side: see *in *adv.* 12 b.

i:nside-ou·tness. [f. *inside out* (Inside A. *sb.* 4) + -ness.] The state of being inside out.

1919 R. Bridges in *S.P.E. Tract* ii. 40 The insideoutness, topsy-turviness, and preposterousness of Mr Jones' method is incredible. **1960** *Encounter* XIV. v. 70 The inside-outness Criticus.

insider. Add: (Earlier and later examples.) Also *attrib.* and *Comb.*

In quot. 1957[1] with play on title of Colin Wilson's work *The Outsider.*

1848 W. Armstrong *Stocks* 7 Insiders are those by whom and through whom all transactions are made in and about the Exchange. **1902** H. L. Wilson *Spenders* xxx. 355 Shepler's back of all three [stocks]. The insiders are buying up now, slowly and cautiously, so as not to start any boom prematurely. **1913** *Q. Rev.* July 256 At any rate, as regards the original 10,000 shares bought by Sir Rufus Isaacs, they took part in it as 'insiders' exploiting the ignorance of the public. **1923** F. Waldo *Down Mackenzie through Gt. Lone Land* 248 The Outsider cannot know: the Insider never can make clear to him the grip that holds, the urge that stirs and never sleeps. **1942** *R.A.F. Jrnl.* 2 May 2 Estimates concerning the output of Japanese airplane industry vary. Insiders consider it to be from 1,500 to 2,500 planes a year. **1957** *Observer* 8 Sept. 10/2 They are fools who compare him [*sc.* Anouilh] with Pinero, a born insider who upheld conformity and bade us compromise with imperfection. **1957** C. Pepler *Riches Despised* ii. 27 To the outsider in fact all these religions would have seemed more or less alike... Indeed the insiders, the Israelites, found themselves all too easily drawn to the high places of the mountains. **1958** *Times Lit. Suppl.* 30 May 293/3 At any moment earnest pedantry may break through to reveal a very young man's novel with nothing much to say and not quite enough 'insider' knowledge to avoid a '*gaffe*'. **1966** *Economist* 12 Feb. 642/2 The main thrust of the Act was to apply to smaller US companies the same financial reporting, proxy-solicitation and insider-trading rules that have long been applied to larger US corporations. **1972** *Observer* 10 Sept. 11/3 The softness of our line compared with that of the US shows up clearly in the area of insider trading. In Britain it is not illegal to use confidential information to make a profit in the stock market. **1973** *Times* 8 June 1/2 The Stock Exchange has reiterated its view that 'insider dealing' in a company's shares should be made a criminal offence. In a memorandum on company law reform presented to the Department of Trade and Industry, it says the police should be empowered to call for the disclosure of true beneficial ownership when they suspect that insider trading has taken place under the cloak of nominee shareholdings.

2. *U.S. slang.* A pocket or pocket-book.

1846 *National Police Gaz.* (U.S.) 12 Sept. 5/1 The mode adopted to get an 'insider' or what may be better understood, the book from an inside coat pocket is as follows. **1896** I. K. Friedman *Lucky Number* 154 Britch is used to designate the front-pocket; gerve, vest-pocket; insider, inside coat-pocket; [etc.]. **1925** H. Leverage in *Flynn's* 7 Feb. 489/2 *Insider* (a double insider), an inside vest pocket. **1955** D. W. Maurer in *Publ. Amer. Dial. Soc.* xxiv. 115 An *insider* is the long flat wallet carried inside the breast-pocket. **1970** C. Major *Dict. Afro-Amer. Slang* 69 *Insiders,* one's pockets.

† **3.** An inside passenger. *Obs.*

1854 B. F. Taylor *Jan. & June* 170 'No Room For Two!' was the exclamation of some insider, the other morning. **1892** *Harper's Mag.* Jan. 257/1 The exhilarating pace, the smooth roads, and the juxtaposition of the insiders tended, in a high degree, to the promotion of enjoyment.

insight, *sb.*[1] Add: **2. d.** *Psychol.* In studies of behaviour and learning, the sudden perception of the solution to a problem or difficulty; applied to animals, giving an indication of their capacity for ideas and reasoning. In *Psycho-analysis,* perception of one's mental condition. Also *attrib.* and in *Comb.,* as *insight-giving, -learning, therapy.*

1909 W. James *Meaning of Truth* xiii. 260 His insistent desire to have a world of that sort is felt by him to be..an altogether peculiar *insight-giving passion* to which..he would be *stupid* not to yield. **1916** R. M. Yerkes *Mental Life Monkeys & Apes* iii. 68 The curve of learning plotted ..would..be described as an ideational, and possibly even as a rational curve; for its sudden drop..to the base line strongly suggests, if it does not actually prove, insight. *Ibid.* 87 This young orang utan..strove persistently, and often vainly, to gain insight. **1925** E. Winter tr. *Köhler's Mentality of Apes* vii. 194 Since, however, we have to decide whether chimpanzees ever behave with insight, [etc.]. *Ibid.* 198 Hence follows this characteristic: to set up as the criterion of insight, the appearance of a complete solution with reference to the whole lay-out of the field. **1949** *Brit. Birds* XLII. 355 These are not necessarily instances of insight learning, but they do represent persistent attempts to reach the milk when the top of the bottle was no longer visible to the bird. **1949** M. Mead *Male & Female* 449 Society is the patient. Those who have been in some way hurt or distorted give us many valuable insights into what is wrong with it. **1956** W. H. Thorpe *Learning & Instinct in Animals* v. 100 Thus insight-learning seems to be a kind of action by hypothesis, and has often been held to be evidence of ideational processes. **1964** M. Argyle *Psychol. & Social Probl.* x. 129 It has been found possible to reduce racial prejudice by means of brief insight-therapy. **1965** A. D. Weisman *Existential Core of Psychoanal.* vi. 139 Insight in psychoanalysis often seems to be the *result* of a resolved conflict, not the *cause* of its resolution. **1967** R. R. Greenson *Technique & Pract. Psychoanal.* I. i. 44 Only rarely does insight lead very quickly to a change in behavior.

insighted, *a.* (Later examples.)

1879 G. M. Hopkins *Let.* 22 Feb. (1955) 71 The thought of the last tercet is truly insighted. **1881** —— *Let.* 16 Sept. (1935) 55 'The Old Bishop' is a fine and insighted picture.

i·nsightful, *a.* [f. Insight *sb.*[1] + -ful.] Characterized by insight. Also **i·nsightfully** *adv.*

1907 Galsworthy *Country House* ii. i. 104 As if she had been guilty of thoughts too insightful, Mrs Pendyce blushed. **1932** *Brit. Jrnl. Psychol.* Jan. 196 The letters so distorted cannot have been insightfully apprehended. **1934** *Ibid.* July 5 When the problem passes the threshold of insightful understanding these answers are chosen more frequently. **1945** *Jrnl. Compar. Psychol.* XXXVIII. 367 (*title*) The relation of previous experience to insightful problem-solving. **1951** *Mind* LX. 518 Behaviour which we might call 'knowing' or 'insightful'. **1955** *Sci. Amer.* Apr. 109/1 Myers was a goose, but he was also brilliant, insightful and high-minded. **1957** R. K. Merton *Student-Physician* 177 Physicians and educators have often commented insightfully on their own experiences. **1967** *Language* XLIII. 744 A sensible and insightful account of the history of linguistic thought. **1970** D. L. Emblen *Peter Mark Roget* (1971) xv. 276 A remarkably insightful —if somewhat cavalier—critic. **1973** *N. & Q.* Jan. 24/1 Mr. Shippey has written an insightful and in many ways exciting study for the non-specialist university student and teacher.

insignia, *sb. pl.* Add: Further examples of *insigne* used (correctly) and of *insignia* used (erroneously) as sing.

¶ The erroneous use is discussed by L. Pound in *Amer. Speech* (1956) XXXI. 156 f.

1912 R. A. Knox in *The Blue Bk.* July 124 The seal, and symbol, and secret of Watson is, of course, his bowler. It is not like other bowlers——it is a priestly vestment, an *insigne* of office. **1948** W. R. Benét *Reader's Encycl.* 850/1 The men of Lord Louis Mountbatten's Southeastern Asia command wore it [*sc.* the figure of a phoenix] as an insigne in World War II. **1971** *Times* 24 Dec. 13/2, I saw not a single racer at Sestrière bearing an insignia that seemed out of place.

insignis (insi·gnis). [a. L. *insignis* remarkable, used as the specific epithet of *Pinus insignis* (D. Douglas in J. C. Loudon *Arboretum et Fruticetum Britannicum* (1838) IV. 2265), the former name of the tree.] The Monterey pine, *Pinus radiata,* which is native to southern California and widely cultivated elsewhere.

[**1866** 'Senilis' *Pinaceæ* iii. 128 Although not so beautiful as Insignis, yet it [*sc.* the radiated-coned pine] is a useful ornamental Pine.] **1920** C. Coltman-Rogers *Conifers* i. 41 The Insignis is a tree that undoubtedly favours sea air. **1931** E. Maxwell *Afforestation in Southern Lands* xxxix. 175 The Insignis thrives well under widely different degrees of rainfall. *Ibid.* 179 The quality of Insignis

timber varies greatly according to the way it has been grown and its age. **1957** *Handbk. Softwoods* (Forest Prod. Res. Lab.) 41 Pine, radiata... Other names. Insignis pine (general), insignis (S. Africa), Monterey pine (U.S.A.).

insinuate, *v.* **8.** Delete †*Obs.*

(Still used in the Commissions issued by the Bishop of Winchester to the Deans of Jersey and Guernsey as his Commissaries.)

insinuendo (insiniu,e·ndo). [A 'portmanteau' blending of INSINUATION and INNUENDO.]

A tasteless word.—Ed.

1885 B. MATTHEWS in *Longman's Mag.* Dec. 151 Could I not damn with faint praise and stab with sharp insinuendo?—to use the labor-saving and much-needed word thoughtlessly invented by the sable legislator of South Carolina. **1906** *N. & Q.* 3 Mar. 171/1 An old Yorkshire friend of mine..used the following words frequently. He thought they were good English:—'Disastrophe' = disaster + catastrophe, 'Insinuendo' = insinuation + innuendo. **1909** *Daily Chron.* 9 June 6/7 It was a sable legislator who howled back with scorn the 'insinuendos' of a political opponent. **1921** C. MACKENZIE *Rich Relatives* ix. 216 Anyone more cunning I've never seen. Nasty insinuendos, enough to make anyone sick! **1966** P. MOLONEY (*title*) A plea for Mersey or the gentle art of insinuendo.

insist, *v.* Add: **3. c.** With quoted words.

1888 MRS. H. WARD *R. Elsmere* II. xxxix. 174 'And rather than try,' he insisted, 'you will go on believing [etc.].' **1906** W. S. MAUGHAM *Bishop's Apron* iv. 47 'Do you care for me at all?' he insisted.

in situ: see *IN *Lat. prep.*

insolubilize (insǫ·liŭbiləiz), *v.* [f. L. *insolūbil-is* INSOLUBLE *a.* + -IZE.] *trans.* To render incapable of dissolving. So **inso·lubilized, inso·lubilizing** *ppl. adjs.*

1897 *Daily News* 4 Oct. 6/4 The colouring matter remaining attached to the paper, and held there by the insolubilised gum. **1904** *Buck's Handbk. Med. Sci.* (rev. ed.) VIII. 351/2 Both the iron and magnesium compounds must be removed from the stomach as soon as possible since the insolubilized arsenic may be again resorbed through the solvent action of the fluids of the body. **1947** *Jrnl. Soc. Chem. Industry* LXVI. 417/2 A small proportion of solids..became insolubilized during boiling. **1962** J. T. MARSH *Self-Smoothing Fabrics* xx. 333 Hence the main effect of heat is to insolubilise the resin. *Ibid.* vii. 100 This compound had some previous application in Germany as an insolubilising agent for the protein binder in the pigment printing process. **1967** E. CHAMBERS *Photolitho-Offset* xiii. 191 The image consists of an organic resin insolubilised by light. **1971** *Nature* 6 Aug. p. iii (Advt.), The world's most comprehensive selection of insolubilized biochemicals. **1972** *Enzymologia* XLII. 275 Treatment with glutaraldehyde could have insolubilized crystalline catalase in two fashions.

Hence **inso:lubiliza·tion,** the process of insolubilizing.

1926 *Chem. Abstr.* XX. 838 According to the French pat. 413,007, addition of an organic acid to a bath containing gelatin and CH_2O prevents the insolubilization, which is restored by NH_3. **1946** *Nature* 28 Dec. 925/2 Reactions of rubber and olefinic systems generally with sulphur and other reagents which are known to produce insolubilization. **1971** *Ibid.* 6 Aug. p. iii (Advt.), Supports for the insolubilization of proteins.

insomniac (insǫ·mniæk). [f. INSOMNI(A + -AC.] One who suffers from insomnia. Also *attrib.* or as *adj.*

1908 *Lancet* 8 Feb. 407/2 The urinary secretion is increased, not diminished. The latter phenomenon is, like all the phenomena of sleeplessness, most evident in the neurotic insomniac. **1930** H. CRICHTON-MILLER *Insomnia* ii. 21 Most insomniacs wish it to be believed that the onus of their insomnia lies with their circumstances and environment. **1939** G. GREENE *Lawless Roads* iv. 126 A Pennsylvanian with pouchy insomniac eyes. **1953** E. HYAMS *Gentian Violet* ix. 176 Jim's absence of mind might cause thousands of back-street chemists to have seven instead of four forms to complete when purchasing barbiturates; and compel insomniac neurotics to pass sleepless nights. **1957** P. I. ROSENTEUR *Morpheus & Me* xvi. 270 Our system of individual enterprise has made it possible for anyone, whatever his original social or economic status, to work and worry himself right into the front ranks of the insomniac army. **1959** *Listener* 23 July 121/2 Baghdad has been an insomniac's paradise. **1973** L. MEYNELL *Thirteen Trumpeters* xiv. 214 A Mickey Finn, guaranteed to put the worst insomniac in the world fast asleep in five minutes.

inspan, *v.* Add: (Earlier examples.)

1834 T. BOWKER *Jrnl.* 25 Dec. in *Towards Dict. S. Afr. Eng.* (Dict. S. Afr. Eng. Dict. Committee) (1971) 43 Arrive at [M]erais after sunset find the waggons inspanned ready for going away. **1838** F. OWEN *Diary* (1926) 118 At length, our oxen being inspanned, the waggon being loaded with the chief necessaries belonging to both families..we left the station.

b. *fig.* or *transf.*

1914 KIPLING in *Geogr. Jrnl.* Apr. 373 One man, apparently without effort, inspans the human equivalent of 'three blind 'uns and a bolter' and makes them do miracles. **1928** *Sunday Express* 8 July 10/5 There are hundreds of keen young players with the player's eyesight available for this lining business. Is it beyond the wit and capacity of the Wimbledon authorities to inspan ... **1939** R. CAMPBELL *Flowering Rifle* I. 15 Our great ..in her car, Which all the way from Portugal to ... inspans in her thundering advance. **1949** *Cape Times* 13 Sept. 8/9 To rescue the Coloured man, all forces will have to be inspanned to raise him economically. **1971** *Rand Daily Mail* 29 June 15 Why, Mrs Barton often gets on the telephone and inspans private householders to help out.

in-spawn (i·n,spǭn), *a.* [attrib. use of the phrase *in spawn* (cf. IN *prep.* 10 b).] That is about to spawn.

1908 *Westm. Gaz.* 14 Mar. 11/3 Netting the in-spawn dace. **1923** *Daily Mail* 13 Feb. 12 After the fish was landed it disgorged an in-spawn trout of 2 lb.

inspection. Add: **1.** (See quots. and cf. *INSPECTORSHIP.)

1861 *Act* 24 & 25 *Vict.* c. 134 § 192 Every Deed or Instrument made or entered into between a Debtor and his Creditors..relating to the Debts or Liabilities of the Debtor, and his Release therefrom, or the Distribution, Inspection, Management, and winding-up of his Estate. **1869** *Act* 32 & 33 *Vict.* c. 71 § 125 (4) The special resolution, together with the statement of the assets and debts of the debtor, and the name of the trustee appointed, and of the members, if any, of the committee of inspection, shall be presented to the registrar. **1883** *Wharton's Law Lex.* (ed. 7) 419/2 Inspection, Deed of.

6. *attrib.* and *Comb.* (Further examples.)

1753 in *Maryland Hist. Mag.* (1908) III. 366 Which made me apprehend they intended some Opposition to the Inspection Law. **1773** *Ibid.* (1907) II. 358 To compel all the Owners or Makers of Tobacco to send it to certain Inspection Houses whence it cannot be again removed till it is put on Board a Ship. *a* **1884** KNIGHT *Dict. Mech.* Suppl. 501/2 *Inspection car*, one used by the officers of a railway while inspecting the track. **1890** *Railways of Amer.* 146 It would require a separate article to give even a brief description of the different kinds of cars which are now used... Inspection-car, [etc.]. **1903** *Westm. Gaz.* 12 Jan. 7/2 The covering of the electrical inspection box at the Thames-street corner of Bennett's-hill was blown off this morning by the fusing of the wires. **1904** GOODCHILD & TWENEY *Technol. & Sci. Dict.* 311/2 *Inspection chamber*, a chamber at the junction of drains to allow of inspection. **1906** *Daily Chron.* 27 Aug. 3/4 To see that these things are observed..the firm employs inspection engineers. **1907** *Westm. Gaz.* 13 Nov. 8/2 Free access to the valves and inspection-doors of the crank chamber is given. **1907** *Ibid.* 11 Dec. 3/2, I have found when towing..that the garage people have a knack of putting difficulties in the way of drivers..using the inspection pits. **1908** *Ibid.* 2 Apr. 4/2 There are two large inspection doors in the crank-case. **1908** *Installation News* II. 87/2 The straight through type of inspection box should be inserted in the conduit run at short intervals. *Ibid.* 148/2 The other remarkable reductions [in price] are..Inspection Fittings [etc.]. **1908** *Westm. Gaz.* 20 Nov. 4/2 At the rear it [*sc.* an automobile] has a large inspection-cover. **1909** *Daily Chron.* 18 Sept. 1/6 The houses were flooded by water and filth from the sewers through the stone slabs covering the inspection chambers being displaced by the flood. **1930** *Engineering* 21 Nov. 658/2 The front inspection lamp consists of an electric bulb with the switch above it. **1946** A. PHELPS *I couldn't care Less* x. 76 Improperly secured inspection panels blew off my wings. **1951** *Good Housek. Home Encycl.* 187/1 Cast-iron manhole covers flush with the ground, technically termed 'inspection covers'. **1967** *Gloss. Sanitation Terms* (*B.S.I.*) 26 *Inspection chamber*, a shallow manhole. **1972** M. GILBERT *Body of Girl* iv. 44 An open-fronted workshop..with two inspection pits.

inspectorship. Add: **b.** *attrib.*, as inspectorship deed (also *deed of inspectorship*), see quots. and cf. *INSPECTION 1.

1861 *Act* 24 & 25 *Vict.* c. 134 § 191 As to Trust Deeds for Benefit of Creditors, Composition and Inspectorship Deeds executed by a Debtor. **1883** *Wharton's Law Lex.* (ed. 7) 419/2 *Inspectorship, Deed of*, an instrument entered into between an insolvent debtor and his creditors, appointing one or more person or persons to inspect and oversee the winding up of such insolvent's affairs on behalf of the creditors. **1902** *Encycl. Brit.* XXX. 151/2 Estates, however, continued to be wound up under deeds of arrangement, whether in the form of an assignment, or composition, or inspectorship deed. **1959** JOWITT *Dict. Eng. Law* I. 980/2 *Inspectorship, Deed of*,..the repealed Bankruptcy Act, 1869.

in-sphere (i·n,sfīəɹ). *Math.* [f. *IN-¹ b + SPHERE *sb.*] A sphere that touches all the faces of a given polyhedron.

1886 G. S. CARR *Synopsis Pure & Appl. Math.* I. II. 890 (Index), In-sphere of a tetrahedron. **1939** H. S. M. COXETER *Ball's Math. Recreations & Ess.* (ed. 11) v. 132 With each of these polyhedra we may associate three concentric spheres: one (the 'circum-sphere') through all the vertices, one touching all the edges, and one (the 'in-sphere') touching all the faces.

inspirate, *v.* Delete †*Obs.* and add later examples.

1939 L. H. GRAY *Foundations of Lang.* 406 They [*sc.* Hottentot and Bushman] are characterised by inspirated consonants. **1964** P. DELATTRE in D. Abercrombie et al. *Daniel Jones* 48 It [sc. *oui*] can be either expirated or inspirated.

inspira·tionalism. [f. INSPIRATIONAL *a.* + -ISM.] = INSPIRATIONISM.

1911 W. DE MORGAN *Likely Story* 343 Authors who may be said to belong to the school of Inspirationalism. **1961** B. R. WILSON *Sects & Society* I. i. 19 Checks on the possibly disruptive tendencies on [*sic*] radical inspirationalism.

inspirator. 1. Delete † *Obs.* and add later examples.

1903 K. M. ABBOTT *Old Paths New Eng.* 99 The first power-loom was set up by Francis Cabot Lowell, the inspirator of cotton manufacture. **1904** *Westm. Gaz.* 19 Nov. 10/3 He might characterise him as the great inspirator of the Opposition.

inspired, *ppl. a.* Add: **5. b.** Phr. *inspired guess*, a guess not based on fact or known information (cf. **educated guess*).

1914 G. B. SHAW *Misalliance* p. xlix, In a single brain.. we get the inspired guess of the man of genius. **1969** J. ARGENTI *Managem. Techniques* 120 Improving the accuracy of a forecast usually calls for the careful and detailed analysis of past records plus an estimate or an inspired guess as to how future trends will differ from those of the past. **1972** N. TINBERGEN in *Proc. R. Soc.* CLXXXII. 389 The effects of other behaviours are so difficult to trace that even now no more than inspired guesses are possible.

inspissator (i·nspisēⁱtəɹ). [f. INSPISSAT(E *v.* + -OR.] An apparatus for thickening or coagulating serum or other body fluids by heat.

1897 MUIR & RITCHIE *Man. Bacteriol.* ii. 48 (*caption*) Blood serum inspissator. **1928** F. W. TANNER *Pract. Bacteriol.* i. 24 Some media..must be sterilized at low temperatures. For this purpose a serum coagulator, or inspissator, is used. The media are heated at from 57° to 60° C. for different lengths of time. **1951** WHITBY & HYNES *Med. Bacteriol.* (ed. 5) iii. 22 A very rich solid medium may be made by coagulating serum or blood into a solid mass. The coagulation is effected by heating to 75° C. in an inspissator.

inst., abbrev. of INSTANT *a.* 2 b.

1771 J. WEDGWOOD *Let.* 7 Sept. (1965) 113 Letters of the 3rd 4th and 5th inst. **1954** CROOKS & DAWSON *Dict. Typewriting* (ed. 6) 146 The principal commercial abbreviations beginning with this letter [*sc.* the letter I] are— ..Inst. [etc.].

install (i·nstǭl), *sb.* [f. INSTALL *v.*¹] Something installed or placed in. (Only G. M. Hopkins.)

1871 G. M. HOPKINS *Jrnl.* (1959) 21 Apr. 207 These are not ribs; they are a 'wracking' install made of these two realities—the frets,..and the whiter field of sky shewing between. **1874** *Ibid.* 23 May 244 True bold realism but quite a casual install of woodland. *Ibid.* 245 Happy use of openings, accidental installs, people's feet, hands etc seen through. *c* **1883** —— *Sermons & Devotional Writings* (1959) II. iii. 146 For accidental being, such as that of the broken fragments of things or things purely artificial or chance 'installs', has no true and intrinsic oneness or true self.

installation. Add: **2.** Also *attrib.*

1898 *Engineering Mag.* XVI. 48 The installation cost is a matter of estimate. **1908** *Installation News* II. 56/2 Competent to act as installation inspector. **1921** *Dict. Occup. Terms* (1927) § 690 *Installation engineer*.., a technical engineer who interviews prospective consumers and points out advantages of electric light or power and advises them as to installation, etc. *Ibid.* § 692 Installation inspector. **1962** *Gloss. Terms Automatic Data Processing* (*B.S.I.*) 52 *Installation time*, time spent in installing, commissioning, testing, and approving equipment.

installer (in Dict. s.v. INSTALL *v.*¹). (Later examples.)

1926 [see **check-back*]. **1968** *Listener* 23 May 683/3 It's worth boring the installer with endless questions when you get any new piece of equipment. **1971** *Sci. Amer.* Sept. 25/1 In Chicago I was successively a telephone installer, a postal clerk, [etc.].

instalment². Add: The spelling *instalment* is now usual in the U.K. and *installment* in the U.S. **3.** *attrib.* (freq. in recent use), as *instalment credit, plan, system*, etc.

1876 *Los Angeles Daily Herald* 4 Oct. 3/6 Lots for Sale on the Installment Plan. **1887** *Courier-Jrnl.* (Louisville, Kentucky) 18 Jan. 3/7 Installment men and agents generally will find just what they need by addressing Installment Dealers' Supply Co. **1894** *Vermont Agric. Rep.* XIV. 94 They..sell the horse on the installment plan, getting enough down to pay all the horse is worth, and holding notes for the rest. **1895** KIPLING *Day's Work* (1898) 156 'It's the Governor,' said the skipper. 'He's been selling her on the instalment plan.' **1904** 'SAKI' *Reginald* 52 They're getting there on the instalment system—so much down, and the rest when you feel like it. **1909** 'O. HENRY' *Roads of Destiny* iii. 47 When they get money they exhibit a strong tendency to spend it..instead of giving it to the instalment man. **1923** R. D. PAINE *Comrades of Rolling Ocean* xi. 187 'This is still a valuable ship,' explained Torrance, 'even if she is floating around the high seas on the installment plan.' **1927** W. E. COLLINSON *Contemp. Eng.* 112 To pay by the instalment system. **1927** *Sat. Even. Post* 24 Dec. 28/2 Upon that premise..is based the vast present-day development of installment selling. **1935** *Economist* 3 Aug. 234/2 The United States itself is the leader of a new, hard, materialistic civilisation..whose priests are the instalment-seller and the advertising expert. **1942** *Short Guide Gt. Brit.* (U.S. War Dept.) 31 *Instalment plan*, hire-purchase system, or hire system. **1948** *Manch. Guardian Weekly* 8 Jan. 4/1 The President says inflation can be beaten..by putting an end to installment buying. **1952** *Ibid.* 15 May 3/1 The Federal Reserve Board was a little tight-lipped in explaining its move..to suspend controls on hire purchase, or what is known here as instalment credit. **1955** *Times* 15 Aug. 11/5 The Federal Reserve..has expressed mild concern over the rapid rise of consumer instalment (hire purchase) debt. **1965** M. SPARK *Mandelbaum Gate* iv. 104 On his discharge he bought a car on the instalment plan. **1967** *N.Y. Times* (International Edition) 11–12 Feb. 3/3

The measures include..more severe installment purchase restraints and reduction in travel allowances. **1972** *Accountant* 17 Aug. 206/2 Instalment credit..group services and group funding, are the subject of special reviews. **1973** *N.Y. Law Jrnl.* 20 Feb., The assumption of installment payments by appellant did not serve to release decedent.

instant, *a.* Add: **4. c.** Of a processed food: that can be prepared for use immediately. Also *transf.* and *fig.*, hurriedly prepared or carried out, etc.

1912 *Ladies' Home Jrnl.* Oct. 71/4 (Advt.), Instant Postum..is regular Postum in concentrated form—made in the cup—no boiling required. **1915** E. B. Holt *Freudian Wish* ii. 87, I wish I had..drunk less of that hot-wash that my wife calls instant coffee. **1924** *Ladies' Home Jrnl.* Oct. 198/1 G. Washington's Delicious Instant Coffee... The coffee ready to drink when dissolved in hot water. **1957** D. Karp *Leave me Alone* xi. 151 Your grand new world of jet airplanes, nylon stockings, frozen food, instant coffee and brain-washing. **1957** *Amer. Speech* XXXII. 313 Instant lather..instant shaving lather. **1958** *Woman* 18 Oct. 4/3 In these days of 'ready-mix' cakes, 'instant puddings' and other time-saving boons to the busy housewife. **1959** *News Chron.* 26 Sept. 3/5, I tried the new instant tea... I measured out a half teaspoonful of the instant powder, poured on hot water and stirred in milk. *Ibid.* 30 Oct. 6/4 British food firms are being chary about introducing 'instant meals'... Instant bread comes as small frozen pebble shapes which fluff up to fresh crisp rolls after a few minutes in the oven. **1961** H. Tracy *Season of Mists* vii. 84 Sit you down, and I'll make the coffee, nice real instant coffee, none of your messy old grounds. **1962** *Listener* 25 Jan. 185/1 Their habit of producing, on all sorts of occasions, bits of what may be called instant poetry. **1962** J. Terraine in *Jrnl. R. United Service Inst.* May 140 There are all too many [historical works] which fall into the category of what I call 'instant history', rapidly composed on the strength of a very fresh approach to the subject, generally devoid of any true period sense, and loaded with comment from false premises. **1963** *Sunday Times* 17 Feb. 29/6 September 3 [*sc.* 1939] is the roundest of capsules: instant peace, instant war, instant history... Instant history may be surface-glossing, but it has a jerky, filmic excitement about it. **1963** *Listener* 7 Mar. 427/3 'This post-war propaganda, piling corpse on corpse, heaping horror on futility, seems bound to fail...' Yet it is back with us now, in the hands of the 'instant historians'. **1965** *Hair Do* July 57/1 Instant curls: for the woman who longs for short, casual curls..the brief luxurious wig is the perfect hair do. **1965** *Punch* 13 Oct. 552/3 A bumper pack of Instant Art for the..young executive—with money. **1966** *Economist* 9 Apr. 161/1 This phrase 'hundred days' is itself out of fashion, because 'instant government' is now condemned as a derogatory term. **1967** *New Scientist* 9 Feb. 352/1 The preparation of instant food is very simple in principle. It consists essentially of precooking the food ..then proceeding to a complete or partial dehydration. **1967** *Observer* 26 Mar. 9 Music and 'instant sex' take subsidiary place to drugs as the real focus of the hippy subculture. **1967** U. Sedgwick *My Learn-to-cook Book* 56 Fruit is an instant food. **1969** *New Yorker* 29 Nov. 167/1 How could Agnew be so confident of the *Register*'s objectivity and so certain that it would find the speech worthy of an editorial—tantamount to 'instant analysis'. **1973** *Times* 22 Feb. 1/3 Rising demand for mueslis and instant porridges.

instant, *sb.* Add: **7.** An 'instant' beverage (see prec.); *spec.* instant coffee.

1954 *N.Y. Times Mag.* 19 Sept. vi. 52 The 'instants'—soluble coffee, soluble cocoa. **1963** 'A. Gilbert' *Ring for Noose* xi. 132 Julie..asked if she could have coffee. 'I'll make you a cup of Instant, dear,' said kind-hearted Sally. **1968** J. Porter *Dover goes to Pott* iii. 40 She offered the two detectives a cup of coffee..with..the assurance that there was plenty more instant in the tin. **1973** 'D. Halliday' *Dolly & Starry Bird* i. 4 He had the kettle on and the Instant on the table.

instantaneous, *a.* Add: **1. b.** *Photogr.* Applied to an exposure whose duration is brief and predetermined by means of a shutter mechanism; orig. applied to those sufficiently brief for a moving object to be photographed (in contrast to the time exposures that were usual), and later to those for which the camera may be held in the hand (see quots.). Also *transf.*, applied to a shutter designed for taking such exposures, a photograph taken with one, etc. Now chiefly *Hist.*

1851 *Athenæum* 6 Dec. 1286/2 (*heading*) On the production of instantaneous photographic images. **1858** Sutton & Worden *Dict. Photogr.* 229 Photographs obtained in a fractional part of a second of time are said to be instantaneous. **1867** Sutton & Dawson *Dict. Photogr.* 156 Mr. England and others use a guillotine sort of shutter, with a slot across it, which falls immediately in front of the sensitive plate... In some respects this is the best instantaneous shutter that has yet been devised. **1884** *Gaiety Theatre Programme* Oct. in L. de Vries *Victorian Advts.* (1968) 99/3 Superior Sets, comprising..Rectilinear Lens, with Instantaneous Shutter, suitable for taking instantaneous pictures of yachts sailing. **1891** W. E. Woodbury *Encycl. Photogr.* 356 Instantaneous dry plates are those coated with a very highly-sensitive emulsion that will become sufficiently impressed by the rapid exposure of the image upon it. An instantaneous lens is one that admits a large amount of actinic light. *Ibid.* 357 Instantaneous Photography.—In the very earliest days of photography this term was applied to what would now be considered very slow work indeed. We now usually apply this term when the exposure does not exceed one second. **1902** *Encycl. Brit.* XXXI. 698/2 It [*sc.* an efficient shutter] should be adjustable for variable instantaneous and for prolonged or 'time' exposures. **1939** Emanuel & Dash *All-in-One Camera-Bk.* 33 It is usual to divide the long series of commonly used exposures into two parts. Exposures of 1/50 or 1/100 second or less belong to the instantaneous group, whereas the slower shutter speeds, such as 1/10 or 1/5 second, and so on, count as time exposures. *Ibid.*, If your hand is reasonably steady you will be able to give an exposure of 1/25 without moving the camera. A picture of this kind, made without the help of a tripod or other fixed support, can be counted as a snap—an instantaneous exposure. **1973** B. Jay *Victorian Cameraman* 57 Instantaneous exposures were not possible when Frith first began his photographic business.

fig. **1867** [in Dict., sense 1].

c. Applied to a gramophone record in which the grooves are made directly by the cutting stylus during recording, and to the making of such records.

1937 *Electronics* Sept. 65/3 (Advt.), Disclube protects the delicate sound impressions in the record groove... A 2 oz. bottle of Disclube will be sent..to any person or firm equipped to make instantaneous recordings. **1949** Frayne & Wolfe *Elem. Sound Recording* xiv. 263 Besides its commercial applications, instantaneous recording finds considerable use in the home and as an adjunct in some of the educational fields, such as voice and music training, although..magnetic recording is becoming a serious competitor in certain fields. *Ibid.* 270 There is little practical difference between the best instantaneous records and the best pressings..when both are played with good light-weight reproducers.

d. *instantaneous (water-)heater* = Geyser 2.

1935 *Plumber & Decorator* Mar. 57/2 Instantaneous water heaters are of two types—the multi-point, supplying hot water to several taps in different parts of the house; the single-point 'geyser' supplying hot water at the place where it is fixed. **1940** *Chambers's Techn. Dict.* 450/2 Instantaneous water-heater. **1959** *Chambers's Encycl.* VII. 258/1 Instantaneous heaters may be multipoint, supplying hot water to a number of taps, or single point for one tap only.

instantial, *a.* Delete *rare* and add later examples. Spec. *instantial premiss* (see quot. 1933). Hence **instantia·lity**, the state of being instantial.

1921 W. E. Johnson *Logic* I. x. 160 This entirely distinct and peculiar use of the term 'existential' has given rise to endless confusion; and..the term should be entirely discarded and replaced by some such term as *instantial*, or, more accurately, indeterminately instantial. **1922** —— *Logic* II. x. 210 The conclusion is a generalisation of a certain premiss or set of premisses which..may be spoken of as 'the instantial premiss'. **1933** C. A. Mace *Princ. Logic* xii. 243 Induction may be defined as a form of inference in which, given instantial premisses (i.e. premisses concerning 'instances' or particular cases), we draw a conclusion involving some measure of generalization of these premisses. **1961** E. Nagel *Struct. of Sci.* iii. 31 The above premisses..contain a number of singular or instantial statements. **1966** J. Ellis in C. E. Bazell *In Memory of J. R. Firth* 81 Contextual meaning is either potential or instantial (or, less unambiguously, 'potential' or 'actual'). *Ibid.*, Between these extremes we might recognize a cline of potentiality/instantiality.

instantiate (instæ·nʃiĕ̆it), *v.* [f. Instance *sb.* (L. *instānti(a)* + -ate[3].] *trans.* To represent by an instance. Also **insta·ntiative** *a.*, of or pertaining to such instances; **insta·ntiating** *ppl. a.*

1946 H. H. Price in *Proc. Brit. Acad.* XXXII. 117 This act of recognizing..is at the same time the verifying of a proposition, the discovering of a fact or truth. The proposition in question is an existential proposition (it might also be called an instantiative proposition). **1949** J. R. Jones in *Philos. Rev.* LVIII. 162 He expressly implies that they are instantiated in the concrete things to which they belong. **1951** J. Holloway *Lang. & Intelligence* ii. 18 Two apples..both instantiate the single universal redness. **1954** I. M. Copi *Symbolic Logic* iv. 100 The instantiating constant '*b*' occurs in the premiss. **1959** P. F. Strawson *Individuals* iv. 130 C is a member of a set of complete concepts K, such that all and only the members of K are, in fact, each uniquely instantiated. **1965** A. Plantinga in M. Black *Philos. in Amer.* 214 God could instantiate *P* by instantiating P_1. **1972** *Language* XLVIII. 350 Thus the ambiguity of the distinctive-feature relations is mirrored by the ambiguity..of the implementation rule, thereby instantiating one of the chief consequences of the iconic function.

instantiation (instænʃiĕ̆ˈi·ʃən). [f. as prec. + -ation.] The action or fact of instantiating; representation by an instance. Also *attrib.*

1949 J. R. Jones in *Philos. Rev.* LVIII. 162 It is the view that instantiation is necessarily a dyadic relation. **1953** H. H. Price *Thinking & Experience* i. 18 It is not easy to see how the doctrine of *universalia in rebus* can make room for this important and familiar notion of instantiation. **1954** A. J. Ayer *Philos. Ess.* i. 18 The ∃x.. has no descriptive force; it serves only to make an instantiation claim. **1954** I. M. Copi *Symbolic Logic* iv. 98 The instantiation rules *UI* and *EI* must be reformulated. **1956** E. H. Hutten *Lang. Mod. Physics* vi. 234 The second alternative, i.e. by instantiation, similarly suggests that we use the law as an empty schema. **1964** M. Black *Compan. to Wittgenstein's Tractatus* lxiii. 293 W. [*sc.* Wittgenstein] modifies the convention by demanding that visibly different variables shall be treated *differently* for the purpose of instantiation. **1972** *Language* XLVIII. 343 But a more difficult task also confronts the linguist: discovering the universal laws underlying language as a whole, of which specific rules are instantiations.

instantize (i·nstăntəiz), *v.* [f. Instant *a.* + -ize.] *trans.* To make (foodstuffs) available in instant form (see *instant *a.* 4 c). So **i·nstantized** *ppl. a.*

1962 R. J. Clarke in *Proc. 1st Internat. Congr. Food Science & Technol.* (1965) IV. 5 'Instantized' milks, with lowered bulk density are making their appearance. **1970** *Americana Ann.* 58 The department contracted..for the purchase of 'instantized' nonfat dry milk for distribution in welfare programs. **1970** *New Scientist* 24 Dec. 560/1 The formulated, instantised, convenience foods will no longer look like meat, milk, cereal or vegetable.

instar (i·nstāɹ), *sb. Ent.* [mod.L. (L. H. Fischer *Orthoptera Europæa* (1853) I. 37), a. L. *instar* form, figure, likeness.] Any of the stages in the life of an insect or other arthropod between successive ecdyses, including the stage between hatching from the egg and the first ecdysis; also (and orig.), an individual arthropod at a particular stage.

1895 D. Sharp in *Cambr. Nat. Hist.* V. v. 158 It may be well to adopt a term suggested by Fischer, and call the Insect as it appears at hatching the first instar, what it is as it emerges from the first ecdysis the second instar, and so on. **1925** A. D. Imms *Gen. Textbk. Entomol.* II. 176 The intervals between the ecdyses are known as stages or stadia, and the form assumed by an insect during a particular stadium is termed an instar. **1932** Metcalf & Flint *Fund. Insect Life* vi. 156 The molts occurring during the growing period divide this life stage..into a number of sharply separated sizes or steps that are called instars. **1964** R. M. & J. W. Fox *Introd. Compar. Ent.* viii. 268 Most spiders provide a cocoon in which the first two instars are spent in passive existence. **1970** *Nature* 24 Oct. 382/1 In Jamaica the fifth instar larvae of the New World hawkmoth..exhibit four basic colours.

in statu nascendi: see *in *Lat. prep.*

in statu pupillari: see *in *Lat. prep.*

instep[1]. Add: **3. b.** The arched part of a boot or shoe between the heel and the sole.

1826 *Kaleidoscope* VI. 223/2 A boot-jack of this description..has an equal purchase on the instep and heel. **1913** E. C. Bentley *Trent's Last Case* v. 106 On each [shoe], in the angle between the heel and the instep, he detected a faint trace of red gravel. **1927** 'E. Bramah' *Max Carrados Mysteries* 160 He slyly inserted a nail in the angle of the instep.

instigatrix. For '† *Obs. rare*[−0]' read '*rare*' and add later example.

1902 *Dublin Rev.* July 105 Lady Macbeth, the instigatrix of the murder.

i·nstinctless, *a.* [Instinct *sb.* + -less.] Without or lacking instinct.

1890 W. James *Princ. Psychol.* I. ii. 77 Schrader gives a striking account of the instinctless condition of his brainless pigeons. **1947** A. Einstein *Mus. Romantic Era* xiii. 181 This return [to antiquity]..was no longer inspired by the reverential Classicism of the 18th century, but rather by the indiscriminate and instinctless 'learnedness' of the 19th.

instinctual (insti·ŋktiuăl), *a.* [f. Instinct *sb.* (L. *instinctu(s)* + -al.] Of or pertaining to, involving or depending upon, instinct.

1924 G. Knox *Land of Afternoon* 294 She possessed the female's instinctual power to project this force. **1925** J. Riviere et al. tr. *Freud's Coll. Papers* IV. 62 A stimulus of instinctual origin does not arise in the outside world but from within the organism itself. **1934** H. C. Warren *Dict. Psychol.* 140/1 *Instinctual fusion*, the theory that every mental process is the result of a fusion of the life instinct and the death instinct. **1937** H. Read *Art & Society* vii. 263 This passage clearly implies an opposition between instinctual (imaginative, creative) activity and practical, mechanical activity. **1945** Koestler *Yogi & Commissar* iii. iv. 228 Its instinctual root is probably the feeling of insecurity. **1955** J. C. Flügel *Stud. Feeling & Desire* iv. 100 In civilised societies suicide is hardly ever considered as occurring as a result of a natural or instinctual impulse. **1957** R. F. C. Hull tr. *Jung's Coll. Works* I. 132 Here it is not so much a lack of ethical feelings..as an excess of instinctual drives. **1966** R. Ardrey *Territorial Imperative* (1967) ii. 46 The pattern..is common to the species and is instinctual.

institute, *sb.*[1] **4.** (Further examples without defining word, esp. as shortened form of *Women's Institute*.)

1924 Kipling *Debits & Credits* (1926) 116 She told me there was a whist-drive that afternoon at the Institute. **1939** M. Spring Rice *Working-Class Wives* v. 111 A woman in another Essex village speaks of 'work for the Institute'. **1959** M. M. Kaye *House of Shade* vi. 74 She misses the Institute and the Girl Guides.

institution. 8. (Further examples.)

1902 *Daily Chron.* 7 May 3/7 Institution life year after year is like pushing a stone uphill. **1905** *Ibid.* 27 Sept. 4/5 To any high-spirited woman, the tyranny of institution life must be almost unbearable. **1930** J. B. Priestley *Angel Pavement* v. 210 That institution atmosphere..was rather depressing. **1956** [see *approved *ppl. a.* 5]. **1960** I. Bennett *Delinquent & Neurotic Children* iv. 129 Failures in the socialization process..will occur more frequently among institution children. **1963** F. F. Laidler *Gloss. Home Econ. Educ.* 48 *Institution administration*, carrying out the management of, or the executive duties concerned with institutions, e.g. Colleges, Hospitals, etc.

institutional, *a.* Add: **1. c.** Of religion: organized into or finding expression through institutions (a church, ordained ministers, ritual). Cf. *INSTITUTIONALISM (*a*).

1908 F. VON HÜGEL *Mystical Element of Relig.* p. vi, The Infinite can still find room for the Historical and Institutional elements in Religion. **1924** A. E. J. RAWLINSON *Authority & Freedom* vi. 136 The Christianity of history is a sacramental and institutional religion. **1941** A. C. BOUQUET *Compar. Relig.* vii. 99 But if the world is unreal, and Deity unknowable, ordinary institutional religion, with its sacrifices and celestial bargaining, becomes a mere fraud.

d. *Linguistics.* (See quots.)

1958 T. HILL in *Orbis* VII. 454 A new branch of systemic linguistics dealing with the types of relation that arise in use between tongues, and between them and their users.. As its aim is to confront tongues and communities as social institutions, it might be called *Institutional Linguistics.* **1964** M. A. K. HALLIDAY et al. *Ling. Sci.* i. 16 There is one aspect [of the study of how language works] ..which does not strictly fall within 'descriptive linguistics': the study of language in relation to those who use it. This, since it is really the study of language as an institution, is recognized as a separate branch of the linguistic sciences and has come to be known as 'institutional linguistics'. *Ibid.*, Whereas in a descriptive statement we may note..that a speaker has used a transitive and not an intransitive clause.., in an institutional statement we may note that he has spoken English and not French.., that he spoke conversationally and not formally.

3. (Later examples.)

1942 *Times Lit. Suppl.* 14 Mar. 127/1 Born in a new country at a time when the desire for freedom from old institutional ways of living..was burning like a flame in many lands. **1960** I. BENNETT *Delinquent & Neurotic Children* vii. 290 Personality was in some ways similar to that of a deprived institutional child. **1963** F. F. LAIDLER *Gloss. Home Econ. Educ.* 50 *Institutional management*, the study of all branches of the administration of large residential or non-residential establishments, including all branches of food service, menu planning, food purchase, preparation and service, equipment and personnel administration. **1966** R. BARTON (*title*) Institutional neurosis. **1972** *Jrnl. Social Psychol.* LXXXVI. 64 The Christian Conservative has a parallel in the 'Institutional Restraint' type in Gordon's analysis. **1972** *Times* 16 Oct. 12/5 In most cases they no longer require medical or nursing care and suffer mainly from 'institutional neurosis' due to their long stay in the protective environment of the hospital ward.

b. Of advertising, etc.: that lays stress on the business firm or institution rather than on the product itself.

1919 T. RUSSELL *Commercial Advertising* 258 Some manufacturers and commercial firms have used what is called 'institutional advertising': instead of advertising their wares they advertised their firm. **1930** *Harvard Advertising Awards, 1924–28* (Harvard Univ. Grad. School of Business Admin.) 75 In 1923, General Motors.. accepted institutional advertising as a business tool. **1957** CLARK & GOTTFRIED *University Dict. Business & Finance* (1967) 10/1 Institutional..Advertising..is aimed at keeping the name of a company or group before the public. **1967** *Economist* 4 Feb. 448/2 A..dignified 'institutional' sales approach.

institutionalism. Add: *spec.*, (*a*) the principles of institutional religion; (*b*) the system of housing people in institutions; the characteristics of life in an institution.

1907 *Daily Chron.* 17 Oct. 8/4 There is nothing of 'institutionalism' about life at the Browning Bethany Homes. **1909** G. TYRRELL *Christianity at Cross Roads* Pref. p. xx, The time has come..for a criticism of categories—of the very ideas of religion, of revelation, of institutionalism, of sacramentalism, of theology, of authority, etc. **1909** *Daily Chron.* 28 Oct. 5/3 The great impediment to success in the work of saving fallen women was the machinery of institutionalism. **1927** *Observer* 21 Aug. 7 The Society has set its face against any tendencies towards 'institutionalism', against any attempt..to take children away from their own homes. **1930** W. R. INGE *Christian Ethics & Mod. Probl.* i. 16 The unquestionable advantages which this fanatical institutionalism confers upon the Church as an organisation. **1958** *Times Lit. Suppl.* 19 Sept. 531/1 Institutionalism is usually followed by repeated further stays in institutions.

institutionalist. Add: Also, one who favours the retention of an institution or institutions.

1920 G. B. SHAW in *New Commonwealth* Suppl. 2 Jan. 3/1 That distinction between the churchman, between the person the Dean of St. Paul's calls the institutionalist, and the genuine out and out Protestant mystic, will always cause a certain division. **1957** O. R. MCGREGOR *Divorce in England* v. 134 'Institutionalists' who insisted on its [*sc.* the matrimonial offence's] retention.

institu:tionaliza·tion. [f. INSTITUTIONALIZE *v.* + -ATION.] The condition or state of being or becoming institutionalized; the action of institutionalizing.

1951 E. E. EVANS-PRITCHARD *Social Anthropol.* iii. 49 This order is brought about by the systematization, or institutionalization, of social activities so that certain persons have certain roles in them and so that the activities have certain functions in the general social life. **1964** M. ARGYLE *Psychol. & Social Probl.* vi. 85 The traditional [mental] hospital was run rather like a prison: inmates ...re treated as if they were incapable of taking an active ...ponsible place in the community, and it has been ...hat the longer they have been inside the more ... from 'institutionalization'—i.e. they become apathetic..and become quite dependent on the hospital. **1964** I. L. HOROWITZ *New Sociol.* 21 If we confront problems of social development, we cannot rest content with their institutionalization in one minuscule town. **1969** H. PERKIN *Key Profession* i. 2 The universities are..the institutionalization of innovation in the arts. **1970** G. GREER *Female Eunuch* 234 The alternative is not the institutionalization of parental functions. **1972** *Physics Bull.* Aug. 445/2 The institutionalization of science has brought it, and particularly its R and D aspects, decisively into the realm of government and politics.

institutionalize, *v.* Delete *rare* and add: (Later examples.) Freq. as *ppl. a.*

1935 B. MALINOWSKI in M. Black *Importance of Lang.* (1962) 80, I have defined magic as the institutionalized expression of verbal optimism. **1952** W. J. H. SPROTT *Social Psychol.* ix. 187 In some simple societies it [*sc.* homosexuality]..is institutionalized;..those showing a persistent preference for their own sex are given a special position. **1959** *Daily Tel.* 3 Apr. 10/2 Only a firm and institutionalised American commitment to Western Europe could achieve this end. **1962** W. NOWOTTNY *Lang. Poets Use* viii. 200 It means that the tears of the saviour have been metamorphosed into an institutionalized church. **1966** *Listener* 17 Nov. 749/3 That it should issue from a highly institutionalized company should not surprise us. **1971** A. QUINTON in A. Bullock *20th Cent.* 261/2 Marxism, institutionalized in the Communist world, has developed in a direction precisely opposite to the one he hoped for.

b. To house, train, or bring up in an institution; to subject (a person) to institutional life. In *pass.*, to show signs of the influence of institutional life.

1905 J. BURNS in *Daily Chron.* 1 Dec. 4/4 He has been 'institutionalised', and I never yet knew the average man survive that pauperising ordeal. **1924** *Glasgow Herald* 24 May 9 The day of the institutionalised boy or girl is past. **1949** M. MEAD *Male & Female* x. 204 Our techniques for diagnosing or institutionalizing the criminally insane are inadequate. **1959** B. WOOTTON *Social Sci. & Social Path.* iii. 119 In which either a parent had been permanently institutionalized or the child concerned had been sent to live with relatives. **1969** *Daily Tel.* 3 May 21/8 Because he was hopelessly institutionalized he was unable to look after himself when free. **1970** G. F. NEWMAN *Sir, You Bastard* v. 150 Sneed's doctor was sympathetic to his views, and thought the best plan was to put the child in an institution and have another. He offered to go and see Angie and help Sneed to institutionalize the infant. **1971** *Oxford Times* 15 Oct. 1/9 [He] had been in approved schools, prison and mental hospitals for much of his life and had become 'institutionalised'.

c. *Linguistics.* Usu. in *pa. pple.* or as *ppl. a.*: recognized or accepted by the speech community.

1949 J. R. FIRTH in *Trans. Philol. Soc. 1948* 128 It is especially helpful that there *are* things called English words and Arabic words..; indeed, English words and Classical Arabic words are firmly institutionalized. **1961** Y. OLSSON *Syntax Eng. Verb* ii. 24 Punctuation..and spacing..mark off units which are institutionalized, that is to say, recognized by the speech community. **1962** *Listener* 27 Sept. 467/2 Both in grammar and vocabulary Pidgin has deeply engrained distinctive features which are quite institutionalized, as we say.

institutionize (institiū·ʃənaiz), *v.* [f. INSTITUTION + -IZE.] *trans.* To render institutional; to institutionalize.

1903 G. TYRRELL *Church & Future* 61 In regarding the 'institutionising' of Christianity as a corruption..Protestantism seems to me to ignore universal and natural laws. **1903** W. JAMES *Mem. & Stud.* (1911) xiv. 335 The institutionizing on a large scale of any natural combination of need and motive always tends to run into technicality and to develop a tyrannical Machine.

i·n-store, *a.* [f. phr. *in store*: cf. *IN *prep.* 17*.] Of or relating to goods, etc., held in store; that is situated or takes place in a store.

1961 *Progressive Grocer* Oct. 38 The in-store advancement training program is given much credit for the success of Safeway Stores in his division. **1968** *Observer* 22 Dec. 11 What are euphemistically described as 'in-store wastages', can mean, he says, 'losing a whole truckload of stuff before it even gets through the loading bay.' The in-store thief could be someone extracting a little money from each till when it is being cashed up, a 16-year-old on the stocking-counter, or a loading bay hand working in collusion with a truck driver. *Ibid.*, There are no niceties about in-store security. **1972** *Police Rev.* 10 Nov. 1467/2 (Advt.), Investigation of all in-store security.

instress (i·nstres), *sb.* [f. IN *adv.* 12 + STRESS *sb.*] In the theories of Gerard Manley Hopkins: the force or energy which sustains an inscape (see quots.). Hence **i·nstress** *v. trans.* and *intr.*; **i·nstressed** *ppl. a.*; **i·nstressing** *vbl. sb.*

1868 [see *INSCAPE *sb.*]. **1873–4** G. M. HOPKINS *Note-bks. & Papers* (1937) 226 You can without clumsiness instress, throw a stress on/a syllable so supported. **1875** —— *Jrnls. & Papers* Feb. (1959) 263 Standing before the gateway I had an instress which only the true old work gives from the strong and noble inscape of the pointed-arch. **1876** —— *Wr. Deutschland* in *Poems* (1967) 53 His mystery must be instressed, stressed. **1881** —— *Note-bks. & Papers* (1937) 349 This song of Lucifer's was a dwelling on his own beauty, an instressing of his own inscape. **1944** W. H. GARDNER *G. M. Hopkins* i. 11 In the vagaries of shape and colour presented by hills, clouds, glaciers and trees he discerns a recondite pattern—'species or individually-distinctive beauty'—for which he coins the word 'inscape'; and the *sensation* of inscape (or, indeed, of any vivid mental image) is called 'stress' or 'instress'. **1948** W. A. M. PETERS *G. M. Hopkins* i. 14 The original meaning of instress..is that stress or energy of being by which 'all things are upheld'..and strive after continued existence.

in-stroke. Add: Also **instroke. 2.** The stroke which carries the piston away from the crankshaft and further into the cylinder of an engine.

1902 *Encycl. Brit.* XXVIII. 183/2 Suction during an entire outstroke of the piston;..compression during the following instroke. **1922** GLAZEBROOK *Dict. Applied Physics* I. 320/1 In the Otto cycle the inlet valve usually opens slightly before the end of the in-stroke of the working piston.

instruction. Add: **4. c.** *Computers.* An expression in a program or routine, or a sequence of characters in a machine language, which specifies an operation (esp. a basic operation) and freq. also one or more operands, and results in its performance by the computer.

1947 GOLDSTINE & VON NEUMANN in J. von Neumann *Coll. Wks.* (1963) V. 82 The control scans the coded instruction in the selectron memory as a rule linearly. **1948** *Math. Tables & Other Aids to Computation* III. 121 The terms defined in the following short glossary are used in their technical sense in this discussion... 2. Word: A group of digits..stored in coded form in a single memory position. .. 5. Instruction: A word directing the machine to perform a particular operation. **1949** D. R. HARTREE *Calculating Instruments & Machines* (1950) 67 A single instruction of this type specifies two locations, one in the store and one in the arithmetical unit, and an operation. **1951** [see *COMMAND *sb.* 1 d]. **1958** M. PHISTER *Logical Design Digital Computers* xi. 342 An instruction (also called a command or an order) is a computer word which identifies which of a limited number of operations the computer is to carry out, and the computer functions by executing a sequence of these instructions, one at a time. **1959** E. M. MCCORMICK *Digital Computer Primer* x. 139 The number of instructions which can be executed by a computer represents a compromise between the designer's and user's requirements. The fewer the instructions, the easier it is to design and build the machine, but the more difficult (at least time-consuming) it is to code for it. *Ibid.* 141 Some computers have two separate instructions in one word... However, most computers, binary or decimal, use one instruction per word. **1962** B. A. GALLER *Lang. Computers* xii. 193 In the IBM 650 computer, for example, a typical [machine] instruction might be 1512150123 in which the first two digits (15) indicate that the contents of the location specified by the next four digits (1215) are to be added to the lower half of the accumulator register. The next four digits (0123) give the address of the location in storage in which the next instruction to be executed is stored. **1967** [see *COMMAND *sb.* 1 d]. **1969** P. B. JORDAIN *Condensed Computer Encycl.* 253 The word instruction is preferable to the words command and order, sometimes used synonymously. Command should be reserved for electrical signals. **1970** O. DOPPING *Computers & Data Processing* vi. 98 When local control units have their own instructions, these instructions can be called commands to distinguish them from the instructions to the central control unit.

5. *attrib.*, as *instruction book.*

1895 *Montgomery Ward Catal.* 123/2 Tissue Paper Flower Outfits...Containing..12 half sheets assorted tissues,..and instruction book. **1926–7** *T. Eaton & Co. Catal.* Fall & Winter 300/3 Easy Method Instruction Books for Various Instruments. **1970** *Which?* Aug. 237/1 The instruction books generally gave good information for setting up and using the machines.

instructional, *a.* Add: **3.** spec. *instructional film* (also ellipt.), *set, television* (U.S.).

1933 (*title*) Guide to instructional and educational films available for use by educational and social organisations in Great Britain (Central Information Bureau for Educational Films). **1944** R. MANVELL *Film* I. 36 The case of the close-up in documentary..is rather different... So also is the obvious importance of close-up in the instructional film, where processes are being explained and emphasised. **1959** HALAS & MANVELL *Technique Film Animation* 13 We are seeing a considerable expansion of the animated film into every kind of use from the television commercial to the highly specialized instructional film. **1962** *Listener* 25 Jan. 193/1 The earnest reportage, the non-theatrical instructionals, and the forward-looking films. **1971** *Jrnl. Gen. Psychol.* Jan. 59 Kazsuk and Bartley supported these findings in a subsequent investigation of the effect of instructional sets on brightness matching. **1972** *Jrnl. Social Psychol.* LXXXVI. 155 For individual cooperative choices, instructional set..and trial blocks.. were significant. **1966** *Sat. Rev.* (U.S.) 19 Nov. 88 After more than a decade of intensive effort and the expenditure of hundreds of millions of dollars, instructional television seems to have arrived. **1968** *Economist* 21 Dec. 31/3 The receiving stations will still fill the rest of the day with instructional television (which is what ITV stands for in America) of a quality which Mr McGeorge Bundy of the Ford Foundation has described as staggeringly mediocre.

instructive, *a.* Add: **b.** Denoting the case used in some languages, e.g. the Ugro-Finnish group, to express means.

1857 *Trans. Philol. Soc.* 34 Nominative..genitive.. dative..instructive..affective. **1890** C. N. E. ELIOT *Finnish Gram.* 22 The instructive is formed by simply adding the letter *n* to a root, and expresses the means by which anything is done. **1896** [see INESSIVE *a.*]. **1954** PEI & GAYNOR *Dict. Ling.* 102 *Instructive*, in certain languages (e.g., Finno-Ugric languages), a case having the same denotation as the English *by means of*.

instructor. Add: **b.** (Earlier and later examples.)

1722 in B. Peirce *Hist. Harvard Univ.* (1833) 232 Voted ..that Mr. Judal Monis be *improved* as an instructor of the Hebrew language in the College. **1873** in *Sci. Amer.* (1973) May 11 There are at present 500 students, and the faculty consists of 40 professors and instructors. **1891** *Univ. Chicago Official Bull.* I. 11 Lecturers and teachers.. shall be classified as follows... (6) The Instructor. **1947** [see *full professor* (*FULL *a.* 12 d)].

Hence **instructo·rial** *a.*

1952 [see **assistant professor*].

instrument, *sb.* Add: **2.** (Further examples.) Also applied to devices whose primary function is to respond to a physical quantity or phenomenon, esp. by registering or measuring it, rather than to accomplish an effect, and which may function with little direct human intervention and be of complicated design and construction.

1672 [see BAROMETER]. **1839** [see INDICATOR 3]. **1845** *Encycl. Metrop.* IV. 68/1 By the term *Electroscope* we understand an instrument which enables us to observe the presence of free electricity. **1864** *Rep. Brit. Assoc. Adv. Sci. 1863* 147 Electric currents are most simply compared by 'electro-dynamometers' (20)—instruments which, unlike galvanometers, are practically independent of the intensity of the earth's magnetism. **1876** [see INDICATOR 3]. **1884** *List of Subscribers* (London & Globe Telephone Co.), The newest and most improved Telephonic Instruments and Apparatus. *Ibid.*, Subscribers..must not allow non-subscribers to use their instruments for the transmission of messages. **1888** S. R. BOTTONE *Electr. Instrument Making* (ed. 2) 116 Ammeters.—These instruments are intended to measure the amount of current in ampères passing through any given circuit. **1889** PREECE & MAIER *Telephone* xxix. 464 An instrument of such marvellous sensitiveness as the telephone. **1910** R. W. A. BREWER *Art of Aviation* xvi. 213 Other instruments will be carried to indicate the speed of the machine relatively to the air and to the land. **1924** P. J. RISDON *Wireless* xxxviii. 304 These bells are kept ringing until the operator gets to his instruments, adjusts his headpiece and is ready to receive the direction signals giving the position of the vessel in distress. **1947** E. W. F. FELLER *Instrument & Control Manual* xii. 280 The primary purpose of an emergency instrument is to sound an alarm or shut down equipment upon some abnormal operation. **1950** A. MARCUS *Radio Servicing* xiii. 585 The vacuum-tube voltmeter..is rapidly becoming one of the most useful instruments employed in radio servicing. **1957** *Encycl. Brit.* XII. 447/1 Instruments which make a record on paper of the magnitude of an electrical quantity with time are available in considerable variety. **1959** K. ULLYETT *Jaguar Compan.* x. 170 Polished figured walnut instrument panel features revolution counter and speedometer..and separate instruments for oil pressure, water temperature, fuel gauge and ammeter. **1963** GODDARD & BROWN *Pract. Chem.* iii. 57 In modern analytical techniques, heavy reliance is placed upon the use of instruments, such as pH-meters, potentiometric titrators,.. spectrographs, polarimeters, refractometers, etc. **1967** D. P. DAVIES *Handling Big Jets* viii. 231 The attitude indicator is the primary flight instrument for turbulence flying.

6. *instrument-carrying* adj.; **instrument board** = **instrument panel*; **instrument panel,** a surface on which gauges, dials, etc., of measuring or indicating instruments are grouped together (as in a motor vehicle or aircraft).

1917 'CONTACT' *Airman's Outings* 18 Not till a pilot can fly his bus unconsciously does he keep place without repeated reference to the throttle and instrument-board. **1926** *Amer. Speech* I. 686/1 Automobile nomenclature... Instrument board [American], facia board [English]. **1930** P. WHITE *How to fly Airplane* iv. 65 The first endeavor of the pilot-instructor is to familiarize the beginner with..the functions of the various controls, and with the instrument board. **1935** *Discovery* Feb. 44/2 The Leningrad University Observatory is stated to be building a high-altitude instrument-carrying rocket for stratospheric work. **1959** *Daily Tel.* 1 May 1/1 The programme will certainly enable Britain to put three or four instrument-carrying satellites into space. **1933** *Discovery* Feb. 59/2 An instrument panel..is incorporated in the camera. **1935** *Economist* 7 Dec. 1140/1 The use of plastics in the motor accessory field will undoubtedly increase considerably in the future... Another noteworthy development with which plastics are connected is the combination instrument panel... By grouping all the instruments in a single panel the space saved can be utilised to give larger storage pockets. **1958** W. R. BARRETT et al. in H. W. Cremer *Chem. Engin. Pract.* V. 126 Large [air-compressor] installations usually have an instrument panel on which are fitted all pressure gauges and a temperature indicator. **1972** E. H. J. PALLETT *Aircraft Instruments* iii. 43 A more effective and standardized grouping has now been adopted; this is known as the 'basic T'... It constitutes a system by which various items of related flight information can be placed in certain standard locations in all instrument panels.

b. With reference to the use of, esp. dependence on, instruments in the flying of aircraft, as *instrument conditions, runway, weather*; **instrument flying,** flying in which the pilot makes no observation of the ground but depends entirely on the instruments in the aircraft; so *instrument flight*; similarly **instrument approach** or **landing,** an approach (*APPROACH *sb.* 13) or landing in which the pilot depends entirely on instruments and a ground-based radio guidance system (an *instrument landing system*).

1947 *Engineering News-Record* 16 Oct. 532/3 Runway E, for instrument approach is 10,000 ft. long and will be paved 8,000 × 200 ft. **1957** *Encycl. Brit.* I. 230/1 During World War II another system was developed for instrument approaches. This..used a talk-down technique. **1957** Instrument conditions [see *instrument landing* below]. **1943** Instrument flight [see *instrument flying* below]. **1956** W. A. HEFLIN *U.S. Air Force Dict.* 270/2 *Instrument flight*, a flight made by using instruments, without visual reference to the ground. **1928** STERLING & KRUSE *Radio Manual* xiii. 506 While instrument flying may enable a pilot to keep his craft at a safe altitude and in a generally correct direction, the hazard of getting far away from the course..is ever present. **1943** *Instrument Flight* (U.S. Bureau of Aeronautics (Navy Dept.)) p. iii, Instrument flying is as logical and easy as contact flying. **1938** *Proc. IRE* XXVI. 681 At present, the major airlines are planning to install a number of instrument landing systems. **1942** J. B. HOAG *Basic Radio* xxxiv. 288 At certain airports, a radio wave is transmitted ..to provide a glider path for 'blind' or instrument landing. **1957** *Encycl. Brit.* I. 230/1 In the United States the Civil Aeronautics administration developed a system for landing approaches under instrument conditions, commonly known as ILS (instrument landing system). **1947** *Shell Aviation News* CXIII. 3/1 It will have three runways: an instrument runway (8,500 ft. × 250 ft.) and two non-instrument runways. **1951** *Gloss. Aeronaut. Terms* (*B.S.I.*) III. 23 *Instrument runway*.., a runway..equipped with non-visual aids for take-off and landing. **1949** *Britannica Bk. of Year 1948* 37/1 Seventy-nine per cent. of all aircraft..landed during instrument weather with no traffic delays.

instrument, *v.* Add: **3.** *trans.* To equip or provide with instruments (for measuring, recording, controlling, etc.).

1949 *Trans. Soc. Instrument Technol.* I. v. 21/1 The extent of instrumentation..is greater than it is in comparable British plants, although the most modern of these are just as comprehensively instrumented as their opposite numbers in the U.S.A. **1959** *Instrument Pract.* XIII. 194/1 The methods [of analysis] are used specifically for production control and merely to instrument them for laboratory use may be to dally unnecessarily halfway. **1961** *New Scientist* 16 Mar. 661/1 The system will be equipped throughout for automatic control and instrumented for safety. **1962** *B.S.I. News* Feb. 27/2 The whole equipment will be scientifically instrumented. **1962** F. I. ORDWAY et al. *Basic Astronautics* iv. 125 Explorer II ..was instrumented primarily to detect and measure high-energy gamma rays. **1970** *Physics Bull.* Mar. 107/1 It would be too costly to instrument and monitor the whole process.

So **i·nstrumented** *ppl. a.*, equipped with or using instruments.

1947 *Shell Aviation News* CIX. 13/1 In a large hangar there [is]..the completely instrumented fuselage of a modern bomber. **1954** *Trans. Soc. Instrument Technol.* VI. 47/1 An analysis of the total number of instruments employed on a well-instrumented ironmaking plant. **1957** *Times* 10 Oct. 10/1 The first fully instrumented satellite was planned for launching in March. **1967** *Guardian* 19 Oct. 1/7 The Russian success in carrying out the first instrumented landing on another planet. **1972** *Lebende Sprachen* XVII. 72/2 This is the launch day scheduled for UK-3, the third British-instrumented satellite to be lifted into orbit by an American scout rocket.

instrumental, *a.* and *sb.* Add: **A.** *adj.* **7.** *Psychol.* A term used to describe the type of learning where a particular response is the instrument by which the organism is taught to alter its environment.

1940 HILGARD & MARQUIS *Conditioning & Learning* iii. 51 When the occurrence of the reinforcement is contingent upon the organism's behavior the procedure may be termed instrumental conditioning. *Ibid.* 52 As a reference experiment for instrumental reward training we may select a study by Grindley. **1956** B. R. BUGELSKI *Psychol. of Learning* iv. 58 'Instrumental' learning covers all other types. It is called 'instrumental' because the organism is learning how to affect its environment to bring about some change. **1964** M. ARGYLE *Psychol. & Social Probl.* x. 128 Instrumental learning consists of the blind stamping-in of rewarded responses. **1969** R. H. SCHUSTER in D. P. Hendry *Conditioned Reinforcement* viii. 194 The complication of three factors is necessary—simple association, instrumental reinforcement, and a decay process. *Ibid.* 195 Whether the stimuli precede or follow an instrumental response. **1971** J. L. GEWIRTZ in R. Glaser *Nature of Reinforcement* viii. 288 He assumes that instrumental conditioning might be more effective for the acquisition of responses connoting complex skills. **1972** *New Yorker* 26 Aug. 32/1 Edward L. Thorndike..is credited with the first rigorous investigation of trial-and-error, or instrumental, learning.

B. *sb.* **4.** (See quot. 1945.)

1940 *Swing* July 17/1 Bob Mersey's *Blue Ink* is another slightly *Wham*-like instrumental. **1945** *Music Library Assoc. Notes* 2nd Ser. VII. 1. 45/1 *Instrumental*, composition written for instrumental performance, solo or group. Also, any performance without benefit of a vocal. **1949** L. FEATHER *Inside Be-Bop* i. 9 Dizzy..changed it from a slow ballad to a jump-tempo instrumental. **1972** *Jazz & Blues* Sept. 11/3 'Jump' instrumentals, normally featuring the tenor of Herb Hardesty.

instrumentalism (instr*u*me·ntăliz'm). *Philos.* [f. INSTRUMENTAL *a.* + -ISM.] The pragmatic theory of John Dewey (1859–1952) that thought exists as an instrument of adjustment to the environment; *spec.* that terms of thought and meaning are relative to the function they perform and that their validity or truth is determined by their efficacy.

1909 *Philos. Rev.* XVIII. 396 By instrumentalism is meant that element of pragmatism which has grown out of the application of the evolutionary method to logical problems. **1929** J. DEWEY *Experience & Nature* iv. 151 'Instrumentalism' is a theory not about personal disposition and satisfaction in knowing, but about the proper objects of science. **1931** A. WOLF in W. Rose *Outl. Mod. Knowl.* 549 Pragmatism, instrumentalism, and fictionism..treat beliefs as instruments of life, and to be valued accordingly. **1948** B. RUSSELL *Human Knowl.* 75 There is another kind of 'meaning', which gives occasion for pragmatism and instrumentalism. **1968** J. J. C. SMART *Between Sci. & Philos.* v. 142 Instrumentalism does allow theoretical concepts to be quite free constructions of the theorist.

instrumentalist. Add: **3.** *Philos.* One who advocates the theory of instrumentalism. Also *attrib.*

1909 *Philos. Rev.* XVIII. 397 From the instrumentalist standpoint, the inquiry, *What is reality?* appears..futile. **1913** W. CALDWELL *Pragmatism & Idealism* i. 17 Professor Dewey has also written many..short studies upon the application of an instrumentalist conception of philosophy to education and to social questions. **1940** B. RUSSELL *Inquiry into Meaning & Truth* viii. 154 There are some schools of philosophy—notably the Hegelians and the instrumentalists—which deny the distinction between data and inferences altogether. **1965** J. D. NORTH *Measure of Universe* App. 421 It would be misleading to describe the views represented in this book as 'pragmatist' or 'instrumentalist'.

instrumentally, *adv.* Add: **3.** *Gram.* In or by the instrumental case.

1846 M. MONIER-WILLIAMS *Elem. Gram. Sanscrit Lang.* 160 Instrumentally Dependent..those [compounds] in which the relation of the first word (being in the crude) to the last is equivalent to that of an instrumental case.

instrumentation. Add: **4.** The design, construction, and provision of instruments for measurement, control, etc.; the state of being equipped with or controlled by instruments; also, such instruments collectively. orig. *U.S.*

1931 *Instruments* Jan. 11 Mr. Schroeder's book..fills an even greater need than that filled by our industrial instrumentation manual. **1932** M. F. BÉHAR *Man. Instrumentation* I. p. xi, I confidently predict the early recognition of Instrumentation as a distinct branch of engineering and as a distinct field of scientific management. **1944** *Jrnl. R. Aeronaut. Soc.* XLVIII. 153 The paper..emphasised quite clearly that instrumentation was coming more and more to the fore in the testing of aircraft. **1949** [see *INSTRUMENT *v.* 3]. **1952** [see *AUTOMATIZE *v.* 2]. **1958** *Engineering* 28 Mar. 387/2 As the age of automation develops it is bound to bring with it increased instrumentation and increased efforts to measure both more rapidly and more accurately by systems of remote control. **1959** *Daily Tel.* 13 Mar. 15/6 The instrumentation on the ground and in the missile recorded the flight satisfactorily. **1959** *Instrument Pract.* XIII. 195/1 In America we find a marked trend towards the instrumentation of a variety of physico-chemical estimations, such as phosphate and sulphur assays. **1963** B. FOZARD *Instrumentation Nucl. Reactors* xiii. 157 Instrumentation of a nuclear power reactor is commonly undertaken on a very large scale. **1973** *Physics Bull.* May 273/3 Josephson's work..has sparked off very fruitful developments in the instrumentation field, leading for example to highly sensitive voltage detectors.

insulant, *a.* Restrict † *Obs. rare* to sense in Dict. and add: **B.** *sb.* Any substance or medium which insulates (electrically, thermally, etc.).

1934 in WEBSTER. **1946** *Electronic Engin.* XVIII. 280/1 The growth of the electronics and high frequencies industries has been phenomenal. With this growth there has been a demand for more efficient insulants. **1959** *Times* 27 Apr. (Rubber Industry Suppl.) p. viii/5 The best thermal insulant is a vacuum. *Ibid.*, Most thermal insulants..work on the principle of trapped air. **1971** *Engineering* Apr. 112/1 (Advt.), A dense yet feather-light carpet of pure mineral fibre... A natural thermal and acoustic insulant.

insular, *a.* Add: **4. b.** *Palæogr.* (See quots.)

1908 W. M. LINDSAY *Contractions in Early Latin Minuscule MSS.* 1 The most fertile source of error..is the unfamiliarity of the writers with the contractions used in the Irish or pre-Carolingian script... The correct term is Insular, for English MSS. are included and Welsh too. **1913** F. W. HALL *Compan. Classical Texts* 167 Insular hands..i.e. Irish and Anglo-Saxon; a peculiar type of the half-uncial developed in the sixth century. **1960** G. A. GLAISTER *Gloss. Bk.* 195/1 *Insular hand*, the name given to the Hiberno-Saxon script widely used in England until the Norman Conquest for non-Latin texts. Its origins may be traced to 6th-century Ireland. An example is the first London Charter, 1066, which may be seen in the Guildhall Library. **1960** E. A. LOWE *Eng. Uncial* 14 By Insular symptoms we mean features and practices peculiar to Anglo-Saxon (and Irish) scribes. **1971** T. A. M. BISHOP *Eng. Caroline Minuscule* p. xiii, The most extensive repertories of Insular abbreviations in Caroline minuscule are MSS. of probably Continental origin.

insulate, *v.* Add: **3.** (Earlier and later examples.) Also used with reference to sound.

1742 J. T. DESAGULIERS *Diss. Electr.* 2 They must be insulated, that is, they must not be suspended from..

any Bodies but what are Electricks *per se.* **1927** DAVIS & KAYE *Acoustics of Buildings* ix. 178 The practice rooms have been so satisfactorily insulated, that it is impossible to hear any sound either through the floors or the partitions. **1955** *Oxf. Jun. Encycl.* XI. 175/2 The need for insulating floors against noise has long been understood.

insulated, *ppl. a.* Add: **3.** (Earlier and later examples.) Also used with reference to heat and sound (cf. INSULATE *v.* 3 in Dict. and Suppl.).

1772 H. CAVENDISH in *Phil. Trans. R. Soc. 1771* LXI. 650 Any number of bodies, insulated and communicating with each other by conducting substances. **1777** T. CAVALLO *Compl. Treat. Electr.* 3 A body resting intirely upon non-conductors is said to be insulated. **1964** W. MARKFIELD *To Early Grave* (1965) x. 176 An appetizing store, where..you can take home their potato salad in an insulated bag. **1970** *Guardian* 24 Aug. 14/2 Insulated containers for the fruit and food trade. **1970** C. DUERDEN *Noise Abatement* vii. 115 Construct a special sound insulated chamber. **1974** A. ROSS *Bradford Business* 75 A length of insulated cable..snaked across the floor to a three-pin socket.

insulating, *ppl. a.* Add: (Earlier and later examples.) Also used with reference to sound.

1767 J. PRIESTLEY *Hist. & Present State Electr.* 200 Upon the subject of insulating bodies, he observes, that when cakes of sulphur..are made use of for this purpose, they ought to be well cooled before they are used. **1893** *Funk's Stand. Dict.*, Insulating tape. **1910** *Hawkins' Electr. Dict.*, 219/1 *Insulating tape*, tape, usually adhesive, rendered non-conducting by being saturated with an insulating compound, for the purpose of covering.. exposed parts of insulated electrical conductors. **1927** DAVIS & KAYE *Acoustics of Buildings* ix. 171 Suitable insulating material can be..interposed between columns, girders, cross-beams etc., to counteract the transmission of sound. **1940** *Chambers's Techn. Dict.* 451/1 *Insulating oils*, special types of oil..used for oil-immersed transformers, circuit-breakers, etc. **1945** *Archit. Rev.* CVI. 308 Roof of steel decking covered with half-inch insulating board and mineral-faced felt. **1955** *Oxf. Jun. Encycl.* VIII. 399/1 The defence against noise lies in planning wisely.. and also in using sound insulating and sound absorbing materials. **1963** H. R. CLAUSER *Encycl. Engin. Materials* 352/1 The selection of the proper insulating varnish for an electrical unit, such as a motor, generator, solenoid coil, or a transformer, is becoming of increasing importance as the efficiency and ratings of electrical units are improved.

insulation. Add: **1.** (Earlier and later examples.) Also, an island.

1848 E. BRYANT *California* xi. 157 The waters surrounding these insulations could be traced between them as far as the eye could reach. **1871** *Scribner's Monthly* II. 7 Their smooth sides, uniform width and height..considered in connection with the courses which had wrought their insulation, excited our wonder and admiration.

3. (Earlier and later examples.) Also used with reference to sound.

1767 J. PRIESTLEY *Hist. & Present State Electr.* 515 It is advisable that there should be no sharp edges or angles about the rubber [of the electrical machine], for that would make the insulation of it..ineffectual. **1913** *Chem. Abstr.* VII. 689 (*heading*) Incombustible and refractory materials for insulation from sound, heat and cold. **1955** *Oxf. Jun. Encycl.* VIII. 399/2 Double partitions, ..'floating floors',..and independent or suspended ceilings are all forms of construction used for sound insulation. **1972** L. L. DOELLE *Environmental Acoustics* xiv. 173 Bare concrete slab..gives satisfactory insulation against airborne noises.

b. (Further examples.)

1927 DAVIS & KAYE *Acoustics of Buildings* ix. 171 Felt-like insulation may..be introduced into the..structure of the building, to assist in isolating noise. **1969** *Sears Catal.* Spring/Summer 963 Fiber glass insulation..keeps water hotter and jacket cooler.

4. *insulation meter, tape, test, tester.*

1909 *Cent. Dict.* Suppl., Insulation-meter. **1920** *Talking Machine News & Jrnl. Amusements* Feb. 77/2 Electrical insulation tape in a metal horn. **1903** *Whittaker's Electr. Engineer's Pocket-Bk.* 276 (*heading*) Insulation tests. **1923** *Nature* 13 Jan. 63/2 The 'Meg' insulation tester.., a remarkably light and cheap megger.

insulative (i·nsiŭlēⁱtiv, -ătiv), *a.* [f. INSULAT(E *v.*: see -IVE.] Of, pertaining to, or as insulation.

1945 *Sci. News Let.* 23 June 397/3 The insulative concretes vary in weight from one-third to one-half that of ordinary gravel concrete. **1971** *Nature* 4 June 331/1 The fur was very spiny with virtually no soft underfur and thus probably offers little insulative protection. This may be an adaptation to the tropical environment. **1973** *Ibid.* 26 Jan. 240/1 Their fur is less than half as long..and has a correspondingly lower insulative quality.

insulator. For 'telegraph wires' read 'telegraph or telephone wires, or power lines'. Also used with reference to sound. (Further examples.)

1814 G. J. SINGER *Elem. Electr.* III. iii. 278 Insulation may..be partially preserved by coating all the glass insulators with sealing wax. **1847** BRETT & LITTLE *Compendium Improvements Electr. Telegraphs* 22 The insulators are made of earthenware, and secured direct to the poles. **1927** DAVIS & KAYE *Acoustics of Buildings* ix. ..e usual principle is to have double walls..and to ..ace..with sound absorbents or insulators. **1950** .. & HARRIS *Acoustical Designing in Archit.* xi. ..rous blocks are not plastered, they may be very poor insulators: sound 'leaks' through the interstices. **1957** *Encycl. Brit.* XIV. 115I/1 On steel tower transmission lines the lightning voltage which can exist on the conductors..depends on the lightning flashover value of the supporting insulators.

insulin (i·nsiŭlin). *Biochem.* Also † **insuline.** [f. L. *insul-a* island (because it is produced by the islets of Langerhans) + -IN¹.] **1.** A polypeptide hormone (the amino-acid composition differing slightly from species to species) which is concerned with carbohydrate metabolism in man and some other vertebrates, being produced by the islets of Langerhans and having effects that include the removal of sugar from the blood (so that a deficiency of insulin causes diabetes mellitus) and the promotion of protein synthesis and fat storage.

The name *insulin(e)* was proposed for the hormone on three separate occasions, each time independently: see quot. 1926.

[**1909** J. DE MEYER in *Archivio di Fisiol.* VII. 96 Le produit de la sécrétion interne du pancréas (non denommé encore).., s'il dérive, comme nous le pensons, des ilots de Langerhans pourrait être appelé *Insuline.*] **1914** E. A. SCHÄFER *Introd. Study Endocrine Glands* 84 The results of pancreas-extirpation and pancreas-grafting can..be best explained by supposing that the islet-tissue produces an autacoid substance which passes into the blood and affects carbohydrate metabolism and carbohydrate storage in such a manner that there is no undue accumulation of glucose in the blood. Provisionally it will be convenient for description purposes to refer to this hypothetical autacoid as insuline. **1916** —— *Endocrine Organs* xvii. 128 The islet tissue produces an autacoid which passes into the blood and affects carbohydrate metabolism...Provisionally it will be convenient to refer to this hypothetical autacoid as insuline. **1922** F. G. BANTING et al. in *Proc. & Trans. R. Soc. Canada* XVI. v. 27 (*heading*) The preparation of pancreatic extracts containing insulin. **1922** F. G. BANTING et al. in *Amer. Jrnl. Physiol.* LXII. 175 Purified alcoholic extracts of pancreas, for which we suggest the name *insulin*, when injected subcutaneously into normal rabbits cause the percentage of sugar in the blood to fall within a few hours. **1923** A. E. HOUSMAN *Let.* 16 May (1971) 213 When I saw the invention of Insulin I..expected to hear you were cured already. **1926** E. A. SCHÄFER *Endocrine Organs* (ed. 2) II. xlix. 343 To this autacoid the name insulin is applied. [*Note*] The term was introduced by de Meyer (Arch. di fisiol., vii., 1909). In ignorance of this it was employed as a convenient term to denote the autacoid of the islet tissue in the first edition of this work, published in 1916. It was independently adopted by the Toronto workers [*viz.* F. G. Banting et al.] in 1922. **1956** *Arch. Biochem. & Biophysics* LXV. 427 The amino acid sequences in pig and sheep insulins were compared with that of cattle insulin...The only differences found were in the three residues occupying positions 8, 9, and 10 in the glycyl chain. **1959** *Ann. N.Y. Acad. Sci.* LXXXII. 340 Most commercial preparations are mixtures of beef and pork insulin. **1968** PASSMORE & ROBSON *Compan. Med. Stud.* I. xxv. 43/1 Insulin promotes all the known pathways of glucose disposal and transformation including glycogen storage, fat formation, total oxidation and the use of the hexose-monophosphate pathway.

2. *attrib.* and *Comb.*, as **insulin shock**, hypoglycæmia resulting from excessive insulin in the body, producing nervousness, weakness, sweating and in extreme cases coma, **insulin coma**; **insulin (shock) treatment**, a treatment for mental illness consisting of a course of artificially produced insulin comas (see quot. 1951).

1942 M. DICKENS *One Pair of Feet* viii. 167 A policeman, who had mistaken an Insulin coma for a drunken stupor. **1959** *Times* 26 Mar. 15/5 Not for them the hashish-dream and the insulin-coma. **1972** *Chem. Abstr.* LXXVII. 135684 After more than 45 min in an insulin coma, administration of glucose..to the affected animals did not interrupt the coma. **1925** *Ann. Clin. Med.* III. 381/1 In diabetics whose blood sugars were high, that is above 300 mgm., symptoms of insulin shock frequently have been observed when their blood sugars were rapidly reduced to within usual normal range. **1936** *Jrnl. Nerv. & Mental Dis.* LXXXV. 504 Insulin shock stimulates metabolism in general and liver function in particular. **1938** *Arch. Neurol. & Psychiatry* (Chicago) XXXIX. 1 (*heading*) Insulin shock treatment of schizophrenic patients. **1951** F. HOPKINS in E. N. Chamberlain *Text-bk. Med.* ix. 692 Insulin shock treatment..consists of the induction of coma by the injection of insulin. When the optimum dose for the individual case has been ascertained, a coma is induced each day for five or six days a week until a course of 50 or thereabouts has been given. **1958** H. BECKMAN *Drugs* xxxiv. 351/2 Epinephrine is used adjuvantly in combating insulin shock. **1940** *Ann. Internal Med.* XIV. 393 The insulin treatment of schizophrenia owes its origin to an accidental observation made by Sakel in his treatment of morphine addicts. **1958** I. MURDOCH *Bell* xxvi. 302 Catherine had been having insulin treatment and was continually under the influence of drugs.

Hence **i·nsulinase** [*-ASE], an enzyme or enzyme system that breaks down insulin; **i·nsulinized** *ppl. a.*, treated with insulin.

1928 *Amer. Jrnl. Physiol.* LXXXIV. 571 In both of these fishes the normal sugars are often even lower than the reduced sugars of the insulinized trout, scup and menhaden. **1949** MIRSKY & BROH-KAHN in *Arch. Biochem.* XX. 8 Pending further investigation, it is proposed..to characterize the active principle in these extracts as 'insulinase'. **1959** *Metabolism* VIII. 99 The liver is rich in an enzyme system designated 'insulinase', which causes cleavage of insulin; this system may be comprised of more than one enzyme. **1966** *Chem. Abstr.* LXV. 1157 The increased sensitivity of aged humans and animals towards hypoglycemics is probably due to decreased insulinase activity. **1969** *Physiol. Chem. & Physics* I. 355 (*heading*) The subsequent accumulation of labeled glucose by insulinized frog muscle at 0°C.

insult, *sb.* Add: **1. d.** *Med.* Anything which tends to cause disease in or injury to the body or to disturb normal bodily processes; also, the resulting reaction, lesion, or injury.

[Cf. quots. 1603, 1610 for sense 1.] **1904** STEDMAN *Dunglison's Dict. Med. Sci.* (ed. 23) 581/1 *Insult*, injury; trauma exciting a morbid process. **1959** S. DUKE-ELDER *Parsons' Dis. Eye* (ed. 13) xvii. 228 The avascularity of the sclera and the lack of reaction of its dense fibrous tissues to insult whether traumatic or infective, make diseases of this tissue relatively rare. **1961** *Acta Psychiatrica et Neurol. Scand. Suppl.* CL. 110 Patients with cerebrovascular insults. *Ibid.* 112 It was possible that the insult had been provoked by the anti-hypertensive therapy. **1962** HARRIS & GRUBER in A. Pirie *Lens Metabolism Rel. Cataract* 373 Changes in the level of inorganic and organic phosphate within the lens may follow certain metabolic insults. *Ibid.* 375 The older the lens, the less is it able to withstand the insult which cold induces. **1970** G. R. TAYLOR *Doomsday Bk.* vii. 158 The US population was exposed to 'severe chronic lead insult' (insult being a technical term in medicine). **1971** *Nature* 23 July 276/2 Left handedness may be caused by neurological insults associated with prenatal or birth trauma. **1971** *Sci. Amer.* Oct. 118/2 Congenital heart abnormalities are the most serious of the commoner defects. Often caused by rubella or similar insults in the early months of pregnancy, they affect about one birth in 60.

2. Freq. in phr. *to add insult to injury.*

1748 E. MOORE *Foundling* v. v. 60 This is adding Insult to Injuries. **1805** *Deb. Congress U.S.* 31 Jan. 1072 It was adding insult to injury, and expenses to both, as it regarded the claimants. **1807** *Ibid.* 18 Nov. 933 Were the laws of a free and respectable State to be evaded by such shameful expedients as these? This was adding insult to injury. **1853** H. T. RILEY tr. *Phædrus' Fables* 429 You wanted to revenge the sting of a tiny insect with death; what will you do to yourself who have added insult to injury? **1928** A. HUXLEY *Point Counter Point* ix. 155 It shocked him that one should lie in bed while other people were up and working. To get up late was somehow to add insult to injury. **1970** B. SPOCK *Decent & Indecent* 19 The behavioural sciences then added insult to injury. Psychologists have given man the impression that he responds like a laboratory rat. **1972** *Times* 12 Dec. 22/7 They submitted defective contracts, made arithmetical errors adding up to several thousand pounds and, to add insult to injury, charged their fees on the wrong and higher scale.

4. Used *attrib.* in expressions denoting contests in verbal insult, characteristic of U.S. Blacks.

1964 *Amer. Folk Music Occasional* I. 81 One of the standard routines of both the Negro and blackface minstrel show was the insult-dialogue. Though this theatrical expression is no longer widely current, this kind of dialogue has retained an interest... Here..is an insult-routine used in a street corner situation. **1968** P. OLIVER *Screening Blues* vi. 246 Dr Abrahams makes acknowledgment of the dozens as played by young Negroes in the army but had not himself noted much use of the insult game among females or adults generally. **1969** *Language* XLV. 602 The children I studied engaged in constant verbal play..(for instance, their ritualized insult game).

insurance. Add: **4. e.** The act or system of insuring employed persons against sickness or unemployment, esp. in accordance with the National Insurance Acts of 1911, 1920, 1946, and 1965, which require certain wage-earners to make weekly payments supplemented by their employers, in return for which they are entitled to State assistance in sickness, unemployment, etc.

1878, etc. [see *National Insurance* s.v. *NATIONAL *a.* 5]. **1911** *Times* 28 Mar. 10/3 The preparation of the Sickness and Invalidity Insurance Bill. *Ibid.* 5 May 14/3 If he had divided his bill into two—one dealing with unemployment and one with invalidity insurance. *Ibid.* 14/5 The burden imposed by State insurance must necessarily fall on manufacturers. **1911** *Act 1 & 2 Geo. V* c. 55. 337 National Health Insurance. **1912** [see sense *5]. **1920** *Act 10 & 11 Geo. V.* c. 30 § 48 (1) This act may be cited as the Unemployment Insurance Act, 1920.

5. (sense 4) *insurance adjuster, agency, agent, commissioner, company* (examples), *man, officer, policy* (examples), *premium*; (sense *4 e) *insurance act, benefit, card, committee, stamp.*

1755 Insurance premium [see ASSURANCE 5]. **1784** in H. M. Brooks *Days of Spinning-Wheel in New Eng.* (1886) 62 The Gentlemen forming this Insurance Company, whose names are inserted in each Policy. **1866** C. N. EMERSON *Internal Revenue Guide* 73 Insurance agents shall pay ten dollars. **1869** 'MARK TWAIN' *Innoc. Abr.* xxxviii. 409 If her [*sc.* Smyrna's] 'crown of life' had been an insurance policy, she would have had an opportunity to collect on it. **1874** B. F. TAYLOR *World on Wheels*, etc. II. ii. 199 He was an insurance agent—a retired doctor, who growing weary of saving lives with pills, had taken to insuring lives with policies. **1879** *Harper's Mag.* July 215 The insurance men..would insure the lives of the hands who were at work there. **1881** *Instructions to Census Clerks* (1885) 83 Insurance Company's officer, manager, actuary, secretary,..clerk. **1883** 'MARK TWAIN' *Life on Mississippi* xliii. 436 Insurance-agency business, you know; mighty

irregular. **1889** *Cent. Dict.*, *Insurance commissioner*, in some of the United States, a State officer who in behalf of the public maintains a supervision over the affairs of insurance companies. **1911** *Act* 1 & 2 *Geo. V.* c. 55 § 15 The regulations made by the Insurance Commissioners. *Ibid.*, The Insurance Committee for each county or county borough. *Ibid.* § 115 This Act may be cited as the National Insurance Act, 1911. **1912** *Chemist & Druggist* LXXX. 950/2 Cards and stamps for health insurance under the National Insurance Act are now procurable at post offices. **1912** *Punch* 31 July 99/3 Mr. Masterman has laid it down that it is the wife's duty, and not that of the husband, to lick the servants' insurance stamps. **1913** *Ibid.* 15 Jan. 49/1 As the 15th of January approaches, bringing fulfilment of 9d. for 4d. through operation of Insurance Act. *Ibid.* 13 Aug. 148/3 Somebody come to see about an insurance card or something. **1915** W. Owen *Let.* 22 June (1967) 189 Am feeling quite independent of Insurance Policies just now. **1923** D. H. Lawrence *Birds, Beasts, & Flowers* 86 Ah Phoenix, Phoenix, John's Eagle! You are only known to us now as the badge of an insurance Company. **1926** Fowler *Mod. Eng. Usage* 741/1 The injustice of throwing on the landlord in whose house they happen to be resident the cost of a large additional insurance benefit for those who are sick. **1929** J. B. Priestley *Good Companions* I. i. 32 He..threw an insurance card and some money on the table. **1930** *Morning Post* 7 Aug. 11 The employers at four factories agreed to take upon themselves the charge of the insurance stamp which the men refuse to pay. **1933** Insurance agent [see *confidence *sb.* 10]. **1933** *Radio Times* 14 Apr. 98/1 Meltonian Cream..is..an insurance policy for shoes. **1934** Insurance adjuster [see *adjuster]. **1945** N. L. McClung *Stream runs Fast* xii. 99 But one day, an insurance man, hearing that Wes had sold his drug store came out to offer him an agency, and Wes became an agent for the Manufacturers' Life Insurance Company. **1958** *Listener* 23 Oct. 634/2 The insurance officer denied that this was an industrial accident. **1961** *Ibid.* 10 Aug. 219/2 An insurance adjuster who also acts as a private detective. **1972** J. Gores *Dead Skip* (1973) xiv. 101 Harvey E. Wyman was red-faced and jovial... He was also, unlike so many small insurance agents Ballard had met, very smart. **1973** W. McCarthy *Detail* i. 56 You should check the people you choose more carefully... They must also have special diets. Just an insurance policy.

insure, *v.* Add: **4. d.** (Cf. *insurance 4 e.)
1911 *Act* 1 & 2 *Geo. V* c. 55 § 1 All persons so insured (in this Act called 'insured persons').

‖ **insurrecto** (insʊre·kto). [Sp.] An insurgent or rebel. Also *attrib.* or as *adj.*
1907 *Cablenews* (Manila, Philippines) 21 Aug. 5/7 Villa, then Colonel of the insurrecto army. **1910** *Sat. Even. Post* 15 Oct. 17/2 I'll declare an amnesty for him and all his insurrectos. **1930** J. Dos Passos *42nd Parallel* I. 1 Up to where them insurrectos was afightin' fit to kill. **1947** *Sat. Even. Post* 8 Mar. 18/3 Later he saw a bit of fighting in the Philippines, north of Manila, against Aguinaldo's insurrectos.

inswept (i·nswept), *a.* [f. In *adv.* + Swept *ppl. a.*] Of the frame of a motor vehicle: narrowed at the forward end or at the side.
1907 *Westm. Gaz.* 12 Nov. 12/3 The frames will be inswept from the dash. **1908** *Ibid.* 30 Jan. 4/1 The frame.. is inswept in front and gracefully upturned in the rear.

inswinger (i·nswi:ŋəɹ). *Cricket.* [In *adv.*] A ball bowled with a swerve or swing from the off to leg in its flight; also, the bowler of such a ball. So **i·nswing,** the swerve or swing imparted to such a ball; a ball bowled in this manner; as vb., to bowl an inswinger; hence **i·nswi:nging** *ppl. a.*
1920 *Times* 29 May 7/2 He [*sc.* Mr. Robertson-Glasgow] again seemed to rely too much on his 'inswinger' on the leg side, and he would surely do very much better if he could be certain of pitching his inswinging ball on the off stump. **1920** E. R. Wilson in P. F. Warner *Cricket* 67 The first right-handed 'in-swinger'..who was in-swinging as early as 1895. **1924** N. Cardus *Days in Sun* 49 Jacques, of Hampshire..was a bowler commanding an in-swinging flight and an off-break. *Ibid.* 254 Nor would it be accurate to describe this ball as an in-swinger, for the true in-swinger swings from almost the first few yards of its flight through the air. **1927** *Observer* 17 Apr. 17/3 Last year he [*sc.* Mr. Allom] specialised in the 'inswing'. **1933** *Times* 28 Jan. 11/5 The leg-theory has been bowled in this country for a number of years, starting with 'in-swing' bowling. **1953** R. Warner *Escapade* 74 He bowls in-swingers himself, though as a matter of fact he takes most of his wickets with his leg-breaks. **1955** *Times* 5 July 4/1 D. J. Smith, in spite of an in-swinger's action, was making the ball move from leg, and C. S. Smith was finding umpire Pothecary hard to satisfy. **1958** *Times* 22 Oct. 14/1 As it is, it may be many a long day before he has better figures as a medium-pace inswinger. **1962** *Times* 2 Aug. 3/3 Buxton, who bowled his inswing deceptively.

‖ **intacta** (intæ·ktă). [fem. of L. *intactus* (see Intact *a.*).] A shortening of L. *virgo intacta* a woman of inviolate chastity, used as adj. to denote: unaffected, not spoiled or sullied, esp. in *fig.* senses.
1941 H. G. Wells *You can't be too Careful* III. xvi. 198 Edward Albert attempted an ironical whistle, but Mrs Butter held her position, intacta. **1960** A. West *Trend is Up* (1961) vi. 244 There's no sex angle to it. The kid is *intacta*, so's the woman for that matter. **1966** *New Statesman* 25 Feb. 255/3 The *People*'s 5½ million readers found their favourite Sunday paper *intacta* this week: the carefully balanced mixture of sex, exposure and sport ..had not been tampered with.

intaglio. Add: **3.** *attrib.* as *intaglio cylinder, engraving, impression, method, principle, printer, process, type, work*; **intaglio print,** an impression of a plate cut in intaglio; **intaglio printing,** the group of processes used to print intaglio plates.
1859 *Abridgments of Specifications relating to Printing* (Patent Office) 354 The invention consists..in producing intaglio-graphic printing and other plates from forms of intaglio types by taking a casting in plaster of Paris, or other suitable material. *a* **1877** Knight *Dict. Mech.* II. 1192/1 *Intaglio-type*, a process..depending upon the production of a friable surface of oxide of zinc on a metallic plate under hydraulic pressure... At drying, the surface is brushed over,..leaving an intaglio impression. **1886** R. A. M. Stevenson tr. *Delaborde's Engraving* iii. 55 It is his [*sc.* Finiguerra's] invention..of the art of printing intaglio engravings, or rather of the art of engraving itself, that has made him immortal. **1888** C. T. Jacobi *Printers' Vocab.* 66 *Intaglio*, printing, such as from copper-plate—the reverse of 'relief' printing. **1914** E. H. Richter *Prints* i. 8 The different intaglio processes produce their blacks in different ways. **1917** E. Pound *Lustra* 181 Give up the intaglio method? **1921** *Dict. Occup. Terms* (1927) § 529 *Intaglio printer*..places metal intaglio cylinder in position in machine, sets roll of paper and adjusts machine for even printing. **1930** D. Strang *Printing of Etchings & Engravings* 1 The term 'etchings' will often..be intended to include all the other processes which are commonly employed by the artist in the making of intaglio prints. **1933** T. S. Barber in W. Atkins *Art & Pract. Printing* IV. i. 8 Printing was done by the intaglio method of inking and wiping. **1959** *Chambers's Encycl.* V. 341/2 Intaglio work, when the design is cut into the block or plate. **1965** Zigrosser & Gaehde *Guide to Collecting Orig. Prints* iv. 46 Intaglio Process... A general term descriptive of all techniques employing the intaglio principle of duplication, where the design is incised below the surface of the plate. **1967** V. Strauss *Printing Industry* i. 28/1 Intaglio printing is the name of a process family comprising a variety of printing methods which all use printing-image carriers with the printing areas sunken, or embedded, in the depth of the carrier material. **1972** W. Chamberlain *Thames & Hudson Man. Etching & Engraving* i. 11 In the context of intaglio printmaking, the term 'etching' normally refers to both the action of corroding lines, etc. into a metal plate with acid, and the inked, paper impression taken from the surface of the plate.

intake, *sb.* For 'Chiefly *Sc.* and *north. dial.*' read 'orig. *Sc.* and *north. dial.*' Add: **1.** (Further examples.)
1940 *Economist* 9 Nov. 590/1 Thanks to the heavy intake of raw wool this year..it has been possible to meet military and almost all export requirements without stinting the home consumer. **1955** *Times* 10 May 18/3 The intake of orders for the first four months is higher than ever before. **1971** *Nature* 2 July 63/3 Thus there is the intake and evaluation in one computerized centre of duplicate magnetic tapes from many sources.
b. (One of) a group of entrants to the army, a school, a trade, etc.
a **1943** B. Webb *Our Partnership* (1948) ii. 79 It was.. among educational ladders..the most elaborate in its organisation of 'intakes' and promotions. **1943** *Times* 10 Dec. 2/1 That is evident from the moment when new intakes arrive and at once are interviewed by the.. commanding officer. **1946** *News Chron.* 8 Aug. 1/4 It is understood that they will be part of the new intake of the U.S. Army. **1958** *Technology* May 66/2 The intake pattern can be worked out for transfer at appropriate stages. **1970** *Nature* 28 Nov. 798/1 The school should be functioning by 1975, with an intake of 100 students.
3. *attrib.*, as *intake crib, tunnel, well.*
1909 *Daily Chron.* 21 Jan. 1/7 A fire which occurred at the construction works of a waterworks intake crib on Lake Michigan. **1909** *Westm. Gaz.* 21 Jan., This new intake tunnel was thrust further out into the lake. **1964** R. Perry *World of Tiger* xi. 160 A tiger had attacked a tapir at a reservoir near Kuala Lumpur, and..both had fallen into the dry 'intake' well.
4. b. Short for *air-intake* (*air *sb.*[1] B. II).
1946 *Flight* 1 Aug. 115/2 (*caption*) A Heinkel single-jet proposal with the intake between two nacelles. **1959** *Listener* 30 July 164/1 He dealt with the ice that started forming on the engine intakes of the Vickers Vimy machine.
7. *attrib.* and *Comb.* (see also 3 above).
1921 *Dict. Occup. Terms* (1927) § 449 *Intake man*, grain intake man (grain milling); at a signal from men on ship, barge, etc., alongside wharf that suction pipe is inserted in grain, starts air pump, which draws up grain through pipe by suction. **1940** *Chambers's Techn. Dict.* 451/2 *Intake belt course*, a projecting course of stone or bricks, serving as an intake at a place where the thickness of a wall is diminished. **1941** *B.B.C. Gloss. Broadc. Terms* 15 *Intake report*, analysis summarizing the content of broadcasts directed to listeners in a particular country, in its own language, from a selected number of stations. **1957** *Times* 2 July (Agric. Suppl.) p. vi/2 A typical old barn now houses the grain intake pit, cleaner, pre-dry bin, continuous dryer, and sectional storage bins. **1958** *U.S. Dept. Agric. Yearbk.* 1957 760/2 *Intake rate*, the rate, usually expressed in inches per hour, at which rain or irrigation water enters the soil. **1961** B. Fergusson *Watery Maze* v. 127 Those ports on the West Coast which had become intake valves for our life's blood from across the Atlantic. **1966** Intake chimney [see *Cordtex]. **1972** *Classification of Occupations & Directory Occupational Titles* (Department of Employment) III. 478/1 *Intakeman* (grain, sugar and similar materials). Checks supplies of grain, sugar and similar materials into storage silos, transfers materials to processing departments and maintains stock records.

intaker. Restrict † *Obs.* to sense in Dict. and add: **2.** (See quot. 1921.)
1921 *Dict. Occup. Terms* (1927) § 368 *Drawer*, drawer-in,..healder, in-taker,..attaches weaving beam to drawing-in frame, and draws each warp yarn, separately, with a hook, through eye (or loop) of heald, and through dent of reed in loom. **1960** *Classification of Occupations* (General Register Office) 49/3 In-taker.

intaking, *vbl. sb.* Restrict † *Sc. Obs.* to senses in Dict. and add later examples in senses 1 and *1 b of Intake *sb.*
1905 C. Kernahan *Visions* 283 The soft intaking of a baby's breath. **1959** *Listener* 5 Mar. 402/2 A period of intensive learning—of intaking rather than outputting. **1966** I. Jefferies *House-Surgeon* iv. 88, I just went to the intaking chief.

intangibility. Add: **b.** Inviolability.
1783 C. J. Fox *Memorials & Corr.* (1853) II. 102, I beg of gentlemen to be aware of the lengths to which their arguments upon the intangibility of this charter may be carried. **1929** *Times* 13 Aug. 10/2 There has been too much talk..of the intangibility of the Young Plan.

intangible, *a.* Add: **B.** *sb.* Anything intangible; spec. (in *pl.*) = *intangible assets*, i.e. assets (e.g. goodwill, rights, etc.) which cannot easily or precisely be measured.
1914 *Cycl. Amer. Govt.* III. 496/1 The term 'personal property'..includes..visible property and intangibles. **1930** *Economist* 29 Mar. 710/1 Net tangible assets may be defined as total assets less 'intangibles' (goodwill, patents, etc.), current liabilities, and funded debt. **1933** *Discovery* Oct. 313/2 Scientific changes were coming in so thick and fast that other factors in social life—the intangibles of credit, the improvements in political and international ideas—were unequal to the task of accommodating them. **1949** *Here & Now* (N.Z.) Oct. 30/3 The intangibles—the many local developments—being not reducible to statistics, the food of all bureaucracy, count for nothing. **1957** *Economist* 19 Oct. (Suppl.) 1/2 The success of individual motor producers will depend mainly upon intangibles such as the success of their design policy.

‖ **intarsia** (intā·ɹsiă). Also **-io.** [It. *intarsio.*] = Tarsia. Also *attrib., transf.* and *fig.* So **intarsiatore** (intā:ɹsiătōᵊ·re), a worker in intarsia; **intarsiatura** (intā:ɹsiătūᵊ·ră), pl. **-e,** = *intarsia.
1863 A. Jameson *Legends of Monastic Orders* (ed. 3) 275 The fine intarsiatura in the Choir of San Francesco di Assisi. **1867** *Ecclesiologist* XXVIII. 216 Hidden under the intarsio pavement. **1868** C. C. Perkins *Italian Sculptors* 262 A celebrated wood-carver and 'intarsiatore' named Luchino Bianchini..helped them to carve the presses for the sacristy. *Ibid.*, Luchino Bianchini..made the woodwork about its great portal, as well as the intaglios and intarsiature of the choir at San Lodovico. **1892** A. M. Clerke *Familiar Stud. Homer* x. 266 Some rusty dagger-blades..skilfully ornamented in coloured metallic intarsiatura. **1894** *Daily News* 6 Dec. 5/2 Humorous intarsia showing Polyphemus..feeling the backs of the sheep. **1896** *Q. Rev.* Oct. 471 The intarsias of the choir-stalls of S. Maria Maggiore at Bergamo. **1906** *Westm. Gaz.* 4 July 2/1 The Brunellese looked critically at the intarsia chests of drawers. **1913** Mrs. H. Ward *Mating of Lydia* iv. xix. 389 The gleaming reflections on lacquer and intarsia, on ebony or Sèvres. **1919** H. F. Jones *Samuel Butler* II. 67 The seats of the stalls in the church of Santa Maria Maggiore at Bergamo are ornamented with intarsia work. **1945** *Burlington Mag.* Aug. 191/2 The treatment of the *intarsia* is closely paralleled in the panelling of coeval rooms in Swiss museums. **1957** *Textile Terms & Defs.* (Textile Inst.) (ed. 3) 54 *Intarsia.* (1) Weft-knitted plain, rib or purl fabrics containing designs in two or more colours... (2) A motif design in stitch and/or colour. **1958** *Listener* 11 Sept. 388/3 Of the poems, with their tessellated intarsia of natural scenery, natural passion and liturgical imagery, perhaps the most revealing on the subject of Zhivago's destiny is the first. **1970** *Times* 28 Feb. (Sat. Suppl.) p. vii/4 The most startling form of marquetry was perspective picture making in wood, known as intarsia. **1973** *Guardian* 10 Apr. 13/3 Sweater with intarsia thistle motif.

integral, *a.* and *sb.* Add: **A.** *adj.* **1.** (Further examples of uses in technical contexts.)
1923 Glazebrook *Dict. Appl. Physics* V. 165/1 This cylinder has an open-ended steel barrel with integral fins. **1958** *Chambers's Techn. Dict.* 987/1 *Integral stiffeners*, the stiffening ridges left when an aircraft skin panel is machined from a solid billet. **1968** *Gloss. Formwork Terms* (*B.S.I.*) 16 *Integral facing*, a special facing concrete or mortar cast simultaneously with the backing concrete so as to be monolithic with it. **1972** [see *integrally *adv.* b].
2. (Further examples of uses in technical contexts.)
1945 H. D. Smyth *Gen. Acct. Devel. Atomic Energy Mil. Purposes* xii. 132 Two 'integral experiments' (experiments on assembled or integrated systems comprising fissionable material, reflector, and perhaps moderator also) may be described. **1953** C. Wallace *Photographer's Pocket-Bk.* 112 In modern colour materials the colours are achieved by building up on a suitable base..an 'integral tri-pack' of three separate emulsions.
4. d. *integral domain*: see *domain *sb.* 4 d.

integralism (inte·grăliz'm). [f. Integral *a.* 1 + -ism.] A name sometimes adopted for a philosophical or political, etc., doctrine or theory which involves the concept of an integral whole.
1871 S. P. Andrews *Primary Synopsis Universology* xii. 178 Integralism is the new and final philosophy; the

all-sided and complete reconciliation of all possible sectarian divisions in all spheres; not as extinguishing individual differences, but as softening, co-ordinating, and utilizing them. **1939** *Times* 18 Feb. 17/4 The counterpart of the Nazi movement—Integralism—has its supporters. **1964** D. G. MacRae in J. H. Plumb *Crisis in Humanities* 127 By 'integralism' is meant a set of beliefs that involve one in claiming that social structures form a 'seamless web' in which every institution and social position is linked to every other and is part of a unique, interconnected configuration. **1969** D. M. Smith *Italy* (ed. 2) vii. xxi. 255 The Rome party congress of 1906 had recorded a victory for 'integralism'..yet revolutionary socialism continued to spread.

integralist (inte·grălist), *sb.* [f. Integral *a.* 1 + -ist.] One who favours a policy or doctrine of integralism. Also *attrib.* or as *adj.* Cf. *integrist.

1907 I. Zangwill *Ghetto Comedies* 412 Russia is to be saved..by the Integralists, who alone maintain the purity of the Social Revolutionary programme. **1922** *Glasgow Herald* 23 Jan. 11 The so-called 'integralists' who held that every good Catholic should see eye to eye with the Holy Father in everything. **1930** *Times Educ. Suppl.* 3 May 197/2 The schools or coteries of the last few decades—the symbolists,..integralists,..and so forth. **1938** *Sun* (Baltimore) 12 May 1/1 To smash completely the outlawed integralist Greenshirt organization. **1967** C. Seton-Watson *Italy from Liberalism to Fascism* vii. 267 His [*sc.* Ferri's] contribution to the restoration of party unity was ..inspired by the 'integralist' formula of 'Neither to right nor to left, but straight ahead'. *Ibid.* xi. 437 So far from being an integralist, he had during his years at Bologna come under suspicion of modernist sympathies. **1968** R. K. Merton *Social Theory* (rev. ed.) iii. xv. 529 He [*sc.* Sorokin] adopts an 'integralist' conception of truth.

integrally, *adv.* **b.** Delete † and add later examples.

1936 Colvin & Stanley *Turning & Boring Pract.* ix. 131 Gisholt lathes have been materially changed in design and construction. Headstocks are now cast integrally with the bed. **1952** S. E. Rusinoff *Forging & Forming Metals* iv. 55 Small steam hammers have the anvil and frame cast integrally, but large hammers have a separate anvil. **1972** *Sci. Amer.* Jan. 49/2 (Advt.), An integral peak-reading meter lets you optimize record level without using a scope. Options include a 5 to 30 foot loop adaptor, an interrupting voice channel, and an inverter for 12 or 28 VDC..all integrally mounted.

integrand (i·ntĭgrænd). *Math.* [ad. L. *integrand-us*, gerundive of *integrāre* (see Integrate *v.*): see *-and[2].] An expression that is to be integrated.

1897 H. F. Baker *Abel's Theorem* xviii. 561 The integrand of the Abelian integral u_r is single-valued on the Riemann surface. **1937** *Proc. Cambr. Philos. Soc.* XXXIII. 374 It is natural to approximate by expanding the integrand in powers of z. **1968** Fox & Mayers *Computing Methods for Scientists & Engineers* ix. 178 We illustrate this process..by considering the computation of the integral $I = \int_0^1 (0{\cdot}92 \cosh x - \cos x)\, dx$... Table 9.3 gives the tabulated values of the integrand and its differences.

integraph (i·ntĭgrɑf). [ad. F. *intégraphe* (B. Abdank-Abakanowicz 1885, in *La Lumière électr.* 17 Oct. 111/1), f. *intégral* Integral *a.* and *sb.*, *intégrer* to Integrate *v.*: see -graph.] Any of various kinds of apparatus which mechanically draw a curve representing the variation in the integral of some given curve or function as a limit or parameter varies.

1885 *Min. Proc. Inst. Civil Engin.* LXXXII. 162 The machines that he [*sc.* B. Abdank-Abakanowicz] had called briefly 'Integraphs' traced these curves mechanically. **1902** *Encycl. Brit.* XXX. 582/1 While an integrator determines the value of a definite integral, hence a mere constant, an integraph gives the value of an indefinite integral, which is a function of x. **1927** *Jrnl. Franklin Inst.* CCIII. 64 Mechanical integrators usually evaluate the definite integral between given fixed limits... The present machine, which we have called an integraph, since it records the result of an integration in the form of a plot or graph, has therefore been developed to evaluate $F(x)$ against x from the expression $F(x) = \int_a^x f_1(x) f_2(x) dx$ where f_1 and f_2 are known functions, formal or empirical. **1931** *Ibid.* CCXII. 77 The Photo-Electric Integraph..extends the range of practical solution of mathematical problems through its usefulness in the evaluation of integrals having a variable parameter within the integrand. **1961** S. Fifer *Analogue Computation* IV. xxv. 968 The development of the harmonic analyzer is closely associated with the development of two devices, (1) the planimeter,..and (2) the integraph, which draws a graph of the indefinite integral of a function.

integrate, *a.* Add: **2.** *Psychol.* Of, pertaining to, or designating people with strong eidetic imagery (particularly in the theories of Jaensch).

1930 O. Oeser tr. *Jaensch's Eidetic Imagery* iii. 93 In these individuals functions that later are separate still interpenetrate one another to a high degree and influence each other. That is why we call them 'integrate'. The integrate type is an earlier one from the evolutionary point of view. *Ibid.* 105 The integrate and disintegrate types are true fundamental forms of human existence corresponding, in a sense, to the fundamental forms dis-[illegible]d by biology. **1931** *Brit. Jrnl. Psychol.* July 94 [illegible]he child is in an integrate state, it should not be [illegible]ehave in a disintegrate manner. **1943** H. Read [illegible]h *Art* iv. iv. 81 Younger children and primitive peoples belong to an earlier evolutionary type which Jaensch calls 'integrate'.

integrate, *v.* Add: **2. b.** To bring (racially or culturally differentiated peoples) into equal membership of a society or system; to cease to segregate (racially). Also *intr.*, to become integrated. (See *integration 1 c.)

1948 *Richmond* (Virginia) *Times-Dispatch* 5 Aug. 1/8 (*headline*) Democrats 'integrate' Negroes for campaign. **1949** W. E. Barker in *Jrnl. Racial Affairs* I. i. 25 In the same way it can be seen that were South Africa to try to integrate her widely differing races, she would only create far greater problems than such a policy could ever solve. **1962** *Daily Tel.* 2 Aug. 10/2 It might be supposed that in doing these things for its people [i.e. of Tristan da Cunha], something had also been done to them: that they had.. been 'integrated'. Not so. They want to go home, with an intensity and unanimity of desire. **1964** Mrs. L. B. Johnson *White House Diary* 10 June (1970) 163 A girl who was one of the first students to be integrated at Little Rock was praised by her counselor. **1964** L. Nkosi *Rhythm of Violence* 46 Why don't Indians in this country ever 'integrate'? **1966** *New Statesman* 22 Apr. 575/1 Those children who came knowing some English integrated well, but, when we threw those who knew none into the maelstrom, they sank... No one was going to integrate without first being able to communicate. **1969** *Times* 30 Apr. 8/3 The Americans intend to make the scheme permanent ..but we advised the experiment to see how well they integrate. **1972** *Nature* 24 Mar. 133/1 Old people, sick people and isolated people need access to a telephone if they are to be fully integrated with the rest of society.

integrated, *ppl. a.* Add: Also of a personality in which the component elements combine harmoniously.

1941 *Brit. Jrnl. Psychol.* Apr. 298 Among the individuals studied..it was possible to distinguish..*integrated* personalities, in which conflicting drives had been reconciled and were now functioning in harmony with each other. **1945** *Psychol. Rev.* LII. 65/2 Later we shall see that an integrated personality does indeed have a kind of 'autonomy' which gives it a certain limited immunity to the Law of Effect. **1950** O. H. Mowrer *Learning Theory & Personality Dynamics* i. ii. 59 When, however, opposing impulses are more nearly matched, the submerged one is likely to exert its influence..by diminishing the smoothness and efficiency of the main stream of integrated behavior. **1954** G. W. Allport *Nature of Prejudice* v. xx. 339 What vanishes in an integrated personality are the racial bogies and traditional scapegoats who have nothing, really, to do with life's woes. **1963** A. Heron *Towards Quaker View of Sex* v. 48 Idealism can be a sign of spontaneous and selfless devotion in an integrated personality. **1973** *Lancet* 24 Feb. 441/2 The plaintiff was well integrated and had learned to live with the problem.

b. Uniting in one system several constituents previously regarded as separate; *integrated circuit*, a small unit or package, often no larger than a button, which is made as a single indivisible structure (such as a chip) and is electrically equivalent to a conventional circuit of many separate components.

1947 F. C. Simmons in *Jrnl. Forestry* XLV. 347/2 At the roadside, or at the using plant, the electric chain-saw, or one of the highly efficient circular-saw cutting-up plants,..can divide these tree lengths into raw material for the products to which they are best suited. This type of logging, which we call 'integrated logging' should result in higher returns from the logging job. **1954** Webster Add., *Integrated logging*, a system of logging planned to remove in one cutting all usable timber and to separate the primary products and distribute them to industries where they will bring the highest returns. **1958** J. T. Wellmark in *Aviation Age Res. & Devel. Technical Handbk. 1958–1959* F-6/1 One promising technique uses the 'integrated electronic device' concept. *Ibid.*, The true 'integrated device' can do the jobs of both active and passive components. **1959** *IRE Trans. Electronic Computers* VIII. 103/1 Some specific examples of integrated logic circuits..are shown in the figures below. **1962** *Electronics, Reliability & Microminiaturization* I. 184/1 In integrated circuits the [circuit] element may be a region in a block of the material rather than a separate device. **1962** A. Battersby *Guide to Stock Control* x. 96 Looking ahead in the field of Integrated Data Processing, we can foresee the situation in which the machine will prepare the advice note and invoice, classify and analyse the sales, calculate ROL and ROQ for each item and go on to send out orders automatically. **1964** *Times Rev. Industry* Apr. 49/2 It will be an integrated mill—trees will go in one end and fine paper will emerge from the other. **1967** *Times Rev. Industry* Mar. 46/1 Where once the circuit designer had to employ comparatively large components mounted on some sort of backing sheet..now he can often put in an integrated circuit, in which the separate components are commonly created in miniscule form on the surface of thin wafers of silicon by complex processing. **1969** A. C. Tickle *Thin-Film Transistors* i. 3 The first advanced all-thin-film integrated circuit, in which *both* active and passive devices were produced by thin-film deposition techniques, was produced by Weimer in 1965. It was designed for scanning an image sensor and contained 360 thin-film transistors, 180 diodes, 360 resistors, and 180 capacitors. **1970** F. C. Fitchen et al. *Electronic Integrated Circuits* i. 4 The monolithic integrated circuit is an IC whose [circuit] elements are formed in situ upon or within a semiconductor substrate with at least one of the elements formed within the substrate... In a multichip integrated circuit, the elements are formed on or within two or more semiconductor chips that are separately attached to a substrate. **1970** 'J. Earl' *Tuners & Amplifiers* i. 16 The majority of Class B and Class AB amplifiers..are of the so-called 'integrated' kind. This means that the preamplifiers and control unit..are built into the same housing—usually on the same chassis—as the power amplifiers and that a common power supply feeds both sections. **1973** *Physics Bull.* May 297/3 The continual recurrence of the same names in different fields of study is..in no way to be confused with, or used to justify, the contemporary rush to some illusory 'integrated science' concept.

c. Of institutions, groups, etc., which are not divided by considerations based on race or culture (see *integrate *v.* 2 b).

1948 *Richmond* (Virginia) *Times-Dispatch* 5 Aug. 1/8 This will be an integrated rather than a segregated operation. **1956** *N.Y. Times* 1 Oct., Approximately 2,400,000 Negro and 6,500,000 white pupils remained in segregated classes. Integrated school districts numbered 780; segregated numbered 3,000. **1958** *Newsweek* 29 Sept. 22 (*title*) Integrated schools or none. **1959** *Spectator* 11 Sept. 319/1 The newly integrated junior high school at Little Rock reopened, but not before three bombs had gone off. **1965** B. Sweet-Escott *Baker St. Irreg.* vi. 167 My assignment at A.F.H.Q. was with the planners. It was my first introduction to a really integrated staff... It was difficult to have a word in private with any of the British members of it because it was a rule that Americans and British should share rooms. **1974** *Times* 14 Jan. 12/4 Southern schools are now more integrated than their northern counterparts.

integrating, *vbl. sb.* and *ppl. a.* (in Dict. s.v. Integrate *v.*). Add: (Further examples.) *integrating circuit* Electr., a circuit whose output is the integral, with respect to time, of the input; *integrating factor* Math., an expression by which a differential equation may be multiplied to turn it into an exact equation (and therefore integrable as it stands); *integrating meter*, a meter which indicates the total amount of one quantity (e.g. electric charge passed) by effectively integrating, with respect to time, another (e.g. electric current).

1948 L. Jánossy *Cosmic Rays* ii. 43 Some authors make use of an integrating circuit which allows [one] to read the average counting rate at any instant. **1961** H. J. Reich *Functional Circuits & Oscillators* iv. 18 Integrating circuits find applications in..electronic instruments and controls,..in analog computers and in circuits for the generation of linearly rising voltages. **1973** M. Woodhouse *Blue Bone* iii. 24 The integrating Dekatron counter I was designing. **1859** G. Boole *Treat. Differential Equations* iv. 55 To every differential equation of the form $Mdx + Ndy = 0$, pertain an infinite number of integrating factors, all of which are included under a single functional expression. **1962** T. M. Apostol *Calculus* II. v. 241 A differential equation may have more than one integrating factor. **1902** *Encycl. Brit.* XXX. 597/1 All the above forms of house meters are called continuously integrating meters, in that the operation of recording or obtaining the time-integral of the current or power is continuous. **1943** *Gloss. Terms Electr. Engin.* (*B.S.I.*) 75 *Integrating frequency meter* (master frequency meter), an instrument for integrating the number of cycles through which the supply voltage has passed, and enabling this to be compared with the number through which it would have passed had the frequency been maintained at the prescribed value. **1952** E. Molloy *Electr. Instruments* 37 The induction disc principle is now adopted as the basic pattern for all types of alternating current integrating meters throughout the world.

integration. Add: **1. b.** *Psychol.* The combining of diverse parts into a complex whole; a complex state the parts of which are distinguishable; the harmonious combination of the different elements in a personality. Also *attrib.*

1855 H. Spencer *Princ. Psychol.* iii. xiv. 481 Progress in integration has been a necessary accompaniment of progress in speciality and complexity. **1893** J. M. Baldwin *Elem. Psychol.* 36 Integration, therefore, represents a structural change in the direction both of simplicity and of complexity. **1931** *Brit. Jrnl. Psychol.* July 25 A more adequate psychological theory..speaks of the 'integration' of the constituent sensations into a perception. **1937** L. T. Hopkins *Integration* i. 2 Integration must be the shorthand word to describe the process involved in this intelligent ongoing, interacting, adjusting behavior. **1938** L. P. Thorpe *Psychol. Found. Personality* ix. 434 Perhaps we are warranted then in using the word integration with the understanding that it stands for a wholeness in personality which gives direction to the coordination of parts. **1943** H. Read *Educ. through Art* iv. iv. 81 Jaensch's next step is to relate his classification to the degree of integration which the individual establishes between his mental imagery and the external world. **1963** Langner & Michael *Life Stress & Mental Health* xvi. 460 Integration involves the incorporation of the 'thou shalt nots' as well as the 'thou shalts', the acceptance of the middle-class rules of the game as well as the goal of winning.

c. The bringing into equal membership of a common society those groups or persons previously discriminated against on racial or cultural grounds.

1940 T. J. Haarhoff *S. Afr. & Crisis Mod. Civilization* 19 For the great task that awaits us in South Africa is a task of integration, of making the Union into a unity. **1949** *Jrnl. Racial Affairs* I. i. 25 Although..assimilation would destroy the racial differences in South Africa, it would necessitate the prior integration of the cultures—a very difficult and uncertain process. Apart from that one argument, there is practically no other logical reason in support of either racial or cultural integration. **1951** J. D. L. Kruger *Bantustan: Study in Pract. Apartheid* iii. 15 In fact it is difficult if not impossible to think of a

single aspect of integration which could be regarded as beneficial to the white population. **1955** *Ann. Amer. Acad. Pol. & Social Sci.* CCCII. 25/1 The frontier for race relations has been shifting more and more to the housing field... The degree of integration in the schools now depends very largely on the residential pattern. **1968** *Listener* 26 Dec. 855/3, I define integration not as a flattening process of assimilation but as equal opportunity accompanied by cultural diversity in an atmosphere of mutual tolerance. **1970** *Times* 23 Mar. 13/3 It seemed that all we had to do to achieve integration was to sit down at enough lunch counters together.

integrational (intĭgrēi·ʃənăl), *a.* [f. INTEGRATION + -AL.] Of or pertaining to integration.

1937 G. W. ALLPORT *Personality* (1938) III. xiii. 354 From each condensed portrait (called by the experimenter 'integrational hypothesis'), the judges predicted what responses the eight subjects would make. **1957** V. W. TURNER *Schism & Continuity in Afr. Soc.* p. xxi, Ndembu ritual..compensates for the integrational deficiencies of a politically unstable society. **1960** J. B. CARROLL in Saporta & Bastian *Psycholinguistics* (1961) 339/2 She tested decoding..and encoding functions with respect to semantic, grammatical, and integrational responses.

integrationist (intĭgrēi·ʃənist), *sb.* and *a.* [f. INTEGRATION + -IST.] **A.** *sb.* An adherent or advocate of integration, esp. political or racial.

1955 *N.Y. Times* 1 June 29/3 The initial reaction, including segregationists and integrationists, overridingly stressed the court's ruling. **1956** *Atlantic Monthly* Nov. 49/1 It is because there the adolescent and 'unprejudiced' mind can be reached that the integrationists have chosen the Southern schools as their primary target. **1959** *Listener* 27 Aug. 305/1 It is becoming less and less possible for the 'integrationists' to paper over the cracks by references to General de Gaulle's 'silences'. **1963** *Economist* 23 Feb. 695/2 This racial appeal is disliked by integrationists. **1971** *Black Scholar* Jan. 52/1 In the work of black authors who are integrationists a tacitly separatist or ethnically independent element appears frequently.

B. *adj.* Of, or pertaining to, persons or policies favouring integration, esp. political or racial.

1956 *Newsweek* 21 May 17/1 A political unknown named Sumter Lowry, who ran on the single plank of preserving segregation, got 130,000 votes. An integrationist candidate got 5,000. **1958** *Times* 11 Nov. 8/1 The solitary list is strongly integrationist, and is led by Azem Ouali, a prominent member of the Algeria-Sahara public safety committee. **1968** *Ann. Amer. Acad. Pol. & Social Sci.* CCCLXXVI. 199/2 These Negroes fervently embraced an integrationist ideology. **1973** *Black World* Mar. 34 The integrationist tendencies of the Negro intellectuals. **1973** E. BULLINS *Theme is Blackness* 4 The militant integrationist syndrome.

integrative, *a.* (Later examples.)

1906 C. S. SHERRINGTON (*title*) The integrative action of the nervous system. **1937** [see *DOMINATIVE *a.* 1 c]. **1937** G. W. ALLPORT *Personality* (1938) II. v. 138 Whatever condition makes for mental health is called 'integrative', whatever condition makes for mental difficulty is called 'disintegrative'. **1953** J. S. HUXLEY *Evolution in Action* iv. 91 What we may call integrative emotions, like love. **1957** M. BANTON *W. Afr. City* ix. 179 Up to this point the integrative effects of the companies have been stressed. **1967** *Amer. Pol. Sci. Rev.* LXI. 91 Far from finding a stagnation of integrative processes since 1958, I would argue that..European integration may have moved into full gear only *since* 1958. **1972** *World Archaeol.* III. 231 He [*sc.* V. G. Childe] saw culture as an essentially integrative device.

integrator. (Earlier and later examples.)

1876 W. THOMSON in *Proc. R. Soc.* XXIV. 269, I have made many attempts to plan a mechanical integrator which should give solutions by successive approximations...We have the instrument founded on my brother's disk-, globe-, and cylinder-integrator. **1884** S. P. THOMPSON *Dynamo-Electr. Machinery* iv. 59 Fig. 48 gives the curve as integrated..for me from Fig. 47 by the aid of the very ingenious curve integrator of Mr. C. Vernon Boys. **1931** *Jrnl. Franklin Inst.* CCXII. 450 There has been an enormous change in technique since the time when Sir William Thomson first suggested..that the integrators developed by his brother could be connected together and thus forced to produce solutions of differential equations. **1938** *Math. Gaz.* XXII. 343 Integrators... Any continuously variable gear can act as an integrating mechanism. **1955** T. L. MARTIN *Electronic Circuits* 618 Waveform relationships in integrators and differentiators. **1964** *Ann. N.Y. Acad. Sci.* CXV. 571 Until recently, analog computers have depended on the use of relays for mode control, switching, and resetting of integrators.

integrist (i·ntegrist). Also **intégriste.** [F. *intégriste.*] = *INTEGRALIST. Hence **i·ntegrism** = *INTEGRALISM.

1907 *Dublin Rev.* Jan. 38 The Carlists and Integrists, who muster half a dozen deputies between them. **1938** *Downside Rev.* LVI. 154 Benedict XV..told Cardinal Billot that he wanted to hear no more talk of 'integrism'. He demanded that..where Rome had not decided, all should be free to state their views without being attacked as heretical. **1969** R. MANHEIM tr. *Corbin's Creative Imagination in Ṣūfism* Introd. 41 We shall let Ibn 'Arabī describe the encounter between the integrist Aristotelian master and the young man. **1970** J. ARDAGH *New France* xi. 577 The tradition of integrism will not die easily in France. *Ibid.*, The unreconciled integrists represent only a small proportion of practising Catholics. **1971** *Month* May 146/2 [The] silent assembly of *intégristes* at Versailles in November 1970. *Ibid.* July 17/1 The French *intégriste* who attended one of the sessions and refused the kiss of peace.

integro-differential (i:ntĭgro͵difĕre·nʃăl), *a.* *Math.* [ad. It. *integro-differenziale* (V. Volterra 1909, in *Atti d. r. Accad. dei Lincei: Rendiconti* (*Classe di sci. fisiche*) XVIII. I. 167).] Involving both integral and differential quantities.

1914 *Trans. Amer. Math. Soc.* XV. 215 A large part of the theory of integral and integro-differential equations may be reduced to the corresponding theory of algebraic and differential equations by the introduction of convenient symbolism. **1923** *Bull. Amer. Math. Soc.* XXIX. 210 Integro-differential invariants of one-parameter groups of Fredholm transformations. **1930** M. LONG tr. *Volterra's Theory of Functionals* 31 As it has the characters of both integral and differential equations, it will be called an integro-differential equation. **1958** E. M. GRABBE et al. *Handbk. Automation, Computation, & Control* I. ix. 18 The method..is applicable to 'integro-differential equations' such as the following: $a_0 dx/dt + a_1 x + a_2 \int_0^t x dt = f(t)$. **1964** N. N. HANCOCK *Matrix Analysis of Electr. Machinery* v. 70 The fundamental equations of an electro-dynamic system are inherently integro-differential equations.

intellectual, *a.* and *sb.* Add: **A.** *adj.* **1. b.** (Further examples.)

1786 A. SEWARD *Let.* 25 Mar. (1811) I. 130 Those who are not interested in its anecdotes, can have little intellectual curiosity and no imagination. **1881** *Atlantic Monthly* May 597/1 He talked in a way..lively enough to sap his own intellectual integrity. **1891** A. JAMES *Diary* 24 June (1965) 216 Owing to my curious, given my inheritance and surroundings, complete absence of intellectual curiosity. **1891** W. JAMES *Let.* 21 Sept. in R. B. Perry *Tht. & Char. of W. James* (1935) II. 174 What a strange thing an intellectual *atmosphere* is! **1896** —— *Will to Believe* (1897) 9 Mr. Balfour gives the name of 'authority' to all those influences, born of the intellectual climate, that make hypotheses possible or impossible for us. **1903** G. B. SHAW *Man & Superman* II. 50 That tone of intellectual snobbery. **1933** *Week-end Rev.* 11 Feb. 142/1 Intellectual integrity is necessary precisely in proportion as it is difficult. **1939** L. MACNEICE *Autumn Jrnl.* xii. 49 Spiritually bankrupt Intellectual snobs. **1965** H. A. GLEASON *Ling. & Eng. Gram.* 35 In the intellectual climate of the late nineteenth century this was most attractive. **1971** D. CRYSTAL *Ling.* iv. 187 We must..take account of the intellectual climate of the time.

B. *sb.* **4.** (Further examples.)

1847 J. J. RUSKIN *Let.* 2 Sept. in M. Lutyens *Ruskins & Grays* (1972) vi. 50, I want you to stand well with Lockhart and the Intellectuals. **1903** *Sat. Rev.* 19 Dec. 760/2 We are compelled to rank higher the mind of the average young man of fashion than the mind of the average 'intellectual' at those literary tea-parties. **1931** [see *CULTURE *sb.* 5 d]. **1937** [see *BRAIN TRUST, BRAINS TRUST]. **1960** *Times Lit. Suppl.* 12 Aug. 553/2 The English have a great respect for brute facts; and the intellectual in politics often looks to them like a man busily engaged in brushing unpleasant facts under the carpet. **1974** *Times* 15 Feb. 15/8 Russian history has set a pattern of alienated intellectuals.

intellectualist. Now freq. attrib. or as adj.

1890 W. JAMES *Princ. Psychol.* II. xxii. 325 The traditional intellectualist philosophy has always made a great point of treating the brutes as wholly irrational creatures. **1941** J. S. HUXLEY *Uniqueness of Man* ii. 76 Men..of an intellectualist and academic type.

intellectualistic, *a.* Add: So **intelle:ctuali·stically** *adv.*

1907 W. JAMES *Pragmatism* iii. 121 Yet dark tho they be in themselves [*sc.* the words *God, free-will,* etc.], or intellectualistically taken, when we bear them into life's thicket with us the darkness *there* grows light about us. **1909** —— *Pluralistic Universe* ii. 72 The substituted conceptions are treated intellectualistically, that is as mutually exclusive and discontinuous. **1927** L. STEIN *A.B.C. of Æsthetics* i. 10 No one can get much good out of my book who reads it intellectualistically.

intellectually, *adv.* Add: Used with an adj. as a quasi-Comb.

1859 J. A. SYMONDS *Let.* Oct. (1967) I. 211, I want to get Puller to organize a club with me, introducing 5 other intellectually-pursuited men. **1923** J. S. HUXLEY *Ess. Biologist* i. 8 Intellectually-minded men. **1941** *Mind* L. 236 Mr. Clive Bell in his excellent and intellectually snobbish book *Civilization*..makes this blunder. **1951** M. MCLUHAN *Mech. Bride* 58/2 The intellectually creative man with whom the future of mankind always rests.

intellectualness. In quot., for '1884' read '1854'.

intelligence, *sb.* Add: **7. a.** *spec.* Information of military value.

1799 G. HARRIS *Diary* 4 Apr. in Wellington *Disp.* (1837) I. 24 If our intelligence is true, his [*sc.* Tippoo Sultaun's] whole army are in a complete state of terror. **1818** [in Dict.]. **1899** *McClure's Mag.* Mar. 473/2 The swift single cruisers, the purveyors of intelligence. **1925** FRASER & GIBBONS *Soldier & Sailor Words* 125 'Intelligence', *i.e.* information of military value. The use of the word as a military technical term dates from the 16th Century, but in the War of 1914–18 it was used to denote specially the department of the General Staff dealing with information. **1974** *Times* 15 Jan. 14/3 The first question that everybody asked was why the intelligence of the Arab armies massing on the borders..was misread?

c. Delete † and add later examples.

1915 KIPLING *France at War* 21 The Intelligence with its stupefying photo-plans of the enemy's trenches. **1949** A. CHRISTIE *Crooked House* xii. 95 A person who has something to hide can't really afford to talk *at all*. The blokes knew that in Intelligence during the war. **1957** [see *COURIER *sb.* 1 b]. **1963** A. ORLOV *Handbk. Intelligence* i. 10 Stalin in 1932 ordered intelligence to discontinue sending him quarterly surveys of foreign countries. **1974** *Listener* 31 Jan. 142/1 Tizard has managed to get it through that someone should be seconded to British Intelligence for a while.

d. (sense 7 c in Dict. and Suppl.) *intelligence agency, corps, officer, operator, service*; **intelligence department**, a department of a state organization or of a military or naval service whose object is to obtain information (esp. by means of secret service officers or a system of spies).

1951 Intelligence Agency [see *C.I.A.* s.v. *C III. 3]. **1960** J. BLISH *Galactic Cluster* 116 This intelligence agency is my sole source of income... I have every right to operate a private investigation bureau. **1963** A. ORLOV *Handbk. Intelligence* i. 7 The American intelligence agencies monitor as many as five million words daily from foreign radio broadcasts alone. **1961** Intelligence Corps [see *intelligence operator* below]. **1974** P. MCCUTCHAN *Call for Simon Shard* xiv. 132 Hedge had been in the war, a captain in the Intelligence Corps. **1875** *Encycl. Brit.* II. 573/1 The Intelligence Department [of the Army]..under a Deputy-Adjutant-General. **1895** *Whitaker's Almanack* 230 Naval Intelligence Department. **1928** W. S. MAUGHAM *Ashenden* i. 2 The Colonel..was known in the Intelligence Department..by the letter R. **1885** Intelligence officer [in Dict.]. **1901** *Westm. Gaz.* 31 Dec. 10/1 You are intelligence officer to the new cavalry brigade. **1914** R. BROOKE in E. Marsh *Rupert Brooke* (1918) 132 Intelligence Officer in H.M.S. *Vengeance*. **1946** E. M. ZACHARIAS (*title*) Secret mission: the story of an intelligence officer. **1961** *Times* 12 Sept. 2/6 The Intelligence Corps... Vacancies exist for training in the trades of:—Staff Intelligence Operator and Counter Intelligence Operator. **1930** B. MIALL tr. *Berndorff's Espionage* i. 16 At Nice..he continued to work for the French Intelligence Service. **1932** R. H. B. LOCKHART *Mem. Brit. Agent* IV. iii. 234 A Colonel in our Intelligence Service. **1956** A. L. ROWSE *Early Churchills* 262 Of this Marlborough, whose intelligence-service was always of the first order, was well aware. **1974** *Listener* 31 Jan. 142/1 The Führer..said he had a secret weapon. Immediately Neville Chamberlain..asked the Intelligence Services what the secret weapon was.

8. *attrib.* and *Comb.*, as **intelligence quotient** [ad. G. *intelligenz-quotient* (W. L. Stern, 1912)], a number arrived at by means of intelligence tests and intended to express the degree of intelligence of an individual in relation to the average for the age-group, which is fixed at 100; abbrev. *I.Q.* (*I. III); so **intelligence test, tester, testing.**

1921 C. BURT *Mental & Scholastic Tests* 151 If a child's mental age be divided by his choronological age, the quotient will state what fraction of ability the child actually possesses... This fraction may be termed..the child's 'intelligence quotient'. **1922** R. S. WOODWORTH *Psychol.* xii. 274 Brightness or dullness can also be measured by the intelligence quotient. **1944** H. READ *Educ. Free Men* iii. 13 Truth, we say, is not found exclusively in the possession of those with a high 'intelligence quotient'. **1953** *Sci. News* XXIX. 45 Isolated concepts, from sex-motivation to intelligence quotients, are taken up, puffed up, and what may be limited but useful notions become ridiculed, because of the disproportionate importance attached to them. **1971** *Nature* 2 Apr. 306/1 The worship of the Intelligence Quotient, mercifully a-dying, is still not entirely dead. **1972** KAGAN & HAVEMANN *Psychol.* (ed. 2) xiv. 473 The intelligence quotient, or I.Q., is simply the relationship of mental age to chronological age; it is obtained by the formula I.Q. = MA/Chronological age × 100...This is the general principle for computing the I.Q. on the Stanford–Binet. In actual practice..the I.Q. is usually determined from tables that make it possible to compare the child's raw score with the scores made by other children of the same age. This latter method is also the one used with all other intelligence tests... This statistical method of computing the I.Q. is valuable because the concept of mental age..is not meaningful for adults. **1914** *Eugenics Rev.* Apr. 42 General ability, estimated by intelligence tests, is largely hereditary. **1957** *Technology* Mar. 10/1 The trade school, however, is well equipped to sort wheat from chaff—each candidate is given the latest types of intelligence and aptitude tests. **1927** A. HUXLEY *Proper Stud.* 65 The intelligence-testers would isolate..the sum of the activities of the whole mind. **1962** H. J. EYSENCK *Know your own I.Q.* 31 From the point of view of the intelligence tester it is very undesirable to have mixed groups to deal with. **1972** J. L. DILLARD *Black English* i. 28 Some intelligence testers..have suffered from lack of valid information about Black English in standard sources on American dialects. **1919** *Elem. School Jrnl.* Sept. 26 (*title*) Intelligence testing as an aid to supervision. **1958** [see *child welfare* (*CHILD *sb.* 22)]. **1972** J. L. DILLARD *Black English* i. 28 An intelligence-testing procedure which is completely invalid because of its cultural and linguistic bias.

intelligentsia (intelidʒe·ntsiă; formerly also intelige·ntsiă). Also (formerly) **intelligenzia.** [f. Russ. *intelligéntsiya*, ad. L. *intelligentia* INTELLIGENCE *sb.*] The part of a nation, orig. in pre-revolutionary Russia, that aspires to intellectual activity; the class of society regarded as possessing culture and political initiative.

1907 M. BARING *Year in Russia* vii. 77 They [*sc.* the revolutionaries] fear that if the question of a Republic is brought forward there will be a general massacre of the

educated bourgeoisie, the so-called 'Intelligenzia'. **1910** —— *Landmarks Russian Lit.* iii. 68 Chekov has depicted the pessimism and the ineffectiveness of the 'intelligenzia'. **1914** *Round Table* Dec. 115 The importance and meaning of the so-called *intelligentsia.* **1916** H. G. Wells *Mr. Britling* I. ii. 62 They are the sort of equivalent of the Russian Intelligentsia, an irresponsible middle class with ideas. **1921** A. Huxley *Let.* 31 May (1969) 197 The English colony [at Florence] is a queer collection; a sort of decayed provincial intelligentsia. **1922** C. E. M. Joad *Highbrows* vi. 224 Those waifs and strays of the intelligentsia who had resolutely refused to participate in the war. **1922** C. Sidgwick *Victorian* xxviii. 211 He told me ..that he belonged to the Intelligentsia and that he was out to shoot capitalists. **1924** Galsworthy *White Monkey* I. ix, It was not the intelligentsia, but just intellectual society, which was gathered there. **1940** Wodehouse *Eggs, Beans & Crumpets* 75 It was a painful shock to the intelligentsia..when they discovered that their old friend was not going to prove the geyser of easy money they had anticipated. **1949** I. T. Sanders *Balkan Village* i. 7 The intelligentsia, as they were called by the [Bulgarian] peasants, were the most influential group in the community... I was sure to find several of them playing cards... The mayor..could watch..the municipal building... The priest could look..to the church just beyond. The village doctor's husband was near in case his wife needed him. **1956** R. Redfield *Peasant Society & Culture* ii. 61 To the administrative and cultural intermediaries between local life and wider life the word 'intelligentsia' has long been applied. **1971** H. Seton-Watson in A. Bullock *20th Cent.* 139/1 The revolutionary propensity of the intelligentsia has been definitely correlated with the extent of the cultural gap between the educated élite and the mass of the people.

Intelsat (i·ntelsæt). Also **INTELSAT.** [An acronym f. the name of the organization, *In*ternational *Tel*ecommunications *Sat*ellite Consortium.] **a.** An international organization of member countries formed in 1964 to establish and operate a worldwide system of commercial communication satellites. **b.** A communication satellite owned by this organization.

1966 *Aviation Week* 7 Mar. 125/3 International Telecommunications Satellite Consortium (Intelsat) is already on the road to becoming a profit-making venture by 1970. It now includes 48 nations... U.S.'s Communications Satellite Corp. serves as manager for the consortium. **1967** *Wall Street Jrnl.* 6 Jan. 4/3 The successful weekend orbiting of Intelsat II. **1969** *Listener* 5 June 779/1 In communications we have accepted INTELSAT, for example, a global organisation which runs the satellite communications system. **1971** *New Scientist* 3 June 552/1 The settlement now reached mostly meets the criticism.. that Intelsat was American dominated. **1972** *Sci. Amer.* Sept. 111/1 The latest Intelsat has a capacity of 5,000 voice channels or 12 television channels.

intemporal, *a.* Delete † *Obs. rare*$^{-1}$ and add later examples.

1911 J. Ward *Realm of Ends* xiv. 306 The intemporal world of ideas. **1962** tr. *J. L. Borges's Labyrinths* (1964) 262 There was no other sound than the intemporal one of the crickets.

intendant, *sb.* Add: **3.** The administrator of an opera house or theatre (cf. G. *intendant*); see also quot. 1903.

1903 R. Hughes *Mus. Guide* I. 174/2 *Intendant*,.. director, conductor. **1958** *Spectator* 1 Aug. 166/1 The vital demarcation between *intendant* and administrator is overgrown by the cult of the amateur run riot. **1961** *Times* 30 Jan. 14/2 In each city, the fortunes of opera, ballet, and drama depend largely on an intendant who occupies his position for a comparatively few years before moving elsewhere. **1966** *New Statesman* 18 Nov. 758/2 Very often the Intendants hardly understand the meaning of the word 'choreography',..and automatically scrap each ballet at the end of the season. **1973** *Times* 11 Apr. 12/5 In most of the big towns the Intendant can attract the audience he needs only with a fairly rapid turnover of plays.

intendedly, *adv.* (Later example.)

1972 *Daily Tel.* 3 Feb. 14 Your implication that priests present at the illegal, though intendedly peaceful, protest march have no right to be 'mixed up' with their people is absurd.

intense, *a.* Add: **4. b.** Also, manifesting intense emotion or excitability, esp. in æsthetic or intellectual contexts.

1817 Keats *Let.* 28 Dec. (1931) I. 76, I..went..to see 'Death on the Pale Horse'. It is a wonderful picture, when West's age is considered; but there is nothing to be intense upon, no women one feels mad to kiss, no face swelling into reality. **1879** W. D. Howells in *Atlantic Monthly* Jan. 38/2 'Why Miss Blood you are intense!' 'I don't know what you mean by that,' said Lydia. 'You like to take things seriously. You can't bear to think that people are not the least in earnest, even when they least seem so.' **1880** G. du Maurier *Eng. Soc. at Home* pl. 49 Fair Æsthetic (suddenly, and in deepest tones, to Smith, who has just been introduced to take her in to Dinner). 'Are you *Intense*?' **1897** H. Ellis *Stud. Psychol. Sex* I. 88 Miss M., aged 29, the daughter of English parents (both musicians) who were both of what is described as 'intense' temperaments. **1925** *Punch* 6 May 487 *Intense Lady.* 'Tell me—have you ever been psychoed?'

intensifier. Add: (Further examples.) *spec.* (*a*) *Gram.* = Intensive *sb.*; (*b*) = *hydraulic intensifier* (s.v. *hydraulic *a.* and *sb.* A. 2); (*c*) = *image intensifier* (s.v. *image *sb.* 8).

1892 *Lockwood's Dict. Mech. Engin.* (ed. 2) 429 *Intensifier*, a device frequently employed in place of the hydraulic accumulator, for converting a low water pressure into a higher. **1915** E. H. Barton *Introd. Mech. Fluids* xii. 191 In connection with an hydraulic pressure system an intensifying accumulator or intensifier may be used. In this device a piston works in the low-pressure cylinder and a connected piston rod, or ram, in the high-pressure cylinder. ..The pressure is magnified in the ratio of the areas of ram and piston. *Ibid.*, The intensifier presents an analogy to the hydraulic press. **1931** G. Stern *Meaning & Change of Meaning* 338 Intensifiers used ironically instead of down-toners. 'A lot you know about that!' **1939** L. M. Myers *Electron Optics* viii. 449 The term amplifier, in contradistinction to converter, indicates an increase in intensity. With the same reasoning we might term the device an image intensifier. Perhaps the term intensifier may be the best of all. However, we shall employ the usually accepted term converter, because there does exist a conversion effect. **1940** C. C. Fries *Amer. Eng. Gram.* 205 The pressure to add *-ly* to intensifiers modifying adjectives is especially strong in Standard English. **1951** W. Empson *Struct. Complex Words* i. 26 The modern feeling about *quite* is entirely different from that about a discredited intensifier (*awfully, frightfully*). **1959** *Proc. IRE* XLVII. 907/2 Although the resolution obtainable is obviously much too low for military use, it is still of interest to the nuclear physicist as a simple and inexpensive intensifier for scintillation photography. **1964** *Language* XL. 39 Intensifier is the name given here to a small class of modifiers, e.g. *mere, utter.* **1970** R. H. Warring *Fluids for Power Syst.* i. 17 Intensifiers are almost invariably used for the production of pressures over 50 000 psi. **1971** G. Ansre in J. Spencer *Eng. Lang. W. Afr.* 162 The word classes: adjective, quantifier, specifier, pluraliser and intensifier respectively.

intensify, *v.* Add: **inte·nsifying** *ppl. a.* esp. in **intensifying screen,** a fluorescent screen placed in contact with the film or plate when a radiograph is taken in order to increase the effect on it of the X-rays.

1866 R. W. Thomas *Mod. Pract. Photogr.* 14 (*heading*) Intensifying solution. **1878** W. Abney *Treat. Photogr.* x. 71 These intensifying solutions may be applied to the image either before or after fixing. **1879** [see Developer b]. **1903** Pusey & Caldwell *Pract. Application Röntgen Rays* vi. 144 The ratio of the exposure necessary with a single intensifying screen and photographic plate to that which is necessary with the same plate without the screen is about 1 to 4 or 5. **1940** K. S. Low *Metall. & Industr. Radiol.* iv. 30 Intensifying screens when placed in contact with the film will by fluorescence under the action of x-radiation supplement the action of x-rays on the film, and thus shorten exposure periods. **1968** *Kodak Med. X-Ray Catal.* 8 High speed, fine grain X-ray film for use with intensifying screens.

intensional (inte·nʃənăl), *a. Philos.* [f. Intension 5 + -al.] Related or pertaining to the intension, or the attributes contained in a concept. Cf. *extensional *a.* 2.

1883 F. H. Bradley *Princ. Logic* 162 Dismissing for the present the intensional reading, let us consider interpretation in *Extension.* **1903** B. Russell *Princ. Math.* vi. § 66. 67 Thus every predicate (provided it can be sometimes truly predicated) gives rise to a class. This is the genesis of classes from the intensional standpoint. **1949** S. I. Hayakawa *Lang. in Thought & Action* (1952) xv. 253 By intensional orientation, 'capitalist', 'Bolsheviks', 'farmers', and 'working men' 'are' what we *say* they are. **1956** A. Church *Introd. Math. Logic* (rev. ed.) I. 28 We shall not have occasion to use variables whose values are propositions, but we would suggest the term intensional propositional variable for these. **1970** *Philos. Q.* XX. 52 The star notation can be made the groundwork of a system of intensional propositional logic in which a wide class of formal principles can be proved.

intensionalist (inte·nʃənălist), *a.* and *sb. Philos.* [f. prec. + -ist 3 b.] **A.** *adj.* Of or pertaining to the intensional attributes of a concept. **B.** *sb.* One who considers a concept from the standpoint of its inner attributes.

1948 *Mind* LVII. 198 No one, I think, ever intended to deny the interdependence of meaning and deducibility in this sense..although some 'intensionalists' have spoken as if it *were* denied. *Ibid.*, The confusion just described is a mild and limited form of what we might describe as the 'intensionalist error'. **1962** *Times Lit. Suppl.* 16 Mar. 187/3 In a level-headed and sometimes ingenious discussion..the authors show themselves uncompromisingly 'intensionalist'. **1963** R. Carnap in P. A. Schilpp *Philos. R. Carnap* 919 The basic ideas underlying my intensionalist thesis are simple.

intensionality (intenʃənæ·liti). *Philos.* [f. *intensional *a.* + -ity.] The state or fact of being intensional. Cf. *extensionality.

1937 A. Smeaton tr. *Carnap's Logical Syntax of Lang.* iv. § 71. 259 The difference between the extensionality and intensionality of a language has nothing to do with the difference between the formal and the material treatment. **1944** K. Gödel in P. A. Schilpp *Philos. B. Russell* 138 Chwistek..has shown that the system of simple types becomes contradictory if one adds the 'axiom of intensionality' which says (roughly speaking) that to different definitions belong different notions.

intensionally (inte·nʃənăli), *adv. Philos.* [f. *intensional *a.* + -ly².] By way of intension, in an intensional manner.

1883 F. H. Bradley *Princ. Logic* 161 If again you emphasize the connection of the differences, you take the judgement intensionally. **1903**, etc. [see *extensionally *adv.*]. **1953** K. Britton *J. S. Mill* vi. 189 This judgement also must be understood intensionally: i.e. as a connexion of universals which holds without reference to the mere spatio-temporal positions of the instances. **1970** *Philos. Q.* XX. 43 We may take it that the expression so obtained is formally valid intensionally.

intensity. Add: **1.** (Further examples.)

1834 *Phil. Trans. R. Soc.* CXXIV. 222 The term intensity..is immediately referable to..the operation of either a part, or the whole of the total force in a given direction up to the point of discharge. **1879** [see Saturation 4]. **1933** L. Bloomfield *Lang.* ix. 156 The second more specialized type of connotation..is intensity. The most characteristic intense forms are exclamations. **1939** Brooks & Warren *Understanding Poetry* ii. 167 The effect of this condensation in poetry is a sense of greater intensity than is usually found in prose fiction. **1961** J. H. Goodier *Dict. Painting & Decorating* 143 *Intensity*, the purity of a colour, sometimes called the 'saturation' or, in American terminology, the 'chroma'.

b. (Later example.)

1896 G. F. Stout *Analytic Psychol.* I. i. v. 110 The word 'intensity' in..psychology..is usually regarded as synonymous with the liveliness or vivacity of which Hume has so much to say.

3. *attrib.* and *Comb.*

1844 in H. M. Noad *Lect. Electr.* (ed. 2) ix. 401 The trifling decomposing effect from the intensity-inductor. *a* **1877** Knight *Dict. Mech.* II. 1192/1 An intensity battery is one in which the elements are coupled up together, to give a current known as high-tension. **1927** E. G. Richardson *Sound* x. 238 Beside the frequency limits there are intensity limits to the sounds which the ear can perceive. **1932** D. Jones *Outl. Eng. Phonetics* (ed. 3) xxxi. 277 Contrast-emphasis may be applied to almost any word, but intensity-emphasis can only be applied to certain words expressing qualities which are measurable. **1940** *Chambers's Techn. Dict.* 452/1 *Intensity modulation*, modulation of a luminosity of the fluorescent screen of a cathode ray tube by variation of the current carried in the beam. **1947** *Radiology* XLIX. 284/2 Our data also suggest that an intensity factor exists. Daily exposures of very short duration over long periods of time should therefore be avoided. **1964** J. C. Catford in D. Abercrombie et al. *Daniel Jones* 31 Fricative *hiss*,.. intensity-modulated by voice. **1972** *Science* 16 June 1236/1 The audio frequency Doppler signals from the detector were amplified sufficiently to provide a 30- to 40-volt signal for intensity-modulating the cathode-ray tube.

intensive, *a.* (*sb.*) Add: **5. b.** Suffixed to sbs. to form adjs. with the sense 'intensively using the thing specified', as *capital-intensive, labour-intensive.*

1957 K. A. Wittfogel *Oriental Despotism* vi. 218 The replacement of labor-intensive irrigation farming by labor-extensive cattle breeding. **1959** *Listener* 22 Oct. 666/1 We have the highly capital-intensive process of textile manufacture. **1970** *Times* 2 June (Container Suppl.) p. iii/4 The latest sophisticated container systems add up to a capital-intensive system of some magnitude. **1972** *Guardian* 29 June 15/5 The developing world..is beginning to see the case for labour-intensive farming. **1973** *Nature* 6 Apr. 378/2 Economies of scale have been operating in capital-intensive and graduate-intensive industries like chemicals, oil, electric power, steel, and computers. *Ibid.* 382/3 Intelligence-intensive biology would take its place alongside this intelligence-intensive cosmology.

8. *intensive care*: a form of medical treatment in which a patient is kept under concentrated and special observation; so *intensive-care unit*, etc.

1963 *Lancet* 19 Jan. 169/2 Our medical staff found the medical intensive-care unit so valuable that they requested..a separate surgical intensive-care unit. **1965** *Math. in Biol. & Med.* (Med. Res. Council) i. 40 He felt that patient monitoring was essential in the operating theatre and the intensive-care unit. **1965** *Listener* 16 Sept. 401/1 We would like to see intensive-care units in all large modern hospitals. **1967** *Spectator* 11 Aug. 159/2 This method of dealing with a serious cardiac emergency ..is known as intensive care. **1972** J. Gores *Dead Skip* (1973) ii. 14 Bart's at Trinity Hospital in intensive care, a single-bed room with a private nurse. **1973** J. Goodfield *Courier to Peking* x. 123 First, one of the general wards..and then to our new intensive care unit.

intention, *sb.* Add: **6. b.** In literary criticism: the aim or design which a critic detects in a writer's work.

1946 Wimsatt & Beardsley in *Sewanee Rev.* LIV. 469 Intention has obvious affinities for the author's attitude toward his work, the way he felt, what made him write. **1959** *Times Lit. Suppl.* 20 Feb. 97/1 Intention, in Mr. Wimsatt's use of the word, does not mean what it means in Dr. Richards's distinction between sense, tone, feeling, and intention... It means what we might have reason to think that the author thought he was up to.

12. b. (Further examples.)

1886 *Echo* 30 Nov., In the Communion Service a '*special intention*' was made known by the introduction of words implying that the 'sacrifice was received in memory' of the dead. **1966** *New Statesman* 22 Apr. 608/1 The text of the Mass itself, with its special intention in capitals.

15. Special Comb.: **intention movement** [tr. G. *intentionsbewegung* (O. Heinroth)], a movement or action on the part of an animal which itself performs no function except to reveal

or signal that a further movement or action may follow or is contemplated; **intention tremor**, a tremor which is manifested when a voluntary action is performed.

[**1910** O. Heinroth in *Jrnl. für Ornith.* LVIII. 122 Eine Modifikation des eigentlichen Locktones, wie sie kurz vor dem Auffliegen hervorgebracht und dann mit den oben beschriebenen Intentionsbewegungen verbunden wird, ist ein langes und fein ausklingendes 'Hu'.] **1950** K. Z. Lorenz in *Symposia Soc. Exper. Biol.* IV. 242 We know of two phyletically distinct ways, by which non-social, mechanically effective endogenous activities may develop into social releasers: in one case the so-called 'intention movement' (*Intentionsbewegung*, Heinroth), in the other the so-called 'displacement activities'. *Ibid.* 243 Intention movements..are..very reliable indicators for the present 'mood' of an animal. **1953** N. Tinbergen *Herring Gull's World* xvii. 153 A bird may rapidly change from pecking to the intention-movement of brooding. **1961** A. J. Berger *Bird Study* v. 136 The first intention movement preceding walking or hopping often is a 'bow'. **1887** Vickery & Knapp tr. *A. von Strümpell's Textbk. Med.* 593 The tremor in multiple sclerosis comes on only with intended movements, 'intention tremor'. **1969** *Times* 8 Feb. 4/1 All but one suffered from defects in their nervous systems. The commonest of these seems to have been intention tremors, which are tremors occurring when a voluntary movement is made.

intentional, *a.* Add: **1.** *intentional fallacy*: in literary criticism, the fallacy that the meaning or value of a work may be judged or defined in terms of the writer's intention.

1946 Wimsatt & Beardsley in *Sewanee Rev.* LIV. 482 The question of 'allusiveness', for example,..is certainly one where a false judgement is likely to involve the intentional fallacy. **1948** [see *affective *a.* 7 c]. **1954** W. K. Wimsatt *Verbal Icon* i. 6 It is not so much a historical statement as a definition to say that the intentional fallacy is a romantic one. **1958** *Listener* 9 Oct. 578/2 A studied defence of what has been labelled—and dismissed—as the 'intentional fallacy'.

intentionalism (inte·nʃənăliz'm). [f. Intentional *a.* + -ism.] The doctrine that a literary work or some other work, etc., is the result of conscious intention or design. So **inte·ntionalist**, one who propounds such a doctrine; **intentionali·stic** *a.*, of, pertaining to, or characterized by intentionalism.

1878 W. Affleck tr. *Janet's Final Causes* i. vi. 215 God has come forth from Himself as well in pantheism as in creationism or intentionalism. **1946** Wimsatt & Beardsley in *Sewanee Rev.* LIV. 485 Allusiveness in poetry is one of several critical issues by which we have illustrated the more abstract issue of intentionalism. *Ibid.* 486 Allusiveness would appear to be in some recent poems an extreme corollary of the romantic intentionalist assumption. **1952** *Essays in Crit.* II. i. 106 But does the 'intentionalist' assert that no lyric can ever be abstracted from a longer work? **1954** W. K. Wimsatt *Verbal Icon* i. 11 The use of biographical evidence [in criticism] need not involve intentionalism. **1958** *Listener* 16 Oct. 595/1 There is a suspicious silence on the whole issue of intentionalism among the classical English critics. **1958** I. P. Hungerland *Poetic Discourse* vi. 162 The Intentionalists have neglected such situations. **1958** M. C. Beardsley *Aesthetics* 27 There are other critics who tend to shift back and forth between the work and its creator, never quite clear in their own minds when they are talking about the one or the other. They mingle the evidences of intention with the evidences of accomplishment, and sometimes decide what the work is or means primarily on external evidence. This is to practice intentionalistic criticism.

inter, L. prep. Add: *inter partes* (Law), of an action: relevant only to the two parties in a particular case (see quots. 1966); of a deed or the like: made between two parties; *inter se* (later examples); *inter vivos*, between living persons (esp. of a gift as opposed to a legacy).

1816 Maule & Selwyn *Rep. Cases King's Bench* III. 308 A deed *inter partes* cannot operate as a release to strangers. **1906** *Daily Colonist* (Victoria, B.C.) 16 Jan. 10/2 Mr. Bodwell..contended that this must not be considered an action inter partes; in form it may have been, but in substance it was a propounding of the will. **1960** *Times* 4 Aug. 11/5 On July 19 the injunction was granted in an *inter partes* form. **1966** Black & Brown *Outl. Eng. Law* vi. xvii. 160 In modern terms actions are either *Actions in Rem* or *Actions in Personam* or *Inter Partes*. *Ibid.* 161 An action..*inter partes* produces a judgment which is binding only as between the parties to the case and not upon third parties. **1968** *Law Rep.* 106 The old common law rule that in an indenture inter partes the covenantee must be named as a party to the indenture to take the benefit of an immediate grant or the benefit of a covenant. **1971** *Mod. Law Rev.* XXXIV. vi. 605 The Court gives decisions on preliminary points of law..when such questions are referred to it by municipal courts or tribunals in the course of proceedings *inter partes*. **1888** G. F. Stout *Stud. Philos. & Psychol.* (1930) i. 42 Forms of combination among presentations other than those by which sense-perceptions are connected *inter se*. **1971** *Mod. Law Rev.* XXXIV. vi. 598 Suppose that..the *inter se* doctrine of Commonwealth relations had emerged as a credible body of legal principle. **1972** *Times* 14 Mar. 12/2 The essential link between members of a volunteer unit was not their contractual relationship *inter se* but their common military service to the Crown. **1837** T. Lewin *Pract. Treat. Law Trusts & Trustees* vi. 86 The Bank of England cannot be made a trustee, for the Company will not enter notice of instruments *inter vivos* upon their books. **1949** W. B. Leach *Cases Law of Wills* 30 In 1931 decedent had created a large inter vivos trust. **1955** *Times* 8 June 4/3 Transfer of property through inheritance or *inter vivos* gifts or settlements should reckon as realization. **1963** *Economist* 16 Mar. 976/1 Death duties are..largely avoided by transfers *inter vivos*. **1969** *Daily Tel.* 1 Oct. 20/6 Half the Seafield 'empire' is owned by Lord Reidhaven following his mother's foresight in transferring the property outside the *inter vivos* period, which exonerates the assets from death duty. **1972** *Accountant* 28 Sept. 381/3 Benefits..should be mentioned in reply to the question in the Inland Revenue Affidavit about gifts *inter vivos*.

inter., inter (i·ntəɹ), abbrev. of Intermediate *a.* = *intermediate examination* (in arts, etc.), often used in ordinary colloquial speech.

1891–2 *London Univ. Guide* 29 Inter. Arts Honours. *Ibid.* 40 Inter. Science and Prel. Sci. Exams. **1913** W. Owen *Let.* 28 Sept. (1967) 199 He was a student of Nottingham College, but failed to pass Inter-Arts. **1948** L. Walmsley *Master Mariner* ii. i. 134 He had entered for a degree in science, had passed his 'inter' with the same ease as he'd passed his matric, and was sitting for his final in the coming term.

inter-, *prefix.* Add: **1. a.** *interfile* (*interfiling* vbl. sb.), *-lot* vbs.

1950 J. Lawler *H. W. Wilson Co.* vii. 111 Specially trained women..handle the task of interfiling the metal linotype slugs. *Ibid.* 112 The Production Department staff interfiles the new and old slips of copy. **1962** Y. Malkiel in Householder & Saporta *Probl. Lexicogr.* 15 Interfiling..of authentic word cards. **1967** Cox & Dews in Cox & Grose *Organiz. Bibliogr. Rec. by Computer* ii. 16 Anonymous works are frequently interfiled by title in author catalogues. **1967** C. J. Duncan *Ibid.* 41 The insertion of special sorts or 'pi-characters' has been the traditional inter-filing solution adopted. **1933** *Bulletin* (Sydney) 22 Nov. 28/1 'Inter-lotting', a practice gratuitously rendered by woolbrokers, consists in selecting a number of what would be star lots, and bracketing them into one big lot to sell as such.

b. *inter-influence* (vbl. sb. *-influencing*), *-lend* vbs.

1921 E. Sapir *Lang.* viii. 184 In many such cases it is perfectly clear that there could have been no dialectic interinfluencing. **1961** L. F. Brosnahan *Sounds of Lang.* x. 215 Genetic and linguistic interinfluencing of such groups favours the reverse trend. **1968** *Listener* 5 Sept. 319/2 Two of the very few important libraries which do not 'inter-lend' are those of Oxford and Cambridge.

2. a. *inter-availability, -behaviour, -celebration, -fertility, -influence, -racialism, -substitutability*; *inter-available, -behavioural, -fertile, -responsive, -sterile, -substitutable* adjs.

1920 *Glasgow Herald* 1 July 6 The issue of a circular cancelling the inter-availability of practically all railway tickets between Scotland and England. **1923** *Ibid.* 27 Jan. 11 The deputation intends..to press for the inter-availability of these tickets on all systems. **1935** *Punch* 21 Aug. 204/3 'Interavailability of Tickets between the G.W., L.M.S. and L. & N.E. Companies'.—*G.W.R. Pamphlet.* **1972** *Daily Tel.* 26 Feb. 2/6 Tickets are inter-available and British Rail fares will now reflect the London Transport increase. **1939** *Mind* XLVIII. 111 Linguistic phenomena are forms of inter-behaviour with stimulus objects. **1952** W. J. H. Sprott *Social Psychol.* 1 By social situation is meant what might be called the 'inter-behaviour' of one human being with one or more other human beings. **1938** J. R. Kantor in *Jrnl. Philos.* XXXV. 449 The interbehavioral hypothesis signifies that all human phenomena..consist of the concrete interbehavior of specific individuals with things. **1939** *Mind* XLVIII. 111 The inter-behavioural hypothesis encourages us properly to evaluate every form of scientific and logical work. **1921** *Spectator* 26 Mar. 391/2, I should be glad to see inter-communion, but not, under present circumstances, inter-celebration. **1969** *Daily Tel.* 30 May 20/6 For inter-celebration of services there must be a solution of the problems over the ministry which the proposals evaded. **1916** *Mem. N.Y. Bot. Garden* VI. 352 Two seedling varieties derived from the same variety may be inter-fertile to some degree. **1971** J. Z. Young *Introd. Study Man* xxvii. 387 Leopard frogs (*Rana pipiens*) from the north and south of the United States are only partially interfertile when they are crossed. **1924** *Genetics* IX. 36 The inter-fertility relationships of these 27 classes are indicated. **1953** *Jrnl. Gen. Microbiol.* VIII. 72 Some forty strains of *Bact. coli*..which either out-cross with K-12 mutants or show inter-fertility. **1948** *Q. Rev.* Apr. 180 The cant inter-influence among all English-speaking countries has been considerable. **1959** C. L. Wrenn *Word & Symbol* (1967) 17 Oghams and Runes came into use at about the same period..and the possibility of their mutual relationship and inter-influence has continued to tease the brains of scholars. **1960** Partridge *Charm of Words* i. 23 This interinfluence is unavoidable. **1931** *Amer. Speech* VII. 78 A writer in the *Congregationalist* says 'Interracialism, like love, service, and brotherhood, is a splendid word which has been cheapened by overuse.' How many acquaintances have you whose diction suffers from over-use of the word interracialism? **1906** *Macm. Mag.* Apr. 434 The mystic net-work, inter-responsive as a delicate system of nerves. **1955** R. Blesh *Shining Trumpets* (ed. 3) ii. 30 It is a thing..as sensitively inter-connected and inter-responsive, as the branches of a tree. **1916** *Mem. N.Y. Bot. Garden* VI. 352 It was found that at least three varieties are strongly inter-sterile. **1956** *Nature* 21 Jan. 142/1 The mating type of the hybrid shows no change, that is, the hybrid males remain intersterile with *O* females, as in the original strain *H*. **1954** I. M. Copi *Symbolic Logic* vii. 224 Of the list of elementary valid argument forms..the last ten were equivalences whose intersubstitutability was assumed. **1957** P. Geach *Mental Acts* 90 We cannot define synonymy as a supreme degree of equivalence, intersubstitutability *salva veritate* in all contexts. **1954** I. M. Copi *Symbolic Logic* iii. 44 The list contains all those logical equivalences which are certified as intersubstitutable. **1957** P. Geach *Mental Acts* 101 In an 'extensional' logic..predicates or relative terms would be freely intersubstitutable provided that they held good of the same objects.

3. a. *interglyph, -mutule.*

1875 *Encycl. Brit.* II. 404/1 The interglyphs are each one-seventh of the whole tablet or triglyph. *c* **1863** *Dict. Archit.* (Archit. Publ. Soc.) III. 149/1 The temple to Ceres at Pœstum has no mutules or triglyphs. The example at Albano has no intermutules. **1901** R. Sturgis *Dict. Archit.*, *Intermutule*, the space between two mutules, as in an architrave.

4. a. *inter-cavernous, -consonantal, -electronic, -follicular, -marginal, -micellar, -morainic, -nebular, -villous* adjs.

1890 Webster, Inter-cavernous. **1968** Passmore & Robson *Compan. Med. Stud.* I. xxi. 9/1 The two cavernous sinuses intercommunicate across the midline by means of the anterior and posterior intercavernous sinuses. **1931** *Amer. Speech* VII. 19 His inter-consonantal *u* is perhaps Southern. **1964** J. W. Linnett *Electronic Struct. Molecules* i. 12 In chromium..the six electrons are spread among the five 3*d* and one 4*s* orbital to reduce the effect of inter-electronic repulsion. **1888** *Syd. Soc. Lex.*, *Inter-follicular*, situated between follicles. **1968** J. H. Burn *Lect. Notes Pharmacol.* (ed. 9) 88 Thyrocalcitonin is a hormone formed in the interfollicular cells of the thyroid gland. **1858** *Phil. Trans. R. Soc.* CXLVIII. 280 Intermarginal cavities [of sponges]. **1900** E. R. Lankester *Treat. Zool.* III. xiv. 246 In some genera intermarginal plates occur between these two series. **1907** J. H. Parsons *Dis. Eye* x. 171 The palpebral conjunctiva is said to commence at the anterior margin of the edge of the lid, but from this point to the posterior margin of the edge (the intermarginal strip) and for about 2 mm beyond (to the sulcus subtarsalis) there is a transitional zone. **1937** *Chem. Abstr.* XXXI. 5155 The diam. of the inter-micellar spaces decreases considerably on shrinkage. **1962** J. T. Marsh *Self-Smoothing Fabrics* xv. 257 They..concluded that the resin must be in the inter-micellar spaces of the cellulose. **1894** J. Geikie *Gt. Ice Age* (ed. 3) xxxv. 593 The inter-morainic lakes which occupy similar positions at the base of the Alps in North Italy. **1957** G. E. Hutchinson *Treat. Limnol.* I. i. 90 A few inter-morainic bogs still exist but the lakes in general have disappeared. **1929** J. H. Jeans *Universe around Us* ii. 142 The vast stretches of internebular space. **1957** *Jrnl. Brit. Interplanetary Soc.* XVI. 22 Calculations on the feasibility of long-range interstellar travel—including internebular journeys. **1890** Billings *Med. Dict.* I. 710/2 Intervillous lacunæ, irregular vascular spaces connected with the maternal blood-vessels, surrounding the fœtal villi in the placenta. **1962** *Gray's Anat.* (ed. 33) 115 In the early stages of placental development the blood in the foetal vessels is separated from the maternal blood in the intervillous space.

b. *inter-testamental* adj.

1956 *Jrnl. Theol. Stud.* VII. 292 Professor Stauffer..is apt to find in the N.T. references to lost intertestamental literature [etc.]. **1973** *Times Lit. Suppl.* 7 Dec. 1516/2 Dr Vermes begins by ransacking the inter-testamental and rabbinic literatures (especially the Dead Sea Scrolls, the Targumim and the Palestinian Talmud).

c. *inter-African, -American, -cameral, -Caribbean, -coastal, -cultural, -dialectal, -ecclesiastical, -ethnic, -generational, -governmental, -perceptual, -professional, -racial* (later examples; so *-racially* adv.), *-regional, -territorial* (later examples).

1956 *Nature* 25 Feb. 366/2 An Inter-African Committee for Social Sciences. **1960** *Guardian* 6 Oct. 10/6 An expression of inter-African solidarity. **1973** *Black World* May 61/2 Those whom the truth would incriminate hid behind the made-in-Hilton Hotel masks of amnesty, reconciliation and inter-African dialogue. **1938** *Sun* (Baltimore) 5 Dec. 2/5 In this and in other matters of inter-American interest, I anticipate working with the representatives of Ecuador. **1961** *Ann. Reg. 1960* 532 The Inter-American system is incompatible with any form of totalitarianism. **1964** *Illustr. London News* 18 Jan. 81 President Johnson..sent his Assistant Secretary of State for Inter-American Affairs..to the Canal Zone. **1972** *Buenos Aires Herald* 4 Feb. 7/1 Bruno Quijano met yesterday with Charles Meyer, assistant secretary of state for inter-American affairs. **1973** *Sunday Advocate-News* (Barbados) 25 Feb. 13/7 Barbados strongly opposes any case of racial discrimination..and for this reason opposes the admission of Portugal in the Inter American system. **1929** *Times* 29 Oct. 16/1 Nobody believes that the question will..go to the intercameral conference before the Special Session ends. **1935** *Economist* 13 July 62/2 The Public Utility Holding Company Bill..has been returned to the Senate, which has sent it to an inter-cameral conference. **1971** *Jamaican Weekly Gleaner* 10 Nov. 5/5 Mr. Arnold Foote..lauded the function as a 'gesture of inter-Caribbean friendship'. **1973** *Caribbean Contact* Jan. 6/3, I believe that this magazine would help bridge the gap between Caribbean peoples and so foster inter-Caribbean harmony. **1927** *Contemp. Rev.* Oct. 493 Already in inter-coastal traffic New York is surpassed. **1969** *Jane's Freight Containers 1968–69* 57/2 Intercoastal Services via the Port of New York. **1937** *Theology* XXXV. 347 Our present consideration of intercultural contacts. **1955** *Sci. Amer.* Apr. 84/2 In the interest of intercultural understanding various U.S. Government agencies have hired anthropologists. **1972** *Ibid.* Nov. 82/1 If pictorial recognition is universal, do pictures offer us a lingua franca for intercultural communication? **1959** M. Schlauch *Eng. Lang. in Mod. Times* i. 28 An inter-dialectal survey. **1920** *Q. Register* Nov. 339 A great moment of international and inter-ecclesiastical opportunity. **1959** H. Wolff in *Anthropol. Ling.* Mar. 34 (*title*) Intelligibility and inter-ethnic attitudes. **1971** *Sunday Nation* (Nairobi) 11 Apr. 13/3 There was one section of the population in Uganda,

inter-ethnic in composition, which was not using English as the primary qualification for professional ascent. This section was the armed forces of Uganda. **1964** S. LIEBERSON in J. A. Fishman *Readings Sociol. of Lang.* (1968) 551 We find intergenerational linguistic unity of nationality groups is less than the unity within the immigrant groups themselves. **1968** *Listener* 29 Feb. 259/1 The intergenerational differences amount to a mutation. **1971** *Black Scholar* June 29/2 The black revolution will then become an intergenerational revolution. **1927** *Glasgow Herald* 20 Jan. 8 When it came to negotiation, agreement could not be obtained by inter-Governmental intervention. **1946** J. S. HUXLEY *Unesco* ii. 48 This important group of human activities..has never previously been adequately dealt with by any inter-governmental organisation. **1969** *Jane's Freight Containers 1968–69* 142/3 Some of the problems requiring action at the inter-governmental level ..have been indicated above. **1973** *Times* 21 May 4/7 The inter-governmental convention establishing the European University Institute was signed by the six founding members of the Community in April, 1972. **1932** W. T. STACE *Theory of Knowledge & Existence* vii. 160 What it is or is not during inter-perceptual periods makes no difference to me as a practical person. **1934** *Mind* XLIII. 151 Why must we believe that causation continues to operate during inter-perceptual intervals? **1960** *Times* 15 Feb. 11/7 The third Interprofessional Conference in March will examine some cardinal moral issues. **1971** *Optometry Today* (Amer. Optometric Assoc.) 13 Naturally, interprofessional referrals are a two-way street. **1905** *Athenæum* 30 Sept. 430/1 Inter-racial cordiality. **1953** E. H. BROOKES *S. Afr. in Changing World* v. 105 Thus the services of Americans to South Africa in the interracial field are spanned across a century. **1960** *Spectator* 22 July 128 There is a large, brand-new 'inter-racial' hotel. **1968** *Blues Unlimited* Dec. 12 The local interracial Dirty Blues Band. **1972** *Publishers Weekly* 7 Feb. 37 (Advt.), Grace Halsell..describes what happens to interracial couples when they are joined in a love affair or marriage. **1964** *Punch* 26 Aug. 290/1 Anger..fomented internally and directed inter-racially. **1972** *Publishers Weekly* 14 Aug. 40/2 He hustled a basketball scholarship, lost it for dating interracially. **1945** Interregional [see *EXPRESSWAY]. **1962** H. R. LOYN *Anglo-Saxon Eng.* ii. 77 Gold was the essential commodity for interregional exchange in the Mediterranean context. **1964** *Ann. Reg. 1963* 102 Agreement..that joint authorities..would continue to provide services on an inter-territorial basis was reached. **1967** *Economist* 17 June 1234/2 The main points of the treaty are: the establishment of an East African development bank; interterritorial tariffs on goods originating in one country and exported to another, [etc.].

5. *inter-arrival, -bank(s), -borough, -caste, -centre, -church, -city* (examples; also *absol.*), *-class* (examples), *-dealer, -electron, -faith, -family, -fibre, -library, -nucleon, -office, -particle, -party, -species, -stream, -trial, -union, -university* (later examples), *-valve, -village, -zone.*

1962 J. RIORDAN *Stochastic Service Syst.* i. 3 For this, as for the Poisson, the intervals between demands (inter-arrival intervals) are independent random variables. **1968** P. A. P. MORAN *Introd. Probability Theory* iii. 179 Much more complicated queueing systems with general inter-arrival and service time distributions are considered. **1907** *Daily Chron.* 29 Sept. 9/2 The Inter-Banks Team Race, in which sixteen banks in London were represented. **1966** *Economist* 12 Nov. 718/2 The big broker in unsecured 'interbank' sterling deposits. **1973** *Daily Tel.* 9 Feb. 21 Overnight money in the interbank market rose to a peak of 13 p.c. earlier this week. **1905** *Westm. Gaz.* 8 Nov. 5/1 The officials of the inter-borough railways. **1928** *Daily Express* 19 May 9/5 The first inter-borough competition of its kind ever organised in London. **1908** *New Reformer* II. 62 It is a case of inter-caste and inter-provincial marriage. **1925** E. S. JONES *Christ of Indian Road* xiii. 243 We sat down to an intercaste dinner—a hundred high-caste Hindus, a hundred outcastes, a hundred Indian Christians, a few Mohammedans, and several of us of the West. **1964** *Ann. Reg. 1963* 358 Among social measures which came into force were the banning of polygamy and permission for inter-caste marriages. **1946** *Nature* 20 July 97/2 Each centimetre on the plotting-board of the apparatus corresponds with 'the cone intercentre distance', that is, the distance between the centre of one foveal cone and that of its next-door neighbours. **1970** *New Scientist* 31 Dec. 596 Saturation signalling involves a large volume of inter-centre communication. **1905** *Daily Chron.* 22 Nov. 1/7 At an inter-Church Conference in New York 17,000,000 Church members of all denominations were represented. **1926** *Brit. Weekly* 22 July 327/1 Dr. Clark has toured the world to build this inter-church, international organisation. **1909** *Westm. Gaz.* 3 June 14/1 In the first inter-city match played between Edinburgh and Glasgow. **1940** A. L. ALBERT *Electr. Communication* (ed. 2) vii. 174 Connections are made between the two exchanges by means of toll lines... In some locations this has been designated intercity service. **1955** *Railway Mag.* May 334/1 The 9 a.m. 'Inter-City' from Paddington averaged 18¼ min. late at Snow Hill. **1968** *Daily Tel.* 12 Nov. 26/7 A three-months' trial scheme..was introduced by British Railways on inter-city trains in September. **1970** A. DEKKER *Divers Diamonds* xxii. 145 The GPO intercity microwave link towers. **1972** *Guardian* 13 Mar. 13/1 The expression 'Inter-City' was a British invention and its success is demonstrated by the adoption of the title in such countries as Germany, Japan, Holland, and now the United States, to describe express business trains. **1973** *Times* 29 Oct. 14/8 On the inter-city to Sunderland I was one of the first people in the dining car. **1909** *Post-Intelligencer* (Seattle) 18 Apr. 1/2 The interclass crews and girls' crews work at other hours during the day. **1950** T. H. MARSHALL *Citizenship & Social Class* I. iv. 57 A divided educational system, by promoting both intra-class similarity and inter-class difference, gave emphasis..to a criterion of social distance. **1971** P. J. KEATING *Working Classes in Victorian Fiction* iii. 71 A romance of corrupted character and inter-class love. **1972** *Listener* 27 July 107/2 Venice was untouched by the inter-class antagonisms..that troubled the domestic peace of other states. **1968** *N.Y. Times* 19 Feb. 60 It appears to be technically feasible to use a central computer to record and report interdealer quotations. **1970** *Washington Post* 30 Sept. D 11/4 The following..are representative interdealer prices. **1964** J. W. LINNETT *Electronic Struct. Molecules* i. 11 Clearly, for the lowest energy state, it is advantageous to reduce inter-electron repulsion as much as possible. **1967** *Economist* 6 May 574/2 It is joining with 39 other firms and an interfaith group to provide 1,500 new jobs. **1970** *Toronto Daily Star* 24 Sept. 37/1 An interfaith group which supports tough anti-obscenity laws. **1973** *Jewish Chron.* 2 Feb. 13/5 The Israel Interfaith Committee. **1946** *Nature* 10 Aug. 204/2 The successful production of hybrid plants from interspecific, intergeneric, and even inter-family crosses has naturally led to investigation of the events which occur in some of the crosses which habitually fail. **1965** J. E. CROSS in *English Studies* Apr. 96 The provincial and interfamily strife..between..Deira and Bernicia. **1962** J. T. MARSH *Self-Smoothing Fabrics* iv. 39 In a fabric with a high cover factor, *i.e.* a tightly woven material, the friction between fibres is apt to be high enough to restrict inter-fibre movement. **1928** J. A. MCMILLEN *(title)* Selected articles on interlibrary loans. **1938** *Times* 1 Jan. 10/1 All England and Wales is now covered by schemes for the inter-library lending of books. **1968** *Language* XLIV. 211 The publications..are available to any American library on inter-library loan. **1953** *Physical Rev.* XCI. 1529/2 The meson theory, which predicts strong internucleon interactions. **1934** WEBSTER, Inter-office. **1938** *Times* 29 Sept. 19/1 War Loan..was being quoted 95 middle in inter-office dealings. **1969** *New Yorker* 20 Sept. 181/1 An interoffice memo cast in cablese. **1972** *Accountant* 6 Apr. 456/1 On the sports side, it was hoped to revive the inter-office cricket tournament and play matches with other students' societies and the law students. **1946** *Nature* 6 July 13/1 The resistance increased, indicating that the width of the inter-particle contacts had diminished. **1953** *Physical Rev.* XCI. 1527 The leading term..depends only on the interparticle distances. **1962** W. B. THOMPSON *Introd. Plasma Physics* vii. 148 The simple theory presented here may be extended by including in a phenomenological way the effect of interparticle collisions. **1909** *Westm. Gaz.* 8 Mar. 2/1 A break in the party seems inevitable. The issue of this inter-party struggle will be one of great moment for South Africa. **1957** C. HUNT *Guide to Communist Jargon* xxx. 103 He [*sc.* Marx] held that, under the capitalist system, parliaments were simply the instruments by means of which the bourgeoisie maintained its domination, and that inter-party conflicts within this framework had no real significance. **1920** *Proc. Amer. Soc. Hort. Sci. 1919* 50 *(heading)* Inter species pollination of plums. **1962** *Punch* 14 Mar. 443/1 The possible consequences of inter-species communication between man and dolphin. **1902** WEBSTER Suppl., *Interstream* a. (Phys. Geog.), between streams. **1968** D. S. SIMONETT in R. W. Fairbridge *Encycl. Geomorphol.* 559 Many geomorphologists today use the term [*sc.* interfluve] for the interstream area to imply a discrete landscape or geomorphic unit. **1971** *Jrnl. Gen. Psychol.* Jan. 125 Within each order, 21 plates consisting of three different spatial arrangements of each level of number were also shown randomly with an intertrial interval of 10 seconds. **1972** *Jrnl. Social Psychol.* Dec. 225 The timer was preset so that the signals for all shock options were of three seconds duration, with a 15-second intertrial interval. **1969** *Daily Tel.* 10 Feb. 19/5 Because of bitter inter-union rivalry, the original purpose of the strike..has become almost totally obscured. **1973** *Times* 17 Jan. 16/8 Eliminating the possibility of inter-union disputes in one factory. **1956** *Nature* 3 Mar. 405/1 In 1944 the Secretary of State for the Colonies invited British universities to set up an Inter-University Organization to assist the development of higher education in the Colonies. **1970** *Internat. & Compar. Law Q.* XIX. I. 181 Dr. Verheul is now Head of the private international law department of the T. M. C. Asser Institute in The Hague, an inter-university institute which is engaged in comprehensive documentation in the field of international law. **1909** *Cent. Dict.* Suppl., *Inter-valve*, in steam-engines, noting the space which is between the throttle- and slide-valves. **1921** *Wireless World* 2 Apr. 17/2 The 5-step Amplifier, with intervalve resistance couplings, is of the usual type. **1921** *Ibid.* 14 May 120/1 Substitute an intervalve transformer for your telephone transformer. **1949** M. MEAD *Male & Female* 413 The biggest inter-village economic exchange. **1960** Inter-zone [see *DUST *v.*[1] 12 c]. **1961** *Times* 8 June 5/2 They gained a 5–1 winning lead over Denmark in the inter-zone final.

6. interacinar (-æsinăɹ) = *interacinous* (s.v. INTER- 6); **intera·trial,** situated between the atria of the heart; **inter-ca·rdinal,** of points of the compass: lying midway between the cardinal points; also as *sb.*; **interco·rtical,** situated within the (or a) cortex (properly **intracortical*); **interge·nic** [*GENIC *a.*], taking place or existing between neighbouring genes; **interpa·lpebral,** situated between the eyelids; **interpla·nar** *Cryst.*, existing between the planes of a crystal lattice; **interplical** (-plǝi·kăl), situated between folds (see PLICA 2); **interpopula·tional,** occurring or existing between populations or groups; **interpro·ximal** *Dentistry*, situated between adjacent teeth; on or affecting the surfaces bounding such a region; **interpu·pillary,** existing between the pupils of the eyes; **interto·nic,** occurring between two tones or stresses; **intertube·rcular,** placed or situated between tubercles; **intervari·etal,** formed or obtained from, or occurring between, (members of) different varieties (VARIETY 6 b); **intervei·nal** *Bot.*, situated or occurring between the veins of a leaf; **interxy·lary** *Bot.*, situated within the secondary xylem.

1900 *Bull. Johns Hopkins Hosp.* XI. 205/2 Interacinar cell islets have been studied by Harris and Gow. **1961** *Lancet* 29 July 258/2 A high prevalence of pancreatic arteriosclerosis..could have caused the associated insular and interacinar fibrosis and hyalinisation. **1911** STEDMAN *Med. Dict.* 431/1 *Interatrial*, between the atria of the heart. **1967** G. M. WYBURN et al. *Conc. Anat.* iii. 89/1 On the interatrial septum there is a shallow depression, the fossa ovalis. **1909** WEBSTER, Intercardinal, adj.—n., an intercardinal point. **1961** F. H. BURGESS *Dict. Sailing* 121 *Inter-cardinal points*, the half-cardinals. **1969** *Gloss. Terms Magnetic Compasses & Binnacles (B.S.I.)* 5 *Intercardinal points.* These are north-east, south-east, south-west, north-west and may be marked with the capital letters NE, SE, SW, and NW respectively. **1902** *Proc. Zool. Soc.* II. 215 Cortex [of the sponge] fibrous throughout,..without intercortical cavities. **1924** R. M. OGDEN tr. *Koffka's Growth of Mind* ii. 55 According to Edinger, morphological changes in the brain are indicated by..the growth of intercortical pathways. **1933** J. ROSETT *Intercortical Syst. Human Cerebrum* iv. 26 In the course of cerebral evolution the intercortical systems increase in number and in bulk. **1941** *Cold Spring Harbor Symp. Quant. Biol.* IX. 161/1 The breaks of minute rearrangements would in all probability differ from them in being only intergenic. **1951** G. H. BOURNE *Cytol. & Cell Physiol.* (ed. 2) v. 225 It..assumes that there are no non-genic portions of the chromosome (matrix, intergenic connexions). **1968** *Canad. Jrnl. Genetics & Cytol.* X. 50 A UV-sensitive mutant of *Aspergillus rugulosus* unrelated to intergenic crossing over. **1892** A. DUANE tr. *Fuchs' Textbk. Ophthalm.* xii. 467 That part of the cornea and of the scleral conjunctiva which ordinarily is not covered by the lids is called the interpalpebral zone... When the eyes are a little screwed together..the interpalpebral zone diminishes in size. **1934** E. WOLFF *Path. Eye* ii. 29 Pinguecula, or interpalpebral spot, is a slightly raised yellowish area placed next to the inner or outer margin of the cornea. **1932** *Amer. Mineralogist* XVII. 549 *(caption)* The values given are the calculated interplanar spacings. **1948** K. LONSDALE *Crystals & X-Rays* iii. 77 There is now, however, no way of measuring interplanar angles. **1970** A. J. C. WILSON *Elem. X-Ray Crystallogr.* ii. 19 All the interplanar spacings capable of producing lines in an X-ray powder photograph can be obtained by consideration of the distance between successive planes of the lattice points. **1900** *Proc. U.S. Nat. Museum* XXIII. 398 The term interplical ridge has been applied to the summit of the radial convexities of the wing and interplical groove the bottom of the alternating concavities. **1903** *Phil. Trans. R. Soc.* B. CXCV. 161 The thickened chitin bands, which..are in contact by those edges directed towards the interplical space, are here divaricated. **1971** *Listener* 30 Dec. 907 There are no known IQ tests which are capable of overcoming the *inter*populational cross-cultural barrier. **1971** *McGraw-Hill Yearbk. Sci. & Technol.* 253 Interpopulational developmental comparisons..helped to clarify what in the past seemed to be an aberrant course of leaf development. **1897** E. C. KIRK *Amer. Textbk. Operative Dentistry* iii. 97 The counteraction of the tongue and cheek..drives the finer particles of the food into the interproximal spaces. **1908** G. V. BLACK *Operative Surg.* 211 *(heading)* Interproximal wear and its treatment. *Ibid.* 213 If there has been much loss of interproximal gum tissue..watch the case for a few weeks. **1960** KERR & ASH *Oral Path.* vii. 115 Interproximal caries involve all of the teeth, but the molars and bicuspids are involved more frequently than the incisors. **1972** S. GARFIELD *Teeth* iv. 88 The small spaces between adjacent teeth around the contact points are called Contact Areas or Interproximal Spaces. *Ibid.* ix. 133 Inside the ridges between the roots of each adjacent tooth the bone is called Interproximal Bone. **1907** J. H. PARSONS *Dis. Eye* xxvi. 525 With an interpupillary distance of 60 mm. this angle is about 2°. **1962** L. S. SASIENI *Princ. & Pract. Optical Dispensing* v. 106 *(heading)* Inter-pupillary distance. **1909** *Cent. Dict.* Suppl., Intertonic. **1953** K. JACKSON *Lang. & Hist. in Early Brit.* II. 268 Syncope of intertonic syllables in Vulgar Latin. **1893** *Jrnl. Anat. & Physiol.* XXVII. 260 The level which is expressed by our inter-tubercular line. **1967** G. M. WYBURN et al. *Conc. Anat.* ii. 53/1 The muscle is inserted..into the lateral lip of the intertubercular groove on the front of the humerus. **1916** *Mem. N.Y. Bot. Garden* VI. 352 No essential differences were noted in intervarietal fertility and fruitfulness. *Ibid.*, Intervarietal crosses. **1951** *New Biol.* XI. 115 In *Paramecium aurelia* there are seven varieties, and each variety contains types I and II... Intervarietal mating takes place very rarely and then only between type I of one variety and type II of the other. **1934** WEBSTER, Interveinal. **1946** *Nature* 9 Nov. 663/2 The virus strain used produced a bright yellow interveinal mottle in the tomato. **1970** *Bot. Gaz.* CXXXI. 152/1 This strip [of leaf] was five interveinal areas wide at the upper margin. **1889** *Ann. Bot.* III. 293 The phloëm-islands, or interxylary phloëm-strands, are formed centripetally by certain portions of the normal cambium. **1969** K. ESAU *Phloem* vi. 213 In..the interxylary or included phloem, the cambium..forms periodically some phloem increments towards the interior of the stem so that the phloem becomes embedded in the xylem.

interacinar: see *INTER- *pref.* 6.

interact, *sb.* Add: *attrib.*

1908 *Daily Chron.* 3 July 3/5 At the 'private' or roofed theatres, the performance of interact music was the rule. **1909** *Morning Leader* 29 May 4/6 At the 'private theatres', such as the Blackfriars, they not only had interacts but interact music.

interact, *v.* (Further examples.)

1967 M. ARGYLE *Psychol. Interpersonal Behaviour* viii. 144 Children and adolescents are very limited in their social techniques, and may be able to interact with other children, and parents, but not with other adults... Most mental patients apart from schizophrenics are able to interact, but are much less successful in forming permanent relationships. **1972** *Jrnl. Social Psychol.* LXXXVII. 7 Very few Ss [*sc.* subjects] left their chair in order to

interact with *E* [*sc.* the examiner]; those who did were ignored.

interaction. Add: (Further examples.) *spec.* in *Physics*, referring to the action between atomic and subatomic particles. Also *attrib.*
1930 *Proc. R. Soc.* A. CXXIX. 4 The simplified interaction which couples the nuclear system and the electron. **1951** T. PARSONS et al. in Parsons & Shils *Toward Gen. Theory Action* II. iv. 190 The specific interaction systems of ego. **1955** H. B. G. CASIMIR in W. Pauli *Niels Bohr* 130 The electrostatic interaction energy is e^2/a where *a* is a distance between electrons. **1959** *Listener* 9 July 52/1 There are four distinct types of force through which the manifold transformations of matter and energy arise. These forces are known as the strong, the electromagnetic, the weak and the gravitational interactions. **1964** *Language* XL. 242 An interaction cycle between the mother and child that amounts to a pair of reciprocal transformations. **1967** M. ARGYLE *Psychol. Interpersonal Behaviour* vii. 128 If A presents himself as an upper-class person but B reacts to him as a working-class person, interaction will not proceed smoothly.

interactionism (intəræ·kʃəniz'm). *Philos.* [f. INTERACTION + -ISM.] The theory that in the causal relations between mind and body the causal influence runs in both directions, in sensation from body to mind and in volition from mind to body. So **intera·ctionist** *sb.*, an adherent of interactionism; *adj.*, of or pertaining to this doctrine.
1902 *Pop. Sci. Monthly* 459 Interactionism has to maintain, in this concrete form of the 'survival theory', that the mental process as such is an aid to evolution. **1903** C. A. STRONG *Why the Mind has a Body* 5 Whether this interactionist tendency in biology be significant or ephemeral, we need not inquire. *Ibid.* 23 What the interactionist..takes for an action of mind on body is..an action of the brain upon the rest of the body. *Ibid.* 33 Interactionism seems almost to necessitate two juxtaposed realities exchanging influences, and thus to imply a metaphysical dualism. **1934** *Brit. Jrnl. Psychol.* Jan. 273 The annoyance may not be a response to being struck with a pin... We will not try here to settle the quarrel between such a parallelistic interpretation and the interpretation of an interactionist. **1941** *Mind* L. 86 He argues for interactionism, as against psychophysical parallelism. **1956** J. O. URMSON *Philos. Analysis* II. vii. 110 One [metaphysician] advocates psycho-physical parallelism, the other interactionism. **1972** *Jrnl. Social Psychol.* Aug. 214 Pursuing the explanations of the symbolic interactionist somewhat further, Mead's theory suggests..maximum category overlap.

interactive, *a.* (Later examples.)
1972 *Computers & Humanities* VI. 195 A method which will provide the student with a rapid interactive feedback. **1972** *Science* 2 June 1019/1 A complicated and interactive set of physical, chemical, biological and human processes act in concert to yield a spectrum of measured values.

inter-African: see *INTER- *pref.* 4 c.

inter-agency. (Later examples.)
1969 *R. & E. Coordinator* (Res. & Engin. Council Graphic Arts Industry) Apr. 4/1 The Government uses millions of microfiche internally for storage and retrieval systems and for interagency communications. **1973** *Times* 24 May 8/4 On July 5, 1970, Mr Nixon said, he appointed Mr Hoover chairman of an inter-agency committee to discuss a need for better intelligence operations.

inter alia: see INTER Lat. prep.

inter-allied (intəræ̆ləi·d, -æ·ləid), *a.* [f. INTER- 1 b + ALLIED.] Existing or constituted between allies or allied forces. So **inter-ally** (-æ·ləi), *a.*
1919 J. M. KEYNES *Econ. Consequences Peace* 96 The supreme authority is to be in the hands of an Inter-Allied Rhineland Commission. *Ibid.* 240 The settlement of inter-Ally indebtedness. **1925** A. TOYNBEE *Survey Internat. Affairs 1920–23* 1 The four Treaties..had provided for the establishment of a number of inter-Allied bodies to perform temporary or permanent executive duties. **1942** W. S. CHURCHILL in *Hutchinson's Pict. Hist. War* 18 Mar.–9 June 30/2 The task of national self-preservation and of inter-allied duty. **1973** *Times* 29 Oct. 15/2 This public airing of an inter-allied dispute on a day of acute international tension was tactless to say the least.

inter-American: see *INTER- *pref.* 4 c.

interanimate, *v.* Add: Hence **interanima·-tion,** mutual animation.
1925 I. A. RICHARDS *Princ. Lit. Crit.* xxxi. 237 Conflicts, resolutions and interanimations. **1966** *English Studies* XLVII. 200 The interanimation of the complex parts.

inter-arrival, -atrial, -availability, -available, -bank(s): see *INTER- *pref.* 5, 6, 2 a, 5.

interbed, *v.* (Earlier example.)
c **1806** D. WORDSWORTH *Jrnl.* (1941) I. 252 These two islands..were intermingled with the water, I might say interbedded and interveined with it.

inter-behaviour, -behavioural: see *INTER- *pref.* 2 a.

interbellum (intəɪbe·lŏm), *a.* Also **interbella.** [f. INTER- 4 b + L. *bellum* war.] Of or with reference to a period between two wars, e.g. between the wars of 1914–18 and of 1939–45. So **interbe·lline** *a.*
1940 BEERBOHM *Mainly on the Air* (1946) 82, I feel sure that even in the inter-bella period a river would have done Bloomsbury no end of good. **1958** *Oxf. Mag.* 22 May 454/1 The interbelline English Don..did his best not to take 'Eng. Lit.'..too seriously. **1961** *Ann. Reg. 1960* 462 Nathalie Sarraute..was noticeably closer than he to the English experimental novel of the interbelline years. **1969** P. ANDERSON in Cockburn & Blackburn *Student Power* 231 The German emigration, coming from a philosophical culture that was quite distinct from the parish-pump positivism of interbellum Vienna, avoided this island.

inter-borough: see *INTER- *pref.* 5.

intercalarium (i:ntəɪkălēə·riŏm). *Zool.* Pl. **-ia.** Also **interca·lare, interca·lary.** [mod.L., neut. sing. of L. *intercalārius* INTERCALARY *a.*] **1.** An element found between adjacent neural arches in the vertebral column of elasmobranchs and certain other fishes.
1887 *Proc. Zool. Soc.* 31 Intercalaria are absent in the hæmal tube [of the shark, *Carcharodon rondeletii*]. **1922** J. F. DANIEL *Elasmobranch Fishes* iii. 49 Each dorsal intercalary [is perforated] by the dorsal root of the same [*sc.* spinal] nerve. **1925** J. S. KINGSLEY *Vertebr. Skeleton* 28 (*caption*) Intercalaria. *Ibid.*, The ring with arches is called the centrum, the one without is an intercentrum or intercalare. **1967** *Jrnl. Linn. Soc.* (*Zool.*) XLVII. 186 In *Polyodon*, dorsal intercalaries may be absent in the abdominal region, but they are usually present in the caudal.
2. In cypriniform fishes, an ossicle forming part of the Weberian apparatus linking the inner ear with the swimbladder.
1893 *Phil. Trans. R. Soc.* B. CLXXXIV. 83 Like the scaphium [in Macrones] the intercalarium consists of ascending and horizontal processes united at nearly a right angle. **1962** K. F. LAGLER et al. *Ichthyol.* viii. 248 These ossicles are derived from the apophyses of anterior vertebrae; the hindmost of them, the tripus, touches the anterior wall of the gas bladder and is connected with a ligament to the next bone, the intercalare. **1970** *Amer. Mus. Novitates* No. 2428. 16 The intercalarium is attached to the tripus by a very dense, elongate ligament.

intercalate, *v.* Add: **3.** *intr.* To become part of a sequence or array as an extraneous interpolation; to become intercalated *in* or inserted *into.*
1960 UBBELOHDE & LEWIS *Graphite* vi. 141 The easy exchange that is observed between halogen atoms when iodine monochloride or monobromide intercalate in graphite lends some support to this suggestion. **1970** *Nature* 24 Oct. 322/2 The dye, ethidium bromide, which intercalates into DNA, binds to tRNA chiefly at one site. **1973** *Sci. Amer.* Apr. 22/1 Large numbers of ethidium bromide molecules can intercalate in a nicked duplex loop or a linear duplex.

intercalate (intəɪkæ·lēit), *sb.* [f. the vb.] **a.** An atom or molecule, or a substance, that enters between the layers of the crystal lattice of another substance, esp. graphite. Freq. *attrib.*
1964 *Proc. R. Soc.* A. CCLXXIX. 291 Fuller understanding of interaction forces between the intercalates and the macro-aromatic molecules is..needed to interpret some highly interesting properties of crystal compounds in the direction of the *c* axis. **1966** *Ibid.* CCXCI. 332 Short range order within any single layer of intercalate clearly resembles that in a liquid or glass. **1968** *Ibid.* CCCIV. 26 Entry of intercalate molecules from the edge of basal planes of crystallites must be kept sufficiently slow to mitigate mechanical strains..before the intercalate has spread uniformly through any layer. **1971** *Nature* 2 July 43/2 Hindrances to charge wandering across the layers in the *c*-axis direction of such crystal compounds must depend extensively on the electron affinity and the local repulsion potentials of the intercalate molecules.
b. A compound formed by foreign atoms or molecules entering between the layers of a crystal lattice, esp. of graphite.
1968 *Proc. R. Soc.* A. CCCIV. 26 First sequence intercalates may eventually be formed on saturation. **1969** *Ibid.* CCCIX. 300 For preparing intercalates with quite low anion uptakes..the mounted specimen was actually immersed in concentrated nitric acid.

inter-cameral, -cardinal, -Caribbean, -caste, -cavernous, -celebration: see *INTER- *pref.* 4 c, 6, 4 c, 5, 4 a, 2 a.

intercellular, *a.* Add: Hence **interce·llularly** *adv.*, between cells.
1935 E. A. BESSEY *Text-bk. Mycol.* (1939) x. 251 The mycelium is long, slender and branching, growing intercellularly within the host. **1950** J. C. WALKER *Plant Path.* viii. 346 The fungus develops in the epidermal wall..and it also proceeds intercellularly.

intercept, *sb.* Add: **1.** *spec.*, of a ball passed or thrown to an opponent.
1954 in WEBSTER Add. **1960** T. MCLEAN *Kings of Rugby* xi. 143 Meredith made an intercept.
3. *Navigation.* The angular difference between the calculated and the observed zenith distances of a heavenly body.
1901 J. R. WALKER *Explanation Method Obtaining Position at Sea* 15 Let the difference between the calculated and observed zenith distance be *k* miles nearer (say) at the first observation and *l* miles further at the second. Let the extremities of these intercepts be A and B. **1939** *Geogr. Jrnl.* XCIV. 254 Nowadays the best way of obtaining latitude and longitude with a theodolite is the quadrantal and intercept method. **1969** G. RICHARDS *Sextant Observations* iii. 92 The difference in value between the true altitude and the tabulated altitude is the intercept, and it can be 'Towards' (the body) or 'Away' (from the body).
4. A conversation, message, code, etc., that is picked up or discovered by the use of a concealed microphone, by listening to a radio communication, etc.; a device for achieving this.
1942 *Sun* (Baltimore) 10 Dec. 1/3 Distributing these copied excerpts to Government departments and officials who might have an interest in such 'intercepts', as they are called. **1945** *Ibid.* 30 Nov. 3 In the War Department.. the intercepts were shown only to Secretary Henry L. Stimson, [etc.]. **1958** *Manch. Guardian* 13 Jan. 4 The 'intercepts' (transcripts of recordings obtained by wire-tapping)..were used as evidence in the hearing. **1967** 'W. HAGGARD' *Conspirators* xii. 123 We can't monitor every wavelength round the clock..but we've picked up one or two intercepts between Kaunas and this diplomat. **1972** R. LUDLUM *Osterman Weekend* i. 32 Intercepts have been placed on all telephones. **1973** *N.Y. Times* 22 June 35 Given torrents of intercepts..cryptanalysts could not reach a solution for thousands of years.

interception. Add: **1. d.** The action of closing in on and trying to destroy an enemy aircraft or missile. Also *attrib.*
1941 in R. W. Zandvoort et al. *Wartime English* (1957) 102 The toll of enemy raiders increases as the R.A.F. improves its methods of interception. **1955** *Bull. Atomic Sci.* Mar. 79/2 There is a great deal more that can be done to set up an effective warning and interception system. **1955** *Sci. News Let.* 15 Oct. 243/1 Once in the air, the missile's miniature radar and its own electronic computer—a baby version of the one that launched it—would keep it on an interception course. **1958** C. C. ADAMS et al. *Space Flight* 64 Surface-to-surface and intercontinental missiles are, generally, a means for delivering atomic and hydrogen bombs as a sort of 'interception-proof' air weapon.

interceptor. Add: **b.** *Aeronaut.* A fast aircraft which is designed specifically for the interception of hostile aircraft. Also *attrib.*, as *interceptor fighter, 'plane.*
1930 *Flight* 27 June 691/2 For a normal fighter, tanks to carry fuel for a flight of..2½ hours are sufficient. The new class of 'interceptor fighters' require even less endurance than that. **1934** *Times* 26 June *Air Suppl.* p. xvi/1 The modern interceptor was evoked by the fast day bomber. **1935** *Economist* 12 Oct. 708/1 There is no direct defence against air attack—'the bomber will always get through'—there never can be an adequate force of interceptor 'planes. **1948** 'N. SHUTE' *No Highway* xii. 294 One of the jet interceptor fighters coming into squadron use. **1966** *Electronics* 17 Oct. 104 The considerations will be presented in terms of a typical modern interceptor system. **1973** *Times* 14 May 12/6 The Warsaw Pact is also superior in light bombers, interceptors, and ground attack aircraft.

interchange, *sb.* Add: **1. b.** *Cytology.* Reciprocal exchange of chromosome segments, esp. between non-homologous chromosomes.
1927 *Jrnl. Genetics* XVIII. 198 In other words, chromosomes I and IX seem to have undergone interchange of a terminal segment in the ancestry of the isomorphic *B* strain. **1963** LEWIS & JOHN *Chromosome Marker* I. iii. 66 Individuals which are heterozygous for an interchange are known as interchange heterozygotes. **1968** R. RIEGER *Gloss. Genetics & Cytogenetics* 440 An interchange of segments between homologous chromosomes is called 'fraternal', while one between nonhomologous chromosomes is called 'external'.
5. A junction of two or more highways on separate levels, allowing vehicles to change from one to another without lines of traffic crossing.
1944 *Sun* (Baltimore) 6 Dec. 7-0 An accident on the Pennsylvania Turnpike near the New Stanton interchange. **1954** HEWES & OGLESBY *Highway Engin.* viii. 207 An interchange not only offers grade separation between the two traffic arteries, but in addition provides easy routes for vehicles transferring from one through facility to the other. **1958** H. M. SHERRARD *Austral. Road Pract.* xix. 365 Much ingenuity has been displayed in the design of such intersections or 'traffic interchanges'. **1962** *Amer. Speech* XXXVII. 267 A multilevel freeway interchange. **1968** *Listener* 29 Aug. 267/3 It was an important junction and interchange. **1970** *Daily Tel.* 14 Nov. 1/7 The Berrygrove interchange of the A41 and the M1. **1973** D. WESTHEIMER *Going Public* ix. 127 A four-mile long.. traffic jam..backing up to the San Diego Freeway interchange.

interchanger. Add: **2.** A heat exchanger.
1896 A. J. WALLIS-TAYLER *Refrigerating & Ice-Making Machinery* viii. 136 An interchanger was also sometimes provided, wherein the air that had done duty in the storage or cold chambers was utilised for further reducing the temperature of the compressed air. **1949** M. DAVIES *Physical Princ. Gas Liquefaction* vi. 86 The tubular type of interchanger carrying the compressed gas through a

pipe mounted within a wider one which carries the expanded gas, is..more common..than the Hampson Spiral.

inter-church, -city, -class, -coastal: see *INTER- *pref.* 5, 4 c.

intercolonial, *a.* (Earlier and later examples.)
1843 J. OSBORNE *Guide Madeiras* 199 (*heading*) Intercolonial voyages. **1905** *Daily Chron.* 14 July 5/5 The Intercolonial Railway to Montreal.

intercolumn. (Later example.)
1934 H. P. CLUNN *Face of London* (ed. 5) 28 The City of London Club, built in 1832–3 with..a Doric order of seven inter-columns.

intercom (i·ntəɹkǫm). Also **inter-com, inter-comm** (with hyphen), **intercomm.** [Colloq. abbrev. of INTERCOMMUNICATION.] A system of intercommunication by radio or telephone between or within aircraft, offices, vehicles, etc. Also *attrib.*
1940 C. OLSSON in Michie & Graebner *Their Finest Hour* iv. 61 The others behind me were gossiping as usual on their 'intercoms'. **1941** [see *DECK *sb.*[1] 3 e]. **1941** *War Illustr.* 20 Oct. 215/1 The rear gunner, I remember, called up on the inter-com., and said, 'I hope you chaps see the next one before I do.' *Ibid.* 30 Dec. 383/1 Unable to talk to the others over the 'intercom,' because my mouthpiece was not working, I stuck to the controls. **1942** T. RATTIGAN *Flare Path* I. 101 He even moaned to me over the intercomm. because he'd shot down a Messerschmitt. **1943** *Electronic Engin.* XVI. 140 A is valve set for three-fold communication: tank–commander; tank–tank; intercomm. in tanks. **1949** *Ibid.* XXI. 109 Electricians will welcome new chapters on Intercoms (loud-speaking telephones). **1951** J. STEINBECK *Log from 'Sea of Cortez'* (1958) p. xxv, An intercom phone between the basement and the upstairs office. **1964** M. MCLUHAN *Understanding Media* II. xxiv. 236 The close teamwork and tribal loyalty now demanded by electrical intercom again puts the Japanese in positive relation to their ancient traditions. **1967** [see *INTERCOMMUNICATION 4]. **1972** G. DURRELL *Catch me a Colobus* iv. 73 The intercom system that we have all over the zoo. **1972** J. POTTER *Going West* 8 The intercom announced the departure of Flight BA 531.

intercombination (i:ntəɹkǫmbinēi·ʃən). [f. INTER- + COMBINATION.] (See INTER- 2 a.) *spec.* in *Physics,* an electronic transition between atomic states of different multiplicities (i.e. having different spin quantum numbers); also *ellipt.* for **intercombination line,** a spectral line so produced.
1930 RUARK & UREY *Atoms, Molecules & Quanta* xx. 705 When intercombination lines occur, the intensity rules considered in this section must be modified. **1934** O. W. RICHARDSON *Molecular Hydrogen* iii. 46 There may be intercombination lines between the singlet and triplet states but if so they must be very faint. **1937** J. W. T. SPINKS tr. *Herzberg's Atomic Spect. & Atomic Struct.* ii. 79 Terms of the triplet system of He practically do not combine with the terms of the singlet system, and conversely. That is, a prohibition of intercombinations is observed. **1941** *Rev. Mod. Physics* XIII. 75 Intercombinations may occur with appreciable intensity only if the molecule contains some heavier atoms. **1950** *Discussions Faraday Soc.* IX. 16 To identify spectroscopically the long-lived luminescence and converse absorption bands as intercombinations, use is made of the characteristics of the spin-orbit coupling process. **1970** G. K. WOODGATE *Elem. Atomic Struct.* vii. 132 When S changes one speaks of intercombination lines.

intercommunal (intəɹkǫ·miunăl), *a.* [f. INTER- 4 c + COMMUNAL *a.*] Existing or occurring between communities or races. Hence **interco·mmunalism.**
1909 in WEBSTER. **1960** S. FOOT *Emergency Exit* xii. 98 The inter-communal strife was at its worst. Turk and Greek were going for each other. **1971** *Black Scholar* June 51/1 With the establishment of society through inter-communalism, the entire social contract must be altered. **1973** *Black World* Dec. 19/2 We believe in intercommunalism—the relatedness of all people. **1974** *Black Panther* 9 Feb. 8/3 The Maryland Pen Intercommunal Survival Collective is calling for a community-based united front to halt the injustices and tortures before it is too late.

intercommunication. Add: **4.** *attrib.* Cf. *INTERCOM.
1911 M. HIRD in L. Weaver *House & its Equipment* 124 With an 'intercommunication' system of telephones in the house, room after room can be..easily 'rung up'. **1967** *Lebende Sprachen* XII. 137/1 *Intercommunication system* (*intercom*), a system of wiring which enables two-way communication between teacher and student(s).

intercommunion. Add: **3.** Participation in the sacrament of Holy Communion by members of different religious denominations.
1921 [see *inter-celebration* s.v. *INTER- 2 a]. **1931** W. TEMPLE *Thoughts on Probl. of Day* iii. 99 It is perfectly clear that the authors of the Memorandum never contemplated such action as formal Intercommunion. **1936** A. M. RAMSEY *Gospel & Catholic Ch.* i. 8 To the one 'intercommunion' is meaningless without unity of outward order; to the other 'intercommunion' seems the one sensible and Christian way towards unity. **1966** *Church of Eng. Newspaper* 3 June, The laity expressing disquiet at what may generically be described as 'acts of intercommunion'. **1971** *World Council of Churches: Faith & Order, Louvain* 63 The whole area of question has generally been referred to in the past as the question of 'intercommunion', but that one word cannot cover the whole range and has become seriously ambiguous. It will be better to find terms which can exactly describe the different practices and their ecclesiological significance, among which the term 'intercommunion' may find its precise and particular place. **1973** *Times* 17 May 21/3 (*heading*) Bishops a stumbling block in intercommunion talks.

i:nterconne·ctedness. [f. *interconnected,* pa. pple. of INTERCONNECT *v.* + -NESS.] The property or state of being interconnected.
1922 A. G. HOGG *Redemption from this World* vi. 191 We labour hardest to perceive the interconnectedness of events. **1952** *Mind* LXI. 285 Logical interconnectedness ..is the mark of genuine knowledge. **1952** S. SPENDER *Learning Laughter* xi. 149 The inter-connectedness of Western and Eastern influences. **1959** *Africa* Apr. 142 The inter-connectedness of political and ritual status.

interconne·ctor. [f. INTERCONNECT *v.* + -OR.] Something that interconnects, *spec.* (see quot. 1940).
1930 *Engineering* 13 June 771/3 The substitution of a supply from Ardnacrusha..has necessitated the erection of a sub-station..into which three of the inter-connectors from Fleet-street to Pigeon House Fort are looped. **1940** *Chambers's Techn. Dict.* 452/1 *Interconnector,* a feeder which serves to interconnect two substations or generating stations, and along which energy may flow in either direction. **1962** *Newnes Conc. Encycl. Electr. Engin.* 598/2 An attempt to adjust..power flow only on the tie between two generating stations will result in an undesirable change of power on the remainder of the interconnectors. **1971** *Nature* 13 Aug. 470/1 (*caption*) Photograph of four diodes in a monolithic array... Contact is made to the devices by aluminium interconnectors.

inter-consonantal: see *INTER- *pref.* 4 a.

intercontinental, *a.* Add: **b.** Capable of travelling or of being sent from one continent to another; esp. in the designation *intercontinental ballistic missile* (abbrev. **I.C.B.M.*).
1956 *Spaceflight* I. 22/2 The terrible threat implicit in the alliance of inter-continental ballistic missiles and thermonuclear warheads, to which the whole world will stand utterly defenceless, is evident for all to see. **1957** *Jane's Fighting Ships 1957–58* 478 The combination of Regulus I guided missiles and submarines has given the United States Navy an intercontinental missile capability today instead of in the years to come. **1968** *Times* 16 Dec. 7/2 The second stage of the Saturn V rocket, with a thrust of one million lb., was comparable with the thrust of the Atlas rocket first developed as an inter-continental ballistic missile. **1969** *Guardian* 23 June 10/2 The Russians did not have a true intercontinental bomber until 1954.

interconversion (intəɹkǫ̈nvə·ɹʃən). [INTER- 2 a + CONVERSION.] The process of converting each of two or more things into the other(s).
1865 *Fortn. Rev.* I. 441 It shall be shown..in what these molecular movements themselves consist..and how their mutual interconversion is effected. **1911** *Ann. Rep. Progr. Chem.* VIII. 65 The interconversion of the hydroxy-acids was realised in accordance with the following scheme. **1946** *Nature* 2 Nov. 610/2 These reaction systems..which must include the interconversions of dietary, bacterial and protozoan protein, through the agency of ciliates. **1970** P. J. WHEATLEY *Chem. Consequences Nucl. Spin* iv. 80 The half-life of interconversion [of ortho- and para-hydrogen] is not known accurately.

interconvert (intəɹkǫ̈nvə·ɹt), *v.* [f. INTER- 1 b + CONVERT *v.*, or as back-formation from prec.] *trans.* To convert into one another.
1953 S. F. MASON *Hist. Sci.* xviii. 167 The ordinary and extraordinary rays were interconverted when the crystals were placed at right angles. **1955** *Sci. News Let.* 7 May 297/1 Other enzymes in the muscle interconvert these two forms [of phosphorylase] and keep them in equilibrium. **1971** *Sci. Amer.* Aug. 47/1 Lester Friedman and John G. Miller..'interconverted' *R*-carvone and *S*-carvone into their enantiomers and then back again.

intercooler (i·ntəɹkūləɹ). Also **inter-cooler.** [INTER- 2 b.] An apparatus for cooling gas heated by compression, esp. before it is compressed a second time (as in a multi-stage compressor or the cylinders of a supercharged engine).
1900 *Engin. Mag.* XIX. 679 A complete system of jacket water and a very large intercooler are used, the total capacity of the machine being 3,000 cubic feet of free air per minute compressed to 125 pounds' pressure. **1903** [see *AFTERCOOLER]. **1932** CHATFIELD & TAYLOR *Airplane & its Engine* (ed. 2) viii. 234 Compressing air by a supercharger..increases its temperature considerably and it is sometimes desirable to cool this air before it reaches the engine. This is accomplished by means of an intercooler which usually takes the form of a small radiator inserted in the air passage between the supercharger and the engine. **1944** [see *AFTERCOOLER]. **1963** A. W. FARRALL *Engin. for Dairy & Food Products* viii. 202 The booster compressor..discharges its gas into an intercooler, which in turn is piped to the suction of a standard high-pressure refrigeration machine. **1970** *Motor Boat & Yachting* 16 Oct. 39/2 By installing a type of heat exchanger, called an intercooler, the mixture leaving the turbo-charger is cooled before it enters the cylinder and this increases the efficiency.

intercooling (i·ntəɹkūliŋ), *vbl. sb.* Also **inter-cooling** (with hyphen). [f. the vb. *intercool* contained in prec. + -ING[1].] The cooling of gas between successive compressions; the use of an intercooler.
1902 G. D. HISCOX *Compressed Air* xii. 187 The value of proper intercooling. **1923** J. M. FORD *Compressor Theory & Pract.* viii. 153 The intercooling of the air or gas..is imperfect in that the temperature is not reduced to the initial value between the several stages. **1951** COHEN & ROGERS *Gas Turbine Theory* i. 7 If..the compression process is carried out in two or more stages with intercooling, the work of compression may be reduced appreciably. **1970** *Commercial Motor* 25 Sept. 56/3 Output of about 350 bhp, naturally aspirated, would be possible with 600 bhp when turbocharged with inter-cooling.
Hence (as a back-formation) **i·ntercool** *v. trans.*, to equip or provide with an intercooler; **i·ntercooled** *ppl. a.*
1944 E. W. F. FELLER *Air Compressors* x. 348 (*caption*) Power saved by intercooling a multistage centrifugal compressor. **1947** *Shell Aviation News* No. 109. 22/3 A wide range of performance at both moderate and high altitudes is provided by the..inter-cooled and after-cooled supercharger. **1970** *Motor Boat & Yachting* 16 Oct. 39/2 A number of diesel engines these days are offered in turbo-charged form, which pushes up their horsepower, and then intercooled as well as turbocharged for a further increase in power. **1971** *Engineering* Apr. 103 (Advt.), The five stage intercooled turbo compressors absorb 1555 bhp delivering 22,700 Kg/hr.

intercorrelate (intəɹkǫ·rĭlēit), *v.* [f. INTER- 1 b + CORRELATE *v.*] *trans.* and *intr.* To correlate with one another.
1909 *Amer. Jrnl. Psychol.* XX. 368 We find..that efficiency in marking A's on a sheet of printed capitals, efficiency in finding circles or hexagons or isosceles triangles on a sheet of printed geometrical forms and efficiency in finding misspelled words are in adults all very closely intercorrelated (to ·8 or more), but are by no means so closely correlated to general intellect. **1955** T. H. PEAR *English Social Differences* 11 These [types] are so intercorrelated that they can be separated only abstractly. **1970** *Jrnl. Gen. Psychol.* LXXXII. 171 If the DAS correlates as highly with each of these scales as they intercorrelate with each other, then it could be argued that the DAS measures anxiety in general rather than death anxiety in particular. **1971** *Nature* 25 June 538/1 Faculty responses to each of these items were highly intercorrelated. **1972** *Jrnl. Social Psychol.* LXXXVII. 69 Tests were intercorrelated, and factor analyses carried out.

intercorrelation (i:ntəɹkǫrĭlēi·ʃən). *Statistics.* [f. INTER- 2 a + CORRELATION.] Correlation (sense *1 c) that relates each of a number of variates with one another.
1901 *Psychol. Rev.* VIII. 540 The laboratory mental tests show little inter-correlation in the case of college students. **1904** *Amer. Jrnl. Psychol.* XV. 92 The three observations of the same objective series presented the extraordinarily small inter-correlation of 0·22. **1922** *Jrnl. Exper. Psychol.* V. 68 Intercorrelations of a number of variables may be efficiently solved on the adding machine by means of transmutation of gross scores into class numbers with the aid of standard grouping tables. **1935** [see *FACTORIALLY *adv.*]. **1961** *Lancet* 12 Aug. 359/2 Intercorrelations were calculated between the four types of test set. **1970** *Jrnl. Gen. Psychol.* LXXXIII. 125 The usual statistical information regarding the tests was obtained, including means, standard deviations,..and intercorrelations.
Hence **i:ntercorrela·tional** *a.*
1970 *Jrnl. Gen. Psychol.* LXXXIII. 157 These additional data..plus the original measures were subjected to an intercorrelational analysis.

intercortical: see *INTER- *pref.* 6.

intercourse, *sb.* **2. d.** (Later examples.)
1919 M. K. BRADBY *Psycho-Anal.* III. ix. 118 Witches were examined during their trials for evidence of their fleshly intercourse with the devil. **1922** JOYCE *Ulysses* 402 He..did not scruple..to attempt illicit intercourse with a female domestic. **1963** A. HERON *Towards Quaker View of Sex* i. 6 The incidence of extra-marital intercourse is great. **1973** S. FISHER *Female Orgasm* i. 26 Some of the decline in intercourse frequency and responsiveness..may be caused by the..physiological decline of their husbands.

intercrop (intəɹkrǫ·p), *v.* [INTER- 1.] To raise a crop among plants of a different kind, usually using the space between rows. Hence **intercro·pping** *vbl. sb.*; **i·ntercrop** *sb.*, a crop so raised.
1898 W. ROBINSON *Eng. Flower Garden* (ed. 6) v. 94 Some kind of inter-cropping would give an excellent result in the flower garden also. **1935** H. F. MACMILLAN *Tropical Planting & Gardening* (ed. 4) iv. 30 The inter-crop or catch-crop may retard the growth of the principal crop. **1945** in R. W. Zandvoort et al. *Wartime English* (1957) 133 In a West-country orchard..rows of inter-cropped potatoes flourish beneath the fruit trees. **1951** J. S. DOUGLAS *Hydroponics* vi. 89 Any well-planned hydroponicum will allow plenty of scope for careful intercropping. **1966** WEBSTER & WILSON *Agric. in Tropics* x. 230 An intercrop is clearly undesirable on account of competition for soil moisture. **1969** G. WRIGLEY *Tropical Agric.* (ed. 2) ii. 119 The production of an acre inter-cropped was equivalent to an acre and a half cultivated in a pure stand.

intercrystalline (intəɹkri·stăləin), *a.* [INTER- 4 a.] Situated or occurring between crystals, esp. those which form a metal.

1901 *Phil. Trans. R. Soc.* A. CXCV. 295 Where the quantity of impurity present is sufficiently great, this eutectic can be seen under the microscope forming an inter-crystalline cement. **1923** GLAZEBROOK *Dict. Appl. Physics* V. 361/2 Intercrystalline cracking near the melting-point sometimes takes place under very low stresses. **1962** *Science Survey* III. 329 The final failure of the metal is essentially mechanical and it usually occurs by the propagation, through the body of the metal, of intercrystalline (or intergranular) cracks.

inter-cultural: see *INTER- *pref.* 4 c.

intercut, *v.* Restrict † *Obs. rare* to sense in Dict. and add: **2.** *Cinematogr. trans.* To insert (a scene or shot) into an existing one by cutting. Const. *with.* Also *intr.* and *transf.* So **i·ntercutting** *vbl. sb.*

1953 K. REISZ *Technique Film Editing* i. 33 Inter-cut with a number of slow-moving shots of Kerensky proudly ascending the stairway, are separate titles describing Kerensky's rank. *Ibid.* ii. 133 The explosion itself is conveyed by the rapid intercutting of frames of the submarine and of a cone of water thrown up by a depth-charge. **1954** *Encounter* Aug. 52/1 Frank Norris.. employed the method of ironic contrast, intercutting the death of a destitute widow from starvation with descriptions of the sumptuous dinner given by a rail-road-king obliquely responsible for her condition. **1957** MANVELL & HUNTLEY *Technique Film Music* ii. 38 The military advance to drum taps and trumpet, beautifully intercut in track and picture to a rising string crescendo for the masses. **1958** *Listener* 6 Nov. 750/2 There was an intrusive guitar, an impromptu balladist, a ticking clock, and much elaborate montage, inter-cutting street voices with voices on the radio. **1962** *Ibid.* 27 Sept. 474/2 *La Notte* abounds with high-angled shots intercut with the reverse low angles which create a complex of vertiginous effects. **1966** *Punch* 9 Nov. 692/1, I intended to do all the characters' complete dialogue before I attempted inter-cutting (the TV phrase). **1970** I. C. JARVIE *Towards Sociol. of Cinema* ix. 128 Resnais..intercuts scenes from the heroine's memories..with her present *affaire.*

interdefinable (intəɹdĭfəi·năb'l), *a. Logic.* [f. INTER- 2 a + DEFINABLE *a.*] Of constants, etc.: that can be defined interchangeably with each other. Hence **interdefinabi·lity,** the state or quality of being interdefinable; **interdefini·tion,** one of two or more definitions that are interchangeable.

1948 AMBROSE & LAZEROWITZ *Fund. Symbolic Logic* iii. 41 With the exception of '∼', which is absolutely primitive, all the symbols for the logical constants are interdefinable. *Ibid.* 36 The possibilities of interdefinition of the relatively primitive constants. **1951** *Mind* LX. 265 The interdefinability of the constants of the system. **1955** A. N. PRIOR *Formal Logic* i. 9 Evaluation of truth-functional forms, and the inter-definability of truth functions. **1958** H. B. CURRY et al. *Combinatory Logic* I. v. 155 (*heading*) Interdefinability of simple combinators. **1965** *Philos. Rev.* LXXIV. 522 'Ought' and 'must' are interdefinable. **1972** H. B. CURRY et al. *Combinatory Logic* II. xiii. 222 In § 2 we considered interdefinitions among the basic arithmetical combinators.

interdental, *a.* Add: **2.** (Later examples.)

1933 L. BLOOMFIELD *Lang.* vi. 98 Contact..can be made against the edges of the upper teeth (interdental position). **1943** K. L. PIKE *Phonetics* II. vii. 123 An interdental sound is one in which the tip of the tongue is placed between the upper and lower teeth.

B. *sb. Phonology.* A sound formed by placing the tip of the tongue between the teeth.

1953 C. E. BAZELL *Ling. Form* iv. 45 The distribution of voiced and voiceless inter-dentals in English is quite different from that of other voiced/voiceless pairs. **1961** R. B. LONG *Sentence & its Parts* xix. 430 This obstruction can occur..at the front teeth, as for the interdentals.

interdentally (intəɹde·ntăli), *adv.* [f. INTERDENTAL *a.* + -LY².] In an interdental position; between the teeth.

1910 *Practitioner* Jan. 115 The neck of the tooth..is embraced by a thin shallow flap of gum, continuous interstitially (interdentally) with the gum pad. **1939** I. BIRSCHFELD *Toothbrush* i. 4 Irregular occlusal openings to the interproximal spaces developed, through which food was forced interdentally.

interdepartmentally (intəɹdīpāɹtme·ntăli), *adv.* [f. INTERDEPARTMENTAL + -LY².] Between or among departments.

1901 *Westm. Gaz.* 7 June 2/2 This is the bane of Government offices, both departmentally and interdepartmentally. **1906** *Ibid.* 30 Oct. 2/1 But there are strong grounds for believing that the question of the attitude of the Government towards the proposals now before the Berlin Conference has not been made a Cabinet question; in other words, that it has been dealt with interdepartmentally. **1963** *Times* 18 Apr. 9/4 One result is that interdepartmentally External Affairs staff frequently display a lack of understanding of other departments and programmes. **1966** *Economist* 10 Dec. 1155/1 In actual fact the case is still being argued interdepartmentally.

inter-dialectal: see *INTER- *pref.* 4 c.

interdiction. Add: **4.** The interruption of supply operations by aerial bombing. Freq. *attrib.*

1944 *B.B.C. War Rep.* 1 Nov. (1946) xiv. 283 The enemy railways were harassed day and night by what was known as 'interdiction'—or, in other words, rail-cutting by air attack. **1955** *Bull. Atomic Sci.* Feb. 56/3 The inability of the Air Force interdiction campaign—Operation Strangle—to bring about the collapse of Communist armies in Korea has obscured the true potential of air interdiction. **1963** *Listener* 21 Feb. 331/1 Overwhelming air support, invaluable as it was in an interdiction role, sometimes proved a clumsy weapon when used in close co-operation with ground forces. **1966** *Guardian* 26 Sept. 9/1 Using a bombing technique known as 'interdiction in depth', Navy planes had destroyed two locomotives, 225 goods wagons. **1973** *Times* 19 Apr. 18/8 Sensitive Washington spokesmen do not like the term bombing. They find it jarring. In Vietnam it was interdiction, armed reconnaissance and protective reaction.

interdigital, *a.* Add: **2.** *Electronics.* Having the form of or consisting of two similar series of parallel strips, those of each series forming part of a single structure and interdigitating with those of the other series: used of a kind of transducer.

1967 *IEEE Trans. Electron. Devices* XIV. 185/2 The operation of an interdigital pattern whose fundamental frequency was 15 MHz has been observed at odd integral multiples up to the seventh on AT-cut quartz. **1968** *Ibid.* XV. 586 (*heading*) Frequency response of an interdigital transducer for excitation of surface elastic waves. **1972** *Sci. Amer.* Oct. 52/3 In recent years the technology of acoustic waves has expanded rapidly with the development of the interdigital transducer, an efficient type of transducer for converting the electrical signal into an acoustic surface wave and reconverting the acoustic wave back into an electrical signal.

interdigitate, *v.* **2.** Delete *rare*⁻⁰ and add to def.: In *Geol.* = INTERSTRATIFY *v.* 1. (Examples.)

1969 BENNISON & WRIGHT *Geol. Hist. Brit. Isles* viii. 160 In north Devon marine and non-marine beds occur in the same sequence. They are interdigitated due to alternating expansions and contractions of the area of marine deposition. **1974** *Sci. Amer.* Feb. 64/1 The last step..involves interdigitating a set of thick filaments in the spaces between the thin filaments.

interdine (intəɹdəi·n), *v.* [INTER- 1 a.] *intr.* Of members of different castes and tribes: to eat a meal together.

1932 G. S. GHURYE *Caste & Race in India* iv. 73 Evidently interdining, like intermarrying, was a mark of equality. **1933** RAHMAT ALI *Now or Never* (1934) 4 We [*sc.* Muslims] do not inter-dine [with Hindus]; we do not inter-marry. **1960** KOESTLER *Lotus & Robot* II. x. 228 In India, inter-marriage, and even inter-dining, between different castes was unthinkable.

interdisciplinary (intəɹdi·siplinări), *a.* [INTER- 4 c.] Of or pertaining to two or more disciplines or branches of learning; contributing to or benefiting from two or more disciplines.

1937 *Jrnl. Educ. Sociol.* Dec. 251 Programs of study submitted should provide..for training of an interdisciplinary nature. **1956** J. LOTZ in L. White *Frontiers of Knowledge in Study of Man* 217 There is also considerable interest in interdisciplinary studies involving structural linguistics. **1957** E. BOTT *Family & Social Network* ii. 35 Ten years ago interdisciplinary research was very much in vogue. **1965** *Listener* 18 Nov. 788/2 The work..is again interdisciplinary and does not fall into any of the established academic categories. **1970** *Guardian* 12 Nov. 5/6 The academic policies put forward—essentially a two-year general interdisciplinary degree. **1972** *Language* XLVIII. 487 Child language acquisition has proved to be one of the more important interdisciplinary areas of the past decade.

inter-dominion (intəɹdomi·nyən), *a.* [f. INTER- 5 + *DOMINION 2 b (*c*).] Occurring, or carried on, between the self-governing dominions of the British Commonwealth.

Used esp. in Australia and N.Z.

1949 *Australia 1949* 776/1 Totalisator investments for the three days of the Auckland Inter-Dominion Championships totalled £506,498/10/–. **1950** *Sydney Morning Herald* 12 Jan. 10/7 Sir Nigel will now go to Melbourne for the inter-Dominion championships in February. **1966** *Weekly News* (N.Z.) 27 Apr. 39 (*caption*) Australian and New Zealand crews competed for an interdominion championship under conditions similar to those at the Cowes Regatta. **1968** *Wanganui* (N.Z.) *Chron.* 15 Nov. 6/9 The 1971 inter-Dominion championship series have been allocated to the New Zealand Metropolitan Trotting Club.

inter-ecclesiastical: see *INTER- *pref.* 4 c.

inter-electrode (i:ntərĭle·ktrōud), *a. Electr.* Also **interelectrode.** [INTER- 5.] Existing between two or more electrodes; said esp. of electrical quantities pertaining to the space between electrodes.

1922 GLAZEBROOK *Dict. Appl. Physics* II. 902/1 Certain types of valve are constructed to reduce the inter-electrode capacity to a minimum. **1925** E. B. WEDMORE *Electr. Engineers' Data Bks.* III. 162 For high frequency amplification it is desirable to use valves having a low interelectrode capacity and also a low amplification factor. **1930** *Daily Express* 9 Sept. 11/1 The new..Valve has a greater effective amplification because its inter-electrode capacity is lower. **1962** W. B. THOMPSON *Introd. Plasma Physics* v. 76 In order to relate the resistance to the resistivity of the plasma, the tube was filled with a solution of known conductivity and the inter-electrode resistance measured. **1964** CHODOROW & SUSSKIND *Fund. Microwave Electronics* ii. 19 When the cathode is heated, the negative charge of the emitted electrons depresses the potential in the interelectrode region.

inter-electron: see *INTER- *pref.* 5.

interest, *sb.* Add: **11.** (sense 4) *interest-bound* adj.; (sense 7) *interest-awaking, -compelling* adjs.; (sense 10) *interest-equalization, -rate; interest-free* adj.; **interest group,** a group of individuals possessing a common identifying interest.

1901 *Daily Chron.* 18 Nov. 6/3 The 'great retrograde, tyrannical, interest-bound party'. **1902** *Ibid.* 17 July 6/4 Its interest-awaking value. **1902** *Ibid.* 6 Aug. 3/2 As interest-compelling..as the amour of a mediæval queen. **1908** A. F. BENTLEY *Process Govt.* xii. 300 The deeper-lying interest groups of society. **1936** WIRTH & SHILS tr. *Mannheim's Ideology & Utopia* III. i. 136 The hitherto constantly emphasized interest-bound nature of political thought. **1943** E. BLUNDEN *Return to Husbandry* iii. 18 This demands ample credit of an interest-free nature. **1957** M. SWAN *Brit. Guiana* iv. 78 Houses which had been built with interest-free loans or with other forms of estate assistance. **1959** E. POUND *Thrones* xcviii. 42 Byzance lasted longer than Manchu because of an (%) interest-rate. **1962** *Economist* 25 Aug. 685/2 The authors see signs of change..in the growth of interest-group organisations. **1963** *Daily Tel.* 2 Oct. 23/8 The interest-equalisation tax to raise the cost of foreign borrowing in New York. **1964** R. WILKINSON *Gentlemanly Power* iv. 48 The parliamentary Conservative party has come to represent different interest-groups, farmers..manufacturers, small professional men..stockbrokers, shopkeepers and elderly widows. **1966** *Times* 28 Feb. (Canada Suppl.) p. vii/5 The United States's interest-equalization tax of 15 per cent, to be paid by any United States resident buying foreign stocks. **1972** *Sat. Rev.* (U.S.) 6 May 38/3 The company store charged exorbitant prices, but extended interest-free credit. **1974** *Times* 18 Feb. 14/5 It may..be difficult with such a budget deficit to prevent interest rates from rising.

interesterification (i:ntərˌesterifikēi·ʃən). [f. INTER- 2 a + *ESTERIFICATION.] The exchange of alkoxy or acyl groups between an ester and another compound, sometimes used to modify the properties of margarine and other fats.

1941 T. P. HILDITCH *Industr. Chem. Fats & Waxes* (ed. 2) IV. ii. 305 Suggestions have..been made.. with the objects either of interchanging the acyl radicals between the triglyceride molecules of the mixture of fats used, or of introducing a certain amount of butyroglycerides into the margarine fats. Brief reference may be made to these 'interesterification' processes. **1961** *Times Rev. Industry* July 8/2 Interesterification..brings about a molecular rearrangement in the fat. This manifests itself in changes both in melting characteristics and crystal type.

Hence (as a back-formation) **i:ntereste·rify** *v. trans.* and *intr.*, to subject to or undergo interesterification; **i:ntereste·rified** *ppl. a.*

1950 KIRK & OTHMER *Encycl. Chem. Technol.* V. 817 Some esters will interesterify with methanol at 100°C. or lower with no catalyst added. **1958** C. PLACEK in *Mod. Chem. Processes* V. 84/2 In baking performance, directly interesterified lard has all the desirable properties of vegetable shortening. *Ibid.* 88/3 Until operating conditions (equilibrium) are reached, material appearing at the end of the run is usually not interesterified to the desired point and is recycled after catalyst separation.

interesting, *ppl. a.* Add: **3.** (*to be*) *in an interesting condition, situation, state*: (to be) pregnant; also, *to be interesting*; *interesting event*: a birth.

1748 SMOLLETT *R. Random* II. lxix. 335 So that I cannot leave her in such an interesting situation, which I hope will produce something to crown my felicity. **1838** DICKENS *Nickleby* (1839) xxix. 286 Mrs. Lenville (who, as has been before hinted, was in an interesting state). **1848** [see SITUATION 7 b]. **1899** *Westm. Gaz.* 27 June 6/3 'Interesting event' at Peterhof. Another daughter! **1928** W. B. MAXWELL *We Forget because we Must* II. iii. 44 I'm afraid I seem to make heavy weather of my interesting condition. **1930** GALSWORTHY *On Forsyte 'Change* 171 Winifred, beginning to be 'interesting', owing to the approach of a little Dartie, kept her eyes somewhat watchfully on 'Monty'. **1970** K. GILES *Death in Church* ii. 49 Her little maid got into An Interesting Condition and the young fellow was willing to solemnise it.

interestingly, *adv.* Add: Used as a sentence adverb.

1972 *Times* 13 May 10/4 Interestingly Balanchine is no longer called a director of New York City Ballet. **1973** *Nature* 18 May 118/1 Interestingly, the results presented were not in accord with the rather precise quantum calculations.

inter-ethnic: see *INTER- *pref.* 4 c.

interface. Add: **2.** *transf.* and *fig.* **a.** A means or place of interaction between two systems, organizations, etc.; a meeting-point or common ground between two parties, systems, or disciplines; also, interaction, liaison, dialogue.

1962 M. McLuhan *Gutenberg Galaxy* 141 (*heading*) The interface of the Renaissance was the meeting of medieval pluralism and modern homogeneity and mechanism. 1962 *Evening Star* (Washington, D.C.) 18 Aug. 1/6 Interface..seems to mean the liaison between two different agencies that may be working on the same project. *Ibid.* 1/7 The Defense Communications Agency.. was made responsible for the resolution of interface problems. 1964 A. Battersby *Network Analysis* viii. 116 Interfaces: events should be established at stages where the work passes from one department to another—these stages are known as interfaces. 1965 H. I. Ansoff *Corporate Strategy* (1968) vi. 107 Functional organizations, such as research, development, finance, and marketing, have a strong interface with the outside environment. 1965 *Internat. Sci. & Technol.* Oct. 30/1 The advantages of high-speed transport were piddled away at the nodes or interfaces: from bus to train, train to train, city terminal to airport terminal, check-in counter to loading gate, and so on. 1967 *Technology Week* 23 Jan. 75/1 The interface across which the engineer-scientist and the biologist can interact is a broad one. 1967 *Times Rev. Industry* Feb. 27/1 The third interface between government and the marketing system is with the intermediate firm supplying either other intermediate firms or the consumer. 1967 *Economist* 16 Sept. p. ix/1 The North Sea and Channel ports form the biggest frontiers in world trade—or the biggest interface, in the language of the modern transport man, meaning the place where the greatest quantity of international cargo changes its mode of transport. 1970 *Nature* 23 May 684/1 The interface between physics and music is of direct relevance to..the psychological effects of hearing. 1970 *Interior Design* Dec. 767/4 Educationalists are convinced that the need for the interface of lecturer and student will not diminish. 1972 *Sci. Amer.* Nov. 51/3 The issue of insanity as a defense in criminal cases..is at the interface of medicine, law and ethics.

b. (An) apparatus designed to connect two scientific instruments, devices, etc., so that they can be operated jointly.

1964 *Ann. N.Y. Acad. Sci.* CXV. 574 The collection of components which connects the analog and digital computers to each other, and which controls and converts the data, is generally termed the 'interface'. 1966 *Electronics* 3 Oct. 130 If a flight carries special equipment, then modular interfaces can easily be designed to adapt the general-purpose computer to the equipment. 1973 T. Allbeury *Choice of Enemies* xvi. 79 Programs are written in a computer language... If you wanted to use one of the IBM languages on an ICL machine, you'd have to have what's called an interface to make the two different things compatible. 1973 *Physics Bull.* Apr. 242/3 Scobie and Wellum..have built interfaces for two pulse height analysers.

interface (i·ntəɹfēⁱs), *v.* [f. the sb.] **1. a.** *trans.* To connect (scientific equipment) *with* or *to* so as to make possible joint operation.

1969 *Computers & Humanities* IV. 76 Professor Louis Delatte..publishes..various computer-prepared indices to classical texts, using a Selectric typewriter interfaced with his own local computer. 1969 *Physics Bull.* Sept. 367/2 The prospect of interfacing each device specifically with each computer on each application becomes formidable in these circumstances in terms of effort and cost. This is avoided using the CAMAC technique of interfacing the device to the dataway, via a module, and the dataway to the computer, via the controller. 1970 *Sci. Jrnl.* Mar. 17/4 Their movements were monitored by a series of illuminated photoconductor cells, which were interfaced to the PDP-8/S computer. 1973 *Nature* 6 Apr. 402/2 A 'Perkin-Elmer 900' and a 'Hewlett Packard 7610A' chromatograph,..interfaced with a 'Perkin-Elmer PEP-1' gas chromatography data system, were used. 1973 *Physics Bull.* Apr. 240/2 The memory uses 'static' circuitry and no clocking is required which makes it easy to use and interface to any system.

b. *intr.* for *pass.*

1969 *New Yorker* 11 Jan. 42 Inflated space units, which have to 'interface'—a space-age verb meaning, roughly, to coordinate—with equipment in the cabin. 1971 *Physics Bull.* Jan. 42/3 The minimum system can be attached to 16 devices..; the largest can 'interface' with about 2000 remote sensing/control devices.

2. *intr.* To come into interaction *with*.

1967 M. McLuhan *Medium is Massage* 88 A strange bond often exists among antisocial types in their power to see environments as they really are. This need to interface, to confront environments with a certain antisocial power, is manifest in the famous story 'The Emperor's New Clothes'. 1968 *Lebende Sprachen* XIII. 4/1 Before turning to a discussion of how this management system..interfaces with functional organization let us try to define what we mean by project management. 1973 *LSA Bull.* Mar. 14 Mr. Hamp, the LSA delegate to UNESCO, reported on ways which he felt the Linguistic Society could interface with the United States National Commission.

interfacing (i·ntəɹfēⁱ:siŋ), *vbl. sb.* [f. Inter- 2 a + Facing *vbl. sb.*; cf. prec.] The action of the verb *interface; also *concr.* (see quot. 1964). Also *attrib.* or as *ppl. a.*

1964 Margolis *Compl. Bk. Tailoring* 180 An interfacing is a reinforcing or shaping fabric used between the outer fabric and the facing or the lining. 1968 J. Ironside *Fashion Alphabet* 89 Very similar to interlining but interfacing is usually only placed along edges or in collars, cuffs, etc. 1968 *Lebende Sprachen* XIII. 4/1 There will be a large or small group, depending on the complexity of the interfacing problems. *Ibid.* 104/1 (*heading*) Terms in PERT planning interfacing network. 1969 *Physics Bull.* Sept. 367/1 The use of a common highway permits many sources and acceptors of data (devices) to be connected to the computer..via the CAMAC compatible modules. This type of interfacing would be unnecessary..if the number of devices were small and the computer had sufficient input-output channels which were already matched to each device.

inter-faith, -family: see *inter- *pref.* 5.

interfere, *v.* Add: **2.** Also in *Broadcasting*: to transmit a signal which is received simultaneously *with* the signal sought; to cause or emit interference (sense 4* a). (Further examples.)

1904 in J. Erskine-Murray *Handbk. Wireless Telegr.* (1907) x. 179 From 11.27 till noon the receiving ship 'Hancock'..and the experimental station in building §75..interfered continually. 1928 L. S. Palmer *Wireless Princ. & Pract.* iii. 49 Stations transmitting on the same wavelength but lying in different directions from the receiving station can be prevented from interfering. 1940 L. R. Lohr *Television Broadcasting* iii. 37 If television images were capable of being received beyond the horizon, the received images..would interfere with the transmissions of other stations. 1960 *Which?* Apr. 72/2 Does it [*sc.* the vacuum cleaner] interfere with radio or TV?

4. c. *Chess.* Of a piece: to obstruct the line of action of another piece. (Cf. *interference 1 b.)

1913 A. C. White *Sam Loyd* 303 The White pieces can interfere in all kinds of ways with the Black pieces, and the Black pieces can interfere with each other with varied and beautiful results. 1926 H. Weenink *Chess Probl.* 38 It will be noticed that..Re6 in turn interferes with the line of force of the Bg4, shutting off its command of d7 and c8. 1930 White & Hume *Valves & Bi-Valves* 139 The moves of the checking Valve interfere, not..on an actual line of the Black Queen, but on her possible (potential) line of check next move. 1937 T. R. Dawson *Caïssa's Wild Roses in Clusters* vi. 24/2 One Black piece..interferes on two squares on the line of another piece... Each of two Black pieces..interferes with the other.

d. Const. *with*: to molest or assault sexually.

1948 D. Ballantyne *Cunninghams* (1963) iii. 22 The former Mayor..who was kicked out of his church for interfering with a youngster in a Sunday School class. 1956 L. McIntosh *Oxford Folly* viii. 119 'All the girls I used to fall for,' said Julian, 'were incredibly beautiful, and as hard as nails. But they tolerated me, because I was much too timid ever to "interfere" with them.' 1968 A. MacLeod *Dam* v. 51 She had reason to suspect that Sandra had been 'interfered' with. 1972 *Observer* 3 Sept. 33/1 In a few cases, like Byron's, a nanny sexually 'interfered' with her charge.

6. *U.S. Football.* To interpose between the player with the ball and a would-be tackler so as to help the former. *Baseball.* To obstruct a runner between two bases; also, to obstruct a catcher or fielder who is trying to take or throw the ball. (Cf. *interference 1 c.)

1920 W. Camp *Football without a Coach* 51 The full-back and the right half must interfere for their companion. 1969 *Official Baseball Rules* 39 The batter..is entitled to first base without liability to be put out..when..the catcher or any fielder interferes with him.

interference. Add: **1. b.** *Chess.* Obstruction of the line of action of one piece by another. Also *attrib.*

1913 A. C. White *Sam Loyd* 303 There are many forms of interference play which have nothing to do with avoiding stalemate... But interference has a far wider scope than the cutting off of one White man by another. 1926 H. Weenink *Chess Probl.* 39 In both problems there is mutual interference of the black Rook and Bishop. 1931 G. Hume in A. C. White *Probl. by my Friends* 210 By forgoing the interference of the Black Bishop with the Black Pawn, a second flight-square has been obtained. 1947 T. R. Dawson *Caïssa's Fairy Tales* 7/2 Rc4, which is Black interference permitting 2 Sb6 mate... The interference and pin ideas create nice new task record objectives. 1963 J. Bochkor tr. *Bán's Tactics of End-Games* ii. 115/2 We can also make use of line interference by sparing a hostile piece that is closing a line and is thus harmful to its own camp.

c. *U.S. Football.* (*a*) The act of interposing between a runner and a tackler to obstruct the latter; (*b*) see quot. 1895; (*c*) a player or players who obstruct the tackler or tacklers. *Baseball.* The act of obstructing a runner between two bases.

1894 *Outing* (U.S.) XXIV. 112/2 The special feature of American Rugby arises from the principle of interference to aid the man running with the ball. 1895 G. J. Manson *Sporting Dict.* 61 *Interference*, using the hands or arms in any way to obstruct or hold a player who has got the ball. 1920 W. Camp *Football without a Coach* 59 To amount to anything at all interference must be perfectly timed... On a play between tackle and guard..the interference must reach that point prepared to take care of the tackle, the guard and even the backfield men, too. 1922 D. Canfield *Rough-Hewn* xxvi. 241 Where *was* the ball? Sometimes it came straight through and the next minute on the same formation swung outside—and Neale uselessly buried under the interference. 1927 H. G. Salsinger in *Secrets of Baseball* 147 Interference plays, too, are scored as they probably have been made. 1969 *Official Playing Rules Nat. & Amer. Football Leagues* 68 Interlocked interference means the grasping of one and another by, or encircling body to any degree with, hands or arms by offensive players.

d. Sexual assault or molestation.

1968 M. Culpan *Vasiliko Affair* v. 63 You'll get the pathologist to examine the body. But I'd say no interference. 1972 J. Symons *Bloody Murder* xii. 160 Before the War..the rape would have been mentioned delicately. 'Any sign of—interference?' 1973 'D. Shannon' *No Holiday for Crime* (1974) ii. 27 Not raped, for ninety-nine per cent sure—no interference.

4*. Various scientific and technical senses.

a. *Broadcasting* and *Telecommunications.* Disturbance of the transmission or reception of signals by the intrusion of extraneous signals; hence, signals collectively or radiation which causes such disturbance, or the effects by which it is perceived (e.g. unwanted sounds in radio reception).

1887 *Electrician* 7 Oct. 462/1 Strong signals were received on the copper [telephone] wires, although they were completely isolated from any possible interference. 1888 *Operator & Electr. World* XII. 140 (*heading*) Dynamo current interference with telephone systems and means of relief. 1899 *Electrician* 17 Nov. 106/2 Before beginning the experiments, Mr. Marconi wrote to the Commission stating that he had an instrument which would render interference practically impossible. 1902 *Windsor Mag.* May 720/2 Two messages were sent, one in English and one in French. Both were received at the same time on the same wire at Poole..without the least interference. 1926 *Encycl. Brit.* I. 459/1 The atmosphere is nearly always filled with vagrant radio waves which enter the receiving set, producing noises called 'interference'. 1932 R. W. Hallows *Finding Foreign Stations* xiv. 113 Other kinds of apparatus which are apt to radiate interference are refrigerators..and flashing signs. 1943 A. L. Albert *Fund. Telephony* xiii. 314 When two or more telephone circuits parallel each other, electric energy may be transferred from one to the other, causing..inductive interference. 1962 J. H. & P. J. Reyner *Radio Communication* viii. 311 The interference is conducted by the mains.. to the point where the receiver is located. 1964 R. F. Ficchi *Electr. Interference* ii. 9 Interference is an electrical disturbance created by equipment in one part of a system which is carried into equipment in another part of the system, causing malfunctioning of the latter part. 1966 *B.B.C. Handbk.* 133 On the television screen the interference is seen as patterns of lines, white flashes or bands of light. 1967 E. L. Gruenberg *Handbk. Telemetry & Remote Control* xi. 11 Some of the remedies for interference are the use of shielded line between signal source and input section of the data-acquisition equipment, [etc.].

b. *Engin.* (i) The collision of the tips of the teeth of one gear-wheel with the flanks of those of the mating wheel which occurs if the teeth are not cut to a suitable profile.

1914 A. E. Ingham *Gearing* i. 32 If, however, pinions having a low number of teeth are constructed, they are much more undercut below the base line than is consistent with strength or with tooth contact. This 'undercut' or 'interference' is clearly shown in Fig. 11. 1926 Bradford & Eaton *Machine Design* viii. 149 Contact will have taken place between the tip of the driven tooth and the radial flank of the driving-gear tooth. Since the latter is not the conjugate involute of the former the two curves will not run together and interference takes place. 1948 Parkinson & Dawney *Gears* iv. 39 (1) Involute interference..is avoided by making the whole working profile of involute form, (2) tip interference..is avoided by making the diameter of the spur pinion a sufficient amount smaller than that of the internal gear. 1966 G. W. Michalec *Precision Gearing* xi. 591 It is important to avoid even the most isolated interference points because they cause wear that results in rapid degradation of precision quality.

(ii) The amount by which the external dimension of a part exceeds the internal dimension of the part into which it has to fit.

[1919: see *interference fit* below.] 1930 L. S. Marks *Mech. Engineers' Handbk.* (ed. 3) 896 In Table 47 is given a summary of the allowances, allowances plus tolerance, and average interferences for the various classes of fits, as recommended tentatively by the A.S.A. Interference here denotes negative allowance. 1950 T. Nuttall *Nat. Cert. Workshop Technol.* xv. 124 The force required to pass in the shaft will be much greater with the maximum interference; for this reason the modern tendency is to specify very close limits for both hole and shaft when interference fits are required. 1969 M. Haslehurst *Manuf. Technol.* xiii. 320 This gives a maximum interference of 0·056 mm and a minimum interference of 0·025 mm.

c. *Genetics.* The action of one cross-over in reducing or increasing (orig. only reducing) the chance of a second cross-over occurring along the same chromosome, the effect being generally proportional to distance.

1916 H. J. Muller in *Amer. Naturalist* L. 288 In a sense, then, the occurrence of one crossing-over interferes with the coincident occurrence of another crossing-over in the same pair of chromosomes, and I have accordingly termed this phenomenon 'interference'. 1969 G. W. Burns *Sci. Genetics* vii. 115 Interference appears to be unequal in different parts of a chromosome... In general, interference appears to be greatest near the centromere and at the ends of a chromosome.

d. *Aeronaut.* (See quot. 1940.)

1932 *Gloss. Aeronaut. Terms* (*B.S.I.*) (Proofs) iii. 3 *Interference*, the aerodynamic influence of two or more bodies on one another. 1940 *Chambers's Techn. Dict.* 452/2 *Interference*, the aerodynamic influence of one body upon another. Usually, the head resistance, or drag, of two bodies placed close together will be greater than the total of their separate drags, because of interference.

e. *Biol.* and *Med.* The action of a virus of one kind in inhibiting a virus of another kind in the same host.

1937 *Jrnl. Path. & Bacteriol.* XLIV. 420 In plant viruses the phenomenon of interference is only seen in connection with those viruses that are generically related. 1970 Passmore & Robson *Compan. Med. Stud.* II. xviii. 108/2 If the viruses are inoculated at different times, the second may not replicate. This is known as interference.

f. *Philol.* (See quot. 1953.) Also *attrib.*

1940 *Language* XVI. iii. 219 Thus, in describing the

difficulty of pronouncing foreign sounds (5), there is no mention of the interference of the speaker's native phonemic habits. **1953** U. WEINREICH *Lang. in Contact* i. 1 Those instances of deviation from the norms of either language which occur in the speech of bilinguals as a result of their familiarity with more than one language..will be referred to as interference phenomena. *Ibid.* 11 In speech, interference is like sand carried by a stream; in language, it is the sedimented sand deposited on the bottom of a lake. **1962** W. F. MACKEY in J. A. Fishman *Readings Sociol. of Lang.* (1968) 569 The foregoing characteristics of degree, function, and alternation determine the interference of one language with another in the speech of bilinguals. Interference is the use of features belonging to one language while speaking or writing another. *Ibid.* 570 In the speech of bilinguals the pattern and amount of interference is not the same at all times and under all circumstances... Interference also varies with the style of discourse used—descriptive, narrative, conversational, etc. **1964** E. PALMER tr. *Martinet's Elem. Gen. Ling.* v. 160 Interference..may have the result of increasing the range of phoneme variation. **1965** *Amer. Speech* XL. 63 Galinsky deals less with regular interference phenomena than with occasional borrowings of language-conscious individuals. **1972** J. L. DILLARD *Black English* i. 36 *Interference* is the term for the influence of one's native language on a language acquired later.

5. *interference pattern*; (sense 4* a) **interference-free** *a.*, not causing or not affected by interference; † **interference preventer**, an apparatus for reducing interference at a radio receiver; **interference suppressor**, an electrical device designed to prevent or reduce the production of interference by the apparatus to which it is fitted; (sense 4* b (ii)) **interference fit** *Engin.*, a fit between two mating parts for which, within the specified tolerances, there is always an interference between them.

1919 *Engineer* 23 May 511/2 The following three classes of fit would be needed, *i.e.*, running fits, transition fits, and interference fits. **1973** A. PARRISH *Mech. Engineer's Ref. Bk.* vii. 31 The magnitude of the interference fit will depend upon the conditions required, i.e. axial, torsional or radial holding ability. **1950** *Engineering* 3 Feb. 140/2 A range of waterproofed and interference-free [electrical] components is being produced. **1965** *B.B.C. Handbk.* 49 Reception in the overcrowded medium- and long-wave bands continues to be difficult in many areas, in marked contrast to the interference-free reception which VHF can provide. **1933** *Discovery* May 151/2 As a typical example, I need only mention the interference patterns which appear when light from one source can travel to a screen along two different paths. **1973** *Nature* 12 Oct. 297/1 The only consistent difference between cross-over and non-cross-over events, apart from the presence or absence of an exchange of homologous segments of chromatids, is in their interference pattern. **1905** Interference preventer [see *ATMOSPHERICS *sb. pl.*]. **1914** R. STANLEY *Text-bk. Wireless Telegr.* xix. 292 Marconi patented an interference preventer which involved the use of two aerials and a rotating machine. **1951** *Gloss. Terms Plastics Industry* (*B.S.I.*) 41 Interference suppressor. **1966** *B.B.C. Handbk.* 133 It has for some years been compulsory for all new vehicles and stationary engines using spark ignition to have interference suppressors fitted.

interferer. Add: **b.** *U.S. Football.* One who interposes between a runner and a tackler.

1897 *Encycl. Sport* I. 424/2 Interference..once established,..the query was immediately raised of how much aid the interferers could give the runner. **1922** D. CANFIELD *Rough-Hewn* xxvi. 243 Neale could see Rogers rock a second, undecided, on tip-toe; side-step an interferer; and then shoot his body like a projectile into the play.

interfering, *ppl. a.* Add: **b.** That causes or constitutes interference (sense 4* a).

1914 R. STANLEY *Text-bk. Wireless Telegr.* xix. 292 If the International Rules are duly observed an interfering station should be one which considers itself out of range. **1954** E. MOLLOY *Radio & Television Engineers' Ref. Bk.* XXXIII. 10 As with all forms of interference, the effect will largely depend upon the ratio of the levels of the interfering signal to the picture signal.

interferogram (intəɹfiə·rogræm). [f. INTERFER(E *v.* + -O + -GRAM.] A pattern formed by the interference of radiation, esp. one represented in a photograph or diagram.

1921 *Trans. Optical Soc.* XXII. 185 Fig. 12 represents an interferogram as seen on one of the lens interferometers described, the thick lines representing dark bands. **1949** *Jrnl. R. Aeronaut. Soc.* LIII. 637/2 The interferograms give the density variation across the mixing zone. **1959** *Physics of Fluids* II. 165 (*caption to photograph*) Monochromatic interferograms taken simultaneously at λ = 4122 A and 5463 A of an ionizing shock wave in argon... The fringes move upward with increasing refractivity. **1965** E. B. BROWN *Mod. Optics* viii. 440 The intensity plots..are referred to as interferograms, and the interferometers used in this fashion are often called interferometer modulators. **1966** D. G. BRANDON *Mod. Techniques Metallogr.* 27 For first-order interference at λ = 5,500 Å with a high refractive index oil between the plates..the cone angle α that can be tolerated is..about 25°, corresponding to a 0·65 *NA* objective, and critical illumination can be used to form the interferogram.

interferometer. Substitute for def.: Any instrument in which the interference of waves (e.g. of light) from a common source is employed to make precise measurements of (linear or angular) length or displacement in terms of the wavelength. (Add earlier and later examples.)

1897 *Physical Rev.* IV. 480 An application of the Michelson 'interferometer' to the measurement of the small linear movements of the electrometer disk. **1897** *Phil. Mag.* XLIV. 91 To these two methods of measuring angular motions we must now add a third, the interferometer method, first suggested by Michelson. **1921** *Discovery* July 181/2 Betelgeux, the size of which was measured in December last at Mount Wilson by interferometer methods, has a diameter of 273,000,000 miles. **1932** HARDY & PERRIN *Princ. Optics* xxviii. 592 These interferometers are often used in the analysis of a mixture of gases to determine the proportion in which the components are present. **1957** *New Scientist* 15 Aug. 14/1 At the Cambridge radio-observatory four aerials with a total area of one acre are placed at the corners of a rectangle to form a double interferometer which was used in 1954 to plot the positions of nearly 2,000 radio stars. **1969** C. A. RONAN *Invisible Astron.* vi. 83 For mapping radio sources..the radio interferometer has become widely adopted. This is based on the same principles as that of the stellar interferometer.., and at its simplest uses two antennae separated by as large a distance as is convenient, the signals being fed into an electronic mixing unit and then passed to the radio telescope receiver.

interferometric (i:ntəɹferome·trik), *a.* [f. prec. + -IC, after *barometric*, etc.] Of or pertaining to interferometry; employing or of the nature of an interferometer.

1932 HARDY & PERRIN *Princ. Optics* xvii. 378 Lens-bench methods [of measuring aberrations of lenses], the Hartmann method, and the interferometric method yield this information in different ways. **1951** *Engineering* 18 May 589/1 Dr. J. S. Courtney-Pratt has used interferometric methods to study the uniformity and thickness of thin films adsorbed on solid surfaces. **1954** *Oxf. Univ. Gaz.* 15 June 1036/1 Spectra for the interferometric determination of wavelengths. **1957** *New Scientist* 24 Oct. 11 An interferometric radio telescope consists of two separate aerials each joined to the same receiver whose output measures, in effect, the difference in the distances from the source to each of the aerials. **1974** *Times* 12 Jan. 14/7 He carried interferometric methods to an extreme degree of precision.

Hence **i:nterferome·trically** *adv.*, by means of interferometry.

1959 *Physics of Fluids* II. 166/2 Photomultiplier observations through 4122-A and 4515-A interference filters show the appearance of peak luminosity to be closely associated with the attainment of interferometrically observable ionization. **1972** *McGraw-Hill Yearbk. Sci. & Technol.* 388/2 Along with the recent development of stable lasers..have come interferometrically ruled gratings practically free of 'ghosts'. **1973** *Physics Bull.* May 307/3 The longitudinal and transverse curvatures of a plate subjected to a bending moment are determined interferometrically.

interferometry (i:ntəɹfĕrǫ·mĕtri). [INTERFEROMETER: see -METRY.] The action or art of measuring interference phenomena; the study and use of the interferometer.

1911 C. BARUS in *Publ. Carnegie Inst. Washington* CXLIX. I. p. iii, I came across a principle of interferometry which seemed of sufficient importance to justify special investigation. **1946** *Nature* 12 Oct. 519/2 It is possible to evaluate an approximate crystal lattice spacing with visible light waves by virtue of multiple beam interferometry. **1950** *Endeavour* IX. 196 Multiple-beam interferometry offers a delicate method of detecting extremely small imperfections in surfaces. **1962** *Punch* 29 Aug. 298/2 The distinguished custodian of Jodrell Bank is well up in the cepheid variables, interferometry and the Laplace hypothesis. **1971** *Physics Bull.* July 397/2 Several of these laboratories..are now using laser interferometry for calibration purposes.

interferon (intəɹfiə·rǫn). *Biol.* [f. INTERFER(E *v.* + *-on*.] A protein released by an animal cell, usu. in response to the entry of a virus, which has the property of inhibiting further development of viruses of any kind in the animal (or in others of the same species).

1957 ISAACS & LINDENMANN in *Proc. R. Soc.* B. CXLVII. 263 To distinguish it from the heated influenza virus we have called the newly released interfering agent 'interferon'. **1961** *New Scientist* 13 July 81/1 It looks as if ..interferon is capable of blocking the multiplication of virtually all the animal viruses that have been tested. **1961** *Lancet* 23 Sept. 680/2 Recently there has been growing evidence that interferon may play an important part in recovery from virus infections. **1963** *Ann. Reg. 1962* 393 The investigation of Interferon, a chemical substance produced in men and animals and believed to act as the body's first line of defence against a wide range of virus infections, passed a critical stage in May 1962. **1968** B. D. DAVIS et al. *Princ. Microbiol. & Immunol.* IV. xxvi. 789 Purified interferons from various sources consist of small proteins usually stable at low pH... Interferons are not virus-specific but cell-specific in both their production and their effects. **1970** PASSMORE & ROBSON *Compan. Med. Stud.* II. xviii. 109/2 Interferon has many of the properties of an ideal antiviral agent but its present clinical applications are limited by difficulties associated with the production of large quantities of purified human interferon and the assessment of its activity in man.

inter-fertile, -fertility: see *INTER- *pref.* 2 a.

inter-fibre, interfile *v.*: see *INTER- *pref.* 5, 1 a.

interfi·nger, *v. Geol.* [INTER- 1 b.] *intr.* Of strata, sediments, etc.: to interdigitate (*with*). So **interfi·ngering** *ppl. a.*

1921 A. W. GRABAU *Textbk. Geol.* II. xxxvi. 441 (*caption*) The source of the black mud is the land on the south from which it was repeatedly washed into the sea, interfingering with clastics derived from the east. **1960** *New Scientist* 23 June 1609/1 Detailed geological mapping of interfingering and overlapping lava flows. **1965** G. J. WILLIAMS *Econ. Geol. N.Z.* xiii. 205/2 The granitic facies of the Hawks Crag Breccia nearby and the interfingering facies containing both granite and greywacke components were quickly found to contain uranium minerals. **1971** *Nature* 28 May 247/1 The lower part of this lacustrine sequence interfingers with about 20 m of fluvio-deltaic sediments.

inter-firm, *a.* [INTER- 5.] Carried on between two or more business firms.

1949 *Collier's Year Bk.* 132 The rulings..disapproved secondary boycotts affecting interfirm activities. **1961** *Times* 2 May 2/5 The growing volume of interfirm comparison work. **1964** *Economist* 21 Mar. 1067/1 Confidential interfirm comparisons. **1967** *Ibid.* 7 Jan. 24/3 What sort of mergers, and what sort of inter-firm co-operation, does Britain want? **1972** *Times* 31 Oct. 25/2 'Interfirm comparison' is one of those rare animals, a management technique which the British have managed to sell to the Americans.

Interflora (intəɹflōə·ră). Name of the Florists' Telegraph Delivery Association, an international agency which organizes the delivery of flowers to order; also the trade name of the British branch of this association.

1949 *Sell's Directory of Registered Telegraphic Addresses* 795/2 Taylor William (florist), .. Worthing, Sussex. Interflora Worthing. **1951** G. LEWIS in *Mod. Florist* xxiii. 229 The four large groups..are closely connected and compose the overall organisation Interflora, set up in 1946 to control and develop the interchange of overseas orders. **1960** L. JOHNS in *Retail Florist's Handbk.* xxii. 250 The clearing house at Interflora headquarters is an impressive sight. **1966** *Guardian* 4 Oct. 8/2, 22 million Interflora orders were sent world-wide last year. **1971** N. FREELING *Over High Side* I. 51 The ladies of Belgrave Square had sent long emotional telegrams and Interflora wreaths. **1972** F. WARNER *Maquettes* 30, I arrange bouquets for Interflora.

interfluve (i·ntəɹflūv). [Back-formation from next.] A region lying between (the valleys of) adjacent watercourses, esp. one between the valleys of a dissected upland.

1902 in WEBSTER Suppl. **1913** *Bull. Geol. Soc. Amer.* XXIV. 206 In an early stage of the new cycle the fault-line scarp will be highest near the incised valleys of transverse streams, and it may remain for a time undeveloped on the interfluves. **1937** *Geogr. Jrnl.* LXXXIX. 356 A cross-section of a typical portion of deltaic country from river to interfluve. **1956** D. L. LINTON *Sheffield* 29 Here are some eighty or more square miles where dips are gentle and the grits build broad tabular interfluves swathed in peat and separating deep valleys with benched sides. **1968** R. W. FAIRBRIDGE *Encycl. Geomorphol.* 559 *Interfluve*... Many geomorphologists today use the term for the interstream area to imply a discrete landscape or geomorphic unit, composed of uni- or polycyclic slope facets. Interfluve almost always appears in a phrase explicitly or implicitly denoting its dissection.

interfluvial (intəɹflū·viăl), *a.* [f. INTER- 4 a + FLUVIAL *a.*] Situated between (the valleys of) adjacent watercourses.

1830 *New Monthly Mag.* III. *Hist. Reg.* Jan. 6/2 Returning from Bagdad across the interfluvial country, he took up his quarters at Hillah. **1903** *Sci. Amer. Suppl.* 14 Feb. 22679/1 A deposit of the flooded rivers during a stage of abundant ice melting, with considerable redistribution over the interfluvial upland areas by winds. **1933** *Antiquity* VII. 27 Beech Bottom and the Verulamium Devil's Dyke were relics of a transverse *limes* covering the whole tract of interfluvial country. **1971** [see *HUM *sb.*[4]].

inter-follicular: see *INTER- *pref.* 4 a.

intergalactic (intəɹgălæ·ktik), *a.* [INTER- 4 a.] Situated between the galaxies; of, pertaining to, or occupying the regions between galaxies.

1928 *Nature* 6 Oct. 556/1 In other words, in interstellar or intergalactic space. **1930** R. A. MILLIKAN *Sci. & New Civilization* iv. 106 We think that the atom-building processes that give rise to the observed cosmic rays can take place only under the extreme conditions of temperature and pressure existing in interstellar, or intergalactic, space. **1953** J. S. HUXLEY *Evolution in Action* i. 13 The whole of space intergalactic as well as interstellar. **1969** *Times* 29 May 12/8 Extremely far away even by intergalactic standards. **1971** *Nature* 29 Jan. 305/2 At these energies both the interstellar and the intergalactic gas should become gradually opaque.

inter-generational: see *INTER- *pref.* 4 c.

intergene·ric, *a.* [INTER- 4 c.] Formed or obtained from (individuals of) different genera.

1921 *Genetics* VI. 380 Intergeneric crosses between genera only distantly related. **1926** *Jrnl. Agric. Res.* XXXIII. 101 (*heading*) Intergeneric hybrids in Aegilops, Triticum, and Secale. **1946** *Nature* 10 Aug. 204/2 The successful production of hybrid plants from interspecific, intergeneric and even interfamily crosses. **1973** W. J.

BEAN *Trees & Shrubs Hardy in Brit. Isles* (ed. 8) II. 103 It is difficult to agree..that these plants [*sc.* varieties of *Erica cinerea*] are intergeneric hybrids between the bell-heather and *Calluna vulgaris*.

intergenic: see *INTER- *pref.* 6.

interglacial, *a.* Add: Also *absol.*, an interglacial period.

1922 *Bull. Geol. Soc. Amer.* XXXIII. 421 In the terraces corresponding to the First Interglacial of the Alps he holds that there is no Scandinavian material. **1939** G. CLARK *Archaeol. & Society* v. 137 An extra long gap, which..would be equivalent to the Mindel-Riss inter-glacial. **1970** I. CORNWALL *Ice Ages* iii. 69 This down-cutting formed the bench..on which the deposits of the following Interglacial were laid down.

Interglossa (intəɹglǫ·sä). [f. INTER- + Gr. γλῶσσα tongue.] An artificial auxiliary language devised by Lancelot Hogben (b. 1895).

1943 L. HOGBEN *Interglossa* 7 The author of *Interglossa* does not flatter himself with the hope that it will ever become the common language of international communication. **1946** H. JACOB *On Choice of Common Lang.* iii. 36 The potential extent of the Interglossa vocabulary will be many times greater than the number of terms contained in its vocabulary. **1954** PEI & GAYNOR *Dict. Ling.* 103 *Interglossa*, an artificial language proposed by Hogben, based on Greek and Latin roots with a system of syntax resembling that of Chinese.

interglyph, inter-governmental: see *INTER- *pref.* 3 a, 4 c.

intergranular, *a.* Delete *Anat.* and add to def.: occurring between granules or grains; intercrystalline. (Further examples.)

1932 *Jrnl. Iron & Steel Inst.* CXXV. 680 Intergranular corrosion of a chromium-nickel steel. **1946** *Nature* 24 Aug. 275/1 It is suggested that the migrations responsible for metasomatism occur partly by ionic diffusion through the crystal lattices and partly by molecular and/or ionic diffusion through the interstices ('intergranular film' of Wegmann) between the minerals. **1962** *Science Survey* III. 329 The final failure of the metal is essentially mechanical and it usually occurs by the propagation, through the body of the metal, of intercrystalline (or intergranular) cracks. **1971** *Nature* 30 July 327/1 It is quite likely that fluids have been able to flow through these rocks by means of both intergranular and fracture channels.

intergroup (i·ntəɹgrūp), *a.* [INTER- 5.] Situated, distributed, carried on, etc., between groups. Also as *sb.* So **intergrou·ping** *vbl. sb.* and (as a back-formation) **intergrou·p** *v.*

1883 W. ROBINSON *Eng. Flower Garden* p. cx/2 Breadth of mass and intergrouping. **1931** *Economist* 11 Apr. 783/1 The formation of an 'intergroup' for mutual benefit in connection with the coming contest at the polls. **1936** *Discovery* May 160/1 Inter-group relations..are cemented by an elaborate exchange of gifts. **1943** WYNDHAM LEWIS *Let.* 17 Aug. (1963) 365 The inter-group and interracial quarrels seem to grow in number. **1965** *Math. in Biol. & Med.* (Med. Res. Council) III. 87 (*caption*) The centres are at points representing the average intergroup distance. **1970** G. F. NEWMAN *Sir, You Bastard* i. 17 The fifteen recruits..were moved and taught en masse, intergrouped with students further advanced and those who followed them in. **1972** *Accountant* 17 Aug. 191/2 Inter-group dividends may thus be paid gross.

interim, *adv., sb.,* and *adj.* Add: **B.** *sb.* **5.** An interim dividend.

1930 *Daily Express* 6 Nov. 14/2 An interim of 5 per cent. actual was declared in May. **1935** *Economist* 14 Sept. 527/2 Associated Portland Cement had decided to pay the first interim in its history, at the rate of 5 per cent. **1964** *Financial Times* 10 Feb. 8/1 On Wednesday an interim is expected from Triplex Holdings.

C. *adj.* (Further examples.)

1869 *Bradshaw's Railway Manual* XXI. 247 The interim dividend of gross receipts. **1905** *Daily Chron.* 21 June 4/3 The Committee should..be invited to present an interim Report. **1950** T. S. ELIOT *Cocktail Party* III. 145 We have just drawn up an interim report. **1968** J. LOCK *Lady Policeman* xviii. 149 A four-week interim order was made so that enquiries could continue. **1972** *Accountant* 17 Aug. 197/1 What would happen if that same company deferred the interim dividend.

‖ **Interimsethik** (i·ntərimzē:tik). *Theol.* Also in anglicized forms **interim-ethic, interim ethic.** [G. (Schweitzer, 1901, 1906) *interims-*, comb. form of *interim*, provisional, temporary + *ethik* ethics, ethical values, principles.] The moral principles laid down by Jesus, interpreted as formulated for the guidance of men expecting the imminent end of the world; hence, a code of behaviour for use in a specific, temporary situation.

1910 W. MONTGOMERY tr. *Schweitzer's Quest Historical Jesus* xix. 352 What this repentance, supplementary to the law, the special ethic of the interval before the coming of the kingdom (*Interimsethik*) is,..He explains in the Sermon on the Mount. [**1915** A. HALL *Jesus & Christianity in 20th Cent.* iii. 43 Schweitzer..perceives the difficulty, and endeavours to overcome it by describing this side of the message and character of Jesus as 'the ethic of the interim'.] **1918** *Encycl. Relig. & Ethics* X. 733/1 Many NT students argue that the ethics of Jesus is conditional, an *Interimsethik*, and was proclaimed in indissoluble connexion with the eschatological expectation of a state of perfect blessedness to be supernaturally brought about. **1946** R. KNOX tr. *Epistles & Gospels* 270 But Matthew makes it more plain than Luke that we are not merely dealing with what Schweitzer called an *interimsethik*, a scale of values only appropriate to a world which is shortly to go up in smoke. **1947** G. SEAVER *Albert Schweitzer* II. xiii. 183 Our Lord's teaching was an *interim-ethic*, that is to say it was conditioned by His conviction of the nearness of the supernatural Kingdom. **1960** N. SYKES *Sixty Yrs. Since* 7 It was in the light of this eschatology that all the ethical teaching of the Gospels must be understood..and the whole was an *Interimsethik*. **1961** *Times Lit. Suppl.* 17 Feb. p. x/3 He also points out..that their advocacy of toleration was intended only as an *Interimsethik*, until reconciliation..had been attained. *Ibid.* p. xii/3 Schweitzer's thorough-going eschatology and his consequent estimate of the ethical teaching of Jesus as *Interimsethik*. **1964** M. RATTER *Schweitzer* 116 The teaching of Jesus is seen to be an 'Interim Ethic'.

interindividual (-indivi·diu,ăl), *a.* [INTER- 5.] Subsisting, carried on, taking place, or forming a communication between, individuals. So **interindivi·dually** *a.*

1922 JOYCE *Ulysses* 651 The converse domain of interindividual relations. **1951** T. PARSONS et al. in Parsons & Shils *Toward Gen. Theory Action* I. i. 24 These selections cannot be inter-individually random in a social system. **1953** N. TINBERGEN *Herring Gull's World* xvi. 122 The female's posture is identical with the submissive posture which the species has developed for other kinds of interindividual conflict. **1965** *Philos. Rev.* LXXIV. 181 According to Kant interindividual inferences concerning existence are impossible by analytic means. **1971** *Jrnl. Gen. Psychol.* Oct. 175 The actual conditioning procedures should be introduced only after interindividual differences have been reduced to a minimum.

inter-influence: see *INTER- *pref.* 1 b, 2 a.

interionic (intəɹəi,ǫ·nik), *a.* [INTER- 4 a.] Existing or occurring between ions.

1903 *Nature* 19 Nov. 65 The interionic forces..probably exert an effect even at dilutions at which the intermolecular forces are negligible. **1929** *Jrnl. Chem. Soc.* 1487 The influence of interionic attractions. **1965** PHILLIPS & WILLIAMS *Inorg. Chem.* I. v. 153 The observed interionic distances and the sums of the radii for the alkali halides with the NaCl structure are given in Table 5. VII.

interior, *a.* and *sb.* Add: **A.** *adj.* **3.** Special collocations, as **interior monologue** (cf. F. *monologue intérieur*), a form of writing in which the inner thoughts of a character are presented; **interior spring** (also **interior-sprung**) **mattress,** one with coiled springs within.

1922 tr. V. Larbaud in *Criterion* I. 103 It is of course especially in the interior monologues..that sexual instinct and erotic revery emerge. **1933** JOYCE *Let.* 17 Mar. (1966) III. 270 The other [is] going to Rome to lecture on the Interior Monologue. **1952** A. WILSON *Emile Zola* iii. 66 The Impressionist approach which he [*sc.* Zola] used could have led to a development of the interior monologue, as it did for Tolstoy. **1971** *Guardian* 27 May 8/7 Eight ward-inmates of an old people's home describe themselves in interior monologue that rambles on. **1959** *Spectator* 9 Oct. 498/2 A fridge, interior spring mattresses, even a bath. **1948** BINNIE & BOXALL *Housecraft* (ed. 4) xvii. 197 Interior sprung beds..may occasionally be turned from side, to side or from end to end. **1951** *Good Housek. Home Encycl.* 187/2 Interior-sprung mattresses do not require such frequent turning. **1961** *Countryman* LVIII. 601 The stretcher felt like an interior-sprung mattress.

B. *sb.* **1. c.** (Earlier and later examples.) Also, in a theatre, a 'set' consisting of the inside of a building or room.

1829 H. FOOTE *Compan. to Theatres* 57 A few interiors, two or three streets, and about the same number of country views, would last as stock scenery for several seasons. **1858** GEO. ELIOT *Jrnl.* 20 May in J. W. Cross *George Eliot's Life* (1885) II. viii. 40 The two interiors of Westminster Abbey by Ainmueller admirable. **1898** W. ARCHER *Theatr. 'World' 1897* 180 Mr. and Mrs. Alfred Wigan at the Olympic, made great strides towards realism in the dressing of modern plays and setting of everyday 'interiors'. **1916** J. R. TOWSE *Sixty Yrs. Theater* ii. 23 There were no elaborate and costly interiors, no enclosed box scenes, flats and wings were shifted before the eyes of the spectators. **1966** J. POTTS *Footsteps on Stairs* (1967) i. 9 She does the most divine interiors.

d. The internal parts of the body, esp. the digestive system. *colloq.*

1835 DICKENS *Let.* 4 Nov. (1965) I. 87 A..Pill—which ..is performing such singular evolutions in my interior. **1906** JOYCE *Let.* 18 Oct. (1966) II. 183 It [*sc.* wine] had not the least effect upon..'my interiors'. **1922** —— *Ulysses* 622 Mr Bloom..noticed when he stood up that he had two flasks of presumably ship's rum sticking one out of each pocket for the private consumption of his burning interior.

interior decoration (intīᵊ·riəɹ dekərēⁱ·ʃən). [f. INTERIOR *sb.* 1 c + DECORATION 1.] The planned co-ordination for artistic effect of colours and furniture, etc., in a room or building. So **interior de·corator,** one who practises interior decoration. Also **interior-de·corate** *v. trans.*, to paint and furnish (a room or the inside of a building) in accordance with an artistic design; *interior-decorated* ppl. adj.; *interior decorating* vbl. sb. Also *attrib.* and *fig.* (see also quot. 1926).

1807 T. HOPE (*title*) Household furniture and interior decoration. **1861** C. M. YONGE *Young Step-Mother* vii. 83 She was..too fond of out-of-door occupation, to regard interior decoration as one of the domestic graces. **1867** D. R. HAY (*title*) The interior decorator, being the laws of harmonious coloring adapted to interior decorations. **1906** *Dress* Oct. p. xxvi/1, I am a student of interior decoration—have had splendid success in this direction. It will pay you to consult me as to your plans for home beautifying. **1921** W. S. MAUGHAM *Circle* II. 51 Arnold should have been an interior decorator. **1926** MAINES & GRANT *Wise-Crack Dict.* 9/2 *Interior decorator*, bartender. **1930** E. FERBER *Cimarron* xxiii. 373 Fascinating little.. interior decorating shops. **1933** *Burlington Mag.* Aug. p. xv/1 Arranging flowers for interior decoration. **1935** *Discovery* Nov. 326/2 Ideal for interior decoration work. **1935** S. LEWIS *It can't happen Here* ii. 24 The bar-room had been professionally interior-decorated by a young New York gentleman. **1943** F. L. WRIGHT *Autobiogr.* (1945) III. 160 John was to regale the inner man, interior-decorate him. **1950** E. H. GOMBRICH *Story of Art* iv. 77 The painters and interior decorators of Pompeii obviously drew freely on the stock of inventions made by the great Hellenistic artists. **1960** *House & Garden* July 4/3, I wonder if there are any courses in Interior Decorating that can be studied at home. I am thinking of starting a small interior decorating business. **1967** E. SHORT *Embroidery & Fabric Collage* i. 18 Texture is a factor which plays a very important part in modern architecture and interior decoration. **1972** L. P. BACHMANN *Ultimate Act* i. 9 The library..was as interior-decorated as the rest of the house.

interior design (intīᵊ·riəɹ dĭzəi·n). [f. INTERIOR *sb.* 1 c + DESIGN *sb.* 7.] The design of the interior of a building, including wall-paper, furniture, fittings, etc., according to artistic and architectural criteria. So **interior designer,** one whose business is to plan such interiors. Cf. prec. entry.

1927 T. P. BENNETT *Archit. Design in Concrete* 13 The effect of this adjustment of proportion and detail upon interior design is..in some ways more fundamental than the effect of the new proportions upon exterior designs. **1938** *Decorative Art* p. xxxii, The favourable attention of all leading Interior Designers can be secured..through a single publication, 'Interior Design and Decoration'. **1957** *Encycl. Brit.* XII. pl. x (*caption*) Living room by Ain, Johnson and Day, showing relationship of interior and exterior design. **1962** H. STEPHENSON *Design & Decoration in Home* 7 There is more to interior design than just putting furniture in a room and paint on a wall. **1967** E. SHORT *Embroidery & Fabric Collage* iii. 64 Good interior designers sometimes go as far as having carpets specially designed and manufactured. **1972** *Guardian* 17 May 9/4 She turned to interior design.

interiority. (Later examples.)

1890 W. JAMES *Princ. Psychol.* II. xvii. 43 It is surely subjectivity and interiority which are the notions *latest* acquired by the human mind. **1934** E. BOWEN *Cat Jumps* 51 Voices came out from some dark interiority. **1941** *Theology* XLII. 156 The characteristic of the new period was, as Hegel put it, interiority. **1967** *Listener* 26 Oct. 552/1 Alan Bates as Gabriel Oak suffers..from Schlesinger's reluctance to suggest, as Hardy might put it, interiority. **1973** *Times Lit. Suppl.* 2 Nov. 1348/4 For all its imaginative ambitiousness, the volume lacks a certain human interiority.

interiorize (intīᵊ·riərəiz), *v.* [f. INTERIOR *a.* + -IZE.] *trans.* To connect with the soul, as distinguished from the body; also, to locate within the mind.

1906 *Academy* 20 Oct. 392/2 To 'interiorise' the struggle, to place it on the stage of the soul, with eternity for background. **1916** STANFORD & FORSYTH *Hist. Mus.* xvi. 329 The second [feature in American life] is the interiorizing and democratic habit-of-mind which partly connotes the term *Americanism*. **1934** *Mind* XLIII. 89 In so far as habits of co-operation have convinced the child at a later age of the necessity of not lying, rules will become comprehensible and interiorised. **1937** G. W. ALLPORT *Personality* (1938) p. viii, From this point of view culture is relevant only when it has become *interiorized* within the person as a set of personal ideals, attitudes, and traits. **1971** *Jrnl. Gen. Psychol.* Apr. 206 The child interiorizes what he already understands.

Hence **interioriza·tion.**

1941 *Theology* XLII. 156 To discover anew the meaning of authority *in* their immanent freedom, by making it itself immanent within them by a process of interiorization. **1956** *Scottish Jrnl. Theol.* IX. 74 Hence he is unable to rise to the thought of suffering as the gift of divine love, as a sacramental medium through the purifying effect of which man attains a deeper realisation and interiorisation of God. **1961** J. N. FINDLAY *Values & Intentions* i. 40 Our talk about thoughts, decisions, etc., is always largely an 'interiorization' of our talk about words. **1966** L. JONES in A. Chapman *New Black Voices* (1972) 465 The Black man must seek a Black politics, an ordering of the world that is beneficial to his culture, to his interiorization and judgment of the world. **1971** *Jrnl. Gen. Psychol.* Apr. 206 Since these interiorizations are not sufficient for the child, he gradually proceeds to representations based upon more logical..principles of operation.

interkinesis (intəɹkəinī·sis). *Cytology.* [ad. F. *intercinèse* (V. Grégoire 1905, in *La Cellule* XXII. 226): see INTER- 2 b and *KINESIS.] A stage which sometimes intervenes between

the first and second divisions of meiosis; also, any stage between mitoses.

1906 *Jrnl. R. Microsc. Soc.* 283 The daughter-chromosomes..preserve their autonomy during the interkinesis. **1925** E. B. WILSON *Cell* (ed. 3) i. 28 The central body.. retains its morphological identity during the interkinesis or vegetative (non-mitotic) condition of the cell. **1965** PENNY & WAERN *Biol.* xlii. 775 In some cases the chromosomes decondense as in ordinary mitosis, and there is a brief pause before the second division commences. This stage, if it occurs, is called interkinesis.

Hence **interkine·tic** *a.*

1927 *Protoplasma* II. 189 The interkinetic nuclear substance is devoid of any structural element. **1931** J. GRAY *Text-bk. Exper. Cytol.* viii. 141 A 'resting' or interkinetic nucleus in the living condition is usually optically homogeneous. **1960** L. PICKEN *Organization of Cells* iv. 101 (*heading*) The interphasic, interkinetic, 'resting', or non-mitotic nucleus.

interlace, *v.* Add: **6.** *Television.* (*trans.*) To present (scanning lines) so that alternate lines of a picture form one sequence and are followed by the intervening lines in a second sequence; to present (dots) similarly so that several fields of regularly spaced dots go to form each picture. Also, to combine (two or more fields), or form (a picture or raster), in this way. Freq. as pa. pple. Cf. also *INTERLACED ppl. a.*

1927 M. LATOUR *Brit. Pat.* 267,513, The elements of the image transmitted by each system AB are..the ones within the others, or interlacing each other. **1936** [see *FRAME sb.* 12 c]. **1955** D. G. FINK *Color Television Standards* iii. 92 Dot interlace, in which minute dots..of different primary colors, produced adjacent to each other during the color-scanning process, are interlaced in various repeated and prearranged sequences. **1966** G. H. HUTSON *Television Receiver Theory* I. xii. 187 If these conditions are met the resulting raster must be interlaced. **1967** [see *FIELD sb.* 16 d]. **1972** *Sci. Amer.* Sept. 132/2 Every other line is scanned in just under a sixtieth of a second and the missing lines are interlaced in the next sixtieth of a second.

interlace (i·ntəɹlěis), *sb.* [f. the vb.] The action or result of interlacing.

1904 GOODCHILD & TWENEY *Technol. & Sci. Dict.* 312/2 *Interlace.* This relates to the crossing of warp and weft, the order of the interlacing in a weave prescribing the structure of the cloth. **1923** *Daily Mail* 19 Mar. 1 The upturned brim has fancy straw interlace, giving a ribbon effect. **1936** A. W. CLAPHAM *Romanesque Archit.* iii. 61 The acanthus-scroll..commonly has a stem composed of three strands, a trick of the carver which was probably inherited from the universal use of the triple strand interlace in Italy at an earlier date. **1948** N. GRAY in *Papers Brit. Sch. Rome* XVI. 116 The cross is carved with a foliage pattern on one side..and an interlace on the other. **1973** *Country Life* 29 Nov. 1761/1 Strap-work and interlace patterns on plain velvet.

b. *spec.* in *Television* (see *INTERLACE v.* 6).

1936 O. S. PUCKLE tr. *M. von Ardenne's Television Reception* i. 5 The line component and the frame component of scanning are regularly recurrent, the interlace being derived from the fractional relationship between line and frame frequencies. **1937** *Electronics* June 15/2 At the end of each half-frame or 'interlace', the frame synchronizing impulses are imposed in a similar manner. **1961** *Listener* 2 Nov. 725/3 The television service reopened on June 7, 1946, using the pre-war system (405-lines, 25 pictures per second with 2:1 interlace, positive modulation and AM sound). **1966** G. H. HUTSON *Television Receiver Theory* I. xii. 192 The alternate scanning field is ¼ line late in starting. This causes very poor interlace.

interlaced, *ppl. a.* (in Dict. s.v. INTERLACE *v.*). Add: Also stressed *i·nterlaced.* **b.** *Television.* Applied to scanning in which the lines or the dots of the picture are interlaced (see *INTERLACE v.* 6), so that each is built up from two or more fields; composed or combined in this way.

1935 R. W. HUTCHINSON *Television Up-to-Date* v. 131 It has been suggested that a system of interlaced scanning, as it is called, should be adopted: in this, lines 1, 3, 5, 7, etc., would first be scanned, and then the intermediate ones, 2, 4, 6, 8, and so on. **1936** O. S. PUCKLE tr. *M. von Ardenne's Television Reception* i. 21 With the resulting 50 pictures per second, the flicker of the interlaced picture is almost entirely avoided. **1953** H. A. CHINN *Television Broadcasting* i. 5 In order to conserve bandwidth without sacrificing freedom from flicker, the standard television system employs a system of interlaced scanning. **1961** *New Scientist* 26 Jan. 199/3 The British system transmits 25 complete pictures per second, forming each from 405 horizontal lines laid down in two interlaced sequences of 202½ lines each.

interlacing, *vbl. sb.* (Further examples.)

1927 *Jrnl. Genetics* XVIII. 182 There is interlacing of the chromatids. **1935** R. W. HUTCHINSON *Television Up-to-Date* v. 132 Both Baird and E.M.I. have experimented with interlacing. **1936** *Proc. IRE* XXIV. 573 The difference between the amplitude of the alternate discharges is somewhat critical for perfect interlacing. **1974** J. ROBINSON *Penguin Bk. Sewing* xii. 328/2 Interlacing..consists of horizontal stitches interlaced with the herring bone stitch.

interlacustrine (intəɹlăkʋ·strin), *a.* [f. INTER-4 a + LACUSTRINE *a.*] Lying between lakes.

1900 *Geogr. Jrnl.* Feb. 179 This region forms part of the great interlacustrine plateau. **1958** E. WINTER in Middleton & Tait *Tribes without Rulers* 158 The other Interlacustrine kingdoms of which the best known is Buganda.

interlaminar, *a.* Add: **2.** Situated or occurring between the reinforcing layers or components of a laminate or composite.

1963 *Symposium Standards for Filament-Wound Reinforced Plastics, 1962* (Amer. Soc. Testing Materials STP 327) 17 In this method, a bending test is conducted with a short span to induce failure in horizontal ('interlaminar') shear. **1964** *Plastics Inst. Trans. & Jrnl.* XXXII. 292/2 Creep effects in the composite thus become limited principally to the resin interlaminar planes. **1966** K. L. LOWENSTEIN in L. Holliday *Composite Materials* v. 200 The consensus of opinion is that failure [of composites] occurs by interlaminar shear, *i.e.* fracture of resin between reinforcing fibres followed, as a secondary step, by the fracture of individual fibres themselves. **1971** *New Scientist* 8 July 70/1 Composites of [carbon] fibres in resin having the expected high tensile strength and modulus..had a low interlaminar shear strength of only 2500 lb/sq in.

interlanguage (i·ntəɹlæ̈ŋgwèdʒ), *sb.* [INTER-2 a.] An artificial auxiliary language. Also *attrib.*

1927 E. S. PANKHURST *Delphos* vii. 86 The Interlanguage cannot be the creation of Governments. **1928** O. JESPERSEN *Internat. Lang.* I. 45 The Delegation and the Ido academy have left their indelible mark on the interlanguage movement. **1929** T. C. MACAULAY in *S.P.E. Tract* (1930) XXXIV. 462 Interlanguage will have no idiomatic tradition of its own. **1960** E. DELAVENAY *Introd. Machine Transl.* iv. 47 Georges Mounin rightly distinguishes between pseudolanguages—of which Esperanto is the classic example—intended to be *speakable*, and interlanguages, designed for use as auxiliary languages, such as the *interlingua* of Peano or that of Gode and Blair.

interla·nguage, *a.* [INTER- 5.] Between or relating to two languages.

1953 U. WEINREICH *Lang. in Contact* i. 8 Interference resulting from such inter-language identification. **1964** E. A. NIDA *Towards Sci. Transl.* vii. 147 In an attempt to describe these interlanguage and intercultural factors, we must reckon with differences of time.

interlay (i·ntəɹlěi), *sb.* [Back-formation f. the vb.] That which is intercalated; esp. in *Printing.*

1901 *Westm. Gaz.* 10 Oct. 2/2 A delicate Chantilly lace mounted over cream satin, with an interlay of cream chiffon. **1940** *Chambers's Techn. Dict.* 453/2 *Interlay,* paper inserted between a printing plate and its mount in order to raise the plate to type height. **1948** H. MISSINGHAM *Student's Guide Commercial Art* II. 82 *Interlay,* paper placed between the mount and the metal plate to raise those portions of the block, representing usually the dark tones and solids.

interlayer (i·ntəɹlěi·əɹ), *sb.* and *a.* [f. INTER- + LAYER *sb.*] **A.** *sb.* [INTER- 2 b.] A layer situated between two other layers.

1936 *Brit. Pat.* 453,578, The polymer..is..dried in vacuo and may be mixed with a suitable amount of an appropriate plasticiser..compressed to form a block either of rectangular or of cylindrical shape, and..cut into sheets ready for use as a laminated safety glass interlayer. **1960** *Nature* 16 July 262/1 The laboratory introduction of aluminium interlayers into montmorillonite and vermiculite produced clays that resembled the chloritized soil clays in their 14-Å. spacing. **1962** L. S. SASIENI *Princ. & Pract. Optical Dispensing* xiii. 329 The three laminae are joined under heat and pressure, and if one or both of the layers of glass are broken by impact..the pieces of glass remain adherent to the interlayer. **1972** *Soil Sci.* CXIII. 172/2 It was anticipated that the removal of interlayer liquid in K-saturated illite might be similar to montmorillonite and vermiculite, where entire interlayers are usually lost abruptly.

B. *adj.* [INTER- 5.] Situated or occurring between two layers.

1956 *Nature* 4 Feb. 239/2 A flake of magnesium vermiculite, which has been partially dehydrated to the phase containing single sheets of interlayer water molecules. **1970** *Proc. Soil Sci. Soc. Amer.* XXXIV. 201/1 Interlayer swelling of the soil clays.

inter-lend, *v.*: see *INTER- pref.* 1 b.

interlevel (i·ntəɹlevĕl). *Linguistics.* [INTER-2 a.] A 'level' of language serving to relate other linguistic levels (see quots.).

1961 M. A. K. HALLIDAY in *Word* XVII. 269 Context is an interlevel in a different sense, since it relates language to something that is not language. **1963** R. M. W. DIXON *Ling. Sci. & Logic* i. 23 An interlevel will itself contain theories which will perform the necessary level-relating. **1964** R. H. ROBINS *Gen. Ling.* p. xix, Both treat phonology as an 'interlevel' serving to relate statements made at the level of grammar with those made at the level of phonetics. **1966** J. ELLIS in C. E. Bazell *In Memory of J. R. Firth* 79 This classification of levels is represented by the diagram showing the levels of subst......form and situation and interlevels of phonology/graphology and context.

inter-library: see *INTER- pref.* 5.

interline (intəɹləi·n), *a.* [f. INTER- 5 + LINE *sb.*[2]] Of or pertaining to transport: using more than one route, service, etc.

1946 T. C. BIGHAM *Transportation* iii. 96 Service may be local or interline. **1957** *Encycl. Brit.* XVIII. 940 (*heading*) Joint or interline rates. **1969** *Jane's Freight Containers 1968–69* 48/1 The New York Port District may be likened to the centre of a web of gleaming steel rails.. of ten long-haul railroads which, through interline connections, serve the entire nation, Canada and Mexico. **1970** *Daily Tel.* 30 June 24 Logically the first flight after the official connecting time would be the correct interline connection.

interlinearly, *adv.* Delete *rare* and add later examples.

1906 *Hibbert Jrnl.* Apr. 682 A distinction that is indeed repeatedly suggested interlinearly in Mr Mallock's pages. **1955** C. E. WRIGHT in *Bald's Leechbook* Pref. 11 One manuscript, the later of the two, is a volume of small format..(glossed interlinearly).

Interlingua (intəɹli·ŋgwă). Also **interlingua.** [f. INTER- + L. *lingua* tongue.] An artificially devised international language; *spec.* one promoted by the International Auxiliary Language Association of New York.

Several invented languages have been so named.

1922 A. L. GUÉRARD *Short Hist. Internat. Lang. Movement* v. 127 Those which, like Neutral, Ido, Interlingua, present themselves as the collective work of some 'Academy' bear..the mark of one master mind. **1927** E. S. PANKHURST *Delphos* iv. 38 'Interlingua is the standard of the insurrection against the routine of red tape and the tyranny of the ancient grammarian', thus wrote Kerchoffs, the first director of the Volapük Academy, in 1886. Giuseppe Peano..was presently to translate those words into a language scheme, and to adopt Interlingua as its title. **1928** O. JESPERSEN *Internat. Lang.* I. 45 This 'interlingua' is now employed in the publication of *Academia pro Interlingua.* **1953** J. B. CARROLL *Study of Lang.* iv. 127 A recent attempt to rationalize an artificial language by making maximal use of elements common to the most widely used natural languages is Interlingua, the work of the International Auxiliary Language Association of New York. **1955** *Sci. News Let.* 29 Jan. 79/2 Interlingua is a language composed of elements common to Spanish, Portuguese, French, Italian and other Romance languages. *Ibid.* 22 Oct. 258/2 Interlingua is no overnight creation of one linguist or even one group of linguists. No one sat down and theorized as to what an international language should be. Instead three decades ago, in 1924, an ambassador-to-be, a chemist, several radio engineers, several educators, editors and linguistic experts started a long and detailed inquiry into what an international language should be. **1956** J. WHATMOUGH *Lang.* iv. 59 An interlingua needs more than expletives and exclamations. **1960** [see *INTERLANGUAGE sb.*].

interlingual, *a.* Delete *rare* and add later examples. So **interli·ngually** *adv.*

In quot. 1931 *spec.* = of or relating to an artificial interlanguage (cf. *INTERLANGUAGE sb.*).

1931 *Mod. Lang. Notes* XLVI. 18 Those who..have paid little attention to the interlingual movement. **1941** P. B. GOVE *Imaginary Voy. Prose Fiction* I. i. 8 The term is in some degree interlingual; occasionally to German writers it seems so apposite that it is not translated. **1951** W. EMPSON *Struct. Complex Words* xxi. 397 The confusion of translation equivalents is so great that many students have been warned against the interlingual dictionary. **1958** J. BERRY in J. A. Fishman *Readings Sociol. of Lang.* (1968) 741 Is it..preferable to follow the orthographic practice of the trade language or that of an interlingual notational inventory such as The Africa Script? **1964** *Language* XL. 243 A minimum of inter-lingual interference. **1966** *Publ. Amer. Dial. Soc.* XLVI. 5 Whenever two interlingually identified forms are similar in sound and..meaning,..we have a homologous diamorph.

interlinguist (-li·ŋgwist). [INTER- 2 a.] One versed in or an adherent of an interlanguage or interlanguages.

1928 O. JESPERSEN *Internat. Lang.* I. 12 What then we interlinguists are thinking of, is..what another inventor of an artificial language, Bollack, took as his motto: The second language to everybody. **1934** *N. & Q.* 8 Sept. 168/1 The true interlinguist..contends that a suitable auxiliary language must be an efficient medium for the communication of thought internationally. **1947** H. JACOB *Planned Auxiliary Lang.* I. i. 31 Leopold Einstein, a well-known interlinguist.

interlinguistic, *a.* Delete *rare* and add: **2.** Of or relating to an interlanguage; between or relating to two languages.

1947 H. JACOB *Planned Auxiliary Lang.* III. xiv. 131 For the purposes of interlinguistic discussion they have been termed the naturalistic school and the autonomistic school. **1962** P. S. RAY in J. A. Fishman *Readings Sociol. of Lang.* (1968) 756 We might speak, instead of 'closure' and 'opening', of intra-linguistic and interlinguistic uniformity.

interlinguistics (-liŋgwi·stiks). [INTER- 2 a.] The study of the relationships of two or more languages, e.g. for the purpose of devising an interlanguage. Hence **interlinguisti·cian** = *INTERLINGUIST.*

1931 O. JESPERSEN in H. N. Shenton et al. *Internat. Communication* iii. 95 A new science is developing, Interlinguistics. **1934** *N. & Q.* 8 Sept. 168/1 The new or coming science of 'interlinguistics' is based upon certain fundamental principles of its own. **1938** *Encycl. Brit. Bk. of Yr.* 673/2 In recent years, interlinguisticians have been feeling their way to an average, as it were, of existing languages. **1947** H. JACOB *Planned Auxiliary Lang.* I. iii. 70 In interlinguistics the term *pleonastic endings* has been used to describe specific grammatical terminations. **1953** M. WEINREICH in J. A. Fishman *Readings Sociol. of*

Lang. (1968) 394 As the raw material..is drawn from the most divergent sources: Persian.., Arabic, Slavic, Greek, several Romance languages, Teutonic, Jewish interlinguistics should prove the comparativist's delight.

interlining, *sb.* (Earlier and later examples.)
1881 C. C. HARRISON *Woman's Handiwork* I. 76 Lay the work upon the interlining of canton flannel, and turn the edges down. **1959** [see *IRON-ON *a.*]. **1974** J. ROBINSON *Penguin Bk. Sewing* v. 133 Interlining..used in tailoring ..consists of the introduction of a section of tailor's canvas, Vilene, [etc.]..to stiffen the fabric.

interlink, *v.* Add: So **interli·nkage.**
1904 *Westm. Gaz.* 3 Dec. 16/3 The phenomena to be seen in the living being, their inter-linkage, their apparent adaptation to an end. **1930** *Times* (Empire Press No.) 31 May p. xi/4 An Empire broadcasting system... A total problem that includes both interlinkage with the United States and [etc.]. **1957** V. W. TURNER *Schism & Continuity in Afr. Soc.* x. 301 The..values shared by all Ndembu are prominently displayed..in the ritual association of those who have suffered regardless of their kinship or other interlinkages.

interlocal, *a.* (Example.)
1920 A. C. PIGOU *Econ. of Welfare* II. vi. 171 So soon as people become thoroughly familiarised with town-planning, local patriotism and inter-local emulation will make resort to external pressure from the central Government no longer necessary.

interlock, *v.* Add: **4.** *Cinemat.* To connect (the electric motors of cameras or the like) electrically in such a way that they rotate in synchronism with one another.
1928 *Trans. Soc. Motion Picture Engin.* XII. 704 It has been necessary..to develop a motor drive equipment which will satisfactorily interlock the camera and the recording machine... It is essential that the interlock should hold..during acceleration and deceleration. **1931** B. BROWN *Talking Pictures* ix. 206 Where we have cameras working in conjunction with sound recorders.. there is absolute necessity for both devices to be interlocked or driven together, so that sound and photograph are always exactly in phase. **1953** L. J. WHEELER *Princ. Cinematogr.* ii. 68 When all was ready to take the scene the camera was interlocked with the sound recorder so that, on starting up, both camera and recorder would rotate in synchronism.

interlock, *sb.* Restrict *rare* to senses in Dict. and add: **2. a.** *Cinemat.* Synchronism between two or more electric motors (e.g. in a camera and in sound-recording apparatus); also, the mechanism by which this is effected. Freq. *attrib.*
1928 [see *INTERLOCK *v.* 4]. **1931** B. BROWN *Talking Pictures* ix. 206 Gaumont coupled the armature of his projector motor, and using a common power supply, obtained synchronism. To-day we use a similar type of arrangement known as the 'electrical interlock'. **1938** *Motion Picture Sound Engin.* (Acad. Motion Pict. Arts & Sci.) viii. 118 Another commonly used driving system employs the Selsyn type of motor and is known as the interlock system. This is virtually an electrical gear system, whereby all the motors connected together on several separated units will start together, come up to speed at the same rate, and continue to run at identical speeds. *Ibid.* 119 Field rheostats for each motor are located in one place and all speeds are adjusted to maintain interlock at the estimated camera and recorder loads. **1949** FRAYNE & WOLFE *Elem. Sound Recording* xxiv. 477 Because the three-phase interlock windings are interconnected with the d-c windings voltage appears on the interlock circuit as soon as the d-c leads are excited. **1962** E. L. LEVITAN *Animation Technique* I. 70/1 The process whereby the picture reel and the sound track are run and projected at the same time is called the interlock.
b. A mechanism for preventing a set of operations from being performed in any but the prescribed sequence.
1934 in WEBSTER. **1945** *Rev. Sci. Instruments* XVI. 57/2 There are two mechanical interlocks on the controls... The selector switch is locked so that it cannot be moved unless the Variac is set to zero. **1955** *Archit. Rev.* CXVII. 142/3 The most important piece of equipment associated with lift doors is the inter-lock, an electro-mechanical device which ensures that the lift cannot move until both car and landing doors are locked in position. **1958** *Engineering* 28 Feb. 261/3 To prevent incorrect operation, electrical interlocks are provided to ensure that the hopper can only be tilted when all the pressing rams are clear and the box is open..and that the ejection door cannot be closed until the final pressing ram has been withdrawn. **1958** *Newnes Compl. Amat. Photogr.* 54 It is common nowadays for even simple cameras to have a shutter-film wind interlock which prevents blank negatives or double exposures. **1963** B. FOZARD *Instrumentation Nucl. Reactors* xiii. 170 Interlocks must be fitted to ensure that the chambers cannot be inserted under high flux conditions.
B. *attrib.* or *adj.* Esp. designating woven material in which the stitches are woven together.
1928 *Daily Mail* 25 July 3/6 (Advt.), The merits of Meridian Interlock Underwear. **1935** *Economist* 23 Nov. 1003/1 Considerable progress..was made with the development of spun yarns for..pyjama cloths and for underwear fabric manufactured on circular interlock knitting machines. **1969** *Sears Catal.* Spring/Summer 26 Cardigan sweater interlock knit of Orlon acrylic.

interlocutor[1]**.** Add: **c.** The compère in a troupe of nigger minstrels; the man in the middle of the minstrel line who questions the end men.
1880 E. JAMES *Amat. Negro Minstrel's Guide* 2 Interlocutor or Middle Man, in the Center. **1884** [see BANJOIST]. **1957** W. C. HANDY *Father of Blues* xxi. 276 Henry Troy acted as the interlocutor, with Tom Fletcher and Laurence Deas as end men.

interlot, *v.*: see *INTER- *pref.* I a.

interludial (intəɹliū·diăl), *a.* [f. INTERLUDE *sb.* + -IAL.] Of, pertaining to, or of the nature of an interlude.
1884 *Encycl. Brit.* XVII. 94/1 Admitted for interludial purposes in a fabrication styled *intermezzo* that was played between the acts of a serious composition, comedy became [etc.]. **1922** S. GREW *Art of Player-Piano* 75 The interludial figure is extended to lead into a *forte.*

inter-marginal: see *INTER- *pref.* 4 a.

intermat (intəɹmæ·t), *v.* [INTER- I b.] *trans.* and *intr.* To mat together.
1904 GOODCHILD & TWENEY *Technol. & Sci. Dict.* 312/2 *Intermat* (Textile Manufac.), the term applied to the felting or shrinking of cloths, the fibres intermatting or felting together. **1927** *Daily Express* 18 Apr. 3/7 As the hair grows, it is worked into a kind of felt by intermatting it.

intermede. 2. Now current in alien form *intermède* (æ̃ntɛrmɛd).
1887 *Gentl. Mag.* June 540 The singularly appropriate *intermède* arranged by Beaumarchais for performance between the acts of his 'Eugenie'. **1931** *Times Lit. Suppl.* 6 Aug. 606/2 The inclusion between the first and second acts of an *intermède* of song and dance. **1970** *Oxf. Compan. Mus.* (ed. 10) 517/2 It was as *intermezzo* or *intermède* that the comic opera grew up.

intermedial, *a.* and *sb.* Delete † *Obs.* and add later example in sense A. *adj.* I.
1942 *Mind* LI. 80 Part II is a systematic and richly illustrated description of generic and special forms, of inter-medial and intra-medial forms.

intermediate, *a.* and *sb.* Add: **A.** *adj.* **d.** (Further examples.) Also *intermediate education, school.*
1842 E. LAZARUS *Let.* 19 July in N. E. Eliason *Tarheel Talk* (1956) 278 There are the primary & the intermediate schools, & the high-school. **1882** W. D. HAY *Brighter Britain* I. ii. 57 It doesn't matter twopence *how* you go out, whether saloon, intermediate, or steerage, so far as your future prospects are concerned. **1886** KIPLING *Plain Tales from Hills* (1888) 120 The four constables saw him safe to Umritsar in an 'intermediate' compartment. **1889** *Act* 52–54 *Vict.* c. 40 (*title*) An Act to promote Intermediate Education in Wales..sect. 1. This Act may be cited for all purposes as the Welsh Intermediate Education Act, 1889. *Ibid.* sect. 17 The expression 'intermediate education' means a course of education which does not consist chiefly of elementary instruction.. but which includes instruction in Latin, Greek, the Welsh and English language and literature,..mathematics, natural and applied science. **1893** *Harper's Mag.* Apr. 806 Oh, she was a rose half-budded, in the intermediate school, And her face and form I studied twice as much as task or rule. **1945** C. V. GOOD *Dict. Educ.* 223 Intermediate school: a school that enrolls pupils in intermediate grades, usually comprising the fourth, fifth, and sixth years of schoolwork. **1974** *Times* 1 Apr. (Yorkshire & Humberside Suppl.) p. i/2 Yorkshire and Humberside is classified as an 'intermediate area'. As such, while enjoying the benefits of financial inducements available to incoming and expanding industry, it does not rank for the benefits available in the other two types of aided regions.
2. Specific techn. uses.
a. *Petrol.* Of a rock: having a silicate content that falls between that of the acidic and that of the basic rocks (cf. ACIDIC *a.* 2, BASIC *a.* 2 b); often *spec.* having a silicate content between 52 and 66 per cent by weight.
1888 J. J. H. TEALL *Brit. Petrogr.* viii. 253 The basic rocks shade into the intermediate rocks, and these again into the acid rocks, in the most gradual manner. **1892** F. H. HATCH *Text-bk. Petrol.* (ed. 2) vi. 107 In respect to the percentage of silica, igneous rocks fall naturally into four groups, viz.:—(1) An acid group with 65–80% of silica... (2) An intermediate group with 55–70% of silica. .. (3) A basic group with 45–60% of silica... (4) An ultra-basic group with silica between 35 and 50%. **1909** *Ibid.* (ed. 5) III. i. 152 Arranged in the order of their silica contents, the plutonic rocks can be divided into three groups: 1. Acid, with silica contents above 66 per cent. 2. Intermediate, with silica contents between 66 and 52 per cent; and 3. Basic, with silica contents below 52. **1939** A. JOHANNSEN *Descr. Petrogr. Ign. Rocks* (ed. 2) I. 181 (*gloss.*) *Intermediate rocks*, rocks intermediate between the 'acid' and 'basic' groups. Syn. Neutral rocks, mediosilicic. Cf. Acid. **1968** B. BAYLY *Introd. Petrol.* vi. 53 The second system is chemical rather than mineralogical, being based on the weight percentage of SiO_2 in the rock; thus if SiO_2 percentage is: over 66, rock is acid; 52–66, rock is intermediate; 45–52, rock is basic; under 45, rock is ultrabasic.
b. *Nuclear Physics.* Applied to neutrons with less energy than fast neutrons but more than thermal neutrons, and also to nuclear reactors in which such neutrons are the chief cause of fission.
1947 *Rep. U.S. Atomic Energy Commission* A-4315 (*title*) A multi-group method for computing critical masses of intermediate piles. **1949** *Nucleonics* Dec. 41/1 Intermediate piles may operate with neutrons at any energy level between thermal and fission or even at several different energy levels. **1956** GLASSTONE *Princ. Nucl. Reactor Engin.* i. 15 In nuclear reactor work, the term *fast neutrons* is applied to neutrons having energies of about 0·1 Mev, i.e., 10^5 ev, or more. Those with energies from 10^5 ev down to 1 ev are called intermediate neutrons. **1959** L. F. CURTISS *Introd. Neutron Physics* i. 18 Less information has been accumulated about intermediate neutrons than about neutrons of lower energies because of [the] difficulty of finding efficient detectors. **1966** *McGraw-Hill Encycl. Sci. & Technol.* XI. 358/1 An example of an intermediate reactor is the first propulsion reactor for the submarine USS *Seawolf*. The fuel core consisted of enriched uranium with beryllium as a moderator.
3. Specific collocations: **intermediate boson:** see *BOSON; **intermediate frequency** *Electronics*, the frequency to which an incoming carrier wave is converted by the frequency changer of a superheterodyne receiver; abbrev. **I.F.*; **intermediate host** *Zool.*, an organism infected by a parasitic animal which then goes on to complete its life cycle in another host; **intermediate-range,** used *attrib.* of a ballistic missile of medium range (less than 'intercontinental').
1924 *Proc. IRE* XII. 540 Three intermediate frequency amplifiers. **1947** D. G. FINK *Radar Engin.* x. 504 The [radar receiver] system which avoids the foregoing difficulties is the superheterodyne, which introduces an initial change from radio frequency to a lower frequency (intermediate frequency) followed by a high-gain amplification at this frequency. **1968** B. P. LATHI *Communication Syst.* iii. 202 The advantage of conversion to an intermediate frequency is that to receive different stations it is necessary to tune only the first stage (and the local oscillator). All of the amplification is achieved at a constant intermediate frequency and needs no tuning. **1878** *Jrnl. R. Microsc. Soc.* I. 377 The ultimate form assumed by the larvae whilst still within the body of the intermediate host. **1892** [see HOST *sb.*[2] 3]. **1901** *Practitioner* Mar. 273 It is parasitic in man and in a certain genus of mosquito (Anopheles); the former is its intermediate host and the latter its definitive host. **1925** A. D. IMMS *Gen. Textbk. Ent.* III. 365 The latter issue from the galls and are divisible into winged *gallicolæ migrantes* (migrantes), which fly to the intermediate host, and *gallicolæ non-migrantes* which remain on the spruce and give rise to further fundatrices. **1971** E. R. & G. A. NOBLE *Parasitol.* (ed. 3) xxiv. 528/1 As a generalization, there is less host specificity when there are two intermediate hosts than when only one is employed. **1956** *Newsweek* 30 Jan. 27/1 Developing a 1,500-mile intermediate-range ballistic missile (IRBM) is now largely a question of 'straightforward engineering'. **1957** *Economist* 30 Nov. 774/2 The Polaris, the intermediate range ballistic missile to be launched from submarines. **1959** *Listener* 18 June 1053/1 Intermediate-range ballistic missiles—in other words, medium-range rockets.
B. *sb.* **1. c.** *Chem.* and *Biochem.* A compound which after being produced by one reaction participates in another; *esp.* one manufactured from naturally occurring materials for use in the synthesis of dyes, plastics, or other substances.
1919 E. DE B. BARNETT *Coal Tar Dyes* I. ii. 29 Aniline. —This is the most important intermediate, and is invariably manufactured by the reduction of nitrobenzole. *Ibid.* 31 Factories preparing their own intermediates. **1938** *Nature* 30 July 203/2 Mr. F. P. Garvan's appreciation of the dependence of the United States on Germany for dyes, intermediates, photographic chemicals, medicinals, etc., led him to organize the Chemical Foundation. **1953** *Nature* 27 June 1160/2 (*heading*) Occurrence of hydroxylamine in lake waters as an intermediate in bacterial reduction of nitrate. **1961** *Times* 30 May (I.C.I. Suppl.) p. xvi/1 All of them are 'intermediates'—the raw materials of other products such as Terylene or plastics. **1962** J. HINE *Physical Org. Chem.* (ed. 2) vii. 163 In most of the S_N1 reactions that have been studied kinetically the carbonium ion is a very reactive intermediate that is rapidly transformed into the final product. **1962** [see *HOMOCYSTEINE].

intermediateness. (Examples.)
1854 GEO. ELIOT tr. *Feuerbach's Essence Christianity* xii. 123 Thoughts of intermediateness and dependence. **1909** W. R. SORLEY *Interpretation of Evolution* 28 The characteristics of life, indeed,..have a certain appearance of intermediateness. **1958** P. A. M. DIRAC *Princ. Quantum Mech.* (ed. 4) i. 13 The probability of a particular result for the state formed by superposition is not always intermediate between those for the original states..so there are restrictions on the 'intermediateness' of a state formed by superposition.

intermedin (intəɹmī·din). *Physiol.* Also **-ine.** [a. G. *intermedin* (Zondek & Krohn 1932, in *Klin. Wochenschr.* 5 Mar. 406/1), f. mod.L. (*pars*) *intermed(ia* the intermediate part (of the hypophysis) + -IN[1].] = **melanocyte-stimulating hormone.*
1932 *Q. Cumulative Index Medicus* XI. 900/1 Red coloring of European minnow as test of intermedin from pars intermedia. **1948** G. H. PARKER *Animal Colour Changes* vi. 194 The intermedine system in amphibians is assumed to operate in the following manner. **1963** M. FINGERMAN *Control Chromatophores* vi. 103 Two general types of intermedin have been found. **1964** E. J. W. BARRINGTON in Pincus & Thimann *Hormones* IV. v. 327 The particular hormone involved, formerly known as intermedin, or B-substance, but now more usually termed melanocyte-stimulating hormone, or MSH.

intermedio-lateral (intəɹmīːdiǫlæ·təɹăl), *a.* *Anat.* Also **intermediolateral.** [ad. mod.L. *intermedio-lateralis*, f. mod.L. *intermedio-*, comb. form of L. *intermedius* intermediate + L. *lateralis* lateral.] Both intermediate and lateral: applied *spec.* to the tract of nerve cells which constitutes the lateral grey column of the spinal cord.

[**1859** J. L. Clarke in *Phil. Trans. R. Soc.* CXLIX. 446 This tract..was first pointed out by myself in 1851. I shall call it, on account of its position, the *tractus intermedio-lateralis.*] **1875** *Encycl. Brit.* I. 866/2 Lockhart Clarke has described an intermedio-lateral group of nerve cells. **1906** *Fifth Rep. Carnegie Trust Scotland* 20 Pathology of the intermedio-lateral tract of the spinal cord. **1972** J. Minckler *Introd. Neuroscience* xxii. 382 The preganglionic fibers arise in the intermediolateral column of cells of the ventral horn from segments T1 to L2.

intermesh (intəɹme·ʃ), *v.* [f. Inter- 1 b + Mesh *v.* 3 b.] *intr.* Of gears, etc.: to mesh or interlock with one another. Also *fig.*

1909 in Webster. **1928** *Daily Tel.* 27 Mar. 7 (Advt.), The light yarns are vibrated to cause them to intermesh in the fabric. **1948** M. J. Herskovits *Man & his Works* xiv. 215 To achieve some expression of the unities in culture by indicating how trait and complex and pattern ..intermesh, as the gears of some machine to constitute a smoothly running, effectively functioning whole. **1955** J. G. Davis *Dict. Dairying* (ed. 2) 153 The cylinders have square-cut threads which intermesh. **1957** G. E. Hutchinson *Treat. Limnol.* I. iii. 201 These chains form an intermeshed net and run in any direction in the free liquid. **1971** *Flying* Apr. 92/3 Medical records..are not yet intermeshed with airman records. **1971** T. F. Mitchell in *Archivum Linguisticum* II. 39 It should perhaps be said again that the aspects of meaning we are distinguishing intermesh and often meet in one text, in one sentence, even in one word or syllable.

intermetallic (intəɹmĭtæ·lik), *a.* Also **inter-metallic** (with hyphen). [f. Inter- 4 c + Metallic *a.* and *sb.*] Applied to compounds formed from two or more metals. Hence as *sb.*, an intermetallic compound.

1900 *Rep. Brit. Assoc. Adv. Sci. 1900* 131 Most students of alloys are now convinced that they often contain definite chemical compounds, yet these 'intermetallic' compounds are still passed over in silence by..books on descriptive chemistry. **1923** U. R. Evans *Metals & Metallic Compounds* I. 198 Inter-metallic compounds are rarely—if ever—formed between two metals belonging to the same group of the periodic table. **1937** *Chem. & Industry* XV. 677/1 A consideration of the formulæ of typical intermetallic compounds..shows at once that their formation is not governed by the simple rules of valency. **1956** *Nature* 10 Mar. 487/1 Its analysis is complicated by the presence of..intermetallics. **1962** Simpson & Richards *Junction Transistors* iii. 36 E.g. InP and GaAs among the intermetallic compounds. **1967** *New Scientist* 27 Apr. 209/2 Intermetallics are compounds of two or more metals, and are commonly found in alloys. **1972** *Sci. Amer.* Aug. 46/3 They have successfully synthesized intermetallic compounds in which the hydrogen is held in the form of hydrides.

intermezzo. 1. (Earlier example.)

1771 [see *bad *a.* 1 c].

inter-micellar: see *inter- *pref.* 4 a.

interministerial, *a.* Add: **2.** Involving the participation of two or more ministers or of the representatives of two or more departments of state; constituted from members of different departments of state.

1937 *Times* 30 Dec. 10/1 After a day of almost incessant inter-Ministerial consultation..the Government decided to take a firm line with the strikers. **1967** *Economist* 29 Apr. 477/1 A secret report on the labour market by the commissioner-general for national planning, M. Francois-Xavier Ortoli, is to be discussed by a special interministerial committee within the next 10 days. **1970** *Nature* 8 Aug. 544/2 In most countries..there is an inter-ministerial committee for science and technology.

intermission[1]. Add: **2.** *spec.* = the interval between the parts of a play, film, concert, etc. Chiefly *U.S.*

1927 *N.Y. World* 24 July, *Intermission*, interval. **1933** H. Footner *Ring of Eyes* xv. 104 When the curtain descended for the intermission, [etc.]. **1955** Keepnews & Grauer *Pict. Hist. Jazz* xvi. 197 Nick Rongetti..loved to join the intermission pianist. **1956** B. Holiday *Lady sings Blues* (1973) iii. 37 In between ups,..there was Garland Wilson at the piano for intermission. **1961** *Listener* 7 Dec. 1002/2 *Rocco* does have an intermission, but when a film is [etc.].

intermitotic (intəɹmaitǫ·tik), *a.* *Cytology.* Also **inter-mitotic.** [f. Inter- 4 b + Mitotic *a.*] Occurring or existing between mitoses; capable of dividing again. Also *absol.*, a cell which is capable of dividing again.

1942 E. V. Cowdry *Probl. Ageing* (ed. 2) xxiv. 627 The daughter epidermal cells that retain a basal location.. are comparatively undifferentiated and may be called vegetative intermitotics. *Ibid.*, The cells that are formed from vegetative intermitotics, and begin to differentiate, may also be intermitotic with lives extending from one mitosis to the next. Their lives are, however, different insofar that they exhibit increasing specialization. Consequently they may be designated differentiating intermitotics. **1948** W. Andrew tr. *E. D. P. de Robertis's Gen. Cytol.* xii. 324 Cowdry has classified cells into four groups on the basis of their degree of differentiation and ability to divide. The first group, vegetative intermitotic cells, comprises those undifferentiated cells which have the capacity to multiply continually. **1962** L. von Sallmann et al. in A. Pirie *Lens Metabolism Rel. Cataract* 449 The intermitotic, or turnover, time was estimated as 19 days for the equatorial zone..of the lens epithelium of young rats. **1964** G. H. Haggis et al. *Introd. Molecular Biol.* i. 13 The appearance of the inter-mitotic nucleus in living cells. **1968** M. W. Strickberger *Genetics* ii. 13 As compared to the period of active mitosis..the interphase or 'intermitotic' period of most cells is usually many times longer.

intermittency. Add: **2.** Special Comb.: **intermittency effect** *Photogr.*, the difference in the density of an emulsion when it is exposed intermittently from that resulting from a continuous exposure (the total light received being the same in both cases).

1907 Sheppard & Mees *Investigations Theory Photogr. Process* II. vi. 223 The intermittency effects are all in good agreement with this view, since the reverse reaction would have the greater effect, (*a*) the longer the pause, and (*b*) the more numerous the pauses, a pause being the period of no illumination. **1958** H. Baines *Sci. of Photogr.* xiv. 172 Another phenomenon now known to be closely connected with reciprocity failure is the intermittency effect.

intermittent, *a.* (*sb.*). Add: **A.** *adj.* **1. a.** *intermittent claudication*: see *claudication.

b. *intermittent movement* (see quot. 1959); *intermittent sterilization*, a microbiological procedure which accomplishes sterilization without using the high temperatures required to kill spores outright, and which involves alternately maintaining the materials to be sterilized at a temperature high enough to kill vegetative cells and at a much lower temperature during which germination of spores occurs (producing new vegetative cells to be killed during the next high-temperature period).

1893 tr. *W. Migula's Introd. Pract. Bacteriol.* ii. 41 The test-tubes containing the blood serum may be now subjected to 'fractional or intermittent sterilisation', by exposing them for an hour a day for eight days to a temperature of 58°C. **1959** W. S. Sharps *Dict. Cinematogr.* 104/1 *Intermittent movement*, the term used for the method of film transport in a camera, projector or printer, whereby the film is moved intermittently and only exposed to light when stationary. **1969** S. T. Lyles *Biol. Microorganisms* v. 130 Intermittent sterilization may be accomplished by boiling or steaming in the autoclave at O pressure.

intermodal (intəɹmōu·dăl), *a.* Also **inter-modal** (with hyphen). [f. Inter- + Mod(e *sb.* 4 + -al.] Of the conveyance of goods: making use of differing modes of transport during the journey between the place of dispatch and the destination. Hence **intermo·dally** *adv.*

1963 A. H. Norling *Future U.S. Transportation Needs* (NASA Rep. N-64-25006) VIII-4 The elimination of the wasteful, duplicative handling now required in the intermodal transfer of goods will call for the increased use of containerized shipments. **1967** *Containerization* (McKinsey & Co.) 27 Low-cost intermodal transfer makes it economic to switch modes to take advantage of the lowest cost alternative. **1968** *Economist* 14 Sept. p. xxxiv, The sea-going container will fit nicely into the big aircraft, and hey presto we have real 'intermodal' transport. **1969** *Jane's Freight Containers 1968–69* 3/2 This subject is part of the legal issues arising in connection with combined or inter-modal transport in general. **1970** *Commercial Motor* 25 Sept. 133/1 The exhibition is by no means limited to container traffic and equipment, but will deal with all the intermodal systems currently available. **1970** *Times* 16 Sept. (Road Haulage Suppl.) p. vii/8 By the mid 1970s, more than 1 m. containers will be circulating intermodally on an international basis. **1971** Johnson & Garnett *Econ. of Containerisation* i. 11 It [*sc.* containerization] has been standardised, making it intermodal: i.e. a container can be carried by almost any mode of transport and easily transhipped between modes. **1972** *Times* 29 Sept. 20/6 The association gives a warning that attempts to take over small ports are likely to result in 'some quite extraordinary distortions of the inter-modal transport patterns'.

intermodulation (iːntəɹmǫdiulē·ʃən). *Electr. Engin.* [f. Inter- 2 a + Modulation.] Modulation of the sinusoidal components of a signal or wave-form by one another, a kind of distortion that produces new components with frequencies equal to the sums and differences of those already present. Freq. *attrib.*, esp. in *intermodulation distortion.*

1931 *Inst. Radio Engin. Year Bk.* 50 Intermodulation is the production, in a non-linear circuit element, of frequencies corresponding to the sums and differences of the fundamentals and harmonies of two or more frequencies which are transmitted to that element. **1940** *Chambers's Techn. Dict.* 454/1 Intermodulation distortion. **1950** K. Henney *Radio Engin. Handbk.* (ed. 4) xvii. 854 These frequencies resulting from intermodulation are generally inharmonic or discordant and also likely to fall in the middle or upper portion of the audio range, both of which conditions make them quite objectionable. **1958** *Engineering* 31 Jan. 160/2 If two musical tones are applied, both appear at the output with all their combination tones (intermodulation products). **1964** R. F. Ficchi *Electr. Interference* iii. 24 The mixing of at least two signals in a nonlinear device which causes intermodulation distortion and results in the generation of harmonics should not be permitted. **1971** *Sci. Amer.* Sept. 178/1 (Advt.), That's 250 watts..over the whole power-pushin' listening range. Right through from 20 Hz to 20,000 kHz [*sic*] with total harmonic and intermodulation distortion at less than 0·1%!

intermolecular, *a.* Add: Hence **intermole·cularly** *adv.*, between molecules.

1936, 1971 [see *intramolecular *a.*]. **1973** *Nature* 13 Apr. 473/2 In a condensed phase, initially formed vibrational excited 'states' are coupled intra- and intermolecularly..to a quasi-continuum of other vibrational 'states'.

intermontane (intəɹmǫ·ntēin), *a.* [f. Inter- 4 a + Montane *a.*] Situated or lying between mountains. Also **i·ntermont, intermou·ntain** *adjs.*

1807 J. Mease *Geol. Acct. U.S.* 59 Whatever of saline.. the soil of the upland contains, is thus floated or rolled along to the low lands, and constitutes with proportional diversity and mixture, the intermontane soil. **1828** Webster, Intermontane. **1900** *Congress. Rec.* 24 Jan. 1147/2 Polygamy..was taught by the Mormon Church throughout the whole of the intermountain country as a religious duty. **1901** *Science* 8 Mar. 396/1 The erosion of narrow valleys in the floor of the weak-rock intermont peneplains. **1902** *Encycl. Brit.* XXV. 362/2 The intermontane basins and the piedmontese plains that slope eastward from the Rocky Mountains in middle latitudes are treeless. **1903** *Science* 12 June 950/1 The study of the anthropology of the Indian races in this intermountain region. **1911** J. L. Myres *Dawn of History* iv. 91 We are ..concerned..with the intermont plains and upland valleys which sustained the old Medes and Persians. **1920** L. V. Pirsson *Textbk. Geol.* (ed. 2) I. 269 Intermontane Plateaus. **1927** *Glasgow Herald* 21 May 8 This fungus.. attacks both the green or Oregon and the blue or Colorado Douglas [fir], as well as the intermountain variety. **1936** *Geogr. Jrnl.* LXXXVII. 27 Coarse detritus which came to rest in the intermont basins. **1959** Wooldridge & Morgan *Outl. Geomorphol.* (ed. 2) xx. 285 Plains are here in a much less dominant rôle; we have an intermont-basin landscape as compared with a true Inselberge landscape. **1962** G. MacEwan *Blazing Old Cattle Trail* xxv. 167 Ranching of western Canada's prairie, foothill and intermountain ranges was just two or three decades old. **1965** G. J. Williams *Econ. Geol. N.Z.* xviii. 297/1 The Tertiary-filled intermontane basin is 50 miles long and averages 15 miles in width.

inter-morainic, -mutule: see *inter- *pref.* 4 a, 3 a.

intern. B. *sb.* For *U.S.* read Chiefly *U.S.* Also **interne.** Now usu., a recent medical graduate who is working under supervision in a hospital (and often living there) as part of his training, prior to entering general practice or becoming a resident. (Broadly equivalent to a houseman in Great Britain.) Also *transf.*, used of individuals in other professions (esp. teaching) who are receiving practical experience under supervision. (Examples.)

Freq. pronounced with stress on first syllable.

[**1699** M. Lister *Journey to Paris* (ed. 3) 74 Monsieur du Pes Surgeon Interne of the Hôtel-dieu.] **1879** in Webster Suppl. **1889** *Kansas City* (Missouri) *Times & Star* 16 Oct., Convalescent women and young nurses are given too much freedom with the internes. **1890** W. James *Princ. Psychol.* I. x. 385 His brother, Dr. Jules Janet..was *interne* at the Salpêtrière Hospital. **1914** M. Gerry *Masks of Love* 123 The young interne..had alarmed them. **1938** *Amer. Speech* XIII. 228/1 *Resident* ranks over *intern* by reason of experience, but both are medical school graduates studying in the hospital. **1955** W. Gaddis *Recognitions* I. i. 41 Physicians, technicians, and internes X-rayed the boy from every possible angle. **1961** J. Heller *Catch-22* (1962) xviii. 175 In the morning a helpful young English intern popped in to ask him about his liver. **1963** A. Beales *Educ. under Penalty* I. ii. 18 In the field of lay education the loss caused by the dissolution was less than formerly supposed, since the monasteries had long ceased, most of them, to teach any but interns. **1967** Mrs. L. B. Johnson *White House Diary* 14 Mar. (1970) 497 One intern was giving remedial reading. **1969** *Eugene* (Oregon) *Register-Guard* 3 Dec. 1A/3 Representing Springfield teachers are Rita Castleberry, Lee Elementary School instructor; Roy Van Horn, principal at Mt. Vernon Elementary School, and Moore, who is intern teacher supervisor at Lee Elementary School. **1970** *Toronto Daily Star* 24 Sept. 31/6 (Advt.), Broderick Crawford..gives young intern Steve Brooks some food for thought. **1972** *Nature* 4 Feb. 291/2 Doctor of medicine and intern of the hospitals of Lyon, in 1908 Professor Lacassagne entered the Laboratory of Histology to work under the direction of Claudius Regaud.

Hence **inte·rnship, interneship,** the position or station of an intern; the period of such a position. Chiefly *U.S.*

1904 *Jrnl. Amer. Med. Assoc.* 13 Aug. 469/2 From one to two years of what might be called practical apprenticeship is the privilege sought by the earnest [medical] student. To gain this privilege he..delays for the period of his interneship his start in the world and his establishment

in his profession. **1924** *Scribner's Mag.* Feb. 183/1 My father, who had the practice..told me the story in professional confidence... I was at that time just finishing my internship. **1934** A. WOOLLCOTT *While Rome Burns* 46 The fiery young doctor, in the days of his interneship, had already tasted the experience of spending two months in the lockup. **1938** *Internships & Residences in N.Y. City, 1934–1937* p. xxvii, An internship is a period of service as a member of the hospital staff while residing in the hospital and receiving a period of formal education subsequent to graduation from medical school. **1948** *Training of a Doctor* (B.M.A.) xxxii. 127 This prescribed period of compulsory pre-registration house-appointments corresponds to the post known in America as an 'internship', and the period is called 'the intern year'. **1957** KENDALL & SELVIN in R. K. Merton *Student-Physician* 155 Nearly every medical student is required to take an internship when he has completed medical school, regardless of his plans for his later career. **1968** *Globe & Mail* (Toronto) 17 Feb. 50 (Advt.), The internship plan for the training of elementary school teachers. **1968** *New Scientist* 14 Nov. 388/2 One suggestion is very similar to the principle of our sandwich systems, under the more anaesthetised name of an 'internship'. **1971** *Black Scholar* June 62/1 (Advt.), An individually tailored, accelerated career program which begins with a two-year internship and leads to positions of increasing responsibility in the developing countries. **1971** *Nature* 1 Oct. 301/1 The money will be used to establish internships in federally funded laboratories for some 420 young unemployed scientists and engineers who hold advanced degrees.

intern, *v.* Add: **4.** (Usu. pronounced with stress on first syllable.) *intr.* To act as an intern. *U.S.*

1933 S. KINGSLEY *Men in White* I. i. 24 You interned here? **1969** *Eugene* (Oregon) *Register-Guard* 3 Dec. 5D/1 He..interned at Cook County Hospital in Chicago for one year. **1971** 'D. SHANNON' *Murder with Love* (1972) v. 83 Harlow interned at the General... He had the makings of a very fine surgeon.

internal, *a.* and *sb.* Add: **A.** *adj.* **1. a.** *internal object*: in *Psychoanalysis*, the inward image formed of an object invested with the emotional energy which would normally have been expended on the object itself.

1940 *Internat. Jrnl. Psycho-Anal.* XXI. 280 (*title*) Temper tantrums in early childhood in their relation to internal objects. **1949** *Brit. Jrnl. Med. Psychol.* XXII. 13 Thus we see the internal object represents also the child himself. **1973** H. SEGAL *Introd. Work M. Klein* (new ed.) ii. 12 These internal objects are not 'objects' situated in the body or the psyche: like Freud, Melanie Klein is describing unconscious phantasies which people have about what they contain.

2. a. *spec.* in *Philos.*, as *internal property, relation*: a property or relation which belongs essentially to an object or proposition.

1883 F. H. BRADLEY *Princ. Logic* 432 As the material supplied is in each case different, so again the product is not the same. In one case the whole precedes and is followed by its internal relations. **1920** G. E. MOORE in *Proc. Aristotelian Soc.* XX. 40 (*title*) External and internal relations. *Ibid.* 41 And I shall maintain that, if we give to the assertion that a relation is 'internal' the meaning which this proposition would give to it, then..*some* relations are 'internal'. **1922** tr. *Wittgenstein's Tractatus* 4. 122 Instead of property of the structure I also say 'internal property'; instead of relation of structures 'internal relation'. **1937** A. SMEATON tr. *Carnap's Logical Syntax of Lang.* v. § 79. 304 The numerous discussions and controversies about external and internal properties and relations. **1959** R. WOLLHEIM *F. H. Bradley* iii. 92 The most important of them all, the doctrine of Internal Relations. **1966** *Amer. Philos. Q.* III. 45/1 This forces one to acknowledge that a thing changes when what it is related to changes. In short one is involved with *internal relations.*

b. *internal revenue*: revenue derived from duties and taxes imposed on domestic trade and commerce; inland revenue. *U.S.*

1796 *Deb. Congress U.S.* 26 Feb. 379 Mr. W. Smith moved the order of the day on the report of the Committee of Ways and Means on the Internal Revenue. **1873** *Newton Kansan* 2 Jan. 2/1 The most important bills ..are those reducing the internal revenue force. **1959** *Chambers's Encycl.* VII. 417/1 In the United States collection is made by the Bureau of Internal Revenue. **1972** *Lebende Sprachen* XVII. 34/1 US internal revenue—BE inland revenue.

5. Special collocations: **internal clock,** a person's innate sense of time; = **biological clock*; **internal-combustion,** used *attrib.* to designate any engine in which combustion of the fuel takes place inside it in the chamber where the force is developed (or a part continuous with it); also *fig.*; **internal conversion** *Physics*, (*a*) the process whereby the whole energy of a gamma-ray photon emitted by a nucleus is given up to an orbital electron, causing its emission from the atom; (*b*) (see quot. 1972[2]); **internal energy,** the energy possessed by a physical system in consequence of the positions and relative motions and interactions of its component parts: a function of its state (usu. of undefined absolute magnitude) such that any change in the function is equal to the sum of the heat absorbed by the system and the work done on it; **internal friction,** resistance to the deformation or flow of a substance that occurs inside it with the production of heat, and arises from the relative motion of adjacent parts; **internal medicine** = MEDICINE *sb.*[1] 1 (in the 'more restricted sense'); **internal phloem** (see quot. 1933); **internal pressure,** the pressure which exists within a fluid arising from intermolecular attraction; **internal secretion** *Physiol.* [tr. F. *sécrétion interne* (C. Bernard *Leçons sur les Propriétés physiol. des Liquides de l'Organisme* (1859) II. xvii. 408)], any secretion that is delivered into the internal environment of the body, esp. into the blood stream; *spec.* a hormone; also, the process of secreting in this manner; **internal stress,** stress that arises inside a substance (e.g. as a result of differential heating of different parts) and is not imposed from without; **internal wave,** any transverse wave occurring within a fluid either along the interface between layers of different density or within a layer having a vertical density gradient.

1960 I. JEFFERIES *Dignity & Purity* vi. 123, I suppose he works according to his own internal clock. **1974** *Guardian* 28 Jan. 8/3 If a programme is on too late for our internal clocks, we would almost rather it were not shown at all. **1884** H. C. F. JENKIN in *Heat in its Mech. Applications* (Inst. Civil Engin.) (1885) 105 The internal combustion engine..is really the fore-runner of the gas-engine. **1921** W. H. BERRY *Mod. Motor Car Pract.* i. 14 In effect liquid fuel made the internal combustion motor practicable for locomotive purposes, its essential qualities being that it can be easily stored and carried, and be readily converted into an explosive gas ignitable within the cylinder. **1949** D. G. SHEPHERD *Introd. Gas Turbine* i. 1 The gas turbine, in common with other forms of internal combustion engines, converts heat into work by a cycle using a gas as the working medium, the processes being compression, addition of heat and expansion, and requiring continuous flow of the gas during these changes of state. **1951** M. MCLUHAN *Mech. Bride* 113/2 What Kipling was to the aggressive British imperialists, these ads are to our domestic economy. They act as a sort of firing spark in the internal combustion engine. **1967** E. DELMAR-MORGAN *Maintenance Inboard Engines* i. 19 Within the broad category of the internal-combustion engine there are the spark-ignition engine (petrol and paraffin) and the compression ignition (diesel). **1927** *Proc. R. Soc.* A. CXVI. 491 (*heading*) The internal conversion of γ-rays. **1927** *Proc. Cambr. Philos. Soc.* 718 The homogeneous groups in the β-ray spectra are due to the conversion of the γ-rays, and the intensities of these groups depend not only on the intensities of these γ-rays but also on the extent to which they are converted, that is the magnitude of the internal conversion coefficient. **1949** P. PRINGSHEIM *Fluorescence & Phosphorescence* iii. 272 Since no light emission accompanies the transition from the higher electronic state to the emitting state, the transition must correspond to a process of internal conversion. **1955** R. D. EVANS *Atomic Nucleus* i. 23 The second general class of nuclear transitions which invariably result in X-ray-emission spectra is the internal-conversion transitions... Internal conversion..often predominates over γ-ray emission if the nuclear excitation energy is small and the angular-momentum change is large. **1959** *Q. Rev.* XIII. 5 The strong fluorescence indicates that internal conversion does not take place as often as would be expected. **1972** H. A. ENGE et al. *Introd. Atomic Physics* xii. 386 Internal conversion competes with gamma emission, and the ratio of the probabilities of the two processes depends strongly upon the multipolarity. **1972** C. H. J. WELLS *Introd. Molecular Photochem.* iii. 34 Internal conversion (ic) is the term given to the radiationless process whereby a molecule transfers from one electronic state to another electronic state of the same multiplicity. **1887** *Encycl. Brit.* XXII. 480/1 Since the gas had neither gained nor lost heat, and had done no work, its internal energy was the same at the end as at the beginning of the experiment. **1921** A. W. JUDGE *Automobile & Aircraft Engines* ii. 60 The internal energy of a given quantity of gas depends only upon its temperature. **1927** H. S. TAYLOR *Elem. Physical Chem.* ii. 64 The internal energies of the gas in the two states may include the energy resultant from such factors as motion and position of the molecules, molecular attraction, intramolecular forces, intra-atomic vibrations, chemical and other unknown forces. We therefore note that the absolute magnitudes..are not ascertainable. The change of internal energy, ΔU, is definite and measurable. **1966** *McGraw-Hill Encycl. Sci. & Technol.* VII. 209/1 The change in internal energy is fixed by the initial and final states, and is independent of the path by which the change in state is accomplished. **1972** A. L. RUOFF *Introd. Materials Sci.* iv. 159 The change in internal energy associated with stress, electric and magnetic fields is due to the work done on the material. **1860** *Phil. Mag.* XIX. 20 The internal friction of gases. **1875** *Encycl. Brit.* III. 39/2 The compressed gas expanded to twice its volume, and the work of expansion..was soon converted into heat by the internal friction of the gas. **1922** GLAZEBROOK *Dict. Appl. Physics* I. 351/1 The characteristics of the internal friction of fluids when the general motion is eddying or turbulent. **1931** [see *internal wave* below]. **1958** *Jrnl. Iron & Steel Inst.* CXC. 93/2 Stress relaxation across grain boundaries and phase interfaces, an important source of internal friction, is considered. [**1894** GOULD *Dict. Med.* 735/1 On the European continent it is customary to divide medicine into internal and external, the former implying the restricted sense of the term, or the study of diseases of internal organs.] **1904** STEDMAN *Dunglison's Dict. Med. Sci.* (ed. 23) 583/2 *I[nternal] medicine*, that branch of medicine which has to do with diseases of the body not amenable to operative treatment; medicine as contrasted with surgery. **1968** TALSO & REMENCHIK (*title*) Internal medicine, based on mechanisms of disease. **1933** *Tropical Woods* XXXVI. 3 Internal Phloem.—Primary phloem internal to the primary xylem. (To replace *Intraxylary Phloem.*) **1953** K. ESAU *Plant Anat.* xii. 268 In angiosperms the internal phloem is initiated somewhat later than the external. **1967** S. BROIDO-ALTMAN tr. *Fahn's Plant Anat.* xi. 167 The internal phloem may be present as separate strands on the border of the pith. **1911** *Trans. Faraday Soc.* VII. 94 It is therefore immaterial..whether we fix our attention on the internal pressure or on the thermal pressure, which acts in the opposite sense. **1940** GLASSTONE *Text-bk. Physical Chem.* vii. 472 The internal pressure of naphthalene is about 3600 atm., so that the forces of cohesion in liquids are evidently very large. **1973** A. W. ADAMSON *Textbk. Physical Chem.* iv. 151 The internal pressure is zero for an ideal gas and for most real gases it is small compared to *P* [*sc.* the measured pressure]. **1895** *Brit. Med. Jrnl.* 10 Aug. 341/1 On the other hand, some secreted materials are not poured out upon an external surface at all, but are returned to the blood. These may be termed internal secretions. **1921** I. G. COBB *Organs Internal Secretion* (ed. 3) i. 19 The term hormone is in more or less general use to denote an internal secretion. **1924** A. LIPSCHÜTZ *Internal Secretions Sex Glands* p. vi, Prof. Starling suggested the term 'hormone' for the active principles of those internal secretions which act as chemical messengers. **1926** J. S. HUXLEY *Ess. Pop. Sci.* 203 Claude Bernard introduced physiology to the general idea of internal secretion. **1941** R. G. HOSKINS *Endocrinol.* i. 20 Usually, however, formal credit for first demonstrating the process of internal secretion is given to Claude Bernard, who in 1848 reported the discovery that sugar stored in the liver in the form of glycogen is discharged as dextrose directly into the blood rather than through the ducts of the organ after the fashion of an ordinary secreting gland. The term 'internal secretion' is no longer applied to substances like sugar, but is restricted to those having a more specific regulatory function. **1966** W. S. HOAR *Gen. & Compar. Physiol.* ii. 34 As a matter of fact, the first internal secretion conclusively demonstrated was the hormone secretion produced by the wall of the gut. **1904** GOODCHILD & TWENEY *Technol. & Sci. Dict.* 313/1 Internal stress. **1906** *Jrnl. Iron & Steel Inst.* LXXII. 608 (*heading*) Internal stresses and strains in iron and steel. **1923** GLAZEBROOK *Dict. Appl. Physics* V. 344/1 Carpenter and Edwards argue that in quenching steel these internal stresses cause internal straining of the metal. **1950** *Jrnl. Iron & Steel Inst.* CLXIV. 166/2 In a partially transformed steel, the volume changes accompanying transformation presumably set up a system of internal stresses. **1931** *Rapports et Proc.-Verb. des Réunions Conseil Perm. Internat. Explor. Mer* LXXVI. 5 (*heading*) On internal waves. *Ibid.* 10 Free internal waves must abate owing to internal friction and eddy-viscosity. **1966** *McGraw-Hill Encycl. Sci. & Technol.* XIV. 417/2 Internal waves have been found in the atmosphere as lee waves (waves in the wind stream down-wind from a mountain) and as waves propagated along an inversion layer. **1966** R. W. FAIRBRIDGE *Encycl. Oceanogr.* 402 Internal waves are subsurface waves found between layers of different density or within layers where vertical density gradients are present. They can exist in any stratified fluid and can be caused by flow over an irregular bottom, atmospheric disturbances, tidal forces, and shear flow.

internalization. (Later examples.)

1942 *Internat. Jrnl. Psycho-Anal.* XXIII. 8 (*title*) A contribution to the problem of sublimation and its relation to processes of internalization. **1952** GERTH & MARTINDALE tr. *Weber's Anc. Judaism* IV. xii. 328 For Jeremiah this internalization..went hand in hand with the formation of quite modest external hopes. **1954** T. GRYGIER *Oppression* I. i. 8 Civilization takes certain measures to check it [*sc.* aggression]. The most important is the introjection or internalization of aggressiveness. **1964** M. ARGYLE *Psychol. & Social Probl.* i. 20 Such people often behave differently when away from the group—they are showing overt compliance without internalization, and we should only speak of learning taking place when there is also internalization. **1970** P. KELVIN *Bases of Social Behaviour* ix. 281 'Internalization' here refers to the process and condition whereby the norms of the group or society become the individual's own norms, whether of behaviour or of values. **1971** *Sci. Amer.* Sept. 192/3 One method of fostering the incorporation of technology assessment into their decisional processes would involve the internalization of costs. **1973** *Nature* 20 Apr. 488/1 The most economical way of controlling both pollution and congestion in cities must depend on what the economists call an internalization of the externalities—making the motorist bear not merely the costs of operating his vehicle but the costs of what he does to other people.

internalize, *v.* Add: *spec.* **a.** *Psychol.* To transfer to a subjectively formed image (the emotions connected with some object) (see also *INTROJECT *v.*); to adopt or incorporate as one's own (the values, etc., of a social group).

1942 *Internat. Jrnl. Psycho-Anal.* XXIII. 15/1 The atonement for guilt is here carried out by internalizing the attacked external object. **1950** BETTELHEIM & SYLVESTER in P. Greenacre et al. *Psychoanal. Study Child* V. 330 While their own actions are motivated by 'what will get by'..they demand that he himself be guided by 'what is right'... The child who tries to internalize these discrepant demands is confronted by a seemingly insoluble conflict. **1958** M. ARGYLE *Relig. Behaviour* v. 42 The suggestion that Protestants internalize the super-ego to a greater extent. **1960** KOESTLER *Lotus & Robot* II. viii. 203 The chances are that his aggressive impulses.. will be internalized and deflected against himself. **1968** J. M. ZIMAN *Public Knowl.* v. 77 He must internalize the scientific attitude so that he cannot even conceive of, say, ..recording the epoch of an eclipse by reference to the age of the reigning monarch. **1971** *Black Scholar* June 7/1 Some [black women] even internalize white society's low regard for black men.

b. *Linguistics.* To acquire knowledge of (a

set of rules in a given language): used esp. of the language-learning procedures of a child.

1965 [implied in quots. for *INTERNALIZED *ppl. a.*]. **1968** CHOMSKY & HALLE *Sound Pattern Eng.* 3 The person who has acquired knowledge of a language has internalized a system of rules. **1971** D. CRYSTAL *Ling.* iii. 104 We have mastered ('internalized' is a word often used here) a technique for breaking each new sentence up.

c. *Econ.* To incorporate (costs) as part of the internal cost structure, esp. 'social' costs, resulting from the use or manufacture of a particular product.

1971 *Sci. Amer.* Aug. 44/3 The first is the alteration of the ground rules and incentives under which the market operates by such devices as taxes, subsidies, and judicial actions to internalize (i.e., make explicit) social costs. *Ibid.* Sept. 194/2 A consideration of means whereby the legal system can internalize costs that power companies have been allowed to treat as external and therefore to exclude from their cost-benefit calculations.

internalized (intə·ɹnăləizd), *ppl. a.* [f. the vb.] Made internal, acquired or mastered internally. Also in other senses of the vb.

1932 A. STRACHEY tr. *Klein's Psycho-Anal. Children* vii. 169 The boy could not maintain this alliance with a cruel external super-ego against his id and his internalized objects. **1942** *Internat. Jrnl. Psycho-Anal.* XXIII. 9/2 The connection between her phantasies about internalized objects and her artistic productivity. **1959** *Psychiatry* XXII. 290 The successfully treated patient comes to be his own critic, using in relation to himself evaluations previously consensually validated with the therapist and hence perpetuating the relationship in an internalized form. **1964** M. ARGYLE *Psychol. & Social Probl.* iv. 54 There is considerable evidence that the stronger the forces which are restraining aggression—whether external fear of punishment or internalized anxiety about aggression—then the more remote the displaced aggression will be. **1965** N. CHOMSKY *Aspects of Theory of Syntax* 21 Few hearers may be aware..that their internalized grammar ..provides at least three structural descriptions for this sentence. **1965** H. A. GLEASON *Ling. & Eng. Gram.* 476 This means strengthened competence in the student's internalized grammar of literary English. **1968** CHOMSKY & HALLE *Sound Pattern Eng.* 3 New utterances..are formed and interpreted by the same grammar, the same internalized system of rules. **1971** *Sci. Amer.* Sept. 194/2 The company may merely pay the internalized costs (whether they are in the form of a judgment for damages, a tax or a negotiated payment), absorbing the payment or passing it on to customers.

international, *a.* (*sb.*) Add: **A.** *adj.* **1. a.** (Later examples.)

1948 *Written Statement U.K.* 11 Dec. in *I.C.J. Pleadings* I. v. 25 Does the United Nations possess international personality? **1959** R. A. GRAHAM *Vatican Diplomacy* vii. 185 After 1870... Could the papacy..be properly regarded as a member of the international community of the law of nations? This was tantamount to asking whether the papacy had 'international personality'. **1963** T. TULLETT *Inside Interpol* ii. 22 What is, in actual fact, an 'international criminal'? The definition of this type of wrongdoer is not based on any legal concept.. but simply on practical convenience. **1970** D. W. GREIG *Internat. Law* iii. 73 The brief statement that an international person is an entity having the power of independent action on the international plane has the obvious advantage of including not only states, but also communities like 'protected states'. **1971** *Mod. Law Rev.* XXXIV. VI. 599 A country may be sovereign in the sense that it satisfies the international law criteria for independent statehood and is recognized as independent by the international community. *Ibid.* 613 The sovereignty of the United Kingdom as an international person has been abridged..a..formidable camel for a court to swallow. **1974** *Times* 15 Feb. 14/1 Renegotiation of our membership of the European Community..will add yet another uncertainty to international relations.

c. Applied to various units of physical quantities (now mostly obsolete) agreed upon by different nations, and in some cases forming part of the formal name of a unit, so as to distinguish it from a unit numerically similar but differently defined; *international system* (*of units*) (usu. with capital initials) [tr. F. *système international d'unités*], a system of physical units (together with a set of prefixes indicating multiplication or division by a power of ten) based on the metre, kilogramme, second, ampere, kelvin, candela, and mole as independent basic units, with each of the derived units defined in terms of these without any multiplying factor.

Quot. 1932 represents an isolated and fortuitous use of *international system of units*, unrelated to the later Système International.

1893 *Electrician* 29 Sept. 578/2 To distinguish these units as now defined from the definitions given by previous meetings or Congresses, they are denominated the 'international' ohm, the 'international' ampere, &c. **1908** *Nature* 29 Oct. 678/2 The international ohm is the resistance offered to an unvarying electric current by a column of mercury at the temperature of melting ice, 14·4521 grams in mass, of a constant cross-sectional area, and of a length of 106·300 centimetres. *Ibid.* 679/1 The difference between the ohm and the international ohm remains a matter for experiment. **1909** *Engineering* 17 Sept. 397/2 The British Committee..now have the honour to submit..that the name 'International Candle' be adopted. **1924** A. W. SMITH *Electr. Measurements* (ed. 2) i. 3 In practical measurements the electron current is measured in international amperes. **1932** *Phil. Mag.* XIV. 292 The international system of [electrical] units differs but little from the practical system, and the two may be taken as identical for the present purpose. **1934** *Brit. Inst. Radiol. Year Bk.* 39 The International Unit of X-radiation shall be called the 'Röntgen'. **1937** *Discovery* Sept. 285/2 Last month, the first international conference on acoustics met in Paris...Thanks in particular to the conciliatory attitude of the delegates of Germany and the United States the 'phon' and the 'decibel' become international units. **1938** G. P. HARNWELL *Princ. Electr. & Electromagn.* 602 It is evident that 1 international volt is equal to 1·00043 absolute volts, 1 international joule is equal to 1·00034 absolute or mechanical joules, etc. [**1957** *Proc.-Verb. du Comité Internat. Poids et Mesures, 1956* 81 Après discussion, la Commission adopte la dénomination de 'Système International d'Unités'.] **1957** *Nature* 21 Dec. 1388/1, 1 A. becomes, by definition, equal to 10^{-10} m. exactly. It may be recalled that the value λ_R = 6438·4696 A. was adopted as the spectroscopic reference standard in 1907 and thereby became the means of defining the international angstrom—the unit that has since served for all spectroscopic measurements of wave-length. **1961** *Ibid.* 21 Jan. 196/2 Among other scientific resolutions adopted by the Conference [*sc.* the eleventh General Conference of Weights and Measures] are the following... Approval of a detailed list of the international system of units (designation *SI*) founded on six basic units (metre, kilogram, second, ampere, degree Kelvin and candela). **1967** A. J. LISSAMAN *Metrology* i. 5 The U.K., U.S.A., Canada, Australia, New Zealand and South Africa have agreed to adopt an international yard based upon the metre. **1971** P. VIGOUREUX *Units & Standards for Electromagn.* ii. 11 The hour, the day and the year, so long established and in such common use, will undoubtedly outlive the International System.

2. Special collocations: **International Brigade,** a body of volunteers, raised internationally by foreign Communist parties, although open to non-Communists, with the purpose of fighting for the Republic in the Spanish Civil War of 1936–39; also *transf.*; hence **International Brigader; international code,** a code of signals by which seamen of all nations can hold communication at sea; **international copyright,** the protection of literary and artistic property by international agreement, particularly the Berne Convention of 1885, which led to the foundation of the International Copyright Union, and the Universal Copyright Convention of 1952; **International Court of Justice,** a judicial court of the United Nations which replaced the Cour Permanente de Justice in 1945; **international date-line,** the date-line (see DATE *sb.*[2] 8) in the Pacific Ocean; **international driving licence, permit,** a licence allowing the holder to drive a specified class of vehicle in foreign countries; **international Gothic,** name given to a style of Gothic art which spread across western Europe in the late 14th and early 15th centuries; also called *international style*; **International Monetary Fund,** an organization having a monetary pool on which member nations can draw, established in 1945 to promote international trade and stabilization of currencies; **international orange,** a bright orange colour, visible from a great distance; **International Phonetic Alphabet,** a set of phonetic symbols for international use, introduced in the late 19th century by the International Phonetic Association: constructed on the basis of the Roman and Greek alphabets with the addition of some special symbols and diacritical marks; **international style,** name given to a naturalistic style of twentieth-century architecture associated esp. with Walter Gropius (1883–1969) and his associates; also (*rare*) = **international Gothic*; **international unit,** (*a*) *Physics* (see sense *A. c above); (*b*) *Biol.* and *Med.*, a unit of activity or potency of sera, hormones, vitamins, etc., defined individually for each substance in terms of the activity of a standard quantity or preparation.

1937 'G. ORWELL' *Let.* 9 May in *Coll. Ess.* (1968) I. 267 Owing partly to an accident I joined the POUM militia instead of the International Brigade, which..meant that I have never seen the Madrid front. **1968** K. MARTIN *Editor* x. 214 The International Brigade..came from every part of Europe and America. **1968** *N.Y. Rev. Books* 11 Apr. 42/3 Genuine American patriots must.. work for the downfall of American imperialism even if this means joining international brigades should the Vietnamese request them. **1972** *N.Y. Times* 3 Nov. 2/2 Well-known as a writer, Mr. Popovic studied philosophy in Paris before World War II and later fought in the International Brigades during the Spanish Civil War. **1949** KOESTLER *Promise & Fulfilment* vi. 57 This same argument..has served the Soviet Government as a constant pretext for refusing to admit..International Brigaders.. into Soviet territory. **1885** H. PAASCH *From Keel to Truck* 161/1 *Signal*,..international code of signals. **1961** F. H. BURGESS *Dict. Sailing* 121 *International code of signals*, the system of signals adopted for use between ships and shore stations of all nations, with simplicity of use in coding and decoding in any language. **1838** *Act* 1 *& 2 Vict.* c. 59 An act for securing to Authors, in certain Cases, the Benefit of International Copyright. **1844** *Act* 7 *& 8 Vict.* c. 12. § 1 Which Act [*sc.* 1 & 2 Vict. c. 59] is herein-after, for the sake of Perspicuity, designated as 'the International Copyright Act'. **1894** in H. Paasch *From Keel to Truck* (ed. 2) (title-page), Protected by International Copyright. **1901** *Empire Rev.* May 364 A book is subject to national copyright..and also to international copyright in the several countries admitting that right. **1942** *Times Lit. Suppl.* 14 Nov. 559/3 The last International Copyright Convention, signed at Berne in 1908, afforded a very considerable degree of protection to the literary and artistic property belonging to the nationals of those countries which signed it. **1971** E. P. SKONE JAMES *Copinger & Skone James on Copyright* (ed. 11) xxiv. 435 International copyright is concerned with treaties or conventions between nations requiring their signatories to respect, in their own countries, the copyright of nationals of other signatories. **1945** *Times* 10 Sept. 2/5 The nomination of candidates to the posts of Judge of the International Court of Justice. **1972** *Mod. Law Rev.* XXXV. I. 52 In the North Sea Continental Shelf Cases the International Court of Justice had the opportunity of considering this phenomenon. **1973** *Times* 15 May 6/4 Mr van der Stoel is in favour of increasing the powers of the International Court of Justice at The Hague so that countries which accept its jurisdiction in principle cannot, as Iceland has done recently and France now threatens to do, disregard the court's competence to judge a case which may turn out wrongly for them. **1910** *Encycl. Brit.* II. 134/1 The so-called 'International Date Line'..is..practically only due to American initiative. **1957** VON ENGELN & NETSCHERT *Gen. Geogr.* iv. 71/2 The international date line does not coincide with 180° meridian..but zigzags to give portions of the same political territories the same date. **1966** MRS. L. B. JOHNSON *White House Diary* 2 Nov. (1970) 453 Sometime in the dark hours over the Pacific we had crossed the International Dateline. **1931** *Automobile Assoc. Foreign Touring Guide* 19 The International Driving Permit acts as a driving licence in all the countries recognising the International Certificate for Motor Vehicles. **1966** R. E. PICKERING *Himself Again* x. 67 Do you have an international driving licence? **1966** A. A. RANDALL *Flashpoint* ii. 41 The two men book a passage on the Car Sleeper Express from Boulogne to Narbonne... You bring the Car Temporary Exportation Certificate, International Driving Permits and Insurance Green Card. **1951** M. DAVIES *Nat. Gallery Catal. Earlier Italian Schools* 280 They [*sc.* works by Master of the Bambino Vispo] are somewhat related to Lorenzo Monaco in style, and are even more markedly in the 'International Gothic' current. **1959** P. & L. MURRAY *Dict. Art & Artists* 199 Masolino may have worked under Ghiberti on the First Baptistry Doors..and this would explain his normal International Gothic style. **1961** H. E. SCOTT tr. *Chiarelli's European Painting 15th Cent.* 10 In international Gothic painting there is a contrast between a growing interest in naturalism..and..a transference of natural forms into abstract figures which are frankly decorative and heraldic. **1970** *Oxf. Compan. Art* 584/1 International Gothic..first distinguished by Louis Courajod in 1892. *Ibid.* 584/2 International Gothic was nurtured in the cosmopolitan courts of France and Burgundy from the soil of the French aristocratic court style. **1944** H. MORGENTHAU in *U.N. Monetary & Financial Conference* p. iii, The International Monetary Fund agreed upon at Bretton Woods will help remedy this situation [*sc.* economic tactics which contribute to world-wide depression and war]. **1955** *Times* 4 July 13/4 The International Monetary Fund has agreed to a change in the par value of the Nicaraguan cordoba from five to seven a United States dollar. **1957** *Economist* 21 Dec. 1075/2 The British Government this week decided to extend for 12 months its $738,530,000 standby credit with the International Monetary Fund. **1958** *Colour Index* (Soc. Dyers & Colourists) (ed. 2) IV. 4323 International Orange 2221... C.I. Pigment Orange 21. **1967** 'G. CARR' *Lewker in Tirol* vi. 85 The cagoule is in the colour we call 'international orange'... It is the colour that can best be seen from a distance, so that climbers in difficulties can quickly be found and rescued. **1969** *New Yorker* 12 Apr. 110/3 The dial is coated with a luminous orange paint called International Orange, a psychedelic color that is glaringly visible against the milky-white experiment. **1898** *Mod. Q. Lang. & Lit.* I. I. 69/2 It is of the utmost importance that, for the more advanced students of languages, we should adopt an international phonetic alphabet. **1912** *Princ. Internat. Phonetic Assoc.* 1 In 1888, after consulting the opinion of its members, the Association drew up an *International Phonetic Alphabet*, by means of which the pronunciation of any language may be accurately represented. **1962** A. C. GIMSON *Introd. Pronunc. Eng.* iv. 35 The International Phonetic Alphabet..provides symbols to denote the sound types occurring in languages. **1964** J. DOWNING *Initial Teaching Alphabet* p. ix, Some educational reformers..favour an alternative type of 'rational orthography' or 'systematized notation' such as the International Phonetic Alphabet. **1932** HITCHCOCK & JOHNSON *Internat. Style* i. 20 There is, first, a new conception of architecture as volume rather than mass. Secondly, regularity rather than axial symmetry serves as the chief means of ordering design. These two principles, with a third proscribing arbitrary applied decoration, mark the productions of the international style. **1937** *Archit. Rev.* LXXXI. 133/2 This natural phenomenon, specifically variegated in each of these regions, constitutes a severe impediment in considering the rational mode of design as quickly resulting in a so-called 'International Style'. **1937** *Time* 8 Feb. 32/1 Walter Gropius, one of the founders of the concrete-pipe-and-plate-glass school of architectural modernism known as the 'International Style'. **1950** E. H. GOMBRICH *Story of Art* xiii. 178 Until round about 1400, art in different parts of Europe had developed on similar lines... The style of the Gothic painters and sculptors of that period is known as the International Style. **1922** *Internat. Conf. Standardisation of Sera & Serological Tests 1921* (League of Nations) 6 The Sub-Committee for investigating methods for testing the potency of anti-diphtheritic and anti-tetanic sera considers it both possible and

desirable to fix for both these sera an antitoxin unit which could be generally accepted and acknowledged as an International Unit. **1944** L. E. H. WHITBY *Med. Bacteriol.* (ed. 4) xxv. 234 Staphylococcus: an 'international unit' is the specific antitoxic activity contained in 0·5 mg. of dry standard serum preserved at the National Institute of Medical Research, London. **1961** *Brit. Med. Dict.* 1500/2 *International unit of male hormone*, the specific activity contained in 0·1 milligram of pure androsterone. .. *International unit of vitamin C*, the antiscorbutic activity contained in 0·05 mg. of pure ascorbic acid. **1970** *Daily Tel.* 12 Oct. 3/2 The Medical Research Council now requires that all influenza vaccines should contain 600 of the new international units of virus to each human dose.

B. *sb.* **a.** (Later examples.) Also, an international contest.

1890 *North British Daily Mail* 7 Apr. 6/6 Their goal was again and again besieged in a way never before seen at the close of an international. **1905** A. CONAN DOYLE *Return of Sherlock Holmes* 330 The defeat of the Light Blues may be entirely attributed to the unfortunate absence of the crack International, Godfrey Staunton, whose want was felt at every instant of the game. **1942** *R.A.F. Jrnl.* 30 May 33 It was like..Wembley or Hampden Park after an international. **1959** *Times* 21 Sept. 3/6 The British Lions were given but a faint hope of defeating the world champion All Blacks in the fourth and final international of their tour at Eden Park yesterday. **1971** *Leader* (Durban) 7 May 1/2 Efforts were being made for the Mauritian team to play a series of games including 'internationals' against South African Indian, Coloured and African elevens. **1973** *Times* 7 Feb. 15/4 It is no wonder, she feels, that so many former internationals never stay on in the sport.

b. (Earlier and later examples.) Also **Internationale.** Spec. **First International,** founded in London by Karl Marx in 1864 for promoting the joint political action of working classes in all countries, and dissolved in Philadelphia in 1876; **Second International,** an organization founded at Paris in 1889 to celebrate the 100th anniversary of the French Revolution; **Third International,** founded at Moscow in 1919 by delegates from twelve countries to promote communism and support the Russian Revolution, and dissolved in 1943; also called **Communist International** (abbrev. *COMINTERN); **Fourth International,** founded in 1936 by followers of Trotsky.

1871 *Observer* 9 Apr. 6/4 Most of the decrees are the work of illiterate members of the *Internationale*; they consist of candid attacks on the rights of property,.. such as you may expect from vulgar Socialists. **1871** G. M. HOPKINS *Let.* 2 Aug. (1935) 27, I feel inclined to begin by asking whether you are secretary to the International... I am always thinking about the Communist future. **1919** Communist International [see *COMMUNIST 1 b]. **1919** G. B. SHAW *Matter with Ireland* (1962) 193 The number of branches of The International formed in France in the 1860s by the police agents of Napoleon III must have filled the Castle with envy. **1920** B. RUSSELL *Pract. & Theory Bolshevism* 6, I do not believe that the methods of the Third International can lead to the desired goal. **1935** C. ISHERWOOD *Mr. Norris changes Trains* vi. 89 My association with..the representatives of the Third International..have even excited favourable comment in certain quarters in Moscow. **1937** E. SNOW *Red Star over China* iv. 154 In 1920, M. Martin, an energetic and persuasive representative of the Third International.. came to Shanghai. **1950** THEIMER & CAMPBELL *Encycl. World Politics* 430/1 Trotsky's adherents in a number of countries, recruited from discontented left-wing communists, tried to found a Fourth International. *Ibid.* 430/2 The Fourth International, a shadowy organization which held conferences in Paris in 1936 and 1948. **1951** W. PICKLES in *Political Q.* XXII. 335 June 30th, 1951..was the fourth occasion in less than 100 years on which a Socialist International has been founded..and the longest-lived of these ancestors, the Second International of 1889, survived for only 25 years. **1959** *Chambers's Encycl.* VII. 684/1 The first International spread rapidly, sections being founded in France, Belgium, Germany, Switzerland, Italy, Spain and other countries. **1967** N. MCINNES in R. P. Arnot et al. *Impact Russ. Revolution* 85 The Communist International having been disbanded by Stalin in 1943, the only socialist international in existence was the Fourth, demonstrating again that Trotskyism was the last refuge of several of socialism's discarded illusions. **1968** K. MARTIN *Editor* xi. 234 'I tell you,' he [*sc.* Trotsky in 1937] said, 'that in three to five years from now the Fourth International will be a great force in the world.' **1969** *Listener* 27 Mar. 429/1 If the ILP had joined the Communist International, as its French and German equivalents did, and as the Scottish divisional council wanted it to, a powerful Communist Party might have come into existence on British soil. **1972** *Guardian* 10 Mar. 3/2 The Fourth International (FI) arose after the disintegration under Stalin of the Third International.

c. *pl.* International bonds.

1909 *Westm. Gaz.* 17 Sept. 12/2 Internationals featureless.

d. *The International* = next.

1912 *Songs for Socialists* (Fabian Soc.) 2 The International. **1928** A. HUXLEY *Point Counter Point* xxiii. 413 Organized singing of the International.

Internationale (-næʃiǒnā·l, ‖ æ̃ntęrnasyonal). [Fr. (sc. *chanson* song).] A revolutionary hymn composed by Eugène Pottier in 1871 and adopted by French socialists and subsequently by others. Also *fig.*

[**1912** H. M. HYNDMAN *Further Reminisc.* 124 We all left Paris regretfully, with the strains of 'L'Internationale' ringing in our ears.] **1920** S. LEWIS *Main St.* i. 9 A Russian Jewess who sang the Internationale. **1933** *Morning Post* 30 Mar. 11/3 Communists..waved red flags and sang the 'Internationale'. **1938** I. GOLDBERG *Wonder of Words* p. vii, This *internationale* of poverty in a West-End slum. **1949** I. DEUTSCHER *Stalin* xii. 491 The Internationale, the hymn of the Labour movement of the world. **1974** *Times* 7 Mar. 16/8 Cardew had intended to end the programme with the *Internationale.*

internationalism. (Earlier and later examples.)

1851 M. TUPPER in D. Hudson *Martin Tupper* (1949) x. 121 [President Fillmore..received me] very kindly and cordially, and avowing himself a great lover of my works and my Internationalism. **1955** *Times* 17 May 10/7 Internationalism seems to have become by now an accepted thing even in trades far less easily internationalized than ours. **1971** *World Archaeol.* III. 226 In Childe's view, it was..the Iron Curtain which abruptly severed this age-old tradition of internationalism. **1973** *Times* 16 Apr. 4/6 No city has done more than Coventry since the war to further the cause of internationalism.

internationalist. Add: (Further examples.)

1916 A. HUXLEY *Let.* 19 Mar. (1969) 94, I get extraordinarily irritated with some of these Internationalists, who conscientiously object. **1955** H. HODGKINSON *Doubletalk* 60 In practice it is enough to discover what the USSR considers her own interests to be to show to the 'proletarian internationalist' his own. **1965** M. BRADBURY *Stepping Westward* i. 47 They were avaricious internationalists, evidently, their legs turned nutmeg by a sun that had come to find them daily in different places. **1973** *Listener* 17 May 636/1 A little-known Maoist organisation known as the Internationalists, founded in Vancouver in March 1963.

c. *attrib.* or as *adj.*

1941 J. S. HUXLEY *Uniqueness of Man* xiv. 288 The nationalistic element in socialized religion will be subordinated or adjusted to the internationalist. **1955** KOESTLER *Trail of Dinosaur* 190 Socialism has lost its claim to represent the internationalist trend of humanity.

Hence **internationali·stic** *a.*

1930 A. FLEXNER *Universities* i. 13 This present-day world, compounded of tradition, good and bad, racial mixtures, nationalistic and internationalistic strivings. **1973** M. TRUMAN *Harry S. Truman* x. 204 Arthur Vandenberg, leader of the internationalistic Republicans, fulminated against what was happening in Poland.

inter-nebular: see *INTER- *pref.* 4 a.

internee (intɜːnī·). [f. INTERN *v.* 2 + -EE[1].] One who is interned; an interned person.

1918 *Rep. Detenus & Internees Bengal* 2 in *Parl. Papers* (Cd. 9198) VIII. 106 The cases of the State prisoners and internees. **1920** *Observer* 5 Dec. 13/4 Lorries with military guards..removed the internees to the camp. **1941** WODEHOUSE *Let.* 13 Aug. in *Performing Flea* (1953) 179 We are elderly internees, most of us with corns and swollen joints. **1972** *Daily Tel.* 4 Mar. 32/6 A policy to end imprisonment without trial by a phased programme of releases of every detainee and internee.

interneuron (intəɹniūᵊ·rǫn). *Physiol.* Also **interneurone.** [f. INTER(NUNCIAL *a.* + NEURON.] Any of the neurons which transmit nerve impulses from receptor neurons to effector neurons; an internuncial neuron.

1939 R. LORENTE DE NÓ in *Jrnl. Neurophysiol.* II. 402 Following the example of Prof. Gerard the simple term 'interneuron' will henceforth be used instead of the rather cumbersome designation 'internuncial neuron'. **1963** S. OCHS in E. E. Selkurt *Physiol.* v. 104 (*caption*) Sensory fibers terminate upon interneurons within the spinal cord which, by multiple branches, engage a large number of motoneurons. **1971** *Jrnl. Exper. Biol.* LV. 727 The DCMD (descending contralateral movement detector) neurone is a monocular visual interneurone..which sends a large axon down the contralateral connective to the thoracic ganglia. **1971** VILLEE & DETHIER *Biol. Princ. & Proc.* xx. 619 Interneurons are those that connect two or more neurons. They usually lie wholly within the central nervous system.

interneuronal (intəɹniūᵊrōᵘ·năl), *a. Physiol.* [Partly f. prec. + -AL, partly f. INTER- 4 a + *NEURONAL *a.*] **a.** Of, pertaining to, or affecting an interneuron. **b.** Occurring or existing between neurons.

1948 E. GARDNER *Fund. Neurol.* viii. 174 The afferent tracts of the cord evolve from such interneuronal pools. **1952** J. D. HARDY et al. *Pain Sensations* i. 15 Lorente de Nó..inferred that all interneuronal connections fall into two categories. **1959** *Jrnl. Amer. Chem. Soc.* LXXXI. 4347/1 In quite a few of the compounds analgesic activity is accompanied by marked interneuronal blocking action. **1969** *New Scientist* 6 Feb. 278/1 The *specificity* of this interneuronal communication, every neuron making contact with other, often carefully specified, neurons.

internist (intɜ̄·ɹnist). *U.S.* [f. **intern*(*al medicine* + -IST.] A general physician; also, a specialist in internal medicine.

1904 *Science* 29 Apr. 696/1 Many internists ('general physicians') of experience and authority. **1910** [see *HYPOPARATHYROID *a.*]. **1918** *Nation* (N.Y.) Feb. 170/1 A maternity bureau composed of expert obstetricians and competent internists. **1961** *Brit. Jrnl. Clin. Pract.* June 510/2 The role of the internist is different. He grasps intuitively the whole of the patient—the 'gestalt' —and combines the various organic findings. **1970** *Sci. Amer.* Mar. 60/3 The British surgeon is a consultant who sees only patients referred to him by a general practitioner or internist. **1972** *Science* 5 May 489/1 The use of antidepressants by general practitioners, internists and psychiatrists.

internment. Add: **b.** *attrib.*, as **internment camp**, a detention camp for prisoners of war and aliens.

1916 *Daily Colonist* (Victoria, B.C.) 26 July 1/3 Brandon, Man. July 25.—The internment camp here is to be closed at the end of this month. **1941** *Star* 10 Apr. 8/3 A revolt at an internment camp at Vernet les Bains.

internuclear, *a.* Add: **2.** *Physics.* Existing between atomic nuclei.

1946 *Nature* 17 Aug. 224/1 The carbon chain must then be coiled to the same extent if normal internuclear distances are to be maintained. **1949** KOESTLER *Insight & Outlook* xi. 156 The integrative tendencies in the various forms of attracting or binding forces: internuclear, gravitational, electromagnetic, and so on. **1962** *Science Survey* III. 36 Typical known values for atomic masses and approximate values for typical inter-nuclear distances.

3. *Phonetics.* Situated between nuclei.

1961 Y. OLSSON *On Syntax Eng. Verb* ii. 23 In pre-, inter-, and post-nuclear sections, 4/S-units and 4/0-units may occur in various combinations.

inter-nucleon: see *INTER- *pref.* 5.

interoceanic, *a.* Add: (Earlier U.S. example.) So **intero·cean** *a.*

1850 *Clayton–Bulwer Treaty* 19 Apr. 8 Interoceanic communication. **1913** *Chambers's Jrnl.* Jan. 22/2 The isthmus ..became a centre of attraction for interocean transit. **1969** *Jane's Freight Containers 1968–69* 93/1 Parcel Tankers, Inc. Agent: Interocean Steamship Corp.

interoceptor (iːntərose·ptǭɹ). *Physiol.* [perh. f. INTER(IOR *a.* and *sb.* + -O + RE)CEPTOR, after *EXTEROCEPTOR.] Any sensory receptor which receives stimuli arising within the body, or *spec.* within the viscera. So **intero·ce·ptive** *a.*

1906 C. S. SHERRINGTON *Integrative Action Nervous Syst.* ix. 317 This [inner] surface of the animal may be termed the intero-ceptive. *Ibid.* 352 Spinal shock hardly at all affects the nervous reactions of the intero-ceptors (visceral system). **1930** L. T. TROLAND *Princ. Psychophysiol.* II. IV. xiii. 14 The visceral or interoceptive systems include those for the feelings of hunger, thirst, nausea. **1940** FRAENKEL & GUNN *Orientation of Animals* (1961) iii. 33 The interoceptors in the alimentary canal which are responsible for belly-aches. **1971** D. J. AIDLEY *Physiol. Excitable Cells* xv. 307 Exteroceptors are sensitive to stimuli originating outside the body, and interoceptors are excited by stimuli inside the body. **1972** C. H. HOCKMAN *Limbic Syst. Mechanisms & Autonomic Function* viii. 128/2 Intracellular recording in awake, sitting squirrel monkeys have shown a differential effect of interoceptive and exteroceptive inputs on the excitability of hippocampal neurons.

inter-office: see *INTER- *pref.* 5.

interoperable (iːntərǫ·pərăb'l), *a.* [f. INTER- 2 a + OPERABLE *a.*] Able to operate in conjunction.

1969 *Nature* 29 Nov. 839/1 Skynet is inter-operable with the IDCSP system and is intended to be inter-operable with its successor now in view. **1970** *Sci. Jrnl.* Mar. 13 In other respects the two nations' forces are working in parallel and Skynet [the Royal Navy's military satellite communications system] is compatible and interoperable with the US Defence Communication Satellite system. **1970** *Fremdsprachen* XIV. 220/1 Sometime in the mid-1970s the communications..will not only be interoperable among themselves, but with United States, Canadian and Australian services also.

inter-palpebral, -particle, -party: see *INTER- *pref.* 6, 5, 5.

inter partes: see *INTER L. prep.

interpellate, *v.* Add: Also and now more usually with pronunc. (intɜ̄·ɹpĕlēit).

inter-perceptual: see *INTER- *pref.* 4 c.

interpermeate (intəɹpɜ̄·ɹmi,ēit), *v.* [INTER- 1 b.] To pervade or penetrate reciprocally. Hence **interpermea·tion.**

1909 in *Cent. Dict.* Suppl. **1926** *Blackw. Mag.* Oct. 518/2 It [*sc.* the Vital Principle] came into being by the interpermeation of air and water. **1954** *Jrnl. Theol. Stud.* V. 54 It is surely more intelligible to postulate a personal unity in which persons coinhere and interpermeate in a way unknown to us on earth.

interpersonal (intəɹpɜ̄·ɹsənăl), *a. Psychol.* [f. INTER- 4 c + PERSONAL *a.* 5.] Between persons; *spec.* a term introduced by H. S. Sullivan (1892–1949) to describe behaviour between people in any encounter. So **interpersona·lity,** the state or fact of being interpersonal; **interpe·rsonally** *adv.*, in an interpersonal manner.

1842 [see INTER- 4 c]. **1938** H. S. SULLIVAN in *Psychiatry* I. 121 Psychiatry seeks to discover and formulate the laws of human personality...Its peculiar field is the study of interpersonal phenomena. Personality is made mani-

fest in interpersonal situations, and not otherwise. It is to the elucidation of interpersonal relations, therefore, that psychiatry applies itself. **1946** C. MORRIS *Signs, Lang. & Behavior* 39 (*heading*) The interpersonality of the language sign. **1947** P. L. HARRIMAN *Dict. Psychol.* 184 *Interpersonal relationships*, the reciprocal influences which persons exert upon one another in primary (face-to-face) social groups. **1949** M. MEAD *Male & Female* x. 212 The specific interpersonality of the sexual act. *Ibid.* ii. 39 Using the understanding not interpersonally but personally. **1959** H. BONNER *Group Dynamics* II. iii. 90 An important feature of interpersonal aggression is that it is usually accompanied by the members' insight into their own behavior. **1962** U. WEINREICH in Householder & Saporta *Probl. in Lexicogr.* 43 Lexicography as a descriptive (rather than a normative) discipline must also take the criterion of interpersonality seriously. **1963** *Dissertation Abstr.* XXIII. 3484/1 He was impulsive, emotionally and interpersonally immature, and not emancipated from his parents. **1964** M. ARGYLE *Psychol. & Social Probl.* xv. 183 Sociological field studies of neighbourhoods, factories and families can disclose facts about inter-personal behaviour and relationships. **1971** M. COOK (*title*) Interpersonal perception. *Ibid.* 11 That area of social psychology—variously called interpersonal perception, person perception and impression formation. **1972** *Jrnl. Social Psychol.* LXXXVI. 177 The 15-year-old boy..was involved in interpersonal conflicts with his stepfather.

interphase (i·ntəɹfēiz), *sb.* and *a.* [f. INTER- + PHASE.] **A.** *sb.* [INTER- 2 b.] **1.** *Cytology.* [a. G. *interphase* (H. Lundegårdh 1912, in *Arch. f. mikrosk. Anat.* LXXX. 27).] A stage in the cycle of nuclear division which intervenes between one mitosis and the next; also, a stage between the first and second division of meiosis. Also *attrib.* or as *adj.*

1925 E. B. WILSON *Cell* (ed. 3) 1134 *Interkinesis...* (*Interphase* of Lundegårdh, 1912). **1932** C. D. DARLINGTON *Recent Adv. Cytol.* iv. 90 The chromosomes may form two daughter-nuclei at the poles and pass into a resting stage, the interphase. **1961** *Lancet* 26 Aug. 488/1 Any X chromosomes in excess may produce a sex-chromatin body in the interphase nucleus. **1968** M. W. STRICKBERGER *Genetics* ii. 13 As compared to the period of active mitosis..the interphase or 'intermitotic' period of most cells is usually many times longer. *Ibid.* 21 The chromosomes pass into a short interphase before the second meiotic division begins.

2. *Physical Chem.* The region between two phases in which the properties are significantly different from the bulk properties of either phase.

1933 *Phil. Mag.* XVI. 849 In recent years attention has been concentrated once more on the electro-chemistry of the interphase between mercury and an aqueous solution containing electrolytes. *Ibid.* 864 The surface tension of a liquid–liquid interphase is defined in such a way as to be applicable to any desired boundary in an interphase of finite thickness. **1955** E. J. PRYOR *Introd. Mineral Dressing* xvii. 428 In the solid–fluid interphase, forces of each phase meet and merge through a transition stage. **1970** BOCKRIS & REDDY *Mod. Electrochem.* I. i. 2 An interface formed by two phases..is an apparent surface because..there is a *region* in which there is a continuous transition from the properties of one phase to the properties of the other. If one aims to refer specifically to this three-dimensional transition region, then it is more appropriate to use the term interphase. **1972** BOCKRIS & DRAŽIĆ *Electro-Chem. Sci.* ii. 22 An interphase is a less sharply definable region, which will range over at least two molecular diameters, but may extend over thousands of ångströms.

B. *adj.* [INTER- 5.] **1.** Occurring or existing between two phases or states of matter.

1933 *Jrnl. Chem. Physics* I. 8/1 The equilization [*sic*] of spreading force *f* in different phases within one field may take place in 3 ways: (a) Interphase mobility by which adatoms cross the phase boundary [etc.]. **1959** *Times* 22 Jan. 2/5 (Advt.), The work will include calculation of interphase reactions in which water or steam is normally one phase. **1967** B. P. NICOLSKY et al. in G. Eisenman *Glass Electrodes for Hydrogen* vi. 175 We shall agree to regard the interphase potential as the electrical potential of the solid phase as compared with the liquid one.

2. *Electr. Engin.* Applied to an inductor used to connect two or more polyphase rectifiers so that they operate in parallel with the current divided between them.

1935 *Gen. Electric Rev.* XXXVIII. 499/1 Polyphase rectifiers usually have an interphase transformer which serves to divide the anodes into two or more groups which operate in parallel. **1952** ERIKSON & BRYANT *Electr. Engin.* xxiv. 431 The presence of the interphase transformer is necessary to allow conduction in two tubes ..at any given time. **1970** J. SHEPHERD et al. *Higher Electr. Engin.* (ed. 2) xxv. 804 By the addition of an interphase reactor to the simple 6-phase connexion it is possible to obtain rectifier action with the smoothness of normal 6-phase rectification and the utilization factor of 3-phase rectification.

interphasic (intəɹfēi·zik), *a. Cytology.* [f. prec. + -IC.] Of or pertaining to interphase.

1948 W. ANDREW tr. *E. D. P. de Robertis's Gen. Cytol.* vii. 134 Every cell passes..through two periods: one being interphasic or metabolic and the other being mitotic, or a period of division. **1960** [see *INTERKINETIC *a.*].

i:nterpheno·menon. *Physics.* Pl. **-phenomena.** [INTER- 2 b.] Reichenbach's name for a phenomenon that cannot (even in principle) be inferred or demonstrated straightforwardly from observations in accordance with the laws of classical physics. Hence used for any unobserved phenomenon.

1944 H. REICHENBACH *Philos. Found. Quantum Mech.* I. § 6. 21 We..shall consider as unobservable all those occurrences which happen between the coincidences, such as the movement of an electron, or of a light ray from its source to a collision with matter. We call this class of occurrences the interphenomena. Occurrences of this kind are introduced by inferential chains of a much more complicated sort; they are constructed in the form of an interpolation within the world of phenomena, and we can therefore consider the distinction between phenomena and interphenomena as the quantum mechanical analogue of the distinction between observed and unobserved things. **1956** —— *Direction of Time* v. § 25. 217 The terms 'particle' and 'wave' both belong to the language of interphenomena. They assert something about what happens between the localized phenomena. **1956** E. H. HUTTEN *Lang. Mod. Physics* v. 195 In classical physics..the unobserved phenomena are supposed to follow the same laws as the observed phenomena. The idealised character of measurement in classical theory allows us to speak about these interphenomena. *Ibid.*, The uncertainty principle makes it impossible to introduce interphenomena.

interphone (i·ntəɹfōun). orig. *U.S.* [f. INTER- 2 a + PHONE *sb.*[2]] An intercommunication system whereby telephones are used to connect points within a small area, as a building, aeroplane, etc.

1942 *Time* 20 Apr. 25/2 During the same fracas, the pilot inquired over the [Flying] Fortress interphone: 'Are you firing at the enemy?' **1958** J. CANNAN *And be a Villain* v. 118 Pelly was speaking on his interphone. **1961** 'B. WELLS' *Day Earth caught Fire* viii. 119 He was urgently dialling his inter-phone. **1962** *Punch* 5 Dec. 816/1 You'll need a Home Interphone, to communicate with the party in the other rooms.

interplanar: see *INTER- *pref.* 6.

interplane (i·ntəɹplēin), *a. Aeronaut.* [f. INTER- 5 + PLANE *sb.*[3]] Situated between or connecting the upper and lower 'planes' or wings of a biplane.

1916 H. BARBER *Aeroplane Speaks* 96 Interplane struts ..have to keep the lifting surfaces or 'planes' apart. **1920** *Blackw. Mag.* Nov. 565/1 Great lanky beasts with double interplane engines, heavy bombers of freak aspect. **1969** K. MUNSON *Pioneer Aircraft 1903–14* 152/2 The rigid construction of the wings needed no tie-wires, the sole bracing consisting of two I-type interplane struts on each side.

interplanetary, *a.* Add: Also, existing between planets or pertaining to travel between planets.

1897 *Pearson's Mag.* July 116/1 Cylinder followed cylinder in its interplanetary flight. **1901** *Daily News* 7 Jan. 5/1 Dreams of inter-planetary communication. **1931** D. LASSER *Conquest of Space* 13 Ignorance and prejudice.. surround the 'interplanetary rocket' question. **1936** 'J. BEYNON' *Planet Plane* iii. 28 Mr. Curtance is going to try to win the Keuntz Prize for the inter-planetary flight. **1943** C. S. LEWIS *Perelandra* vi. 91 In obscure works of 'scientification', in little Interplanetary Societies and Rocketry Clubs. **1950** *Jrnl. Brit. Interplanetary Soc.* IX. 300 Should be able to take the Interplanetary Age, when it comes, without hysteria. **1957** *Economist* 2 Nov. 377 The artificial satellite circling the earth was to be a proud reminder of the distance covered along the road from the wooden plough to the inter-planetary rocket. **1960** *Analog Science Fact/Fiction* Oct. 30/1 Maybe they were bravely defending their own planet by hunting down an interplanetary raider. **1962** [see *COSMIC *a.* 3 b].

interplant (intəɹplɑ·nt), *v.* [f. INTER- 1 a + PLANT *v.*] *trans.* To plant (land) so that it is occupied by a mixture of plant species; to plant (a specified crop) *with* another crop. Hence **interpla·nting** *vbl. sb.* So **i·nterplant** *sb.*, a plant growing among others of different species.

1927 *Daily Tel.* 11 May 3/4 Included in the 1,442 acres of rubber were 98 acres which were interplanted with coffee. **1942** *R.A.F. Jrnl.* 30 May 27 Fill every inch of space by inter-planting one crop with another. This principle has already been illustrated by interplanting early potatoes with winter greens. **1950** *N.Z. Jrnl. Agric.* LXXX. 539/1 Other interplants are chiefly peaches. **1966** WEBSTER & WILSON *Agric. in Tropics* x. 230 Interplanting with suitable crops, in a manner which maintains fertility and avoids competition, may be profitable. **1969** G. WRIGLEY *Tropical Agric.* (ed. 2) ii. 119 On the fertile soils of East Africa bananas are interplanted with coffee. **1971** *Countryman* LXXVI. IV. 109 Interplant them with dark purple tulips, or white splashed with purple, to give spring interest.

interplical: see *INTER- *pref.* 6.

interpluvial (intəɹplū·viăl), *a.* and *sb.* [f. INTER- 4 b + PLUVIAL *a.*] **A.** *adj.* Designating any of the periods of generally drier conditions in equatorial latitudes during the geological past (esp. the Pleistocene) which alternated with pluvial periods in a cycle which may be correlated with or related to the better-known cycle of interglacial and glacial periods in more polar latitudes. **B.** *sb.* An interpluvial period.

1907 *Bull. Geol. Soc. Amer.* XVIII. 362 The time when a thesis occurs is a thesial epoch, which may be described as interglacial, or interfluvial, and so forth, when the agents which modify the earth's surface are considered, or as intervegetal, interpluvial, and so forth, when other phases are considered. **1931** L. S. B. LEAKEY *Stone Age Cultures Kenya Colony* ii. 13 During the dry inter-pluvial periods..the lakes in the Rift Valley dried up. *Ibid.*, One would expect that the prehistoric tribes moved to the high land..during the inter-pluvials. **1940** *Geogr. Jrnl.* XCVI. 333 There have been very long wet and dry phases, the so-called pluvials and interpluvials. **1957** G. E. HUTCHINSON *Treat. Limnol.* I. i. 133 Such deposits are supposed to be the result of water-borne material, washed toward the pan in pluvial times, becoming cemented during the following interpluvial. *Ibid.*, Interpluvial periods of deflation. **1963** D. W. & E. E. HUMPHRIES tr. *Termier's Erosion & Sedimentation* i. 9 In Equatorial Zones it is now suspected that the pluvial phases were hot times and interpluvial (dry) phases were equivalent to the glacial epochs. **1973** *Nature* 16 Mar. 187/1 It seems.. that the tectonic movement which caused the tilting of the Ubeidiya Formation occurred some time within the Mindel-Riss Interpluvial and is younger than 640,000 yr.

Interpol (i·ntəɹpǫl). [abbrev. of *Inter*national *pol*ice.] The International Criminal Police Commission (founded in 1923), with headquarters in Paris.

1952 SÖDERMAN & O'CONNELL *Mod. Criminal Investigation* (ed. 4) ii. 24 All national bureaus of the ICPC have adopted the telegraphic address of 'Interpol'. **1955** *Times* 7 July 7/5 They have issued the description of a man of about 45..whom they would like to interview. This has been circulated through the international police organization, Interpol, since it is thought likely that the man may have gone abroad. **1957** *Times* 24 June 10/2 Wire-tapping was one of the subjects discussed at the Lisbon meeting of the International Criminal Police Commission (Interpol) which ended yesterday. **1958** *Daily Mail* 31 July 1/5 British police last night sent a call to Interpol, the international police organisation, for help in solving the riddle of a British airman whose father believes he is still alive 15 years after he was shot down over Germany. **1964** J. CRAMER *World's Police* VI. 442 The word 'Interpol' was originally the telegraphic address of the I.C.P.O. but it became so well known that it is now part of the official title of the organization.

interpolability (intə̄·ɹpŏlăbi:lĭti). [f. INTERPOLAB(LE *a.* + -ILITY.] The state or quality of being interpolable.

1938 *Nature* 12 Nov. 852/2 Attention is paid everywhere to interpolability, and the volume ends with a number of tables of interpolation coefficients. **1971** T. F. MITCHELL in *Archivum Linguisticum* II. 46 Other points of contrast with the other examples include the interpolability before *off* of the 'adverbial' forms *straight* or *right*, the substitutability of *away* for *off*, [etc.].

interpolant (intə̄·ɹpŏlănt). *Math.* [f. L. *interpolant-em*, pres. pple. of *interpolāre* (see INTERPOLATE *v.*), or INTERPOL(ATE *v.* + -ANT[1].] A value or expression (given or calculated) used in finding some other value by interpolation.

1920 *Tracts for Computers* II. 17 Forward difference formulae, central difference formulae and Lagrangian formulae, when the interpolants are spaced equally apart are really different aspects of the same process, i.e. running a parabola of the $(n-1)$th order through n points. **1946** *Phil. Mag.* XXXVII. 260 A function value interpolated in this way may indeed be more accurate than any of the eight values used to obtain it. For in a perfect table the rounding-off errors of the eight interpolants have uniform probability distributions between −0·5 and 0·5 in units of the last decimal, and it may be shown that the probability of the resulting error of the interpolate is very nearly normally distributed with standard deviation 0·12. **1965** A. RALSTON *First Course Numerical Analysis* iii. 57 An important advantage of finite-difference interpolation formulas..would seem to be the property..that enables a term to be added to them merely by adding one tabular point and computing an additional row of differences... This enables us to generate a sequence of interpolants each involving one more tabular point than the previous one.

interpolate, *v.* Add: **3. c.** (With the words spoken as object.) To interpose orally.

1881 MRS. J. H. RIDDELL *Senior Partner* I. vii. 151 'I have not a word to say against Effie,' began..Robert... 'If ye had, ye'd best not say it before me,' interpolated his father. **1908** *Smart Set* June 142/1 'I suppose I may claim some eminence as physicians go.' 'Top notch of the whole bunch, dad!' interpolated Keene. **1922** JOYCE *Ulysses* 614 What year would that be about? Mr Bloom interpolated.

6. (Further examples.) Also *absol.* or *intr.*, to use or perform interpolation. Also *fig.*

1888 *Encycl. Brit.* XXIX. 8/2 The reciprocal of a number of five figures is therefore taken out at once, and two more figures may be interpolated for as in logarithms. **1905** [see *EXTRAPOLATE *v.* 2 b]. **1928** *Monthly Notices R. Astron. Soc.* LXXXVIII. 506 The Lagrangian method of interpolating to fixed sub-divisions of an interval. **1968** FOX & MAYERS *Computing Methods for Scientists & Engineers* i. 11 Interpolating for $y(2{\cdot}5)$, from given values at $x = 2$ and $x = 3$, the formula gives $y(2{\cdot}5) = 22y(3)/35 + 18y(2)/35$.

interpolate (intə̄·ɹpŏlĕt), *sb. Math.* [f. L. *interpolāt-us*, pa. pple. of *interpolāre* (see

INTERPOLATE *v.*): see -ATE[1] b.] A value arrived at by interpolation.

1920 *Tracts for Computers* II. 17 As a rule the interpolation formulae work, but once in a while bitter experience forces us up against cases in which increasing the number of differences..is quite ineffectual as a method of obtaining accurate interpolates. **1932** *Proc. Edin. Math. Soc.* III. 56 For example, a linear interpolate $u_{0 \cdot 683}$ can be computed from u_0 and u_1 as $u_{0 \cdot 683} = 0{\cdot}317u_0 + 0{\cdot}683u_1$. **1946** [see *INTERPOLANT]. **1956** F. B. HILDEBRAND *Introd. Numerical Analysis* ii. 35 If more reliable interpolates are desired, it is clearly necessary to make use of more information than that consisting merely of tabulated values (ordinates) of a function, corresponding to two successive abscissas.

interpolation. Add: **3. b.** (Later examples.) Freq. *attrib.*

1872 [see *EXTRAPOLATION]. **1888** *Encycl. Brit.* XXIII. 13/1 All tables of proportional parts may be regarded as interpolation tables. **1928** *Monthly Notices R. Astron. Soc.* LXXXVIII. 511 The interpolation formula known as Bessel's, but really discovered by Newton. **1968** FOX & MAYERS *Computing Methods for Scientists & Engineers* viii. 147 Moreover the 'interpolation coefficients'..are available in tabular form,..and our interpolation process is reasonably straightforward. **1970** O. DOPPING *Computers & Data Processing* xvi. 256 The computer calculates a first approximation to the desired address by interpolation between the known minimum and maximum values of the argument.

interpolator. Add: **2.** A mechanical contrivance for securing correct retransmission from a submarine cable of any consecutive letter-elements having the same sign.

1902 *Encycl. Brit.* XXXIII. 226/2 The special form of curb sender mentioned, termed the 'Interpolator'. **1958** *Economist* 1 Nov. 425 (Advt.), The Interpolator is the essential part of the mechanism used to re-form signals automatically at the end of their journey through a long cable, before they are sent into another.

3. *Engin.* A device or apparatus which, when fed with a set of datum points defining a curve, produces a continuous output for guiding a tool over the curve.

1953 *IRE Trans. Industr. Electronics* I. 29 The interpolator output provides a continuous angular rotation whose instantaneous angular position represents the radius vector of the machine tool's cutter locus. **1961** S. FIFER *Analogue Computation* IV. xxx. 1279 The function of the analogue interpolator is to compute a continuous curve from the discrete set of digital information and to position a mechanical lathe accordingly. **1973** tr. *W. Simon's Numerical Control Machine Tools* ii. 43 The cost of the control equipment located on the machine tool itself is considerably reduced, since the machine no longer has its own interpolator.

interpolatory (intɜ̄·ɹpǒlătəri), *a.* [f. INTERPOLAT(E *v.* + -ORY[2].] Serving to interpolate.

1946 *Mind* LV. 201, I would suggest approaching the matter from the Quantum Analogue angle and boldly taking the line that the latter were Interpolatory expressions. **1965** W. S. ALLEN *Vox Latina* iii. 72 The interpolatory nature of the '*gnus*' passage.

interpole (i·ntəɹpōᵘl). *Electr.* [INTER- 2 b.] In an electric motor or generator having a commutator, each of a set of auxiliary poles situated between the main poles and connected in series with the armature, the function of which is to facilitate commutation of the current by cancelling the induced e.m.f. in the coils that tends to hinder it.

1907 H. H. NORRIS *Introd. Study Electr. Engin.* x. 280 The function of the commutating or 'inter' pole is to produce a reversing field for the coil undergoing commutation. **1927** H. H. BROUGHTON *Electr. Winders* iii. 82 Sparkless commutation can be obtained by means of interpoles alone. **1964** R. F. FICCHI *Electrical Interference* vii. 108 If interpoles or compensating windings are introduced in the design, the commutation process will usually become more efficient and interference will be minimized.

interpolymer (i·ntəɹpǫ:liməɹ). *Chem.* [INTER- 2 b.] (See quot. 1966.)

1936 *Chem. Abstr.* XXX. 6478/2 Mixts. of polymers or interpolymers of these compds. **1950** *Thorpe's Dict. Appl. Chem.* (ed. 4) X. 87/2 The product is not a mixture of polymers A-A-A-A-A-A-...with B-B-B-B-B-B-..., but an interpolymer, e.g. A-B-A-A-B-A-B-A-A-..., the order in which the units are arranged not being readily determinable. **1955** *Jrnl. Polymer Sci.* XVIII. 129 A general method of producing graft and block interpolymers between elastomers is therefore indicated. **1966** M. L. MILLER *Struct. Polymers* ix. 426 Polymers made up of molecules containing two or more types of monomer units are called copolymers or interpolymers...The terms 'copolymer' and 'interpolymer' are essentially equivalent but the term 'interpolymer' is more restrictive because it implies an intimate distribution of monomer units in the molecule while the term 'copolymer' has no such implication.

Hence **interpo·lymerize** *v. trans.* and *intr.*, to combine so as to form an interpolymer; **i:nterpolymeriza·tion.**

1950 *Thorpe's Dict. Appl. Chem.* (ed. 4) X. 87/2 Vinyl acetate is interpolymerised with vinyl chloride to give plastics which are lower softening and more soluble than polyvinyl chloride. *Ibid.* 88/1 There are monomers.. which do not give high molecular-weight polymers by themselves but may readily interpolymerise with a second component... Interpolymerisation may even be effected in cases where neither component is separately polymerisable.

interpopulational: see *INTER- *pref.* 6.

interpose, *v.* Add: **1. c.** *Chess.* To move (a man) so as to obstruct the line of action of an opposing piece, esp. when the latter is giving check. Also *absol.*, or with the interposed man as subject.

1761 E. HOYLE *Ess. Game of Chess* 2, 6 B. The Queen gives Check. W. The Bishop interposes. **1765** R. LAMBE *Hist. Chess* 107 If the B. Bp. instead of retreating, checks your K. you must interpose your Bp. **1808** J. H. SARRATT *Treat. Game of Chess* I. 49 If he interpose his King's Knight, you must take his Rook with your Queen. **1844** W. LEWIS *Treat. Game of Chess* 19 Sometimes a piece or pawn, which before was out of play, may be interposed, and force the piece that checks to retire. **1861** *Chambers's Encycl.* II. 799/2 The king..must either move out of check or interpose some one of his subjects, unless the checking piece can be captured. **1876** *Encycl. Brit.* V. 593/1 If..the king, being thus in check, cannot move to another square.. and there is no piece or pawn which can be interposed, and the checking piece or pawn cannot be taken, then it is 'checkmate'. **1950** *Hoyle's Games Modernized* (ed. 20) 366 The player may..interpose one of his own men between the King and the attacking piece.

interpret, *v.* Add: **1. d.** To obtain significant information from (a photograph), used esp. of aerial photographs taken for military purposes.

1950 A. LEE *Soviet Air Force* vii. 154 Photographs, developed in mobile front-line vans, were interpreted and the main points signalled..to army and corps headquarters. **1958** C. B. SMITH *Evidence in Camera* i. 21 Although the art of interpreting air photographs had been developed quite a long way in the First World War, in the summer of 1939 there was precisely one experienced interpreter.

interpretability. (Earlier and later examples.)

1854 G. BOOLE *Investigation Laws of Tht.* 67 The same conditions of interpretability. **1956** E. H. HUTTEN *Lang. Mod. Physics* ii. 64 It is not translatability but interpretability in terms of an empiricist language that can establish meaning.

interpretant (intɜ̄·ɹprĕtănt). *Philos.* [f. INTERPRET *v.* + -ANT[1].] Peirce's term for the effect of a proposition, or sign-series, upon its interpreter, the person who understands it; thus, the meaning, in one sense.

c **1905** C. S. PEIRCE *Coll. Papers* (1931) I. III. 147 Now the relation of every sign to its object and interpretant is plainly a triad. *a* **1910** W. JAMES *Some Probl. Philos.* (1911) iv. 71 The interpretants are then substituted for the sensations, which thus get rationally conceived. **1939** *Mind* XLVIII. 480 The class of interpretations of the kind described in L will be called the *interpretant* of that sign. **1946** C. MORRIS *Signs, Lang. & Behavior* i. 17 The disposition of an interpreter to respond, because of the sign,..will be called an interpretant. **1947** H. REICHENBACH *Elem. Symbolic Logic* vii. 280 These psychological processes are sometimes called the *interpretant* of a sentence. **1964** *Language* XL. 234 The relationship between linguistic signs and their users, the relationship which Morris calls the 'interpretant'.

interpretation. Add: **1. c.** The technique of obtaining information from a photograph, esp. an aerial photograph. Cf. *INTERPRET *v.* 1 d.

1948 CARLING & ROSS *Brit. Surg. Pract.* V. 276 The interpretation of the pyelogram may be difficult. **1958** C. B. SMITH *Evidence in Camera* i. 21 Interpretation was supposed to be a job that any Station Intelligence Officer could be trained for in a week or two.

5. *attrib.*: **interpretation clause,** a clause in an Act of Parliament which defines the meaning of certain terms for the purposes of the Act.

1897 *Bouvier's Law Dict.* I. 1107/2. **1971** *Halsbury's Statutes Eng.* (ed. 3) XXXII. 363 *Interpretation sections.* Most modern Acts contain an interpretation clause which states the meanings which particular expressions used in the Act in question are to bear or include.

interpretatively, *adv.* **a.** Delete *rare* and add later examples.

1950 E. E. EVANS-PRITCHARD *Ess. Social Anthropol.* (1962) i. 22 He then lives the experiences over again critically and interpretatively in the conceptual categories and values of his own culture. **1969** *Daily Tel.* 17 Dec. 10/8 It was already obvious that we were to be treated to playing which was free of all technical cares, and which developed interpretatively with disciplined spontaneity.

interpretativeness (intɜ̄·ɹprĭtătivnės). [f. INTERPRETATIVE *a.* + -NESS.] The quality or condition of being interpretative.

1932 *Mind* XLI. 216 The several associations of 'meaning' with intellectual interpretativeness, value-carrying, and purposefulness are being confounded. **1957** D. L. BOLINGER in *Publ. Amer. Dial. Soc.* XXVIII. 26 The interpretativeness may be indicated merely by accent.

interpreter. Add: **1. d.** One who interprets (sense *1 d) photographs.

1950 A. LEE *Soviet Air Force* ii. 55 Large flying units.. had photographic interpreter specialists. **1958** [see *INTERPRET *v.* 1 d].

5. *Computers.* **a.** A machine that prints on a punched card fed into it the alphabetic or numerical equivalent of the pattern of holes.

1949 E. C. BERKELEY *Giant Brains* iv. 47 The chief IBM punch-card machines are: the key punch, the verifier, the sorter, the interpreter, the reproducer, the collator, the multiplying punch, the calculating punch, and the tabulator. **1970** O. DOPPING *Computers & Data Processing* iii. 54 If the cards have no text, a special machine, an 'interpreter', can be used to read the cards and print their contents on the top line.

b. An interpretive routine (see *INTERPRETIVE *a.* b).

1954 *Computers & Automation* Dec. 15/2 *Interpreter*, an executive routine which, as the computation progresses, translates a stored program expressed in some machine-like pseudo-code into machine code and performs the indicated operations, by means of subroutines, as they are translated. **1958** GOTLIEB & HUME *High-Speed Data Processing* xiv. 291 If a complete translation of the program is prepared *before* the initiation of its operation the system is a compiler; if the pseudo-code is retranslated each time it is used during operation, the system is an interpreter. **1964** [see *INTERPRETIVE *a.* b].

interpretive, *a.* Delete *rare* and add later examples.

1953 D. CECIL in W. de la Mare *Private View* p. vi, In his critical essays, Mr. de la Mare had not the scope for his interpretive genius to display itself so freely. **1955** *Bull. Atomic Sci.* June 218/3 There will be some 200 to 300 supplementary and interpretive books on atomic energy provided by American publishers. **1966** J. J. KATZ *Philos. of Lang.* iv. 111 Both the phonological and semantic components are, therefore, purely interpretive. **1966** MEIER & ELLIOTT (*title*) From plantation to ghetto: an interpretive history of American negroes. **1969** A. B. CALLOW (*title*) American urban history: an interpretive reader with commentaries. **1970** A. CAMERON et al. *Computers & O.E. Concordances* 107, I will admit that what follows will be interpretive. **1971** *World Archaeol.* III. 197 The field of interpretive functions which archaeologists call upon their pottery collections to sustain. **1973** *Studies in Eng. Lit.: Eng. Number* (Tokyo) 65 This is a highly controversial analysis, and has been much criticized by the so-called Interpretive Semanticists.

b. *Computers.* Applied to a routine that executes a source program by translating each instruction into machine language and then executing it (by means of subroutines) before proceeding to the next instruction; of or pertaining to the operation of such a routine.

1951 M. V. WILKES et al. *Preparation of Programs for an Electronic Computer* I. iv. 34 There are in the library a number of subroutines which, when called in, execute series of operations according to sets of parameters in the store... These subroutines are usually called in by the method used for the closed type, the parameter following the orders which call in the routine. The routines do, however, form a distinct class, and have been labelled 'interpretive'. **1957** W. D. BELL *Managem. Guide Electronic Computers* viii. 148 The availability of already established libraries is an important consideration in selecting a data system. And then there are 'interpretive routines', 'pseudo coding', 'compilers', and many other specialized programming methods and techniques. **1964** F. L. WESTWATER *Electronic Computers* ix. 143 As the number of subroutines available increased..whole programs could be written without any machine code being necessary. The coded orders were read in and a special routine (called the interpretive program or 'interpreter') selected each required subroutine in turn. **1970** O. DOPPING *Computers & Data Processing* xix. 306 Nowadays, the interpretive systems are used mainly for simulating a computer *B* using another computer *A* with other programming characteristics.

interproximal: see *INTER- *pref.* 6.

interpulse (i·ntəɹpʌls), *a.* and *sb.* Also **inter-pulse.** [f. INTER- + PULSE *sb.*[1]] **A.** *adj.* [INTER- 5.] Existing or occurring between one pulse and the next.

1948 G. N. GLASOE in Glasoe & Lebacqz *Pulse Generators* iv. 119 For such a succession of pulses, it is generally desired that the interpulse intervals, as well as the pulses, be of controlled duration. **1962** SIMPSON & RICHARDS *Physical Princ. Junction Transistors* xvii. 444 The interpulse period must be long enough to allow C_1 to replenish its charge before another sweep begins. **1966** *Jrnl. Exper. Psychol.* LXXI. 881/1 As the interpulse intervals increase the threshold for the gap monotonically increases. **1971** *Jrnl. Gen. Psychol.* LXXXIV. 86 It is possible that pairs of photic pulses of the proper durations and appropriate interpulse intervals would provide impairment of visual resolution. **1971** *Sci. Amer.* Jan. 50/1 The amplitude of the pulses from the objects was observed to be very uneven, but the interpulse spacing was quite regular.

B. *sb. Astr.* [INTER- 3.] A weaker pulse occurring between the main pulses of radiation from some pulsars.

1969 *Nature* 8 Feb. 525/2 The interpulse trails the main pulse by 14·0 ms. **1971** *New Scientist* 1 July 6/2 In many pulsars..there is a weak 'interpulse' roughly halfway between main pulses.

interpupillary: see *INTER- *pref.* 6.

interquartile (intəɹkwǭ·ɹtəil), *a. Statistics.* [f. INTER- 5 + QUARTILE *sb.*] Situated between the first and third quartiles of a distribution.

1882 F. GALTON in *Rep. Brit. Assoc. Adv. Sci. 1881* 245 This gave the upper and lower 'quartile' values, and consequently the 'interquartile' range (which is equal to twice the 'probable error'). **1944** *Mind* LIII. 175 Does a statistical description in terms of mean, mean deviation, interquartile range, describe well enough the individuals we have examined? **1952** *New Biol.* XII. 23 The interquartile range will be about 7 per cent of the median. That is to say, if we take 101 teeth, and arrange them in order for the particular length measured, the difference in length between the 26th and the 76th will be about 7 per cent of the length of the 51st.

inter-racial, -racialism: see *INTER- *pref.* 4 c, 2 a.

interrelate, *v.* Delete *rare* and add later examples. Also *intr.*

1964 R. JOHNSTON in *Oceanogr. & Marine Biol.* II. 100 Because the conductivity-chlorinity relationship has been shown to be somewhat variable, one cannot interrelate density, chlorinity and conductivity. **1964** M. MCLUHAN *Understanding Media* (1967) II. xiv. 149 Money becomes..the principal means of interrelating the ever more specialist activities of literate society. **1973** *Times Lit. Suppl.* 23 Mar. 320/3 The essays do not interrelate very adequately.

interrenal, *a.* (Further examples.)

1902 *Nature* 18 Sept. 516 On the interrenal bodies of Plagiostomes, by M. Ed. Grynfeltt. **1929** *Physiol. Abstr.* XIII. 530 The interrenal organ is essential to life in Selachians. **1940** *Chambers's Techn. Dict.* 455/2 *Interrenal body*, in selachian Fish, a ductless gland which lies between the kidneys and corresponds to the cortex of the suprarenal gland of higher Vertebrates. **1965** LEE & KNOWLES *Animal Hormones* iv. 69 The term adrenal cortex can be retained for all the vertebrate classes, but in the fish in view of the anatomical position the synonym interrenal may be preferred.

inter-responsive: see *INTER- *pref.* 2 a.

interrogate, *v.* Add: **4.** *trans.* **a.** To cause (a transponder, or a vehicle or craft fitted with one) to transmit a signal, usually coded to give information about the device or its surroundings, by transmitting a triggering signal to it.

1945 R. WATSON-WATT in *Nature* 15 Sept. 319/2 The 'H' and 'Oboe' systems, in which the primary radio pulses 'interrogating' the mobile craft automatically release from it a series of reinforced, coded, and conveniently frequency-displaced reply pulses. **1951** *Engineering* 3 Aug. 151/3 The aircraft would carry a transponder which, when interrogated would give the aircraft's identity and possibly other information such as height. **1953** *Electronic Engin.* XXV. 416/1 As the balloon ascends into the upper air, its airborne transponder is interrogated from the ground station by radar pulses. **1960** *Electronics Weekly* 23 Nov. 20/1 It..allows the control stations to interrogate each repeater for checking its operational condition. **1961** *Observer* 19 Feb. 11/1 The Russians have said they will 'interrogate' the rocket every five days. **1970** *Sci. Jrnl.* Apr. 52/1 Orbiting satellites interrogate the moving platforms..as they pass over them, using a coded VHF signal, and receive back the data measured by sensors carried by the platforms.

b. To cause (a computer memory or memory element) to give a signal that corresponds to or reveals information contained in it.

1964 T. W. MCRAE *Impact of Computers on Accounting* i. 7 A system whereby one can interrogate any record (or group of records) directly without having to process all of the previous records is called a random access storage system. **1971** *Nature* 19 Mar. 156/2 It is now possible, in principle, for the user to interrogate the computer store directly. **1971** *Publishers' Weekly* 9 Aug. 25/3 The customer's file will be interrogated to determine his credit status. **1972** *Nature* 31 Mar. 206/1 The memories are interrogated (read) by much lower voltage signals.

interrogatee. (Later example.)

1964 D. F. GALOUYE *Counterfeit World* i. 11 'I won't answer any questions,' Siskin said...The pollster frowned. 'You must. You are an officially registered interrogatee.'

interrogating (inte·rǒgēitiŋ), *ppl. a.* [f. INTERROGAT(E *v.* + -ING².] Of a radio signal: intended to cause a transponder to emit a signal.

1946 *Jrnl. Inst. Electr. Engin.* XCIII. IIIA. 332/1 In the earliest radar beacon systems the responder replied on the same frequency as the radar interrogating pulse. **1953** *Electronic Engin.* XXV. 416/1 The interrogating pulses are received by the balloon-borne unit.

interrogation. Add: **2. b.** *note of interrogation*: also *fig.*

1889 W. B. YEATS *Let.* 7 May (1954) 125, I have no theories about her. She is simply a note of interrogation. **1897** G. B. SHAW *Our Theatres in Nineties* (1932) III. 130 The ending of the play is not on the face of it particularly tragic: the alleged 'note of interrogation' is a sentimental fancy. **1931** H. G. WELLS *Work, Wealth & Happiness of Mankind* (1932) xv. 747 The note of interrogation which is born in the nature of every human being has been released. **1944** —— *'42 to '44* 116 No battle is a foregone conclusion, and so I must end with a note of interrogation. Will this thing be done now, rapidly?

3. The process of obtaining a signal from a transponder by transmitting an appropriate 'interrogating' signal to it; also, an interrogating signal.

1946 *Jrnl. Inst. Electr. Engin.* XCIII. IIIA. 487/2 The earlier varieties of I.F.F. all used direct interrogation. *Ibid.*, Each display..showed one echo fixed in position for each aircraft, due to its station's own interrogation. **1947** L. N. RIDENOUR *Radar Syst. Engin.* viii. 258 The interrogations were at 10 cm, the replies at 1·5 m. **1959** K. HENNEY *Radio Engin. Handbk.* (ed. 5) xix. 112 The moving craft sends out the interrogation and the beacon returns the reply. **1966** *Guardian* 19 Aug. 16/6 The new Interrogation Recording and Location System..to be embodied in future Nimbus satellites. **1970** *Sci. Jrnl.* Apr. 52/2 Direct interrogation of the package is made from the satellite using normal VHF interrogation telecommunications.

4. *attrib.* (sense 1), as *interrogation centre, room.*

1973 *Freedom* 2 June 3/1 Always there are the Chicago-style shootings from passing cars, the churches bombed or burned, the homes gutted by fire and watching over it all the army with its own State-sponsored violence, the interrogation centre, the beatings-up, [etc.]. **1944** *Sat. Even. Post* 15 July 19, I went into the interrogation rooms with these pilots and listened to the laconic reports they were relating to the Intelligence officers. **1971** 'O. BLEECK' *Thief who painted Sunlight* (1972) ix. 79 We were in one of those small, brown interrogation rooms at Homicide South. **1972** H. C. RAE *Shooting Gallery* iii. 142 Surely, sir, you've *seen* them round here, in the Interrogation Room, at the desk?

interrogator¹. Add: **2.** A radio or radar transmitter designed to transmit interrogating signals to a transponder; also (more fully *interrogator-responsor, -responder*), one that in addition receives the resulting signals from the transponder.

1945 *Nature* 15 Sept. 324/1 Pulses from an airborne or shipborne interrogator. **1945** *Electronic Engin.* XVII. 735/3 Aircraft and other moving vehicles could now carry small questioning transmitters ('interrogators'). **1946** *Jrnl. Inst. Electr. Engin.* XCIII. IIIA. 331/2 (*heading*) Introduction of an independent interrogator-responder system. **1947** A. ROBERTS *Radar Beacons* ii. 28 An interrogator-responsor can be so designed as to be useful as a radar. **1962** *Aeroplane & Commercial Aviation News* 29 Mar. 27/1 The aerial system..was delivered in February and the interrogator-responsor is now being shipped. An airborne transponder is also being obtained.

in terrorem: see IN *Lat. prep.* in Dict. and Suppl.

interrupt (intěrʊ·pt), *sb. Computers.* [f. the vb.] The action (usu. automatic) of interrupting the execution of a program as a result of the need for the immediate execution of another program, after which the original program is automatically resumed.

1957 *Computers & Automation* VI. 17/2 The interrupt feature of the 1103A will no doubt be embodied in many future computers. **1967** *Technology Week* 23 Jan. 11/1 (Advt.), Sigma 5 can deal with foreground real-time interrupts in 6 microseconds. **1969** P. B. JORDAIN *Condensed Computer Encycl.* 257 Some interrupts are initiated by the computer operator when he wants to give a command, or by a remote user who wishes to request service. **1970** O. DOPPING *Computers & Data Processing* vi. 106 In older computers, the response to an error discovered by the built-in checks was usually to stop... In modern machines, the response usually is an interrupt.. which automatically gives a branch to a special routine for analyzing and, if possible, correcting the error. *Ibid.* ix. 126 During these time intervals, the computer can run a background program which is not a real-time job. When a transaction has been input, perhaps over a telecommunication line, an interrupt signal causes the CPU to hand over control to the real-time program. When the transaction is dealt with.., a return jump to background takes place.

interrupter, -or. Add: **b.** (Earlier U.S. example.)

1851 C. CIST *Cincinnati* 302 It has been represented that Prof. Locke had merely invented a new species of 'electrical interrupter'.

c. *attrib.* **interrupter gear,** a timing device attached to machine-guns in aeroplanes to prevent the discharge of bullets when the propeller is in the line of fire. Also *transf.*

1928 C. F. S. GAMBLE *Story N. Sea Air Station* x. 150 The Fökker monoplane, which was equipped with a mechanical interrupter gear. **1932** *Discovery* Oct. 323/2 A very great advance..has been made in reducing the attrition of fabrics during washing, by an invention of the Research Association, called the Interrupter Gear. **1940** *Flight* 4 Jan. 7/1 That machine was..fitted with a rather crude but serviceable type of interrupter gear.

interruptible, *a.* Delete *rare* and add later examples. Also **interruptable.**

1939 H. NICOLSON *Diary* 4 Feb. (1966) 390 Compared with a film, it [*sc.* television] is a bleary..interruptible thing. **1961** R. B. LONG *Sentence & its Parts* xvii. 389 *Awhile*, of course, is readily interruptible: *I waited a long while* is common alongside *I waited awhile*. **1961** *Economist* 2 Dec. 910 A supply of gas that is interruptible. **1966** *Ibid.* 14 May 734/1 So customers prepared to accept 'interruptable' electricity and have their power cut at peak hours can buy electricity very cheap indeed—possibly too cheap. **1971** *Daily Tel.* 4 Mar. 14/3 Supplies will be on an interruptible basis, so that a cold-weather surge in domestic demand for gas might be met by cutting off supplies to industrial users such as Tunnel.

intersection. Add: **2.** *spec.* = CROSS-ROAD 2. Chiefly *N. Amer.*

a **1864** [in Dict.]. **1931** W. FAULKNER *Sanctuary* xxiv. 231 He whipped the car in and out of traffic.., shooting recklessly across inter-sections. **1953** W. BURROUGHS *Junkie* (1972) ii. 31, I had to pull over to the side of a road and wait until the weed wore off. I could not tell how far away anything was or when to turn or put on the brakes for an intersection. **1970** *Rand Daily Mail* 28 Feb. 7/4 In the same way it does not matter that South Africans should say..'intersection' for cross roads. **1970** *Globe & Mail* (Toronto) 25 Sept. 2/4 Two girls, 14 and 15 years old, were killed last night when struck by a car at the intersection of Park and Cherry Streets.

3. b. *Logic* and *Math.* The set which comprises all the elements common to two or more given sets, and no others; also, the operation of forming such a set.

1909 in WEBSTER. **1941** BIRKHOFF & MACLANE *Survey Mod. Algebra* xi. 313 Intersection and union are related to each other and to inclusion by a fundamental principle of *Consistency*: The three conditions $X \leqslant Y$, $X \cap Y = X$, and $X \cup Y = Y$, are mutually equivalent. **1950** W. FELLER *Introd. Probability* I. i. 14 In the theory of probability we can describe the event *AB* in words as the simultaneous occurrence of *A* and *B*. In standard mathematical terminology *AB* is called the (logical) intersection of *A* and *B*. **1952** F. B. FITCH *Symbolic Logic* iv. 101 For any two classes F and G there is a class [F ∩ G] known as the intersection of F with G and having as members just those things which belong to both F and G. **1963** ANDERSON & HALL *Sets, Sequences, & Mappings* iii. 50 A point is in the intersection of a collection of sets iff it is a member of every set in the collection. **1968** E. T. COPSON *Metric Spaces* i. 9 Let *A*, *B*, *C* be subsets of a given set *E*. Then the operations of union, intersection and complementation have the following properties: (*a*) $A \cup A' = E$, $A \cap A' = \emptyset$. [Etc.]

intersegment. Restrict *rare* to sense in Dict. and add: **2.** *Zool.* In certain animals, for example earthworms or caterpillars, the part of the body between two segments.

1901 *Proc. Zool. Soc.* 211 Papillæ with the arrangement just described were only found in one example [of the earthworm, *Benhamia gambiana*]; in another the intersegment xv./xvi. bore but a single median papilla.

intersegmental, *a.* (in Dict. s.v. INTER- *pref.* 4 a). Add: (Examples.) Used esp. in *Zool.* and *Linguistics.*

1894 *Jrnl. R. Microsc. Soc.* 545 Miss Platt describes.. three longitudinal ectodermic ridges, which become connected by intersegmental transverse ridges. **1906** J. B. SMITH *Explanation Terms Entomol.* 69 Intersegmental: = interarticular. **1925** A. D. IMMS *Gen. Textbk. Entomol.* I. 11 The flexible infolded portion of the cuticle between adjacent segments is the intersegmental membrane. **1952** *New Biol.* XIII. 86 The abdomen when empty is flat (hence the name 'mahogany flat') and the intersegmental membranes are telescoped under the segments. **1964** *Language* XL. 220 One could speak of this intersegmental dependency as a form of redundancy. **1970** I. M. MACKERRAS in *Insects of Australia* (Commonwealth Sci. & Industr. Res. Organization) i. 5/2 When sclerotization develops [in insect skeletons], it does so in dorsal and ventral plates extending from just anterior to each intersegmental groove. **1972** *Language* XLVIII. 46 In intersegmental variation, different values for a feature are distributed in different contexts.

Hence **intersegme·ntally** *adv.*

1909 *Cent. Dict.* Suppl., Intersegmentally. **1941** JOHANNSEN & BUTT *Embryol. of Insects & Myriapods* xv. 242 At about the 112-hour stage the neuroblasts of the median cord..at first lying intersegmentally shift forward. **1957** S. POTTER *Mod. Ling.* v. 105 Sentences may be described..intersegmentally in respect of the prosodeme of syllabic transition or juncture.

intersensory, inter-sensory (intəɹse·nsǒri), *a.* [f. INTER- 4 + SENSORY *a.*] Registered by two or more senses, e.g. sight and hearing. Hence **intersenso·rial** *a.*, **interse·nsorily** *adv.*

1933 *Proc. Brit. Acad.* XIX. 71 This [protocol-] language is inter-subjective and inter-sensory. **1934** M. BLACK tr. *Carnap's Unity of Sci.* 62 Physical determinations are valid inter-sensorily. **1935** *Brit. Jrnl. Psychol.* XXV. 468 A perception is produced by sensations of different modalities, which often create intersensorial patterns. **1964** M. CRITCHLEY *Developmental Dyslexia* xiii. 79 The evolution of behaviour can be 'conceptualised' as the process of development of intersensory patterning. **1973** *Jrnl. Genetic Psychol.* Sept. 115 (*title*) Effects of training on intersensory communication by three- and five-year olds.

intersertal (intəɹsə̄·ɹtăl), *a. Petrogr.* [a. G. *intersertal* (F. Zirkel *Untersuch. über Basalt.* (1870) iv. 111), f. L. *intersert-*, ppl. stem of *interserere* (see INTERSERT *v.*): see -AL.] Applied to the texture of igneous rocks containing a relatively small proportion of glass, augite, or other minerals in interstices between feldspar laths.

1893 A. GEIKIE *Text Bk. Geol.* (ed. 3) II. vii. 168 Under the name of Tholeite some interesting augite-andesites have been described, in which the felspar prisms form a network filled in with granular augite and interstitial matter (intersertal structure). **1916** A. JOHANNSEN tr. *Weinschenk's Fund. Princ. Petrol.* x. 199 Among the basic melaphyres there occurs a texture analogous to the ophitic, namely the intersertal. **1962** READ & WATSON *Introd. Geol.* vii. 412 Pyroxenes often include both

augite and pigeonite; they occupy the spaces between the feldspars and are sometimes granular giving the intersertal texture. **1972** *Science* 2 June 977/1 Sample 14310 is an intersertal plagioclase-rich basalt.

inter-service(s) (intəɹsə̄·ɹvis, -sə̄·ɹvisėz), *a.* [INTER- 5 + *SERVICE¹.] Existing or constituted between, or common to, the armed services.

1942 *Aircraft Recognition* Sept. 2, I am very pleased to write a preface to the first edition of the *Inter-Services Journal on Aircraft Recognition* which is being launched by my Department. **1946** *Daily Tel.* 24 Sept.,Fortunately, experience since 1939 has destroyed many inter-Service prejudices without modifying the legitimate pride each Service takes in its corporate spirit. **1958** 'P. BRYANT' *Two Hours to Doom* 74 In the few weeks he had been President he had already experienced one major inter-service row and three or four minor squabbles. **1958** *Times* 19 May 11/3 Coordinating purchases by the formation of inter-service supply committees. *Ibid.*, Inter-service differences revolve largely round the allocation of finance and resources.

intersex (i·ntəɹseks). *Biol.* [ad. G. *intersexe* (R. Goldschmidt 1915, in *Biol. Centralblatt* XXXV. 566): see INTER- 2 b and SEX *sb.*] In a diœcious species, an abnormal form or individual having characteristics of both sexes; the condition of being of this type.

[**1910** X. MAYNE (*title*) The intersexes, the history of similisexualism as a problem in social life.] **1917** R. GOLDSCHMIDT in *Endocrinology* I. 437 We have proposed the use of the terms intersexe, intersexual, intersexuality instead of sex-intergrades. **1920** *Science* 26 Mar. 326 The intersex gene itself has been found not to be sex-linked. **1930** G. R. DE BEER *Embryol. & Evolution* iii. 22 Animals which have switched over from a period of development in one sex to a period of development in the other are called intersexes. **1955** T. DOBZHANSKY *Evolution, Genetics & Man* xi. 262 This progeny consists of ordinary diploid females, diploid males, triploid females, and three new sexual types known as intersexes, superfemales, and supermales. **1956** *Nature* 21 Jan. 144/1 The birds were found to be six males, ten females and one intersex. **1962** D. J. B. ASHLEY *Human Intersex* p. vii, I have been interested in the problems of intersex particularly from the viewpoint of my own discipline. *Ibid.* p. viii, Gonadal tumours present a difficult problem in the intersex patient. **1971** *Daily Tel.* (Colour Suppl.) 10 Dec. 18/2 There are four main criteria involved in diagnosing and assigning the true sex of an individual: the chromosome sex, the sex of the gonads, the sex of the genitalia and the psychological sex. Dr Armstrong has defined intersex as the state in which any of these fail to agree.

So **i·ntersexed** *a.* = *INTERSEXUAL *a.* 2.

1939 *Ann. Reg. 1938* 372 The production of feminized males and intersexed rats by antenatal administration of oestrogens. **1968** R. J. STOLLER *Sex & Gender* ii. 17 (*heading*) The intersexed patient with normal gender identity.

intersexual (intəɹse·ksiuăl), *a.* [f. INTER- 4 c + SEXUAL *a.*] **1.** Existing between the sexes.

a **1866** J. GROTE *Treat. Moral Ideals* (1876) viii. 108 The intersexual feeling which belongs to all animals. **1897** in H. Ellis *Stud. Psychol. Sex* I. 183 This is quite as true of intersexual..love. **1904** G. S. HALL *Adolescence* I. iii. 223 A subtle but potent intersexual influence is among the strongest factors of all adolescent sport.

2. *Biol.* Typified by or having both male and female characteristics; having some characteristics proper to the other sex. Also *absol.* as *sb.*, an intersexual individual.

1916 [see *INTERSEXUALITY]. **1917** R. GOLDSCHMIDT in *Endocrinology* I. 438 With the male of race P, all would-be females will be high grade intersexuals, almost transformed into males. **1926** J. S. HUXLEY *Ess. Pop. Sci.* 51 Intersexual males—*i.e.* animals which have started as males and been forced to finish their development as females. **1962** D. J. B. ASHLEY *Human Intersex* xxi. 289 When the diagnosis of an intersexual state is deferred. **1965** *Punch* 10 Nov. 691/1 The intersexual goats are sterile. **1970** *Guardian* 7 Jan. 7/3 With..intersexuals, the problem begins at birth, for in rare cases it is uncertain from the genital organs whether a baby is a boy or a girl.

intersexuality (i:ntəɹseksiuæ·lĭti). *Biol.* [ad. G. *intersexualität* (R. Goldschmidt 1915, in *Biol. Centralblatt* XXXV. 566): see INTER- 2 b and SEXUALITY.] The state or condition of being intersexual; intersexual character.

1916 R. GOLDSCHMIDT in *Amer. Naturalist* L. 708 It seems advisable to use another term for these forms, which in general represent a definite step between the two sexes. The phenomenon shall therefore be called intersexuality. Further experiments now proved that intersexuality segregates, F_2 giving normal and intersexual animals. **1930** G. R. DE BEER *Embryol. & Evolution* iii. 22 A series of degrees of intersexuality can be established from very slight to complete sex-reversal. **1965** *Punch* 10 Nov. 691 Goat-breeders have tried to maximise hornlessness..but in so doing they have unwittingly increased the frequency of the gene for intersexuality. **1966** K. L. MOORE *Sex Chromatin* xiv. 229 Intersexuality occurs about as frequently in cattle, swine and goats as it does in humans.

inter-species: see *INTER- *pref.* 5.

interspecific, *a.* Add: Also, formed or obtained from (individuals of) different species. (Further examples.)

1913 *Amer. Naturalist* XLVII. 243 Interspecific hybrids seldom show the typical Mendelian behavior. **1946** [see *INTERGENERIC *a.*]. **1968** H. HARRIS *Nucleus & Cytoplasm* v. 93 If somatic cells derived from the two species of animal are fused together with inactivated virus, the resultant interspecific hybrids not only multiply, but actually overgrow the two parent cells.

Hence **interspeci·fically** *adv.*, between species, from one species to another.

1970 *Nature* 10 Oct. 189/2 The number of cellular enzymes known to differ interspecifically, for example, between mouse and man, is increasing rapidly.

interstadial (intəɹstē̆i·diăl), *sb.* and *a. Geol.* [a. G. *interstadial*, ad. F. *interstadiaire* adj. (A. Penck et al. 1894, in *Bull. de la Soc. d. Sci. nat. de Neuchâtel* XXII. 81): see INTER- and *STADIAL.] **A.** *sb.* A minor period of ice retreat during a glacial period, less pronounced than an interglacial. **B.** *adj.* Pertaining to or characteristic of such a period.

1914 W. B. WRIGHT *Quaternary Ice Age* vii. 156 It is, of course, extremely difficult to distinguish between interstadial and interglacial. This can only be done with certainty when the flora of the deposit in question indicates an oscillation of the snow-line of too great a magnitude to be regarded as interstadial. **1922** *Bull. Geol. Soc. Amer.* XXXIII. 421 Baltic interstadial (= Achen recession). **1946** L. D. STAMP *Britain's Struct.* xiv. 163 Arkell attributes the Aurignacian buried channel period to an 'interstadial' period in the midst of the Fourth or Final Glaciation rather than to the Third Interglacial. **1953** *Proc. Prehist. Soc.* XIX. 181 The additional notch at about 5 m. may correspond to the Epi-Monastirian beach of the First Interstadial of the Last Glaciation. **1968** ERICSON & WOLLIN *Ever Changing Sea* iv. 139 We may be living during a short interval of mild climate, or interstadial, within the last ice age. **1969** *Proc. Geol. Soc.* Aug. 155 Includes Upton Warren interstadial complex. **1973** *Times Lit. Suppl.* 1 June 607/3 (Advt.), The evidence for high interstadial sea levels.

i·nterstage, *a.* [INTER- 5.] Situated or occurring between successive stages of an apparatus.

1929 R. F. YATES *ABC of Television* v. 89 This interstage shielding is further insurance against audio-frequency regeneration. **1933** A. HUND *High-Frequency Measurement* viii. 255 This happens..when interstage transformers are used in amplifiers. **1958** W. R. BARRETT et al. in H. W. Cremer *Chem. Engin. Pract.* V. 125 The interstage relief valves protect the compressor against excessive interstage pressures. **1970** V. O. STOKES *Radio Transmitters* xi. 147 The most suitable method of interstage coupling when driving a final amplifier in a grounded-cathode arrangement is a *Π* circuit. **1972** *Physics Bull.* Oct. 583/1 In the manufactured version of this pump the interstage pressure is raised to about 0·1 Torr.

interstate, *a.* For *U.S.* read orig. *U.S.* Change def. to read: Lying, extending, or carried on between independent states, or between states belonging to a Union, Federation, etc. Also as *sb.*, a road between states. (Add further examples.)

1887 *Statutes at Large U.S.A.* XXIV. 383 A Commission is hereby created and established to be known as the Inter-State Commerce Commission. **1928** *Manch. Guardian Weekly* 31 Aug. 75/1 The problem of inter-State legal aid was bound to throw light upon the larger question of international legal aid. **1943** WYNDHAM LEWIS *Let.* 21 Aug. (1963) 367, I hate to think how much inter-state competition there is going to be after this war. **1953** A. UPFIELD *Murder must Wait* iv. 30 Such matters as State boundaries [in Australia] and inter-State jealousies wouldn't register with Bony. **1968** *Globe & Mail* (Toronto) 3 Feb. 33/5 Here in Georgia where Interstate 75 slices through the heart of a peanut, cotton and general farming area. *Ibid.* 17 Feb. B2/3 The U.S. Food and Drug Administration proposes to ban the interstate shipment of products containing carbon tetrachloride because of health hazards. **1969** *Jane's Freight Containers 1968–69* 115/1 During 1967, the Interstate Commerce Commission approved the merger of the company with the Chicago Great Western Railway. **1969** *Sydney Morning Herald* 24 May 35/4 (Advt.), Interstate carrier requires hauliers. **1971** *Sunday Australian* 8 Aug. 8/3 Builders and interstate truckdrivers, always high on the bankruptcy lists, continue to provide more than their share of debtors. **1971** D. E. WESTLAKE *I gave at the Office* (1972) 84 The shipments..traveled via truck on Interstate 40 and US 64 to a small town near Little Rock. **1972** *Times of India* 28 Nov. 10/7 Referring to inter-state disputes, Dr. Gajendragadkar urged the government to set up an inter-state council under Art. 263 to deal with such disputes instead of attempting to solve them on a political plane. **1973** J. M. WHITE *Garden Game* 173 The five-hour drive along Interstate 10 from Phoenix to Los Angeles. **1973** *Sun-Herald* (Sydney) 26 Aug. 73/4 As NSW champion she would have been the first player picked in the State team for the interstate series.

inter-sta·tion, *a.* [INTER- 5.] Occurring (in a radio) between two stations or tuning positions.

1940 *Chambers's Techn. Dict.* 456/1 *Inter-station interference*, interference which arises from the presence of another transmitter on the same (or on an adjacent) wavelength as that to which a receiver is tuned. **1946** C. A. QUARRINGTON *Mod. Pract. Radio & Television* I. xxvii. 225 Another unpleasant inter-station noise is experienced when tuning off one station and when tuning on to the next. **1970** J. EARL *Tuners & Amplifiers* i. 24 Other features found in tuner-amplifiers..are automatic mono/stereo switching..and an inter-station muting device which in the 'on' position deadens the audio channels on weak signals..and on noise signals between stations, thus making it possible to tune over the f.m. band without the annoyance of a high background noise, the tuner audio channels only being activated when a transmission of a useable strength is tuned.

interstellar, *a.* Add: (Further examples.) Also, relating to matter or to travel in interstellar space; occurring in such regions.

1926 A. S. EDDINGTON *Internal Constitution of Stars* xiii. 377 Fixed calcium lines..are formed either in an envelope surrounding the whole system or during the passage of the light through interstellar space. *Ibid.* 379 The question..arises whether, granting that there is a cloud extending through interstellar space, the fixed lines are produced uniformly during the transit of the light from the star to the earth. **1930** *Astrophysical Jrnl.* LXXII. 199 A star at a distance of 200 parsecs from the sun should show an interstellar K line of intensity 2. **1936** S. ROSSELAND *Theoret. Astrophysics* xxiii. 345 An intensive study of interstellar absorption is a necessary feature of stellar spectroscopy. **1937** *Physical Rev.* LII. 762/1 A third hypothesis..seems to point toward a physical relationship between space reddening (presumably caused by interstellar dust) and the formation of the spectral line. **1937** WHIPPLE & GREENSTEIN in *Proc. Nat. Acad. Sci.* XXIII. 178 The energy density in the galactic nucleus will be considerably increased, resulting in an increased temperature and emission for the interstellar particles. **1946** A. HUXLEY *Let.* 18 Mar. (1969) 539 People either wanted to talk about themselves, their job and their country; or else they couldn't stick to the point at issue, but wandered off into interstellar space. **1950** [see *COSMONAUTICS]. **1950** O. STRUVE *Stellar Evolution* II. 106 All indications are that interstellar matter can and does condense into protostars which later form real stars. **1952** LOVELL & CLEGG *Radio Astron.* ii. 34 The current belief about the remaining mass is that it is concentrated in the dust and gas which permeates interstellar space. By terrestrial standards this interstellar material is highly attenuated. **1953** *Mag. Fantasy & Sci. Fiction* I. II. 95 The cruiser *Ilkor* had just gone into her interstellar overdrive beyond the orbit of Pluto. **1966** *McGraw-Hill Encycl. Sci. & Technol.* VII. 221/1 Interstellar lines can be distinguished from the stellar atmospheric lines by their extreme narrowness. **1969** *Times* 16 Jan. 4/7 Measurements of the radio signals from sulphur hydride may be a valuable check of estimates of the amount of sulphur in interstellar space. **1973** *Times* 28 Dec. 10/8 Amino acids ..are formed when three of the chemicals known to be present in the interstellar clouds..are mixed in a flask and subjected to an electric spark.

inter-sterile: see *INTER- *pref.* 2 a.

interstice. Add: **1. b.** *Physics.* The space between adjacent atoms or ions in a crystal lattice. Cf. *INTERSTITIAL *a.* 2 e.

1933 [see *INTERSTITIAL *a.* 5]. **1940** F. SEITZ *Mod. Theory Solids* xiv. 496 The interstices of metals forming substitutional alloys usually are much smaller than the atomic size. **1942** SNEED & MAYNARD *Gen. Inorg. Chem.* xlvii. 1108 The interstices in a metal lattice are small, hence only the smallest metalloid atoms, C, N, B and H, can form such compounds and solid solutions. **1972** GROSS & WISEALL *Princ. Phys. Chem.* xix. 339 The holes or interstices formed between the layers of spheres in close-packed structures are of two different types, (a) tetrahedral interstices and (b) octahedral interstices.

interstitial, *a.* Add: **2. e.** *Physics.* Situated between the normally occupied points of a crystal lattice. Cf. sense *5.

1938 *Trans. Faraday Soc.* XXXIV. 851 Motion..is possible by jumps of ions from one interstitial position to the neighbouring one... An interstitial ion takes the place of a neighbouring lattice ion. **1940** F. SEITZ *Mod. Theory Solids* xiv. 496 Semi-conductors, such as zinc oxide, that have interstitial atoms. **1966** C. R. TOTTLE *Sci. Engin. Materials* iv. 92 There may be interstitial atoms present in a lattice as impurities.

5. Containing atoms or ions in interstitial positions: cf. sense *2 e.

1933 W. H. & W. L. BRAGG *Crystalline State* I. vii. 158 The atoms of H, N, C, or B are placed in the interstices of the metallic structures... Such structures are called *Einlagerungsstrukturen* by Hägg, and will be referred to here as 'interstitial structures'... All hydrides and nitrides [of transition elements], and some carbides, fall within the first category of interstitial compounds. **1948** *Acta Crystallogr.* I. 180/1 A large number of metals form metal-like phases with hydrogen, boron, carbon, nitrogen, and occasionally oxygen... Following suggestions of Hägg, these phases are generally regarded as interstitial solutions of the small, light elements in the metals. **1967** B. L. SHAW *Inorg. Hydrides* xi. 101 It is now known that the metal lattice often does change when the hydrogen is absorbed so that the term 'interstitial hydride' is not a good one.

B. *sb. Physics.* An interstitial atom or ion.

1961 *Physical Rev.* CXXIV. 669/2 If the interstitial is displaced slightly from its position in configuration '*B*' toward surrounding crowdion, 'body-centred' or '*A*' interstitial positions the calculations show that the interstitial returns to its position in configuration '*B*'. **1969** [see *DISLOCATION 1 e]. **1972** *Physics Bull.* July 400/1 At the temperatures relevant to the operation of fast reactors both vacancies and interstitials, produced as a consequence of radiation damage, are able to migrate under thermal activation.

interstitialcy (intəɹsti·ʃălsi). *Physics.* [f. INTERSTITIAL *a.* + -CY, after *vacancy.*] A kind of imperfection in a crystal lattice, characterized by an interstitial atom able to displace an atom from an adjacent lattice position so

that it becomes the interstitial in its turn, able to displace another atom.

1950 F. Seitz in *Acta Crystallogr.* III. 361/1 The lattice imperfection which is the inverse counterpart of a lattice vacancy is an interstitial atom which moves by jumping into a normal lattice site and forces the atom that is there into a neighboring interstitial site...We shall term it an interstitialcy. *Ibid.* 361/2 The interstitial atom associated with a passing interstitialcy at any point in its migration may be either an *A* atom or a *B* atom. **1956** *Physical Rev.* CI. 1210/2 The effects discussed here may be useful in distinguishing experimentally between interstitialcy and vacancy migration in other crystals. **1967** F. C. Brown *Physics of Solids* x. 315 In the silver halides the interstitial ion moves by an interstitialcy mechanism. **1968** J. R. Manning *Diffusion Kinetics for Atoms in Crystals* i. 6 Two jumps of the interstitialcy are required to move an atom from one lattice site to another.

interstitially, *adv.* (Examples in *Biol.* and *Physics.*)

1913 F. H. Humphris *Electro-Therapeutics for Practitioners* xvi. 115 Antiseptic chemicals..interstitially diffused throughout the growth. **1938** *Trans. Faraday Soc.* XXXIV. 851 Some ions exist interstitially within the normal lattice. **1965** *Nuclear Instruments & Methods* XXXVIII. 158/2 Interstitially located impurities. **1972** *Sci. Amer.* Nov. 45/1 In silver halide many cations wander interstitially through the lattice.

interstrain, inter-strain (i·ntəɹstrēⁱn), *a. Biol.* [f. Inter- 5 + Strain *sb.*[1]] Occurring or existing between one strain (Strain *sb.*[1] 7) and another; formed by crossing two strains.

1950 *Amer. Jrnl. Bot.* XXXVII. 631/1 Exceptions to the relatively ready inter-strain crossability among the strains hybridized were 109 × 105 and 109 × 110. **1955** *New Biol.* XIX. 52 Livesay's interstrain F_1 hybrids should be genetically uniform. **1965** *Jrnl. Gen. Microbiol.* XLI. 7 The progeny of inter-strain crosses.

inter-stream: see *inter- *pref.* 5.

intersubjective (intəɹsɒ̆bdʒe·ktiv), *a. Philos.* [Inter- 4 c.] Existing between conscious minds. Hence **intersubje·ctively** *adv.*, in an intersubjective manner; **intersubjecti·vity**, the fact or state of being intersubjective.

1899 J. Ward *Naturalism & Agnosticism* II. 170 It seems to depend upon three elements or conditions which are consequences of intersubjective intercourse. **1925** J. E. Turner *Theory Direct Realism* iv. 44 Intersubjective communication. **1934** M. Black tr. *Carnap's Unity of Sci.* iii. 42 It will be proved..that the physical language is inter-subjective and can serve as a *universal* language. *Ibid.* iii. 51 In such a case p will be said to have sense (for those persons) inter-subjectively. **1938** *Mind* XLVII. 133 Propositions about private experiences are inter-subjectively understood. **1938** C. Morris *Found. Theory of Signs* § 12. 125 The thesis of the potential intersubjectivity of every meaning. **1945** K. R. Popper *Open Soc.* II. xxiii. 205 Scientific objectivity can be described as the inter-subjectivity of scientific method. **1945** *Psychol. Rev.* LII. 258/2 Concepts which are to be of value to the factual sciences must be definable by operations which are..intersubjective and repeatable. **1956** *Essays in Crit.* VI. 10 The validation for the new myth philosophy ..plunges, in the vast reservoir of racial unconsciousness, for an intersubjective base for universality. **1957** C. La Drière in N. Frye *Sound & Poetry* 97 The acknowledged intersubjectivity of meaning is a kind of objectivity. **1963** R. Carnap in P. A. Schilpp *Philos. R. Carnap* 52 One of the most important advantages of the physicalistic language is its intersubjectivity, i.e., the fact that the events described in this language are in principle observable by all users of the language. **1967** W. Sellars *Philos. Perspectives* xv. 371 Universals are..identities not only with respect to their many instances, but also with respect to the many minds which think in terms of them... This inter-subjective and inter-linguistic character must be accounted for by any adequate theory of abstract entities.

intersubstitutability, -substitutable, -territorial, -testamental: see *inter- *pref.* 2 a, 2 a, 4 c, 4 b.

interti·llage. *U.S.* [Inter- 1.] Intercropping. So **interti·lled** *a.*

1912 L. A. Morehouse in *Bull. Bureau Plant Industry, U.S. Dept. Agric.* No. 260. 55 The alfalfa roots give some trouble at times, especially with the first cultivations of an intertilled crop, but this difficulty does not seem to be encountered when the cantaloupe or the cucumber is selected as the initial crop in the rotation. *Ibid.* 60 Regular intertillage can not be omitted without incurring losses. **1914** *Rep. Brit. Assoc. Adv. Sci.* 270 The intertilled crop has in many sections largely taken the place of fallow. **1973** *Times Lit. Suppl.* 21 Dec. 1572/3 The schemes of the Altai region to replace fallow and grass with intertilled crops (sugar-beet, maize, and fodder beans).

intertonic: see *inter- *pref.* 6.

intertrade (i·ntəɹtrēⁱd). [Inter- 2 a.] Reciprocal trade. Also *attrib.*

1915 E. Carpenter *Healing of Nations* xi. 168 Merchants and dealers came in and effected the exchange, and so an intertrade has sprung up. **1929** *Daily Tel.* 15 Jan. 6/4 The variations in the curve of consumer demand are much less than the curve of inter-trade demand.

intertranslatable (intəɹtrɑnslēⁱ·tăb'l), *a.* [Inter- 2 a.] Capable of being translated from one language to another and vice versa. Also *transf.* Hence **intertranslatabi·lity.**

a **1866** J. Grote in *Jrnl. Philol.* (1872) IV. 58 We assume that all languages are pretty accurately intertranslatable. **1951** *Mind* LX. 93 There is thus no genuine intertranslateability. **1960** W. V. O. Quine *Word & Object* ii. 76 An illusion that our so readily intertranslatable sentences are diverse verbal embodiments of some intercultural proposition or meaning. **1969** *Canad. Jrnl. Linguistics* XV. 47 From these (and other) approaches, therefore, we are forcefully reminded that linguistics now has more facets than ever—and that we must be on guard to maintain a degree of integration and inter-translatability among its schools.

intertrial, -tubercular: see *inter- *pref.* 5, 6.

Intertype (i·ntəɹtəip). [f. name of the *International Type*setting Machine Company, which manufactured the first machines of this type.] The proprietary name of a composing machine which produces type in whole lines rather than individual letters; cf. *Linotype, *Monotype.

1913 *Official Gaz.* (U.S. Patent Office) 1 Apr. 242/2 International Typesetting Machine Company, New York, N.Y. Intertype—Type Casting, Setting, and Composing Machines. **1916** Legros & Grant *Typogr. Printing-Surfaces* 437 *The Intertype*..closely resembles the two-letter, single-magazine Linotype... The constructors have given special attention to speed of operating... It appears to be virtually a copy of American model 5 Linotype. **1932** *Year Bk. Printing Dept. North-Western Polytechnic 1931–2* (Intertype Section, *subtitle*) Examples of Intertype composition composed by students in the Intertype Classes, and printed direct from the slugs. **1946** A. Monkman in H. Whetton *Pract. Printing & Binding* iii. 35/2 The Intertype... These [machines] are designed to produce a wide variety of composition, in the form of slugs. **1959** *Times* 14 Jan. 12/4 The great bulk of typesetting is achieved..by keyboard-operated Monotype, Linotype, and Intertype. **1967** V. Strauss *Printing Industry* ii. 74/1 The Intertype casts lines of type or slugs instead of individual types.

inter-union, -university: see *inter- *pref.* 5.

interurban, *a.* Add: (Later examples.)

1898 *Engineering Mag.* May 163/1 A finely-illustrated description of an English inter-urban street railway. **1901** *Westm. Gaz.* 15 Feb. 4/3 The Minister of the Interior [in Spain] has prohibited inter-urban telephonic communication. **1903** *Ibid.* 14 May 16/3 In the provision of means of inter-urban transport, London was originally..not inferior to any other city. **1962** *Coast to Coast 1961–62* 72 The cameras zoomed to a middle-aged man alighting from an inter-urban Hovercraft. **1971** *Selling Today* Sept. 4/3 Inter-urban motorways.

b. Ellipt. as *sb.*, an interurban railway or train. *U.S.*

1912 *Out West* Mar. 204/1 There is no more beautiful road..than the Los Angeles interurban through Azusa. **1948** *Daily Ardmoreite* (Ardmore, Okla.) 11 Apr. 1/6 Fifty persons were hurt..when two interurbans smashed head-on.

interval, *sb.* Add: **2. c.** *Physics.* A quantity *ds*, invariant under the Lorentz transformation, that represents the separation of two events in space-time and is defined by $ds^2 = dx^2 + dy^2 + dz^2 - c^2dt^2$ (or by the negative of the right-hand side), where *dx*, *dy*, *dz*, and *dt* are the differences in the space and time coordinates of the events and *c* is the speed of light.

1918 A. S. Eddington *Rep. Relativity Theory Gravitation* ii. 15 In the four-dimensional continuum the interval δs between two point-events..is unaffected by any rotation of the axes, and is therefore invariant for all observers. **1929** W. C. D. Dampier-Whetham *Hist. Sci.* ix. 422 Just as the distance between two points in the continuous space of Euclidean geometry is the same however measured, so, in the new continuum of space-time, two events may be said to be separated by an 'interval', involving both space and time. **1952** C. Møller *Theory of Relativity* iv. 99 This expression for the line element or the interval defines the geometry in (3+1)-space. **1959** J. Aharoni *Special Theory of Relativity* i. 25 When the interval is time-like it is always possible to find a system of coordinates in which the events appear in the same place.

6*. *Math.* **a.** A range between one number and another; *spec.* that between successive values of the argument in a mathematical table.

1838 *Penny Cycl.* XII. 508/2 The smaller the tabular interval, the more correctly will a given number of differences serve to make the interpolation. **1911** *Encycl. Brit.* XIX. 862/2 The actual calculation of the number of primes in a given interval may be effected by a formula constructed and used by D. F. E. Meissel. **1928** [see *interpolate *v.* 6]. **1946** *Nature* 12 Oct. 504/1 The basic sequence is the integration procedure for one interval of the integration, which is a sequence of operations starting from the initial values for that interval and giving final values which become the initial values for the next interval. **1968** Fox & Mayers *Computing Methods for Scientists & Engineers* i. 8 If $1{\cdot}5 \leqslant x \leqslant 2{\cdot}5$, then $y = x^{10}$ is in the approximate interval $57{\cdot}6 \leqslant y \leqslant 9536{\cdot}7$. **1974** *Nature* 26 Apr. 739/1 The grain temperature..is determined by the emissivity between 4 and 15 μm. We have carried out calculations..over this spectral interval.

b. A set composed of all the numbers between two given numbers, which may be either included in the set (a *closed interval*) or excluded (an *open interval*); an analogously defined subset of any partially ordered set.

The distinction made in quot. 1949 is not usual.

1902 *Encycl. Brit.* XXVIII. 545/2 This domain may be an 'interval', i.e., it may consist of two terminal numbers, all the numbers between them and no others. **1949** S. Lefschetz *Introd. Topology* i. 27 If the real line *L* is parameterized by means of a parameter *u*, then an interval is a set: $a < u < b$, and a segment is a set $a \leqslant u \leqslant b, a < b$. **1962** B. H. Arnold *Intuitive Concepts Elem. Topology* viii. 164 It is easy to see that a set $A \subset R$ is an interval if and only if it contains all points which lie between any two of its members. **1965** A. Abian *Theory of Sets* iv. 184 Let $(P, \leq)$ be a partially ordered set. For every two elements *a* and *b* of *P*, the set of all elements of *P* such that $a \leq x \leq b$ is called a closed interval and is denoted by $[a, b]$, and the set of all elements *x* of *P* such that $a < x < b$ is called an open interval and is denoted by (a, b).

7. (sense 1) *interval music, prose*; also **interval running,** in *Athletics*, a method of training by running set distances at pre-determined speeds (opp. *fartlek); so **interval training;** (sense 2) **interval signal** *Broadcasting* (see quot. 1941).

1951 *Catal. of Exhibits, South Bank Exhib., Festival of Britain* 176 Recordings for Interval Music. **1967** *Daily Tel.* 12 May 20/6 The unchanging interval-music. **1970** *Listener* 8 Jan. 60/2 The material..provided interval prose of just the right emotional tone between two parts of a good concert. **1957** *Oxf. Pocket Bk. Athletic Training* (ed. 2) 22 *Interval running*,..a series of runs over a particular distance each in a certain time..linked up by jogging between each. **1932** *B.B.C. Year Bk.* 373 The sudden failure of the programme..is likely to cause the listener to think his set has become faulty. The radiation of the interval signal relieves all anxieties on this account. **1941** *B.B.C. Gloss. Broadcasting Terms* 16 *Interval Signal*, particular sequence of sounds used by a broadcasting organization to fill short intervals between programmes, and to enable listeners to identify its transmissions. **1962** *Times* 9 Apr. 5/7 Oxford's application of interval training, on the other hand, may have been at fault.

intervallary (intəɹvæ·lări), *a. rare.* [See Intervallic *a.* and -ary[2].] = Intervallic *a.*

c **1864** G. M. Hopkins *Jrnls. & Papers* (1959) 76 The division then is of abrupt and gradual,..of intervallary and chromatic..and qualitative beauty. **1889** *London Med. Recorder* 20 Aug. 310/2 Herr Pfeiffer recommends in the intervallary treatment of gout the Wiesbaden baths.

intervalometer (intəɹvălǫ·mītəɹ). *Photogr.* [f. Interval *sb.* + -ometer.] An attachment for a camera that enables photographs to be taken automatically at set intervals.

1933 *Discovery* Feb. 60/1 The photographer works out the intervals that he must allow between exposures, so as to secure a 60 per cent. overlap, and sets the required interval on the intervalometer on the remote control. **1971** *Amat. Photographer* 13 Jan. 51/3 Time-lapse devices known as Intervalometers (repeating timers giving various ranges of delays between 0·2 sec. and 10 min.). With these the camera can be left unattended for indefinite periods (for motion analysis of such things as plant growth, etc.).

inter-valve, -varietal, -veinal: see *inter- *pref.* 5, 6, 6.

intervening, *ppl. a.* (in Dict. s.v. Intervene *v.*). *spec.* in *Psychol.*, *intervening variable*, a factor, such as individual memory, desire, or habit, which may affect the results of psychological tests or experiments in a way which is hard to predict.

1935 E. C. Tolman in *Philos. of Sci.* II. 365 The nature of this their resulting behavior is determined by a set of intervening variables to be conceived as lying in the organism... The molar behaviorist seeks to state the intervening variables as specific types of behavior-readiness. **1951** *Mind* LX. 50 The methodological device of the 'intervening variable' (drive, habit, demand, etc.). **1963** A. Pap *Introd. Philos. of Sci.* v. xx. 383 Human behavior also has mental determinants, such factors as memories, expectations, desires, [etc.]. But since these 'intervening variables' were supposed to be inaccessible to scientific investigation, the tendency developed to interpret them as certain *dispositions* to overt behavior.

intervention. Add: **1. b.** *Law.* The action of one, not originally a party, who intervenes in a suit.

1860 *Act* 23 & 24 *Vict.* c. 144 § 7 The said Proctor.. may..intervene in the Suit, alleging such Case of Collusion..and it shall be lawful for the Court to order the Costs..arising from such Intervention, to be paid by the Parties. **1864** G. Browne *Treat. Princ. & Pract. Court for Divorce & Matrimonial Causes* 152 There are two kinds of intervention, one 'by any person' under the first branch of the section, the second by the Queen's proctor under the latter branch... It appears that at any time before a decree for dissolution of marriage is made absolute, it is competent for one of the public to intervene.

Ibid. 153 The Court will not act on an intervention, when satisfied that it is made at the instance of the respondent or co-respondent. **1883** [see INTERVENER¹]. **1952** *Stroud's Judicial Dict.* (ed. 3) II. 1500 Intervention in divorce proceedings (generally by the King's Proctor) is for (*a*) collusion, or (*b*) suppression of a material fact.

Hence **interve·ntionism**, the principle or policy of intervening, esp. in international and economic affairs; **interve·ntionist**, also, one who favours a doctrine of intervention; one who favours intervention with the course of a disease on medical grounds (*Cent. Dict.*); also as *adj.*

1915 *Morning Post* 19 Apr. 8/4 Interventionist, and, in some places, neutralist meetings were held yesterday at Milan. **1921** *Glasgow Herald* 22 July 7 M. Tchitcherin sees in this fact another 'interventionist' manœuvre. **1923** *Ibid.* 29 Mar. 5 The methods of interventionism..are contrary to the spirit of cooperation. **1930** *Times Lit. Suppl.* 14 Aug. 648/2 The 'interventionist' conception of miracle has passed out of fashion. **1940** *Economist* 6 July 2/2 It was not primarily because of this advocacy of support for Britain that Mr Willkie was nominated...We cannot go further than to say that Mr Willkie's interventionism did not prevent his success. Moreover, there are severe limitations on interventionism even of the Willkie type...For example, there is the almost universal qualification that aid must stop 'short of war'. **1945** K. R. POPPER *Open Soc.* II. xvii. 117 We must demand that *laissez-faire capitalism* give way to an *economic interventionism*. *Ibid. Notes* 318, I suggest using the name *laissez-faire capitalism* for that period which Marx analysed..and the name *interventionism* for our own period. The name 'interventionism' could indeed cover the three main types of social engineering in our time: the collectivist interventionism of Russia; the democratic interventionism of Sweden and the 'Smaller Democracies' and the New Deal in America. **1962** *Listener* 20 Dec. 1040/1 The long-standing tradition [*sc.* in France] of an active, confident, and interventionist civil service. **1967** *Economist* 30 Sept. 1162/1 The new interventionism is an economic theory that came into vogue with some Labour intellectuals about three years ago, and with some core of justification. Its kernel was the entirely true argument that the governments of some countries with successful postwar economic records (e.g. France, Japan, Italy) have had greater scope for influencing the course of major industrial investment than have the less successful governments of postwar Britain. **1969** *Observer* 26 Jan. 8/4 America has never swung back..to isolationism and Russia has never regressed to all-out revolutionary interventionism. **1970** *Times* 2 July 8/3 It will not be easy to persuade the country to prefer government interventionism to the freedom which is Mr. Heath's aim. **1971** *Physics Bull.* June 261/2 Interventionists such as Joan of Arc, Ralph Nader, Ghandi [*sic*] and Sir Alan Herbert. **1973** *Financial Times* 28 Feb. 27/2 The contrast between the philosophy of the Conservative Government that believed so earnestly in the miraculous powers of laissez-faire in 1970 and the interventionist Conservative Government of today.

interview, *sb.* Add: **1. c.** Similarly in broadcasting.

1956 B. PAULU *Brit. Broadcasting* vii. 176 The BBC prefers straight talks to interviews, believing that talks are more apt to be carefully worked out. **1965** *Listener* 18 Feb. 260/2 The right interview..has to be used in the right place with the right person if the programme is to be craftsmanlike. **1974** *Radio Times* 21 Feb. 5/5 The background to my interviews is firmly in my head, though I still face the interviewer's perennial problem of..when to change the topic.

4. *interview room* (in a police station or prison).

1967 E. GRIERSON *Crime of one's Own* xvi. 135 Donald was called..to the interview room on the ground floor [of the prison]. **1969** J. GARDNER *Compl. State of Death* v. 76 Interview room. Usual. Stone walls and glossy paint. Table. Three chairs. **1974** J. WAINWRIGHT *Evidence I shall give* xxxiii. 188 He..left the Murder Room and found a telephone in one of the Interview Rooms, where he couldn't be overheard.

interview, *v.*² Add: Now *spec.*, to talk with or question (a person) for a programme broadcast on radio or television.

1933 *Radio Times* 14 Apr. 96/1 Three speakers..will interview experts in design before the microphone on behalf of listeners. **1957** G. HARDING *Along my Line* xvi. 159 One or two of the guests whom I had agreed to interview had gone to the trouble to notify their friends and relations across the width and breadth of Canada. **1974** *Radio Times* 21 Feb. 41/2 Robin Day interviewing those making the news.

interviewee. (Later examples.)

1959 F. GRISEWOOD *My Story of B.B.C.* xii. 190 The laborious business of discovering exactly how many.. interviewees watched or listened to each of more than a hundred programmes a day. **1965** *Listener* 20 May 756/2 It [*sc.* a radio programme] seemed to have caught some of the town-hall atmosphere, tersely described by a teenage interviewee as 'dead'. **1970** *Nature* 8 Aug. 641/1 Hammerton might contemplate the exact nature of the questions he asked his interviewees. **1973** *Guardian* 17 Apr. 15/1 The interviewee usually remembers the one-to-one relationship with the reporter.

interviewer. Add to *spec.* sense: also, a person employed by a broadcasting organization to perform a similar function.

1939 *Radio Times* 25 Aug. 20/2 'Come and be televised.' Interviewer, Elizabeth Cowell. **1941** *B.B.C. Gloss. Broadcasting Terms* 16 *Interviewer*, person whose role is to interrogate a broadcaster at the microphone and to elicit his story. **1969** *Times* 24 Nov. 17/3 Praise the Lord for a television interviewer who does not ram his personality down our throats. **1974** [see *INTERVIEW *sb.* 1 c].

interviewing, *vbl. sb.* (Later examples.)

1949 *Radio Times* 15 July 9/2 As compère, Brian Reece returns to the job in which he first showed his flair for radio—that of interviewing, 'gagging', and knitting a programme together. **1960** *20th Cent.* May 458 There is no substitute for direct contact through intimate interviewing. **1968** *Guardian* 26 Apr. 9/1, I wish I had some interviewing officers who could interview.

inter-village, -villous: see *INTER- *pref.* 5, 4 a.

Intervision (i·ntəɹviʒən). [f. *Inter*national tele*vision*.] (See quot. 1962².)

1961 *Listener* 2 Nov. 729/2 Other countries in the Intervision (East European) network. **1962** *Ibid.* 20 Dec. 1042/2 It [*sc.* the speech] was also carried by Intervision for viewers in Finland, Denmark, and Sweden. **1962** *B.B.C. Handbk.* 25 International co-operation between BBC engineers, Eurovision, and its Eastern counterpart, Intervision.

inter vivos: see *INTER L. prep.

intervocal, *a.* Add: So **intervoca·lically** *adv.*

1950 D. JONES *Phoneme* 22 Double k occurs only intervocalically. **1964** R. H. ROBINS *Gen. Ling.* viii. 327 Cockney speakers often have glottalized stops intervocalically. **1972** *Language* XLVIII. 465 Whatever analysis is adopted, the patterning of these segments is admittedly anomalous. They occur only intervocalically.

inter-war, *a.* [INTER- 5.] Of a period occurring between wars; *spec.* of the period 1919 to 1939 between the two world wars.

1939 O. LANCASTER *Homes Sweet Homes* 74 The inter-war period through which we have just passed. **1944** W. TEMPLE *Church looks Forward* v. 39 There must be no slipping back into the self-seeking and self-indulgence of the interwar years. **1959** *Encounter* Aug. 47/1 In the inter-war period [in Hungary] a limited number of Government and Opposition newspapers could be printed. **1973** *Listener* 25 Jan. 104/3 *Mein Kampf* is a vital document of the inter-war period.

interweft (i·ntəɹweft). *rare.* [f. INTER- 2 a + WEFT *sb.*¹] = INTERWEFTAGE.

1927 R. FRY *Cézanne* 80 In nature such a scene gives an effect of a confused interweft. **1939** —— *Last Lectures* 19 We begin to yield ourselves to the rhythmical movements of Botticelli's linear design, to its mazy interweft of curves.

interxylary: see *INTER- *pref.* 6.

interzonal (intəɹzōᵘ·năl), *a.* [INTER- 4 a, c.] Existing or carried on between zones.

1881 E. L. MARK in *Bull. Mus. Compar. Zool. Harvard* VI. II. 198 When seen lengthwise of the spindle, the numerous..thickenings appear arranged..in the form of a ring...Between the two zones of thickenings are stretched delicate nearly parallel threads, which I shall designate as interzonal filaments. **1920** L. DONCASTER *Introd. Study Cytol.* iii. 32 As the chromosomes travel to the poles, the interzonal spindle-fibres are seen still running continuously from pole to pole. **1956** *Ann. Reg. 1955* 229 In interzonal trade [in Germany] the volume reached little more than half the target figure for the year. **1959** *Ann. Reg. 1958* 263 Dr Adenauer..warned the East Germans that interzonal trade..would meet with difficulties if there were any interference with West Berlin's supplies.

inter-zone: see *INTER- *pref.* 5.

intestinal, *a.* **1.** *fig.* (Later examples.)

1945 *N.Y. Times Mag.* 21 Oct. 18/4 (*caption*) Edgar Bergen—'That guy has a lot of intestinal fortitude.' Charlie McCarthy—'I know a quicker way to say that.' **1961** J. S. MAYER *Restorative Art* (ed. 4) 21 This is the time for intestinal fortitude and determination.

in-thing: see *IN *a.* 2.

‖ **intichiuma** (intitʃi,ū·mă). Pl. **intichiuma.** [Native name.] Sacred ceremonies performed by some Central Australian Aborigines with the purpose of increasing the totemic plants or animals, and thus ensuring a good food supply.

1899 SPENCER & GILLON *Native Tribes Cent. Austral.* vi. 170 It sometimes happens that the members of the totem, such as..the rain or water totem, will hold their *Intichiuma* when there has been a long drought and water is badly needed. **1911** J. G. FRAZER *Golden Bough* (ed. 3) I. iii. 85 The general result supposed to be accomplished by these magical totemic ceremonies, or *intichiuma*, as the Arunta call them, is that of supplying the tribe with food and other necessaries. **1950** J. STRACHEY tr. *Freud's Totem & Taboo* ix. 139 The *intichiuma* ceremonies of the Central Australian tribes.

intilted (i·ntiltėd), *ppl. a.* [IN *adv.* 11 b.] Tilted inwards.

1940 F. SMYTHE *Adventures Mountaineer* viii. 117 At the base of the buttress lay a big intilted granite slab. **1956** M. STEWART *Wildfire at Midnight* x. 87 He climbed.. easily, making for the next stance, which was an in-tilted ledge some fifteen feet above him.

intimacy. 1. b. Delete 'illicit' and add further examples.

1906 B. WEBB in S. Hynes *Edwardian Turn of Mind* (1968) iv. 114 Friendship between particular men and women..is practically impossible..without physical intimacy...There remains the question whether, with all the perturbation caused by such intimacies, you would have any brain left to think with? **1907** *Westm. Gaz.* 14 Dec. 11/2 She stayed the night with Wood at his father's house. ..Intimacy took place on that occasion. **1963** A. HERON *Towards Quaker View of Sex* 71 *Intimacy*, close friendship, but also as a synonym for sexual intercourse.

intimal (i·ntimăl), *a. Biol.* [f. INTIM(A + -AL.] Of the intima.

1907 *Buck's Handbk. Med. Sci.* (rev. ed.) II. 98/2 A ligated vessel may be occluded by intimal proliferation without thrombosis taking place. **1961** *Lancet* 22 July 187/1 Numerous small systemic arteries can be seen and some of these show intimal hypertrophy.

intimate, *a.* **3. b.** Delete 'illicit' and add later examples.

1926 R. MACAULAY *Crewe Train* II. vi. 139 Some of them were..what newspapers call intimate together, without having undergone marriage. **1963** 'E. MCBAIN' *Ten Plus One* (1964) xiv. 162 Do you mean that you and the other two girls were *intimate* with these boys? **1969** *Times* 15 Nov. 3/2, I ripped her dress off. She was lying on her face. I was intimate with her.

d. Used allusively of women's underclothing.

1904 P. GIBBON *Souls in Bondage* i. 5 Clothes hung on lines in all directions, intimate linen flapped in the wind. **1970** *Globe & Mail* (Toronto) 28 Sept. 32/4 (Advt.), Next week we'll be highlighting panti hose and the week after it will be Intimate Apparel week in our Foundations Departments. **1973** *Tucson* (Arizona) *Daily Citizen* 22 Aug. 10 (Advt.), Intimate Apparel, mall level.

e. Of a theatrical performance, esp. a revue: that aims at establishing familiar and friendly relations with the audience. Also of a theatre itself.

1915 H. K. MODERWELL *Theatre To-Day* xvi. 309 The [Manchester Repertory] theatre happens to work mostly with the modern 'intimate' or 'realistic' play, and so is enabled to get along with one company of actors, albeit a large one. **1919** A. HORNBLOW *Hist. Theatre Amer.* II. xxxi. 343 The new method is to build a smaller house, or *théâtre intime*, allowing of an auditorium with limited capacity so that no seat will be very far from the stage. Among these theatres may be mentioned..the Maxine Elliott, one of the first of the intimate theatres. **1929** *N.Y. Times* 1 May 28/5 The Little Show. An intimate revue in two acts and twenty-seven scenes. **1930** *Nation* (N.Y.) 24 Sept. 331/1 The place and the popularity of the intimate music show is assured. People are delighted if it sounds like an impromptu affair. **1948** *Penguin Music Mag.* VI. 51 A series of intimate opera to be given at La Scala with a small audience seated on the stage. **1952** GRANVILLE *Dict. Theatr. Terms* 102 *Intimate revue*, a smart, topical revue played in a small (*intimate*) theatre. **1959** *Times* 22 Jan. 3/2 Intimate revue, at a glance, appears to be the theatre's gift to television. **1961** A. BERKMAN *Singers' Gloss. Show Business* 52 The Intimate Position of the head is that in which both the face and the eyes are directed squarely toward the other person. **1974** *Times* 27 Aug. 8/5 That quiet British archness which put the phrase Intimate Revue into the language.

‖ **intime** (æ̃ntīm), *a.* Examples of the French word revived in modern English use.

1857 W. BAGEHOT in *National Rev.* V. 411 The real, rougeless, *intime* Flicflac we know not. **1947** *Ballet Ann.* I. 73 *Ballet intime* bears the same relation to *Ballet Russe* as chamber music bears to a symphony. **1963** J. WIESENFARTH *Henry James* iii. 60 Another carriage ride introduces Maisie to an intime relationship between her father and her governess. **1968** W. GARNER *Deep, Deep Freeze* vii. 87 She..patted the sofa, 'Come and sit here. It is more *intime*.' **1973** *New York* 26 Mar. 21/2 Intime restaurant with continental cuisine.

intimism (i·ntimiz'm). Also ‖ **intimisme.** [ad. F. *intimisme.*] (See quot. 1959.)

1903 *Daily Chron.* 19 Dec. 3/2 The great result of the emancipation of French art from Italian influence is what he [*sc.* C. Mauclair] calls 'intimism'. **1959** P. & L. MURRAY *Dict. Art & Artists* 164 *Intimisme*, a form of Impressionist technique applied to the depiction of everyday life in domestic interiors rather than to landscape. The work of Bonnard and Vuillard is usually meant. **1960** *Times* 16 Feb. 14/7 To paint a group of television viewers would be a caricature of 'intimisme'.

Hence **i·ntimist,** ‖ **i·ntimiste** *a.*, relating to intimism. Also *transf.* Also as *sb.*, a painter following the principles of intimism.

1903 P. G. KONODY tr. *Mauclair's French Impressionists* ix. 196 Simon Bussy is decidedly the most personal of that young generation of 'Intimists' who seem to have retained the best principles of the Impressionist masters. **1937** *Times* 7 Oct. 12/3 In artistic slang they [*sc.* Bonnard and Vuillard] are grouped together as 'intimists', and the name serves well enough to describe..their habit of dwelling upon their material so as to extract from it the last possibilities in subtle colour relationships. **1959** *Listener* 21 May 898/1 The modified impressionism of Vuillard, a style especially suitable for such *intimiste* themes. **1967** *Ibid.* 18 May 654/1 Károly Ferenczy's 'Sunny Morning' of 1905 and the *intimiste* paintings of about the same period by..an associate of Bonnard in Paris. **1968** *Ibid.* 23 May 680/1 Jiri Menzel has everywhere been praised, like other Czech directors, as *intimiste*. **1973** *Times* 20 Mar. 9/7 The gallery shows a mixture of contemporary art and regular *Paris–Londres* exhibitions together with minor impressionists and intimists.

into, *prep.* Add: **23.** Interested or involved in; knowledgeable about. *colloq.*

1969 *Rolling Stone* 28 Jan. 19/1, I tend to like the stuff the rock groups are doing because they're creative and original, and that's something I'm very much into. **1969** *Down Beat* 20 Mar. 17/1 She is a Libra, for those of you who are into that. **1969** *It* 4–17 July 15/3 He was basically into being a hustler, which he was very, very good at. **1971** *Ink* 12 June 19/1 This should have been the highlight of the evening, but the audience just wasn't into it. **1971** *New Yorker* 11 Sept. 48 First I was into Zen, then I was into peace, then I was into love, then I was into freedom, then I was into religion. Now I'm into money. **1973** *Listener* 15 Feb. 209/1 Margaret is 'into' astrology, and consults the *I-Ching* each morning.

B. *adj. Math.* Used to designate a mapping (of one set 'into' another (Into *prep.* 6 a)) that is not necessarily 'onto'.

1949 S. Lefschetz *Introd. Topology* 215 (Index), Into transformation. **1958** K. S. Miller *Elem. Mod. Abstr. Algebra* i. 21 Since the mapping is into, there may exist elements in $\bar{S}$ which have no preimage in *S*. **1968** E. T. Copson *Metric Spaces* vii. 85 Every 'onto' mapping is 'into' but not all 'into' mappings are 'onto'.

intolerant, *a.* Add: **1. b.** *Ecol.* Of trees or other plants: unable to flourish in deep shade.

1898 G. Pinchot *Adirondack Spruce* 5 The Poplar, a tree very intolerant of shade..rapidly takes possession of the soil. *Ibid.* 22 If the intolerant species can get the start, being often rapid of growth, they may hold their position by growing above the other trees about them. **1929** Weaver & Clements *Plant Ecol.* xiv. 320 The leaves of intolerant trees can not make food in weak, diffuse light. **1952** P. W. Richards *Tropical Rain Forest* iii. 42 Of the young trees in this patch of undergrowth the more light-demanding (intolerant) species respond more quickly than the shade-bearing (tolerant) species. **1965** G. L. Clarke *Elem. Ecol.* (rev. ed.) vi. 233 Plants that require strong illumination and will not survive or develop in reduced light are referred to as intolerant species.

‖ **intombi** (intǫ·mbi). [Xhosa, Zulu *i-ntombi* maiden.] (See quot. 1913.)

1809 R. Collins *Jrnl.* in D. Moodie *Record: Papers Native Tribes S. Afr.* (1842) v. 46 Cattle are never given for a Tumbee, but her father or brother is supplied with assagays by her keeper. **1833** S. Kay *Trav. Caffraria* xviii. 470 'That,' said he, 'contains the body of an *intombi* (young woman) who was killed by lightning from heaven, about two years ago.' **1855** J. W. Colenso *Ten Weeks in Natal* 26 There is another special one [*sc.* reason] for the young men wishing to go home from time to time—namely, to make acquaintance with the *intombies*, or young women, where they will one day acquire for wives. **1913** C. Pettman *Africanderisms* 228 *Intombi*,..a girl or young unmarried woman. **1947** L. Hastings *Dragons are Extra* vi. 118 The little girls, the intombis, were busy with bunches of twigs tidying up the huts.

intonation[1]. Add: **4.** (Later examples.)

1935 M. Schubiger *Role of Intonation in Spoken Eng.* 2 Word-order can remain unaltered, and then the different intonation, the rising instead of the falling tune, is the sole bearer of the interrogative relation. **1965** W. S. Allen *Vox Latina* 6 It is important to distinguish tone from intonation. The former refers to the pitch-patterns operative within individual words, whereas 'intonation' refers to the pitch-pattern operative over the whole clause or sentence.

5. *attrib.* and *Comb.*, as *intonation change, morpheme*; **intonation contour**, a succession of levels of pitch extending over an utterance; **intonation curve**, the rising and falling of pitch within an utterance; **intonation pattern**, a pattern of variations in pitch; **intonation phoneme** = *intoneme; **intonation tune** (see quot. 1964); **intonation turn**, the point, usually at a prominent part of an utterance, at which the intonation rises or falls.

1964 C. Barber *Present-Day Eng.* iii. 50 There are intonation-changes inside the syllable which require a certain length of vowel to manifest themselves. **1946** K. L. Pike *Intonation Amer. Eng.* iii. 20 All speakers of the language use basic pitch sequences in similar ways under similar circumstances. These abstracted characteristic sentence melodies may be called *Intonation Contours.* **1960** [see *attitudinal *a.*]. **1964** R. A. Hall *Introd. Ling.* xix. 114 An intonation contour does not..make any difference in the 'dictionary meaning' of an utterance. **1970** Intonation contour [see *contour *sb.* 1 e]. **1936** H. Mulder *Cognition & Volition in Lang.* ii. 65 Wishes, commands, and questions introduced by interrogative pronouns, can be communicated on the same intonation-curve as plain statements. **1965** *Language* XLI. 498 In refusing to consider intonation-curves as subject to division into significant units, Martinet alleges that every modification..of a melodic curve brings with it a corresponding modification of meaning. **1953** *Internat. Jrnl. Amer. Ling.* XIX. ii. Suppl. 29 Hjelmslev requested a metalinguistic analysis of the English intonation morphemes which Smith had demonstrated earlier so as to make clear the difference between differential meaning and the meaning in general of the intonation patterns. **1966** G. N. Leech *Eng. in Advertising* ii. 18 The relationship of apposition between elements is marked in speech by tone-concord, or equivalent intonation patterns on each element. **1971** D. Crystal *Ling.* Interlude 134 A noun phrase may not have any separate intonation pattern at all. **1948** Intonation phoneme [see *intoneme]. **1934** J. J. Hogan *Outl. Eng. Philol.* i. v. 31 Its [*sc.* a verse's] accompanying intonation-tune suffers modification by the regular tune which is what the line always retains of its character as a sentence or clause. **1964** R. H. Robins *Gen. Ling.* iv. 148 Intonations or intonation *tunes*, as they are often called, are regular sequences of pitch differences coextensive with a whole sentence or with successive parts thereof, and constituting an essential feature of normal spoken utterance. **1935** M. Schubiger *Role of Intonation in Spoken Eng.* 9 If the psychological predicate consists of several words the most important gets the intonation turn.

Hence **intona·tional** *a.*, relating to intonation; **intona·tionally** *adv.*, in an intonational manner.

1895 J. Osgood in *Forum* June 503 The misused intonational 'twist', technically noted as the circumflex inflection. **1949** E. A. Nida *Morphol.* (ed. 2) 62 In English the sentence-final glides which follow the last intonationally stressed syllable constitute morphemes. **1952** *Trans. Philol. Soc.* 91 Differences of intonational relationship between stem and ending. **1957** *Publ. Amer. Dial. Soc.* xxviii. 6 We might start intonationally with Qs [*sc.* questions] classed as upmoving and downmoving. **1958** C. F. Hockett *Course in Mod. Ling.* 45 Certain types of speech..show..a total loss of intonational contrasts. **1964** R. H. Robins *Gen. Ling.* iii. 112 The different ways in which pitch differences are exploited intonationally and tonally. *Ibid.* iv. 149 In English..stressed syllables carry more intonational weight than unstressed syllables. **1971** D. Crystal *Ling.* 133 The intonational movement over the noun phrase as a whole must be indicated.

intoneme (intōᵘ·nīm). [Short for **intonation phoneme*: see *-eme.] An intonation pattern that contributes to the meaning of an utterance.

1948 K. L. Pike *Tone Lang.* v. 60 One may choose to call the key pitches *intonation phonemes* or *intonemes.* **1965** *Language* XLI. 498 Intonation-curves..can nevertheless be classified into contrasting units (call them 'tonemes' or 'intonemes' if you like). **1967** *Word* XXIII. 473 To turn again to my son's efforts to communicate, it was possible to isolate at the age of four months two intonemes, the one for desiderative and the other for deictic purposes. **1968** *Language* XLIV. 82 These two intonemes operate in the high range in the intonation system.

intorsion. Add: Also *spec.* in *Ophthalm.* (see quots.).

1899 A. Duane tr. *Fuchs's Text-bk. Ophthalm.* (ed. 2) xiv. 578 It [*sc.* the superior rectus muscle] also rolls the eye in such a way that the upper extremity of its vertical meridian is inclined inward (intorsion). **1964** [see *extorsion].

in toto: see In *L. prep.* in Dict. and Suppl.

Intourist (i:ntūə·rist). [Russ. *Inturist*, abbrev. of *inostránnyĭ turist* foreign tourist.] Name of the State Travel Bureau of the U.S.S.R. Also *attrib.*

1932 *Intourist's Pocket Guide to Soviet Union* 581 The State Joint-Stock Company for Foreign Tourists—*Intourist*—was established in 1929 jointly by the People's Commissariat for Foreign and Domestic Trade, the People's Commissariat for Ways and Communications and the Soviet Mercantile Fleet. **1935** N. Mitchison *We have been Warned* ii. 194 All arrangements in the competent hands of the Intourist Office, who undertook all Russian travel. **1940** H. G. Wells *Babes in Darkling Wood* iii. ii. 251, I suppose they were packing off most of the Intourist people. **1949** F. Maclean *Eastern Approaches* i. iii. 35, I walked into the local branch of Intourist and informed the seedy little Armenian clerk behind the counter that I wished to book a passage across the Caspian to Central Asia. **1952** M. McCarthy *Groves of Academe* (1953) ix. 169 He took you through that session like a regular Intourist guide with a party of dumb fellow-travellers. **1958** J. Gunther *Inside Russia Today* i. 29 You go to any travel agency that has an arrangement with Intourist, the official Russian agency..and apply for a tourist visa. **1973** T. Allbeury *Choice of Enemies* xix. 95 The failed ballerinas seconded to Intourist as easy lays for Western salesmen.

in-town. Restrict *Sc.* to sense in Dict. and add: **2.** *adj.* and *adv.* Within (the central part of) a town.

1817 J. Keats *Let.* 16 May (1958) I. 147, I am glad to hear of Mr T's health and of the Wellfare of the In-town-stayers. **1941** W. Stevens *Let.* 25 Mar. (1967) 388 Today, as I walked in-town, I heard..song sparrows. **1958** S. Spender *Engaged in Writing* i. 24 A concourse of canals that formed a minute intown harbour. **1967** *Boston Herald* 1 Apr. 22/1 Three intown congregations..will join in worship here at 11 a.m. Sunday.

intra (i·ntrǎ), *prep.* [L., = within.] **1.** In phr. *intra vires*, within the powers or legal authority (*of* a person, etc.). Cf. Ultra *prep.* 1.

1877 S. Brice *Treat. Doctrine Ultra Vires* (ed. 2) ii. ii. 56 It will be best to retain the secondary use of the term Ultra Vires, and..to deal only with those proceedings which are bad in reference to matters admitted to be Intra Vires in both meanings. **1884** *Law Times* LXXVIII. 110 (Stanford), If this were *intra vires*, the other securities which they had accepted were not *bonâ fide* ones. **1930** A. Palmer *Company Secretarial Pract.* 185 Excess borrowing *intra vires* of the company but *ultra vires* of the directors may be ratified by ordinary resolution. **1966** *Rep. Comm. Inquiry Univ. Oxf.* I. 256 We have already explained..the methods by which this power may be kept *intra vires.* **1970** *Internat. & Compar. Law Q.* 4th Ser. XIX. ii. 244 It would seem that, at least in New Zealand municipal law, if the Antarctica Act is *intra vires*, the Dependency includes the high seas south of 60° S.

2. intra vitam, during life; while still living. Freq. *attrib.*, = *intravital *a.*

1881 *Bull. Mus. Compar. Zool. Harvard* VI. ii. 264 Whether the intranuclear network was present as a structure *intra vitam.* **1898** *Jrnl. Microsc. Soc.* 133 Herr A. M. Przesmycki has made a long series of experiments on *intra-vitam* staining. **1965** *Acta Med. Scand.* CLXXVIII. 155 (*heading*) Intra-vitam diagnosis of oxalosis.

intra-, *prefix.* Add: **1. intra-amnio·tic**, taking place, situated, or administered within the amnion; so **intra-amnio·tically** *adv.*, within the amnion; **intra-arterial** (further examples); also, administered into an artery; **intra-arte·rially** *adv.*, (by injection) into an artery; **intra-arti·cular**, situated within or passing into a joint of the body; **intracapi·llary**, existing within a blood capillary; **intraca·rdially** *adv.*, into the heart; **intra-cerebral** (earlier and later examples); **intrace·rebrally** *adv.*, in or into the cerebrum; **intraciste·rnal**, occurring within or (of an injection) administered into a cistern of the body, esp. one in the brain; hence **intraciste·rnally** *adv.*; **intracoa·stal**, situated close to the coast; **intraco·ronal** *Dentistry*, placed or performed within the crown of a tooth; hence **intraco·ronally** *adv.*; **intraco·rtical**, situated or occurring within the cortex of the brain; **intracru·stal** *Geol.*, situated within the earth's crust; **intracry·stalline** *Min.*, occurring within a crystal; **intracu·ltural**, occurring within a culture; hence **intracu·lturally** *adv.*; **intracuta·neous** = *intradermal* (below); hence **intracuta·neously** *adv.*; **intracytopla·smic**, situated or occurring within the cytoplasm of a cell; **intra-departme·ntal**, done or occurring within a department; **intrade·rmal, -de·rmic**, situated or applied within the skin; hence **intrade·rmally** *adv.*; **intradu·ctal**, situated or applied within a duct (of a breast); **intradu·ral**, situated or performed within the dura mater; hence **intradu·rally**; **intraepide·rmal, -epide·rmic**, situated or occurring within the epidermis; **intra-Europe·an**, occurring or carried on within Europe; **intra-experie·ntial**, within experience; **intrafasci·cular** *Bot.*, situated within a vascular bundle; **intraforma·tional** *Geol.*, formed or occurring within a geological formation; **intrafu·sal** [L. *fusus* spindle], situated or occurring within a muscle spindle; **intraga·stric**, applied, existing, or situated within the stomach; hence **intraga·strically** *adv.*, into the stomach; **intragene·ric**, occurring or existing within a genus or between individuals of a single genus; **intrage·nic** [*genic *a.*], occurring within a gene; **intragla·cial** = *englacial *a.*; also, lying upon or within, or being, the terrain formerly occupied by a glacier or ice-sheet; **intragla·ndular**, existing or carried out within a gland; **intraglute·al**, administered into the gluteal muscles; **intragovernme·ntal**, occurring within the institutions or branches of a government; **intralenti·cular** *Ophthalm.*, situated within the lens of the eye; **intra-li·ngual**, (*a*) *Med.*, situated or occurring in the substance of the tongue (*New Syd. Soc. Lex. Med.* 1888); (*b*) of communication, etc.: within a given language; within the bounds of language; **intra-lingui·stic** = **intralingual* (*b*); **intralu·minal**, existing within a lumen, esp. that of the intestine; **intrama·mmary**, existing or applied within a breast; **intra-me·ntal**, occurring within the mind; so **intra-menta·lity**; **intramorphe·mic**, occurring or existing within a morpheme; **intramuscular** (further examples); also, administered into a muscle; hence **intramu·scularly** *adv.*, (by injection) into a muscle; **intrana·sally** *adv.*, through, in, or into the nose; **intrana·tal**, taking place at the time of birth; **intrana·tional**, occurring or carried on within a nation-state; **intraneu·ral**, situated or occurring within a nerve; **intranucleolar** (-niukliōᵘ·lǎɹ, -niūklī·ǒlǎɹ), situated or occurring within a nucleolus; **intra-orga·nic, -organi·smal, -organi·smic**, within an organism; **intra-pe·rsonal**, occurring inside a person's mind or character; **intra-psy·chic, -psy·chical**, occurring or existing within the psyche; **intrapulmo·nic** = *intrapulmonary* (in Dict.); **intrara·cial**, within, or occurring within, a race; **intrare·gional**, occurring within a region; **intrasegme·ntal** *Zool.* and *Linguistics*, occurring within a 'segment'; **intrase·minal** *Bot.*, occurring or existing within a seed; **intrasoma·tic** [Gr. σῶμα body], situated or occurring

within the body; **intraspi·nally** *adv.*, within the spinal cord; **intra-subje·ctive,** of a reaction, response, etc., which occurs within a person; **intratesti·cular,** existing or carried out within, or administered into, a testicle; hence **i:ntra-testi·cularly** *adv.*; **intrathecal,** (*b*) going into or occurring within the spinal theca; hence **intra-the·cally** *adv.*; **intratra·cheally** *adv.*, within the trachea; **intra-ty·pical,** occurring within one type; **intravaginal,** (*b*) *Bot.*, within the sheath of a leaf; **intravari·etal,** occurring or existing within a variety (VARIETY 6 b), or between individuals of the same variety; **intravehi·cular,** of, pertaining to, or used within a space vehicle; **intrave·rbal,** within a word; **intra-ve·rtebral,** situated within a vertebra; hence **intrave·rtebrally** *adv.*

1960 *Biol. Abstr.* XXXV. 1865/2 (*heading*) The lipids in the coating layer of the epidermis during the intra-amniotic life. **1973** *Nature* 26 Jan. 280/1 The observed periodicity in response to the intra-amniotic injection of $PGF_{2\alpha}$ must..be related to endocrine and/or other rhythmic metabolic changes. **1961** *Lancet* 5 Aug. 279/1 If the endocrine condition of one uterine horn is altered experimentally (..by injecting progesterone intra-amniotically into one horn) the two horns deliver at different times. **1973** *Nature* 26 Jan. 280/1 Intra-amniotically injected $PGF_{2\alpha}$ appears to be slowly transferred from the amniotic compartment. **1946** *Ibid.* 17 Aug. 238/1 Buchtal and Kahlson have pointed out that the close intra-arterial injection of 5 μgm. acetylcholine after introduction of adenosine triphosphate increases the intensity and duration of the mechanical response of muscle. **1962** *Lancet* 29 Dec. 1338/1 Substances given by intra-arterial infusion. **1938** *Coll. Papers Mayo Clinic* XXIX. 533 Histamine phosphate..and acetyl β-methylcholine..were injected intra-arterially. **1964** W. G. SMITH *Allergy & Tissue Metabolism* ii. 26 Doses of antigen given intra-arterially or intravenously. **1890** BILLINGS *Med. Dict.* I. 711/1 Intra-articular. **1908** *Practitioner* Apr. 516 There was much intra-articular effusion into both knee-joints. **1961** *Lancet* 29 July 266/2 Intra-articular cartilage is avascular. **1879** *Jrnl. Physiol.* II. 336 The relation which exists between the intracapillary pressure and the degree of dilation of these delicate tubes. **1961** *Lancet* 16 Sept. 664/2 A higher intracapillary hydrostatic pressure is presumably related to a greater leakage of protein and fluid. **1917** *Jrnl. Immunol.* II. 141 Römer..injected guinea pigs sensitized to horse serum intracardially with diphtheria antitoxin. **1958** *Immunology* I. 104 Injections were made intracardially. **1881** G. SIGERSON tr. *Charcot's Lect. Dis. Nervous System* II. 281 An intra-cerebral focus of hæmorrhage. **1890** W. JAMES *Princ. Psychol.* I. iii. 100 He found very regularly an immediate deflection of the galvanometer, indicating an abrupt alteration of the intra-cerebral temperature. **1964** S. DUKE-ELDER *Parsons' Dis. Eye* (ed. 14) xxxiii. 530 They spread slowly within the sheaths, and death is due to intracerebral extension. **1910** *Jrnl. Exper. Med.* XII. 253 Inoculated intracerebrally with spinal cord. **1937** *Jrnl. Path. & Bacteriol.* XLIV. 418 The strain of fowl pest virus..was only very slightly pathogenic for mice when inoculated intraperitoneally or even intracerebrally. **1970** *European Jrnl. Cancer* VI. 173/1 Inbred Swiss/Ry-female mice were inoculated intracerebrally with Ehrlich carcinoma. **1932** DORLAND & MILLER *Med. Dict.* (ed. 16) 642/1 *Intracisternal*, within a cistern, especially the cisterna magna. **1958** *Technology* Jan. 384/3 By intracisternal injection *nor*-morphine was rather more active than morphine. **1964** G. H. HAGGIS et al. *Introd. Molecular Biol.* v. 141 One hour after the first meal following starvation..the endoplasmic reticular cavities of the basal zone..are distended and contain small granules (intracisternal granules). **1934** *Physiol. Abstr.* XIX. 481 Histamine.., acetylcholine, and padutin have no influence upon the blood pressure when injected intracisternally. **1971** *Nature* 5 Mar. 54/1 Intracisternally injected radioactive noradrenaline. **1928** *Daily Tel.* 26 June 10/6 Houston['s]..hinterland is shortly to be widened by the construction of the intra-coastal canal from New Orleans. **1964** *Times Rev. Industry* Mar. 86/1 Between Jacksonville and Palatka..there is a navigable channel in the St. Johns River forming part of the Atlantic Intra-coastal waterways. **1972** *Countryman* Winter 41 Fifty miles along the intracoastal canal to the Aransas wildlife sanctuary [in Texas]. **1940** S. D. TYLMAN *Theory & Pract. Crown & Bridge Prosthesis* xix. 177 Retainers are classified into three types: The first is the intracoronal, or inlays... As the name indicates, the prepared cavity and its cast retainer lie largely within the body of the coronal portion of the tooth. **1963** C. R. COWELL et al. *Inlays, Crowns & Bridges* ii. 4 A gold inlay is an intracoronal restoration for a vital tooth. *Ibid.* vi. 60 Tooth substance may have been lost to such an extent that a restoration cannot be retained intracoronally. **1890** W. JAMES *Princ. Psychol.* II. xix. 128 The normal forward irradiation of intra-cortical excitement through association-paths is checked. **1970** *Jrnl. Physiol.* CCX. 57P (*heading*) Relation of movements induced by intracortical stimulation to receptive fields of points in the perirolandic and parietal cortex of the monkey. **1933** Intracrustal [see *BYSMALITHIC *a.*]. **1921** *Sci. Papers U.S. Bureau of Standards* XVI. 215 The fracture of normal material is, in general, intra-crystalline; that is, it consists of a break across the grains rather than of a separation between them. **1955** *Soil Sci.* LXXX. 425 The intracrystalline swelling of montmorillonite. **1973** *Nature* 3 Aug. 277/1 The increase in intra-crystalline slip..may lead to the elongation of the recrystallized grains. **1937** R. H. LOWIE *Hist. Ethnol. Theory* (1938) xiii. 237 As soon as functionalism is reduced to what it is—a worthy programme for ascertaining what intracultural bonds may exist—the neglect of other methods appears as solely a matter of personal preference. **1956** GARVIN & MATHIOT in J. A. Fishman *Readings Social. of Lang.* (1968) 366 In intra-cultural terms, different segments of a speech community can be compared as to the degree to which the standard language has penetrated them, just as different subcultures of the same culture can be compared in terms of different degrees of penetration by urban elements. **1956** LENNEBERG & ROBERTS *Language of Experience* 4 Not all hypotheses can be verified intra-culturally. **1972** *Jrnl. Social Psychol.* LXXXVII. 13 The study of values both intraculturally and cross-culturally has a long, and..distinguished history. **1885** M. HAY tr. *H. von Ziemssen's Handbk. Gen. Therapeutics* II. 391 We may characterise all such procedures, in contradistinction to the epidermic method, as the endermic or intracutaneous administration of remedies. **1905** HYDE & MONTGOMERY *Pract. Treat. Dis. Skin* (ed. 7) 96 Hypodermatic and intracutaneous injections. **1956** D. M. PILLSBURY et al. *Dermatol.* xv. 139 Scratch or intracutaneous tests are routinely employed to detect the presence of skin-sensitizing antibodies. **1925** *Jrnl. Immunol.* X. 729, 0·1 cc. was the amount intracutaneously injected in each case. **1927** *Proc. Soc. Exper. Biol. & Med.* XXV. 97 An injection..was given intracutaneously. **1961** *Jrnl. Amer. Med. Assoc.* 29 July 279/2 Alum-precipitated toxoids were injected intracutaneously. **1916** *Jrnl. R. Microsc. Soc.* 307 The chromatic margin of the undulating membrane represents an intracytoplasmic posteriorly-directed flagellum. **1971** *Biol. Abstr.* LII. 2029/1 In other organs..secretory granules may undergo intracytoplasmic lysis without destruction of their limiting membrane. **1961** P. FLEMING *Bayonets to Lhasa* xxiii. 291 The fruits of intradepartmental research. **1967** A. BATTERSBY *Network Analysis* (ed. 2) iii. 42 The single activity..might well be a summary of an intra-departmental arrow diagram. **1900** DORLAND *Med. Dict.* 327/2 Intradermal. **1946** *Nature* 31 Aug. 311/2 The intradermal test [for tuberculosis] is conceded to be eminently satisfactory in cattle. **1964** W. G. SMITH *Allergy & Tissue Metabolism* i. 8 A patient who developed a local reaction to an intradermal injection. **1926** *Amer. Year Bk. 1925* 951/1 The time required for the disappearance of intradermally injected salt solution. **1937** *Jrnl. Path. & Bacteriol.* XLIV. 410 Four rhesus monkeys were inoculated intradermally on the inner side of the left thigh with 0·2 c.c. of a 20 per cent. suspension of mouse brain. **1962** *Lancet* 26 May 1107/2 Sarcoid tissue..was..inoculated intradermally into 4 patients with suspected sarcoidosis. **1888** *Syd. Soc. Lex.* III, Intradermic. **1966** *Amer. Jrnl. Vet. Res.* XXVII. 541/1 The cervical region of cattle is the most responsive site for applying intradermic tuberculin tests. **1953** L. C. DE LEBORGNE tr. *R. A. Leborgne's Breast in Roent. Diagn.* i. 14 When contrast mammography shows intraductal lesions..we collect the liquid that has been injected, by softly expressing the breast (intraductal rinse). **1961** *Lancet* 29 July 241/2 Prolactin activity was detected and assayed semiquantitatively by the localised lactogenic response of the mammary gland of the pseudo-pregnant rabbit to intraductal injections. **1971** *Amer. Jrnl. Obstetr. & Gynecol.* CX. 505/1 In our study of 20 intraductal papillomas of the breast, the similarity of these lesions to the papillary hidradenoma of the vulva was striking. **1890** BILLINGS *Med. Dict.* I. 711/1 Intradural. **1901** J. COLLINS in Hektoen & Riesman *Text-bk. Path.* xi. 618 Intradural tumors arise either from the inner surface of the dura or the pia. **1950** *Jrnl. Neurosurg.* VII. 1 Intradural granulomas are very rare and may be intramedullary or extra-medullary. **1971** *Ibid.* XXXIV. 378/1 We therefore think that the intradural approach..is not more hazardous than the extradural approach. **1944** *Brit. Jrnl. Ophthalm.* XXVIII. 328 Some surgeons again approach the ganglion intradurally. **1960** *Cleveland Clinic Q.* XXVII. 198 When this extradural treatment fails..we have injected corticosteroids intradurally by lumbar puncture. **1971** *Jrnl. Neurosurg.* XXXIV. 378/2 No facial palsy occurred in more than 1000 patients, most of whom were operated on intradurally. **1904** F. P. FOSTER *Appleton's Med. Dict.* 1161 Intraepidermal. **1951** J. J. & W. D. ELLER *Tumors Skin* (ed. 2) vii. 336 (*heading*) Intra-epidermal and superficial carcinomatous changes. **1971** *Dermatologica* CXLII. 29 (*heading*) On benign intra-epidermal follicular acanthomas. **1904** F. P. FOSTER *Appleton's Med. Dict.* 1161 Intraepidermic. **1910** *Practitioner* June 871 An intra-epidermic abscess. **1949** *Time* 11 Apr. 39 They had launched the Intra-European Payments plan also as 'the little ECA'. **1962** H. O. BEECHENO *Introd. Business Stud.* i. 4 The European countries felt that there was no further danger of another intra-European War. **1967** *Guardian* 15 May 6/6 Intra-European bilateral contacts continue to proliferate benignly. **1973** *Nature* 16 Mar. 150/2 Designed for intra-European communication the satellite will handle telephone, telegram, telex and television channels. **1895** W. JAMES *Meaning of Truth* (1909) ii. 45 Mental images..are one phenomenal fact; the tigers are another; and their pointing to the tigers is a perfectly commonplace intra-experiential relation. **1909** W. M. URBAN *Valuation* vi. 188 For Ehrenfels the real test of the rationality of the desire is not an intra-experiential test. **1900** B. D. JACKSON *Gloss. Bot. Terms* 137/1 Intrafascicular (*fasciculus*, a bundle), within a bundle. **1914** M. DRUMMOND tr. *Haberlandt's Physiol. Plant. Anat.* ii. 97 So-called fascicular or intrafascicular cambium forms a strip which extends tangentially right across the bundle. **1917** *Ann. Bot.* XXXI. 45 The existence of this vestigial, intrafascicular cambium indicates that Monocotyledons have been derived from a dicotyledonous stock. **1960** W. B. R. LAIDLAW *Guide Brit. Hardwoods* 228 *Interfascicular*, between bundles..(cp. intrafascicular—cambium inside a bundle). **1894** C. D. WALCOTT in *Bull. Geol. Soc. Amer.* V. 192 An intra-formational conglomerate is one formed within a geologic formation of material derived from and deposited within that formation. **1938** HATCH & RASTALL *Petrol. Sedimentary Rocks* (ed. 3) iv. 76 Remarkable beds of intraformational breccia and conglomerate are found in some limestone and dolomite formations. **1940** E. S. HILLS *Outl. Structural Geol.* i. 15 When a slumped mass slides down on to undisturbed sediments it may later be covered by younger deposits. Severely disturbed beds will then be found between undisturbed strata, an arrangement that is known as intraformational contortion or corrugation. **1963** D. W. & E. E. HUMPHRIES tr. *Termier's Erosion & Sedimentation* x. 194 False unconformities and intraformational unconformities can often be explained by the effect of 'creep'. **1894** C. S. SHERRINGTON in *Jrnl. Physiol.* XVII. 240 Its own contained muscle-fibres, or as they may be termed the intrafusal muscle-fibres, always however run parallel with the long axis of the spindle itself. **1905** J. S. FERGUSON *Normal Histol.* ix. 136 The bundle of intrafusal muscle fibres is again surrounded by a delicate axial sheath of connective tissue. **1968** PASSMORE & ROBSON *Compan. Med. Stud.* I. xxiv. 12/2 A muscle spindle..contains a few short and very slender striated muscle cells; these are the intrafusal fibres which contrast with the main mass of extrafusal fibres. The intrafusal fibres receive motor nerve terminals. **1970** F. J. SCHULTE in U. Stave *Physiol. Prenatal Period* II. xxv. 805 In kittens, the intrafusal activity..seems to be less tonic than in adult cats. **1900** DORLAND *Med. Dict.* 327/2 Intragastric. **1903** G. HERSCHELL *Man. Intragastric Technique* vii. 107 The intragastric needle-douche..may be described as the application of fine jets of fluid under considerable pressure to the interior of the stomach. **1926** J. A. RYLE *Gastric Function* I. i. 15 When the stomach is filled and the intragastric tension thereby raised, the tension..quickly falls again. **1972** *Nature* 21 Apr. 385/2 Contractions of the body of the stomach of an anaesthetized rat measured from pressure changes in an intragastric balloon. **1959** *Proc. Amer. Assoc. Cancer Res.* III. 63/2 (*heading*) Relationship of dose of intragastrically administered methylcholanthrene to incidence of breast cancer in rats. **1971** *Nature* 16 Apr. 461/1 Propane sultone administered intragastrically at two dose levels gave rise chiefly to gliomas. **1947** *Biol. Abstr.* XXI. 2107/2 The role of intra- and intergeneric hybridization in the breeding of cultivated plants. **1971** *Nature* 22 Oct. 526/1 They approach the limits of intrageneric relationship when compared with other fish taxa. **1937** *Ibid.* 30 Oct. 760/2 These are changes of 'balance', and rank with intra-genic changes and position changes as one of the three effective means of variation. **1971** *Ibid.* 10 Dec. 337/1 One or more amino-acids have been deleted, probably during intragenic crossing over. **1895** J. D. DANA *Man. Geol.* (ed. 4) 957 Nearly all transported debris of the glacier was confined at first to its lower part... It was intraglacial, as now in Greenland. *Ibid.*, The term englacial..is not here adopted because it is half Greek. Intraglacial accords with Latin usage. **1896** *Amer. Geologist* XVIII. 153 Intraglacial..is here used for drift deposited in the field occupied by the ice, in contradistinction to extraglacial drift which has come to rest on ground not actually covered by the ice when it was deposited. According to Prof. Dana's use of this term, however, it would be synonymous with englacial, as Prof. Chamberlin designates the drift enclosed in the lower part of the ice-sheet. **1898** *Q. Jrnl. Geol. Soc.* LIV. 205 The débris-bands and intraglacial material with which the lower part of the glacier is so richly charged. **1966** *Geogr. Abstr.* A. 287 In the intraglacial zone are found: forms of marginal dissection, numerous eskers and kames. **1892** *Amer. Jrnl. Med. Sci.* CIII. 466 The author believes that in circumscribed growths, in the future, the only operation that will be admissible will be the bloodless intra-glandular method. **1909** *Practitioner* Nov. 682 Intraglandular enucleation.. should be performed. **1969** *Cancer* XXIV. 765/2 The intraglandular dissemination of thyroid cancer was seen in a very high proportion in follicular adenocarcinoma. **1940** BECKER & OBERMAYER *Mod. Dermatol. & Syphilol.* xlviii. 798/1 Intragluteal injection should be made in the upper outer quadrant of the buttock. **1961** *Lancet* 29 July 268/2 They were given 125 units of chorionic gonadotrophin daily by deep intragluteal injection. **1964** P. WORSLEY in I. L. Horowitz *New Sociol.* 388 The institutional norms..intra-governmental and intra-social. **1967** *Time* 10 Feb. 58 An ugly intragovernmental feud over the creation of an electronics and broadcasting giant. **1944** *Amer. Jrnl. Ophthalm.* XXVII. 1427/1 A case of intra-lenticular foreign body is presented. **1962** HARRIS & GRUBER in A. Pirie *Lens Metabolism Rel. Cataract* 383 If.. there are capsular and intralenticular barriers to diffusion ..localized accumulation of fluid could occur. **1937** O. JESPERSEN *Analytic Syntax* II. xxix. 109 In the case of ..the German or Latin masculine the correspondence with the extralingual quality 'male sex' is far from being pure: here the extralingual and the intralingual are inextricably mingled. *Ibid.*, When the preterit is used for 'the shifted present time' in indirect speech this cannot in the same way be said to refer to something outside the linguistic expression: it is intralingual. **1956** J. WHATMOUGH *Lang.* 63 For intralingual purposes (i.e. communication within a single language) every language is a good language for those who actually use it. **1964** E. A. NIDA *Toward Sci. Transl.* i. 3 'Intralingual' translation..consists essentially in rewording something within the same language. **1965** *Language* XLI. 505 Meaning refers to the intralingual relations contracted by linguistic units. **1937** J. R. FIRTH *Tongues of Men* iii. 34 For the vast majority of mankind clicks are extra-linguistic sounds, but for..Zulus they are intra-linguistic—that is to say, they form part of grammatical words. **1945** *Mind* LIV. 149 Morris' 'syntactics'.. deals only with relations among expressions in a language and thus with an entirely intra-linguistic subject-matter. **1962** U. WEINREICH in Householder & Saporta *Probl. Lexicogr.* 35 Over-schematized though it may be, ad hoc intralinguistic considerations suggest that 'c_1 and c_2' should have been considered a single condition. **1936** STEDMAN *Med. Dict.* (ed. 13) 555/2 *Intraluminal*, intra-tubal. **1943** *Jrnl. Clin. Invest.* XXII. 225/1 The clinical importance of intra-luminal pressure measurements in hollow viscera is well exemplified by the syndromes of hyper- and hypotension in the cardiovascular system. **1961** *Lancet* 30 Sept. 738/2 This flora may have utilised a relatively large part of the intraluminal nutrients during their logarithmic rate of growth. **1971** *Gut* XII. 268 Intraluminal pressure measurements may be a useful guide for the treatment of achalasia by pneumatic dilatations. **1892** *Amer. Jrnl. Med. Sci.* CIV. 96 (*heading*) The treatment of intra-mammary abscesses. **1960** *Farmer & Stockbreeder* 8 Mar. 107/1 His vet bill was too high... The balance was for drugs—almost entirely expensive intra-mammary antibiotics. **1971** *Jrnl. Endocrinol.* LI. p. xiii, The myoepithelial cells of the mammary gland contract in response to oxytocin and this results in a rise in intra-mammary pressure. **1904** *Jrnl. Philos., Psychol. & Sci. Methods* I. 300 The intra-mental and the extra-mental objects..differ only in position and in relational context. **1935** *Mind* XLIV. 356 Purely intra-mental causation. **1958** Intra-mental [see *extra-mental* (*EXTRA- 1)]. **1946** *Mind* LV. 372 Notwithstanding his insistence on the intra-mentality of objects, he keeps 'what is in the mind "intirely distinct" from the mind itself'. **1962** A. TIETZE in House-

holder & Saporta *Probl. Lexicogr.* 272 It has no intra-morphemic changes. **1973** A. H. SOMMERSTEIN *Sound Pattern Anc. Greek* ii. 22 Words containing intramorphemic clusters /pm bm p^{h}m/..all, historically, underwent assimilation. **1946** *Nature* 17 Aug. 242/2 The present data ..cover some twenty-six treatment schedules with intra-muscular penicillin. **1962** LUNTZ & WRIGHT in A. Pirie *Lens Metabolism Rel. Cataract* 317 These persons,..when given a desensitizing course of intramuscular injections.., rapidly improved. **1909** *Practitioner* Dec. 871 Digalen.. can be used by the mouth, by the rectum, intravenously, intramuscularly, and hypodermically. **1933** *Discovery* Jan. 4/2 This could be safely injected intramuscularly and intravenously. **1961** *Ann. N.Y. Acad. Sci.* XCIV. 917 A carcinoma had been transplanted intramuscularly, intra-peritoneally, or into the lungs. **1933** *Jrnl. Amer. Med. Assoc.* 24 June 2014/1 These agents were given intra-nasally. **1961** *Lancet* 23 Sept. 680/2 Swiss white mice.. were infected intranasally with..egg cultures of influenza viruses. **1971** *Infection & Immunity* IV. 738 Statolon.. when instilled intranasally (IN) protects mice infected with lethal doses of influenza virus. **1902** *Encycl. Brit.* XXXI. 304/1 The causes of the high death-rate among infants, whether due to ante-natal, intra-natal, or neo-natal conditions, come under..observation. **1922** *Rep. Public Health & Med. Subjects* (Ministry of Health) No. 7. 8 Death during labour—intra-natal fœtal death. **1963** D. G. W. CLYNE *Textbk. Gynaecol. & Obstetr.* xxxvii. 875 The intranatal care of the premature infant has been summarized. **1923** G. O'BRIEN *Ess. Econ. Effects Reformation* iv. 179 It is an institution at once intranational and international. **1940** A. HUXLEY *Let.* 15 Dec. (1969) 464 Two satisfactory alternatives, either voluntary international and intranational co-operation, or balance of power. **1901** *Buck's Handbk. Med. Sci.* (rev. ed.) II. 110/1 Foci of degeneration in the nerves were found to correspond to nodules upon intraneural arterial branches. **1936** H. MULDER *Cognition & Volition in Lang.* iii. 118 A bit of intraneural behavior in the brain of the man who coined it. **1954** ZACHARY & ROAF in H. J. Seddon *Peripheral Nerve Injuries* II. 73 Complete palsies have been caused by the accidental intraneural injection of a noxious substance. **1879** *Jrnl. R. Microsc. Soc.* II. 138 Finally, the ordinary intranucleolar network is produced, marking the completion of the division process and the entrance of the nuclei into a state of quiescence. **1970** *Jrnl. Cell Biol.* XLV. 584 (*heading*) Aberrant intranucleolar maturation of ribosomal precursors in the absence of protein synthesis. **1894** A. C. FRASER in Locke *Hum. Und.* II. IV. xi. 327 An odd and inadequate illustration; for 'writing' and 'moving the hand', although intraorganic, as much need to have their reality indicated as the sight of black or white does. **1962** S. K. LANGER *Philos. Sk.* i. 9 Sentience is a phase of vital process itself, a strictly intraorganic phase, i.e., an appearance which is presented only within the organism in which the activity occurs. **1941** J. S. HUXLEY *Uniqueness of Man* xi. 241 Analogy may very readily mislead. Weismann sought to apply this same analogy of intra-organismal struggle and selection to the units of heredity; but the analogy happens not to hold good. **1952** *Brit. Jrnl. Psychol.* XLIII. 245 The production of a neurosis in a cat by a method that is of special interest in that a difficult discrimination of intraorganismal cues was involved. **1955** Intraorganismic [see *extra-organismic* (*EXTRA- 1)]. **1909** W. M. URBAN *Valuation* x. 286 The terms of estimation are..wholly intra-personal, within the ego. **1935** G. K. ZIPF *Psycho-Biol. of Lang.* (1936) 297 The occasions of inter-personal conflict are often occasions for intra-personal conflict as well. **1955** R. JAKOBSON in H. Werner *On Expressive Lang.* 79 A competition of both devices is manifest in any symbolic process, either intrapersonal or social. **1917** C. R. PAYNE tr. *Pfister's Psychoanal. Method* viii. 169 The sleeping state lowers the power of the intra-psychic censor. **1954** J. A. C. BROWN *Social Psychol. of Industry* ix. 252 Frustration, whether intrapsychic or due to external factors. **1935** *Mind* XLIV. 215 The interplay of conflicting intra-psychical forces. **1923** *Amer. Jrnl. Physiol.* LXV. 229 Blood pressure changes are..complicated by the increased intrapulmonic pressure interfering with filling of the heart. **1968** *Biol. Abstr.* XLIX. 2076/2 Excess intrapulmonic pressure in the abdominal and thoracic cavities. **1903** *Biometrika* Feb. 152 The interracial correlation of the mean numbers of stamens and pistils is very much greater than the mean intraracial correlation between stamens and pistils. **1922** JOYCE *Ulysses* 717 Intraracial inhibition. **1957** *Antiquity* XXXI. 196 These two groups [of early Man] are in effect intra-racial variants. **1964** *Ann. Reg. 1963* 204 Intra-regional trade increased. **1966** *B.B.C. Handbk. 1966* 51 These intra-regional services are directed..to the region as a whole. **1909** WEBSTER, Intrasegmental. **1940** *Chambers's Techn. Dict.* 456/2 *Intrasegmental*, said of vertebrae which arise by the fusion of the cranial and caudal elements of the same somite. **1953** C. E. BAZELL *Ling. Form* 3 It is to be noted however that the intra-segmental range of a suprasegmental phoneme has normally no distinctive relevance. **1972** *Language* XLVIII. 46 In intra-segmental variation, as has been seen, different values for a feature are distributed over different portions of one and the same segment. **1895** S. H. VINES *Students' Text-bk. Bot.* II. III. 440 The intra-seminal stage includes the whole of the development which the embryo undergoes during the conversion of the ovule into the ripe seed. **1902** *Nature* 3 Apr. 519/1 Seeds from infected plants are entirely free from disease, thereby proving fairly conclusively the impossibility of intra-seminal sources of infection. **1930** *Ann. Bot.* XLIV. 772 The germination of the seed [of *Garrya elliptica*] is reported as 'intra-seminal'. **1932** H. H. PRICE *Perception* viii. 257 The revival of kinaesthetic and other intra-somatic data..is..far less common. **1938** [see *EXTRASOMATIC *a.*]. **1939** *Mind* XLVIII. 517 His treatment of intrasomatic sense-perception is equally precise. **1948** *Mind* LVII. 246 Any 'map' which may be elaborated at this level has a purely 'intrasomatic' significance. **1906** *Jrnl. Physiol.* XXXIV. 31 The reflex arcs from separate areas of the receptive field are closely knit together intraspinally. **1970** *Biol. Abstr.* LI. 7775/1 (*heading*) Clinical trials with the use of 5% phenol intraspinally in the treatment of cancer pain. **1914** MYERS & VALENTINE in *Brit. Jrnl. Psychol.* VII. I. 72 Bullough's..physiological aspect has here been extended to include not merely the sensory effects and the changes in feeling..but also the experiences of self-activity which the sounds may produce in the subject; in consequence, the word 'intra-subjective' will be substituted for this aspect. **1921** E. BULLOUGH *Ibid.* XII. I. 86 After the experiments of C. S. Myers..I would adopt the term 'intra-subjective' proposed by him, in place of 'physiological', which..was found by him to be too narrow, when applied to musical experiences. **1955** *Times* 26 May 3/4 Bruckner was a late romantic and as such was concerned with intra-subjective emotion as the material of his art. His fondling of an idea, then dropping it, at a silent pause and picking up another involves no incongruity. **1959** W. V. QUINE in R. A. Brower *On Translation* II. 159 Intrasubjective synonymy ..is intrasubjective in that the synonyms are joined for each subject by sameness of stimulus meaning for him;.. intrasubjective synonymy is in principle just as objective, just as discoverable by the outside linguist, as is translation. **1888** *Syd. Soc. Lex.*, Intratesticular. **1921** *Brain* XLIV. 168 In case XXIX an intratesticular injection of 3 c.c. [was given]. **1958** *Immunology* I. 4 For intratesticular grafting, the right testis was delivered through the smallest possible incision in the scrotum. **1970** *Sci. Jrnl.* June 68/2 The spermatozoa..are transferred through an uninterrupted system of ducts which originate from a complex network of intratesticular ducts. **1942** *Cancer Res.* II. 288 After the blood examinations had been concluded, the animals were inoculated intratesticularly with the Brown–Pearce tumor. **1971** *Lipids* VI. 706/1 Fatty acid synthesis was studied in testes of young and adult rats either injected intratesticularly or incubated with 1-^{14}C acetate. **1921** *Brain* XLIV. 168 In Case III an intrathecal injection of 1·5 c.c. cerebrospinal fluid was given. **1960** P. W. DAYKIN *Vet. Appl. Pharmacol. & Therapeutics* iv. 36 Administration by the intrathecal route involves the penetration of the dura mater, and the route is not frequently used in veterinary practice. **1971** *Jrnl. Path.* CIV. 141 An intrathecal lipoma of the filum terminale..was found in a 2-yr-old female infant dying from extensive burns. **1928** L. E. H. WHITBY *Med. Bacteriol.* xxiii. 236 The most popular method is to inject 500 units intrathecally immediately the diagnosis is made. **1972** *Lancet* 30 Dec. 1401/2 An account of the toxicity of antifolate drugs given intrathecally. **1923** *Jrnl. Exper. Med.* XXXVII. 793 (*caption*) Protocols of rabbits treated intratracheally and intraperitoneally with killed cultures of hog-cholera bacillus. **1930** *Jrnl. Laboratory & Clin. Med.* XVI. 87 (*heading*) A new apparatus for administering volatile anesthetics intratracheally without tracheotomy. **1973** *Nature* 16 Mar. 203/2 Turkey poults were inoculated intratracheally. **1934** *Mind* XLIII. 74 An intra-typical variable is a variable all of whose arguments are of one type. **1959** P. F. STRAWSON *Individuals* I. i. 53 The cases in which this intra-typical identification is possible are severely restricted. For they require that the parties to an identifying reference should be operating with one and the same type-homogeneous referential framework. **1900** I. B. BALFOUR tr. *Goebel's Organogr. Plants* II. 359 The intravaginal squamules are organs which secrete mucilage for the protection of the bud. **1951** MCLEAN & IVIMEY-COOK *Textbk. Theoret. Bot.* I. xxii. 993 The first [leaf structures] are called intravaginal scales because they appear in the axil within the leaf sheath or vagina of certain Monocotyledons... They take the form of small tooth-like scales. **1916** *Mem. N.Y. Bot. Garden* VI. 352 The marked self-sterility of individual plants, the intra-varietal sterility, and the cases of inter-varietal sterility are not due to 'any inherent weakness of either ovaries or pollen grains'. **1970** *Euphytica* XIX. 382 (*heading*) Intra-varietal variation of yield in two varieties of *Lolium perenne* L. **1969** *Encycl. Sci. Suppl.* (Grolier) 329 The intravehicular space suit consists of: fecal containment subsystem, constant wear garment, [etc.]. **1970** N. ARMSTRONG et al. *First on Moon* iii. 62 There were two kinds of suits... Mike Collins had the lighter 'intra-vehicular' version. **1909** WEBSTER, Intraverbal. **1953** C. E. BAZELL *Ling. Form* 87 On the level of the sememe itself, all such facts as congruence, rection, extra-verbal as opposed to intra-verbal formation, are excluded. **1957** B. F. SKINNER in Saporta & Bastian *Psycholinguistics* (1961) 229/2 A comparable minimal repertoire was found to be lacking in intraverbal behavior. **1855** R. G. MAYNE *Expos. Lex. Med. Sci.* (1860) 535/2 Intra-vertebral chord. **1896** *Phil. Trans. R. Soc.* B. CLXXXVII. 10 One of the last changes of importance is the appearance of intra-vertebral cartilage. *Ibid.* 12 In all Amphibia and Amniota each spinal nerve lies intravertebrally, *i.e.* issues behind the dorsal arch of its vertebra.

2. intra-class, -party, -state, occurring within a class, political party, state. Also **intracloud,** within a cloud; **intra-day,** occurring within one day; **intra-list** *Psychol.*, occurring between lists (of words, numbers, etc.) within a test situation; **intra-sentence,** occurring within a sentence.

1950 Intra-class [see *inter-class* (*INTER- 5)]. **1971** *Jrnl. Gen. Psychol.* Apr. 306 The intraclass correlation was significant but small. **1970** *Sci. News* 28 Mar. 320 Zeroing in on intracloud lightning. **1973** J. L. MARSHALL *Lightning Protection* II. 31 The higher frequency radiation is dominant in intracloud discharges. **1972** *Daily Tel.* 11 Nov. 17/4 The previous intra-day high for this most illustrious of all stock market indices was 1,001·11 which was reached more than six-and-a-half years ago on Feb. 9, 1966. **1972** *Korea Times* 16 Nov. 3/5 The Dow topped 1,000 on an intraday basis—a compilation of the day's highs for all component issues. **1942** *Jrnl. Exper. Psychol.* XXX. 185 (*heading*) Intra-list generalization as a factor in verbal learning. **1958** G. A. MILLER in Saporta & Bastian *Psycholinguistics* (1961) 213/2 The redundant strings show greater intralist similarity. **1970** *Jrnl. Gen. Psychol.* Oct. 256 The last letter being thus the only characteristic by which the entire series was to be differentiated..would reduce the level of intralist interference. **1971** *Ibid.* Apr. 194 Overt intralist intrusions were scored as if stimuli had been clustered for both groups. **1923** *Glasgow Herald* 24 Apr. 8/4 Mr Harding proposed to the Senate that the United States should accept membership of the Court of International Justice at The Hague... Present indications are that he will refuse to retreat, and will make participation in the Court the issue of the preliminary intra-party campaign. **1963** *Economist* 20 July 257/1 This is nothing less than an intraparty revolt. **1969** *Sunday Statesman* (Calcutta) 27 July 12/3 The intra-party quarrel of the SSP deepens. **1969** *Computers & Humanities* IV. 129 Investigation of intra-sentence parallelism in present-day American prose. **1903** E. JOHNSON *Amer. Railway Transportation* 370 In 1886 the Supreme Court in the Wabash decision..limited the authority of the State strictly to the intrastate traffic and excluded that moving from one State to another. **1969** *Jane's Freight Containers 1968–69* 37/2, 101 inter- and intra-state motor freight lines serving the Port of Toledo. **1971** M. TAK *Truck Talk* 90 *Intrastate shipping*, any transportation of goods that has its origin and destination within the same state.

intra-amniotic to **intra-articular:** see *INTRA- *pref.* 1.

i:ntra-ato·mic, *a.* [INTRA- 1.] Occurring or existing within an, or the, atom.

1904 *Nature* 16 June 151/2 Enormous orbital velocities due to intra-atomic rearrangement. **1946** *Nature* 23 Nov. 726/1 For 'chemical process' is suggested the definition: 'a process in which a product is formed by a re-arrangement or re-distribution of atoms of chemical elements present in the starting materials, or by intra-atomic change'. **1955** *Bull. Atomic Sci.* Mar. 92/1 The possibility of releasing very large reserves of intra-atomic energy appeared suddenly a few months after the discovery by Hahn and Strassmann of the neutron fission of uranium atoms. **1971** B. A. LENGYEL *Lasers* (ed. 2) iii. 212 The general laws of emission and absorption of radiation are as valid for recombinations [of electrons and holes in semiconductors] as they are for ordinary intra-atomic transitions.

intra-capillary to **intracortical:** see *INTRA- *pref.* 1.

intra-class, intracloud: see *INTRA- *pref.* 2.

intracranial, *a.* Add: Hence **intracra·nially** *adv.*, in or within the cranium.

1908 *Practitioner* Aug. 296 Rabbits were inoculated intracranially with the fluid. **1971** *Biol. Abstr.* LII. 7922/2 A large stick remained intracranially for a long time without clinical neurological deficit.

intracrustal to **intracytoplasmic:** see *INTRA- *pref.* 1.

intrada (intrā·dă). *Mus.* [Modified f. It. *intrata*, older form of *entrata* entry, prelude.] An introduction or prelude; = ENTRÉE 3 b.

1740 J. GRASSINEAU *Mus. Dict.* 113 *Intrada*, an entry, much the same as prelude, or overture. **1801** BUSBY *Dict. Mus.*, *Intrada*, the old Italian name for an opera overture, or prelude. **1883** GROVE *Dict. Mus.* III. 756/1 In Purcell's suites, for instance, which date from the last 10 or 20 years of the 17th century, besides the Allemande and Courante..in one case the group also comprises a Sarabande, Cebell, Minuet, Riggadoon, Intrade, and March. **1954** *Grove's Dict. Mus.* (ed. 5) IV. 525/1 These intradas usually form part of a suite of dances. The term is seldom found after the middle of the 17th century, being replaced by the French term *entrée*, though Bach, Mozart..and Beethoven..still used it.

intra-day: see *INTRA- *pref.* 2.

intra-departmental to **intragovernmental:** see *INTRA- *pref.* 1.

intragroup (i·ntrăgrūp), *a.* [INTRA- 2.] Existing or occurring within a group or between the members of a group.

1918 *Genetics* III. 477 Intra-group competition. **1952** C. P. BLACKER *Eugenics* iv. 90 If we owe as much to the social instincts and co-operativeness of our forebears as to their competitive success in a struggle for existence, how far, we may ask, is the continued strife between man and man necessary for the further development of the race? Diverse answers were given by the controversialists of the period, and discussion turned much on the effects of two kinds of struggle—that *inside* social groups and that *between* social groups—or, as they were called *intra*-group and *inter*-group struggle. **1958** W. J. H. SPROTT *Human Groups* ix. 141 The organized group displayed much more intra-group aggression than did the unorganized group. **1963** C. S. JOHNSON in M. M. Grossack *Mental Health & Segregation* 44 For the Negro youth, the tensions inherent in the intra-group class struggle become extremely important. **1965** *Math. in Biol. & Med.* (*Med. Res. Council*) III. 86 The degree of variation within the groups was estimated by the average intragroup distance. **1972** *Accountant* 23 Mar. 384/1 The accounting practice persists whereby we defer profits on all intra-group sales and chalk up another defeat for reality.

intralenticular to **intra-mentality:** see *INTRA- *pref.* 1.

intra-list: see *INTRA- *pref.* 2.

intramolecular, *a.* Add: Hence **intramole·cularly** *adv.*, within a molecule.

1936 G. M. KLINE *Organic Plastics* (U.S. Bureau of Standards Circular C411) 6 Condensations may take place intramolecularly, as in the case of the formation of phthalic anhydride from phthalic acid, or intermolecularly. **1962** WALKER & STRAW *Spectroscopy* II. 181 Dipole attachment occurs between the intramolecularly hydrogen bonded

and the solvent molecule. **1964** N. G. Clark *Mod. Org. Chem.* x. 195 It undergoes a Cannizzaro reaction with sodium hydroxide; this occurs intramolecularly, i.e. within the same molecule. **1971** *Biochemistry* (Easton, Pa.) X. 925/1 Is the S–S polylysine intramolecularly or intermolecularly cross-linked?

intramorphemic: see *intra- *pref.* 1.

intramurally (-miū͡ə·răli), *adv.* [Intra- 1.] Within the walls or boundaries; inside a particular community, institution, etc.

1927 [see *extramurally *adv.*]. **1952** *Facilities for Advanced Study Univ. Oxf.* 29 Research studies in all branches of agricultural economics have been conducted both 'in the field', extra-murally, and intra-murally by means of records. **1968** *Sat. Rev.* (U.S.) 2 Nov. 32 Older families, with their own special and intramurally recognized ways of walking, talking and thinking.

intramuscular to **intraneural:** see *intra- *pref.* 1.

intra·nsigeance. *rare.* [Fr.] = Intransigence.

1899 J. W. Mackail *Life W. Morris* II. 291 Socialism.. from extreme intransigeance..had swung back to something approaching opportunism. **1909** *Daily Chron.* 20 July 3/2 The loves of Jeanne-Jeannette and the young man from Montpellier are threatened by the intransigeance of their respective ancestors.

intransigeantly (intrɑ·nsidʒăntli), *adv.* [f. F. *intransigeant* (see Intransigent *a.* and *sb.*) + -ly².] Uncompromisingly.

1921 *Contemp. Rev.* Sept. 331 The peasants are intransigeantly anti-Karlist. **1925** *Glasgow Herald* 17 Mar. 8 The advocates of an intransigeantly nationalist policy.

in-tra·nsit, intransit, *a.* [f. *in *prep.* 17* + Transit *sb.*] Of or pertaining to people, goods, etc., that are in transit; being in transit.

1918 Johnson & Huebner *Princ. Ocean Transportation* III. xx. 309 The granting of in-transit privileges on all-rail routes. **1951** *Manila Daily Bulletin* 26 Mar. 1–P, The ship had seven intransit passengers and around 1,741 tons of transit cargo. **1967** V. S. Naipaul *Mimic Men* III. vii. 279 There were no aeroplanes..that day... Sixteen intransit hours awaited me. **1969** *Jane's Freight Containers 1968–69* 102/2 The in-transit time between UK/Europe and the Far East could be considerably reduced by transporting containers by rail across the North American continent. **1971** *Jamaican Weekly Gleaner* 17 Nov. 38/4 Miss Milford Rohrbaugh, 53, an American tourist slipped and fell in the intransit lounge of the Palisadoes Airport yesterday on her way to board an aircraft to Miami, Florida.

intransitable, *a.* (U.S. and later examples.)

1838 'Texian' *Mexico v. Texas* 9 In that singular region of Mexico..there extends..a desert..so utterly devoid of water and vegetation as to be intransitable. **1897** *Geogr. Jrnl.* X. 64 A road along the coast would become lost in intransitable gorges of the coast range of mountains.

intransitive, *a.* Add: **3.** *Logic.* Of a relation: such that if the relation holds between a first and a second item, and also between the second and third, it cannot hold (or more widely, does not hold) between the first and the third.

1870 C. S. Peirce in *Mem. Amer. Acad.* (1873) IX. 369 Repeating relatives may be divided (after De Morgan) into those whose products into themselves are contained under themselves, and those of which this is not true. The former are well named by De Morgan transitive, the latter intransitive. **1881** J. Venn *Symbolic Logic* xix. 403 Relations..may be divided into those which are 'transitive' and those which are 'intransitive'. **1903** B. Russell *Princ. Math.* xxvi. 218 Relations which do not possess the second property I shall call not transitive; those which possess the property that *xRy*, *yRz* always exclude *xRz* I shall call intransitive. All these cases may be illustrated from human relationships... *Spouse* is symmetrical but intransitive;..*father* is both asymmetrical and intransitive. **1930** L. S. Stebbing *Mod. Introd. Logic* vii. 113 Symmetry and transitiveness..are independent, so that relations can be symmetrical and either transitive or intransitive; asymmetrical and either transitive or intransitive. **1964** E. Bach *Introd. Transformational Gram.* vii. 155 *Equal*, *Smaller* are transitive; *Father* is an intransitive relation; *Friend* is non-transitive if you are my friend and have friends who are not my friends.

4. *Math.* Of a group: not transitive (see Transitive *a.* (*sb.*) 6 and quot. 1889).

1889 *Amer. Jrnl. Math.* XI. 195 If a substitution-group *I* is intransitive, the letters upon which it operates can be distributed into 'systems of intransitivity', x_1, x_2...; y_1, y_2...; z_1, z_2... such that the substitutions of *I* interchange among each other only the letters x_1, x_2...; the letters y_1, y_2...; the letters z_1, z_2..., and so on, and connect transitively the letters of each system. **1940** D. E. Littlewood *Theory Group Characters* iii. 42 In an intransitive group the symbols are divided into transitive sets, the symbols of each set being permuted amongst themselves. **1971** Powell & Higman *Finite Simple Groups* vii. 234 If the union of these is Ω, they form a fixed trio, and if not, the group is intransitive.

intransitivity (i:ntrɑnsiti·viti). [f. Intransitiv(e *a.* + -ity.] The property or quality of being intransitive (in any sense).

1889 [see *intransitive *a.* 4]. **1933** Chapman & Henle *Fund. Logic* 3 We have chosen four logical properties of certain relations—transitivity and intransitivity, symmetry and asymmetry. **1950** W. V. Quine *Methods of Logic* (1952) 177 A dyadic relative term is called..intransitive..according as it fulfils:..(x)(y)(z)(Fxy.Fyz.⊃ – Fxz) (intransitivity). **1971** *Archivum Linguisticum* II. 104 Aspect, as well as transitivity, intransitivity, expression of cause, wish, etc., are secondary developments and more recent than the use of *s* to denote tense or mood.

intransitivize (intrɑ·nsitivəiz), *v. Gram.* [f. Intransitiv(e *a.* + -ize.] *trans.* To make intransitive. Chiefly as **intra·nsitivizing** *ppl. a.*

1949 E. A. Nida *Morphol.* (ed. 2) iii. 68 In Tzeltal there is an intransitivizing verbal infix -h-. **1964** *Language* XL. 76 The intransitivizing stem formative -di.

intransmissibility (i:ntrɑnsmisibi·liti). [f. Intransmissible *a.* + -ity.] The state or quality of being intransmissible.

1913 H. Goudy in P. Vinogradoff *Ess. Legal Hist.* 225 The passive intransmissibility of actions of Debt and Account.

intransparency (intrɑnspē͡ə·rĕnsi, -pæ·r-). [f. Intransparent *a.*: see -ency.] The quality of being opaque; also, an instance of this.

1902 *Encycl. Brit.* XXXI. 570/1 This intransparency caused by a mere infiltration generally clears away in the course of time. *Ibid.*, Centrally placed intransparencies, which cover the pupil, are relatively the most disturbing.

intranucleolar to **intra-personal:** see *intra- *pref.* 1.

intra-party: see *intra- *pref.* 2.

intrapluvial (intrăplū·viăl), *a.* and *sb.* [f. Intra- 1 + Pluvial *a.*] **A.** *adj.* Of, pertaining to, or designating relatively short, drier periods (less marked than interpluvials) that may have occurred during pluvials. **B.** *sb.* An intrapluvial period.

1934 E. J. Wayland in *Jrnl. R. Anthrop. Inst.* LXIV. 344 In each of them [*sc.* pluvials] there is a break, or intrapluvial period. **1939** T. P. O'Brien *Prehist. Uganda* i. 9 The evidence in support of the intrapluvial in Pluvial I was provided by local, though not intense, soil reddening, selenite beds within Pluvial I deposits and by talus accumulations. **1940** *Geogr. Jrnl.* XCVI. 333 There have been very long wet and dry phases, the so-called pluvials and interpluvials; there have been shorter intrapluvials and epipluvials; and there have been short-period oscillations. ..The intrapluvial oscillations are measured in terms of one hundred years. **1946** F. E. Zeuner *Dating Past* viii. 247 The succession of pluvials with intrapluvials and separated by interpluvials, however, appears at present to be somewhat uncertain.

intrapolation (intræ:pŏlē͡i·ʃən). [f. Intra- 3 + *-polation*, after *extrapolation.*] = Interpolation 3; also more widely, (an) inference within the scope or framework of what is known.

1923 C. D. Broad *Sci. Thought* xi. 428 Like all extrapolations, this argument is weaker than an intrapolation. **1949** Koestler *Insight & Outlook* xxv. 352 The listener is forced to complete its pattern himself, by a process of intrapolation and extrapolation. **1956** E. H. Hutten *Lang. Mod. Physics* v. 195 This intrapolation between observations is not, as such, required as support for the theory. **1969** D. F. Horrobin *Sci. is God* iv. 49 This is known as intrapolation because..the process operates only within the range..actually measured.

So **intra·polate** *v.* = Interpolate *v.* 6 (in Dict. and Suppl.).

1956 E. H. Hutten *Lang. Mod. Physics* v. 189 In classical mechanics we are able to intrapolate between observations and to say that, between the space-time points where it is observed, the particle follows a definite path.

intra-psychic to **intrasomatic:** see *intra- *pref.* 1.

intra-sentence: see *intra- *pref.* 2.

intraspe·cies, *a.* [Intra- 2.] = next.

1927 *Techn. Bull. N.Y. State Agric. Exper. Stat.* No. 127. 5 During the past 18 years many intra- and inter-species crosses of *Prunus* have been made. **1953** *New Biol.* XIV. 9 Intraspecies fighting is different from inter-species fighting. **1963** *Language* XXXIX. 461 The whistles, squeals, chirps, clicks, rasps, and other noises of marine mammals have suggested three areas of inquiry: orientation by echolocation, intraspecies communication, and interspecies communication. **1973** *Sci. Amer.* Aug. 29/1 This interspecies difference contrasts with remarkable intraspecies similarity.

intraspeci·fic, *a.* [f. Intra- 1 + Specific *a.*, as adj. from *species.*] Produced, occurring, or existing within a (taxonomic) species or between individuals of a single species.

1919 *Genetics* IV. 501 (*heading*) An analysis of certain cases of intraspecific sterility. **1929** *Hereditas* XIII. 185 Partial sterility in intra- and interspecific crosses. **1937** A. Huxley *Ends & Means* xiv. 265 Progress is dependent on the preponderance of intra-specific co-operation over intra-specific competition. **1953** N. Tinbergen *Herring Gull's World* x. 88 Species are known in which the reproductive season brings much intraspecific strife. **1966** M. Latzke tr. *Lorenz's On Aggression* iii. 18 The survival value of inter-specific fights is much more evident than that of intra-specific contests. **1968** R. D. Martin tr. *Wickler's Mimicry* xvi. 227, I have given the term intraspecific mimicry to this form of self-imitation within a species. **1969** *Daily Tel.* 13 Feb. 22/4 Mankind's allegedly instinctive affection for weaponry and intraspecific killing has been a selling subject.

intraspinally to **intra-typical:** see *intra- *pref.* 1.

intra-state: see *intra- *pref.* 2.

intra-uterine, *a.* Add: Also **intrauterine.** Applied *spec.* to contraceptive devices for placing in the uterus. (Further examples.)

1931 F. W. S. Browne tr. *T. H. van de Velde's Fertility & Sterility in Marriage* xiv. 354 The intra-uterine appliances were based on the same principle as the vaginal; but they soon completely changed their mechanism and structure. **1969** N. W. Pirie *Food Resources* 15 The contraceptive ideal is a treatment of some sort that makes one or other sex infertile until it is reversed. The closest approach to this ideal so far is the intrauterine device. **1972** *Guardian* 10 July 9/2 Asking, at a Family Planning Association branch, for an intra-uterine device.

intravaginal, -varietal: see *intra- *pref.* 1.

intravascular, *a.* Add: Hence **intrava·scularly** *adv.*, within the vascular system.

1906 [see *anti-¹ 7 c]. **1971** *Nature* 5 Feb. 412/2 For preservation, dog brain was perfused intravascularly with 3% glutaraldehyde for 5–20 min.

intravehicular: see *intra- *pref.* 1.

intravenous, *a.* Add: Also as *sb.*, an intravenous injection or feeding.

1960 J. G. Ballard in D. Knight *100 Yrs. Sci. Fiction* (1969) 355 Took me half an hour to steady myself enough for an intravenous. **1970** *New Yorker* 21 Nov. 66/2 You have intravenouses going in both your hands.

intraventricular, *a.* Add: Hence **intraventri·cularly** *adv.*, into or within a ventricle.

1951 *Year Bk. Drug Therapy* 218 Trial of streptomycin intraventricularly..seems indicated. **1955** *Brit. Jrnl. Pharmacol.* X. 373/1 Bulbocapnine, when injected intraventricularly, produces its characteristic effects in doses a fraction of those effective on subcutaneous injection. **1961** *Lancet* 22 July 178/1 The sodium salt of polymyxin B methane sulphonic acid..is well tolerated intraventricularly. **1972** *Science* 29 Sept. 1213/2, 6-HDA administered intraventricularly can produce several aspects of the classical lateral hypothalamic syndrome.

intraverbal: see *intra- *pref.* 1.

intraversable, *a.* Add: (Later example.) Also **intraversible.**

1900 W. James *Let.* 26 Sept. (1920) II. 137 It must seem strange to you that the way from the mind to the pen should be as intraversable as it has been in this case of mine. **1923** R. F. Horton *Mystical Quest Christ* III. xxiv. 255 The vast universe seems so homeless, so comfortless; its spaces of darkness so intraversible.

intravertebral, -vertebrally: see *intra- *pref.* 1.

intravital (intrăvəi·tăl), *a. Biol.* [f. Intra- 1 + Vital *a.*, perh. suggested by *intra vitam* (see *intra *prep.* 2).] Performed on, applied to, or occurring in something alive.

1890 in Billings *Med. Dict.* 712/1. **1922** *Proc. R. Soc.* B. XCIV. 138 On intra-vital staining by polychrome methylene blue, some of these granules are stained blue, others red. **1938** *Biochem. Jrnl.* XXXII. 381 The distribution of the lyochromes in the kidneys of frogs and rats was studied by intravital microscopy. **1963** *Lancet* 19 Jan. 152/2 The technique of intravital staining of the motor end plate..is of limited diagnostic value.

Hence **intravi·tally** *adv.*, during life, in a living organism.

1930 *Biol. Abstr.* IV. 3299/3 (Index), Iron lactate, storage intravitally. **1937** *Acta Med. Scand.* XCI. 350 It has been demonstrated intravitally in retinal vessels in cases of stasis provoked by pressure on the eye.

intra vitam: see *intra *prep.* 2.

in-tray (i·ntrē͡i). [Cf. In *adv.* 12 a.] In an office, etc.: a tray for incoming correspondence and other papers; = *in-basket. Cf. *out-tray.

Sometimes written as two separate words with *in* regarded adjectivally.

1941 *Punch* 25 June 602/2, I found the first one lying quietly in my IN tray (or IN wire-basket). **1943** W. S. Churchill *Second World War* (1951) IV. 852 A habit of having secret papers placed in 'In' or 'Out' trays on the desks of important officers. **1958** *New Statesman* 25 Jan. 112/3, I hope some copies reach the In-trays of the Indian officials who refused to support him at Oxford. **1968** P. McKellar *Experience & Behaviour* vi. 163 In an office, some item waiting to be dealt with in the older man's in-tray may seem to him to wait only a short time. **1970**

New Scientist 30 Apr. 239/1 The issue of industrial noise is finding its way to the political in-trays.

intrazonal (intrăzōᵘ·năl), *a. Soil Sci.* [a. F. *intrazonal* (N. Sibirtsev 1897, in *Compt. Rend. de la VIIᵉ Session, Congr. géol. internat.* (1899) II. III. v. 83): see INTRA- 1 and ZONAL *a.*] Designating any soil which occurs within a major soil zone but differs from the characteristic soil of that zone owing to the overriding influence of relief, parent material, or other local factor.

[**1908** *Jrnl. Agric. Sci.* III. 84 In all these zones also certain interzonal soils are sure to occur, which owe their peculiarities to special conditions of topography alone. *Ibid.*, Such soils constitute the six..interzonal types enumerated by Sibirtzev.] **1927** C. F. MARBUT tr. *Glinka's Great Soil Groups* 28 Intrazonal soils originate, according to Sibirceff, where local soil forming forces predominate over the general or zonal forces. **1946** LUTZ & CHANDLER *Forest Soils* xi. 385 Intrazonal soils have more or less well-defined characteristics which reflect the dominating influence of some local factor, such as relief, parent material, or age, over the normal effect of climate and vegetation. **1965** B. T. BUNTING *Geogr. Soils* i. 18 The soils of the world have been considered as belonging to one of the three major orders—zonal, azonal and intrazonal—each divisible into many groups.

intrigue, *v.* Add: **5.** *trans.* To excite the curiosity or interest of; to interest so as to puzzle or fascinate. Also *absol.* (A modern gallicism.)

1894 *Month* May 122 The publishers often become so intrigued by these claims of authorship, that we find them at times passing by the matter altogether. **1896** [in Dict., sense 1]. **1900** *Westm. Gaz.* 5 Dec. 2/2 We do agree most heartily, but the observation intrigues us not a little. **1909** H. G. WELLS *Ann Veronica* iii. 78 The New Woman and the New Girl intrigue me profoundly. **1918** A. QUILLER-COUCH *Stud. in Lit.* 1st Ser. 147 These theological poets and preachers of the seventeenth century..were intrigued ..by man's lapse from a state of innocence. **1924** W. M. RAINE *Troubled Waters* xxi. 225 The conspiracy she proposed intrigued his interest. **1957** PARTRIDGE *English gone Wrong* i. 9 Such words as..'to be *intrigued*' for 'deeply or much interested'..have degenerated from definite sense to indefinite nonsense.

intriguing, *ppl. a.* Add: Also, in sense of prec. Hence **intri·guingly** *adv.*

1909 *Daily Chron.* 29 Apr. 3/2 A brisk, intriguing, and entertaining story. **1920** *Isis* (Oxf.) 27 Oct. 2/1 Edited.. by three members of Oriel..with a longish and intriguing introduction by Mr. John Masefield. **1922** *Blackw. Mag.* June 778/2 The line of alders on the far bank was intriguingly punctuated with squatting figures. **1935** W. S. MAUGHAM *Don Fernando* x. 190, I would say boldly then that no great artist is more intriguing than El Greco. **1970** *Daily Tel.* (Colour Suppl.) 30 Oct. 15/1 She was a mine of intriguingly useless information. **1974** *Observer* 10 Feb. 32/8 Even more intriguing than the sociology of fashion is its psychology.

intrinsic, *a.* Add: **3. d.** *intrinsic factor*, a substance (perhaps a mucoprotein) which is secreted in the gastric juice and makes possible the absorption by the body of vitamin B_{12} ('extrinsic factor').

1930 [see *EXTRINSIC *a.* 3 c]. **1961** *Lancet* 26 Aug. 483/2 Vitamin-B_{12} deficiency through lack of intrinsic factor (I.F.), as in pernicious anæmia, has stimulated efforts to purify and isolate I.F. **1965** A. DOSCHERHOLMEN *Stud. Metabolism Vitamin B_{12}* 4 The intrinsic factor has not yet been isolated in pure form.., but it is believed to be a mucoprotein or mucopolypeptide... The purpose of the intrinsic factor is to bring about the absorption from the food, by some mechanism still unknown.., of the small amount of cyanocobalamin needed.

e. *Physics.* Of a semiconductor: owing its electrical conductivity to thermally excited electrons from the principal substance present, rather than to electrons from impurity atoms. Hence applied to conduction that arises in this way.

1933 R. H. FOWLER in *Proc. R. Soc.* A. CXL. 507 Semiconductors without impurities owe their conductivity and other electrical properties to thermal excitation of electrons from band 2 to band 1. These we shall refer to as intrinsic semi-conductors. **1945** *Jrnl. Appl. Physics* XVI. 562/2 The atoms of the bulk material hold their valence electrons at low temperatures but become thermally ionized at elevated temperatures. An electronic conductivity of this type is called intrinsic. **1948** TORREY & WHITMER *Crystal Rectifiers* iii. 47 Intrinsic semiconduction occurs in materials that have a band structure similar to that of insulators..but with the difference that the gap in energy between the highest filled band and the lowest empty band is relatively small. **1962** SIMPSON & RICHARDS *Physical Princ. Junction Transistors* viii. 167 The region near the collector is practically intrinsic and under proper operating conditions the transition region (depletion region) of the collector barrier occupies the whole of it. **1966** C. R. TOTTLE *Sci. Engin. Materials* ii. 46 Intrinsic semiconductors..are insulators below a given temperature and conductors with a negative temperature coefficient above it. Silicon and germanium are examples of this type of semiconductor.

intro, intro., colloq. abbrev. of INTRODUCTION.

1923 *Daily Mail* 17 July 12 (Advt.), It's extraordinary the number of fellows who..write to us..thanking me for the intro! **1928** *Melody Maker* Feb. 195/3 The sixth and eighth bars of the intro. worried me a little. **1929** J. B. PRIESTLEY *Good Companions* III. ii. 515 You'd never see him if you hadn't an intro, but when you do see him, 's'business. **1949** L. FEATHER *Inside Be-Bop* ii. 17 The intro and coda of *Ko-ko*. **1964** *Listener* 17 Dec. 987/2 The intro film's symbols..appear to be so dully strange that they induce an uneasy feeling. **1968** *Blues Unlimited* Dec. 6 Al Smith compered. Not very imaginatively, in fact he started off two intros word for word the same. **1973** J. JONES *Touch of Danger* xx. 116 Fred Tarkoff..gave me a letter of intro to her. **1974** *Melody Maker* 13 Apr. 50/2 There are guitar intros and solos.

introducing, *vbl. sb.* (In Dict. s.v. INTRODUCE *v.*) Add: Also *attrib.*, as † **introducing house** (see quots.). *Obs.* exc. *Hist.*

1846 *Swell's Night Guide* 41 French introducing houses. These accommodation cribs have become so numerous, that it requires some tact and *nous* to discover them. **1857** W. ACTON *Prostitution* vii. 97 The establishments of certain procuresses..vulgarly called 'introducing houses'..are worth notice as the leading centres of the more select circles of prostitution here. **1861** MAYHEW *Lond. Labour* (1862) Extra vol. 214/1 Under this head [*sc.* brothels] we must include introducing houses, where the women do not reside, but merely use the house as a place of resort in the daytime. **1955** C. PEARL *Girl with Swansdown Seat* ii. 36 The Victorian 'introducing house' where the pleasant ceremony of introducing wealthy amateurs to willing girls was carried out with dignity and delicacy.

introduction. Add: **1. d.** The issuing of new shares by a company not directly to the public but through the medium of the Stock Exchange.

1929 *Economist* 27 July 175/1 The Stock Exchange 'introduction' (as distinct from the issue by prospectus or offer for sale) will fill an increasingly important *rôle*. **1966** P. A. S. TAYLOR *New Dict. Econ.* 152 *Introduction*, the offer of a new issue to the public, not directly but through the Stock Exchange... This method does away with part of normal new issue procedure, but necessitates that there should be a large body of shareholders, securities available to start the market, and no large 'deal' involved in the marketing of the securities. **1970** G. D. NEWBOULD *Business Finance* III. 193 Two less common techniques are the public issue and the introduction... The *introduction* is unique, since there is no formal issue of shares...The introduction can be used only where there are a sufficient number of shareholders to ensure a market when quotation is granted. **1971** J. BATES *Financing Small Business* (ed. 2) vi. 95 The Stock Exchange introduction is effectively an application by the issuing house on behalf of the shareholders for shares to be quoted on a Stock Exchange.

5. b. (Earlier and later examples.)

1801 C. WILMOT *Let.* 13 Dec. in *Irish Peer* (1920) 14 Mr. Holcroft, to whom Lady Mount Cashell had a letter of introduction. **1816** JANE AUSTEN *Emma* II. xiv. 267 The idea of her being indebted to Mrs. Elton for what was called an *introduction*—of her going into public under the auspices of a friend of Mrs. Elton's. **1885** A. EDWARDES *Girton Girl* III. xv. 267 It was well for her, she said, to.. look at Newnham and Girton from without, before delivering her letters of introduction. **1949** *Radio Times* 15 July 6/3 The BBC's New York office has given me introductions to the broadcasting people in Montreal. **1969** L. HELLMAN *Unfinished Woman* vii. 81, I had sent off a few letters of introduction, but..they weren't answered.

c. (Earlier example.)

1808 JANE AUSTEN *Let.* 26 June (1952) 200 They have nice weather for their introduction to the Island.

introessive (-e·siv), *a. Gram.* [f. L. *intrō* within + *esse* to be + -IVE.] Designating the case which expresses 'motion into'.

1903 *Amer. Anthropologist* Jan.–Mar. 13 Besides a general locative some of the most frequently occurring are inessive, superessive, introessive, ablative, and terminative.

introgress (intrǫgre·s), *v. Biol.* [Back-formation from next.] *intr.* To be transferred by introgression *into* another species. So **introgre·ssed** *ppl. a.*, (*a*) transferred in this way; (*b*) produced as a result of introgression; **introgre·ssing** *ppl. a.*

1958 F. C. ELLIOTT *Plant Breeding & Cytogenetics* ix. 267 Genes from one species introgress into another. **1963** E. MAYR *Animal Species & Evolution* vi. 124 Introgressing hybrid swarms. *Ibid.*, They are introgressing hybrid populations between *D. middendorfiana*, *D. schoedleri*, and *D. pulex*. **1965** D. ZOHARY in Baker & Stebbins *Genetics Colonizing Species* 415 Introgressed types are quickly fixed by self-pollination. **1968** J. A. SERRA *Mod. Genetics* III. xx. 198 This introduction of alien loci or introgressed loci may be of as much interest as the introduction of entire alien chromosomes. **1972** *Science* 22 Sept. 1076/2 Where the introgressed maize at Tehuacán came from is not known.

introgre·ssion. [See s.v. INTRO-.] **1.** (In Dict. s.v. INTRO-.)

2. *Biol.* The transfer of a small amount of genetic material from one (usu. plant) species to another as a result of hybridization between them and repeated back-crossing.

1938 ANDERSON & HUBRICHT in *Amer. Jrnl. Bot.* XXV. 399 We conclude that there is a strong introgression of *T. canaliculata* into *T. occidentalis*. **1950** G. L. STEBBINS *Variation & Evolution in Plants* vii. 265 In this instance, therefore, frequent interspecific hybridization is not accompanied by introgression of genes across the barrier formed by partial sterility of the F_1 hybrid. **1963** LEWIS & JOHN *Chromosome Marker* IV. iv. 373 Low sterility and open pollination will favour introgression. **1971** V. GRANT *Plant Speciation* iv. 52 If the introgression goes far enough, it may obliterate the morphological and ecological distinctions between the original species.

introgressive (intrǫgre·siv), *a. Biol.* [f. INTROGRESS(ION + -IVE.] Characterized by, bringing about, or resulting from introgression; *introgressive hybridization*, introgression; hybridization leading to introgression.

1938 ANDERSON & HUBRICHT in *Amer. Jrnl. Bot.* XXV. 396 We have therefore given it a distinctive name, introgressive hybridization. *Ibid.* 398 The introgressive effect of *T. canaliculata.* **1950** G. L. STEBBINS *Variation & Evolution in Plants* vii. 263 The habitat provides an ecological niche for the establishment of the introgressive types. **1968** J. A. SERRA *Mod. Genetics* III. xx. 199 The introgressive introduction of some loci of *Nicotiana plumbaginifolia* into *N. tabacum.* **1970** *Watsonia* VIII. 85 (*heading*) Introgressive hybridisation between British annual *Senecio* species. **1971** V. GRANT *Plant Speciation* iv. 51 Such bridging populations of hybrid origin fall into two general classes: hybrid swarms and introgressive populations. **1971** G. L. STEBBINS *Chromosomal Evolution Higher Plants* v. 149 The phenomenon of introgressive hybridization or introgression is a sequence of three processes: hybridization, back crossing, and natural selection of back cross derivatives in a habitat where they are superior to either of the original parents.

introject (introdʒe·kt), *v. Psychol.* [Back-formation f. next.] *trans.* To incorporate an inward image of (an external object, or the values and attitudes of others) into oneself. Cf. *INTROJECTION 2, 3. Hence **introje·ctive** *a.*, that is introjected; **introje·cted** *ppl. a.*

1925 J. RIVIERE et al. tr. *Freud's Coll. Papers* IV. 78 The objects presenting themselves, are absorbed by the ego into itself, 'introjected'. **1932** *Brit. Jrnl. Psychol.* Oct. 156 Between the ages of 1 and 2½ his [the child's] mentality alternates between an introjective psychotic pattern..and a projective psychotic pattern. **1935** *Internat. Jrnl. Psycho-Anal.* XVI. 145 From the beginning the ego introjects objects 'good' and 'bad', for both of which the mother's breast is the prototype—for good objects when the child obtains it and for bad when it fails him. **1937** 'C. CAUDWELL' *Illusion & Reality* viii. 158 A blue rose, which was in the *speaker's* perceptual world,..has been formed in the common perceptual world and introjected into the hearer's perceptual world. **1952** W. J. H. SPROTT *Social Psychol.* ix. 169 We are familiar with a theory that we 'introject' our version of our parents. **1962** *Sci. & Psychoanal.* V. 74 Second, the problem was said to be related to the *cathexis* of a deceased sister now existing as an 'introjected object'. **1964** GOULD & KOLB *Dict. Social Sci.* 353/2 It is more probable that as a result of the powerful oral medium of the initial object-relations, identification may assume a more or less oral-cannibalistic, incorporative, and therefore introjective terminology. **1967** M. ARGYLE *Psychol. Interpersonal Behaviour* vii. 123 Children introject their parents' love and admiration of themselves. If they are never loved they will come to reject themselves and suffer from low self-esteem in later life.

introjection (introdʒe·kʃən). [Cf. INTRO-. In senses 2 and 3, ad. G. *introjektion.*] **1.** (In Dict. s.v. INTRO-.)

2. *Philos.* A theory whereby external objects are images of elements within the consciousness of the individual. Hence **introje·ctionism**, belief in a theory of introjection, **introje·ctionist** *a.*, pertaining to introjection.

1899 J. WARD *Naturalism & Agnosticism* II. xvi. 172 The term 'introjection' we owe..to the late Richard Avenarius of Zurich. *Ibid.*, Thus while my environment is an external world for me, his experience is for me an internal world in him. This is introjection. **1903** A. E. TAYLOR *Elem. Metaphysics* II. i. 81 Subjectivism is thus the last step in the development of the fallacy which begins with what Avenarius calls 'introjection'. *Ibid.* IV. i. 304 To translate it into the introjectionist psychology. **1912** *Mind* XXI. 10 The theory appears..to be really a piece of lingering introjectionism. **1931** G. F. STOUT *Mind & Matter* 291 Ward finds this in a supposed process ..which, following Avenarius, he calls Introjection.

3. a. *Psycho-analysis.* A term used by S. Ferenczi (1909 *Jahrb. f. Psychoanalyt. Forschungen* I. 422–57) to denote the forming of a subjective image of an object and the transfer to it of emotional energy previously given to the object itself.

1916 E. JONES tr. *Ferenczi's Contrib. Psycho-Anal.* ii. 40 One might give to this process, in contrast to projection, the name of *Introjection.* **1917** C. R. PAYNE tr. *Pfister's Psychoanal. Method* xii. 387 In the projection, one feels subjective processes producing discomfort as influences of the outer world; in the introjection, inversely, processes of the outer world as one's own. **1922** J. STRACHEY tr. *Freud's Group Psychol.* 65 First, identification is the original form of emotional tie with an object; secondly, in a regressive way it becomes a substitute for a libidinal tie, as it were by means of the introjection of the object into the ego. **1946** *Mind* LV. 83 This growth of the super-ego has four main features, 'narcissism', 'introjection', 'nemesism', and 'sado-masochism'. **1963** *Listener* 7 Mar. 431/2 The ego has incorporated (by means of introjection ..) certain fantasy figures acquired in infancy (such as the image of the breast).

b. *Psychol.* The forming of an inward image of the attitudes, values, and expectations of

people or groups by whom one is anxious to be accepted.

1931 J. C. FLÜGEL in W. Rose *Outl. Mod. Knowl.* ix. 384 An introjection into the self of the earliest external moral forces, i.e. the moral attitudes and precepts of parents. **1955** M. KLEIN *New Directions in Psycho-Anal.* i. 21 External and internal situations are always interdependent, since introjection and projection operate side by side from the beginning of life. **1962** *Listener* 21 June 1055/2 When a child's parents have habitually reacted to his behaviour in a certain way—for instance, being shocked if he cheats—then after a time the child begins to react in this way towards himself. This is the process sometimes described as 'introjection'. **1967** M. ARGYLE *Psychol. Interpersonal Behaviour* vii. 121 A process of *introjection*, whereby children adopt the perceptions, attitudes, and reactions to themselves of parents and others.

intropunitive (intrōpiū·nitiv), *a. Psychol.* Also **intrapunitive.** [f. L. *intrō* inwardly (cf. INTRO-) + PUNITIVE *a.*] Blaming oneself rather than other people or events; of or pertaining to an unreasonable feeling of responsibility for frustrations or the like. Contrasted with *EXTRAPUNITIVE *a.* and *IMPUNITIVE *a.*

1938 S. ROSENZWEIG in H. A. Murray *Explorations in Personality* vi. 587 He may react with emotions of guilt and remorse and tend to condemn himself as the blameworthy object. This type of reaction may be termed 'intropunitive'. **1954** G. W. ALLPORT *Nature of Prejudice* xxvii. 437 This inwardness and ability to know and to laugh at oneself make for the intropunitive tendency that we examined... Self-blame takes the place of projected external blame. **1958** [see *IMPUNITIVE *a.*]. **1965** B. I. MURSTEIN *Handbk. Projective Techniques* xxxii. 575 These criteria included diagnostic council ratings.., Rosenzweig Extrapunitive and Intrapunitive Scores, and the self-ratings of the subject. **1969** [see *EXTRAPUNITIVE *a.*].

Hence **intropu·nitiveness**, the condition of being intropunitive.

1943 *Psychol. Abstr.* XXVII. 99/2 Nonhypnotizability is associated with other defense mechanisms.., and with other reactions to frustration, such as intropunitiveness and extrapunitiveness. **1958** M. ARGYLE *Relig. Behaviour* xii. 161 There is no evidence concerning the intropunitiveness or private religious activities of sect members, but the above three findings confirm the application of the reduction of guilt theory to sects. **1969** M. D. VERNON *Human Motivation* ix. 145 One of the most frequently occurring types of intropunitiveness is anxiety.

introscope (i·ntrŏskōup). [f. INTRO- + -SCOPE.] An instrument designed to be inserted into tubes so as to permit a visual examination of their interiors, and provided with a light source and some kind of optical system.

1937 *Nature* 27 Feb. 380/2 Charles Baker showed an 'introscope', an instrument for inspecting the interiors of boiler tubes, ship shaftings, oxygen bottles and aeroplane spars, etc. By means of this instrument, it is possible to illuminate and examine microscopically surfaces which cannot easily be inspected in other circumstances. **1958** *Ann. Rep. Chief Insp. Factories for 1957* (Cmnd. 521) 27 Entry into the reactor vessel itself will not be possible. Accordingly,..great attention is being given to the developments of introscopes..which will allow remote inspection of internal surfaces. **1962** *Punch* 18 Apr. 604/2 There are men who spend their best years bending pipes; ..others who peer inside them, with the aid of introscopes and boroscopes capable of seeing round four or five corners. **1973** A. PARRISH *Mech. Engineer's Ref. Bk.* viii. 3 Introscopes, Endoscopes, Borescopes, etc. (The Trade name depending on the manufacturer) are forms of rigid, narrow, long industrial telescopes which introduce light and permit visual examination through small apertures e.g. down a small bore tube. They range from 2–50 mm in diameter and, in special cases, may be made from small sections up to 50 m long.

introspectible (introspe·ktĭb'l), *a.* Also **-able.** [f. INTROSPECT *v.* + -IBLE.] Of a thought, sensation, experience, or other mental phenomenon: capable of being examined by introspection.

1925 C. D. BROAD *Mind & its Place* ix. 419 How little of this..is introspected or is introspectible! **1937** *Mind* XLVI. 22 We must include, under the psychological responses which the words tend to produce, not only immediately introspectable experiences, but *dispositions* to react in a given way with appropriate stimuli. **1940** *Philosophy* Jan. 10 Show me the impression, the sensible or introspectible datum.., from which your general symbol derives its meaning. **1959** A. J. AYER *Logical Positivism* 17 The prevailing view was that these [elementary] statements referred to the subject's introspectible or sensory experiences. **1971** A. QUINTON in A. Bullock *20th Cent.* 257/2 The introspectible facts of mental life.

introspectionism (introspe·kʃəniz'm). *Psychol.* [f. INTROSPECTION + -ISM.] Introspective psychology (see *INTROSPECTIVE *a.*); also, more generally, = INTROSPECTION 2.

1922 R. S. WOODWORTH *Psychol.* ii. 21 Without caring to attach ourselves exclusively to either introspectionism or behaviourism. **1931** *Psyche* Jan. 68 Straightforward introspectionism, on the whole, judged by the contents of this book, has very little status in modern psychology. **1965** N. CHOMSKY *Aspects of Theory of Syntax* 193 Introspectionism—should one make use of introspective data in the attempt to ascertain the properties of these underlying systems? **1967** *Lancet* 11 Nov. 1050/1 Behaviourism..arose as a reaction to the even less fruitful introspectionism of the late 19th century.

introspectionist. Add: **c.** *attrib.* or as *adj.*

1934 in WEBSTER. **1949** KOESTLER *Insight & Outlook* xiii. 184 Behaviourism has rendered a service to science by its puritan intolerance towards introspectionist debauch.

introspectioni·stic, *a.* = prec.

1943 *Mind* LII. 133 The methodologically correct use..of introspectionistic terms..is not impugned.

introspective, *a.* Add: *introspective psychology*, psychology based on introspection and on the direct observation of one's own mental states.

1878 W. JAMES in R. B. Perry *Tht. & Char. W. James* (1935) II. LIII. 29 Those whose highest flights are articles in the *Popular Science Monthly* will talk of the exploded superstitions of introspective psychology. **1931** R. S. WOODWORTH *Contemp. Schools Psychol.* ii. 17 What we do find..is..more precise formulation of the aim of introspective psychology. *a* **1942** B. MALINOWSKI *Sci. Theory of Culture* (1944) vii. 71 Whether we use introspective psychology, and say that understanding means identification of the mental processes, or whether, as behaviourists, we affirm that his response to the integral stimulus of the situation follows lines familiar to us from our own experiences, does not change the argument profoundly. **1951** E. E. EVANS-PRITCHARD *Social Anthropol.* iii. 44 Other anthropologists were later left in a similar way in the fashion of introspective psychology.

introsusception. 2. (Earlier example.)

1786 J. C. LETTSOM (*title*) The history of an extraordinary introsusception... With an account of the dissection. By..Whately.

‖ **introuvable** (æ̃ntruvāb'l), *a.* [Fr.] Unfindable, undiscoverable; *spec.* of books. Also as *sb.*

1824 *Edin. Rev.* Mar. 2 We are by no means of opinion that it [*sc.* a correct standard of national prosperity] is really *introuvable.* **1856** *Newsp. & Gen. Reader's Compan.* II. § 1436 Give me a mere *annonce* of any thing, that can tell me of your *introuvable* friend. **1895** H. B. FORMAN in Nicoll & Wise *Lit. Anecdotes 19th Cent.* I. 67 The almost introuvable tract *Prothanasia and other Poems.* **1963** *Times Lit. Suppl.* 15 Feb. 116/3 A potential *introuvable* to future collectors.

introversion. Add: **1. b.** The tendency to turn psychic energy inwards and to withdraw from the external world; opp. *EXTRAVERSION 2, *EXTROVERSION 3.

1912 *Psychol. Bull.* IX. 159 So that when in later life there occurs an introversion (in the sense of Jung), it consists of a harking back to regressive, reminiscent, infantile material. **1915**, etc. [see *EXTRAVERSION 2]. **1935** C. G. JUNG *Analytical Psychol.* (1968) ii. 41 The psychological mechanism of introversion of the conscious mind into the deeper layers of the unconscious psyche. **1955** *Sci. News Let.* 19 Mar. 185/2 Patients with this disease are at times completely withdrawn from the world around them and give the picture of the very extreme of introversion. **1964** M. ARGYLE *Psychol. & Social Probl.* vi. 75 Eysenck has suggested the three dimensions of neuroticism, psychoticism and introversion–extraversion.

introversive. Add: **1. c.** Characterized by introversion (sense *1 b).

1923, **1932** [see *EXTROVERSION 3]. **1970** *Jrnl. Gen. Psychol.* July 65 Rorschach writes:..all of these findings indicate a more introversive type. **1972** *Daily Tel.* (Colour Suppl.) 25 Aug. 31/1 Indoor flying is one of the world's most esoteric and introversive hobbies.

introvert, *sb.* Add: **2.** *Psychol.* A person characterized by introversion; a withdrawn or reserved person; opp. *EXTROVERT *sb.* Also *attrib.* and as *adj.* Also **i·ntrovertish** *a.*, said of such a person, his activities, etc.

1918, etc. [see *EXTROVERT *sb.* (and *a.*)]. **1925** C. FOX *Educational Psychol.* 254 The introvert abstracts from the object and deals with it by concepts concentrating upon the inner world of thought. **1934** *Brit. Jrnl. Psychol.* July 26 They were noticeably more introvert, schizoid and desurgent in temperament. **1946** R. P. BASLER in W. S. Knickerbocker *20th Cent. English* III. 392 In the snugness of introvertish isolation, there is always time, an eternity for continual deception and indecision. **1955** L. LANGSTROTH *Struct. of Ego* vii. 82 This question of the relative strength of the social and biological selves suggests at once Jung's broad division of personalities into two main types: the introvert and the extrovert. **1957** H. J. EYSENCK *Dynamics Anxiety & Hysteria* vi. 213 The introvert, as we have seen, is socialized. **1960** *Encounter* XV. 47 The introvert-intellectual is the hero of several of Buchan's works. **1967** M. ARGYLE *Psychol. Interpersonal Behaviour* iii. 50 Experiments with schoolchildren show that introverts respond better to praise.

introverted, *ppl. a.* **1.** Add to def.: esp. in *Psychol.*

1915 [see *EXTRAVERSION 2]. **1916** C. E. LONG tr. *Jung's Coll. Papers Analytical Psychol.* 348 The introverted type is characterised by the fact that his libido is turned towards his own personality to a certain extent. **1923** [see *EXTROVERT *sb.* (and *a.*)]. **1957** H. J. EYSENCK *Dynamics Anxiety & Hysteria* i. 31 We may take dysthymics on the one hand, and hysterics and psychopaths on the other, as examples of our introverted and extroverted groups. **1968** C. RYCROFT *Critical Dict. Psychoanal.* 48 There is a tendency to equate 'introverted' with 'withdrawn' or 'schizoid'. **1974** *Country Life* 17 Jan. 76/3 Dorothy Osborne... This witty and introverted girl.

intrude, *v.* **5.** For † *Obs. rare* substitute: *Obs. rare* except in *Geol.* To be forced or thrust into. (Add later examples.)

1925 J. JOLY *Surface-Hist. Earth* viii. 130 Both these [series], together with a series mainly of basaltic eruptives .., were finally intruded by vast uprisings of granites (largely batholithic). **1932** W. H. EMMONS et al. *Geol.* xii. 361 This sill intrudes limestone, is nearly flat lying, and in general is almost parallel to the beds it intrudes. **1955** *Econ. Geol.* L. 715 Four locations where sills, dikes, and stocks intrude or cut off the phosphate-bearing beds. **1957** *Mineral. Mag.* XXXI. 588 This block is intruded by three stock-like masses of fine-grained granite. **1966** C. O. DUNBAR *Earth* iv. 61 Remnants of the oldest sedimentary formations were intensively deformed and intruded by the underlying granite. **1971** I. G. GASS et al. *Understanding Earth* ii. 48/2 A small igneous intrusion.. which intruded a fossiliferous sediment.

intruder. Add: **3.** An aeroplane (or its pilot) that invades the enemy's aerodromes to interfere with his operations. Also *attrib.*, as *intruder attack, raid.*

1941 *Aeroplane Spotter* 9 Oct. 174 *The Intruder.* 'Night intrusion' is the name of one type of operation on which Douglas Havocs are earning distinction. The Havocs fly out over enemy aerodromes when the night bombers are returning and shoot them down over their home stations. *Ibid.* 6 Nov. 205 Messerschmitt Me 110 two-motor fighters are now being used with Ju 88s for night defence over Germany and 'intruder' work over Great Britain. **1943** *Times* 22 Dec. 4/5 R.C.A.F. intruders destroyed two enemy aircraft. **1944** *Times* 6 Nov. 4/4 Night fighters and intruder aircraft of Bomber Command supported the bombers. **1966** M. R. D. FOOT *SOE in France* iv. 82 But 418 was an ordinary Canadian intruder squadron.

intrusion. Add: **1. b.** (Earlier example.)

1839 R. I. MURCHISON *Silurian Syst.* v. 78 This intrusion having taken place on a line of ancient volcanic eruption, the origin of which cannot be understood without a previous acquaintance with the history of the Silurian System, the account of this new red trap dyke is necessarily deferred.

3. *spec.* in contexts of Journalism.

1958 *Spectator* 18 July 110/3 Newspaper intrusion into private lives. **1960** *New Statesman* 15 Oct. 556/2 The intrusion and impertinence of some of the gossip writers.

intrusive, *a.* Add: **B.** *sb. Geol.* An intrusive rock or rock mass.

1895 A. HARKER *Petrol.* vii. 87 Acid intrusives. The acid intrusive rocks embrace a considerable range of varieties. **1925** N. E. ODELL in E. F. Norton *Fight for Everest, 1924* 300 Yet the character of the former [*sc.* the limestone series] may be entirely due to its proximity to the hard crystalline rocks and its alteration brought about by pressure against them, if not also by their igneous intrusives. **1962** W. T. HUANG *Petrol.* iii. 51 It [*sc.* magma] may be solidified at great depth, forming such large intrusives as batholiths, stocks, and lopoliths. **1968** J. GILLULY et al. *Princ. Geol.* (ed. 3) xviii. 435 (*caption*) Devil's Tower, Wyoming, probably a volcanic plug, but perhaps part of a roofed intrusive.

intuit, *v.* Add: **2.** (Later example.)

1968 J. C. HOLMES *Nothing more to Declare* 105 You had to be able to intuit on the bias, to hear music *being* music.

b. (Later examples.)

1926 A. HUXLEY *Two or three Graces* 85 You intuit things that aren't there at all. **1968** *Times* 13 Jan. 20/3 We may intuit his reality, but we cannot share it. **1972** *Times Lit. Suppl.* 18 Feb. 178/1 What Johnson intuited and asserted in 1765, that of the Folios only the first had any textual authority, was demonstrated by Malone in 1790.

intuitable (intiū·ităb'l), *a.* [f. INTUIT *v.* + -ABLE.] That can be known by intuition.

1887 G. T. LADD tr. *Lotze's Outl. Logic* § 64 'Abstraction' makes the content of the concept intuitable only as a whole. **1904** J. H. MUIRHEAD in J. E. Hand *Ideals of Sci. & Faith* 91 If the mere absence of intuitable continuity were the only difficulty in the way of assimilation, we might ignore it. **1932** H. H. PRICE *Perception* vi. 168 The intuitable characteristics of the sense-datum now sensed. **1971** R. HARROD *Sociol.* 51 In the case of lying, there is no question of its having a certain innate intuitable quality.

intuited (intiū·itĕd), *ppl. a.* [f. INTUIT *v.* + -ED[1].] Arrived at or known by intuition.

1886 A. WEIR *Hist. Basis Mod. Europe* xii. 481 The mathematical sciences..drew their conclusions from intuited figures and series. **1890** W. JAMES *Princ. Psychol.* I. 630 Meanwhile, the specious present, the intuited duration, stands permanent, like the rainbow on the waterfall, with its own quality unchanged by the events that stream through it. **1924** H. J. W. HETHERINGTON *Life & Lett. Sir H. Jones* I. 64 Even intuited truth is not reality. **1967** *Listener* 4 May 593/1 Some felt or intuited absolute ethical standard. **1973** S. HENDERSON *Understanding New Black Poetry* 10 Fidelity to the observed or intuited truth of the Black Experience in the United States.

intuition. 5. c. (Earlier example.)

1796 F. A. NITSCH *Gen. View Kant's Princ. concerning Man* 75 Those ideas which immediately arise in consequence of our external sense being affected are external perceptions or external intuitions.

intuitionism. Add: **3.** *Math.* The theory put forward by L. E. J. Brouwer (1908) that

mathematics is founded on extra-linguistic constructs based on pure intuition (in the Kantian sense, cf. INTUITION 5 c); that space geometry is reducible to arithmetic and that therefore the law of the excluded middle, applying to finite classes, might not be valid for infinite classes. Cf. *FORMALISM 3.

1913 tr. L. E. J. Brouwer in *Bull. Amer. Math. Soc.* XXV. 86 From the present point of view of intuitionism.. all mathematical sets of units..can be developed out of the basal intuition, and this can only be done by combining a finite number of times the two operations: 'to create a finite ordinal number' and 'to create the infinite ordinal number ω'. **1940** [see *FORMALISM 3 a]. **1941** COURANT & ROBBINS *What is Math.?* i. 87 Some distinguished mathematicians have recently advocated the more or less complete banishment from mathematics of all non-constructive proofs... The school of 'intuitionism', which has adopted this program, has met with strong resistance. **1959** E. W. BETH *Found. Math.* xv. 413 One of the most spectacular features in Brouwer's intuitionism is..his rejection of the unrestricted application of the principle of the excluded third in mathematical reasoning. **1965** KLEENE & VESLEY *Found. Intuitionistic Math.* i. 1 Modern intuitionism, founded by Brouwer, constitutes a vigorous manifestation of the constructive tendency. **1973** *Sci. Amer.* Mar. 103/2 Three modern schools of mathematical thought: logicism, formalism and intuitionism.

intuitionist. Add: **1.** *attrib.* (Earlier example.)

1872 MILL *Exam. Hamilton's Philos.* (ed. 4) xiv. 339 This..is the staple of the Intuitionist argument.

2. (Later examples.) Used esp. in *Math.* Cf. *INTUITIONISM 3. Also *attrib.*

1913 *Bull. Amer. Math. Soc.* XXV. 86 The intuitionist can never feel assured of the exactness of a mathematical theory by such guarantees as the proof of its being non-contradictory, the possibility of defining its concepts by a finite number of words or the practical certainty that it will never lead to a misunderstanding in human relations. **1926** *Proc. London Math. Soc.* 2nd Ser. XXV. 339 Apart from formalism, there are two main general attitudes to the foundation of mathematics: that of intuitionists or finitists..and that of the logicians. **1933** M. BLACK *Nature of Math.* 195 The intuitionist recognises only the existence of denumerable sets. **1941** [see *FORMALIST 5]. **1952** R. M. HARE *Lang. Morals* iii. 30 The word 'good' is treated in the fashion that many intuitionists have treated it. **1959** E. W. BETH *Found. Math.* xv. 421 The intuitionist..can point to the edifice of intuitionistic mathematics which has been built alongside classical mathematics. **1967** S. C. KLEENE *Math. Logic* § 36. 196 To prove an existence statement ∃xA(x), an intuitionist insists that it be shown how to find an *x* such that A(*x*). **1973** *Sci. Amer.* Mar. 103/2 As for intuitionists, they have in effect returned to the Pythagorean position that the natural numbers must be accepted without further analysis as the foundation of mathematics.

b. *attrib.* or as *adj.* Of or pertaining to intuitionism.

1926 [see *FORMALIST B]. **1933** M. BLACK *Nature of Math.* 11 Intuitionist doctrines require the larger part of mathematics to be rewritten. *Ibid.*, The intuitionists.. are beginning to produce an intuitionist formal logic. **1960** S. KÖRNER *Philos. of Math.* vi. 131 The intuitionist logic is a *post factum* record of the principles of reasoning which have been employed in mathematical constructions. *Ibid.*, Every intuitionist proposition *p*, whether or not the (intuitionist-)negation occurs in it, is the record of a construction. **1970** A. KINO et al. *Intuitionism & Proof Theory* 19 That is the general way of accepting-on-faith in the domains of religion and philosophy, and in traditional intuitionist or constructivist mathematics also.

intuitionistic *a.* (later examples); also **intuitioni·stically** *adv.*, in an intuitionistic manner.

1940 *Mathematical Rev.* Nov. 323/1 The treatment is 'intuitionistic' in the sense that it is purely algebraic, involving reference to order, absolute value, boundedness, etc., but not to limiting processes. **1942** D. D. RUNES *Dict. Philos.* 150 The resulting disjunction becomes intuitionistically acceptable. **1944** *Mathematical Rev.* Sept. 198/2 The author proves intuitionistically seven theorems concerning the full product of a finite or denumerable number of virtually ordered sets, generalizing some results of Brouwer concerning the full products of sets of integers. **1945** E. T. BELL *Devel. Math.* (ed. 2) xxiii. 560 The 'objects' with which intuitionistic mathematics is concerned are said to be immediately apprehended in thought. **1946** *Nature* 7 Sept. 323/1 Nevertheless, if ethics is to be scientific in this sense, some possible theories, particularly those commonly called intuitionistic, are excluded. **1957** *Encycl. Brit.* XV. 82B/1 Most theorems of classical arithmetic can be established intuitionistically. **1962** B. MELTZER tr. *Gödel's On formally Undecidable Propositions* 60 The following is demonstrated in an intuitionistically unobjectionable way. **1965** KLEENE & VESLEY (*title*) The foundations of intuitionistic mathematics. **1967** S. C. KLEENE *Math. Logic* § 44. 257 The consistency proof by a truth definition can even be managed intuitionistically. **1971** R. SCHOCK *Quasi-Connectives* vi. 58 The resulting quasi-connectives satisfy all the axioms of the intuitionistic sentential calculus, but not the principle of the excluded middle.

intuitive, *a.* Add: **3. b.** (Earlier example.)

1833 MILL *Let.* 5 July (1910) I. ii. 54, I conceive that most of the highest truths are..intuitive; that is, they need neither explanation nor proof, but if not known before are assented to as soon as stated.

6. (Earlier example.)

1852 MILL in *Westm. Rev.* LVIII. 362 If it is alleged that the intuitive school require, as an authority for the feeling, that it should *in fact* be universal, we deny it.

B. *sb.* One who works by intuition.

1907 *Westm. Gaz.* 28 Nov. 2/1 Poincaré divides mathematicians into analysts and geometers—i.e., into logicians and 'intuitives'. **1927** A. HUXLEY *Proper Stud.* 207 Intellectuals and intuitives.

intuitively, *adv.* Add: **3.** *Logic.* By, or to, unaided reflection; without the use of any technique of logic.

1942 J. C. COOLEY *Primer of Formal Logic* vi. 218 Most of the statements excluded by the theory of types would probably be avoided intuitively because they do not make sensible English sentences.

intuitivism. 1. (Earlier example.)

a **1866** J. GROTE *Exam. Utilitarian Philos.* (1870) i. 21 That doctrine, hostile to utilitarianism, to which he has given the name of 'intuitivism'.

intuitivist, *a.* (Earlier example.)

a **1866** J. GROTE *Exam. Utilitarian Philos.* (1870) x. 168 The..description of conscience which Mr. Mill gives.. seems to me, if anything is, intuitivist.

inturn, *sb.* Add: **4.** *Curling.* An inward turn of the elbow made in delivering a stone.

1890 [see *OUT-TURN c]. **1897** *Encycl. Sport* I. 262/1 The inturn is made when the curl is to be toward the right. **1923** G. RAE *Langsyne in Braefoot* iv. 42, I want the in-turn, an' I want ye here. Dinna lie back for ony sake. **1969** R. WELSH *Beginner's Guide Curling* xi. 83 Almost all beginners are taught first to play the in-turn.

inturned, *ppl. a.* (Later examples.)

1906 R. H. BENSON *Queen's Tragedy* III. iv. 367 She.. touched the palms of her hands with her in-turned fingers. **1923** D. H. LAWRENCE *Birds, Beasts & Flowers* 6 The fig-fruit: Involved, Inturned, The flowering all inward and womb-fibrilled. **1967** *Antiquaries Jrnl.* XLVII. 256 The ditch as now defined with its right-angle turn near the western corner of the Arbour and its possible inturned entrance is best interpreted as the defence or boundary work of a Belgic *oppidum*.

intussuscept, *v.* (Earlier example.)

1802 *Med. & Physical Jrnl.* VII. 36 The part of the intestine inflated by Mr. Muir, was an intus-suscepted portion.

intussusception. Add: **3. a.** (Earlier and later examples.) Also, the mass of intestine involved in this.

1802 *Med. & Physical Jrnl.* VII. 36 Intestinal intus-susceptions vary much in their extent, situation, and other circumstances. **1838** *Guy's Hosp. Rep.* III. 332 There were four intus-susceptions of the small intestines. **1960, 1970** [see *INTUSSUSCEPTUM]. **1970** H. M. SPIRO *Clin. Gastroenterol.* xxii. 356/1 At laparotomy, the intussusception is easily recognized and reduced or..resected.

intussusceptum (i:ntɒs,sɒse·ptɒm). *Med.* [mod.L., neut. sing. of *intussusceptus*: see INTUSSUSCEPT *v.*] The middle and the innermost tubes of intestine (taken together) of the three present in an intussusception; also (less commonly), the innermost tube alone.

1857 DUNGLISON *Dict. Med. Sci.* (rev. ed.) 507/2 It [sc. *intussusceptio*] means the introduction of one part of the intestinal canal—*intussusceptum*—into another, which serves it as a sort of vagina or sheath. Generally, it is the upper part of the small intestine, which is received into the lower—*intussuscipiens*—when the intussusception is said to be progressive. **1884** F. TREVES *Intestinal Obstructions* viii. 168 The external of the three layers is known as the intussuscipiens, the sheath, or the receiving layer... The innermost cylinder is known as the entering layer..and the middle one as the returning layer... Taken together, these two layers form the intussusceptum. **1960** JONES & GUMMER *Clin. Gastroenterol.* iii. 93 An intussusception when fully developed is made up of three layers of intestine. The innermost or entering portion of the gut is called the intussusceptum... The middle or returning layer..is referred to as the resceptum and the outermost or ensheathing layer is the intussuscipiens. **1965** LUMSDEN & TRUELOVE *Radiol. Digestive Syst.* xv. 497 The barium may penetrate between the intussuscipiens and the intussusceptum, thus outlining the apex of the intussusceptum. **1970** H. M. SPIRO *Clin. Gastroenterol.* xxii. 353/2 Intussusception is the telescoping of the wall of one segment of the bowel into the adjacent distal portion. ..In formal circles, the invaginated segment is known as the intussusceptum, the receiving segment is the intussuscipiens.

intussuscipiens (i:ntɒs,sɒsi·pienz). *Med.* [mod.L., pres. pple. of *intussuscipere*: cf. prec.] The outermost of the three tubes of intestine which are present in an intussusception, and into which the other two are inserted.

1857, etc. [see prec.].

Inuit, var. *INNUIT.

inulase (i·niulēiz, -s). *Biochem.* [f. INUL(IN + *-ASE.] An enzyme which hydrolyses inulin to fructose, found esp. in some fungi.

1893 J. R. GREEN in *Ann. Bot.* VII. 90 This transformation has been found to be due to a special enzyme, to which the name inulase may be given. It is a different body from diastase, for it has no action upon starch-paste. **1931** E. C. MILLER *Plant Physiol.* xi. 628 Inulase may occur with diastase but has no action whatsoever upon starch. **1965** FLORKIN & STOTZ *Comprehensive Biochem.* (ed. 2) XIII. 136 Systematic name: β-2, 1-Fructan fructanohydrolase. Recommended trivial name: Inulase.

inundatal (i·nɒndēităl), *a. Ecol.* [irreg. f. INUNDATE *v.* + -AL.] Of plants: growing in areas subject to flooding.

1847 H. C. WATSON *Cybele Britannica* I. 65 Inundatal. Plants of places liable to be inundated in wet weather, but often dry in summer. **1897** G. C. DRUCE *Flora Berkshire* 575 Water Whorl Grass... Native. Inundatal. On the muddy margins of ditches, ponds, &c. **1926** *Nat. Hist. Oxford District* 88 Paludal flora (including uliginal and inundatal species).

inurn, *v.* Add: **inu·rnment,** the process of placing the ashes of a cremated body into an urn.

1934 *Amer. Speech* IX. 317/1 Olivet Memorial Park provides every service for Entombments, Inurnments, Interments. **1948** E. WAUGH *Loved One* 36 Normal disposal is by inhumement, entombment, inurnment or immurement, but many people..prefer insarcophagusment.

in utero, in vacuo: see *IN *Lat. prep.*

invalid. Add: **B.** *sb.* **3.** (Further examples.)

1822 M. EDGEWORTH *Let.* 28 May (1971) 402 Her own invalid breakfast as she called it, a glass of Seltzer-water and milk! **1847** W. M. THACKERAY *Vanity Fair* (1848) xli. 375 Sir Pitt's invalid-chair was wheeled away into a tool-house in the garden. **1859** DICKENS in *N.Y. Ledger* 27 Aug. 5/5 The hand-carriage was spinning away ..at a most indecorous pace for an invalid vehicle. **1861** MRS. BEETON *Bk. Househ. Managem.* 893 (*heading*) Invalid cookery... A few rules to be observed in cooking for invalids. **1862** *Illustr. London News* 1 Nov. 473/1 An elongated invalid-chair is shown which is capable of being arranged as an ordinary easy-chair and of being extended into a camp bedstead. **1873** C. M. YONGE *Pillars of House* I. iii. 38 Wilmet could..do invalid cookery. **1876** —— *Three Brides* II. xiv. 259 He diverged to the invalid-carriage he had secured. **1880** Invalid furniture [see *carrying-chair* (*CARRYING *vbl. sb.* 4)]. **1902** 'MARK TWAIN' *Let.* 23 Oct. in C. Clemens *Mark Twain* (1932) 95 We brought Mrs. Clemens through successfully in an invalid car. **1911** *Daily Colonist* (Victoria, B.C.) 27 Apr. 6/1 (Advt.), Wiese & Brohn's Oporto Invalid Port, best on the market. **1934** T. S. ELIOT *Rock* I. 15 And political religion is like invalid port: you calls it a medicine but it's soon just a 'abit. **1953** 'N. BLAKE' *Dreadful Hollow* I. ii. 28 She's got an electric invalid-carriage. **1967** *Guardian* 12 June 6/4 As an Oxford undergraduate with a muscular dystrophy, I am grateful for a Ministry of Health invalid tricycle. **1972** K. BONFIGLIOLI *Don't point that Thing at Me* i. 1 Invalid Port of an unbelievable nastiness. **1972** *Guardian* 4 Sept. 11/8 The middle-aged spina bifida sufferer who, after having saved to buy an invalid car, lost his job.

invalidity. Add: **3. b.** *attrib.*

1906 *Daily Chron.* 18 Nov. 3 A State scheme of invalidity insurance would lead to the destruction of the successful voluntary system. **1907** *Ibid.* 15 July 3/2 [Germany] The invalidity pensions go to all those of any age who are unfitted for relief. **1908** *Ibid.* 16 June 5/7 There is a great deal to be said for the German invalidity scheme. **1969** *Daily Tel.* 25 July 23 The new 'invalidity pension' will be introduced as part of the proposed earnings related retirement pension scheme..due to come into force in 1972. *Ibid.*, The new invalidity pension is designed to take over after a person has been away from work through illness for more than 28 weeks.

invalidy (i·nvălĭdi), *a. colloq.* [f. INVALID *sb.* + -Y¹.] Of the nature of an invalid.

1894 MRS. H. WARD *Marcella* III. 9 She's fussy, you know, and invalidy, and has to be wrapped up in shawls. **1912** 'R. DEHAN' *Between two Thieves* 626 We invaded the Crimea with a weakly, invalidy, or crippled army.

Invar (i·nvāɹ). Also **invar.** [a. F. *invar* (M. Thury *Nouveau Pendule Compensateur* (1897) 4), f. *invar*(*iable* invariable.] The proprietary name of an alloy of iron or steel (about 64%) and nickel (about 36%), which has a very small coefficient of expansion.

1902 *Encycl. Brit.* XXXIII. 805/2 For ordinary standards of length Guillaume's alloy (invar) of nickel (35·7 per cent.) and steel (64·3 per cent.) is used, as it is a metal that can be highly polished, and is capable of receiving fine graduations. **1928** J. E. HASWELL *Horology* iii. 29 The more recent discovery of the nickel-steel alloy, 'Invar', by Dr. C. E. Guillaume has, however, to a considerable extent revolutionised compensated pendulums. **1929** J. A. RATCLIFFE *Physical Princ. Wireless* iii. 50 The oscillating system..is not an electrical circuit, but is a tuning-fork made of 'invar' metal, whose frequency remains very constant under all conditions. **1955** [see *GRAVIMETER 2]. **1962** J. G. TWEEDDALE *Metall. Princ. for Engineers* iv. 106 Nickel may be used to reduce the coefficient of thermal expansion of steel, 36% reducing the coefficient practically to zero at room temperature when the carbon is 0·2% and manganese 0·5% (this alloy is sold in this country under trade names such as 'Invar' and 'Nilo 36'). **1971** R. J. P. WILSON *Land Surveying* viii. 134 Invar tapes are more delicate than steel tapes and cannot stand up to everyday survey use. Also the degree of accuracy they can provide is unnecessary on most survey work. However, they are invaluable on precise base measurements, all the British bases being measured with 100-ft invar tapes.

invariance. Add: Hence applied to a similar property with respect to any transformation or operation. Also *attrib.*

1910 [see *Galilean *a.*² b]. **1919** A. N. Whitehead *Enquiry Princ. Nat. Knowl.* 41 This invariance, with these formulae for transformation, does not extend to Maxwell's equations for the electromagnetic field. **1941** Courant & Robbins *What is Math.?* iii. 159 A particular consequence of the invariance of angle under inversion is that two circles or lines that are orthogonal, i.e. that intersect at right angles, remain orthogonal after an inversion. **1969** *Observer* 13 Apr. 1 These rules [*sc.* conservation laws of physics] are based on much more fundamental ideas about nature, called invariance principles. *Ibid.* 2/6 The conservation of energy is a direct result of the principle of 'time invariance'. This says that the laws of nature do not change with time.

2. *gen.* The property of remaining unaltered or of being the same in different circumstances; an instance of this, an invariant.

1939 *Mind* XLVIII. 50 This (heuristic) principle of ethical invariance is what I wish to oppose to the principle of ethical relativity. **1956** Jakobson & Halle *Fund. of Lang.* iii. 28 The study of invariances within the phonemic pattern of one language must be supplemented by a search for universal invariances in the phonemic patterning of language. **1962** F. I. Ordway et al. *Basic Astronautics* xiii. 525 Drugs..might also minimize the psychological problems of space flight by reducing the tensions associated with sensory deprivation or invariance. **1964** *Language* XL. 202 Concepts concerning the invariance of linguistic units. **1973** [see *invariant *a.* a].

invariant, *a.* and *sb.* Add: **A.** *adj.* (Further examples.)

1957 G. E. Hutchinson *Treat. Limnol.* I. ix. 634 The relatively invariant climatic conditions of the equatorial regions. **1964** M. Argyle *Psychol. & Social Probl.* i. 14 These so-called 'first-order factors' are not a satisfactory final solution, since they will reflect the numbers of tests of different kinds which have been used, and fail to yield a stable or 'invariant' set of factors. **1966** [see sense B. 2 below]. **1973** *Sci. Amer.* Feb. 26/1 The locations of nerve cells, the trajectories of nerve fibers and the spatial arrays of synaptic connections are invariant in all individuals of the same species. This invariance is termed neuronal specificity.

b. *Physical Chem.* Having no degrees of freedom (see *freedom 10 b).

1899 R. A. Lehfeldt *Text-bk. Physical Chem.* v. 208 Such systems may conveniently be called invariant, univariant, divariant, &c., according as they possess no, one, two, &c., degrees of freedom. **1923** A. C. D. Rivett *Phase Rule* i. 25 When $F = 0$ the system is said to be invariant, since none of its variables may be altered at will without destroying the system in the sense of altering the number of coexisting phases. **1971** F. A. Bettelheim *Exper. Physical Chem.* xxvii. 259 Phase diagrams of ternary systems that are plotted on a triple co-ordinate graph have two important features: an invariant point, *O*, and the solubility curves.

c. *Math.* and *Physics.* Unchanged by a specified transformation or operation. Const. *under.*

1908 H. Hilton *Introd. Theory Groups of Finite Order* v. 62 If every element of a group *G* transforms an element *g* of *G* into itself, so that *g* is permutable with every element of *G*, *g* is called a normal, self-conjugate, or invariant element of *G*... Similarly, if every element of *G* transforms a subgroup *H* into itself, *H* is called a normal, self-conjugate, or invariant subgroup of *G*. **1914** L. Silberstein *Theory of Relativity* iv. 111 The principle of relativity excludes all such laws as are not invariant with respect to the Lorentz transformation. **1919** A. N. Whitehead *Enquiry Princ. Nat. Knowl.* 39 They [*sc.* Newton's equations] are invariant for the spatio-temporal transformations from one such set to another within the Newtonian group. **1941** Birkhoff & MacLane *Survey Mod. Algebra* vi. 153 A subgroup *S* of a group *G* is normal (in *G*) if and only if it is invariant under all inner automorphisms of *G* (i.e., contains with any element all its conjugates). **1955** W. Pauli *Niels Bohr* 34 The theory is invariant with respect to space or time reflection separately. **1968** [see *covariant B].

B. *sb.* Also *attrib.*

1908 J. E. Wright *Invariants of Quadratic Differential Forms* Pref., The aim of this tract is to give..an account of the invariant theory connected with a single quadratic differential form. **1940** J. L. Coolidge *Hist. Geom. Methods* II. ii. 156 The invariant idea, thus launched, was eagerly seized on, especially..by the great twin brethren, Cayley and Sylvester.

b. Any quantity or expression which is invariant under a specified transformation or operation.

1908 H. Hilton *Introd. Theory Groups of Finite Order* vii. 99 An expression is an invariant of [a substitution-group] *G* if it is not altered when we perform on it every one of a set of substitutions which generate *G*. **1914** L. Silberstein *Theory of Relativity* iv. 112 It may be expressed shortly by saying that $x^2 + y^2 + z^2 - c^2t^2$..is a relativistic invariant. **1956** E. M. Patterson *Topology* i. 11 Such entities are called topological invariants, because they are the same for all topologically equivalent spaces. **1959, 1967** [see *covariant].

2. *gen.* An invariant property or feature.

1939 *Mind* XLVIII. 39 There is a widespread view that the sole invariant of morals is their sociological function to secure the preservation and welfare of a social group. **1960** E. Delavenay *Introd. Machine Transl.* iii. 28 In 1949 Weaver pointed out that..one discovers statistical invariants, as found in cryptography.., semantic invariants,..and logical invariants. **1966** J. J. Katz *Philos. of Lang.* ii. 9 The study of language in general provides us with generalizations expressing the invariant features of language which we may particularize as the requirement that an empirically correct description of a natural language represents such invariants.

invasion. Add: **1. c.** *Path.* The spreading of pathogenic microorganisms or malignant cells that are already in the body to new sites.

1891 F. P. Foster *Med. Dict.* III. 2011/2 *Invasion*, the process by which a particular organ or part becomes affected with disease or parasites existing elsewhere in the organism. **1892** G. M. Sternberg *Man. Bacteriol.* III. i. 221 The invasion of the blood which occurs in anthrax and in various forms of septicæmia in the lower animals, induced by subcutaneous inoculation with pure cultures of certain pathogenic bacteria, does not generally immediately follow the inoculation. **1924** R. Muir *Text-bk. Path.* xii. 332 Incision of the capsule may permit of renewed invasion by the tumor. **1949** H. T. Karsner *Human Path.* (ed. 7) 312/2 Although certain normal cells may infiltrate into neighboring structures,..yet infiltration and invasion are properties of neoplastic cells. **1965** T. F. Nealon *Managem. Patient with Cancer* i. 13/2 Extension or invasion is the spread of a cancer by direct involvement of surrounding structures, lymphatics, or blood vessels.

2. Esp. in phr. *invasion of privacy.*

1890 *Harvard Law Rev.* 15 Dec. 198 The common law recognizes and upholds a principle applicable to cases of invasion of privacy. **1912** Kipling *Divers. Creatures* (1917) 2 Any complaint of invasion of privacy needs immediate investigation. **1967** H. McCloy *Further Side of Fear* i. 3 He would have no motive for coming by stealth ... Besides, it was impossible to associate Mr. Erskine with any invasion of privacy.

4. *Ecology.* The spread of a plant or animal population into an area formerly free of the species concerned.

1905 F. E. Clements *Res. Methods Ecol.* iv. 210 By invasion is understood the movement of plants from an area of a certain character into one of a different character, and their colonization in the latter. **1932** Fuller & Conard tr. *Braun-Blanquet's Plant Sociol.* xiii. 308 The colonization of new unoccupied land by plant disseminules may be either by centrifugal or by marginal invasion. **1940** H. F. Witherby et al. *Handbk. Brit. Birds* I. 31 The slender-billed nutcracker... Not confined to conifer woods in its 'invasions' of Europe. **1958** C. Elton *Ecol. of Invasions* vi. 111 We have to accept the proposition that invasions of animals and plants and their parasites—and *our* parasites—will continue. **1964** Gould & Kolb *Dict. Social Sci.* 354/1 The process which occurs when one kind of population begins to occupy a territory (or an occupational niche) already occupied by another, or it increases its rate of occupancy... In human ecology *invasion* is restricted to this..meaning.

5. *attrib.*

1915 Mrs. Belloc Lowndes *Let.* 10 Mar. (1971) 57 No, I do *not* believe in either Zeppelins or an invasion... There is an invasion scare but I don't believe in that. **1923** W. S. Churchill *World Crisis* (1938) I. xix. 404 An invasion scare took a firm hold of the military and naval authorities. **1941** *Times* (Weekly ed.) 15 Oct., One of the heaviest attacks of the war was made on the invasion coast. **1942** *R.A.F. Jrnl.* 3 Oct. 8 The men..who would fly tomorrow's dawn patrol along the invasion coast. *Ibid.* 18 A tradition which was..renewed in France in 1939..; over the 'invasion ports' of Northern France in 1940 and 1941.

invasive, *a.* Add: **2. c.** *Path.* Of, exhibiting, or characterized by invasiveness.

1926 H. T. Karsner *Human Path.* xii. 332 It is probable that nearly all tumors begin originally as a somewhat invasive growth...The invasive character depends very largely upon the multiplication of the cells in the margin of the tumor. **1948** R. A. Willis *Path. Tumours* ix. 148 While proliferation is an important factor in invasive growth, it is certainly not the only or even the most essential one. **1970** [see *invasiveness]. **1971** *Brit. Med. Bull.* XXVII. 4/2 The attempt is made to relate the number of cases of carcinoma-in-situ entering a population to the number leaving it to become cases of invasive cancer.

invasiveness (invē̆i·zivnės). *Path.* [f. Invasive *a.* + -ness.] The ability of pathogenic microorganisms or malignant cells that are already in the body to spread to new sites.

1937 R. W. Fairbrother *Text-bk. Med. Bacteriol.* vii. 69 The term *invasiveness* is sometimes erroneously used as synonymous with virulence; it, however, applies strictly to the power of the organism to invade the tissues of the host. **1949** *Cancer Res.* IX. 559/1 Evidence was found indicating that the invasiveness of the cancer cells depended on their lessened adhesiveness. **1967** R. A. Willis *Path. Tumours* (ed. 4) ix. 149 The factors determining invasiveness are still uncertain. Continued excessive proliferation is one of them. **1970** Passmore & Robson *Compan. Med. Stud.* II. xviii. 28/1 Virulence may involve invasiveness or toxigenicity; some pathogenic organisms are typically invasive, e.g. the causative organisms of typhoid fever.

inveigle, *v.* Now also with pronunc. (invē̆i·g'l).

inventory, *sb.* Add: **2. b.** *spec.* in *Linguistics.*

1945–49 *Acta Linguistica* V. 88 The graphemes become manifested in concrete letters and letter-attributes. ..These items make up what may be called the graphic inventory of the given language, which has..its counterpart in the phonic inventory of the same language. **1954** U. Weinreich in *Word* X. 394 One thing is certain: In the study of language contact and interference..a clear picture of differences in inventory is a prerequisite. *Ibid.* 395 We are not told whether in the phoneme inventory of Southeastern American English, the /æy/ of *pass* does or does not correspond as an inventory item to the /æ/ of other varieties. **1971** B. Mafeni in J. Spencer *Eng. Lang. W. Afr.* 109 It is possible that a number of nasalised vowel phonemes may be included in the vowel inventories of some of the conservative varieties of Nigerian Pidgin spoken in certain parts of the country.

3. b. *spec.* The quantity of material, etc., in use or held in stock in an installation at any one time. Also *attrib.*

1955 *Proc. Internat. Conf. Peaceful Uses Atomic Energy* (United Nations) III. 4/2 The inventory is the total of all separated fissile fuel supplied to the reactor or system other than produced internally in the reactor, less the amount assignable to the steady rate of make-up. **1963** *Chem. Engineer* 292/1 Returns..may range from inventory statements to quality control rights. *Ibid.*, The problem of maintaining minimum inventories at minimum cost to the company. **1970** *New Scientist* 25 June 628/2 Freezing also wins over evaporating as the 'heat inventory' is far lower—the latent heat of fusion is far less than the latent heat of evaporation. **1970** *Supervisor* XXI. 65/2 Vehicles are built for inventory in slack sales periods in anticipation of the peak sales periods. Production hours can thus be stored as physical inventory.

4. (Further *attrib.* examples.)

1906 *Daily Chron.* 1 Feb. 5/1 An attempt to enforce the inventory clause of the new separation law was responsible for serious conflict between the police and the people in many quarters of Paris to-day. **1927** Carr-Saunders & Jones *Survey Social Struct. Eng. & Wales* 107 There is a distinction between what we may call the 'going concern' and the 'inventory' methods of estimating wealth. **1943** N. J. Silberling *Dynamics of Business* xviii. 443 Manufacturing and mining industries are now able to operate more freely on a rational inventory-valuation method that unquestionably will introduce greater stability in income statements. *Ibid.* xvi. 367 Speculation in raw materials or merchandise or what is known as 'inventory write-up'. **1951** A. H. Hansen *Business Cycles & National Income* II. ix. 122 What is happening..to inventory accumulation..throws light on how business activity, employment, and income are likely to unfold. **1958** *Spectator* 7 Feb. 186/1 One would expect the present cyclical-type recession [in the U.S.A.] to last longer than the previous inventory-type recession of twelve to sixteen months. **1962** A. Battersby *Guide to Stock Control* p. vii, Not only do excessive stocks immobilize our capital resources: they can generate the so-called 'inventory recession'. **1969** J. Argenti *Managem. Techniques* 137 That aspect of inventory control concerned with how large a consignment of any given item one puts into stock at a time.

inventory, *v.* Add: **2.** *intr.* and *trans.* To amount to or be worth (so much) on an inventory.

1902 G. H. Lorimer *Lett. Merchant* ix. 113 The last time I saw her, she inventoried about $10,000 as she stood. **1905** *Springfield* (Mass.) *Weekly Republ.* 20 Oct. 12 The late Senator Platt left an estate which inventories at $20,880.

inverse, *a.* and *sb.* Add: **A.** *adj.* **5.** *inverse spelling*, an unetymological spelling based on the spelling of another word containing an element that is no longer pronounced, e.g. *limb* from OE. *lim* after *lamb* (from OE. *lamb*).

1933 L. Bloomfield *Lang.* xvii. 294 So-called inverse spellings tell the same story... When we find the word *deleite*..spelled *delight*, then we may be sure that the [x] was no longer spoken in words like *light*. **1956** N. E. Eliason *Tarheel Talk* v. 194 Occasionally inverse spellings occur, for example *forks* for *folks*,..and *polk* for *pork*.

6. *Cryst.* Designating a spinel structure, $B[AB]O_4$, in which half the B (trivalent) cations are in tetrahedral holes and the A (bivalent) cations together with the other half of the B cations are in octahedral holes in the array of oxide ions (in contrast to the normal structure $A[B_2]O_4$).

[**1947** Verwey & Heilmann in *Jrnl. Chem. Physics* XV. 175/2 For the sake of convenience, the first arrangement will be indicated as characteristic for 'normal spinels', the Barth and Posnjak arrangement as that of 'inversed spinels'.] **1957** *Jrnl. Physics & Chem. Solids* III. 313 These energies..may be sufficient to determine whether a given spinel shall be normal or inverse. **1970** R. G. Burns *Mineral. Applications Crystal Field Theory* vi. 112 Ni^{2+} and Cu^{2+} have a strong tendency to form inverse spinels. Ions such as Fe^{3+} and Mn^{2+}, which have zero octahedral site preference energies, form both normal and inverse spinels.

B. *sb.* **3.** *Rouge et Noir.* The section at the end of the table in which are placed bets wagering that the colour of the card that wins the coup will not be the same as that first dealt for a colour.

1850 *Bohn's Hand-bk. Games* 343 If the player..be determined to try his luck on the inverse, he must place his money on a yellow circle, or rather a collection of circles, situated at the extremity of the table. *Ibid.*, The punters place on the Rouge, the Noir, the Couleur, or the Inverse, the sum they wish to risk. **1909** [see *couleur 2]. **1950** *Hoyle's Games Modernized* (ed. 20) 291 The *tailleur* never mentions the words 'Black' or 'Inverse', but always says that Red wins or Red loses, and that the colour wins or the colour loses.

4. *Math.* An element which, when combined with a given element by a given operation, produces the identity element for that operation.

E.g. the inverse of any number with respect to multiplication is the reciprocal of that number, and with respect to addition the negative of it.

1900 *Ann. Math.* II. 48 For every element T_K exists an element (denote it by T_K^{-1}) such that $T_K T_K^{-1} = T_K^{-1} T_K = 1$. T_K^{-1} is called the inverse of T_K. **1905** *Trans. Amer. Math. Soc.* VI. 187 The identity, *z*, of this group, is

called the zero-element of the field, and is denoted by 0; while the inverse of an element *a* is here called the negative of *a*, and is denoted by $-a$. **1951** N. JACOBSON *Lect. Abstr. Algebra* I. i. 22 If the operation in 𝔊 is denoted as +, we denote the identity as 0. The inverse of *a* if it exists is written as $-a$. **1953** BIRKHOFF & MACLANE *Survey Mod. Algebra* (ed. 2) vi. 122 Hence $\phi\psi = I$ and ψ is a right-inverse of ϕ. **1965** PATTERSON & RUTHERFORD *Elem. Abstr. Algebra* i. 19 Let $\wedge$ be the closed binary operation in R defined by $x \wedge y = x + y - 2x^2y^2$... Show..that every..non-zero element *x* of R such that $x > -\frac{1}{2}$ has two inverses but that if $x < -\frac{1}{2}$, then *x* has no inverse.

inversion. Add: **2. f.** *Meteorol.* In full, *temperature inversion*. An increase of temperature with height in part of the atmosphere (the reverse of the usual situation); a layer of air having such a temperature gradient; also, more widely, an analogous deviation from the normal temperature gradient in bodies of water.

1902 *Sci. Abstr.* V. 285 There are instances of temperature inversion, ascribed to insulation of the clouds. **1903** *Sci. Abstr.* A. VI. 491 Temperature inversions were observed..mostly between altitudes 200 and 1,500 m. **1906** W. MARRIOTT *Hints to Meteorol. Observers* (ed. 6) 66/2 *Inversion of temperature*, a warmer stratum of air above a colder one. **1928** D. BRUNT *Meteorol.* vi. 59 An inversion is most readily produced during a clear night in winter. **1957** G. E. HUTCHINSON *Treat. Limnol.* I. vii. 487 Slight temperature inversions of the order of 0·1° to 0·2°C often occurred in the temperature curves at the bottom of two Austrian lakes. **1969** *Courier-Mail* (Brisbane) 16 Sept. 2/3 New York's skyscraper skyline is now badly clouded ..only when the city is trapped under what is called an 'inversion'. **1971** *Nature* 26 Feb. 583/2 It is only a decade since old people in their hundreds were killed off in northern cities when sulphur dioxide and other noisome products were trapped beneath inversion layers.

g. Philol. *inversion-compound*, a compound place-name in which the second element is a personal name, or a word designating a person, in the genitive (or genitive-equivalent) case, as the property-name *Kuikobba* (in Kirkwall), f. ON. *kvi Kobba* sheep-pen of Kobbi.

1918 E. EKWALL *Scandinavians & Celts in N.-W. Eng.* i. 15 In inversion-compounds the second element is a necessary ingredient, which can be absent only owing to ellipsis. **1963** C. MATRAS in Brown & Foote *Early Eng. & Norse Stud.* xii. 148 'Inversion-compounds' can serve as a criterion for classifying a settlement as Norwegian (as distinct from Danish).

h. *Biol.* A reversal of the order of the genes in a chromosome segment as compared with the corresponding segment of a normal homologous chromosome; a chromosome segment exhibiting such a reversal.

1921 A. H. STURTEVANT in *Proc. Nat. Acad. Sci.* VII. 236 The simple inversion of a section of a normal chromosome. **1939** C. H. WADDINGTON *Introd. Mod. Genetics* iv. 93 Pairing may be more nearly complete in flies heterozygous for very long inversions. **1964** G. H. HAGGIS et al. *Introd. Molecular Biol.* x. 258 The term mutation embraces stable chromosomal variations..including..the turning of an interstitial segment back to front (inversion). **1969** G. W. BURNS *Sci. Genetics* xii. 221 Inversions act chiefly as so-called crossover suppressors. **1972** W. V. BROWN *Textbk. Cytogenetics* xiv. 204/2 In most interbreeding populations inversions are eliminated because of the numerous types of inviability they produce. *Ibid.* 205/1 *Drosophila pseudoobscura* is unusual for the number of different inversions within especially the third chromosome of the species.

i. *Electr.* The conversion of direct current into alternating current: the opposite of rectification.

1926 L. B. W. JOLLEY *A.C. Rectification* (ed. 2) xix. 443 The problem of inversion, viz. the conversion from direct to alternating current. **1964** *New Scientist* 2 Apr. 25/1 Thyristors can also be used to convert d.c. to a.c.—a process known as 'inversion'. **1967** F. G. SPREADBURY *Electr. Inverters* i. 2 The choice of a current converter for inversion purposes will, of course, depend on the magnitude of the output voltage, current and frequency required.

j. *Telecommunications.* Reversal of the order of the component frequencies of a signal: cf. *INVERT *v.* 2 g.

1930 *Engineering* 14 Nov. 625/3 Though the simple inversion..is satisfactory on short waves, it is not so effective on long waves, since, as only one side band is present, it is immaterial whether the transmission is inverted or not, provided the oscillator at the receiving end injects a local carrier of the correct frequency. **1933** K. HENNEY *Radio Engin. Handbk.* x. 273 To insure secrecy of transmission, frequency inversion or frequency scrambling methods are used. **1967** D. H. HAMSHER *Communication Syst. Engin. Handbk.* x. 23 A reduction in interfering energy of about 3 db is realized by frequency inversion.

k. *Computers.* The conversion of either of the two binary digits or signals into the other; negation.

1955 R. K. RICHARDS *Arithmetic Operations in Digital Computers* ii. 32 The 'not' operation, or inversion, is symbolized by a block labeled with the letter *I*. **1970** O. DOPPING *Computers & Data Processing* ii. 39 The number that is somewhat inappropriately called the 1-complement of x is obtained simply by inversion, i.e. by substituting zeroes for all ones and vice versa. **1972** B. H. VASSOS *Analog & Digital Electronics for Scientists* viii. 207 There are two other basic gates.., called NOR and NAND, respectively. They cannot be implemented by simple diode logic, because inversion is required, which can only be produced by an active device.

1. *Physics.* In full *population inversion.* A transposition of the relative numbers of atoms or molecules occupying certain energy levels.

1961 *Physical Rev. Lett.* VI. 106/1 Population inversions are achieved between several Ne levels by means of excitation transfer. **1968** E. L. STEELE *Optical Lasers in Electronics* iv. 135 In the limit when total inversion occurs the ground state is entirely empty. **1973** *Sci. Amer.* Feb. 92/3 The condition of having more atoms in the upper state is called a population inversion (because it goes against the normal processes of nature, which tend to keep more electrons at lower energies than at higher energies).

3. c. *Math.* The process of finding a function $g(y)$ which either (*a*) yields a variable *x* when its argument is a given function $y = f(x)$ of that variable, or else (*b*) yields a given function when transformed by a given transformation.

1880 *Encycl. Brit.* XIII. 66/2 We have mentioned.. the problem of inversion which leads to elliptic functions, viz., that if $u = F(\kappa, \phi)$, then $\phi = \mathrm{am}\ u$. **1934** *Trans. Amer. Math. Soc.* XXXVI. 107 $f(x) = \int_0^\infty e^{-xt} d\alpha(t)$... By the inversion of the integral we mean the determination of the function $\alpha(t)$ in terms of the function $f(x)$. **1962** D. R. COX *Renewal Theory* i. 11 Suppose that we have calculated the Laplace transform $k^*(s)$ of an as yet unknown function $k(x)$. The problem of finding $k(x)$ from $k^*(s)$ is called the inversion problem. *Ibid.* 13 We shall commonly find that, although we can find a quite simple expression for the Laplace transform, $k^*(s)$, of the function $k(x)$ in which we are interested, the inversion cannot be done explicitly in simple terms. **1968** P. A. P. MORAN *Introd. Probability Theory* vi. 250 $\phi(t)$ [$= \int_{-\infty}^{\infty} e^{itx} dF(x)$] is uniquely determined by $F(x)$. We shall show that the reverse is true by obtaining an explicit expression, the inversion formula, for $F(x)$ in terms of $\phi(t)$.

5. b. In full, *Walden inversion* [tr. G. *Walden'sche umkehrung* (E. Fischer 1906, in *Ber. d. Deut. Chem. Ges.* XXXIX. 2895), named after P. von *Walden* (1863–1957), Latvian chemist]. Originally, the reversal of the direction of optical rotation observed in certain substitution reactions. Now interpreted as a change of configuration (from D to L or vice versa) occurring when a reactant enters along the axis of the bond between a central atom and the leaving group and causes the other substituents on the central atom to pass through a plane perpendicular to this axis; hence extended to other substitution reactions in which there is such a reversal of configuration, regardless of whether the molecule is optically active or the direction of activity reversed.

1899 *Jrnl. Chem. Soc.* LXXVI. II. 540 If..the sign of the rotatory power alone is considered, then optical inversion occurs in the action of phosphorus pentachloride and pentabromide..and the only 'normal' action in which no inversion occurs is the hydrolysis by means of silver oxide. **1911** *Ann. Rep. Progr. Chem.* VIII. 64 Most cases of the Walden inversion have been observed in transformations of α-substituted acids and their derivatives. **1937** F. C. WHITMORE *Org. Chem.* xxi. 480 In the Walden inversion, the process takes place on a *single* carbon atom instead of with a system of several atoms. **1962** E. L. ELIEL *Stereochem. Carbon Compds.* xiii. 375 In most cases the covalent attachment occurs from the side opposite to the one from which X had departed..and the stereochemical course is therefore predominantly inversion. **1964** D. A. SHIRLEY *Org. Chem.* ix. 202 The molecule of methyl bromide is said to undergo inversion in its conversion to methyl alcohol. **1966** MORRISON & BOYD *Org. Chem.* (ed. 2) xiv. 473 Paul Walden..discovered the phenomenon of inversion in 1896 when he encountered one of the exceptional reactions in which inversion [of configuration] does *not* take place. **1968** J. MARCH *Adv. Org. Chem.* x. 254 The Walden inversion has been found at a primary carbon atom..and at a sulfur (in sulfoxides), a silicon, and a phosphorus atom.

6*. *Physical Chem.* A transformation of a substance, esp. an enantiotropic one, from one solid form to another; **inversion temperature**, the temperature at which the two forms can coexist in equilibrium.

1903 M. H. FISCHER tr. *Cohen's Physical Chem.* vii. 111 This temperature, above which the Glauber's salt is transformed into the anhydride, is designated the inversion temperature of the Glauber's salt. **1904** A. FINDLAY *Phase Rule* iii. 34 If the vapour phase [of sulphur] is absent and the system maintained under a constant pressure..there will also be a definite temperature at which the two solid forms are in equilibrium... This temperature..is known as the transition temperature or inversion temperature. **1928** *Jrnl. Physical Chem.* XXXII. 1205 When quartz is subjected to a uniform hydrostatic pressure..the temperature of its high-low inversion is raised. **1947** R. H. BOGUE *Chem. Portland Cement* vii. 125 The α–β inversion temperature of C_2S was found to be 1456°. **1966** W. A. DEER et al. *Introd. Rock-forming Min.* 129 It [*sc.* pigeonite] then later inverts to an orthorhombic pyroxene and the inversion is accompanied by the exsolution of a second generation of augite lamellae.

8. c. *Anat.* (See quots.)

1869 G. V. ELLIS *Demonstrations Anat.* (ed. 6) ix. 762 In inversion the great toe is adducted, the inner border of the foot is shortened, and is raised from the ground so that the sole looks inwards, whilst the outer border is depressed. **1902** D. HEPBURN in D. J. Cunningham *Text-bk. Anat.* 304 By inversion we mean the raising of the inner border of the foot so that the sole looks inwards, while the toes are depressed towards the ground. **1971** D. L. KELLEY *Kinesiology* vi. 75 Inversion lifts the medial border of the foot to turn the sole inward.

10. In full, *sexual inversion.* Homosexuality (see also quot. 1958).

1895 A. BEARDSLEY *Let.* 15 May (1971) 85 [*To André Raffalovitch*] Your study of inversion is I think quite brilliant. **1897** H. ELLIS *Stud. Psychol. Sex* I. ii. 27 In Italy, also, Ritti, Tamassia, Lombroso, and others began to study these phenomena, and it seems to have been in Italy that the convenient term 'sexual inversion' was first used. When the matter was taken up in France, the same term was used. **1901** J. A. GODFREY *Sci. Sex* v. 206 Sexual inversion—that is, the turning-in of the sex instinct towards individuals of the same sex—is an abnormal phenomenon. **1927** *Scots Observer* 1 Oct. 15/3 It will help to approach the problems of inversion with knowledge and charity. **1958** *Amer. Jrnl. Orthopsychiatry* XXVIII. 424 Many workers fail to distinguish between homosexuality and sexual inversion, or more accurately, sex-role inversion. Freud..himself..equated the two terms. *Ibid.*, The following distinction is offered: homosexuality refers to sexual activity or the desire for such activity between two members of the same sex, while the criterion of inversion is a personality in which a person's thinking, feeling, and acting are typical of the opposite sex. **1965** J. MARMOR (*title*) Sexual inversion.

11. Special Comb.: **inversion temperature,** (*a*) *Physics,* the temperature (for any particular gas) at which the Joule–Thomson effect changes sign, so that the gas is neither heated nor cooled when allowed to expand without doing any work; (*b*) (see sense 6* above).

1902 *Phil. Mag.* III. 536 It had been deduced by Wilkowski..by assuming the thermodynamic coincidence of the inversion temperatures for hydrogen and for air. **1940** S. GLASSTONE *Text-bk. Physical Chem.* iv. 285 The inversion temperature, as derived from the van der Waals equation, should be twice the Boyle point... The observed inversion temperature for hydrogen is about 190°K. **1971** *Nature* 20 Aug. 519/1 For every gas, however, there is at a given pressure an inversion temperature above which throttled expansion results in a temperature increase. (The inversion temperature decreases with increasing pressure.)

invert, *v.* Add: **2. g.** *Telecommunications.* To subject (a signal) to a heterodyning process that reverses the order of the component frequencies (either completely or in a restricted range) prior to modulation for transmission, those at the two extremes being interchanged.

1930 *Engineering* 14 Nov. 625/1 The risk of important conversations being overheard..has still further been reduced by using a complex heterodyning process, which inverts and mixes the signals. *Ibid.* 626/1 The original speech-frequency range is divided into a number of bands. ..These bands can then be inverted as explained above, and re-arranged in transposed bands. **1933** K. HENNEY *Radio Engin. Handbk.* x. 274 To obtain an intelligible signal at the receiving end, it is necessary to again invert the modulation frequencies by the reverse process. **1966** *McGraw-Hill Encycl. Sci. & Technol.* X. 624/2 The first method employs equipment for inverting speech to make overseas telephone conversations unintelligible to the casual listener.

5*. *intr.* Of a substance: to undergo inversion.

1887 [see *CARAMEL *v.*]. **1933** *Amer. Jrnl. Sci.* XXV. 284 It would..be possible for β-solid solutions to invert to the γ-form. **1966** [see *INVERSION 6*].

9. *Geom.* (*intr.*) To be transformed by inversion *into.*

1865 R. TOWNSEND *Chapters on Mod. Geom.* II. xxiv. 384 Every two circles invert into two whose radii have a constant ratio from every point on any third circle coaxal with themselves. **1916** J. L. COOLIDGE *Treat. Circle & Sphere* i. 22 Points within the circle of inversion other than the centre will invert into points without, points without will always invert into points within. **1966** J. H. CADWELL *Topics in Recreational Math.* v. 42 Hence the locus..is a circle centre C_1. We note that C_1 is not the inverse of *C*, i.e. centres do not invert into each other.

invert, *sb.* Add: **2.** *Psychol.* One whose sex instincts are inverted. (Cf. *INVERSION 10; *INVERTED *ppl. a.* 3 c.)

1897 H. ELLIS *Stud. Psychol. Sex* I. 12 Caesar was proud of his physical beauty, and like many modern inverts he was accustomed carefully to shave his skin. *Ibid.* 144 The sexual invert is specially liable to suffer from a high degree of neurasthenia. **1911** R. W. CHAMBERS *Common Law* i. 29 This world is full of pale, enraptured artists;..full of unwashed little inverts. **1957** L. DURRELL *Justine* II. 96 At least the invert escapes this fearful struggle to give oneself to another. **1957** *Observer* 1 Sept. 11/5 For once, the hero is not wrongly but rightly accused: he is an irrevocable invert. **1971** R. REISNER *Graffiti* (1974) viii. 115 The inverts (a word preferred by homosexuals to perverts) attempt to win converts.

invert, *a.* Add: Also *ellipt.*

1910 *Encycl. Brit.* IV. 508/2 This method is more suited to the preparation of invert in the brewery itself than the acid process. **1940** H. L. HIND *Brewing* II. xxii. 545 The sugars must be pale in colour and carefully selected in accordance with the flavour required in the

beer. No. 1 and No. 2 inverts and other sugars of somewhat similar character are suitable. **1971** J. S. HOUGH et al. *Malting & Brewing Sci.* xi. 296 The solid invert can be added directly to the copper or dissolved in liquor before addition.

b. **invert soap** [tr. G. *invertseife* (Kuhn & Bielig 1940, in *Ber. d. Deut. Chem. Ges.* LXXIII. 1080)]. A soap whose surface-active ion is a cation (rather than the more usual anion): a cationic detergent.

1941 *Chem. Abstr.* XXXV. 3596 K. and B. intended to study the mechanism of the bactericidal action of Zephirol (mixt. of alkyldimethylbenzylammonium chlorides) and other quaternary ammonium, sulfonium and phosphonium salts by means of expts. on the interaction of these 'invert soaps'..with proteins, chromoproteids, ferments, symplexes and genes. **1947** CONANT & BLATT *Chem. Org. Compounds* (ed. 3) x. 213 Another group of detergents consists of the invert soaps... These are quaternary ammonium salts containing at least one large alkyl group. **1966** SMITH & CRISTOL *Org. Chem.* xl. 765 Cationic detergents or invert soaps are used mainly for germicidal properties.

invertase (i·nvəɹt-, invə̄·ɹtēiz, -s). *Biochem.* [f. INVERT(IN + *-ASE.] = INVERTIN.

1887 *Jrnl. Chem. Soc.* LI. 60 Solutions of invertase and diastase were prepared from Mr. O'Sullivan's specimens. **1949** [see *FICIN]. **1964** N. G. CLARK *Mod. Org. Chem.* xvi. 330 Hydrolysis is also brought about by the enzyme, invertase. **1970** *Sci. Jrnl.* Mar. 19/3 A 1 ml sample of this water is then treated with the enzyme invertase, which converts any of the sugar sucrose..into a mixture of glucose and fructose.

inverted, *ppl. a.* Add: **1. c.** (Later examples.)

1902 [see *CACUMINAL *a.*]. **1918, 1934** [see *CEREBRAL *a.* 2].

3. c. *Psychol.* spec. of the sex instincts.

1897 H. ELLIS *Stud. Psychol. Sex* I. 16 The painter Bazzi seems to have been radically inverted. *Ibid.* 156 Social opinion is most amply adequate to deal with the manifestations of inverted sexuality. **1958** *Amer. Jrnl. Orthopsychiatry* XXVIII. 428 Inverted females would be expected to show..a relatively complete identification with the masculine role. **1974** *Times Lit. Suppl.* 1 Feb. 109 A telling parody of inverted sexist trends in our own society.

9. Special collocations: *inverted comma* (see also COMMA 4), *engine* (see quot. 1961), *loop, pleat*; **inverted snob,** one who dislikes, or avoids contact or association with, the upper classes; one who tries to appear to be a member of, or sympathetic to, the lower classes; so *inverted snobbery, snobbism*; **inverted spelling** = *inverse spelling* (*INVERSE *a.* 5).

1789 J. ROBERTSON *Ess. Punctuation* 130 Two inverted commas are generally placed at the beginning of a phrase or a passage, which is quoted or transcribed from some author, in his own words. **1927** R. B. MCKERROW *Introd. Bibliogr.* 316 Inverted commas were, until late in the seventeenth century, frequently used at the beginnings of lines to call attention to sententious remarks... They were not especially associated with quotations until the eighteenth century. **1933** *Week-End Rev.* 28 Oct. 439/1 'Dunky Fitlow'! What a name! One could hardly ask for it without embarrassment, without qualifying it by inverted commas in the voice. **1956** A. S. C. ROSS in M. Black *Importance of Lang.* (1962) 95 It is non-U to place the name of a house in inverted commas. **1963** AUDEN *Dyer's Hand* 520 One has a sense, and nowhere more strongly than in the songs [of *Twelfth Night*], of there being inverted commas around the 'fun'. [**1885** *List of Subscribers, Classified* (United Telephone Co.) (ed. 6) 236 High-class..stationary engines. Beam, Compound Condensing, Inverted, Vertical.] **1933** *Meccano Mag.* Feb. 109/2 It is fitted with three de Havilland 'Gipsy III' inverted engines. **1961** WEBSTER, *Inverted engine*, an engine whose crankshaft is above the cylinders. **1940** *Chambers's Techn. Dict.* 458/1 *Inverted loop*, a manœuvre of an aeroplane consisting of a complete revolution about a lateral axis, with the normally upper surface of the machine on the outside of the path of the loop. Must be commenced while flying inverted. **1915** *T. Eaton & Co. Catal.* Spring & Summer Suppl. 1/2 The smart patch pockets are finished with stitched inverted pleats. **1964** *McCall's Sewing* ii. 30/1 *Inverted pleat*, two side pleats which turn toward each other. **1971** 'D. HALLIDAY' *Dolly & Doctor Bird* iii. 29 For golf, I have always worn an Orkney tweed skirt with a low inverted pleat at the back. **1943** N. MARSH *Colour Scheme* vi. 99 Don't call me Mr. Bell. I'm afraid you're an inverted snob. **1955** KOESTLER *Trail of Dinosaur* II. 87 Only an inverted snob will pretend..that 'the aristocracy'..is devoid of value. **1966** *Guardian* 14 May 7/6 But, gosh, don't be an inverted snob! Subculture is fun! **1883** R. L. STEVENSON *Silverado Squatters* 176 His book..was a capital instance of the Penny Messalina school of literature; and there arose from it..a rank atmosphere of..sickening, inverted snobbery. **1930** R. LEHMANN *Note in Music* III. 108 Inverted-snobbery complex, Clare would have called it. **1937** L. BROMFIELD *Rains Came* I. xxxviii. 159 It was that eternal, inverted snobbery of his, that hatred of anyone born with the things he had never achieved. **1958** *Times* 25 Jan. 7/3 Inverted snobbery, we are told, is rampant in Cambridge. **1971** *Lancet* 23 Apr. 918/2 The curious inverted snobbery of the use of 'Mr.' by surgeons (even if they have an M.D. or a PH.D. as well as their M.B.),..with all its regional and specialty variations, is well worth the attention of a sociologist. **1939** A. THIRKELL *Before Lunch* vi. 160 The inverted snobbism that at once overcame her against her will. **1958** G. L. BROOK *Hist. Eng. Lang.* v. 102 Another contributory cause of the confusion of Modern English spelling is to be found in what are called inverted spellings. **1970** B. M. H. STRANG *Hist. English* II. v. 291 Inverted spellings, e.g. *y* for *e* in districts suspected to be *y*-less, are as revealing as direct *e* for *y* spellings.

inverter. Restrict *rare* to sense in Dict. and add: **2.** That which inverts, or produces inversion. **a.** *Electr.* Also **invertor.** Any apparatus which converts direct current into alternating current.

1926 L. B. W. JOLLEY *A.C. Rectification* (ed. 2) xix. 444 In an inverter such as is shown in Fig. 324 a direct current generator G is supplying a steady current to two three-electrode valves and the primary of a transformer. **1947** P. KEMP *Alternating Current Electr. Engin.* (ed. 7) xxviii. 498 Inverters are used for regenerative braking on electric railways. **1961** *Listener* 9 Nov. 773/1 The valve serves not only as a rectifier..but—at the other end of the direct current link—as an invertor, turning direct current into alternating current. **1962** A. SHEPARD in *Into Orbit* 103 Inverters are used to convert the DC current which comes from the batteries into the AC current required to power some of the systems in the booster. **1970** J. SHEPHERD *Higher Electr. Engin.* (ed. 2) xxv. 817 D.C. links (with a rectifier at one end and an invertor at the other end of the link) are now commonly used to connect two a.c. power distribution systems together. **1973** *Wireless World* June a7 (Advt.), Models 107A and B are precision built inverters providing 240 volts a.c. from 12 and 24 volt battery systems.

b. *Telecommunications.* A device that inverts a signal (see *INVERT *v.* 2 g).

1930 *Engineering* 14 Nov. 625/3 The inverter is usually inserted at the point where the transmitting and receiving signals are combined.

c. *Computers.* A device which converts either of the two binary digits or signals into the other.

1955 R. K. RICHARDS *Arithmetic Operations in Digital Computers* ii. 32 If the input to an inverter is A, the output is $\bar{A}$. **1960** T. C. BARTEE *Digital Computer Fund.* iv. 63 Because of its high input resistance, low output resistance, and voltage- and current-gain characteristics, the inverter is one of the most commonly used transistor configurations in digital systems. **1972** MILLMAN & HALKIAS *Integrated Electronics* vi. 164 The output of an inverter is relatively more positive if and only if the input is relatively less positive.

invertible, *a.*[2] Add: **2.** *Math.* Of an element of a set: having an inverse in the set (*spec.* an inverse for multiplication).

1956 C. CHEVALLEY *Fund. Concepts Algebra* ii. 27 Let G be the set of all invertible elements of a monoid A. **1963** G. D. MOSTOW et al. *Fund. Struct. Algebra* vi. 141 Invertible elements are divisible only by invertible elements. *Ibid.* xii. 341 An element a is called invertible if there is an element a' in A such that $aa' = a'a = e$. **1965** PATTERSON & RUTHERFORD *Elem. Abstract Algebra* iv. 122 An element $x \in R$ is said to be invertible if it has an inverse with respect to multiplication: that is, if there exists y such that $xy = e = yx$.

Hence **invertibi·lity.**

1963 H. B. CURRY *Found. Math. Logic* v. 249 Ketonen ..showed the invertibility of his classical propositional rules. **1973** J. J. ZEMAN *Modal Logic* iii. 50 The number of rules we must examine for invertibility.

invertor. Add: **2.** *Anat.* A muscle which turns a part (as the foot) inwards.

1903 [see *EVERTOR]. **1967** ROWE & WHEBLE *Conc. Textbk. Anat. & Physiol.* (ed. 2) v. 258 The invertors of the foot are:—*Tibialis posterior* [and] *Tibialis anterior.* **1969** MACCONAILL & BASMAJIAN *Muscles & Movements* xiii. 254 The tibialis posterior is an invertor in non-weightbearing movements of the foot.

3. *Electr.* var. *INVERTER 2 a.

invest, *v.* Add: **2. c.** To embed in or surround *with* investment (sense *2 b).

1892 C. HUNTER *Man. Dental Laboratory* viii. 107 We.. apply the little plaster-mould to the face of the model and settle the tooth in it, cement tooth to auxiliary plate, then carefully remove from denture, invest and solder. **1946** *Foundry* Aug. 85/1 Precision casting is a somewhat abused term often employed to designate the lost wax investment casting process... Properly, the phrase *investment casting* is the most suitable for use in defining the lost wax investment casting process since it is characterized primarily by the use of a molding material which completely enrobes or invests an expendable pattern. **1964** S. CRAWFORD *Basic Engin. Processes* xii. 255 This casting process involves the use of a heat-disposable wax pattern which is invested with refractory material forming a mould (or shell).

9. c. To lay out money in betting on a horse race, or in football pools, etc.

1951 'H. CECIL' *Painswick Line* ix. 107 He went to the £5 tote windows and invested (as they euphemistically call it) £100 on Maiden Aunt. **1958** *Punch* 27 Aug. 265/1 Your skill can put you on top of the world when it's invested with ——'s [Pools]. **1973** *Times* 21 Apr. 12/1 In bookie parlance, one does not bet on a horse; one invests.

investible, *a.* [f. INVEST *v.* + -IBLE.] = INVESTABLE *a.*

1931 *Economist* 18 July 110/2 Central Banks..should take steps..to counteract any tendency which their own nationals may show either to keep their investible resources excessively liquid or to undertake excessive long-term commitments. **1968** *Daily Tel.* 21 Nov. 3 These funds form a pool of investible money.

investigational (investigēi·ʃənăl), *a.* [f. INVESTIGATION + -AL.] Of or pertaining to investigation.

1905 *Science* 29 Sept. 387/1 Investigational apparatus of great importance. **1930** *Aberdeen Press & Jrnl.* 4 Sept. 7/3 An unprecedented demand for botanical specialists to fill investigational and advisory posts. **1946** *Nature* 12 Oct. 522/1 This would be sufficient for the investigational purposes now envisaged by the Board. **1971** *Mod. Law Rev.* XXXIV. VI. 651 What..is to be the future of the social sciences as part of the normal decisional or investigational equipment of lawyers?

investigative, *a.* (Later examples.)

1925 [see *FLAIR[1] 2]. **1955** *Sci. News Let.* 16 Apr. 249/2 The pathologists can and will assume their part in this investigative obligation and I'm sure that practicing physicians will do likewise. **1972** *Village Voice* (N.Y.) 1 June 37/1 What is vitally needed is more investigative reporting on this growing national phenomenon. **1975** *Times* 24 Jan. 14/5 Some suggest that I should turn my investigative powers to other vanishing drinks.

investigator. (Later examples.)

1971 *Nature* 15 Oct. 469/2 Other investigators who have scanned the North Polar spur and portions of other galactic spurs..at large solar zenith angles have not observed any enhancement at soft X-ray energies. **1972** *Daily Tel.* 21 Jan. 7/1 Department of Employment investigators, only 30 for the whole country, are too few to catch offenders.

investigatory, *a.* (Later examples.)

1966 *Punch* 23 Feb. 276/3 During his editorship, Sam Campbell, as he was known to most of Fleet Street, added more than one and a half million paying readers to his paper by sustained crusading investigatory journalism of a kind unequalled since W. T. Stead. **1969** *Listener* 27 Mar. 436/2 *World in Action* has an aggressive investigatory policy. **1969** *Daily Tel.* 31 Oct. 1/4 The judges said they believed it was desirable to have the inquest kept secret to 'protect its integrity, investigatory character and effectiveness'. *Ibid.*, Inquest proceedings are not accusatory and..they should be regarded as investigatory.

investment. Add: **2. b.** Refractory material which can be used to embed or surround an object and then is allowed to harden, so that soldering can be carried out (in *Dentistry*) or a mould made from it; freq. *attrib.*, as *investment material*; **investment casting,** a technique for making small, accurate castings from alloys having high melting points, the mould being made by investing a pattern of wax or similar material that can be removed from the investment by melting it.

1892 C. HUNTER *Man. Dental Laboratory* viii. 115 If the new tooth must be soldered, an hour-and-a-half, from the time the case is ready to be put in the investment, is not too much for its safe accomplishment. **1942** *Iron Age* 9 July 39 Production of castings..by a modern modification of the lost-wax process is described herein. This method utilizes a refractory investment which makes possible the casting of stainless and other alloy steels. **1946** Investment casting [see *INVEST *v.* 2 c]. **1947** J. C. RICH *Materials & Methods Sculpture* vi. 140 For the solid casting of small bronze statuettes, the Greeks employed a simple technique. The work was modeled in wax and incased in a containing negative mold composed of sand and earth-clay. When this investment material was dry, an opening was made and the entire mass was heated until the wax ran off. **1956** J. N. ANDERSON *Appl. Dental Materials* xvii. 191 A wax pattern may be expanded directly by using warm water to mix the investment. **1963** C. R. COWELL et al. *Inlays, Crowns & Bridges* ii. 3 Modern inlay waxes and investment techniques make dimensional control possible. **1964** S. CRAWFORD *Basic Engin. Processes* xii. 255 Precision casting, investment casting, and the lost-wax process, are various names given to the process by which small intricate castings can be produced to a high grade of dimensional accuracy and surface finish in materials which prove difficult or impossible to cast and subsequently machine by the more traditional methods... The principle of the process..has been in use in the jewellery and dental trades for many years.

5. b. *attrib.* (Further examples.) Also **investment currency,** the currency resulting from the sale of foreign securities or used for their purchase when such transactions are controlled and channelled through a market separate from the market in foreign exchange; **investment trust,** a trust (TRUST *sb.* 7 a) whose business is the investment of money; also *attrib.*

1885 *List of Subscribers, Classified* (United Telephone Co.) (ed. 6) 213 American Investment Trust Co. **1924** B. D. NASH *Investment Banking in Eng.* 3 The function of investment banking is to gather together the savings and surplus capital of individuals and companies and to turn this accumulation into the hands of others for use in the construction of fixed plants. **1924** L. M. SPEAKER *Investment Trust* 3 The investment trust in its characteristic form is an institution mainly of British origin. It is essentially a corporation, the business of which consists chiefly of judicious investment of its capital. **1929** *Observer* 17 Nov. 2/3 Among the many high-class securities which have had to be sold to meet the demand for money caused by the depressed conditions have been the junior stocks of the large investment trust companies. **1933** B. ELLINGER *This Money Business* iv. 33 There are a number of firms and brokers connected with trust and investment companies. **1935** *Economist* 5 Jan. 23/1 The extent of the..movement may be appreciated from

the following table of representative values and yields based on the Actuaries' Investment Index. **1951** R. W. Jones *Thomson's Dict. Banking* (ed. 10) 346/1 Investment Ledger. A separate account is opened in this ledger for each different investment. **1961** 'E. Lathen' *Banking on Death* (1962) iii. 21 Robichaux had..surprised his friends and relations by becoming an astute and competent investment banker. **1963** *Listener* 31 Jan. 191/1 Bankers have looked with jaundiced or favourable eye on the investment bank. **1965** D. Greenwald et al. *McGraw-Hill Dict. Mod. Econ.* 274 The first real investment trust was the Foreign and Colonial Trust, which was established in London in 1868. Its purpose was to give small investors the same advantage, diversification, that large capitalists had. **1967** *Spectator* 21 July 85/3 Investment trusts are closed portfolios. Selling or buying shares in such trusts neither increases nor decreases the size of the portfolio. **1969** *Times* 30 Apr. 30/6 Investment companies qualify, so do unit trusts, and a company is eligible for relief if the interest would have been eligible when payable by an individual. **1969** *Times* 5 May (Suppl.) p. vi/5 Now the insurance companies have joined the fight for this part of the investment dollar. **1971** *Mod. Law Rev.* XXXI. vi. 699 The second chapter..contains a detailed practical account of the work of American investment bankers. **1972** D. Lees *Zodiac* 117 He's among the top six investment consultants in the world today. **1973** *Country Life* 12 July 120/3 It is necessary to buy what is known as investment currency, which is a pool of funds created by the sale of British investments abroad. **1973** *Times* 17 Dec. 14/3 Investment funds..went too much into property or overseas, too little into productive industry.

investor. Add: **2. b.** One who bets on a horse race, or in football pools, etc. Cf. *INVEST *v.* 9 c.
1958 [see *BANKER[2] 5].

inviable (invəi·ăb'l), *a. Biol.* [f. IN-[3] + VIABLE *a.*[1]] Unable to survive; unable to germinate, grow or develop; unable to perform its proper biological role.
1918 *Genetics* III. 476 The disadvantage of so many individuals being rendered sterile or inviable. **1946** *Nature* 12 Oct. 520/2 Among 986 seeds collected in 1941 from chimeral plants there were found six triploid ones, three of which proved inviable. **1948** *Mind* LVII. 297 He found that within one 'species' of frog..ranging from lat. 45° N. to 27° N. in the United States, representatives of the northern and southern ends of the range gave inviable hybrids, though parents not too far apart geographically gave normal development. **1955** *New Biol.* XIX. 21 More usually an unbalanced and inviable nucleus is formed [from an irregular mitosis] in which some chromosomes are represented twice, others once or not at all. **1956** *Nature* 31 Mar. 626/2 Damage arising from inviable recombinations of broken chromosome ends. **1962** *Lancet* 29 Dec. 1384/2 Since the O-sperm, if functional, leads to the Turner zygote which is in great deficit in the general population, it seems likely that O-sperm are inviable and that the Turners are due to a phenomenon other than fertilisation by O-sperm.
So **inviabi·lity**, the state or condition of being inviable.
1918 *Genetics* III. 614/2 (Index), Inviability. **1929** *Encycl. Brit.* XI. 495/1 The inviability of most gametic and zygotic combinations. **1972** [see *INVERSION 2 h].

in vino veritas: see *IN *Lat. prep.*

inviscid, *a.* Add: **2.** Not possessing viscosity.
1913 *Phil. Mag.* XXVI. 1001 (*heading*) On the stability of the laminar motion of an inviscid fluid. **1930** *Flight* 3 Jan. 29/1 The practically useful theory of Prandtl comes from considering air as frictionless or inviscid. **1938** L. M. Milne-Thomson *Theoret. Hydrodynamics* i An inviscid fluid is a continuous substance which will yield instantly to any shearing stress however small. **1971** *Nature* 6 Aug. 427/1 The problem of the plane transonic flow of an inviscid gas.

invisible, *a.* Add: **1. c.** *invisible college* (further examples).
1962 D. J. de S. Price *Science since Babylon* (new ed.) v. 99 Collaborative work now exceeds the single-author paper, and the device of prepublication duplicated sheets circulated to the new Invisible Colleges has begun to trespass upon the traditional functions of the printed paper in a published journal. *Ibid.,* The new Invisible Colleges, rapidly growing up in all the most hard-pressed sections of the scholarly research front, might well be the subject of an interesting sociological study. **1967** Garvey & Griffith in De Reuck & Knight *Communication in Sci.* 25 Once an author submits his manuscript the dissemination of this piece of work is small and usually only to members of his invisible college. **1971** Halsey & Trow *Brit. Academics* xiii. 362 Here is evidence of the 'invisible college' having its greatest importance.
d. *invisible exports, imports*: those items which do not appear in returns of exports and imports for which payment has to be accepted from or made to a foreign country, such as shipping services, insurance, profits on foreign investment, money spent by visitors from a country with a different currency, etc. Also *invisible earnings, trader, transaction*, etc.
1911 C. G. Robertson *Eng. under Hanoverians* ii. iv. 344 Prior to the Industrial Revolution the seaborne and carrying trades, with their invisible exports, are an expanding source of wealth, but are not indispensable. **1919** J. A. Todd *Mech. Exchange* (ed. 2) xiv. 174 An invisible export is something which enables a country to import goods without paying for them directly by the export of other goods, and conversely, an invisible import is something which makes it necessary for a country to export

goods without receiving payment directly in other goods. **1923** *Westm. Gaz.* 24 Feb., Depressed shipping means less insurance, less banking, and a smaller earning in freights —all the things we mean when we speak of our invisible exports. **1935** *Economist* 12 Oct. 712/2 Among 'invisible' traders with Italy, the shipping lines with Mediterranean routes would suffer some inconvenience. **1957** *Encycl. Brit.* VIII. 991/2 Invisible exports are of vital importance to countries whose limited resources..make them dependent on large imports. Italy's high percentage is due to foreign tourists' expenditure and to a steady flow of remittances from Italians living abroad. **1958** *Economist* 18 Oct. 256/1 The..government deficit on invisible account. **1963** *Ann. Reg. 1962* 479 Net earnings on invisible transactions improved somewhat. **1969** *Times* 27 Nov. 6/6 The rapid growth of invisible earnings. **1971** *Daily Tel.* 24 Apr. 2 The works of songwriters and composers are now one of Britain's major 'invisible' exports.
e. *invisible man*: used esp. with direct or implied allusion to H. G. Wells's novel *The Invisible Man* (1897).
1911 Chesterton *Innocence of Father Brown* v. 120 (*title*) The invisible man. **1940** 'G. Orwell' in *Horizon* Mar. 191 The one theme that is really new is the scientific one. Death-rays, Martians, invisible men, robots. **1959** N. Polsky in N. Mailer *Advts. for Myself* (1961) 313 Even in the world of the hipster the Negro remains essentially what Ralph Ellison called him—an invisible man. **1963** D. B. Hughes *Expendable Man* (1964) v. 139 He's safe only so long as he's the invisible man. I'm going to have to..find out who he is. **1966** J. Wainwright *Evil Intent* 123 He isn't The Invisible Man. Somebody must have seen him. **1973** E. Berckman *Victorian Album* 144 Dancey'll work out how to be the invisible man, it's just up his street.
f. *invisible mending*: repair of material, clothing, etc., so carefully executed that little or no sign of the repair can be seen. So *invisible mender*, one who undertakes such repairs; *invisibly-mend* v. trans.
1921 *Dict. Occup. Terms* (1927) § 419 Invisible mender, ..repairs tears, by hand, using stoating, finedrawing, or rentering process, according to kind of tear and material. **1931** W. Holtby *Poor Caroline* i. 33 She complained of the price of invisible mending. **1937** E. Price *Enter—Jane* i. 1 Until you have paid the invisible-mending bill..you shan't have your threepence a week pocket-money! **1959** G. Freeman *Jack would be Gent.* i. 16 Sitting in the shop window invisibly-mending nylons with a little hook. **1969** D. Francis *Enquiry* xv. 201 My coat would cost a fortune at the invisible menders. **1970** *— Rat Race* xv. 199 My coat was soaked...Have to get it cleaned, and the slit invisibly mended.
3. (Further examples.)
1834 E. E. Perkins *Lady's Shopping Manual* 103 Invisible Wire for Lace and Nett Caps. **1881** *Queen* 12 Mar. (Advt.), Invisible fringe nets made of hair. **1895** *Montgomery Ward Catal.* 87/1 Invisible Hairpins, about 50 in a box. **1897** *Sears, Roebuck Catal.* 322/2 Invisible Hair Pins made of Good Wire. **1901** Invisible stitch [see STOAT *v.*]. **1964** *McCall's Sewing* ii. 30/1 *Invisible stitch*, used for hems and attaching facings and interfacings in tailoring. **1966** J. S. Cox *Illustr. Dict. Hairdressing* 83/2 Invisible pins, very fine hairpins which are difficult to see when placed in the hairdress. **1967** J. Caird *Murder Scholastic* xiv. 190 Mabel Glossop had worn her thick, beautiful white hair in a bun, over which she put a fine 'invisible' net. **1973** *Times* 19 Oct. 3/1 (Advt.), Without these foils such modern marvels as 'invisible' hearing aids or heart pacemakers simply could not exist.
B. *sb.* **3.** Usu. in *pl.* Invisible exports and imports. Cf. sense *1 d of the adj.
1958 *Economist* 18 Oct. 256/1 Net earnings from commercial services ranked as invisibles also rose. **1962** H. O. Beecheno *Introd. Business Stud.* xv. 143 These 'invisibles' arise mainly from services which we supply to other countries. **1964** *New Statesman* 3 Apr. 514/1 Angola and Mozambique provide one-third of all Portuguese exports, valued at £50 million, and this sum does not include invisibles from tourism, shipping and railways. **1973** *Daily Tel.* 13 July 19 The average deficit for the latest three months, excluding invisibles, is £22 million lower than in May at £133 million.

invita Minerva (invəi·tā minə·ivā), *advb. phr.* [L., = 'Minerva (the goddess of wisdom) unwilling'.] When one is not in the vein or mood; without inspiration.
1584 R. Scot *Discov. Witchcr.* XII. iii. 219 It should be vnto them (*Inuita Minerua*) to banket or danse with Minerua. **1626** Bacon *Sylva* § 292 That nothing bee done *Inuitâ Minervâ*, but *Secundum Genium*. **1848** Geo. Eliot *Let.* Feb. (1954) I. 250, I have tired myself with trying to write cleverly 'invita Minerva'. **1954** 'M. Cost' *Invitation from Minerva* 126 It is always a mistake to do anything invita Minerva... Briefly, against the grain.

invitation. Add: **2. b.** *Bridge.* (See quot. 1964.)
1928 A. E. M. Foster *Auction Bridge for All* i. i. 22 There still lurks amongst a number of players the notion that a bid of a minor suit by their partner is what they call 'an invitation to a No Trumper'. Again and again I have heard said: 'I responded to your invitation, partner.' **1958** *Listener* 23 Oct. 669/3 With his excellent controls it is easy for West to accept the slam invitation. **1964** *Official Encycl. Bridge* 265/1 Invitation, a bid which encourages the bidder's partner to continue to game or slam, but gives him the option of passing if he has no reserve values in terms of high-card strength or distribution.
3. (Further examples.)
*c*1855 in M. Johnson *Amer. Advertising, 1800–1900* (1960), Invitation notices, and every arrangment for funerals personally attended to with correctness and dispatch. **1902** A. Bennett *Grand Babylon Hotel* vi. 71 The invitation-list..contained no reference to any such person.

1931 A. E. M. Foster *Auction Bridge made Clear* 124 An original bid of Two of a suit is by them reserved as a 'Demand' or 'Invitation' bid. That is, a demand or invitation to partner to show his quick tricks. *Ibid.* 125 Z has..a hand of over seven tricks but under eleven—the 'Invitation Area'... Z bid 'Two Hearts' as an 'Invitation'. **1968** *Radio Times* 28 Nov. 27/1 Invitation concert... Recorded before an invited audience.

invitational (invitēi·ʃənǎl), *a.* [f. INVITATION + -AL.] Characterized by invitation. Also as *sb.*, an invitational tournament (? only *N. Amer.*).
1922 *Chambers's Jrnl.* Aug. 543/1 Philip walked the room's length with invitational pauses. **1957** *Publ. Amer. Dial. Soc.* XXVIII. 58 Somebody like to help me?..someone in the context..would sound more factual..than invitational. **1958** *Listener* 23 Oct. 669/3 A cue bid of Five Hearts would be too strongly invitational. **1964** *Official Encycl. Bridge* 265/1 *Invitational bid*, bid indicating strong game prospects, which requests partner to continue if he has some reserve strength. **1964** N. Squire *Bidding at Bridge* ii. 17 Your partner..will give an invitational raise to 2NT. **1968** *Globe & Mail* (Toronto) 3 Feb. 35/5 Yesterday Sinclair's mixed rink of his wife, Betty, Don Maclellan and Mildred Maclellan advanced to the quarter-finals of the Thornhill mixed invitational tournament. *Ibid.* (*headline*), 2 Thornhill rinks survive club's mixed invitational. **1972** *Evening Telegram* (St. John's, Newfoundland) 27 June 11/1 John Hamilton won the June Invitational on his first try Monday, despite a desperate charge by two Corner Brook golfers on the final day of the tournament.

invite, *v.* Add: **1. a.** Also, *to invite in*: to ask (a person) to come into one's house.
1875 *Harper's Mag.* Aug. 417 She found a house where she was invited in. **1888** Mrs. H. Ward *R. Elsmere* II. iii. xxii. 213 It was evidently the Squire's purpose to come in, so Robert invited him in. **1899** Skeel & Brearley *King Washington* 37 Being occupied in a nice calculation whether or not her breakfast menu would stand the strain of an extra appetite should Mr. Ettrick..invite the captain in. **1974** 'M. Underwood' *Pinch of Snuff* xi. 94 'I doubt whether we need a warrant,' Sergeant Ellis remarked. 'After all, he invited us in.'

invite, *sb.* Add: **1.** (Later examples.) Now usu. with stress on first syllable.
1937 *Times* 28 Dec. 7/5 This little servant girl, who.. believed that she would some day receive an 'invite' to a royal ball and marry the prince, [etc.]. **1968** *Listener* 13 June 770/1 Is it just an invite from the colonel for a working week-end? **1970** G. F. Newman *Sir, You Bastard* v. 143 The four detectives didn't await an invite into the house.

invitee. Add: **b.** *spec.* (See quot. 1913.)
1913 *Law Rep. King's Bench* I. 410 The duty of the owner or occupier to use care..is..never very definitely measured... More care, though not much, is owed to a licensee—more again to an invitee. The latter term is reserved for those who are invited into the premises by the owner or occupier for some purpose of business or of material interest. Those who are invited as guests..are not in law invitees but licensees. **1953** *Times* 14 Nov. 2/7 Their Lordships now held that the plaintiff was himself to blame for the accident, and that he was not an 'invitee' because the business on which he was engaged was not one in which the defendant had a common interest. **1965** *Mod. Law Rev.* XXVIII. v. 519 A finding that a workman was *sciens* was sufficient to defeat his claim as an invitee, even if he was not *volens*. **1971** *N.Y. Law Jrnl.* 23 Nov. 19/3 In England the distinction between licensees and invitees have [*sic*] been abolished by statute.

in vitro, in vivo: see *IN *Lat. prep.*

invoice, *v.* Add: (Further examples.) Also, to send or submit an invoice to (a person).
Rarely occurs in written English, but common in speech. The contextual sense in quot. 1939 is not certain.
1939 Joyce *Finnegans Wake* (1964) iii. 623 You invoiced him last Eatster so he ought to give us hockockles and everything. **1956** *Invoicing Methods* (Brit. Inst. Managem.) xv. 124 An opaque signal is placed over the ledger folio on the customer record in order to prevent subsequent orders from the customer being inadvertently stamped with the ledger folio as a sign that they may be invoiced in the ordinary way. **1972** *Daily Tel.* 12 July 11 (Advt.), I enclose my remittance of £6 for the first ingot, and agree to pay for each subsequent ingot upon being invoiced on a monthly prepayment basis.

involatile, *a.* **2.** (Further examples.)
1962 Simpson & Richards *Physical Princ. Junction Transistors* xii. 263 When wetted with an involatile (silicone) oil the mica may introduce a resistance of some 0·5°C/watt. **1965** Phillips & Williams *Inorg. Chem.* I. xvii. 623 Many of the compounds of this section are very high-melting solids, while many others are relatively involatile solids or oils.

involute (i·nvŏliᵘt), *v.* [Back-formation from INVOLUTED *a.*] *intr.* **a.** 'To return to a normal condition' (*Cent. Dict.* Suppl.). **b.** To undergo involution (sense 4). Hence **i·nvoluting** *ppl. a.*
1904 *Buck's Handbk. Med. Sci.* (rev. ed.) VII. 782/2 A circular scaly pink patch that spreads peripherally with a pinkish border, and clears up or involutes in the central portion. **1910** *Practitioner* July 106 The uterus had involuted normally. **1968** *Amer. Jrnl. Obstetr. & Gynecol.* CII. 33/1 Deeper arteries and veins contract and are compressed from without by the involuting muscle mass of the uterus. **1971** *Jrnl. Insect Physiol.* XVII. 857 These..

glands reach the peak of their metabolic and synthetic activity shortly before rapidly involuting, leaving only a small remnant.

involuted, *a.* Add: **1. b.** *fig.*
a **1910** 'MARK TWAIN' *Speeches* (1910) 290 Whatever moral..you put into a speech,..gets diffused among those involuted sentences. **1972** *Times Lit. Suppl.* 22 Dec. 1552/1 Clothed in orthodoxy, that could be no more than an involuted way of saying that God is love.

involution. Add: **6. c.** A function or transformation that is equal to its inverse.
1916 E. KASNER in *Amer. Jrnl. Math.* XXXVIII. 177 It is easy to determine all regular transformations of period 2. In the direct type $Z=f(z)$ the functional equation is $f(f(z))\equiv z$, that is, $f^2=1$; in the reverse type $Z=f(z_0)$ the functional equation is $f(f_0(z))\equiv z$, that is, $ff_0=1$, where f_0 denotes the series whose coefficients are the conjugates of the coefficients of series f. We shall call a transformation of the former type (excluding the identical transformation) a conformal involution, and one of the latter type a conformal symmetry. **1969** F. M. HALL *Introd. Abstr. Algebra* II. ii. 31 If θ is a 1–1 correspondence between elements of A and itself such that $\theta=\theta^{-1}$, then θ is said to be an involution.

involutional (invǒli*ū*·ʃənăl), *a. Psychol.* [f. INVOLUTION + -AL.] Of or pertaining to the bodily change of involution (sense 4), or to mental disturbances associated with this change.
1910 *Rev. Neurol. & Psychiatry* VIII. 8, I refer to the work of Dreyfus, who, after reviewing Kraepelin's own cases of involutional melancholia, concludes that the involutional depression is a mixed form of manic-depressive insanity. **1934** P. BOTTOME *Private Worlds* 111 It's not an ordinary melancholic case. She hasn't had any attacks before; and it is not involutional; she is only thirty. **1945** E. DAVIDOFF in O. J. Kaplan *Mental Disorders Later Life* viii. 189 There may be a qualitative as well as a quantitative difference between the nonpsychotic involutional syndrome and the involutional psychosis. **1950** J. ZINKIN tr. *Bleuler's Dementia Praecox* II. 242 Kraepelin was the first to draw attention to the high incidence of cases who develop an apparently common melancholia during the involutional period. **1965** FOULDS & CAINE *Personality & Personal Illness* II. iv. 67 We do not have much difficulty in understanding what is meant by an involutional melancholia with obsessional features. **1968** *Amer. Jrnl. Obstetr. & Gynecol.* CII. 29/1 Pronounced involutional atrophy occurred in the..myometrium at 7 weeks post partum. **1969** *Biochem. Jrnl.* CXII. 641/1 Oestradiol might not have a differential effect on two separate involutionary processes, but might just decrease the water content of the treated uteri.

involutionary (invǒli*ū*·ʃənări), *a.* [f. INVOLUTION + -ARY[1].] Characterized by involution; retrograde.
1920 *Discovery* Nov. 338/2 Our conceptions of psychical ..'regression'.., the backward or involutionary path of mental processes to more infantile conditions. **1942** *Mind* LI. 146 The infinite series of causes to which *Ethices I, xxviii* [of Spinoza] refers is not a temporal regress to an impossible 'first' cause, but the involutionary sequence of eternal causes to a necessary First Cause.

involutory (invǒli*ū*·təri), *a. Math.* [f. L. type **involūtōri-us*: see INVOLUTORIAL *a.* and -ORY[2].] That is an involution (sense *6 c).
1941 BIRKHOFF & MACLANE *Survey Mod. Algebra* viii. 203 The correspondence $A\leftrightarrow A'$ therefore preserves sums and inverts the order of products, so is sometimes called an anti-automorphism. Since $(A')'=A$, this anti-automorphism is called 'involutory'. **1971** J. H. CONWAY in Powell & Higman *Finite Simple Groups* vii. 217 The p objects permuted by $L_2(p)$..can in each case be taken as p involutory permutations of the set Ω. **1972** F. J. BUDDEN *Fascination of Groups* viii. 81, 2-groups always arise as subgroups of larger groups whenever there is an 'involutory' element present, that is, an element whose square is equal to the identity.

invulnerability. (Later examples.)
1900 *Daily News* 4 Sept. 6/1 The superstition of their [*sc.* the Boxers'] invulnerability to cannon shot... The Empress-Dowager..is said to have been deceived by the invulnerability superstition. **1962** *Listener* 29 Mar. 540/1 'Invulnerability' suggests, first of all, protecting your missiles under concrete, or hiding missiles and bombers and submarines by having them moving about. But 'invulnerability' also includes having too many missile sites for your enemy to be able to knock out even with a perfectly executed first strike; it includes having a mixed deterrent of bombers and land-base missiles and sea-going missiles, and it includes the case where your enemy knows that you are sure to have enough warning to launch your missiles and get your bombers aloft. This business of warning introduces serious ambiguities in the idea of 'invulnerability'. **1972** *Sci. Amer.* July 14/2 As a result of this possibility each country will be concerned to maintain the invulnerability of its submarine-based strategic missiles, which are essentially immune to attack from land-based weapons.

invulnerable, *a.* **1.** (Later examples.)
1962 *Listener* 29 Mar. 540/1 It is essential, isn't it, to have what are called 'invulnerable strategic forces'? *Ibid.* 554/1 The speediest possible development of 'invulnerable' nuclear retaliatory power. *Ibid.*, The 'increasingly invulnerable' missile.

inward, *adv.* **3.** (Further examples.)
1850 J. G. WHITTIER *Songs of Labor* 59 Still dreamed my inward-turning eye. **1890** W. JAMES *Princ. Psychol.* I. x. 320 The more utterly 'selfish' I am in this primitive way, the more blindly absorbed my thought will be in the objects and impulses of my lusts, and the more devoid of any inward looking glance. **1910** KIPLING *Rewards & Fairies* p. x, These shall cleanse and purify Webbed and inward-turning eye. **1946** KOESTLER *Thieves in Night* 207 She sipped her dry Martini with an inward-turned look. **1961** A. MILLER *Misfits* xii. 131 His eyes are sightless, inward-looking. **1963** *Times* 28 Jan. 5/2 Yet Schumann's poetry has its feet on German earth, and it was possible to feel that Mr. Richter's presentation of it was just a little too disembodied and wraithlike, his interpretation a little too inward-looking. **1968** *Guardian* 15 Apr. 9/6 Pressure from inward-looking, anti-national groups.

in-winter (i·nwintəɹ), *v.* [IN- *pref.*[1]] *trans.* To protect (animals, particularly sheep) by keeping them indoors during severe weather and providing food for them. So **in-wi·ntered** *ppl. a.*, **in-wi·ntering** *sb.*
1961 *2nd Rep. Hill Farming Res. Organisation 1958–61* 25 Hoggs have been in-wintered experimentally in improvised cattle courts... In-wintered Blackface hoggs.. thrived normally on diets of hay... Indoor wintering is quite satisfactory. **1962** *Times* 26 Nov. 17/6 The in-wintering of in-lamb ewes. **1965** COOPER & THOMAS *Profitable Sheep Farming* viii. 69 The main interest today ..is the inwintering of breeding ewes on lowland farms. *Ibid.* 70 A hundred six and seven-crop Mule ewes..were inwintered in a Dutch barn. **1971** *Farmer & Stockbreeder* 16 Feb. 25/3 In-wintered ewes should also be dosed two weeks after being brought in.

inwit. 1, 2. Used as a conscious archaism by some modern writers.
In Joyce's *Ulysses* adopted from Dan Michel's title *Ayenbite of Inwyt* (1340); so also in quots. 1967 and 1968. Cf. AYENBITE.
1922 R. BRIDGES *Coll. Ess.* (1928) III. 68 If..such good old English words as *inwit* and *wanhope* should be rehabilitated (and they have been pushing up their heads for thirty years), we should gain a great deal. **1922** JOYCE *Ulysses* 17 They wash and tub and scrub. Agenbite of inwit. Conscience. **1955** E. POUND *Classic Anthol.* III. 150 Designing in his heart felicity From inwit to his act moved ever so straight He got in sovereignty the whole Quadrate. *Ibid.* 174 There is no light in your conscience And your acts shed, therefore, no light In your inwit. **1967** *Punch* 12 July 72/1 There's this dedicated, totally frenetic fumble under the skin of the times' underbelly.. for the agenbite of inwit. **1968** *Listener* 28 Mar. 411/3 Very probably Bond fans will be able to turn a blind eye to the bites and agenbites of new-Bond's *inwit.*

in-word, -work: see *IN *a.* 2 b, *prep.* 10 a.

inworker. Add: **2.** One who works on the premises of a shop or factory.
1909 *Fabian News* XX. 75/1 A minimum wage for both inworkers and outworkers.

‖ **inyanga** (inya·ŋă). *S. Afr.* Also **enyanga, inyanger.** [Zulu.] A medicine-man (see also quot. 1826).
1826 N. ISAACS *Jrnl.* 1 Apr. in *Trav. E. Afr.* (1936) I. vi. 82 The 'inyangers', or water doctors, arrived to take us across the river. *Ibid.* 83 The inyangers from their great muscular power, and experience in their occupation, kept us above the water. **1862** G. H. MASON *Zululand* xiv. 180 An 'Enyanga', as the said professor is called, is a formidable foe; merely as being master of the most deadly poisons in the world. **1946** *Archit. Rev.* C. 22/1 Before the first stick or stone is cleared the headman has the new site approved and then treated by an inyanga—a specialist in various types of native medicine, a man usually labelled by the ethnocentric European as 'magician'. **1954** H. GIBBS *Background to Bitterness* II. ii. 66 He [*sc.* Dingaan] decided to spare Owen and a few American missionaries in Natal—the next morning his inyangas told Owen they would be spared. **1970** *Golden City Post* 28 June, Millionaire inyanga Sethuntsa Khotso, who last year threw the bones and successfully tipped Naval Escort, says that Golden Jewel will win the Durban July next Saturday.

inyoite (i·nyōᵘəit). *Min.* [f. the name of *Inyo* County, California + -ITE[1].] A hydrated calcium borate, $Ca_2B_6O_{11}.13H_2O$, found as colourless rhombic crystals.
1914 W. T. SCHALLER in *Jrnl. Washington Acad. Sci.* IV. 355 Inyoite and Meyerhofferite, two new Calcium Borates from Death Valley, Inyo County, California, belong to the Colemanite series. **1921** *Bull. Geol. Survey Canada* XXXII. 2 The crystals of inyoite from Hillsborough are remarkably well developed and clear. **1959** *Acta Crystallogr.* XII. 162 Polyions of inyoite are connected to one another and to neighboring water molecules by bonding through calcium ions and by hydrogen bonds.

io[2] (əi·ōᵘ). [mod.L., the specific name of the insect, a Gr. Ἰώ, daughter of the river god Inachus.] In full, *io moth.* A large yellow North American moth, *Automeris io*, distinguished by prominent ocelli on the hind wings.
[**1869** *Canad. Entomologist* II. 20 These caterpillars.. proved to be the very familiar larvae of what is commonly known as the Io Emperor-moth.] **1870** *Canada Farmer* 15 Sept. 336/2 The beautiful, pale yellowish-green caterpillar..is the larva of the handsome Io-moth. **1873** C. V. RILEY in *5th Ann. Rep. Missouri State Entom.* 133 The Io Moth..is one of our most beautiful moths, receiving its name from two conspicuous eye-spots on the hind wings, in allusion to the ancient Greek heroine, Io. **1912** G. STRATTON-PORTER *Moths of Limberlost* viii. 207 Mr. Eisen presented me with a pair of *Hyperchiria Io*... Because the Io was yellow, I wanted it. **1954** BORROR & DELONG *Introd. Study Insects* i. 6 A few caterpillars, such as the saddleback and the larva of the io moth, have stinging hairs.

iod-. Add: **iodargyrite** (examples); see quot. 1971; **iode·mbolite** *Min.* [EMBOLITE], the name now given to IODOBROMITE.
1868 A. RAMSAY *Rudiments of Mineral.* v. 143 Iodargyrite readily fuses, colours the flame red, and yields a globule of silver when reduced. **1950** *Thorpe's Dict. Appl. Chem.* (ed. 4) X. 766/1 Silver iodide, AgI, occurs in Chili, Peru, Mexico, and Spain as the mineral iodargyrite in citron-yellow hexagonal crystals. **1971** *Mineral. Mag.* XXXVIII. 104 Recommendations of the Commission [on New Minerals and Mineral Names of the International Mineralogical Association] on minerals for which more than one name is in common use... Iodargyrite, not iodyrite. **1902** PRIOR & SPENCER in *Mineral. Mag.* XIII. 176 Since the name [*sc.* iodobromite] is a particularly misleading one..we propose to refer to the varieties of the cerargyrite group which contain all three halogens as iodiferous embolites or briefly iodembolites. **1944** *Mineral. Abstr.* IX. 59 At Maikan, near Pavlodar, iodembolite and embolite occur in native sulphur.

iodimetry (əiˌǒdi·mĕtri). *Chem.* [f. IODI(NE *sb.* + -METRY.] The titrimetric analysis of an oxidizing or reducing agent using the iodine/iodide redox system; *spec.* the quantitative analysis of a solution of a reducing agent by titration with a standard solution of iodine. Cf. *IODOMETRY.
1897 *Jrnl. Chem. Soc.* LXXII. II. 342 (*heading*) Barium thiosulphate as basis for iodimetry. **1907** LINCOLN & WALTON *Exerc. Elem. Quantitative Chem. Analysis* 78 The methods of determination in iodimetry may be divided into three general classes: 1. The titration of..reducing agents. 2...oxidizing agents... 3. Free chlorine. **1939** A. I. VOGEL *Text-bk. Quantitative Inorg. Analysis* iii. 401 Iodimetry covers titrations *with* a standard solution of iodine. Iodometry deals with the titration *of* iodine liberated in chemical reactions. **1960** R. J. WINTERTON in C. L. & D. W. Wilson *Comprehensive Analytical Chem.* IB. vii. 249 Iodine..may be used as a standard solution and titrated into the reducing solution, or it may be liberated from potassium iodide or some other compound of iodine by an oxidising agent in solution, and titrated with thiosulphate solution...The use of standard iodine is called direct iodimetry, and the other method indirect iodimetry.
So **iodime·tric** *a.*, of or pertaining to iodimetry; **iodime·trically** *adv.*, by means of iodimetry.
1887 *Jrnl. Chem. Soc.* LII. 997 The iodimetric method serves well for the assay of commercial sodium sulphide. *Ibid.* 998 Ferrous and ferric oxides, in hydrochloric acid solution, can be determined iodimetrically. **1931** JENKINS & DUMEZ *Quantitative Pharmaceutical Chem.* viii. 123 Iodimetric methods include some of the most exact processes of volumetric analysis, because..the presence of one part of iodine in several million parts of solution can be recognised by means of starch indicator solution. **1963** SKOOG & WEST *Fund. Analytical Chem.* xx. 458 The first [category] is made up of procedures that use a standard solution of iodine to titrate easily oxidized substances. These are termed direct or iodimetric methods and have rather limited applicability since iodine is a relatively weak oxidizing agent. **1969** H. T. EVANS tr. *Hägg's Gen. & Inorg. Chem.* xxi. 534 Since many oxidizing agents oxidize iodide ion to iodine, such substances can also be determined iodimetrically.

iodinate (əi·ǒdinēit), *v.* [f. IODIN(E *sb.* + -ATE *suffix*[3].] *trans.* **a.** To introduce an iodine atom into (a compound or molecule) in place of a hydrogen atom. **b.** To treat with iodine. Hence **i·odinated** *ppl. a.*, **i·odinating** *vbl. sb.*
1908 *Jrnl. Chem. Soc.* XCIV. 778, *m*-Nitroaniline is readily iodinated by adding iodine..to a solution of the base. **1917** *Jrnl. Amer. Chem. Soc.* XXXIX. 444 The xylenols are not so readily iodinated as the lower members. **1921** *Biochem. Jrnl.* XV. 320 The monochloride of iodine has been used before as an iodinating agent. **1926** *Chem. Abstr.* XX. 596 (*heading*) Iodinated pyrrole derivatives. **1948** *New Biol.* IV. 138 Similar improvements in the yields of cows can be obtained by injecting the thyroid hormone—thyroxine—or by feeding the closely related substances known as iodinated proteins. **1964** N. G. CLARK *Mod. Org. Chem.* xiv. 275 They are then all iodinated three times on the methyl group. **1968** *Canad. Jrnl. Physiol. & Pharmacol.* XLVI. 449 The effects of increasing or decreasing the endogenous secretion of thyroid-stimulating hormone on the iodinating activity of the rat thyroid gland were investigated. **1969** *Nature* 23 Aug. 778/2 Thomas [etc.]..have measured..the uptake of radioactive iodine in twenty-two adults before and after swimming in an iodinated pool.

iodination (əiˌǒdinēi·ʃən). *Chem.* [f. IODIN(E *sb.* + -ATION.] **a.** The replacement of a hydrogen atom in a compound or molecule by an iodine atom.
1873 *Chem. News* 26 Sept. 167/2 (*heading*) On the chlorination and iodination of anthracen. **1919** *Jrnl. Chem. Soc.* XLI. 293 Iodobenzene on iodination with the required quantity of iodine and nitric acid gives *p*-diiodobenzene. **1971** *Jrnl. Chem. Educ.* XLVIII. 508/1 Iodination by molecular iodine occurs only with phenols and amines.
b. Addition of iodine (e.g. to a water supply).
1966 *Jrnl. Clin. Endocrinol. & Metabolism* XVI. 620/1 Prior to iodination of the water. **1969** *Arch. Environmen-*

tal Health XIX. 127/1 Iodination of a public water supply has proven to be technically and commercially feasible.

iodine, *sb.* Add: **2. d.** Other *attrib.* uses, as **iodine number, value** [tr. G. *jodzahl* (A. Hübl 1884, in *Dingler's polytechn. Jrnl.* CCLIII. 287)], the proportion of unsaturated matter present in a substance as measured by the number of grammes of iodine which can be taken up by 100 grammes of the substance; **iodine scarlet,** mercuric iodide, HgI_2, a brilliant red powder.

1885 *Analyst* X. 123 About everything on the list which might be used to adulterate or be substituted for butter, gave iodine numbers so far removed from that for genuine butter that no difficulty would occur. **1969** J. R. HOLUM *Introd. Org. & Biol. Chem.* ix. 302 Oleic acid has an iodine number of 90, linoleic acid 181, and linolenic acid 274. **1835** G. FIELD *Chromatography* x. 94 Iodine scarlet is a new pigment of a most vivid and beautiful scarlet colour, exceeding the brilliancy of vermilion. **1885** *Encycl. Brit.* XIX. 87/2 From mercury combined with iodine is prepared a pigment of unequalled vivacity and brilliance, Iodine Scarlet, but unfortunately as fugitive as it is bright. **1969** R. MAYER *Dict. Art Terms & Techniques* 198/1 *Iodine Scarlet,* mercuric iodide; a dangerously poisonous inorganic pigment of the most brilliant scarlet hue. It is useless as a paint pigment because it fades to a pale yellow. **1898** *Analyst* XXIII. 241 Purified allyl alcohol has a theoretical iodine value of 435. **1921** *Biochem. Jrnl.* XV. 319 Resins also show great variations in iodine values according to the conditions of the determination. **1953** J. DAVIDSOHN et al. *Soap Manuf.* I. xviii. 365 In order to produce a hard soap, a fat charge with low iodine value and low saponification value should be selected.

iodine *v.* (examples other than in *Photogr.*).

1929 C. C. MARTINDALE *Risen Sun* 173 His grooms.. were iodining his abrasions. **1936** A. HUXLEY *Eyeless in Gaza* li. 571 How I regret those cretins one used to see in Switzerland when I was a child! They've iodined them out of existence now.

i·odinized, *ppl. a.* [f. IODINE *sb.*: see -IZE.] Of a material: treated or impregnated with iodine.

1919 *Chem. Abstr.* XIII. 2254 (*heading*) Iodinized emulsion. **1962** *Jrnl. Laboratory & Clin. Med.* LIX. 118 (*heading*) Effects of iodinized contrast media upon electrophoretic mobilities of blood proteins. **1963** *Neurology* XIII. 492/1 All the water-soluble iodinized contrast media currently used in diagnostic procedures..have been reported to cause side effects and complications.

iodipin (əiˌōu·dipin). *Pharm.* [ad. G. *jodipin,* f. *jod* iodine + L. *adip-, adeps* fat: see -IN[1].] A liquid obtained by treating sesame oil with iodine, formerly used in treating syphilis and scrofula and as a contrast medium in radiography.

1899 *Brit. Med. Jrnl. Epitome* 18 Nov. 81/1 Iodipin, apart from its uses as a test is, as an iodine preparation, also therapeutically active. **1907** WOOD & BACHE *Dispensatory U.S.A.* (ed. 19) 1532/1 Iodipin.—A yellow, oily fluid, of a purely oleaginous taste. **1930** *Biol. Abstr.* IV. 2568/2 Injection of a medicinal iodine compound ('Iodipin') into the uterine cavity promises to yield clinical diagnostic results of some value by outlining the uterine cavity and the Fallopian tubes. **1940** H. A. MCGUIGAN *Appl. Pharmacol.* 190 Iodipin is iodized sesame oil. The dose of 10 per cent iodipin is 4 to 8 Gm.

iodization (əiːŏdəizēi·ʃən). [f. IODIZ(E *v.* + -ATION.] The process or practice of iodizing; the addition of iodine or an iodine compound to a substance.

1909 *Jrnl. Chem. Soc.* XCVI. II. 919 The species specificity of a protein is considerably modified as regards its biological action by iodisation. **1956** *Nature* 24 Mar. 562/2 Iodine metabolism and the iodization of food will first be considered. **1971** *Sci. Amer.* June 97/1 This aspect of thyroid physiology, together with increasing reports of severe iodine toxicity..elicited strenuous opposition to the iodization of table salt.

iodized, *ppl. a.* (Later example.)

1933 *Radio Times* 14 Apr. 112/2 Finest iodised table salt.

iodo-. Add: In combination stressed *i·odo-* or *io·do-*. **a. iodoacetic** *a.*, now the usual form of *iodacetic* adj. (s.v. IOD-); (examples); hence **iodoa·cetate,** an ester or salt of iodoacetic acid; **iodopro·tein,** any protein containing iodine; **iodopyracet** (-pəiə·räset) *U.S.* [f. di-*iodo-pyr*idone-*acetic*], the diethanolamine salt, $C_{11}H_{16}N_2O_5I_2$, of 3,5-di-iodo-4-pyridone-*N*-acetic acid, used in radiography as a contrast medium, principally for intravenous urography and for measuring renal plasma flow; called *diodone* in the U.K.; **iodopy·rin(e** *Pharm.*, a crystalline iodinated derivative, $C_{11}H_{11}N_2OI$, of antipyrin, used as an antipyretic; **iodothy·rin** = *thyro-iodine* (s.v. THYRO-). **b.** Delete **iodometric, iodometry** and see *IODOMETRY; **i·odo-, io·dophil(e** [-PHIL, -PHILE], **iodophi·lic** *adjs.*, readily stained by iodine.

1902 *Jrnl. Chem. Soc.* LXXXII. I. 585 By the condensation of ethyl iodoacetate with citraldehyde, a mixture of substances is apparently obtained. **1931** *Times Lit. Suppl.* 9 July 550/3 Sodium iodoacetate prevents a similar breakdown of methylglyoxal by its inhibition of the enzyme glyoxalase. **1964** W. G. SMITH *Allergy & Tissue Metabolism* ii. 25 Inhibition of histamine and SRS-A release by antigen was noted with iodoacetate. **1888** *Syd. Soc. Lex.*, *Iodo-acetic acid*, see Iodacetic acid. **1948** *Jrnl. Biol. Chem.* CLXXVI. 88 The irreversible toxic action of the inhibitor toward yeast cells is proportional to the concentration of undissociated iodoacetic acid. **1962** *Lancet* 15 Dec. 1275/1 Although iodoacetic acid and acetoacetate might have a different action on the metabolism of the heart muscle, both seem to inhibit contractions. **1902** *Encycl. Brit.* XXXII. 817/2 The Myxobolidæ.., which have an iodophile vacuole. **1927** THAYSEN & BUNKER *Microbiol. Cellulose* viii. 218 Henneberg's statement that most of the cellulose-decomposing organisms found in the intestine are iodophil..disagrees with all previous observations. **1942** *Nature* 23 May 582/1 Both the rumen in ruminant and the cæcum in non-ruminant Herbivora support an abundant iodophile microflora: that is, an association of taxonomically diverse species exhibiting, in consequence of the decomposition within them of bacterial starch or granulose, the common characteristic of giving a blue colour with iodine. **1948** *Jrnl. Bacteriol.* LV. 197 In the majority of instances iodophilic colonies were frequent on the sucrose agar plates containing penicillin. **1971** HAWKER & LINTON *Micro-Organisms* xv. 543 Cellulose decomposition is associated with iodophilic bacteria (i.e. organisms which reveal starch-like substances when stained with iodine). **1909** *Jrnl. Chem. Soc.* XCVI. II. 919 The behaviour of iodoproteins as regards the formation of specific antisubstances was investigated. **1951** *Adv. Protein Chem.* VI. 253 (*heading*) Natural and artificial iodoproteins. **1963** *Lancet* 5 Jan. 12/1 Very rare examples of absent T_3 suppression in patients not having hyperthyroidism have been recorded when a thyroid nodule with autonomous iodine uptake synthesises abnormal iodoproteins. **1947** *Dispensatory U.S.A.* (ed. 24) 584/2 The iodopyracet injection is warmed to body temperature and 20 cc.., containing 7 Gm..of the drug, is injected slowly intravenously. **1951** A. GROLLMAN *Pharmacol. & Therapeutics* xxxii. 751 Iodopyracet may be injected into the aorta in order to visualize the renal arteries; or into the brachial vein to visualize the chambers of the heart in the diagnosis of congenital cardiac lesions. **1971** *Amer. Jrnl. Obstetr. & Gynecol.* CX. 566/1 Following injection of radioactive iodopyracet into the fetal circulation radioactivity moved equally rapidly into amniotic fluid in preparations involving nephrectomized or normal fetuses. **1892** *Brit. Med. Jrnl.* 2 Jan. 22/1 Iodopyrin. This product is a chemical compound of iodine with antipyrin, in which an atom of hydrogen is replaced by iodine. It occurs in colourless crystals. **1909** H. A. HARE et al. *National Stand. Dispensatory* (ed. 2) 201 Iodopyrine presents the combined physiological action of iodine and an antipyretic, and has been recommended in bronchial asthma and tertiary syphilis. **1961** L. MARTIN *Clinical Endocrinol.* (ed. 3) iii. 68 There are also certain other therapeutic substances which will produce a simple goitre... These include..iodopyrine (..found in Felsol powders which are used for asthma). **1897** *Jrnl. Chem. Soc.* LXXII. II. 330 The animal was taking..diet to which was added either fresh thyroid or iodothyrin. **1909** H. A. HARE et al. *National Stand. Dispensatory* (ed. 2) 855 Iodothyrine is a white or yellowish-white powder, having a sweet taste, and is prepared..by boiling fresh thyroid glands..with dilute sulphuric acid. **1932** *Discovery* Mar. 96/2 The flattened gilled water newt called the Axolotl [is] changed into a smaller differently shaped land newt in the course of a few weeks by feeding it with thyroid. In this case the active substance can be extracted from the gland and chemically analysed; it is termed iodothyrin.

iodometry (əiŏdǫ·mĕtri). *Chem.* [f. IODO- + -METRY.] The titrimetric analysis of an oxidizing or reducing agent using the iodine/iodide redox system; *spec.* the quantitative analysis of a solution of an oxidizing agent by the addition of excess iodide followed by titration of the iodine so liberated with thiosulphate or arsenite solution. Cf. *IODIMETRY.

1883 *Chem. News* 6 Apr. 166/1 (*heading*) Preparation of a durable starch solution for iodometry. **1916** *Chem. Abstr.* X. 730 (*heading*) Differential iodometry. I. Determination of periodates, iodates, bromates and chlorates in the presence of each other. **1928** *Ibid.* XXII. 2901 Reaction between iodic and hydriodic acids in very dilute solution and the titration of the liberated iodine with thiosulfate... An investigation of reactions involved in iodometry. **1939** [see *IODIMETRY]. **1973** *Chem. Abstr.* LXXVIII. 23524 Iodometry can be employed for detn. of small amts. of Zn, Cu, Cd, Co and Hg.

So **iodome·tric** *a.*, of or pertaining to iodometry; **iodome·trically** *adv.*, by means of iodometry.

1856 *Q. Jrnl. Chem. Soc.* VIII. 194 We have employed the much more accurate and convenient iodometric method, which..gives a degree of accuracy attainable by very few analytical processes. **1891** *Jrnl. Chem. Soc.* LX. 614 The facility with which pure potassium iodate is prepared renders it an admirable basis for iodometric analysis. **1928** A. W. WELLINGS *Volumetric Analysis* v. 102 Nitrites may also be estimated iodometrically. **1957** G. E. HUTCHINSON *Treat. Limnol.* I. xiii. 769 The excess chromate, equivalent to the original sulfate, is determined iodometrically. **1960** *Limnology & Oceanogr.* V. 343 (*heading*) A note on a stabilized starch indicator for use in iodometric and iodimetric determinations. **1971** G. D. CHRISTIAN *Analytical Chem.* xv. 238 Sodium thiosulfate solution is standardized iodometrically against a pure oxidizing agent such as $K_2Cr_2O_7$, KIO_3, $KBrO_3$, or metallic copper.

iodonium (əiˌŏdōu·niŏm). *Chem.* [f. IOD- + *-ONIUM.] The name of cations of the type $RR'I_2^+$ where R and R′ are (different or the same) alkyl or aryl radicals, or part of a ring. Usu. *attrib.* or as a formative element.

1894 *Jrnl. Chem. Soc.* LXVI. I. 242 Diphenyliodonium iodide, $I \cdot IPh_2$. *Ibid.* 243 Phenyl, which does not form ammonium and sulphonium bases, forms iodonium bases. **1922** J. MELLOR *Comprehensive Treat. Inorg. & Theoret. Chem.* II. 108 The iodonium bases and salts resemble those of lead and silver but particularly those of thallium. **1950** N. V. SIDGWICK *Chem. Elements* II. 1257 The free iodonium bases $Ar_2I \cdot OH$ are only known in solution, being made from the halides with silver oxide. **1962** P. J. & B. DURRANT *Introd. Adv. Inorg. Chem.* xxiii. 931 Diphenyliodonium hydroxide $[(C_6H_5)_2I]OH$. **1966** *Chem. Abstr.* LXV. 8872 (*heading*) Chemistry of heterocyclic iodonium compounds.

iodophor (əiˌōu·dǫf-, əi·ŏdǫfǭɹ). [f. IODO- + *-PHOR.] Any substance in which iodine is combined with a surface-active agent to render it more soluble and chemically stable in aqueous solution, and so more suitable for use (in solution) as a disinfectant.

1952 TERRY & SHELANSKI in *Mod. Sanitation & Building Maintenance* IV. 62/2 This combination of iodine with a carrier is called a halophor (or more specifically it could be referred to as an iodophor). **1962** *Lancet* 22 Dec. 1330/2 A convenient way of using iodine would be to employ an iodophor, which, incidentally, would add a little cleaning power to the water. **1963** *Surg., Gynecol. & Obstetr.* CXVI. 363 The iodophor solutions were all pleasant to use. They did not irritate the skin, eyes, or nasal passages. **1967** *Biol. Abstr.* XLVIII. 10833/1 The percentage dissociation of the iodine complex in 16 commercial iodophors at use dilution was calculated from the partition coefficients. **1972** *Dairy Sci. Abstr.* XXXIV. 205/2 The development and use of foamless iodophors, particularly for cleaning milking equipment..and in combatting mastitis when used as a teat dip.

iodoso(-) (əiŏdōu·so), used in *Chem.* as comb. form of IODOUS *a.* to indicate the presence of an IO— group in a compound, as in **iodo:sobe·nzene,** C_6H_5IO, a yellow amorphous powder which disproportionates to iodobenzene and iodoxybenzene, and explodes when heated. Also as quasi-*adj.*

1892 *Jrnl. Chem. Soc.* LXII. 1460 On heating the solution for some seconds, cooling, and pouring into water, a precipitate of iodosobenzoic acid, $C_7H_5IO_3$, separates. **1893** Iodosobenzene [see next]. **1893** *Jrnl. Chem. Soc.* LXIV. I. 508 All attempts to obtain iodoso-derivatives from meta- and para-iodobenzoic acid have been without success. **1935** *Ibid.* 1671 Other reactions of iodoso-compounds point to the vulnerability of their I–O link to addition. **1936** *Chem. Abstr.* XXX. 6662 (*heading*) Use of iodosobenzene in developers and emulsions. **1950** N. V. SIDGWICK *Chem. Elements* II. 1249 The iodoso-compounds are greyish-white, amorphous substances, with a very characteristic penetrating 'iodoso smell'. **1968** Iodosobenzene [see next].

iodoxy(-) (əiŏdǫ·ksi), *prefix.* [f. IOD- + OXY-2.] Used in chemical names to indicate the presence of the radical IO_2— (or, formerly, IO—), as in **i:odoxybe·nzene,** a compound, $C_6H_5IO_2$, forming colourless needles and obtained by disproportionation of iodosobenzene. Also as quasi-*adj.*

1865 *Jrnl. Chem. Soc.* XVIII. 308 A combustion made of the pure acid gave numbers leading to the formula of iodoxybenzoic acid $C_7H_5IO_3$. **1889** *Ibid.* LVI. 1150 The authors are inclined to regard it as an iodoxydiiodobenzene, $C_6H_3I_2 \cdot OI$. **1893** *Ibid.* LXIV. I. 506 Iodoxybenzene, $C_6H_5IO_2$, when treated with hydrochloric acid in aqueous solution, is converted into iodosobenzene hydrochloride. **1905** *Jrnl. Soc. Chem. Industry* 31 Jan. 104/1 (*heading*) Iodoxy compound (*p*-iodoxyphenol ester): and process of making same. **1935** *Jrnl. Chem. Soc.* 1669 The present summary of several of our investigations, dealing particularly with the iodoxy-group IO_2. **1950** N. V. SIDGWICK *Chem. Elements* II. 1251 The iodoxy-compounds hold their oxygen more firmly than the iodoso, and they are not such strong oxidizing agents. **1968** R. O. C. NORMAN *Princ. Org. Synthesis* xvi. 535 Iodoxybenzene may be obtained in over 90% yield by steam-distilling iodosobenzene to remove the iodobenzene formed by the disproportionation.

ion. Add: (Further examples.) In modern use, any individual atom, molecule, or group having a net electric charge (either positive or negative), whether in an electrolytic solution or not.

In the def. in Dict. *element* is to be understood in the sense 'component substance' (ELEMENT *sb.* 2), not 'chemical element'.

1834 W. WHEWELL *Let. to Faraday* 5 May in I. Todhunter *William Whewell* (1876) II. 182 For the two together you might use the term *ions.* **1834** FARADAY in *Phil. Trans. R. Soc.* CXXIV. 79 Finally, I require a term to express those bodies which can pass to the electrodes... I propose to distinguish these bodies by calling those anions which go to the anode of the decomposing body; and those passing to the cathode, cations; and when I have occasion to speak of these together, I shall call them ions. [*Note*] Since this paper was read, I have changed some of the terms which were first proposed. *Ibid.* 112 A body decomposable directly by the electric current, i.e. an electrolyte, must consist of two ions. *Ibid.*, Compound ions are not necessarily composed of electro-chemical equivalents of simple ions. For instance, sulphuric acid,

boracic acid, phosphoric acid, are ions, but not electrolytes, i.e. not composed of electro-chemical equivalents of simple ions. **1856** W. A. MILLER *Elem. Chem.* II. xviii. 1110 When a binary compound, such as a fused chloride, ..is submitted to electrolysis, the ions or components of the compound are separated at the respective electrodes in equivalent proportions. **1879** *Encycl. Brit.* VIII. 107/1 Sodium acetate and silver chloride are therefore electrolytes of which Ag, Cl, Na, $C_2H_3O_2$ are the respective ions. **1896** W. R. WHITNEY tr. *Le Blanc's Elem. Electrochem.* iii. 60 Only those substances conduct which are at least partly dissociated, and therefore the conductivity is due to the dissociated parts; to the latter, which were called by him the 'ions', Arrhenius ascribed electric charges. **1896** RUTHERFORD & THOMSON in *Phil. Mag.* XLII. 405 We have made..experiments with the view to seeing whether there is any polarization when a current of electricity passes through a gas; we have not, however, been able to satisfy ourselves of the existence of this effect. The absence of polarization implies, however, that the ions are able to give up their charges to the metal electrodes. **1899** RUTHERFORD in *Ibid.* XLVII. 112 The theory has been put forward that the rays in passing through the gas produce positively and negatively charged particles in the gas, and that the number produced per second depends on the intensity of the radiation and the pressure... The term ion was given to them from analogy with electrolytic conduction, but in using the term it is not assumed that the ion is necessarily of atomic dimensions; it may be a multiple or submultiple of the atom. **1927** N. V. SIDGWICK *Electronic Theory of Valency* vi. 91 In a crystal like calcium carbonate we find the same kind of relation between the calcium ion and the CO_3 ion, but a different one for the constituent atoms of the CO_3 group;..this may be taken as evidence that the calcium and the CO_3 are themselves ions, but that the atoms of the CO_3 group are covalently linked to one another. **1962** P. J. & B. DURRANT *Introd. Adv. Inorg. Chem.* xii. 346 An ionic crystal is one in which the units of crystal structure are the ions of a salt. **1967** *New Scientist* 30 Nov. 531/1 The normal electrode separation is less than 1 mm, so there is a very strong electric field which ionizes the gas atoms, giving ions and electrons.

2. Special Comb.: **ion beam**, a current of ions moving in a fixed direction; **ion bombardment**, the process of bombarding a surface with ions (usu. of an inert gas), so breaking up the surface, used to remove impurities; hence **ion-bombarded** *a.*; **ion burn**, the damaging of the phosphor of a cathode-ray tube by negatively ionized gas molecules produced by the electron beam and focused on to the screen; also, an ion spot so produced; **ion chamber**, an ionization chamber; **ion drive**, (*a*) = **ion propulsion*; (*b*) = **ion engine*; **ion engine**, a rocket engine that employs ion propulsion; **ion etching**, the controlled removal of extremely thin layers of material from the surface of an object by the use of an ion beam; **ion gun**, a device in which ions are produced (usu. by the ionization of a gas) and emitted in a beam; **ion implantation**, the implantation of ions in a crystalline material (see *IMPLANTATION 7); **ion pair**, (*a*) a pair of oppositely charged ions held together in a solution by electrostatic attraction; (*b*) a negative ion (or an electron) and a positive ion formed from a neutral atom or molecule by the action of radiation; **ion propulsion**, a mode of rocket propulsion in which thrust is produced by the ejection of ions produced inside the engine and accelerated by an electric field; **ion rocket**, (*a*) = **ion engine*; (*b*) a rocket in which an ion engine is the means of propulsion; **ion source**, a device for producing ions, *spec.* an ion gun; **ion spot**, (*a*) a dark spot in the middle of the screen of a cathode-ray tube where the phosphor is damaged as a result of ion burn; (*b*) a white spot in a television picture produced as a spurious signal when ionized gas molecules strike the target of a television camera tube; **ion trap**, a device designed to catch ions; *spec.* one in a cathode-ray tube or television camera tube that prevents ionized molecules from reaching the screen or the target and causing an ion spot. Also *ION EXCHANGE.

1932 *Physical Rev.* XL. 33 Intense high speed ion beams. **1951** *Jrnl. Brit. Interplanetary Soc.* X. 253 The acceleration of a space ship by an ion beam seems to offer no particular difficulties. **1970** *New Scientist* 5 Feb. 256/1 The ion beam, projected at a small area of the sample, consists of heavy, positively charged ions of inert gas, which remove atoms from the specimen's surface layers. **1959** *Jrnl. Chem. Physics* XXX. 926/2 The relative ease of removal of oxygen can therefore not be explained by the assumption that the ion-bombarded and annealed surface is partially oxygen contaminated. **1930** *Rev. Mod. Physics* II. 186 'Sputtering', or disintegration of an electrode subjected to positive ion bombardment is a well known and often troublesome phenomenon. **1952** *Trans. Faraday Soc.* XLVIII. 747 As a general procedure for cleaning surfaces, the inert gas ion-bombardment has some advantages: its main disadvantage is that there is sputtering of the metal on to the walls of the vessel. **1960** *Jrnl. Appl. Physics* XXXI. 1516 (*title*) Ion-bombardment etching of synthetic fibers. **1954** E. MOLLOY *Radio & Television Engineers' Ref. Bk.* xxiv. 27 The third technique of preventing ion burn is by protecting the screen with a layer of aluminium. **1956** [see *ion spot* below]. **1963** J. R. DAVIES *Understanding Television* ii. 62 Ion burns normally show up as brown circles an inch or so in diameter, the discoloration being greatest at the centre of the burn. In some cathode ray tubes, protection against ion burn is achieved by mounting part of the electron gun assembly at an angle, and..applying across the tube neck a fixed magnetic field which causes electrons only to be deflected across the screen. **1955** *Bull. Atomic Sci.* June 213/3 An ion chamber, however, is a device which directly measures the dose to the air volume it encloses. **1962** F. I. ORDWAY et al. *Basic Astronautics* iv. 121 Solar radiation intensities in the Lyman-alpha experiment were measured by a photo-sensitive ion chamber. **1958** C. C. ADAMS et al. *Space Flight* xiv. 346 Both rubidium and cesium have been considered as the propellant for the ion drive. **1960** *Aeroplane* XCVIII. 776/2 Ion-drive cannot be used in propelling space-vehicles from the Earth's surface because of their inherently low thrust. **1962** F. I. ORDWAY et al. *Basic Astronautics* x. 424 The three basic elements of the ion drive are the emitter, the accelerator, and the beam neutralizer. **1960** *Aeroplane* XCVIII. 776/2 (*heading*) Experimental ion engine. **1961** [see *ion rocket* below]. **1971** *Jrnl. Brit. Interplanetary Soc.* XXIV. 573 The use of pulsed plasma thrusters rather than ion engines for attitude control has..become a distinct possibility. **1965** *Chem. Abstr.* LXII. 3491 (*heading*) Ion etching: an effective method for the elimination of foreign layers in ultra vacuum. **1968** *Times* 13 Nov. 16/1 The inside appearance of a red blood cell has been revealed for the first time by the novel combination of two physical techniques, scanning electron microscopy and ion etching... Ion etching has so far been used chiefly to study the structure of metals. The specimen is bombarded with a stream of high energy ions and the inner structure of the material is revealed as successive layers are stripped off. **1970** *New Scientist* 5 Feb. 256/2 It has been possible to use ion etching to penetrate the cuticular layers of insects. **1952** *Jrnl. Brit. Interplanetary Society* XI. 179 Any rocket system requiring the conversion of electric to kinetic energy will require one or more ion guns. **1957** *Physical Rev.* CVII. 642/1 The performance of the spectrometers was tested with an electron gun and with an ion gun. **1967** *New Scientist* 30 Nov. 531/1 The apparatus..consists of two ion sources (ion guns) which direct beams of ions at shallow angles on to the centres of the faces of a disc-like sample of ceramic. **1965** *Nuclear Instruments & Methods* XXXVIII. 169 (*heading*) Doping of silicon by ion implantation. **1970** *Times* 23 Jan. 27/8 This makes a low-temperature method of doping the silicon, such as ion implantation, an attractive approach to..flexible circuit fabrication. **1970** *New Scientist* 15 Oct. Suppl. 16/1 In ion implantation, the necessary impurities are accelerated by an electric field to an energy sufficient to embed them into the silicon to the depth required. **1972** *Physics Bull.* Oct. 612/3 Ion implantation can be helpful in understanding already known damage centres by careful choice of bombarding isotope. **1933** *Jrnl. Amer. Chem. Soc.* LV. 477 The changes in the properties of the solvent..caused by the presence of undissociated (non-conducting) ion pairs will be neglected. **1941** *Proc. 7th Internat. Congr. Genetics* 246 At 0·01 r. per min. there is on the average only one ion pair produced in a sperm nucleus every 27 min. and since the ion pairs produced by γ-rays are rather far apart, it is now more difficult than ever to avoid the conclusion that individual mutations arise from individual ionizations and that there is no threshold intensity. **1963** B. FOZARD *Instrumentation Nucl. Reactors* ii. 13 When a charged particle of high energy is introduced into the sensitive volume of a gas ionisation detector it undergoes large numbers of ionising and exciting collisions... In suitable conditions the whole of this energy is expended within the sensitive volume. In such cases the total number of ion pairs produced is a direct measure of the particle energy. **1964** BLACK & WAGNER *Dynamic Path.* xi. 231 The different types of ionizing radiation produce the same fundamental change in matter, that is, the ejection of planetary electrons from atoms or molecules, leading to the formation of ion pairs. **1957** *Jrnl. Brit. Interplanetary Soc.* XVI. 233 A system which may ultimately utilize power from fusion is that of ion (or plasma) propulsion. *Ibid.*, Much serious attention is being given to the ion-propulsion problem in the U.S.A. **1966** *McGraw-Hill Encycl. Sci. & Technol.* VII. 245/2 The space charge represents one of the serious obstacles of any ion-propulsion system. **1949** *Jrnl. Brit. Interplanetary Soc.* VIII. 64 These techniques form the basis for what we shall here call the 'ion rocket', the jet of which might more correctly be termed an exhaust beam. **1951** *Ibid.* X. 248 The use of ion rockets as a means for propelling vehicles between satellite stations. **1953** *Ann. Reg. 1952* 406 The 'most feasible project' was described as consisting of space stations circling the most important planets with ion rockets plying between them. **1961** *Flight* LXXIX. 330/2 The earliest ion rockets to be considered for spaceflight will have a thrust of one-tenth of a pound and will be powered by 30kW SNAP-8 nuclear reactors after first-stage launch by Atlas-Centaur or Saturn C-1 boosters. Higher-powered ion engines (up to one megawatt) will also be considered. **1971** *Nature* 6 Aug. 357/1 What was called space technology—the design and operation of solar cells, ion rockets and the like. **1955** *Gloss. Terms Radiology (B.S.I.)* 43 *Ion source*, a device in which gas ions are produced, focused and accelerated, and emitted as a narrow beam. **1966** *McGraw-Hill Encycl. Sci. & Technol.* VII. 245/1 The ionizer or ion source converts the propellant from its original stored form to a system of charged corpuscles. **1967** Ion source [see *ion gun* above]. **1940** D. G. FINK *Princ. Television Engin.* viii. 341 If magneto-static focusing is used, the ion spot is spread over a much larger area (often the full area of the screen) and is much less troublesome, whether electric or magnetic deflection is used. **1953** AMOS & BIRKINSHAW *Television Engin.* I. v. 93 Spurious signals in the form of a white ion spot are eliminated by use of an ion-trap mesh situated close to the target. **1953** H. A. CHINN *Television Broadcasting* ii. 69 Occasionally, a white spot..may be observed in the center of the picture. Such a spot, especially if it is visible on the monitor with the camera lens capped, is probably an ion spot. **1956** M. SLURZBERG et al. *Essent. Television* x. 375 A concentrated bombardment of the fluorescent screen by the heavy ions produces a small brown circle in the centre of the picture screen, called an ion burn or ion spot. **1905** BRAGG & KLEEMAN in *Phil. Mag.* X. 321 An arrangement which we find to be of great importance is the ion-trap which is placed under the gauze of the ionization chamber. **1940** D. G. FINK *Princ. Television Engin.* viii. 342 The ion spot may..be eliminated by an ingenious construction in the electron gun known as an 'ion trap'. **1953** Ion-trap [see *ion spot* above]. **1954** E. MOLLOY *Radio & Television Engineers' Ref. Bk.* xxiv. 27 The successful operation of..ion traps depends upon the different paths followed by the electrons and negative ions under the action of magnetic fields. **1967** WHARTON & HOWORTH *Princ. Television Reception* iv. 59 A small permanent magnet known as the ion trap magnet was mounted on the neck of the tube to deflect the electrons so that they travelled axially and landed on the screen.

-ion, *suffix*[2], the ending of INION[1], proposed by P. Broca, 1875 (in *Bull. de la Soc. d'Anthrop. de Paris* X. 346), as a suffix for forming the names of other craniometric points (as *GNATHION, *GONION).

-ion, *suffix*[3], the word ION added to abbreviated forms of the names of elements and radicals to form the names of their ions, as *chlorion*, *HYDRION, *nitrion*, *sodion*.

-ion, *suffix*[4]. (See quot. and ALLIANCE *sb.* 6.)

1930 F. R. BHARUCHA tr. *Braun-Blanquet's Vocab. Plant Sociol.* 23 For designation of Alliances, the suffix '*-ion*' is added to the radical of the name of one of the principal associations of the alliance. Ex. *Ammophilion-Genisteto-Vaccinion.*

ionamine (əiˌǫ·nămīn). *Dye Chem.* Also **Ionamine.** [f. ION + AMINE.] Any of various [(arylazo)arylamino] methanesulphonates, $X \cdot N_2 \cdot Y \cdot NRCH_2SO_3Na$ (where X and Y are (substituted) benzene nuclei), formerly used as specific dyes for acetate silk.

1922 *Glasgow Herald* 24 Apr. 10 The 'ionamines' will have nothing to do with this homely fibre [*sc.* cotton]. They will only dye silk, either real or artificial. **1923** GREEN & SAUNDERS in *Jrnl. Soc. Dyers & Colourists* XXXIX. 12/1 Those Ionamines which are derived from primary amido compounds or contain free amido groups are capable of being diazotised upon the fibre, and in combination with various developers produce a wide range of shades from orange to scarlet, red, maroon, violet, blue and black. **1946** S. R. & E. R. TROTMAN *Bleaching, Dyeing & Chem. Technol. Textile Fibres* (ed. 2) 474 The chief advantages of the ionamines are (i) ready solubility, and (ii) miscibility with direct dyestuffs. **1971** R. L. M. ALLEN *Colour Chem.* i. 12 Systems in which the solubilising groups are eliminated by hydrolysis during or after dyeing have also been used in dyes such as the Ionamine (British Dyestuffs Corp.) and Neocotone..ranges, but these have now been superseded.

ionene (əi·ŏnīn). *Chem.* [ad. G. *ionen* (Tiemann & Krüger 1893, in *Ber. d. Deut. Chem. Ges.* XXVI. 2693), f. Gr. ἴον violet: see -ENE.] 1,1,6-Trimethyltetralin, $C_{13}H_{18}$; a bicyclic oily liquid obtained on elimination of a water molecule from α- or β-ionone.

1894 *Jrnl. Chem. Soc.* LXVI. I. 82 When heated with hydriodic acid and phosphorus, it [*sc.* ionone] loses water, and yields ionene, $C_{13}H_{18}$, which boils at 106–107° (10 mm.)... It resembles irene very closely. **1933** *Jrnl. Amer. Chem. Soc.* LV. 4680 That ionene is a true 1,1,6-trimethyltetralin is evidenced by its smooth sulphonation and nitration, and by the oxidation products obtained from ionene. **1960** *Jrnl. Chem. Soc.* 3128 *Ionene.*—This hydrocarbon was prepared in 53% yield from β-ionone.

ion exchange. The interchange of ions of like charge between an insoluble solid and a solution in contact with it. Freq. *attrib.* (usu. hyphenated), as **ion-exchange resin**, any synthetic resin or polymer suitable for use as an ion exchanger, characterized in general by a cross-linked molecular network which allows the penetration of solvent and ions (causing swelling) and has ionized or ionizable groups weakly attached to it.

1923 *Chem. Abstr.* XVII. 578 (*heading*) The ion exchange between the blood corpuscles and the serum. **1943** *Industr. & Engin. Chem.* Aug. 858 (*heading*) Ion exchange resins. New tools for process industries. **1946** *Jrnl. Amer. Leather Chemists' Assoc.* XLI. 555 The present work is an attempt to explore the possibilities of utilizing ion exchange resins in the analysis of some chromium liquors of various types. **1949** [see *ion exchanger* below]. **1950** *Sci. Amer.* Nov. 51/3 Ion exchange has provided a tool for fascinating studies of the constituents of cell nuclei—nucleic acids and nucleotides—which are so similar to one another that they are nearly impossible to separate by conventional means. **1951** J. E. MAUDRU in R. A. McGinnis *Beet-Sugar Technol.* x. 289 Ion exchange..is another type of juice purification which has recently been applied to the beet-sugar industry. This process consists of passing dilute juice..through beds of active synthetic resinous material, which removes ionized impurities. **1952** *Sci. News* XXVI. 83 Ion-exchange resins are usually marketed in the form of coarse or spherical granules, about 1–2 millimetres in diameter... The major use of these resins is in the complete removal of salts from water

by ion-exchange. **1963** *Guardian* 28 Feb. 18/1 The Government had decided to establish an experimental pilot plant to examine the problems in the removal of strontium 90 from milk by an ion-exchange process. **1964** *Oceanogr. & Marine Biol.* II. 149 The amino acid compositions of phytoplankton and pure cultures of phytoplanktonic species have been determined by paper chromatography and by ion-exchange chromatography.

Also **ion exchanger**, a solid involved or used in ion exchange; also, an apparatus for effecting ion exchange.

1941 *Jrnl. Franklin Inst.* CCXXXII. 317 It is possible ..that the characteristics of an ion exchanger are conditioned by the nature of the ion with which it was last saturated. **1949** H. F. Walton in F. C. Nachod *Ion Exchange* 4 In the materials which find practical use as ion exchangers, such as the synthetic aluminosilicates, synthetic resins, or sulfuric acid-treated coals, nearly all of the ion exchange takes place in the interior of the granules, which have a gel structure, something like a sponge on the molecular scale. **1950** *Sci. Amer.* Nov. 50/2 During the war compact little ion exchangers were used in life-raft emergency kits for making drinking water from sea water. **1960** R. Kunin *Elem. Ion Exchange* iii. 24 Only the zeolite minerals have a sufficiently satisfactory combination of the above-mentioned characteristics..to permit their use as ion exchangers on a commercial scale.

Ionic, *a.*[1] and *sb.* Add: **B.** *sb.* **4.** *Typogr.* A type face distinguished by prominent serifs and a high degree of legibility.

1842 H. Caslon *Specimen of Printing Types* in *Two Centuries of Typefounding* (Caslon Letter Foundry) (1920) 71 (*caption*) Diamond two-line Ionic. **1934** A. F. Johnson *Type Designs* viii. 205 Ionic in some cases appears to be only another name for Egyptian. **1954** *Archit. Rev.* CXVI. 119/1 Ionic, or Clarendon, is familiar to all readers of *The Architectural Review* as a type face. It can also be pleasing and useful as an architectural letter. **1970** W. P. Jaspert et al. *Encycl. Type Faces* (ed. 4) 121 The first Ionic was a bold face cut by Caslon and shown 1842... It has been revived as a suitable newspaper type... Linotype Ionic was introduced in 1926 in the *Newark Evening News*.

ionic, *a.*[2] Add to def.: composed of or containing ions; that is an ion. (Further examples.)

1913 *Q. Rev.* July 122 A knowledge of the total mass of water precipitated by the expansion enabled Mr. Wilson.. to estimate the number of ionic nuclei required to form the cloud. **1914** J. J. Thomson in *Phil. Mag.* XXVII. 761 Molecules of this type, which I shall call ionic molecules. **1936** *Discovery* June 197/2 A description of ionic clouds formed in electrolytes is given. **1936** *Jrnl. R. Aeronaut. Soc.* XL. 594 Experiments on ionic crystals have determined the weakening effect of minute cracks. **1962** [see *ion 1]. **1966** C. R. Tottle *Sci. Engin. Materials* ii. 33 Magnesium..will form an ionic compound with two chlorine atoms, $MgCl_2$, by donating its two 3*s* electrons, one to each of two chlorine atoms. The magnesium will be doubly charged (positive) and will therefore take up a position in the crystal lattice in which for each magnesium atom there are two chlorine atoms.

b. Brought about by, employing, or depending on ions; applied *spec.* to an electrovalent bond.

1907 *Brit. Med. Jrnl.* 14 Sept. 631/1 The study of ionic medication—the subject of Professor Leduc's paper —has been in many respects the most fruitful of modern times. **1910** E. R. Morton *Essent. Med. Electr. & Radiogr.* (ed. 2) v. 120 The advantages of the ionic method are very obvious... We can introduce a drug exactly where it is required. **1930** [see *heteropolar *a.* 3]. **1938** R. W. Lawson tr. *Hevesy & Paneth's Man. Radioactivity* (ed. 2) xxiv. 261 The phenomenon of the 'ionic wind'... When the air between the plates of an ionization chamber is ionized, then on applying an electric field the air between the plates is set in motion. **1939** L. Pauling *Nature Chem. Bond* i. 4 We describe the interactions in this crystal by saying that each ion forms ionic bonds with its six neighbors, these bonds combining all of the ions in the crystal into one giant molecule. **1958** C. C. Adams et al. *Space Flight* ix. 236 When atomic energy, ionic drive, and light beams have been harnessed for propulsion, combined perhaps with anti-gravity, flight to the stars may be possible. **1966** C. R. Tottle *Sci. Engin. Materials* vi. 127 In solid materials ionic conduction is strongly structure-sensitive, particularly with respect to impurities and flaws or defects in the lattice. **1972** *Physics Bull.* Nov. 651/3 The atomic bonding within the network is partly covalent, partly ionic.

ionically (əiˌǫ·nikăli), *adv.* [f. Ionic *a.*[2]: see -ically.] By means of ions or an ionic bond; as regards or in terms of ions.

1912 *Marconigraph* II. 340/1 The author's own observations on the influence of ordinary cloud on signals proved that the ionically turbulent belt was above the ordinary cloud level. **1925** H. H. U. Cross *Electro-Therapy & Ionic Medication* vi. 172 The efficacy of introducing drugs ionically depends..upon the fact that a drug introduced by ionic medication does not quickly pass out of the tissues which surround the point of introduction. **1965** Phillips & Williams *Inorg. Chem.* I. xv. 567 The electrical conductivity of liquid SO_2 has been commonly interpreted as due to the doubly-charged ions SO^{2+} and SO_3^{2-}, which would mean that a typical acid-base reaction would be written ionically as $SO^{2+} + SO_3^{2-} \rightarrow 2SO_2$. **1972** *Nature* 4 Feb. 262/1 The passage of dyes and small molecules between excitable cells which are ionically coupled has also been observed.

ionicity (əiˌǒni·siti). *Chem.* [f. Ionic *a.*[2]: see -icity.] Ionic character (in a chemical bond or a crystal).

1946 *Nature* 26 Oct. 592/2 The absence of a similar fall in the C—O bond-breaking energy passing from methyl to ethyl alcohol can be satisfactorily explained in terms of the increased ionicity of the C—O bond in ethyl alcohol relative to C—O in methyl alcohol. **1952** C. A. Coulson *Valence* v. 123 The asymmetry of charge, i.e. the polar character of the bond, sometimes called the degree of ionicity. **1960** *Nature* 13 Aug. 590/1 In discussions..regarding bonding in inorganic semiconducting (or insulating) crystals there seems to be some confusion between bond ionicity on one hand and charge separation effects due to electronegativity differences on the other. **1966** *Bull. Amer. Physical Soc.* XI. 187/1 The large hyperfine parameter for the NaCl structure is consistent with the expected greater ionicity.

ionium (əiˌōu·niŏm). *Chem.* [f. Ion + -ium: see quot. 1907.] A radioactive isotope of thorium with mass number 230, produced by the α-decay of uranium 234. Symbols Io, ^{230}Th.

1907 B. B. Boltwood in *Amer. Jrnl. Sci.* XXIV. 372 The name 'Ionium' is proposed for this new substance... This name is believed to be appropriate because of the ionizing action which it possesses in common with the other elements which emit α-radiations. **1930** *Engineering* 4 Apr. 461/2 The elements ionium and thorium were actually found to have the same chemical properties, though differing in mass. **1954** K. Rankama *Isotope Geol.* lxxxiii. 410 The age of deep-sea sediments younger than approximately $0{\cdot}5 \times 10^6$ years may be determined from their ^{230}Th (ionium) content. A plot of the ionium content against the depth in these sediments reveals the decay of the 80 000-year ^{230}Th, and from this graph the age of the sediment at a given depth may be calculated... This is the ionium method for dating deep-ocean sediments. **1970** *Geochim. et Cosmochim. Acta* XXXIV. 389 (*heading*) A system for detection of ionium, thorium and protactinium to date deep-sea cores.

ionizable (əi·ǒnəizăb'l), *a.* [f. Ioniz(e *v.*[2] + -able.] Capable of being ionized.

1907 *Jrnl. Chem. Soc.* XCII. ii. 560 In the haloid salts all the halogen is in an ionisable state. **1946** *Nature* 7 Sept. 325/2 One notable change in this edition is that the 1940 table of 'available' (ionizable) iron contents has been dropped. **1968** R. F. Steiner *Life Chem.* ii. 27 Each amino acid in the free state contains at least two ionizable sites. **1972** *Exper. Cell Res.* LXX. 122/1 The pI of the cells would..give information about the nature of ionisable groups present on the surface.

ionization[2] (əi:ǒnəizēi·ʃən). [f. Ion + -ization.] **1.** The state of being ionized, or the process of ionizing.

1891 G. F. Fitzgerald in *Rep. Brit. Assoc. Adv. Sci. 1890* 327, I object to the term dissociation as applied to the ions in an electrolyte... I would..appeal to both sides to adopt some neutral term such as 'ionisation' to express the state of ions in electrolytes. **1898** *Nature* 8 Dec. 142/1 The measurements of the ionisation produced by Röntgen rays in fourteen gases showed that the ionisation was connected with the chemical composition in a very simple manner. **1908** *Westm. Gaz.* 13 Mar. 2/1 Paulsen urges that the aurora is due to an immense ionisation of the upper layers of the air. **1926** A. S. Eddington *Internal Constitution of Stars* i. 10 In the actual conditions of a star the ionisation is not quite complete. **1938** R. W. Lawson tr. *Hevesy & Paneth's Man. Radioactivity* (ed. 2) i. 12 This kind of ionization of a gas, in which the ions initially produced gain sufficient energy by their acceleration in the electric field to produce fresh ions by collision, is called 'ionization by collision'. **1947** Glasstone *Elem. Physical Chem.* xiii. 422 It is essential to distinguish between 'dissociation' and 'ionization'... The term 'ionization' applies to the total number of ions, irrespective of whether they are free or are held in ion-pairs. **1962** *Newnes Conc. Encycl. Electr. Engin.* 161/2 The ionization of an atom by the removal of an outermost electron (or electrons) requires a definite amount of energy.

2. *Med.* = *cataphoresis a.

1908 *Practitioner* June 785 The modern zinc mercury ionisation treatment is a very definite way of directly applying powerful drugs to a diseased area. **1909** [see *iontophoresis]. **1934** E. P. Cumberbatch *Lect. Med. Electr.* iii. 32 Ionization is a form of treatment in which ions possessing therapeutic properties are made to migrate into the body by the agency of electro-motive force. **1944** E. B. Clayton *Electrotherapy* xi. 171 The patient should receive the ionisation reclining on a couch. **1960** B. Savage *Pract. Electrotherapy* iv. 63 Histamine ionization is used whenever there is need for a marked increase in local circulation.

3. *Comb.*: **ionization chamber**, an instrument for measuring the intensity of ionizing radiation by collecting and measuring the charge on the ions which the radiation produces in a volume of gas; **ionization constant** *Physical Chem.* = *dissociation constant* (*dissociation 2); **ionization current,** an electric current arising out of the movement, under the influence of an electric field, of ions and electrons produced in a gas; **ionization energy** = **ionization potential*; **ionization gauge,** an instrument for measuring the pressure in an evacuated vessel by ionizing the residual gas and measuring the resulting ionization current; **ionization potential,** the potential difference through which an electron must be accelerated in an electron impact experiment, or the energy required, to remove an electron in its lowest energy state from an atom or molecule of a gas.

1904 *Phil. Mag.* VIII. 721 In Rutherford's experiment ..the radioactive material was scattered over the floor of the ionization chamber. **1919** J. A. Crowther *Ions, Electrons & Ionizing Radiations* ii. 15 The gas under investigation is contained in a metal box which is connected to earth... The box and its electrodes forms what is known as an ionization chamber. **1945** *Electronic Engin.* XVII. 405 These experiments were carried out by means of ionization chambers, like most of the early investigations on cosmic rays. **1966** *McGraw-Hill Encycl. Sci. & Technol.* VI. 92/1 If the voltage is too low, the electron avalanche never builds up, and the [Geiger] counter operates only as an ionization chamber (a device which gives the total ionization produced in the gas) or proportional counter, in which the output pulses are much smaller. **1904** T. S. Moore in R. A. Lehfeldt *Electro-Chem.* I. ii. 101 For binary electrolytes, in comparing the ionisation-constants, we are comparing the concentration necessary to produce a given degree of dissociation. **1924** J. R. Partington in H. S. Taylor *Treat. Physical Chem.* I. xi. 538 The ionization constant of water..increases very rapidly at lower temperatures, passing through a maximum about 218°. **1972** Moeller & O'Connor *Ions in Aqueous Solutions* iv. 74 Inasmuch as numerical values for ionization constants are available for many weak acids and bases, it is possible to calculate ion concentrations in solutions containing these substances under a variety of conditions. **1902** *Phil. Mag.* IV. 375 The time taken to pass over 100 divisions of the scale is taken by a stop-watch. The rate of movement is a measure of the ionization-current between the plates. **1956** Hine & Brownell *Radiation Dosimetry* i. 18 The determination of dose in roentgens requires the measurement of an ionization current under saturation conditions. **1928** F. J. Fuchs tr. *Gerlach's Matter, Electr., Energy* v. 69 On account of its large diameter and high ionization energy.., this singly charged helium atom appropriates to itself very rapidly a second electron. **1940** Glasstone *Text-bk. Physical Chem.* i. 52 The ionization energy is the work required to remove an electron from its lowest level to infinity. **1973** *Sci. Amer.* Feb. 91/1 Each kind of atom has a different ionization energy depending on the number of protons, neutrons and electrons it has. **1934** *Physical Rev.* XLV. 611/2 The pressure within the vacuum chamber as recorded by an ionization gauge..is often less than 10^{-6} mm Hg. **1966** *McGraw-Hill Encycl. Sci. & Technol.* VII. 253/2 In another type of ionization gage, the gas is ionized by high-energy alpha particles emitted by a radioactive source such as radium. **1914** *Phil. Mag.* XXVIII. 753 (*heading*) Note on the ionization potential of mercury vapour. **1927** *Physical Rev.* XXIX. 287 The second ionization potential of lithium, the amount of work required in order to remove one further electron from the singly ionized lithium atom, Li^+, in the normal state 1S, has not been directly determined by the method of electron impact. **1935** J. N. Friend *Text-bk. Physical Chem.* II. viii. 362 Upon raising the P.D. still more, gaseous ionisation occurs, the lowest potential producing this being known as the ionisation potential. **1950** W. J. Moore *Physical Chem.* x. 262 The alkali metals have low ionization potentials; the inert gases, high ionization potentials. **1972** C. E. Brion in A. Maccoll *Mass Spectrometry* iii. 61 PES [*sc.* photoelectron spectroscopy] is a detector of direct photoionisation and as a result has proved to be the best and most prolific source of both inner and outer ionisation potentials.

ionize, *v.*[2] Add to def.: to produce ions in (a substance or medium). Also *absol.* (Further examples.)

1901 B. Blount *Pract. Electro-Chem.* i. 16 Solutions of moderate strength..behave as if a portion of the molecules were ionised and a portion were present as ordinary molecules. **1915** *Proc. R. Soc.* XCI. 485 The minimum energy required to ionise an atom of mercury is that acquired by an electron in passing through a fall of potential of 4·9 volts. **1916** *Physical Rev.* VIII. 386 None of the electrons emitted by the cathode are able to ionize until they have moved a fraction V_0/V of the distance toward the anode. **1927** N. V. Sidgwick *Electronic Theory of Valency* i. 10 Whenever an atom is ionized, whether by chemical combination, or by exposure under suitable conditions to the action of light, heat, or electricity, it gains or loses one or more electrons. **1947** *Sci. News* IV. 55 Through the action of various radiations the gas in this region is ionised, *i.e.*, split into electrically positive or negative particles. **1956** Hine & Brownell *Radiation Dosimetry* i. 2 Electromagnetic radiations, having energies above a few kev, ionize by virtue of the secondary electrons released when they are absorbed. **1963** C. A. McDowell *Mass Spectrometry* xii. 507 Electrons with sufficient energy can ionize molecules by the following process.

2. *intr.* To dissociate into ions; to become converted (wholly or partly) into ions.

1904 T. S. Moore in R. A. Lehfeldt *Electro-Chem.* ii. 130 Those di-acid bases which ionise in stages show the same relation between the first and second ionisation as the dibasic acids. **1930** Field & Weill *Electro-Plating* vii. 92 Copper sulphate ionises as follows: $CuSO_4 \rightleftarrows Cu^{\cdot\cdot} + SO_4^{--}$. **1966** *McGraw-Hill Encycl. Sci. & Technol.* VI. 60/1 At..the breakdown voltage, the nearly conducting gas ionizes and becomes a good conductor, and a self-sustained discharge is established. **1968** R. O. C. Norman *Princ. Org. Synthesis* ii. 63 There is an increase in stabilization energy when acetic acid ionizes.

3. *Med.* (*trans.*) **a.** To introduce (a substance) *into* tissue by means of medical ionization. **b.** To treat by medical ionization.

1909 *Lancet* 13 Mar. 756/2 If a person ionises cocaine into himself..the skin becomes anæsthetic. *Ibid.*, I have placed under the microscope a piece of skin ionised with calcium. **1913** H. L. Jones *Ionic Medication* iii. 84 They [*sc.* corns] should have a thorough preliminary soaking.., and then may be ionized. **1936** J. N. Dyson *Pract. Ionization* iv. 51 For certain reasons the ulcer was ionized

in two parts. **1949** *Brit. Jrnl. Physical Med.* XII. 144/2 Penicillin was 'ionized' into the skin covering the paronychia.

Hence **i·onized** *ppl. a.*; **i·onizing** *vbl. sb.* and *ppl. a.*; † *ionizing potential* = *ionization potential* (s.v. *IONIZATION[2] 3); *ionizing radiation*, radiation which produces ionization in matter through which it passes.

1899 *Nature* 30 Nov. 114/1 The only ionising inorganic solvents hitherto found in addition to water are nitric acid and liquefied ammonia. **1902** *Phil. Mag.* IV. 704 The ionization observed in gases may be due..to the emission of an ionizing radiation from the walls of the containing vessel. **1914** *Proc. R. Soc.* A. XC. 398 It appeared to be of interest to measure the ionising potential for negative corpuscles under experimental conditions somewhat different from those previously adopted. **1919** J. A. CROWTHER (*title*) Ions, electrons, and ionizing radiations. *Ibid.* v. 52 We have already seen..that the current through an ionized gas increases with increasing electric field up to a certain maximum value known as the saturation current. **1924** S. DUSHMAN in H. S. Taylor *Treat. Physical Chem.* II. xvi. 1110 This accounts for the production of arcs in gases at voltages below the ionizing potential. **1935** *Brit. Jrnl. Radiol.* VIII. 479 The Hospital Physicist is required to measure ionising radiations covering the vast range of intensities from many röntgens per second down to comparatively weak intensities. **1935** *Discovery* Mar. 76/2 It was clear that the sun is the ionising agent. **1937** *Ibid.* Jan. 5/2 (*caption*) The transmitter sends out 50 pulses per second, which after travelling to the ionised layers are reflected and received by the receiver. **1956** A. H. COMPTON *Atomic Quest* 42 He had perfected to a high degree the Geiger counters that have become so valuable for measuring ionizing radiations. **1969** R. & E. BRECHER *Rays* xxvi. 416 Of special interest during the 1960's were the studies of what happens when ionizing radiation is absorbed by human cells. **1970** D. W. TURNER et al. *Molecular Photoelectron Spectroscopy* i. 2 This instrument possessed the advantage of..intimate juxtaposition of ionizing region and analyser entrance slit.

ionizer (əi·ǒnəizəɹ). [f. prec. + -ER[1].] That which produces ionization.

1901 *Smithsonian Contrib. Knowl.* No. 1309. 27 Instead of a single tube, two or more ionizers..are used simultaneously, each of them being charged with phosphorus. **1905** *Phil. Mag.* X. 207 An α particle is nearly twice as efficient an ionizer as the electron at its maximum efficiency. **1933** *Discovery* Apr. 107/2 This recoiling nucleus, on the other hand, is an efficient ionizer. **1967** S. W. TROMP et al. *Biometeorol.* II. ii. 1025 Unavoidable by-production of chemical compounds, and poor knowledge of ion distribution around emitting electrodes, have largely hampered the design and practical use of electrical ionizers. *Ibid.*, Sufficient ion concentration can be achieved in the centre of a room by inconspicuous ionizers.

iono- (əi·ǒno-, əiˌǫ·no-), used as comb. form of (*a*) ION, (*b*) *IONOSPHERE.

ionogen (əi·ǒnodʒěn, əiˌǫ·nodʒěn). *Physical Chem.* [f. *IONO- + -GEN 1.] Any compound which exists as ions when dissolved in a solvent.

1906 A. SMITH *Introd. Gen. Inorg. Chem.* xvii. 296 The substances of the three classes which alone are ionized may be designated ionogens... The electrolytic property of ions is only one amongst many special properties of electrolytes, and the majority of these properties are chemical and have nothing to do with electrolysis. Hence we have preferred the more general word 'ionogen'. **1922** *Chem. Abstr.* XVI. 1890 (*heading*) Nature of the ionogen linkage. **1935** J. N. FRIEND *Text-bk. Physical Chem.* II. vii. 217 The undissociated molecules and the ions of an ionogen in aqueous solution constitute a system in equilibrium. **1943** *Gloss. Terms Electr. Engin.* (*B.S.I.*) 91 The term 'ionogen' has been suggested as an alternative to the term 'electrolyte' when used with this meaning [*sc.* a substance which, when dissolved in a specified solvent, produces a conducting medium].

ionogenic (əiˌǫ:nodʒe·nik), *a. Chem.* [f. *IONO- + *-GENIC.] † **a.** [ad. G. *ionogen* (O. Hinsberg 1911, in *Jrnl. f. prakt. Chem.* LXXIV. 179).] Of an atom or radical: promoting ionization elsewhere in the molecule of which it forms part. *Obs.*

1912 *Chem. Abstr.* VI. 351 (*heading*) Ionogenic atomic groups and atoms.

b. Capable of being ionized chemically.

1922 J. LOEB *Proteins & Theory Colloidal Behavior* ii. 34 If we wish to prepare gelatin or casein free from ionogenic impurities, we must bring these proteins..to the isoelectric point and then wash them. **1955** *Federation Proc.* XIV. 735/1 The electrophoretic mobility of a given protein is a function of the net electric charge and hence of the number of ionogenic groups. **1967** *Jrnl. Cell. Physiol.* LXIX. 287/1 It appears likely..that ionogenic groups of RNA, i.e. phosphate groups, are present at the electrokinetic surfaces of the two cell types. **1972** *Materials & Technol.* V. x. 275 Of the water-soluble surface-active agents.., some undergo ionization when dissolved in water whereas others do not ionize. On this basis, they are divided into two broad groups, namely ionogenic, or ion-forming, and non-ionogenic.

ionogram (əiˌǫ·nogræm). [f. *IONO- + -GRAM.] **1.** A record of radio pulses received by an ionosonde following their reflection by the ionosphere.

1955 *Sci. Amer.* Sept. 128/2 To make an ionosonde record (ionogram) the transmitter and receiver are tuned rapidly through a range of frequencies. The echoes received are displayed on a cathode ray oscilloscope and photographed. **1963** *Times* 15 Feb. 7/7 Some 70,000 'ionograms'—graphs of frequency against depth of reflection below the satellite—have so far been obtained and are of good quality. **1967** *Encycl. Dict. Physics* Suppl. II. 240 The resulting 'ionogram', showing time delay as a function of frequency, can be interpreted as electron density as a function of 'virtual height' in the atmosphere.

2. *Chem.* The result of an ionographic separation, usually a series of spots or bands on the support medium.

1955 *Federation Proc.* XIV. 736/2 To determine the location of the various zones on an ionogram occupied by the individual components of a mixture, a number of procedures have been developed. **1963** *Proc. 17th World Veterinary Congr.* II. 1107 The ionogram of serum represents the electrolytic compounds of extracellular fluid in dogs. **1970** *Biol. Abstr.* LI. 354/1 Pre- and post-operational ionograms should be examined, in patients with a funnel-shaped deformation of the thorax.

ionography (əiˌǒnǫ·grăfi). *Chem.* [f. *IONO- + -GRAPHY.] The migration of ions or charged colloidal particles in a buffer solution held on a support (usu. filter paper) under the influence of an electric field, esp. as used to separate the components of a mixture; = *electrochromatography* (s.v. *ELECTRO-).

1950 H. J. McDONALD et al. in *Science* 25 Aug. 228/1 It is suggested that the term *ionography* be used to describe the technique. *Ibid.* 228/2 The isoelectric point of proteins can be determined, and..amino acids and proteins can be separated by ionography. **1955** *Federation Proc.* XIV. 736/2 Although paper has been used as the stabilizer in over 95% of the published articles on ionography, the use of starch has been found to have certain advantages in special cases. **1957** *Texas Rep. Biol. & Med.* XV. 235 An investigation into the lipoprotein levels of serum from patients was undertaken, using the technique of ionography.

Hence **ionogra·phic** *a.*, of or pertaining to ionography.

1955 *Federation Proc.* XIV. 733/1 The term 'ionographic apparatus' will refer to the instrument used in carrying out ionographic separations. **1968** *Compar. Biochem. & Physiol.* XXV. 727 The ionographic properties of the hemoglobins from ten species of *Peromyscus* have been compared.

ionomer (əiˌǫ·nǒməɹ). [f. *IONO- + *-MER.] Any of a class of thermoplastics in which there is ionic bonding between the polymer chains.

1964 *Mod. Plastics* Sept. 98/1 E. I. du Pont de Nemours & Co. Inc. has finally announced the introduction of an exciting new transparent thermoplastic it calls 'ionomer'. *Ibid.* 98/2 The tensile strength of many grades of ionomers is higher than that of any commercial polyolefin. **1967** H. F. MARK et al. *Encycl. Polymer Sci. & Technol.* VI. 395 Another class of copolymers with exceptional properties are the ionomers, which are essentially the metal salts of ethylene-acrylic acid copolymers. The resulting ionic bonding makes these materials a special class. **1967** *Times Rev. Industry* May 76/2 Among the newer plastics materials offered for use in packaging are ionomer and ethylene/vinyl acetate (EVA) films for meat and other retail produce.

ionone (əi·ǒnōᵘn). *Chem.* [ad. G. *ionon* (Tiemann & Krüger 1893, in *Ber. d. Deut. Chem. Ges.* XXVI. 2693), f. Gr. ἴον violet + -ONE.] **a.** Either of two liquids (*α-ionone* and *β-ionone*) that are used in perfumery for their strong odour of violets and are isomeric cyclic ketones, $(CH_3)_3C_6H_6CH{:}CH{\cdot}CO{\cdot}CH_3$, differing only in the position of the double bond in the C_6H_6 ring.

Ionone is a proprietary name in the U.S.

1894 *Jrnl. Chem. Soc.* LXVI. I. 82 When pseudoionone is heated with dilute sulphuric acid and a little glycerol, it is converted into the isomeric ionone... This substance boils at 126–128° at 12 mm. **1900** *Ibid.* LXXVIII. II. 375 In order to separate and detect the α- and β-ionone, the crude ketones are boiled with a little alcohol and an aqueous solution of sodium sulphite. **1929** *Encycl. Brit.* VIII. 721/1 Ionone, derived from citral isolated from oil of lemongrass,..is the basis of all violet scents, and perhaps the most important of all synthetic perfumes. **1943** *Jrnl. Amer. Chem. Soc.* LXV. 2062/2 The resolution of *dl*-α-ionone was accomplished by means of *l*-menthydrazone. **1957** T. MOORE *Vitamin A* x. 100 The synthesis of vitamin A from β-ionone obviously requires the formation of a longer side chain to the trimethylcyclohexenyl ring. **1971** *New Scientist* 6 May 351/2 The pleasant-smelling ionones are breakdown products of carotenoids.

b. *ψ*-**ionone** (*pseudoionone*), $C_{13}H_{20}O$, a third isomer which can be cyclized to form α- and β-ionones.

1897 *Jrnl. Chem. Soc.* LXXII. I. 538 Ionone is..easily prepared by the action of sulphuric acid on *ψ*-ionone, the latter substance being produced from geranaldehyde by condensation with acetone. **1969** W. TEMPLETON *Introd. Chem. Terpenoids & Steroids* iii. 46 Similarly *ψ*-ionone.., obtained by condensation of citral with acetone, cyclizes under acidic conditions to α- and β-ionones, which are found in Nature.

ionophone (əiˌǫ·nofōᵘn). [f. *IONO- + *-PHONE.] A type of loudspeaker using the vibrations of a volume of ionized air in place of those of a diaphragm.

1955 *Sci. News Let.* 23 July 63/3 The vibrating pocket of air in the new loud speaker, called the Ionophone, will create the sound without this setback, the designers say. **1962** A. NISBETT *Technique Sound Studio* 257 *Ionophone*, a type of loudspeaker which has no moving parts.

ionophore (əiˌǫ·nofōəɹ). *Biol.* [f. *IONO- + -PHORE.] An agent which is able to transport ions across a lipid membrane in a cell. So **ionopho·rous** *a.*

1967 B. C. PRESSMAN et al. in *Proc. Nat. Acad. Sci.* LVIII. 1954 It is our conclusion that both the valinomycin and the nigericin classes of antibiotics induce alkali ion permeability in mitochondrial and other systems by carrying ions across lipid barriers as lipid-soluble complexes. Accordingly we propose to classify them generically as ionophores or ionophorous agents. **1970** *Jrnl. Biol. Chem.* CCXLV. 5606 (*heading*) Effect of nucleotides on the transport of alkali metal cations catalyzed by ionophorous antibiotics across mitochondrial membranes. **1971** *Nature* 5 Nov. 12/2 Cyclic peptides such as gramicidin-S or alamethecin which can act as ionophores ..in membranes.

ionophoresis (əiˌǫ:nofǒrī·sis). *Biochem.* [f. *IONO- + *-PHORESIS.] The migration of ions in solution under the influence of an electric field, esp. as used to separate the components of a mixture. Hence **io:nophore·tic** *a.*

1945 *Adv. Protein Chem.* II. 31 We propose to use *ionophoresis* to describe processes concerned with the movement in an electric field of relatively small ions, *electrophoresis* for movement of large molecules and particles. *Ibid.* (*heading*), Ionophoretic methods. **1949** ABRAHAM & HEATLEY in H. W. Florey et al. *Antibiotics* I. ii. 106 An apparatus in which ionophoretic separation takes place in a slab of silica jelly, the substances under investigation being inlaid in a gutter at right angles to the length of the slab. **1956** *Nature* 25 Feb. 393/2 A number of primary aliphatic amines can readily be separated.. by ionophoresis on paper at *p*H 7 using collidine acetate buffer, and the spots revealed with ninhydrin. **1967** *Biol. Abstr.* XLVIII. 895/2 (*heading*) Detection of metal cations in soil by chromatographic and ionophoretic techniques. **1971** *European Jrnl. Biochem.* XIX. 125/1 Ionophoresis in the second dimension was carried out on an 85×45 cm sheet of DEAE-cellulose paper..in 7% formic acid.

ionosonde (əiˌǫ·nosǫnd). [f. *IONO- + *SONDE.] An instrument for obtaining information about the ionosphere by transmitting a succession of radio pulses into it at different frequencies and recording their echoes.

1955 *Sci. Amer.* Sept. 128/2 The instrument used to explore the ionosphere is called an ionosonde. **1962** *Flight International* LXXXI. 681/2 The 95 (US) tons of water ballast was released by explosion of the vehicle at a height of about 65 miles 160 sec after lift-off, and a large white cloud of ice particles was formed... Observations were made by ground-based cameras, aircraft at various altitudes, ground radars and ionosondes. **1971** *New Scientist* 18 Mar. 598/2 Reflections of a swept-frequency pulse of radio waves by the ionosphere—the ionosonde technique—provide information about the distribution and density of its constituent electrons. **1972** *Science* 5 May 464/1 Lightweight ionosondes have been placed in satellites.

ionosphere (əiˌǫ·nǒsfīəɹ). [f. *IONO- + *-SPHERE.] A region of the outer atmosphere, beginning at a height of 50–80 km. (30–50 miles), which contains many ions and free electrons and is capable of reflecting radio waves; also, a corresponding region above other planets.

1926 R. A. WATSON-WATT *Let.* 8 Nov. in *Nature* (1969) 13 Dec. 1096/1 We have in quite recent years seen the universal adoption of the term 'stratosphere'..and.. the companion term 'troposphere'... The term 'ionosphere', for the region in which the main characteristic is large scale ionisation with considerable mean free paths, appears appropriate as an addition to this series. **1929** —— in *Q. Jrnl. R. Meteorol. Soc.* LV. 278, I have suggested the name ionosphere to make the systematic group troposphere, stratosphere, ionosphere, but meanwhile the term 'upper conducting layers' seems to hold the field. **1932** E. V. APPLETON in *Jrnl. Inst. Electr. Engin.* LXXI. 642 (*heading*) Wireless studies of the ionosphere. [*Note*] This is a convenient term, suggested by Mr R. A. Watson Watt, connoting the ionized regions of the upper atmosphere. **1934** *Times* 23 Feb. 20/2 Beyond lies the ionosphere, and of the layers in this we learn from the paths of radio-waves. **1947** *Sci. News* IV. 55 Sir Edward Appleton, whom one might call the Master of the Ionosphere, distinguishes in it the following layers: the complex F-layer 250 kilometres (150 miles) above the earth (also called the Appleton layer), the E- or Heaviside layer at about 100 km., and further down the D layer which is little noticeable in normal times, but whose ionisation is considerably increased as long as a solar flare is visible. **1955** *Times* 15 June 5/5 The ionosphere, a belt of gases ionized.. by ultra violet rays from the sun and lying between 70km. and 300–400km. above the earth, makes medium and short wave radio propagation possible by reflecting signals back to earth. **1959** DAVIES & PALMER *Radio Stud. Universe* iv. 66 This is difficult to explain if Jupiter is surrounded by an ionosphere similar to the Earth's. **1973** *Physics Bull.* Feb. 93/3 Spacecraft observations of the ionospheres of Venus and Mars.

ionospheric (əiˌǫ:nosfe·rik), *a.* [f. prec. + -IC.] Of, pertaining to, or involving the ionosphere.

1933 *Proc. Physical Soc.* XLV. 673 (*heading*) On two

methods of ionospheric investigation. **1937** *Discovery* Jan. 3/2 (*heading*) The base hut in Brandy Bay..with the wireless and ionospheric research masts behind. **1955** *Sci. News Let.* 28 May 339 Most of the radio frequency power in the new method is lost, but some is scattered by the lower part of the E region... This portion is received hundreds of miles away by high-gain antennas aimed at the exact spot. The system is called either forward scatter, or FPIS, for forward propagation by ionospheric scatter. **1958** *Times* 8 Nov. 4/7 Assurances that the ionospheric forward-scatter radio station..will not represent a radiation hazard to the public have now been given officially. **1966** *Electronics* 3 Oct. 181 Boelkow has designed a fixed-wing rocket—intended for ionospheric studies—that can be recovered from 48 miles.

Hence **io:nosphe·rically** *adv.*, by the ionosphere.

1955 *Proc. IRE* XLIII. 1174 Ionospherically propagated waves. **1971** *Nature Physical Sci.* 5 Apr. 125/1 There is no fading such as occurs in ionospherically reflected sky waves.

ionospherist (əiˌǫ:nosfe·rist). *rare.* [f. as prec. + -IST 4 b.] One who studies the ionosphere. Also **io:nosphe·ricist**, in the same sense.

1933 *Proc. R. Soc.* A. CXLI. 715, I should be most disappointed if time permitted only those whom I might call the professional ionospherists to take part in the discussion. **1955** *Jrnl. Brit. Interplanetary Soc.* XIV. 19 Moving concentrations of electrons account for the other main type of irregularity [in the ionosphere]; ionospherists seem never to grow tired of studying them. **1971** *Nature* 1 Jan. 15/3 The angle of arrival of radio waves is determined by ionosphericists using spaced receivers.

ionotropy (əiǒnǫ·trǒpi). *Chem.* [f. *IONO- + Gr. -τροπ-ία turning (f. τρέπειν to turn) + -Y³.] **1.** Tautomerism or tautomeric change, regarded as occurring through the detachment of an ion from the molecule concerned followed by a redistribution of the charge in the resulting molecular ion and reattachment of the ion to a different part of it. *rare.*

[**1926** T. M. LOWRY in *Inst. Internat. de Chimie Solvay: Deuxième Conseil de Chimie..1925..Rapports et Discussions* 151 Les transformations dans lesquelles des radicaux autres que l'hydrogène se déplacent peuvent..être formulées comme comportant une *migration d'ions* et peuvent être désignées sous le terme d'*ionotropie*.] **1928** *Ann. Rep. Progr. Chem. 1927* XXIV. 107 Lowry has also used the word 'ionotropy' (Report of the Second Solvay Conference 1925, p. 182). **1955** *Chem. Abstr.* XLIX. 40 Reactions of acids and bases can be described by assuming the fundamental reaction of 'ionotropy'.

2. [ad. G. *ionotropie* (H. Thiele 1947, in *Naturwiss.* XXXIV. 123/2.] The ordering of particles in a gel that results when an electrolyte is added to a colloidal suspension.

1949 *Chem. Abstr.* XLIII. 4539 Usually the sign of the ionotropy is the same as that of flow anisotropy. **1958** *Jrnl. Physical Chem.* LXII. 1277/1 The phenomenon of ionotropy can be simply demonstrated by placing a thin layer of 2% suspension of salt-free Wyoming bentonite on a glass slide and then placing a crystal of sodium chloride on the layer of suspension.

Hence **ionotro·pic** *a.*, exhibiting ionotropy (sense *2).

1944 *Handbk. Descr.* in *Chem. & Chem. Engin.* (U.S. Manpower Comm.) Nov. 66 Polarity, ionotropic change and conjugation. **1954** H. THIELE in *Discussions Faraday Soc.* XVIII. 295 Since ionotropic gels are formed by chemical or electrical forces the degree of order decreases with decreasing dissociation of the ionic groups of the colloid particles. **1969** *Jrnl. Biomed. Materials Res.* III. 432 The ordered ionotropic structure of the fibers of the polyelectrolyte directs the mineralization and calcification in the same manner as in biological tissue.

iontophoresis (əiˌǫn:tofǒrī·sis). *Med.* [f. Gr. ἰοντ-, ἰόν pr. pple. of ἰέναι to go + -O + *-PHORESIS.] = *CATAPHORESIS a.

1909 *Lancet* 13 Mar. 756/1 By medical ionisation, or, as it is called abroad..'iontophoresis', we mean the introduction of ions of different sorts into the tissues of the human body. **1937** *New Eng. Jrnl. Med.* 5 Aug. 202/2 Iontophoresis is a term used for denoting the act of driving negatively or positively charged ions into the subcutaneous tissues by means of a galvanic or direct current of electricity. **1949** A. HUXLEY *Let.* 26 Feb. (1969) 591 Dr Gustav Erlanger..has developed a method for treating the eyes by iontophoresis and gets remarkable results. **1971** *Jrnl. Physiol.* CCXV. 199 DNP and other metabolic inhibitors were tested on cortical neurones by iontophoresis from micropipettes.

Hence **io:ntophore·tic** *a.*, of, pertaining to, or employing iontophoresis; **io:ntophore·tically** *adv.*, by means of iontophoresis.

1937 *New Eng. Jrnl. Med.* 5 Aug. 204/1 The changes were not of sufficient degree to make us feel that the iontophoretic administration of acetyl β-methylcholine produced constant changes in the blood-sugar level. **1947** ABRAMOWITSCH & NEOUSSIKINE *Treatm. by Ion Transfer* iii. 68 Novocain was introduced iontophoretically. **1955** *Jrnl. Investigative Dermatol.* XXV. 223 It seemed logical to first find out whether or not the thorium X..could be introduced into a test material by the galvanic iontophoretic current. **1964** D. M. GORDON *Med. Managem. Ocular Dis.* iv. 20 Many of the systemic preparations can be..administered iontophoretically. **1971** *Jrnl. Cell. Physiol.* LXXVII. 339/2 Iontophoretic application of materials was accomplished by connecting a variable voltage source with a micropipette containing the material. **1972** *Science* 5 May 515/1 The ACh was applied iontophoretically by a micropipette containing a 4M solution of ACh chloride.

Iowan (əi·ŏwăn), *sb.* and *a.* Also formerly **Iowaian** (from the pronunciation *Ioway* of *Iowa*, which is still heard). [f. *Iowa*, name of one of the United States of America, formerly of a tribe of Indians inhabiting Iowa and Minnesota.] **A.** *sb.* A native or inhabitant of Iowa.

c **1848** W. WHITMAN in *Amer. Speech* (1961) XXXVI. 297 Iowans *Gophers*. **1856** N. H. PARKER *Iowa as it Is* 56 Our ferry is busy all hours in passing over the large canvas-backed wagons, densely populated with becoming Iowaians. **1928** *Glasgow Herald* 6 Apr. 12 Iowans..used to console themselves by telling the world..that their largest city had the greatest consumption of ice-cream per head of population. **1964** MRS. L. B. JOHNSON *White House Diary* 21 Nov. (1970) 208 Just enough places for the Iowans and the kinfolks.

B. *adj.* Of, pertaining to, or designating what was formerly considered the fourth Pleistocene glaciation of North America, but which is now considered the earliest phase of the Wisconsin glaciation. Also *absol.*, the Iowan glaciation or the deposits it produced.

1894 J. GEIKIE *Gt. Ice Age* (ed. 3) xlii. 756 It may..be the equivalent of the next later formation—the East-Iowan. *Ibid.* 760 The East-Iowan till-sheet..is not usually bordered by any definite terminal moraine. *Ibid.*, The designation 'East-Iowan formation' is chosen because it has been most carefully worked out by Mr. McGee in north-eastern Iowa. **1896**, etc. [see *ILLINOIAN *a.*]. **1968** R. W. FAIRBRIDGE *Encycl. Geomorphol.* 292/2 In the Wisconsin phase, the Iowan Lobe was considerably smaller.

ipecacuanha. 5. *ipecacuanha lozenge* (examples).

1847 F. A. KEMBLE *Let.* 7 Mar. in *Rec. Later Life* (1882) III. 173, I..am swallowing ipecacuanha lozenges by the gross. **1926–7** *Army & Navy Stores Catal.* p. xlix, Ipecacuanha lozenges.

ipid (i·pid, əi·pid), *sb.* and *a.* [a. mod.L. *Ipidæ*, f. Gr. ἰπ-, ἴψ woodworm.] **a.** *sb.* A bark-beetle of the family Ipidæ, which is now included in the Curculionidæ. **b.** *adj.* Of or pertaining to a beetle of this type. Cf. *SCOLYTID.

1866 E. C. RYE *Brit. Beetles* xii. 100 The Ipides have a single lobe to the maxillæ. **1922** W. M. WHEELER *Soc. Life Insects* 40 The females of the Ipid ambrosia beetles carry the fungus in the fore part of the stomach.

ipiti (i·piti). *S. Afr.* Also **impiti, ipiete.** [Zulu *i-mpiti*.] The blue duiker, *Cephalophus monticola*, the smallest South African antelope.

1836 R. M. MARTIN *Hist. S. Afr.* I. iv. 138 They [*sc.* the 'Caffres'] display considerable taste in the arrangement of their dress, particularly for the head, which is covered by a turban made of the skin of the '*ipiete*', a species of antelope. **1878** T. J. LUCAS *Camp Life & Sport S. Afr.* viii. 101 Immediately around Pietermaritzberg the game is comparatively scarce, consisting principally of the small Ipite Bok, a graceful little antelope. **1879** R. J. ATCHERLEY *Trip to Boerland* 26, I shot a few small buck known as *impiti*..not much larger than a hare. **1905** D. BLACKBURN *Richard Hartley* xiii. 244 The beautiful little ipiti, no bigger than a toy-terrier and quite as sprightly and alert. **1926** R. LYDEKKER *Game Animals Afr.* (ed. 2) 143 (*heading*) Blue Buck or Blue Duiker... Ipiti, Zulu. **1934** B. I. BUCHANAN *Pioneer Days Natal* ii. 33 Twice we saw some of the fairy bucks—the darling little ipiti—which immediately won our hearts.

ipoh (ī·pǫ). Also **Ipoh.** [Malay.] The upas tree, *Antiaris toxicaria*, or a creeping shrub, *Strychnos ignatii*, both of which are native to SE. Asia and have a poisonous sap; also, the poison itself.

1779 T. FORREST *Voy. New Guinea* I. xviii. 369 They [*sc.* the Sooloos] are acquainted with a subtle poison called Ippoo, the juice of a tree, in which they dip small darts. **1820** J. CRAWFURD *Hist. Indian Archipelago* I. iv. 468 The Malays call this last [shrub] *Ipoh*. **1836** J. LOW *Diss. Soil & Agric. Penang* iv. 206 Many arrows tipped with Ipoh were given to me by the different tribes in Perak. **1839** T. J. NEWBOLD *Pol. & Statistical Acct. Straits of Malacca* I. vii. 444 The Upas tree of the Javanese, or the Ipoh of the Malays, is found though rarely in the forests. *Ibid.* II. xii. 211, I had the greatest difficulty to prevail on one of this wild race to part with..a small quantity of the ipoh poison. **1907** *Q. Rev.* July 190 The poison for their arrows is obtained from the ipoh or upas tree. **1958** J. SLIMMING *Temiar Jungle* v. 78 The poison with which the darts are smeared is a mixture of the saps from the Ipoh tree and the Ipoh creeper. **1965** C. SHUTTLEWORTH *Malayan Safari* ii. 27 Perhaps the most dangerous poison is found in the sap of the ipoh tree from which the aborigines obtain poison for their blowpipe darts.

iproniazid (əiprǫnəi·ăzid). *Pharm.* [f. *i*(*so*)-*pro*(*pyl* (s.v. Iso- b) + *ISO)NIAZID (iproniazid being the isopropyl derivative of isoniazid).] A derivative of isoniazid which was used for a time (usually as the phosphate, a white crystalline powder) in the treatment of tuberculosis and as an antidepressant; 1-iso-nicotinyl-2-isopropyl hydrazine, $(CH_3)_2CH\cdot NH\cdot NH\cdot CO\cdot C_5H_4N$.

1953 *Amer. Rev. Tuberculosis & Pulmonary Dis.* LXVII. 214 A definite pattern of withdrawal has been observed following discontinuance of isoniazid and iproniazid therapy. **1960** *Times* 4 Mar. 15/7 Yet another of the psychotropic drugs now being used, iproniazid, reverses the effect of reserpine. **1968** W. C. BOWMAN et al. *Textbk. Pharmacol.* xxiii. 623 The antitubercular drug iproniazid ..possesses marked antidepressant activity and inhibits MAO [*sc.* monoamine oxidase]... Iproniazid may cause a number of side-effects, the most serious being acute hepatic necrosis which is occasionally fatal. Because of this, the use of iproniazid as an antidepressant has been discontinued. **1971** *Brit. Med. Bull.* XXVII. 28/2 Hypertensive attacks were described in patients who were given iproniazid for tuberculosis.

ipsilateral (ipsilæ·tĕrăl), *a.* Formerly also **ipse-, ipsolateral.** [*ipselateral* f. L. *ipse* self + LATERAL *a.*, after CONTRALATERAL *a.*; *ipsi-*, *ipsolateral* app. formed by alteration.] Belonging to or occurring on the same side of the body; connecting two parts on the same side.

1907 *Jrnl. Physiol.* XXXVI. 187 On then eliciting the ipselateral 'flexion-reflex' this latter will..appear in the full diphasic form. **1910** *Ibid.* XL. 30 This reflex contraction is readily seen to be inhibited by stimulation of the ipsilateral musculo-cutaneous nerve. **1911** STEDMAN *Med. Dict.* 438/1 Ipsolateral. **1917** *Jrnl. Physiol.* LI. 405 The ipsilateral hind-foot is brought forward to scratch the stimulated part. **1962** J. W. PATTERSON et al. in A. Pirie *Lens Metabolism Rel. Cataract* 413 The initial cataract was contralateral in 9 animals, ipsilateral in 4 animals, and in 3 animals it developed simultaneously in both eyes. **1972** *Sci. Amer.* Aug. 84/3 The rabbit, with only a tiny binocular portion in its visual field, has a very small number of ipsilateral, or uncrossed, fibers in the optic chiasm.

Hence **ipsila·terally** *adv.*, on the same or on one side of the body.

1950 *Merck's Man. Materia Med.* (ed. 8) 300 It [*sc.* the pain] may be referred ipsilaterally to the ear or to an adjacent tooth. **1962** J. W. PATTERSON et al. in A. Pirie *Lens Metabolism Rel. Cataract* 413, 14 developed cataracts contralaterally and 2 ipsilaterally. **1968** A. SOULAIRAC et al. *Pain* 39 A number of fibers which ascend ipsilaterally to their origin.

ipsissima verba (ipsi·simă vɜ̄·ɪbă). [L.] The precise words used by a writer or speaker.

1807 SOUTHEY *Lett.* (1856) II. 40 Last night I was in too much haste to look for the *ipsissima verba* of Fuller. **1834** *Edin. Rev.* Apr. 151 We..shall, therefore,..treat the reader to our author's *ipsissima verba*. **1886** *Athenæum* 13 Nov. 630/1 An assurance that the extracts contain the *ipsissima verba* of the poet would be..valuable. **1888** W. JAMES *Let.* 2 Jan. in R. B. Perry *Tht. & Char. W. James* (1935) I. 403 Your *ipsissima verba* of latest date were what I required. **1931** *Times Lit. Suppl.* 28 May 416/2 An undergraduate named Brauer,..who..seems to have taken down the *ipsissima verba* of Kant with almost impeccable accuracy. **1937** *Mind* XLVI. 302 Mr. Paton's interpretations..where they exceed Kant's *ipsissima verba*..seem to be careful and reasonable. **1961** A. HUXLEY *Let.* 21 Feb. (1969) 904 D. H. L[awrence]'s *ipsissima verba* are: 'The hot stinging centrality of the goose on the cold shifting flux of mud and waters.' **1972** J. A. W. BENNETT *Piers Plowman* p. ix, Some of my notes may retain vestiges of his *ipsissima verba*.

ipso jure (i·pso dʒūᵊ·ri), *advb. phr.* [L.] By the operation of the law itself.

1909 in WEBSTER. **1913** *Act* 3 & 4 *Geo. V* c. 20 § 97 The act and warrant of confirmation in favour of the trustee shall ipso jure transfer to and vest in him..the whole property of the debtor.

-ir-. *Chem.* [See quot.] A formative element in the names of three-membered heterocyclic ring systems. A systematic nomenclature is generated by appending to *-ir-* a prefix (or prefixes) representing the hetero-atom(s), and one of the suffixes -ANE 2, -ENE, *-IDINE c, or *-INE⁵, to indicate saturation or unsaturation and the presence or absence of a nitrogen atom in the ring. (Cf. *-IRANE, *-IRENE, *-IRIDINE, *-IRINE.)

1928 A. M. PATTERSON in *Jrnl. Amer. Chem. Soc.* L. 3079 With a precedent already set for *et* (four members, compare '*tetra*') and with *ol* (five members) and *in* (six members) already confirmed by usage, it would only be necessary to supply three syllables more to cover all but rare cases. These might be *ir* (from '*tri*', reversed) for three members. *Ibid.*, Examples of the resulting names and combining forms are: ox*irene*, ox*irane* (ethylene oxide).

-irane. *Chem.* [See *-IR-.] A suffix used systematically to form the names of saturated heterocyclic monocyclic compounds having a three-membered ring containing no nitrogen atom. Cf. *-IR-.

Iranian, *a.* and *sb.* Add: **B.** *sb.* **2.** The Iranian language.

1885 *Encycl. Brit.* XVIII. 655/2 Afghan..is at bottom a pure Iranian language, not merely intermediate between Iranian and Indian. **1898** R. BROWN *Semitic Influence Hellenic Mythol.* III. iii. 89 Its truth does not depend upon the fact that Iranian and Greek are two dialects of an

original common speech. **1952** G. Sarton *Hist. Sci.* I. xii. 312 Scythian was probably a form of Iranian, the northwestern branch of it. **1966** *Chambers's Encycl.* VII. 705/2 The nations speaking Iranian are divided linguistically into two main groups.

So **Ira·nicize, Ira·nize** *v. trans.*, to make Iranian in character, etc.

1899 W. Z. Ripley *Races of Europe* xv. 420 The Azerbeidjians..have become much Iranized by contact with the dolichocephalic peoples of this region. **1945** *Jrnl. R. Anthrop. Inst.* LXXV. 74/1 There is some reason to believe that the Daylamites were of pre-Iranian origin, but by the tenth century they were iranicized, although not entirely assimilated to the dominant race. **1948** D. Diringer *Alphabet* 316 They [*sc.* Uighurs]..may conveniently be called Iranized Turks. **1961** L. F. Brosnahan *Sounds of Lang.* viii. 177 A palatalisation.. occurs in most of the Turco-Tartar languages..but not in..the iranised Uzbek dialects.

Iraqi (irā·ki). Also **Iraki.** [Arab.: f. *Irāq* (see def.) + -ī adj. suffix.] A native or inhabitant of Iraq, a republic in the Persian Gulf, formerly (before 23 Aug. 1921) known as Mesopotamia: a kingdom from 1921 until the assassination of Faisal II in 1958 when it became a republic; the capital is Baghdad. Also as *adj.*, of or belonging to Iraq or its inhabitants. Also (now *Obs.*?) **Ira·q(u)ian** *sb.* and *a.*

1777 J. Richardson *Dict. Persian, Arabic & Eng.* I. p. xliv/2 They [*sc.* Arabians] have three principal *perdes* or modes; called the *Isphahani*, which appears to be the original Persian melody; the *Iraki* or the Babylonish; and the *Hejazi* or the Arabian. **1824** J. Morier *Adventures Hajji Baba* II. xi. 163 'Untie the string of your trowsers,' said an old Irâki. **1923** *Glasgow Herald* 9 Apr. 10 The Iraqians declare that it took the British all their time to win. **1924** *Blackw. Mag.* Mar. 345/1 The administration is now in the hands of Iraqis, assisted by a mere handful of British advisers. **1927** *Observer* 7 Aug. 13/5 An addition of Iraqi or Syrian territory to the Turkish Republic would constitute a danger to his State. *Ibid.*, The Iraqi movement towards Westernisation. **1939** L. H. Gray *Foundations of Language* 364 [Arabic] was divided into several dialects, of which only that of Mekkah has survived, this being the parent of a large number of modern vernaculars, notably Arabian.., Irāqian (Baghdādh, Mōsul, Mardīn), [etc.]. **1958** *Economist* 26 July 267 Among Iraqis in general there were..widespread desires to be Arab and to be neutral. *Ibid.* 268 No Iraqi statement has been made concerning withdrawal from the [Baghdad] pact. **1965** *Listener* 17 June 900/1 Zamal, an Iraki..was ..expected to be the life and soul of a diplomatic party. **1973** *Times* 16 Apr. 14/1 Such a flexing of Iraqi muscles would (if taken too far) provide the Shah with ample pretext to cut the Iraqis down to size.

So **Ira·qize** *v. trans.*, to make Iraqi in character, etc.; hence **Iraqiza·tion.**

1959 *Economist* 23 May 751/1 'Iraqisation'..aims at a system in which 'no job is done by a foreigner if an Iraqi can do it as well'. *Ibid.* 752/1 The company is prepared to help in its exploitation on behalf of a fully 'Iraqised' industry. **1961** *Ann. Reg. 1960* 311 Prolonged conversations took place..on..increased 'iraqization' of senior staff. **1964** *Ann. Reg. 1963* 312 Already 633 commercial agencies..had 'Iraqized' themselves by allocating 51 per cent of their shareholding to Iraqis.

Ireland (əiᵊ·ɹlănd). The name of a classical scholarship at Oxford University founded in 1825 by John *Ireland*, D.D. (1761–1842), of Oriel College, Dean of Westminster.

1861 J. A. Symonds *Let.* 13 Mar. (1967) I. 282 We hope to secure the Ireland too this Term. If we do not, we shall be in a poor way. **1877** O. Wilde *Let.* Mar. (1962) 32, I have been in for 'the Ireland' and of course lost it: on six weeks' reading I could not expect to get a prize for which men work two and three years. **1951** M. Kennedy *Lucy Carmichael* II. 80 He really is clever; he got the Ireland or the Hertford, I forget which, at Oxford. **1953** E. Barker *Age & Youth* II. iii. 317 A year later, when I tried my luck for the Ireland, the king of classical scholarships, I had less confidence. **1972** *Oxf. Univ. Cal. 1972–73* 216 Dean Ireland's Scholarship... Value: £120. Awarded annually in Michaelmas Term after an examination... The examination is the same as that for the Craven Scholarships and the person elected to the Ireland Scholarship is, if not already a Craven Scholar, elected to the first Craven Scholarship.

irene (əiᵊ·rīn). *Chem.* [ad. G. *iren* (Tiemann & Krüger 1893, in *Ber. d. Deut. Chem. Ges.* XXVI. 2682), f. G. *ir-on* *irone + *-en* -ene.] A colourless, liquid, bicyclic hydrocarbon, $C_{14}H_{20}$, obtained by the dehydration of irone.

1894 *Jrnl. Chem. Soc.* LXVI. I. 81 When treated with hydriodic acid and phosphorus, irone loses a molecule of water, and forms irene, $C_{13}H_{18}$, which is a colourless oil boiling at 113–115° (9 mm.). **1938** *Jrnl. Amer. Chem. Soc.* LX. 933 The 1, 1, 2, 6-tetramethyltetralin structure for irene..has been supported by the synthesis of this tetralin from *m*-bromotoluene.

-irene. *Chem.* [See *-ir-.] A suffix used systematically to form the names of unsaturated heterocyclic monocyclic compounds having a three-membered ring containing no nitrogen atom. Cf. *-ir-.

iretol (əiᵊ·rĕtǫl). *Chem.* [a. G. *iretol* (De Laire & Tiemann 1893, in *Ber. d. Deut. Chem. Ges.* XXVI. 2015), f. G. *ir-igenin* *irigenin: see -et and -ol.] 2,4,6-Trihydroxyanisole, $C_7H_8O_4$, a crystalline compound obtained by alkaline hydrolysis of irigenin.

1894 *Jrnl. Chem. Soc.* LXVI. I. 48 Iretol, $C_6H_2(OH)_3$·OMe...is ultimately obtained in white needles melting at 186°. **1937** *Jrnl. Amer. Chem. Soc.* LIX. 933/1 Iretol is stable when pure and dry, but readily turns dark if exposed to moisture and oxygen. **1960** *Tetrahedron Let.* v. 8 Iridonitrile and iretol (Hoesch reaction) yielded the deoxybenzoin (I).

Irgun (iːɹgu·n). [mod.Heb., organization; in full *Irgun Zvai Leumi* national military organization (also used).] Name of a militant right-wing Zionist organization. Hence **Irgu·nist**, a member of this organization.

1946 Koestler *Thieves in Night* 243 The new organisation, 'Irgun', was numerically smaller and organised on the conspiratorial lines of a terrorist underground movement. **1947** *Ann. Reg. 1946* 299 The Irgun Zvai Leumi and the Stern Group had worked with the Hagana High Command in certain of these operations. **1949** Koestler *Promise & Fulfilment* II. v. 260 A woman of sixty-five, who escorted her grandson, an Irgunist wanted by the police, across Tel Aviv to a safe hiding place. **1959** *Chambers's Encycl.* XII. 398/1 The immediate post-war years saw such Jewish organizations as the *Irgun Zvai Leumi* and the Stern Gang undertake planned terrorist activities against the mandatory power. **1968** P. Durst *Badge of Infamy* iii. 26 Eichmann..was kidnapped in South America by the Irgun and brought to trial by the State of Israel. **1970** *Observer* 12 Sept. 9/6 Leila Khaled is inspired by the same fanatical devotion..as the Irgun Zvai Leumi and the Stern Group, who fought against the British and the Arabs to establish the State of Israel. **1972** *Guardian* 11 Jan. 11/1 The news agency's stringer was a secret member of the Irgun. **1972** *Times* 23 Sept. 5/1 The district Court here refused a police request to remand Mr Amihai Paglin, the key strategist of the Irgun Zvai Leumi during British rule in Palestine.

Irian (i·riăn), *a.* [Native name.] Of or pertaining to Irian Barat or West Irian, formerly Dutch New Guinea or Netherlands New Guinea, since 1963 a province of Indonesia. Hence **Iriane·se**, a native or inhabitant of this province; also *collect.*

1950 tr. *Rep. Comm. New Guinea* (*Irian*) III. iv. 96 The Netherlands promise that it is prepared to listen to the voice of the original Irian people. **1958** *Times* 9 Sept. 9/3 'West Irian action', meaning the 'liberation' of west New Guinea from the Dutch. **1967** *Guardian* 17 Nov. 12/7 To talk of self-determination for West Irian by 1969 is, of course, unrealistic... To most of the Irianese.. considerations of this sort are academic. **1969** *New Yorker* 31 May 44/2 Suharto..rose steadily... His outstanding military performance was as a co-ordinator of the West Irian campaign in 1961–62.

iridal, *a.* Add: **2.** *Med.* Of or pertaining to the iris of the eye; = *iridic *a.*²

1830 W. Mackenzie *Pract. Treat. Dis. Eye* xix. 770 One anatomist supposes that he has traced branches from the ciliary or iridal nerves, where they lie between the sclerotica and choroid. **1879** *Brain* I. 8 In addition to..absence of iridal susceptibility to influence from the other eye, we have..failure of accommodation. **1965** *Ophthalmologica* CXLIX. 35 Although the iridal tumour revealed no sign of malignancy, it metastasized to the ipsilateral cervical lymph nodes prior to the enucleation of the eyeball.

iridesce (iride·s), *v. rare.* [Back-formation from Iridescent *a.*] *intr.* To exhibit iridescence; to shine in an iridescent manner.

1884 E. Coues *Key to N. Amer. Birds* (ed. 2) III. i. 427 General plumage of metallic lustre, iridescing dark green on most parts. **1905** J. London *Jacket* (1915) 48 Sun-flashed water where coral-growths iridesced from profounds of turquoise deeps.

iridiagnosis (əiᵊ:ridəiăgnōᵘ·sis). [f. Iris *sb.* 4 a + Diagnosis.] Diagnosis of disease from observation of the iris of the eye; iris diagnosis.

1918 F. W. Collins in P. J. Thiel *Dis. diagnosed by Observations of Eye* xvi. 76 See our works under preparation:..'Pathology, Iridiagnosis and Treatment', by F. W. Collins..and Charles F. Haverin. **1919** H. Lindlahr (*title*) Iridiagnosis and other diagnostic methods. **1928** *Sunday Express* 8 Apr. 10/7, I had never come across iridiagnosis before.

iridial (əiri·diăl), *a. Med.* [Irreg. f. L. *īrid-* (see Irid) + -ial.] = *iridal *a.* 2, *iridic *a.*²

1911 Stedman *Med. Dict.* 438/2 *Iridial, iridian*, iridal. **1920** I. F. & W. D. Henderson *Dict. Sci. Terms* 156/2 *Iridial angle*, the filtration angle of the eye; an angular recess at the anterior surface of the attached margin of the eye. **1960** *Anatomical Rec.* CXXXVI. 345/1 The iridial muscles of reptiles.

iridic (əiri·dik), *a.*² *Med.* [f. as prec. + -ic.] Of or pertaining to the iris of the eye; = *iridal *a.* 2.

1891 M. Foster *Textbk. Physiol.* (ed. 5) IV. iii. 717 On the inside the curved circumferential portion of the cornea makes a blunt angle, 'iridic angle', with the outer edge of the more or less horizontal iris. **1907** *Ophthalmoscope* V. 378 A true fistulous passage lined by iridic pigmented epithelium. **1964** S. Duke-Elder *Parsons' Dis. Eye* (ed. 14) i. 6 The third portion of the muscle is composed of a few tenuous iridic fibres..finding insertion in the root of the iris.

iridin (əi·ridin). Also **iridine.** [f. as prec. + -in¹.] **1.** *Pharm.* A substance obtained from the rhizome of the blue flag, *Iris versicolor*, and formerly used as a hepatic stimulant.

1879 *Pharmaceutical Jrnl. & Trans.* IX. 988/2 Iridin is obtained from the fresh rhizome of *Iris versicolor*. It is usually mixed with liquorice, or some other absorbent powder. **1907** *Yesterday's Shopping* (1969) 504/1 Iridin Compound. **1921** *Oxf. Index Therap.* 992 *Iridin*. Dose 1 to 5 grains..in pill...Cholagogue and diuretic in its action.

2. *Chem.* [a. G. *iridin* (De Laire & Tiemann 1893, in *Ber. d. Deut. Chem. Ges.* XXVI. 2011).] 5, 7, 3′-Trihydroxy-6, 4′, 5′-trimethoxyisoflavone 7-glucoside, $C_{24}H_{26}O_{13}$, a crystalline compound occurring in the rhizome (orris-root) of the Florentine iris (*Iris florentina*).

1894 *Jrnl. Chem. Soc.* LXVI. I. 47 The dried roots of the violet (*Iris florentina*) on extraction with alcohol, yield a glucoside iridin, $C_{24}H_{26}O_{13}$; it forms slender, white needles. **1928** *Ibid.* 1027 An alcoholic solution of iridin develops with a trace of ferric chloride a somewhat intense, dull reddish-violet colour. **1966** *Chem. Abstr.* LXIV. 15826 (*heading*) Final structure elucidation and complete synthesis of iridine.

3. *Chem.* [a. G. *iridin* (K. Felix et al. 1951, in *Zeitschr. f. physiol. Chem.* CCLXXXVII. 226).] A protamine or mixture of protamines found in the heads of spermatozoa of the rainbow trout, *Salmo gairdneri* (= *S. irideus*).

1953 *Chem. Abstr.* XLVII. 10018 Fresh spermatozoa heads of *Salmo iridis* [*sic*] and..of herring were shown to consist of nucleoprotamine..[which] contained the protamines iridin and clupein. **1969** *Internat. Jrnl. Protein Res.* I. 221/1 Iridine from rainbow-trout..has been separated by column chromatography..into three main fractions.

-iridine. *Chem.* [See *-ir-.] A suffix used systematically to form the names of saturated monocyclic compounds having a three-membered ring which includes a nitrogen atom. Cf. *-ir-.

iridium. Add: *Comb.*, as *iridium-pointed* adj.

1897 *Sears, Roebuck Catal.* 433 Gold filled and ebony telescopic Holder, with best quality iridium pointed pens. **1908** *Daily Chron.* 27 Feb. 7/3 A gold-iridium-pointed nib. **1926–7** *Army & Navy Stores Catal.* 425 Fountain pens. Fitted with 14-ct. gold nib, iridium-pointed.

irido-. Add: Also before a vowel **irid-. iridencleisis** (-klai·sis) [Gr. ἐγκλείειν to shut up], the trapping of a portion of the iris in an incision of the cornea; **iridople·gia** [*-plegia], paralysis of the iris.

1855 R. G. Mayne *Expos. Lex. Med. Sci.* (1860) 540/2 *Iridencleisis*, old term for strangulation of a prolapsed portion of the iris, between the lips of an incision in the cornea. **1879** *Arch. Ophthalm.* VIII. 497 (*heading*) A case of severe iritis and glaucoma, following iridencleisis. **1964** D. M. Gordon *Med. Managem. Ocular Dis.* xviii. 335 Chandler prefers peripheral iridectomy in acute cases in which the pressure is rapidly brought under control. If the pressure has been elevated for 36 or more hours.., he prefers an iridencleisis. [**1854** W. Mackenzie *Pract. Treat. Dis. Eye* (ed. 4) xxii. 882 (*heading*) Myosis... Iridoplegia pupillam contrahens.] **1878** *Brain* I. 8 Iridoplegia is a term applicable wherever both circular and radiating fibres of the iris are paralysed, and the pupil fails wholly to respond to the stimulus of light. **1970** E. Zagora *Eye Injuries* i. 12/1 Occasionally traumatic iridoplegia and cycloplegia occur as a result of concussion of the eye.

iridocyte (əiᵊ·ridosəit). *Zool.* [a. Fr. *iridocyte* (G. Pouchet 1876, in *Jrnl. de l'Anat. & de la Physiol.* XII. 45), f. Gr. ἰριδ-, Iris *sb.* + κύτος a hollow, cell.] A cell which refracts light to cause iridescence, found in the skin of fishes, cephalopods, and certain other animals.

1893 Cunningham & MacMunn in *Phil. Trans. R. Soc.* B. CLXXXIV. 767 The chief features of the iridocytes are their regularity of outline, and their great reflecting power. **1923** *Glasgow Herald* 23 June 4 The silveriness [of plaice] is due to the reflection of light from minute spangles of a waste-product called guanin, which accumulates in certain skin-cells called iridocytes. **1940** *Proc. Zool. Soc.* A. CX. 19 Throughout the epithelial tissues of the animal [sc. *Sepia officinalis*], lying below the chromatophores, is a layer of immobile reflector cells, the iridocytes or iridophores. **1960** Fox & Vevers *Nature of Animal Colours* x. 150 In scales the guanine crystals may cause iridescence by interference of light and the chromatophores are then called iridocytes.

irigenin (əiridʒe·nin). *Chem.* [a. G. *irigenin* (De Laire & Tiemann 1893, in *Ber. d. Deut. Chem. Ges.* XXVI. 2011), f. G. *iri-din* *iridin 2: see *genin.] A pale yellow crystalline flavonoid, $C_{18}H_{16}O_8$, obtained on acid hydrolysis of iridin, of which it is the aglycone.

1894 *Jrnl. Chem. Soc.* LXVI. I. 47 Iridin undergoes hydrolysis when heated with dilute sulphuric acid at 80–100°, yielding *d*-glucose and irigenin... This substance

crystallises in rhombohedra, melting at 186°. **1928** *Ibid.* 1925 These results prove that irigenin..is consequently 5:7:3′-trihydroxy-6:4′:5′-trimethoxy*iso*flavone. **1960** *Tetrahedron Let.* v. 9 The synthetic irigenin..was identical with the natural product.

-irine. *Chem.* [See *-IR-.] A suffix used systematically to form the names of unsaturated monocyclic compounds having a three-membered ring which includes a nitrogen atom. Cf. *-IR-.

irinite (i·rinəit). *Min.* [ad. Russ. *irinit* (Borodin & Kazakova 1954, in *Doklady Akad. Nauk S.S.S.R.* XCVII. 725), f. the name of *Irin*-a Dmitrievna Borneman-Starynkevich, Russian geochemist: see -ITE[1].] An oxide-hydroxide of sodium, cerium, thorium, titanium, and niobium occurring as red-brown crystals in the Khibiny Massif, U.S.S.R., and belonging to the perovskite group of minerals.

1955 *Mineral. Abstr.* XII. 462 Irinite occurs as combination of cube and octahedron from 0·5 to 1 cm. in size... Formula ABX_3, namely (Na, Ce, Th)$_{1-x}$(Ti, Nb)(O$_{3-x}$, (OH)$_x$) with deficiency of A cations. **1962** W. A. DEER et al. *Rock-forming Min.* V. 51 Irinite, described as a new mineral of the perovskite group..has a high thorium and rare earth content.

iris, *sb.* Add: **4. c.** *Photogr.* = *iris-diaphragm*; also *attrib.* Also **iris-in** *sb.*, **iris-out** *sb.* (see quot. 1959): both used as vbs. Also *transf.* and *fig.*

1911 C. N. BENNETT et al. *Handbk. Kinematogr.* I. iv. 28 In the form of lens attached to kinematograph cameras, alteration of diaphragm is effected by the movement of a ring or pin on the lens mount which causes the 'iris' inside to open and close like the iris of a cat's eye, except that the hole in the middle always remains circular in shape. **1929** I. MONTAGU tr. *Pudovkin's On Film Technique* App. 191 The author gives..the iris-in and iris-out, mentioning what is called the fade only as a variant. **1934** WEBSTER, *Iris*, to operate the iris of a camera so as to fade (a picture). With *in* or *out*. **1958** *Spectator* 6 June 730/3 He can iris himself in and out of the scene at will. **1959** W. S. SHARPS *Dict. Cinematogr.* 104/2 *Iris-in*, the film wipe, in which the image viewed progressively disappears and at the same time is replaced by another, moving from the centre of the frame outwards in the form of a circle. *Ibid.*, *Iris-out*, the film wipe, in which the image viewed progressively disappears and is replaced by another from the outside of the frame, moving inwards in the form of a circle. **1961** K. REISZ *Technique Film Editing* (ed. 9) iii. 246 An iris may on occasion introduce or close a shot in a more telling way than a fade. **1962** *B.B.C. Handbook* 119 The control of the zooming, focusing, and iris setting, of a television camera. **1966** WODEHOUSE *Plum Pie* vii. 177 After a terrific struggle the hood called it a day and irised out. **1968** BLISH & KNIGHT *Torrent of Faces* II. vii. 137 Fongaváro glided silently through the Rest Stop door, which irised shut as silently behind him. **1969** GISH & PINCHOT *Lilian Gish* xi. 145 The scene of Sherman's march to the sea opened with an iris shot—a small area. *Ibid.*, Slowly the iris opened wider to reveal a great panorama. **1972** WODEHOUSE *Pearls, Girls, & Monty Bodkin* vii. 102 When a bunch of flatfeet burst in with their uncouth cry of 'Everybody keep their seats, please,' the thing to do is to iris out unobtrusively through the kitchen.

7. (sense 5) *iris blue, green*; **iris diagnosis** = *IRIDIAGNOSIS; **iris-diaphragm** (earlier examples).

1908 F. TREVES *Cradle of Deep* x. 57 A West Indian island..rising aloft from an iris-blue sea. **1921** *Glasgow Herald* 17 Feb. 9 Iris diagnosis and its relation to true health. **1938** H. ORBELL (*title*) The science of iris-diagnosis. **1867** *Trans. R. Microsc. Soc.* XV. 74 (*heading*) Iris diaphragm proving the circular form whether expanding or contracting. *a* **1877** KNIGHT *Dict. Mech.* II. 1195/2 *Iris-diaphragm*, a contractile diaphragm, simulating the action of the natural iris. **1875** E. SPON *Workshop Receipts* 95/1 *Iris green*, a pigment prepared by grinding the juice of the petals of the blue flag with quicklime. It is very fugitive. **1880** *Encycl. Brit.* XIII. 276/2 From the flowers of *Iris florentina* a pigment—the 'verdelis', 'vert d'iris', or iris-green, formerly used by miniature painters—was prepared by maceration.

Irish, *a.* and *sb.* Add: **A.** *adj.* **2.** *Irish butter, guipure, linen, poplin, tweed, whiskey* (examples).

1741 RICHARDSON *Pamela* IV. xiii. 75 A Piece of Irish or Scotish Linen. **1751** [see POPLIN[2] *attrib.*]. **1780** A. YOUNG *Tour in Ireland* I. 276 The salt for the fish trade [comes] from Rochelle: for butter english and irish. **1785** J. WEDGWOOD *Let.* 3 Oct. (1965) 285 Irish linens in the British market. **1798** C. MORDAUNT *Let.* July in E. Hamilton *Mordaunts* (1965) x. 243, I hope our conduct may gain us credit for discipline, but am terribly afraid of the cheap Irish whiskey. **1805** *Times* 6 Nov. 1/2 (Advt.), The Public supplied, as usual, with pieces of Irish linen, at the wholesale prices, at the Irish Linen Company's, No. 4, Bloomsbury-square, near Hart-street. **1813** JANE AUSTEN *Let.* 15 Sept. (1932) II. 321 Very pretty English poplins at 4*s.* 3*d.*; Irish, ditto at 6*s.* **1828** M. R. MITFORD *Our Village* III. 178 Crockery ware was piled on one side of her door-way, Dutch cheese and Irish butter encumbered the other. **1851** *Illustr. Catal. Gt. Exhib.* III. 516/1 Dowlas is a strong kind of Irish linen, for shirting. *Ibid.* 561/1 Laces: Royal Irish guipure; Irish appliqué. **1855** [see SCOTCH *a.* 2 a]. **1861** MRS. BEETON *Bk. Househ. Managem.* 808 Irish butter sold in London is all salted, but is generally good. **1865** F. B. PALLISER *Hist. Lace* xxxv. 416 Irish Brussels is made at Clones,...Irish guipure at Carrickmacross, in the same Co. **1879** M. E. BRADDON *Vixen* III. 319 She wore Irish poplin, and Irish lace, Irish stockings, and Irish linen. **1892–3** *T. Eaton & Co. Catal.* Fall & Winter 33/1 Boys' Overcoats... In Scotch, English and Irish tweeds. **1895** *Army & Navy Co-op. Soc. Price List* 15 Sept. 1094 Irish poplin. *Ibid.* 1099 Irish lawn... Irish diapers. **1896** *Illustr. London News* 25 Feb. (jacket) 4/3 (Advt.), A three-garment suit for boys... In Scotch and Irish tweeds. **1907** *Yesterday's Shopping* (1969) 12/1 Butter..Irish (finest Creamery)—lb. 1/2. **1909** Irish tweed [see *DONEGAL]. **1966** MRS. L. B. JOHNSON *White House Diary* 17 Mar. (1970) 373 Irish whiskey for St. Patrick's Day, the first time it's been served in the White House, I'll bet, and not a soul wanted tea! **1968** J. IRONSIDE *Fashion Alphabet* 233 *Irish linen*, a very fine light-weight linen woven of Irish flax. *Ibid.*, The linen industry in Ireland now, however, produces all weights of linen and linen mixtures..which are collectively and erroneously referred to as 'Irish' linen. **1968** L. ROSTEN *Joys of Yiddish* p. xiii, Yiddish phrasing and overtones are found in, say, the way an Irish whiskey advertises itself. **1970** J. FLEMING *Young Man, I think you're Dying* viii. 106 There was an Irish tweed jacket for Joe and a toy leprechaun. **1973** P. GEDDES *Ottawa Allegation* viii. 102 In a department store on the Mall she stood and fingered Irish linens.

b. *Irish potato, setter* (see the sbs.); **Irish deer**, the extinct giant deer, *Megaceros giganteus*, whose remains have been found in Ireland and other parts of Europe; **Irish elk** = **Irish deer* (examples); **Irish terrier**, a large wire-haired terrier, with a sandy or reddish-coloured coat; **Irish wolfhound**, a large, rough-coated hound, often grey in colour.

1697 T. MOLYNEUX in *Phil. Trans. R. Soc.* XIX. 505 We shall not have the least Reason to question but these vastly large Irish Deer and the American Moose, were certainly one and the same sort of Animal. **1825** S. HIBBERT in *Edin. Jrnl. Sci.* III. 15 The Irish Elk attracts no small share of attention. **1844** *Rep. Brit. Assoc. Adv. Sci.* 237 The most remarkable of the unquestionably extinct species of the Cervine family is that which is commonly called the Irish Elk. *Ibid.* 238 Mr. Parkinson refers the beams of two antlers found in the till at Walton in Essex, on account of their large size, to the great Irish Deer. **1857** C. KINGSLEY *Two Yrs. Ago* II. viii. 269 Round the burleaf-bed dances a rough, white Irish terrier. **1880** G. A. GRAHAM in H. Dalziel *Brit. Dogs* iii. 34 The Irish wolf-hound, being used for both the capture and despatch of the wolf, it would necessarily have been of greyhound conformation, besides being of enormous power. **1892** H. N. HUTCHINSON *Extinct Monsters* xvi. 224 The 'Great Irish Elk', as it is generally called, deserves special notice. *Ibid.*, The term 'Elk' is misleading, for it is not an elk (*Alces*) at all, but a true *Cervus* (stag). It should be called 'the Great Irish Deer'. **1897** *Encycl. Sport* I. 323/1 It is just twenty years since the Irish terrier first obtained recognition in the Kennel Club Stud Book. **1908** A. J. DAWSON *Finn* vi. 59 Finn had won two special prizes; one, a medal offered by the Irish Wolfhound Club..and another..for the biggest Irish Wolfhound in the Show. **1933** A. S. ROMER *Vertebr. Paleontol.* xviii. 356 Among the more interesting forms was the gigantic 'Irish elk', *Megaceros*, with the largest antlers of any known deer. **1947** J. STEVENSON-HAMILTON *Wild Life S. Afr.* viii. 68 A plucky Irish terrier diverted the pig's attention by attacking it from behind. **1964** G. K. WHITEHEAD *Deer Gt. Brit. & Ireland* xxx. 435 The giant deer—variously called great fallow deer and, quite erroneously, the Irish elk—was undoubtedly the finest deer that has ever inhabited Great Britain. **1969** E. H. HART *Encycl. Dog Breeds* 313 The Irish Wolfhound is remarkable in combining power and swiftness with keen sight. *Ibid.* 521 Origin of the Irish Terrier is a subject likely to provide debate as long as interest in the breed continues.

c. Irish American, an American of Irish origin; as *adj.* (with hyphen), of or pertaining to such a person, or to the Irish community, in the United States; **Irish apricot** *humorous*, a potato; **Irish articles**, articles of belief drawn up by Archbishop Ussher in 1615; **Irish-Australian** *a.*, of or pertaining to an Australian of Irish origin; (as two words) such a person; **Irish bridge**, an open stone drain carrying water across a road (see quots.); **Irish coffee** = **Gaelic coffee*; **Irish confetti** *slang*, stones, bricks, etc., esp. when used as weapons; **Irish crochet** = **Irish lace (a)*; *also attrib.*, as *Irish crochet lace, point*; **Irish Free State**, (from 1921) name of the independent democratic State of Southern Ireland (since 1937 called Eire, and since 1949 the Republic of Ireland); **Irish green**, Connemara marble; **Irish Guards** [GUARD *sb.* 8], an infantry regiment of the British Army formed to signalize the bravery of Irish troops in the Boer War of 1899–1902; **Irish harp** = CLAIRSCHACH; **Irish horse** *slang*, salted meat; **Irish hurricane** *Naut. slang*, see quots.; **Irish Ireland** *a.*, designating a movement to arouse the interest of all Irish people in their own country; **Irish lace**, (*a*) a type of lace that resembles crochet; (*b*) see quot. 1957; **Irish martingale** (see quot. 1958); **Irish pennant** *Naut. slang*, see quot. 1962; **Irish point**, a kind of lace made in Ireland; **Irish Society**, a society founded in the reign of James I to have jurisdiction over the new Protestant settlement in Ulster; **Irish stitch** (earlier and later examples); **Irish Sweep** (or **Sweepstake**), a sweepstake organized by Irish hospitals on the results of English horse-races, esp. the Derby and the Grand National Steeplechase.

The examples are arranged for convenient reference in alphabetical order.

1832 *New-England Mag.* June 490 Irish-American Literature. **1836** T. POWER *Impressions Amer.* I. 185 The accent of the Irish American..differs [little] from that of the settler of a year. **1891** KIPLING *Life's Handicap* 197 My Irish American-Jew boy. **1902** *Irish Rosary* Jan. 77/1 The Irish-American Press should urge upon the Irish in America a sense of their duty in this matter. **1957** P. KEMP *Mine were of Trouble* x. 197 The famous Irish-American plastic surgeon, Eastman Sheean. **1971** *Guardian* 27 Oct. 12/6 The Irish-Americans are interested in Ireland. **1972** T. P. MCMAHON *Issue of Bishop's Blood* (1973) xiii. 188 The nylon-curtain Irish Americans of the Seventies. **1785** GROSE *Dict. Vulgar T.*, *Irish apricots*, potatoes; it is a common joke against the Irish vessels to say they are loaded with fruit and timber, that is, potatoes and broomsticks. **1846** *Swell's Night Guide* 122/2 *Irish apricots*, potatoes. **1973** *Times* 15 Feb. 14/3 Like the Norfolk Capon (a red herring), the Irish Apricot (a potato)..the Welsh Rabbit is a time-honoured joke. **1877** P. SCHAFF *Hist. Creeds of Christendom* I. 664 The Irish Articles are one hundred and four in number. **1967** D. T. KAUFFMAN *Dict. Relig. Terms* 253/2 *Irish articles*, the Calvinistic statement of faith, adopted in 1615 by the Irish Episcopal Church in the form of 104 articles, which became part of the basis of the Westminster Confession. **1907** *Westm. Gaz.* 17 Sept. 1/3 The..Irish-Australian baronet. **1957** P. KEMP *Mine were of Trouble* vi. 106 Peter Lawler, a hard-bitten little Irish-Australian. **1923** W. L. STRANGE *Indian Engin.* xlvi. 205 For lower-class roads..stream crossings may be substituted... The cheapest form is a level crossing...The next higher type is a road dam, or 'Irish bridge', for which two parallel curtain walls are constructed across the stream bed and continued for a short distance as flanks up the approaches; between them is the roadway: the downstream wall should be securely founded. **1969** 'M. INNES' *Family Affair* xv. 167 You cross the river by an Irish bridge... It's just a bridge, but built under the water instead of over it... It's really a reliable sort of ford. **1950** *Social & Personal* Dec. 57/1, I am..drinking Irish coffee, which.. is a mixture of very, very good Power's whiskey and very, very bad coffee. I am deciding that my next drink will be an Irish coffee without the coffee. **1959** D. O'NEILL *Life has no Price* vii. 102 Donal ordered himself an Irish coffee. **1966** 'S. FORBES' *Terror touches Me* iv. 37 Everyone ..had Irish coffee after dinner...He spooned brown sugar into glasses... Over the sugar he poured dollops of Irish whiskey... Next came steaming dark coffee..and.. cream..poured slowly over the back of a spoon. **1969** *Observer* (Colour Suppl.) 30 Nov. 10/1, 17/6 each...The Irish Coffee glass. **1935** A. J. POLLOCK *Underworld Speaks* 62/1 *Irish confetti*, bricks. **1939** G. KERSH *I got References* xii. 161, I learned the use of Irish Confetti, or Brickbats, at a tender age. **1966** *Observer* 19 June 40/1 An American friend in Amsterdam, describing last week's riots there, said: 'There's just a lot of Irish confetti around.' **1966** F. SHAW et al. *Lern Yerself Scouse* 57 *A cargo uv Irish confetti*, a cargo of stone chippings. **1881** C. C. HARRISON *Woman's Handiwork* III. 217 A deep fall of large-patterned Irish crochet lace. **1900** Irish crochet point [see POINT *sb.*[1] A. 31]. **1932** D. C. MINTER *Mod. Needlecraft* 103/1 A fine linen thread is most suitable for Irish crochet. **1965** *Daily Express* 14 Apr. 8/3 Linen..covers her drawing room walls (held down by strips of Irish crochet). **1969** *New Yorker* 31 May 92/2 The attached vestees are done in oyster bolillo lace, which is rather like heavy Irish crochet. **1922** *Act* 13 *Geo. V* c. 2 An Act to make such provisions as are consequential on or incidental to the establishment of the Irish Free State. **1929** *Encycl. Brit.* XII. 628/1 The Irish Free State, with the status of a British Dominion, came officially into being on January 15, 1922. **1937** V. BARTLETT *This is my Life* x. 144 When the Irish Free State was admitted [to the League of Nations]..President Cosgrave made his opening speech in Gaelic. **1959** *Chambers's Encycl.* V. 49/1 The constitution is considered by the *dáil* to apply to the whole of Ireland..but, 'pending the reintegration of the national territory' to have effect only in the area formerly known as the Irish Free State. **1883** *Encycl. Brit.* XV. 529/1 The 'Irish green' of architects is a similar rock from Connemara in western Galway. **1886** Irish green [see *CONNEMARA]. **1902** *Encycl. Brit.* XXXIII. 684/1 The Queen.. issued an order..for a new regiment of Irish Guards to be constituted. **1923** KIPLING (*title*) The Irish Guards in the Great War. **1967** A. FARRAR-HOCKLEY *Death of Army* v. 179 General Landon had sent him the 2nd Grenadier Guards and the Irish Guards. **1611** G. VADIANUS in *Coryat's Crudities* sig. l 2 Torn is an Irish Harpe, whose heart-strings tune As fancies wrest doth straine or slacke his cord. *a* **1700** EVELYN *Diary* an. 1654 (1955) III. 92 My old acquaintance & most incomparable player on the Irish-Harp, Mr. Clarke. **1797** *Encycl. Brit.* VIII. 326/1 There are among us two sorts of this instrument, *viz.* the Welch harp..and the Irish harp. **1879** GROVE *Dict. Mus.* I. 686/1 The beautiful form of the more modern Irish harp is well known from its representation in the royal coat of arms. **1969** *Guardian* 16 Sept. 11/3 They only need to play Irish harps..to complete the absurd romanticism of Free Belfast. **1973** *Country Life* 29 Mar. 861/3 A finished harp costs at least £1,300. Happily.. small Irish harps..made almost entirely of wood..can be bought for £130. They serve as a sort of apprenticeship for would be serious harp players. **1748** SMOLLETT *R. Random* I. xxxiii. 291 Our provision consisted of putrid salt beef, to which the sailors gave the name of Irish horse. **1886** H. BAUMANN *Londinismen* 83/2 *Irish horse*, Pökelfleisch, s. salt horse. **1929** F. C. BOWEN *Sea Slang* 72 *Irish hurricane*, a flat calm with drizzling rain. **1962** *John o' London's* 14 June 571/2 An Irish hurricane is a flat calm. **1904** W. B. YEATS in *Daily Chron.* 18 Mar. 3/4, I went..to tell the Irish of America of what we call the Irish Ireland movement. **1854** C. M. YONGE *Heartsease*

I. xiv. 336 She was..prettily dressed with some Irish lace. **1880** L. HIGGIN *Handbk. Embroidery* v. 51 Tambour work..is now almost confined to the manufacture of what is known as Irish or Limerick lace..made as net.. with a tambour or crochet hook. **1881** C. C. HARRISON *Woman's Handiwork* I. 94 Irish lace, made of flax-thread with a ground-work of crochet. **1895** *Army & Navy Co-op. Soc. Price List* 1126/1 (*heading*) Real Lace Sets.. Irish..per set 4/6 to 20/0. **1907** E. WHARTON *Fruit of Tree* II. ix. 139 Let me lend you my dress with the Irish lace. *a* **1929** L. TROUBRIDGE *Life amongst Troubridges* (1966) iii. 16 We all had new poplin dresses with Irish lace collars. **1957** M. B. PICKEN *Fashion Dict.* 201/2 *Irish lace,* variety of laces made in Ireland. Best known are crochet, net embroideries of Limerick, and Carrickmacross cut work or Irish guipure. **1937** P. RODZIANKO *Mod. Horsemanship* iii. 94 An ordinary Irish martingale has two rings that are connected with a leather strap, of about three inches long. This..prevents the reins going over his [the horse's] head as it catches him under the jaws. **1946** M. C. SELF *Horseman's Encycl.* 272 *Irish martingale.* This is a short strap with a ring at each end. The reins of the snaffle bridle run through the rings and the strap slide up to about six inches from the bit. It gives additional control and prevents the snaffle being pulled too far through the animal's mouth. **1958** J. HISLOP *From Start to Finish* 172 *Irish martingale,* two rings joined by a leather strap, about six inches long, through which the reins are passed. It is the type of martingale most used on racecourses and is more usually called 'rings', sometimes 'spectacles'. **1883** W. C. RUSSELL *Sailors' Lang.* 73 *Irish pennants,* fag-ends of rope, rope-yarns, etc., flying about. **1910** D. W. BONE *Brassbounder* i. 14 'Irish pennants' fluttering wildly on spar and rigging tell of scamped work of those whose names are not on our 'Articles'. **1962** A. G. COURSE *Dict. Naut. Terms* 108 *Irish Pennants or Pendants,* untidy ends of ropes, rope yarns, etc., flying in the wind. It is said that it was originally the name given to a flag with a torn or frayed fly or end. **1865** F. B. PALLISER *Hist. Lace* xxxv. 416 The fabric flourishes, and is known by the name of 'Irish', or 'Curragh point'. **1882** CAULFEILD & SAWARD *Dict. Needlework* 272/1 Irish Point can be worked entirely as old Brussels needle point. **1613** in *Hist. Narr. Irish Soc.* (1916) 163 After all which done information was given by the Governor and Assistants of the Irish Society, that all the monies formerly levied towards that charge is altogether issued. **1846** T. MACNEVIN *Confiscation of Ulster* vii. 214 The Irish Society is a type and symbolical representation of English rule in Ireland from the beginning. **1877** *Encycl. Brit.* VI. 224/2 The separate estates are still held to be under the paramount jurisdiction of the Irish Society. **1634** J. TAYLOR *Needles Excellency* (ed. 10) sig. A2 Fisher stitch, Irish-stitch, and Queen stitch. **1738** C. FIENNES *Journeys* (1947) 364 A 'seatee of Irish stitch'. .. '8 Irish stitch coushons.' **1932** D. C. MINTER *Mod. Needlecraft* 10/1 Intergradating one stitch and colour with another, as is possible with Irish stitch. **1931** F. LENWOOD *Why all this Fuss about 'Sweeps'?* 10 How unsocial it all is may be seen from the excitement over the Irish Sweep and the Derby of 1931. **1933** W. S. MAUGHAM *Sheppey* I. 12 Did you have a ticket for the Irish Sweep? **1937** G. GREENE *Coll. Ess.* (1969) IV. 425 The great muted chromium shadows wait..the novelist's Irish sweep: money for no thought, for the banal situation and the inhuman romance. **1963** 'G. BAGBY' *Murder's Little Helper* (1964) vi. 52 When you people come around, it's never been to tell one of my roomers that he's won the Irish Sweepstakes. **1965** N. GULBENKIAN *Pantaraxia* viii. 152 Although I was not a gambler, I did buy a ticket in the first Irish Sweep. .. One afternoon..the..commissionaire came in..and he said..'You've drawn a horse in the Irish Sweep.' **1974** A. ROSS *Bradford Business* 48 A wad of Irish Sweepstake tickets.

4. *spec.* Used of seemingly contradictory statements. (See also *Irish hurricane* s.v. sense *A. 2 c.)

1820 H. BROUGHAM *Let.* 5 Feb. in H. Maxwell *Creevey Papers* (1903) I. 297 Your advice has been followed by anticipation (to speak Irish). **1838** GEO. ELIOT *Let.* 18 Aug. (1954) I. 6 Isaac and I went alone (that seems rather Irish), and staid only a week. **1843** F. A. KEMBLE *Let.* 25 Aug. in *Rec. Later Life* (1882) III. 36 We are going out of town,..to-morrow at half-past six in the morning, and it is now past midnight, and I have every mortal and immortal thing to pack, with my own single pair of hands, which is Irish, Lord bless us! **1857** MRS. GASKELL *Let.* 7 Dec. (1966) 491 The lecture was not (to me) so very interesting, being a sort of recapitulation of what he was *going* to say (if that's not Irish). **1892** C. H. FRETWELL *Anc. Mariner* 94, I had what sailors call 'an Irish rise', becoming second officer after being for a time commanding officer. **1903** H. C. ROWLAND *Sea Scamps* 4, I was promptly addressed as 'lieutenant', which struck me as being rather an Irish promotion, having once previously served as major. **1926** J. S. HUXLEY *Essays Pop. Sci.* 121 To be Irish, the longer it lives, the sooner it ought to die. **1937** A. UPFIELD *Mr. Jelly's Business* (1938) iii. 28 He doesn't seem to mind me courting his daughter, but he doesn't give me a chance to do any courting. That's Irish, but it's a fact. **1970** R. HILL *Clubbable Woman* vi. 192 'Marcus wouldn't dare to tell a lie like that unless it was true!' 'Irish,' said Pascoe.

B. *sb.* **1. a.** Also, *black Irish,* Irish of Mediterranean appearance.

1888 KIPLING *Soldiers Three* (1890) 82 Those are the Black Oirish an' 'tis they that bring dishgrace upon the name av Oireland. **1953** K. TENNANT *Joyful Condemned* v. 46 His fleshy hooked nose..suggested Jewish blood, but he claimed he was black Irish. **1961** J. B. PRIESTLEY *Saturn over Water* xiv. 201 He was a black Irish type, with centuries of rebelliousness behind him. **1962** *Guardian* 18 July 5/5 That haunted 'Black Irish' face [of Eugene O'Neill]. **1970** K. GILES *Death in Church* vii. 177 Have you ever seen the black Irish?

4. (Earlier and later examples.)

1784 COWPER *Let.* 21 Mar. in *Corr.* (1904) II. 181 Your mother wishes you to buy for her ten yards and a half of yard-wide Irish, from two shillings to two shillings and sixpence per yard. **1834** E. E. PERKINS *Lady's Shopping Manual* 63 The regard to time and other circumstances which has been recommended in choosing Irishes, should be observed in the purchase of all linens. **1889** J. K. JEROME *Three Men in Boat* ii. 29 Harris..proposed that we should go out and have a smile, saying that he had found a place..where you could really get a drop of Irish worth drinking. **1914** [see *APOLLINARIS]. **1972** P. RUELL *Red Christmas* vi. 58 Irish. I drink Irish. Not this muck.

5. Temper; passion. orig. *U.S.* and *dial.*

1834 D. CROCKETT *Narr. Life* iv. 30 Her Irish was up too high to do any thing with her. **1860** BARTLETT *Dict. Amer.* (ed. 3) 217 My friends say that my Irish is getting up, meaning, I am getting angry. **1877** F. ROSS et al. *Gloss. Words Holderness* 80/1 *Iry; Irish,* E. and N., passion; anger; rage; fury. **1933** PARTRIDGE *Words, Words, Words!* I. 9 Both *Irish* and the colloquial *Paddy* are used for anger. **1949** R. HARVEY *Curtain Time* vii. 73 But George's Irish was up. **1972** *Evening Telegram* (St. John's, Newfoundland) 23 June 1/4 'I got my Irish up,' he said, 'and here's a man that's going to fight back.'

Irisher (əiᵊ·riʃəɹ). *colloq.* [f. IRISH *a.* + -ER[1].] A person of Irish origin, an Irishman.

1807 C. SCHULTZ *Let.* 15 July in *Trav. on Inland Voy.* (1810) I. 8 The inhabitants are mostly of German descent, and still, in a great measure, retain their national prejudices, and consider all who do not speak their own language either as Yankees or Irishers. **1832** J. BARRINGTON *Personal Sk. Own Times* (ed. 2) III. 35 What would the poor Irishers have done in owld times? **1854** MRS. GASKELL *North & South* (1855) II. iii. 35 This indignation was tempered..by contempt for 'them Irishers'. **1882** W. D. HAY *Brighter Britain!* II. 283 A big, red-headed Irisher. **1956** H. GOLD *Man who was not with It* (1965) xi. 90 I'm a Wop Irisher from Boston. **1973** M. MACKINTOSH *King & Two Queens* xii. 180 I'm only a no-account Irisher, but I like to pay my debts.

Irishly. Delete *rare* and add later examples.

1907 *Daily Chron.* 23 May 6/4 That solitary English engineer—who is, to speak Irishly, of course, a Scotchman—holds the Nile in fee. **1915** W. OWEN *Let.* 4 Apr. (1967) 329 She is..badly off; and though spending irishly, spends every penny. **1929** E. BOWEN *Joining Charles* 64 Grizelda and Doris were best in the Irish Jig; so saucy, quite Irishly saucy. **1959** R. GRAVES *Coll. Poems* 290 How Irishly you sacrifice Love to pity, pity to ill-humour.

Irishman. Add: **2.** In full, *wild Irishman.* A thorny New Zealand shrub, *Discaria toumatou;* also called MATAGOURI and TUMATAKURU.

1857 C. W. RICHMOND in *Richmond–Atkinson Papers* (1960) I. vi. 317 Besides the grasses there is flax, *tutu* and wild Irishman. **1860** S. BUTLER in H. F. Jones *Samuel Butler* (1919) I. 80 There is a large quantity of Irishman (the name given to a thorny shrub which, in the back country, attains to a considerable size)...A glorious lurid flare marks the ignition of an Irishman. **1883** [see TUMATA-KURU]. **1896** *Australasian* 28 Aug. 407/5 It seems uncivil to a whole nation—another injustice to Ireland—to call a bramble a wild Irishman. **1941** O. DUFF *N.Z. Now* i. 1 If a wild Irishman is grown in a hothouse it loses its spines and develops soft leaves. **1966** G. W. TURNER *Eng. Lang. Austral. & N.Z.* viii. 168 The shrub matogowrie, called Irishman in early writings, is especially common in the South Island where Maori influence is least strong and anglicization is most likely.

3. **Irishman's hurricane** *Naut. slang,* a dead calm (see also quot. 1961); cf. *Irish hurricane* (*IRISH *a.* 2 c); **Irishman's promotion, rise,** reduced wages; cf. *IRISH *a.* 4 (quots. 1892, 1903).

1827 J. F. COOPER *Red Rover* III. v. 107 There was an Irishman's hurricane, right up and down, for a day. **1873** 'VANDERDECKEN' *Yachts & Yachting* xxxi. 264 She is like a hurrah's nest, or a billyboy caught in an Irishman's hurricane! **1889** BARRÈRE & LELAND *Dict. Slang* I. 488/1 *Irishman's rise,*..wages reduced. **1902** C. J. C. HYNE *Mr. Horrocks, Purser* ii. 27 I've a sort of memory that you got Irishman's promotion for a bit of a mistake just recently. **1915** *Truth* 25 Aug. 295/2 The utmost the surveyor might expect from most corporations would be an Irishman's rise. **1957** A. MACNAB *Bulls of Iberia* xiii. 140 He..asked for a job as a picador. His offer was accepted immediately—on condition that he would stand guarantee for any horses that might be killed under him! This would have been an Irishman's rise, even in those days when they used worn-out horses from the U.S.A. at five dollars a head. **1961** F. H. BURGESS *Dict. Sailing* 121 *Irishman's hurricane,* a slight drizzle in a calm. **1972** *Times* 29 Sept. 15/4 For many low-paid workers with children, an extra £2 a week may be no more than an 'Irishman's rise'.

Irishness. (Later examples.)

1902 *Daily Chron.* 12 Sept. 3/3 Mr. Cobb's 'man of sentiment' is an Irishman with a broad brogue, who out-Herods Herod in his Irishness. **1930** H. V. MORTON *In Search of Ireland* vi. 119 At times this Irishness is a rather pleasant melancholy. **1972** 'R. CRAWFORD' *Whip Hand* I. iv. 18 What made Mullins' [a public house] special was its authentic uncompromising Irishness. **1973** *Times* 5 Dec. 18/1 The contemplation of a common Irishness between north and south.

Irishy (əiᵊ·riʃi), *a.* [f. IRISH *a.* and *sb.* + -Y[1].] Like the Irish, somewhat Irish.

1884 'MARK TWAIN' *Lett. to Publishers* (1967) 174 The boy's mouth is a trifle more Irishy than necessary. **1913** D. H. LAWRENCE *Let.* 1 Feb. (1962) I. 182 A reaction against Shaw and Galsworthy and Barker and Irishy (except Synge) people.

irisin (əi·risin). *Chem.* [a. G. *irisin* (O. Wallach 1886, in *Ann. d. Chem.* CCXXXIV. 374), f. G. *iris* IRIS *sb.* + *-in* -IN[1].] A fructan present in the rhizome of the yellow iris, *Iris pseudacorus.*

1887 *Jrnl. Chem. Soc.* LII. I. 26 The rhizome of the water lily, *Iris pseudacorus,* contains a peculiar carbohydrate, called 'irisin' by the author. Irisin..closely resembles inulin. **1925** *Chem. Abstr.* XIX. 2813 Irisin..by the diffusion method shows a mol. wt. of 10,300. **1946** *Ibid.* XL. 550 Of the fructosans, irisin is the most stable to dry heat. **1953** *Q. Jrnl. Exper. Physiol.* XXXVIII. 9 Intravenous administration of low molecular weight grass levan and irisin is unaccompanied by vasomotor and respiratory disturbances.

iris-in, iris-out: see *IRIS *sb.* 4 c.

irk, var. *ERK.

‖ **iroha** (*iro*·ha). Also **irofa, irova.** [Jap., named from the first three syllables *i, ro,* and *ha* or *fa.*] The Japanese kana or syllabary.

1845 *Encycl. Metrop.* XX. 482/2 They..formed a collection of 47 syllables, comprehending all the sounds which are found in their language...This syllabarium, or alphabet, is called *irofa,* from its three first elements. **1868** J. J. HOFFMAN *Japanese Gram.* 9 To facilitate the learning of the Japanese sounds or syllables, they have been so arranged as to compose a couple of sentences, and as these begin with the word *Irová,* that name has been given to the Japanese alphabet. **1890** B. H. CHAMBERLAIN *Things Japanese* 379 The order of the I-ro-ha bears witness to the Buddhist belief of the father of Japanese writing. **1903** C. NOSS tr. *Lange's Text-bk. Colloquial Japanese* Introd. p. xvi, There is another arrangement of the syllabary called *iroha*...This is in the form of a stanza of poetry giving expression to Buddhistic sentiment. **1937** I. NITOBÉ *Lect. Japan* xi. 177 Our language is polysyllabic and is expressed in forty-seven sounds... We call the whole collection a syllab[a]ry instead of an alphabet. In our own language it is called *i-ro-ha* from the first three syllables. **1967** R. A. MILLER *Japanese Lang.* iii. 127 The *kana* symbols have at various times been arranged into mnemonic word lists...One such is the *ame tsuchi* list... A somewhat later example..is the *iroha* list..thought today to have been the work of the priest Kūya (903–972) or of the priest Senkan (918–983).

iroko (irōᵘ·ko). [Yoruba.] A hardwood tree of the genus *Chlorophora,* either *C. excelsa,* which is found across the central part of Africa, or *C. regia,* which grows in the western region; also, the timber from these trees, sometimes called West African or Nigerian teak.

1890 A. MILLSON in *Kew Bull.* 240 The only trees of unusual bulk [in Yorubaland] are the cotton trees and an occasional 'Iroko' tree. **1894** H. M. WARD *Laslett's Timber & Timber Trees* (ed. 2) xxv. 307 Mention may also be made of Iroko, a very valuable and handsome building and cabinet wood. **1939** EGGELING & HARRIS in L. Chalk et al. *Forest Trees & Timbers Brit. Empire* IV. 84 The harder, more durable 'Brown Iroko' is probably *C. excelsa;* the softer, less durable 'Yellow Iroko' *C. regia.* **1955** *Times* 18 July 9/7 The good stout hull, framed with English oak, planked with iroko—a type of teak from Africa—and copper fastened, shows not the slightest sign of movement or decay. **1964** R. W. J. KEAY et al. *Nigerian Trees* II. 188 This [sc. *Chlorophora excelsa*] is a very common large forest tree with dark green foliage and distinctive leaves. It is widely known by the Yoruba name Iroko. **1967** W. SOYINKA *Kongi's Harvest* 58 When a squirrel Seeks sanctuary up the *iroko* tree The hunter's chase is ended. **1974** *Habitat Catal.* 76/3 Work top; warm honey coloured Iroko, a West African hardwood similar to teak.

iron, *sb.*[1] Add: **1. d.** *Geol.* Any meteorite which contains a high proportion of iron.

[**1826** *Phil. Mag.* LXVII. 4 (*heading*) Falls of meteoric stones and masses of iron.] **1842** *Amer. Jrnl. Sci. & Arts* XLIII. 358 The imbedded grains of olivin in the Pallas iron of Siberia, and the Otampa iron of South America. **1868** *Geol. Mag.* V. 75 The bodies which are comprised under the general name of meteorites have long since been arranged under two great divisions, the irons and the stones. **1920** *Mineral. Mag.* XIX. 56 In this scheme [of the author], meteorites are divided into four classes, viz. Irons, Stony-irons, Chondritic Stones, and Non-chondritic Stones. **1962** B. MASON *Meteorites* ix. 130 In total mass the iron meteorites far outweigh the stones, since all large meteorites are irons, and the average mass of an iron is much greater than that of a stone. **1971** I. G. GASS et al. *Understanding Earth* viii. 116/1 The basic division [of meteorites] into irons, stony-irons, and stones is simple and straightforward.

4. g. *slang.* Money. Cf. *IRON-MAN 1 c and d.

1785 GROSE *Dict. Vulgar T., Iron,* money in general. **1906** E. PUGH *Spoilers* i. 5 The iron you're goin' to give me. **1966** C. ROUGVIE *Gredos Reckoning* iii. 50 He was earning a bit of iron.

h. *pl.* Iron supports to correct bow-legs, etc.

1838 DICKENS *Nickleby* (1839) viii. 67 Children..with irons upon their limbs, boys of stunted growth. **1884** W. PYE *Surg. Handicraft* xxv. 319 Wooden splints are.. preferable to 'irons'. **1927** W. E. COLLINSON *Contemp. Eng.* 56 We could see..deformities due to rickets or injuries and the remedies e.g. irons to correct bow-legs.

i. (Usu. in *pl.*) A stirrup. Cf. STIRRUP-IRON 1.

1894 *Country Gentleman's Catal.* 173 Saddles..with girths, stirrup leathers and irons, complete. **1907** *Yesterday's Shopping* (1969) 304 Gentleman's spring-side safety irons, with Prussian sides. **1955** *Times* 30 June 3/7 He bumped Gawthorpe badly, causing Nevett to stand up quickly in his irons. **1963** E. H. EDWARDS *Saddlery* xix. 145 There are two main variations of the basic iron which are the Bent Top iron..and the Kournakoff. **1969** D. M.

GOODALL tr. *Müller's Pocket Dict. Horseman's Terms* 70 *Stirrup/irons*, der Steigbügel.

j. *pl.* Eating utensils. *dial.* and *slang.*

1905 *Eng. Dial. Dict.* Suppl., *Irons*... Cum. Knife and fork, in phr. *to be a good fist with one's irons*, to have a good appetite. **1943** in HUNT & PRINGLE *Service Slang* 40. **1946** J. IRVING *Royal Navalese* 97 *Irons (eating irons)*, the sailor's name for his knife, fork and spoon.

k. *slang.* An old motor vehicle.

1935 *Sun* (N.Y.) 19 Feb. 28/1 'Iron' is the dealer's name for an obsolete [automobile]. **1961** J. STROUD *Touch & Go* xi. 105 'This iron of yours——' began Frank. **1963** *Amer. Speech* XXXVIII. 42 *Iron*, an old truck. **1967** M. REYNOLDS *After Some Tomorrow* 9 Well, it would mean being able to maintain a decent hovercar rather than the..four wheel iron he was currently driving.

l. Used as a form of currency in Sierra Leone.

1936 G. GREENE *Journey without Maps* I. iii. 64 One could speculate in irons: the rate that day was twenty for fourpence.

m. *slang.* A jemmy used in housebreaking.

1941 'V. DAVIS' *Phenomena in Crime* xix. 251 The bishop, cane, iron, or stick. **1962** *John o' London's* 25 Jan. 82/1 Tools for breaking into other people's premises are *irons*.

8*. = *corrugated iron. Austral.* and *N.Z.*

1924 'R. DALY' *Outpost* iii. 28 The Residency was a large iron-and-weatherboard bungalow. **1944** D. STEWART in D.M. Davin *N.Z. Short Stories* (1953) 270 We sat for hours..listening to the rain hammering on the iron roof. **1948** V. PALMER *Golconda* x. 73 Her banter usually glanced off Neda like hail from an iron roof. **1956** G. BOWEN *Wool Away!* (ed. 2) x. 115 Building paper should be used under the iron above the shearing board.

8.** Ellipt. form of *iron hoof*, rhyming slang for 'poof', a homosexual.

1936 J. CURTIS *Gilt Kid* viii. 79 You gets into bed and goes straight off to kip, never touched me you didn't, you great iron. **1938** J. PHELAN *Lifer* iv. 39 Harry had a young iron an' Painter butted in on him. **1961** PARTRIDGE *Adventuring among Words* xii. 58 Gorblimey, 'e's an *iron*, did'n yeh know?

8*.** *Theatr. slang.* Ellipt. form of *IRON CURTAIN I.

1951 R. SOUTHERN in *Oxf. Compan. Theatre* 171/2 Another curtain in the proscenium opening is the Safety or Fireproof Curtain, sometimes nicknamed the Iron. **1952** GRANVILLE *Dict. Theatr. Terms* 102 Iron's down. **1967** N. MARSH *Death at Dolphin* v. 112 'I'll take the Iron up and you can see Jeremy Jones's set for the first act.' He..sent up the elegantly painted fireproof curtain.

11. a. (sense 1 c) *iron pill, tablet, tonic.* **b.** *iron-containing* adj. **c.** *iron-stained* (examples). **d.** *iron-coloured* (later examples), *-like* (later examples), *-red* (examples).

1849 D. G. ROSSETTI *Let.* 27 Sept. (1965) I. 61 The iron-coloured sea. **1909** S. W. BUSHELL *Chinese Art* (ed. 2) II. viii. 26 Bowls and cups with iron-coloured feet and brown mouths. **1901** *Brit. Med. Jrnl.* 23 Nov. 1540/1 It also revealed a yellowish-brown iron-containing substance within the primitive nuclei of red globules. **1926** *Jrnl. Biol. Chem.* LXX. 474 The amounts of iron-containing supplements to be fed. **1946** *Nature* 12 Oct. 516/2 The intensification due to the formation of the iron-containing complex would increase the slope of the density/concentration curves at the lower concentrations of molybdenum. **1908** *Daily Chron.* 17 Sept. 6/3 The discipline is as iron-like as ever. **1963** *Times* 25 Feb. 5/7 Shepherds with Byzantine, iron-like faces protect their flocks against the wolves. **1879** *Family Physician* 809 This condition, known as *chlorosis* or *green sickness*, is readily controlled by the use of iron... The systematic use of the iron pills is almost invariably attended with the most satisfactory results. **1912** *More Secret Remedies* (B.M.A.) 203 The pills were..a form of Blaud's pill, somewhat weaker than the official iron pill. **1820** D. WORDSWORTH *Jrnl.* 11 Aug. (1941) II. 125 Its crags of grey and iron-red hues. **1909** S. W. BUSHELL *Chinese Art* (ed. 2) II. viii. 29 Coral or iron-red *(fan hung)*. **1974** *Country Life* 3/10 Jan. 10/1 Asil game cocks..head and breast enamelled with iron-red flecks over a wash of rouge-de-fer. **1876** MEREDITH in *Fortn. Rev.* 1 June 829 A shape in stone, Sword-hacked and iron-stained. **1915** E. R. LANKESTER *Diversions of Naturalist* vii. 63 A few only iron-stained and yellow. **1957** *Brit. Nat. Formulary* (B.M.A.) (ed. 4) 147 *Ferrous Carbonate Tablets*, B.P.C. Synonyms: Blaud's tablets: iron tablets. **1933** E. C. PEARCE *Short Encycl. for Nurses* 24 Good nourishing food,..combined with the use of iron tonics, is all that is necessary. **1973** J. PORTER *It's Murder with Dover* ix. 88 Getting her daughter to take a dose of iron tonic.

12. iron bacterium, any of various bacteria, found esp. in fresh water, which are capable of oxidizing ferrous salts to ferric hydroxide (perhaps obtaining energy thereby) and storing the end product in their structure; **iron-binding** *a.*, able to combine chemically with iron; *sb.*, combination with iron; also *attrib.*; **iron buff,** hydrated ferric oxide used as a dye for cotton by impregnating the cloth with a soluble iron salt, passing it through an alkali solution, and oxidizing; **iron deficiency,** insufficient iron in an organism or in its food; also *attrib.*, so *iron-deficient* adj.; **iron-fall** (earlier example); **iron gang** *Austral.*, a gang of prisoners working in irons; **iron loss** *Electr.* = *core-loss* (*CORE *sb.*[1] 15); **iron maiden,** an instrument of torture consisting of a coffin-shaped box lined inside with iron spikes, inside which the victim is confined; also *transf.* and *fig.*; also *iron maid*; **iron mask,** a mask, supposedly made of iron, worn by a political prisoner in France at the time of Louis XIV who died in the Bastille in 1703 and whose identity is disputed; hence used as the name of the prisoner himself; also *fig.*; **iron mountain,** a mountain rich in iron ore; **iron play** *Golf*, a specified manner of playing with irons (sense 4 e); so **iron player; iron ration,** *(a)* (usu. *pl.*) an emergency ration of tinned food, esp. as provided in the armed services; *(b)* various extended and *fig.* uses; **iron shot** *Golf*, a shot made with an iron; **iron virgin** = *iron maiden.

1888 *Jrnl. R. Microsc. Soc.* 786 Bacteria which assume a rust-coloured hue were denominated iron-bacteria by Ehrenberg. *Ibid.*, The oxidizing power of the cells of iron-bacteria must be extremely great. **1919** D. ELLIS *(title)* Iron bacteria. **1945** *Science* 23 Nov. 533/1 It seems unreasonable..to conclude that an organism is an iron bacterium or that it is developing as an iron bacterium unless there are far greater quantities of ferric hydrate than cell substance in the accumulated materials resulting from bacterial growth. **1955** K. V. THIMANN *Life of Bacteria* xxi. 598 The iron bacteria are of two types, unicellular and multicellular. **1946** *Science* 11 Oct. 340/1 *(heading)* An iron-binding component in human blood plasma. **1949** *Arch. Biochem.* XX. 170 *(heading)* Carbon dioxide and oxygen in complex formation with iron and siderophilin, the iron-binding component of human plasma. *Ibid.* 172 *(heading)* On the mode of iron binding by siderophilin. **1970** *Clin. Chem.* XVI. 148/1 An automated method has been developed for determining serum iron-binding capacity. **1902** *Encycl. Brit.* XXVII. 564/1 Iron Buff is produced by impregnating the cotton with a solution of ferrous sulphate, squeezing, passing into sodium hydrate or carbonate solution, and finally exposing to air. **1925** S. R. & E. R. TROTMAN *Bleaching, Dyeing & Chem. Technol. Textile Fibres* xxxiii. 517 Iron buffs are fast to light, washing, and alkalis, but are sensitive to acids. **1971** R. J. ADROSKO *Nat. Dyes & Home Dyeing* 49 While one might deduce correctly that iron buff would not necessarily produce a lively color, it was expected to last for the life of the textile. **1923** *Biochem. Jrnl.* XVII. 205 The result was that the symptoms and effects of iron deficiency as described appeared in the pigs. **1929** *Trans. & Proc. N.Z. Inst.* Mar. 51 The theory..that iron deficiency in the pasture was the cause of 'Bush Sickness', was finally adopted. **1956** *Nature* 18 Jan. 336/1 Metal-induced iron-deficiency in crop plants. **1971** *Brit. Med. Bull.* XXVII. 6/2 The detection of iron deficiency anaemia by measuring the haemoglobin content of the blood. *Ibid.* 32/1 Iron deficiency is believed to be common in Great Britain in adult women of all ages. **1932** *Biol. Abstr.* VI. 792/1 'Salt sick' of cattle on certain iron-deficient sandy and residual soils has proved to be a nutritional anemia due to deficiency of Fe, or of Fe and Cu in the forage crops. **1956** *Nature* 14 Jan. 95/1 In iron-deficient plants there is observed an increase of the soluble forms of nitrogen, with a simultaneous decrease of its protein forms. **1846** *Amer. Jrnl. Sci. & Arts* II. 385 We find in the weight of the two iron-falls (Croatia, 1752, and Tennessee, 1835) as set off against that of all the stones.., a ratio approximating that of one (for irons) to twenty (for stones). **1840** *Sydney Gaz.* 8 Feb. in Stewart & Keesing *Old Bush Songs* (1957) 29 I'll tell the Mahers, MacNamaras and McCartys All about iron gangs and road parties. **1848** H. W. HAYGARTH *Recoll. Bush Life Austral.* iv. 35 Had escaped with one or two others from his 'iron gang'. **1945** BAKER *Austral. Lang.* ii. 44 A bullock wagon taking supplies to men in an iron gang. **1894** *Electrician* 14 Dec. 190/2 In the case of certain transformers specially tested for the purpose no time increase in the iron loss takes place. **1931** A. W. HIRST *Direct Current Machine Design* vi. 106 *(heading)* Armature iron losses. **1958** E. H. FROST-SMITH *Theory & Design Magnetic Amplifiers* xiii. 366 Excessive iron losses cause reduced gain. **1951** E. E. CUMMINGS *Let.* 10 Feb. (1969) 211 Later or sooner I always glimpse a miserably exhausted me—tortured in his 'iron maid'—waiting & waiting. **1895** *Brewer's Dict. Phr. & Fable* (new ed.) 662/2 *Iron Maiden of Nuremberg*,..a box big enough to admit a man, with folding-doors, the whole studded with sharp iron spikes. When the doors were pressed-to these spikes were forced into the body of the victim... (German, *Eiserne Jungfrau*.) **1958** J. BALDWIN in W. King *Black Short Story Anthol.* (1972) 278 Then she hated herself; thinking into what an iron maiden of love and hatred he had placed her, she hated him even more. **1962** F. I. ORDWAY et al. *Basic Astronautics* xii. 465 Submerged in this water-filled 'iron maiden'..a subject was able to withstand 31 *G* for a period of 5 sec. **1972** *Daily Tel.* 11 Oct. 19/7 The 'callous and inhuman' treatment of a Moscow Jewish scientist said to have been incarcerated in an 'iron maiden'... He had been held..in a cell measuring 3 ft by 18 inches... The walls of the cell were covered with spikes which prevented him leaning or sitting down. **1752** tr. *Voltaire's Age of Lewis XIV.* II. xxiv. 10 The marshal de Feuillade..has told me, that when his father-in-law [*sc.* Chamillard] was dying, he conjured him..to tell him who this person was, who had been known by no other name than that of the *man with the iron mask.* Chamillard answered him, it was the secret of state, and he had sworn never to reveal it. **1826** G. A. ELLIS *(title)* The true history of the state prisoner commonly called the Iron Mask, extracted from documents in the French archives. **1841** C. FOX *Jrnl.* 20 Apr. (1972) 104 Sterling..believes that Kasper Häuser was an imposter. The Iron Mask much more fascinating, but unluckily there was no prince in Europe missing at the time. **1858** GEO. ELIOT *Let.* 21 Jan. (1954) II. 424 The iron mask of my incognito seems quite painful in forbidding me to tell Dickens how thoroughly his generous impulse has been appreciated. **1869** 'MARK TWAIN' *Innoc. Abr.* (1870) xi. 75 They showed us the noisome cell where the celebrated 'Iron Mask'—that ill-starred brother of a hard-hearted king of France—was confined. **1893** H. L. WILLIAMS tr. *Dumas's Man in Iron Mask* xliii. 332 D'Artagnan..asked himself..why the Iron Mask had thrown the silver plate at the feet of Raoul? **1959** *Oxf. Compan. French Lit.* 460/2 So persistent was the rumour that Monmouth had survived his supposed execution in 1685 that Voltaire thought it necessary to deny..that he was the Man in the Iron Mask. **1968** M. GUYBON tr. *Solzhenitsyn's First Circle* x. 52 At all times the privileged prisoner's cell was in semi-darkness... The other prisoners nicknamed him 'The Man in the Iron Mask'. No one knew his real name. **1838** *Boston Weekly Mag.* 24 Nov. 91/1 Having visited the Iron Mountain in Missouri..I am happy to add my testimony..respecting the remarkable deposites of iron ores. **1846** *Sci. Amer.* 12 Dec. 90/1 The new blast furnace at the iron mountain is again in blast. **1887** *Encycl. Brit.* XXII. 638/2 [Sumatra]. Iron is not unfrequent, and magnetic iron is obtained at the 'Iron Mountain' near Fort van der Capellen. **1969** *Times* 21 Nov. 27/3 The most poignant part of the trip was a visit to Hamersley [in Western Australia] to see Mount Tom Price, the 'iron mountain'. **1892** Iron play [see PUTTING *vbl. sb.*[2] 1]. **1973** *Country Life* 21 June 1806/3 An historic exhibition of iron play by a master of the game [*sc.* golf]. **1909** *Westm. Gaz.* 22 Feb. 12/2 He was also a most accomplished iron player. **1876** VOYLE & STEVENSON *Mil. Dict.* (ed. 3) 20/2 The ordinary iron rations for two days should be 2 lbs. preserved meat and 2 lbs. biscuits, supplemented in such manner as circumstances admit. **1896** FARMER & HENLEY *Slang* IV. 16/1 *Iron-rations* (nautical), tinned meat; specifically boiled salt-beef. **1915** 'I. HAY' *First Hundred Thousand* xvi. 215 A haversack, occupied by his 'iron ration'—an emergency meal of the tinned variety, which must never on any account be opened except by order of the C.O. **1918** E. S. FARROW *Dict. Mil. Terms* 318 Fritz is getting his iron rations. **1925** FRASER & GIBBONS *Soldier & Sailor Words* 128 'Iron rations' was in the War also a colloquial expression in speaking of a hot shell-fire, *e.g.*, 'Jerry is letting them have it, lots of iron rations flying about!' **1951** L. MACNEICE tr. *Goethe's Faust* I. 61 O believe *me*, who have been chewing These iron rations many a thousand year. **1970** R. LOWELL *Notebk.* 235 The new painting has to live on iron rations. **1973** *Daily Tel.* 25 Apr. 36/6 When the boys left on their expedition they took with them only one day's supply of food, and intended to pick up more provisions during their journey. They..included in their packs 'iron rations' of chocolate, raisins and Kendal mint cake. **1909** *Westm. Gaz.* 28 May 12/3 Maxwell..had made a splendid iron shot. *c* **1895** B. STOKER *Squaw* in *B. Stoker Bedside Compan.* (1973) 123 When we got back to the chamber we found Hutcheson still opposite the Iron Virgin. **1906** J. HUNEKER *Melomaniacs* 273 You remember the summer I spent at Nuremberg digging up the old legend, and the numberless times I visited the torture chamber where stands the real Iron Virgin, her interior studded with horrid spikes? **1973** C. OSBORNE in B. Stoker *B. Stoker Bedside Compan.* 11 'The Squaw'..involves a torture device which Bram had examined in Nuremburg, a contraption known as the 'Iron Virgin'.

b. iron-monticellite [tr. G. *eisenmonticellit* (C. Doelter *Handb. d. Mineralchem.* (1914) II. I. 499)], a silicate of calcium and iron, $CaFeSiO_4$, analogous to monticellite, found as a constituent of slag and more recently as a natural mineral (kirschsteinite); **iron pan** (earlier and later examples).

1937 *Mineral. Mag.* XXIV. 613 Iron-monticellite. **1950** *Jrnl. Amer. Ceramic Soc.* XXXIII. 164/2 Iron-monticellite ($CaFeSiO_4$) is a compound that forms an unbroken series of solid solutions with fayalite (Fe_2SiO_4). **1957** *Mineral. Mag.* XXXI. 698 *(heading)* Kirschsteinite, a natural analogue to synthetic iron monticellite, from the Belgian Congo. **1840** *Outl. Flemish Husbandry* in *Brit. Husbandry* III. II. ii. 12 Between the sand and the loam, an indurated crust of earth cemented by carbonate of iron, which is well known to all improvers of poor sands by the name of the iron pan. **1949** *Antiquity* XXIII. 35 A thick layer of the same blue clay..was incorporated in the body of the cairn between two layers of stones: it had been trampled down and iron-pan had formed on it. **1961** *Listener* 12 Oct. 559/1 The soil is a 'podsol', with its contrasting dark, humic, white-leached, and iron-pan layers.

iron, *a.* Add: **3. c.** *iron hand*: in var. phrases with *velvet glove* indicative of firmness or inflexibility combined with apparent softness or gentleness. Also, formerly in Australia, the closure (see quots. 1876, 1883).

1850 T. CARLYLE *Latter-Day Pamph.* ii. 8 Soft of speech and manner, yet with an inflexible rigour of command.. 'iron hand in a velvet glove', as Napoleon defined it. **1876** *Victorian Hansard* 20 Jan. 2002 They [*sc.* the Government] have dealt with the Opposition with a velvet glove; but the iron hand is beneath, and they shall feel it. **1883** G. W. RUSDEN *Hist. Austral.* III. 406 The *clôture*, or the 'iron hand', as McCulloch's resolution was called, was adopted in Victoria, for one session. **1925** WODEHOUSE *Carry on, Jeeves!* i. 14 You have to keep these fellows in their place, don't you know. You have to work the good old iron-hand-in-the-velvet-glove wheeze. **1941** S. WOOD *Murder of Novelist* (1946) xvi. 123 She..runs the town.. with an iron hand. And no nonsense about a velvet glove. **1942** R. A. J. WALLING *Corpse with Eerie Eye* vi. 177 The velvet glove and the iron hand are outmoded. **1963** *Times* 2 Feb. 7/2 Mr. Winston Field, who has so far shown only the velvet glove since he was elected Prime Minister of Southern Rhodesia in December, today revealed the iron hand expected of Rhodesian Front Government when he announced a Bill to introduce the death penalty by hanging for various offences, including the throwing of petrol bombs.

4. a. *iron-jawed, -knobbed, -minded, -railed, -studded, -willed* (examples), adjs.

1883 'MARK TWAIN' *Life on Mississippi* iii. 45 I'm the old original iron-jawed, brass-mounted..corpse-maker from the wilds of Arkansaw! **1926** E. HEMINGWAY *Torrents of Spring* (1933) i. 26 A short, iron-jawed man. **1895** B. M. CROKER *Village Tales* 196 Shut it out by merely closing to the street an iron-knobbed wooden door. **1949** BLUNDEN *After Bombing* 41 At the iron-knobbed

church door. **1897** J. L. ALLEN *Choir Invisible* xii. 168 Fighting it all over in his foolish, iron-minded way. **1944** BLUNDEN *Shells by Stream* 9 Squadrons of gem-eyed hobby-horses Whirr round his iron-minded forces. **1968** *Punch* 28 Feb. 323/2 His blunt, iron-minded relatives in Yorkshire. **1883** 'MARK TWAIN' *Life on Mississippi* xliv. 442 Long, iron-railed verandas running along the several stories. **1964** A. WYKES *Gambling* i. 10 He had set up an iron-railed podium. **1903** *Trawl* May 30 In the wall in front of him was an iron-studded door. **1848** J. R. LOWELL in *National Anti-Slavery Standard* 9 Nov. 96/1 In that far isle, whence, iron-willed, The new-world's sires their bark unmoored. **1951** M. MCLUHAN *Mech. Bride* (1967) 67/1 Thurber's 'Mother' is a flint-eyed, iron-willed, Republican matriarch.

c. iron cap = IRON HAT 2; **iron chink** [*CHINK *sb.*^{5}] (see quot. 1942); **Iron Cross** [G. *das eiserne kreuz*], a German and Austrian decoration awarded for distinguished services in war (founded by Frederick William III of Prussia in 1813, to reward those who served in the wars against Napoleon, and later revived by William I in 1870); **Iron Duke,** a name for the first Duke of Wellington (1769–1852); **Iron Guard,** an anti-Semitic, Fascist, terrorist Rumanian political party developed from the Legion of the Archangel Michael, founded by C. Z. Codreanu (?1899–1938) in 1927; **iron gum(-tree)** *Austral.*, one of several Queensland species of *Eucalyptus* which have particularly strong wood; **iron horse** (earlier and later examples); **iron jubilee,** the seventieth anniversary of an event; **iron law** (of wages), the law or idea that wages tend to sink to the level of mere subsistence; **iron mike** *slang*, a familiar name for the automatic steering device of a ship; **iron oak,** for def. (s.v. sense 12 of the sb.) read: any of several oaks with particularly durable wood, as *Quercus cerris*, *Q. stellata*, etc.; add examples; **iron paper,** extremely thin sheet-iron.

1911 *Chambers's Jrnl.* Mar. 166/1 The indication of a deposit of pyrites is the appearance of an outcrop of oxide of iron more or less honeycombed. This is called the 'iron cap', or in Cornwall 'gossan'. **1913** *Heaton's Guide to Western Canada* 11 In the salmon canneries the introduction of a machine called the 'Iron Chink', for cleaning and cutting the fish has made a great economy in the cost of labor. **1914** *Star* 14 Nov. 4/4 The 'iron chink' cuts off the heads, tails, and fins, dresses the fish at the rate of 3,000 per hour. **1942** H. W. VON LOESECKE *Outl. Food Technol.* vi. 228 The fish..go to the so-called 'iron chink', a machine which automatically severs the head and eviscerates the fish. In the early days of the [salmon] industry, this work was performed by Chinese labor, hence the name 'iron chink' for the machine. **1963** *Vancouver Sun* 5 Apr. 34/1 (Advt.), Fishing company requires qualified iron chink operator. **1871** *Monthly Packet* July 24 Two prints which appeared during the autumn of 1870 in the Illustrated London News, one..of the Crown Prince distributing the Iron Cross. **1902** *Encycl. Brit.* XXXI. 340/2 The Austrian Iron Cross, founded by Napoleon I. as king of Italy in 1805..conferred for personal merit. **1914** *Punch* 11 Nov. 390/2 The Iron Cross. (For German looters.) **1944** V. G. GARVIN tr. *R. Gary's Forest of Anger* xxvi. 114 My Frieda would rather have me back with pox than dead with the Iron Cross! **1850** Iron Duke [see DUKE *sb.* 3 a]. **1852** (*title*) The wisdom of Wellington; or maxims of the Iron Duke. **1882** [see *CORSICAN *a.* and *sb.* 1]. **1928** O. BRETT *Wellington* xix. 278 (*heading*) The Iron Duke. **1957** *Encycl. Brit.* XXIII. 501 As a diplomatist the 'Iron Duke'..was no match for the 'Iron Tsar'. **1965** W. R. BENÉT *Reader's Encycl.* (ed. 2) 1081/1 Wellington, 1st duke of. Arthur Wellesley. Known as the Iron Duke. **1933** *Times* 16 Nov. 13/2 It is reported that the new Government has decided to dissolve the Iron Guard organization..anti-Semitic and pro-Fascist and Hitlerist. **1934** *Ann. Reg. 1933* 210 M. Duca..was assassinated..by a student member of the Iron Guard. **1942** L. B. NAMIER *Conflicts* 46 The Iron Guard, which was indebted to Germany for much of its income and of its revolutionary *élan*, indulged in the extremest forms of anti-Semitism, demanded a complete dictatorship with a social revolutionary programme. **1971** W. LAQUEUR *Dict. Politics* 438 After mounting Iron Guard atrocities and massacres of Gentiles as well as Jews, Antonescu repressed the Iron Guards with German consent. **1879** F. VON MUELLER *Eucalyptographia* 1, s.v. *Eucalyptus Raveretiana*. Vernacularly it passes in the districts of its growth as 'Grey Gum-tree' and 'Iron Gum-tree'. **1888** F. M. BAILEY *Queensland Woods* 63 E[*ucalyptus*] *Raveretiana*...Thozet's Box or Iron Gum-tree. A large tree with a scaly bark persistent on the trunk. **1919** R. T. BAKER *Hardwoods Austral.* 173 *Eucalyptus Raveretiana*, F. von M. 'Thozet's Box' or 'Iron Gum Tree'...close-grained, very hard, and tough; valuable for building purposes. **1957** *N.Z. Timber Jrnl.* Sept. 61/1 *Irongum*: Eucalyptus spp. Australia. The best known is E. maculata Hook, or spotted gum. Weight 64 lbs. **1970** N. HALL et al. *Forest Trees Austral.* 46 Spotted iron gum (Qld) *Eucalyptus maculata*. **1840** D. MARCH *Yankee Land* 23 There were noble steeds in the days of old... But the iron horse, there were none like him! **1846** *Congress. Globe* 6 Feb. 323/3 The iron horse.. with the wings of the wind,..vomiting fire and smoke. **1958** C. ACHEBE *Things fall Apart* xvi. 129 Stories about these strange men [*sc.* missionaries] had grown since one of them had been killed in Abame and his iron horse tied to the sacred silk-cotton tree. **1967** C. O. SKINNER *Madame Sarah* viii. 171 The engineer returned to his iron horse and the train started. **1903** *Westm. Gaz.* 6 Feb. 10/1 Pope Leo XIII. will celebrate..during the present year..his 'Iron Jubilee' as a priest—he was ordained seventy years ago. **1896** R. H. I. PALGRAVE *Dict. Pol. Econ.* II. 568/1 He [*sc.* Lassalle] dwelt on what he called the iron or 'brazen law' (*ehernes Gesetz*) of wages, already laid down by Turgot and Ricardo. **1907** J. S. NICHOLSON in *Cambr. Mod. Hist.* X. 774 Ricardo..was credited with the 'iron law of wages' on the one side and the theories of the continuous growth of rent and the unearned increment on the other. **1913** *Pitman's Commercial Encycl.* IV. 1662/2 The 'iron law'.. of the mere subsistence wage taught that the general rate of wages constantly tends to starvation limit. **1966** A. GILPIN *Dict. Econ. Terms* 219 *Subsistence theory.* Of French origin, this 'iron law' of wages asserted that if wages rose above subsistence level an increase in population would inevitably follow, thus forcing wages down again to subsistence level. **1926** M. CRANE *Yarns from Windjammer* 27 He [*sc.* the quartermaster] will be jealous indeed of the praise bestowed on Iron Mike, an eight-foot high iron box, with complicated electrical 'innards', for the Captain of the liner on which Gyro-pilot—Iron Mike's Sunday name—was tried, stated that the ship saved eight or ten miles a day by superior steering. **1937** *Jrnl. R. Aeronaut. Soc.* XLI. 415 The automatic helmsman or 'Iron Mike' for marine craft was a proved success. **1956** A. G. COURSE *Merchant Navy Today* ix. 130 Now we have a gyro-compass pilot or automatic helmsman—often known as an 'iron mike'—which steers the ship. **1742** W. ELLIS *Timber-Tree Improved* II. i. 15 The white iron or ring Oak has its Name from the long Duration of its Timber. **1810** W. WADE tr. *Michaux's Quercus* 1 *Chêne gris.* Upland white oak, iron oak. **1832** D. J. BROWNE *Sylva Amer.* 275 In Maryland and a great part of Virginia ..it [*sc. Quercus stellata*] is called Box White Oak, and sometimes Iron Oak and Post Oak. **1838** J. C. LOUDON *Arboretum* III. 1846 Q[*uercus*] *Cerris* L. The bitter, or mossy-cupped, Oak...the Turkey Oak; the Iron, or Wainscot, Oak. **1908** N. L. BRITTON *N. Amer. Trees* 342 It [*sc. Quercus stellata*, post oak] is also known as Box white oak, Iron oak [etc.]. **1871** F. KILVERT *Diary* 27 Dec. (1969) II. 101 A new invention, iron paper, as thin as the thinnest tissue paper. The sheets of iron are rolled so thin that 3000 sheets together are only an inch thick.

iron, *v.* Add: **3.** *fig.* (Further examples of *iron out.*)

1905 *Springfield* (Mass.) *Weekly Republ.* 31 Mar. 8 The differences between Chairman Flaherty..and Col. William A. Gaston are in a fair way to be amicably ironed out. **1924** 'L. MALET' *Dogs of Want* v. 122 Mr. Harvey-Noakes plays a ripping game... He has flattened me out,..completely ironed me out. **1929** *Observer* 17 Nov. 3/4 The best practical method of ironing out ups and downs of the business cycle. **1930** *Time & Tide* 28 Mar. 389 The progress of negotiations to 'iron out' differences between Britain, Japan, and America. **1949** F. SWINNERTON *Doctor's Wife comes to Stay* vii. 80 Roly..had married a widow with children,..and been—in the cliché of the day—'ironed out'. **1971** *Daily Tel.* 28 Oct. 29/5 Like the great horseman he is, he patiently ironed out the kinks in plenty of time to catch Hush Money on the flat. **1971** *Guardian* 1 Nov. 6/4 The new computer was delivered.. last week.. Ironing out the bugs will probably take until the new year.

b. *intr.* Of a garment, material, etc.: to respond to ironing, to undergo smoothing or pressing with an iron.

1943 *Mod. Lang. Notes* Jan. 12 They claim that.. 'lingerie *tubs* quickly and *irons* easily'. **1946** *Ibid.* Nov. 444 The use, in advertising, of the 'potential intransitive', in such examples as..'this dress *washes* and *irons* and *packs* easily'.

iron-bark. Add: (Later examples.)

1909 A. E. MACK *Bush Calendar* 4 The blue gums, ironbarks, and turpentines gave way to scribbly gums and banksias. **1911** E. M. CLOWES *On Wallaby* ix. 249 In the Victorian Grampians is to be found for the most part blue gum and messmate, stringy bark, and red and white iron bark. **1967** A. RULE *Forests Austral.* ii. 27 A list of the more valuable species would include the red and the grey ironbarks—those hard, heavy and tremendously tough timbers that make the name ironbark almost synonymous with durability.

d. Passing into *adj.*: hard, unyielding. *Austral.*

1888 'R. BOLDREWOOD' *Robbery under Arms* I. vi. 85, I always thought he was ironbark outside and in. **1945** BAKER *Austral. Lang.* 90 From countrymen in general, *ironbark*, unyielding.

iron-blue. Add: **c.** *sb.* The pigment Prussian blue (PRUSSIAN *a.* 2).

1930 A. W. C. HARRISON *Manuf. Lakes & Precipitated Pigments* ix. 124 The term 'iron blue' covers a number of types and shades of 'Prussian blues'. **1948** S. F. DIMLICH in W. von Fischer *Paint & Varnish Technol.* vi. 93 Iron blue is probably the most important blue pigment used by the paint industry. **1967** KARCH & BUBER *Offset Processes* vii. 268 Iron blue (made in a number of shades, such as milori blue, bronze blue, prussian blue, etc.) is a chemical compound of iron.

iron-cased, *a.* Add: Also in other uses.

1901 L. M. WATERHOUSE *Conduit Wiring* 50 The Simplex iron-cased distributing boards. **1906** *Westm. Gaz.* 29 Aug. 10/1 His tubular iron-cased telephone. **1921** *Wireless World* 25 June 200/1 T_4 and T_5 are fixed audio-frequency transformers, iron-cased and with iron cores.

ironclad, iron-clad, *a.* and *sb.* Add: **A.** *adj.* **1. b.** Applied to electrical apparatus.

1902 *Encycl. Brit.* XXVII. 584/2 The two-poled ironclad type [of field-magnet], so called from the exciting coil being more or less encased by the iron yoke. **1910** *Hawkins' Electr. Dict.*, *Iron-clad dynamo*, a dynamo having an iron-clad armature. **1927** W. WILSON *Electr. Control Gear* xvi. 226 There are..reasonably cheap ironclad types of starting equipment on the market. **1939** READ & CORCORAN *Electr. Engin. Exper.* 91 The iron-clad solenoid can be made more effective by providing it with a stationary iron core which occupies about 20 or 30 per cent of the axial length.

2. *fig.* Also, of plants, able to withstand cold and frost. *U.S.*

1872 *Rep. Vermont Board Agric.* I. 54 Currants and gooseberries are iron clad as regards climate. **1882** *Rep. Maine Board Agric.* XXVI. 336 It is an early winter fruit, the tree not perfectly 'iron clad', notwithstanding its origin, yet hardy enough for most places.

3. (Earlier and later examples.)

1866 *Congress. Globe* 14 Feb. 835/1 Traitors never would be troubled with the 'iron-clad oath', for they never would have a chance to take it. **1868** *Harper's Mag.* Sept. 484/2 [He] was as well reconstructed as a man might be who could not take the iron-clad oath. **1873** J. MILLER *Life amongst Modocs* xxvi. 304 Some hard, iron-clad oaths and then shot after shot. **1911** H. S. HARRISON *Queed* x. 114 He insisted on doing it after an ironclad schedule. **1930** *Observer* 1 June 11 The rationing system..is not so complete or ironclad as those which prevailed in various European countries during the war. **1951** E. KEFAUVER *Crime in America* (1952) xix. 223 The operations of Murder, Inc., finally came to light when..police obtained ironclad evidence against a gangster known as Abe (Kid Twist) Reles.

B. *sb.* **2.** *transf.* and *fig.*

1867 J. N. EDWARDS *Shelby* 483 The West Pointers were the iron-clads in our wooden navy. **1875** 'MARK TWAIN' *Sk. New & Old* (1900) 157 After the Tortoises came another long train of ironclads—stately and spacious Mud Turtles. **1889** —— *Connecticut Yankee* xxxix. 456 Things began to look serious to the iron-clads [*sc.* knights in armour]. **1892** O. F. WHITNEY *Hist. Utah* I. 547 The ravages of the 'iron-clads' [i.e. grasshoppers] were widespread and far-reaching. **1974** *Country Life* 28 Mar. 752/1 Those plants that are always a risk, climatewise, but which do offer rewards..such as the hardy ironclads can never quite match. **1974** *Oxford Times* 19 Apr. 3/3 'Iron clads' are the..term for day-old Chelsea buns.

iron curtain. [f. IRON *sb.*^{1} + CURTAIN *sb.*^{1}] **1.** In a theatre, a curtain of iron which can be lowered between the stage and the auditorium in order to prevent passage or communication, or for protection.

1794 *Times* 13 Mar. 3/2 Besides other precautions, an iron curtain has been contrived, which, on such occasion [of fire], would compleatly prevent all communication between the audience and stage. **1829** H. FOOTE *Compan. to Theatres* 30 As a precaution against fire, an iron curtain was constructed, so as to let down in a moment of danger and separate the audience from the stage. **1891** SCOTT & HOWARD *Life E. L. Blanchard* II. 557 And provision against fire is made [in the Prince of Wales' Theatre] by an iron curtain. **1908** WODEHOUSE & WESTBROOK *Globe by the Way Bk.* 51/2 'The iron curtain,' she gasped, and exerting her full strength, held the actor under the descending sheet of metal.

2. *fig.* Any impenetrable barrier.

After 1946 regarded as a transf. use of sense *2 b.

1819 EARL OF MUNSTER *Jrnl. Route across India 1817–18* iv. 58 On the 19th November we crossed the river Betwah, and as if an iron curtain had dropt between us and the avenging angel, the deaths diminished. **1904** H. G. WELLS *Food of Gods* III. iv. 274 It became evident that Redwood had still imperfectly apprehended the fact that an iron curtain had dropped between him and the outer world. **1915** G. W. CRILE *Mechanistic View War & Peace* iv. 69 Suppose that Mexico were a rich, cultured, and brave nation of forty million with a deep-rooted grievance, and an iron curtain at its frontier. [**1916** E. HOWARD *Potsdam Princes* 250 The war, of course, has made them bitter enemies, and when reminded of her German relations, Queen Elizabeth of Belgium is reported to have said that between her and her people in Bavaria a curtain of iron had fallen.] **1939** J. GLOAG *Word Warfare* xi. 113 In an international crisis Germany can be cut off from the world by an iron curtain of censorship. **1946** J. C. DAVIES *Episcopal Acts Welsh Dioceses 1066–1272* I. 43 Within this iron curtain in the south the princes of Deheubarth maintained a precarious independence until the middle of the thirteenth century. **1959** *Listener* 29 Jan. 198/1 By tact and determination she gradually broke down the iron curtain and mobilized the women into a united Conservative front. **1962** *Daily Tel.* 15 Aug. 13/2 There was no 'Iron Curtain' between them and the consumer. **1967** *Freedomways* VII. 119 Since I don't want the United States to appear like an 'Iron Curtain' to the Vietnamese, I think it would be good for several Vietnamese women to visit this country.

b. *spec.* (usually with initial capitals). A barrier to the passage of information, etc., at the limit of the sphere of influence of the Soviet Union. Cf. **bamboo curtain* (*BAMBOO *sb.* 2), *CURTAIN *sb.*^{1} 3 c. Also in extended use (as quot. 1924).

The *locus classicus* is quot. 1946.

1920 MRS. P. SNOWDEN *Through Bolshevik Russia* ii. 32 We were behind the 'iron curtain' at last! **1924** LORD D'ABERNON *Diary* 14 Sept. in *Ambassador of Peace* (1930) III. iv. 101 Stresemann considered that it was essential for the Rhineland to be frankly part of Germany, also for Danzig to be reincorporated. Without this there could be no permanent peace. I put forward my view of the reciprocal iron curtain or strip of inviolable territory as a protection. [**1945** *Times* 23 Feb. 3/4 (tr. Paul Josef Goebbels, German Minister for Propaganda, from *Das Reich*) If the German people lay down their arms, the whole of eastern and south-eastern Europe, together with the Reich, would come under Russian occupation. Behind an iron screen [*ein eiserner Vorhang*] mass butcheries of peoples would begin.] **1945** *Times* 3 May 4/5 (speech by the German Foreign Minister, Schwerin von Krosigk) In the East the iron curtain behind which, unseen by the eyes of the world, the work of destruction goes on is moving steadily forward. **1945** SIR ST. V.

TROUBRIDGE in *Sunday Empire News* 21 Oct. 2/2 A Curtain Across Europe... Yet at present an iron curtain of silence has descended, cutting off the Russian zone from the Western Allies. **1946** W. S. CHURCHILL in *Times* 6 Mar. 6/1 (Address at Westminster College, Fulton, U.S.A., 5 March) From Stettin, in the Baltic, to Trieste, in the Adriatic, an iron curtain has descended across the Continent. **1953** *Encounter* Oct. 58/1 If they live behind the Iron Curtain they can do none of these things—for, while the Communists agree that knowledge is power, they are persuaded that they are already in essential possession of both. **1953** W. S. CHURCHILL *Second World War* (1954) VI. xxxiv. 498 In these same days I also sent what may be called the 'Iron Curtain' telegram to President Truman.. *Prime Minister to President Truman* 12 May 45..An iron curtain is drawn down upon their front. We do not know what is going on behind. **1971** *Times Lit. Suppl.* 31 Dec. 1621/5 The theory of convergence informs us that societies on both sides of the Iron Curtain are conditioned by similar forces in all essential respects, whatever the differences in kind or degree of individual liberty enjoyed by their members. **1972** *Guardian* 23 Aug. 7/5 The iron curtain that fell on Anglo-Soviet cultural deals when 105 Soviet diplomats were expelled from Britain last year has been lifted. **1973** J. M. WHITE *Gooden Game* 184 One of Harrison's local contacts, an experienced Iron Curtain operator.

irone (aiə·rōᵘn). *Chem.* [ad. *G. iron* (Tiemann & Krüger 1893, in *Ber. d. Deut. Chem. Ges.* XXVI. 2679), f. G. *ir-is* IRIS *sb.* 5: see -ONE.] Orig., an essential oil obtained from orris-root; hence, any of the three isomers (*α*-, *β*-, and *γ-irone*) of which this is composed, which are cyclic ketones, $(CH_3)_4C_6H_5\cdot CH{:}CH\cdot CO\cdot CH_3$, that differ only in the position of the double bond in the C_6H_5 ring and are methyl derivatives of the ionones.

1894 *Jrnl. Chem. Soc.* LXVI. I. 80 The readily-volatile fraction [of iris root] contains the irone or fragrant oil. *Ibid.*, Irone..is an oil which is scarcely soluble in water. **1934** *Chem. Abstr.* XXVIII. 4053 Analyses of irone.. establish the compn. $C_{14}H_{22}O$. **1948** *Ann. Rep. Progr. Chem.* XLIV. 148 While *α*- and *γ*-irone possess a fresh violet odour (the 'irone' odour), the *β*-isomer has an ionone smell. **1952** SIMONSEN & OWEN *Terpenes* (ed. 2) III. 497 It is now recognised that irone is 6-methylionone, and that it can exist in the *α*-, *β*-, and *γ*-forms..each of which has several stereoisomeric modifications. *Ibid.* 503 *γ*-Irone is transformed into a mixture of *α*- and *β*-irones when treated with dilute sulphuric acid. **1963** *Chem. Abstr.* LVIII. 1500 Irones are used in the manuf. of perfumes; and they can be synthesized from dextro-*α*-pinene.

ironer. 1. (Earlier examples.)

1773 *South Carolina Gaz.* 26 July, To be sold...a complete Washer and Ironer, and remarkable for doing up Ladies fine Cloaths. **1820** *Barbados Mercury & Bridge-Town Gaz.* 16 Sept. 4/3 (Advt.), Also for sale, a family of Negroes, consisting of a woman, a complete washer and ironer, [etc.].

ironing, *vbl. sb.* Add: **1.** Further *attrib.* uses, as *ironing blanket, board, machine, room, stool; ironing table* (later examples).

1810 E. WEETON *Let.* 25 Feb. in *Jrnl. of Governess* (1969) I. 232, I flew into the servants' hall for the ironing blanket. **1854** MRS. GASKELL *North & South* (1855) I. iv. 44 Dixon had complained that the ironing-blanket had been burnt again. **1843** *New Mirror* 8 Apr. 4/2 Swapped away for a wash-bench or an ironing-board. **1876** H. E. SCUDDER *Dwellers in Five-Sisters Court* iii. 52 Nicholas will have to carry the ironing-board for her. **1928–9** *T. Eaton & Co. Catal.* Fall & Winter 391/4 Ironing Board Cover..padded with wadding..fits any regulation-sized board. **1969** E. H. PINTO *Treen* 151 Ironing boards..are found in a variety of shapes and sizes, for skirts,.. trousers,..and sleeves. **1972** *Guardian* 30 June 7/7 This superb new Milium Ironing Board Cover..is scorch resistant. **1972** *Sci. Amer.* Dec. 48/3 The development of fine glass yarns..has brought glass fibers into such products as bedspreads and covers for ironing boards. *a* **1877** KNIGHT *Dict. Mech.* II. 1203/2 *Ironing-machine*, one for ironing clothes, etc. **1962** *Which?* June 170/1 We should like to hear from members who have bought a dishwashing machine or an ironing machine during 1960 or 1961. **1894** E. BANKS *Campaigns of Curiosity* 195 The one large room ..should be divided into..three apartments; wash-house, sorting-room, and ironing-room. **1906** *Westm. Gaz.* 5 July 2/1 The hooded fireplace of the ironing-room. **1962** *Guardian* 3 Dec. 4/7 Mothers come..to enjoy working in the little ironing room. **1878** MRS. STOWE *Poganue People* xxv. 268 Will seized her off the ironing stool and, perching her on his shoulder, danced round the table. **1911** F. B. JACK *Woman's Bk.* 273/1 The Ironing Table.—This must be of a good size, strong, and steady, and of a convenient height for working at. *Ibid.* 273/2 In addition to the ironing table, a smaller one for placing the work on will be found a great convenience if space permits. **1959** *Sears, Roebuck Catal.* Spring & Summer 966/2 Ironing Table Designed for stand-up and sit-down ironing. **1974** *J. Frazer Catal.* 739/1 Ironing surface 36″ × 13″ All-metal ironing table..£4.50.

ironize, *v.*[1] Delete † *Obs.* and add later examples.

1906 H. BLAND *Lett. to Daughter* 116 Does one satirise, ironise, slate, bully-rag, and squirt verbal vitriol at the thing one loves? **1933** PARTRIDGE *Words, Words, Words!* III. 184 The tendency either to ironize or to belittle one's fears, sufferings and discomforts. **1969** *Daily Tel.* 13 Feb. 22/4 There is also the ironist, ironising himself.

iron lung. 1. A kind of respirator for giving prolonged artificial respiration mechanically, consisting of a metal case that fits over the patient's chest or trunk with an air-tight aperture for the neck (and limbs), so that air may be forced into and out of the lungs by producing rhythmic variations in the air pressure in the case. orig. *U.S.*

1932 *N.Y. Times* 3 Oct. 19/5 Surgeons revealed today that Birdsall Sweet, 14, of Beacon has just rounded out one year in the artificial respirator or 'iron lung' in Vassar Brothers hospital, Poughkeepsie. **1934** E. PODOLSKY *Medicine marches On* v. xvi. 140 Dr. Drinker's machine was called into service. The patient was placed in the machine that was to do his breathing for him. The iron lung forced air into his paralyzed chest and drew it out again. **1938** *Encycl. Brit. Bk. of Yr.* 406/2 The new type of respirator or iron lung..covers only the upper half of the body and does not involve the insertion of the complete person into the apparatus. **1938** *Times* 12 Aug. 14/4 Eric Baker, aged 11, died at Braintree..from infantile paralysis. He was taken ill on Monday and was placed in an iron lung. **1948** *Electronic Engin.* XX. 4/1 In the modern 'iron lung' bellows are used which take upon them the work usually done by the muscles of chest and diaphragm. *a* **1963** S. PLATH *Ariel* (1965) 78 No fingers to grip, no tongue, My god the iron lung That loves me, pumps My two Dust bags in and out.

2. *slang.* A Nissen hut.

1943 HUNT & PRINGLE *Service Slang* 40 *Iron lung*, Barrage Balloon boys' phrase for Nissen hut.

iron-man. Add: **1. c.** *U.S. slang.* A dollar.

1908 H. GREEN *Maison de Shine* 45 A feller who shells out his six iron men every week. **1926** *Flynn's* 16 Jan. 639/1 Still I can flash a toad-skin now and then, and have a few iron men planted where th' berries grow. **1932** J. DOS PASSOS *1919* 52 He still had more'n fifty iron men. **1945** *This Week Mag.* 21 Apr. 15/2 When I'd given the boys back their dough I had a nice little profit of two hundred iron men. **1970** E. R. JOHNSON *God Keepers* (1971) vi. 62 An ounce should bring a street pusher about two thousand iron men.

d. *slang* (orig. *Austral.*). A pound. Cf. *IRON *sb.*[1] 4 g.

1959 BAKER *Drum* 119 *Iron man*, a £1 note. **1973** J. LEASOR *Host of Extras* i. 16 A nut..to whom I'd sold a Bean Tourer—not the most exciting car..but what did he expect for five hundred iron men? **1974** J. WAINWRIGHT *Evidence I shall Give* xxviii. 141 Ten thousand iron men... We're talking bank-notes.

ironmongery. Add: **1. c.** *slang.* Firearms.

1902 KIPLING *Traffics & Discov.* (1904) 11 They'd all stand to their horses and pile on the ironmongery, and washers, and typewriters, and..they'd sail out..lying down and firing. **1905** A. H. LEWIS *Sunset Trail* (1914) x. 160 All men have their delicate side, and it was Mr. Allison's to regard the open wearing of one's iron-mongery as bad form. **1942** E. WAUGH *Put out More Flags* 275 Their '098 stores arrived; a vast profusion of ironmongery which..included Alastair's mortar. **1960** 'W. HAGGARD' *Closed Circuit* xv. 177 He wasn't armed. He had never carried ironmongery. **1973** J. WAINWRIGHT *Devil you Don't* 112 Shove it. You are only here for the ride. If you hadn't been so damned handy with the ironmongery—.

d. Also in other applications (see quots.).

1892 *Century Mag.* Dec. 218/2 The broad veranda.. had the customary array of..hanging lamps set with bosses of colored glass, and much ironmongery in spirals and curlicues. **1934** H. G. WELLS *Exper. Autobiogr.* II. viii. 568, I tried to make him [*sc.* Gissing] a cyclist..'Get on to your ironmongery,' said I. **1955** *Times* 4 Aug. 8/7 A pike which was already the subject of legend..had broken anglers' tackle seven times..appeared to thrive on a diet of triangles, and snap-tackles, plug-baits, five-inch spoons, and other ironmongery. **1958** *Engineering* 4 Apr. 425/1 No good starting with ironmongery—computers—got to start with systems analysis. **1967** *Guardian* 5 May 6/7 With the 'attached ironmongery', there is a disturbing lack of coordination... The lighting standards are not inelegant, but there are too many of them... Guard-rails, crash barriers, gantries, and direction signs..have the appearance of rushed afterthoughts. **1971** D. HASTON in C. Bonington *Annapurna South Face* xvii. 212, I started off on the chimney. At this time we were badly short of rope and ironmongery. I had about three hundred feet of rope, four pegs and about six karabiners.

i·ron-o·n, *a.* [f. IRON *v.* 3 + ON *adv.*] Such as can be affixed to the surface of a fabric by ironing.

1959 *Times* 12 Jan. 11/5 Woven cotton iron-on interlining. **1966** *Olney Amsden & Sons Ltd. Price List* 35 Iron-on Sheet Markers. **1967** E. SHORT *Embroidery & Fabric Collage* iv. 94 (*caption*) The fabric, previously backed with an iron-on interlining, is cut with a razor blade and pressed. **1970** *Guardian* 10 Sept. 13/3 Sewing on name tapes is a tedious job. Iron-on tapes can cut down the sewing.

iron-sand. 1. (Earlier and later examples.)

1805 D. MCCLURE *Diary* (1899) 29 The soil abounds in iron sand Ore. **1862** W. K. HULKE *Let.* 9 Aug. in *Richmond–Atkinson Papers* (1960) I. 781 Yesterday the battle about the iron-sand leases came off. **1963** *Times* 6 Feb. (N.Z. Suppl.) p. iv/5 New methods have been developed to process the ironsands of the North Island beaches.

ironweed. (Earlier and later U.S. examples.)

1819 D. THOMAS *Trav. Western Country* 231 The *ironweed*, which I first saw above Pittsburgh, extends on clayey lands all the way to the Wabash. **1963** GLEASON & CRONQUIST *Man. Vasc. Plants Northeastern U.S.* 746 *Vernonia* Schreb. Ironweed... Our spp. bloom in late summer and fall.

Iroquoian (i·rǒkwoi,ǎn, -koi-), *a.* and *sb.* [f. *IROQUOI(S *a.* and *sb.* + -AN.] **A.** *adj.* Of or pertaining to the Iroquois, or to the language family defined in sense B a below. **B.** *sb.* **a.** A language family which includes the Iroquois, Huron, Cherokee, and several lesser-known American Indian languages. **b.** A member of this linguistic group.

1697 L. LE COMPTE *Mem. Journey through China* I. v. 124 Iroquian Mathematicians, or Learned Alkonkins. **1888** J. C. PILLING (*title*) Bibliography of the Iroquoian languages. *Ibid.* Pref. p. v, To the Iroquoian perhaps belongs the honor of being the first of our American families of languages to be placed upon record. **1906** *Rep. Brit. Assoc. Adv. Sci.* 679 The Iroquoian tribes of North America possess a word which exactly expresses this potentiality. **1917** W. K. MOOREHEAD *Stone Ornaments Indians* 170 A surface find in the Iroquoian area in New York is no sure indication that the artifact is Iroquoian. **1933** L. BLOOMFIELD *Lang.* iv. 72 The Iroquoian family was spoken in a district surrounded by Algonquian; it includes..the Huron (or Wyandot) language, and the languages of the Iroquois type..; in a detached region to the south Cherokee was spoken. **1934** D. JENNESS *Indians of Canada* (ed. 2) xix. 288 When Jacques Cartier sailed up the St. Lawrence river in 1535 he found Iroquoians cultivating the land and controlling the country around the present site of Montreal. **1959** E. TUNIS *Indians* 19/2 Remnants of the temple-mound culture survived into historical times among the Muskhogean Indians of the Southeast and there are broad hints of a connection between the burial-mound people and the Iroquoians. **1968** F. G. LOUNSBURY in J. A. Fishman *Readings Sociol. of Lang.* (1968) 51 The writer has done intensive field work on a language—Cayuga, one of the languages of the Iroquoian family. **1969** *Observer* (Colour Suppl.) 25 May 53/1 Various groups that spoke dialects of the Iroquoian language.

Iroquois (i·rǒkwoi, -koi *U.S.*, i·rǒkwa *Canad.*), *a.* and *sb.* [Fr., from some Algonquian language, perh. Montagnais (G. Day in E. Tooker *Iroquois Culture* (1967), 57–61).] **A.** *adj.* Of or pertaining to an American Indian group of peoples (the 'Five Nations') encountered esp. in Ontario and central and northern New York State, or to the languages of this group; = *IROQUOIAN *a.* **B.** *sb.* **a.** A member of this group (see *Five Nations* (*FIVE *a.* and *sb.* C. 2)); also as collect. sing., this confederacy. **b.** More widely = *IROQUOIAN *sb.* **c.** The languages of this group.

1666 in *Documents Colonial Hist. New-York* (1853) III. 134 The Irocquois Indians should not cômit any Act of hostilety. **1677** LOCKE tr. *Nicole's Ess.* (1828) 71 There needs not many other thoughts to make up the complete idea of an Iroquois. **1705** [see *ALGONQUIN, -KIN *sb.* and *a.*]. **1710** SHAFTESBURY *Advice to Author* 179 Historys of Incas or Iroquois, written by Friars and Missionarys. **1756** [see *HURON]. **1791** [see *ESKIMO *a.* 1]. **1851** *Harper's Mag.* Aug. 390/2 He fancied he heard her mutter in Iroquois one word—'revenged'! **1852** [see *Five Nations* (*FIVE *a.* and *sb.* C. 2)]. **1866** G. M. WALLACE tr. *Beethoven's Lett.* II. 91, I must also strive to make some future provision for him [his nephew]; being neither Indians nor Iroquois, who, as we know, leave everything to Providence, whereas we consider a pauper's existence to be a very sad one. **1881** [see GYNEOCRACY]. **1922** D. CANFIELD *Rough-Hewn* (1923) i, Neale was silent as an Iroquois. *Ibid.* xxv, His Iroquois mask of insensibility. **1933** [see *CAYUGA]. **1959** [see *Five Nations* (*FIVE *a.* and *sb.* C. 2)]. **1965** *Canad. Jrnl. Ling.* Spring 135 Iroquois speakers remain in New York State;..others remain in the Carolinas (Cherokee). **1969** *Listener* 12 June 834/1 It is curious to think of Winston Churchill having Red Indian blood, but his mother was one-eighth Iroquois.

irradiance. Add: **2.** The flux of radiant energy per unit area, esp. an area normal to the direction of travel through a medium.

1956 A. HOLLAENDER *Radiation Biol.* III. iii. 129 'Irradiance' is the intensity term applicable to the interception of radiant energy by objects and is power per unit area. Frequently 'intensity' is used loosely as a substitute for 'irradiance'. *Ibid.* 136 The U.S. Weather Bureau..still uses the calorie per minute per square centimeter for the specification of solar irradiance. **1966** *McGraw-Hill Encycl. Sci. & Technol.* XII. 105/2 At a depth of 64 m where the irradiance is 0·5 $watt/m^2$.. approximately 0·04 watt of radiant power is absorbed by every cubic meter of sea water. **1969** *Physics Bull.* Oct. 409/2 Outside the earth's atmosphere..the annual mean irradiance of the sun is about 270 $W\,m^{-2}$ on a plane parallel to the earth's surface at latitude 52° N. **1973** *Nature* 9 Feb. 402/1 The total irradiance of the unattenuated light..was approximately $4{\cdot}5 \times 10^3\ \mu W/cm^2$.

irradiate, *v.* Add: **1. d.** To expose to the action of some kind of radiation (other than visible light, as X-rays, ultra-violet radiation, or neutrons).

1901 *N.Y. Med. Jrnl.* 16 Nov. 909/1 The inguinal tumor was removed..and now the inguinal area is also irradiated. **1927** *Jrnl. Biol. Chem.* LXXIII. 383 Cholesterol solutions were also irradiated by the *γ*-rays from radium emanation. **1952** COOK & DUNCAN *Mod. Radiochem. Pract.* v. 203 To obtain the maximum yield of a radio-element by use of a laboratory neutron source it is often of advantage to irradiate an aqueous solution of the absorbing element. **1957** *Technology* Mar. 14/2 Food can be preserved for long periods if irradiated. **1963** BOWEN & GIBBONS *Radioactivation Analysis* ii. 5 When a material is bombarded or irradiated by the nuclear particles produced in a nuclear reactor, particle accelerator, or other

suitable source, some of the atoms present in the sample will interact with the bombarding particles. **1964** M. Pyke *Food Sci. & Technol.* viii. 153 By irradiating frozen whole egg with from 0·1 to 1·0 Mrad, it is possible to destroy certain pathological micro-organisms. **1971** *Nature* 4 June 317/1 When the spores were initially irradiated with γ-rays, the germination rate increased remarkably. **1973** *Sci. Amer.* Apr. 71/1 The diffusion constant can now be determined by irradiating the silicon with slow neutrons and measuring the energy of the alpha particles that emerge.

irradiated, *ppl. a.* Add: **1. c.** Exposed to the action of some kind of radiation (see prec., 1 d).

1915 Colwell & Russ *Radium, X-Rays & Living Cell* iii. 117 The nuclear changes observed in the development of such irradiated ova have been investigated. **1931** *Times* 13 May 17/4 A cheap and effective means of obtaining Vitamin D has been made available in the form of irradiated ergosterol. **1957** Benedict & Pigford *Nucl. Chem. Engin.* i. 17 The most important neutron-absorbing and long-lived fission products in irradiated uranium are listed in Table 1.2. **1958** *Observer* 11 May 8/3 Japanese doctors could draw upon a wealth of medical information gained by systematic examination of men, women and children who had survived the blast, heat and radiation at Hiroshima and Nagasaki. But..knowledge about the treatment of irradiated individuals was woefully inadequate. **1970** *New Scientist* 6 Aug. 284/1 Most countries have banned the sale of irradiated food... However, in the UK the Minister of Health can exempt a particular food..if evidence is submitted to show that irradiation is harmless.

irradiation. Add: **3. b.** *Photogr.* The scattering of light by silver halide crystals in a photographic emulsion causing diffuseness of the image obtained on development.

1924 L. P. Clerc *Ilford Man. Process Work* vi. 53 The effect of irradiation, evidently, is the more marked,..as the exposure is longer. **1940** 'C. I. Jacobson' *Developing* ii. 43 If the exposure is longer, then the light is scattered so that it spreads beyond the area protected by the metal, and hence irradiation takes place. **1968** H. Baines in C. E. Engel *Photogr. for Scientist* i. 20 This scatter from one crystal to others is known as 'irradiation'.

9. Exposure to the action of some kind of radiation (other than visible light, as X-rays, ultra-violet radiation, or neutrons); the (or an) action or process of irradiating something. Also, radiation allowed to be incident upon something.

1901 *N.Y. Med. Jrnl.* 16 Nov. 908/2 Up to today irradiation has been done seven times [on the same patient]. *Ibid.* 909/1 If a strong effect is desired, intense irradiation must naturally be employed. **1915** Colwell & Russ *Radium, X-Rays & Living Cell* iii. 116 Radium, like X rays, does not effect the immediate death of the cell; specimens subjected to three days' continuous irradiation still underwent division. **1935** *Practitioners Libr. Med. & Surg.* VII. v. 158 Ultraviolet irradiation of the skin is effective in preventing or curing rickets. *Ibid.* 159 Short exposures of thin films of milk to ultraviolet irradiation. **1936** B. J. M. Harrison *Textbk. Roentgenology* iii. 52 If he moves out of position the irradiation falls on the protected covers and not upon the patient. **1951** *Jrnl. Sci. Instruments* XXVIII. 191/1 The neutron irradiation of small quantities of material in the pile is often carried out in aluminium foil 'envelopes' or in silica capsules. **1953** Carter & Merritt in Smith & Wermer *Mod. Treatm.* xx. 433/1 Daily shortwave diathermy in combination with infra-red irradiation twice applied to the lumbar area may be of value. **1953** *Cold Spring Harbor Symp. Quant. Biol.* XVIII. 101/2 Irradiation of cultures of lysogenic *Bacillus megatherium* with ultraviolet light greatly increased the proportion of bacteria producing phage. **1957** *Times* 3 Sept. 9/2 Therapeutic irradiation of the pelvic region would certainly involve considerable risk to an embryo in the direct beam. **1972** *Physics Bull.* July 398 The damage produced during irradiations with 20 MeV C ions and 48 MeV Ni ions has been normalized to that produced by 4 MeV protons where we can make reasonably accurate estimates of the number of displaced atoms.

irradiator. (Later example: cf. *irradiate *v.* 1 d.)

1971 *Nature* 12 Mar. 120/2 Corneas were first irradiated for 15 h in a γ-irradiator..delivering 1·2 × 10⁵ rad/h.

irrationalist. Add: Also *attrib.* or as *adj.*

1897 H. M. Cecil (*title*) Pseudo-philosophy at the end of the nineteenth century: an irrationalist trio: Kidd, Drummond, Balfour. **1910** W. James *Mem. & Stud.* (1911) xv. 392 Listen for a moment to such irrationalist deliverances on his part as these.

irrationalistic (iræʃənăli·stik), *a.* [f. Irrational *a.* + -istic.] Characterized by irrationalism; contrary to reason; illogical.

1910 W. James *Mem. & Stud.* (1911) xv. 400, I spoke a while ago of its being an 'irrationalistic' philosophy in its latest phase. **1912** *Q. Rev.* Oct. 364 This brings us to the fundamental difference between the standpoints of history and science, which the theology called 'irrationalistic' appears to have overlooked. **1920** A. S. Pringle-Pattison *Idea of God* (ed. 2) 64, I have dwelt in the latter part of this lecture on the tendency to slip into an anti-intellectualistic, and even irrationalistic, mode of statement in expressing the principle of value. **1934** A. C. Ewing *Idealism* v. 250 The irrationalistic and excessively pluralistic tendencies of the present day. **1963** R. Wellek in N. Frye *Romanticism Reconsidered* 121 He singles out the most irrationalistic writers.

irreconciliation. Delete † *Obs.* and add later examples.

1906 *Daily Chron.* 1 Oct. 5/6 Where..brotherly love and charity [have long been] enemies sworn to irreconciliation. **1927** *Brit. Weekly* 24 Mar. 639/1 Science has its confusions and irreconciliations no less than religion.

irredeemable, *a.* (*sb.*) Add: **1.** Also, *irredeemable debenture* (see quot. 1965).

1900 *Daily News* 3 July 2/5, £800,000 in Four-and-a Half per Cent. Irredeemable Mortgage Debenture stock at £108. **1965** Perry & Ryder *Thomson's Dict. Banking* (ed. 11) 317/1 *Irredeemable debenture*, a debenture which does not contain any provision for repayment of the principal money. Even if irredeemable, it falls to be paid upon the company going into liquidation.

b. (Earlier U.S. example.)

1837 D. Webster in *Niles' Weekly Reg.* 6 May 155/3, I abhor paper; that is to say irredeemable paper, paper that may not be converted into gold or silver at the will of the holder.

B. *sb.* Restrict † *Obs.* to sense in Dict. and add: **b.** Anything that is irredeemable; *spec.* an irredeemable debenture.

1904 *Daily Chron.* 6 Feb. 3/2 The redemption of the irredeemable by woman's sweet and subtle influence the author has spared us. **1952** *Economist* 30 Aug. 514/1 Prices of most stocks at their lowest for twenty years, with irredeemables offering flat yields ranging up to..4⅝ per cent. **1967** *Ibid.* 18 Nov. 785/2 The main effect..would eventually be felt by the long end of the market, especially by the irredeemables. **1973** *Daily Tel.* 24 Nov. 27/4 Most of the irredeemables return over 12 p.c. on income.

‖ **irredenta** (irĭde·ntă). [It. (see Irredentist).] A region containing people who are ethnically related to the inhabitants of one state but are politically subject to another. Also, post-positively, as *adj.*

1914 *Everybody's Mag.* Sept. 333 These million Germans along the Baltic..constitute a Germania Irredenta which is one of the things that Kaiser Wilhelm is after. **1916** *Times Hist. War* 31 Oct. 407/2 Rumanian interests would ..have become wholly identified with those of the Central European *bloc* but for the fact that between them loomed the question of Rumania irredenta. *Ibid.* 408/2 She [*sc.* Rumania] had no territorial irredenta to secure. **1934** A. Huxley *Beyond Mexique Bay* 73 British Honduras still is regarded by the Guatemalans as an *irredenta.* **1938** H. Nicolson *Diary* 22 Aug. (1966) 356 Even if Germany absorbed a portion of the Ukraine, how would it benefit her? It would create an *irredenta* and perpetuate Russo-German enmity. **1967** *Punch* 1 Feb. 141/2 They annexed Tibet, but they had argued themselves into the belief that this was ancient Chinese territory, China *irredenta.*

irredentism. Add: Also in extended use of any policy of seeking the recovery and re-union to one country of a region or regions for the time being subject to another country.

1922 *Encycl. Brit.* XXX. 314/1 Up to the World War there was actually no articulate irredentism among the Austrian Poles. **1932** *Times Lit. Suppl.* 5 May 319/1 Never was 'irredentism' so rampant as it is today; and so far as Germans and Magyars are concerned there does not seem much prospect of their reshaping their minds. **1961** *Listener* 21 Dec. 1057/1 The young African states are..learning that they are no more immune than the wicked old nations from the evils of frontier disputes, irredentism, and even ideological differences. **1973** *Ibid.* 20 Dec. 845/3 The seeds of Japanese irredentism, already latent, will begin to sprout.

irredentist. Add: Also in extended use (see prec.).

1919 G. B. Shaw *Peace Conf. Hints* vi. 75 The French and Italian Jingos have been..making no secret of their determination to annex parts of the Rhineland and the Austrian Tyrol..without regard to the irredentist movements which must follow such annexations. **1920** [see *crab *v.*² 2 b]. **1958** G. Mikes *East is East* 28 Naturally, I instinctively sympathised with Hungary and became a staunch irredentist at the age of six or so. Later..some subversive older friends assured me that irredentism was wrong. **1961** *Listener* 21 Sept. 411/1 The extremist parties [in the German Federal Republic] representing communist, neo-nazi, and irredentist tendencies. **1972** D. Dakin *Unification of Greece* v. 73 The bolder irredentists in Greece had taken the field.

irreducibly, *adv.* (Later example.)

1923 C. D. Broad *Sci. Thought* x. 368 The temporal relations..are really irreducibly triadic.

irreductible, *a.* (Later examples.)

1922 Joyce *Ulysses* 673 What anthem did Bloom chant partially in anticipation of that multiple, ethnically irreductible consummation? **1964** *English Studies* XLV. 98 He described the scientist's labour as a hammering out of truth in the teeth of irreductible stubborn facts.

irredundant (irĭdʌ·ndănt), *a. Math.* [f. Ir-² + Redundant *a.*] Containing no redundant elements.

1925 A. Church in *Trans. Amer. Math. Soc.* XXVII. 318 A set of postulates is irredundant if the postulates are independent and no one of them can be weakened with respect to the set. **1957** *IBM Jrnl. Res. & Devel.* I. 175/2 To be irredundant the statement has to involve the complete list of reasons which are necessary and sufficient to make this prime implicant dispensable. **1965** R. E. Miller *Switching Theory* I. 195 An 'irredundant cover' of a complex has the property that if any cube is eliminated from the cover, the resulting set of cubes is no longer a cover. **1966** *Math. Rev.* XXXI. 37/1 A factorization $a = a_1 a_2 \ldots a_m$ of a into simple factors is irredundant if no product $a_i a_{i+1} \ldots a_{i+p}$, $p > 0$, is simple.

Hence **irredu·ndance, irredu·ndancy** *sbs.*, the property of being irredundant.

1925 *Trans. Amer. Math. Soc.* XXVII. 320 (*heading*) A criterion for irredundance. **1952** *Proc. Amer. Catholic Philos. Assoc.* XXVI. 112, *f* fulfills the irredundancy requirement. **1960** *IRE Trans. Electronic Computers* IX. 248/2 Comparing all the resulting implications for irredundancy.

irreflexive, *a.* Delete *rare* and add: *Logic* and *Math.* Of a relation which no postulate can have to itself. Hence **irrefle·xiveness, irreflexi·vity,** the quality or property of being irreflexive. See also *non-reflexive *a.*, *reflexive *a.*

1933 *Mind* XLII. 36, $a < b$. ⊃. $a \neq b$..gives..the property of irreflexiveness. **1937** A. Smeaton tr. *Carnap's Logical Syntax of Lang.* iv. § 63. 234 A relation P is called irreflexive when no object has this relation to itself. **1942** J. C. Cooley *Primer of Formal Logic* 157 A relation, *f*, is said to be irreflexive when: $(x) \sim fxx$. **1952** S. C. Kleene *Introd. Metamath.* vii. 188 Connexity, irreflexiveness, asymmetry. **1954** I. M. Copi *Symbolic Logic* v. 143 An irreflexive relation is one which no individual has to itself. **1963** W. V. Quine *Set Theory* § 21. 147 Or, better, stipulate the irreflexivity and derive the asymmetry. **1964** E. Bach *Introd. Transformational Gram.* vii. 156 No item precedes itself (irreflexivity). **1967** R. A. George tr. *Carnap's Logical Struct. of World* § 11. 22 A relation is called a *sequence* if it is irreflexive and transitive (and hence asymmetrical) and connected.

irrega·rdless, *a.* and *adv.* Chiefly *N. Amer.* [Prob. blend of *irrespective* and *regardless.*] In non-standard or humorous use: regardless.

1912 in Wentworth *Amer. Dial. Dict.* **1923** *Lit. Digest* 17 Feb. 76 Is there such a word as *irregardless* in the English language? **1934** in Webster (*labelled* Erron. or Humorous, U.S.). **1938** I. Kuhn *Assigned to Adventure* xxx. 310, I made a grand entrance and suffered immediate and complete obliteration, except on the pay-roll, which functioned automatically to present me with a three-figure cheque every week, 'irregardless', as Hollywood says. **1939** C. Morley *Kitty Foyle* xxvii. 267 But she can take things in her stride, irregardless what's happened. **1955** *Publ. Amer. Dial. Soc.* xxiv. 19, I don't think like other people do and irregardless of how much or how little dope would cost me [etc.]. **1970** *Current Trends in Linguistics* X. 590 She tells the pastor that he should please quit using the word 'irregardless' in his sermons as there is no such word. **1971** M. McShane *Man who left Well Enough* iv. 96 The sun poured down on Purity irregardless of the fact that it received no welcome.

irregular, *a.* Add: **II. 8*.** *Astr.* **a.** Of a galaxy: having an irregular shape and lacking any axis of symmetry or central nucleus. Also *ellipt.* as *sb.*

1811 W. Herschel in *Phil. Trans. R. Soc.* CI. 296 By calling the figure of a nebula irregular, it must be understood that I saw no particular dimension of it sufficiently marked to deserve the name of length. **1875** *Encycl. Brit.* II. 821/1 Among the varieties of form may be noted spiral, elliptic, and ring nebulæ, double nebulæ, and irregular nebulæ. **1928** J. H. Jeans *Astron. & Cosmogony* i. 28 The irregular nebulae shew the bright line spectrum which is characteristic of a transparent gas. **1936** E. Hubble *Realm of Nebulæ* ii. 47 About half of the irregulars form a homogeneous group, in which the Magellanic Clouds are typical examples. **1959** *Listener* 31 Dec. 1152/1 There are a few galaxies that do not fit conveniently into this classification of spirals, ellipticals, and irregulars. **1965** J. Muirden *Handbk. Astron.* xxiv. 239 Irregular galaxies seem to be the adolescents; spirals are in the prime of life, while elliptical galaxies are bankrupt.

b. Of a variable star: fluctuating in brightness in a way that lacks any definite rhythm.

1903 A. M. Clerke *Probl. Astrophysics* xxiii. 363 (*heading*) Peculiar and irregular variables. **1955** F. Hoyle *Frontiers Astron.* xi. 190 Certain irregular variables are among the brightest of all stars. **1970** D. H. Menzel et al. *Survey Universe* xxvi. 551 Truly irregular variables, like R Coronae Borealis, suffer brightness changes in abrupt and unpredictable fashion.

irremeable, *a.* (Later example.)

1974 *Encounter* Feb. 54/1 The subject of correctness in language is now tending to be lost in an irremeable labyrinth.

irrepealability. (Earlier U.S. example.)

1802 *Deb. Congress U.S.* 18 Feb. 592 The character of irrepealability was not exclusively attached to this law.

irrepressible, *a.* (*sb.*). (Earlier example.)

1811 Jane Austen *Sense & Sens.* III. ix. 198 His was an involuntary confidence, an irrepressible effusion.

irreption. Delete † *Obs.* and add later examples.

1926 G. W. S. Friedrichsen *Gothic Version of Gospels* 190 Previous to this there had been casual but continued irreptions from the Old Latin. *Ibid.* 249 The Gothic reading could..be explained as a corruption due to the irreption of some parallel or reminiscent passage. **1974** *Encounter* Feb. 54/1 A protection against casual and deplorable irreptions creeping into the language.

irretention. (Later example.)

1963 V. Nabokov *Gift* ii. 85 All this sick irretention of electric light.

irre·ticence. [IR-².] The condition of being irreticent. With *an* and *plural*: an instance of this.

1919 V. WOOLF *Night & Day* xvi. 211 Rodney might begin to talk about his feelings, and irreticence is apt to be extremely painful. *a* **1941** —— *Captain's Death Bed* (1950) 112 Those irreticences and hyperboles which the voice of the speaker corrects in talk.

irreticent, *a.* (Later example.)

1932 V. WOOLF *Let. to Young Poet* 6 Therefore you could afford to be intimate, irreticent, indiscreet in the extreme.

irreversible, *a.* Add: **3.** *Physical Chem.* Of a colloid or colloidal system: incapable of being changed from a gelatinous state into a sol by a reversal of the treatment which turns the sol into a gel or gelatinous precipitate. Of a change of state: characterized by this property.

[**1899** *Jrnl. Physiol.* XXIV. 180 (*heading*) Colloidal mixtures which form irreversible molecular aggregates when they pass into the gel state.] **1900** *Proc. R. Soc.* LXVI. 110 A large number of colloidal solutions..belong to the class of irreversible colloidal mixtures. **1915** M. H. FISCHER tr. *Ostwald's Handbk. Colloid-Chem.* 40 When a change in the state of a colloid may be reversed by reversing the conditions which brought that change about, it is said to be 'reversible'. Thus when a colloid which has been precipitated by a salt goes back into solution on removal of the salt, the colloid change is said to be 'reversible'. On the other hand, if this does not occur it is 'irreversible'. **1930** J. C. WARE *Chem. Colloidal State* ix. 204 When a reversible colloid is evaporated to dryness and later stirred into the fluid which constituted the external phase, a very complete dispersion will again result. With an irreversible colloid, a suspension will not result by mixing with the solvent but one of the regular methods for the preparation of the colloidal state must be applied. **1930** *Engineering* 18 July 61/1 Gels which cannot be converted into sols are 'irreversible'. **1959** K. J. MYSELS *Introd. Colloid Chem.* iv. 82 These different behaviors are quite generally called reversible and irreversible flocculations.

irrigate, *v.* Add: **4.** *intr.* To drink; to take a drink. *slang* (chiefly *U.S.*).

1856 'J. PHOENIX' *Phœnixiana* 104 [He] was invited by the urbane proprietor to irrigate. *c* **1880** in Thornton *Amer. Gloss.* (1912) II. App. 975 'Stranger, do you irrigate?' 'If you mean drink, sir, I do not.' **1905** A. ADAMS *Outlet* xxi. 298 Sponsilier..called every one to the bar to irrigate. **1911** E. M. CLOWES *On Wallaby* viii. 202 There was even a further decrease in drunkenness, people having no money, I suppose, for what out here [*sc.* Victoria] they call 'irrigating'.

irrigation. Add: **4.** *irrigation canal, ditch*; **irrigation-wheel,** a wheel by means of which land is irrigated.

1910 *Encycl. Brit.* XIV. 841/2 When a river partakes of the nature of a torrent,..it is impossible to construct a system of irrigation canals without very costly engineering works. **1923** R. FRY *Let.* 21 May (1972) II. 536 A vast flat plain perfectly green with corn,..and all run by irrigation canals from the Ebro. **1870** Gov. HUNT *Own Story* (MS.) 1 Irrigation ditches were dug for as much of the land as could be covered with water. **1902** O. WISTER *Virginian* vi. 77 One of the irrigation ditches ran under the fence from the hay-field to supply the house with water. **1958** [see *ACEQUIA]. **1974** J. THOMSON *Long Revenge* vi. 67 The only possible cover was that provided by the tall reeds that grew in the deeper irrigation ditches. **1864** J. A. GRANT *Walk Across Afr.* 410 Mr. Aipperly had..made friends with the natives by assisting to put up their irrigation-wheels.

irritable, *a.* Add: **2. b.** *irritable heart,* a syndrome characterized by shortness of breath on exertion, palpitation, fatigue, chest pain, and dizziness, and believed to be psychosomatic; 'soldier's heart'.

1864 J. M. DA COSTA *Med. Diagn.* iv. 280 These statements are not intended to be final. They are but a very short summary of the results of a large number of observations which I have had an opportunity of making on these cases of 'irritable heart', and which elsewhere..will be laid before the profession. **1922** [see *cardiological* adj. s.v. *CARDIO-]. **1971** CONN & HORWITZ *Cardiac & Vascular Dis.* I. xxiv. 600/1 This condition has been known by many names, such as irritable heart, soldier's heart, disordered action of the heart, functional heart disease, effort syndrome, and neurocirculatory asthenia.

irrotationality (i:rotēi·ʃənæ·liti). *Physics.* [f. IRROTATIONAL *a.* + -ITY.] The property or state of being irrotational.

1960 *McGraw-Hill Encycl. Sci. & Technol.* VII. 402/1 For an incompressible fluid, the continuity equation..is div v = 0; hence, combining this relation with irrotationality gives Laplace's equation, div (grad ϕ) = 0. **1967** *Progress Aeronaut. Sci.* VIII. 6 The velocity field is determined by the equation of continuity and the condition of irrotationality.

irrumation (irumēi·ʃən). [f. ppl. stem of L. *irrumāre* to practise fellatio on or L. *irrumātiō, -ōnis* the action of the verb.] (See quot. 1901.) Also **i·rrumate** *v. trans.*, to practise irrumation on (a person); **i·rrumator,** one who practises irrumation.

1887 L. C. SMITHERS tr. *Forberg's Man. Classical Erotology* iii. 72 To put the member in erection into some one's mouth is called to irrumate, a word, which in its proper sense means to give the breast. *Ibid.* 90 Irrumators are less feared by married men. *Ibid.* 97 Erasmus, in his *Sayings*,..does not deny that in his time the obscene practice of irrumation was still known. **1888** tr. *Priapeia* 39 If thou shalt attempt a third theft,..I will sodomise and irrumate thee. **1901** A. ALLINSON tr. *Rosenbaum's Plague of Lust* II. xxi. 3 Very much more abominable and repulsive still is the habit of Irrumation (..to erect the *penis* and insert it into the mouth of another person). *Ibid.* 20 The *irrumator*..takes the *fellator* between his opened thighs. **1947** P. L. HARRIMAN *Dict. Psychol.* 187 *Irrumation,* the act of obtaining an orgasm by the mouth; fellatio or penilingus.

irruption. Add: *spec.* An abrupt local increase in the numbers of a species of animals.

1912 W. E. CLARKE *Stud. Bird Migration* II. xxi. 112 During the remarkable irruption of Crossbills from the Continent in the summer of 1909, Fair Isle received many of the visitors. **1936** A. L. THOMSON *Bird Migration* ii. 42 Apart from all the categories of annual movements, there are movements which occur at irregular intervals in the form of invasions or irruptions... In the spring of certain years the birds have 'irrupted' in large numbers. **1968** *New Scientist* 21 Nov. 425/2 The majority of migrants [*sc.* butterflies] reaching Britain are regularly seen within a few days of an irruption in their home territory.

¶ Confused with ERUPTION. Delete *Obs.* and add later U.S. examples.

1883 'MARK TWAIN' *Life on Mississippi* 244 A filament-obliterating irruption of profanity. **1892** —— *Amer. Claimant* 62 A volcanic irruption.

is. (Properly s.v. *BE *v.*) Infinite vars. of the expression (*a*) — *is a* — *is a* —, on the model of Gertrude Stein's line (see quot. 1922).

1922 G. STEIN *Geogr. & Plays* 187 Rose is a rose is a rose. Loveliness extreme. **1968** *Listener* 5 Sept. 292/1 Trevelyan is Trevelyan is Trevelyan, and film censorship will endure for as long as he keeps on fighting. **1970** *Guardian* 2 Apr. 10/1 There is only one art form common to all sorts and conditions of people: the poster..a hoarding is a hoarding is a hoarding. **1971** 'L. BLACK' *Death has Green Fingers* xiv. 158 Let me adapt the quotation. 'A crook is a crook is a crook.' **1974** *Times* 4 Jan. 12/5 As Miss Gertrude Stein would have said: 'A union is a union is a union.'

is (iz), *sb.* [f. the vb.] That which exists, that which is; the fact or quality of existence.

1897 F. THOMPSON *New Poems* 164 Could I face firm the Is, and with To-be Trust Heaven. **1903** *North Amer. Rev.* Apr. 507 She is not a Has Been, she is an Is. **1951** S. F. NADEL *Found. Social Anthropol.* iii. 37 The blueprint of his culture and society, the 'should-be' rather than the 'is'. **1958** C. PEPLER *Eng. Relig. Heritage* IV. viii. 300 The man is conscious that he *is*, and in comparison to the Is of God, this realisation is itself the greatest sorrow.

I's: see *ISE, I'SE b.

Isabella. 2. b. (U.S. examples of absol. use.)

1846 *Knickerbocker* XXVII. 419 A snaky looking vine.. from which glorious bunches of Catawbas and Isabellas may be gathered. **1864** [see *CONCORD *sb.*² 2]. **1949** *Amer. Photography* Apr. 244/1 *Vitis labrusca*..has furnished the catawba,..the Concord,..and the Isabella.

isacoustic: see *ISO-.

is all. (Properly s.v. *ALL *a.* 8 g.) *U.S.* and *Canad. colloq. phr.*, a shortened form of *that is all.*

1954 G. BREWER *Killer is Loose* iii. 27 You didn't see the bus, is all. **1967** 'W. WRIGHT' *Shadows don't Bleed* vii. 126 I'm not married. Paula looks after the house for me, is all. **1969** C. HIMES *Blind Man with Pistol* xiv. 152, I help you look, just don't call me nigger is all.

isallobar (əis,æ·lobāɹ). *Meteorol.* [f. Gr. ἴσ-ος equal (ISO-) + ἄλλο-ς other (*ALLO-) + βάρ-ος weight, after *isobar.*] A line (imaginary or on a map) connecting points at which the barometric pressure has changed by an equal amount during a specified time. Hence **isalloba·ric** *a.*

1911 N. SHAW *Forecasting Weather* xv. 337 Dr. Nils Ekholm, of Stockholm,..uses charts of isallobars. *Ibid.*, Similar groups of isallobars appear on both maps, so that the isallobaric groups may be regarded as travelling as well as the isobaric groups. **1934** D. BRUNT *Physical & Dynamical Meteorol.* ix. 189 Brunt and Douglas found that the isallobaric component of wind frequently amounted to as much as 5 metres/sec. **1959** S. L. HESS *Introd. Theoret. Meteorol.* xiv. 226 This solution is for the case of isobars and isallobars (lines of constant pressure tendency) which are oriented east-west. **1962** *Course Elem. Meteorol.* (Meteorol. Office) ii. 25 By analogy with isobars we have isallobaric highs and lows, showing centres of rising and falling pressure respectively.

isanomalous, -anomaly: see *ISO-.

isat-. Add: **isa·togen,** any compound containing the bicyclic group $C_8H_4NO_2$ found in isatin; hence **isatoge·nic** *a.*

1882 *Jrnl. Chem. Soc.* XLII. 198 Isatogenic acid is very unstable, and cannot be obtained either from the above salt, or from free orthonitropropiolic acid, as it is immediately converted into isatin. *Ibid.* 620 To ascertain the nature of the isatogen-group, experiments were made on its derivatives. **1889** ROSCOE & SCHORLEMMER *Treat. Chem.* III. v. 262 When the solution is poured into water, the isatogenic acid decomposes instantaneously into carbon dioxide and isatin. **1916** *Chem. Abstr.* X. 1334 The isatogens are typical quinones, forming a new class of *m*-quinoid compds., in which the group N:O plays the role of a CO group. **1948** WENGRAF & BAUMANN tr. *Diseren's Chem. Technol. Dyeing & Printing* I. i. 26 The formation of indigo can be explained by an intermediate rearrangement of the *o*-nitrophenyl propiolic acid into isatogenic acid... The latter product is reduced to indigo by splitting off CO_2. **1965** *Jrnl. Pharmacy & Pharmacol.* XVII. 736 The isatogens..were all effective against Gram-positive organisms. **1972** W. A. REMERS in W. J. Houlihan *Chem. Heterocyclic Compounds* XXV. i. 193 Isatogens..also undergo addition to the 1,2-double bond.

isatoic (əisătōu·ik), *a. Chem.* [See below.] **1.** *isatoic acid* [tr. G. *isatosäure* (H. Kolbe 1884, in *Jrnl. f. prakt. Chem.* XXX. 85): see ISAT-]. † **a.** = *isatoic anhydride* (below). *Obs.* **b.** *N*-Carboxyanthranilic acid, C_6H_4(COOH) (NH-COOH), known only as its derivatives.

1885 *Jrnl. Chem. Soc.* XLVIII. I. 58 Isatin is converted by chromic acid, dissolved in glacial acetic acid, into an acid which the author styles isatoic acid... It is sparingly soluble in cold water and alcohol. *Ibid.* 666 Anthranilcarboxylic acid..has the same composition as isatoic acid. **1899** [see sense *2]. **1930** *Chem. Abstr.* XXIV. 4793 Isatoic acid and its derivs. are obtained by treating congo acid solns. of aromatic *o*-aminocarboxylic acids with $COCl_2$.

2. *isatoic anhydride* [after G. *isatosäure-anhydrid* (E. Erdmann 1889, in *Ber. d. Deut. Chem. Ges.* XXXII. 2163)]. The anhydride,

$$\underbrace{C_6H_4\cdot CO\cdot O\cdot CO\cdot NH}$$,

of isatoic acid, obtained by oxidation of isatin.

1899 *Jrnl. Chem. Soc.* LXXVI. I. 939 'Isatoic acid' is thus not an acid, but the anhydride of a dicarboxylic acid, $COOH\cdot C_6H_4\cdot NH\cdot COOH$. The author calls this dibasic acid isatoic acid, and the anhydride, previously known as isatoic acid he terms isatoic anhydride. **1944** *Jrnl. Org. Chem.* IX. 55 Isatoic anhydride is a convenient reagent for certain anthranoylations. **1971** *Jrnl. Pharmaceutical Sci.* LX. 1252/1 The condensation of isatoic anhydride with primary amines was found to yield the corresponding substituted anthranilamides.

Isaurian (əisǭ·riăn), *sb.* and *a.* [f. *Isauria* (see below) + -AN.] **A.** *sb.* A native or inhabitant of Isauria, an ancient country in Asia Minor, between Cilicia and Phrygia; *spec.* applied to a line of emperors of the Eastern Roman Empire. **B.** *adj.* Of or belonging to Isauria, or to the emperors thus called.

1776 GIBBON *Decl. & F.* I. x. 285 In the heart of the Roman monarchy, the Isaurians ever continued a nation of wild barbarians. **1843** *Penny Cycl.* XXVII. 770/2 The increasing power of the brothers and other Isaurian friends of Zeno. **1880** *Encycl. Brit.* XI. 114/2 The emperors of this time were those of the Isaurian, Armenian, and Amorian dynasties. **1904** W. M. RAMSAY *Lett. Seven Churches* xxvii. 399 The Empire of Rome has been..transformed into a Roman-Asiatic Empire, on whose throne sat successively Phrygians, Isaurians, Cappadocians, and Armenians. **1957** J. M. HUSSEY *Byzantine World* I. ii. 29 The Isaurians were administrators as well as soldiers.

‖ **isba** (izbā·). Also **isbah, izba.** [ad. Russ. *izbá* (related to STOVE *sb.*¹).] A Russian hut or log-house.

1784 J. KING in Cook *Voy. Pacific Ocean* III. 374 These houses consist of three distinct sorts, jourts, balagans, and loghouses, called here isbas. **1833** R. PINKERTON *Russia* 24 These simple articles compose the whole..furniture of a Russian izba. **1883** *Harper's Mag.* Jan. 251/1 Her serfs, if they wanted new isbahs—alias log huts—..would get the priests..to versify their petition. **1892** *Daily News* 22 Jan. 6/7 The meanest Kirghis yourt was more artistically decorated than his grimy, unventilated isba. **1943** E. M. ALMEDINGEN *Frossia* ii. 89, I was twenty-one, married, had my own *izba*, owned my own livestock. **1962** *Observer* 20 May 21/1 We lived in a tiny *isba*, or log cabin, together with three other families.

‖ **isblink** (ī·sbliŋk). Also 8–9 **eis-blink, iisblink.** [Sw. (and mod. Dan.) *isblink*, etc.: see ICEBLINK.] = ICEBLINK 2.

1796 Eis-blink [see ICEBLINK 2]. **1870** *Q. Jrnl. Geol. Soc.* XXVI. 679 Here the 'Iisblink', or the 'ice glance', of the Danes (*i.e.* the projecting glacier—though English seamen use the word iceblink in a totally different sense, meaning thereby the 'loom' of ice at a distance), projects bodily out to sea for more than a mile. **1880** *Encycl. Brit.* XI. 167/2 If..the sea is shallow, the glacier will protrude for a considerable distance, as in the case of the Isblink. **1957** J. K. CHARLESWORTH *Quaternary Era* I. iv. 72 For this type [*sc.* continental ice-sheet] there is almost universal assent: it constitutes O. Nordenskiöld's 'continental glaciers', Hobbs' 'ice-cap type', and the 'inland ice' of Drygalski, Ferrar and Gourdon. Early writers, following H. Rink (1851), named it *Isblink* from the peculiar light seen over the inland ice when approached from the sea.

ischæmia, -emia. Add: Hence **ischæ·mically** *adv.*, by, or as a result of, ischæmia.

1967 *Urologia Internat.* XXII. 381 (*heading*) Electron-microscopic investigation of the action of mannitol in ischemically-damaged rat kidneys. **1970** *Nature* 27 June 1272/1 In 1963 and 1964..a high attrition rate resulted from the use of ischaemically damaged grafts..and

absence of tissue typing facilities. **1972** *Ibid.* 21 Jan. 171/2 We have tried to develop a simple perfusing system with better protection of the organ..and eventually to test this system with ischaemically damaged kidneys.

ischio-. Add: **ischiocaverno·sus** *Anat.* [mod. L. (ad. F. *ischio-caverneux* (J.-B. Winslow *Expos. anat. de la Struct. du Corps Humain* (1732) 571/1)), f. L. *cavernōsus* full of hollows, in *corpus cavernosum* (see CORPUS 2)], either of a pair of small perineal muscles, each of which arises partly from the ischial tuberosity and partly from the ramus of the ischium and is inserted into the crus of the penis (or clitoris) and perhaps helps to maintain erection.

1733 G. DOUGLAS tr. *Winslow's Anat. Expos. Struct. Human Body* II. viii. 198 The first two muscles are commonly termed erectores, but might be more properly named ischio-cavernosi. **1867** *Quain's Elem. Anat.* (ed. 7) I. 264 The ischio-cavernosus, or erector penis muscle, embracing the crus penis, arises from the inner part of the tuber ischii, behind the extremity of the crus penis, and from the pubic arch along the inner and outer sides of the crus. **1967** G. M. WYBURN et al. *Conc. Anat.* i. 17/2 Each crus is covered by the ischiocavernosus muscle.

Ise, I'se. Add: (Later example.)

c **1863** T. TAYLOR in M. R. Booth *Eng. Plays of 19th Cent.* (1969) II. 91 *Waiter.* Beg pardon sir, it's for No. 1. *Brierly.* I'se No. 1.

b. *spec.* in the United States. Also I's.

Freq. in Black English writings.

1852 W. L. G. SMITH *Life at South* iii. 51 I'se tinking wha' jolly time we will hab on Saturday arternoon, down under ole elm trees, on bank ob de riber. **1875** S. & C. LANIER in *Scribner's Monthly* June 240 I'se pow'ful skeered; but neversomeless I ain't gwine run away. *Ibid.*, I's like a word dat someone done said, and den forgotten. **1898** P. L. DUNBAR *Folks from Dixie* 32 No, suh, I's a Babtist myse'f. *Ibid.* 49 I's mighty fond o' fishin', myse'f. **1902** J. D. CORROTHERS *Black Cat Club: Negro Humor & Folklore* i. 14 I'se a genamum, mase'f. *Ibid.* iii. 43, I writes a good han' and I's done read de dictionary. *Ibid.* iv. 56 De kine o' dahkey I'se talkin' 'bout am de feller whut's done bumped his head up ag'inst some college 'tel he cain't talk nothin' but Greek an' Latin, an' cuss you in Trinogometry. **1922** T. W. TALLEY *Negro Folk Rhymes* 135 I'se a bird o' one fedder, w'en it comes to you. **1927** A. P. RANDOLPH in A. Dundes *Mother Wit* (1973) 201/2 Wait a minute, son. I's wid you. *Ibid.*, Suppose des white folks find out I'se jined dis Brotherhood? *Ibid.*, Suppose des white folks ask me whether I'se a member? **1940** J. STREET in *Sat. Even. Post* 6 Jan. 32/2 I knows Ise out-figger'd. I knows I's whupped. **1967** C. HIMES *Black on Black* (1973) 133 'I'se tired as you are,' she said evilly. *Ibid.* 136 Ise already free.

isenthalpic, isentropic, -ally: see *ISO-.

isepiptesis, isopiptesis (əise:pipˈtī·sis, əiso-pipˈtī·sis). *rare.* [a. G. *isepiptese* (A. T. von Middendorff 1855, in *Mém. Acad. Imp. Sci. St. Pétersbourg, 6e série, Sci. nat.* VIII. 8), f. Gr. ἐπίπτησις flying down upon.] A line (either imaginary or on a map) connecting points which migrating birds reach at the same time. Hence **isepipte·sial** *a.*

1875 A. NEWTON in *Encycl. Brit.* III. 768/1 His [*sc.* Middendorff's] chief object has been to trace what he has termed the isepipteses... Assuming that the advance is directly across the isepiptesial lines..the whole course of the migration is thus most accurately made known. **1926** A. L. THOMSON *Probl. Bird-Migration* viii. 132 His [*sc.* Middendorff's] method was to plot out 'isepipteses', or isochronal lines, joining up all localities corresponding with each other as to their average dates for the arrival of particular summer visitors. [**1962** C. D. SHERMAN tr. *Dorst's Migrations of Birds* viii. 233 He [*sc.* Middendorff] plotted these data on a map, linked the localities which migrants reach on the same date and thus obtained a line he called the isopiptes..(this line was later named the isochronal line).]

Isfahan: see *ISPAHAN.

-ish¹. Add: **4.** Added to names of hours of the day or numbers of years to denote: round about, somewhere near (the time or period of) (prob. after *earlyish, latish*).

1916 'PETER' *Trench Yarns* ix. 110 'What time shall I come?' 'Elevenish,' Sam replied. **1925** B. TRAVERS *Mischief* xiv. 209, I shall be going to Shady Nook at about tenish. **1930** J. B. PRIESTLEY *Angel Pavement* iii. 106 Eightish then, next Tuesday, eh? **1941** *Britannia & Eve* Sept. 15/3 Lady Regan was probably thirty. Sir Gerald looked fifty-five-ish. **1950** *Sat. Rev. Lit.* 28 Jan., The ninetyish, gentle Chandler at the reception desk. **1955** E. HYAMS *Slaughterhouse Informer* xiv. 220 'We'll make a party of it.' 'Sixish?' **1967** B. NORMAN *Matter of Mandrake* xx. 174 Will you be in your room about sevenish? **1971** P. PURSER *Holy Father's Navy* iii. 19 Thirtyish furniture in pale, shabby wood. **1972** C. FREMLIN *Appointment with Yesterday* iv. 24 This anxious thirty-five-ish person.

ishan (ī·ʃān). [Pers., = hill, landmark.] A prehistoric mound in Iraq.

1921 *Blackw. Mag.* June 708/1 They had just moved their home to an ishan or mound only some ten or fifteen minutes from the river. **1927** 'FULANAIN' *Haji Rikkan* i. 8 Facing us was a group of the strange mounds or *ishans* which here and there, in the marshes of Southern 'Iraq, stand out high, or seeming high in that vast watery expanse. **1964** W. THESIGER *Marsh Arabs* xix. 173 We passed a bare black mound..known to the Madan as Ishan Waqif, or Standing Island.

Ishihara (iʃihā·rā). *Ophthalm.* The name of Shinobu *Ishihara* (1879–1963), Japanese ophthalmologist, used *attrib.* with reference to a test for colour-blindness (the *Ishihara test*) devised by him in 1917, in which the subject is asked to name the numbers in (or, for illiterates, to distinguish pathways through) a series of printed plates (*Ishihara plates*), in each of which the numbers or pathways are formed of coloured spots in a background of spots of a different colour or colours; so *Ishihara-blind* adj., *method*, etc.

1924 *Amer. Jrnl. Physiol. Optics* V. 269 (*heading*) The Ishihara test for color blindness. **1944** *Amer. Jrnl. Physiol.* CXL. 578 The color vision was tested by the Ishihara method. *Ibid.* 579 Twelve of the 'Ishihara blind' students were trichromats. *Ibid.*, The Ishihara test gave a correct diagnosis. **1968** C. BEARD et al. *Symposium Surg. & Med. Managem. Congenital Anomalies Eye* xvi. 423 In the Ishihara plates the colors of the test symbols and of the background are of such saturation, hue, and brightness that they are regularly confused by either the deutan or protan or both. *Ibid.* 425 The tracing plates in the Ishihara test..are useful for young children and illiterates.

ishikawaite (iʃikā·wăˌəit). *Min.* Also † **ishi-kawite.** [ad. Jap. *ishikawaishi* (K. Kimura 1922, in *Jrnl. Geol. Soc. Tokyo* XXIX. 320), f. *Ishikawa*, the name of a district in Honshu, Japan + *ishi* stone, mineral: see -ITE¹.] A black oxide of various metals, perhaps (U, Fe, Yt, Ce) (Nb, Ta)O_4.

1922 *Jrnl. Geol. Soc. Tokyo* XXIX. No. 347 (contents list), On ishikawite, a new mineral from Ishikawa District. **1923** *Mineral. Abstr.* II. 380 For ishikawaite..new axes are suggested. **1944** C. PALACHE et al. *Dana's Syst. Min.* (ed. 7) I. 766 *Ishikawaite*... The tabular crystals {100} are supposedly orthorhombic.

isidium. Add: [ad. mod.L. generic name *Isidium* (E. Acharius *Lichenographiae Suecicae Prodromus* (1798) 87), formerly used to include all lichens bearing isidia.] Hence **isi·dial** *a.*, of or pertaining to an isidium; **isi·diate, isi·dioid** *adjs.*, bearing isidia.

1921 A. L. SMITH *Lichens* iii. 149 In the genus [*sc. Isidium*] were included the more densely isidioid states of various crustaceous species. *Ibid.* 150 The centre of the isidial tuft [of *Umbilicaria pustulata*] may fall out. **1959** U. K. DUNCAN *Guide to Study of Lichens* 7 *P*[*armelia*] *crinita*... Resembles an isidiate form of *P. trichotera.* **1962** *Lichenologist* II. 3 *P*[*armelia*] *reddenda* is a pseudocyphellate species with peculiar granular or granular-isidiate outgrowths on the upper surface. **1967** M. E. HALE *Biol. Lichens* i. 22 It is not apparent that isidiate species hold any advantage over non-isidiate species. **1970** *Lichenologist* IV. 216 Further development of the isidial initials leads to a definite dorsi-ventral organization.

Islam. Now freq. with pronunc. (izlā·m).

Islamic, *a.* (Earlier example.)

1791 W. ENFIELD *Hist. Philos.* II. 244 Avenpace.. applied it to the illustration of the Islamic system of theology.

Islamitic, *a.* (Earlier example.)

1791 W. ENFIELD *Hist. Philos.* II. 240 Al-Ashari.. applied an extensive knowledge of the Peripatetic philosophy to the explanation of the Islamitic law.

island, *sb.* Add: **1. d.** In specific elliptical uses for some particular island or islands, as the Isle of Wight, the Hebrides, some islands in the western Pacific. Also, by further extension, for a specific prison on an island.

1814 JANE AUSTEN *Mansf. Park* I. ii. 34 She thinks of nothing but the Isle of Wight, and she calls it *the Island*, as if there were no other island in the world. **1817** KEATS *Let.* 17 Apr. (1931) I. 19, I intend to walk over the Island east—West—North South. **1852** C. M. YONGE *Two Guardians* xiii. 239 Suppose I was to take him to Marchmont's grouse shooting place in Scotland, and about among the Highlands and Islands. **1896** CONRAD *Outcast of Islands* I. ii. 15 There was not a white man in the islands, from Palembang to Ternate, from Ombawa to Palawan, that did not know Captain Tom and his lucky craft. **1901** *N.E.D.* s.v. *Isle*, The Isle of Wight is commonly referred to as 'the island'. **1902** *Captain* VII. 141 We used to gather the niggers in from all round the islands [*sc.* Pacific Islands]. *a* **1911** D. G. PHILLIPS *Susan Lenox* (1917) II. vii. 185 He was caught, did a year on the Island before his 'pull' could get him out. **1930** V. PALMER *Men are Human* xxiii. 205 He was tormented by sporadic impulses to scrap his responsibilities and go off to the [Pacific] Islands. **1935** A. J. POLLOCK *Underworld Speaks* 62/2 *Island*, Portland prison, England; Blackwell's Island, N.Y. **1939** J. PHELAN *In Can* iii. 28 He's bin on the Moor and the Island an' in the Ville, but I ain't never heard as he was in *Eton.* **1968** R. C. GALWAY *Assignment Gaolbreak* viii. 71 You're going straight to the island, via the cells at the Old Bailey. **1974** *Times* 9 Mar. 3/1 It was here in the Isle of Wight that the Conservatives last week suffered their biggest electoral disaster... For the past 50 years the island..had been considered a Tory fortress.

2. (Further examples.)

1776 A. HENRY *Trav. & Adv. Canada* (1901) xi. 282 The country was one uninterrupted plain,..a frozen sea, of which the little coppices were the islands. **1834** *Visit to Texas* iv. 41 These groves are called islands, from the striking resemblance they present to small tracts of land surrounded by water. **1843** *Amer. Pioneer* II. 283 An island of timber. **1853** F. W. THOMAS *John Randolph* 61 Islands—that is, great clumps of trees, covering sometimes many acres, appearing just like many islands in an outstretched ocean. **1902** S. E. WHITE *Blazed Trail* ix. 63 The pine there grew thick on isolated 'islands' of not more than an acre or so in extent,—little knolls rising from the level of a marsh. **1930** *19th Cent.* Dec. 713 Now, the draw-back of this plan, from the Zionist point of view, is that it will prevent land purchase for the meantime and the growth of the Jewish 'islands' in the country. **1962** A. FRY *Ranch on Cariboo* iv. 42 The islands were small patches of pine and spruce timber on little rises of high ground that occurred here and there in the several hundred acres of the meadow. **1974** *Country Life* 21 Feb. 350/1 A churchyard..is..perhaps a well-wooded 'island' in an agricultural countryside.

b. *island* (or *Island*) *of Langerhans* = *islet of Langerhans* (*ISLET 2 b); also *ellipt.*

1899 *Jrnl. Exper. Med.* IV. 285 Pigment is frequently abundant in the cells composing the intertubular cell-groups or islands of Langerhans. **1900** *Bull. Johns Hopkins Hosp.* XI. 205 (*heading*) On the histology of the islands of Langerhans of the pancreas. *Ibid.* 207 When the fœtal pancreas is affected by congenital syphillis, the islands..retain their continuity with the secreting structures. **1951** A. GROLLMAN *Pharmacol. & Therapeutics* xxvi. 571 Banting and Best..obtained a preparation which was named insulin, since it is derived from the Islands of Langerhans in the pancreas, and not from the general parenchyma of the gland. **1962** W. H. HOLLINSHEAD *Textbk. Anat.* ix. 140/2 The endocrine tissue of the pancreas, the pancreatic islands (islets) or islands of Langerhans, consists of small groups of cells scattered among the more numerous acini.

c. = REFUGE *sb.* 3 c.

1869 *Spectator* 12 June 695/1 We have already 'refuges', or 'islands', or whatever they are, in most crossings. **1878** *Social Notes* 10 Aug. 358/1 It is only very lately that 'islands'—those necessary havens of refuge—have been placed at the most dangerous portions of the boulevards. **1899** *Daily Tel.* 31 Jan. 6/6 The statue being situated on an 'island', a certain amount of skirmishing was necessary in order to reach it. **1926** C. SIDGWICK *Sack & Sugar* xi. 131, I took Gerda's arm, and was nearly at the island, when the bus swept round a corner and was on us. **1930** L. COOPER *Ship of Truth* ii. 178 He stood on an island in the middle and saw the traffic sweep past him. **1956** D. GASCOYNE *Night Thoughts* 26 Street-crossing islands stand becalmed. **1970** P. LAURIE *Scotland Yard* iii. 72 The cart collided with a concrete bollard and finished up on an island. **1972** *Daily Tel.* 20 Jan. 17/7 The gang lifted a grill on a Shaftesbury Avenue island to gain access to the inspection tunnel.

d. A small isolated ridge or structure between the lines in finger-prints.

1891 *Proc. R. Soc.* XLIX. 545 Any one well-marked characteristic of a minute kind, such as an island, or enclosure, or a couple of adjacent bifurcations. **1930** E. WALLACE *White Face* xii. 183 Before we start discussing whorls, islands and circles..what is this? **1950** *Gross's Criminal Investigation* (ed. 4) v. 127 On Fig. 4 are marked some of the common types of ridge characteristics:—'A' is an enclosure or lake... 'F' is a short independent ridge or island.

e. = **speech island.*

1882 A. J. ELLIS in *Trans. Philol. Soc.* 30 The maps being thus arranged, coloured lines are drawn on them marking boundaries, which sometimes unite and form islands. **1892** *Dialect Notes* I. iv. 225 One of his own students was thinking of a linguistic island in the Tennessee mountains as a field for future work. **1923** A. L. KROEBER *Anthropol.* v. 105 This explains the numerous survivals and 'islands' of speech. **1934** H. KURATH in *Proc. Amer. Philos. Soc.* LXXIV. 239 R-islands still exist in eastern New England.

f. A piece of furniture, in a private house or in a museum, library, etc., surrounded by unoccupied floor space. Freq. *attrib.*

1932 *Museums Jrnl.* June 127 In the vertical island-cases with different displays on opposite sides. **1960** *Guardian* 1 Mar. 3/5 Living and dining space planned round a large island range and barbecue grill. *Ibid.*, Peter Jones and Heal's both show island fireplaces. **1960** *Oxf. Univ. Gaz.* 4 Mar. 806/2 A new island bookcase has been acquired for the library. **1960** *House & Garden* Aug. 65/2 The cooking island screens a small corner used for informal meals. **1968** *Globe & Mail* (Toronto) 13 Feb. 30/1 (Advt.), Huge kitchen with built-ins and double sink plus island sink for children. **1972** *House & Garden* Dec.–Jan. 77 Country-style kitchen..has a central butcher-block island with built-in hot-plates.

g. The superstructure of a ship, esp. an aircraft carrier.

1937 *Jane's Fighting Ships* 497 Adding 2½ feet to the beam..to balance the island superstructure. **1964** *New Scientist* 2 July 22 (*caption*) The 'island' which supports a giant radar scanner on HMS *Hermes.*

3. a. *island fortress, race* (i.e. the British).

1898 H. NEWBOLT (*title*) The island race. **1902** BELLOC *Path to Rome* 51 Some kinds of men begin talking of Dogged Determination, Bull-dog pluck, the stubborn spirit of the Island race, and so forth. **1942** *R.A.F. Jrnl.* 18 Apr. 28 In the strongly defended island fortress of Corregidor. **1958** *Spectator* 14 Feb. 199/2, I could wish that the Island Race as a whole were a little more discriminating in its drooling. **1966** *Listener* 26 May 771/1 Aware of Mr Menuhin's devotion to his adopted country, one felt it matched by the island-race stateliness of Sir Adrian.

4. island arc, any arcuate chain of islands located and aligned in relation to an orogenic belt and characteristically having a deep

trench on the convex side; **Island Carib,** (*a*) the Carib people of the Lesser Antilles; (*b*) the language of this people; **island-hill, -mountain,** a hill or mountain rising out of a plain; **island-hop** *v. intr.* (of the U.S. army in the Pacific during the war of 1941–45), to recapture Japanese-occupied islands one after another; also *transf.*; chiefly in *vbl. sb.*; **island-mountain:** see *island-hill* above; **island plot, site,** a plot of land on a building site surrounded by streets or open spaces; **island-refuge** = *2 c; **island site:** see *island plot* above; **island-universe,** add: [app. tr. G. *weltinsel* (von Humboldt), though the term has been attributed to Sir William Herschel] (earlier and later examples).

1906 H. B. C. & W. J. SOLLAS tr. *Suess's Face of Earth* II. iv. 207 It would be sound geology to draw the western boundary of the Pacific Ocean outside the island arcs from Kamchatka through Japan. **1971** I. G. GASS et al. *Understanding Earth* xix. 271/1 The zone meets the surface close to the line of the deep ocean trench and dips away beneath the island-arc. **1938** D. TAYLOR in *U.S. Bureau Amer. Ethnol. Bull.* No. 119. 140 The most typical product of the Island Carib is..the dugout canoe. **1951** —— *Black Carib of Brit. Honduras* 41 The Black Carib of Central America speak a dialect of Island Carib—of the language, that is to say, spoken by the native Indian inhabitants of the 'Caribee' islands at the time of Breton's stay among them (1635–1653). **1968** *Encycl. Brit.* XXIII. 433/1 These island Carib [of Dominica] have not retained as much of their aboriginal language and culture [as the Black Carib]. **1969** *Word* XXV. 276 In Island-Carib, the plural is employed only with reference to animate..beings. **1839** H. T. DE LA BECHE *Rep. Geol. Cornwall, Devon & W. Somerset* i. 26 The lower island-hills of Pawlet and Chedzoy..rise out of the plain near Bridgewater. **1907** Island-hill [see *INSELBERG]. **1944** *Sat. Even. Post* 28 Oct. 98/3 American air power won the battles for Attu, Kwajalein and Tarawa, and has made possible island hopping. **1946** *Sat. Rev. Lit.* 23 Feb. 33/1 Cant takes us along on the island-hopping campaigns. **1955** in *Amer. Speech* (1956) XXXI. 85 Did you island-hop or did you take the plane directly? **1971** P. DRISCOLL *White Lie Assignment* vii. 61 The caiques are built for coasting and island-hopping. They can't take much rough weather. **1972** *Guardian* 11 Aug. 1/1 The airlift by small, island-hopping aircraft. **1906** *Daily Chron.* 31 Aug. 4/4 They [*sc.* the Malvern Hills] lie precisely north by south, moored like some great island-mountain to the westward of the central plain of England. **1913** *Geogr. Jrnl.* XLII. 149 The fantastic peaks and domes of the rocky island-mountains. **1941** F. H. LAHEE *Field Geol.* (ed. 4) xi. 360 A similar residual type in arid regions is the island mountain, or island mount (German, Inselberg). **1908** *Daily Chron.* 20 Apr. 3/5 On this 'island' plot of land has been erected a building which is certainly an adornment to Great Portland-street. **1922** F. MUIRHEAD *London & Environs* (ed. 2) 8 A busy street should be crossed only at a point where an 'island-refuge' is provided in the middle. **1907** *Westm. Gaz.* 20 Sept. 10/1 Australia and the Strand 'Island Site'. **1936** C. ROUSE *Old Towns* i. 17 The market house or town hall was often built on an island site in those wide streets. **1972** *Accountant* 17 Aug. 206/1 Two important island sites with main frontages to Great Portland Street have been assembled over the course of many years. [**1845** A. VON HUMBOLDT *Kosmos* I. 93 Unter den vielen selbstleuchtenden ihren Ort verändernden Sonnen ..welche unsre Weltinsel bilden.] **1867** A. J. DAVIS *Stellar Key to Summer Land* vi. 32 The expression 'Island Universe' was suggested by the immense distance of the fixed stars from our Sun and Planets; giving the impression that our Solar System occupies an isolated position in the boundless ocean of space. **1887** R. A. PROCTOR *Other Suns than Ours* i. 1 Our 'island universe', as Humboldt poetically called the stellar system. *Ibid.* 11 The results which Sir W. Herschel published in 1817 and 1818 justify the belief that..large numbers of the nebulæ must be regarded as external galaxies. This grand conception fascinated..some who, like Humboldt,..had understood and appreciated the work of the great observer. The idea of 'island universes' strewn throughout the ocean of space impressed the world. **1928** J. H. JEANS *Astron. & Cosmogony* i. 19 These figures amply show that these nebulae and star-clouds are quite outside our system of stars; they constitute what Herschel described as 'island-universes' distinct from the universe which contains our sun. **1959** DAVIES & PALMER *Radio Stud. Universe* i. 2 Many..nebulae were discovered. However, it was not until the 1920's that the problem of their distance and spacing was unravelled by Hubble, who showed that they were very distant island universes (galaxies) of stars many of which were similar to our Milky Way system.

Isle of Wight (əiləvˌwəi·t). The name of an island off the coast of Hampshire, used *attrib.* to designate a disease of bees first found there in 1904, caused by the parasitic mite *Acarapis woodsi*; also called *acarine disease*.

[**1907** A. D. IMMS in *Jrnl. Board Agric.* XIV. 129 (*title*) Report on a disease of bees in the Isle of Wight.] **1909** W. MALDEN in *Jrnl. Board Agric.* XV. 815 In commencing my observations on the Isle of Wight disease, I first endeavoured to ascertain whether, by careful dissections, any characteristic lesions could be discovered in the internal anatomy of the diseased bees. **1932** E. B. WEDMORE *Man. Beekeeping* xvii. 401 In 1920 Miss E. J. Harvey observed a mite in the tracheæ of bees suffering from 'Isle of Wight' disease. **1965** M. HOYT *World of Bees* x. 171 Acarapis is sometimes called Isle of Wight disease.

islet. Add: **2.** Also = *ISLAND *sb.* 2 d.

1921 *Discovery* Oct. 257/2 A dozen guiding marks, consisting of the beginnings of lines, bifurcations and islets.

b. *islet* (or *Islet*) *of Langerhans* [tr. F. *îlot de Langerhans* (E. Laguesse 1893, in *Compt. rend. hebdom. d. Séances et Mém. de la Soc. de Biol.* XLV. 819): named after Paul *Langerhans* (1847–1888), German anatomist, who, in 1869, first described such islets], any of numerous highly vascular islets of tissue in the pancreas, composed of light-staining cells of two principal types, one of which secretes insulin and the other glucagon; also *ellipt.*

1896 *Jrnl. R. Microsc. Soc.* 35 Besides the solid buds which form the first 'islets of Langerhans', they give rise to numerous hollow buds. **1904** *Proc. R. Soc.* LXXIII. 84 The degeneration or absence of the islets in diabetes. **1910** *Practitioner* Jan. 32 Many other pathological conditions.. have been ascribed to abnormalities of other ductless glands; e.g...glycosuria to the loss of the internal secretion formed by the islets of Langerhans in the pancreas. **1968** *Times* 27 Nov. 9/3 Those parts of the organ [*sc.* the pancreas] concerned with carbohydrate metabolism—known as the islets of Langerhans. **1973** *Nature* 23 Mar. 259 Yields of up to 350 Islets per rat pancreas have been achieved using this method.

3. (*attrib.* examples of sense 2 b.)

1914, etc. Islet-tissue [see *INSULIN 1]. **1927** HALDANE & HUXLEY *Animal Biol.* xii. 279 Islet cell of human pancreas. **1962** *Lancet* 12 May 1003/2 The characteristics of the Zollinger–Ellison syndrome are extreme gastric hypersecretion, intractable peptic ulceration..and either hyperplasia or tumour of the islet-cells of the pancreas. **1963** E. J. W. BARRINGTON *Introd. Gen. & Compar. Endocrinol.* iii. 43 We have evidence that islet tissue arose very early in vertebrate evolution. **1965** LEE & KNOWLES *Animal Hormones* vii. 113 Occasionally in man a tumour of the islet cell occurs and there is excessive secretion of insulin.

islomania (əiːlomēⁱ·niă). [f. ISL(AND *sb.* + -O + -MANIA.] A passion or craze for islands.

1962 *Listener* 25 Oct. 693/1, I suffer from acute islomania, and was therefore specially interested in 'Let's Imagine'..which investigated the Channel Island of Herm. **1971** D. CONOVER *One Man's Island* 110 Islomania runs in my blood. I would rather talk about islands than eat, would rather—and often do—think about islands than sleep. **1972** *Times* 4 May 11/6 Psychologists have a word for it—islomania—an insatiable attraction to islands.

ism, *quasi-sb.* (Earlier and later examples.)

1680 'HERACLIO DEMOCRITUS' *Vision of Purgatory* 46 He was the great Hieroglyphick of Jesuitism, Puritanism, Quaquerism, and of all Isms from Schism. **1756** *Monthly Rev.* XIV. 359 Arianism, Socinianism, Arminianism, or any other *ism*. *a* **1773** [see GERMANISM 1]. **1928** G. B. SHAW *Intelligent Woman's Guide Socialism* lxxxiii. 447 The proletarian Isms are very much alike. **1944** J. S. HUXLEY *On Living in Revolution* iii. 29 Democracy could become more dynamic than Fascism or Communism or any other ism or ideology. **1963** F. W. FREY in L. W. Pye *Communications & Political Devel.* xvii. 299 Movement towards..'Communism', or 'totalitarianism', or..whatever one's preferred 'ism'..happens to be. **1968** S. C. HUTCHISON *Hist. R. Acad.* xvii. 183 He saw no place in art for abstractions and 'isms' and had a very low opinion of their adherents. **1974** *Listener* 14 Feb. 220/1 Impressionism became the most successful 'ism' in the history of art.

-ismus, *suffix*, repr. G. *-ismus* or L. *-ismus* (see -ISM), used similarly to -ISM, indicating a typical condition or typical conduct, in nouns formed from proper names, or indicating a system or principle, as in *historismus, mysticismus, Sherlockismus, snobismus*. Freq. with ironical or pejorative overtones.

1912 R. A. KNOX in *Blue Bk.* (Oxf.) July 132 There is a special kind of epigram, known as the Sherlockismus, of which the indefatigable Ratzegger has collected no less than 173 instances. The following may serve as examples: 'Let me call your attention to the curious incident of the dog in the night-time.' 'The dog did nothing at all in the night-time.' 'That was the curious incident,' said Sherlock Holmes. And again: 'I was following you, of course.' 'Following me? I saw nobody.' 'That is what you must expect to see when I am following you,' said Sherlock Holmes. **1948** *Scottish Jrnl. Theol.* I. 142 This kind of unhistorical thinking is neither Biblical nor Christian and.. is allied to the speculations of Philo... *This* is certainly not the way to escape from the errors of *Historismus*. **1952** *Spectator* 14 Mar. 344/2 A sincere and compelling protest against *mysticismus* in power politics. **1959** H. KENNER *Invisible Poet: T. S. Eliot* (1960) v. 241 His exchange with the Third Tempter opens with the figure of rhetoric the late Rev. Ronald Knox christened the Sherlockismus: *Third Tempter*: I am an unexpected visitor. *Thomas*: I expected you. **1961** *Daily Tel.* 23 June 18/5 Of all the practitioners of this new cult of 'Sherlockismus', Mr Starrett is..far the most interesting. **1971** A. QUINTON in A. Bullock *20th Cent.* 260/2 Massive studies of *Historismus* by the historians Troeltsch and Meinecke. **1974** *Times Lit. Suppl.* 1 Feb. 113/2 Perhaps he has also done more than he reckoned to put an end to the tiresome excesses of Sherlockismus. **1974** V. GIELGUD *In Such a Night* xx. 172 His acquaintances accused him of Victorian *snobismus*.

isness. Delete *nonce-wd.* and add earlier and later examples.

1865 J. H. STIRLING *Secret of Hegel* II. III. i. 4 *Seyn*, in Germany, often in Hegel himself, means the abstraction of sensuous Isness. **1884** 'SCOTUS NOVANTICUS' *Metaphysica Nova et Vetusta* VI. 146 The moment of being or is-ness yields identity (A = A); and as this is-ness is given *in concreto* as a determined somewhat which *is*, we have the category of Essence as derivative category from Being. **1918** [see *GOOD A. *adj.* 14 c]. **1942** *Mind* LI. 257 Any one..who sets out along the *via negativa* in this spirit is confessing in the very act that 'is' can never be tortured into 'isness'. **1955** A. HUXLEY *Genius & Goddess* 46 The girl is who she is. Some of her isness spills over and impregnates the entire universe. **1965** L. R. HUBBARD *Scientology Abridged Dict.*, *Is-ness*, one of the four conditions of existence. It is an apparency of existence brought about by the continuous alteration of an As-isness. This is called, when agreed upon, reality.

Isnik (izni·k). The name of a town in Asian Turkey, the classical Nicæa (see NICENE *a.* (and *sb.*)), used *attrib.* to denote pottery or tiles made there, or imitations thereof, from the fifteenth to the seventeenth centuries, characterized by the use of brilliant pigments.

[**1909** F. R. MARTIN in *Burlington Mag.* Aug. 270/2 The splendid blue and white bowls, commonly ascribed to Kutaya, which I am convinced come from Isnik.] **1932** R. L. HOBSON *Guide Islamic Pott. Near East* III. 87 There were doubtless potters at work in other towns in the sixteenth century,..and it is highly probable that they would adapt their wares to the prevailing Turkish taste as expressed by the Isnik pottery. **1939** A. LANE *Guide Coll. Tiles* (V. & A. Mus.) ii. 16 The pure white ground and tense drawing so characteristic of the later Isnik tiles. **1957** —— *Later Islamic Pott.* iii. 60 It will probably never be possible to stop dealers and collectors calling the later Isnik wares 'Rhodian', and the nickname is at any rate a convenient label for the whole class in which the 'sealing-wax red' appears. **1966** J. FOWLES *Magus* xv. 88 A triangular cabinet full of pale-blue and green Isnik ware. **1972** *Daily Tel.* 5 Dec. 12/5 A large Isnik pottery dish of the late 16th century was bought by Eskenazi for ..£8,000 at Sotheby's yesterday.

iso-. Add: **isacoustic** *a.*, (*b*) *Seismology*, applied to a line (imaginary or on a map) connecting places where an equal percentage of observers heard the sound of an earthquake; **isano·malous** *a.*, (of a line) isabnormal; (of a map) depicting such lines; **isanomaly,** add: also **isonomaly;** also used with reference to other kinds of anomaly (see quots.); **isentha·lpic** *a.*, of or denoting equal enthalpy; **isentropic** *a.* (earlier and later examples); also, taking place at constant entropy, involving no change in entropy; *sb.* (examples); hence **isentro·pically** *adv.*, without a change in entropy; **iːsoacce·ntual** *a.*, of verse in which the syllables are of equal length and accent; **isoagglu·tinate** *v. trans.* (also *absol.*), to cause isoagglutination (of); chiefly in **isoagglu·tinating** *vbl. sb.* and *ppl. a.*; **iːsoagglutina·tion** *Immunol.* [a. G. *isoagglutination* (A. Klein 1902, in *Wiener klin. Wochenschr.* XV. 415/1)], agglutination of cells of an individual by a substance obtained from another individual of the same species; so **iːsoagglu·tinative** *a.*, pertaining to or causing isoagglutination; **iːsoagglu·tinin** *Immunol.*, an agglutinin that agglutinates cells of other individuals of the same species as that in which it is found; **iːsoagglu·tinogen** *Immunol.*, a substance that elicits or reacts with an isoagglutinin; **isoallele** (əisoˌæ·līl) *Genetics*, an allele indistinguishable from another allele in its effect on the phenotype except when special techniques are employed; hence **isoalle·lic** *a.*; **isoa·ntibody** *Immunol.*, an antibody elicited by an isoantigen; **isoa·ntigen** *Immunol.*, an antigen in one individual which is capable of eliciting antibody formation only in other, genetically different, individuals of the same species; so **isoantige·nic** *a.*; **i·sobase** *Geol.* [ad. Sw. *isobas* (G. De Geer 1890, in *Geol. Fören. i Stockholm Forhandl.* XII. 72), f. Gr. βάσις stepping, step], a line (either imaginary or on a map) connecting points on the earth which have undergone equal amounts of uplift (or more rarely depression) over a period of geological time; hence **isoba·sic** *a.*; **i·sobath** *sb.* [Gr. βάθος depth], a line (either imaginary or on a map) joining places where water has equal depth; an underwater contour; **isoba·thic** *a.*; **isoca·loric** *a.*, of equal calorific value; hence **isocalo·rically** *adv.*, in a way that leaves the calorific value unchanged; **isoche·mical** *a. Geol.*, taking place with or characterized by constant chemical composition; hence **isoche·mically** *adv.*, without a change in chemical composition; **i·sochlor** (-klǭɹ) [CHLOR(INE *sb.*], a line (imaginary or on a map) connecting points where the concentration of chlorine in the surface water is the same; **isochro·mosome** *Cytology*, an abnormal chromosome having a pair of identical arms; **isoco·lloid** *Chem.* [ad. G. *isokolloid* (W. Ostwald *Grundriss*

der Kolloidchemie (ed. 2, 1911) I. iv. 128)], a colloidal solution in which the disperse phase and the dispersion medium are chemically identical (as ice dispersed in water) or chemically related (as a polymer dispersed in its monomer); **isoco·rtex** *Anat.* [mod.L. (C. & O. Vogt 1919, in *Jrnl. f. Psychol. u. Neurol.* XXV. 293)] = *NEOPALLIUM; **isocy·clic** *a. Chem.* = *homocyclic* adj. s.v. *HOMO-; **iso-e·cho** *a.*, applied to a line on a radar display along which the echo signal (from clouds and the like) has the same strength, and to devices and techniques relating to such lines (as in the detection of rain and atmospheric turbulence); **isoelectric**, delete def. in Dict. and see *ISO-ELECTRIC *a.*; **isoenerge·tic** *a.*, having, denoting, or giving rise to equal amounts of energy; taking place at constant energy; **i·sogel** *Chem.*, an isocolloid in the form of a gel; **i·sograd** *Petrol.* [GRAD(E *sb.*], a line or surface (either imaginary or in a diagram) joining points where the rock originated under the same conditions of pressure and temperature, as indicated by similarity of facies or metamorphic grade; hence **i·sograde, isogra·dic** *adjs.*, that is an isograd; of the same facies or metamorphic grade; **i·sogyre**, a thick band or bow of darkness seen crossing the coloured fringes in an interference pattern; **i:sohæmagglutina·tion** (also **-hem-**) *Immunol.*, isoagglutination of red blood cells; **i:sohæmagglu·tinin** (also **-hem-**) *Immunol.*, an isoagglutinin which agglutinates red blood cells; **i:sohæmoly·sin** (also **-hem-**) *Immunol.*, a hæmolysin that lyses red blood cells of other individuals of the same species as that in which it is found; **isohaline** (-hēⁱ·ləin) *sb. Oceanogr.* [Gr. ἅλινος of salt], a line (imaginary or on a chart), or an imaginary surface, connecting points which have the same salinity; *a.*, connecting such points; also, of a constant salinity throughout; **i·sohel** [Gr. ἥλιος sun], a line (imaginary or on a map) connecting points having the same amount or duration of sunshine; so **isohelic** (-hī·lik), *a.*; **i·sohyet** (-həiĭt) [Gr. ὑετ-ός rain], = *isohyetal* sb. s.v. Iso-; **isohyetal** *a.* and *sb.* (examples); **isoimmu·ne** *a.*, of, producing, or exhibiting isoimmunization; **i:soimmuniza·tion** (an instance of) the development of an isoantibody in an individual against an antigen derived from another individual of the same species; **isokine·tic** *a.*, characterized by no disturbance to the speed and direction of a fluid when it is withdrawn as a sample from a flow; hence **isokine·tically** *adv.*, in an isokinetic manner, i.e. without causing such a disturbance; **isole·cithal** *a.* = *homolecithal* adj. (s.v. *HOMO-); **i·solex** *Linguistics*, a line connecting places in which there is uniformity of vocabulary; hence **isole·xic** *a.*; also **isole·ctic** *a.*; **i·soline** = *ISOPLETH 1; **isoly·sin** *Immunol.* [a. G. *isolysin* (Ehrlich & Morgenroth 1900, in *Berliner klin. Wochenschr.* XXXVII. 455/1)] = *isohæmolysin* above; **isomagne·tic** *a.*, denoting a line (either imaginary or on a map) connecting places which have the same value of a particular parameter of the earth's magnetic field, and a map or chart showing such lines; also as *sb.*, an isomagnetic line; **isonomaly**, var. *isanomaly* (in Dict. and Suppl. s.v. Iso-); **isonu·clear** *a. Chem.* = *HOMONUCLEAR *a.* b; **iso-osmo·tic** *a. Physiol.* = *isosmotic* adj. (below); **isopiestic** *a.* (substitute for def.:) representing, having, or characterized by equal or constant pressure; also as *sb.*, a line in a diagram representing states of equal pressure; (examples); **i·sopor** [Gr. πόρ-ος passage, way], a line (either imaginary or on a map) connecting points at which equal annual changes in some parameter of the earth's magnetic field are observed; hence **isopo·ric** *a.*; **isosmotic** (əisǫzmǫ·tik) *a. Physiol.*, of or having the same osmotic pressure; const. *with*; **i·sostich** (-stik) *Biochem.* [Gr. στίχ-ος line (of poetry)], each of two or more fractions of a polynucleotide that contain the same number of nucleotides; **isostru·ctural** *a. Min.*, having the same or similar crystal structure; const. *with*; **isosylla·bic** *a. Linguistics*, of a metrical structure in which the syllables are of the same length; **isosynta·ctic** *a.* (see quot.); **isosynta·gmic** *a. Linguistics* (see quot. 1954); **i·sotach** [Gr. τάχ-ύς swift], a line on a chart or diagram connecting points where the speed of something, esp. the wind, is the same; **isote·niscope** [irreg. f. TEN(SION *sb.* + -I- + -SCOPE], an instrument for measuring the vapour pressure of a liquid over a range of temperatures, consisting of a bulb for containing the liquid attached to one arm of a U-tube, which is used as a manometer to show when the pressure applied to the other arm is equal to the vapour pressure; **i·sovol** [VOL(ATILE *sb.* and *a.*], a line (either imaginary or on a map) joining places at which the coal has the same ratio of fixed to volatile carbon.

1900 C. DAVISON in *Phil. Mag.* XLIX. 43 An isacoustic line may be defined as a line which passes through all places in which the percentage of persons who hear the sound is the same. **1938** L. D. LEET *Pract. Seismol.* viii. 282 Curves passing through the places at which equal percentages of the observers heard the earthquake sound were drawn in 1899, and Davison, followed by Knott and de Montessus, called them isacoustic lines. **1900** *Geogr. Jrnl.* XV. 662 Maps of isotherms and isanomalous lines for January and July. **1943** G. T. TREWARTHA *Introd. Climate* (ed. 2) i. 56/2 If lines, called isanomals, are drawn on a world map, joining places of equal thermal anomaly, an isanomalous map is the result. **1967** R. W. FAIRBRIDGE *Encycl. Atmospheric Sci.* 985/1 Isanomalous lines drawn on a map..reflect regional distortions of the world patterns. **1930** *Meteorol. Gloss.* (Meteorol. Office) (ed. 2) 109 *Isanomaly.* This word..is used of lines joining all points on a map or chart having equal anomalies, or differences from normal, of a particular meteorological element. **1931** F. H. LAHEE *Field Geol.* (ed. 3) xxiii. 674 Equal anomalies may be connected by flowing lines called isonomalies, or isanomalies, which express in gammas the local variations from the average total magnetic intensities in the area. **1962** F. I. ORDWAY et al. *Basic Astronautics* v. 199 Lines of regional vertical intensity are constructed, as are isonomaly charts expressing in gammas the local variations in the average total magnetic intensity of a given region. **1967** R. W. FAIRBRIDGE *Encycl. Atmospheric Sci.* 507/2 *Isanomaly*, lines or contours of equal anomalies or departures from normal (often used with gravity anomalies, cf. *Isogal*). **1925** *Proc. Amer. Acad. Arts & Sci.* LX. 581 The isenthalpic curves themselves contain valuable information. **1937** M. W. ZEMANSKY *Heat & Thermodynamics* xiv. 245 (*caption*) Isenthalpic states of a gas. *Ibid.* 246 The numerical value of the slope of an isenthalpic curve on a *t–P* diagram at any point is called the Joule–Kelvin coefficient. **1973** J. S. TURTON *Macroscopic Thermodynamics* iv. 81 The process undergone by the gas or vapour in passing through the constriction cannot be represented by an isenthalpic curve. **1873** J. W. GIBBS in *Trans. Connecticut Acad. Arts & Sci.* II. 311 If, however, we..call that quantity entropy..it seems natural to..call the lines in which this quantity has a constant value isentropic. *Ibid.* 327 Although the inclination of the isentropics is independent of the quantity of gas under consideration, the rate of increase of η will vary with this quantity. **1923** LEWIS & RANDALL *Thermodynamics* xii. 137 In such an isentropic compression there will ordinarily be a change in temperature. **1951** C. L. BROWN *Basic Thermodynamics* vi. 88 Two additional relations..relate temperature and volume and pressure and volume for an isentropic. **1956** G. C. McVITTIE *Gen. Relativity & Cosmol.* vii. 123 An equation determining the function *F* in isentropic flow. **1951** C. L. BROWN *Basic Thermodynamics* vi. 89 The gas expands isentropically and is exhausted at 15 psia. **1972** *Nature* 15 Sept. 139/2 The pressure applied to an implosion system does *PdV* work generating kinetic energy which is converted near isentropically to internal energy concentrated in the compressed volume. **1956** H. WHITEHALL in *Kenyon Rev.* 420 There is..in much of Milton, isochronic counterpointed with isoaccentual rhythm. In some poems of Dylan Thomas, we find a most elaborate counterpoint of isoaccentual..and, apparently, isotonic rhythms. **1957** N. FRYE *Sound & Poetry* 143 Isoaccentual, or, as it is often called, isosyllabic rhythm weights with stress. **1904** *Alienist & Neurologist* XXV. 386 The serum from such blood was also isoagglutinating. **1910** *Johns Hopkins Hosp. Bull.* XXI. 70/1 Human beings can be divided into four groups according to the ability of their serum to cause isoagglutination and of their corpuscles to be isoagglutinated. **1921** *Biol. Bull.* XL. 18 The iso-agglutinating power of the egg-water. **1967** D. M. WEIR *Handbk. Exper. Immunol.* iv. 87 The isoagglutinating activity found in this sedimentation region of human serum. **1907** *Jrnl. Med. Res.* XVII. 338 Human bloods may be separated into three rather definite groups as regards isoagglutination. **1921** *Biol. Bull.* XL. 17 In iso-agglutination round solid masses of agglutinated spermatozoa form in a few seconds. **1927** Iso-agglutination [see *A 7]. **1970** *Exper. Cell Res.* LIX. 37 (*heading*) Jelly coat substances of sea urchin eggs. I. Sperm isoagglutination and sialopolysaccharide in the jelly. **1902** *Science* 28 Nov. 858/1 The isoagglutinative and isolytic properties of human serums in health and in disease. **1911** *Jrnl. Exper. Med.* XIII. 537 Isoagglutinative serum is active at a considerable dilution. **1903** DORLAND *Med. Dict.* (ed. 3) 350/1 iso-agglutinin. **1907** [see *isohæmagglutination* below]. **1971** J. A. BELLANTI *Immunol.* iii. 78 All mature individuals possess antibody in their serum, the so-called 'naturally occurring' isoantibodies (isoagglutinins) directed against the antigenic determinant absent from their own erythrocytes. **1926** *Jrnl. Immunol.* XI. 240 The main human iso-agglutinogens A and B are to be detected not only by human serum but also by the sera of animals. **1972** W. E. HAESLER *Immunohematol.* i. 2 Immunohematology deals with hemagglutinogens (isoagglutinogens, immunogens, antigens) that are a natural phenomenon in human beings. **1943** STERN & SCHAEFFER in *Proc. Nat. Acad. Sci.* XXIX. 361 Different alleles indistinguishable except by special tests will be called isoalleles. **1970** *Sci. Amer.* Mar. 104 These slightly different forms of the same gene that perform the same function are called isoalleles. **1944** *Genetics* XXIX. 485 These crosses established the iso-allelic if not identical nature of all seven *pyd* mutants. **1961** *Lancet* 29 July 262/2 An isochromosome carries, on its two symmetrical arms, duplicate gene loci each influencing the same character. These arms can be both isologous and isoallelic. **1919** L. & H. HIRSCHFELD in *Lancet* 18 Oct. 676/1 The antibodies produced within the species which we call isoantibodies..act..only against the differences between the blood of the animal which provides the blood for injection and that of the recipient. **1971** Isoantibody [see *isoagglutinin* above]. **1936** *Jrnl. Immunol.* XXX. 445 (*heading*) Procedure for the determination of isoantigens in saliva. **1971** J. A. BELLANTI *Immunol.* iii. 76 Homologous antigens or isoantigens (alloantigens) are those genetically controlled antigenic determinants which distinguish one individual of a given species from another. **1938** *Jrnl. Path. & Bacteriol.* XLVI. 249 Iso-antigenic factors present in the grafted tissue and absent in the host are capable of eliciting a response which results in the destruction of the graft. **1971** J. A. BELLANTI *Immunol.* iii. 80 New human isoantigenic specificities. **1892** G. DE GEER in *Proc. Boston Soc. Nat. Hist.* XXV. 457 To get a general view of the warping of land..I have used the graphic method of Mr. G. K. Gilbert..and have connected with lines of equal deformation, or as I have called them isobases, such points of the limit as were uplifted to the same height. **1957** J. K. CHARLESWORTH *Quaternary Era* II. xlv. 1289 (*caption*) Map of the sea's greatest area in Baltoscandia (black), with areas of most important glacier-lakes (shaded) and isobases of uplift in metres. **1969** BENNISON & WRIGHT *Geol. Hist. Brit. Isles* xvi. 366 It is still not possible to construct accurate isobases (lines joining points of equal uplift) for Britain, as has been done in the case of Scandinavia. **1932** E. G. WOODS *Baltic Region* x. 121 A glance at such a map with the isobasic lines indicated, shows the late-glacial sea at about its maximum development. **1895** *Rep. Sci. Results Voy. H.M.S. Challenger, Summary* I. 55 Bauche..is..considered as the first to make use of isobaths for the sea. **1938** *Jrnl. Marine Res.* I. 138 (*caption*) Isobaths (light broken lines) for every ten meters depth. **1956** *Trans. Amer. Microsc. Soc.* LXXV. 335 Miner's map is our primary source of that shore line.. just as it is for the contained isobaths. The Commission ..has in no way modified the lakes except to build a bathing beach and boat docks. **1972** *Nature* 4 Feb. 253/2 Thus Corsica makes a good fit with France along the 1,000-metre isobath. **1895** *Rep. Sci. Results Voy. H.M.S. Challenger, Summary* I. 50 These isobathic curves are intended to show that certain elevations of the sea-bottom correspond with the orography of the neighbouring land. **1957** *Encycl. Brit.* VIII. 743/2 The isobathic chart of the Severn estuary..shows a progressive deepening seaward by means of V-shaped lines which become blunter westward. **1922** *Experiment Station Rec.* Sept. 370 The sugar tolerance of the diabetic patient was..more markedly lowered by protein than by isocaloric amounts of fat. **1956** *Biol. Abstr.* XXX. 2208/1 Male Wistar rats were divided into 3 groups receiving an isocaloric diet. **1971** *Jrnl. Gen. Psychol.* LXXXV. 155 Decreasing the amount of protein in the diet, while holding it isocaloric through addition of carbohydrate, resulted in an increase in the 'excitatory process' of rats. **1973** *Lancet* 2 June 1201/2 A programme of work on an isolated group of healthy young men, using isocaloric substitution of glucose syrup..for dietary sucrose. **1971** *Jrnl. Gen. Psychol.* LXXXV. 156 Diets in which carbohydrate and protein were interchanged isocalorically. **1972** *Science* 19 May 795/1 The animals fed alcohol received the identical diet except that ethanol..isocalorically replaced carbohydrate. **1937** *Trans. R. Soc. Edin.* LIX. 218 Correlation between rocks of the same bulk-composition metamorphosed under different physical controls—i.e. isochemical correlation. **1951** TURNER & VERHOOGEN *Ign. & Metamorphic Petrol.* xv. 369 Metamorphism may be considered as commonly approaching, though seldom attaining, the nature of an isochemical change. **1952** T. F. W. BARTH *Theoret. Petrol.* IV. xii. 356 In geological discussions the fact that sediments at the very incipience of metamorphism regularly change their chemical composition has often been neglected. However, these changes are not to be neglected... Isochemical regional metamorphism *senso strictu* [sic].. does not exist. **1969** W. D. JOHNS tr. *Correns's Introd. Mineral.* ix. 298 Transformations in an isochemical system depend on the temperature and pressure to which the system has been subjected. **1964** J. CHALLINOR *Dict. Geol.* (ed. 2) 133/2 A rock changing its mineral composition isochemically remains a closed 'system'. **1973** *Nature* 23 Mar. 243/2 The thickness of halite salt that could be precipitated isochemically from one basinful of Mediterranean waters..is..only about 20 m. **1890** *Rep. on Water Supply & Sewerage Pt. 1: Examinations of Water Supplies & Inland Waters* (Massachusetts State Board of Health) 679 In the accompanying map of normal chlorine of Massachusetts, the points of like normal chlorine have been connected by lines which we will call isochlors. **1943** *Proc. R. Irish Acad.* XLVIII. B. 157 The geochemical data of chlorine are considered with respect to river and surface waters, and equations developed relating the distance of any particular isochlor from the sea coast. **1957** G. E. HUTCHINSON *Treat. Limnol.* I. viii. 545 In Europe a greater proportion of rain is derived from air which has moved in perpendicular to the isochlors than is likely to be the case in North America. **1939** C. D. DARLINGTON in *Jrnl. Genetics* XXXVII. 357 The attached-*X* chromosome has two exactly similar arms united at the centromere. It is what we may call an iso-chromosome. **1972** W. V. BROWN *Textbk. Cytogenetics* xix. 268 The only likely isochromosomes found in human beings are of the long arm of a G-group chromosome, probably No. 21, and of the X chromosome. **1915** M. H. FISCHER tr. *W. Ostwald's Handbk. Colloid-Chem.* iv. 103 We shall term these structures in which disperse phase and dispersion means are chemically isomeric, isocolloids. **1946** J. ALEXANDER *Colloid Chem., Theoret. & Appl.* VI. xxiii. 531 Wolfgang Ostwald considers high-boiling petroleum fractions as isocolloids, in which the dispersed phase and the dispersion medium possess the same or similar chemical constitution. **1934** *Biol. Abstr.* VIII. 1476/1 Myelin reduction, at least in the iso-cortex, is discontinuous. **1937** BEST & TAYLOR *Physiol. Basis Med. Pract.* lxiii. 1418 The laminated cortex, which in man constitutes the remaining eleven-

twelfths [of the cortical area] and in animals is a much smaller fraction of the whole, is called the isocortex. **1951** K. S. Lashley in L. A. Jeffress *Cerebral Mechanisms in Behaviour* 132 In the rat, I have removed..practically every other part of the isocortex without disturbing visual perception or memory. **1970** *Developmental Biol.* XXII. 575 Fetal mouse cerebral isocortex from normal animals ..was dissociated and aggregated. **1900** E. F. Smith tr. *V. von Richer's Org. Chem.* (ed. 3) II. 435 The carbocyclic substances..belong to the class of isocyclic compounds which consist of rings of atoms of one and the same element. **1932** [see *homocyclic* adj. s.v. *homo-]. **1951** I. L. Finar *Org. Chem.* I. 667 The subject matter is divided into four main divisions: (i) Alicyclic compounds. (ii) Isocyclic compounds. (iii) Heterocyclic compounds. (iv) Natural products. **1951** *Jrnl. Meteorol.* VIII. 274/1 The distribution of echo intensity from all points in the two-dimensional cut through a storm may be plotted by use of the contour-mapping techniques suggested by Langille and Gunn or Atlas. The latter techniques produce a contour chart showing isopleths of reflected power throughout the area of the storm. (These isopleths will be referred to as 'isoecho lines' or 'power contours'.) **1959** L. J. Battan *Radar Meteorol.* xv. 141 (*heading*) Isoecho contouring. *Ibid.*, If range differences are negligible, the isoecho contour corresponds to a line of equal cloud reflectivity and equal rain intensity. **1961** *Aeroplane* CI. 573/2 For general weather observation the C.R. 353 has a 12-in. PPI unit incorporating iso-echo circuits which enable the operator to make cloud density determinations. **1969** *New Scientist* 4 Dec. 509/1 A..height-finding radar system has been modified to observe cloud and rain up to 160 miles out to sea..and to plot contours of constant rain intensity (iso-echo contours). **1899** *Ann. Rep. Board of Regents Smithsonian Inst., 1897–8* 543 Two weights of different aliments for which these numerical values are the same are said to be..isoenergetic weights. **1937** *Proc. R. Soc.* A. CLXI. 259 The mean free path in paraffin wax of the iso-energetic neutrons obtained by bombarding heavy hydrogen with deuterium ions has been measured. **1937** M. W. Zemansky *Heat & Thermodynamics* xiv. 281 Show that the slope of an isoenergetic curve on a T–V diagram is equal to [etc.]. **1962** *Jrnl. Aerospace Sci.* XXIX. 400/2 During the first phase of re-entry, the motion is isoenergetic and no significant heating or deceleration problem will exist. **1936** *Trans. Faraday Soc.* XXXII. 124 As a consequence of the..growth of the micelles the resin passes from its (assumed) isogel state..into the infusible *C* stage. **1937** *Jrnl. R. Aeronaut. Soc.* XLI. 531 Phenolformaldehyde resins (at least in their initial stages of condensation) are 'isogels'. **1950** Robitschek & Lewin *Phenolic Resins* iv. 56 As condensation proceeds, crosslinking takes place between some of the largely spherical bigger molecules (micelles) leading to a structure which.. can be likened to a sponge and is termed an isogel. **1924** C. E. Tilley in *Geol. Mag.* LXI. 169 In the terminology suggested above, this line may be said to be an Isograd... In reality an isograd is the intersection of an inclined isograd surface with the earth's surface. **1956** E. W. Heinrich *Microscopic Petrogr.* vi. 173 By joining points on a map that mark the initial appearance of each of the diagnostic minerals, mineral isograds (biotite isograd, sillimanite isograd, etc.) may be defined. **1971** I. G. Gass et al. *Understanding Earth* i. 36/2 The garnet isograd for example is the surface (line on the map) separating the garnet-bearing rocks of the garnet zone (high-grade) from the garnet-free rocks of the biotite zone (low grade). **1924** C. E. Tilley in *Geol. Mag.* LXI. 168 Isograde rocks are those which have originated under closely similar physical conditions of temperature and pressure. **1966** *McGraw-Hill Encycl. Sci. & Technol.* VIII. 298/1 Rocks within the same zone [of metamorphism] may be called..isograde. **1924** C. E. Tilley in *Geol. Mag.* LXI. 168 Rocks which belong to the same facies can be said to be in the same metamorphic grade, and can be referred to by the terms which I now suggest as isofacial or isogradic. **1926** G. W. Tyrrell *Princ. Petrol.* xv. 259 In the green-schist facies, a chlorite-quartz-muscovite-schist is isogradic with a green schist composed of chlorite, epidote, and albite. **1968** F. J. Turner *Metamorphic Petrol.* viii. 376 On this model the isogradic surfaces near the heat source have a reversed dip. **1902** Mann & Millikan tr. *Drude's Theory of Optics* II. II. iii. 354 The whole field of view is now.. traversed by a black curve, the so-called principal isogyre. **1922** N. H. & A. N. Winchell *Elem. Optical Mineral.* (ed. 2) I. xviii. 168 The biaxial optic axis interference figure differs from the uniaxial optic axis interference figure most clearly in the fact that it has only one isogyre instead of two. It also differs..in the fact that the single isogyre is not fixed in position, nor constantly straight, when the crystal is rotated. *Ibid.* 172 As in uniaxial crystals, the isogyres are the locus of all points at which the light emerges with its vibration planes parallel with the planes of the nicols. **1964** Hartshorne & Stuart *Pract. Optical Crystallogr.* v. 203 These interference bands are symmetrically arranged around the optic axis (or axes)...In addition to these bands there are dark 'brushes' or isogyres. **1907** *Jrnl. Med. Res.* XVII. 321 Earlier observers of human isohemagglutination asserted that isoagglutinins occurred only in the sera of pathological states. **1940** *Amer. Jrnl. Physiol.* CXXXI. 205 Breed, sex and age of animals seemed to have no influence on the occurrence of natural isohemagglutination. **1907** *Jrnl. Med. Res.* XVII. 334 Such an experiment, in the case of human isohemagglutinins, does more to prove the strict specificity of each 'bound aggutinin'. **1971** J. A. Bellanti *Immunol.* ii. 44 It is known that isohemagglutinins—the antibody to blood groups—..may develop as a result of exposure to enteric bacilli, containing blood grouplike substances in their structure. **1905** Gould *Dict. New Med. Terms* 318/2 Isohemolysin. **1916** Isohemolysin [see *blood group* s.v. *blood *sb.* 19]. **1972** W. E. Haesler *Immunohematol.* i. 2 Hemolysis is most frequently observed in the detection of the group A and B isohemolysins and the Le^a antibodies. **1902** *Encycl. Brit.* XXXI. 404/2 South of the Tropic of Capricorn the isohalines run nearly east and west. **1964** *Oceanogr. & Marine Biol.* II. 71 In winter the fiord water becomes isothermal and isohaline with average temperature and salinity of −1·76°C and 32·75‰. *Ibid.* 375 (*caption*) The increase in salinity in recent decades has altered..the course of the isohalines given in the chart. **1968** G. Neumann *Ocean Currents* iv. 129 The slope of isobaric surfaces..is small when compared to the slope of isothermal, isohaline (surfaces of equal salinity) and isopycnal surfaces. **1904** Goodchild & Tweney *Technol. & Sci. Dict.* 323/1 *Isohels*, lines connecting places having the same amount of sunshine. **1931** A. A. Miller *Climatol.* 22 The deviation of sunshine (shown on maps by lines of equal duration known as isohels). **1968** J. Gentilli *Sun, Climate & Life* (1971) xiii. 141/2 These lines are called isopleths as a general term, but..more specifically..isobars (equal pressure), isotherms (equal temperature),..isohels (equal sunshine),..etc. **1897** *Geogr. Jrnl.* X. 306 König.. has found sufficient material for a first attempt to draw 'isohelic' lines for Western Europe. **1899** *Nature* 21 Dec. 172/2 Isobars and isohyets indicating monthly and annual distribution of barometric pressure and rainfall. **1911** C. E. W. Bean *'Dreadnought' of Darling* xv. 144 The carpet which covers a country within the ten-inch isohyet (rainfall line) is a pretty ticklish thing to play with. **1967** M. J. Coe *Ecol. Alpine Zone Mt. Kenya* 63 The main peak area has a rainfall of between 30″ and 40″ per annum, the 30″ Isohyet being displaced slightly to the South-west of the peaks. **1889** *Cent. Dict.*, *Isohyetal*, *a.* and *n.* **1895** T. Russell *Meteorol.* vii. 141 A graphic representation of quantity of rainfall by lines through places having equal depths of rainfall are 'isohyetals'. **1909** *British Rainfall 1908* 140 The isohyetal lines are drawn about the 18th of the following month. **1923** *Glasgow Herald* 1 Feb. 6 Most of these features are..illustrated by maps exhibiting them..by isohyetal lines. **1962** W. Stegner *Wolf Willow* IV. iv. 281 She knew nothing about minimal annual rainfall, distribution of precipitation, isohyetal lines. **1938** *Jrnl. Path. & Bacteriol.* XLVII. 234 Fleisher found evidence of iso-immune reactions working with grafts of renal tissue in the guinea-pig. **1967** D. M. Weir *Handbk. Exper. Immunol.* xxx. 991 Isoantigenic differences, though usually detected by isoimmune sera, may in some cases also be picked up with antisera produced by immunization across a species gap. **1969** B. Pirofsky *Autoimmunization* xxi. 479/1 The bulk of knowledge concerning the nature and effect of immune interactions on the erythrocytes has been derived from heteroimmune and isoimmune studies. **1939** *Jrnl. Amer. Med. Assoc.* 8 July 126/1 It would seem to resemble agglutinins resulting from iso-immunization following repeated transfusions. **1971** J. A. Bellanti *Immunol.* iii. 77 Alternatively, isoimmunization can occur during the course of pregnancy when fetal cells..or proteins gain access to the maternal circulation. **1971** *Nature* 29 Oct. 608/1 The human foetus is at greater risk from maternal isoimmunizations than the bovid foetus. **1958** *Engineering* 22 Aug. 230/1 Regular production has..commenced..of the isokinetic sampling apparatus developed by the British Iron and Steel Research Association. **1959** *Brit. Jrnl. Appl. Physics* X. 26/1 The dust concentration calculated from the sample will be correct provided the gas sample is drawn into the nozzle at the same velocity as that of the gas stream. This is known as isokinetic sampling. *Ibid.* 27/2 In the extreme case of isokinetic sampling the nozzle becomes effectively non-existent. **1967** *Ann. Occupational Hygiene* X. 77 Brass nozzles were fitted around the filter retaining ring in order to obtain isokinetic samples at windspeeds from 5·4 m.p.h. to 30 m.p.h. *Ibid.*, 3-in.-long nozzles were attached to the filter holder to allow isokinetic flow into the inlet. **1958** *Engineering* 22 Aug. 230/1 The stainless steel probe faces directly into the stream of dusty gas and a sample is withdrawn isokinetically, that is, it flows into the nozzle in the same direction and with the same velocity as the local undisturbed gas stream. **1972** *Science* 16 June 1232/3 We sampled the suspended fly ash isokinetically at several locations across the outlet duct of the electrostatic precipitator. **1926** Jordan & Kindred *Textbk. Embryol.* v. 31 Since the small amount of yolk is evenly distributed throughout the cytoplasm, it [*sc.* the human egg] may also properly be called an isolecithal egg. **1940** L. H. Hyman *Invertebrates* I. v. 256 When the yolk is slight in amount, it is also more or less evenly dispersed; such eggs are variously termed isolecithal, alecithal, or homolecithal. **1972** P. A. Meglitsch *Invertebr. Zool.* (ed. 2) iv. 81/2 Isolecithal ova usually cleave in a characteristic manner. **1921** *Jrnl. Eng. & Gmc. Philol.* XX. 183 The finding and fixing of the isolectic lines is a task of word geography. *Ibid.* 182 There is danger in delay if certain phases of dialect life are to be recorded at all, and an accelerated pace in registering them would be advisable, especially in establishing the boundary lines of present dialects, with their maze of isophones, isomorphs, isolexes, and isotaxes, i.e., lines connecting places of identical or nearly identical sounds, forms, words, and syntactical peculiarities. **1963** *Amer. Speech* XXXVIII. 127 The regional diversity and the complicated grid of isolexes in the Northern counties. *Ibid.* 128 Any attempt to correlate the isolexes with demographic factors. **1926** *Germanic Rev.* I. iv. 285 The isolexic lines of this word..present a hopeless tangle. **1939** L. H. Gray *Foundations of Lang.* ii. 26 These lines will be isophonic, isotonic, isomorphic, isosyntagmic, or isolexic according as they indicate identical sounds, tones, inflexions, syntax, or vocabulary. **1954** Pei & Gaynor *Dict. Ling.* 107 *Isolexic lines*, lines on a linguistic map, indicating the approximate boundaries of the speech-areas in which a uniformity in the vocabulary of the speakers and in their use of words can be observed. **1944** V. Conrad *Methods in Climatol.* xiii. 167 Isolines..are fully analogous to contour lines, or to the equipotential lines used in physics...Closed isolines surrounding a region indicate that this is either depressed or elevated. **1961** G. T. Trewartha *Earth's Problem Climates* xvi. 237/2 In summer..the isolines of rainfall frequency show a strong zonal arrangement. **1969** *Nature* 29 Nov. 903/1 Vertical sections show that isolines slope steeply to the surface [of the sea] during upwelling, but the slope of the isoline varies with the parameter chosen. **1970** *Biol. Abstr.* LI. 11534/1 The resulting pattern of the isolines can be readily related to the distribution of a particular organism. **1901** Dorland *Med. Dict.* (ed. 2) 333/2 Isolysin. **1910** *Jrnl. Hygiene* X. 186 The injection of goats' blood into other goats resulted as a rule in the formation of isolysins. **1969** L. H. Crisp *Clin. Immunol. & Allergy* (ed. 2) xliv. 433/1 Isohemolysins, isolysins, or antibodies capable of lysis of erythrocytes may be found in the serum in paroxysmal hemoglobinuria. **1898** J. Milne *Seismol.* xii. 225 Slight changes in the isomagnetics of a district. **1899** *Nature* 6 July 236/2 An opportunity will thus be afforded..to obtain some idea of the accuracy with which the isomagnetic lines can be determined. **1940** Chapman & Bartels *Geomagnetism* I. iii. 96 The lines are called isomagnetic lines, and a chart in which the distribution of a magnetic element is thus indicated..is called an isomagnetic chart. **1967** E. H. Vestine in Matsushita & Campbell *Physics of Geomagnetic Phenomena* I. II. ii. 185 The isomagnetic lines for declination *D* or variation of the compass are also called 'isogonic' lines. **1900** E. F. Smith tr. *V. von Richter's Org. Chem.* (ed. 3) II. 390 Isonuclear substitution products with adjacent substituents show in general the same deportment as the ortho-substitution products of benzene. **1951** I. L. Finar *Org. Chem.* I. xxix. 586 Introduction of a second substituent can give rise to homonuclear (isonuclear) substitution..or to heteronuclear substitution. **1908** *Jrnl. Exper. Med.* X. 137 An iso-osmotic physiologically balanced solution. **1971** *Biochem. Jrnl.* CXXI. 261 Protein-polysaccharides of knee-joint cartilage of 9-month-old pigs were extracted sequentially with neutral iso-osmotic sodium acetate. **1873** J. W. Gibbs in *Trans. Connecticut Acad. Arts & Sci.* II. 311 In the same way we may conceive of lines of equal pressure...These lines we may also call..isopiestic. *Ibid.* 313 To prove that the ratio is independent of the shape of the circuit, let us suppose the area..divided up by an infinite number of isometrics..with equal differences of volume *dv*, and an infinite number of isopiestics..with equal differences of pressure *dp*. **1902** *Encycl. Brit.* XXXIII. 283/2 The isothermals..coincide with the isopiestics for a saturated vapour in presence of its liquid. **1940** Glasstone *Text-bk. Physical Chem.* ix. 622 If two vessels containing different solutes in the same solvent are placed side by side in a closed space, vapor will distil from the solution of higher vapor pressure and condense in the one having the lower pressure until, when equilibrium is attained, both solutions are exerting the same pressure, that is to say they are isopiestic. **1966** R. Joel *Basic Engin. Thermodynamics* i. 80 The pressure remains constant throughout the process. It is often referred to as an isobaric or isopiestic process. **1931** *Compt. Rend. de l'Assemb. de Stockholm 1930* (Union Géod. et Géophys. Internat., Sect. de Magn. et Électr. Terr.) 284 In that year the zero-isopor (the line dividing easterly and westerly change) crossed central Siberia. **1963** J. A. Jacobs *Earth's Core* v. 53 Considerable changes take place in the general distribution of isopors even within 20 years. **1931** *Compt. Rend. de l'Assemb. de Stockholm 1930* (Union Géod. et Géophys. Internat., Sect. de Magn. et Électr. Terr.) 280 A consideration of the most recent published results of secular-variation observations..has revealed some very interesting and important conditions governing isoporic movements. **1940** Chapman & Bartels *Geomagnetism* I. iii. 114 The rate of the secular variation in each element at any epoch..can..be represented by..isoporic charts, a term proposed by Harradon. **1973** M. W. McElhinny *Palaeomagnetism & Plate Tectonics* i. 6 Isoporic foci are not permanent, but grow and decay, their lifetime being of the order of 100 years, during which they move on the earth's surface in a somewhat irregular fashion. **1895** C. S. Palmer tr. *Nernst's Theoret. Chem.* I. v. 121 The investigation of solutions having the same osmotic pressure, viz. the so-called is-osmotic solutions. **1905** W. H. Howell *Text-bk. Physiol.* 884 A 0·95 per cent. solution of NaCl is isotonic or isosmotic with mammalian serum. **1967** *Oceanogr. & Marine Biol.* V. 383 In life the muscle cells are probably isosmotic with the interstitial fluid and the plasma. **1964** Shapiro & Chargaff in *Biochim. & Biophys. Acta* XCI. 263 There exist procedures permitting the separation of the hydrolysates [of DNA] into a series of fractions, each comprising the equimunerant oligonucleotide runs of a given length. .. It may be convenient to refer to such a size group as an isostich. **1970** *Nature* 26 Sept. 1296/1 The tracts were fractionated into isostichs by chromatography on DEAE-cellulose. **1971** F. von der Harr et al. in Cantoni & Davies *Procedures Nucleic Acid Res.* II. 682 The isostichs can be further separated into their components, differing in base composition, by paper chromatography. **1906** *Jrnl. Chem. Soc.* LXXXIX. II. 1129 It is conceivable that in the case of two 'isostructural' substances the actual size of the structural unit may be of the greatest importance. **1965** Phillips & Williams *Inorg. Chem.* I. xvi. 576 Tellurium is only known in one form, isostructural with grey Se. **1922** Joyce *Ulysses* 307 The intricate alliterative and isosyllabic rules of the Welsh englyn. **1943** *Jrnl. Theol. Stud.* XLIV. 51 The isosyllabic metre of the Greek homilies of Ephraem, typical of Syriac poetry. **1957** Isosyllabic [see *isoaccentual* adj. above]. **1956** H. Whitehall in *Kenyon Rev.* XVIII. III. 420 Of the non-syllabic rhythms, the first, found typically in Old Testament Hebrew verse and in some, though not all, 'free verse' is *isosyntactic*—the recurrent factor is repetition of the same syntactic construction, usually a phrase or clause, in strictly parallel sequences. **1939** Isosyntagmic [see *isolexic* adj. above]. **1954** Pei & Gaynor *Dict. Ling.* 107 *Isosyntagmic lines*, lines on a linguistic map, indicating the approximate boundaries of the speech-areas in which a uniformity of syntax can be observed. **1957** Isosyntagmic [see *isomorphic *a.* 5]. **1947** *Mineral. Abstr.* X. 159 Isogyres and isotaches (curves of equal velocity) are plotted on a stereographic net. **1955** W. J. Saucier *Princ. Meteorol. Analysis* x. 304/1 The wind field is analyzed by drawing streamlines and isotachs, which give, respectively, the course of flow and its speed. **1970** *Nature* 11 Apr. 133/2 (*caption*) Geostrophic isotachs (in knots) at 500 mbar for 00 GMT November 14, 1968. **1910** Smith & Menzies in *Jrnl. Amer. Chem. Soc.* XXXII. 1420 The purpose of the apparatus being to show when two pressures have become equal, the arrangement may be called an isoteniscope. **1960** *Jrnl. Chem. Education* XXXVII. 533/1 Livingstone suggests the inclusion of a thermometer well in the isoteniscope bulb so that temperature equilibrium can be ascertained at the time of the pressure measurements. **1915** D. White in *Jrnl. Washington Acad. Sci.* V. 198 Lines were then drawn through the points of equal fixed carbon (or volatile matter). Such lines,..which I have termed 'isovols', are drawn to mark each 5 per cent increase in the fixed carbon in the pure coal. **1923** *Glasgow Herald* 11 June 7 The isovols for the Hutton seam take the form of a number of rings with a common centre to the north-west of Durham. **1928** E. R. Lilley *Geol. Petroleum*

& Nat. Gas v. 113 The greater part of the oil of Pennsylvania is produced from pools lying between the isovols.. of 55 and 60%. **1968** MURCHISON & WESTOLL *Coal* xv. 370 Fig. 15 shows lines of equal magnetic vertical intensity and the isovols of the Wealden coals.

b. Add to note:

Iso- was formerly regarded as a separable prefix and printed in italics (often with a hyphen). The International Union of Pure and Applied Chemistry recommendation is that *iso-* should always be directly attached to the remainder of the parent name (and be printed in ordinary type).

Where the isomerism occurs within an alkane or alkyl radical, the prefix *iso-* is used to form the name of the isomer having a $(CH_3)_2CH$— group at the end of an otherwise straight chain: so $CH_3(CH_2)_3CH_3$ (normal or *n*-) pentane, $(CH_3)_2CHCH_2CH_3$ isopentane, $(CH_3)_3CCH_3$ neopentane.

i:soallo·xazine [ALLOX(AN + *AZINE], the hypothetical tricyclic parent compound, $C_{10}H_6N_4O_2$, of the flavins, which has a structure formed of fused benzene, pyrazine, and pyrimidine nuclei and is known only as substituted derivatives; **isoa·myl alcohol** = **isopentyl alcohol*; **isobo·rneol** [a. G. *isoborneol* (Bertram & Walbaum 1894, in *Jrnl. f. prakt. Chem.* XLIX. 1)], a crystalline bicyclic alcohol, $C_{10}H_{18}O$, which is a stereoisomer of borneol and like it yields camphor on oxidation; **isobu·tane**, 2-methylpropane, $(CH_3)_2$-$CH{\cdot}CH_3$, a gaseous hydrocarbon used as a fuel; **isobu·tene** = **isobutylene*; **isobu·tyl**, the radical $(CH_3)_2CH{\cdot}CH_2$—, 2-methylpropyl, as in **isobutyl alcohol,** $(CH_3)_2CH{\cdot}CH_2OH$, a primary alcohol which is a colourless liquid and occurs in fusel oils; **isobu·tylene** († -en), 2-methylpropylene, $(CH_3)_2C{:}CH_2$, an easily liquefied gas used in the manufacture of butyl rubber; **isobu·tyrate,** any of the esters of isobutyric acid, several of which are used as flavourings and in perfumery; **isobuty·ric acid** [tr. G. *isobuttersäure* (H. Kolbe 1864, in *Zeitschr. f. Chem. und Pharm.* VII. 33)], a liquid carboxylic acid, $(CH_3)_2CH{\cdot}COOH$, found in many plants and also obtained by oxidation of isobutyl alcohol; **isoci·trate,** the anion, or an ester or salt, of isocitric acid; **isoci·tric acid** [tr. G. *isocitronsäure* (F. Rochleder 1869, in *Jrnl. f. prakt. Chem.* CVI. 320)], 1-hydroxypropane-1,2,3-tricarboxylic acid, $HOOC{\cdot}CH$-$(OH)CH(COOH)CH_2COOH$, which occurs in blackberry juice and is formed in the Krebs cycle by dehydration of citric acid to *cis*-aconitic acid followed by rehydration; **isocy·anate** [a. F. *isocyanate* (F.-S. Cloëz *Rech. sur Éthers Cyaniques* (Thesis, 1866) 18)], any of the class of compounds containing the group —N:C:O, some of which are used in making polyurethane resins; **isocya·nic acid,** the acid HN:-C:O, which exists in equilibrium with cyanic acid (HO·CN); **isocy·anide,** any member of the class of compounds having the formula R—NC (where R is an alkyl, aryl, etc., radical), which in general are poisonous liquids with a strong unpleasant odour; also called carbylamines, isonitriles; **isoeugenol** (əiso,-yū·dʒĕnǫl) [a. G. *isoeugenol* (Tiemann & Kraaz 1882, in *Ber. d. Deut. Chem. Ges.* XV. 2067)], an aromatic liquid that occurs in ylang-ylang and other essential oils, is produced commercially from eugenol, and has been used in the manufacture of vanillin and in perfumery; 2-methoxy-4-propenylphenol, $CH_3CH{:}CH{\cdot}C_6H_3(OCH_3)OH$; **isofla·vone,** (*a*) the crystalline tricyclic ketone 3-phenylbenzo-4-pyrone, $C_{15}H_{10}O_2$; (*b*) any of the derivatives of this compound, which occur (often as glycosides) in many plants; **isoli·chenin** [a. G. *isolichenin* (F. Beilstein *Handbuch d. Org. Chem.* (1881) I. xxxix. 602)], a water-soluble starch occurring in lichens which yields glucose on hydrolysis; **isoma·ltose** [a. G. *isomaltose* (E. Fischer 1890, in *Ber. d. Deut. Chem. Ges.* XXII. 3688)], 6-*O*-α-D-glucopyranosyl-D-glucose, $C_6H_{11}O_5$·-$O{\cdot}C_6H_{11}O_5$, a syrupy disaccharide formed by the action of acid on glucose; **i:sonicoti·nic acid** [tr. G. *isonicotinsäure* (Weidel & Russo 1883, in *Sitzungsber. d. K. Akad. d. Wissen.* (Math.-Nat. Classe) LXXXVI. II. 1172)], pyridine-4-carboxylic acid, $(C_5H_4N)COOH$, a crystalline compound used in the synthesis of isoniazid; **isonicotinic (acid) hydrazide** = *ISONIAZID; **isoni·trile** = **isocyanide*; **isopa·-raffin,** any branched-chain paraffin, *spec.* one containing the isopropyl group, $(CH_3)_2CH$—, attached to an otherwise straight chain; **isope·ntane,** 2-methylbutane, $(CH_3)_2CHCH_2$-CH_3, a volatile liquid hydrocarbon present in petroleum; **isope·ntyl,** the radical $(CH_3)_2$-$CHCH_2CH_2$—, as in **isopentyl alcohol,** a liquid primary alcohol, $(CH_3)_2CH_2CH_2OH$, which has a disagreeable odour and is obtained from fusel oil; **isophtha·late,** a salt or ester of isophthalic acid; **isophtha·lic acid,** benzene-*m*-dicarboxylic acid, $C_6H_4(COOH)_2$, a crystalline compound made by the oxidation of *m*-xylene and used in the manufacture of polyester and alkyd resins; **isopro·panol** = **isopropyl alcohol*; **isopro·penyl,** the radical $CH_2{:}C(CH_3)$—; **isopro·pyl,** the radical $(CH_3)_2CH$—, as in **isopropyl alcohol,** a liquid secondary alcohol, $CH_3CHOH{\cdot}CH_3$, made by the hydration of propylene and widely used as a solvent and in the production of acetone; **isopropy·lidene,** the bivalent radical $(CH_3)_2C$=, frequently introduced into compounds by reaction with acetone; **isoqui·noline** [ad. F. *isoquinoléine* (Hoogewerff & Van Dorp 1885, in *Rec. des Trav. chim. des Pays-Bas* IV. 128)], a low-melting, crystalline, bicyclic compound, C_9H_7N, found in coal tar and forming the nucleus of many alkaloids; **isovalera·ldehyde,** 2-methylbutyraldehyde, $(CH_3)_2CH{\cdot}CH_2$·-CHO, a liquid which occurs in peppermint, sandalwood, eucalyptus, and other oils; **isova·lerate,** a salt or ester of isovaleric acid; **isovaleria·nic (acid)** = **isovaleric acid*; **isovale·ric acid,** 2-methylbutyric acid, $(CH_3)_2$-$CHCH_2COOH$, a liquid with a disagreeable odour found free in valerian root and as esters in porpoise and dolphin oils; **iso·xazole** [ad. G. *isoxazol* (A. Hantzsch 1888, in *Ann. d. Chem.* CCXLIX. 3)], (*a*) a liquid heterocyclic compound,

CH:CH·O·N:CH,
|____________|

with a penetrating odour; (*b*) a derivative of this compound.

1936 *Chem. Abstr.* XXX. 4512 Isoalloxazines with a substituent, e.g., alkyl, cycloalkyl or aryl, in the 9-position are prepd. by condensing *N*-monosubstituted aromatic *o*-diamines with alloxan. **1953** FRUTON & SIMMONDS *Gen. Biochem.* xiii. 320 In riboflavin, a sugar residue, D-ribitol, is attached to a nitrogen atom of a heterocyclic nucleus, termed an isoalloxazine ring. **1968** I. L. FINAR *Org. Chem.* (ed. 4) II. 556 It appears that *iso*alloxazine, the tautomer of alloxazine, does not exist as such; only when the hydrogen atom is substituted is the *iso*alloxazine form retained. **1886** *Jrnl. Chem. Soc.* XLIX. 770 The value of the ratio [of vapour pressures] of isobutyl and isoamyl alcohol is practically a constant. **1927** *Chem. Abstr.* XXI. 985 Isoamyl alc. is considered as the mother substance of most of the compds. constituting oil of lavender. **1970** *New Phytologist* LXIX. 557 Isovaleric acid and isoamyl alcohol have been identified as metabolites of *Agaricus bisporus*. **1894** *Chem. News* 30 Mar. 156/2 Isoborneol..crystallises out of petroleum ether in thin, feathery leaflets. **1951** P. Z. BEDOUKIAN *Perfumery Synthetics & Isolates* 93 Iso-borneol and its esters, particularly the acetate, are employed in many types of industrial perfumes—for example, in sprays. **1972** G. D. SARGENT in Olah & Schleyer *Carbonium Ions* III. xxiv. 1122 On reduction with lithium aluminium hydride, camphor (34) gives isoborneol (35) in high yield. **1876** *Jrnl. Chem. Soc.* XXIX. 540 When isobutane is heated to 250° with iodine trichloride it gives the same products as propane. **1936** [see *CALOR]. **1959** *Times Rev. Industry* Aug. 98/2 Other processes..include alkylation, in which iso-butane is reacted with olefins to produce high octane material for aviation gasoline and high quality motor spirit. **1876** *Jrnl. Chem. Soc.* XXX. 397 Isobutene combines readily with hypochlorous acid. **1964** N. G. CLARK *Mod. Org. Chem.* viii. 141 t-Butyl alcohol..is obtained from a 2-methylpropene [isobutene] using 65 per cent sulphuric acid. **1870** *Chem. News* 21 Jan. 34/2 (*heading*) Conversion of isobutyl-alcohol into tertiary pseudobutyl-alcohol. **1873** [in Dict.]. **1964** D. A. SHIRLEY *Org. Chem.* x. 251 Isobutyl alcohol..is manufactured by a modification of the carbon monoxide and hydrogen method for synthesis of methanol. **1966** *Nomencl. Org. Chem.* (I.U.P.A.C.) (ed. 2) A. 8 The following names are retained for the unsubstituted radicals only: Isopropyl..Isobutyl..Isopentyl [etc.]. **1872** *Chem. News* 29 Nov. 265/2 Chlorhydric acid behaves with isobutylen in the same manner as iodhydric acid, the result being the formation of a tertiary chloride of butyl. **1913** J. B. COHEN *Org. Chem. Adv. Students* II. ii. 119 Isobutylene when heated with strong sulphuric acid yields a mixture of isomeric diisobutylenes. **1951** *Economist* 29 Dec. 1599/2 It should produce butyl rubber based almost entirely on iso-butylene. **1969** R. F. LANG tr. *Henglein's Chem. Technol.* 576 Cracking gases consist of ethylene, propylene and isobutylene... Isobutylene yields on polymerization a dimer which can be hydrogenated to iso-octane. **1873** *Jrnl. Chem. Soc.* XXVI. 55 Ethylic isobutyrate boils at 113°. **1928** *Chem. Abstr.* XXII. 2809 A table of 23 butyrates and isobutyrates, giving their name, odor and specific use in perfume. **1973** *Proc. Soc. Exper. Biol. & Med.* CXLII. 595/1 Sucrose acetate isobutyrate.. is employed as a flavor-suspending agent in the manufacture of soft drinks. **1871** *Jrnl. Chem. Soc.* XXIV. 126 Isobutyric acid..is scarcely attacked by a mixture of potassium dichromate and dilute sulphuric acid. **1881** ROSCOE & SCHORLEMMER *Treat. Chem.* III. I. 599 Isobutyric acid is found in the free state in the flowers of the *Arnica montana*, as well as in the carob bean, and amongst the acids of croton oil. **1970** *Exper. Parasitol.* XXVII. 408 The branched chain acids, isobutyric and isovaleric, are also excreted by *A. caninum*. **1925** *Jrnl. Amer. Chem. Soc.* XLVII. 572 The ethyl isocitrate obtained from the first lot of blackberries was levorotatory. **1952** *Biochem. Jrnl.* LII. 528/2 The observations are in agreement with Martius's earlier assumption..that *cis*-aconitate is an intermediate in the conversion of citrate into *iso*citrate. **1971** *Jrnl. Biol. Chem.* CCXLV. 4807/1 Studies are reported..which indicate that there is a specific carrier system for the transport of citrate and isocitrate in mitochondria. **1869** *Chem. News* 11 June 287/1 The isocitric acid may be obtained pure..and then exhibits a crystalline mass. **1930** *Jrnl. Amer. Chem. Soc.* LII. 2928 As there are two asymmetric carbon atoms in isocitric acid, and no meso form is possible, four optically active forms and two racemic forms of the acid may exist. **1968** R. F. STEINER *Life Chem.* xii. 219 The reversible transformation of citric acid to *cis*-aconitic acid, and of the latter to isocitric acid, is catalyzed by a single enzyme, aconitase. **1872** *Jrnl. Chem. Soc.* XXV. 446 The first members of the group of compounds, now generally described as the isocyanates and isocyanurates, were discovered by Wurtz in the ethyl and methyl series. **1877** [in Dict.]. **1944** S. J. SMITH *Princ. Org. Chem.* xiv. 312 The alkyl isocyanates are liquids with a powerful stifling odour. **1961** *Times* 30 May (I.C.I. Suppl.) p. xxii (Advt.), Italians need isocyanates for lightweight rigid and flexible polyurethane foams. **1963** in *Amer. Speech* (1964) XXXIX. 146 A dummy man made of material resembling human flesh which has a base of isocyanate rubber. **1891** *Jrnl. Chem. Soc.* LX. I. 282 Hydrocyanic acid and a small quantity of isocyanic acid are evolved. **1919** *Jrnl. Amer. Chem. Soc.* XLI. 381 The reaction between isocyanic acid and benzylidenaniline leads directly to a four-membered cyclic-urea. **1973** J. J. LAGOWSKI *Mod. Inorg. Chem.* xi. 349 Isocyanic acid (mp −86·8°, bp 23·5°) is formed when cyanuric acid is passed through a hot tube; the product reverts to cyanuric acid spontaneously. **1877** Isocyanide [in Dict.]. **1881** ROSCOE & SCHORLEMMER *Treat. Chem.* III. I. 162 Cyanides of the alcohol radicals. These bodies are formed when an alcoholic iodide is heated with silver cyanide... The compounds obtained in this way are usually termed isocyanides or carbamines. **1907** *Daily Chron.* 12 Dec. 5/5 Someone noiselessly discharged several squibs of isocyanide, and two ladies in the audience fled. **1928** *Sunday Dispatch* 16 Dec. 13/5 The new gas, cacodyl isocyanide, which..was..so terrible and destructive..in its effect on life. **1964** N. G. CLARK *Mod. Org. Chem.* xiii. 265 The isocyanides are of no practical value, with the possible exception of the Carbylamine Reaction. However, the elucidation of their structure..has provided an interesting chapter in the development of organic chemistry. **1883** *Jrnl. Chem. Soc.* XLIV. 201 By distilling it [*sc.* homoferulic acid] with lime a body is obtained which is isomeric with eugenol, and termed isoeugenol. **1891** *Jrnl. Soc. Chem. Industry* 31 Oct. 854/1 Iso-eugenol..is prepared from eugenol, or the Essence of Cloves, by heating it with caustic potash in amyl alcohol for 16–24 hours. **1936** A. HUXLEY *Eyeless in Gaza* xviii. 243 That's one of the reasons why your scent costs you so much. The poor..have to be content with plain iso-eugenol. **1965** *Chem. Abstr.* LXII. 6815 Eugenol and isoeugenol were estd. in the smoke at 4 and 14·7 mg./1000 Turkish tobacco cigarets, resp. **1925** *Jrnl. Chem. Soc.* CXXVII. 1981 The occurrence of derivatives of 3-phenylchromone (*iso*-flavone) has not yet been definitely proved. **1948** *Proc. Indian Acad. Sci.* A. XXVII. 36 Hydroxy isoflavones are more toxic than the corresponding flavones. **1951** *Ann. Rev. Biochem.* XX. 508 The..occurrence of the isoflavone (prunetin) along with its isomeric flavone (genkwanin) is a rare example of such association. **1965** T. SWAIN in Pridham & Swain *Biosynthetic Pathways Higher Plants* 33 Isoflavones..are common in other members of the Leguminosae. **1898** *Amer. Jrnl. Physiol.* I. 455 The unusual behavior of isolichenin towards amylolytic enzymes—the formation of dextrins without sugars—recalls the formation (from glycogen) of dystropo-dextrin. **1934** *Chem. Abstr.* XXVIII. 2375 Isolichenin was proved in some varieties of the lichens produced in Japan, such as *Alectoria ochroleuca*... Isolichenin closely resembles amylose. **1967** M. E. HALE *Biol. Lichens* viii. 103 Isolichenin, the rarer of the two major lichen starches, is distinguished by a positive iodine test and consists of D-glucose residues with α-1,3 and α-1,4 glucosidic linkages. **1891** *Jrnl. Chem. Soc.* LX. I. 413 The author has obtained from glucose a new glucobiose, which from its properties is doubtless constituted like maltose, and is hence called isomaltose. **1892** *Jrnl. Soc. Chem. Industry* 30 July 627/2 Iso-maltose is an important constituent of beer and forms 25–30 per cent of beer extract. **1956** *New Biol.* XXI. 12 Maltose appears after two days [during malting], and then maltatriose and isomaltose, as a result of the degradation of starch. **1883** *Jrnl. Chem. Soc.* XLIV. 484 In the form of sulphate it [*sc.* γ-dipyridyl] is easily oxidised by potassium permanganate, yielding pyridine-monocarboxylic or isonicotinic acid... This acid..forms a white crystalline mass melting at 307°. **1952** *Biol. Abstr.* XXVI. 35208 Isonicotinic acid hydrazide..is effective against tuberculosis in the mouse. **1956** *Nature* 25 Feb. 367/2 An active programme of leprosy work at Singapore included a chemotherapeutic trial of isonicotinic hydrazide. **1961** *Biol. Abstr.* XXXVI. 2299/1 (*heading*) Antituberculous activity of isonicotinic acid derivatives in vitro. **1972** *Biochem. & Biophys. Res. Communications* XLVIII. 58 (*heading*) In vitro inhibition of tRNA and protein methylation by nicotinamide and isonicotinic acid hydrazide. **1871** *Jrnl. Chem. Soc.* XXIV. 137 This body [*sc.* a urea], when heated, is resolved into triethylphosphine sulphide and the isonitrile of the allyl series. **1915** R. H. A. PLIMMER *Pract. Org. & Biochem.* 61 To the dilute solution of chloroform in water is added some alcoholic sodium hydroxide and a drop of aniline and the mixture heated. Phenyl isonitrile or carbylamine is formed. **1965** *Chem. Communications* May 181/1 The ability of isonitriles to act as bridging groups has now been demonstrated by the preparation of the iron complex (I). **1971** GREEN & HOFFMANN in I. Ugi *Isonitrile Chem.* i. 1 The term isonitriles is used for the

general class of compounds, whereas the term isocyanide is used for specific designations (e.g., ethyl isocyanide). **1876** *Phil. Mag.* I. 206 The dimethylated and trimethylated paraffins have been distinguished for some time past as normal and isoparaffins respectively. **1889** G. M'Gowan tr. *Bernthsen's Text-bk. Org. Chem.* i. 43 Iso-paraffins, in which one assumes a single branching in the molecule. **1939** Gruener & Lankelma *Introd. Org. Chem.* vi. 85 A tertiary alcohol is obtained only in the case of branching carbon chains, or 'isoparaffins'. **1969** R. F. Lang tr. *Henglein's Chem. Technol.* xxi. 576 The synthesis of antiknock isoparaffins for aviation gasoline is achieved also by chemical means. **1876** *Encycl. Brit.* V. 558/2 Isopentane..is formed by the dehydration of amyl alcohol by means of zinc chloride. **1943** V. A. Kalichevsky *Amazing Petroleum Industry* iv. 55 Natural gasoline contains certain quantities of a hydrocarbon known as isopentane which is a valuable component of high-grade gasolines. **1964** Roberts & Caserio *Basic Princ. Org. Chem.* iii. 92 The chlorination of isopentane at 300° gives all four possible monosubstitution products. **1876** *Phil. Mag.* I. 217 One of the two conceivable isopentyl alcohols would be derivable in this way from pseudobutyl alcohol. **1970** H. E. Nursten in A. C. Hulme *Biochem. Fruits* I. x. 247 Hultin and Proctor..had already found..isopentyl alcohol to be significant as regards the rank odour of over-ripe fruit. **1886** E. F. Smith tr. *V. von Richter's Chem. Carbon Compounds* 566 It [*sc.* the barium salt] is not precipitated by barium chloride from a solution of ammonium isophthalate. **1968** A. L. Waddams *Chemicals from Petrol.* (ed. 2) xii. 182 Isophthalates have many properties in common with the phthalate esters so that the two are in competition to some extent. As the isophthalates are the more expensive their use is limited to more specialized applications. **1870** *Chem. News* 22 Apr. 191/2 (*heading*) On isophthalic acid and some of its derivatives. **1914** H. T. Clarke *Introd. Study Org. Chem.* xxxiii. 399 Isophthalic acid..differs from phthalic acid in being incapable of forming an anhydride or an imide. **1968** A. L. Waddams *Chemicals from Petrol.* (ed. 2) xii. 182 The production of isophthalic acid in the U.S.A. is about 30,000 long tons a year. Its major use is in unsaturated polyester resins (38 per cent of the total). 31 per cent of consumption is for alkyd resins. **1945** *Chem. Abstr.* XXXIX. 349 Isopropanol ..in blood and body fluids can be detd. iodometrically. **1956** *Nature* 11 Feb. 271/1 Fractions of ribonucleic acid were hydrolysed..to mononucleotides, which were separated by paper chromatography in *iso*propanol-water-ammonia. **1972** P. Wiseman *Introd. Industr. Org. Chem.* vi. 218 Acetone is made by the dehydrogenation of isopropanol. **1885** *Jrnl. Chem. Soc.* XLVIII. 645 On heating isopropenyl carbinol with a small quantity of acid, isobutaldehyde is formed. **1950** R. C. Fuson *Adv. Org. Chem.* xv. 347 The conversion of isopropenyl acetate to acetylacetone. **1965** *Nomencl. Org. Chem.* (I.U.P.A.C.) C. 239 Isopropenyl (replacing 1-methylvinyl) (unsubstituted only). **1866** *Jrnl. Chem. Soc.* XIX. 487 We know that isopropyl compounds do not yield propionic acid by oxidation. **1872** *Ibid.* XXV. 237 The production of isopropyl alcohol, instead of the normal alcohol, by the decomposition of normal propylamine nitrite. **1888** [in Dict.]. **1934** H. Hiler *Notes Technique Painting* v. 288 Isopropyl alcohol or petrohol is one of the latest solvents used. It will dissolve most varnishes. **1948** *Economist* 31 July 193/1 American production of isopropyl alcohol (now the principal source of acetone) began in small quantities about fifteen years ago. **1955** H. R. Downs *Chem. Living Cells* xii. 410 Administration of doubly labeled isovaleric acid gives rise to cholesterol in which it appears that the carbons of the isopropyl group of that acid have been incorporated as a unit. **1966** [see *isobutyl* above]. **1970** Passmore & Robson *Compan. Med. Stud.* II. xviii. 40/2 Ethyl alcohol, or better isopropyl alcohol, are used for rapid skin disinfection and are probably the best substances for this purpose. **1900** E. F. Smith tr. *V. von Richter's Org. Chem.* (ed. 3) II. 495 The condensation of the same oxime in the presence of ketones or aldehydes gives rise to isopropylidene and benzylidene methyl isoxazolons, $(C_4H_3NO_2)$:$C(CH_3)_2$ [etc.]. **1932** H. Pringsheim *Chem. Monosaccharides & Polysaccharides* ii. 31 Into the hexoses and pentoses there can be introduced two isopropylidene remainders. **1967** R. J. McIlroy *Introd. Carbohydrate Chem.* v. 52 This displacement of the ring has led to the employment of isopropylidene derivatives in the synthesis of reference compounds of the furanose type. **1886** *Jrnl. Chem. Soc.* L. 78 By adding concentrated sulphuric acid to an alcoholic solution of crude quinoline from coal-tar, the sulphates of quinoline and isoquinoline, C_9H_7N, are precipitated. **1932** I. D. Garrard *Introd. Org. Chem.* xii. 180 Morphine is one of the alkaloids obtained from opium. It is a derivative of isoquinoline. **1960** R. M. Acheson *Introd. Chem. Heterocyclic Compounds* vi. 231 Many alkaloids (*e.g.* papaverine) contain either the aromatic, or the reduced, isoquinoline system. **1972** N. L. Allinger et al. *Org. Chem.* xxviii. 746 Isoquinoline may be synthesized from benzaldehyde by a cyclization reaction known as the Pomeranz–Fritsch synthesis. **1883** *Jrnl. Chem. Soc.* XLIII. 86 The same remark applies to the polymeride obtained..from isovaleraldehyde. **1946** *Chem. Abstr.* XL. 6757 The oil examd., obtained in 1·2% yield by direct steam distn... of *Lavandula delphinensis* plants..had...isovaleraldehyde 0·02[%]. **1970** *Jrnl. Econ. Ent.* LXIII. 1819/1 Bioassay results with 37 terpenoids and related plant constituents indicate that..menthone, isovaleraldehyde, and linalool were among the most attractive to *Anthomus grandis* Boheman. **1882** *Jrnl. Chem. Soc.* XLII. 30 Fraction 3..yielded impure isopentyl isovalerate. **1888** *Ibid.* LIV. 251 Silver isovalerate. **1963** *Chem. Abstr.* LVIII. 4974 Other compds. identified [in nutmeg oil] were.. isoeugenol..and menthyl isovalerate. **1894** *Chem. News* 9 Feb. 66/1 (*heading*) Condensation of isovalerianic aldehyd with ordinary acetone. **1927** *Chem. Abstr.* XXI. 985 By oxidation iso-AmOH gives the aldehyde and isovalerianic acid, all 3 of which have been found in oil of lavender. **1971** *Angewandte Parasitol.* XII. 107 The pure attractants ..valerianic acid and iso-valerianic acid had only a little attraction [for synanthropic flies]. **1882** *Jrnl. Chem. Soc.* XLII. 162 Of the lower homologues of isocaproic acid which contain the isopropyl group, isovaleric acid alone yields an acid similar to the above on oxidation. **1934** *Biochem. Jrnl.* XXXVIII. 401 The porpoise and dolphin depôt fats are unique in containing large amounts of *iso*valeric acid. **1950** J. Bonner *Plant Biochem.* xxv. 393 Fig. 25-3 gives an example of a fractionation conducted on oil of peppermint... Acetaldehyde, acetone, isovaleric acid, and isoamyl alcohol first distil over. **1960** K. S. Markley *Fatty Acids* (ed. 2) II. ii. 55 Isovaleric acid has been reported to occur in the free state in large amounts in valerian root; in lesser amounts in the oils of pineapple and lavender, and among the volatile acids of mutton tallow.., and in the rumen of the sheep. **1891** *Jrnl. Chem. Soc.* LIX. 410 (*heading*) Formation of isoxazoles. **1946** A. A. Morton *Chem. Heterocyclic Compounds* xiv. 421 No naturally occurring isoxazole compounds are known. They are often obtained in the course of laboratory work with nitroso and isonitroso compounds. **1960** R. M. Acheson *Introd. Chem. Heterocyclic Compounds* vii. 272 Isoxazole itself is obtainable from propargyl aldehyde and hydroxylamine; 1,3-dicarbonyl compounds also give isoxazoles with hydroxylamine in a very general synthesis.

isoaccentual, isoagglutination (and derivs.), **isoagglutinin, isoagglutinogen, isoallele, isoallelic, isoantibody, isoantigen, -genic**: see *iso-. **isoalloxazine, isoamyl alcohol:** see *iso- b.

isobar. Add: **1. b.** A line in a diagram that represents states or conditions of equal pressure.

1892 P. Alexander *Treat. Thermodynamics* v. 39 An isobar is a constant pressure thermogram. **1924** A. E. Hill in H. S. Taylor *Treat. Physical Chem.* I. ix. 383 The isobar *ab* drawn at 1 atmosphere pressure intersects the curve *BO* at −78·3°. **1969** S. M. Blinder *Adv. Physical Chem.* viii. 144 In Fig. 8.2, the same data are represented as a series of isobars, plots of *V* versus *t* for fixed *P*.

2. *Physics.* Each of two or more nuclides which have the same mass number but different atomic numbers (and so are different elements). Orig. † **isobare** (*obs.*).

1918 A. W. Stewart in *Phil. Mag.* XXVI. 331 These elements [*sc.* mesothorium and radiothorium] differ completely from one another in chemical character; but they all possess the same atomic weight. For this reason the name isobares..is here suggested for them. **1928** M. Steel *Physical Chem. & Biophysics* ii. 37 Any product of radioactive change due to the loss of a beta particle..is an isobar of the parent element. **1946** *Electronic Engin.* XVIII. 88/2 Neptunium and plutonium are isobares (same atomic mass but different atomic number). **1952** *Sci. News* XXIII. 37 These nuclei are called isobares. **1954** K. Rankama *Isotope Geol.* xxv. 302 The isotope ^{40}K is the active nuclide in the series of the three neighbouring isobars, ^{40}A— ^{40}K— ^{40}Ca. **1955** R. D. Evans *Atomic Nucleus* iii. 99 The chemical properties of isobars are generally dissimilar, but their nuclear properties tend to present many parallel features. **1966** Phillips & Williams *Inorg. Chem.* II. xxxv. 621 We shall use the symbol *Z* for the number of protons in a nucleus (i.e. the atomic number) and *N* for the number of neutrons, so that $A = Z + N$, where *A* is the mass number or 'rounded' atomic weight. All nuclei of the same *Z* are called isotopes, of the same *N* isotones, and of the same *A* isobars.

isobare, obs. var. *isobar 2.

isobaric, *a.* Add: **1. b.** Occurring at or pertaining to a constant pressure.

1903 A. Ogg tr. *Planck's Treat. Thermodynamics* I. i. 7 (*heading*) Behaviour under constant pressure (isopiestic or isobaric changes). **1933** D. J. Martin *Introd. Thermodynamics for Chemists* xiii. 315 The isobaric heat of adsorption corresponds to the heat of a reaction in a condensed system, the amount adsorbed changes while the pressure remains practically constant. **1937** P. S. Epstein *Textbk. Thermodynamics* iii. 46 The heat function acquires a particular importance in the so-called isobaric process, i.e. a process which takes place without change of pressure. **1966** [see *isopiestic* adj. s.v. *iso-].

2. *Physics.* Of, pertaining to, or being isobars (sense *2); *isobaric spin* = *isospin. Const. *with.*

1919 *Nature* 18 Sept. 61/2 Elements can be regarded as divisible into three classes:—(1) Isotopic elements, each set of which have different atomic weights but identical chemical properties; (2) isobaric elements which have identical atomic weights but different chemical properties; and (3) normal elements which differ..both in atomic weights and chemical properties. **1933** F. W. Aston *Mass-Spectra & Isotopes* xii. 158 Spectra were obtained which showed four strong isotopes and two very weak ones, one of which is isobaric with W^{186}. **1948** Glasstone *Textbk. Physical Chem.* (ed. 2) ii. 171 With the development of the study of artificial radioactivity it has become apparent that there are more than seventy pairs of such isobaric isotopes, now known as isomeric nuclei. **1953** D. R. Inglis in *Rev. Mod. Physics* XXV. 395/2 One finds the states listed according to the usual quantum numbers *L* and *S* of the (*LS*)-coupling scheme and also according to the isobaric spin quantum number *T* (or isotopic spin as it has been less aptly called since it was named long ago by Wigner, who agrees to this renaming of his child). **1971** *Physics Bull.* Mar. 137/1 Isobaric spin was first introduced into nuclear interactions by Heisenberg purely as a mathematical convenience.

3. *Med.* Of, pertaining to, or designating a solution for spinal anæsthesia having the same density as the cerebro-spinal fluid.

1930, 1946 [see *hyperbaric *a.* a]. **1947** J. Adriani *Techniques & Procedures Anesthesia* v. 222 A 2½% solution of procaine in distilled water is nearly isobaric. **1962** —— *Chem. & Phys. Anaesthesia* (ed. 2) xxxi. 653/1 The results obtained with isobaric techniques are unpredictable and variable. **1971** P. C. Lund *Princ. & Pract. Spinal Anesthesia* vii. 371 Isobaric solutions have not been popular..because of the difficulty of achieving predictable levels of anesthesia. *Ibid.*, An adaptation of isobaric spinal anesthesia for anorectal surgery was introduced by Jacoby et al. in 1965.

B. *sb.* = *isobar 1 b.

1903 *Engineer* 24 July 83/3 The isobarics of evaporation happen to be isothermals. **1937** M. W. Zemansky *Heat & Thermodynamics* iv. 56 The series of short isobarics and isovolumics from *i* to *f* and the continuous curve from *i* to *f* represent other possibilities.

isobarically (əisobæ·rikăli), *adv.* [f. prec. + -ly².] At constant pressure, without a change in pressure.

1951 R. B. Montgomery in D. E. Kerr *Propagation Short Radio Waves* iii. 186 Wet-bulb Temperature.—This may be defined as the temperature at which saturation would occur if the air were cooled isobarically and adiabatically by means of contact with a water surface.

isobase, isobasic, isobath *sb.*: see *iso-.

isobestic, var. *isosbestic *a.*

isoborneol, isobutane, isobutene, isobutyl, isobutylene, isobutyrate, isobutyric acid: see *iso- b. **isocaloric, -calorically:** see *iso-.

isocarboxazid (əi:sokāɹbǫ·ksăzid). *Pharm.* [f. *isocarbox-* (by rearrangement of part of the chemical name: see quot. 1959) + *hydr)a-zid(e.] A whitish powder that is a hydrazine derivative, $C_6H_5CH_2NH{\cdot}NHCO{\cdot}C_3HNO{\cdot}CH_3$, and is used as an antidepressant.

1959 *Diseases Nervous Syst.* XX. 269/1 An analog of iproniazid, isocarboxazid.., has been used in pharmacological studies which show it to be a more potent amine oxidase inhibitor than its progenitor. Its chemical formula is 1-benzyl-2-(5-methyl-3-isoxazolylcarbonyl)-hydrazine. **1963** *Jrnl. Amer. Med. Assoc.* 16 Mar. 952/1 It is the opinion of the Council that isocarboxazid seems to be effective in the depressed phases of anxiety and manic-depressive states as well as in certain involutional, obsessive, and dissociative reactions. **1965** J. Pollitt *Depression & its Treatment* iv. 56 The monoamine oxidase inhibitors include several members, among them phenelzine (Nardil), iproniazid (Marsilid), isocarboxazid (Marplan).

isocentre (əi·sosentəɹ). Also (*U.S.*) **-center.** [f. Iso- + Centre *sb.*] In aerial photography, the point at which the bisector of the angle between the optical axis of the camera and the vertical at the inner nodal point of the lens meets the plane of the camera plate or film (or the corresponding object point where the bisector meets the ground).

1931 C. M. Hotine *Surveying from Air Photogr.* v. 63 We may, therefore, consider the plate isocentre as the centre of tilt distortions, in that images are displaced radially from the isocentre from the positions they would occupy if the photograph had not been tilted. **1950** L. G. Trorey *Handbk. Aerial Mapping* i. 3 Any photograph is angle true with respect to the isocentre for all points in the plane of the isocentre. **1970** J. A. Howard *Aerial Photo-Ecology* ix. 102 The isocentre and nadir are very important due to their relation to tilt and radial displacement.

isochar (əi·sokāɹ). [f. Iso- + Char(acter *sb.* rendering G. *isopsepher* (W. Rothmaler 1938, in *Beih. Rep. Spec. Nov. Reg. Veg.* C. 90), f. Gr. ψῆφος number + ἦρος sign.] A line (imaginary or on a map) linking areas containing plants showing similar numbers of distinguishing characteristics.

1963 Davis & Heywood *Princ. Angiosperm Taxon.* ix. 317 The second procedure involves the drawing of *Isopsepheren*, a term which we can anglicise to *isochars*. These are based on the largest possible number of contrasting character expressions found in the taxa being studied... We are grateful to Dr. W. T. Stearn for suggesting this term.

isochemical, -chemically, isochlor: see *iso-.

isochromatic, *a.* Add: **1.** Substitute for def.: Of a single colour or tint: applied to a fringe in an interference pattern obtained with birefringent material, such as a biaxial crystal or material used in photoelastic experiments (when such a fringe corresponds to points where the difference between the principal stresses is the same). Also, representing or depicting such fringes. (Further examples.)

1931 Coker & Filon *Treat. Photo-Elasticity* iii. 248 The integrated tint remains the same over the whole of this locus, and it is for this reason that such lines are called lines of equal tint or isochromatic lines. **1932** Hardy & Perrin *Princ. Optics* xxix. 617 Although the values of *p* and *q* themselves can be computed from the isoclinic and isochromatic patterns, the operations are extremely tedious. **1966** *McGraw-Hill Encycl. Sci. & Technol.* X. 150/1 Utilizing equations for the difference of the principal stresses from the isochromatic fringe orders, the

stresses may be found by solving the two equations for the two principal stresses.

2. (Examples.)

1884 *Philadelphia Photographer* Oct. 315/1 (*heading*) Isochromatic gelatin plates. **1885** *Jrnl. Franklin Inst.* CXIX. 368 It was..the only truly isochromatic process ever discovered. Dr. Vogel's new process was not only no better in any respect, but the plates were insensitive to scarlet and ruby-red. *Ibid.* 371 Truly isochromatic photography. **1903** A. M. CLERKE *Probl. Astrophysics* II. iii. 191, D appeared conspicuously on Professor Campbell's isochromatic plates. **1904** *Westm. Gaz.* 19 Nov. 16/2 Not much has been heard of late about isochromatic plates, and it is to be feared that among amateurs their use is not on the increase. Generally speaking, the more recent advances in orthochromatic photography have been in the direction of increasing rather than lessening the difficulties. **1932** *Discovery* Sept. 292/1 The extension of the sensitivity of photographic emulsions..has given rise to three..types of colour sensitive material. The first type includes materials in which the sensitivity has been extended to cover the green; such materials are generally known as 'orthochromatic' or 'isochromatic'. **1955** H. & A. GERNSHEIM *Hist. Photogr.* xxiii. 268 Vogel and others had transformed the hitherto colour-blind emulsion into one which was more accurately sensitive for most colours—i.e. the so-called iso- or orthochromatic plates.

B. *sb.* An isochromatic fringe or line.

1924 *Rep. Brit. Assoc. Adv. Sci. 1923* 354 The disc carried a network of reference lines and the appearances were projected on a screen, upon which the isoclinics and isochromatics were traced with a pencil. **1948** M. M. FROCHT *Photoelasticity* II. iv. 139 The fringes or isochromatics..all pass through the points of application of the loads. **1958** CONDON & ODISHAW *Handbk. Physics* III. vi. 86/2 With a white light source the stress patterns consist of colored bands, called isochromatics, which form in the order of yellow, red, and green followed by similar cycles.

isochromosome: see *ISO-.

isochron (əi·sokrǫn), *a.* and *sb.* Also **isochrone** (-krōᵘn). [f. Gr. ἰσόχρον-ος (see ISOCHRONAL *a.*).]

A. *adj.* (In form *isochrone*) = ISOCHRONOUS *a.*

1697, etc. [in Dict. s.v. ISOCHRONAL *a.*].

B. *sb.* † **1.** An isochronal line. *Obs.*

a **1774** [in Dict. s.v. ISOCHRONAL *a.*].

2. A line (imaginary or on a map) connecting points at which a particular event occurs or occurred at the same time.

1881 F. GALTON in *Proc. R. Geogr. Soc.* III. 658 Along the coast of West Africa..the ports are regularly served by steamers that touch at every one of them..and which consequently occupy more than forty days to reach even the mouth of the Congo, whereas steamers occasionally sail direct to one or other of those ports in considerably shorter time than these mail steamers. This particular difficulty is met and explained by the sea isochrones, which in this case do not conform to those of the land. **1909** *Cent. Dict.* Suppl., *Isochrone*, n., a line connecting points at which the same events occur simultaneously. Thus the isochrone of travel is the line connecting points attainable by a person riding or an army marching from a given center forward during a given interval of time; the phenological isochrone, the line connecting points at which plants of any species attain simultaneously the same stage of development. **1948** *Antiquity* XXII. 114 While all competent authorities will agree that the practice of producing food..must have spread in some such way as this map shows, there will be differences of opinion... We expect for instance that the bulge made by the isochrones to include Anau and no more is largely artificial. **1955** W. J. SAUCIER *Princ. Meteorol. Analysis* xii. 389/1 If the weather occurs along a line, successive positions (isochrones) will be curves on the map. **1956** *Nature* 24 Mar. 571/1 The plots of radio blackout distribution in the North American and North Atlantic region..agree with the isochrons of the 'morning' maximum of magnetic disturbance in the Arctic region. **1970** *Ibid.* 17 Jan. 224 The map depicts..the course of withdrawal of the ice sheet from its greatest extent some 18,000 years ago... The detailed isochrons, separated in places by as little as 100 years, graphically depict the north–south corridor that had opened up to the east of the Rocky Mountains about 7,000 years ago.

3. A line (imaginary or on a map) connecting points at which some chosen time interval has the same value.

1940 C. A. HEILAND *Geophysical Explor.* ix. 548 Adjusted times are plotted against the location of depth points; points with equal time differences are connected by isochrons which, barring velocity variations and steep dips, give a true picture of the depth contours of the structure. **1945** *Electronic Engin.* XVII. 713/2 Sets of lines can be drawn, joining all the points having the same time-differences; and it has been agreed to call these lines 'isochrones', analogous to the 'isobars' of a weather-map. In general, these 'isochrone' lines are hyperbolae. **1952** F. H. LAHEE *Field Geol.* (ed. 5) xxiii. 779 On the assumption that velocity values [of seismic waves] are essentially constant and that reflecting horizons are continuous over a given area, the differences in arrival time from two such horizons can be plotted at each station and then lines of equal time difference (isochrons) can be drawn to produce an isochron map. **1958** *Jrnl. Brit. Interplanetary Soc.* XVI. 340 We have expressed the duration of the voyage in terms of *q*, *ε* and *n* only. In our diagram we can now draw lines of equal duration, which we call isochrones. In Fig. 9 are shown the isochrones for voyages from the Earth to Venus in days.

4. In the isotopic dating of rock, a straight line whose gradient is taken to represent the time since the isotopic content of a sample was fixed (e.g. by crystallization), and obtained by plotting the ratio of the amount of a radiogenic isotope to that of a non-radiogenic isotope against a corresponding ratio for a second radiogenic isotope and the same non-radiogenic one in two or more samples having the same history but different ratios.

1953 F. G. HOUTERMANS in *Nuovo Cimento* X. 1624 By dividing (3b) by (3a) the equations of 'isochrones' are obtained... These are a number of straight lines, intersecting at the point α_W, β_W corresponding to the isotopic constitution of 'primeval lead' at the time *w*. **1963** K. RANKAMA *Progr. Isotope Geol.* lxxxvii. 543 When the $^{207}Pb/^{204}Pb$ ratio was plotted against the $^{206}Pb/^{204}Pb$ ratio, the slope of the $^{207}Pb = f(^{206}Pb)$ isochron yielded the age 4·55 Gy for meteoritic matter, and the isotopic constitution of rock lead fell close to the isochron. **1969** BENNISON & WRIGHT *Geol. Hist. Brit. Isles* iii. 41 This data can also be presented as isochrons.., the slope of a whole-rock isochron being proportional to the age of initial crystallization and the slope of the mineral isochron to that of the metamorphism. **1971** *Nature* 25 June 500/1 Bofinger..has carried out extensive radiometric dating on illitic sedimentary rocks..; he produced eight separate total-rock Rb-Sr isochrons from seventy-two samples.

5. A line (imaginary or on a map) connecting points on the sea-floor formed at the same time.

1968 *New Scientist* 30 May 452/2 American workers hope eventually to produce a complete 'isochron' (lines of equal age) map of the world's oceans. **1972** *Nature* 8 Dec. 339/2 The discharge curve for Iceland was constructed..by extrapolating seafloor spreading isochrons from the ocean floor immediately southwest of the aseismic ridge.

isochronal, *a.* Add: **2.** Of a line: connecting points at which a particular event occurs or occurred at the same time. Of a diagram: depicting such lines. Also as *sb.*, = *ISOCHRON 2.

1926 [see *ISEPIPTESIS, ISOPIPTESIS]. **1937** D. KENNEDY tr. *Imamura's Theoret. & Appl. Seismol.* iv. 42 If a line is passed through places where a certain phase of the earthquake motion..appears simultaneously..a line resembling an isoseismal is obtained. It is the coseismal, or the isochronal of some recent writers. **1948** R. B. HOUNSFIELD *Traffic Surveys* vi. 39 Another type of diagram used in planning is the 'isochronal' diagram. *Ibid.* 40 (*caption*) Isochronal diagram showing accessibility of different areas. **1962** C. D. SHERMAN tr. *Dorst's Migrations of Birds* vii. 236 The influence of temperature, revealed in this parallelism between isochronal lines and isotherms, may be less apparent because of other factors which also govern migration.

isochronic, *a.* (in Dict. s.v. ISOCHRONAL *a.*). Add: **2.** = *ISOCHRONAL *a.* 2; *spec.* (see quots. 1881, 1959).

1881 F. GALTON in *Proc. R. Geogr. Soc.* III. 657 By 'isochronic' passage-charts, I mean charts constructed to show the extreme distances that can be traversed in 'equal times' from a common starting point. *Ibid.* 658 Isochronic maps might be..constructed for Continental travel or for home excursions. **1948** *Antiquity* XXII. 114 The second [map]..covers the Old World and shows the spread of the food-producing economy from five possible independent centres. The date at which food-production first appeared is shown by isochronic lines. These are an ingenious invention which show 'equal dates' exactly as contours show equal heights and isobars equal pressure. **1959** L. M. HARROD *Librarians' Gloss.* (ed. 2) 155 *Isochronic map*, one which shows possible progress of travel in all directions from a given centre in certain specified time intervals.

3. *Prosody.* Equal in metrical length.

1956 H. WHITEHALL in *Kenyon Rev.* XVIII. III. 418 Unlike such 'syllable-timed' languages as Spanish, English is 'stress-timed' or *isochronic*. **1959** *PMLA* LXXIV. 587/1 Mr. Whitehall distinguishes a type of 'rhythm' which he calls the isochronic: it 'depends on equal time lapses between primary stresses'.

isochronism. Add: **2.** *Prosody.* The character or property of being isochronous.

1942 WELLEK & WARREN *Theory of Lit.* 166 The artistic rhythm of prose..must not reach an apparent isochronism (that is, a regularity of time intervals between rhythmical accents). **1956** H. WHITEHALL in *Kenyon Rev.* XVIII. III. 418 Isochronism is produced not only by accelerating and crushing together the syllables between primary stresses but also by increasing or decreasing the pauses. **1959** *PMLA* LXXIV. 587/1 If isochronism *were* a general principle, or even an approximate principle, of all English speech, it would clearly be a different thing from meter. **1966** M. PEI *Gloss. Ling. Terminol.* 133 *Isochronism*, a term applied to verse in which the amount of time between two primary stresses tends to be the same, irrespective of the amount of material between them. **1973** *Studies in Eng. Lit.: Eng. Number* (Tokyo) 31 Hopkins has nowhere upheld a principle of absolute isochronism.

isochronous, *a.* Add: *spec.* in *Prosody*, equal in metrical length.

1784–1822 [in Dict.]. **1857** C. PATMORE in *North Brit. Rev.* XXVII. 149 A metre which, totally abandoning the element of natural syllabic quantity, takes the isochronous bar for the metrical integer. **1942** J. C. POPE *Rhythm of Beowulf* 9 Isochronous measures are the rule..and it is easy to produce them in *Beowulf* by means of limited quantitative variation. **1948** *Mod. Philology* XLVI. 75 There is..no reason to suppose that, *if* the *Beowulf* was chanted to a real musical accompaniment, the lines were therefore delivered in isochronous groups. **1971** *Times Lit. Suppl.* 1 Oct. 1179/3 Its technique of isochronous rhythm—a metrical sequence which remains constant for a given part, though the pitch relationships change—is comparable with the Oriental tala.

2. *Palæont.* [ad. G. *isochron* (E. Mojsisovics *Die Cephalopoden der Hallstätter Kalke* (1893) II. 5).] Originating or formed at the same period.

1895 [see *HOMŒOMORPHY]. **1913** [see *HETEROCHRONOUS *a.* b]. **1952** R. C. MOORE et al. *Invertebr. Fossils* vi. 218/1 Such contemporaneous or near-contemporaneous forms he [*sc.* Buckman] designated as isochronous homeomorphs.

isochrony (əisǫ·krŏni). [f. as ISOCHRONISM, after *synchrony*, etc.] Isochronism; the character or property of being isochronous.

1953 *Word* Apr. 3 [The] tendency toward word isochrony whereby every simple word gets two moras either in one long syllable or in two short ones. **1961** *Brno Studies in English* III. 48 In his [*sc.* A. Martinet's] opinion, 12th century English achieves what he ca'ls isochrony, i.e. the state of things resulting from the elimination of vocalic quantity as a phonematic feature. **1961** *Rev. Eng. Stud.* XII. 342 There exist all sorts of musical rhythms very different from the isochrony which has dominated European music for so long a time. **1966** J. C. POPE *Rhythm of Beowulf* (rev. ed.) p. x, Isochrony and initial rests are.. vital, in my opinion, for the achievement of an adequate sense of order in opposition to the extraordinary variety of syllabic patterns in the verses. **1973** *Word 1966* XXII. 5 It is a whole chapter of the history of isochrony, the process through which the quantitative pattern of Proto-Indo-European was reorganized in most of the languages of that family.

isocitrate, isocitric: see *ISO- b.

isoclasite (əisoˌklē·səit, -zəit). *Min.* [f. G. *isoklas* (F. Sandberger 1870, in *Jrnl. f. prakt. Chem.* II. 125, f. Gr. κλάσ-ις fracture) + -ITE[1].] A colourless or white hydrated phosphate and hydroxide of calcium, $Ca_2(PO_4)(OH).2H_2O$, known from a single locality in Bohemia.

1872 G. J. BRUSH in J. D. DANA *Syst. Min.* (ed. 5) App. I. 7 Isoclasite. **1955** M. H. HEY *Index Min. Species* (ed. 2) 231 Isoclasite.

isocli·nally, *adv. Geol.* [f. ISOCLINAL *a.* + -LY[2].] In the manner of isoclinal strata (see ISOCLINAL *a.* 2).

1936 *Bull. Geol. Soc. Amer.* XLVII. 720 Straight, seemingly undeformed layers of marble enclose isoclinally folded and dismembered fragments of stronger rocks. **1970** *Nature* 23 May 691/2 Greenstones..and associated serpentinites and stratiform basic complexes have been isoclinally folded on NNW-trending axes.

isoclinic, *a.* and *sb.* Add: **A.** *adj.* **2.** Corresponding to or depicting the locus of points in a body where each of the principal stresses is in some fixed direction.

1915 FILON & COKER in *Rep. Brit. Assoc. Adv. Sci. 1914* 203 The lines of principal stress are parallel to the axes of the Nicols... These may be called the lines of equal inclination or isoclinic lines. **1939** *Jrnl. Appl. Physics* X. 254/1 The direction of the stresses are taken from the isoclinic sketch. **1966** *McGraw-Hill Encycl. Sci. & Technol.* X. 150/1 Isoclinic fringes are a different set of interference patterns made by using white light, removing the quarter wave plates and rotating the polarizer and analyzer a fixed number of degrees. These fringes represent lines making known angles with the principal planes of stress.

B. *sb.* **2.** An isoclinic line or curve.

1924 L. N. G. FILON in *Rep. Brit. Assoc. Adv. Sci. 1923* 352 Consider a point A..through which passes the isoclinic of parameter *φ*. *Ibid.* 353 The isoclinics are usually well-defined brushes, of which the direction, at any point, can be observed with considerable accuracy. **1948** M. M. FROCHT *Photoelasticity* II. iv. 147 All isoclinics above the X axis pass through the point of application of the downward load and those below the X axis pass through the point of application of the upward load. *Ibid.* 150 The isoclinics are all horizontal where they intersect the boundary of the disk. **1958** CONDON & ODISHAW *Handbk. Physics* III. vi. 86/2 Isoclinics stand out more sharply against colored backgrounds.

isocolloid: see *ISO-.

isocolon. (Earlier and later examples.)

1550 R. SHERRY *Treat. Schemes & Tropes* sig. D5 Isocolon. Compar, euen or equall, is when the oracion hath in it the partes of the whyche we spake before (Articulus, Dialyton), and that they be made of euen number of sillables: but thys equalitie must not stand by numbryng of them, but by perceyuyng of it in the mynd. **1941** *English Studies* XXIII. 16 When we start looking for Pettie's isocolon we do find an average of 8·5 words in a sentence, but there is much more irregularity than in Lyly. **1962** [see *AGNOMINATION 2].

isocortex, isocyclic: see *ISO-. **isocyanate, isocyanic, isocyanide:** see *ISO- b.

isodose (əi·sodōᵘs). [f. ISO- + DOSE *sb.*] An imaginary line or surface, or a graphical representation of one, connecting points, esp. points in the body, that receive equal doses

of radiation; now always used *attrib.*, esp. of such lines and surfaces and of diagrams depicting them.

1922 H. Schmitz tr. *Kroenig & Friedrich's Princ. Physics & Biol. Radiation Therapy* 249 To render a graphical presentation of the distribution of the dose in radiated tissue one proceeded with the conception that the equal intensity curves of like doses in a body, which we may term 'isodoses', are spheres which surround the center of the preparation concentrically. *Ibid.*, The isodoses of such strong capsules as are used in deep therapy must deviate from the circular or cylindrical forms. **1923** O. Glasser in *Amer. Jrnl. Roentgenology* X. 405 (*heading*) Isodose charts. *Ibid.* 405/2 The curves are called 'isodoses', a name I gave first to these curves in connection with radium five years ago. **1939** *Brit. Jrnl. Radiol.* XII. 263/1 The isodose curves or dose contours cut out in space complex solids whose surfaces are 'isodose surfaces'. **1950** *Rev. Sci. Instruments* XXI. 363/1 The automatic isodose recorder..satisfies the demand for tracing radiation fields with a good accuracy in a short length of time. *Ibid.* 365/1 Both the speed of the isodose tracing and the accuracy..are quite adequate. **1956** Hine & Brownell *Radiation Dosimetry* xii. 573 (*caption*) Isodose contours for cancer of the esophagus obtained by combining six 6 × 15-cm fields using Co^{60}. **1966** R. D. Cadle *Particles in Atmosphere & Space* iv. 104 Fallout patterns are maps consisting of families of isodose rate lines or contours. **1968** *Brit. Med. Bull.* XXIV. 242/1 The computer produced a mass of figures..which were easily converted with an x–y plotter to an isodose distribution form, with which all radiotherapists are familiar.

isodrin (əi·sǫdrin). [f. Iso- b + *al)drin.] An insecticide that is a stereoisomer of aldrin, $C_{12}H_8Cl_6$.

1953 *Rev. Appl. Entomol.* XLI. 144 Isodrin is defined by the Committee as 1,2,3,4,10,10-hexachloro-1,4,4a,5,8,8a-hexahydro-1,4,5,8-endo-endo-dimethanonaphthalene. **1955** *Jrnl. Hort. Sci.* XXX. 181 Isodrin and endrin are newer insecticides, but show great promise in their versatility of action; control of such completely different insects as aphids and cut-worms has been obtained by their use. **1971** *Jrnl. Agric. & Food Chem.* XIX. 5/1 Homogenates prepared from the excised roots of bean seedlings..oxidized isodrin, producing a compound corresponding chromatographically to endrin ketone.

isoelectric (əiso,ɪ̆le·ktrik), *a.* [f. Iso- + Electric *a.*] **1.** Equal in electrical potential; containing or indicating no potential difference.

1877 [in Dict. s.v. Iso-]. **1901** J. H. Raymond *Human Physiol.* (ed. 2) 445 A normal muscle in a condition of rest is iso-electric—*i.e.*, it is 'equally electric throughout, and hence has no electric current'; the same is true of dead muscle. **1940** Scherf & Boyd *Clin. Electrocardiogr.* 2 The two waves are separated from each other by a short isoelectric line. **1972** T. P. Forde in R. G. Sanderson *Cardiac Patient* iv. 149 The electrocardiographic tracing is flat or isoelectric during this event.

2. (Composed of particles) having no net electric charge; equal as regards electric charge; chiefly in *isoelectric point*, the point (usually *p*H value) at which an amphoteric molecule or a colloidal particle is electrically neutral in a solution.

1900 W. B. Hardy in *Proc. R. Soc.* LXVI. 112 It is clear that there exists some point at which the particles and the fluid in which they are immersed are iso-electric. This iso-electric point is found to be one of great importance. As it is neared, the stability of the hydrosol diminishes until, at the iso-electric point, it vanishes, and coagulation or precipitation occurs. **1922** J. Loeb *Proteins & Theory Colloidal Behavior* i. 6 The conception of the 'isoelectric point' of proteins was introduced before its chemical meaning was recognized and it attracted attention because it was connected with the precipitation of colloids. *Ibid.* iv. 42 When an acid, *e.g.*, HCl, is added to isoelectric gelatin (or any other isoelectric protein), an equilibrium is established between free HCl, protein chloride, and non-ionogenic (or isoelectric) protein. **1946** P. H. Mitchell *Textbk. Biochem.* iv. 107 Crystallization of a protein is usually carried out at its isoelectric point. **1958** Packer & Vaughan *Mod. Approach Org. Chem.* xiii. 433 In a solution at the isoelectric point, amino acid molecules will not migrate in the electric field created by the introduction of a cathode and an anode. **1966** *Acta Chem. Scand.* XX. 821 The peptides isoelectric between pH 5·0 and 6·5 proved to possess poor carrier ampholyte properties.

b. Carried out or occurring at the isoelectric point.

1961 *Acta Chem. Scand.* XV. 326 Isoelectric analysis and fractionation by electric transport is based on sending a direct current through a system of electrolytes such that the pH increases gradually from anode to cathode... Proteins and other ampholytes will..collect in a region where the local pH is identical with the isoelectric point of the ampholyte. **1971** *European Jrnl. Biochem.* XXI. 110/1 One might expect the 'isoelectric coagulation'..to represent a polymerization reaction based on unaltered native molecules.

Hence **isoele·ctrically** *adv. Biochem.*, by making use of the different isoelectric points of the components of a mixture (in order to separate them).

1966 *Acta Chem. Scand.* XX. 834 Viruses with an average molecular weight of 20 × 10⁶ can be expected to be isoelectrically resolvable only about three times more effectively than myoglobins. **1970** *Zeitschr. Klin. Chem. Klin. Biochem.* VIII. 383 Iron-free transferrin was separated isoelectrically into 2 components with isoelectric points at pH 5·8 and 5·4.

isoelectronic (əi:so,ɪ̆lektrǫ·nik), *a. Chem.* and *Physics.* [f. Iso- + *electron² + -ic.] (Composed of atoms or molecules) having the same number of electrons. Const. *with*.

1928 *Chem. Rev.* V. 155 Vertical lines represent atoms having the same number of external electrons ('isoelectronic systems'). **1929** *Physical Rev.* XXXIII. 538 The succeeding elements calcium, scandium, titanium, vanadium, etc., are made iso-electronic (that is, having the same number of electrons) with potassium by removing one electron from calcium, two electrons from scandium,..etc. **1946** *Nature* 5 Oct. 480/2 In particular, they have assigned the line at 1,400 $cm.^{-1}$ to NO_2^+, comparison with the isoelectronic molecule CO_2 having shown that a polarized Raman frequency would be expected to appear in this region. **1964** C. Chandler *Atomic Spectra* (ed. 2) ix. 138 Ions which have only one electron outside an inert gas shell and are therefore isoelectronic with the alkalis. **1971** *Internat. Jrnl. Quantum Chem.* V. 335 Wave functions of the ^1S (ground state), ^3P and ^1P states for the beryllium isoelectronic sequence have been obtained.

isoenergetic: see *iso-.

isoenzyme (əi·so,e:nzəim). *Biochem.* Also **iso-enzyme.** [f. Iso- + *enzyme.] One of two or more chemically different forms of an enzyme (see quot. 1968). Cf. *isozyme.

1960 *New England Jrnl. Med.* 15 Sept. 531 (*heading*) Isoenzymes and myocardial infarction. **1964** *Oceanogr. & Marine Biol.* II. 220 Species- and tissue-specific forms of enzymes (iso-enzymes) have been reported in animal material. **1968** Latner & Skillen *Isoenzymes in Biol. & Med.* i. 1 It is now well recognized that a large number of enzymes exist in multiple forms. This applies not only to tissues and tissue extracts but also to enzyme proteins which have been isolated in the crystalline state and are really mixtures. Isoenzymes are examples of these multiple forms. Precise definition of the word 'isoenzyme' is, however, rather difficult. Different tissues of the same individual or even of different species may possess closely similar enzymes, which are not really isoenzymes. For the time being, most authorities believe that a broad definition such as 'different proteins with similar enzymatic activity' best suits the current state of our knowledge. It is customary, for the most part, to limit this definition to multiple enzymes obtained from one tissue of one individual animal or plant or possibly a small organ, or a culture of a unicellular organism. An exception would be the major multiple forms of human alkaline phosphatase. They are nevertheless referred to as isoenzymes. **1970** *Nature* 30 May 862/1 The enzyme glucose-6-phosphate dehydrogenase..exists in several different forms (isoenzymes) in the human erythrocyte... The structural differences between the isoenzymes lead to different enzymatic activities.

Hence **isoenzy·mic** *a.*

1968 *Brit. Med. Bull.* XXIV. 222/2 Chemical differences between individuals have been much studied..for example..the occurrence of isoenzymic variants of a number of well-known enzymes.

isoetes (əisō^u·ɪ̆tīz, əiso,ɪ̆·tīz). [mod.L. (Linnæus *Skånska Resa* (1751) 417), f. Gr. *ἰσοετής*, f. *ἴσος* equal + *ἔτος* year: the plants are evergreen.] An aquatic plant of the genus so called; = *quill-wort* (s.v. Quill *sb.*¹ 8 b).

1886 *Encycl. Brit.* XX. 431/2 An Isoetes plant was produced on the leaf instead of a sporangium. **1910** *Rep. Brit. Assoc. Adv. Sci.* 784 The whole axis of the *Isoëtes* plant can be compared with that of *Lepidodendron*. **1965** R. F. Scagel et al. *Evolutionary Survey Plant Kingdom* xix. 375/1 One of the most distinctive vascular plants, *Isoetes*, consists of a thick mass of tubular to strap-shaped leaves borne in a rosette on a very short stem.

isoeugenol, isoflavone: see *iso- b.

isoflor (əi·soflō^ə.ɪ). [f. Iso- + Flor(a rendering G. *isoporie* (W. Rothmaler 1938, in *Beih. Rep. Spec. Nov. Reg. Veg.* C. 89), perh. f. Gr. *πορεία* load.] A line (imaginary or on a map) linking areas containing equal numbers of plant species.

1944 S. A. Cain *Found. Plant Geogr.* xii. 163 Isoflors, lines delimiting regions with equal numbers of species (within the circle of affinity), can be drawn for the generic area as a whole. **1960** N. Polunin *Introd. Plant Geogr.* vii. 208 Sometimes a fair one [*sc.* indication of a centre of origin] may be given by isoflors, which are lines delimiting regions supporting equal numbers of species. **1963** Davis & Heywood *Princ. Angiosperm Taxon.* ix. 317 In the construction of isoflors, it is not the distribution of the individual species that is important, but only the number of species occurring together at any one point. In order to produce the isoflor map, a grid is drawn on the map and the number of taxa noted which occur in each quadrat.

isogam (əi·sogæm). [app. f. Iso- + Gam(ma.] **1.** A line (imaginary or on a map) connecting points where the acceleration due to gravity has the same value. Freq. *attrib.*

1928 *Science* 13 July 37 *Isogam*, surface or line of equal gravitative attraction. **1931** F. H. Lahee *Field Geol.* (ed. 3) xxiii. 661 *Isogam* is the name applied to lines of equal value of relative or absolute gravity. Isogam maps..are used to picture the variation of gravity. **1940** *Geogr. Jrnl.* XCV. 135 The gravity pendulum..cannot produce a survey of gravity in which isogams at 2 milligal intervals can be drawn with confidence. **1954** *Geophysical Suppl. Monthly Notices R. Astron. Soc.* VI. 180 The easiest approach to the problem..is to prepare a chart of density anomalies..and next an isogam chart of the gravity effect of these density anomalies.

2. [cf. *gamma 1 c (iv).] An isodynamic line.

1940 L. L. Nettleton *Geophysical Prospecting for Oil* viii. 163 Contours, or lines of equal magnetic intensity, are commonly called 'isogams'. **1965** G. J. Williams *Econ. Geol. N.Z.* xix. 354/2 A recent magnetic survey revealed a group of high values corresponding fairly well with the inferred position of the anticline; the trend of the isogams and of the high axis is almost parallel to that of the axis.

isogamy. Add: (Later examples.) **isogamete, isogamous** *a.* (earlier and later examples).

1889 Bennett & Murray *Handbk. Cryptogamic Bot.* 272 The only known sexual mode of reproduction [in the Confervoideae] is an isogamous one between two masses of protoplasm. **1935** F. E. Fritsch *Struct. & Reprod. Algae* I. 43 Isogamy (i.e. the fusion of morphologically identical gametes) is very usually..combined with an absence of differentiated organs for the production of the sexual cells or gametes. *Ibid.* 46 Isogametes are commonly positively phototactic. **1938** G. M. Smith *Cryptogamic Bot.* I. ii. 21 All green algae in which both gametes are nonflagellated..are isogamous. **1952** C. J. Alexopoulos *Introd. Mycol.* i. 17 We use the terms isogametangia and isogametes..to designate gametangia and gametes which are morphologically indistinguishable. **1964** E. J. H. Corner *Life of Plants* vi. 85 The process is called isogamy or the union of outwardly similar gametes. **1968** Bell & Woodcock *Diversity of Green Plants* ii. 39 The gametes [of *Stigeoclonium*] are noticeably smaller than the zoospores, and copulation is isogamous.

isogel: see *iso-.

isogeneic (əisodʒenɪ̆·ik, -ē^i·ik), *a. Immunol.* [f. Iso- + Gr. *γενε-ά* race, stock + -ic.] = *syngeneic *a.*

1963 Humphrey & White *Immunol. for Students of Med.* xi. 359 When grafts are made..from one animal to another isogeneic animal they are 'isografts'. *Ibid.* 365 Since surgeons rarely have the opportunity of working with isogeneic patients, successful grafting has been largely limited to autografts. **1973** *Nature* 23 Mar. 259/2 An animal strain in which inbred immunologically isogeneic lines are available, making possible transplantation studies uncomplicated by rejection problems.

isogenic (əisodʒe·nik, əisodʒɪ̆·nik), *a. Biol.* [ad. G. *isogen* (W. Johannsen *Elem. d. exakten Erblichkeitslehre* (ed. 2, 1913) xii. 208), f. Iso- + *gen(e + -ic.] Having the same genotype (*genotype *sb.*²).

1933 *Biochem. Jrnl.* XXVII. 6 In all the work discussed in this paper we have, unless otherwise stated, compared only isogenic animals (animals of the same sex and from the same litter). **1943** *Proc. Nat. Acad. Sci.* XXIX. 361 Three homozygous stocks were obtained, which were isogenic except for the fourth chromosome. **1950** *Jrnl. Exper. Zool.* CXIII. 123 To obtain a culture isogenic with the recessive parent, employ the usual backcross procedure. **1956** *Nature* 7 Jan. 42/2 Males of a wild-type ('Canton-S') stock of *Drosophila melanogaster*, which had been made isogenic some time before the experiments, were crossed to homozygous *ci ey^R* females. **1970** *Ibid.* 7 Feb. 557/1 This method..is especially suitable for characters in which the distributions of the isogenic parental strains are not clearly dichotomous. **1973** *Ibid.* 9 Feb. 383/2 The relatively uniform appearance and behaviour of the aggressive isolates suggest that these are highly isogenic, possibly with a recent origin from a single clone.

isogloss (əi·soglǫs). [a. G. *isogloss* (A. Bielenstein *Die Grenzen des Lettischen Volksstammes* (1892) 397, f. Iso- + Gloss *sb.*¹] In Linguistic Geography, the boundary of an area of local concentration or dominance of a significant feature (as of vocabulary or pronunciation). Also, a line plotted on a map indicating the area in which such a feature is concentrated or is dominant. Hence **isoglo·ssic** *a.*

1925 O. Jespersen *Mankind, Nation & Individual* iii. 41 As a rule we find that the frontiers for one phenomenon do not exactly coincide with the frontiers for another, so that the 'isoglosses' (as such frontiers of single phenomena are called) sometimes agree, sometimes run somewhat parallel with one another, but fairly often cross one another in the most distracting manner. **1927** L. Bloomfield in *Mod. Philology* Nov. 220 The boundaries of successive linguistic changes (isogloss lines) do not coincide... Isoglosses may be bundled along barriers to communication; if the barrier (e.g., a political boundary) is removed, the isoglossic bundle may be overlaid by later linguistic development. **1933** —— *Lang.* iii. 51 Within a dialect area, we can draw lines between places which differ as to any feature of language. Such lines are called isoglosses. **1949** H. Kurath *Word Geogr. Eastern U.S.* 11 In figure 2 the focus of each of the more distinctive subareas of the Eastern States is set off by a single word line or isogloss. **1953** J. B. Carroll *Study of Lang.* ii. 59 The purpose of linguistic geography is to make a detailed analysis of local linguistic variations... Efforts are made to establish isoglosses, which may be described as cartographic lines separating the geographical localities which show a difference with respect to a specific linguistic item. **1955** *Publ. Amer. Dialect Soc.* xxiii. 40 When it [*sc.* a form] is found within a sharply defined area, one may draw a line called an isogloss, to indicate the boundaries of the area in which this form occurs. **1958** *Ibid.* xxx. 3 But a number of lexical terms do not occur in geographical patterns corresponding to the isogloss divisions for known Northern and Midland features. **1964** H. B. Allen in A. A. Marckwardt *Stud. Lang. & Ling. in*

Honor C. C. Fries 305 The major isogloss bundle is shown on the map by the 1–1 line. **1968** *Amer. Speech* XLIII. 185 It is separated from other dialects of Yiddish by a bundle of grammatical, phonological, and lexical isoglosses. **1968** W. S. ALLEN *Vox Graeca* i. 12 The ττ of pure Attic is part of an isogloss having its probable point of origin in Boeotian. **1972** H. KURATH *Stud. Area Ling.* 60 The location of some representative isoglossic lines..is shown in Figure 21.

Hence also **isoglo·ttal, -glottic** *adjs.*

1932 *Missouri Alumnus* Apr. 232/1 The American Council of Learned Societies is financing a 'Dialect Atlas of the United States and Canada', and already the workers are making a survey of New England. They have a 'work-sheet' of 800 questions which bring to light the notable speech variations, and from the information so gathered they construct maps with 'iso-glottal' lines like those on a topographic map. **1939** L. H. GRAY *Foundations of Lang.* ii. 26 Such lines are termed isoglottic lines or isographs. **1954** *Word* X. 375 The location of different isoglottic lines did not coincide in one linguistic area.

isogonic, *a.*[2] Read: *Biol.* [ad. Fr. *isogonique* (A. Pézard 1918, in *Bull. Biol. de la France et de la Belgique* LII. 24).] Of an organ, growing at the same rate as its parent body. So **iso·gony,** growth of this kind.

1924 J. S. HUXLEY in *Nature* 20 Dec. 895/1 Pézard.. has styled the growth of such an organ heterogonic..as opposed to isogonic. **1932** —— *Probl. Relative Growth* i. ii. 8 An organ which..is growing at the same rate as the body..must be styled isogonic. *Ibid.* iii. 38 It is justifiable to regard isogony as a special case of heterogony, with growth-coefficiency unity. **1945** RICHARDS & KAVANAGH in Clark & Medawar *Ess. Growth & Form* 219 Isogonic growth is a special case of isotropic growth in which the specific growth-rate in length is the same at every point throughout the organism.

isograd, isograde, isogradic: see *ISO-.

isograft (əi·sograft), *sb. Med.* and *Biol.* [f. ISO- + GRAFT *sb.*[1]] **a.** = *HOMOGRAFT. Now *rare* or *obs.*

1909 *Jrnl. Exper. Med.* XI. 194 Three isografts were placed. **1919** J. S. DAVIS *Plastic Surg.* iv. 50, I have thought for some time that the success or failure of isografts may be dependent on the similarity or dissimilarity of blood groups of the host and donor. **1942** J. P. WEBSTER in F. Christopher *Textbk. Surg.* (ed. 3) xxxv. 1587 Successful free corneal isografts have been reported with maintenance of transparency. **1950** F. SMITH *Plastic & Reconstruction Surg.* i. 27 Homograft, homologous graft and isograft are synonymous terms indicating tissue transplanted from one to another person of the same species.

b. A graft taken from an identical twin of the recipient or from an animal of the same inbred strain.

1958 *Immunology* I. 1 Adrenal cortical grafts transplanted between members of an inbred strain of mice ('isografts') are held to be successful when they empower adrenalectomised mice to subsist on a diet low in NaCl. *Ibid.* 6 Homografts transplanted to the brain and testis were significantly inferior to isografts. **1963** HUMPHREY & WHITE *Immunol. for Students of Med.* xi. 359 Isografts usually also take permanently, although even within a pure line of mice male skin may be rejected by a female recipient, by virtue of the fact that the Y chromosome can carry sex-linked genetic differences. **1970** *Microvascular Res.* II. 91 The vascular dilation and petechiae, which were observed in the skin isografts in animals treated with cortisol, were similar in the allograft group.

isograft (əi·sograft), *v. Med.* and *Biol.* [f. ISO- + GRAFT *v.*[1] or f. prec.] *trans.* **a.** To transplant from one individual to another of the same species; = *HOMOTRANSPLANT *v.* **b.** To transplant between identical twins or animals of the same inbred strain. So **i·sografted** *ppl. a.*, **i·sografting** *vbl. sb.*

1909 *Jrnl. Exper. Med.* XI. 194 The following day the isografting was made. **1919** J. S. DAVIS *Plastic Surg.* iv. 50 Care must be taken when isografting is contemplated, not to transmit disease to a healthy person. **1959** *Proc. Soc. Exper. Biol. & Med.* CII. 651/1 (*caption*) Light-dark synchronized activity rhythm whether or not pituitaries were isografted. **1962** *Dissertation Abstr.* XXII. 2829/1 The sex of the recipient animal had no effect on the survival of isografted fetal tissue. **1970** *Zeitschr. für Anat. & Entwickl.-Gesch.* CXXXII. 318, 92 mammary duct-segments..were excised..and microdissected for isografting into the fourth mammary gland-free fat pads of the 46 female hosts.

isograph (əi·sograf). [f. ISO- + -GRAPH.] **1.** A drawing instrument (see quots.).

1838 *Civil Engin. & Arch. Jrnl.* I. 349/1 These are a set of triangular rulers, drawing paper, with the lines and ellipses described upon it, and the isograph which consists of a number of rulers, made of brass or ivory, the fiducial edge of each being an inch apart, and parallel to each other. **1909** WEBSTER, *Isograph*, an instrument consisting of two short straightedges connected by a large circular joint marked with angular degrees, used with a T square on a drawing board and combining the functions of a protractor and a set square. **1926–7** *Army & Navy Stores Catal.* 456/1 Isograph. 12 in. boxwood, brass joint.

2. *Linguistics.* (See quots.)

1939 L. H. GRAY *Foundations of Lang.* ii. 26 Certain features of any one of the dialects will be common to some of the rest..so that it will be possible to draw upon a map lines indicating at least the approximate boundaries of these features... Such lines are termed isoglottic lines or isographs. **1954** PEI & GAYNOR *Dict. Ling.* 106 *Isograph*, any line on a linguistic map, indicating a uniformity in the use of sounds, vocabulary, syntax, inflexion, etc.

isogyre, isohæmagglutination, isohæmagglutinin, isohæmolysin, isohaline, isohel, isohelic: see *ISO-.

isohydric (əisohəi·drik), *a.* [ad. G. *isohydrisch* (S. Arrhenius 1887, in *Ann. d. Physik u. Chem.* XXX. 54): see ISO- and HYDRIC *a.*] **a.** *Physical Chem.* Having the same hydrogen ion concentration; maintaining the same hydrogen ion concentration after mixing; also used with reference to other ions.

1887 *Jrnl. Chem. Soc.* LII. I. 415 The molecular conductivity of a mixture of butyric and acetic acid solutions in any proportions is always the sum of the molecular conductivities of the constituent solutions. Each electrolyte behaves as if the other were absent. Such solutions are termed by the author [*sc.* S. Arrhenius] 'isohydric'. **1899** J. WALKER *Introd. Physical Chem.* xxv. 288 Let there be prepared isohydric solutions of the different salts, NaCl being made isohydric with NaBr, by getting the sodium ions of the same concentration in both solutions. **1930** GLASSTONE *Electrochem. Solutions* viii. 151 Solutions of acids which do not change their ionization on mixing are said to be isohydric with one another. **1952** J. E. RICCI *Hydrogen Ion Concentration* ii. 26 We shall here examine the conditions for the validity of the theorem of isohydric solutions, that isohydric solutions (solutions of the same *H*) mix without change of *H*.

b. *Physiol.* Occurring without causing any change in the *p*H of the blood: applied to the reactions by which carbon dioxide is removed from the tissues and taken up by the blood.

1920 *Proc. Soc. Exper. Biol. & Med.* XVII. 181 Curves ..have been obtained, showing an isohydric shift of base between hemoglobin and the other constituents of the blood. **1946** J. F. FULTON *Howell's Textbk. Physiol.* (ed. 15) xxxix. 887 This series of chemical reactions in the erythrocyte has been designated as the isohydric cycle because the uptake of CO_2 and the release of O_2 is accomplished without the production of an excess of H^+. **1954** A. WHITE et al. *Princ. Biochem.* xxvi. 691 The isohydric shift entails formation of about 0·7 meq. of bicarbonate for each millimole of oxygen which dissociates from oxyhemoglobin. **1970** R. W. MCGILVERY *Biochem.* xxv. 612 This action of the Bohr effect to permit the blood to take up CO_2 without a change in pH is known as the isohydric carriage of CO_2.

isohyet, isohyetal, isoimmune, isoimmunization: see *ISO-.

isoionic (əiso,əi,ǫ·nik), *a. Physical Chem.* and *Biochem.* [f. ISO- + IONIC *a.*[2]] Of a solute or solution: giving rise to or containing no non-colloidal ions other than those formed by dissociation of the solvent; *isoionic point*, † *reaction*, the point (usually *p*H value) at which the average number of hydrogen ions attached to the basic groups of solute molecules is equal to the average number dissociated from the acidic groups.

This is the 'theoretical' definition of *isoionic point*; for the 'practical' definitions, see quot. 1959.

1926 LINDERSTRØM-LANG & LUND in *Compt. Rend. Lab. Carlsberg* XVI. v. 22 We will therefore define isoionic reaction as the value of pa_H, pa_H^0 at which h [*sc.* the specific hydrogen ionisation of the ampholyte] is 0. **1934** *Biochem. Jrnl.* XXVIII. 1257 At 0°, the isoionic point of crystallised haemoglobin was at p_H 7·6. **1943** J. D. EDSALL in Cohn & Edsall *Proteins* xx. 446 If the protein binds no other ions than protons, the isoionic point may correspond to the isoelectric point of the protein... If the protein combines with other ions also, the isoelectric and isoionic points are different. **1949** *Jrnl. Physical & Colloid Chem.* LIII. 88 Operationally we may define the isoionic material as the limit approached by successful electrodialysis. *Ibid.* 95 We may..calculate the change in pH of a solution which is not isoionic. **1959** LINDERSTRØM-LANG & NIELSEN in M. Bier *Electrophoresis* I. ii. 63 According to the first definition the isoionic point is the pH of the protein solution which does not change on the addition of more isoionic protein. According to the second definition the isoionic point is the pH of a solution of the isoionic protein in water, or in a solution which does not produce H^+ or OH^- ions when dissolved in water alone. Thus a mixture of proteins may be isoionic. **1969** OTTAWAY & IRVINE tr. *Netter's Theoret. Biochem.* vi. 192 Amino acids and proteins are usually characterised by their isoelectric or isoionic point.

isokinetic, -kinetically: see *ISO-.

isokite (isōu·kəit). *Min.* [f. *Isok-a*, name of a small town in Zambia: see -ITE[1].] A white, buff, or pinkish phosphate and fluoride of calcium and magnesium, $CaMgPO_4F$.

1955 DEANS & MCCONNELL in *Mineral. Mag.* XXX. 681 The mineral, for which the name isokite is now proposed, occurs in the carbonatite plug which forms Nkumbwa Hill (lat. 10°10′ S. long. 32° 51′ E), 15 miles east of Isoka (pronounced Isōka) in Northern Rhodesia. *Ibid.* 686 The analysis leaves no doubt that isokite is essentially $CaMgPO_4F$. **1968** I. KOSTOV *Mineral.* II. 463 Tilasite and isokite are monoclinic (*C*2/*c*), isostructural with sphene.

isolable, *a.* (Later examples.)

1926 A. R. LORD *Princ. Pol.* v. 147 Democracy is no isolable, dead element in the composition of social and political humanity. **1965** W. LAMB *Posture & Gesture* vii. 97 We can demonstrate, however, that there is a distinctly isolable quality of children's physical behaviour.

isolatable (əisolēi·tăb'l), *a.* = ISOLABLE *a.*

1936 *Chem. Abstr.* XXX. 6354 G[rundmann] has attempted to apply the reaction to certain substituted phenols in order to obtain aliphatic polyene polycarboxylic acids, *o*-Coumaric acid gave, as the only isolatable product, *I* in very small amt. **1949** E. A. NIDA *Morphol.* (ed. 2) ii. 60 The morphemes *cran-*, *rasp-*, and *cray-* are isolatable because the elements *berry* and *fish* occur in isolation or in other combinations. **1957** N. FRYE *Anat. Criticism* 198 Romance, like Comedy, has six isolatable phases. **1964** R. H. ROBINS *Gen. Ling.* vii. 277 The bound morpheme..is likely to be a much less semantically isolatable unit. **1971** *Jrnl. Gen. Psychol.* LXXXIV. 169 Personality is the name for something that is not 'time-bound': that is, it is not an event that occurs in a limited period of time and is not isolatable in the way other categories are.

Hence **i:solatabi·lity.**

1949 E. A. NIDA *Morphol.* (ed. 2) 59 On the basis of the first condition of isolatability we may identify as morphemes such forms as *boy*, *cow*..since it is possible to utter..these forms in isolation.

isolate, *a.* (*sb.*) Add: (Later examples.)

1923 D. H. LAWRENCE *Kangaroo* vii. 151 In the visible world I am alone, an isolate instance. **1956** R. REDFIELD *Peasant Soc. & Cult.* 8 Little isolate societies. *a* **1963** S. PLATH *Ariel* (1965) 26 These are the isolate, slow faults That kill, that kill, that kill. **1967** T. GUNN *Touch* 33 Drops are isolate on leaves. **1973** *Archivum Linguisticum* IV. 14 'Am' is a bound form, a pronoun which only occurs as an object and never as an isolate form.

B. *sb.* Add to def.: Esp. something abstracted from its normal context for study. (Further examples.)

1934 *Nature* 8 Dec. 889/2 The method of science to search for useful isolates may easily lead the scientific worker to overlook the reactions of his social environment on his own scientific work. **1937** D. J. B. HAWKINS *Causality & Implication* iii. 57 Perhaps it will be best to use the term *isolate*, meaning what is *isolated* in thought but referring specifically to the factual element which is thus isolated. *Isolate* is an appropriate name for any conceptual object in itself, whether it be a simple character or a complex of characters. **1950** J. E. L. FARRADANE in *Jrnl. Documentation* June 87 An item of knowledge will thus be an object..or an abstract..which is clearly and, at its own level of complexity, uniquely definable, as far as may be possible. Any other item would in reality be composed of two or more concepts, leading to logical confusions. Let us call these items, as defined, isolates. **1951** S. F. NADEL *Found. Social Anthropol.* v. 75 In this sense no legitimate isolate can be discovered more basic than that of a standardized pattern of behaviour rendered unitary and relatively self-contained. **1956** R. REDFIELD *Peasant Society & Culture* 7 The primitive isolate, the community that is a whole all by itself,..became the model of research. **1958** *Antiquity* XXXII. 148 Cultural isolates from archaeological material. **1961** *Encounter* May 74 'Homosexuality' is a false isolate, a term covering a number of conditions. **1964** C. D. NEEDHAM *Organizing Knowl. in Libraries* vii. 71 The isolates now need grouping so that those which are related are proximate. **1969** A. C. FOSKETT *Subject Approach to Information* I. v. 56 Copper as a topic taken out of context is an isolate, but if we place it in a facet in a particular basic class we can refer to it as a focus. **1972** *Jrnl. Social Psychol.* LXXXVI. 109 *Ss* reported that the isolate reduced the homogeneity.

b. *Perfumery.* A compound which is isolated in a more or less pure condition from a natural essential oil for use in perfumery.

1923 W. A. POUCHER *Perfumes & Cosmetics* iii. 214 It is usual to combine both with a natural isolate of rose odour such as geraniol. **1949** R. W. MONCRIEFF *Chem. Perfumery Materials* I. ii. 29 Most of the alcohols used in the perfume industry are isolates rather than synthetics. **1957** E. SAGARIN *Cosmetics* xxxiii. 743 Of the chemical bodies used in perfumery, the isolates from plant oils bear the strongest resemblance to the plant materials themselves.

c. *Biol.* A group of like micro-organisms obtained by isolation or culturing for study or experiment; *esp.* a pure culture.

1931 W. B. BRIERLEY in *Ann. Appl. Biol.* XVIII. 421 The procedure I adopt in my *Botrytis* work is as follows. Each separate pure culture made by direct isolation from fresh material, whether a number of cultures are made from a single lesion or from one or more host plants, I term an Isolate. If the first culture direct from the diseased tissue contains, as is very often the case, two or more types, the pure or single-spore isolations from this mixture and not the first impure culture are the isolates. Each isolate is an individual line and sub-cultures are merely duplicates or replicates of that isolate or line. The isolate is the nearest equivalent to Lotsy's 'species'. **1949** H. W. FLOREY et al. *Antibiotics* I. i. 66 Many surveys for antibiotic activity have been performed on type-culture collections of fungi and on new isolates. **1958** *New Biol.* XXVII. 63 It seems to be no easier to establish experimental infections with isolates of *Candida albicans* derived from epidemic outbreaks than with isolates from any other source. **1971** *E. Afr. Standard* (Nairobi) 13 Apr. 9/8 Identification of isolates and antisera received from associate laboratories in Senegal..continued. **1972** *Nature* 17 Mar. 122/1 In an investigation of this increased severity, isolates of *Ceratocystis ulmi* were made from infected trees in the outbreak regions.

d. *Soc. Psychol.* A person who, either from choice or through separation or rejection, is

isolated from normal social interaction; also occas. an animal separated from its kind.

1942 *Psychol. Bull.* XXXIX. 458 Differences in interpersonal capacity for participation with others, differences which are revealed when the personalities of isolates and leaders are studied. **1953** J. L. Moreno *Who shall Survive?* I. 100 A rough classification of the position of the individual in the groups was possible—the isolates, the pairs, and the bunch that clung to the leader. **1963** T. & P. Morris *Pentonville* vii. 174 The retreatist is difficult to detect because he *is* an isolate. **1966** T. Pynchon *Crying of Lot 49* v. 113 Nobody knows anybody else's name... We're isolates, Arnold. Meetings would destroy the whole point of it. **1968** *Observer* (Colour Suppl.) 14 Apr. 36/1 Woolly monkeys..who..live on as 'pets' become desocialised, isolates. **1969** *Sunday Times* (Colour Suppl.) 16 Mar. 23/4 Social isolates..often become so careless of their own welfare that they become undernourished. **1970** *New Scientist* 14 May 319/1 In previous attempts at social rehabilitation, normal monkeys of the same age as the isolates were placed in the cage with them. But the isolate ignored its visitor.

e. *Biol.* A group of plants or animals which has developed characteristics distinct from those of the parent species through the operation of an **isolating mechanism*.

1948 G. Dahlberg in *Adv. Genetics* II. 92 Recessive mutations will come to the fore more quickly in a population built up of small isolates than in one composed of large ones. **1967** M. E. Hale *Biol. Lichens* iv. 62 The form and appearance of colonies of different mycobionts and even different isolates of the same mycobiont vary considerably. **1969** E. Mayr *Princ. Systematic Zoology* iii. 49 Isolates are frequently of sufficient difference to merit subspecies rank.

f. *Linguistics.* A word, or words, or other linguistic feature(s) abstracted from context for special study. Also, a word or short phrase that functions as a clause.

1949 *Trans. Philol. Soc. 1948* 128 For the purpose of distinguishing prosodic systems from phonematic systems, words will be my principal isolates. **1961** R. B. Long *Sentence & its Parts* i. 20 Isolates sometimes take adjunct modifiers, much as nucleuses do. Adjuncts are italicized in the following sentences. Thanks *very much.* Good night, *Marian.* **1965** W. S. Allen *Vox Latina* 7 In French, stress is a feature of the word only as an isolate (in which case it falls on the final syllable). **1972** Hartmann & Stork *Dict. Lang. & Ling.* 119/2 *Isolate,* (*a*) a single word functioning as a clause.., (*b*) a term used occasionally as an alternative to segment.

isolate, *v.* **4.** Add: Also *absol.*

1888 Mrs. H. Ward *R. Elsmere* II. iii. xxi. 178 Three cases of diphtheria..I must go for..a nurse, and we must isolate and make a fight for it.

isolated, *a.* Add: *isolated pawn*: see quots.

1842 C. Pearson *Chess Exemplified* 27 An isolated pawn is one that has no comrade on the same or either adjoining file, so that he requires the support of a Piece. **1847** H. Staunton *Chess-Player's Handbk.* 23 A Pawn which stands alone, without the support or protection of other Pawns, is termed an isolated pawn. **1950** S. Tartakover in R. N. Coles *Chess-Player's Week-End Bk.* 153 An isolated pawn spreads gloom all over the chess-board. **1957** Cunnington & Du Mont *Chess Traps & Stratagems* ii. 75 An isolated pawn is normally weak, a pawn supported by its neighbours is a strong asset.

isolating (əi·sŏlēitiŋ), *ppl. a.* [f. Isolate *v.* + -ing[2].] **1.** *Linguistics.* Designating languages (e.g. Vietnamese) in which (for the most part) words do not vary in form according to their grammatical functions in sentences, as contrasted with agglutinating and inflecting languages.

1860 [see Inflexional, inflectional *a.*]. **1861** Max Müller *Lect. Sci. Lang.* 1st Ser. viii. 274 Languages belonging to this first or Radical Stage, have sometimes been called Monosyllabic or Isolating. **1868** —— *Sel. Ess. Lang.* (1881) I. 44 We find it repeated again and again in most works on Comparative Philology, that Chinese belongs to the isolating class, the Turanian languages to the combinatory, the Aryan and Semitic to the inflectional. **1885** *Encycl. Brit.* XVIII. 774/2 Such languages, constituting the small minority of human tongues, are wont to be called 'isolating', i.e., using each element by itself, in its integral form. **1921** E. Sapir *Lang.* vi. 133 More justifiable [than the traditional classification of linguistic types as i) isolating, ii) agglutinative, iii) inflective] would be a classification according to the formal processes most typically developed in the language. Those languages that always identify the word with the radical element would be set off as an 'isolating' group against such as either affix modifying elements..or possess the power to change the significance of the radical element by internal changes. **1953** C. E. Bazell *Ling. Form* i. 2 In languages of so-called 'isolating' structure the syllable may often be regarded as the minimal unit having independent morphological relevance.

2. *Biol.* **isolating barrier, mechanism,** a geographical, ecological, seasonal, physiological, or other factor which limits or prevents interbreeding between groups of plants or animals.

1913 W. Bateson *Probl. Genetics* vi. 119 In one remarkable case the season of appearance plainly acts as the isolating barrier. **1937** T. Dobzhansky in *Amer. Naturalist* LXXI. 405 The expression 'isolating mechanisms' seems to be a convenient general name for all the mechanisms hindering or preventing the interbreeding of racial complexes or species. **1973** I. H. Herskowitz *Princ. Genetics* xxxvi. 564 It is expected..that natural selection would favor isolating mechanisms that operate prior to mating.

isolation. Add: **2. a.** *Psychol.* and *Sociol.* The separation of a person or thing from its normal environment or context, either for purposes of experiment and study or as a result of its being, for some reason, set apart. Also *attrib.* or as *adj.*

1890 C. L. Morgan *Animal Life & Intelligence* viii. 322 We may call the process by which we select a certain quality, and consider it by itself to the neglect of other qualities, *isolation.* **1902** *Amer. Jrnl. Sociol.* VIII. 37 Thus isolation, apparently confined to a single person, consisting in the negation of sociality, is really a phenomenon of very positive sociological significance. **1934** *Ibid.* XL. 157 The hypothesis is that the cause of schizophrenia is isolation of the person. **1950** K. H. Wolff tr. *Simmel's Sociol.* iii. 119 Isolation thus is a relation which is lodged within an individual but which exists between him and a certain group or group life in general. **1961** D. O. Hebb in P. Solomon et al. *Sensory Deprivation* ii. 7 The isolation procedure seems to be contributing to more effective interrelations between psychiatry and psychology. **1964** Gould & Kolb *Dict. Social Sci.* 355/2 Isolation is regarded as one of the dynamic variables in the failure to acquire personality. **1969** Zigler & Child in Lindzey & Aronson *Handbk. Social Psychol.* (ed. 2) III. xxiv. 523 That early isolation increases later aggression is an especially interesting phenomenon which has also been found in mice..and monkeys. **1970** G. A. & A. G. Theodorson *Mod. Dict. Sociol.* 216 The prolonged isolation of an individual from satisfying social..involvement with others usually leads to or is a result of a mental disorder. **1971** *Jrnl. Gen. Psychol.* LXXXV. 107 Isolation fails to enhance total list acquisition. *Ibid.* 157 Operant tasks were performed in an isolation chamber. **1972** *Jrnl. Social Psychol.* LXXXVI. 106 The results of the experiment showed an isolation effect to the name 'Cecil'.

b. *Psychoanal.* A defence mechanism whereby a particular wish or thought loses emotional significance by being isolated from its normal context.

1926 *Brit. Jrnl. Med. Psychol.* VI. 125 In obsessional neurosis the isolation is given magical motor reinforcement—motor isolation is a guarantee for rupture of thought connections. **1937** tr. *Freud's Gen. Sel. Works* 280 Our attention has..been drawn to a process of 'isolation' (whose technique cannot as yet be elucidated) which has direct symptomatic manifestations of its own. **1946** O. Fenichel *Psychoanal. Theory of Neurosis* ii. ix. 155 Another mechanism of defense prevalent in compulsion neuroses and of very general significance for psychopathology is isolation. **1951** P. M. Symonds *Ego & Self* xii. 181 The compulsive neurotic may use the mechanism of isolation in which a portion of his personality is walled off through lack of feeling. **1964** H. Hartmann *Ess. Ego Psychol.* i. iii. 48 A tendency toward isolation ('good' things must not be contaminated with 'bad' things [etc.]). **1970** P. Chodoff in H. S. Abram *Psychol. Aspects Stress* 54 Isolation of affect [among concentration camp inmates], which could be so extreme as to involve a kind of emotional anesthesia, seemed to have functioned particularly to protect the ego.

3. *Biol.* The limitation or prevention of interbreeding between groups of plants or animals by geographical, ecological, seasonal, or other factors, leading to the development of new species or varieties.

[**1859** Darwin *Origin of Species* iv. 105 Isolation, by checking immigration and consequently competition, will give time for a new variety to be improved at a slow rate.] **1913** W. Bateson *Probl. Genetics* vi. 119 The distinctness of the two forms [of the moth *Tephrosia bistortata*] in the places where they co-exist is maintained by the seasonal isolation. **1929** *Biol. Abstr.* III. 1621/1 If foreign hereditary elements are mixed in a population, correlations will be established, partly through polymery, partly through isolation. **1937** T. Dobzhansky *Genetics & Origin of Species* viii. 230 The mechanisms that prevent the interbreeding of groups of individuals, and consequently engender isolation, are remarkably diversified. **1973** I. H. Herskowitz *Princ. Genetics* xxxvi. 563 Although cross breeding may occur naturally or experimentally between closely related species, each maintains its unique gene pool via reproductive isolation.

isolationism (əisŏlēi·ʃəniz'm). [f. Isolation + -ism.] The policy of seeking (political or national) isolation: with special reference to the U.S.A. Also *transf.*

1922 *19th Cent.* Nov. 731 Her isolationism..discovered that the strain of a formidable advance against freedom was more than it could bear. **1930** *Headway* June 112/2 Add to this the fact that half the people..who have emigrated to America in the last generation or so are Europeans who have left Europe because they wanted to get away from Europe, and the secret of America's 'isolationism' is very largely explained. **1931** *Time & Tide* Suppl. 4 July, However much an instructed minority in America might be in favour of the abandonment of isolationism and a larger co-operation with Europe. **1934** [see *autarky b]. **1953** *Manch. Guardian Weekly* 27 Aug. 1 He was now ready to say that 'unilateralism is the new face of Isolationism'. **1955** *Bull. Atomic Sci.* Oct. 274 Apparently, the period of enforced scientific isolationism imposed on them for several years has not destroyed this tradition. **1956** K. Clark *Nude* v. 167 The rigid isolationism of the Parthenon metopes. **1969** *Nature* 8 Feb. 524/2 One of the lamentable consequences of intellectual isolation is isolationism—the unconscious fear of exposing the inadequacy of one's achievement to one's fellow scientists. **1973** *Guardian* 25 Apr. 11/1 The difference.. between the old isolationism and the new was that whereas the United States felt itself too good for the world in the 1930s, it now felt it was not good enough.

isolationist. Add: Also *transf.*

1901 *Rep. Brit. Assoc. Adv. Sci.* 676 This way of accounting for progress in one or more directions may prove as inadequate as the one suggested by isolationists. **1929** *Times* 31 Oct. 16/1 If a grave crisis were ever to arise on the western borders of Russia, the isolationists might be swept off their feet. **1962** [see *comparatist]. **1969** *Guardian* 6 Feb. 10 A teacher cannot be an isolationist. He has to go out and meet the people whose opinions matter in education.

b. *attrib.* or as *adj.*

1921 *Glasgow Herald* 21 Apr. 8 Regarding the future policy of the United States...The isolationist attitude.. is..much less obvious. **1922** *Ibid.* 30 Dec. 7 Senator Borah has been regarded as the foremost advocate..of the isolationist policy. **1930** *New Statesman* 26 Apr. 69/2 When Mr. Hoover signed last year the prospect was good, but the prolonged bickerings in London have stiffened the isolationist sentiment of the interior. **1958** *Punch* 1 Jan. 75/1 They go further and speculate about the future of an isolationist Britain. **1958** M. West *Second Victory* iii. 56 You know what these mountain people are —irredentist, isolationist, intolerant of foreigners and officials alike.

Hence **isolationi·stic** *a.*; **isolationi·stically** *adv.*

1943 E. W. Hall in *Mind* LII. 232, I shall speak of them as the 'primitivistic', the 'isolationistic', and the 'semantical' usages, respectively. **1964** *Economist* 7 Nov. 567 To be..isolationistically independent and..internationally dominant.

isolative (əi·sŏlētiv), *a.* [f. Isolate *v.* + -ive.] **a.** *Phonology.* Of a sound-change: taking place without reference to neighbouring sounds: opp. *combinative *a.* 3.

1888 H. Sweet *Hist. Eng. Sounds* 17 Isolative changes are those which affect a sound without any reference to its surroundings. *Ibid.* 26 Isolative change of s into ʃ is regular in Gm initial *s* followed by a cons., as in *schwan, stein.* **1906** H. C. Wyld *Hist. Study Mother Tongue* iv. 73 Sound changes are conveniently divided into two main classes: *Isolative Changes,* which take place independent of other neighbouring sounds in the word or sentence, and uninfluenced by them; and *Combinative Changes.* **1972** Hartmann & Stork *Dict. Lang. & Ling.* 212/2 A sound change is said to be..isolative, autonomous, spontaneous, sporadic when it is in no way dependent on its environment but occurs in all positions in which the sound in question occurs.

b. *gen.* Tending to isolate.

1957 *Antiquity* XXXI. 189 Natural selection and isolative mechanisms. **1968** G. Jones *Hist. Vikings* ii. i. 69 The axe-resisting, isolative forests of central Sweden.

‖ **isolato** (isolā·to). [It.] An isolated person, an outcast.

The spelling in quot. 1950 is *erron.*

1851 H. Melville *Moby Dick* I. xxvi. 191 They were nearly all Islanders in the *Pequod, Isolatos* too, I call such, not acknowledging the common continent of men,..yet ..what a set these Isolatos were! **1950** Auden *Enchafèd Flood* i. 35 What it feels like to be such an isolatoe, who ..is left standing there alone in the wide waste. **1958** *New Statesman* 6 Sept. 322/2 What most of them failed to see..was that the Negro was also, primarily, an American and faced many of the same problems as the displaced isolato, the white American.

isolecithal, isolectic: see *iso-.

Isolette (əisole·t). *N. Amer.* Also **isolette.** [f. Isol(ation + -ette.] The proprietary name of a type of infants' incubator.

1949 *Official Gaz.* (U.S. Patent Office) 7 June 45/2 [Trade-mark] No. 542,499 Air Shields, Inc., Hatboro, Pa... Isolette. For Infant Incubators. **1950** *Collier's* 1 Apr. 71/2 Through the isolettes the baby can be seen at all times, yet need never be moved or exposed. **1951** *Trade Marks Jrnl.* 21 Feb. 182/1 Isolette... Incubators for the care of infants. Airshields, Inc.., Hatboro,..Pennsylvania, United States of America; Manufacturers. **1962** *Jrnl. Pediatrics* Aug. 306/1 Four model C 77 Isolette incubators were used. Two of these were equipped with an Infant Servo-Controller. **1970** *Daily Colonist* (Victoria, B.C.) 27 Feb. 23/2 Mrs. Margaret Kienast..got her first look at her brood [*sc.* quintuplets] last Wednesday when she was brought from her room to the isolette in the centre's babies hospital.

isoleucine (əisoliū·sīn). *Biochem.* [ad. G. *isoleucin* (F. Ehrlich 1903, in *Zeitschr. Ver. d. Deut. Zucker-Ind.* LIII. 821), f. *iso-* Iso- b + *leucin* Leucin.] An amino-acid of which the dextrorotatory or L-form is an essential nutrient and a general constituent of proteins; 1-amino-2-methylvaleric acid, $CH_3CH_2CH(CH_3)CH(NH_2)COOH$.

1903 *Jrnl. Chem. Soc.* LXXXIV. i. 796 The author has isolated leucine and a new compound, *d isol*eucine, isomeric with it. *d-iso*Leucine crystallises in shining rods or leaflets. **1936** *Jrnl. Biol. Chem.* CXIV. 89 Leucine and isoleucine have been isolated in considerable quantities by extracting the dried, defatted mycelium of *Aspergillus syndowi* with acetone. **1962** *Lancet* 6 Jan. 26/1 They demonstrated a marked elevation of four amino-acids in the blood and urine—namely, the three branched-chain aminoacids (leucine, isoleucine, and valine) and also methionine.

isolex, -lexic, isoline: see *ISO-. **isolichenin:** see *ISO- b.

isologue (əi·sǫlǫg). *Org. Chem.* Also (*U.S.*) isolog. [a. F. *isologue* (C. Gerhardt *Traité de Chim. Org.* (1853) I. II. 127): see Iso- and -LOGUE.] Each of two or more isologous compounds.

1889 in *Cent. Dict.* **1924** *Chem. Abstr.* XVIII. 2158 Preparation of the thiopene isolog of cocaine. **1949** G. B. BACHMAN *Org. Chem.* xi. 110 Propanoic, propenoic, and propynoic acids are isologs of each other. **1965** *Jrnl. Med. Chem.* VIII. 846/1 While the former compound has a pK_a of 7·7, that of its selenium isolog was found to be 4·68± 0·05. **1970** *Tetrahedron* XXVI. 2151 (*heading*) NMR studies on the conformation of acetylcholine isologues.

isologous, *a.* Add: [First formed as F. *isologue* (C. Gerhardt *Traité de Chim. Org.* (1853) I. II. 127).]

b. Applied to each of two or more chemically similar compounds having some difference in composition other than a multiple of CH_2; now usu. applied *spec.* to compounds which have different atoms of the same valency at some position(s) in the molecule but are otherwise of identical molecular structure.

1884 *Jrnl. Chem. Soc.* XLVI. 12 In the author's results differences of Br_2 in isologous compounds, as allyl and dibromopropyl alcohols, correspond with differences of specific volume varying from 49·96 to 59·14. **1931** F. J. MOORE *Hist. Chem.* (ed. 2) xiv. 163 By isologous compounds Gerhardt understood substances of analogous function like acetic and benzoic acids whose formulæ showed some other difference than CH_2. **1959** *Jrnl. Amer. Chem. Soc.* LXXXI. 6272/1 (*heading*) Partition of isologous oxygen, sulfur and selenium compounds between buffers and organic solvents. **1964** *Jrnl. Med. Chem.* VII. 229/1 Selenoacyl compounds undergo aminolysis much more readily than isologous thioacyl compounds.

2. *Med.* and *Biol.* Genetically identical, esp. with respect to immunological factors; derived from another individual that is genetically identical or belongs to the same inbred strain; carried out between such individuals.

1955 *Jrnl. Nat. Cancer Inst.* XV. 1023 Lorenz, Congdon and Uphoff have increased the 30-day survival time of mice..by the injection of isologous, homologous and, in some cases, heterologous bone marrow. **1959** *Folia Biologica* V. 24/1 An isologous combination..fulfils the conditions for reciprocal tolerance between the host and the haematopoietic tissue graft. **1961** [see *isoallelic* adj. s.v. *ISO-]. **1962** *Cancer Res.* XXII. 947 Sera from mice which had been rendered resistant against the isologous transplantation of Gross virus-induced lymphomas.. were found to be cytotoxic. *Ibid.*, Admixture of lymph node cells from isologous mice..inhibited the outgrowth. **1971** *Nature* 1 Oct. 310/2 Human antibodies..against diphtheria toxoid likewise disappear rapidly when injected into isologous human skin.

isolux (əi·sǫlɒks), *a.* Also **iso-lux.** [f. Iso- + L. *lux* light.] = *ISOPHOTAL *a.*

1911 A. P. TROTTER *Illumination* iv. 47 (*heading*) Contour lines of equal illumination or iso-lux curves, due to two lights at a distance apart equal to four times their height. **1926** J. W. T. WALSH *Photometry* iv. 99 An iso-lux diagram may be used to obtain a mental conception of the effect of a given system of light sources of known distribution. **1934** *Archit. Rev.* LXXV. 66 (*caption*) Isolux diagram. This should be read similar to a contour map, the rings representing foot candle intensities on a plane 2 ft. 6 in. above the floor. **1967** E. CHAMBERS *Photolitho-Offset* xi. 164 With the glass screen the unit dots grow by exposure to a graded pattern formed by diffraction effects and..their contour shapes follow the isolux lines of equal intensity.

isolysin, isomagnetic: see *ISO-. **isomaltose:** see *ISO- b.

isomer. Add: **2.** *Physics.* A nucleus having the same atomic number and mass number but different radioactive properties, as a result of being in a different, long-lived, energy state from which a transition is inhibited; *esp.* one in a metastable excited state rather than the ground state. Also called *nuclear isomer.*

1934 *Physical Rev.* XLV. 729/2 The introduction of isomers may be of help for the removal of existing contradictions in the estimation of neutronic mass from different nuclear reactions. **1950** GLASSTONE *Sourcebk. Atomic Energy* x. 278/1 The second class consists of genetically related isomers,..in which the metastable state decays to the ground state with a definite half life. **1955** R. D. EVANS *Atomic Nucleus* iii. 97 Isobaric isotopes with distinguishable nuclear properties are called isomers. **1968** F. B. MORINIGO tr. *H. von Buttlar's Nucl. Physics* xiv. 478 If the half-life is larger than 1 msec, the state is called a nuclear isomer (the choice of 1 msec for this definition is arbitrary).

isomerase (əisǫ·mərēiz, -s). *Biochem.* [f. ISOMER + *-ASE.] Any enzyme which brings about an isomerization reaction; orig. applied to two particular enzymes (see quots. 1943, 1944).

1943 I. BANGA in *Stud. Inst. Med. Chem. Univ. Szeged* III. 67 When ADP had been incubated with isomerase, the product was split by actomyosin which suggested that isomerase had changed the molecular structure of ADP. It was for this reason that the name isomerase was given to the new protein. **1944** *Jrnl. Biol. Chem.* CLVI. 109 Triose phosphate isomerase (or more briefly isomerase) is an enzyme..which catalyzes the reaction glyceraldehyde phosphate ⇌ dihydroxyacetone phosphate. **1953** *Ibid.* CCI. 83 *Escherichia coli* contains an adaptive isomerase catalyzing the equilibrium, D-arabinose ⇌ D-ribulose. **1963** C. H. DOERING tr. *Karlson's Introd. Mod. Biochem.* ix. 173 Two enzyme systems are involved in the biosynthesis of uroporphyrin III from porphobilinogen: a deaminase and an isomerase. **1972** J. R. WHITAKER *Princ. Enzymol. for Food Scientists* xiv. 417 The 'isomerases' are enzymes which bring about an isomerization of the substrate. The name is formed on the order 'substrate prefix-isomerase'. The prefix indicates the type of isomerization involved, e.g., 'maleate *cis-trans*-isomerase'.

isomeric, *a.* Add: **1. b.** *Physics.* Of, pertaining to, or designating nuclear isomers; *isomeric transition,* a radioactive transition from a metastable state to a lower energy state of the same nuclide.

1934 *Physical Rev.* XLV. 729/1 Another consequence of the introduction of negative protons is the possibility of the existence of isomeric nuclei, that is, nuclei with the same charge and mass but different internal structure. **1937** *Ibid.* LI. 1011 The 18 minute, 4·2 hour, and 35 hour activities must all belong to Br^{80} and Br^{82}, i.e. one of these isotopes appears to exist in two isomeric forms, from which it decays with different periods. **1950** GLASSTONE *Sourcebk. Atomic Energy* x. 276/1 Over seventy examples of nuclear isomerism have been discovered, and the phenomenon of decay by isomeric transition, that is, by the spontaneous conversion of one nuclear isomer into another, has been elucidated. In most instances there are isomeric pairs only, but triple isomerism has been observed in a few cases. **1955** R. D. EVANS *Atomic Nucleus* vi. 231 By the usual definition, an isomeric level is one whose half-period is 'measurably' long. **1970** MARMIER & SHELDON *Physics of Nuclei & Particles* II. xv. 1276 Those nuclei whose ground-state configuration is modified by the preferential-filling rule would be expected to display low-lying excited states whose configuration corresponds to that of an unmodified ground state; because of the large spin change occasioned by this effect, the excited state is usually an isomeric state.

isomerism. Add: **b.** *Physics.* The fact or condition of being nuclear isomers.

1938 R. W. LAWSON tr. *Hevesy & Paneth's Man. Radioactivity* (ed. 2) x. 124 This isotope of silver..has two half-value periods, 24·5 m. and 8·2 d., the former being associated with positron emission, and the latter with the emission of β- and γ-rays... Here we are confronted with the phenomenon of nuclear isomerism. **1950** [see *ISOMERIC *a.* 1 b].

isomerization (əisǫ:mĕrəizēi·ʃən). *Chem.* [f. *ISOMERIZ(E *v.* + -ATION.] The conversion of a compound into an isomer of itself.

1891 *Chem. News* 27 Nov. 274/1 The isomerisation is complete at 140°–170°. **1946** *Industr. Chemist* XXII. 45/1 Since 1944 Tide Water Associated Oil Company, California, has operated a liquid-phase pentane isomerisation plant of the Shell type. **1971** *Sci. Amer.* Dec. 48/3 Isomerization increases the compactness of gasoline molecules, thereby improving the fuel's antiknock quality.

isomerize (əisǫ·mĕrəiz), *v. Chem.* [f. ISOMER + -IZE I.] *trans.* and *intr.* To change *into* or *to* an isomer (of the original substance).

1891 *Chem. News* 27 Nov. 274/1 Monosubstituted acetylenes with primary alkyl radicles are isomerised to bisubstituted acetylenes. **1903** *Notices Proc. R. Inst.* (1906) XVII. 100 It is isomerised into the quinonoid form by the addition of water. **1920** *Biochem. Jrnl.* XIV. 185 The free oxonium base (III) which more or less easily isomerises into the colourless pseudo-base (II). **1924** *Jrnl. Chem. Soc.* CXXV. II. 2545 These cycloids isomerise to hydroxyamidines at the moment of their formation. **1955** PINES & MAVITY in B. T. Brooks et al. *Chem. Petroleum Hydrocarbons* III. xxxix. 44 Incapable of isomerizing to a six membered ring compound, cyclopentane showed quite low reactivity in the presence of aluminium chloride. **1971** *Sci. Amer.* Dec. 48/3 The straight-chain saturated hydrocarbons can be catalytically isomerized to more compact structures.

Hence **iso·merized** *ppl. a.*, having undergone isomerization; **iso·merizing** *ppl. a.* and *vbl. sb.*

1908 *Chem. Abstr.* II. 1970 The velocity and the limits of the isomerizing power of a solvent are independent of each other. **1941** *Jrnl. Amer. Chem. Soc.* LXIII. 519 The question arises whether these catalysts have any isomerizing properties. **1942** *Canad. Chem. & Process Industries* XXVI. 637/2 The most outstanding recent development allied with fatty acids lies in the field of synthetic drying oils. Of these, two are outstanding—dehydrated castor oil, and the isomerized oils with conjugated double bond structure. **1954** Isomerized [see *CYCLIZE *v.*]. **1963** *Agric. & Biol. Chem.* XXVII. A4/1 (*heading*) Identification and cultural conditions of glucose isomerizing bacteria. **1965** NYLÉN & SUNDERLAND *Mod. Surface Coatings* iii. 99 Isomerized linseed oil dries more rapidly than the normal oil.

isometric, *a.* Add: **4.** Delete the reference to ISOTONIC *a.* 2 and substitute: [ad. G. *isometrisch* (A. Fick *Mech. Arbeit u. Wärmeentwickelung bei d. Muskelthätigkeit* (1882) vii. 112).] Of, pertaining to, or designating muscular action in which tension is developed but appreciable shortening of the muscle is prevented. (Examples.)

1891 A. D. WALLER *Introd. Human Physiol.* ix. 330 If a muscle contracts against a large resistance..so that it can shorten very little, the curve described by a lever attached to it is termed 'isometric'. **1895** *Proc. R. Soc.* LVII. 423 The shortening of the muscle is prevented by resistance (isometric contraction of Fick). **1900** [see ISOTONIC *a.* 2]. **1920** *Jrnl. Physiol.* LIV. 85 During the development of tension in an isometric contraction both heat and potential energy are being produced by the muscle. **1951** [see *ISOTONIC *a.* 3]. **1969** *New Yorker* 20 Dec. 43/2 He neither drinks nor smokes, and he devotes an hour a day to yoga and isometric exercises. **1971** [see *ISOTONIC *a.* 3]. **1973** *Sci. Amer.* Mar. 83 Whereas a machine only performs mechanical work when a force moves through a distance, muscles consume energy when they are in tension but not moving (doing what is sometimes called 'isometric' work).

5. *Physics.* Indicating, or taking place under, conditions of constant volume.

1873 J. W. GIBBS in *Trans. Connecticut Acad. Arts & Sci.* II. 311 The points associated with states of equal volume will form lines, which..we may also call isometric. **1912** G. A. GOODENOUGH *Princ. Thermodynamics* (ed. 2) ii. 22 Lines of constant volume [are called] isometric lines. **1957** V. M. FAIRES *Thermodynamics* (ed. 3) v. 69 For a reversible steady flow isometric process..we have the energy equation from equation (7A).

6. *Biol.* = *ISOGONIC *a.*[2]

1950 J. S. HUXLEY in *Proc. R. Soc.* B. CXXXVII. 467 In an isometric organ we find no change in the proportions of its parts with increase in its absolute size.

7. *Math.* That is an isometry; related by an isometry. Const. *to.*

1952 C. C. KRIEGER tr. *Sierpinski's Gen. Topology* vi. 100 Two metric spaces consisting of the same elements but with different metrics may be isometric. **1959** L. F. BORON tr. *M. A. Naimark's Normed Rings* i. 38 Two metric spaces X, X' are said to be isometric if there exists an isometric mapping of X onto X'. **1966** J. H. CADWELL *Topics in Recreational Math.* xi. 117 A pattern is characterised by the set of isometric motions that bring it into self-coincidence, and this set forms a discrete group. **1968** E. T. COPSON *Metric Spaces* iv. 53 If the points **a, b** of A^* correspond to the points a and b of M, we have proved that $\rho^*(\mathbf{a}, \mathbf{b}) = \rho(a, b)$, so that A^* is isometric to M.

B. *sb.* **1.** *Physics.* A line in a diagram that corresponds to or represents states of equal volume.

1873 [see *isopiestic* adj. s.v. *ISO-]. **1936** *Industr. & Engin. Chem.* Feb. 261/2 Not only are the isometrics of the pure substances themselves substantially straight, but the same is also true for mixtures. **1963** OBERT & GAGGIOLI *Thermodynamics* (ed. 2) x. 215 For the real gas, the isometrics are displaced from the origin and are either straight or slightly curved.

2. *pl.* A system of stationary physical exercises in which muscles are exercised isometrically by pitting one against another or against an unyielding object. orig. *U.S.*

1962 *Scholastic Coach* Nov. 31/1 This concludes a series of three comprehensive articles on isometrics. **1964** *Life* 17 Apr. 47/1 In 1921 Atlas began preaching the muscle-building system he called Dynamic Tension, which pits one muscle against another. Now variations of his system, in which muscles struggle against immobile objects, are the latest U.S. exercise fad. Scientists lump the systems under one fancy word, isometrics. **1970** *New Scientist* 20 Aug. 365/1 Isometrics, but recently hailed as the key to the good life, have also now been condemned for dangerously rocketing the blood pressure.

isometrically, *adv.* (in Dict. s.v. ISOMETRICAL *a.*). Add: **2.** *Physiol.* Under isometric conditions (see *ISOMETRIC *a.* 4).

1920 *Jrnl. Physiol.* LIV. 84 When a muscle is stimulated isometrically it passes gradually into a new elastic condition. **1945** *Amer. Jrnl. Physiol.* CXLIV. 477 Strings were tied to the tendons and the contractions were recorded isometrically under an initial tension of 50 grams. **1973** *Nature* 23 Feb. 537/2 The muscle twitch was measured isometrically.

3. *Math.* By means of or in the manner of an isometry.

1959 L. F. BORON tr. *Naimark's Normed Rings* ii. 181 Two normed rings R and R' are said to be isometrically isomorphic if there exists an isometric isomorphism of R onto R'. **1971** E. C. DADE in Powell & Higman *Finite Simple Groups* viii. 318 The map $\phi \to \phi^*$ sends x_+ isometrically into x_-.

isometry (əisǫ·mĭtri). [ad. Gr. ἰσομετρία equality of measure (f. μέτρος measure): see -Y[3].] **1.** *Math.* A one-to-one transformation of one metric space into another that preserves the distances or metrics between each pair of points.

1941 BIRKHOFF & MACLANE *Survey Mod. Algebra* vi. 128 An obvious example is furnished by the symmetries of the cube. Geometrically speaking, these are the one–one transformations which preserve distances on the cube. They are known as 'isometries', and are 48 in number. **1965** S. LANG *Algebra* xiv. 356 If σ is a linear isomorphism, and is metric, then we say that σ is an isometry. **1966** J. H. CADWELL *Topics in Recreational Math.* xi. 113 A fundamental property of isometries is that any two carried out in succession define a third. Thus if isometry U takes figure F into figure F', while V takes F' into F'', their combined effect, taken in this order, is an isometry carrying F into F''.

2. *Biol.* = *ISOGONY (s.v. *ISOGONIC *a.*[2]).
1950 J. S. HUXLEY in *Proc. R. Soc.* B. CXXXVII. 465 Isometry is used of the special case when the organ grows at the same rate as the body.

isomorph. Add: **2.** *Linguistics.* A line in a linguistic atlas connecting places exhibiting identical or nearly identical morphological forms; a morphological isogloss.
1921 E. C. ROEDDER in *Jrnl. Eng. & Germ. Philol.* XX. 182 The boundary lines of present dialects, with their maze of..isomorphs,..and isotaxes, i.e., lines connecting places of identical or nearly identical..forms,..and syntactical peculiarities. **1926** *Germanic Rev.* I. iv. 303 Like the larger dialects, they would have to be portioned off against each other by isophones, isomorphs, isolexes, and isotaxes, i.e., lines of agreement in sound, form, word (meaning), and syntax. **1937** J. ORR tr. *Iordan's Introd. Romance Ling.* iii. 215 Val d'Ajol alone offers certain well-marked individual features... A group of 'isophones' and 'isomorphs' passes exactly through the point where the two valleys..investigated join each other.

isomorphic, *a.* **2.** (Also *Logic* and *Linguistics.*) For 'groups' read 'groups or other sets' and add to def.: related by an isomorphism; that is an isomorphism. Const. *to, with.* (Earlier and later examples.)
1892 F. N. COLE tr. *Netto's Theory of Substitutions* iv. 83 If to every substitution of *G* correspond *q* substitutions of 𝔊, and to every substitution of 𝔊 *p* substitutions of *G*, then *G* and 𝔊 are said to be (*p-q*)-fold isomorphic, or if *p* and *q* are not specified, manifold isomorphic. If $p = q = 1$, the groups are said to be simply isomorphic. **1900** *Ann. Math.* II. 48 Two abstract groups *G, H* which are 1–1 isomorphic are evidently, as far as structure goes, not distinct. **1934** J. A. ELDRIDGE *Physical Basis of Things* xxviii. 372 The scientist studies the infinite variety of nature's processes, acquaints himself with nature's group of operations, and then attempts to find a representation, in models or symbols, which is isomorphic therewith. **1937** A. SMEATON tr. *Carnap's Logical Syntax of Lang.* IV. 224 If S_1 is reversibly transformable in S_2 in respect of symbols, then S_1 and S_2 are called isomorphic. **1952** H. B. VEATCH *Intentional Logic* I. iii. 36 Whether it is necessary and proper that the structure of logical entities should correspond to, or be isomorphic with, or be similar to the structure of the facts which they are supposed to signify or represent. **1962** C. O. FRAKE in J. A. Fishman *Readings Sociol. of Lang.* (1968) 437 The items and arrangements of a structural description of the language code need not be isomorphic with the categories and propositions of the message. **1965** PATTERSON & RUTHERFORD *Elem. Abstr. Algebra* ii. 51 In other words, G_2 is isomorphic to G_1 if G_1 is isomorphic to G_2. **1968** J. LYONS *Introd. Theoret. Ling.* ii. 55 To the degree that the meanings of one language can be brought into one-to-one correspondence with those of another we will say that the two languages are semantically isomorphic (have the same semantic structure). **1971** *Nature* 22 Jan. 233/2 We can imagine the state of the whole system described by the states $S_1, S_2,..S_n$ of its S_n components. These values will determine a unique point in the *n* dimensional phase-space *S* such that there is an isomorphic correspondence between points in the space and the states of the system. **1973** J. HINTIKKA *Logic, Lang.-Games & Information* ii. 28 In order for anything to be an isomorphic representation of anything else, they must both have a certain structure.
3. *Biol.* Of the same or an analogous form.
1888 *Nature* 20 Dec. 180/1 Dicholophus..has assumed peculiar Raptorial characters isomorphic with those of Gypogeranus, which is a true bird of prey.
4. *Bot.* In algæ and certain fungi, designating a type of alternation of generations in which the two forms are morphologically similar.
1935 F. E. FRITSCH *Struct. & Reprod. Algae* I. 52 Isomorphic (homologous) alternation occurs in each of the three largest classes of the Algae. **1951** M. O. P. IYENGAR in G. M. Smith *Man. Phycology* iii. 59 In the third type of life-cycle [of Chlorophyta], there is an alternation of two generations both externally similar... This kind of alternation has been called by Fritsch isomorphic alternation. *Ibid.* 60 Isomorphic types very probably originated from haploid types. **1964** E. J. H. CORNER *Life of Plants* vi. 93 Their [*sc.* slender brown seaweeds'] life-cycle is an isomorphic alternation of diploid sporophyte with haploid gametophyte. **1964** J. S. KARLING *Synchytrium* iii. 51 In 1905 Lowenthal described fusion of two motile isomorphic cells in *S[ynchytrium] taraxaci* and illustrated what appears to be a binucleate zygote. **1970** RAVEN & CURTIS *Biol. Plants* vi. 438/2 In *Ulva*, the alternation is isomorphic—that is, the mature sporophytes are morphologically identical to mature gametophytes.
5. *Linguistics.* Similar in morphological structure, having similar morphological forms.
1950 *Language Learning* III. iii. 93 The presentation of such items seems to be indicated in terms of lists the members of which are isomorphic (i.e. show similar differences between morpheme alternants). **1954** PEI & GAYNOR *Dict. Ling.* 107 *Isomorphic lines*, lines on a linguistic map, indicating the approximate boundaries of the speech-areas in which a uniformity in grammatical forms, inflections, etc. can be observed. **1957** S. POTTER *Mod. Ling.* vi. 134 On more detailed [linguistic] maps we might construct different kinds of lines called isophonic, isotonic, isomorphic, or isosyntagmic, which would record differentiating features of sound, tone, word-form and clause-structure respectively.
Hence **isomo·rphically** *adv.*, by an isomorphism (sense 2); in an isomorphic manner.
1935 *Amer. Jrnl. Math.* LVII. 434 By means of $P_i \rightarrow P^*_i$ we thus map the algebra 𝔄 reduced modulo $(1-u)$ isomorphically upon itself. **1960** BROWN & GILMAN in J. A. Fishman *Readings Sociol. of Lang.* (1968) 266 There are a large number of expressions of subordination which are patterned isomorphically with *T* [*sc.* a familiar pronoun such as *tu*] and *V* [*sc.* a polite pronoun such as *vous*]. **1971** E. C. DADE in Powell & Higman *Finite Simple Groups* viii. 258 R_i sends the algebra A_i isomorphically onto $\text{Hom}_F(I_i, I_i)$ for all $i = 1,..., k$.

isomorphism. **2.** (Also *Logic* and *Linguistics.*) For 'groups' read 'groups or other sets' and add to def.: An exact correspondence as regards the number of constituent elements and the relations between them; *spec.* a one-to-one homomorphism. (Examples.)
1892 F. N. COLE tr. *Netto's Theory of Substitutions* iv. 83 The correspondence of two groups as just defined is called isomorphism. **1897** W. BURNSIDE *Theory of Groups of Finite Order* xi. 222 A correspondence between the operations of a group, such that to every operation *S* there corresponds a single operation *S'*, while to the product *ST* of two operations there corresponds the product *S'T'* of the corresponding operations, is said to define an isomorphism of the group itself. **1941** W. V. QUINE in P. A. Schilpp *Philos. A. N. Whitehead* 160 The theory of relation numbers is the general theory of isomorphism, i.e., of structural identity among relations. **1949** HUTTEN & REICHENBACH tr. *H. Reichenbach's Theory of Probability* vi. § 41. 207 By showing that both the frequency interpretation and the geometrical interpretation satisfy the axioms of the formal system of probability..we have demonstrated the isomorphism, or structural identity, of the two interpretations. **1956** E. M. PATTERSON *Topology* iv. 81 An isomorphism ϕ between two groups G_1, G_2 is a one–one transformation ϕ: $G_1 \rightarrow G_2$ of G_1 onto G_2 which preserves the group operation. **1962** *Anthropol. Ling.* June 26 An analysis of the special uses that an individual may make of other dialects..may tell us something about the range of prestige variants and the relative isomorphism of prestige scales that are involved in inter-dialect interchange. **1963** J. LYONS *Structural Semantics* ii. 17 In so far as semantic and distributional criteria converge on the establishment of the same [grammatical] units, this is due to the admitted partial isomorphism between the 'expression-plane' and the 'content-plane' of language. **1965** PATTERSON & RUTHERFORD *Elem. Abstr. Algebra* iii. 77 An isomorphism of a ring R_1 onto a ring R_2 is a one–one mapping *f* of R_1 onto R_2 such that, for all $x_1, x_2 \in R_1$, we have $f(x_1 + x_2) = f(x_1) + f(x_2), f(x_1x_2) = f(x_1)f(x_2)$... In a similar manner, we define isomorphisms between integral domains and fields. **1971** *Sci. Amer.* Aug. 96/3 Boole.. noticed that there was a considerable similarity (in fact a mathematical isomorphism) between the rules that govern the use in logic of the connectives 'and', 'or' and 'not', and the operations on sets of, respectively, intersection, union and complementation. **1973** J. HINTIKKA *Logic, Lang.-Games & Information* ii. 42 The basic idea of Wittgenstein's picture theory is the idea of an isomorphism obtaining between language and reality.., an isomorphism which can be established by any correlation or mapping.
3. *Biol.* A similarity of appearance displayed by organisms having different genotypes.
1902 *Encycl. Brit.* XXVI. 255/2 A few fundamental characters are better indications of the affinities of given groups of birds than a great number of agreements if these can be shown to be cases of isomorphism or heterophyletic, convergent analogy. **1920** I. F. & W. D. HENDERSON *Dict. Sci. Terms* 158/1 *Isomorphism*, apparent similarity of individuals of different race or species.
4. *Psychol.* The correspondence assumed to exist between mental perception and physiological processes.
1930 W. KÖHLER *Gestalt Psychol.* ii. 46 But I should have ever so much difficulty in trying to relate definite experiences to definite processes so long as I failed to assume one specific relationship between the two orders, viz., that of *congruence or isomorphism in their systematic properties.* This principle is sometimes formulated more explicitly in a number of 'psycho-physical axioms'. **1937** R. H. THOULESS *Gen. & Social Psychol.* (ed. 2) xii. 241 One of the boldest of the Gestalt speculations has been that of the 'isomorphism' of brain processes and mental processes. **1951** R. B. MACLEOD in Rohrer & Sherif *Social Psychol. at Crossroads* 223 In the doctrine of isomorphism, however, it is asserted that the all-important parallel to perceptual organization is to be found not in the patterning of stimulus processes but rather in the immediately underlying organization of brain activities. **1970** H. C. SHANDS *Semiotic Approaches to Psychiatry* xviii. 290 The evidence suggests strongly that at every level there is an isomorphism between physiological and psychological mechanisms [in cancer patients] when both are abstractly considered.

isomorphously (əisǫmǭ·ɹfəsli), *adv. Min.* [f. ISOMORPHOUS *a.* + -LY[2].] In such a way as to produce isomorphous substances.
1901 *Mineral. Mag.* XIII. 45 Miersite..mixes isomorphously with marshite (CuI) on the one hand, and on the other forms intimate intergrowths with iodyrite. **1906** *Jrnl. Chem. Soc.* LXXXIX. II. 1148 Chlorine and fluorine sometimes replace each other isomorphously. **1928** *Amer. Mineralogist* XIII. 52 $AlAlO_3$ may enter $CaMgSi_2O_6$.. isomorphously to as much as 25 per cent. **1947** *Q. Rev.* I. 254 When it is found that F' can replace OH' isomorphously, as in the apatites..this can be taken as strong presumptive evidence that the OH..is ionic. **1963** *Geochemistry* 1173 Manganese..is associated with the bivalent iron and calcium which it replaces isomorphously in the rock-forming minerals.

isoniazid (əisonəi·ăzid). *Pharm.* [f. *isoni(cotinic acid* (s.v. *ISO- b) + *HYDR)AZID(E.] A white or colourless crystalline compound, $C_5H_5N \cdot CO \cdot NH \cdot NH_2$, which has bacteriostatic properties against mycobacteria and is used esp. in the treatment of tuberculosis.
1953 *Jrnl. Pharmacol. & Exper. Therap.* CVII. 219 Isonicotinic acid hydrazide (Nydrazid), generically designated as isoniazid, has been shown to be an effective chemotherapeutic agent against experimental..and human tuberculosis. **1962** *Lancet* 29 Dec. 1364/2 In the second phase, since the bacilli are no longer multiplying rapidly and resistant mutants are therefore unlikely to appear, a single drug only—isoniazid—need be continued to kill off those remaining. **1970** PASSMORE & ROBSON *Compan. Med. Stud.* II. xx. 32/2 Isoniazid (isonicotinic acid hydrazine INH) is the most powerful and effective antituberculous drug. **1973** TURNER & RICHENS *Clin. Pharmacol.* xiv. 186 Isoniazid can interfere with the metabolism of pyridoxine and can cause peripheral neuritis when prolonged courses are given.

isonicotinic, isonitrile: see *ISO- b. **isonomaly:** see *ISO-.

isonomia (əisonōu·miă). = ISONOMY.
1853 E. CREASY *Rise & Progress Eng. Constitution* xiii. 198 There is no part of our constitution so admirable as this equality of civil rights, this *isonomia*, which the philosophers of ancient Greece only hoped to find in democratical government. **1926** *Contemp. Rev.* Oct. 485 It was the *name* 'isonomia' that so commended a democracy.

isonuclear: see *ISO-.

isooctane (əiso,ǫ·ktēin). Also **iso-octane.** [f. ISO- + OCTANE.] † **a.** 2-Methylheptane, $CH_3 \cdot (CH_2)_4 \cdot CH(CH_3) \cdot CH_3$, a liquid hydrocarbon that occurs in petroleum. *Obs.*
1909 L. CLARKE in *Jrnl. Amer. Chem. Soc.* XXXI. 107 In this paper are described the preparation and properties of iso-octane or 2-methyl heptane... Iso-octane is the ninth hydrocarbon to be prepared in the series C_8H_{18}. **1911** *Ibid.* XXXIII. 524 2-Methylheptane (or iso-octane) has the boiling point 116°. [**1966** *McGraw-Hill Encycl. Sci. & Technol.* I. 249/1 Although the name isooctane correctly designates 2-methylheptane, it should be avoided because of the unfortunate use of the misnomer 'isooctane' in the petroleum industry to represent 2,2,4-trimethylpentane.]
b. 2,2,4-Trimethylpentane, $(CH_3)_3C \cdot CH_2 \cdot CH(CH_3) \cdot CH_3$, a colourless liquid hydrocarbon which is used in aviation fuels and as a solvent and which, because of its good anti-knock properties, is taken as a standard in the determination of octane numbers (being assigned the number 100).
This use of the name does not conform to the convention for using *iso-* described s.v. *ISO- b.
1932 *Bureau of Standards Jrnl. Res.* (U.S.) IX. 269 As a criterion for the purity of commercial 'iso-octane', it is desirable to have a reliable value for the freezing point. **1938** *Jrnl. Chem. Soc.* 239 *iso*Octane..is now produced commercially for blending purposes from *iso*butylene via di*iso*butylene. **1946** *Industr. Chemist* XXII. 519/1 This small yield of *iso*octane was the backbone of the 87 octane no. finished aviation grade produced commercially before the war. **1954** D. M. DESOUTTER *All about Aircraft* vii. 120/2 A fuel of 130 octane is one which allows a standard test engine to give 30 per cent more power than it would when using pure iso-octane. **1962** *Biochim. & Biophys. Acta* LXI. 467 It occurred to us that the use of an organic solvent to detach lipid and lipoprotein from rat-liver microsomes might be possible, and this note presents results of the successful use of isooctane. **1971** R. J. & J. S. FESSENDEN *Basis Org. Chem.* ii. 36 At one time, the branched-chain alkane erroneously named isooctane was the best antiknock fuel known. It was given an octane number of 100.

iso-osmotic: see *ISO-.

isopach (əi·sopæk). [f. ISO- + Gr. παχ-ύς thick.] **1.** *Geol.* = *ISOPACHYTE.
1918 *Private Let. U.S. Geol. Survey* (G. & C. Merriam Co. files) 10 May, *Isopach, isopachous*—noun and adjective, referring to lines on a map that shows equal thicknesses of beds, e.g. coal beds. **1925** *Bull. Amer. Assoc. Petroleum Geologists* IX. 890 The term 'isopach' is used to designate lines through points of equal thickness. *Ibid.*, The isopachs swing from a general east-and-west direction to the north. **1957** *Bull. Geol. Survey Gt. Brit.* XII. 55 The total stratigraphical thickness in feet at each locality was plotted and isopachs drawn through points of equal thickness. **1969** *Nature* 8 Nov. 536/2 The measured thickness of the pyroclastic deposits at various localities and the proposed isopachs are shown in Fig. 2. The isopachs generally extend south-eastwards from the eruptive centres, indicating distribution under the influence of a prevailing north-westerly wind.
2. = *ISOPACHIC *sb.*
1936 *Jrnl. R. Aeronaut. Soc.* XL. 55 An isopach is defined..as lines along which the sum of the principal stresses is constant. **1962** J. C. JAEGER *Elasticity, Fracture & Flow* (ed. 2) iv. 182 Isopachs are curves of constant mean stress $\sigma_1 + \sigma_2$.

isopachic (əisopæ·kik), *a.* and *sb.* [f. as prec. + -IC.] **A.** *adj.* Corresponding to or depicting the locus of points in a body where the sum of the principal stresses has the same value.
1931 COKER & FILON *Treat. Photo-Elasticity* ii. 178 By observations with the lateral extensometer we can..obtain..the curves for which $P+Q$ has an equal value. These may be briefly referred to as Isopachic curves, or curves of equal thickness. **1950** M. HETÉNYI *Handbk. Exper. Stress Analysis* xvii. 910 If the isochromatic and isopachic lines for a given model and loading are known, it

becomes..simple..to evaluate the two principal stresses at any point by direct addition and subtraction of the equivalent values. **1972** *Phys. Bull.* May 276/3 The use of double exposure holography to obtain isopachic–isochromatic fringe patterns in the reconstructed image has also been reported.

B. *sb.* An isopachic line or curve.

1931 Coker & Filon *Treat. Photo-Elasticity* ii. 179 The lines of equal *P* are..obtained by taking successive intersections of isochromatics and isopachics, the parameters of the isochromatics going up one at a time, those of the isopachics going down one at a time; or conversely. **1958** Condon & Odishaw *Handbk. Physics* iii. vi. 88/1 Curves of constant $p+q$ are called isopachics.

isopachous (əisopæ·kəs, əisǫ·păkəs), *a. Geol.* [f. as prec. + -ous.] Depicting or pertaining to isopachs (sense *1); that is an isopach.

1913 *Bull. U.S. Geol. Survey* No. 537. 89 (*caption*) Sketch map showing lines along which a coal bed is of equal thickness (isopachous lines), drawn for use in valuation of coal land. **1938** *Bull. Amer. Assoc. Petroleum Geologists* XXII. 425 (*heading*) Thinning of Devonian shown by isopachous lines. **1940** *Ibid.* XXIV. 2151 (*heading*) Isopachous studies in Michigan. **1968** Harbaugh & Merriam *Computer Applications in Stratigr. Analysis* v. 87/1 A thickness map (also termed an isopachous map)..portrays the interval between two stratigraphic horizons.

isopachyte (əisopæ·kəit). *Geol.* [f. Iso- + Gr. παχύτ-ης thickness.] A line on a map or diagram joining points below which a particular stratum or group of strata has the same thickness.

1912 *Compt. Rend. XI Congrès Géol. Internat.* I. 250 A series of maps was prepared..and on them were drawn isopachytes, or lines marking points of equal thickness. **1946** *Nature* 13 July 49/2 The detailed stratigraphy of the Coal Measures, shown by isopachyte maps and many other data, gives an insight into the development of this sedimentary series. **1969** Bennison & Wright *Geol. Hist. Brit. Isles* iv. 77 Isopachytes for the Cambrian as a whole ..must be interpreted with caution.., but they provide some indication of the form of the Cambrian geosyncline in Wales.

isoparaffin, isopentane, isopentyl: see *iso- b.

isophane (əi·sofēin), **isophene** (-fīn). [f. as next; cf. Phen-, pheno-.] A line (imaginary or on a map) linking places in which seasonal biological phenomena (the flowering of plants, etc.) occur at the same time. Hence **isopha·nal, isophe·nal** *adjs.*

1918 A. D. Hopkins in *U.S. Dept. Agric. Monthly Weather Rev. Suppl.* IX. 8 (*caption*) Isophenal map of North America. *Ibid.* 9/1 Taking base maps of North America and of the major and minor political divisions, parallel lines (designated as isophanes) are drawn on them to define, according to the bioclimatic law, theoretical lines and zones of equal phenomena as to time of occurrence and equal bioclimatic conditions, at the same level. **1929** V. E. Shelford *Lab. & Field Ecol.* i. 15 An isophenal map was prepared with isophenes drawn through equal-event dates at the same altitude. **1931** *Trans. Entomol. Soc. Lond.* LXXIX. 183 Local conditions.. cause considerable departures in the actual dates of seasonal events from those indicated by isophanes. *Ibid.*, Instead of basing the isophanal map on degrees of latitude and longitude, he [*sc.* Znamenskii] made use of the mean annual isotherms. **1947** R. F. Daubenmire *Plants & Environment* iv. 219 From phenologic data maps can be drawn with lines (isophenes) connecting locations where plants are in the same stage of development at the same time. **1963** E. Mayr *Animal Species & Evolution* xiii. 362 This north–south cline is crossed by the isophenes, lines connecting all populations with the same phenotype.

isophane (əi·sofēin), *a. Pharm.* [f. Iso- + Gr. -φανης showing, appearing (f. φαίνειν to show, cause to appear).] **a.** Designating that ratio of protamine to insulin which, in a solution made by mixing solutions of the individual substances, gives rise to equal turbidity in two equal samples taken after a precipitate has been allowed to form when one sample has sufficient insulin added to it to precipitate all the protamine in it and the other a sufficient amount of protamine to precipitate all the insulin.

1946 Krayenbühl & Rosenberg in *Rep. Steno Memorial Hosp.* I. 65 The proportion of protamine to insulin must be nearly isophane. At isophane proportions the formation of crystals is rapid. **1950** *Federal Register* (U.S.) 2 Nov. 7363/2 The isophane ratio shall be expressed as milligrams of protamine per 100 U.S.P. Units of insulin. **1955** *Dispensatory U.S.A.* (ed. 25) 686/2 The most useful of these mixtures, for many patients, proved to be the 2:1 mixture of regular insulin and protamine zinc insulin. In this mixture protamine is present to the extent of about 0·5 mg. per 100 units of insulin, which is the combining proportion, or so-called isophane ratio, of protamine and insulin.

b. Applied to a crystalline mixture of insulin and protamine in the isophane ratio with zinc, which has longer-lasting effects than pure insulin. Also *ellipt.* as *sb.*

1954 A. Grollman *Pharmacol. & Therapeutics* (ed. 2) xxvi. 606 (*table*) NPH Insulin (Isophane). **1955** *Dispensatory U.S.A.* (ed. 25) 686/2 In preparing Isophane Insulin Injection, sufficient insulin is used to provide either 40 or 80 U.S.P. Insulin Units for each ml. of the Injection. **1955** *Brit. Med. Jrnl.* 19 Feb. 478/2 Having used isophane.. since November, 1953, and in more than 60 diabetics, I find it easily the most satisfactory one-shot-a-day insulin available. **1966** *Lancet* 24 Dec. 1389/2 A 20-year-old diabetic patient, who was poorly controlled on 45 units isophane insulin in the morning and 35 units isophane insulin in the evening, was admitted in diabetic ketoacidosis. **1968** Pond & Oakley in W. G. Oakley et al. *Clin. Diabetes* xxiii. 602 A comparable method of control by a single morning injection is the use of a mixture of isophane (NPH) and SI.

isophone (əi·sofōᵘn). *Linguistics.* [f. Iso- + Phone *sb.*[1]] A phonetic isogloss; also, a phonetic feature shared by speakers in contiguous areas. Hence **isopho·nic** *a.*

1921 E. C. Roedder in *Jrnl. Eng. & Germ. Philol.* XX. 182 The boundary lines of present dialects, with their maze of isophones,..and isotaxes, i.e., lines connecting places of identical or nearly identical sounds,..and syntactical peculiarities. **1926** *Germanic Rev.* I. iv. 286 A map of France with all isophonic lines would show the wildest maze and confusion. **1926** [see *isomorph 2]. **1932** W. L. Graff *Lang.* 364 There were isoglosses and isophones which contained the germs of later developments. **1935** *Univ. Mich. Publ. Lang. & Lit.* XIII. 23 We believe ..that these isophonic lines do reflect roughly at least approximate boundaries for eleven of the most important characteristics of the regional dialects of Middle English as they existed about the middle of the fourteenth century. *Ibid.* 32 The physiographical boundaries are an interpretation of the isophones and are therefore subject to the modifications that additional documentary evidence may bring. In some cases these modifications will result in a closer approximation of the isophones to the corresponding physiographical boundaries. **1936** *Trans. Philol. Soc. 1936* 79 It certainly raises the question as to how far the delimitation of dialects and dialect features in Middle English by means of 'isophones' can really be reliable. **1937** *Year's Work Eng. Stud. 1935* 42 The country marked out by 'isophonic' lines into ten areas, each of which presents a more or less distinct complex of dialect-characteristics. **1955** W. S. Avis in *Amer. Speech* XXX. 7 In a very loose way this boundary approximates an *r*-isophone. **1970** *English Studies* LI. 445 The new and very clear ā/ǭ isophone there [*sc.* in Lincolnshire] is an important result of the investigation.

isophot, var. *isophote.

isophotal (əisofōᵘ·tăl), *a.* [f. as next + -al.] Applied to an isophote and to a diagram depicting isophotes. Also as *sb.*, = *isophote.

1904 D. Burnett in *Trans. Amer. Inst. Electr. Engin.* XX. 74 The impression they convey would much more nearly accord with what actually occurs if the curves showed not the intensity of light in the various directions, but the lines along which the lighting is equal at any point. Such curves may be called 'isophotals', and while they are of the same general shape as intensity curves, their dimensions are as the square root of the radii. *Ibid.*, The tendency of enclosing an arc.., either in the interior gas globe or more particularly in the outer diffusing globe, is to make such an isophotal curve approach more nearly a circle. **1930** *Astrophysical Jrnl.* LXXI. 365 The total luminosity of the entire nebula out to the distance *r*/*a* is found by integrating successive elliptical rings on the assumption that the isophotal contours are all similar ellipses. **1964** *Jrnl. Geophysical Res.* LXIX. 487/1 These regions were characterized by systems of isophotal contour lines, sometimes occupying virtually the whole observed area. *Ibid.* 487/2 Isophotal sky maps. **1964** A. Cox *Syst. Optical Design* ix. 367 The contour lines are 'isophotals' mapping areas of equal intensity.

isophote (əi·sofōᵘt). Also **-phot** (-fǫt). [f. Iso- + Gr. φῶς, φωτ- light.] A line (imaginary or in a diagram) connecting points where the brightness or the illumination is the same. Also *transf.* (of radiation other than light).

1909 *Cent. Dict.* Suppl., Isophote. **1937** *Nature* 2 Oct. 577/1 The successive isophotes of the corona round the sun are nearly circular. **1957** G. E. Hutchinson *Treat. Limnol.* I. vi. 373 (*caption*) Isophots in 1000 cal. cm.$^{-2}$ received during April, May, June, and July on the Scandinavian Peninsula. **1959** Davies & Palmer *Radio Stud. Universe* iv. 47 In some cases the radio isophotes are far more extensive than their optical counterparts. **1966** E. Harrison-Jones in Hewitt & Vause *Lamps & Lighting* xxix. 466 In planning general window lighting of this kind..isophot diagrams are used to determine direct illumination. **1973** *Physics Bull.* July 417 (*caption*) Intensity map of elliptical galaxies NGC 4278 and 4283, showing the outermost faint isophotes.

isophotic (əisofōᵘ·tik), *a.* [f. as prec. + -ic.] = *isophotal *a.*

1931 *Nature* 14 Mar. 418/2 Diagrams are given, showing the isophotic lines in the two [Magellanic] clouds. **1935** E. A. Milne *Relativity, Gravitation & World-Struct.* xiv. 279 The circular shape of the observed isophotic contours near a nebular nucleus. **1971** *Jrnl. Astron. Soc. Canada* LXV. 251 (*heading*) Monochromatic photographs and isophotic contours of planetary nebulae.

isophthalate, isophthalic: see *iso- b. **isopiestic:** see *iso-.

isoplasty (əi·soplæsti). *Med.* and *Biol.* [f. Iso- + -plasty.] = *homoplasty, *homotransplantation. Hence **isopla·stic** *a.* = *homoplastic *a.* 2.

1923 Isoplasty, -plastic [see *homografting *vbl. sb.*]. **1929** *Ann. Surg.* XC. 926 Homoplasty, homeoplasty and isoplasty mean tissue transplantation from one individual to another of the same species.

isopleth (əi·sopleþ). [ad. Gr. ἰσοπληθ-ής equal in quantity, f. πλῆθος multitude, quantity.] **1.** [ad. G. *isoplethe* (C. A. Vogler *Anleitung zum Entwerfen graph. Tafeln* (1877) i. 7).] A line (either imaginary or on a map or diagram) connecting points for which some chosen quantity has the same value, the points (if on a diagram) being defined by two variables of which one is usually distance and the other either distance or time.

1909 in *Cent. Dict.* Suppl. **1911** N. Shaw *Forecasting Weather* 4 Isobars are isopleths of pressure, isotherms are isopleths of temperature, and so on. **1935** *Geogr. Jrnl.* LXXXV. 145 Isopleths of population density are drawn. **1950** Conrad & Pollak *Methods in Climatol.* (ed. 2) iii. 69 The curves z = const., called isopleths, thus show the relationship of the two variables x and y only for selected values of the third variable z, which is constant for each curve. **1957** G. E. Hutchinson *Treat. Limnol.* I. ix. 630 Three days later a still more striking deflection of the oxygen isopleths downward at the upper end of the basin was noted. **1971** *Sci. Amer.* Sept. 92 (*caption*) Mean radiation of the earth is portrayed by isopleths..that give the net radiation in terms of calories per square centimeter per minute.

2. *Physical Chem.* A line or surface (in a diagram) joining points that represent mixtures of the same composition.

1924 G. Edgar in H. S. Taylor *Treat. Physical Chem.* I. ix. 400 Assume a complex containing 60 per cent phenol to be warmed from 10° to 70°; the process can be followed by drawing a line of equal concentrations, *ab*, called an isopleth. **1950** W. J. Moore *Physical Chem.* vi. 136 Let us follow the sequence of events as the pressure is gradually reduced along the line of constant composition, or isopleth, *xx′*. **1951** J. E. Ricci *Phase Rule* iii. 59 The representation of the melting point region may be completed by a constant composition section, the isopleth shown in Fig. 3–12.

Hence **i·sopleth**al (-plīþăl) *a.*, carried out or occurring at constant composition.

1924 G. Edgar in H. S. Taylor *Treat. Physical Chem.* I. ix. 411 The general diagram..may be used to illustrate the effect of isothermal and isoplethal changes. **1951** J. E. Ricci *Phase Rule* ix. 189 Isoplethal or Synthetic Methods. These involve the measurement of the temperature of phase transition or of the curve of a miscibility gap, upon complexes of known composition.

isopor, isoporic: see *iso-.

isoprenaline (əisopre·nălīn). *Pharm.* [f. the chemical name N-*isopr*opylnoradr*enaline*.] A sympathomimetic amine, $C_6H_3(OH)_2CH$-$(OH)CH_2NHCH(CH_3)_2$, that is a derivative of adrenaline and is used (usu. as the hydrochloride or sulphate, both whitish, bitter-tasting powders) either sublingually or in an aerosol for the relief of bronchial asthma and pulmonary emphysema.

This is the name in the *British Pharmacopœia*: cf. *isoproterenol.

1951 *Brit. Jrnl. Pharmacol.* VI. 295 The amines used were *l*-adrenaline..and *dl*-isopropyl-*nor*adrenaline hydrochloride (isoprenaline). **1965** *Lancet* 19 June 1301/2, 75 patients with symptoms due to heart-block were treated with a long-acting formulation of isoprenaline. **1966** Dunlop & Alstead *Textbk. Med. Treatm.* (ed. 10) 716 Isoprenaline given by inhalation is effective within a few minutes and, although the relief is relatively short-lived, this form of treatment has a useful place in the treatment of episodic asthma. **1971** *Brit. Med. Bull.* XXVII. 27/1 Death might be caused by the excessive use of aerosol inhalers containing..isoprenaline.

isoprene (əi·soprīn). [f. Iso-, perh. + Pr(opyl)ene.] **a.** 2-Methyl-1,3-butadiene, CH_2:C-$(CH_3)CH$:CH_2, a colourless liquid obtained by the destructive distillation of rubber and from petroleum and used in the manufacture of certain synthetic rubbers.

1860 C. G. Williams in *Phil. Trans. R. Soc.* CL. 244, I have given the substance thus examined the name of isoprene. *Ibid.* 249 Isoprene combines explosively with bromine. *Ibid.* 255 The isolation of isoprene, $C^{10}H^8$. **1867** Bloxam *Chem.* 481 Heated in a retort, caoutchouc is decomposed into several hydrocarbons, one of which, called isoprene, boils at about 100°F. **1906** *Westm. Gaz.* 8 Sept. 10/2 In forming caoutchouc from isoprene, the great problem is already practically solved. **1957** *Technology* July 176/3 By the use of Ziegler catalysts..Goodrich-Gulf were able to synthesize from isoprene a polymer almost identical with natural rubber. **1972** P. Wiseman *Introd. Industr. Org. Chem.* vii. 253 More important than high molecular weight homopolymers of isobutene are copolymers with 1·5 to 4·5% of isoprene, known as butyl rubber.

b. *attrib.*, as **isoprene rule**, the rule that the carbon skeleton of a terpene is made up of isoprene units linked together; **isoprene unit**, the arrangement of five carbon atoms found in the isoprene molecule (the single or double nature of the bonds between them being disregarded).

1926 C. K. INGOLD in *Proc. Leeds Philos. & Lit. Soc. (Sci. Sect.)* I. 11 It is known..that the carbon skeletons of all terpenes of established constitution can empirically be built up from the skeleton of isoprene, the common product of thermal degradation of almost all terpenes. Divisibility into isoprene units may therefore be regarded as a *necessary* condition to be satisfied by the structure of any plant-synthesised terpene product. **1931** J. L. SIMONSEN *Terpenes* I. p. xii, An apparent exception to the 'isoprene rule', the hydrocarbon, sylvestrene, has been shown not to be a plant product. **1942** FUSON & SNYDER *Org. Chem.* xxvii. 358 Caoutchouc is composed of the isoprene unit repeated over and over. *Ibid.*, The occurrence of isoprene units is so general that investigators of the structures of natural products generally consider the most probable formula of an unknown compound to be that which contains the maximum number of isoprene units. **1959** L. RUZICKA in *Proc. Chem. Soc.* 343/2 Up to 1921, the idea that the higher terpenes are structurally composed of isoprene units was not used as an accepted working hypothesis. **1967** *Nature* 18 Nov. 642/2 The occurrence of a series of hydrocarbons, with structures based on the C_5H_8 isoprene unit, has been invoked as evidence for life-forms in Pre-Cambrian times. **1971** J. D. ROBERTS et al. *Org. Chem.* xxix. 779 The empirical isoprene rule resulted from Ruzicka's observation that the majority of the terpene families could be considered as arising from head-to-tail combinations of isoprene units.

isoprenoid (əi·sǒprĭnoid, əisoprī·noid), *a.* and *sb. Chem.* [f. prec. + -OID.] **A.** *adj.* Containing or designating the isoprene unit; having a molecular structure composed of such units. **B.** *sb.* An isoprenoid compound.

1945 *Chem. Abstr.* XXXIX. 5887/1 Other isoprenoid hydrocarbons, as isoprene, diterpenes, triterpenes, sesquiterpenes, are either entered at their trivial names or named systematically. **1958** *Proc. Nat. Acad. Sci.* XLIV. 167 Squalene synthesis from branched-chain subunits will be treated as a two stage process, namely (a) the condensation of three 'isoprenoid' units to a sesquiterpene (C_{15}) [etc.]. **1965** *New Scientist* 24 June 867/2 The branched-chain compounds called isoprenoids, which have a branch every fourth carbon atom. **1971** *Nature* 24 Dec. 449/1 Pristane (2,6,10,14-tetramethylpentadecane) and phytane (2,6,10,14-tetramethylhexadecane), isoprenoid hydrocarbons, which probably arise from diagenetic degradation of algal chlorophylls, were present [in the sediment] in trace amounts. **1972** *Science* 9 June 1121/2 After 2 years, isoprenoids..and alicyclic and aromatic hydrocarbons remained prominent in the polluted sediments.

isopropanol, isopropenyl, isopropyl, isopropylidene: see *ISO- b.

isoproterenol (əi:soprotěrī·nǫl). *Pharm.* [f. the chemical name N-*isopro*pylar*terenol*.] The name in the *United States Pharmacopeia* for *ISOPRENALINE.

1957 *Jrnl. Pharmacol. & Exper. Therap.* CXIX. 253 Isoproterenol..produces vasodilation and a marked increase in heart contractile force. **1961** *Lancet* 9 Sept. 574/1 Isoproterenol hydrochloride..was administered intravenously, and the nodal pacemaker gradually increased in rate with sudden re-emergence of ventricular fibrillation. **1972** R. HAIAT et al. in J. Han *Cardiac Arrhythmias* v. 91 Although some authors reported satisfactory medical management of chronic heart block, long-term drug therapy with isoproterenol is often unreliable and even hazardous.

isopycnal (əisopi·knăl). *Oceanogr.* [f. Iso- + Gr. πυκν-ός dense + -AL.] A line (imaginary or on a chart) or an imaginary surface connecting points which have the same density. Also *attrib.* or as *adj.*

1927 *Geofysiske Publikasjoner* IV. II. 18 We may therefore assume the chief cause of the variations in the depth of the isopycnals to have been oscillations of the water-masses. **1962** C. A. M. KING *Oceanogr. for Geographers* iv. 119 A line joining points of equal density is called an 'isopycnal'. **1968** G. NEUMANN *Ocean Currents* iv. 129 The slope of isobaric surfaces..is small when compared to the slope of isothermal, isohaline (surfaces of equal salinity) and isopycnal surfaces. *Ibid.* 168 In the case of frictionless ocean currents and without mixing a non-accelerated current must always be parallel to the isobars and to the isopycnals.

isopycnic (əisopi·knik), *a.* and *sb.* [f. as prec. + -AL.] **A.** *adj.* (Connecting points) of the same density or of constant density; also, in *Biochem.*, used with reference to ultracentrifugal separative techniques which rely on differences in density between the components of a mixture.

1890 WEBSTER *s.v.*, An isopycnic line or surface. **1910** V. BJERKNES et al. *Dynamic Meteorol. & Hydrogr.* I. iii. 39 We may represent the distribution of mass by drawing surfaces of constant value of the density, or isopycnic surfaces. **1930** N. SHAW *Man. Meteorol.* III. vi. 262 (*caption*) The isothermic, isobaric, isopycnic lines. **1955** *Exper. Cell Res.* IX. 457 Isopycnic gradient centrifugation for the stratification and separation of marine egg halves and quarters was first described by the Harveys. **1962** *Aeroplane* CII. 179/1 The isopycnic level at about 25,000 ft., known to meteorologists for its relative constancy, is being suggested as an accurate reference level for shifting safely from pressure instrument to density altimeter set according to the standard atmosphere. **1964** *Jrnl. Appl. Meteorol.* III. 292/2 A thick isopycnic zone might reasonably be said to exist there [in the equatorial region] from about 5–14 km. **1964** C. J. O. R. & P. MORRIS *Separation Methods in Biochem.* xxi. 807 On the application of the centrifugal field each particle migrates to a position in the gradient corresponding to its own density (the isopycnic point). Particles initially situated below their isopycnic level float upwards to it. *Ibid.* 809 The apparent density..found from isopycnic measurements. **1971** *Nature* 29 Jan. 299/3 Preparing material entirely uncontaminated by cytoplasmic ribosomes, by isolating the mitochondria by isopycnic centrifugation through sucrose gradients.

B. *sb. Meteorol.* A line (imaginary or on a map) or an imaginary surface connecting points at which the density is the same.

1890 WEBSTER, *Isopycnic* n., a line or surface passing through those points in a medium, at which the density is the same. **1924** *Q. Jrnl. R. Meteorol. Soc.* L. 32 In all probability the concentration of the isopycnics takes place over the antarctic continent. **1930** N. SHAW *Man. Meteorol.* III. vi. 260 (*table*) Isobars..Isotherms..Isopycnics.

isopycnosis (əi:sopiknōᵘ·sis). *Cytology.* Also **-pyknosis.** [f. Iso + *HETERO)PYCNOSIS.] The character or condition of having such a degree of condensation and staining as is typical of the majority of chromosomes or chromosomal regions within a particular nucleus. Hence **i:sopycno·tic** *a.*

1950 G. ÖSTERGREN in *Hereditas* XXXVI. 511 Heteropycnosis is a term in current use in chromosome studies... It might be useful to have a term for the opposite effect to that called heteropycnosis. Since such a term might actually have a function to fulfil, I suggest that the term isopycnosis be introduced. *Ibid.* 512 That a chromosome region is isopycnotic should then mean simply that it does not differ from the majority of the chromosome regions of the cell in its appearance. **1962** *Lancet* 29 Dec. 1384/1 In female meiosis the two X chromosomes may show complete or partial isopyknosis according to the type of pairing. **1967** U. MITTWOCH *Sex Chromosomes* xii. 242 Both X-chromosomes of the female become isopycnotic [during gametogenesis].

isoquinoline: see *ISO- b.

isorhythm (əi·sorið'm). Also **isorr-.** [f. Iso- + Gr. ῥυθμ-ός measured motion.] The rhythmic structure of isorhythmic music.

1954 *Grove's Dict. Mus.* IV. 551/1 *Isorhythm*, the main feature of the French motet in the 14th and early 15th centuries. **1959** *Times* 13 Feb. 13/5 The hockets and isorrhythms of the Middle Ages. **1963** *Listener* 17 Jan. 141/1 A set of variations using the medieval technique of isorhythm (the repetition throughout of a certain rhythmic pattern, in the manner of a passacaglia).

isorrhythmic, *a.* Add: Now more usually **isorhythmic.** **3.** *Mus.* 'A modern musicological term applied to fourteenth-century choral works in which the tenor *canto fermo* (or sometimes an upper part) is many times repeated as to its rhythmic features, the pitch of the notes, however, being varied each time it appears' (*Oxf. Compan. Mus.* ed. 9). Also in more general use.

1954 *Grove's Dict. Mus.* IV. 551/1 The isorhythmic motet came to life shortly before 1316. **1957** *Listener* 26 Dec. 1086/1 An aria..on an isorrhythmic bass, that is to say, a 'ground' whose recurrencies begin on different beats in the bar. **1962** *Ibid.* 20 Sept. 453/1 Whether the demonstration is of isorhythmic patterns, classical thematic structures or rotations of a twelve-note succession, it rarely does more than rationalize a unity already intuitively experienced. **1963** *Medium Ævum* XXXII. 151 The elaborate iso-rhythmic setting of *O potores exquisiti* from the Carmina Burana. **1972** *Daily Tel.* 23 Feb. 11/7 To pinpoint some isorhythmic features when a given sequence of durations, though not of pitches, is reiterated in one or more parts. **1972** *Composer & Conductor* Aug. 6/1 Friedrich Ludwig proposed the term Isorhythmic to designate identical rhythmic patterns of different melodies in medieval motets.

isosbestic (əiso,sbe·stik), *a. Physical Chem.* Also erron. **isobestic.** [ad. G. *isosbestisch* (A. Thiel et al. 1924, in *Fortschr. d. Chem.* XVIII. 116), f. Gr. ἴσος equal + σβεστ-ός extinguished (f. σβεννύναι to quench, extinguish): see -IC.] *isosbestic point*: a wavelength at which the absorption of light by a liquid remains constant as the acidity varies or, more generally, as the state of equilibrium between two interconvertible substances or states shifts.

1925 *Chem. Abstr.* XIX. 2180 Photometric measurements of the absorption spectra were plotted for equal degrees of acidity and these curves intersected in general in the 'isobetic' point [*sic*: rendering G. *isosbestischer Punkt*.]. **1943** W. R. BRODE *Chem. Spectroscopy* (ed. 2) ix. 249 (*caption*) Spectrophotometric determination of hydrogen-ion concentration; mixed indicator (methyl red + bromothymol blue). (Note isosbestic points at 467 and 500 mμ.) **1954** *Trans. Faraday Soc.* L. 802 The ionized form exhibits absorption at a longer wave-length (251 mμ) than the non-ionized (209 mμ) and there is an isosbestic point at 245 mμ. **1958** MEITES & THOMAS *Adv. Analytical Chem.* viii. 277 The spectra of a number of solutions having equal formal concentrations of bromthymol blue but different pH values will all intersect at 501 mμ. Such a point is known as an isosbestic point, and the appearance of such a point on a family of spectra is a necessary (but not quite sufficient) criterion of the presence of two and only two forms of the absorbing substance in equilibrium with each other. **1960** *Jrnl. Biol. Chem.* CCXXXV. 1026/2 Each of the absorption maxima and isosbestic points is essentially the same for normal as well as for sickle cells and homozygous C hemoglobins. **1962** R. E. DODD *Chem. Spectroscopy* v. 299 The absence of an isobestic point indicates a more complex system. **1971** F. A. BETTELHEIM *Exper. Physical Chem.* xiii. 144 The absence of an isosbestic point is definite proof of the presence of more than two absorbing species. **1972** *Nature* 24 Mar. 140/2 Control measurements are made at an isosbestic point for the rhodopsin and the product.

¶ Other anomalous forms (with quot. 1939 cf. quot. 1943 above).

1939 W. R. BRODE *Chem. Spectroscopy* ix. 206 There will be a point..where the extinction curves should have a common value at any *p*H concentration. Such a point is known as an isobastique point. **1949** A. C. CANDLER *Pract. Spectroscopy* iv. 90 As one absorption curve fades, another develops, while the absorption at an intermediate wavelength, called by Brode the isobastic point, remains unaltered. *Ibid.* 91 The indicator should be of standard strength, but slight variations may be corrected if the absorption at both the centre of the absorption band and at the isobastic point are measured.

isosmotic: see *ISO-.

isospin (əi·sospin). *Physics.* [Contraction of **isotopic spin*, **isobaric spin*.] A vector quantity associated with elementary particles and atomic nuclei which is used to give mathematical expression to the fact that the strong interaction is independent of electric charge; its quantum number (symbol T or I, $T = 0$, $\pm\frac{1}{2}$, ± 1, $\pm\frac{3}{2}$, etc.) is assigned on the basis of there being $2T+1$ particles in a charge multiplet, each with the same value of the quantum number T but differing in the value of the third component of isospin T_3 (or T_z) according to the charge of each particle, with the result that these can be treated as different states of a single particle.

1963 S. TOLANSKY *Introd. Atomic Physics* (ed. 5) xxiii. 395 The decay of a particle is controlled by a quantity T which has been called the isotopic spin vector or more simply, the isospin. **1965** H. MUIRHEAD *Physics Elem. Particles* i. 14 The isospin of a system is formally similar to angular momentum but is linked to the charge states of the system. **1970** *Physics Bull.* Jan. 22/1 These hadrons and their compounds (the atomic nuclei) appeared as charge multiplets, the members of which had essentially the same mass and the same strong interactions, but different charge values, these being the $(2I+1)$ values $(\frac{1}{2}B-I)e$, $(\frac{1}{2}B-I+1)e$, ..$(\frac{1}{2}B+I)e$ where B is the baryon number..and I (called the isospin) is characteristic of the multiplet. **1971** P. E. HODGSON *Nucl. Reactions* xix. 575 The isospin T of a nucleus is the sum of the isospins t_i of its constituent nucleons...The isospins t of the nucleons have the same mathematical properties as the spin vectors σ, that is $t^2\chi = t(t+1)\chi$, $t_z\chi = \pm\frac{1}{2}\chi$, where $t_z = +\frac{1}{2}$ refers to neutrons and $t_z = -\frac{1}{2}$ to protons. Here the *z* component refers to isospin space and not to ordinary space.

isostasy. Also **isostacy** (*rare*). Add to def.: The condition thought to exist within the earth's crust of approximate hydrostatic equilibrium between portions of different density, the land masses being supported by underlying denser material that yields or flows under their weight and those parts of them that reach to a greater height also extending to a greater depth, any (large) part slowly rising (or falling) if matter is removed from (or added to) its surface. (Earlier and later examples.)

1889 C. E. DUTTON in *Bull. Philos. Soc. Washington* XI. 53 For this condition of equilibrium of figure, to which gravitation tends to reduce a planetary body, irrespective of whether it is homogeneous or not, I propose the name isostasy...We may also use the corresponding adjective isostatic. **1893** *Ann. Rep. U.S. Geol. Survey 1891–2* II. 280 The condition of isostasy prevailing in the earth's mass demanded that compensation should be made to the continental area for the load taken from it. **1914** [see *ASTHENOSPHERE]. **1923** *Discovery* Dec. 315/2 The suggestion which has gained most favour, and seems to fit in with many observations, is the theory of Isostacy, which contends that all visible land is composed of the lighter parts of the Earth's crust and is floating upon the components of greater density. **1944** A. HOLMES *Princ. Physical Geol.* iii. 34 It must..be clearly realized that isostasy is only a state of balance; it is not a force or a geological agent. It is the disturbance of isostasy by denudation and deposition, earth movements and igneous activity, that brings into play the gravitational forces that restore isostasy. **1950** *Antiquity* XXIV. 43 The dating of these sites involves the post-Algonquin changes in Great Lakes water-levels through isostasy and drainage. **1960** *New Scientist* 19 May 1278/2 The gravity variations are generally consistent with the theory of isostasy, according to which mountains 'float' in hydrostatic equilibrium in the dense mantle as do icebergs in the sea.

isostatic, *a.* Substitute for def.: Pertaining to, produced by, or characterized by isostasy. (Examples.)

1889 [see *ISOSTASY]. **1893** *Ann. Rep. U.S. Geol. Survey 1891–2* II. 280 During the period of sedimentation, which ultimately set up isostatic adjustment, there had been continuous shrinkage of a nucleus cooling beneath the accumulating strata. **1927** PEAKE & FLEURE *Apes &*

Men v. 80 There may have been a slight compensating, or as it is called isostatic, uprise in Denmark and other regions around the margin of the ice sheet. **1937** *Proc. Prehist. Soc.* III. 181 The isostatic emergence of the land from the sea since the last glacial maximum. **1944** A. Holmes *Princ. Physical Geol.* xi. 189 While the crust was being thus unloaded by denudation, slow isostatic uplift must have been continuously in progress. **1955** *Antiquity* XXIX. 181 The complex eustatic and isostatic movements which determine the part played by land movements on one hand and changes of sea-level on the other. **1960** [see *isostatically *adv.* a]. **1960** B. W. Sparks *Geomorphol.* xiv. 311 Large ice sheets caused an isostatic depression of the areas they occupied and a subsequent rise as the ice melted away.

2. Performed under or involving conditions in which equal pressure is applied from all directions.

1957 *Ceramic News* Apr. 20 (*heading*) Unique 'isostatic process' marks manufacture of Coors famous high density grinding media. **1965** Hove & Riley *Ceramics for Adv. Technologies* iii. 79 In isostatic pressing, the powder material is compacted under uniform pressure. **1967** M. Chandler *Ceramics in Mod. World* vi. 163 (*caption*) New ceramic materials demand new forming techniques, such as this isostatic press for making ceramic spark plug insulators.

isostatically (əisostæ·tikăli), *adv.* [f. prec.: see -ically.] **a.** *Geol.* As regards isostasy; by, or as a result of, isostatic forces.

1901 *Geogr. Jrnl.* XVIII. 517 The elevation of the land caused an ice-sheet to form gradually over it until the surface was depressed, isostatically, by the weight of accumulated ice. **1924** J. G. A. Skerl tr. *Wegener's Orig. Continents & Oceans* xi. 160 It [*sc.* the map] shows us immediately the mass-defect under mountain chains through which the latter are isostatically compensated. **1957** G. E. Hutchinson *Treat. Limnol.* I. i. 8 The rebound of the southern part of the recently deglaciated Scandinavia, which rose isostatically more rapidly than the postglacial eustatic rise in sea level. **1960** *New Scientist* 19 May 1278/3 Considerable local departures from isostatic equilibrium are known, but an area forming a considerable fraction of a continent is in general found to be isostatically compensated. **1969** *Nature* 21 June 1120/1 Continents and continental margins respond isostatically to pressure variations of ten bars or less.

b. By (means of) pressure applied equally from all directions.

1960 *Times Rev. Industry* Feb. 24/2 Silicon nitride.. powder may be formed to the required shape by..slip casting, or pressing either in steel dies, or isostatically in a thin walled rubber sac. **1972** *McGraw-Hill Yearbk. Sci. & Technol.* 332/2 The table shows a comparison of some of the properties achieved by hot isostatically pressed alloys compared to those of cast products of the same composition.

isoster: see *isostere 2.

isostere (əi·sostīəɹ). [f. Iso- + Gr. στερε-ός solid.] **1. a.** [ad. G. *isoster* (A. R. v. Miller-Hauenfels *Theoret. Meteorol.* (1883) i. 2).] A line or surface (either imaginary or on a map or diagram) connecting points where some substance has an equal specific volume.

1900 V. Bjerknes in *U.S. Dept. Agric. Monthly Weather Rev.* XXVIII. 436/2 The upper isosteres surround the whole earth, whereas the lower ones intersect the earth's surface along the isosteric curves. **1944** H. R. Byers *Gen. Meteorol.* ix. 217 The lines of constant specific volume, called isosteres, slope upward toward the pole. **1957** G. E. Hutchinson *Treat. Limnol.* I. v. 287 It is probable that in all cases in stratified lakes the deep water currents do not represent steady-state circulation systems maintained by a more or less constant wind stress, but rather continually changing readjustments to the changing position of the isosteres.

b. *Physical Chem.* [ad. G. *isoster* (H. Freundlich *Kapillarchemie* (1909) A. ii. 102).] A line on a graph showing the pressure of a gas required to produce a given amount of adsorption at different temperatures.

1919 *Proc. R. Soc.* XCVI. 289 It is..difficult to obtain observations of an adsorption isostere over a very wide stretch of temperature. **1940** Glasstone *Text-bk. Physical Chem.* xiv. 1173 The isostere for log p against $1/T$ is linear, as it should be if the van't Hoff equation is applicable. **1970** A. J. B. Robertson *Catalysis Gas Reactions by Metals* ii. 22 Such isosteres can be derived from isotherms at different temperatures.

2. Also **isoster**. *Chem.* Each of two or more isosteric molecules or ions (see *isosteric *a.* 4).

1919 I. Langmuir in *Jrnl. Amer. Chem. Soc.* XLI. 1544 Compounds showing a relationship to one another like that between carbon dioxide and nitrous oxide will be called isosteric compounds or isosteres. **1924** J. A. Cranston *Struct. Matter* viii. 160 The tabulation of isosteres is of special value in the study of the crystalline forms of compounds. **1958** A. Albert in *Current Trends in Heterocyclic Chem.* (Chem. Soc.) viii. 64 Thiazole and pyridine are another pair of isosteres said to resemble one another closely in properties. **1968** *European Jrnl. Cancer* IV. 222 The carcinogenic activity of 10 heteropolycyclic substances, of which 7 were sulfur-containing isosters, and 3 were isomers.

isosteric (əisoste·rik), *a.* [f. as prec. + -ic.] **1.** (In Dict. s.v. Iso-.)

2. Indicating equal specific volume.

1900 V. Bjerknes in *U.S. Dept. Agric. Monthly Weather Rev.* XXVIII. 436/1 This distribution can be expressed with the help of surfaces of equal specific volume, or isosteric surfaces. **1934** D. Brunt *Physical & Dynamical Meteorol.* viii. 166 Any isosteric surface is also isopycnic. **1957** G. E. Hutchinson *Treat. Limnol.* I. v. 263 When isosteric surfaces or surfaces of equal density or specific volume do not correspond to the equigeopotential or level surfaces, a current must be flowing.

3. *Physical Chem.* Of a heat of adsorption: corresponding to a constant amount of adsorbed material as the pressure and temperature vary (equilibrium being maintained).

1918 *Proc. R. Soc. Edin.* XXXVIII. 31 Freundlich.. considers an 'isosteric' heat of adsorption where α [= number of mols. of gas adsorbed per grm. adsorbent, adsorbing at p, T] is constant, p and T variables... But it is difficult to see how we can have an isosteric heat of adsorption per mol. adsorbed, for under the defined conditions nothing is adsorbed. We have merely a readjustment of p and T. **1933** D. J. Martin *Introd. Thermodynamics for Chemists* xiii. 314 The isosteric heat of adsorption is such that the amount adsorbed is kept constant while the pressure and temperature are varied. **1970** *Biopolymers* IX. 1531 A comparison between calorimetric and isosteric heats of sorption..will indicate the degree of irreversibility of the sorption process.

4. *Chem.* Having the same number of valence electrons arranged in a similar manner.

1919 [see *isostere 2]. **1921** F. H. Loring *Atomic Theories* xv. 134 Methane is isosteric with the ammonium ion. **1938** *Jrnl. Amer. Chem. Soc.* LX. 2628/1 In a few cases, isosteric compounds are interchangeable in serological reactions. **1971** *Arch. Biochem. & Biophysics* CXLIII. 252 These overall studies support the concept that the 1,4-cyclohexadienyl group is an effective isosteric replacement for a phenyl group.

isosterism (əisostīə·riz'm). *Chem.* [f. as prec. + -ism.] The condition of being isosteric (sense *4).

1919 I. Langmuir in *Jrnl. Amer. Chem. Soc.* XLI. 1545 The isosterism of the cyanate and trinitride ions applies of course also to compounds derived from them. **1935** J. N. Friend *Text-bk. Physical Chem.* II. ix. 384 (*caption*) Isosterism of CO_2 and N_2O. **1963** *Pharmaceutica Acta Helv.* XXXVIII. 706 The two most important postulates for isosterism were there: similarity in shape and polarity.

isostich, isostructural, isosyllabic, isosyntactic, isosyntagmic, isotach: see *iso-.

isotactic (əisotæ·ktik), *a. Chem.* [f. Iso- + Gr. τακτ-ός arranged, ordered + -ic, as ad. It. *isotattico* (G. Natta 1955, in *Atti d. Accad. Naz. d. Lincei, Mem.* (*Classe d. Sci. fis.*) 8th Ser. IV. ii. 69), f. Attic τάττ-ειν (= Gr. τάσσειν) to arrange.] Having or designating a polymeric structure in which all the repeating units have the same stereochemical configuration.

1955 *Chem. Abstr.* XLIX. 12912 The designation 'isotactic' is applied to chain polymers contg. alternating CH_2 and asym. C groups of identical configuration. **1963** *Times* 11 June 19/1 The entry into production of the Brindisi plant..considerably increased output of the isotactic polypropylene plastic ('Moplen'), now becoming popular in many countries throughout the world. **1964** *New Scientist* 23 Jan. 225 These arrangements, known as 'isotactic' and 'syndiotactic' configurations.., have now been realised with most of the common vinyl monomers. **1972** *Physics Bull.* Nov. 666/1 Isotactic polypropylene is a useful commercial plastic noted for its high strength/weight ratio.

Hence **isotacti·city**, the quality of being isotactic.

1959 Natta & Danusso in *Jrnl. Polymer Sci.* XXXIV. 7 All the arrangements which may compose the isotacticity must be only repetitive arrangements. **1968** *Ibid.* A-2. VI. 1495 The isotacticity and the crystallizability of the original sample remain unchanged after degradation.

isoteniscope: see *iso-.

isotherm. Add: Also, a similar line (either imaginary or in a diagram) connecting points other than on the earth's surface. (Further example.)

1973 *Nature* 16 Feb. 446/2 A pressure-sensing float and a barrier driven by a motor, each fencing the film and connected to a recorder.., made it possible..to obtain isotherms of films.

b. = *isothermal *sb.* b.

1895 C. S. Palmer tr. *Nernst's Theoret. Chem.* ii. ii. 192 The behaviour of gaseous and liquid carbon dioxide was studied very exactly by Andrews for those temperatures the isotherms of which are plotted. **1924** A. E. Hill in H. S. Taylor *Treat. Physical Chem.* I. ix. 383 The result of changing the pressure at constant temperature can be deduced by following a line drawn parallel to the pressure axis, and called an isotherm, or isothermal line. **1961** M. Tribus *Thermostatics & Thermodynamics* viii. 205 There is shown a line of constant temperature which is tangent to the top of the vapor–liquid region. This line represents the critical isotherm, since it represents the temperature above which only one phase exists. **1971** F. A. Bettelheim *Exper. Physical Chem.* xli. 378 In the graphic representation of the adsorption isotherm, one usually plots the amount of component 1 adsorbed on the surface of the solid per gram (or per unit surface area) of the solid against the equilibrium composition of the solution.

isothermal, *a.* and *sb.* Add: **A.** *adj.* **1. c.** Applied to a line in a diagram that represents states or conditions of equal temperature.

1873 J. W. Gibbs in *Trans. Connecticut Acad. Arts & Sci.* II. 311 In the same way we may conceive of lines..of equal temperature... These lines we may also call..isothermal. **1922** Glazebrook *Dict. Appl. Physics* I. 930/1 When a perfect gas expands isothermally PV is constant, and hence its isothermal line on the pressure–volume diagram, for any assigned temperature, is a rectangular hyperbola. **1949** F. Tyler *Intermediate Heat* vii. 146 The relative slopes of the isothermal and adiabatic curves passing through the point P_1..may be obtained as follows.

2. Occurring at a constant temperature; pertaining to or involving a constancy of temperature with time.

1887 *Encycl. Brit.* XXII. 481/1 During isothermal expansion a gas must take in an amount of heat just equal to the work it does. **1937** M. W. Zemansky *Heat & Thermodynamics* xiii. 231 The isothermal compressibility of a gas may be calculated from an empiric equation expressing the dependence of V upon P at constant temperature. **1957** *Encycl. Brit.* VIII. 123/2 Under ordinary conditions the adiabatic constants for a solid substance are practically the same as the corresponding isothermal constants. **1967** A. H. Cottrell *Introd. Metall.* xx. 373 Decisive progress [in the heat-treatment of steel] came only after the development of the technique of isothermal transformation..in which specimens are quenched into a bath of molten lead or salt at some pre-determined temperature and the course of their transformation at this fixed temperature is then determined.

3. Of the same temperature throughout.

1909 *Rep. Brit. Assoc. Adv. Sci. 1908* 591 Permit me to open the discussion on the Isothermal Layer, and the inversions of temperature which are found there. **1912** H. N. Dickson *Climate & Weather* iii. 77 At heights greater than about nine miles the temperature..remains nearly constant at about −70°F at all levels... In this 'isothermal layer'..there would seem to be..little movement. **1951** J. A. Hynek *Astrophysics* xiv. 662 It is possible that at this stage..the star develops a small isothermal core at the center. **1964** *Oceanogr. & Marine Biol.* II. 71 In winter the fiord water becomes isothermal and isohaline with average temperature and salinity of −1·76°C and 32·75‰.

B. *sb.* **b.** A line in a diagram that is isothermal (sense *A. 1 c).

1873 J. W. Gibbs in *Trans. Connecticut Acad. Arts & Sci.* II. 323 In that part of any diagram which represents a mixture of vapor and liquid, the isopiestics and isothermals will be identical, as the pressure is determined by the temperature alone. **1879** *Amer. Jrnl. Sci.* XVIII. 463 In Diagram A, are drawn Isothermals, curves of equal temperature, in which the abscissæ are wave lengths, the ordinates intensities. **1937** P. S. Epstein *Textbk. Thermodynamics* iii. 49 The slope of the adiabatic ($dp/dv = -\gamma p/v$) is always steeper than the slope of the isothermal ($dp/dv = -p/v$) passing through the same point. **1968** Wallace & Linning *Basic Engin. Thermodynamics* 458 At very low pressures all isothermals tend towards a value of the compressibility function equal to unity, i.e. towards perfect gas behaviour.

isothermally (əisoþə̄·ɹmăli), *adv.* [f. prec. + -ly².] At a constant temperature, without a change in temperature.

1886 *Proc. R. Soc. Edin.* XIII. 79 Steam might be condensed isothermally to supersaturation without condensing. **1897** [in Dict. after Isothermal *a.* and *sb.*]. **1922** [see *isothermal *a.* 1 c]. **1952** *New Biol.* XII. 75 In a system such as this the simultaneous dismantling and assembly can be described as 'energy-linked'; and since no heat is lost or gained the changes occur isothermally, that is, at constant temperature. **1967** A. H. Cottrell *Introd. Metall.* xx. 374 Over the range in which the austenite decomposes isothermally the time of transformation follows a *C*-curve like that of Fig. 20.2.

isothermic (əisoþə̄·ɹmik), *a.* [f. Iso- + Gr. θέρμ-η heat, θερμ-ός hot + -ic.] **a.** = Isothermal *a.* 1 (in Dict. and Suppl.).

1879 *Amer. Jrnl. Sci.* CXVIII. 466 Such an error, in order to produce such an effect in *all* the isothermic curves, must be looked for either in my comparison of the sun's spectrum with that of the platinum wire, or in Lamansky's measurements of the sun's heat. **1881** *Proc. R. Geogr. Soc.* III. 657 Fall of temperature as we proceed in different directions is shown by means of isothermic lines. **1930** [see *isopycnic *a.*].

b. = *isothermal *a.* 2.

1936 *Jrnl. Iron & Steel Inst.* CXXXIV. 265 A, A certain lowering of the tensile strength and limit of proportionality is revealed between certain temperature limits after isothermic treatment. **1951** R. A. Dutcher et al. *Introd. Agric. Biochem.* xix. 383 Hydrolyses are characterized by no perceptible heat changes and..are known as isothermic reactions. **1965** B. E. Freeman tr. *Vandel's Biospeleol.* xxx. 474 The humus of these mountains possesses an isothermic climate.

c. = *isothermal *a.* 3.

1963 S. W. Tromp *Med. Biometeorol.* i. 22 Above the troposphere lies a region known as stratosphere..divided into three layers: a lower cold isothermic layer 12–35 km above sea level with fairly constant temperatures..a warm layer..and a very cold upper layer.

isotone (əi·sotōᵘn). *Physics.* [a. F. *isotone* (K. Guggenheimer 1934, in *Jrnl. de Physique et le Radium* V. 253), coined by replacing the *p* of *isotope* (the initial letter of *proton*) by *n* for *neutron*.] Each of two or more nuclides

having the same number of neutrons (but usually different numbers of protons).

1934 *Sci. Abstr.* A. XXXVII. 734 It is proposed that elements having the same number of neutrons, but different atomic numbers shall be termed 'isotones'. **1952** *Sci. News* XXIII. 39 There is an exceptionally large number of nuclei all containing 20 protons (isotopes of calcium)... Nuclei containing 20, 50 or 82 neutrons also have a large number of isotones. **1966** [see *ISOBAR 2]. **1972** *Physics Bull.* Mar. 148/3 The isotone shift differs from the isotope shifts in that the former measures the energy difference of atoms when protons are added to the nucleus with the number of neutrons remaining the same, whereas for the latter the role of protons and neutrons are reversed. The study of isotope as well as isotone shifts reveal the nuclear shell structure.

isotonic, *a.* **2.** Delete '(See quot. 1900.)' and substitute: [ad. G. *isotonisch* (H. de Vries 1884, in *Jahrb. f. wiss. Bot.* XIV. 427).] Of, pertaining to, or (of a solution) having the same osmotic pressure as some particular solution (usually that in a cell, or a body fluid). Const. *with.* (Earlier and later examples.)

Quot. 1900 in Dict. belongs to sense 3 below.

1895 [see *HYPERTONIC *a.* 2]. **1902** POYNTING & THOMSON *Text-bk. Physics: Properties of Matter* xvi. 190 A series of solutions can be prepared which are isotonic with each other. **1936** A. P. MATHEWS *Princ. Biochem.* xxxiv. 364 Practically all the secretions of the body, except the urine, as for example the bile, the pancreatic juice, the saliva and so on, have the same osmotic pressure as the blood. They are isotonic with the blood. **1951** H. DAVSON *Textbk. Gen. Physiol.* vii. 159 For marine eggs the isotonic concentration will generally be approximately 0·5 M salts or 1 M non-electrolyte. *Ibid.* 158 In isotonic glycerol solution the cell is unstable because no osmotic equilibrium is possible. **1969** J. H. GREEN *Basic Clin. Physiol.* vi. 37/1 The sodium chloride is present in plasma to the extent of 0·9 g. per 100 ml. A solution containing this amount of sodium chloride in water is termed normal, isotonic, or physiological saline, and it has the same electrolyte strength as blood. Such a solution.. could be run into the veins of a patient, whereas pure distilled water would destroy the red blood cells by the process of haemolysis. **1972** *Nature* 17 Mar. 117/2 Each animal received an intraperitoneal injection of ethanol (4 g kg^{-1}, 25% v/v solution in isotonic saline).

3. *Physiol.* [ad. G. *isotonisch* (A. Fick *Mech. Arbeit u. Wärmeentwickelung bei d. Muskelthätigkeit* (1882) vii. 112).] Of, pertaining to, or designating muscular action in which the muscle contracts more or less freely against a small, constant resistance.

1891 A. D. WALLER *Introd. Human Physiol.* ix. 330 If a muscle contracts against a small and constant resistance, so as to be extended by a constant force during its contraction, the curve described by a light lever attached to it is termed 'isotonic'. **1900** [in Dict., sense 2]. **1939** *Jrnl. Physiol.* XCVI. 63 The relation between applied force and speed of isotonic shortening was studied in frog and tortoise muscle. **1951** H. DAVSON *Textbk. Gen. Physiol.* xvii. 481 A record of an isometric twitch is thus a record of changes in tension of the muscle, whilst that for an isotonic twitch is a record of changes in length. **1971** A. C. GUYTON *Basic Human Physiol.* vii. 77/1 In comparing the rapidity of contraction of different types of muscles, isometric recordings..are usually used instead of isotonic recordings, because the duration of an isotonic recording is almost as dependent on the inertia of the recording system as upon the contraction itself.

isotonically (əisotǫ·nikăli), *adv. Physiol.* [f. prec.: see -ICALLY.] Under isotonic conditions (see *ISOTONIC *a.* 3).

1953 A. SZENT-GYÖRGYI *Chem. Physiol. Contraction in Body & Heart Muscle* ix. 52 Fig. 8..sums up the experience..on a widely varied material, registered both isotonically and isometrically, excited in different ways. **1970** *Nature* 16 May 656/1 The muscular activity was recorded isotonically on a kymograph. **1971** A. C. GUYTON *Basic Human Physiol.* vii. 77/2 Muscles can contract both isometrically and isotonically in the body, but most contractions are actually a mixture of the two.

isotonicity (əi:sotǫni·siti). *Physiol.* [f. as prec. + -ITY.] The property or state of being isotonic (sense *2); equality of osmotic pressure; also, degree of osmotic pressure (of the blood).

1896 T. L. STEDMAN *20th Cent. Pract.* VII. 284 After twelve or twenty-four hours the solution which is exactly isotonic is determined..and the isotonicity of the blood corpuscles..determined at the same time. *Ibid.*, The isotonicity of the corpuscles is 0·45. **1906** *Amer. Jrnl. Physiol.* XV. 366 Every degree of dilution from isotonicity down to distilled water acts as a stimulus to the heart ganglion of Limulus. **1909** R. J. M. BUCHANAN *Blood in Health & Dis.* ix. 182 The isotonicity of the plasma is rather below normal. **1939** A. KROGH *Osmotic Regulation Aquatic Animals* 196 The isotonicity normally present between tissue cells and the surrounding medium need not mean, however, that the sum of free ions on both sides of the cellular membrane is the same. *Ibid.* 66 Schwabe (1933)..observed a definite hypotonicity for [the crab] *Pachygrapsus marmoratus* amounting to 57mM., while he confirmed the absolute isotonicity for *Portunus corrugatus*. **1951** [see *HYPERTONIC *a.* 2]. **1974** *Nature* 4 Jan. 50/1 The concentration of calcium was varied from 0 to 2·5 mM (isotonicity was kept constant by appropriate adjustments in the concentration of NaCl).

isotope (əi·sǫtōup). [f. Iso- + Gr. τόπ-ος place.] **1.** A variety of a chemical element (strictly, of one particular element) which is distinguished from the other varieties of the element by a different mass number but shares the same atomic number and chemical properties (and so occupies the same position in the periodic table); freq. used to denote any individual variety without reference to identity of atomic numbers (see quot. 1947 and cf. *NUCLIDE).

1913 F. SODDY in *Nature* 4 Dec. 400/1 The same algebraic sum of the positive and negative charges in the nucleus, when the arithmetical sum is different, gives what I call 'isotopes' or 'isotopic elements', because they occupy the same place in the periodic table. They are chemically identical, and save only as regards the relatively few physical properties which depend upon atomic mass directly, physically identical also. **1915** *Rep. Brit. Assoc. Adv. Sci. 1914* 301 Sir E. Rutherford (replying) said that the chemical inseparability of certain isotopes was, indeed, derived from experiments with small quantities, but the methods used were very delicate. **1923** *Glasgow Herald* 7 Apr. 7 Another entirely revolutionary factor in chemical theory has been the discovery that the majority of the chemical elements are mixtures of isotopes. **1927** N. V. SIDGWICK *Electronic Theory of Valency* i. 11 What Soddy has called an isotope—an element of the same atomic number but a different atomic weight. *Ibid.*, The one element of which the isotopes can be obtained in any quantity in a state of approximate purity..is lead. **1942** J. D. STRANATHAN *'Particles' of Mod. Physics* v. 205 Hertz, employing gaseous diffusion at low pressure through a special porous material, succeeded in producing a real separation for the isotopes of Ne. *Ibid.* 207 By this method the isotopes H^2, Li^7, C^{13} and N^{15} have been produced in significant concentration. **1947** *Amer. Jrnl. Physics* XV. 356/2 There is at present no word in the English language to express the concept of a particular species of atom, differing from all others in the constitution of its nucleus... In recent years the word *isotope* has come into use for this purpose, less by design than by default. According to its definition [by Soddy], this general usage is incorrect, since *isotope* properly refers to a species of a particular and designated element, and emphasizes its relationship to other isotopes of that element. It is analogous to such words as *brother* and *colleague*. **1959** *New Biol.* XXX. 96 Radioactive isotopes behave chemically in identical fashion with the normal isotopes, but can be distinguished by means of their radioactivity. **1962** *Nature* 19 May 621/2 There are about 300 naturally occurring isotopes, and several hundred additional isotopes can be prepared artificially. **1963** D. W. & E. E. HUMPHRIES tr. *Termier's Erosion & Sedimentation* i. 4 The isotopes O^{16}, O^{17} and O^{18} of oxygen are in different proportions in atmospheric and sea water, the latter being rich in heavy isotopes as a result of differential evaporation. **1966** *McGraw-Hill Encycl. Sci. & Technol.* VII. 291/2, 20 elements possess no isotopes; each of these consists of one type of atom only. **1966** C. R. TOTTLE *Sci. Engin. Materials* i. 23 Hydrogen has three isotopes, the two heavier ones being known as deuterium (originally called heavy hydrogen), with one neutron per atom, and tritium, with two neutrons per atom.

b. In the usage of biologists and biochemists: a less common, usually radioactive, isotope of an element as used in tracer or other studies, in contradistinction to the common, naturally occurring isotope of the element; freq. without *the.*

1945 *Jrnl. Biol. Chem.* CLIX. 697 Isotopic analyses were usually made on these inorganic salts, thus avoiding the dilution of the isotope [*sc.* C^{13}] by non-isotopic carbon. **1954** A. WHITE et al. *Princ. Biochem.* xiv. 307 By degradation of the product and determination of the distribution of isotope among its atoms, one may often procure information as to the mechanism of the transformation. **1954** CANTAROW & SCHEPARTZ *Biochem.* xiv. 352 The assay of stable isotopes is based upon the difference in atomic weight between the normal element and the isotope used. **1971** MAZUR & HARROW *Textbk. Biochem.* (ed. 10) iv. 99 Synthesis of physiologically important compounds, containing isotopes in place of the normally occurring elements, furnishes the worker with a 'tag' that can easily be followed. **1972** *Science* 2 June 1032/1 Swiss albino mice were labeled with ^{45}Ca by injection with 10 μc of isotope 1 day after birth.

2. Special combs.: **isotope dilution**, a diminution of the concentration of one isotope (or isotopically labelled compound) by the addition or presence of another isotope of the same element (or of the unlabelled compound); *esp.* as a technique for measuring the amount of an element or compound in a system by introducing a known amount of a different isotope (or a labelled compound) and then measuring its concentration in a sample withdrawn from the system after mixing; **isotope effect**, a variation in some physical or chemical characteristic between one isotope of an element and another; **isotope shift**, a small difference in the wavelength of corresponding spectral lines of different isotopes of an element owing to the different masses and charge distributions of their nuclei.

1940 RITTENBERG & FOSTER in *Jrnl. Biol. Chem.* CXXXIII. 737 (*heading*) A new procedure for quantitative analysis by isotope dilution. *Ibid.* 744 A new method (isotope dilution procedure) for the analysis of complex mixtures is described. **1956** *Nature* 28 Jan. 159/1 Isotope-dilution analysis, a technique which is now being increasingly applied in geology, agriculture, metallurgy and biology. **1971** *Metabolism* XX. 1099 (*heading*) Kinetics of potassium distribution in man using isotope dilution and whole-body counting. **1972** *Chemico-Biol. Interactions* IV. 103 This finding suggested that the decreases in specific activity were a result of isotope dilution rather than inhibition of protein synthesis. **1923** *Science* 31 Aug. 164/2 (*heading*) The vibrational isotope effect in the band spectrum of boron nitride. **1956** *Nature* 28 Jan. 159/2 Most properties of solids depend on the atomic masses, and the study of isotope effects can be a powerful means of testing the validity of theories. **1967** A. H. COTTRELL *Introd. Metall.* xxiv. 503 The importance of the lattice ions in superconductivity is shown by the isotope effect. Different isotopes of mercury (also tin) are found to have different critical temperatures, proportional to $M^{-\frac{1}{2}}$, where M is the atomic mass of the isotope concerned. **1968** A. WHITE et al. *Princ. Biochem.* (ed. 4) xiii. 288 Distinct isotope effects, *e.g.* differential rates of reaction between normal and tritiated compounds, have been observed. **1932** *Physical Rev.* XLII. 350 It appears that this determination fits in with the magnitude of the isotope shift. **1958** *Oxf. Mag.* 8 May 418/1 Work on high resolution optical spectroscopy is now mainly directed towards the study of 'isotope shifts'. **1971** *Physics Bull.* Oct. 583/2 Isotope shifts occur when the energy levels of different isotopes are slightly shifted with respect to one another, resulting in an apparent splitting of the 'line' if two or more isotopes are present in the source.

isotopic (əisǫtǫ·pik), *a.* [f. prec. + -IC.] **a.** Of, pertaining to, or being an isotope or isotopes of an element; *isotopic number*, the number of neutrons in a nucleus minus the number of protons.

Before Soddy coined the word in 1913, *isotopic* had previously (unknown to him) been used in a different sense (see quot. 1904), but this use did not gain currency.

[**1904** COHEN & MILLER in *Jrnl. Chem. Soc.* LXXXV. 1624 Supposing the bromine in the ortho- and meta-positions to retard oxidation more than the chlorine in these positions, the effect should become apparent when the isotopic dichloro-, chlorobromo-, and dibromo-toluenes are oxidised together. [*Note*] We propose..to employ the word 'isotopic'..in place of the rather awkward expression 'similarly substituted'.] **1913** [see *ISOTOPE 1]. **1919** F. SODDY in *Jrnl. Chem. Soc.* CXV. 18 The chemistry of actinium has been enormously simplified by the discovery that mesothorium-2 is isotopic with it, for the latter may be used as an indicator to show in what way the actinium distributes itself after any chemical treatment. **1920** *Glasgow Herald* 7 Oct. 8 It had now been found that certain elements which hitherto had been stated to have atomic weights fractional were mixtures of isotopes, and such isotopic elements had atomic weights as whole numbers on the oxygen scale. **1921** W. D. HARKINS in *Nature* 14 Apr. 202/2 Let us specify the atoms of this important class as those of isotopic number 0. Then the isotopes of magnesium of atomic weights 24, 25, and 26 will have isotopic numbers 0, 1, and 2. *Ibid.*, The isotopic number *n* is the number which, when added to twice the atomic number, gives the atomic weight. **1933** F. W. ASTON *Mass-Spectra & Isotopes* xiv. 176 Atoms of isotopic number 0, such as C^{12}, O^{16}, Mg^{24}, etc., predominate in a marked degree. Abundance is much less for isotopic number 1 such as F^{19}, Na^{23}, Al^{27}, decreases again for 2:—N^{14}, Ne^{22}, and becomes practically zero for 3:—Cl^{37}. **1942** J. D. STRANATHAN *'Particles' of Mod. Physics* v. 200 Considerable isotopic data has been obtained from studies of hyperfine structure. **1954** *Sci. News* XXXIV. 51 The next simplest use of the mass spectrometer is to measure the quantity of one isotope of an element compared with another—the isotopic ratio as it is called. **1956** A. H. COMPTON *Atomic Quest* i. 52 The isotopic separation of U-235 from U-238. **1957** G. E. HUTCHINSON *Treat. Limnol.* I. viii. 549 A study of the isotopic constitution of the sulfur in the sulfate of rain. **1971** J. Z. YOUNG *Introd. Study Man* v. 82 Many of the elements exist in isotopic forms, which break down spontaneously.

b. Of, pertaining to, or designating isospin; orig. and chiefly in *isotopic spin* = *ISOSPIN.

1937 E. WIGNER in *Physical Rev.* LI. 106/2 W. Heisenberg..considered protons and neutrons as different states of the same particle. Heisenberg introduced a variable τ which we shall call the isotopic spin, the value -1 of this variable can be assigned to the proton state of the particle, the value $+1$ to the neutron state. *Ibid.* 107/1 The Pauli principle requires that the wave function $\Psi(r_1 s_1 \tau_1, r_2 s_2 \tau_2, \ldots, r_n s_n \tau_n)$ be antisymmetric with respect to the simultaneous interchange of Cartesian, spin and isotopic spin variables of any pair of heavy particles. This fact is quite analogous to the similar statement for ordinary spin. *Ibid.* 117/1 Terms with different ζ components of the isotopic spin have the same energy in approximation 2. These are, of course, terms of different isobaric nuclei, and a total isotopic spin T will be a term with the same binding energy for all nuclei with isotopic numbers from $-T$ to T. **1953** M. GELL-MANN in *Physical Rev.* XCII. 833/2 Let us suppose that the new unstable particles are fermions with integral isotopic spin and bosons with half-integral isotopic spin. For example, the V_1 particles may form an isotopic triplet, consisting of $V_1{}^+$, $V_1{}^0$, and $V_1{}^-$. The τ^+ and $V_4{}^0$ may form an isotopic doublet, which we may call τ^+ and τ^0. **1963** K. W. FORD *World of Elem. Particles* viii. 235 For a group of nucleons, a rotation of the total isotopic-spin vector in I space corresponds to changing from one nucleus to another without changing the total number of nucleons. *Ibid.*, New particles..were found to come in closely linked groups, like proton and neutron. There were three pions which formed a triplet and could be described as three states of a single pion with one unit of isotopic spin. **1965** *Listener* 2 Sept. 332/1 Abstract quantities known as 'isotopic spin' and 'hypercharge'. **1969** D. H. WILKINSON *Isospin* i. 3 It is clear that Wigner gave the isotopic spin that name because it is a vector whose z-projection, $\frac{1}{2}(N-Z)$, distinguished one isotope from another along an isobaric multiplet. In fact Wigner often called T_z itself the isotopic spin and T 'the total isotopic spin quantum number'. Others felt that a stronger case could be made to call the new quantum

number the isobaric spin because its magnitude was constant along an isobaric multiplet.

c. Containing or being a less common or special isotope, e.g. as a label. Cf. *ISOTOPE 1 b.

1942 J. D. STRANATHAN *'Particles' of Mod. Physics* v. 209 Heavy water..is one of the few compounds which can be produced in practically pure isotopic form. **1953** FRUTON & SIMMONDS *Gen. Biochem.* xxviii. 641 The administered isotopic glycine had 'mixed' with nonisotopic glycine already present in the body of the animal. **1954** A. WHITE et al. *Princ. Biochem.* xiv. 306 The isotopic material may be administered and, from the subsequent analyses for the appropriate isotope in the various tissues.., the distribution of the isotopic atom may be ascertained. **1958** *Oxf. Univ. Gaz.* 5 June 1127/1 Studies on intermediary metabolism in whole animals using isotopic carbon.

d. Employing or depending on isotopes; obtained by such methods.

1956 A. H. COMPTON *Atomic Quest* v. 326 As of 1956, three hundred American companies are using isotopic thickness gauges. **1962** *Newnes Conc. Encycl. Nucl. Energy* 365/2 Another example of the application of the isotopic tracer technique..is furnished by the use of radioactive iron to investigate the economy of haemoglobin iron. **1969** BENNISON & WRIGHT *Geol. Hist. Brit. Isles* ii. 26 While isotopic dating does provide a system of dating of this kind, giving dates in millions of years, it is too imprecise to be relevant to this problem. **1971** I. G. GASS et al. *Understanding the Earth* ii. 42/1 Laboratory techniques for determining so-called radioisotope, isotopic or radiometric ages of rocks (which used to be erroneously called absolute ages) are extremely complex.

isotopically (əisǒtǫ·pikăli), *adv.* [f. prec.: see -ICALLY.] **a.** As regards isotopes or isotopic constitution.

1933 in *O.E.D.* Suppl. **1940** *Jrnl. Biol. Chem.* CXXXIII. 737 A deuteropalmitic acid is added to a mixture of isotopically normal fatty acids. **1960** *New Scientist* 14 July 136/3 For an age determination it is not sufficient only to analyse the mineral for uranium, thorium and total lead, but the lead must also be analysed isotopically. **1963** G. TROUP *Masers & Lasers* (ed. 2) viii. 136 The electrons were localized on donor (Phosphorus) atoms in isotopically pure silicon of atomic weight 28 which has no nuclear magnetic moment. **1970** *Nature* 23 May 738/2 The solar wind may actually deposit isotopically heavier carbon on the lunar surface. **1970** D. W. TENQUIST et al. *University Optics* II. v. 190 Isotopically pure elements must therefore be used.

b. By means of isotopes or isotopic methods.

1954 *New Biol.* XVI. 74 The behaviour of isotopically labelled molecules. **1959** *Times* 15 May 3/3 (Advt.), Vacancies for Chemists to work on the following projects: ..c) the synthesis of isotopically labelled compounds. **1964** G. H. HAGGIS et al. *Introd. Molecular Biol.* ii. 33 Many steps in the metabolic pathways of cells have been discovered or confirmed using isotopically labelled compounds. **1969** BENNISON & WRIGHT *Geol. Hist. Brit. Isles* xii. 272 The rarity of isotopically datable rocks in the Triassic System of Britain and north-western Europe presents a further problem.

isotopy (əisǫ·tǒpi). [f. *ISOTOP(IC *a.* + -Y[3].] The fact or condition of being isotopic.

1919 F. SODDY in *Jrnl. Chem. Soc.* CXV. 18 Its [*sc.* actinium's] definite location in the periodic table, by virtue of its isotopy with mesothorium-2. **1925** J. JOLY *Surface-Hist. Earth* ix. 150 Isotopy is not peculiar to the uranium and thorium groups of elements. **1926** R. W. LAWSON tr. *Hevesy & Paneth's Man. Radioactivity* xvi. 125 (*heading*) Isotopy and the displacement laws in the light of atomic constitution. **1966** *McGraw-Hill Encycl. Sci. & Technol.* VII. 291/2 The occurrence and degree of isotopy among the 83 elements that are found in nature in significant amounts have been ascertained by means of mass spectrometer studies.

Also **i·sotopism** (in the same sense).

1914 F. SODDY *Chem. Radio-Elements* II. 17 The new data are the isotopism of mesothorium II and actinium, and of radio-actinium and thorium. **1938** *Chem. Abstr.* XXXII. 8925 Evidence is offered that the discovery of the existence of isotopism in nonradioactive elements is another confirmation of O.'s nuclear law of 4.

isotransplant (əisotra·nsplɑnt). *Med.* and *Biol.* [f. ISO- + TRANSPLANT *sb.*] A piece of tissue transplanted from one individual to another of the same inbred strain.

1953 G. D. SNELL in Homburger & Fishman *Physiopath. Cancer* xiv. 358 There exists in the case of isotransplants a possibility for genetic difference between tumor and host that is not found in autotransplants. **1966** *Nature* 23 Apr. 429/2 There was a significantly higher number of acceptances of tumour isotransplants in mice which were pre-treated with 'Cytoxan'. **1971** *Radiology* XCIX. 187/1 The autotransplants were irradiated when they reached an average of approximately 1 cm diameter, significantly larger than the isotransplants.

Hence **isotranspla·nted** *ppl. a.*

1967 *Jrnl. Nat. Cancer Inst.* XXXIX. 1 (*heading*) Morphologic studies of lymphoid tissues during the growth of an isotransplanted mouse tumor. **1970** *Biol. Abstr.* LI. 3130/2 (*heading*) Role of the immune system in the growth of an isotransplanted urethan-induced lymphosarcoma.

isotransplantation (əi:sotrɑnsplɑntē[i]·ʃən). *Med.* and *Biol.* [f. ISO- + TRANSPLANTATION.] † **1.** = *HOMOTRANSPLANTATION. *Obs.*

1909 *Jrnl. Exper. Med.* XI. 194 Of 35 isotransplantations in 17 dogs.., thirty-two parathyroids were either absorbed or necrotic.

2. The operation of transplanting tissue from one individual to another of the same inbred strain.

1962 *Cancer Res.* XXII. 955 A state of relative resistance can be built up in highly inbred skin-compatible C3H mice against the isotransplantation of lymphomas recently induced in the same strain. **1963** *Exper. Cell Res.* XXXII. 618 (*heading*) Resistance against isotransplantation of mouse tumors induced by Rous sarcoma virus. **1966** *Cancer Res.* XXVI. 127/2 Spontaneous loss.., induced loss.., and even gain of antigens..can occur on isotransplantation.

isotron (əi·sotrǫn). [f. ISO- (repr. *isotope*) + *-TRON.] A machine for separating isotopes emitted as ions from an extended source by accelerating them by means of a varying electric field, which causes ions of like mass to bunch together, and applying a transverse radio-frequency field synchronized with the arrival of the bunches, so that the ions are deflected by an amount dependent on their mass.

1945 H. D. SMYTH *Gen. Acct. Devel. Atomic Energy Mil. Purposes* xi. 112 The objective..shifted to the effecting of large-scale separation of uranium isotopes by electromagnetic methods... Of the many electromagnetic schemes suggested, three soon were recognized as being the most promising: the 'calutron' mass separator, the magnetron-type separator.., and the 'isotron' method of 'bunching' a beam of ions. *Ibid.* 118 The device which resulted from Wilson's idea was given the deliberately meaningless name 'isotron'. **1946** *Electronic Engin.* XVIII. 153/3 Another method, dispensing altogether with a magnetic field, makes use of the klystron bunching principle and the device has been called the isotron. *Ibid.*, It is understood from publications on the subject that the isotron method has not yet been fully developed.

isotropic, *a.* Add: Also **isotro·pically** *adv.*, equally in all directions.

1885 *Electrician* 24 Jan. 220/1 If μ = constant, all space equally magnetisable isotropically, then B is the same multiple of H everywhere. **1946** *Nature* 5 Oct. 483/1 The crystal structure of silver is cubic and it expands isotropically. **1970** G. K. WOODGATE *Elem. Atomic Struct.* vi. 98 The electrons are moving freely, with no forces acting on them, and their translational momenta can be taken to be directed isotropically in momentum space.

isotype (əi·sotəip). [f. ISO- + Gr. τύπ-ος TYPE *sb.*[1]; cf. Gr. ἰσότυπος shaped alike.] † **1.** *Biol.* (In Dict. s.v. Iso-.) *Obs.*

1881 [in Dict. s.v. Iso-]. **1905** *Bull. U.S. Nat. Museum* No. 53. 16 Isotypes (*equal* or *like* and *form*): Forms common to different countries; *e.g.* the Shrews are isotypes in Europe and North America.

2. *Min.* Any mineral which is isotypic with another; an assemblage of minerals of which all the members are isotypic with one another.

1901 *Mineral. Mag.* XIII. 52 These minerals are placed by F. Rinne in the 'magnesium type' of his isotypes. **1943** *Science* 22 Jan. 99/1 A more complex type formula is necessary to cover the phosphates, arsenates and hydrates which are now recognized as isotypes. **1947** *Mineral. Abstr.* X. 52 With substitution of Si by other elements various isotypes are illustrated.

3. *Bot.* A duplicate of the *HOLOTYPE.

1919 F. W. PENNELL in *Torreya* XIX. 13 To meet this need [for a term for a duplicate type] I suggest the term isotype. **1943** *Rhodora* XLV. 485 If a type specimen is lost or unavailable an isotype is in general much more important than a paratype for the interpretation of a name. **1966** *Internat. Code Bot. Nomencl.* ii. 19 An isotype is any duplicate (part of a single gathering made by a collector at one time) of the holotype.

4. Also **Isotype.** [f. *I*nternational *s*ystem *o*f *ty*pographic *p*icture *e*ducation.] The name of an international picture language devised by O. Neurath (1882–1945): used esp. to display statistical information in a convenient visual form.

1936 O. NEURATH *Internat. Picture Lang.* 17 We have made *one* international picture language..into which statements may be put from all the normal languages of the earth. We have given it the name 'isotype'. **1945** G. WILLIAMS *Women & Work* 10 Isotype charts..illustrate and elaborate the argument. **1948** *Sunday Times* 15 Feb. 2/6 A record in powerful and sometimes horrifying images of misery, interrupted by only a few isotypes. **1950** NEURATH & LAUWERYS *Living in Early Times* 1 These Isotype symbols..are always kept as simple and clear as possible. **1966** *Chambers's Encycl.* IX. 792/2 He [*sc.* O. Neurath] developed the 'isotype', a system of visual linguistics... His isotype films, e.g. *World of Plenty*, attracted wide attention. **1966** M. PEI *Gloss. Ling. Terminology* 135 *Isotype*, a system of writing that uses non-phonetic symbols of universal significance, designed as a medium of education, but also to convey information in ready visual form (the picture of one soldier to indicate an army division).

isotypic (əisoti·pik), *a.* [f. prec. + -IC.] **1.** (In Dict. s.v. Iso-.)

2. *Min.* [ad. G. *isotyp* (F. Rinne 1894, in *Neues Jahrb. f. Mineral., Geol. u. Palaeontol.* I. 55).] Having the same or similar crystal structure (i.e. isostructural) and, with some authors, having in addition analogous chemical formulæ; exhibiting such similarity. Const. *with*.

1929 H. L. BOWMAN *Miers's Mineral.* (ed. 2) 251 Substances which thus have the same type of composition and resemble one another in their angles and structure have been described by F. Rinne as 'isotypic'. **1942** *Mineral. Abstr.* VIII. 220 It [*sc.* berlinite] is therefore identical with artificial $AlPO_4$..and isomorphous with $AlAsO_4$.., which are isotypic with quartz. **1943** *Amer. Mineralogist* XXVIII. 598 Na_2BeF_4 was shown by them to be isotypic with γ-Ca_2SiO_4. **1943** *Science* 22 Jan. 98/2 Investigations..have revealed new isomorphic and isotypic relationships among silicates and phosphates. **1959** W. H. DENNEN *Princ. Mineral.* iii. 104 Isotypic minerals are those with both isostructural characteristics and chemical similarity. *Ibid.*, The members of an isomorphous series are isotypic, but..isotypic minerals are not necessarily isomorphous. **1959** W. F. DE JONG *Gen. Crystallogr.* 182 If the structures of two compounds are entirely or nearly equal, and if the ratios of the dimensions do not differ much, the structures are called isotypic. NaCl and PbS form isotypic structures. **1968** MASON & BERRY *Elem. Mineral.* (new ed.) iii. 83 Sometimes the terms isostructural or isotypic are used instead of isomorphous.

isotypy (əi·sotəipi). *Min.* [ad. G. *isotypie* (F. Rinne 1894, in *Neues Jahrb. f. Mineral., Geol. u. Palaeontol.* I. 55): see *ISOTYPE and -Y[3].] The character or state of being isotypic (sense *2); isotypic relationship. Also **isoty·pism** (in the same sense).

1938 *Mineral. Abstr.* VII. 92 A list of similar isotypism between other silicates and phosphates (or arsenates) is given. **1942** *Chem. Abstr.* XXXVI. 694 (*heading*) Isotypy between phosphates of general composition $MLiPO_4$ and silicates of the olivine-monticellite series. **1943** *Science* 22 Jan. 98/2 The isotypism of $AlPO_4$ and SiO_2. **1943** *Amer. Mineralogist* XXVIII. 598 O'Daniel and Tscheischwili consider the isotypy of Ca_2SiO_4 and Na_2BeF_4 as limited to the low-temperature modifications. **1959** W. F. DE JONG *Gen. Crystallogr.* 182 (*heading*) Isotypism. **1967** Isotypy [see *FLINKITE].

isovaleraldehyde, isovalerate, isovalerianic, isovaleric, isoxazole: see *ISO- b. **isovol:** see *ISO-.

isozyme (əi·sozəim). *Biochem.* [f. ISO- + *EN)ZYME.] = *ISOENZYME.

1959 MARKERT & MØLLER in *Proc. Nat. Acad. Sci.* XLV. 753 We propose, therefore, to use the term *isozyme* to describe the different molecular forms in which proteins may exist with the same enzymatic activity. **1968** T. WIELAND in Thoai & Roche *Homologous Enzymes & Biochem. Evolution* iii. 3 The second group of multiple forms consists of the so called 'isozymes'. They may be defined as the multiple molecular forms of an enzyme existing within a single organism. *Ibid.* 9 Isozymes are multiple forms of enzymes, which occur in one cell or—less strictly defined—in one organ of an organism. **1968** *New Scientist* 21 Mar. 649/2 LDH exists in five very slightly different forms... Each version is known as an isozyme of LDH, and each will catalyze the final glycolysis step.

Hence **isozy·mic** *a.*

1959 MARKERT & MØLLER in *Proc. Nat. Acad. Sci.* XLV. 756 The relative enzymatic activity disposed in each isozymic band. **1973** *Nature* 3 Aug. 261/2 The genes for isozymic forms of various enzymes are often not linked to each other.

ispaghul (i·spagūl). Also **ishabgul, ispagool, ispughool, isubgol.** [Hind., a. Pers. *asp* horse + *gol* ear, in allusion to the shape of the leaves or seeds.] A plantain, esp. *Plantago ovata*, native to India and Persia, the dried seeds of which are used medicinally.

1810 J. FLEMING in *Asiatick Researches* XI. 174 *Plantago Ispaghul* (Roxb. MS.) *Ispaghul*, H[industani]... *Ispughool* [Sanskrit]. **1820** W. ROXBURGH et al. *Flora Indica* I. 404 *Ispagool*, the Hindee and Persian name, and that by which it is most generally known in Bengal and on the coast of Coromandel. **1880** BENTLEY & TRIMEN *Medicinal Plants* III. § 211 Ispaghŭl seeds have long been highly valued in India and other parts of the East for their cooling and demulcent properties. **1889** G. S. BOULGER *Uses of Plants* II. 111 The mucilaginous seeds of *Plantago decumbens*, Forsk., Ispaghúl, or Spogel, are used in India as a demulcent drink, especially in dysentery. **1931** M. GRIEVE *Mod. Herbal* II. 643/1 Plantain, Ispaghul. *Ibid.* 643/2 The seeds of the Indian species, *Plantago Amplexicaulis*, are sold in the bazaars as Ispaghula. **1953** B. MUKERJI *Indian Pharmaceutical Codex* I. 124 Commercial samples of ishabgul consist of the seeds of *P. arenaria* Waldst., *P. lanceolata* Linn., *P. major* Linn. besides *P. ovata* Forsk. and *P. psyllium* Linn. **1969** *Wealth of India* (Council Sci. & Industr. Res. India) VIII. 151/1 The efficacy of isubgol is due entirely to the large quantity of mucilage present in the husk.

Ispahan (i·spăhān). Also **Isfahan.** The name of a province and town in West Central Persia, used *attrib.* and *ellipt.* to designate a type of hand-woven rug, the most distinguished of which were produced there in the 16th century.

1931 A. U. DILLEY *Oriental Rugs & Carpets* ii. 32 From the succeeding court came, during the sixteenth century, the 'Ispahan' rugs so greatly esteemed by collectors. *Ibid.* iii. 61 A fourth group of superior rugs, distinguished by pattern of palmette and now called Ispahan. **1960** H. HAYWARD *Antique Coll.* 149/2 *Ispahan carpets*, Persian carpets or rugs, often employing medallion or vase designs..in a wide range of colours, the composition being very well balanced. **1969** 'W. HAGGARD' *Doubtful Disciple*

xv. 166 The dealers call them Isfahans and..know they're Heratis. **1969** B. Weil *Dossier IX* v. 38 A carpet that.. Asher could see was an Isfahan. **1970** V. Canning *Great Affair* iv. 50 He took the heavy Passavant carpet from the floor..added a smaller Ispahan rug.

‖ **ispravnik** (ispra·vnik). *Hist.* Pl. **ispravniki, ispravniks.** [Russ., lit. 'executor'.] A chief of police in a rural district in Czarist Russia.

1886 *Encycl. Brit.* XXI. 70/2 The organs of the central government..are..the *stanovoys* and *ispravniks* (chiefs of the police) in the districts. **1898** J. Y. Simpson *Side-Lights on Siberia* 90 The *ispravnik* of the district happened to be in the village. **1906** *Daily Chron.* 24 Aug. 5/6 The police informed the ispravnik (chief of rural police). **1911** *Encycl. Brit.* XXIII. 876/1 As organs of the central government there are further, the *ispravniki*, chiefs of police in the districts into which the governments are divided. **1952** H. Altschuler tr. *Gorky's Artamonovs* i. 156 The ispravnik shook a threatening finger, and shouted: 'Hush, fool!' **1967** H. Seton-Watson *Russ. Empire* I. i. 20 The chief executive officer at the *uezd* level was the *ispravnik*, who was elected by the nobility, and presided over the local court which was an administrative rather than a judicial body.

Israel. Add: **3.** An independent Jewish State established in 1948 in the country formerly called Palestine. Also *attrib.*

1948 *Manch. Guardian* 15 May 5/1 The Jews yesterday proclaimed in Tel Aviv the new State of Israel. **1957** L. F. R. Williams *State of Israel* 13 The Israel Government has been kindness personified in helping me with my researches. *Ibid.* 17 The modern state of Israel occupies part of territory which in ancient times formed a link between the civilizations of Egypt, Asia Minor and Mesopotamia. **1958** *Economist* 26 July 300/2 The western armies cannot stay in the Middle East indefinitely, while Israel must live in the region forever. **1972** *Encycl. Judaica* I. 12 According to official government usage, Israel (and not Israeli) is the adjective relating to Israel: Israeli is a citizen (or permanent resident) of the State of Israel. **1972** *Times* 24 Mar. 10/4 Israel has decided to recall its military experts from Uganda. **1974** *Times* 17 Apr. 14/7 Israel newspaper correspondents were given preferential treatment. *Ibid.* 14/8 The ban remained for Israel-based reporters... The Israel government has followed a curious policy.

Hence **Isra·eli** *sb.*, (*a*) a native or inhabitant of the State of Israel; (*b*) the language spoken by the inhabitants of the State of Israel (more usually called *Modern Hebrew*). Also **Israeli** *a.*, relating to the State of Israel, its inhabitants, etc.

1948 *Daily Tel.* 23 June 1/1 A coastal vessel of the Israeli Navy stood by. **1948** *N.Y. Times Mag.* 5 Dec. 4/3 Shortly after the proclamation of the new State of Israel.. Moshe Shertok announced that its citizens would be called Israelis. **1949** Koestler *Promise & Fulfilment* II. ii. 222 His English is good with a specific Israeli-*sabra* accent. **1949** H. Nicolson *Diary* 25 July (1968) 173 George Weidenfeld..has been asked by [Chaim] Weizmann to become his personal assistant. The problem is whether he should become an Israeli and get a definite job in the Israeli civil service. **1958** *Economist* 26 July 300/1 The Israeli government has asked Britain to order another course for the airflight to Jordan. **1964** R. MacGregor-Hastie *Pope Paul VI* x. 215 The Pope greeted Dr. Shazar in Israeli—'Shalom, Shalom!' **1967** *Listener* 8 June 741/1 The Israelis, with their small country and just over two million population, can never conquer the Arab States. **1972** [see 3 above].

iss (is), *adv.* Dial. var. Yes *adv.* (*sb.*[2]); also used to represent an inaccurate pronunciation of 'yes' by a speaker whose native language is not English.

1795 'P. Pindar' *Royal Visit to Exeter* II. 17 Iss, iss, he'll do the feat. **1829** G. Griffin *Collegians* (ed. 2) I. xii. 259 'Erra, no!' 'Iss, dear knows.' **1853** Mrs. Gaskell *Ruth* I. vi. 154 One servant-girl..was wearied out of what little English she had knowledge of..and could only answer, 'Iss, indeed, ma'am,' to any question. **1890** A. Gissing *Village Hampden* I. i. 19 Iss, Miss—but 'ere he be. *a* **1966** C. S. Forester *Hornblower & Crisis* (1967) vii. 71 'You boy!..D'you want to earn a shilling?' 'Iss, that do I.'

issuance. (Earlier and later examples.)

1863 *National Almanac & Ann. Rec.* 545/2 A proclamation of neutrality..was issued by Victoria, Queen of England... A brigade of British Volunteers..enlisted in the North..disbanded after its issuance. **1905** *Westm. Gaz.* 11 Jan. 1/3 The new canon insists on at least a year's delay after the issuance of a decree of divorce before any marriage can take place. **1931** G. T. Clark *Leland Stanford* vii. 214 The Supreme Court rendered another decision..to compel the issuance of the bonds voted by the people of San Francisco. **1967** *Boston Sunday Herald* VI. 5/1 (Advt.), You save 25% on the issuance charge. **1972** *Science* 12 May 640/2 Overzealous concern with style and format of writing imposed by the issuance, first in 1909, of the Survey's style manual. **1972** *N.Y. Law Jrnl.* 22 Aug. 12/1 A brother..filed objections and cross-moved for issuance of letters to him.

issue, *sb.* Add: **13*.** *the* (*whole*) *issue*: everything, the lot. *colloq.*

1919 W. H. Downing *Digger Dial.* 29 *Issue*, 1. A portion; 2. 'to get one's issue'—to be killed; 3. 'to get the whole issue of a shell'—to be struck bodily by a shell. **1925** Fraser & Gibbons *Soldier & Sailor Words* 129 Not a soul got back; the whole issue were done in last night. **1930** Brophy & Partridge *Songs & Slang 1914–18* 131 *The issue* was also used for 'the whole lot', e.g. 'There's no rum tonight. The sergeant's snaffled the issue.' **1941** Baker *Dict. Austral. Slang* 38 *Issue*, all, everything, the lot. **1960** K. Amis *Take Girl like You* i. 10 He put a metal flint-scratcher into the mouth of the geyser and went clicking away... 'Now the water... Funny. The whole issue should light up now.' **1966** 'L. Lane' *ABZ of Scouse* 53 Yer've buggered up ther 'ole issue.

14. b. (Of books and periodicals: examples.)

1833 *Penny Mag.* Monthly Suppl. Nov.–Dec. 511/1, 12,000 copies of each number (the quantity required for the first issue of the volume [*sc.* of the *Penny Magazine*]) will have been delivered to two book-binders. **1895** B. Wood in *Brontë Soc. Trans.* I. i. 4 Many of the editions of the Brontë Works are merely reprints of previous issues. **1910** C. Shorter in E. Brontë *Compl. Poems* p. vi, It is a curious irony of circumstance that this little volume [*sc.* the Brontë *Poems*]..now sells..for more money than the whole issue cost Charlotte Brontë and her sisters when they had it published at their own expense. **1929** J. L. Young *Bks. from MS. to Bookseller* viii. 93 Quite a considerable proportion of the issue of every book is given away for one purpose or another. **1954** *Willing's Press Guide* p. vii, With this issue..we announce important policy developments... As from this edition special supplements will be issued. **1962** M. Toase *Guide Current Brit. Periodicals* p. viii, Information given in the entries. .. Date of first issue. **1974** *Leisure Painter & Craftsman* Aug. (verso front cover), We have invited Mr. Harry Richardson to outline, in this issue, his..approach to the problem.

(ii) *Bibliogr.* In bibliogr. classification and description, a subdivision of an edition (or of an impression [see *impression *sb.* 3 d] of an edition), denoting a distinct form, planned and put on sale by the publishers, of the edition (or impression) sheets; a new issue is normally indicated by the provision of a new title-leaf, with or without other changes.

In some cases the precise application of *issue* in this sense remains subject to discussion.

1928 M. Sadleir *Trollope: a Bibliogr.* p. xiii, It would be well to distinguish clearly between an 'issue' and a 'binding-up'. An 'issue' represents an order from the publishers for a definite effort in publication... It is a *piece of publishing*, and reflects some definite intention in the publishers' mind. A 'binding-up', on the other hand, is a mere replenishment of the stock in a publisher's warehouse. **1949** F. Bowers *Princ. Bibliogr. Descr.* ii. 41 *Issue* is included within *edition* and itself includes only *state*. *Ibid.* 78 Removed from consideration [*sc.* of issue] are all alterations made during continuous printing of the original sheets, as well as alterations made after public sale had begun which are largely for the purpose of constructing an 'ideal copy'. We must take it as a fundamental assumption that, except in the most uncommon circumstances, sheets will not be re-issued without a change of title-page... It is impossible to set up any standards for issue [*sc.* for hand-printed books] which have any likelihood of uniform and logical application unless the title-page is taken as the prime evidence. *Ibid.* xi. 403 Sadleir's correct refusal to admit as issues those bindings-up exhibiting small variants in the binding not the result of a publisher's order helps sweep away the majority of the ridiculously conceived modern 'issues' but still leaves various ambiguities. *Ibid.* 419 Alterations to the text [*sc.* of 19th- and 20th-century books] are a cause of re-issue even if the title-page is unaffected, providing they go beyond the standards of *ideal copy* and were not made during the course of printing the impression affected... At the publisher's request, the text of D. H. Lawrence's.. *White Peacock* (1911) was altered in certain respects by the substitution of two cancellans leaves..causing re-issue... In *The White Peacock*..the second issue is found in a second state. **1952** J. Carter *ABC for Bk.-Collectors* 108 Since differences of issue are bibliographically tidier and more straightforward than differences of state, and since the term falls much more pleasingly on the priority-conscious ear, a good many undeterminable cases have been, and no doubt will continue to be, given the benefit of the doubt. **1960** G. A. Glaister *Gloss. Bk.* 200/1 Before the term 'issue' can first be applied, copies of the work without any of the changes now involved must have already been published. Bibliographers then speak of a 'first issue' and a 'second issue' of the 'first edition'. The term is less precisely used in the book trade. **1969** E. W. Padwick *Bibliogr. Method* xvi. 206 Both *issue* and *state* are included within *impression*... Basically, *issue* should be regarded as an act of intent by the publisher to effect some change in the yet unbound copies of an impression after the publication of some copies has taken place. **1972** P. Gaskell *New Introd. Bibliogr.* 317 The term 'edition' has always been used in the trade for 'impression' or 'issue' as well as for edition in the bibliographical sense; a book that is advertised as a 'new edition'..may be.. simply a reissue of the original sheets with a new title-page.

c. An item or amount of something given out or distributed. orig. *U.S.*

1861 *Regulations Army U.S.* 283 His descriptive list.. on which the surgeon shall enter all payments, stoppages, and issues of clothing to him in hospital. **1881** *Rep. Indian Affairs* (U.S.) 10 They agreed to go as soon as the issue of beef..had been made. **1882** *Cassell's Family Mag.* June 399/1 He is also responsible that the proper issues of bread and meat are made to the men. **1899** T. W. Hall *Tales* 109 Then our..aching bodies are loaded down with a further issue of ammunition. **1911** H. Quick *Yellowstone Nights* xii. 305 'You represent the Elkins interests in the matter of supplying for the issue do you not?' says he. *Ibid.* 321 She hove in sight of the issue. **1919** *Athenæum* 8 Aug. 727/2 Anything supplied by the Army was an 'issue'. **1940** 'Gun Buster' *Return via Dunkirk* I. ii. 20 His beard..had all the luxuriance of a ten-days unhampered growth...Some of our gunners began to give themselves a morning shave...His face..said..'Do as you please. I'm sticking to mine. I'm not likely to get a better issue.' **1942** E. E. Dale *Cow Country* 163 They [*sc.* Amerindians] could not subsist upon the present issue of eighty thousand pounds a week.

15. (sense 11) *issue roll*; (sense *14 c) *issue boot, cigarette, day, house, mess tin, shoe.*

1927 *Daily Express* 4 Oct. 3 Men..running up and down perpendicular 4-inch steel stairs in issue boots without arriving in hospital. **1925** Fraser & Gibbons *Soldier & Sailor Words* 129 An 'Issue' cigarette..was a ration cigarette, in contradistinction to one bought at the Canteen. **1874** R. Glisan *Jrnl. Army Life* xxxi. 447 They gave the white physicians much annoyance by coming for medicine only on issue or ration day. **1878** *Rep. Indian Affairs* (U.S.) 39 Other mechanics are putting up new store and issue-houses. **1911** H. Quick *Yellowstone Nights* xii. 316 The way we..hit the trail f'r the Issue House was a high-class piece o' teamin'. **1944** *Living off Land* vii. 145 The Australian issue mess tin is light, durable and well-suited to bush cooking. **1886** *Encycl. Brit.* XX. 312/1 The judgment rolls pass through three stages—first, they are plea rolls; then, when the parties join issue, issue rolls; and lastly,..judgment rolls. **1946** *R.A.F. Jrnl.* May 155, I put on a pair of R.A.F. issue shoes which I had grabbed.

issue, *v.* Add: **9.** (Of books and periodicals: earlier and later examples.)

1833 *Penny Mag.* Monthly Suppl. Oct.–Nov. 472/1 Twenty million 'Penny Magazines' have been issued from the commencement. **1876** 'Mark Twain' *Lett. to Publishers* (1967) 95 It is going to rush you too tight to do your canvassing and issue 'Tom' [sc. *Tom Sawyer*] in the middle of April isn't it? **1954** [see *issue *sb.* 14 b]. **1966** (*title*) The English catalogue of books..1963–1965, giving..the size, price, date of publication, and publisher of books issued in the United Kingdom.

11. To give things out to (a person); to supply (a person) *with*. (Cf. *issue *sb.* 14 c.)

1925 T. G. Bruce in E. F. Norton *Fight for Everest, 1924* 344 Every man in the Expedition should be issued with one blanket either in Kalimpong or Phari. **1927** *Daily Tel.* 27 Sept. 8/6 Infantry battalions were issued with two weighted dummies apiece. **1928** *Sunday Express* 18 Mar. 3/2 The extraordinary experience of being twice in a year issued by the same bank with a faulty £1 Treasury note. **1929** F. A. Pottle *Stretchers* (1930) 37 Before we were issued our heavy trench shoes. **1953** *Listener* 6 Aug. 224/2 Then, the idiom 'issued with': 'He was issued with' a rifle, and a packet of cigarettes, or what not. I suppose this horror has come to stay. It is undeniably convenient. **1961** *Oxford Times* 15 Dec. 14/9 He stated that he had not been issued with a licence previously when, in fact, one had been issued by Surrey County Council earlier that year.

issuing, *vbl. sb.* Add: **3. issuing house**: see quot. 1965.

1929 *Issuing House Year Bk.* 3 The requirements of an Issuing House in the production of a Prospectus are more exacting than for almost any other work the printer is called upon to undertake. **1932** *Daily Tel.* 8 Oct. 2/3 Regarding the continued default on City of Riga 4½ p.c. Bonds,..what is inexplicable is that the bondholders have shown such apathy and negligence in this matter respecting the negotiations between the issuing house and the City of Riga. **1965** Perry & Ryder *Thomson's Dict. Banking* (ed. 11) 317/2 The main function of an issuing house is to obtain from the public capital for the expansion of existing companies, for new public companies, or for private companies being converted into public concerns.

‖ **istana** (istā·na). Also **astana, astanah.** [Mal. *istana*, ad. Skr. *ā-sthāna* place, site, assembly.] In Malay kingdoms, a ruler's palace.

1839 T. J. Newbold *Pol. & Statistical Acct. Straits of Malacca* II. viii. 90 He married Tuanku Itam..and proceeded to his astánah in Srimenanti. **1907** F. A. Swettenham *Brit. Malaya* xiii. 315 The Sultan's *astâna* or palace ..surrounds on three sides a court of sand. **1927** R. J. H. Sidney *In Brit. Malaya Today* xxiii. 271 His [*sc.* the Sultan's] *Istana* at Klang is filled with work done by his own hand. **1965** *Festival Malaysia 1965: Calendar of Events* 6/1 The Investiture Ceremony held in the afternoon at the Istana in Sri-Menanti is followed by a Garden Party in the evening. **1972** *Sunday Times* (Kuala Lumpur) 30 Apr. 5/2 The Yang di-Pertuan Agong today presented awards to 76 people at an investiture ceremony at the Istana Negara. **1972** *Straits Times* (Malaysia ed.) 24 Nov. 20/6 This Istana in the village of Bandar was the residence of Sultan Abdul Samad in the middle of the nineteenth century.

Istrian (i·striăn), *a.* and *sb.* [f. *Istria*, a peninsula near the head of the Adriatic sea; see -an.] **A.** *adj.* **1.** Of or belonging to Istria.

1607 Topsell *Four-f. Beasts* 288 The Istrian Horsses are of good able feete. **1881** E. A. Freeman *Sk. Subject Lands Venice* 98 The Istrian shore has lost its beauty. **1920** *Glasgow Herald* 16 Apr. 8 The 'conversation' broke down solely on the question of the Istrian frontier. **1967** C. Seton-Watson *Italy from Liberalism to Fascism* xi. 426 A new and energetic Minister of War, General Vittorio Zupelli, of Istrian origin, took the job of military preparation systematically in hand.

2. Special Comb.: **Istrian marble, stone,** a fine limestone resembling marble; also *ellipt.*; **Istrian pointer,** a hunting dog (in Yugoslavia).

1611 Coryat *Crudities* 163 Stately pillers made partly of white stone, and partly of Istrian marble. **1947** J. C. Rich *Materials & Methods Sculpture* viii. 228 Istrian marble, which is found on the Istrian peninsula and on some of the Dalmatian islands, is a large-grained, buff marble that compares favorably with the Greek marbles. **1971** *Country Life* 18 Feb. 16F Suppl., A most important 17th century Italian Istrian marble wall fountain. **1948** A. Lokar in B. Vesey-Fitzgerald *Bk. Dog* II. 536 The Istrski Brak (Istrian Pointer) has a wide range in Yugoslavia. **1888** *Encycl. Brit.* XXIV. 149/2 This Istrian stone

has for most architectural purposes all the beauty of the finest white marble. **1962** *Listener* 27 Dec. 1105/3 The sculptor is not above counterpointing the folds of a drapery or the positioning of a hand with the natural pressure lines in a fine piece of green Istrian. **1972** *Country Life* 6 Jan. 16/1 This colonnade..culminates in an early baroque Italian fountain of Istrian stone.

B. *sb.* A native or inhabitant of Istria.

1880 *Encycl. Brit.* XIII. 433/2 The Istrians..were only subdued by the Romans in 177 B.C. after two wars. **1974** *She* Jan. 28/2 The Istrians are hospitable and friendly.

it, *pron.* Add: **1. d.** Sexual intercourse. Now *slang* or *colloq.* Cf. *DO *v.* 16 b.

1611 COTGRAVE *Dict.*, *Fretiller*..to..lust to be at it. **1896** FARMER *Vocab. Amatoria* 118/1 *Faire*, to copulate; 'to do it'. **1922** JOYCE *Ulysses* 747 Gardner said no man could look at my mouth and teeth smiling like that and not think of it. **1923** T. WOLFE *Lett.* (1956) 45, I have been reading the *Amores* of Ovid this morning. It is beautiful Latin and beautiful poetry—although it is altogether concerned with two topics: How am I going to get it and How fine it was when you let me have it. **1941** H. G. WELLS *You can't be too Careful* III. xi. 161 Edward Albert knew.. of venereal disease, clumsy 'precautions' and the repulsive aspects of the overwhelming desire for 'It'. **1949** N. MITFORD *Love in Cold Climate* I. xi. 119, I was lugged off to their secret meeting-place..to be asked what IT was like. **1972** F. WARNER *Maquettes* 16 He doesn't even know I'm overdue. And he hasn't had it for a week.

e. In emphatic predicative use: the actual or very thing required or expected; that beyond which one cannot go; the *ne plus ultra*; the acme. (In 20th-c. use from U.S.)

a **1834** C. LAMB *Dramatic Ess.* (1891) 52 Lovegrove.. revived the character..and made it sufficiently grotesque; but Dodd was *it*, as it came out of Nature's hands. **1896** ADE *Artie* i. 4, I didn't do a thing but push my face in there about eight o'clock last night, and I was 'it' from the start. **1900** *Dialect Notes* II. I. 42 Did he know his Greek? I should say so. He was *it*. **1904** F. LYNDE *Grafters* xxx. 397 Mrs. Hepzibah..thinks you are It. **1906** *Daily Chron.* 5 Mar. 6/6 There is in America a curious use of the word 'it' conveyed by emphasis. Pre-eminently Roosevelt is 'it'. Next after Roosevelt an American would say 'Shaw is it'. **1915** 'I. HAY' *First Hundred Thousand* xx. 307 You can't go anywhere in London without running up against him. He is It. **1916** 'TAFFRAIL' *Pincher Martin* vii. 111 On board his ship he had a very poor time; but ashore he was absolutely *it*, so far as the ladies were concerned. **1923** D. H. LAWRENCE *Birds, Beasts & Flowers* 206 Red Men still stick themselves over with bits of his fluff, And feel absolutely *it*. **1930** H. M. SMITH *Inspector Frost in City* III. v. 103, I have some new plus-fours which are 'it'. **1963** P. WILLMOTT *Evolution of Community* i. 8 People were making themselves out to be something they weren't... They thought they were it.

f. In children's games, the player who has the task of catching or touching the others. Also *transf.* and *fig.*

1842 R. CHAMBERS *Pop. Rhymes Scotl.* 62/2 The tig usually catches and touches some one upon the crown before all are *in*—otherwise he has to be *it* for another game. **1888** [see *COUNT *v.* 15 b]. **1923** KIPLING *Land & Sea Tales* 279 As the sides are chosen and all submit To the chance of the lot that shall make them 'It'. **1949** J. B. PRIESTLEY *Delight* 137 The boy who was 'it' retrieved the can and replaced it in the circle. **1950** C. S. LEWIS *Lion, Witch & Wardrobe* iii. 30 They decided to play hide-and-seek. Susan was 'It' and..the others scattered to hide. **1969** I. & P. OPIE *Children's Games* i. 18 They do whatever they can to avoid being..the one who, as they express it, is..'it'. **1970** G. JACKSON *Let.* 23 Mar. in *Soledad Brother* (1971) 188 It's us against them, hide and seek. They're always it and getting caught means getting dusted. **1974** S. GULLIVER *Vulcan Bulletins* 111 'I'm not helping to get him knocked off to suit..the CIA.' 'That's too bad, Lee,' said Selby quietly, 'because you're it.'

g. 'Sex appeal.'

1904 KIPLING *Traffics & Discoveries* 352 'Tisn't beauty, so to speak, nor good talk necessarily. It's just It. Some women'll stay in a man's memory if they once walk down a street. **1927** E. GLYN '*It*' i. 10 He had that nameless charm, with a strong magnetism which can only be called 'It'. **1930** G. B. STERN *Mosaic* III. i. 205 The Viennese composer made his first awed acquaintance with the words pep, kick, body-urge, sex-appeal, a hundred-per-cent. stuff, spin it along, put it over, and It. **1932** *Bystander* 23 Mar. 546 A film star who has proved to producers and film public alike that she is blessed with that undefinable quality called 'It'. **1972** L. P. BACHMANN *Ultimate Act* i. 16 She really had 'It', as it was called.

2. e. *this is it* colloq. phr.: used when something previously spoken about or foreboded has come to pass or is about to happen.

[**1908** G. MURRAY tr. *Aristophanes' Frogs* I. iii. 34 That's it, sir. These are the Initiated Rejoicing somewhere, just as he told us.] **1942** *Newsweek* 27 July 23/3 Finucane tried to settle the rocking plane onto the water. It hit the waves, then sank like a rock. Just before, Paddy spoke into the two-way radio: 'This is it, chaps.' **1959** *Sunday Times* 5 Apr. 15/7 He heard the sound of countless aircraft overhead. This is it, he thought.

f. *that's it* (and similar colloq. phrases): there is no more to it than that.

1966 P. WILLMOTT *Adolescent Boys E. London* v. 88 You got no encouragement. They'd look at the report at the end of term and that was about it. *Ibid.* 92 We just sat about..doing half-witted things. You only had to find a weak teacher and that was it. **1968** *Listener* 31 Oct. 574/3 Really I think the Brummie likes to stay at home. And work. And shop in Birmingham. Holiday in Majorca —and that's it. **1968** *New Yorker* 2 Nov. 163 They are excellent musicians (except for one of the girls, whose function is obscure; she shakes a tambourine now and then, but that's about it). **1972** *Observer* (Colour Suppl.) 13 Feb. 18/1 Adoption agencies are wary..of any people who want to adopt for any reason other than that they love children, that they have homes and that there are children who need homes. To put it briefly, parents are parents and that's it.

3. f. (Later examples.)

1840 K. H. DIGBY *Mores Catholici* x. vii. 171 In Saxon histories... Thus it says. **1894** G. F. X. GRIFFITH tr. *C. Fouard's St. Paul* xv. 352 From the sequel, as it reads in the Acts, it would seem [etc.]. **1902** H. K. MANN *Lives of Popes* I. II. 234 'In mense Junius Indictione ii,' or x., as by mistake it reads in the *Chronicle*. **1932** CHESTERTON *Chaucer* iii. 108 Chaucer was a man for whom the world teemed with quiet fun, as it says in the comic opera. **1955** tr. *William of Rubruck's Journey* in C. Dawson *Mongol Mission* xxxvii. 212 In Isaias it says that they fled into the land of Ararat.

g. (Later examples of *were it not* or *had it not been for*, *if it were not*, etc., *for*.)

1710 SWIFT *Jrnl. to Stella* 30 Sept. (1948) I. 47 They may talk of the *you know what*; but, gad, if it had not been for that I should never have been able to get the access I have had. *a* **1732** J. GAY *Fables* (1738) II. xiii. 118 Were it not for this cursed show'r, The park had whil'd away an hour. **1736** J. BUTLER *Analogy of Relig.* II. v. 200 Assistance which they would have had no Occasion for, had it not been for their Misconduct. **1780** *Mirror* No. 102 The misapplication of the term is so completely ridiculous, as to be beneath contempt, were it not for the mischief that I am convinced has been occasioned by it. **1864** G. MEREDITH *Emilia in England* II. v. 69, I feel better already, if it weren't for my legs. **1974** *Times Lit. Suppl.* 5 Apr. 375/2 Disaster that would have been total had it not been for the conventional crime-writer's beginning and end.

It, it (it), *sb.* See *gin and it* s.v. *GIN *sb.*² 2 b.

ita (i·tă). Substitute for entry ITA-PALM: Also **eta, ite.** [f. Arawak *ite*.] In full, *ita palm*. The tropical South American fan-palm, *Mauritia flexuosa*, or the drink made from its fermented sap; cf. *ETA².

1845 *Encycl. Metrop.* XX. 6/2 The Eta, a smaller kind of this [cabbage] palm, furnishes nuts. **1860** MAYNE REID *Odd People* 360 The *itá* is a true palm-tree. **1866** [in Dict. s.v. ITA-PALM]. **1904** W. H. HUDSON *Green Mansions* xxii. 292 Even the Ita palm and mountain glory..had lost all grace and beauty. **1922** W. E. ROTH tr. *Schomburgk's Trav. Brit. Guiana* I. 150 There was..a considerable supply of a rarer drink, the Ite, manufactured by the Indians from the juice of *Mauritia flexuosa*. **1957** M. SWAN *Brit. Guiana* x. 152 An outcrop of sandy soil has produced a cluster of ite palms, those 'trees of life' found all over the coastal areas.

‖ **itai-itai** (i·təiˌi·təi). [Jap., lit. 'ouch-ouch'.] A disease, first reported in Japan in 1955, caused by the ingestion of cadmium and characterized by severe pain particularly in the back.

1969 *Keio Jrnl. Med.* (Tokyo) XVIII. 181 (*title*) Causation of ouch-ouch disease (Itai-Itai byō). **1970** *Biol. Abstr.* LI. 4256/1 Rice straw samples used were 2 kinds of stubble grown in the 'Itai-itai' disease epidemic district. **1973** *Biol. Conservation* V. 143 *Itai-itai* originated in the prefectures of Toyama and Gumma, in north-western Japan. The cause of the affliction, however, is world-wide: rivers poisoned by effluence from smelters.

Italian, *a.* and *sb.* Add: **A.** *adj.* **4.** *Italian clover, paper, vermouth*; **Italian cypress,** *Cupressus sempervirens* var. *stricta*; **Italian earth,** the colour sienna; **Italian garden,** a formal garden, characterized by clipped trees, box-edged beds of flowers, paved paths, statues, fountains, etc.; often arranged in terraces linked by steps and balustrades; **Italian paste,** the paste from which macaroni and vermicelli are made; **Italian pink** = **Dutch pink*; **Italian quilting** (see quots.); **Italian stitch,** a form of CROSS-STITCH *sb.*

1840 C. DEWEY in Dewey & Emerson *Rep. Herbaceous Plants & Quadrupeds Mass.* 66 *Trifolium incarnatum*, Italian clover. **1908** *Animal Managem.* 109 'Valerian', 'Italian' or 'Crimson clover', commonly called 'Trifolium'. **1838** J. C. LOUDON *Arboretum* IV. 2464 The common, or evergreen, Cypress... Synonymes...the Italian Cypress. **1923** L. H. BAILEY *Cultivated Evergreens* II. 208 Italian Cypress... Much planted since ancient times in southern Europe particularly in its columnar form. *Ibid.*, Columnar Italian C[ypress]... With erect branches, forming a narrow, columnar head. The classical cypress of the Greek and Roman writers. **1969** T. H. EVERETT *Living Trees of World* 35/1 The Italian cypress is really a horticultural form of venerable ancestry, its exact origin unknown. **1854** F. W. FAIRHOLT *Dict. Terms Art* 260/1 *Italian earth*, a pigment known as burnt Italian earth. **1897** *Sears, Roebuck Catal.* 361/2 Pastel Crayons..Burnt Sienna..Italian Earth..Purple Brown. **1969** R. MAYER *Dict. Art Terms & Techniques* 200 *Italian earth*, an old name for sienna. [**1822** J. C. LOUDON *Encycl. Gardening* I. 16 He [*sc.* Volkman] considers the Italian gardens as inferior to those of France in point of superb alleys, lofty clipt hedges, and cabinets of verdure.] **1883** W. ROBINSON *Eng. Flower Garden* p. vi/2 It has been affirmed that none but an Italian garden would have suited South Kensington. **1928** L. ARCHER-HIND tr. *Gothein's Hist. Garden Art* II. xvi. 329 We feel the resemblance to the parterre of the Doria Pamfili when we walk through an 'Italian garden' at an English country seat. **1942** A. E. W. MASON *Musk & Amber* i. 10 The Italian garden.., an oblong of grass paths and glowing flower beds, of box trees and hedges, of stone seats..and..a ridiculous charming little temple with open pillars. **1961** G. MASSON *Italian Gardens* 274 Within the space of two hundred and fifty years, Italian gardens had been introduced into France, developed and expanded until they represented a national style that became the model for Europe, and then via Spain returned to their point of departure, the Neapolitan Realm, as a foreign innovation. **1924** A. HUXLEY *Let.* 25 Feb. (1969) 228 The best form, I think, would be something small, cheap and pretty. Covers of Italian paper or something of the kind. **1930** *Times Lit. Suppl.* 6 Feb. 108/4 A large variety of Italian papers. **1845** E. ACTON *Mod. Cookery* i. 4 All the ingredients used for soups should be fresh,..particularly Italian pastes of every kind (maccaroni, vermicelli, &c.). **1907** *Army & Navy Stores Catal.* 1246/2 Italian paste, for soups. **1957** *Encycl. Brit.* XIV. 544/2 *Macaroni*...The same substance in different forms is also known as *vermicelli*, *pasta* or Italian pastes, *spaghetti*, *taglioni*, *fanti*, etc. **1835** Italian pink [see **English pink*]. **1934** H. HILER *Notes Technique Painting* ii. 111 *Italian pink*, *quercitron lake*, etc., organic pigments prepared from Turkish or Avignon berries, quercitron bark, etc. **1971** *Country Life* 10 June 1428/3 This leads into the north-facing hall, which has been painted an Italian pink as a background to full-length portraits. **1937** E. HAKE *Eng. Quilting* iii. 16 Italian quilting..was as prevalent in England as in any other European country during the seventeenth and eighteenth centuries. **1955** *Oxf. Jun. Encycl.* XI. 323/1 Italian quilting consists of two layers of cloth sewn together in a design built up entirely of parallel lines. A padding of soft wool or piping cord is then threaded between the narrow channels. **1967** E. SHORT *Embroidery & Fabric Collage* ii. 47 In Italian quilting the design is worked entirely in parallel lines of running or back stitch, which are then padded by inserting a thick wool from the back. **1882** Italian stitch [see *HOLBEIN]. **1913** M. K. GIFFORD *Needlework* xvii. 262 *Italian stitch* can be worked either open or close. The latter makes a very solid filling. **1957** M. B. PICKEN *Fashion Dict.* 185/2 *Italian-stitch*, running stitch done twice on the same line. **1896** *T. W. Stapleton & Co. Wine List* Dec., Vermouth, Italian—36/-. **1925** TOYE & ADAIR *Drinks Long & Short* 12 Three and a half glasses of gin, one and a half of Italian Vermouth. **1967** A. LICHINE *Encycl. Wines* 541/1 Vermouth was certainly being made in Italy in the seventeenth century, and now it is produced all over the world, and the two main types are 'French' and 'Italian'.

B. *sb.* **5.** Ellipt. for *Italian cloth*. Also *attrib.*

1897 *Sears, Roebuck Catal.* 177/1 Fine Italian lining in fancy figured effects. **1900** *T. Eaton & Co. Catal.* Mid-winter Sale 13/2 Ladies' black boucle curl cloth jackets.., lined throughout with mercerized Italian. **1907** *Yesterday's Shopping* (1969) 743/1 Jackets..in serges and cloths, lined Italian. **1960** *Textile Terms & Definitions* (Textile Inst.) (ed. 4) 82 *Italian*,..a cloth of 5-end sateen weave with a lustrous finish, used chiefly as a lining material.

6. = **Italian vermouth*. Chiefly in phr. *gin and Italian*. Cf. *GIN *sb.*² 2 b.

1929 J. B. PRIESTLEY *Good Companions* II. i. 264 Couldn't you take some cocktails—gin and Italian or sherry and bitters or something—upstairs to those people. **1957** G. BELLAIRS *Death in High Provence* vii. 80 Two long Italians with some ice and perrier, please.

italic, *a.* and *sb.* Add: **A.** *adj.* **4.** Pertaining to the older Latin version of the Bible known as *Vetus Itala*.

1861 C. D. GINSBURG tr. *Coheleth* App. I. 501 The Old Italic Version forms the basis of the one on which St. Jerome wrote the *Commentarium ad Paulam et Eustochium*. **1957** *Oxf. Dict. Chr. Ch.* 981/1 It has been generally supposed that there are two main types—the 'Italic' (represented by the MSS. *f*..and *q*..) and the 'European'.

B. *sb.* **2.** Add to def.: Also, a modern adaptation of the old Italic hand. Hence **ita·licist,** one who favours or practises this style.

1955 W. BLUNT *Handwriting* 9 Many firms..produce fountain-pens designed for Italic. **1956** *Jrnl. Educ.* July 304/1 Having myself been lambasted more than once by the Italicists because I dared to qualify my praise of their handwriting. *Ibid.* 304/2, I know of *no* school where italic is given a disproportionate share of the timetable. **1963** A. FAIRBANK *How to teach Italic Hand* 14 The following remarks relate to pen-and-ink italic.

Italo-. Add: **Italo-Celtic, Italo-Keltic,** a postulated common parent language of Italian and Celtic; also as *adj.*, of, pertaining to, or characteristic of this language; **I·talophi:l, -phi:le** *a.*, friendly to Italy or to what is Italian; *sb.*, one who is Italophile; **I·talopho:be,** one affected with **I:talopho·bia,** intense dislike or fear of Italy.

1877 J. RHYS *Lect. Welsh Philol.* i. 5 Some subdivide the Southern division into an Italo-Celtic and a Hellenic group, while others prefer to suppose a Celtic and a Greco-Italic group. **1888** J. WRIGHT tr. *Brugmann's Elem. Compar. Gram. Indo-Gmc. Lang.* I. 3 The Italo-Keltic hypothesis has perhaps the best prospect of attaining a greater degree of probability in the future. **1906** *Daily Chron.* 28 Mar. 5/4 The appointment of the Italophile reactionary Miushkovitch Ministry. **1920** G. E. BUCKLE *Life Disraeli* V. iii. 130 Protestant and Italophil England rejoiced. **1921** *Contemp. Rev.* Oct. 494 Some Italophobe Germans. **1922** *Ibid.* Sept. 302 The official state of hostility between the Vatican and Italy and the periodical protests against it..maintain in the Catholic masses a feeling of Italophobia. **1927** *Scots Observer* 26 Mar. 12/5 Italy found it easier to buy Ahmed Zogu, turn him into an Italophil. **1932** W. L. GRAFF *Lang.* 375 Italo-Celtic was probably once a common group of closely related dialects. **1933** L. BLOOMFIELD *Lang.* iv. 62 Some scholars believe that Italic and Celtic are connected.., so as to form an

Italo-Celtic sub-group within the Indo-European family. **1958** N. Gordimer *World of Strangers* 20 She..was a passionate Italophile, scattering her speech with *cara mia*'s. **1966** E. P. Hamp in Birnbaum & Puhvel *Anc. Indo-European Dial.* 116 Germanic and..Italo-Keltic have *-yo/ī*, almost leveled out for both verb types. **1967** C. Seton-Watson *Italy from Liberalism to Fascism* x. 378 The Italophil Prime Minister of Bulgaria, Gueshov, offered an alliance. **1973** *Times Lit. Suppl.* 5 Oct. 1151/1 Such an experienced Italophile.

ita-palm: see *ita.

itatartaric (itătaɹtæ·rik), *a. Chem.* [tr. G. *itaweinsäure* itatartaric acid (T. Wilm 1867, in *Ann. d. Chem. u. Pharm.* CXLI. 33), f. *ita-* (in *itaconsäure* itaconic acid (see Itaconic *a.*)) + *weinsäure* tartaric acid.] *itatartaric acid*: dihydroxyitaconic acid, $CH_2OH \cdot C(OH)$-$(COOH) \cdot CH_2COOH$. Hence **itata·rtrate**, a salt of this acid.

1872 Watts *Dict. Chem.* Suppl. 762 Pure itatartaric acid is amorphous, vitreous, smells like honey when gently heated, deliquesces in the air, dissolves easily in alcohol, and does not volatilise perceptibly at 100° with aqueous vapour. *Ibid.*, Calcium itatartrate..forms crystalline masses sparingly soluble in water. **1945** *Jrnl. Biol. Chem.* CLXI. 739 (*heading*) Itatartaric acid, a metabolic product of an ultraviolet-induced mutant of *Aspergillus terreus*.

itch, *v.*[1] **3.** Delete † *Obs.* and add later examples. Also *refl.* and *fig.*

1900 J. London *Let.* 16 June (1966) 107 It is a fascinating subject. It has itched me for long, and it is often all I can do to keep away from writing on it. **1922** Joyce *Ulysses* 748 My hole is itching me always when I think of him. **1947** *Penguin New Writing* XXIX. 12 With long sensuous strokes he smoothed a patina of paint down the chairlegs, then itched with fussing dabs the corners and underneath. **1951** R. Campbell *Light on Dark Horse* vi. 99 The thick super-salty water of the Mediterranean, which itches and itches the naked eye. **1951** L. MacNeice tr. *Goethe's Faust* II. I. 171 The dice already itch me in my pocket. **1954** S. Beckett *Waiting for Godot* II. 46 Then I can keep it [*sc.* a hat]. Mine irked me... How shall I say? ..It itched me. **1973** *Welcomat* (Philadelphia) 10 Oct. 4/2 The sticker that itches her most is the one that says: 'School's Open. Drive Carefully.'

ite (əit). [The suffix -ite[1] used as an independent word: cf. Ism *quasi-sb.*] A person or thing that is or may be designated by a sb. in *-ite*.

1852 *Blackw. Mag.* Aug. 260/1 The right honourable gentleman has shown that he is neither a Derby-*ite* nor a Russell-*ite*. Then what *ite* are you? **1906** *Westm. Gaz.* 1 Dec. 9/2 A big factory for explosives, holding dynamite, ballistite, cordite..Heaven knows what 'ites'—sufficient to wreck half the world. **1926** R. W. Hutchinson *First Course Wireless* viii. 138 Most of the 'ites' on the market.. are galena subjected to various treatments.

ite: see *ita.

-ite, *suffix*[1]. Add: **2. b.** Also used more widely in *tektite*, and hence in the names of tektites from different regions (as *australite*, *indochinite*).

item, *adv.* and *sb.* Add: **B.** *sb.* **2.** (Further examples.)

1961 *Lancet* 12 Aug. 358/2 Questions [set]..included items that the undergraduate who had read something more..than an introductory text could be expected to answer. **1970** *Jrnl. Gen. Psychol.* LXXXII. 63 A person may agree with an item and its opposite because he believes statements worded in the dogmatic (authoritarian) direction but agrees with a reversed item because of the high social desirability of this item.

c. *Computers.* Any quantity of data treated as a unit, such as a field, a group of fields, or a record.

1954 *Computers & Automation* May 17/2 *Item*, a set of one or more fields containing related information. **1958** *Computer Jrnl.* I. 71/1 Let us call the units which are to be sorted items. *Ibid.* 71/2 If every item of data has a unique key, complete sorting will result in each place holding no more than one item. *Ibid.* 72/2 A typical item in commercial data is an 80-column punched card. **1964** A. Lytel *Fund. Data Processing* (1965) iv. 108 Information is stored in variable-length memory areas called fields... Consecutive fields can be combined to form a larger unit of information called an item. Grouping fields to form an item simplifies the manipulation of related-data fields, and minimizes the number of instruction executions required to move consecutive fields within the main memory. **1967** B. S. Walker *Introd. Computer Engin.* vi. 157 The field or item is typically a group of letters or numbers, in association, to mean a name, or reference number, or a heading of some kind. **1971** *Computers & Humanities* VI. 67 Each item file is composed of an open-ended sequence of variable length records called 'items', every item being the description of one entity.

d. A member of a set of linguistic units.

1954 *Word* X. 230 'Items'..are either morphemes or sequences of morphemes, but still one has to contend with the independent status of order, constructions, and hierarchical structure. Even so, there is a clear difference between taking some phonemic material as 'root' (= item) and some as 'marker' of processes. **1964** R. A. Hall *Introd. Ling.* vi. 34 The first group [of linguistic analysts] wish to limit their description strictly to an enumeration of items and the arrangements or sequences in which they are found... The other group..take into account the passage of time when the observer moves from one part of his material to another... This approach is based on a listing of items involved and of 'processes' which the items 'undergo'. *Ibid.* 35 In some respects, the item-and-process (IP) approach is closer to our traditional type of grammatical description than is the item-and-arrangement (IA) approach. **1964** M. A. K. Halliday et al. *Ling. Sci.* ii. 24 In English..'chair' is a lexical item: it operates as an item in open set choices. 'the', 'chair', the '-s' in 'chairs', 'in case'..are grammatical items. **1970** *Canad. Jrnl. Linguistics* XV. 95 This system grew out of a union of the item-and-process approach to linguistics with automata theory. **1971** T. F. Mitchell in *Archivum Linguisticum* II. 64 In the English-speaking world of linguists little more than ten short years ago, the talk was of grammatical models labelled 'Item and Arrangement', 'Item and Process', and 'Word and Paradigm'.

C. *attrib.* and *Comb.*

1859 E. H. N. Patterson in L. Hafen *Overland Routes to Gold Fields* (1942) 68 This..is one of those cases, probably, that will remain a mystery only to be solved when the great item book of the recording angel shall be opened to justify the final sentence. **1961** *Lancet* 12 Aug. 359/2 Item analysis showed that there were fairly large differences between the groups on a few questions, and these were seen to be due to specific differences in teaching. **1970** *Jrnl. Gen. Psychol.* LXXXII. 166 Item–item and item–test correlations were computed. **1972** *Jrnl. Social Psychol.* LXXXVI. 221 An item analysis technique was used to select those items that discriminated between the high and low scores by 20 percentage points.

iterate, *v.* Add: **4.** *intr. Math.* To employ iteration; to make repeated use of a formula by substituting in it each time the result of the previous application.

1953 A. S. Householder *Princ. Numerical Analysis* ii. 45 Since the 'approximation' x_0 with which one may start an iteration does not necessarily need to be close, it is sometimes advantageous to..start with an arbitrary x_0, perhaps $x_0 = 0$, and iterate until the approach is sufficiently close. **1957** L. Fox *Numerical Solution Two-Point Boundary Probl.* iv. 81 As an example..of an uncommon but convenient iterative procedure consider the solution of the differential equation $y'' - (1/x^4 - 2/x^3)y + 1/x^2 = 0$... We iterate according to the scheme $y_{n+1} = x^2(1 + x^2y''_n)/(1 - 2x)$, with $y_0 = 0$.

iterate (i·tĕrĕt), *sb. Math.* [f. the vb., or ad. L. *iterāt-us*, pa. pple. of *iterāre* (see Iterate *v.*): see -ate[1].] A quantity arrived at by iteration.

1941 R. J. Schmidt in *Phil. Mag.* XXXII. 370 Denote the *n*th approximation to the value of any unknown x_r by $x_r^{(n)}$. To solve these [simultaneous] equations by the method of successive approximations, we assume approximations $x_2^{(0)}$, $x_3^{(0)}$,... $x_m^{(0)}$ to the unknowns x_2, x_3,.. x_m. Making use of these values we then use the first equation to find $x_1^{(1)}$, the first approximation to x_1. As the approximations will not always converge to the value of the unknowns, we shall, in future, call the numbers $x_s^{(r)}$ iterates. **1956** F. B. Hildebrand *Introd. Numerical Analysis* x. 449 The error t_k in the *k*th iterate will be approximately the *square* of that in the preceding iterate, and will be of opposite sign. **1968** Fox & Mayers *Computing Methods for Scientists & Engineers* i. 10 In the days of machine saturation it is tempting to take 25 iterates even though 250 are really necessary. **1968** N. Bourbaki *Theory of Sets* iii. 186 The mapping f^n is called the *n*th iterate of the mapping *f*.

iteration. 1. b. Add: *esp.* The repeated application of a formula devised to provide a closer approximation to the solution of a given equation when an approximate solution is substituted in the formula, so that a series of successively closer approximations may be obtained; a single application of such a formula; also, the formula itself.

1924 Whittaker & Robinson *Calculus of Observations* vi. 79 In 1674 a method depending on a new principle, the principle of iteration, was communicated in a letter from Gregory to Collins. **1941** *Phil. Mag.* XXXII. 374 After a few iterations the values of ϵ_r much less than unity will hardly affect the results. **1960** G. N. Lance *Numerical Methods for High Speed Computers* i. 8 Whichever criterion is used to determine the end of the iteration, it is clear that the orders to evaluate $f(x_r)$ and $f(x_{r+1})$ are identical except that x_{r+1} is used instead of x_r. This kind of modification is made extremely simple on high-speed computers. **1968** E. T. Copson *Metric Spaces* viii. 115 The Newton–Raphson iteration $x_{n+1} = x_n - f(x_n)/f'(x_n)$ for solving the equation $f(x) = 0$.

iterative, *a.* Add: **1. c.** *Math.* Of the nature of or employing iteration.

1924 Whittaker & Robinson *Calculus of Observations* vi. 81 A pleasing characteristic of iterative processes may be observed..that a mistake in the performance of the numerical work does not invalidate the whole calculation. **1943** *Phil. Mag.* XXXIV. 409 Iterative methods have found favour with computers, despite an outward semblance of clumsiness which masks their solid advantages from the casual critic. **1949** *Proc. Cambr. Philos. Soc.* XLV. 230 Iterative methods seem very suitable, in principle, for application in large automatic calculating machines. **1953** A. S. Householder *Princ. Numerical Analysis* ii. 44 Generally speaking, an iterative method for solving an equation or set of equations is a rule for operating upon an approximate solution x_p in order to obtain an improved solution x_{p+1}, and such that the sequence $\{x_q\}$ so defined has the solution *x* as its limit. **1968** E. T. Copson *Metric Spaces* viii. 115 The iterative process $x_{n+1} = f(x_n)$ leads to a solution of the equation $x = f(x)$ when the mapping of the real line into itself is a contraction mapping.

B. *sb. Philol.* **a.** An iterative verb or aspect. **b.** A word expressing repetition of an action, sound, etc.

1853, 1884 [see *aspect *sb.* 9 b]. **1934** Priebsch & Collinson *German Lang.* I. i. 13 Formation of distributive numerals in Latin by adding *-no* to the iteratives. *Ibid.* II. iii. 225 Verbs in *-ern*. Some are..iteratives.. e.g. *flattern*. **1961** F. G. Cassidy *Jamaica Talk* iv. 69 In Standard English one finds three kinds of iteratives: the simple ones like *hush-hush*..; those with vowel gradation like *ding-dong*..; and the rhyming ones like *handy-dandy*.

ithel (i·þel). Also **athel, athleh, atl, ithil.** [Local Arab.] A tamarisk, *Tamarix aphylla*, bearing panicles of pink flowers and minute leaves, native to western Asia and north-east Africa.

1838 W. Ainsworth *Res. Assyria* 125 The common tamarisk of the country, the Athleh or Atle of Sonnini, is the Tamarix orientalis of Forskahl. **1875** *Encycl. Brit.* II. 236/2 Of plants there is an endless variety [in Arabia]. ..The tamarisk or 'Talh', the southern larch or 'Ithel', the chestnut, the sycamore, and several other trees. **1881** A. Blunt *Pilgrimage to Nejd* I. 84 The Ithel, a tree grown in every village of Central Arabia. *Ibid.* 85 The roof was of ithel beams. **1924** *Blackw. Mag.* Mar. 351/1 Mackintosh..was watching them from the shelter of a clump of *ithil* bushes. **1949** L. H. Bailey *Man. Cultivated Plants* (rev. ed.) 678 *T*[*amarix*] *aphylla*... Athel Tamarisk. Shrub or small tree... Useful as a windbreak in desert regions. **1963** F. von Breitenbach *Indigenous Trees Ethiopia* (ed. 2) 150 *Tamarix aphylla*... Atl (Arabic)... Leaves reduced to a minute triangular tooth on a sheathing base.

ithomiid, ithomiine, *sb.* and *a.* (iþōᵘ·mi,id, -īn). [f. mod.L. family and subfamily names *Ithomiidæ*, *Ithomiinæ*, f. the generic name *Ithomia* (J. Hübner *Verzeichniss bekannter Schmetterlinge* (1816) 9), f. Gk. ἰθύς straight + ὦμος shoulder.] A tropical Central or South American butterfly belonging to the family Ithomiidæ, or this group treated as the subfamily Ithomiinæ of the family Nymphalidæ; of or pertaining to an insect of this kind.

1899 D. Sharp in *Cambr. Nat. Hist.* VI. vi. 346 The Ithomiides are peculiar to tropical America. **1912** G. B. Longstaff *Butterfly-Hunting* vi. 312 The hour was earlier and the Ithomiines were not so closely packed. **1930** *Proc. Entomol. Soc. London* V. 91 An Ithomiine butterfly and its Heliconine mimic taken flying together in NW. Peru. **1972** Brown & Heineman *Jamaica & its Butterflies* 97 The number of ithomiids found in Central America is limited. *Ibid.* 99 *Greta* is among the most advanced in structure of all ithomiid genera.

I-thou (əi·ðau). [tr. G. *ich-du* (M. Buber (1923) *Ich und Du* 9), f. I *pers. pron., 1st sing. nom.* + Thou *pers. pron., 2nd sing. nom.*] Used *attrib.* of a personal relationship between man and God. Also *transf.*

1937 R. G. Smith tr. *Buber's I and Thou* I. 3 The primary words are not isolated words, but combined words. The one primary word is the combination *I-Thou*. The other primary word is the combination *I-It*. *Ibid.*, If *Thou* is said, the *I* of the combination *I-Thou* is said along with it. **1958** *Church Times* 14 Feb. 10/3 Am I really prepared to obey God, in the utter loneliness of the 'I-Thou' relationship, even if it means the actual hatred of other people? **1961** *English Studies* Oct. 323 But Dr Esch also stresses the differences: while the other of the love-poetry is an equal partner, his God is *totaliter aliter*, which makes for a completely different I-Thou relation. **1967** C. Davis *Question of Conscience* 223 We may first take the I-Thou relationship of deep personal commitment. **1967** *Guardian* 19 May 9/1 When any chorus stands up to sing..it is so much more an I-Thou affair than opera.

ithyphallic, *a.* and *sb.* Add: So **ithypha·llus,** an erect phallus.

1889 in *Cent. Dict.* **1967** *Listener* 28 Sept. 401/2 The fathers..exhibit their ithyphalluses. **1968** *Punch* 27 Mar. 469/3 The spike (Laius's sword) Jocasta steadily presses through her womb is replaced by a golden ithyphallus ten foot tall.

Iti (əi·təi), *sb.* and *a.* Also **Itie, Ity.** [Dim. of Italian *a.* and *sb.*] Used with disparaging overtones: **A.** *sb.* An Italian. **B.** *adj.* Italian. Cf. *Eyetie *sb.* and *a.*

1941 R. Moore in Michie & Graebner *Lights of Freedom* x. 130 Ity planes were circling overhead. *Ibid.* 131 How surprised the Ities would be to see us. **1942** *E. Afr. Ann. 1941–2* 109/1 The Itis ran away with it all, fancy even taking the macaroni, poor devils. **1944** A. Jacob *Traveller's War* xiv. 246 We thought you were Iti. *Ibid.* xviii. 278 The petulant Itie or the solid Boche. **1947** [see *brush *sb.*[5]]. **1959** G. Jenkins *Twist of Sand* iv. 68 Those Itie destroyers will have to come mighty close. **1965** *Economist* 4 Dec. 1100/3 With all these Ities and squareheads and Greeks around, it might be worth remembering. **1973** *Times* 1 Jan. 14/4 I'm going to be a German, an Iti, a Dutchman.

itis (əi·tis), *sb.* [The suffix -itis used as an independent word.] A bodily condition, affection, or disease that is or may be described or designated by a word ending in *-itis*.

[1896: cf. Dict. s.v. -ITIS.] **1909** *Practitioner* Nov. 706 It must be remembered that the complaint referred to [*sc.* mucous colitis] is not, strictly speaking, an *itis* at all.

-itis. Add: In irregular trivial use applied to a state of mind or tendency fancifully regarded as a disease.

1903 ASQUITH in *Westm. Gaz.* 19 Oct. 5/1 All the people were suffering from a new disease—the disease of fiscalitis. **1906** *Ibid.* 27 Apr. 4/2 Several members of Parliament are suffering from a slight attack of Suffragitis. **1912** *Q. Rev.* Oct. 504 Cricket has just suffered from so severe an attack of 'testitis' as to render it highly improbable [etc.]. **1944** F. CLUNE *Red Heart* 68 Those were the days when the nor'-west of New South Wales was agog with bushranger-itis. **1945** W. S. CHURCHILL *Victory* (1946) 186 It was impossible to go on in a state of 'electionitis' all through the summer and autumn. **1969** *Sunday Express* 28 Dec. 24/3 As the year wears on, politicians' electionitis will have more influence on events than central bankers' views.

itisket, itasket (i·tiskėt i·taskėt). A vocal utterance in verses accompanying any of several children's games, esp. 'Drop the handkerchief'.

1926 D. LA SALLE *Play Activities Elem. Sch.* II. 71 Itisket, itasket, a green and yellow basket. I lost a letter to my love and on the way I found it... (Drop and pick up the handkerchief.) **1969** R. D. ABRAHAMS *Jump-Rope Rhymes* p. xviii, This game [*sc.* drop the handkerchief] is found with a number of accompanying chants, including 'Itisket, Itasket'.

-itol (itǫl). *Chem.* [f. -IT(E[1] 4 + -OL 1.] A suffix used to form the names of polyhydric alcohols other than di- or trihydric alcohols.

Such compounds were formerly given names terminated by *-ite*, as in *dulcite, inosite, mannite.* These names were later modified by the addition of *-ol* to express their alcoholic nature, giving e.g. *dulcitol, inositol, mannitol.* Hence in mod. use *-itol* has become an independent suffix, as in *hexitol.*

I told you so. [TELL *v.* 8.] *Phr.* used to remind the person addressed that he has previously been warned that his actions would incur misfortune. As *sb.*, a person who uses this expression or adopts this attitude; such an expression or attitude; used *attrib.* (as *I-told-you-so*) to denote such an attitude. Also used as a kind of quasi-vb.

1609 [see TELL *v.* 8]. **1823** BYRON *Don Juan* XIV. l. 3 Sadder than owl-songs or the midnight blast, Is that portentous phrase, 'I told you so'. **1919** W. DE MORGAN *Old Madhouse* xxviii. 435 Perhaps I'm only I-told-you-soing. **1926** WHITEMAN & MCBRIDE *Jazz* iii. 49, I really did debate whether I hadn't better give up and let the I-told-you-so's, who said jazz would bring me to no good end, have it their own way. **1930** J. DOS PASSOS *42nd Parallel* IV. 299 Alice had an Itoldyouso manner. **1954** W. FAULKNER *Fable* (1955) 43 His I-told-you-so to the elders. **1959** A. LEJEUNE *Crowded & Dangerous* xi. 125 She'll.. put on that disapproving I-told-you-so look.

itsy-bitsy (i·tsi͵bi·tsi), *a. colloq.* [Baby-form of LITTLE *a.* + *BITSY *a.*: see -SY.] Small, (charmingly) insubstantial, tiny; also, used disparagingly: arty-crafty, twee. So **i·tsy-bi·tsiness.** Cf. *ITTY-BITTY *a.*

1938 I. GOLDBERG *Wonder of Words* viii. 162 Itsy-bitsy (little bit). **1939** R. CHANDLER *Trouble is my Business* (1950) 23 The same clerk was nuzzling at the same itsy-bitsy moustache. **1953** P. JONES in *Plays of Year* IX. 567 You should be allowed to revolve radiantly at some cocktail party..a dry martini in one hand and an itsy-bitsy little thing on a stick in the other. **1957** P. WILDEBLOOD *Main Chance* 197 An itsy-bitsy tot of vodka and a teeny-weeny tranquilliser. **1958** *Observer* 15 June 11/2 The rather sentimental and itsy-bitsy patterns that used to be considered suitable for wear by the young. **1967** *House & Garden* Mar. 74/1 The Peter Pan statue..is the embodiment of all sentimental itsy-bitsiness. **1972** 'H. HOWARD' *Nice Day for Funeral* iii. 45 If Frankie was here he'd break you into itsy-bitsy pieces. **1972** *Lady* 29 June 1052/1 Country accessories are also bold, far less itsy-bitsy than many town-worn ones.

itty (i·ti), *a. colloq.* Also **ittie.** [Baby-form of LITTLE *a.* + -Y *suffix*[6].] Used hypocoristically for 'little' (chiefly in reference to babies or small domestic animals).

1798 JANE AUSTEN *Let.* 27 Oct. (1932) I. 10 My dear itty Dordy's remembrance of me is very pleasing to me. **1853** MRS. GASKELL *Cranford* vii. 132 Come down stairs with me, poor ittie doggie, and it shall have its tea. **1938** D. RUNYON *Furthermore* viii. 159 He..starts whispering, 'There, there, there, my itty oddleums.' **1964** *Guardian* 30 Oct. 13/3 Now, ah reckon Lady Bird an' ah will git ahselves an itty bit o' sleep.

i·tty-bi·tty, *a.* = *ITSY-BITSY *a.*

[**1938** *Amer. Speech* XIII. 314/1 Itty bitty kitty from the city, a country yokel who tries to be a cat.] **1940** R. CHANDLER *Farewell, my Lovely* xxxiii. 253 Itty-bitty frame houses on the wrong side of town. **1959** H. HOBSON *Mission House Murder* xiii. 89 No big swallows now. Itty-bitty sips—and take your time. **1968** W. GARNER *Deep, Deep Freeze* v. 62 I'll move every ittybitty piece on that goddammed fancy board. **1969** L. KENNEDY *Very Lovely People* i. 35, I felt, here I am in this itty-bitty tropical village, a tremendous long ways from anywhere.

Ity, var. *ITI *sb.* and *a.*

-ium, *suffix.* Add: **b.** Used to form the names of various protonated, mostly organic, bases, as *anilinium, benzenium, ethenium, flavylium, guanidinium, hydrazinium, imidazolium, pyrylium.* Cf. *-ONIUM.

This usage of the suffix derives from AMMONIUM. For rules governing the application of the suffix see *Nomenclature of Organic Chemistry* and *Nomenclature of Inorganic Chemistry*, published by the International Union of Pure and Applied Chemistry.

i-umlaut: see *I I. 2 b.

Ivan (əi·văn, ī·vā·n). [Russ., = John.] Used for: a Russian, esp. a Russian soldier (as typical of the Russian army).

[**1870** *Brewer's Dict. Phr. & Fable* 448/1 *Ivanovitch*, a lazy, good-natured person, the national impersonation of the Russians as a people, as *John Bull* is of the English. **1890** WEBSTER, *Ivan Ivanovitch*, an ideal personification of the typical Russian or of the Russian people;—used as 'John Bull' is used for the typical Englishman.] **1925** FRASER & GIBBONS *Soldier & Sailor Words* 129 *Ivan*, the everyday name in the Russian Army, at any rate down to 1916, for a private soldier, equivalent to our 'Tommy Atkins'. **1959** M. CROSLAND tr. *Rovan's Germany* 51 The Russian 'Ivan' is the brutal sub-man and the giant with the kind, noble and spontaneous heart..[to] the German spectator. **1968** 'B. MATHER' *Springers* xii. 128 We'd knocked off quite a few of their side so far, and even dedicated Ivans could be expected to show a little exacerbation under the circumstances. **1971** C. EGLETON *Last Post for Partisan* xvii. 174 So long as the Ivan kept on coming he wasn't worried. **1972** *Guardian* 8 Sept. 12/4 A situation in which Ivan continues to come a lot cheaper than GI Joe.

ivi (ī·vi). Also **eevie, ifi, ihi.** [Fijian *ivi*, Samoan *ifi.*] The Tahitian chestnut, *Inocarpus fagiferus* (*I. edulis*), a leguminous evergreen tree bearing spikes of white or yellow flowers and dark red, edible fruit.

1862 B. SEEMANN *Viti* xvi. 318 The Ivi, or Tahitian chestnut,..is one of the common trees [in Fiji]. **1874** LINDLEY & MOORE *Treas. Bot.* II. Suppl. 1308/1 Ivi (Feejee). *Inocarpus edulis.* **1881** C. F. CUMMING *At Home in Fiji* I. 275 A group of eevie trees appears like one gigantic mass of lovely trailing foliage. **1888** W. HILLEBRAND *Flora Hawaiian Islands* 109 Here [*sc.* among the Caesalpinieae] also must be given a place to the anomalous *Inocarpus edulis*, Forst., or Tahitian Chestnut, the Ivi or Mapê. **1894** B. THOMSON *S. Sea Yarns* 7 He repaired to the mainland to consult a rival oracle named *Na-ivi* (the ivi-tree). **1935** *B. P. Bishop Mus. Bull.* (Honolulu) CXXX. 119 The native names [of *Inocarpus edulis*] are *ihi* or *mape* in Nukuhiva and Hivaoa of the Marquesas. **1964** C. S. BELSHAW (*title*) Under the ivi tree. Society and economic growth in rural Fiji. **1970** W. R. SYKES *Contrib. Flora Niue* 156 No ifi trees were seen growing in places other than those connected with man's activities.

Ivicene (i·visīn), *sb.* and *a.* [f. *Ibiza, Iviça*, one of the Balearic Islands + Sp. *-eño*, -ENE.] A type of hound, said to be descended from ancient Egyptian hunting dogs, native to the island of Ibiza and characterized by large, pointed, pricked ears and white, fawn, or reddish-brown colouring; also as *adj.*; also called **Ibizan* or *Balearic hound.*

1929 *Morning Post* 5 Feb. 15/3 The Ivicene Described. *Ibid.*, The Ivicene dog, a breed which has never before been seen in this country. **1929** *Dog World* 8 Feb. 912/1 Pedro of Chardia, Ivecine [*sic*], Greyhound type, wants time and should do well, rare and undeveloped at the moment. **1948** C. L. B. HUBBARD *Dogs in Brit.* III. xv. 124 The correct name of Cà Eivissenne is loosely pronounced as 'Ivicene', which led to considerable publicity in Britain about 1930, giving the dog the breed name of Ivicene. **1964** E. F. DAGLISH tr. *Schneider-Leyer's Dogs of World* 165 (*heading*) Balearic Hound or Ivicene.

-ivity (in Dict. s.v. -IVE *suffix*). Add: (See quot. 1895.)

1885 O. HEAVISIDE in *Electrician* 4 Sept. 311/1 Thus, 'specific resistance' may well be called 'resistivity', and specific conductance 'conductivity', referring to the unit volume. Resistivity is the reciprocal of conductivity, and resistance of conductance. **1895** *Rep. Brit. Assoc. Adv. Sci.* 197 That the termination *-ance* be used in general for words expressing the properties of a definite body or piece of matter; *e.g.*, resistance, conductance, inductance, permeance, reluctance, &c.; and that the termination *-ivity* or *-ility* or the like be used for words expressing the specific properties of a material; *e.g.*, conductivity, resistivity, inductivity, refractivity, permeability, &c.

-ivore, usual comb. form of the suffix *-VORE.

ivoried, *a.* (Later examples.)

1893 *19th Cent.* Nov. 843 On thy bare and ivoried shoulder. **1928** HARDY *Coll. Poems* 156, I borrowed deep to carve the screen And raise the ivoried Rood. **1945** W. DE LA MARE *Burning-Glass* 76 Tipped arrow, ivoried bow, and rain-soaked quiver.

-ivorous, usual comb. form of the suffix -VOROUS.

ivory. Add: **5. d.** *collect. sing.* and *pl.* The keys of a piano or similar instrument. *colloq.*

1818 KEATS *Let.* 18 Dec. (1958) II. 13 She plays the Music without one sensation but the feel of the ivory at her fingers. **1854** THACKERAY *Newcomes* I. xi. 114 It is a wonder how any fingers can move over the jingling ivory so quickly as Miss Cann's. **1918** [see *JAZZ *v.* 2]. **1940** *S.P.E. Tract* LV. 196 Tickle the ivories. **1962** *Times* 10 Feb. 4/2 'Ivory-tickling' has become an outmoded and faintly derogatory description of piano-playing. **1974** *Times* 15 Feb. 14/7 Its cover portrays the Prime Minister, seated at the organ, tinkling one lot of ivories and flashing the other lot.

10. ivory-bill (earlier U.S. examples); **ivory board,** a kind of pasteboard with both surfaces smooth; **ivory dome** *U.S. slang*, a stupid person; **ivory (nut) palm,** a South American palm of the genus *Phytelephas*, or a Micronesian one of the genus *Metroxylon*, both of which bear nuts yielding vegetable ivory; **ivory plum** *U.S.*, the wintergreen, *Gaultheria procumbens*, or the creeping snowberry, *Chiogenes hispidula*, or their fruit; **ivory-wood** *Austral.*, the tree *Siphonodon australe*, or its timber, which is used for drawing-instruments, etc.

1787 *Ellicott Almanac 1788* (Winchester, Virginia) sig. B2, The land fowls [of Kentucky] are turkeys, pheasants, ..the perraquet, ivory-bill, woodcock, and the great owl. **1872** E. COUES *Key to N. Amer. Birds* 191 The ivory-bill and the flicker stand nearly at extremes of the family. **1926** *Paper Terminol.* (Spalding & Hodge) 14 *Ivory boards*, superfine cardboard highly finished by means of bees-waxed rolls. **1962** F. T. DAY *Introd. to Paper* iv. 46 A large variety of boards is produced by the paper maker, in grades ranging from high class Bristol and Ivory boards to the cheaper kind of Triplex board. **1923** Ivory dome [see *DOME *sb.* 4 d]. **1844** W. PURDIE *Let.* 14 Dec. in *Compan. Bot. Mag.* (1847) LXXIII. 11 The *Phytelephas* (Vegetable Ivory Palm) is procurable at Sta. Martha. *Ibid.* 12, I think of ascending the Magdalena, and myself collecting growing plants and seeds of the Ivory Palm. **1871** C. KINGSLEY *At Last* I. viii. 303 The ripe fruit [of the Moriche palm] contains first a rich pulpy nut, and at last a hard cone, something like that of the vegetable ivory palm. **1916** *Jrnl. Bombay Nat. Hist. Soc.* XXIV. 682 Names of the Tree [sc. *Phytelephas macrocarpa*]. English: Large-fruited Ivory Plant, Ivory Palm, Ivory nut Palm, Vegetable Ivory Plant. **1951** J. H. KRAEMER *Trees W. Pacific Region* 10 In this genus [sc. *Metroxylon*] are the sago palms and the ivory-nut palms. **1966** E. J. H. CORNER *Nat. Hist. Palms* xiii. 315 This anomalous species is the Caroline ivory-nut palm, *M*[*etroxylon*] *amicorum* of Micronesia. **1828** J. NEAL *Rachel Dyer* 55 The more brilliant ivory-plumbs or clustered bunch-berries rattled among the withered herbage. **1891** *Jrnl. Amer. Folk-Lore* IV. 149 *Gaultheria procumbens* seems to have an almost endless variety of epithets...The berries are called Ivory Plums. **1892** *Ibid.* V. 99 *Chiogenes serpyllifolia*, ivory plums. **1887** *Colonial & Indian Exhib. Rep. Col. Sect.* 429 Ivory-wood. **1888** F. M. BAILEY *Queensland Woods* 29 Ivory-wood. A tall tree with straight erect stem, the bark of a light colour... Found in the dense scrubs both north and south in Queensland, and also in New South Wales. **1932** R. H. ANDERSON *Trees New South Wales* 145 Ivorywood..is sometimes known as Native Guava. **1965** *Austral. Encycl.* II. 310/1 Though widely spread in coastal New South Wales and Queensland, the ivorywood is a comparatively rare tree.

ivory tower. [tr. F. *tour d'ivoire* (see below).] A condition of seclusion or separation from the world; in general, protection or shelter from the harsh realities of life. Also (with hyphen) *attrib.* Hence *ivory-towered* adj., *ivory-toweredness; ivory-towerish* adj., somewhat ivory-towered; *ivory-towerism, -towerist.*

[**1837** SAINTE-BEUVE *Pensées d'Août, à M. Villemain* 152 Et Vigny, plus secret, Comme en sa tour d'ivoire, avant midi rentrait.] **1911** BRERETON & ROTHWELL tr. *Bergson's Laughter* iii. 135 Each member [of society] must be ever attentive to his social surroundings..he must avoid shutting himself up in his own peculiar character as a philosopher in his ivory tower. *a* **1916** H. JAMES *Ivory Tower* (1917) II. iii. 142 Doesn't living in an ivory tower just mean the most distinguished retirement? **1922** H. CRANE *Let.* 10 Dec. (1965) 108, I have grown accustomed to an 'ivory tower' sort of existence. **1936** E. POUND *Let.* Jan. (1971) 277 Ivory tower aesthetes. **1938** R. G. COLLINGWOOD *Princ. Art* vi. 120 The tendency was for each artist to construct an ivory tower of his own: to live, that is to say, in a world of his own devising. **1940** H. G. WELLS *New World Order* § 9. 133 We want a Minister of Education who can..electrify and rejuvenate old dons or put them away in ivory towers, and stimulate the younger ones. **1945** A. HUXLEY *Let.* 2 Apr. (1969) 518 Between ivory-towerism and art for art's sake on the one hand and direct political action on the other lies the alternative of spirituality. **1947** J. HAYWARD *Prose Lit. since 1939* 46 If [literature] fails in this task it will be reduced to the status of an art pursued for art's sake by isolated groups of writers, segregated from the world in their ivory towers and 'private worlds'. **1953** G. VANN *Water & Fire* iii. 50 That ivory-tower æstheticism which averts its gaze from the squalors of humanity. **1954** 'N. BLAKE' *Whisper in Gloom* vii. 94 I'm going to plunge you into reality, my little Ivory-Towerist. **1959** *20th Cent.* Nov. 401 British governments..have been badly informed..and Britain's ivory-towered embassies may have to bear some of the blame. **1963** M. MCCARTHY *Group* vi. 120 We called you the Ivory Tower group. Aloof from the battle. **1963** *Daily Tel.* 12 Oct. 8/7 Pity the poor parson!..If he eschews all worldly contact, he's accused of being ivory-towerish and out of touch. **1963** *Economist* 26 Oct. 355/1 Every don..however attached to

academic ivory-toweredness. **1967** P. Nokes *Professional Task in Welfare Pract.* vii. 113 When I began teaching at the Prison Staff College..I soon became aware of a well established tradition that what was taught there was 'ivory-towered'. **1968** J. J. C. Smart *Between Sci. & Philos.* 17 It would be unwise to think that philosophy is exclusively a subject for inhabitants of ivory towers. **1972** *Science* 19 May 769/3 New realities which make it impossible for them to think and perform in such ivory-tower isolation.

ivy, *sb.* Add: **1. c.** *U.S.* = *poison ivy* (see sense 2).
    1788 J. May *Jrnl.* 9 June (1873) 65, I have been clearing land for eight days, and now begin to feel the effects of poison—from ivy, doubtless. **1849** F. Parkman *Calif. & Oregon Trail* xiii. 205 In the morning Shaw found himself poisoned by ivy.

ivy-berry. Add: (Later example.)
    1971 *Country Life* 25 Mar. 667/3 The woodpigeons.. had been on the ivy berries and the clover fields.
    b. *U.S.* The wintergreen or checkerberry, *Gaultheria procumbens.*
    1840 *Southern Lit. Messenger* VI. 518/2 There were the fringed polygala, the buttercup, wild geranium, bunch-plum, ivy-berry. **1892** *Jrnl. Amer. Folk-Lore* V. 100 *Gaultheria procumbens,* ivy-berry.

ivy-leaf. Add: **b.** *attrib.* = Ivy-leaved *a.*
    1909 *Daily Chron.* 5 June 9/5 Ivy-leaf geraniums can be depended on to produce a long succession of blooms. **1939** E. Bowen *Coll. Impressions* (1950) 64 A window-box gay with pink ivy-leaf geraniums. **1957** *Encycl. Brit.* X. 205/2 The ivy-leaf geranium, derived from *P[elargonium] peltatum,* has given rise to an important class of both double- and single-flowered forms adapted especially for pot culture, hanging baskets, [etc.].

Ivy League. Name given to a group of long-established eastern U.S. universities; also *attrib.* of the social and intellectual prestige or other characteristics of these universities, or of, relating to, or characteristic of the members or former members of these universities. So **Ivy Leaguer,** a member or former member of an Ivy League university.
    [**1933** S. Woodward in *N.Y. Herald Tribune* 16 Oct. 18/1 The fates which govern [football] play among the ivy colleges and academic boiler-factories alike seem to be going around the circuit.] **1939** *Princeton Alumni Weekly* 29 Sept., The 'Ivy League' is something which does not exist and is simply a term which has been increasingly used in recent years by sports writers, applied rather loosely to a group of eastern colleges. **1943** K. P. Kempton in *Sat. Even. Post* 22 May 14 (*title*) Ivy Leaguer. **1949** S. Woodward *Sports Page* xii. 132 For many years the colleges seemed to feel that there was something not quite nice about the press. It was fashionable, especially in the hallowed precincts of the Eastern Ivy League, to snub and bamboozle the sports writers. **1951** J. D. Salinger *Catcher in Rye* xii. 103 My father wants me to go to Yale, or maybe Princeton, but I swear, I wouldn't go to one of those Ivy League colleges. *Ibid.* xvii. 133 The jerk had one of those very phoney, Ivy League voices, one of those very tired, snobby voices. **1959** *Listener* 12 Feb. 283/1 Hemingway's sense of Ivy-League social life and its

complex snobberies. **1962** 'S. Ransome' *Without Trace* v. 49 He could drop his natural guttersnipe talk and sound like an Ivy Leaguer whenever it suited him. **1965** *Times Lit. Suppl.* 25 Nov. 1053/1 James Purdy's Ivy-league rapist. **1970** *Daily Tel.* 28 Apr. 4/6 Rising costs are driving away middle-income students from some of America's Ivy League universities, turning the campuses into places for the poor, supported by scholarships, and the rich, admissions officers say. *Ibid.,* The Ivy League colleges are Brown, Columbia, Cornell, Dartmouth, Harvard, Pennsylvania, Princeton and Yale. **1973** S. Alsop *Stay of Execution* (1974) II. 171 Waspish Ivy Leaguers like Roosevelt or Welles.

ixodid (iksōu·did), *sb.* Pl. **ixodides.** [f. mod.L. family name *Ixodidæ,* f. the generic name *Ixodes* (P. A. Latreille 1795, in *Magazin encyclopédique* IV. 15), f. Gk. ἰξώδης sticky.] A tick of the family Ixodidæ. Also *attrib.* or as *adj.,* of or pertaining to a tick of this type.
    1911 G. H. F. Nuttall et al. *Ticks* II. 105 Leach called the Acarina *Monomerosomata,* and divided them into 11 families, one of which, Ixodides, included *Argas, Ixodes* and *Europoda. Ibid.* 113 The Argasid and Ixodid ticks are recognized as possessing very distinctive features. **1935** T. H. Savory *Arachnida* xiii. 146 The Ixodides possess a soft-skinned opisthosoma capable of great distension necessary for the alternate gorging and fasting that is inseparable from the life of a tick. **1952** Baker & Wharton *Introd. Acarology* iv. 144 The majority of ixodids usually parasitize different hosts in the immature and mature stages. *Ibid.,* Heavy infestation with ixodid ticks can cause anemia in domestic animals. **1965** B. E. Freeman tr. *Vandel's Biospeleol.* xv. 256 An ixodid parasitic on bats has been found frequently in Europe, Asia and Africa.

ixora (iksō·rǎ). [mod.L. (Linnæus in J. Burmann *Thesaurus Zeylanicus* (1737) 125), ad. *Iswara,* name of a Hindu divinity, = Skr. *íśvara* lord, master: so named because the flowers of some species are used as votive offerings.] An evergreen shrub or small tree of the genus so called, mostly native to tropical Africa and Asia and bearing clusters of white or brightly-coloured flowers.
    1816 *Bot. Reg.* II. 154 (*heading*) Large-flowered scarlet Ixora. **1846** J. Lindley *Veget. Kingd.* 764 The fragrance or beauty..of the Gardenias, Hindsias, Posoquerias, Ixoras..&c. is unsurpassed. **1871** C. Kingsley *At Last* I. vii. 231 The air was..almost too heavy with the fragrance of the 'white Ixora'. **1926** D. H. Campbell *Outl. Plant Geogr.* vi. 214 In the upper forest [of Sarawak], a handsome Ixora..was abundant. **1961** *Amateur Gardening* 21 Oct. Suppl. 29/3 For those with plenty of heat in the greenhouse the ixoras are well worth growing.

Iyyar (ī·yā.ɪ). Also **Iyar, Jiar, Jyar, Yiar.** [ad. Heb. *iyyār.*] The post-exilic name of one of the Jewish months, being the eighth of the civil and second of the ecclesiastical year; its pre-exilic name was *Zif.*
    1737 W. Whiston tr. *Josephus' Works* 910 The Romans began to raise their banks on the twelfth day of the month Artemisius (Jyar). **1738** A. Cruden *Compl. Concordance Holy Scriptures* s.v. *month,* Zif..is the second month of the holy year, and..answers to that which after-

wards had the name *Jiar,* or *April.* **1902** *Encycl. Brit.* XXVI. 43/2 In 746 B.C. Calah rebelled, and on the 13th of Iyyar (April), in the following year, Pulu or Pul..seized the throne. **1962** *New Jewish Encycl.* 229/2 Most of the *Sefirah* days occur during the month of Iyar. **1973** *Jewish Chron.* 9 Feb. 29/2 On May 7 this year the State of Israel will be 25 years old. (The Hebrew date is the fifth day of the month of Iyar.)

Izarra (izā·rɑ). Also **Izzara.** [Basque, lit. 'star'.] A liqueur from the Pyrenees, brandy-based and flavoured with herbs.
    1926 E. Hemingway *Sun also Rises* xix. 243 The waiter recommended a Basque liqueur called Izarra.. made of the flowers of the Pyrenees..It looked like hair-oil and smelled like Italian *strega.* **1965** R. Postgate *Plain Man's Guide to Wine* (ed. 2) ix. 149 Name Izarra. Flavour Wild herbs. Origin France. **1971** *Good Food Guide* 397 Grapefruit sorbet with Izarra.

izba, var. *Isba.

Izod (əi·zǫd). The name of E. G. *Izod* (fl. 1903), British engineer, used *attrib.* with reference to a kind of impact test devised by him in which a notched specimen fixed at one end is broken by a blow from a pendulum hammer and the energy absorbed determined by the decrease in the swing of the pendulum.
    1904 *Proc. Inst. Mech. Engin.* IV. 1225 A single-blow test of the Izod type. **1922** Glazebrook *Dict. Applied Physics* I. 206/1 The brittleness in steel resulting from a high percentage of sulphur and phosphorus is well marked by the Izod test. *Ibid.,* The form of notch selected, and sometimes called the Izod notch, is a 45° vee, 2 mm. deep, with a root radius of 0·25 mm. **1939** E. C. Rollason *Metall. for Engineers* i. 11 As a material with a low Izod figure offers a poor resistance to the development of a crack, a low Izod value indicates that in service there will be a greater chance of final failure before the crack is discovered. **1954** A. R. Bailey *Text-bk. Metall.* xiii. 457 The Izod test..is standard in Great Britain. **1968** D. R. Cliffe *Technical Metallurgy* vii. 152 The Izod machine is a cantilever type with the knife-edge of the hammer striking the specimen at the horizontal at a point 22 mm above the plane of gripping.

|| **izzat** (i·zʊt). Also **izzut.** [Urdu, ad. Arab. *'izzah* glory.] Honour, reputation, credit, prestige.
    1857 H. Lawrence *Let.* 26 Feb. in Edwardes & Merivale *Life Sir H. Lawrence* (1872) II. xviii. 279 Man can but die once, and if I die in Oude, after having saved some poor fellow's hearths, or skins, or *izzut* (reputation), I shall have no reason for discontent. **1893** Kipling *Many Inventions* 207 Thou hast done great wrong, and altogether lost thy *izzat* and thy reputation. **1922** *Blackw. Mag.* Feb. 201/1 *Izzat,* too, generally prescribes that he should be an hour or two late. **1924** E. M. Forster *Passage to India* iii. 31 The educated native..[is] trying to increase his izzat—in plain Anglo-Saxon, to score. **1953** —— *Hill of Devi* 27 In every remark and gesture, does not the Indian prince either decrease his own 'izzat' or that of his interlocutor? **1968** J. Barzun *Amer. University* (1969) viii. 252 We saw how much faculties want presidents 'prestigious'. I suggest that instead of prestige we use the Hindi word *izzat* and see how absurd we are: 'Has he *izzat*? Have we enough *izzat* in the house? Our friends across the way are getting ahead of us in *izzat.*' Newspapers could then rank institutions *izzat*-wise.

J

J. Add: **II. 6. b.** In *Electr.* *j* is used (in place of the mathematical symbol *i*, which is used for electric current) to represent $\sqrt{(-1)}$, or an angular displacement of 90°.

1893 *Electrician* 15 Sept. 522/2 The next Paper was by Mr. C. P. Steinmetz on 'Complex Quantities and their Application in Electrical Engineering'. This Paper contained a novel method of the treatment of alternating currents.. The device is to introduce the letter *j* in the expression of the sine curve, at first simply as a distinguishing index without mathematical meaning, and afterward as $j = \sqrt{(-1)}$. **1907** FRANKLIN & ESTY *Elem. Electr. Engin.* II. v. 90 It can be shown..by ordinary trigonometry that the components of a line whose length is $I\sqrt{R^2+X^2}$ and which is θ degrees ahead of *I*, where θ is the angle whose tangent is X/R, are $e_1 = Ri_1 - Xi_{11}$ and $e_{11} = Xi_1 + Ri_{11}$. Therefore the term j^2Xi_{11}..must be equal to $-Xi_{11}$, or, in other words, we must have: $j^2 = -1$. **1945** '*Electr. Engineer*' *Ref. Bk.* I. 67 Considering *j* as a vector-operator, it is a means whereby a length in one direction is rotated anticlockwise by 90°. **1961** R. B. ANGUS *Electr. Engin. Fund.* xiii. 341 Since $j^2A = -A$.., then $j^2 = -1$ or $j = \sqrt{(-1)}$. *Ibid.* 343 The *j* is always placed to the left in the product. This practice helps avoid the overlooking of a *j*-term when real and *j*-terms are being grouped.

c. In *Physics* J and j represent quantized angular momentum.

j was first used by A. Sommerfeld (in *Ann. d. Physik* (1923) LXX. 33), in place of n_J, which had been used by W. Heisenberg (in *Zeitschr. f. Physik* (1922) VIII. 274) in place of Sommerfeld's original symbol n_i, which he introduced (in *Atombau und Spektrallinien* (ed. 3, 1922) vi. 446 and *Zeitschr. f. Physik* (1922) VIII. 269) as an empirical 'inner' quantum number (G. *innere Quantenzahl*) in describing the Zeeman effect. As this was interpreted in terms of later theory, *j* became the quantum number of the total angular momentum of an electron, corresponding to the resultant of its spin s and orbital momentum l; *J* is used similarly for an assemblage of electrons, and in molecular spectroscopy is the quantum number for angular momentum due to rotation of a molecule as a whole. Apart from these specific uses, j and J are often used as symbols for a general angular momentum.

jj-coupling, an approximation used in the quantum theory of the atom when the spin–orbit interaction of individual electrons is large compared with the remaining electrostatic interaction between one electron and another, so that spin and orbital angular momenta may be coupled to give a resultant j for each electron, and the resultants in turn coupled to give the total angular momentum J of the electrons. Cf. **LS-coupling*.

1924 *Phil. Mag.* XLVIII. 720 The X-ray atomic levels may be conveniently classified by means of three quantum numbers—*n* (total), *k* (azimuthal), and *j* (inner). **1929** *jj*-coupling [see *COUPLING *vbl. sb.* 6 f (ii)]. **1930** *Physical Rev.* XXXVI. 613 The resultant angular momentum of the molecule (quantum number *J*). **1955** TOWNES & SCHAWLOW *Microwave Spectroscopy* i. 5 As *J* increases and the molecule rotates faster, it stretches. **1957** M. E. ROSE *Elem. Theory Angular Momentum* i. 11 Consider the case of two spins (or angular momenta) j_1 and j_2. **1970** G. K. WOODGATE *Elem. Atomic Struct.* vii. 140 In the lower-lying configurations of neutral atoms the *j–j* coupling approximation is not often found, in other words the conditions for small electrostatic interaction are not often satisfied, even in heavy elements.

III. J, joule; J.A., Judge Advocate; Justice of Appeal; J.C.R., Junior Common Room; j.n.d., just noticeable difference; J.P. (examples).

1951 *Symbols, Signs & Abbreviations* (R. Soc.) 14 Joule..J. **1967** W. H. HAYT *Engin. Electromagn.* (ed. 2) ii. 32 The volt..having the label of joules per coulomb (J/C) or newton-meters per coulomb.., we shall..measure electric field intensity in..volts per meter (V/m). **1881** D. JONES *Notes Mil. Law* p. vii, *J.A.*, Judge Advocate. *Ibid.* v. 67 The J.A. and prosecutor must not be the same person. **1918** E. S. FARROW *Dict. Mil. Terms* p. x, *J.A.*, Judge Advocate. **1883** *Wharton's Law Lexicon* (ed. 7) 432 *J.A.*, Justice of Appeal. **1972** *Mod. Law Rev.* XXXV. I. 45 The dictum already referred to of Watermeyer J.A. came at the end of his judgment. **1892** *Isis* (Oxf.) 8 June 35/2 Only the Pres. of the J.C.R. and the Captain of the Eleven retain their equanimity. **1914** C. MACKENZIE *Sinister St.* II. III. viii. 656 The editor rejected the frivolous attentions of his audience, and left the J.C.R. **1968** *Listener* 1 Aug. 147/1 The Student Council received the support..of the vast majority of JCRs. **1929** *Encycl. Brit.* VII. 420/1 The just noticeable difference, often called the 'j.n.d.', between the stimuli of two sensations. **1948** *Sci. News* VII. 14 Rubbers could be compared with one another with about three times as small a j.n.d. as that found for bitumens. **1732** *Calendar State Papers Amer. & W. Indies* (1939) 48 A dispute arising between two of his men on shore, Francis Squib and Jacob Taverner, J.P's in that harbour, put them in the stocks. **1869** *Bradshaw's Railway Manual* XXI. 328 Directors..Sir Benjamin Morris, J.P. **1972** P. JOHNSON *Offshore Islands* v. 291 The Local Government Act of 1888..replaced the old Quarter Sessions of JPs by democratically elected County Councils.

jab, *v.* Add: **d.** *trans.* To give (a person) a stabbing blow with the fist. Also *fig.*

1901 R. FITZSIMMONS *Physical Culture & Self-Defense* 114 Jab him, if you can, with your left. **1915** E. CORRI *30 Yrs. Boxing Referee* 38 Time and again he jabbed and patted Smith cleverly on the nose with his left hand. **1959** *Amer. Speech* XXXIV. 155 One may be shafted or jabbed by the opposite sex, a professor..or anyone else for any real or imagined injury.

e. *trans.* and *intr.* To inject or inoculate (a person) with a hypodermic needle; to use (a hypodermic needle) to make an injection. So **ja·bbing** *vbl. sb. slang* (orig. *U.S.*).

1926 *Flynn's* 16 Jan. 638/2 Some stiffs uses mud but coke don't need any jabbin', cookin', or flops. You can hit it an' go. **1938** *Amer. Speech* XIII. 186/1 *To jab*, to take drugs hypodermically. **1948** PARTRIDGE *Dict. Forces' Slang* 100 *Be jabbed*, to be inoculated or vaccinated. **1956** S. LONGSTREET *Real Jazz* xviii. 114 Not all jazz-players smoke marijuana or opium, or sniff snow or jab a vein. **1968** J. R. ACKERLEY *My Father & Myself* xiii. 146 Dr Wadd..dashed in with a hypodermic syringe of digitalis and jabbed it so hastily, though successfully, into the back of one of his hands that it raised a large lump. **1968** 'L. BLACK' *Outbreak* ix. 82 Smith-road primary was jabbed. Why not our school?

jab, *sb.* Add: **b.** An injection with a hypodermic needle. *slang* (orig. *U.S.*).

1914 JACKSON & HELLYER *Vocab. Criminal Slang* 48 *Jab*, current amongst morphine and cocaine fiends. A hypodermic injection. **1959** *Punch* 13 May 658/3 Receiving the hypodermic jab intended for the bullock. **1972** G. DURRELL *Catch me a Colobus* i. 11 Can't you give me a jab of something to keep me going? **1973** *Times* 17 Apr. (Liberia Suppl.) p. ii/2 The visitor must..take precautions and submit to a variety of jabs.

2. A radio signal of momentary duration. *colloq.*

1932 *News Chron.* 23 Sept. 10/7 Another film I saw was of the flight of a jab of wireless energy on its journey from the East End to King's College, Strand. **1945** *Electronic Engin.* XVII. 679/3 For this purpose they devised a radio transmitter which sent out very short pulses, or jabs, of radio energy.

jabal, var. *JEBEL.

jabbers, jabers (dʒæ·bəɹz, dʒēⁱ·bəɹz). Also jap(p)ers. Corruption of *Jesus*, used expletively (see *BEJAB(B)ERS *int.*).

1821, etc. [see *BEJAB(B)ERS *int.*]. **1934** A. P. HERBERT *Holy Deadlock* 311 'Be Jabers!' said the girl, 'is that the way you feel?' **1970** *Alberta Hist. Rev.* XVIII. III. 18/2 'Can you hit that man?' The gunner replied, 'Be japers, I'll ate what's left of him.'

jabberwock (dʒæ·bəɹwǫk). The name of the fabulous monster in Lewis Carroll's poem *Jabberwocky*. Hence in allusive and extended uses, esp. 'incoherent or nonsensical expression'. So **ja·bberwocky,** invented language, meaningless language, nonsensical behaviour; also as *adj.*, nonsensical, meaningless, topsy-turvy. Also **ja·bberwock(y)** *v. intr.*, to write, speak, etc., in jabberwocky style.

1871 'L. CARROLL' *Through Looking-Glass* i. 22 The Jabberwock, with eyes of flame, Came whiffling through the tulgey wood. **1902** J. BUCHAN *Watcher by Threshold* iii. 38 It was the strangest jumble of vowels and consonants I had ever met.. It was some maniac talking Jabberwock to himself. **1908** *Daily Chron.* 10 Apr. 4/7 Those exceptional modern folk who write with equal ease in the ordinary left-to-right manner and in 'Jabberwocky' fashion..right to left. **1917** [see *CHRISTMAS-TREE 2]. **1926** *Glasgow Herald* 7 Oct. 5 From 'Jabberwocky' it is but a short step to the old-fashioned nursery-rhyme. **1931** E. WILSON *Axel's Castle* vi. 227 The dreaming mind does not usually speak—and when it does, it is more likely to express itself in the looking-glass language of 'Jabberwocky' than in anything resembling ordinary speech. **1939** *Times* 25 Feb. 15/5 It is all very Jabberwocky, and so far the writers of the movement [surrealism] have the advantage of the artists. **1953** H. MILLER *Plexus* (1963) ii. 57 Realizing in a short time that I was not in the least interested in all this jabberwocky, and thinking of Mona waiting for me to lunch with her, I suddenly interrupted him. **1959** *Listener* 29 Jan. 226/1 His [*sc.* Skelton's] tendency to jabberwock (like Pound or Eliot, Skelton was a polylingual versifier). **1963** *Guardian* 22 July 5/5 He jabberwockied, pulling furiously at his ear-lobe as he talked. **1964** A. SWINSON *Six Minutes to Sunset* vi. 126 Sometimes, to confuse the issue,..he would indulge in his own subtle form of jabberwocky. **1970** J. FLEMING *Young Man, I think you're Dying* xii. 164 He was going to wear her down, intimidate her, tame and train her to obey, and a whole lot of other jabberwocky which he couldn't..remember now. **1972** *Collector's Guide* Aug. 12/1 (Advt.), Worcester first period teapot stand 'Jabberwocky pattern'.

jabiru. Also *Austral.* **jaberoo, jabiroo.** Add later examples of the Australian name for the black-necked stork, *Xenorhynchus asiaticus*, which is closely related to the tropical American *Jabiru mycteria*.

1912 A. SEARCY *By Flood & Field* viii. 60 There were also Jaberoo, Spoonbill, Ibis and Spur-wing Plover. **1943** W. E. HARNEY *Taboo* 158 The jaberoo struts along its sands. **1946** I. L. IDRIESS *In Crocodile Land* xxxiii. 237 The call of the jabiru. **1952** *Coast to Coast 1951* 211 He had ridden up quietly, and the big, black-and-white, dark-blue-necked jabiroo, pacing slowly on its red-yellow legs at the further end of the lagoon, had not flown away. **1965** G. MCINNES *Road to Gundagai* viii. 125 The brick walls dissolved into..polygonum swamps over which the long legged jabiroo flew creaking on its way. **1965** *Austral. Encycl.* V. 114/1 Sometimes the jabiru is quite solitary, hence perhaps the term 'policeman-bird', by which it is known in North Queensland.

Jablochkoff (yā·blǫχkǫf). The name of Paul *Jablochkoff* (1847–94), Russian physicist, used *attrib.* and in the possessive to denote an electric arc lamp invented by him (now obsolete) in which carbon rod electrodes were placed side by side and separated by an insulating material such as plaster of Paris, which gradually melted as the electrodes burned away.

1877 *Jrnl. Franklin Inst.* CIV. 295 Jablochkoff's electric candles burn for two or three hours without interruption. **1884** J. E. H. GORDON *Pract. Treat. Electr. Lighting* vii. 99 The lighting of the Avenue de l'Opera in Paris in 1878 by Jablochkoff candles first demonstrated the possibility of street lighting by electricity. **1894** R. M. WALMSLEY *Electr. Current* xii. 508 Because of the difference in the rate of burning of the positive and negative carbons in the ordinary arc, the Jablochkoff candle has to be supplied with alternate currents. **1922** S. G. STARLING *Electricity* vi. 85 In that year [*sc.* 1876] Jablochkoff employed two parallel carbon rods, separated by an insulating material. ..These were called Jablochkoff's candles. They soon gave place to more convenient arc lamps.

jaboticaba (dʒabǫtikā·bă). Also **jabuticaba.** [Tupi.] An evergreen Brazilian tree, *Myrciaria* (or *Eugenia*) *cauliflora*, of the family Myrtaceæ, which bears clusters of white flowers and purple fruits directly on the trunk and branches; also, the fruit of this tree.

1824 H. E. LLOYD tr. *Spix & Martius's Trav. Brazil* II. III. ii. 85 A light and agreeable wine is also prepared from the fruits of the jabuticaba (*Myrtus cauliflora*). **1862** *Chambers's Encycl.* IV. 161/1 *E*[*ugenia*] *cauliflora*, a Brazilian species,..yields a very fine fruit of a black colour, about the size of a greengage plum, called the Jabuticaba. **1931** B. MIALL tr. *Guenther's Naturalist in Brazil* iv. 79 In the Jaboticaba, a myrtle-tree, even the trunk looks as though beaded with the blue-black fruits, about the size of a damson, that seem to be nailed on to the bark. **1974** F. N. HOWES *Dict. Useful Plants* 132 Jaboticaba (Braz[il]) *Myrciaria*, esp. *M. cauliflora*, (Braz. grape), fr[uit] ed[ible], used for wine and jelly.

jacal (hăkā·l). Also **hackal, jackal(l), jucal.** [Mexican Sp., ad. Nahuatl *xacalli.*] A hut constructed of erect poles or stakes filled in with wattle and mud, a type common in Mexico and the south-western United States; an adobe house; also, the material or method used in building such a hut.

1838 'TEXIAN' *Mexico v. Texas* 249 It was a little *Jacal*, or cabin, built with large unburnt bricks, called *adobes*, in the language of the country. **1844** J. J. WEBB *Adventures in Santa Fe Trade* (1931) 104 In a valley..where the herders had a temporary corrall and *jacal* made of bushes laid upon poles. *Ibid.* 105 The *jacal* was *full*, packed so thick it was impossible to count them. **1850** J. W. AUDUBON *Western Jrnl.* (1906) 230 We..saw a comfortable (for this country), log and jacal built house. **1897** *16th Ann. Rep. U.S. Bureau Amer. Ethnol. 1894–95* 108 This method is known to the Mexicans as '*jacal*', and much used by them. It consists of a row of sticks or thin poles set vertically in the ground and heavily plastered with mud. **1900** R. B. C. GRAHAM *Thirteen Stories* 127 A straw-thatched jacal. **1947** *Chicago Sun Bk. Week* 8 June 2/2 In the back alleys..are to be found..primitive jacals.

J-acid. *Dye Chem.* A crystalline dye intermediate, 2-amino-5-naphthol-7-sulphonic acid, $C_{10}H_9NO_4S$, used in coupling reactions with diazotized amines to form direct azo dyes.

1914 F. W. ATACK tr. *A. Wahl's Manuf. Org. Dyestuffs* vii. 66 The third [*sc.* compound] is obtained by alkaline fusion of 2-naphthylamine-5:7-disulphonic acid, and is called 'J acid'. **1917** FORT & LLOYD *Chem. Dyestuffs* xvi. 159 There are certain peculiarities about J-acid and its azo derivatives. Thus coupled with diazobenzene derivatives cotton-dyeing properties are absent, but with diazonaphthalene derivatives are strongly marked. **1937** *Chem. Abstr.* XXXI. 3281 Absorption by cotton cellulose of J acid..was studied. **1971** R. L. M. ALLEN *Colour Chem.* v. 57 About 35 monoazo direct dyes are in use, most of them containing either a thiazole or a J acid residue.

jacinth. Add: **1. e.** = *HYACINTH 3 b.

1854 L. A. MEALL *Moubray's Treat. Poultry* 288

Jacinth,..slaty-blue, and pied on back and wings with white.

jacitara (dʒæsitā·rǎ). [Tupi.] In full, *jacitara palm*. A prickly climbing palm, *Desmoncus macroacanthus* or *D. orthacanthos*, native to the Amazon region.

1853 A. R. WALLACE *Palm Trees of Amazon* 74 The 'jacitara' never loses its hold, and it is only by deliberately extracting its fangs that the intruder can expect to depart unhurt. **1860** MAYNE REID *Odd People* 52 The grated pulp [of manioc]..is afterwards put into a long elastic cylinder-shaped basket or net, of the bark of the 'jacitara' palm. **1863** H. W. BATES *Naturalist on River Amazons* I. ii. 48 There is even a climbing genus of palms (*Desmoncus*), the species of which are called, in the Tupí language, Jacitára. *Ibid.* vii. 322 When the rolls [of tobacco] are sufficiently well pressed they are bound round with narrow thongs of remarkable toughness, cut from the bark of the climbing Jacitára palm tree. **1878** *Chambers's Encycl.* Suppl. X. 579/1 Jacitara palm, (*Desmoncus macroacanthus*), a palm found in the forests of the low lands of the Amazon district in South America. **1927** R. R. GATES *Botanist in Amazon Valley* vii. 167 Among climbers collected here was a small climbing palm called *jacitara* (*Desmoncus sp.*). The slender stem bears sharp spines in pairs, projecting backwards. **1931** B. MIALL tr. *Guenther's Naturalist in Brazil* v. 92 In Brazil there is another climbing palm, the Jacytára. I found it in Pernambuco, and was quite intimidated by its armament, which has earned it the name of 'the terrible'.

Jack, *sb.*[1] Add: **1. d.** Used as a form of address to an unknown person. *colloq.* (orig. *U.S.*).

1889 BARRÈRE & LELAND *Dict. Slang* I. 490/2 *Jack* (American), it is common among schoolboys in Philadelphia to address a stranger as *Jack*. **1933** PARTRIDGE *Words, Words, Words!* I. 71 *Jack* is still very frequent among 'the common people' when, in addressing a stranger, one wishes to avoid the abruptness caused by omitting the unknown name. **1943** *N.Y. Times* 9 May II. 5/4 Jack, that man had them rolling in the aisles. **1966** S. KELLY in F. Shaw et al. *Lern Yerself Scouse* 76 Dawn taps yer winder [*sc.* window]..another day before yiz [*sc.* you], Jack. **1970** C. MAJOR *Dict. Afro-Amer. Slang* 70 *Jack*, term of address by one male to another.

2. d. A policeman or detective; a military policeman. Cf. *JOHN 1 c. *slang*.

1889 CLARKSON & RICHARDSON *Police!* xxiii. 320 *A policeman*, a fly, Jack,..crusher, peeler. **1899** *Birmingham Daily Mail* 1 Nov., A couple of men who were in plain clothes in the tap-room of a public-house, and were suspected by the 'gaffer' of being 'Jacks'. **1919** W. H. DOWNING *Digger Dial.* 29 *Jack*, a military policeman. **1930** *Bulletin* (Sydney) 1 Jan. 11/2 Blue..looked up and saw two Jacks waiting. 'Where are you going?' demanded one M.P. **1941** *Argus* (Melbourne) *Week-End Mag.* 15 Nov. 1/4 *Jacks*, military police. **1946** F. SARGESON *That Summer* 102 We all had to stand there with a crowd of jacks in plain clothes standing round. **1967** J. GARDNER *Madrigal* viii. 199 You're not going to believe it. I haven't told all to the jacks naturally. **1971** J. WAINWRIGHT *Dig Grave* 45 These county coppers..couldn't get their minds unhooked from the words 'New Scotland Yard'—as if every jack in the Metropolitan Police District worked from *there*.

e. Slang phr. *on one's jack* = on one's own, alone (short for *on one's Jack Jones*: see 34 e below).

1931 'G. ORWELL' *Coll. Ess.* (1968) I. 71 *Jack, on his*: on his own. **1935** —— *Clergyman's Daughter* iii. 197 Michael went off on his jack an' left me wid de bloody baby. **1936** [see *GRASS *sb.*[1] 11*]. **1968** M. WOODHOUSE *Rock Baby* ix. 93 You're off on your jack then? **1973** R. PARKES *Guardians* x. 193, I thought I could go sneaking in there all on my jack and bring out the evidence.

3. b. Phr. *Jack ashore*: see quot. 1909. *slang*.

[**1875** R. ROWE (*title*) Jack afloat and ashore.] **1909** J. R. WARE *Passing Eng.* 158/2 *Jack ashore*, Jack elevated—practically drunk, and larky. **1920** CONRAD *Victory* (1921) Author's note p. xviii, It was long after the sea-chapter of my life had been closed, but it is difficult to discard completely the characteristics of half a lifetime, and it was in something of the Jack-ashore spirit that I dropped a five-franc piece into the sauceboat. **1970** E. MCGIRR *Death pays Wages* iv. 90 Jack Ashore does not check bills.

c. Colloq. phr. *I'm all right, Jack*: a saying indicating selfish complacency on the part of the speaker.

1910 D. W. BONE *Brassbounder* iii. 37 It's 'Damn you Jack—I'm all right!' with you chaps. **1919** F. NINETTE *Tiddley Sailors* 26 They dodged as much work as possible and generally assumed the manner 'I'm all right Jack'. **1958** A. HACKNEY (*title*) Private life *or* I'm all right Jack. **1960** *News Chron.* 2 May 4/6 This 'I'm all right, Jack' attitude towards such relatives is deplorable. **1970** *Times* 17 Feb. 3/2 He adopted an 'I'm all right, Jack' attitude in leaving his convoy. **1971** JOHN & HUMPHRY *Because they're Black* (1972) x. 105 Right now it is, as I said before, dog eat dog... I'm all right, Jack, damn you.

4. b. Colloq. shortening of *lumberjack* (LUMBER *sb.*[1] 4). *N. Amer.*

c **1900** in F. Rickaby *Ballads & Songs Shanty-Boy* (1926) 97 Every jack's a cant-hook man... They do some heavy loggin'. **1913** *Collier's* 18 Jan. 21/1 The breaking up of the lumber camps and the streaming southward of thousands of 'jacks'. **1947** *Sat. Even. Post* 8 Mar. 20/1 The red-bearded jack came on again, head low and shielded. **1961** W. E. GREENING *Ottawa* 101 The jacks who felled the trees and the workers who stripped them were called *piqueteurs*. **1973** L. GUTTERIDGE *Killer Pine* iv. 46, I had to fire thirty Jacks last fall... Lumberjacks.

5. b. *California jack* (examples). Also *Californian jack*.

1882 J. W. STEELE *Frontier Army Sk.* (1883) 50 Here is the down-east Yankee..turning his native cunning to account at poker and California jack. **1893** W. RALEIGH *Let.* 28 July (1926) I. 177 His losses at Californian Jack.. were my gains. **1921** C. E. MULFORD *Bar-20 Three* iii. 39 For two hours they sat and played California jack in plain sight of the street.

15. d. Substitute for def.: A socket or receptacle having one or more pairs of terminals and designed so that insertion of a suitable plug enables a device to be quickly introduced into a circuit. (Examples.)

1891 J. POOLE *Pract. Telephone Handbk.* vii. 128 The effect of inserting a plug in one of the jacks is that the end of the plug lifts the line spring R from pin Y. **1905** PREECE & SIVEWRIGHT *Telegraphy* (new ed.) xi. 233 The home sections and the multiple panels are made up of 'jacks', mounted in strips. *Ibid.* 234 The 'jacks' consist of two springs of unequal length and a collar or socket. **1926** J. L. PRITCHARD *Broadcast Reception* xi. 185 The last three jacks have filament controlling contacts by which the insertion of the plug automatically lights the filaments. **1970** *Toronto Daily Star* 24 Sept. 38/2 (Advt.), Lloyd's AM/FM digital clock radio... Features..earphone jack and solid-state circuitry. **1971** R. THOMAS *Backup Men* xiii. 119 Is there another jack in this room?.. Can you get another phone and plug it in?

18. b. = JACK-STONE; usu. *pl.*; also, a game played with these (see also quot. 1908).

1900 S. R. CROCKETT *Little Anna Mark* xii. 97 Playing at quoits, tops, marbles, tic-tac-toe, jacks, knucklebones. **1908** *Dialect Notes* III. 323 *Jack*,..a piece of metal with five tines or protuberances, used in the game of jacks. *Jacks*, an indoor catching game played with small five-tined metal pieces. **1922** A. C. SIES *Spontaneous & Supervised Play* xix. 293 'Jacks' is a game in which throwing and catching are not the main centers of interest; rather are the attention and interest focussed on what is done between catches. **1960** H. MILLER *Nexus* (1964) i. 11 Do you know how to skate?..Did you ever play jacks?

19. c. Money. *slang* (orig. *U.S.*).

1890 M. TOWNSEND *Index U.S.A.* 427 The..verbal wealth of the United States language is illustrated in an inquiry for a loan of money; by using any of the following words in conjunction with the inquiry, *Have you any*.. Jacks, [etc.]. **1920** *Collier's* 28 Aug. 33/2 The fans which paid their jack to see a *fight* would be gypped. **1932** J. DOS PASSOS *1919* 24 This way every bastardly tourist with a little jack thinks he can hire you. **1945** 'N. SHUTE' *Most Secret* 111, I hadn't that much jack... I worked a passage home. **1960** A. PRIOR in *Pick of Today's Short Stories* XI. 184, I asked him..to think of the new suits he could get..when the jack came in.

d. *slang.* Also *jacks, jax.* Five pounds; a five-pound note. Cf. *Jack's alive* s.v. sense *36.

1958 F. NORMAN *Bang to Rights* III. 150 I'll bet you a jacks that I nick you. **1968** *Gloss. Brit. Argot, Jack,* five pounds. **1968** *Guardian* 13 Apr. 7/3 'That one,' says the dealer from Islington, 'that one we *know* she died in; so it'll cost you a jax.'..Five quid for a shroud; cheap at the price. **1970** G. F. NEWMAN *Sir, You Bastard* viii. 230 'Couldn't lend me a Jack's, Terry, could you?' 'Sure.' He gave the DS a fiver. **1972** K. ROYCE *Miniatures Frame* v. 64 From under a pottery sugar jar..protruded two jacks.

25. (Examples.) Also *jack boat*.

1891 *Rep. U.S. Comm. Fish & Fisheries 1887* App. VI. 529 The jack varies from 5 to 15 tons; is schooner-rigged, carrying three sails as a rule. **1895** *St. Nicholas* Apr. 448/2 The gashers [were] dashing in and out among the punts and jacks (stoutly built two-stickers larger than gashers). **1908** *Daily Chron.* 8 Jan. 3/3 A little jack (much the same in rig as our North Sea smacks). **1937** *Beaver* June 29/2 Bill had a nice little jack (small fishing schooner, in this case with outriggers on the quarters instead of booms). **1951** *Maine Coast Fisherman* Oct. 26 A typical Newfoundland jack seen in the cruise to the Bras D'Or Lakes. **1954** *9th Census of Canada 1951* IX. Table 4 Jack boats... Bateaux 'Jack'. **1965** *National Fisherman* Mar. 24/2 The 'jack schooners' or 'jack boats' (so-called in Cape Breton), or 'two-spar boats' (as they are known in Newfoundland) were 40′ to 50′ from stemhead to taffrail. They were gaff-rigged on both masts and they usually carried a longish bowsprit. **1969** H. HORWOOD *Newfoundland* xx. 157 The sons of men who had built windjammers were confined to building trap skiffs and jack boats.

26*. A tablet of heroin. *slang*.

1967 M. M. GLATT et al. *Drug Scene* 115 *Jack*, heroin tablet. **1971** R. BUSBY *Deadlock* xii. 177 He's been cranking up on horse [*sc.* heroin]. His last jack is wearing off, and he's grovelling on the floor for another fix.

29. c. *Austral.* A laughing jackass, a kookaburra. Cf. *JACKO, *JACKY 1 c.

1898 MORRIS *Austral Eng.* 216/1 The bird is generally called only a *Jackass*, and this is becoming contracted into the simple abbreviation of *Jack*. **1934** *Bulletin* (Sydney) 14 Feb. 26/2 Jack came to the conclusion that it was, as tucker, a washout, and departed. **1949** *Geogr. Mag.* Feb. 374/1 Hence such names for the kookaburra as *laughing jackass, jack*.

33. a. jack-hammer, jackhammer, a portable rock-drill worked by compressed air; **jack-ladder,** (*b*) = *JACK-CHAIN 2; **jack-plug** *Electr.*, a single-pronged plug for use with a jack (sense *15 d); **jack-pot** (earlier and later examples); also, any large prize, as from a lottery or a gambling machine; often, a prize that accumulates until it is won; *to hit the jack-pot*: to win such a prize; to have an extraordinary stroke of luck; (*b*) (see quot. 1914); **jack-roller** (see quots.); so *jack-roll* v. trans., *jack-rolling*; **jack shaft,** any of various kinds of auxiliary or intermediate shafts which are driven by another shaft or by a set of gears, esp. in locomotives and motor vehicles (see quots.); **jack-socket** *Electr.* = *JACK *sb.*[1] 15 d.

1930 *Engineering* 24 Oct. 511/2 A battery of about 45 jackhammers..drilled two lines of holes. **1936** *Economist* 12 Oct. 714/1 While this may be possible with machine drills in development faces, it is difficult at the moment to see how such appliances could be used with mobile jackhammers in stoping. **1971** *Daily Tel.* 2 Aug. 20/5 A specially-designed percussion drill similar to a jack-hammer. **1972** *Southerly* XXXII. 102 He works a ship and has about the delicacy of a jackhammer. **1886** *Encycl. Brit.* XXI. 345/1 From the rear end of the mill.. a 'jack ladder' is constructed of heavy timber. **1929** *Ibid.* XIV. 482/1 An endless spiked conveyor known as a jack ladder. **1931** MOYER & WOSTREL *Radio Handbk.* 874 (Index), Jack plugs. **1953** W. MACLANACHAN *Television & Radar Encycl.* 103/2 *Jack and Jack plug*, a socket with two or more contacts..into which a jack plug with corresponding contacts can be inserted. **1973** Jack plug [see *jack socket* below]. **1881** *Harvard Lampoon* 6 Apr. 40/2 Poker-playing is not to be learned in one evening, and Jack Pots are often a snake in the grass. **1884** *Virginia* (Nev.) *Chron.* 1 Oct. 3/3 Old Bill [the warden] just lays back until there is a good jack-pot of trout in hand, and then he makes a bold bluff and walks off with it. **1886** 'M. KERSHAW' *Colonial Facts & Fictions* 229 They call this [growing poker] pool a Jack Pot. **1887** *Grip* (Toronto) 21 May 10/2 What was written of..was a jack-pot. **1902** L. MCKEE *Land of Nome* 123 On the occasion of his getting into a 'jack-pot' (some trouble) he had hunted Nome after me for legal advice. **1914** JACKSON & HELLYER *Vocab. Criminal Slang* 48 *Jackpot*, a dilemma; a difficult strait; a retribution; trouble; an arrest. **1923** G. ADE *Let.* 24 Oct. (1973) 97, I..have been rather interested to learn that the Governor did not show you any degree of gratitude for your work in organizing the jackpot. **1944** *Newsweek* 25 Dec. 67/1 The 'Vick's Vaper' had indeed hit the jack-pot. **1949** *Radio Times* 15 July 6/3 We saw our first American audience-participation show. The prizes included a diamond wrist watch... The jackpot was 1,250 dollars! **1956** N. STREATFEILD *Judith* II. 150 Those sort of weak good looks..quite often hit the jackpot. **1959** *Maclean's Mag.* 4 July 34/3 Canada House receives SOS messages from 'distressed Canadians', the official designation for those who get themselves into various jackpots. **1962** *Sunday Times* Suppl. 10 June 10 There is always the chance that one or other number or artist will hit the jackpot. **1963** *Listener* 28 Mar. 568/3 Cabinet Ministers are hauled out in front of the cameras and asked increasingly impertinent leading questions. A week or two ago Mr Butler copped one of these jackpots from Robert Mackenzie: did he, or did he not, want to be Prime Minister? **1967** *Times* 18 Dec. 5/6 A jackpot may be opened by any player who holds a pair of jacks or a higher ranking hand. **1970** *New Scientist* 14 May 341/1 Rolls-Royce landed a jack-pot order from the USA for the supply of aircraft engines. **1973** 'M. INNES' *Appleby's Answer* i. 10 It was nice to be fairly widely read... It would be even nicer if one day she contrived to hit the jackpot. **1923** N. ANDERSON *Hobo* i. 5 The 'jack roller',.. the man who robs his fellows, while they are drunk or asleep. *Ibid.* iv. 51 'Jack rolling' may be anything from picking a man's pocket in a crowd to robbing him while he is drunk or asleep. **1926** *Flynn's* 16 Jan. 638/1 Jack rollin' th' workstiffs was like takin' candy from th' kids. **1930** C. R. SHAW *Jack-Roller* vii. 85, I was in a predicament, for I had no money, and you can't enjoy life without dough. My buddy, being an old 'jack-roller', suggested 'jack-rolling' as a way out of the delima [*sic*]. **1955** *Publ. Amer. Dial. Soc.* XXIV. 171 Thieves who specialize..on lumberjacks or other seasonal workers who get paid off in a lump sum at the end of the season are called jack rollers. **1896** T. THORNLEY *Cotton Spinning Calculations* II. 70 The jack shaft of the frame makes 298 revolutions per minute. **1901** J. BLACK *Illustr. Carpenter & Builder Ser.: Scaffolding* 72 The electric motor..with jack-shaft and friction drive. **1907** R. B. WHITMAN *Motor-Car Princ.* ix. 146 The jack shaft..is a shaft passing across the car, and bearing on its ends the sprockets by which the wheels are driven. **1925** A. W. JUDGE *Mechanism of Car* vii. 105 The object of the differential is to enable either jack shaft to rotate at a different speed to the other..whilst transmitting the drive. **1936** W. STANIAR *Mech. Power Transmission Handbk.* v. 144 The jackshaft is used for ratio purposes and also to break up long center distances. *Ibid.* 145 Jackshafts. Location.—Either between head and line shafts, or between line- and countershafts. **1940** *Chambers's Techn. Dict.* 465/2 *Jack shaft*, an intermediate shaft used in locomotives having collective drive; the jack shaft is geared to the motor shaft and carries cranks which drive the coupling rods on the driving wheels. **1950** *Engineering* 23 June 699/2 The final drive is through reduction gearing to a jackshaft which is fitted with pressed-on balanced cranks; thence the drive is by rods to the crankpins of the middle coupled wheels [of the Diesel locomotive]. **1962** *Diesel Traction* (Brit. Railways Board) 266 *Jackshaft*, a shaft with cranks at each end mounted across the frames for driving the road wheels through connecting rods. **1966** *McGraw-Hill Encycl. Sci. & Technol.* XII. 240/2 A countershaft, especially when used as an auxiliary shaft between two other shafts, is termed a jack shaft. **1970** J. EARL *Tuners & Amplifiers* i. 14 Modern amplifiers are often equipped with a jack socket wired to accommodate stereo headphones. **1973** *Radio & Electronics Constructor* XXVI. 700/2 A suitable circuit for a miniature 2·5 mm. or 3·5 mm. switched jack socket is given in Fig. 4, and this causes the speaker to be silenced when the jack plug is inserted.

34. b. (Further examples.)

1903 [see *DOGIE, DOGY]. **1942** G. MITCHELL *Laurels are Poison* xvii. 181 It'll be all over College before you can say Jack Robinson. **1956** N. MITFORD *Noblesse Oblige* 43 That picture will appear at Christies before you can say Jack Robinson, though there is no necessity whatever for such a sale.

c. *Jack Scott* = *Jock Scott* (see JOCK[1] 1).

1908 R. BAGOT *Anthony Cuthbert* xxix. 378 'There are some grilse come up. What do you think would be a good fly to use?'..'I should put on a small Jack Scott.' **1915** J. WEBSTER *Dear Enemy* 167 He..got out his case of fishing-flies, and gallantly presented Betsy and me with ..a 'Jack Scott'..to make hat-pins.

d. *Jack Johnson* [from the name of a noted American Negro boxer, whose nickname was 'The Big Smoke'], = *BLACK MARIA 2.

1914 *Illustr. London News* 10 Oct. 504/1 The German 'Jack Johnson' siege-guns. *Ibid.* 505 The gigantic projectile which on bursting makes the black smoke called 'Jack Johnson'. **1919** [see *BLACK MARIA 2]. **1962** J. B. PRIESTLEY *Margin Released* II. iii. 101 The German heavy batteries..dropped 'Jack Johnsons' among us.

e. *Jack Jones*: rhyming slang for 'alone'; usu. in phr. *on one's Jack Jones*: on one's own; alone. Cf. sense 2 e above.

1925 FRASER & GIBBONS *Soldier & Sailor Words* 130 Jack Jones, alone. **1935** 'G. ORWELL' *Clergyman's Daughter* ii. 156 A good night's kip all alone... All on your Jack Jones. **1958** P. SCOTT *Mark of Warrior* II. 168 You're on your jack jones again. What do you do? **1972** A. DRAPER *Death Penalty* xx. 134 You're on your Jack Jones. Ben's deserted you.

35. Jack Dusty *Naut. slang* (see quots.); **Jack Mormon** *U.S.*, a non-Mormon on friendly terms with Mormons; also, a nominal or backsliding Mormon; **Jack Shalloo, Shilloo** *Naut. slang* (see quots.); **Jack Strop** *Naut. slang* (see quots.).

c **1931** W. N. T. BECKETT *Few Naval Customs* 18 The junior member of the Paymaster's Victualling staff is known as The Dusty Boy or Jack Dusty. **1938** 'GIRALDUS' *Merry Matloe Again* 263 *Jack Dusty*, a ship's steward's assistant, *i.e.* any member of the supply branch below the rating of a petty officer. **1974** P. WRIGHT *Lang. Brit. Industry* x. 85 In the Second World War, destroyers had a *Jack Dusty*, a supply assistant who kept ledgers listing all the stocks. **1845** *Quincy* (Ill.) *Whig* 30 Oct. 2/1 Jack Mormons, and sympathizers abroad may croak and groan over the poor Mormons. **1846** Jack-mormon [see *BIG-HEAD 3 b]. **1890** *Congress. Rec.* 2 Apr. 2941/2 In our country we have a *genus homo* called 'Jack-Mormon',..a class of individuals who do not belong to the Mormon church,..yet who are ever found doing the bidding of Mormon priests. **1947** *Time* 21 July 21/1 The number of backsliding 'jack-Mormons' is increasing. **1904** E. P. STATHAM *Story of 'Britannia'* iv. 70 This lad [*sc.* an officer cadet]..was already rather a favourite, being of the breezy type, which sailors call a 'Jack-shilloo'. **1929** F. C. BOWEN *Sea Slang* 73 *Jack Shalloo*, a braggart according to its old naval meaning. Nowadays it is applied to a happy-go-lucky, careless officer and hence a slack ship is called a Jack Shalloo ship. **1962** GRANVILLE *Dict. Sailors' Slang* 65/1 *Jack Shalloo*, naval officer whose aim in life is to be popular with the men. A corruption of *John Chellew*, an officer who earned himself the title Popularity Jack. **1945** BAKER *Austral. Lang.* viii. 162 *Jack Strop*, a new recruit who tries to pass himself off as an old hand. **1946** J. IRVING *Royal Navalese* 98 *Jack Strop*, the Mess Deck's sobriquet for a conceited, opinionated sort of man.

36. *Jack in the basket* Naut., a type of warning beacon (see quot. *a* 1865); *Jack of the dust* (examples); *Jack's alive*, (*b*) rhyming slang for 'five'; also, a five-pound note; *Jack the Painter*, a kind of acrid green tea formerly used in the Australian bush; *Jack the Ripper*, popular name for a murderer of women in London in 1888, who mutilated the bodies of his victims; also used *allusively*.

a **1865** SMYTH *Sailor's Word-Bk.* (1867) 407 *Jack in the basket*, a sort of wooden cap or basket on the top of a pole, to mark a sand-bank or hidden danger. **1921** *Yachting Monthly* Mar. 299/1 How comfortingly the cocoa boiled on an even keel at dawn with Jack-in-the-basket in sight! **1941** *Beaver* Sept. 38/1 Jack-in-the-Basket. A beacon. The Moose River was well buoyed, and the many shoals were marked with high poles surmounted with long wicker baskets, or broom heads of willows. **1878** *Detroit Free Press* (Suppl.) 12 Jan. 2/4 Forward, on the gun-deck, the Paymaster's Steward, and his assistant, the Jack of the Dust, were serving out small stores. **1882** J. W. DANENHOWER *Narr. 'Jeannette'* II. 41 He was doing duty at the time as paymaster's yeoman, or 'Jack of the Dust'. **1931** BROPHY & PARTRIDGE *Songs & Slang 1914–18* (ed. 3) 322 *Jacks alive*, the number 5, especially at House. **1938** F. D. SHARPE *Sharpe of Flying Squad* 331 *Jack's Alive*, a five-pound note. **1852** G. C. MUNDY *Our Antipodes* I. x. 329 Another notorious ration tea of the bush is called 'Jack the Painter'. This is a *very* green tea indeed. **1878** *Australian* I. 418 The billy wins, and 'Jack the Painter' tea Steams on the hob, from aught like fragrance free. **1945** BAKER *Austral. Lang.* iv. 83 *Jack the painter*..from the stain left round the drinker's mouth or in the billy (at least, that is the approved explanation). **1890** *Pall Mall Gaz.* 7 Mar. 5/1 A Jack the Ripper outrage at Moscow. **1902** *To-Day* XXXV. 99/2 Now we know 'oo Jack the Ripper was! **1919** C. P. THOMPSON *Cocktails* 17 If only the officer would let him have a whack at her over the open sights, he'd do the Jack-the-ripper act on her in half a tick. **1958** HAYWARD & HARARI tr. *Pasternak's Dr. Zhivago* II. ix. 268, I expected to see a bashi-bazook or a revolutionary Jack the Ripper, but he was neither. **1959** 'H. CARMICHAEL' *Stranglehold* i. 13, I had to obtain a Home Office permit. And in case you still think I'm Jack the Ripper, here it is. **1972** A. E. LINDOP *Journey into Stone* (1973) ii. 21 There's a *lousy* fog... It's a Jack the Ripper's paradise.

37. Jack Russell (terrier), a small terrier named after John Russell (1795–1883), the so-called 'sporting parson'; **jack salmon**, read: *U.S.*, a large freshwater fish, *Stizostedion vitreum*, also called walleyed pike; **jack-sharp**, a northern dialect name for the STICKLEBACK; **jack-spaniard** (earlier and later examples).

1907 R. LEIGHTON *New Bk. Dog* xxix. 317/1 In another decade or so the neglected Sealy Ham Terrier,..and the almost forgotten Jack Russell strain, may have claimed a due recompense for their long neglect. *Ibid.* 318/1 'I have kept the Jack Russell type of terrier for nearly twenty years,' says Mr. Reginald Bates, 'and have used them for fox and badger digging.' **1931** *Times Lit. Suppl.* 13 Aug. 620/4 Perhaps the most popular is the 'Jack Russell' which..may now be considered a breed. **1965** B. VESEY-FITZGERALD *Dog Owner's Encycl.* 125 Jack Russell terrier. A small working terrier, named (for no very sound reason) after a West Country parson [*sc.* the Rev. John Russell of Devonshire] who, a century ago, was renowned for his working terriers. Any small Hunt terrier may be called a Jack Russell... There is no distinct type and the breed is not recognised by the Kennel Club. **1973** 'I. DRUMMOND' *Jaws of Watchdog* i. 13 A little tubby man..with..the look of an overfed Jack Russell terrier. **1871** *Game Laws* (Pennsylvania) in *Fur, Fin & Feather* (1872) 122 The species commonly known as Susquehanna salmon, pike, perch, jack salmon..shall henceforth not be taken..during their spawning time. **1920** *Outing* (U.S.) May 118/2 We always hope..to catch a few jack salmon. **1811** A. CLARKE *Jrnl.* 12 June in *Acct. Life A. Clarke* (1833) II. 261, I went into the grounds where I had often sported, read, talked, searched for birds' nests, and caught jack-sharps. **1876** I. BANKS *Manchester Man* I. v. 81 He mun larn to tak' care on himsel' th' next time he marlocks among th' Jack-sharps. **1901** *Westm. Gaz.* 24 Apr. 8/1 A boy of ten was attempting to catch jacksharps when he fell from the embankment into the stream... (South-country readers will be interested to learn that jacksharps are the little fishes known to them as sticklebacks or tittlebats.) **1925** J. T. JENKINS *Fishes Brit. Isles* 124 There are numerous local names for this fish [*sc.* the three-spined stickleback], such as Jack Sharp, Prickleback, [etc.]. **1974** P. WRIGHT *Lang. Brit. Industry* vii. 63 The worker pursuing his week-end hobby of angling may find round a pond *cockies* or *jacksharps*, 'sticklebacks' to the uninitiated. **1833** *Chambers's Edin. Jrnl.* 21 Sept. 269/3 The jack-spaniard may be called the wasp of the West Indies; it is twice as large as a British wasp. **1867** J. K. LORD *At Home in Wilderness* xviii. 299 A hornet, called by the packers a 'Jack-Spaniard',..builds a circular paper nest. **1938** *Trans. R. Entomol. Soc.* LXXXVII. 181 *Polistes* Latreille. Four species of this genus were collected in Trinidad. *P. canadensis* (L.). Typical form. 'Jack Spaniard'. Common throughout all settled areas. **1963** D. M. DOUGLASS *Saba's Treasure* i. 14 You could as well discover the particular jack-spaniard that stung you a week ago.

38. jack bean, a sub-tropical, climbing, leguminous plant of the genus *Canavalia*, esp. *C. ensiformis*; **jack-go-to-bed-at-noon** (examples); **Jack-in-the-bush**, (*a*) (example); (*b*) = JACK-IN-THE-GREEN 1; **jack-in-the-hedge** = *Jack-by-the-hedge*, the hedge-garlic, *Alliaria petiolata*; **jack-in-the-pulpit** (earlier and later examples); **jack oak** (earlier and later examples); **jack-pine**, any of several species of pine, esp. the Banksian pine, *Pinus banksiana*.

1885 'C. E. CRADDOCK' *Prophet Gt. Smoky Mts.* xv. 280 He sat upon the cabin porch beneath the yellow gourds and the purple blooms of the Jack-bean. **1951** *Dict. Gardening* (R. Hort. Soc.) I. 382/1 Jack Bean. Chickasaw Lima Bean... The young beans (about 4 to 6 in. long) are sometimes used like Scarlet Runners; the ripe seeds are said to be used as a substitute for coffee. **1853** A. PRATT *Wild Flowers* II. 47 The leaves and stems are often the only portions of the plant [*sc.* Yellow Goat's Beard] to attract the eye of the wanderer, for the flower is closed by mid-day. Several of its country names refer to this peculiarity, as Noontide, and Jack-go-to-bed-at-noon. **1931** M. GRIEVE *Mod. Herbal* I. 360/1 The Goat's Beard opens its blossoms at daybreak and closes them before noon, except in cloudy weather, hence its old country name of 'Noon-flower' and 'Jack-go-to-bed-at-noon'. **1951** W. DE LA MARE *Winged Chariot* 9 How punctual they!.. As testifies 'Jack-go-to-bed-at-noon'. **1807** R. SOUTHEY *Lett. from Eng.* I. xiii. 146 A more extraordinary figure is sometimes in company, whom they call Jack-in-the-Bush; as the name indicates, nothing but bush is to be seen, except the feet which dance under it. The man stands in a frame-work which is supported upon his shoulders, and is completely covered with the boughs of a thick and short-branched shrub. **1872** F. KILVERT *Diary* 10 May (1939) II. 196 He [*sc.* the sawyer] said wild garlic, called Jack-in-the-Bush, is a famous pot herb. **1875** Jack-in-the-hedge [in Dict.]. **1925** W. DE LA MARE *Broomsticks* 312 Young spring flowers—primroses, violets, jack-in-the-hedge, stitchwort—in palest blossom starred the banks. **1941** A. L. ROWSE *Poems of Decade* 111 The many and various scents of the flowers, Cuckoo-pint, cow-parsley and jack-in-the-hedge. **1837** H. MARTINEAU *Society in Amer.* I. II. 211 Fine specimens of Jack-in-the-pulpit, and the moccassin-flower. **1906** *N.Y. Even. Post* (Suppl.) 16 June 2 In these woods I made acquaintance with Jack-in-the-pulpits, or, as the English call them, 'Lords and Ladies'. **1949** *Nature Mag.* Apr. 178 A few of these, like Indian turnip or jack-in-the-pulpit, cowslip and milkweed, may be considered mildly inedible. **1972** T. MCHUGH *Time of Buffalo* viii. 91 Soups were popular, some brewed with..buffalo meat, berries, fat, and the roots of jack-in-the-pulpits. **1816** U. BROWN *Jrnl.* in *Maryland Hist. Mag.* (1915) X. 266 Jack Oaks and other Scrub Wood. **1836** D. B. EDWARD *Hist. Texas* iv. 68 The post-oak and Jack-oak are considered in Texas as every man's property. **1901** DUNCAN & SCOTT *Hist. Allen & Woodson Counties, Kansas* 581 The 'jack oak hills' have been fenced. **1883** G. O. SHIELDS *Rustlings in Rockies* xxxi. 285 This [country] is now grown up with scattering dwarf pines or, as the settlers call them, jack-pines. **1925** *Chambers's Jrnl.* June 381/2 The jack-pine grows low and twisted. **1957** J. KEROUAC *On Road* (1968) II. ix. 55, I..looked up and saw jackpines in the moon. **1965** G. MCINNES *Road to Gundagai* xii. 210, I saw, moving majestically towards me and looming over the head of the crowd like a Douglas fir among jackpine, a prematurely grey giant about nine feet tall. **1969** T. H. EVERETT *Living Trees of World* 51/1 The range of the jack pine (*P. banksiana*), the most northern of eastern American pines, extends south from near the Arctic Circle to New York and Minnesota.

jack, *sb.*[4] Add: (Further examples.)

1820 J. CRAWFURD *Hist. Indian Archipelago* I. IV. 122 Of the Jack fruit..two species occur in the Indian islands. ..The Jack is highly nutritious. **1824** H. E. LLOYD tr. *Spix & Martius's Trav. Brazil* I. II. i. 175 Brazil is indebted to the intercourse of the Portuguese with the East Indies..for the excellent fruits of the jaca, the mango, and the jambos. **1839** T. J. NEWBOLD *Pol. & Stat. Acct. Straits of Malacca* ii. 53 In the valley grow various fruit-trees, such as..the jack. **1919** *Nature* 25 Sept. 78/2 The native of the country is content with the fruit that is easily produced there and is already well known (in this case the durian, mango, sapodilla, mangosteen, jak, etc.). **1931** B. MIALL tr. *Guenther's Naturalist in Brazil* iv. 80 The fruits of the Jaca, as large as a man's head, seem to grow directly from the trunk and boughs. **1969** *Oxf. Bk. Food Plants* 114/2 Jak or Jack Fruit (*Artocarpus integrifolia*) is a related species with enormous fruits which can weigh up to 70 lb. each. In spite of their very strong odour, they are relished especially in Asia and may be eaten cooked or raw.

b. (Further examples.)

1869 A. R. WALLACE *Malay Archipelago* I. xvi. 362 There were also great numbers of a wild Jack-fruit tree (Artocarpus), which bore abundance of large reticulated fruit. **1900** W. W. SKEAT *Malay Magic* vi. 563 To dream about eating jack-fruit (*nangka*)..is an indication of great trouble impending. **1908** E. J. BANFIELD *Confessions of Beachcomber* I. i. 43 We have..Jack fruit..in plenty. **1920** *Outward Bound* Oct. 44/1 The shameless stranger..issued from the saffron sunset, somewhere behind the spiky line of the mission jack fruit trees. **1921** E. M. FORSTER *Let.* 4 June in *Hill of Devi* (1953) 92 The Jack Fruits are ripening a little—they are extraordinary, with crocodile scales. **1947** *E. Afr. Ann. 1946–7* 23/2 Doors, mostly of local jack-fruit tree wood, are still being carved by Swahili craftsmen. **1962** *Housewife* (Ceylon) Apr. 23 The rich green foliage of mature plaintain and jak trees. **1966** D. FORBES *Heart of Malaya* ii. 27 A Malay kampong stands..half hidden by an assortment of fruit trees—durian, jack-fruit, mangosteen and rambutan. **1967** SINGHA & MASSEY *Indian Dances* xx. 175 It is said that he once had a vision in which Krishna asked him to carve his image from the wood of a certain jack-fruit tree. **1972** A. AMIN tr. *Ahmad's No Harvest but Thorn* ii. 13 The handle of his *parang*, which was made of the heart-wood of a jack-fruit tree.

jack, *v.*[1] Add: **1.** (Further examples.)

1971 J. D. MACDONALD *Seven* (1974) iii. 46 When we decided to give up the apple stand, I said it might make a nice little cabin. My husband Ralph jacked it up and put it on a flatbed wagon and tractored it up through the west orchard. **1973** *Country Life* 18 Oct. 1190/1, I enjoy reminiscing over early motoring days... Jack up the back tyre to ensure easier starting.

b. *transf.* and *fig.* To raise, increase; to force or bolster *up*. *colloq.* (orig. *U.S.*).

1904 *N.Y. Tribune* 8 May 10 The management thought it saw a chance to jack up rents, and made a sudden announcement of a raise. **1939** J. P. MARQUAND *Wickford Point* x. 126 She had jacked up the price on the table d'hôte ten francs. **1959** *Economist* 7 Feb. 504/1 At his first trial, Cho Bong-Am got only five years, but a second trial jacked this up to capital punishment. **1964** *Ann. Reg. 1963* 44 Mr Heath unveiled the plans to jack up the punctured local economies. **1971** *Daily Tel.* 26 July 15/7 Reinvestment would then jack up earnings per share and hence the value of the equity.

c. To arrange, organize, fix *up*; to put right, spruce *up*. *N.Z. slang.*

1942 *2 N.Z.E.F. Times* 12 Oct. 6/5 *Jack-up*, a term meaning to achieve the apparently impossible or to bring out of chaos; to arrange, inveigle, wangle or bolster up (a) Any transport (b) any alibi (c) leave (d) ED pay—usually without the prior knowledge or consent of authority. **1943** *Ibid.* 16 Aug. 6/5 Some of the pubs could do with a jacking up... Not enough service and civility. **1944** J. H. FULLARTON *Troop Target* xxvi. 187 I've jacked up a hot snack for the end of the shoot. **1945** E. G. WEBBER *Johnny Enzed in Middle East* 13/3 May take a year to jack it up again. **1956** D. M. DAVIN *Sullen Bell* I. iii. 24 I've jacked it up to stay the night with a friend of mine. **1960** B. CRUMP *Good Keen Man* 59 Harry decided to try his hand at jacking up a home brew. **1963** *Weekly News* (Auckland) 8 May 39/3 We jacked it up between ourselves that one evening we'd get Honey's gloves. **1971** *N.Z. Listener* 22 Mar. 13/1 I'll see you right at a boardin' place until you get jacked up.

4. Slang phr. *to jack in*: to abandon, leave, give up, stop. Freq. in phr. *to jack it in*.

1948 A. BARON *From City from Plough* i. 12 'What's your ol' woman do to you, Charlie?' 'Jacked me in for a civvy. I got home; no one there, no furniture, nothing.' **1958** F. NORMAN *Bang to Rights* III. 77 There was only fifteen of us on the hunger strike, I suppose the others must have got hungrey anyway they jacked it in. **1963** 'A. GARVE' *Sea Monks* v. 130, I ain't goin' to jack it all in now for Chris or anyone. **1972** K. ROYCE *Miniatures Frame* ix. 123 I'm beginning to wonder if it's worth it... Let me jack it in. **1973** *Times* 31 May 10/7 Private landlords jack-in the shaky business of letting.

5. *to jack off* (intr.): (*a*) to go away, depart; (*b*) to masturbate. *slang.*

1935 'G. ORWELL' *Clergyman's Daughter* ii. 109 Flo and Charlie would probably 'jack off' if they got the chance of a lift. *a* **1950** —— *Coll. Ess.* (1968) I. 71 *Jack off, to,* to go away. **1959** W. BURROUGHS *Naked Lunch* 74 He plummets from the eyeless lighthouse, kissing and jacking off in face of the black mirror. **1971** R. A. CARTER *Manhattan Primitive* (1972) xxiv. 237 You miserable little queer... You can jack off in Llewellyn's best hat for all I care. **1972** V. FERDINAND in A. Chapman *New Black Voices* 472 We might as well be jacking off, masturbating for our own self-gratification.

jack (dʒæk), *a. Austral. slang.* [f. JACK *v.*[1] 3.] Tired *of* (something or someone); bored.

1901 E. DYSON *Gold Stealers* iv. 41 Oh, well, Twitter's jack of it, an' I don't think it's much fun. **1944** J. DEVANNY *By Tropic Sea & Jungle* xviii. 155 Too much of it makes you jack of it quick. **1959** BAKER *Drum* vi. 50 He was clearly a bore and they were jack of him. **1969** *Coast to Coast 1967–8* 4 He was willing to bet she'd get jack of it.

ja·ckal, *v.* [f. the sb.] *intr.* To play the jackal (see JACKAL 2); to do subordinate work or drudgery.

1900 KIPLING in *Daily Mail* 21 Apr. 4/5 For three months she had jackalled behind the army..and in that time had carried over thirteen hundred sick and wounded. **1914** A. DOBSON *18th Cent. Stud.* 204 Johnson..lost many of the papers lent to him by Percy. Malone, who jackalled for him, lost others. **1940** V. WOOLF *Writer's Diary* 6 Apr. (1953) 331, I..brooded quietly till the tyre punctured: we had to jackal in mid-road.

jackal(l), varr. *JACAL.

jackaroo, jackeroo. Add: (Earlier and later examples.) Now esp. a cadet or novice on a sheep-station or cattle-station.

1878 'R. BOLDREWOOD' *Ups & Downs* vii. 72 If these here fences is to be run up all along the river, any Jackaroo can go stock-keeping. **1911** C. E. W. BEAN '*Dreadnought' of Darling* xi. 99 In the bachelors' quarters there will probably live..one or two 'jackeroos'—young Australians, or sometimes young Englishmen, learning the work of a sheep run by taking an ordinary part in it. **1918** *Chambers's Jrnl.* Apr. 267/2 The tracker's methods are noted in the following true story of a lost 'jackeroo' (a 'new chum' learning station work). **1936** I. L. IDRIESS *Cattle King* xxxii. 287 Some of the blacks told me he was coming with a couple of young jackeroos. **1956** 'N. SHUTE' *Beyond Black Stump* ii. 45 At the age of sixteen David had gone as a jackeroo upon a sheep station, to learn the business. **1962** *Coast to Coast 1961–62* 28 Coorabin's Royal Hotel had afforded her plenty of practice in turning on a stare that caused the invitations of commercial travellers, boundary-riders and jackaroos to trail off before they were half spoken. **1968** *TV Times* (Austral.) 28 Aug. 30/1 Jackaroo. 45 min. documentary. The jackaroo is..an apprentice to the rural industry, and in theory is in training to become a manager or owner. **1969** *West Australian* 5 July 58/2 (Advt.), 2 Jackaroos or Junior Stockmen with riding experience 16/18 years for West Kimberley Cattle Station.

jackaroo, jackeroo *v.* (earlier and later examples).

1878 'R. BOLDREWOOD' *Ups & Downs* xix. 239 A year or two more Jackerooing would only mean the consumption of so many more figs of negro-head. **1911** C. E. W. BEAN '*Dreadnought' of Darling* xxxiv. 302 A houseful of bachelors—three or four young fellows jackerooing (that is to say, learning colonial experience) under a bachelor manager. **1936** A. RUSSELL *Gone Nomad* ii. 12 My graduation in jackerooing, or, as I usually call this period of my life, my 'pack-mule and damper days', had begun. **1967** *Coast to Coast 1965–6* 161 Young and old..jackerooed for thirty bob and tucker.

jackass, *sb.* Add: **4. b.** (Examples.)

1891 in H. PATTERSON *Illustr. Naut. Dict.* **1907** A. T. MAHAN *From Sail to Steam* iv. 96 The absurd-sounding, but legitimate, message to have the jackasses put in the hawse-holes. **1918** F. RIESENBERG *Under Sail* ii. 29 'Jackasses' were then bowsed into the hawse holes *for fair.* **1948** R. DE KERCHOVE *Internat. Maritime Dict.* 368/1 Jackasses are a most effective method of making hawseholes watertight in ships using stocked anchors.

5. jackass barque, a sailing ship having the same sails as a barquentine but rigged in a manner varying in some respect from the orthodox barquentine rig; **jackass brandy** *U.S. slang,* home-made brandy; **jackass brig** (examples); **jackass-rigged** *a.,* substitute for def.: of a schooner, having three masts with square sails set on the foremast and having no main topmast; add further example; **jackass schooner,** a schooner which is jackass-rigged.

1861 *Mitchell's Maritime Reg.* 890 On the 10th instant there was launched from the building-yard of Messrs. J. and J. Hall, at Arbroath, a beautifully modelled jackass barque, named the Princess Alice, of 190 tons N.N.M. **1923** F. C. BOWEN *Ships for All* ii. 39 The sails of a barquentine and of a jackass barque are precisely the same. **1969** B. LANDSTRÖM *Sailing Ships* 178 It sometimes occurred that a ship was rigged, for example, with a fore-and-aft sail on the lower mainmast and square sails on the top and topgallant masts... In England all such types of pseudo-barques were called *jackass barques.* **1920** *Federal Reporter* (U.S.) CCLXXVIII. 42 Intoxicating liquors, to wit, one pint bottle of jackass brandy. **1921** *Dialect Notes* V. 109 *Jackass brandy,* a home-made brandy with a powerful 'kick'. **1923** *San Francisco Examiner* 18 Feb. 16/7 A still in operation and a stock of jackass brandy close by. **1883** R. B. DIXON *Fore & Aft* 191 The potatoes would have to be paid for before that 'jackass brig' could sail. **1887** G. DAVIS *Recoll. Sea Wanderer's Life* 231 She is what is called a jackass brig. She has one mast square rigged and the other is schooner rigged, with topsail. **1926** *Sea Breezes* VIII. 214 There was a jackass brig, no main course, main yard high up, rigged like a topsail schooner on main mast. **1898** A. ANSTED *Dict. Sea Terms* 239 There is another class of trading schooner, with three masts...When it sets square sails on the foremast it is sometimes called *jackass* rigged. **1929** H. W. SMYTH *Mast & Sail* (new ed.) 520 *Jackass schooner,* still used occasionally of a schooner without main-topmast. **1951** H. BENHAM *Down Tops'l* v. 71 'Jackass' schooners.. were so called because they were square rigged forward like a tops'l schooner, but had a ketch's mizzen. **1961** F. H. BURGESS *Dict. Sailing* 122 A 'jackass schooner' has no main topmast.

jack boat: see *JACK *sb.*[1] 25.

jack-boot, jackboot. Add: Also, those worn by German soldiers during the Nazi regime.

1942 *R.A.F. Jrnl.* 2 May 36 Either the British way shall survive or the Nazi jackboot and whip shall take its place. **1955** *Times* 13 June 8/5 There were jackboots to be seen, iron crosses were pinned to the pockets of a few green shirts.

b. *fig.* Military oppression; rough bullying tactics. Also *attrib.*

1768 J. MORDAUNT *Let.* 10 May in E. Hamilton *Mordaunts* (1965) ix. 215 Some insults were offer'd to some of the Lords & Commons in their Coaches as they went down with a Cry of Wilkes & Liberty & no Jack Boot. **1910** *Westm. Gaz.* 14 Feb. 5/1 A large numerical majority..excluded from power and honour by a mere jack-boot minority. **1968** *Sat. Rev.* 26 Oct. 36 The writers' trials and the jackboot on Prague have made it quite clear that Brezhnev and Kosygin's views on liberalism are akin to Stalin's. **1968** 'R. SIMONS' *Death on Display* vii. 105 He also objected strongly to what he called your jackboot methods when you interviewed Mrs Hurd. **1970** *Times* 18 Mar. 26 This..attempt by the Government to bludgeon this Bill through with jackboot tactics.

Hence **ja·ck-booted** *a.*

1846 R. FORD *Gatherings from Spain* xxii. 300 The clumsy look of a French jackbooted postilion. **1939** 'N. BLAKE' *Smiler with Knife* iv. 60 Silent, jack-booted watchers standing outside frightened houses. **1946** *R.A.F. Jrnl.* May 175 The once-jackbooted Germans. **1972** J. ROSSITER *Rope for General Dietz* ii. 28 He stood..with his jackbooted legs apart..as if to underline what they'd done in the name of Nazi justice.

jack-chain. Add: **2.** *Logging.* (See quot. 1905.)

1905 *Terms Forestry & Logging* (U.S. Dept. Agric. Bureau Forestry) 40 *Jack chain,* an endless spiked chain, which moves logs from one point to another, usually from the mill pond into the sawmill. **1957** in *Brit. Commonwealth Forest Terminol.* II. 97.

jacker. Add: **b.** *jacker-off, -up*: see quots. 1921.

1881 in *Instructions to Census Clerks* (1885) 70. **1904** *Westm. Gaz.* 28 Apr. 4/1 It was in the lace factory that the lad was set to work as a 'jacker-off'. **1921** *Dict. Occup. Terms* (1927) § 399 *Jacker-off* (lace); takes off from bobbins, waste lengths of unused threads, and winds them on to large wooden bobbins, using a small winding machine. *Ibid.* § 688 *Jacker-up* (lead pencil making); places a number of glued pencils together in a clamp, and screws down clamp to make glueing secure; removes pencils when clamping is complete. **1924** J. MARCHANT *Dr. John Clifford* i. 5 Three-fourths of the children were jackers-off or 'piecers'.

jackeroo: see JACKAROO in Dict. and Suppl.

jacket, *sb.* Add: **1. f.** See also DUST *v.*[1] 6 b in Dict. and Suppl.

†**g.** *Mil. colloq.* (See quots.) *Obs.*

1898 *Geogr. Jrnl.* May 556 Lieut. Tanner obtained his 'jacket', and was the *beau ideal* of a horse-artillery officer. **1908** *Westm. Gaz.* 15 Oct. 5/3 Until 1895..a 'jacket'—i.e., a post in the Royal Field Horse Artillery—might be given to an officer of Field Artillery or of Garrison Artillery. **1909** J. R. WARE *Passing Eng.* 158/2 *Jacket* (Military), a soldier who wears a jacket (chiefly cavalry or horse artillery). **1925** FRASER & GIBBONS *Soldier & Sailor Words* 130 *Jacket, to get the*: colloquial for an appointment to the Royal Horse Artillery.

2. b. See also *dust-jacket* (*DUST *sb.*[1] 8 e).

d. *Ordnance.* A coil or cylinder of wrought iron or steel placed around the barrel of a gun to strengthen or protect it.

1876 *Engineering* XXI. 17 This improvement consists in the addition of a steel jacket to the body of the gun from the breech to beyond the trunnions. **1888** O. E. MICHAELIS tr. *Monthaye's Krupp & De Bange* ii. 24 The tube..is encircled by a single band or jacket (Mantel, in German), shrunk on. **1902** *Kynoch Jrnl.* Apr.–May 79/2 A second gun..having a jacket of cast steel. **1972** *Internat. Defense Rev.* Feb. 61 Sheathing the gun tube in an insulating jacket of cloth, plastic material or aluminum plate.

4. jacket crown *Dentistry,* a crown (*CROWN *sb.* 28 b), often of porcelain or vinyl, fitted over an existing natural crown, which is usually ground down to receive it; **jacket potato,** a potato cooked in its jacket, i.e. unpeeled.

1903 H. J. GOSLEE *Princ. & Pract. Crowning Teeth* viii. 129 The so-called jacket crown is often a most useful style of construction. **1963** [see *bridge-work* (*BRIDGE *sb.*[1] II b)]. **1966** L. DEIGHTON *Billion-Dollar Brain* xix. 197 One of my jacket crowns is loose. [**1902** WRIGHT *Eng. Dial. Dict.* (s.v. *jacket*), *Jackutty-taters,* potatoes boiled with their skins on.] **1928** GALSWORTHY *Swan Song* I. v. 37 A young woman was handing him 'jacket' potatoes. **1967** M. SUMMERTON *Memory of Darkness* iv. 56 You'll fare better on Rosie's stew and my baked jacket potatoes.

jacket, *v.* Add: **1. c.** To enclose (a person) in a strait-jacket.

1856 C. READE *Never too Late* I. xv. 276 He found himself surrounded, jacketed, strapped, and collared. **1905** J. LONDON *Jacket* (1915) 52 They told me plainly that they would jacket me to death if I did not confess.

Jackfield (dʒæ·kfīld). The name of a village in Shropshire, used *attrib.* to denote a kind of black-glazed pottery of a type manufactured there in the 18th century. Also *ellipt.* as *sb.*

1904 A. H. CHURCH *Eng. Earthenware* (rev. ed.) xv. 115 Collectors of English earthenware are generally inclined to assign the black so-called 'Jackfield ware' to Whieldon. Possibly the black glaze..may have been added at Jackfield. **1967** *Sunday Times* 5 Mar. 47/1 Leeds pottery dates from about 1750, and though the creamware is the commonest product, the factory also produced some rather nasty shiny black earthenware called 'Jackfield'. **1968** *Canad. Antiques Collector* Oct. 5/2 A smaller exquisitely modelled Jackfield ware jug.

jack-fruit: see JACK *sb.*[4] b (in Dict. and Suppl.).

jack-knife, *sb.* Add: **1.** (Earlier Amer. example.)

1711 *Official Rec. Springfield, Mass.* (1898–9) IX. 39 One Dozen of Jack Knives, at six pence the knife.

3. *Swimming.* In full, *jack-knife dive.* A kind of dive executed by first doubling up and then straightening the body before entering the water.

1922 *Country Life* (U.S.) July 60/3 All variety dives fall into four main groups—somersaults, twists, gainers, jack-knives. **1928** *Radio Times* 11 May 274/2 Doing jack-knife and swallow dives from incredible heights. **1942** J. D. CARR *Seat of Scornful* xiv. 191 That's not a jack-knife, you ass... A jack-knife dive is where you bend double and touch your toes in mid-air, and then straighten out before you hit the water. **1956** J. SYMONS *Paper Chase* x. 60 His long legs drawn up like those of a jack-knife-diving swimmer.

4. The accidental folding up of an articulated lorry.

1966 *Times* 29 Sept. 11/6 A 'jack-knife' is an ugly complaint of 'artics' as these articulated monsters [*sc.* lorry and trailer] are known familiarly in the trade. The trailer and lorry fold up like a Boy Scout's jack-knife.

jack-knife, *v.* Add: (*a*) (Earlier U.S. example.) (*b*) (Earlier and later examples.) *spec.* Of the sections of an articulated lorry: in an accident, to fold together like a jack-knife. (*c*) To do a jack-knife dive. So **ja·ck-knifing** *vbl. sb.*

1806 *Balance* (Hudson, N.Y.) 22 July 228 (Th.), A sailor..Jacknifed (as he termed it) the poor creature [*sc.* a cat] in several places about the head. **1888** *Century Mag.* June 251/2 The practice..of dodging shots, 'jack-knifing' under fire. **1920** T. S. ELIOT *Ara Vos Prec* 22 The sickle motion from the thighs Jackknifes upward at the knees Then straightens down from heel to hip. **1949** *Sun* (Baltimore) 4 Aug. 1/8 An automobile crashed into a tractor-trailer truck that jackknifed in a driving rain. **1955** T. STERLING *Evil of Day* v. 50 He..jack-knifed into a chintz armchair. **1958** *Times* 12 Apr. 7/7 Nobody envies Joe Cree his new 'artic.', for there is always the danger that, on ice, the rear will swing round, or jack-knife. **1964** [see *FIN *v.* 4]. **1968** *New Scientist* 14 Mar. 573/3 Jack-knifing accidents to articulated vehicles are all too common...The vehicle folds up—jack-knifes—at the kingpin, which is the hinge between the two parts. **1971** *Rand Daily Mail* 27 Mar. 8/2 This was particularly so in the case of drivers, when jackknifing of the upper torso onto the steering wheel rim could lead to serious injuries. **1971** *New Scientist* 12 Aug. 359/2 Commercial vehicles..need them [*sc.* antilock brakes] most urgently because of their widely varying states of load and their tendency to jack-knife if articulated.

jack-leg, jackleg (dʒæ·kleg), *a.* and *sb. U.S. colloq.* and *dial.* [f. JACK *sb.*[1] + *-leg* as in BLACK-LEG 2, 3.] Used as a term of contempt or depreciation: **A.** *adj.* Incompetent, unskilled; unscrupulous, dishonest. Freq. used of lawyers and preachers. **B.** *sb.* An incompetent or unskilled or unprincipled person.

1850 *Amer. Rev. Mag.* XI. 465/2 A party of some twenty of the most notorious rode up, headed by what is there [*sc.* in Texas] known as a 'jack-leg' lawyer. **1853** 'P. PAXTON' *Stray Yankee in Texas* xiii. 137 A sorter jack-leg lawyer. *Ibid.* xxviii. 284 In the Texan vocabulary, all men who have a mere inkling of any trade or profession are called 'jack-legs'. *Ibid.*, These men were 'jack-leg' carpenters. **1891** *Harper's Mag.* June 160/1 Once I was called a jack-leg and shyster. **1902** W. N. HARBEN *Abner Daniel* ii. 16 The Atlanta jack-leg lawyer is akin to the Tompkins family some way. **1943** R. OTTLEY *New World A-Coming* 86 The cultists were augmented by a number of herb doctors, clairvoyants, and 'jackleg' preachers. **1958** P. OLIVER in P. Gammond *Decca Bk. Jazz* i. 19 The wandering evangelists, and 'Jack-leg'

preachers. **1974** *Amer. Speech 1971* XLVI. 70 One innovation possibly attributable to population shift is *jackleg preacher*, which Carlson heard from a black informant in Roxbury.

So **ja·ck-legged** *a.*

1839 *Congress. Globe* App. 127 A set of jack-legged pettifogging lawyers. **1892** *Congress. Rec.* 27 May 4777/1 He goes away, and a jack-legged [army] officer could do nothing except to mark him as a deserter.

Jacko (dʒæ·ko). *Austral. slang.* [f. *JACK *sb.*[1] 29 c + *-O[2].] A kookaburra (= *JACK *sb.*[1] 29 c).

1941 BAKER *Dict. Austral. Slang* 38 *Jacko*, a kookaburra. **1942** C. BARRETT *On Wallaby* iv. 80 Were they only having a close-up view, having mistaken the moving figure among the dunes for a Jacko?

Jack-o'-lantern, *sb.* **3.** (Examples.)

1837 HAWTHORNE *Twice-Told Tales* 222 Hide it [*sc.* the great carbuncle] under thy cloak, say'st thou? Why, it will gleam through the holes, and make thee look like a jack-o'lantern! **1959** I. & P. OPIE *Lore & Lang. Schoolch.* xii. 269 As soon as it is dark on Hallowe'en they take the lighted 'Jack-o-lanterns' and put them on their gateposts.

jack-pot: see JACK *sb.*[1] 33 a (in Dict. and Suppl.).

jack-rabbit. Add: (Earlier and later examples.) Also *attrib.* and *fig.*

1863 N. S. KEITH *Let.* 24 Aug. in *Colorado Mag.* (1940) XVII. 69 We saw wolves, buffalos, antelopes, jack-rabbits, prairie-dogs innumerable, deer, and birds of various sizes. **1906** *Chambers's Jrnl.* July 538/1 For miles one may ride without seeing a living thing larger than a jack-rabbit. **1929** W. FAULKNER *Sartoris* III. iv. 206 The mules flapped their jack-rabbit ears. **1961** 'E. LATHEN' *Banking on Death* (1962) vii. 57 He was thrown backward by a jack-rabbit start from a stop sign. **1962** *Amer. Speech* XXXVII. 269 *Jack rabbit*, a motorist who is proficient at watching the cross-street traffic light; when it turns yellow, he starts up and is into the intersection before the light in front of him has turned green. **1963** D. P. MANNIX *All Creatures Great & Small* xi. 180 We saw our first live jackrabbit just at dawn while crossing the plains of Nebraska. A big, white-tailed jack with black-and-white squares like signal flags on his long ears bolted across the road. **1972** *Guardian* 16 Dec. 10/1 You surely have hit the jack-rabbit on the head with a fire-iron.

Jacksonian (dʒæksōu·niăn), *a.*[1] [See -IAN.] Pertaining to or characteristic of Andrew Jackson (1767–1845), seventh president of the United States, a prominent leader of the Democratic party. Also as *sb.*, a follower of Jackson. Hence **Jackso·nianism.**

1824 *Amer. Sentinel* (Georgetown, Ky.) 18 Oct. 3/1 At Mount-sterling..they collected together six Jacksonians. **1824** *Commentator* (Frankfort, Ky.) 23 Oct. 3/2 The old Jacksonian aristocratic leaven of the Adams faction. **1906** W. CHURCHILL *Coniston* v. 51 He..preached the word of Jacksonian Democracy in all the farmhouses round about. *Ibid.* 57 The conscientious Jacksonians who were misguided enough to believe in such a ticket. **1929** *Encycl. Brit.* I. 156/2 Up to this point Adams's career had been almost uniformly successful, but his presidency (1825–29) was in most respects a failure, owing to the virulent opposition of the Jacksonians. *Ibid.* IV. 585/1 Calhoun,..during the remainder of the Jackson regime, was a severe critic of Jacksonianism. **1966** AUDEN *About House* 16 A Proustian snob or a sound Jacksonian Democrat. **1973** *New Yorker* 28 Apr. 146/2 Douglas's creed was Jacksonianism, which to him meant a United States expanding over the whole continent and demonstrating that a democracy could not only survive but prosper.

Jacksonian (dʒæksōu·niăn), *a.*[2] *Med.* [f. the name of John Hughlings *Jackson* (1834–1911), English physician and neurologist: see -IAN.] Designating a form of epilepsy (and the associated convulsions, fits, etc.) in which the seizures are usually confined to one side of the body (in which case consciousness is retained) and begin at one site (usually a digit or the angle of the mouth), progressing from there to neighbouring parts.

1877 *Brit. & Foreign Med.-Chirurg. Rev.* LIX. 51 The epithet 'Jacksonian' is even being introduced in France by Charcot to be applied to epilepsy or convulsions of a localised and partial character. **1878** *Glasgow Med. Jrnl.* X. 92 Dr Robertson showed a patient who suffers from Jacksonian Epilepsy. **1878** *Brit. Med. Jrnl.* 28 Dec. 959/1 (*heading*) Jacksonian convulsions. **1890** *Jrnl. Nerv. & Mental Dis.* XVII. 56 The Jacksonian spasm confined chiefly to the left hand and arm. **1933** W. R. BRAIN *Dis. Nervous Syst.* iii. 224 Jacksonian attacks may occur at long intervals, or with great frequency, even up to several hundreds a day—serial Jacksonian epilepsy. **1960** W. G. LENNOX *Epilepsy* I. vii. 212 Most authorities, including Penfield.., use the term Jacksonian to cover all forms of local motor seizures. **1969** H. H. JASPER et al. *Basic Mechanisms Epilepsies* xix. 517/1 Particular interest was centered in Jacksonian seizures.

jacksy (dʒæ·ksi). *slang.* Also **jacksie, jacksy-pardo, -pardy, jaxey, jaxie.** [f. JACK *sb.*[1] + -SY.] The posterior, backside, arse.

1896 FARMER & HENLEY *Slang* IV. 33/1 *Jacksy-pardy*, the posteriors. **1943** HUNT & PRINGLE *Service Slang* 40 *Jacksie*, service slang for 'rear', 'tail', or 'bottom'. **1959** K. WATERHOUSE *Billy Liar* v. 78 Why don't you tell the boring little man to stick the job up his jacksy? **1963** *Sunday Times* 15 Sept. 29/8 Tonbridge boys many years ago said 'a root on the Jaxie (or Jacksie)' for 'a kick in the pants'. **1966** B. NAUGHTON *Alfie* xxxvi. 206 She's sitting there on her jacksie, reading one of those colour things out of a newspaper. **1970** A. DRAPER *Swansong for Rare Bird* i. 9 The amount of love in our house you could stick up a dog's jacksie and he wouldn't even yelp.

jack-up (dʒæ·kˌʊp). [f. JACK *v.*[1] 1.] In full, *jack-up rig.* A type of drilling rig for use in an offshore oil-field the legs of which are lowered to the sea bed from the operating platform.

1965 *Oil & Petroleum Year Bk.* 511 (Advt.), Santa Fe's offshore operations now include drilling services from fixed platforms, jack-ups and the semi-submersible Blue Water No. 2. **1967** *Ocean Industry* Dec. 11/1 Husky's New Jack-up Rig Designed for North Sea Husky Oils new $10-million jack-up *Gulftide* was christened October 6. **1970** *New Scientist* 29 Oct. 219/2 In the North Sea.. of the dozen or so mobile rigs usually operating the most common types are the semi-submersible and the jack-up. *Ibid.*, Jack-ups are..very vulnerable when jacking up or down to move location. **1972** *Times* 23 Nov. 23/2 The discovery was made by the new jack-up rig Zapata Nordic which is under long term contract to Shell.

Jacky. Add: **1.** (Further examples in sense 'a sailor'.)

1893 *Funk's Stand. Dict.*, *Jacky*, a sailor. **1909** *Daily Chron.* 1 Oct. 1/6 The place of honour..was given to the British 'jackies', who were easily the most popular.

b. Also *Jacky-Jacky.* A white man's name for an Aboriginal. *Austral. slang.*

1928 'BRENT OF BIN BIN' *Up Country* ii. 35 He was.. going to..outdo Jacky-Jacky as a swell. **1944** W. E. HARNEY *Taboo* (ed. 3) 87 Such was the view of the boss—not how good a cattle-man you were, but how cheap and good were your methods with the 'jackies'—the name given to the natives out there. **1969** *Sun-Herald* (Sydney) 13 July 52/1 'Jackie Jackie' is dead. There is a new and growing spirit in the Aboriginal community.

c. *Austral.* A kookaburra. Cf. *JACK *sb.*[1] 29 c.

1934 *Bulletin* (Sydney) 11 July 21/2 Jacky left hurriedly and didn't return for his dinner. *Ibid.* 17 Oct. 20/4 Cockatoos are the latest-feeders among the bush birds, bar the jacky.

3. Jacky (or **Jackie**) **Howe** (see quot. 1965); also **Jimmy Howe** *Austral.* and *N.Z. slang*; **Jacky Winter** *Austral.*, the brown flycatcher, *Micrœca fascinans.*

1930 *Bulletin* (Sydney) 9 Apr. 19/2 It took nine bars of soap to wash his 'Jacky Howe' flannel. **1937** E. HILL *Great Austral. Loneliness* xl. 301 A weird figure in a flour-bag, Jimmie Howe, with shoes of raw-hide laced with pandanus, Leng carried no luggage. **1948** V. PALMER *Golconda* xi. 85 In his sleeveless Jackie Howe he swaggered around showing the punctures on his burly arm. **1965** *N.Z. Listener* 26 Feb. 15/2 *Jackie Howe*, the familiar navy or black woollen singlet worn by Australian and New Zealand shearers and bushmen. It is named after Jackie Howe, an Australian shearer who in 1892 established a world shearing record by shearing 321 Merinoes with hand shears in 8 hr 40 min. **1898** MORRIS *Austral Eng.* 218/2 Jacky Winter..the vernacular name in New South Wales of the Brown Flycatcher, *Micrœca fascinans*, a common little bird about Sydney. **1911** LUCAS & LE SOUËF *Birds Austral.* 272 Jacky Winter is indeed seldom molested by even the thoughtless schoolboys. **1936** F. D. DAVISON *Children of Dark People* 5 Jacky winters..flitted among the bushes. **1969** A. BELL *Common Austral. Birds* (ed. 2) 22 Post Boy, Jacky Winter, Spinks—half-a-dozen unofficial names suggest the friendly feeling towards this quiet, confidential, contented bird.

jackyard. (Earlier and later examples.)

1873 'VANDERDECKEN' *Yachts & Yachting* 186, I have never seen a jack yard used with a jib-headed gaff-topsail. **1931** *Rudder* Mar. 82/2 The topsail might be termed half a club topsail, having a jack yard or club at the luff only.

Jacob. Add: **4.** [f. Genesis 30:40 A.V. 'Jacob did separate the lambs, and set the faces of the flocks toward the ring-straked'.] A variety of two- or four-horned piebald sheep, believed to have been introduced from Spain in the eighteenth century, and since used as an ornamental park breed.

1913 H. J. ELWES *Guide Primitive Breeds of Sheep* 30 'Spanish' or Piebald Sheep...These sheep are called by various names—'Syrian', 'Persian', 'Zulu', 'Barbary', 'Jacobs', and 'Spotted'. **1970** *Observer* (Colour Suppl.) 26 Apr. 35/2 The black and white Jacobs..are another rare breed of sheep. **1972** *Kent Life* July 28/2 Ten years ago the number of Jacob Sheep in Britain could be counted in dozens. Today the National Agricultural Centre calculates that there are more than 3,000 sheep in 132 flocks. **1973** *Times* 14 Apr. 14/5 Most horned breeds are hill breeds. Exceptions are Dorset..and Jacob.

jacobæa (dʒækŏbī·ă). [mod.L. (R. Dodoens in *Trium Priorum de Historia Stirpium* (1553) 15), perh. f. G. popular name of the plant *S. Jacobs kraut.*] **1.** The ragwort, *Senecio jacobæa*, formerly called St. James's wort, or a related purple-flowered species from South Africa, *S. elegans.*

[**1578** H. LYTE tr. *Dodoens's Niewe Herball* 69 Jacobea. S. James' worte. Jacobea marina. S. James' worte of the Sea...The first kinde of S. James worte, hath long, browne, red, crested or straked stalkes. **1728** R. BRADLEY *Dictionarium Botanicum* I. s.v., Jacobæa, in English, Ragwort, is of different Sorts. *Ibid.*, James-wort, or Ragwort, is Jacobæa, which see.] **1789** W. AITON *Hortus Kewensis* III. 193 Elegant Groundsel, or Purple Jacobea. Nat[ive] of the Cape of Good Hope. **1884** W. MILLER *Dict. Eng. Names Plants* 69/2 Jacobæa, Purple. *Senecio elegans.* c **1903** E. T. COOK *Cent. Bk. Gardening* 27/1 The botanical name of the Jacobaea is Senecio elegans. **1972** W. T. STEARN in *A. W. Smith's Gardener's Dict. Plant Names* (rev. ed.) 371/3 Jacobea. *Senecio jacobaea.*

2. jacobæa lily: see JACOBEAN *a.* 2 b.

1752 P. MILLER *Gardeners Dict.* (ed. 6) s.v. Amaryllis. The third Sort, which is commonly called Jacobæa-lily, is now become pretty common. **1760** [see JACOBEAN *a.* 2 b]. **1789** W. AITON *Hortus Kewensis* I. 416 Jacobea Lily. Nat[ive] of South America. Cult[ivated] 1658, in the Oxford garden. **1864** L. H. GRINDON *Brit. & Garden Bot.* 644 Perhaps the commonest [Amaryllid] is the 'Jacobæa-lily', *Amaryllis formosissima*, easily told by its dark hue. **1962** *Jrnl. Roy. Hort. Soc.* LXXXVII. 284 (*title*) The Jacobaea Lily—*Sprekelia formosissima.*

Jacobean, *a.* Add: **1. b.** In the furniture trade, designating wood of the colour of dark oak, or the colour itself; also denoting furniture made in mock-Jacobean style.

1918 *Heal & Son Catal.* 28 Jacobean refectory table in dark oak. **1928** *Daily Mail* 31 July 1/2 It can be obtained in Light Brown or Jacobean coloured solid oak. **1930** *Daily Express* 8 Sept. 2 This fine Chest is..finished Jacobean colour. **1974** *Times* 8 Apr. 13/3 Philips can provide you with a colour television set in a Jacobean chest. *Ibid.* 18 May 5/5 (Advt.), Reproduction styling in Jacobean oak, walnut, white or ivory and gilt finishes.

3. Of or pertaining to Henry James (1843–1916), American novelist and critic.

1906 M. BEERBOHM *Around Theatres* (1953) II. 442, I cannot imagine two minds..more divergent than the Shavian and the Jacobean. Mr James must excuse my invention of this adjective. **1932** Q. D. LEAVIS *Fiction & Reading Public* III. iii. 264 Those interested will even find a telegram in Jacobean English in *The Great Good Place.* **1958** *Times* 6 Mar. 13/5 The masterly Jacobean answer to this insult is laid up in the Lubbock volumes of James's letters.

Jacobethan (dʒækŏbī·þăn), *a.* [Blend of JACOBEAN *a.* and ELIZABETHAN *a.*] Of design: that displays a combination of the Elizabethan and Jacobean styles. Also *transf.* and *ellipt.* as *sb.*

1933 J. BETJEMAN *Ghastly Good Taste* iv. 53 The style in which Gothic predominates may be called, inaccurately enough, Elizabethan, and the style in which the classical predominates over the Gothic, equally inaccurately, may be called Jacobean. To save the time of those who do not wish to distinguish between these periods of architectural uncertainty, I will henceforward use the term 'Jacobethan'. *Ibid.* 54 To me the appeal of Jacobethan is indeed remote... Jacobethan architecture may be ugly, but it is never dull. **1945** *Archit. Rev.* Nov. 124/3 Westcombe Park Road..shows an early tendency towards those ornamental features which long afterwards gave the names of 'sham Tudor' and 'Jacobethan' to a rather pathetic phase in domestic design. **1966** *Listener* 22 Dec. 928/1 The hacienda-Jacobethan garage with which the inhabitants of Sompting are so rightfully delighted. **1969** J. GROSS *Rise & Fall Man of Lett.* i. 13 Archaisms, hand-picked quotations, artful Jacobethan echoes. **1974** *Times Lit. Suppl.* 7 June 602/4 The specimen quoted is a pseudo-archaic piece of 'Jacobethan' prose, modelled on the style of the King James Bible.

Jacob Evertsen (ya·kŏb ē·vəɹtsən). *S. Afr.* Also **Jacob Evertson, jacopever.** [Name of a 17th-c. Dutch sea-captain.] Any of several marine food fishes distinguished by reddish skin and large eyes, esp. *Sebastichthys capensis.*

1727 J. G. SCHEUCHZER tr. *Kæmpfer's Hist. Japan* I. I. xi. 136 *Ara* is what the Dutch in the Indies call *Jacobs Ewertz.* **1798** S. H. WILCOCKE tr. *Stavorinus's Voy. E. Indies* II. II. iii. 352 There is likewise, it is said, a large fish near the pier-head at Amboyna, to which the name of Jacob Evertsen has been given. **1801** J. BARROW *Acct. Trav. S. Afr.* I. i. 31 The *Scorpæna Capensis*, here called Jacob Evertson, is a firm, dry fish, but not very commonly used. **1853** L. PAPPE *Synopsis Edible Fishes Cape of Good Hope* 14 *Sebastes Capensis*... Called Jacob Evertsen, after a Dutch Captain, remarkable for a red face and large projecting eyes. **1927** *Ann. S. Afr. Mus.* XXI. 908 *Sebastichthys capensis* (Gmel.). Jacob Evertson; Jacopever... Red, shading to orange below; several silvery-white or pinkish irregular spots on sides. *Ibid.* 910 *Sebastosemus capensis* (G. and v. B.). Spiny Jacopever. **1973** *Farmer's Weekly* (S. Afr.) 18 Apr. 102 In the very early days of the Colony, the Dutch East India Company had as captain of one of its ships a certain Jacob Evert. When the local fishermen caught a fish with a red face, bulging eyes and thick lips they named it jacopever.

Jacobite, *sb.*[4] and *a.*[2] Add: **B.** *adj.* **2. b.** Of glass or pottery: bearing inscriptions and emblems which indicate Jacobite sympathies.

1936 *Burlington Mag.* Oct. p. xxiii/1 There are also many specimens of engraved glasses including Jacobite specimens with their symbolic references. *Ibid.* 175/1 A series of Jacobite glasses. **1957** MANKOWITZ & HAGGAR *Conc. Encycl. Eng. Pott. & Porc.* 117/2 Jacobite pottery. **1960** H. HAYWARD *Antique Coll.* 150 *Jacobite glasses*, propaganda glasses bearing emblems and mottoes of a cryptic character associated with the Jacobite cause. **1970** *Canad. Antiques Collector* Oct. 29/2 The emblems to

be found on these Jacobite glasses include a rose..and the Latin word 'Fiat'.

Jacobite (dʒæ·kŏbəit), *sb.*[5] [f. as JACOBITE *sb.*[4]] An admirer of Henry James (1843–1916). Cf. *JACOBEAN *a.* 3.

1909 BEERBOHM *Around Theatres* (1953) II. 541 There, in those six last words, is quintessence of Mr James; and the sound of them sent innumerable little vibrations through the heart of every good Jacobite in the audience. **1961** L. AUCHINCLOSS *Reflections of Jacobite* p. vii, I have called myself a Jacobite because so much of my lifetime's reading has been over the shoulder of Henry James.

Jacob's ladder. Add: **5.** An elevator consisting of a series of bucket-shaped receptacles fixed upon an endless chain.

1845 G. DODD *Brit. Manuf.* 5th Ser. ii. 31 The hops are raised to the boiler by a contrivance something like the buckets of a dredging-machine; it is called a 'Jacob's ladder'. **1853** *Househ. Words* VII. 491/1 The malt.. being precipitated up a curious contrivance called a 'Jacob's ladder'. **1860** *Ure's Dict. Arts* (ed. 5) II. 589 It [*sc.* the bloom] is squeezed four times before it leaves the rolls and falls upon the Jacob's ladder. **1884** W. H. GREENWOOD *Steel & Iron* xvi. 303 The puddled ball.. falling from the bottom shoot of the machine on to a Jacob's ladder or other elevator.

Jacobson (dʒē·kəbsən). The name of Ludwig Levin *Jacobson* (1783–1843), Danish anatomist and physician, used in the possessive or with *of*-adjunct to designate structures investigated by him, as **Jacobson's nerve,** the tympanic nerve, a branch of the glossopharyngeal (ninth cranial) nerve; **Jacobson's organ,** an organ which is only vestigial in adult man but is a well-developed olfactory organ in many vertebrates, notably snakes and lizards, occurring as (one of) a pair of sacs or tubes in communication with the mouth (or in some cases the nose).

1836–9 R. B. TODD *Cycl. Anat. & Physiol.* II. 495/2 The most important of these is a small branch which proceeds from the ganglion into the tympanum (*ramus tympanicus nervi glosso-pharyngei*; nerve of Jacobson). **1860** GRAY *Anat.* (ed. 2) 524 The tympanic branch (Jacobson's nerve), arises from the petrous ganglion. **1871** T. H. HUXLEY *Man. Anat. Vertebrated Animals* ii. 72 In the latter case they are the canals of Stenson...Glandular diverticula of the mucous membrane, supplied with nervous filaments from both the olfactory and the fifth pair, may open into these canals. They are called..the 'organs of Jacobson'. **1888** W. R. GOWERS *Man. Dis. Nervous Syst.* II. 212 The gangliform enlargement also receives a twig from the nerve (small petrosal) which connects the otic ganglion, through the nerve of Jacobson, with the glosso-pharyngeal. **1896** KIRKALDY & POLLARD tr. *Boas's Text Bk. Zool.* 333 In some Reptiles and most Mammals, there is a peculiar saccular or tubular paired organ, Jacobson's organ, in close connection with the olfactory apparatus. **1951** C. K. WEICHERT *Anat. Chordates* vi. 254 Although the function of Jacobson's organ is obscure, it is believed to aid in the recognition of food, since it is best developed in animals which hold food in their mouths. **1954** T. L. PEELE *Neuroanat. Basis Clin. Neurol.* ix. 217/2 By way of the tympanic branch of the glossopharyngeal (Jacobson's nerve) sensory fibers are supplied to the medial surface of the ear drum, to the tympanic cavity, to the eustachian tube in part, and to mastoid cells. **1965** R. & D. MORRIS *Men & Snakes* viii. 195 Snakes, like lizards, possess a..Jacobsen's [*sic*] Organ. This is a scent-sensitive pair of pits lying in the roof of the mouth.

Hence † **Jacobso·nian** *a.* (*obs.*).

1878 A. MACALISTER *Introd. Syst. Zool. & Morphol. Vertebr. Animals* iii. 16 In connexion with this 5th pair [of nerves] there may be six separate ganglia:..5th, Cloquet's, on the Jacobsonian organ. **1893** GUNN & HENSMAN in H. Morris *Treat. Human Anat.* VII. 928 In the septal cartilage above the opening of Stenson's canal there is a small pouch which presents a minute opening below. This is the representative of the Jacobsonian organ. A strip of cartilage underneath this..is known as the Jacobsonian cartilage.

Jacqueminot (ʒa·kmino). [Name of the Vicomte J. F. *Jacqueminot* (1787–1865), French soldier.] In full *Général Jacqueminot.* A red-flowered, hybrid perpetual variety of rose; also, formerly used for a colour resembling that of the flower.

1857 T. RIVERS *Rose Amateur's Guide* (ed. 6) 98 We must not forget to rank under our crimson flag General Jacqueminot, which..is so glorious in its colour. **1881** C. C. HARRISON *Woman's Handiwork* I. 12 Contrast the works of art of quondam florists..with the sumptuous modern assembling of Maréchal Neil [*sic*] or glowing Jacqueminot roses. **1893** W. ROBINSON *Eng. Flower Garden* (ed. 3) 644/2 General Jacqueminot and many other H.Ps. do not usually bloom after the month of August. **1895** *Montgomery Ward Catal.* 6/3 French crepon... Colors: Beige,..heliotrope, magenta or jacqueminot. **1908** *Daily Chron.* 10 Mar. 3/2 English roses have ..arrived.., and include the beautiful Jacqueminot. **1920** E. WHARTON *Age of Innocence* I. ix. 69 He tried to analyse the trick, to find a clue to it in..the fact that only two Jacqueminot roses (of which nobody ever bought less than a dozen) had been placed in the slender vase. **1955** C. C. HURST in G. S. Thomas *Old Shrub Roses* ix. 87 In 1852 'Jules Margottin' and the famous 'Général Jacqueminot' arrived... 'The General', with its brilliant scarlet-crimson flowers and damask fragrance was a fertile tetraploid.

jacu (dʒăkū·). [Pg., f. Tupi *jacú.*] A large, turkey-like, South American game bird of the genus *Penelope*, esp. *P. marail* or *P. jacquacu*; cf. GUAN.

1824 H. E. LLOYD tr. *Spix & Martius's Trav. Brazil* II. IV. ii. 227 Several species of wood-hens, particularly the pretty Jacú (*Penelope Marail, leucoptera*). **1876** *Encycl. Brit.* IV. 227/2 The gallinaceous *jacús*, the *hoccus*, and different kinds of pigeons, haunt the woods [of Brazil]. **1933** P. FLEMING *Brazilian Adv.* I. xvi. 137 There were a lot of the birds called *jacú*, a kind of stringy, dowdy pheasant with subfusc plumage. **1964** A. L. THOMSON *New Dict. Birds* 175/2 There are 12 species of guans, some of them with the names 'jacu' and 'camata'.

jacutinga (dʒækiuti·ŋgă). Also 9 jaco-. [f. Pg. *jacutinga* (formerly *jacú-tinga*), Brazilian name of a kind of guan (*jacu*) (probably the black-fronted piping guan, *Pipile jacutinga*) whose plumage the ore is said to resemble.] A name given to various kinds of soft gold-bearing iron ore found in Brazil (see quot. 1963).

1846 *Trans. R. Geol. Soc. Cornwall* VI. 227 In both mines [*sc.* Itabira and Santa Anna, in Brazil] the directions and inclinations of the gold-bearing beds conform to the configuration of the neighbouring mountain, as well as to the structure of the contiguous rock;—a circumstance of common occurrence in jacotinga formations. **1851** *Edin. New Philos. Jrnl.* L. 61 These [strata] are followed by the *Jacotinga*, the principal auriferous rock, which is for the most part composed of specular iron-ore and oxide [*printed* oixide] of manganese. **1869** R. F. BURTON *Explor. Highlands Brazil* I. 301 The mysterious Jacutinga. The name is evidently derived from the well-known Penelope called Jácu-tinga (P. Leucoptera) from the white spots upon its crested head and blue-black wings. This substance of iron-black, with metallic lustre, sparkles in the sun with silvery mica... The constituents are micaceous iron schist and friable quartz mixed with specular iron, oxide of manganese, and fragments of talc. **1908** J. M. MACLAREN *Gold* 649 With the itabirite are associated thin beds..of sandy micaceous and limonitic iron-ore containing yellowish talc and earthy oxides of manganese. These beds are generally friable, and appear to be a decomposition product of itabirite. The rock is locally known as jacutinga. **1934** BAIN & READ *Ores & Industries S. Amer.* vi. 112 In places this [*sc.* itabirite] contains narrow veins of native gold, or of gold-bearing quartz, giving rise to what are known as jacutinga ores, which are peculiar to Minas Geraes. **1963** *Prof. Papers U.S. Geol. Survey* No. 341-C. 104/2 The term 'jacutinga' is now used indiscriminately for soft high-grade hematite, soft itabirite, or both, depending entirely upon the locality within the Quadrilátero Ferrífero. In short, it has only a local, not a general meaning and should not be used in scientific description without precise definition.

‖ **jadam** (dʒa·dam). [Malay.] A type of silver or brass niello ware from the Malay Peninsula and Sumatra: used esp. for decorating belt-buckles.

1907 F. SWETTENHAM *Brit. Malaya* vii. 138 The most original and artistic work of all is called *chûtam* or *jâdam*, and it was made originally in the Province of Ligor. **1908** L. WRAY in A. Wright *20th Cent. Impressions Brit. Malaya* 244/1 The art of enamelling is also known to the Malays. The ware is called *Jadam*, which is equivalent to niello in England. **1910** C. W. HARRISON *Illustr. Guide Federated Malay States* II. 166 *Jadam* is the fashion in Rembau where the women wear large belt-buckles of it called *pinding*, but it is also made in boxes of all shapes. It may be of silver or of brass filled with enamel. **1953** C. A. GIBSON-HILL *Malay Arts & Crafts* § Silverwork, A form of silverware called *Jadam*, in which the hollows of the pattern were filled in with black enamel to give a smooth surface, used to be made in the western Malay states, principally in Negri Sembilan. The art is said to have come from Sumatra... In Malaya *jadam* work was used mostly for the production of decorated waist buckles.

jade, *sb.*[2] Add: **1. c.** A colour resembling that of jade; jade-green. Also *attrib.*

1921 H. WALPOLE *Young Enchanted* IV. iv. 391 The faint jade of the fading light. **1926** M. LEINSTER *Dew on Leaf* iii. 42 The jade rabbit (moon) nibbles the clouds. **1928** *Manch. Guardian Weekly* 31 Aug. 175/3 A faint breeze blowing in from a North Sea of misty jade. **1972** *Guardian* 5 Dec. 11/2 Toga dress..in..midnight blue, jade, red, sapphire.

2. b. *jade-coloured* adj.

1868 G. M. HOPKINS *Jrnl.* 19 July (1959) 178 The Aar sallow and jade-coloured. **1926** A. HUXLEY *Essays New & Old* 17 The brown or jade-coloured water.

jadeite. Add: Hence **jadeitic** (dʒēidi·tik) *a.*, approximating to jadeite in composition.

1965 *Prof. Papers U.S. Geol. Survey* No. 525. 25 (*heading*) Composition of jadeitic pyroxene from the California metagraywackes. **1971** I. G. GASS et al. *Understanding Earth* viii. 116/1 A notable feature of the overall mineralogy of meteorites is the absence of phases, such as..jadeitic pyroxenes, indicative of high pressure.

jadoo (dʒā·dū). Also **jadu.** [Hind. *jādū* enchantment.] Magic, conjuring. *Comb.* **ja·doo-wa:llah** [WALLAH], a Hindu conjurer.

1886 KIPLING *Plain Tales from Hills* (1888) 126 If there was any *jadoo* afoot. **1890** *Q. Rev.* July 244 The Indian conjurers, or Jadoo-walla. **1924** J. A. TYSON *Barge of Haunted Lives* iv. 93 These took me before a jaboowallah [*sic*], who..had performed some of his tricks before me at Rajiid.

‖ **j'adoube** (ʒadūb). *Chess.* [Fr., = I adjust.] An expression used when a player wishes to touch a chessman without making a move.

1808 J. H. SARRATT *Treat. Game of Chess* I. 3 If a player *touch* one of his adversary's pieces, without saying '*J'adoube*', he may be compelled to take it. **1847** H. STAUNTON *Chess-Player's Handbk.* 36 A Piece or Pawn touched must be played, unless at the moment of touching it the player say '*J'adoube*', or words to that effect. **1967** *Chess* 11 Dec. 99/2 You may adjust a piece if you previously warn your adversary you are going to do so by saying 'j'adoube'.

Jaeger[1] (yē·gəɹ). The proprietary name of an all-wool clothing material manufactured originally by Dr. [Gustav] Jaeger's Sanitary Woollen System Co. Ltd.; also, a garment made of this material. Also *attrib.* and *fig.*

1887 G. B. SHAW *Let.* 8 Feb. (1965) 163 Seeing me arrive, clad in an irresistible new Jaeger samite. **1893** K. SANBORN *Truthful Woman in S. California* 121, I really suffered during a drive, although encased in the heaviest of Jaeger flannels. **1905** CHESTERTON *Heretics* x. 140 Those who talk to us with interfering eloquence about Jaeger and the pores of the skin. **1925** *Trade Marks Jrnl.* 7 Oct. 2200 Jaeger... Cloths and stuffs of wool, worsted or hair. The Jaeger Company, Limited,.. London,..merchants. **1932** THORNE SMITH *Bishop's Jaegers* (1934) 2 If they could not be called things of beauty, these brave long jaegers of the Bishop's, they did ..represent the highest expression of the drawers-maker's craftsmanship. **1936** R. LEHMANN *Weather in Streets* I. i. 12 A grubby jaeger shroud lay over the first suburbs. **1942** N. BALCHIN *Darkness falls from Air* vii. 127 The inspector was wearing a roll-necked Jaegar [*sic*] pull-over. **1973** A. MORICE *Death & Dutiful Daughter* v. 53 Betsy's old Jaeger dressing-gown.

Jaeger[2] (yē·gəɹ). The name of E. R. *Jaeger* von Jastthal (1818–1884), Austrian ophthalmologist, used in the possessive (or occas. *attrib.*) to designate a series of short passages printed in type-faces of different sizes and used for testing visual acuity at reading distances.

1869 *Trans. Amer. Ophthalm. Soc., 4th and 5th Ann. Meeting* 68 In Jaeger's Schrift-Scalen the numbering is altogether arbitrary and irregular. **1884** G. HARTRIDGE *Refraction Eye* iii. 45 Snellen and Jaeger's are the types most commonly in use. **1897** NORRIS & OLIVER *Syst. Dis. Eye* II. 28 Jaeger's Schriftscalen consisted of a very complete set of reading tests printed in several languages. **1907** J. H. PARSONS *Dis. Eye* ix. 161 Jaeger's near test types..are simply the ordinary printers' founts of type, from the smallest upwards (nonpareil, minion, etc.). **1962** H. C. WESTON *Sight, Light & Work* (ed. 2) viii. 224 Another series of test types has been selected by the British Faculty of Ophthalmologists and either this or the Jaeger series is readily obtainable.

Jaffa (dʒæ·fă). The modern name of Joppa, a port in Israel, used *attrib.* or *absol.* to designate an oval, thick-skinned variety of orange first cultivated near Jaffa, and later introduced to other parts of Israel and suitable regions elsewhere.

1881 A. H. MANVILLE in T. W. Moore *Treat. & Handbk. Orange Culture in Florida* (ed. 2) 110 Jaffa and other recently imported varieties have not been fruited long enough in the State to determine their qualities. **1909** *Westm. Gaz.* 20 Apr. 7/2 The practice of 'faking' oranges by boiling and greasing them and selling them as Jaffas. *a* **1916** 'SAKI' *Toys of Peace* (1919) 134 We have some very fine Jaffa oranges. **1943** WEBBER & BATCHELOR *Citrus Industry* I. v. 511 In Florida, however, the Jaffa develops a fruit of very good quality. **1962** J. FLEMING *When I grow Rich* xix. 207 Oven-hot rolls, ice-cold Jaffa juice, fragrant hot coffee. **1973** 'D. JORDAN' *Nile Green* xx. 76 The orange-juice they serve..in the Beirut St Georges isn't Israeli but I'm sure they'd produce the Jaffas if you insisted. **1974** W. GARNER *Big Enough Wreath* IV. 43 El Al's flying in fresh-picked Jaffa oranges. *Ibid.*, Miss Cleverley's..face showed no more emotion than a Jaffa.

jag, *sb.*[2] Add: **1. c.** (Earlier and later examples.) For *U.S.* read *dial.* and *colloq.* Also, a drinking bout; the state or a period of being drunk.

1678 J. RAY *Coll. Eng. Proverbs* (ed. 2) 87 Proverbiall Periphrases of one drunk... He has a jagg or load. **1872** J. GLYDE *Norfolk Garland* I. 149 He has got his jag, *i.e.*, as much drink as he can fairly carry. **1894** [see *GIN *v.*[3]]. **1895** *N.Y. Dramatic News* 26 Oct. 7/2 An ability to acquire a 'jag' in a wonderfully short space of time and with a single drink. **1904** [see *HANG-OVER 2]. **1921** E. WALLACE *Law Four Just Men* iv. 112 He had been on a jag the night before and had finished up in what he called an opium house. **1924** [see *CROOK *v.*[1] 1 d]. **1934** WODEHOUSE *Right Ho, Jeeves* xix. 250, I took the whole thing as a great compliment, proud to feel that any drink from my cellars could have produced such a majestic jag. **1966** *Listener* 28 Apr. 619/1 Sid Chaplin's *Saturday Saga*, the account of two miners on a memorable jag.

d. *transf.* and *fig.* A period of indulgence in a particular pastime, emotion, interest, etc.; = FIT *sb.*[2] 4 a; freq. with defining word

prefixed, as *crying jag*; *spec.* (see quot. 1946). *colloq.* (orig. *U.S.*).

1913 J. London *Valley of Moon* (1914) I. xv. 119 'Aw, it's only one of his cryin' jags,' Mary said. **1924** P. Marks *Plastic Age* xix. 213 One had a 'crying jag'. *Ibid.* xxii. 254 A girl got a 'laughing jag' and shrieked with idiotic laughter. **1933** S. Howard *Alien Corn* III. 97 Isn't seventy-one fifty cheap for the jag I've got to-night? **1945** S. Lewis *Cass Timberlane* (1946) xlix. 347 Now you're beginning to get over your love-jag, maybe you can see that Jinny is as..tricky and grabbing as a monkey. **1946** Mezzrow & Wolfe *Really Blues* 375 *Jag*, a state of extreme stimulation, produced by marihuana or some other stimulant. **1958** *Spectator* 4 July 15/2 The British public are on an enormous clean-clothes jag. **1972** *New Yorker* 26 Aug. 38/3 A neurotic habit..may be overt, like a temper tantrum or a crying jag. **1973** *Times Lit. Suppl.* 8 June 631/3 The Kennedy years..launched the Americans on a jag of hope and fear.

Jag (dʒæg), *sb.*³ Colloq. abbrev. of *Jaguar* (the proprietary name of a make of motor car). See also *gin-and-Jag* s.v. *gin *sb.*² 2 b.

1959 J. Drummond *Black Unicorn* xxi. 146 'He will meet us opposite the clock-tower in Point Road. I gave him a little word-picture of the Jag.' The Jaguar was a long cream drop-head. **1962** *Times Lit. Suppl.* 19 Oct. 805/4 Stephen, the boss's son, with his Jag, to Wilf, the miner's son, with his typewriter. **1968** J. Fleming *Kill or Cure* vii. 88 People with lots of money, living in the Jag belt. **1974** T. Allbeury *Snowball* x. 55 They've bought a car. A Jag—second-hand.

Jagatai (dʒægătā·i). [The native name of Turkestan, f. *Jagatai*, a son of Jenghiz Khan, who inherited it.] The branch of the Turkic group of languages spoken in Turkestan. Also *attrib.* Also **Jagata·ic**. Hence **Jagata·ian** *a.*, pertaining to Turkestan or the dialects spoken there.

1843 *Penny Cycl.* XXV. 406/1 Jagatâï, [spoken] in the greater part of independent Turkistán... The Jagatâï language has a valuable literature. **1867** *Chambers's Encycl.* IX. 589/2 The former [*sc.* Eastern Turkish] is mainly represented by the Uigur (Jagatai). *Ibid.* 590/1 The Eastern [Turkish] or Jagataian [literature]. **1908** T. G. Tucker *Introd. Nat. Hist. Lang.* 134 (*d*) *Uiguric*, including *Uigur* proper, *Jagataic*, and *Turkoman*, the dialects spoken in the parts of Turkestan not occupied by the Kirghiz. **1929** *Encycl. Brit.* XXII. 920/1 The Uzbeg (Jagatai Turkish) tongue. **1962** A. Tietze in Householder & Saporta *Probl. Lexicogr.* 266 Jagatai and other non-Ottoman Turkic languages.

jagatī (dʒʌ·gătī). Also **gagatî**. [Skr.] A Vedic metre of twelve syllables.

1843 [see *gāyatrī]. **1869** Max Müller tr. *Rig-Veda-Sanhita* p. cxxx, I maintain by no means that this was the actual origin of Gagatî metres... Theories..would wish us to look upon the hendecasyllabic Trishtubh as originally a dodecasyllabic Gagatî, only deprived of its tail. **1937** M. D. Shastri *Ṛgveda-Prātiśākhya* III. 137 All that is light by nature is related to light syllables, and a Jagatī, one should know, has light syllables. **1969** *Language* XLV. 251 A cadence of four or five syllables depending on whether the pāda is in triṣṭubh meter (typically 11 syllables) or jagatī (12 syllables).

jagged (dʒægd), *a.*² *slang* (chiefly *U.S.*). [f. *jag *sb.*² I c + -ed².] Drunk, intoxicated.

1737 *Pennsylvania Gaz.* 6–13 Jan. 1/3 He's Jagg'd. **1902** *Telegram* (Winnipeg) 20 Aug. 7/4 Miller was pretty well jagged. **1904** 'O. Henry' in *N.Y. World Mag.* 1 May 8/2 What I want is a masterful man that slugs you when he's jagged, and hugs you when he ain't jagged. **1956** *Amer. Speech* XXXI. 279 *Jagged*, adj. In the sense of intoxicated..[it] is probably not of American origin.

b. Intoxicated by, or under the influence of, drugs.

1938 C. Himes *Black on Black* (1973) 175 She made him smoke pot and when he got jagged..she put him out on the street. **1973** Boyd & Parkes *Dark Number* xiii. 151 Solange is—was—God help her, a heroin addict. When we first met, she was all jagged up. She was a reject on the junk heap.

‖ **jagt** (yakt). [a. Da. *jagt* (cf. Norw., Sw. *jakt*) Yacht *sb.*] In Scandinavia, a small single-masted coastal vessel, rigged either with square sails or as a cutter or sloop.

1861 J. Lamont *Seasons with Sea-Horses* ii. 22 We saw two small vessels, which we made out to be a brig and a sloop, or 'jagt', at some distance amongst the ice. **1906** H. W. Smyth *Mast & Sail* iii. 44 Square-rigged Nordland jaegts which formerly were so characteristic a feature of the Norwegian coastline. *Ibid.* 51 The old Nordland 'jaegt' which formerly did so much of the coast-wise trade of Norway. **1925** A. Moore *Last Days Mast & Sail* vi. 181 Amundsen's ship, the *Gjoa*, in which he made the North-West Passage, was described in the English papers as a sloop, and she was one according to the old definition; but in the list of the Bureau Veritas for 1907 she is called a *Jagt*. **1971** *Mariner's Mirror* LVII. 152 In Schleswig-Holstein the *Jachten* doubtless were of the classical Danish *jagt* design in hull and rig; carvel-built keel craft with transom stern and outside rudder, convex stem, and pole-masted gaff sloop rig.

jaguarondi. Add: Also **jaguarundi, yaguarundi.**

1906, 1955 [see *eyra]. **1959** A. S. Leopold *Wildlife Mexico* 482 Little is known of the jaguarundi. **1964** L. S. Crandall *Managem. Wild Mammals in Captivity* 368 The jaguarundi is a shy, secretive creature.

jai alai (hɘi·lɘi, hɘi·ălɘi, hɘiˌălɘi·). [Sp., f. Basque *jai* festival + *alai* merry.] = Pelota.

1910 I. A. Wright *Cuba* i. 7 (*caption*) Ball Players on the Court. General Leonard Wood, a Jai Alai enthusiast among them. **1923** W. Stevens *Let.* 4 Feb. (1967) 234 In the evening I went to see a game of jai alai, the Spanish national game. **1947** M. Lowry *Under Volcano* i. 9 Its jai-alai courts are grass-grown and deserted. **1972** *Times* 8 Aug. (Asian Suppl.) p. vii/8 Do not forget to see a game of *jai-alai* [in the Philippines]. **1973** *Times* 28 May (Macao Suppl.) p. iii/3 The fast and furious Basque ball and racquet game of Jai Alai (or Pelota Basque in Portuguese) is the latest of Macau's diversions for the visitor. The opulent new Jai Alai Centre on the Outer Harbour offers the last word in de luxe comfort for fans or gamblers betting on the matches, plus nightclub, restaurant and bar facilities.

‖ **Jai Hind** (dʒɘi hind), *int.* [Hindi, f. *jai* long live! + *Hind* India.] In India, a salutation: used in exchange of greetings, at a public meeting, etc.

1948 A. Moorehead *Rage of Vulture* v. 76 The Indians ..raised their cry of 'Jai Hind', and it really meant 'Expel the British'. And finally they have expelled us. They go on crying 'Jai Hind', and now it means exactly what it says—'Long Live India'. **1969** *Commerce* (Bombay) 26 July 170/3 We remain committed to the freedom and progress of the people of this great country. Jai Hind.

jail, gaol, *sb.* Add: **2. jail-bait** *slang* (orig. *U.S.*), a girl who is under the legal age of consent; **jail-break** orig. *U.S.*, the act of escaping from a jail.

1934 J. T. Farrell *Calico Shoes* 48 She's not hard on the eyes but she's jail bait. **1957** J. Braine *Room at Top* xxiv. 198 I'm not interested in little girls. Particularly not in jail-bait like that one. **1972** A. Draper *Death Penalty* vi. 45 She looks young enough to be jail bait. **1910** J. Hart *Vigilante Girl* xix. 266 Hamlin did not yet know of the jail-break. **1952** J. Steinbeck *East of Eden* 440 Not with her holding that jail-break over him. **1973** E. Hyams *Final Agenda* ii. 24 He..led a jail-break of seventeen political prisoners.

Jaipur (dʒɘi·pūᵊɹ). The name of a former Indian native state and its capital city, now capital of the State of Rajasthan, used *attrib.* to designate products of this State. Hence **Jaipuri**, the dialect of this region.

1889 Kipling in *Macm. Mag.* Dec. 152/1 The cedar sliding doors were fitted with hasps of translucent Jaipur enamel. **1901** *Jrnl. R. Asiatic Soc.* 787 Sixteen real dialects spoken over the area in which Rājasthānī is a vernacular..fall into four main groups, which may be called Mēwātī, Mālwī, Jaipurī, and Mārwārī. *Ibid.* 788 Jaipurī may be taken as representing the dialects of Eastern Rājputānā, as far east as Gwāliōr. **1931** A. U. Dilley *Oriental Rugs & Carpets* Pl. 37 (*caption*), Agra copy of Jaipur plant rug. **1957** *Encycl. Brit.* XVIII. 957/2 Rajasthani language..has several dialects, the principal of which are Jaipuri, Marwari, Mewati and Malvi. **1963** *Listener* 28 Feb. 365/2 Then there is Jaipur work.

jak, var. Jack *sb.*⁴ (in Dict. and Suppl.).

jake (dʒēⁱk), *sb.*¹ *U.S. colloq.* [Prob. the personal name *Jake*, abbrev. of *Jacob*.] A rustic lout or simpleton: usually *country jake*.

a **1854**, etc. [see *country jake* s.v. *country 16]. **1884** G. W. Peck *Peck's Boss Bk.* 68 A masher, like many of the Jakes of the present day. **1915** *Dialect Notes* IV. 199 He's no jake even though he did come from a Nebraska farm. **1941** H. S. Truman *Let.* 5 Oct. in M. Truman *Harry S. Truman* (1973) viii. 142 You'd think I was Cicero or Cato. But I'm not. Just a country jake who works at the job.

jake (dʒēⁱk), *sb.*² *slang* (orig. *U.S.*). [Abbrev. form of **Jamaica* (*ginger*).] An alcoholic beverage made from Jamaica ginger. **b.** Methylated spirits used as an alcoholic drink.

1926 [see *hip *a.*]. **1932** *Fortn. Rev.* Mar. 324 Over twenty-five per cent. are 'jake' or 'feke' drinkers... They drink methylated spirits. **1935** H. Neville *Sneak Thief on Road* ii. 162 That's pure meths... They call it Blue Billy or jake, and it's known among all tramps and kip-houses and wherever men have empty lives. **1939** J. Steinbeck *Grapes of Wrath* x. 131 He would drink jake or whisky until he was a shaken paralytic.

jake (dʒēⁱk), *a. slang* (orig. *U.S.*). [Origin obscure.] Excellent, admirable, fine, 'O.K.'

1914 Jackson & Hellyer *Vocab. Criminal Slang* 48 As an adjective 'jake' means good; satisfactory; acceptable; all-right. **1921** P. & T. Casey in *Adventure* (U.S.) 18 May 40/2 Well, if it *is* Jerrold, everything's jake. **1924** P. Marks *Plastic Age* xxii. 247 She said the whole college seemed jake to her. **1924** Wodehouse *Bill the Conqueror* vi. 130 Everything was jake with Horace. **1930** [see *by *prep.* 33 e]. **1943** *2 N.Z.E.F. Times* 10 May 5/1 She'll be Jake on the counter. **1947** D. M. Davin *Gorse blooms Pale* 190 We'll just give [the tea] a minute to draw and she'll be jake. **1958** R. France *Race* 100 'Will you be all right..if I lie down in the wheelhouse?'..'I'm jake. You have a rest.' **1958** 'A. Gilbert' *Death against Clock* viii. 105 'If it's about the election we vote conservative here.' 'Jake by me,' said Mr. Crook politely. **1967** *Southerly* XXVII. 149 'Is she [*sc.* a train] on time?'.. 'She's jake tonight mate.' **1970** *N.Z. Listener* 12 Oct. 12/4 Long as there's plenty of beer, she'll be jake.

So **jake(a)loo, jakerloo** *a. Austral.* and *N.Z. slang*, in the same sense.

1919 W. H. Downing *Digger Dial.* 29 Jake-aloo. **1936** N. Marsh *Death in Ecstasy* xvii. 211 It'll all come out what the Australians call 'jakealoo'. **1936** 'R. Hyde' *Passport to Hell* xi. 174 Jakeloo, Starkie; she's a little beauty, clean through my arm. **1938** X. Herbert *Capricornia* xii. 169 'Lambkin, you're not wounded, are you?'..'Na—ow! I'm jakerloo.' 'You're what?' she demanded, looking scared. 'Jakerloo Mum, jakerloo.' 'What—not a disease, my darling?' 'Na—ow—that's French for "I'm good-o".' **1965** G. McInnes *Road to Gundagai* viii. 123 Jakeloo! Let's have the names then, *and* the addresses.

jakes. 1. (Later examples.)

1913 L. Woolf *Village in Jungle* iv. 54 The headman's brother is to marry a sweeper of jakes! **1922** Joyce *Ulysses* 68 He kicked open the crazy door of the jakes. **1969** *Listener* 26 June 902/3 He is at his best when not occupied with symbols..but concerned to tell how the keeper of an 'underground jakes' mistakes a police stool-pigeon for a real poof.

jakkalsbessie (ya·kălsbe:si). *S. Afr.* [Afrikaans, f. *jakkals* jackal + *bessie* berry.] Either of two trees, the evergreen *Diospyros mespiliformis* or *Sideroxylon inerme*, or their fruit. Also *attrib.*

1854 L. Pappe *Silva Capensis* 22 *Sideroxylon inerme.* Lin. (*Melkhout.*)... The fruit (*Jackalsbesjes*) are edible. **1917** R. Marloth *Dict. Common Names of Plants* 42 Jakkalsbessie. *Diospyros mespiliformis*, but also *Sideroxylon inerme* (milkwood). **1932** Watt & Breyer-Brandwijk *Medicinal & Poisonous Plants S. Afr.* 137 The Zulus take an infusion of the bark of *Sideroxylon inerme* L., White milkwood, Wit melkhout, Jakkals-bessie..to dispel bad dreams. **1953** [see *geelhout]. **1963** S. Cloete *Rags of Glory* 377 Here and there a giant tree, a baobab, jakkals-bessie, or fig, stood out—a blob dropped on the carpet. **1969** T. H. Everett *Living Trees of World* 285/1 A fine African member of the genus [*Diospyros*] is the jakkalsbessie, West African ebony or Transvaal ebony (*D. mespiliformis*), which becomes 70 feet tall with a trunk diameter of 3 feet. **1973** Palmer & Pitman *Trees of Southern Africa* III. 1795 The bar at Leydsdorp is made out of a solid piece of jakkalsbessie timber.

Jakun (dʒakū·n). [Native name.] An aboriginal people of the southern part of the Malay peninsula; a member of this people; also, their language. Also *attrib.* or as *adj.*

1839 T. J. Newbold *Pol. & Stat. Acct. Straits of Malacca* I. vii. 421 The Jakuns do not differ materially from the Malay in colour or physiognomy. **1883** *Encycl. Brit.* XV. 323/2 The aborigines..are divided into a great many tribes, of which the best known are the Jakuns, widespread in the south. **1906** Skeat & Blagden *Pagan Races Malay Peninsula* I. ii. v. 235 An old Jakun, who was singularly free from superstition. *Ibid.* II. iii. vi. 196 In the Semang tribes the office of chief medicine-man appears to be generally combined with that of chief, but amongst the Sakai and Jakun these offices are sometimes separated. *Ibid.* iv. i. 405 It may be that before their decay, the other Jakun dialects resembled it [*sc.* Kenaboi] more than they do now... Kenaboi must be regarded either as the best specimen of Jakun recorded or else as not being Jakun at all. **1935** *Discovery* Sept. 262/2 The Jakun, straight haired and akin to the Malay, occupy Southern Johore. **1947** R. O. Winstedt *Malays* 14 A Jakun (or Proto-Malay) marriage ceremony..requires the groom to walk or run after his bride three or seven times round a hillock. **1958** *Listener* 13 Nov. 793/3 Ethnically, they [*sc.* the aborigines of Malaya] were divided into Jakun (proto-Malays), Negritos, and a group that was primarily Caucasoid. **1972** A. Amin tr. *Ahmad's No Harvest but Thorn* iii. 18 If the *jakuns* come out what can we say?

jāl, var. *jol.

jalapinolic (dʒæ:lăpinǫ·lik), *a. Chem.* [tr. G. *jalappinolsäure* jalapinolic acid (W. Mayer 1854, in *Ann. d. Chem. u. Pharm.* XCII. 128), f. *jalappin* (now *jalapin*) Jalapin + -ol -ol: see -ic.] *jalapinolic acid*: the dextrorotatory form of 11-hydroxyhexadecanoic acid, $CH_3(CH_2)_4CHOH(CH_2)_9COOH$, a crystalline derivative of palmitic acid obtained by hydrolysis of jalapin.

1855 *Chem. Gaz.* 15 Mar. 115 The oxidation of convolvulinolic and jalapinolic acids by nitric acid. **1928** *Jrnl. Amer. Chem. Soc.* L. 1749 The resin from Orizaba root yields on hydrolysis an hydroxyhexadecanoic acid, jalapinolic acid. **1964** *Phytochemistry* III. 289 The aglycons most frequently obtained from convolvulaceous glycosidic acids have been (+)-11-hydroxyhexadecanoic acid (jalapinolic acid) and convolvulinolic acid.

‖ **jaleo** (hale·o). [Sp., lit. 'halloo'.] A lively Andalusian dance, or the clapping that accompanies it.

1865 H. O'Shea *Guide to Spain* p. xlv, The dances differ in each province... Andalucia is the land of the *jaleo de Jerez*. **1893** *Funk's Stand. Dict.*, *Jaleo*, a vivacious Spanish dance. **1967** 'La Meri' *Spanish Dancing* (ed. 2) v. 69 Probably because of the centuries of dancing to a percussive sound, the *jaleo* accompanying the dance has developed into an art in itself.

jalopy (dʒălǫ·pi). *colloq.* (orig. *U.S.*). Also † **gillopy, jalapa, jollopy; jallopy, jaloppi(e), -y.** [Origin unknown.] A battered old motor vehicle; also, an old aeroplane.

1929 HOSTETTER & BEESLEY *It's a Racket!* 229 *Jaloppi*, a cheap make of automobile; an automobile fit only for junking. **1936** J. STEINBECK *In Dubious Battle* vi. 90 Mac and Jim circled the buildings and went to the ancient Ford touring car. 'Get in, Jim. You drive the gillopy.' **1937** *Time* 17 May 35/1 They announced they would burn..used cars at the fair grounds... The huge pile of jalopies was touched off while firemen..looked on. **1938** P. GALLICO in *Sat. Even. Post* 8 Oct. 8/3 He..made a living out of the Red Arrow Hangar down at one end of the field, teaching beginners how to hoist a couple of training jalopies around the field without killing themselves. **1941** AUDEN *New Year Let.* III. 68 And in jalopies there migrates A rootless tribe from windblown states. **1951** WODEHOUSE *Old Reliable* xxi. 233 This afternoon we'll go out in my jalopy and start pricing ministers. **1955** M. E. B. BANKS *Commando Climber* vi. 114 Perhaps a succession of broken down jalopies has impaired my faith in the internal combustion engine. **1973** A. HUNTER *Gently French* ii. 22 He'd get in the jalopy beside him, start trying to pressure him.

jalousie. (Earlier and later examples.)

1766 DUCHESS OF NORTHUMBERLAND *Diary* 23 Oct. (1926) 76, Rows of Seats with Jalousies in Front that they [*sc.* the women] may not be seen. **1961** I. FLEMING *Thunderball* xxiv. 254 Inside the small room, the jalousies threw bands of light and shadow over the bed. **1974** K. BENTON *Craig & Tunisian Tangle* v. 47 Tall windows shielded against the sun by wooden jalousies.

jalpaite (dʒæ·lpă͵əit). *Min.* [ad. G. *jalpait* (A. Breithaupt 1858, in *Berg- und hüttenmännische Zeitung* 17 Mar. 85/2), f. *Jalpa*, the name of a locality in Mexico (probably the town of that name in southern Zacatecas): see -ITE[1].] A sulphide of silver and copper, Ag_3CuS_2, of a light metallic-grey colour when freshly fractured.

1868 J. D. DANA *Syst. Min.* (ed. 5) ii. 39 Jalpaite is a cupriferous silver-glance from Jalpa, Mexico. **1925** *Mineral. Abstr.* II. 519 Jalpaite.., as narrow veins in hornstone, gave analyses agreeing closely with the formula $3Ag_2S.Cu_2S$. **1968** *Amer. Mineralogist* LIII. 1539 Jalpaite from Silver Plume and Boulder County, Colorado probably formed at some temperature below 117°C.

jam, *sb.*[1] Add: **1.** (Further examples.) Also, *spec.* in logging, an accumulation of logs in a river. Also *attrib.*

1805 *Deb. Congress U.S.* 7 Apr. 1076 Its overflowing [is] occasioned by a jam of timber choking the river. **1836** *Bytown* (Ottawa) *Gaz.* 9 June 4/3 A canoe with nine men..were engaged in taking some timber in a jam at the head of Colton's shoots. **1905** *Terms Forestry & Logging* (U.S. Dept. Agric. Bureau Forestry) 40 *Jam, to break a*, to start in motion logs which have been jammed. **1910** S. E. WHITE *Rules of Game* I. xii. 69 'Where's the drive, doctor?' asked the lumberman. 'This is the jam camp,' replied the cook. 'The jam's upstream a mile or so.' **1929** *Encycl. Brit.* XIV. 482/1 A log jam in the Montreal river, Ontario, Canada. **1955** *Times* 31 May 4/3 From all around the capital came reports of traffic jams. **1968** R. M. PATTERSON *Finlay's River* 32 So they made a risky crossing of the Parsnip [River] on a jam, wondering as they did so whether the ice-bridge over the deepest water would not give way beneath them. **1971** *Daily Tel.* (Colour Suppl.) 22 Oct. 22/1 There would be fewer frayed tempers and thus far fewer accidents—not to mention fewer jams.

b. Also *fig.*, an awkward or difficult situation; trouble; = FIX *sb.* 1; freq. in phr. *in a jam. colloq.* (orig. *U.S.*).

1914 *San Francisco Call* 26 Oct. 7, I knew we'd get in a jam coming here. **1926** *Clues* Nov. 159/1, I think some one single-duked us, but if so I'll shiv the heel. There'll be plenty of jam. **1927** WODEHOUSE *Small Bachelor* vi. 93 'I've gone and got myself into the devil of a jam.' 'A position of embarrassment?' 'You said it!' **1938** R. D. FINLAYSON *Brown Man's Burden* 81 Henare would give his whole-hearted sympathy and his last shilling to anyone in a bit of a jam. **1950** [see *CLEANER 2]. **1958** *New Statesman* 12 Apr. 459/3 He knew instinctively that in a jam it was not done to let down one's own side.

2. Jamming (of broadcasts, devices, etc.), or an instance of this. Hence **ja·m-proof** *a.*, proof against jamming. Cf. *JAM *v.*[1] 3 c.

1914 P. VAUX *Sea-Salt & Cordite* 129, I don't like this wireless jam! **1927** W. E. COLLINSON *Contemp. Eng.* 113 The trouble caused by jams, atmospherics, and howlings. **1964** *Ann. Reg. 1963* 185 It was said..that the needles in orbit round the earth could provide an inexpensive and jam-proof global communications system. **1972** *Sci. Amer.* June 17/1 These communications must be jam-proof; the potential attacker cannot be allowed to hope that a communications failure might prevent a retaliatory strike.

3. (This sense may belong to JAM *sb.*[2]) *colloq.* Jazz or similar music simultaneously extemporized by a number of performers; a period of playing such music. Freq. *attrib.*, esp. as **jam session**, a gathering of musicians to improvise jazz; also *transf.* and *fig.*

1929 *Melody Maker* Jan. 75/3 There are many variations on this rhythm..which make excellent breaks—or 'jams' as they now call them when they are taken by the whole band, the word 'break' being used only when it is intended to signify that it is played by one instrument or a section moving together or unaccompanied. **1933** *Fortune* Aug. 90/1 The jazz musicians' jam sessions where the players vie with one another in hot solos. **1935** *Swing Music* July 120/2 The best Chicagoans very often had 'jam' sessions. **1935** *Vanity Fair* (N.Y.) Nov. 71/3 Extremely hot ensemble improvisations are *jams*. **1937** *Amer. Speech* XII. 46/2 A jam band depends entirely on improvisation, using no written music. **1944** *Theology* XLVII. 278 This contemporary jam session gives enormous pleasure to the participants. But we [*sc.* the Church of England] have had little enough success in charming the ear of the nation to the extent of persuading it to come and join the band. **1949** *Chicago Daily News* 25 Mar. 33/2 One of his ambitions reportedly was to sit in on a jam session with some of our jazz musicians. **1959** R. GANT *World in Jug* 116 Everyone sat back to hear Mitch give a muted chorus which had them roaring again as we went into a final jam. **1967** 'LA MERI' *Spanish Dancing* (ed. 2) vi. 78 Martinez called bulerias 'the Cachucha of the gitanos', while Argentinita described it as a 'flamenco jam-session'. **1969** S. GREENLEE *Spook who sat by Door* xx. 170 He..moved to the stereo. 'Let's see if I can remember the jams you dig.' **1972** *Jazz & Blues* Feb. 18/3 Several musicians told me how much they enjoyed the jam sessions.

jam, *sb.*[2] Add: **b.** (Further examples.) Colloq. phrases: *to have* (or *like, want*) *jam on it*: to have, etc., something exceedingly pleasant or easy; *jam tomorrow*: something pleasant promised or expected for the future, esp. something that one never receives; *money for jam*: see *MONEY *sb.* 6 h.

1871 'L. CARROLL' *Through Looking-Glass* v. 94 The rule is, jam to-morrow and jam yesterday—but never jam to-day. **1874** HOTTEN *Slang Dict.* 268 *Real jam*, a sporting phrase, meaning anything exceptionally good. **1919** *Athenæum* 8 Aug. 727/2 'Having jam on it' (*i.e.*, something nice and easy, a 'cushy' job). **1925** FRASER & GIBBONS *Soldier & Sailor Words* 130 'You want jam on it', *i.e.*, You expect too much. **1936** J. CURTIS *Gilt Kid* 23 You want jam on it, you do. **1939** A. HUXLEY *After Many a Summer* II. iii. 201 The entire capital outlay had already been amortized, so that everything from now on would be pure jam. **1946** J. IRVING *Royal Navalese* 99 The ironical suggestion made to a sailor already 'moaning' about his job—'Do you want jam on it?' **1951** 'J. WYNDHAM' *Day of Triffids* xii. 225 Just put the Americans into the jam-tomorrow-pie-in-the-sky department awhile. **1962** *Listener* 29 Nov. 925/1 Dr Leavis sees C. P. Snow as a gross materialist concerned only with jam tomorrow. **1970** *Times* 21 Feb. 6/8 Freedman says he can break even during the 10 weeks, with the jam to follow in the summer. **1972** *Daily Tel.* 30 Mar. 22/6 Ultramar has ever been the 'jam tomorrow' stock par excellence, with not a penny paid out in dividends. Instead, shareholders get scrip issues. **1973** G. MITCHELL *Murder of Busy Lizzie* i. 14 'I think Greece might be a very good idea—later on.' 'Never jam today!' muttered Margaret. **1974** O. MANNING *Rain Forest* I. vi. 87 Hugh.. was free to leave at six... Pedley..said: 'You've got jam on it: walking home in the sunset.'

c. *jam-making* (examples), *-pudding, -tin*; **jam-buttie, -butty**, a butty (*BUTTY[2]) spread with jam; **jam-jar**, (*a*) a jar designed for holding jam; (*b*) rhyming slang for 'motor-car' (see also quot. 1943).

1927, 1965 Jam-buttie, butty [see *BUTTY[2]]. **1970** *Times* 29 Jan. 9/8 You could have knocked us all down with a jam buttie when she [*sc.* Gracie Fields] first took up with those foreigners. **1972** *Observer* (Colour Suppl.) 16 Jan. 17/4, I am sluggish and sapped of energy and living on an occasional 'jam butty'. **1895** *Army & Navy Co-op. Soc. Price List* 785 [Cut glass] Jam Jar. **1902** M. BARNES-GRUNDY *Thames Camp* iv. 67 Jane went on with her jam-jar trap [for wasps]. **1934** P. ALLINGHAM *Cheapjack* xiii. 163 Have you got a jam-jar—a car? **1943** C. H. WARD-JACKSON *It's a Piece of Cake* 38 *Jam jars*, armoured cars. **1962** R. COOK *Crust on its Uppers* i. 23 Parking this dreadful great orange-and-cream jamjar..slap under a no-parking sign. **1967** N. FREELING *Strike Out* 81 A few brushes in a jam-jar. **1908** G. JEKYLL *Children & Gardens* ii. 12 In the kitchen the children..learn the elements of even more serious cookery, such as jam making. **1968** P. JENNINGS *Living Village* 122 Most wives buy cakes and preserves, a few still do their own baking and jam-making. **1841** THACKERAY *Gt. Hoggarty Diamond* (1849) ix. 100 My dear wife..vowed she would cook all the best dishes herself (especially jam pudding, of which..I am very fond). **1906** E. DYSON *Fact'ry 'Ands* xii. 161 Gets 'is quid a week..solderin' jam-tins. **1956** *Coast to Coast 1955–6* 59 He had one of the jam-tins in his hand.

2. Affected manners; self-importance; freq. in phr. *to lay* (or *put*) *on jam. Austral. slang.*

1882 *Sydney Slang Dict.* 5/1 *Jam* (*putting on*), assuming fast airs of importance. **1901** 'M. FRANKLIN' *My Brilliant Career* (1966) xxvi. 159 People who knew how to conduct themselves properly, and who paid one every attention without a bit of fear of being twitted with 'laying the jam on'. **1924** LAWRENCE & SKINNER *Boy in Bush* 46 Don't y' get sidey..puttin' on jam an' suchlike. **1945** BAKER *Austral. Lang.* vi. 119 Terms like..jam and guiver, connoting 'side' or affectation.

Jam, *sb.*[4] Substitute for def.: A hereditary title of certain princes and noblemen in Sind, Kutch, and Saurashtra. Add earlier and later examples.

1727 A. HAMILTON *New Acct. E. Indies* I. xi. 115 The *Jams* to the Eastward, who being Borderers, are much given to Thieving, and they rob all whom they are able to master. **1913** A. G. GARDINER *Pillars of Society* 293 And so, 'hats off' to the Jam Sahib—the prince of a little State, but the king of a great game. **1958** L. F. R. WILLIAMS *Black Hills* 70 Certain chiefs..whose original early title of Jam is by tradition associated with the mighty Iranian monarch Jamshed.

jam, *v.*[1] Add: **3. c.** *trans.* To cause interference with (radio or radar signals) so as to render them unintelligible or useless, esp. deliberately; to prevent reception of (a transmitter or station) by such means. Also *transf.*

1914 P. VAUX *Sea-Salt & Cordite* 46 Communications became regularly jammed. *Ibid.* 47 We'll stop this jamming, wherever it's coming from. **1914** *Wireless World* July 246/1 Electricity in our language..is not 'juice'; neither is radio interference 'jamming'. **1920** *Discovery* Apr. 116/2 When the reception of a message is thus interfered with by other messages being sent at the same time, the message is said to be 'jammed'. *Ibid.*, The jamming of a message may also be caused by stray ether disturbances in the atmosphere itself. **1920** *Telegraph & Telephone Jrnl.* VI. 165/1 As the number of aeroplanes multiplied 'jambing'—the great drawback of wireless—became more acute. 'Jambing'..refers to the general mix up which results from the reception of two or more sets of signals at once in the same instrument. **1926** E. F. SPANNER *Naviators* x. 124 The Admiral had answered the Japanese C.-in-C. by sending out jamming signals immediately the British scout had been driven down. **1939** *War Illustr.* 7 Oct. 126/2 Gramophone records of pledges given by Hitler in his public speeches have been broadcast from France—and jammed by the Germans! **1947** *Amer. Speech* XXII. 154/1 Allied bombers jammed (rendered ineffective) German radar equipment by dropping quantities of metal foil when over enemy targets. **1947** *Jrnl. R. Aeronaut. Soc.* LI. 432/2 We developed a jamming screen for the purpose of blinding the enemy's early warning system and so preventing him from obtaining information of our approach. **1955** *Times* 18 Aug. 9/2 In 1933 the Vienna transmitters were put on to jam Nazi attacks on the Dolfuss Government from the Munich transmitters. Between 1934 and the outbreak of the war the device was copied wholesale. **1959** *Ann. Reg. 1958* 235 Jamming of Western broadcasts continued. **1970** *Daily Tel.* 16 Apr. 1 The Post Office is jamming broadcasts by the pirate radio ship North Sea International. **1971** *Sci. Amer.* June 132/2 Any sonar can be jammed, and clever moving jammers would pretty surely beat the art of beam shaping. **1971** *New Scientist* 2 Sept. 536/3 In 1942 they investigated the severe jamming of army radar stations, and concluded that radio waves of amazing intensity are emitted by the Sun.

5. b. To apply or put (a brake) *on* violently.

1925 *Morris Owner's Manual* 11 Jambing on the brakes at the last moment.

6. *intr.* To play in a 'jam' or 'jam session' (see *JAM *sb.*[1] 3); to extemporize. Also *trans.*, to improvise (a tune, etc.). *colloq.* (orig. *U.S.*).

1935 *Stage* Sept. 46/2 *Jam*, to improvise hot music, usually in groups. **1936** *Delineator* Nov. 11/2 He just comes on in here once in a while because he likes to jam. **1951** E. PAUL *Springtime in Paris* xi. 203 Pierre Braslavsky could sit in anywhere old-school jazzmen are jamming. **1955** L. FEATHER *Encycl. Jazz* 132 He was seen in the Norman Granz film, *Jamming the Blues*. **1958** R. HORRICKS in P. Gammond *Decca Bk. Jazz* ix. 115 This became an important factor in Kansas City jamming. *Ibid.* 117 The legendary Art Tatum loved to jam with the resident jazz musicians. **1960** *Melody Maker* 31 Dec. 5/3 They just wanted me to jam a blues for the fourth number. **1971** *It* 2–16 June 19/1 They've been jamming together at a studio in Greenwich Village.

jam, *v.*[2] Add: **2.** To make into jam. Hence **jammed** *ppl. a.*[2]; **ja·mming** *vbl. sb.*[2]

1854 THOREAU *Walden* 256 The cranberries,..destined to be *jammed*. **1905** *Daily Chron.* 2 Dec. 4/4 Apples, pears, plums, berries, &c. (fresh or dried, or jammed, or tinned, or bottled). **1949** *Hansard Commons* 16 May 12 'Jamming sugar' is a term very frequently used by housewives. **1969** *Islander* (Victoria, B.C.) 21 Sept. 8/1 In many kitchens there is jamming, jelly and pickle making, perking.

jam (dʒæm), *adv.* and *a.* orig. *U.S.* Also **jamb.** [f. JAM *v.*[1]] **A.** *adv.* **1.** Closely; in close contact or with firm pressure. Often with *up* (*against*).

1825 J. NEAL *Bro. Jonathan* II. 52 He had been sitting, for two or three hours,..'jam up' in a back seat. **1842** *American Pioneer* I. 184 The next moment the sloop ran jamb against it. **1852** MRS. STOWE *Uncle Tom's Cabin* I. 49 'It'll stand, if it only keeps jam up agin de wall!' said Mose. **1932** *Kansas City* (Missouri) *Star* 24 May 18 His Chevrolet..[ran] jam up against a house.

2. *jam up*: thoroughly, perfectly, excellently; right up *to*; so *jam-full* adj.: packed full, completely filled; *jam-packed* adj.: tightly packed; closely crowded or squeezed together; hence (as a back-formation) *jam-pack* v. trans., to pack tightly, fill.

1835 D. CROCKETT *Acct. Col. Crockett's Tour* 192 [Andrew Jackson] went jam up for war; but the cabinet got him down to half heat. **1846** *Congress. Globe* 22 May 852 Their notion is that we go jam up to 54° 40′, and the Russians come jam down to the same. **1858** S. A. HAMMETT *Piney Woods Tavern* xiv. 146 The regular stage was jam full, and there was an extra put on, and that was jam full, and a leetle more. **1866** C. H. SMITH *Bill Arp* 61 Linton played his part of the programme jam up. **1893** G. B. SHAW *Let.* 27 Apr. (1965) 392 Friday & Saturday are jam full. **1925** R. LARDNER in *Liberty* 28 Mar. 5/1 This place is jam-packed Saturdays, from four o'clock on. **1928** WODEHOUSE *Money for Nothing* v. 96 How can you be poor, when that gallery place you showed us round yesterday is jam full of pictures worth a fortune an inch? **1936** F. CLUNE *Roaming round Darling* xxi. 214 Eventually we were jampacked in, with the ladies alternately sitting on the Poet's knees. **1938** *State Jrnl.* (Lincoln, Nebr.) 5 May 14 The foursome finally got a chance to try the floor of the ballroom before the crowd, which later jampacked it, got there. **1947** J. BERTRAM *Shadow of War* 262 It was jam-packed with neglected cargo. **1958** *Archit. Rev.* CXXIV. 383 In surprising and welcome contrast to the jam-packed streets. **1970** N. ARMSTRONG et al. *First on Moon* xiii. 322 They passed the rock boxes through to me, and I handled them as if they were absolutely jam-packed with rare jewels.

B. *adj.* Usu. *jam-up.* Excellent, perfect; thorough. *colloq.*

1832 *Boston Transcript* 6 Aug. 1/1 Do you like jam spruce beer, Miss? **1839** F. Trollope *Dom. Manners Amer.* (ed. 5) 270, I must have everything jam. *Ibid.* 273 That's a jam gal. **1841** *Southern Lit. Messenger* VII. 54/2 Introduced him to the 'jam-up little company' in his command. **1855** T. C. Haliburton *Nat. & Human Nat.* II. ix. 261 In Paradise..connubial bliss, I allot was rael [*sic*] jam up. **1946** Mezzrow & Wolfe *Really Blues* i. 4, I got my first chance to play in a real man-size band, with jam-up instruments.

jama² (dʒā·mă). Colloq. abbrev. of *pyjama*. Usu. *pl.*

1960 *Galaxy Mag.* Feb. 120/2, I groped under the bed for the paper bag that had my jamas in it. **1969** E. Gébler *Shall I eat you Now?* 59 She pulled her skirt on up over her pyjama trousers, and rolled the jama legs up. **1969** *Guardian* 26 Aug. 7/1 Pyjamas..in the language of lingerie..are now called 'jamas.

jama, jamabandi, varr. *jumma, **jumma-bundi.*

Jamaica. Add: *Jamaica bark, bilberry, cherry*: examples; *Jamaica shorts*; **Jamaica ginger,** white ginger (see Ginger *sb.* 1).

1801 T. Dancer *Med. Assistant* 363 *Jamaica bark*... These [species] are indigenous species of the Jesuits or Peruvian bark. **1811** W. J. Titford *Sk. Hortus Bot. Amer.* 60 Jamaica bilberry, or Whortle Berry. **1942** A. L. Simon *Conc. Encycl. Gastron.* V. 40/2 Jamaica Bilberry. The edible berry of a Jamaica mountain shrub. *Ibid.*, Jamaica Cherry. A West Indian Fig, globose and no bigger than a cherry. **1946** Jamaica cherry [see *ceriman]. **1818** *Public Ledger* LVIII. 4/5, 20 Bags and 10 Casks Jamaica Ginger. **1870** Jamaica ginger [see Ginger *sb.* 1]. **1920** *T. Eaton & Co. Catal.* Spring & Summer 367/3 Ginger, Jamaica, powdered. **1959** *Sears, Roebuck Catal.* Spring/Summer 333/3 Jamaica shorts. One pocket. **1972** *Evening Telegram* (St. John's, Newfoundland) 23 June 2/6 (Advt.), 500 only Ladies Jamaica Shorts.

b. *ellipt.* for *Jamaica coffee, rum,* etc.

1899 *T. Eaton & Co. Catal.* Spring & Summer 171/3 Coffees...Finest Santos and Jamaica with chicory. **1910** S. R. Crockett *Dew of their Youth* ii. xviii. 142 My grandfather got his ale, of the sort just then beginning to be made—called 'Jamaica', because a quantity of the cheap sugar refuse from the hogsheads was used in its production. **1938** S. V. Benét *Thirteen o'Clock* 206 He bought his Jamaica personal and in the jug. **1964** *Women's Wear Daily* 30 Nov. 36 From short-shorts to slacks—with Jamaicas, Nassaus, Bermudas, knee pants in between. **1969** *Sears Catal.* Spring/Summer 41D Package of 3 Jamaicas [*sc.* shorts]. (Above-the-knee length.)

Jamaican (dʒămē̆i·kăn), *sb.* and *a.* [f. Jamaica + -an.] **A.** *sb.* A native or inhabitant of Jamaica; the form of English spoken there.

1693 *Truest & Largest Acct. Earthquake in Jamaica* 23 God curb'd their Malice, restrain'd their Power, and gave the Jamaicans a Signal Victory over them. **1770** W. Guthrie *New Geogr. Gram.* 613 The Jamaicans were undoubtedly very numerous, until reduced by earthquakes. **1902** J. D. Hooker in L. Huxley *Life J. D. Hooker* (1918) II. 408 The Jamaicans do not deserve the sacrifice England is making in respect of its fruit trade. **1960** R. B. Le Page *Jamaican Creole* x. 116 'English with a Jamaican accent' ..one could well call Standard Jamaican. *Ibid.* 120 The grammar of Standard Jamaican is not very greatly different from that of Standard English. **1970** *Sunday Times* (Colour Suppl.) 6 Dec. 39/1 Everyone's English accent..had lapsed comfortably into Jamaican during the flight. **1971** I. F. Hancock in J. Spencer *Eng. Lang. W. Afr.* 114 *Jamaican Creole*: spoken in one form or another by about one million Jamaicans.

b. A Jamaican cigar.

1964 I. Fleming *You only live Twice* ii. 27 The best of the Jamaicans are quite up to the Havanas these days. They've got the outer leaf right at last. **1971** 'A. York' *Infiltrator* x. 144 Lucinda carefully pierced his cigar... 'I like these stogies... Better than your Jamaicans.'

B. *adj.* Of or pertaining to Jamaica or the Jamaicans.

1881 *Handbk. Jamaica* iv. 131 The Calipeva or 'Jamaica Salmon'..ranks among three specially Jamaican dainties. **1907** W. Jekyll (*title*) Jamaican song and story. **1913** [see *gros Michel* s.v. *gros *a.*]. **1955** *Caribbean Q.* IV. ii. 125, 4 Jamaican plums, hard round sugar sweets, a roast corn. **1971** [see the *sb.*, above]. **1972** 'B. Graeme' *Tomorrow's Yesterday* xiv. 145 He..pushed a box of cigars across the table. 'Do you smoke these? They are not too bad. Jamaican.'

Hence **Jamai·canism,** a Jamaican word or idiom.

1961 [see *chinchy *a.*]. **1963** *Amer. Speech* XXXVIII. 136 The cultural and historical setting in which these Jamaicanisms have developed. **1967** F. G. Cassidy in *Amer. Speech* XLII. 190 (*title*) Some new light on old Jamaicanisms.

jaman. Add: (Further examples of the forms *jamoon* and *jamun*.) Also *attrib.*

1914 *Indian Forester* XL. 268 *Eugenia Jambolana*, Lam. Jam, Jamun, H[indi]. **1958** J. Carew *Black Midas* x. 206 Get you mango,..soursop, starapple and sweet jamoon. **1965** 'Lauchmonen' *Old Thom's Harvest* x. 133 Everybody make their cake and ginger-beer and jamoon and rice wine. **1969** S. M. Sadeek *Windswept & Other Stories* 32 Rance lay under the jamoon tree.

jambalaya (dʒæmbăl*ē*i·ă). orig. *U.S.* Also **jambalayah, jambolaya.** [Louisiana Fr., f. Provençal *jambalaia*.] A dish composed of rice together with shrimps, chicken, turkey, etc. Also *fig.*

1872 *New Orleans Times* 28 June, Those who brought victuals, such as gumbo, jambalaya, etc., all began eating and drinking. **1905** 'O. Henry' in *Munsey's Mag.* July 467/2 Terrapines,..jambolaya, and canvas-covered ducks. **1916** *Dialect Notes* IV. 269 The show was a regular jambalaya of stunts. **1949** B. A. Botkin *Treas. S. Folklore* iv. i. 552 Louisianians [grow lyrical] over the superiorities of the Cajun and Creole cuisine—gombo, jambalaya, bouillabaisse. **1961** *Listener* 14 Dec. 1050/2 *Jambalaya*..is based on a creole mixture of ham chunks, prawns, and rice, highly flavoured and simmered in chicken stock. **1973** L. Hellman *Pentimento* (1974) 78 The dinner was wonderful: jambalaya, racoon stew, and wild duck.

jambone (dʒæ·mbōᵘn). *Euchre.* ? *Obs.* (See quots.)

1864 W. B. Dick *Amer. Hoyle* (1866) 83 A party who plays Jambone plays a lone hand with his cards exposed upon the table. **1886** *Euchre: how to play It* 42 A Jambone is to play a lone hand with the cards exposed on the table, and to give to that adversary who is entitled to the lead, or whose first play it is, the privilege of calling one of the exposed cards to the first trick played, or if the jambone player has the lead, to call upon him to lead any one of the exposed cards.

jamboree. For *U.S. slang* read 'orig. *U.S. slang*'. Add earlier and later examples.

1868 *N.Y. Herald* 10 July 8/3 The Seventh regiment has gone on a jamboree to Norwich, Connecticut. **1955** H. Spring *These Lovers fled Away* iii. 90 There was some jamboree or other at the Assembly Rooms. **1959** *Economist* 27 June 1144/1 This is sufficiently important, and difficult, to warrant a top-level western conference this year—not merely another Atlantic jamboree. **1960** A. Huxley *Let.* 17 July (1969) 893 Meet me in Boston with the Microbus and drive me..to Hanover, where you might stay for all or part of the Jamboree (at which I am to receive an honorary degree). **1973** G. Scott *Water Horse* (1974) v. 33 Even the most respectable souls milled around the countryside..holding all sorts of jamborees.

b. *Euchre.* A lone hand containing the five highest cards. ? *Obs.*

1886 *Euchre: how to play It* 45 *Jamboree* signifies the combination of the five highest cards, as, for example, the two Bowers, Ace, King, and Queen of trumps in one hand, which entitles the holder to count sixteen points. The holder of such a hand simply announces the fact, as no play is necessary; but should he play the hand as a Jambone, he can count only eight points, whereas he could count sixteen if he announced it as a Jamboree.

c. The name given to the 1920 International Rally of Boy Scouts, and now applied to any large scout rally. Also *attrib.*

1919 *Times* 17 Oct. 9/6 The Council of the Boy Scouts Association announce that a 'Jamboree' will be held at Olympia, for about eight days next August. **1931** *Mag. Univ. Students' Union* Apr. 2 The Jamboree spirit was marvellous. **1955** *Times* 20 Aug. 9/3 The four-year cycle for jamborees is being broken in order to commemorate in 1957 the fiftieth anniversary of scouting.

jambu: see Jambo.

James Bond (dʒē̆i:mz bǫ·nd). The name of the hero of a series of novels by the British writer Ian Fleming (1908–64), used allusively (freq. *attrib.* or as *adj.*) of adventurous, sophisticated men resembling the hero, or of situations similar to those in the novels. So **James Bo·ndish** *a.*

1966 *Economist* 19 Mar. 1115/1 There was nothing James Bondish about his arrival, for Mr Smith's external relations department was informed well in advance. **1967** *Guardian* 23 Dec. 14/2 The escape itself was James Bond with the merest trace of Keystone Cops. **1968** *Ibid.* 23 Feb. 7/4 This fast James Bond stuff doesn't blend happily with the more realistic comedy. **1968** K. Bird *Smash Glass Image* iv. 54, I should love to deck myself out as a two-fisted James Bond because that would impress you. **1970** *Motoring Which?* Apr. 43/2 Aston Martin DB5—very powerful James Bond car. **1972** G. Lyall *Blame the Dead* vii. 47 People who..go running around France playing James Bond with unlicensed Walthers.

Jamesian (dʒē̆i·mziăn), *a.* (*sb.*) [f. *James* + -ian.] **1.** Of or pertaining to the American philosopher and psychologist William *James* (1842–1910) or his works. Also as *sb.*, a follower or admirer of William James.

1875 C. Wright *Let.* 18 July in R. B. Perry *Tht. & Char. W. James* (1935) I. 532 He rather attracts me by the Jamesian traits. **1935** R. B. Perry *Tht. & Char. W. James* II. 668 While there are very few pure Jamesians, in the sense of direct descent, the world is full of mixed Jamesians, who acknowledge their common relationship to him without feeling any bond with one another. **1955** Koestler *Trail of Dinosaur* 249 The Jamesian view that a transcendental faith was a biological necessity for man. **1964** *Amer. Philos. Q.* I. 115/1 Elements in the German phenomenology of the 1930's..are clearly repugnant to the post-Jamesian American philosophical temper.

2. Of or pertaining to the American (later naturalized British) writer Henry *James* (1843–1916) or his works. Also as *sb.*, a follower or admirer of Henry James.

1905 *Daily Chron.* 7 Sept. 3/1 The plot..is Jamesian.. in its tenuity. **1954** *Essays in Crit.* IV. 371, I am not a good enough Jamesian to decide the other claim. **1958** *Listener* 17 July 98/1 For Jamesians, it is the first thrilling scent of the great chase. **1972** J. Symons *Bloody Murder* xvi. 235 The motivations of his characters seem at times to be of Jamesian complexity.

James–Lange (dʒē̆i·mz,læ·ŋə). *Psychol.* The names of W. *James* (1840–1900) and C. G. *Lange* (1834–1900), used *attrib.* to designate a theory propounded by each of them separately that the response to an emotional stimulus is, in the first place, an organic reaction rather than a mental awareness of the emotion.

1909 H. R. Marshall *Consciousness* i. App. A. 109 It is not correct to say either that the emotions cause the instinctive reaction..nor to say that the instinctive reactions cause the emotions, as the common statement of the James–Lange theory implies. **1914** M. Prince *Unconscious* xiv. 423 The James–Lange theory is disregarded here as untenable. **1918** E. Jones *Papers on Psycho-Anal.* (ed. 2) xxvii. 485 The occurrence of the abortive anxiety attacks..stands in direct conflict with the James–Lange hypothesis. **1933** G. Murphy *Gen. Psychol.* v. 75 Such evidences might even lead to a partial confirmation of the James–Lange view. **1949** D. O. Hebb *Organization of Behavior* x. 237 Just such an inconsistency of thought has led to an endless, and pointless, debate on the James–Lange theory of emotion. **1970** H. C. Shands *Semiotic Approaches to Psychiatry* xx. 307 The James–Lange notion is an interpretation of a communicational process involving feedback from one's own behavior.

Jameson (dʒæ·misǫn, dʒē̆i·-, dʒi·-). The proprietary name of a brand of Irish whiskey. Also, a drink of this whiskey.

[**1877** *Trade Marks Jrnl.* 28 Feb. 568/1 W. Jameson & Co. Distillers. Dublin. William Robertson, on behalf of self and partners, William Jameson and James Jameson, trading as Wm. Jameson and Co.,..Dublin; whisky distillers.] **1922** Joyce *Ulysses* 176 We'll take two of your small Jamesons after that. **1948** W. Stevens *Let.* 7 Sept. (1967) 613 Perhaps if I could have that bottle of Jameson..on the reading stand, I could really get somewhere. **1965** *Trade Marks Jrnl.* 24 Mar. 414/1 Jameson..Irish whiskey..John Jameson & Son Limited, ..Dublin.

Jamie Green (dʒē̆i·mi grīn). *Naut.* [Proper name, orig. unknown.] The name of a type of sail found on tea-clippers. Cf. *Jimmy Green* (*Jimmy 8).

1866 Capt. Keay *Jrnl.* 20 June in B. Lubbock *China Clippers* (1914) App. H. p. xxi, About 5.30 a.m., all staysails and fore-topmast and topgallant stunsails set and Jamie Green. **1927** G. Bradford *Gloss. Sea Terms* 109/2 *Jamie Green*, a sail set beneath the bowsprit and jib-boom of a tea clipper. The halyard hauled the sail to the end of the jib-boom and the tack to the lower end of the martingale boom. **1934** P. Mitchell *Deep Water* i. xxiii. 184 They..had..Jamie Greens for under the jib boom, ringtails, watersails, and an extra flying jib. **1961** F. H. Burgess *Dict. Sailing* 123 *Jamie Green*, a sail set under the jib-boom, to the dolphin striker.

jammer (dʒæ·məɹ). [f. Jam *v.*¹ + -er¹.] A transmitter used for jamming.

1947 *Jrnl. R. Aeronaut. Soc.* LI. 428/1 We could.. dispose our limited number of transmitters along the tracks usually followed by the beam-flying enemy bombers and site our relatively low-powered jammers where they would produce their greatest effect. **1957** *B.B.C. Handbk.* 39 Jamming by the Communist authorities is more efficient than the wartime efforts of the Germans and Italians, but except in certain centres of population where local jammers are used, it is not completely effective. **1965** H. Kahn *On Escalation* vii. 141 The Soviets might even use shipboard jammers. **1971** [see *jam *v.*¹ 3 c].

jammy (dʒæ·mi), *a.* [f. Jam *sb.*² + -y¹.] Covered with jam, sticky. Also *fig.* (*colloq.*), excellent; very lucky or profitable; easy, 'soft'. Hence **ja·mminess.**

1853 D. G. Rossetti *Let.* 2 Nov. (1965) I. 161 The frame for my water-colour..is..jammy, nobby, stunning, jolly, splendacious. **1895** *Punch* 12 Oct. 180/1 The way as that Sam chewed the rag was just jammy **1899** Kipling *Stalky & Co.* 228 Jam for the Sixth! Jam for us! Either way it's jammy! **1908** 'I. Hay' *Right Stuff* xi. 205 We had disposed of grouse sandwiches..and jammy scones. **1915** D. O. Barnett *Lett.* 170 If I get a 'jammy' one as it is called, I shall be back pretty soon. **1920** *Chambers's Jrnl.* X. 862/2 She was aroused by the..jammy caresses of her blue-eyed nephews. **1929** W. Deeping *Roper's Row* 179 There was a jamminess about these meals and about the ladies' fingers. **1932** A. J. Worrall *Eng. Idioms* 32, I don't know any one like him. He's jammy. **1955** M. Allingham *Beckoning Lady* x. 137 The twins, jammy-faced and excited. **1973** 'Trevanian' *Loo Sanction* (1974) 130 'I almost always win. Isn't that odd?' The Sergeant regarded the slim body... 'I'd say you were bloody jammy.'

jam-packed, *a.*: see *jam *adv.* 2.

jams (dʒæmz), *sb. pl.* [Shortened from Pyjamas, pajamas *sb. pl.*] A garment, derived from Pyjamas, worn as leisure-wear, and *spec.* as a type of swimming-trunks.

1966 *Telegraph* (Brisbane) 3 Feb. 18 It's the season of the hubba hubba jams—and that's..a patio fashion stopper. It is snug..just-above-the-knee jams worn with

a covered camisole top...Jams can be worn with a bikini top or a frilly feminine flip-top style. **1968** *N.Y. Times* 22 Jan. 36 There will also be ascots (which can double as belts), walking shorts, swim trunks and surfers' 'jams', knee-length trunks with drawstring waists. **1970** *New Yorker* 14 Mar. 34/3 He wore His-'n-Hers flowered at-home jams. **1971** *Telegraph* (Brisbane) 29 Dec. 31 (Advt.), Boys' cotton floral swim jams... Cord tie at waist. Hip pocket detail.

jam-tree. Also **jamwood.** = *raspberry jam tree* (s.v. RASPBERRY 4). *Austral.*

1934 T. WOOD *Cobbers* vii. 91 Jam trees grow here [*sc.* in Western Australia], and blackboy, that strange fascination. **1941** *Coast to Coast* 46 The wheat..rippled up the hillside and lost itself..in the shadow of a jam-tree belt. **1947** *Coast to Coast 1946* 202 Old Tom Caseley had just finished whittling the fifty-seventh link in his jamwood chain when he died. **1962** A. UPFIELD *Will of Tribe* iv. 39 He..dismounted and neck-roped the horse to a stout desert jamwood. **1965** *Austral. Encycl.* IX. 219/2 Myall wood has a peculiar violet-like fragrance, while jamwood is reminiscent of raspberries.

jam-up, *sb. colloq.* [JAM *sb.*[1] + UP *adv.*[1]] = JAM *sb.*[1] 1 (in Dict. and Suppl.).

1941 J. M. CAIN *Mildred Pierce* xi. 229 To forestall the possibility of another jam-up. **1961** *Time* 14 Apr. 105/3 The jam-up at the post-office when the social security checks arrive. **1970** *Globe & Mail* (Toronto) 28 Sept. 22/4 Larry Foubert of Weston ended up on the infield grass after a jam-up at the north end of the track. **1973** 'D. JORDAN' *Nile Green* xi. 46 There was the usual jam-up.. and the auto horns blared in frustration.

janapa (dʒæ·năpă). Also **-um.** [Tamil.] = SUNN.

1851 *Illustr. Catal. Gt. Exhib.* IV. 882/2 *Crotolaria juncea*..is cultivated in most parts of India for its fibre, which..is called *sun* and *sunnee* in different parts of India, but, in the Madras peninsula, *janapum*. **1866** LINDLEY & MOORE *Treas. Bot.* II. 635/1 *Janapa*, an Indian name for Sunn Hemp.

Jane, jane[2] (dʒēⁱn). *slang* (orig. *U.S.*). [Female Christian name.] A woman, girl, girl-friend.

1906 *Dialect Notes* III. 142 'It's the magazine over yonder with a red Jane on it.' 'Going to take your Jane to the show?' **1916** C. J. DENNIS *Moods of Ginger Mick* 79 She's like some fat ole Jane 'oo loves to smile. **1923** [see *DAME 2 c]. **1924** P. MARKS *Plastic Age* 149, I met a bunch of janes down at Bar Harbour. **1929** 'G. DAVIOT' *Man in Queue* iii. 30 He has a new 'jane'. He probably wants money. **1941** *Coast to Coast* 129, I was trailing round with a high-class little jane in those days. **1958** 'A. GILBERT' *Death against Clock* x. 145 She didn't see that it could, and for once I agree with a jane. **1967** E. S. GARDNER *Case of Queenly Contestant* (1973) xiii. 150 'Who was this jane' Anybody I know?' 'No one you know... She had been a nurse in San Francisco.'

Janeite (dʒēⁱ·nəit). Also **Jane-ite, Janite.** [f. the Christian name of *Jane* Austen (1775–1817), novelist + -ITE[1].] = *AUSTENITE[1].

1896 G. SAINTSBURY *Hist. 19th Cent. Lit.* 129 It did not apparently occur to this critic that he (or she) was in the first place paying Miss Austen an extraordinarily high compliment—a compliment almost greater than the most enthusiastic 'Janites' have ventured. **1924** KIPLING *Debits & Credits* (1926) 147 (*title*) The Janeites. **1927** *Observer* 5 June 6/3 Clearly he is *not* a Janeite. **1928** *Daily Tel.* 7 Aug. 3/3 The best page of her book by far is her spirited defence of Jane Austen, which will endear her to the 'Jane-ites' for all time. **1947** W. J. BLYTON in *Eng. Lang. & Lit.* vii. 111/1 Men as masculine as Scott and Kipling have been Jane-ites and have been enthralled by her sly humour and fidelity to reality. **1972** N. FREELING *Long Silence* II. 149 Arlette was not a Janeite, and..it was accidentally that she let slip..that Piet used to call her 'Bates'.

jang(g)a, varr. *JONGA.

janitor. Add: **1. b.** A caretaker of a building, esp. a school, who has charge of the cleaning, heating, etc., of it. Also *attrib.*

1708 C. MORTHLAND *Acct. Govt. Church of Scotl.* 18 When a Student enters the University [of Edinburgh] he must pay Half a Crown to the Porter or Janitor and Seven Pence to his Servant. **1835** DR. NEILL in J. J. Audubon *Ornith. Biogr.* III. 313 A cock-heron..had been..kept for some weeks in a cellar in the old College, and then presented to me by the late Mr John Wilson, the janitor. **1868** *Mich. Agric. Rep.* VII. 22 Expenses for wood, furniture, janitor work, &c. **1884** H. BUTTERWORTH *Zigzag Journeys Western States* 50 He was employed merely as janitor at Yule [school]. **1952** *Manch. Guardian Weekly* 4 Dec. 13 The Civil Service now protects janitors and chauffeurs. **1954** *Press & Jrnl.* (Aberdeen) 7 Apr., The Education Committee..had recommended that a janitor be appointed, and that he be responsible for all janitorial and cleaning work at the school, including maintenance of the gardens. **1961** *Evening Standard* 12 Sept. 19/1 Janitor required for building in W.1. area. **1968** *Globe & Mail* (Toronto) 13 Feb. 31/6 (Advt.), Prestige offices, full janitor services.

janizary, janissary. Add: **4. janizary music** [G. *janitscharenmusik*] = *Turkish music* (TURKISH *a.* 2 b); **janizary pedal,** a pedal attached to some old pianofortes, etc., having an arrangement of drums and cymbals connected with it, by which a sound as of martial music was produced.

1888 F. MOSCHELES tr. *Mendelssohn's Lett. to I. & C. Moscheles* 54 He must have a cradle song with drums and trumpets and janissary music. **1896** A. J. HIPKINS *Descr. & Hist. Pianoforte* 106 Drum and triangle (for Janissary music). **1922** J. RIVIERE tr. *Freud's Introd. Lect. Psycho-Anal.* 75 The little bells, shaken violently, begin their familiar janizary music. **1900** *Pall Mall Gaz.* 21 May 4/2 Even Mozart condescended to employ the 'Janissary pedal' in one or two of his sonatas.

‖ **janken** (dʒa·ŋken). [Jap.] A Japanese children's game played with the hands. Now principally used in sport to decide ends, etc.

1936 E. K. VENABLES *Behind Smile in Real Japan* viii. 269 The ceremony which is the Oriental equivalent of tossing up... *Jan-ken-poh*, as it is called, is used in all such cases of decision by chance. **1964** *Japan* (Jap. Nat. Commission for Unesco) 831/2 *Janken* is the only form of the game which remains today as a means to decide the dealer in card games, the server in a match, and so on. **1967** D. & E. T. RIESMAN *Conversations in Japan* 157 *Janken* (games of three: paper, scissors, and stone). **1972** *Nat. Geographic* CXLI. 689/2 There was the ritual with children of *jan ken pon*, a game in which fist and fingers represent paper, rock, or scissors.

jankers (dʒæ·ŋkəɪz). *Services' slang.* [Origin unknown.] Punishment for defaulters; the defaulters themselves; the cells in which they are placed. Also *attrib.* (occas. in *sing.* form).

1916 J. N. HALL *Kitchener's Mob* 35 The 'jankers' or defaulters' squad was always rather large. **1919** *Athenæum* 25 July 664/2 The advent of the Royal Navy Division introduced to the Army the sailor's slang word 'jankers', the equivalent of the soldier's 'clink', punishment cells. *Ibid.* 8 Aug. 727/2 When doing C.B. or 'time' he [*sc.* the soldier] was doing 'jankers' or 'Paddy Doyle'. *a* **1935** T. E. LAWRENCE *Mint* (1950) II. xxii. 160 A week before my last jankers. **1936** F. RICHARDS *Old-Soldier Sahib* ii. 54, I was now a defaulter, or 'on jankers' as the troops called it. **1946** *Penguin New Writing* XXVII. 72, I stepped into the hall of B.H.Q. over two janker-wallahs. *Ibid.* 73 He broke off to bawl out the jankermen. **1960** T. RATTIGAN *Ross* I. ii. 20 None of your lip, Parsons, now —unless you want a dose of jankers. **1965** J. PORTER *Dover Two* ix. 122, I pulled her leg about it a bit, you know, said something about having her put on jankers if she was late again. **1971** *Sunday Mail Mag.* (Brisbane) 25 July 6/2 Jankers can be painful. It usually means confined to barracks and menial tasks. *Ibid.*, My first jankers was for causing a fire.

jann (dʒān). Also **jan.** [a. Arab. *jānn* demon.] = JINN *sb.*

1777 J. RICHARDSON *Dict. Persian, Arabic & Eng.* I. 667 That race of creatures called by the Arabians *Jan* or *Jinn.* **1891** E. S. HARTLAND *Sci. Fairy Tales* x. 256 Hasan is favoured with the sight of 'ten virgins'... He fell madly in love with the chief damsel, who turns out to be a daughter of a King of the Jann. **1931** A. WILSON in E. S. Stevens *Folk Tales Iraq* p. xiv, Stories in which *jānn*, or fairy-folk, don at will the appearance of birds.

janney (dʒæ·ni). *Newfoundland.* Also **janny, jenny, johnny.** [Prob. var. JOHNNY, JOHNNIE.] A Christmas mummer in Newfoundland. Hence as *v. intr.*, to act as a janney; to dress *up* as a janney.

1896 *Jrnl. Amer. Folklore* IX. 36 *Old teaks* and *jannies*, boys and men who turn out in various disguises and carry on various pranks during the Christmas holidays. **1925** *Dialect Notes* V. 335 *Johnnies*, Christmas mummers. Also *jennies.* **1964** *Canad. Jrnl. Linguistics* Fall 44 At Christmas time it was usual for people to..'janny up'—dress up as mummers. **1969** J. D. A. WIDDOWSON in Halpert & Story *Christmas Mumming in Newfoundland* 218 Janneys 'janney up', but mummers 'rig out' or 'dress up'.

January. Add: **2.** *attrib.*, as *January sale.*

1896 in G. Eley *Ruined Maid* (1970) 24/1 A friend of mine..bought at a January sale six yards of brocade in pale electric blue. **1936** *Discovery* Oct. 320/2 A rush.. which must have equalled the January sales of our own days. **1967** E. G. COUSINS *Death in Quiet Place* xiv. 177 Mollie's getting so used to Town that she's threatening to stay on over the January Sales.

Janus. Add: **2.** Designating materials with a double facing, or things having a two-way action, as *Janus-beaver, -cloth, -cord, -lock.*

1851 *Illustr. Catal. Gt. Exhib.* III. 486/2 Fur Janus beaver. *Ibid.* v. 1468/2 Janus locks. *a* **1877** KNIGHT *Dict. Mech.* II. 1210/2 *Janus-cloth*, a fabric having each side dressed, and different colors on the respective sides. Such fabric is used for reversible garments. **1881** in A. Adburgham *Shops & Shopping* (1964) vi. 64 Mourning materials such as Victoria Cords, Janus Cords, Cashmere, and so on. **1960** CUNNINGTON & BEARD *Dict. Eng. Costume* 259/2 *Janus cord*, a black rep of wool and cotton, the fine cord showing equally on both sides. Much used for mourning.

b. *Dye Chem.* Applied to a group of basic azo dyes that contain a quaternary ammonium group, often with safranine as the diazo component, and are capable of dyeing cotton directly; **Janus** (also **janus**) **green (B),** either of the two basic dyes obtained by coupling diazotized safranine or dimethylsafranine with dimethylaniline, of little importance as dyes but extensively used as biological stains.

1898 *Jrnl. Soc. Dyers & Colourists* XIV. 146 The first eight patterns..were dyed with Janus Colours on Union linings. *Ibid.* (Table), Janus Black I. Janus Blue R... Janus Green G. Janus Green B. **1926** *Stain Technol.* I. 35 The use of janus green to stain mitochondria has long been known. While using it to study the mitochondria in *Trichomonas buccalis* it was found to stain flagella also. **1928** C. E. MULLIN *Acetate Silk* x. 142 Some of the Janus dyes are also applicable to acetate silk, however most of them give rather dull shades. **1949** N. G. HEATLEY in H. W. Florey et al. *Antibiotics* I. iii. 118 The test organism was *Welchii perfringens* strain HA, the indicator wss janus green. **1971** D. R. BAER in K. Venkataraman *Chem. Synthetic Dyes* IV. iv. 165 Derivatives of (*m*-aminophenyl)trimethylammonium chloride..formed part of the Janus range of colors which were of limited use on rayon, silk–wool unions, and on cotton. **1971** E. GURR *Synthetic Dyes* 128 There are apparently two types of Janus green B, one from the USA and the other of European origin. *Ibid.* 129 Both types of Janus green are employed as oxidation-reduction indicators.

Jap, *sb.* Add: (Later examples.) Also as *adj.*; spec. *Jap silk* = *HABUTAI.

As *sb.* and *adj.* the word *Jap* has strong derogatory connotations and is now falling into disuse.

1895 *Montgomery Ward Catal.* 37/3 Ladies' short silk waists, made of plain colored Habutai Jap silk. **1900** in *American Mail Order Fashions* (1961) 18 Jap braid edge. **1902** *To-Day* 14 May 95/1 Printed Jap silks are lovely. **1914** *Dialect Notes* IV. 136 This is a Jap Kimona. **1921** [see *CHOW *sb.* 1]. **1936** *Times* 3 Jan. 10/3 The most jealously limited edition of an unacted Swinburne drama, 50 copies only on jap vellum. **1940** [see *DAGO, DAGO]. **1944** *Living off Land* viii. 156 The Jap pearlers have landed on his coasts. **1951** *Good Housek. Home Encycl.* 251/2 Many attractive natural silk fabrics..jap and spun silks and ninons. **1959** [see *JEW *sb.* 3 a]. **1970** G. F. NEWMAN *Sir, You Bastard* viii. 211 Nice little tape-recorder... Snazzy Jap job.

jap (dʒæp), *v. U.S. slang.* [f. JAP *sb.*] *trans.* To make a sneak attack on; also, to queer the pitch of (a person).

In restricted use.

1957 *New Yorker* 21 Sept. 135/1 'They japped us,' a third boy said, meaning that the Cherubs had taken them by surprise. **1958** H. E. SALISBURY *Shook-up Generation* (1959) ii. 29 An uncertain area where one side or another may at any sudden moment 'jap' an unwary alien. **1971** D. E. WESTLAKE *I gave at the Office* 170 Joe would hate me forever and would probably jap me with Mr. Clarebridge.

Japan, *sb.* Add: **6. Japan anemone,** one of several varieties or hybrids of *Anemone hupehensis*, bearing large pink or white flowers; **Japan camphor** = *tub-camphor* (see TUB *sb.* 10); **Japan cedar** = *CRYPTOMERIA; **Japan current** = KUROSHIWO; **Japan lacquer (tree)** (see LACQUER *sb.* 2 b, 4); **Japan lily,** any of several species of *Lilium* native to Japan, esp. *L. japonicum*; **Japan paper** = **Japanese paper*; **Japan pepper** = *Japanese pepper* (see PEPPER *sb.* 3); **Japan quince** (see *JAPONICA); **Japan rose,** a name once used for the camellia; later = **Japanese rose*; **Japan varnish (tree)** = *varnish sumach* (see VARNISH *sb.*[1] 5); = **Japan lacquer*; **Japan wax** = **Japanese wax.*

1847 *Curtis's Bot. Mag.* LXXIII. 4341 (*heading*) Japan Anemone. **1870** W. ROBINSON *Wild Garden* I. 28 The Japan Anemone and A. hybrida..grow so strongly that they will take care of themselves. **1882** [in Dict.]. **1908** G. JEKYLL *Colour in Flower Garden* ix. 81 The pink colourings are the wide-headed *Sedum spectabile*, pink Japan Anemone and a few pale pink Gladioli. **1882** R. BENTLEY *Man. Bot.* (ed. 4) 642 Commercial camphor is derived entirely from the island of Formosa and Japan,.. the latter [being known] as *Japan* or *Dutch Camphor.* **1852** Japan cedar [see *CRYPTOMERIA]. **1900** M. THORN in W. D. Drury *Bk. Gardening* xi. 488 *C. japonica* (Japan Cedar) is a charming tree. **1865** D. PAGE *Handbk. Geol. Terms* (ed. 2) 263 *Japan current*, that branch of the equatorial current of the Pacific which trends northwards along the Japan coasts. **1885** [see KUROSHIWO]. **1936** RUSSELL & YONGE *Seas* (ed. 2) x. 231 The Japan Current or 'Kuro Shiwo' corresponding to our Gulf Stream. **1835** W. J. HOOKER *Compan. Bot. Mag.* I. 268/1 The so much celebrated Japan lacquer or varnish. **1880** C. E. BESSEY *Bot.* XX. 535 Japan Lacquer, so much used by the Japanese in the manufacture of many wares, is obtained..from *Rhus vernicifera*, and probably other species. **1884** W. MILLER *Dict. Eng. Names Plants* 241/1 Japan Lacquer-, or Varnish-, Tree. **1911** *Encycl. Brit.* XXVI. 70/2 *Rhus vernicifera* is the Japan lacquer or varnish-tree. **1813** *Curtis's Bot. Mag.* XXXVIII. 1591 (*heading*) White one-flowered Japan Lily. **1854** C. M. YONGE *Heartsease* I. iv. 56 You should go and look at the Japan lilies. **1625** PURCHAS *Pilgrimes* III. II. v. 339 Nothing gave him such content as two Bookes of Iapon paper, smooth and hard bound in Europæan manner. **1914** *Photo-Era* Feb. 102/1 There are certain tricks to produce a soft print from a sharp negative, one of which is to put a piece of Japan paper between the plate and the sensitive paper in the printing-frame. **1974** *Country Life* 17 Jan. 75/1 The exquisite *Le Bain* of 1905, a dry point (an impression from the edition of 27 or 29 on Japan paper). **1866** Japan pepper [see PEPPER *sb.* 3]. **1914** W. J. BEAN *Trees & Shrubs Hardy in Brit. Isles* II. 692 *Z*[*anthoxylum*] *piperitum*, De Candolle. Japan Pepper... The seeds when ground are used by the Japanese as pepper. **1850** W. HOWITT *Year-bk. Country* 24 In gardens..come forth the vernal crocus, various hellebores, the Japan quince. **1916** L. H. BAILEY *Pruning-Manual* 222 *Chænomeles japonica* (Japan quince) **1789** W. AITON *Hortus Kewensis* II. 460 Camellia. .. Japan Rose. **1793** B. EDWARDS *Hist. Brit. Colonies W. Indies* I. 204 *Camellia japonica*, Japan Rose. **1895** W. ROBINSON *Eng. Flower Garden* (ed. 4) 732/1 It [*Rosa acicularis*] has a showy fruit, which differs from that of the Japan Rose, for, instead of being roundish and smooth, it is long and Pear-shaped. [**1727** J. G. SCHEUCHZER tr.

Kæmpfer's Hist. Japan I. I. ix. 114 The *Urusi* or *Varnish-Tree* is another of the noblest and most useful Trees of this country.] **1789** J. Belknap *Let.* 13 Mar. in W. Parker & J. P. Cutler *Life M. Cutler* (1888) II. 252, I have sent for the seeds of the Japan varnish tree. **1843** *Penny Cycl.* XXVI. 147/2 The Japan varnish of Kæmpfer and Thunberg is Rhus vernix. **1889** W. Robinson *Eng. Flower Garden* (ed. 2) 788/2 Others in cultivation..include *R[hus] vermicifera*, or Japan Varnish Tree. **1859** Japan wax [see *Japanese wax* s.v. *Japanese *a.* b]. **1887** *Colonial & Indian Exhib. Rep. Col. Sect.* 275 Myrtle wax..which, like Japan wax, is rather a fat than a true wax. **1969** R. Mayer *Dict. Art Terms & Techniques* 201/2 Japan wax is sometimes called vegetable wax.

Japanese, *a.* and *sb.* Add: **A.** *adj.* **b.** Special collocations: **Japanese anemone** = **Japan anemone*; **Japanese ape** = **Japanese monkey*; **Japanese artichoke** = **Chinese artichoke*; **Japanese beetle,** a scarabæid beetle, *Popillia japonica,* which has become a pest of foliage and grasses in eastern North America; **Japanese camphor** = **Japan camphor*; **Japanese cedar** = *cryptomeria; **Japanese cherry,** an ornamental flowering tree belonging to a variety or hybrid of several species of *Prunus* native to Japan; **Japanese current** = Kuroshiwo; **Japanese flower,** a piece of coloured paper which unfolds like a flower when placed in water; **Japanese garden,** a garden in which clipped shrubs, water, bridges, rocks, stepping-stones, raked gravel, stone lanterns, etc., are used in a formal design, without masses of bright colour; **Japanese gold thread** (see quot. 1880); **Japanese iris,** a variety of *Iris kæmpferi* or *I. lævigata*; **Japanese lantern** = *Chinese-lantern* (see Chinese *a.* 2); **Japanese larch,** *Larix leptolepis,* which was introduced to Britain in 1861; **Japanese lily** = **Japan lily*; **Japanese macaque** = **Japanese monkey*; **Japanese maple,** a variety of *Acer palmatum* or *A. japonicum,* cultivated esp. for its decorative foliage; **Japanese medlar** = Loquat; **Japanese monkey,** a large monkey, *Macaca fuscata,* which is native to Japan; **Japanese pagoda tree,** *Sophora japonica,* the scholar tree; **Japanese paper,** paper made by hand, originally and chiefly in Japan, from the bark of the mulberry-tree; **Japanese pepper** (see Pepper *sb.* 3); **Japanese print,** a coloured print made in Japan from a wood-block; **Japanese quince** = *japonica; **Japanese rose,** any of several species of *Rosa* native to Japan, esp. *R. rugosa*; **Japanese screen,** an embroidered screen made in Japan; **Japanese silk** = **Jap silk*; **Japanese spaniel,** a breed of small, black-and-white or brown-and-white, long-coated dog; **Japanese stitch** (see quot. 1880); **Japanese tissue (paper),** a type of strong thin transparent paper; **Japanese vellum** (see quot. 1923); **Japanese waltzing mouse,** a mutant of *Mus musculus bactrianus,* a house mouse native to Central and Eastern Asia; also **Japanese waltzer; Japanese wax,** a yellow wax obtained from the berries of certain plants of the genus *Rhus*; **Japanese wolf,** *Canis lupus hodophylax,* a subspecies of the common wolf.

c **1908** E. J. Cook *Century Bk. Gardening* 71/1 The Japanese Anemone..was originally seen only in its pink-blossomed form. **1913** C. Mackenzie *Sinister St.* I. I. vi. 87 All along the paths were masses of flowers, phloxes and early Michaelmas daisies and Japanese anemones. **1969** H. R. Fletcher *Story R. Hort. Soc.* x. 151 All the 'Japanese anemones'..are now grouped under the hybrid name of *A.* x *elegans.* **1883** *List Animals* (Zool. Soc.) (ed. 8) 22 *Macacus speciosus*... Japanese Ape. **1966** R. & D. Morris *Men & Apes* i. 18 The famous three wise monkeys, See-no-evil, Hear-no-evil and Speak-no-evil.. are based on the Japanese ape (*Macaca fuscata*), a delightful monkey with a short, stumpy tail and a bright pink face that flushes scarlet when the animal is sexually active. **1905** tr. *Vegetable Garden* (Vilmorin-Andrieux et Cie) 671 Chinese or Japanese Artichoke... These rhizomes ..are white, watery, and tender. **1970** Simon & Howe *Dict. Gastron.* 40/2 Artichokes, Japanese or Chinese. These are small tubers which one writer describes as looking like 'petrified worms'. **1919** *Rev. Appl. Entomol.* A. VII. 101 Eradication work in connection with a Japanese beetle (*Popillia japonica*) has been systematically undertaken. **1922** *Jrnl. Econ. Entomol.* XV. 303 An efficient contact spray will no doubt have considerable application in the control of the Japanese beetle at this time. **1936** *Discovery* XVII. 36/1 The Japanese Beetle (*Popillia japonica*)..accidentally introduced into America in the larval stage in a shipment of Japanese iris in 1916, has now invaded the eastern coastal states. **1972** Swan & Papp *Common Insects N. Amer.* xx. 431 The Asiatic Garden Beetle..is similar in habits to the Japanese beetle ..but it flies only at night. **1727** J. G. Scheuchzer tr. *Kæmpfer's Hist. Japan* I. 179 Japanese boil'd Camphire may be had for one single Catti of the true Bornean Camphire. *Ibid.*, The Japanese Camphire-tree. **1880** *Encycl. Brit.* XIII. 574/2 *Cryptomeria* (Japanese cedar). **1954** *New Biol.* XVI. 97 The Japanese Cedar or Sugi, a tree found in China and Japan and, in the latter country, an important and abundant timber tree. **1901** L. H. Bailey *Cycl. Amer. Hort.* III. 1452/2 Japanese Flowering Cherry. **1913** W. P. Wright *Garden Trees & Shrubs* xxvi. 215 The double Japanese Cherries..have beautiful rosy flowers. **1925** *Jrnl. R. Hort. Soc.* L. 73 (*title*) Notes on Japanese cherries. **1951** *Dict. Gardening* (R. Hort. Soc.) II. 1085/2 It is only comparatively recently that the Japanese Cherries have been widely planted. **1972** G. Chadbund *Flowering Cherries* i. 16 As far as we know none of the upright garden varieties of Japanese cherries were introduced into the western world until 1894. **1926** *Daily Colonist* (Victoria, B.C.) 16 Jan. 1/3 Similar conditions..gave rise to the belief that the Japanese current had changed its course. **1972** *Islander* (Victoria, B.C.) 26 Mar. 16/1 The fickle Japanese current which sweeps in a circular motion across the Pacific. **1917** N. Douglas *South Wind* xxii. 271 Those Japanese flowers..those paper flowers, I mean, which we used to put in our finger-bowls... They look like shrivelled specks of cardboard. But in the water they begin..to unfold themselves into unexpected patterns of flowers of all colours. **1968** D. Hopkinson *Incense-Tree* iv. 42 A Japanese flower in a glass of water slowly uncurling to reveal its coloured pattern. **1863** R. Alcock *Capital of Tycoon* I. iv. 103 We ..gained a fine suite of apartments looking on to as beautiful a specimen of Japanese garden..as can well be conceived. **1902** C. H. Townsend in G. Brown *European & Japanese Gardens* 162 The composition of the Japanese garden depends chiefly upon the arrangement of its trees, boulders, paths, streams, bridges and other artificial structures. It is, least of all, a flower garden, and is probably best understood when regarded as a reduced copy of the scenery of a country—conveying the impression produced by a picture. **1912** Mrs. B. Taylor *Japanese Gardens* iv. 53 Seldom does a Japanese garden lack water, or the appearance of water, in its scenery. **1920** W. J. Locke *House of Baltazar* i. 13 The Japanese garden with its pond of great water-lilies and fairy bridge across. **1957** M. G. Sims tr. *Yoshida's Gardens of Japan* i. 7 Much in the Japanese garden is merely symbolical of nature. *Ibid.* 9 The Japanese garden is monochrome, the European polychrome. **1971** S. Eliovson *Gardening the Japanese Way* 26 Another misconception is that Japanese gardens are composed only of sand and stone. **1972** T. Ito (*title*) The Japanese garden—an approach to nature. **1880** L. Higgin *Handbk. Embroidery* i. 8 '*Japanese gold thread*', which has the advantage of never tarnishing, is..made of gilt paper twisted round cotton thread. **1883** W. Robinson *Eng. Flower Garden* 155/2 *I[ris] Kæmpferi* (Japanese Iris). The large number of varieties in cultivation under this name have sprung from *I. lævigata* and *I. setosa.* **1900** L. H. Bailey *Cycl. Amer. Hort.* II. 822/1 There are few handsomer flowers than good forms of the white Japanese Iris. **1936** *Discovery* XVII. 86/2 An iris garden with special emphasis on Japanese Iris. **1895** *Brit. Warehouseman* Feb. 26/1 Japanese lanterns and Kakemonos (wall-pictures) are shown. **1901** *Daily Colonist* (Victoria, B.C.) 2 Oct. 10/2 There, added to the the effect of the bunting drapings and clusters of flags, three long strings of Japanese lanterns stretch from the roof. **1966** G. Baxt *Queer Kind of Death* (1967) xii. 174 The garden will be festooned with Japanese lanterns. **1861** *Gardeners' Chron.* 12 Jan. 23/1 The Japanese larch, *A[bies] leptolepis* of Zuccarini, is represented with cones four times larger than those sent home by Mr. Veitch. **1914** W. J. Bean *Trees & Shrubs Hardy in Brit. Isles* II. 8 The Japanese larch has been almost, although not wholly, immune from the attacks of larch canker. **1957** M. Hadfield *Brit. Trees* 46 In Britain the European and Japanese larches have been planted extensively. **1870** J. C. Patteson *Let.* 21 Dec. in C. M. Yonge *Life J. C. Patteson* (1874) II. xii. 488, I have *such* Japanese lilies making ready to put forth their splendours. **1943** R. Godden *Rungli-Rungliot* 45 What else is there in the garden? Wild coffee flowers, roses, Japanese lilies. **1894** H. O. Forbes *Hand-bk. Primates* II. 14 Nothing is known of the habits of the Japanese Macaque. **1967** J. R. & P. H. Napier *Handbk. Living Primates* 405 Japanese macaque. Yellowish-brown shaggy fur. **1898** W. Robinson *English Flower Garden* (ed. 6) 379/1 The varieties of the Japanese Maple (*A. palmatum*) and its numerous forms..have been found of much interest for the garden. **1904** *Jrnl. R. Hort. Soc.* XXIX. 328 The popularly known 'Japanese Maples' are varieties of the two species *Acer palmatum* and *Acer japonicum.* **1973** C. Lloyd *Foliage Plants* x. 172 The beautiful but slow growing Japanese maple of the golden foliage is the corner piece at the back. **1866** Lindley & Moore *Treas. Bot.* I. 462/1 The Loquat, or Japanese Medlar..is a native of Japan and the southern parts of China. **1950** G. Brenan *Face of Spain* iv. 80 The Japanese medlars with their fish-shaped leaves and thick snake-like branches. **1972** A. F. Simmons *Growing Unusual Fruit* 179 It [*sc.* the loquat] arrived in the Mediterranean area in the nineteenth century, under the name of the Japanese medlar. **1872** *Proc. Zool. Soc.* 780 (*heading*) Observations on the Macaques.—IV. The Japanese Monkey. **1932** S. Zuckerman *Social Life Monkeys* xix. 310 The Japanese monkeys are confined together. **1961–2** *Primates* (Inuyama, Japan) III. II. 3 The Japanese monkey is an endemic species which usually inhabits the thick forests of the mountains which cover the greater part of the Japanese Islands. **1924** L. H. Bailey *Man. Cultivated Plants* 413 Japanese Pagoda-Tree. Round-headed deciduous tree attaining 60 ft., with spreading branches. **1973** *Times* 20 Feb. 16/3 The 152-year-old scholar tree, or Japanese pagoda tree, at Oxford University Botanic Garden is being felled because it is dying. **1727** J. G. Scheuchzer tr. *Kæmpfer's Hist. Japan* II. App. ii. 25 The Japanese paper is very tight and strong, and will bear being twisted into ropes. **1822** F. Shoberl tr. *Titsingh's Illustr. Japan* II. 319 Two hundred and thirty-four different flowers, painted with great truth on thin Japanese paper. **1877** *Trans. Asiatic Soc. Japan* V. 77 The kites are constructed of Japanese paper which is both thin and strong. **1905** F. H. Collins *Author & Printer* 190/2 *Japanese paper*, hand-made in Japan with vellum surface. Used for proofs of etchings and engravings. **1958** J. R. Biggs *Woodcuts* 90 The best Japanese papers are made from the fibres of the mulberry tree. *a* **1963** S. Plath *Ariel* (1965) 59 My head a moon Of Japanese paper. **1861** R. Bentley *Man. Bot.* II. 503 The fruit of *X[anthoxylum] piperitum* is employed by the Chinese and Japanese as a condiment... It is commonly termed in commerce, Japanese Pepper. **1972** Y. Lovelock *Vegetable Bk.* III. 344 The most important among these [members of the genus *Zanthoxylum*] include Chinese pepper (*Z. bungei*) and Japanese pepper (*Z. aromaticum*). *c* **1895** A. Beardsley *Lett.* (1971) 98 All the books I have left behind are at your disposal. Also a set of erotic Japanese prints. *a* **1922** T. S. Eliot *Waste Land Drafts* (1971) 33 line 140 A touch of art is given by the false Japanese print, purchased in Oxford Street. **1972** *Country Life* 5 Oct. 805/1 William Burges was collecting Japanese prints in the 1850s. **1900** L. H. Bailey *Cycl. Amer. Hort.* I. 427/1 Rarer kinds..are grafted in the greenhouse in early spring, on stock of the Japanese or common Quince. **1972** A. F. Simmons *Growing Unusual Fruit* 152 A species known often as *Cydonia sinensis* and classed with the Japanese quince or japonica ..does not, however, belong to the same genus. **1883** W. Robinson *Eng. Flower Garden* 244/1 The palm for hardiness and decorativeness in exposed situations must be given to another Japanese Rose (Rosa rugosa). **1922** T. G. W. Henslow *Rose Encycl.* xiv. 176 The Japanese Rose (*R. Rugosa*). These roses are gaining in popularity every day. **1956** B. Park *Collins Guide to Roses* xi. 196 *R[osa] rugosa.* The Ramanas Rose. The Japanese Rose. The typical form has deep purplish-pink single flowers. **1872** D. G. Rossetti *Let.* 18 Dec. (1967) III. 1108 If you could look in at Hewitt's one day, would you see what Japanese screens he has, and what he wants for them? **1881** C. C. Harrison *Woman's Handiwork* III. 151 A Japanese screen in the house is a liberal education to the follower of art-needlework. **1935** C. Isherwood *Mr. Norris changes Trains* xv. 254 In addition to the etchings and the Japanese screen, Arthur gave her three flasks of perfume. **1973** *Country Life* 22 Nov. 1691 A few delectable painted Japanese screens..averaged about £750 each. **1873** *Young Englishwoman* May 258 How to clean a white Japanese silk, which has got soiled in the wearing. **1895** *Montgomery Ward Catal.* 79/3 Ladies' Japanese Silk Chemisette. [**1863** R. Alcock *Capital of Tycoon* I. xv. 309 First I am to find a pair of well-bred Japanese dogs, 'with eyes like saucers, no nose, the tongue hanging out at the side, too large for the mouth, and white and tan if possible'.] **1880** H. Dalziel *Brit. Dogs* III. 444 At the New York Dog Show..they [*sc.* Japanese pugs] were classed as Japanese spaniels. **1894** R. B. Lee *Hist. & Descr. Mod. Dogs Gt. Brit. & Ireland* (*Non-Sporting Division*) xiii. 302 These little dogs are now called and identified as Japanese spaniels because they are supposed to have originally been brought from Japan. **1948** C. L. B. Hubbard *Dogs in Brit.* 253 The native Japanese spaniel is quite distinct from the Pekingese of China. **1971** F. Hamilton *World Encycl. Dogs* 524 One such rarity is what is known in its country of origin, Japan, as the Chin; in Britain as the Japanese; and in the Americas as the Japanese Spaniel. **1880** L. Higgin *Handbk. Embroidery* v. 51 *Japanese Stitch* is a modification of stem..taking very long stitches, and then bringing the needle back to within a short distance of the first starting-place. **1900** *Knowledge* 1 Dec. 285/1 Japanese tissue paper used by dentists. **1936** *Discovery* May 157/2 Paste a good quality Japanese tissue on to both sides of the document. **1888** C. T. Jacobi *Printers' Vocab.* 68 *Japanese vellum paper*, thick hand-made paper with a vellum surface manufactured in Japan. **1923** H. A. Maddox *Dict. Stationery* 41 *Japanese Vellum*, a stout toned printing or cover paper with smooth surface and of exceptional strength made from long Japanese fibre by natural methods. **1952** J. Carter *ABC for Bk.-Collectors* 109 Japanese vellum is a very costly paper, hand-made in Japan from the inner bark of the mulberry tree. **1902** *Biometrika* II. 101 (*title*) Note on the results of crossing Japanese waltzing mice with European albino races. **1904** [see Waltzing *vbl. sb.* and *ppl. a.*, Waltzer b]. **1943** H. Grüneberg *Genetics Mouse* iv. 50 Most stocks of Japanese waltzing mice are homozygous for it [*sc.* the gene for 'recessive' or piebald spotting]. *Ibid.* 85 Japanese waltzers differ slightly, but significantly, from albino mice in their temperature of choice. **1964** G. Durrell *Menagerie Manor* vii. 141 Rich people who do nothing all day long but revolve from one cocktail party to another, like a set of Japanese waltzing mice. **1859** L. Oliphant *Narr. Earl of Elgin's Mission China & Japan* II. 257 Hitherto the most successful cargo brought to this country from Japan has been one of Japanese wax. Mr. Simmonds..gives the following account of Japan wax:—'Rhus succedanea, the species which furnishes the Japan wax, has long been grown in our greenhouses, having been introduced from China nearly a century ago.' **1951** Japanese wax [see *heneicosane]. **1878** *Proc. Zool. Soc.* 788 Judging from the present specimen the Japanese Wolf, although nearly allied to *Canis lupus*, would seem to be a distinct species, to be recognized by its smaller size and shorter legs. **1968** R. & A. Fiennes *Nat. Hist. Dog* 160 Japanese wolves are very like the common northern wolves, but they are smaller.

Japaneseness (dʒæpănī·znes). [f. Japanese *a.* + -ness.] The quality or state of being Japanese, or of displaying Japanese characteristics.

1965 *New Statesman* 19 Mar. 462/2 There is no point in trying to skirt the sheer Japaneseness of Ozu's film. **1967** D. & E. T. Riesman *Conversations in Japan* 8 The wife being the one to bear the burden of Japaneseness.

Japanesery (dʒæpănī·zəri). [f. Japanese *a.* and *sb.* + -ery, after F. *japonaiserie* (see *japonaiserie).] Japanese characteristics or fashion; also *pl.*, Japanese ornaments, knick-knacks, etc.

1885 *Daily News* 30 Apr. 4/8 The 'Mikado' may even bring in a little agreeable Japanesery. **1894** W. J. Locke *At Gate of Samaria* ix. 103 Cheap Japaneseries that had lent it the suggestion of artistic atmosphere the girl of eighteen had craved. **1906** E. Nesbit *Man & Maid* viii. 179 Bright, picturesque cushions and screens and Japaneseries. **1929** Blunden *Near & Far* Pref., Those, however, who go from England to Japan without succumbing first to Japanesery will find that there is no great gulf

between the old experiences and the new. **1958** *Spectator* 14 Feb. 204/2 One very soon starts longing for a bit of simple Japanesery without all that *obtrusive* local detail.

Japanesey, Japanesy (dʒæpǣnī·zi), *a.* [f. JAPANESE *a.* and *sb.* + -Y[1].] Having or inclining to a Japanese character.

1890 B. H. CHAMBERLAIN *Things Japanese* 144 Criticism is not at all a 'Japanesey' thing. **1891** S. J. DUNCAN *Amer. Girl in London* 55 Her parlour was Japanesy, too, in places. **1901** 'C. HOLLAND' *Mousmé* xxiii. 328 He..has referred to..their figures as '*petite*' and Japanesy. **1923** E. F. WYATT *Invis. Gods* I. ii. 17 The Japanesy shadows of the black scrub pine. **1925** *Glasgow Herald* 8 May 10 High-art, Japanesy tenements. **1941** *Penguin New Writing* X. 23 The stained Japanesey walls. **1971** *Country Life* 16 Dec. 1720/3 A trifle too fussy, too obviously Japanesey?

Japanned, *ppl. a.* Add: **3.** *Japanned leather* (see quot. *a* 1877); *Japanned peacock, peafowl,* the black-winged peafowl, *Pavo cristatus* mut. *nigripennis.*

1814 R. HERON *Jrnl.* in *Proc. Zool. Soc.* (1835) 54 The hens..would not suffer a japanned peacock to touch them. **1851** *Illustr. Catal. Gt. Exhib.* IV. 1252/1 Japanned leather, grained calf-skin for boots and shoes, and trimmings. **1855** J. C. MORTON *Cycl. Agric.* II. 698/2 The Japanned pea-fowl, as it ought to be styled, instead of the *Japan* pea-fowl. *a* **1877** KNIGHT *Dict. Mech.* II. 1211/1 *Japanned leather*, leather treated with several coats of Japan varnish and dried in a stove. **1894** A. NEWTON *Dict. Birds* III. 699 The 'japanned' Peacock, often erroneously named the Japanese or Japan Peacock,..has received the name of *P[avo] nigripennis*, as though it were a distinct species. *Ibid.* 701 The 'japanned' bird is not known to exist anywhere as a wild race.

Japano- (dʒæ·pǣno), used as combining form of JAPANESE, esp. in adjs. meaning 'belonging to Japan (and some other country)'. Also **Ja·panophile,** a lover of Japan or the Japanese.

1904 *Daily Chron.* 10 May 5/2 The Japano-Russian war. **1905** D. SLADEN *Playing Game* II. iii. 185 Under the influence of the Japanophile Jevons. **1906** *Daily Chron.* 21 May 7/5 The Japano-Korean treaty. **1910** *Westm. Gaz.* 3 Feb. 3/1 The Japano-Chinese war of 1894–5. **1973** *Record* (Oxf. Univ. Press) XVIII. 5/1 We..made our way to..Tokyo where TK greeted us in his Japano-Oxford accent and bore us off to the Palace Hotel.

Japlish (dʒæ·pliʃ). [f. JAP(ANESE *sb.* + ENG)LISH *sb.*] A blend of Japanese and English spoken in Japan: either the Japanese language freely interlarded with English expressions or the English language spoken in an unidiomatic way by a Japanese speaker. Also *attrib.* or *adj.*

1960 *N.Y. Times* 25 Dec. 3/5 (*caption*) New traffic nstructions, written in 'Japlish', cause linguistic bewilderment. **1963** *Harper's Mag.* Jan. 54 A great many Japanese speak English nowadays (or at least 'Japlish', as the American colony calls it), and their words are usually understandable. **1966** *Time* 22 July 30 Japanese sometimes sounds like Japlish: *masukomi* for mass communications, *terebi* for TV, *demo* for demonstration and the inevitable baseballisms *pray bollu, storiku* and *hitto.* **1970** *Times* 26 Nov. 12 A word of warning to tourists and others: the Japlish veneer can be deceptive. The Japanese may use more English words, but they still think like Japanese. **1970** *Bull. Inst. Res. Lang. Teaching* (Tokyo) CCXCIII. 13 There are, moreover, hosts of 'Japlish'..words and expressions, such as '*old miss*'..(meaning 'old maid' or 'spinster').

‖ **japonaiserie** (ʒaponẹzri). [Fr.] = * JAPANESERY.

1896 S. R. CROCKETT *Cleg Kelly* xxvii. 195 The little alcove..was cobwebbed with the latest artistic Japonaiseries of the period. **1902** *Westm. Gaz.* 11 Aug. 12/2 His earlier passion for Gothic art had been succeeded by one for *japonaiseries.* **1905** W. STEVENS *Let.* 21 Aug. (1967) 84 The japonaiserie of the pines. **1966** *New Statesman* 8 July 64/2 This..enthralling piece of contemporary *japonaiserie* [*sc.* a film] circles round a gentle young wife.

japonica (dʒăpǫ·nikă). [mod.L., fem. of *japonicus* pertaining to Japan.] A name used for various plants originally native to Japan, esp. formerly the camellia (*C. japonica*); now usually designating a spring-flowering, deciduous shrub of the genus *Chænomeles*, esp. *C. japonica*, the Japanese quince, or its fruit.

1819 KEATS *Let.* 13 Mar. (1931) II. 309, I would put it [*sc.* a globe of gold-fish] before a handsome painted window and shade it all round with myrtles and Japonicas. **1851** H. MELVILLE *Moby Dick* I. xli. 299 Whiteness refiningly enhances beauty,..as in marbles, japonicas, and pearls. **1859** A. VAN BUREN *Jottings of Sojourn in South* 134 That richest and sweetest blossomed of tropical shrubs—the japonica—that never blossoms only in winter. **1910** 'O. HENRY' *Strictly Business* (1917) ix. 91 You put me in mind of a japonica in a window. **1933** A. OSBORN *Shrubs & Trees for Garden* xxxv. 318 *C[ydonia] japonica* (Japanese Quince), of which there are varieties with flowers of many shades of white, yellow, pink and red, is often known as 'Japonica'. **1963** W. BLUNT *Of Flowers & Village* 46 The japonica has had no less than five different names during my lifetime. **1969** *Listener* 9 Jan. 45/2 The Japonica is strangled with convolvulus.

b. The fruit of the Asian plant *Zizyphus jujuba* (*Z. sinensis*); cf. JUJUBE.

1874 LINDLEY & MOORE *Treas. Bot.* II. Suppl. 1308/1 Japonica. A market name for the fruits of *Zizyphus sinensis*, which are occasionally sold in Covent Garden as dessert fruits. **1887** R. BENTLEY *Man. Bot.* (ed. 5) II. 517 Another Japanese species, *Z[izyphus] sinensis*, yields the fruits known as Japonicas.

Hence **japo·nicadom** *U.S.* (see quot. 1860). *Obs.*

1851 A. O. HALL *Manhattaner* 123 The general society of New Orleans is still in a chaotic state, and she has no located, acknowledged empire of Japonicadom. **1860** BARTLETT *Dict. Amer.* (ed. 3), *Japonicadom*, a word invented by N. P. Willis to denote the upper classes of society.

jar, *sb.*[1] Add: **V. 9.** *attrib.* and *Comb.*, as **jar ramming** *Founding* = *jolt ramming* (s.v. *JOLT *sb.* 5).

1909 *Iron Age* LXXXIV. 1165/1 The working foundryman has carried this development, especially as applied to what are known as jolt or jar ramming machines, far beyond what was anticipated. **1912** *Jrnl. Iron & Steel Inst.* LXXXVI. 546 A jar-ramming moulding-machine with a roll-over device, which also lowers the mould away from the pattern, is described. **1934** LAING & ROLFE *Man. Foundry Pract.* v. 102 (*heading*) Jolt- or jarramming.

jar, *sb.*[2] Add: † **2. b.** *Electr.* A unit of capacity (see quot. 1920[1]). *Obs.*

[**1834** W. S. HARRIS in *Rep. Brit. Assoc. Adv. Sci. 1833* 387 The unit of measure consists of a small electrical jar, having a discharging electrometer. **1889** A. W. POYSER *Magn. & Electr.* xiii. 139 Harris's unit jar.—This instrument is used for measuring the charge given to a Leyden jar.] **1920** *Admiralty Handbk. Wireless Telegr.* iii. 68, 1 farad = . . 9 × 10[8] (nine hundred million) 'jars'. *Ibid.*, The jar is a Service unit, and is very useful when dealing with small capacities. *Ibid.* viii. 245 Provide a condenser composed of two elements of 100 jars each. **1932** *Admiralty Handbk. Wireless Telegr. 1931* vi. 338 The low reactance of even minute capacities and the easy shunt paths they provide..may best be realised by giving a comparative table of the reactances of a capacity of 1 jar and an inductance of 100 microhenries at various frequencies.

c. A drink (of beer, etc.). *colloq.*

1925 S. O'CASEY *Juno & Paycock* I, in *Two Plays* 42 *Boyle.* An' now, Mr. Bentham, you'll have to have a wet. *Bentham.* A wet? *Boyle.* A wet—a jar—a boul! **1941** BAKER *Dict. Austral. Slang* 38 *Jar*, a pint or 'handle' of beer. **1961** C. WILLOCK *Death in Covert* i. 8 'Have a jar, Goss,' he said, and poured him at least three fingers of whisky. **1966** P. MOLONEY *Plea for Mersey* 56 Whan lads frae Scotty Road gang far, Untae the boozer for a jar. **1969** V. CANNING *Queen's Pawn* iii. 41 Hot morning. Care for a jar? They keep good beer. **1972** *Observer* 26 Nov. 26/4 The painter, Raymond Piper, took us for a jar at his local. **1973** *New Society* 6 Sept. 563/1 A great place to meet old friends and make new ones, to knock back the jars and sit gossiping into the early hours.

jar (dʒɑːɹ), *v.*[2] [f. JAR *sb.*[2]] *trans.* To preserve (fruit) in a jar; to bottle. Also *transf.*

1747 H. GLASSE *Art of Cookery* xviii. 152 (*heading*) To jar Cherries. **1962** *Guardian* 24 Dec. 4/3 There's no point in jarring it away. You have to buy clothes with anything you get.

‖ **jarabe** (hără·be). Also **jarave.** [Amer. Sp., a. Sp. *jarabe* syrup.] One of several Mexican pair dances in which the man dances the zapateado steps.

1834 A. PIKE *Prose Sk. & Poems* 103 In the jarabes, or singular dances of the fandango, her first partner was always Rafael. **1903** C. LUMHOLTZ *Unknown Mexico* II. xxii. 382 Professional male and female dancers, engaged as special attractions, execute the national dance, *jarave.* **1932** H. CRANE *Let.* 12 Apr. (1965) 408 Someone dances a *jarabe*, a dance that is all vibrant gristle. **1964** *Spectator* 3 Apr. 450/1 The typical dance [of Mexico], the *Jarabe*, slightly Spanish in origin.

jardinière. Add: **2.** *Cookery.* (See quot. 1877). So *jardinière soup*, vegetable soup.

1841 THACKERAY in *Fraser's Mag.* June 723/1 They..served us..Jardinière cutlets (particularly seedy). **1846** A. SOYER *Gastronomic Regenerator* 40 [Sauces.] Jardinière. **1846** C. E. FRANCATELLI *Mod. Cook* 234 Fill the centre of the *entrée* with a *jardiniere* of vegetables. **1877** *Cassell's Dict. Cookery* 338/1 Jardinière.—This is a garnish made of cooked vegetables, which gives its name to the dish with which it is served. Thus, fillet of beef à la jardinière, mutton à la jardinière, goose à la jardinière, simply mean fillet of beef, mutton, and goose served with a garnish à la jardinière. *Ibid.*, Jardinière Soup. **1907** G. A. ESCOFFIER *Guide Mod. Cookery* 357 Prepare the fillet as directed under 'Filet de Bœuf Jardinière'. Set it on a long dish and surround it with a *Macédoine* garnish. The latter comprises the same ingredients as the '*Jardinière*'. *Ibid.* 512 *Sauté* the *suprêmes* in butter. Dish and surround with small heaps of vegetables, arranged very neatly, as explained in the case of the *Jardinière* garnish. **1969** R. & D. DE SOLA *Dict. Cooking* 128/1 Vegetables served in a savory sauce or soup, usually labelled *à la jardinière.*

jargoneer (dʒāɹgəniə·ɹ). [f. JARGON *sb.*[1] + -EER.] One who uses jargon.

1913 A. QUILLER-COUCH *On Art of Writing* (1916) 90 A Jargoneer would have said that 'among the beneficent qualities of sleep its capacity for withdrawing the human consciousness from the contemplation of immediate circumstances may perhaps be accounted not the least remarkable'. **1923** *19th Cent.* Nov. 786 Your true jargoneer must have at least two languages in the same word. **1947** I. BROWN *Say Word* 92 Among the jargoneers of our time..the advertisers of women's garments have a notable place. **1973** *N.Y. Law Jrnl.* 4 Sept. 5/1 Another miserable heritage of Watergate has been the bilge loosed on the public by..psychopathic jargoneers..and belly-achers.

jarlite (yā·ɹləit). *Min.* [f. the name of C. F. *Jarl*, 20th-century Danish mining official: see -ITE[1].] A colourless to greyish-white fluoride of sodium, strontium, and aluminium, $NaSr_3Al_3F_{16}$, found as monoclinic crystals at Ivigtut, Greenland.

1933 R. BØGVAD in *Meddelelser om Grønland* XCII. VIII. 3 The mineral has been named jarlite, after Mr. C. F. Jarl, by whose courtesy I have been enabled to carry out the present investigations. **1949** *Amer. Mineralogist* XXXIV. 386 Jarlite..occurs as colorless, flat crystals about 1 mm. in size, often fused in the shape of a fan and growing with thomsenolite in vugs in the cryolite.

jarool (dʒărū·l). Also **jarul.** [Hind., a. Bengali *jarūl.*] A deciduous tree, *Lagerstrœmia speciosa*, of the family Lythraceæ, which is native to tropical Asia and bears large panicles of purple flowers; also, the wood of this tree.

1850 J. D. HOOKER *Himalayan Jrnls.* (1854) II. xxxi. 327 These forests are frequented by timber-cutters, who fell jarool (*Lagerstrœmia Reginæ*), a magnificent tree with red wood, which, though soft, is durable under water, and therefore in universal use for boat-building. **1889** G. S. BOULGER *Uses of Plants* VII. 188 Among numerous proposed teak substitutes we can..mention..the Jarúl. **1922** J. S. GAMBLE *Man. Indian Timbers* (ed. 2) 373 The Jarúl tree is never likely to be important beyond its use for local requirements. **1962** *Wealth of India* (Council Sci. & Industr. Res. India) VI. 24 Jarul is a constructional timber of considerable commercial importance, particularly in North-East India.

jarovization (yæːrovəizēⁱ·ʃən). Also **iarovization.** [ad. Russ. *yarovizátsiya*: see *VERNALIZATION.] = *VERNALIZATION.

[**1933** WHYTE & HUDSON in *Bull. Imperial Bureau Plant Genetics* No. 9. 3 The Russian word 'Jarovizatzia', referred to in German publications as 'Jarowisation', has here been translated by the latinized equivalent 'vernalization' in consultation with the School of Slavonic Studies, London, and Miss M. V. Cytovich.] **1934** *Biol. Abstr.* VIII. 1655/2 Discussion is given of..the process of vernalization (or iarovization) by means of which an early development of the reproductive phase of many plants..was obtained. **1946** *Nature* 19 Oct. 548/1 Vol. 1, No. 1 [of *Genetica Agraria*] contains papers on such subjects as ..Jarovization of the potato and resistance to rust in wheat.

jas, var. *JAZZ *sb.*

jasbo, var. *JAZZBO.

jasmine. Add: **3. jasmine tea,** tea perfumed with jasmine; also *ellipt.*

1933 N. WALN *House of Exile* I. iii. 44 We finished our meal with..cups of jasmine tea..served without milk or sugar. **1967** V. C. CLINTON-BADDELEY *Death's Bright Dart* 64 Neither Lapsang..nor Jasmine, was what he wanted. **1967** S. KNIGHT *Window on Shanghai* 119 Just broke off to..make myself a cup of jasmine tea which smells delicious. **1972** *Korea Herald* 17 Nov. 5/1 Between sips of jasmine tea they haggle.

jaspé (dʒɑ·spe, ‖ ʒaspe). Also **jaspe.** [Fr., pa. pple. of *jasper* to marble.] Resembling jasper; mottled or variegated.

1851 *Illustr. Catal. Gt. Exhib.* III. 500/2 Printed and embroidered 'jaspé' cashmere. **1908** *Ladies' Field* 24 Oct. 318/1 The Ghiberti damask has a *jaspé* ground. **1923** *Weekly Dispatch* 11 Feb. 16 Harmonising shades of Pink, Blue, Mauve, Brown and Green on Cream, Jaspe, Black or Grey backgrounds. **1931** *Daily Express* 23 Sept. 4/1 New clasp in Imitation Jaspe Shell. **1961** J. I. M. STEWART *Man who won Pools* 36 Crossing the jaspé lino. **1968** J. ARNOLD *Shell Bk. Country Crafts* 274 Products of horn are obtainable in four colours:—a mottled horn called 'Jaspé', [etc.].

jasper (dʒæ·spəɹ), *sb.*[2] *U.S. colloq.* [Male Christian name.] A person, fellow: usu. with contemptuous overtones; *spec.* a rustic simpleton, 'hick'. Also (with capital initial) used as a nickname (see quots. 1929, 1952).

1896 H. M. BLOSSOM *Checkers* x. 229 After supper..I went over to the only shanty in the place that looked like a store, and opened the door. There were a lot of 'Jaspers' sitting around the stove, chewing Tobacco and swapping lies. **1914** 'B. M. BOWER' *Flying U Ranch* 174 Some uh you boys help me rope him—like him and that other jasper over there done to Andy. **1929** T. GORDON *Born to Be* 236 *Zigaboo, Dingo, Jasper*, nicknames for Ethiopians. **1952** GRANVILLE *Dict. Theatr. Terms* 103 *Jasper*, the traditional name for the villain of the piece in melodrama. **1963** 'M. CORRIGAN' *Why do Women — ?* xxiii. 173 If that dark jasper calls on you again, try and keep him here. **1970** *New Yorker* 17 Oct. 40/3 What's with those jaspers?

jasperoid, *a.* Add: (Further example.)

1965 G. J. WILLIAMS *Econ. Geol. N.Z.* xii. 176/1 The lode..lies immediately alongside and to the south-east of a belt of banded jasperoid chert.

B. *sb. Petrol.* A rock in which silica, in the form of fine-grained quartz or chalcedony, has replaced some of the original constituents (usually the carbonate of limestone).

1898 J. E. SPURR in *Monogr. U.S. Geol. Survey* XXXI. 219 He [*sc.* the writer] has become impressed with the widespread occurrence of this variety of quartz, which arises from the replacement of some original rock, ordinarily limestone or dolomite, by silica from circulating waters; and there seems to be need of some term which may specifically indicate it. For this use the word 'jasperoid' is suggested. Jasperoid may then be defined as a rock consisting essentially of cryptocrystalline, chalcedonic, or phenocrystalline silica, which has formed by the replacement of some other material, ordinarily calcite or dolomite. **1928** W. LINDGREN *Mineral Deposits* (ed. 3) xiii. 207 Silicification of limestone, argillaceous shale and rhyolite is..a very common process taking place frequently with preservation of texture. The quartz will usually be fine-grained. Silicified limestones are called jasperoids. **1944** *Proc. Prehist. Soc.* X. 12 The cherts and jasperoids probably came from the conglomerates at Bankrom. **1968** *Prof. Papers U.S. Geol. Survey* No. 600-B. 112/1 Sixty-eight samples of jasperoid associated with base- and precious-metal ore deposits in 25 western mining districts..were analysed for gold.

jass, var. *JAZZ *sb.*

jassid (dʒæ·sid), *a.* and *sb.* [f. mod.L. family name *Jassidæ* f. the generic name *Iassus* (*Jassus*) (J. C. Fabricius *Systema Rhyngotorum* (1803) 85), f. L. *Iāsus* a town in Asia Minor.] **A.** *adj.* Of or pertaining to a homopterous insect of the family Jassidæ, sometimes considered equivalent to the Cicadellidæ, and including several pests of cereals, fodder crops, etc. **B.** *sb.* A leaf-hopper, a small, jumping insect of this kind, which attacks the leaves of plants.

1892 *Trans. Amer. Entomol. Soc.* XIX. 307 Mr. Howard Ewarts Weed..has brought to light many new and interesting members of the little-known Jassid fauna of the 'Mississippi Bottoms'. **1895** *Insect Life* VII. 323 The half-clothed jassid (*Eutettix seminudus* Say) was often taken on the stalk of the cotton, and was observed to feed upon the juices of the plant. **1918** *Agric. Gaz. New South Wales* 568 (*title*) The apple-leaf Jassid (*Empoasca australis*). **1926** *Proc. U.S. Nat. Museum* LXVIII. 1 (*title*) Revision of the American leaf hoppers of the Jassid genus *Typhlocybe.* **1956** *Nature* 11 Feb. 282/2 The influence of sprayed areas in reducing populations of jassids infesting adjacent unsprayed cotton was elucidated recently.

Jat[1] (dʒāt). Also 7 **Jett, Jutt,** 8 **Jaut.** [Hindi *Jāṭ.*] A member of an Indian tribe settled in the Punjab, Sind, and North-West Provinces. Also *attrib.*

1622 in W. Foster *Eng. Factories India 1622–3* (1908) 90 [There] goeth with the carts 27 Jutts, etc. for their safer passadge. *Ibid.* 111 A Jett whome some tymes you have [app]roved off for trusty. **1787** C. HAMILTON *Hist. Relation of Rohilla Afgans in N. Provinces of Hindostan* 104 By similar means he procured the assistance of Soorâj Mull with a number of Jâts. **1797** *Encycl. Brit.* VIII. 529/1 The Jauts, or Jats. **1845** *Encycl. Metrop.* XXIII. 781/2 The Ják'har, Shiyág'hs and Punyás..are all of Jat origin. **1880** *Encycl. Brit.* XIII. 597/2 Early Jat settlements on the shores of the Persian gulf. **1901** *North Amer. Rev.* Feb. 301 The Jats are the most important people in the Punjab. **1946** J. H. HUTTON *Caste in India* I. iv. 33 The Jats who form perhaps the most important element in the population of the Punjab may be either Hindu or Sikh or Muslim, though..the typical Punjab Jat is probably a Sikh. The Jat is a typical yeoman, devoted to agriculture and..takes a lower social level than the Rajput. *Ibid.* 34 The Sikh of Rajput or Jat origin. **1956** SINGH & SETI in Aiyappan & Ratnam *Soc. in India* xxii. 241 The Sardars.. have been converted from the higher castes of Hindus and Jats. **1964** A. SWINSON *Six Minutes to Sunset* iii. 49 Some retired Jat and Sikh police officers. **1972** *Nat. Geographic* Oct. 535/1 Each of the three basic divisions of the Sikhs—Jats, non-Jats, and untouchables—lives behind boundaries that the others cross with difficulty.

jat[2] (dʒāt). Also **jāt, jāti.** [Hind. *jāt.*] A caste, tribe, sect.

[**1855** H. H. WILSON *Gloss. Judicial & Revenue Terms* 234 *Ját,* H., and in most dialects; corruptly, *Jaut...* Caste, clan, tribe, occupation, kind, sort.] **1873** E. BALFOUR *Cycl. India* (ed. 2) III. 151/2 *Jat* or Jet or Jut or Zat, pronounced thus variously in different parts of India, means a race, a tribe, a clan, a manner, a kind. **1894** M. DYAN *All in Man's Keeping* I. i. 5 Are they not all one jât or caste? **1909** M. DIVER *Candles in Wind* viii. 80 She's another 'jāt' [*note,* class] from us altogether. **1931** N. K. DUTT *Orig. & Growth Caste in India* i. 6 Many castes or jatis were produced by a series of crosses..between members of the four varnas. **1960** A. C. MAYER *Caste & Kinship in Cent. India* III. viii. 152 *Jat,* the general word for species, is the most commonly used term for 'caste'... You ask a man..'what is your *jat*'. **1971** *Illustr. Weekly India* 4 Apr. 11/3 Besides, they have helped in removing a number of malpractices in the community like child marriage, polygamy and in settling *Jati* disputes.

jat' (yat^y), *sb.*[3] Also **ěti, iet, jat, jet', yat,** etc. [ad. OSl. *jatĭ*; cf. quot. 1964.] The name of the characters Ⱑ and ѣ of the Slavonic Glagolitic and Cyrillic alphabets; the sound represented by these characters, or the Common Slavonic sound from which it developed.

1763 W. MASSEY *Origin & Progress of Letters* (*tables facing* 114) Yat..iet. **1883** I. TAYLOR *Alphabet* II. 196 (*table*) Yet. **1887** M. GASTER *Ilchester Lectures on Greeko-Slavonic Lit.* 214 (*table*) ěti. **1950** *Slavistična Revija* III. 257 In both alphabets *jat'* as a letter is distinct from the other vowel-symbols. **1955** R. JAKOBSON *Slavic Languages* (ed. 2) 14, *ě* (called *jat'*, the reflex of *ē* and *oi*). **1964** M. SAMILOV *Phoneme jat' in Slavic* 11 One of the main reasons for disagreement is the extreme diversity of the reflexes of *jat'* (as the Glagolitic and Cyrillic letter for the sound **ě* has been called)... The old name for the Glagolitic Ⱑ and Cyrillic ѣ seems to have been *ědĭ* or *jadĭ* 'food'. **1965** G. Y. SHEVELOV *Prehist. of Slavic* xi. 164 Long *eᵃ* has traditionally been denoted in Slavistics by *ě* (and known as *jat'*).

Jataka (dʒā·tăkă). [Skr. *jātaka* engendered by, born under, f. *jātá,* pa. pple. of *jan* to produce.] In Buddhist literature, a story of one or other of the former births of the Buddha; also, the name of the Pāli collection of these stories. Also *attrib.*

1828 *Asiatic Researches* XVI. 427 *Játaka,* treat of the actions of former births. **1861** V. FAUSBÖLL *Five Játakas* Pref., We.., in the Játaka, meet with some of the Comical stories that are well known all over Europe under different names. **1876** *Encycl. Brit.* IV. 430/1 Jātaka stories..containing..the oldest known versions of many of the nursery songs, and fairy tales, and comic stories, and fables, which are the common property of Europe in the present day. **1876** J. FERGUSSON *Hist. Indian & Eastern Archit.* I. 88 Bas-reliefs..representing some scene or legend of the time, and..inscribed..with the title of the jataka or legend. **1951** G. DE *Significance of Jātakas* p. xii, Prof. Rhys Davids..has observed..that a typical Jātaka is one which has..an introductory episode,..the story of the past being the Jātaka proper in prose. **1956** M. WICKRAMASINGHE *Buddhist Jataka Stories & Russ. Novel* p. ix, The linguistic, religious and sociological aspects of the Jataka Stories have attracted the attention of Western Orientalists. *Ibid.* i. 3 There are two kinds of narratives in the Jataka Book.

jatha (dʒā·tă). *India.* Also **jathā.** [Hind. *jathá.*] An armed or organized band, *spec.* of Sikhs.

1922 *Glasgow Herald* 9 Sept. 9 There is no waning in Sikh fanaticism, and organised jathas, or companies, come forward increasingly. A jatha of Sikh women wearing daggers has been formed. **1924** *Ibid.* 31 Mar. 11 A continuous procession of martyr jathas from Amritsar to Jaito. **1964** H. SINGH *Heritage of Sikhs* xviii. 156 A Jatha of 150 Sikhs came to make obeisance at the Gurdwara. **1964** A. SWINSON *Six Minutes to Sunset* x. 181 The Sikh leaders [in 1947] sat at the feet of Master Tara Singh and listened as he roused them to violence. His plan was to form murder gangs known as *jathas.* **1966** K. SINGH *Hist. Sikhs* II. IV. xiii. 203 *Jathās* of 100 Akalis each were formed. They first took an oath..to remain non-violent.

jati, jâti (dʒā·ti). [Skr. *jāti.*] (See quots.)

1891 C. R. DAY *Mus. & Mus. Instruments S. India* iii. 36 The different degrees of time are termed Tâlas, of which there are seven, each being sub-divided into five 'jâtis', or kinds; so that there are in use no less than thirty-five distinct measures. **1914** A. H. F. STRANGWAYS *Mus. Hindostan* iv. 112 There are seven modes (*mūrchaṇā*) of each of the two *grāmas,* i.e. fourteen in all; but only seven of these fourteen are in practical use under the name of *jātis,* species. **1967** SINGHA & MASSEY *Indian Dances* ii. 42 The adavus are combined in the tirmanas with complex rhythm patterns known as *jatis.* Jatis are a combination of long and short syllables. **1968** A. DANIÉLOU *Rāga-s of N. Indian Mus.* ii. 55 The classes obtained by grouping the modes according to the number of their notes are sometimes known as *jāti-s.*

jāti, var. *DJATI, *JAT[2].

jato (dʒēi·to). *Aeronaut.* orig. *U.S.* Also **Jato, JATO.** [f. the initial letters of *jet-assisted take-off.*] **a.** A take-off assisted by a jato unit. **b.** An auxiliary, usually detachable, unit of one or more jet engines (usually rockets) for providing temporary extra thrust when an aircraft takes off. Usu. *attrib.,* esp. in *jato unit.*

1944 *Sci. News Let.* 7 Oct. 229/3 Of particular value on the restricted area of carrier flight decks, JATO, as jet-assisted take-offs are known in the Navy, will also be extremely useful for lifting heavily-laden flying boats from the water. **1950** J. V. CASAMASSA *Jet Aircraft Power Syst.* v. 94 The application of the 1,000-lb thrust of a single JATO rocket motor to an aircraft traveling at a take-off speed of 115 mph at sea level is equivalent to an additional 395 engine-brake-horsepower for the duration of the thrust. **1951** COGGINS & PRATT *Rockets, Jets, Guided Missiles & Space Ships* iv. 35/1 When the Jato unit burned out the pilot could push a release lever and drop the empty cylinder. *Ibid.* 35/2 Jatos were being used to help Navy fighters go almost straight up into the air. **1962** F. I. ORDWAY et al. *Basic Astronautics* ii. 21 During World War II he worked for the U.S. Navy on propellant pumps, jatos, and liquid propelled engines. **1965** C. N. VAN DEVENTER *Introd. Gen. Aeronaut.* vi. 125/1 JATO (jet-assisted takeoff) is sometimes used to accelerate to the required flying speed. **1967** *Propulsion* (Amat. Rocket Assoc. U.S.) ii. 39 Jato units permit aircraft to take off with a heavier payload or to utilize unusually short airfields. **1973** W. T. GUNSTON *Bombers of West* i. 36 We flew an F-80 jet at Muroc.., and with it also experienced JATO take-offs.

jatoba (dʒatŏbā·). [Tupi.] = COURBARIL.

1890 BILLINGS *Med. Dict.* I. 726/1 *Jatoba,* resin of *Hymenæa courbaril.* **1933** P. FLEMING *Brazilian Adv.* II. ii. 191 We landed on a beach strewn with *jatobá* nuts, of which we subsequently made a dish as nauseous as any I have ever tasted.

jaul, var. *JOL.

jaundy, var. *JAUNTY *sb.*

jaune, *a.* Add: **b.** In the names of pigments: *jaune brill(i)ant,* cadmium yellow (alone or in a mixture with white lead); *jaune jonquille* (see quot. 1960).

1851 H. WATTS tr. *Gmelin's Hand-bk. Chem.* V. 57 Sulphide of Cadmium.—Found native in the form of Greenockite. Prepared as a pigment known by the name of *Jaune brillant.* **1895** *Montgomery Ward Catal.* 252/3 Artists tube oil colours...Jaune Brilliant. **1910** B. RACKHAM *Bk. of Porc.* iv. 56 On a ground of yellow (*jaune jonquille*) are rococo-bordered panels. **1924** F. W. WEBER *Artists' Pigments* 30 Mixtures of Cadmium Yellow and Lead White are offered under the name *Jaune Brilliant.* **1948** KIRK & OTHMER *Encycl. Chem. Technol.* II. 736 Cadmium sulfide (cadmium yellow, jaune brillant). **1960** R. G. HAGGAR *Conc. Encycl. Cont. Pott. & Porc.* 234/2 *Jaune jonquille,* a yellow ground colour introduced at Sèvres in 1753. It is of great intensity and beauty and somewhat different from the shade of yellow employed at Meissen.

Jaune Desprez (ʒōn deprɛ). The name of Monsieur *Desprez,* nineteenth-century French horticulturist, used to designate a variety of yellow climbing rose developed by him about 1830.

1837 T. RIVERS *Rose Amateur's Guide* 82 Jaune Desprez, or the new French Yellow Noisette, is a well-known and much esteemed rose... This was originated by M. Desprez about seven years since. **1867** H. KINGSLEY *Silcote of Silcotes* I. x. 93 Clinging to the house itself, hung the deep dark porch..with festoons of Jaune d'Esprez, and Dundee Rambler. **1869** S. R. HOLE *Bk. about Roses* ix. 134 Jaune Desprez, Noisette.—Phoebus, what a name!..Yellow Desprez, moreover, is not yellow, but buff or fawn colour, deliciously fragrant. **1955** C. C. HURST in G. S. Thomas *Old Shrub Roses* ix. 82 In 1830 'Lamarque' and 'Jaune Desprez' appeared...yellowish Noisettes which, selfed, gave Yellow Climbing Teas.

jaunty (dʒǭ·nti), *sb. Naut. slang.* Also **jaundy, jonty.** [Said to be a sailor's corruption of GENDARME.] The master-at-arms on board ship.

1902 KIPLING *Traffics & Discov.* (1904) 197 The other jaunty is now pursuin' us on his lily feet. **1903** 'L. YEXLEY' *Grog Time Yarns* 3 The Chief of the Police—the Master-at-Arms—is always referred to as the 'Jonty'. **1909** J. R. WARE *Passing Eng.* 159/2 *Jaundy,* master-at-arms. **1927** *Blackw. Mag.* Oct. 457/1 Mounting the rope ladder in that awful sea..proved a bit of a task to the unaccustomed Jonties. **1928** *Weekly Dispatch* 27 May 14 The sailor spun a yarn that would make the hardest-hearted jonty (master-at-arms) weep.

Java. Add: **Java ape-man** = **Java man* (below); **Java canvas,** a loosely-woven linen cloth with an even mesh used in embroidery; **Java man,** the fossil hominid, *Homo erectus* (formerly *Pithecanthropus erectus*) whose remains were first found by E. Dubois in Java in 1891; cf. PITHECANTHROPE b.

1931 STUBBS & BLIGH *Sixty Centuries Health & Physick* 3 Pithecanthropus, the Java ape-man. **1872** *Omen* 26 Oct. 342/2 Antimacassar (Java canvas). **1878** *Cassell's Family Mag.* 494/2 The materials used for these curtains are many—velvet, .., Java canvass, .. and serges. **1882** CAULFEILD & SAWARD *Dict. Needlework* 278/1 *Java canvas,* a close make of canvas, having an appearance of being plaited, and made in many sizes and degrees of fineness. *Ibid., Java canvas work,* this Embroidery is named from the material upon which it is worked and is used for mats, work cases, music cases. **1932** D. C. MINTER *Mod. Needlecraft* 246 Two 4″ squares of Java canvas. [**1896** E. DUBOIS in *Nature* 16 Jan. 247/1, I could find no place for the fossil Javanese form, which I consider as intermediate between Man and the Anthropoid apes.] **1911** A. KEITH *Anc. Types of Man* xiv. 136 One is compelled to believe that the human brain had attained a greater size than that of the Java man at the end of the Pliocene Period. **1945** *Anthropol. Papers Amer. Mus. Nat. Hist.* XL. 62/2 Considering..the complexity of the problem of Java man..I deem it best to put aside the Sangiran Mandible of 1939 for the present. **1965** M. H. DAY *Guide to Fossil Man* 224 The features of this femur.. suggest strongly that Java man was capable of standing and walking erectly.

b. *ellipt.* Coffee from Java; also (*slang*) any sort of coffee.

1850 L. H. GARRARD *Wah-to-Yah* xiii. 169 Partaking of the nectar-like Java. **1926** J. BLACK *You can't Win* vi. 67 We went back to the fire and discussed breakfast. 'Nothing but Java,' said the bum that had the coffee. **1945** G. MILLAR *Maquis* ii. 29 Later on, to wake you up a bit.., we'll give you a nice cup of Java, strong and hot. **1956** H. GOLD *Man who was not with It* (1965) xxv. 235 Lots a guys come in for chatter and java, friend.

javaite (dʒā·vă,əit). *Geol.* [f. JAVA + -ITE[1], rendering Du. *javaniet* (see etym. of *JAVANITE).] Any tektite from the tektite field of Java.

1938 *Mineral. Abstr.* VII. 78 The tektites ('javaites') from Solo in central Java..have the form of balls or

drops. **1961** *Sci. Amer.* Nov. 63/1 Those [tektites] from Java, Indo-China and the Philippines are designated javaites, indochinites and philippinites respectively. **1964** *Geochim. & Cosmochim. Acta* XXVIII. 761 Rhenium and osmium abundances have been determined in two australites, two javaites, one philippinite, two indochinites, two moldavites and one bediasite.

Javan, *a.* and *sb.* (Further examples.)

1817 [see *BANTENG, BANTING]. **1892** in G. T. Wrench *Restoration of Peasantries* (1939) v. 59 The Javans have escaped the fatal gift of proprietary right which has been the ruin of so many tens of thousands of our peasantry in India. **1893** W. B. WORSFOLD *Visit to Java* x. 172 The average size of the Javan coffee plantation is from 400 to 500 acres. **1910** *Encycl. Brit.* VII. 795/2 The Javans are perhaps unique in their distinct and graceful gestures of the hands and fingers [in dancing]. **1939** G. T. WRENCH *Restoration of Peasantries* v. 58 They [*sc.* the Dutch] made no effort to impose the methods of their civilization upon the Javans for their good. *Ibid.*, They stood aside from indifference and lack of interest in their Javan subjects. **1962** *Times* 20 Dec. 9/6 Some such as..the Javan Rhinoceros are on the verge of extinction. **1964** R. PERRY *World of Tiger* xiii. 192 The reputations of some Javan tigers as man-eaters have served to scare poachers away from the haunts of the lesser one-horned rhino. **1965** R. MCKIE *Company of Animals* xiii. 184 Two species of rhinoceros..have lived in the jungles of Malaya for thousands of years. One, known as the Javan, has one horn on its snout. **1966** C. A. W. GUGGISBERG *S.O.S. Rhino* v. 125 The 300 to 400 bantengs (*Bibos javanicus*) and the numerous Javan deer (*Rusa timorensis*)..frequent the more open parts of the reserve.

‖ **javanais** (ʒavanɛ). [Fr.] A form of French *argot* or slang in which *av* or *va* is introduced after each syllable of a word.

1925 P. RADIN tr. *Vendryes's Lang.* 255 French children often employ *javanais* in the school. **1939** L. H. GRAY *Foundations of Lang.* 31 The relatively recent French *loucherbème* and *javanais*.

Javanese, *a.* and *sb.* Add: Now normally with pronunc. (dʒæv-). (Further examples.)

1836 N. WISEMAN *Twelve Lect. Sci. & Revealed Relig.* I. i. 47 Among these languages [*sc.* the vernacular Indo-Chinese languages on the continent] he [*sc.* J. Leyden] reckons the Bugis, Javanese, Malayu,..and others. *Ibid.* 48 Javanese..is peculiarly deficient in grammatical forms. **1847** F. A. KEMBLE *Let.* 23 June in *Rec. Later Life* (1882) III. 204 Patagonians, Javanese, from the Cordilleras, from Peru..—the flower tribes of the whole earth. **1869** *Month* June 612 Javanese servants and porters. **1933** [see *FORMOSAN *a.* and *sb.*]. **1961** P. KEMP *Alms for Oblivion* v. 85 The peoples of Indonesia, many of whom differed widely in language, religion and culture from the Moslem Javanese. *Ibid.* 86 The full fury of Javanese chauvinism was reserved for the Eurasians. **1964** R. PERRY *World of Tiger* ii. 26 A Javanese tiger..carried off a girl. **1969** *Word* XXV. 323 All masculine names are either first names (in Javanese terminology *nama alit*, little names) or second names. **1973** D. MAY *Laughter in Djakarta* i. 7 He peered into the warm Javanese night from the betjak—the bicycle rickshaw—in which he was riding. *Ibid.* 18 The other, Subekto, evidently a Javanese like Sumitro, laughed softly.

javanicin (dʒāvæ·nisin, dʒāvănəi·sin). *Pharm.* [f. mod.L. *javanic-um* (f. JAVA), specific epithet (see def.) + -IN[1].] A red, crystalline, bicyclic compound, $C_{15}H_{14}O_6$, isolated from the fungus *Fusarium javanicum* and having antibacterial properties.

1946 H. R. V. ARNSTEIN et al. in *Nature* 16 Mar. 333/2 One pigment formed red laths with a coppery lustre, m.p. 208° (decomp.)... It had the molecular formula $C_{15}H_{14}O_6$, and as it does not seem to have been encountered before, the name 'javanicin' is proposed for it. **1949** ABRAHAM & FLOREY in H. W. Florey et al. *Antibiotics* I. vii. 306 Germination of lettuce seeds was entirely suppressed by a concentration of 1 in 20,000 of javanicin. **1967** E. PARYSKI tr. *T. Korzybski's Antibiotics* II. iii. 1320 Gram-negative micro-organisms..are very slightly sensitive to javanicin.

javanite (dʒā·vănəit). *Geol.* [f. JAVAN *a.* and *sb.* + -ITE[1]; before coining the word in Eng. von Koenigswald had previously coined its Du. equivalent, *javaniet*, in *Natuurkundig Tijdschrift voor Nederlandsch-Indië* (1936) XCVI. 285.] = *JAVAITE.

1957 G. H. R. VON KOENIGSWALD in *Proc. Kon. Nederl. Akad. van Wetensch.* B. LX. 371 Here for the first time we will give a survey of the types we can distinguish among the javanese tektites, for which the name 'Javanites' is proposed. *Ibid.* 380 The Javanites (nom. nov.) from Java. **1963** J. A. O'KEEFE *Tektites* i. 1 Accepted varieties [of tektites] are..javanites from Java. **1964** *Geochim. & Cosmochim. Acta* XXVIII. 793 Forty-two tektites and two 'amerikanites' were..analysed for major elements. Included were 7 moldavites, 1 bediasite, 2 javanites, 15 philippinites, 12 indochinites and 5 australites.

javelin, *sb.* Add: **4. javelin-throwing,** the throwing of a javelin as an athletic field event; also *ellipt.* as *javelin.*

1902 *Daily Chron.* 7 Apr. 3/1 Professors in a university to teach javelin-throwing. **1906** *Westm. Gaz.* 3 May 10/2 Very pretty was the javelin-throwing, the long thin spear being launched high into the air. **1958** *Times* 20 Aug. 2/6 Mrs. Zatopkova..won the women's javelin with a new European record of 183 ft. 9½ in. **1964** J. J. WALSH *Understanding Paraplegia* xix. 128 Throwing and catching a medicine ball, javelin-throwing, and shot-putting, were all of use. **1974** *Country Life* 14 Feb. 292/1 The big breakthrough..came from young Charles Clover in the javelin as he threw 278 ft 7¼ in.

Javelle (ʒave·l). Also **Javel, javelle.** [ad. *Javel*, name of the village near (now a suburb of) Paris where the solution was first made as a bleach.] *eau de Javelle* (also *water of Javelle, Javelle('s) water*): an aqueous solution containing potassium hypochlorite and used as a bleach or a disinfectant; also applied to a similar solution of sodium hypochlorite, which has largely replaced it in modern use. Cf. *LABARRAQUE.

1807 J. A. CHAPTAL *Chem. Arts & Manuf.* III. v. 98 What is known at Paris by the name of *eau de javelle*, is oxy-muriatic acid, combined with an alkali. It is used for taking out the stains of fruit, &c. from linen. **1815** S. PARKES *Chem. Ess.* IV. xii. 57 Some manufacturers at Javelle near Paris announced..that they had discovered a particular liquor which they called the Lye of Javelle, having the property of bleaching cloth by a few hours immersion. This composition..was found to be..a solution of the oxy-muriate of potash. *Ibid.* 61 The manufacturers of Javelle,..having been disappointed in their commercial prospects at home, came over to England, and settled at Liverpool for the purpose of manufacturing the solution of oxy-muriate of potash, which they proposed to sell to the English bleachers in bottles, and which they still denominated the Liquor de Javelle. **1875** *Ure's Dict. Arts* (ed. 7) I. 787 When a weak solution of caustic potash or soda is saturated with chlorine, it affords a bleaching liquor, still used by some bleachers and calico-printers for delicate processes. The chloride of potash is known as Water of Javelle, and the chloride of soda as Labarraque's Liquor... These so-called chlorides are now generally considered to be mixtures or compounds of chlorides and hypochlorites. **1888** J. P. REMINGTON *Pract. Pharmacy* xxxii. 422 Solution of chlorinated soda.. is sometimes substituted for *Eau de Javelle* (Javelle's water), a French preparation made with potassium carbonate instead of sodium carbonate. **1892** A. BROTHERS *Photogr.* iv. 260 As a reducing agent for negatives which are too dense and for removing the last traces of sodium thiosulphate, the following solution, which forms *eau de javelle*, may be used:—Chloride of lime 2 ounces. Potassium carbonate 4 ounces. Water 40 ounces. **1928** *Daily Express* 19 Dec. 5 Javelle water, made by dissolving half a pound of washing soda in a quart of cold water, adding four ounces of bleaching powder. **1951** A. GROLLMAN *Pharmacol. & Therapeutics* xxv. 517 Compounds which give off chlorine have long been used as disinfectants, e.g., potassium hypochlorite (Javelle water), alkaline sodium hypochlorite (Labarraque's solution). **1958** L. DURRELL *Balthazar* vi. 117 It's all right..and smells fashionably of armpits and *eau de javel.* **1967** *Martindale's Extra Pharmacopoeia* (ed. 25) 314/2 Eau de Javel (Fr[ench] P[harmacopoeia]) is a concentrated solution of sodium hypochlorite. **1969** B. WEIL *Dossier IX* iii. 22 The bathroom with shower, redolent of *Eau de Javel.*

jaw, *sb.*[1] Add: **1. b.** The parts of certain invertebrates used for the ingestion of food.

1870 H. A. NICHOLSON *Man. Zool.* 163 The Medicinal Leech (*Sanguisuga officinalis*)..has its mouth furnished with three crescentic jaws. **1877** T. H. HUXLEY *Man. Anat. Invertebr. Animals* i. 56 In the Arthropoda, what are usually termed jaws are modified limbs. **1902** *Encycl. Brit.* XXV. 696/1 The jaws of Peripatus are formed by the axis or corm itself. **1932** BORRADAILE & POTTS *Invertebrata* xviii. 567 The lantern [of echinoids] consists of five composite jaws, each clasping a tooth. **1971** J. E. SMITH et al. *Invertebr. Panorama* iv. 55 The gut [of leeches] has a muscularized blood-sucking pharynx often armed with piercing jaws.

6. (Further examples.) Also, a long talk, incessant chatter.

1842 F. J. FURNIVALL in *F. J. Furnivall: Personal Rec.* (1911) p. xi, Had a jaw with Young, which ended, as it began, in nothing. **1846** *Swell's Night Guide* 123/1 *Jaw*, abusive language. **1861** D. G. ROSSETTI *Lett.* (1965) II. 387 We would go to a theatre afterwards or else have a jaw here. **1916** G. B. SHAW *Pygmalion* I. 115 Come with me now and lets have a jaw over some supper. **1964** *Guardian* 2 Mar. 7/6 So before the show starts the promoter gives me a bit of a jaw. **1968** J. R. ACKERLEY *My Father & Myself* viii. 79 He invited the two of us into the billiard-room of Grafton House..for a 'jaw'. **1972** *Times Lit. Suppl.* 14 Apr. 420/3 Without these things, committee work is just endless jaw and empty substitute.

7. *jaw-line, -muscle, -opening*; **jaw clutch,** a claw clutch or a dog clutch; **jaw-jerk** *Med.*, a jerk (JERK *sb.*[1] 2 b (*a*)) of the lower jaw elicited by a downward blow on it when the mouth is open; **jaw-piece,** read: † (*a*) = JOWPY, JOPY; (*b*) (see quot. 1886); **jaw-process** = *GNATHOBASE; **jaw-smith, jawsmith** *U.S. slang*, a talkative person; esp. a loud-mouthed demagogue.

1893 LANGMAID & GAISFORD *Elem. Less. Steam Machinery* vi. 62 A common form of this fitting is the jaw clutch. **1907** Jaw clutch [see *change-speed* (*CHANGE *sb.* 12 a)]. **1911** *Encycl. Brit.* XVIII. 927/1 A clutch of this description can be made to engage without difficulty, there being no fixed positions or steps such as one associates with the ordinary jaw-clutch. **1936** W. STANIAR *Mech. Power Transmission Handbk.* vii. 267 Jaw Clutches.—This type of clutch is employed for moderate and heavy rough driving... It consists of a square or spiral jaw portion which is keyed to the driving shaft and a sleeve portion equipped with square or spiral jaws into which the driving portion can be engaged. With this type of clutch..the pick-up is instantaneous, resulting therefore in shock. **1966** *McGraw-Hill Encycl. Sci. & Technol.* III. 224/1 Although square jaw clutches are the strongest and most elementary to construct, the difficulty of engagement limits their use... A modification..to permit more convenient engagement and to provide a more gradual movement of the mating faces toward each other produces the spiral jaw clutch. **1886** A. DE WATTEVILLE in *Brain* VIII. 518 It does not appear to be generally known that a 'jaw-jerk' can be readily elicited... The phenomenon is clearly of the same nature as that of the 'knee-jerk', and is due to the sudden stretching of the masseter and other muscles of mastication. Hence the name I have ventured to give to it, in preference to the longer and less accurate term mandibular (or masseteric) tendon-reaction (or reflex). **1968** PASSMORE & ROBSON *Compan. Med. Stud.* I. xxiv. 12/2 This jerk [*sc.* the knee jerk] is one of a whole family of tendon jerks... They include the Achilles tendon or ankle jerk..the biceps and triceps jerks.., and the masseter-temporalis or jaw jerk. **1936** J. CURTIS *Gilt Kid* xiv. 144 Perhaps his jaw-line was a little tenser. **1971** *Chatelaine* Aug. 41/2 Tweezing stragglers over nose bridge and applying tawny blusher from brows to jawline livened her skin and slimmed her face. **1890** W. JAMES *Princ. Psychol.* I. x. 301 In *effort* of any sort, contractions of the jaw-muscles and of those of respiration are added to those of the brow and glottis. **1929** W. FAULKNER *Sound & Fury* 140 My jaw-muscles getting numb. **1958** E. FISCHER-JØRGENSEN in Saporta & Bastian *Psycholinguistics* (1961) 131/2 Slow jaw-opening might rather be combined with a fortis–lenis difference. **1886** WILLIS & CLARK *Archit. Hist. Univ. Cambr.* I. 283 A 'jaw-piece' or triangular piece of wood.. interposed between [the principal] itself and the spars forming the roof. **1881** Jaw process [see *GNATHOBASE]. **1902** *Encycl. Brit.* XXV. 697/1 The usual uni-ramose limb found in the various classes of Arthropoda..varies as to the presence or absence of the jaw-process. **1887** *Chicago Tribune* 13 May 5/2 George Schilling, Socialist and jawsmith. **1910** Jawsmith [see *HOT AIR 2]. **1942** BERREY & VAN DEN BARK *Amer. Thes. Slang* § 422 Talker,..*jawsmith* (esp. a public speaker).

‖ **jawan** (dʒăwā·n). Also **juwan.** [a. Urdu *jawān.*] An Indian soldier.

1839 M. TAYLOR *Confessions of Thug* I. i. 6 Chumpa was busy cooking and the Juwans were all out of the way. **1923** *Blackw. Mag.* July 22/1 The cool deliberately-aimed fire of the jawans lashed them each time. **1962** *Listener* 29 Nov. 895/2 For the public, the cult of the Indian soldier, the Jawan, remains unshaken. **1965** P. ROBINSON *Pakistani Agent* i. 9 A *jawan* in a dark-green uniform.. was resting upright against the wall of the cargo shed, with his rifle propped up next to him. **1969** *Amrita Bazar Patrika* 5 Aug. 1/1 Ten persons, including five Security Force personnel, were killed and three jawans were wounded in two incidents of ambush in far-flung areas of the State in the last 48 hours. **1971** *Sunday Times* 13 June 12/2 One of the *jawans* (privates) crouched in the back of the Toyota Land Cruiser called out sharply: 'There's a man running, Sahib.'

jawbation: see JOBATION (in Dict. and Suppl.).

jaw-bone, jawbone. Add: **2.** An animal's jaw-bone used as a musical instrument; also, castanets or a jew's harp.

[**1790** W. BECKFORD *Descr. Acct. Jamaica* II. 387 Their musical instruments..consist of..the jaw-bone of an animal, from which is produced a harsh and disagreeable sound.] **1844** in C. Cist *Cincinnati Misc.* (1845) I. 14/2 Fowler..found the truant..at a dance house..playing the *jaw bones* or Castanets. **1952** B. ULANOV *Hist. Jazz in Amer.* (1958) v. 46 By the end of the 1880s New Orleans Negro musicians were no longer playing jawbones, hide-covered casks, or bamboo tubes. **1970** P. OLIVER *Savannah Syncopators* 109 *Jawbone*, jawbone of a mule, ass, cow or other domestic animal used as a rattle. A North American plantation instrument. The jawbone was also struck or played with a nail or length of iron.

3. Credit. *N. Amer.* (orig. *Canadian*) *slang.*

1862 *Times* 21 Oct. 9/4 Individuals who, in digger's parlance, live on jawbone (credit). **1885** A. S. HILL *From Home to Home* 413 His ready money gone, he has nothing to live on but 'jawbone', *i.e.* credit. **1941** J. SMILEY *Hash House Lingo* 33 *Jawbone*, credit. **1970** *New Yorker* 31 Oct. 130/3 A young Canadian..started this film on a small grant..and apparently finished it on jawbone and by deferring processing costs. **1971** A. P. MCINNES *Dunlevy* 54 No jaw-bone credit is allowed and all bets must be matched with goods.

Hence **jawboning** *U.S. slang*, name applied to a policy, first associated with the administration of President Lyndon Johnson (1963–1969), of urging management and union leaders to adopt a policy of restraint in wage and price negotiations. Also in extended use. Also (as a back-formation) **jaw-bone** *v.*

1966 *N.Y. Times* 2 Jan. iv. 2 Every price increase that happens to catch the public's eye must be 'jawboned' to death by the Government. **1969** *Time* 19 Sept. 32 Since June, Feather has been jawboning his union chiefs on the virtues of labor discipline on the shop floor. **1969** *Time* 10 Oct. 57 As for jawboning, Nixon's Republican advisers consider it unfair and almost immoral to single out individual companies or industries. **1970** *Daily Tel.* 19 June 15 Policy will almost certainly concentrate on 'jawboning', the American tactic of trying belatedly to talk both sides of industry out of outlandish wage and price increases. **1970** *Harper's Mag.* Mar. 48 Lecturing business and labor on their responsibilities to hold down prices and wages—jawboning as it was called in the Johnson Administration—has been foregone. **1970** *Times* 7 Nov. 7/1 He criticized the Nixon Administration's decision on coming to office to drop the practice of 'jawboning', or presidential persuasion, on the prices and wages front.

Jawi (dʒā·wi). [Malay.] Formerly, the Malay vernacular; now, the Malay language written in Arabic script.

1808 *Asiatick Researches* X. iii. 164 The *Basa Jawi* or written language of composition, is nearly the same in all [dialects]. **1812** W. Marsden *Gram. Malay Lang.* p. xiv, *Jāwi* or *bhāsa jāwi* is..employed in writings to denote the vernacular language of the Malays, especially that of books, as distinguished from all foreign languages. **1920** R. O. Winstedt *Colloquial Malay* (ed. 2) 138 The Malay word spelt in Arabic characters is a puzzle to be solved by the possession of a large vocabulary. And it is impossible to draw up a logical system of *Jawi* spelling. **1964** M. Taib bin Osman in Wang Gungwu *Malaysia* III. xv. 210 Traditional literature as known today is the literature written in the Perso-Arabic script known as *Jawi*. **1972** *Straits Times* (Malaysian ed.) 24 Nov. 21/1 A tombstone found in the same area has inscriptions in Jawi, stating that it was erected in 1292.

jaw-jaw (dʒǭ·dʒǭ), *v.* [Redupl. form of Jaw *v.*[1]] *intr.* To talk in a tedious manner or at great length.

Quot. 1831 is an isolated early example.

1831 M. Edgeworth *Let.* 14 Apr. (1971) 523 Mrs. Sotheby is *jaw-jawing* in the drawing room to that poor victim Fanny. **1954** *Times* 28 June 8/1 [W. S. Churchill at a White House lunch] Eden's two words are pretty good words. To jaw-jaw is always better than to war-war. **1969** *Manch. Guardian Weekly* 13 Dec. 12 The novelty of the reaction to the latest call for a European Summit is not in any changed assessment of the super-Powers' intentions, but in the feeling that it is time at last to start jaw-jawing.

jaw-jaw (dʒǭ·dʒǭ), *sb.* [Redupl. form of Jaw *sb.*[1] 6.] Talking, often with the implication of lengthy and sterile discussion.

1958 *Times* 31 Jan. 6/7 He [*sc.* Mr. H. Macmillan] believed, in the words of Sir Winston Churchill, that 'jaw jaw is better than war war'. **1960** *Economist* 22 Oct. 326/3 The easy going jaw-jaw policy introduced to Lancaster House by Mr Macleod has been successful enough so far. **1963** *Daily Tel.* 7 Aug. 10/2 We seem to be entering an era of 'jaw-jaw'. **1969** *Listener* 10 July 59/2 Here..is one idea..which might actually enliven the jaw-jaw on Radio-4.

jawl, var. *jol.

jawless, *a.* (Later examples.)

1968 *Times* 19 Dec. 4/8 Lampreys, like hagfish, are surviving members of the jawless fishes, the first group of vertebrates to evolve. **1972** *Sci. Amer.* Nov. 61/3 Primitive jawless ostracoderms belonging to the orders Anaspida and Thelodonti.

jaw's harp, jaws harp, varr. Jews' harp.

1880 Grove *Dict. Mus.* II. 34/1 *Jew's-harp*, possibly a corruption of Jaw's-harp. **1927** *Melody Maker* Aug. 811/1 When I tune my 'Jaws Harp' as a 'Jujulele', I do not seem to get the *full* banjolic effect. **1958** P. Oliver in P. Gammond *Decca Bk. Jazz* i. 23 Cheap guitars, jaw's harps and harmonicas became available in greater numbers in the 'nineties.

jax: see *Jack *sb.*[1] 19 d; **jaxey, jaxie,** varr. *Jacksy.

jay. Add: **1. b. blue jay,** read: (*a*), a North American jay, *Cyanocitta cristata* (earlier and later examples); (*b*) = Roller *sb.*[2] 1.

(*a*) **1709** *Gleanings Anc. Rec. Bristol, R.I.* 18 Mar. in *Narragansett Hist. Reg.* (1885) III. III. 211 The same order shall extend to the killing of blew Jawes [*sic*]. **1731** M. Catesby *Nat. Hist. Carolina* I. 15 The Blew Jay is full as big, or bigger than a Starling. **1792** J. Belknap *Hist. New Hampshire* III. 173 The blue jay, the wood pecker and the partridge..are then seen flying. **1886** *Harper's Mag.* Nov. 877/2 The bell note of the blue-jay comes up from some mysterious haunt. **1961** O. L. Austin *Birds of World* 226/2 Essentially a woodland species fond of open forest, the Blue Jay has become a common resident of the parks and suburbs of most North American cities. (*b*) **1878** T. J. Lucas *Camp Life & Sport S. Afr.* vi. 83 Conspicuous among them [*sc.* the birds] were..the beautiful blue jay, and the Kaffir finch. **1896** H. A. Bryden *Tales S. Afr.* viii. 185 Please don't forget the blue jay [*fn.* the 'roller' is usually called 'blue jay' by colonists] feathers. **1911** *Encycl. Brit.* XV. 298/1 The birds known as blue jays in India and Africa are rollers. **1964** A. L. Thomson *New Dict. Birds* 411/2 'Blue Jay' is a misnomer in India for *Coracias benghalensis*.

3. d. Also *attrib.* or as *adj.*, dull, unsophisticated; inferior, poor. *U.S. colloq.*

1889 *Daily Even. Bulletin* (San Francisco) 13 July 1/6 Smith has a poor opinion..of St. Joseph, which he alludes to as a 'jay' town of the worst description. **1891** H. C. Bunner *Short Sixes* 91 'T ain't neuralogy, you jay pill-box, she's *cooked*! **1900** Ade *More Fables* (1902) 185 It was a Shame to String these Jay Amateurs. *a* **1911** D. G. Phillips *Susan Lenox* (1917) II. ii. 23 Gee, what awful jay things we work off on them, sometimes! They can't see the dress for the figure. **1916** H. L. Wilson *Somewhere in Red Gap* viii. 348 Them jay New York newspapers would fall for it. **1942** Berrey & Van den Bark *Amer. Thes. Slang* § 21/10 Small; insignificant,..*jay*. *Ibid.* § 30/4 Poor; mean; contemptible,..*jay*. *Ibid.* § 45/3 Small country town; 'hick' town,..*jay town*.

jay-bird. (Earlier and later Amer. examples.)

1661 *Early Rec. Dedham, Mass.* (1894) IV. 41 En Dani Fisher is creditor to the Towne for his sonne catching of Jaybirds. **1832** J. P. Kennedy *Swallow Barn* II. iii. 55 A scream of jay-birds heard at intervals. **1896** J. C. Harris *Sister Jane* 84, I hear a flutter in the chaney-berry tree and look up and see a jaybird. **1972** D. Delman *Sudden Death* (1973) iii. 74 The corpus was naked as a jaybird.

Jaycee (dʒēi·sī·). orig. *U.S.* [f. J + C, initial letters of *junior chamber*.] A colloquial name for a member of a junior chamber of commerce. Also **Jaycee-ette, Jaycette,** a female member of such an organization. Also *attrib.*

1946 in *Amer. Speech* XXI. 295. **1952** *Ibid.* XXVII. 75 *Jaycee-ettes* are the wives of Jaycees—members of the United States Junior Chamber of Commerce. **1969** *Sun-Herald* (Sydney) 13 July 77/1 Blue and white—Jaycee colours—was the theme for decorations at Menzies Sydney Hotel when the Combined Sydney Metropolitan Jaycees held their 2nd annual ball last night. **1971** *Illustr. Weekly India* 25 Apr. 20/3 Through his association with the Jaycees he met Paru, a fellow-Jaycee, whom he married. **1972** *Malay Mail* 25 May 2/3 (*headline*) Four Malaysian Jaycees for Asian youth voyage. **1973** *Sunday Advocate-News* (Barbados) 25 Feb. 14/1 Mrs. Hazel Ann Edwards..[was] named the 1972 Jaycette of the Year... Mrs. Edwards..received her award at the annual Jaycees of Barbados Awards dinner. **1974** *Ibid.* 3 Mar. 5/7 Yesterday Mr. Mann toured projects of the Jaycees and met members of the State Board, Bridgetown Jaycees and Jaycettes at Viamede.

jay-walker (dʒēi·wǭkəɹ). orig. *U.S.* [f. Jay 3 d + Walker *sb.*[1]] A pedestrian who crosses a street without regard to traffic regulations. Hence **jay-walk** *v. intr.*; **jay-walking** *vbl. sb.*

1917 *Harper's Mag.* June 70/2 The Bostonian..has reduced 'a pedestrian who crosses streets in disregard of traffic signals' to the compact *jaywalker*. **1919** S. Lewis *Free Air* 257 He had..been cursed by a policeman for jaywalking. **1933** *Bulletin* (Sydney) 1 Nov. 23/4 His car brushed plaintiff, who was jay-walking. **1937** *Times* 25 Jan. 8/2 In many streets like Oxford Street, for instance, the jaywalker wanders complacently in the very middle of the roadway as if it was a country lane. **1957** C. Brooke-Rose *Lang. of Love* 15 She jay-walked through the traffic-jam of St. Giles, vaguely hoping to be run over. **1970** P. Laurie *Scotland Yard* v. 123 A quarter of all London's accidents involve pedestrians—we have no effective jay-walking law. **1972** *Police Rev.* 24 Nov. 1528/3 Realising his mistake, [he] pulls back quickly, narrowly missing the jay-walker. **1973** *Scotsman* 7 Aug. 8/3 Although there are penalties for jay-walking they do not seem to be much needed. Indeed a friend of mine from another part of Canada once jay-walked in the city I refer to and said that she would never do so again because she had been so embarrassed when all the traffic stopped for her.

jazz (dʒæz), *sb.* orig. *U.S. slang.* Also † **jas, jascz, jass, jasz, jaz.** [Origin unknown: see quots. for some of the many suggested derivations. Cf. *jazzbo.] **1.** A kind of ragtime dance (see quot. 1919[2]); hence, the kind of music to which this is danced; (the usual sense) a type of music originating among American Negroes, characterized by its use of improvisation, syncopated phrasing, a regular or forceful rhythm, often in common time, and a 'swinging' quality (see quots.); loosely, syncopated dance-music.

Connection with Amer. Eng. *jasm* 'energy, enthusiasm' (see Mathews *Dict. Amer.* s.v.) cannot be demonstrated.

1909 C. Stewart *Uncle Josh in Society* (*gramophone-record*), One lady asked me if I danced the jazz. **1913** *Bulletin* (San Francisco) 6 Mar. 16 The team which speeded into town this morning comes pretty close to representing the pick of the army. Its members have trained on ragtime and 'jazz'. **1917** *Sun* (N.Y.) 5 Aug. III. 3/6 Variously spelled Jas, Jass, Jaz, Jazz, Jasz and Jascz. The word is African in origin. It is common on the Gold Coast of Africa and in the hinterland of Cape Coast Castle. *Ibid.* 3/7 Jazz is based on the savage musician's wonderful gift for progressive retarding and acceleration guided by his sense of 'swing'. **1918** *Era* 11 Sept. 21 John Lester's Frisco Five. The Jollities of 'Jazz'. **1919** *Punch* 12 Mar. 193/1 'Whitehall,' says a society organ, 'has succumbed to the Jazz, the Fox-trot and the Bunny-hug.' **1919** 'Monsieur Pierre' *How to Jazz* 7 The Jazz is a three-step dance done to four-beat time. The three steps fall on the first three beats of the bar, the third being prolonged to last two beats, namely, the third and fourth. There are three distinct movements, which may be described as the Straight Jazz, the Side Jazz and the Jazz-Roll. **1920** V. Lindsay *Daniel Jazz* 1 Daniel was the chief hired man of the land. He stirred up the jazz in the palace band. **1921** W. Le Queux *Secret Telephone* 48, I was thoroughly enjoying a delightful jazz with the child. **1922** C. Engel *Discords Mingled* (1931) 147 Jazz is rag-time, *plus* 'blues', *plus* orchestral polyphony; it is the combination, in the popular music current, of melody, rhythm, harmony, and counterpoint. **1925** *Amer. Mercury* Sept. 7 According to tradition, jazz has taken its name from Jasbo Brown, an itinerant Negro player along the Mississippi, and later, in Chicago cabarets. **1927** [see *Beethovenized *ppl. a.*]. **1928** Galsworthy *Swan Song* I. iv. 26 'The faster you can move your legs, the more you think you're dancing.'..'You don't like jazz?' queried the young lady. 'I do not,' said Soames. **1930** Auden *Poems* 41 In a hot room with the sagging melody of jazz. **1933** *Fortune* Aug. 47/2 Their use of 'jazz' includes both Duke Ellington's Afric brass and Rudy Vallée crooning *I'm a Dreamer, Aren't We All?* **1934** S. R. Nelson *All about Jazz* i. 23 It has been suggested that jas, jass, jaz, jazz, jasz, or jascz were originally part of the patois of the Negro in his native Africa. **1937** *Amer. Speech* XII. 180 Mr. Preston Jackson, negro trombonist of note, says that the 'Creole Jazz Band' was in New Orleans in 1911. Almost as early as that was the 'Original Dixieland Jass Band' which was the first of the lot to have the name printed on a phonograph record, 1917..The word 'Jass' was a verb of the negro patois meaning 'to excite' with an erotic and rhythmic connotation. Later becoming pronounced 'Jazz', it was used attributively to describe bands which by the intensity of their rhythm produced excitement. **1950** *N.Y. Times* 30 June 21 Dr. Bender.. was stumped by the word 'jazz'. In..three years..he.. tracked it to the West Coast of Africa, the contact point for the slave trade with colonial America. He said that the word meant 'hurry up' in the native tongue, and was first applied in the Creole dialect to mean 'speed up' in the syncopated music in New Orleans. **1952** B. Ulanov *Hist. Jazz in Amer.* viii. 82 When..[Brown's] band came to Chicago, directly from New Orleans, the word 'jass' had a semi-sordid sexual connotation. Chicago Musicians Union officials..thought that labeling this group a jass or jazz band would be a very successful smear. But.. the term caught on, and Brown's Dixieland Band became Brown's Dixieland Jass Band. **1955** L. Feather *Encycl. Jazz* 50 Improvisation has always been the life blood of jazz. There are critics today who still claim that true jazz cannot be written down. This is not literally true, but it is true that orchestrated jazz, if it is to remain jazz, must retain the same rhythmic feeling, the same concept of phrasing, that is inherent in improvised jazz... Just as the three basic elements of music as a whole are melody, harmony and rhythm, the three additional elements essential to jazz may be said to be syncopation, improvisation and inspiration. **1955** J. Jones in Shapiro & Hentoff *Hear Me Talkin' to Ya* 358 What is jazz? The closest thing I can get to saying what jazz is, is when you play what you feel. All jazz musicians express themselves through their instruments and they express the types of person they are, the experiences they've had during the day, during the night before, during their lives. D. Brubeck *Ibid.* 361 When there is not complete freedom of the soloist, it ceases to be jazz... If it's spontaneous, it's going to be rough, not clean, but it's going to have the spirit which is the essence of jazz. **1956** M. Stearns *Story of Jazz* (1957) xxii. 282 We may define jazz tentatively as a semi-improvisational American music distinguished by an immediacy of communication, an expressiveness characteristic of the free use of the human voice, and a complex flowing rhythm; it is the result of a three-hundred-years' blending in the United States of the European and West African musical traditions. **1968** A. Dankworth *Jazz* 1 Most jazz is in the form of melodic or rhythmic variations upon a theme. The theme is usually a twelve-bar blues melody, the chorus of a popular dance-tune, or a specially composed theme. **1970** *Melody Maker* 12 Sept. 35/1 The essential motive of all jazz, at least through the end of the 1950s, was to relate to the audience through a steadily pulsing improvisational concept—in other words, to swing. Today we find young jazzmen effecting radical alterations in this objective. Much of the jazz presented by today's innovators avoids the free-flowing 4/4 or 3/4 essence in favour of a beat that is often heavier though not necessarily cruder.

† **b.** A piece of jazz music. *U.S. Obs.*

1920 *Harvey's Weekly* 24 July 14/2 That isn't a keynote; it's a jazz. **1921** *Ladies' Home Jrnl.* Jan. 50 All the latest popular hits..all this season's jolliest jazzes.

c. *spec.* A passage of improvised music in a jazz performance.

1926 [see *break *sb.*[1] 9 c].

2. *transf.* Energy, excitement, 'pep'; restlessness, excitability.

1913 *Bulletin* (San Francisco) 6 Mar. 16 What is the 'jazz'? Why it's a little of that 'old life', the 'gin-i-ker', the 'pep', otherwise known as the enthusiasalum. **1922** *Dialect Notes* V. 142 *Jazz*,..animation, animal good spirits. 'She's just full of jazz.' **1923** L. J. Vance *Baroque* vi. 34 Only about enough heroin to give every man, woman and child in N'York the jazz for a week. **1924** Galsworthy *White Monkey* II. iii. 145 With all the jazz there is about, she'd appreciate somebody restful. **1928** 'J. Sutherland' *Knot* xii. 163 'What is really the matter?' she asked. 'You look extraordinarily queer, and you ought to be full of jazz.'

3. Meaningless or empty talk, nonsense, rot, 'rubbish'; unnecessary ornamentation; anything unpleasant or disagreeable.

1918 *Dialect Notes* V. 25 *Jazz*, talk; 'gas'. College students. **1930** E. Pound *XXX Cantos* vii. 27 'Toc' sphinxes, sham-Memphis columns, And beneath the jazz a cortex, a stiffness or stillness, Shell of the older house. **1936** *Harper's Mag.* Apr. 567 The word jazz has been used to describe every disagreeable phenomenon since the year 1916, when it came into common use. **1944** *Metronome* Apr. 22 Some of them [*sc.* swing musicians] use the noun 'jazz' to denote corn, especially those who are opposed to the Dixieland type of music and sum it up derogatorily with the word 'jazz'. **1953** D. Wallop *Night Light* III. 153 What do you call that jazz, alpaca or something? **1958** 'E. McBain' *Killer's Choice* (1960) iii. 31 'How was school today, darling?' 'Oh, the same old jazz,' Monica said. **1962** M. Barrett *Return of Cornish Sailor* x. 129 All this jazz about your poppa and..his old ship, all that stuff. **1969** C. F. Burke *God is Beautiful, Man* (1970) 20, I asked one of the young men if he understood what had been read from the Bible. His response was that he 'didn't get that jazz'. **1971** B. Malamud *Tenants* 165, I read all about that formalism jazz in the library and it's bullshit.

b. Colloq. phr. *and all that jazz*: and all that sort of thing; et cetera.

1959 F. Astaire *Steps in Time* (1960) i. 3 But it's nice to hear, 'How does the old boy do it..why isn't he falling apart?' And all that jazz. **1960** *Punch* 9 Mar. 345/1 Politics, world affairs, film stars' babies and all that jazz, the things that the adult world seems obsessed with, do not interest us at all. **1968** B. Turner *Sex Trap* ix. 69 Always been a good girl and all that jazz, but a bit stage-

struck. **1972** J. PORTER *Meddler & her Murder* x. 132 Come to identify the body..and all that jazz.

4. *slang.* Sexual intercourse. Cf. *JAZZING *vbl. sb.* 2.

[**1924** *Étude* Sept. 595/3 If the truth were known about the origin of the word 'Jazz' it would never be mentioned in polite society... The vulgar word 'Jazz' was in general currency in those dance halls thirty years or more ago.] **1927** *Jrnl. Abnormal & Social Psychol.* XXII. I. 14 The word *jazz*... Used both as a verb and as a noun to denote the sex act,..has long been common vulgarity among Negroes in the South, and it is very likely from this usage that the term 'jazz music' was derived. **1950** A. LOMAX *Mister Jelly Roll* (1952) 47 Winding Boy is a bit on the vulgar side. Let's see—how could I put it—means a fellow that makes good jazz with the women.

5. *attrib.* and *Comb.*, as *jazz ballet, band, banjo, club, cult, dance, -dancing, drum, -drummer, -drumming, fan, festival, joint, king, -land, -lover, music, musician, opera, orchestra, -player, queen, record, scene, -singer, song, tune*; *jazz-conscious, mad* adjs.; *jazz-loving, -minded, -oriented, -struck, -tinged* ppl. adjs.; **jazz age** (freq. with capital initials), the era of jazz; *spec.* (see quot. 1959); **jazz baby**, a girl who is interested in jazz; a flapper; **jazz poem**, a poem that is read aloud to the accompaniment of jazz; so *jazz poetry*; **jazz–rock**, music that has the characteristics of both jazz and 'rock' music. Also *JAZZMAN.

1922 F. SCOTT FITZGERALD (*title*) Tales of the jazz age. **1926** WHITEMAN & MCBRIDE *Jazz* vii. 137 The jazz age has been the subject of profound and careful condemnation. **1959** T. GRIFFITH *Waist-High Culture* (1960) iii. 31 In the years between the Armistice and the stock-market crash, came the period we used to call..the Jazz Age. **1920** F. SCOTT FITZGERALD in *Metropolitan* Oct. 65/2 Evylyn and Ben followed singing a drowsy song about a Jazz baby. **1964** M. MCLUHAN *Understanding Media* (1967) II. xxxi. 348 Baseball..will always remain a symbol of the era of the hot mommas, jazz babies..and the fast buck. **1961** WEBSTER, Jazz ballet. **1972** *Times* 16 May 14/8 We have a jazz ballet by a Canadian choreographer, set to music that uses a string quartet and a rock quartet. **1916** *Ragtime Rev.* Oct. 6/3 The 'Jaz' bands that are so popular at the present time. **1916** *Variety* 27 Oct. 12/4 The Jazz Band is composed of three or more instruments and seldom plays regulated music. **1917** *Era* 20 Aug. 20 Holborn Empire... Frank Powell and The Magleys and the Jazz Band. **1919**, etc. [see *DIXIE^2 1 c]. **1956** M. STEARNS *Story of Jazz* (1957) vii. 71 The 101 Ranch, a cabaret which employed many jazz-bands, was particularly famous. **1923** Jazz banjo [see *BANJOLIN]. **1917** *Spiker* 25 Dec. 10/3 H. Williams, Rickard, Putney, Short, Hermann and Duncan were the Jazz Club entertainment committee. **1958** *New Statesman* 25 Jan. 102/3 Our native music..still flourishes nightly in the jazz-clubs, though best in those where musicians..like to drop in for a little drinking, gossiping, watching the dancers..and perhaps sitting in with the band. **1968** A. DIMENT *Great Spy Race* vii. 114 Past the pub with built-in Jazz Club. **1956** M. STEARNS *Story of Jazz* (1957) xxiii. 286 With the arrival of jazz-conscious American troops, the murmur of interest grew to a rhythmic roar. **1933** *Fortune* Aug. 47/3 The jazz cult is apathetic to nine-tenths of modern dance music. **1919** *Punch* 30 Apr. 333/3 An early bather was seen executing the Jazz-dance on the beach at Ventnor on Easter Monday. **1963** *Spectator* 27 Dec. 852/1 In America the jazz-dance..has a validity as..a pop-art expression of one side of the national culture. *Ibid.*, The so-called jazz-dancing which has insidiously crept into our ballet repertory. **1919** *Observer* 16 Mar. 14/4 There has been a good deal of curiosity concerning the origin of the term 'Jazz'. Authorities on Jazz dancing say it is a word used by niggers to denote a scramble. **1922** *Encycl. Brit.* XXX. 796/1 The music..consists of various combinations, the most common of which perhaps is:—piano, violin, alto or tenor saxophone, banjo and jazz-drum. **1925** *Chambers's Encycl.* VI. 302/2 The jazz-drummer, a sort of one-man band, provides the characteristic feature of jazz, which is noise. **1930** *Melody Maker* Feb. 123/2 Murray Pilcer—Britain's first 'jazz' drummer and still going strong. **1956** B. EDWARDS in S. Traill *Play that Music* vi. 59 There have been five major stages in jazz-drumming during the last three and a half decades. **1958** D. HALPERIN in P. Gammond *Decca Bk. Jazz* xx. 241 Calling the young man..a jazz-fan would be off-centre; he is, rather, a jazz convert. **1961** *Observer* 16 July 5/5 He caught on, first with his fellow college intellectuals and jazz fans (whom he still calls 'my people') and then with a wider audience. **1959** 'F. NEWTON' *Jazz Scene* xi. 184 'Jazz festivals'—in Newport, Conn., in Nice, Cannes, San Remo and other European holiday resorts. **1970** *New Statesman* 9 Oct. 454/3 The crowd was very similar..to the audience that came to the Beaulieu jazz festivals. **1942** BERREY & VAN DEN BARK *Amer. Thes. Slang* § 366/4 Dance hall,..*jazz joint*. *Ibid.* § 576/27 *Jazz King*, Paul Whiteman, jazz orchestra leader. **1920** *Quill* Sept. 6 They're the best jazz kings in the jazzy world. **1958** *Daily Herald* 24 Mar. 2/4 Gladys Hampton, wife of jazz-king Lionel, arrived in London yesterday. **1942** BERREY & VAN DEN BARK *Amer. Thes. Slang* § 578/2 *Jazzland*, the world of jazz. **1947** *Penguin Music Mag.* May 30 'You can't make a gentleman out of jazz'—a perfectly true statement, and one which all jazz-lovers will applaud. **1974** *Guardian* 22 Mar. 14/6 The European jazz lover can go to Harlem or New Orleans. **1956** M. STEARNS *Story of Jazz* (1957) xvii. 201 Jazz-loving record buyers wore out the grooves. **1924** 'J. SUTHERLAND' *Circle of Stars* xxvi. 273 Far more dangerous to a silly, headstrong child than the jazz-mad boys she chose as habitual companions. **1955** L. FEATHER *Encycl. Jazz* vii. 141 A style that was found palatable by many non-jazz-minded people. **1917** *Sun* (N.Y.) 5 Aug. III. 3/7 Jazz music is the delirium tremens of syncopation. **1922** W. J. LOCKE *Tale of Triona* v. 51 The crash of jazz music welcomed them. **1941** B. SCHULBERG *What makes Sammy Run?* iii. 46 It made me realize again how true jazz music was, how it echoed everything that was churning inside us. **1973** *Listener* 19 Apr. 522/2 The excitement in jazz music is usually concerned with nerve. **1917** *Sun* (N.Y.) 5 Aug. III. 3/7 The jazz musicians and their auditors have the most rhythmic aggressiveness. **1969** Jazz musician [see *BIT *sb.*^{2} 4 i]. **1924** *N.Y. Times* 18 Nov. 23/1 Irving Berlin, Jerome Kern and George Gershwin might submit..a jazz opera to..the Metropolitan Opera House. **1970** *New Yorker* 29 Aug. 22/2 Recently, I [*sc.* Rolf Liebermann] commissioned a jazz opera, because I think that is a way to make contact with..young people. **1916** *Variety* 27 Oct. 12/4 The low cost makes it possible for all the smaller places to carry their Jazz orchestra. **1925** *Scribner's Mag.* July 45/1 The faint echo of a jazz orchestra in the background. **1955** KEEPNEWS & GRAUER *Pict. Hist. Jazz* xv. 155/2 The personnel were primarily jazz-oriented musicians. **1918** *Quill* June 31 (Advt.), Music and Entertainment by the original Jackson Jazz Players. **1958** *New Statesman* 25 Jan. 102/3 Jazz-players and promoters.. are so much more difficult to handle than the good old-fashioned pit and palais musicians. **1960** *Guardian* 21 Nov. 7/7 A 'jazz poem' read at a recital of modern poetry and jazz. **1959** *Listener* 26 Mar. 567/3 In the current craze for jazz poetry a mistaken attempt is made to bend the verse to the last of the music. **1922** *Canad. Mag.* June 96 What will they make of a literature which is garnished with references to 'snuggle puppers' and 'jazz queens' and 'flappers' and 'face dancers'? **1923** H. CRANE *Let.* 5 Dec. (1965) 159 We had a Victrola... Lots of jazz records, etc. **1970** *Americana Ann.* 578 The year [*sc.* 1969] was flooded with such new combinations as jazz-rock, folk-rock, and country-rock. **1974** *Down Beat* 18 July 26/3 Here are two exploratory jazz-rock albums. **1959** 'F. NEWTON' (*title*) The jazz scene. **1969** Jazz scene [see *BIT *sb.*^{2} 4 i]. **1927** (*film-title*) The jazz singer. **1929** A. HUXLEY *Do what you Will* 57 He is employed as a jazz-singer on the music-hall stage. **1923** H. CRANE *Let.* 9 May (1965) 133 Marvelous jazz songs, jokes, etc. **1947** R. DE TOLEDANO *Frontiers of Jazz* vii. 82 The jazz-struck kids who are today the core of the non-commercial white bands. **1955** L. FEATHER *Encycl. Jazz* vii. 227 A honey-toned, jazz-tinged, original song stylist. **1918** F. HUNT *Blown in by Draft* vi. 144 This, he felt deep in his heart, might be a fighting army, but it was a jazz tune army. **1926** [see *CLASSIC *sb.* 1 c].

6. *attrib.*, passing into *adj.* Of grotesque or fantastic design, marked by vivid or riotous colouring; also, lively, sophisticated, unconventional.

1919 *Punch* 7 May 357 Jazz stockings are the latest thing. **1919** *Current Opinion* Aug. 98/3 Boston is only slightly Jazz. **1922** *Glasgow Herald* 14 Dec. 5 He has some justification for using this jazz language. **1923** *Daily Mail* 5 May 8 Jazz patterns in dress. **1927** R. H. WILENSKI *Mod. Movement in Art* III. 165 The 'jazz' curtains and sunshades..and the prevalence of bright tints in the theatre. **1928** E. WEEKLEY *Eng. Lang.* 76 The rather jazz-patterned idiom which is now spoken. **1930** J. COLLIER *His Monkey Wife* xiv. 198 Drawing a jazz silk dressing-gown about her shoulders, she went to the bathroom. **1938** S. M. BESSIE (*title*) Jazz journalism: the story of the tabloid newspapers. **1957** H. CROOME *Forgotten Place* 15 A jazz-patterned carpet on the floor.

jazz (dʒæz), *v.* orig. *U.S. slang.* [Cf. prec.] **1.** *trans.* To speed or liven *up*; to render more colourful, 'modern', or sensational; to excite.

1917 *Sun* (N.Y.) 5 Aug. III. 3/6 In the old plantation days when the slaves were having one of their rare holidays and the fun languished some West Coast African would cry out, 'Jaz her up', and this would be the cue for fast and furious fun... Curiously enough the phrase 'Jaz her up' is a common one to-day in vaudeville and on the circus lot. **1919** *Amer. Mag.* Nov. 69/1 For ways that is dark and tricks which is vain, the daughters of Eve is peculiar, to jazz up a line of Bret Harte's. **1923** *Daily Mail* 27 Mar. 8 My colour scheme is rather fetching, don't you think? X—a famous artist—jazzed it up for me. **1923** WODEHOUSE *Inimitable Jeeves* xv. 195 It's rather too late to alter the thing [*sc.* a little fairy play] entirely, but at least I can jazz it up. **1926** [see *GAS *sb.*^{2}]. **1959** *Times Lit. Suppl.* 2 Oct. 557/3 The 'honesty' and the depth of the rejection here carry no conviction and the attempt to jazz it up leads Mr. Sillitoe where we would expect it to lead him—to bluster and sentimentality. **1967** *Surfabout* IV. III. 33/2, I could hardly sleep at all; man, I was jazzed just listening to the hissing swells as they smoothly broke through the night. **1974** *Guardian* 13 June 10/5 He..jazzes the mixture up with a series of film-makers' cliches that one can only describe as stylised film school.

b. To play (music, or an instrument) in the style of jazz. Freq. const. *up*.

1919 E. SCOTT *All about Latest Dances* 76 The nigger bands at home 'jazz' a tune; that is to say, they slur the notes, they syncopate, and each instrument puts in a lot of little fancy bits on its own. **1922** C. SANDBURG *Slabs of Sunburnt West* 6 Listen while they jazz the classics. **1934** *Hound & Horn* VII. 599 The saxaphone..can be as 'hot' as the clarinet when it is 'jazzed up'. **1934** C. LAMBERT *Music Ho!* II. 74 A Frenchman or an Italian might have felt some embarrassment about jazzing up the classics. **1965** *Listener* 20 May 738/2 He had jazzed up Weill's music in the modern American manner.

2. *intr.* To play jazz; to dance to jazz music. Hence *transf.*, to move in a grotesque or fantastic manner; to behave wildly (see also quot. 1918^2).

1918 F. HUNT *Blown in by Draft* vi. 143 Ole Hen Sauser..started, walking up and down the black and white ivories until he had the brown box rocking and swaying and jazzing like eight electric pianos. **1918** *Dialect Notes* V. 25 *To jazz*. 1. To talk to kill time. 2. To walk about to kill time. Rare. 'I *jazzed* around all forenoon.' **1919** E. SCOTT *All about Latest Dances* 80 When the band is 'jazzing' along. **1919** *Punch* 23 Apr. 318/1 She did not ask whether I could jazz, mainly, I think, because I had already danced with her. **1922** *Dialect Notes* V. 142 You mustn't expect to pass your quizzes if you keep jazzing around like this. **1923** *Daily Mail* 18 Apr. 8 There are a good many present-day books that just give the reader a view of the protagonists jazzing across the pages in a vivid pattern of action, passion or crime. **1934** S. SPENDER *Vienna* ii. 23 Where radio crazily jazzes. **1966** 'J. HACKSTON' *Father clears Out* 19 Chester..waltzed, jazzed, did Catherine wheels, [etc.].

3. *trans.* and *intr.* To have sexual intercourse (with). *slang.*

1927 [see *JAZZ *sb.* 4]. **1929** T. WOLFE *Look Homeward, Angel* (1930) II. xiv. 176 Jazz 'em all you like,..but get the money. **1930** J. T. FARRELL in *This Quarter* July–Sept. 193 'She's cute. I jazzed her too,' O'Keefe said. **1931** G. IRWIN *Amer. Tramp & Underworld Slang* 109 *Jazz*,.. to have intercourse. **1948** H. MACLENNAN *Precipice* (1949) I. 81 My sister was being jazzed by half the neighbourhood cats by the time she was fifteen. **1968** B. FOSTER *Changing Eng. Lang.* ii. 114 The original verb 'jazz' denoting the human male's most important generic activity (itself probably an African word).

jazzbo (dʒæ·zbo). *U.S. slang.* Also **jasbo, jazz-bo.** [Origin unknown; perh. a corruption of the name *Jasper*; cf. *JAZZ *sb.*] (See quots.)

1917 *Sun* (N.Y.) 5 Aug. III. 3/7 'Jasbo' is a form of the word [*sc.* jazz] common in the varieties, meaning the same as 'hokum', or low comedy verging on vulgarity. **1919** *Quill* June 9 Have you heard Jazzbo the chocolate syncopated Hobohemian at the Moulin Rouge Cave? **1923** H. C. WITWER *Fighting Blood* ix. 272, I merely commence to stutter an apology, when the old jazzbo [= fellow] shuts me off kind of angrily. **1923** *N.Y. Times* 9 Sept. VII. 2/1 *Jazzbo*, bladder and slapstick comedy. **1926** WHITEMAN & MCBRIDE *Jazz* v. 122 Sousa..says jazz slid into our vocabulary by way of the vaudeville stage, where at the end of a performance, all the acts came back on the stage to give a rousing, boisterous *finale* called a 'jazzbo'. **1942** BERREY & VAN DEN BARK *Amer. Thes. Slang* § 438/1 Dissolute person,..*jazz-bo*. *Ibid.* § 583/18 *Jazz-bo, jazzbo*, a negro performer, esp. in a minstrel show. *Ibid.* § 868/3 *Jazzbo*, a colored American soldier. **1944** [see *JIGABOO]. **1957** J. KEROUAC *On Road* (1958) II. i. 113 He dodged a mule wagon; in it sat an old Negro plodding along... He slowed down the car for all of us to turn and look at the old jazzbo moaning along.

jazzed (dʒæzd), *ppl. a.* [f. *JAZZ *v.* + -ED^1.] Played in the style of jazz; hence, enlivened; made more colourful, 'modern', or sensational. Freq. with *up*.

1919 E. SCOTT *All about Latest Dances* 75 Certain steps and movements already in practice may be more or less adaptable to 'jazzed' music. **1926** *Bulletin* 9 June 5 Some of our own jazzed thoroughfares. **1929** *Musical Times* Feb. 129 The music is jazzed-up, restless stuff. **1958** E. BORNEMAN in P. Gammond *Decca Bk. Jazz* xxi. 270 The real Cuban rumba..had next to nothing to do with the jazzed-up sones which had passed under the name 'rumba' in the U.S. **1969** *Listener* 16 Jan. 85/2 Denouncing his inaugural lecture at the University of Malaya (or rather, a tendentious and jazzed-up version of part of the lecture which had appeared in the local Singapore press). **1972** *Country Life* 7 Dec. 1587 (Advt.), Jazzed up drinks aren't quite our style.

jazzer (dʒæ·zəɹ). orig. *U.S. slang.* [f. *JAZZ *v.* + -ER^1.] One who plays or dances to jazz; a jazz fan.

1919 *Current Opinion* Aug. 99/3 The 'klaxon' in particular..as one of the Jazzers explains,..reminds them that they have an automobile. **1922** *Public Opinion* 5 May 418/2 The son of an agricultural labourer has won the second prize as the best jazzer in the village. **1927** *Musical Times* Nov. 978 In the hands of jazzers, syncopation is a ruthless and mechanical defiance of strict time. **1928** A. HUXLEY *Point Counter Point* xxiii. 418 A real complete human being. Not a newspaper reader, not a jazzer, not a radio fan. **1935** *Punch* 22 May 620/2 D'ye think the earliest jazzer Who coined the ragtime strain Was the ill-starred Belshazzar, Or was it Tubal Cain? **1973** *Melody Maker* 31 Mar. 18 Most of the musical action for jazzers is, then, in the studios, away from the public gaze.

jazzetry (dʒæ·zĕtri). [f. *JAZZ *sb.* + PO)ETRY.] The reading aloud of poetry accompanied by jazz; a recital of poetry accompanied by jazz.

1959 *Daily Mail* 17 Feb. 4 A hybrid art-form..known variously as jazzetry, jazz-poetry readings or..just J. & P. **1959** C. LOGUE in *Encounter* June 86 A jazzetry, using two narrative poems of mine and some short epigrammatic fables will have been given at the Royal Court. **1963** *Spectator* 26 July 113 A new art form had been developed called (by Lindsey Anderson) 'jazzetry' and consisting of poetry read to a jazz accompaniment.

jazzify (dʒæ·zifəi), *v.* [f. *JAZZ *sb.* + -IFY.] *trans.* To render jazzy; = *JAZZ *v.* 1 a and b. So **ja:zzifica·tion**; **ja·zzified** *ppl. a.*

1922 [see *crazy flying* s.v. *CRAZY *a.* 5]. **1927** *Daily Express* 9 Nov. 9 In 'Hit the Deck',..British bluejackets kneel down, and, with arms uplifted to heaven, jazzify a negro spiritual. **1928** *Daily Tel.* 28 Feb. 15/1 We had already seen our musical taste jazzified, and our British standards of art and life were being jazzified by foreign films. **1958** E. BORNEMAN in P. Gammond *Decca Bk. Jazz* xxi. 270 The mambo, of course, was part of the gradual 'jazzification' of Cuban folk-music that had begun with the so-called 'rumba'.

jazzily, jazziness: see *JAZZY *a.*

jazzing (dʒæ·ziŋ), *vbl. sb.* (and *ppl. a.*). orig. *U.S. slang.* [f. *JAZZ *v.* + -ING^{1,2}.] **1.** The playing of jazz music; jazz dancing. Also *attrib.* or as *ppl. adj.*

1918 *Red Cross Mag.* Oct. 53/1 When I was singing this, one poor fellow..endeavored to keep time to my jazzing by wiggling his toes! **1919** *Lit. Digest* 26 Apr. 28/1 The negro loves anything that is peculiar in music, and this 'jazzing' appeals to him strongly. **1920** P. GIBBS *Realities of War* VIII. v. 437 There was an epidemic of dancing, Jazzing, card-playing, theatre-going. **1920** *Glasgow Herald* 26 Feb. 9 This business woman of 1920 has nothing of the jazzing featherhead about her appearance. **1920** *Chambers's Jrnl.* 28 Aug. 617/1 Good jazzing partners were scarce. **1922** CHESTERTON *Ballad St. Barbara* 75 Of earth's other tributes are plenty to choose, Tobacco and petrol and Jazzing and Jews. **1928** D. L. SAYERS *Unpleasantness at Bellona Club* vii. 80 They had a much better time than they have now, with all this jazzing and short skirts and pretending to have careers. **1938** *Life* 26 Dec. 52/2 Whiteman's new-fangled jazzing of the classics.

2. Sexual intercourse. *slang.*

1958 MURTAGH & HARRIS *Cast First Stone* xiv. 205 She asked if I wanted to do a little jazzing... I said, 'How much?' 'Two dollars,' she said.

jazzist (dʒæ·zist). orig. *U.S.* [f. *JAZZ *sb.* + -IST.] = *JAZZER.

1926 WHITEMAN & MCBRIDE *Jazz* viii. 181 Jazzists chuckle over lowbrows who say they can't abide classical music and highbrows who squirm when they hear jazz. **1927** *Radio Times* 1 July 1/1 Whether the jazzist ever listens to oratorio with an appreciative ear is possibly a doubtful point. **1941** *New Yorker* 1 Mar. 44/2 Basie makes effective use of tone-shading, a technique which some of our noisier jazzists might do well to cultivate.

jazzman, jazz man (dʒæ·zmæn). orig. *U.S.* [f. *JAZZ *sb.* + MAN *sb.*^{1}] A man who plays jazz.

1926 *Amer. Mercury* Apr. 392/1 Alfredo Casella..bore public testimony in writing that the American jazz men have invented effects that he and his colleagues never dreamt of. **1935** *Vanity Fair* (N.Y.) Nov. 38/1 Our jazzmen have had no attention. **1939** W. HOBSON *Amer. Jazz Mus.* 30 Traditionalists accuse the jazz players..and the jazz men accuse the traditionalists. **1970** [see *JAZZ *sb.* 1]. **1972** J. L. DILLARD *Black English* vi. 262 New Orleans jazzmen.

jazzophile (dʒæ·zofəil). *U.S.* [f. *JAZZ *sb.* + -O + -PHIL, -PHILE.] A devotee of jazz.

1941 *Jazz Information* Nov. 24/2 Many hardshelled jazzophiles. **1959** *Look* 21 July 76/2 But 3,000 brave jazzophiles sat patiently through three hours of liquefied jazz.

jazzy (dʒæ·zi), *a.* orig. *U.S.* [f. *JAZZ *sb.* + -Y^1.] Pertaining to or resembling jazz; characterized by jazz; spirited, lively, exciting; vivid, gaudy. Hence in more pejorative senses: 'corny', false, phoney.

1919 *Quill* Apr. 8 Gil Boag promises the Jazziest dance of the season. **1920** *Collier's* 13 Mar. 57/2 Bergstrom's two-piece orchestra was in the throes of its jazziest fox-trot number. **1922** *Dialect Notes* V. 142 She's the jazziest girl in Pem East. **1924** GALSWORTHY *White Monkey* I. ix. 76 'Whom do you think to meet him, besides Alison?' 'Nothing jazzy.' *Ibid.* III. iii. 238, I should like to change my bedroom curtains to blue... The present curtains really are too jazzy. **1925** *Chambers's Jrnl.* 466/2 To sing some jazzy stuff called 'Alexander's Rag Time Band'. **1925** D. H. LAWRENCE *Refl. Death Porcupine* 82 Inside it, the worms will jig the same jazzy dances. **1928** 'J. SUTHERLAND' *Knot* xv. 204, I may be frivolous and modern and jazzy and all the things you clever people hate. **1934** [see *CORNINESS]. **1937** *Amer. Speech* XII. 46/2 *Jazzy*, outmoded, showy, ostentatious style of playing. **1944** *Metronome* Apr. 22 Most musicians use the adjective 'jazzy' to denote 'corny'. **1957** *Sunday Mail* (Glasgow) 10 Feb. 11 Poor ole-fashioned jazz is almost a dirty word with the kids. So Jazzy means phoney or false. **1959** *Times Lit. Suppl.* 2 Oct. 556/3 The jazzy ebullience of the United States seems curiously out of date. **1961** C. MCCULLERS *Clock without Hands* vii. 149 Hard as it was for Jester to make up jazzy hurtful remarks, he was learning to do it. **1963** N. & J. KANTROWITZ in A. Dundes *Mother Wit* (1973) 351 *Jazzy motherfucker*..describes someone fluent, glib, animated. **1967** E. SHORT *Embroidery & Fabric Collage* ii. 54 Beach clothes can take bold areas of really 'jazzy' colours. **1967** *Melody Maker* 27 May 10/3 The material he works over on eleven tracks isn't the jazziest ever. **1971** *Homes & Gardens* Aug. 32 Jazzy colours are confined to the bathrooms and kitchen, where they make a vibrant contrast to the other rooms. **1973** B. BROADFOOT *Ten Lost Years* xxvii. 311 He bought a new car, the jazziest in Calgary.

Hence **ja·zzily** *adv.*; **ja·zziness.**

1921 J. C. LINCOLN *Galusha the Magnificent* xv. 253 They danced jazzily in the hotel parlor and on the porches. **1927** *Melody Maker* Sept. 847/2 Quite as full of jazziness of song and dance as it is now. **1928** *Ibid.* Feb. 183/2 The slow tempo and complete absence of 'jazziness' is the ideal treatment for a melody number. **1928** *Gramophone* VI. 300/1 With a musically artistic legato rhythmic swing and not 'jazzily'. **1951** *Archit. Rev.* CIX. 220/2 The freedom of handling, the faith in elementary cubic forms, the occasional jazziness of detail. **1959** *Encounter* Nov. 60/1 When the ballets met with resistance, it often hinged on this question of jazziness. **1968** D. E. ALLEN *Brit. Tastes* v. 126 These jazzily unnerving designs and patterns.

J-curve: see *J-SHAPED *a.*

jean. Add: **2. b.** (Earlier and later examples.) Now usu. close-fitting trousers of this (or other) material. See also *blue-jean* s.v. *BLUE *a.* 13.

1843 R. S. SURTEES *Handley Cross* I. xiii. 276 Septimus arrived flourishin' his cambric, with his white jeans strapped under his chammy leather opera boots. **1846** S. F. SMITH *Theatr. Apprenticeship* 48 My friend in the jeans and white hat. **1873** 'MARK TWAIN' & WARNER *Gilded Age* (1874) i. 19 They were dressed in homespun 'jeans', blue or yellow. **1904** G. V. HOBART *Jim Hickey* ii. 35 Wouldn't we be a nice pair of turtles to stand around with coin in our jeans and see a nice girl like Amy getting the ice? **1923** J. GALSWORTHY *Captures* 62 He wore, not white ducks, but blue jeans. **1936** WODEHOUSE *Laughing Gas* xvii. 187 No doubt this fiend in butler's shape was even now on his way east with the stuff in his jeans, gone beyond recall. **1957** *Times* 12 Nov. (Canada Suppl.) p. xv/4 For miles and miles of suburban area you will rarely see a young woman out of blue jeans, shorts or slim-jim pants during the day. **1958** *Economist* 11 Jan. 94/1 Girls in tight jeans and dazzle socks. **1958** *Daily Herald* 24 Mar. 2/6 In bright red jeans and thick nautical sweater, secretary Fiona stood on the deck of her Thames-side barge. **1969** I. & P. OPIE *Children's Games* xi. 317 Little girls, dressed in T-shirts and jeans.

c. *jean boot, trousers* (examples); **jean-age** [cf. *TEEN-AGE *a.*], the age at which a young person is likely to wear jeans; so *jean-aged* adj.; *jean-ager.*

1960 *Guardian* 15 Sept. 9/1 A full-house audience, ranging from the peerage to the jean-age. **1967** *Observer* (Colour Suppl.) 30 Apr. 34/2 (*heading*) Up to jean-age. *Ibid.*, The most comprehensive analysis yet of the difficult jean-age years. **1962** *Times Lit. Suppl.* 18 May 359/2 Mr. Kerouac is..far more than the mere apostle of jean-aged, teen-aged..American youth. **1959** *Design* Oct. 29/2 Pony-tailed jean-agers. **1961** *Times Lit. Suppl.* 1 Dec. p. iv (*heading*) Tales for jean-agers. **1849** THACKERAY *Pendennis* I. xxiv. 231 His jean-boots, with tips of shiny leather. **1860** *Observer* 16 Sept. 3/6 The disinterested and brave liberator of Italy, in his red shirt, in a dirty pair of jean trowsers, and worn-out boots. *c* **1871** J. ALBERY *Dramatic Works* (1939) I. 234 He..wears..brown, soiled jean trousers.

Hence **jeaned** *a.*, clad in jean trousers.

1970 'E. LINDALL' *Gathering of Eagles* iii. 30 Van Jordan stood up and looked down at him, legs wide and hands on her jeaned hips. **1971** D. WALLIS *Bad Luck Girl* I. i. 8 She forked out a length of jeaned thigh to fall against his own.

jean(n)ette (dʒăne·t). Also **jean(n)et.** [f. JEAN + -ETTE.] A name for various types of material resembling jean (see quot. 1950).

1785 *Daily Universal Reg.* 1 Jan. 4/2 Half-ell printed jeanets. **1862** *Illustr. Catal. Internat. Exhib., Industr. Dept., Brit. Div.* II. No. 3667 Spinners and manufacturers of jeannettes. **1882** CAULFEILD & SAWARD *Dict. Needlework* 278/2 *Jeanette*, a variety of jean, coarser in quality, yet not so closely woven. Some Jeanettes are twilled. **1950** '*Mercury*' *Dict. Textile Terms* 286 *Jeanettes*, a cloth similar to jean, but usually finer yarns... There is very little difference between jeans and jeanettes. Many makers make no distinction at all. *Jeannet*, a strong coarse fabric, made with cotton warp and wool weft in a twill weave, especially for working clothes for use in cold weather.

jebel (dʒe·bel). Also **djebel, djibel, gebel, jabal.** [a. colloq. Arab. *jebel*, classical Arab. *jabal* mountain.] A hill or mountain; freq. in specific names.

[**1600** J. PORY tr. *Leo Africanus' Geogr. Hist. Afr.* II. 58 (*heading*) Of the mountaine of Iron, commonly called Gebelelhadih. **1834** *Penny Cycl.* II. 210/1 The mountainous region in the interior is distinguished by the appellation of Jabal, 'the Hills'.] **1844** A. W. KINGLAKE *Eothen* xxvii. 387 For a part of two days I wound under the base of the snow-crowned Djibel el Sheik. **1848** H. MARTINEAU *Eastern Life* I. iv. 53 It [*sc.* the causeway] extends from the river bank to the town, and thence on to the Djebel (mountain) with many limbs from this main trunk. **1920** *Blackw. Mag.* Nov. 667/1 An enormous waste of rocky jebels and broad sandy plains. **1924** *Ibid.* Oct. 562/1 The mountains or gebels, to give them their local name, are honeycombed with caves. **1927** *Chambers's Jrnl.* 535/1 A low-lying bank of white mist wound itself round the gaunt jabal. **1942** F. STARK *Lett. from Syria* 186 He thought I was referring to the Intelligence in the Jebel Druse! **1968** *New Scientist* 30 May 447/3 Swarms of desert locusts have whirled up like djinns from the moist jebels on both sides of the Red Sea. **1970** *Guardian* 3 Aug. 3/1 The annual monsoon..hits the Jebel, the mountain range behind Salala.

jeep (dʒīp), *sb.* orig. *U.S.* [f. the initials *G.P.* (dʒī pī) '*g*eneral *p*urpose', prob. influenced by the name 'Eugene the Jeep', a creature of amazing resource and power, first introduced into the cartoon strip 'Popeye' on 16 March 1936 by his creator E. C. Segar.] A small, sturdy, four-wheel-drive army vehicle, used chiefly for reconnaissance; a similar vehicle in non-military use; hence (*colloq.*) any vehicle. Also *attrib.* and *Comb.*

For an earlier application in 1937 of the term to a commercial motor vehicle, see 1944 *Amer. N. & Q.* May 26/2 and June 43/1.

1941 *Amer. Speech* XVI. 166/2 *Jeep*, a term applied to bantam cars, and occasionally to other motor vehicles; in the Air Corps, the Link trainer; in the Armored Force, the 1½ ton command car. **1941** J. DANIELS *Tar Heels* 47 Beer wagons moved on the road with the brown jeeps of soldiers and marines. **1942** *News Chron.* 7 Apr. 4/5 The light armoured car which hauls the gun and carries the gun crew is called a jeep. **1942** *R.A.F. Jrnl.* 3 Oct. 24 The Canadians..put their dollars on a Jeep. There were a few of these contraptions beetling about the countryside. **1943** *Archit. Rev.* XCIV. 52 The Jeep is no family car, but it has points that private-car designers might well study. **1945** *Trade Marks Jrnl.* 22 Aug. 423/2 Jeep... Motor cars, and parts thereof..Willys-Overland Motors Inc., Toledo, State of Ohio, United States of America; manufacturers. **1946** *R.A.F. Jrnl.* May 174 The men and machines, drivers and Jeeps..have finished their job. **1950** G. GREENE *Third Man* iv. 37 A jeep came tearing round the corner and bowled him over. **1952** MORIN & SMITH tr. *Herzog's Annapurna* ii. 30 The jeep now took us along a dusty stony road. **1954** D. DODGE *Lights of Skaro* vi. 213 We were picked up by a jeep-load of soldiers. **1955** *Sci. News Let.* 18 June 396/3 The cosmetic preparations women use to remove superfluous hair might help speed recovery from jeep disease. This is the slow-healing painful infection at the base of the spine which thousands of World War II soldiers developed from riding in jeeps. Doctors called it pilonidal sinus. **1958** *Punch* 22 Jan. 141/1 We flew over more icebergs and then landed at Gander, Newfoundland, where people in woolly tartan jackets drove around in jeeps. **1960** *Guardian* 25 Feb. 9/4 The arrival of jeep-loads of armed police. **1966** F. SHAW et al. *Lern Yerself Scouse* 64 Here comes the police jeep. **1967** WODEHOUSE *Company for Henry* ix. 155 Repeated inquiries as to whether his darned jeep couldn't do more than three miles an hour. **1971** *Country Life* 19 Aug. 431/1 There are no paths, pony tracks or jeep roads to this inaccessible spot. **1973** *Daily Mirror* 24 Jan. 15 On the US side, ADSIDS (air delivered seismic intrusion detectors) dropped by plane, could tell a Communist jeep from a truck. **1973** J. LEASOR *Host of Extras* vii. 127 The Jeep driver started his engine... The Jeep shuddered.

jeep (dʒīp), *v.* orig. *U.S.* [f. the sb.] *intr.* To travel by jeep. So **jee·ping** *vbl. sb.*

1942 *Time* 28 Sept. 57 Yanks: drinking English tea; jeeping in the Middle East. **1945** *Picture Post* 14 Apr. 7 Sometimes, it took us hours to jeep a few miles. **1959** *Times Lit. Suppl.* 27 Feb. 115/4 Jeeping across the mountains on sheep tracks, ingeniously harrying the Germans. **1966** M. R. D. FOOT *SOE in France* xii. 406 An attempt to harass the impending German retreat by jeeping and ambushing.

jeepable (dʒī·păb'l), *a.* [f. *JEEP *sb.* + -ABLE.] Negotiable by jeep.

1944 *Daily Tel.* 12 July 4/6 A new word is now being used on the maps of the South-East Asia Command. It designates tracks impassable to vehicles other than jeeps. These are marked as 'jeepable'. **1946** G. HANLEY *Monsoon Victory* vii. 71 The infantry battalions took off their jackets and started to lay thousands of logs across the mud in an endeavour to make the road even 'Jeepable'. **1960** D. MORAES *Gone Away* 195 There are two passes into Tibet: the Jelep La and the more strategically important Nathu La, to which a jeepable road has been constructed from Gangtok. **1967** *Guardian* 19 Jan. 9/4 Now at least many roads are jeepable.

jeepers (dʒī·pəɪz), *int. slang* (orig. *U.S.*). Also **jeepers-creepers** (-krī·pəɪz). [Corruption of JESUS.] = *JEEZ(E *int.*

1929 W. D. EDMONDS *Rome Haul* ii. 24 Jeepers! A cat would n't stand no show at all. *Ibid.* 30 Spinning swore. 'I'll bet that's right. Jeepers Cripus! How can they expect us to help a marshal if he don't let us know who he is?' **1930** *Amer. Speech* VI. 98 *Jeepers*, an expression of astonishment. 'By Jeepers!' **1937** *Sat. Even. Post* 13 Feb. 13/2 Jeepers Creepers! Where are you going to find a couple of goats and a red wagon on Christmas Eve in three hours? *Ibid.* 82/2 Jeepers, what a story! **1938** MERCER & WARREN (*song-title*) Jeepers creepers. **1939** A. HUXLEY *After Many a Summer* II. ix. 265 'Jeepers Creepers!' he said to himself, remembering the expression on Mr. Stoyte's face. **1940** 'N. BLAKE' *Malice in Wonderland* I. vii. 94 'I think you're very pretty.' 'Jeepers-creepers! Put some conviction into your voice, my pet.' **1959** C. MACINNES *Absolute Beginners* 57, I put my head around the door, and jeepers-creepers, nearly had a fit. **1972** J. AIKEN *Butterfly Picnic* vii. 129 Jeepers, Fernand, we had a bullfight... It was real great!

jeepney (dʒī·pni). *Philippine Islands.* [f. *JEEP *sb.* + *JIT)NEY.] A jitney bus converted from a jeep.

1961 in WEBSTER. **1963** *New Yorker* 8 June 137 A flock of jeepneys—United States Army surplus jeeps the Filipinos have converted into buses. **1972** *Asian* 26 Nov.–2 Dec., The Philippine *jeepney*, the jeep bus (which derives its name from the New Orleans *jitney*, or five cent ride..).

jeerga, var. *JIRGA.

Jeeves (dʒīvz). The name of a character in the novels of P. G. Wodehouse represented as the perfect valet, used allusively. Hence **Jee·vesian, Jeeves-like** *adjs.*, resembling Jeeves.

1930 E. WAUGH *Labels* iii. 46 The stewards..maintained a Jeeves-like standard of courtesy and efficiency. **1952** 'R. GORDON' *Doctor in House* xiii. 149 I'll..get my evening clothes out, and appear as the Jeeves of the chafing dish. **1957** M. SUMMERTON *Sunset Hour* i. 7 That dummy Jeeves we've hired for the evening. **1962** *Observer* 24 June 24/8 A periphrastic and Jeevesian repetition. **1970** *Times* 8 Apr. 18/3 (Advt.), Jeeves required to attend the needs of wealthy bachelor. **1972** *Listener* 27 Jan. 125/2 His Jeeves-like valet. **1972** E. ROUTLEY *Puritan Pleasures of Detective Story* xii. 140 Wimsey is buried in a trench and rescued by his batman. The batman becomes his Jeeves. In Bunter there is about 70 per cent Jeeves.

Jeez(e) (dʒīz), *int. slang* (orig. *U.S.*). Also Geez(e), **Jese, Jez,** and with lower-case initial. [Corruption of JESUS.] = *GEE *int.*²

1923 G. EMERY in A. H. Quinn *Contemp. Amer. Plays* 252 Gee-z—it's a cold night, I'll tell the world. **1930** J. DOS PASSOS *42nd Parallel* I. 73 Jez we got to get us women. **1932** L. GOLDING *Magnolia St.* III. vi. 546 'Jeeze!' he said. 'It's going to be a swell party!' **1934** J. BROPHY *Waterfront* i. 17, I wish you wouldn't say, Jeez. **1937** N. MARSH *Vintage Murder* xxi. 238 'Aw, Geeze!' said Wade disgustedly. 'What a case!' **1939** I. BAIRD *Waste Heritage* iii. 40 He muttered, 'Jese, Eddy, I don't know whether I ought to apologise to you or turn you over to the cops.' **1946** 'S. RUSSELL' *To Bed with Grand Music* iii. 45 Jeez, I certainly am proud to be seen out with you. **1965** D. LODGE *Brit. Mus. is falling Down* x. 164 Geeze, was that you? What were you doing up there? **1968** A. HAILEY *Airport* I. iii. 43 At an adjoining table, a woman said loudly, 'Geez! Lookit the time!' **1970** *Private Eye* 2 Jan. 12 Jeez, that's nice of you to say so. **1971** *Melody Maker* 18 Dec. 30/6 Jeez, this travels.

jeff (dʒef), *sb.*² Also **Jeff Davis.** [f. *Jefferson Davis* (1808–89), president of the Confederate States 1861–5.] A derogatory term for a man, usu. a 'hick' or a bore; esp. used by American Blacks of white men. Also *attrib.*, as *jeff artist, hat.*

1870 O. LOGAN *Before Footlights* 202, I thought perhaps they imagined I was a female Jeff Davis, and were going to make a '*charge a la bayonette*' instanter. **1917** E. E. CUMMINGS *Let.* 4 June (1969) 26, I escaped repairing with the bums, mutts and Jeffs. **1938** C. CALLOWAY *Hi De Ho* 16 *Jeff*, a pest, a bore, an icky. **1946** MEZZROW & WOLFE *Really Blues* (1957) 375 *Jeff Davis*, an unenlightened person, a hick from down South; sometimes shortened to *jeff.* **1952** BERREY & VAN DEN BARK *Amer. Thes. Slang* (ed. 2) (1954) 391/3 *Jeff Davis, jeff*, a Southern 'hick'. **1969** *Publ. Amer. Dial. Soc.* LI. 29 Names used exclusively by Negroes..jeff, jeffer, jeff davis, jeff artist. **1970** C. MAJOR *Dict. Afro-Amer. Slang* 70 *Jeff*,..a white person;..a dull person; a horrible square. **1973** *Black World* Apr. 57 He wears a jeff hat and a light raincoat.

jeff, *v.* Add: (Earlier and later examples.) Hence **je·ffing** *vbl. sb.*

1837 *Baltimore Commercial Transcript* 7 Nov. 2/1 (Th.), We move that the printers of the U.S. divide off in halves, and 'jeff' to see which shall go to digging ditches or picking stone coal for a living. **1841** W. SAVAGE *Dict. Art of Printing* 428 *Jeff.* See *Throw.* **1875** J. SOUTHWARD *Dict. Typogr.* (ed. 2) 58 *Jeffing*, throwing with quads... One of .. [the party interested] takes up the quads, shakes them ..and throws them..after the manner of throwing dice, when the number of quads with the nicks appearing uppermost are counted,..the highest thrower being the winner. **1884** J. GOULD *Letter-Press Printer* (ed. 3) 166/1 *Jeff*, to throw for a choice with quadrats instead of dice. **1892** A. POWELL *Southward's Pract. Printing* (ed. 4) lxv. 577 In the old companionship system, the fat [*sc.* easy work] is distributed by 'jeffing', or 'throwing quads'. **1942** BERREY & VAN DEN BARK *Amer. Thes. Slang* § 526 *Jeff*, to play dice with em quadrates. **1947** E. HOWE *London Compositor* 24 A custom [*sc.* playing at quadrats] known in the nineteenth century as 'Jeffing'. **1967** F. J. M. WIJNEKUS *Elsevier's Dict. Printing & Allied Industr.* 177/2 *Jeffing*, gambling with nine one-em quadrats, i.e., to throw quards [*sic*] like dice, using the nick side, appearing uppermost, representing one and the other sides blanks. It is a very old custom, but now almost entirely out of practice.

Jeffersonian, *a.* and *sb.* Add: **A.** *adj.* (Earlier and later examples.)

1800 *Connecticut Courant* 6 Oct. 1/3 The Jeffersonian party boast, that the increase of Jacobinism has been great in the Northern part of the United States, within the last year. **1806** *Balance* (Hudson, N.Y.) V. 35/3 Occlusion.. is a Jeffersonian word. **1813** *Niles' Reg.* IV. Suppl. 65/1 This is true Jeffersonian, Madisonian, democratic economy. **1838** *U.S. Mag. & Democratic Rev.* Jan. 145 Jeffersonian republicanism. **1972** *Science* 16 June 1223/3 The group takes a Jeffersonian view of the virtues of rotation in office and recommends that a committee member's service be limited to a 3-year term. **1972** *Listener* 21 Dec. 858 They didn't say: 'Yessir, Mr Jefferson, we are going to conquer the North-West for Jeffersonian democracy.'

B. *sb.* (Earlier and later examples.)

1799 *Spectator* (N.Y.) 3 Apr. 1/1 Rouse, ye insurgents, rioters, refugees, and deserters! Ye friends to liberty and equality... Ye Jeffersonians, Gallatonians, Nicholites. **1803** *Fredericktown* (Maryland) *Herald* 30 Apr. 3/3 A thorough going Jeffersonian. **1948** *Antioch Rev.* Spring 10 American Federalists openly sympathized with British Tories and American Jeffersonians with French Girondists.

Jeffrey (dʒe·fri). The name of John *Jeffrey* (d. ?1854), British plant-collector, used *attrib.* or in the possessive to designate *Pinus jeffreyi*, a large pine with a spreading head of drooping branches, collected by him in California in 1852.

1858 G. GORDON *Pinetum* 198 *Pinus Jeffreyii*, Hort. Jeffrey's Pine... A noble tree, growing 150 feet high. **1908** N. L. BRITTON *N. Amer. Trees* 25 Black Pine, *Pinus Jeffreyi* A. Murray, also known as Jeffrey's pine..occurs on dry volcanic mountains from southern Oregon through California. **1931** *Discovery* XII. 92/1 The insect [*sc.* the pandora moth] attacks only pines, its principal hosts being western yellow pine (*Pinus ponderosa*) and Jeffrey pine (*P. jeffreyi*). **1942** N. A. BOWERS *Cone-bearing Trees Pacific Coast* 107 As compared with the Yellow Pine, the Jeffrey cones are much denser; they are shaped like the old-fashioned beehive. **1965** *Listener* 20 May 742/3 There are a good many specimen trees of considerable age—Jeffrey's pine, the Bishop pine. **1967** N. T. MIROV *Genus Pinus* iii. 159 *Pinus jeffreyi*, commonly known as 'Jeffrey pine', has been considered by some botanists as a variety of *P. ponderosa*, while other specialists maintain it to be an independent species.

Jehoshaphat (dʒīhǫ·ʃăfæt, -săfæt). orig. *U.S.* Also **Jehosaphat,** etc. A biblical name (2 Sam. viii. 16, etc.) used interjectionally as a mild expletive. Freq. *jumping Jehoshaphat.*

1857 S. A. HAMMETT *Sam Slick in Texas* xxiv. 161 'Jehosophat!'.. 'Easy over the stones, Joe,' ses I. **1866** MAYNE REID *Headless Horseman* vi. 39 Geehosofat! what a putty beest it air! *Ibid.* xviii. 100 By the jumpin' Geehosofat, what a gurl she air sure enuf! **1876** [see GREAT *a.* 12 c]. **1898** J. D. BRAYSHAW *Slum Silhouettes* 123 'Oh, Jehosephat!' cried the old man, with a chuckle. **1935** G. HEYER *Death in Stocks* iv. 41 'Great jumping Jehoshaphat!' he exclaimed. 'Who did it?' **1972** *Guardian* 16 Dec. 10/1 Why Jeehosophat, Houston, you surely have hit the jack-rabbit on the head.

Jehovah. Add: **2.** *Jehovah's Witness*, a member of a fundamentalist millenary sect, the Watchtower Bible and Tract Society, founded *c* 1879 (under the name 'International Bible Students') by Charles Taze Russell (1852–1916), which rejects institutional religion and refuses to acknowledge the claims of the State when these are in conflict with the principles of the sect. Occas. *Jehovah Witness.*

[**1932** J. F. RUTHERFORD *Health & Life* (Watchtower Bible & Tract Soc.) 7 This commandment is written, in Isaiah 62:10, directed to Jehovah's faithful witnesses.] **1933** M. S. CZATT (*title*) The International Bible Students, Jehovah's Witnesses. **1941** H. G. WELLS *You can't be too Careful* IV. i. 223 A single declared Fascist or Communist or Jehovah's Witness or Single Taxer. **1944** G. B. SHAW *Everybody's Pol. What's What?* v. 46 May he choose..a tribal idol as the sect called Jehovah's Witnesses now do? **1955** W. GADDIS *Recognitions* II. i. 305 It's like Jehovah's Witnesses when you sit down at a table there, everybody comes over. **1961** *Times* 5 May 20/6 A rhesus-positive baby whose father, a Jehovah Witness, refused to consent to a blood transfusion. **1962** *Lancet* 7 Apr. 747/2 Jehovah Witnesses will usually accept their own blood at operation, though they would not take that of a donor. **1973** *Guardian* 14 Mar. 7/4 A mother who divorced her husband because of his adultery is to lose her children because of her religious beliefs. She is a Jehovah's Witness. *Ibid.*, To bring up the children under the Jehovah Witness cult would tend to isolate them.

jejuno-. Add: **jeju:noi·leum** [prob. ad. F. *jéjuno-iléon* (J. Cruveilhier *Traité d'Anat. path.* (1849) I. 718)], the small intestine exclusive of the duodenum; the jejunum and ileum considered together; **jeju:nojejuno·stomy** [*-STOMY], the operation of joining, and creating a passage between, two parts of the jejunum so that the intervening part is bypassed; **jejuno·stomy** [*-STOMY], the operation of attaching the jejunum to the abdominal wall and making an opening, through which the patient may be fed, directly into the jejunum from the exterior; also, the opening thus made.

1876 DUNGLISON *Dict. Med. Sci.* (rev. ed.) 561/2 Jejunoileum. **1955** R. T. SHACKELFORD *Bickham-Callander Surg. Alimentary Tract* II. vii. 999 The jejunoileum..is coiled in a complicated fashion. **1925** DORLAND *Med. Dict.* (ed. 13) 595/2 Jejunojejunostomy. **1955** R. T. SHACKELFORD *Bickham-Callander Surg. Alimentary Tract* I. ii. 330 Most surgeons do not perform jejunojejunostomy routinely with antecolic gastrojejunostomy. **1885** *Brit. Med. Jrnl.* 5 Dec. 1063/2 For the operation of jejunostomy, as he [*sc.* C. H. Golding-Bird] termed the one that he detailed, he claimed that..it was..the best palliative operation for pyloric cancer. **1948** T. H. SOMERVELL *Surg. Stomach & Duodenum* xxvii. 500 The patient is well nursed, and nourished through the jejunostomy. **1971** CAREY & ALBERTIN *Ellison's Atlas Surg. Stomach & Duodenum* ix. 125 Even though parenteral hyperalimentation has decreased the need for jejunostomy, it remains a valuable procedure. *Ibid.* 130 Feedings through the jejunostomy should not be attempted until the return of normal bowel activity.

Jekyll (dʒe·kil, dʒe·k'l). The name of the hero of R. L. Stevenson's story, 'Strange Case of Dr. Jekyll and Mr. Hyde' (published 1886), who appears as a benevolent and respectable character under the name of *Jekyll* and the opposite under the name of *Hyde*: used allusively in reference to opposite sides of a person's character or to persons or things of a dual character, alternately good and evil. Also *attrib.* (Cf. *HYDE.)

?**1885** F. STEVENSON *Let.* in J. Pope-Hennessy *R. L. Stevenson* (1974) ix. 179 While one side represents an angel, the devil must have posed for another... Plainly Jekyll and Hyde. **1887** *Puck* (U.S.) XXII. 188 Is that you, Livingston?.. No, m' dearsh, it'sh Doct' Hyde. Mist' Jekyll didn't..g-g' out t'night! **1902** *Daily Chron.* 22 May 3/4 While the left lobe is the Jekyll of the intellect, the right, on occasion at least, is apt to play the part of Hyde. **1905** *Strand Mag.* Apr. 455/2 Meeting a young and winsome feminine counterpart of Dr. Jekyll and Mr. Hyde in real life is a very pleasant, if novel, experience. **1915** 'I. HAY' *First Hundred Thousand* xiv. 187 When he is good he is very good indeed, and when he is bad he is horrid. He is either Jekyll or Hyde. *Ibid.*, But we encountered surprisingly few Hydes. Nearly all were Jekylls —Jekylls of the most competent and courteous type. **1929** W. J. LOCKE *Ancestor Jorico* xviii. 253 Suppose it pleased him to lead a Jekyll and Hyde sort of life? **1931** *Times Lit. Suppl.* 2 July 522/1 Turner was a case of Jekyll and Hyde in real life and oscillated continuously between the Victorian respectability of Bloomsbury..and the Rabelaisian society of the London Docks. **1945** A. J. P. TAYLOR *Course German Hist.* 146 A Jekyll and Hyde policy, the bureaucrat Jekylls confident until too late that they could always shake off the Pan-German Hyde at their convenience. **1971** L. P. DAVIES *Shadow Before* xi. 128 We are all a mixture of good and evil, Jekyll and Hyde, if you like.

jeldi, var. *JILDI.

jell, *v.* For *U.S. colloq.* read orig. *U.S. colloq.* (Add further examples.) Also *fig.*, to take definite or satisfactory shape; = CRYSTALLIZE *v.* 5. Cf. *GEL *v.* Hence **jelled** *ppl. a.*

1869 L. M. ALCOTT *Little Women* II. 60 The jelly won't jell. **1902** *Fortn. Rev.* June 1021 (*heading*) Why a nerve tends to 'jell'. **1908** *Daily Chron.* 20 Mar. 3/3 [He] remarked of his countrywomen's minds that they 'didn't jell'; but he possibly, and mistakenly, thought he was talking American. **1937** *Maclean's Mag.* 15 Apr. 17/3 Davis shook his head, but the look of innocent disclaimer in his cherubic eyes didn't quite jell. **1956** K. FARRELL *Cost of Living* 138 'Not going well?' 'Hardly going at all. Even the cat book doesn't quite jell.' **1958** K. AMIS *I like it Here* ix. 113 His uncertainty..now felt more or less permanently jelled. **1958** *Observer* 18 May 10/5 Let jell in cool larder. **1959** P. H. JOHNSON *Unspeakable Skipton* iv. 26 They did the music by itself, later, at the Wigmore Hall, but it didn't jell. **1970** *Times* 5 Dec. 21/1 The present Parliament is only two parliamentary months old.., and although it will jell in time, it has not yet done so. **1972** *Times Lit. Suppl.* 12 Jan. 45/5 Somehow his case against RTZ as a sort of Hydra does not quite jell. **1972** *Village Voice* (N.Y.) 1 June 24/3 These detective novels were written very fast, read extremely well, and, as Himes told me: 'They worked. They jelled.'

2. *trans.* = JELLIFY *v.* 1. Also *fig.*, to give shape to; to make clear and definite.

1905 *Dialect Notes* III. 62 *Jell*, make or turn into jelly. **1935** *Forres Gaz.* 6 Nov. 4/5 To jell (to firm jelly). **1941** A. J. CRONIN *Keys of Kingdom* (1942) ii. 20 The tea was delicious, the scones and bannocks home-made, the preserves jelled by Elizabeth's own hands. **1948** *Newsweek* 10 May 58/3 The studio also ordered that no scripts be bought unless it was certain they could be jelled onto film. **1968** J. M. ZIMAN *Public Knowl.* v. 91 The course work is too rich a diet, and the knowledge it contains has been jelled too soon.

jell (dʒel), *sb.* orig. *U.S.* [f. the vb.] A jelly or gel.

1870 'F. FERN' *Ginger-Snaps* 262 My excellent country friends put up pounds and quarts of 'jell' every fall. **1951** *Good Housek. Home Encycl.* 423/1 Allow it to boil briskly, without stirring, until a jell is obtained on testing. **1959** *Listener* 11 June 1043/1 The sticky jells given by other starches such as tapioca and arrowroot.

jellaba(h), jellibee, varr. *GALABIYA. Cf. JELAB.

1904 A. E. W. MASON *Truants* xxv. 233 A black jellaba and cap, such as the Jews must wear in Morocco. **1922** JOYCE *Ulysses* 742 Longbearded jews in their jellibees. **1964** *Punch* 19 Feb. 278/3 'He had always a bottle of whisky under his jellaba,' Si Mohammed went on. **1969** *Daily Tel.* (Colour Suppl.) 24 Jan. 17/2 A girl called Susy in a jellabah like John Hanson in *Desert Song.*

jellied, *a.* Add: **3.** Coated with jelly; made or cooked inside jelly.

1895 'M. RONALD' *Century Cook Bk.* iv. 171 Jellied veal ..a good cold dish to use with salad. *Ibid.* v. 182 Jellied boned chicken. A braised boned chicken may be..jellied as follows. **1907** *Daily Chron.* 6 June 5/5 'Jellied eel! 'Ave a plate; lovally jelly,' shouts a third. **1908** *Ibid.* 6 July 3/4 She..knows the secrets of jellied eels. **1911** *Daily Colonist* (Victoria, B.C.) 26 Apr. 10/5 (Advt.), Jellied Ham per lb. 40¢. **1960** *Good Housek. Cookery Bk.* (rev. ed.) 84/2 Jellied eels. *Ibid.* 157/2 Jellied sheep's tongues. *Ibid.* 524/1 Jellied eggs.

Jell-o, Jello (dʒe·lo). Chiefly *N. Amer.* [f. JELLY *sb.*] The proprietary name of a powder used to make a fruit-flavoured gelatin dessert; loosely (with lower-case initial), jelly.

1934 *Trade Marks Jrnl.* 11 July 907 *Jell-o.* Brand of Jelly Powder... Jell-o can be placed in the refrigerator as soon as dissolved... The Jell-o Company of Canada Limited..Montreal, Canada; Manufacturers. **1936** *Amer. Speech* XI. 40 *Nervous pudding, Shivering Liz*, or *Shimmy* for jello..describe neatly. **1945** *New Yorker* 1 Dec. 36/2 Carola..learned to prefer salt fish and bean curd..to Jello and cereal. **1961** *Guardian* 29 Mar. 12/4 All the side dishes of salad and jello were there. **1971** *Black Scholar* Sept. 44/2 Her firm young breasts quivering like a dish of molded jello. **1972** *Sat. Rev.* (U.S.) 27 May 7/2 Herb Edelman's well-turned contribution as the agent with a heart of jello.

jelly, *sb.*¹ Add: **1. c.** A table-jelly.

1728 E. SMITH *Compleat Housewife* (ed. 2) 146 *To make Riben Jelly*.. run the Jelly into little high Glasses..one

Colour must be thorough cold before you put another on.. colour red with Cochineal, green with Spinage..and sometimes the Jelly by it self. **1845** E. ACTON *Mod. Cookery* (ed. 2) xx. 438 A great variety of..excellent jellies for the table may be made with clarified isinglass, clear syrup, and the juice of..fresh fruit. **1851** *Illustr. Catal. Gt. Exhib.* III. 650/1 Moulds for jellies, cakes, &c. **1916** *Punch* 6 Dec. 394/2 He shook all over like a badly-set jelly. **1930** C. MACKENZIE *April Fools* vii. 152 Mr. Wenlow, balanced like a pale jelly on the edge of a chair in the drawing-room. **1974** *Radio Times* 4 Apr. 42/4 (Advt.), Rowntrees strawberry flavour jelly.

2. *glycerin(e) jelly*, any of various mixtures of glycerol and gelatin, principally used as mounting media in microscopy; cf. JELLY *sb.* 2 d; *royal jelly*, the secretion produced by honey bees to feed the larvae of the colony, esp. those that will become queens.

1817 KIRBY & SPENCE *Introd. Entomol.* II. xix. 130 They will select one or more to be educated as queens; which..being fed with royal jelly for not more than two days..will come forth complete queens. **1859** *Q. Jrnl. Microsc. Sci.* VII. 257 The bottle of glycerine jelly is put into a cup of hot water, until liquefied. **1880** *Amer. Monthly Microsc. Jrnl.* I. 208/1, I have used such a medicine dropper to hold and apply glycerin jelly, with great satisfaction. **1886** F. R. CHESHIRE *Bees* I. vi. 82 In the case of the queen larva..that secretion, commonly, though, as I hold, erroneously, called royal jelly, is added unstintingly. **1954** C. G. BUTLER *World of Honeybee* iv. 46 It has come to be believed that any female honeybee larva..that is fed exclusively on royal jelly always develops into a queen bee. **1958** J. R. BAKER *Princ. Biol. Microtechnique* xiii. 255 Preparations mounted in glycerine-jelly, balsam, or other commonly-used media. **1973** L. HELLMAN *Pentimento* (1974) 230 He was always having mysterious operations... He took royal jelly.

e. *slang.* A pretty girl; a girl-friend.

1889 BARRÈRE & LELAND *Dict. Slang* I. 496/1 *Jelly*, or *All jelly*, a buxom, good-looking girl. **1931** W. FAULKNER *Sanctuary* iii. 23 Gowan goes to Oxford a lot...He's got a jelly there. He takes her to the dances. *Ibid.* iv. 36 Don't think I spent last night with a couple of your barbershop jellies for nothing.

f. A gelatinous contraceptive substance.

1931 F. W. S. BROWNE tr. *T. H. van de Velde's Fertility & Sterility in Marriage* III. xiv. 348 The most important chemical contraceptives are the lubricant jellies. **1935** E. F. GRIFFITH *Mod. Marriage* iv. 84 There are numberless chemical substances, made up either in the form of tablets or jellies... These are introduced into the vagina and are intended to kill the sperms. **1937** —— *Voluntary Parenthood* iii. 46 Many other devices have been invented to carry the chemical, such as jellies, ointments, foaming tablets and foaming jellies... All these solubles, jellies and tablets are unsatisfactory and if used by themselves are liable to fail in a high percentage of cases. **1943** in T. H. van de Velde *Ideal Marriage* (1947) 148 Arrangements have now been made for the manufacture of Dr. Van de Velde's Jellies ('Eugam'): Lubricant, Contraceptive and Proconceptive. **1949** *New Gould Med. Dict.* 529/1 *Contraceptive jelly*, any one of a number of viscous substances introduced into the vagina to prevent conception. **1970** *Which? Contraceptives Suppl.* (ed. 3) 58 (*heading*) Spermicidal creams, jellies and pastes. **1972** *Guardian* 9 June 5/5 Her doctor..prescribed a diaphragm and a contraceptive jelly but the jelly was seized by the [Irish] customs authorities.

4. *jelly-boned* adj.; **jelly baby**, a soft gelatinous sweet in the shape of a baby; **jelly bean** orig. *U.S.*, (*a*) a bean-shaped sweet with a gelatinous centre and a hard sugar coating; (*b*) *slang*, an unpleasant, weak, or dishonest person; *spec.* a pimp; **jelly-belly**, a fat person; hence **jelly-bellied** *a.*; **jelly paint**, a non-drip paint with the consistency of jelly; **jelly powder**, (*a*) a kind of explosive (see quot. *a* 1884); (*b*) a crystalline powder used in the preparation of table-jellies; **jelly roll** *U.S.*, a cylindrical cake containing jelly or jam; freq. in *transf. slang* senses: (*a*) a lover; (*b*) sexual intercourse; (*c*) the female genitalia or vagina.

1945 DYLAN THOMAS in *Listener* 20 Dec. 734/2 A bag of moist and many-coloured jelly-babies. **1950** 'R. CROMPTON' *William—the Bold* i. 13 'Jelly babyth are nithe, too,' said the small shrill voice behind them. **1972** *Guardian* 27 Dec. 9/1 A lady going round Europe buying..jelly babies. **1905** *Chicago Daily News* 5 July 11/5 Jelly beans, assorted, per lb., 9 c. **1919** *Dialect Notes* V. 65 Mary is such a jelly-bean that she never gets her lessons. **1923** WODEHOUSE *Adv. Sally* 223 What's the idea, you jelly bean? **1929** W. FAULKNER *Sound & Fury* 202 Are you hiding out in the woods with one of those damn slickheaded jellybeans? **1935** A. J. POLLOCK *Underworld Speaks* 63/2 *Jelly bean*, a pimp (jellyjay eanbay). **1940** C. MCCULLERS *Heart is Lonely Hunter* (1943) I. iii. 32 She..took from her shirt pocket a blue-coloured jelly bean. **1972** M. J. BOSSE *Incident at Naha* i. 56, I went into the kitchen for jelly beans, which taste good after you've been blowing grass. **1899** KIPLING *Stalky & Co.* 214 He was..a Flopshus Cad, an Outrageous Stinker, a Jelly-bellied Flag-flapper (this was Stalky's contribution). **1938** *Times Lit. Suppl.* 26 Nov. 753/2 The most jelly-bellied of them is Nabucet, a flowery and despicable humbug. **1950** M. LOWRY *Let.* 23 June (1967) 213 She [*sc.* Russia]..lives in a state of constant 'war effort', with its attendant..'jelly-bellied flag-flapping'. **1896** FARMER & HENLEY *Slang* IV. 44/1 *Jelly-belly*, a fat man or woman. **1903** [see *EH *int.* 3]. **1935** L. A. G. STRONG *Tuesday Afternoon* 88 If ever I want a ginger-chinned jelly-belly's advice,..I'll ask for it. **1912** D. H. LAWRENCE *Let.* 3 July (1962) I. 134 Curse the blasted, jelly-boned swines. **1961** *Spectator* 17 Nov. 698 It is so spineless and 'jelly-boned'. **1958** *Listener* 28 Aug. 323/1 If anyone were to ask me what has been the most interesting new development for the do-it-yourself painter over the last year or two I think I would say the dripless, or jelly, paints... Some complain that the jelly paints do not cover up the surface underneath. *a* **1884** KNIGHT *Dict. Mech.* Suppl. 511/2 *Jelly powder*, so called from its resemblance to calf's-foot jelly. It consists of 94% or 95% of nitro-glycerine and 5% or 6% collodion cotton, so mixed as to assume a gelatinous form. **1895** *Army & Navy Co-op Soc. Price List* 16 Table Jelly powder..in packets. **1921** *Daily Colonist* (Victoria, B.C.) 6 Apr. 6/1 Lipton's and Shirriff's Jelly Powders, per packet..10¢. **1895** 'M. RONALD' *Century Cook Bk.* xxi. 468 *Jelly Rolls.* Make a layer of Genoese..press it through a pastry bag in lines onto the tins... Before it has had time to cool, cut off the hard edges, spread it with..any jelly or jam, and roll it up evenly; then roll it in paper and tie, so it will cool in a round, even shape. **1914** W. C. HANDY *St. Louis Blues* (song), I'm most wile 'bout mah Jelly-Roll. **1919** S. & C. WILLIAMS (*song-title*) I ain't gonna give nobody none o' this jelly roll. **1927** *Jrnl. Abnormal & Social Psychol.* XXII. 13 By far the most common of these terms is *jelly roll*. As used by the lower class Negro it stands for vagina, or the female genitalia in general, and sometimes for sexual intercourse. *Ibid.* 14 Angels in heaven do the sweet jelly roll. **1929** T. WOLFE *Look Homeward, Angel* (1930) xxii. 324 'What yo' want?' she asked softly. 'Jelly roll?' **1964** *Amer. Folk Music Occasional* I. 12 Negro blues where women are sweet food (*biscuit-roller..jelly roll baker*). **1970** G. GREER *Female Eunuch* 265 If a woman is food, her sex organ is for consumption also, in the form of..*cake-* or *jelly-roll*. **1971** B. MALAMUD *Tenants* 205 Irene Lost Queen I miss To be between Your Jelly Roll. **1974** *Amer. Speech 1971* XLVI. 79 Jelly-filled doughnut, *bismarck, jelly roll.*

jelly (dʒe·li), *sb.*[2] *slang.* Also **gelly.** [Shortening of the pronunciation of GELIGNITE, influenced by its jelly-like appearance.] Gelignite.

1941 in BAKER *Dict. Austral. Slang.* **1948** D. L. G. MUNDY *There's Gold in them Hills* x. 128 Put a charge of 'gelly' under it. **1955** [see *CREEP *v.* 5 b]. **1960** *Observer* 24 Jan. 5/2 A hut where they knew gelly was kept. *Ibid.* 5/3 There was always the gelly and oxy-acetylene if necessary. **1971** *Guardian* 28 Aug. 1/1 Stolen 'gelly' found.

jelly-fish. 2. b. (Further examples.)

1910 [see *GABFEST]. **1928** [see *FACE *v.* 6]. **1966** C. ACHEBE *Man of People* viii. 88 Max's unfortunate.. presentation of me as a kind of pitiable jellyfish.

jellygraph (dʒe·ligrɑf). [f. JELLY *sb.* + -GRAPH.] An appliance used for multiplying copies of writing, etc., of which the essential part is a sheet of jelly. Also *attrib.* Hence **je·llygraph** *v. trans.*, to copy with a jellygraph; **je·llygraphed** *ppl. a.*

1900 H. G. WELLS *Love & Mr. Lewisham* xxv. 241 A letter of atrociously jellygraphed advices from Messrs. Danks & Wimborne. **1902** WODEHOUSE *Pothunters* xii. 182 On Sunday we jellygraph it—it'll have to be a jellygraphed number this time. **1904** *Sat. Rev.* 9 Jan. 40 It is better 'jellygraphing' questions for some one else's form than [etc.]. **1919** *Brit. Jrnl. Photogr. Alm.* 615/1 Jellygraph mixture for enlarging easel. **1936** 'G. ORWELL' *Keep Aspidistra Flying* iii. 58 They ran an unofficial monthly paper..duplicated with a jellygraph. **1972** W. A. PANTIN *Oxf. Life* iv. 52 We can trace the belated triumph of the typewriter..over the older methods of manuscript, jellygraph, and printed fly-sheet.

jelutong (dʒelū·tǫŋ). Also 9 **jolo-, julu-**; 20 **jela-, jelo-**. [Malay.] A Malaysian tree of the genus *Dyera*, esp. *D. costulata*, which produces a latex when tapped; the latex or the light-coloured wood from a tree of this kind.

1836 J. LOW *Diss. Soil & Agric. Penang* iv. 205 *Julutong*—very white. These woods are used chiefly by undertakers. **1885** *Spons' Mechanics' Own Bk.* 164 Jolotong... Well adapted for patterns and mouldings, excellent for carving purposes. **1900** W. W. SKEAT *Malay Magic* 205 Other haunted trees..are the Jawi-jawi, the Jĕlotong, and Bĕrombong. **1904, 1927** [see *GUTTA[2] 2]. **1940** E. J. H. CORNER *Wayside Trees Malaya* I. 144 The *Jelutong* is deciduous partly or wholly. **1947** H. BARRON *Mod. Rubber Chem.* (ed. 2) iii. 27 Jelutong is obtained by tapping. **1970** *Timber Trades Jrnl.* 21 Mar. 54/1 Few sales of jelutong or kapur have been made, but meranti is said to be selling fairly well.

‖ **je m'en fiche** (ʒəmaṅfiʃ), *phr.* [Fr.] I couldn't care less; I don't care at all. Hence **je-m'en-fich(e)ism(e)**, indifference.

1889 E. DOWSON *Let.* 10 Mar. (1967) 48 As for *esprit*—je m'en fiche—there never was a woman spirituelle before she was thirty. **1902** W. JAMES *Varieties Relig. Experience* ii. 36 *Je m'en fiche* is the vulgar French equivalent for our English ejaculation 'Who cares?' And the happy term *je m'en fichisme* recently has been invented to designate the systematic determination not to take anything in life too solemnly. **1905** A. BENNETT *Sacred & Profane Love* III. iii. 251 'Oh!' with a disdainful gesture. '*Je m'en fiche.* Let him go.' **1916** A. HUXLEY *Let.* Dec. (1969) 117 Old Birrell came down..professing an almost total je-m'en-ficheisme about the war. **1921** GALSWORTHY *To Let* II. ii. 139 Why want to know anything of that 'small' mystery—*Je m'en fiche*, as Profond says? **1923** A. HUXLEY *Antic Hay* v. 69 His divining eyes pierced through the veil of cynical *je-m'en-fichisme* to the bruised heart beneath. **1968** W. GARNER *Deep, Deep Freeze* ix. 240 As they say in this part of the world, *je m'en fiche.* **1970** R. HAUGHTON *Love* i. 25 The school of Anglo-Saxon 'je m'en fiche-ism'.

‖ **je m'en fous** (ʒəmaṅfu), *phr.* [Fr.] = prec. Hence **je-m'en-foutism(e).**

1918 A. BENNETT *Pretty Lady* xxi. 134 'But, madame, it is raining terribly.' '*Je m'en fous.* Run for a taxi.' **1936** 'G. ORWELL' *Keep Aspidistra Flying* x. 269 At the bottom of all his feelings there was a sulkiness, a je m'en fous in the face of the world. **1954** *Landfall* VIII. I. 27 The Sydneysider's traditional lounging *jemenfoutism.* **1959** *Guardian* 5 Nov. 6 France..has gone from despair and j'menfoutisme to optimism. **1964** *Ibid.* 4 Dec. 11/3 There is a species of *je m'en foutisme* in Godard that I like. **1966** *Ibid.* 9 Dec. 7/3 Happiness, they appear to say, is square, happiness is corny—and *je m'en fous.*

Jemima, jemima (dʒĕmai·mă). [Female Christian name.] **1.** A made-up tie. Also *attrib.*

1899 SOMERVILLE & 'ROSS' *Some Experiences Irish R.M.* v. 97 We indulged in..'Jemima' ties with diagonal stripes. **1920** *Glasgow Herald* 3 Apr. 4, I have never learned the knack of fixing a dress tie, and I have not the moral courage to wear a jemima.

2. *pl.* Elastic-sided boots; the British name for *Congress boots.*

1902 *M.A.P.* 29 Mar. 323/1, I spoke of Mr. Chamberlain's having fallen from sartorial grace to the extent of wearing 'Jemimas'. **1906** *Westm. Gaz.* 31 Dec. 3/1 A pair of well-preserved 'jemimas'. They are a kind of footgear the immortal Teufelsdröckh himself might have worn, unless he had a weakness for bluchers. **1927** *Glasgow Herald* 24 Aug. 8 The old-fashioned, long obsolete elastic-sided boots, known for some obscure reason as 'Jemimas'. **1961** *Times* 2 Oct. 13/4 The..Dame would at last be caught in the mangle out of whose rollers protruded the struggling feet in the supposedly ludicrous Jemimas.

Jemmy O'Goblin, var. *Jimmy O'Goblin* (s.v. *JIMMY 5).

1889 in BARRÈRE & LELAND *Dict. Slang.*

Jena (yē̆i·nă). The name of a city in East Germany, used *attrib.* to designate glass made there, which originated in the experiments of Ernst Abbe and Otto Schott and became famous for its high quality and the special kinds that were developed.

1892 *Work* IV. 145/2 The new Schott Jena glass. **1902** J. D. & A. EVERETT tr. *Hovestadt's Jena Glass* i. 20 The introduction of Jena glass into practical optics was initiated by Abbe, who was now enabled, with the help of the technical resources of Zeiss' optical works, to realise his long-cherished plans for the improvement of the microscope. *Ibid.* vii. 189 Results for 29 different Jena glasses. **1902** [see *ANASTIGMAT]. **1908** W. ROSENHAIN *Glass Manuf.* i. 7 Another instance of these refractory glasses is to be found in the Jena special thermometer glasses..; the best of these glasses show little or no plasticity at temperatures approaching 500°C. **1941** *Jrnl. Inst. Petroleum* XXVII. 434 The solution was sucked off via a Jena-glass immersion filter. **1954** G. W. MOREY *Properties Glass* (ed. 2) iii. 78 The first Jena 'Geräte' glass, made before 1910.., differed from the ordinary soda-lime glass in the substitution of magnesia and zinc oxide for lime, and in having a small content of B_2O_3. Later..the soda content was reduced and the magnesia largely removed, with increase in the zinc oxide, alumina and boric oxide.

Jennerian (dʒenīə·riăn), *a. Med.* [f. the name of Edward *Jenner* (1749–1823), English physician, who in 1796 vaccinated a subject with cow-pox against small-pox and thereby laid the foundations of vaccination in medicine and of the science of immunology: see -IAN.] Of, pertaining to, or commemorating Jenner; made by or following the methods of Jenner.

1801 *Med. & Physical Jrnl.* VI. 5 The Jennerian Inoculation is universally adopted by the medical gentlemen of this town and neighbourhood. **1805** W. ROWLEY *Cow-Pox Inoculation No Security against Small-Pox* p. v, The names of..those who formed the principals in the Royal Jennerian Institution, etc. are omitted. **1824** MILL *Prefaces to Liberty* (1959) 72 The great spiritual physicians who would vaccinate the nation with hypocrisy to prevent the eruption of infidelity, are not acting on a true Jennerian analogy. **1911** G. B. SHAW *Doctor's Dilemma* p. lxvi, To this day the law which prescribes Jennerian vaccination is carried out with an anti-Jennerian inoculation because the public would have it so. **1951** W. R. LEFANU *Bio-Bibliogr. E. Jenner* ii. 59 The text was included in Jones' and Crookshank's Jennerian collections.

jer (yer). Also **ier, yeer, yer(r).** Pl. **jers, jery.** [ad. OSl. *jerŭ* and *jerĭ*, Russ. *er* (pl. *éry̆*) and *er'*.] The name of either member of the pairs of characters ꙑ, ꙗ and ъ, ь of the Slavonic Glagolitic and Cyrillic alphabets, sometimes distinguished according to their Slavonic names as **jerŭ** (**yerŭ, jer**) and **jerĭ** (**yerĭ, jer'**) respectively; one or both of the sounds represented by these characters, or the Common Slavonic sounds from which they developed. Also *attrib.* (**Jerek, Yerek** in quots. 1861, 1883, referring to the second member of each pair, are from the deriv. seen in Russ. *érik*.)

1763 W. MASSEY *Origin & Progress of Letters* (*tables facing* 114) Yerr... Yeer... ier. **1861** *Grammatography*

Based on the German compilation of F. Ballhorn 58 (*table* Jer... Jerek. *Ibid.* 61 (*table*) Yerr... Yer. **1883** I. Taylor *Alphabet* II. 196 (*table*) Yer... Yerek. **1949** *Archivum Linguisticum* I. 158 The left-to-right characters, viz. *jestŭ, kako, onŭ, ukŭ*, and the left-inclined, *jerŭ* and *jerĭ*.. are significant. **1949** Entwistle & Morison *Russian & Slavonic Languages* 66 Peter the Great's Russian 'civil alphabet'..retained the two *jers* which had no longer an alphabetical value. *Ibid.* 82 In Russian the *jers* continued to be distinguished as back/front vowels, and so developed into the open vowels *o/e* respectively. **1952** *Word* VIII. 323 Leskien..thought that the spellings indicated a change in the quality of the consonant preceding the jer-letter. *Ibid.* 325 The category of jer-phonemes had been sharply reduced as to occurrence. **1955** H. G. Lunt *Old Church Slavonic Gram.* 30 A jer is weak in a syllable followed directly by a non-reduced vowel or pause... A jer is strong only in a syllable directly before a weak jer... When the jers were lost as a category, the weak jers simply disappeared, and the strong jers were replaced by another vowel. **1969** *Language* XLV. 558 The rule specifying sequences of obstruents as fricative + stop was eliminated by the time the jers were lost.

Jeremiah (dʒerĭmai·ă). The name of a Hebrew prophet (see Jeremiad), used allusively to denote a person given to lamentation or woeful complaining.

1781 Gibbon *Decl. & Fall* III. 620 The vague and tedious lamentations of the British Jeremiah [*sc.* Gildas]. **1902** *Daily Chron.* 15 Oct. 3/1 This talk about the rate-payers only came from municipal Jeremiahs. **1905** *Ibid.* 1 Sept. 5/7 The Jeremiahs have been on the rampage; the dismal and the doleful would-be experts [etc.]. **1928** *Daily Express* 23 Feb. 3/5 There are always Jeremiahs who go about saying that we have never had such bad times. **1928** *Observer* 22 July 16/3 The Socialists are..bound to be confirmed Jeremiahs by the necessity of their propaganda. **1963** *Times* 22 Apr. 8/5 Mr. Selwyn Lloyd..wanted to see Young Conservatives 'rise up in protest against the Jeremiahs, defeatists, pessimists, denigrators', [etc.]. **1973** *Listener* 15 Nov. 655/1, I am not going to try to play the role of prophet, least of all Jeremiah.

Jeremianic (dʒe:rĭmai,æ·nik), *a.* [f. *Jeremiah, after *Messianic*.] Of or pertaining to the prophet Jeremiah or the book of the Old Testament which bears his name.

1880 *Encycl. Brit.* XIII. 628/1 Brought into its present form by a captivity prophet, working on a Jeremianic basis. **1891** T. K. Cheyne *Orig. Psalter* 151 A group of literary works which we may call Jeremianic. **1921** J. Moffatt *Approach to New Testament* ii. 62 The Jeremianic prediction of the new covenant has been fulfilled in Christianity.

jerk, *sb.*[1] Add: **2. b.** (*a*) (Examples of the unqualified use.)

1895 G. N. Stewart *Man. Physiol.* xii. 625 The interval which elapses between the tap and the jerk ($\frac{3}{100}$ to $\frac{4}{100}$ second) is distinctly shorter than the reflex time of the extremely rapid lid-reflex. **1936** M. G. Eggleton *Muscular Exercise* viii. 181 The jerk is equally readily obtained if the skin has been de-sensitized by application of a local anæsthetic. **1968** Passmore & Robson *Compan. Med. Stud.* I. xxiv. 14/1 The presence of a normal jerk shows that the receptors are sensitive..and the responding muscle is in order.

d. Colloq. phr. *physical jerks*, physical or gymnastic exercises.

1919 [see sense 2 e below]. **1930** E. Raymond *Jesting Army* I. i. 7 It was the parade for 'Physical Jerks'. *Ibid.* 14 Now the whole family party must go out into the garden to do physical jerks. **1966** A. Sachs *Jail Diary* ii. 24 In the afternoon, I am busy doing physical jerks. *Ibid.* 25 My physical jerks period.

e. Colloq. phr. *to put a jerk in it*, to act vigorously, smartly, or quickly.

1919 *Athenæum* 25 July 664/2 'Physical jerks' dates from war-time, as does also the admonition 'put a jerk in it', which is the equivalent of the ante-bellum 'jump to it'. **1921** N. Kent *Quest M. Harland* II. viii. 241 'I like to see young people enthusiastic. Put a jerk in it, can't you?' 'A—a *what*?' stammered Anthea, tottering. 'Put a jerk in it,' repeated Roger. **1939** C. Day Lewis *Child of Misfortune* III. ii. 271 Put a jerk in it. I'm meeting my boy at the second house at the Royal. **1974** 'J. Ross' *Burning of Billy Toober* xv. 147 If you put a jerk into it, you'll probably have something for me by lunchtime.

f. The name of a dance characterized by jerking movements.

1966 *N.Y. Times Mag.* 9 Jan. 106/2 There is the Watusi, basically a side-to-side stumble, the Shake, and the Jerk—whose movements come as no surprise to old fans of burlesque. **1969** N. Cohn *AWopBopaLooBop* (1970) ix. 85 Dance-crazes bossed pop right up until the Beatles broke... The Jerk and the Block. **1972** T. Kochman *Rappin' & Stylin' Out* 161 Names for dances (Rock and Roll,..Jerk, and Black Power Stomp) all embody kinetic elements.

5. *slang* (orig. *U.S.*). Someone of little or no account; a fool, a stupid person. Cf. *jerkwater b.

1935 A. J. Pollock *Underworld Speaks* 63/2 *Jerk*, a boob; chump; a sucker. **1938** *New Republic* 7 Sept. 129/1 A jerk not only bores you but pats you on the shoulder as he does so. **1945** *Daily Express* 11 Sept. 2/4 See this lighter? A dying Jerry gave it to me. I gave the jerk a smoke from my last cigarette. **1950** [see *brown-noser* s.v. *brown *a.* 7]. **1956** L. McIntosh *Oxford Folly* 85 Julian sounds a dismal little jerk when you sum him up like that. **1958** *Listener* 15 May 802/1 If..the sponsors get eight letters saying that their comedian is an idiot, or a foul-mouthed jerk, they're terrified. **1971** J. Ball *First Team* (1972) xxiv. 382 '*I say* you're a nigger!'..'And I say that you're a goddamned jerk.'

6. *Physics.* Rate of change of acceleration (with respect to time).

1955 J. S. Beggs *Mechanism* iv. 122 Since the forces to produce accelerations must arise from strains in the materials of the system, the rate of change of acceleration, or jerk, is important. **1964** A. G. Fadell *Calculus* vii. 195 In the automobile industry the concept of a jerk is used as a 'comfort index'. *Ibid.*, Free fall has an ideal comfort index, namely zero of jerk. **1973** *Nature Physical Sci.* 19 Feb. 140/1 Large values of jerk (third derivative of the position of *m*) can occur if *M* is sufficiently large.

jerk, *v.*[1] Add: **7.** *trans.* To serve (soda, beer, etc.) at a soda-fountain, bar, etc. Cf. **soda-jerker*. *U.S. colloq.*

1883 G. W. Peck *Peck's Bad Boy* xiii. 126 Well, I must go down to the sweetened wind factory, and jerk soda! **1884** J. Miller *Memorie & Rime* 20 They stared at me, but went on jerking beer behind the counter. **1935** *Amer. Mercury* May 102/1 They had spent their tender years jerking sodas. **1949** Wodehouse *Uncle Dynamite* iv. 54, I also jerked soda.

8. *to jerk off* (trans. and intr.), to masturbate. *slang.*

1937 in Partridge *Dict. Slang.* **1947** A. Bernstein *Home is the Hunted* 152 Big enough for a bush and jerking off like crazy, disconcerted and embarrassed by the riches of manhood flooding through your bones, veins, and gizzard. **1969** P. Roth *Portnoy's Complaint* 177 She will jerk off one guy, but only with his pants on. **1971** B. Malamud *Tenants* 202 The mother..dies unattended, of malnutrition, as Herbert jerks off in the hall toilet.

jerkin[1]. Add: (Later examples.) In modern use, usu. a sleeveless jacket or waistcoat (see quots.).

1935 E. Weekley *Something about Words* 44 Until the War one vaguely associates *jerkin* with the costume of Robin Hood, but after the War 'army jerkins' were to be had cheap. **1957** M. B. Picken *Fashion Dict.* 187/2 *Jerkin*, jacket, short coat, or doublet, sometimes of leather. Occasionally, waistcoat without sleeves. Also straight woolen pull-over. **1963** *Austral. T.V. Times* 18 Apr. 10/1 *Jerkin*, a sort of zipper jacket. **1974** *Guardian* 4 Apr. 11/2 It is legal to shoot clouts, which used to be the jerkins of longbowmen hung on a stick.

jerking, *vbl. sb.* Add: **b.** The action of *jerk *v.*[1] 8. Also with *off*.

1889 Barrère & Leland *Dict. Slang* I. 497/2 *Jerking*, masturbation. **1960** E. L. Wallant *Human Season* ix. 94 Another thing bothers me is your jerking off in bed at night. **1969** F. Norman *Banana Boy* 108 'Ninety-nine change hands,' he would laugh when he came into the kitchen after a hard night's jerking-off. **1972** *Screw* 12 June 12/1 Such sexual behavior as homosexuality, jerking off, [etc.].

jerk-line (dʒə·ɹk,ləin). *N. Amer.* [f. Jerk *v.*[1] 2.] A rope used in place of reins to guide a team of horses, etc. Also *attrib.*

1888 M. Grigsby *Smoked Yank* xix. 156 The driver rode on the nigh wheel mule, and drove the leader with a jerk-line. **1907** S. E. White *Arizona Nights* III. iv. 287, I bet that Sang would get a wiggle on him.., if he had a woman ahold of his jerk line. **1910** J. Hart *Vigilante Girl* x. 140 This train of animals was driven by a 'jerk line' instead of reins. **1937** J. Steinbeck *Of Mice & Men* ii. 61 He was a jerkline skinner..capable of driving ten, sixteen, even twenty mules with a single line to the leaders. **1960** A. Downs *Wagon Road North* 43 Sometimes there were so many horses or mules hitched to a freight wagon that the use of reins was impractical. Under these circumstances a 'jerk-line' was used. This was a single line connected to the bridles of the lead horses.

jerk-off (dʒɔ̄·ɹk,ǫf), *a.* [f. vbl. phr. *to jerk off* (*jerk *v.*[1] 8).] Erotic; encouraging masturbation.

c **1957** in N. Mailer *Advts. for Myself* (1961) 310 They turn their backs..on..the grandeurs of the past, restrict their horizon to..tripe..jazz magazines and jerk-off magazines. **1965** *New Society* 30 Dec. 21/1 It would prove Screeches was not a 'jerk-off' press but was serious.

jerk-off (dʒɔ̄·ɹk,ǫf), *sb.* [Perh. f. prec. but cf. *jerk *sb.*[1] 5.] = *jerk *sb.*[1] 5.

1968–70 *Current Slang* (Univ. S. Dakota) III–IV. 75 *Jerk off*,..a rustic; a simpleton. **1972** J. Mills *Report to Commissioner* 145 I'm sitting there alone..feeling like the biggest jerk-off in the history of the world. **1972** R. A. Wilson *Playboy's Bk. Forbidden Words* 172 A jerk or jerk-off is a fool. **1973** W. Sheed *People will always be Kind* I. xiv. 182 You know perfectly well that the jerk-offs do all the talking at meetings.

jerkwater (dʒɔ̄·ɹk,wǭ:təɹ). *U.S.* [f. Jerk *v.*[1]] In full, *jerkwater train*. A train on a branch railway (see quot. 1945). Also *attrib.*

1878 F. H. Hart *Sazerac Lying Club* 16, I wish I may be run over by a two-horse jerk-water if there was a sage-hen in sight. **1905** *Dialect Notes* III. 84 The St. Paul branch is a jerkwater railroad. *Ibid.*, *Jerkwater* (*train*), train on a branch railway. 'Has the jerkwater come in yet?' **1909** *Sat. Even. Post* 15 May 9/3 The farther along Thorpe got in the list the more disgusted he became with the prospect of living on jerk-water trains. **1920** *Bulletin* 22 June 10/1 This Oriental who, with perfect self-possession..descended from the jerk-water train carrying a modern suitcase. **1926** J. Black *You can't Win* xx. 303, I followed the pay-roll aboard the jerkwater train that carried it to the waiting miners. **1941** *Sun* (Baltimore) 7 Mar. 12/7 In the early days of railroads the small boilers of the locomotives required frequent refilling, and water tanks were very few. Every train crew carried a leather bucket on a long rope with which they 'jerked water' from the streams along their track. As locomotives increased in size the small 'jerk-water' engines were relegated to branch-line service. Today no train crew carries a bucket, but the name 'jerk water' still sticks and has become part of our national heritage of American slang. **1945** J. L. Marshall *Santa Fe, Railroad that built an Empire* 68 The Santa Fe was the Jerkwater Line—because train crews, when the water got low, often had to stop by a creek, form a bucket brigade and jerk water from the stream to fill the tender tank.

b. Used *attrib.* or as *adj.* in sense 'small, insignificant, inferior'. *colloq.*

1897 *Chicago Tribune* 25 July 15/2 John J. Ingalls regards the Swiss Mission as a jerkwater job, and would not take it if it were offered to him. **1911** H. S. Harrison *Queed* xviii. 225 The spring found West stronger and more contented with his lot as president of a jerkwater college. **1923** J. Dos Passos *Streets of Night* 130 Perkinville, a little jerkwater town back in South Dakota. **1936** *Jrnl. Genetic Psychol.* XLIX. 492 It was one of those jerkwater towns that have one lawyer, one drug store and no traffic cops. **1950** Blesh & Janis *They all played Ragtime* (1958) 3 Vaudeville teams—from the jerkwater acts to specialists like Ben Harney. **1970** R. Lockridge *Twice Retired* (1971) v. 68 It won't be easy for him to get another job if he's fired... Maybe at some jerkwater college at half what he's getting now.

jerrican, jerrycan (dʒe·rikæn). Also **jerry can, jerry-can.** [f. *Jerry *sb.*[2] + Can *sb.*[1]] A five-gallon (usu. metal) container for petrol, water, etc., of a type first used in Germany and later adopted by the Allied forces in the war of 1939–45.

1943 *Hutchinson's Pict. Hist. War* 17 Feb.–11 May 258 Mules carrying 'jerricans' to British troops... Jerricans are a special type of petrol container for transporting water. **1944** [see *Jerry *sb.*[2]]. **1944** *Times* 25 Nov. 8/3 The Germans had a very efficient five-gallon petrol can. The Eighth Army captured some of the cans. They were sent back to England, and the British started manufacturing them. They were called jerricans. **1955** M. E. B. Banks *Commando Climber* v. 87 We counted our burden of spuds a privilege in comparison to the jerrycan of red wine which was foisted on to one unfortunate. **1958** *Punch* 9 July 60/2 It [*sc.* sea-water] is collected *each week*..and rushed to Paris in white plastic jerricans. **1969** *New Yorker* 4 Oct. 55/1 Foreigners flying into Biafra now bring their own food and, if the pilot permits it, their own gasoline in jerry cans. **1972** D. Haston *In High Places* x. 109 Water is the only problem: you have to bring big jerry-cans in from Cassis.

Jerry (dʒe·ri), *sb.*[2] *colloq.* (orig. *Mil. slang*). [Prob. alteration of German *a.*[2] and *sb.*[2], perh. infl. by Jerry *sb.*] A German; *spec.* a German soldier; a German aircraft; also, the Germans or German soldiers collectively. Also *attrib.* or as *adj.* Cf. *Fritz[1].

1919 J. B. Morton *Barber of Putney* ii, There was three Jerries waiting for 'im to get tired and chuck it. **1925** Fraser & Gibbons *Soldier & Sailor Words* 131 *Jerry over*, 'Lights out!' The word passed along the lines at the Front at night on the nearing overhead of an enemy aeroplane. *Ibid.*, *Jerry up*, a warning call on the approach of a German aeroplane. **1929** E. W. Springs *Above Bright Blue Sky* 272 If you have many chaps like him, it won't take long to chase Jerry back to the Rhine. **1931** W. V. Tilsley *Other Ranks* 8 The way they referred to the Germans—almost affectionately. Old Fritz, or Old Jerry! Might be an ally! **1941** *Southern Daily Echo* (Southampton) 26 Mar., Last time the enemy was generally called the *Hun* by the people at home, and *Jerry* by the soldiers. The latter is the term which remains in use in the present war. **1942** *Tee Emm* (Air Ministry) II. 58 Net result: all square—instead of one Jerry down. **1943** [see *bag *sb.* 17 (*c*)]. **1944** G. Netherwood *Desert Squadron* xii. 118 The well known Jerry boat, the canvas and leather affair, was soon put into active service by our men and also the petrol container known as the 'Jerrycan'. **1955** J. Thomas *No Banners* xx. 198, I thought you were a Jerry, trailing me. **1961** W. Vaughan-Thomas *Anzio* viii. 185 They almost felt a sympathy for the Jerries under that merciless rain of explosions. **1972** *Daily Mail* 4 May 3/3 Give us a Jerry paper, love... There's a German bloke on top wants one.

jerry (dʒe·ri), *sb.*[3] *slang.* [Prob. abbrev. of Jeroboam.] A chamber-pot.

[**1827** W. Maginn *Whitehall* II. iv. 140 The naval officer ..came into the Clarendon for a Jerry [= jeroboam] of punch. **1850** *Sessions Papers Cent. Criminal Court* (Surrey cases) May 124, I went into the *jerry* [= water-closet], but they had got there before me.] **1859** Hotten *Dict. Slang* 53 *Jerry*, a chamber utensil. **1932** J. Cary *Aissa Saved* xvii. 96 A thin handsome young man carrying a tin jerry in his hand and a broken kettle among the tatters on his back. **1939** 'G. Orwell' *Coming Up for Air* IV. vi. 271 A bed not yet made and a jerry under the bed. **1968** *Canad. Antiques Collector* Dec. 10/1 Young English ladies and gentlemen were beginning to find it offensive to have the old man keep a jerry in the side-board.

jerry (dʒe·ri), *sb.*[4] *Austral.* and *N.Z. slang.* [Cf. *Jerry *a.*[2] and *v.*] Phr. *to take a jerry* (*to*): to investigate and understand (something), to 'tumble' *to* (something).

1919 W. H. Downing *Digger Dial.* 30 *Take a jerry*, change (for the better) one's course of conduct. **1937** Partridge *Dict. Slang* 437/1 *Jerry*,..a recognition, discovery, 'tumble'. **1969** *Landfall* XXIII. 328 It was time this country—ah! Took a jerry to itself. Ha ha.

jerry (dʒe·ri), *a.*[2] *U.S. slang.* [Origin unknown.] Phr. *to be* (or *get*) *jerry* (*on, on to, to*): to be aware (of); to be 'wise' (to); to understand.

1908 K. McGaffey *Sorrows of Show Girl* 200 She accepted the attentions of the comedian which his wife was not supposed to be jerry to. **1921** *Adventure* (U.S.) 18 May 25/1 I've got a strong hunch that thousand bucks is all stowed away, neat as pie, in the pendulum box o' that clock. I'm wise, Kid; I'm jerry. **1926** *Flynn's* 16 Jan. 639/1, I know that th' fly was jerry because he gave me th' once over as I was comin' out. **1942** Berry & Van den Bark *Amer. Thes. Slang* § 149/7 Know; be aware of, *be hep, —jerry, — on, — onto, — wise to. Ibid.* § 149/12 Knowing; cognizant; aware of,..*jerry.*

jerry (dʒe·ri), *v. slang* (chiefly *Austral.* and *N.Z.*). [Cf. *Jerry *sb.*[4]] *intr.* To understand, realize; to 'tumble' *to* something.

1917 *Digger* 4/3 The excuse was so full of Mer(r)it that the officer failed to 'Jerry' to it. **1918** *Chrons. N.Z.E.F.* 21 June 221/1 Unless the sergeant jerries to your lurk. **1925** Fraser & Gibbons *Soldier & Sailor Words* 131 *Jerry, to,* to understand, *e.g.*, 'Do you Jerry it, man?' **1959** G. Slatter *Gun in my Hand* viii. 91 Tried to cut me out with me sheila. Hadn't jerried to it before.

jerry-built, *a.* Add: Also *fig.*

1901 *Daily Chron.* 13 Aug. 3/2 In an age of jerry-built books it is refreshing to come across a volume that has taken forty years to compile. **1903** *Ibid.* 20 Feb. 3/2 Fiction, he said, was now jerry-built. **1933** J. Baillie *And Life Everlasting* (1934) i. 15 That great cataclysm undoubtedly came as a rude shock to many jerry-built philosophies of life.

jerrycan: see *Jerrican.

Jersey[1]**.** Add: **1.** (Further examples.) Also used of fine machine-knitted fabric generally.

1881 *Queen* 8 Jan. (Advt.), Boy's jersey suit. **1938** D. Baker *Young Man with Horn* I. iv. 38 His brother Henry..was selling jersey knits. **1959** *Observer* 22 Mar. 18/4 Some lovely short evening dresses were in silk jersey and had to be bought therefore, a little surprisingly, in the jersey wear department. **1966** *Economist* 9 Apr. 175/1 Acrylics (woolly, fluffy fibres used in knitwear mostly) and polyesters (mostly used in wool mixes, now bulked in jersey-knits) are bound to follow the same course as nylon. **1969** N. Freeling *Tsing-Boum* vi. 36 A nearly new jersey cocktail dress with the boutique label of a couturier. **1972** *Sci. Amer.* Dec. 4/2 The fabric is a plain knitted jersey... It was knitted..of a spun, staple yarn.

4. Also *attrib.* or as *adj.*

1842 *Guide to Island of Jersey* v. 94 The English reader need scarcely be told in what great estimation the Jersey Cows and Heifers are held... The Jersey cow is small and slender in its make, with short crumpled horns. **1845** *Jrnl. R. Agric. Soc.* V. 47 The Jersey cow is a singularly docile and gentle animal. **1875** [see *Alderney]. **1964** G. Durrell *Menagerie Manor* ii. 35 You have vivid mental pictures of an escaped tiger stalking your pedigree herd of Jersey cows.

5. (sense 4) *Jersey cream, milk*; **Jersey elm,** *Ulmus stricta* var. *sarniensis,* a variety of elm of more erect growth than the parent species; **Jersey lily,** a nickname for Li(l)lie or Lily Langtry (1852–1929), an actress born in Jersey.

1895 *Montgomery Ward Catal.* 110/1 Williams' Medicated Jersey Cream Toilet Soap; contains pure, rich cream from Jersey Cows. **1971** 'J. J. Marric' *Gideon's Art* iv. 35 The butler..offered more of the delicious apricot and peach flan, more of the rich Jersey cream. **1838** J. C. Loudon *Arboretum* III. 1376 The Jersey Elm: is a free-growing variety, differing very little from the species. **1914** W. J. Bean *Trees & Shrubs Hardy in Brit. Isles* II. 620 A yellow-leaved form of the Jersey elm originated in the nurseries of Messrs Dickson at Chester in 1900. **1957** M. Hadfield *Brit. Trees* 242 The Jersey Elm is not infrequently seen planted as a street or ornamental tree, but is believed to be indigenous only to the Channel Islands. **1971** *Country Life* 8 Apr. 823/1 It should be widely known that the Jersey elm (*Ulmus stricta sarniensis*) is not immune to elm disease. **1882** W. Hamilton *Aesthetic Movement* 103 *La bella Donna della mia Mente* exists, but she is not the Jersey Lily, though I have grovelled at her feet. **1895** M. Beerbohm in *Yellow Bk.* IV. 275 To have strained my eyes for a glimpse of the Jersey Lily. **1930** W. S. Maugham *Cakes & Ale* xii. 145 She had..a fringe on the forehead with a bun at the nape of the neck as you may see in old photographs of the Jersey Lily. **1972** *Times* 3 July 14/8 The Millais portrait ..showed her [*sc.* Lily Langtry] holding a lily in one hand which earned her the nickname 'Jersey Lily'. **1881** *Jrnl. R. Agric. Soc.* 2nd Ser. XVII. 234 Jersey milk is considered too rich [for a calf]. **1970** E. McGirr *Death pays Wages* vi. 115 Her own breakfast..was Jersey milk and sliced banana.

Jersey[2] (dʒɜ̄·ɹzi). *U.S.* = *New Jersey,* the name of the state situated south of New York, used *attrib.* and *Comb.* to denote people or things coming from or associated with New Jersey, as *Jersey girl, maid*; *Jersey-built, -made* adjs.; **Jersey blue,** (*a*) a colonial New Jersey soldier (so called from his blue uniform); (*b*) a native or inhabitant of New Jersey; (*c*) a breed of chicken; **Jersey justice,** strict or severe justice; **Jersey lightning** *colloq.*, a strong kind of apple-jack, peach-brandy, or whisky; **Jersey pine,** the scrub pine, *Pinus virginiana*; **Jersey tea,** the red-root, *Ceanothus americanus,* the leaves of which were used as a substitute for tea; **Jersey wag(g)on,** a light carriage formerly used in New Jersey.

1758 C. Rea *Jrnl.* 16 July in *Essex Inst. Hist. Coll.* (1881) XVIII. 110 Excepting ye Yorkers and Jersy Blews all ye Provincials didn't loose more than 100 men. **1849** J. F. Cooper *Sea Lions* I. i. 3 Distinctions..exist between the eastern and the western man,..the Buckeye or Wolverine, and the Jersey Blue. **1850** D. J. Browne *Amer. Poultry Yard* 77 The Jersey-Blue Fowl..is another large mongrel of a bluish cast. **1942** C. Weygandt *Plenty of Pennsylvania* 277 We have no native breeds of fowls in Pennsylvania as New Jersey had its Jersey Blues. **1829** R. C. Sands *Writings* (1834) II. 121 Trim Jersey-built wagons. **1770** *Boston Gaz.* 7 May (Th.), A likely active Jersey girl. **1903** *N.Y. Tribune* 18 Oct. 8 Even with a faithful judge..'Jersey justice' did not shine as brilliantly as usual. **1948** *Collier's* 20 Nov. 78/3 Pellechia is having dealings with Jersey justice. **1852** *Alta California* (San Francisco) 23 Aug. 2/5 The rumsellers dealt out Jersey lightning by the gallon. **1872** G. P. Burnham *Mem. U.S. Secret Service* p. vi, *Jersey lightning,* a peculiar New Jersey drink; 'blue ruin'. **1970** *Observer* 19 Apr. 9/4 This urbane and sophisticated man came to believe that after repeal Jersey Lightning would capture the fancy of the whole country, and become a standard national drink. **1778** *Boston Gaz.* 25 Aug. 373 Handy, light, Jersey made waggon. **1713** *Boston News-Let.* 5 Oct. 2/2 A Jersey Maids times for four years and an half very good Servant to be disposed of. **1743** J. F. Gronovius *Flora Virginica* 191 The common Jersay-Pine. **1908** N. L. Britton *N. Amer. Trees* 46 Jersey Pine—*Pinus virginiana* Miller... This tree grows in poor rocky or sandy soil from southern New York to Indiana. **1971** *Country Life* 23 Dec. 1773/1 A singular collection of conifers, some species such as the Jersey pine (*Pinus virginiana*) being planted in considerable numbers. **1759** P. Miller *Gardeners Dict.* (ed. 7) s.v. Ceanothus. New Holland Dogwood with female cornel leaves commonly called New Jersey Thea grows naturally in most Parts of North America, from whence great Plenty of the Seeds have been of late Years brought to Europe, by the Title of New Jersey Thea, where I have been informed the inhabitants dry the leaves of this Shrub to use as Thea. **1808** H. Muhlenburg *Let.* 5 July in E. Rowland *Life W. Dunbar* (1930) 203 Red Root or Jersey Tea we call the Ceanothus americanus a little shrub with white Flowers, cordate leaves—Some times the sanguinaria is called so. **1870** *Amer. Naturalist* IV. 583 The *Ceanothus*, or Jersey tea, is a frequent inhabitant of the prairies. **1948** *Green Bay* (Wisconsin) *Press-Gaz.* 13 July 11/4 Jersey tea, the shrub whose leaves were the 'tea' used by the colonists after the Boston tea party. **1811** R. Sutcliff *Travels N. Amer.* p. viii, Jersey waggons..are made very light, hung on springs with leather braces, and travel very pleasantly. **1835** J. J. Audubon *Ornith. Biogr.* III. 606 Fishermen gunners passed daily..with Jersey wagons, laden with fish, fowls, and other provisions. **1944** *Sat. Rev.* (U.S.) 14 Oct. 24/2 The vagabond Reverend Mason Weems 'bumping along in his Jersey wagon'.

Jerseyman (dʒɜ̄·ɹzimǣn), *sb.*[1] Now *rare.* A native or inhabitant of New Jersey, U.S.A.

1679 *Rec. Early Hist. Boston* (1881) VII. 58 Thomas Begretia [entertained] at James Wardens, Jersiman. **1839** *Southern Lit. Messenger* V. 800/2 A Jerseyman is pre-eminently calculated to make a good traveller. **1873** C. G. Leland *Egypt. Sk.-Bk.* 45 The last number of the *Anglo-American* contains the names of half-a-dozen as veritable Jerseymen as ever drank apple-jack. **1878** *Harper's Mag.* 318/2 'Pretty hard times,' said the Jerseyman; 'but I want three hundred dollars in cash.' **1949** *Hist. & Philos. Soc. Ohio Bull.* Apr. 74 They were especially obnoxious to the Pennsylvanians and Jerseymen.

Jerseyman (dʒɜ̄·ɹzimǣn), *sb.*[2] A native or inhabitant of Jersey (one of the Channel Islands).

1825 J. C. Loudon *Encycl. Agric.* 1129/2 The treasure highest in a Jersey-man's estimation, is his cow. **1842** *Guide to Island of Jersey* x. 144 There is an independence of character in a Jerseyman. **1973** A. Grey *Some put their Trust in Chariots* v. 23 Jerseymen turn every statement into a question with that little word 'Ay?'

Jerusalem. Add: **Jerusalem cherry** = Winter cherry 1 b.

1884 W. Miller *Dict. Eng. Names Plants* 251 *Solanum Pseudo-Capsicum.* Jerusalem Cherry, Winter-Cherry Capsicum. **1887** G. Nicholson *Illustr. Dict. Gardening* III. 455/1 S[*olanum*] *Pseudo-capsicum* (false Capsicum). Jerusalem Cherry. A few handsome hybrids have been raised from this species. **1902** L. H. Bailey *Cycl. Amer. Hort.* IV. 1679/1 [*Solanum*] *Pseudo-Capsicum,* Linn. Jerusalem Cherry... An old-fashioned plant..grown for its showy berry-like fruits, which persist a long time. **1969** *Northwest* (*Sunday Oregonian Mag.*) 14 Dec. 19/3 Christmas potted plants are just as important a part of the scene. Poinsettias, cyclamens, chrysanthemums, Christmas peppers, Jerusalem cherries, foliage plants, dish gardens, and others are among them.

2. *fig.* An ideal or heavenly city; *spec.* = City 3 b; freq. *the new Jerusalem.*

1382, etc. [see City 3 b]. **1535** [see New *a.* 5 c]. **1601** *Song of Mary Mother of Christ* 38 Ierusalem my happy home, when shall I come to thee. **1804–8** W. Blake *Milton* Pref., in *Compl. Writings* (1972) 481, I will not cease from Mental Fight, Nor shall my Sword sleep in my hand Till we have built Jerusalem In England's green & pleasant Land. **1933** J. Buchan *Prince of Captivity* I. ii. 70 For the first time Adam told another of..his childhood home and its lonely peace... 'Ah,' he said, 'it is as I guessed. We have each our Jerusalem.' **1959** A. Huxley *Let.* 10 Jan. (1969) 863 The nature of these visions is often paradisal and the descriptions of them remind one irresistibly of the description of the New Jerusalem in the Apocalypse. **1968** *Listener* 21 Mar. 377/3 Both men indeed looked forward to the same new Jerusalem—a society in which the state would wither away, bureaucracy would be no more.

3. Used as an exclamation, usu. of surprise.

1840 *Spirit of Times* 8 Aug. 276/2 By Jerusalem! **1868** Reade & Boucicault *Foul Play* III. xvii. 199 'What is your name, when you are ashore?' 'Robert Penfold. The Reverend Robert Penfold.' 'The Reverend!—Jerusalem.' **1872** [see *Geewhillikins *int.*]. **1898** J. D. Brayshaw *Slum Silhouettes* 179 Jee-roosalem! You can't stand there; the police won't allow it. **1914** Chesterton *Wisdom of Father Brown* i. 19 'Jerusalem!' ejaculated Brown suddenly. **1968** J. F. Straker *SIN & Johnny Inch* i. 19 He consulted his watch. 'Jerusalem! It's nearly three hours.' **1974** P. Lovesey *Invitation to Dynamite Party* ii. 27 'He kept..buying me whisky.' Jerusalem! Cribb blinked. 'You were on spirits that night, then?'

jes, jes' (dʒes), colloq. shortening of Just *adv.*; freq. in American (esp. Black English) writings. Cf. *Jest.

1851 Mrs. Stowe *Uncle Tom's Cabin* (1852) I. iv. 41 Missis let Sally try to make some cake t'other day, jes to *larn* her, she said. **1886** in H. Baumann *Londinismen* 85/2. **1895** *Southern Workman* XXIV. 15/3 Ef I was starvin' an' had jes one ginger-cake, I would give you half. **1925** Odum & Johnson *Negro & his Songs* ii. 39 Ef you want to see old Satan run, Jes fire off dat gospel gun. **1929** *Amer. Mercury* XVIII. 48/1 This big sargent wus jes' too mean to live. **1938** R. E. Bass in B. A. Botkin *Treas. S. Folklore* (1949) III. i. 457 He jes rared back and 'lowed, 'I ain't never told a lie in my life.' **1962** *Jrnl. Amer. Folklore* LXXV. 311 They thinks that science has solved jes' about ever'thin. **1966** *Massachusetts Rev.* VII. 659 He be sittin' theah at crop time, jes' afigurin' an' areckonin'. **1969** 'J. Morris' *Fever Grass* vi. 65 You jes talked a whole lotta sense.

Jesse[2] (dʒe·si). *U.S. slang.* (? *Obs.*). Also **jesse, jessie, jessy.** [Perh. derived from a jocular interpretation of 'There shall come a rod out of the stem of Jesse' (Isa. xi. 1).] *To give* (a person) *Jesse*: to treat or handle severely; to beat or scold soundly. Similarly *to catch* or *get Jesse.*

1839 *Spirit of Times* 19 Oct. 396/3 If I thought he had been shot and creesed in that savigerous sorta fashion, I'd give him jessy with my butcher knife. **1840** *Daily Even. Transcript* (Boston) 12 Feb. 1/1 If any of you ever come to Saco, I kalkilate you'll get *jesse.* **1846** *Spirit of Times* 4 July 223/3 One of the combatants 'caught Jessie'. **1846** D. Corcoran *Pickings* 126 Threatening to give Miss Martin 'jessy' when she would next meet her. **1865** A. H. Stephens *Diary* 29 Sept. (1910) 518 While I thought I was giving you Jesse on hearts, you were giving me fits on spades. **1946** *Amer. Speech* XXI. 153/1 Thornton's latest citation for *give him Jesse* is from 1865... In February, 1946, I heard the expression used in a game of bridge by a player from Sidney, Nebraska, when her partner was ruffing an opponent's suit.

Jessie (dʒe·si). *colloq.* Also **Jessy,** and with lower-case initial. [Female proper name.] A cowardly or effeminate man; a male homosexual.

1923 G. Blake *Mince Collop Close* i. 20 He was a big Jessie, ...but she liked him. **1938** [see *go-round]. **1958** K. Amis *I like it Here* ii. 31 Darling, you really don't have to convince me that you're not a jessie. **1958** M. Dickens *Man Overboard* iv. 59 Don't listen to those timid old Jessies at Southampton. **1971** G. Sims *Deadhand* II. ii. 88 Duff had been scathing about 'soft jessies who couldn't get their fat heads down'. **1973** D. Lees *Rape of Quiet Town* xix. 153 The implication that J. Plummer Esquire was a soft jessie—because he had a rotten objection to getting himself killed.

jest (dʒest), colloq. and dial. var. Just *adv.* Cf. *Jes, jes'.

1815 D. Humphreys *Yankey in Eng.* I. 22 I'm rather in a strait, jest now. **1890** Kipling *Barrack-Room Ballads* (1892) 19 Jest send in your Chief an' surrender. **1896** in G. F. Northall *Warwickshire Word-Bk.* 119. **1908** A. J. Dawson *Finn* xix. 293 Jest you remember, my boy, that where I sleeps I breakfast. **1971** M. Babson *Cover-up Story* x. 112 Hell, it was jest a thought. **1973** *Black World* June 63 Jest git on da good foot.

Jesuit, *sb.* Add: **1.** (Further examples.)

For note in Dict. read:

The object of the Society of Jesus was to support the Roman Church in its struggle with the 16th c. Reformers and to propagate the faith among the heathen. Hated and feared by Protestants, the Order, with its authoritarian constitution and its principle of total obedience to papal commands, became suspect to many in Roman Catholic countries too—more especially when Jesuit schools and confessionals came to exercise great influence on rulers and high society. By their enemies, the Jesuits were accused of teaching that the end justifies the means, and the lax principles of casuistry put forward by a few of their moralists were ascribed to the Order as a whole, thus giving rise, not only in English but in French and other languages, to sense 2, and to the opprobrious sense attached to *Jesuitical, Jesuitry,* and other derivatives.

1846 W. F. Hook *Church Dict.* (ed. 5) 491 The Jesuits assume neither the name, quality, nor way of living, of monks. They call themselves an *order of priests*... The end of their institution is the salvation of souls: they preach, instruct youth, read lectures, and dispute and write against heretics. **1913** G. P. Gooch *Hist. & Historians in 19th Cent.* xxvi. 530 Renan sharply castigates the futility of the Priestly Code and the sterile scholasticism of its commentators. Nehemiah is described as the first Jesuit, who turned Jerusalem into a tomb. **1914** [see

*BOYO]. **1932** E. BEVAN *Christianity* ix. 191 Jesuits were trained by a severe discipline, not to live in retirement from the world, but to mingle with the world in order to conquer it for the Church. **1934** H. H. GOWEN *Hist. Relig.* xxxix. 598 The Jesuits as a body, by their splendid training, their broad-minded knowledge of human nature, and by their extraordinary personal devotion, did much to win for the Roman Churches territory far larger in area than..had been lost. **1939** [see *ICONOLOGY 1]. **1953** J. E. NEALE *Elizabeth I & her Parliaments* VII. i. 370 The Jesuits came, as it were, direct from England's capital enemy, the Pope. **1959** L. HANKE *Aristotle & Amer. Indians* viii. 108 The efforts of another Jesuit, Antonio Vieira, in the seventeenth century to protect the natives of Brazil. **1972** J. P. KENYON *Popish Plot* i. 22 The Jesuits..aimed to draw England into the revitalized Church Universal of the Counter-Reformation.

2. (Further examples.) Also *fig. depreciatory.*

[**1852** THACKERAY *Esmond* I. v. 99 Father Holt wore more suits of clothes than one. All Jesuits do. You know what deceivers we are, Harry.] **1855** C. KINGSLEY *Westward Ho!* III. ii. 34 Eustace is a man no longer; he is become a thing, a tool, a Jesuit. **1856** J. W. CARLYLE *Jrnl.* 11 Apr. in *Lett. & Memorials* (1883) II. 271 'I'll tell you what to do,' said this Jesuit of a baker; 'Go and join the Methodists' chapel for six months; make yourself agreeable to them, and you'll soon have friends that will help you in your object.' *c* **1879** E. DICKINSON *Poems* (1955) III. 1015 The Jesuit of Orchards He cheats as he enchants. **1907** G. B. SHAW *Major Barbara* III. 285 Charles Lomax: you are a fool. Adolphus Cusins: you are a Jesuit. Stephen: you are a prig. Barbara: you are a lunatic. **1923** D. L. SAYERS *Whose Body?* ii. 40 Gentlemen, we are not Jesuits, we are straightforward Englishmen. You cannot ask a British-born jury to convict any man on the authority of a probable opinion. **1947** V. S. PRITCHETT in *Horizon* May 241 Rubashov and Gletkin are a sad pair of Jesuits consumed and dulled as human beings by their casuistry. **1948** D. SHUB *Lenin* vii. 152 In July 1916, Viacheslav Menzhinsky, later chief of the Soviet secret police,..wrote: Lenin is a political Jesuit who over the course of many years has molded Marxism to his aims of the moment.

4. a. *adj.* (Further examples.)

1874 J. R. GREEN *Short Hist. Eng. People* vii. 402 The torture and death of the Jesuit martyrs sent a thrill of horror through the whole Catholic Church. **1922** JOYCE *Ulysses* 220 Father Conmee..thought ..of the book that might be written about jesuit houses. **1939** *Times Lit. Suppl.* 14 Jan. 20 One of the most heroic members of one of the most heroic bodies in the history of the world, the Jesuit mission to the Hurons. **1950** *Chambers's Encycl.* VIII. 273/1 In 1872 supervision of schools was reserved exclusively for the government of Prussia and the Jesuit Order was banned from Germany altogether. **1953** J. E. NEALE *Elizabeth I & her Parliaments* VII. i. 370 The Jesuit mission to England led by two distinguished and contrasting men, Parsons and Campion. **1956** *Atlantic Monthly* Nov. 43/2 It was a form of answer well known to the examiners—the famous Jesuit equivocation. **1966** D. JOHNSON *France & Dreyfus Affair* xiii. 220 The tighter the organisation of the group, Assumptionist or Jesuit, the greater the hostility towards Dreyfus. **1972** J. P. KENYON *Popish Plot* vi. 182 The suspicion that he had designs on the family estate, which should have descended to his Jesuit brother, now in Newgate.

c. Used *attrib.* to designate a type of Chinese 18th-century export porcelain decorated with religious pictures copied from European designs.

1882 W. W. OLD *Indo-European Porc.* 5 Dealers as a rule calling it [*sc.* Indo-European porcelain] 'Jesuit china', a general impression has prevailed that it was the work of the converts to the early Romish missions in China and Japan. **1898** W. G. GULLAND *Chinese Porc.* 12 Christianity has left little mark on the ceramics of China;..few pieces display biblical subjects or Christian emblems, and such are known as 'Jesuit China'. **1900** F. LITCHFIELD *Pott. & Porc.* vii. 114 This is called 'Jesuit china', because it is said that it was painted to the order of..the Jesuit missionaries. **1927** W. B. HONEY *Guide Later Chinese Porc.* viii. 67 'Jesuit china' was..probably copied from designs supplied by the merchants. **1952** M. ANDERSON *Story Chinese Porc.* 46 Flat-edged plates with biblical subjects painted in a grey-black are the usual features of these 'Jesuit' pieces. **1962** D. IMBER tr. *Beurdeley's Porc. E. India Co.* 141/2 The Roman Catholic creed was foremost in Europe at the time, but the great reformers, Calvin and Luther, are also represented on different plates and servers. The British Museum has a plate representing John of Leyden, the leader of the Anabaptists. It will be clear, then, that the title *Jesuit porcelain* cannot be maintained in the light of the facts.

Jesuitical, *a.* Add: **1.** (Further examples.)

1848 *Jesuitism in Church* iv. 41 Jesuitical principles are by no means confined to those who openly adhere to the rule of Loyola. *c* **1905** H. A. HENDERSON *Shall we tolerate Jesuits?* vii. 24 An influx of Jesuitical religious Orders. **1932** G. F.-H. BERKELEY *Italy in Making* I. xvi. 238 The head of a Jesuitical society, the *Amicizia cattolica.* **1943** H. J. MULLER *Sci. & Crit.* 195 It has therefore incorporated the Jesuitical principle that the end justifies the means. **1947** C. J. CADOUX *Philip of Spain & Netherlands* vii. 147 The need of money for..launching his Jesuitical seminaries..caused the pope great financial difficulty.

2. (Further examples.) Often used in sense 'hair-splitting', keenly analytical.

1829 *Jesuitism & Methodism* I. viii. 119 She trusted..to preserve Cordelia from being perverted, by Jesuitical craft, from the true light. **1925** T. DREISER *Amer. Trag.* (1926) II. III. xxvi. 327 'Hesitating fatally but not criminally at the one time in his life when he should not have hesitated'—a really strong if jesuitical plea which was not without its merits and its weight. **1932** E. BEVAN *Christianity* ix. 192 Two things especially brought odium upon the name of Jesuit. One is the suspicion of vast subterranean intrigue carried on to gain worldly power..; and the other is the belief that the Jesuits cultivate an immoral casuistry—whence the adjective 'jesuitical'—and especially teach that a good end justifies any kind of means. **1950** *Nation* (N.Y.) 16 Dec. 595 If they insist on debating jesuitical verbal formulas instead of effective and enforceable agreements..then no worth-while end would be served by attempting to bargain with them. **1971** M. HASTINGS *Jesuit Child* I. i. 14 People only call a man jesuitical when they are beaten in an argument. **1972** *New Yorker* 29 Apr. 112/2 The film ['Loot'] is made up of people who regard themselves as lone wolves with a unique hold on sense who have to put up with the Jesuitical twitterings of everybody else. **1974** *Daily Tel.* 17 Dec. 12 An argument of such Jesuitical subtlety that one would have thought it could impress no one of moderate common sense or sanity.

jesuitically, *adv.* (Later examples.)

1946 *Protestant* (Boston, Mass.) Oct.–Nov. 48 Yet so jesuitically has the argument of 'discrimination' been presented that it has taken in even some well-intentioned progressive citizens. **1962** *Punch* 7 Feb. 253/3 'It's an ancient highway, a bit of old England,' he pleads jesuitically, caring nothing for the means so that his end be achieved. **1974** I. MURDOCH *Sacred & Profane Love Machine* 240 Monty in black linen jacket and white shirt, his dark hair well combed and neat, his black shoes ludicrously well polished, was looking his most jesuitically untouchable.

Jesuitism. 1, 2. (Further examples.)

1749 J. WESLEY *Jrnl.* 2 June (1912) III. 404 A gentlewoman informed me that Dr. B had averred to her..that it [*sc.* Methodism] was all Jesuitism at the bottom. Alas for poor Dr. B.! **1829** *Jesuitism & Methodism* I. xi. 187 Had he been present,..spite of Jesuitism and priestly pride, it is probable his secret would have escaped him. **1897** J. MCCABE *Twelve Yrs. in Monastery* ix. 187, I have met very many priests who quite accept the Protestant Alliance version of Jesuitism. **1901** W. C. COPELAND *Empire's Greatest Danger* is. 58 How can one prove that the origin of this particular 'genius' of Jesuitism belongs to Mussulman monasticism? *c* **1905** H. A. HENDERSON *Shall we tolerate Jesuits?* viii. 32 Jesuitism is too deadly a danger for us as a Protestant nation to tolerate. **1913** J. MCCABE *Candid Hist. Jesuits* vii. 167 (*heading*) The first century of Jesuitism. **1956** *Time* 2 Jan. 58/2 Her plans to give 'freedom' to Bavaria were blocked by what she called 'the cloven foot of Jesuitism'. **1970** *Guardian* 25 July 7/2 Both Catholics and Communists suffered from Jesuitism, from a belief that the ends justified the means, and the Church would be willing to come to agreement when the terms suited its books.

Jesuitry. 1. (Further examples.)

1901 W. C. COPELAND *Empire's Greatest Danger* vi. 40 Belgium cleared its borders of Jesuitry in 1818. **1911** *Encycl. Brit.* XV. 340/1 A certain characteristic, which soon began to manifest itself in an impatience of episcopal control, showed that the quality of 'Jesuitry', usually associated with the Society, was singularly lacking in their dealings with opponents. **1944** *Atlantic Monthly* Nov. 75/1 Humanism considered as an intellectual discipline-for-discipline's-sake..is a prime specific for such ills as bigotry and puritanism and jesuitry and vulgarity.. and the complacency of the bourgeois mind. **1951** R. HALL *Short Hist. Ital. Lit.* 261 The words *Jesuitry* and *Jesuitical* have become proverbial in reference to dishonestly subtle dialectics and hypocritical condonement of evil practice. **1972** *Times Lit. Suppl.* 22 Dec. 1551/1 Casuistry like Jesuitry is a perfectly respectable word, but it has acquired a sinister connotation.

Jesus. Add: **1. b.** Used as (or as part of) an oath or as a strong exclamation of surprise, disbelief, dismay, or the like; also in various phrases, as *by Jesus, Jesus (H.) Christ, Jesus wept.* Cf. *GEE *int.*[2], *JEEZ(E *int.*

1377, 1676 [in Dict., sense 1]. **1592** SHAKS. *Rom. & Jul.* II. iv. 31 Iesu a very good blade, a very tall man. *Ibid.* v. 29 Iesu what hast? can you not stay a while? **1753** GRAY *Long Story* in *Six Poems* 22 Jesu-Maria! Madam Bridget, Why, what can the Viscountess mean? **1922** JOYCE *Ulysses* 38 Jesus! If I fell over a cliff. *Ibid.* 39 Yes, sir. No, sir. Jesus wept: and no wonder, by Christ. *Ibid.* 131 By Jesus, she had the foot and mouth disease and no mistake! **1923** *Dialect Notes* V. 212 *Jesus Christ*, an expletive or exclamation common to both men and women and considered by neither as in any wise profane. **1924** *Ibid.* 264 Jesus Christ, Jesus H. Christ, holy jumping Jesus Christ. **1936** S. SASSOON *Sherston's Progress* IV. iii. 273 Someone gasping by, carrying a bag of rations—'Jesus, ain't we there yet?' **1943** 'C. DICKSON' *She died a Lady* xvi. 135 Have we heard about him?.. Jesus H. Christ! **1966** A. LA BERN *Goodbye Piccadilly* vi. 66 It's you she's describing, your clothes, everything. Oh, Jesus wept! **1968** B. HEALEY *Murder without Crime* iii. 59 Jesus! It's murder out there. **1970** T. LEWIS *Jack's Return Home* 223 'Jesus Christ!' he says softly. 'Jesus H. Christ.' **1974** I. MURDOCH *Sacred & Profane Love Machine* 94 He's so spineless... He just wants to be let off and I let him off. Jesus wept!

3. b. Used *attrib.* or *Comb.* to designate a fervently evangelical type of Christian, or a group of such people, or things characteristic of them.

1970 *Catholic Worker* Feb. 2/3 He still spoke contemptuously of Jesus-shouters. **1970** *N.Y. Times* 22 Feb. 64 They gladly accept the name Jesus Freaks and have long hair and other marks of hip culture. **1971** *New Scientist* 3 June 588/1 Its Jesus shops, symbols of the brand of freaked-out Christianity that has replaced Flower Power as a culture. **1971** *Listener* 9 Sept. 324/1 The Jesus people, offering religion as a substitute for the drug cult among young people, arrived from America. **1971** *Daily Colonist* (Victoria, B.C.) 12 Dec. 4/1 Certainly the sect seems to have outfreaked all its competitors in the 'Jesus Freak' movement. **1972** *Sat. Rev.* (U.S.) 6 May 58/2 (*heading*) Meditations on the Jesus Movement. *Ibid.*, The Jesus revolution is simply the most recent, popular, and obvious expression of that need. *Ibid.*, The Jesus-cults..offer the young..an instantaneous and push-button forgiveness. **1972** *Awake!* 8 Nov. 3/1 Also called 'Jesus freaks', or 'Street Christians', they put up Jesus posters, wear Jesus buttons, and emblazon their car bumpers with stickers that say: 'Honk, if you love Jesus.' **1973** *Times* 3 Mar. 6/3 Dr Ramsey said: 'I welcome Jesus Freaks as a genuine religious movement.'

jet, *sb.*[3] Add: **III. 4. c.** *Astr.* (i) A thin, well-defined stream of luminous material extending from the nucleus in the head of a comet.

1866 W. LOCKYER tr. *Guillemin's Heavens* (ed. 2) 293 If we look at the drawings..of the comet of 1862..we shall be astonished at the rapidity of the changes of position and form of the luminous jets which successively were emitted from the nucleus... M. Chacornac was able to distinguish the formation of thirteen..jets, similar to jets of steam. **1888** C. A. YOUNG *Textbk. Gen. Astron.* (1889) xvii. 404 In the case of a very brilliant comet, its head is often veined by short jets of light which appear to be continually emitted by the nucleus. **1931** *Publ. Lick Observatory* (Univ. Calif.) XVII. 481 Secondary nuclei were found showing all the properties of the primary nucleus, namely, halos, jets, and streamers. **1966** *McGraw-Hill Encycl. Sci. & Technol.* III. 314/1 At smaller distances [from the sun] (less than 0·5 AU) there may be profuse emission of material but distinguishable features, such as jets, are seldom observed.

(ii) A spicule or similar structure in the solar chromosphere.

1948 *Astrophysical Jrnl.* CVIII. 130 An interpretation of the chromospheric spicules as a system of superthermic jets is presented. **1951** *Monthly Notices R. Astron. Soc.* CXI. 630 The solar chromosphere exhibits an intricate fimbriate structure that consists of very small prominences in contact with the photosphere. For brevity, these chromospheric details will be called 'jets'. *Ibid.*, 'Spicule', introduced by W. O. Roberts.., apparently refers to the largest of the jets that appear in the Sun's polar regions. **1953** G. P. KUIPER *Sun* v. 212 The chromosphere seems composed of a more or less homogeneous layer, from which emerge fine streaks or spikes... Roberts has introduced the name spicules for these fine details, Lyot and Mohler call them jets.

(iii) A narrow strip extending radially outwards from some galaxies and quasars and usually differing from the rest of the galaxy or quasar in the radiation it emits.

1954 *Astrophysical Jrnl.* CXIX. 221 NGC 4486 has a unique peculiarity which has been known for a long time. In the center of the nebula..is a straight jet, extending from the nucleus in position angle 290°...Several strong condensations are in the outer parts of the jet, which extends about 20″ from the nucleus and has an average width of about 2″. **1966** *Nature* 13 Aug. 698/2 The synchrotron radiation of the jet of 3C 273 is detectable optically but not in the radio wave-lengths. **1967** *Internat. Astron. Union Symposium* XXXI. 442 A well-known feature of M87 is a jet, about 1000 pc long, emitting polarized light via the synchrotron mechanism. **1972** *Physics Bull.* Apr. 202/2 An example is galaxy M87, the famous 'jet' galaxy showing a high velocity jet of matter flying from its centre.

d. = *JET STREAM.

1953 *Q. Jrnl. R. Meteorol. Soc.* LXXIX. 236 The wind components perpendicular to this axis were evaluated on each sounding at 50-mb intervals below and above the level of the jet. **1957** *Ibid.* LXXXIII. 222 The local and shallow nature of the near-discontinuity surface compared to the upper-temperature gradients in the jet certainly suggests a minor role for the front in the overall mechanics of the waves. **1963** tr. *E. R. Reiter's Jet-Stream Meteorol.* iv. 167 (*heading*) The structure of the frontal zone in the region of the polar-front jet. **1968** *Jrnl. Atmospheric Sci.* XXV. 1169/1 An equatorial jet can be driven by a convergence of momentum flux. **1970** *Nature* 17 Jan. 254/2 Thermal convection on a global scale in the lower atmosphere of Jupiter redistributes angular momentum so as to produce a well defined westerly jet at high level astride the equator... On Earth, equatorial jets are found in the lower stratosphere and in the oceans.

5. (Further examples.)

1887 *Encycl. Brit.* XXII. 500/2 The oil is injected in the form of a spray..by a steam jet arranged in such a way that air will be drawn into the furnace along with the petroleum. **1901** *Motor-Car World* II. 42/1 Sometimes the jet gets stopped up, causing the engine to cease working. **1929** NEWTON & STEEDS *Motor Vehicle* vii. 108 [In a Diesel engine] the jet must also be so disposed and directed that a stream of liquid is not likely to impinge on the cylinder wall or piston, where rapid carbonization would occur. **1943** A. P. FRAAS *Aircraft Power Plants* vii. 116 The simple carburetor has been used to meter fuel to gasoline engines from the time they first came into use. Essentially, it consists of two orifices in parallel. The first, the air venturi, meters the air flow. The second, the fuel jet, meters the fuel flow. **1963** C. CAMPBELL *Sports Car Engine* vi. 97 This is a simple auxiliary carburettor with an air jet and a fuel jet feeding into a passage leading to the engine side of the throttle plate.

c. [Ellipt. use.] A jet plane or a jet engine.

1944 *Flight* 10 Feb. 153/2 The advantages of the jet are so great that I am sure their development will be rapid. **1944** *Collier's* 22 Apr. 13/3 The jet..is capable of faster flight at low altitudes than any airplane with conventional engines and propeller. **1948** 'N. SHUTE' *No Highway* i. 7 The Mark I model..had radial engines, though now they all have jets. **1957** *Economist* 31 Aug. 697/1 In military air weapons, the jet is now giving way to the rocket motor. **1973** *Observer* 14 Jan. 7/2 The enormous capacity of the latest generation big jets can be filled only by promotional and concessionary fares.

9. *jet speed, velocity*; **jet boat** *N.Z.* (see quot. 1968); **jet engine**, an engine utilizing jet

propulsion to provide forward thrust, esp. an aircraft engine that takes in air and ejects hot compressed air and exhaust gases; so *jet-engined* adj.; **jet flap** *Aeronaut.*, a jet of gas from a jet engine ejected downward as a sheet through a slot in the trailing edge of an aircraft wing, so as to act as a flap and increase the lift; **jet injector** *Med.*, an instrument for giving injections without breaking the skin by means of a fine jet of fluid forced through it under pressure; **jet motor** = *jet engine* above; **jet pipe**, a pipe or duct from which a jet of fluid is expelled; *spec.* the exhaust duct of a jet engine; **jet turbine**, a turbojet engine. Also *JET STREAM.

1964 Jet boat [known to Editor]. **1967** A. & D. REID *Paddle Wheels on Wanganui* p. x, Canoes, rafts and jet-boats notwithstanding, there can be no equal to the experience of shooting a long twisting rapid in the lumbering, flat bottomed, inelegant work-horse that was a Wanganui riverboat in its heyday. **1968** *Times* 31 Aug. 7/5 The jet boat is..a simple enough contraption—a strong glass fibre hull..; a powerful and reliable inboard engine; and..a highly developed water pump. Water is sucked in through a flat grating..and projected violently out the back to supply propulsion and steering. **1970** *N.Z. Listener* 27 Feb. 1 (*caption*) The experimental jetboat on the Waimakariri River, 1951. **1975** *N.Z. News* 8 Jan. 9/3 Another development of consequence in New Zealand has been the invention of the jet boat... Propelled and steered by its water jet, the [Sir William] Hamilton jet boat can make 180-degree turns in its own length. **1943** *Jrnl. R. Aeronaut. Soc.* XLVII. 413 In general, the jet engine performance is given not in h.p. but in kg. of thrust. **1950** *Sci. News* XV. 72 The ordinary jet engine uses oxygen from the air, but the rocket carries its own oxygen supply with it in some form. **1952** A. Y. BRAMBLE *Air-Plane Flight* x. 156 There are, at present, three types of air-plane jet 'engine'—(*a*) rocket, (*b*) turbo-jet, (*c*) athodyd. **1969** *Jet Engine* (Rolls-Royce Ltd.) (ed. 3) i. 4/1 Although a rocket engine..is a jet engine, it has one major difference in that it does not use atmospheric air as the propulsive fluid stream. **1952** *Lancet* 15 Nov. 967/2 In jet-engined aeroplanes the high sonic frequencies predominate. **1960** *Guide Civil Land Aerodrome Lighting* (*B.S.I.*) 30 Where a runway is used by large jet-engined aircraft, blister type fittings are advisable as elevated fittings can be blown over by the jet efflux. **1958** *Spectator* 7 Feb. 160/3 The vast amount of British work on blown flaps, jet flaps, jet lift and boundary layer control. **1963** *Engineering* 5 Apr. 493/1 The principle of the jet flap was..patented in 1952 by the National Gas Turbine Establishment and is a technique whereby the power of jet engines installed for propulsion can also be used greatly to increase the wing lift at low speeds. **1947** *Current Res. Anesthesia & Analgesia* XXVI. 223 Figure 2 shows position of the jet injector for anesthetizing the skin preparatory to insertion of lumbar puncture needle. **1965** *Brit. Med. Jrnl.* 25 Dec. 1541/1 High-pressure jet injectors..throw the material to be injected with considerable force through a very fine nozzle. **1973** *Lancet* 28 Apr. 927/2 Contacts of the early cases were vaccinated by intradermal injection, but two jet injectors were ordered for the vaccination of the 5 and 6-year-old children. **1944** *Discovery* Nov. 346/2 This is the Whittle aircraft, with a gas-turbine jet-motor. **1950** J. V. CASAMASSA *Jet Aircraft Power Syst.* v. 89 The Aerojet motor is a true rocket, since its propellent charge contains both the fuel and the oxygen necessary to burn it. Consequently, this jet motor delivers its rated power independent of altitude or atmospheric conditions. **1946** *Jrnl. R. Aeronaut. Soc.* L. 317/1 After compression in the compressor, the air is circulated through a radiator or heat exchanger situated in the jet pipe of the engine. **1966** *McGraw-Hill Encycl. Sci. & Technol.* X. 227/2 Jetting consists of displacing the soil at the pile tip by means of a quantity of water or air through an internal or external jet pipe, which also lubricates the sides of the pile as it rises to escape. **1966** D. STINTON *Anat. Aeroplane* vii. 126 The thrust of a turbojet is frequently augmented by burning additional fuel in the jetpipe, thus utilizing unburnt air. **1934** *Aircraft Engineering* VI. 170/2 At the maximum pressure end the difference between the static pressure inside the [wind] tunnel and atmospheric at a jet speed of 200 ft./sec. is about 45 lb./sq. ft. **1945** *Sci. Amer.* June 365 Jet turbines have extremely low oil consumption ratings. **1949** *Punch* 14 Sept. 286/3 Emerging miraculously from its dive, the monster..flashes low across the runway, the whiffling roar of its jet-turbine manfully pursuing. **1935** in *Aeronaut. Jrnl.* (1970) LXXIV. 130/2 The jet velocity resulting from a useful heat drop of 250 units is..2320 ft/s. **1966** *McGraw-Hill Encycl. Sci. & Technol.* XIV. 159/1 Under these conditions, afterburning to an exhaust temperature of 3460°R provides an increase in jet velocity of..1·5.

IV. 10. Combs. in which *jet* represents 'jet engine', as *jet efflux, fuel*; *jet-assisted, -powered* adjs.; esp. in the designations of aircraft (and occas. other forms of transport) powered by jet engines, as *jet aeroplane, aircraft, air liner, airplane, bomber, fighter, lifter, liner, plane, tanker, trainer*. Also **jet lift**, lift (vertical thrust) provided by a jet engine. (For *jet engine, motor*, etc., see sense *9.) Also *JET PROPULSION.

1951 'J. WYNDHAM' *Day of Triffids* ii. 36 Also I must buy an aeroplane—a jet aeroplane, very fast. **1944** *Flight* 3 Feb. 130/1 Now about the jet aircraft. Instead of the jets coming out of the tail, shape the aircraft like an orange pip and have several jets coming out of the shoulders, pressing air against and all round the fuselage. **1954** *Economist* 11 Sept. 12/2 On multi-engined jet aircraft the horizontal tail must also be placed away from the jet blast. **1959** *Daily Tel.* 23 Feb. 11/8, I have seen films of man's experience of weightlessness in a jet aircraft. **1970** *Times* 25 Feb. 8/6 The first Whittle jet was tested three years later [*sc.* in 1937].., and the first British jet aircraft flew in 1941. **1947** *Jrnl. R. Aeronaut. Soc.* LI. 178/2 With regard to the comfort of jet air liners, he wondered whether people were being misled. **1959** *Daily Tel.* 2 Mar. 16/4 The new large jet airliners are probably as fast, and can fly as high, as most jet bombers now in service. **1944** *Collier's* 22 Apr. 13/1 Few standard conveniences for upper stratosphere flying had yet been built into the jet airplane. **1944** Jet-assisted [see *JATO]. **1957** *Jane's Fighting Ships 1957–8* 413 The missile is using jet-assisted rocket bottles to launch it. **1952** *Oxf. Jun. Encycl.* X. 56/2 One of the first tactical jet bombers to go into service was the English Electric *Canberra*. **1965** H. KAHN *On Escalation* x. 200 In a jet-bomber and ballistic-missile age, events go so fast. **1960** Jet efflux [see *jet-engined* adj. in *9]. **1966** D. STINTON *Anat. Aeroplane* 244 The position of the fin was an initial argument against mounting the engine above the boom, because of the hot jet efflux playing on the surfaces. **1944** *Sat. Even. Post* 6 May 20/2 The British had flown a jet plane successfully, and now the USAAF proposed to develop a twin-engined jet fighter of its own. **1955** *Ann. Reg. 1954* 149 An outstanding item in Canadian mutual aid within N.A.T.O...was the transfer of 164 Sabre jet fighters to Greece and Turkey. **1964** M. MCLUHAN *Understanding Media* II. xxvii. 272 The two pilots of one Canadian jet fighter. **1953** *Ann. Reg. 1952* 164 Agreement was also reached on financing the first half of the..programme for air-fields, communications, and jet-fuel supplies. **1966** *McGraw-Hill Encycl. Sci. & Technol.* I. 178/2 Volatility is the most important consideration in the selection of jet fuels; combustion qualities are of secondary concern. **1958** Jet lift [see *jet flap* in *9]. **1968** *New Scientist* 25 July 167/1 Jet lift, as a means of personal mobility, has been a tempting idea since Rolls-Royce began using the Flying Bedstead about 15 years ago... This invites speculation as to whether paratroopers, deployed from a transport aeroplane, might subsequently be gathered back into it with the help of their individual jet-lift belts. **1954** P. MASEFIELD in *Listener* 30 Sept. 511/2 The commercial jet-lifters are yet to come. **1967** *Times Rev. Industry* Feb. 68/2 As long as a decade ago, technically competent enthusiasts were saying that another form of vertical take-off and landing (VTOL) transport, the jet-lifter, was just round the historical corner. **1949** *Birmingham* (Alabama) *News-Age-Herald* 13 Nov. A. 18/3 But there is much work yet to be done before the combination of the jetliner and the helibus can be fully utilized. **1961** A. MILLER *Misfits* i. 12 A great jet liner roars over, flying quite low. **1970** *New Scientist* 23 Apr. 172/2 The cruising speed would be competitive with current jetliners at Mach 0·93. **1971** *Daily Tel.* (Colour Suppl.) 30 July 25 This frenetic era of automated jetliners and impersonal airports. **1944** G. SMITH *Gas Turbines & Jet Propulsion for Aircraft* (ed. 3) 104 He believed the jet plane would be used in the near future. **1944** *War Illustr.* 10 Nov. 404/3 The first enemy jet-plane to fall in Allied lines was shot down over Nijmegen on October 5 by six R.A.F. Spitfires; it was a Me 262. **1964** M. MCLUHAN *Understanding Media* II. xviii. 177 The effect of..jet-plane speeds. **1956** W. A. HEFLIN *U.S. Air Force Dict.* 281/1 *Jet-powered*, powered by one or more jet engines. **1957** *Encycl. Brit.* I. 246/2 Aeroplanes are either propeller driven or jet powered. **1959** *Daily Tel.* 2 Mar. 16/4 The United States Air Force already has a large number, probably about 400, Boeing KC-135 jet tankers. **1967** *Times* 28 Feb. (Canada Suppl.) 27 Jet tankers are also needed for long distance inflight refuelling of the CF5. **1959** *Daily Tel.* 23 Feb. 11/8 The first such experiments were conducted by a pilot and a doctor in a T-33 jet trainer.

11. In numerous combinations (in which *jet* represents 'jet plane') relating to locomotion by means of jet aircraft, as *jet route, transport, transportation, travel, traveller*; *jet-borne* adj. Also **jet age**, the age or era of travel by jet aircraft; **jet hop**, a short or rapid flight by a jet aircraft; also as *v. intr.*; **jet lag**, the delayed effects (esp. temporal disorientation) suffered by a person after a long flight on a (jet) aircraft; **jetport** [after *AIRPORT], an airport served by jet aircraft; **jet set**, a smart set of wealthy people who conduct business by jet travel, or who make frequent journeys, e.g. to holiday resorts, by jet aircraft; also in weakened senses; so **jet-setter**.

1952 R. WALKER (*title*) Jet age. **1953** *Sci. News Let.* 21 Feb. 122/1 A weird-looking, skin-tight 'space suit' now clothes the jet-age test pilot. **1958** *New Statesman* 21 June 804/2 The uppermost deck of this air-pier or jet-age jetty is an open public area—'waving base' in official terminology—that gives one a grandstand or pierhead view of the comings and goings. **1963** *PMLA* LXXVIII. I. p. v, Air France ground hostesses threaten to work in civilian clothes unless their employer comes up with jet age fashions. **1971** *Guardian* 12 June 12/3 You can cleanse yourself immediately of most jet-age pollution in the..local Turkish bath. **1968** *N.Y. Times* 21 Apr. IV. 1 Johnson..climbed aboard his jetborne White House for the flight back to his Texas ranch. **1963** *Times* 26 Feb. 8/6 A certified real Orient just a jet-hop away. **1969** J. MANDER *Static Soc.* i. 27 As he jet-hops from country to country, it is the similarities that strike him. **1969** A. CADE *Turn up Stone* i. 23 The long journey, jet-lag and the heat had given him a headache. **1971** *Times* 16 Apr. 7 (Advt.), A team of scientists has researched the phenomenon of 'jet lag' thoroughly. The disorientation of a jet flight has been proved to upset..decision-making. **1972** *Sat. Rev.* (U.S.) 10 June 15/2 The news of Nixon—booked into Salzburg to fight jet lag for a weekend on his way to the summit meeting in Moscow. **1973** *Observer* 3 June 29/1 They had the dazed, sleep-walking look of people still confused by jet-lag. **1961** *N.Y. Times* 1 June 37/1 (*caption*) New study backs jetport in Morris. **1972** *Fortune* Jan. 40D/3 (Advt.), A fourth major jetport to serve the New York metropolitan area. **1970** *Times* 27 Feb. 3/8 (*heading*) Windsor on jet route. **1951** *San Francisco Examiner* 5 Aug. 5/1 You're strictly jet set.. if you stake your claim in the dunes..*never* descend to ocean level except for a quick dunk. **1956** *N.Y. Times Mag.* 4 Nov. 14 This is the Soviet 'Jet Set', an element of the younger generation... The term was originated by a young member of a foreign embassy staff in Moscow and refers to the Soviet youth who are attracted by things foreign. **1963** *Amer. Speech* XXXVIII. 206 *Jet set* (analogous to *smart set*), rhyming slang term referring to the sophisticated, well-to-do skiers who go abroad by jet just for skiing vacations in the best known resorts. **1964** *Sat. Rev.* (U.S.) 10 Oct. 70/1 The Jet Set..has rediscovered St. Tropez. **1966** *Daily Tel.* 24 Oct. 13/6 Clothes for the jet set, for you who seek the sun in winter. **1970** *Americana Ann.* 694 His campaign managers created a new image of him [*sc.* Pierre Trudeau] as the youthful, debonaire, 'with-it' man of the jet-set age. **1972** *House & Garden* Dec.–Jan. 126/2 Even in the jet-set hotels..local dishes are presented. **1965** *N.Y. Times* 13 June 17 (*caption*) Jet-setter Mrs...and model..prepare for ABC's fall special, 'The Wild, Wild East'. **1966** *Time* 9 Dec. 88/3 In swarmed the jet-setters (Gloria Guinness, Lee Radziwill, Count and Countess Rudolfo Crespi). **1973** *Daily Tel.* 22 Sept. 19/8 The crowd..naturally included show business celebrities and jet-setters who had paid £40 for court-side seats. **1949** *Flight* 29 Sept. 438/2 A large jet transport might take five years to develop to the production stage. **1961** L. MUMFORD *City in Hist.* xvi. 505 Jet transportation brings an area twelve hundred miles away as near as one sixty miles distant today. **1962** *Daily Tel.* 13 June 11/1 What with jet travel, the Common Market and [etc.]. **1964** M. MCLUHAN *Understanding Media* II. x. 94 The jet traveler..might just as well be in a cocktail lounge.

jet, *v.*[2] Add: **9.** *trans. Building.* To loosen and remove (sand, gravel, etc.), or to sink (a pile), by the technique of jetting (see *JETTING *vbl. sb.*[2] 4).

1956 H. L. NICHOLS *Mod. Techniques Excavation* v. 58/2 In peat, the points are jetted down and sand pumped in the hole around them. *Ibid.* vi. 25/2 If the cover should be left off, and the vertical pipe filled with dirt.., it may be jetted out by the use of an engine-driven water pump.

jet (dʒet), *v.*[3] [f. JET *sb.*[3]] *intr.* To travel by jet plane. Also *trans.* (and *refl.*), to convey by jet plane or jet engine. So **je·tted** *ppl. a.*

1946 *All Hands* June 50 A Martin Marauder was jetted into the air for the scientist-spectators. **1949** *Sat. Rev.* (U.S.) 8 Jan. 17, I rather think Captain Osborne will be the first of us to go jetting to the moon. **1951** A. C. CLARKE *Sands of Mars* vii. 81 They jetted themselves slowly out across the surface of Deimos. **1965** F. POHL *Alternating Currents* (1966) 96 We can't jet home through normal space because we don't have the fuel. **1959** *Time* 23 Mar. 20/3 Jetting home to Moscow..Krushchev exuded confidence. **1962** *Daily Tel.* 13 June 11/1 There's no rest for the 'jetted' British businessman. **1966** *Guardian* 7 June 12/6 In the last few days, Brown has jetted over an area the size of Europe. **1968** *Daily Tel.* 28 Sept. 9/6 (Advt.), Clarksons jet you to top resorts like Alpbach, Auffach, [etc.]. **1971** *Radio Times* 21 Oct. 71/3 Perhaps I'd been lucky to catch him in today, before he jetted off to Tokyo or the Bahamas? **1973** *Daily Tel.* (Colour Suppl.) 10 Aug. 7/2 But Beer now jets between Santiago and his Surrey home.

jetavator (dʒe·tăvēⁱtəɪ). *Astronautics.* Also **jetevator.** [f. (irreg., in the case of *jetavator*) JET *sb.*[3] + EL)EVATOR.] A ring-shaped deflector surrounding the exit nozzle of a rocket engine which can be swivelled into the exhaust gases to divert them and so alter the direction of the thrust.

1960 *Aeroplane* XCVIII. 176/2 The missile is powered by a solid-propellent Aerojet rocket motor fitted with 'jetavator' deflectors of the kind developed for Polaris. **1961** *Flight* LXXIX. 13/2 The use of swivelling nozzles is claimed to be lighter than the Polaris system of fixed nozzles plus jetevators, and undoubtedly minimizes drag. **1967** *Propulsion* (Amat. Rocket Assoc. U.S.) ii. 45 A jetavator consists of a ring surrounding the exhaust-nozzle exit. The ring is mounted so that it can be moved into the jet exhaust as needed.

‖**jeté** (ʒəte). Also erron. **jété, jetée, jetté.** [F. *jeté*, pa. pple. (sc. *pas* step) of *jeter* to throw.] A ballet-step in which one leg is moved forwards, backwards, or sideways while a quick leap is made with the other foot. So **jeté en tournant** (an turnan), a leap executed with a turning movement. Cf. *GRAND JETÉ.

1830 R. BARTON tr. *Blasis' Code of Terpsichore* II. vi. 78 *Entrechats* are generally begun with an *assemblé*, *coupé*, or *jetté*. **1877** [see *CONTRETEMPS 3]. **1927** *Dancing Times* Apr. 9 All dancers know that the coupé cannot be done alone, as the position of the foot which is being 'cut-away' depends entirely upon the step which follows the coupé. I am therefore taking the 'coupé-dessous', followed in the first instance by a 'posé', and afterwards the 'coupé-dessous' followed by a 'jeté'. **1930** CRASKE & BEAUMONT *Theory & Pract. Allegro in Classical Ballet* 95 Execute a *Jeté en Tournant*, that is:—With a slight spring, change the position of the feet so that the *right* foot is *sur le cou de pied devant*. **1953** *Ballet Ann.* VII. 59 She took off with a wonderful *jeté* and landed only a few inches from his nose. **1958** *Observer* 28 Sept. 18/5 A special salute is due to Yelle Bettencourt's splendid *jétés*. **1961** *Times* 28 Dec. 12/7 M. Jean-Paul Andreani is quite electrifying with his *jétés en tournant*.

jetevator, var. *JETAVATOR.

jeton (dʒe·tən). [See JETTON.] **1.** = JETTON.
1933 H. G. WELLS *Shape of Things to Come* II. § 11. 229 Today our museums contain hundreds of thousands of specimens of these improvised European coins of lead, nickel, tin and all sorts of alloys, *jetons* or checks of wood. **1969** R. C. BELL *Board & Table Games* II. x. 138 Many of these casting-counters, or *jetons*, simulated coins, and cause difficulty to collectors of medieval money.

2. (ʒetoṅ). A metal disc used, chiefly in France, instead of a coin for insertion in a public telephone box. Also *attrib.*
1942 E. PAUL *Narrow St.* xi. 82 In order for a client to use the phone he had to buy from her a metal disc or *jeton*. **1957** *Times* 16 Oct. 11/7 The French *jeton* system for calls from public telephone boxes. *Jetons* were introduced in France because of frequent changes in the local call tariff (15 changes in 20 years) and in the diameter and material of the coinage. **1962** A. WILLIAMS *Long Run South* VI. ii. 193 An old crone sold him a jeton and he dialled the number of the house in the Viale Piemonte. **1972** *Times* 4 Jan. 14/8 (*heading*) Use the nickel sixpence as a jeton [for telephone coin boxes].

jet propulsion. [JET *sb.*[3]] The ejection of a usu. high-speed jet of gas (or liquid) as a source of propulsive power, esp. for aircraft.
1867 *Ann. Rep. Aëronaut. Soc.* 50 In spite of the costly experiments..made to revive the system of jet propulsion, it was clear to him that the screw propeller must be much superior. **1877** C. B. MANSFIELD *Aerial Navigation* II. xiii. 453 One of the great advantages attending the system of pump or jet propulsion in the air is that, however the force be generated, the direction in which it is applied may be instantly altered, without shifting the position of the actual instrument of motion. **1886** *Ann. Rep. Aëronaut. Soc.* 67 (*heading*) Jet propulsion for aëronautical purposes. **1892** J. H. COTTERILL *Appl. Mech.* (ed. 3) 572 The efficiency of jet propulsion [of ships] can hardly be estimated as greater than ·33. **1920** *Chambers's Jrnl.* June 415/1 In the case of life-boats liable to ground on sandbanks..jet-propulsion has obvious advantages. **1935** BALMER & WYLIE *After Worlds Collide* iv. 75 The most energetic members of the colony were working upon a small metal jet-propulsion [air]ship. **1944** *Time* 24 Jan. 66 This..drawing illustrates..the operation of a propellerless, jet-propulsion airplane. **1945** *Daily Express* 4 June 4/8 America's car manufacturers are secretly experimenting to produce the first jet-propelled car, using exhaust gases from the present car to boost power by jet propulsion. **1953** J. Y. COUSTEAU *Silent World* xi. 106 The octopus was downright terrified... It made off by slow jet propulsion, exuding spurts of its famous ink. **1962** F. I. ORDWAY et al. *Basic Astronautics* x. 392 Jet propulsion may be divided into two categories: ducted or air-breathing engines and rocket engines.

So **jet-propelled** *a.*, having or employing a means of jet propulsion; also *fig.*, very fast, frenzied; also (as a back-formation) **jet-propel** *v. trans.* (chiefly *fig.*).
[**1867** J. BOURNE *Treat. Screw Propeller* (new ed.) p. cxix/3 Johnson's jet propeller.] **1877** W. H. WHITE *Man. Naval Archit.* xiv. 612 Jet-propelled vessels, when moving ahead at full speed, derive their steering power from the reaction of the water in the wake upon the rudder. **1904** R. KENNEDY *Mod. Engines & Power Generators* I. ii. 104 The Viper and Vixen, twin screw vessels of about the same tonnage..were built as fair competitors with the jet propelled Waterwitch. **1922** *Flight* XIV. 276/2 *Many* of the inventions imagined by Jules Verne..have already been realised, so who shall say that the design for a jet-propelled monoplane seaplane described by M. Maurice Armende..will not materialise—some day? **1936** *Daily Sketch* 17 Nov. 13/4 In visualising a jet-propelled aeroplane of the future, the mind immediately thinks of a large hole in the tail, from which would come a blast of whatever gases were being released. **1944** A. HUXLEY *Let.* 9 July (1969) 507 One can be safe in betting that, within ten years, there will be rockets, or jet-propelled flying bombs,..capable of flying any distance up to five thousand miles. **1945** F. WHITTLE in *Proc. Inst. Mech. Engin.* CLII. 422/2 At the beginning of 1940 the Air Ministry.. began to work on the assumption that there was a good chance of getting jet propelled fighter aircraft into production for use in the war. **1947** *Sci. News* IV. 35 When Sir Malcolm Campbell makes his next attempt on the world's speed record, he will be using a true 'jet-propelled' speedboat. **1949** *Sat. Rev.* (U.S.) 25 June 17/2 It was that courage..that jet-propelled her onward and upward to stardom and marriage to Florenz Ziegfeld, Jr. **1950** in *Amer. Speech* (1956) XXXI. 285 They have learned to jet-propel bodies, but they haven't taken the first step in jet-propelling the human spirit. **1954** 'N. BLAKE' *Whisper in Gloom* I. i. 15 If the jet-propelled craft he had built failed to jet-propel itself. **1958** A. HUXLEY *Let.* 22 June (1969) 850 Time, as one advances in life, seems to become jet propelled. **1959** *Encounter* Aug. 35 He was lit up and jet-propelled by a sort of crazy, electric frenzy. **1960** *Times* 6 Aug. 9/5 On the same disc..is Mendelssohn's concerto which Heifetz carries by assault. He lays into the triplets of the first movement.., plays the slow movement with a fair amount of elbow-power, and jet-propels the fairies through the last. **1962** *Economist* 19 May 672/1 Dr Nkrumah's phrase about achieving a 'jet-propelled' rate of economic growth. **1969** *Daily Tel.* 13 Feb. 22/8 The book conveys the period of music-making in the 1920s and 1930s and its air of domesticity far removed from today's jet-propelled bustle.

jet stream. [f. JET *sb.*[3] + STREAM *sb.*] **a.** A fast-moving, relatively narrow stream of fluid that is present as a current in an atmosphere or ocean; *spec.* in *Meteorol.*, a strong wind confined to a narrow region of the atmosphere, esp. one in the upper troposphere at middle latitudes that blows in an approximately horizontal direction, predominantly from west to east.
1947 *Bull. Amer. Meteorol. Soc.* XXVIII. 255 During periods of reasonably straight west wind circulation over the North American continent, there exists normally, at levels between 5 km and 15 km above sea level, a fairly narrow zone of extremely strong west wind circulation (jet stream), reaching its maximum intensity and sharpness at the tropopause level. **1950** *Time* 29 May 70/2 Six miles up, where the air is thin and cold, a fearful wind zigzags round the earth at 200 m.p.h. Meteorologists call it the 'jet stream'. **1957** G. E. HUTCHINSON *Treat. Limnol.* I. iv. 225 The jet-stream mechanisms believed to maintain circulation in the region of the westerlies. **1963** tr. *E. R. Reiter's Jet-Stream Meteorology* iv. 271 (*heading*) Jet streams in the oceans. *Ibid.*, The current does not spread out..but it remains concentrated in a narrow band of high velocities—the oceanic jet stream. **1971** *New Scientist* 8 Apr. 90/2 In the tropopause..there is a meandering hemispheric band of high speed westerly winds, called the jet streams.

b. A jet of fluid (JET *sb.*[3] 4), esp. one ejected by a jet engine.
1955 *Sci. News Let.* 5 Mar. 160/3 Graphite lubricant is propelled in a jet-stream reaching many often inaccessible trouble spots. **1955** *Ibid.* 26 Mar. 200/1 These air whirlpools are not caused by either the propeller backwash or jet stream, but by the action of the plane's wings. **1959** S. N. SAMBUROFF tr. *Feodosiev & Siniarev's Introd. Rocket Technol.* vii. 232 The presence of the jet stream.. introduces certain specific peculiarities into rocket aerodynamics. **1962** H. E. NEWELL *Express to Stars* iii. 29 It takes a force to expel material into a jet stream..and by Newton's law of reaction there must be a reaction force.

‖ **jettatura** (yetătūə·ră). [ad. It. *iettatura.*] The evil eye (see EVIL *a.* 6); bad luck. So **jettato·re** [ad. It. *iettatore*], a person who brings bad luck.
1855 MRS. GASKELL *Accursed Race* in *Househ. Words* 25 Aug. 78/2 Their glance, if you meet it, is the jettatura, or evil eye. **1882** C. M. YONGE *Unknown to Hist.* II. iii. 34 'Tis not only the *jettatura* wherewith the Queen Mother used to reproach me. Men need but bear me good will, and misery overtakes them. **1892** A. LANG *Bks. & Bookmen* (new ed.) 122 The superstitious might have been excused for crediting him with the gift of *jettatura*,—of the evil eye. **1921** *Glasgow Herald* 29 July 6 This simple remedy is much in use throughout Italy to-day as an antidote to the evil power of the Jettatore.

jetted (dʒe·ted), *a.*[2] *Tailoring.* [app. f. JET *v.*[2]] Of a pocket: having no flap, but an outside seam on either edge, called the **jetting**.
1923 *Daily Mail* 23 Apr. 8 The skirt pockets, which are finished in jetted fashion. **1928** [see *FLAPLESS *a.*]. **1933** J. E. LIBERTY *Pract. Tailoring* v. 38 *Jettings.* These are strips of material about 9 in. long and 2 in. wide. They.. are made up in two forms, flat jettings,..and as a narrow piping.

jetting, *vbl. sb.*[2] Add: **2. b.** (See quot. 1957.)
1941 *Nature* 5 Apr. 422/2 Work in Britain has been concentrated mainly on chemical means of protecting the host by the use of dips. Jetting has been tried in Scotland, but protective dusts have not been experimented with on a large scale. **1957** *New Biol.* XXII. 99 Mr A. J. Gillespie, a woolgrower in Queensland, suggested jetting. This consisted of spraying the breech of the sheep with a jet of fluid delivered at a pressure of up to 120 lb per square inch from a nozzle whose aperture varied between 3/64 and 5/64 of an inch. A solution of sodium arsenite was the most popular jetting fluid.

4. *Building.* The loosening and removal of sand, gravel, etc., by directing jets of water or compressed air on to it, esp. so as to make a hole for pile-driving; the sinking of a pile by this means.
1942 *Amer. Speech* XVII. 280/1 *Jetting*, the act of pushing aside the mud or sand at the foot of a pile by a jet of compressed air or water. **1948** D. W. TAYLOR *Fund. Soil Mech.* xx. 647 Jetting often aids greatly in getting piles to the desired final grade. **1951** G. P. TSCHEBOTARIOFF *Soil Mech.* xv. 445 It is not always possible to drive piles.. through a compact layer of sand without serious damage to the piles... Jetting of the piles has to be used then. **1956** H. L. NICHOLS *Mod. Techniques Excavation* v. 60/1 Jetting with high pressure water, or less commonly, compressed air, is used in making deep narrow holes for setting piles, installing vertical drains, obtaining soil samples, and for various other purposes. **1966** *McGraw-Hill Encycl. Sci. & Technol.* X. 228/1 Open-type piles are usually cleared of soil by jetting.

je·tting, *vbl. sb.*[3] [f. *JET *v.*[3] + -ING[1].] Travelling in a jet plane.
1966 in WEBSTER. **1971** *Guardian* 9 Sept. 11/3 It is work which involves much jetting about,..lecture tours across the States, visits to North Vietnam.

jettison, *v.* Add: **b.** To release or drop from an aircraft or spacecraft in flight; *spec.* to drop (a bomb) intentionally from an aircraft elsewhere than over an assigned target.
1934 [implied in *JETTISONABLE *a.*]. **1942** D. M. CROOK *Spitfire Pilot* 66 Enemy bombers showed a much greater tendency to jettison their bombs. **1942** *R.A.F. Jrnl.* 18 Apr. 14 'C for Charlie's' pilot jettisoned his guns rather too near the wife of a senior officer who happened to be below. *Ibid.* 34 The crew went to their ditching stations. ..No fuel was jettisoned. **1946** TAYLOR & ALLWARD *Spitfire* 101/1 The hood..could be jettisoned. **1955** *Times* 10 Aug. 8/7 The world's fastest aircraft..was jettisoned by its mother aircraft after an explosion at 30,000 ft. **1974** *Flight International* 29 Aug. (Suppl.) 11/1 Surface-to-air missiles often use a booster to produce a high initial acceleration and push the missile clear of its launcher, the booster then being jettisoned.

2. *intr.* To drop off, or fall away from, an aircraft or spacecraft in flight.
1962 J. GLENN in *Into Orbit* 138 The escape tower, which we would not need once we got above the atmosphere, would jettison when the boosters dropped off and lighten the load even more.

jettisonable (dʒe·tisənăb'l), *a.* [f. JETTISON *v.* + -ABLE.] Capable of being **jettisoned** from an aircraft or spacecraft; designed to be readily detachable in flight.
1934 *Shell Aviation News* No. 34. 18/1 As a result, the machine can be used for a variety of purposes... It is fitted with a 'jettisonable' fuel tank riveted with duralumin. **1946** *Aeroplane Spotter* 14 Dec. 290/1 The pilot and test engineer are housed in a conical nose section which is jettisonable and contains a decelerating parachute in case of emergency. **1956** *Spaceflight* I. 24/1 The second stage ..is a new rocket; the final stage and the satellite package are enclosed within its jettisonable nose. **1961** E. BROWN *Wings on my Sleeve* x. 113 The undercarriage consisted of a retractable skid mounted on the jettisonable two-wheel chassis which was automatically dropped when the skid was retracted on take-off. **1963** A. SMITH *Throw out Two Hands* v. 52 The balloon commander is all,..the passenger is nothing more than jettisonable ballast.

jettisoning, *vbl. sb.* (*Fig.* and *Aeronaut.* examples.)
1950 *Engineering* 10 Feb. 158/1 Landing operations.. could take the form of 'jettisoning' operations. **1957** J. S. HUXLEY *Relig. without Revelation* ix. 209 This wholesale jettisoning.

jeu. Add: **c. jeu de paume** (ʒö də pōm) [Fr., lit. 'game of palm (of the hand)']: tennis (not lawn-tennis); also, a tennis court; also *fig.*
1789 A. YOUNG *Jrnl.* 20 June in *Trav. France* (1792) I. 115 The resolution..was to assemble instantly at the *Jeu de paume*, and there the whole assembly took a solemn oath. **1880** GEO. ELIOT *Let.* 7 Oct. (1956) VII. 329 Johnnie gets a game of real tennis—jeu de paume—every day. **1910** *Encycl. Brit.* X. 450/1 Fives and racquets are probably both descended from the *jeu de paume*, of which they are simplified forms. **1939** A. TOYNBEE *Study of Hist.* IV. 161 Warfare now is no longer just a *jeu de paume* among a party of kings. **1940** E. POUND *Cantos* lviii. 74 Playing at jeu de paume and escrime. **1970** *Guardian* 3 June 9/2 The story that the *jeu de paume* has been played by members of the opposing army with a living infant as the ball, goes back hundreds..of years.

d. jeu de règle (ʒö də rẹgl') [Fr., lit. 'game of rule']: in the game of *Écarté* (see quot. 1963).
1850 *Bohn's Hand-bk. Games* 261 On this principle all '*Jeux de Regles*' are played without changing (although there be a few which can scarcely reckon in their favor 2 to 1). **1934** *Neuphilol. Mitt.* XXXV. III/IV. 132 Écarté.. *jeu-de-règle*, hand which should be played without taking cards. **1963** G. F. HERVEY *Handbk. Card Games* 61 There are certain stock hands, called *jeux de règle*, holding which a player should play and not propose, and equally refuse the opponent's proposal.

e. jeu de société (ʒö də· sosiete) [Fr., lit. 'game of society']: (freq. in *pl.*) a game or amusement at a party.
1827 *Edin. Rev.* XLVI. XCII. 382 To these pantomimes succeeded ballets, and such *jeux de société* as 'La Peur'.. a sort of dumb show. **1854** THACKERAY *Newcomes* I. xxviii. 271 These little diversions and *jeux de société* can go on anywhere. **1932** H. NICOLSON *Diary* 1 Jan. (1966) 104 He..had been kept up doing *jeux de société* till 8 am. **1963** A. ZAINA in B. Sewell *Two Friends* 78 The two duologues..were obviously destined to be a *jeu de société*... Perhaps it was performed at one of the Raffalovich parties.

jeuk skei: see *JUKSKEI.

‖ **jeune fille** (ʒön fīy). [Fr.] A young girl. Used *attrib.* or as *adj.*: characteristic of an *ingénue*.
1802 H. ECKERSALL *Jrnl.* 4 July in Malthus *Trav. Diaries* (1966) 296 Les jeunes filles who were sitting near us were much diverted but did not look as if they would take his advice. *a* **1855** C. BRONTË *Professor* (1857) I. xii. 191, I took these sketches in the second-class school-room of Mdlle. Reuter's establishment, where about a hundred specimens of the genus 'jeune fille' collected together, offered a fertile variety of subject. **1888** E. DOWSON *Let.* 13 Nov. (1967) 19 It is not les filles de l'opéra or horizontales that I protest against—it is les jeunes filles de société. **1892** [see *ENFANT GÂTÉ]. **1903** H. JAMES *Ambassadors* VI. xiv. 189 It will really be a chance for you..to see the *jeune fille*—I mean the type—as she actually is. **1926** C. BEATON *Diary* in *Wandering Yrs.* (1961) 110 Miss Wilberforce plays safe in a *jeune fille* frock. **1928** D. H. LAWRENCE *Phoenix II* (1968) 519 Talking to an intelligent girl, the famous '*jeune fille*'..you find..that she, the innocent girl in question, is flinging all sorts of fierce questions at your head. **1946** 'S. RUSSELL' *To Bed with Grand Music* ix. 115, I always think romance is rather *jeune fille*. **1974** *Times* 30 Apr. 8/6 The dresses are ravishing—*jeune fille* dresses of the right sort, drifting and romantic.

‖ **jeune premier** (ʒön prəmye). [Fr., lit. 'first young man'.] An actor who plays the part of the principal lover or young hero. So **jeune première** (prəmyẹr), the performer of the corresponding female part.

1852 *Blackw. Mag.* Nov. 600/2 The *prima donna* and *jeune premiere* of the troop. **1877** *Sat. Rev.* 24 Nov. 662/2 What the *jeune premier* would necessarily be when acting the part of a ruined country gentleman. **1888** *Athenæum* 3 Nov. 588/2 Theology always plays a part, albeit in the form of the *jeune premier*, the handsome curate with Broad Church instead of agnostic views. **1896** MRS. H. WARD *Sir G. Tressady* xiii. 283 Ancoats always seems to me the *jeune premier* in his own play. **1902** *Sat. Rev.* 13 Sept. 329/2 [He] plays him with no more intelligence than would suffice for the part of a quite ordinary jeune premier. **1924** 'R. CROMPTON' *William—the Fourth* iv. 71 William..has eloped with a *jeune première* and a bear-skin. An entire Christmas pantomime is searching the village for him. **1946** MRS. BELLOC LOWNDES *Let.* 1 Jan. (1971) 269 Lord Rosebery..was the *jeune premier* of that generation. **1958** L. DURRELL *Mountolive* xv. 272 Mountolive was now irradiated by an appalling sense of futility as he sat (like some ageing *jeune premier*) and listened to the torrent of Nur's excuses. **1960** *Guardian* 20 May 8/4 He..became a highly successful jeune premier in light comedy and revue.

‖ **jeunesse** (ʒœnɛs). [Fr.] Young people; the young.

1781 H. WALPOLE *Let.* 25 July (1904) XII. 31 All the *jeunesse* strolled about the garden. We ancients..retired from the dew. **1858** TROLLOPE *Doctor Thorne* II. xv. 309 'La jeunesse' was beginning to get a lesson; experience.. sometimes comes early in life. **1884** H. JAMES in *Atlantic Monthly* Sept. 310/2 In the early days of October when the whole *jeunesse* of the country is going back to school. **1947** *Horizon* Oct. 11 As if the wonderful *jeunesse* of America were suddenly to retain their idealism.

‖ **jeunesse dorée** (ʒœnɛs dore). [Fr., lit. = gilded youth.] Orig. applied in France to the group of fashionable counter-revolutionaries formed after the fall of Robespierre; now *gen.*, young people of wealth and fashion.

1830 W. HAZLITT *Life Napoleon Buonaparte* I. viii. 383 The volatile genius of this people [*sc.* the French] ..decked out the youth of the city [*sc.* Paris] (*La Jeunesse Dorée*) in the Chouan uniform. **1836** *Edin. Rev.* LXIII. 460 The indefatigable opponents of the ancient rudeness, the *jeunesse dorée* of Germany. **1837** [see GILT *ppl. a.* 2]. **1845** *Encycl. Metrop.* XIII. 374/1 These young men, who were commonly known as the 'Jeunesse dorée', no longer permitted the Jacobins to hold assemblies in the public places. *Ibid.*, The Jeunesse dorée and the Thermidorians had on their side the tradesmen. **1886** *Athenæum* 11 Sept. 329/2 We shall not envy the *jeunesse dorée* of the period these so-called sports. **1888** *N. & Q.* 7th Ser. V. 190/1 *Jeunesse dorée* answers, perhaps, rather to Disraeli's expression of 'curled darlings' than to 'dandy'. **1910** D. SCHWANN *Bk. Bachelor* 47 Mason..received the guests, who were the fine flower of dramatic and critical Bohemia, with a sprinkling of the *jeunesse dorée* of Society and high finance. **1939** N. MONSARRAT *This is Schoolroom* I. i. 28 One of the favourite children, the *jeunesse dorée*. **1965** *New Statesman* 9 Apr. 568/2 The *jeunesse dorée* would have to go out and work for their living. **1969** J. MANDER *Static Soc.* v. 134 Those Country Clubs where the *jeunesse dorée* of Lima, Caracas and Bogota cavort. **1974** D. SMITH *Look back with Love* x. 90 The love-life of the Old Trafford *jeunesse dorée*.

Jew, *sb.* **1.** Read: A person of Hebrew descent; one whose religion is Judaism; an Israelite. (Add further examples.)

Orig. a Hebrew of the kingdom of Judah, as opposed to those of the ten tribes of Israel; later, any Israelite who adhered to the worship of Jehovah as conducted at Jerusalem. Applied comparatively rarely to the ancient nation before the exile (cf. HEBREW *sb.* 1), but the commonest name for contemporary or modern representatives of this group, now spread throughout the world. The word 'Jew' is also applied to groups, e.g. the Falashas in Ethiopia, not ethnically related to persons of the main European groups, the Ashkenazim and the Sephardim.

1710 etc. [see *FALASHA]. **1940** AUDEN *Another Time* 116 He [*sc.* Sigmund Freud] Was taken away from his old interest To go back to the earth in London, An important Jew who died in exile. **1956** I. MURDOCH *Flight from Enchanter* ix. 126 'Of course, you realize that I could rescue you with my little finger,' said Mrs Wingfield. 'I'm as rich as a Jew!' **1968** L. ROSTEN *Joys of Yiddish* 142 Relentless persecution of Jews, century after century, in nation after nation, left a legacy of bitter sayings: 'Dos ken nor a goy.' ('That, only a *goy* is capable of doing'). **1970** R. D. ABRAHAMS *Positively Black* iii. 76 The Englishman is arrogant and overbearing, the American is a check-writing millionaire who doesn't mind the cost, the Jew tries to push down the entry price into heaven. **1970** *Times* 28 Jan. 10/4 At the heart of the matter lies the rabbinical definition of a Jew: a person born of a Jewish mother, or a person who has converted to Judaism according to rabbinical law. **1971** B. MALAMUD *Tenants* 50 The Jews got to keep us bloods stayin weak. **1974** J. R. BAKER *Race* xiv. 232 In various parts of the world today there are communities that practise the Jewish faith in one form or another, but are ethnically distinct from the Jews of Europe and North America. *Ibid.* 234 From the traditional religious point of view, a Jew was a person born of a Jewish mother, but this formula suffers from the defect that the defined word is included in adjectival form in the definition. The same flaw occurs in part of the new definition enacted by the Israeli Parliament in..1970, according to which a person is a Jew if he or she is the offspring of a Jewish mother or has been converted to the Jewish faith by the Orthodox Rabbinate or by the Rabbis of the Jewish Reform Movement or by the Rabbis of the Jewish Conservative Movement.

c. *Black Jew* (see quot. 1967); also = *FALASHA.

1807 C. BUCHANAN *Jrnl.* 4 Feb. in *Christian Res. in Asia* (1811) 192 The resident Jews are divided into two classes, called the Jerusalem or *White* Jews; and the Ancient or *Black* Jews. The White Jews reside at this place [*sc.* Cochin]. The Black Jews have also a Synagogue here; but the great body of that tribe inhabit towns in the interior of the province. *a* **1817** T. DWIGHT *Trav. New-Eng.* (1823) III. 174 The black Jews in Hindostan. **1822** *Imperial Mag.* IV. 358 A copy of the Hebrew Pentateuch ..found in one of the Black Jews' Synagogues, at Cochin. **1843** J. C. MAITLAND *Lett. from Madras* xviii. 178, I told him about the first preachers, the Black Jews, the Syrian Christians, &c. **1892** G. M. RAE *Syrian Church in India* x. 150 These black Jews are converts to the faith from among the people of the land. **1907** I. ZANGWILL *Ghetto Comedies* 155 The black Jews..surrounded by all those millions of Hindoos. **1930** H. NORDEN *Africa's Last Empire* 185 The black Jews among whom he works. **1964** [see *FALASHA]. **1967** D. T. KAUFFMAN *Dict. Relig. Terms* 77/1 *Black Jews*, in India, term applied to brown-skinned Jews to distinguish them from a group known as 'White Jews'. Sometimes used also for Negro Jewish groups. **1974** J. R. BAKER *Race* xiv. 232 The Falasha or 'black Jews' of Ethiopia are members of the Aethiopid subrace, a hybrid taxon.

d. A ship's tailor. Hence also **jewing** *vbl. sb.* and *ppl. a. Naut. slang.*

1916 *Chambers's Jrnl.* May 278/2 They [*sc.* ships' tailors] were still known as 'jews'. *Ibid.*, The term 'jewing', as sewing is still called. **1945** 'TACKLINE' *Holiday Sailor* x. 102 There was the 'Jewing-bloke', who undertook tailoring repairs. *Ibid.*, The 'Jewing-bloke' had a rather ancient Singer sewing machine, bought when ashore at Alexandria with..pay in his pocket. **1946** J. IRVING *Royal Navalese* 100 A sailor-tailor is known as a 'Jew'. **1962** GRANVILLE *Dict. Sailors' Slang* 66/1 *Jewing firm*, ship's tailoring 'firm' run by one or more ratings who repair and make clothing.

2. Read: *transf.* and *offensive.* As a name of opprobrium: *spec.* applied to a grasping or extortionate person (whether Jewish or not) who drives hard bargains. (Add further examples.)

In medieval England, Jews, though engaged in many pursuits, were particularly familiar as money-lenders, their activities being publicly regulated for them by the Crown, whose protégés they were. In private, Christians also practised money-lending, though forbidden to do so by Canon Law. Thus the name of Jew came to be associated in the popular mind with usury and any extortionate practices that might be supposed to accompany it, and gained an opprobrious sense.

1846 *Swell's Night Guide* 123/1 *Jew*, an overreaching fellow. *c* **1861** E. DICKINSON *Poems* (1955) I. 160 'Twould be 'a Bargain' for a *Jew*! *Say*—may I have it—Sir? **1906** J. M. SYNGE *Lett. to Molly* (1971) 31 What have I done that you should write to me as if I was a dunning Jew? **1920** T. S. ELIOT *Ara Vos Prec* 14 The jew is underneath the lot. Money in furs. **1931** T. R. G. LYELL *Slang* 428 Why waste your time asking him for a subscription? He's a perfect Jew where money's concerned. **1944** *Britannica Bk. of Year* 693 In March 1943 there were tirades from Bangkok radio against the 'Jews of Siam' (probably Chinese), who were accused of profiteering. **1952** G. BONE *Came to Oxf.* xi. 34 There is a curious fallacy, rather wide-spread, that a borrower of money is an innocent and hapless person, while a lender is a shark, a harpy, a 'Jew'. **1964** H. BROTZ *Black Jews of Harlem* iii. 54 Occasionally the Black Jews forget they are Jews when complaining about the fact that 'the Jews' own all or most of Harlem!

b. A pedlar.

In this use not depreciatory.

1803 G. COLMAN *John Bull* III. ii. 32 Here is two poets, and a poll-parrot, the best image the Jew had over his head, over the mantle-piece. **1963** 'E. MCBAIN' *Ten Plus One* (1964) iv. 42 There was a guy who used to come around to the door selling stuff, and my mother called him 'The Jew'... For her, 'Jew' was synonymous with pedlar. **1970** J. H. GRAY *Boy from Winnipeg* 43 For us, however, 'Jew' was just another generic word that often included the peddlers who were Greek or Italian. When we scrounged bottles it was to sell to 'the Jew', who was anybody that came along buying junk.

3. a. *Jew boy* (examples), *girl, man.*

Such expressions now mainly in offensive use but not originally opprobrious.

1796 P. COLQUHOUN *Treat. Police of Metropolis* (ed. 3) vi. 125 Jew Boys..go out every morning loaded with counterfeit Copper, which they exchange for bad Silver, to be afterwards coloured anew, and again put into circulation. **1817** M. EDGEWORTH *Harrington* iii. 45 Mowbray easily engaged me to join him against the Jew boy; and a zealous partizan against Jacob I became. **1873** TROLLOPE *Eustace Diamonds* II. liii. 361 You used to be very wicked, and say he was once a Jew-boy in the streets. **1929** D. H. LAWRENCE *Let.* 10 Oct. (1962) II. 1208, I do hate John's Jewish nasal sort of style—so uglily moral. ..Spring doesn't only come for the moral Jew-boys—for them perhaps least. **1948** J. BALDWIN in *Commentary* Oct. 334/2 Jules Weissman, a Jewboy, had got the room for me. **1954** Jewboy [see *IKEY *sb.* and *a.*]. **1959** N. MAILER *Advts. for Myself* (1961) 50 Jewboy, blond Jewboy Wexler perched by the cellar window, tackling Japs with machine-gun bullets. **1968** *Daily Mail* 9 Feb. 3/3 Angry viewers rang the BBC last night to complain about an 'anti-Semitic' remark on the TV programme *Softly, Softly*. In last night's episode..the detective tells the man: 'You always were a great one for putting things in your wife's name, Bob, just like a Jewboy heading for bankruptcy.' **1972** *Observer* 7 May, Mrs Lane Fox dismisses what she calls the country set, who call their children 'the brats', talk about 'thrashing them into shape', support Enoch Powell and still refer to 'jew boys'. **1974** *New Society* 3 Jan. 11/2 A car's desirability also creates the opposite reaction, in that envy is easily turned to resentment and aggression towards, for instance, the 'jewboy', the 'poser', the 'toffee nose' and the 'business classes' who sport expensive and powerful cars. **1796** E. WYNNE *Diary* 11 Dec. (1937) II. ix. 139 Before having ever seen us she declared that we were all excepting the youngest, like little crows and Jew girls. **1930** E. POUND *XXX Cantos* x. 45 Wives, jew-girls, nuns. **1971** B. MALAMUD *Tenants* 50 Jewgirls are the best whores. **1905** JOYCE *Let.* 29 Oct. (1966) II. 127 For a Jewman it's better than having to bathe. **1922** —— *Ulysses* 336 I'll brain that bloody jewman for using the holy name. **1938** W. B. YEATS *John Kinsella's Lament* in *London Mercury* Dec. 114 Though stiff to strike a bargain Like an old Jew man.

c. Jew-baiter (later examples); **Jew-baiting** *sb.* and *a.* (later examples); **Jew plum** = OTAHEITE APPLE; **Jew Tongo,** a language spoken among Bush Negroes in Surinam, possessing a structure largely derived from West African languages and a vocabulary largely derived from English.

1907 I. ZANGWILL *Ghetto Comedies* 85 She's honest... She won't fall back on the old Jew-baiter. **1945** W. S. CHURCHILL *Victory* (1946) 145 Julius Streicher, most notorious of Jew-baiters, was captured by the Americans. **1960** C. DAY LEWIS *Buried Day* vi. 116 The same herd instinct that produces Teddy Boys, Jew-baiters and Ku-Klux-Klansmen. **1974** G. MITCHELL *Javelin for Jonah* xi. 133 Benjy was unlucky enough to fall foul at school of a ring of young Jew-baiters. **1922** JOYCE *Ulysses* 202 Shylock chimes with the jewbaiting that followed the hanging. **1939** *Ann. Reg. 1938* 203 The brutalities began on April 23, and it was clear that the scheme of Jew-baiting had been worked out in readiness for the 'Anschluss'. **1969** J. MANDER *Static Soc.* iii. 99 The American, however ugly, is no Jew-baiting *Gauleiter*. **1913** W. HARRIS *Notes Fruit & Veg. in Jamaica* 18 The Jew Plum..was introduced to Jamaica in 1782 and again in 1792. **1920** W. POPENOE *Man. Tropical & Subtropical Fruits* iv. 156 Jew-plum is another name for the ambarelle, used in Jamaica. **1971** *Caribbean Q.* XVII. II. 14 Different name, same referent..golden apple / Jew plum / pomme-citerre. **1933** L. BLOOMFIELD *Lang.* xxvi. 474 Two creolized forms of English are spoken in Suriname (Dutch Guiana). One of these.., more divergent from ordinary types of English, is known as Jew-Tongo. **1968** W. J. SAMARIN in J. A. Fishman *Readings Sociol. of Lang.* 666 Amerindian pidgins... Saramakan (Jew Tongo, Ningre-Tongo).

Jew, jew, *v.* Add: (Further examples.) Also, to drive a hard bargain. Also *intr.*, to haggle. Phr. *to jew down*, to beat down in price; also *transf.*

These uses are now considered to be offensive.

1824 C. HARDING *Diary* 29 Apr. in *Sketch* (1929) 75 He is a country clergyman; and, from his Jewing disposition, I should judge he had more taste in tithes than pictures. **1825** *Constitutional Adv.* (Frankfort, Kentucky) 15 Dec. 3/1 We hope, for the honour and character of the state, that neither the legislature nor the people, will Jew the items of expence. **1833** L. DOW *Dealings of God* (1849) 189 If they [*sc.* the Jews] will *Jew* people, they cannot flourish among Yankees, who are said to '*out-jew*' them in trading. **1848** W. BAGLEY *Let.* 14 Mar. in N. E. Eliason *Tarheel Talk* (1956) 279, I Jewed old Galloway down to 1·50 for ploughs. **1851** H. MAYHEW *London Labour* I. 368/1 Some of the ladies in the squares..sets to work Jewing away as hard as they can, pricing up their own things, and downcrying yourn. **1870** *Congress. Globe* 7 July 5340/1 This bill supposes that Congress..is ready to commence jewing down the pay of its General. **1872** *Chicago Tribune* 14 Oct. 8/2 The prices [for lodging] asked vary—the lodger being generally asked as much as it is thought he will give. If he jews, he will get it for comparatively little. **1883** G. M. HOPKINS *Let.* 6 Dec. (1938) 195 You will I know say..that Jew is a reproach because the Jews have corrupted their race and nature, so that it is their vices and their free acts we stigmatise when we call cheating 'jewing'—and that you mean that Disraeli in 1871 overreached and jewed his constituents. **1897** [see *HIGHLAND *a.* 2 b]. **1908** *Dialect Notes* III. 32[illegible] *Jew*, to beat down the price. 'I tried to jew him, but he wouldn't jew.' **1926** *Market Growers Jrnl.* 1 July 3, I make my retail prices about half way between grocery store wholesale and retail prices, and do not stand for any 'jewing' down. **1937** *Scribner's Mag.* Apr. 25 Thought we might get the divorce a little under fifty dollars. Maybe we might jew the young man down. **1939** A. POWEL[illegible] *What's become of Waring* v. 140 Then we can meet again and jew each other down. **1946** W. G. HAMMOND *Remembrance of Amherst* 121 Both here and at the mountain top we were unmercifully jewed for all the refreshments. **194[illegible]** L. Z. HOBSON *Gentleman's Agreement* i. 9 Now she was describing the large new house she and Dick wanted to buy. 'Did you close the sale on the old place?' Mrs. Green asked. 'Not yet. That cheap Pat Curran keeps trying to Jew us down.' **1968** L. ROSTEN *Joys of Yiddish* 142 Just as some Gentiles use 'Jew' as a contemptuous synonym for too-shrewd, sly bargaining ('He tried to Jew the price down,' is about as unappetizing an idiom as I know), so some Jews use *goy* in a pejorative sense. **1970** R. LOWELL *Notebk.* 69 This embankment, jewed—No, yankeed—by the highways down to a grassy lip. **1971** R. THOMA[S] *Backup Men* xxi. 184, I say how much and he says this much and I say it's not enough so we jew around with each other until we make a price. **1972** *Harper's Mag.* May 83 Jew the fruitman down for his last Christmas tree. **1972** *New Society* 11 May 301/1, I got jewed down in Tesco's over the cheap offer.

jewel, *sb.* Add: **3.** *jewels of the crown*, a rhetorical phrase for the colonies of the British Empire. *temporary.*

1901 P. MANSON in *Daily Mail Year Bk.* 101, 10 or 1[illegible] years hence that region [*sc.* West Africa] would be regarded as one of the richest jewels in the crown of England. **1931** *N. & Q.* 5 Sept. 166/2 Those irritations against tyranny and stupidity which lost us those jewels of the Crown [*sc.* the American colonies].

5. d. jewel-weed, read: *U.S.*, either of two annual herbs, *Impatiens capensis*, with orange flowers, or *I. pallida*, with yellow flowers native to eastern and central North America.

1818 A. Eaton *Man. Bot.* (ed. 2) 283 *Impatiens.. nolitangere* (jewel-weed, touch-me-not). **1869** J. G. Fuller *Uncle John's Flower-Gatherers* 223, I have seen.. the wild jewel-weed in our meadow. **1884** [in Dict.]. **1907** *St. Nicholas* July 842/2 A sudden thrust of the lantern into this clump of jewel weed near our path, produces a shower of miniature drops. **1951** R. Frost *Coll. Poems* 143 It will be found Either to have gone groping underground..Or flourished and come up as jewel-weed. **1968** *Herb Grower Mag.* (Falls Village, Connecticut) XXI. II. 23 Jewelweed is our favorite [name] for the plant which makes its own gleaming droplets, poised to defy gravity even on leaves tipped downwards, out of rain, dew or even tap water that falls upon the foliage.

jeweller, -eler. Add: *jeweller's* (or *jewellers'*) *rouge*, a fine preparation of ferric oxide used as rouge.

1839 [see Rouge *sb.*[1] 2]. **1886** *Encycl. Brit.* XXI. 13/2 Jeweller's rouge for polishing gold and silver plate is a fine red oxide of iron prepared by calcination from sulphate of iron. **1947** J. C. Rich *Materials & Methods Sculpture* vii. 210 For the final stages of polishing, a chamois skin can be used to apply a fine buffing powder or jeweler's rouge.

Jewess. (Later examples.)

1922 Joyce *Ulysses* 756 As if we met somewhere I suppose on account of my being jewess looking after my mother. **1927** E. O'Neill *Lazarus Laughed* II. ii. 84 And why should you plead for them, Jewess? **1936** G. B. Shaw *Millionairess* II. 39 'Are you..[an] Italian aristocrat..?'..'My ancestors were moneylenders to all Europe ..we are now bankers to all the world.'..'Jewess, eh?' **1970** J. Updike *Bech: a Book* 35 'Is she also a typical Rumanian beauty?' 'I think..she is a typical little Jewess.'

Jewessy (dʒiū·ėsi), *a. depreciatory.* [f. Jewess + -y[1].] Resembling or characteristic of a Jewess.

1930 J. B. Priestley *Angel Pavement* iv. 151 And there were two or three [girls] worth looking at, the flashy young Jewessy type.

Jew-fish. (Earlier and later examples.)

1679 T. Trapham *Discourse State of Health in Jamaica* 65 The Jew fish crowds to be one of the first three of our most worthy Fish. **1968** J. E. Randall *Caribbean Reef Fishes* 60 Jewfish. *Epinephelus itajara*... Tropical western Atlantic and eastern Pacific... Highly esteemed as food. 1972 *Nature* 7 Apr. 266/2 The groupers (some species are known as jewfishes and hinds) are well represented in American warmer seas.

Jewhil(l)iken(s), -kin(s), varr. *Geewhillikins.

Jewish, *a.* Add: **1.** (Later examples.)

1925 P. Gibbs *Unchanging Quest* xiv. 109 These peasants think the Duma will..kill all the *Koulaks*, or Jewish moneylenders. **1935** [see *Armenoid *a.*]. **1941** *Time* 24 Feb. 102/3 Alfred Rosenberg last fortnight opened in Frankfurt am Main what Nazis call 'the biggest library in the world dealing exclusively with the Jewish problem'. **1951** A. Powell *Question of Upbringing* ii. 96 Yes— and have you seen it? A Jewish old clothes man would think twice about wearing it. **1957** *Oxf. Dict. Chr. Ch.* 1093/2 The Jewish problem arose at a later date than in Spain, and it was not until 1536 that, under the influence of the civil power, the Inquisition was set up. **1968** L. Rosten *Joys of Yiddish* 141 It is important to note that the idea of respect for others and the values of a pluralistic society form an old, integral part of Judaism and Jewish tradition. **1970** I. Sieff *Memoirs* vi. 113 In February we submitted a memorandum to the Peace Conference. It asked that Palestine 'Shall be placed under such political, administrative, and economic conditions as will ensure the establishment therein of the Jewish national home.' **1970** *Times* 24 Jan. 7/1 It is now declared that under the law of Israel a person may be of Jewish nationality although not of Jewish religion, whereas under Rabbinic law the two are inseparable. **1973** *Times* 17 July 15/2 PLO leaders seek to identify a community of culture interest between the Palestinian Arabs and these oriental Jews whom they call 'Jewish Arabs'. **1973** *Daily Mail* 4 Oct. 4/5 The strain of anguish and uncertainty shows in the face of this Jewish woman as she waits with her grandson at a railway station before going to Schoenau transit camp in Austria. **1974** [see *Jew *sb.* 1]. **1974** *Publishers Weekly* 18 Feb. 12/2, I do not see why writers should be given ethnic identities when the habit of so designating individuals has been abandoned generally. I suppose it is because of the new use of the term 'Jewish writers'. But those are writers—I believe—who concentrate on the experience of being Jewish in America.

Jewy (dʒiū·i), *a. depreciatory.* Also **Jewey.** [f. Jew *sb.* + -y[1].] Resembling or characteristic of a Jew or the Jews; having the characteristics attributed to Jewish people. Also as *sb.*

1904 Fowler & Felkin *Kate of Kate Hall* xvii. 194 They [*sc.* the noses] are as like as two peas, and both, to my mind, a bit Jewy. **1914** E. Pugh *Cockney at Home* 67 You're a dirty, bloomin' tyke, Jewey. **1919** 'W. N. P. Barbellion' *Jrnl. Disappointed Man* 154 That mean, Jewy, secretive, petty creature, J. M. W. Turner. **1922** Joyce *Ulysses* 287 Jesus, I had to laugh at the little jewy getting his shirt out. *Ibid.* 299 I'm told those Jewies does have a sort of a queer odour coming off them for dogs. **1930** J. B. Priestley *Angel Pavement* iv. 184 A neat dark Jewy sort of chap.

Jeyes(') fluid (dʒēⁱz). [f. *Jeyes*, the name of the manufacturing company.] The proprietary name of a disinfectant consisting of a saponified solution of phenols, resins, and other ingredients. Also *Jeyes(') disinfecting fluid.*

[**1888** *Trade Marks Jrnl.* 18 July 995/2 [In] sickness always use Jeyes' disinfectants...Jeyes' Sanitary Compounds Company, Limited,..London,..manufacturers.] **1900** *Encycl. Medica* III. 31 Cresol or methyl phenol with its derivatives forms the chief constituent of..'Jeyes' Fluid' and a host of similar mixtures. **1911** *T. Eaton & Co. Catal.* Spring & Summer 175/4 Jeyes' Disinfecting Fluid. **1933** D. L. Sayers *Murder must Advertise* iv. 72 'It's the boy that goes round with the disinfectant, sir.' 'Ah, of course! Spray with Sanfect and you're safe.' 'That's right, sir, except that they use Jeyes' Fluid.' **1957** S. Locket *Clin. Toxicol.* xix. 490 Phenolic substances and cresols are contained in a number of disinfectants, e.g...Izal, Jeyes' Disinfecting Fluid and Creolin. For sanitary purposes varying mixtures with soap and alkali are used. **1973** *Times* 19 June 1/3 Jeyes Fluid will rise by a maximum of 20 per cent.

jhoom, jhum, varr. Joom, Júm.

1886 Yule & Burnell *Hobson-Jobson* 351/2 Jhoom, Jhūm. **1895** W. R. Fisher *Schlich's Man. Forestry* IV. 350 Jhuming, or the thorough burning of branchwood on the soil. *Ibid.* 543 In *jhums*, or cultivations on forest clearings, where the branches and undergrowth are burned. **1921** J. H. Hutton *Angami Nagas* II. 72 Good jhum land, cleared once in twelve or fifteen years. *Ibid.*, The Lhotas, Semas, Aos, and trans-Dikhu and trans-Tizu tribes cultivate only by 'jhuming'. **1927** *Blackw. Mag.* June 816/2 Crops are grown by a simple method known as 'Jhoom'. *Ibid.*, A fresh patch of jungle is then cut down, and the 'Jhooming' process repeated. **1936** *Nature* 5 Sept. 408/1 A fisher folk, who..practised a rude form of agriculture, comparable to jhuming, but not terracing or systematic irrigation. **1937** *Times Lit. Suppl.* 20 Feb. 123/2 The low-caste Indian addicted to *jhum* cultivation. **1946** Ali & Lambert *Assam* 16 One or two tribes have adopted terrace cultivation, but the others depend on the *taungya* or *jhuming* system, which is very wasteful.

jhula (dʒū·la). *India.* Also **joolah.** [Hind., Hindi *jhūlā* swing, swing-rope.] A simple suspension bridge used in the Himalayas.

1830 A. S. H. Mountain *Mem. & Lett.* (1857) 114 Our chief object in descending to the Sutlej was to swing on a Joolah bridge. **1844** J. C. Stocqueler *Hand-bk. India* 458 The rustic bridge is supplanted..by *jhulas*, formed by ropes stretched across, constituting a species of loose parapet. **1923** *Blackw. Mag.* Aug. 259/2 A *jhula* or swinging rope-bridge.

jiao (dʒau). Also **chiao.** [Chinese.] A unit of currency and coin of China.

1949 *Whitaker's Almanack* 905/2 By Presidential Decree of August 19, 1948, the Chinese National Dollar currency ..was replaced by a new currency named the *Gold Yuan*. ..The subsidiary coinage consists of *fen* (cents) and *Chiao* (tenths of a *yuan*). **1962** R. A. G. Carson *Coins* 544 The coinage of Nationalist China in Formosa, issued since 1949 in various values of the chiao in aluminium and bronze. **1971** *Whitaker's Almanack* 980 China—*Renminbi* or *Yuan* of 10 *Jiao* or 100 *Fen.* **1973** *Times* 21 Mar. (China Trade Suppl.) p. iii/6 The subsidiary units are jiao (10 jiao = 1 yuan).

jib, *sb.*[1] Add: **3. jib topsail** (see quot. 1961).

a **1865** in Smyth *Sailor's Word-Bk.* (1867) 411. **1866** Capt. Keay *Jrnl.* in B. Lubbock *China Clippers* (1914) App. H. p. xxii, Again bent the spare flying-jib for a jib topsail set on fore-royal stay well up. **1892** *Rudder* Sept. 202 The Princess had her jib topsail hoisted. **1927** G. Bradford *Gloss. Sea Terms* 92/2 *Jib-topsail*, a light jib set aloft in a similar manner to other head sails. It is hoisted on the outer of the head stays with its tack well up above the jib-boom instead of being fast to it. **1929** A. J. Villiers *Falmouth for Orders* 219 There were rumours that the captain intended to bend royal-stays'ls and a jib-tops'l, and a water-sail under the bowsprit. **1936** B. Adams *Ships & Women* xi. 239 While Pat O'Brien went out to the boom end to furl the jib topsail I stood on the forecastle head. **1961** F. H. Burgess *Dict. Sailing* 123 *Jib topsail*, a light triangular sail, set above the jib; it is hanked to the topmast stay and sometimes called 'jib o' jib'.

jib (dʒib), *sb.*[4] *slang.* Also **gib, jibb.** [Origin unknown.] A first-year student at Trinity College, Dublin.

Unknown to the present generation of TCD students (1973).

1827 in J. E. Walsh *Trinity College in 19th Cent.* (1901) 21 About a hundred young jibbs..forced the gates and sallied out into the streets. **1839** C. J. Lever *Confessions H. Lorrequer* xiii. 99 During all this melée tournament, I perceived that the worthy jib as he would be called in the parlance of Trinity, Mr. Cudmore, remained perfectly silent. **1902** W. M. Dixon *Trinity College, Dublin* vi. 137 It was a proud thing for a 'gib' to present himself to a crowd round the door, hear many a cry, 'Make way for the gentleman of the College!' **1922** Joyce *Ulysses* 160 And the Trinity jibs in their mortarboards.

jibbah. (Earlier and later examples.)

1848 J. Richardson *Trav. Sahara* I. xiv. 386 Feel glad I took the advice of the Governor of Ghadames, and purchased a quantity of warm woollen clothing, heik, bornouse, and jibbah. **1922** [see *Abaya].

jibber, *sb.* Add: **b.** One who jibs.

1936 F. D. Davison *Children of Dark People* x. 147 He said you'd got lost and he'd been sent out by the elders of the tribe to look for you; the old jibber! **1961** F. H. Burgess *Dict. Sailing* 123 *Jibber*, one who has second thoughts about attempting something, and then refuses to make the effort.

jibber, *v.* Add: Also **jibber-jabber** *sb.* and *v.*

1922 A. Haddon *Green Room Gossip* ix. 240 The jibber-jabber was entertaining, not because the utterances were those of ordinary human beings, but because they were the voice of Shaw. **1945** L. Shelly *Jive Talk Dict.* 26 *Jibber jabber*, senseless talk. **1948** *Bulletin* (Philadelphia) 23 Mar. 24/5 Time for Congress to quit jibber-jabbering.

jibe, *v.* For '*U.S.*' read 'Chiefly *U.S.*' Add later examples.

1959 [see *Gybe]. **1970** *New Yorker* 28 Nov. 101/1, I didn't jibe with my mother as a personality, but there was no other woman..I could relate to. **1973** *Word 1970* XXVI. 16 The first does not jibe with the patterning of meanings.

‖**jicara** (hī·kără). Also **jicaro.** [Amer. Sp. *jícara, jícaro*, ad. Nahuatl *xicalli*.] A Central American name for the *calabash-tree* (s.v. Calabash 7) or its fruit (Calabash 2).

1859 J. Froebel *Seven Years' Travel in Central Amer.* I. vi. 91 On the market place..many interesting and highly creditable articles of Indian skill and industry are offered for sale..*jicaras* and *guacales* (cups and basins made of calabashes) ornamented with reliefs. **1892** C. F. Lummis *Tramp across the Continent* 149 Each bore upon her head a big, flaring basket—the rush *chiquihuite* of home make, or the elegantly woven Apache *jicara*. **1924** *Chambers's Jrnl.* Sept. 615/1 They saw a woman carrying a jicara gourd. **1927** D. H. Lawrence *Mornings in Mexico* 73 He bargained..for a carved *jicara*. **1943** Record & Hess *Timbers of New World* 78/2 The shells [of calabash fruits] are used by the natives for making cups, dishes, and other household utensils, and some of them are ornately carved or painted... Common names: Calabash ..jícaro. **1964** Little & Wadsworth *Common Trees Puerto Rico & Virgin Islands* 490/2 Calabash-tree... Widely planted in Puerto Rico and through the tropics for the fruits... Other common names..jícaro, jícara (Central America).

Jicarilla (hīkarī·lyă). Also **Jiccarilla.** [Mexican Sp. (dim. of prec.).] In full, *Jicarilla Apache.* An Apache people in New Mexico and nearby states; a member of this people; also, the name of their language. Also *attrib.* or as *adj.*

1850 *Ex. Doc. 31st U.S. Congress 1 Sess. Senate* No. 64. 57 The vocabulary as distinctly shows the kindred character of the language of the Navajos and of the Ticorillas [*sic*] branch of the Apache. **1858** D. C. Peters *Life Kit Carson* xv. 416 The Jiccarillas..had broken out in open defiance of the authorities. **1871** *Republican Rev.* (Albuquerque, New Mexico) 1 Apr. 2/1 News also came on Sunday of the murder of Francisco, the lawyer of the Jicarilla Apache tribe. **1911** *Anthropol. Papers Amer. Mus. Nat. Hist.* VIII. 8 A large number of texts was secured from Cas Miria, a Jicarilla now about seventy years of age and nearly blind. *Ibid.*, This shift..has taken place in the Lipan, Jicarilla, and Kiowa-Apache. **1944** J. Adair *Navajo & Pueblo Silversmiths* vi. 97 The Jicarilla Apache move down to the southern edge of their reservation in the winter. **1971** *Observer* 24 Jan. 32/5 The land-rich Jicarilla tribe in New Mexico. *Ibid.*, The Jicarillas didn't ask for an *anti*-Western with a trendy social message.

jiffle, *v.* Add: (Later examples.) Also as *sb.*

1963 S. Marshall *Exper. in Educ.* iii. 93, I have usually been aware of a discreet rustling (and jiffling) among my audience, and..little note-books and pencils have appeared. **1968** G. J. Barrett *Guilty, be Damned!* ix. 104 Fenton's stomach squirmed, and he jiffled in his seat. **1971** B. W. Aldiss *Soldier Erect* 13 Ann was working our gramophone,..and Sylvia was standing beside her, jiffling to the tunes. *Ibid.*, I prowled round the perimeter of the little conversations, attracted by Sylvia's jiffle.

jiffy. Add: **2.** *Comb.* The proprietary name *Jiffy* in **Jiffy (book) bag,** a type of large envelope padded to protect the contents; also *fig.*; also *ellipt.* as *Jiffy*; **Jiffy pot,** a type of small pot in which seeds may be sown (see quot. 1972); also **jiffy-quick** *adv.*, in a jiffy.

1956 *Library Jrnl.* 1 June 1384/1 Book handling equipment... Mailing bags: Jiffy, Triangle. *Ibid.* 1388/1 Jiffy book bag. **1968** *New Scientist* 10 Oct. 77/1 Dr. Pratt has recently been using 'Jiffy bags' for his outer-jackets—those patent padded envelopes used for mailing books. **1969** *Trade Marks Jrnl.* 2 July 1084/2 Jiffy... Padded paper bags, cushioned paper pads and padded paper in sheet or roll form, all being wrapping and packaging materials for industrial use, for protecting goods in transit. Jiffy Packaging Company Limited,.. Winsford, Cheshire; manufacturers. **1973** 'D. Halliday' *Dolly & Starry Bird* xvi. 249 Maurice..had backed discreetly into a Jiffy bag of deliberate ignorance. **1957** *Trade Marks Jrnl.* 4 Dec. 1278/1 Jiffapot [*sic*]... Hormonal peat in the form of propagating pots for plants. **1959** *Greenhouse* IV. IV. 243 (Advt.), These tomato plants grew up side by side,..'B' in a standard clay pot,'A' in a Jiffy Pot... Exhibit 'A' forged ahead... Ideal for root cuttings too—hyacinths start evenly in Jiffy Pots. **1965** G. V. Williams *Econ. Geol. N.Z.* xvi. 256/2 It is of interest to note that 25 million 'jiffy pots' are used annually for horticultural purposes in New Zealand. **1968** *Trade Marks Jrnl.* 27 Mar. 484/2 Jiffypots... Flower, planting and transplanting pots made of peat. Odd Smaaberg Melvold and Leif Fraas Koxvold, trading as Me-Kox Industri Melvold & Koxvold, Østre Akers Vei 210 Grorud, near Oslo, Norway; manufacturers and merchants. **1972** *Guardian* 16 Dec. 12/7 Jiffy pots are ..made of peat and wood pulp, through which plant roots can grow. **1927** *Ladies' Home Jrnl.* Dec. 34/3 A waxed

surface that..you can dust up jiffy-quick promises spick-and-span floors with but little trouble.

jig, *sb.*[1] Add: **1.** *Irish jig* (earlier example). Also as *v. intr.*

1780 A. YOUNG *Tour in Ireland* II. xvii. 75 The irish jig, which they can dance with a most *luxuriant* expression. **1919** [see *FOX-TROT *v.*].

5. (Earlier U.S. and later examples of *the jig is up*.) Also, *the jig is over*.

1777 *Maryland Jrnl.* 17 June (Th.), Mr. John Miller came in and said, 'The jig is over with us.' **1800** *Aurora* (Philadelphia) 17 Dec. (Th.), As the Baltimore paper says, 'The Jigg's up, Paddy.' **1923** E. WALLACE *Missing Million* xii. 100 It was almost like the last spiteful act of a man who knew the jig was up. **1961** WODEHOUSE *Service with a Smile* (1962) ix. 134 You're in the soup, Miss Briggs. The gaff has been blown, and the jig is up. **1965** *New Yorker* 18 Sept. 56 O.K., Frankie, the jig's up! **1974** *Nature* 15 Feb. 420/3 The weight of opinion seems to be that the jig is up for the map's supporters.

6. b. (Earlier and later examples.)

1849 *Ex. Doc. 31st U.S. Congress 1 Sess. House* No. 5. III. 479 Assay and analysis of the washed metals from the jigs at the Boston and Pittsburg Company's mine. **1953** F. B. MICHELL in *Symposium Recent Devel. Mineral Dressing* (Inst. Mining & Metall.) 263 The jig is by no means obsolete and in the United States, indeed, it is finding increased use for the treatment of those fractions which are too fine for economical concentration by dense media.

c. (Earlier U.S. example.)

1846 *Knickerbocker* XXVII. 513 See that your jigs are in perfect order, for if we do get hold of 'em, our lines and hooks will have to take it, I guess, for a spell.

e. A device for accurately guiding and positioning a drill or other tool in relation to the workpiece, or for positioning the parts of an object during assembly, and used when a large number of similar articles have to be made with high precision; = TEMPLET[1] 2 b.

1894 W. L. LINEHAM *Text-bk. Mech. Engin.* vi. 274 Jigs are an extension of the template principle. Instead of thin plates, castings of an inch or so in thickness are used, supplied with holes where needed, the object being to guide the drill to its proper place on the work without the necessity of lining-out. **1903** W. H. VAN DERVOORT *Mod. Machine Shop Tools* xxvii. 410 Jigs are manufacturing tools of, as a rule, high first cost and their economy depends very largely on the number of pieces to be drilled. **1912** R. W. A. BREWER *Motor Car Construction* ii. 13 Modern competition has made jig work absolutely essential. **1942** B. A. SHIELDS *Princ. Flight* iii. 91 The airplane fuselage is built in a jig. **1947** BRYANT & DICKINSON *Jigs & Fixtures for Mass Production* i. 4 In the machine shop, a jig is usually an appliance which guides a cutting tool... In the automotive industry, a jig is a work-holding device wherein all positions for assembly or fabrication operations are prelocated. **1967** M. CHANDLER *Ceramics in Mod. World* iv. 127 (*caption*) Assembling a large post insulator in a jig.

f. *Dyeing* = *JIGGER *sb.*[1] 5 n.

1942 WHITTAKER & WILCOCK *Dyeing with Coal-Tar Dyestuffs* (ed. 4) iv. 67 The jig or jigger is a machine designed for dyeing piece goods at full width. **1963** MEITNER & KERTESS tr. *Schmidlin's Preparation & Dyeing Synthetic Fibres* xii. 108 High-temperature pressure jigs are mainly used for heavier fabrics.

8. jig borer, (*a*) a machine for drilling holes in or machining the surfaces of a component (esp. a jig (sense *6 e)), usually having a vertical spindle mounted above a table which can be accurately positioned relative to the spindle; (*b*) (see quot. 1972); so **jig-boring** *vbl. sb.*; hence (as a back-formation) **jig-bore** *v. trans.*, to drill (a hole) by means of a jig borer; **jig box,** the box or sieve of a jig (sense 6 b); **jig-brow** (earlier example); **jig button,** a steel bush used for accurate positioning of a jig plate when making jigs on a lathe; **jigman,** one who works an ore-dressing jigger; **jig plate,** (a part of) a jig consisting of a steel plate which carries the bushes which guide the drill; **jig-time,** *colloq.* (chiefly *U.S.*) in phrase *in jig-time* expressing a very short space of time.

1939 C. B. COLE *Tool Making* 258 The bushing plate is made from cold-rolled steel, and this is laid out carefully and the hole jig-bored for the drill bushing. **1967** A. J. LISSAMAN *Metrology* vi. 71 The holes in the plate would be jig-bored prior to the fitting of the bushes and the centre distances would need to be checked, both after jig-boring, and after the fitting of the drill bushes. **1932** GWIAZDOWSKI & LORD *Econ. Tool Engin.* xiii. 189 A Swiss firm..developed a large jig borer that derives its accuracy from its lead screws. **1941** W. C. DURNEY *Machine Shop Pract.* v. 149 In the majority of modern engineering establishments, manufacturing jigs and fixtures in any quantity, these pieces of vital auxiliary apparatus are usually machined up in jig borers. **1959** *Times* 5 Oct. (Switzerland Suppl.) p. vii/3 Over one thousand SIP jig-borers are installed in the United Kingdom to-day. **1972** *Classification of Occupations & Directory Occupational Titles* (Department of Employment) III. 290/2 *Jig borer*, [one who] sets up and operates a jig boring machine to drill and bore holes in workpieces to fine limits of accuracy. **1932** GWIAZDOWSKI & LORD *Econ. Tool Engin.* xiii. 183 (*heading*) Jig-boring methods. **1935** H. J. DAVIES *Precision Workshop Methods* vii. 115 A large proportion of the time occupied in jig-boring..is taken up in the initial setting up of the discs or buttons on the work. **1970** W. J. PATTON *Mod. Manuf.* vii. 157 Jig-boring machines are not production machines but toolmaking

equipment for the accurate location and drilling of holes. **1902** *Encycl. Brit.* XXXI. 371/2 The pulsating current is obtained by placing a vertical longitudinal partition.. extending part of the way down to the bottom of the jig box. **1951** A. F. TAGGART *Elem. Ore Dressing* x. 190 The supporting reactions of the relatively rigid screen and sidewalls of the jig box are familiar. **1877** Jig-brow [see *DIP *sb.* 5 b]. **1932** GWIAZDOWSKI & LORD *Econ. Tool Engin.* xiii. 184 (*caption*) Toolmaker's jig buttons. **1964** S. CRAWFORD *Basic Engin. Processes* v. 134 Fig. 19 (*a*) shows a sectional view of a jig-button, a small cylindrical steel bush accurately ground on the circumference and end faces, the hole being about ⅛ inch larger in diameter than the retaining screw. These buttons can be set by end measurement. **1849** *Ex. Doc. 31st U.S. Congress 1 Sess. House* No. 5 III. 469 The heavier metals are thrown out to be farther cleansed by the Jigmen. **1921** *Dict. Occup. Terms* (1927) 18/1 *Jigger, jigman*; controls by levers and generally attends to jig, i.e., water concentration machine used to separate larger portions of ore from rock, stones, etc., with which it is found. **1929** F. H. ROLT *Gauges & Fine Measurement* II. vi. 108 Three discs are.. attached to the jig plate by screws passing through loosely fitting holes. **1970** W. J. PATTON *Mod. Manuf.* v. 79 Drill bushings are inserted into a jig plate and used to guide the drill bit. **1916** H. L. WILSON *Somewhere in Red Gap* vii. 314 Kate has about four more of 'em licked to a standstill in jigtime. **1922** JOYCE *Ulysses* 313 Confident of knocking out the fistic Eblanite in jigtime. **1947** S. J. PERELMAN *Westward Ha!* (1949) x. 123 We completed the return journey in jig time; some mysterious metamorphosis..had endowed me with the agility of a lizard. **1962** K. ORVIS *Damned & Destroyed* xiv. 100 Then he gets it out of his possession in jig-time. **1968** L. W. ROBINSON *Assassin* (1969) xvi. 203 If I was you, I'd see Gracie Hutchinson.. She'd solve your problem in jig time.

jig (dʒig), *sb.*[2] *U.S. coarse slang.* Also **jigg(s.** [Origin unknown, but perhaps the same word as prec.] A Negro.

Like *JIGABOO, a term that gives offence.

1924 F. J. WILSTACH *Slang Dict.* Stage (Typescript in N.Y. Public Libr.), *Jiggs*, Negro actor. **1927** K. NICHOLSON *Barker* III. i. 128 You go along and give 'em a hand, too. Nat Brody's there and a crew of jigs. **1931** *Amer. Mercury* Nov. 352/2 *Jig*, a Negro.—*Jigband*, the sideshow band. **1932** J. T. FARRELL *Young Lonigan* iii. 113 Janitor's jobs were for jiggs, and Hunkies, and Polacks, anyway. **1933** *Fortune* Aug. 47/1 A couple of jigs got on the bus with a doghouse. **1935** E. HEMINGWAY *Green Hills Afr.* (1936) II. vi. 163 This jig we call Othello falls in love with this girl. **1939** *New Yorker* 7 Oct. 22/3 He said if a jig band..could be a big success in Paris why not a fellow like you. *Ibid.*, They even made this jig a lieutenant [*sic*]. **1950** BLESH & JANIS *They all played Ragtime* (1958) i. 23 Tom Ireland recalls that up to that time ragtime piano was called 'jig piano', and the syncopating bands, like Joplin's were called 'jig bands'. This term, taken from jig dances, even came a little later to be a designation for the Negro himself. **1969** S. GREENLEE *Spook who sat by Door* xiii. 116, I don't have to worry about no jig lieutenants! **1972** 'H. HOWARD' *Epitaph for Joanna* iv. 51 The photograph..showed..a Negro orchestra... I'd never seen the jig band before.

jig, *v.* Add: **9.** *trans.* To provide or equip with jigs (sense *6 e). Also *absol.*

1900 *Machinery* (N.Y.) Dec. 130/1 There are many other considerations..which cannot be overlooked when the question of 'To jig or not to jig' arises. **1927** *Observer* 16 Oct. 26 A sound financial scheme always includes writing off the heavy cost of jigging and tooling up a factory to manufacture a given type during the first year of its production. **1957** *Times* 23 Aug. 3/6 There was lying idle floor space jigged and tooled to produce six Britannia fuselages a month.

jigaboo (dʒi·gǎbū). *U.S. coarse slang.* Also **jiggabo, jijjiboo, zigabo,** etc. [Related to *JIG *sb.*[2] after BUGABOO.] A Negro.

Like *JIG *sb.*[2], a term that gives offence.

1909 WESTON & BARNES *I've got Rings on my Fingers* (song), So come to your na-bob, and next Pat-rick's Day Be Mis-tress Mum-bo Jum-bo Jij-ji-boo J. O'Shea. **1929** *Sat. Even. Post* 13 Apr. 54/4 Jigaboo (underworld). **1929** T. GORDON *Born to Be* 236 Zigaboo, Dinge, Jasper, nicknames for Ethiopians. **1930** *Amer. Mercury* Dec. 456/1 Me broad's squawkin' the jigaboo hop tries to make her. **1935** J. T. FARRELL *Studs Lonigan* iv. 87 Yes, but the pupils are all jigabooes, and the parish is very poor now, I guess. **1935** D. RUNYON *Money from Home* 6, I will take Follow You and that zigaboo jock of his in the Gold Vase for mine against any horse and any amateur rider in the world. **1940** W. R. BURNETT *High Sierra* vi. 35 'Yeah,' said Red, 'I think the zigaboo has got your cabin all set.' **1944** *Amer. Speech* XIX. 174 Such vulgar synonyms for Negro as..jazzbo, jigabo (with the variants, jibagoo, jig, zigabo, zigaboo, zig). **1961** J. H. GRIFFIN *Black like Me* (1962) 57 The Negro..hearing himself referred to as nigger, coon, jigaboo! **1970** L. SANDERS *Anderson Tapes* lix. 160 The tall one..was a jigaboo. **1973** *Washington Post* 11 Mar. 6/6 'All that is left back there is a bunch of boos'—short for 'jigaboos', a derogatory term for blacks.

jig-a-jig. Add: Also **jig-jig.** Used in sense 'sexual intercourse'; also as *vb.*, to copulate. *slang.*

1896 FARMER & HENLEY *Slang* IV. 54/2 *Jig-a-jig*, to copulate. **1932** L. GOLDING *Magnolia St.* II. xiv. 468 This was..the red lamp district... The women stopped... 'Jig-a-jig, Johnny? Very nice!' they said. **1935** AUDEN & ISHERWOOD *Dog beneath Skin* i. v. 58 Come wiv me. Good Jig-a-Jig. **1935** A. J. POLLOCK *Underworld Speaks* 64/1 *Jig-jig*, a lewd act. **1948** G. GREENE *Heart of Matter* I. I. i. 2 The boys' refrain... 'Captain want jig jig, my sister pretty girl school-teacher, captain want jig jig.' **1953**

A. BARON *Human Kind* xvii. 124 He put his hand on her knee. 'You like jig-a-jig?' **1966** 'E. LINDALL' *Time too Soon* (1967) iv. 49 This woman's master has jig-a-jig with my blood sister. **1971** B. W. ALDISS *Soldier Erect* 125 'Hello, sweetheart. You like jig-jig?' 'That's the idea. Let's look at you first.'..She said something—... All we had in common was the word, the call-sign, 'jig-jig'.

jigger, *sb.*[1] Add: **1. b.** In full, *jigger coat.* A woman's short loosely-fitting jacket.

1957 M. B. PICKEN *Fashion Dict.* 190/2 *Jigger coat*, short semi-tailored, informal coat. **1966** *Olney Amsden & Sons Ltd. Price List* 30, 50 numbers Pinarettes, Aprons and Jiggers. **1968** J. IRONSIDE *Fashion Alphabet* 36 *Jigger*, a jacket popular in the 1930s—loose, finger-tip length, often with a tuxedo front. **1974** *Times* 12 Feb. 11/7 I thought this little mink jigger..was a coming look.

c. *N.Z.* (See quot. 1971.)

1961 *Countryman* LVIII. iii. 500 The axeman has to insert at least two 'jiggers' or steps. **1966** *Wanganui* (N.Z.) *Photo News* 4 June 43/2 (*caption*) Champion axeman Sonny Bolstad is watched by the Queen Mother as he competes in a jigger chop. **1971** F. C. FORD-ROBERTSON *Terminol. Forest Sci.* 252/2 *Jigger(-board)* (New Zealand) .., a short board or plank, its end notched into the bole on which the cutter stands so as to enable him to fell the tree at a level not reachable from the ground.

4. Also, in ice-fishing. *Canad.*

1946 *Beaver* June 17/1 The jigger is a wooden plank with a slot in the middle through which a wooden arm controlled by a metal lever, moves. **1972** D. PRYDE *Nunaga* i. 16 The ice is eight feet thick on the lakes and it's almost impossible to set a net without a jigger. We had a jigger in here once and showed the Eskimos how to use it to string a net under the ice, but no one ever bothered to make one.

5. Other specific applications:

l. Any small mechanical contrivance; a 'thingummy' *U.S. colloq.* **m.** *Golf.* A short iron-headed club used for approaching shots. **n.** *Dyeing.* A device for dyeing piece goods by passing them back and forth through a dye-bath over a set of rollers. **o.** A bicycle or small motor vehicle or hand-car. † **p.** *Radio.* A high-frequency transformer used in early spark transmitters to couple the aerial circuit to the circuit in which the oscillations were generated; an oscillation transformer. *Obs.* **q.** A light vehicle, esp. one that moves on rails. *dial.* and *N.Z.* (see *E.D.D.*, sense 4. **r.** A ouija. **s.** A device for administering electric shock (see quot. 1973).

l. **1874** HOTTEN *Slang Dict.* 203 Jigger has many meanings, the word being applied to any small mechanical contrivance. **1926** *Amer. Speech* I. 628/2 The term jigger has long been used of small mechanical devices... In America, jigger is often used as an indefinite name, not too dignified, of the same order as thingumbob. **1942** H. WENTWORTH *Amer. Dial. Dict.* 328 *Jigger*, thingema-jig.

m. **1893** H. G. HUTCHINSON *Golfing* 21 The learner will probably do better..to employ.—supposing that he finds he cannot play the short approaches with sufficient dead loft off an ordinary iron—a much-laid-back approaching cleek. On some links these are a great deal used, under the name of jiggers. **1931** *Punch* 1 July 717/2 *Full-equipped Visitor*. This looks a weird sort of hole. What on earth does one take here? *Local player*. One takes a jigger, if that's all one has. **1970** H. TAYLOR *Golf Dict. Jigger*, an iron club, of value in all kinds of golfing situations.

n. **1893** E. KNECHT et al. *Man. Dyeing* II. ix. 694 The modern jigger consists of a wooden or cast-iron dye vessel heated by steam and provided with water supply and waste-pipe. In the vessel are three rollers..at the top and two..at the bottom, which guide the pieces in their passage through the dye-liquor. **1915** T. BEACALL et al. *Dyestuffs & Coal-Tar Products* iv. 82 The machine most frequently met with in the dyeing of cotton cloth is the jigger. In this machine the cloth in full width is passed through the dye liquor several times over guide rollers. **1963** MEITNER & KERTESS tr. *Schmidlin's Preparation Dyeing Synthetic Fibres* xi. 90 Although a discontinuous machine the automatic jigger is very suitable for de-sizing boiling-off, bleaching and dyeing of heavy fabrics sensitive to creasing.

o. **1897** H. G. WELLS in *Humours of Cycling* 7 'Pretty Jigger!' said the Bounder... 'Nice-looking machine you've got.' **1930** 'E. BRAMAH' *Little Flutter* iv. 52 My little jigger is no good for a job like this. **1958** *Globe Mail* (Toronto) 9 Aug. 18/1 A jigger carrying eight men came belting around the mountains and ran smack into a moose. **1973** *Courier-Mail* (Brisbane) 28 July 17/11 It takes little time, too, to absorb the antique public school language... Jigger—a bicycle.

p. **1902** *Encycl. Brit.* XXXIII. 230/2 The plugs of the sensitive tube..are joined to the terminals of the secondary circuit S'S' of a small transformer, called a 'jigger'. **1906** J. A. FLEMING *Princ. Electr. Wave Telegr.* vii. 4 If the oscillation transformer, or jigger, is not wound suit the wave length employed, so far from being a benefit it prevents any signals being received at all. **1924** P. R. RISDON *Wireless* xii. 116 The oscillating current in the primary circuit induces, through the 'jigger' coils, as they we called, another current of the same frequency in the aerial circuit. **1937** in 'DECIBEL' *Wireless Terms Explained* 4

q. **1904** 'G. B. LANCASTER' *Sons o' Men* 158 Two men sat on the little iron jigger that straddled the wooden tram-line. **1918** *N.Z.E.F. Chrons.* 8 Nov. 179/1 At last I commenced the second stage—this time on a 'jigger', a frame on two rubber-tyred wheels which holds the stretcher. **1949** E. DE MAUNY *Huntsman in Career* Chancey..went off on the jigger down the narrow track into the bush each morning.

r. **1916** O. LODGE *Raymond* 186 Jigger. (A kind Ouija.)

s. **1972** *Sunday Sun* (Brisbane) 26 Nov. 1/2 Battery operated jiggers are being used on mentally retarded children..to bring them into line. The electric shock treatment is followed by..lollies if they behave. **1974** *Sunday Mail Mag.* (Brisbane) 25 Feb. 14/1 Occasionally a blue spark would flash forth as a recalcitrant beast was touched with the 'jigger' (a battery-operated dev-

carried over the shoulder and imparting an electric shock through an insulated rod held in the hand).

6. c. A passage between or at the back of houses; a back entry or alley. *Merseyside.*

1902 in *Eng. Dial. Dict.* **1966** [see *knee-trembler* s.v. *KNEE *sb.* 13]. **1966** P. MOLONEY *Plea for Mersey* 21 'A seen a scuffer up a jigger wid a rozzer' ('I saw two policemen in the side entry'). **1967** A. HENRI in *Penguin Mod. Poets* X. 16 A Polish gunman..collapses down a back jigger.

7. b. (Earlier examples.) Also, a small glass or metal cup, a measure used in mixing cocktails; the contents of such a glass or measure.

1836 W. O'BRYAN *Narr. Trav. U.S.* 107 These canal labourers have a boy to supply them with Whiskey, called a *Jiggar boss*, who goes on the canal and carries a half gill (half noggin) of Whiskey to every man sixteen times a day! **1870** J. H. B. NOWLAND *Early Reminisc. Indianapolis* 361 By jiggers was meant a small cup of whisky, say about a gill; they had cups made on purpose for this use. **1879** *N.Y. Herald* 21 Nov. 8/2 A jigger..is a conical metal cup in which to mix fancy drinks. **1946** E. HOLDING *Innocent Mrs. Duff* 17 On a shelf there was a fine array of bottles, with jiggers of two sizes, swizzle sticks, glass mixers. **1946** 'P. QUENTIN' *Puzzle for Fiends* (1947) viii. 62 A jigger of liquor clutched between thumb and first finger. **1952** S. KAUFMANN *Philanderer* (1953) vii. 114 What I came out to ask you is, do you have any gin in the house and could you spare me a jigger? **1971** R. DENTRY *Encounter at Kharmel* ix. 148 A baker's dozen perversions for a jigger of vodka.

8. (senses 5 a, b) *jigger-boy*; (sense *1 c) **jigger-board** *N.Z.* = *JIGGER 1 c; **jigger-saw** = JIG-SAW *sb.*

1944 R. GILBERD in *N.Z. New Writing* III. 55 We would have given you..nerves to stand the narrow insecurity of the jigger-board. **1961** B. CRUMP *Hang on a Minute* 42 During the next few weeks Jack learned about scarfing, backing, limbing, deeing, sniping, jigger-boards, platforms, toms, strops, drives, triggers, and saw and axe sharpening. **1963** N. HILLIARD *Piece of Land* 176 The best thing of the day to watch, the three-tier jigger-board chop. **1869** *Good Words* 1 Mar. 172/2 A plaster-of-Paris cast is placed on a disc which a handle-turning 'jigger-boy' causes to revolve. **1921** Jigger boy [see *JIGGERER]. **1888** *Lockwood's Dict. Mech. Engin.* 197 *Jigger saw*, or *jig saw*. **1957** *N.Z. Timber Jrnl.* Sept. 61/1 *Jigger saw*, a reciprocating saw. A fret or scroll or jig saw, used for pierced and tracery work.

jigger, *sb.*^{2} Also jigger flea (examples). The Latin name of the insect is now *Tunga penetrans.*

1947 H. VAUGHAN-WILLIAMS *Visit to Lobengula* xxvii. 176 Arthur's feet suffered badly from jigger fleas—horrid little tiny insects that burrow under the skin and lay a bunch of eggs there in a capsule. **1953** *New Biol.* XIV. 120 *Tunga penetrans*, the tropical jigger flea of man, is the best-known of these [burrowing fleas]. **1962** GORDON & LAVOIPIERRE *Entomol. for Students of Med.* xxxv. 217 Both the male and the female jigger flea are blood-suckers.

jigger, *v.*^{1} Add: **2.** orig. *pass.*, usu. with *up*: to be tired out, exhausted; so, to be 'done for', devitalized. Also *actively*: to break, destroy, ruin. *dial.* and *slang.*

1862 C. C. ROBINSON *Dial. Leeds* 332 *Jigger'd up*, Av tramp'd a matter o' fotty mile to-daay, an' am fair jigger'd up. *a* **1865** SMYTH *Sailor's Word-Bk.* (1867) 412 *Jiggered-up*, done up; tired out. **1885** B. BRIERLEY *Ab-o' th-Yate in Yankeeland* v. 42 A generation or two would see it jiggered up if it wurno' for th' fresh blood that's bein sent into it. **1895** 'G. MORTIMER' *Like Stars that Fall* xii. 167 Bates will jigger us if he can... I wouldn't trust that fellow. **1896** *Yorks. Weekly Post* 6 June 6/8 T'chap wor reight jiggered up. **1923** *Daily Mail* 13 June 12 I've 'jiggered' up my Rolls-Royce. **1949** E. DE MAUNY *Huntsman in Career* 150 He jiggered up his ankle last Saturday. **1969** *Telegraph* (Brisbane) 19 May 8/1 The firing pin's jiggered and the sights are sloppy.

jigger, *v.*^{2} Add: Also ji·ggering *ppl. a.* and intensive *adv.*

1903 *Daily Chron.* 14 Sept. 3/3 Once you've made up your mind, as you may say, about a young man, you've got to be jiggerin' well careful you don't go and lose him. **1950** X. HERBERT in Murdoch & Drake-Brockman *Austral. Short Stories* (1951) 301 Take the lot. Take the lintin' jiggerin' lot!

ji·gger, *v.*^{4} *Pottery.* [f. JIGGER *sb.*^{1} 5 a.] *trans.* To shape with a jigger.

1931 W. H. WARBURTON *Hist. Trade Union Organization in Potteries* xi. 208, I will try and get the price you want for this article, but you must remember that this.. is being jiggered by a firm in the next town at a much less price. **1967** M. CHANDLER *Ceramics in Mod. World* ii. 63 Shaping methods..include..throwing, jollying or jiggering, plastic pressing, and extrusion.

ji·gger, *v.*^{5} *Book-binding.* [? f. JIGGER *sb.*^{1}] *trans.* To rub (a tool) backwards and forwards along a line or other impression in a leather binding, in order to polish it. Hence **ji·ggering** *vbl. sb.*

1880 J. W. ZAEHNSDORF *Art of Bookbinding* xxii. 114 The lines impressed on the back must now have their gloss given to them. This is done by *jiggering* the pallets over them. **1901** D. COCKERELL *Bookbinding* xv. 224, I have found that a tool guided by a straight-edge, and 'jiggered' backwards and forwards, makes by far the best lines for blind-tool work. **1946** E. DIEHL *Bookbinding* II. xxiii. 352 It [*sc.* the fillet] is then pushed over the line a few times with a 'jiggering' motion, until the line is polished. **1951** L. TOWN *Bookbinding by Hand* x. 229 The tool can be put down again and rocked slightly. This gives a polished surface as well as a darkened one, and is known as 'jiggering'. **1963** B. C. MIDDLETON *Hist. Eng. Craft Bookbinding Technique* xii. 167 The tools are usually rocked or jiggered to produce a polish.

jiggerer (dʒi·gərəɹ). [f. JIGGER *sb.*^{1} 5 + -ER^1.] One who uses or works with a jigger (in various trades).

1881 *Instructions to Census Clerks* (1885) 84 Coal Miner... Loader, Jiggerer, Trammer, Hooker-on. *Ibid.* 88 China, Porcelain, Manufacture:..Jigger or Gigger Turner, Jiggerer. **1921** *Dict. Occup. Terms* (1927) § 043 *Jigger, jigger boy, jiggerer*..attaches or detaches tubs, singly or in pairs, to or from endless rope, by placing rope in fork of 'jigger', or double crook, in socket at one side or end of tubs. *Ibid.* § 105 *Jigger, jiggerer*, makes flat-ware such as plates, saucers; presses bat of clay on top of mould, already revolving on vertical spindle. **1931** W. H. WARBURTON *Hist. Trade Union Organization in Potteries* xi. 205 By this scheme his hollow-ware pressers would employ female assistants in the same way as did his hollow-ware jiggerers and 'jolliers'.

jiggery-pokery (dʒi·gəri,pōu·kəri). *colloq.* [Cf. Sc. *joukery-pawkery* (see JOUKERY, JOOKERY b).] Deceitful or dishonest 'manipulation'; hocus-pocus, humbug.

1893 in DARTNELL & GODDARD *Gloss. Words Wiltshire* 86. **1926** E. F. SPANNER *Naviators* ix. 104, I thought.. it was some more jiggery-pokery to keep down the expenditure this financial year. **1943** *Mind* LII. 304, I share with Gray the feeling that there's some *jiggery pokery* here and that what you are doing is not what one tends to feel you are doing. **1973** G. MITCHELL *Murder of Busy Lizzie* ii. 23 Business reasons could make any alliance respectable..so long as there was no jiggery-pokery.

jigging, *vbl. sb.* **2.** (Examples in the sense of *JIG *v.* 9.)

1903 W. H. VAN DERVOORT *Mod. Machine Shop Tools* xxvii. 410 No class of work in the manufacturing shop presents as many possibilities for jigging as does the work handled in the drilling machine. **1945** LEA & SIMONS *Machining of Steel* xii. 107 A fraction of a minute per part saved in large-scale production by better jigging soon outweighs any appreciable resultant increase in the cost of the jig.

jiggoty, var. JIGGETY *a.*

1876 H. E. SCUDDER *Dwellers in Five-Sisters Court* ii. 30 Mr. le Clear appeared and received the jiggoty Miss Pix's welcome in a smiling and well-bred manner.

‖ **jigotai** (dʒigotai·). *Judo.* [Jap.] In Judo, a defensive posture.

1950 E. J. HARRISON *Judo* 102 *Jigotai*, self-defensive posture. **1957** TAKAGAKI & SHARP *Techniques Judo* i. ii. 12 *Jigo-tai*..is assumed by spreading your legs wide apart and bending your knees to lower your body.

jig-saw, *sb.* Add: For '*U.S.*' read 'orig. *U.S.*' Also **jigsaw.** (Later example.) Also *attrib.*, of a type of architectural decoration using fretwork patterns.

1892 KIPLING *Lett. of Travel* (1920) 21 The jig-saw days, when it behoved respectability to use unlovely turned rails and pierced gable-ends. **1928** E. O'NEILL *Strange Interlude* III. 86 The room is one of those big, misproportioned dining rooms that are found in the large, jigsaw country houses scattered around the country as a result of the rural taste for grandeur in the eighties. **1966** M. M. PEGLER *Dict. Interior Design* 245 *Jigsaw detail.* a cutout or fretwork design made with a jigsaw. It was used for the enhancement of buildings of the mid and late 19th century. The bargework was often made with a jigsaw. The 'gingerbread' or 'steamboat Gothic', late Victorian period was jigsaw work in its most aggravated form. **1968** J. ARNOLD *Shell Bk. Country Crafts* 274 Salad-forks, for example, are cut without previous marking by a hand jig-saw.

b. In full, *jig-saw puzzle.* A puzzle formed by cutting into small irregular pieces (orig. with a jig-saw) a picture mounted on a sheet of wood, cardboard, or the like. (Now the usual sense.) So *jig-saw map.* Also *transf.* and *fig.*

1909 *Daily Mirror* 17 Aug. 4/4 A jigsaw map of England. *Ibid.*, These jigsaw geography puzzles should be introduced into all the Council schools in London. **1910** *Punch* 9 Mar. 172 (*caption*) What if the jig-saw epidemic spreads? **1915** *Morning Post* 15 Apr. 2/4 A kind of verbal jig-saw. **1919** E. SHACKLETON *South* i. 11 Pack-ice might be described as a gigantic and interminable jigsaw-puzzle devised by nature. **1935** W. S. MAUGHAM *Don Fernando* x. 213 The various particulars fit like the pieces of a jig-saw puzzle. **1947** *People* 22 June 4/3 How can this jigsaw be pieced together? Many of the facts are now known as a result of most painstaking police inquiries. **1955** A. HUXLEY *Let.* 25 Sept. (1969) 766 All this jigsaw work entailed in shaping a play for stage production is extremely boring. **1964** M. CRITCHLEY *Developmental Dyslexia* ix. 57 Constructional tasks which embrace spatial concepts include the assembling of jigsaw puzzles, a game which may not be easy for some of these dyslexics. **1972** *Oxford Times* 11 Aug. 3 As the excavation proceeds more and more tiny pieces of the archaeological jigsaw puzzle will be discovered. **1974** G. MARKSTEIN *Cooler* xl. 149 Sylvia was turning into the little jigsaw piece that often remained the hardest one to find.

jig-saw *v.*, also, to fit together the pieces of a jig-saw puzzle. Freq. *fig.*

1938 *Times* 2 Feb. 13/4 Jig-sawing is one of the few pastimes in which bludgeoning methods definitely do not pay. **1963** *Harper's Bazaar* Jan. 29/3 It taxed all Miss Molesworth's expertise to jigsaw the requirements into a pleasing ensemble. **1966** *Punch* 18 May 720 I've often cut his articles into line sentences, mixed them up, and tried to jigsaw them together, a most difficult thing to do until you've caught the drift of his mind. **1967** *Listener* 9 Feb. 207/3 The interviews through which Lowry's character was jigsawed together were wholly fascinating. **1973** *Guardian* 27 Feb. 11/5 We..jig-sawed our bits together into one consecutive piece, typing on maddening French machines.

jildi (dʒi·ldi). *Mil. slang* (orig. *Anglo-Indian*). Also **jeldi, jildy, juldie,** and other varr. [ad. Hind. *jaldi* quickness.] Haste, as in phrases *on the jildi*, in a hurry, and to *do* or *move a jildi*. So **jildi** *a.*, quick; **jildi, juldily** *adv.*, quickly; **jildi** *v. trans.* and *absol.*, to hurry.

1890 KIPLING *Barrack-Room Ballads* (1892) 24 You put some *juldee* in it Or I'll *marrow* you this minute. **1919** W. H. DOWNING *Digger Dial.* 59 *Jeldi*, hurry; run. *Ibid.* 30 *Jeldy* (Hind.), quickly. **1926** *Scots Observer* 30 Oct. 21/1 Wullie..would have seen..that the rabbits were moving juldie into the thistles and long grass as he came along. Juldie! What's that? Hindustani for quick. **1929** [see *FUCK *v.* 3]. **1930** R. BLAKER *Medal without Bar* vii. 47 Come on. We'll catch 'im if we jildi. **1930** BROPHY & PARTRIDGE *Songs & Slang 1914–18* 132 *Jildi*, quick, look sharp, hurry. Also used in the phrase 'on the jildi', e.g. 'Get them bags filled on the jildi.' **1948** PARTRIDGE *Dict. Forces' Slang* 102 *Jildi*, hurry! Also *get a jildi on.* (Indian Army.) *Ibid.*, *Do a jildi move*, to beat a hasty retreat. General Army slang... Among tank men: to take evasive action. **1957** M. K. JOSEPH *I'll soldier no More* (1960) 14 Hey, Antonio, where's me rooty? And make it juldy, see? **1972** J. BROWN *Chancer* i. 12, I went out jilty..and there he was.

jill (dʒil), *v.* [Presumably var. of GILL *v.*^{2}: cf. quot. 1855 s.v.] *intr.* Of a boat: to move *about*, to move *around*; to idle around.

1955 *Times* 18 July 9/6 In the early morning light Falmouth bay looked as lovely as ever, with its rounded green hills and little fishing boats jilling about under sail off the Manacles. **1956** W. GOLDING *Pincher Martin* i. 18 Survivors, a raft, the whaler, the dinghy, wreckage may be jilling about only a swell or two away hidden in the mist and waiting for rescue with at least bully and perhaps a tot. **1964** F. CHICHESTER *Lonely Sea & Sky* xxix. 303 After breakfast I took over for an hour or two until we had cleared the point, when I gratefully lowered all sail and *Gipsy Moth* jilled along. **1972** *Guardian* 23 Sept. 5/4 Bosun dinghies jilling around the windless Medway... Picture by Peter Johns.

jillaroo (dʒilarū·). *Austral.* Also **jilleroo.** [Jocular formation from JACKAROO *sb.*] A female station-hand. So as *v. intr.*, to work as a jillaroo.

1945 BAKER *Austral. Lang.* iii. 62 The past few years have given us a variant [of jackeroo] in *jillaroo*, a female station-hand.., especially used during World War No. 2 for a Land Girl. **1945** *Salt* 26 Feb. 16/1 Miss Garraty is our new 'jilleroo'. **1964** *Pix* 22 Aug. 41 Dr. Davies said *Pix* should have called Miss Lukis a jenniroo or jennyroo. That might be all right for West Australians but the word used in the Eastern States is jillaroo. **1969** *Courier-Mail* (Brisbane) 15 Aug. 7/3 A part-time model, jilleroo and cattle judge was named the top under-21 Rural Youth member yesterday. **1970** *Sunday Mail Mag.* (Brisbane) 28 June 6/2 Isabel has been jillarooing all over Australia for the last four years.

jillion (dʒi·lyən). orig. *U.S.* [Fanciful formation after BILLION, MILLION.] Very many, a great many.

1942 BERREY & VAN DEN BARK *Amer. Thes. Slang* § 18/6 *Indefinite number*, jillion. **1945** L. SHELLY *Jive Talk Dict.*, *Jillion*, a lot of people or money. **1950** *Time* 13 Feb. 10/1 After Spindletop, in the superlatives of the oilfields, came a jillion jackpots—roaring booms at Electra, Ranger, Burkburnett, Desdemona and Mexia proved that oil was where you found it. **1957** *New Yorker* 2 Nov. 141/1 'Oh, I've got a jillion,' he replied. 'A jillion ties and no wife. I have ties from many parts of the world.' **1963** 'R. L. PIKE' *Mute Witness* (1965) vi. 100, I bet I've hit about a jillion travel agencies today. **1971** *Physics Bull.* Nov. 682/3 Gamesters with 'game theories' of a jillion different maliciously fixable kinds.

jills (dʒilz). *slang.* [Shelta.] Used with a possessive pronoun: *my jills* = 'I', *his jills* = 'he', etc.

1906 E. DYSON *Fact'ry 'Ands* ix. 117 'They thort his jills had done er get,' said the packer. **1940** *N. & Q.* 15 June 421/1 In the current slang of the Variety profession and other Bohemian circles, 'jills', coupled with a possessive pronoun, stands for 'I', 'you', 'he', etc., according to the possessive pronoun prefixed... So 'my jills', 'your jills', 'his jills'.

jim (dʒim). *Austral. colloq.* [f. **Jimmy O'Goblin*.] A pound, a pound note.

1906 E. DYSON *Fact'ry 'Ands* xvi. 214 He was tearin' ratty t' raise another jim. **1919** V. MARSHALL *World Living Dead* in Baker *Austral. Lang.* (1945) xvii. 310 Half a jim (10s.). **1959** BAKER *Drum* 120 *Jim*, the sum of £1.

Jim-crow. Substitute for entry:
Jim Crow[1], Jim-crow, jim crow (dʒi·m,krōu·). [From the refrain of a popular old Negro song, 'Wheel about and turn about and jump Jim Crow'.]

Orig. *U.S.*, but the main current senses (1 f, and its *attrib.* and verbal uses, with *Jim Crowism*) are used throughout the English-speaking world, although chiefly in U.S. contexts.

1. The name of a Negro plantation song of the early nineteenth century; also, a stage presentation of a song and dance first performed by Thomas D. Rice (1808–60) and subsequently by other actors dressed as 'nigger minstrels'.

1828 T. D. RICE *(title)* Jim Crow. Celebrated comic song or ballad. **1832** *Amer. Sentinel* (Philadelphia) 11 Sept. 3/1 (Advt.), Mr. Rice will appear and sing Jim Crow. **1835** *Vade Mecum* (Philadelphia) 28 Mar. 2/7 'Ditanti Palpita', 'Jim Crow', 'Old Hundred', with two or three waltzes played in *different* keys usually form the *Hotchpotchiana* of their delicious entertainment. **1837** *New Yorker* 16 Dec. 610/2 The impulse of despair must have tempted them to strike up 'Jim Crow'. **1841** THACKERAY in *Britannia* 15 May 315/4 The organ-man.. struck up two beautiful melodies, viz., 'Getting up Stairs', and 'Jim Crow'. **1926** *N.Y. Times* 26 Dec. VII. 8/2 From 'Old Jim Crow' to 'Black Bottom', the negro dances..are African in inspiration.

b. Phr. *to jump Jim Crow*: to execute the dance that was part of a theatrical (or street) performance of Jim Crow; to jump about. Also *fig.*, to change one's political principles, to desert one's party.

1833 *Sk. & Eccentr. D. Crockett* 41 You nebber get to Heben till you jump Jim Crow. **1836** *Louisville* (Kentucky) *Jrnl.* 16 Sept., A Mr. Collier of Virginia has 'jumped Jim Crow'. **1840** *Log Cabin Song-Bk.* 38 Fo he's the man to jump Jim Crow, And prove that black is white. **1857** *Observer* 12 Apr. 2/4 A street clown once told him (Mr. Mayhew) that..he jumped 'Jim Crow' for twelve hours in the mud and wet of the streets, and he carried home..the sum of 15d. **1922** GALSWORTHY *Windows* I. 19 Not much balance about us. We just run about and jump Jim Crow.

c. A Negro character in the Jim Crow song; T. D. Rice or another performer of the Jim Crow act; in England, a street performer of this type of act (see b).

1835 *Vade Mecum* (Philadelphia) 24 Jan. 3/7 Jim Crow is in the town, about to 'wheel about' for the edification of the Brandywine. Daddy Rice will surprise them. **1851** H. MAYHEW *London Labour* I. 4/1 The street-actors—as clowns, 'Billy Barlows', 'Jim Crows', and others. **1861** *Ibid.* III. 121/1 A few minutes afterwards I saw this man dressed as Jim Crow, with his face blackened, dancing and singing in the streets as if he was the lightest-hearted fellow in all London. **1867** *Atlantic Monthly* Nov. 608/2 As a national or 'race' illustration, behind the footlights, might not 'Jim Crow' and a black face tickle the fancy of pit and circle?

d. A turncoat. (Cf. the *fig.* sense of b.)

1837 *New Yorker* 16 Dec. 610/2 An engraving of the veritable Jim Crow is to be seen in every print-shop, with the exception that the face of Lord Lyndhurst usurps that of Rice, his lordship being placed in that peculiar attitude which the Liberals denominate 'turning about—wheeling about' from political consistency and common sense. **1840** J. ROMILLY *Diary* 13 Nov. (1967) 204 The blackgds in the gallery hooted & called him Jim Crow.

e. A Negro. *depreciatory.*

1838 'UNCLE SAM' in *Bentley's Misc.* IV. 582 Don't be standing there like the wooden Jim Crow at the blacking maker's store. **1841** H. PLAYFAIR *Hugo Playfair Papers* I. 3 A portmanteau and carpet-bag..were snatched up by one of the hundreds of nigger-porters, or Jim Crows, who swarm at the many landing-places to *help* passengers. **1948** *Sat. Rev.* (U.S.) 27 Mar. 36/1 Jim Crow works at the depot.

f. Racial discrimination, *spec.* against Negroes in the U.S. More usually *attrib.*, or as *Jim Crowism* (below).

1943 R. OTTLEY *New World A-Coming* 69 Negro soldiers had suffered all forms of Jim Crow, humiliation, discrimination, slander, and even violence at the hands of the white civilian population. **1946** J. H. BURMA in A. Dundes *Mother Wit* (1973) 625/2 To the Negro any joke is particularly humorous if it shows Jim Crow 'backfiring' on a Southerner. **1958** J. ASMAN in P. Gammond *Decca Bk. Jazz* xiv. 166 The difficulties facing any studio recordings by Negro artists are almost insurmountable in the Southern States, where Jim Crow is predominant, even to the present time. **1969** *N.Y. Times* 16 Jan. 40/5 Those of them who are young and loud want segregated colleges... It's Jim Crow when we want it... Why don't they think of it as James Eagle? **1971** *Black Scholar* June 4/1 The historical literature..suggests that Jim Crow was directed more at the black male than the black female. **1973** A. DUNDES *Mother Wit* 231 Since white southerners obviously spoke in dialect..this practice was little more than another insidious form of Jim Crow. **1973** *Freedomways* XIII. 30 One hundred years of frustration and battle have not resulted in victory over Jim Crow and racism.

2. In various technical senses. (Dict. sense 1, *jim-crow planing-machine* in Dict. sense 2.)

3. *attrib.*, as (sense 1 a) *Jim Crow song*; (sense 1 c) *Jim Crow boots, dance, hat*; (sense 1 e) *Jim Crow line*; (sense 1 f) *Jim Crow bill, car, college, conditions, law, school, town.* Also (with possessive case) **Jim Crow's nose** = *John Crow('s) nose* (*JOHN CROW).

1835 *Knickerbocker* V. 47 Some jolly slaves..were waiting to take us into a ferry-boat, which they rowed, singing some Jim Crow song. **1842** *Liberator* (Boston) 21 Jan. 10/1 It is this spirit that compels the colored man to ..ride in the 'Jim-Crow car'. **1847** *Chicago Jrnl.* 7 Oct., We do not mean *Jim Crow* dances and poor songs worse sung. **1851** G. S. COOPER *Jrnl. Expedition Auckland to Taranaki* 58 A man in a common shooting jacket, a Jim Crow hat, trowsers rather the worse for wear and a pair of moustaches. **1851** MRS. STOWE *Uncle Tom's Cabin* (1852) II. xx. 33, I thought she was rather a funny specimen in the Jim Crow line. **1866** LINDLEY & MOORE *Treas. Bot.* II. 638/1 Jim Crow's nose. A West Indian name for *Phyllocoryne.* **1887** C. B. GEORGE *40 Yrs. on Rail* viii. 160 An educated colored man..found, on going from Boston to Salem, his home, that he must ride in the Jim Crow car. **1902** A. H. LEWIS *Wolfville Days* xvi. 235 An' whyever don't you-all wear leather chapps that a-way, instead of them jimcrow boots an' trousers? **1903** *Sun* (N.Y.) 29 Nov. 7 The members of the committee have arranged with the parents of negro children to send them all to the Jim Crow school, thus entirely separating the white and negro pupils. **1904** *Nation* (N.Y.) 17 Mar. 202 The Jim Crow bills now before the Maryland Legislature. **1904** *Richmond* (Virginia) *Times-Despatch* 25 May 10 Violating the Jim Crow law by allowing negroes to ride in the same car with whites. **1926** A. NILES in W. C. Handy *Blues* 20 'Jim Crow' songs with syncopated airs..were current long before the Civil War. **1931** W. FAULKNER *Sanctuary* xix. 167 It was full too, the door between it and the jim crow car swinging open. **1949** L. FEATHER *Inside Be-Bop* i. 3 Big band jazz had been played by Negro orchestras, frequently under Jim Crow conditions. **1957** W. C. HANDY *Father of Blues* xiv. 195 Having spent much time in Jim Crow towns, I was under the illusion that these Negro musicians would jump at the chance to patronize one of their own publishers. **1960** *New Left Rev.* Sept.–Oct. 39/2 The Uncle Tom presidents of the captive Jim Crow colleges. **1971** *Black World* Mar. 75/1 Black people will continue to see themselves under jim crow conditions. **1973** A. DUNDES *Mother Wit* 397 Riding on Jim Crow cars could literally make a Negro sick.

So **Jim Crow** *v. trans.*, to segregate persons ethnically, to discriminate against (Negroes or other non-whites); so **Jim Crowing** *vbl. sb.*; **Jim Crowism**, the institution of segregation, the practice of 'racial' discrimination; also, the act of deserting one's political party.

1837 *N.Y. Mirror* 7 Oct. 118/1 Then, to counterbalance this good, you have entailed upon those British islands the curse of Jim Crowism. **1841** *Times* 21 June 5/6 His propensities to what they call 'Jim Crowism' in politics. **1921** *United Free Ch. Miss. Rec.* Jan. 2/1 [S. Africa] The picture he gives of the 'jimcrowing' and ostracizing of the natives in public places and the working of the pass-laws up-country is dark enough. **1923** *Nation* (N.Y.) 15 Aug. 155 But they are not 'jim crowed'. **1925** *Amer. Mercury* Jan. 87/2 In his celebrated Atlanta speech he justified all the forms of Jim-Crowism. **1932** E. WILSON *Devil take Hindmost* iii. 17 The Negroes..are discriminated against by a general policy of Jim Crowism. **1942** C. HIMES *Black on Black* (1973) 216 Out of the bootings and the lynchings and the jim-crowings..will come our strength. **1948** *Sat. Rev.* (U.S.) 24 July 16/3 It is to his eternal credit that he ripped through the Jim Crowism of our national game by giving a fine Negro athlete a chance to play in organized baseball. **1955** L. FEATHER *Encycl. Jazz* i. 22 The Negro musician was Jim Crowed from the day he first became aware of music. **1969** C. HIMES *Blind Man with Pistol* i. 16 It was obviously a jim-crowed convent, and no one ever dreamed that white Catholics would act any different from anyone else who was white. **1971** *Rand Daily Mail* (Johannesburg) 4 Dec. 4/2 Since I visited South Africa, the Government has opened the door to dozens of prominent Blacks and ensured that they were not Jim Crowed. (Jim Crowed means treated like Blacks in the old segregationist United States South.)

Jim Crow[2] (dʒi·m,krōu·). *colloq.* [Coined by W. S. Churchill; cf. CROW *sb.*[1] 8 and CROW'S NEST.] A roof-top spotter of enemy aircraft; also his look-out post (see also quot. 1943).

1940 W. S. CHURCHILL *Into Battle* (1941) 278 Our plan must be to use the siren..as an alert and not as an alarm, and to have a system of highly trained what I may call Jim Crows or look-out men, who will give the alarm when immediate danger is expected at any point. **1941** *Battle of Britain Aug.–Oct. 1940* (Ministry of Information) 21 Except when roof-watchers—the Prime Minister's 'Jim Crows'—signalled that danger was imminent, life went on as usual and still does. **1943** HUNT & PRINGLE *Service Slang* 41 *Jim Crow*, normally used to describe the corps of roof-spotters guarding our large buildings. Now taken into service slang to denote the man on watch when 'unofficial business', such as cards, is being transacted. **1952** R. SHERBROOKE-WALKER *Khaki & Blue* v. 43 An anti-aircraft post, with a good view of the sky, had already been installed on top of one of the forts. To convert this into 'Jim Crow', it was turned into a post de luxe.

ji·m-da·ndy, *sb.* and *a.* *U.S. colloq.* [Cf. DANDY *sb.*[1] (and *a.*).] **A.** *sb.* An excellent person or thing. **B.** *adj.* Remarkably fine, outstanding.

1887 *Courier-Jrnl.* (Louisville, Kentucky) 12 Jan. 2/1 Dear Sir: Though a stranger to you (yet a Democrat), let me say you are a 'Jim Dandy'. **1888** *Inter-Ocean* (Chicago) 14 Feb. (Farmer), George C. Ball came upon the floor yesterday arrayed in a jim-dandy suit of clothes. **1902** O. WISTER *Virginian* xxvii. 346 He must have been a jim-dandy of a boy. **1904** W. N. HARBEN *Georgians* ix. 87 Right thar I baked pies—open-top jim dandies, too. **1912** *Collier's* 21 Dec. 23/2 Prince Albert rolls up the jim dandiest cigarette. **1919** H. L. WILSON *Ma Pettengill* iv. 119, I bet you made a jim-dandy good report. **1941** J. STUART *Men of Mountains* 154 He said the blue-tick hound was a jim-dandy possum dog. **1953** *New Yorker* 7 Feb. 92/2 When one suffers from headaches,..Anacin is the jim-dandy remedy. **1963** *Spectator* 12 July 45 The new GPO tower building is a jim-dandy, it excites and pleases me. **1972** B. GARFIELD *Line of Succession* (1974) ii. 128 Your voting record on foreign affairs was fine, jim-dandy.

ji·m-hi·ckey. [Cf. *HICKEY *sb.*] = prec. *sb.*

1895 S. CRANE *Red Badge of Courage* xxi. 207 Th' lieutenant, he ses: 'He's a jimhickey,' an' th' colonel, he ses: 'Ahem! ahem! he is, indeed, a very good man.' **1907** J. MASEFIELD *Tarpaulin Muster* xii. 131 Them topsails had a good look along the yard..or there was a jim hickey of a stink raised.

jiminy. Substitute for entry:
jiminy, jimminy, now the usual form of GEMINI (sense 4). Used esp. in phrases *jiminy Christmas* (see *CHRISTMAS *sb.* 1 c) and *jiminy cricket.*

1803 G. COLMAN *John Bull* I. i. 5 *Den.* A customer... *Mrs. B.* Jemmeny! and so there is. *c* **1816** [see CRIMINE, -INY *int.*]. **1848** in *Amer. Speech* (1935) X. 40 *By Jiminy Cricket*, an exclamation of surprise. **1863** [see GEMINI 4]. **1890** *Dialect Notes* I. 49 Jimminy Cripes! and Jimminy Christmas! are forms of oaths overheard. **1894** J. T. MOORE *Songs & Stories from Tennessee* (1897) 18 Jiminy! But didn't we hab a good time on de road? **1897** [see *CHRISTMAS *sb.* 1 c]. **1930** J. DOS PASSOS *42nd Parallel* II. 147 Jimminy criskets [*sic*], what I couldn't do to a watermelon, Joe. **1934** W. SAROYAN *Daring Young Man* (1935) 123 He was telling her. Jiminy crickets. **1940** N. MARSH *Surfeit of Lampreys* (1941) x. 139 'I am completely baffled.' 'Jiminy cricket!'

jim-jam. **1.** Delete † *Obs.* and add later example.

1890 KIPLING *Phantom 'Rickshaw* 85 There was half a dozen big stone idols. Dravot he goes to the biggest.. and says: 'That's all right..all these old jim-jams are my friends.'

3. b. *pl.* The fidgets, jitteriness; a fit of depression. *colloq.*

1896 'MARK TWAIN' in *Harper's Mag.* Sept. 537 They gave me the jimjams and the fantods and caked up what brains I had. **1904** *Strand Mag.* Dec. 770/2 By Gosh, look there. Enough to give a fellow the jim-jams, isn't it? **1926** GALSWORTHY *Silver Spoon* I. vi. 44 Who was the old buffer?..he gave me 'the jim-jams'. **1931** C. MACKENZIE *Buttercups & Daisies* xiii. 169, I reckon if you put him in the upper circle at *Charley's Aunt* he'd give half the audience the jim-jams and upset the whole piece. **1946** K. TENNANT *Lost Haven* (1947) xix. 332 'There *is* someone out there,' he said. 'Or else I'm giving myself the jim jams.' **1961** R. M. PATTERSON *Buffalo Head* vi. 223 Th sides gave me the jim-jams merely to look at them: o the south, sliding rock and then a drop of 2000 feet down

jimmies, *sb. pl. colloq.* = JIM-JAM 3 and *3 b

1900 J. C. HARRIS *On Wing of Occasions* 42 Take 'in to the hospital, Tim; 'tis the only way to clear the jimmie from his head. **1921** A. MASON *Flying Bo'sun* xxvi. 21 Riley,..you drank too much Scotch last night; be carefu that you don't get the Jimmies and jump overboard. **192** *New Yorker* 22 Dec. 18/3 Him popping down the chimne —well, frankly, it gives me the jimmies. **1945** BAKE *Austral. Lang.* x. 199 *Britts up, to have the*, to be alarmed From 'to have the wind up' and 'have the sh-ts', b rhyming slang on the name of the former lightweigh boxing champion of the world, Jimmy Britt, who wa on vaudeville tour in Australia during World War No. *To have the jimmies* is an extension. **1961** P. WHIT *Riders in Chariot* xi. 415 She was not accustomed to se the grey light sprawling on an empty bed; it gave her th jimmies.

jimmy, dial. and colloq. pronunciation c JEMMY *sb.* Add: Now the more usual forn in the U.S. (Examples.) Also as *v. trans.*, t open with a jemmy.

1848 G. W. M. REYNOLDS *Mysteries of London* IV cxcv. 369/1, I have got my own clasp-knife..and a sma jimmey. **1854** *Alta California* (San Francisco) 23 Feb Officer Powers,..upon examining the lock, found it ha been broken open with a 'jimmy'. **1893** J. HAWTHORN *Confessions of Convict* iii. 49 We took the safe..and ca ried it..to the basement... We jimmied it open in n time. *Ibid.* xi. 172, I have drilled holes in large safes s accurately that the bolts could be 'jimmied' without lea ing a mark. **1904** G. H. LORIMER *Old Gorgon Graham* vi 159 You can't break a big merchant with a jimmy and stick of dynamite. **1905** *N.Y. Even. Post* 22 Dec. 3 Th thieves jimmied the front door. **1922** R. PARRISH *Case Girl* xxxii. 247 Finally we jimmied open the back door this garage. **1973** 'E. MCBAIN' *Let's hear It* xiii. 194 Th patrolman..was examining a door and jamb for jimm marks. **1973** *Sat. Rev. Society* (U.S.) May 42/2 An attempt to jimmy the doors, hood, or trunk will cause th horn to begin sounding. **1973** P. B. AUSTIN tr. *Sjöwall Wahlöö's Locked Room* v. 24 The door was equippedwith jimmy-proof lock. *Ibid.* xxiii. 186 [He] had brought wit him every thinkable jimmy and other tool for opening th door.

Jimmy (dʒi·mi). [A male personal name, pet form and familiar equivalent of the nam JAMES.] In various transferred senses:

1. In full, **Jimmy Grant.** Rhyming slang fo *immigrant* or *emigrant.* *Austral.*, *N.Z.*, an *S. Afr.*

1845 E. J. WAKEFIELD *Adventure N.Z.* I. xi. 337 Th profound contempt which the whaler expresses for th 'lubber of a *jimmy-grant*', as he calls the emigrant. **18** *McLean Papers* VIII. 177 (MS.), I consider Davy h done a foolish thing in selling his farm... I am glad it h

ot as usual fallen into the hands of 'Jimmies', usurpers the soil. **1859** H. KINGSLEY *Recoll. G. Hamlyn* II. ix. 54 'What are these men that we are going to see?' Why one,' said Lee, 'is a young Jimmy (I beg your pardon, i, an emigrant), the other two are old prisoners.' **1878** . AYLWARD *Transvaal of To-Day* xi. 216, I was a raw migrant, and still what Natalians call a '*Jimmy*'. **1922** *aily Mail* 11 Dec. 8 With his wife and child he had just ome over as a 'Jimmie-grant'. **1948** F. IRVINE-SMITH *treets of my City* ii. 32 At the close of 1840, there were 500 settlers, or in whaler parlance, 'Jimmy Grants', pon its shores.

2. Jimmy Ducks, Jimmy Dux. Also **Jemmy)ucks.** A sailor who had charge of the live-tock carried on merchant ships to serve as ood on long voyages. *Naut. slang* (*Obs.* exc. *Hist.*).

1849 H. MELVILLE *Redburn* I. ix. 97 He in the rudest ind of manner laughed aloud in my face, and called me 'Jimmy Dux'. **1850** —— *White Jacket* I. iii. 12 These llows are all Jimmy Duxes—sorry chaps, who never ut foot in ratlin, or venture above the bulwarks. **1890** . C. LESLIE *Old Sea Wings* xiii. 177 The ship's butcher nd his mate, 'Jemmy Ducks', formed an important part the economy of our old East Indiamen. *Ibid.* 182 A gay ooster, after an exciting chase round the decks by Jemmy ucks, escaped overboard. **1928** J. MASON *Before Mast Sailing Ships* 13 One of our men had deserted an Orient iner in Sydney, and had been a 'Jimmy Ducks' on that essel. **1938** W. E. DEXTER *Rope-Yarns* v. 32 'Sails' or immy Ducks' was the first one to get round.

3. Jimmy Low *Austral.*, a name for red nahogany, *Eucalyptus resinifera*.

1887 *Colonial & Indian Exhib. Rep. Col. Sect.* 428 immy Low is usually a large tree, yielding timber of a ch red colour. **1888** F. M. BAILEY *Queensland Woods* 65 immy Low'. Forest Mahogany of N.S.W. Usually a ery large tree with a rough, reddish, fibrous bark. **1904** . H. MAIDEN *Forest Flora N.S.W.* I. 67 In Queensland it c. *Eucalyptus resinifera*] is often called 'Jimmy Low', fter the late Mr. James Low, of Maroochie River, a lo-ality for some of the finest specimens in that State. **1945** AKER *Austral. Lang.* xii. 215 Among popular names for arious trees noted by Morris were Jemmy Donnelly, immy Low and Roger Gough.

4. Jimmy (also **Johnny**) **Wood(s, Woodser,** solitary drinker; a drink taken on one's wn; also *transf.*; so **Jimmy Woods** *nonce vb.*, o drink alone. *Austral.* and *N.Z. slang*.

The usual form is *Jimmy Woodser*.

1892 B. H. BOAKE in *Bulletin* (Sydney) 7 May 15/1 At he thought the heart beats quicker Than an old Bohe-iian's should... Bah! I'll go and have a liquor With the enial 'Jimmy Wood'. **1898** *Ibid.* 17 Dec. Red Page/2 The se of Christian names in this form of slang seems to have riginated the Australian..*Jimmy-Woodser*, a solitary rinker. **1900** H. LAWSON *Verses Pop. & Humorous* 67 The old Jimmy Woodser comes into the bar, Unwelcomed, nnoticed, unknown. **1928** J. DEVANNY *Dawn Beloved* . xxxiv. 307 Duke preferred to drink alone.., Jimmy Voods-ing, as the miners called it. **1930** *Bulletin* (Sydney) 9 Feb. 51/4 'You have your holiday.' 'Oh, no,' she told im..'I'm getting too old for Jimmy Woodsers, thanks.' 933 *Press* (Christchurch, N.Z.) 28 Oct. 17/7 *Jimmy* or *ohnny Woodser*, slang. A drink by yourself. It is a ommon expression up-country in New Zealand. **1942** *N.Z.E.F. Times* 21 Dec. 18/2 You'll find me lonesome i a Naafi, a-drinkin' to me sins, A-sippin' like a Jimmy Voodser. **1945** BAKER *Austral. Lang.* ix. 171 A *Jimmy Voodser* is not only a lone drinker, but also a drink con-umed by such a person. **1957** D. NILAND *Call me when ross turns Over* i. 9 I'm a real Jimmy Woodser now. On iy own. The first bird on the family tree and the last.

5. In full, **Jimmy O'Goblin** (also with lower-ase initials). Rhyming slang for 'sovereign', wenty shillings. Cf. *GOBLIN², *JEMMY)'GOBLIN. *slang*.

1899 A. E. W. MASON *Miranda of Balcony* xv. 206, I ant one thousand jimmies per annum. **1931** T. H. DEY *eaves from Bookmaker's Bk.* xi. 180 Here's another story a lost 'Jimmy o' Goblin'. **1932** D. L. SAYERS *Have is Carcase* xi. 128 Three hundred golden sovereigns... hree hundred round, golden jimmy o' goblins. **1934** . WAUGH *Handful of Dust* ii. 35 He had won five Jimmy-goblins at ten to three at Chester. **1956** C. SMITH *eadly Reaper* xiv. 108 Her first husband left her half million. Yes, sir, five hundred thousand jimmy o'goblins. 959 *Spectator* 3 July 5/2 The proposed sale of the Wat-rd firm S. G. Brown Ltd., at present owned by the Ad-iiralty..is a most unlikely haunt of businessmen, if the iirty-eight million jimmy-o'goblins they were wasting on bsolete warships a month or so ago is anything to go by. 967 C. WATSON *Lonelyheart 4122* xv. 149 'The money's aid in—five hundred nice shiny Jimmy O'goblins.' (Dear od! Where had she last come across that one? Sapper? enty?) **1973** *Times* 28 June 16/2 He..had made a profit some six million jimmy-o-goblins.

6. In full, **Jimmy the One.** First Lieutenant. *Naut. slang.* Also in various other applica-ions (see quots.).

1916 'TAFFRAIL' *Pincher Martin* viii. 147 Th' Bloke, an' immy the One, an' most o' th' other officers made a bit o. **1935** WODEHOUSE *Luck of Bodkins* viii. 80 'By ghts I ought to just go to Jimmy the One.'..'The chief eward, sir?' **1945** [see *FLANNEL *sb.* 1 f]. **1953** E. HYAMS *entian Violet* v. 76 He became second in command of a ery old destroyer and as such he was perhaps the only immy-the-One in the Royal Navy who was not detested y the ship's company. **1962** 'E. PETERS' *Funeral of igaro* i. 10 He was..used to being Number One or immy the One [in a theatre]. **1970** *Guardian* 19 Aug. 5/8 Smith told Petty Officer David Lewis, 'We are oing to have a sit-in and give the "Jimmy" a hard time.'

7. dismal Jimmy: see *DISMAL *a.* 7.

8. Jimmy Green = *JAMIE GREEN; a sail under the jib-boom.

1913 E. K. CHATTERTON *Ships & Ways of Other Days* xii. 265 The reader will remember we called attention some time back to those spritsails which seem so curious to us moderns. They were also known as 'water sails' and as 'Jimmy Greens', both appellations being due, obviously, to the unhappy knack they possessed of scooping up the sea. **1933** *Sea Breezes* XVII. 186 A 'Jimmy Green' was set along the bowsprit and jibboom under the head sails. **1944** J. MASEFIELD *New Chum* 155 Once one came by with an odd triangular yardless topsail, then, very rare, but now in use again. We were told that it would be called a Jimmy Green if set above a royal.

9. In full, **Jimmy Riddle.** Rhyming slang for *piddle*.

1937 in PARTRIDGE *Dict. Slang.* **1959** R. FULLER *Ruined Boys* i. 10 Come and have a Jimmy Riddle. **1964** J. SYMONS *End of Solomon Grundy* I. ii. 34, I must do a Jimmy Riddle before I go. **1966** 'L. LANE' *ABZ of Scouse* 56 Said of a person with a weak bladder: 'e's got ther jimmy riddles. **1971** D. CLARK *Sick to Death* vii. 154 Mrs D. was in there having a jimmy.

jimsonweed. Also jim(p)son, jimpsonweed. = JAMESTOWN-WEED.

1812 *Cramer's Almanac 1813* (Pittsburgh) 26 James'-town weed..also known by the name of Jimson, and Thorn-Apple. **1842** *Amer. Pioneer* I. 314 She said her principal dressings were made of..the leaves of stramo-nium, or 'jimson'. **1880, 1892** [see JAMESTOWN-WEED]. **1911** C. HARRIS *Eve's Second Husband* xiv. 299 Clumps of sweet jimson and borders of balsam and pinks. **1930** R. BASS in A. Dundes *Mother Wit* (1973) 382 He cures.. headaches with a poultice of jimson-weeds. **1934** *Amer. Ballads & Folk Songs* 23 Mike was pilin' ties near the ditch by the road Out among the jimpson where the boys ain't mowed. **1943** R. PEATTIE *Great Smokies* 118 Jimson root for ulcers. **1954** C. J. HYLANDER *Macmillan Wild Flower Book* 360 Jimsonweed is a stout plant, growing to a height of five feet, with ovate lobed leaves and white or violet, trumpet-shaped flowers up to four inches in length.

jimswinger (dʒi·mˌswiŋəɹ). *Southern U.S.* Also **jim swinger, jim-swinger.** [Origin un-known.] In full, *jimswinger coat*. A swallow-tailed coat, esp. a frock-coat.

1890 *Dialect Notes* I. 389 *Jim-swinger*, long-tailed coat, especially a 'Prince Albert'. **1898** P. L. DUNBAR *Folks from Dixie* 52 He walked to church, flanked on one side by Aunt Caroline..and on the other by her husband stately in the magnificence of an antiquated 'Jim-swinger'. **1912** H. & W. B. CRUMPTON *Adv. Two Alabama Boys* 78, I was a tall, slim, awkward lad, about eighteen years old, thin as a match, pale as a ghost and had on a long Jim Swinger. **1933** C. MILLER *Lamb in Bosom* v. 47 If you were a lawyer, ..you wore a jimswinger coat. **1950** *Publ. Amer. Dial. Soc.* XIV. 75 *Cut-away and Jim swinger*, formal clothes. Suwannee backwoods. **1951** E. PAUL *Springtime in Paris* i. 9 She wore indoors and out a strictly tailored swallow-tail coat, the kind American Negroes call a 'Jimswinger'. **1972** *News & Observer* (Raleigh, North Carolina) 30 Dec. 4/1 Jim-swinger coat..and brogans have almost vanished.

Jina (dʒi·nă). Also **Gina.** [Skr.: see JAIN.] Title given to Mahavira or to any other of the twenty-four Jain tirthankars or to one of the five Dhyani Buddhas; a sculptured representa-tion of such a saint.

1807 *Asiatick Researches* IX. 303 The first chapter [of a vocabulary of synonymous terms, by an author of the Jaina sect] begins with the synonyma of a *Jina* or deified saint. **1833** *Ibid.* XVII. 250 Notwithstanding the same-ness of the general character and identity of generic attri-butes, the twenty-four *Jinas* are distinguished from each other in colour, stature, and longevity. Two of them are red, two white, two blue, two black, the rest are of a golden hue, or a yellowish brown. The other two peculiar-ities..observe a series of decrement from *Rishabha*, the first *Jina*, who was five hundred poles in stature, and lived 8,400,000 great years to Mahávira the 24th, who had degenerated to the size of man, and was not more than forty years on earth. **1875** M. WILLIAMS *Indian Wisdom* vii. 129 Twenty-four Jinas or 'perfect saints' raised to the rank of gods have appeared in the present Avasarpini cycle. **1884** *Sacred Bks. East* XXII. I. 201 The Venerable One had become an Arhat and Gina, he was..omniscient. **1901** V. A. SMITH *Jain Stûpa of Mathurâ* xviii. 46 The Jina shown in the plate is Pârśvanâth. **1915** A. M. STEVEN-SON *Heart of Jainism* iii. 39 Mahāvīra now added to his titles those of *Jina* (or Conqueror of the Eight Karma, the great enemies), from which Jainism derives its name, [etc.]. **1924** B. BHATTACHARYA *Indian Buddhist Iconogr.* i. 2 The Jinas (victorious ones) are Vairocana, Ratnasam-bhava, Amitābha, Amoghasiddhi and Akṣobhya, whose colours respectively are white, yellow, red, green and blue. **1971** *Illustr. Weekly India* 11 Apr. 8/1 (*caption*) Risabha and Vardhamana are the most honoured among the twenty-four Tirthankaras and the Jain scriptures narrate in detail the life of these two Jinas.

Jindyworobak (dʒi:ndiwǫ·robæk). [Austral. Aboriginal word.] A member of a group founded in 1938 by R. C. Ingamells (1913–55) to promote Australianism in literature, art, etc. Also *attrib.* or as *adj.*

1938 (*title*) Jindyworobak anthology. **1958** *N. & Q.* Oct. 459/1 Roland Robinson, the Jindyworobak, is a perspicuous observer of natural beauty. **1959** *Times Lit. Suppl.* 2 Jan. 9/1 This book demonstrates that, while in the direct Jindyworobak line, he is no fanatic.

jing, *sb.*² Add non-*Sc.* examples.

1809 [see *GOOD *a.* 19]. **1881** 'MARK TWAIN' *Let.* 16 Dec. (1917) I. 412 By jings! the postman will be here in a minute. **1925** T. DREISER *Amer. Tragedy* II. iii. 184 Well, by jing, if it ain't Tom. **1941** BAKER *Dict. Austral. Slang* 39 *By jings!*, an exclamation, derived from 'by jingo!'

jingle, *sb.* Add: **2. b.** *Austral. slang.* Money. Cf. *jingle-boy*.

1906 E. DYSON *Fact'ry 'Ands* viii. 99 Ther Elder dug in 'n' brought up er 'andful iv jingle. **1941** BAKER *Dict. Austral. Slang* 39 *Jingle*, money.

3. b. A short verse or song in a radio or tele-vision commercial or in general advertising.

1930 A. FLEXNER *Universities* I. xxv. 165 Let the psychologists study advertising..in order to understand what takes place when a jingle like 'not a cough in a carload' persuades a nation to buy a new brand of cigarettes. **1949** *Life* 28 Mar. 36/1 She abhors the jingle's suggestion that she be taken home and squeezed. **1959** *Punch* 10 June 769/1 He says I can't possibly get on in the jingles business without going to Oxford. *Ibid.* 17 June 815/2 Channel 9 already gets into hot water when its 'natural breaks' happen to clip a speech in mid-sentence: its life would not be worth living if it saw fit.. to substitute a jingle for the heavyweight's knock-out hook. **1968** *Listener* 26 Sept. 421/3 Certainly those hideous jingles could go: it made good sense for Radio London or Radio Caroline, as new, commercial stations, to tell us that they were wonderful, but the BBC could spare itself that reassurance. **1972** D. RAMSAY *Little Murder Music* 76 Colby was working a jingle date. *Ibid.*, The jingle, a singing commercial for a detergent, was being recorded.

4. Also in Cornwall.

1874 A. I. THACKERAY *Let.* 12 July (1924) viii. 158 You come to a most detestable little object called Bude.. and then you..come home in a little thing called a Jingle. **1906** *Daily Chron.* 10 Mar. 4/4 When I asked one of the drivers how to reach the Cornish border, he offered to convey me..in a jingle-cart. **1924** C. MACKENZIE *Heavenly Ladder* ii. 34 He saw the black-coated train toiling up Pendhu hill,..some leading the ponies in the jingles. **1942** A. L. ROWSE *Cornish Childhood* vii. 189, I was sent to put the donkey into the shay or jingle.

jingled (dʒi·ŋg'ld), *ppl. a. U.S. slang* (now *rare*). [f. JINGLE *v.* + -ED¹.] Intoxicated, fuddled.

1908 G. H. LORIMER *Jack Spurlock* xii. 315 Old Mrs. Corliss was purple with pleasure at having so plausible a pretext for getting comfortably jingled. **1917** [see *BLOTTO *a.*] **1942** in BERREY & VAN DEN BARK *Amer. Thes. Slang* § 106/7.

jingling, *ppl. a.* Add: **jingling Johnny,** (*a*) *slang* = *Chinese pavilion*; (*b*) *Austral.* and *N.Z. slang*, one who shears sheep by hand; *pl.* hand shears.

a. 1904 H. G. FARMER *Mem. R. Artillery Band* ii. 51 An instrument known as the 'Jingling Johnnie', and tambourines were employed. **1920** G. B. SHAW *How to become Mus. Critic* (1960) 311 Every scorer of ballets could scatter pearls from the *pavillon chinois* (alias Jingling Johnny) over the plush and cotton velvet of his harmonies. **1970** *Times* 24 Aug. 20/5 (Advt.), French Pavillon Chinois (jingling Johnny) for sale. Recently restored. £100 o.n.o.

b. 1934 L. G. D. ACLAND in *Press* (Christchurch, N.Z.) 20 Jan. 15/7 *Jingling Johnnies*, old time slang term for hand shearers. **1941** BAKER *Dict. Austral. Slang* 39 *Jingling johnnies*, hand shears. **1945** [see *DAGGER *sb.*² a]. **1965** J. S. GUNN *Terminol. Shearing Industry* I. 33 *Jingling Johnny*, originally a swagman or bagman but in many districts this was also another name for a hand-shearer.

jink, *sb.*¹ Add: **1.** Used esp. of a tricky turn in Rugby Football, or in Aeronautics. Also *transf.* and *fig.*

a **1914** J. E. RAPHAEL *Mod. Rugby Football* (1918) 122 [Poulton Palmer's] 'jink' is all by itself in modern-day Rugger. **1921** E. H. D. SEWELL *Rugby Football* vi. 126 The defender..moves to *his* left as the dummy pass is made, thus making wider the gap which the attacker widens still further by his jink to the defender's right. **1943** HUNT & PRINGLE *Service Slang* 41 *Jinks*, quick turns in the air, a form of aerobatics and of avoiding action. **1959** V. FUCHS *Antarctic Adv.* xii. 168 Suddenly, ..below them, they spotted vehicle tracks in the snow. From the outward flight they remembered that except for one 'jink' these led in a straight line from South Ice—and the 'jink' was only about a quarter of a mile from the station. **1969** P. DICKINSON *Pride of Heroes* 164 A jink in his train of thought made Pibble wonder who the next heir was.

3. high jinks. Hence **high-ji·nking.**

1891 *Pall Mall Gaz.* 22 Oct. 2/1 On board we were very jovial and had much high jinking. **1904** *Daily Chron.* 13 July 8/1 It is evening—eight o'clock—and the festival is at its very top notch of high-jinking.

jink, *v.*¹ For 'Chiefly *Sc.*' read 'orig. *Sc.*' Add later examples of senses 1 and 2, esp. in Rugby Football and Aeronautics; cf. *JINK *sb.*¹ 1. Also *to jink one's way*, to advance by means of jinks.

a **1914** J. E. RAPHAEL *Mod. Rugby Football* (1918) 103 This is a method which..should not be copied by the ordinary performer—except perhaps when 'jinking'. **1927** WAKEFIELD & MARSHALL *Rugger* 93 A curious jinking side-step. **1932** *Daily Tel.* 19 Mar. 17/2, I can see him jinking his way past our mid-field players. **1940** *Aeroplane*

30 Aug. 235/2 One example of Air Ministry verbosity is the continual use of the phrase 'took evasive action', instead of saying 'dodged' or 'jinked'. **1942** *R.A.F. Jrnl.* 18 Apr. 3 You boost and you dive and you jink. **1942** E. WAUGH *Put out More Flags* iii. 243 If they come in now from the rear the cars may jink round and give the other companies a chance to get out. **1944** *R.A.F. Jrnl.* Aug. 288 The aircraft crossed in front of them, jinking steadily at high speed. **1959** V. FUCHS *Antarctic Adv.* xii. 169 The visibility was about a hundred yards, but where the tracks jinked sharply right, he closed the throttle. **1961** R. JEFFRIES *Evidence of Accused* i. 14 A rabbit..jinked away under a rhododendron bush. **1963** I. FLEMING *On H.M. Secret Service* xvii. 189 Bond..put on all the speed he could, crouching low and jinking occasionally to spoil the man's aim. **1969** G. MACBETH *War Quartet* 35 Untailed, I jinked, Flipped over in a half-roll. **1973** *Times* 1 Jan. 17/2 Hales scored two tries, but I only saw the first of them, and a good one it was as he jinked inside his man.

jinker². Add: (Later examples.) Also, in *Trotting*, a sulky.

1916 J. B. COOPER *Coo-oo-ee* i. 1 Often the wheels of the jinkers bogged in a soak on the track. **1941** BAKER *Dict. Austral. Slang* 39 *Jinker*, a trotting sulky. **1941** *Coast to Coast* 185 Then would come a decision, a harnessing of the old horse to the jinker and a trip to the township. **1966** 'J. HACKSTON' *Father clears Out* 15 We hated the horse that was tied to the man's jinker.

jinker, *v. Austral. trans.* To manipulate with a jinker (see JINKER²).

1903 R. BEDFORD *True Eyes & Whirlwind* 240 Waiting for a fine day to jinker those trees out of the bush.

jinny. 1. (Earlier example of *jinny-road.*)

1877 [see *DIP *sb.* 5 b].

jintawan (dʒintā·wăn). [Malay.] A kind of caoutchouc derived from *Urceola elastica*, a woody climbing plant of the family Apocynaceæ; also, the plant itself.

1851 *Illustr. Catal. Gt. Exhib.* IV. 877/2 Raw caoutchouc from Assam, Singapore (*Urceola elastica*, the Jintawan of the Malays). **1853** URE *Dict. Arts* (ed. 4) I. 984 The said apparatus may be used also for purifying caoutchouc and jintawan. **1880** *Encycl. Brit.* XII. 817/1 Besides the orange ..we have the rambutan,..the jintawan,..and the jambosa.

jinx (dʒiŋks). orig. *U.S.* Also **ginks, jinks.** [app. f. JYNX 2.] A person or thing that brings bad luck or exercises evil influence; a hoodoo, a Jonah. Also *attrib.* and *Comb.*

1911 *Chicago Daily News* 19 Sept. 6/3 Dave Shean and 'Peaches' Graham..have not escaped the jinx that has been following the champions. **1919** *Oxf. Mag.* 7 Mar., Will some one remove the jinx? On Friday, February 28, we lost to Oriel and Merton by 3 goals to nil. On Saturday, March 1,..we lost to Queen's by 1–0. **1926** ANDERSON & STALLINGS *What Price Glory* III, in *Three American Plays* 88 This town is a jinx for me. **1927** A. MILLER *Colfax Bk.-Plate* xiv. 172, I thrust that jinx of a book back into the lowest left-hand drawer. **1931** *Collier's* 26 Sept. 57/3 They say he is a jinx to them and they cannot beat him in any manner, shape, or form. **1932** J. T. FARRELL *Young Lonigan* iv. 157 Young Corbett who was born with a horse shoe in his hands..put a jinx on Terrible Terry. **1948** MENJOU & MUSSELMAN *It took Nine Tailors* 96 There has never been such a jinx picture as that one. **1955** E. POUND *Classic Anthol.* III. 179 Jinx on the remnants everywhere. **1958** *Times Lit. Suppl.* 24 Jan. 41/4 The family jinx, in this case dark strangers who erupt into the bourgeois marriages of three generations, leaving behind an illegitimate child and the torturing memory of a bliss that might have been. **1962** *Times* 19 Feb. 3/7 A jinx-ridden Thomas somehow contrived to miss the kick. **1969** *Daily Colonist* (Victoria, B.C.) 30 Nov. 8/4 A man and two boys went fishing Friday, and Mary went along. The boat capsized, and apparently she alone survived. 'I'm either a jinx, or very lucky,' she says. **1972** 'E. LATHEN' *Murder without Icing* (1973) xxiii. 198 I'm beginning to think that damned team is a jinx... It's been a bad-luck team from the beginning.

So **jinx** *v. trans.* (freq. *pass.*) to cast a spell on, to bring bad luck upon; **jinxed** *ppl. a.*

[**1912** C. MATHEWSON *Pitching in a Pinch* xi. 244 He outjinxed our champion jinx killer.] **1917** *Amer. Mag.* Apr. 43/1 What do you mean—humming love songs when their darn pitcher is forcing in runs? You jinxed my ball club. **1934** J. T. FARRELL *Young Manhood* iv. 61, I know they ain't loaded. But use these ones. Them damn things is jinxed! **1946** E. O'NEILL *Iceman Cometh* (1947) III. 147 I's an ole gamblin' man and I knows bad luck when I feels it!.. But it's white man's bad luck. He can't jinx me! **1956** D. BARNHAM *One Man's Window* 26 He told me he was 'jinxed'. He explained that on his last three trips [in a fighter aircraft] he had been in trouble. **1962** K. ORVIS *Damned & Destroyed* xi. 73 I'm jinxed. No fix. All blew up. **1972** G. DURRELL *Catch me a Colobus* vii. 152 I'm damned if I'm going to take up all my animals and myself and my wife in a jinxed plane. No, I'm afraid I'll have to get another charter flight.

jipijapa (hī·piˌhā·pă). Also **jipi-japa, jippa-jappa, jippi-jappa.** [Name of a town in Ecuador.] **a.** The palm-like tree, *Carludovica palmata*, native to tropical America, or the fibre produced from its leaves. **b.** A Panama hat. Also *attrib.*

1858 P. L. SIMMONDS *Dict. Trade Products* 273/2 (s.v. *Panama-hats*), In Central America where they are made, the palm is called Jipijapa. **1877** *Encycl. Brit.* VI. 155/1 Straw hats, usually known as jipijapa or Panamá hats. **1901** *Amer. Anthropologist* III. 206 Ecuador is the real home of the hats wrongly designated under the name of 'panama'... Everywhere in Latin America the hat is known under the name of *jipijapa*, in honor of the city where its manufacture was first started. **1901** *Daily Chron.* 7 Feb. 4/6 The Jippi-Jappa plant, known sometimes as 'the broom thatch'. **1953** V. BELL in *Caribbean Anthol. Short Stories* 72 He could almost see her there in her usual seat at the back of the church in her white linen dress and her jippi-jappa hat. **1961** F. G. CASSIDY *Jamaica Talk* vi. 115 The best known Jamaica-made hat is the *jipi-japa*..from the name of the town..in Ecuador. **1965** I. FLEMING *Man with Golden Gun* iv. 51 There were only two other passengers..Cubans, perhaps, with jippa-jappa luggage. **1972** D. SALE *Love Bite* iv. 52 Shops crammed with liqueur, tweeds, English doeskin, jippa-jappa straw goods.

jipper (dʒi·pəɹ). *dial.* Also **gipper.** Gravy; dripping; stew. So as *v. trans.*, to baste.

1822 SCOTT *Fortunes of Nigel* III. vi. 176 This man Gregory is not fit to jipper a joint with him. **1886** W. H. LONG *Dict. Isle of Wight Dial.* 31 Thee'st lat all the jipper out of the pudden. **1896** FARMER & HENLEY *Slang* IV. 59/2 *Jipper* (nautical), gravy. **1900** *N. & Q.* 9th Ser. V. 295 The *chef de cuisine* was an old navy pensioner, and his instructions were: 'Mind you jipper them [*sc.* thrushes] well.' From him I learned to call gravy 'jipper', and bread and dripping 'bread-and-jipper'. **1904** *Daily Chron.* 12 Aug. 3/7 The mysteries of Irish stew, or 'gipper', as it is mysteriously termed in camp. **1909** H. G. WELLS *Tono-Bungay* II. iii. 195 They [*sc.* shavings] might be anything. Soak 'em in jipper,—Xylo-tobacco!

jippo². = *GIPPO².

1929 *Papers Mich. Acad. Sci., Arts & Lett.* X. 303 *Jippo*, fat. **1931** W. V. TILSLEY *Other Ranks* 119 Every morning, a good thick slice of bread and toasted cheese or bacon. Plenty of jippo (if you were pally with the orderly man). **1937** D. JONES *In Parenthesis* v. 118 He's with his longe ladel To test the jippo.

jirga (dʒiə·ɹgă). Also **jeerga, jirgah.** [Pushtu.] An assembly or council of the headmen of Pathan or Baluchi tribes.

1843 F. SALE *Jrnl. Disasters Afghanistan* p. xii, *Jeerga*. An assembly or council—a diet. **1894** M. DYAN *All in Man's Keeping* I. iv. 75 All large issues had to be referred to his Jeerga. **1906** *Westm. Gaz.* 14 May 3/2 They can..mobilise as easily as a Pathan jirga. **1908** *Ibid.* 24 Feb. 7/1 Afridis other than Zakka Khels are collecting at Chora for a jirgah. **1926** *Chambers's Jrnl.* Apr. 293/2 He eyed the elders of Pir Mahommed, assembled in *jirga*. **1935** *Pathfinder* July 125/1 The 'jirga', that is the council of the headmen of each tribe, would meet us at each new boundary..to..see if they would let us pass or not. **1967** A. SWINSON *N.-W. Frontier* xv. 326 This triumph seemed to expend the tribesmen's energy and soon the jirgas came in to sue for peace. **1972** *Times of India* 28 Nov. 11/5 The paper quoted Mr. Bhutto as telling a tribal jirga at Landikotal..that unfortunately Pakistan did not accept this offer.

jism (dʒiz'm). *slang* (orig. *U.S.*). Also **chism, gism, jizz,** etc. [Origin unknown.] **a.** Energy, strength. **b.** Semen, sperm.

In sense b often regarded as a taboo-word.

1842 *Spirit of Times* 29 Oct. 409/3 At the drawgate Spicer tried it on again, but his horse was knocked up—'the gism' and the starch was effectively taken out of him by the long and desperate struggles he had been obliged to maintain. **1899** B. W. GREEN *Word-bk. Virginia Folk-Speech* 85 *Chism, chissum*, seminal fluid. **1937** J. WEIDMAN *I can get it for you Wholesale!* xxxii. 314 'Step on it, will you?' 'Sure..' 'All right,..but put a little jism into it, will you?' **1942** C. MORLEY *Thorofare* (1943) xxxvii. 137 One of the same fields that the Major said had had the jizzum leached out of it by tobacco. **1955** T. STERLING *Evil of Day* vii. 76 The man had more jisum than he'd counted on. **1959** W. BURROUGHS *Naked Lunch* 90 The Moslems must have blood and jissom... See, see where Christ's blood streams in the spermament. **1967** S. BECKETT *Stories & Texts for Nothing* 85 A week will be ample, a week in spring, that puts the jizz in you. **1968** J. UPDIKE *Couples* iv. 311 Georgene would wash herself before and after. Said his jizz ran down her leg, too much of it. **1969** P. ROTH *Portnoy's Complaint* 132 You've got to..walk round downtown Newark dripping gissum down your forehead. **1972** *Screw* 12 June 35/3 At last I felt my gism rushing up like electricity and I..felt the love bolt burst out of my cock into her vacuum-sucking mouth.

jist (dʒist), colloq. and dial. var. JUST *adv.* Cf. *JEST.

c **1820** in *Amer. Speech* (1941) XVI. 157/1 *Jist*, just. **1835** A. B. LONGSTREET *Georgia Scenes* 29 His eyes don't look like it; but he *jist as live go agin* the house with you, or in a ditch, as anyhow. **1839** [see *LOP *v.*² 2 b]. **1848** TROLLOPE *Kellys & O'Kellys* II. iii. 69 You must do more than jist ask her. **1931** D. L. SAYERS *Five Red Herrings* xxv. 283 'I was jist thinkin', then,' said Duncan, '..whether it was not, after all, possible.' **1941** *Sat. Even. Post* 10 May 36/2 Jist taste a grain o' patience. *Ibid.* 112/3, I jist saw a quare thing.

jit¹ (dʒit), abbrev. *JITNEY 1.

1913 *Awgwan* (Univ. of Nebraska) 3 June 10 We went to the second jit show. **1915** G. BRONSON-HOWARD *God's Man* IV. iv. 264 Keeping tab on you and knowing how much you snatch to the last jit. **1926** J. BLACK *You can't Win* xx. 318 A 'jit', as the Southern negro affectionately calls his nickel. **1931** J. T. FARRELL in *New Rev.* (Paris) I. 24 Say Vinc lemme take a nickel will yuh?.. You'll lemme take a jit won'tcha?..I'll give yuh the jitney back with a nickel interest. **1946** B. TREADWELL *Big Bk. of Swing* 124/2 Jit, five-cent piece.

jit² (dʒit). *U.S. slang. depreciatory.* [Origi unknown.] A Negro.

1931 G. IRWIN *Amer. Tramp & Underworld Slang* 11 *Jit*... A negro, or, more usually, a negress, and seeming a term of derision. **1936** MENCKEN *Amer. Lang.* (ed. 296 For Negro..jit. **1942** BERREY & VAN DEN BAR *Amer. Thes. Slang* § 385/14 *Negro*, jit.

jitney (dʒi·tni). *N. Amer.* [Origin unknown. **1.** A five-cent piece, a nickel. *slang.*

1903 *Cincinnati Enquirer* 2 May 11/5 [In St. Louis] 'crown guy' is a policeman, a 'gitney' is a nickel, an 'mug's landing' is the Union Station. **1915** *Nation* (N.Y 4 Feb. 142/1 The word 'jitney'..is the Jewish slang ter for a nickel. **1916** *Chambers's Jrnl.* June 400/1 Five cen ..is the charge for any distance, and as the colloqui name for this coin is a 'jitney', this form of traffic ha become known as 'jitney competition'. **1931** 'D. STIF *Milk & Honey Route* 177 Beer or wine at a jitney a thro **1947** W. SAROYAN *Jim Dandy* I. i. 11 Call that money A jitney? A nickel?

2. In full *jitney bus, omnibus.* An omnibu or other motor vehicle which carries passenger for a fare, orig. five cents. So, on account o the low fare or the poor quality of these buses used *attrib.* to denote anything cheap, impro vised, or ramshackle.

1914 *Let.* 28 Nov. in *Nation* (N.Y.) (1915) 14 Jan. 50/ This autumn automobiles, mostly of the Ford variety have begun in competition with the street cars in th city [*sc.* Los Angeles]. The newspapers call them 'Jitne 'buses'. **1915** *N.Y. Even. Post* 16 Apr., The jitney wea out the streets and should contribute to their repair. **191** *Daily Colonist* (Victoria, B.C.) 6 July 4/5 The dail jitney service between Nanaimo and South Wellingto has been discontinued. Hereafter cars will run on Satu days only and the fare has been raised from 25 cents t 50 cents. **1916** H. L. WILSON *Somewhere in Red Gap* 59 He..sells these jitney pianos and phonographs an truck like that. **1917** E. FROST *Lett.* (1972) 13, I hire McGrath, the jitney driver, to bring us home. **191** M. A. VON ARNIM *Christopher & Columbus* xxxi. 400 H had come in the jitney omnibus to the nearest point. **192** [see *DAIQUIRI]. **1921** *Daily Colonist* (Victoria, B.C.) 2 Mar. 2/4 The decision of the Provincial Legislature t prohibit the sale of near beer will affect 58 jitney bars i this city, according to City Licence Inspector Charle Jones. **1923** F. PARSONS *Everybody's Business* 215 A the jitney operators on the line. **1925** *Amer. Speech* 152/1 That bastard word 'jitney' is still used in outlyin places, where a 'jitney dance' means a nickel dance. **193** *N.Y. Herald Tribune* 5 Dec. 17/3 We refer to the jitne economists, the boys who play the money tunes only b ear. **1946** E. O'NEILL *Iceman Cometh* (1947) I. 36 He neve worries in hard times because there's always old friend from the days when he was a jitney Tammany politicia **1947** E. A. MCCOURT *Music at Close* 108 He would go t the jitney dance held in the big open space behind th town hall unless an outdoor floor had been set up. **1967–** *Bahamas Handbk. & Businessmen's Ann.* (ed. 7) 19 There are jitneys on New Providence..which travel ov unscheduled and not necessarily prescribed routes pickin up and dropping off passengers. **1973** *Philadelphia In quirer* (Today Suppl.) 7 Oct. 8/2 From the museum jitney carries visitors to the Mills.

jito (dʒī·to). Also **gito.** [Jap.] In the Japan ese feudal system: a military land stewar (see also quot. 1974).

1845 *Encycl. Metrop.* XX. 472/2 A military commande ..appoints the *gitos*, or revenue officers,..who ar stationed in every township to levy the portion of the pr duce claimed by the Crown. **1902** L. HEARN *Kottō* viii. 6 The Jitō of the district, with a hunting party. **197** *Encycl. Brit. Macropædia* X. 64/2 In 1185..Yoritom appointed military governors (*shugo*) in all the province and military stewards (*jitō*) in both public and privat landed estates... The *jitō* collected taxes, supervised th management of landed estates, and maintained publi order.

jitter (dʒi·təɹ), *sb. colloq.* [Origin unknown. **1.** *pl.* (usu. *the jitters*). Extreme nervousness nervous incapacity; a state of emotional an (often) physical tension; agitation.

1929 P. STURGES *Strictly Dishonorable* II. 123 *Isabell* Willie's got the jitters—. *Judge.* Jitters? *Isabell* You know, he makes faces all the time. **1930** *N.Y. Pres* 2 Apr. 6/4 The game is played only after the mugs an wenches have taken on too much gin and they arrive a the state of jitters, a disease known among the commo herd as heebie jeebies. **1931** *Charlottesville* (Virgini *Progress* 23 Mar. 12/8 Swift moving elevators and rolle coasters also give her the jitters. **1931** *Harper's Mag.* Ma 420/2 How much of a price did we pay next day for a n very good party? How many kinds of hangovers a there? How much do you have to drink to get 'jitters' I know my hostess called me up to say she had the jitte and her husband an awful hangover. **1932** E. WILSO (*title*) The American jitters. **1933** *Passing Show* 15 Ju 14/1 Oh Heck, tell some photographer I can't be phot graphed. The very sight of a camera nowadays gives m the jitters. **1934** *Redbook Mag.* June 38/2 You begin t have the 'jitters'. Your placid disposition has given wa to irritability, sarcasm and dissatisfaction. **1936** 'I QUENTIN' *Puzzle for Fools* vi. 44 My old jitters had r turned and I had started to shake. **1937** *Daily Herald* Jan. 15/5 All this chatter about rough play has been t give players..the jitters. **1939** F. M. FORD *Let.* 23 Ma (1965) 324 All the publishers here have the jitters s badly that they won't look at anything new at all. **194** *Univ. of Colorado Stud.* Ser. B. II. iv. 42 The cures General Semantics are not limited, fortunately, to thos suffering from platform jitters. **1957** *Economist* 7 Sep 759/1 The recession jitters now afflicting significa numbers of economists..seem to be better founded o

economic evidence than did the others. 1971 B. W. ALDISS *Soldier Erect* 229 The signal came, the machine-gun fire stopped... Geordie was next to me, not showing a sign of his earlier jitters.

b. **jitter party** *Mil. slang* (see quot. 1948).

1948 PARTRIDGE *Dict. Forces' Slang 1939–45* 102 *Jitter party*, a party of Japanese sneaking around the perimeter of a camp and trying to cause panic with strange noises and grenades. 1956 W. SLIM *Defeat into Victory* xviii. 430 Only a few jitter parties prowled about the perimeter. 1962 *Times* 16 Oct. 14/6 Still less was anyone to return the unaimed small-arms fire so often indulged in after nightfall by Japanese 'jitter-parties'.

2. Chiefly *Electronics*. Random or irregular variation in the shape or timing of a regularly repeated pulse; the resulting unsteadiness of an image in a cathode-ray tube. Also in *Cinemat.*, jerkiness of the picture.

1943 *Electronic Engin.* XVI. 55/2 Absence of 'jitter' or hum derived from fluctuations of the H.T. supply potential. 1954 *Ibid.* XXVI. 37/2 V_6..failed to fire properly.. and caused considerable 'jitter' in the output pulse length. 1959 MALAS & MANVELL *Technique Film Animation* xix. 231 The main danger of rostrum tracks and pans is strobing, or jitter. *Ibid.* 339 *Jitter*, uncontrolled movement on the screen caused by faulty animation, tracing or camera work. 1960 J. D. HAIGH *Radiolocation Techniques* v. 76 If the displayed picture is to be..free from 'jitter' echoes must appear in exactly the same position at each recurrence of the time-base. 1966 *Jrnl. Acoustical Soc. Amer.* XXXIX. 920 The principal experimental parameters are the mean interval between pulses and root-mean-square deviation or jitter about this interval. 1966 R. J. ROSS *Television Film Engin.* i. 5 Very slight errors in registration cause vertical or horizontal unsteadiness in screen presentations, commonly known as jitter or weave.

So **ji·tteriness**; **ji·ttery** *a.*, nervy, jumpy, upset, 'on edge'; also *transf.*

1931 H. CRANE *Let.* 1 May (1965) 369 I'm too jittery to write a straight sentence. 1936 'P. QUENTIN' *Puzzle for Fools* iv. 26 A slight return of jitteriness. 1937 *Daily Mirror* 27 Feb. 10/4 Stop being so jittery. What if we have missed the bus? There will be another later. 1941 *Penguin New Writing* X. 23 Jittery light sprang on the screen. 1946 *Mind* LV. 137 There is the effect of their [*sc.* the Wittgensteinians'] therapy upon ordinary philosophers. Under its attack, the latter tend, in general, to become 'jittery' and to retreat into worried silence. 1950 H. E. BATES *Scarlet Sword* ii. 17 An atmosphere of tense and growing jitteriness. 1957 *Listener* 12 Dec. 968/2 An impression of weakness and jitteriness. 1963 A. ROSS *Australia 63* viii. 153 Barrington made 33, in his more jittery manner, before flicking at an outswinger and being caught at slip. 1970 B. W. ALDISS *Moment of Eclipse* 47 Nobody gets jittery down there? 1972 *Jrnl. Social Psychol.* LXXXVIII. 279 Clutched-up, jittery, stirred-up, fearful.

jitter (dʒi·təɹ), *v. colloq.* [Origin unknown.] **1.** *intr.* To move in an agitated manner; to exhibit alarm, to act in a nervous way, to get the 'jitters'.

1931 A. M. MACKENZIE *Cypress in Moonlight* IV. iv. 226 Her lace cap jittered tremulously till her earrings rattled. 1932 *Brevities* (N.Y.) 5 Dec. 16 (*heading*) Jittering junkies sniff sexy joy flakes. 1936 M. ALLINGHAM *Flowers for Judge* xxi. 301 You've been jittering around the Continent like an agitated tourist. 1938 *N. & Q.* 5 Mar. 172/1 My daily paper this morning points out that the total of the workless is higher, and adds, 'But don't jitter!' 1959 'P. QUENTIN' *Shadow of Guilt* vii. 67 My thoughts jittered around Chuck. 1960 'S. HARVESTER' *Chinese Hammer* vi. 64 There was a funny atmosphere about him. He jittered. 1966 *Electronics* 17 Oct. 109 If the error signal during the measurement period is too low, the antenna may jitter. 1970 *New Yorker* 28 Feb. 73/1 He sat there quietly, taking part in the dinner, but I knew that under the table his leg was jittering wildly.

2. *trans.* To propel by nervous energy; to fluster.

1932 E. HEMINGWAY *Death in Afternoon* ii. 18 His effort to be statuesque while his feet jittered him away out of danger was very funny to the crowd. 1951 C. SIMAK *Time & Again* (1956) xvi. 78 He knew that I would catch and he thinks he can jitter me.

3. *trans.* To subject (a series of pulses, or some characteristic of it) to rapid variation. So **ji·ttered** *ppl. a.*

1960 J. D. HAIGH *Radiolocation Techniques* xvii. 251 In order that an aircraft might be able to identify the responses to its own transmissions its pulse recurrence frequency was 'jittered' automatically. 1966 *Jrnl. Acoustical Soc. Amer.* XXXIX. 920/2 Jittering the interval between pulses might also eliminate perceptual differences. *Ibid.* 922/1 Assumptions of ideal distributions were used to obtain power-density spectra of jittered pulse-train signals.

jitterbug (dʒi·təɹbɒg), *sb.* orig. *U.S.* Also **jitter bug, jitter-bug.** [f. *JITTER *v.* + *BUG *sb.*² 4a.] **1.** A jittery or nervous person; an alarmist; an attack of the jitters. Also as *adj.*

1934 C. CALLOWAY et al. (*song title*) Jitter bug. 1934 —— in *Song Hits Mag.* (1939) Nov. 19 They're four little jitter bugs. He has the jitters ev'ry morn, That's why jitter sauce was born. 1939 *Times* 30 Jan. 13/5 It [*sc.* the Government] is the only body capable of giving the information which would largely dispel the apprehensions of the 'Jitter-bugs', who, though perhaps few in number, are vocal and often influential. 1941 N. MARSH *Death & Dancing Footman* (1942) iv. 65 One man will keep his head in a crisis where another will go jitter-bug. *Ibid.* 76 Nick had a jitter-bug and wanted to make off. 1944 [see *bomb-happiness]. 1966 E. H. JONES *Margery Fry* xiv. 193 Sir Samuel Hoare denounced the 'jitterbugs' who feared war... Five days after..German troops moved unresisted into Czechoslovakia.

2. A jazz musician; a devotee of jazz; a person who dances the jitterbug.

1937 *Down Beat* Feb. 9/4 (*heading*) 'Jives of the jitter-bugs.' High and low-down on the swing men. 1938 *Manch. Guardian Weekly* 2 Sept. 188/3 A 'jitterbug' is a person keen on swing. 1939 *Times* 27 Jan. 7/5, I am told that in the U.S.A. there is a class of people who sit listening in hysterical excitement to what is called 'hot-music' and waiting for the final crash. Americans in their forcible language call them the 'Jitter-bugs'. There are many people in Europe to-day who seem to be behaving in much the same way. 1942 *Dancing Times* May 411/2 Equally pleasing to Jitterbugs and some rhythm dancers will be 'Russian Salad'. 1951 E. PAUL *Springtime in Paris* xii. 218 On the corner, the Nest of Vipers nightly harboured jitterbugs and Lindy hoppers whose antics shamed the praying mantis.

3. A dance, popular esp. in the early 1940s, performed chiefly to boogie-woogie and swing music, and consisting of a few standardized steps augmented by much improvisation.

1939 R. CHANDLER in *Sat. Even. Post* 14 Oct. 11/1 This jitterbug music gives me the backdrop of a beer flat. I like something with roses in it. 1943 *Dancing Times* Sept. 560/1 The wildest Jitterbug yet is danced by Dorothy Lamour. 1969 N. COHN *AWopBopaLooBop* (1970) ix. 81 With old favourites like the jitterbug and the jive.. the girls spun like tops and everyone got fast flashes of knicker. 1971 *Daily Tel.* 1 Nov. 9/1 To pop music..she performed movements reminiscent of the jitterbug of a generation ago.

ji·tterbug, *v.* orig. *U.S.* [See prec., sense 3.] *intr.* To dance the jitterbug.

1939 *Amer. Mag.* Sept. 160 Susy Shag..begins thinking seriously of marrying the guy she's been jitterbugging with. 1949 N. MARSH *Swing, Brother, Swing* v. 77 D'you jitter-bug? 1951 J. D. SALINGER *Catcher in Rye* x. 80 The band was starting a fast one. She started jitterbugging with me. 1955 C. FOX in *Jazzbook 1955* 4 They jitterbugged down the aisles to the exhilarating music, horrifying their parents and bringing worried frowns to the faces of the jazz purists of those days. 1972 *Jazz & Blues* Nov. 5/1 They jitterbugged to 'One O'Clock Jump' and stomped their feet to 'Maple Leaf Rag'. 1973 *Washington Post* 5 Apr. B.2 The happiest part..is a salute to the big bands of the '40s, with Miss Adams in a snood and Candoli jitterbugging in a zoot suit.

Hence **ji·tterbugging** *vbl. sb.* and *ppl. a.*

1938 *Call-Bulletin* (San Francisco) 8 Dec. 17/1 'Jitter-bugging is just a phase,' he said... 'It isn't music. This town wants real music and nothing else will do.' 1939 *San Francisco Examiner* 17 Sept. 2/2, I love ballroom dancing and I usually do just that, but at times I find it a job to express my joy of living by doing a little jitter-bugging. 1940 GRAVES & HODGE *Long Week-End* xxii. 390 Jitterbugging had then [1939] just come over from the United States..an ecstatic mode of dancing to fast swing music in which the two partners could perform absolutely any..acrobatic feat they liked. 1942 A. P. JEPHCOTT *Girls growing Up* iii. 63 The slick, apparently assured, smoking, jitterbugging town girl of sixteen still regards friendliness as the all-important feature of any group with which she intends to associate. 1952 M. MCCARTHY *Groves of Academe* (1953) ii. 20 He did not dance, but..vigorously nodded with approval when a jitter-bugging pair desisted. 1973 G. DURRELL *Beasts in my Belfry* v. 105 The only folk dances I have ever witnessed were danced by elderly, aesthetic ladies with fringes and strings of beads and they were nothing like the gnus' wild jitterbugging.

jiu-jitsu, -jutsu, varr. *JU-JITSU *sb.*

jiva (dʒī·vă). *Hindu* and *Jain Philos.* [Skr. *jīvá* living being, life, the highest personal principle of life.] Life, the soul, the self; the vital principle.

1807 *Asiatick Researches* IX. 290 The *Jainas* conceive the soul (*Jíva*) to have been eternally united to a very subtil material body. 1885 E. BALFOUR *Cycl. India* (ed. 3) II. 442/2 *Jiva*. Sansk. Life, the soul. 1887 W. J. WILKINS *Mod. Hinduism* viii. 101 All beings possessed of jiva are of two kinds: those who can move and those who cannot. 1915 A. M. STEVENSON *Heart of Jainism* 176 As long as the jīva or ātmā is fettered by karma, so long must it undergo rebirth, and it must be remembered that karma is acquired through good as well as through evil actions. 1951 H. ZIMMER *Philosophies of India* III. i. 229 Jainism regards the life-monad (*jiva*) as pervading the whole organism; the body constitutes, as it were, its garb; the life-monad is the body's animating principle. *Ibid.* 277 Some vegetables, such as trees, are provided with a collectivity of jīvas. 1971 *Times Weekender* (Ceylon) 3 Oct. 4/3 As the macrocosmic reality it is called Braman and its manifestation through human beings is the microcosmic reality known as the atman or soul or jiva.

Jivaro (hī·văro). [ad. Sp. *jíbaro*, f. a native name.] An Indian people of Ecuador and Peru; a member of this people; also, the language of this people or a group of related languages of which this is the principal. Also *attrib.* or as *adj.* So **Ji·varan, Jivaro·an** *adjs.*

1862 *Intellectual Observer* Mar. 134 On the eastern side of the Republic of Ecuador..live a tribe of Indians called Jívaros. *Ibid.* 135 It is in the forests among these rivers that the Jívaro Indians now make their homes. 1902 *Encycl. Brit.* XXV. 374/1 The families of..South America are..Jivaroan, [etc.]. 1927 K. G. GRUBB *Lowland Indians of Amazonia* v. 77 The Jivaro live in communal houses divided into numerous sub-tribes. *Ibid.*, The Jivaro language has been attested by a variety of documents. 1934 WEBSTER, Jivaran. 1957 *Encycl. Brit.* VII. 941/1 The Cayapa-Colorados and the Jivaro [languages] still survive owing to their existence in inaccessible regions. *Ibid.* XIII. 69/2 *Jivaran*, an independent linguistic stock of South American Indians, so called from the best known tribe, the Jivaros. The Jivaran tribes live in eastern Ecuador and the adjacent portions of Peru. 1962 N. MAXWELL *Witch-Doctor's Apprentice* i. 3 That was my first long jungle trip and I was lucky enough to get to a tribe of Jívaros who had never seen a white woman before. 1969 *Times* 24 Jan. 6/7 Jivaro give the seeds to refractory children so that during their visions the ancestral spirits may come to admonish them.

jive (dʒəiv), *sb. slang* (orig. *U.S.*). [Origin unknown.] **1.** Talk or conversation; *spec.* talk that is misleading, untrue, empty, or pretentious; hence, anything false, worthless, or unpleasant; vaguely, 'stuff'; = *JAZZ *sb.* 3 a.

1928 R. FISHER *Walls of Jericho* 301 *Jive*, pursuit in love or any device thereof. Usually flattery with intent to win. 1929 T. GORDON *Born to Be* 236 *Jive*, a misleading remark. 1932 MUSE & ARLEN *Way down South* 50 Thus the enamoured customer completed his meal, without ever having taken his eyes off that tantalizing brown, with her suave Birmingham jive. 1935 *Swing Music* Autumn 55/2 Maybe you think that that is all jive. You are wrong if you do. It is the way I felt about these new records. 1946 MEZZROW & WOLFE *Really Blues* iii. 37, I used to hear a lot of medical jive. *Ibid.* 375 *Jive* n., confusing doubletalk, pretentious conversation, anything false or phony. *Jive that makes it drip*, clouds that produce rain. 1954 L. ARMSTRONG *Satchmo* x. 150 There was lots of just plain common shooting and cutting. But.. that jive didn't faze me at all. *Ibid.* xii. 193, I bought a lot of cheap jive at the five and ten cents store to give to the kids. 1956 M. STEARNS *Story of Jazz* (1957) v. 50 The attitude of several modern jazzmen, born and bred in the South, is striking: 'This hoodoo jive is nowhere,' they say, 'but man, watch out!' 1960 in P. Oliver *Blues fell this Morning* vii. 197 I'm evil and mean and funny, so don't come back with that line of jive. 1972 M. J. BOSSE *Incident at Naha* iii. 152 Maybe some of his Christian sentiments sound corny today, but..he had cut through a lot of the jive of his own time, and he had, like, the balls to fight injustice. 1973 *Black World* Oct. 36/2 Everything that we do must be aimed toward the total liberation, unification and empowerment of Afrika... Anything short of that is jive.

2. Jazz, esp. a type of fast, lively jazz; 'swing'.

1928 (*title of gramophone record by Cow Cow Davenport*) State Street Jive. 1937 *New Yorker* 17 Apr. 31/3 The music of hot bands..is referred to as *swing* or *jive*, of which, in turn, there are several kinds. 1939 *San Francisco News Let.* 1 Sept. 12/2 Fats Waller..is the King of Jive and gets off some fine stuff. 1946 *N. & Q.* 13 July 20/1 Mr. Mitchell Parish, the American song-writer,.. told me that he uses *jive* to describe syncopated music played noisily, and (usually) fast, with great emphasis on rhythm. 1959 'F. NEWTON' *Jazz Scene* i. 12 In Sophiatown and the rest of the South African ghettoes the 'jive bands' play what is patently jazz. 1960 *Down Beat* 9 June 15 Regarding the word jive, Wilson said, it is nothing more than an obsolete slang term for jazz.

b. Lively and uninhibited dancing to dance-music or jazz; *spec.* 'jitterbugging'.

1943 *Dancing Times* Dec. 117/1 The rhythm of the Jive is not an entirely new one. 1957 C. MACINNES *City of Spades* I. iv. 24 I'll teach you..bop steps, and jive, and all. 1958 *Listener* 20 Nov. 848/1 Jive and tribal dancing. 1969 H. HORWOOD *Newfoundland* x. 69 The jive..is still the universal dance of..outport youngsters.

3. A variety of American English associated with the Harlem area of New York; slang used by American Blacks, or by jazz musicians and their followers. Also *attrib.*, as *jive talk*.

1938 C. CALLOWAY *Hi De Ho* 16 *Jive*. 1. Harlemese speech or lingo. 2. To kid along, to blarney, to give a girl a line. 1943 *Time* 26 July 56/2 A jive-talk glossary that is strictly Dracula has been put out by Parents' Institute. 1944 D. BURLEY (*title*) Original handbook of Harlem jive. E. CONRAD in *Ibid.* 5 Jive is one more contribution of Negro America to the United States. *Ibid.* 6 Jive talk may have been originally a kind of 'Pig Latin' that the slaves talked with each other, a code—when they were in the presence of whites. 1960 *Time & Tide* 24 Dec. 1599/2 Jive-talk is nothing new. It goes back at least to the thirties when for the first time a brand of jazz, swing, grew to be a cult. Jive was originally the patois of Harlem, not jazz musicians' slang; but with time the distinction was lost. 1965 *Economist* 4 Sept. 888/2 Some common American jive-words (nappy, funky) are left out [of the *Penguin English Dictionary*]. 1971 *Black World* June 92/2 All the rest of that jive talk about white liberals and Rhett Butler is part of another conversation, Sam. 1971 *Melody Maker* 13 Nov. 31/1 That is if you forget the usual jive phrases that whittle their way into his conversation. 1973 *Times Lit. Suppl.* 1 June 604/4 A narrative tone which frequently coincides with the fast, obscene jive-talk of his characters.

4. Marijuana, or a cigarette containing it.

1938 *Call-Bulletin* (San Francisco) 19 Mar., The cigarettes are variously called sticks, reefers, tea gyves, Mary Anns and goofy butts. 1952 *N.Y. Times* 29 Apr. 25 So Diane smoked jive, pod, and tea. 1955 *U.S. Senate Hearings* (1956) VIII. 4168 'Sticks', 'reefers', 'jive sticks'. 1963 'D. RUTHERFORD' *Creeping Flesh* ii. 124 'Jive' originally meant marijuana. 1972 *Lancet* 16 Sept. 565/1 She was convinced that only in the institution could she 'make it without jive', for she invariably used heroin whenever she was sent home.

jive (dʒəiv), *v. slang* (orig. *U.S.*). Also **gieve.** [Cf. prec.] **1. a.** *trans.* To mislead, to deceive,

to 'kid'; to taunt or sneer at. Also *intr.*, to talk jive, to talk nonsense, to act foolishly.

1928 L. ARMSTRONG (*title of gramophone record*) Don't jive me. **1929** W. THURMAN *Blacker the Berry* 128 But I jived her along, so she ditched him, and gave me her address. **1934** *Amer. Speech* IX. 26/2 *Gieve*.., to mislead with words; to take into one's confidence. *Ibid.* 27/1 *Jive*, see *gieve*. **1938** *Ibid.* XIII. 317/1 *To jive around*,.. 'to fool around'. **1939** J. DOLLARD in A. Dundes *Mother Wit* (1973) 281/2 Willy kept 'jiving' him until Jimmy finally left. **1944** D. BURLEY *Orig. Handbk. Harlem Jive* 71 Jive is a distortion of that staid, old respectable English word 'jibe'... In the sense in which it came into use among Negroes in Chicago about the year 1921, it meant to taunt, to scoff, to sneer. *Ibid.*, A highly effective manner of talking about each other's ancestors and hereditary traits..called 'Jiving' someone. **1946** MEZZROW & WOLFE *Really Blues* vi. 70 Monkey wasn't jiving about that bartender. **1950** A. LOMAX *Mr. Jelly Roll* (1952) iv. 170, I..jived the expressman to hank my trunks to the station by telling him my money was uptown. **1969** J. MCPHERSON in A. Chapman *New Black Voices* (1972) 162, I don't need no money. Nobody's jiving me. I'm jiving them. You know I can still pull in a hundred in tips in one trip [as a waiter on a train]. **1973** *Black World* Mar. 57 Lawd, don't jive Miz Jackson,..Ride on King Jesus!

b. *intr.* To make sense; to fit in. *U.S.* Cf. JIBE *v.*

1943 *Amer. Speech* XVIII. 153/2 *Doesn't jive*, doesn't make sense. **1955** W. GADDIS *Recognitions* II. i. 308 His analyst says he's in love with her for all the neurotic reasons in the book. It don't jive, man. **1973** *To our Returned Prisoners of War* (Office of U.S. Secretary of Defense) 7 *Jive*, verb meaning fit in, go with, to make sense.

2. *intr.* **a.** To play 'jive' (*JIVE *sb.* 2 a).

c **1938** N. E. WILLIAMS *His Hi De Highness of Ho De Ho* 35/2 'Jiving', meaning to improvise. **1942** BERREY & VAN DEN BARK *Amer. Thes. Slang* § 579/9 Play 'hot jazz'; 'swing',..*jive*. **1947** AUDEN *Age of Anxiety* (1948) ii. 44 The juke-box jives rejoicing madly.

b. To dance the 'jive' (*JIVE *sb.* 2 b).

1939 *San Francisco News Let.* 1 Sept. 12/2 If you should dance to the rhythms of either gentleman you will be jiving. **1957** *Observer* 13 Oct. 3/4 Young people from the East End and the West End came there [the Humphrey Lyttelton Club] to jive or listen. **1958** *New Statesman* 4 Jan. 10/2 A couple began a little hesitantly to jive.

Hence **ji·ver**, one who jives; **ji·ving** *vbl. sb.* and *ppl. a.*

1936 *N.Y. World-Telegram* 6 Oct. 16/1 High jiving—tall, if you know what I mean, talk. *c* **1938** [see 2 above]. **1939** BLIND BOY FULLER (*song title*) Jivin' Big Bill Blues. **1939** *San Francisco Examiner* 18 Aug. 3 (*heading*) Jiving deluxe. **1943** *N.Y. Times* 9 May II. 5/7 I'm a jivin jitterbug. **1943** *Gramophone* Aug. 47/2 Lawd, don't cut out 'Jazz'! I'll write you as many letters as Robert Mackenzie likes, but..don't forget the 'jiver', sir, don't forget the 'jiver'! **1944** S. J. PERELMAN *Crazy like Fox* (1945) 163 A jiving, hot-hosing jitterbug. **1947** M. H. BOULWARE *Jive & Slang of Students in Negro Colleges*, *Jiver*,..a flatterer. **1951** 'A. GARVE' *Murder in Moscow* iii. 46 Her daughter.. had won a prize for jiving at some South London *palais*. **1959** *Spectator* 12 June 856/1 One..finds the jazz virtuoso Stephane Grapelly performing to an admiring crowd of jivers. **1973** *Black World* Mar. 85 Jiving, bopping, napping, signifying, sounding—all modes of Afro-American expression—seek to affirm the vitality of the Black American experience. *Ibid.* May 84/1 He comes down hard on white racists, but he also attacks Black 'jivers' who seek to exploit their brethren under the guise of Blackness.

jive (dʒəiv), *a.* *U.S. slang.* [f. the sb.] Used, chiefly by American Blacks, in the primary sense 'not acting correctly' but with a wide range of connotations ('pretentious', 'deceitful', etc.).

[**1959** *Esquire* Nov. 70] *Jive*, to fool, to kid. The adjective is bogus.] **1971** E. E. LANDY *Underground Dict.* 112 *Jive*,..not acting right; doing something wrong—e.g. *You never showed up. You're a jive dude.* **1973** E. BULLINS *Theme is Blackness* 131 Kiss ma ass ya jive mathafukker! **1973** *Black World* June 61 Huh? Awh, Sistuh, u sho is jive. *Ibid.* 79/1 The hero..is 'hip', but not 'jive'. *Ibid.* Sept. 53, I been confused, fucked up, scared, phony And jive To a whole/lot of people.

jive-ass (dʒəi·væs, -ɑ̄s). *U.S. slang.* Also **jiveass.** [f. *JIVE *sb.* + ASS (= ARSE *sb.*).] **a.** A person who loves fun or excitement. **b.** A deceitful or pretentious person. Freq. *attrib.*

A word of fluid meaning and application.

1964 R. S. GOLD *Jazz Lexicon* 169 Jive-ass motherfucker. **1969** C. BROWN in A. Chapman *New Black Voices* (1972) 181 'You jiveass nigger,' Reb said, laughing. 'No, I'm telling the truth.' *Ibid.* 184 He became a hustler, a jiveass, a jazz player. **1970** *New York* 16 Nov. 42/1 This happens to be a jive-ass af-*flu*-ent neighborhood. **1973** *Black World* Aug. 55/2 Silly-ass so-called hangups of jive-ass white folks. *Ibid.* 67/1 Jive-ass jivers. Stupid. Looking clever.

jivey (dʒəi·vi), *a.* *slang* (chiefly *U.S.*). Also **jivy.** [f. *JIVE *sb.* + -Y[1].] Jazzy, 'swinging', lively (see also quot. 1954); also, misleading, phoney, pretentious.

1944 [in the popular song *Mairzy Doats* by M. Drake, A. Hoffman, and J. Livingston]. **1953** BERREY & VAN DEN BARK *Amer. Thes. Slang* (1954) § 149/13 'Knowing'; 'hep' (manifesting knowledge of what is proper or fashionable)..*jivey*. **1955** KEEPNEWS & GRAUER *Pict. Hist. Jazz* xv. 187 Stuff Smith, one of the jiviest. *Ibid.* xix. 248 Bassist Slam Steuart was..primarily a jivey Swing man who hummed solos loudly as he played. **1972** M. J. BOSSE *Incident at Naha* ii. 85 I'm not sure I would have accepted that sort of jivey explanation, but Mrs. Halliday did. **1972** *Jazz & Blues* Dec. 28/1 This coupling finds him in jivey mood.

jiwan (dʒiwā·n). [Skr. *jīvana* a son; cf. Hindi *jawān*.] = *JAWAN; also, an Indian youth.

1914 KIPLING *New Army* (1915) 49 The trouble in India was that all the young men—the mere *jiwans*—wanted to come out at once. **1924** *Blackw. Mag.* Aug. 227/1, I met the Gurkha officer in the back of beyond with two or three of his *jiwans*. *Ibid.* 232/2, I ruled over as jolly a crowd of students as a Principal of a College can hope to collect, north-country lads—Sikh, Muhammadans, and Hindus... At cricket..we had an English professional..who coached them... He became attached to my *jiwans*.

Jixi, Jixie (dʒi·ksi). *temporary.* [f. *Jix*, nick-name of *J*oynson-H*icks* (see below) + *-i*, after TAXI.] A two-seater taxi-cab licensed in 1926 while Sir William Joynson-Hicks (1865–1932) was Home Secretary.

1926 *Westm. Gaz.* 7 Apr., Jixi is the name given by the Westminster Gazette, and now used by everyone, to 2-seater taxicabs. **1926** *Punch* 21 Apr. 438/2 The Home Secretary explained to Sir F. Meyer that the police have licensed two types of 'Jixi'. **1927** *Observer* 3 Apr. 9 The first 'Jixie' or two-seater taxicab will probably be seen on the streets of London at the end of the present week.

jizz (dʒiz). [Etym. unknown.] The characteristic impression given by an animal or plant.

GUISE *sb.* 5 is coincident in sense but the phonetic relationship remains unexplained and the two words may therefore be unrelated.

1922 T. A. COWARD *Bird Haunts & Nature Memories* 141 A West Coast Irishman was familiar with the wild creatures which dwelt on or visited his rocks and shores; at a glance he could name them, usually correctly, but if asked how he knew them would reply 'By their "jizz".' What is jizz?..We have not coined it, but how wide its use in Ireland is we cannot say...Jizz may be applied to or possessed by any animate and some inanimate objects, yet we cannot clearly define it. A single character may supply it, or it may be the combination of many. *Ibid.* 143 Jizz, of course, is not confined to birds. The small mammal and the plant alike have jizz. **1950** *Brit. Birds* XLIII. 29 Miss Quick obviously looks at her birds more than once and does so with an artist's eye for those peculiarities of shape, outline and stance which give a species its 'jizz'. **1960** *Times* 14 June 14/7 The boy could name any bat at a glance..(an indefinable accomplishment which the late T. A. Coward..once described as 'jizz' when speaking of bird identification). **1966** D. MCCLINTOCK *Compan. Flowers* ix. 117, I know only too well the problem of trying to express what there is in a plant that enables me, or you, to tell it from another at sight. The word I use for these intangible characteristics, that defy being put into words, is jizz

jizz, var. *JISM.

‖ **jnana** (dʒənā·nă). *Hinduism.* Also **jnyana.** [Skr. *jñāna*, f. *jñā* to know.] Spiritual knowledge, as a means of salvation.

1827 *Trans. R. Asiatic Soc.* I. 576 *Vásudéva*, or *Bhagavat*,..has six especial attributes,..1st. Knowledge (jnyána), or acquaintance with everything animate or inanimate constituting the universe. **1875** M. WILLIAMS *Indian Wisdom* iii. 59 Jnāna, 'knowledge of universal truth'. **1916** T. A. GOPINATHA RAO *Elem. Hindu Iconogr.* II. I. 273 Śiva was seated facing south when he taught the *rishis yōga* and *jñāna*. **1945** A. HUXLEY *Let.* 10 Apr. (1969) 520 There is gnosis or jnana after death only for those who have chosen to pay the price..of gnosis during life. **1971** *Illustr. Weekly India* 11 Apr. 15/4 The essence of the world is religion..the essence of religion is knowledge (*jnana*).

b. *Comb.*, as **jnana-marga** [Skr. *mārga* road, path], the way to salvation through spiritual knowledge or asceticism.

1877 M. WILLIAMS *Hinduism* i. 11 Popular Hindûism.. though supposed to accept this creed as the way of true knowledge (*Jnāna-mārga*)..adds to it two other..ways. **1883** —— *Relig. Thought & Life in India* iii. 63 The way of love and faith (bhakti-mārga)..superseded the other two ways of salvation—knowledge and works (jñāna-mārga and karma-mārga). **1937** [see **bhakti-marga*]. **1945** A. HUXLEY *Let.* 21 Jan. (1969) 513 The three types of religion enumerated in the *Bhagavad Gita*, (karma marga, the way of works or action; Bhakti marga, the way of devotion; and jnana marga, the way of knowledge) correspond precisely to the three extremes of somatotonic, viscerotonic and cerebrotonic temperament. **1963** *Listener* 28 Mar. 550/2 In earliest times, in pre-Buddhist texts such as the first *Upanisads* is described what later became known as *Jnana-marga*, or the way of knowledge, in which the realization of the identity of the individual self or soul with the Universal, the absolute, Brahma, was sought.

‖ **jnani** (dʒənā·ni). *Hinduism.* [Skr., f. *JNANA.] A worshipper or devotee of *jnana-marga.*

1885 E. BALFOUR *Cycl. India* (ed. 3) II. 442/2 *Jnani*, or divine Buddhas, are five. **1916** T. A. GOPINATHA RAO *Elem. Hindu Iconogr.* III. I. 242 The silent *jñānis* destroying the threefold bond..behold the sacred and are filled with bliss. **1962** BRAHMACHARINI USHA *Ramakrishna-Vedanta Wordbk.*, *Jnani*. 1. One who follows the path of knowledge and discrimination to reach the impersonal Reality; a non-dualist. 2. A knower of Brahman. **1969** *Indian Music Jrnl.* V. Suppl., Arunagiri completed the song, got cured of his ailments and became a Jñānī and a yōgēśvara.

Joachimite (dʒōu·ăkimәit). *Ch. Hist.* [f. the name of *Joachim*, abbot of Fiore in Calabria (*c* 1132–1202) + -ITE[1].] A heretical follower of the Italian mystic, Joachim of Fiore. Also **Jo·achimist, Jo·achist, Jo·achite, Jo·achitist;** so **Jo·achimism, Jo·achism.**

1797 *Encycl. Brit.* IX. 290/2 *Joachimites*, in church history, the disciples of Joachim, a Cistertian monk. **1842** K. H. DIGBY *Mores Catholici* XI. xiii. 478 The execrable book, entitled the eternal Gospel,..whose adherents, termed Joachimites, as it was ascribed to Joachim, were again condemned by the Council of Arles. **1874** J. H. BLUNT *Dict. Sects* 242/1 As early as 1260 the Council of Arles spoke of the Joachitist error as spreading like a cancer. **1906** G. G. COULTON *From St. Francis to Dante* 104 The Pope..insisted on his resignation, partly on account of his Joachism. *Ibid.* 108 A great orator and a great Joachite. **1913** E. G. GARDNER *Dante & Mystics* vi. 192 The Joachists went considerably beyond what Joachim himself had taught. **1913** A. G. F. HOWELL *S. Bernardino of Siena* i. 10 They cultivated the Joachite literature. **1926** E. HUTTON *Franciscans in Eng.* ix. 141 A sect of Joachists had arisen among the 'spiritual' party within the Franciscan Order. **1929** E. C. MESSENGER tr. *Guiraud's Mediæval Inquisition* v. 143 In 1247, a friar with Joachimist tendencies, John of Parma was elected minister general of the Order. *Ibid.*, Peter John Olivi.. expounded a modified Joachimism which was henceforth the doctrine of the Spirituals. **1931** H. BETT *Joachim of Flora* v. 112 These Joachites maintain that the future age of the Holy Spirit shall be enlightened with a more perfect law. **1932** *Speculum* VII. 260 These works.. beside throwing some lights on several problems of the Joachite tradition, were..useful in awakening more interest in the subject. *Ibid.* 267 Grundmann's work is.. epoch-making in the studies on Joachim and Joachism. **1947** H. R. WILLIAMSON *Arrow & Sword* x. 158 The Joachists..had taken their master's ideas to their logical conclusion. *Ibid.*, It is possible that the *Divine Comedy*.. is the classic Joachist apologia.

joanna (dʒoæ·nă). Also **joano, johanna,** and other varr. Rhyming slang for 'piano'.

1846 *Swell's Night Guide* 34 As a sort of whipper-in, music is provided—viz.,..a joano. **1912** A. N. LYONS *Clara* iii. 28 All the time a party down below was bangin' out a song called 'Bedelia' on a old johanner. **1923** J. MANCHON *Le Slang* 168 *Johannah, johanner*, un piano. **1961** S. PRICE *Just for Record* ix. 89 He gets up from the joanna-stool. **1972** *Listener* 20 July 92/2 The old Jo-anna intrudes its amateurish thumpings.

joaquinite (wā-, wokī·nәit, dʒō·ăkwinәit). *Min.* [f. *Joaquin*, the name of a ridge in San Benito County, California: see -ITE[1].] A honey-yellow to brown silicate of sodium, barium, iron, and titanium that occurs as small, isolated, orthorhombic crystals.

1909 G. D. LOUDERBACK in *Bull. Dept. Geol. Univ. Calif.* V. 376 Joaquinite... A honey yellow or light brown substance in small generally individual crystals or crystal grains..which is believed to be a new mineral. **1932** *Amer. Mineralogist* XVII. 308 (*heading*) The chemical nature of joaquinite. *Ibid.* 312 There are, therefore, 4 molecules of composition $NaBa(Ti, Fe)_3Si_4O_{15}$ in the unit cell of joaquinite. **1967** *Ibid.* LII. 1762 An apparently new rare-earth mineral of the joaquinite group occurs in nephelin–syenite pegmatites of Ilimaussaq alkaline massif (S. Greenland). Optical and X-ray properties are the same, as for standard joaquinite Na Ba Ti_3 Si_4 O_{15} from California, but the chemical analysis is quite different... The formula is $NaBa_2Fe^{2+}Ce_2Ti_2Si_8O_{26}(OH)$.

joar, var. *JOHAR.

job, *sb.*[2] Add: **1. c.** (Earlier and later examples.)

1795 *Let. of Compositors of London* in E. Howe *London Compositor* (1947) i. 76 That all jobs, not exceeding one sheet, be paid at the rate of six pence per thousand. **1841** W. SAVAGE *Dict. Art of Printing* 428 Any thing which printed does not exceed a sheet, is termed a Job, and is paid for extra to the compositor, because there is no return of furniture or of letter: he has generally to put up fresh cases, and has some additional trouble in getting the right letter, and in making up the furniture. **1960** P. M. HANDOVER *Printing in London* vii. 183 In general, however, both the Bagford and Johnson Collections [*sc.* of ephemera] reveal that during the eighteenth century the letterpress printers made little effort to extend the range of jobs.

3. *jobs for the boys*: see *BOY *sb.*[1] 6 d.

4. a. *spec.* A paid position of employment, a situation (sense 6 b).

1858 in *Amer. Speech* (1965) XL. 130 But when he gets a good fat job For dat am all he cares. *a* **1861** T. WINTHROP *Edwin Brothertoft* (1862) 38, I will find you a fat job and plenty of pickings! **1883** [see FAT *a.* 9 b]. **1931** *Daily Express* 13 Oct. 5/2 When I got my job as social secretary..I got a large salary and lived in luxury. **1940** G. D. H. & M. COLE *Counterpoint Murder* xv. 237 He was in the same job up to about a week ago. **1974** *New Statesman* 17 May 701/3 After the Tory general election defeat of 1964, the outgoing Chancellor of the Exchequer..told a newspaper gossip writer: I shall have to get a job and earn some money.

b. *bad job* (earlier and later examples); *job of work*: a task, piece of work; *to have a job (to)*: to have difficulty (in doing something); similarly, *to be a job*: to present difficulties;

also, (*to be*) *the devil's* (*own*) *job*; *to get on with the job* [Get *v.* 63 f], to proceed with one's work, to continue with one's affairs; *just the job* (colloq.): exactly what is wanted, the very thing.

1557 in A. Feuillerat *Documents Revels Court Ed. VI & Q. Mary* (1914) 236 Doinge certen Iobbes of woorke. **1862** Borrow *Wild Wales* I. xix. 210 The minister of the parish..had frequently entered into argument with him, but quite unsuccessfully and had at last given up the matter, as a bad job. **1873** Trollope *Eustace Diamonds* I. xix. 252 Arthur did not go on the search, because he had a job of work to do. *Ibid.* III. lxxii. 251 The barrister who will have the cross-examining of her..will have a job of work on his hand. **1878** [see *coast *v.* 14]. **1887** G. H. Devol *Forty Yrs. a Gambler* 267 For ten or fifteen years during my early life, the sporting men of the South tried to find a man to whip me, but they couldn't do it, and finally gave it up as a bad job. **1907** J. M. Synge *Tinker's Wedding* I. 1 It's the divil's job making a ring. **1922** F. H. Burnett *Robin* xviii. 154 'You propose to suggest that she shall marry *you*?'..'Yes. It will be the devil's own job..she has abhorred me all her life.' **1928** M. Walsh *While Rivers Run* xx. 279 'A sound job of work!' boasted Alistair. 'We have arriven.' **1931** A. Huxley *Let.* 24 Aug. (1969) 351 It has been a job writing the book and I'm glad it's done. **1931** 'P. Williams' *Word of To-morrow* iv. xvi. 263 Tramps..who wouldn't do an honest job of work not if it was offered them. **1935** *Punch* 21 Aug. 208/3, I had a job to find the meter, and I can't think why they want to hide it behind a table. **1941** *London Opinion* June 48 (*caption*) I'll have a job explaining things to my wife. **1942** 'A. Bridge' *Frontier Passage* viii. 131 Why the hell couldn't all the extremists ..allow sensible people..to get on with the job?—the job being to live the good life. **1943** Hunt & Pringle *Service Slang* 42 *Just the job*, if you see anything that you like, whether it is something in a shop window or a new billet, this is what you say, meaning of course that it suits you all right. **1944** R. Lehmann *Ballad & Source* 55 My riding lessons had been given up as a bad job. **1959** 'J. Ross' *Boy in Grey Overcoat* ii. 21, I thought..she'd be just the job. **1960** H. Pinter *Dumb Waiter* 148 Just the job. We should have used it before. **1966** *Listener* 1 Sept. 300/2, I have had quite a job to get a copy [of a book]. **1969** *Ottawa Commons Debates* 24 July 11570/2 If the opposition accords so little respect to parliament that it defines governing as evil, that getting on with the job is regarded as tyranny, then I am happy to be given the chance to join issue. **1973** E. Page *Fortnight by Sea* ix. 98 If Mrs Barratt could possibly see her way to letting us stay on..it really would be just the job.

c. A consignment of goods to be sold cheaply as bargains, a job lot.

1858 *Illustr. News World* I. 257/3 Butcher's meat, the week's gathering, to be sold by the job. **1905** *Daily Chron.* 18 Nov. 3/7 As soon as a girl can do a corset, which is at all passable, even if we have to put it into the 'jobs'—that is, lots for selling cheap—she can earn much more.

d. *on the job*: (*a*) hard at work, busy (also in extended senses, committing a crime, engaged in sexual intercourse, etc.); (*b*) (of a racehorse) out to win and well backed; (*c*) = *by the job* (in Dict., sense 1 d); (*d*) used as *attrib. phr.* (hyphenated): done or occurring while a person is at work.

1882 W. Burnot *Old Mother Goose* iii. 12 He will have to hide his nob. Come along, we're on the job. *a* **1889** in Barrère & Leland *Dict. Slang* (1889) I. 502/1 Trainers and jockeys..very easily gathered whether a particular horse..was 'out for an airing' or was on the job. **1890** Lloyd George *Let.* 7 Aug. (1973) 32, I am on the job Saturday or Monday. **1891** *Licensed Victuallers' Gaz.* 23 Jan. (Farmer & Henley), There was a long wrangle over the choice of referee, for no one cared to occupy that thankless post when the Lambs were on the job. **1892** E. J. Milliken *'Arry Ballads* 3 'Arry is fair on the job. **1901** *To-Day* 22 Aug. 115/1 'This cook..is very good.' 'She is, but she is only here on the job.' **1909** *Post & Paddock* 22 Nov. 1/3 Their denunciations of horses 'not trying', being 'out for an airing', or 'not on the job' on every occasion when their speculations go wrong. **1914** G. Atherton *Perch of Devil* I. iv. 22 She was 'on the job' every minute until the cottage was 'on wheels'. **1922** Joyce *Ulysses* 466 Mother Slipperslapper. (*Familiarly.*) She's on the job herself tonight with the vet. **1922** *N. & Q.* 9 Sept. 206/2 To be 'on the job' is for a horse to be 'busy', to be 'out', *i.e.*, backed and trying. **1937** *Burlington Mag.* June p. xxvi/1 The slippery pickpocket is depicted 'on the job'. **1947** [see *biotechnology]. **1958** *Times* 24 Mar. (Careers in Industry Suppl.) p. vi/4 Everyone should receive the training appropriate to his particular aptitude—which may range from the on-the-job training to a university course. **1966** 'L. Lane' *ABZ of Scouse* 78 *On ther job*: engaged in sexual intercourse. **1971** *Optometry Today* 17 On-the-job accidents and injuries could be appreciably reduced if every worker had maximum visual efficiency for the task at hand. **1972** *Daily Tel.* (Colour Suppl.) 16 Nov. 94/3 'Why the hell did you play Eric Clapton's *Easy Now*?..Didn't you realise it was all about some guy on the job?' And I said, 'Yeah. How many songs aren't?' **1973** *Amer. Speech 1969* XLIV. 243 This approach..falls short of giving the reader an accurate idea of the large role that railroad language plays in on-the-job communication.

e. A commission to back a racehorse; so, a horse on which such bets are placed.

1889 Barrère & Leland *Dict. Slang* I. 502/1 'He has got the job', he has the putting on of the stable money. **1907** *Favourite* 16 Nov. 9/2 Elfin Revel was a big starting-price job for the Croxteth Plate. **1911** *Turf* 10 Oct. 1/1, I am not now referring to s.p. jobs.

f. *colloq.* A term of wide application, often with suggestions of excellence, to describe something, esp. something manufactured (as a motor vehicle, aircraft, etc.); also *joc.* of persons, esp. a pretty girl.

1927 D. Hammett in *Black Mask* May 14/2 She's a tough little job who was probably fired for dropping her chewing gum in the soup the last place she worked. **1928** *Daily Mail* 7 May 6/4 [U.S. slang] *A job*, always used when a particular aeroplane is mentioned. **1930** 'A. Armstrong' *Taxi* xii. 164 The fare is 'the rider' or 'the job'. **1930** *Engineering* 18 July 79/3 The motorship press would hail with delight the figures given..as showing the fuel cost of Diesel engines to be almost half that of any of the steam jobs. **1938** *Harper's Mag.* Jan. 141/2 There was an antiquated high-wing monoplane job. **1939** *Ottawa Jrnl.* 25 July 7/3 He was just about to sit down to a good breakfast in Texas opposite a young woman who was a first class job. **1942** Berrey & Van den Bark *Amer. Thes. Slang* § 81.2 *Automobile*,..job. **1942** *R.A.F. Jrnl.* 30 May 23 The bath was a limited affair: a quick sponge job from a gallon or so of warm water. **1942** *Gen* 1 Sept. 12/2 A 'ropey job' is likely as not to be a blonde who proved uncollaborative. **1946** Brickhill & Norton *Escape to Danger* v. 50 A rather imposing moustache. It was one of those bushy black jobs. **1948** C. Day Lewis *Otterbury Incident* i. 2 It [*sc.* a chronometer] was one of those super Swiss jobs. **1964** 'A. Gilbert' *Knock, knock, who's There?* i. 9 You make good contacts in a pub... There was a job called the Admiral Box where I'd never been. **1972** G. Lyall *Blame the Dead* xvii. 117 The only desk was Steen's own oiled-teak job. **1973** *Daily Tel.* 22 June 9 (Advt.), Its suspension's almost identical to that of a £2,966 Mercedes 220. (Not to mention a few other equally pricey jobs.)

5. *good job, bad job*: (later examples).

1923 *Spectator* 9 June 972/2 The novel ends, therefore, with Derek making the best of a bad job. **1930** J. B. Priestley *Angel Pavement* ii. 65 Girls *are* a bit silly..and it's a good job for the men they are. **1942** *Punch* 9 Sept. 215 (*caption*) It's a good job that pig-headed old fool of a farmer ignored our instructions, or we'd have been running on ploughed land. **1950** T. S. Eliot *Cocktail Party* ii. 111 *Edward*: Lavinia, we must make the best of a bad job. That is what he means. *Reilly*:..The best of a bad job is all any of us make of it.

7. *attrib.* and *Comb.* (now chiefly in sense *4), as *job assessment, assignment, centre, content, -counselling, definition, description, discrimination, displacement, enlargement, enrichment, evaluation, -hungry* adj., *hygiene, insecurity, mobility, opportunity, placement, reservation, -rich* adj., *rotation, satisfaction, security, -seeking, situation, specification, structuring, study*. Also **job analysis,** analysis of the essential factors of a particular piece of work and the necessary qualifications of the person who is to perform it; so *job analyst*; **job-buyer,** one who buys job lots; **job case** (*Printing*), a type case used in job printing with boxes for both upper- and lower-case types; **Job Corps** *U.S.*, 'an organization..that operates rural conservation camps and urban training centers for poor youths' (Random House Dict.); **job fount, font** (*Printing*), see quots. 1888, 1894; **job-hopping,** the act or practice of changing from one job to another; so **job-hop** *v. intr.*; **job-hopper; job house** (*Printing*), = *job-office*; **job-office** (*Printing*) (examples); **job press** (*Printing*), a small press designed for job-printing; **job-print, -printing,** the printing of job-work (see sense 1 c); **job-printer** (examples); **job sheet,** a sheet on which are recorded details of a job that has been done; **job shop,** (*a*) a workshop where small pieces of work are performed; (*b*) = *job-office*; (*c*) (see quot. 1972); **job-type** (examples); **job-work,** (*b*) the printing of jobs (sense 1 c).

1923 J. D. Hackett in *Managem. Engin.* May, *Job analysis*, the determination of the essential factors in a specific kind of work and of the qualifications of a worker necessary for its competent performance. **1929** *Encycl. Brit.* XIII. 78/2 This 'questionnaire method' has received severe condemnation from scientists and should be used sparingly by investigators in the field of job analysis. **1962** H. C. Weston *Light, Sight & Work* (ed. 2) viii. 239 This is subsequently fitted to a job visual standards profile based on the results of job-analysis. **1946** R. H. Warnhoff *Automobile Accessory Industry* 18 *Job analyst.* Performs detailed job analysis and job evaluation studies. **1971** *State Service* Nov. 340/2 The job analyst..assesses the post. **1959** *Gloss. Terms Work Study* (*B.S.I.*) 26 *Job assessment*, the process of ascertaining the relative value of a job by examination of the job analysis and job description. **1964** G. L. Cohen *What's Wrong with Hospitals?* i. 17 Through job-assignment, nurses gain expertise but also become frustrated. **1903** *Daily Chron.* 7 Oct. 10/1 E. H...described as a 'Job buyer'. **1894** *Amer. Dict. Printing & Bookmaking* 308/2 *Job case*, a lower case condensed into two-thirds of its usual width, half of the boxes in the upper case being placed by its side. **1946** A. Monkman in H. Whetton *Pract. Printing & Binding* ii. 20/1 The two best double cases are the California Job Case..and the Improved Double Case. **1972** *Jrnl. Printing Hist. Soc. 1971* VII. 39 By 1860 the full size job case was generally available as a printers' supplier's stock item on both sides of the Atlantic. **1972** *Times* 8 Sept. 15/1 Forget about the Government employment exchanges..think about the bright, new offices with a new image and a sign outside saying job centre. **1973** *Guardian* 23 May 6/4 Britain's first Job Centre will be opened this afternoon. Job Centres are the modern version of what have..been called employment exchanges or..labour exchanges. **1969** J. Argenti *Managem. Techniques* 153 The use of a computer to analyse trends in job content. **1965** Mrs. L. B. Johnson *White House Diary* 3 Feb. (1970) 234 Dr. Otis Singletary..director of the Job Corps..says that applications to join are coming in about six thousand a day. **1965** *Economist* 4 Sept. 884/1 Over forty of the Job Corps centres are already in operation. **1970** *Times* 1 June 9/1 The separation of benefit from job counselling. **1967** A. Battersby *Network Analysis* (ed. 2) iv. 68 It will always be more convenient to go on using existing job-definitions for which data on performance and cost are already known. **1951** J. M. Fraser *Psychol.* ii. xi. 126 Once we have drawn up a complete and realistic description of a job we can work out from it a specification of the kind of person who is likely to do it satisfactorily. It is very important that..each quality laid down in it should be linked with some aspect of the actual duties shown in the job description. **1972** *Accountant* 28 Sept. 385/1 Essential records are..those for employee turnover, performance appraisals, dynamic job descriptions/specifications. **1970** G. Greer *Female Eunuch* 297 A protest against job discrimination. **1964** Job displacement [see *across *prep.* 2 c]. **1954** *Time* 12 Apr., Job enlargement (a phrase coined by Yale's Human Relations Expert Charles R. Walker) was formally born in 1943. On a trip through International Business Machine Corp.'s plant at Endicott, N.Y., I.B.M. President (now Chairman) Thomas J. Watson spotted a young woman standing idly by a milling machine. She explained that she was waiting for the 'machine inspector' (there was a 'setup man', whose task it was to adjust the machine for each new operation, and an inspector, who okayed the adjustment). Actually, she was able to adjust the machine herself, but it was against the plant rules to do so. **1966** T. Lupton *Managem. & Social Sci.* ii. 32 It might well be possible to look at individual jobs to see whether it is possible to make them less rigidly paced and repetitive and not lose output, by 'job enlargement' for example. **1972** *Listener* 7 Sept. 301/1 A growing interest in the idea of work-structuring or 'job enrichment'. **1957** *Encycl. Brit.* XXIII. 272/1 Where job evaluation wage rate systems prevail jobs are analyzed and defined in terms of basic attributes and requirements. **1973** *Times* 17 Jan. 13/3 Some techniques that until recently were virtually unheard of in the [hotel] industry are now beginning to make their appearance, such as job evaluation and formal performance appraisals. **1888** C. T. Jacobi *Printers' Vocab.* 68 *Job fount*, a small fount of type used for displaying purposes. **1894** *Amer. Dict. Printing & Bookmaking* 308/2 *Job font*, a small font of type used for display, distinct from a book font. **1972** *Jrnl. Printing Hist. Soc. 1971* VII. 39 A more efficient use of the full size case in accommodating the caps, figures and points only job fonts came with the devising of the treble case. **1970** *Time* 19 Jan. 43 He job-hopped, serving briefly as operating vice president of Servo-mechanisms Inc. and later organizing his own law firm in Los Angeles. **1967** *Time* 13 Oct. 63 Boyden's prospects are rarely aware that Boyden is aware of them as potential job hoppers. **1953** *Britannica Bk. of Year* 639/2 *Job-hopping*, a policy of changing jobs so as to place a higher value on one's services. **1972** *Times* 22 Sept. 22/6 Increased job-hopping tendencies among young male graduates. **1825** T. C. Hansard *Typographia* 700 But, that it [*sc.* a kind of printing machine] could be introduced into a book-work house, or even a job-house, to execute all the variety of sizes of works and pages, was a thing which I could never believe. **1841** W. Savage *Dict. Art of Printing* 428 *Job house*, a printing office, the general run of business in which is the printing of Jobs; namely, cards, shop bills,..play bills,..and all other things of a similar description. **1888** C. T. Jacobi *Printers' Vocab.* 68 *Job house*, a term applied to printing offices distinct from book or newspaper offices. **1894** *Amer. Dict. Printing & Bookmaking* 309/1 *Job house*, a term applied in England to printing-offices where the chief kind of work done is in jobs. **1946** Job-hungry [see *gadget 2]. **1966** T. Lupton *Managem. & Social Sci.* iii. 63 Good environmental conditions—so called 'job hygiene', i.e. good welfare facilities, meals, lighting, heating, good mates. **1959** *Listener* 25 June 1095/2 The very notion of a job insecurity..is alien to the Russians. **1966** I. Jefferies *House-Surgeon* iii. 26 Rosalind..was used to even more job-mobility than most people would regard as desirable. **1972** *Accountant* 12 Oct. 441/2 To cope with the problems presented by job mobility it was proposed to concentrate employees' records in ten computer centres. **1882** T. MacKellar *Amer. Printer* (ed. 13) 301 A useful thing to have in a job office is Ame's Paper and Card Scale. **1894** *Amer. Dict. Printing & Bookmaking* 309/2 *Job office*, a printing-house where the chief work is in jobs. **1971** *Wall St. Jrnl.* 22 July iv. 1/1 While thousands of 1971 graduates pound the pavements in pursuit of jobs, an exclusive little group here has found alluring job opportunities popping up on all sides. **1963** *New Society* 7 Nov. 7/2 The private employment agencies, who handle a lucrative job-placement business. **1894** *Amer. Dict. Printing & Bookmaking* 309/2 *Job press*, a press on which job-work is done. It is, however, in practice usually limited to the treadle-machines, which do not print a sheet larger than 14 or 15 by 21 [inches]. **1936** Greenhood & Gentry *Chronol. Bks. & Printing* (rev. ed.) 111, 1850..Gordon of New York is awarded a patent for first 'job' press. **1971** R. W. & E. W. Polk *Pract. Printing* (ed. 7) xv. 115 Most of the small presses for general job work are of the platen type. These presses are often classified as job presses. **1921** C. E. Mulford *Bar-20 Three* vi. 77 A hard-riding courier, relaying twice, carried the work of the job-print toward Mesquite. **1884** J. Gould *Letter-Press Printer* (ed. 3) 132 For job-printers the small platen machines are invaluable. **1960** P. M. Handover *Printing in London* vii. 194 Without the lavish production of publicity material fashionable since the second world war many job printers would be unable to meet the necessary cost of new machines and the rising cost of labour and rent. **1825** *New Lisbon* (Ohio) *Patriot* 29 Oct. 1/4 Job Printing, Neatly and expeditiously done at this office. **1859** *Abridgments of Specifications relating to Printing* (Patent Office) 365 The main object of this invention is to carry on 'job printing'.. without the necessity of employing skilled labour. **1892** A. Powell *Southward's Pract. Printing* (ed. 4) xxix. 266 Bookwork is almost always executed in black ink; while in job printing any colour is permissible. **1924** *Southward's*

Mod. Printing (ed. 5) I. Job Design Suppl. 2 (following p. 336), Fine book and job printing a speciality. **1960** P. M. HANDOVER *Printing in London* viii. 196 As job printing in London followed a course separate from that of periodicals,..so the course of book printing was equally distinct. **1969** *Times* 19 Nov. 30/2 Some form of job reservation [in South Africa] imposed either by legislation or custom will persist for some time to come. **1971** *Sunday Express* (Johannesburg) 28 Mar. 4/3 Sir Francis de Guingand..said he found job reservation difficult to understand. **1972** *Sat. Rev.* (U.S.) 6 May 39/1 Industrialized and job-rich Morgan City. **1963** R. STEWART *Reality of Management* II. vii. 119 The companies which use job rotation as a conscious policy are likely to have a general policy of moving people in their early years and later to practise selective job rotation. **1955** BRAYFIELD & CROCKETT in *Psychol. Bull.* LII. 397/1 We have not attempted to define such terms as job satisfaction or morale. Instead, we have found it necessary to assume that the measuring operations define the variables involved. **1972** *Accountant* 21 Sept. 346/1 Prinny.. would attend the first course to assess its suitability in terms of personal job-satisfaction. **1959** *Listener* 25 June 1095/1 A number of other attitudes towards job security. **1972** *Sat. Rev.* (U.S.) 6 May 39/1 Job-seeking itself can be costly. **1970** P. LAURIE *Scotland Yard* v. 116 The ambulance crew which we met on the way are in Sister's office drinking tea and filling out their job-sheets. **1974** 'J. ROSS' *Burning of Billy Toober* xvi. 149 Completing job sheets and questionnaires. **1851** H. MELVILLE *Moby Dick* III. xl. 233 When I kept my job-shop in the Vineyard. **1963** *Times* 15 Feb. 7/1 The west coast and international editions of the *New York Times* are printed in 'job shops', commercial printing offices working on a contract basis. **1967** *Electronics* 6 Mar. 28 (Advt.), Whether you have an in-plant plating operation or a job shop, we'll help you select a process. **1972** *Times* 7 June 27/5 The Butts Centre..will feature a job shop—the officially approved title of a room full of advertising boards where people can browse. **1951** J. M. FRASER *Psychol.* II. xi. 120 We are confronted then with two variables, the job and the individual... Our task is to match up one with the other, to find the individual who will fit neatly into the job situation. **1923** J. D. HACKETT in *Managem. Engin.* May, *Job specification*, a record of the essential factors in a given piece of work and of the human qualifications necessary for its performance. **1970** *Times* 11 May 9/1 The company has begun the groundwork for job structuring. **1951** J. M. FRASER *Psychol.* II. xi. 128 The job-study provides a complete factual description of the job and the conditions in which it is carried out. **1882** T. MACKELLAR *Amer. Printer* (ed. 13) 304 Capitals and lower-case job types should not be laid together in the same boxes. **1888** Job type [see *book type* (*BOOK *sb.* 18)]. **1892** A. POWELL *Southward's Pract. Printing* (ed. 4) viii. 53 Job types are laid in upper and lower cases, in double cases, or in half cases, according to the extent of the founts. **1832** *Reg. Deb. Congress U.S.* 5 May 2766 The occasional advertising and job-work for the Government. **1859** *Abridgments of Specifications relating to Printing* (Patent Office) 390 This invention relates to an arrangement of machinery intended chiefly for printing 'job work' with great expedition. **1892** A. POWELL *Southward's Pract. Printing* (ed. 4) xxix. 266 It is obvious that there is hardly any limit to the modes in which job work may be executed. **1948** *Words into Type* 543 *Job work*, miscellaneous printing—all except newspaper, magazine, or book work. **1966** BERRY & POOLE *Ann. Printing* 256/1 The extravagant style of American job work.

Job, *sb.*[4] Add: **2.** **Job's cat, turkey** *U.S. joc.*, used as types of poverty.

1854 S. SMITH *Way down East* 184, I should rather be as poor as Job's cat all the days of my life. **1824** *The Microscope* 22 May 42/2 We have seen fit to say 'the patience of Job's turkey', instead of the common phrase, 'as patient as Job'. **1871** E. EGGLESTON *Hoosier Schoolmaster* (1872) iv. 22 But laws! don't I remember when he was poorer nor Job's turkey! **1951** *Publ. Amer. Dial. Soc.* xv. 58 Poor as Job's turkey.

job, *v.*[2] Add: **6.** *to job off*: to sell goods at very low prices.

1903 *Lett. that bring Business* 68 We have had some very unpleasant experiences in the past through our goods being held on consignment for months, and then jobbed off at suicidal prices. **1936** *Economist* 22 Feb. 400/1 Motor spirit..has been comparatively easy to sell, while heavier oils have either been 'jobbed off' or used for 'cracking' into lighter oils. **1955** *Times* 22 Aug. 7/6 The bottom has dropped out of the rice market and hard decisions are being taken about jobbing off as cattle fodder a million tons of surplus rice.

c. *to job backwards*: to engage retrospectively in calculations, e.g. of profits on Stock Exchange transactions, that presume knowledge of subsequent events. Freq. *transf.*

1919 D. LLOYD GEORGE *Let.* 8 July in A. J. P. Taylor *My Darling Pussy* (1975) 27 The election was muddled but it is no use jobbing backwards. **1931** *Economist* 21 Mar. 621/1 Calculations based on 'jobbing backwards' on a Fixed Trust holding are altogether illusive. **1939** *War Illustr.* 18 Nov. p. ii/1, I notice that in his [*sc.* Lloyd George's] writings about this later, and quite possibly greater, War he shows a sad inclination to 'job backwards', as they say on the Stock Exchange. By jobbing backwards I have no difficulty in proving how I could have been worth £20,000,000, whereas if I die, or get bombed, before this war finishes I shall figure for ever so much less than that, having lost a considerable fortune by declining values of stocks and shares. **1959** *Times* 4 Sept. 11/4 Did he [*sc.* the Prime Minister] not actually say 'We never job backwards'? This is a Stock Market term meaning, in this context, 'We let bygones be bygones.' **1959** *Observer* 11 Oct. 15/3 Meanwhile, jobbing backwards, how much was one inclined to overestimate the effect of those excellently produced Labour Party telecasts? **1968** J. M. ZIMAN *Public Knowl.* iii. 31 All too often it becomes an exercise in 'jobbing backwards': it tells us how we ought to have derived our result if only we had known the answer before we began.

10. To cheat; to betray; = *FRAME *v.* 10. *slang* (orig. *U.S.*).

1903 A. H. LEWIS *Boss* viii. 100 Twelve honest dullards who called themselves a jury, despite his protestations that he was 'being jobbed', instantly declared him guilty. **1904** *McClure's Mag.* Nov. 64/1 Now she was coming back, swearing she'd been 'jobbed', the judge had been bought, and the jury corrupted. **1926** J. BLACK *You can't Win* xxiii. 353 It has always been a question with me where this framing and jobbing started; whether the defense originally began it..or whether it was the other way round. *Ibid.* 366, I was in the district attorney's office ..and I know you got 'jobbed'. I'll take your case for nothing. **1972** C. DRUMMOND *Death at Bar* v. 110 Funny you not minding Alwyn jobbin' your mum, not to mention your lawful wedded hubby. **1972** J. PHILIPS *Vanishing Senator* (1973) I. ii. 11 'Peter is troubled by the possibility that Jeremy Lloyd was jobbed by the Justice Department.'.. 'You think Lloyd is innocent?' **1973** K. GILES *File on Death* ii. 28 You want to watch or they'll job you on that.

jobation. Add: (Later examples of *jawbation.*) Also, a long discussion.

1916 'TAFFRAIL' *Pincher Martin* v. 75 Well, after a lot of jawbation we got him into the boat. **1925** P. GIBBS *Unchanging Quest* vii. 51, I used to watch Katherine while all this jawbation was in progress. **1938** H. G. WELLS *Apropos of Dolores* iv. 227 They aren't happy until the hand's been played [*sc.* at bridge] and the jawbation begins.

jobbing, *vbl. sb.*[2] Add: **1.** (*Spec. printing*), the printing of jobs (JOB *sb.*[2] 1 c.); also *attrib.* and *Comb.* as JOB *sb.*[2] 7, *jobbing case, fount, office, press, printer, printing, type, work.*

1841 W. SAVAGE *Dict. Art of Printing* 428 Jobbing is an extensive business in London. **1861** [in Dict.]. **1872** *Printers' Register* Apr. 114/1 The difficulty often experienced in laying Jobbing Founts. **1884** J. GOULD *Letter-Press Printer* (ed. 3) 78 Every compositor should endeavour to make himself acquainted with the composition of miscellaneous work, as it is a great source of annoyance to find that a man who is put on to assist cannot earn his wages, but is in fact a hindrance to others in a jobbing office. **1888** C. T. JACOBI *Printers' Vocab.* 68 *Jobbing cases*, double cases made with upper and lower in one. They are sometimes made treble. **1892** A. POWELL *Southward's Pract. Printing* (ed. 4) vi. 41 Jobbing Type is so called because it is used for 'jobs', i.e., for work like cards, circulars, letter headings, and advertisements. **1924** *Southward's Mod. Printing* (ed. 5) I. ii. 9 (*caption*) Small jobbing office. *Ibid.* v. 37 The ordinary arrangement causes the 49 boxes, in seven rows, for the capitals, to be much too small for jobbing founts. For this reason, double cases are now being made with only five or six rows of boxes. *Ibid.* li. 328 Jobbing work is a term applied to every kind of printing except book-work and newspaper work. **1946** A. MONKMAN in H. Whetton *Pract. Printing & Binding* vii. 75/1 There is still a wide variety of work available to the general or jobbing printer. **1960** P. M. HANDOVER *Printing in London* vii. 172 (*heading*) Jobbing. *Ibid.* vii. 173 The range of jobbing is so great that it would be possible to confine the following pages to a single subject, such as printed games. **1960** G. A. GLAISTER *Gloss. Bk.* 204/1 *Jobbing types*, types used for jobbing printing. **1966** BERRY & POOLE *Ann. Printing* 236/2 This [*sc.* Gordon's 'Alligator' Press 1851] was a jobbing press with a platen standing fixed at an angle of 45 degrees. *Ibid.* 248/2, 1870..A collection of 'artistic' jobbing work..the work of Oscar H. Harpel..was published in Cincinnati. *Ibid.* 253/2, 1880..The [Printers' International Specimen] Exchange was commenced with the object of fostering good jobbing printing. **1972** *Jrnl. Printing Hist. Soc.* 1971 VII. 38 *Double case, improved double case, improved jobbing case*, British terms for full size job cases which put the lower case letters in the left two thirds and the capitals in the right third of the case. *Ibid.*, Most printers both in America and in Britain were forced to add more and more of the new letters to their stores of type in order to remain competitive in the jobbing printing business. *Ibid.*, J. L. Ringwalt [and others]..offer succinct but accurate accounts of the forces that brought about the design and production of these new jobbing types. **1973** *Univ. of Stirling Press Room* (Univ. of Stirling Library), The Press Room contains a large assortment of printing types, jobbing cases, galleys, chases, composing sticks, rules and leads. **1973** *Times Lit. Suppl.* 7 Dec. 1500/3 These principles underlie the construction of most of the presses now operating, from jobbing presses to the largest newspaper machine.

3. (Earlier example.)

1780 A. YOUNG *Tour in Ireland* II. ix. 41 Lists and tables of the names of all persons who have obtained presentments,..should be given freely by the jurymen, to all their acquaintance, that every man might know, to whose carelessness or jobbing, the public wes indebted for bad roads.

jobbing-master. (Later example.)

1960 G. E. EVANS *House in Furrow* xv. 193 A jobbing-master at The Rampant Horse, kept about six horses for use in broughams and so on.

jo·b-hunter. *colloq.* [f. JOB *sb.*[2] + HUNTER 1 b.] One who seeks employment. So **jo·b-hunting** *vbl. sb.* and *ppl. a.*, and (as back-formations) **jo·b-hunt** *v.* and *sb.*

1928 *Daily Tel.* 13 Nov. 9/3 His abrupt departure without returning to Washington will serve as a notice to job-hunters..that he intends to make up his own mind about all important appointments. **1930** H. CRANE *Let.* 16 Mar. (1965) 349 I've really never known so discouraging a time job-hunting. **1946** *Vogue* June 88/2 Hardly anyone's prepared to job-hunt till they've had their demobilisation leave. **1956** W. H. WHYTE *Organization Man* (1957) ix. 113 Job-hunting seniors. **1965** H. WAUGH *Girl on Run* (1966) x. 63 If the idea falls through, then you can job hunt. **1970** *Physics Bull.* Mar. 106/1, I launched into my own 'job hunt': the only way to see the full picture was to go out and see industry for myself. **1972** M. JONES *Life on Dole* II. v. 120 Every day, they.. study the advertisements. Then they go job-hunting. **1973** *Sci. Amer.* Apr. 63/2 (Advt.), How to job hunt for a 20% to 50% salary increase.

jobless, *a.* Restrict *rare* to sense in Dict. and add: **2.** Out of work, unemployed. Also as *sb. collect.* So **jo·blessness**, the state of being out of work.

1923 *Public Opinion* 30 Mar. 304/1 He means not the fear of foremen so much as the fear of joblessness. **1923** *Glasgow Herald* 25 Oct. 7 The demand that would ensue for land users would mean jobs for jobless men. **1937** *Times Lit. Suppl.* 16 Oct. 755/2 The later episodes showing the graduates of the college being set free into a jobless world full of depression are not so agreeable. **1958** *Economist* 1 Nov. 415/1 One-sixth to one-fourth of the labour force has been jobless for several months. **1964** *Economist* 11 Jan. 110/1 The realities behind joblessness. **1970** *Times* 7 Sept. 16 (*headline*) Jobless total must go higher says Paish. **1971** *Nature* 8 Oct. 369/2, 4·4 per cent of the engineers who do not possess a degree of any kind were jobless in the summer.

Jo block, colloq. abbrev. of *Johansson block* (see *JOHANSSON). Also *fig.*

1936 H. D. BURGHARDT *Machine Tool Operation* (ed. 2) I. xi. 274 Size blocks may be used also instead of the pin gauge for spacing the holes. The most accurate of these gauges are the Johansson gauge blocks or 'Jo-blocks', which measure accurately in millionths of an inch. **1942** F. H. COLVIN *Gages* viii. 96 Standard measuring blocks, once known largely as 'Jo' blocks from the name of the first maker, Johannsen. **1957** R. A. HEINLEIN *Door into Summer* (1960) ii. 41, I had known Ricky half her life and if there ever was a human being honest as a Jo block, Ricky was she. **1966** G. W. MICHALEC *Precision Gearing* xi. 564 Using a very accurate input for positioning the carriage, such as master Jo-blocks.., the output can be observed and plotted.

jo·bmongering, *vbl. sb. rare.* [f. JOBMONGER + -ING[1].] The action or practice of a jobmonger.

1901 *Daily Chron.* 18 Dec. 5/1 Has Tammany no synonym? Or what about jobmongering? **1927** *Glasgow Herald* 24 Mar. 4 The intriguing and jobmongering of the Base.

jobster (dʒǫ·bstəɹ). [f. JOB *sb.*[2] + -STER.] = JOBBER[2].

1892 W. W. GREENER *Breech-Loader* 117 If unable to send [a damaged gun] to the makers, avoid advertising jobsters. **1897** *N.Y. Times* 15 Nov., The Hawaiian jobsters are astir again...They seem to feel sure of the administration. **1901** *Westm. Gaz.* 7 May 2/2 All the jobsters, speculators, South African financiers, all the coal and steel owners, who in 1899 cheered on the war. **1913** R. M. LA FOLLETTE *Autobiogr.* 167 He was not in favor of the spoilsman or the jobster. **1964** R. M. BUCK *Grim Truth about Fluoridation* iv. 23 (*heading*) Federal jobsters disagree.

Jocism (dʒōu·siz'm). [ad. F. *Jocisme*, acronym from the initial letters of *Jeunesse Ouvrière Chrétienne*, Christian working youth, set up by Joseph Cardijn in Belgium in 1924, and subsequently extended in Europe: see -ISM.] An organization which aimed at spreading Christianity amongst working people. So **Jo·cist** *sb.* and *a.*

1935 *Catholic Worker* Nov. 3/2 It is necessary to have study circles exclusively for the young wage-earners... Let us see how the Jocists (Catholic working youth) run theirs. **1939** *Theology* XXXIX. 432 Jocism has as its final end the conquest of the entire working class, the whole world, for Christ and His Church. *Ibid.* 437 The apex of the Jocist organization. **1951** *Scottish Jrnl. Theol.* IV. 160 This theory, sometimes derided by its opponents as 'Jocist romanticism', has been the main support, particularly in Anglo-Catholic circles, of much Christian social doctrine. **1960** *Rev. Politics* XXII. 339 From the beginning Mounier was against any political movement by a specifically confessional group (such as the Jocist movement).

Jock[1]. Add: **1. b.** A Scottish (or † northern English) sailor; a Scottish soldier or a member of a Scottish regiment; any Scotsman. Freq. as a nickname. *slang.*

1788 GROSE *Dict. Vulgar T.* (ed. 2), *Jock*,..a jeering appellation for a north-country seaman, particularly a collier. *a* **1865** SMYTH *Sailor's Word-Bk.* (1867) 413 *Jocks*, Scotch seamen. **1914** R. HODDER *Brit. Regiments* 17 'The Jocks.' The origin of this name for the Scots Guards is obvious. **1918** H. MATTHEWS in Murdoch & Drake-Brockman *Austral. Short Stories* (1951) 242 And he had to admit that some of the Jocks and Tommies from France were fine fellows. **1925** FRASER & GIBBONS *Soldier & Sailor Words* 132 *Jocks*, Scotsmen in general. Men of a Highland regiment. **1930** BLUNDEN *De Bello Germanico* 17 An interminable stream of displeased and ejaculatory Jocks repeat the act. **1952** 'J. TEY' *Singing Sands* vii. 101 Mr. Mackay had been in North Africa with the Jocks. **1965** *New Statesman* 16 Apr. 606/3 Why can't the Jocks support their team without dressing up like that? **1968** *Scottish Field* Feb. 35/1 All the infantry officers..attached tremendous importance to the Scottishness of their regiments. Kilts, trews, bonnets, pipe bands..have helped

enormously to make the Jock the man he is. *Ibid.* 37/2 The Scots Guards could be described as typical Jocks. **1970** G. M. FRASER *General danced at Dawn* 46 Who knows your Jocks aren't my matelots?

jock². Add: Also as colloq. abbrev. of **disc-jockey*.

1952 in Wentworth & Flexner *Dict. Amer. Slang* (1960) 294/1 Already the jukes and jocks are dinning our ears with Christmas songs. **1972** *Islander* (Victoria, B.C.) 9 Jan. 14/4 Jocks..are pretty much a thing of the past.

jock³ (dʒǫk). *coarse slang.* [Origin unknown; perh. f. an old slang word *jockum, -am* penis (Farmer & Henley).] The genitals of a man (or † of a woman). So † **jock-gagger**, a man living upon the earnings of a prostitute (*Obs.*).

a **1790** H. T. POTTER *New Dict. Cant & Flash* (1795) 36 *Jock*, private parts of a man or woman. **1809** G. ANDREWES *Dict. Slang & Cant, Jock-gagger*, a sort of fellows who live on the prostitution of their wives, &c. **1846** *Swell's Night Guide* 123/1 *Jock*, man's privates. **1960** J. CROSS *Backward Sex* iii. 73 Sprigs clattering on the floor, knees, jocks, backsides and shouting as everybody dressed. **1966** 'L. LANE' *ABZ of Scouse* 56 *Jocks*, testicles. **1972** *Dict. Contemp. & Colloq. Usage* (Eng.-Lang. Inst. Amer.) 17/1 *Jock*,..*vulgar*, the penis.

jock⁴ (dʒǫk). *dial.* and *slang.* [Origin unknown.] Food. (See also *E.D.D.*)

1879 *Yorkshireman's Comic Ann.* 33 Monny a shift he wor put to to get jock eniff. **1881** B. PRESTON *Dial. & Other Poems* 3 An' bumps 'em dahn i' t'corner chair, An' gloars reyt hard at t'jock. **1966** H. SHEPPARD *Dict. Railway Slang* (ed. 2) 7 *Jock*, food. **1974** P. WRIGHT *Lang. Brit. Industry* vi. 59 Food becomes..*jock*.., and contrasts oddly with officialese.

jock⁵ (dʒǫk). *N. Amer. slang.* **1.** Abbrev. of *JOCK-STRAP I.

1952 B. MALAMUD *Natural* (1963) 68 He located his jock, with two red apples in it, swinging from a cord. **1973** W. MCCARTHY *Detail* ii. 87 He found the Beretta..as well as the jock strap. He quickly took off his trousers, put on the jock.

2. Abbrev. of *JOCK-STRAP 2.

1963 [see *JOCK-STRAP 2]. **1968** *N.Y. Times* 12 May IV. 13 An obstacle to such trust is the attitude of some students and faculty members who, for example, smear all anti-strike students with the blanket label of 'jocks'. **1969** C. DAVIDSON in Cockburn & Blackburn *Student Power* 351 The administration will try by a whole range of 'divide and rule' tactics such as fostering the 'Greek-Independent Split', sexual double standards, intellectuals *vs* 'jocks', [etc.]. **1970** *Globe Mag.* (Toronto) 26 Sept. 2/1 On the sundeck are the clubbers, the sweats, the jocks. **1972** *Time* 2 Oct. 41/2 Rocks for jocks, elementary geology course popular among athletes at Pennsylvania.

jocker (dʒǫ·kəɹ). *N. Amer. slang.* [f. *JOCK³ + -ER¹.] **a.** A tramp who is accompanied by a youth who begs for him or acts as his catamite. **b.** A male homosexual.

1893 'J. FLYNT' in *Cent. Mag.* Nov. 107/2 Subject to the whims and passions of various 'jockers', or protectors. **1913** 'A No. 1' *Trail of Tramps* 72 A simple-faced chap.. played the deaf and dumb game, for which purpose his jocker had forced him to learn the sign language. **1923** [see *GUNSEL I]. **1931** 'D. STIFF' *Milk & Honey Route* iii. 34 While it is true that the punk serves the jocker..it is not accurate to call this exploitation. *Ibid.* xiv. 161 Whenever a man travels around with a lad he is apt to be labeled a 'jocker' or a 'wolf'. **1935** A. J. POLLOCK *Underworld Speaks* 64/2 *Jocker*, one who practices sodomy (ockerjay). **1950** H. E. GOLDIN *Dict. Amer. Underworld Lingo* 111/1 *Jocker*, an active pederast. **1972** B. RODGERS *Queens' Vernacular* 156 *Jocker* is synonymous with wolf: his role in prison parodies the husband's relationship in a marriage. **1972** J. WAMBAUGH *Blue Knight* (1973) iv. 54 Roxie hustles the guys who want a queen, and the kid goes after the ones who want a jocker. This jocker would probably become a queen himself.

jockette (dʒǫke·t). [f. JOCK² + -ETTE.] Occas. used for: a female jockey.

1969 *N.Y. Times* 17 Jan. 21/3 The male riders, determined not to let the so-called jockettes compete against them, continue to follow 'Vive la Différence!' **1972** *Sunday Express* 11 June 16/4 That leaves Mr. Rippon about as much chance of displacing him as jockette Miss Meriel Tufnell has of dislodging Lester Piggott from his chosen mount in the St. Leger. **1973** *Times* 17 Oct. 13/3 We have now reached the stage when theoretically a 'jockette' could ride in the 1975 Derby.

jockey, *sb.* Add: **5. b.** *transf.* A driver of a motor vehicle. Freq. preceded by a *sb.* used *attrib.* So *garage jockey*, a garage attendant. Chiefly *N. Amer.*

1912 *Collier's* 28 Sept. 11/2 Some are, so to speak, 'gentlemen jockeys', and own, enter, and drive their own cars for the fun of the thing. **1929** D. RUNYON in *Hearst's International* Nov. 72/2 Jerking me into the cab and telling the jockey to go to the Penn Station. **1936** *Daily Herald* 5 Aug. 8/4 Here is a short list of busmen's slang phrases:.. *Jockey* (*Driver*). **1942** BERREY & VAN DEN BARK *Amer. Thes. Slang* § 723/2 *Automobile racer*, auto or buzzer jockey, ..speed jockey,..suicide jockey. *Ibid.* § 723/4 *Motorcycle racer*, broadsider, jockey,..motor jockey. *Ibid.* § 765/2 *Commercial driver* (*bus, taxicab, truck*),..jockey, motor jockey. *Ibid.* § 765/5 *Truck driver*, truck jockey or spinner. .. *Spec.* juice jockey, a gasoline-truck driver; grunt-and-squeal jockey, a stock hauler;..suicide jockey, a nitroglycerine hauler. **1945** *Amer. Speech* XX. 148/1 *Jeep jockey*, truck driver. **1954** *Chicago Tribune* 20 July A. 17/1 Trolley jockey gets even with slowpokes. **1968** *Drive* Spring 113 The driver of any heavy-load vehicle is known as the pilot or jockey. **1970** *Globe & Mail* (Toronto) 25 Sept. 37/3 (Advt.), Executive 2 bedroom, 2 baths professionally decorated, overlooking rose garden, pool treed ravine. Doorman and car jockey. **1972** *Nat. Geographic* Aug. 209/1 Sweat-streaked truck jockey. **1973** J. CLEARY *Ransom* i. 33 There had been no trouble with the garage jockey. He had been lounging in a chair in the tiny office.

c. = **disc-jockey*.

1963 B. W. ALDISS *Airs of Earth* 69 We stayed with the jocular jockey, hoping to catch a news bulletin, as I drove south. **1971** *Daily Tel.* 5 Jan. 10/1 The same 30 turns. Different jockeys. Different stations, but no real choice. **1972** P. BLACK *Biggest Aspidistra* III. iv. 179 *Housewives' Choice*, a favourite shop-window for records and jockeys from 1946 to 1967.

7. [Shortening of *jockey-sleeve*.] *Fashion.* (See quot. 1960.)

1896 *Godey's Mag.* Feb. 211/1 Jockeys cut in fanciful shape are set into the shoulders of many of the sleeves. **1960** CUNNINGTON & BEARD *Dict. Eng. Costume* 118/2 *Jockey*,..a flat trimming applied over the outer part of the shoulder of a dress and having the lower border free. **1963** A. GERNSHEIM *Fashion & Reality* I. 27 By 1841 tight sleeves were..often headed by a *mancheron* (later called jockey).

8. a. (*b*) *jockey-back, -leg*: applied to a style of boot.

1909 *Boot Catal.*, Gentleman's brown calf lace, whole golosh, jockey back. **1862** *Illustr. Catal. Internat. Exhib., Industr. Dept., Brit. Div.* II. No. 4658, Skins, kips, fronts, shoe legs, jockey legs, cordovan, grained calf.

9. jockey briefs, shorts, short under-drawers for men; **jockey club,** (*b*) a toilet-water releasing chiefly rose and jasmine scents; **jockey spider** *Austral.*, a venomous black spider, *Latrodectus hasseltii*, the female of which is distinguished by a red stripe on the upper side of its abdomen; also = KATIPO; also ellipt. *jockey*; **jockey-stick** *U.S.* (see quots.); **jockey strap** = *JOCK-STRAP I ?*Obs.*; **jockey-wheel,** (*b*) a small adjustable wheel at the nose of a caravan.

1966 J. GARDNER *Amber Nine* ix. 130 He stripped to his jockey briefs. **1855** G. W. S. PIESSE *Art of Perfumery* 122 Jockey Club Bouquet. **1859** in Bartlett *Dict. Amer.* (1860) 396, I..used cologne, hair oil, and scented my handkerchief with 'jockey-club'. **1907** *Yesterday's Shopping* (1969) 521/1 Highly concentrated Essences... Jockey Club, Maiglöckchen, [etc.]. **1941** W. A. POUCHER *Perfumes, Cosmetics & Soaps* (ed. 6) II. vii. 281 Jockey Club...Bergamot oil...Jasmin...Rose...Tuberose...Mace oil... Civet extract. **1973** *Sat. Rev. World* (U.S.) 6 Nov. 29/2 The following..of our own exclusive scents..are presently available: 1 Jockey Club, 2 Number Six, [etc.]. **1951** G. MARX *Let.* 18 Jan. (1967) 194, I remember in 1932 telling Truman to stick to the haberdashery business, that there was a fortune in shirts and jockey shorts. **1968** J. R. ACKERLEY *My Father & Myself* 210, I took to wearing tight jockey shorts. **1971** B. MALAMUD *Tenants* 210 The bridegroom, in a smoked raffia skirt from waist to knees over his jockey shorts. **1933** *Bulletin* (Sydney) 15 Nov. 20/4 *Latrodectus*, which we call the 'redback' or 'jockey'. **1936** K. C. MCKEOWN *Spider Wonders Austral.* xi. 155 In the Jockey Spider the red stripe is a direct and unmistakable warning. **1942** C. BARRETT *On Wallaby* ii. 30 An infant bitten by a 'jockey'..died six hours later. **1944** *Living off Land* vi. 129 The red-back spider, or katipo, also called the 'jockey' spider, definitely is harmful. **1965** *Austral. Encycl.* VIII. 236/2 The best-known Australian member [of the comb-footed group of spiders] is the red-back, red-spot, or jockey spider, *Latrodectus hasseltii*, with a distribution from Arabia to New Guinea, the whole of Australia, the Pacific Islands, Hawaii and New Zealand; in the last-named country it is called 'katipo' (night-stinger). **1887** E. B. CUSTER *Tenting on Plains* xii. 352 [In driving a prairie schooner] a small hickory stick, about five feet long, called the jockey-stick, not unlike a rake-handle, is stretched between a pilot [mule] and his mate. **1968** R. F. ADAMS *Western Words* (rev. ed.), *Jockey stick*, in freighting, a hickory stick,..stretched between a pilot mule or horse and its mate. **1896** *Crescent* (Brooklyn, N.Y.) 1 Dec. 33/1 (Advt.), Suspensories, Jockey Straps. **1909** *Spalding's Athletic Library* (N.Y.) Group XV. No. 333 (Advt.), Bike Jockey Strap Suspensory. **1952** *Motor Manual* (ed. 34) xiii. 248 Car and caravan can be connected or disconnected in a matter of a few seconds. To help this operation, the forward end of the van chassis is provided with a jockey wheel to take the forward weight. **1966** *Caravanning* ('Know the Game' Series) 12 The nose weight of a caravan can vary from a few pounds to over a hundredweight. On most vans there is a telescopic jockey wheel to facilitate raising the nose.

jockey, *v.* Add: **1. d.** Freq. in phr. *to jockey for position*, to try to gain an advantageous position (in a race, contest, etc.).

1908 *Daily Chron.* 16 July 8/1 The fastest time was that by J. Matthews..but that counts for little in a cycle race owing to the..jockeying..for position in the final sprint. **1955** *Times* 27 July 6/7 In Alberta when there was no jury, congestion was caused by lawyers jockeying for position in order to appear before the right judge. **1969** AUDEN *City without Walls* 105 They're jockeying for position round the first bend.

jockeying, *vbl. sb.* **2.** (Earlier Amer. example.)

1779 G. WILLIAMS *Let.* 28 Feb. in *Essex Inst. Hist. Coll.* (1907) XLIII. 202 The Makers of Money sent it to there servants to purchas goods and thay knew it was to be out of circulation in a few months. It would be called by some Jockeing.

Jocko. (Earlier examples.)

1777 P. THICKNESSE *Year's Journey* II. xl. 68 My monkey..rode postilion upon my sturdy horse... Jocko put whole towns in motion. **1778** *Ibid.* (ed. 2) II. xlv. 106, I have seen an animal of the Jocko kind, when chained to a spot, contrive to get his food, which was out of his reach, by an address which many human creatures would have perished for want of abilities to put in practice.

jock-strap (dʒǫ·kˌstræp). [f. *JOCK³ + STRAP *sb.*] **1.** A supporter or protector for the male genitals, worn esp. by sportsmen; also (occas.), a *CACHE-SEXE.

1897 *U.S. Patent Office Index* 27 Bennett, Charles F., Chicago, Ill. Combined jock-strap and suspensory. **1911** *T. Eaton & Co. Catal.* Spring & Summer 179/2 Athletic Support. Sharp & Smith's Bike-Jock Strap, being made entirely of elastic. **1929** T. WOLFE *Look Homeward, Angel* (1930) II. xiv. 191 The checking of overcoats, evening wraps, jock-straps, and jewellery. **1933** E. E. CUMMINGS *eimi* 52 Do I seriously..seem to see your human mind squatting in your magic jockstrap, freely watching Hitchy Goomy Gitchie Koo (the sickest medicine-man of them all) turn your ailments into formulas? **1935** *New Statesman* 14 Sept. 357/1 (Advt.), The Linia Belt, including a Linia Jock Strap. **1936** H. MILLER *Black Spring* 247 The night is cold but the queen is naked save for a jock-strap. **1947** 'A. P. GASKELL' *Big Game* 15, I had to undo my pants and look to see whether I'd put on my jock-strap. **1954** *Dancing Times* Mar. 400 Articles for Sale. Jock straps for either sex in pink, white or black. **1960** *Guardian* 23 Sept. 26/7 A Nubian chauffeur in a leopard-skin jockstrap. **1969** *Daily Tel.* 7 Mar. 21/1 It is the first play in which I remember to have encountered an actor with a jockstrap which squeaks when pushed.

2. An athletic (as distinguished from an æsthetic or intellectual) man (esp. one at a university); a 'hearty'. *N. Amer. slang.*

1956 *Amer. Speech* XXXI. 192 A healthy, athletic young man addicted to sports may wince under the pointed *jockstrap marine*. **1963** *Ibid.* XXXVIII. 169 A college athlete: jock (81), animal (32)...The full synecdoche itself, jockstrap, was also reported once.

Hence **jo·ck-strapped** *a.*; **jo·ck-strapper.**

1960 *Spectator* 23 Sept. 432 Even prints biographical notes on its jock-strapped heroes. **1967** N. MAILER *Cannibals & Christians* I. 14 Scranton had none of the heft of a political jockstrapper like Goldwater.

jodhpurs (dʒǫ·dpŭəɹz, dʒōᵘ·d-), *sb. pl.* Also **jodhpor, jodpor(e, judhpur,** etc. [Name of a town and district in Rajasthan, a state in north-western India.] **1. a.** Riding-breeches reaching to the ankle, combining breeches and gaiters. Also *attrib.* in *sing.* **b.** Indian trousers cut loosely at the top but close-fitting below the knee.

1899 G. W. STEEVENS *In India* iv. 28 The Jodhpur riding-breeches—breeches and gaiters all in one piece, as full as you like above the knee, fitting tight below it, without a single button or strap..are on the way to be world-famous. **1913** E. M. FORSTER *Let.* 1 Jan. in *Hill of Devi* (1953) 21 My legs were clad in Jodpores made of white muslin. **1925** *Vogue* 1 Sept. 66 Judhpur. **1927** *Daily Express* 14 Nov. 5/2 These ski-ing suits are made with a plain, well-cut coat and jodhpurs or trousers. **1928** *Ibid.* 2 May 13 Finding some new jodhpors in his room, [he] could not resist trying them on. **1931** *Times* 7 May 17/5 Princess Elizabeth of York is shown dressed for a ride with her fair curls shining and wearing a yellow jumper pulled down over her jodhpurs. **1952** R. S. SUMMERHAYS *Elements of Riding* (ed. 3) xv. 87 Jodhpurs ..are less expensive than breeches. **1957** *Encycl. Brit.* XIII. 80/2 The Jodhpur style of riding breeches (also seen, made of cotton, as normal walking garb in northern India) comprises breeches and gaiters in one. **1969** G. GREENE *Travels with my Aunt* I. iii. 19 Men..in tweed coats..split horsily behind, gathered round a girl in jodhpurs. **1973** 'B. MATHER' *Snowline* xvii. 203 The Ismailis..dress in a distinctive style—jodhpurs, silk frock-coats and small embroidered skull-caps.

2. jodhpur boot, an ankle-high boot, orig. as worn with jodhpurs.

1939 E. HEMINGWAY *Fifth Column* II. iii. 61 *Dorothy Bridges*, wearing..a tweed skirt, wool stockings and jodhpur boots. **1972** *Police Rev.* 10 Nov. 1472/1 (Advt.), Angel (Reg. Brand) Best Jodhpur Boot.

Hence **jo·dhpured** *a.*, wearing jodhpurs.

1969 *Daily Tel.* 8 Sept. 10/5 Small, pig-tailed Thelwell girls in voluminous riding-macs that flap round the bottoms of their plump, jodhpured legs. **1971** D. FRANCIS *Bonecrack* vii. 94, I watched the trim jodhpured figure walk off.

Jōdo (dʒōᵘ·do). Also **Jō-do.** [Jap., lit. 'purified land'.] **a.** A Japanese Buddhist sect which teaches salvation through absolute faith in the Buddha Amida and constant repetition of a formulaic prayer invoking his name. **b.** One of the heavens of Buddhist faith; *spec.* the Western Paradise, where the Buddha Amida resides. Also *attrib.* or as *adj.*

1727 J. G. SCHEUCHZER tr. *Kæmpfer's Hist. Japan* I. IV. iii. 287 Zealous persons, chiefly the followers of the Sect of *Siodo*. **1886** B. NANJIO *Short Hist. Twelve Jap. Buddhist Sects* ix. (*title*) The Jō-do-shū, or Pure Land sect. **1895** W. E. GRIFFIS *Relig. Japan* ix. 268 The Japanese technical term, *'tariki'*, or relying upon the strength of another, renouncing all idea of *ji-riki* or self-power is the substance of the Jō-dō doctrine. **1911** B. H. CHAMBERLAIN *Jap. Poetry* IV. 215 *Jōdo*, literally, 'the Pure Land',

is one of the Buddhist heavens fabled to exist in the West. **1938** D. T. Suzuki *Zen Buddhism & its Influence on Jap. Culture* I. iii. 37 The Jōdo appeals naturally more to plebeian requirements because of the simpleness of its faith and teaching. **1970** J. W. Hall *Japan from Prehist. to Mod. Times* vi. 74 In the tenth century new and more accessible teachings began to gain currency among the aristocracy. Among these was the worship of Amida, the Buddha of the Pure Land (Jōdō) or Western Paradise.

jods (dʒǫdz, dʒōᵘdz), *colloq.* abbrev. of *JODHPURS *sb. pl.* Also (in *sing.*) *attrib.*

1959 J. Verney *Friday's Tunnel* xxvii. 258, I had nothing on but a sopping shirt and jods. *Ibid.* 259 The thought of riding reminded me of gob-stoppers. I found three left in my jod pocket. **1960** E. H. Clements *Honey for Marshal* ii. 43 Better take her jods! Your children do ride, don't they?

Joe, *sb.*[2] Add: **1. b.** phr. *not for Joe* (*Joseph*), by no means, not on any account.

1844 C. Selby *London by Night* (1886) II. i. 9/1 *Jack.* Who's to pay? *Ned.* Whichever you please. *Jack.* Oh! in that case you may as well settle it. *Ned.* Not for Joseph! You asked me to tea. *c* **1867** *Broadside Ballad* in Farmer & Henley *Slang* (1896) IV. 76/2 Not for Joe... Not for Joseph, if he knows it. **1928** Galsworthy *Swan Song* II. xiii. 219 Not if he knew it—not for Joe.

c. *int.* (See quots. 1855[1] and 1862.) So as *v. trans.* (See quot. 1861.) *Austral.* and *N.Z. slang.*

1855 W. Howitt *Land, Labour & Gold, or Two Yrs. in Victoria* I. xxii. 400 The well-known cry of 'Joe! Joe!'..which means..one of the myrmidons of Charley Joe, as they familiarly style Mr. [Charles Joseph] La Trobe [Governor of Victoria]. **1855** C. R. Thatcher in Stewart & Keesing *Old Bush Songs* (1957) 111 Should a body 'Joe' a body For having on a hat? **1861** T. McCombie *Austral. Sk.* 135 To 'Joey' or 'Joe' a person on the diggings, or anywhere else in Australia, is grossly to insult and ridicule him. **1862** E. Hodder *Memories N.Z. Life* 188 As [the diggers] descried us approaching on the rocks, a simultaneous cry of 'Joe! Joe!' was raised. This is a popular cry on the New Zealand diggings and is used to hail any 'new chums' who may appear. It had its origin at the Australian diggings, where licenses were granted to all who held claims... When the police came upon the ground, to inspect licences, the cry of 'Joe!' was raised. **1871** C. L. Money *Knocking about in N.Z.* vii. 103 The word 'Joe' expresses derision usually bestowed on new chums on the diggings, or any man acting, or dressing, or speaking in any way considered as outré by the diggers themselves. *Ibid.*, Among the first to 'Joe' me at the beginning. **1917** 'H. H. Richardson' *Fortunes R. Mahony* I. i. 11 An odd figure..crying at the top of her voice: 'Joe, boys!—Joe, Joe, Joey!'

5. *colloq.* A fellow, 'guy', chap; (in certain countries) an American. Cf. **G.I. Joe*, **Holy Joe*.

1846 *Swell's Night Guide* 123/1 *Joe*, an imaginary person, nobody, as Who do those things belong to? Joe. **1906** E. Dyson *Fact'ry 'Ands* viii. 92 Why, man, it's meat 'n' beer t' them Joes what go in fer bringin' ther wanderers 'ome. **1932** *Amer. Speech* June 333 *Joe*, term used to designate anyone whose real name is unknown. When used with a place or profession 'Joe' indicates a perfect example of the type connected with that place or profession. **1945** 'A. Boucher' in M. & G. Gordon *Pride of Felons* (1964) 80 The customers are mostly elderly Italian businessmen who are good Joes. **1947** *Amer. Speech* XXII. 55/1 *Joe*, name given by the natives [in the Pacific] to any American. **1952** S. Selvon *Brighter Sun* iv. 55 In Trinidad... All Americans..are known as 'Joes'. **1957** J. Osborne *Entertainer* viii. 71 While everyone else is sitting on their hands you're the Joe at the back cheering. **1962** E. Lacy *Freeloaders* vii. 133 Way I see it, Gil is an American... We joes have to stick together. **1969** M. Pugh *Last Place Left* xvi. 110 A few of his men were Irish moleskin joes from the hydro-electric operation. **1972** J. Burmeister *Running Scared* xii. 169 Be a good Joe and take the pills. Please. **1973** *Publishers Weekly* 26 Mar. 65/2 The average Joe probably thinks that cyclists..are eccentric folk.

b. Joe College. 'A college boy; *esp.* one devoted to amusement' (Webster, 1961).

1932 *Amer. Speech* June 333 'Joe College' is a perfect specimen of the college man. Often used with 'himself'. **1964** *Ibid.* XXXIX. 193 The net effect of the publications on college slang has been to encourage the image of perky Joe College.

c. Joe Bloggs, Joe Blow (*U.S.*), **Joe Do(a)kes:** names applied to a hypothetical average or ordinary man.

c **1941** Kendall & 'Viney' *Dict. Army–Navy Slang*, Joe Blow...means any soldier. **1943** *Amer. Speech* XVIII. 109 *Joe Doakes*, generic term for all ball players. **1945** L. Lane *How to become a Comedian* x. 92 He would ask the conductor if he had seen 'Joe Dokes' last night. **1956** B. Holiday *Lady sings Blues* (1973) ix. 90 But just let me walk out of the club one night with a young white boy of my age, whether it was John Roosevelt, the President's son, or Joe Blow. **1968** *Jazz Monthly* 15/1 All these items are essentially jazz-tinged versions of Joe Doakes's favourite melodies. **1969** *Guardian* 6 Mar. 7/2 LSD can be taken by Joe Bloggs on a lump of sugar. **1970** C. Major *Dict. Afro-Amer. Slang* 71 *Joe Blow*,..horn-blowing musician..came to mean any male person. **1971** *Daily Tel.* 27 July 13/5 In too many cases these forms arrive on the desk of a busy executive who concludes that Joe Bloggs down the corridor must have signed the order. **1973** K. Giles *File on Death* iv. 98 Joe Bloggs, the honest garage mechanic.

d. Joe Soap: name applied to a 'dumb' person, a mug; also, more generally, a quite ordinary person, any person.

1943 Hunt & Pringle *Service Slang* 41 *Joe Soap*, the 'dumb' or not so intelligent members of the forces. The men who are 'over-willing' and therefore the usual 'stooges'. **1966** 'L. Lane' *ABZ of Scouse* 56 *Joe Soap*, whozit, whatzisname. When asked by the police to account for the possession of a stolen article the answer often is *I got guv it by Joe Soap.* **1968** 'B. Mather' *Springers* xi. 111, I sat there like Joe Soap on guard; feeling guilty if I dozed off. **1969** *Guardian* 31 Mar. 15/8 Socialists have become..over-eager to find out what Joe Soap is doing in order to tell him not to do it. **1972** J. Brown *Chancer* ix. 118 Who do you think I am, moosh? Joe Soap?

6. Joe Blake. *Austral. rhyming slang.* A snake.

1927 M. Terry *Through Land of Promise* ix. 123 I'll bet you what you like there are Joe Blakes in this camp. **1934** *Bulletin* (Sydney) 22 Aug. 20/2 At Bob's prompting Billy sneaked up quietly and quickly behind Joe Blake, and, seizing the tail firmly, gave a terrific swing round his head. **1970** *Sunday Mail Mag.* (Brisbane) 11 Jan. 3/1 We've camped..with the Joe Blakes, the goannas, the flies, and 4000 skinny jumbucks.

7. A French Canadian. *Canad. slang.*

1968 R. I. McDavid in *Mencken's Amer. Lang.* 368 Frog is not applied in Canada to a French Canadian, who is a Canuck or simply Joe, and prefers to be called a Habitant. **1966** *Globe & Mail* (Toronto) 19 Apr. 6/6 Their waspish counterparts in Quebec always refer to 'pea-soupers' or 'Joes'. The word 'Frog' in that connection went out of fashion 50 years ago.

joe (dʒōᵘ), *sb.*[3] *U.S. colloq.* [Origin unknown.] Coffee.

1941 J. Smiley *Hash House Lingo* 34 *Joe*, coffee. **1944** K. D. McCracken *Baby Flat-Top* 87 Quartermasters.. are inexhaustible in furnishing the Officer of the Deck with anything from the true wind and the relative humidity to a flashlight and a pot of Joe. **1953** C. M. Kornbluth *Syndic* (1964) viii. 80 Get me a mug of joe, sailor... Go get the coffee. **1963** 'E. McBain' *Ten plus One* (1964) v. 48 'Would you like some coffee?' Carella asked. 'Is there some?' 'Sure... Can we get two cups of joe?'

joe-pye weed. *N. Amer.* Also **joe pye.** [See quot. 1893.] Either of two tall, perennial herbs, *Eupatorium purpureum* or *E. maculatum*, belonging to the family Compositæ, and bearing clusters of purplish flowers.

1818 A. Eaton *Man. Bot.* (ed. 2) II. 245 *Eupatorium.. purpureum* (purple thoroughwort, or joe-pye). *Ibid.* *Eupatorium..verticillatum* (joe-pye's weed). **1866** Lindley & Moore *Treas. Bot.* II. 638/1 Joe-pye weed. An American name for *Eupatorium purpureum*. **1893** F. T. Dana *Wild Flowers* iii. 210 Joe-Pye-Weed. Trumpet-Weed. *Eupatorium purpureum*... 'Joe Pye' is said to have been the name of an Indian who cured typhus fever in New England by means of this plant. **1895** K. D. Wiggin *Village Watch-Tower* 42 Purple asters and gay Joe Pye waved their colors by the road-side. **1903** E. C. Waltz *Pa Gladden* vii. 144 In other Septembers the slope ..was lovely with..joepye-weed. **1949** *Nature Mag.* Apr. 187/2 Later the cowslips are replaced by purple loosestrife and that butterfly magnet, Joe-pye weed. **1954** C. J. Hylander *Macmillan Wild Flower Bk.* 412 Joe-Pye-weed is found from New England south to North Carolina and New Mexico.

joes (dʒōᵘz), *sb. pl. Austral. slang.* [Origin unknown.] Depression of spirits, the blues.

1916 C. J. Dennis *Moods of Ginger Mick* 27 'E's got the joes reel bad. *a* **1938** —— in *Penguin Bk. Austral. Ballads* (1964) 235 It gimme Joes to sit an' watch them two! **1957** V. Palmer *Seedtime* xx. 138 What I saw in the sugar country gave me the joes.

joey[1]**.** Restrict † *Obs.* to sense in Dict. and add: **2.** A threepenny bit. *slang.*

1936 'G. Orwell' *Keep Aspidistra Flying* i. 7 A Joey. He took out the miserable little threepenny-bit. **1945** Baker *Austral. Lang.* v. 109 *3d.*,..joey. **1965** *Australasian Post* 4 Mar. 46 *Threepence*, 'joe' or 'joey', though these..two words are now rarely heard. (A 'joey' was originally London slang for a fourpenny bit; and later was transferred to the English threepence). **1966** F. Shaw et al. *Lern Yerself Scouse* 33 *Joey*, threepence.

Joey[3] (dʒōᵘ·i). *colloq.* [Familiar abbrev. of the name of the clown *Joseph* Grimaldi (1779–1837).] A clown.

1896 G. B. Shaw *Our Theatres in Nineties* (1932) II. 105 Its [*sc.* philosophic comedy's] common Joeys with red-hot poker and sausages. **1926** *Amer. Speech* Feb. 283/2 I'm through with bein' a joey. Gettin' too old, thought I would never troupe again. **1962** D. H. Laurence in G. B. Shaw *Platform & Pulpit* p. xiii, Thus was created a paradox of the public simultaneously decrying Shaw for playing a 'Joey' rôle and seeking desperately to set a jester's cap upon his head. **1973** J. Wainwright *Devil you Don't* 121 A pensioner—gnarled hand gripping a walking-stick, grey hair peeping from beneath an old-fashioned flat cap, pullover, frayed jacket and baggy trousers—like a Joey, without make-up.

jog, *sb.*[1] Add: **2. b.** (Further examples in sense 'a slow measured trot or run'.)

1948 *Oxf. Pocket Bk. Athletic Training* iii. 32 A very slow jog, where the runner lands flat-footed with a slight jarring action. **1969** [see *JOG *v.* 4].

jog, *sb.*[2] Add: **3.** *Cryst.* A step in a dislocation where it passes from one atomic plane to another.

1951 N. F. Mott in *Proc. Physical Soc.* LXIV. B. 733 Supposing one of the expanding dislocation loops..cuts a screw dislocation, pictured as perpendicular to the plane of the paper. This will normally happen several times in the expansion of a loop in a real crystal. The loop will then necessarily contain what we call a 'jog', i.e. a point where the dislocation jumps from one slip plane to an adjacent one. **1955** *Rep. Conf. Defects Crystalline Solids 1954* (Physical Soc.) 391 If the section of the dislocation between the two parallel planes has a length of the order of the atomic distance, it is called a dislocation jog. **1960** *New Scientist* 6 Oct. 915/3 There is a theory based on the strain fields round the dislocations and the way they attract and repel each other, and a theory based on the way they get kinky ('jogs' is the technical word) when they cut through each other. **1966** C. R. Tottle *Sci. Engin. Materials* iv. 98 If the jog climbs, by moving into another slip plane, point defects are created, but the screw dislocation containing the jog can continue to slip.

jog, *v.* Add: **4.** Later examples in sense 'to run at a gentle pace' (esp. as part of a 'keep-fit' schedule).

1968 'E. V. Cunningham' *Margie* ix. 156 Fenton, who was jogging in place to keep his circulation up, explained that they were in a local elevator. **1969** *Age* (Melbourne) 24 May 17/4 Latest to join the 'jog' set is Sir Reginald Sholl, who was seen jogging around Fawkner Park. **1970** N. Armstrong et al. *First on Moon* ii. 37 There would be little time..to read or jog on the beach.

c. (Later example with *along*.)

1847 A. Brontë *Agnes Grey* xxii. 325 They're jogging along as usual, I suppose.

jogah (dʒōᵘ·gă). *slang.* Also **jogar.** [Origin unknown.] = *BUSKER[2].

1928 *Radio Times* 2 Nov. 302/1 'Varda the polone,' murmurs a 'jogah'. **1952** Granville *Dict. Theatr. Terms* 104 *Jogar*, a street-singer, or queue entertainer.

jogee, jogi, varr. Yogi.

1864 J. A. Grant *Walk across Afr.* 317 Like mad 'jogees' or devotees. **1899** *Folk-Lore* X. 394 The struggle for local supremacy between a Musalman saint and his rival and counterpart, a Hindu *jogi*. **1922** *Chambers's Jrnl.* 29 Apr. 343/2 Other *jogis* there are, with heavy iron rings in their ears.

‖ **joget** (dʒǫ·gĕt). Also *erron.* **jogget.** [Mal. *joget.*] A Malay popular dance, in which a couple improvises to the accompanying music. Also *attrib.*, and *transf.*, the place where such dancing occurs.

1895 F. A. Swettenham *Malay Sk.* vii. 45 Dancing girls..perform what is called the 'Jôget'—a real dance with an accompaniment of something like real music, though the orchestral instruments are very rude indeed. **1900** W. W. Skeat *Malay Magic* vi. 513 The *Joget*, a kind of dramatic and symbolical dance. **1910** R. J. Wilkinson *Papers on Malay Subjects: Life & Customs* III. 22 The *ronggeng*, *gamboh* and *joget* come from Java. **1959** P. Brown *As Far as Singapore* vi. 125 'It is the Malayan *jogget* dancing.'.. It was rather like an Oriental version of jiving, with the boy and girl facing each other and executing intricate steps to the rhythmic music, but never actually touching each other. **1963** J. Kirkup *Tropic Temper* xv. 163 The place where the dancing is done is called a joget. **1966** D. Forbes *Heart of Malaya* vii. 89 We were shown..an entertainment at court, providing the occasion for more music and for *joget* dances. **1972** M. Sheppard *Taman Indera* 92 (*caption*) The Trengganu palace *Joget* dancers in an 18th century dance. **1972** *Straits Times* (Malaysian ed.) 23 Nov. 4/4 Among the dances to be performed are..Joget.

jogged, *a.* Restrict ? *Obs.* to sense in Dict. and add: **b.** *Cryst.* Having a jog or jogs.

1962 *Phil. Mag.* VII. 83 Jogged dislocations can advance only if the jogs glide conservatively along the Burgers vector direction or by producing lines of point defects. **1973** *Nature* 3 Aug. 276/2 Bowed, looped and jogged dislocations.

jogger. Add: (Examples of 'one who jogs at a gentle pace for physical exercise'.)

1968 *Times* 24 May (N.Z. Suppl.) p. viii/5 The caption refers to the runner as 'a jogger out for his morning run'. In New Zealand the noun jogger is an acceptable..word because so many people..run for fitness. **1968** *Chicago Tribune* 9 July I. 12/1 Joggers have become an almost familiar sight thruout America in the last year. **1969** *Age* (Melbourne) 24 May 17/4 Ken Myer is a well-known jogger around the Toorak area.

jogging, *vbl. sb.* (Later examples.)

1948 K. S. Duncan *Oxf. Pocket Bk. Athletic Training* iii. 33 The runner should start any piece of jogging with the slow jog style. **1968** *Courier-Mail* (Brisbane) 4 May 4/6 Jogging enthusiasts say that it improves posture and waistline. **1972** *Publishers Weekly* 3 Apr. 64/1 His whole-hearted commitment to jogging..on five mile jaunts around New York's Central Park.

joggling-table (s.v. Joggle *v.*[1]). Add: (U.S. example); (*b*) *Printing* (see quot. 1947).

1849 *Ex. Doc. 31st U.S. Congress 1 Sess. House* No. 5. I. 435 It is probable that a set of joggling and sleeping tables will be added to the washing machinery. **1947** *Jrnl. R. Aeronaut. Soc.* LI. 319/1 Offset lithographic process...The mat surface is obtained by placing the template on a joggling table...When the table is joggled or agitated by a lever.., the constant scouring action.. produces a delicate mat surface.

jog-trot, *v.* **1.** (Later example.)

1968 *Courier-Mail* (Brisbane) 4 May 4/6 The latest American keep-fit craze—jogging. The idea is to jog-trot for 50 yards, then walk 50 yards and repeat this sequence until you are tired.

johachidolite (dʒohæ̆tʃi·dŏləit). *Min.* [f. *Jōhachidō*, Japanese name for the village of Sāngpal-dong in Kilchu Co., North Hamgyong Province, Korea: see -LITE.] A colourless hydrous fluoborate of sodium, calcium, and aluminium, $Na_4Ca_6Al_8B_{10}O_{25}(OH, F)_{20}$.

1942 IWASE & SAITO in *Sci. Papers Inst. Physical & Chem. Res.* (Tokyo) XXXIX. 302 Investigation on chemical composition and determination of some physical constants convincingly demonstrate that the blue fluorescent mineral here studied is a new mineral species for which we would like to present the name jōhachidōlite after Jōhachidō district, where we have come across it. **1968** *Amer. Mineralogist* LIII. 2082 (*heading*) Johachidolite, a revised chemical formula.

Johannean, *a.* (Earlier example.)

1847 W. SMITH tr. *Fichte's Characteristics Present Age* 98 The Johannean Jesus knows no other God than the true God.

Johannes, Joannes. (Earlier example.)

1758 *Essex Inst. Hist. Coll.* (1881) XVIII. 102, I this day delivered one Johannes to Major Gage.

Johannisberger. Delete (?) *erron.* -**berg** and add later examples of the form *Johannisberg*.

1853 S. WHITING *Mem. Stomach* 112 From the Johannisberg, with the golden seal..down to the poverty-stricken Marsala. **1888** *Century Mag.* Apr. 875/1 This brief but finished composition stood in the same relation to the usual 'magazine story' that a glass of Johannisberg occupies to a draught of table d'hôte *vin ordinaire.* **1958** A. L. SIMON *Dict. Wines* 93/2 Plain Johannisberg..is never one of the best wines of Johannisberg. **1967** A. LICHINE *Encycl. Wines* 437/1 The estate-bottled (*Original-abfüllung*) Schloss Johannisberg is divided into three grades of quality and price.

johannsenite (dʒohæ·nsənəit). *Min.* [f. the name of Albert *Johannsen* (1871–1962), American geologist: see -ITE¹.] A brown, greyish, or greenish silicate of calcium and manganese, $CaMnSi_2O_6$, which often occurs with partial substitution of ferrous iron for manganese.

1932 *Amer. Mineralogist* XVII. 575 The Mineralogical Society of America...List of papers to be presented Wednesday, December 28, 1932...W. T. Schaller.—Johannsenite, a new manganese pyroxene. **1963** W. A. DEER et al. *Rock-Forming Min.* II. 75 Johannsenite, the manganese analogue of diopside and hedenbergite, occurs in metasomatized limestones, and is found less frequently as a vein mineral.

Johansson (yohæ·nsən). Also erron. **Johannson, Johannsen.** The name of Carl E. *Johansson*, 20th-century Swedish armaments inspector, used *attrib.* to designate a type of steel block originated by him which is made with flat, parallel faces and of a designated length to a high degree of accuracy, and forms one of a set of different sizes used in making up standard lengths.

1918 D. T. HAMILTON *Gages* i. 3 (*heading*) Johansson reference blocks. **1920** *Proc. Inst. Mech. Engin.* Nov. 1102 A gauge of known length is made up by wringing together a series of Johansson gauges. **1932** HARDY & PERRIN *Princ. Optics* xxviii. 577 A set of Johansson gauges used in conjunction with a plane test glass..can be used for the extremely accurate measurement of thickness. **1935** O. W. BOSTON *Engin. Shop Pract.* II. ix. 448 So-called master gage blocks with very hard, smooth, flat, and parallel surfaces in the form of Johansson gages..which are known as Swedish gages as they were made in Sweden, but which are now owned and made by the Ford Motor Company. **1941** A. W. JUDGE *Aircraft Engines* II. iv. 141 The inside walls..receive a micro-finish..guaranteed to be accurate within 2 micro-inches..longitudinally; this corresponds to the surface finish of Johansson gauge blocks. **1943** S. H. LEBOWITZ *Pre-Service Course Machine Sci.* vi. 149 When two adjoining surfaces of solids are sufficiently smooth and plane, they cohere from relatively slight pressure. This fact can be demonstrated with Johansson gage blocks. **1968** J. A. RANKIN *Workshop Processes & Materials* II. ix. 156 Slip gauges, often called Johannsen gauges after their originator, are rectangular blocks of steel with a cross-section of about 1¼ in. by ⅜ in. which are hardened before being finished to size.

johar (dʒō̆u·haɪ). Also **jauhar, joar.** [ad. Hindi *jauhar*, f. Skr. *jatu-griha* a house built of combustible materials.] The sacrificial burning of Rajput women to avoid their being captured by the enemy.

1802 C. JAMES *New Mil. Dict.*, *Joar*, a general massacre of the women and children, which is sometimes performed by the Hindoos, when they find they cannot prevent the enemy from taking the town. **1907** *Westm. Gaz.* 27 Nov. 2/1 The last siege of Chitor, terminated by the greatest of the Johars. **1919** V. A. SMITH *Oxf. Hist. India* 350 The women were immolated on funeral pyres to save them from dishonour, a dread rite known as *jauhar*, and usually practised by Rājpūts when hard pressed. **1965** *Handbk. for Travellers India* (ed. 20) p. xlviii, Three times Chitor suffered the horrors of sack. Time after time, when all hope was lost, the fatal *johar* was commanded. The women committed their bodies to the flames, and the men, arrayed in bridal robes of saffron, sallied out and died fighting.

johl, var. *JOL.

John. Add: **1. c.** A policeman; (less commonly) a detective. In full, **johndarm** (dʒǫ·ndāɹm) [ad. F. *gendarme*]. Also with suffixed quasi-surname, as *John Dunn* (Austral.), *John Hop* (Austral. and N.Z.), *John Law* (U.S.). Cf. *JONNOP. [Austral., N.Z., and U.S. *john* perh. shortened directly from *John Hop* (rhyming slang for COP *sb.*⁵) and *John Law.*] *depreciatory.*

1633 [in Dict., sense 1 b]. **1858** S. A. HAMMETT *Piney Woods Tavern* vi. 63 He larnt that time to let the John Darmes hunt thar own varmint. **1901** *Westm. Gaz.* 18 Sept. 8/2 'George Johns are sure to visit the old girl to see if anyone has got to her... Brake the cab then shift it again as the John will be sure to tell the porter of that.'.. Detective-sergeant Stevens said the word 'Johns' on the paper signified 'detectives'. **1905** *Munsey's Mag.* July 466/2 Somebody hollers that the johndarms are coming. **1906** E. DYSON *Fact'ry 'Ands* viii. 99 'Twas near two hours afore I see His Whiskers steamin' back, 'n' he had er John in tow...Ther policeman was fer me. **1907** J. LONDON in *Cosmopolitan* May 17/2 A lot of my brother hoboes had been gathered in by John Law. **1918** *Chrons. N.Z.E.F.* 19 July 280 In view of the fact that the camp 'John Hops' were off duty. *Ibid.* 22 Nov. 206 'Never mind about that,' said the John—and dumped him in the cell. **1925** [see *FINK *sb.*²]. *c* **1926** 'MIXER' *Transport Workers' Song Bk.* 94 'Tis us..The wily 'John Hop' loves to track. **1933** *Bulletin* (Sydney) 31 May 12/3 Even on beat duty a John Hop..can cogitate. **1939** H. HODGE *Cab, Sir?* xv. 222 A policeman is the usual cockney 'Grass'...Or sometimes 'Johndarm'—thus proving we know French. **1940** R. CHANDLER *Farewell, my Lovely* xxxix. 302 'The johns tied me to it?' 'I don't know.' **1941** BAKER *Dict. Austral. Slang* 39 *John Dunns*, policemen. **1941** W. G. DAVIS *Phenomena in Crime* xix. 254 Bogies, busies, gendarmes, johns...Detectives. **1961** P. WHITE *Riders in Chariot* xi. 380 'I'll fetch the johns in the mornin'!' she shrieked. 'Layin' into a white woman!' **1965** G. MCINNES *Road to Gundagai* xi. 187 Then we would climb the steps, leaving our bicycles chained to a lamp post (courtesy of the John Hops). **1965** M. SHADBOLT *Among Cinders* xxi. 202 Bill Halloran... He's the local john. **1968** K. WEATHERLY *Roo Shooter* 23, I didn't tell the John to sweep your cell out.

d. (With lower-case initial.) A lavatory, water-closet. *slang* (chiefly *U.S.*).

[**1735** *Harvard Laws* in W. Bentinck-Smith *Harvard Bk.* (1953) 146 No freshman shall mingo against the College wall or go into the fellows' cuzjohn.] **1932** *Amer. Speech* VII. 333 *John, johnny*, a lavatory. **1946** 'J. EVANS' *Halo in Blood* xvi. 181, I..made a brief visit to the john. **1959** C. MACINNES *Absolute Beginners* 54 'You poor old bastard,' I said to the Hoplite, as he sat there on my john. **1972** *Last Whole Earth Catalog* (Portola Inst.) 247/3 Every time you take a dump or a leak in a standard john, you flush five gallons of water out with your piddle. **1973** *Black World* June 19 They gave me my Status Symbol The key to the white Locked John.

e. In full, *John Chinaman.* A Chinaman; the Chinese collectively. *depreciatory.*

1818 B. HALL *Acct. Voy. Corea* ii. 92 This interpreter is called 'John' by all the parties. **1826** *Ibid.* (rev. ed.) i. 37 The seamen..not caring whether John Chinaman, as they called him, understood them or not. **1834** *Amer. Railroad Jrnl.* III. 189/1 They are required to..ascertain the height of John Chinaman in a breath. **1853** *Alta California* (San Francisco) 20 Apr. 2/2 The May Adams brought 118 'Johns' from the terrestrial kingdom of heaven. **1854** C. A. CORBYN *Sydney Revels of Bacchus, Cupid & Momus* 125 They came to the determination of giving wretched John Chinaman such a dose that prussic acid is fool to it. They committed John for trial at the Quarter Sessions. **1858** *Brit. Colonist* (Victoria, B.C.) 27 Dec. 4/3 The Johns had a high time, drinking brandy and eating fried hog. **1865** *Dunedin Punch* 16 Sept. 119 John Chinaman is to immigrate here. **1869** J. R. BROWNE *Adv. Apache Country* 308 John Chinamen, with long tails rolled up on the backs of their heads, running distractedly through the crowd in search of their lost bundles. **1872** [see CHINAMAN 2]. **1921** R. WATSON *Spoilers of Valley* 310 John always was a better truck farmer anyway. **1933** *Bulletin* (Sydney) 8 Mar. 10 Old John Chinaman, patient, hardworking, scrupulously honest. **1970** *Brewer's Dict. Phr. & Fable* (rev. ed.) 591/2 *John Chinaman*, a Chinaman or the Chinese as a people.

f. A ponce; the client of a prostitute. *slang* (orig. *U.S.*).

a **1911** D. G. PHILLIPS *Susan Lenox* (1917) II. vi. 154 A John's a sucker—a fellow that keeps a girl. **1928** [see *CREEP *v.* 5 b]. **1953** W. BURROUGHS *Junkie* (1972) ii. 27 Mary was describing the techniques she used to get money from the 'Johns' who formed her principal source of revenue. **1967** M. M. GLATT et al. *Drug Scene* 117 *John*, prostitute's customer. **1972** *New York* 24 Apr. 38/3 Many working girls, when they are new in the city, spend at least a few months with a madam to meet the better johns. **1973** *Times* 22 Mar. 8/7 The customers (Johns or tricks) are the usual solitary, bored, out-of-town..men.

g. Abbrev. of **John Thomas* (*b*).

1934 *Neuphilol. Mitt.* XXXV. 130 Here [at public-school] his first linguistic experience will be with mumfordish and swear-words (e.g...*john* 'penis'..). **1948** D. BALLANTYNE *Cunninghams* II. xvi. 241 How often did the nurse find him with his old john lying limply? **1972** C. MURRY *Private View* I. 33 The tip of old John brushed against the inside of my thigh.

4. John Barleycorn: see BARLEY-CORN 1 b; **John Birch Society** (see *BIRCHER); hence **John Bircher** = *BIRCHER; **John boat** (also **Jon boat**) *U.S.*, a small, flat-bottomed boat for use principally on inland waterways; **John Citizen,** the ordinary man (esp. considered as a member of the community); **John Collins,** a Collins (see *COLLINS²) made with a base of gin or whisky; a **Tom Collins*; **John Doe,** also in *U.S. Law*; (*b*) name given to an ordinary or typical citizen (see also quot. 1942); **John Down,** a Newfoundland name for the fulmar; **John Hancock** *U.S. colloq.*, a signature; **John Henry** *U.S. local slang* = prec.; **John Innes (compost),** one of a group of composts prepared according to formulæ developed at the John Innes Horticultural Institution in the late 1930s; **John Q. Public** *U.S. colloq.*, the general public, or a member of this; **John Roscoe,** a gun (*U.S. slang*); see also *ROSCOE; **John Thomas,** (*b*) *slang*, the penis.

1961 John Bircher [see *BIRCHER]. **1961** *Listener* 20 Apr. 684/1 The patriots of the right—and they seem to be mushrooming belligerent societies round the country, as witness the sudden, and alarmingly widespread, rise of the John Birch Society. **1963** *Ibid.* 21 Feb. 350/2 The line taken by the interviewer, whose questions might have been drafted by the John Birch Society, so puritanical did they sound. **1967** *Boston Sunday Herald* 30 Apr. I. 1/1 A strange hybrid bird is hovering..over the town of Lincoln. Is it a dove? Is it a hawk? No, it's a John Bircher who may be somebody's pigeon. **1973** W. MCCARTHY *Detail* iii. 201 We have covered every John Bircher and nut that has sworn to kill the President. **1905** *N.Y. Even. Post* (Sat. Suppl.) 2 Sept. 3/1 Two men came down the Mississippi in an Illinois Jon-boat, paddling slowly with rough-whittled boards. **1917** H. KEPHART *Camping & Woodcraft* II. 134 We..hit upon what we conceived to be a brilliant scheme for transporting a gallon of whiskey inconspicuously in our John-boat. **1921** *Rudder* Feb. 7 Their scope of understanding..ranges from the 150-foot schooner to the ten-foot 'john boat'. **1965** A. J. MCCLANE *Standard Fishing Encycl.* 441/2 The original john boat.. was made of clear pine boards 20 feet long and 18 inches wide. **1924** H. H. CURRAN (*title*) John Citizen's job. **1931** T. E. GREGORY in W. Rose *Outl. Mod. Knowl.* 626 If John Citizen buys a house out of his own savings, [etc.]. **1937** *Evening News* 12 Mar. 8/1 No Government department has yet thought of issuing a pamphlet extolling the virtues of John Citizen, who, as taxpayer, every year takes a stronger weight and never complains. **1958** *Daily Tel.* 8 Aug. 11/4 When all is quiet John Citizen says what a great humanitarian he is. **1965** MRS. L. B. JOHNSON *White House Diary* 13 July (1970) 296, I would depend upon that man if I were John Citizen looking on from my living room. **1865** *Australasian* 25 Feb. 8/7 That most angelic of drinks for a hot climate—a John Collins... Take a bottle of sodawater, a wineglassful of gin, a lump of sugar, a piece of ice, with a slice of lemon—mix well together. **1913** R. BROOKE *Let.* 3 Aug. in *Coll. Poems* (1918) p. lxxxvi, I believe I could do a deal in Real Estate, ..over a John Collins, with a clean-shaven Yankee. **1928** T. M. HEALY *Lett. & Leaders* I. x. 142 Two barmen who.. served me with a 'John Collins' [in U.S.]. **1962** John Collins [see *COLLINS²]. [**1825** 'O'HARA FAMILY' (*title*) Tales, containing..John Doe.] **1852** DICKENS *Bleak Ho.* (1853) xx. 195 It is reported at the public offices that his father was John Doe. **1900** (*title*) The bridge manual..by John Doe [pseudonym of Francis Reginald Roe]. **1928** M. H. WESEEN *Crowell's Dict. Eng. Gram.* 355 John Doe. Properly used in legal actions as the name of a fictitious plaintiff. Richard Roe is the corresponding name of a fictitious defendant. By extension these names are used loosely as substitutes for real names in other affairs. **1932** John Doe [see *JONES 1]. **1935** M. M. ATWATER *Murder in Midsummer* xxi. 196 Serve on them one of the John Doe warrants with which you have been provided. **1938** S. ROBERTSON in *For Men Only* Feb. 50 (*heading*) John Doe... crosses the Styx. **1940** L. E. FRAILEY *How to write Better Business Lett.* ii. 14 You start thinking: 'Here's a salesman, John Doe.' **1941** *N.Y. Times* 13 Mar. 25/2 (*title*) Meet John Doe, screen play by Robert Riskin... 'John Doe'.. Gary Cooper. **1942** BERREY & VAN DEN BARK *Amer. Thes. Slang* § 442/3 *One whose name is not known,..*Joe Doe, Joe Zilch, John Doe, John Henry, John Smith. **1957** B. & C. EVANS *Dict. Contemp. Amer. Usage* 259/2 John Doe is a fictitious person in legal proceedings, usually the plaintiff. The corresponding fictitious defendant is Richard Roe. **1972** *N.Y. Law Jrnl.* 31 Oct. 15/4 USA v. Jose Valenzuela-Correa,..John Doe. **1973** *Washington Post* 18 Apr. 1H. 1/8 They didn't include any small guys struggling down here. I think they should have had some John Doe on there. **1852** *Arctic Miscellanies* 10 On the banks of Newfoundland, where this bird is known by the name of 'John Down', it attends the fishing vessels for the offal of the cod fish. **1893** A. NEWTON *Dict. Birds* II. 471 John-Down, the name given to the Fulmar by Newfoundland fishermen. **1917** T. G. PEARSON *Birds of America* I. 80 Fulmar. *Fulmarus glacialis glacialis*... [Also called] Molly Hawk; John Down; Sea Horse. **1957** W. L. MCATEE *Folk-Names Canad. Birds* 4 Fulmar... John Down (Sailor's name, significance unknown. Nfld.). [**1846** HOLMES in R. W. Griswold *Passages from Corr.* (1898) 221 Avoiding..the pretentious boldness of John Hancock..I subscribe myself Yours very truly.] **1903** ADE *People you Know* 150 After he got through filling in the Blank Spaces with his John Hancock, he didn't have a Window to hoist or a Fence to lean on. **1937** *N. & Q.* 6 Mar. 178/1 There is also a popular phrase for signature, 'John Hancock', as in, 'Go ahead. Put down your John Hancock.' **1937** *Greensboro* (N. Carolina) *News* 23 Dec., Lindberg's *John Hancock* is worth ten to twenty-five dollars on the market. **1972** *Listener* 7 Dec. 784/1 Even today an American handing you a contract is apt to say: 'And now if you will just give us your John Hancock.' **1914** *Dialect Notes* IV. 109 *John Henry* or *John Hancock*, autograph. **1951** *Publ. Amer. Dial. Soc.* xv. 56 Put your John Henry on that. **1974** T. BARLING *Shooter Man* iii. 20 Sign your John Henry there... Your name is Balkin. You'd better get used to it. **1939** *Ann. Rep. John Innes Hort. Inst. 1938* XXIX. 17 A great many enquiries about the John Innes composts have been received. The John Innes Base Fertiliser is now being widely used. **1939** LAWRENCE & NEWELL *Seed & Potting Composts* 9 These composts are the outcome

of experiments to meet the practical needs of cultivation at the John Innes Horticultural Institution. *Ibid.* 10 In the John Innes composts the gardener has soil mixtures which, properly used, always give excellent results. **1951** *Good Housek. Home Encycl.* 94/2 The compost for..practically all house plants should be that known as 'John Innes'. **1959** *Listener* 12 Nov. 850/1 The standard John Innes compost is excellent. **1970** *Nature* 25 July 377/1 These results show that fertilizer is crucial for satisfactory growth, particularly slow acting types such as John Innes base. **1973** *Country Life* 29 Mar. 864/3 Acidanthera corms are being potted..in 7 or 8 in. pots of John Innes No. 2 compost. **1937** *N. & Q.* 6 Mar. 177/2 'John Citizen'..is not so frequent in American usage as 'John Q. Public'... It is probably a play on the name of an early president, John Q(uincy) Adams. **1938** S. Chase *Tyranny of Words* xiv. 175 There is no 'public'... Calling it 'John Q. Public' does not help. **1972** M. Kaye *Lively Game of Death* ix. 49 My main concern at that moment was to play John Q. Public by phoning the cops. **1938** D. Runyon *Furthermore* iii. 54 The joke is, I will not be asleep in the sack, and my hands will not be tied, and in each of my hands I will have a John Roscoe, so..I pop out blasting away. **1973** A. S. Neill *Neill! Neill! Orange Peel!* (rev. ed.) ii. 130 The USA.., where anyone can carry a gun, or, to be topical, should I say a Betsy or a John Roscoe? **1879–80** *Pearl* (1970) 76 As around her fair form I a firm hold took, And John Thomas I silently buried. **1928** D. H. Lawrence *Lady Chatterley* xiv. 253 'John Thomas! John Thomas!' and she quickly kissed the soft penis. **1957** L. Durrell *Justine* 249 She had neatly tied his dresstie to his John Thomas, a perfect bow. **1972** *Times Lit. Suppl.* 7 July 783/3 The grotesquely coy accounts of sex, during which Tony tells us that his 'John Thomas' was 'up and raring to go'.

John Canoe (dʒɒn kănū·). *W. Indies* (and †*U.S.*). Also (with various local pronunciations) **John Connú, Johnkannau, joncanoe, jonkanoo,** etc. [f. a W. African lang.] **a.** The chief dancer, or one of several dancers, in a Christmas celebration. **b.** Any of various masks or structures worn or carried on the head by the dancer at Christmas time. **c.** The celebration itself.

See also Cassidy and Le Page *Dict. Jamaican Eng.* s.v.

1774 E. Long *Hist. Jamaica* II. iii. iii. 424 The masquerader..dances at every door, bellowing out *John Connú!* **1816** M. G. Lewis *Jrnl. W. India Proprietor* (1834) 51 The John-Canoe is a Merry-Andrew..bearing upon his head a kind of pasteboard house-boat. **1825** R. Bickell *W. Indies as they Are* 214 The crowds of Slaves..making John Canoe, as they term it, according to the customs of Africa. **1826** A. Barclay *Pract. View Slavery W. Indies* 11 One or two Joncanoe-men, smart youths, fantastically dressed. **1826** C. R. Williams *Tour through Jamaica* 25 This [model of a] house is called the Jonkanoo. **1844** W. Bagley *Let.* 18 Dec. in N. E. Eliason *Tarheel Talk* (1956) 279 On Christmas day..four young fellows blacked themselves & dressed up in negro clothes ..& the fiddler would play & the rest dance. They acted the part of 'John Cunners' very well. **1861** H. Jacobs *Incidents Life Slave Girl* 179 Every child rises early on Christmas morning to see the Johnkannaus. **1929** M. Beckwith *Black Roadways* ix. 155 The instruments which I saw used in the John Canoe performance [were] identical with those accompanying the myal dance. **1952** M. Kerr *Personality & Conflict in Jamaica* 144 These dances..are usually called the John Canoe Dance. **1961** F. G. Cassidy *Jamaica Talk* xii. 256 The John Canoe dancing, recently revived, has had a complex history, and the meaning of the name is uncertain. **1962** S. Wynter *Hills of Hebron* ii. 36 The mask on the face of a 'junkonoo' dancer, striped black and white with slits for eyes and huge white teeth. **1966** *Punch* 5 Jan. 27/2 The wild revelry of the Junkanoo Parade. **1972** E. Hargreaves *Fair Green Weed* xii. 172 John Kanoos...They're rather like old-fashioned mummers. they go round at Christmas time.

John Crow (dʒɒn krōᵘ). [Reduction, in folk pronunciation, of *carrion crow.*] In Jamaica, a name for the red-headed turkey vulture, *Cathartes aura.* Hence **John Crow('s) nose,** a parasitic plant, *Scybalium jamaicense,* which bears bright red flowers.

Entered in Dict. s.v. John 4 without examples.

1826 C. R. Williams *Tour through Jamaica* 82 The dead carcass of a mule, on which a score of john-crows were holding an inquest. **1864** A. H. R. Grisebach *Flora Brit. W. Indian Islands* 785 John-Crow's-nose. **1893** A. Newton *Dict. Birds* ii. 470 In Jamaica, within a few years, the John-Crow, though there protected by human law, has been nearly extirpated by the introduction of the Mongoose. **1963** Robertson & Gooding *Bot. for Caribbean* xvi. 122 In the rain-forests of the West Indies, several members of the family Balanophoraceae occur as parasites on the roots of trees. An example is the John Crow Nose (*Scybalium jamaicense*), which occurs in Jamaica, Cuba and Puerto Rico. **1963** A. L. Thomson *New Dict. Birds* 867/1 The Turkey Vulture *Cathartes aura* (also called 'Turkey Buzzard' and 'John Crow' in the United States) is regarded as a pest on the Peruvian guano islands. **1972** E. Hargreaves *Fair Green Weed* viii. 88 The john-crows hadn't yet caught sight of him, and given warning by their insistent, wheeling flight.

Johne (yō·nə). The name of Heinrich Albert *Johne* (1839–1910), German veterinary surgeon, used in the possessive to designate **Johne's bacillus,** *Mycobacterium johnei,* first recognized by him in 1895, which causes **Johne's disease,** an infectious enteritis of cattle and sheep, characterized by diarrhœa and progressive emaciation.

1907 J. M. Fadyean in *Jrnl. Compar. Path. & Therapeutics* XX. 53, I have therefore ventured to suggest that in this country the disease might in future be known as Johne's disease. Similarly, the causal organism would be known as the bacillus of Johne's disease. **1910** *Proc. R. Soc.* B. LXXXIII. 158, I have also succeeded in isolating and growing the acid-fast bacillus found in the intestine of cows in Jöhne's [*sic*] disease... Jöhne's bacillus grows somewhat more easily than Hansen's lepra bacillus. **1913** Twort & Ingram *Monogr. Johne's Dis.* iii. 29 'Johne's disease' should be the name given to the disease of sheep produced by an infection of Johne's bacillus in the gut and mesenteric glands. **1943** *Jrnl. Compar. Path. & Therapeutics* LIII. 140 Lesions could be produced with various saprophytic acid fast bacilli and killed cultures of Johne or tubercle bacilli suspended in saline. **1945** *Ibid.* LV. 41 (*title*) Ovine paratuberculosis (Johne's disease of sheep). **1972** *Jrnl. Compar. Path.* LXXXII. 333 (*title*) *Corynebacterium renale* as a cause of reactions to the complement fixation test for Johne's disease.

Johnny, Johnnie. Add: **1.** (Further examples.)

1865 R. H. Kellogg *Life & Death in Rebel Prisons* 194 The 'cheekiest' thing that had been done by the 'Johnnies' ..was an attempt to secure the services of our men as artillerists. **1900** [see *crumpet 4 b]. **1930** [see *cool *v.* 3 e]. **1960** M. Spark *Bachelors* i. 9 He felt himself to be, not the amiable johnnie he had by then..affected to be. **1965** A. Nicol *Truly Married Woman* 42 Why are you always trying to be fair, you Johnnies?

b. [Cf. *John 1 c.] A policeman. Also *Johnny Darby, Johnny Hop. slang.*

a **1852** H. Mayhew *London Labour* (1861) II. 154/1 The 'Johnnys' on the water are always on the look out, and..we has to cut our lucky. **1886** *Graphic* 30 Jan. 130/1 Constables used to be known as 'Johnny Darbies', said to be a corruption of the French *gensdarmes*, and they are still occasionally called 'Johnnies'. **1898** W. T. Goodge in M. Davitt *Life & Progress Australasia* xxxv. 192 A policeman is a 'johnny', Or a 'copman' or a 'trap'. **1923** D. H. Lawrence *Kangaroo* xvi. 357 Somers knew that Johnny Hops was Australian for a policeman. **1935** H. Neville *Sneak Thief on Road* 347 Johnny, a policeman. A Lincoln johnny, a stupid and impudent policeman.

c. (*a*) = *John 1 e; (*b*) a soldier of the Indian Army (before 1947); (*c*) a Gurkha; (*d*) = **Johnny Turk*; (*e*) an Arab; (*f*) an onion-seller from Brittany.

1857 T. B. Gunn *Physiology of N.Y. Boarding Houses* 275 He's seed the *Johnnies* goin' into that there doorway next block. **1858** *Leisure Hour* 27 May 326/1 Sepoys..known as Johnnys. **1888** Kipling *Wee Willie Winkie* (1889) 103 The Highlander..turning to a Gurkha, said, 'Hya, Johnny!' **1897** I. Scott *How I stole over 10,000 Sheep in Austral. & N.Z.* 46 His name was Lim Hung Ching...this Johnny knowing he would have no show in such a scotch town if he sent in his tender with his own name,..signed it Angus McPherson. **1916** *Anzac Book* 50 What should we do at Anzac have done without 'Johnnie' and his sturdy little mules? **1925** Fraser & Gibbons *Soldier & Sailor Words* 132 *Johnny*, a Turk. (As a Service nickname, dating from the Crimean War.) **1948** Partridge *Dict. Forces' Slang* 103 *Johnny*, soldiers' word for Arab. It rebounded, as Arabs also used the name for British soldiers. **1960** *Guardian* 8 Mar. 8/7 Any time now we shall have the Johnnies [from Brittany] coming around in small vans. **1967** J. Caird *Murder Scholastic* xi. 130 She heard the knock at the door...It could be a tradesman.. or Onion Johnny, or a tramp. **1969** S. Mays *Fall out Officers* xxii. 173 'Now we are all the fighting brothers,' said Johnny with delight.

2. b. Read: A sailor's name for a penguin, *Pygoscelis papua,* the Gentoo (*sb.*²). (Earlier and later examples.)

1879 H. N. Moseley *Notes by Naturalist on 'Challenger'* vii. 175 One [sort] was a penguin called by the sealers the 'Johnny' (*Pygoscelis tæniata*), the 'Gentoo' of the Falklands. **1893** A. Newton *Dict. Birds* ii. 471 Johnny, the South-Sea sealers' name for a Penguin, *Pygoscelis papua* or *tæniata*, one of the widely-distributed species. **1954** W. B. Alexander *Birds of Ocean* (ed. 2) 155 At the Falkland Islands it [*sc.* the gentoo penguin] is usually known as the 'Johnny'.

3. *Johnny Armstrong* joc. slang (see quot. 1962); *Johnny-come-lately* orig. *U.S.*: (*a*) a newcomer; (*b*) = *Johnny Raw*; (*c*) *fig.* and *attrib.*; *Johnny Crapaud* [i.e. toad], also *Johnny Crapeau*: (*a*) nickname for a Frenchman or French Canadian; (*b*) (*Obs.*) the French nation; *Johnny Head-in(-the)-Air*: nickname for a man with 'his head in the clouds', unconscious of his surroundings; *Johnny Magorey* (see quots.); *Johnny Newcome*: (*a*) = *Johnny Raw*; (*b*) a newcomer of any kind; *Johnny-on-the-spot*: a person who is available when needed, or 'at the psychological moment'; quasi-*adj.*, present, in readiness; *Johnny Reb*: a *U.S.* (Northern) name for a 'rebel' or Confederate soldier in the American Civil War; *Johnny Turk*: a Turkish soldier; any Turk; *Johnny Woodser* = *Jimmy Woodser* (*Jimmy 4).

1922 *N. & Q.* 9 Sept. 206/2 *Johnny Armstrong*, the action of 'pulling' or restraining a horse. **1962** Granville *Dict. Sailors' Slang* 66/2 *Johnny Armstrong*, any hard work involving pulling or hauling. **1839** C. F. Briggs *Adv. H. Franco* I. 249 'But it's Johnny Comelately, aint it, you?' said a young mizzen topman. **1924** 'R. Daly' *Outpost* xiv. 139 He may be an old barbarian, but he's entitled to more consideration than these Johnny-come-lately's who cruise along the coast after trade. **1933** *Press* (Christchurch, N.Z.) 28 Oct. 17/7 *Johnny-come-lately*, nickname for a cowboy or any newly-joined hand or recent immigrant. **1946** M. Shulman *Zebra Derby* iii. 22 Postwar planning in these United States was no Johnny-come-lately. **1952** E. Coxhead *Play Toward* iii. 88 The Midlands are..all Johnny-come-latelys who coined money out of the war. **1953** *Amer. Scholar* XXIII. 17 The excessive power and renown of many Johnny-come-lately anti-Communists. **1972** *Listener* 16 Nov. 671/2 Here [in Utah] man himself is a Johnny-come-lately. [**1818** 'A. Burton' *Adv. Johnny Newcome* iii. 131 Jean Crappeau's mighty stout, He surely means to fight it out.] **1834** W. N. Glascock *Naval Sketch-Bk.* 2nd Ser. II. 137 Mister Bull and Johnny Crappo..have..suddenly taken for each other..a fit of affection. **1839** *Spirit of Times* 31 Aug. 312/1 Poor Johnny Crapeau has been the favorite mark for every shaft of ridicule. **1840** J. F. Cooper *Pathfinder* II. vi. 201 We are no Johnny Crapauds to hide ourselves behind a..fort on account of a puff of wind. **1851** J. F. W. Johnston *Notes N. Amer.* II. 6 These Ayrshire emigrants appear to be shrewd enough to buy out Johnny Crapaud. **1887** *Gentl. Mag.* Feb. 135 Those vessels went armed, too, as befitted the majesty of the bunting under which old Dance had gloriously licked Johnny Crapeau. **1915** G. Parker *Money Master* xxiii. 323 Yet, raging as he was, and ready to take the Johnny Crapaud..by the throat, he was not yet sure that Jean Jacques was not armed. **1919** W. A. Fraser *Bulldog Carney* 70 Them Johnnie Crapeaus from Quebec. **1965** G. R. Stevens *Incompleat Canadian* 142 'Johnny Crapeau', esteemed alike for his good temper..and ebullient spirits. **1848** Johnny Head-in-Air [see *head *sb.* 39*]. **1913** C. Mackenzie *Sinister St.* I. i. ii. 23 Much of his morning walk was passed in a dream... Nanny used to jeer at him, calling him Little Johnny Head-in-Air. **1929** C. Day Lewis *Transitional Poem* i. 14 What happier place For Johnny Head-in-Air, Who never would hear Time mumbling at the base? **1942** [see *head *sb.* 39*]. **1958** B. Nichols *Sweet & Twenties* xvi. 225 Yet he was not a Johnny-Head-in-the-Air; he had a shrewd grasp of the contemporary scene. **1870** G. M. Hopkins *Jrnl.* 4 Apr. (1959) 198 The following Irish expressions..Johnny Magoreys (seeds of the hip). **1922** Joyce *Ulysses* 172 Poisonous berries. Johnny Magories. **1815** (*title*) The military adventures of Johnny Newcome, with an account of his campaigns on the Peninsula and in Pall Mall. **1818** 'A. Burton' (*title*) The adventures of Johnny Newcome in the navy; a poem, in four cantos. **1833** *United Service Jrnl.* XI. i. 59 On first landing at Port Royal, a Johnny Newcome (as all strangers are there called)..will at once imagine himself transported into the community of Bedlamites. **1839** Barham *Ingol. Leg.* (1840) 1st Ser. 308 Now to young 'Johnny Newcome' she seems to confine hers, Neglecting the poor little dear out at dry-nurse. **1865** J. H. A. Bone *Petroleum & Petroleum Wells* 40 The Johnny Newcomes had to fight their way back to the bar, and deposit seventy-five cents for the bit of blue pasteboard. **1961** F. H. Burgess *Dict. Sailing* 125 *Johnny Newcome*,..a new hand or a landsman, unused to the sea. **1896** Johnny-on-the-spot [see *case *sb.*² 1 d]. **1902** 'D. Dix' *Fables of Elite* 43 Because they had never Tried it, they thought they were Johnny on the Spot, and could do anything. **1914** Wodehouse *Man Upstairs* 102 'I must be close at hand. I must be—what's your expression?—' 'Johnny-on-the-spot.' **1916** *Daily Colonist* (Victoria, B.C.) 23 July 7/5 We have our eyes on some splendid billets, and will be 'johnny on the spot' when the present residents move out. **1944** E. Bennett-Bremner *Front-Line Airline* (1945) viii. 50 Qantas Empire Airways have been called upon to conduct searches for missing aircraft, and it was only natural, therefore, that being 'Johnny-on-the-spot' they should be asked to join in when aircraft went missing. **1961** J. McCabe *Mr. Laurel & Mr. Hardy* (1962) ii. 57 Suddenly they needed a fat boy for a comedy sequence. He was Johnny-on-the-spot and he was hired at $5 a day. **1968** *Globe & Mail* (Toronto) 13 Jan. 42/7 He..was johnny-on-the-spot to rap in Mike Walton's rebound. **1865** *Nation* (N.Y.) I. 584 They said he was a Johnny Reb. **1948** Johnny Reb [see *grey, gray *sb.* 1 c]. **1919** *Mr. Punch's Hist. Gt. War* 24 Now it is the turn of 'Johnny Turk', who has had his knock on the Suez Canal. **1972** E. Ambler *Levanter* ii. 22 'Johnny Turk is a gentleman,' he used to say. **1933** Johnny Woodser [see *Jimmy 4].

4. (With lower-case initial.) = *John 1 d. *slang* (chiefly *U.S.*).

1932 [see *John 1 d]. **1934** J. O'Hara *Appointment in Samarra* (1935) iv. 98 Kitty Hofman came in the johnny. **1946** C. S. Archer *China Servant* ii. 32 He left a smell of stale tobacco where-ever he went. Even in the johnny. **1969** L. Greenbaum *Out of Shape* (1970) xviii. 136 You're not going to find me in aisle four next to the toilet paper and the johnny mop. **1971** D. Conover *One Man's Island* 65 Why, oh, why, do little boys (and big ones) rush to a johnny when nature provides opportunity everywhere?

5. johnny-jump-up *N. Amer.*, a name used for several kinds of wild or cultivated pansy or violet; **Johnny penguin** = *Johnny 2 b.

1842 *Knickerbocker* XIX. 115 Mr. Ketchup had now kissed little Chip and stuck a johnny-jump-up in his cap. **1872** E. Eggleston *End of World* i. 12 Julia..was hoeing a bed in which she meant to plant some johnny-jump-ups. **1929** F. A. Pottle *Stretchers* (1930) iii. 48 Under foot the ground teemed with lupine and phlox and those large scentless violets which the natives call 'Johnny-jump-ups'. **1972** T. A. Bulman *Kamloops Cattlemen* xii. 75 Green grass, buttercups and Johnny-jump-ups were much in evidence. **1879** H. N. Moseley *Notes by Naturalist on 'Challenger'* viii. 189 The whole beach of Christmas Harbour [in Kerguelen's Land] was covered with droves of the Johnny Penguin. **1882** *Encycl. Brit.* XIV. 49/1 All parts of the coast [of Kerguelen's Land] and even the lower slopes are covered with penguins of various species, mainly the Johnny penguin..rock-hopper..and king penguin. **1968** Shackleton & Stokes *Birds Atlantic Ocean* 20/2 Affectionately known as 'Johnny' penguin, the gentoo is the only penguin with white on top of its head.

Johnny-cake. Add: **a.** Also *W. Indies*, a scone or dumpling (cf. quot. 1831 in Dict.). (Earlier and later examples.)

1739 *S. Carolina Gaz.* 22 Dec. 4/2 (Advt.) (Th. Suppl.),

New Iron Plates to cook Johnny Cakes or gridel bread on. **1893** in C. SULLIVAN *Jamaica Cookery Bk.* **1952** S. SELVON *Brighter Sun* vi. 109 Over there, nastiness and poverty, a tin cup of weak tea and a johnny cake or a roti. **1972** J. HEWITT *N.Y. Times Heritage Cook Bk.* 96 Massachusetts johnnycakes usually have wheat flour and corn meal in them.

Johnson (dʒǫ·nsən). A common surname, used in *low slang* to designate: **a.** The penis. Also *Jim Johnson.*

1863 W. B. CHEADLE *Jrnl. Trip across Canada* (1931) 108 Neck frozen. Face ditto; thighs ditto; Johnson ditto, & sphincter vesicae partially paralyzed. **1972** *Screw* 12 June 10/3 So I went to take my turn with the hopes of somehow getting my *Jim Johnson* wet.

b. A man who is kept by a prostitute or prostitutes, a ponce.

1960 'J. ASHFORD' *Counsel for Defence* v. 66 You got Legs off... He was a Johnson.

Johnson bar (dʒǫ·nsən bāɪ). *U.S.* [Origin unknown.] A long heavy lever used to reverse the motion of a steam locomotive. Also *transf.* (see quot. 1971).

1930 *Railroad Man's Mag.* II. 471/1 *Johnson bar*, reverse lever on a locomotive. **1943** *Railroad Mag.* XXXIV. 58/1 He jerked two short ones from his chime, eased the Johnson bar down to the first corner and dropped his left hand on the throttle. **1959** P. RANSOME-WALLIS *Conc. Encycl. World Railway Locomotives* 508 *Johnson bar*, reversing lever. **1971** M. TAK *Truck Talk* 93 *Johnson bar*, the emergency brake handle.

Johnsoniana (dʒǫnsōᵘniēⁱ·na, -ā·nă). [f. *Johnson* (see JOHNSONIAN *a.* and *sb.*) + *-IANA.] Sayings, etc., of or about Dr. Samuel Johnson; matters connected with Dr. Johnson.

1776 (*title*) Johnsoniana; or, a collection of Bon Mots, etc., by Dr. Johnson and others. **1909** *Daily Chron.* 14 Sept. 3/2 [Mr. Reade's] latest compilation of Johnsoniana. **1928** *Daily Tel.* 12 June 17/3 Miss Anna Seward's delightful Johnsoniana. **1952** *Bull. John Rylands Libr.* XXXV. 211 (*title*) Johnsoniana from the Bagshawe muniments.

Johnson noise. *Electronics.* [Named after John Bertrand *Johnson* (b. 1887), naturalized U.S. physicist, who published an account of it in 1928.] Electrical noise caused by the random thermal motion of conduction electrons.

1931 *Proc. IRE* XIX. 1407 Finally..an irreducible minimum of noise is encountered, commonly referred to as 'Johnson' or circuit noise. **1947** [see *flicker noise* (*FLICKER *sb.*[3] 4)]. **1958** CONDON & ODISHAW *Handbk. Physics* v. iii. 31/1 This voltage fluctuation, called Johnson noise, which places a limit on the ultimate sensitivity of amplifiers, provides a method for measuring thermodynamic temperature. **1973** *Physics Bull.* Oct. 596/2 Any electrical resistor exhibits a Johnson noise voltage, with a mean square amplitude proportional to absolute temperature.

johnstrupite (yǫ·nstrᵘpəit, dʒǫ·nstrŭpəit). *Min.* [ad. G. *johnstrupit* (W. C. Brögger 1890, in *Zeitschr. f. Krystallogr. u. Mineral.* XVI. 75), f. the name of J. F. *Johnstrup* (1818–1894), Danish geologist: see -ITE[1].] A brownish green hydrous silicate and fluoride of several metals.

1890 *Jrnl. Chem. Soc.* LVIII. 1077 In addition to the minerals previously known, the author [*sc.* Brögger] has found..johnstrupite. **1906** J. P. IDDINGS *Rock Minerals* II. 458 Mosandrite and johnstrupite occur in nephelite-syenites and closely related rocks, chiefly in the region of the Langesund fjord, Norway; also in the aphanitic and lava equivalents in other localities. **1959** *Mineral. Abstr.* XIV. 105/1 Calculations of the unit cell contents.. give the following formulae:..johnstrupite (Ca, Na, Ce)$_{12}$ (Ti, Mg, Al, Zr)$_8$Si$_7$O$_{31}$H$_2$F$_{4-5}$... The authors conclude that mosandrite and johnstrupite are varieties of the same species. **1965** *Ibid.* XVII. 287/1 Selective concentration of B..has been observed in specimens of..mosandrite and johnstrupite.

Johnswort. = *St. John's-wort* (JOHN 5).

1753 J. HEMPSTEAD *Diary* (1901) 611 Wee pulld up the yellow Blossoms (alias Johnsworth) in the upper end & back Side the Lot. **1819** *Mass. Hist. Soc. Coll.* 2nd Ser. VIII. 170 In July the lover of plants is gratified with.. two species of pyrala, the small geranium, several species of hypericum or John's wort. **1874** *Rep. Vermont Board Agric.* II. 390 It is very desirable that the dairyman's pastures should be well stocked with good nutritious grasses, not wild grass of the low boggy pasture, or johnswort, or daisies, but June or blue grass and clover.

‖ **joie de vivre** (ʒwa də vīvr). [Fr., = joy of living.] A feeling of healthy enjoyment of life; exuberance, high spirits.

1889 E. DOWSON *Let.* 1 Apr. (1967) 58, I do not suppose 'la joie de vivre' will be revealed to me any more at Limehouse than in the Temple. **1901** 'L. MALET' *Hist. R. Calmady* III. v. 204 The hungry all-compelling *joie de vivre* which is begotten whensoever youth thus seeks and finds youth. **1907** *Westm. Gaz.* 5 Feb. 4/2 The new *joie de vivre* of motoring. **1917** S. MCKENNA *Sonia* vi. 263 It was only when the twanging banjos changed to rag-time that the majority of our neighbours sheepishly unbent and put forth an assumption of *joie de vivre.* **1925** A. P. HERBERT *Laughing Ann* 82 The simple mind and manly air, Not Brains so much as Breeding, With *joie de vivre* and *savoir faire*, Are constantly succeeding. **1935** *Discovery* Jan. 28/2 Song is an outlet for any of a bird's emotions.., but chiefly *joie de vivre.* **1944** *Burlington Mag.* Sept. 216/2 Many delightful travel impressions have also been noted by him in spirited pen and wash drawings, glistening with *joie-de-vivre.* **1955** *Times* 16 Aug. 5/3 She is excitable, but rather in the sense of joie de vivre. Children play with her, ride on her back, twist her tail and do anything that might aggravate a ferocious dog. **1964** R. CHURCH *Voyage Home* i. 10 Suffering acutely from the effort to ignore the bursts of *joie-de-vivre* from the corridors. **1974** I. MURDOCH *Sacred & Profane Love Machine* 96 He had laughed at Sophie's spiteful jokes, of which the sheer *joie de vivre* had seemed to lessen the bite.

join, *sb.* Add: Also *join-up.*

1945 A. LUNN *Third Day* v. 47 If we are expected to accept the hypothesis of a second-century compiler who worked his heterogeneous materials into an artistic unity with..skill we may ask why the join-ups between the 'we' sections and the rest of the *Acts* are so inartistic. **1969** *Sun* 22 July 1/2 On the join-up, Eagle and Columbia ended their separate existences [as space vehicles] and became Apollo-11 again.

join, *v.*[1] **6. b.** Delete † *Obs.* and add later examples.

1882 R. L. STEVENSON *New Arabian Nights* I. 95 You join yourselves to persons of condition..for no other purpose than to escape the consequences of your crimes. **1904** S. J. WEYMAN *Abbess of Vlaye* ii. 41 Had I known of what sort they were to whom I was joining myself.

15. d. *to join up*: to enlist in the army.

1916 'BOYD CABLE' *Action Front* 5 Just joined up to get a finger in the fighting? **1922** D. H. LAWRENCE *England, my England* 40 Egbert went and joined up immediately as a private soldier. **1934** J. T. FARRELL *Young Manhood* i. 20 He stepped up to a beefy-faced sergeant... 'We came to join up.' **1943** J. B. PRIESTLEY *Daylight on Saturday* xxxviii. 301, I wish you'd leave here —join up or something.

22. *to join the ladies*: to go into the room to which the ladies have retired after dinner.

1848 *Punch* XIV. 204/1 (*caption*) Walter, I think you had better join the ladies. **1921** J. M. BARRIE (*title*) Shall we join the ladies? **1956** N. MARSH *Off with his Head* (1957) x. 212 'Join the ladies?' Dr. Otterley suggested, and they did so. **1974** N. FREELING *Dressing of Diamond* 95 And that, thought Richard grinning, will be denounced as' sexual fascism'... And shall we now join the ladies?

23. *if you can't beat them, join them*: a semi-proverbial assertion applied to a situation where a person crosses to another side or party because he is unable to defeat them by opposition alone.

1955 [see *EPISTEMOLOGICAL *a.*]. **1970** *Times* 26 Nov. 12/3 Gale will also be applying for a ticket to the Parliamentary lobby for himself: 'If you can't beat them, join them.'

joiner, *sb.* Add: **1. b.** One who makes a habit of joining societies, etc. Cf. JOIN *v.*[1] 15 b. *colloq.* (orig. *U.S.*).

1890 *Ann Arbor* (Mich.) *Reg.* 13 Mar., Ypsilanti is a good place for 'jiners'. There are..100 societies and organizations that a person can join. **1923** R. MACAULAY *Told by Idiot* 36 That was Stanley's headlong manner of entering into movements. She was a great and impetuous joiner. **1957** *Times Lit. Suppl.* 15 Nov. 690/2 He is not a 'joiner', that [is] he resists the temptation to cash in on stock fashionable attitudes. **1967** W. MURRAY *Sweet Ride* vii. 109 I'm not a joiner, you know? I mean, all they do is party, party, party all the time. **1971** *Guardian* 6 July 8/5 You could not see Bogart as a marcher or a singer or a joiner—he was strictly solo. **1973** C. MULLARD *Black Brit.* III. vii. 78 Sadly, this meant that people who were not 'joiners', but who might have been active in race relations, were not considered.

joint, *sb.* Add: **4. c.** *Bookbinding.* The flexible cloth or leather which forms the junction between the spine and the sides of the binding of a book; also the projection along the edge of this junction.

1835 J. HANNETT *Bibliopegia* 104 The volume being laid upon the table or press, with the head towards the workman and the upper board open, the guard or false end paper must be removed and all other substances cleared out of the joint with the folder. **1861** *Chambers's Encycl.* II. 226/2 Coming to his hands flat and solid, and with its joints well formed. **1894** *Amer. Dict. Printing & Bookmaking* 313/2 *Joints*, the projection formed in backing to admit the millboards. The leather or cloth placed from the projection to the millboard is called a joint. **1901** D. COCKERELL *Bookbinding* xii. 165 Ensure that there is enough leather in the turn-in of the joint to allow the cover to open freely. **1951** L. TOWN *Bookbinding by Hand* xvi. 203 If a slight amount of moisture is still present the leather will bed itself very neatly into position in the joint. **1967** V. STRAUSS *Printing Industry* x. 673/2 Backing does not give the book a new back but provides the joints of the back.

11. b. *flat joint, set joint, strong joint*: see the adjs. in Suppl.

14. More generally, a place; a house. (Earlier and later examples.)

1821 *Real Life in Ireland* xvii. 199, I had my education at the boarding-school of Phelim Firebrass..; and when I slipt the joint, and fang'd the arm, he strengthened the sinews. **1877** *Sessions Papers Cent. Criminal Court* 25 Oct. 631 The *joints*—that means the offices where the swindle was carried on—that is a cant word. **1880** *Weekly Times* 4 Jan. 8/3 They soon found him a 'joint' to do... Doing a 'joint' means effecting a burglarious entrance. **1904** *Sun* (N.Y.) 6 Mar. 7/4 Of course, there are no saloons in Kansas; no one would dream of calling them by that name. They are all 'joints', whether the drinks are passed over a polished counter by a white aproned attendant, or shoved through a hole in the wall by a dirty fist. **1905** 'H. MCHUGH' *You can search Me* 20, I took Clara J. to the St. Regis to dinner... It's a swell joint, all right. **1912** *Maclean's Mag.* Sept. 69/2 Mr. Kelley, to whom few streets were unfamiliar, knew the place exteriorly as a 'Dago joint'. *a* **1922** T. S. ELIOT *Waste Land Drafts* (1971) 59 line 50 So the men..thought Of home, and dollars, and the pleasant violin At Marm Brown's joint, and the girls and gin. **1925** H. L. FOSTER *Trop. Tramp with Tourists* 32 Been to Havana? Good Lord! I've been to that damned joint with Cook, Clarke, Frank, Raymond-Whitcomb, and the American Express. **1934** WODEHOUSE *Right Ho, Jeeves* xiv. 167 Hanging out in a joint called Kingham Manor. **1935** A. SQUIRE *Sing Sing Doctor* v. 73 In cities the market for brothels, gambling joints, & narcotic dens is better. **1946** F. SARGESON *That Summer* 55, I found a joint that was kept by a Mrs. Clegg. **1953** G. LAMMING *In Castle of my Skin* xiv. 282, I see one or two things change round this joint... I mean the village. **1959** 'A. GILBERT' *Death takes Wife* xv. 198 Put down money for a joint you didn't frisk in advance. **1959** 'M. M. KAYE' *House of Shade* iii. 31 He turns the joint upside down until he finds it. **1974** *Listener* 13 June 766/2 A rather pokey, smokey little jazz joint in San Francisco.

b. *Fairground slang.* A stall, tent, etc., in a circus or fair; a concession stand. orig. *U.S.*

1927 *Amer. Speech* June 414 A carnival concession is known as a joint or store. **1931** *Amer. Mercury* Nov. 353/1 *Joint*, any concession stand, or novelty spindle. **1934** P. ALLINGHAM *Cheapjack* ii. 16 'You can build up yonder... Where's your joint?'.. It took some time to discover that by a 'joint' he meant my tent. **1968** D. BRAITHWAITE *Fairground Archit.* 22 The tober is a composite of many elements—roundabouts, booths, joints, and transport vehicles. *Ibid.* 68 Joints fall into roughly three categories—round ones, generically termed hoop-las, side-stuff,..and casual stalls for vending.

c. A marijuana cigarette; also, hypodermic equipment used by drug addicts.

1935 A. J. POLLOCK *Underworld Speaks* 65/1 *Joint*, a complete hypodermic outfit consisting of syringe and needles (ointjay). **1938** *Amer. Speech* XIII. 186/1 *Joint.* The hollow needle, or a substitute... The hypodermic outfit including all accessories...The opium smoker's outfit complete. **1952** G. MANDEL *Flee Angry Strangers* 171 You got a couple of joints to take along?..I know I'll want to get on. Take some pod, Dinch. **1967** M. M. GLATT et al. *Drug Scene* i. 5 In Britain, cannabis is..almost always smoked in the form of a cigarette which is referred to as a smoke, joint or reefer. **1970** *Times* 28 Apr. 10/8 (*caption*) Please fasten your seat belts and extinguish your joints. **1971** *Black Scholar* Sept. 33/1 When the shower stopped he lit two joints and went to the bathroom. **1972** *Daily Tel.* 3 Apr. 8 The making of the joint seemed to be as much a part of the ritual as smoking it.

d. Prison. *U.S. slang.*

1953 W. BURROUGHS *Junkie* (1972) xii. 124 He said even the best thieves spend most of their time in the joint. **1969** C. F. BURKE *God is Beautiful, Man* (1970) 27 She made things so rotten for him that the king threw him in the joint. **1972** J. WAMBAUGH *Blue Knight* (1973) i. 28 He was a no-good asshole and belonged in the joint.

15. (sense 5) *joint-face, -filling, -surface*; **joint bolt**, a bolt for holding together the two parts of a joint; *spec.* (see quots. *a* 1884, 1964); **joint box**, a junction-box, esp. one designed to be filled with an insulating material; **joint mouse** *Med.* [tr. G. *gelenkmaus* (see quot. 1886)], a loose fragment (as of cartilage or bone) floating in the cavity of a joint; usu. *pl.*; **joint-plane** *Geol.*, a plane in rock in which a joint exists or is liable to form; also, an exposed surface that was once such a plane; **joint set** *Geol.*, a group of parallel joints; **joint system** *Geol.*, a group of two or more intersecting joint sets; **joint-vetch**, a leguminous plant of the genus *Æschynomene*, so called from its jointed seed pods.

1844 H. STEPHENS *Bk. Farm* II. 75 The top bar..swells out in the middle, where it is perforated for the joint-bolt of the lever. *a* **1884** KNIGHT *Dict. Mech.* Suppl. 514/2 *Joint bolt*, a bolt used for fastening two timbers, one endwise to the other... Used commonly as a fastening for a bed-rail to the bed-post. **1964** J. S. SCOTT *Dict. Building* 159 *Handrail bolt* or *joint bolt*, a bolt threaded at both ends. **1901** *Chambers's Jrnl.* Dec. 845/2 A new form of joint-box for forming connections. **1907** J. F. C. SNELL *Distrib. Electr. Energy* v. 269 Joint boxes must be used to connect lengths of cables or conductors equivalent to, or larger than 7–16 S.W.G. **1929** G. W. STUBBINGS *Underground Cable Systems* v. 50 A cast-iron joint box must provide a compound-tight chamber for the filling compound. **1966** J. F. WHITFIELD *Electr. Installations & Regulations* vi. 120 There is some saving in cable but extra man-hours are needed for joint-box connections. **1912** *Jrnl. Geol.* XX. 76 The cliff face is in many parts composed of projecting and re-entrant angles formed by the joint faces of large area meeting in obtuse angles. **1931** *Times Lit. Suppl.* 11 June 466/2 A block of which the bounding joint-faces slope downwards and towards each other will be squeezed upwards. **1961** *Amer. Jrnl. Sci.* CCLIX. 502 The convergence of plumose and radial structures toward the center of the joint face strongly suggests that joints are fractures initiated at a point. **1916** F. H. LAHEE *Field Geol.* viii. 223 By their shape and relations to the surface of unconformity, these joint fillings may indicate something of the original character and arrangement of the fractures in which they were formed. **1965** G. J. WILLIAMS *Econ. Geol. N.Z.* xiv. 230/1 Soft white

veinlets and joint-fillings of crystalline laumontite are abundant in greywackes throughout New Zealand. **1886** H. MARSH *Dis. Joints* xv. 185 On account of the manner in which these bodies change their site, and slip out of reach, the Germans have suggestively called them 'joint-mice' (*gelenk-mäuse*). **1920** R. STOCKMAN *Rheumatism & Arthritis* ix. 115 'Joint-mice', if present, can be felt, and slip from under the fingers in a very characteristic fashion. **1952** E. F. TRAUT *Rheumatic Dis.* ix. 194 A detached portion of the internal meniscus constitutes a loose body or joint mouse. **1961** R. D. BAKER *Essent. Path.* xxi. 560 (*caption*) Aching, weakness and locking, inability to extend left knee, began 11 years previously, following which joint mice were removed on two occasions. **1855** J. PHILLIPS *Man. Geol.* ii. 44 The cleavage and joint planes in these beds are not parallel to the general cleavage. **1905** J. GEIKIE *Struct. & Field Geol.* x. 144 Common household coal..is divided by three sets of planes disposed at right angles to each other: namely (*a*) planes of bedding..and (*b*) and (*c*) joint-planes. **1944** A. HOLMES *Princ. Physical Geol.* vi. 76 The joint pattern may also control the course of rivers, the joint planes themselves commonly forming the walls of steep-sided gorges and canyons. **1970** R. J. SMALL *Study of Landforms* iv. 122 The spectacular cliffs on the east side of the A'Chir ridge coincide with near-vertical joint-planes. **1931** C. M. NEVIN *Princ. Struct. Geol.* v. 144 That it [*sc.* tension] is the effective stress which caused the actual break has not been proven for dip and strike joint sets. **1942** *Bull. Geol. Soc. Amer.* LIII. 392 The relationships of the joint sets to other structures indicates their age. **1965** P. C. BADGLEY *Struct. & Tectonic Princ.* iv. 117/1 A close relationship exists between these lineament patterns and regional joint sets. **1943** *Bull. Geol. Soc. Amer.* LIII. 396 On most of the more planar joint surfaces featherlike or flamelike markings..are found. **1961** *Amer. Jrnl. Sci.* CCLIX. 493 Freshly exposed joint surfaces commonly are marked with faint ridges that form plume-like or radial patterns. **1973** E. E. WAHLSTROM *Tunneling in Rock* v. 102 Joint surfaces that are smooth..commonly display slickensides and contain crushed materials. **1929** C. R. LONGWELL *Pirsson's Textbk. Geol.* (ed. 3) I. xii. 315 In many places there are two prominent sets of joints, approximately at right angles to each other and each set nearly vertical. Such a combination of two or more intersecting sets constitutes a joint system. **1952** VON ENGELN & CASTER *Geology* xiv. 191 Joint systems are commonly much more distinctively and conspicuously developed in sedimentary than in other classes of rocks. **1973** E. E. WAHLSTROM *Tunneling in Rock* v. 99 Regional geological studies often reveal a systematic geometrical relationship between joint systems and faults and folds. **1829** J. C. LOUDON *Encycl. Plants* 1284 *Arthrolobium*...Joint-Vetch. **1884** W. MILLER *Dict. Eng. Names Plants* 156/1 *Æschynomene..hispida.* Sensitive Joint-Vetch.

joint, *a.* Add: **2.** (Further examples.)

1828 P. BINGHAM *Rep. Court Common Pleas* IV. 70 (Adamson v. Jarvis 1827), The Plaintiff and Defendant.. must..be both considered as joint tort feasers, and the present action is nothing else but an attempt by one tort feaser to recover contribution from another. **1886** [see TORTFEASOR]. **1908** J. C. MILES in E. Jenks *Digest Eng. Civil Law* II. i. 337 Persons are joint tort-feasors when one aids, counsels, or joins the other in the commission of a tort. **1920** H. CRANE *Let.* 28 Jan. (1965) 32, I am enraged at Mencken and Nathan..the joint authors. **1925** J. A. HOLDEN *Bookman's Gloss.* 63 Joint author, a person who writes a book in collaboration with one or more associates. **1935** *Act* 25 & 26 *Geo. V* c. 30 § 6 Any tort-feasor liable in respect of..damage may recover contribution from any other tort-feasor who is..liable in respect of the same damage, whether as a joint tort-feasor or otherwise. **1957** J. G. FLEMING *Law of Torts* xxviii. 744 The common law..does attach some significance to the distinction between 'joint' and 'several' tortfeasors. **1967** *Anglo-Amer. Catal. Rules: Brit. Text* 267 *Joint author*, a person who collaborates with one or more associates to produce a work in which the contribution of each is not separable from that of the others. **1971** *Mod. Law Rev.* XXXIV. vi. 674 The accessory after the fact has become, perhaps more appropriately, something more like the joint-tortfeasor.

b. *joint family*, a type of extended family in which married children share the family home, living under the authority of the head of the family. Also *attrib.*

1876 W. K. SULLIVAN in *Encycl. Brit.* V. 799/2 Beside the 'joint and undivided family' there was another kind of family which we might call the 'joint family'. This was a partnership composed of three or four members of a sept whose individual wealth was not sufficient to qualify each of them to be an aire, but whose joint wealth qualified one of the co-partners as head of the joint family to be one. **1889** C. N. STARCKE *Primitive Family* II. ii. 139 Polyandry belongs to the category of facts which have to do with the ordinary family communism, and especially with the joint family group. **1937** *Jrnl. R. Anthrop. Inst.* LXVII. 137 Members of the owner's joint-family and lineage. **1953** J. H. WEAKLAND in Mead & Métraux *Study of Culture at Distance* x. v. 423 Dissent among the brothers of a Chinese joint family is concealed from the public. **1957** *Encycl. Brit.* XII. 235/2 The striking feature of Hindu society and Hindu law is the joint family. It is the form, no doubt, in which the Aryan patriarchal family has survived. **1968** G. D. MITCHELL *Dict. Sociol.* 77 Extended family is sometimes used not merely to include but as a synonym for joint family. It is more useful to restrict this last term to a form of family which has a number of distinctive characteristics: co-residence, commensality and often some common family cult. **1971** *Illustr. Weekly India* 11 Apr. 23/2 (*caption*) The house was full of Tagore relatives who all lived together as a traditional Bengali joint-family.

3. (Further examples.)

1778 *N.Y. Laws* 27 Mar., The joint Committee..[shall] canvas and estimate the votes. **1869** *Bradshaw's Railway Manual* XXI. 80 The companies should enter into a joint purse agreement with the Irish North Western. **1884** Joint account [see ACCOUNT *sb.* 2, def.]. **1886** G. C. BRODRICK *Hist. Univ. Oxf.* xviii. 213 A vote of censure on Dr. Hampden..was defeated in Convocation by the Proctors' joint-veto. **1909** WEBSTER, Joint sitting. **1936** T. S. ELIOT *Coll. Poems 1909–1935* 138 The fletchers and javelin-makers and smiths Have appointed a joint committee to protest against the reduction of orders. **1937** *Discovery* May 139/1 The formal invitation of the Indian Science Congress Association for the British Association to send a party to hold a joint session in India. **1942** N. BALCHIN *Darkness falls from Air* x. 184 You'll want some money... Use the joint account. **1952** H. NICOLSON *King George V* ix. 132 It was agreed..that if..an irreconcilable conflict arose between the House of Commons and the House of Lords, the matter should be settled by a Joint Sitting of both Houses. **1964** W. DUFF *Indian Hist. Brit. Columbia* I. 73 Of great and growing importance in recent years has been the development of 'joint' or 'integrated' schools. **1965** H. I. ANSOFF *Corporate Strategy* ii. 16 Joint-venture opportunities. **1966** *Rep. Comm. Inquiry Univ. Oxf.* I. 83 A statutory 'joint' committee of Council, the General Board, and the Council of the Colleges. **1966** T. LUPTON *Managem. & Social Sci.* iii. 63 The term Joint Consultation is usually used to describe the formal machinery through which the managers and the workers in a firm..discuss their common problems. **1972** WODEHOUSE *Pearls, Girls, & Monty Bodkin* iv. 50 He and his wife have a joint account, and he can't draw a cheque without her approval. **1973** *Oxf. Univ. Gaz.* 16 May 866/1 A universal system of joint appointments is in my view unnecessary.

b. *joint denial*: the negation of each of two or more stated propositions; 'neither..nor..'.

1940 W. V. QUINE *Math. Logic* i. 45 A joint denial, e.g. 'Neither is Jones away nor is Smith ill',..is true just in case its components are both false. *Ibid.* 49 The definability of denial, conjunction, and alternation in terms of joint denial was first pointed out by Sheffer in 1913. **1954** I. M. COPI *Symbolic Logic* viii. 256 The other operator which suffices for a functionally complete logic is that of 'joint denial'. **1960** S. KÖRNER *Philos. of Math.* ii. 40 All truth functions..can be introduced by definition if we start either (a) with the single notion of alternative denial .., or else (b) with the single notion of joint denial.

joint, *v.* Add: **1. d.** (Earlier U.S. example.)

1815 *Niles' Reg.* IX. 36/1 The power is given by one or two horses, which with a man and a boy can dress and joint..the staves necessary for one hundred barrels.

4. *intr.* To form joints.

1772 *Carroll Papers* in *Maryland Hist. Mag.* (1919) XIV. 287, I am apprehensive it will be too thick and Joint if the weather proves warme. **1904** *Topeka* (Kansas) *Daily Capital* 1 June 8 Wheat has not done well, though it is jointing now.

jointed, *a.* Add: **1.** (Examples in *Geol.*: cf. JOINT *sb.* 5.)

1821 J. MACCULLOCH *Geol. Classification of Rocks* viii. 129 In a few instances, from the extreme shortness of the prisms, the columnar passes to a tabular, or a lamellar and jointed structure. **1863** D. T. ANSTED *Gt. Stone Bk.* ix. 133 The harder kinds of sand-rock are always jointed. **1968** R. W. FAIRBRIDGE *Encycl. Geomorphol.* 489/2 The contrast between granite that is widely jointed and that which is closely jointed and generally shattered is easily seen in many localities.

3. *Bot.* Having or appearing to have joints; separating readily at the joints; as a specific vernacular name.

1597 Iointed Glassewoort [see GLASSWORT]. **1793** T. MARTYN *Lang. Bot.* s.v. Jointed...Applied to the root.. —to the stem or culm, in corn and grasses—to the leaves, when one leaflet grows from the top of another. **1821** S. F. GRAY *Nat. Arrangement Brit. Plants* II. 160 Leaves ..knotty, jointed, or smooth. **1839** J. LINDLEY *Sch. Bot.* 4 If a stem is swelled at the part where the leaves grow, and capable of being snapped across, or apparently so, it is called *articulated* or *jointed*, as in Stellaria Holostea, and Geraniums. **1843** C. C. BABINGTON *Man. Brit. Bot.* 31 *Raphanus Raphanistrum* (L.)..Jointed Charlock. **1913** C. PETTMAN *Africanderisms* 234 Jointed cactus, *Opuntia pusilla*, a dangerous weed. **1971** J. E. LOUSLEY *Flora Isles of Scilly* 268 *J*[*uncus*] *articulatus* L. Jointed Rush. Native.

jointer[2]. **1. a.** (Further examples.)

1885 J. RICHARDS *Wood-Working Machinery* 147 The first and leading tools are bench planes, a set of which should consist of one 26-inch jointer..one 24-inch jointer ..one 22-inch foreplane [etc.]. **1900** C. G. WHEELER *Woodworking for Beginners* xvi. 448 The jointer..is more accurate for making a surface level and true, or for shooting the edges of boards. **1953** W. COVENTON *Woodwork Tools* ii. 48 The trying plane..will be used for finishing the jointing, unless there is much jointing to do in hardwood, when it will pay to follow with a steel panel and jointer plane. **1958** G. H. LOVE *Theory & Pract. Woodwork* ii. 28 Working on the assumption that the longer the surface, the longer the plane required to true it, we have the jointer, a plane which is even longer than the trying plane. **1959** *Handyman & Home Mechanic* I. 36/2 Steel trying planes are often known as jointers, and are similar to steel jack planes except in length.

joint-grass. (U.S. examples.)

1835 W. G. SIMMS *Partisan* 55 Rebellion grows like joint-grass when it once takes root. **1894** J. M. COULTER *Bot. W. Texas* III. 499 Joint grass...Moist places throughout Texas and across the continent.

jointless, *a.* Add: **b.** In one piece; without a seam or joint of any kind.

1909 *Prosp. Rubber-Tanned Leather Co.* 2 May, Automobile tyres in seamless and jointless bands. **1921** *Dict. Occup. Terms* (1927) § 571 'Composition' or jointless floors.

joint stock, joint-stock. Add: **2.** *attrib. joint-stock bank, -company* (earlier and later examples). Also *joint-stock-companyship.*

1776 Joint-stock company [see COMPANY *sb.* 7]. **1843** *Ainsworth's Mag.* IV. 110 It is a pleasant privilege of the honourable corps..that a sort of joint-stock-companyship prevails among them. **1853** MRS. GASKELL *Cranford* xii. 225 Her poor opinion of joint-stock banks in general. **1964** GOULD & KOLB *Dict. Social Sci.* 550/1 The modern business corporation or joint stock company originated in the 18th century. **1969** *Lebende Sprachen* XIV. 97/2 Clearing arrangements have been agreed with the joint stock banks, so that money can be readily transferred from a giro account to a bank account. **1972** *Accountant* 5 Oct. 413/1 Sweden's national pension fund, it has been recommended, should be free to invest approximately 1 per cent of its resources in selected joint-stock companies.

joint-worm. 2. Substitute for def.: The larval form of several species of chalcid flies belonging to the genus *Harmolita* (or *Tetramesa*), which forms galls near joints on grain stems, causing them to bend. (Examples.)

1851 *Southern Planter* (Richmond, Virginia) July 197/2 Joint worm has injured White Flint most, Early Purple Straw next, and Mediterranean least. **1851** A. FITCH in *Cultivator* VIII. 322/1, I first observe, lying upon the infested stalk, the insect to which you allude in your letter, as perhaps having been hatched from the joint-worm. **1852** T. W. HARRIS *Insects Injurious to Vegetation* (ed. 2) 443 The ravages of the joint-worm in the wheat-fields of Virginia are said to have been first observed in Albemarle county, about four or five years ago. **1882** *Illinois Entomol. Rep.* XI. 81, I have obtained another specimen of this species from a gall in a stalk, produced evidently by the regular joint-worm. **1918** *U.S. Dept. Agric. Farmers' Bull.* No. 1006. 2 This jointworm can be controlled in Virginia, Tennessee, and Kentucky by plowing down wheat stubble deeply after harvest. **1972** SWAN & PAPP *Common Insects N. Amer.* xxi. 537 The Rye Jointworm, *T*[*etramesa*] *secale*, occurs in eastern U.S., westward to Utah and Alberta.

Jokari (dʒǒkā·ri). The proprietary name of a game played with bat and ball.

The name is registered for a number of games, etc. (see quot. 1973).

1953 *N.Y. Times* 2 Aug. 43L (Advt.), Jokari requires little space. You use paddles and a ball that's fastened to the Jokari center control box on a long rubber cable. **1960** 'A. GARVE' *Golden Deed* xxiv. 161 A bald, plump man..was playing Jokari with an equally plump youth on the grass outside the door... Mellanby waited till the ball had come to rest. **1961** B. W. ALDISS *Primal Urge* ii. 34 That podgy creature who..played Jokari from a sitting position. **1963** I. FLEMING *On H.M. Secret Service* i. 11 Two golden girls in exciting bikinis packed up the game of Jokari which they had been so provocatively playing. **1973** *Trade Marks Jrnl.* 4 Apr. 665/1 Jokari... Games (other than ordinary playing cards), playthings, gymnastic and sporting articles (other than clothing), and parts..of all the aforesaid goods. R. & J. Travis Limited, Fenbright Works,..Berkhamsted, Hertfordshire; manufacturers and merchants.

joke, *sb.* Add: **1.** *practical joke* (earlier and later examples); *a joke is a joke*: a joke is not to be taken seriously (freq. with the implication that the matter referred to is too serious for jokes); *joke over*: the joke is finished (usu. implying that the speaker is not amused by the words or behaviour of the person addressed).

1804 M. WILMOT *Let.* 4 June in *Russ. Jrnls.* (1934) I. 104 Such are the practical Jokes of the Great. **1824** J. HOGG *Private Mem. Justified Sinner* 356 Nane o' your practical jokes on strangers an' honest foks. **1837** DICKENS *Sk. Boz* 2nd Ser. 123 A joke's a joke: and even practical jests are very capital in their way, if you can only get the other party to see the fun. **1838** T. C. HALIBURTON *Clockmaker* 2nd Ser. xvii. 253 A joke is a joke, but that's no joke. **1849** [see PRACTICAL *a.* 1]. **1892** [see **bear-fight*]. **1930** R. GORE-BROWNE *By Way of Confession* vi. 52 'Goes too far, 'e does!' agreed an elder with a walrus mustache. 'A joke's er joke.' 'And politics is politics!' The retort came from a skinny-necked man. **1941** [see *COD *v.*[3]]. *a* **1953** E. O'NEILL *Long Day's Journey* (1956) I. 25 No, Mary, a joke is a joke, but—. **1961** PARTRIDGE *Dict. Slang* Suppl. 1153/2 Joke over! or when do we laugh? **1965** G. M. WILSON *Devil's Skull* ix. 112 'Telephone!' He laughed again. 'All right, joke over,' said Lovick, nettled. **1967** C. WATSON *Lonelyheart 4122* xviii. 180 All right. Joke over. Now just what is it you think you're up to? **1972** *Listener* 2 Nov. 614/1 Midnight feasts, practical jokes and all the fun of the dormitory.

b. *black joke* (see quot. 1796). Also *coal-black joke. slang.*

The *c* 1710 example in Dict. should be dated not earlier than 1734 (*Amer. Speech* (1963) XXXVIII. 152).

1729 C. COFFEY *Beggar's Wedding* I. iv. 17 (*heading*) Hunter with Musick. Air X. Coal-black Joak. **1748** SMOLLETT *R. Random* II. liii. 186 He whistled one part and hummed another of Black Joke. **1796** GROSE *Dict. Vulgar T.* (ed. 3) *Black Joke*, a popular tune to a song, having for the burden, 'Her black joke and belly so white': figuratively the black joke signifies the monosyllable. **1808** S. W. RYLEY *Itinerant* I. iv. 91 A blind fiddler, mounted on a three footed stool, rasped away very *seriously* the black *Joke*. *c* **1835** [in Dict., sense 1]. **1970** P. O'BRIAN *Master & Commander* ix. 252 He decided..to sit it out until the drum beat to quarters,..humming the Black Joke.

4. *joke book, shop.*

1951 J. STEINBECK *Burning Bright* 23 His malformed wisdom, his pool-hall, locker-room, joke-book wisdom.

1973 T. TOBIN *Lett. of George Ade* 174 This rare pamphlet is in the Ford joke book tradition. **1947** K. P. KEMPTON *Short Story* 189 At a joke shop in town he had bought one of those spark-plug bombs with the idea of hitching it to a friend's jalopy. **1951** J. M. FRASER *Psychol.* iii. 28 Any 'joke-shop' will furnish examples of similar bits of apparatus designed to suggest a misleading total situation. **1967** V. C. CLINTON-BADDELEY *Death's Bright Dart* 122 Sinister in the silence gleamed the window of the Joke Shop. **1973** E. PAGE *Fortnight by Sea* ix. 101 One of those joke shops, you know, rubber poached eggs, exploding cigars.

joke, *v.* Add: **1. b.** *you are* (or *have got to be*) *joking*, etc.: in phrases indicative of incredulity. Cf. also *HAVE *v.* 7 d.

1907 G. B. SHAW *John Bull's Other Island* II. 36 Youre joking, Mr. Keegan: I'm sure yar. **1967** PARTRIDGE *Dict. Slang* Suppl. 1204/2 *You're, he is*, etc. *joking, of course.* A c.p. of modified optimism. **1967** N. LUCAS *C.I.D.* xiii. 195 'Norman, would you be interested in meeting Charlie de Silva?' 'Probably,' I replied, 'but where do I have to go, Paris, New York...' 'You're joking. He's skint.' **1968** M. STEWART *Wind off Small Isles* i. 26 'If I've got to turn on sand—' 'You could reverse up.' 'You've got to be joking.' **1972** *Times* 29 Sept. 15/5 'We can consider ourselves fortunate in the character of the Prime Minister.'.. In the parlance of the day, you must be joking, mate.

joker. Add: **1.** (Earlier and later examples of *practical joker.*)

1830 G. COLMAN *Random Rec.* II. vi. 205 It convinced me that he was no practical joker. **1899** BEERBOHM *More* 70 Scores of licensed practical jokers. **1926** A. CONAN DOYLE *Hist. Spiritualism* I. vii. 153 The contemptible crew of practical jokers and ill-natured researchers who visited her found her a ready victim. **1950** T. S. ELIOT *Cocktail Party* II. 104 Are you a devil Or merely a lunatic practical joker?

2. esp. *Austral.* and *N.Z.*

1868 *Auckland Punch* No. 2. 7/1 If Louis Napoleon could be prevailed on to bring over his Zouaves, and join the mounted marines, together with some Indian jokers. **1888** J. C. WICKHAM *Ramblings* xv. 92 The driver of this coach was the joker that wanted to charge me a shilling. **1895** [see *BEST *a.* 5 b]. **1941** *Coast to Coast* 197 We'd get tired of tramping around the mines listening to well-fed jokers say 'No'. **1949** [see *CLEAN *v.* 6 b]. **1951** *Landfall* V. 21 There are about a dozen brush in the place and about three times as many jokers. **1963** *Australasian Post* 14 Mar. 51/2 Mr Dingleton turned out to be a tall, rather thin, pleasant-looking joker with big feet. **1970** *N.Z. Listener* 12 Oct. 13/5 Their benevolent guff's even harder for a decent-spirited joker to accept.

3. b. Also in fig. phr. *joker in the pack*: a person whose behaviour is unexpected or unpredictable.

1963 *Times* 25 Feb. (Canada Suppl.) p. ii/2 Mr. Caouette is a joker in the pack; his group's tally of 26 federal seats reflects a morbid situation. **1973** G. SIMS *Hunters Point* vi. 47 Fred Wheeler may be the joker in the pack. He might have got Dave involved in something wild. **1974** *Times* 9 May 4/1 Although the Government has a majority of four votes over the Conservatives, there are 37 'jokers in the pack'.

4. A clause unobtrusively inserted in a legislative enactment and affecting its operation in a way not immediately apparent. Also *transf.* of a clause, etc., in a contract, administrative order, etc., which frustrates its intention or puts one of the parties at a disadvantage; *fig.*, a drawback, a 'snag', a trick. *U.S.*

1904 *N.Y. Even. Post* 11 May 1 They are all nervous over the possibility that there may be a hitherto unperceived joker in the present bill. **1906** *Ibid.* 30 Apr. 6 The Malby 'joker' to the Adirondack Reserve bill. **1914** S. H. ADAMS *Clarion* 241 Even her simple mind grasped the joker in the contract. **1928** *Daily Express* 17 July 8/2 The surtax was slipped into the Finance Act of 1927 very much as a 'joker' is occasionally insinuated into an American Tariff Act—that is to say, surreptitiously, without anybody except those in the know being aware of the significance of what was happening. **1935** A. J. POLLOCK *Underworld Speaks* 65/1 *Joker* (*nigger in the wood pile*), laws, investigations, vice abatements, controversies, political appointments, newspaper articles, speeches or contracts arranged for..so that the looters in on the in will be financially benefited. **1942** E. PAUL *Narrow St.* xiv. 100 Early in 1926 Painlevé introduced a bill to reorganize the French army from thirty-two to twenty divisions. To this was attached a joker, increasing the term of universal compulsory military service from one year to eighteen months. **1947** *Harper's Mag.* Nov. 441/1 The order also contains this crucial joker: The charges shall be stated as specifically and completely as..security conditions permit. **1953** *Congress. Rec.* XCIX. App. A5292/2 A postal rate increase bill..had within it a 'joker' which seriously affected the nonprofit publications of organized labor in all parts of America.

jokery. Delete † and add later example.

1970 *Daily Tel.* 21 May 6/5, I could find very little to make me laugh..although it has all the ingredients of current jokery.

jokey: see *JOKY *a.*

jokiness (dʒōᵘ·kinės). [f. JOKY *a.* + -NESS.] A joking style or manner.

1869 D. G. ROSSETTI *Let.* 26 Aug. (1965) II. 720 His letters remind one by their ponderous jokiness of Holman Hunt. **1966** *Punch* 26 Jan. 138/3 Very short chapters and much coy jokiness about methods of fiction add to the Shandean charm. **1971** *Daily Tel.* (Colour Suppl.) 8 Jan. 6/2 The jokiness at a first night of an amateur theatrical company. **1974** *Times* 11 May 9/8 The self-conscious jokiness and triviality that is the bane of newscasting on British television.

joking, *vbl. sb.* Add: (Earlier examples of *practical joking.*) Phr. *joking apart* [APART *adv.* 5 b].

1745 S. CIBBER *Let.* 18 July in D. Garrick *Private Corr.* (1831) I. 35 But joking apart, I long till you come that we may consult together. **1841** J. ELLIOTSON *Let.* 4 Aug. in Dickens *Lett.* (1969) II. 345 Joking apart, you make me ashamed with your overflowing of the *milk* of kindness. **1853** MRS. GASKELL *Cranford* vi. 101 The captain of the school in the art of practical joking. **1860** Practical joking [see BITE *sb.* 9]. **1918** C. MACKENZIE *Early Life Sylvia Scarlett* II. i. 256 No, joking apart, I think it would be a great effort. **1931** 'G. TREVOR' *Murder at School* xiii. 254 Joking apart, you had some ingenious ideas. **1973** *Times* 17 Nov. 11/8 Joking apart, this is the kind of show difficult to write about without..spoiling the jokes.

b. *joking relationship* (Anthropol.), a relationship of familiarity between specific persons which is sanctioned in certain tribal groups.

1920 R. H. LOWIE *Primitive Soc.* (1921) v. 95 Of a distinct character is the joking-relationship of the Crow and Hidarsa. **1933** E. E. EVANS-PRITCHARD *Ess. Social Anthropol.* (1962) vii. 151 One way in which intimacy and equality are expressed between the partners [*sc.* blood-brothers] is by each publicly insulting the other, a custom commonly described by ethnologists as a 'joking relationship'. *Ibid.* 152 A 'joking relationship' may grow up between two clans. **1958** A. R. RADCLIFFE-BROWN *Method in Social Anthropol.* I. v. 119 The expression of opposition between the moieties may take various forms. One is the institution to which anthropologists have given the not very satisfactory name of 'the joking relationship'. **1964** GOULD & KOLB *Dict. Social Sci.* 358/1 A joking relationship is a relationship between two persons (sometimes between two groups) in which one is by custom permitted (and in some cases obliged) to tease or make fun of the other, who must take no offence...Obscenity.. and the taking of property are common forms.

jokist. (Earlier U.S. example.)

1873 'MARK TWAIN' & WARNER *Gilded Age* xxxvi. 331 And here is The Jokist's Own Treasury.

joky, *a.* Add: Freq. **jokey.** Also, subject to jokes, ridiculous. (Later examples.)

1964 'N. BLAKE' *Sad Variety* viii. 149 'Leake,' I said, 'your mind's as jokey as your clothes.' **1970** *Homes & Gardens* May 145/1 Despite the jokey reputation that middle-class British hotels enjoy, they compare very well indeed for comfort with their European and US counterparts. **1972** *Times Lit. Suppl.* 1 Sept. 1014/4 Crops up again in less joky moments. *Ibid.* 1021/1 A jokey 'textbook' tricked out with comic diagrams. **1974** *Times Lit. Suppl.* 11 Oct. 1142/4 The use of anachronism..is now a joky, selfconscious device.

‖ **jol** (dʒōᵘl). Also **djōl, jāl, jaul, jawl, johl, jōl.** [Arab.] The local name (often with capital initial) for a barren, much dissected, limestone plateau south of Wadi Hadhramaut in the Arabian peninsula; also applied (often with capital initial) to different regions within this plateau, and (with lower-case initial) to the individual blocks of tableland into which the whole plateau is dissected.

By some writers the plateau itself is designated by the plural form.

1904 D. G. HOGARTH *Penetration of Arabia* II. ix. 217 The guides conducted Hirsch through the cultivated coastal district..up to a bare down-land, 'Jol', rising to six thousand five hundred feet. *Ibid.* 219 At the head of this [*sc.* a valley] he found himself once more on the downs of the Jol, a wild, arid, broken country. **1921** *Handbk. Arabia* (Admiralty, Naval Intelligence Div.) I. vii. 218 Physically the Hadhramaut may be divided into four main horizontal belts:..(*b*) a broad belt of downs or plateaux (jāl) diversified by a few outstanding peaks. **1932** VAN DER MEULEN & VON WISSMAN *Ḥadramaut* iii. 53 Our way now led over the *djōl* as far as Wādī Dōᶜan. The *djōl* consists of vast table-lands of reddish-brown limestone. *Ibid.* xvi. 210 This *djōl* differed little in character from that which we had crossed on our way to Wādī Dōᶜan. **1936** F. STARK *Southern Gates Arabia* ix. 87 The Jōl has usually been dismissed by travellers as a piece of dull dreariness, a plateau where heat and cold are alike unbearable. **1940** —— *Winter in Arabia* iii. 14 Our lorry ..began to climb long broken ridges that lead to the tilted plateau of the jōl. *Ibid.*, Jōl—waterless steppe plateau. **1945** *Antiquity* XIX. 189, I expect that these stone-age people lived very much the life that the Beduins of the northern jols of the Hadhramaut on the edge of the Rub'al Khali live today. **1946** *Western Arabia & Red Sea* (Geogr. Handbk. Ser. B.R. 527, Admiralty, Naval Intelligence Div.) ii. 32 To the north the land rises to 3,500 feet between the wadi and the desert, but to the south altitudes of 6,000 feet and more are attained. These barren *jōls* are dissected into detached blocks of tableland by an extraordinarily intricate network of canyons and valleys. **1958** *Geogr. Jrnl.* CXXIV. 165 This is Wādī Ḥadramaut..which is enclosed by the precipices of the limestone strata of a wide and barren table land, the Jaul. **1961** *U.S. Board on Geogr. Names, Gazetteer no. 54: Arabian Peninsula* p. vi, Jawl..plateau, plain. **1966** J. LUNT *Barren Rocks Aden* ix. 139 We were now on the *johl*, as the Arabs call the mountainous plateau which lies between the coast and the Wadi Hadhramaut, and between the Wadi Hadhramaut and the Empty Quarter. **1966** W. C. BRICE *S.-W. Asia* xii. 253 Further inland, in the districts known as the Jols, the limestone surface..is scored with a maze of ravines.

‖ **jolie laide** (ʒoli lɛ̄d). [Fr., fem. sing. of *joli* pretty + *laid* ugly.] A woman or girl who is attractive in spite of not being pretty. Occas. *joli laid* (lɛ̄), applied to a man.

1894 LADY MONKSWELL *Diary* 12 May in E. C. F. Collier *Victorian Diarist* (1944) I. 243 Mrs. Flower is a 'jolie laide' of about 50, rather charming. **1949** N. MITFORD *Love in Cold Climate* I. viii. 87 One was a beauty or a *jolie-laide* and that was that. **1960** D. HOLMAN-HUNT *My Grandmothers & I* i. 6 The lazy young ladies who came to stay were called *jolies laides.* **1961** *Times* 10 Oct. 16/1 The arrival in the house..of a jolie-laide innocent looking for the Y.W.C.A. **1966** *Observer* 20 Mar. 25/4 He has the *joli-laid* face of a boxer. **1972** *Times* 22 June 12/5 Sexual teases like *jolie-laide* Israeli Drora. **1973** R. RENDELL *Some lie & Some Die* xi. 95 He had an ugly attractive face, *joli laid.*

jolley (dʒǫ·li). *Pottery.* Also **jolly.** [Of unknown origin.] A variety of jigger (see JIGGER *sb.*[1] 5 a). So **jo·lleying, jo·llying** *vbl. sb.*, the act of using a jolley; **jo·llied** *ppl. a.*, manufactured by jolley; **jo·llier**[1], **jollyer,** one who makes pottery by means of a jolley.

1881 *Instructions to Census Clerks* (1885) 88 Earthenware..manufacture... Jollier. Jolly Maker. **1891** *Pop. Sci. Monthly* Dec. 168 A 'jolly'..consisting of a table on which is a revolving mold [etc.]. **1901** W. P. RIX tr. *Bourry's Treat. Ceramic Industries* iv. 182 In jollying, the body is compressed, and forced to become stretched out by means of a profile, having the outline of the article to be made. *Ibid.* 213 The heads of jolleys are arranged so as to receive the moulds, the placing and removal of which must be done very rapidly. **1915** A. B. SEARLE *Clays & Clay Products* xv. 118 As plates and saucers are always made 'upside down' the profile forms the 'bottom' of the plate. The machines used for this work are known as *jiggers* and *jolleys.* **1921** *Dict. Occup. Terms* (1927) § 105 *Bowl maker*,..a jollier who makes bowls by jolleying process. *Ibid.*, *Cup maker*, a jollier who makes cups on a single or double cup jolley. **1934** J. B. PRIESTLEY *Eng. Journey* 213 If Bennett had been either a master potter on the one hand, or a 'thrower' or 'jollyer' on the other. *Ibid.* 220 If you work at the stuff [*sc.* potter's clay] inside a mould, you are, I believe, either 'jollying' or 'jiggering'. **1951** *Electronic Engin.* XXIII. 337 Automatic jollying machines have now been developed for the production of plates, cups and saucers. **1960** H. POWELL *Beginner's Bk. Pott.* I. i. 14 A good investment for a fairly small cash outlay is the jigger, or jolley (no one seems to know which name is correct). **1972** N. FRENCH *Industr. Ceramics: Tableware* iii. 26 The extreme precision and expense of mould-making normally offsets the advantages of jolleying.

jo·llier[2]. *U.S.* [f. JOLLY *v.* 2 c.] One who 'jollies' or flatters others; a jovial or sociable person.

1896 ADE *Artie* ix. 78 He's one o'f the biggest jolliers that ever come over the hills. **1901** MERWIN & WEBSTER *Calumet 'K'* i. 12 Oh, he's a good-looking young chap... He's a great jollier. **1904** 'No. 1500' *Life in Sing Sing* 250/1 Jollier, flatterer. **1905** *N.Y. Even. Post* 12 Oct. 2 He was talkative, and as the attendants say, 'quite a jollier'. **1946** W. A. WHITE *Autobiogr.* 443, I was errand boy, peacemaker, jollier, fixer, horse-trader.

jollo (dʒǫ·lo). *Austral. slang.* [app. f. JOLL(IFICATION + Austral.termination *-o[2].] A party, esp. one at which liquor is drunk. Cf. *JOLLY *sb.*[4]

1934 *Bulletin* (Sydney) 25 July 46/3 Most..came to the wedding jollo to drink the beer and admire the bride's new fawn coat-and-skirt. **1966** BAKER *Austral. Lang.* (ed. 2) xi. 230 Australians have a fair selection of terms to describe drinking and drinking bouts, such as..jollo [etc.].

Jollof, Jolof, varr. *WOLOF.

jollop (dʒǫ·ləp), *sb.*[2] *slang.* [See JALAP *sb.*] **a.** A purgative, a medicine. **b.** Strong liquor, or a drink of this.

1920 *Contemp. Rev.* Aug. 250 We may imagine them [*sc.* smugglers *c* 1820] stowing away their precious booty in *caches*, then a jollop of brandy all round. **1955** D. NILAND *Shiralee* 146 He nutted out some jollop for her cough. **1961** C. WILLOCK *Death in Covert* ii. 32 'Tell 'em up at the house to bring out the jollop.' The keeper uttered this in a tone that made it quite clear that he considered serving refreshment something completely outside his duties. **1966** 'L. LANE' *ABZ of Scouse* 57 If yer don't wallop yer jollop yer'll get ther beezers in yer belly.

jollopy, var. *JALOPY.

jolly, *a.* Add: **5. b.** *jolly roger*: see ROGER[2] 4.

13. b. Also *ironically.*

1916 GALSWORTHY *Sheaf* i. 13 'Jolly for my new coat!' I said.

C. jolly-tail *Austral.*, a small fresh-water fish of the genus *Galaxias*, esp. *G. attenuatus.*

1892 P. L. SIMMONDS *Commercial Dict. Trade Products* (rev. ed.) Suppl. 463/2 *Jolly-tail*, a small fresh-water fish of Australia..highly esteemed as a delicacy for the table. There are several species. **1898** E. E. MORRIS *Austral Eng.* 224/1 Jolly-tail, *n.* a Tasmanian name for the larger

variety of the fish *Galaxias attenuatus*, Jenyns, and other species of *Galaxias*. **1951** T. C. ROUGHLEY *Fish Austral.* (rev. ed.) 156 It [*sc.* whitebait] is composed mainly of the young fry of small fish known as minnows or jollytails (*Galaxias attenuatus*). **1965** *Austral. Encycl.* V. 141/2 Jollytails, small freshwater fishes (*Galaxias*) rarely attaining a length of 8 inches.

Jolly (dʒǫ·li, yǫ·li), *sb.*[3] The name of P. von *Jolly* (1809–1884), German physicist, used *attrib.* († or in the possessive) to denote a balance invented by him, used esp. in determining the specific gravities of minerals, in which the elongation of a helical spring when a body is hung on it indicates the weight of the body.

1882 A. GEIKIE *Text-bk. Geol.* II. ii. 93 Jolly's spring balance is a simple and serviceable instrument. **1906** J. P. IDDINGS *Rock Minerals* ii. 92 By means of a Jolly balance or spring..the specific gravity of a crystal may be found with approximate accuracy. **1964** J. SINKANKAS *Mineral. for Amateurs* vii. 187 In the homemade Jolly balance shown.., a specimen attached by thread to the lower hook of the spring carries it down a certain distance which can be measured.

jolly, *sb.*[4] *colloq.* Short for JOLLIFICATION; so, a thrill of enjoyment or excitement, as in phr. *to get one's jollies*. Also *jollyo, jolly-up*. Cf. *JOLLO.

1905 in *Dialect Notes* (1908) III. 325 Justice Brewer's jolly. **1907** F. H. BURNETT *Shuttle* xxiii. 237 If you can give 'em a jolly and make 'em laugh, they'll listen. **1920** *Spectator* 4 Dec. 740/1 Every age must be allowed an occasional 'jolly'. **1921** GALSWORTHY *To Let* II. iv. 154 Come and have a 'jolly' with us. **1924** M. NEWMAN *Consummation* IV. xv. 197 Troops fed to the teeth with.. relentless routine, broken only by the occasional horror of a 'show' (what Bossy called a 'jolly'). **1927** *Amer. Speech* II. 277/1 *Jolly-up*, informal dance. **1932** E. WAUGH *Black Mischief* iv. 140 Why can't the silly mutt go off home and leave us to have a jolly up. **1957** M. SHULMAN *Rally round the Flag, Boys!* (1958) ix. 100 If she wasn't so goddam busy..then he wouldn't be thinking about getting his jollies elsewhere! **1962** in Wentworth & Flexner *Dict. Amer. Slang* Suppl. (1967) 686/1 The owner of this place gets his jollies by walking around most of the day in a Sioux war bonnet. **1963** *Daily Tel.* 3 Oct. 20/2 Many parents rejoice inwardly at..their sons being immured under a régime of spartan rigour, but if the compensating jolly-up in the holidays is carried beyond a certain point the whole exercise becomes..unrealistic. **1966** D. FRANCIS *Flying Finish* v. 64 You couldn't just go up alone for an afternoon's jolly in an airliner. **1968** *Surfer Mag.* Jan. 18/2 The announcer acted like this is where all of the surfers go after dark to get their jollies. **1970** V. C. CLINTON-BADDELEY *No Case for Police* iv. 78, I had gone for a jollyo to one of the rather swell hotels. **1971** 'W. HAGGARD' *Bitter Harvest* xiv. 145 It would be a splendid wedding, the sort of big jolly Charles Russell enjoyed.

jolly, *v.* Add: **2. a.** (Later example.)

1924 H. DE SELINCOURT *Cricket Match* vii. 219 Their main effort seems not to be..jollied out for a depressing total.

c. For '*U.S.*' read 'orig. *U.S.*' (Earlier and later examples.) Also with *impers.* obj.

1890 H. PALMER *Stories of Base Ball Field* 81, I jollied him along as strong as I could. **1901** *Daily Colonist* (Victoria, B.C.) 19 Oct. 2/5 It is now asserted that the message was an artful device of the astute Mr. Bratnober, who wanted to keep Mr. Macdonald 'jollied up' until the time should come to dispense with his services. **1908** G. H. LORIMER *Jack Spurlock* v. 91 Our customers expect the boys to have a little snap and jolly their grub along. **1929** E. WILSON *I thought of Daisy* iv. 253, I thought that I'd jolly him along a little. **1938** E. WAUGH *Scoop* II. i. 124 We've got to..make contacts, dig up some news sources, jolly up the locals a bit. **1943** J. B. PRIESTLEY *Daylight on Saturday* xi. 68 He had seen himself arranging sports and entertainments..and generally jollying everybody along. **1958** 'A. GILBERT' *Death against Clock* 10 Her clothes were varying shades of brown, jollied up with a purple scarf. **1959** *Times* 28 July 11/2 Mr. Maurice Browning..jollies things along briskly enough, with enthusiastic aid from the audience. **1973** H. MCCLOY *Change of Heart* iv. 40 He protested, he argued, he even tried to jolly them along. They only became bolder.

jolt, *v.* Add: **2. b.** To startle, to surprise. Cf. *JOLT *sb.* 2 b.

1872 'MARK TWAIN' *Roughing It* (1873) ii. 27 She would launch a slap at him that would have jolted a cow. **1875** —— in *Atlantic Monthly* Feb. 219, I said I didn't know. 'Don't know?' His manner jolted me. **1919** H. CRANE *Let.* 27 Dec. (1965) 28 Yes, the last word will jolt you. **1972** *Guardian* 23 Dec. 17/2 Those mega-million pound takeover bids which jolt the City.

jolt, *sb.* Add: **2. b.** *fig.* A surprise; a shock which disturbs one's mental composure.

1884 'MARK TWAIN' *Huck. Finn* v. 30, I was scared now,..but in a minute I see I was mistaken. That is, after the first jolt,..he being so unexpected. **1905** D. G. PHILLIPS *Plum Tree* 3 I'd like to give him a jolt. **1924** H. T. LOWE-PORTER tr. *Mann's Buddenbrooks* I. vi. 208 Oh, no! I know they gave you a jolt yesterday—a very, very stimulating jolt.

c. A blow in boxing. Also in phr. *to pass a jolt*, to deliver a blow. Also *fig.*

1908 S. E. WHITE *Riverman* xvii. 160 Murphy blocked, ducked, and kept away, occasionally delivering a jolt as opportunity offered. **1912** [see *HAY-MAKER 4]. **1916** C. J. DENNIS *Songs Sentimental Bloke* 124 *Jolt, to pass a*, to deliver a short, sharp blow. **1950** J. DEMPSEY *Championship Fighting* vii. 26 Best of all the punches is the 'stepping straight jolt'. **1954** F. C. AVIS *Boxing Reference Dict.* 60 *Jolt*, a kind of jab punch that brings up short an advancing opponent.

4. a. A drink of liquor. *slang* (chiefly *U.S.*).

1904 *McClure's Mag.* Mar. 560/2, I stopped at a blacksmith's shop..and had my arm dressed and a big jolt of whiskey. **1920** F. SCOTT FITZGERALD *This Side of Paradise* (1921) II. iv. 252 We'll take you to some secluded nook and give you a wee jolt of Bourbon. **1935** G. BLUNDEN *No More Reality* xxxiii. 344 'Take another jolt, sport,' said Clarrie with a grin. **1957** A. MACNAB *Bulls of Iberia* xii. 125 'You've been drinking.'..'I shoved in a couple of jolts on the way here.' **1959** T. GRIFFITH *Waist-High Culture* (1960) 231 Jolts of whiskey or vodka. **1973** R. THOMAS *If you can't be Good* (1974) xvi. 145 She took two green plastic glasses... I poured a generous jolt into both of them.

b. A prison sentence. *slang* (orig. *U.S.*).

1912 D. LOWRIE *My Life in Prison* ii. 17 A professional 'pete' man had..returned exultingly to the jail with a six-year 'jolt'. **1926** J. BLACK *You can't Win* xii. 197 He was in good spirits and condition after 'stopping his jolt' in the stir and anxious to start 'rooting'. **1928** [see *BOOK *sb.* 9 d]. **1936** 'D. HUME' *Meet Dragon* ix. 96 They are only too ready to turn King's evidence...you'd take a very stiff jolt.

c. = *BANG *sb.*[3]; a quantity of a drug in the form of a cigarette, tablet, etc. *slang* (chiefly *U.S.*).

1916 T. BURKE *Limehouse Nights* 19 A little later he would take a jolt of opium at the place at the corner of Formosa Street. **1926** J. BLACK *You can't Win* xii. 162 He wouldn't give us a jolt if we had the horrors... Given a sufficient quantity of hop, no fiend is ever at a loss for a sound reason for taking a jolt of it. **1929** D. HAMMETT *Dain Curse* (1930) xxi. 233 You can take your jolt in front of me. I won't blush. **1955** *U.S. Senate Hearings* (1956) VIII. 4164 Terms used in the traffic pertaining to the alkaloid morphine are as follows:..jolt,..a dose. **1970** K. PLATT *Pushbutton Butterfly* (1971) vi. 58 Her LSD cap would cost about two dollars and fifty cents for the jolt.

5. *attrib.* and *Comb.*, as **jolt ramming** *Founding*, a method of packing the sand around a pattern in which the moulding box, pattern, and sand are repeatedly lifted by machine and allowed to fall; freq. *attrib.*; **jolt-squeeze** *Founding*, simultaneous or successive jolting of a moulding box and 'squeezing' of the sand in it (i.e. application of pressure at the top), as a means of packing the sand around a pattern; usu. *attrib.*

1909 *Iron Age* LXXXIV. 1165/1 Today we have pneumatic jolt-ramming machines in successful service with lifting capacities from 10 to 15 tons. *Ibid.* 1165/2 How to adapt our foundry methods to this new principle of jolt-ramming green sand molds. **1926** *Jrnl. Iron & Steel Inst.* CXIII. 568 The whole of the mould and core are rammed on a Mumford jolt ramming machine. **1950** J. S. CAMPBELL *Casting & Forming Processes* xii. 104 Jolt ramming packs the lower portions of the sand next to the pattern best. **1931** *Jrnl. Iron & Steel Inst.* CXXIII. 602 (*heading*) A novel combination jolt-squeeze moulding machine. **1955** HEINE & ROSENTHAL *Princ. Metal Casting* iv. 53 Match-plate molding using jolt-squeeze machines is perhaps the simplest method of speeding up the molding of small castings. **1971** W. B. PARKES *Clay-Bonded Foundry Sand* viii. 235 For most moulds, all that is needed is a simultaneous jolt-squeeze of a few seconds.

jolter, *sb.*[1] (Further example.)

1843 *Knickerbocker* XXI. 39 The traveller has but to express a wish to visit a distant plantation, and his.. luggage is placed in the donkeyed jolter.

jo·ltiness. [f. JOLTY *a.* + -NESS.] The condition of being jolty.

1891 'L. MALET' *Wages of Sin* IV. iii. 78 Oh! the joltiness of this conversational road. **1905** *Westm. Gaz.* 9 May 4/2 The existing motor-'buses..with their perpetual pulling up, their joltiness, and malodorousness.

Joly (dʒǫ·li). The name of John *Joly* (1857–1933), Irish physicist, used *attrib.* and in the possessive to denote apparatus and processes devised by him, as **Joly('s) method, process** *Photogr.*, a process of colour photography using a screen (*Joly screen*) ruled with a repeating sequence of adjacent orange, blue-green, and blue lines placed in front of the plate in the camera and a screen similarly ruled with red, green, and blue lines placed in contact with the transparency when it is being projected; **Joly's steam calorimeter,** a device for determining the specific heat of a substance by measuring the weight of steam that condenses on a known mass of the substance in raising its temperature to that of the steam.

1894 T. PRESTON *Theory of Heat* v. 236 (*heading*) Joly's steam calorimeter. **1902** *Encycl. Brit.* XXXI. 686/1 (*heading*) Joly's process. **1906** E. J. WALL tr. *König's Natural-Color Photogr.* 20 In 1904 Professor Wood improved his process and applied it to positives obtained by the Joly process... Gratings were ruled with three sets of lines in bands corresponding to the width of the red, green, and blue lines of the Joly screen. **1909** S. E. BOTTOMLEY *Photogr. in Princ. & Pract.* xxvi. 207 At the time the Joly process was put on the market, a suitable panchromatic emulsion was not obtainable, and to this cause alone must be ascribed its non-success. **1938** W. J. SPARROW *Heat* vii. 139 Joly's steam calorimeter may be used (*a*) to find the specific heat of a solid.., (*b*) to determine the specific heat of a gas at constant volume. **1940** *Chambers's Techn. Dict.* 469/1 *Joly screen*, a colour mosaic consisting of ruled lines. **1958** H. BAINES *Sci. of Photogr.* xx. 246 Fig. 6 illustrates the reproduction of a red colour by the Joly and similar methods...The Joly experiments showed the possibility of colour photography using a mosaic screen. **1963** A. E. E. MCKENZIE *Second Course Heat* ii. 32 Joly's steam calorimeter measures heat in terms of the mass of steam condensed on a body.

Jomon (dʒōu·mǫn). Also **Jōmon.** [Jap.] Used *attrib.* in *Jomon pottery* to denote a kind of very early hand-made Japanese pottery; hence applied to the early neolithic or pre-neolithic culture which is characterized by this pottery.

1946 G. B. SANSOM *Japan* (rev. ed.) i. 1 Two main types of neolithic culture are distinguished. One is known as the Jōmon ('rope-pattern') type, because the pottery which characterises it was made by coiling or has a coil as conventional decoration. **1957** *Encycl. Brit.* XII. 901/1 The Jomon is classified as Neolithic. *Ibid.*, The Jomon ('cord-pattern') cultures have handmade pottery with patterns formed by rolling or pressing a cord-wrapped stick..into the still wet clay. **1960** B. LEACH *Potter in Japan* vii. 156 The earliest Jomon pots are long pre-Ainu and are estimated to be upwards of 6,000 years old. **1970** J. KIRKUP *Japan behind Fan* 27 Rare Haniwa and Jomon figures.

Jon (dʒǫn), abbrev. *JONATHAN 3.

1931 *Daily Tel.* 21 May 5/1 Jons 10s 6d–12s 6d.

Jonathan. Add: **3.** A red-skinned variety of dessert apple, first introduced in the United States.

1831 J. BUEL in *Gardeners' Mag.* VII. 239 Besides the Newton, I know of none except the Aesopus, the Pownal, the White and the New, or Jonathan. **1831** *Catal. Fruits in Garden of Hort. Soc.* (ed. 2) 18 Apples... Jonathan. **1845** A. J. DOWNING *Fruits Amer.* 113 The Jonathan is a very beautiful dessert apple... The original tree of this new sort is growing on the farm of Mr. Philip Rick, of Kingston, New York. **1879** *Chicago Tribune* 3 May 10/3 Our best winter apples are..Jeniton, Jonathan, Red Canada, Wythe. **1924** *Glasgow Herald* 23 Dec. 5 In 1922 the price realised for Jonathans did not pay the cost of packing. **1932** [see *DELICIOUS *a.* 2 b]. **1950** SMOCK & NEUBERT *Apples & Apple Products* ix. 233 Jonathan spot occurs primarily on Jonathan apples. **1959** [see *DELICIOUS *a.* 2 b]. **1963** A. LUBBOCK *Austral. Roundabout* 68 The crimson-cheeked Jonathan apples.

Jones (dʒōunz). **1.** One of the commonest British family names, used esp. in the plural to designate one's neighbours or social equals, as in phrase *to keep up with the Joneses*: see *KEEP *v.* 57 j; now usu. with allusion to this phrase.

1879 E. J. SIMMONS *Mem. Station Master* (1974) vi. 83 There is a considerable amount of importance attached to this public place of meeting—the railway station. The Jones's who don't associate with the Robinsons, meet there. Mr Jones would not like the station master to touch his cap to the Robinsons, and pass him without notice. **1932** E. C. HARWOOD *Cause & Control of Business Cycle* x. 124 Why..does John Doe choose to speculate on margin?.. An ages-old desire to get something for nothing; keeping up with the Joneses; [etc.]. **1955** J. CANNAN *Long Shadows* vii. 106 On a higher scale you're simply outdoing the Joneses. **1959** 'L. GIBB' (*title*) The Joneses: how to keep up with them. **1959** *Times* 18 Sept. 14/5 By addressing Mr. and Mrs. Jones through The Reader's Digest, you thus exert a selling leverage [etc.]..that's Jonesmanship. **1962** *Friend* 29 June 801/1 What we decide will be affected by whether we think morals are something stuck on to people by outside pressure (law, custom, tradition, and 'what the Joneses do') or whether they are an outcome of our nature. **1967** *Guardian* 3 Jan. 4/7, I pretended not to hear..but in the end you follow the Joneses. **1967** G. HOUSEHOLD *Courtesy of Death* 38 Dunton..avoided any nonsense of competing with Joneses.

2. *slang.* A drug addict's habit.

1968 *Sun Mag.* (Baltimore) 13 Oct. 19/4 Soon you're out to keep from getting the Jones. **1970** C. MAJOR *Dict. Afro-Amer. Slang* 71 *Jones*, a fixation; drug habit; compulsive attachment. **1971** *Black World* Mar. 54/1, I don't have a long jones. I ain't been on it too long. **1971** E. E. LANDY *Underground Dict.* 113 *Jones*, the habit of a drug addict—eg. *His jones is heavy*. **1974** *Publishers Weekly* 12 Aug. 50/2 Knows the reality of Detroit's heroin sub-culture as few of those who are not 'Jones men' do. ('Jones' stands for both heroin and the habit.)

Jonesian (dʒōu·nziăn), *a.* [f. name of Daniel *Jones* (1881–1967), English phonetician + -IAN.] Used to designate the phonetic system or the system of classifying phonemes adopted by Daniel Jones. Hence as *sb.*, an adherent or follower of Jones.

1951 *Language* XXVII. 334 Neither 'pure' phonetics nor Jonesian phonemics stands the ghost of a chance. **1953** A. MARTINET in *Anthropol. Today* 578 A Jonesian origin of the Bloomfieldian phoneme might account for the opinion. **1964** Y. R. CHAO in D. Abercrombie et al. *Daniel Jones* 40 Linguists trained under the Jonesian cardinal vowels. **1965** *Language* XLI. 308 Linguists who are neither Firthians nor Jonesians. **1969** *Ibid.* XLV. 109 A reaction against Jonesian and Bloomfieldian phonemics.

jong[1] (yǫŋ). *S. Afr.* [Afrikaans *jong* a coloured servant, f. Du. *jong* a young person.] Formerly, a young male slave; now a coloured male servant; also used as a familiar term of address to any person.

1615 W. PEYTON in R. Raven-Hart *Before Van Riebeeck* (1967) 71 One of the Condemned menn (with twoe other of the Peppercornes companye) caryed awaye her pinasse the next night, at which instant twoe yeongers of my Shipps companye allsoe conserted to carry awaye my boat. **1812** A. PLUMPTRE tr. *Lichtenstein's Trav. S. Afr.* I. viii. 119 A Hottentot..takes it extremely amiss if he is addressed by the words *Pay* or *Jonge*, as the slaves are. **1846** J. C. BROWN tr. *Arbousset & Daumas's Narr. Tour N.-E. of Cape Good Hope* xxiii. 253 Tied his *jong*, or young bushman slave, to the wheel of his wagon, where he was severely flogged. **1886** G. A. FARINI *Through Kalahari Desert* xvii. 279 These slaves were called 'yungs' or 'boys'. **1912** *East London* (Cape Province) *Dispatch* 13 Feb. 3 (Pettman), Presently a couple of jongs came along with dainty cigarettes in their mouths. **1926** E. LEWIS *Mantis* I. v. 88 And then, another time (so Dan wrote to his father), he'd make you feel a piccanin yourself, a proper little *jong* that'd never been beyond the dorp. **1939** S. CLOETE *Watch for Dawn* v. 65 Where is your whip, jong? **1953** J. COLLIN-SMITH *Locusts & Wild Honey* II. iv. 155, I..shouted into the house for the 'jong', the coloured houseboy, to bring me coffee. **1956** A. G. MCRAE *Hill called Grazing* vii. 55 Now look here, *jong*, I've got all these pigs yere on my farm, man. *Ibid.*, Now, if I can't get a permit to sell them, man *jong*, I'll have to drive them up on to the main road. **1960** D. LYTTON *Goddam White Man* i. 10 The sergeant at the police station says—'Watch it jong.' **1973** *Sunday Tribune* (Durban) 1 Apr. 20 Jong, I've had enough of this!

jong[2] (dʒǫŋ). Also **dzong.** [ad. Tibetan *rdzoṅ* fortress.] A Tibetan building (also, a territorial and administrative division) constituting a prefecture, freq. also serving as a fortress, a monastery, or both. Hence **dzo·ngpön, jo·ngpen, jong-pon,** a prefect; **jong-nyer,** a sub-prefect.

[**1888** *Encycl. Brit.* XXIII. 340/2 A valley to the south-east..contains the towns of Pena-jong and Gyangtse-jong.] **1904** *Times* 11 May 5/1 The Tibetans have strongly fortified the jong. **1904** *Daily Chron.* 21 May 5/4 The collection and equipment of the local levies are conducted by various Jongpen. **1911** *Encycl. Brit.* XXVI. 922/1 The administrative subdivisions of the Lhasa country..are called *jong*, or 'prefecture', each of which is under the rule of two *jong-pon*. *Ibid.*, There are 123 sub-prefectures under *jong-nyer*. **1921** *Glasgow Herald* 13 July 9 The Jongpen of the district rode out to meet us with a few followers. **1938** F. S. CHAPMAN *Lhasa* iii. 33 The *Dzongpön* (fort commander) of Phari came in for tea. *Ibid.* iv. 49 The dzong is..on the summit of a volcano-like rock six or seven hundred feet high. *Ibid.* v. 83 He is..magistrate, or dzongpön, of a district called Purang. **1960** 'S. HARVESTER' *Chinese Hammer* xi. 99 Phari Dzong, Hog Fort, a large square grey fortress. **1960** *Times* 9 June 15/6 The castle-monastery (the *dzong*) which rears high above the floor of the wide valley. **1966** *Times* 17 June 13/5 The great *dzong*..rears up on the side of the valley, inward-leaning walls around a keep.

jonga (dʒǫ·ŋgă). Also **jangga.** [f. Doulla-Bakweri (Cameroons) *njaŋga* crayfish.] In Jamaica, a small freshwater prawn, *Macrobrachium jamaicensis.*

See Cassidy & Le Page *Dict. Jamaican Eng.* s.v. *jangga* for oral uses of the word.

1893 C. SULLIVAN *Jamaica Cookery Book* 4 Jonga Soup. *Ibid.* 8 Jongas are a kind of small cray-fish which are often found in our mountain rivers. **1929** M. W. BECKWITH *Black Roadways* 51 Fresh-water shrimps, called *jonga*, from the mountain streams. **1967** *Amer. Speech* XLII. 191 *Jangga*, the river prawn *Macrobrachium jamaicense* [sic]. This word is usually found in print as *jonga*, an unfortunate misrepresentation which has probably led would-be explainers astray. Its actual pronunciation among the folk may always be respelled *jangga*. **1969** 'J. MORRIS' *Fever Grass* iii. 31 They're even canning *jongas* from the head-waters of the Martha Brae. **1971** E. JONES in J. Figueroa *Caribbean Voices* I. 4 Up in de hills, where de streams are cool, An' mullet an' janga swim in de pool.

joning (dʒōᵘ·niŋ), *vbl. sb.* [Origin unknown.] A name given by American Blacks to a game characterized by the exchange of insults; 'playing the dozens'.

1970 H. E. ROBERTS *Third Ear* 12/2 *Signifying*,..language behavior that makes direct or indirect implications of baiting or boasting, the essence of which is making fun of another's appearance, relatives or situation. Variations include joning, playing the dozens. **1971** C. M. KERNAN in A. Dundes *Mother Wit* (1973) 312 The verbal insult game known in other regions as..'Joning'. **1972** J. L. DILLARD *Black English* vi. 260 There are, of course, some characteristic topics, speech styles, and modes of discourse. One of the more interesting is called *jonin'* by the Washington community—*sounding* or *the dozens* elsewhere.

jonnop (dʒǫ·nəp). *Austral. slang.* [Contraction of *John Hop* (*JOHN I c).] A policeman.

1938 X. HERBERT *Capricornia* xxiv. 353 But even the jonnops don't treat the Binghis anything like they used to. **1963** A. LUBBOCK *Austral. Roundabout* 45 He's not a bad sort for a jonnop. **1966** BAKER *Austral. Lang.* vii. 142 England was originally responsible for the word cop, which Australia elaborated into the now-obsolete copman and copperman and which, by a process of rhyme, gave us the popular Australianisms john hop, jonnop and hop.

Jonsonian (dʒǫnsōᵘ·niăn), *a.* [f. the name of Ben *Jonson* (?1573–1637), English dramatist + -IAN.] Of, pertaining to, or characteristic of Jonson or his works. So **Jonso·nianly** *adv.*, in the manner of Jonson or his works.

1886 J. A. SYMONDS *Ben Jonson* 153 The most truly Jonsonian of all these places..was the Old Devil Tavern at Temple Bar. **1909** G. G. GREENWOOD *In re Shakespeare* ii. 76, I here leave the Jonsonian riddle. **1928** C. J. SISSON *Eliz. Dramatists* iv. 43 The Jonsonian comedy of humour. **1931** *Times Lit. Suppl.* 21 May 405/1 But the 'laws of dramatic art' have already ceased to look Aristotelian or Jonsonian. **1947** *Partisan Rev.* Mar.–Apr. 176 They are monsters in the Jonsonian manner; a human trait has been carried in them to the point of inhumanity. **1948** F. R. LEAVIS *Great Tradition* v. 235 Bounderby..remains Jonsonianly consistent in his last testament and death. **1959** *Times* 26 Nov. 6/5 Mr. Raymond Raikes's production took pleasure in the Jonsonian tumult. **1973** M. R. BOOTH *Eng. Plays of 19th Cent.* IV. 2 The father..may be a traditional Jonsonian 'humours' character with a dominant eccentricity.

jonty, var. *JAUNTY *sb.*

Jonval (ʒo·nval). *Engin.* The name of Nicolas Joseph *Jonval*, nineteenth-century Frenchman, used *attrib.* and *absol.* to denote an obsolete kind of reaction turbine (see quots.), patented by him in 1841.

1851 *Jrnl. Franklin Inst.* LII. 419 The advantage of the Jonval Turbine over the over-shot wheel, using the same amount of water, is consequently seven per cent. **1894** W. J. LINEHAM *Textbk. Mech. Engin.* xi. 724 The Jonval turbine, like the Fourneyron, is a pressure turbine; but while the latter works best above tail water, the Jonval is always drowned or else connected to tail water by a 'suction' tube. **1909** H. LOUIS *Dressing of Minerals* xii. 491 For lower falls turbines are best employed; a twin Jonval parallel-flow turbine..offers many advantages, amongst which may be reckoned the fact that the turbine itself may be situated 10 to 15 feet above the level of the tailwater. **1957** *Encycl. Brit.* XXII. 580/2 In..the Fourneyron, the guide vanes were inside the runner, and the water flowed outward. This was followed by the Jonval turbine, in which the guide vanes are above the runner and the water flows axially into and through the wheel. Both types are now obsolete.

jook, var. *JUKE *sb.*

Jordan[2] (dʒǭ·ɹdăn). The name of a river in Palestine, the crossing of which is used (after Num. 33:51) in pietistic language to symbolize death.

1684 BUNYAN *Pilgr.* II. 222 Mr. Stand-fast..went down to the River..he said..my Foot is fixed upon that, upon which the Feet of the Priests..stood while Israel went over this Jordan. **1707** I. WATTS *Hymns & Spiritual Songs* II. No. LXV. 139 Could we but climb where Moses stood, And view the Landskip o're, Not Jordan's Stream, nor Death's cold Flood Should fright us from the Shore. **1772** W. WILLIAMS *Hymn, 'Guide me, O Thou Great Jehovah'*, When I tread the Verge of Jordan. **1786** S. STENNETT (*title of hymn*), On Jordan's stormy banks I stand. *c* **1871** in J. W. Johnson *Bk. Amer. Negro Spirituals* (1925) 63, I look'd over Jordan, an' what did I see... A band of angels comin' after me. *a* **1890** in Barrère & Leland *Dict. Slang* (1890) II. 368/1 (s.v. *T'other*), And I saw a mighty charret a comin'.., To take us to de odder side of Jordan... Jordan am a hard road to trabble. **1944** D. VAN DE VOORT in B. A. Botkin *Treas. Amer. Folklore* v. 682 Everybody thought that when Wiley's pappy died he'd never cross Jordan because the Hairy Man would be there waiting for him.

Jordan[3] (dʒǭ·ɹdăn). *Math.* [Name of Marie Ennemond Camille *Jordan* (1838–1922), French mathematician.] *Jordan curve,* any curve that is topologically equivalent to a circle, i.e. is closed and does not cross itself; so *Jordan('s) (curve) theorem,* the theorem that any Jordan curve in a plane divides the plane into just two distinct regions having the curve as their common boundary.

1900 W. F. OSGOOD in *Trans. Amer. Math. Soc.* I. 310 By a Jordan curve is meant a curve of the general class of continuous curves without multiple points, considered by Jordan, *Cours d'Analyse*, vol. I, 2d edition, 1893, p. 90. **1919** *Ann. Math.* XXI. 180 (*heading*) A proof of Jordan's theorem about a simple closed curve. **1939** M. H. A. NEWMAN *Elem. Topology of Plane Sets of Points* vi. 132 Theorem 2·3. (Jordan's Theorem for a polygon.) A simple polygon determines two domains, of each of which it is the frontier. **1947** COURANT & ROBBINS *What is Math.?* (ed. 4) v. 246 The Jordan curve theorem is quite simple to prove for the reasonably well-behaved curves, such as polygons or curves with continuously turning tangents, which occur in most important problems. **1965** S. BARR *Exper. Topology* i. 13 A Jordan curve can be drawn on the side of the torus and still divide it into two, but not if it circles, or goes through the hole.

Jordanian (dʒǭɹdēⁱ·niăn), *a.* and *sb.* [f. *Jordan* + -IAN.] **A.** *adj.* Of or pertaining to the Hashemite kingdom of the Jordan (see *JORDAN[2]), formerly Transjordan. **B.** *sb.* A native or inhabitant of Jordan. Hence **Jo·rdanize** *v. trans.*, to render Jordanian in character; **Jo:rdaniza·tion.**

1950 *Encycl. Brit. Bk. of Year* 371/1 On Aug. 26 the Jordanian minister in London announced that a firm of British irrigation engineers..were now engaged in drafting practical schemes of irrigation for the Jordan valley. **1953** *Daily Tel.* 10 Mar. 6/5 The refugees, sometimes aided by Jordanian..officials, 'infiltrate' into Israel. **1955** *Times* 12 May 11/7 As totally inaccessible to Jordanians as Siberia or Tibet. **1959** *Chambers's Encycl.* XIII. 745/1 There is..a national guard, to which all Jordanians between 20 and 40 years of age are liable to be called for service. **1960** A. RAMATI *Rebel against Light* v. 110 Then the Jordanian guns opened fire again, but this time at another part of the city. **1962** *Oxf. Univ. Gaz.* 9 Mar. 776/2 The British School in Jordanian Jerusalem, where a further lecture was given. **1969** *Listener* 6 Mar. 305/1 The dignity, pride, reticence..of the Jordanian and Palestinian Arab. **1970** *Times* 13 May 11/2 Israel hawks have often spoken of the 'Jordanization' of Lebanon. **1972** *Times* 27 June 9/1 They asserted that the main aim of the 'Israeli aggressors' was to 'Jordanize' Lebanon. **1972** *Guardian* 11 Oct. 4/2 Jordanians, like Israelis, wanted..peace, the newscaster assured viewers.

Jordanite[2]. [f. the proper name *Jordan* (see below) + -ITE[1].] A believer in the doctrines of Jordan, a 20th-century Jamaican preacher who found followers in Guyana.

1934 E. WAUGH *Ninety-two Days* ii. 43 The Jordanites are one of the many queer sects that flourish among negroes. They derive their name not..from the river, but from a recently deceased Mr. Jordan from Jamaica. **1958** J. CAREW *Black Midas* iv. 60 Processions of torch bearing Jordanites passed by the house. **1965** 'LAUCHMONEN' *Old Thom's Harvest* ix. 113 Brother Polo..was done up in flowing white cotton gown like the Jordanite sect wear.

Jordanon (dʒǭ·ɹdănǫn). [f. the name of Alexis *Jordan* (1814–1897), French botanist.] = *MICROSPECIES.

1916 J. P. LOTSY *Evolution by Means of Hybridization* i. 23 Forms from which we know nothing else than that they breed true to type, may consequently not be designated as species but must receive another name; as such I propose *Jordanons*. **1963** DAVIS & HEYWOOD *Princ. Angiosperm Taxon.* xi. 378 The formation of numbers of morphologically uniform populations, all easily separable from each other and eligible for consideration as distinct taxa..is well known to the practising taxonomist who often refers to the populations as microspecies or Jordanons after the nineteenth-century French botanist who described so many breeding lines as distinct 'true' species.

jordisite (dʒǭ·ɹdisəit, yǭ·ɹd-). *Min.* [ad. G. *jordisit* (F. Cornu 1909, in *Zeitschr. f. Chem. u. Ind. d. Kolloide* IV. 190/2), f. the name of E. F. A. *Jordis* (1868–1917), German chemist: see -ITE[1].] A black amorphous sulphide of molybdenum, MoS_2.

1910 *Mineral. Mag.* XV. 423 Jordisite... A black, powdery, colloidal form of molybdenum sulphide. **1951** *Amer. Mineralogist* XXXVI. 614 The present study..indicates that Cornu was correct in his statement that ilsemannite is derived from a black colloidal molybdenum sulfide, and although Cornu did nothing to establish the name 'jordisite', the occurrence in Oregon should confirm the name as a valid one for the mineraloid. **1966** *Prof. Papers U.S. Geol. Survey* No. 550-B. 120/1 Much of the jordisite occurs in medium-grained to coarse-grained sandstone.

joree (dʒōrī·). *U.S.* [Echoic, from the call of the bird.] = *ground robin* (*GROUND *sb.* 18 b).

1884 J. C. HARRIS *Mingo* 179 We seem to agree, Brother Brannum, like the jay-bird and the joree—one in the tree and t'other on the ground. **1938** M. K. RAWLINGS *Yearling* iv. 35 Jorees flew from the denseness. **1955** *Sci. News Let.* 23 Apr. 271/2 Other names by which he [*sc.* the towhee or ground robin] is known include swamp robin, joree, bush-bird and turkey sparrow.

jornada. Add: **2.** Also **journada, -ado.** (Earlier examples of forms.)

1828 in *Missouri Hist. Rev.* (1914) VIII. 190 At 4 p.m. we entered *Jornada.* **1844** J. J. WEBB *Adv. Santa Fe Trade* 156 Stopping over for a few hours..to prepare for the journey of fifty miles to the Arkansas, without water, [we] started into the *jornada*. *Ibid.* 119 Whether..to..travel a longer distance and through two *jornadas.* **1845** J. C. FRÉMONT *Rep. Exploring Expedition* 260 The caravans sometimes continue below to the end of the river, from which there is a very long *jornada* of perhaps sixty miles. **1859** [in Dict.].

‖ **joro** (dʒōᵘ·ro). [Jap. *jorō, jōro*, a prostitute.] In Japan: a prostitute.

1884 [see *HININ]. **1891** A. M. BACON *Jap. Girls & Women* x. 289 Below the géisha in respectability stands the jōrō, or licensed prostitute. **1899** J. LONDON *Let.* 22 Feb. (1966) 17 My last posed foto was taken in sailor costume with a Joro girl in Yokohama. **1959** N. MAILER *Advts. for Myself* (1961) 109 The Americans..did not want geisha girls. They wanted a *joro*, a common whore.

‖ **jōruri** (dʒōᵘ·ruri). [Jap., f. the name of Lady *Jōruri*, whose story was one of the most popular subjects for recitation.] **1.** A type of dramatic recitation to musical accompaniment, associated with the Japanese puppet theatre. Also *attrib.* or as *adj.*

1890 B. H. CHAMBERLAIN *Things Japanese* 342 The plays given at these [kabuki] theatres originated..partly in marionette dances accompanied by explanatory songs, called *jōruri* or *gidaiyū*. **1911** *Encycl. Brit.* XV. 170/1 The Jōruri is a dramatic ballad, sung or recited to the

accompaniment of the *samisen* and in unison with the movements of puppets. **1965** W. Swaan *Jap. Lantern* xv. 175 *Joruri* singing or chanting or recitation derives from an ancient form of metrical story-telling analogous to that of the Greeks and the mediaeval bards.

2. In full, *ningyo-jōruri* [Jap. *ningyo* doll]. The Japanese puppet drama.

1950 *Chambers's Encycl.* VIII. 60/2 The *jōruri* (puppet play) arose from recitations..which were combined in the early 17th century with marionette performances. **1954** F. Bowers *Jap. Theatre* i. 30 The word *Joruri* applies specifically to musical dramas which developed from this style of chanting, and which retain for their accompaniment a combination singer-narrator and one or more samisen players. **1959** E. Ernst *Three Jap. Plays* 36 It is not clear when the puppets were added to jōruri, but it is thought that puppet *jōruri* performances were given in 1596 in the city of Kyoto. **1966** C. J. Dunn *Early Jap. Puppet Drama* 4 The name *bunraku* has widely displaced *jōruri* as the name of the puppet drama.

Joseph. Add: **4.** A violin made by Joseph Guarnieri del Gesù (1698–1744). Cf. *Guarnerius.

1875 G. Hart *Violin* vi. 95 How is this 'Joseph', unaccustomed to elbow his legitimate namesakes in the world of fiddles, to maintain the character he has assumed? **1879** Grove *Dict. Mus.* I. 637/2 The value of a good 'Joseph' now varies from £150 to £400. **1968** *Encycl. Brit.* X. 986/2 It was not until Paganini played on the 'Joseph' that the taste of amateurs turned from the sweetness of the Amati and the Stradivari violins in favour of the more robust tone of the Giuseppe Guarneri.

josephinite (dʒōᵘ·zĕfinəit, dʒōᵘzĕfī·nəit). *Min.* [f. *Josephine*, the name of the county in south-western Oregon where it was first found: see -ite¹.] The terrestrial (as opposed to meteoric) alloy of nickel and iron, having about 67 to 77 per cent of nickel.

1892 W. H. Melville in *Amer. Jrnl. Sci.* CXLIII. 509 (*heading*) Josephinite; a new nickel-iron. *Ibid.* 514 The placer gravel, in which josephinite is found. **1905** *Ibid.* CLXIX. 415 It is seen from a glance at the analyses of the alloys from the five different localities, that there is a certain uniformity in composition, but that they are not a definite compound of iron and nickel is evident, nor would this be expected... It seems unfortunate that so rare a substance should have received three distinct names, awaruite, josephinite, and souesite, and it is urged that awaruite, which has priority, should alone be used. **1950** *Mineral. Mag.* XXIX. 390 The occurrences of native nickel-iron regarded as magmatic secretions from peridotites (awaruite, josephinite, souesite, &c.) are certainly formations of extremely low temperatures.

Josephite¹ (dʒōᵘ·zĕfəit). [f. the name *Joseph* (see below) + -ite¹.] A member of either of two orders of St. Joseph, the Priests of the Mission of St. Joseph (founded *c* 1640), or a teaching institute founded in 1817 by Constant-Guillaume van Crombrugghe (1789–1865). Also *attrib.* or as *adj.*

1846 in N. French *Works* I. p. lvi, At the end of the street, there is a large building yet occupied as a school, and now held by the Josephites. **1897** Addis & Arnold *Cath. Dict.* (ed. 5) 531/2 *Josephites.* Two communities bear, or have borne, this name. The first was founded by Jacques Cretenet at Lyons... At the Revolution it was suppressed. The second.., founded in 1817 at Grammont in Belgium. **1898** C. H. Bowden *Simple Dict. for Catholics* 18 *Josephites*, a teaching institute..for the education of the commercial and industrial classes. **1973** *Daily Colonist* (Victoria, B.C.) 28 June 43/1 The 50-year-old former Josephite priest was parolled last December.

Josephite² (dʒōᵘ·zĕfəit). Also **Josephine.** [f. the name of St. *Joseph* (1439–1515), Abbot of Volokolamsk, a Russian zealot.] A member of an ascetic and caesaro-papist party formed among Russian Orthodox monks in the sixteenth century. Hence **Josephism²**, **Josephitism**, the doctrines of this party.

1944 B. H. Sumner *Survey Russ. Hist.* iv. 187 The Josephines won the day in the church council of 1503. **1946** G. P. Fedotov *Russ. Relig. Mind* p. xii, The study of the conflict between the Josephites and the Trans-Volgans led at least one of our scholars to deeper inquiry. **1947** R. M. French tr. *Berdyaev's Russ. Idea* i. 7 Fedotov explains this as due to the fatal influence of 'Josephism' which has distorted the portrait of Christ among the Russian people, so that the Russian people wants to take shelter from the frightful God of Joseph Volotsky behind Mother Earth. **1950** G. P. Fedotov *Treas. Russ. Spirituality* p. xiii, Josephitism degenerated into static ritualism. **1953** K. S. Latourette *Hist. Christianity* xxvii. 618 Probably it was inevitable that the Josephites and the Non-Possessors should clash. *Ibid.* xl. 905 The Josephites..believed in the possession of property by the monasteries and the Church. They were ascetic, approved works of charity, and stressed ritual... The Josephites believed in the maintenance of a close tie between Church and State. **1963** T. Ware *Orthodox Church* vi. 117 Russia needed both the Josephite and the Transvolgian forms of monasticism.

Josephson (dʒōᵘ·zĕfsən). *Physics.* The name of Brian David *Josephson* (b. 1940), British physicist, used *attrib.* to denote an effect predicted by him in 1962, whereby an electric current (*Josephson current*) can flow from one superconducting metal to another with no potential difference between them if they are separated by a sufficiently thin layer of an insulator (owing to tunnelling by coherent pairs of electrons), the application of a potential difference causing the current to oscillate with a frequency equal to the voltage multiplied by $2e/h$ (e = the electronic charge, h = Planck's constant). So **Josephson junction**, a metal–insulator–metal junction exhibiting this effect.

1963 Anderson & Rowell in *Physical Rev. Lett.* X. 231/1 There are..four experimental points suggesting that this is indeed the Josephson effect. **1966** *Physical Rev.* CXLI. 366/2 The Josephson junction behaves as a parametric inductance element in which the voltage is proportional to the frequency. **1966** *McGraw-Hill Encycl. Sci. & Technol.* XIII. 301/2 If a very small voltage difference is maintained between the two sides of the barrier..the Josephson current should oscillate. Its frequency should be $4{\cdot}836 \times 10^{14}$ cycles per second per volt of potential difference. **1969** J. E. Mercereau in R. D. Parks *Superconductivity* I. viii. 399 Such structures of two superconductors nearly in contact (weakly connected) are now called Josephson junctions... The device provides a unique opportunity to study the coupling of electromagnetic and quantum waves. **1972** *Physics Bull.* Aug. 457/1 The Josephson effects have led to new types of galvanometer, magnetometer and computer memory elements, to new methods of harmonic mixing of two frequencies and of harmonic generation, and to simple oscillators.

josh, *v.* Add: Also **joss.** For '*U.S. slang*' read '*slang* (orig. *U.S.*)'. (Earlier and later examples.)

1852 *Lantern* (N.Y.) I. 199/2 The squint eyed chap's been jossin' ye. **1921** Wodehouse *Indiscretions of Archie* vi. 54 Are you trying to josh me? **1927** J. Devanny *Old Savage* 30 They jossed him in the usual way about his proverbial amours. **1940** L. A. G. Strong *Sun on Water* 58 Though every now and then she'd remember and clap a hand to her mouth, we'd soon josh her out of it. **1950** C. M. Kornbluth in D. Knight *100 Yrs. Sci. Fiction* (1969) 249 A humorous sergeant, the Mindworm was pleased to note, joshed the loafer out of his temper. **1972** P. H. Kocher *Master of Middle-Earth* (1973) v. 107 When Pippin and Merry are reunited with their comrades.. Gimli joshes them over and over as 'truants' who had to be rescued.

2. *intr.* To indulge in banter or ridicule.

1845 *St. Louis Reveille* 19 Apr. 2/4 Look out in future, and if you must *Josh*, why, give a *private* one. **1887** F. Francis *Saddle & Mocassin* 185 He..liked nothing better than to..chin and josh [*note*, chat and joke] with them in his funereal fashion. **1905** *Amer. Illustr. Mag.* Dec. 214, I was jus' joshin', mother, 'cause I 'spect all your plans are made. **1958** J. G. MacGregor *North-West of 16* xiv. 195 Each, according to his outlook on life, grumbled or whined, laughed or 'joshed'. **1963** *Guardian* 25 Jan. 9/4 The bearded Alberts tootle and joss with a goon-like ebullience. **1966** J. Dos Passos *Best Times* (1968) i. 13 I'd huddle in acute misery while he joshed with the waiters.

Hence **jo·sher, jo·shing** *vbl. sb.* and *ppl. a.*, **jo·shingly** *adv.*

1864 in *Ohio Arch. & Hist. Q.* LII. 175 The Bay was rough; thirty minutes out and the boys began to get sick. There was a good deal of joshing. **1899** F. Norris *McTeague* iv. 57 What a josher was this Marcus! Sure, you never could tell what he would do next. **1909** R. A. Wason *Happy Hawkins* xxii. 263 Dick was smilin' now.. an' makin' funny, joshin' remarks. **1921** *Daily Colonist* (Victoria, B.C.) 25 Mar. 4/3 Indifference is blazingly conspicuous by the small audiences that attend pre-election meetings; also the joshing manner in which the electors speak to and about the candidates. **1924** Wodehouse *Bill the Conqueror* xvii. 273 Miss Stryker formally stamped him with the seal of her approval as 'a good kid'. And..it is but a step from being a good kid to being..a great old josher. **1948** V. Palmer *Golconda* xi. 85 It was only Donovan's energy and easy joshing that carried the day with them. **1957** —— *Seedtime* 122 Donovan had said joshingly to the..conductor..'Well, how's this strike of yours going?' **1959** J. Thurber *Years with Ross* ii. 21 The intramural joshing turns up everywhere in the crumbling documents. **1966** H. Marriott *Cariboo Cowboy* viii. 75 This P.G.E., or 'Please Go Easy' as some smart joshers called it, started its way at Squamish on Howe Sound. **1970** B. Spock *Decent & Indecent* 18 There has been a trend in social gatherings to substitute loud joshing and playful insults for conversation. **1972** P. Dickinson *Lizard in Cup* xi. 172 Buck maintained his peculiar brand of joshing bonhomie.

josh (dʒǫʃ), *sb. U.S. slang.* [f. the vb.] A piece of banter or badinage; a good-natured or bantering joke. Also as *adj.*, ridiculous.

1878 F. H. Hart *Sazerac Lying Club* 57 Be there anything in this..or aint it only one of them 'joshes' they get up in the *Reveille* sometimes? **1896** Ade *Artie* iii. 30 That ain't no josh, neither. **1908** G. H. Lorimer *Jack Spurlock* iii. 40 First, I sat there chuckling, but by and by I began to forget the josh end of it I had joined [the union] for, and to remember my own grievances against the house. **1948** *Sat. Rev.* (U.S.) 12 June 19/1 We found him tired-eyed and peaked,..not a man for josh and chatter. **1959** J. Thurber *Years with Ross* ii. 20, I shall spare you the *New Yorker's* prospectus, drawn up in..1924, except for.. 'There will be a personal mention column... This will contain some josh.'

Joshua¹ (dʒǫ·ʃuă). [f. the Christian name of Sir *Joshua* Reynolds (1723–92), English painter.] In full, *Sir Joshua.* **a.** A portrait painted by Reynolds. **b.** A woman resembling those depicted in the portraits of Reynolds.

[**1866** A. J. Munby *Diary* 6 July in D. Hudson *Munby* (1972) 227 One [girl] with a rose in her bosom..looked like a masterpiece of Sir Joshua.] **1875** G. H. Lewes *Diary* 8 July in Geo. Eliot *Lett.* (1956) VI. 155 Lady Clementina Mitford—quite a Gainsborough or Sir Joshua —charmed me with her beauty. **1972** 'M. Innes' *Open House* xi. 102 It's a poor class of thing to my eye—me 'aving been in places with Joshuas and the like on the walls.

Joshua² (dʒǫ·ʃuă). *U.S.* [prob. f. the name of the Old Testament leader of the Israelites, in allusion to the branching shape of the tree, compared with that of Joshua brandishing a spear: see Josh. 8:18.] In full **Joshua palm, tree,** or **yucca.** A small evergreen tree, *Yucca brevifolia*, bearing clustered white flowers and found in western, desert regions.

1867 W. H. Jackson *Diary* 15 Feb. (1959) I. 134 Sage brush is used for cooking and the cactus or Joshuas, as I hear them called, for other fires. **1897** G. B. Sudworth *Nomencl. Arborescent Flora U.S.* 106 *Yucca arborescens*... Joshua Yucca... Common names... The Joshua (Utah). Joshua Tree (Utah, Ariz., N. Mex.). **1946** E. S. Gardner *D.A. Breaks Seal* 3 Joshua palms, thrusting up grotesque spine-covered arms, made the scenery resemble some fantastic reconstruction of life on another planet. **1948** A. Huxley *Ape & Essence* (1949) 12 A strangely gesticulating Joshua-tree, rough-barked, or furred with dry prickles. **1955** *Sci. Amer.* Apr. 69 (*caption*) Joshua trees (Yucca brevifolia) grow among the fantastic rock formations of the Joshua Tree National Monument in southern California east of Los Angeles. These plants are characteristic of high steppe-desert vegetation in the southwestern U.S. **1964** Gleason & Cronquist *Nat. Geogr. Plants* xxii. 408 Some of the most interesting plants of the Sonoran Floristic Province are giant Joshua (*Yucca brevifolia*) [etc.].

joss. Add: Also, (*colloq.*) luck: *bad, good, joss.*

1913 *Chambers's Jrnl.* Aug. 590/2 This comprises a good 'joss' for the voyage, and may be likened to a system of 'blessing'. **1915** Kipling *Fringes of Fleet* 48 Mines are all Joss. You either hit 'em or you don't. **1948** Partridge *Dict. Forces' Slang* 104 Bad joss your leave being stopped.

b. joss-man, a priest of a Chinese religion; *slang*, of any other religion (see also quot. 1948); **joss-pidgin,** a religious ceremony; **joss-pidgin-man,** a minister of religion; **joss-stick** (earlier and later examples).

1845 J. R. Peters *Misc. Remarks upon Chinese* 111 Every one has a shrine and Jos, or representation of one, before which a jos stick is kept continually burning. **1876** C. G. Leland *Pidgin-Eng. Sing-Song* 43 Burnee joss-stick, talkee plitty. **1879** I. L. Bird *Let.* 4 Jan. in *Golden Chersonese* (1883) 49 There is a recess outside each shop, and at dusk the joss-sticks..fill the city with the fragrance of incense. **1886** Yule & Burnell *Hobson-Jobson* 354/1 Joss-house-man or Joss-pidgin-man is a priest, or a missionary. *a* **1889** *Mary Coe* in Barrère & Leland *Dict. Slang* (1889) I. 508/1 Allo tim he make joss-pidgin, Wat you fan-kwei cālly 'ligion. *a* **1889** *The Rebel Pig* in *Ibid.* I. 508/1 When dey talkey pig look all-samee like he joss-pidgin-man. **1913** *Chambers's Jrnl.* Aug. 590/2 A missionary is known as a European 'joss-man'. **1926** M. Leinster *Dew on Leaf* iv. 45 He do joss-pidgin. **1948** Partridge *Dict. Forces' Slang* 104 *Jossman*, a term used on China-side for Plymouth gin... (From the picture of the monk on the bottle.) All holy men are 'jossmen' to the Chinese. **1964** *Navy News* Nov. 12/4, I was watch aboard and tried to get a sub, but no joy. I asked the Jossman if I could go ashore, and he told me to go to ... **1970** *Islander* (Victoria, B.C.) 17 May 5/2 The jossman picked up hammer and nails and, with great care, fixed the eyes, exactly 15 feet from the bow [of a junk]. **1974** *Times* 15 Aug. (India Suppl.) p. iv/9 The sandalwood-based joss sticks.. were produced to the tune of 5,000 tonnes last year.

joss² (dʒǫs). *dial., Austral.,* and *N.Z.* [Eng. dial., of unknown origin.] = Boss *sb.*⁶

c **1860** in H. Maxwell *Evening Memories* (1932) xviii. 323 Come where the boss is a deuce of a joss, Come to the pub next door! *a* **1876** E. Leigh *Gloss. Words Dial. Cheshire* (1877) 111 *Joss*, a foreman. Used in Macclesfield. **1877** F. Ross et al. *Gloss. Words Holderness* 81/2 *Joss*, a head man; a superior. *a* **1922** H. Lawson in *Penguin Bk. Austral. Ballads* (1964) 149 Must I turn aside from my destined way For a task your Joss would find me? **1948** V. Palmer *Golconda* iv. 28 'Then why don't you go to the Golconda Mining Company?' asked Donovan slyly. 'Tilburg Kloss is there, a big joss from down south.' **1955–6** —— in *Coast to Coast* 36 A big joss among the young bucks and gins.

joss, var. *josh *v.*

josser (dʒǫ·səɹ). *slang.* [f. Joss + -er¹.] **1.** A clergyman or minister of religion, 'padre'. *Austral.*

1887 J. Farrell *How he Died* 22 The reverend josser.. hammering the pulpit. **1889** Barrère & Leland *Dict. Slang* I. 507/1 *Josser*,...a priest... Australian slang designated those who ministered in them [*sc.* joss-houses] *jossers*, and then extended this term it had created to mean ministers of any religion. **1941** Baker *Dict. Austral. Slang* 40 *Josser*, a parson. **1973** G. Rose *Clear Road to Archangel* iii. 35 The old josser, all black robe and beard and upside-down hat and silver cross, addressed himself to me. In German.

2. a. A simpleton; a soft or silly fellow. So, in flippant or contemptuous use, a fellow, an (old) chap (see also quots. 1933 and 1946).

1886 *Broadside Ballad*, '*I took it On*' in Farmer & Henley *Slang* (1896) IV. 77/1, I took it on, Of course I was a josser. **1890** *Punch* 22 Feb. 85/2 These 'Equality' jossers would spile it; if arf their reforms they can carry. **1894** WILKINS & VIVIAN *Green Bay Tree* I. vii. 176 The josser next me, who had won his money. **1901** *Westm. Gaz.* 30 Mar. 8/2 The old josser asked me where the fire was, and I said: 'Jolly well go and find out yourself, you old bounder!' **1902** STRONG & OSBOURNE *Memories of Vailima* (1903) 61 Though he had known and liked Mr. Stevenson all this time, it was only the other day..that it came over him all of a heap—'*he's* the josser that wrote *Treasure Island*'. **1904** 'G. B. LANCASTER' *Sons o' Men* 184 There's a big josser at Gatefield—Hunt, I s'pose. He gits what he wants. **1911** G. B. SHAW *Getting Married* 244 *Reginald*: Boxer is rather a fine old josser in his way. **1933** E. SEAGO *Circus Company* iii. 29 One of their number would speak of a subject not meant for a 'gajo's' ears, to be checked immediately..'Nante palari before the josher [*sic*] cul.' *Ibid.* 294 *Josser*, outsider. **1936** F. CLUNE *Roaming round Darling* vi. 53 Meanwhile, a hard-boiled josser, with beard and gun complete, has seated himself on a post to see we didn't get away with his wire fence (for a towline). **1938** 'R. HYDE' *Nor Years Condemn* xv. 270 Some josser with a necktie tells 'em he's got a job waiting. **1946** G. TYRWHITT-DRAKE *Eng. Circus & Fair Ground* vi. 67 A 'josser' is an amateur, or in fact any one of the public who does not belong to the profession.

b. *attrib.*

1891 *Daily News* 29 June 2/4 Any 'josser' policeman would be enabled..to pry into their show. **1893** *Standard* 29 Jan. 2 (Farmer & Henley), Now suppose we are on the road..and we meet a josser policeman?

‖ **jota** (hōˑtă). [Sp.] A Spanish folk dance in $\frac{3}{4}$ or $\frac{3}{8}$ time. Also, the music of this dance.

1846 A. ROBINSON *Life in California* iii. 23 Singing or whistling the air of some favorite '*jota*'. **1850** E. G. BUFFUM *Six Months in Gold Mines* 143 Often have I seen little girls, scarce six years of age, flying through a *cotillon*..or dancing with great skill their favourite *jotah* or *jarabe*. **1902** *Encycl. Brit.* XXVII. 374/2 The *Jota* is the national dance of Aragon. **1912** J. E. C. FLITCH *Mod. Dancing & Dancers* xiii. 195 The Spanish dance is intensely national. The snapping of the castanets, the short and insolent skirt, the exciting rhythm of the music, do not alone suffice for the performance of the *jota* or *fandango*, as some foreign artists would appear to suppose. **1922** J. HERGESHEIMER *Bright Shawl* (1923) 12 The air.. was Liszt's Spanish Rhapsody. The accent of its measure, the jota, was at once perceptible and immaterial. **1960** *Spectator* 16 Dec. 988 Antonio's own solo numbers have vitality, and the company's final *jota* is attractive. **1967** 'LA MERI' *Spanish Dancing* (ed. 2) ii. 36 It is said that the Jota, 'the fastest dance in the world', is less a dance than an endurance contest.

jotter (s.v. JOT *v.*²). Add: **2.** A small pad or writing-book used for jotting down notes, memoranda, etc.; a memorandum book.

1882 OGILVIE *Imp. Dict.*, *Jotter*,..the book in which notes or memoranda are made. **1916** A. S. NEILL *Dominie's Log* xii. 132 More attention..should be paid to neatness of method and penmanship in copybooks and jotters. **1930** *Times Educ. Suppl.* 29 Nov. 487/2 The present practice is to supply to all primary schools a sufficient supply of 'Second' readers and jotters sufficient for free issue to all pupils. **1968** M. WOODHOUSE *Rock Baby* vii. 75 A scribbled list on a desk jotter.

‖ **joual** (ʒwāl). *Canada.* [Dialectal Canad. Fr., ad. F. *cheval* horse.] 'Uneducated or dialectal Canadian French considered as debased or inferior by educated French Canadians, characterized by regional pronunciations, non-standard grammar, and often, especially in cities, by numerous English words and syntactical arrangements' (*Dict. Canadianisms*).

[**1959** *Le Devoir* (Montreal) 21 Oct. 4/6 Faut-il expliquer ce que c'est que *parler joual*?... Tout y passe: les syllabes mangées, le vocabulaire tronqué ou élargi, toujours dans le même sens, les phrases qui boitent, la vulgarité virile, la voix qui fait de son mieux pour être canaille.] **1962** M. CHAPIN tr. *Impertinences of Brother Anonymous* 27 Our pupils talk joual, write joual, and don't want to talk or write any other way. Joual is their language. *Ibid.* 30 To be understood, I often must have recourse to one or another joual expression. **1963** *Maclean's Mag.* 16 Nov. 54/3 [I] have less trouble with workers' *joual* than with Montreal cabdrivers. **1965** *New Statesman* 10 Dec. 931/1 The uneducated [in Quebec] often speak a *patois* which is not even a genuine dialect so much as a lazy slurring—it is known as *joual*, which reproduces the pronunciation of *cheval*. **1972** *Evening Telegram* (St. John's, Newfoundland) 5 Aug. 36/7 Michel Tremblay's play, Les Belles-Soeurs, done in the joual. **1972** *Islander* (Victoria, B.C.) 15 Oct. 15/1 The French is mere tokenism, too; a few words or sentences of high-school français and joual sandwiched between paragraphs of English. **1973** *N.Y. Times* 22 Apr. 14/3 There are six million Canadians whose native language is French, but much of what they say would be baffling to a Parisian because many of them speak a patois known as '*Joual*', its name drawn from the way some rural people in Quebec pronounce the word 'cheval' or horse. **1975** *Canadian Forum* (Toronto) Oct. 7/2 In some of his books he lapses into *joual*.

jouk, var. *JUKE *sb.*

Joule. Add: The pronunc. (dʒūl) is now usual for the name of the unit and the physicist.

Although some people of this name call themselves (dʒaul) and others (dʒōᵘl) (D. Jones *Everyman's Eng. Pronouncing Dict.* (ed. 11, 1956), G. M. Miller *BBC Pronouncing Dict. British Names* (1971)), it is almost certain that J. P. Joule (and some at least of his relatives) used (dʒūl). For evidence on this point see *Nature* (1943) CLII. 354, 418, 479, 602.

Add to def.: Later adopted as the M.K.S. unit of energy and work in non-electrical contexts also; it is equal to 10 million ergs, and is now incorporated in the International System of Units, in which it is given the equivalent definition of the work done when the point of application of a force of one newton is displaced through a distance of one metre in the direction of the force. Usually written **joule.** (Further examples.)

1886 J. A. FLEMING *Short Lect. to Electr. Artisans* v. 87 An amount of work equal to 10 million ergs is called one joule. Hence one foot-pound = 1·356 joules, or one joule = ·7373 foot-pound. **1889** *Rep. Brit. Assoc. Adv. Sci. 1888* 56 It was also agreed to adopt the name 'Joule' for 10^7 C.G.S. units of work. Thus a Joule is equal to 10^7 ergs. It is the work done in one second by a power of one Watt. **1893** *Operator & Electr. World* 2 Sept. 175/1 The several governments represented by the delegates of this International Congress of Electricians..hereby recommended to formally adopt as legal units of electrical measure the following... As a unit of work the joule, which is 10^7 units of work in a C.G.S. system. **1896** *Rep. Brit. Assoc. Adv. Sci. 1896* 154 The amount of heat required to raise the temperature of 1 gramme of water 1° C. of the scale of the hydrogen thermometer, at a mean temperature which may be taken as 10° C. of that thermometer, is 4·2 Joules. **1923** N. SHAW *Forecasting Weather* (ed. 2) i. 24 Observations for nine stations within greater London, comprising measures of atmospheric pollution at Richmond and South Kensington, total solar radiation at South Kensington in joules, and its average and maximum rate in milliwatts. **1949** *Nature* 19 Mar. 428/1 It was also agreed [by the ninth International Conference of Weights and Measures] that the unit of heat should be the 'Joule'. **1951** *Engineering* 11 May 577/1 The international units, as realised in the various national laboratories, differed by small amounts, but it has been agreed that the mean international joule of the various laboratories is equal to 1·00019 absolute joules. *Ibid.* 577/3 If the value of the 15-deg. calorie is taken as 4·1855 absolute joules, a B.Th.U. is equal to 1054·54 absolute joules. **1963** [see *CALORIE]. **1970** *Daily Tel.* 4 May 3 Adoption of the metric system and loss of the calorie as a unit of energy may increase the hazard of obesity, Prof. J. B. M. Coppock, an expert on nutrition, said yesterday... There was a danger of losing the calorie for another unit, the joule, which was little understood outside physics and engineering... It would be years before the public..could adjust to a new jargon.

2. Used *attrib.* and in the possessive as the personal name to designate quantities, effects, etc., discovered by Joule or arising out of his work: **Joule** († or **Joule's**) **effect,** (*a*) the heating effect of an electric current flowing through a resistance (described by *Joule's law* (*a*)); (*b*) a change in the linear dimensions (esp. length) of a body when it is subjected to a magnetic field; **Joule's equivalent** (examples); **Joule heating,** the heating that occurs when an electric current flows through a resistance; **Joule's law,** (*a*) the law that the heat produced by an electric current i flowing through a resistance R for a time t is proportional to i^2Rt; (*b*) a law concerning ideal gases, now usually given in the form: the internal energy of a given mass of a gas depends only on its temperature.

¶ See also *JOULE–KELVIN, *JOULE–THOMSON.

1879 *Encycl. Brit.* VIII. 57/2 In general the Peltier effect is..mixed up with Joule's effect, and makes itself felt by producing a disturbance at the junction. **1914** *Physical Rev.* IV. 499 If the change in length of AC is measured as the field, H, is varied, we have the ordinary longitudinal Joule effect, whereas if DB or the length normal to the page is measured we have the transverse Joule effect. **1931** S. R. WILLIAMS *Magn. Phenomena* ii. 108 In the Joule effect the changes in length are..very small. *Ibid.* 111 (*heading*) Transverse Joule effect—change in dimensions normal to the magnetic field. **1933** J. E. PHILLIPS *Intermediate Magn. & Electr.* xiii. 303 The Peltier effect..is proportional to the first power of the current, while the Joule effect varies as the square of the current. **1939** L. F. BATES *Mod. Magn.* x. 303 The existence of a Joule effect in non-ferromagnetic substances was first proved by Kapitza. **1966** F. BRAILSFORD *Physical Princ. Magn.* vi. 143 Additional to the high-field volume change is the Joule effect involving changes in linear dimensions in relatively low fields, which in most cases may be 10 to 100 times greater than those due to the volume magnetostriction. **1853** W. J. M. RANKINE in *Trans. R. Soc. Edin.* XX. 192 This last quantity..is.. one-ninth of the value according to Mr Joule's equivalent. W. THOMSON in *Ibid.* 298 In terms of Joule's mechanical equivalent of heat. **1912** H. A. PERKINS *Introd. Gen. Thermodynamics* ii. 19 The numerical constant connecting heat energy..and mechanical energy..is known as 'Joule's equivalent'. **1958** A. J. WOODALL *Heat* v. 99 Joule's equivalent is, of course, expressible in different units. **1929** J. A. RATCLIFFE *Physical Princ. Wireless* iv. 57 The known forms of A.C. galvanometer, which depend on Joule heating. **1971** *Physics Bull.* Apr. 207/3 Some of the power generated is wasted by joule heating within the element. **1855** W. THOMSON in *Proc. Philos. Soc. Glasgow* III. 286 We thus have an equation between the diminution of the electrical energy in any infinitely small time, and the expression according to Joule's law for the heat generated in the same time in the discharges multiplied by the mechanical equivalent of the thermal unit. **1879** *Encycl. Brit.* VIII. 57/1 The current of the battery heats the pile in part uniformly according to Joule's law. **1887** *Ibid.* XXII. 480/1 Joule's law... When a gas expands without doing external work, and without taking in or giving out heat, its temperature does not change... We must therefore conclude that the internal energy of a given mass of a gas depends only on its temperature, and not upon its temperature or volume. **1945** R. H. FRAZIER *Elem. Electr.-Circuit Theory* i. 21 Ohm's law and Joule's law are interdependent; either can be derived from the other. **1951** C. L. BROWN *Basic Thermodynamics* vi. 83 For a perfect gas the internal energy is a function of temperature only. This statement, known as Joule's law after its formulator, can be expressed symbolically as $u = f(T)$.

joulean, Joulean (dʒūˑliăn), *a. Physics.* Chiefly *U.S.* [f. prec. + -AN.] Of or pertaining to Joule heating.

1891 *Electrician* 27 Feb. 507/2 The waste in Joulean heating. **1903** C. O. MAILLOUX tr. *Boy de la Tour's Induction Motor* p. xii, Joulean effect. This term is used ..to denote the loss of power (watts), and the heating, due to ohmic resistance. **1937** M. W. ZEMANSKY *Heat & Thermodynamics* xiv. 268 A phantom experiment in which the two irreversible phenomena, namely, Joulean dissipation and heat conduction are absent. **1952** A. HUND *Short-Wave Radiation Phenomena* I. i. 3 The electric field component along the conductor surface accounts for the joulean heat loss in the conductor. *Ibid.* II. ix. 1196 This energy is dissipated in the thin skin as joulean heat. **1960** E. M. & E. W. PUGH *Princ. Electr. & Magn.* vi. 179 The joulean heat produced in the windings of an electromagnetic generator.

Joule–Kelvin (dʒūl keˑlvin). [See next.] = next.

1909 *Cent. Dict.* Suppl. s.v. *Effect*, Joule-Kelvin effect. **1916** I. B. HART *Student's Heat* xvi. 320 The liquefaction of hydrogen is achieved as a result of the fact that at 200 atmospheres and a temperature of −200° C. the Joule-Kelvin effect changes from a heating to a cooling. **1937** M. W. ZEMANSKY *Heat & Thermodynamics* xiv. 246 One of the most important commercial applications of the Joule-Kelvin effect involves the transition of a liquid at room temperature and at high pressure (15 to 20 atm) into a mixture of liquid and vapor at a temperature about 30°C colder. **1965** W. C. REYNOLDS *Thermodynamics* viii. 216 Show that the Joule-Kelvin coefficient for a perfect gas is zero.

Joule–Thomson (dʒūl tǫˑmsən). The names of James Prescott *Joule* (1818–89), English physicist, and Sir William *Thomson*, Lord Kelvin (see *KELVIN), used *attrib.* with reference to an effect discovered jointly by them, viz. the change of temperature of a gas that occurs when it expands through a porous plug or a throttle without doing external work, the gas being heated or cooled according as it is initially above or below its inversion temperature (which is above room temperature for most gases).

1899 *Proc. Physical Soc.* XVI. 454 He desires to indicate the relation which must exist between the formula assigned to the Joule-Thomson effect, considered as a function of the temperature, and the particular form adopted for the characteristic equation of a gas. *Ibid.* 464 The Joule-Thomson results..were necessary for the establishment of the thermodynamic scale [of temperature]. **1930** *Engineering* 7 Feb. 163/3 The first commercial pure oxygen which Carl Linde put on the market in 1902 was prepared by the application of the Joule-Thomson effect. **1957** G. E. HUTCHINSON *Treat. Limnol.* I. iii. 207 The amount of change in temperature per unit change of pressure is known as the Joule-Thomson coefficient. **1966** D. G. BRANDON *Mod. Techniques Metallogr.* 221 Miniaturized liquid-hydrogen refrigerators based on Joule–Thomson cooling are now available commercially.

jounce, *v.* Add: **1.** (Later U.S. examples.)

1967 C. O. SKINNER *Madame Sarah* viii. 171 The train ..swayed, rocked, jounced and hustled a couple of passengers from their seats. **1969** *New Yorker* 12 Apr. 118/3 The drill, which is a percussive one, jounces up and down. **1971** D. E. WESTLAKE *I gave at the Office* (1972) 55 The two trucks jouncing off along the narrow dirt road through the swamp.

2. (Later U.S. examples.)

1902 H. L. WILSON *Spenders* xiv. 148 Then I jounced Hank. **1910** *N.Y. Even. Post* 4 Aug. (Th.), The raft was jounced about so severely that it broke its anchorages. **1972** *Time* 17 Apr. 40/3 The rover's seat belts have been redesigned to anchor passengers more comfortably during the jouncing ride in the moon's weak gravity.

jour. Add: **2.** (Earlier and later examples.)

1865 F. B. PALLISER *Hist. Lace* xiii. 181 Twined among them appear a variety of 'jours', filled up with patterns of endless variety, the whole wreathed and garlanded like the decoration of a theatre. **1953** M. POWYS *Lace & Lace-Making* iv. 27 *Binche*, Modern Belgian Lace... As a filling in the center is the Fond à la Mariage or honeycomb, mode or jour.

3. jour de fête = *fête-day*.

1806 C. WILMOT *Let.* 21 Oct. in *Russ. Jrnls.* (1934) II. 234 The gift of their Wives on such a *Jour de Fête* or *Jour de Nom*. **1864** MRS. GASKELL *French Life* in *Fraser's Mag.* Apr. 439/2 The gowns they wear on jours de fêtes. **1869** C. SCHREIBER *Jrnl.* 17 May (1911) I. 4 Jour de Fête, no shops open.

jour[2] (dʒūr), U.S. colloq. abbrev. of JOURNEYMAN.
1835 *Gent's. Vade-Mecum* (Philadelphia) 27 June 3/1 The *jours* are in the habit of *spouting* their work from one week to another. **1854** B. P. SHILLABER *Life & Sayings Mrs. Partington* 146 'I wouldn't be so bothered about *my* meals,' said a jour printer to a brother typo. **1868** E. E. HALE *If, Yes & Perhaps* 35, I stopped at one or two cabinet-makers, and talked with the 'jours' about work. **1898** *Milwaukee Sentinel* 16 Jan. II. 2/7 Where the hundreds of old time-honored 'jours'..have gone to, no one seems able to decide.

journal, *sb.* Add: **11. b.** (senses 2 and 4) **journal-letter,** a letter written as a diary. (Cf. sense 11 a, quot. 1742.)
1756 J. HANWAY *Jrnl. Eight Days Journey from Portsmouth* III. 9 You see I have begun my Journal Letters, with the solemnity of a dedication. **1869** L. M. ALCOTT *Little Women* II. x. 141, I shall keep a journal-letter, and send it once a week. **1906** *Daily Chron.* 26 Oct. 3/3 Fanny's journal-letters to her dear 'Daddy Crisp'..are delightful and vivid effusions. **1964** *Listener* 17 Dec. 983/2 Sir Edward Marsh's long journal-letters..reveal that he was often silly.

journey, *sb.* Add: **3. e.** The travelling of a vehicle along a certain route between two fixed points and at a stated time.
1851 *Illustr. London News* 25 Oct. 526/1 If they.. obtained..12 passengers at 2d. each per journey, the profit would be 19s. 3d. per diem. **1878** *Porcupine* XX. 507/2 The conductor..shouts, 'Journey's end.' **1908** *Daily Chron.* 4 Jan. 1/7 London Motor Bus Strike...The company is determined to insist on the journey system of payment. **1909** *Westm. Gaz.* 8 Sept. 2/1 The journey-time to Glasgow is 8¾ h. **1954** *Gloss. Highway Engin. Terms* (*B.S.I.*) 55 *Journey time*, the overall time taken to travel between two specified points on a route, excluding the times of any stoppages other than those due to interruptions of traffic.

10. c. A set of trams in a colliery.
1883 W. S. GRESLEY *Gloss. Terms Coal Mining* 144 *Journey*, a train or set of trams all coupled together running upon an engine plane. **1896** MRS. H. WARD *Sir G. Tressady* xxiv. 553 The 'journey' of trucks..was standing laden in the entrance of the mine. **1901** *Daily Chron.* 8 Nov. 11/3 He was caught by the 'journey' and killed. **1921** *Dict. Occup. Terms* (1927) § 043 *Journey rider*,.. rides on trams or tubs on haulage planes. **1967** *Gloss. Mining Terms* (*B.S.I.*) x. 14 *Train* (*journey, set, trip*), a number of tubs or cars coupled together.

11. journey-money, read: travelling expenses; (later examples); **journey-pride** *dial.*, excitement or alarm occasioned by the prospect of travelling; so **journey-proud** *a.*
1914 'I. HAY' *Lighter Side School Life* iv. 95 You've been a long time getting your journey-money. **1936** 'R. HYDE' *Check to your King* vii. 84 Vigneti is parcelled off to Guadeloupe, supplied by his Sovereign Chief with a thousand francs journey-money. **1960** G. E. EVANS *Horse in Furrow* v. 69 Wagoners and horsemen on long journeys..even where they had adequate journey-money, ..often preferred to sleep out. **1902** *Eng. Dial. Dict.*, *Journey-proud*, excited like children, at the prospect of a journey. **1908** *Daily Chron.* 5 Nov. 4/7 In Cheshire,.. a village good-wife, describing her farm-labourer husband's first visit to Manchester, declared that he was 'that journey-proud that he couldn't eat a bite o' breakfast'. **1938** *Times* 21 Dec. 10/4 'Journey-pride'..will be familiar to your west-country readers. The adjective is still more useful, for 'feeling-upset-physically-and-mentally-with-anticipatory-excitement-and/or-anxiety' can all be expressed by 'journey-proud'. **1956** *Sunday Times* 3 June 2/6 The lengthy German phrase for holiday anxiety...People who suffered from it used to be described in Yorkshire..as being journey proud.

journeyman. Add: **3. b.** = *impulse dial* (*IMPULSE *sb.* 5 b).
1904 GOODCHILD & TWENEY *Technol. & Sci. Dict.* 384/1 *Master clock*, the timepiece controlling and actuating by electricity a series of dial works, or 'journeymen', at different points in the circuit. **1923** [see *impulse clock* (*IMPULSE *sb.* 5 b)]. **1938** J. W. PLAYER *Britten's Watch & Clock Maker's Handbk.* (ed. 14) 159 Secondary clocks, sometimes called impulse clocks, dial works, or journeyman clocks, are simple constructions.

jowler[2]. *Merseyside slang.* = *JIGGER *sb.*[1] 6 c.
1961 PARTRIDGE *Dict. Slang* Suppl. 1154/1 *Jowler*, a lane between back-to-back houses: Liverpool. **1966** S. KELLY in F. Shaw et al. *Lern Yerself Scouse* 80 When I was young half of me time was spent Up jowlers.

joy, *sb.* Add: **1. g.** *colloq.* Result, satisfaction, success. Esp. with negative, and freq. *ironical.*
1945 *Tee Emm* (Air Ministry) V. 53 There's even less joy in sending us the money. **1945** C. H. WARD-JACKSON *Piece of Cake* (ed. 2) 40 *Joy*, satisfaction. Thus, 'Johnnie took the new kite up this morning—had bags of joy', or 'no joy at all'. **1946** BRICKHILL & NORTON *Escape to Danger* xxxiii. 294 At 9.15 the workers had been down nearly forty minutes and still 'no joy'. **1961** S. PRICE *Just for Record* ii. 17, I..tried to get a taxi. No joy, so back into the studio. **1961** H. R. WILLIAMSON *Wicked Pack Cards* ix. 94 Did you get any joy at the picture gallery? **1971** D. BAGLEY *Freedom Trap* vii. 147 He reported, 'No joy!' *Ibid.* viii. 178 'Any joy there?' She looked up. 'There's not much more than I told you last night.' **1972** R. FIENNES *Ice Fall in Norway* vi. 86 It was becoming late—we tried to locate Patrick's position again, but without joy. **1973** *Scotsman* 7 Aug. 8/2 Parking the car in this bay we started to look for a path and a break in the barbed wire—again with no joy.

10. *joy-night*; **joy-firing**: delete (*nonce-wd.*) and add later example in sense: the firing of celebratory shots (cf. FEU DE JOIE 2); **joy-flight,** an aerial joy-ride; so **joy-flying**; **joy-house** *slang*, a brothel; **joy juice** *U.S. slang*, alcoholic drink; **joy-plank,** a plank leading from the stage to the audience in a theatre, for the use of performers; **joy-popper** *slang* (orig. *U.S.*), an occasional taker of illegal drugs; hence [back-formations] **joy-pop,** (an inhalation or injection of) a drug; **joy-pop** *v. intr.*, **joy-popping** *vbl. sb.*; **joy-stick** *slang*, the control-lever of an aeroplane; the controls of another vehicle; also *attrib.*, *transf.*, and *fig.*; **joy-wheel,** a form of amusement consisting of either (*a*) a gigantic wheel-shaped structure, as on a fairground, on which passengers are carried in cars rotating round the axis, or (*b*) (see quot. 1954).
1926 T. E. LAWRENCE *Seven Pillars* (1935) cxvii. 635 The shooting he heard was joy-firing. **1923** *Daily Mail* 7 Aug. 8/2 The 'joy flights' in three-seater Avros, at 5s. a time. **1928** *Daily Express* 3 July 12 Strict regulations were made against joy-flights during the war. **1940** R. CHANDLER *Farewell, my Lovely* iii. 24, I ain't been in a joy house in twenty years. **1970** 'B. MATHER' *Break in Line* iii. 43 All right—so you're a sailor in a joy-house with a sore foot. **1960** WENTWORTH & FLEXNER *Dict. Amer. Slang* 297/2 *Joy-juice*, liquor. **1974** *Black World* Mar. 56/2 He could hear the others as in a dream, laughing, telling dirty jokes, playing cards and swizzling joy-juice. **1925** T. DREISER *Amer. Tragedy* I. I. viii. 53 Being invited by them to a joy-night supper—a 'blow-out' as they termed it..he decided to go. **1928** *Daily Mail* 7 Aug. 12/7 It was a 'joy night', although many people were still unable to believe that they could..buy a packet of cigarettes openly. **1924** *Illustr. London News* 27 Dec. 1265/2 The picture of the Grand Ballet at Florence in 1616.. shows a method of presentation which was in vogue here in Revues a year or two ago, and is still continued in the Cabarets; performers leaving the stage by means of steps and 'joy-planks'. **1970** J. B. PRIESTLEY *Edwardians* III. 247 (*caption*) Shirley Kellogg leading the chorus along the joy plank in *Hullo Ragtime!* at the London Hippodrome in 1912. **1939** *Detective Fiction Weekly* 18 Mar. 59/1 If you should happen to hear anybody speaking of a sueypow or a joy-pop or of gowing out the lemon bowl,.. bring him right here. **1951** *Time* 26 Feb. 24/3 A sniff of heroin is a 'snort of horse', and an injection under the skin a 'joy pop'. **1954** BECKHARDT & BROWN *Violators* viii. 238 Every now and then he would 'joy-pop' (take an occasional injection) but he thought he could avoid the 'hook' (addiction) by 'spacing his shots'. **1962** K. ORVIS *Damned & Destroyed* v. 41, I take a joy-pop once in a while. *Ibid.* vii. 51 So you're handling a bit of hot stuff as well as joy-popping? **1964** D. WARNER *Death of Dreamer* I. i. 8 Each junkie is taking an average of twenty joy-pops a day. The joy-pops are sold in one-grain packets, called decks by the junkies. **1936** *Amer. Speech* XI. 123/1 *Joy-popper*, a person, not a confirmed addict, who indulges in an occasional shot of dope. However, joy-popping is usually the beginning of a permanent addiction. If the joy-popper has trouble establishing the desire and pleasure from indulging it, he is called a student. **1949** N. ALGREN *Man with Golden Arm* I. 24 They called those using the stuff only occasionally 'joy-poppers' and wished them all great joy. For the 'joy-poppers' had no intention of becoming addicts in the true sense. **1972** J. BROWN *Chancer* ii. 30 The weekend ravers and joy-poppers..for whom smoke and amphetamines alone were not enough. **1910** R. LORAINE *Diary* 9 Apr. in W. Loraine *Robert Loraine* (1938) vi. 105 In order that he shall not blunder inadvertently into the air, the central lever—otherwise the *cloche*, or joy-stick is tied well forward. **1916** Joy-stick [see **control lever*]. **1932** AUDEN *Orators* II. 52 *Joystick*—Pivot of power And responder to pressure And grip for the glove. **1936** *Amer. Speech* XI. 123/1 *Joy stick*, an opium pipe. **1948** PARTRIDGE *Dict. Forces' Slang* 104 *Joysticks*, the two levers by which the steering of tanks and some other tracked vehicles was controlled. **1950** G. BARKER *News of World* 44 My love, my love, lift up your joystick hand. Dismiss the dividing Grief. **1952** A. TUSTIN *Automatic & Manual Control* 467 Both hands held at approximately elbow height a joystick that could be rotated or deflected about a universal coupling, to control the spot movement in elevation and traverse. *Ibid.* 468 The joystick controlled the movements of the spotlight. **1964** S. DUKE-ELDER *Parsons' Dis. Eye* (ed. 14) x. 98 (*caption*) Joystick lever for horizontal course and fine adjustments. **1967** *Times Rev. Industry* Mar. 43/3 The system is simply operated by a keyboard and joystick—no computer programming knowledge is needed. **1969** G. MACBETH *War Quartet* 34 Easing the joy-sticks to their mid-riffs. **1911** *Oxford Times* 9 Sept. 10/6 A new form of amusement to Oxford, known as the 'Joy Wheel'. **1942** 'M. INNES' *Daffodil Affair* I. i. 7 Perhaps twenty times it passed to and fro, as if outside some great joy-wheel were oscillating idly in a derelict amusement park. **1954** *Engineer* 27 Aug. 282/2 A once-popular novelty, now obsolete, was the 'Joywheel', or 'Devil's Disc'. This consisted of a power-driven spinning disc, slightly domed and having a smooth surface. It was surrounded by a stationary padded circular platform, which in turn was surrounded by a padded wall. Riders sat on the disc while it was stationary and, as it accelerated, were eventually thrown off against the padding. **1968** D. BRAITHWAITE *Fairground Archit.* 65 A panoramic 'Joy Wheel' using kinetoscope effects to create the illusion of a race between motor-car and train.

Joycean (dʒɔi·siăn), *a.* and *sb.* Also **Joycian. A.** *adj.* Of, pertaining to, or characteristic of the Irish writer James *Joyce* (1882–1941), or his work. **B.** *sb.* An admirer or follower of Joyce.
1927 *New Republic* 20 July 236 Joycean passages and bursts of purple lyricism. **1932** *Times Lit. Suppl.* 26 May 386/3 The modified 'Joycean' language is clever and expressive. **1935** *Discovery* Dec. 378/2 The verbatim description of one 'disturbed case' by another, with its progressive lapse into Joycian language. **1938** PARTRIDGE *World of Words* vi. 161 The Joyceans are artificial, but, except at the cost of a highly gymnastic cerebration, unintelligible. **1953** M. LOWRY *Lett.* (1967) 330 Even Bernard de Voto had to interpolate that he was 'a good Joycean—he hoped'. **1965** *Times Lit. Suppl.* 11 Mar. 199/3 This particular 'deviation' has a rather Joycean flavour to it, as it combines the meaning and the effect of exorbitance in one word. **1966** *Listener* 2 June 805/3 The hero's name, Strumienski, would delight any Joycean: it is derived from 'stream'. **1971** *Ibid.* 16 Sept. 381/2 There was a fine Joycian slide into a muck wake. **1971** *Daily Tel.* (Colour Suppl.) 3 Dec. 9/2 The lecturer..led his summer school audience down the howling avenues of Joycean puns.

joyful, *a.* Add: **4.** *o* (or *oh*) *be joyful*, an alcoholic drink. *slang.*
1823 P. EGAN *Grose's Dict. Vulgar T.* (rev. ed.), *O be joyful*, good liquor; brandy. *Sea term.* **1830** *Greensborough* (N. Carolina) *Patriot* 4 Aug. 4/2 They didn't come to, till the old woman and her darter poured some o be joy full down their throates. **1846** L. CRAWFORD *Hist. White Mts.* iv. 45, I was loaded..with a plenty of what some call..'O-be-joyful'. **1865** *London Jrnl.* 8 Apr. 222/3 Like a great many other clever fellows, he was too much addicted to the 'O be joyful!' **1934** T. S. ELIOT *Rock* ii. 77 Well, boys, what do you say to a pint of Oh be Joyful? **1968** *Listener* 21 Mar. 369/3 It's a lively scene on this part of the Oldham Road: some very jolly pubs, Dutton's O Be Joyful ales in little bottles.

joy-ride (dʒɔi·rəid), *sb. colloq.* (orig. *U.S.*). [f. JOY *sb.* + RIDE *sb.*[1]] A pleasure trip in a motor car, aeroplane, etc., often without the permission of the owner of the vehicle. Also *transf.* and *fig.* Hence **joy-ride** *v. intr.*, to go for a joy-ride; *trans.*, to convey (as) on a joy-ride; **joy-rider,** one who goes on a joy-ride; **joy-riding** *vbl. sb.*; also *attrib.*
1908 W. S. BLUNT *Diary* 5 Aug. (1920) II. 217 Joy-riders..light-hearted Londoner folk concerned with nothing but their own pleasure. **1909** *N.Y. Even. Post* (Semi-weekly ed.) 15 July 2 [The] Acting Mayor vetoed the ordinance passed last week to prevent city officers from taking 'joy rides'. *Ibid.* 2 Sept. 8 'This was no haphazard expedition,' he said, 'no intensified Arctic joy ride, undertaken on nerve.' **1910** *National Police Gaz.* 2 July 3/4 As a rule there isn't much chance of joy riding in a taxi. **1913** *Aeroplane* 17 Apr. 455/2 The pilots of machines already qualified naturally took no risks of damaging their mounts by 'joy riding'. **1913** *Collier's* 27 Dec. 9 (*heading*) With the joy-riding fleet. **1915** D. O. BARNETT *Let.* 6 July 206 We joined forces and captured a motor-ambulance which joy-rided us back here. **1915** *Amer. Mag.* Oct. 28/2 You take your dago friend 'n' joy-ride with the gang all night. **1918** H. HAYENS *Lords of Air* 41 Unfortunately I was not joy-riding, but bent on serious business. **1919** *Aeroplane* 5 Feb. 555/1 There are two million people in this country who wish for what is vulgarly called a joy-ride in an aeroplane. *Ibid.* 555/2 Joy-riders will not be taken aloft one at a time but in half-dozens and dozens, in big flying boats..and multiple-engined land machines. **1922** F. HARRIS *My Life & Loves* I. ix. 187 'Aren't you tired?'..'No,' I replied, 'I feel no fatigue, indeed, I feel the better for our joy ride!' **1922** JOYCE *Ulysses* 497 You once nobble that, congregation, and a buck joy ride to heaven becomes a back number. **1925** *Flynn's* 14 Feb. 664/2 *Joy-ride*, intoxication resulting from use of drugs. **1925** *Times* 26 Sept., For the third year..no fatal accident involving passengers in other flying for hire, mainly 'joy ride' flights. **1930** E. POUND *XXX Cantos* ix. 36 With three pages of secret instructions To the effect: 'Did he think the campaign was a joy-ride?' **1952** C. DAY LEWIS tr. *Virgil's Aeneid* XII. 280 Around them..The hostile formations are pressing..While you're joy-riding over these empty fields. **1972** J. BROWN *Chancer* xii. 161 That's what you need now, he says—need a joy-ride, man... No danger neither, he says, on the joy-pop. **1972** *N.Y. Law Jrnl.* 10 Oct. 20/6 The annotation..dealing with elements of the offense defined in 'joyriding' statutes fails to disclose any case in which the person using a rented vehicle with the consent of the custodian has been held guilty of unauthorized use. **1973** *Scottish Sunday Express* 5 Aug. 7/8 A man who drove away two cars for a 'joy ride' was fined £75.

J-shaped (dʒēi·,ʃēipt), *a.* Having the shape of the letter J; used *esp.* of a graph or of a variable expressed by it. Also **J-curve,** a J-shaped curve.
1911 G. U. YULE *Introd. Theory Statistics* II. vi. 98 The extremely asymmetrical, or 'J-shaped', distribution, the class-frequencies running up to a maximum at one end of the range. **1927** H. L. RIETZ *Math. Statistics* iii. 57 Type III would be J-shaped if $\gamma\alpha$ were negative. **1939** *Amer. Jrnl. Sociol.* XLIV. 975 He [*sc.* Professor Allport] advances the 'J-curve hypothesis of conforming behavior'. **1950** S. A. STOUFFER *Measurement & Prediction* i. 41 In general, as predicted, a *J*-shaped or *U*-shaped curve was obtained with attitude data. **1968** P. MCKELLAR *Experience & Behaviour* xi. 304 If..the situation is changed by the introduction of a traffic light we have J-curve behaviour. **1973** *Times* 7 May 16/4 The notion of the post-devaluation 'J-curve', according to which an initial deterioration in the balance of payments is followed by a more-than-offsetting improvement as the volume of

exports responds over time to the gain in price competitiveness.

Ju (dʒū). [ad. *Ju Chou*, the name of a town in Honan, China.] Used to designate pottery with buff body and blue-green glaze produced in Ju Chou in the 12th century.

1906 W. BURTON *Porcelain* vi. 57 Dr. Bushell mentions a fine piece of *Ju-Yao* in his possession, which, however, has a delicate greenish glaze with no trace of blue. **1936** *Burlington Mag.* 4/1 The original Ju ware was made at the potteries at Ju Chou. **1949** G. SAVAGE *Ceramics for Collector* ii. 44 The kiln was in operation only for about twenty years, and at one time the '*ying ch'ing*' type was identified with Ju ware. **1969** *Times* 9 Dec. (Taiwan Suppl.) p. vii/2 The 24 items of Ju ware are the best of the porcelain. **1972** *Collector's Guide* June 95 Ju ware, only identified as recently as 1936 by Sir Percival David, is much rarer than Ting.

jube³ (dʒūb), abbrev. of JUJUBE 2.

1937 PARTRIDGE *Dict. Slang* 445/2 *Jube*, a coll. abbrev. of *jujube* (the lozenge). **1967** E. & M. A. RADFORD *No Reason for Murder* iii. 16 He bought..bars of chocolate and jubes. **1970** J. CLEARY *Helga's Web* vii. 118 Do you have any menthol jubes?

jube⁴ (dʒūb). [Persian.] An open watercourse in Iranian cities.

1948 in *Punch's Almanack* 2. **1953** A. SMITH *Blind White Fish in Persia* iii. 48 By every pavement ran the jube, a stream of water which had doubtless been clean at the top of the town but did not remain so for long. **1959** T. GRIFFITH *Waist-High Culture* (1960) ix. 115 Tehran, its streets vivid with sidewalk hawkers, the flow of filth in the jubes.

jubilee, *sb.* Add: **5. c.** A Negro folk-song of an optimistic and joyful kind, often having a religious basis; freq. *attrib.*, esp. *jubilee singer, song.*

1872 *N.Y. Tribune* 17 Feb. 3/6 Unique Vocal Concert by the Jubilee Singers. *c* **1872** T. F. SEWARD (*title*) Jubilee songs as sung by the Jubilee Singers, of Fisk University. **1873** G. D. PIKE *Jubilee Singers* 163 The excellent rendering of the Jubilee Band is made more effective..by the comparison of their former state of slavery..with the present prospects and hopes of their race. **1922** *Jrnl. Amer. Folk-Lore* XXXV. 248 Every Time I Feel the Spirit. This is one of the most thrilling of the later jubilee songs. **1946** S. H. HOLBROOK *Lost Men Amer. Hist.* 133 The Chautauqua offered no such strong meat as the Lyceum, but went in for bell ringers, jubilee singers, preachers..and assorted stuffed shirts. **1949** B. A. BOTKIN *Treas. S. Folklore* v. i. 701 Besides his 'jubilee' and 'sorrow songs', the Negro has his 'sinful' songs. **1956** M. STEARNS *Story of Jazz* (1957) xii. 133 The next step in this blending, which produced both ring-shout and spiritual, is the jubilee. Jubilees are both cheerful and rhythmic, usually announcing some sort of good news. **1961** J. JAHN in A. Dundes *Mother Wit* (1973) 99/1 The hymns of Christian European origin used by the missions are Africanized, producing jubilees. **1968** P. OLIVER *Screening Blues* Introd. 7 Blues recordings accounted for nearly half the total output in the 'twenties whereas religious issues, including those by solo evangelists and jubilee groups, totalled only a fraction over a sixth of the number. *Ibid.* ii. 81 The gospel, or jubilee, quartets performed all their songs in harmonized style which smoothed out the differences between the blues, popular and gospel song forms.

jubjub (dʒʌ·bdʒʌb). [Invented by 'Lewis Carroll' (C. L. Dodgson); perh. a portmanteau word or formed after such representations of bird-cry as *jug-jug* (JUG *sb.*³).] An imaginary bird of a ferocious, desperate and occasionally charitable nature, noted for its excellence when cooked.

1871 'L. CARROLL' *Through Looking-Glass* i. 22 Beware the Jubjub bird, and shun The frumious Bandersnatch. **1876** —— *Hunting of Snark* 44 Should we meet with a Jubjub, that desperate bird, We shall need all our strength for the job! *Ibid.* 58 The song of the Jubjub recurred to their minds, And cemented their friendship for ever! **1962** M. GARDNER in 'L. Carroll' *Annotated Snark* 104 Their common fear of the *Jubjub Bird* is interesting. Philologically..Jubjub is a 'portmanteau bird', compounded of *jabber* and *jujube*... It flashed across me that the Jubjub was Society itself.

jucal, var. *JACAL.

Judæan, Judean (dʒudī·ăn), *a.* and *sb.* [f. L. *Jūdæus*, a. G. Ἰουδαῖος, f. Ἰουδαία, f. Ἰούδας, ad. Heb. *Jehūdah* Judah, name of a son of Jacob.] **A.** *adj.* Of or pertaining to Judæa or southern Palestine. **B.** *sb.* A native or inhabitant of this region.

In Shakes. *Oth.* v. ii. 347 the first Folio has the doubtful reading *Iudean*; the other Folios and the Quartos have *Indian.*

1652 HEYLIN *Cosmogr.* III. 89 Accaron, on the South of Gath, of great wealth and power, and one that held out notably against the Danites and Judæans. **1832** J. BELL *Syst. Geogr.* IV. 206 Judean Holy Mountains. **1852** H. W. DULCKEN tr. *Pfeiffer's Visit Holy Land* 103 The foreground of the picture is formed by the Judæan mountains. **1880** *Encycl. Brit.* XIII. 410/1 A Judæan, Amos of Tekoa. **1922** A. E. GARVIE *Beloved Disciple* x. 210 The Synoptic record is incomplete as regards the Judæan ministry. **1931** *Times Lit. Suppl.* 5 Nov. 853/1 A preliminary survey of Judaean sites. **1955** R. W. MILLAR tr. *Daniel-Rops's Jesus in his Time* 57 Eleven of the disciples were Galileans, the one Judean was Judas. **1965** M. SPARK *Mandelbaum Gate* ii. 22 She..had driven northward through the Judean hills to Galilee. **1973** *Times* 3 Dec. 17/6 David Ben-Gurion..took a leading part..in recruiting for the Judaean battalions of the Royal Fusiliers.

Judæo-, Judeo- (dʒudī·o), used as comb. form of L. *Judæus* *JUDÆAN, JUDEAN *a.* and *sb.*, designating persons or things pertaining to Judæa and hence (more widely) to the Jews; often = Jewish (and); **Judaeo-German,** Yiddish.

1823 *Christian Observer* App. 828/1 The New Testament in German-Hebrew, and Judeo-Polish. **1851** *Illustr. Catal. Gt. Exhib.* III. 552/1 Judæo Spanish, Old Testament. *Ibid.* 552/2 Judæo Arabic, four books of New Testament. **1863** *Chambers's Encycl.* V. 712/2 The number of Judæo-Greek fragments..which have survived. *Ibid.* 721/2 Numerous authors wrote in Hebrew,..and Judæo-German. **1899** *Lit. Guide* 1 Oct. 146/1 The total abandonment of the Judæo-Christian 'continuity' theory. **1900** tr. *J. Deniker's Races of Man* 424 Particular kinds of jargon, the most common of which is the Judeo-German. **1906** *Westm. Gaz.* 17 Aug. 10/2 The Judæo-Spanish world of the Levant. **1910** *Ibid.* 12 Mar. 2/1 'The Judæo-Masonic and Protestant coalition' which now governs France. **1910** *Encycl. Brit.* VI. 494/1 The Clementine literature throws light upon a very obscure phase of Christian development, that of Judaeo-Christianity. **1937** *Times Lit. Suppl.* 16 Jan. 37/2 Irrelevances about the world hegemony of Judaeo-Masonry. **1939** *New English Weekly* 27 July 237/2 The Judaeo-Christian scheme of morals. **1939** L. H. GRAY *Foundations of Language* 349 The two chief forms of creolised languages of the Teutonic group, in addition to those already noted for English.., are *Afrikaans*..; and *Yiddish*, or *Judaeo-German*, based upon a Franconian German dialect of the fourteenth century with many Hebrew words, and spoken by Jewish communities in Lithuania, Poland, Russia, and parts of Rumania as well as by Jewish emigrants from those areas. **1948** D. DIRINGER *Alphabet* II. iv. 267 Judezmo or Judæo-Spanish, called also Ladino, contains many Hebrew words, but is principally based on Old Spanish or Castilian. **1952** KOESTLER *Arrow in Blue* xxv. 234 Immune against German chauvinism through a hereditary judeo-cosmopolitan touch. **1957** N. FRYE *Anat. Criticism* 145 The appearance of the Judaeo-Christian deity in fire. **1960** *Encounter* Mar. 34/2 The religious zeal of Judeo-Christianity. **1964** *Language* XL. 282 Mediaeval Judaeo-French. **1974** R. A. HALL *External Hist. Romance Languages* 24 Judaeo-Spanish or 'Ladino'. *Ibid.* 30 Judaeo-Italian, now dying out, has been attested in some medieval documents, and in scattered remnants in modern Italian dialects.

Judahite (dʒū·dăˌəit), *a.* and *sb.* [f. *Judah* name of an ancient Hebrew tribe and kingdom + -ITE¹.] **A.** *adj.* Of or pertaining to the tribe or the kingdom of Judah. **B.** *sb.* A member of the tribe, or an inhabitant of the kingdom, of Judah.

1899 J. HASTINGS *Dict. Bible* II. 792/2 Five Judahite clans were in the course of time formed. **1901** R. L. OTTLEY *Short Hist. Hebrews* vi. 137 In the early stages of the conquest we find the Kenites coalescing with the Judahites. **1932** T. H. ROBINSON *Hist. Israel* I. II. viii. 170 In Judges xv...Judahites are introduced into the story of Samson. *Ibid.*, An old Judahite tradition of the capture of Hebron..is transferred to Caleb. **1950** H. H. ROWLEY *From Joseph to Joshua* i. 5 We find a Levite.. who regarded Benjamites equally with Judahites as associated peoples. **1971** *Catholic Biblical Q.* July 394, 5 and 8a describe a Judahite defeat.

Judas. Add: **4.** *Judas kiss* (earlier and later examples); **Judas goat,** an animal used to lead others to destruction; also *transf.*; **Judas priest** *int.*, a euphemism for *Jesus Christ* in an oath.

1941 *Amer. Speech* XVI. 236/1 Sheep are led to the shackling pen by a Tony or Judas goat. **1964** *Punch* 19 Feb. 283/2 Irene only used Billy as a 'judas goat' to catch Des. **1972** D. ANTHONY *Blood on Harvest Moon* xxv. 220 Not dead. Not me as the Judas goat. *c* **1400** R. LAVYNHAM *Litil Tretys* (1956) 11 Hate of herte is whan a man spekyth litil & menyth moche malyce..& at þe laste wᵗ a iudas kesse schewith a love y fayned. **1860** GEO. ELIOT *Mill on Floss* III. VI. i. 15 A woman who was loving and thoughtful for other women, not giving them Judas-kisses with eyes askance. **1942** 'G. ORWELL' *Diary* 28 Sept. in *Coll. Ess.* (1968) II. 449 A special prayer 'for the people of Stalingrad'—the Judas kiss. **1947** E. SITWELL *Shadow of Cain* 18 When the last Judas-kiss Has died upon the cheek of the Starved Man Christ. **1973** R. LEWIS *Blood Money* ix. 146 Candour shone from his eyes, as insincere as a Judas kiss. **1914** 'HIGH JINKS, JR.' *Choice Slang* 13 *Judas Priest*, an exclamation of surprise. **1922** S. LEWIS *Babbitt* ix. 126 Judas Priest, I could write poetry myself if I had a whole year for it. **1972** J. D. BUCHANAN *Professional* xi. 123 Judas Priest! What the hell are you saying?

judder (dʒʌ·dəɹ), *v.* [Imit.; cf. SHUDDER *v.*] *intr.* To shake violently, esp. of the mechanism in cars, cameras, etc.; also of the voice in singing, to oscillate between greater and less intensity. Hence **ju·ddering** *vbl. sb.* and *ppl. a.*

1931 A. J. CRONIN *Hatter's Castle* I. xii. 213 The train entered this tunnel. It entered slowly,..juddering in every bolt and rivet of its frame as the hurricane assaulted [it]. **1933** AUDEN in M. Roberts *New Country* 197 His [*sc.* a motorcyclist's] back wheel juddered; he was off with a roar. **1958** 'P. BRYANT' *Two Hours to Doom* 122 He felt the onset of compressibility vibration... The juddering stopped. **1960** *New Scientist* 21 Apr. 1015/2 The drum must run perfectly true and not 'judder' at its circumference more than 1/1,000 inch. **1962** *Times* 28 Feb. 14/6 All day long the school has been juddering and shuddering in the hysterical blasts of north-west wind. **1965** *Punch* 3 Feb. 175/1 As the train juddered a few yards back towards Westminster, he flung a huge arm round my shoulder to steady himself. **1970** *Times* 1 May 2/7 Driver Gwynn started the engine..with much.. cranking and juddering. **1970** *Motoring Which?* July 85/1 During our track tests the front brakes vibrated and juddered when used hard. **1971** B. W. ALDISS *Soldier Erect* 120 Beggars with heroic deformities lay juddering in the gutter. **1973** *Weekly News* (Glasgow) 11 Aug. 3/3 A sustained campaign has been under way on behalf of crippled people who are provided with those juddering little three-wheeled cars to get about in.

judder (dʒʌ·dəɹ), *sb.* [f. prec.] An instance or state of juddering.

1935 *Practical Motorist* 26 Oct. 993/1 (*heading*) Curing clutch judder. **1946** F. C. FIELD-HYDE *Vocal Vibrato, Tremolo & Judder* iii. 10 Judder consists of marked, rapid changes in intensity during the emission of tone, due to involuntary variations..of the vocal tension. **1952** *Times* 18 Dec., A pronounced judder was felt..and in spite of two corrective movements of the control column [of the aircraft] the judder continued. **1956** *Sunday Times* 28 Oct. 13/3 There is a little 'judder' from the steering wheel at speed, but it is not worrying. **1958** *Times Rev. Industry* May 31/1 The coupling operates with the smoothness and absence of jerk or judder found in hydraulic devices. **1960** O. SKILBECK *ABC of Film & TV*, *Judder*, violent vertical unsteadiness of picture due to faulty camera motion. **1972** *Daily Tel.* 12 Apr. 13/5 It is not difficult to get a touch of wheelspin and axle judder by fierce acceleration in the lower gears.

juddite (dʒʌ·dəit). *Min.* [f. the name of John Wesley *Judd* (1840–1916), English geologist: see -ITE¹.] A mineral of the amphibole group (see quots.).

1908 L. L. FERMOR in *Rec. Geol. Survey India* XXXVII. 212 The optical characters of the mineral leave no doubt that it is a new variety of the amphibole group; I propose to name it juddite in honour of Professor J. W. Judd, F.R.S., and as a respectful tribute from a former student. **1963** W. A. DEER et al. *Rock-Forming Min.* II. 369 Although Bilgrami (1955) considered it appropriate to classify the manganese-rich alkali amphibole juddite.. with the richterite group, it has been included here in the eckermannite-arfvedsonite series. The mineral has a high content of Na..and high Fe^{+3}, as well as high Mn, and the formula $(Na_{2\cdot5}Ca_{0\cdot5})(Mg_{2\cdot5}Mn_{1\cdot0}Fe^{+3}_{1\cdot0})Si_{7\cdot5}Al_{0\cdot5}O_{22}(OH)_2$ is typical of the eckermannite-arfvedsonite group: it is suggested that the mineral may be adequately characterized by the name manganarfvedsonite. **1970** *Mineral. Mag.* XXXVII. 708 It may thus be concluded that the juddites generally refer to (manganoan) magnesioriebeckite compositions.

‖**Judenhetze** (yū·dənhetsə). [G., = Jew-baiting.] Systematic persecution of the Jews.

1882 *19th Cent.* Aug. 254 Those forces which Europe has confessed are too powerful for it to deal with, and which have led to persecution in Russia and to *Judenhetze* in Germany.

‖**Judenrat** (yū·dənrat). [G., = Jewish council.] A council representing a Jewish community in a locality controlled by the Germans during the war of 1939–45.

1950 J. HERSEY *Wall* I. i. 20 The *Judenrat* had been formed a month earlier, to the day. The Germans told us then that the *Kehilla*, or Community Council, would henceforth become the *Judenrat* and would be the instrument of German authority over the Jews. **1959** M. LEVIN *Eva* 20 In the very first days after the Germans came, they had ordered the Jews to select a Judenrat. **1960** H. AGAR *Saving Remnant* v. 146 In the Ghettos of Eastern Europe the Germans invariably set up a *Judenrat*: a Council of Jews to transmit orders to the community. **1967** *Sat. Rev.* (U.S.) 15 Apr. 20/2 Krüger sent his blood-spattered uniform and boots to the *Judenrat*, the community council.

‖**judenrein** (yū·dənrəin), *a.* [G., = free of Jews.] Of a society or organization: without Jewish members, out of which Jews have been expelled.

1942 *New Republic* 21 Dec. 817 It is not merely central and eastern Europe which are being 'purged', or rendered 'Judenrein', as the Nazis like to say. **1951** H. ARENDT *Origins of Totalitarianism* i. 4 When Hitler came to power, the German banks were already almost *judenrein.* **1960** H. AGAR *Saving Remnant* vii. 188 A country which was becoming almost Hitlerianly *Judenrein.* **1969** C. ROTH *Short Hist. Jewish People* (rev. ed.) VI. xxxi. 444 The survivors..were rounded up and sent to the death camps, Warsaw being now *judenrein.*

judge, *sb.* Add: **1. c.** Phrases, *as grave, sober, as a judge.*

1650 COWLEY *Guardian* II. ii. sig. B3/2 If I look not as grave as a Judge upon the bench, let me be hanged for't. **1734** FIELDING *Don Quixote in England* III. xiv. 57, I am as sober as a Judge. **1842** DICKENS *Let.* 28 Mar. (1938) I. 423, I remained as grave as a judge. **1856** [in Dict., sense 1 a]. **1866** MAYNE REID *Headless Horseman* xliv. 210 I'm as sober as a judge. **1889** [see GRAVE *a.*¹ 3].

d. *Judges' Rules*: (see quot. 1965²).

1925 *Criminal Appeal Rep.* XVIII. 47 The Judges' Rules for the guidance of the Police discussed. **1931** D. L. SAYERS *Five Red Herrings* vii. 80 Between the Judges' Rules..and his anxiety to pull off a coup, he felt his position to be a difficult one. **1965** J. PORTER *Dover Two* iv. 54 And don't start quoting the Judges' Rules to me... The only time you need bother about the Judges' Rules is when the accused person's likely to

know more about 'em than you do. **1965** *Stone's Justices' Manual* (ed. 97) I. 368 The Judges' Rules, made by Her Majesty's judges of the Queen's Bench Division, are concerned with the admissibility in evidence against a person of answers, oral or written, given by that person to questions asked by police officers and of statements made by that person. **1973** 'M. INNES' *Appleby's Answer* xix. 167 Miss Pringle wondered whether..she would.. perhaps receive some caution required by what are called Judges' Rules.

10. judge-made *a.* (earlier and later examples).

1824 J. S. MILL in *Westm. Rev.* I. 510 The common judge-made definition of a public libel, is, any thing which tends to bring the constituted authorities into hatred and contempt. **1965** *Mod. Law Rev.* XXVIII. v. 510 The clash between democracy and judge-made law.

judgement, judgment. Add: **13.** judgement sample *Statistics* (see quot.).

1947 W. E. DEMING in *Jrnl. Marketing* Oct. 145/1 *Judgment-samples*, wherein the biases and sampling errors cannot be calculated from the sample, but instead must be settled by judgment.

judgemental, judgmental (dʒʌdʒme·ntăl), *a.* [f. JUDGEMENT, JUDGMENT + -AL.] Involving the exercise of judgement; inclined to make moral judgements.

1909 W. M. URBAN *Valuation* ii. 40 Whether exclusively judgmental or not is a question to be determined. **1952** S. KAUFFMANN *Philanderer* (1953) ix. 154 'Russell,' she said with a queer grin that was friendly and yet vaguely judgemental, 'you puzzle me.' **1964** *Philos. Rev.* LXXIII. 373 There is also..a 'judgmental' constituent of perceptual experience. **1965** HALL & HOWES *Church in Social Work* xv. 246 A criticism sometimes made of moral welfare workers..is that they are 'judgmental' in the approach to clients. **1969** *Sci. Jrnl.* Feb. 64/1 Jenny was described rather well and the more quantitative structure analysis (versus content analysis by judgmental methods) yielded greater amounts of information about this woman. **1972** *Jrnl. Social Psychol.* LXXXVI. 13 Conforming behavior was produced..with the use of a two-choice judgmental task. **1973** *Times* 16 July 13/4 As one who is entirely unconvinced about the usefulness of boycotts—of any kind—and a little suspicious of judgmental attitudes to South Africa [etc.].

So **judg(e)me·ntally** *adv.*

1971 J. B. CARROLL et al. *Word Frequency Bk.* p. xli, If the citations..are gathered in a number of separate judgmentally biased ways, the significance of each.. must be assessed individually.

‖ **judicatum** (dʒūdikēⁱ·tŏm, -ātŏm). *Philos. rare.* Pl. **-ata.** [L. *jūdicātum* judgement, pa.pple. of *jūdicāre* to judge.] (See quots.)

1913 *Mind* XXII. 15 As I use the term, the proposition is what the logicians call the import of the judgment or proposition. It is the *propositum* or *judicatum*. I do not use it as equivalent either to the act of judging or the verbal sentence. **1935** *Mind* XLIV. 365 A judgement *to the effect that* A is B seems to be just a judgement (act of judging) whose *object* or *judicatum* is that A is B. **1936** H. H. PRICE *Truth & Corrigibility* 17 The relation is between *judicata* or *judicabilia*, or—as some call them—'propositions'.

judo (dʒū·do). Also formerly **jiudo, ju-do.** [Jap., f. *ju* gentleness, ad. Chinese *jou* soft, gentle + Jap. *dō*, ad. Chinese *tao* way.] A refined form of ju-jitsu introduced in 1882 by Dr. Jigoro Kano, using principles of movement and balance, and practised as a sport or form of physical exercise. Also *attrib.*

1889 *Trans. Asiatic Soc. Japan* XVI. 192 The art of Jiujutsu, from which the present Jiudo..has sprung up. *Ibid.* 204 In Judo, which is an investigation of the laws by which one may gain by yielding, *practice* is made subservient to the *theory*. **1892** *Trans. & Proc. Japan Soc.* I. 9 It is due to the study of *Jū-do* that the Japanese police.. are so skilful in seizing malefactors. **1905** HANCOCK & HIGASHI *Compl. Kano Jiu-Jitsu* p. xi, *Jiudo* is the term selected by Professor Kano as describing his system more accurately than *jiu-jitsu* does. **1921** *Glasgow Herald* 1 Jan. 9/1 This 'Judo' is practised all over Japan. **1931** E. V. GATENBY in *Studies in Eng. Lit.* (Tokyo) XI. 515 There is at least one jûdô society in London. **1953** *Encounter* Oct. 24/1 She ties it in front like a judo jacket. **1958** *Radio Times* 7 Feb. 9/4 A judo club. **1971** R. BUSBY *Deadlock* xiii. 193 A pair of judo pyjamas. **1972** *Oxford Mail* 1 Aug. 10/4 Judo is a way of learning to control yourself and your opponent. *Ibid.*, The first judo club in England was founded in 1918 in London.

Hence **ju·dogi,** the costume worn for judo; **ju·doka,** one who practises, or is expert in, judo.

1952 *Time* 22 Dec. 40/2 France, center of the European cult, now has 150,000 judo wrestlers (called judoka). **1954** E. DOMINY *Teach yourself Judo* 190 *Judogi*,..Judo costume. **1961** *New Statesman* 22 Sept. 402/2 The thrower's..right hand lifts the lapels of the Uke's judogi—his canvas wrestling-jacket. **1964** *Sunday Mail Mag.* (Brisbane) 1 Mar. 7 The only major expense in Judo is £3 for the uniform, which is known as a judogi. *Ibid.*, The examiners..award various gradings to the different judoka. **1974** *Times* 9 Jan. 14/5 With tough agility, however, the British *judoka* emerged from a tight corner.

judoist (dʒū·doist). [f. prec. + -IST.] An expert in judo; one who practises judo.

1950 *Chambers's Encycl.* XIV. 757/1 Whatever the attacker's movement the judoist yields to it in order to lure him into a weakened stance or position. **1966** *Times* 29 Nov. 4 Mr. Gleeson [is] one of the most experienced judoists in this country, and national coach to the British Judo Association. **1969** S. GREENLEE *Spook who sat by Door* iii. 26 Soo thinks him one of the finest natural judoists of his experience.

judy. Add: Now somewhat less disparaging than indicated in Dict. (Further examples.)

Often used colloq. simply to mean 'a girl, woman'.

1929 *Papers Mich. Acad. Sci. Arts & Lett.* X. 303/1 *Judies*, girls. **1932** KIPLING *Limits & Renewals* 244 'We began to bustle our people over the bows before she went to pieces. You'll admit Paul was a help there, Red?' 'I dare say he herded the old judies well enough.' **1934** G. B. SHAW *Too True to be Good* III. 83 *The Sergeant*... [*He kisses her*] How does that feel, Judy? **1938** J. MASEFIELD *Dead Ned* 284 You'd ought to be careful with the judy. It's best to keep in her good books. **1944** *Penguin New Writing* XIX. 105 I'm off the beer, but I could use a judy for a battering-ram against any wall in creation. **1963** [see *GEAR *sb.* 5 e]. **1966** F. SHAW et al. *Lern Yerself Scouse* 25 Me judy, me tart, me gerl. My lady-friend; my fiancée; my wife. **1973** *Guardian* 31 May 13/7 During a strike a man whose judy is working is obviously better off than the man with a wife and three kids about the house.

jug, *sb.*² Add: **1. c.** A jug used as an instrument in a jazz band. So *jug-blower*, etc. See *jug band* (sense 3 below).

1946 R. BLESH *Shining Trumpets* (1949) v. 104 Exotic instruments may be utilized as well, such as harmonica, kazoo, jug, washboard, wood blocks and musical saw. **1956** M. STEARNS *Story of Jazz* (1957) xiv. 157 He didn't even get a chance to team up with washboard beaters, jug blowers, kazoo players, tub thumpers, or alley fiddlers. **1960** *20th Cent.* Dec. 556 The hillbilly form..is played on ..the twelve-string guitar, the jug, the jew's harp. **1964** *Amer. Folk Music Occasional* I. 95 Horses of many different colors run loose in this album, the common denominator being the use by all of a jug, which (blown like a coke bottle) produces rich, booming sound, able to take the bass part. **1968** *Blues Unlimited* Nov. 8 In Memphis, we recorded Dewey Corley, who used to blow jug with the Memphis Jug Band.

2. (Earlier U.S. example.)

1815–16 *Niles' Reg.* IX. Suppl. 190/1 A full grown villain, who with an accomplice, were shortly after safely lodged in the jug.

b. A bank. *slang.*

1845 *National Police Gaz.* 15 Nov. 97/3 Jim Morgan.. disdained no branch of business, from 'craking a jug' (entering a bank) to picking a pocket. **1862** *Cornh. Mag.* Nov. 648 It is all in single pennifs on the England jug... It is in 5*l* notes on the Bank of England. **1904** [see *BOX *sb.*² 3 i]. **1935** G. INGRAM *Cockney Cavalcade* viii. 121 Give me time to go to the 'jug'. **1960** *Observer* 24 Jan. 5/1 If a villain had seriously suggested screwing a jug (breaking into a bank).

3. jug and bottle, used *attrib.* of the bar of a public house at which alcoholic liquors are sold for consumption off the premises; **jug band,** a jazz band in which jugs (sense 1 c above) are used; **jug handle,** the handle of a jug; also *attrib.* and *fig.*, shaped like a jug handle; hence **jug-handled** *a.*, (*a*) *lit.* placed on one side, as the handle of a jug; (*b*) *fig.* (*U.S.*) unilateral, one-sided, unbalanced.

1894 G. MOORE *Esther Waters* xxx. 236 The public entrance and the jug and bottle entrance were in a side street. *Ibid.* xlii. 327 Journeyman was surprised to see Ketley sitting quite composedly in the jug and bottle bar. **1909** *Daily Chron.* 31 Mar. 1/3 A 'jug and bottle' department..does not come within the definition of an open bar. **1932** L. GOLDING *Magnolia St.* I. ix. 144 She got her pint from the Jug and Bottle Department. **1953** *Word for Word: Encycl. Beer* (Whitbread & Co.) 11/2 *Jug-and-bottle bar*, specially reserved for the purchase of drinks for consumption off the premises; only to be found in older pubs. **1946** R. BLESH *Shining Trumpets* (1949) xi. 253 The southern 'jug' band typical of Tennessee and Mississippi. **1970** P. OLIVER *Savannah Syncopators* 63 The recordings of some of the jug bands. **1970** *Western Folklore* XXIX. 229 The..'gutbucket'..is generally played in ensembles such as jug and skiffle bands. **1846** S. F. SMITH *Theatr. Apprenticeship* 118 Not perceiving the entire justice of this arrangement, it being somewhat on the jug-handle principle, all on one side. **1900** E. GLYN *Visits of Elizabeth* 245 She has a jug-handle chignon. **1955** M. E. B. BANKS *Commando Climber* iii. 38 A final wall, almost vertical but amply provided with the largest of jug-handles, remained. **1961** L. MUMFORD *City in Hist.* xvi. 506 To ensure the continuous flow of traffic,..immense clover leaves and jug handles are designed. **1967** R. J. SERLING *President's Plane is Missing* (1968) ii. 27 He was one of those homely men whose virile masculinity masked such features as a big nose and jug-handle ears. **1970** A. BLACKSHAW *Mountaineering* (rev. ed.) vi. 163 A large incut hold (a 'jug-handle') in good rock is the most secure of all holds. **1881** *Congress. Rec.* 8 Dec. 60/2 English reciprocity in pleasure travel,..like their often proposed commercial reciprocity, is comparatively jug-handled. **1904** *Boston Herald* 28 Sept. 6 The trade between Canada and the United States is..jug-handled.

jug (dʒʌg), *sb.*⁵ Slang abbrev. of JUGGINS.

1914 D. H. LAWRENCE *Let.* 18 Dec. (1962) I. 299 But he is a jug...Don't bother anymore. **1956** H. GOLD *Man who was not with It* (1965) xi. 96 It was nice to find the born jug of the continent and to decide even about him: he knows what he wants.

Jug (dʒūg, yūg), *a.* and *sb.*⁶ Abbrev. of *JUGOSLAV(IAN.

1949 V. GIELGUD *Fall of Sparrow* xvii. 168 I've been down among the Jugs during this last week or two. **1958** P. KEMP *No Colours or Crest* x. 218 If Cairo's relations with the Jug Partisans are really so important,..why the hell didn't they warn us off before? **1961** R. B. AMOS *Wasp in Web* vii. 74 A Jug friend of mine was standing next to me. **1967** L. FORRESTER *Girl called Fathom* iv. 33 Most..are based here all the time..the nursing sister, Radik the Jug.

jug (dʒʌg), *sb.*⁷ *West Indies.* Also **jug-jug.** [Origin unkn.] A savoury Barbadian dish served esp. at Christmas (see quots.).

1945 E. P. CLARK *West Indian Cookery* xix. 80 *Jug Jug*... Clean, cut up, and season the beef and pork... Stew the pork.., then add beef and peas and stew..until peas are soft. **1957** F. A. COLLYMORE *Notes for Gloss. Barbadian Dial.* (ed. 2) 49 *Jug, jug-jug*, a famous Christmas dish. **1958** B. HAMILTON *Too Much of Water* iv. 74 A real Barbadian breakfast.., sweet potatoes, an' jug-jug, an' okras. **1970** M. SLATER *Caribbean Cooking* 142 'Jug' is a Bajan Christmas speciality, served with turkey. Jug-Jug came to Barbados..via the Scottish 17th Century exiles, in an attempt to produce something resembling haggis. **1973** *Advocate-News* (Barbados) 25 Dec. 4/6 The specialities of the Yuletide dinner—the turkey, the ham, the plum pudding; the pudding and souse; the peas and rice; the jug-jug; and even caviar.

jug, *v.*¹ Add: **4.** *intr.* To fish with a bait attached to a floating jug (see *jug-fishing* s.v. JUG *sb.*² 3). *U.S.*

1872 *Kansas Mag.* Feb. 178 Jugging for catfish in the chutes of the Missouri and the Kaw. **1947** *Life* 15 Sept. 155 The boys go jugging for catfish. They tie their fishing lines to jugs and haul them in when the jug bobs in the water.

‖ **juge** (ʒüʒ). [Fr.] A judge. *juge d'instruction*, an examining magistrate, a police magistrate.

1882 *Standard* 25 Dec. 3/2 After giving their names and addresses they were permitted to retire, but were informed that they would be called up for examination by a *juge d'instruction*. **1911** CHESTERTON *Innocence of Father Brown* i. 2 How he turned the *juge d'instruction* upside down and stood him on his head, 'to clear his mind'. **1964** *Ann. Reg. 1963* 51 One of Lord Shawcross's solutions was recourse to an examining magistrate, on the lines of a continental *juge d'instruction*. **1973** M. CATTO *Sam Casanova* ii. 22 You're going to have a *juge d'instruction* on your back.

‖ **Jugendstil** (yū·gənt,ʃtīl). [G., f. *jugend* youth (the name of a German magazine started in 1896) + *stil* style.] The German equivalent of *art nouveau*. Also *attrib.* (occas. with lower-case initial).

1928 *Minutes of G. & C. Merriam Co. Editorial Board* III. 707 Note the expression *Jugend Stil*, meaning nouveau art. **1950** B. S. MYERS *Mod. Art in Making* 254 In the works of the *Jugendstil* painters in Germany.., those ideas found their expression. **1958** M. L. WOLF *Dict. Painting* 148 *Jugendstil*, in Germany, the name applied to the *art nouveau* movement, popular from 1890 to 1905, and affecting all of the visual arts. **1960** *Times* 4 May 16/6 The individual stature of the two leading figures of the *jugendstil* period represented in this exhibition. **1963** *Listener* 24 Jan. 160/2 The Jugendstil was much more exuberant, much more demonstratively independent of any past style, and much more violent. **1967** A. WILSON *No Laughing Matter* III. 369 'Not our happiest sort of architecture, I'm afraid.' 'No? I suppose it's the usual Jugendstil of its period.' **1972** *Guardian* 16 Mar. 14/4 In Cracow there's a political cabaret 80 years old, with hair-raising original *Jugendstil*. décor. **1974** *Times Lit. Suppl.* 11 Oct. 1116/2 Sheer frustration may have thrown up a Jugendstil *Parsifal*.

jugful. (Earlier U.S. and further examples.)

1831 *Boston Transcript* 14 Nov. 2/1 'Vote on your side!' says another: 'Not by a jug full.' **1865** DICKENS *Mut. Fr.* II. IV. vii. 217 Mr. Riderhood..fetched his jug-full of water. **1967** WODEHOUSE *Company for Henry* xii. 220 Did your heart melt? Not by a jugful. You gave him the sleeve across the windpipe and kicked him out. **1971** —— *Much Obliged, Jeeves* vi. 57 'Then why is Tuppy short of cash? Didn't he inherit them?' 'Not by a jugful.'

juggernaut, *sb.* Add: **3.** A large heavy vehicle; *spec.* a heavy lorry.

In quot. 1927 prob. just an ordinary motor car.

1841 THACKERAY *Second Funeral of Napoleon* iii. 58 Fancy, then,..the body landed at day-break..and transferred to the car; and fancy the car, a huge Juggernaut of a machine. **1927** W. G. M. DOBIE *Game-Bag & Creel* 20 How gladly would I have him killed or shot, That blind, fat fool who drove the Juggernaut! **1946** G. TYRWHITT-DRAKE *Eng. Circus & Fair Ground* xvii. 198 In 1919 I bid £900 for one of these juggernauts [*sc.* a traction engine] to use for hauling my circus equipment. **1969** *Evening Star* (Ipswich) 28 Apr. 16/2 Experienced colleagues of mine are concerned about container lorries—the 30-ton juggernauts—which are completely disregarding speed limits. **1972** *Guardian* 30 Nov. 32/6 (*headline*) No entry for juggernauts. *Ibid.*, The juggernaut lorry will be kept out. **1972** *Oxford Mail* 11 Dec. 3/3 A plan to banish the juggernaut lorry from many Oxfordshire village roads is being prepared. **1973** *Press & Jrnl.* (Aberdeen) 7 Aug. 8/6 (*caption*) Sunshine and shade in the Church Square, Ballater. Continental juggernauts, on their way to the west coast, would certainly change this peaceful scene. **1973** *Daily Tel.* 10 Aug. 3, French police were last night interviewing 27 Asians—17 Pakistanis and 10 Indians found in Calais under a false floor in a juggernaut bound for Britain.

ju·ghead. *slang* (chiefly *U.S.*). [f. JUG *sb.*² + HEAD *sb.*] **a.** A mule; also, a stubborn horse. **b.** A foolish or stupid person; also, as a mere term of abuse.

1926 L. H. NASON *Chevrons* iii. 86 'Unload everything,' he says. Hear that, you jugheads? At four-thirty! **1936** D. MCCARTHY *Lang. Mosshorn, Jughead*, a horse which seemingly has no brains. **1942** *Sat. Even. Post* 3 Oct. 36/1 Unloose dat jughead jaw! **1966** *Publ. Amer. Dial. Soc.* 1964 XLII. 18 Hardtail, a derogatory name for a mule. Others were *jarhead* and *jughead*. **1971** *Illustr. Weekly India* 25 Apr. 67/5 Jughead, what took you so long?

juglet (dʒʌ·glėt). *Archæol.* [f. JUG *sb.*² + -LET.] A small vessel of jug shape.

1932 *Discovery* Sept. 305/1 The small juglets were commonly made in two halves and imperfectly joined together, though no mark was visible on the outer surface. **1942** *Antiquity* XVI. 187 The juglet with elongated stump base is not among the earliest types of Bronze Age pottery. **1957** K. KENYON *Digging up Jericho* 98 Out of a total of 251 vessels..111 are juglets with a round base, a wide mouth and a rather high loop-handle.

juglone (dʒū·-, dʒʌ·glōᵘn). *Chem.* Also † juglon. [ad. G. *juglon* (C. Reischauer 1877, in *Ber. d. Deut. Chem. Ges.* X. 1542), f. L. *iūglans* walnut: see -ONE.] 5-Hydroxy-1,4-naphthoquinone, $C_{10}H_6O_3$, a reddish-yellow crystalline compound obtained from the green shells of walnuts and having fungicidal properties.

1878 *Jrnl. Chem. Soc.* XXXIV. 233 Juglone (Nucin)... This body, prepared from the green shells of walnuts (*Juglans regia*), has been analysed by the author, who assigns to it the empirical formula, $C_{36}H_{12}O_{10}$. **1887** *Chem. News* 9 Nov. 214/1 'Juglon'. An extended series of analytical results with regard to this body. **1892** ROSCOE & SCHORLEMMER *Treat. Chem.* III. VI. 138 About 150 grms. of juglone are thus obtained from rather more than 100 kilos. of walnut-shells. **1925** *Phytopathology* XV. 783 Juglone..is an irritant causing violent sneezing and has been found..to be especially valuable as a medicant for skin diseases. **1949** E. P. ABRAHAM in H. W. Florey et al. *Antibiotics* I. xiv. 619 Brissemoret and Michaud (1917) reported the use of juglone in clinical cases of eczema, impetigo, and other skin diseases. **1971** R. H. THOMSON *Naturally Occurring Quinones* (ed. 2) iv. 222 Finely powdered juglone is an effective sternutator and like many other quinones has weak fungicidal and bactericidal properties.

Jugoslav, Jugoslavian: see *YUGOSLAV, etc.

jugular, *a.* and *sb.* Add: Now usually pronounced (dʒʌ·giŭlăɹ).

jugulo- (dʒū·-, dʒʌ·giŭlo), combining form of JUGULAR *a.* and *sb.*, JUGULUM, in a few anatomical terms, as **ju:gulodiga·stric** *a.*, designating a pair of lymph nodes (sometimes also including several smaller associated nodes) in the neck (see quots.); **ju:gulo-omohy·oid** *a.*, designating either of a pair of lymph nodes in the neck (see quots.). See also JUGULO-CEPHALIC *a.*

1920 JAMIESON & DOBSON in *Brit. Jrnl. Surg.* VIII. 80 Examined from in front, certain members are particularly conspicuous.., and merit special mention: these are a large gland and a variable number of smaller nodes lying in a triangle formed by the posterior belly of the digastric, common facial vein, and internal jugular vein. These may be called the jugulodigastric glands. **1967** G. M. WYBURN et al. *Conc. Anat.* iv. 120/1 The lymph node at the angle of the jaw, the jugulodigastric, drains the tonsil. **1972** C. R. & T. S. LEESON *Human Struct.* xxix. 151/1 Jugulodigastric. This node (or nodes) lies where the deep chain is crossed by the posterior belly of the digastric muscle. **1920** JAMIESON & DOBSON in *Brit. Jrnl. Surg.* VIII. 80 One gland..situated on or just above the omohyoid, frequently presents at the anterior border of the sternomastoid... From its connection with all parts of the tongue we have to refer to it frequently, and suggest the name jugulo-omohyoid gland. **1963** TOBIAS & ARNOLD *Man's Anat.* II. xv. 120 The jugulo-omohyoid node lies on the internal jugular vein just above the tendon of the omohyoid.

jugum. Add: **2. a.** *Zool.* In certain brachiopods with hinged shells, a process of the dorsal valve. **b.** *Ent.* In certain Lepidoptera, a lobe on the fore wing which is able to link it to the hind wing. Hence **ju·gal, ju·gate** *adjs.*

1888 ROLLESTON & JACKSON *Forms Animal Life* (ed. 2) 693 One valve may have depression or sinuses to which correspond elevations or juga on the other. **1893** J. H. COMSTOCK in *Wilder Quarter-Century Bk.* 43 There are two distinct ways of uniting the two wings of each side in the Lepidoptera; they may be united by a frenulum or..by a jugum. *Ibid.* 84 In this genus [sc. *Hepialis*]..they [*sc.* the wings] are joined by a membranous lobe extending back from near the base of the inner margin of the fore wing. To this lobe I have applied the name jugum. **1895** J. H. & A. COMSTOCK *Man. Study Insects* xviii. 215 This projecting lobe is named the jugum or yoke; and the moths possessing this organ are termed the Jugatæ or the Jugate Lepidoptera. **1952** R. C. MOORE et al. *Invertebr. Fossils* vi. 213/1 A variously shaped crossbar between the spiralia is called [the] jugum; it has considerable importance in classifying some groups of spine-bearing brachiopods. **1957** RICHARDS & DAVIES *Imms's Gen. Textbk. Ent.* (ed. 9) 538 Wing-coupling apparatus of jugate type, the jugal lobe elongate and resting upon the hind wing. **1969** R. F. CHAPMAN *Insects* x. 175 The Hepialidae have a strong jugal lobe which lies beneath the costal margin of the hind wing so that this is held between the jugum and the rest of the fore wing.

juice, *sb.* Add: **1. b.** Also more generally, alcoholic liquor. *U.S. slang.*

1932 *Evening Sun* (Baltimore) 9 Dec. 31/4 *Juice*, whisky. **1940** D. ELLINGTON in *Swing* May 10/3 Everybody in our band at that time was a juice-hound, juice meaning any kind of firewater. **1956** B. HOLIDAY *Lady sings Blues* (1973) xix. 157 There was no place I could work in New York—not if they sold juice there. **1961** R. RUSSELL *Sound* 22 'Nuthin' at all like juice, either,' Hassan said. 'No hangover.' **1971** *Harper's Mag.* May 83 But they need their juice, for their kind of tension would not be relieved by the head-lightening stuff, they need the down-deep sleep of the intelligence that comes with liquor.

c. (*a*) The liquor from the sugar cane; (*b*) this made ready for evaporation.

(*a*) **1697** *Phil. Trans. R. Soc.* XIX. 381 The Juice of the Cane. **1784** P. H. MATY in *New Rev.* Sept. 194 To..cut the cane,..to have the juice expressed, and boiled into sugar. **1812** J. TAYLOR *Arbores Mirabiles* 39 The season continues..about six weeks, when the juice is found to be too thin and poor to make sugar. **1830** G. R. PORTER *Nature & Properties Sugar Cane* 17 The cane contains three sorts of juice, one aqueous, another saccharine, and the third mucous.

(*b*) **1839** URE *Dict. Arts* 1202 Where canes grow on a calcareous marly soil, in a favourable season the saccharine matter gets so thoroughly elaborated, and the glutinous mucilage so completely condensed, that a clear juice and a fine sugar may be obtained without the use of lime. **1887** *Encycl. Brit.* XXII. 626/1 Wetzel's pan,..and similar devices for the efficient evaporation of juice..are also in use.

d. Electricity, electric current. *slang.*

1896 *Boston Herald* 25 Dec. 4/5 Now we know what a blessing the trolley is—when the juice isn't turned off. **1903** *Electrical Engineer* 28 Aug. 327/2 The first he asked, a councillor Whose town had got the juice. **1916** 'TAFFRAIL' *Pincher Martin* xiii. 238 Call her up by wireless... Don't make our name, but use all the juice you can, so that they'll think we're very close. **1928** U. SINCLAIR *Boston* (1929) xxiv. 724 The juice was turned off, and Vanzetti was officially pronounced dead. **1934** J. M. CAIN *Postman always rings Twice* ii. 18 They got neon signs, they show up better, and they don't burn as much juice. **1966** H. SHEPPARD *Dict. Railway Slang* (ed. 2) 9 *On the juice*, running on electrified lines—particularly LTE.

e. Petrol. *slang.*

1909 *Installation News* III. 52/2 We are not faced with a threepenny tax on each gallon of 'juice'. **1918** E. M. ROBERTS *Flying Fighter* 281 Then I discovered that the tank was nearly empty. That meant that I would have to go in search of 'juice'. **1959** *N.Z. Listener* 12 June 20/4 'Turn the juice on!' He felt sheepish as he twisted the key. **1968** K. WEATHERLY *Roo Shooter* 56 The Rover had him worried. If she ran out of juice..he had to walk in. **1973** *Nation Rev.* (Melbourne) 24–30 Aug. 1399/6 'Tis cheaper to slow down—you use less juice then, be it petroleum or gastric.

f. A drug or drugs. *slang.*

1957 [see *gang-bang* s.v. *GANG *sb.*¹ 12]. **1972** H. C. RAE *Shooting Gallery* iii. 187, I wasn't interested in him. I mean, when you shoot juice, you lose the other thing.

4. c. Political influence (exercised by or on behalf of criminals); money paid to obtain immunity from prosecution, or lent at a usurious rate of interest, or the interest thus extorted; money acquired by corruption, gambling, or threats. Also *attrib. U.S.*

1935 A. J. POLLOCK *Underworld Speaks* 65/1 *Juice*, corrupt influence (shake-down) for protection to operate unlawfully. **1951** [see *ICE *sb.* 4 e]. **1961** *Chicago Daily Tribune* 12 Aug. 1 William ('Action') Jackson..a 'juice man' (loan collector) for syndicate hoodlum bosses. **1962** A. BUCHWALD *How Much is that in Dollars?* 75 'Well, use some juice,' Mr Cahn said. 'Juice' is a Hollywood expression which means influence. **1963** P. WYDEN *Hired Killers* xii. 196 'Juice'—usurious interest of up to twenty per cent—was known to fester at the root of some of these assassinations. The juice racket has been flourishing for decades. **1964** [see *COSA NOSTRA]. **1968** *N.Y. Times* 9 June 1. 29 At least two murders and perhaps more have been connected to the loan shark, or 'juice' racket, as it is called here, as well as beatings and threats. **1969** *Time* 11 July 24 This Las Vegas is..a venal demimonde in which the greatest compliment that can be paid a man is to say that he has 'juice' (influence in the right places). **1970** E. R. JOHNSON *God Keepers* (1971) xiv. 146 Vito Lucchese was involved in the case and..he had a certain amount of juice around the city. **1971** *Ink* 12 June 14/2 His high-paid whizkid managers weren't whizzing too well so he went after some extra juice.

6. juice-head *slang*, an alcoholic; **juice-joint** *N. Amer. slang*, a bar, club, or stall serving either alcoholic or non-alcoholic liquor.

1955 S. WHITMORE *Solo* 247 The juiceheads..got so fractured [i.e., drunk] that they wouldn't show up for a date. **1967** *New Yorker* 9 Sept. 41 If anybody wanted to get stoned the guy who owned the pad made them go up on the roof. Juice-heads drank Red Mountain. **1969** A. H. CAIN *Young People & Drugs* 159 *Juice head*, one whose hang-up is booze; an alcoholic. **1927** K. NICHOLSON *Barker* 149 *Juice joint*, soft drink stand. **1932** *Evening Sun* (Baltimore) 9 Dec. 31/4 *Juice-joint*, speakeasy. **1958** G. LEA *Somewhere there's Music* iv. 35 Six lonely nights a week in a juice joint. **1960** WENTWORTH & FLEXNER *Dict. Amer. Slang* 298/2 *Juice-joint*. 1. A soft-drink tent, stand, booth, or concession. Carnival and circus use. 2. A speakeasy; a bar or nightclub. Orig. 1920 use. **1970** C. MAJOR *Dict. Afro-Amer. Slang* 72 *Juice joint*, tavern, bar, cabaret.

juice, *v.* Add: **2.** To animate, liven *up*, inspire. *slang.*

1964 *Time* 23 Oct. 61 A thing like that can really juice you up. **1972** J. MILLS *Report to Commissioner* 259 The departmental surgeon asked Jackson if he wanted him to give Lockley a shot of something, he meant juice him up a little, keep him from passing out.

juiced, *a.* Add: **2.** Drunk. Also const. *up. slang.*

1946 C. HIMES *Black on Black* 260 She was an old wino used to come there every night and get juiced up. **1955** D. W. MAURER in *Publ. Amer. Dial. Soc.* XXIV. x. 170 Men sufficiently *juiced up* to be robbed without much interference. **1956** B. HOLIDAY *Lady sings Blues* (1973) ii. 17 The doctor said if her man had even come to enough to raise the window and let in some air he could have saved her. But he was too juiced even for that. **1968** A. YOUNG in A. Chapman *New Black Voices* (1972) 149 Chicken Hawk and Wine, well-juiced, eased quietly up the back steps. **1969** *Time* 24 Oct. 70 Later Marvin apologized: 'I'm sorry I was so rotten this afternoon. I was a little juiced.' **1971** 'S. RANSOME' *Trap 6* (1972) xiii. 147 He was sitting at the bar brooding over a drink—not making any trouble, not getting juiced up.

juice-harp. Corrupted form of JEWS' HARP.

1942 BERREY & VAN DEN BARK *Amer. Thes. Slang* § 577/22 Jews'-harp, jaw-harp, juice-harp. **1950** BLESH & JANIS *They all played Ragtime* (1958) vi. 109 The childhood band he led, consisting of two tin whistles, jew's-harp ('juice-harp'), and triangle, was a country rag band. **1959** M. STEARNS in M. T. Williams *Art of Jazz* (1960) ii. 9 Sonny Terry listened to his father's harmonica and 'juice' harp. **1968** *Publ. Amer. Dial. Soc.* XLIX. 15 The decline of *juice harp* and *jew's harp* and the students' use of *mouth harp*.

juicer (dʒū·səɹ). [f. JUICE *sb.* + -ER¹.] **1.** An electrician. *slang.* (Cf. *JUICE *sb.* 1 d.)

1928 *Amer. Speech* III. 366 'Juicers' have a most juicy vocabulary of their own. Thanks to them Hollywood has 'kliegs' (klieg lights). **1934** *Tit-Bits* 31 Mar. 12/2 Here are some more studio terms. 'Juicers' are electricians. **1950** B. SCHULBERG *Disenchanted* (1951) i. 11 Assistant directors, cutters, bit players, second cameramen, sound men, juicers, grips, special effects men, Hollywood's exclusive proletariat. **1957** V. J. KEHOE *Technique Film & Television Make-up* i. 18 He directs the..juicers to place the lights in the most effective positions.

2. An appliance used to extract juice from fruit and vegetables.

1938 *Cooperative Distributors Catal.* in *Amer. Speech* (1942) XVII. 272/1 A well constructed juicer for oranges. **1945** *Archit. Rev.* XCVII. 152 (*caption*) The 'Dazey' super juicer..in aluminium. **1961** *Listener* 31 Aug. 331/2 Self-contained grinders, liquidizers, juicers and meat mincers are also made. **1972** *New York* 1 May 27/2 Juicers—used to extract the juice of fresh vegetables and fruits.

3. An alcoholic. *U.S. slang.*

1967 *New Yorker* 13 May 40 The difference between the juicers and the heads is that the juicers sometimes get a little obstreperous but the heads go sit quietly in a corner someplace. **1970** *Ibid.* 28 Feb. 31/1 'Forget him, he's catatonic.' 'Forget him, he's a juicer.'

juicily (dʒū·sili), *adv. slang.* [f. JUICY *a.* + -LY².] **a.** Excellently, vigorously, well. **b.** Suggestively.

1916 E. F. BENSON *David Blaize* vi. 118 [He] hit it juicily to square leg. **1927** WODEHOUSE in *Sunday Express* 18 Oct. 9 Abstemious cove though I am as a general thing ..on this occasion..I had been doing myself rather juicily. **1969** *Daily Tel.* 3 Dec. 13/8 The hand-outs asked juicily whether the girls who took on these jobs were really on the first step to the harem and white slavery.

juicy, *a.* Add: **2. c.** Suggestive, esp. in a sexual way; piquant, racy, sensational. *colloq.*

1883 J. GREENWOOD *Odd People* 59 'Let me play you a tune, then,' said the frightened lad... 'All right, then. Play us something juicy,' exclaimed the ruffian. **1908** KIPLING *Lett. of Travel* (1920) 153 They interpolated no juicy anecdotes of murder or theft among their acquaintance. **1920** S. LEWIS *Main St.* ix. 102 The gang..gathered in a snickering knot to listen to the 'juicy stories'. **1923** A. BENNETT *Riceyman Steps* I. ii. 4 Accounts of bloody crimes and juicy sexual irregularities. **1929** [see *duck soup* s.v. *DUCK *sb.*¹ 12]. **1953** [see *gang-bang* s.v. *GANG *sb.*¹ 12]. **1958** B. NICHOLS *Sweet & Twenties* 106 Extracting what he was pleased to call 'the juicy bits'. **1965** 'O. MILLS' *Dusty Death* xix. 177 'Aren't you going to give us a look at it?' 'Not this one, no. Far, far too juicy.' **1972** J. MCCLURE *Caterpillar Cop* xiii. 218 His parents sound the sort who'd run a mile before they'd say the word 'sex'. They wouldn't have any juicy books in the house either.

d. Excellent, vigorous, first-rate; serious; profitable.

1916 E. F. BENSON *David Blaize* vi. 119 It didn't often happen that the first ball of an innings was slogged for six. Juicy hit, too! **1922** G. ADE *Let.* 8 Mar. (1973) 80 The author who has only a few stories ready to market can see no prospect of juicy returns. **1934** *Time & Tide* 8 Sept. 1122/2 But still, with this juicy price in prospect, the shrewd professionals are hesitant. **1948** PARTRIDGE *Dict. Forces' Slang* 104 *Juicy*, (of targets) easy, or well worth the trouble of destroying. **1962** *Times* 18 Oct. 6/3, I have been thinking of some very juicy ways of how we can use the South Carriage Drive in one of the royal parks.

ju-jitsu (dʒū:dʒi·tsu), *sb.* Also formerly jiu-jitsu, -jutsu, ju-jitzu, -jutsu; and as one unhyphenated word. [ad. Jap. *jūjutsu*, f.

jū (Chinese *jou*: see *JUDO) + *jutsu* (Chinese *shu*, *shut* art, science).] A Japanese system of wrestling and physical training, characterized by the use of certain techniques and holds to overcome an adversary. Cf. *JUDO. Also *attrib.*

1875 *Japan Mail* 10 Mar. 133/1 *Jiu-jitsu* (wrestling) is also taught, but not much practised by gentlemen. **1889** [see *JUDO]. **1891** L. HEARN *Let.* Nov. in E. Bisland *Life & Lett. L. Hearn* (1906) II. 70 A building in which jū-jutsu is taught by Mr. Kano. **1893** —— *Let.* 13 Oct. (1910) 183, I am working out an essay—a philosophical essay on 'Jiujutsu'. **1895** J. INOUYE *Wrestlers & Wrestling* 3 These methods were adopted and extensively practised by *Samurai*, and were finally developed into what is now known as *Jujitsu*. **1905** *Daily Chron.* 21 Feb. 7/4 Their gymnasium is often visited by ju-jitsu wrestlers. **1910** H. G. WELLS *Hist. Mr. Polly* vii. 238 A combination of something romantic called 'Ju-jitsu' and..the 'Police Grip'. **1925** N. VENNER *Imperfect Impostor* xvi, Jos Polkins ..enwrapped him in a benevolent jiu jitsu grip that left him powerless to move. **1946** R. BENEDICT *Chrysanthemum & Sword* (1947) xii. 277 He perfects himself in jujitsu or sword play.

fig. **1906** R. WHITEING *Ring in New* xxix. 206 To lay him flat on his back by a sort of intellectual jiu-jitsu. **1928** F. ROMER *Numbers Up!* 11 'Revenge?'..'nothing of the kind. I shall merely practise Moral Jiu-jitsu.' **1942** WYNDHAM LEWIS *Let.* 15 July (1963) 334 There are omens of promise—in much that Mr. Roosevelt has done, or in the splendid massive jujitzu of the Russians. **1965** K. BRIGGS in Battiscombe & Laski *Chapelet for C. Yonge* 25 Practising a kind of spiritual ju-jitsu, in which by falling with the misfortune you overcome it.

Hence **ju-ji·tsu** *v. trans.*, to overcome by means of ju-jitsu; **ju-ji·tsian, ju-ji·tsuist**, one who teaches or practises ju-jitsu.

1905 D. SLADEN *Playing Game* II. iv. 202 The wiry little Japanese having Jujitsu'd the three biggest men on the Russian flag-ship. **1905** HANCOCK & HIGASHI *Compl. Kano Jiu-Jitsu* p. v, Those famous *jiu-jitsians*, Hoshino and Tsutsumi. **1905** *Westm. Gaz.* 23 Nov. 4/2 He..issued ..a challenge to all jiu-jitsuists of the world. **1928** *Observer* 4 Mar. 15/2 They seem to me to put up no fight at all, and to be very easily ju-jitsued by the Japanese servants.

ju-ju[2] (dʒū·dʒū). *slang.* [redupl. form of *MARI)JU(ANA.] A marijuana cigarette. Also *attrib.*

1940 R. CHANDLER *Farewell, my Lovely* xi. 83 'I knew a guy once who smoked ju-jus,' she said. 'Three high balls and three sticks of tea and it took a pipe wrench to get him off the chandelier.' **1963** N. FREELING *Because of Cats* x. 163 'He had juju cigarettes too; like Russians, with a big mouth piece and pretty loose...' 'The jujus are—you feel very clever.'

juke (dʒūk), *sb. slang* (orig. *U.S.*). Also **jook, jouk.** [Prob. f. Gullah *juke, joog* disorderly, wicked, of W. Afr. origin; cf. Wolof *dzug* to live wickedly.] **1.** A roadhouse or brothel; *spec.* a cheap roadside establishment providing food and drinks, and music for dancing. In full *juke-house, juke-joint.*

1935 Z. N. HURSTON *Mules & Men* I. iii. 82 They talked and told strong stories of Ella, Wall, East Coast Mary,.. and lesser jook lights around whom the glory of Polk County surged. **1936** *Scribner's Mag.* Dec. 27/2 Jim's daddy owned the General Store and a nigger jook. **1937** in *Florida Rev.* (1938) Spring 28/1 Back yonder a 'juke' was a place, usually a shack somewhere off the road, where a field negro could go for a snort of moonshine. *Ibid.*, There were negro juke-joints as far back as I can remember. **1941** J. FAULKNER *Men Working* ii. 39 The glow from the lights of the jook house at the lake appeared above the trees. **1956** S. LONGSTREET *Real Jazz* xviii. 151 *Juke* from juke box came from juke house—which was once a whorehouse. **1958** P. OLIVER in P. Gammond *Decca Bk. Jazz* i. 23 The crude, wood-frame dance-halls called 'jooks' (or jukes). **1964** *Amer. Folk Music Occasional* I. 93 You go into the bars and the juke joints and you ask around. **1968** *Blues Unlimited* Nov. 6 Now Ike told Dave that he cut Elmore's 'Dust my broom' at a Canton juke-joint. **1971** *Black World* June 72/2 Had done sent Lueta and Carol Ann to every juke joint in Greenwood askin bout you.

2. juke-box (occas. **juke-organ**), a machine that automatically plays selected gramophone records when a coin is inserted; also ellipt. as *juke*. Also *attrib.*, *transf.*, and *fig.*

1937 in *Florida Rev.* (1938) Spring 25/3 The screeching of the 'jook' organ. **1939** *Time* 27 Nov. 56/2 Glenn Miller attributes his crescendo to the 'juke-box', which retails recorded music at 5 ¢ a shot in bars, restaurants and small roadside dance joints. *Ibid.* 25 Dec. 3/1 To the Florida Man such an instrument is a jook organ. **1942** D. POWELL *Time to be Born* (1943) x. 241 Corinne put a quarter in the juke-box to play 'Let's Be Buddies' five times. **1944** AUDEN *For Time Being* (1945) 65 War has become Like a juke-box tune that we dare not stop. **1947** *Gramophone* Dec. 95/1 It is the Petrillo thesis that records which are played in juke-boxes and broadcast over the radio..are monsters which have threatened the musicians' very existence. **1947** [see *JIVE *v.* 2 a]. **1954** *Archit. Rev.* CXVI. 92/2 The stupefying juke-box façade of the Wertheim project. **1959** C. MACINNES *Absolute Beginners* 83 See all the kids jam-packed in there beside the jukes? **1961** L. MUMFORD *City in Hist.* viii. 224 Pennsylvania Station in New York retains this noble quality—or did until that structure was converted..into a vast jukebox. **1968** J. WINEARLS *Mod. Dance* (ed. 2) vi. 143 There emerges a constant from which the immediate must not depart. Our teenage Juke Box Juries demonstrate this ably. **1973** C. BONINGTON *Next Horizon* xvii. 244 A coffee bar for teenagers, complete with juke box. **1973** *Nation Rev.* (Melbourne) 31 Aug. 1453/4 The America they traverse, of fibro suburbs and prison farms and jukebox bars, is..correctly and compassionately observed.

juke (dʒūk), *v. slang* (orig. *U.S.*). Also **jook, jouk.** [Cf. prec.] *intr.* To dance, esp. at a juke-joint or to the music of a juke-box (see also quot. 1958). So **ju·king** *vbl. sb.*

1933 W. ROLAND (*title of disc*) Jookit Jookit. **1937** C. R. COOPER *Here's to Crime* ix. 190 In the 'jukin' joints' there is, of course, the prime requisite of liquor. **1941** *Amer. Speech* XVI. 319/2 'Let's jouk' is an invitation to dance, but 'let's go joukin'' is a request for a date. **1958** T. WILLIAMS *Orpheus Descending* I. 28 I'd like to go out jooking with you tonight...That's where you get in a car and drink a little and drive a little and stop and dance a little to a juke box. **1960** *20th Cent.* Aug. 144 But living, in these terms, is reduced to jooking. **1967** *Daily Tel.* 15 May 12/8 To juke also came to mean to dance and to go pub-crawling.

jukskei (yǒ·kskēi). *S. Afr.* Also **jeuk skei, jukschei.** Pl. **jukskeie, jukskeis.** [Afrikaans, f. *juk* yoke + *skei* pin, SKEY *sb.*[2]; cf. *yoke-skey*.] **1.** A yoke-skey.

1822 W. J. BURCHELL *Trav. S. Afr.* I. viii. 151 The yokes are straight, and pierced with two pair of mortices to receive the *jukschei* which fits in loosely, and answer to what in English husbandry are called the *bows*. **1871** LORD & BAINES *Shifts & Expedients Camp Life* ix. 452 Near each end are two mortices..through which to pass the 'jeuk skeis', or yoke keys, which keep it in place on the neck of the ox. **1971** *Evening Post Mag.* (Port Elizabeth) 27 Feb. 2 A stinkwood yoke, with 'jukskeis', serves as a hatstand.

2. A quoits-like game; the bottle-shaped 'quoit' used in this game.

[**1934** C. P. SWART *Africanderisms* (M.A. Thesis, S. Afr.), *Jukskeigooi*, a game, very similar to quoits, played by the Boers, a skey being used instead of the customary circular ring.] **1942** *Cape Times* 10 Nov. 4/2 Saturday's Jukskei results were as expected. **1947** *Ibid.* 21 Apr. 7 The jukskeis were brought..by Mr. Tom Naude. **1950** S. DE WET *Hour of Breath* ix. 69 In the late afternoon we used to play Jukskei on the river bank below our houses. **1956** *Cape Times* 26 Jan. 1/1 A few minutes after throwing about six practice *jukskeie* at the Newlands circus grounds.. Mr. P. A. Meiring..dropped dead. **1971** *Progress* (Cape Town) May 2/4 No one has challenged us at jukskei.

juldie, var. *JILDI.

julienite (dʒū·liĕnəit, yūli,ēi·nəit). *Min.* [ad. Flemish *juliëniet* (A. Schoep 1928, in *Natuurwet. Tijdschr.* X. 58), f. the name of Henri *Julien* (d. 1920), Belgian geologist: see -ITE[1].] A hydrous thiocyanate of sodium and cobalt, $Na_2Co(SCN)_4.8H_2O$, that occurs as minute blue needles and has been made artificially; orig. wrongly regarded as a cobalt chloro-nitrate.

1928 *Mineral. Mag.* XXI. 567 Julienite... Hydrated chloro-nitrate of cobalt as minute blue needles, presumably hexagonal and isomorphous with buttgenbachite: from Katanga. **1954** *Mineral. Abstr.* XII. 337 Needles of julienite.., prepared by digesting Na-Co nitrite with an aqueous solution of Na sulphocyanide, are tetragonal. **1969** I. KOSTOV *Mineral.* 117 The interesting mineral julienite..is obtained during the exogenetic decomposition of primary cobalt sulphides.

julienne. Add: **2.** Applied *attrib.* or as *adj.* to vegetables cut into small thin strips.

1889 A. B. MARSHALL *Cookery Bk.* ii. 31 *Julienne Garnish.*—Peel and cut the vegetables, such as carrots, turnips, etc., into strips about an inch long. **1906** A. FILIPPINI *Internat. Cook Bk.* 228 Cut with a sharp knife—if no julienne-shaped potato cutter is at hand—into even julienne, match-like strips. **1920** [see *cornflakes* sb. pl. s.v. *CORN *sb.*[1] 11]. **1971** *Salads* (Cordon Bleu Cookery School) 100/2 Wash, peel and slice celeriac, cut across into julienne strips (about 1½–2 inches long).

Juliet (dʒū·liĕt). [Female personal name (F. *Juliette*, It. *Giulietta*), dim. of *Julia*.] *Juliet cap* (see quot. 1957).

1909 *Westm. Gaz.* 9 Feb. 8/3 Their Juliet caps were composed of violets. **1930** *Daily Tel.* 7 Apr. 7/6 The 'Juliet' cap idea is to be found in the little theatre hats worn abroad. **1957** M. B. PICKEN *Fashion Dict.* 49/2 *Juliet cap*, small, round cap of wide, open mesh, usually decorated with pearls or other jewels, similar to that worn on the stage by Shakespeare's Juliet. Worn chiefly for evening. **1973** *Times* 15 Nov. 6/3 The bridesmaid..wore a pinafore dress and a jewelled Juliet cap.

jum, júm: see JOOM.

jumar (dʒū·mǎɹ). *Mountaineering.* [Swiss name.] A clip which when attached to a fixed rope automatically tightens when weight is applied and relaxes when it is removed, thus facilitating the climbing of the rope; also, a climb using jumars. Hence as *v. intr.*, to climb with the aid of jumars; **ju·maring** *vbl. sb.*, the action of so doing.

1966 *Climbers' Club Jrnl.* 77 Somebody spotted him dangling from his Jumars, half-way down one of the fixed ropes. **1968** P. CREW *Encycl. Dict. Mountaineering* 73/1 Jumars are the most effective device for prusiking, but they have the disadvantage of not working well on iced ropes. **1969** *Sunday Times* (Colour Suppl.) 16 Feb. 38/3, I dreamed that I was on the ropes setting off for the summit by myself and I was jumaring all night without getting anywhere. **1971** C. BONINGTON *Annapurna South Face* viii. 90 Once the ropes are in place, the climbers no longer move roped together, but simply clip onto the rope, using on the upward sections a device called a jumar clamp. This is a metal handle, with a knurled lever which is fitted over the rope. It works on a ratchet principle, sliding easily up the rope, but biting into it when put under tension. *Ibid.* xi. 125 This was the first time that this type of free jumaring had ever been necessary at this altitude in the Himalayas. **1971** D. HASTON in *Ibid.* xvii. 214 The sun was two hours away from the gully when we started the upward jumar. **1972** —— *In High Places* 2 Onward, outward, creeping on jumars and rimed ropes. It is cold... Dachstein-mitted hands freeze in jumar clutch. *Ibid.* ix. 104 The hook fitted, a quick move, and I was up. Mick jumared and I pushed on again. **1973** C. BONINGTON *Next Horizon* ix. 141 Later, I learned that an essential precaution for any jumaring is to tie a knot in the rope, so that if the jumars do slip on the rope, you don't slide straight off the end.

jumbal, jumble. (Later examples.)

1892 *Mrs. Beeton's Bk. Househ. Managem.* xl. 1125 California jumbles... sugar,..butter,..flour,..grated lemon-peel..whites of 4 eggs. **1923** CHESTERTON *Fancies versus Fads* ii. 21 It involved eating jumbles (a brown flexible cake now almost gone from us). **1974** *Daily Tel.* 29 Apr. 16/7 Miss Lane mentions the absence from the glossary of such terms as cracknells, jumbells, trencher-bread, etc.

jumbee, jumbi, jumbie, varr. *JUMBY.

jumble, *sb.*[1] Add: **1. b.** *collect. sing.* Articles for a jumble-sale; also, a jumble-sale or sales. *colloq.*

1931 *Times* 16 Mar. 1/3 Maternity Hospital, holding annual Jumble Sale.—Please deluge us with jumble. **1932** *Daily Tel.* 17 Mar. 1/2 Do please help us with our Easter Jumble on March 18th by sending anything saleable, old or new. **1962** [see *FÊTE *sb.* 1 b]. **1966** *Listener* 20 Oct. 570/1 This feat of administration, this orgy of jumble and whist. **1973** J. BURROWS *Like Evening Gone* ii. 27 When did the scouts have their jumble? I'd have thought every gloryhole..was empty.

Jumble (dʒʌ·mb'l), *sb.*[2] *slang.* [Corruption of JOHN BULL.] A black man's nickname for a white man. Also *attrib.* or as *adj.*

1957 C. MACINNES *City of Spades* I. iii. 17 'You're a Jumble, man... That's what we call you... It's cheeky, perhaps, but not so very insulting.' 'May I enquire how it is spelt?' 'J-o-h-n-b-u-l-l.' '..But pronounced as you pronounce it?' 'Yes: Jumble.' **1957** *Listener* 12 Sept. 402/1 Jumble, a happy corruption of John Bull, is the Englishman's nickname in the mouths of the thousands of Africans and West Indians who have flocked to London since the war. *Ibid.*, The Jumble capital. *Ibid.*, An alien and uncomprehending Jumble world. **1961** M. DICKENS *Heart of London* II. 190 Get all you can out of the Jumbles. *Ibid.* III. 294 He feeling his way about the Jumbles, he got no time to worry about Trinidad.

ju·mble-bead. [Alteration of *jumby-bead* (see *JUMBY b), prob. after *mumble*.] The parti-coloured seed of the jequirity.

1855 R. G. MAYNE *Expos. Lex. Med. Sci.* (1860) 554/2 *Jumble beads*, an irreverent name for the seeds of the *Abrus precatorius*, from the purpose they are applied to in forming rosaries. **1887** [see JEQUIRITY]. **1951** A. NELSON *Medical Bot.* xxiii. 456 The seeds [of *Abrus precatorius*] may be referred to as Abrus, Jequirity, Jumble beads or Prayer beads, and are known to contain two poisonous principles.

jumbo. Add: **1. b.** (Earlier and later examples.) Also *Comb.*, as **jumboburger** *U.S.*, a large hamburger; **jumbo jet**, a large jet aeroplane with a seating capacity of several hundred passengers; **jumbo-size(d)** *a.*, of a large size.

1897 *Sears, Roebuck Catal.* 12/2 Peaches, Jumbo California, halves. **1916** *Amer. City* Apr. 373/1 Large jumbo peanuts were bought, instead of culls. **1940** S. LEWIS *Bethel Merriday* i. 19 The three children..supped on a jumbo malted milk. **1949** *Sat. Even. Post* 2 Apr. 116/3 Davis..is a jumbo-sized (six feet two, 202 pounds) man of forty-six. **1958** *Daily Express* 1 Apr. 1/4 You and your jumbo Martinis!! **1959** *Observer* 8 Nov. 3/5 We can expect the kind of hamburger proliferation that exists in America, with beefburgers, eggburgers, cheeseburgers, jumbo burgers, superior 'Hamburger Heavens'. **1960** *Guardian* 9 Sept. 8/4 The jumbo-sized plastic bone. **1964** *Punch* 15 July 79/3 The silly girl spends most of her time eating jumboburgers. **1964** *Economist* 19 Dec. 1317/2 Some.. airlines do not expect..an American supersonic airliner ever to go into production. Jumbo-jets, with 500 seats and two decks,..look much cheaper to fly. **1965** *Teacher's World* 18 June 5/4 The shelves of the local supermarket are full of 'king-sized', 'giant economy' and 'jumbo' packages. **1965** *Business Weekly* 25 Dec. 31 Nosing into the Jumbo jet race: Lockheed, Boeing and Douglas. **1968** 'R. RAINE' *Night of Hawk* xxvii. 126 The meal was avocado salad, a jumbo-size steak, and a mountain of ice cream. **1969** *Listener* 13 Nov. 683/3 They can replace two flights on conventional aircraft with a single jumbo jet flight. **1970** *Drum* (E. Afr. ed.) Feb. 31/3 This airport will be capable of handling jumbo jets and is ideally situated in the heart of the safari country. **1972** J. ROSSITER *Rope*

for General Dietz iii. 34 The shrill rasping of a jumbo-size cicada..woke me. **1973** *Sun* 18 Jan. 6 The Prime Minister handled his jumbo Press conference amid the splendour of Lancaster House with poise and style.

c. *Engin.* Any of various large types of equipment used in drilling, lifting, dumping, etc.

1908 *Sat. Even. Post* 7 Nov. 11/3 Nearest the portal was the 'jumbo', a great, movable platform through which the 'muckers' dumped their barrow-loads to cars beneath. **1909** WEBSTER, *Jumbo*,..a large traveling carriage for transporting excavated material, as in tunnel driving. **1950** *Engineering* 10 Mar. 264/3 The method is well illustrated in the Stockholm tunnel, using a truck-mounted jumbo. **1951** *Ibid.* 12 Jan. 34/2 The concrete was placed from a travelling frame or 'jumbo', as it is termed in American practice. This straddled the pipe and travelled on rails laid in an excavated trench.

d. (See quot. 1948.)

1912 *Outing* Aug. 629/2 The pilot schooners when lying at their stations, the sail carried being jumbo or forestaysail, foresail, and reefed mainsail. **1916** F. W. WALLACE *Shack Locker* (1922) i. 22 Slack off that jumbo an' the foresheet! **1927** *Canad. Fisherman* 141/2 A gigantic sea boarded the vessel and broke about fifteen feet up the jumbo stay. **1932** J. BARBOUR *48 Days Adrift* vii. 94 'Hard, down hard,' I cried; 'haul over the jumbo sheet. If we are not careful we will all be lost this time.' **1948** R. DE KERCHOVE *Internat. Maritime Dict.* 377/1 *Jumbo* (U.S.). 1. The forestaysail on fore-and-aft-rigged vessels. 2. A triangular sail which sets, point downward, on the foreyard of a square-rigged vessel or a topsail schooner in place of the regular foresail. **1956** A. F. LOOMIS *'Hotspur' Story* x. 117 The weather looked a little threatening and I set the jumbo and storm jib.

e. Short for **jumbo jet.*

1966 *New Statesman* 22 Apr. 591/2 The competitors.. need only a small handful of jumbos..on the popular long-distance routes. *Ibid.*, A rival jumbo designed by Douglas. **1971** *Daily Tel.* (Colour Suppl.) 8 Jan. 15/4 A collision between two jumbos on the approaches to Heathrow could produce a deathroll of thousands. **1972** H. OSBORNE *Pay-Day* III. 154 They can't get him on a plane before tonight. They want someone to go down on the Jumbo today. **1973** *Guardian* 12 Mar. 10/4 Jumbo-loads of Soviet immigrants. **1974** *Observer* (Colour Suppl.) 29 Sept. 65/1 The visitors who disembarked from our jumbo at Kai Tak Airport.

jumboize (dʒʌ·mbo͵aiz), *v.* [f. JUMBO + -IZE.] *trans.* To enlarge a ship, esp. a tanker, by inserting a new middle section between the bow and stern. So **ju·mboized** *ppl. a.*; **ju·mboizer**; **ju·mboizing** *vbl. sb.*

1956 *N.Y. Times* 23 Dec. S11/7 (*heading*) Concern to build ten and 'jumboize' nine. *Ibid.*, 'Jumboizing' consists of building an entire new center section for a tanker. The existing vessel is then cut off at the bow and stern which are later joined to the new section. **1957** *Sun* (Baltimore) 4 Apr. 16 We're 'jumboizing' present tankers. *Ibid.*, First completed 'jumboized' oil tanker. **1957** *New Yorker* 14 Sept. 33/3 In language controls, the trend is toward bastardization, if you ask us, and we wish the National Association of Manufacturers would call in all the jumboizers and miniaturizationists and bang their heads together. **1961** *Economist* 28 Jan. 366/1 Conversions and jumboizing within 56 days. *Ibid.*, The Schlieker yard had 'jumboized' on the spot the T2 tanker *Kaposia*. **1973** *Daily Colonist* (Victoria, B.C.) 10 Feb. 25/2 Ferries on this route currently do not have the double kitchens of the jumboized ships on the Shwartz Bay–Tsawassen service.

jumbuck. Add: (Earlier and later examples.) Also *N.Z.*

1824 W. WALKER *Let.* 26 Jan. in W. S. Ramson *Austral. Eng.* (1966) vi. 107 They smacked their lips and stroked their breasts, 'boodjerry patta! murry boodjerry!—fat as jimbuck!!' i.e. good food, very good, fat as mutton. **1871** C. L. MONEY *Knocking about in N.Z.* i. 7 A pivot.. shot the unsuspecting 'jumbucks' into the water below. **1896** H. TICHBORNE *Noqu Talanoa: Stories S. Seas* 95 Our girls very often possess fathers who own considerable stretches of 'jumbuck' property. **1933** L. ACLAND in *Press* (Christchurch, N.Z.) 28 Oct. 17/7 *Jumbuck*, slang for sheep..has always been in common use here. **1934** [see *GUTS *v.*]. **1967** *Sunday Mail Mag.* (Brisbane) 16 Apr. 2 The swagman who shoved a jumbuck in his tucker bag was stealing a sheep.

jumby (dʒʌ·mbi). Chiefly *West Indies.* Also **jumbee, jumbi, jumbie, zumbi.** [ad. Kongo *zumbi* fetish.] A ghost or evil spirit among American and West Indian Negroes. Cf. *ZOMBIE.

1871 C. KINGSLEY *At Last* II. x. 56 Out of the mud comes up—not jumbies, but—a multitude of small stones. **1876** R. F. BURTON *Two Trips Gorilla Land* II. 124 There was no danger of the Zumbi, or ghost. **1887** W. H. BENTLEY *Dict. & Gram. Kongo Lang.* 505 The fetish Zumbi is supposed to bring good luck with it. It sometimes consists of a bundle of charms, at others it is an image, or even an animal. **1891** 'J. EVELYN' *Baffled Vengeance* iv. 60 The 'jumbies' (evil spirits) that haunted the ill-omened spot. **1894** 'A. SPINNER' *Study in Colour* iv. 47 To tremble over the terrible tales of the Jumbi and Duppies, that..terrify belated travellers. **1918** C. W. BEEBE *Jungle Peace* (1919) vii. 138 Sam had formerly been a warden in the Georgetown jail, and rumour had it that he left because he saw 'jumbies' in the court where one hundred and nine men had been hanged. **1951** E. A. MITTELHOLZER *Shadows move among Them* I. ii. 18 A pencil drawing of an ugly face—the face of a jumbie as imagined by Berton. *Ibid.* II. ix. 239 Believe in fairies and ghosts and jumbies and goblins. **1955** *Caribbean Q.* IV. I. 32 Caribs..delight in telling as a matter of fact how they met a certain 'jumby' in the road after dark. **1973** *Daily Tel.* (Colour Suppl.) 21 Sept. 25/3 To comb your hair at night is an open invitation for the Jumbies to call. (Jumbies are West Indian ghosts.)

b. *attrib.*, as **jumby-bead**, the hard seed of any of several West Indian plants; **jumby-bean** = **jumby-tree*; **jumby-bird**, a bird of ill omen, esp. an owl; **jumby-tree**, any of several West Indian trees, esp. the lead tree, *Leucæna glauca.*

1802 H. SWINBURNE *Let.* 17 Feb. in *Courts of Europe* (1841) II. 339, I gathered to-day, a handful of Jumbee beads. **1871** C. KINGSLEY *At Last* II. xiii. 197 Hedges of dwarf Erythrina, dotted with red jumby beads. *Ibid.* xvi. 276 The scarlet flowers of the Jumby-bead bush. **1934** J. RHYS *Voy. in Dark* I. vi. 66 The niggers say that jumbie-beads are lucky, don't they? **1956** *Caribbean Q.* IV. III. 198 They also sold charms made of 'Jumby beads' (*abrus precatorius* and allied species). **1920** BRITTON & MILLSPAUGH *Bahama Flora* 162 *Leucaena glauca*... Probably native of continental tropical America. Jumbie Bean. **1871** C. KINGSLEY *At Last* II. xiii. 206 The obnoxious bird was not an owl, but a large goat-sucker, a Nycteribius, I believe, who goes by the name of jumby-bird among the English Negros. **1893** A. NEWTON *Dict. Birds* II. 471 Jumby-bird, a Negro name for almost any kind that is of bad omen, but especially for an Owl. **1923** E. INGERSOLL *Birds in Legend* 168 The 'jumbie-bird', or 'big witch', of the West Indian region..is the dead-black ani, a kind of cuckoo. **1960** J. BOND *Birds W. Indies* 120 Barn Owl *Tyto alba.* Local names: Owl; Screech Owl; Night Owl; Death Owl; Death Bird; Jumbie Bird. **1928** M. SUMMERS *Vampire* 265 The occult silk-cotton tree (*bombax ceiba*, often known as the Devil's tree or Jumbie tree).

Jumeau (dʒū·mo). [Proprietary name.] The name of Pierre François and Émile *Jumeau*, 19th-century French doll-makers, used to designate a doll manufactured at their establishment; freq. *attrib.*

[**1888** *Official Gaz.* (U.S. Patent Off.) 27 Nov. 950/2 Dolls. Emile Jumeau, Paris, France. Application filed Oct. 8, 1888. Used since 1840. 'The words "Bébé Jumeau".'] **1897** *Pearson's Mag.* July 60/1 The Bébé Jumeau is known all over the world. *Ibid.* 65/1 The Jumeau dolls serve two purposes, the one being to amuse children and the other to instruct ladies..in the latest phases of Parisian fashion. **1951** E. ST. GEORGE *Dolls of Three Centuries* iii. 27 The Jumeau doll is still being made... The present day Jumeau bears little or no resemblance to the old, collector's Jumeau. **1962** G. WHITE *Dolls of World* 192 By 1862, the Jumeau dolls were quite famous; their well-modelled heads, waxen complexions, life-like eyes and movable joints attracted much attention. **1972** *National Observer* (U.S.) 27 May 9/4 (Advt.), Antique dolls, mint condition dressed and wigged. Guaranteed no reproductions. German or French, many rare French dolls, Jumeaus all sizes. **1973** *Times* 31 July 23/3 (*caption*) A late 19th century Jumeau doll, papier mâché with bisque head, height 20½ inches.

jumma (dʒʌ·mă). Also **jama, jummah.** [ad. Hind. *jama* collection, amount, account, a. Arab. *jama'* total, aggregate.] During British rule in India, the assessment for land revenue from an estate or division of country. So **jummabu·ndi** [Pers.-Arab. *jama'bandī* (Hind. *bandī*, a. Pers. *bandi* a tie, band; Skr. *bandh* bind)], the settlement of the revenues; the document recording this settlement.

1772 H. VERELST *View of Bengal* 214 The rents of the province, according to the Jummabundy, or rent-roll... The amount..was taken at a considerable discount from the former Jumma or valuation. **1800** *Asiatic Ann. Reg., Proc. Parl.* 38/1 The collections on the current jumma have fallen short 16,875l. **1845** *Encycl. Metrop.* XXI. 672/1 Jumma-bundee Customs. **1851** *Illustr. Catal. Gt. Exhib.* IV. 926/2 Model of a Jamma Bundi. Collector making the annual jambundi. **1858** J. B. NORTON *Topics for Indian Statesmen* 269 When he reached the station he found the magistrate absent on jumabundy. **1892** B. H. BADEN-POWELL *Land-Syst. Brit. India* I. I. i. 24 To say that the 'jama' of village A. is Rs. 300 means that the Government Land Revenue demand on the village as a whole is Rs. 300 each year. *Ibid.* II. IV. i. 563 The 'jamabandī' is perhaps the most generally useful of all the papers.

jump, *sb.*[1] Add: **1. c.** A descent on a parachute.

1922 *Encycl. Brit.* XXX. 14/2 The parachute..is of little use unless the jump is made over 200 ft. from the ground. **1935** C. G. BURGE *Compl. Bk. Aviation* 490/1 Jumps have been made from heights up to 30,000 ft., the descent taking about 40 min. **1970** *Times* 9 Dec. 16/1 The man..made his astonishing parachute jump into allied territory.

d. A journey, trip. *slang* (orig. *U.S.*).

1923 N. ANDERSON *Hobo* v. 83 He likes to tell of making 'big jumps' on passenger trains as from the coast to Chicago in five days, or from Chicago to Kansas City or Omaha in one day. **1932** E. SMITH *Satan's Circus* 17 The performers..amused themselves, during the tedium of long 'jumps', by making him sing to them. **1956** B. HOLIDAY *Lady sings Blues* (1973) viii. 77 We were playing big towns and little towns, proms and fairs. A six-hundred-mile jump overnight was standard. **1967** C. O. SKINNER *Madame Sarah* xii. 268 On sleeper jumps after the star had got to bed, it was Pitou's nightly duty to hear her read the lines of a role.

e. Jazz music with a strong beat; a jazz tune with a strong rhythm. Freq. *attrib.* orig. *U.S.*

1937 *Metronome* Sept. 32/2 Count Basie. *John's Idea*; *One O'Clock Jump.* **1943** R. BLESH *This is Jazz* 30 You have left only the intolerable monotony of 'jump' (riff) phrases played over and over. **1946** MEZZROW & WOLFE *Really Blues* xvii. 325 This mechanical swing-band age of jump, organ-grinder riffs, mop-mop and rip-bop. **1946** R. BLESH *Shining Trumpets* (1949) xii. 279 Jump-swing, that aptly named music which cannot be danced to but must be jumped to. *Ibid.* 282 The small jump bands that are constantly forming and disbanding. *Ibid.*, Exploiting jump rhythms. **1955** C. FOX in A. J. McCarthy *Jazzbook 1955* 6 Ellington..produced jazz in the 'twenties, 'swing' during the 'thirties, 'jump' in the early 'forties. **1971** *Melody Maker* 9 Oct. 17/4 In a way, his band was a 1940's jump band with amplifiers. **1972** *Jazz & Blues* Sept. 10/3 The West Coast 'jump' style adopted by artists like Roy Milton and Joe Liggins. *Ibid.* 11/3 'Jump' instrumentals.

f. An act of copulation; sexual intercourse. *slang.*

1934 J. O'HARA *Appointment in Samarra* (1935) vii. 212 Then you get cockeyed and take her out for a quick jump and ruin the whole works. **1970** G. GREER *Female Eunuch* 249 A wank was as good as a jump in those days.

5. b. *Contract Bridge.* A bid higher than is necessary in the suit concerned. Also *attrib.*

1927 M. C. WORK *Contract Bridge* (1928) 24 One more trick than would be required in Bridge to justify a raise or jump. *Ibid.* 56 With Ace-King-Queen..make a jump denial by bidding three. **1931** E. CULBERTSON *Contract Bridge at Glance* 11 A jump bid in a new suit by Opening bidder, after a minimum response by partner, is a Forcing Re-bid. **1933, 1959, 1970** [see *FORCING *ppl. a.*]. **1970** *Globe & Mail* (Toronto) 26 Sept. 51/4 The jump to three diamonds shows 13 to 16 points. **1973** *Country Life* 27 Dec. 2184/1 The jump bid in the opponents' suit is to show that he really has them.

7. *on the jump* (earlier and later examples); also (*b*) abruptly; swiftly; (*c*) in a nervous condition; *all of a jump* (orig. *U.S.*), in a jumpy or nervous state; (*at a*) *full jump* (*U.S.*), at full speed; *at one jump* (*U.S.*), in one go; *at the jump* = *at the first jump*; *for* (or *on*) *the* (*high*) *jump, for the jumps*, up for trial, on a charge for misdemeanour; due for punishment, *spec.* hanging; *to get* (or *have*) *the jump on* (orig. *U.S.*), to gain a lead on, get an advantage over (someone); *one jump ahead*, one step in front *of* (someone or something); just avoiding a pursuer or the like (*lit.* and *fig.*).

1825 J. NEAL *Bro. Jonathan* II. 291 What's the matter with you,—all of a jump! **1854** M. J. HOLMES *Tempest & Sunshine* i. 12 What you ridin' Prince full jump down the pike for? **1859** *Southern Lit. Messenger* XXVIII. 143, I run down stream, an I meets Bill on the jump. **1870** DE B. R. KEIM *Sheridan's Troopers* vi. 39 The irate quadruped made for our party, coming at a 'full jump'. **1884** 'MARK TWAIN' *Huck. Finn* xviii. 162 My nigger had a monstrous easy time..but Buck's was on the jump most of the time. **1896** ADE *Artie* xvi. 147, I put up a holler right at the jump. **1899** 'MARK TWAIN' in *Century Mag.* Nov. 76/1 It was my idea to spread [a name] all over the world, now, at this one jump. **1905** J. C. LINCOLN *Partners of Tide* vi. 106 When one of us three says, 'Nickerson, do thus and so,' you *do* it, and do it on the jump. Don't stop to think 'bout it. **1912** ADE *Knocking Neighbors* 123 Rufus was sinfully Rich, but nevertheless Detestable, because his Family had drilled into him the low-down Habit of getting the Jump on the Other Fellow. **1912** F. M. HUEFFER *Panel* III. i. 289 That elderly gentleman was exceedingly 'on the jump', as nervous as a man well could be. **1914** 'HIGH JINKS JR.' *Choice Slang* 21 Only about three jumps ahead of a young conniption. **1919** *Athenæum* 1 Aug. 695/2 'He's for the high jump' is a favourite expression meaning that someone is to be charged before his company or commanding officer. *Ibid.* 8 Aug. 727/2 'For the jumps' (up for trial). **1921** C. MULFORD *Bar-20 Three* xviii. 230 Hurrying men pulled thick planks from the pile..and hauled them, on the jump, to windows and doors. **1922** E. O'NEILL *Anna Christie* (1923) 29, I didn't go wrong all at one jump. **1925** FRASER & GIBBONS *Soldier & Sailor Words* 119 *High jump, on the*, a term used of a man entered on a 'Crime sheet', and for trial for a military offence; the suggestion being that the accused would need to jump very high to get over the trouble. **1936** E. AMBLER *Dark Frontier* xi. 173 If we fall down on this job..it's me for the high jump. **1936** G. GREENE *Gun for Sale* i. 23 He sounded all of a jump. **1940** WODEHOUSE *Eggs, Beans & Crumpets* 103 If ever I saw a baby that looked like something that was one jump ahead of the police..it is this baby of Bingo's. Definitely the criminal type. **1942** 'N. SHUTE' *Pied Piper* 247 I'm for the high jump. They got the goods on me all right. **1956** 'A. GILBERT' *And Death came Too* xiv. 145, I can't afford to act for someone who's going to be found guilty. And.. it looks to me remarkably likely Mrs. Appleyard is going to find herself for the high jump. **1960** D. LYTTON *Goddam White Man* xi. 183 He thinks he has the jump on us. **1963** J. PRESCOT *Case for Hearing* viii. 123 All of the accused are for the high jump. **1971** M. SINCLAIR *Sonntag* ii. 14 Someone is for the jump, I can tell you. Misinformed, that's what I was. **1972** *Real Estate Rev.* Winter 22/1 Each of these new developers hopes to get the jump on the other by adding more square footage to the units and giving more in amenities. **1972** J. PHILIPS *Vanishing Senator* (1973) I. iv. 37 Get over here on the jump... Step on it, will you? **1973** *Sun* 18 Jan. 6 That would allow the Government to permit wage rises to keep one jump ahead of prices.

8. A robbery (see quots.). *slang.*

1777 in Partridge *Dict. Underworld* (1949) 374/1 *The jump...* The dusk of the evening is the time allotted for this, as it prevents any one at a distance from observing what passes; a great number of rogues then gets lurking about, taking advantage of the unpardonable neglect of others; every window they come near that has no light in,

they open, if it happens not to be fastened; they then take what is most valuable out of that room, and very often go into others in the same house. **1781** G. PARKER *View of Soc.* II. i. 140 As soon as they have completed this robbery, the *Jumper* descends...The *Jump* being thus completed, they sheer off immediately. **1788** GROSE *Dict. Vulgar T.* (ed. 2), The jump, or dining room jump; a species of robbery effected by ascending a ladder placed by a sham lamp-lighter, against the house intended to be robbed. It is so called, because, should the lamp-lighter be put to flight, the thief who ascended the ladder has no means of escape but that of jumping down. **1901** 'LINESMAN' *Words by Eyewitness* (1902) 293 They are sure to see a 'jump' in everything, even in concessions. *Note* : South African euphemism for a robbery.

9. *Comb.* (sense *1 c), as **jump boot**, a parachutist's boot; **jump-master**, a man in charge of parachutists; **jump-sack** *slang*, a parachute; **jump-suit, jump suit** orig. *U.S.*, a parachutist's one-piece garment; also, a similar garment worn by other people.

1948 *Amer. Speech* XXIII. 319 *Jump boots*, paratroopers' shoes. **1972** *Daily Colonist* (Victoria, B.C.) 4 Aug. 1/6 She ran to her husband's prostrate body, unlaced his jump boots and pulled them off. **1942** *Look* 3 Nov. 43/2 (*caption*) The jumpmaster..cries, 'Stand in the door!' and the men crowd forward, waiting for the electrifying order: 'Jump!' **1970** N. ARMSTRONG et al. *First on Moon* xiv. 353 It's like riding an airplane, getting ready to jump. Anything could go wrong. Something could happen to the airplane.., the jumpmaster. **1973** *Daily Colonist* (Victoria, B.C.) 20 May 30/5 She was standing on the wing of the airplane hanging on and waiting for the jumpmaster to say 'go'. **1942** 'B. J. ELLAN' *Spitfire!* p. x, A parachute is called a *brolly* or a *jumpsack*. **1948** *Amer. Speech* XXIII. 319 *Jump suit*, uniform worn when jumping from airplane. **1965** *Guardian* 7 May 10/1 Rayon linen jump-suit with turn-up trousers and Orlon fish-net midriff. **1965** H. KANE *Devil to Pay* (1966) xxii. 129 Nora was slender and graceful in a crisp white narrow-legged jump suit. **1969** *New Yorker* 30 Aug. 73/1 Three parachutists in jump suits. **1971** *Black World* Apr. 38/2 We worry over horsepower (no pun intended) and power steering, fashionable jump suits and Afro haircuts. **1972** *Time* 17 Apr. 58/2 He..sews conservation patches all over his jumpsuit.

jump, *v.* Add: **1. c.** *to jump out of one's skin*: see SKIN *sb.* 5 f.

d. Colloq. phr. *to jump* (or *go* (*and*) *jump*) *in the lake*: to go away and cease being a nuisance; usu. *imp.* as a contemptuous dismissal.

1912 [see *GO *v.* 32 a]. **1937** E. S. GARDNER *Case of Lame Canary* vii. 67 Suppose she tells us to go jump in the lake? **1946** H. CROOME *Faithless Mirror* ix. 97 'I'm here to stop that particular change.' 'You and what ten other fellows? Go jump in the lake.' **1966** M. WOODHOUSE *Tree Frog* xviii. 129 There was no real reason why I shouldn't have told Andy to jump in the lake as soon as he'd got us through Customs at Heathrow. **1968** [see *FRUIT *sb.* 2 e]. **1974** D. GRAY *Dead Give Away* xxii. 202 She smelt pot in his room... He destroyed the evidence, and told her to jump in the lake.

e. *to jump to the eye(s)* [tr. F. *sauter aux yeux*]: to be noticed; to be obvious or prominent.

1926 FOWLER *Mod. Eng. Usage* 311/1 *Jump to the eye(s)* is a bad Gallicism. **1929** G. GOODWIN *Conversations with G. Moore* xxvii. 174 The fact that the Banquo scene in 'Macbeth'—a scene which jumps to the eye—was overlooked, encourages me, obliges me, to think that no one reads Shakespeare. **1931** M. D. GEORGE *England in Transition* iii. 59 Things jump to the eyes of the reader of this passage which have yet been ignored.

f. *to jump rope*: to skip with a skipping-rope. Cf. *jump-rope* s.v. *JUMP-. *N. Amer.*

1934 in WEBSTER. **1961** *Western Folklore* July 179 If only two children are jumping rope, one end of the rope may be tied to a tree, the other end being turned by one of the children. *Ibid.* 193/1 When she died she told me this, When I jump rope I always miss. **1972** *Nat. Geogr.* Sept. 414 When they aren't shooting marbles or jumping rope, the youngsters lurch about on..stilts.

g. To jump out of an aeroplane.

1935 C. G. BURGE *Compl. Bk. Aviation* 490/1 After jumping and pulling the release cord the parachutist finds that the parachute opens fully in about 1½ sec. **1942** [see *jump-master* s.v. *JUMP *sb.*¹ 9]. **1969** A. WHITE *Long Drop* 220 Ben jumped. His parachute failed to open.

h. Of jazz or similar music: to have a strong or exciting rhythm; to 'swing'; so of a place, esp. a place of entertainment: to pulsate with activity; to be full of excitement or enjoyment. *colloq.* (orig. *U.S.*).

c **1938** N. E. WILLIAMS *His Hi de Highness of Ho de Ho* 16 *The joint is jumping*, the place is lively, the club is leaping with fun. **1943** H. A. SMITH *Life in Putty Knife Factory* vi. 89 He then called up a couple of his friends.. and they came, and before long the joint was jumpin'. **1944** *Needle* July 23/2 The jumping-jive Harlem musicians who think that to obtain any semblance to rhythmic excitement they must leave the theme and become lost altogether. **1946** MEZZROW & WOLFE *Really Blues* (1957) vi. 71 Indiana Harbor was small but it jumped like mad. **1946** F. STACY in Rosenthal & Zachary *Jazzways* 49/2 The meaning of a 'jump tune' should be clear enough from the term itself; literally, it jumps. **1959** 'F. NEWTON' *Jazz Scene* v. 86 Nobody minded what was played so long as it 'jumped'. **1968** J. SANGSTER *Foreign Exchange* i. 31 The place was really jumping. It took me three minutes to locate the bar through the smoke haze. **1972** *Jazz & Blues* Sept. 12/1 We should give some mention to the jumping instrumentals which Fats and the band were committing to wax during the early 50's.

i. *to jump up.* To dance the 'jump-up' (***JUMP-UP 2**). *West Indies*.

1959 'M. UNDERWOOD' *Arm of Law* xiv. 165 Glad to see you enjoying carnival. But why aren't you jumping up? **1968** C. NICOLE *Self Lovers* v. 71 'Alex!..I don't suppose you'd care to jump up.'..'I'd love to.' He took her in his arms. The tempo changed to a calypso beat. **1973** *Sunday Advocate-News* (Barbados) 21 Jan. 6/6 Barbadians will have the opportunity to 'jump up' in real carnival fashion at the Barbados Cruising Club's annual carnival dance which will take place at Culloden Farm on Saturday, March 3.

4. b. Also *to jump on.*

1887 *Lantern* (New Orleans) 1 Oct. 2/1 The idea of two big chaps jumping on one man. **1891** [in Dict.]. **1917** D. CANFIELD *Understood Betsy* (1922) viii. 153 If you had to live the way he does, you'd be dirty!..And then you go and jump on him! **1939** I. BAIRD *Waste Heritage* xxi. 292 I'm sorry, Eddy, I didn't mean to jump on you that way. **1973** 'M. INNES' *Appleby's Answer* xvi. 138 She jumped on the butler for misunderstanding something about the drinks.

c. *to jump down one's throat*: see THROAT *sb.* 3 a.

d. *to jump to it*: to make an energetic start upon something; to take prompt action; usu. *imp.* Also occas. *to jump to* = to obey readily. *colloq.* (orig. *Mil.*).

[**1886** F. T. ELWORTHY *West Somerset Word-Bk.* 390 *Jump*, to readily accept an offer. 'Not her hab'm? Let-n ax o' her, that's all; I tell ee her'd jump to un.'] **1917** W. OWEN *Let.* 12 Feb. (1967) 434 He does nothing off his own bat, and doesn't always 'jump to' my orders! **1919** [see *JERK *sb.*¹ 2 e]. **1929** *Morning Post* 13 July 16 He does not know whether the service will come to his fore- or his back-hand; but he is ready to 'jump to it', whatever happens. **1956** J. MASTERS *Bugles & Tiger* xiv. 178 A P.&O. run like a warship, where the passengers would do as they were told and jump to it, and like it. **1974** M. BABSON *Stalking Lamb* xvi. 121 When you hear my signal—jump to it!

6. b. Also, to leave (a place or thing) suddenly; *spec.* of a seaman: to desert (his ship) before his contract expires. orig. *U.S.*

1875 J. MILLER *First Fam'lies Sierras* vii. 47 Even the head man of the company..jumped a first-class poker game..to come in and weigh out dust. **1883** *American* VI. 40 This evasion of imperative duty affords impunity to the men, if they jump the boat on the route. **1921** C. E. MULFORD *Bar-20 Three* vii. 88 I'm admittin' I'm walkin' soft, an' ready to jump th' country right quick. **1923** R. D. PAINE *Comrades of Rolling Ocean* xiv. 260, I told you about jumping the town because I had stove up a limousine. **1939** G. GREENE *Lawless Roads* 302 He thought perhaps he'd jump the ship at Lisbon—but..he was carried remorselessly on. **1957** 'N. SHUTE' *On Beach* iv. 131 Most of them would probably jump ship.

d. *to jump the bite* (Dentistry): to correct a faulty occlusion or 'bite', esp. one due to a retracted mandible, by bringing the mandible forward as a whole.

1880 [see *BITE *sb.* 1 f]. **1901** SMALE & COLYER *Dis. & Injuries Teeth* (ed. 2) iv. 158 If..the patient can be made to acquire the permanent habit of bringing the mandible forward so as to make the teeth articulate normally, the bite will have been 'jumped'. **1951** J. M. SCHWEITZER *Oral Rehabilitation* xxxv. 830 Nearly 80 years ago Class II, Division 1 (Angle), cases were treated by 'jumping the bite'... An attempt was made to reposition the mandible in an anteroposterior as well as a vertical and lateral direction.

e. *Contract Bridge.* To raise (a bid) higher than necessary in the suit concerned. Also *intr.*

1927 M. C. WORK *Contract Bridge* (1928) 33 If the partner jump, it must be with three cards of a suit. *Ibid.* 55 Cases of one No Trump jumped to two, and two of a Major jumped to three. **1929** —— *Complete Contract Bridge* i. 7 His proper procedure may be to shift to another declaration, or it may be to jump the original bid. **1963** G. F. HERVEY *Handbk. Card Games* 142 If responder has a count of 12 points he can jump straight to three No-Trumps.

8. c. (Earlier examples.)

1836 *Southern Rose* 10 Dec. 57/3 The boys were ordered to stick close to the dogs, and if they jumped the buck to catch him. **1839** *Southern Lit. Messenger* V. 377/1, I would go, but I am a going to jump mullet to-night. **1874** J. W. LONG *Amer. Wild-Fowl Shooting* 205 The most successful method of hunting ducks is identical with..'jumping them up' along the creeks.

10. *to jump one's bail*: for *U.S. slang* read orig. *U.S. slang*, and add earlier and later examples. Freq. *to jump bail*.

1859 G. W. MATSELL *Vocabulum* 47 *Jumped his bail*, run away from his bail. **1872** G. P. BURNHAM *Memoirs U.S. Secret Service* 55 Pete's friend Fred Biebusch had hid himself, after jumping his bail. **1911** L. J. VANCE *Cynthia* 177 He's jumped bail on a bigamy indictment. **1973** M. RUSSELL *Double Hit* xxii. 165, I shan't jump bail. They'll see me..back in court. **1974** *Guardian* 25 Jan. 24/1 [He] was given a three years' sentence in his absence, after he had jumped bail.

b. To drive past (traffic lights) when they indicate that one should stop. Also *transf.* orig. *U.S.*

1938 *Words* Mar. 44/2 *Jump*, v.t., to anticipate (the go signal of a traffic director). **1958** *Listener* 6 Nov. 731/1 Cutting in, jumping the lights, blind corners at sixty,.. they're things I'd never dream of doing. **1961** J. BARLOW *Term of Trial* II. ii. 160 She stared at the conflict of traffic. 'Good God!' she protested... 'They jump the lights!' **1970** J. PORTER *Rather Common Sort of Crime* iv. 42 She jumped a red light..it was a damned silly place to have traffic lights. **1973** *Daily Tel.* 5 Jan. 2/7 The driver of the local train..said he had jumped a red signal light.

c. *to jump the gun*: see *GUN *sb.* 6 e; *to jump the queue*: to go unfairly to or near the front of a queue of people; to push forward out of one's turn; also *fig.*, to gain an unfair advantage or preferential treatment.

1947 *Hansard Commons* 9 Dec. 951 There is no local authority who can clear these camps by allowing the people in them to jump the queues. **1955** L. P. HARTLEY *Perfect Woman* viii. 82 He distrusted the quality of imagination; it was a rogue quality that jumped the queue. **1955** *Times* 27 June 8/2 The Port of London Authority gave permission for the ship to 'jump the queue' of other vessels waiting in the river for berths. **1958** HAYWARD & HARARI tr. *Pasternak's Dr. Zhivago* II. ix. 273 There was always a queue in the street... Of course I didn't try to jump the queue, I didn't say I was his wife. **1958** P. TOWNSEND in N. Mackenzie *Conviction* 118 Choosing whether to dodge some taxes..or jump the queue at the hospital. **1973** 'M. INNES' *Appleby's Answer* v. 49 One of the women makes a gesture, indicating that you should jump the queue.

jump-. Add: **jump-ball, jump ball** *Basketball*, a ball thrown between two opposing players by the referee; **jump-cut, jump cut** *Cinemat.* and *Television* (see quot. 1953); also *transf.*, *attrib.* and as *v. trans.* and *intr.*; **jump-jet, jump jet**, a vertical take-off/landing jet aircraft; **jump jockey** *Horse racing*, a jockey who rides in steeplechases; **jump-rope, jump rope** (chiefly *N. Amer.*), a skipping-rope; **jump-seat, jump seat**, (b) a folding seat in a motor car; also *transf.*; **jump-shot, jump shot**, (a) *Billiards*, etc., a shot which causes the ball to jump; (b) *Basketball* (see quot. 1961); **jump-spark, jump spark**, a spark produced by the application of a potential difference to two electrical conductors separated by a narrow gap; usu. *attrib.*, designating devices or methods employing this; **jump take-off** *Aeronaut.*, a vertical take-off; **jump-turn, jump turn**, a turn made while jumping; *spec.* in *Skiing*.

1924 W. E. MEANWELL *Sci. of Basket Ball* 62 During scrimmage watch the tip-off formations and also those for jump ball and from out of bounds. **1939** JOURDET & HASHAGEN *Mod. Basketball* xi. 63 Cover your man well on all jump balls. If you are jumping someone else's man, make sure he covers yours. **1969** *Eugene* (Oregon) *Register-Guard* 3 Dec. 3D/1 The game had started on a technical foul when the Beavers were awarded a free throw instead of the usual jump ball. **1953** K. REISZ *Technique Film Editing* 280 *Jump cut*, cut which breaks continuity of time by jumping forward from one part of an action to another obviously separated from the first by an interval of time. **1962** *Listener* 9 Aug. 223/1 The eye-jerking, ear-jarring jump cuts which result when the commercials are removed from imported American programmes. **1962** *Punch* 19 Sept. 428/1 Harsh jump-cuts that might almost be breaks in the film. **1964** *Observer* 12 July 25/5 A jump-cut speeded-up sequence mostly shot from a helicopter. **1965** *Time* 18 June 80 He recklessly jump-cuts from scene to scene, using gimmicky transitions. **1966** *Punch* 6 July 26/2 The restless, jump-cutting style is sometimes disconcerting—one takes a second or two to realise that an expected bridging passage has been waived. **1968** P. DICKINSON *Skin Deep* vii. 130 The soft lines of the black visage jump-cut into wary maturity. **1972** *Times Lit. Suppl.* 9 June 649/4 A series of frenzied incidents..a matter of jump-cuts and unfinished sentences suggestive of a painful collaboration between Ken Kesey and Ford Madox Ford. **1974** *Ibid.* 14 June 629/4 The reader adjusts soon enough to the breakneck jump-cuts of the first few pages. **1975** *New Yorker* 20 Jan. 79/1 Once Trintignant takes over as the filmmaker, the movie loses its playful movie-within-a-movie spirit, and the technique, which had been a sprinting, jump-cutting shorthand that didn't take itself too seriously, turns glassy smooth. **1964** *Sunday Times* 12 Jan. 1/4 The Ministry of Defence delays ordering the revolutionary Hawker P. 1154 'jump jet' fighter. **1970** *New Scientist* 19 Feb. 362/1 The trials that the RAF and RN are now conducting on the employment at sea of the Harrier 'jump-jet'. **1973** *Guardian* 18 Apr. 24/5 A command cruiser designed to carry jump-jet aircraft. **1970** J. LEACH *Rider on Stand* ix. 89 Jump jockeys are a devil-may-care bunch. They accept the hazards of their profession in a happy-go-lucky manner. **1972** *Times* 29 Nov. 1/1 Michael Eddery, the jump jockey,..had his right leg amputated. **1973** *Scotsman* 7 Aug. 15/6 Barry Brogan's dispute with the Jockey Club over renewal of his jump jockey's licence ended amicably. [**1805** G. McINDOE *Poems & Songs* 40 At three year auld he crys for whips,..And guns, and girrs, and jumpin'-rapes.] **1834** EMERSON *Jrnl.* (1964) IV. 359 Thus is one reminded of the children's prayers who in confessing their sins, say, 'Yes, I did take the jumprope from Mary.' **1869** L. M. ALCOTT *Little Women* II. x. 147 Mr. Bhaer down on his hands and knees..Kitty leading him with a jump-rope. **1969** R. D. ABRAHAMS (*title*) Jump-rope rhymes. **1973** *Islander* (Victoria, B.C.) 8 Apr. 8/1 Spring brings activity —jacks and jump ropes pop up with the flowers. **1931** *Automotive Abstr.* Aug. 238/2 Treatment of the jump-seat explains unique problems presented by this accessory. **1963** MRS. L. B. JOHNSON *White House Diary* 24 Nov. (1970) 8 We all got into the same limousine—Mrs. Kennedy and Lyndon in the back seat, the Attorney General and I in the jump seats. **1972** *Guardian* 18 Sept. 14/1, I was sitting in the jump seat... We were racing through the city. **1973** *Black Panther* 6 Oct. 10/1 Only the jump seat for stewardesses was behind him. **1909** P. A. VAILE

Mod. Golf 92 This shot has its exact counterpart on the billiard table in the useful jump-shot. **1966** MILLER & THORP *Croquet* 174 *Jump shot*, a shot in which the ball is struck so that it leaves the ground. **1961** J. S. SALAK *Dict. Amer. Sports* 250 *Jump shot* (basketball), a shot taken with both feet off the floor. It can be made with one or two hands with the one-handed shot in general use in the National Basketball Association. **1969** *New Yorker* 14 June 79/1 You go through Harlem and you'll see kids less than five feet tall with pretty good jump shots and hook shots. **1974** *Anderson* (S. Carolina) *Independent* 20 Apr. 8A/1 New York's Julius Erving, known as Dr. J., drilled the 20-foot jump shot that gave the Nets their 3-0 margin in the series with an 89-87 victory at Louisville on Wednesday. **1908** J. H. ADAMS in Onker & Baker *Harper's How to understand Electr. Work* 340/2 *Jump-spark*, a disruptive spark excited between two conducting surfaces in distinction from a spark excited by a rubbing contact. **1911** *Daily Colonist* (Victoria, B.C.) 20 Apr. 8/1 A regal Marine Engine... Jump spark or make-and-break ignition. **1922** A. F. COLLINS *Bk. Wireless Telegraph & Telephone* i. 6 The spark-coil, or induction coil,..is used to change the battery current into a current of high pressure to make jump sparks. **1938** A. W. JUDGE *Automobile Electr. Maintenance* ii. 27 A brass plate at the end of the arm..passes very close to the brass contacts..as it rotates, so that a spark leaps across the small air gap. This is known as the jump spark method. **1963** BIRD & HUTTON-STOTT *Veteran Motor Car* 8 'Jump-spark' ignition in American usage generally, though not always, referred to high tension coil and battery apparatus with a mechanical contact-breaker and non-trembling coil, but in English usage, at one time, 'jump-spark ignition' meant any form of H.T. ignition with spark-gaps or 'intensifiers' included in the circuit. **1939** *Jrnl. R. Aeronaut. Soc.* XLIII. 62 A sustaining rotor for a gyroplane of the 'jump take-off' type. **1924** *Tourist* Winter Sports No. 12/1 *Jump turn*, a method of changing direction or stopping. **1949** SHURR & YOCOM *Mod. Dance* v. 147 Add a jump in place after each landing, before executing jump-turn movement in air. **1972** M. YORKE *Silent Witness* ii. 13 He did a quick jump turn and took the narrow track, running fast along the twisting *piste*.

jumped, *ppl. a.* Add: **b.** *jumped-up*: that has newly or suddenly risen in status or importance (often with an implication of conceit or arrogance). Also *transf.*

1835 'T. TREDDLEHOYLE' *Bairnsla Ann.* 35 (E.D.D.), A bit ov a jumpt up dress-macker, wot reckans ta be t' biggest beauty it taan. **1867** E. WAUGH *Tufts of Heather* 23 What a stark, starin', jumped-up foo aw wur to send tho up theer! **1895** *Punch* 24 Aug. 93 You jumped-up, cheap, Coventry bagman. **1919** J. C. SNAITH *Love Lane* xxxiv. 189 Democracy. Between you and me, Gert, it's mainly a name for a lot of jumped-up ignoramuses. **1934** J. B. PRIESTLEY *Eng. Journey* 380 It has flourished as the big city in the minds of men for generations. It is no mere jumped-up conglomeration of factories, warehouses and dormitories. **1942** L. A. G. STRONG *Slocombe Dies* xxvii. 127 The better class despise me as a jumped-up chap with too good a conceit of himself. **1972** J. WILSON *Hide & Seek* i. 19 That jumped-up tarty little madam who couldn't even keep her own husband. **1973** J. WAINWRIGHT *Pride of Pigs* 177 He didn't like being talked to.. as if he was some moss-green recruit..by a jumped-up C.I.D. clown from headquarters.

jumper, *sb.*[1] Add: **1. b.** A ticket-inspector or ticket-collector. *slang.*

1900 [in Dict., sense 1]. **1906** *Daily Chron.* 24 July 3/7 It was not a fact that unless the 'jumpers'—travelling ticket inspectors—made a certain number of reports they were discharged. **1931** *Evening Express* (Aberdeen) 4 Apr., It is not at all uncommon for a 'jumper' to find that fifty per cent. of the occupants of a second class compartment have only third class tickets. **1937** *Daily Express* 21 Jan. 3/4 If you use a second [class carriage] with a 'third' ticket, watch for the 'jumpers', ready to pounce and demand excess. **1966** H. SHEPPARD *Dict. Railway Slang* (ed. 2) 7 *Jumper*, travelling ticket collector.

c. *Basketball.* A jump-ball or jump-shot; a player of such a ball or shot.

1937 F. C. ALLEN *Better Basketball* II. xiii. 182 Any jumper must keep his eyes fixed upon the ball until it is tapped. He must always play the ball and not the other jumper. *Ibid.* 188 Many jumpers are taught illegally to jump sooner than their opponent in order to get above him. **1958** F. MCGUIRE *Offensive Basketball* ii. 75 Getting possession of the ball depends upon a number of items which are more or less related. First comes the leaping and timing ability of the jumper. *Ibid.* 112 The two-hand overhead jump shot is made in the same manner as the one-hand jumper except that the ball is carried above the head instead of over the shoulder. **1969** Z. HOLLANDER *Mod. Encycl. Basketball* 121/2 Lucus..could also score on jumpers from the corner. **1969** *Eugene* (Oregon) *Register-Guard* 3 Dec. 3D/4 The Vikings took the lead on Snider's free throw with 46 seconds left, but Steve Halberg hit a 15-foot jumper to put the Irish back on top and North couldn't come up with an equalizer.

3. b. In full, *jumper ant.* An Australian ant of the genus *Myrmecia.*

1907 W. W. FROGGATT *Austral. Insects* 92 The 'Jumper', *Myrmecia albo-cincta*..is one of the smaller species, about ½ an inch in length. *Ibid.* 436/2 (*index*) Jumper ant. **1926** R. J. TILLYARD *Insects Austral. & N.Z.* xxii. 287 The genus *Myrmecia*..contains the huge Bull-dog Ants and the smaller Jumpers..which swarm out of their nests and advance to the attack in a series of jumps or springs. **1970** E. F. REEK in *Insects of Australia* (Commonwealth Sci. & Industr. Res. Organization) xxxvii. 956/1 Forms such as the bulldog or jumper ants..feed largely on nectar and honey-dew as adults.

6. d. For *Telegraphy* read *Electr.* and add examples.

1906 T. E. HERBERT *Telegraphy* xviii. 586 When any cross is necessary, the cross-connecting or 'jumper' wires between the vertical and horizontal sides of the frame are altered, so avoiding the necessity for disturbing the cabling. **1931** MOYER & WOSTREL *Radio Handbk.* xi. 560 A temporary jumper may be used to close the circuit. **1948** *Aircraft Power Plants* (Northrop Aeronaut. Inst.) ix. 216/2 Test the switch by placing heavy jumpers across the terminals. In other words, close the circuit through the switch with temporary conductors. **1967** *Electronics* 6 Mar. 282/3 The mode selector..includes a 'battery' position that enables checking the condition of the battery without removing it or connecting jumpers. **1972** G. H. REED *Refrigeration* xiii. 120 A single wire 'jumper' lead.. is useful both for by-passing faulty controls or for incorporating a capacitor in the test cord.

7. Also *Canad.*

1834 J. LANGTON *Let.* 2 Feb. in *Early Days Upper Canada* (1926) 81 A jumper..is a most admirable conveyance and most properly called a jumper...It sticks at nothing; wherever the horses can scramble the jumper can leap after them. **1902** A. C. LAUT *Story of Trapper* xv. 221 The rutted marks of a 'jumper' sleigh cut the hard crust. **1903** B. W. CARR-HARRIS *White Chief of Ottawa* 119 They had not gone far when the Indian drew their attention to the tracks of a jumper in the snow. **1941** *Beaver* June 28 We loaded twelve hundred pounds of freight into a canoe, besides the dogs and a jumper sleigh. **1964** E. C. GUILLET *Pioneer Days Upper Canada* 74 Early settlers from the vicinity of Meaford and Owen Sound brought their grists in home-made sleighs called jumpers, which were hauled by oxen. **1971** J. McDOUGALL *Parsons on Plains* i. 5 Then, in winter, with our little white pony and jumper, we would make the same trips.

jumper, *sb.*[2] Add: **3.** = JERSEY 3 a; also, a loose-fitting blouse worn over a skirt; (see also quot. 1968).

1908 *Sears, Roebuck Catal.* 1149/4 The jumper is made in surplice effect. **1908** *Dialect Notes* III. 326 *Jumpers*, a one-piece garment for children to play in, 'rompers'. **1909** *Public Ledger* (Philadelphia) 24 June 7/6 One-piece & jumper styles. **1909** *Westm. Gaz.* 7 Aug. 15/2 For smaller girls the jumper still holds its own. **1925** W. DEEPING *Sorrell & Son* i. 13 The modiste had received a consignment of silk 'jumpers'. She was unpacking them and hanging them up on the stands in her showroom where they glowed brilliantly like jewels in a case. **1928** GALSWORTHY *Swan Song* II. ix. 181 He came on Anne herself, without a hat, sitting on a gate, her hands in the pockets of her jumper. **1930** *N. & Q.* 14 June 431/1 Some five years ago the fashion-mongers gave the name of jumper to the knitted blouses ladies had been wearing under the name of sports coats. **1945** *Wales* IV. vi. 44 He turned up the cuff of his jumper and showed her the word 'Sue' tattooed with a border of foliage on his forearm. **1965** *Australian* 13 Apr. 5 She also prefers casual clothes like the jumper and skirt she is wearing here. **1968** J. IRONSIDE *Fashion Alphabet* 61 *Jump-suit.* This is an abbreviation of 'jumpers', another name for rompers (i.e. top and bloomers in one) worn by children.

b. *U.S.* A pinafore dress. Also *jumper dress.*

1939 M. B. PICKEN *Lang. Fashion* 84/3 *Jumper-dress*, sleeveless, one-piece garment worn with guimpe. **1967** *Boston Sunday Herald* (Mag.) 16 Apr. 6/1 (Advt.), Wear as a jumper over blouses. **1971** *New Yorker* 11 Dec. 3 (Advt.), Wear a jumper to dinner!

c. *Comb.*, as **jumper suit**, (*a*) a pinafore dress; (*b*) a woman's suit consisting of a jumper and skirt made of the same material, freq. wool.

1908 *Sears, Roebuck Catal.* 1149/1 An unusually pretty jumper suit made of soft striped taffeta silk. **1925** *Times* 29 Dec. 7/6 Sports stockinette jumper suits. **1931** E. RAYMOND *Mary Leith* III. ii. 225 Mary was in a jumper suit of primrose silk. **1973** *Country Life* 2 Aug. 335/2 Soft jumper-suits in fine printed wools.

jumper, *v.*[2] (s.v. JUMPER *sb.*[1]). Add: **2.** *Electr.* To connect by means of a jumper (sense 6 d).

1929 *Post Office Electr. Engineers' Jrnl.* XXII. 79/1 From the cable terminal tag blocks all lines are jumpered *via* protecting apparatus to the 'line' tag blocks of the test boards. **1968** T. HOWARD *Black Light* xxi. 183 He made no attempt to force the locked ignition, but simply 'jumpered' the ignition wiring so that it by-passed the locked switch.

jumping, *vbl. sb.* Add: **b. jumping-board,** a spring-board; also *fig.*; **jumping jockey** = *jump jockey* s.v. *JUMP-; **jumping-off board** = **jumping-board*; **jumping-off ground, place** (earlier and later examples); also *transf.* and *fig.*; (*b*) *N. Amer.*, a place regarded as being the farthest limit of civilization or settlement; a very remote place; the extreme limit of the earth; also *fig.*; (*c*) a starting-point for aircraft or the like; so *jumping-off point, spot*; **jumping-pole,** a long pole used in jumping long distances or in making pole-vaults; **jumping-wire,** on a submarine: see quot. 1974.

1878 H. H. JACKSON *Bits Trav. at Home* 53 There are public gardens..with little ponds, and boats, and targets, and jumping-boards. **1909** *Athenæum* 21 Aug. 218/2 A jumping-board for the imagination to spring from. **1947** W. BEBBINGTON *Rogues go Racing* xviii. 115 There are some [jockeys] who are known to me as habitual gamblers. Particularly is this so with certain of our 'jumping' jockeys. **1914** *Eng. Rev.* Sept. 237 Salonika..was to be the German jumping-off board to Asia Minor. **1931** *Musical Times* 1 June 497/2 His studies abroad had given him a stock of admirably nurtured gifts, but no jumping-off board such as that offered by a career in an English institution. **1934** R. MACAULAY *Going Abroad* xi. 82 That's abso*lute*ly the best jumping-off ground for the new life. **1959** P. MOYES *Dead Men don't Ski* vi. 74 Tangiers is a convenient jumping-off ground. **1826** T. FLINT *Recoll.* 366 Being, as they phrase it, the 'jumping off place', it is necessarily the resort of desperate, wicked, and strange creatures who wish to fly away from poverty, infamy, and the laws. **1834** H. M. BRACKENRIDGE *Recoll.* x. 111, I had no jumping off or jumping up place, like those who prepare their exordium and perorations, and leave the body of the speech to take care of itself. **1847** W. I. PAULDING in J. K. & W. I. Paulding *Amer. Comedies* 197, I *have* hunted all over them parts, almost clean out to the jumping off place of creation. **1899** B. TARKINGTON *Gentleman from Indiana* xv. 266 He had come to a jumping-off place in his life—why had they not let him jump? **1909** F. ASH *Trip to Mars* xvii. 131 A narrow platform which had been erected as a 'jumping-off place' for fliers. **1922** *Encycl. Brit.* XXX. 14/2 The Governments demanded that their aeroplanes should be transported in crates, or towed with folded wings to their jumping-off places. **1930** G. B. SHAW *Apple Cart* I. 37 Today the nation would be equally amazed if a man of his ability thought it worth his while to prefer the woolsack even to the stool of an office boy as a jumping-off place for his ambition. **1953** F. STARK *Coast of Incense* 242 The way to carry out an adventure is to organize the jumping-off place as near to its borders as possible. **1964** D. JENNESS *Eskimo Admin.* II. 14 Archdeacon Stuck described Herschel Island during the whaling period as 'the world's last jumping-off place, where no law existed and no writs ran'. **1927** R. H. WILENSKI *Mod. Movement in Art* I. 13 An emotional reaction as the sole jumping-off point. **1958** G. LASCELLES in P. Gammond *Decca Bk. Jazz* viii. 100 It is not unnatural.. for New York to have been the proving ground and the jumping-off point for a new sort of music. **1909** *Daily Chron.* 8 Sept. 1/4 To reach the neighbourhood of Cape Columbia.., his elected jumping-off spot for the Pole. **1966** *Beautiful Brit. Columbia* Spring 23/1 Prince Rupert ..is a jumping-off spot for the Queen Charlotte Islands. **1873** L. TROUBRIDGE *Life amongst Troubridges* (1966) vi. 47 We..jumped loads of ditches, and when we came to a very large one we made a bridge of our jumping poles. **1972** *Listener* 31 Aug. 274/2 We had jumping-poles and we jumped from one rock to another. **1919** *Jane's Fighting Ships* 318 Jumping wires were added to French submarines. **1940** 'N. SHUTE' *Landfall* iii. 73 'Did you notice how many jumping-wires she had?' 'That's the wire that runs from bow to stern over the conning-tower, isn't it?' 'That's right. Did she have one or two?' **1974** G. JENKINS *Bridge of Magpies* xv. 223 Her jumping-wire—the thick cable designed to slice through undersea objects like mine mooring—which runs from bow to stern via the conning-tower.

jumping, *ppl. a.* Add: **b. jumping deer,** substitute for def.: either of two North American animals, the pronghorn, *Antilocapra americana*, or the mule deer, *Odocoileus hemionus* (examples); **jumping-shrew** (examples).

1806 A. HENRY *Jrnl.* 14 July in E. Coues *New Light Hist. Greater Northwest* (1897) I. ix. 305 Herds of cabbrie or jumping deer were always in sight. **1831** R. COX *Adv. Columbia River* II. 364 The jumping-deer, or chevreuil, ..frequent the vicinity of the mountains in considerable numbers. **1908** J. W. TYRRELL *Across Sub-Arctics of Canada* (ed. 3) xxi. 243 Jumping Deer are found in more or less abundance throughout the timbered country about southern parts of the [Hudson] Bay. **1936** D. McCOWAN *Animals Canad. Rockies* xxxi. 265 The Mule deer is most common... In some parts of Canada the animal is called Jumping deer, this from its well known habit of progressing when alarmed in a series of immense leaps and bounds. **1961** R. P. HOBSON *Rancher takes Wife* vii. 108 There were the tiny little white-tailed jumping deer that would make about four meals for one man. **1900** H. A. BRYDEN *Animals Afr.* ii. 16 The typical Cape jumping shrew has a long, proboscis-like nose, large ears, long, thin hind legs, which enable him to take enormous leaps for his size, and a long, rat-like tail. **1920** F. W. FITZSIMONS *Nat. Hist. S. Afr. Mammals* IV. 2 There are several species or kinds of Jumping or Elephant Shrews inhabiting South Africa. **1971** D. J. POTGIETER et al. *Animal Life S. Afr.* 346/2 The elephant-shrews or jumping shrews (*Macroscelidea*) are insect-eaters, and the whole order is confined to Africa.

c. jumping-bean (examples); (*b*) a toy consisting of a small bean-shaped capsule containing a weight such as a lead ball which causes it to move unaided down a sloping surface; **jumping-seed** (examples).

1889 *Cent. Dict.*, Jumping-bean. **1896** *Chambers's Jrnl.* 18 Apr. 249 A new botanical curiosity..has lately been brought into notice in England under the name of 'A Jumping Bean'. **1910** *Boy's Own Paper* 15 Jan. 256 *Tommy* (who has been watching the jumping beans for some time): 'Oi'm waitin' to see them sticks walk.' **1972** F. WARNER *Maquettes* 14 Along they go, like jumping beans from a toy factory. **1972** SWAN & PAPP *Common Insects N. Amer.* 312 The wriggling larva of an olethreutid moth, *Laspeyresia saltitans*, is the activator of the Mexican 'jumping bean', the seed of a species of *Croton.* **1876** *Field & Forest* II. 53 These so-called jumping seeds received from California. **1889** *Wesley Naturalist* III. 22 Those are the only 'jumping seeds' of which I had even heard until I met with these of Natal.

jump-off (dʒʌ·mpǫf). [f. *to jump off.*] **1.** A precipitous descent; a place from which a person must jump. *U.S. colloq.*

1873 [see *BED *sb.* 12 f]. **1884** C. PHILLIPPS-WOLLEY *Trottings of Tenderfoot* v. 129 The broad stem of a fallen giant gives you 150 feet of splendid wooden road; but.. you find you have been gradually ascending, and now stand on what the Americans would call a 'jump off'. **1909** R. A. WASON *Happy Hawkins* ii. 26 The lantern shed a splash o' light on the shelf, but the jump-off looked like the mouth o' the pit.

b. The start of a military operation or campaign. *U.S. slang.*

1918 [see *H-Hour* s.v. **H. III]. **1944** *Daily Progress* (Charlottesville, Va.) 12 May 1/8 The Fifth and Eighth armies have launched the greatest drive in Mediterranean warfare in the jump-off of Allied spring offensives. **1945** *Sun* (Baltimore) 23 Feb. 1/6 (*heading*) Canadians find going toughest since jumpoff.

2. *Aeronaut.* A vertical take-off.

In quot. 1969 'jump off point' = **jumping-off point*. **1939** *Jrnl. R. Aeronaut. Soc.* XLIII. 110 (*heading*) Possibilities of the jump-off autogyro. *Ibid.*, The available kinetic energy in the rotor system for 'jump-off' is directly proportional to the weight of the blades and to the square of the rotational speed of the rotor. **1969** *Daily Tel.* 16 Jan. 1/6 A space station in permanent orbit round the earth..could..be used as a 'jump off' point for travel to the moon.

3. *Show-jumping.* A final round to resolve or determine a tie.

1947 H. DISSTON *Equestionnaire* (rev. ed.) 77 In the event of a jump off over triple bars, how is the obstacle altered? **1954** P. SMYTHE *Jump for Joy* vii. 113 The final jump-off included a high wall with a pole on top. **1969** *Times* 10 May 6/5 Alan Oliver..justified..the odds laid on him in the..competition yesterday. Riding Pitz Palu, who was made favourite at 7–2 and shortened to 2–1 for the jumpoff, he..made the running from start to finish.

jump-up (dʒɒ·mpɒp). *colloq.* [f. *to jump up*.] **1.** An escarpment. *local Austral.*

1927 M. TERRY *Through Land of Promise* 85 We had been looking at the 'jump-up' marking the extremity of the Barkly Tableland. **1969** 'A. GARVE' *Boomerang* i. 32 There's a sharpish rise from the plain to the tableland, with a steep edge—what we call the 'jump-up'.

2. An informal West Indian dance.

1955 *Caribbean Q.* IV. ii. 102 Children and adults dancing in the shuffling manner of the Trinidad Carnival 'jump-up'. **1959** 'M. UNDERWOOD' *Arm of Law* xiv. 164 Some might be found doing a traditional mid-day jump-up. **1965** 'LAUCHMONEN' *Old Thom's Harvest* vii. 96 A few people..gathered around the calypsonian... Saul was doing a real jump-up in the centre. **1971** *Sunday Times* 13 June 9 You have some rum and a bloody good lunch, then you have a jump-up, and a proper shindig. **1973** *Advocate-News* (Barbados) 17 Feb. 6/1 With the carnival fever in the air, the students at the Cave Hill campus will stage their pre-carnival jump-up and calypso tent at the campus tomorrow, beginning at 5 p.m.

jumpy, *a.* **2. a.** Add to def.: nervous, apprehensive. (Add further examples.)

1918 *Wine, Women & War* (1926) 10 No trip for anybody with jumpy nerves. **1935** [see **GOOEY a.*]. **1957** *Sat. Even. Post* 21 Sept. 94 One of our pals in the nightclub business is jumpy and he needs a bodyguard tonight. **1974** G. MARKSTEIN *Cooler* xlvi. 167 She was jumpy about the blackout too... She *is* on edge, he decided.

jun. (Examples.)

1708 [see JUNIOR *a.* 1]. **1837** DICKENS *Sk. Boz* 2nd Ser. 222 Mr. Green, sen., and his noble companion entered one car, and Mr. Green, jun., and *his* companion the other. **1922** JOYCE *Ulysses* 391 Dixon jun., scholar of my lady of Mercy. **1955** *Times* 8 July 6/7 On June 8, continued counsel, Thomas Foote, jun., saw a bank official carrying out two bags of silver to a car. **1974** *Country Life* 11 Apr. (Suppl.) 66 John Frederick Herring Jun. A farmyard scene.

junction, *sb.* Add: **1. c.** In Jespersen's terminology, a group of words consisting of a primary word and an adjunct (**ADJUNCT sb.* 5 b).

1924 O. JESPERSEN *Philos. Gram.* vii. 97 If..we compare the combination *a furiously barking dog*..with *the dog barks furiously*..there is a fundamental difference between them, which calls for separate terms for the two kinds of combination: we shall call the former kind *junction*, and the latter *nexus*. *Ibid.* viii. 115 In a junction a secondary element (an adjunct) is joined to a primary word as a label or distinguishing mark. **1935** *Jrnl. Eng. & Germ. Philol.* XXXIV. 415 Two entirely different classifications are involved: (1) an assignment of importance within the frame of a sentence.. (2) a scrutiny of subordination within a group ('junction'). **1966** M. PEI *Gloss. Ling. Terminol.* 136 *Junction*, a grammatical unit formed by qualified and qualifying terms (*the red barn*).

2. b. *Electronics.* A transition zone in a semiconductor between two regions of different conductivity type (usually *n*-type and *p*-type).

1949 W. SHOCKLEY in *Bell Syst. Techn. Jrnl.* XXVIII. 435 Silicon and germanium may be either *n*-type or *p*-type semiconductors... If, in a single sample, there is a transition from one type to the other, a rectifying photosensitive *p-n* junction is formed. *Ibid.* 436 We shall use the word *junction* to include all the material near the transition region in which significant contributions to the rectification process occur. **1959** R. A. SMITH *Semiconductors* xii. 444 *p-n* junctions are generally much more stable mechanically than fine metal point contacts and the modern tendency is to use them whenever possible. **1962** SIMPSON & RICHARDS *Physical Princ. Junction Transistors* iii. 43 If the change from *n⁺*-type to *n*-type is sufficiently gradual, electrons diffusing from the *n⁺*-type material will recombine with holes before reaching the *n*-type material and the *n⁺-n* junction will be non-rectifying. **1965** BURFORD & VERNER *Semiconductor Junctions & Devices* vii. 91 All junctions in semiconductors are inherently rectifying. To make such a *p-n* junction into an operable rectifier, we merely attach leads to the *p* and *n* regions and protect the active element..by suitable encapsulation.

4. junction-box, a closed, rigid box or casing used to enclose and protect the junctions of electric wires or cables; junction diode *Electronics*, a diode consisting essentially of a piece of semiconductor containing a rectifying *p-n* junction; junction rectifier *Electronics* = **junction diode*; junction transistor *Electronics*, a transistor consisting essentially of a piece of semiconductor containing two (or more) junctions that divide it into three (or more) regions.

1885 E. S. FARROW *Mil. Encycl.* II. 147/1 In submarine mining, when it is necessary to employ a multiple cable, a junction-box is used to facilitate the connection of the several separate wires diverging from the extremities of such a cable. **1934** *Archit. Rev.* LXXV. 141/3 Junction boxes are arranged at close intervals all over the floor before the blocks or floorboards are put down. **1958** M. DICKENS *Man Overboard* ii. 28 He tripped over a large metal junction-box, where several thick cables met in a writhing tangle. **1972** *Police Rev.* 10 Nov. 1453/3 A security van..crashes into an electric junction box at the side of the road. **1952** *Proc. IRE* XL. 1348/1 This paper describes..a new type of silicon diode, namely, the *p-n* junction diode prepared by alloying. **1970** J. EARL *Tuners & Amplifiers* ii. 28 Very few tuners are now being made with valves. The vast majority employ semiconductor devices, and of these many use transistors and junction diodes, but the trend is also towards the use of ICs. **1951** *Physical Rev.* LXXXI. 475/1 The holes move mainly under the influence of diffusion in a manner similar to that discussed in connection with carriers injected across the junction in a *p-n* junction rectifier. **1962** SIMPSON & RICHARDS *Physical Princ. Junction Transistors* iii. 35 While it is possible to produce junction rectifiers and transistors from many different semiconductors, the devices in successful commercial production are.. made from either germanium or silicon. **1949** W. SHOCKLEY in *Bell Syst. Techn. Jrnl.* XXVIII. 435 (*heading*) The theory of *p-n* junctions in semiconductors and *p-n* junction transistors. **1959** R. A. SMITH *Semiconductors* xii. 449 The first type of transistor to be used was the point-contact transistor, but this has been almost entirely replaced by the junction transistor. **1962** SIMPSON & RICHARDS *Physical Princ. Junction Transistors* i. 1 The extraordinary technological growth that has taken place since that time [*sc.* 1948] has established the junction transistor as a device of major engineering and economic importance.

junction (dʒɒ·ŋkʃən), *v.* [f. the *sb.*] *intr.* To form a junction; to join *with* or *on to*.

1904 *Electrical Investments* IV. 771/2 Railway companies whose lines junctioned with each other did not always give either the passenger or goods traffic the advantages that the physical junctions rendered possible. **1909** R. A. WASON *Happy Hawkins* xxvii, Deuced if I ever could see where your trail could have junctioned onto the Clarenden family. **1936** I. L. IDRIESS *Cattle King* xii. 105 This line..gradually draws in towards the Diamantina until it junctions with it here, just above the South Australian border. **1959** *Tararua* XIII. 47 New Zealanders and Australians occasionally use the verb *junction with* of rivers, though why this is necessary when there is the verb *join* is hard to say.

junctive (dʒɒ·ŋktiv), *a.* *poet. rare.* [ad. L. *junctīv-us*, f. *junct-*, pa. ppl. stem of *jungĕre* to join.] Having the quality of joining.

1898 HARDY *Wessex Poems* 28 So may I live no junctive law fulfilling, And my heart's table bear no woman's name.

juncture. Add: **2. c.** *Linguistics.* The transition between two linguistic segments or between an utterance and preceding or following silence; the phonetic feature that marks such a transition. Also *attrib.*

[**1934** PRIEBSCH & COLLINSON *German Lang.* iii. 210 When a stem-vowel or declensional suffix in its crude form occurs in the first components of compound substantives and adjectives, it is called the 'Fugenvokal', i.e. juncture vowel.] **1941** *Language* XVII. 224 Those [phonemes] that relate to the way in which utterances begin and end.. we call juncture phonemes... A logical order of exposition ..will begin with the juncture phenomena... The present study..will deal with junctures, stresses, [etc.]. *Ibid.* 225 The transition from a pause preceding an isolated utterance to the first segmental phoneme, and from the last segmental phoneme to the following pause, we call open juncture. **1942** BLOCH & TRAGER *Outl. Ling. Analysis* ii. 35 Phenomena relating to the way in which sounds are joined together are summarized under the term *juncture*. **1946** E. A. NIDA *Morphol.* 94 When two items are combined, there are potentially several different types of junctures, or seams, at the point of contact. **1957** S. POTTER *Mod. Ling.* iii. 73 No less elusive than intonation.. are the related features of *juncture* and *pause*. Where precisely does one syllable end and another begin? **1969** *English Studies* L. 292 They regard juncture as a special type of phoneme, neither segmental nor prosodic, causing sub-significant changes in the environment. **1972** R. WARDHAUGH *Introd. Linguistics* 64 We can say that such words as *nitrate, night rate*, and *Nye trait* require the postulation of a juncture phoneme to show the difference.

Hence ju·nctural *a.*, ju·ncturally *adv.*

1942 *Language* XVIII. 14 A suprasegmental phoneme is junctural if each member phone has a determining starting-point (or a determining end-point). **1964** [see **DEMARCATIVE a.*]. **1965** *Language* XLI. 499 A separate phoneme..(which is subject to frequent loss, mainly but not wholly juncturally conditioned). **1966** W. S. ALLEN in C. E. Bazell *In Memory of J. R. Firth* 11 This ..would have been contrary to Greek junctural principles (being characteristic of close and not open juncture).

June, *sb.* Add: **2.** June-berry (earlier and later examples); also used for other trees or shrubs of the genus *Amelanchier*, or their fruit; June-bug (earlier and later examples); June grass (examples); June Week, at Durham University, the last week of the summer term, Commemoration week.

1832 D. J. BROWNE *Sylva Amer.* 217 The wood of the June berry is of a pure white. **1854** MAYNE REID *Young Voyageurs* 356 The berries..are known as..'June-berries' [or] 'service-berries'. **1914** I. COWIE *Company of Adventurers* 327 A grizzly bear [was] found among the saskatoon (Juneberry) bushes. **1928** J. E. LeROSSIGNOL *Beauport Road* 274 The chief attraction..was along the fences and hedgerows where, in season, were strawberries, June berries..dew berries. **1969** R. C. HOSIE *Native Trees Canada* (ed. 7) 234/1 Mountain Juneberry..and Saskatoon-berry..occasionally become trees. **1829** in *Amer. Speech* (1965) XL. 132 *Jim Crow*... Dere's possum up de gumtree, An Raccoon in de hollow, Wake Shakes for June Bugs Stole my half a dollar. **1836** *Congress. Globe* 5 May 349/2 They hopped upon it, to use a homely phrase, like a duck on a June-bug. **1906** W. CHURCHILL *Coniston* xv. 189 June-bugs hummed in at the high windows. **1972** L. E. CHADWICK tr. *Linsenmaier's Insects of World* 162/3 (*caption*) An American June beetle, the June bug, having completed development but still in its underground cavity. **1855** *Trans. Mich. Agric. Soc.* VI. 160 A stiff June grass sod plat. **1919** *Maine, my State* (Maine Writers Research Club) 336 How fair her fields when June-grass waves! **1970** *Alberta Hist. Rev.* Winter 1/2 Prairie wool, a nutritious blend of..June grass..and other grasses. **1889** *Durham Univ. Jrnl.* IX. 1 The end of last term was signalised by what was called by some 'Commemoration' and by others 'the June Week'. **1900** *Ibid.* XIV. 229 Those who have visited the race-course during the June Week.

june (dʒūn), *v.* *U.S. colloq.* and *dial.* [? f. the *sb.*] **a.** *intr.* To move in a lively fashion, hurry; to be restless or aimless; to wander *around.* **b.** *trans.* To drive briskly. *rare.*

1869 *Overland Monthly* III. 127 A trig, smirk little horse is a 'lace-horse', and he often has to 'june' or 'quill'. **1892** *Dialect Notes* I. 230 *June-in'*, running fast. 'She came a-june-in'.' **1895** W. C. GORE in *Inlander* Nov. 61 *June around*, to be busy but not accomplish anything. **1903** A. ADAMS *Log of Cowboy* xiv. 228 To june a herd of cattle across in this manner would have been shameful. **1948** *Amer. Speech* XXIII. 305/1 You stay here and I'll go down and june around awhile.

jungar, var. JANGAR.

‖ **Junggrammatiker** (yu·ŋ₊gramā:tikər), *sb. pl. Philol.* [G.] A name given to members of a late 19th-century school of historical linguistics who held that phonetic changes (sound laws) operated without exceptions. The name was accepted by the persons concerned and by others, and has been anglicized as 'neogrammarians'. Hence **junggrammatisch** *a.*

1922 O. JESPERSEN *Language* iv. 93 The 'blind' operation of phonetic laws became the chief tenet of a new school of 'young-grammarians' or 'junggrammatiker' (Brugmann, Delbrück, Osthoff, Paul, and others). **1936** J. R. KANTOR *Objective Psychol. Gram.* viii. 108 The *Junggrammatiker*..believed themselves to have discovered absolute phonetic laws. **1936** *Language* XII. 58 There is another point of view,..an organic development..of the essential core of truth in the Junggrammatiker doctrine. **1938** *Year's Work Eng. Stud.* 1936 30 Wilhelm Havers..well summarizes the history of the changing attitude towards 'sound-laws' since the first confident days of the *Ausnahmslosigkeit* of the *Junggrammatiker*. **1953** J. B. CARROLL *Study of Lang.* ii. 50 In opposition to the neogrammarians (*Junggrammatiker*), as Leskien, Osthoff, and Brugmann came to be called, Schuchardt (1885), Curtius, and Ascoli pointed to what seemed to be exceptions to phonetic laws. **1958** A. S. C. ROSS *Etym.* 8 It is certainly quite impossible for anyone to understand Laryngeal Theory without being thoroughly familiar with junggrammatisch Ablaut. **1965** *Language* XLI. 187 Brugmann.. accepted the originally humorous epithet *Junggrammatiker* and used it as a rallying cry.

Jungian (yu·ŋiăn), *a.* [See -IAN.] Of or pertaining to Dr. Carl Gustav *Jung* (1875–1961), the Swiss leader of the school of analytic psychology, or his teaching. Also *sb.*, a follower or adherent of Jung. Hence Ju·ngianism, the teaching or system of Jung; a characteristic specimen of this.

1933 D. C. DAKING (*title*) Jungian psychology and modern spiritual thought. **1942** K. W. BASH tr. *Jacobi's Psychol. C. G. Jung* iii. 59 Jungian psychotherapy is no analytical procedure... It is..a 'way of healing'. **1947** *Downside Rev.* 35 For the Jungian the whole position is altered... The historical causality of complexes is not denied, and the methods of releasing these complexes, as discovered by Freud, are recognized. **1956** *Essays in Crit.* VI. 417 How we can now avoid Jungianism is a difficult problem. **1958** *Times Lit. Suppl.* 1 Aug. 438/5 The church has a resident Jungian psychiatrist. **1959** *Ibid.* 20 Mar. 164/5 To non-Jungians..this will seem merely another Jungian book. **1964** M. McLUHAN *Understanding Media* (1967) II. xx. 207 Myth and Jungian archetypes.

jungle, *sb.* Add: **2. a.** (Further examples.) Also, a place of bewildering complexity or confusion; a place where the 'law of the

jungle' prevails; a scene of ruthless competition, struggle, or exploitation; esp. with qualification, as **blackboard jungle* in schools, *asphalt jungle, concrete jungle* in cities.

1906 U. Sinclair (*title*) The Jungle. **1920** Ade *Hand-Made Fables* 83 After the newly arrived Delegate from the Asphalt Jungles had read a Telegram..he..sauntered back to the Bureau of Information. **1924** A. D. Sedgwick *Little French Girl* II. vi. 150 The jungle itself was part of the order, since the *demimondaine* was taken as much for granted as the *femme du monde.* **1949** W. R. Burnett *title*) The asphalt jungle. **1954** [see *blackboard]. **1956** 'E. McBain' *Cop Hater* (1958) viii. 70 Their front page.. shouted 'The Police Jungle—What Goes On In Our Precincts.' **1958** [see *blackboard]. **1969** D. Morris *Human Zoo* 8 The city is not a concrete jungle, it is a human zoo. **1971** *Sunday Times* 30 May 31/5 Namier.. fitted especially ill in the academic jungle. **1971** *Times* 17 July 5/2 New York seemed to me infernal... By night the streets become concrete jungles, their occupants hysteric, terrified of predators. **1972** *Guardian* 14 Feb. 10/5 The Minister lit up some lurid corners of the taxation jungle. **1974** *Black World* Jan. 38 The Waikiki jungle is kind of a—you might call it a ghetto surrounded by high-rise buildings in Waikiki.

b. *pl.* Shares in West African concerns. Also *attrib.* ? *Obs.*

1904 *Daily Chron.* 2 Dec. 1/7 Kaffirs weakened, but Jungles moved upward. **1906** *Ibid.* 9 Feb. 2/3 Jungle shares were..firm. **1908** *Westm. Gaz.* 10 Dec. 15/4 A Jungle Dividend.

c. A camp for hoboes, tramps, or the like. Also *attrib. slang* (orig. *U.S.*).

[**1908** C. Johnson *Highways & Byways Pacific Coast* 215 My companions spoke of the grove they were in as the 'Hoboes Jungle'.] **1914** *Sat. Even. Post* 4 Apr. 10/3 It followed the two along the tracks and into the jungle. *Ibid.* 11/3 Frisco Red slouched into the jungle. **1915** *N.Y. World Mag.* 9 May 14 *Jungle buzzard*, a tramp who sneaks around hobo or tramp camps to get a free meal. *Ibid.*, *Jungle court*, a make-believe court held in woods by hoboes. **1923** N. Anderson *Hobo* ii. 21 Most 'jungle buzzards', men who linger in the jungles from season to season, take an interest in the running of things. **1926** J. Black *You can't Win* vi. 65 'This is a pretty snide jungle,' he said, 'no cans.' *Ibid.* 82 There was a grand jungle by a small, clean river where they boiled up their verminous clothes. **1971** *Islander* (Victoria, B.C.) 4 Apr. 12/1 During the depression in the 1930s gangs of youths ranged across the country, riding the rails and sleeping in jungles, and caused us concern.

3. *jungle craft.*

1942 *R.A.F. Jrnl.* 27 June 24 Even an expert can make mistakes in jungle craft. **1946** W. S. Churchill *Secret Session Speeches* 59 The Japanese armies..having added their jungle-craft..have established themselves..in the whole of these wide regions.

b. jungle-bashing *slang* [*bashing *vbl. sb.* 3], movement through a jungle, esp. by soldiers; so *jungle-basher*; **jungle bunny** orig. *U.S.*, a term used by some white people to designate Negroes, Australian Aborigines, etc.; **jungle green,** a dark green colour; clothes of this colour; also *attrib.*; **jungle gym** (formerly a registered trade mark in the U.S.), a type of climbing frame; **jungle juice** *slang*, alcoholic liquor, esp. liquor that is either very powerful or that has been prepared illicitly or amateurishly; also *transf.*; **jungle law,** the 'law of the jungle' (see *law *sb.*[1] 16 c); **jungle rot** *slang*, name given to a tropical skin disease; **jungle war,** a war fought in jungle; also *fig.*; so *jungle warfare.*

1963 *Times* 24 May 14/6 All the poor 'jungle-bashers' could offer by way of city reminiscence was the egregious Calcutta. **1954** V. Bartlett *Rep. from Malaya* iii. 46 A man does an average of 700 hours 'jungle-bashing' before he kills a Communist. **1969** J. M. Gullick *Malaysia* ii. 113 British, Malay and other Commonwealth troops spent many weary hours on patrol, 'jungle-bashing' as they called it, with the object of contacting terrorists. **1966** *Publ. Amer. Dial. Soc. 1964* XLII. 27 Both middle-aged informants giving *jungle bunny*.. work with adolescents. **1968–70** *Current Slang* (Univ. S. Dakota) III–IV. 76 *Junglebunny, n.* Negro (derogatory). **1973** *Sunday Times* (Colour Suppl.) 10 June 51/3 Australians in the Territory can be grossly insensitive to the pride of the local people, using terms like 'jungle bunnies'. **1974** *New Society* 14 Mar. 627/2 White South Africans who wanted to gamble, buy *Playboy*..and go to bed with a 'jungle bunny'. **1946** *Nature* 14 Sept. 386/2 Land Army hose, sea-boot stockings, R.A.F. socks and jungle-green pullovers also came under the scheme. **1947** Jungle green [see *cobber *sb.*[2]]. **1973** D. Lees *Rape of Quiet Town* iii. 53 A commanding figure in jungle green with a Lüger pistol in his hand. **1923** *Official Gaz.* (U.S. Patent Off.) 30 Jan. 844/2 Junglegym, Inc., Chicago, Ill. Filed Nov. 14, 1921. Junglegym... Playground Apparatus, in Particular Climbing Frames. **1925** *Playground* Mar. 721 (Advt.), 22 Units—Now in the New York City Playgrounds... Junglegym is six years old this spring. **1929** L. F. Zwarg *Study of Hist. Apparatus Physical Educ.* i. 81 Many odd contrivances [of physical education apparatus] of former years have disappeared entirely, others have from time to time been rediscovered or reinvented. The climbing tower (jungle gym) and the teeter ladder, are examples of this. **1931** *Recreation* May 97 The low climbing device (which is known as the Junglegym). **1951** W. van Hagen et al. *Physical Educ. Elem. Sch.* v. 93 Monkey rings... Manufactured under various names, such as climbing trees, junglegyms, climbing towers, castle towers, and climbing maze. **1963** Barnard & Lauwerys *Handbk. Brit. Educ. Terms* 115 *Jungle gym*, a simple gymnastic apparatus on which children in an infant school can climb or swing as part of their free activity curriculum. **1967** J. Redgate *Killing Season* (1968) II. vii. 104 Through the kitchen window he could see the children laughing and wrestling with each other inside their jungle gym. **1973** *Washington Post* 3 Oct. B1/4 (*heading*) Recreation 1973: Everything from jungle gyms to the Bataca bromb. **1945** Baker *Austral. Lang.* viii. 157 *Jungle juice*, any alcoholic beverage concocted by servicemen in the tropics. *Ibid.* 158 *Jungle juice*, poor quality petrol. **1958** R. Stow *To Islands* i. 19 The cartoons.. about going troppo and drinking jungle juice. **1960** *News Chron.* 9 Mar. 7/4 The draught cider and gin they drink in the West of England and call 'jungle juice'. **1967** O. Norton *Now lying Dead* vi. 99 Oh, I know what our ale can do! Jungle-juice, as the lads call it. **1894** Kipling *Jungle Bk.* 63 One of the beauties of Jungle Law is that punishment settles all scores. **1957** M. Kennedy *Heroes of Clone* III. vi. 204 It was awkward having to explain jungle law to someone who had never..emerged from a well-kept shrubbery. **1971** *Daily Nation* (Nairobi) 10 Apr. 13/2 The Obote regime had turned the country into 'a political jungle ruled by jungle law' whereby some people earned their living by putting others into prison. **1944** *Amer. N. & Q.* Mar. 183/1 Can somebody identify a tropical disease called 'jungle rot'? Is it a new name for an old illness? **1945** Jungle rot [see *crud 2 b]. **1958** *Times* 28 Oct. 4/5 (*headline*) N.A.L.G.O. fear 'jungle war' —arbitration move opposed. **1955** E. Waugh *Officers & Gentlemen* I. vi. 70 They put me in charge of a jungle warfare school. **1972** D. Bloodworth *Any Number can Play* viii. 61 He had forgotten more about jungle warfare than a fellow like that would learn in a lifetime. *Ibid.* xix. 194 It has..a big tangle of forest and swamp for jungle-warfare training.

c. Passing into *adj.* = characteristic of the jungle; savage, untamed; *spec.* designating a style of jazz music characterized by primitive sounds redolent of the jungle.

1908 A. Noyes *William Morris* 118 Torn by the savage jungle-cries of the elemental passions. **1909** *Daily Chron.* 22 Jan. 3/3 These wild poems of fierce jungle-passion and horror. **1935** *Vanity Fair* (N.Y.) Nov. 71/3 The savagery of their rhythm calls forth the terms '*shake music*' and '*jungle music*'. **1955** Keepnews & Grauer *Pict. Hist. Jazz* xiii. 141 Cootie Williams..produced a fine, muted 'jungle' sound. **1955** L. Feather *Encycl. Jazz* vii. 133 Early Ellington orchestral characteristics included the use of what he originally called 'jungle style' effects, through the use of plunger mutes. **1957** *Times Lit. Suppl.* 25 Oct. 637/2 A clearly truthful account of the lives and jungle-fights of those cold-hearted career-women who make fortunes from knocking pounds of unnecessary weight off sad fat ladies without love. **1972** *Jazz & Blues* Feb. 20/2 Duke's 'jungle' sounds.

jungle (dʒʌ·ŋg'l), *v.* [f. *Jungle *sb.* 2 c.] *intr.* To prepare a meal at a hoboes' camp; to form such a camp; to join forces with another person. Usu. with *up.*

1922 J. Tully *Emmett Lawler* 252 The fire was built in the improvised furnace, and water was carried from the brook. They returned laden with meat and eggs, potatoes, and coffee... The method is called 'jungling up' by tramps. **1924** 'Digit' *Confessions 20th Cent. Hobo* 12 *Jungle up*, bivouac in the weeds and clean up generally. **1926** J. Black *You can't Win* vi. 70 You're welcome to travel with me, kid, if you want to jungle-up for a month or two. **1931** U. Ledoux *Mr. Zero's Scrapbk.: Ho-bo-ho Medley No. 1* 11 Hoboes and Yeggs never mix and jungle in separate camps. **1937** J. Steinbeck *Of Mice & Men* i. 8 Tramps who come wearily down from the highway in the evening to jungle-up near water.

jungli (dʒʌ·ŋgli), *a.* and *sb.* [f. Jungle + *-i*, adj. suffix as in *Hindi*, etc.] **A.** *adj.* = Jungly *a.* 2; (see also quot. 1927[1]). **B.** *sb.* An inhabitant of the jungle.

1920 *Blackw. Mag.* Oct. 463/1 Just oneself with half a dozen of one's men and some jungli villagers. **1927** *Chambers's Jrnl.* 29 Jan. 138/2 Already he ceases to be jungli. *Note*, Wild and boorish, a clodhopper or uneducated peasant. **1927** *Blackw. Mag.* Mar. 290/1 His crew of two junglis managed to make him understand. **1928** *Ibid.* Jan. 1/2 A system of small flying columns kept the junglis from the inertia which breeds mischief.

Junian, *a.* Delete *rare* and add later examples.

1963 *Times Lit. Suppl.* 25 Jan. 67/1 Candidates for the Junian crown of laurels. **1964** *Language* XL. 87 A word count of the Junian material.

2. Of or pertaining to Francis Junius (1589–1677), philologist and antiquary.

1826 J. J. Conybeare in W. D. Conybeare *Illustr. Anglo-Saxon Poetry* 197 The Junian Cædmon. **1840** J. Petheram *Hist. Sk. Progress Anglo-Saxon Lit. in England* 73 The copy used was the Junian transcript in the Bodleian. **1892** S. A. Brooke *Hist. Early Eng. Lit.* II. 67 Archbishop Ussher..found this manuscript and gave it to Francis Dujon, a scholar of Leyden, who is known in literature as Junius, and from whom the manuscript derives its name of the *Junian Caedmon.* **1897** F. A. Blackburn in *Anglia* XIX. 91 The same device is found in other manuscripts, for example in the Genesis and the Exodus of the Junian MS. in the Bodleian. **1914** *PMLA* XXIX. 146 This book was printed at Dort from the famous and beautiful Junian types representing the Gothic and Anglo-Saxon alphabets, which Junius later presented to the University of Oxford.

junior, *a.* (*sb.*) Add: **3. b.** Designating something intended for children or young people; also applied to a product, device, etc., that is smaller than the normal size.

1860 (*title*) The junior atlas, for schools; fourteen maps selected from the college atlas. **1884** *Chambers's Hist. Readers* (*title*) Junior English history. **1941** *Tennessean* (Nashville) 12 Aug. 9 (Advt.), Handyhot junior electric washer. **1948** (*title*) Oxford junior encyclopaedia. **1948** *Tennessean Mag.* (Nashville) 7 Nov. 23 The idea that 'Junior is a size, not an age', has been plugged with rather half-hearted vigor for several years..in clothes in the 9 to 17 size range. **1967** L. B. Archer in Wills & Yearsley *Handbk. Managem. Technol.* 125 It will be an important design consideration to know whether the product is to be presented as one of a family of different products.. and/or one of a family of similar products (standard, de luxe, junior, and portable models?). **1967** M. Drabble *Jerusalem the Golden* vii. 172 She had been in the afternoon to the chemist's to buy some Junior Aspirin. **1972** *Practical Motorist* Oct. 212/1 A full-size hacksaw won't fit into the average tool box, nor will it work in tight corners. A 'junior' frame saw is a useful back-up, since it's small enough to travel with any tool kit.

5. Special collocations: *junior college* (in *U.S.*), 'a college, operating as a separate institution or as part of a standard college, which does not offer courses more advanced than those of the sophomore year' (D.A.E.); also, a similar institution in Britain and elsewhere; *junior high* (*school*) (*N. Amer.*), a school intermediate between elementary school and high school; *junior miss* (orig. *U.S.*), a young teen-aged girl; = Miss *sb.*[2] 4; also *attrib.*; *junior school*, (*a*) in the state educational system, a school for children aged roughly between 7 and 11; a primary school; (*b*) the lower forms of some fee-paying schools; *junior service*, the Army; *junior stock* (see quot. 1914); *junior technical school*, a school providing a technical and secondary education for boys.

1899 *Univ. Chicago Reg. 1898–99* 37/1 The Faculties of the Schools of Arts, Literature, and Science have been organized as follows: (1) The Faculty of the Junior Colleges; [etc.]. **1949** *Manch. Guardian Weekly* 7 Apr. 8 You will not learn what are the ambitions of the students at a junior college. **1957** *Encycl. Brit.* XX. 258/1 Some schools extended secondary education upward by offering two years of additional work of 'junior college' type. **1963** *Higher Educ.: Rep. Comm. under Ld. Robbins 1961–3* 148 in *Parl. Papers 1962–3* (Cmnd. 2154) XI. 639 Other witnesses..advocated the creation of separate junior or preparatory colleges to undertake the later stages of sixth form work and the first year of university work. **1971** *English Studies* LII. 569 The action..takes place in a classroom of a Southern Californian junior college. **1909** *Ann. Rep. Bd. Educ.* (Columbus, Ohio) 168 The Board has declared itself in favour of the Junior High School System. **1929** *Encycl. Brit.* XX. 258/1 The junior high school has also been a vehicle for innovations in teaching methods. **1948** *Daily Ardmoreite* (Ardmore, Okla.) 12 Oct. 10/1 They met in the ninth grade in junior high. **1968** *Globe & Mail* (Toronto) 13 Feb. 30/2 (Advt.), Convenient to public, junior high and separate schools. *Ibid.* 33/6 (Advt.), Experienced Junior High, social studies and science teacher required. **1927** *Vogue* 15 Jan. 106/2 Junior Misses' Frock. **1950** M. Allingham *Take Two at Bedtime* 17, I was still wearing the junior-miss dresses I had had at school. **1965** *Harper's Bazaar* May 75 *Both* dresses £1 19s. 11d. by Marks & Spencer Junior Miss. **1871** *Minutes of School Board for London* I. 156 Public elementary day schools are conveniently classified into infant schools, for children below seven years of age; junior schools, for children between seven and ten years of age; and senior schools, for older children. **1902** *Captain* VII. 221/1 Workington passed out of the Junior school. **1971** *Times Educ. Suppl.* 5 Feb. 41/4 (Advt.), Small groups of immigrant pupils in Junior Schools, who need additional language instruction. **1915** E. Wallace *Man who bought London* viii. 81 She had a son in the army, and she bore the junior service a grudge in consequence. **1914** H. Halford *Dict. Stock Market Terms* 50 *Junior stocks*, ordinary and deferred stocks ranking for dividend after debentures and preference stocks. **1932** *Daily Tel.* 8 Oct. 2/4 The current quotations of the junior stocks remove the likelihood of an issue in that form. **1929** *Encycl. Brit.* VII. 988/2 Its lower grades have shown a considerable increase, whether in junior technical schools, art schools or evening classes. **1931** *Education Outlook* June 183/1 Its pupils [*sc.* of the new senior school] are distinguished from their contemporaries in grammar schools, modern schools, and junior technical schools.

B. *sb.* **a.** More generally (chiefly *U.S.*), a child, esp. a young boy. Freq. with capital initial.

1946 *Sun* (Baltimore) 14 Dec., Lest the joy of Christmas be marred by..Junior's nipping his pal's arm with an arrow from his archery set, [etc.]. **1951** O. Nash *Family Reunion* 31 But you take ingenuous Junior, and it's just a radio to him. **1968** *Globe & Mail* (Toronto) 13 Jan. 25/6 (Advt.), Enclosed is cheque..for..adults..and.. juniors. **1970** G. Greer *Female Eunuch* 230 If junior finds out that his parents are going out, he'll scream.

2. A barrister who has not taken silk; a junior barrister.

1837 [in Dict., sense B. *sb.* b]. **1842** Dickens *Amer. Notes* I. iii. 127 The counsel who interrogated the witness ..was alone and had no 'junior'. **1872** G. H. Lewes *Let.* 5 Jan. in Geo. Eliot *Lett.* (1956) V. 234 We had..Bowen (the junior in the Tichborne case on whom Coleridge mainly relies),..and had..lots of fun. **1958** S. Hyland *Who goes Hang?* xlix. 260 Oliver Passmore K.C., M.P. And there was a 'junior' with him called Mortimer. **1972** 'W. Haggard' *Protectors* iii. 26 This barrister was..a strong Junior at the criminal bar, and he'd defended Martiny's friend.

junk, *sb.*[2] Add: **1. d.** (Earlier and later

examples.) Also, second-hand or discarded articles of little or no use or value; rubbish.

1842 *Congress. Globe* 23 Feb. 261 Champagne was charged for under the head of 'old junk'. **1913** V. Steer *Romance of Cinema* 30 The life of a film is very short. It is 'first run' to-day and 'junk' a few short weeks hence. **1924** Galsworthy *White Monkey* I. v. 33 His 'junk', however, was not devoid of the taste and luxury which overflows from the greater houses of England. **1935** A. Christie *Death in Clouds* xi. 118, I have my collection ..that all connoisseurs know—and also I have—well, frankly, Messieurs, let us call it junk! **1940** *Punch* 3 Apr. 386/2 A great deal of ecclesiastical junk which the Vatican ..would have obvious difficulty in dispersing. **1952** R. Finlayson *Schooner came to Atia* 112 The boat was found battered to junk in a pool. **1974** *Woman* 4 May 5/1 Collecting junk for creative work is a way of life at school.

e. Any narcotic drug, esp. heroin; also, such drugs collectively. Also *attrib. slang* (orig. *U.S.*).

1925 *Writer's Monthly* June 487/1 *Junk*, dope. **1930** *Liberty* 5 July 24/1 When he has the junk in him there is no telling what he'll do. **1933** 'J. Spenser' *Limey* iii. 37 You shoulda seen him when he was only half light with a shot o' the junk (dope) he used. **1937** B. Reitman *Sister of Road* (1941) vii. 74 She was full of junk, which she had received in her mail. **1938** [see *connect *v.* 5 b]. **1953** W. Burroughs *Junkie* (1972) vii. 66 It doesn't take the manager long to spot a bookie or a junk-pusher. *Ibid.* x. 108 You cannot escape from junk-sickness any more than you can escape from junk-kick after a shot. *Ibid.* xii. 120 Lupita got her start with one gram of junk and built up from there to a monopoly of the junk business in Mexico City. **1957** P. Frank *Seven Days to Never* vii. 204 Pretty slick way to carry your junk... You're a junkie, aren't you? **1960** J. Gelber *Connection* I. 25 You cats ought to smoke pot instead of using junk. It would make you more agreeable. **1963** A. Trocchi *Cain's Book* 73 One must go where the junk is and one is never certain where the junk is, never sure that where the junk is is not the anteroom of the penitentiary. **1966** *Listener* 17 Mar. 401/2 Burroughs's position is explicit: junk—*i.e.*, all narcotic drugs, as opposed to hallucinogenic ones like hashish and mescalin—are purely evil. **1972** J. Brown *Chancer* ix. 85 You do anything for junk... Cheat. Lie. Steal.

5. (sense 1 d) *junk car, cart, collector, -heap, merchant, -pile, -room, -stall, store, -yard*; **junk art** (see quot.); so *junk artist*; **junk jewellery** = **costume jewellery*; **junk mail** *N. Amer.*, circulars, advertisements, etc., sent by post to a large number of addresses; **junk-playground** = **adventure playground*; **junk sculpture** = **junk art*; so *junk sculptor*; **junk-shop** (further examples).

1966 *Britannica Bk. of Year* (U.S.) 807/1 *Junk art*, three-dimensional art made from discarded material (as of metal, mortar, glass, or wood); junk artist, *n.* **1954** *Amer. Speech* XXIX. 99 *Junk car* or *junker*, a car in poor condition that has been made to look like a hot rod. Usually used sarcastically of any car ready for the junk yard. **1967** *Boston Sunday Herald* 26 Mar. II. 9/2 Thirty-five junk cars hauled away. **1879** *Scribner's Monthly* May 34/1 These piers..are too narrow even for the circulation of a junk-cart. **1934** Webster, Junk collector. **1956** J. M. Mogey *Family & Neighbourhood* 10 Junk-collectors' yards. **1906** *Westm. Gaz.* 26 Oct. 2/1 He [*sc.* Hearst]..took hold of a junk-heap relic of Pacific-coast journalism called the *Examiner*. **1917** R. L. Alsaker *Eating for Health* II. xiii. 195 You and I..have to conform to the laws of nature, or else we are thrown into the junk heap. **1953** C. Day Lewis *Italian Visit* iii. 34 It would take three life-times to cover The glorious junk-heap. **1973** *Guardian* 23 Mar. 12/4 In Plymouth once they raided the local junk-heap to supplement the props which they had brought with them. **1939** *Sun* (Baltimore) 8 May 17 The Duchess of Kent..envies American women their smart 'junk jewelry' (costume stuff). **1960** *Sunday Express* 21 Feb. 14/3 American women have..loaded themselves with so much 'junk' jewellery they jangle as they walk. **1954** *Reader's Digest* Oct. 37/1 The argument for junk mail is that sorting requires little time—the postman simply delivers one throwaway to each home. **1967** *Economist* 23 Dec. 1227/1 These high charges are necessary to subsidise third class bulk mail, often called 'junk' mail, which includes millions of unsolicited advertisements sent out to lists of names as well as mail order catalogues. **1972** *Edmonton* (Alberta) *Jrnl.* 26 June 5/5 Within the first few months of their baby's life, the Duncans had received more than 1,000 pieces of junk mail. **1901** *Westm. Gaz.* 8 July 3/2 Twenty tons of unsold copies of a well-known cheap magazine were sold for waste-paper to junk merchants. **1880** *Harper's Mag.* June 67/1 The junk pile in the barn is invaded, and the rusty plough abstracted. **1912** J. H. Moore *Ethics & Educ.* 10 They should be sent without sighs or lamentations to the junk-pile. **1957** *Economist* 5 Oct. 28/2 That lively social experiment the Grimsby 'shanty town', a junk-playground which has evolved into a children's community. **1936** M. Allingham *Flowers for Judge* xiv. 207 They didn't keep anything valuable there. It's a sort of junk-room. **1966** *Time* 14 Jan. E1 Long before the *tachiste* painter or the junk sculptor, the American Indian shaped art from sand, bone, feathers—whatever he had at hand. **1969** *Harper's Mag.* Sept. 14 Students interested in musicology, junk sculpture, the Theater of the Absurd. **1970** *Times* 7 Mar. p. iv/6 He [*sc.* Brion Gysin] had time on his hands and became one of the pioneers of junk sculpture. **1841** 'Dow, Jr.' *Short Patent Sermons* 77 Trash, that wouldn't fetch two cents in the market of heaven, and but a trifle more in the junk-shops of hell. **1879** *Scribner's Monthly* May 33/2 New York is bordered with rat-holes and rotten cribs, gin-mills and junk-shops. **1881** C. C. Harrison *Woman's Handiwork* III. 171 She confessed to having purchased from a junk-shop the charming little gilt-framed oblong mirror. **1939** C. Day Lewis *Child of Misfortune* I. v. 70 Lady Gresham's mind was dark, dusty and furtive as a junk-shop. **1951** M. Kennedy *Lucy Carmichael* III. i. 157, I saw it..in a tray in a junk shop. **1969** *Listener* 17 Apr. 533/1 The Metropolitan Museum in New York was a really dismal junk shop 40 years ago. **1962** *John o' London's* 11 Jan. 40/3 Oddities off junk-stalls. **1882** J. D. McCabe *New York* 583 They..sell it to the junk and rag stores. **1908** Kipling *Lett. of Travel* (1920) 197 We went to look at a marine junk-store. **1880** G. W. Cable *Grandissimes* 192 You may still..see one [*sc.* a villa] standing..among..junk-yards, and long-shoremen's hovels. **1952** W. R. Burnett *Vanity Row* (1953) vi. 50 All about loomed gas tanks, warehouses, junk yards. **1953** *Manch. Guardian Weekly* 27 Aug. 7 Suffocating in a junkyard of chairs. **1966** T. Pynchon *Crying of Lot 49* i. 14 If it had been an outright junkyard, probably he could have stuck things out, made a career. **1974** M. Hastings *Dragon Island* ix. 77 The only reason this floating junkyard's still in service is that the Chinese perishers that own her can't even give her away.

junk, *v.* Add: **2.** To treat as junk or rubbish; to discard, abandon; to 'scrap'.

1916 B. Hall *Diary* 11 Oct. in Hall & Niles *One Man's War* (1929) 196 When he got home his ship was a complete wreck. It will be junked. **1922** H. Titus *Timber* xxxii. 281 Perhaps he had friends..who are junking their mills now and getting ready to move. **1930** *Time & Tide* 20 Sept. 1164 Jugo-Slavia will not disband a soldier, scrap a gunboat, or junk a gun while Italy menaces her. **1945** [see *cow-country* s.v. *cow *sb.*[1] 7]. *a* **1963** S. Plath *Crossing Water* (1971) 33 The roses in the Toby jug Gave up the ghost last night...You should have junked them before they died. **1972** *Listener* 21 Dec. 860/2 The free-wheeling teams..might have to junk their wagons and stumble on foot down the western slopes of the Sierra. **1973** K. Giles *File on Death* vi. 149, I dare say you can pick up junked bits of weapons. **1973** *Times* 21 Mar. 9/4 The story of a man who junked his education and went after the short-term riches of sport.

junkanoo, junkonoo: see *John Canoe.

Junker[1]. Add: Also *transf.*

1914 G. B. Shaw *What I really wrote about War* (1931) 25 The Junker is by no means peculiar to Prussia...Lord Cromer is a Junker. **1916** *Ibid.* 159 British Junker stupidity. **1919** W. H. Downing *Digger Dial.* 30 *Junker*, a superior staff-officer. **1920** E. Antonelli *Bolshevist Russia* I. ii. 32 A delegation of 'Junkers' (pupils of the Military Schools) appeared before Kerensky. *Ibid.* 35 Some Junker and regimental delegations..received no reply.

junker[2] (dʒʊ·ŋkəɹ). *Austral.* and *N.Z.* = Jinker[2].

1888 P. W. Barlow *Kaipara* xiii. 94 He mounted the 'junker'... The unhappy [horse] gave a feeble shake with one hind leg. **1924** Lawrence & Skinner *Boy in Bush* 236 'What's a junker, Tom?' 'A low, four-wheeled log hauler, with a long pole.'

junker[3] (dʒʊ·ŋkəɹ). *U.S. slang.* [f. *junk *sb.*[2] 1 e + -er[1].] A drug-addict; a drug-peddler.

1922 E. F. Murphy *Black Candle* II. xvii. 276 One must ..be known as a 'junker' or addict to make the purchase. **1930** *Detective Fiction Weekly* 15 Nov. 473/2 He got the poppy gum from the smugglers and turned it over to the chemists at a good profit, getting back half in cash and half in drugs, which his junkers peddled. **1930** C. R. Shaw *Jack Roller* xii. 161 Next to me in the hospital was Herbie, a junker, who was taking the cure. **1949** 'J. Evans' *Halo in Brass* (1951) iv. 29 No slim-waisted junker with a snapbrim hat and a deck of nose candy for sale to the right guy.

junket, *sb.* Add: **4.** Also *transf.* and *fig.*; *spec.* (see quot. 1886). Chiefly *U.S.*

1886 *Detroit Free Press* 4 Sept. 4/2 The term 'junket' in America is generally applied to a trip taken by an American official at the expense of the government. **1946** R. Blesh *Shining Trumpets* (1949) vii. 162 The first recording junket of modern times. **1954** Koestler *Invis. Writing* xxxi. 326 Bloomsbury and Greenwich Village went on a revolutionary junket. **1966** *Telegraph* (Brisbane) 13 Apr. 51/1 United States delegates to the Inter-Parliamentary Union conference in Canberra are upset that their trip has been described as a junket. **1966** *Sunday Times* 11 Dec. 3/2 A week here as a member of a gambling junket. **1973** *Black World* Apr. 96 On a junket to L.A. and New York looking for scripts. **1973** *Times* 18 Aug. 14/1 The only way I could get to see the countries about whose politics I would write so knowledgeably was to get myself attached to groups of travel writers on facility trips, or what the Americans call junkets.

junketeer (dʒʊːŋkėtīə·ɹ). orig. *U.S.* [f. Junket *sb.* + -eer.] = Junketer.

1939 *Amer. Speech* XIV. 237/1 Junketeer is a term used in the press in these days. **1963** *Economist* 1 June 902/2 The 'junketeers' need not submit any receipts or documents. **1969** *Daily Tel.* 21 Feb. 19/6 Most of the junketeers have been Americans with personal credit ratings of 2,000 dollars upwards.

junkie (dʒʊ·ŋki). *slang* (orig. *U.S.*). Also **junkey, junky.** [f. *junk *sb.*[2] 1 e + -ie.] A drug-addict; also occas., a drug-peddler. Also *attrib.* or as *adj.* (chiefly in form *junky*).

1923 [see *gun *sb.* 3 e]. **1929** *Flynn's* 2 Feb. 125/2 He's a confirmed 'junkie' and, of course, he'll get hold of it if he can. **1930** *Time & Tide* 20 Sept. 1181 He became a recognised junky and earned his living as a useful subordinate member of a drug-traffic gang. **1930** *Detective Fiction Weekly* 20 Dec. 362 (*heading*) Undercover man Murray follows the junkey trail into the greatest city's street of evil. **1949** N. Algren *Man with Golden Arm* 25 You're not a student any more... Junkie—you're hooked. **1951** *N.Y. Times* (City ed.) 27 June 19/5 An addict who sells narcotics, for which he usually gets his own daily supply, is called a 'junkie', he explained, and they hang out in taverns and cafes until the police raid them. **1959** W. Burroughs *Naked Lunch* 13 He would suck the juice right out of every junky he ran down. *Ibid.* 53 He spoke in his dead, junky whisper. **1959** C. MacInnes *Absolute Beginners* 68 If you have a friend who's a junkie..you soon discover there's no point whatever discussing his addiction. **1969** *Daily Tel.* (Colour Suppl.) 16 May 33/2 Combined with my appetite-killing pills and my tranquillisers I was possibly the junkiest man on the [ski] slopes. **1970** *Times* 22 Sept. 10/4 Over-prescribing by the notorious junkie doctors. **1971** *Daily Tel.* 18 June 17/3 They plan to tour villages showing a film about 'junkies' and giving lectures to youngsters about the dangers of drugs. **1972** J. Brown *Chancer* iv. 59 Lacerated hands, the hands of junkies, scarred where needles had searched for veins. **1973** *Black World* May 47 Talk about how to get more money, how to get educated, how to have scientists for children rather than junkies.

junkman[2]. For *U.S.* read orig. *U.S.*, and add earlier and later examples.

1872 E. Crapsey *Nether Side N.Y.* 39 The shop of a junkman selected..as the purchaser of the plunder. **1879** *Scribner's Mag.* May 37/2 He is a licensed junkman; he holds a license for running a boat and buying and selling old refuse articles of any kind—a kind of water-ragman. **1963** H. Garner in R. Weaver *Canad. Short Stories* (1968) 2nd Ser. 38 The two of them helped the junkman load his truck. **1972** R. K. Smith *Ransom* iv. 150 The old pawnbroker watched the junkman.

junky (dʒʊ·ŋki), *a.* [f. Junk *sb.*[2] + -y[1].] **1.** Worthless, valueless, rubbishy.

1946 'G. Orwell' *Coll. Ess.* (1968) IV. 92 The kind of junky books..that accumulate in the bottoms of cupboards. **1966** *Punch* 27 July p. vii, Dealing in junky but odd bric-à-brac and more expensive furniture. **1972** *N.Y. Times* 3 Nov. 16/8 'Those are junky schools,' she declared. 'They have riots up there every day.' **1974** *New Yorker* 25 Feb. 62/3 Not necessarily cheap junk, however. In the past couple of years, an extraordinary demand for junky furniture seems to have arisen in London.

2. See *junkie.

junr. (Examples.)

1813 Jane Austen *Let.* 16 Sept. (1952) 326 The Letter you forwarded from Edwd Junr has been duly received. **1819** M. Edgeworth *Let. c* 1 Jan. (1971) 154 Mr. Brooke Boothby (Junr.) and Mr. Henry Vernon dined here.

‖ **junshi** (dʒu·nʃi). *Hist.* [Jap.] In Japan, suicide at the death of one's lord, self-immolation.

1871 A. B. Mitford *Tales Old Japan* II. 57 The ancient Japanese custom of *Junshi*; that is to say 'dying with the master'. **1904** L. Hearn *Japan: Attempt at Interpretation* iv. 47 With the rise of the military power there gradually came into existence another custom of *junshi*, or following one's lord in death,—suicide by the sword.

jupati (dʒū·-, hū·păti). [Pg., a. Tupi.] A Brazilian palm, *Raphia tædigera*, bearing large leaves whose long stalks are used locally as a building material.

1856 B. Seemann *Popular Hist. Palms* 331 *Raphia tædigera* Mart., the Jupati of the Lingoa Geral, is one of the many noble Palms which grow on the rich alluvium of the Amazon. **1863** H. W. Bates *Naturalist on River Amazons* I. v. 196 The moon now broke forth and lighted up..the leaves of monstrous Jupatí palms which arched over the creek. **1908** in R. Spruce *Notes of Botanist on Amazon & Andes* II. 521 Glossary of native names... Jupati. *Rhaphia* [sic] *tædigera*. A short-stemmed but noble palm with immense leaves. **1972** Y. Lovelock *Vegetable Bk.* 302 Palms are to be found spanning the equatorial belt around the world. They include..the Japanese [*sic*] jupati palm.

Jupiter. Add: **1. b.** *Jupiter Pluvius*, Jupiter as the dispenser of rain; hence used trivially in reference to a fall or storm of rain.

1864 G. A. Sala *Quite Alone* I. ii. 39 'Take my advice, and..borrow somebody else's umbrella.'..'Are you, too, ready for the wrath of Jupiter Pluvius?' **1874** G. H. West *Rugby Union Football Ann.* 62 But 'Jupiter Pluvius' and the Fates were against it. **1922** Joyce *Ulysses* 598 It cleared up after the recent visitation of Jupiter Pluvius.

Jura (dʒūᵊ·ră, ‖ ʒūra). [Name of the range of mountains on the borders of France and Switzerland that gave its name to the Jurassic system; in this use prob. a. Ger. *Jura*, *Jura*-Jurassic (sb. and adj.).] Jurassic rocks or strata; the Jurassic system. Also *attrib.*, = Jurassic *a.*

Lower or *Black Jura* = Lias 2; *Middle* or *Brown Jura* = Dogger[3] 2; *Upper* or *White Jura* = Malm *sb.* 1 a.

1829 *Proc. Geol. Soc.* I. 94 On the descent to Sospello [near Nice] are found, in a regular descending series, green-sand, Jura, oolitic (or younger Alpine) limestone, lias, red-marl, and older Alpine limestone or dolomite. **1851** *Q. Jrnl. Geol. Soc.* VII. II. 42 (*heading*) On the comparison of the German Jura formation with those of France and England. *Ibid.* 46 In the Jura, or in the lower land of Berne, where the 'black Jura' is developed, there is no great extension in width. *Ibid.* 47 The Marne, Seine,.. Indre, &c., all of which flow westward, descend from the Lias to the 'brown Jura', and thence to the 'white'; whilst in the German 'Jura' the rivers flow from the heights of the 'white Jura' through the 'brown' and the

'black'. *Ibid.* 85 The 'Jura'-formations in northern Asia. **1893** P. Lake tr. *E. Kayer's Text Bk. Compar. Geol.* 241 In England the Jura forms a broad zone striking N.N.E. **1895** *Jrnl. Geol.* III. 380 During all this time the Upper Jura of South America..retained its central European character. **1900** *Jrnl. Geol.* VIII. 216 The rocks of the region represent..remnants of formations belonging to the Algonkian, Cambrian, Silurian, Carboniferous, Jura-trias, Cretaceous, and Eocene periods. **1929** *Bull. Geol. Soc. Amer.* XL. 176 (*heading*) Delimitation of Jura and Trias in British Columbia. **1955** G. G. Woodford tr. *M. Gignoux's Stratigr. Geol.* vii. 314 In describing the Swabian Jura, Quenstedt and Leopold von Buch distinguished three successive groups of rocks, to which they gave the names Black Jura, Brown Jura, and White Jura, in accordance with their appearance in outcrops. These three groups correspond approximately to what we now call the Lower Jurassic or Lias, the Middle Jurassic or Dogger and the Upper Jurassic or Malm.

‖ **Jurançon** (ʒüraṅsoṅ). [Name of a commune in the Basses Pyrénées.] The white wine produced in Jurançon.

[**1833** C. Redding *Hist. Mod. Wines* v. 138 The first growths of Jurançon and Gan bring two hundred francs the hectolitre.] **1920** A. L. Simon *Blood of Grape* ix. 243 Fine wines..from the Mediterranean Coast and the Pyrénées (..*Rivesaltes, Jurancon*, etc., etc.). **1926** P. M. Shand *Bk. Wines* v. 64 Like all fine wines, Jurançon owes its quality to one supreme and informing vine. **1969** L. Orizet *Wine Bk.* 144 The production seldom exceeds 400,000 gallons of genuine white Jurançon a year, and a few gallons of red wine.

Jurassic, *a.* Add to def.: Also applied to the period itself and to flora and fauna found in Jurassic formations. (Earlier and additional examples.)

1831 *Proc. Geol. Soc.* I. 241 The Jurassic and Alpine limestones. **1847** *Q. Jrnl. Geol. Soc.* III. 117 A succession of deposits..formed during the Jurassic period. **1851** *Ibid.* VII. 179 But for the 'plant-beds' at Gristhorpe, Cloughton, Kiburn, and Whitby, we should know little of the ancient vegetation of the Jurassic period. These localities have supplied, in fact, the types of the Jurassic Flora. **1909** Chamberlin & Salisbury *Geol.: Shorter Course* xxiv. 712 (*caption*) A group of Jurassic ammonites. **1938** L. D. Stamp *Physical Geogr. & Geol.* xiii. 207 At the close of the Jurassic period the sea retreated and left a great lake in south-eastern England. **1968** D. A. Robson *Sci. Geol.* ix. 242 The succession is reminiscent of that of the Carboniferous Coal Measures, except for its distinctive Jurassic flora.

b. *absol.* as *sb.* The Jurassic system or the Jurassic period.

1831 *Proc. Geol. Soc.* I. 241 Chalk does not exist in the Carpathians, nor could the author recognise it at Cracow, the limestone of which he refers to the Upper Jurassic. **1873** [in Dict.]. **1902** A. J. Jukes-Browne *Student's Handbk. Stratigr. Geol.* xiv. 331 The Upper Jurassic, again, is an argillaceous series. **1938** A. K. Wells *Outl. Hist. Geol.* xv. 153 The Lower Jurassic is co-extensive with the Lias, a formation..splendidly exposed in parts of the English coast that enjoy a measure of popularity as seaside resorts. **1956** W. J. Arkell *Jurassic Geol. of World* i. 3 In the popular imagination the Jurassic is the period of great marine reptiles and flying dragons. **1973** *Nature* 13 July 92/1 Rifting probably started in the Triassic and by the Jurassic a reasonably large Tethyan Ocean was in existence.

juriballi (yūᵊribæ·li). Also **euri-, youraballi.** [Arawak (Makuchi).] Any of several trees belonging to the family Meliaceæ, especially a species of *Trichilia*, the bark of which was formerly used as a febrifuge; also, the bark itself.

1834 J. Hancock in *Trans. Medico-Botanical Soc. 1832–33* 36 (*title*) Remarks on the Juribali, or Euribali. **1846** J. Lindley *Veget. Kingd.* 462 Juriballi bark, a Demerara product..is described as being a potent bitter and astringent, far superior to Peruvian bark in fevers of a typhoid and malignant nature. **1851** *Illustr. Catal. Gt. Exhib.* IV. 982/1 Youraballi. **1903** *Imperial Inst. Techn. Rep.* 285 The Crabwood and Euriballi would have shown fair results.

jurimetrics (dʒūᵊrime·triks). [f. L. *juris*, gen. of *jūs* law + *-metrics*, as in *biometrics, econometrics*.] The use of scientific methods in the study of legal matters. So **jurimetri·cian, jurime·tricist**, a student of, or expert in, jurimetrics.

1949 L. Loevinger in *Minnesota Law Rev.* XXXIII. 483 The next step forward in the long path of man's progress must be from jurisprudence (which is mere speculation about law) to *jurimetrics*—which is the scientific investigation of legal problems. **1964** *Jrnl. Politics* XXVI. 915 Professor Spaeth's view of what jurimetrics may hope to accomplish. **1966** *Sci. Amer.* Sept. 296 Being, in this enterprise, jurimetricists and not legal historians, they chose the molds of analytic rather than historical jurisprudence for the ordering of their materials. *Ibid.* 295 The fruit of the union of jurisprudence and social science has inevitably been christened 'jurimetrics'. **1970** *Encycl. Sci. Suppl.* (Grolier) 287 Polimetricians, psychometricians, jurimetricians are all rapidly proliferating species of a genus of mathematically minded scholars.

jurist. 1. For † *Obs.* read *Obs.* exc. *U.S.*, and add further examples. Also, a judge.

1905 E. B. Holt tr. *H. Münsterberg's Americans* iv. 88 Sixty-one of them [*sc.* members of the Senate] were jurists... As to the jurists, they are not men who are still active as attorneys or judges. **1931** W. G. McAdoo *Crowded Years* iii. 41 A well-known jurist at that time was Judge Trewhitt. **1936** *S. P. E. Tract* XLV. 188 Even more important is the divergence between the English and American uses of *jurist*, which is not restricted in the United States to the meaning of an expert in the science of law. It is commonly applied to any one who has obtained the qualifications required for legal practice. **1973** N. W. Schur *British Self-Taught* 211 In America *jurist* is synonymous with *judge*. Unfortunately not all *jurists* (in the American sense) are *jurists* (in the English sense).

jury, *sb.* Add: **6.** *jury service, system*; **jury-fixer** *U.S.*, one who bribes or otherwise illegally influences a jury or juror; so *jury-fixing*; **jury-woman**, (*b*) a female juror.

1882 *Washington Post* 18 Mar. (Th.), There might be some scope in the proceedings before the Grand Jury for a 'jury fixer'. **1931** *Blue Valley Farmer* (Okla. City) 24 Dec. 1/6 Fill the town with secret service men to catch the jury fixers. **1887** *Library Mag.* Apr. 531/2 Bribery and jury-fixing would speedily disappear. **1946** C. McWilliams *Southern California Country* 245 The long and sordid aftermath, involving jury-fixing, bribery, and murder. **1955** *Radio Times* 22 Apr. 28/3 Jury Service is often regarded as a tiresome duty. **1973** E. McGirr *Bardel's Murder* i. 26, I got caught for jury service, six horrible days of it. **1875** W. Stubbs *Constitutional Hist. Eng.* I. xiii. 611 Many writers of authority have maintained that the entire jury system is indigenous in England. **1974** *Times* 2 May 18/6 The acquittals..demonstrate the strength of a jury system which acquits when there is reasonable doubt. **1927** *Daily Tel.* 24 May 17/6 The manner in which the recalcitrant jurywoman is eventually brought round is not altogether convincing. **1962** *Punch* 21 Nov. 733/2 One of the two jury-women who made up our twelve disappeared completely during the last day's hearing.

jus, jus', colloq. and dial. shortening of Just *adv.*

1801 T. Tenney *Female Quixotism* II. xiv. 145 He kill us all, one after toder, jus as easy as we kill chickens. **1884** J. C. Egerton *Sussex Folk* iii. 33, I jus should be glad if you could get rid an 'em for me. **1935** Z. N. Hurston *Mules & Men* (1970) I. i. 28 Jus' go wid Gabriel. **1973** *Black World* July 56/2 We jus' laid on the corner and watched. *Ibid.* Aug. 55/1 He walked over to the Village an' dug a backdoor with a lock jus' beggin' to be picked.

‖ **jus cogens** (dʒʊs kōᵘ·genz). [L., compelling law.] A principle of international law which cannot be set aside by agreement or acquiescence. So, in modern use, as laid down by the Vienna Convention on the Law of Treaties (1969), 'a peremptory norm of general international law'. (See quots.)

1895 W. H. Rattigan *Private Internat. Law* vi. 163 A *jus cogens* regulating rights of this description is a product of modern commercial and intellectual activity, and finds no place, for instance, in the jurisprudence of the Roman Empire. **1937** *Amer. Jrnl. Internat. Law* XXXI. 571 The answer to this question depends on the preliminary question, whether general international law contains rules which have the character of *jus cogens*. **1945** M. Wolff *Private Internat. Law* III. 168 Savigny..clearly showed that the rules of an absolute, imperative character (the *ius cogens*) to be found in any legal system are of two kinds. There are first of all those rules 'that are enacted merely for the sake of persons who are the possessors of rights', such as the laws limiting the capacity to act on account of age or sex, or laws concerning the transfer of property; and secondly the rules that are not made solely for the benefit of single individuals but rest on moral grounds, or on the 'public interest'... *ius cogens privatorum pactis mutari non potest.* **1957** G. Schwarzenberger *Internat. Law* (ed. 3) I. xx. 352 In this respect, the rules governing the principle of the freedom of the seas are not *jus cogens* which as such is unalterable, but as much *jus dispositivum* as any of the other rules of international law. **1960** F. A. Mann in *Brit. Year Bk. Internat. Law 1959* 45 Lord McNair must allow the *jus cogens* of the proper law to override the general principles which are merely incorporated into it. **1965** *Texas Law Rev.* XLIII. 455 The problem of international *jus cogens* can be stated in a simple question: Are there rules of international law which, by consent, individual subjects of international law may not modify? **1969** *Vienna Convention on Law of Treaties* 18 in *Parl. Papers 1968–9* (Cmnd. 4140) LV. 395 Treaties conflicting with a peremptory norm of general international law (jus cogens). A treaty is void if, at the time of its conclusion, it conflicts with a peremptory norm of general international law. For the purposes of the present Convention, a peremptory norm of general international law is a norm accepted and recognized by the international community of States as a whole as a norm from which no derogation is permitted and which can be modified only by a subsequent norm of general international law having the same character. **1971** M. Akehurst *Mod. Introd. Internat. Law* (ed. 2) iii. 60 The technical name now given to the basic principles of international law, which states are not allowed to contract out of, is 'peremptory norms of general international law', otherwise known as *jus cogens*.

‖ **jus gentium** (dʒʊs dʒe·nʃiʊ̆m). [L.] = *law of nations* (see Law *sb.*[1] 4 c).

1548 Hooper *Declar. Commandm.* iii. 31 They shuld observe the commune lawes vsyd among all people whiche is callid ius gentium. **1682** Evelyn *Let.* 19 Sept. in *Diary & Corresp.* (1906) 666 The right of passes, and petitions thereupon, were formed upon another part of the *Jus Gentium*, than our pretended dominion of the seas. **1771** 'Junius' *Lett.* (1772) II. lxi. 285 Any law that contradicts or excludes the common law of England; whether it be *canon, civil, jus gentium*, or *levitical*. **1839** *Penny Cycl.* XIII. 361/2 According to their [*sc.* Roman lawyers'] phraseology,..*jus gentium* consists of those rules of law which are common to all nations. **1856** Bouvier *Law Dict.* (ed. 6) I. 685 Among the Romans by *jus civile* was understood the civil law, in contradistinction to the public law, or *jus gentium*. **1880** *Encycl. Brit.* XIII. 191/1 The ambiguity of the phrase *jus gentium* enabled the early founders of international law to apply the principles of the *jus naturæ* to the conduct of states *inter se* in a way of which there is no example in the Roman law-books. **1959** Jowitt *Dict. Eng. Law* II. 1035/1 *Jus gentium*, the law of nations.

jusi (hū·si). Also **husi, jussi.** [a. Sp. *jusi*, ad. Tagalog *husi*.] A delicate fibrous fabric woven in the Philippine Islands.

1851 *Illustr. Catal. Gt. Exhib.* IV. 1344/1 Piece of 'jusi', and a shawl of 'jusi'. *Ibid.*, Pieces of striped jusi dresses. **1902** *Encycl. Brit.* XXXI. 667/1 Beautiful fabrics called 'piña' and 'jusi', the former woven of pineapple-leaf fibre and the latter of this fibre mixed with silk.

‖ **jus primæ noctis** (dʒʊs prəi·mi nǫ·ktis). [L., right of the first night.] = *droit du seigneur* (see *Droit[1] 1 b).

1887 F. K. Wischnewetzky tr. *Engels's Condition of Working-Class in England in 1844* 99 Factory servitude.. confers the *jus primæ noctis* upon the master... If the master is mean enough,..his mill is also his harem. **1911** *Encycl. Brit.* XV. 593/1 *Jus primae noctis* or *droit du seigneur*, a custom alleged to have existed in medieval Europe, giving the overlord a right to the virginity of his vassals' daughters on their wedding-night... The *jus*, it seems, is a myth, invented no earlier than the 16th or 17th century. **1923** A. Huxley *Antic Hay* xviii. 250 It was on a splendid subject—the 'Jus Primæ Noctis, or Droit du Seigneur'. **1933** 'G. Orwell' *Down & Out* xxxiv. 256 He had heard..of..the *jus primae noctis* (he believed it had really existed). **1970** G. Greer *Female Eunuch* 228 No serf, writhing under the law of *jus primae noctis*,..ever had it worse. **1971** *Black Scholar* Dec. 13/1 The integration of rape into the sparsely furnished legitimate social life of the slaves harks back to the feudal 'right of the first night', the *jus primae noctis*.

‖ **jusqu'au bout** (ʒüskobu), *adv. phr.* [Fr.] To the end, to the conclusion, to completion; to the bitter end; *spec.* in the war of 1914–18, used in the context of carrying on fighting until a conclusive victory has been gained. Hence **jusqu'auboutisme**, the policy of carrying on to the bitter end; **jusqu'auboutist(e** (also without apostrophe), an advocate of *jusqu'auboutisme*.

1917 A. Huxley *Let.* 30 Sept. (1969) 134 Are the French socialists going to make much fuss at Bordeaux? I think and hope we are all Jusquauboutistes here. **1918** G. B. Shaw *What I really wrote about War* (1931) 280 In Constantinople it will be a matter of fighting *jusqu'au bout*. *Ibid.* 282, I am a Jusqu'auboutist. I do not want this war to be compromised as long as it will be possible for any of the belligerent Powers afterwards to pretend that if it had only gone on for another year it would have won. **1933** A. Huxley *Let.* 13 Aug. (1969) 372, I have never more passionately felt the need of using reason jusqu'au bout. **1968** *Listener* 4 July 12/1 The rhetoric of the klieg-lit European student leaders spouting mocking *jusqu'auboutisme* like post-Marxist Beatles.

Jussiæan (dʒʊsi,ī·ăn), **Jussieu(e)an** (dʒʊsiyū·-ăn), *a.* Also **Jussiean.** [f. mod.L. *Jussiæus*, or its origin, the French surname *Jussieu* + -an.] Of or pertaining to Bernard de Jussieu (1699–1777) and his nephew Antoine Laurent de Jussieu (1748–1836), or to the natural system of botanical classification devised by them.

1824 J. C. Loudon *Encycl. Gardening* (ed. 2) 47 All the hardy plants..arranged in groups, according to the Jussieuean system. **1857** A. Henfrey *Elem. Bot.* § 392 The Jussieuan System. **1865** G. Bentham *Handbk. Brit. Flora* p. viii, The so-called Linnæan or Jussiæan systems. **1876** *Encycl. Brit.* IV. 81/1 It [*sc.* the Linnæan method] was superseded by the Jussiean method.

just, joust, *sb.*[1] Now usu. spelt joust and pronounced (dʒaust).

just, joust, *v.*[1] Now usu. spelt **joust** and pronounced (dʒaust).

just, *adv.* Add: **1. c.** *just so* (earlier and later examples); also, (*b*) in the required or appropriate manner; (*c*) very close or friendly; (*d*) neatly and tidily; also as *adj.*; *just-so story*, a story which purports to explain the origin of something; a myth.

1751 Richardson in Johnson *Rambler* No. 97. ¶ 24 When I courted and married my Lætitia, then a blooming Beauty, every Thing passed just so! **1794** *Massachusetts Spy* 3 Sept. (Th.), A few years ago, every body supposed that if people did not behave just so, they ought to be punished. **1824** 'A. Singleton' *Lett.* 18 Their *just so* garb, which, when adopted, was the court costume of the time, makes them [*sc.* Quakers] appear like antediluvians. **1831** J. Constable *Let.* 4 Dec. (1966) IV. 361 Was it *now* in its first state, I would rejoice to publish it *just so*. **1886** *Lantern* (New Orleans) 15 Sept. 4/2 It looks as though the contractors and the aldermen are just so, and fully understand each other. **1887** Parish & Shaw *Dict. Kentish Dial.* 85 He's not a bad master, but he will have everything done just-so; and you wunt please him

without everything is just-so. **1902** Kipling (*title*) Just so stories. **1922** J. Strachey tr. *Freud's Group Psychol.* x. 90 This is only a hypothesis..a 'Just-So Story'. **1930** *Times Lit. Suppl.* 27 Feb. 155/2 The charm of an album of Just-so stories, such as proves that even the humblest members of the human race possess..the saving grace of vision. **1952** L. MacNeice *Ten Burnt Offerings* 76 Reposed on a Sunday lap in the just-so room. **1960** R. Pound *Selfridge* i. 8 He always looked as if he had just come out of the bandbox. His mother..kept him just so. **1969** E. Bishop *Compl. Poems* 198 A raccoon..was the executioner. He was very fastidious and did everything just so. **1969** R. A. Noblett *Stavin' Chain* 5 Now Stavin' Chain wuz a man just so: When he got good whiskey, he would gurgle it slow. **1973** *Times Lit. Suppl.* 25 May 576/2 At first sight *My Country* is another of these just-so stories.

g. Delete 'in *U.S.*' and add later U.K. examples.

1960 R. A. Knox *Occasional Sermons* 227 Many who value the name of Christian still find it reasonable to believe that he did just that. **1971** *You* Sept. 24/1 Doctors and researchers are spending their energies and our money on finding out just how the female body ticks. **1974** *Times Lit. Suppl.* 8 Mar. 243/5 One wonders just how biased a view we develop of the human ecology of tropical Africa.

6. Delete 'Chiefly *Sc.* and *dial.*' and add further examples.

1937 A. Huxley *Ends & Means* xii. 199 In the abstract this scheme seems good enough; but in practice it just doesn't work. **1962** *Listener* 18 Jan. 135/1 The functionalist revolution just doesn't seem to have reached architectural photography. *Ibid.* 25 Oct. 694/2 It is just not true that cultivated people are able to pronounce equally on films, books, paintings, the theatre. **1972** *Newsweek* 10 Jan. 34/1 Now most businessmen think they just have to have a guard.

b. Delete 'in *Sc.* and *north. dial.*' and add further examples.

c **1863** T. Taylor in M. R. Booth *Eng. Plays of 19th Cent.* (1909) II. 119 Ain't it a bore, just! *c* **1875** 'Brenda' *Froggy's Little Brother* (new ed.) iv. 41 'Now, haven't we 'ad a supper *just?*' exclaimed Froggy with satisfaction. **1894** Kipling *Let.* 28 July in C. E. Carrington *Rudyard Kipling* (1955) ix. 217 Won't New York be hot—just! **1903** A. Bennett *Leonora* viii. 228 'He's a good dancer.' 'I should think he was!..Isn't he just, mother?' **1904** E. Nesbit *Phoenix & Carpet* v. 94 'Luv us!' said Ike, 'ain't it been taught its schoolin', just!' **1930** J. B. Priestley *Angel Pavement* i. 16 She let herself go all right, didn't she just! **1943** K. Tennant *Ride on Stranger* (1968) iv. 36 'I don't believe you'd do that anyway yourself. Just grab money.' 'Wouldn't I just,' her mentor said exultantly.

c. *just too bad*, unfortunate but inevitable.

1935 H. L. Ickes *Secret Diary* (1953) I. 270 If, in the course of his investigation, Glavis runs across your brother or my son, that will be just too bad, but it will be in the line of his duty. **1938** Auden & Isherwood *On Frontier* ii. 75 If some one's mistaken or lying or mad, Or if we're defeated, it will be just too bad. **1962** J. F. Powers *Morte d'Urban* ix. 199 Well, isn't that just too bad? **1962** 'S. Woods' *Bloody Instructions* viii. 87, I admit you'll come in for some rough handling, and that's just too bad.

7. c. Also *S. Afr.* [tr. Afrikaans *netnou*].

1939 'D. Rame' *Wine of Good Hope* i. iii. 40 'Well, eat then,' said Lowell. 'I'll come just now.' **1953** N. Gordimer *Lying Days* ii. ix. 92 'Well,' I said, 'I'll open it just now—.' **1966** A. Sachs *Jail Diary* xvi. 143 'Would you mind switching off the light after you lock up.' 'The men on cell duty will do that just now.'

‖ **juste milieu** (ʒüst' milyö). [Fr., lit. 'the right mean'.] The happy medium, the golden mean; judicious moderation, esp. in politics.

1833 Mill *Lett.* (1910) I. 76 The Enfantin portion.. have become *juste milieu* men in politics. **1866** Mrs. Gaskell *Wives & Daughters* II. xxvii. 279 Now I hope that man in the garden is the *juste milieu,*—I'm that myself, for I don't think I'm vicious, and I know I'm not virtuous. **1875** J. G. Saxe *Leisure-Day Rhymes* 261 For me, the *juste milieu* I seek; I fain would leave alone The girl who rudely slaps my cheek Or volunteers her own! **1882** E. W. Hamilton *Diary* 13 June (1972) I. 289, I suppose between the extremes there must be a *juste milieu*, but as to where it is I am at sea. **1936** E. Sitwell *Victoria of Eng.* iii. 48 It was the *juste milieu* that ruled her life. **1945** A. J. P. Taylor *Course of German Hist.* 13 One looks in vain in their history for a *juste milieu*, for common sense.

Justicialism (dʒʊsti·ʃăliz'm). Also in Sp. form **Justicialismo** (hustisiali·zmo), and with small initial. [f. Sp. *justicia* justice + -al + *-ismo* -ism.] The name given by Juan Domingo Perón (1895–1974), President of Argentina (1946–55 and 1973–4), to his political doctrine: a combination of Fascism and socialism. Cf. *Peronism. So **Justi·cialist**(a *adj.*

1949 tr. *J. Perón's Speech at Opening 83rd Parl. Session Nat. Congr.* 7 The year that has gone by will be recorded in the Argentine history as the year of the 'justicialist' Constitution. [**1950** R. A. Mende (*title*) El Justicialismo.] **1952** *Time* 12 May 28/3 If we take advantage of this historic moment, we shall impose Justicialism on the world and the coming century will be Justicialist. **1953** G. I. Blanksten *Perón's Argentina* xii. 276 The current label [for Perón's system] is *Justicialismo.* **1955** G. Pendle *Argentina* vi. 107 The basis of 'justicialist philosophy' was never more clearly expressed, perhaps, than in the following presidential assertion: 'For us there is nothing fixed and nothing to deny. We are anti-Communist because Communists are sectarians, and anti-capitalist because capitalists are sectarians. Our Third Position is not a central position. It is an ideological position which is in the centre, on the right or on the left, according to specific circumstances.' **1971** A. Hennessy in A. Bullock *20th Cent.* 120/2 In spite of..exaggerated claims for the ideology of 'justicialism' as a Third Position —neither capitalism nor communism—Peronism's impact outside Argentina was limited. **1972** *Buenos Aires Herald* 3 Feb. 9/2 A Justicialista Party executive committee member. **1972** *Times* 17 Nov. 16/2 Justicialismo, a vague word described as a middle way between communism and capitalism. *Ibid.* 16 Dec. 4/5 The candidate will be a Justicialist civilian.

jut, *sb.*^{2} Add: **3.** *Comb.*, as **jut-jawed** *a.*, having a jutting jaw.

1943 *Commonweal* (N.Y.) 11 June 195 The company sergeant-major, a tough, jut-jawed, red-faced, bull-necked veteran of the last war. **1952** T. Pyles *Words & Ways Amer. Eng.* v. 94 The dour, thin-lipped, jut-jawed righteousness of his [*sc.* N. Webster's] later portraits. **1959** *Daily Mail* 21 Mar. 6/4 That jut-jawed Marshal of the R.A.F.

jutia, var. *hutia.

jutka (dʒʊ·tkā). [f. Hindi *jhaṭka* a jerk, jolt, lurch.] In southern India, a light two-wheeled vehicle drawn by a horse.

1886 Yule & Burnell *Hobson-Jobson* 362/2 *Jutka*,.. the native cab of Madras, and of Mofussil towns in that Presidency; a conveyance only to be characterised by the epithet *ramshackle*... It consists of a sort of box with venetian windows, on two wheels, and drawn by a miserable pony. It is entered by a door at the back. **1907** B. M. Croker *Company's Servant* xxxi. 318 She..got her baggage on a jutka and drove away. **1927** *Scots Observer* 16 Apr. 3/2 All afternoon jutkas and carts..are arriving. **1947** R. K. Narayan *Astrologer's Day* 4 *Jutka* drivers swore at their horses. **1961** K. Nagarajan *Chron. Kedaram* 117 It was so reminiscent of a *jutka* pony.

jutty, *a.* Delete *rare*$^{-1}$ and add later examples.

1868 G. M. Hopkins *Jrnl.* 19 July (1959) 178 Lying in jutty bends. **1922** A. S. M. Hutchinson *This Freedom* ii. 23 He swung round and pushed his dark face and jutty nose into the face of Bolas. **1937** G. M. Young *Daylight & Champaign* 93 Driving away the birds who nest in the jutty frieze.

juve (dʒūv). Colloq. abbrev. of **juvenile lead.* Also *attrib.*

1935 *Variety* 17 Apr., Jones is a good-looking juve and possesses a corking tenor. **1968** P. Loraine *Dead Men of Sestos* viii. 115 I'm the young tenor, the juve, the one with the tennis racket. **1974** *Observer* 25 Aug. 22/3 The cherished tradition which demands that the worst thing about the Hammer horror [film]s shall be their juve leads.

Juvenal (dʒū·vənăl), *sb.*^{2} Anglicized form of the cognomen of the Roman satirist Decimus Junius *Juvenalis*, used gen. to designate a satirist.

1592 Greene *Groats W. Wit* sig. F1, With thee I ioyne yong Iuuenall [*sc.* Nashe], that byting Satirist. **1693** Dryden tr. *Juvenal's Satires* p. vii, I might find in France, a living Horace and a Juvenal, in the person of the admirable Boileau. **1841** I. D'Israeli *Amenities of Lit.* III. 132 Jonson, the Juvenal of our drama. **1885** *Brewer's Dict. Phrase & Fable* (ed. 17) 469/1 The English Juvenal. John Oldham... The Juvenal of Painters. William Hogarth. **1902** *Daily Chron.* 20 Feb. 3/2 The art of satire is dead in England... The Juvenals of Fleet-street are no more.

juvenile, *a.* and *sb.* Add: **A.** *adj.* **1.** *spec.* Designating young offenders against the law, or the offences committed by them; esp. in *juvenile delinquency, delinquent*; also *juvenile adult*, a person below the legal age of responsibility and above a certain minimum age, who is held to be punishable for breaking the law (the term was discontinued by the Family Law Reform Act of 1969).

1816 *Rep. Soc. investigating Causes Increase in Juvenile Delinquency* 5 It was found that Juvenile Delinquency existed in the metropolis to a very alarming extent. **1817** *Observer* 14 Sept. 1/3 Your Committee have anxiously sought for information as to the number of juvenile delinquents who are annually committed to the different prisons in the metropolis;..the greater part of these Juvenile Offenders..are mixed indiscriminately with old offenders of all ages. **1837** Dickens *Let.* *c* 2 Oct. (1965) I. 315 Many thanks for your statistical Magazine, which contains some tables concerning juvenile delinquency. **1837** —— *O. Twist* (1838) I. xix. 321 Then the Juvenile Delinquent Society comes, and takes the boy away. **1847, 1854** [see Offender]. **1902** [see *Borstal, borstal]. **1916** *Lancet* 2 Feb. 365/1 (*title*) Juvenile crime. **1917** C. Leeson (*title*) The child and the war, being notes on juvenile delinquency. **1926** *Encycl. Brit.* I. 411/1 In 1894 two public inquiries into the administration of prisons and of Home Office schools arrived..at the same.. conclusion, viz: 'that the age 16–21 was the dangerous age; that we must concentrate on that; on the incipient criminal' or, as he was officially christened, the juvenile adult. **1958** *New Statesman* 25 Oct. 551/1 Some years ago when the current crop of juvenile delinquents were being labelled in the press as cosh-boys, I had written an article that contained interviews with some live specimens, hand-picked for me by an underworld acquaintance. **1959** Jowitt *Dict. Eng. Law* II. 1041/1 *Juvenile adult*, a person not less than sixteen and not more than twenty-one. **1964** M. Argyle *Psychol. & Social Probl.* v. 59 Juvenile delinquency is one of our most pressing social problems. *Ibid.* xv. 187 The rate of juvenile crime has risen rapidly during the decade, particularly since 1955.

b. *juvenile lead* = Juvenile *sb.* 2; *spec.* an actor who plays the leading youthful part in a play, etc.; the rôle so played. So *juvenile leading.*

1870 [see *heavy *a.*^{1} 21]. **1885** J. K. Jerome *On Stage* (1891) xi. 102 Juvenile Lead's opinion is that the stage manager is a fool. **1897** G. B. Shaw *Our Theatres in Nineties* (1932) III. 210 This is not human nature or dramatic character; it is juvenile lead, first old man, heavy lead, heavy father. **1910** M. Beerbohm *Around Theatres* (1924) II. 460 The 'ingénue' and 'juvenile lead' of old-fashioned commercial drama. **1946** G. Millar *Horned Pigeon* i. 7 The part..might lead to great things, even to juvenile leads. **1973** J. Porter *It's Murder with Dover* xvi. 160 MacGregor flashed his juvenile lead smile.

2. *juvenile court*, a court of law for the trial of young offenders.

1899 *Illinois Laws* 132 A special court room, to be designated as the juvenile court room, shall be provided ..and the court may, for convenience, be called the 'Juvenile Court'. **1908** *Act* 8 *Edw. VII* c. 67 § 111 A court of summary jurisdiction when hearing charges against children..shall..sit either in a different building ..or on different days.., and a court of summary jurisdiction so sitting is in this Act referred to as a juvenile court. **1944** *Ann. Reg. 1943* 381 More attention than usual was focussed on the work of the Juvenile Courts. **1972** *Daily Tel.* 5 May 13/1 The Scots..abolished juvenile courts and replaced them with a system of children's panels.

3. *Geol.* [tr. G. *juvenil* (E. Suess 1902, in *Verh. d. Ges. deutsch. Naturf. u. Ärzte* 141).] Originating within the earth (or another planet) and brought to the surface for the first time.

1907 *Econ. Geol.* II. 266 Many mineral springs may be of magmatic origin, but since their starting points are inaccessible they can be proved to be juvenile only by showing that they cannot be meteoric. **1909** H. B. C. & W. J. Sollas tr. *Suess's Face of Earth* IV. xv. 549 [The hot springs] of Carlsbad..bring yearly to surface a million kilogrammes of juvenile salt. *Ibid.* 559 We must assume that the juvenile gases are originally liberated beneath the Sal mantle. **1944** *Bull. Geol. Soc. Amer.* LV. 1375 Clearly one cannot hold that the volcano was kept alive merely by free juvenile gas rising from an abyssolithic injection. **1955** [see *connate *a.* 5]. **1973** *Sci. Amer.* Jan. 56/2 One speculation is that deep permafrost is involved, associated perhaps with the arrival near the surface of juvenile water preceding and accompanying the rise of molten rock near the surface of the planet during the volcanic episode apparent to the west.

4. Special collocations: **juvenile foliage, leaf**, a type of foliage characteristic of the immature stages of certain trees, shrubs, or woody climbers, differing in shape, colour, etc., from the adult form; **juvenile hormone** *Ent.*, the hormone that controls the development of larval characteristics in insects; **juvenile wood**, an inner core of wood in a tree, distinguished by particularly small cells.

1957 M. Hadfield *Brit. Trees* 96 The juvenile foliage [of *Cryptomeria*] is spreading, with flatter and softer leaves than the adult. **1971** T. T. Kozlowski *Growth & Devel. Trees* I. iii. 95 Plants derived from needle-leaved cuttings [of *Chamæcyparis pisifera*] retained juvenile foliage if the source tree did so. **1940** V. B. Wigglesworth in *Jrnl. Exper. Biol.* XVII. 221 In previous papers the 'inhibitory hormone' was so called because in its presence the production of imaginal characters at moulting is suppressed. But in view of its probable mode of action through the activation of the nymphal system at the expense of the imaginal, it might be preferable to refer to this hormone as the 'nymphal' or 'juvenile' hormone. **1965** Lee & Knowles *Animal Hormones* xiii. 161 Normal development depends on changes in the relative amounts of ecdysone and the juvenile hormone which are available to the tissues. **1967** *New Scientist* 20 Apr. 154/1 Juvenile hormone..is necessary for the normal growth of immature insects—caterpillars and grubs, for example. **1970** *Daily Tel.* 16 Nov. 6/1 Many South American plants contain similar substances to insect juvenile hormone. **1910** L. Cockayne *N.Z. Plants* iv. 60 After a few weeks its [*sc.* a veronica's] new growth will be of the juvenile form, and juvenile and adult leaves will be on the plant at the same time. **1946** A. B. Jackson *Identification of Conifers* 2 In many cases the juvenile leaves differ in form, attachment or arrangement from those on the adult tree. **1956** F. W. Jane *Struct. Wood* ix. 191 Juvenile wood often has cells of smaller dimensions, often much smaller, than those of the trunk. **1971** T. T. Kozlowski *Growth & Devel. Trees* I. iii. 109 The wood in the region of the pith, which is formed early ..is termed juvenile (sometimes called core or pith) wood.

B. *sb.* **2.** (Later examples.)

1898 G. B. Shaw *Our Theatres in Nineties* (1932) III. 307 Ferdinand Gadd, the leading juvenile of The Wells. **1933** P. Godfrey *Back-Stage* iv. 46 His legs are too short or too long..for him to be a successful male juvenile. *Ibid.* vi. 72 Dramatists, like stage juveniles, are considered young until they are past the age of forty. **1973** *Times* 17 Nov. 11/5 I'm going to be your juvenile next season.

3. A book written for children. Freq. *pl.* Also *attrib.*

1849 *Mother Goose in Hieroglyphics* (1963) (Advt.), Pictures from the history of the Swiss... A very instructive and entertaining Juvenile, designed for children from ten to fifteen years of age. **1908** *Daily Chron.* 27 Nov. 3/5 What would John Newbery say if he were to.. see his old shop..filled with this season's 'juveniles'? **1930** *Publishers' Weekly* 5 July 28 We announce 10 juveniles. **1947** *Times Lit. Suppl.* 15 Nov. 593/2 (Advt.), The exacting and critical Juvenile public in this country.

juvenilia (dʒūvĭni·liă), *sb. pl.* [L., neut. pl. of *juvenilis* JUVENILE *a.*] Literary or artistic works produced in the author's youth (freq. as a title of such works collected). Also *transf.*

1622 G. WITHER (*title*) Ivvenilia: a collection of those poemes which were heretofore imprinted and written by George Wither. **1633** DONNE (*title*) Iuuenilia: or certaine paradoxes and problemes. **1693** DRYDEN tr. *Juvenal's Satires* p. ix, His *Juvenilia*, or Verses written in his Youth. *a* **1849** H. COLERIDGE *Ess. & Marginalia* (1851) II. 265 Whatever effect these juvenilia may have produced at the time, they are quite worthless now. **1896** in Tennyson *Works* 2 Juvenilia. **1929** *Sunday Dispatch* 13 Jan. 10/5 Not that I belong to the school which would trace, in these innocent juvenilia of our nation, an anthropological or historical origin. **1952** *Brontë Soc. Trans.* XII. 126 Prose and verse by Charlotte and Branwell [in M. Christian's 'Census of Brontë Manuscripts in the United States'] classified as unpublished are mostly in the *Juvenilia* category. **1971** W. GÉRIN in C. Brontë *Five Novelettes* 7 Charlotte Brontë wrote the following novelettes between the years 1836 and 1839, from the time when she had just turned twenty until her twenty-third year. They cannot, therefore, be technically reckoned as belonging to her juvenilia. **1973** *Times Lit. Suppl.* 23 Nov. 1453/1 It is always difficult to judge the literary merit of juvenilia.

juvescence (dʒūve·sĕns). *rare.* [irreg. f. JUVE(NILE *a.* and *sb.*: see ADOLESCENCE.] The state of becoming young, juvenescence.

1920 T. S. ELIOT *Ara Vos Prec* 11 In the juvescence of the year Came Christ the tiger. **1948** S. SPENDER in *Time & Tide* 10 Jan. 33/1 That kissing of steel furies Preparing a world's childless juvescence.

juvey, var. *JUVIE.

juvia (dʒū·-, hū·viă). [Amer. Sp.] The Brazilnut. Also *attrib.*

c **1840** W. RHIND *Hist. Vegetable Kingdom* xxxix. 387 The triangular grains which the shell of the juvia incloses, are known in commerce under the name of Brazil nuts. **1852** T. Ross tr. *A. von Humboldt's Personal Narr. Trav. Amer.* II. xxiii. 390 Juvia-trees, which furnish the triangular nuts called in Europe the almonds of the Amazon, or Brazil-nuts. **1858** W. BAIRD *Cycl. Nat. Sci.* 69/1 The natives are very fond of this nut, and celebrate the harvest of the *Juvia* with great rejoicings. **1860** MAYNE REID *Odd People* 142 The splendid fruits of the *Bertholetia excelsa*, or juvia-tree, known in Europe as 'Brazil nuts'.

juvie (dʒū·vi). *U.S. slang.* Also **juvey.** [Colloq. shortening of JUVENILE *a.* and *sb.*] A juvenile or juvenile delinquent; also, a detention centre or a court for juvenile delinquents.

1941 J. SMILEY *Hash House Lingo* 34 *Juvie,* child. **1966** *Time* 2 Dec. 52/3 Los Angeles County police went after the 'juvies' (minors under 18), began carting them off by the busload. **1967** *New Yorker* 25 Feb. 128/3 But the teacher at juvey said, 'You have to finish it.' **1967** E. B. NICKERSON *Kayaks to Arctic* vii. 58, I wondered..if we would have to bail them out of the Canadian equivalent of 'Juvies'. **1970** P. STADLEY *Autumn of Hunter* (1971) viii. 115 Just where would you take me, little juvie? To a drive-in movie?

juxta-. Add: **ju:xta-arti·cular** *a. Anat.*, situated near a joint.

1900 in DORLAND *Med. Dict.* **1910** CASTELLANI & CHALMERS *Man. Trop. Med.* lviii. 1137 (*heading*) Juxta-articular nodules. **1940** *Q. Bull. Northwestern Univ. Med. Sch.* XIV. 270/1 Juxta-articular nodes are non-inflammatory, painless, fibrous, subcutaneous growths.

juxtaglomerular (dʒʊ:kstăglǫme·rŭlăɹ), *a. Anat.* [f. JUXTA- + GLOMERULAR *a.*] Situated next to a glomerulus of the kidney; *juxtaglomerular apparatus,* a structure variously considered to comprise (i) a juxtaglomerular body alone, (ii) one of these bodies and a *macula densa,* or (iii) (also *juxtaglomerular complex*) one of each of these, together with lacis cells and the afferent and efferent arterioles of a glomerulus; *juxtaglomerular body,* a mass of tissue scattered along the wall of the afferent arteriole of a glomerulus, composed of cells (*juxtaglomerular cells*) with conspicuous cytoplasmic granules, believed to be the site of renin secretion.

1935 *Biol. Abstr.* IX. 2181/2 The neuro-myo-arterial juxtaglomerular segments of the kidney. **1939** *Proc. Soc. Exper. Biol. & Med.* XLII. 227 The media of these vessels [*sc.* the interlobular and glomerular arteries] is composed not only of ordinary smooth muscle cells but also of larger, more afibrillar and probably less contractile cells. In the kidney these cells are found all along the arterial vascular tree and accumulate in groups at the vascular poles of the glomeruli to form the 'juxta glomerular apparatus' or 'polkissen'. **1942** J. F. A. McMANUS in *Lancet* 3 Oct. 394/2 (*heading*) The juxtaglomerular complex. *Ibid.,* There are an increasing number of references ..to a structure termed the 'juxtaglomerular apparatus'. By this term we mean a group of apparently specialised structures in relation to, and including, the afferent and efferent arterioles of the glomerulus. The term 'complex' is used here in preference to Goormaghtigh's term 'apparatus', since he restricts the meaning to the vascular and perivascular arteriolar structures. *Ibid.* 395/1 Ruyter in 1925 saw granular, afibrillar cells in the juxtaglomerular portion of the afferent arteriole in the mouse. **1952** A. C. ALLEN *Kidney* ii. 32/1 The macula densa in combination with the juxtaglomerular body is referred to as the juxtaglomerular apparatus. **1958** *Amer. Jrnl. Path.* XXXIV. 863 (*heading*) The juxtaglomerular cells in man. **1968** PAGE & McCUBBIN *Renal Hypertension* i. 40 (*heading*) Structure of the juxtaglomerular apparatus. **1968** E. L. BECKER *Struct. Basis Renal Dis.* i. 34 The juxtaglomerular apparatus..is considered to consist of four portions: the specialized portion of the afferent arteriole containing characteristic granules; the first portion of the distal convoluted tubule, or macula densa; the cushion of cells at the vascular pole, continuous with the mesangium, termed the polkissen 'lacis' cells; and the efferent arteriole.

juxtaposition. Add: † **b.** *spec.* in *Cryst.* Contactual union between twinned crystals; *juxtaposition twin,* a composite crystal of two (or more) crystals joined along a plane; a contact twin. *Obs.*

1883 *Encycl. Brit.* XVI. 366/1 In aragonite the crystals are partly interpenetrating, and partly merely in juxtaposition. **1890** G. H. WILLIAMS *Elem. Crystallogr.* ix. 185 Two individual crystals in twinning position are usually, though by no means always, united in a plane, which may or may not coincide with the twinning plane. Twins of this sort are called contact or juxtaposition twins. **1911** A. E. H. TUTTON *Crystallogr.* xxvi. 420 In the case of 'juxtaposition twins' the plane of union, whether the twin plane or not, is known as the 'plane of composition'. **1917** F. M. JAEGER *Lect. Princ. Symmetry* vii. 171 The classification of twins into such as are produced by juxtaposition or by penetration, may have certain advantages from a practical standpoint.

juxtapositive (dʒʊkstăpǫ·zĭtiv), *a. Gram.* [f. JUXTAPOSIT(ION + -IVE.] The designation of a case expressing juxtaposition.

1880 A. H. SAYCE *Introd. Sci. Lang.* I. v. 370 Steinthal, however, goes on to divide his formless languages into 'juxta-positive' and 'compositive'. **1890** A. S. GATSCHET *Klamath Indians* 1. 490 Juxtapositive case in -tana.

K

K. Add: **3. b.** In *Physics* *k* (or *K*) is the symbol of thermal conductivity. [Introduced by J. B. J. Fourier, 1822.]

[**1822** J. B. J. FOURIER *Théorie anal. de la Chaleur* i. 54 Nous avons choisi ce même coëfficient K, qui entre dans la seconde équation, pour la mesure de la conducibilité spécifique de chaque substance.] **1850** in *Trans. R. Soc. Edin.* (1864) XXIII. 137 The specific heat of the metal being known, we can convert this amount of heat or flux across *x* into absolute measure; for the Flux is = – K *dv/dx* and *dv/dx* is known... Thus every experiment becomes an independent means of finding K. **1880** *Encycl. Brit.* XI. 579/2 Let *k* be the thermal conductivity of the substance and *c* its thermal capacity per unit bulk. **1947** *Sci. News* IV. 147 With glass..the heat conductivity (*k*) is 0·002. *Ibid.* 148 Steel (*k* = 0·10). **1969** *Jane's Freight Containers 1968–69* 239/1 The k-value according to choice of insulating material is about 0·4 to 0·5 kcal/m² h°C.

c. *Physics.* The designation of one of the strongest Fraunhofer lines, situated in the extreme violet at a wavelength of 3934 Å and due to absorption by calcium ions.

1879 *Proc. R. Soc.* XXVIII. 367 The calcium line with wave-length 4226..appears more or less expanded with a dark line in the middle..; the remaining bright lines of calcium are also frequently seen in the like condition, but sometimes the dark line appears in the middle of K (the more refrangible of Fraunhofer's lines H), when there is none in the middle of H. **1897** *Ibid.* LXI. 437 The H and K lines have become thin and defined. **1967** R. G. GIOVANELLI in J. N. Xanthakis *Solar Physics* xii. 353 The Balmer lines and the *H* and *K* lines of ionized calcium are..strong Fraunhofer absorption lines.

d. In *Physics* and *Chem.* *k* is the symbol of Boltzmann's constant.

1901 *Sci. Abstr.* IV. 230 For a comparison of his own reasoning with that of Boltzmann on gas molecules, the author deduces from *k* an estimate ($6{\cdot}175 \times 10^{23}$) for the number of molecules in the gramme molecule of any element. **1915**, etc. [see *BOLTZMANN]. **1962** W. B. THOMPSON *Introd. Plasma Physics* ii. 17 A temperature of 11,600°K is needed to give an energy kT of 1 eV so that the mean kinetic energy of a molecule, $\frac{3}{2}kT$, reaches 1 eV only when $T = 7{,}730$°K.

e. In *Physics* *K* is used to designate the series of X-ray emission lines of shorter wavelength obtained by exciting the atoms of any particular element (cf. *L 6* a); these arise from electron transitions to the innermost, lowest-energy atomic orbit, of principal quantum number 1, which is thus termed the *K-shell*, and electrons in this shell *K-electrons*. **K(-electron) capture**, the capture by an atomic nucleus of one of the *K*-electrons.

1911 C. G. BARKLA in *Phil. Mag.* XXII. 406 It is seen that the radiations fall into two distinct series, here denoted by the letters K and L. [*Note*] Previously denoted by letters B and A... The letters K and L are, however, preferable, as it is highly probable that series of radiations both more absorbable and more penetrating exist. **1923** H. L. BROSE tr. *Sommerfeld's Atomic Struct. & Spectral Lines* iii. 144 If the excitation occurs through the agency of cathode rays, it is easy to imagine that the tearing-off of the 'K-electron' is effected by the impact of a cathode-ray particle that has penetrated into the atom. **1923** E. N. DA C. ANDRADE *Struct. Atom* vi. 100 Moseley identified in the *K* series the two lines which he called α and β. ..In the *L* series he identified five lines. **1938** L. B. LOEB *Atomic Struct.* iii. 83 A tube with 1,470 volt electrons may excite *K* x-rays of Al, while it takes 60,600 volt electrons to excite the *K* x-rays of tungsten. **1946** H. SEMAT *Introd. Atomic Physics* (ed. 2) viii. 342 Probably the most clear-cut example of *K*-electron capture is the radioactive disintegration of vanadium, $_{23}V^{49}$, into titanium, $_{22}Ti^{49}$, with the capture of a *K* electron by the vanadium nucleus to form a titanium atom in the *K* state. **1951** J. DOUGALL tr. *Born's Atomic Physics* (ed. 5) vii. 220 *K*-capture should therefore compete with β-decay. **1970** HURST & TURNER *Elem. Radiation Physics* ii. 24 A few nuclei..capture an atomic electron from outside the nucleus, most often from the K-shell, and emit a neutrino.

f. *Physics* and *Chem.* In the old quantum theory *k* is the azimuthal or subordinate quantum number (introduced by N. Bohr 1920, in *Zeitschr. f. Physik* II. 445), which determines the shape of electronic orbits of the same *n*; (now superseded by the quantum number *l*). In molecular spectroscopy *K* is a quantum number which in diatomic and linear molecules represents the total angular momentum apart from electronic spin (now usu. replaced by *N*), and in polyatomic molecules represents the component of the total momentum about an axis of symmetry.

1922 A. D. UDDEN tr. *Bohr's Theory of Spectra* II. iii. 44 The perturbations are periodic, so that we may assume that to each energy value of a stationary state of the unperturbed system there belongs a series of discrete energy values of a whole number *k*. *Ibid.* III. iii. 85 Where it is necessary to differentiate between orbits corresponding to various values of the quantum number *k*, a central orbit, characterized by given values of the quantum numbers *n* and *k*, will be referred to as an n_k orbit. **1930** R. S. MULLIKEN in *Physical Rev.* XXXVI. 613 In [Hund's] case *b*, $\Lambda h/2\pi$ and the nuclear angular momentum combine to give a quantised resultant... For the corresponding quantum number..the designation *K* is now recommended. The possible values of *K* are Λ, $\Lambda+1$, $\Lambda+2$... There is usually a small magnetic field in the molecule parallel to *K*, so that *K* and *S* form a resultant *J*. **1934** H. L. BROSE tr. *Sommerfeld's Atomic Struct. & Spectral Lines* (ed. 3) ii. 115 In wave mechanics the azimuthal quantum number, our n_ϕ or Bohr's *k*.., becomes replaced by the quantity $l = n_\phi - 1$, $l = 0, 1, 2...$ **1961** POWELL & CRASEMANN *Quantum Mech.* i. 24 A perturbation of the force, such as might be produced by the presence of other electrons, has the effect of removing the degeneracy, so that states with the same value of *n* but different values of *k* have different energies. **1962** P. J. & B. DURRANT *Introd. Adv. Inorg. Chem.* vii. 226 Paschen-Back effect [for diatomic molecules] (strong magnetic field)... **K** and **S** are not coupled together but are coupled directly to the field. **1966** C. N. BANWELL *Fund. Molecular Spectroscopy* iii. 94 Parallel Vibrations [of Symmetric Top Molecules]. Here the selection rule is: $\Delta v = \pm 1$, $\Delta J = 0, \pm 1$, $\Delta K = 0$.

g. *Psychol.* The letter chosen to represent the spatial factor, or aptitude for remembering form and structure, in some ability-tests.

1935 *Brit. Jrnl. Psychol.* Monogr. Suppl. xx. vii. 65 In order to distinguish these eight tests from the rest of the table they may for convenience be called the *K* tests. *Ibid.* 75 Therefore there is in them [*sc.* specific correlations], over and above '*g*', *one group factor*; this we name the *K* factor. **1944** L. L. THURSTONE *Factorial Study Perception* iii. 117 It is quite likely that the factor *K* is determined by experimental dependence. **1950** SPEARMAN & JONES *Human Ability* xii. 132 For the first time, the spatial test does, in some degree, measure K. **1969** P. E. VERNON *Intelligence & Cultural Environment* ix. 59 Embedded Figures and the Kohs Block test are good measures of the *k* factor of British psychologists..and this is much the same as Thurstone's original *S* (spatial) factor.

h. [From its use as an abbrev. for *kilo-*.] In connection with *Computers* K or k is used to represent 1,000 (or 1,024: see quot. 1970).

1966 P. D. REYNOLDS *Computer ABC* 54 The internal storage of computers is commonly arranged..to hold a quantity of data which is some power of 2, for example, 4096 characters, bytes or words, which is 2^{12}. The convention is to refer to this number as 4K. 64K..amounts to 65,536(2^{16}). **1967** COX & GROSE *Organiz. Bibliogr. Rec. by Computer* II. 2 It seemed desirable..wherever possible to ignore the limitations of the computer available to us (a KDF 9 with a store size of 16 K 48-bit words). **1970** O. DOPPING *Computers & Data Processing* ii. 35 Sometimes, a 'K' is used for a number which is either 1,000 or 1,024, depending on whether the context calls for integral powers of 10 or 2. If we say that a certain computer has a memory capacity of 4 K words, then, this means either 4,000 or 4,096 words, depending on whether the computer in question has a decimal or binary address system. However, the usage is a little loose: the number $2^{16} = 65{,}536$ is written either as 64 K or 65 K. **1971** *Daily Tel.* 21 July 20 (Advt.), I.B.M. programmers... Sal. from £1,600 to £2·4k. **1971** *New Scientist* 9 Sept. 569/1 Typically, a minicomputer has a minimum memory of between one and eight K words.

4. b. K.H.B. *colloq.* (see quot. 1925); K.O.S.B., King's Own Scottish Borderers. **c.** K used *colloq.* for *knighthood*; also K.B.E., Knight Commander of the Order of the British Empire; K.B.S., Knight of the Blessed Sacrament; K.C.B. (examples); K.C.V.O., Knight Commander of the Victorian Order; K.G. (examples); K.S.G., Knight of the Order of St. Gregory the Great. **e.** Also many other abbreviations of names of units in which *k* represents *kilo-*, as kcal., kcal, kilocalorie(s); kHz, kilohertz; kVA (also kv.-a., etc.), kilovolt-ampere(s); kW (also K.W., kw., etc.), kilowatt(s); kWh, kilowatt-hour(s). **f.** In miscellaneous abbreviations, as °K, K, (degree) Kelvin (see *KELVIN, KELVIN 3 b); K.E., k.e., kinetic energy; K.G.B. [Komitet Gosudarstvennoĭ Bezopasnosti] = Committee of State Security (U.S.S.R.); K.i.H., K.I.H., Kaisar-i-Hind; K.K.K., Ku Klux Klan; K.L., Kuala Lumpur; K.L.M. [Koninklijke Luchtvaart Maatschappij], Royal Dutch Airlines; K.M.T., Kuomintang; K.O., k.o. = knock(ed) out (cf. *KAYO *v.* and *sb.*); K.P. (*U.S.*), kitchen police(man); K.P.D. [Kommunistische Partei Deutschlands], German Communist Party; k.p.h., kilometres per hour; K *ration* [f. the initial letter of the surname of Ancel *K*eys (1904–   ), American physiologist], a package of concentrated food; KWIC = *key-word-in-context* (*KEY *sb.*¹ 17).

1911 *Physical Rev.* XXXIII. 226 The value of the ice point..was taken as 273·2°K. **1937** M. W. ZEMANSKY *Heat & Thermodynamics* xiii. 232 The isothermal compressibility of copper is plotted against the Kelvin temperature in Fig. 72. Above about 100°K the rise..is approximately linear. **1959** *Sci. News* LI. 11 The lowest temperature that can conveniently be obtained by evaporating helium under reduced pressure is about 1°K. **1970** *Nature* 10 Oct. 144/2 The coolest spectrum recorded over the Antarctic plateau indicates a surface temperature of 190 K (– 83° C). **1972** *Amat. Photographer* 12 Jan. 38 Household Bulbs...150 watts is usually the maximum, with a colour temperature of around 2,700 to 2,900°K. **1910** *Lett. Lord Kilbracken & Gen. Godley* (*c* 1932) 13 Long may you live to wear your honours, and I hope that 'the coming K' will not be long deferred. **1966** J. BETJEMAN *High & Low* 70 That very near miss for an All Souls' Fellowship, The recent compensation of a 'K'. **1968** *Listener* 13 June 770/3 A 'K' isn't certain any more, even if you're a civil servant. **1973** *Times* 24 Aug. 12/8 There might not have been much merit in a political knighthood, but there was no harm in it... The 'K', when it came, was a boon to the Member's wife, and a blessing to the Member himself. **1952** 'W. COOPER' *Struggles of Albert Woods* IV. i. 206 They tell me your Principal got a plain K and was hoping for K.B.E. **1968** *Listener* 12 Dec. 787/3 He was given a KBE for his efforts. **1916** *Let.* 12 June in *Knights of Blessed Sacrament* (Catholic Truth Soc.) (1918) 14, I have started the K.B.S. among my men here. **1923** A. O'CONNOR *Knight in Palestine* ii. 11 The K.B.S. and another Catholic made ready the altar. **1954** R. T. SANDERSON *Introd. Chem.* iv. 43 Larger quantities of heat are measured in kilocalories, which are 1000 calories each. They are sometimes abbreviated as Cal with a capital C; more commonly they are simply kcal. **1964** N. G. CLARK *Mod. Org. Chem.* iii. 29 The energy required to bring about this rotation is seen to be 5 kcal, a relatively trivial amount capable of being supplied by the thermal motion of neighbouring molecules. **1849** THACKERAY *Three Sailors* in S. Bevan *Sand & Canvas* xxv. 341 There's the British fleet a riding at anchor, With Admiral Napier, K.C.B. **1880** E. W. HAMILTON *Diary* 29 Aug. (1972) I. 40 Loch, the Governor of the Isle of Man, is to be a KCB. **1904** *Westm. Gaz.* 8 Jan. 6/2 Lord Lawrence used to speak of England's aggressive policy in India as the 'K.C.B.' mania. **1972** *Times* 6 May 1/4 Sir James..was appointed KCB in the New Year Honours. **1897** *Whitaker's Almanack* 108 The Royal Victorian Order. Instituted 21st April, 1896... Knights Grand Cross. G.C.V.O... Knights Commanders. K.C.V.O. **1968** *Listener* 29 Aug. 278/1 His sufferings..were not assuaged by a KCVO. **1888** A. AVELING *Mech. & Exper. Sci.: Mech.* xiii. 137, *k.e.* of the two masses after collision = $mv^2/2$. **1909** JACKSON & ROBERTS *First Dynamics* 88 The gain of K.E. equals arithmetically the work done by the forces. **1965** VAN WYLEN & SONNTAG *Fund. Classical Thermodynamics* v. 84 *E* = Internal energy + Kinetic energy + Potential energy or $E = U + KE + PE$. **1876** TROLLOPE *Prime Minister* IV. iv. 52 (*heading*) The new K.G. **1880** E. W. HAMILTON *Diary* 23 Aug. (1972) I. 37 A Garter is vacant by death of Lord Stratford de Redcliffe ..Lord Palmerston is a precedent for a commoner receiving a KG. **1904** K.G. [see *GUNNER 1 c]. **1972** *Whitaker's Almanack 1973* 463 The Viscount Montgomery of Alamein K.G., G.C.B., D.S.O. **1960** *Analog Science Fact/Fiction* Oct. 122/2 The KGB was once again checking on every foreigner. **1966** J. PORTER *Sour Cream* v. 58 The K.G.B. is willing to shell out a small fortune in roubles for me, dead or alive. **1972** K. BENTON *Spy in Chancery* i. 8 The Russian who's made the approach..isn't the type of KGB operative one would expect to make a run for it. **1916** 'TAFFRAIL' *Pincher Martin* iv. 62 He was a K.H.B., and they were not sorry to be rid of his presence. **1925** FRASER & GIBBONS *Soldier & Sailor Words* 134 *A K.H.B.*: a King's Hard Bargain. A worthless or incorrigible fellow. (Old Service term.) **1955** *Proc. IRE* XLIII. 880/3 A happy solution would be more widespread use of the term 'hertz', meaning cycle-per-second. Thus the units of frequency would be hertz (or hz), khz, and Mhz. **1974** *Electronics* 26 Dec. 48E A portable a-m signal generator..covers 85 kHz to 100 MHz. *a* **1912** W. T. ROGERS *Dict. Abbrev.* (1913) 108/2 K.I.H., Kaiser-i-Hind (Emperor of India). **1942** PARTRIDGE *Dict. Abbrev.* K.i.H. or K.I.H., the Kaisar-i-Hind Medal; for useful service in India. **1973** *Daily Tel.* 20 Sept. 36/7 Alice Headwards-Hunter, K.I.H., F.R.C.S.E., D.C.H., formerly of Calcutta. **1872** in W. L. Fleming *Documentary Hist. Reconstruction* (1907) II. 132 We advanced upon the supposed K.K.K.'s. **1877** J. M. BEARD *K.K.K. Sk.* 35 The horses of the raid were.. furnished with all those *cap-a-pie* appointments of K.K.K. regalia. **1952** *N.Y. Times* 1 Aug. 16/2 For conspiracy to flog a Negro woman, the so-called 'Imperial Wizard' of the local KKK has been given..four years. **1970** G. JACKSON *Let.* Apr. in *Soledad Brother* (1971) 48 I've already mentioned that most of them are K.K.K. types. **1961** 'G. BLACK' *Suddenly, at Singapore* ix. 129 From there we could have been going to K.L. or anywhere in Malaya. **1973** *Observer* 7 Oct. 36/6 Here is the capital, Kuala Lumpur, which the old Malay hands called KL and now everybody does. **1933** *Meccano Mag.* Mar. 193/1 A pilot flying on the K.L.M. route to Batavia. **1968** *Listener* 28 Nov. 704/3 KLM suggest you come to Amsterdam just to see the airport. **1959** *Times Lit. Suppl.* 8 May 270/4 Two months later Chiang struck again by excluding Communists from any higher posts in the K.M.T. **1969** J. M. GULLICK *Malaysia* ii. 85 At one time the Chinese middle class gave its support to the Kuomintang, an effective if externally orientated nationalist movement, but the KMT was ground between..British restrictions.. and..communist penetration of the Chinese working class. **1972** 'M. HEBDEN' *Killer for Chairman* I. ix. 115, I last saw you in Canton... There was one of the K.M.T.

generals still hiding there. 1922 T. Burke *London Spy* 209 As a youth the ring attracted him... A few k.o.'s put an end to that. 1923 H. Cox *Dogs & I* xxii. 209 The Field Spaniel has received the 'K.O.' and taken the count! 1927 *Observer* 25 Dec. 12/6 His record..includes a k.o. victory over Paul Berlenbach. *Ibid.*, Knut Hansen, who k.o. Phil Scott in the first round. 1928 *Daily Express* 25 June 17/7 Young Stanley..was then k.o. by a right swing to the jaw. 1951 'J. Wyndham' *Day of Triffids* viii. 142 Coker an' another chap was giving them the k.o. as they tripped. 1971 *Weekend World* (Johannesburg) 9 May 1/2 Morodi said he was not upset by the defeat—the first k.o. he has suffered in 70 fights. 1909 *Who's Who* p. xi/1 K.O.S.B. King's Own Scottish Borderers. 1914 F. W. Spicer *Diary* in P. Young *Brit. Army* (1967) xv. 203 On our right was the 13th Infantry Brigade, with the 2/K.O.S.Bs. joining up with our right Company. 1924 *Cricketer Ann. 1923–4* 82 The band and pipers of the K.O.S.B.'s. 1964 'T. Carew' *Vanished Army* II. 128 The K.O.Y.L.I. saw strange faces in their depleted ranks—men of the Suffolks, K.O.S.B. and Manchesters. 1917 D. C. Falls *Army & Navy Information* 84 K.P., Kitchen Police. A mild form of punishment. 1921 J. Dos Passos *3 Soldiers* I. 10 The men..filed by the great tin buckets at the door, out of which meat and potatoes were splashed into each plate by a sweating K.P. in blue denims. 1929 [see *kitchen police* s.v. *kitchen *sb.* 7]. 1956 B. Holiday *Lady sings Blues* (1973) xviii. 143 After all the big personnel experts got together to figure out a job that was right for a city girl like me, I was cast for the part of Cinderella of Cottage No. 6. This was nothing but a fairy-tale name for permanent K.P. 1973 *Publishers Weekly* 25 June 70/2 For an uncertain spell he struggles through the miserable childhood of 'Norma Jean' in a welter of secondhand conjectures—Mailer doing biographical KP. 1922 *Encycl. Brit.* XXXI. 280/2 The violent agitation conducted by the central committee of the K.P.D. in Berlin. 1935 C. Isherwood *Mr Norris changes Trains* vi. 98, I am not a member of the Communist Party..I merely sympathize with the attitude of the K.P.D. to certain non-political problems. 1964 *New Statesman* 28 Feb. 332/1 Relations with Germany—and with the German Communist Party, the KPD—stood at the centre of the picture. 1966 G. B. Mair *Kisses from Satan* ix. 106 They were doing over a hundred k.p.h. on a snaky road. 1972 W. Garner *Ditto, Brother Rat!* xxiii. 172 The speedo needle crept past the 150 kph mark. 1944 *R.A.F. Jrnl.* Aug. 283 We get American 'K' rations, with a few extras. 1967 'T. Carew' *Korea* ii. 19 A K ration consisted of a tin of compressed meat hash, coffee, powdered milk, a fruit bar, cigarettes, chewing gum, and toilet paper. 1909 Webster, K.S.G. 1905 S. P. Thompson *Dynamo-Electr. Machinery* (ed. 7) II. iii. 173 An 8-pole, 60 KVA three-phase generator. 1930 *Engineering* 14 Mar. 355/1 Supplies to the villages will be..through pole transformers with capacities of 50, 20 and 10 kv.-a. 1959 *B.S.I. News* June 9/1 The standard applies to power transformers, reactors and earthing transformers having windings insulated with four different classes of insulating material, with single-phase ratings of 1kVA and above or polyphase ratings of 2kVA or above. 1905 A. H. Bate *Princ. Electr. Power* iii. 34 Electrical power can thus be expressed in either of three units, namely:—The watt, equal to 1 volt multiplied by 1 ampere. The kilowatt (K.W.), equal to 1000 watts. And the electrical horse-power. 1930 *Engineering* 23 May 667/1 The maximum load in the area during 1928–29 was 26,059 kw., [etc.]. 1959 *Chambers's Encycl.* V. 93/2 Central power stations for public electricity supply may range in capacity from the comparatively small size of 40,000 kW to the very large capacity of 500,000 kW or more. 1930 *Engineering* 28 Feb. 299/2 The best yearly record has been reduced to as low as 12,500 B.Th.U. per kw.-h. sent out. 1963 *Times* 3 June 12/1 The Minister expressed his belief that in 1968–70 30,000m. kWh of a total electricity production of 260,000m. kWh will be produced by France's atomic plants. 1959 H. P. Luhn in *IBM Corporation ASDD Rep.* RC-127 (*title*) Keyword-in-context index for technical literature (KWIC index). 1967 Cox & Grose *Organiz. Bibliogr. Rec. by Computer* vi. 154 It has been decided not to produce a KWIC index at this stage. 1969 *Computers & Humanities* III. 166 An obvious prerequisite for this kind of dictionary construction is large key-word-in-context (KWIC) lists drawing on large samples of the language.

ka (kā), *sb.* Also **kaa.** The name given by the ancient Egyptians to a spiritual part of a human being or a god which survived after death and could reside in a statue of the dead person.

a 1892 Tennyson in A. G. Weld *Glimpses Tennyson* (1903) 119, I believe that beside our material body we possess an immaterial body, something like what the ancient Egyptians called the Ka. 1905 E. F. Benson *Image in Sand* i. 11 Somebody's Ka—his ghost, you know, or his astral body. 1923 *Glasgow Herald* 22 Feb. 4 The Princess has a Ka, or better self. 1952 J. M. White *Anc. Egypt* 40 The Ka lived in the tomb with the mummy. 1968 V. Ions *Egyptian Mythol.* 123 The *ka*, the vital principle of a man or of a god. 1972 *Daily Tel.* (Colour Suppl.) 3 Mar. 29/4 The Ancient Egyptians, whose civilisation goes back earlier than 3,000 BC, believed that the *ka* or spirit of a man could only survive if his body was preserved.

kaaba, kaabeh, varr. Caaba.

Kababish (kăbā·biʃ). Also 8 **Cubbabeesh,** 9 **Kobabeish.** [Arab. *ḳabābīš*, pl. of *ḳabbāšī*.] A nomadic Arab people of the northern Kordofan and Dongola provinces of the Sudan. Also *attrib.*

1790 J. Bruce *Trav.* IV. viii. x. 515 Lately the Beni Gerar, Beni Faisara, and Cubba-beesh, have expelled the ancient Arabs of Bahiouda. *a* 1817 J. L. Burckhardt *Trav. Nubia* (1822) 438 The Djerar, Kobabeish, and Feysara live to the north and north-east. 1861 J. Petherick *Egypt, Soudan & Cent. Afr.* xvii. 282 The entire Kababish nomade tribe inhabiting the northern confines of the province emigrated to Darfour. 1891 F. R. Wingate *Mahdiism & Egyptian Sudan* ix. 288 The Kababish, who lived in the desert west of Dongolee. 1898 Alford & Sword *Egyptian Soudan* I. ii. 26 The earliest and most important revolt against the Khalifa was the rising of the Kababish Arabs. 1918 C. G. & B. Z. Seligman in *Harvard Afr. Stud.* II. 105 The Kabâbîsh constitute the richest and most powerful of the Arab tribes of the Anglo-Egyptian Sudan. 1954 H. A. MacMichael *Sudan* vii. 74 Little tribal authority survived except among those nomadic tribes, such as the Kababish. 1960 A. Tibble *With Gordon in Sudan* ii. 48 Those camel-owning nomads whom Gordon would meet between Dongola and Metemma were the Kababish.

kabad(d)i (kăbā·di). [Tamil.] A game popular in northern India and Pakistan played between two teams of nine boys or young men (see quot. 1935). Also *attrib.*

1935 W. M. Ryburn *School Organization* 278–80 Kabaddi... 3. Each team consists of nine players... 5. The members of each team remain in their respective semicircles... 10. A player scores a point for his team if he succeeds in getting back to his semicircle after touching some opponent (with the hand only) or after pushing some opponent out of his semicircle provided that he holds his breath all the time. He will say that word 'kabaddi' over and over to show that he is holding his breath... An attempt by a player to touch an opponent is known as a kabaddi. 1943 Moraes & Stimson *Introd. India* (ed. 3) 171 Among Indian games *kabadi* (*hu-tu-tu*) and *kho-kho* are prominent (they are too complicated to describe here). 1965 E. Linton *World in Grain of Sand* x. 172 There was volley ball, tug of war and 'kabadi'. Kabadi, the Indian wrestling game, is fascinating to watch. 1969 *Femina* (Bombay) 26 Dec. 45/1 The versatile collegians of Bombay lifted the Inter-Varsity table tennis, kabaddi and swimming titles. *Ibid.* 45/4 (*caption*) Rajkumari Jain..during the inter-varsity kabaddi tourney. 1971 *Illustr. Weekly India* 11 Apr. 51/1 (*caption*) A variety of Indian games (like *khokho* and *kabaddi*) find play here. 1974 *Dawn* 17 Apr. 4/3 Special attention was being paid to the popularization of indigenous games like Kabaddi and even a National Kabaddi Federation had been formed.

Kabaka (kăbā·kă). The Bantu title which was given to the ruler of the province of Buganda in Uganda. Hence **Kaba·kaship,** the office of Kabaka.

1878 H. M. Stanley *Through Dark Continent* I. 189 General jack-of-all-trades for the *Kabaka*. 1925 J. W. Mackail *J. L. Strachan-Davidson* 90 The choice of an English tutor for the eight-year-old Kabaka of Uganda. 1954 *Ann. Reg. 1953* 123 The U.K. Government had withdrawn recognition from the Kabaka of Buganda. 1960 *Economist* 8 Oct. 136/2 The public esteem for the institution of the Kabakaship in Buganda. 1966 *Ibid.* 9 July 139/1 Mr Obote seems to intend to maintain the Kabakaship. *Ibid.* 139/2 Any descendant of Mutesa I is eligible for selection as Kabaka. 1971 *Sunday Nation* (Nairobi) 11 Apr. 6/2 Mutesa was their last Kabaka and..Uganda is to stay a Republic.

kabane (kăbā·ne). Also **kabané.** [Jap.] In ancient Japan, a series or system of titles of rank.

1890 B. H. Chamberlain *Things Japanese* 252 The *kabane* or *sei*, a very ancient and aristocratic sort of family name, but now so widely diffused as to include several surnames in the narrower sense of the word. 1904 L. Hearn *Japan: Attempt at Interpretation* xii. 260 Caste would not seem to have developed any very rigid structure in Japan; and there were early tendencies to a confusion of the kabané. 1931 G. B. Sansom *Japan* I. ii. 39 An integral part of the clan system..was the system of titles, or *kabane*. 1970 J. W. Hall *Japan from Prehist. to Mod. Times* v. 36 A more precise set of titles of rank (*kabane*) had also been evolved.

kabaragoya (kabaragōᵘ·yă). Also **kabragoya.** [Etym. unknown.] The water monitor, *Varanus salvator*, a large lizard found in south-eastern Asia.

1681 R. Knox *Ceylon* I. vii. 30 There is a Creature here called *Kobberaguion*, resembling an Alligator. The biggest may be five or six foot long, speckled black and white. 1892 C. F. G. Cumming *Two Happy Years in Ceylon* (ed. 4) II. xx. 176 A gigantic lizard, or rather iguana, of a greenish-grey colour, with yellow stripes and spots, called by the natives kabragoya, awoke from its midday sleep. ..The kabragoya is amphibious. 1960 H. W. Parker tr. *Mertens's World of Amphibians & Reptiles* x. 181 In south-eastern Asia the large Kabara Goya (*Varanus salvator*), despite its timidity, prefers to be associated with man.

Kabardian (kăbā·ɹdiăn), *sb.* and *a.* Also **Kabard, Kabardan, Kabardin(e), Kabardinian.** [f. Russ. *Kabarda* (place-name) + -ian.] **A.** *sb.* **a.** A member of one of the peoples inhabiting the Kabardino-Balkarian Republic in the northern Caucasus, related ethnically to the Circassians, of Caucasian race but non-Indo-European in language. **b.** The north-western Caucasian language of this people.

1824 *Encycl. Brit.* III. 166/2 The most remarkable are the Kabardines,..the Kisti, the Ossetes. 1888 *Ibid.* XXIII. 514/2 Kabards, Circassians, Osses, and Karapapakhs. 1931 G. C. Wheeler tr. *Nansen's Through Caucasus* 43 The Kabardians live on the north side of the Caucasus along the Terek. 1956 J. Lotz in Saporta & Bastian *Psycholinguistics* (1961) 10/1 In Kabardian, also of the Caucasus. 1960 A. H. Kuipers *Phoneme & Morpheme in Kabardian* 8 The Kabardians differed from their Western relatives in that they formed a well-developed feudal ceremony. 1965 D. Fidlon tr. *Trunov's Trip N. Caucasus* 11 'The place swarms with birds,' the Kabardinian continued.

B. *adj.* Of, pertaining to, or characteristic of the Kabardians or their language.

1902 [see *Ingush]. 1940 J. F. Baddeley *Rugged Flanks Caucasus* II. xxii. 220 This ceremonial observance is..a point of honour with the Kabardán nobility. 1950 D. Jones *Phoneme* 222 The Kabardian language of the Caucasus. 1965 D. Fidlon tr. *Trunov's Trip N. Caucasus* 14 She was a graceful Kabardinian girl with a healthy suntan.

kabeljou (kā·bəlyau, kǫ·bəlyau, ‖ ka·bəlyōᵘ). *S. Afr.* Also **cabaljao, cabeliau, kabbeljou, kabeljaauw, -jauw, -jouw, kobeljauw, -jouw** and, abbreviated, ***kob**[2] [Afrikaans, = Du. *kabeljauw* (see Cabilliau).] A large marine food fish, *Johnius hololepidotus*, of the family Sciænidæ.

1731 [see Cabilliau]. 1838 J. E. Alexander *Expedition Interior Afr.* II. iv. 83 We got a great prize in a stranded cabaljao, fifty pounds weight, like a huge salmon. 1912 J. T. Cunningham *Reptiles, Amphibia, Fishes* 277 The name kabeljaauw [= cod]..in South Africa has been transferred to a fish of a very different species,..the maigre, *Sciaena aquila*. 1913 C. Pettman *Africanderisms* 271 Kobeljauw or Kabeljauw. 1930 C. L. Biden *Sea-Angling Fishes of Cape* 109 The kabeljou is often mistaken for the geelbek. 1950 *Cape Times* 17 Nov. 13/8 Last week-end kobeljouw catches were kept down by the difficulty of casting into the teeth of the wind. 1952 *Ibid.* 7 Nov. 3/5 Fishing-boats brought home the first few kabbeljou of the season. 1959 *Ibid.* 16 Nov 2/5 A..visitor..landed a 94-pound Kabeljouw in the Klein Rivier lagoon. 1973 *Farmer's Weekly* (S. Afr.) 13 June 102 The species being tagged include grunter and white steenbras, elf (shad), kob (kabeljauw or Cape Salmon in Natal) haarders (mullet) and leervis (garrick).

Kabistan (kæbistā·n). Also **Cabistan.** Erron. for *Kubistan* after the district of Kuba in Azerbaijan, used *attrib.* or *absol.* to designate a finely woven, short napped rug or carpet with intricate geometric design made in that area; also called *Kuba.

1900 J. K. Mumford *Oriental Rugs* ix. 111 In the Kabistans the weft and sometimes the warp is of cotton cord. 1904 M. B. Langton *How to know Oriental Rugs* iii. 117 The Cabistan rug is a most desirable, moderate-priced rug, of artistic worth. 1913 G. G. Lewis *Pract. Bk. Oriental Rugs* (rev. ed.) x. 128 S Forms..are very common in the Caucasian fabrics, especially in the Kabistans and Shirvans. 1931 A. U. Dilley *Oriental Rugs & Carpets* Pl. 52 (*caption*) Kabistan or Hila. Geometric adaptation of Persian pattern. 1964 *Sunday Times* (Colour Suppl.) 19 Jan. 24 Cabistan. Similar to Shirvan rugs in weave and colour. 1970 J. Franses *European & Oriental Rugs* 44 (*caption*) Antique Kabistan rug. 1972 [see *Kuba].

kabouri (kabu·ri). *Guyana.* Also **kaboura, kaburi.** [Origin unknown.] A fly of the genus *Simulium.*

1899 J. Rodway *In Guiana Wilds* xi. 161 The great pest was the kaburi, which raised a blister in every spot where its venomous proboscis was inserted. 1917 W. G. White in C. W. Beebe et al. *Trop. Wild Life Brit. Guiana* I. xxxiv. 486 No one can know the district without knowing the kabouri fly... It is a blood-sucker, which marks one as with fine pocks... I am told that there are two species of kabourie; *Simulium guianense*, and *Simulium amazonicum*. 1954 G. Durrell *Three Singles to Adventure* iv. 92 We were fiercely attacked by great numbers of tiny black flies a little larger than a pin-head but with a kaboura fly's bite that was out of all proportion to their size...'They're kaboura flies...' The kabouras continued their assault on us.

‖**kabouter** (kăbau·təɹ). [Du.] A gnome, goblin, or dwarf; *transf.*, used for a member of an anti-establishment political movement in Holland.

1961 T. Henrot *Belgium* 182 Each region has its familiar spirits..the dwarves kindly and quarrelsome—*Nûtons* in the grottoes of Namur, *Kabouters* on Campine's heaths, *Sotâis* of the Amblève. 1970 *Guardian* 6 June 11/4 Remember the Provos, Amsterdam's pacifist rebels..? Their successors, the Kaboute [*sic*] or Elves, have gone one better. They campaigned in the nude for this week's city council elections. 1970 *Daily Tel.* 30 June 16 *World in Action* (ITV) introduced the Kabouter, the gnomes of Amsterdam, an anti-establishment movement who wear pointed hats..and, to general astonishment, have won five seats on the city council. 1971 *Guardian* 13 Apr. 11/4 The Kabouters—the Dutch street action group. 1973 *Reader's Digest* Apr. 97/1 What city would have a political movement called the *kabouters*, or pixies?

Kabuki (kăbū·ki, ‖ kabuki). Also with small initial. [Jap., f. *ka* song + *bu* dance + *ki* art, skill.] A traditional and popular form of Japanese drama which employs highly stylized singing, miming, and dancing in addition to acting, and in which (since *c* 1650) all the parts are played by males. Also *attrib.* Hence **Kabukie·sque** *a.*, in the style or manner of the Kabuki theatre.

1899 W. G. Aston *Hist. Jap. Lit.* VI. iii. 288 Kabuki theatres, which had men for actors, had been established there before the middle of the seventeenth century. **1928** *Daily Tel.* 4 Dec. 8/4 The Kabuki affords freedom for old and favourite plays, for new ones on Western lines, and for adaptations of Western drama. **1951** *Oxf. Compan. Theatre* 411 The present day Japanese theatre takes three distinct, although related forms, the *Nō* or lyrical drama, *Ningyō-shibai* or marionettes, and *Kabuki*, the popular theatre. **1954** F. Bowers *Jap. Theatre* vii. 224 Another woman who lies down to offer herself as a substitute for the married woman—a postwar Kabukiesque 'substitution'. **1960** B. Leach *Potter in Japan* viii. 190 The merchant class with its popular arts of the Kabuki theatre and the colour print. **1970** *Oxf. Compan. Art* 1171 Favourite subjects were theatre scenes, which began to appear along with the development of the popular *Kabuki* theatre in the 17th c. **1972** *Nat. Geographic* Sept. 378 Man in maiden's guise charms theatergoers in the classical drama known as Kabuki. **1972** *Mainichi Daily News* (Japan) 6 Nov. 3/5 Collection and sale of kabuki dolls.

Kabuli (kăbū·li), *a.* and *sb.* Also **Cabuli, Kabulian. A.** *adj.* Of, pertaining to, or characteristic of the city or province of Kabul in Afghanistan.

1887 Kipling *Plain Tales from Hills* (1888) 173 Baskets of fruit and pistachio nuts and Cabuli grapes. **1893** —— *Day's Work* (1898) 3 A little switch-tailed Kabuli pony. **1909** *Westm. Gaz.* 2 Feb. 5/1 These Cabuli rooks do not visit us every winter. **1966** P. King *Afghanistan* 64 (*caption*) Kabuli carpet seller.

B. *sb.* A person or animal from Kabul; also, the Iranian language of some of the people of this area or its script.

1895 Kipling *Day's Work* (1898) 188 You're to take one of Sir Jim's horses. There's a gray Cabuli here. **1909** M. Diver *Candles in Wind* xi. 112 He urged the Kabuli forward. **1948** D. Diringer *Alphabet* 301 The Kharoshthi, which is called also Bactrian..Kabulian..and so forth. **1964** H. H. Paper tr. *Shafeev's Short Gram. Outl. Pashto* 1 Until 1936 the official language of Afghanistan was Kabuli, one of the dialects of Tajik.

kaburi, var. *Kabouri.

Kabyle (kăbəi·l). Also **Kabail, Kabile, Kabyl.** [Arab. *ḳabā'il*, pl. of *ḳabīla* tribe.] A member of a group of Berber peoples inhabiting northern Algeria and Tunisia; these peoples collectively; also, the Berber (Hamitic) language of these peoples. Also *attrib.* *Kabyle dog* (see quot. 1945).

1738 T. Shaw *Trav. Barbary* i. 8 The several Portions and Districts..are chiefly known and distinguished by the particular Names of the Kabyles..or African Families, who respectively possess them. **1818** E. Blaquière tr. *Pananti's Narr. Residence Algiers* 181 The Bedouins are divided into many scattered tribes, called *Kabiles*, and vulgarly *Nege.* **1861** *Chambers's Encycl.* II. 44/1 In Algeria, where they [*sc.* Berbers] usually are termed Kabyles, they are yet unconquered by the French. **1868** L. Wingfield *Under Palms in Algeria & Tunis* I. iv. 84 He told us many things about the 'interieur' of Kabyle life. **1882** F. W. Newman *Libyan Vocab.* 3 The Libyan language..was but one, according to St. Augustine. Now there are at least four, the Kabail in Algeria, the Shilha in the mountains of Morocco, the Tuarik..beyond the Atlas, and the Ghadamsi at Ghadames. *Ibid.* 38 Kabail verbs and verbals, including adjectives. **1900** A. Wilkin *Among Berbers of Algeria* 178 Cheek by jowl the villages of Frenchmen and Kabyles stand. **1900** *Knowledge* 1 Aug. 173/2 The various Kabyle tribes. **1924** *Glasgow Herald* 14 Aug. 7 The Kabyles are agricultural Berbers living in the uplands of Morocco and Algeria. **1945** C. L. B. Hubbard *Observer's Bk. Dogs* 176 Kabyle Dog..a sheepdog native to the Kabyle Mountains. **1963** *Guardian* 9 Oct. 11/1 President Ben Bella..does not speak Kabyle and many Kabyles do not understand Arabic. **1969** E. Gellner *Saints of Atlas* i. 14 A Kabyle worker in France..has also kept his Berber speech. **1974** *Times* 30 May 10/5 Sons are what Kabyl husbands demand... Sterility and daughters alike are no good, and Kabyl women know it.

Kach(ch)eri, var. Cutcherry, cutchery.

1903 *Oxf. Mag.* 11 Feb. 208/1 The Kachcheri..is the centre of official life in the province. **1913** L. Woolf *Village in Jungle* vii. 179 He was standing..frightened, on the Kachcheri verandah. **1926** *United Free Ch. Miss. Rec.* Sept. 391/2, I can't have the Kacheri turned into a pawnshop.

kach(h)a, var. Cutcha *a.*

1920 *Blackw. Mag.* Oct. 921/1 My friend transported me over three extra miles of 'kacha' road. **1975** *Bangladesh Times* 20 July 2/5 A good number of kacha houses were damaged.

Kachin (kătʃi·n). [Burmese.] A member of a Tibeto-Burman ethnic group inhabiting the mountainous regions of north-east Burma; its language group, which includes Chingpaw, Atsi, Maru, etc. Also *attrib.*

1892 W. R. Winston *Four Yrs. Upper Burma* 102 In the north of Burma..are found the Kachins, a warlike hill people. **1903** G. A. Grierson *Linguistic Survey of India* III. ii. (*title*) Specimens of the Bodo, Nāgā, and Kachin groups. **1906** O. Hanson (*title*) A dictionary of the Kachin language. **1925** *Blackw. Mag.* Dec. 864/1 The reiterated word accented in Kachin is most descriptive. **1934** 'G. Orwell' *Burmese Days* xiv. 211 Producing two green pigeons from his Kachin bag. **1962** [see *Chin *sb.*[3]]. **1963** C. Maxwell-Lefroy *Land & People of Burma* vii. 47 Warm green tea,..shyly handed to us by a pretty Kachin girl. **1970** F. S. V. Donnison *Burma* ii. 47 The Kachins are nine-tenths Animists and the rest Christians.

kachina (kătʃī·nă). Also **cachina, katc(h)ina,** and with capital initial. [Hopi *qacina* supernatural.] In North American Pueblo Indian mythology, one of the deified ancestral spirits which periodically visit the pueblos, to bring rain, etc. Also in *Comb.*, as *kachina dance*, a dance performed at annual ceremonies by masked and elaborately costumed men impersonating the kachinas whom they seek to invoke; *kachina doll*, a doll representing a kachina, given to children at the annual ceremonies by the kachina dancers.

1888 S. Wallace *Land of Pueblos* 47 The *cachina* dance, which they celebrate at certain seasons of the year. **1907** F. W. Hodge *Handbk. Amer. Indians* I. 638/1 Kachina. A term applied by the Hopi to 'supernatural beings impersonated by men wearing masks'. **1910** G. W. James *Grand Canyon* 122 For use in the katchina dances, katchina baskets are made. **1948** *Seattle Sunday Times* (Mag.) 26 Sept. 3/4 The masked dancers who impersonate deities, or katchinas, in the great rain rites and rituals. **1959** E. Tunis *Indians* 126/2 He saw the sacred kachinas, and he was given dolls dressed like them to play with. **1968** N. Benchley *Welcome to Xanadu* ii. 29 Harry was a Hopi Indian, and..he sold silverware and pottery and kachina dolls. **1972** *Sat. Rev.* (U.S.) 3 June 33/2 The high-voltage transmission towers..march across the desert like giant skeletal Kachinas—Hopi ceremonial figures—carrying the white man's electricity.

kack-handed, var. *Cack-handed *a.*

1955 M. Allingham *Beckoning Lady* vi. 91, I never met such a kack-handed jackass in all my born days. **1964** S. Jepson *Fear in Wind* i. 17 A series of kack-handed manœuvres..designed to keep one end of a stick on the ground.

kackle, var. Cackle *v.*[2] *Naut.*

1883 *Man. Seamanship for Boys' Training Ships R. Navy* (Admiralty) (1886) 128 The cable is then served, or, as is termed, kackled with 2½-in. rounding, for the distance of 9 ft. from the eye.

Kadet, var. *Cadet[2].

Kadiak, var. *Kodiak.

‖ **kadin** (kā·din). Also **kadine.** [Turk.; the form *kadine* is prob. through Fr.] A lady of the Sultan's harem.

1843 *Penny Cycl.* XXV. 394/2 The women of the harem are divided into five classes:—1, 'Kádin', or 'wives of the Sultan', in number from four to seven. **1896** *Westm. Gaz.* 16 Sept. 1/3 He seldom notices any woman in his harem except the chief kadine. **1937** *Times Lit. Suppl.* 16 Jan. 36/2 He [*sc.* the Sultan] was content with four *kadins.*

kadir, var. *Khadar.

kadish (ka·diʃ). Also 9 **gedish.** [Arab. *kadīš*, f. O.Turk. *igdiş* a cross-breed, f. *igid-* to feed, rear; cf. Turk. *idiş* gelding.] An Arabian horse that is not a thoroughbred; a cross-bred horse, a nag; a gelding.

a **1817** J. L. Burckhardt *Trav. Syria & Holy Land* (1822) 295 A man with two or three is esteemed wealthy; and such a one has probably two camels, perhaps a mare, or at least a Gedish (a gelding), or a couple of asses. **1879** A. Blunt *Let.* 6 May in Lady Wentworth *Authentic Arabian Horse* (1945) 26 They have made my horses vulgar 'Kadishes'. **1924** *Blackw. Mag.* Mar. 346/2 Others less generous or more cautious sent *kadish* horses, only fit for the plough. **1945** Lady Wentworth *Authentic Arabian Horse* i. 34 All Oriental potentates regarded the Arabian as the only Horse and the rest as 'Kadishes', a word which exactly corresponds to the word 'cur' in English. It was the excellence of these Arabians..whose fame earned for the country-bred Kadishes a reflected radiance. **1970** A. Dent tr. *Schiele's Arab Horse in Europe* 24 If there were the tiniest lacuna or unknown quantity in its ancestry, it was no longer regarded as 'asil' and was demoted to the status of 'kadish'.

‖ **kadkhoda** (kadkō·dă). Also **kadkhuda,** and with capital initial. [Pers. *kadkhudá.*] The head man of an Iranian village.

1934 F. Stark *Valleys of Assassins* 56 We..were welcomed by the *kadkhuda* and a dozen tribesmen or so. **1953** A. Smith *Blind White Fish in Persia* v. 80 The Kadkhoda, the bailiff of the village, blows out his lamp and retires to bed. **1963** *Times* 6 Feb. 12/6 The *kadkhoda*, or head man.

KADU, Kadu (kā·du). [f. the initials of the words *K*enya *A*frican *D*emocratic *U*nion.] The name of a Kenyan political party.

1962 *Listener* 12 Apr. 643/3 The two main African parties, Kadu and Kanu. **1964** *Ann. Reg. 1963* 107 During the campaign rifts appeared in KADU.

kæmmererite, obs. var. *Kämmererite.

kaempferol (kæ·-, ke·mpfĕrǫl). *Chem.* Also **kampherol** (kæ·mfĕrǫl). [f. mod.L. *Kaempferia*, generic name of the plant (*K. galanga*) from which it was first obtained, f. the name of Engelbert *Kaempfer* (1651–1716), Ger. physician and traveller: see -ol.] A yellow crystalline flavonoid, $C_{15}H_{10}O_6$, that occurs alone and in glycosides in various plants; 3,4′,5,7-tetrahydroxyflavone.

1897 H. M. Gordin *On Crystallised Substances contained in Galangal Root* (Dissertation, Univ. of Berne) 37 Demethylised kampherid or kampherol as we agreed to call it crystallises from alcohol in light yellow needles. It contains one molecule of water of crystallisation. **1900** *Proc. Chem. Soc.* XVI. 183 The colouring matter has properties resembling those assigned to kampherol. **1923** *Nature* 17 Nov. 747/2 Four different species of Acacia.. have been examined... The water soluble yellow pigment was a glucoside of kæmpferol. **1963** *Brit. Pharmaceutical Codex* 718 The drug [*sc.* senna leaf] also contains rhein, aloe-emodin, kæmpferol and isorhamnetin in the free state and combined as glycosides. **1969** Kirk & Othmer *Encycl. Chem. Technol.* (ed. 2) XIX. 743 China tea, *C. sinensis*, contains relatively large amounts of triglycosides of quercetin and kaempferol.

kaersutite (kēᵊɹsu-təit). *Min.* [ad. Da. *kaersutit* (J. Lorenzen 1884, in *Meddelelser om Grønland* VII. 27), f. *Kaersut*, name of the locality (on the shore of Umanak Fiord on the west coast of Greenland) where it was first found: see -ite[1].] A dark brown or black kind of hornblende characterized by a high titanium content and occurring as a constituent of many volcanic rocks.

1886 *Jrnl. Chem. Soc.* L. 519 Analyses of minerals from Greenland... Kærsutite, colour black, streak brown. **1939** *Trans. & Proc. R. Soc. N.Z.* LXIX. 305 It appears that in the Dunedin district brown monoclinic amphiboles occur very generally in the only slightly alkaline basalts and trachybasalts of the first and second volcanic phases, and prove to be basaltic hornblendes which in the two samples analysed have just sufficient content of TiO_2 to permit their being classed as kaersutite. **1966** W. A. Deer et al. *Introd. Rock-Forming Min.* ii. 177 Kaersutite is a typical constituent of alkaline volcanic rocks, and occurs as phenocrysts in trachybasalts, trachyandesites, trachytes..and alkali rhyolites; in the more silica-rich rocks it occurs also as a groundmass constituent. **1968** *Mineral. Mag.* XXXVI. 1001 Aoki (1963) considered an amphibole from a trachyte with 4·36% TiO_2 (0·49 Ti) as not a typical kaersutite...It is clear that any lower limit of titanium for kaersutite must be an arbitrary one.

Hence **kaersuti·tic** *a.*, of the nature of or resembling kaersutite.

1968 *Mineral. Mag.* XXXVI. 1001 The data..strongly suggest that upper mantle amphibole is probably a kaersutitic hornblende.

‖ **kafenion** (kæfĕnī·ən). [Gr. καφενεῖον.] A Greek coffee-house or café.

In the Greek word the final -*n* is often dropped in the spoken form (thus quot. 1939). The Gk. pl. form is καφενεῖα.

1939 E. Ambler *Mask of Dimitrios* iv. 63 It took another week, a week of waiting, of sitting in *kafenios*, of being introduced to thirsty gentlemen with connections in the municipal offices. **1964** *Punch* 24 June 925/2 They overflowed the local kafenion. **1967** J. Eastwood *Little Dragon from Peking* xiii. 130 The kind of reception accorded to a woman unaccompanied in, say, a male-dominated, male-preserve Kafenion in rural Greece. **1974** 'M. Yorke' *Mortal Remains* i. vii. 24 There was a Kafenion on the water-front, so he sat at a table..and ordered coffee.

‖ **kaffeeklat(s)ch** (ka·feklatʃ). Also with hyphen or as two words, and with capital initial(s). [G., f. *kaffee* coffee + *klatsch* gossip.] Gossip over coffee cups; a coffee party; cf. *coffee klatsch* (s.v. *Coffee *sb.* 5 b). Hence **kaffeeklatscher** *sb.*, **kaffeeklatsching** *vbl. sb.* Cf. *Klatsch.

1888 in A. Randall-Diehl *2000 Words & Definitions.* **1903** *Current Opinion* Aug. 205/2 She usually operates as an amateur, appearing at *Kaffeeklatsches.* **1906** S. Ford *Shorty McCabe* 111 He let it out one day after we'd had our little kaffee klatch with the gloves. **1911** *International* (N.Y.) July 35/2 Theatrical *Kaffeeklatsch* has now absorbed the space where once the redoubtable Charles Edward fought his battles. **1919** F. Hurst *Humoresque* 322 They're a darn sight better than the wads of respectability I see waddlin' in here to swap *Kaffee Klatsches* with you! **1936** H. Miller *Black Spring* 134 It's the hour of the kaffee-klatchers sitting around the family table. **1956** W. H. Whyte *Organization Man* (1957) xxii. 286 Dot will be *Kaffee-klatsching* and sun-bathing with the girls. **1958** M. West *Second Victory* i. 5 They came in summer to take the waters, to sit on the terrace for *Kaffeeklatsch.* **1969** R. Lockridge *Murder in False Face* ix. 112 If [he]..wants a morning kaffee-klatch it's all right with me. **1972** J. Williams *Home Fronts* xiii. 233 The traditional friendly *Kaffeeklatsch*—the afternoon coffee party with friends.

Kaffir. Add: **1.** (Earlier example.)

1790 J. Bruce *Trav.* IV. viii. ix. 497 Why did not you tell those black Kafrs..to stay a little longer.

2. (Further examples.) Also, usu. disparagingly, with reference to any black African. Also *transf.*, as a term of opprobrium, a white man who associates with or is thought to favour black Africans.

1792 E. Riou tr. *J. van Reenen's Jrnl. Journey from Cape Good Hope* 22 We saw several Kaffers. **1852** Godlonton & Irving *Narr. Kaffir War* iii. xv. 180 The other teachers ..who could speak Kaffir. **1926** S. G. Millin *S. Africans* 209 In the old days..men, thrusting their ancestry, their traditions..completely behind them, became what people sometimes call in South Africa 'white Kafirs'. They

merged themselves with the natives, stayed for ever with the wives they had bought and with their African children. **1949** [see *HOTNOT]. **1949** *Cape Argus* 9 July 3/5 'Did you think he was a perfectly reliable person to give information to?'—'I would have given the statement to a Kaffir if someone had sent a Kaffir along.' **1959** *New Statesman* 2 May 62/3 How, for instance, does one describe negroid South Africans? The early missionary word 'kaffir', meaning heathen, has become a term of abuse. **1960** *Cape Times* 6 Sept. 7 A mob which swore at the police, called them 'white Kafirs', and hurled bottles at them. **1961** L. van der Post *Heart of Hunter* I. iii. 62 Kaffir is the term used by Europeans to describe all black people in Africa irrespective of their race and origin. **1967** [see *COOLIE, COOLY 2 b]. **1973** *Deb. Senate S. Afr.* 17 May 2777 When we..were young people the word 'kaffir' meant nothing more than to indicate a Black man... It has deteriorated to such an extent that it offends people with a dark coloured skin and..we try to avoid it. *Ibid.* 2798, I have heard people when I visit a farm call out 'Kaffir' and a wife appears, and he says 'my kaffir, prepare food for us'..; but, if I called my friend the hon. Senator.., 'You are a kaffir', then it has another meaning.

3. Substitute for def.: Usu. **Kafir.** A member of a people inhabiting the Hindu Kush mountains of north-east Afghanistan; **Kafir harp,** a primitive harp with four or five strings used by this people.

1961 A. Baines *Mus. Instruments* 43 In the Kafir harp the lower end of the bow reappears above the skin.

4. Kaffir beer, an alcoholic beverage brewed from Kaffir corn by the black inhabitants of S. Africa; **Kaffirboetie** (kæ·fəɪbūti) *S. Afr.* [partial tr. Afrikaans *Kafferboetie*, f. *Kaffer* Kaffir + *boetie* little brother], an opprobrious term for a Negrophil; **Kaffir-boom** (earlier and later examples); **Kaffir bread** (earlier and later examples); **Kaffir Circus** *Stock Exchange slang*, the body of brokers who operate in 'Kaffirs', or the place where they operate; **Kaffir corn** (earlier and later examples); **Kaffir crane,** a name formerly used for the crowned crane, *Balearica pavonina regulorum*, which is grey with a tuft of black feathers on top of its head; **Kaffir finch, fink,** the red bishop-bird, *Pyromelana oryx*, or a closely related bird of the sub-family Ploceinæ; **Kaffirland,** the land of the Kaffirs; **Kaffir lily,** a herb of the family Iridaceæ, *Schizostylis coccinea*, bearing spikes of gladiolus-like flowers; also = *CLIVIA; **Kaffir (water-)melon,** either of two species of melon, *Citrullus caffer* or *C. vulgaris*; **Kaffir orange,** a shrub or small tree of the genus *Strychnos*, esp. *S. pungens*, or its fruit; **Kaffir piano,** a S. African marimba or xylophone; **Kaffir pot,** an iron cooking-pot usu. on three short metal legs; **Kaffir tea** (examples); **Kaffir('s) tree** (earlier example); **Kaffir truck** *S. Afr.*, term applied to small miscellaneous general goods for barter or sale.

1837 R. B. Hulley in F. Owen *Diary* (1926) 174 About a hundred pots filled with Kaffir beer were brought and placed before the..men. **1905** *Transvaal Agric. Jrnl.* Jan. 314 Kaffir beer, which..is not..a bad drink for natives. **1952** L. Marquard *Peoples & Policies S. Afr.* iv. 101 Africans may..drink kaffir beer. This is a traditional African drink, brewed by African women from fermented kaffir corn and containing a maximum of 2 per cent of alcohol. **1968** M. Pyke *Food & Society* iv. 43 It is a very great error..to assume..that this Kaffir-beer is simply and solely an intoxicating drink. **1939** R. F. A. Hoernlé *S. Afr. Native Policy* p. vii, For a member of the White group to be concerned about the impact of white domination on the non-European population of the Union..is to earn for himself the title of 'negrophilist', *kafir-boetie*, or—most scathing of all—'liberal'. **1942** P. Abrahams *Dark Testament* I. xiii. 71 One's got to live. I can't let the other fellows call me a 'Kaffir boetie'. **1947** A. Keppel-Jones *When Smuts Goes* ii. 20 The disgruntled factions of trade unionists and liberals, Indians and 'Kafferboeties', seemed very small fry. **1958** N. Gordimer *World of Strangers* v. 115 You must be Communist or Anti-Communist, Nationalist or Kaffirboetie. **1965** *Punch* 24 Feb. 272/3 Multi-racialists, educationalists, Kafir-boeties. **1827** G. Thompson *Trav. & Adv. S. Afr.* I. i. ii. 18 The stakes of this fence, consisting chiefly of Caffer-boom (*Erythrina Caffra*) which grows abundantly in the neighbourhood, had in numerous instances struck root. **1949** *Cape Argus* 15 Oct. 4/5 The Alexandria forests, red with giant kaffirbooms. **1953** J. Packer *Apes & Ivory* xv. 160 The red flowers of the *kaffir-booms* flamed in the hard clear light. **1964** A. Rothmann *Elephant Shrew* 19 There was a big clump of wild bananas in this camp, and also two large, spreading kaffirbooms. **1801** J. Barrow *Acct. Trav. S. Afr.* I. iii. 189 The *zamia cycadis*, or Kaffer's bread-tree, growing on the plains. **1958** L. G. Green *S. Afr. Beachcomber* 14 Beyond the Buffalo River lies the Wild Coast, with the frangipane and kaffir-bread trees growing down to the beaches. **1896** M. Donovan *Kaffir Circus* 96 A big boom is on in the Kaffir Circus, and Laure's shares are worth £15,000. **1901** C. Duguid *How to read Money Article* 121 The market in which they are dealt in the Stock Exchange is often called the 'Kaffir Circus'. Term does not comprise Rhodesians. **1902** *Encycl. Brit.* XXXII. 865/1 At first..the 'Kaffre circus', as it was called, was regarded with contempt by the older *habitués* of the Stock Exchange. **1928** *Daily Chron.* 9 Aug. 8/6 Otherwise the Kaffir Circus presented a very idle appearance. **1785** G. Forster tr. *Sparrman's Voy. Cape Good Hope* II. x. 10 The kind of corn which they sow, is..known to yield abundantly. The colonists call it caffer-corn. **1792** Kaffir corn [see *black bean* (*BLACK *a.* 19)]. **1954** R. St. John *Through Malan's Afr.* i. 14 Indian millet is called Kaffir corn. **1973** *Farmer's Weekly* (S. Afr.) 13 June 3 (Advt.), Prevent fallen kaffir corn and other crops from being double cut. **1834** A. Smith *Diary* 15 Nov. (1939) I. 137 Saw several Caffer cranes. **1853** F. Fleming *Kaffraria* iii. 68 The handsomest of these [birds] to be met with is the Kaffir Crane..a species of the *Anthropoides-Pavonia* or Crowned-Demoiselle. **1906** W. L. Sclater *Birds S. Afr.* IV. 279 *Bugeranus carunculatus.* Wattled Crane..sometimes 'Kaffir Crane' of Colonists. *Ibid.* 284 *Balearica regulorum.* Crowned Crane. ..'Kaffir Crane' of some. **1822** W. J. Burchell *Trav. S. Afr.* I. i. 20 In the aviary I saw..the *Kaffers Fink.* **1834** [see *FINK *sb.*[1]]. **1844** J. Backhouse *Narr. Visit Mauritius & S. Afr.* xiv. 202 The Caffer Finch of this part of the country is *Ploceus spilonotus.* **1897, 1908** [see *FINK *sb.*[1]]. **1931** Kaffir fink [see *bishop-bird*]. **1973** A. P. Brink *Birds* 4 You're so cocky. What are you—a kaffir finch? **1821** E. Blount *Notes on Cape Good Hope* 137 A poet of great respectability..was ready to invoke the muse of Kaffer-land. **1853** *Househ. Words* 11 June 338/1 Let us.. see what the noble savage does in Zulu Kaffirland. **1900** W. D. Drury *Bk. Gardening* x. 348 *Schizostylis coccinea* (Crimson Flag; Kaffir Lily) is a lovely iridaceous subject with bright crimson gladiolus-like spikes of flower. **1946** M. Free *All about House Plants* xii. 94 *Clivia miniata*, Kafir Lily. Give only enough water to keep leaves from wilting. **1951** *Dict. Gardening* (R. Hort. Soc.) IV. 1904/1 *S[chizostylis] coccinea.* Crimson Flag; Kaffir Lily. **1970** M. Allan *Tom's Weeds* ii. 27 A feature of Number 1 greenhouse was the imantophyllum or Kaffir lily, renamed clivea by John Lindley in honour of the Duchess of Northumberland (of Syon House) who was a member of the Clive family. **1886** G. A. Farini *Through Kalahari Desert* xii. 199 Close by were a lot of young gourds growing which Kert said were Kaffir melons; they were quite unlike our English watermelons; nor were they like a pumpkin. **1950** *Cape Times* 1 June 7/6 The National Parks Board has authorized expenditure on kafir melons with which to feed the elephants in summer-time. **1859** R. J. Mann *Colony of Natal* viii. 159 The 'Kafir orange' of the sea-coast-bush is a 'strychnos' and has strychnine in its seeds. **1907** T. R. Sim *Forests & Forest Flora Cape Good Hope* 274 *Strychnos spinosa* (Kafir Orange..). An evergreen shrub 8–10 feet high, seldom a small tree... Fruit size of an orange, or larger, with rind green when young, yellow when ripe, hard shell, and numerous flat seeds lying in acidulous edible pulp. **1932** Watt & Breyer-Brandwijk *Medicinal & Poisonous Plants S. Afr.* 140 The pulp of the fruit of *Strychnos pungens* Solered., Wild orange, Kaffir orange..is acidulous from the presence of citric acid, and is very refreshing. **1952** S. Cloete *Curve & Tusk* (1953) xiii. 112 There were patches where the marsala or kaffir orange grew, its round, hard-shelled fruit a favourite dish of the baboon and kudu. **1891** Monteiro *Delagoa Bay* 253 (Pettman), The song had a rapidly played accompaniment on the Kaffir piano. **1897** J. Bryce *Impressions S. Afr.* xiv. 251 The so-called 'Kaffir piano', made of pieces of iron of unequal length fastened side by side in a frame. **1931** J. Mockford *Khama* xxiii. 157 To the throb and wail of these kafir pianos the big-bodied, lusty mine-boys dance freely in two long lines. **1948** H. V. Morton *In Search of S. Afr.* x. 311 A native band was thrumming on 'Kaffir pianos', instruments like large xylophones. **1896** H. A. Bryden *Tales of South Africa* 260 The *kaptein* ..persuaded the *vrouw* to follow his own example, and roast wild duck or a joint of springbok in a Kaffir pot. **1922** S. G. Millin *Adam's Rest* III. x. 254 Over the fire stood a big black tripod Kaffir-pot. **1959** A. Fullerton *Yellow Ford* xiii. 177, I use a kaffirpot, a three-legged thing made of cast iron. **1851** J. J. Freeman *Tour S. Afr.* xv. 362 One kind hearted woman..prepared a Kaffir meal for us—a pot of sour-milk, some Kaffir corn bread and some Kaffir tea. **1899** G. Russell *Hist. Old Durban* 96 An indigenous herb both nutritive and refreshing, which is known to us as *Kaffir tea.* **1949** L. G. Green *In Land of Afternoon* 55 Bush tea is popular in the fashionable cafes of the United States. They call it 'Kaffir tea' over there. **1792** E. Riou tr. *J. van Reenen's Jrnl. Journey from Cape Good Hope* 38 We interred the body of our friend, under a large kaffer-tree standing alone. **1855** G. H. Mason *Life with Zulus* 133 (Pettman), This portion of South Africa is dependent entirely on the P. M. Berg traders for..*caffre truck.* **1900** J. Robinson *Life Time in S. Afr.* 279 (Pettman), Glass, beads, knives, scissors, needles,..small looking-glasses—such are the chief staples of *Kaffir truck.* **1948** E. Rosenthal *Afr. Switzerland: Basutoland* vii. 83 Basuto, who crowd a quaint kiosk loaded with what is called 'Kaffir Truck' in South Africa—bangles, beads, mirrors, combs, and the like. **1951** D. Lessing *This was Old Chief's Country* ix. 198 He had gone into town and was down among the kaffir-truck shops buying a supply of aprons for his houseboys. **1832** *Graham's Town* (Cape Province) *Jrnl.* 1 June 92 All the Caffers..were dispatched forward, that they might get Caffer water melons to make soup. **1838** W. H. Harvey *Genera S. Afr. Plants* 105 The water-melon of which two colonial species *C. Caffer* (Kaffir-water-melon) and *C. amarus*..are described. **1932** Watt & Breyer-Brandwijk *Medicinal & Poisonous Plants S. Afr.* 180 *Citrullus vulgaris* Schrad is known as Water-melon, Wild water-melon, Kaffir water-melon.

B. *adj. S. Afr. slang.* Bad, unreliable.

1934 'N. Giles' *Ridge of White Waters* II. vii. 266 'Another kaffir bargain!' said Sir Alfred wearily. **1961** *Spectator* 14 July 53 'That was a real Kaffir shot.'.. This ..was the first time I had come across Kaffir, *adj.*: bad, clumsy, inferior..etc.

Kaffrarian, var. *CAFFRARIAN *a.*

Kafkaesque (kæfkă͵e·sk), *a.* Also with hyphen. [See -ESQUE.] Of or relating to the Austrian writer Franz *Kafka* (1883–1924) or his writings; resembling the state of affairs or a state of mind described by Kafka. Hence **Kafkae·squely** *adv.*

1947 *New Yorker* 4 Jan. 61/1 Warned, he said, by a Kafka-esque nightmare of blind alleys. **1954** Koestler *Invis. Writing* x. 120 Long before the Moscow purges revealed that weird, Kafka-esque pattern to the incredulous world. **1958** *Spectator* 24 Jan. 114/2 An authentic Kafkaesque atmosphere of despair and horror. **1958** E. Dundy *Dud Avocado* I. viii. 147 Postcards and wires to the Paris Embassy were all Kafkaesquely re-routed to that powerful Man in Charge. **1963** *Times* 23 May 6/7 Kafkaesque in its grip and pitiless in its exposition of the cruellest of tortures, that of hope. **1972** *Newsweek* 10 Jan. 51/2 The Kafkaesque self-abnegation of the infamous 'show trials' [in Russia].

Also **Ka·fka** *sb.* used *attrib.*, **Ka·fkan, Ka·fkaish, Ka·fkian** *adjs.* = *KAFKAESQUE *a.*

1936 M. Lowry *Let.* (1967) 11 This is the perfect Kafka situation. **1951** S. Spender *World within World* v. 272 They became more Kafkaish than ever. **1959** *N. & Q.* Oct. 381/1 A *re*-statement of the Kafkan anguish. **1962** tr. *J. L. Borges's Labyrinths* (1970) 234 The moving object and the arrow and Achilles are the first Kafkian characters in literature. **1962** *Guardian* 26 Sept. 8/6, I..had wondered if the whole project would turn out to be a Kafka nightmare. **1966** *New Statesman* 25 March 437/1 All the Kafkan stuff..gone seedy and suicidal in a back-street rooming-house. **1971** N. Freeling *Over High Side* II. 82 So little of what one did made any sense. One lived in a Kafka world.

kaftan, var. CAFTAN (in Dict. and Suppl.) (further examples).

1965 [see *CAFTAN 2]. **1967** *Daily Mail* 10 Aug. 4/7 I'd like to see men in this country wearing kaftans—those long cotton robes—to relax at home. **1969** *Daily Nation* (Nairobi) 31 Oct. 19/2 It comprises a Kaftan, slit on either side to the knees to reveal pencil slim hipster pants. **1972** J. Wilson *Hide & Seek* ii. 37 Her wedding dress..had been an all enveloping Kaftan because she'd been hugely pregnant.

kafuffle, var. CURFUFFLE *sb.*, *GEFUFFLE, *KERFUFFLE.

1946 F. Sargeson *That Summer* 94, I bet it [*sc.* the domestic row] ended up in a good old kafuffle.

kagg: see *CAG *sb.*[3]

‖ **kagura** (kā·gură). [Jap.] A sacred dance performed at Shinto festivals, one of the oldest dances of Japan; also, one performed at a village shrine on a festive day.

1884 Satow & Hawes *Handbk. for Travellers Cent. & N. Japan* (ed. 2) 63 At some temples young girls fill the office of priestess, but their duties do not appear to extend beyond the performance of the pantomimic dances known as *Kagura*, [etc.]. **1899** W. G. Aston *Hist. Jap. Lit.* v. iii. 197 The drama in Japan was in its beginnings closely associated with religion. Its immediate parent was the Kagura, a pantomimic dance, which is performed at this day to the sound of fife and drum at Shinto festivals. **1936** K. Nohara *True Face of Japan* v. 191 Dances and festival plays were performed in front of Shinto shrines, which were called *Kagura*, or 'Joys of the Gods'. **1946** R. Benedict *Chrysanthemum & Sword* (1947) v. 90 Watching wrestling matches or exorcism or *kagura* dances, which are liberally enlivened by clowns. **1966** P. S. Buck *People of Japan* (1968) xii. 132 At special times the Shinto priests perform their own religious dance, the *kagura.*

‖ **Kahal** (kā·hal). [Heb. *ḳāhal* assembly, community.] One of the former localized Jewish communities in Europe; also, the governing body of such a community.

1901 *Daily Chron.* 14 June 3/4 The power of the *Kahal* —the court of the congregation. **1907** I. Zangwill *Ghetto Comedies* 342 The very Rabbi was petrified; the elders of the *Kahal* stood dumb. **1916** H. Sacher *Zionism & Jewish Future* 19 In every Kahal (community) many youths..studied. *Ibid.* 20 A Kahal of fifty families. **1937** Wyndham Lewis *Blasting & Bombarding* v. v. 280, I took no further interest in this cowboy songster, said to be a young sprig of the Kahal. **1971** *Encycl. Judaica* V. Gloss., *Kahal*, Jewish congregation; among Ashkenazim, *Kehillah.*

kahawai (kā·wai, ka·hawai). Also **kawai.** [Maori.] A perciform, marine, food fish, *Arripis trutta*, found in shoals in New Zealand and south-eastern Australian waters.

1838 J. S. Polack *New Zealand* I. 322 The *káháwai*, or colourless salmon. **1845** E. J. Wakefield *Adventure N.Z.* I. 92 A shoal of *kawai* came into that part of the bay. The *kawai* has somewhat of the habits of the salmon. **1849** W. T. Power *Sketches in N.Z.* ix. 76 The kawai is not unlike the salmon in size and shape, and, like it, comes up the rivers in shoals in the spring. **1870** R. Taylor *Te Ika a Maui* (ed. 2) 623 The Kahawai..is one of the most abundant, and is called mackerel by the settlers. **1927** *Daily Express* 26 Feb. 1 The Duchess returned to the Renown with seventeen 'schnapper' and one 'kahawai'. **1962** *Antiquity* XXXVI. 272 *Fish-hooks*.. another type of lure with barbed point notched for lashing (the *kahawai* lure). **1962** G. W. Jackson *N.Z. Beach & Boating Bk.* viii. 82 The bait is..a bundle of sprats or a whole kahawai. **1963** *Evening Post* (Wellington, N.Z.) 30 Nov., Stripping fillets of kahawai and baracouta we cut them into fish shapes and the reaction was immediate, the big fellows accepting them as readily as they had the rock cod earlier.

kahika (kā·͵ikă). [Maori.] = KAHIKATEA.

1921 H. Guthrie-Smith *Tutira* x. 71 Close to this orchard grew..three tall white pines, survivors of the kahika grove, from which the flat had probably taken its name. **1949** P. Buck *Coming of Maori* (1950) IV. i. 450

She [*sc.* Hinewaoriki] gave birth to twins in the form of the *kahika* and *matai* trees.

kahili (kăhī·li). [Hawaiian.] A feather standard, mounted on a tall pole, symbolic of royalty in Hawaii and used on ceremonial occasions.

1866 'MARK TWAIN' *Lett. from Hawaii* (1967) 180 A dozen or more of these gaudy kahilis were upheld by pallbearers. **1883** C. F. G. CUMMING *Fire Fountains* I. 35 At the door of the mausoleum are placed tall *kahilis*, honorific symbols, which to irreverent foreign eyes are suggestive of gigantic feather-brushes, or rather bottle-brushes. **1915** W. A. BRYAN *Nat. Hist. Hawaii* 61 In the hand is a small kahili with ivory and tortoise shell handle. **1937** D. & H. TEILHET *Feather Cloak Murders* xv. 267 The Baron was next to find two rotted kahilis, ancient feather standards. **1948** KUYKENDALL & DAY *Hawaii* xi. 108 In the shadow of somber *kahilis* (royal standards) his ministers and his subjects marched past. *Ibid.* xvi. 166 He stood beside..the *kahili*, symbolic of Hawaiian chieftainship.

Kahn (kān). *Med.* The name of Reuben Leon *Kahn* (b. 1887), Lithuanian-born U.S. bacteriologist, used *attrib.* and *absol.* to designate a diagnostic test for syphilis devised by him in 1922, in which serum or spinal fluid that has been inactivated by heating is shaken with a suspension of antigen obtained from beef heart and the mixture examined for flocculation (usually after a period of incubation).

1922 *Jrnl. Amer. Med. Assoc.* 9 Sept. 874/1 The clinical application of the Kahn precipitation test compares favorably in sensitiveness with the standard Wasserman reaction. *Ibid.* 873/1 In the serums examined from patients with late bone and joint involvement, the Kahn reaction again compares very favorably with the two Wasserman reactions. **1950** R. R. WILLCOX *Text-bk. Venereal Dis.* ix. 115 As a verification test the Kahn performed at different temperatures..has not proved entirely satisfactory. **1953** *Med. Ann.* LXXI. 7 Positive Wassermann and Kahn reactions may be given, for a time, by the serum of patients recovering from glandular fever. **1964** KING & NICOL *Venereal Diseases* vii. 95 Of the many flocculation tests available, the Kahn test has been the most widely used, but in recent years the Price precipitation test (PPR) has increased in popularity in Great Britain.

kahuna (kahū·nă). [Hawaiian.] **a.** A Hawaiian priest or minister; an expert or wise man. **b.** *Surfing.* (With capital initial.) A term adopted to designate a 'god' of surfing.

1886 H. H. GOWEN *Let.* 6 Dec. in *Paradise of Pacific: Hawaii* (1892) viii. 85 The *Kahunas* advised him to stave off the calamity by getting rid of the *white power*. **1915** W. A. BRYAN *Nat. Hist. Hawaii* 54 A numerous class of more irregular priests or Kahunas, that were little more than sorcerers. **1920** *Nature* 15 July 628/1 A much longer paper..deals with the functions of the *Kahuna* 'the priest-hood called the Order of Sorcery'. The word in varying forms (*tahuna, tahunga, tauna*) is used throughout the Eastern Pacific to denote possessed of varying degrees of wisdom from priesthood to sorcery. **1948** KUYKENDALL & DAY *Hawaii* i. 8 The *kahunas* (priests, doctors, sorcerers, navigators, and experts in various other lines) comprised a class closely associated with the chief. **1962** *Austral. Women's Weekly* (Suppl.) 24 Oct. 3/2 Kahuna..the god of the Californian and Hawaiian board-riders. **1970** *Studies in English* (Univ. Cape Town) I. 25 The word 'kahuna' has been personified into *Kahuna*, the god of surfing.

kai (kai). *N.Z.* [Maori.] Food, victuals.

[**1838** J. S. POLACK *New Zealand* I. 289 There is a much larger variety of this esculent [*sc.* potato] called *kai pakehá*, or white man's food.] **1845** E. J. WAKEFIELD *Adventure N.Z.* I. 265 The determination of the natives not to move till all the *kai* was exhausted. **1925** FRASER & GIBBONS *Soldier & Sailor Words* 134 *Kai*, food. (A Maori word, used among the New Zealand troops in the War.) **1927** T. E. DONNE *The Maori, Past & Present* 95, I kep in te whare for tree day, but no *kai* (food). **1952** R. FINLAYSON *Schooner came to Atia* iii. 17, I can take Tua smokes and good kai. **1970** *N.Z. Listener* 12 Oct. 12/1 Some kai would go nicely now. Empty bellies do things to people.

So (in reduplicated form) **kaikai** (kaikai), food; feasting; a feast.

[**1807** J. SAVAGE *Some Acct. N.Z.* xi. 75 *Kiki*..food.] **1845** E. J. WAKEFIELD *Adventure N.Z.* I. 29 He explained ..that there would be much *kai kai* or feasting. **1894** STEVENSON & OSBOURNE *Ebb-Tide* I. iv. 60 There shall be no growling about the kaikai, which will be above allowance. **1901** A. C. HADDON *Head-Hunters* 39 One afternoon some of us went to a *kaikai*, or feast. **1941** BAKER *N.Z. Slang* 26 In early records the 'pidgin' forms kaikai or kiki are often discovered. **1969** *Coast to Coast 1967–68* 48 No, she didn't say tucker. The kanakas said kai-kai.

‖ **kaïd.** Add: (Earlier and later examples.) Also **kayed, kaid.** Hence **kai·dship.**

1816 'ALI BEY' *Trav.* I. 5, I handed it [*sc.* my passport] to the captain, who ordered that no one should come on shore, and went away to shew my passport to the *Kaïd*, or Governor. *a* **1817** J. L. BURCKHARDT *Trav. Nubia* (1819) 364 The Shikh of the tribe is never the commander..of the armed parties, which the tribe sends out against an enemy. He may join the expedition, but the command of it is in the Kayed, or leader, a dignity which is always hereditary in the same family. **1920** *Glasgow Herald* 23 Sept. 6 Kaid of Tangier. **1920** *Blackw. Mag.* Dec. 742/2 His half-brother was already nominated to the kaidship. **1925** *Ibid.* Nov. 622/2 Presently the Kayed will appear, walking with his chief villagers.

kaik, var. ***KAINGA**.

kaikomako (ka,ikomā·ko). *N.Z.* [Maori.] A New Zealand tree, *Pennantia corymbosa*, which bears panicles of fragrant white flowers.

1832 G. BENNETT in *London Med. Gaz.* 22 Sept. 794/2 (*heading*) Kaiko-mako tree of the natives of New Zealand. ..This tree..attains the elevation of twenty-five to thirty feet...The wood of the..Kaiko-mako, is only used by the natives for procuring fire. **1882** W. D. HAY *Brighter Britain!* II. 198 The Kaikomako..will be much cultivated as a garden ornament. **1910** L. COCKAYNE *N.Z. Plants* iii. 37 *Pennantia corymbosa* (the kaikomako) vies in its purity with any bridal flower. **1963** POOLE & ADAMS *Trees & Shrubs N.Z.* 122 *P*[*ennantia*] *corymbosa*... Kaikomako. Tree reaching 12m... Flowers small, dioecious, fragrant.

‖ **kain** (ka·,in, kɔin). [Malay.] Cloth, a piece of cloth. Usu. with defining word following (see quots.).

1783 W. MARSDEN *Hist. Sumatra* 44 The *cayen sarrong* is not unlike a Scots highlander's plaid..being a piece of party colored cloth about six or eight feet long, and three or four wide, sowed together at the ends. **1848** H. LOW *Sarawak* v. 143 Their dress..consists of the kain tapé, or cloth, which has been described as a wide sack open at both ends. **1910** C. W. HARRISON *Illustr. Guide Federated Malay States* II. 206 The great majority of sarongs are of cotton cloth known as *kain plekat*. **1919** P. MIJER *Batiks* i. 7 'Kains' can be bought as cheaply as a dollar each. **1947** R. O. WINSTEDT *Malays* viii. 148 The obsolescent 'lime' pattern (kain limau)..reminds one of Indian designs. *Ibid.*, Patani, Pahang and Selangor produce cloths (*kain telepok*) gilded by a technique practised also in the Punjab. **1958** H. FORSTER *Flowering Lotus* ii. 25 Formal Javanese wear, for gentlemen as for ladies, was the *kain batik*. This was a simple length of cotton cloth, decorated with an elaborate pattern. **1963** J. KIRKUP *Tropic Temper* iv. 41 There are many ways of folding the big, starched kerchief in a form of head-dress... On the East Coast it is called kain satangan. *Ibid.* xv. 167 Round their waists they wore vivid red or purple kain songket which is a silver or gold-threaded sarong reaching down to the knees and tied on the left hip in an especially intricate knot. **1967** F. MULLALLY *Prizewinner* ii. 39 Indonesians in bosom-moulding *kabajas* and *batik kains*. **1971** *Carry Singapore in your Pocket* (Singapore Tourist Promotion Board) (ed. 3) 53 *Kain songket*, spun silk woven on cottage handlooms highly prized for its dazzling beauty of gleaming motifs in gold or silver. **1972** M. SHEPPARD *Taman Indera* 117 *Kain lepas*, unsewn sarong-length, often of gold thread silk. *Ibid.* 118 (*caption*) Part of a length of *Kain Limar*, from Kelantan. Fine silk cloth with a rose red warp and a mosaic pattern. **1972** *Sunday Times* (Kuala Lumpur) 25 June 7/4 The Queen was given a kain kebat—a dress resembling the sarong.

kainga (kā,i·ngă, ‖ kaiŋa). *N.Z.* Also (*South Island*) **kaik.** [Maori.] A place of residence; a settlement, village.

1820 *Gram. & Vocab. Lang. N.Z.* (Church Missionary Soc.) 157 Káinga...A place of residence, a home, &c. **1838** J. S. POLACK *New Zealand* I. 66 These animals were a disgrace to the *kaingá*, or village, of which they formed part. **1879** [see *gum-digging* (*GUM *sb.*[2] 9)]. **1884** *Maoriland* 84 The drive may be continued from Portobello to the Maori kaik. **1904** 'G. B. LANCASTER' *Sons o' Men* 56 He had..fallen foul of many native kiangas [*sic*] where the pakeha was unwelcome. **1905** W. B. *Where White Man Treads* 281 And so to-day: when you see small square potato patches dot the landscape near his kaingas, this meagre husbandry is no sign of improvidential laziness. **1926** J. COWAN *Trav. N.Z.* I. 114 They are places for the artist, these out-of-the-way *kaingas*. **1938** R. D. FINLAYSON *Brown Man's Burden* 49 The Maori just sits in his kaianga and takes what comes to him. **1944** *Mod. Jun. Dict.* (Whitcombe & Tombs) 229 Kaik, kainga... A Maori village; 'kaik' in the South Island only. **1967** A. & D. REID *Paddle Wheels on Wanganui* 12 The excitement of the riverside Maoris as the ship passed their lonely kaingas.

kainite. Add: Also kainit.

1877, 1882 Kainit [in Dict.]. **1950** *Engineering* 4 Aug. 101/2 Among the interesting and unusual cargoes which had been shipped from time to time, there were some which had been described, respectively, as praff, shooks, kainit, and thiolith. **1971** *Farmers Weekly* 19 Mar. 38/3 This week we have been dressing beet ground with kainit, a cheap source of potash and salt.

kainosite (kɔi·-, kǣ·nǒsəit), the usual spelling of *CENOSITE.

1888 [see *CENOSITE]. **1925** *Mineral. Mag.* XX. 356 Unless obviously in error, species names should be accepted in as nearly as possible the same form as that given by the first author... As an example, take the two names Kainosite and Kainite, originally given in Swedish and German in the forms Kainosit and Kainit respectively, and both derived from the Greek καινός, new. The first was altered by Dana (1892) to Cenosite, which is scarcely recognizable even in English. **1968** I. KOSTOV *Mineral.* 306 Nordite and kainosite are orthorhombic.

kairoline (kɔi·rolin, -īn). *Chem.* [ad. G. *kaïrolin* (Hoffmann & Konigs 1883, in *Ber. d. Deut. Chem. Ges.* XVI. 740), f. *kaïrin* KAIRINE with insertion of *-ol* -OL.] 1,2,3,4-Tetrahydro-*N*-methylquinoline: an oily liquid, $C_{10}H_{13}N$, with antipyretic properties.

1883 *Pharmaceutical Jrnl.* XIV. 384 The chinolinmethylhydride (kairoline) of Konigs and Hoffmann..[was] tried and also found to have antipyretic properties. Kairoline is built up in precisely the same way as kairine, except that one atom of H is replaced by HO. **1953** *Jrnl. Amer. Chem. Soc.* LXXV. 3030 Following the procedure of Gilman and Banner kairoline was prepared from freshly distilled 1,2,3,4-tetrahydroquinoline..and freshly distilled dimethyl sulfate.

‖ **kairos** (kɔi·rɒs). [Gr. καιρός right or proper time.] Fullness of time; the propitious moment for the performance of an action or the coming into being of a new state.

1936 E. L. TALMEY tr. *Tillich's Interpretation of Hist.* II. ii. 129 We call this fulfilled moment, the moment of time approaching us as fate and decision, *Kairos*. In doing this we take up a word that was, to be sure, created by the Greek linguistic sense, but attained the deeper meaning of fullness of time, of decisive time, only in the thinking of early Christianity and its historical consciousness. **1939** V. A. DEMANT *Religious Prospect* viii. 220 A teaching that all man can know is how to respond to the Unconditioned at each moment of decision, which he calls the Kairos. **1948** J. L. ADAMS tr. *Tillich's Protestant Era* (1951) I. iii. 47 Every kairos is..implicitly..an actualization of the unique kairos, the appearance of the Christ. *Ibid.* 48 We are convinced that today a kairos, an epochal moment of history, is visible. **1963** AUDEN *Dyer's Hand* III. 140 The Greek notion of *Kairos*, the propitious moment for doing something, contained the seed of the notion of punctuality.

Kaiser. Add: **Kai·serate, Kai·serdom** = KAISERSHIP; **Kai·serish** *a.*; **Kai·serism,** absolutism as exhibited in the rule of the German emperor; **Kai·serist,** an adherent of the absolutist political system of the German emperor, *esp.* that of Wilhelm II (ruled 1888–1918); so **Kaiseri·stic** *a.*; **Kaisership** (earlier U.S. example).

1848 J. R. LOWELL *Fable for Critics* 73 Two dozen of Italy's exiles who shoot us his Kaisership daily. **1881** R. ADAMSON *Fichte* 81 Even the shadowy bond which seemed to unite the German States had been dissolved by the Austrian emperor's renunciation of the Kaiserate. **1905** *Westm. Gaz.* 27 Apr. 2/2 We confess to finding his speech..distinctly Kaiserish. **1914** C. BRERETON *Who is Responsible?* 101 In order to smash and pulverize Kaiserdom and all that it stands for in the world. **1914** T. ROOSEVELT in *N.Y. Herald* 5 Sept. 8/2 The American people will countenance nothing..that resembles.. Kaiserism. **1915** *Morning Post* 13 Feb. 6/7 The Revolutionaries, who declare that 'Kaiserism' is as deadly a form of 'Absolutism' as any that can be encountered. **1919** *New Appeal* (Girard, Kansas) 18 Jan. 4/6 The Tribune's editorials..have generally been in a Kaiseristic vein. **1920** B. CRONIN *Timber Wolves* vii. 121 A more flagrant example of business Kaiserism never happened. **1920** *Glasgow Herald* 10 June 4 The curious relations between Kaiserists and anarchists. **1923** *Ibid.* 23 May 7 The Kaiserist system of political autocracy. **1972** *Times Lit. Suppl.* 27 Oct. 1272/5 A brilliant imperial stroke in the defence of world liberty against Kaiserism.

2. *Comb.* **Kaiser moustache** (also **Kaiser Bill moustache, Kaiser Wilhelm moustache**): see quot. 1966; **Kaiser's war,** the war of 1914–18.

1938 J. CARY *Castle Corner* 108 His small, reddish moustache was curled up at the ends. It was not a Kaiser moustache. **1946** G. MILLAR *Horned Pigeon* xvi. 213 The clientèle favoured cropped hair and either Hitler or Kaiser Wilhelm moustaches. **1952** 'M. INNES' *Private View* iv. 70 Absolutely trustworthy—my batman..in the Kaiser's war. **1958** P. KEMP *No Colours or Crest* (1960) x. 205 The one appointed as our personal bodyguard was a bibulous, red-faced fellow with an enormous 'Kaiser Bill' moustache. **1963** BIRD & HUTTON-STOTT *Veteran Motor Car* 16 Before the Kaiser's war famous firms made cars in Scotland. **1966** J. S. COX *Illustr. Dict. Hairdressing* 86/1 *Kaiser Moustache*, a moustache of which the ends are turned up in the manner of William II, Emperor of Germany, the Kaiser. **1971** A. PRICE *Alamut Ambush* x. 118 The war the wheelwright was remembering was the Kaiser's, not Hitler's. **1974** A. ROSS *Bradford Business* 20 The man..was tall..with a shock of white hair and a Kaiser Bill moustache.

‖ **kaitaka** (kaitā·kă). *N.Z.* [Maori.] A flaxen cloak worn by Maoris.

1882 W. D. HAY *Brighter Britain!* II. 148 The kaitaka, a toga with a silky gloss and texture, was very highly esteemed. **1884** M. MARTIN *Our Maoris* vi. 84 The kaitaka, made of the finest flax and ornamented by a handsome border. **1949** P. BUCK *Coming of Maori* (1950) II. v. 173 The plain cloaks with *taniko* borders divide into two classes. 1. *Parawai* or *Kaitaka*... 2. *Paepaeroa*.

‖ **kajang** (kā·dʒæŋ). Also **cajang, kadjan, kedgang.** [Malay *kājang*.] Matting made from the leaves of palms or pandanus.

1821 J. LEYDEN tr. *Malay Annals* viii. 261 Raja Ahmed..flew a huge kite, as big as a cajang, (or tent folding screen). **1839** T. J. NEWBOLD *Pol. & Statistical Acct. Straits of Malacca* I. vi. 369 The Rhio gambier is often adulterated with sago, and rendered heavier by the Chinese purposely packing it in baskets lined with wet cajangs. **1845** J. BROOKE *Jrnl.* 1 Feb. in H. Keppel *Expedition Borneo* (1846) II. vi. 131 The number of fallen trees..obliged us to quit our boat, and remove all the kajang covers. **1848** F. S. MARRYAT *Borneo* 63 The Malay war-boat..is built of timber at the lower part, the upper is of bamboo, rattan, and kedgang (the dried leaf of the Nepa palm). **1901** A. C. HADDON *Head-Hunters* 299 The roof was covered with *kajangs* from the boats. **1904** E. H. GIGLIOLI tr. *Beccari's Wanderings Gt. Forests Borneo* 223 Sampans have generally a roofing of 'kadjan', a sort of matting made with palm or pandanus leaves. **1922** *Chambers's Jrnl.* 503/1 Under the *kajang* (native rush matting) covering. **1959** 'M. DERBY' *Tigress* iv. 161 The *kajang*-maker, who wove waterproof strips of matting of screw-pine leaves for roofing boats and carts.

Kajar (kā·dʒāɹ). Also **Kadjar, Qajar.** [Pers. *ḳājār*.] A member of a northern Iranian people of Turcoman origin, who formed the ruling dynasty of Persia from 1794 to 1925. Also *attrib.*

1883 *Encycl. Brit.* XV. 651/2 Branches of the royal Afsháre and Kájár tribes of Túrki descent. **1902** P. M. SYKES *Ten Thousand Miles in Persia* 121 Baluchis call all Persians *Gajar*, a corruption of Kájár, the reigning dynasty. **1932** A. T. WILSON *Persia* v. 103 Under the Qajars, roads and caravansarais were allowed to decay. **1968** R. SANGVHI *Aryamehr: Shah of Iran* xxiii. 232 Power sprang originally from their association with the Qajar monarchy. **1973** *Country Life* 31 May 1548/1 Those pictures are of a kind made in large numbers, mostly at Isfahan and Shiraz, throughout the Qajar period.

kajat, var. *KIAAT.

kajatenhout: see *KIAAT.

‖ **kakahi** (kā·kăhi). *N.Z.* [Maori.] The freshwater mussel, *Hyridella menziesi.*

1921 H. GUTHRIE-SMITH *Tutira* viii. 55 The shallows of the lake were paved with mussel-beds—kakahi. **1949** P. BUCK *Coming of Maori* (1950) II. viii. 235 The rake was lowered from a canoe on to the shoals with beds of the fresh-water clam termed *kakahi.* **1962** *Post-Primary School Bull.* XV. I. 19 Kakahi are to be found embedded in the muddy and sandy bottoms of rivers and lakes. **1966** *Encycl. N.Z.* II. 616/1 These bivalve shellfish are..the kakahi of the Maoris.

‖ **kakaho** (kā·kaho). *N.Z.* [Maori.] **a.** The dry flower-stalk of the *toetoe raupo* (*Arundo conspicua*), used for thatching and the making of mats and cloaks. **b.** From its use for cloaks, a general term for clothing.

1832 A. EARLE *Narr. Residence N.Z.* (1966) 59 They were clothed in mats, called Ka-ka-hoos. **1936** *Punch* 14 Oct. 443/1 Pingao and kakaho, which are used in tuku-tuku work. **1949** P. BUCK *Coming of Maori* (1950) II. ii. 122 The walls were sometimes lined with *kakaho* reeds but without cross stitch designs. *Ibid.* v. 166 The general term for clothing is *kakahu* or *kahu* but the different types of garments have received specific names. **1974** *Nat. Geographic* Aug. 209/1 Mrs. Emily Schuster, supervisor of women's work, showed me how her girls put together a *kakahu*, the magnificent feathered cape for ceremonial occasions.

kaki. (Earlier and later examples.)

1727 J. G. SCHEUCHZER tr. *Kæmpfer's Hist. Japan* I. I. 116 There are three different sorts of Fig-trees growing in Japan. One is call'd *Kaki*, if otherwise it may be called a Fig-tree, it differing from it in several particulars. **1795** tr. *C. P. Thunberg's Trav. Europe, Afr. & Asia* (ed. 2) III. 61 Another cause [of diarrhœa] supervened, viz. the excessive eating of the fruit of the Kaki (*Diospyros kaki*) which was at this time ripe. *Ibid.* IV. 38 For the desert [*sic*], they have kaki-figs. **1892** F. T. PIGGOTT *Garden of Japan* 43 The golden clusters of tiny flowers of *Diospyros kaki* give promise of a rich harvest of luscious fruit in the autumn—the *Kaki* loved of the Japanese. **1920** W. POPENOE *Man. Tropical & Subtropical Fruits* xii. 353 (*heading*) The Kaki or Japanese Persimmon. *Ibid.* 354 The kaki is a deciduous tree growing up to 40 feet in height. *Ibid.* 355 From Japan the kaki has been carried around the world. **1936** K. NOHARA *True Face of Japan* v. 162 The fruiterer with apples, mandarines and *kaki* fruits. **1951** *Dict. Gardening* (R. Hort. Soc.) II. 688/1 D[*iospyros*] *Kaki.* Kakee or Chinese Persimmon. *Ibid.* III. 1098/1 Kaki. See *Diospyros Kaki*, Japanese name. **1965** J. OHWI *Flora Japan* 725/1 *Diospyros kaki* Thunb...—Kaki-no-ki.

Kakiemon (kākiˌemǫn). [f. the name of Sakaida *Kakiemon*, a 17th-c. Japanese potter.] A Japanese porcelain first made by Kakiemon at Arita, characterized by asymmetrical designs, large areas of undecorated porcelain, and the use of iron red enamel, with blue, green, and yellow enamels as foils; also, any porcelain in the style of Kakiemon, which was widely imitated in Europe. Also *attrib.*

1890 J. L. BOWES *Jap. Pott.* 171 (*heading*), Arita wares. Kakiyemon ware.... A tea bowl. **1902** T. J. LARKIN in W. G. Gulland *Chinese Porc.* II. 322 The shapes and decoration..never were appreciated..by them with the exception of the Kakiemon porcelain. **1906** R. L. HOBSON *Porcelain* xx. 187 The enamel painting was largely in the Kakiemon style,..a pattern consisting of one or two birds..and a spray of bamboo or plum. **1932** W. A. THORPE tr. *Schmidt's Porc. as Art* 20 The decoration which best kept the equivalence of white ground and coloured design was the type known as Kakiemon. **1965** FINER & SAVAGE in J. Wedgwood *Sel. Lett.* viii. 151 The Chelsea mark rarely appears on their extremely close copies of Japanese Kakiemon porcelain. **1970** *Oxf. Compan. Art* 610 For refinement of shape, material, and decoration these *kakiemon* wares fully equal their Chinese counterparts. **1970** *Times* 11 Mar. 12/6 Ten years ago Meissen copies of Kakiemon wares fetched about ten times the Japanese originals.

‖ **kakke** (kæ·ke). Also **kakké.** [Jap., f. *kyaku, kaku* leg + *ki, ke* illness, disease.] The Japanese name for beriberi.

1874 *Boston Med. & Surg. Jrnl.* XC. 361 We have received a late number of the *Japan Mail*, containing an interesting description..of a species of endemic disease, known as *kak-ke*, peculiar to the Islands of Japan. **1893** A. M. BACON *Jap. Interior* ix. 153 Had I died of kakke the year before last, there would have been no help, would there? **1906** *Practitioner* Nov. 695 In her previous wars, Japan saw her armies practically prostrate with beri-beri or kakké. **1930** A. C. REED *Trop. Med. in U.S.* vii. 311 This [belief] would relate wet or edematous beriberi..to the 'kakke' of the Labrador fisherman..and certain forms of ship beriberi. **1951** E. R. WHITMORE in R. B. H. Gradwohl *Clin. Trop. Med.* lxi. 1333 Kakké is mentioned in a Chinese pamphlet of the second century B.C...: it is recorded as occurring in Japan in the ninth century.

kakoto·pia. [f. KAKO- + EU)TOPIA, U)TOPIA.] = *DYSTOPIA. Cf. CACOTOPIA.

1915 P. GEDDES *Cities in Evolution* ii. 74 The material alternatives of real economics, which these obsessions of money economics have been too long obfuscating, are broadly two, and each is towards realising an ideal, a Utopia. These are the paleotechnic and the neotechnic—Kakotopia and Eutopia respectively. **1970** *New Yorker* 10 Oct. 100/3, I use 'kakotopia'..as the opposite of 'utopia', to describe a misplanned and ugly urbanoid place. **1970** L. MUMFORD *Pentagon of Power* 49 This nightmarish conclusion..has been a recurrent theme of later technological kakotopias.

kakur (kā·kuəɹ). Also **kakar, karkur.** [prob. f. Hindi *kākar*.] The muntjak or barking deer, *Muntiacus muntjak.*

1876 A. A. A. KINLOCH *Large Game Shooting* II. 26 The Kakur is one of the smallest Deer, not being much more than eighteen inches in height. **1887** J. M. BROWN *Shikar Sk.* 254 The harsh roar of a karkur rang out close to us. **1925** A. G. ARBUTHNOT in G. Burrard *Big Game Hunting* 141 The flesh of kakur is excellent. **1946** J. CORBETT *Man-Eaters of Kumaon* (ed. 2) 185, I..went to sleep listening to a kakar barking in the scrub jungle behind my tent. **1964** R. PERRY *World of Tiger* iv. 56 Occasionally in India, and more frequently in Burma and Malaya, the little kakar, the muntjac or barking deer, is preyed upon.

Kalá, var. *KULLAH.

kala azar (kālă-, kælăˌāzā·ɹ). *Path.* Also with hyphen. [Assamese, f. *kālā* black + *āzār* disease.] A febrile disease of tropical and subtropical regions caused by the protozoan *Leishmania donovani* and transmitted by sand flies of the genus *Phlebotomus*: usually associated with emaciation, enlargement of the spleen and liver, and often bronzing of the skin. Also known as visceral leishmaniasis.

1883 J. J. CLARKE in *Ann. Sanitary Rep. Assam 1882* 36 As far back as 1869, the attention of administrative officers in Assam became directed to a peculiar disorder (called 'Kala Azar', the 'Black Disease', from the singular bronzing of the skin so often observed with it), the ravages of which decimated..numerous villages in the district of the Gáro Hills. **1908** L. ROGERS *Fevers in Tropics* i. 31 Kala-azar is the epidemic manifestation of a fever, endemic in extensive areas of India, which has spread slowly for thirty years up the Assam valley. **1930** ROGERS & MEGAW *Trop. Med.* ii. 81 The name kala-azar ..was in use in Bengal and Assam long before the nature of the disease was known. **1932** GAIGER & DAVIES *Vet. Path. & Bacteriol.* xxiii. 346 Visceral leishmaniasis is known in human beings as kala-azar, and is found frequently in dogs.., especially on the shores of the Mediterranean. **1966** 'HAN SUYIN' *Mortal Flower* i. 35 The German pension..was run by Mrs Apelt, whose husband was dying of kala-azar acquired in Manchuria. **1970** PASSMORE & ROBSON *Compan. Med. Stud.* II. xix. 8 *Leishmania donovani* causes kala azar or visceral leishmaniasis in man and animals, and the disease occurs in certain parts of all continents except Australia.

kalanchoe (kæ:lănkōᵘ·i). [Fr. (M. Adanson *Familles des Plantes* (1763) II. 247), ult. f. Chinese.] A sub-shrub of the genus so called, belonging to the family Crassulaceæ, native to Africa and southern Asia, and distinguished by succulent leaves and red, pink, or white flowers borne in terminal panicles; often cultivated as a house or greenhouse plant.

1830 J. C. LOUDON *Hortus Britannicus* 160 *Kalanchoe* Adan. Kalanchoe. (Chinese name). **1864** *Curtis's Bot. Mag.* XC. 5460 (*caption*) Large-flowered Kalanchoe. **1915** L. H. BAILEY *Stand. Cycl. Hort.* III. 1732/2 Any number of kalanchoës may appear in the collections of fanciers. **1942** *E. Afr. Ann. 1941–2* 44/1 Kalanchoes, with their large heads of four-petalled flowers are very showy. **1951** *Dict. Gardening* (R. Hort. Soc.) III. 1098/1 Kalanchoes require a good, well-drained soil. **1970** M. ALLAN *Tom's Weeds* xix. 150 There were plenty of interesting plants.. [including] the pretty little kalanchoe which Rochford's are now popularizing.

kalashi, kalashy, kalas(s)i, varr. *KHALASI.

‖ **kalashnikov** (kălæ·ʃnikǫf, kălă·ʃnikǫf). [Russ.] The name of a type of rifle or submachine gun made in the U.S.S.R. Also *attrib.*

1970 *N.Y. Times* 30 Oct. 41 A ragtag group of *fedayeen* bearing *kalashnikovs*, hand grenades and often Pepsi-Cola bottles, swarms around the headquarters area. **1971** E. LUTTWAK *Dict. Mod. War* 19/2 AK-47 (Avtomat Kalashnikov). Soviet rifle (includes AKM and RPK). **1972** *Times* 12 Jan. 10 They consist of forays across the border by from 40 to 100 men armed with Russian mortars, rockets, recoilless guns and kalashnikov automatics. **1973** *Times* 11 Apr. 1/8 He ran to get his *kalashnikov* (a Russian assault weapon) but when he returned, the Israelis had burst through the door.

kale. Add: **2*.** *N. Amer. slang.* Money.

1912 J. SANDILANDS *Western Canad. Dict.* 26 Kale, money, or wealth. **1922** [see *funfest* s.v. *FUN *sb.* 3 b]. **1926** *Flynn's* 16 Jan. 638/1 The kale is cut up an th' biggest corner goes to th' brains. **1927** *Daily Express* 23 Sept. 1 Enough 'kale' (prize-fighters' name for money) has been received..to assure the promoters a profit of approximately £100,000. **1946** B. TREADWELL *Big Bk. of Swing* 124/2 *Kale*, paper money.

kalei·doscope, *v.* [f. the sb.] To present the appearance of a brightly coloured and constantly changing pattern; to cause to come together or coalesce with pleasing results. Hence **kalei·doscoping** *ppl. a.* and *vbl. sb.*

1891 *Daily News* 5 Mar. 5/3 The spectators in the gallery cheered heartily when some particularly effective kaleidoscoping of colours happened amongst the dancers on the floor below. **1894** *Ibid.* 1 Feb. 3/1 If the ladies and gentlemen so industriously kaleidoscoping below only cared, they might do something better on these carnival nights than play at devils and clowns. **1900** *Literature* 14 July 25/1 In 'Isis'..Villiers kaleidoscoped from his memory and imagination what he had read in many Oriental and medieval books. **1933** *Discovery* July 218/2 The sitting-rooms, parlour, drawing-room, morning room, study, library, ballroom and so on have all been kaleidoscoped into the living room. **1971** *Guardian* 4 Jan. 9/2 These days of kaleidoscoping time.

kalgan (kā·lgăn). [f. *Kalgan*, name of the capital of Chahar Province, China.] Used *attrib.* or *absol.* to designate a fur obtained from the kalgan lamb.

[**1930** M. BACHRACH *Fur* iii. 35 Kalgan in Chihli, northern China, is a junction city on the Kiachta–Peiping route, and furs offered from that city are taken in the districts just mentioned.] **1960** *Guardian* 22 Apr. 8/3 Furs..never..seen in London before. Among them were ..Kalgan lamb gill. **1970** *Ibid.* 18 Nov. 13/2 A wild suede coat may be trimmed with shaggy Kalgan. **1972** *Times* 28 July 10/4 (*caption*) Tank top and battle jacket lined in white kalgan lamb.

Kali[2] (kā·li). *Hinduism.* Also **Cali.** [Skr. *kālī* fem. of *kālā* black, dark; also taken as fem. of *Kālà* time (as destroyer), one of the names of Siva.] The name given to the Hindu mother-goddess Devi, consort of Siva, in her most terrible form as goddess of destruction and death, when she is depicted as black-skinned, smeared with blood, and wearing a necklace of skulls and a girdle of snakes.

1798 W. C. BLAQUIRE tr. in *Asiatick Researches* V. 369 Let the sacrificer say *Hrang, hring.* Ca'li, Ca'li, O horrid-toothed goddess; eat, cut, destroy all the malignant. **1810** E. MOOR *Hindu Pantheon* 145 Of the many names of the goddess..those of Parvati, Bhavani, Durga, Kali, and Devi..are the most common. **1832** C. COLEMAN *Mythol. Hindus* vii. 92 Kali is also called the goddess of cemeteries, under which form she is described dancing with the infant Siva in her arms. **1882** W. J. WILKINS *Hindu Mythol.* vii. 257 Kālī (the black woman), or, as she is more commonly called Kālī Mā, the black mother, with the aid of Chandi, slew Raktavija, the principal leader of the giant's army. **1917** A. COOMARASWAMY in Coomaraswamy & Duggirala tr. *Mirror of Gesture* 8 Kālī..dances in the burning ground..to signify the heart of the devotee made empty by renunciation. **1933** E. A. PAYNE *Śāktas* ii. 13 Hibiscus flowers have become a favourite present to Kālī, probably because they are the colour of blood. **1952** S. SELVON *Brighter Sun* vii. 130 Don't know Indian people haveam own god?..To pray Kali for rain? **1971** 'G. BLACK' *Time for Pirates* i. 9 They were Moslems, which meant that there shouldn't have been a place in their faith for a worship of Kali, the Destroyer.

kalicine (kæ·lisīn). *Min.* [a. F. *kalicine* (F. Pisani 1865, in *Compt. Rend.* LX. 919), irreg. f. *kali*, mod.L. *kalium* (see KALI 2), old names for potassium + *c* + *-ine* -INE[5].] Potassium bicarbonate, $KHCO_3$.

1892 E. S. DANA *Dana's Syst. Min.* (ed. 6) 294 Kalicine. .. Potassium bicarbonate. **1922** J. W. MELLOR *Comprehensive Treat. Inorg. & Theoret. Chem.* II. xx. 774 The corresponding potassium hydrocarbonate, $KHCO_3$, was reported by F. Pisani to occur at Chypis (Canton Wallis) as a mineral which he called kalicine or kalicinite. **1965** *Chem. Abstr.* LXIII. 1514 Investigations on various blast furnaces showed the destructive effects of alkali metals, Zn, Pb, and C on the refractory shaft lining... Alkali metal and Zn compds...form a no. of minerals, such as kalicine, kalsilite,..and zincite. **1968** I. KOSTOV *Mineral.* 530 Kalicine and teschemacherite occur as finely crystalline white masses.

kalicinite (kæli·sinəit). *Min.* [f. prec. + -ITE[1].] = prec.

1922 *Mineral. Mag.* XIX. 343 Kalicinite...Variant of Kalicine..for monosymmetric $HKCO_3$. **1971** *Mineral. Rec.* II. 130/1 Buetschliite, kalicinite, carbonaceous material, and quartz are constituents of fused wood-ash clinkers formed as a result of the burning of a dead, but still standing chestnut-oak tree near Long Shop, Montgomery County, Virginia.

‖ **kalimba** (kăli·mbă). [Bantu.] A musical instrument played with the thumbs, consisting of metal strips along a small, hollow piece of wood.

1968 *Sat. Rev.* (U.S.) 26 Oct. 89 Buckley blends unusual 'noises' into the music: clinks, kalimba, calliope, gunfire, and an odd assortment of rhythm instruments. **1971** *Ink* 12 June 19/2 Toni Brown wrote most of the songs, sings lead on a couple of them, and plays keyboards..and something called a kalimba.

kalistrontite (kælistrǫ·ntəit). *Min.* [ad. Russ. *kalistrontsit* (M. L. Voronova 1962, in *Zap. Vsesoyuz. Mineral. Obshch.* XCI. 712), f. *káli-ĭ* potassium (cogn. w. KALI) + *strónts-iĭ* STRONTIUM + *-it* -ITE[1].] A sulphate of potassium and strontium, $K_2Sr(SO_4)_2$, found as colourless hexagonal crystals.

1963 *Mineral. Abstr.* XVI. 183/2 A new potassium and strontium sulphate found in saline anhydrite rocks from a borehole near the village of Alshtan, Bashkir, A.S.S.R., is named kalistrontite. **1968** I. KOSTOV *Mineral.* 504 Kalistrontite is trigonal, isostructural with palmierite $K_2Pb(SO_4)_2$.

kallidin (kæ·lĭdin). *Biochem.* [a. G. *kallidin* (E. Werle 1948, in *Angew. Chem.* LX. A. 53), f. G. *kall-ikrein* *KALLIKREIN + *pept-id* *PEPTIDE: see -IN[1].] † **a.** A supposed hypotensive peptide, released from a globulin by the enzyme kallikrein, which stimulates the uterus and intestine; later shown to be a mixture of two such peptides, bradykinin and kallidin (sense *b). *Obs.*

1950 *Chem. Abstr.* XLIV. 5476 Kallidin (previously called DK substance) is a low-mol.-wt. peptide. **1959** *New Scientist* 16 Apr. 856/1 When its properties were studied, bradykinin showed itself to be extremely similar to the peptide kallidin, whose existence was first demonstrated in Germany between the wars.

b. (Also *kallidin II.*) The peptide having the same sequence of constituent amino-acids as bradykinin except for an additional lysergic acid residue at the hydrogen end.

1961 PIERCE & WEBSTER in *Biochem. & Biophys. Research Communications* V. 353 The present report describes the isolation of two kallidins from the incubation of human urinary kallikrein with acid-treated human plasma. *Ibid.* 354 Two peaks of activity [on a chromatograph] were obtained. These were designated kallidins I and II. *Ibid.* 356 These data indicate that kallidin I is identical with bradykinin and that kallidin II is a decapeptide. **1965** *Jrnl. Physiol.* CLXXVI. 1 Bradykinin and kallidin II are respectively, a nona- and a deca-peptide, which occur in man and other species... Kallidin II (hereafter referred to as kallidin), which is converted from kallidinogen by the enzyme kallikrein, appears to be the immediate precursor of bradykinin. **1970** PASSMORE & ROBSON *Compan. Med. Stud.* II. xvii. 1 The name kallidin now refers specifically to lysyl-bradykinin.

kallikrein (kæ·likri,in, -krīn). *Biochem.* Also † **callicrein.** [a. G. *kallikrein* (H. Kraut et al. 1930, in *Zeitschr. f. physiol. Chem.* CLXXXIX. 99), f. Gr. καλλίκρε-ας sweetbread (f. καλλι-, comb. form of κάλλος beauty + κρέας flesh): see -IN[1].] **a.** An enzyme found in the human pancreas and elsewhere in the body, which releases kallidin from a plasma precursor and has been used therapeutically as a vasodilator and hypotensive agent.

1930 *Chem. Abstr.* XXIV. 4541 The name *callicrein*, taken from a Greek synonym for pancreas, is proposed for this circulatory hormone. **1967** *Martindale's Extra Pharmacopoeia* (ed. 25) 1440 Kallikrein is a dilator of the peripheral blood-vessels... It has been used in the treatment of vasospastic circulatory disorders, including.. chilblains. **1956** ROBSON & KEELE *Recent Adv. Pharmacol.* (ed. 2) xiv. 480 Kallidin is formed by the proteolytic action of a widely distributed (in saliva, serum, urine, pancreas, etc.) enzyme called Kallikrein, which under the name Padutin has been used therapeutically.

b. Any enzyme which liberates a kinin from a protein.

1966 M. E. WEBSTER in E. G. Erdös *Hypotensive Peptides* 650 A kallikrein is defined as an endogenous enzyme which rapidly and specifically liberates a kinin from kininogen... In view of the many known chemical and physical differences between the kallikreins, each kallikrein should be identified by species and source, e.g. hog pancreatic kallikrein. **1969** *Physiol. Rev.* XLIX. 510 The kallikreins (kininogenases) are a group of enzymes... They have marked actions on blood vessels and smooth muscles in vivo that..are due to the rapid enzymatic cleavage of a specific substrate, an α_2 globulin present in plasma and lymph.

ka·llipyg. *rare.* [Cf. CALLIPYGIAN *a.*] A person with finely developed buttocks.

a **1913** F. ROLFE *Desire & Pursuit of Whole* (1934) xvii. 178 Some bulgy kallipyg with swung skirts and cardboard waist.

kallitype (kæ·litəip). *Photogr.* [f. Gr. καλλι-, comb. form of κάλλος beauty + -TYPE.] A disused photographic printing-process using either paper coated with a ferric salt and silver nitrate which is developed in a solution of borax and Rochelle salt, or paper sensitized with a ferric salt and developed in silver nitrate solution.

1890 *Brit. Jrnl. Photogr.* 23 May 335/2 We may here state that we have received..two specimens of kallitype. **1941** *Ibid.* LXXXVIII. 445 Owing to the present scarcity of printing material it seemed worth while canvassing some of the old abandoned processes of photographic printing; the most probably useful seemed to be Kallitype. This was widely used before the days of P.O.P. and bromide. **1965** J. KOSAR *Light-Sensitive Syst.* i. 39 In the past, silver-iron printing papers were employed also for producing continuous-tone prints. This process was named 'Kallitype'; its attractive feature was the possibility of toning the prints with toning baths.

kalloscope (kæ·loskōᵘp). *Disused.* [Irreg. f. Gr. κάλλος beauty + -SCOPE.] A type of STEREOSCOPE.

1901 *Daily Chron.* 10 Aug. 5/6 The suppression of what are known as kallascopes [*sic*], stereoscopes and similar machines. **1902** *Ibid.* 3 May 4/5 The 'Automatic Kalloscope'..which attracted the attention of the police.

kalmia (kæ·lmiă). [mod.L. (Linnæus *Nova Plantarum Genera* (1751) no. 1079), f. the name of Pehr *Kalm* (1716–1779), Swedish botanist + -IA[1].] An evergreen shrub of the genus so called, belonging to the family Ericaceæ, native to North America, and bearing clusters of pink or white flowers; also called mountain laurel or calico-bush.

1765 J. BARTRAM *Diary* 6 Sept. in *Trans. Amer. Philos. Soc.* (1942) XXXIII. 24/1 Here grows most northward trees here [*sic*] except..white pine & our 3 calmias. **1785** H. MARSHALL *Arbustrum Americanum* 72 Narrow leaved Kalmia..delights in moist or swampy places. **1838** *Boston Weekly Mag.* 22 Sept. 17/2 The *Rhodora* is followed in succession by the *Honeysuckles*, the *Kalmias* or *Laurels*, the *Azalea.* **1878** R. T. COOKE *Happy Dodd* 347 With.. glittering clusters of Kalmia leaves..she adorned all the rooms. **1900** L. H. BAILEY *Cycl. Amer. Hort.* II. 854/1 The Kalmias thrive well in a sandy, peaty or loamy soil. **1955** *Sci. News Let.* 21 May 334/2 Kalmia, or mountain laurel, is a most attractive plant at any time, for its dark shining leaves are evergreen...Its clusters of closed starflowers, pink..are things for poets to write sonnets about.

Kalmuck (kæ·lmɒk). Also 8 **-muc,** 9 **-muk, -myk,** 7–9 **Calmuc(k.** [Russ. *kalmýk.*] **1. a.** A member of a Mongolian people living on the north-west shores of the Caspian Sea. Also *attrib.* or as *adj.*

1613 PURCHAS *Pilgrimage* IV. xiii. 358 Master Ienkinson mentioneth a Nation liuing among the Tartars, called Kings; which are also Gentiles, as are also the Kirgessen.. and the Colmackes, which worship the sunne, **1617** *Ibid.* (ed. 3) IV. xv. 482 There are some..which are not Mahumetans, nor shaue their haire of their heads after the Tartarian manner; and therefore they call them Calmuck or Pagans. **1757** J. DYER *Fleece* IV. 126 The Cossac there, The Calmuc, and Mungalian, round the bales In crouds resort. **1783** W. TOOKE tr. *Georgi's Russia* IV. 121 The dwellings of the heathenish and christian Kalmucs. *Ibid.* 125 The Kalmuc hords on the Volga. **1822** BYRON *Don Juan* VII. lviii. 273 Suwarrow, who was standing in his shirt Before a company of Calmucks. **1882** R. L. STEVENSON *New Arabian Nights* (ed. 2) II. 66 His broken nose and high cheekbones gave him somewhat the air of a Kalmuck. **1902** *Encycl. Brit.* XXX. 8/2 Kalmyk, or Kalmuck Steppe, a territory or reservation belonging to the Kalmyks. **1903** LD. R. GOWER *Rec. & Reminisc.* 430 A man..with a rather Kalmuk-featured face and white curly hair. **1963** V. NABOKOV *Gift* ii. 114 The compact, sturdy Kalmuk ponies walk in single file forming echelons. **1972** J. POYER *Chinese Agenda* (1973) xiii. 180 A caravan of Kalmuck traders. *Ibid.* 181 These Kalmucks are strictly traders.

b. The language of this people, belonging to the Ural-Altaic group.

1883 *Encycl. Brit.* XVI. 750/2 The Kalmuk and East Mongolian dialects do not differ much...In Kalmuk..the guttural can only be traced through the lengthening of the syllable. **1947** [see *BURIAT].

2. (With small initial letter.) A kind of shaggy cloth, resembling bearskin (see also quot. 1940).

1860 S. JUBB *Hist. Shoddy-Trade* 40 A cloth called calmucks..has..replaced 'short ends'. **1940** *Chambers's Techn. Dict.* 128/1 *Calmuc*, a coarse type of wool, from the Khirghiz district, Central Asia.

Hence **Kalmu·ckian** *a.*

1727 J. G. SCHEUCHZER tr. *Kæmpfer's Hist. Japan* I. I. vi. 90 The Prince of the Calmuckian Tartars.

‖ **kalokagathia** (kæ:lokægæ·þiă, kēi:lo-). [Gr. καλοκαγαθία, f. καλοκάγαθος = καλὸς κἀγαθός for καλὸς καὶ ἀγαθός beautiful and good (the perfect character).] Nobility and goodness of character.

1921 tr. *W. Rathenau's New Soc.* x. 102 The Greeks.. adopted as their highest law..that impulse of the will which they called *Kalokagathia.* **1930** N. MITCHISON in *Time & Tide* 14 June 773/1 The formal kalokagathia of that incredible time.

kalsilite (kæ·lsiləit). *Min.* [f. the letters *KAlSi* in its chemical formula + -LITE.] A rare silicate of potassium and aluminium, $KAlSiO_4$, that is chemically and physically similar to nepheline and occurs in some potassium-rich lavas.

1942 A. HOLMES in *Mineral. Mag.* XXVI. 198 Mr. Bannister's results, supplemented by micro-chemical analyses made by Dr. M. H. Hey, are recorded in the communication which follows this paper. The new data indicate that the mineral is..a hitherto unrecognized polymorph of $KAlSiO_4$ for which the appropriately mnemonic name kalsilite is proposed. **1942** BANNISTER & HEY in *Ibid.* 221 It is proposed to name the new mineral kalsilite after its composition $KAlSiO_4$. **1967** *Nature* 24 June 1322/1 Kalsilite ($KAlSiO_4$) occurs as a major constituent of a large sedimentary xenolith metamorphosed to the sanidinite facies within the gabbro of Brome Mountain, Quebec. Kalsilite is extremely rare and has previously been found only as an igneous mineral in three volcanic areas. **1972** M. H. BATTEY *Mineral. for Students* II. 292/2 The ratio of K to Na in nepheline varies and there is a series towards kalsilite $KAlSiO_4$ which is a rare mineral found in certain potassic lavas on the Uganda–Congo border.

kalsomine (kæ·lsomain). For 'erron.' read 'orig.' Add examples. Also as *v. trans.* and *intr.*, to whitewash with kalsomine. Hence **ka·lsomined** *ppl. a.*, **ka·lsominer, ka·lsomining** *vbl. sb.*

1840 *Athenæum* 20 June 502 Kalsomine. **1858** W. A. BUTLER *Two Millions* 42 From lowest basement up to topmost attic, The whole was gorgeous, glaring and prismatic; Pannelled and kalsomined. **1883** *Harper's Mag.* Mar. 503/2 Paint and kalsomine can not be counted upon. **1884** H. G. CARLETON *Thompson St. Poker Club* 20 An extensive kalsomining contract **1888** *Pall Mall Gaz.* 3 Mar. 11/1 Over face, arms, neck,..and bosom she spreads a coat of liquid white... In plain words, she, as it were, kalsomines herself. **1891** H. C. BUNNER *Zadoc Pine* 166 White kalsomined bedrooms. **1893** K. A. SANBORN *Truthful Woman S. California* 81 Those who feel an unctuous joy in painting the lily, kalsomining the calla, and adding perfumes to the violet. **1904** 'O. HENRY' *Cabbages & Kings* xiv. 248 Let me kalsomine you a little mental sketch to consider. **1916** H. L. WILSON *Somewhere in Red Gap* iv. 128 He was a painter and grainer and kalsominer and paperhanger. *Ibid.* 135 He..began to paper and paint and grain and kalsomine. **1924** *Spectator* 1 Nov. 640 These walls can be whitewashed or covered with vines on the outside and kalsomined within. **1936** L. C. DOUGLAS *White Banners* iii. 57 The specifications for improvements: a new sink, repair of the hot-water machine, kalsomining in the kitchen. **1945** B. MACDONALD *Egg & I* (1946) 49 We laid new floors; put in windows; kalsomined the walls.

Kalydor (kæ·lidōᵊɪ). Also **kalydor.** (The proprietary name of) a type of skin tonic of which almond oil forms the basis.

1824 *Advt.* in C. W. Cunnington *Feminine Attitudes 19th Cent.* (1935) 309 The Kalydor..a never-failing specific for all cutaneous deformities. **1828** tr. *L. af Holberg's Journey to World under Ground* 239 The fourth attended with a bottle of kalydor, for the improvement of the complexion. **1861** [see AMANDIN(E]. **1876** *Trade Marks Jrnl.* 13 Dec. 993 Rowland's Kalydor for improving and beautifying the complexion. Eradicates all cutaneous eruptions... Henry Edward Rowland and George William Rowland, trading as Alexander Rowland and Sons,.. Hatton Gardens, Middlesex. **1901** C'TESS C. *Beauty's Aids* 242 (Advt.), Rowland's Kalydor..successfully opposes the attacks of the hot summer sun or damp chilly weather..allays all smarting irritations..removes freckles, tan, sunburn, prickly heat..imparts a luxuriant beauty to the complexion, and arrays the neck, hands, and arms in matchless whiteness. **1907** *Yesterday's Shopping* (1969) 539/2 Rowland's Kalydor bot. 2/0. **1939–40** *Army & Navy Stores Catal.* 438/3 Rowland's Kalydor—bot. 2/6.

kamachili (kāmătʃi·li). Also **camanchile, guamachil, kamachile, kamachilis.** [Tagalog: see quot. 1923.] A tree, *Pithecolobium dulce*, of the family Leguminosæ, native to tropical America and naturalized in the Philippines, having edible pods and bark that yields a yellow dye. Also *attrib.*

1866 LINDLEY & MOORE *Treas. Bot.* II. 898/2 *P[ithecolobium] dulce*..produces cylindrical irregularly swollen pods, curled at the top, containing a sweet edible pulp, which the Mexicans, who call the tree Guamachil, boil and eat. **1903** E. D. MERRILL *Dict. Plant Names Philippine Islands* 44 Camachilis, T[agalog]. Pithecolobium dulce Benth. **1915** *Philippine Jrnl. Sci.* A. X. 353 The price of air-dried camanchile bark has risen. **1923** E. D. MERRILL *Enumeration Philippine Flowering Plants* II. 243 *Pithecolobium dulce*... Throughout the Philippines... Introduced from Mexico; now pantropic. Local names:.. kamachili (Tag.); kamachilis (Tag.)..all corruptions or modifications of the Aztec *kwamochitl.* **1937** *Nature* 16 Oct. 687/1 Several trees growing in the Philippine Islands yield liquors suitable for tanning purposes. The betel nut, *Areca Catechu*..and kamachile, *Pithecolobium dulce*, are.. the most important trees. **1954** W. H. BROWN *Useful Plants of Philippines* II. 154 Camanchile bark is used almost exclusively by Filipino tanners.

kamagraph (kæ·măgrɑf). [f. next.] **a.** A painting reproduced by kamagraphy. **b.** A printing press which produces kamagraphs.

1967 *Time* 23 June 49 Each kamagraph looks as though the artist had painted it by hand. **1968** *Collier's Encycl. Year Book* 131 Max Ernst, the well-known dada and surrealist painter; Edouard Pignon, a French abstractionist; and the late René Magritte, the extraordinary Belgian surrealist who died this year, have all executed special work for the kamagraph.

Hence **kama·grapher, kamagra·phic** *a.*

1970 *Britannica Bk. of Year* (U.S.) 798/2 *Kamagraphy*, a process for making multiple copies of a painting produced by an artist on a specially treated canvas in which

the copies retain the texture of the brushstrokes of the original but the original is destroyed in the process; *kamagraph, kamagrapher*; *kamagraphic, adj.*

kamagraphy (kămæ·grăfi). [ad. F. *kamagraphie*.] A process for making copies of original paintings, using a special press and treated canvas, which reproduces exactly the colour and texture of the brushstrokes.

1967 *Time* 23 June 49 Kamagraphy faithfully produces 250 perfect copies of a painting on a special press, destroying the original in the process. **1968** *Collier's Encycl. Year Book* 131 A French process called kamagraphy has been developed by engineer André Cocard, with the backing of art collector and vintner Alexis Lichine. **1970** [see prec.].

kamahi (kā·măhī, kā·məi). *N.Z.* Also **kaamahi, karmahi, karmai.** [Maori.] A forest tree, *Weinmannia racemosa*, belonging to the family Cunoniaceæ, and bearing racemes of small, cream flowers.

1867 J. D. Hooker *Handbk. N.Z. Flora* II. 765/2 Karmahi, *Hector*. *Weinmannia silvicola* and *racemosa*. **1868** J. Hector in *Trans. N.Z. Inst.* I. iii. Essay 4 The flat land and low spurs are covered with the common species of Pines and Birch, such as Rimu, Totara, Weinmannia (Karmahi), and Fagus (Tawai). **1868** J. Buchanan in *Ibid.* Essay 37 Towai, or Karmai (*Weinmannia racemosa*). A beautiful large tree, especially when in flower. **1899** T. Kirk *Students' Flora N.Z.* 140 *W[einmannia] racemosa*, Linn. f. A shrub or large tree, often from 70 ft.–90 ft. high... *Kamahi.* **1953** *Landfall* VII. 122 He had played his violin under a kamahi tree. **1963** B. Pearson *Coal Flat* iv. 59 In a little clearing in the kaamahi and fuchsia and young bush..was Mrs Seldom's little house. **1966** *Weekly News* (Auckland) 22 June 44 The kamahi present on this charming little hill is a hardy tree.

Kamakura (kā·măkūᵊrā). The name of a town in central Japan, used *attrib.* to designate the art of the period (1192–1333) during which Kamakura was the seat of government.

[**1890** B. H. Chamberlain *Things Japanese* 227 The grandest example of..colossal bronze-casting is the *Daibutsu* (literally, 'great Buddha') at Kamakura.] **1902** F. Brinkley *Oriental Series: Japan* VII. iii. 110 Nearly four hundred years may be regarded as the Kamakura epoch from the point of view of the sculptor's art, and may also be regarded..as the final era of vigorous originality in religious sculpture. **1912** E. F. Fenollosa *Epochs Chinese & Jap. Art* I. ix. 197 Several phases of Kamakura art..went on parallel to the main stream of secular makimono painting. **1952** L. Warner *Enduring Art Japan* iv. 52 Kamakura scrolls seemed to epitomise the other changes. **1970** *Oxf. Compan. Art* 606/2 Works of the spiritual stature of the Tempyō sculptures or the Kamakura portraits were isolated incidents rarely attained.

Kamares (kămā·rīz). Also **Kamarais.** [Gr. Καμάραις, name of a cave-sanctuary of the Minoans on Mt. Ida in Crete, where the pottery was first found.] A type of Minoan pottery from the Middle Bronze Age, characterized by the use of red, white, and yellow ornaments on a black ground, depicting abstract or stylized plant designs. Also *attrib.*

1895 *Proc. Soc. Antiquaries London* XV. 356 The red.. on very thin black-glazed ware, is exactly of the Kamárais tint, while the drawing has the Kamárais touch. *Ibid.*, We may consider that the Kamárais pottery began at least as early as 2300 B.C. **1902** *Encycl. Brit.* XXXI. 56/1 This ware, known as 'Kamáres', from a cave near a village on the south-east of Mount Ida. **1948** A. Lane *Greek Pott.* iv. 22 The 'Kamares' style named after a cave in Crete where many examples were found. **1949** W. F. Albright *Archaeol. of Palestine* v. 93 There was nothing in Palestine like the delicate Kamares ware of Middle Bronze Crete, which was in great demand in Egypt. **1960** T. Burton-Brown *Early Medit. Migrations* i. 1 Certain classes of pottery..were believed to indicate direct contacts between the peoples of Egypt and those of the Aegaean area. Amongst these are sherds of polychrome painted fabrics, some of which may be either Kamares wares from Crete, or related wares. **1970** *Oxf. Compan. Art* 725/2 The 'egg-shell' Kamares ware..bears some of the very best of Minoan decoration, with some floral motifs possibly derived from geometric forms rather than copied from nature.

kamarezite (kămā·rəzəit). *Min.* [ad. G. *kamarezit* (K. H. E. G. Busz 1893, in *Verh. d. naturhist. Vereins* L. *Sitzungsber. d. naturwiss. Sekt.* 84) f. *Kamareza*, name of the place in Greece where it was first found: see -ite[1].] A grass-green basic sulphate of copper, originally thought to be $Cu_3(SO_4)(OH)_4.6H_2O$, but later found to be identical with brochantite, $Cu_4SO_4(OH)_6$.

1895 *Jrnl. Chem. Soc.* LXVIII. ii. 506 Kamarezite... This new mineral from Kamareza, Laurium, Greece, is grass-green and shows a crystalline structure. **1951** C. Palache et al. *Dana's Syst. Min.* (ed. 7) II. xxxi. 588 *Kamarezite*...Orthorhombic (?). In minute crystals. **1965** *Amer. Mineral.* L. 1456 The optical, physical, crystallographic, and chemical evidence that have been presented ..is (*sic*) strong support for the contention that the mineral described as kamarezite by Busz (1893, 1895) is brochantite. *Ibid.* 1457 We recommended that kamarezite be removed from the list of accepted mineral species; this recommendation has been accepted by..the Commission on New Minerals and Mineral Names.

kamassi (kama·si). *S. Afr.* Also **camassie, kamasse, kamassie.** [Afrikaans *kammassie*, f. native name.] A South African evergreen tree, *Gonioma kamassi*, of the family Apocynaceæ, or its hard yellow wood. Also *attrib.*

1793 tr. *C. P. Thunberg's Trav. Europe, Afr., & Asia* II. 110 Camassie wood (Camassie-hout), is merely a shrub, and consequently produces small pieces only, which serve for veneering. **1814** R. B. Fisher *Importance of Cape Good Hope* 84 The kamasse, a sort of bark, being the rhind or shavings of the tree of that name. **1907** T. R. Sim *Forests & Forest Flora Cape Good Hope* 323 The Knysna export under the name of Boxwood was all, or mostly, Kamassi-wood, without any Boxwood. **1924** Record & Mell *Timbers Tropical Amer.* 506 One of the two South African woods known to the world trade is the so-called Knysna or Kamassi boxwood. **1935** L. Chalk et al. *Forest Trees & Timbers Brit. Empire* III. 15 Kamassi attains about 40 ft. in height and generally a maximum girth of 2 to 3 ft. *Ibid.* 17 Kamassi is one of the two timbers exported from South Africa regularly in small quantities. **1951** *Dict. Gardening* (R. Hort. Soc.) II. 908/2 *G[onioma] Kamassi.* Evergreen shrub... Yields the hard Kamassi wood of S. Africa. **1973** Palmer & Pitman *Trees S. Afr.* III. 1905 Kamassi occurs in numbers in the Midland forests of the Cape. *Ibid.* 1906 It is exported in small quantities, as is Cape box for which kamassie is often mistaken.

Kama Sutra (kā:mă sʊ·tră). Also (as one word) **Kamasutra.** [Skr. *kāma* love + *sūtra* (see Sutra).] The title of an ancient Sanskrit treatise on the art of love and sexual techniques; hence used allusively.

1883 Burton & Arbuthnot *Kama Sutra of Vatsyayana* 3 In the present publication it is proposed to give a complete translation of what is considered the standard work on love in Sanscrit literature, and which is called the 'Vatsyayana Kama Sutra', or Aphorisms on Love, by Vatsyayana. *Ibid.* iii. 24 Man should study the Kama Sutra and the arts and sciences subordinate thereto... Even young maids should study this Kama Sutra. **1915** *Encycl. Relig. & Ethics* VIII. 450/1 The *Kāmasūtra* permits love matches generally. **1960** 'S. Harvester' *Chinese Hammer* xix. 172 A large illustration of many-armed embrace whose postures owed more to the Hindu *Kamasutra* than to a depiction of a Tibetan *Dukor* with his bejewelled *shakti*. **1961** C. Willock *Death in Covert* iii. 73 Individual pillars were decorated with some rather questionable designs. Whynne..said: 'Don't worry. We shall be building an outdoor Espresso Bar..round the most Kama Sutra of those.' **1964** *Listener* 26 Nov. 848/3 For its delineation of the almost innumerable techniques for handling a locomotive, *The Train* must be accounted the *Kama Sutra* of the permanent way. **1970** J. Boland *Big Job* xii. 100 The things I've taught that girl. Proper little Kama Sutra, I am. **1972** R. Quilty *Tenth Session* 93 He'll be bursting in any minute. Kama Sutra lips—ready for the last waltz.

Kamba (kæ·mbă). [Bantu.] A Bantu-speaking people of central Kenya, related ethnically to the Kikuyu; a member of this people; their language.

1885 J. T. Last *Gram. Kamba Lang.* 14 Probably the cardinal numbers are seldom used by the Kambas beyond *iyana*, 100. *Ibid.* 31 The simplest form of the verb is used in Kamba, as in Swahili and English, for the second person singular of the imperative. **1938** W. M. Hailey *Afr. Survey* ii. 24 Among the Kikuyu and Kamba, a whole age-grade of boys is initiated at one time. **1959** B. Bernardi *Mugwe* i. 2 They share this tradition with the other bordering Bantu peoples, the Kikuyu,..the Mbere and the Kamba. **1963** *Times* 31 May 10/2 Mr. Sagini is a Kisii, Mr. Mwanyumba (Works) is a Taita and Mr. Mwendwa (Labour) is a Kamba.

Kamba, var. *Khamba.

Kamchadal (kæ·mtʃădæl). Also **Kamtchat(ka)dale, Kamt(s)chadale.** [Russ.] **a.** A member of a Mongoloid people inhabiting the Kamchatka peninsula on the Pacific coast of Siberia. **b.** The language of this people.

1764 J. Grieve tr. *Krasheninnikov's Hist. Kamtschatka* iii. iii. 175 Thus it appears likely, that the Kamtschadales lived formerly in Mungalia beyond the river Amur, and made one people with the Mungals. **1790** tr. *J. B. B. de Lesseps's Trav. Kamtschatka* I. 134 It is observed..that Kamtschadales of either sex, do not live longer than Russians. **1824** J. D. Cochrane *Narr. Journey Russia & Siberian Tartary* (ed. 2) II. xi. 43 The number of real Kamtchatdales who retain their ancient usages is small. **1855** *Eng. Cycl.: Nat. Hist.* III. 557 The Kalan of the Kamtchatkadales. **1871** E. B. Tylor *Primitive Culture* I. iii. 98 This spiritualistic belief among the Kamchadals is, no doubt, the key to their superstition as to rescuing drowning men. **1909** *Westm. Gaz.* 28 Aug. 10/2 The Kamchadals, one of the numerous tribes inhabiting the North of Siberia. **1933** L. Bloomfield *Lang.* iv. 70 The Hyperborean family..consists of Chukchee..Koryak..and Kamchadal. **1937** R. H. Lowie *Hist. Ethnol. Theory* ii. 15 The Kamchadal cooked meat in wooden troughs filled with water into which they threw heated rocks. **1956** [see *Gilyak].

Kamchatkan (kæmtʃæ·tkăn), *sb.* and *a.* Also **Kamschatkan, Kamskatchan, Kamt(s)chatkan.** [f. *Kamchatka* (place-name); see -an.] **A.** *sb.* A person from the peninsula of Kamchatka in Siberia; often = prec. **B.** *adj.* Of or pertaining to Kamchatka.

1797 *Encycl. Brit.* IX. 429/2 The southern Kamtchatkans commonly build their villages in thick woods. **1833** W. L. Mackenzie *Sk. Canada & U.S.* 25 Even the wild Greenlander, the grim Kamschatkan, and the desolate Siberian love their barren wastes. **1865** Dickens *Mut. Fr.* II. iv. v. 201 [She] sometimes might have issued her directions to equal purpose in the Kamskatchan language. **1871** *Month* May–June 552 The marvellous fertility and floweriness of a Kamchatkan summer. **1888** *Athenæum* 3 Mar. 270/3 An Eskimo offshoot, though mixed with Tuski or Kamtchatkan blood. **1890** J. G. Frazer *Golden Bough* II. iii. 110 It was a principle with the Kamtchatkans never to kill a land or sea animal without first making excuses to it. **1917** W. M. Salter *Nietzsche* 263 The Kamschatkans required that snow should never be scraped off with a knife. **1937** *Times* 30 Dec. 9/3 By a Convention signed in 1928 Japan was given extensive fishing rights in Russian waters off the Kamchatkan and other eastern coasts.

kameel (kămī·l). *S. Afr.* [Afrikaans, a. Du. *kameel* camel.] The giraffe, *Giraffa camelopardalis*.

1839 W. C. Harris *Wild Sports S. Afr.* 373 *Camelopardalis Giraffa*. The Giraffe. Kameel of the Cape Colonists. **1896** H. A. Bryden *Tales S. Afr.* 70 As..we wanted meat, I rammed the spurs in and galloped headlong for the kameels. **1900** W. L. Sclater *Fauna S. Afr.* I. 264 The name giraffe..is practically unknown in South Africa where the term 'kameel' is always used. **1925** F. C. Slater *Shining River* 234 Kameel—The Southern giraffe, formerly found throughout the country north of the Orange River.

kameeldoorn (kămī·lduᵊɹn). *S. Afr.* Also **kameeldoring.** [Afrikaans, ad. Du. *kameel* camel + *doorn* thorn.] = *camel-thorn* (*b*) (s.v. *Camel *sb.* 5).

1822 W. J. Burchell *Trav. S. Afr.* I. xviii. 453 A large solitary tree of *Kameel-doorn* (Camel-thorn, or the tree on which, generally, the Camelopardalis browses), the first I had seen of the species, was standing here. **1896** H. A. Bryden *Tales S. Afr.* 44 Groves of giraffe acacia (*kameel doorn*), through which still wander freely in these pathless, waterless solitudes the tall giraffe. **1937** S. Cloete *Turning Wheels* 53 Passing the big group of kameel-doorns that were a landmark, they turned slightly west. **1948** [see *gompaauw, gompauw]. **1957** *Cape Times* (Mag. Section) 20 July 2/7 Ghani got out lazily.. stationing himself beneath a shady kameeldoring overlooking the hotel yard. **1972** *S. Afr. Garden & Home* Oct. 33 The striking crimson-breasted shrike..seen perched on a *kameel-doring*.

kameez(e, var. Camise, camiss.

1966 J. & R. Godden *Two under Indian Sun* iii. 73 A coat and trousers instead of dhoti and kameeze. **1971** *Femina* (Bombay) 2 Apr. 51/2 An off-shoot of the same idea is a two-piece unit, basically a kameez and gharara, but the kameez-sleeves being of the same material as the gharara, extra colourful, while the body of the kameez itself is a plain dark self-colour. **1972** 'E. Peters' *Death to Landlords!* i. 21 She had taken to the *shalwar* and *kameez* of the Punjabi women.

kamerad (kæ·mĕrăd, ‖ kamĕrā·t). [G., ad. F. *camarade* Comrade.] Comrade, companion: the exclamation used as an appeal for quarter by a German-speaking soldier on surrendering. Hence jocularly as *v. intr.*, to say 'kamerad', express one's wish to surrender.

1914 *Illustr. London News* 10 Oct. 497 How the enemy surrenders, saying, 'Kamerad..Pardon!' **1916** 'Boyd Cable' *Action Front* 63 'Nein, nein!' answered Ainsley. 'You kamarade—sie kamarade.' The other, in somewhat voluble gutturals, insisted that Ainsley must 'kamarade', otherwise surrender. **1917** P. MacGill *Brown Brethren* vii. 105 'Kamerad! Kamerad!' they whined, their arms shaking as if stricken with palsy. **1917** *Times Hist. War* XIV. 199/2 Then Gardener shouted to the others..'You're late. Everybody else has Kameraded.' **1918** *Daily News* 21 Sept. 5/2 When our men came down the steps of the dugout the card-players perfunctorily held up their hands and 'Kameraded'. **1923** *Westm. Gaz.* 3 July, Sir W. Joynson-Hicks cried 'Kamerad' at once. He tried to let himself down lightly by saying that he had expected a unanimous acceptance. **1930** Kipling *Limits & Renewals* (1932) 259 'Kamerad, Bull! I'll come in,' said Loftie. Vaughan's hands had gone up first. **1973** C. Egleton *Seven Days to Killing* viii. 89 He threw his weapon aside, held up his hands and yelled Kamerad.

kami. Add: (Earlier and later examples.) Also **kami-dana** = *god-shelf* s.v. God *sb.* 16 *a*.

1616 R. Cocks *Diary* (1883) I. 131 Micarna Camme Samme, the Emperours sonns sonne. **1663** R. Manley tr. *Caron & Schouten's True Descr. Kingdoms Japan & Siam* 115 *Owarny Cammy Samma*, the old Emperors Brother. **1876** [see *god-shelf]. **1904** L. Hearn *Japan: Attempt at Interpretation* viii. 150 The domestic god-shelf —*Kamidana*. **1931** G. B. Sansom *Japan* i. iii. 46 At one end of the scale the Sun Goddess, that Heaven-Shining-Great-August Deity is a *kami*, and at the other mud and sand and even vermin are *kami*. **1965** W. Swaan *Jap. Lantern* iii. 33 Mirrors are sacred objects associated with *kami* (spirits). **1970** J. W. Hall *Japan from Prehist. to Mod. Times* iv. 32 Often translated as 'god', 'deity', or 'spirit', *kami* can best be described as localized spiritual forces. **1972** *Guardian* 23 Sept. 10/3 He spends twenty minutes in personal prayer to the 'kami' of the shrine, who in this case are the Emperor Meiji, the monarch who presided over the modernisation of Japan in the late nineteenth century, and his consort, Empress Shoken.

kamik (kæ·mik). Also **kammik.** [Eskimo.] A long boot of sealskin worn by the Eskimos.

1891 L. GIBSON *Jrnl.* 15 Aug. in R. E. Peary *Northward over Gt. Ice* (1898) I. iii. 109 The [Eskimo] woman made us a pair of Kamiks. **1900** *Scribner's Mag.* Sept. 297/1 Seal-skin kammiks, or top boots. **1910** R. E. PEARY *North Pole* xiv. 128 The *kamiks*, or boots, of seal-skin, soled with the heavier skin of the square-flipper seal. **1922** *Chambers's Jrnl.* 425/1 Untying the upper part of his *kamik*, or long boot. **1933** J. BUCHAN *Prince of Captivity* iii. 106 Their reindeer-skin kamiks had been worn into holes. **1945** D. LEECHMAN *Eskimo Summer* 29 Nearly all of them [*sc.* Eskimo girls] were wearing sealskin *kamiks*, but one or two girls actually had on silk stockings and shoes with medium high heels. **1969** *Daily Tel.* (Colour Suppl.) 18 Apr. 11/4 Eskimo wives stitching parkas and *kamiks*, or sealskin boots, which they trade at the local co-op store.

‖ **kamikaze** (kæmɪ̆kā·zi). Also with capital initial. [Jap., 'divine wind', f. *kami* god, KAMI + *kaze* wind.]

The word was originally used in Jap. lore with reference to the supposed divine wind which blew on a night in August 1281, destroying the navy of the invading Mongols.

A. *sb.* **1.** 'The wind of the gods' (see small-type note above).

1896 L. HEARN *Kokoro* x. 137 That mighty wind still called *Kami-kazé*,—'the Wind of the Gods', by which the fleets of Kublai Khan were given to the abyss. *Ibid.*, But ..the Kami-kazé did not come. **1970** J. W. HALL *Japan* vii. 93 The 'divine wind' (*kamikaze*) which Japan's protective *kami* had generated against its enemies.

2. One of the Japanese airmen who in the war of 1939–45 made deliberate suicidal crashes into enemy targets (usu. ships). **b.** An aircraft, usu. loaded with explosives, used in such an attack. Also *transf.*

1945 *Newsweek* 27 Aug. 25 As a British task force was hoisting victory pennants a Kamikaze darted out of the clouds toward the ship. **1952** *Time* 22 Dec. 17/1 No land-based bomber—including the Japanese *Kamikaze*—has ever sunk a U.S. carrier while the carrier was traveling in a task group. **1954** *Time* 4 Jan. 67/1 Fleets of Kamikazes plunged out of the sky, their suicidal pilots aiming their bomb loads at the destroyers. **1959** *Sunday Times* 5 Apr. 13/5 The Kamikaze hit the bridge, killing thirty and wounding eighty-seven. **1964** *Sun-Herald* (Sydney) 21 June 28/2 Three Australian guards and more than 200 kamikazes died. **1971** *Observer* 28 Nov. 3/6 The stand of the *kamikazes* means that in any critical division the Government is assured of a working majority.

3. *Surfing.* (See quots.)

1963 *Pix* 28 Sept. 62/3 Kamikaze: riding the nose with the hands in cross across chest. **1967** J. SEVERSON *Great Surfing* Gloss., *Kamikaze*, a planned wipe-out; taken on purpose with no hope of saving the board or avoiding the swim. **1970** *Studies in English* (Univ. of Cape Town) I. 32 A *kamikaze* occurs when the surfer takes a wipe-out fair on the nose of his surfboard.

B. *adj.* **1.** Of, pertaining to, or characteristic of a *kamikaze* (sense 2, above).

1946 *Chem. & Engin. News* XXIV. 1030/2 The Army and Navy..provided protective [smoke] screens against the Kamikaze attack of the Japanese. **1954** P. K. KEMP *Fleet Air Arm* 203 A Kamikaze, or suicide, plane dived into the base of H.M.S. *Indefatigable*'s island. **1956** A. H. COMPTON *Atomic Quest* iv. 225 Japan's one great new weapon was her 'kamikaze' planes, loaded with bombs and guided to their targets by heroic suicide pilots. **1960** *Spectator* 3 June 803 With the suicidal self confidence of kamikaze pilots ramming an aircraft-carrier. **1966** *New Scientist* 11 Aug. 305/3 After the mobilization of the bedbugs for guard duties in Vietnam comes news of *kamikaze* porpoises. **1974** *Illustr. London News* Feb. 25/3 Newspaper speculation that *kamikaze* dolphins, with explosives strapped to them, had been trained to ram and destroy enemy craft.

2. *transf.* and *fig.* Reckless, dangerous, or potentially self-destructive (*lit.* and *fig.*).

a **1963** S. PLATH *Ariel* (1965) 23, I have taken a pill to kill The thin Papery feeling. Saboteur, Kamikaze man. **1963** *Punch* 16 Jan. 81/3 One of the *Kamikaze* apes at the RAF's Central Ape School. **1964** J. H. ROBERTS *Q Document* (1965) viii. 198 The Ginza was crowded... The kamikaze cabs did not seem to be affected..by the condition of the streets. They followed the same erratic courses through the staggered lines of more cautious drivers. **1966** L. COHEN *Beautiful Losers* (1970) I. 92 Kamikaze insects splashed against the glass. **1967** *Telegraph* (Brisbane) 5 Apr. 8/1 No one is too anxious to be a 'Kamikaze kid', and take on a seat without hopes. **1968** *Evening Standard* 29 Aug. 13/3 He developed a contempt for the kamikaze liberals who prefer glorious defeat to sensible accommodation. **1974** D. SEAMAN *Bomb that could Lip-Read* xi. 88 The Royal Army Ordnance Corps—not normally looked upon as a kamikaze outfit—supplies two such [bomb disposal] units, the only ones in the whole British Army.

Kamilaroi (kă̆mi·lăroi). [Austral. Aboriginal.] A group of Australian Aboriginal peoples living between the Gwydir and Lachlan rivers in New South Wales; also, their language.

1856 W. RIDLEY (*title*) Kamilaroi and other Australian languages. **1877** L. H. MORGAN *Anc. Society* II. i. 51 The Kamilaroi are divided into six gentes, standing with reference to the right of marriage, in two divisions. **1911** J. G. FRAZER *Golden Bough: Magic Art* (ed. 3) I. iii. 101 The Cammeroi of whom Collins speaks are no doubt the tribe now better known as the Kamilaroi. **1952** A. G. MITCHELL in *Chambers's Shorter Eng. Dict.* Suppl., *Kamilaroi*,..one of the New South Wales aboriginal tribes. **1972** *Talanya* I. 21 The Wiradjuri language..met Kamilaroi on the north.

‖ **kamish** (kă̆mi·ʃ). [ad. Russ. *kamýsh* reed.] The common reed, *Phragmites communis.*

1902 *Westm. Gaz.* 25 Jan. 3/1 As we advanced the mountainous country changed gradually into desert, and the desert again into steppes overgrown with kamish, or reeds, where good water could be dug out almost anywhere. **1964** R. PERRY *World of Tiger* i. 2 The vast beds of kamish reeds..which stretch for miles from the slow flood of the Kuban to the Persian shore of the Caspian.

kämmererite (ke·m-, kæ·mərərəit). *Min.* Also † **kæm-, kam-.** [ad. Sw. *kæmmererit* (N. Nordenskiöld 1842, in *Acta Soc. Sci. Fennicæ* I. 486), f. the name of August Alexander *Kämmerer* (1789–1858), Prussian surveyor of mines: see -ITE[1].] A mineral of the chlorite group that is a chromiferous variety of pennine and occurs as soft, flaky, pale violet crystals.

1854 J. D. DANA *Syst. Min.* (ed. 4) II. 292 Kæmmererite occurs in hexagonal prisms, of a reddish violet color... Found with chromic iron at Bissersk, Siberia; also at Texas, Lancaster Co., Pennsylvania. **1926** *Amer. Jrnl. Sci.* CCXI. 284 Chlorite includes as end members.. (7) $H_4Mg_2Cr_2SiO_9$ (kämmererite or Kr). **1928** *Q. Jrnl. Geol. Soc.* LXXXIII. 647 The most extensively-developed chromiferous silicate in the Shetlands is the chrome-chlorite (kämmererite). **1958** *Amer. Mineralogist* XLIII. 954 Chromium substitutes into both the octahedral and tetrahedral positions of chlorite. Above 2 per cent chromic oxide content, the former are termed kammererite, and the latter kotschubeite.

Kampa, var. *KHAMBA; **kampherol,** var. *KAEMPFEROL.

kampong. Add: Also **kampung.**

1972 *Straits Times* (Malaysian ed.) 23 Nov. 13/7 A kampung worker..was sentenced to 18 months' jail today. *Ibid.* 24 Nov. 19/8 (*heading*) Elephant visits keep a whole kampung on edge.

Kamschatkan, Kamskatchan, varr. *KAMCHATKAN *sb.* and *a.*

Kamtchat(ka)dale, Kamt(s)chadale, varr. *KAMCHADAL.

Kamt(s)chatkan, varr. *KAMCHATKAN *sb.* and *a.*

kana (kā·nă). Also 8 **canna, kanno.** [Jap.] Japanese syllabic writing, the chief varieties of which are *HIRAGANA and *KATAKANA.

1727 J. G. SCHEUCHZER tr. *Kæmpfer's Hist. Japan* I. I. iv. 68 The Names of the Provinces..are only in their *Canna*, or common Writing. *Ibid.* IV. iv. 305 Publish'd in the vulgar characters, call'd *Kanno.* **1874** *Trans. Asiatic Soc. Japan* I. 104 The invention of the Japanese syllabic *kana* ten centuries ago. **1879** *Ibid.* VII. 101 It is supposed that he is responsible for the *kana* readings given by the side of the Chinese text. *Ibid.* 230 The *kana* in the Kozhiki and Nihongi are the earliest examples of the use of Chinese characters by the Japanese as phonetic symbols. **1931** H. O. YARDLEY *Amer. Black Chamber* 194 Every time I..saw this benevolent-faced whiskered old missionary as he puzzled over Japanese words, *kana* and code groups. **1965** W. SWAAN *Jap. Lantern* vi. 74 Each of the symbols, known as *kana*, represented either a vowel or a syllable. **1968** *Encycl. Brit.* XII. 882 These syllabaries or *kana*, originally consisting of about 50 syllables, greatly stimulated the development of literature. **1973** *Physics Bull.* May 279/2 Japanese is normally written, typed or printed in a mixture of Chinese and Japanese Kana characters. The simplest set of these, the 'education set', already contains 881 Chinese characters and the 'daily use' and 'standard' sets contain 1850 and 2669 characters respectively. The dictionary set amounts to between 10 000 and 15 000 characters.

kanae (ka·nəi). *N.Z.* Also **kanai.** [Maori.] A grey mullet, *Mugil cephalus*, found in New Zealand waters.

1820 *Gram. & Vocab. Lang. N.Z.* (Church Missionary Soc.) 158 *Kanáe*,..the mullet fish. **1838** J. S. POLACK *New Zealand* I. 322 Some deep banks lie off the east coast, on which the *kanai*, or mullet..abound. **1860** A. S. ATKINSON *Jrnl.* 25 Dec. in *Richmond–Atkinson Papers* (1960) I. 671 Magnificent breakfast of kanae & oysters. **1888** in E. E. Morris *Austral Eng.* (1898) 229/1 The months of December, January, and February in each year are here prescribed a close season for the fish of the species of the mugil known as mullet or kanae. **1966** *Encycl. N.Z.* II. 600/2 Mullet, grey (*Mugil cephalus*), or kanæ of the Maoris, is an excellent food fish, rich in fat and protein, and especially suitable for smoking.

kanaff, var. *KENAF.

‖ **kanaima** (kănai·mă). [Native name.] The name given by the Indians of Guyana to an evil avenging spirit.

1951 E. MITTELHOLZER *Shadows move among Them* I. i. 8 The Genie might lure you away—or a *kanaima. Ibid.* xiii. 115 A *kanaima* bit me... He's a terrible Indian man who stalks through the jungle looking for people to attack.

Kanaka. Add to def.: Also, the Hawaiian language. *Obs.*

1866 'MARK TWAIN' *Lett. from Hawaii* (1967) 68, *k* and *t* are the same in the Kanaka alphabet. *Ibid.* A white chief clerk..handed the document to Bill Ragsdale.. who translated and clattered it off in Kanaka.

Hence **Kanakaland,** Queensland; **Kanakalander,** an inhabitant of Queensland. *Obs.*

1945 BAKER *Austral. Lang.* x. 186 Kanakalanders... Used during the closing decades of the last century when many Pacific island natives were imported. *Ibid.*, 187 Queensland: *Bananaland, Kanakaland* (now obsolete) and *the Nigger State* (now obsolete).

Kanam (kă̆nā·m). The name of a place in Kenya, on the south shore of the Kavirondo gulf of Lake Victoria, used *attrib.* in **Kanam jaw, man, mandible,** to designate the fossil hominid remains found there by L. S. B. Leakey in 1932.

1933 L. S. B. LEAKEY in *Man* XXXIII. 200 (*title*) The status of the Kanam mandible and the Kanjera skulls. **1935** —— *Stone Age Races Kenya* ii. 11 Further examination of the Kanam mandible has led me to separate it from the species *Homo sapiens* and to give it a new specific name *Homo kanamensis. Ibid.* 148/2 (*index*) Kanam Man. **1952** M. R. SAHNI *Man in Evolution* x. 246 If the evidence of the Kanam jaw from East Africa were relied upon, it would take us back to the Lower Pleistocene. **1965** M. H. DAY *Guide to Fossil Man* 145 Kanam man. *Ibid.* 147 Originally Keith thought..that the Kanam mandible was evidence of the early development of a modern type of man... Later Keith said that the small front teeth of the Kanam jaw suggested a closer relationship to the australopithecines than to modern man. **1968** P. V. TOBIAS in G. Kurth *Evolution & Hominisation* (ed. 2) 180 A re-assessment of the morphology of the Kanam mandibular fragments convinced me that...the specimen clearly contains a number of archaic features which relate it most closely to the Upper Pleistocene mandible from Dire-Dawa, in the Harrar district of Ethiopia.

kanamycin (kænămai·sin). *Pharm.* [f. mod.L. *kanamyc-eticus*, specific epithet (see def.) + -IN[1]; cf. *-MYCIN.] (One of) a mixture of antibiotics, chemically related to neomycin, which are produced by the bacterium *Streptomyces kanamyceticus* and are effective against a wide range of bacteria.

1957 H. UMEZAWA et al. in *Jrnl. Antibiotics* (Tokyo) A. X. 188 An antibiotic was isolated from a streptomyces which was assigned to a new species *S. kanamyceticus, n. sp.* Okami et Umezawa... This antibiotic was named kanamycin. **1958** *Ann. N.Y. Acad. Sci.* LXXVI. 27 Paper chromatography of kanamycin preparations revealed a second antibiotic, designated kanamycin B, which has been isolated and characterized. **1958** *Observer* 3 Aug. 9/4 A new antibiotic, kanamycin, discovered and developed by Professor Umezawa and his colleagues..of Tokyo, is now being marketed in the United States. It is active against staphylococcus... It also appears to be highly effective in acute gonorrhea in males. **1963** *Brit. Pharmaceutical Codex* 414 Toxic effects occur with sufficient frequency to make kanamycin useful only when the infecting organisms are resistant to other antibiotics. **1969** H. SMITH *Antibiotics in Clin. Pract.* vii. 97 Chemically, kanamycin is related to neomycin, consisting of two amino sugars linked to a deoxystreptamine. This polybasic water soluble antibiotic in commercial preparations consists..of kanamycin A and B... It is a white crystalline powder dissolving easily in water. **1969** KIRK & OTHMER *Encycl. Chem. Technol.* (ed. 2) 42 The kanamycins are produced by selected strains of *Streptomyces kanamyceticus.*

Kanarese (kænărī·z), *a.* and *sb.* Also **Canarese.** [f. *Kanara* + -ESE.] **A.** *adj.* Of or pertaining to Kanara in western India, or its people. **B.** *sb.* **a.** A native of Kanara. **b.** The language of Kanara, belonging to the Tamulic class of the Dravidian family, closely allied to Telugu; also called Karnata, and now generally and officially Kannada.

1838 KRISHNAMACHARYA (*title*) A grammar of the modern Canarese language. **1847** *Jrnl. Asiatic Soc. Bengal* XVI. II. 1142 The same effect is observable even in Telugu and Canarese. **1856** [see *KARNATA *a.* and *sb.*]. **1875** *Encycl. Brit.* III. 513/2 Maráthi and Kanarese are both spoken. **1880** *Ibid.* XII. 428/2 In the different parts of the [Hyderabad] territory the Marathí, the Kanarese, and Telugu languages are spoken. **1920** *Publ. Opinion* 26 Nov. 521/2 Instruction in the following tongues, Hindustani, Kaffir, Kanarese. **1921** *Q. Rev.* Oct. 328 That Indian Kings were deified after death is placed beyond doubt by a Kanarese inscription. **1939** L. H. GRAY *Foundations of Lang.* 30 The languages of South India (Tamil, Telugu, Kanarese, etc.). **1969** *Enactment* (Delhi) Nov. 12/1, I do not hurl abuses and acid bulbs on my neighbours because they speak..Kanarese and I speak Konkani. **1971** *Hindustan Times Weekly Rev.* (New Delhi) 4 Apr. p. iv/5 (Advt.), Please send me a free set of recipes in..Malayalam/ Gujarati/Marathi/Kanarese.

‖ **kanat** (kanā·t). Also **kanát, kanaut,** etc. [Pers., a. Arab. *ḳanāt.*] A gently sloping underground channel or tunnel, usu. *spec.* in Persia, leading water from the interior of a hill to a village in the valley below, and provided at regular intervals with a series of vertical shafts communicating with the surface of the ground to assist in its construction and maintenance.

1855 *Q. Jrnl. Geol. Soc.* XI. I. 252 Subterraneous canals called Konáts, for irrigation derived from the river, have been cut by Persian perseverance for miles through the gravel at a great depth below the surface. Their course is traceable by the heaps of pebbles thrown out at regular intervals through walls. **1861** *Jrnl. R. Geogr. Soc.* XXXI. 37 By means of a subterranean passage—the excavated earth being thrown up, forming these cannauts..—water

is brought sometimes 5 and 6 miles across the plain. **1865** *Ibid.* XXXV. 180 The Afladj is not a province of itself, but, as its name denotes, is that portion of Dowasser which is watered by kanaats, or underground water-ducts. **1874** *Ibid.* XLIV. 185 For irrigation the plains and valleys depend on the mountains, and at the base of these are 'kanats', or underground channels. **1894** G. BELL *Safar Nameh Persian Pict.* 81 A kanat which is carrying water to many gardens. **1902** P. M. SYKES *Ten Thousand Miles in Persia* iv. 44 A heavy shower or a sandstorm frequently choking up the *kanát*. **1902** EARL OF RONALDSHAY *Sport & Politics under Eastern Sky* 364 Our road took us along the *karez* or *kanat* which brought water from the mountains at the head of the plain. **1968** *Encycl. Brit.* X. 949 Teheran and Marrakesh are among the many modern cities whose water is supplied by kanats.

Kandh, var. *KHOND.

Kandyan (kæ·ndiăn), *a.* and *sb.* Also Kandian. [f. *Kandy, Candy,* in Sri Lanka; see -AN.] **A.** *adj.* Of, pertaining to, or characteristic of the town or kingdom of Kandy, or of its inhabitants. **B.** *sb.* A native or inhabitant of Kandy; the language of the Kandyans.

1849 in T. Skinner *Fifty Yrs. Ceylon* (1891) 220 Robberies and bloodshed became familiar to the Kandyan. **1883** J. FERGUSON *Ceylon in 1883* 129 The Kandyan Buddhist temples. *Ibid.* 138 Of nothing is the elephant so much afraid as of fire, and with nothing will a Kandyan approach a wild elephant so readily. **1891** T. SKINNER *Fifty Yrs. Ceylon* 30 My raw untaught Kandians. **1892** C. F. G. CUMMING *Two Happy Years in Ceylon* I. 255 Most of the chiefs who attended the reception could talk more or less English, but the ladies were as deficient therein as we were in Kandyan. **1923** A. GIBSON *Cinnamon & Frangipanni* 23 Some of the real old Kandyan brass. **1933** P. FLEMING *Brazilian Adventure* ii. 20 He spent all his.. money on a fruitless search..for the buried treasure of the Kandyan Kings. **1942** H. A. J. HULUGALLE *Ceylon* 10 The up-country Sinhalese are loosely called Kandyans. **1956** R. PIERIS *Sinhalese Social Organization* 3 The Kandyan kingdom maintained its independence under the kings of Kandy from Vimala Dharma Sūrya I (reg., A.D. 1591–1604) to the deposition of Śrī Vikrama Rājasimha by the British in 1815. **1969** *Femina* (Bombay) 26 Dec. 5/4 She also excels in the Kandyan dances of Ceylon. **1971** *Weekend* (Ceylon) 12 Sept. 4/1 (Advt.), Father Burgher Mother Kandyan Goigama Buddhist seek partner for their pretty educated homely daughter.

Kanesian (kănī·ʒən). [Irreg. f. *Kanesh,* ancient city of Asia Minor + -IAN.] The principal dialect of Hittite, also called Kaneshite.

1921 [see *NESITE]. **1928** C. DAWSON *Age of Gods* xiii. 302 The official language of the [Hittite] empire has been named by its discoverers Nashili or Kanesian. **1950** H. L. LORIMER *Homer & Monuments* i. 4 Lydian, the language of the Lemnian inscription, and Etruscan are all three closely interrelated and belong, like Kanesian, to that early (though post-Luvian) stage of I.-E.

kang, var. CANGUE, CANG.

1928 H. LAMB *Genghis Khan* 27 Targoutai..commanded that a *kang* be put upon him—a wooden yoke resting on the shoulders and holding the wrists of a captive prisoned at both ends.

kanga[1] (kā·ŋă). *N.Z.* Also **kaanga.** [Maori.] Indian corn, *Zea mays.*

1843 E. DIEFFENBACH *Trav. in N.Z.* II. III. 366 *Kanga,* corn, maize. **1905** W. B. *Where White Man Treads* 2 Plantations of..Kaanga (Indian corn). **1949** P. BUCK *Coming of Maori* (1950) II. i. 111 Indian corn.. received the name of *Kanga,* the Maori form of the word corn... A unique method of utilizing it as food was evolved... The unhusked cobs were placed in fenced enclosures in still water where the grain became soft. **1959** *Economic Botany* XIII. 321/2 The vernacular name covering all maize is *kaanga.*

kanga[2] (kæ·ŋgă). *Austral. colloq.* [Shortened form of *kangaroo.*] = KANGAROO *sb.* 1.

[**1926** A. A. MILNE *Winnie-the-Pooh* vii. 91 Christopher Robin..said that a Kanga was Generally Regarded as One of the Fiercer Animals. *Ibid.* 93 Kanga never takes her eye off Baby Roo, except when he's safely buttoned up in her pocket.] **1942** C. BARRETT *On Wallaby* iv. 73 'Leaves a kanga cold,' Tim declared after seeing a jerboa in action. **1969** *Sun* (Melbourne) 12 July 9/3 (*heading*) Kangas: all are to blame.

kanga, var. *KHANGA.

|| **kangany** (kăngā·ni). Also **canganeme, cangany, kangani.** [f. Tamil *kaṅkāṇi,* f. *kaṇ* eye + *kāṇ* to see.] An overseer or headman of a gang of local labourers in Sri Lanka, southern India, and Malaya.

1817 'PHILALETHES' *Hist. Ceylon* lvi. 324 *Canganeme.* This officer musters the people of the village, and calls them together when there is any work to be done. *Ibid.* 336 Canganys, corporals under the aratsches. **1886** R. W. JENKINS *Ceylon in Fifties & Eighties* 78 Kangani, head of a gang of coolies. **1903** *Westm. Gaz.* 30 May 4/3 The kanganies (head coolies)..say if their coolies are not given work they must remove them to another estate. **1923** *Glasgow Herald* 21 Apr. 4/1 When the tasks are all filled the tappers go to work..under the native overseers or Kanganies. **1926** *Blackw. Mag.* Apr. 507/1 Several Tamil headmen—Kanganies—are sent to India with recruiting licenses. Each Kangany will go to his own village in South India. **1964** K. G. TREGONNING *Hist. Mod. Malaya* 199 As indentured labour diminished in importance..it was replaced by the *kangany* system, whereby a foreman or senior labourer from the estate was sent back to India, empowered to recruit in his old village... The *kangany* system was abolished in 1938.

kangaroo, *sb.* Add: **3. g.** Applied to a form of Parliamentary closure by which some amendments are selected for discussion and others excluded.

1913 *Q. Rev.* Apr. 551 The 'kangaroo' or selection by the Chairman of Committee of the amendments to be discussed. **1927** [see *guillotine resolution* s.v. *GUILLOTINE *sb.* 4].

h. A system of containerized freight transportation by railway in which a loaded road trailer complete with wheels is carried on a flat rail car; also called 'piggyback'.

1967 *Guardian* 3 July 6/3 On the European continent.. there has recently been a very rapid increase in 'Kangaroo', the system of piggyback for road trailers and semi-trailers developed by French railways. **1969** *Jane's Freight Containers 1968–69* p. iii/2 Rolling stock and terminals designed for containers should be owned or operated, or..TOFC ('piggyback' or 'kangaroo') equivalent should be owned or operated. *Ibid.* 178/1 Vehicles available: T.I.R. flat and kangaroo trailers.

4. b. kangaroo closure (see *3 g); **kangaroo court** orig. *U.S.,* an improperly constituted court having no legal standing, e.g. one held by strikers, mutineers, prisoners, etc.; **kangaroo justice,** the trying of a person by an unauthorized court, as a kangaroo court; also, the decision of such a court, taken with a disregard for normal legal procedures and criteria; **kangaroo mouse** (earlier examples); **kangaroo paw,** an Australian herb belonging to the genus *Anigozanthos* of the family Hæmodoraceæ; **kangaroo ship** (see quot.); **kangaroo-shoot,** a hunting expedition to shoot kangaroos; hence **kangaroo-shooter, -shooting.**

1930 *Times Educ. Suppl.* 22 Nov. p. i/1 It will be necessary to further restrict the rights of private members of the House of Commons by use of what is known as 'The Kangaroo Closure'. **1853** 'P. PAXTON' *Stray Yankee in Texas* 205 By a unanimous vote, Judge G—— was elected to the bench and the 'Mestang' or 'Kangaroo Court' regularly organized. **1895** *Harper's Mag.* Apr. 718/2 The most interesting of these impromptu clubs is the one called in the vernacular the 'Kangaroo Court'. It is found almost entirely in county jails. **1931** 'DEAN STIFF' *Milk & Honey Route* 209 *Kangaroo court,* mock court held in jail for the purpose of forcing new prisoners to divide their money. **1935** A. J. POLLOCK *Underworld Speaks* 66/1 *Kangaroo Court,* a jail tribunal comprised of inmates which collects money from prisoners awaiting trial to supply the needy with tobacco, food and a few luxuries—its decision regarding disputes is final. **1966** *Times* 14 Mar. 10/1 Shop stewards at Theale are to meet tomorrow to consider paying back the sums levied by a kangaroo court. **1971** *Times* 20 Jan. 15/3 Citizens who live in the riotous areas [of N. Ireland] deserve protection from.. kangaroo courts. **1973** C. MULLARD *Black Brit.* III. vii. 81 Such practices are surely more like those of a kangaroo court than those that the Race Relations Board should encourage. **1909** *Daily Chron.* 15 Jan. 6/7 It seems to me to be something like Kangaroo justice. **1966** *Oxford Mail* 11 Mar. 1/6 The unconstitutional strike at B.M.C. Service, Cowley, and the 'kangaroo justice' to which seven men were subjected. **1867** *Amer. Naturalist* I. 394 They are known in the vernacular as 'Kangaroo' or 'Jumping' Rats and Mice, and are entirely confined to Transmississippian regions. **1875** J. MILLER *First Fam'lies Sierras* (1876) xxx. 243 Wood-rats, kangaroo-mice..had gone into winter-quarters under the great logs. **1902** *Western Austral. Year-Bk. 1900–01* I. II. ix 304 Some of the most remarkable flowers in the flora of Western Australia [are].. Kangaroo Paws, of which there are nine species altogether. **1949** D. WALKER *We went to Austral.* 184 With the kangaroo paw it is the stalk that is scarlet and the blending of the colours peculiar. **1966** *Times* 11 Nov. (W. Austral. Suppl.) p. iv/2 The red-and-green kangaroo paw (*Anigosanthus manglesii,* the state's floral emblem) is a barbaric cluster of rich green-and-gold, paw-like flowers on a regal three-foot stem of deep scarlet, yet it is only one of nine species known to exist in the state. **1919** H. JENKINS *John Dene of Toronto* (1920) ii. 32 'A "mother",' he explained, 'is a kangaroo-ship, a dry-dock ship for salvage and repair of submarines.' **1933** *Bulletin* (Sydney) 11 Oct. 11/3 The royal pair had been participating in a kangaroo-shoot. **1902** J. H. M. ABBOTT *Tommy Cornstalk* i. 11 Indeed, it is doubtful whether there is any better shot in the world than the kangaroo-shooter. **1963** A. LUBBOCK *Austral. Roundabout* 15 The kangaroo-shooters go out at night in cars, and the kangaroos..are shot down. **1888** A. C. GUNTER *Mr. Potter* vi. 80 The Australian has been accustomed to kangaroo-shooting.

Hence **kangaroo·er,** one who hunts kangaroos.

1909 in *Cent. Dict.* Suppl. **1936** A. RUSSELL *Gone Nomad* viii. 63 That night we hobbled out at a kangarooer's camp.

Kang-Hai, Kang-He, Kang-Hi, erron. forms of next.

1910 *Encycl. Brit.* V. 747/1 On the finely prepared K'ang-hi wares much more striking and brilliant colour effects were obtained. **1911** in C. Schreiber *Jrnls.* II. (plate facing p. 16), Powdered blue..bottle of the Kang-He period. **1966** S. MORROW *Moonlighters* xvi. 166 A.. game of hide-and-seek which had toppled an irreplaceable K'ang Hai pot from his mother's desk.

K'ang-Hsi (kæŋʃī). [Royal name of Hsüan-Yeh, emperor of China 1661–1722.] Used *attrib.* with ref. to the Chinese pottery and porcelain of the latter half of the seventeenth century and the first quarter of the eighteenth, notable for very fine blue-and-white wares and the development of *famille verte* and *famille noire* enamels.

1906 S. W. BUSHELL *Chinese Art* II. viii. 33 The use of cobalt as a ground wash, foreshadowing the greater triumphs of the coming K'ang Hsi epoch. **1934** *Burlington Mag.* Mar. p. xv/1 The K'ang Hsi figures of *Kuan-yin* ..are especially remarkable. **1937** E. LINKLATER *Juan in China* xii. 213 A small flower-painted black vase. 'K'ang-hsi,' she said. **1943** D. WELCH *Maiden Voy.* xxii. 188 The K'ang-Hsi blue and white which the Dean was buying for his grey-walled room at home. **1965** D. TORR *Diplomatic Cover* vi. 103 Powder blue Chinese vases, a Sèvres biscuit group, a Nevers faience jug and the precious little Kang Hsi figures.

|| **kangri** (ka·ŋgri). [Hindi *kaṅgrī;* cf. Kashmiri *kangurü.*] A small wicker-covered clay-lined pot filled with glowing charcoal, carried esp. by Kashmiris next to the skin to warm the air beneath the clothing.

1911 *Allbutt's Syst. Med.* (ed. 2) IX. 591 Scars due to burns (compare the kangri carcinoma of Thibet). **1912** *Med. Ann.* 197 A form of cancer..in the natives of Kashmir,..due to their habit of carrying a portable fire-basket (kangri) beneath their clothes in contact with the abdominal skin. **1956** LD. AMULREE in A. Pryce-Jones *New Outl. Mod. Knowl.* 214 Among the Indians it has been shown that cancer of the skin is associated with the use of kangri heaters applied to the abdomen. **1968** *Daily Tel.* (Colour Suppl.) 20 Dec. 27 (*caption*) She keeps warm with a kangri, a pot filled with hot embers. **1972** *Times* 5 Aug. 11/1 If it is cold..a Kashmiri may offer the visitor his kangri... The kangri is a small wicker basket with a metal pan filled with glowing coals.

kanickanick, etc. = KINNIKINIC.

1839 J. K. TOWNSEND *Narr. Rocky Mts.* ii. 146 He smokes the article called *kanikanik,*—a mixture of tobacco and the dried leaves of the poke plant. **1847** C. LANMAN *Summer in Wilderness* xiv. 87 A bag of ka-nick-a-nick and tobacco was circulated and a cloud of fragrant smoke ascended to the sky.

Kanjar (kæ·ndʒaɪ). A generic term for certain small gypsy communities which wander about India.

1875 *Encycl. Brit.* III. 508/1 The aboriginal tribes consist of the Bhars, Cherus, Dhángars, Kanjhárs, Kharwárs, Kols. **1885** *Ibid.* XVIII. 72/1 The Nats and Kanjars wander like gipsies over the country. **1916** R. V. RUSSELL *Tribes & Castes Cent. Provinces India* III. 333 The Kanjars and Berias are the typical gipsy castes of India. **1924** *Chambers's Jrnl.* Aug. 497/2 Dulloc..was nothing better than an outcast Kanjar. **1931** E. A. H. BLUNT *Caste System of N. India* 150 All Kanjars, however, are not criminals; many are poor and fairly respectable hunters and *shikaris.*

|| **kanji** (ka·ndʒi). [Jap., f. *kan* Chinese + *ji* letter, character.] **a.** The corpus of borrowed and adapted Chinese ideographs which forms the principal part of the Japanese writing system. Cf. *KANA. **b.** Any one of these ideographs. Used esp. *attrib.*

1920 W. M. MCGOVERN *Colloq. Japanese* 7 The *Honji* or *Kanji* consist of the ideographs taken over from China. **1960** *New Scientist* 21 Apr. 1014/3 The Japanese newspaper contains roughly 50 per cent. kanji or Chinese characters, 40 per cent. kana letters or phonetic signs, and 10 per cent. Arabic figures and other signs. **1964** M. CRITCHLEY *Developmental Dyslexia* iv. 14 More difficulty was experienced in reading the syllabary Kana script than the ideographic Kanji symbols of Chinese origin. **1965** W. SWAAN *Jap. Lantern* vi. 74 The immense prestige of the *kanji* (Chinese characters) proved irresistible. **1972** *Mainichi Daily News* (Japan) 6 Nov. 17/4 (Advt.), Plastic Kanji Cards... All the 1,900 symbolic characters now used in Japanese newspapers and magazines, in Plastic Cards. *Ibid.,* An easy method to learn the 1,900 Chinese-Japanese characters (Kanji) now used.

kankerbos, kankerbossie (ka·ŋkəɪbǫs, -bǫːsi). *S. Afr.* [Afrikaans.] = *cancer bush* (*CANCER *sb.* 5).

1913 C. PETTMAN *Africanderisms* 248 Kanker boschje. —*Sutherlandia frutescens, R. Br.* is so named in the Riversdale district. **1931** *Farming in S. Afr.* Sept. 216 They preferred by far the 'klein kankerbos'. **1949** L. G. GREEN *In Land of Afternoon* 50 There is the kankerbos, which has failed to provide a cure for cancer. **1953** *Cape Times* 14 July 2/7 These [*sc.* existing plantings] will be followed by the introduction of more woody species, such as bitou, blombos, kankerbossie and waxberrie.

Kannada (kæ·nădă). Now the official and the more usual name for *KANARESE *sb.* b.

1856 [see *KARNATA *a.* and *sb.*]. **1877** A. HOVELACQUE *Sci. of Lang.* 78 The *Kanarese,* or *Kannada,* occupies the north Dravidian district. **1942** MORAES & STIMSON *Introd. India* ii. 16 Other widely spoken languages are the southern group—Tamil, Telugu, Kannada and Malayalam. **1959** *Clarendonian* June 46 New editions of the *First Aid* textbook have recently been published in Arabic, Greek, Turkish, Chinese, Gujarati, Kannada, and Bengali.

1969 *Filmfare* (Bombay) 1 Aug. 23/4 There is friction between distributors, exhibitors and the State Government regarding exhibition of Kannada films in Bangalore.

‖ **káns** (kāns). *India.* [a. Hindi *kans*, f. Skr. *kāśa*.] A large grass, *Saccharum spontaneum*.
1874 E. F. T. Atkinson et al. *Statistical Acct. N.-W. Provinces India* I. 89 The very destructive weed *káns*.. yields a good coarse grass for thatching. **1884** *Encycl. Brit.* XVII. 234/2 Cultivators dare not leave their lands fallow, even for a single year, for the ground would be immediately occupied by rank *káns* grass. **1918** R. N. Parker *Forest Flora Punjab* 535 *Saccharum spontaneum* ... Vern. *káns, káhi, kán.* Throughout the plains of the Punjab.

Kansa (kæ·nză). Also **Kansas, Kanzas,** etc. [Native name.] A Siouan Indian people formerly of Kansas and now in Oklahoma; also known as *Kaw; a member of this people; the name of their language. Also *attrib.* or as *adj.*
1722 D. Coxe *Descr. Carolana* i. 11 The Southerly of these two Rivers, is that of the Ousoutiwy upon which dwell..the Kansæ, Mintou, Erabacha and others. **1806** Wilkinson in Z. M. Pike *Acct. Expeditions Sources Mississippi* (1810) 108 You may attach to this deputation ..the same number of Kanses chiefs. **1847** D. Coyner *Lost Trappers* (1859) 41 They were informed of the trade made by Captain Williams and the chief of the Kansas village. **1848** E. Bryant *California* 41, I asked him if he was a Kansas. **1907** F. W. Hodge *Handbk. Amer. Indians* I. 654/1 The Kansa figured but slightly in the history of the country until after the beginning of the 19th century. **1933** L. Bloomfield *Lang.* iv. 72 The Siouan family includes many languages, such as..Kansa. **1957** *Encycl. Brit.* XX. 714/1 The principal Siouan tribes were..in the west, Dakota and Assimiboin,..tribes speaking Dhegiha, viz., Omaha, Ponca, Kansas, [etc.].

Kansan (kæ·nzăn), *sb.* and *a.* [f. *Kansas*, the name of one of the United States: see -an.] **A.** *sb.* A native or inhabitant of the State of Kansas; = *Kansian.
1868 J. N. Holloway *Hist. Kansas* 574 At a favorable opportunity the Kansans seized the Ruffians,..and held them for trial. **1924** M. Cretcher (*title*) The Kansan. **1964** *Amer. Folk Music Occasional* 1. 40 Now I am teamed up with another singer. He's a Kansan like myself. **1973** *Times* 9 Nov. 12/1 The editor of the *Journal* of Salina, Kansas..suggests Kansans are longing for Mr Nixon to make a last-minute comeback.

B. *adj. Geol.* Of, pertaining to, or designating the second Pleistocene glaciation of North America, which was probably contemporary with the Mindel glaciation in the Alps. Also *absol.*, the Kansan glaciation or the deposits it produced.
1894 J. Geikie *Gt. Ice Age* (ed. 3) xlii. 755 While the formation in Kansas is subordinately divisible, it appears to be an essential unity, and therefore the name *Kansan formation* is selected..as a convenient designation of the outermost drift sheet. **1896, 1934, 1957** [see *Illinoian *a.*].

Kansas City. [City in Missouri, U.S.A.] Used *attrib.* with ref. to a style of big-band jazz which evolved in Kansas City in the 1930s.
1946 *Hollywood Q.* July 449 We have..Kansas City jazz. **1955** L. Feather *Encycl. Jazz* i. 22 Kansas City jazz was brewing in the bands of Benny Moten and Andy Kirk. **1958** P. Gammond *Decca Bk. Jazz* ix. 116 A further facet of Kansas City jazz: the singularity of the beat which it evolved to underline the inspiration of its soloists, and of its principal orchestral exponent, the Count Basie band. **1959** M. T. Williams *Art of Jazz* (1960) xviii. 188 Charlie Parker is an exponent of the Kansas City style in and general Lester Young in particular.

† **Kansian** (kæ·nziăn). *Obs.* [f. as *Kansan *sb.* + -ian.] = *Kansan *sb.*
1855 W. Whitman *Leaves of Grass* 58 Not only the free Utahan, Kansian, or Arkansian. **1873** J. H. Beadle *Undevel. West* 214 It was laid out by a town company of ambitious Kansians. **1878** —— *Western Wilds* ix. 133 Discount sixty per cent when a Kansian talks about snakes. **1879** W. Whitman *Specimen Days* (1882–3) 141 We found a train ready and a crowd of hospitable Kansians to take us on to Lawrence.

Kantean *a.*, var. Kantian *a.*

‖ **kantele** (ka·ntĭli). [Finn.] A form of zither used in Finland and Lithuania.
1921 *Glasgow Herald* 24 Nov. 8 Eastern Karelia, where the kantele players still survive, is the home of the most characteristic Finnish music. **1960** G. Taylor *Mortlake* iii. ix. 272 The kantele..was a large wooden box, pentagonal and tapering at one end. The five strings were stretched the length of the instrument. **1969** *Listener* 24 July 124/1 The best bits were musical: a lovely Lapp pentatonic chant, a zither-like instrument called a *kantele*, and, of course, liberal doses of Sibelius.

kantharos: see *cantharus.

Kantian. Add: Also **Kantean.** **A.** *adj.* (Earlier examples.)
1796 F. A. Nitsch *Gen. View Kant's Princ. concerning Man* 1, I venture to address the Learned and Philosophers, on the Kantean principles. **1798** A. F. M. Willich *Elem. Critical Philos.* 22 Plattner..has employed rational scepticism against the Kantian system. **1811** H. C. Robinson *Diary* 29 Mar. (1967) 3, I doubt the concurrence of this explanation of a general idea with the Kantian theory.

B. *sb.* (Earlier examples.)
1799 Coleridge *Notebooks* (1957) I. 390 Brown was no Kantian & probably held nothing but high degrees of Probability possible. **1805** J. Mackintosh in R. J. Mackintosh *Mem. Life Sir J. Mackintosh* (1836) I. 260, I own to you that I am not a whit more near being a Kantian than I was before.

KANU, Kanu (kā·nu). [f. the initials of the words *K*enya *A*frican *N*ational *U*nion.] The name of a Kenyan political party.
1960 *Times* 6 June 6/5 Kenyatta was recently elected as President of Kanu. **1961** *Economist* 17 June 1244/1 The divisional and provincial boards..are manned by officials and trusty Africans of the old school. KANU branches have asked..to have representation on these boards. **1962** [see *KADU, Kadu]. **1969** *Reporter* (Nairobi) 13 June 5/2 The KANU Government had been sustained by the faith and confidence of the people. **1971** *Daily Nation* (Nairobi) 10 Apr. 2/3 The people of Kisumu District are fully behind him, the Government and Kanu.

Kanuck, var. *Canuck.

kanuka (ka·nukă). *N.Z.* [Maori.] A small, white-flowered, evergreen tree, *Leptospermum ericoides*; also called white tea-tree.
1906 T. F. Cheeseman *Man. N.Z. Flora* 161 *L[eptospermum] ericoides*... Abundant from the North Cape to the Bluff... Kanuka; Maru. **1929** W. Martin *N.Z. Nature Bk.* II. 84 The endemic Kanuka or Tea-tree.. is restricted to low levels. **1963** *Weekly News* (Auckland) 26 June 28 (*caption*) Kanuka plants being lined out in rows in the outdoor section of the nursery. **1966** *Ibid.* 1 June 16/3 Smoke is drifting, blue and hazy, through the kanukas above the campfire. **1966** *Encycl. N.Z.* II. 406/2 Kanuka grows into a small tree up to 40 or more feet high.

Kanuri (kănū·ri). [Native name.] A group of Negroid peoples living in the region of Lake Chad, in north-eastern Nigeria; their language, which belongs to the Central Saharan group.
1876 *Encycl. Brit.* IV. 61/1 The leading people of the country, called Bornuese or Kanuri, present a perfect specimen of the negro form and features. **1888** *Ibid.* XXIII. 334 Barth on linguistic grounds grouped them with the Kanuri of Bornu, who are undoubtedly Negroes. **1932** W. L. Graff *Lang.* 434 Kanuri, of the Nilo-Chadian group. **1959** *Listener* 29 Oct. 740/1 The..Kanuri of Nigeria. **1966** J. H. Greenberg *Languages of Africa* (ed. 2) 132 In agreement with Eastern Sudanic Kanuri has a *tə-* prefix for the causative in a few verbs of the 'strong' conjugation.

‖ **kanzu** (ka·nzū). [Swahili.] A long white cotton or linen robe as worn by East African men.
1902 *Westm. Gaz.* 24 Nov. 2/1 Dressed in a white kanzu, or long shirt, with a tweed coat over it,..he was an attractive little figure. **1920** *Chambers's Jrnl.* Sept. 572/2 He wears..the white linen Kanzu or long robe rather like a nightgown. **1966** B. Kimenye *Kalasanda Revisited* 17 He was wearing a kanzu in deference, no doubt, to the Sabbath, instead of his week-day costume. **1970** *Times* 20 May 7/1 He was wearing a kanzu (cotton robe) over his shirt.

kaoliang (kē·oˌlyæŋ). [Chinese; lit. 'high grain'.] The Indian millet, *Sorghum vulgare*.
1904 *Westm. Gaz.* 5 Sept. 7/1 The kao-ling (millet). **1909** *Official Hist. Russo-Jap. War* (ed. 2) I. vi. 56 The advanced guard..erected screens of *kao-liang* and trees at every point. **1923** *Chambers's Jrnl.* 40/2, I found the god of rain..glaring at me from the middle of a parched kaoliang patch. **1928** *Brit. Chem. Abstracts* B. 443 A relatively easy-bleaching soda pulp can be obtained from the stalk of 'Kaoliang'. **1945** R. Hargreaves *Enemy at Gate* 265 The field of fire was invariably obscured by meadows of high-standing *kao-ling*. **1958** A. N. Steward *Man. Vasc. Plants Lower Yangtze Valley* 485 *Sorghum vulgare*..(Kao Liang; Tall Millet)... Cultivated in warm countries.

kaolinitic (kēiŏlini·tik), *a. Min.* [f. Kaolinit(e + -ic.] Of the nature of or containing kaolinite.
1885 *Nature* 8 Oct. 559/1 The interstitial dusty, siliceous, and kaolinitic paste has only crystallised in part. **1940** *Mineral. Abstr.* VII. 427 The formation of kaolinitic-nontronitic clays is primarily due to the hydrothermal processes. **1965** G. J. Williams *Econ. Geol. N.Z.* xx. 364/2 Clay from well-weathered greywacke, transported and deposited in fresh water is kaolinitic and of fine grain size. **1971** *Nature* 6 Aug. 371/2 The thin, curious, kaolinitic bands called tonsteins discovered more recently in the coalfields of Western Europe.

kaon (kēi·ǫn). *Nuclear Physics.* Also † **kayon.** [f. *ka(y)*- (repr. the pronunc. of the letter *K* in *K(-)meson, *K(-)particle) + *-on[1].] Any of a group of mesons which have masses several times those of the pions and non-zero hypercharge, and on decaying usually produce two or three pions or else a muon and a neutrino.
1958 *Phil. Mag.* III. 330 Writing $m_K{}^+$, $m_\pi{}^+$, $m_\pi{}^0$, m_μ, for the kayon, charged pion, neutral pion, and muon masses. **1958** *Proc. 2nd U.N. Internat. Conf. Peaceful Uses Atomic Energy* XXX. 44/2 When the newly produced kaons disintegrate, only half of them should exhibit the short lifetime 10^{-10} sec. **1960** *Rev. Mod. Physics* XXXII. 479/1 Kayons were clearly observed at least as early as 1947. **1960** *McGraw-Hill Encycl. Sci. & Technol.* IV. 543 *K*-meson (kaon). **1963** K. W. Ford *World of Elem. Particles* vi. 180 The weak interactions.. act in their own leisurely fashion and bring about the kaon decay after about 10^{-10} sec. **1968** *New Scientist* 18 Jan. 144/2 It has generally been supposed that cosmic-ray muons are the product of the radioactive decay of the mesons known as pions and kaons. **1972** G. L. Wick *Elem. Particles* iv. 77 Both the lambda and the kaon decay into strongly interacting particles, but the lifetimes are very long.

Hence **kao·nic** *a.*, of or pertaining to a kaon, or an atom having a kaon orbiting the nucleus.
1965 *McGraw-Hill Yearbk. Sci. & Technol.* 181/1 (In table), Kaonic state. **1969** *Physical Rev. Lett.* XXII. 1238/1 The ultimate ability of kaonic x rays to yield information on the nuclear-size parameters requires the accurate determination of the kaon-nucleus potential. **1972** *Physics Bull.* Mar. 149/3 The study of kaonic atoms may provide us with information about the extreme surface region of the nucleus. **1972** *Sci. Amer.* Nov. 106/3 Increasing the charge of the nucleus shrinks the kaonic orbits and brings the kaons closer to the nucleus.

‖ **kapa,** another form of Tapa.
1909 in *Cent. Dict.* Suppl. **1913** R. Brooke *Let.* 28 Oct. (1968) 521 Their women held up pieces of 'kapa'—which is bark beaten into a stiff cloth, and covered with a brown pattern.

‖ **kapai** (kæ·pəi), *a.* and *adv. N.Z.* Also **carpi, ka pai.** [Maori *ka pai*.] Good, fine; also as an exclamation of pleasure or approval.
1836 W. B. Marshall *Personal Narr. Two Visits N.Z.* ii. 256 'Kapai! Good!' being the only vocable by which satisfaction at the receipt of kindness is communicable. **1840** E. Hobson *Let.* 29 June in A. Drummond *Married & gone to N.Z.* (1960) 50 My dear husband..is on excellent terms with the natives, who call him the Carpi (good) Governor. **1861** *Taranaki Punch* 2 Jan. 2/1 The pudding turned out *kapai* until we came to cut it. **1918** *N.Z.E.F. Chrons.* 27 Feb. 37/1 The evening was simply 'kapai'. **1933** F. E. Baume *Half-Caste* v. 55 You're looking kapai, Ngaire. **1938** R. D. Finlayson *Brown Man's Burden* 30 They can do South Sea hulas... Ka pai! they're very good. **1960** N. Hilliard *Maori Girl* ii. xiii. 153 '*Kapai!*' shouted Henry.

‖ **kaparrang, -ring** (kăpā·răŋ, -riŋ). *S. Afr.* Also **caparran, kaproen.** [ad. Jav. *gamparan*.] A wooden sandal worn by the Cape Malays.
1867 M. Kollisch *Mussulman Population Cape Good Hope* 23 Both sexes in some instances carefully ignoring the use of shoes, rather preferring clogs, called *kaparrans* (which is a small piece of wood with two slips joined underneath, and a wooden knob on the upper side). **1870** *Cape Monthly Mag.* Aug. 109 A Malay beauty..clatters upon '*caparrans*' (a species of wooden buskin). **1911** *State* Dec. 596 (Pettman), The old coloured woman walking carefully in *kaproens*. **1953** *Cape Argus* (Mag. Section) 28 Feb. 3/6 Malays, with 'Kapparings' on their feet,..were our fish vendors. **1972** I. D. Du Plessis *Cape Malays* (ed. 3) iii. 33 Kaparrings (probably from the Javanese gamparan: wooden sandals with a knot to push between the big and second toes) are still in use in the Mosques.

‖ **Kapenaar** (kā·pənār). *S. Afr.* Also **Kaapenaar.** [Afrikaans *kapenaar*, f. *kaap* Cape + *-enaar* pers. suffix.] **1.** An inhabitant of Cape Town or of the Cape Peninsula and its environs.
1834 *Cape of Good Hope Lit. Gaz.* IV. 180 (Pettman), The Capenaars have..attempted to justify the holding of human flesh in bondage by appeals to Scripture. **1902** *Dowey's Early Annals of Kobstad* 99 (Pettman), He was a Kaapenaar. **1946** *Spotlight* (Johannesburg) 13 Dec. 2b Kapenaars..feel that the Cabinet is really learning something of agricultural economy. **1959** *Cape Times* 9 Mar. 10/5 A statement more pleasing to..all true Kapenaars than that the long battle for the preservation of the building has been won. **1973** *Ibid.* 22 Jan. 5 Is it the mountain which makes Kaapenaars so allergic to change?

2. A large, silver-coloured, marine, food fish, *Argyrozona* (or *Polystegamus*) *argyrozona*, of the family Denticidæ.
1902 J. D. F. Gilchrist in *Trans. S. Afr. Philos. Soc.* XL. 223 At Port Elizabeth it is called not Silver-fish, but Kapenaar. **1913** W. W. Thompson *Sea Fisheries of Cape Colony* 154 *Dentex argyrozona*... Silver-fish; Kaapenaar (Port Elizabeth). **1947** K. H. Barnard *Pictorial Guide S. Afr. Fishes* 157 Silverfish, Kapenaar (*Polystegamus argyrozona*)... Table Bay to Natal, down to 70 fathoms. One of the best known, and economically important South African fishes. As well as being sold fresh, it is cured and smoked and sold as 'haddock'. **1962** *Pretoria News* 5 Jan. 4/2 The Japanese come for what they call red bream, or 'red fish', which includes the red roman, 74, kaapenaar and silver fish.

kapok. Add: Now usu. with pronunc. (kēi·pǫk). Substitute for def.: A large tropical tree, *Ceiba casearia*; silk cotton, the fibre produced from the soft covering of the seeds within its fruit, used to stuff mattresses, cushions, etc. Also *attrib.* (Earlier and later examples.)

1735 T. SALMON *Mod. Hist.* XXVII. vi. 186 There is also [in Guinea] the Capot Tree, that bears a sort of Cotton. **1795** tr. *C. P. Thunberg's Trav. Europe, Afr. & Asia* II. 284 The cotton which encloses the seed in the capsule, is called Kapock, and is not used for spinning, but for making mattrasses, bolsters, and pillows. **1907** *Yesterday's Shopping* (1969) 692/2 Life belts. 'Kapok' pillow belt. **1940** E. J. H. CORNER *Wayside Trees Malaya* I. 436 The Kapok is grown mainly for the wool obtained from the fruits. **1958** J. SLIMMING *Temiar Jungle* v. 77 Chabok..raised his blow-pipe, quickly inserting a dart into the mouthpiece and packing the end with a small twist of raw kapok. **1963** J. KIRKUP *Tropic Temper* 33 It had a good firm mattress stuffed with locally-grown fresh kapok. *Ibid.* 127 The kapok tree's gaunt appearance with its thin branches stuck out at right-angles to the dead-straight trunk, has earned it the nickname of P.W.D. tree. (Because people think it resembles a telegraph pole erected by the Public Works Department.) **1966** D. FORBES *Heart of Malaya* vi. 66 The kapok tree, called the midnight horror, with its long seed pods hanging down like drooping fingers, and the fan palm were common enough. **1974** L. DEIGHTON *Spy Story* xx. 209 We stood around..wearing kapok-lined white snow-suits.

kappa (kæ·pă). [Gr. κάππα.] **1.** The tenth letter of the Greek alphabet, *K*, κ.

c **1400** [see LAMBDA 1]. **1746** T. NUGENT tr. *De Port Royal's New Method of Learning Gk. Tongue* I. ii. 3 The Greeks have 24 Letters, whose Figure, Name, and Power are as followeth:..Thêta..Iôta..Cappa..Lambda [etc.]. *Ibid.* xi. 41 *Κάππα*, *Kappa*, from the Hebrew *Cap* or *Caph*, or rather from the ancient *Kappa*. **1791** R. P. KNIGHT *Analytical Ess. on Gk. Alphabet* i. 5 After the invention of the Kappa, the simple Gamma seems to have fallen into disuse in some dialects. *Ibid.*, The harshest and most emphatical palatial consonant..is the Kappa. **1871** [see *CHAPTER *sb.* 5 b]. **1948** D. DIRINGER *Alphabet* II. viii. 453 The *qoph*, which expresses the Semitic emphatic *k*, was adopted [*sc.* into the Greek alphabet] as *koppa*, differentiated from *kappa*.

2. *Biol.* An agent in some strains of *Paramecium aurelia* that confers on cells possessing it the property of producing a substance toxic to *Paramecium* cells lacking it, and exists as small cytoplasmic particles (*kappa particles*) capable of reproducing independently of the cell containing them and of infecting other *Paramecium* cells; these particles collectively. Freq. *attrib.*

1945 T. M. SONNEBORN in *Amer. Naturalist* LXXIX. 319 The alternative characters, killer and non-killer, are determined by a pair of allelic genes, K and k, and a cytoplasmic factor, which may be called kappa. Clones are killers only when both the dominant gene K and the cytoplasmic factor kappa are present; they are non-killers when kappa is absent, regardless of genic constitution. *Ibid.* 332 How can the unequal division of kappa at fission be accounted for? **1947** *Genetics* XXXII. 106 Under conditions in which the concentration of kappa decreases, two methods may be used to find the number of kappa particles per original killer cell. **1951** G. H. BOURNE *Cytol. & Cell Physiol.* (ed. 2) ii. 91 The factor kappa can reproduce itself in the cytoplasm but only if the gene *K* is present in the nucleus. **1965** PEACOCKE & DRYSDALE *Molecular Basis Heredity* ii. 7 These so-called kappa particles are probably best regarded as self-determining invaders and not as part of the normal cell. **1969** J. R. PREER in *Res. Protozool.* 174 Kappa itself has been shown..to respire and utilize glucose and sucrose *in vitro*. The presence in kappa of the biochemical apparatus required for such a sophisticated metabolism clearly eliminates the possibility that it is a virus. *Ibid.* 183 The kappas of stocks 7 and 51.

‖ **kappie** (ka·pi). *S. Afr.* Also 9 cappie, kap(p)je. [Afrikaans, = Du. *kapje* dim. of *kap* hood.] A sun-bonnet or coal-scuttle bonnet.

1834 A. SMITH *Diary* (1939) I. 92 All that a farmer's daughter can do or ever does is to make cappies. **1871** J. MACKENZIE *Ten Yrs. North of Orange River* iv. 62 Her taste as to colours and shapes in kapjes, handkerchiefs and dresses. **1883** 'R. IRON' *Story Afr. Farm* I. ii. 26 Em took off her big brown Kappje and began..to fan her red face with it. **1902** *Daily Chron.* 18 Mar. 3/4 Women, in big, flapping kapjes, were at work on household business. **1939** S. CLOETE *Watch for Dawn* iii. 47 In her anger she had pulled her kappie from her head. **1966** E. PALMER *Plains of Camdeboo* xviii. 295 In burst Hannie Rafferty, her blue kappie askew, her round face red. **1974** *Africana Notes & News* Sept. 93 The strong contrast of her black kappie against the white kappie of the woman at her side.

‖ **kapu** (ka·pu), *a.* and *sb.* [Hawaiian.] = TABOO, TABU *a.* and *sb.*

1933 *Ancient Hawaiian Civilization* (Bishop Museum, Honolulu) 35 The kapu was the ancient social and religious law of Hawaii... The word itself can best be translated 'forbidden'. The king and all his family, his clothes, and his possessions, were kapu because of the ali'i's sacredness. All the rules and prohibitions established by the ali'i..were called the 'kapu system'. *Ibid.* 71 These prayers and the feast removed the kapu on the new dwelling. **1954** J. SHERIDAN in J. Macdonald *Lethal Sex* (1959) 151 That room is *kapu*. Definitely not the background for the sort of shindig his wife throws. **1968** *Awake!* 8 May 21/1 Under this [Polynesian] pagan religious system there was a set of taboos called *kapu*,.. that controlled almost every action of every person.

kapur (ka·pŭɹ). [Malay.] A large dipterocarp timber tree of the genus *Dryobalanops*, esp. *D. aromatica*, native to Malaya, Sumatra, and Borneo; also, the wood of a tree of this kind.

1935 I. H. BURKILL *Dict. Econ. Products Malay Peninsula* I. 863 There is probably a total of more than 500,000 acres of 'kapur' forest in the Peninsula. **1940** E. J. H. CORNER *Wayside Trees Malaya* I. 212 The *Kapur* may form almost pure forests, and it is at once distinguished by its beautiful, open, fine-leafed crown. **1956** *Handbk. Hardwoods* (Forest Prod. Res. Lab.) 125 Kapur grows to a height often exceeding 200 ft. **1963** *Engineering* 25 Oct. 525/2 Beams composed of four species, western hemlock, European redwood, jarrah and kapur. **1972** *Timber Trades Jrnl.* 13 May 39/2 Of the lesser species merbau and kapur are readily available.

kaput (kăpu·t), *a.* (in pred. use). *slang.* Also kaputt. [ad. G. *kaputt*, f. Fr. (*être*) *capot* (to be) without tricks in the card-game of piquet; see CAPOT *sb.*[1]] **a.** Finished, worn out; dead or destroyed. **b.** Rendered useless or unable to function.

1895 W. M. CONWAY *Alps from End to End* iii. 59 The thing would then go *wie's Donnerwetter* and the man would be *kaput* at once. [**1914** DUCHESS OF SUTHERLAND *Six Weeks at the War* p. xiv, When Prussian military despotism is 'Kaputt'—to use the Germans' favourite word about their foe, meaning 'done'.] **1924** *Glasgow Herald* 11 Dec. 7 The intellectual consciousness is kaput. *a* **1930** D. H. LAWRENCE *Last Poems* (1932) 286 So self-willed, self-centred, self-conscious people die The death of nothingness, worn-out machines, kaput! **1955** E. POUND *Classic Anthol.* I. 19 North gate, sorrow's edge, Purse kaput, nothing to pledge. **1959** J. BRAINE *Vodi* iv. 63 He could now see that his whole life was *kaputt*. **1972** *New Yorker* 9 Sept. 30 It's a real American tragedy—Wunderkind at twenty, Übermensch at thirty, kaputt at forty. **1975** J. SYMONS *Three Pipe Problem* xix. 220 Sherlock Holmes is finished. Finito. Kaput.

‖ **kar, Kar** (kāɹ). *Physical Geogr.* Pl. kare, kars; also *erron.* kar, karen. [G.] = CIRQUE 2, *CWM.

1893 *Geogr. Jrnl.* I. 352 The direct erosive action of ice in forming 'glacier-pots' (Karen) and inland lakes. **1905** *Jrnl. Geol.* XIII. 2 Above the shoulders the valley slopes are far from being regular; often they form cirque-like niches, at the bottoms of which little tarns occur. These are the *Kar* of the Alps, the 'corries' of Scotland. *Ibid.* 16 Now and then we find here mountains with a single corrie or *Kar. Ibid.*, There is a sharp crest line which separates the corries or *Kare* of opposite sides. **1957** G. E. HUTCHINSON *Treat. Limnol.* I. i. 59 Such amphitheaters are called *cirques* in the French-speaking parts of the Alps, *Kars* in the German-speaking regions, *cwms* in Wales, and *corries* in Scotland. All four terms have achieved some degree of international usage, but the first seems to have been the most widely employed. **1963** D. W. & E. E. HUMPHRIES tr. *Termier's Erosion & Sedimentation* v. 128 The heads of the fjords formed in this way are called *botn*, *dalbotn* or *saekkedaler*..and differ from the true glacial cirque or *fjeldbotn*. They are almost the equivalent of the *trogschluss* or *kar* of the Alps.

Karabagh (kæ·răbā). Also **Carabagh.** The name of a region in the Soviet republic of Azerbaijan used *attrib.* or *ellipt.* to denote a thick knotted carpet or rug (orig.) made there, usually with a floral but occas. an animal pattern.

1900 J. K. MUMFORD *Oriental Rugs* ix. 118 The production of Karabaghs..has of late been pushed forward without stint. **1962** C. W. JACOBSEN *Oriental Rugs* 227 Karabagh Rugs...Also spelled Carabagh...Where made: In the southern part of what used to be called Caucasia, now the Russian States of Armenia, Azerbaijan, and Nakichevan. **1973** *Country Life* 6 Dec. (Suppl.) 40g Karabagh rug... Caucasus dated 1876.

karabiner (kæræbī·nəɹ). *Mountaineering.* Also **carabiner**, *erron.* **karibiner.** [Shortened form of G. *karabiner-haken* spring-hook.] A coupling device consisting of a metal oval or D-shaped link with a gate protected against accidental opening. Cf. *KRAB.

1932 *Amer. Alpine Jrnl.* 526 (*caption*) Safety snap (carabiner). **1933** G. D. ABRAHAM *Mod. Mountaineering* x. 182 Light pitons..are used and karibiners. The latter are special oval-shaped rings with a hinge or swivel somewhat like that found on the end of a watch chain. **1942** K. A. HENDERSON *Amer. Alpine Club's Handbk. Amer. Mountaineering* vi. 124 *Snap-rings*, sometimes called by their German name, *karabiner*, are used to fasten the rope to the piton. They come in both oval and pear-shaped form. **1946** J. E. Q. BARFORD *Climbing in Brit.* ii. 25 These are called karibiners in Germany..and consist of an oval steel ring with a spring loaded hinged link on one side. **1959** W. H. MURRAY *Five Frontiers* iv. 93 Round my waist I tied a loop of rope, clipped on a karabiner (a steel ring with a spring clip, used in rock-climbing). **1965** *New Scientist* 22 July 205/3 The karabiner is basically a hook which is closed by a pivoted arm that may or may not snap home on the latch. **1972** D. HASTON *In High Places* i. 7 Oval metal snaplinks, called carabiners. **1973** C. BONINGTON *Next Horizon* xii. 169 A jerk—you drop three inches... But you're alive! The knot in the sling attached to the karabiner in your waist harness had jammed on the gate of the karabiner, and had then freed itself, letting you drop those few inches.

‖ **karaburan** (kærăbiū^ə·răn). [Turk., f. *kara* black + *buran* whirlwind.] A hot dusty wind in Central Asia.

1903 J. T. BEALBY tr. *Hedin's Cent. Asia & Tibet* I. xx. 331 The first real *kara-buran*, or 'black tempest',.. came..early... Drift-sand and dust swept down the Tarim and made the air so thick that we were unable to see the steep dune which faced us. **1931** A. A. MILLER *Climatol.* xiii. 243 Strong winds from almost any point of the compass spring up by day, carrying clouds of dust and sand... The *karaburan* is of this type, blowing strongly from the north-east in the Tarim basin. **1949** W. MOORE *Dict. Geogr.* 90 The sand blown along by the karaburan is one of the principal causes of the changes in the courses of rivers through the desert.

Karadagh, Kara Dagh (kæ·rădā). The name of a range of mountains in north-western Iran, used *attrib.* or *ellipt.* to denote a thick woollen carpet or rug (orig.) made there and knotted with either a geometrical or a floral pattern.

1900 J. K. MUMFORD *Oriental Rugs* xi. 180 The Kara Dagh weavings are not often seen in market. **1962** C. W. JACOBSEN *Oriental Rugs* 228 If there are any rugs coming to Ardebil or Tabriz as Karadaghs, it will be news to most buyers in Tabriz. What little information is available describes these as being very much like the Caucasian Karabaghs, thick rugs with both geometric and floral designs... The new Ardebil rugs are successors to the Karadaghs.

karaji, var. *KORADJI.

karaka. (Earlier and later examples.)

1834 G. BENNETT *Wanderings New South Wales* I. xvii. 336 The Karaka tree, (*Corynocarpus lævigata*,) of New Zealand, was in thriving condition, having reached the elevation of from six to nearly fourteen feet, and borne fruit. **1905** W. B. *Where White Man Treads* 16 And of nuts—the karaka, with its coating of soft yellow pulp. **1921** H. GUTHRIE-SMITH *Tutira* xii. 102 Single plants of karaka (*Corynocarpus lævigatus*) grew also. **1938** R. D. FINLAYSON *Brown Man's Burden* 77 Herding the cows down by the karaka trees. **1949** E. DE MAUNY *Huntsman in Career* 72 He could see the red karaka berry. **1957** J. FRAME *Owls do Cry* II. xv. 67 Green as karaka leaf.

Karakalpak, Kara-Kalpak (ka·răkălpa·k), *a.* and *sb.* [Kirghiz, f. *kara* black + *kalpak* cap.] **A.** *adj.* Of or pertaining to a Turkic people inhabiting a region south of the Aral Sea. **B.** *sb.* **a.** This Turkic people; a member of this people. **b.** (Also **Kara-Kalpaki.**) The Turkic language of the Karakalpak people.

1832 [see *KAZAKH]. **1865** J. & R. MICHELL tr. *Valikhanof's Russians Cent. Asia* ii. 24 The Mission was met by four deputies... These were the Karakalpak Prince Istleu [etc.]. **1875** G. R. ABERIGH-MACKAY *Notes W. Turkistan* 79 Karakalpaks offer allegiance to Russia..1723. **1882** *Encycl. Brit.* XIV. 94/1 The Kipchaks, forming a connecting link between the nomad and settled Turki peoples of Ferghana and Bokhara, and the Kara-Kalpaks on the south-east side of the Aral Sea. **1888** *Encycl. Brit.* XXIII. 661/2 Tatar dialects (..Kumi, Karatchai, Kara-Kalpaki). **1959** E. H. CARR *Socialism in One Country* II. xx. 270 The Kara-Kalpak autonomous region of the Kazakh autonomous SSR. **1970** *Encycl. Brit.* XXII. 399/1 Kara-Kalpak, which is hardly more than a Kazakh dialect, is used..by the Kara-Kalpaks living in Afghanistan.

‖ **karakia** (karăkī·ă). *N.Z.* Pl. **-kia, -kias.** [Maori.] An incantation (see quot. 1949).

1832 H. WILLIAMS *Jrnl.* 6 Jan. in H. Carleton *H. Life Williams* (1874) I. 111 If they should be where they cannot land, everyone immediately ceases talking, and they commence *karakia* [their incantations]. **1843** E. DIEFFENBACH *Trav. N.Z.* II. i. vii. 114 The 'Karakia' (prayers).. are most powerful when coming from a priest who is distinguished by high birth. **1862** A. S. ATKINSON *Jrnl.* 10 Sept. in *Richmond–Atkinson Papers* (1960) I. xiii. 791 We got there just after the flag had been hoisted & while the karakia were being chanted. **1874** J. C. JOHNSTONE *Maoria* 191 *Karakia*, incantations. In their use of this word the Maoris had no idea of prayer, and it is a mistake to attach that meaning to Karakia. **1905** W. B. *Where White Man Treads* 38 [The Maori's] 'karakia' (incantations) were invocations to his gods to preserve him from the Unknown. **1921** H. GUTHRIE-SMITH *Tutira* x. 70 Preparing herself..by the recitation of proper *karakias*—incantations. **1949** P. BUCK *Coming of Maori* (1950) IV. iii, The priests established oral communication with their gods by means of *Karakia*. A *Karakia* may be defined as a formula of words which was chanted to obtain benefit or avert trouble... They cover a range which exceeds the bounds of religion. It is therefore impossible for one English word to cover adequately all the meanings of *Karakia*. All *Karakia* are chants but there are a number of chants,..which are not *Karakia*... Probably incantation is the nearest in general meaning. **1959** TINDALE & LINDSAY *Rangatira* iv. 41 The karakia ceremony in which the canoe said farewell to the stump on which it had grown. **1968** *Landfall* XXII. 255 Underneath, Back, back The old life seeths, Sound of old chants, Of karakias In my skin.

Hence as *v. trans.*, to put a spell on (a person or object) by chanting or reciting *karakia*; also *intr.*, to chant or recite *karakia*.

1833 H. WILLIAMS *Let.* in H. Carleton *Life H. Williams* (1874) I. 134 His old superstition was too strong, though he did not submit to be *karakia'd* previous to dissolution. **1836** J. A. WILSON *Jrnl.* in *Missionary Life & Work N.Z.* (1889) III. 42 They invited me to hold afternoon prayers.. I reminded them of the cruel and bloody war they had long waged... They..again pressed me to *karakia*. **1874** H. CARLETON *Life H. Williams* I. 41 The natives said he had '*Karakia'd*' us—a term they apply to our religious worship.

Kara-Kirghiz (ka·rā,kiəɪgī·z). [Native name, f. *kara* black + *Kirghiz.] = *Kirghiz *sb.* and *a.*

1879 *Encycl. Brit.* IX. 85/2 The nomads are mainly Kipchaks and Kara Kirghiz. **1959** E. H. Carr *Socialism in One Country* II. xx. 268 The Kirgiz (here called Kara-Kirgiz) population was to form a new autonomous region within the RSFSR. **1967** D. S. Parlett *Short Dict. Lang.* 73 *Kirgiz* (Kara-Kirgiz).., apparently one of the oldest (or oldest attested) Turkic tribes. **1971** *Whitaker's Almanack 1972* 966 In 1924, a Kara-Kirghiz Autonomous Province was formed within the R.S.F.S.R.

karakul (kæ·răkŭl). Also **caracul(e), carakul, karacul.** [Russ., f. *Karakul,* name of a province and lake in Bokhara, where the breed originated.] **a.** A breed of sheep with coarse wiry fur; a sheep of this breed. **b.** The glossy curled coat of a young karakul lamb, valued as fur. Also *attrib.*, as *karakul cloth,* a kind of cloth made in imitation of karakul.

1853 M. Arnold *Sohrab & Rustum* in *Poems* 10 And on his head he plac'd his sheep-skin cap, Black, glossy, curl'd, the fleece of Kara-Kul. **1894** *Westm. Gaz.* 20 Sept. 3/3 Here is fashion's forecast for the winter season:—Blue the leading colour... Caracule the popular fur. *Ibid.* 4 Oct. 3/3 The most striking of this season's productions is caracule-cloth, which closely resembles the fur of that name. **1894** *Queen* 27 Oct. 735/3 A 'Caracule' plush, which simulates that fashionable fur. **1895** *Army & Navy Co-op. Soc. Price List* 1095 Astrachans, &c... Black Caracul. **1898** *Daily News* 15 Oct. 6/4 A tight-fitting caracul with revers of chinchilla. **1913** *Illustr. Technical World* XIX. 700/1 The Karakul is a desert sheep native to Bokhara, Central Asia. **1929** *Daily Express* 26 Jan. 5/3 The smarter coats are generally collared with a flat fur. These include astrachan, krimma, and caracul, in black, beige, or grey. **1930** *Economist* 4 Jan. 10/2 There have also been established in the prairie provinces karakul sheep farms, from which astrakhan and broadtail are secured. **1948** L. G. Green *To River's End* viii. 88 On both sides of the river the karakul lamb is flourishing. *Ibid.* x. 111 Glossy black karakul skins drying on their frames. **1949** *Amer. Speech* XXIV. 95 Lambs from China or the interior of Asia possess pelts distinguished by a flat, open, wavy curl and give their name to a common variety of skin very common in the industry called *karacul,* also spelled *carakul.* **1957** V. Nabokov *Pnin* v. 134 The warm rose-red silk lining of her karakul muff. **1960** *Times* 31 May (S. Afr. Suppl.) p. vi/7 Wool, of course, is a major export and is well supported by karakul pelts.

karakurt (ka·răkūəɪt). [Turki, f. *kara* black + *kurt* wolf.] A venomous, black spider, *Latrodectus tredecimguttatus,* found in southern Russia and eastern Europe; = Malmignatte.

[**1909** A. Petrunkevitch in *Sci. Amer.* 22 May 395/3 Like other species of *Latrodectus, Karakurt* does not show much inclination to attack.] **1932** E. Nielsen *Biol. Spiders* I. i. 43 One of the most poisonous spiders is the Russian *Karakurt* (*Lathrodectus lugubris*), which causes great damage in the steppes of South Russia in the hot months of the summer.

karamat, var. *kramat.

Karamojo (kærāmōu·dʒo). Also **Karamojong.** [Native name.] **a.** A Nilotic people of north-eastern Uganda; a member of this people. **b.** The language of this people.

1911 *Encycl. Brit.* XXVII. 559/1 (*heading*) Nile negroes (Aluru,..Turkana and Karamojo). **1959** A. Moorehead *No Room in Ark* vii. 137 The Karamojong is a warrior and a herdsman of cattle. *Ibid.* 144 The Karamojong warrior wears the kind of accessories a well-dressed western woman might have, but without the clothes. **1961** Webster, *Karamojong,* a Nilotic language of the Karamojong people. **1964** C. Willock *Enormous Zoo* i. 3 In the north-east [of Uganda] lay the Karamoja,..a semi-desert peopled by the Karamojong, a group of nomadic, pastoralist tribes. **1966** J. H. Greenberg *Lang. Afr.* (ed. 2) v. 86 The Eastern Sudanic family has the following..branches: ..Nilotic:..Eastern: Dodoth, Karamojong, Teso. *Ibid.*, We may compare Nilo-Hamitic..Karamojong *ano,* Kakwa *an* with Nilotic Shilluk *an,* Anuak *ana.*

karana (kărā·nă). *India.* [Skr. *kárana* doing, making, (hence) position, posture.] One of the 108 basic postures in Indian dance, details of which were set out in the *Natya Sastra* by the sage Bharata Muni, traditionally after instruction from the god Siva, lord of the dance.

1936 B. V. N. Naidu et al. tr. *Bharata's Taṇḍava Lakṣaṇam* ii. 19, I shall now enumerate..the Karaṇas and Rēcakas... A Karaṇa in dance is the co-ordination of movements of the hands and feet. **1948** G. Venkatachalam *Dance in India* 132 *Karana,* a fundamental pose. **1956** P. Banerji *Dance of India* (ed. 5) iv. 51 The Karanas are single postures, the special feature of them being that the left hand is generally put on the breast while the right hand follows the movements of the feet. *Ibid.* 52 A Karana is the source and origin of all the movements. **1965** E. Bhavnani *Dance in India* iii. 17 In the Nataraja temple at Chidambaram..there are carvings of the 108 *Karanas* or basic dance postures. **1967** Singha & Massey *Indian Dances* ii. 41 Just as in Bharata's time the basic unit of dance was the karana, so it is generally agreed that today this unit is the *adavu,* which seems to have evolved from the karana. **1969** *Weekly Mail* (Madras) 26 July 10/4 Karanas can be classified as those which are anukaranas (imitations)..and those which are abstract meant only for aesthetic (internal) pleasure.

Karankawa (kăræ·ŋkăwă). Also **Carancahua, Carancoway, Carankoua.** [Native name.] **A.** *sb.* An Indian people of the Gulf coast of Texas; a member of this people; also, their language. **B.** *adj.* Of or pertaining to this people. Also **Kara·nkawan.**

1806 J. Sibley in *Message from President of U.S., communicating Discoveries made in exploring the Missouri by Captains Lewis & Clark* 72 Carankouas, live on an island, or peninsula, in the bay of St. Bernard. **1823** W. B. Dewees *Lett. from Early Settler Texas* (1852) 30 During their absence the Carancoway Indians attacked the vessel. **1891** *7th Ann. Rep. U.S. Bureau Amer. Ethnol. 1885–6* 82 (*heading*) Karankawan [linguistic] family. (*text*) The Karankawa formerly dwelt upon the Texan coast. **1907** F. W. Hodge *Handbk. Amer. Indians* I. 657/1 Karankawa... The signification of the name has not been ascertained. **1948** *True* May 126/2, I hear the Carancahuas been putting on war paint down south of here. **1957** *Encycl. Brit.* XII. 203 A/1 Powell classification (1891)..Language family..Karankawan (Extinct). *Ibid.* 203 B/2 (*heading*) Sapir arrangement (1929). (*text*) Coahuiltecan *a.* Tonkawa. *b.* Coahuilteco. *c.* Karankawa. **1966** C. F. & F. M. Voegelin *Map N. Amer. Indian Langs.* (*caption*) Language isolates and families with undetermined phylum affiliations... Karankawa Language Isolate.

karanteen (kæ·răntīn). *S. Afr.* Also **-ine.** Either of two marine fishes of the family Sparidae, *Crenidens crenidens,* or the larger *bamboo-fish* (*bamboo *sb.* 2), *Sarpa salpa,* also known, in Natal, as the striped karanteen.

1905 *Natal Mercury Pictorial* 334 (Pettman), The fish pictured today is a Karantine. It is a local species. **1913** [see *bamboo-fish*]. **1930** C. L. Biden *Sea-Angling Fishes of Cape* 62 Mackerel, mullet, sardine, and bamboo-fish (Natal karanteen) are the best lures. **1947** K. H. Barnard *Pict. Guide S. Afr. Fishes* 152 White Karanteen (*Crenidens crenidens*)... Silvery, greenish or bluish above, narrow dark longitudinal stripes. *Ibid.* 156 Striped Karanteen (Natal) (*Sarpa salpa*)... Silvery, greenish or bluish above, yellow-orange longitudinal stripes. **1953** J. L. B. Smith *Sea Fishes S. Afr.* (rev. ed.) 274 *Sarpa salpa*... Striped Karanteen, Bamboo Fish (Natal)..is said to occur right round Africa. *Ibid.* 275 *Crenidens crenidens*... Karanteen... Comes from Indian waters, extends to Durban. **1970** *Albany Mercury* (S. Afr.) 29 Jan. 15 Smaller fish—such as mullet and karanteen—making up his [*sc.* the leerfish's] staple diet.

karat. Delete obs. and add U.S. examples.

1901 *Manufacturing Jeweler* 28 Feb. 244 (Advt.), Our rose gold, green gold, Roman and karat gold..are well known and universally used. **1903** 'O. Henry' in *Ainslee's Mag.* Mar. 125/1 There stood..a first-class looking little man, with a four-karat diamond on his finger. **1945** *Jewelers' Dict.* 124/2 In U.S. usage *karat* designates the proportion of fine gold in an alloy; while *carat* is applied to the weight of a stone. **1972** *Newsweek* 10 Jan. 15/1 (Advt.), *Cross* pens and pencils are recognized as fine writing instruments. Available in lustrous chrome, sterling silver, gold filled and solid fourteen karat gold, they are purchased with pride. **1972** *Sci. Amer.* Dec. 8/1 (Advt.), Exclusive, extra-large, 18-karat gold point with etched facing assures super-smooth writing action.

karate (kărā·ti), *sb.* [Jap., lit. 'empty hand'.] A Japanese system of unarmed combat in which hands and feet are used as weapons. Also *attrib.*, esp. **karate chop,** a sharp slanting blow with the hand.

1955 E. J. Harrison *Fighting Spirit Japan* (ed. 2) vii. 74 Karate resembles both jujutsu and judo. *Ibid.*, A single karate technique..is capable of inflicting fatal injury upon its victim. **1962** *Movie* Dec. 35/3 The interest of the karate techniques employed. **1964** *Guardian* 11 Jan. 5/1 Her unsporting habit of dispatching people of both sexes with a carefully rehearsed Karate blow. **1964** I. Fleming *You only live Twice* x. 127 Your judo and karate are special skills requiring years of practice. **1966** J. Porter *Sour Cream* ix. 126 She probably knew the lot: unarmed combat, judo, karate. **1970** *New Yorker* 5 Dec. 49 'I'm Larry Taylor,' a breathless, sharp-featured young man said, offering a karate-chop handshake to Jay Steffy. **1971** *Ink* 12 June 17/4 He floored the guard with a karate chop.

Hence ‖ **karateka** (kărā·tikă), an exponent or devotee of karate, a karate expert.

1966 *New Scientist* 7 July 8/1 Karatekas, those fearsome exponents of the Japanese technique of self-defence called Karate..often display their prowess by breaking..bricks with their bare hands. **1972** *Straits Times* (Malaysian ed.) 26 Sept. 3/2 Some 700 karatekas from the Police Reserve Unit..will be attending. **1972** D. Lees *Zodiac* 122 The other guy was making like a karateka. **1973** [see *kata].

karate (kărā·ti), *v.* [f. prec.] *trans.* To strike or beat with karate blows. Also **karate-chop** *v.*, to strike with a karate chop.

1966 T. Pynchon *Crying of Lot 49* v. 134 'I'm unarmed. You can frisk me.' 'While you karate-chop me in the spine, no thank you.' **1968** *New Yorker* 14 Sept. 129 A wolf was bugging me, so I..karated him, and called the fuzz. **1970** *Time* 11 May 62 The wife..can karate-chop hell out of her husband.

karaya (kărai·ă). [ad. Hind. *karāl, karāyal* resin.] In full, *karaya gum, gum karaya.* A gum exuded by the Indian tree *Sterculia urens* when the bark is pierced: used industrially, esp. as a substitute for gum tragacanth.

1893 G. Watt *Dict. Econ. Products of India* VI. iii. 365 The gum [of *Sterculia urens*], under the name of *karai-gond,* is largely used in Bombay in the manufacture of native sweetmeats (*Dymock*). **1916** *Sci. Amer. Suppl.* 16 Dec. 393/2 (*heading*) What is karaya gum? **1918** *Jrnl. Amer. Pharmaceutical Assoc.* VII. 789 Karaya gum is used extensively in India as a substitute for tragacanth in the preparation of sweetmeats, and also locally as a demulcent in the treatment of throat affections. **1947** C. L. Mantell *Water-Soluble Gums* iii. 50 Karaya gum has been used in the United States since the latter part of the 19th century, but the large scale use in the United States dates from World War I, when the price of tragacanth was high. Karaya is frequently sold as tragacanth. **1954** Kirk & Othmer *Encycl. Chem. Technol.* XIII. 883 Gums derived from Irish and Iceland moss, karaya, algin, and quince seeds have received limited applications in textile finishes. **1962** M. G. DeNavarre *Chem. & Manuf. Cosmetics* (ed. 2) II. 119 Although karaya has sometimes been used as a tragacanth adulterant, its acidity, odor, color, negative starch reaction, and ability to swell in 60% alcohol will quickly differentiate it from tragacanth. Gum karaya has found its widest cosmetic use in making finger-waving concentrates for subsequent dilution to proper consistency with water. **1974** *Daily Colonist* (Victoria, B.C.) 20 Oct. 2/3 Mrs. Wallace decided to experiment with Karaya vegetable gum powder made from the extract from a tree grown in India, in an effort to promote healing of Nunn's wound.

karbi (kā·ɪbi). *Austral.* [Aboriginal name.] A small, dark, stingless, native bee, *Trigona carbonaria.*

1884 H. J. Hockings in *Trans. Entomol. Soc. London* 149 Of these stingless bees of Australia two varieties only have come under my immediate observation..'Karbi' or 'Keelar' and 'Kootchar' are the names given to them by the natives. *Ibid.* 150 'Karbi' gather but little honey. **1932** *Victorian Naturalist* (Melbourne) XLVIII. x. 185 The aborigines were familiar with several species, and.. *Trigona cassiæ* Ckll. is known as 'Koochee', and *Trigona carbonaria* Smith, as 'Koobee', or 'Karbi'. **1948** *Bull. Amer. Mus. Nat. Hist.* XC. 22/1 The spiral staircase type of nest was recorded by Hockings..in the case of an Australian *Trigona* known as 'karbi' or 'keelar' that he believed to be *carbonaria* F. Smith.

karee, var. Karree (in Dict. and Suppl.).

karela (ka·rēlă). Also **kareli, kurilla.** [Hindi.] The balsam pear or bitter gourd, *Momordica charantia,* a climbing plant of the family Cucurbitaceæ, native to south-east Asia and tropical Africa, and cultivated in India for its edible, rough-skinned, yellow or white fruit, which is lemon-shaped and may be as much as eight inches long.

1839 J. W. Masters in *Trans. Agric. & Hort. Soc. India* III. 200 *Karilla,* annual, propagated by seeds. **1881** J. A. Murray *Plants & Drugs of Sind* 41 (*heading*) Momordica balsamina. ..The Balsam Apple. Vernacular —Karelo-Jangro, *Sind.* Fruit ovoid, smooth,..tapering at both ends. Eaten in pickle. **1893** G. Watt *Dict. Econ. Products India* V. 256 The rainy season kind, called *kareli,* has rather smaller fruits and is more esteemed than the hot-weather variety, known in some districts under the name of *karela.* **1895** Kipling *Second Jungle Bk.* 81 The Karela, the vine that bears the bitter wild gourd. **1962** J. F. Dastur *Medicinal Plants India & Pakistan* (ed. 2) 112 (*heading*) *Momordica charantia* Linn. Family: Cucurbitaceae. *Local names*: Karela, karvel. *English names*: African Cucumber, Bitter Gourd. **1969** *Sunday Statesman* (Calcutta) 27 July 4 Vegetable vendors have lao sag at 30 paise a bundle... Tinda, french beans and karela are all Re 1 a kg.

Karelian (kărī·liăn), *sb.* and *a.* Also **Carelian.** [f. *Karelia,* name of a region in Eastern Finland and of a republic in the adjoining parts of the U.S.S.R.] **A.** *sb.* **a.** A native or inhabitant of Karelia. **b.** The Finno-Ugric language of this people.

1855 R. Sears *Illustr. Descr. Russ. Empire* iii. 94 The district of the government traversed by this canal is inhabited by a tribe of Carelians. **1879** *Encycl. Brit.* VIII. 700/1 Finnic or Ugrian represented by (*a*) Finnish proper or Suonic, (*b*) Karelian. **1882** *Ibid.* XIV. 307/2 The Karelians were pressing on the Eastern Lapps. **1921** *Glasgow Herald* 21 Nov. 10 The Karelians want..to open ..peace negotiations. **1931** K. M. Stewart-Murray *Conscription of a People* vii. 75 The conscription of 30,000 Karelians for lumbering early in 1931. **1935** Huxley & Haddon *We Europeans* vii. 220 The east [of Finland is inhabited] by Karelians. **1942** K. W. Deutsch in J. A. Fishman *Readings Sociol. of Lang.* (1968) 600 Seven of these [smaller nations] reached some form of statehood between 1900 and 1941: Albanians, Irish, Byelo-Russians, Karelians, Moldavians—the three last-named only as 'Union Republics' within the federal framework of the U.S.S.R., [etc.]. **1961** L. F. Brosnahan *Sounds of Lang.* viii. 177 In Finno-Ugrian it [*sc.* palatalisation opposition] is present in eastern dialects of Finnish and Estonian, southern Karelian, and in all the languages of this family which occur to the east. **1967** E.-L. Wuorio *Midsummer Lokki* iii. 93 Kalle Koli, Finnish war-hero, Karelian, ex-gentleman farmer, and now an evacuee.

B. *adj.* Of or relating to Karelia, the Karelians, or their language.

1879 *Encycl. Brit.* IX. 218/2 It was Torkel Knutson who conquered and connected the Karelian Finlanders in 1293. **1920** *Glasgow Herald* 29 Oct. 9/2 The Karelian population in the governments of Archangel and Olonets will enjoy the right to national self-determination. **1954** *Chambers's World Gazetteer* 357/1 The great Finnish epic

Kalevala is of Karelian origin. **1967** E.-L. Wuorio *Midsummer Lokki* iii. 72 The heavy Karelian accent made it difficult for Luke to understand. **1969** E. H. Pinto *Treen* 331 Karelian birch cigar cases..enjoyed quite a vogue in the first 30 years of this century. **1974** *Sci. Amer.* Sept. 101/1 After World War II some 2·7 million Sudeten Germans were transferred to Germany and 415,000 Karelian Finns were moved to Finland.

karelianite (kărī·liănəit). *Min.* [f. prec. + -ite[1].] An oxide of vanadium, V_2O_3.

1963 J. V. P. Long et al. in *Amer. Mineralogist* XLVIII. 40 Electron microprobe analyses and the crystallographic data obtained suggest the existence of a new vanadium mineral, V_2O_3, isostructural with hematite, eskolaite and corundum. The name karelianite, after the region of Finland in which the Outokumpu mine is situated, is proposed for this mineral, the name to be applied to the pure end member. **1967** *Mineral. Abstr.* XVIII. 282/2 Three principal minerals compose the dominantly vanadiferous ores [at Mounana, Gabon]—karelianite, montroseite, and roscoelite. Karelianite, rarely more than 0·5 mm in size, occurs as grains in the grit cement or as blades forming 60° stars in quartz.

Karen (kăre·n), *sb.* and *a.* Also † **Carayner, Carian(er), Carianner.** [f. Burmese *ka-reng* wild, dirty, low-caste man.] **A.** *sb.* **1.** One of a group of non-Burmese Mongoloid tribes scattered throughout Burma, esp. to the east; a member of one of these tribes.

c **1759** in A. Dalrymple *Oriental Repertory* (1793) I. 100 This Country contains two Nations, the Bûraghmahns, and Peguers... There is another People in this Country called Carianners, whiter than either. **1800** M. Symes *Acct. Embassy to Kingdom of Ava* vi. 207 Carayners, or Carianers..inhabit different parts of the country. **1833** W. Tandy tr. *Sangermano's Descr. Burmese Empire* vi. 34 The Carian, a good and peaceable people. **1833** Bennett *Let.* 11 Nov. in F. Mason *Karen Apostle* (1847) v. 45 Four of the Karens were yesterday baptized. **1885** [see *crow-flight* s.v. *crow *sb.*[1] 11]. **1910** *Jrnl. R. Soc. Arts* LVIII. 701/2 The Karen undoubtedly had his original home in China. **1922** W. G. White *Sea Gypsies of Malaya* i. 18 Upon the 'backbones' of Burma live the Karens... The Karens are..monolatrists, if not monotheists. **1937** R. H. Lowie *Hist. Ethnological Theory* (1938) vii. 84 He [*sc.* Tylor] definitely ascribes the latter view only to Algonkians, Fijians, and Karens. **1962** [see *Chin *sb.*[2]]. **1965** B. Sweet-Escott *Baker St. Irreg.* viii. 236 Hitherto we had been compelled to discourage widespread guerrilla activity among the loyal tribes such as the Karens. **1972** *Nat. Geographic* Feb. 270/1, I knew that a handful of Karens had moved into these hills about 125 years ago and now far outnumbered the native Lua.

2. The language of this people.

1861 J. Wade *Karen Vernacular Gram.* p. iii, Without this knowledge no one can determine, with confidence, what is good..Karen, and what is mere colloquial jargon. **1871** C. M. Yonge *Pioneers & Founders* vi. 161 She tried to learn Karen, but never had time, and..she could always have an interpreter. **1887** D. M. Smeaton *Loyal Karens Burma* ii. 73 Reduplication of words in Karen conveys an adverbial signification. **1961** *Dental Practitioner* XI. 369/1 Indeed, 'PAT' has now been programmed to produce phrases in English, Swedish, Polish, and Karen (a language of Burma). **1970** M. Pereira *Pigeon's Blood* vii. 81, I can speak ten dialects of Chinese, but not a word of Karen or Shan.

B. *adj.* Of or relating to the Karens or their language.

1839 [see *fine-tooth *a.*]. **1885** A. R. Colquhoun *Burma & Burmans* i. 11 The White Karen chief of Western Karennee. **1887** D. M. Smeaton *Loyal Karens Burma* ii. 73 The Karen language is monosyllabic. **1892** W. R. Winston *Four Yrs. Upper Burma* x. 99, I have.. listened in Upper Burma to..glees, choruses and solos, rendered by Karen young men and maidens. **1948** D. Diringer *Alphabet* vii. 412 The Karen character is a modern adaptation of the Burmese script to the Karen tongue. **1959** *Listener* 30 Apr. 746/1 The Karen rebels. **1972** *Nat. Geographic* Feb. 270/1 We found our Karen neighbors bore their troubles in a cheery, resilient, and generally relaxed way.

‖ **karez** (kā·rez). Also **kareze.** [Pers. (whence Pushtu) *kārez.*] In Afghanistan and Baluchistan = *kanat.

1875 *Encycl. Brit.* I. 232/1 The water of the *kârez*, or subterranean canals. **1880** *Ibid.* XIII. 836/2 Irrigation by 'karez' is also largely resorted to. **1902** [see *kanat]. **1920** *Blackw. Mag.* Feb. 246/2 Then I planned a *kareze*, a subterranean water-cut. **1924** *Glasgow Herald* 29 May 9 The Persian husbandmen had even begun to repair and refit their wonderful 'karezes'. **1969** B. L. C. Johnson *South Asia* iv. 95/1 A karez system consists of a near horizontal tunnel driven from the level of the cultivable land near the centre of an intermontane basin to intersect the water-table in the gravelly detritus which constitutes the fans along the mountain foot... At the lower end of the tunnel emerges a small stream of water which is led to the fields. An important advantage of the karez is that the water travels most of its way underground, and so with the minimum risk of loss by evaporation.

‖ **karezza** (kăre·tsă). Also **carezza.** [It. *carezza* caress.] Sexual union in which ejaculation or complete orgasm is avoided (see quot. 1896); = **coitus reservatus*.

1896 A. B. Stockham *Karezza* ii. 22 Karezza consummates marriage in such a manner that through the power of will, and loving thoughts, the final crisis is not reached, but a complete control by both husband and wife is maintained throughout the entire relation. **1953** [see *coitus reservatus* s.v. *coitus c]. **1956** A. Huxley *Adonis & Alphabet* 276 He advocated Male Continence and what Dr Stockham was later to call *Karezza*. **1970** W. W. Robson *Mod. Eng. Lit.* v. 105 Late in his life.. he [*sc.* Aldous Huxley] speculated optimistically on the benefits of a technique of sexual intercourse known as *carezza*. **1970** B. Walker *Sex & Supernatural* ix. 83 In time 'karezza' was believed to bestow extraordinary.. blessings.

Karitane (kæritā·ni). *N.Z.* [f. *Karitane*, a township in the South Island of New Zealand.] Used *attrib.*, of or pertaining to the system of ante- and post-natal care for mothers and babies initiated by Sir F. Truby King (1858–1938).

1913 F. T. King *Feeding & Care of Baby* 43 What has been achieved..on a relatively small scale at the Karitane Hospital is reflected enormously magnified in the district work. **1917** W. Wrench *Let.* in M. King *Truby King* (1948) xxiv. 234, I am convinced that our greatest need in this country is a Training Centre on Karitane lines. **1930** *Bulletin* (Sydney) 26 Mar. 42/3 The Karitane Training Centre in Nelson-street, Woolahra, has appointed Sister May Richardson as its matron. **1945** R. M. Burdon *N.Z. Notables* 2nd Ser. iv. 62 [Truby King] had long wished to build a proper Karitane Hospital in Wellington where, as yet, there was only a mothercraft home. **1947** 'A. P. Gaskell' *Big Game* 122 Margaret had started training as a Karitane nurse. **1948** M. King *Truby King* xv. 107 The word 'Karitane' has become famous in connection with Truby King Mothercraft work; but its origin is far removed from babies. The Huriawa or Karitane Peninsula lies at the south end of the wide Waikonaiti Bay. **1958** *N.Z. News* 11 Mar. 3/1 As an example, he [*sc.* Sir Truby King] successfully treated thirteen neglected infants in his own home, and ultimately six model 'Karitane' homes were founded throughout the Dominion. **1966** *Encycl. N.Z.* II. 222/2 A nurse was needed for the first Karitane baby.

Karlowitz(er), varr. *Carlowitz.

karma. Add: Also with pronunc. (kā·ɹmă). (Further examples.) Also in Hinduism.

Latterly adopted by Western popular 'meditative' groups.

1827 H. T. Colebrooke in *Trans. R. Asiatic Soc.* I. 111 The next head in Canáde's arrangement, after quality, is action (*carme*). **1830** —— *Ibid.* II. 38 Questions most recondite, which are agitated by theologians, have engaged the attention of the *vêdántins* likewise..such as.. efficacy of works (*carman*). **1881** A. P. Sinnett *Occult World* 132 Every thought of man upon being evolved passes into the inner world... It survives as an active intelligence..so man is continually peopling his current in space with a world of his own... The Buddhist calls this his 'Shandba'; the Hindu gives it the name of 'Karma'. **1899** L. Hearn *In Ghostly Japan* iii. 28 The destruction of Karma by virtuous effort is likened to the burning of incense by a pure flame. **1915** A. M. Stevenson *Heart of Jainism* viii. 175 While Hindus think of karma as formless (*amūrta*), Jaina believe karma to have shape. **1948** N. Micklem *Relig.* ii. 45 Thus the doctrine of *karma* (*literally* 'action') or transmigration is intimately associated with the philosophy of the *Upanishads*. **1962** T. C. Lethbridge *Witches* x. 133 The individual's choice of a future earthly body is limited however by what is known as the 'Law of Karma'. **1969** *Surfer* IX. vi. 38 May your destiny always be flavoured with good—good karma in this life. *Ibid.* 62 This is a bad Karma contest. **1971** *Nat. Geographic* Mar. 321/2 Officials, too, are subject to the law of karma—that sooner or later every action brings its retribution, in this existence or in one to come. **1971** *Rolling Stone* 24 June 32/2 John Sebastian's recording career has been plagued with an unusually bad karma. **1972** *Last Whole Earth Catalog* (Portola Inst.) 407/2 Because the karma is a little slower when you're not stoned, but it's the same karma and it works the same way.

Hence **ka·rmic** *a.*, pertaining to, relating to, or concerning *karma*.

1883 A. P. Sinnett *Esoteric Buddhism* xii. 195 Thus, on a careful examination of the matter the Karmic law.. will be seen not only to reconcile itself to the sense of justice, but to constitute the only imaginable method of natural action that would do this. **1931** L. H. Myers *Prince Jali* vi. 63 Would not a good Buddhist see in her only a link in the long karmic chain? **1949** S. Barbanell *Silver Birch Speaks* xiii. 142 One limit imposed, and always imposed, is what I would call the karmic debt of the patient, the relationship between mind and body determined by that individual's spiritual growth and attainment. **1974** *Publishers Weekly* 29 Apr. 47/2 Brodsky begins with an introduction to current genetic theory and proceeds to relate that to Eastern karmic understanding.

‖ **karmadharaya** (kaɹmădā·răyă). *Linguistics.* [Skr., f. Karma + *dhāraya* holding, bearing.] A compound in which the first member describes the second, as *highway* (adjective + noun), *steamboat* (attrib. noun + noun).

1846 M. Williams *Elem. Gram. Sanscrit Lang.* ix. 158 Native grammarians class compound nouns under five heads:..The 3d, *Karmadháraya*, or those composed of an adjective and substantive. **1933** L. Bloomfield *Lang.* xiv. 235 The Hindus found it convenient to set off..a special class of syntactic attribute-and-head compounds (*Karmadharaya*), such as *blackbird*. **1957** S. Potter *Mod. Ling.* iv. 92 That important type of compound called *karmadharaya* by Indian grammarians is represented by E *blackbird*, consisting of attribute + substantive.

‖ **karma-marga** (kā:ɹmă,mā·ɹgă). *Hinduism.* [Skr., f. Karma + *mārga* road, path.] A strict following of Hindu precepts as a means of attaining a better life in one's next incarnation; the way of works or action (contrasted with **bhakti-marga* and **jnana-marga*).

1877 M. Williams *Hinduism* i. 11 Belief in the efficacy of works, penances, and austerities,..is the *Karma-mārga*, 'way of works'. **1883** [see *jnana b]. **1937** [see *bhakti b]. **1945** [see jnana b].

Kármán (kā·ɹmān, -ăn). Also **Karman.** [Name of Theodore von *Kármán* (1881–1963), Hungarian-born physicist and aeronautical engineer who investigated the phenomenon.] *Kármán* (*vortex*) *street*, or *Kármán street of vortices*: a vortex street in which the vortices of one line are situated opposite points midway between those of the other line, an arrangement which is stable in certain conditions.

1928 *Proc. R. Soc.* A. CXX. 34 (*heading*) The characteristics of the Karman vortex street in a channel of finite breadth. **1929** *Phil. Trans. R. Soc.* A. CCXXVIII. 275 The following investigations deal with a Kármán street of vortices, or unsymmetrical double row, in a channel of finite width. **1936** *Proc. R. Soc.* A. CLIV. 68 Some very fine photographs of Kármán streets have been taken..in the water tank at the Aeronautical Research Laboratory of the Imperial College. **1949** O. G. Sutton *Sci. of Flight* iii. 64 In certain conditions the eddies detach themselves alternately from either edge of an obstacle placed across stream and as they break away they form in the wake the pattern known as the Kármán vortex street. **1956** A. A. Townsend *Struct. Turbulent Shear Flow* vii. 149 The eddies occur alternately in each half of the wake (as in a Kármán vortex street).

Karman, var. *Kirman.

‖ **karma-yoga** (kā:ɹmă,yōᵘ·gă). *Hinduism.* [Skr., f. Karma + Yoga.] The attainment of perfection through disinterested action. So **ka:rma-yo·gi**, an adherent or devotee of *karma-yoga*.

1896 'Vivekānanda' *Addresses Vedânta Philos.* I. 19 The Karma Yogî..is the man who understands that the highest ideal is non-resistance, but who also knows that it is the highest manifestation of power. *Ibid.* 55 Karma Yoga is the Yoga of work, to reach the goal of perfection by means of work. **1960** Koestler *Lotus & Robot* i. i. 36 Vinoba Bhave could be described as a Karma-Yogi—a person who seeks fulfilment by action. **1962** A. Huxley *Island* vi. 78 It's a real yoga... As good as raja yoga, or Karma yoga, or bhakti yoga. **1969** *Indo-Asian Culture* Oct. 42 Gandhiji's philosophy of action is *karmayoga*.

karmic: see *karma.

Karnata (kaɹnā·tă), *a.* and *sb.* Also **Carnataca, Carnati(c), Karnatak(a), Karnatakam, Karnatic, Kurnata.** [f. *Karnata* (Kanara), a region of south-west India; also var. of *Carnatic* (Karnatak), the name given, under British rule, to a region of southern India in the presidency of Madras.] **A.** *adj.* Of or pertaining to Karnata or the Carnatic. **B.** *sb.* **a.** The music of southern India, purer in form and more ancient than the Hindustani music of the north. † **b.** *Obs.* The native language of Karnata and the Carnatic; = *Kanarese *sb.* b.

1792 W. Jones in *Asiatick Researches* III. 82 On the formulas exhibited by Mirzakhan I have less reliance; but, since he professes to give them from *Sanscrit* authorities, it seemed proper to transcribe them: (*heading*) Dipaca:..*Netta*:..*Cédari*:..*Carnati*. **1801** H. T. Colebrooke *Ibid.* VII. 227 Carnáta, or Cánara, is the ancient language of Carnátaca. **1814** W. Carey *Gram. Telinga Lang.* p. i, The languages of the south of India, i.e. The Telinga, Kurnata, Tamul, Malayala, and Cingalese. **1820** J. McKerrell *Gram. Carnataca Lang.* p. i, The Carnátaca Language..is nearly the universal Language of all the dominions of the late Tippoo Sultan. **1855** H. H. Wilson *Gloss. Judicial & Revenue Terms* p. ix, In Karnáta, *kuḷ* is a payer of government revenue. **1856** R. Caldwell *Compar. Gram. Dravidian Lang.* 6 The Kannadi or Karnâtaka..is spoken throughout the plateau of Mysore. ..'Karnâtaka'..is defined to mean primarily 'a species of dramatic music', or 'comedy': it is used secondarily in Telugu as an adjective to signify 'native', 'aboriginal' ..it then became the common designation of the Telugu and Canarese, or 'native' languages: and, finally, was restricted still further, and became the distinctive appellation of the Canarese alone. **1892** A. M. Chinnaswami Mudaliyar *Oriental Mus. in European Notation* 9 The unfettered use of accidentals in European Music is regarded by the Karnāta musician as due to want of principle and system. *Ibid.* 12 The primary distinction is into two classes, Mārga (celestial) and Dēsi (terrestrial); the latter is now broadly divided into Hindustani and Karnāta. **1914** A. H. F. Strangways *Mus. Hindostan* 15 The Carnatic system frankly ignores the niceties..of intonation. **1920** E. Clements *Rāgas of Tanjore* 43/2 The Chaturdandi Prakāshikā..is said to be the principal treatise followed by modern Karnatic musicians. **1929** E. Rosenthal *Story Indian Mus.* i. 10 There is a wide diversity between the classification of *rágas* in the northern or Hindustani system, and in the southern or Carnatic system. **1948** G. Venkatachalam *Dance in India* x. 90 Carnatic music had its origin in the Telugu country. **1952** P. Sambamoorthy *Dict. S. Indian Mus. & Musicians* p. vi, A few pictures are from the valuable collection of musical instruments in the Central College of Karnataka

Music,..Madras. **1968** *Jrnl. Musical Acad. Madras* XXXIX. 49 Is the wealth of Karnataka music preserved and handed down to posterity? **1971** *Shankar's Weekly* (Delhi) 4 Apr. 25/1 There is much more honesty..in a Jon Higgins submitting himself to the discipline of Karnatak music wholeheartedly. **1972** P. HOLROYDE *Indian Mus.* iii. 84 The Karnatakam remained uninfluenced... South Indian music, properly known as Carnatic, and South Indian dance, survived therefore in more-or-less pure form.

Karnaugh (kā·ɹnǭ). [The name of Maurice *Karnaugh* (b. 1924), U.S. physicist, who published an account of the diagram in 1953.] *Karnaugh map* or *diagram*: a diagram that consists of a rectangular array of squares each representing a different combination of the variables of a Boolean function (used, e.g., to find by inspection a simpler equivalent function).

1958 M. PHISTER *Logical Design Digital Computers* 405 (Index), Karnaugh map. **1960** W. C. IRWIN *Digital Computer Princ.* xiv. 76 The most elementary Karnaugh map represents a function of two variables. **1968** HILL & PETERSON *Introd. Switching Theory* vi. 87 The Karnaugh map is essentially a diagrammatic form of truth table, and..the Venn diagram concepts of union and intersection of areas aid us in setting up or interpreting a Karnaugh map. **1970** O. DOPPING *Computers & Data Processing* i. 28 When the number of sets is large, the overall view is improved by using a kind of modified Venn diagrams called Karnaugh diagrams or Veitch diagrams. **1973** *Math. Teaching* Sept. 48/1 The Karnaugh map takes the place of a truth table.

karo (kā·ro). *N.Z.* [Maori.] An evergreen shrub or small tree, *Pittosporum crassifolium*, which bears crimson flowers.

1853 J. D. HOOKER *Bot. Antarctic Voy.: Flora Novæ-Zelandiæ* I. 23 *Pittosporum cornifolium*... Nat[ive] name, 'Karo'. **1868** W. COLENSO in *Trans. N.Z. Inst.* I. III. Essay. 5 Of our shrubs and smaller timber trees, several are of strikingly beautiful growth, or blossom, or foliage; and are often seen to advantage in some clear glade..and, on the sea-coast,..the Karo, *Pittosporum crassifolium*. **1928** COCKAYNE & TURNER *Trees N.Z.* 104 *Pittosporum crassifolium*... Karo. A small tree, 15–30 ft. high, or frequently a dense shrub. **1950** *N.Z. Jrnl. Agric.* Dec. 533/1 The native karo (*Pittosporum crassifolium*) will thrive in heavy shade and will stand strong salt winds and much drier soil conditions than boxthorn, but it requires permanent double fencing to protect it from stock. **1963** J. T. SALMON *N.Z. Flowers & Plants in Colour* 53 The rich sweet scent of karo flowers fills the air of a calm evening when the tree is in flower.

Karok (kărɑ·k). Also † **Cahroc, Kahruk.** [f. Karok *káruk* upstream.] **a.** An Indian people of the Klamath river valley in northwestern California. **b.** The language of this people. Also *attrib.*

1851 G. GIBBS *Jrnl.* 12 Oct. in H. R. Schoolcraft *Hist. & Stat. Information Indian Tribes* (1853) III. 151 They do not seem to have any generic appellation for themselves, but apply the terms 'Kahruk', up and 'Youruk', down, to all who live above or below themselves. **1872** *Overland Monthly* Apr. 328/2 The Cahrocs are probably the finest tribe of Indians in California. *Ibid.* 330/2 The Cahroc language, though rich in its vocabulary, is said to contain no expression for 'virtue'. **1877** *Contrib. N. Amer. Ethnol.* III. 32 The Karok language is said by those acquainted with it to be copious, sonorous, and rich in new combinations. **1903** G. W. JAMES *Indian Basketry* (ed. 3) 53 The Karoks (often spelled Cahrocs) are a fine, vigorous people. **1913** [see *HOKAN]. **1921** E. SAPIR *Lang.* ix. 220 'Hokan' languages (Shasta, Karok). **1940** *Oregon Guide* 34 The southern part of Oregon was occupied by..two 'spill-overs' from California—the Shastas and Karoks. **1962** J. J. GUMPERZ in J. A. Fishman *Readings Sociol. of Lang.* (1968) 467 Certain Californian Indian tribes (the Yurok, Karok and Hupa). **1971** *Language* XLVII. 830 The Karok shift suggests consonant frequency raising in addition to palatalization.

karoro (ka·roro). *N.Z.* [Maori.] The southern black-backed gull, *Larus dominicanus.*

1861 A. S. ATKINSON *Jrnl.* 18 Jan. in *Richmond-Atkinson Papers* (1960) I. 680 Saw another noteworthy sight..a young karoro just out of the nest, running along in a curious human way all by himself. **1888** W. L. BULLER *Hist. Birds N.Z.* (ed. 2) II. 47 *Larus dominicanus*. (Southern Black-backed Gull.)..Native names. Karoro; the young bird distinguished as Ngoiro, Koiro, and Punua. **1930** W. R. B. OLIVER *N.Z. Birds* 260 Black-backed Gull. Karoro..[is] one of the most common and conspicuous birds on our coasts. **1966** R. A. FALLA et al. *Field Guide to Birds N.Z.* 154 Southern black-backed gull *Larus dominicanus*... Maori name: Karoro.

karper, var. *KURPER.

karpinskyite (kāɹpi·nski,əit). *Min.* [ad. Russ. *karpinskiit* (L. L. Shilin 1956, in *Dokladȳ Akademii Nauk SSSR* CVII. 737), f. the name of A. P. *Karpinsky* (1847–1936), Russ. geologist: see -ITE[1].] A hydrous alumino-silicate of sodium, beryllium, zinc, and magnesium, $Na_2(Be,Zn,Mg)Al_2Si_6O_{16}(OH)_2$, occurring as radial aggregates of white, needle-shaped crystals.

1956 *Dokladȳ Akademii Nauk SSSR* CVII. 628 (*table of contents*) Karpinskyite—a new mineral. **1958** *Mineral. Mag.* XXXI. 963 Karpinskyite. **1968** I. KOSTOV *Mineral.* 406 Leifite..is similar to cancrinite, and so also is karpinskyite.

karree. Also karee (now the usual form). Substitute for def.: Either of two South African trees of the genus *Rhus*, *R. lancia* or *R. viminalis*, of the family Anacardiaceæ. (Earlier and later examples.)

1815 A. PLUMPTRE tr. *Lichtenstein's Trav. S. Afr.* II. xliv. 223 Mimosas,..willows, and *karree bushes*. Among the latter the colonists include several sorts of *rhus*. **1834** A. G. BAIN *Let.* 18 Dec. in *Jrnls.* (1949) 151 It was actually two large karee trees with large pools of rain-water around them. **1898** W. C. SCULLY *Vendetta of Desert* xviii. 177 They quickened their paces so as to reach a long, low ridge dotted with *karee* bushes. **1934** L. VAN DER POST *In a Province* viii. 110 Noon beats on tattered parasols of karee-thorn over them. **1939** S. CLOETE *Watch for Dawn* xxviii. 418 Behind a thick clump of karee boom a Kaffir squatted motionless. **1958** L. VAN DER POST *Lost World of Kalahari* i. 15 In the rivers and streams he constructed traps beautifully woven out of reeds and buttressed with young karee wood or hardekool. **1966** E. PALMER *Plains of Camdeboo* xvii. 287 Along the river-beds across the plains are thorn trees and karees. *Ibid.* 288 The karee trees, with their round crowns of yellow-green drooping foliage, were a welcome sight to the travellers.

‖ **karren, Karren** (ka·rən), *sb. pl. Geomorphol.* [G.] The furrows, fissures, or grikes of a *karrenfeld*; also, = *karrenfelder.*

1894 *Geogr. Jrnl.* III. 322 The chief features of such limestone regions are those known as *karren, dolinen,* blind valleys, and *poljen*. The *karren*, or surfaces composed of blocks of limestone separated by narrow fissures, are dealt with very briefly. **1898** *Ibid.* XII. 90 Karren are peculiar fissures in the rocky surface of some mountainous regions. **1902** LD. AVEBURY *Scenery of Eng.* xiii. 437 In calcareous districts the surface is sometimes quite bare and intersected by furrows... Such districts are known on the Continent as 'lapiées' or 'karren'. **1924** *Geogr. Rev.* XIV. 27 Lapiés are found at all altitudes from sea level to lofty mountain summits. They were first observed and described in the limestone Alps in Switzerland, where in the cantons of German speech they are called *Karren* or *Schratten*. **1960** B. W. SPARKS *Geomorphol.* vii. 155 The surface of the limestone..is often conspicuously furrowed and fretted (clints, grykes, lapiés, rascles, Schratten, Karren). **1971** J. N. JENNINGS *Karst* iv. 41 Very many *Karren* in central and western Europe must be regarded as stripped.

‖ **karrenfeld, Karrenfeld** (ka·rənfelt, -feld). *Geomorphol.* Pl. **-felder, -felds.** [G., f. *karren* (see prec.) + *feld* field.] An area or landscape, usu. of limestone bare of soil, which has been eroded by solution of the rock giving an extremely dissected surface with conspicuous furrows and fissures, often separated by knife-like ridges.

1885 A. GEIKIE *Text-bk. Geol.* (ed. 2) III. ii. 322 Limestones frequently assume a remarkable channelled rugose surface, with projecting knobs, ridges and pinnacles especially developed in high bare tracts of ground. (Karrenfelder.) **1922** *Geol. Mag.* LIX. 394 In Switzerland, notably in the canton Glarus, these bare surfaces known as *Karrenfelder* have been the subject of detailed studies by Heim. **1923** *Nature* 9 June 787/1 These have originated in guano, which gathered in the hollows of a 'karrenfeld', worn out of upraised coral-limestone. **1948** C. A. COTTON *Landscape* (ed. 2) xxiii. 445 It has been suggested that all karrenfelds are such surfaces stripped of soil in recent times. **1957** G. E. HUTCHINSON *Treat. Limnol.* I. i. 100 In some cases a *karrenfeld*, consisting of small pinnacles separated by crevices, may form.

Karri-Kot: see *CARRY-COT.

‖ **karrozzin** (kărǫ·tsin). Also **carozzi, carrozzi, karrozin.** [Maltese, f. It. *carrozza* carriage.] A horse-drawn cab used in Malta. Also *attrib.*

1926 E. SHEPHERD *Malta & Me* vii. 53, I..preferred the dreary carozzi. *Ibid.* xvi. 129 The roads leading to Valletta are black from early morning with carozzis. **1943** *Epic of Malta* 25 (*caption*) The picture above shows a 'carrozzi' (Maltese cab) at its usual..stand. *Ibid.* 89 (*caption*) In the picture below Maltese ponies are seen sheltering beside their 'carozzis' (cabs). **1960** *Sunday Express* 6 Nov. 19/4 You can ride in a horse-drawn cab (called a *karrozin*). **1964** G. BUTLER *Coffin in Malta* iii. 66 The flower-sellers and the karrozzin drivers in the square. **1968** *Clarendonian* XXII. 269 One could get up into town by a lift up the cliff face for 2½d...or by karrozzin, the Maltese name for the colourful horse and buggy. **1972** *Daily Tel.* (Colour Suppl.) 21 Jan. 21 (Advt.), They're horse-drawn 'karrozzins', and each one is so beautifully painted you get the feeling all the owners are in earnest competition. Hire one, and go for a ride through Malta's tiny winding streets, at a good steady trot.

karrusel (karuse·l). *Horology.* Also **karussell.** [Da., = *CAROUSEL 2.] (See quot. 1962.)

1892 B. BONNIKSEN *Brit. Pat. No. 21,421* 24 Nov., The drawing accompanying this following description, is an illustration of what I have named a position-equalizing-karrusel (hereinafter termed' karrusel'; the word 'karrusel' means the same as a 'roundabout') its purpose is to make the balance of..any..portable timepiece, turn round itself in any given time. **1929** G. H. BAILIE *Watches* xix. 347 A different type of tourbillon was invented by Bonniksen of Coventry in 1892 and called by him a Karussell. **1962** E. BRUTON *Dict. Clocks & Watches* 98 *Karrusel*, arrangement similar to the tourbillon in which the escapement revolves every 52½ minutes.

karsey, var. *KARZY.

Karshuni, var. *GARSHUNI.

karst, Karst (kāɹst). **1.** The name (*the Karst*, G. *der Karst* (= Serbo-Croat *Kras*)) of a high barren limestone region south of Ljubljana in N.W. Yugoslavia that has given its name to a kind of topography typified there (see 2); used *attrib.* in *Geomorphol.* (now usu. with small *k*) to designate similar regions and scenery, features, and phenomena associated with them, etc.; **karst land, karstland,** karstic land; a karstic region.

1894 *Geogr. Jrnl.* III. 321 Under the general designation *Karst-phenomena*, physical geographers in Germany include a variety of land-surface features, all characteristic of limestone regions, which, when the features in question are present, are known as 'Karst-regions'. *Ibid.* 509 A monotonous limestone plateau almost without water and vegetation, and occasionally exhibiting the very worst Karst features. **1898** Karst-land [see *BLIND *a.* (and *adv.*) 11 c]. **1903** *Westm. Gaz.* 10 Feb. 3/1 The latter [*sc.* Herzegovina], although fertile in parts and well cultivated, is a Karst country, warm and southern. **1908** H. B. C. & W. J. SOLLAS tr. *Suess's Face of Earth* III. vi. 231 In the Shan states of Burma, several of the coulisses which approach from the north and north-east disappear beneath a karst-like plateau of Palaeozoic limestone. **1909** CHAMBERLIN & SALISBURY *Geol.: Shorter Course* xxiii. 689 The limestone and dolomite are much more resistant than the associated shales, and as a result, erosion has developed a distinctive topography (Karst topography) at several points in the southern Alps. **1921** *Geogr. Rev.* XI. 594 In a region where karst topography is fully developed the water circulates almost entirely underground. *Ibid.* 631 To Penck and others we owe something for their development of the idea of the karst cycle. **1922** *Geol. Mag.* LIX. 394 Karst phenomena are not infrequent in the Alpine limestone districts. **1924** *Glasgow Herald* 25 Aug. 4 Karakul sheep were also introduced..in the Austrian 'karst land', in the mountains between Croatia and the Adriatic. **1932** W. H. EMMONS et al. *Geol.* v. 80 In the United States similar topography is developed in limestone areas in central Tennessee and Kentucky and is referred to as Karst topography. **1939** BAILEY & WEIR *Introd. Geol.* xxxi. 183 Karst land is rare in Scotland. **1954** W. D. THORNBURY *Princ. Geomorphol.* xiii. 349 Whether there exists a distinct cycle of land-form evolution in limestone terrains which we may designate as a karst cycle or whether what has been so designated is better considered as the karst phase of a fluvial cycle is a disputed question. **1957** G. E. HUTCHINSON *Treat. Limnol.* I. i. 107 Along the southwestern shore of the lakes where the karst topography is best developed, there are not only many islands but also very deep holes. **1958** *Geogr. Jrnl.* CXXIV. 184 (*heading*) The karstlands of Jamaica. **1963** 'M. ALBRAND' *Call from Austria* xvii. 145 He might have fallen into one of those *karst* holes you can't spot until it's too late. **1963** D. W. & E. E. HUMPHRIES tr. *Termier's Erosion & Sedimentation* xiv. 316 A karst-eroded surface. **1971** *Guardian* 5 June 9/2 This is Italy's deep south, karst country, hot and dry, split with canyons.

2. (With small *k*.) A kind of topography of which the Yugoslavian Karst is typical, found in areas of readily dissolved rock (usually limestone) and predominantly underground drainage and marked by numerous abrupt ridges, fissures, sink-holes, and caverns; a region dominated by this kind of topography.

In quot. 1902 the Karst in Yugoslavia is referred to.

1902 *Geogr. Jrnl.* XX. 429 The uvala is a large, broad sinking in the karst with uneven floor. **1916** H. F. CLELAND *Geol.* iii. 72 Karst is used as a descriptive term for any limestone region which has been etched and eroded by water into a rough surface. **1922** *Geol. Mag.* LIX. 394 The south of France where the karst attains its greatest development in Western Europe. **1937** WOOLDRIDGE & MORGAN *Physical Basis Geogr.* xix. 289 The surface of a well-developed karst has lost all semblance of normal water-modelled forms. It is a stone desert, a chaos of pits, elongated hollows, and ridges. **1958** *Geogr. Jrnl.* CXXIV. 192 Considerable areas of degraded karst occur in northern and central Jamaica. **1963** D. W. & E. E. HUMPHRIES tr. *Termier's Erosion & Sedimentation* vi. 148 Bauxites occur very frequently on karsts. **1966** J. C. PUGH in G. H. Dury *Ess. Geomorphol.* 135 Some workers prefer to regard cockpit country and tower karst as typical of karst in general, holding that in the past too much emphasis has been placed on solution and on associated collapse of passages, and too little on surface features of solution which are not restricted to tropical regions. **1968** R. W. FAIRBRIDGE *Encycl. Geomorphol.* 682/2 The terrace surface is a deeply etched karst ('karrenfeld'), with pinnacles 15 feet high, alternating with deep crevices, partly filled with red soil. **1972** J. ROGLIĆ in Herak & Stringfield *Karst* i. 6 Following Cvijić, he considered the doline a basic feature ('Leitform') of karst.

Hence **ka·rstic** *a.*, of or characteristic of karst; that is (a) karst.

1925 *Geogr. Rev.* XV. 72 The poljes have been formed by karstic and fluvial erosion. *Ibid.* 140 They occur in volcanic and karstic terrains. **1933** *Geogr. Jrnl.* LXXXI. 275 Karstic drainage occurs in limestone, dolomite, gypsum. **1957** G. E. HUTCHINSON *Treat. Limnol.* I. i. 19 In common with the other large lakes of the region [*sc.* the Balkans], both show some karstic features. **1963** D. W. & E. E. HUMPHRIES tr. *Termier's Erosion & Sedimentation* vi. 148 The karstic form of the limestone has thus acted

as a trap for the transported sediment. **1970** R. J. SMALL *Study of Landforms* iv. 152 Enclosed depressions in karstic areas are usually attributed either to (i) slow downward development by solution processes..or to (ii) collapse of rock above an underground passage or cavern.

karstification (kāːɹstifikēⁱ·ʃən). *Geomorphol.* [f. prec. + -IFICATION.] Development of karst or karstic features; alteration into karst. So **ka·rstify** *v. trans.*, to subject to karstification; **ka·rstified, ka·rstifying** *ppl. adjs.*

1958 *Geogr. Jrnl.* CXXIV. 186 'Karstification' of the White Limestones began..after the mid-Miocene movements. **1968** R. W. FAIRBRIDGE *Encycl. Geomorphol.* 582/2 For a karst to develop fully or for an area to become karstified, the region must possess the following set of features. **1972** *Science* 12 May 664/2 The book is a bit thin on chemistry, considering that karstification is mainly a chemical process. **1972** F. DARÁNYI in Herak & Stringfield *Karst* viii. 283 Karst surfaces in Hungary occupy an area of some 3,000 km². The contributions of the various epochs are, however, very different, being dependent on stratigraphic position, thickness, tectonic setting, and karstifying agents. *Ibid.*, On the present-day surface of the western half of the Mecsek, the 400 m thick Anisian sequence has been karstified.

karsting (kā·ɹstiŋ), *vbl. sb. Geomorphol.* [f. as prec. + -ING¹.] = *KARSTIFICATION.

1921 *Geogr. Rev.* XI. 597 In youth, the surface of the land is still principally drained by the rivers which flow on the former surface of the land before the limestone subject to karsting was laid bare. **1956** D. L. LINTON *Sheffield* ii. 27 Our knowledge of the 'karsting' of the limestone plateau of the southern Pennines is still elementary.

karsto·logy. *Geomorphol.* [f. as prec. + -OLOGY.] The study of karst.

1968 R. W. FAIRBRIDGE *Encycl. Geomorphol.* 560/2 There are furthermore several national and international organizations that promote congresses and publications in Speleology and Karstology. **1972** HERAK & STRINGFIELD *Karst* i. 2 The classical connection of karstology with the Dinaric karst was not accidental.

kart. Restrict † *obs.* to sense in Dict. and add: **2.** = *GO-KART. Hence **ka·rting** *vbl. sb.*, the sport of driving or racing a kart.

1959 *Motor* 9 Sept. 111/1 The whole affair may well seem reprehensible to those who feel that an injustice has been wrought on the children or that karting is too juvenile for adults, but after trying a kart, although one must admit that they are a joke, there is no doubt that they are one of the very best jokes to come out of the U.S.A. since Thurber's dogs. After 10 minutes' karting the cynic is invariably asking where he can get one. **1961** *Sunday Express* 1 Jan. 15/3 '*Karting clothes*' the newest fad. **1964** K. WHEELER *Sport* 123 The newest motor sport is Karting. In the late 1950s the first little midget cars were seen on the tracks... Now karting is much faster, and an officially recognised sport with its own trophies and its own champions... A kart can cost as little as £80. **1968** *Times* 2 Aug. 13/2 Her tiny 100 c.c. machine is capable of 80 m.p.h. She has been driving since she was 13, the minimum age for kart racing in this country.

‖ **karuna** (kărū·nă). *Buddhism.* [Skr. *karuṇā* charity, compassion.] Loving compassion, as that sought and attained by a *Bodhisattva*.

1850 R. S. HARDY *Eastern Monachism* xx. 246 When we see any object in distress, we feel kampáwíma, agitation, in the mind; and from this arises karuná, pity or compassion. **1960** A. HUXLEY *Let.* 17 July (1969) 893 Then no me any more and a kind of *sat chit ananda*, at one moment without *karuna* or charity. **1962** —— *Island* ix. 152 A fair chance..of eventual *prajnaparamita* and *karuna*, eventual wisdom and compassion.

karyo-. Add: **karyo·gamy** [*-GAMY], fusion of cell nuclei; **ka·ryomere** [Gr. μέρος part], a vesicular chromosome enclosed in a nuclear membrane of its own, such as forms at telophase in the division of some cells; **karyoplasma·tic, -pla·smic** *adjs.*, of or pertaining to karyoplasm; **karyothe·ca** *rare*, the nuclear membrane.

1891 *Jrnl. R. Microsc. Soc.* 49 In *Hydatina*, as in some Hymenoptera, there is established between arrhenotoky (parthenogenetic production of males) and fecundating karyogamy, a relation so necessary that the second is impossible without the first. **1901** G. N. CALKINS *Protozoa* iii. 97 It is quite possible that many cases of so-called conjugation are only instances of plastogamy, or fusion of the cell-body, and are not followed by union of the nuclei (karyogamy), as in fertilization. **1970** J. WEBSTER *Introd. Fungi* 187 Karyogamy (i.e. nuclear fusion) occurs within certain of the binucleate cells. **1912** *Jrnl. Acad. Nat. Sci. Philadelphia* XV. 525 The most general results of increased temperature are:...(4) Formation of numerous karyomeres from these scattered chromosomes; indeed by slight increase of temperature almost every chromosome may be caused to remain distinct from every other one, and to give rise to a separate chromosomal vesicle. **1934** L. W. SHARP *Introd. Cytol.* (ed. 3) x. 136 Of considerable interest are those nuclei in which every chromosome of the telophase group forms an individual vesicle, or karyomere. In some cases the karyomeres may eventually fuse partially or completely, but in others they remain separate although in contact, forming what is virtually a group of small nuclei containing one chromosome each. *Ibid.* 146 The limits of the several chromosomes remain visible through this stage [*sc.* between mitoses] in certain nuclei; in extreme cases the nucleus is virtually a group of separate elementary nuclei, or karyomeres. **1969** BROWN & BERTKE *Textbk. Cytol.* xvii. 318/2 Karyomeres are rather like micronuclei except that they are normal and become associated to form a 'compound' nucleus. **1920** L. DONCASTER *Introd. Study Cytol.* ii. 16 Hertwig regards a disturbance of the normal karyo-plasmatic ratio as the immediate cause of cell-division, and supposes that the unequal rate of growth of nucleus and cytoplasm brings about a condition of 'karyo-plasmatic strain' leading to cell-division and a consequent restoration of the normal ratio. **1909** *Cent. Dict.* Suppl., Karyoplasmic. **1924** E. V. COWDRY *Gen. Cytol.* VI. 351 Hertwig's karyoplasmic relation hypothesis. **1925** E. B. WILSON *Cell* (ed. 3) iii. 237 These various facts show on how precarious a basis rest theories of senescence and rejuvenescence which refer these processes to changes in the karyoplasmic ratio. **1948** R. A. R. GRESSON *Essent. Gen. Cytol.* i. 2 It has been found that a quantitative relationship exists between nuclear mass and cytoplasmic mass; this is known as the karyoplasmic ratio. **1966** D. M. KRAMSCH tr. *Grundmann's Gen. Cytol.* ii. 66 The optical appearance of the karyoplasmic area is homogeneous and frequently seems to be empty. **1896** E. B. WILSON *Cell* 337 *Karyotheca*, the nuclear membrane. **1948** W. ANDREW tr. *E. D. P. de Robertis's Gen. Cytol.* iii. 45 Between the two parts of this heterogeneous system.., there is found the karyotheca or nuclear membrane.

karyogram (kæ·riogræm). *Biol.* [f. KARYO- + -GRAM.] **a.** A karyotype or idiogram.

In quot. 1952 (by a Jap. writer) perh. an error for *karyotype*, which is used throughout the paper (in sense *1 a).

1952 *Cytologia* XVII. 311 (*heading*) Karyogram studies in birds. **1965** *Amer. Jrnl. Bot.* LII. 968 (*caption*) Karyogram from untreated apical and nodal cells..showing chromosome length greater than that in pretreated antheridial filament cells. **1971** *Nature* 9 Apr. 368/1 (*caption*) A typical karyogram of Chinese hamster strain *wg* 3 *IMP*⁻: twenty-two chromosomes, all but one (bottom right) distinguishable from those of mouse strain *3T3 TK*⁻.

b. A diagram in which each chromosome of a set is represented by a point positioned with respect to a vertical and a horizontal axis, these axes corresponding to two numerical characteristics of the chromosomes.

1960 K. PATAU in *Amer. Jrnl. Human Genetics* XII. 255 A chromosome characterized by two quantities is best represented by a point in a two-dimensional co-ordinate system. The choice of these quantities—total length and arm index or two arm lengths, is in principle irrelevant... Let the percent length, l, of the longer arm serve as abscissa and the percent length, s, of the shorter arm as ordinate. The scatter diagram obtained by plotting in this manner all chromosomes of the given complement will henceforth be referred to as a 'karyogram'. **1966** STEWART & KILLEAN in Darlington & Lewis *Chromosomes Today* I. 211 In the production of karyograms the basic data are taken from a photographic enlargement of the chromosome plate to be analysed. **1969** *Nature* 22 Nov. 801/2 The results of a chromosome analysis can be displayed in several ways. The methods commonly used are the karyotype..and the karyogram, in which each chromosome is represented by a point in a bivariate coordinate system.

karyology (kæriǫ·lŏdʒi). *Biol.* [f. KARYO- + -LOGY.] **a.** The distinctive or characteristic features (esp. as regards chromosomes) of a particular cell nucleus, or of the nuclei of a particular species, strain, etc. **b.** The study of cell nuclei, esp. the chromosomes they contain.

1895 *Ann. Bot.* IX. 631 Wager ('89) has carefully investigated the karyology of *Peronospora parasitica*. **1932** *Symbolae Bot. Upsalienses* I. 150 The chromosomes have individuality or genetic continuity from one cell generation to another. This conception..may be considered as the foundation of all comparative karyology. **1948** W. ANDREW tr. *E. D. P. de Robertis's Gen. Cytol.* vii. 134 There was considerable progress in karyology, which is a branch of cytology dealing with the nucleus or karyosome, to the detriment of the study of the cytoplasm or cytosome. **1965** *Jrnl. Nat. Cancer Inst.* (U.S.) XXXV. 766/1 This..indicates a significant difference between the general karyology of the normal cell and of the tumor cell population. **1970** *Cytologia* XXXV. 294 (*heading*) Karyology of *Sequoia sempervirens*: karyotype and accessory chromosomes. **1971** *Daily Colonist* (Victoria, B.C.) 24 Dec. 4/2 Karyology, or the study of the number, shape, and size of chromosomes, is Dr. Wiens' specialty.

Hence **karyolo·gic** (chiefly *U.S.*), **-lo·gical** *adjs.*, of or pertaining to karyology; **karyolo·gically** *adv.*, as regards or in relation to karyology.

1927 *Trudy̆ po Prikladnoĭ Botanike i Selektsii* XVII. III. 64 Presence, shape and size of the satellite are characters of much importance in karyological systematics. *Ibid.* 65 The plates given..represent races which are karyologically most sharply different. **1929** *Cytologia* I. 76 (*heading*) Karyological studies in *Hemerocallis*. **1935** *Experiment Station Rec.* LXXII. 754 Karyologic and genetic studies with Fragaria. **1962** *Exper. Cell Res.* XXVI. 434 (*heading*) Karyologic studies on polyoma virus induced mouse tumors. **1962** *Lancet* 27 Jan. 219/1 Karyologically the cells with 47 chromosomes were typically mongoloid, and those with 46 chromosomes were normal. **1970** *Nature* 11 July 169/1 The karyological properties of MRC-5 cells conform to those required of a diploid cell of human origin to be used for producing viral vaccines intended for human use. **1974** *Ibid.* 5 Apr. 504/2 A unique possibility of investigating RSV production on a permanent cell line which is well defined karyologically.

karyosome. Substitute for def. (in Dict. s.v. KARYO-): **1.** [ad. G. *karyosoma* (M. Ogata 1883, in *Arch. f. Anat. u. Physiol.* (Physiol. Abt.) 414).] **a.** A body of chromatin in a nucleus resembling a nucleolus but distinguished from the 'true' nucleolus or plasmosome. **b.** Any densely staining central body of a nucleus.

1889 [see *hyalosome* s.v. *HYALO-]. **1890** [in Dict. s.v. KARYO-, where for *Soc.* read *Sci.* in the title]. **1896** E. B. WILSON *Cell* i. 24 The bodies known by this name [*sc.* nucleolus] are of at least two different kinds. The first of these, the so-called true nucleoli or plasmosomes.., are of spherical form... Those of the other form, the 'net-knots' (Netzknoten), or karyosomes, are either spherical or irregular in form, stain like the chromatin, and appear to be no more than thickened portions of the chromatic network. **1901** G. N. CALKINS *Protozoa* v. 146 In most cases they [*sc.* the nuclei of Sporozoa] consist of a firm and resisting membrane containing a single large chromatin reservoir or karyosome. **1920** L. DONCASTER *Introd. Study Cytol.* ii. 18 The karyosome or chromatic nucleolus is a mass of chromatin of varying size... It appears to serve as a reservoir of chromatin from which the chromosomes..may draw part at least of their supply when nuclear division is approaching. **1926** G. N. CALKINS *Biol. Protozoa* ii. 60 The centrally placed intranuclear body is generally described under the name karyosome, a term which has been so widely used by students of the Protozoa and for so many obviously different structures that it is practically synonymous with endosome or Binnenkörper. **1948** W. ANDREW tr. *E. D. P. de Robertis's Gen. Cytol.* iii. 59 In the fixed nucleus one can distinguish:..(4) in some nuclei there are found larger and denser flakes of chromatin situated in the chromonemata, the chromocenters or karyosomes, also called false nucleoli or chromatin nucleoli. **1961** MACKINNON & HAWES *Introd. Study Protozoa* i. 12 The term karyosome (the endosome of some authors) is here used descriptively as the name of any conspicuous, deeply staining body lying in the nuclear sap, without regard to its constitution. Undoubtedly some karyosomes are really nucleoli (*Trichomonas vaginalis*) and they disappear during mitosis; others play an important part in that process (*Naegleria*) and some are Feulgen positive (*Trichomonas sanguisugae*). **1969** BROWN & BERTKE *Textbk. Cytol.* xvii. 320/1 The terms 'karyosome', 'endosome', and 'central body' are applied to nucleolus-like nuclear organelles that are permanent structures... Karyosomes, etc. are probably permanent nucleoli that undergo division and are found in numerous algae, protozoa, and some fungi.

† **2.** = NUCLEUS *sb.* 6 a. *Obs.*

1894 S. WATASÉ in *Biol. Lect. Marine Biol. Lab. Wood's Holl 1893* 84 An animal cell may be described as composed of two sharply distinct organs: the cell body (cytosome), and the nucleus (caryosome). **1948** [see *KARYOLOGY].

karyotin (kæ·riotin). *Biol.* Also **-ine.** [a. G. *karyotin* (H. Lundegård 1910, in *Svensk bot. Tidskr.* IV. 177), f. *karyo-* KARYO- + *-tin* (after *chromatin*).] The stainable material of a cell nucleus; the substance of which the nuclear reticulum is composed.

1925 E. B. WILSON *Cell* (ed. 3) i. 90 Such considerations led Lundegårdh ('10) to propose that the term 'chromatin' be replaced by 'karyotin' (caryotin), the substance thus designated appearing in either a basichromatic or an oxyphilic phase. **1934** L. W. SHARP *Introd. Cytol.* (ed. 3) iii. 55 Only future research can decide whether karyotin ('chromatin' in the wide sense) is a true chemical compound. **1948** W. ANDREW tr. *E. D. P. de Robertis's Gen. Cytol.* vii. 138 Other authors admit the existence of two distinct phases: the karyolymph, which is considered as a colloid sufficiently stable to be precipitated only with acids and fixatives, and the karyotin, a more labile and complex colloid dispersed in the karyolymph, which would precipitate with great facility. **1966** D. H. KRAMSCH tr. *Grundmann's Gen. Cytol.* ii. 66 The nucleus was..regarded as a solution, a sol in which little droplets, the so-called karyotine droplets, representing a somewhat more solid 'phase', were dispersed.

karyotype (kæ·riotəip), *sb. Biol.* and *Med.* [ad. Russ. *kariotip* (L. N. Delone (Delaunay) 1922, in *Vestnik Tiflisskogo botanicheskogo Sada* 2nd Ser. I. 49): see KARYO- and -TYPE.

Orig. coined by Delaunay in sense 2, but according to quot. 1931 it was later coined independently (again in Russ.) by Lewitsky (1924), in sense 1 a.]

1. a. The chromosomal constitution of a cell (and hence of an individual, species, etc.) as determined by the number, size, shape, etc., of the chromosomes (usually, as observed at metaphase during cell division).

1929 *Amer. Jrnl. Bot.* XVI. 415 In studying the karyotypes of different varieties of *Hyacinthus orientalis* which have chromosomes with permanent secondary constrictions, de Mol (1927) found correlation between the number of chromosomes with constrictions and the number of nucleoli. **1931** G. A. LEWITSKY in *Trudy̆ po Prikladnoĭ Botanike i Selektsii* XXVII. I. 221, I have proposed myself, independently from Delaunay, the same term 'Karyotype', but merely for designation of nuclear peculiarities of a given organism or systematical unit. **1934** L. W. SHARP *Introd. Cytol.* (ed. 3) ix. 128 The diagrammatic representation of a karyotype..is called an idiogram. *Ibid.* 129 Groups of related genera, as well as the related species of a genus, often have the same general karyotype. **1956** *Nature* 18 Feb. 336/1 In species of *Hemerocallis*, etc., different individuals of the same species differ in the karyotypes of the normal cells, even if these do not differ in chromosome number. **1957** C. P. SWANSON *Cytol. & Cytogenetics* xiii. 449 It is from a close study of related species ..that the evolution of the karyotype has been to a limited

extent unravelled. **1957**, etc. [see *IDIOGRAM]. **1961** *Lancet* 29 July 263/2 The mother..and the father..were also examined by fibroblast tissue culture and their karyotypes were apparently normal. **1964** M. HARRIS *Cell Culture & Somatic Variation* iv. 239 In these materials, normal chromosome complements were reported to predominate, with abnormal karyotypes appearing ordinarily only in tumors of large size or after transplantation. **1971** *Nature* 31 Dec. 506/3 It should now be possible, in theory at least, to eradicate Down's syndrome (mongolism) by recognizing its karyotype in foetal cells, and aborting the foetuses concerned.

b. A systematized representation of the chromosomes of a cell or cells, esp. a photographic one (cf. *IDIOGRAM).

1950 in WEBSTER Add. **1960** *Lancet* 14 May 1063/1 In contemporary publications the terms, karyotype and idiogram, have often been used indiscriminately. We would recommend that the term, *karyotype*, should be applied to a systematised array of the chromosomes of a single cell prepared either by drawing or by photography, with the extension in meaning that the chromosomes of a single cell can typify the chromosomes of an individual or even a species. **1969** *Nature* 22 Nov. 801/2 The results of a chromosome analysis can be displayed in several ways. The methods commonly used are the karyotype, 'a systematized array of the chromosomes of a single cell', and the karyogram. **1970** *Sci. Jrnl.* June 76/3 The best way we know of detecting abnormalities is to cut out each chromosome from a photomicrograph and pair them up like a jigsaw. This array, known as a karyotype, is constructed according to an international convention. **1970** J. D. BURKE *Cell Biol.* ix. 267 (*caption*) The mitotic metaphase chromosomes of a somatic cell of a male, arranged in a karyotype. **1973** *Lancet* 24 Feb. 420/1 Strictly speaking the actual pictures are karyotypes, and an idiogram is a diagram of the chromosome state of an individual.

† **2.** [After the original meaning of the Russ.] A group of species having similar karyotypes (sense *1 a). *Obs. rare.*

1931 *Trudy po Prikladnoĭ Botanike i Selektsii* XXVII. I. 221 [*Referring to the work of L. N. Delaunay.*] The variations from species to species within the indicated genera, or 'karyotypes' are, as it were, quantitative. In most cases it is but the length of the arms of the chromosomes..which undergoes variation. **1932** H. G. BRUUN in *Symbolae Bot. Upsalienses* I. 111 The species [of *Primula*] can be divided according to their nuclear constitution into different cytological types..called 'karyotypes'. *Ibid.* 117 Allied species as a rule also belong to the same karyotype. *Ibid.* 195 In agreement with this [statement of Delaunay's], 'Karyotypus' has been defined as a taxonomical conception, for which reason its use is made impossible in discussing the relation between taxonomy and cytology. ..In this work..the unconditional term 'cytological type' has had to be employed instead. But there exists an obvious need of a term to include all the species with nuclei of similar type, independent of taxonomical considerations, and in this sense I suggest that the term 'karyotype' be used... The karyotype should, therefore, be founded exclusively on chromosome-morphology.

karyotype (kæ·riotəip), *v. Biol.* and *Med.* [f. prec. sb.] *trans.* To determine or investigate the karyotype of.

1963 *Lancet* 24 Aug. 417/1 The more cells examined (karyotyped) the greater the chance of encountering neoplastic cells. **1971** *Nature* 11 June 387/1 Ninety-seven of these modal cells were karyotyped according to the Denver–London system. **1972** *Lancet* 29 July 213/2 Newborn infants who were suspected of having an anomalous cytogenetic constitution of any kind have been photographed, X-rayed, and karyotyped.

Hence **ka·ryotyped** *ppl. a.*, **ka·ryotyping** *vbl. sb.*

1963 *Lancet* 24 Aug. 417/1 We have undertaken..the karyotyping of cells obtained by lumbar puncture. **1966** *New Scientist* 3 Nov. 217/1 Foetal karyotyping would not, of course, reveal all genetic defects. It would show up gross chromosome abnormalities. **1971** *Nature* 2 July 25/1 In the karyotyped cells, all the normal chromosomes could be separated into pairs on the basis of their distinctive patterns of fluorescence.

karyotypic (kærioti·pik), *a. Biol.* and *Med.* [f. as prec. + -IC.] Of or pertaining to a karyotype. Also **karyoty·pical** *a.*, in the same sense.

1931 *Trudy po Prikladnoĭ Botanike i Selektsii* XXVII. I. 236 The lowest type of karyotypical variations are certainly the polyploid multiplication of sets. **1959** *Cytologia* XXIV. 390 No work has yet been carried out to find out how far karyotypic changes..have contributed to the origin of these varieties. **1963** *Canad. Jrnl. Genetics & Cytol.* V. 132 The idiogram can also be considered as a standard for detecting potential karyotypical alterations. **1964** M. HARRIS *Cell Culture & Somatic Variation* iv. 201 Various neoplasms among a series of related tumors were found to share these features, although individual differences were found in the detailed karyotypic patterns. **1968** *New Scientist* 2 May 219/2 Karyotypic analysis, or biochemical tests for the presence of sex-linked genes.., might be employed as alternative methods of sexing.

Hence **karyoty·pically** *adv.*, as regards karyotype.

1965 *Canad. Jrnl. Genetics & Cytol.* VII. 358 Karyotypically abnormal cells. **1972** *Science* 23 June 1333/1 Differences in..chromosome lengths between two karyotypically divergent groups of *Peromyscus maniculatus* are taken as evidence for an addition–deletion mechanism of chromosomal variation. **1972** *Nature* 8 Sept. 88/2 Several HAT-resistant clones were karyotypically male.

karzy (kā·ɹzi). *slang.* Also **carsey, carsy, karsey, karzey.** [Corruption of It. *casa* house.] = WATER-CLOSET.

1961 PARTRIDGE *Dict. Slang* Suppl. 1029/1 *Carsey*,..a w.c. **1965** *Daily Mail* 2 Oct. 5/4 Where do you spend a penny? (a) Toilet..(d) Karzy. **1966** D. FRANCIS *Flying Finish* ix. 118, I was in the cockpit most of the time... I went aft to the karzy once. **1967** J. BURKE *Till Death us do Part* v. 84 Have you seen the carsy? Just a bucket with a seat on top. **1968** T. E. B. CLARKE *Trail of Serpent* xiii. 122 You made a real thorough search? Everywhere? Outhouses, karzey, the lot? **1969** K. GILES *Death cracks Bottle* iv. 38 Apart from a working pee none of my ladies nor me got out of here. There's only one door to the carsey. **1970** G. F. NEWMAN *Sir, You Bastard* 262 Visits to the karsey.

kasbah (kæ·zbā). Also **casbah, cashbah, cassaubah, kasba, kasbar.** [ad. F. *casbah*, f. N. Afr. Arab. dial. *ḳaṣba* fortress.] **a.** A North African castle or fortress. **b.** The Arab quarter surrounding a castle or fortress in a North African town, esp. that of Algiers.

1738 T. SHAW *Trav. Barbary & the Levant* 313 They made an unsuccessful Attempt upon the Government, by endeavouring to seize upon the *Cassaubah*. **1844** J. H. DRUMMOND HAY *Western Barbary* 113 We paced with measured steps to the *Kasba*, or citadel, wherein is situated the '*Dar-al-Kebeer*', the residence of the governor. **1857** H. BARTH *Travels* I. 147 The little kasbah, which is never wanting in any of these towns, was in tolerable condition. **1867** 'OUIDA' *Under Two Flags* II. i. 12 Singing her refrain,..as she bounded over the picturesque desolation of the Cashbah. **1890** G. W. HARRIS *Pract. Guide Algiers* I. 41 This Casbah, in the good old days of Algerian predominance, was a magnificent palace fitted with all the luxury and refinement of the epoch. **1902** *Westm. Gaz.* 9 Dec. 3/1 Algiers.., with its quaint Kasbah, or native quarter, its Citadel,..and its interesting suburbs. **1930** E. WAUGH *Labels* viii. 189 Five Scots people..were caught by a very shady guide who took them up to the Kasbar in a taxi-cab. **1958** *Times Lit. Suppl.* 11 July 393/4 The kasbah country south of the Atlas *is* on the tourist route, and well organized. **1961** *Times* 6 May 9/7 In Algiers the Casbah is entirely without romance. **1969** R. LANDAU *Kasbas S. Morocco* 11 The first kasbas (qasbas, more precisely) were built by the Almohad dynasty in the thirteenth century; they were not simply fortresses, but were the walled-in section of the ruler's capital, a complex with palace, main mosque, .. and various state offices. **1971** *Country Life* 28 Oct. 1120 The kasbahs, or mud fortresses, of the pre-Saharan oases in southern Morocco are virtually unique as a form of defensive architecture.

‖ **kasha**[1] (kæ·ʃă). Also **casha.** [Russ.] **1.** A gruel or porridge made from cooked buckwheat or other meals or cereals.

1808 M. WILMOT *Jrnl.* 5 July in *Russ. Jrnls.* (1934) III. 356 Their Casha is very like *Stirabout*, & this is a favourite dish. **1903** [see *BLINTZE]. **1958** HAYWARD & HARARI tr. *Pasternak's Dr. Zhivago* II. ix. 270 I'll get Uncle Yury to stay to dinner and take the kasha out of the oven. **1961** N. FROUD et al. tr. *Montagné's Larousse Gastronomique* 554 Kasha is the Russian for cooked buckwheat. **1966** N. BEHN *Kremlin Let.* xiv. 141 Breakfast..consisted of one small bowl of kasha..the [Russian] equivalent to American hot cereals. **1971** *New Statesman* 1 Jan. 8/3 Rents are low in Russia..and the basic necessities—bread, potatoes and *kasha* flour—are not dear. **1973** *Times* 3 Feb. 13/5 You can try the kneidlach soup (with matzo-meal dumplings), the kasha (buckwheat) and the tzimmes.

2. A beige colour resembling that of buckwheat groats.

1957 M. MCCARTHY *Memories Catholic Girlhood* viii. 200 She had an outfit made..in a new colour called 'kasha'. **1971** *Guardian* 19 Jan. 9/3 Principal colours are navy, 'Kasha' (a Russian buckwheat porridge beige), and 'smoke'.

Kasha[2] (kæ·ʃă). Also **kasha.** The proprietary name, originated by Rodier, a French textile manufacturer, of a soft napped fabric made from wool and hair. Also in various *Combs.* (see quots.). Also applied to a cotton lining material.

1920 *Queen* 10 Apr. 466 Dress with very wide skirt in pale green kasha. **1923** *Daily Mail* 12 Feb. 15 White Kasha cloth. **1926** *Queen* 17 Feb. 10 A modified Inverness coat made by Lelong in the new kasha with the slightly spongy surface—kashatoile. **1926** G. G. DENNY *Fabrics* (ed. 2) II. 53 *Kasha*, (a) fine, soft, napped wool dress fabric originated with Rodier Freres, Paris. (b) Cotton plain weave napped on reverse side, for linings. **1928** *Observer* 4 Mar. 20/4 The couturiers..give prominence to jersey, crêpella, Kashatoil, Kashangora, and a host of other materials. **1941** R. STOUT *Red Threads* i. 6 He must have the natural kasha, the one with nubs, by tomorrow. **1942** G. G. DENNY *Fabrics* (ed. 5) I. 37 *Kasha*, fine, soft napped wool dress fabric with crosswise streaked effect in dark hairs... Similar textures in wool and cotton now made in United States called Kasha. **1967** *Boston Sunday Globe* 23 Apr. (Advt. Suppl.), Roomy enough to sleep 2 or separate into two single full size sleeping bags. Top, bottom and snap-on canopy made of cotton duck, with kasha flannel lining. **1968** J. IRONSIDE *Fashion Alphabet* 234 *Kasha*, very soft pale beige fabric made from goat-hair and wool.

Kashan (kăʃā·n). Also **Keshan.** The name of a province and town in central Iran, used (freq. *attrib.*) to designate a finely woven rug, usu. of wool or silk, made there.

1905 M. C. RIPLEY *Oriental Rug Bk.* 305 Kashan rugs. **1920** C. J. D. MAY *How to identify Persian Rugs* v. 61 *Sarouks*... The student may regard these merely as a slightly inferior grade of Kashan. **1931** A. U. DILLEY *Oriental Rugs & Carpets* iv. 122 Kashan rugs, always important, were so far unrecognized as a separate weaving thirty years ago that no mention of them was made in the first modern rug books. **1960** H. HAYWARD *Antique Collecting* 157/1 *Kashan carpets*, Persian carpets in which medallion and prayer designs predominate, woven in wool or silk. **1962** *Times* 12 June 20/1 (Advt.), A beautiful and rare carved silk Keshan rug...a superb natural Keshan carpet. **1962** C. W. JACOBSEN *Oriental Rugs* II. 230 In the 20 nearby villages..Kashans are woven which are equal to those made in the city itself. **1963** L. DEIGHTON *Horse under Water* xxxviii. 150 I'm leaving before I vomit over your beautiful Kashan carpet. **1967** J. MORGAN *Involved* 126 Thomas looked up from an all-silk Kashan rug he was lying on.

Kashgai (kæ·ʃgəi). Also **Kashkai, Qashgai, Qashqai.** A Turkic-speaking people living around Shiraz in Persia; a member of this people. Also *attrib.*

1885 *Encycl. Brit.* XVIII. 625/1 The Kashgais, or those wandering semi-Turkish tribes brought down from Turkestan to the neighbourhood of Shíráz, have the credit of possessing good steeds. **1921** *Glasgow Herald* 19 April 5 Among the most important questions were the relations with the Kashgais and other nomad tribes. The Kashgais were about 135,000 strong. **1937** *Sunday Times* 29 Aug. 7/5 The region is occupied by scattered and turbulent Qashgais upon whom the Tehran Government has only very recently imposed its authority. **1957** H. H. VREELAND *Iran* ix. 105 The Qashqa'i tribesmen are important in this area. *Ibid.* x. 128 The Qashqa'i have firmly resisted conscription, and no tribal members have yet been taken into the army.

b. Used *attrib.* or *absol.* to designate a type of nomad rug made by them.

1922 KENDRICK & TATTERSALL *Hand-Woven Carpets* 196 Kashkai carpets. **1931** A. U. DILLEY *Oriental Rugs & Carpets* iv. 95 Both Afshar and Kashgai rugs are Caucasian nomad transplants. **1962** C. W. JACOBSEN *Oriental Rugs* II. 257 Plate 104 is a typical design found in many Qashqai (Mecca Shiraz) but no two designs are exactly alike. *Ibid.* III. 403 The correct technical name is 'Qashqai Prayer Rug'.

Kashgar (kā·ʃgāɹ). **1.** A language or dialect of the central Turkic or Turco-Tatar group of Altaic languages, spoken in Kashgar. Also *attrib.* or as *adj.*

1875 R. B. SHAW *Sk. Turki Lang.* p. xv, An examination of the Yarkánd and Káshghar dialect accounts for them in another way. **1918** G. W. HUNTER *Examples Turki Dial.* III. 1 Under this section is included Kashgar Turki and Kirghese Turki as they have much in common... Kashgar Turki is spoken by the Sart..people of Chinese Turkestan. **1948** D. DIRINGER *Alphabet* 568 Kashgar Turkish, spoken between the T'ien Shan mountains and northern Tibet. **1954** PEI & GAYNOR *Dict. Ling.* 113 *Kashgar*, an Asiatic language; member of the Central Turkic group of the Altaic sub-family of the Ural-Altaic family of languages.

2. The name of a city and district of Sinkiang-Uighur (formerly East Turkestan), used *attrib.* or *absol.* to designate a type of Turkoman carpet.

1900 J. K. MUMFORD *Oriental Rugs* (1901) 273 Kashgar rugs. **1931** A. U. DILLEY *Oriental Rugs & Carpets* x. 224 Kashgar and Yarkand rugs..are attributed more or less arbitrarily. *Ibid.* pl. 69 (*caption*) Kashgar, Disc–Star–Seal Pattern. **1962** C. W. JACOBSEN *Oriental Rugs* II. 232 Kashgars are more like a Chinese rug than a Bokhara. None are available, and I have seen a few rugs that were called Kashgar but there is not enough definite information on these rugs... We seldom come across the name.

Kashmir (kæ·ʃmiᵊɹ, kæʃmiᵊ·ɹ). [var. CASHMERE.] **1.** Used *attrib.* in the sense: of or pertaining to Kashmir. Also as *sb.*, a native or inhabitant of Kashmir. Hence **Kashmi·rian** *sb.*

1876 C. F. G. CUMMING *From Hebrides to Himalayas* II. 309 Kashmerians, Persians, Paharis, Hindus of every possible sect. **1882** F. M. CRAWFORD *Let.* 21 July in M. H. Elliott *My Cousin F. M. Crawford* (1934) vi. 136 The Tibetans have no postage stamps, but the Kashmirs have. **1887** J. M. BROWN *Shikar Sk.* 237 The Kashmir stag—cervus Cashmeriensis. **1925** A. G. ARBUTHNOT in G. Burrard *Big Game Hunting* 126 A very old Kashmir shikari. **1971** R. RUSSELL tr. *Ahmad's Shore & Wave* i. 15 Courtiers..who had been..patiently gazing at the Kashmir carvings on the wooden columns.

2. Also **Cashmere.** Used *attrib.* of a Caucasian pileless carpet, characterized by the many loose yarn ends on the back resembling a Cashmere shawl. Also *ellipt.*

1900 J. K. MUMFORD *Oriental Rugs* (1901) ix. 119 It is the shaggy ends of the colored nap-yarns, left loose at the back of these rugs, which has given them the name of 'Kashmir'... The true name of the so-called 'Kashmir' rugs is Shemakha, derived from the city where they are marketed. **1904** M. B. LANGTON *How to know Oriental Rugs* iii. 127 The Cashmere or Soumak rugs are not from the Vale of Cashmere, in India,..but are made by the nomad tribes in and about Shemakha, the old capital of Shirvan. **1931** A. U. DILLEY *Oriental Rugs & Carpets* vii. 179 Soumak rugs, formerly called Kashmir,..derive their true name from the town of Shemakha. **1962** C. W. JACOBSEN *Oriental Rugs* II. 297 Rugs are generally called Soumak or Kashmirs...The distinguishing feature of this rug is the loose ends of stitch yarn at the back of the rug, about the same effect as we find in the Cashmere shawl.

Kashmiri (kæʃmīə·ri), *a.* and *sb.* Also **Kashmiree.** [f. prec. + *-I.] **A.** *adj.* Of or pertaining to Kashmir, a state in the western Himalayas. **B.** *sb.* **a.** A native or inhabitant of Kashmir. **b.** The Dardic language spoken in Kashmir.

1880 *Encycl. Brit.* XIII. 821/2 The language distinct from Turki, Persian, Hindi, and Kashmiri. **1884** KIPLING *Let.* in C. E. Carrington *Rudyard Kipling* (1955) iv. 56 There came out a Cashmiri girl that Moore might have raved over. **1891** 'L. MALET' *Wages of Sin* III. v. vii. 56 The Kashmiree beauties. **1901** KIPLING *Kim* i. 33 A smooth-faced Kashmiri pundit. **1936** P. FLEMING *News from Tartary* VII. xi. 375 Kashmiri herdsmen camped in grubby tents. **1953** R. GODDEN *Kingfishers catch Fire* xiii. 159 She had to speak to them in Urdu and they probably only knew Kashmiri. **1955** *Times* 27 June 6/3 It is therefore surprising that so little attention is given to the political welfare of the four million Kashmiris. **1971** *Shankar's Weekly* (Delhi) 4 Apr. 5/3 He was taken for a Kashmiri priest. **1974** 'S. HARVESTER' *Forgotten Road* i. 11 He spoke..Hindi and Kashmiri, Tamil and Gujerati and Konkani among the many tongues of India.

Kashrut (kāʃrū·t). Also **Kashres, Kashrus, Kashruth,** and with small initial. [Heb., = fitness, legitimacy (in religion), f. *kāshēr* KOSHER *a.*] The body of Jewish religious laws relating to the fitness of food, and also of persons and objects; the observance of these laws. Also *attrib.*

1907 *Daily Chron.* 7 Dec. 4/7 The word 'Kashruth'.. denotes the dietary laws as laid down by Moses, together with..commentaries and explanations thereof made by the Rabbis in the intervening centuries... 'Questions of Kashruth' concern themselves even with the utensils used in the preparation and serving of the food... [They] can only be decided by the Rabbi. **1953** *Jewish Chron. Trav. Guide* 12 In this group come those establishments in regard to the kashrut of which no information is to hand, or which, while not insisting on strict observance of kashrut, have a special interest for Jewish clients. *Ibid.* 43 The following..are under the official supervision of the Beth Din and Kashrus Commission. **1962** *New Jewish Encycl.* 264 Most Jewish communities the world over set up Kashrut regulations and provide..for the supervision of the slaughtering and distribution of meat. **1970** L. M. FEINSILVER *Taste of Yiddish* 242 *Kashres,* the system of kashruth observance, or 'keeping kosher'... Though the Reform movement originally rejected the binding force of kashruth, some Reform Jews today 'keep kosher'. **1973** *Jewish Chron.* 19 Jan. 8/1 The freedom and the high standards of kashrut which we in Britain enjoy should be shared equally by the Jewish communities in the rest of the EEC. **1973** *Times* 3 Feb. 13/4 The laws of Kashrus, which govern Jewish cooking and give us the label 'Kosher Food'.

Kashube (kāʃū·b). Also **Kashub, Kaszube.** [f. *Kashubia* (Pol. *Kaszuby*), a region of Poland west and north-west of Gdansk.] **a.** A member of the Slavonic people inhabiting Kashubia. **b.** The Slavonic language spoken in this region. Also *attrib.* or as *adj.* So **Cassu·bian, Kashu·bian, Kashu·bish, Kassu·bian** *sbs.* and *adjs.*

1893 W. R. MORFILL *Poland* i. 13 The language of the Kashubes differs in some interesting points from the Polish, having a fluctuating accent..and more nasal sounds. **1919** A. B. BOSWELL *Poland & the Poles* 14 The original Pomeranians were absorbed by German colonists. But in the region west of the Vistula there still dwells a tribe called the Kaszubes who are descended from them... This region of Pomerania..is known to the Poles as the Kaszubian Switzerland. *Ibid.* 26 Lower Polish dialects.. Kaszubian. **1934** PRIEBSCH & COLLINSON *German Lang.* I. i. 11 The Cassubian and almost extinct Slovinzian (brought by Lorentz under the collective name Pomeranian). **1935** *Times Lit. Suppl.* 15 Aug. 506/2 A Slav language, called sometimes Slovincian and sometimes Cassubian. **1936** *Discovery* Mar. 95/1 The Cassubians are an ancient and peculiar tribe who live on the seashore on both sides of the German-Polish frontier line. **1950** A. P. GOUDY in *Cambr. Hist. Poland* i. 9 From the linguistic point of view Slovinzish and Kashubish belong to the Polish group. **1950** [see *LECHITIC *sb.* and *a.*]. **1955** *Archivum Linguisticum* VII. 133 The accent is free in North Kashubian. **1957** *Encycl. Brit.* XIII. 293 *Kashubes,* a Slavonic people living in the northwest of Poland. *Ibid.* In Kashube, as against Polish, all vowels can be nasal instead of *a* and *e* only. *Ibid.* XVIII. 152/1 Linguistically.. two local Pomeranian dialects remained until the 20th century, the Slovince (Slowinski) and the Cassubian (Kaszubski). **1972** W. B. LOCKWOOD *Panorama Indo-Europ. Lang.* 158 The present territory of these Pomeranian Slavs, Kashubs as they call themselves, comprises no more than the north-eastern tip from Lake Leba to the southern outskirts of Gdynja (Gdingen). Its southern border is ill-defined, being followed by a broad band of transitional dialects, basically Kashubian, but already highly polonised.

kasidah, var. *QASIDA.

kas-kas (kɒs,kɒs). *Jamaican.* Also **cuss-cuss, kass-kass, kos-kos, kus-kus.** [f. Twi *kasákàsa* to dispute.] In folk usage: a dispute, quarrel.

Pronunciation perh. influenced by Eng. *cuss* var. *curse.*

1873 C. J. G. RAMPINI *Lett. from Jamaica* 176 Cuss-cuss (calling names) no bore hole in my skin. **1943** L. BENNETT *Jamaican Humour in Dial.* 15 Dat marga gal Wingy Want put me eena kus-kus An big lian story. **1950** —— et al. *Anancy Stories & Dial. Verse* 33 Anancy never like fe se' two people live neutral, so him start fe carry lie and story between dem, and start big kaskas. **1961** F. G. CASSIDY *Jamaica Talk* iii. 29 When Jamaicans become angry and indulge in a *kas-kas,* the lilt is quite lost and the imprecations come pelting in a high-pitched volley. **1971** *Jamaican Weekly Gleaner* 3 Nov. 5/1 She's..fed up of kass-kass with customers.

kasolite (kæ·so-, kēⁱ·zoləit). *Min.* [a. F. *kasolite* (A. Schoep 1921, in *Compt. Rend.* CLXXIII. 1476), f. *Kasolo,* the name of a locality (prob. near Shinkolobwe, west of Likasi) in Katanga province, Zaïre: see -ITE[1].] A yellow, rather soft, hydrous silicate of lead and uranium, $Pb(UO_2)(SiO_4).H_2O$.

1922 *Mineral. Mag.* XIX. 343 Kasolite... Hydrated silicate of uranium and lead, $3PbO.3UO_3.3SiO_2.4H_2O$, forming ochre-yellow, monoclinic crystals. **1958** E. W. HEINRICH *Mineral. & Geol. Radioactive Raw Materials* viii. 294 Kasolite occurs preferentially in dolomitic-graphitic shale.

kassidar, var. *KHASSADAR.

Kassite (kæ·səit), *sb.* and *a.* Also **Cossæan, Kasshi, Kossæan.** [Native name.] **A.** *sb.* A member of an Elamite people from the central range of the Zagros mountains, who ruled Babylon from the 18th to the 12th century B.C.; also, their language. **B.** *adj.* Of or pertaining to the Kassites.

1888 Z. A. RAGOZIN *Assyria* (ed. 2) ix. 300 The next.. expedition, against the very warlike and turbulent mountain tribes of the *Kasshi* (*Cossæans* of classical writers), is of some interest because of the details we are given concerning that most rugged region of the Zagros range. **1894** A. H. SAYCE *Primer of Assyriology* iii. 47 Babylonia was conquered by Kassite princes who ruled over it for 576 years and nine months (B.C. 1806–1229). **1898** C. R. CONDER *Hittites & their Lang.* ii. 41 The Kassites thus became dependent on Assyria. **1902** *Encycl. Brit.* XXVI. 43/1 Babylonia was conquered by Kassites or Kossæans from the mountain of Elam, under Kandis or Gaddas (in 1800 B.C.), who established a dynasty which lasted for 576 years and nine months. **1909** *Daily Chron.* 14 Jan. 4/4 There is a letter to Kadashman-Targu, the Kassite King of Babylon, as to the appointment of a successor. **1928** [see *GUTIAN *sb.* and *a.*]. **1934** A. TOYNBEE *Study of Hist.* I. 116 The Kingdom of the Sea-Land..had been annexed to the barbarian 'successor-state', subsequently established by the Kassites at Babylon, at the turn of the eighteenth and seventeenth centuries B.C. **1938** T. FISH in E. I. J. Rosenthal *Judaism & Christianity* III. ii. 31 In the second millennium Babylonia was Semitic, though the rulers and the court at Babylon were non-Semitic (Kassite) for several centuries. **1939** L. H. GRAY *Found. Lang.* xii. 380 Attempts have been made to connect the language [*sc.* Elamite] with Altaic,..with Kassite, and with Carian... The language of the *Kassites* (or *Cossaeans*) ..is known only from a scanty glossary. **1964** G. ROUX *Ancient Iraq* vi. 79 The Sumerians..and..the Amorites, Kassites, Assyrians and Chaldaeans who, after them, ruled in succession over Mesopotamia.

Kassubian: see *KASHUBE.

kastura (kastū·rǎ). Also **kasturi, kustoorah.** [Hindi *kastūrī.*] The Himalayan musk deer, *Moschus moschiferus.*

1837 T. HUTTON in *Jrnl. Asiatic Soc. Bengal* VI. 936 The Kastúra, or musk deer of these hills is to be found in the deep forest shades of Mahássú throughout the year. **1867** T. C. JERDON *Mammals India* 267 *Moschus moschiferus... Kastúrá,* H.— *Rous* or *Roos* and *Kasturé,* Kashmir. **1884** R. A. STERNDALE *Nat. Hist. Mammalia India & Ceylon* 494 The Musk Deer. Native names—*Kastura,* Hindi;.. *Kasturé,* in Kashmir. **1893** [see MUSK-DEER]. **1904** F. G. AFLALO *Sportsman's Bk. India* 186 Local Names of various Game...Musk deer. Kustoorah. **1951** ELLERMAN & MORRISON-SCOTT *Checklist Palaearctic & Indian Mammals* 353 *Moschus moschiferus* Linnaeus, 1758. Musk Deer (Kastura). **1955** P. BAUER *Kanchenjunga Challenge* IV. ii. 184 The Kasturi is a [Himalayan] musk deer and on this account it has been almost exterminated.

|| **kata** (ka·tǎ). [Jap.] A system of basic exercises or formal practice used to teach and improve the execution of Judo techniques, devised by Prof. Jigoro Kano (1860–1938).

1954 E. DOMINY *Teach Yourself Judo* 190 *Kata,* a prearranged series of movements performed for the purpose of demonstration. **1956** C. YERKOW *Judo Katas* i. 14 This training is called *kata* and means form-practice, both for stand-up techniques and in mat-work. **1961** *New Statesman* 22 Sept. 402/2 Kata is the general technique of posture and balance. **1970** G. JACKSON *Let.* in *Soledad Brother* (1971) 247 It's never bothered me too much before, the sex thing. I would do my exercises and the hundreds of katas, stay busy with something. **1973** *Express* (Trinidad & Tobago) 27 Apr. 31/3 Over 500 karatekas will be competing for titles in..katas (imaginary combat).

kata, shortened f. *KATATHERMOMETER.

katabatic (kætǎbæ·tik), *a. Meteorol.* [f. Gr. καταβατ-ός descending (f. καταβαίνειν to go down) + -IC (or ad. Gr. καταβατικ-ός affording a means of descent).] Of a wind: blowing down a slope, or from an elevated region to a lower one, esp. when caused by the effect of gravity on air cooled by the underlying ground. Cf. *ANABATIC *a.* 2.

1918 *Meteorol. Gloss.* (Meteorol. Office) 182 A local cold wind is called Katabatic if it is caused by the gravitation of cold air off high ground. **1920** W. J. HUMPHREYS *Physics of Air* vii. 111 Where the valley is long and rather steep..the down-flowing air current may attain the velocity of a gale and become a veritable aerial torrent. This drainage flow is known..as the mountain breeze, or mountain wind; also canyon wind, katabatic wind, and gravity wind. **1936** *Geogr. Jrnl.* LXXXVII. 433 The extremely cold katabatic winds blowing off the high Greenland ice-cap..lowered the temperature. **1954** W. D. THORNBURY *Princ. Geomorphol.* xiv. 362 The radially outflowing winds which Hobbs took as evidence of the existence of a permanent anticyclone over the interior of the Greenland ice cap are really katabatic winds or cold air draining downslope under the influence of gravity. **1967** R. W. FAIRBRIDGE *Encycl. Atmospheric Sci.* 1153/1 Foehn... This is a gusty katabatic wind which crosses the Alps..and is characterized by dryness and warmth.

Hence **kataba·tically** *adv.,* as a result of downward motion.

1967 R. W. FAIRBRIDGE *Encycl. Atmospheric Sci.* 1152/2 They consist of more or less cool, dry, continental air, nearly always of anticyclonic source, at times katabatically warmed.

|| **katabothron.** Add: Forms with initial *k* and medial *v* are most usual (with varying endings: see note below). Substitute for etym.: [a. mod.Gr. καταβόθρα swallow-hole, f. κατά down + βόθρος hole.

Katavothra (or *-bothra*) is the correct sing. form, with plurals *-ai* (*-æ*) and *-es* (corresponding respectively to the mod.Gr. pl. forms καταβόθραι and καταβόθρες). *Katavothre* is an erron. sing. formation from *katavothres*; the sing. ending *-on* (pl. *-a, -ons*) corresponds to nothing in mod. or ancient Gr. and prob. arose as a result of mistaking καταβόθρα for a neut. pl.]

(Further examples.)

1892 A. J. JUKES-BROWN *Student's Handbk. Physical Geol.* (ed. 2) xi. 197 The torrents of the Morea are usually charged with reddish mud, sand, and pebbles, when they enter the *katavothra,* but are pure and limpid when they flow out again. **1892** *Proc. R. Geogr. Soc.* XIV. 466 (*heading*) The katavothræ of the Morea. *Ibid.* 467 All these basins are drained by underground channels, to the entrance of which the name katavothra is given. **1937** *Geogr. Jrnl.* XC. 448 Since the water was drawn off, the mouths of twenty-five large katavothrai..have appeared in the sides of the surrounding hills. **1957** G. E. HUTCHINSON *Treat. Limnol.* I. i. 107 Though these variations [in level] can in part depend on rainfall, they are largely independent of it and may be attributed to the silting of the katavothrai or sinks which drain the lake. **1970** *Water-Supply Paper U.S. Geol. Survey* No. 1899-K. 11/2 *Katavothron,* a closed depression or swallow hole. **1971** J. N. JENNINGS *Karst* v. 74 The French name *estavelle* is commonly used for these alternating orifices but they are also well known by the Greek *katavothre.*

katakana (kætǎkā·nǎ). Also 8 **kattakanna,** 9 **katagana.** [Jap., f. *kata* side + *kana* *KANA.] One of the two varieties of the Japanese syllabic writing, the characters of which are more angular than the hiragana, derived from abbreviated forms of Chinese ideographs of the corresponding sounds, and used chiefly in scientific and official documents and in spelling out foreign words adopted into the Japanese language. Cf. *HIRAGANA.

1727 J. G. SCHEUCHZER tr. *Kæmpfer's Hist. Japan* II. v. xiv. 590 The other was a map of the whole world, of their own making, in an oval form, and mark'd with the Japanese *Kattakanna* characters. **1822** F. SHOBERL tr. *Titsingh's Illustr. Japan* 194 These works, published in the learned language, *Gago,* with the *kata-kana,* or women's letters, have been re-printed expressly for them. **1859** A. STEINMETZ *Japan & her People* I. vii. 305 *Katagana* is very simple, each sound having one invariable representative. **1861** G. SMITH *Ten Weeks in Japan* xi. 173 A copy of St. Luke's gospel in the Katagana Japanese character published at Hong-kong. **1880, 1928** [see *HIRAGANA]. **1970** *Jrnl. Gen. Psychol.* LXXXII. 40 The transmission of the Katakana syllabary by electrical signals applied to the skin. **1973** *Physics Bull.* May 280/3 We have also extended the process by including in addition to the 881 Chinese characters, the 50 Japanese Kata-Kana and 50 Hira-Gana characters and 10 numerals.

katalase, var. *CATALASE.

katamorphism (kætǎmǭ·ɪfiz'm). *Petrol.* [f. Gr. κατά down + μορφή form: see -ISM.] Alteration of rocks (usually at or near the earth's surface) characterized by the formation of chemically simpler minerals from more complex ones. Hence **katamo·rphic** *a.*

1904 C. R. VAN HISE in *Monogr. U.S. Geol. Survey* XLVII. 43 The geological factor which in this treatise will serve as the primary basis for a classification of metamorphism is the dominant factor of depth. On this basis metamorphism will be classified into (1) alterations in the zone of katamorphism and (2) alterations in the zone of anamorphism... The zone of katamorphism may be defined as the zone in which the alterations of rocks result in the production of simple compounds from more complex ones. *Ibid.* 162 Katamorphic zone. **1916** F. H. LAHEE *Field Geol.* ix. 230 Any kind of alteration that any rock has undergone, whether katamorphic or anamorphic, comes under the head of metamorphism, but there are many geologists who prefer to restrict the meaning of the more general term so that it does not

include weathering. **1946** *Amer. Mineralogist* XXXI. 288 It is very well known that oxidation is one of the important chemical processes of katamorphism, especially of weathering.

‖ **katana** (kătā·nă). Also 7 **cattan.** [Jap.] A long single-edged sword of the Japanese samurai.

1613 J. Saris *Jrnl.* 11 June in *Voy. Japan* (1900) 79 Either of them had two Cattans or swords of that Countrey by his side. **1615** R. Cocks *Diary* 17 June (1883) I. 10, I delivered Mr. Richard Wickham the rich *cattan* he left in my custody at his departure towardes Siam. **1874** *Trans. Asiatic Soc. Japan* 57 The word 'sword' is invariably rendered by the Japanese word '*ken*', which signifies a long, straight, double-edged sword, as opposed to the '*katana*', of modern times, which has but a single edge, and is slightly curved towards the point. **1890** B. H. Chamberlain *Things Japanese* 328 The Japanese sword of ancient days (the *tsurugi*) was a straight double-edged heavy weapon some three feet long... That of medieval and modern times (the *katana*) is lighter, shorter, has but a single edge, and is slightly curved towards the point. **1906** *Macm. Mag.* Apr. 457 An escort of sturdy little Japanese armed with service rifles and the keen-bladed *katana.* **1959** R. Kirkbride *Tamiko* xvii. 138 He'd cut both our heads off with honourable katana. **1963** *Art of Armourer: Exhib. Armour, Swords & Firearms* (V. & A. Mus.) 97 Blade of the long sword (*katana*) signed.., and dated in the 6th year of the period Yeishō (1509).

katathermo·meter (kæ:tă-). Also **kata thermometer, kata-thermometer.** [f. Kata- + Thermometer.] An alcohol-in-glass thermometer with an enlarged bulb and restricted scale, used for determining the cooling power of ambient air by measuring the time taken for its temperature to fall from one fixed value to another. Also shortened to **ka·ta.**

1914 *Rep. Brit. Assoc. Adv. Sci. 1913* 673 (*heading*) The katathermometer. By Professor Leonard Hill. **1915** L. Hill et al. in *Phil. Trans. R. Soc.* B. CCVII. 185 The katathermometer..is an instrument designed primarily for the measurement of its own rate of cooling when its temperature approximates to that of the human body. **1915** *Ibid.* 191 The heat lost from the kata at body temperature. **1930** W. G. Kendrew *Climate* xxx. 189 The conditions of a perspiring body may be imitated by surrounding the bulb of the kata-thermometer with wet muslin. **1936** *Discovery* Sept. 280/1 When the air conditions of the bakery were tested, the 'Katathermometer' revealed most unsuitable conditions. **1938** *Jrnl. Amer. Med. Assoc.* 18 Nov. 1649/2 The time required for the alcohol meniscus to fall from the 100 to the 95 degree mark is then observed, and the 'kata factor' marked on the stem..is divided by this time in seconds, giving the 'cooling power' of the air. **1948** W. N. Witheridge in F. A. Patty *Industr. Hygiene & Toxicol.* I. x. 346 The kata thermometer has been calibrated as an air-velocity instrument. **1963** Hertig & Belding in C. M. Herzfeld *Temperature* III. iii. xxxii. 348 The thermoanemometer.. and the katathermometer are representative of instruments whose readings are proportional to the rate of heat loss.

Hence **ka:tathermome·tric** *a.*

1923 *Med. Res. Council Special Rep. Ser.* No. 73. 90 (*heading*) A kata-thermometric comparison of methods of heating and ventilation.

katavothra, -vothre, -vothron: see Kata-bothron in Dict. and Suppl.

katc(h)ina, varr. *kachina.

Kate Greenaway (kē̆it grī·năwēi). The name of Kate (Catherine) Greenaway (1846–1901), English artist and illustrator of children's books, used *attrib.* and *absol.* to designate the style of children's clothing modelled on her drawings.

1902 *Little Folks* 153/1 Mothers began to dress their little boys and girls in what they came to call 'Kate Greenaway dresses'. **1907** 'E. Godfrey' *Eng. Children in Olden Time* xvi. 262 The Little Female Academy is supposed to exist about 1770, so by that time the pretty little 'Kate Greeneway' [*sic*] garments prevailed. **1940** Beerbohm *Lett. to R. Turner* (1964) App. B. 294 The Preraphaelite influence, with the Kate Greenaway influence thrown in. **1957** M. B. Picken *Fashion Dict.* 193 (*caption*) Kate Greenaway..Coat, 1890's. **1959** *Times* 21 Sept. 12/3 The child bridesmaid..wore a long Kate Greenaway dress. **1960** S. Kale *Fire Escape* v. 27 Priscilla was naturally chosen to take part in a scene calling for Kate Greenaway fashions. **1965** M. Sharp *Sun in Scorpio* iii. xxv. 131 Elspet was peddling lavender-bags in her Kate Greenaway. *Ibid.* 130 'That's me being bridesmaid in Kate Greenaway,' pointed out Elspet. **1966** J. S. Cox *Illustr. Dict. Hairdressing* 86 *Kate Greenaway style,* hairdresses for young children inspired by the hair fashions depicted in the coloured illustrations by Kate Greenaway published between 1879–1895. **1968** J. Ironside *Fashion Alphabet* 140 *Kate Greenaway,* a child's bonnet of the style illustrated by Kate Greenaway, similar to those worn in the Empire period and with a frill round the face. Still worn by small bridesmaids sometimes.

‖ **κατ' ἐξοχήν** (kăte·ksokīn, -kēin). More usual form of Katexoken. [Gr. phr.] Pre-eminently, par excellence.

1588 A. Fraunce *Lawiers Logike* sig. ¶¶iv The Romayne Lawe, which Iustinian calleth the Cyuill law κατ'εξοχην, (as Homer is called the Poet). **1698** J. Sergeant *Non Ultra* (in *Monist* XXXIX, 1929) 605. § 21 Which Propositions being..most fully and Properly such we do therefore, κατ'ἐξοχην, call Identical. **1841** Mill *Let.* 1 Mar. in *Works* (1963) XIII. 466 Poetry κατ'ἐξοχήν or poet's poetry as opposed to everybody's poetry. **1865** —— *Exam. Hamilton's Philos.* xx. 402 If any general theory of the sufficiency of Evidence and the legitimacy of Generalization be possible, this must be Logic κατ'ἐξοχήν. **1879** W. James *Coll. Ess. & Rev.* (1920) 88 Schopenhauer ..says that Intuition..'is knowledge κατ'ἐξοχήν'.

kathak (kătā·k). [Skr., = professional story-teller.] **a.** A North Indian caste of story-tellers and musicians; a member of this caste. **b.** A North Indian classical dance composed of passages of mime alternating with passages of dance.

1931 E. A. H. Blunt *Caste System of N. India* 244 Kathak.—These religious troubadours carefully preserve their ancient ballads, and allow nobody to tamper with them. **1941** 'La Meri' *Gesture Lang. Hindu Dance* 17 Pantomime is relatively unimportant in Kathak, virtuosity being entirely in the feet. **1957** G. B. L. Wilson *Dict. Ballet* 158 *Kathak,* one of the four main forms of Indian dancing. **1959** *Marg* XII. iv. 10 Thakur Prasad, a Kathak, migrated to Lucknow about the beginning of the 19th century and became the Court Dancer of Wajid Ali Shah. *Ibid.* 12 The contribution which the Jaipur gharana has made to the preservation and spread of the Kathak dance is very considerable. To this school goes the credit of having given us some of our best Kathaks. **1967** Singha & Massey *Indian Dances* xv. 125 The word Kathak, story-teller, derives from 'katha' which means story. **1969** *Amrita Bazar Patrika* 5 Aug. 4/6 The group-dances were generally imposing based on the kathak, and soft touch of Manipuri and choreographer Namita Chatterjee intelligently introduced the various folk-dances—Rajasthani, Manipuri, Garba, Lotus to avoid the spell of monotony. **1969** *Cultural News from India* Nov. 25 To observe the sixtieth birth-day of Ustad Dabir Khan a two-hour Saraswat Veena and Surbahar recital was given... Munawar Ali Khan (vocal), Ustad Bahadur Khan (sarod), Bandana Sen (Kathak dance) and Keramatullah (tabla) were among those who took part in the programme. **1971** *E. Afr. Standard* (Nairobi) 10 Apr. 6/7 Apart from the film songs, there was a delightful Kathak group dance by three very young pupils of Uma Devi.

Kathakali (kātăkā·li). Also **Kadhakali.** [Malayalam *kathakali* drama, f. *katha* story (Skr. *kathā*) + *kali* play.] A South Indian dance-drama based on Hindu literature, and characterized by its stylized costume and make-up, and frequent use of mime.

1900 T. K. Gopal Panikkar *Malabar & its Folk* v. 74 Malabar Drama... Our drama..assumes various forms of which Krishnattom and Ramanattom are the principal ones. The latter is usually called *Kadhakali* and constitutes our drama proper... Our drama is altogether a dumb-show in which the actors never utter a word but do everything by signs and gestures. **1933** R. K. Yajnik *Indian Theatre* iii. 61 The 'Kathākāli' of the Malabar district..fairly gives an idea of what a country drama is like. **1967** *Spectator* 18 Aug. 193/3 At the Saville..we are seeing Kathakali for the first time in its pure form. Dating from the sixteenth century, indigenous to Malabar, it is a dance-drama drawn from the great Indian epics. **1969** *Cultural News from India* Nov. 13 Kanak has devoted her whole heart and soul to the study of Kathakali and defied tradition in the fact that females are traditionally debarred from dancing the genre. **1969** R. Shankar *My Music* iii. 63/2 The noble style of the dance drama, *Kathakali.* **1974** H. R. F. Keating *Bats fly Up* i. 10 The measured-to-a-fingersbreadth gestures of a Kathakali dancer.

katharevousa (kā:þäre·vŭsă). Also **katharevoussa, katharevusa.** [mod.Gr. καθαρεύουσα, fem. of καθαρεύων, pres. pple. of Anc.Gr. καθαρεύειν to be pure, f. καθαρός pure.] The purist form of Modern Greek; the 'official' language as opposed to the spoken and literary *demotic *a.* 1 b.

1912 S. Angus tr. *Thumb's Handbk. Mod. Gr. Vernacular* p. xi, The term 'modern Greek'..designates *two* forms of language—first, the living language..; and, secondly, the literary language, the καθαρεύουσα. **1956** J. Pring *Compan. Greece* 31 Katharevusa is used not only in official and technical matters, but also in public notices, shop signs and the news columns of the press. **1959** *Times Lit. Suppl.* 15 May 288/4 The literary language was..the *katharevousa,* that artificial pseudo-antique speech. **1969** R. Browning *Med. & Mod. Gr.* 150 *Katharevousa,* the learned, archaising form of Modern Greek. **1969** 'E. Lathen' *When in Greece* vi. 63 His Greek was..a shade pedantic. He used the precise formulations of the *Katharevoussa.* **1974** C. Spencer *How the Greeks kidnapped Mrs Nixon* viii. 53 The Greek Prime Minister was..using, as was customary, the official language, *Katharevousa.*

katharometer (kæþărǫ·mĭtəɹ). [f. Gr. καθαρός pure: see -meter.] An instrument for determining the concentration of one gas in another by comparing the rate of heat loss of an electrically heated wire in the mixture with that in the second gas alone.

1917 G. A. Shakespear in *Rep. & Mem. Advisory Comm. Aeronaut.* No. 317. 3 The following is a brief account of a permeability tester..designed for the rapid testing of balloon and airship fabrics... At the centre of the lower part a katharometer (an instrument for measuring directly the percentage of hydrogen in the air) is fixed. **1945** G. R. Noakes *Text-bk. Heat* ix. 354 The conductivity of hydrogen is about seven times as great as that of air under similar conditions, and this has been made the basis of an instrument called the 'katharometer' (or purity tester) originally designed by Shakespear and Daynes for detecting the leakage of hydrogen through balloon fabrics. **1961** *Engineering* 2 June 780/1 One [detector] widely adopted is the katharometer which measures thermal conductivity... It has a zero or constant response so long as carrier gas alone is flowing, but produces a signal each time one of the components emerges from the column. **1971** D. W. Grant *Gas-Liquid Chromatogr.* vi. 116 The katharometer is normally situated in a separately heated air oven, next to the column oven.

kathete (kæ·þīt), anglicized f. *kathetus,* Cathetus.

1912 G. Kapp *Electr.* viii. 210 The well-known Pythagorean axiom that the sum of the squares of the kathetes in a rectangular triangle is equal to the square of the hypotenuse.

Kathi (kā·ði). Also **kathi.** [Malay.] A judge in Islamic law, who also functions as a registrar of Muslim marriages, divorces, etc.

1947 R. O. Winstedt *Malays* 117 The Chief Kathi of Kelantan fined 14 men and 2 women $15 each, with imprisonment in default. **1963** J. Kirkup *Tropic Temper* 31 In religious matters the Kathi or Muslim religious authority exercises magisterial powers. **1967** W. R. Roff *Origins Malay Nationalism* iii. 73 In June 1884 the Council decided to appoint a State Kathi, 'to decide disputes involving Muhammadan Law and Custom', and the appointment of assistant kathis for the districts was ratified in the following year. **1972** M. Sheppard *Taman Indera* 96 He [*sc.* a *Mufti*] can, if requested, conduct a marriage, but this is normally undertaken by a minor official called *Kathi.* *Ibid.* 102 *Kathi,* a Registrar of Muslim marriages. **1972** *Straits Times* (Malaysian ed.) 25 Nov. 13/2 A former school servant, who declared before a kathi that he was a bachelor and married a second time, was jailed for a day and fined $500 or three months' jail yesterday.

‖ **kati** (kæ·ti). Also **katti.** Var. Catty.

1727 J. G. Scheuchzer tr. *Kæmpfer's Hist. Japan* I. iv. viii. 367 Camphire of Baros, a *Katti,* or 1 pound and a qr. *á* 33 *Siumome,* or *Thails.* **1820** J. Crawfurd *Hist. Indian Archipelago* I. iii. i. 273 One hundred katis make a pikul, or 133⅓ lbs. avoirdupois. **1900** W. W. Skeat *Malay Magic* v. 214 Prices varying according to the quality from $15 to $40 per *katti.* **1947** R. O. Winstedt *Malays* 126 One buffalo costing a *kati* of silver. **1969** J. M. Gullick *Malaysia* v. 232 The miners..are expected to recover 6 *katis* (8 lbs.) of tin ore from each cubic yard of soil. **1972** *Straits Times* (Malaysian ed.) 25 Nov. 13/2 Chicken cost $1·20 per kati.

kationoid, var. *cationoid *a.*

katipo. Substitute for def.: A large, black, venomous New Zealand spider, *Latrodectus katipo,* closely related to the Australian *jockey spider* (*jockey *sb.* 9) and the American *black widow* (*black *a.* 19). Add earlier and later examples.

1843 E. Dieffenbach *Trav. N.Z.* II. iii. ix. 366/2 Katipo—a black spider on the seashore, regarded as poisonous. **1915** *Chambers's Jrnl.* May 319/1 The katipo spider..is the Dominion's [*sc.* New Zealand's] one poisonous creature. **1934** *Bulletin* (Sydney) 4 July 21/4, I gathered katipo by the dozen on the sandhills at the entrance of the Wanganui. **1942** C. Barrett *On the Wallaby* ii. 29 The katipo or red-backed spider enjoys a very wide distribution in Australia. **1963** *Evening Post* (Wellington, N.Z.) 20 Dec., The katipo spider..is black with a red stripe on its back.

katjiepiering (ka:tyipi·riŋ). *S. Afr.* Also **catjepiring, katjepeering, katjiepering.** [Afrikaans, f. Malay *katja-piring, kachapiring,* the Cape jasmine, *Gardenia jasminoides.*] A South African evergreen shrub of the genus *Gardenia,* esp. *G. thunbergia,* belonging to the family Rubiaceæ and bearing large, fragrant, white or yellow flowers.

1793 tr. *C. P. Thunberg's Trav. Europe, Afr. & Asia* II. 111 Wild Catjepiring (*Gardenia Thunbergia*) is a hard and strong kind of wood, and on this account used for clubs. **1869** W. G. Atherstone in R. Noble *Cape & its People* 373 The wagons..stand on a bed of wild flowers..fragrant clematis—the 'traveller's joy',—vying in sweetness with the wild 'katjepeering'. **1910** D. Fairbridge *That which hath Been* 269 Friends bring the first daphne of the year, the richest purple violets, the sweetest katjiepierings, until the house is heavy with the perfume of flowers. **1949** *Cape Argus* 3 Dec. 18/5 Gardenias (Katjiepering), flowering, 4s. 6d. each. **1972** *Stand. Encycl. S. Afr.* V. 120/1 Gardenia. Katjiepiering. Genus of evergreen shrubs..which bear sweetly scented white flowers.

katonkel (kătǫ·ŋkəl). *S. Afr.* Also **katonker, katunka, katunker.** [Afrikaans, f. Malay *kentangkai* a kind of fish.] Either of two marine game fishes: (*a*) *Scomberomorus commersoni,* of the family Scomberomoridæ, which may be six feet long, occurs in the Indo-Pacific ocean, and is also called barracuda; (*b*) *Sarda sarda,* of the family Scombridæ, a much smaller fish found in the Atlantic, and also called bonito.

1853 L. PAPPE *Synopsis Edible Fishes Cape Good Hope* 26 Stromateus Capensis. Mihi. N. Sp. (*Katunker*.).. A good table-fish, but not common. It is caught with the hook and net, chiefly East of Table Bay. **1893** H. A. BRYDEN *Gun & Camera S. Afr.* 449 Many of the Cape fish are endowed with the quaintest Dutch names. Here are a few of them: Kabeljouw,..katunka, elftvisch. **1930** C. L. BIDEN *Sea-Angling Fishes of Cape* vii. 144 The word 'Katonkel' has been corrupted from what was known by the Port Elizabeth Malays as 'katunker' or 'katonker' which originated from the original Malay word 'kentangkai', a kind of sea-fish. **1959** *Cape Times* 18 Feb. 2/4 This is the first time in eight years that so many barracuda (katonkels) have been caught at one time. **1974** *Eastern Province Herald* (S. Afr.) 1 Aug. 21 Katankel were a regular summer fishing feature of Port Elizabeth when the harbour breakwater was open to anglers.

katoptrite (kătǫ·ptrəit). *Min.* Also **catoptrite.** [ad. G. *katoptrit* (G. Flink 1917, in *Geol. För. Förh.* XXXIX. 432), f. Gr. κάτοπτρ-ον mirror (alluding to its brilliant lustre): see -ITE¹.] A silico-antimonate of bivalent manganese (partly replaced by magnesium and bivalent iron) and aluminium (partly replaced by trivalent iron) occurring as black, lustrous, monoclinic crystals.

1917 *Chem. Abstr.* XI. 2650 Catoptrite, a new mineral from Nordmarken. **1919** *Jrnl. Chem. Soc.* CXVI. II. 112 Katoptrite occurs as tabular crystals and irregular lumps with magnetite in granular limestone in the Brattfors mine at Nordmark. **1951** C. PALACHE et al. *Dana's Syst. Min.* (ed. 7) II. 1029 Catoptrite. **1966** *Amer. Mineralogist* LI. 1495 The analysis of Flink (1917)..seems to be essentially correct, even considering the peculiar composition of catoptrite. The analysis computes to very nearly $(Mn_{.86},Mg_{.10},Fe_{.04})_{14}{}^{2+}(Al_{.83},Fe_{.17})_4{}^{3+}Sb_2Si_2O_{29}$. **1968** I. KOSTOV *Mineral.* 328 Katoptrite and parwelite are monoclinic.

Kat stitch (kæt stitʃ). [f. *Kat*, abbrev. of Katharine, in ref. to Katharine (Catherine) of Aragon who was thought to have invented the stitch: see STITCH *sb.*¹ 9.] In lace-making, a stitch which forms a star-shaped ground net.

1919 T. WRIGHT *Romance of Lace Pillow* ix. 84 Downton, five miles from Salisbury, produced..a lace with a net..which is similar to Bucks Point, and the Kat Stitch finds favour with the workers. *Ibid.* xiv. 194 Catherine the Saint became confused with Katharine the Queen—that is to say, Katharine of Aragon..of Kat Stitch fame. **1931** M. MAIDMENT *Man. Hand-Made Bobbin Lace Work* x. 158 *Bucks Kat Stitch or Wire Ground.* This stitch is used as a ground net or filling, and it is sometimes varied by the use of plaits. **1960** H. HAYWARD *Antique Coll.* 156/2 *Kat stitch*, a term used in lace-making to describe a *fond chant* ground but frequently found in Bedfordshire lace and given legendary association with Katherine of Aragon.

‖ **katsuo** (ka·tswo). [Jap.] = BONITO, *Katsuwonus pelamis*, an important food fish in Japan, whether fresh or dried. So **ka·tsuobushi,** a dried quarter of this fish.

1727 J. G. SCHEUCHZER tr. *Kæmpfer's Hist. Japan* I. I. 136 The best sort of *Katsuwo* fish is caught about Gotho. **1884** tr. *J. J. Rein's Japan* I. vii. 194 Most conspicuous is the common bonito or Katsu-uwo (Thynnus pelamys), one of the most important and most valued fishes of Japan. **1891** A. M. BACON *Jap. Girls & Women* i. 5 Sometimes a box of eggs, or a peculiar kind of dried fish, called *Katsuobushi*, is sent with this present. **1899** L. HEARN *In Ghostly Japan* xiv. 227 The Yaidzu-fishing-industry, which supplies dried *katsuo* (bonito) to all parts of the Empire. **1965** W. SWAAN *Jap. Lantern* iv. 51 Sticks of *katsuobushi*, a form of *bonito*, a species of striped tunny. **1969** *Guardian* 16 July 16/4 One staple [Japanese food]..is dried bonito (*Katsuobashi*).

‖ **katsura** (katsu·ră). [Jap.] A type of wig worn mainly by Japanese women.

[**1894** L. HEARN *Glimpses Unfamiliar Japan* II. xviii. 421 As soon as the girl becomes old enough to go to a female public day-school, her hair is dressed in the pretty, simple style called katsurashita.] **1908** N. G. MUNRO *Prehistoric Japan* xiii. 567 The word *Katsura* means a vine, such as the Ainu use on certain occasions for personal decoration. In the middle ages it was applied to artificial hair, which meaning is still retained; the evidence scarcely justifies the conviction that wigs were worn by the prehistoric Yamato. **1970** J. KIRKUP *Japan behind Fan* ii. 63, I watched..a display of graceful dances by girls in kimono,..*obi* (belt) and black-lacquered *katsura*, or wig.

‖ **katsuramono** (katsu:rămǫ·no). Also **kazuramono.** [Jap., f. prec. + *mono* piece, play.] One of the categories of Japanese Noh plays in which the chief character is female and the theme romantic. It is usually presented third in the sequence of five plays of different categories which makes up a performance of Noh. Also *ellipt.* **katsura.**

1916 FENOLLOSA & POUND *Noh* 15 Kazura, or Onnamono, 'wig-pieces', or pieces for females, come third. Many think that any Kazura will do, but it must be a 'female Kazura', for after battle comes peace. **1932** B. L. SUZUKI *Nōgaku* 19 A romantic play (*jo* or *katsuramono*), in which the chief character is a woman and the chief motive love. **1948** *Introd. Classic Jap. Lit.* 141 The regular *kazuramono* contains a *jonomai*, a dance consisting of five movements and a prelude. **1964** W. G. RAFFÉ *Dict. Dance* 353/2 They [*sc.* Noh plays] range.. from romantic themes (*katsuramono*) to farce (*kyogen*). **1965** W. SWAAN *Jap. Lantern* xiii. 153 *Katsura-mono* or wig-plays consisting chiefly of posturing by a woman.

Kattern (kæ·təɹn). Also **Cathern, Cattern.** [Corruption of Catherine, in ref. to St. Catherine of Alexandria, the patron saint of spinners, who was martyred in A.D. 307.] Used in the possessive in **Kattern's day,** 25 November, the feast day of St. Catherine, which was formerly celebrated by lace-makers in the Midlands (see also quot. 1849). Also *ellipt.* **Kattern('s).** Hence **ka·tterner; ka·tter(n)ing** *vbl. sb.*

[**1521** in H. Ellis *Brand's Pop. Antiq.* (1813) I. 322 Mem. that reste in the hands of the wyffe of John Kelyoke and John Atye, 4 merkes, the yere of ower Lorde God 1521, of Sent Kateryn mony.] **1730** C. LAMOTTE *Ess. Poetry & Painting* ii. 126 St. Catherine..is held in so much Veneration in the Church of Rome...her Holiday is observed, not in Popish Countries only, but even in many Places in this Nation, young Women meeting on the 25th of November, and making merry together, which they call Catherning. **1849** H. ELLIS *Brand's Pop. Antiq.* (rev. ed.) I. 413 Until within a very recent period, it was the custom of the dean and chapter of Worcester, yearly, on St. Catharine's Day,..to distribute amongst the inhabitants of the college precincts a rich compound of wine, spices, &c., which was..called the Cattern or Catharine bowl. **1862** *N. & Q.* 17 May 387/2 In Buckinghamshire, on Cattern Day..these hard-working people hold merry-makings, and eat a sort of cakes they call 'wigs'. **1865** F. B. PALLISER *Hist. Lace* XXX. 352 To this very day..the lace-makers still hold 'Cattern's day', the 25th Nov., as the holiday of their craft. **1875** W. D. PARISH *Dict. Sussex Dial.* 25 *Catterning*, to go catterning is to go round begging for apples and beer for a festival on St. Catherine's Day, and singing,—'Cattern' and Clemen' be here, here, here, Give us your apples and give us your beer.' **1899** A. M. SHARP *Point & Pillow Lace* vii. 171 Till well within the present century the name-day of the kind but most unhappy lady [*sc.* Catherine of Aragon], St. Catherine's Day,..was annually kept as a treat-day for young lace-makers,..and called 'Kattern's Day'. **1919** T. WRIGHT *Romance of Lace Pillow* xiv. 194 In some parts of Northants, Bucks and Beds, the leading festival [for lace-makers] was Catterns (St. Catharine's Day), Nov. 25th—St. Catharine being the patron saint of the spinners. **1942** W. ROSE *Good Neighbours* xv. 131 The mid-winter turning of the days, with its joyous celebrations, of which the visit of the 'Katterners' or 'Mummers'—as they were called—was an announcement and a beginning. **1950** *Bedfordshire Mag.* II. xv. 254 How many Bedfordshire people have kept Kattern? Yet St. Catherine's day was once an important occasion to pillow-lace makers. **1959** *Times* 4 Dec. 19/1 English 'luck-visits'..take their names from the Christian usage that overlies pagan observance—as souling, katterning (St. Catherine), [etc.].

katti: see *KATI.

katun (kā·tūn). [Maya.] A period of twenty years, each with 360 days, in the calendar of the Mayan Indians.

1902 *Amer. Anthropologist* Jan.–Mar. 135 Moreover, in A3 we find the Katun sign with the number 1, which may be a declaration that the date is in a first Katun or beginning Katun, for I can see no reason why the beginning Cycle, Katun, Tun, Uinal and Kin should not have been called the first. **1934** A. HUXLEY *Beyond Mexique Bay* 212 Each stela marks the close of one of the shorter of the chronological periods, in terms of which they [*sc.* the Mayas] reckoned their position in endless duration—the close of a Katun of 7200 days. **1950** *Caribbean Q.* II. II. 28 Each altar is in fact a huge day glyph marking the end of a Katun (7,200 days). *Ibid.*, The ancient inhabitants..set up beside the altars stelae bearing Long Count glyphs including the altars' Katun numbers, thus setting the Katun dates into their correct positions. **1968** D. BAGLEY *Vivero Let.* vii. 179 It's a stele—a Mayan date-stone. In a given community they erected a stele every katun—that's a period of nearly twenty years.

katydid. Substitute for first part of def.: A large longhorn grasshopper of the family Tettigoniidæ. (Add earlier and later examples.) See also *CATYDID.

[**1751** J. BARTRAM *Observations Pensilvania to Ontario* 70 It was fair and pleasant, and the great green grasshopper began to sing (*Catedidist*) these were the first I observed this year.] **1784** J. F. D. SMYTH *Tour U.S.A.* II. 243 They are named by the inhabitants here *katy did's*, from their note, which is loud and strong, bearing a striking resemblance to those words. **1886** *Outing* (U.S.) IX. 106/2 Soon the chiding katydids mingled their voices with the rush of the foaming river. **1909** *Springfield* (Mass.) *Weekly Republ.* 16 Sept. 1 All around the globe people are like katydids, saying he did and he didn't in an endless reiteration. **1935** M. MOORE *Sel. Poems* 64 The small tuft of fronds or katydid legs above each eye. **1942** E. O. ESSIG *College Entomology* viii. 95 The name 'katydid' has gradually replaced all others. It originated in the United States, having been derived from characteristic stridulatory sounds produced by the males of certain green species, notably *Pterophylla camellifolia*.. whose note, the loudest of all species of the eastern states, simulates 'Katy did, Katy she did'. **1957** L. EISELEY *Immense Journey* 25 The skilled listener can distinguish man's noise from the katydid's rhythmic assertion. **1972** SWAN & PAPP *Common Insects N. Amer.* iii. 74 Katydids are predominantly green, have exceedingly long antennae, are more often heard than seen.

Katyusha (katiū·ʃă). [Russ.] A Russian rocket launcher.

1955 M. REIFER *Dict. New Words* 116/1 *Katyusha*, Soviet counterpart of the bazooka, an anti-tank weapon employing rockets. **1970** *Guardian* 28 Jan. 10/6 To talk of demilitarisation in the days of Katyushas is obsolete. *Ibid.* 2 June 2/5 Arab guerillas fired Russian-made Katyusha rockets into the Northern Israeli town of Beisan. **1972** E. AMBLER *Levanter* vi. 170, I remembered what Barlev had told me about the 120-mm. Katyusha rocket: fifty kilo warhead, range of about eleven kilometres.

katzenjammer (kæ·tsĕndʒæ:məɹ). *U.S. colloq.* [G., f. *katzen* (comb. form of *katze* cat) + *jammer* distress, wailing **a.** A hangover, or a symptom of one.

1849 *Ex. Doc. 31st U.S. Congress 1 Sess. House* No. 5. III. 733 Some of Mr. Hale's men had kept up a drunken frolic all night, general kakenjammer [*sic*], therefore all day. **1877** R. J. BURDETTE *Rise & Fall of Mustache* 291 This 'Centennial Cordial and American Indian Aboriginal Invigorator'..has positively no equal for the cure of.. katzenjammer. **1948** *Life* 5 Apr. 111/2 Attempting to drink himself to death on..vodka and champagne... The result one of the most colossal *Katzenjammers* ever recorded. He was in bed for a week. **1965** P. DE VRIES *Let Me count the Ways* ix. 125 The symptoms classic to hangover persist. Dizziness, nausea, headache—you know that katzenjammer just above the eyes.

b. *transf.* and *fig.* An unpleasant aftermath or reaction; depression, 'blues'; clamour, uproar.

1897 W. W. COOK in *Yellow Kid* 8 May 26/2 He has a deplorable habit of constantly looking for something. Either he is the relict of some individual who was brought up in a sawmill or else he is suffering from a bad attack of katzenjammer. **1900** W. JAMES *Let.* 8 June in R. B. Perry *Tht. & Char. W. James* (1935) II. 198, I am afraid of what the French people may do during the *Katzenjammer* which will inevitably succeed the Exhibition. **1922** W. STEVENS *Let.* 24 Aug. (1967) 228 Nothing has survived the subsequent katzenjammer. **1949** I. DEUTSCHER *Stalin* x. 406 Amid the *Katzenjammer* which befell them after 1933, most leaders of the German left were only too eager to explain away their own failure. **1960** B. KEATON *Wonderful World of Slapstick* (1967) iv. 74 The Katzenjammer spirit of the other acts on the bill inspired them to contribute new plot turns.

c. *Katzenjammer Kids* (or *Children*), mischievous, naughty children; *enfants terribles.* So called from the title of a comic strip, first drawn by Rudolph Dirks in 1897 for the *New York Journal*, featuring Hans and Fritz, two incorrigible children. Also *attrib.*

1897 R. DIRKS in *N.Y. Jrnl.* 12 Dec. 8 (*comic strip title*) Ach, Those Katzenjammer Kids! **1910** M. G. PEDRICK in *Good Housekeeping* (N.Y.) May 625/2 The children are engrossed with the mishaps of Happy Hooligan, Smarty, Gaston or the 'demoniacal ingenuity of the Katzenjammer Kids'. **1947** W. STEVENS *Let.* June (1967) 558 The noisy Katzenjammer children..were upstairs saying their prayers. **1962** *Times Lit. Suppl.* 13 July 511/3 He has no difficulty in matching the varied dialects of the Greek, drawing as required on such rich sources as mint-julep Southern, broad Brooklynese or Katzenjammerkids German.

‖ **kau kau** (kau kau). [Native name.] In New Guinea, the sweet potato.

1937 *Official Handbk. New Guinea* v. 435 In Morobe District, taro, sweet potatoes (*kau-kau*), sugar-cane and bananas furnish the main food, supplemented by yam, coco-nut and sago in certain areas. **1957** M. WEST *Kundu* xiv. 166 They returned laden with taro and kau-kau and sugar-cane. **1964** *Economist* 30 May 985/1 Sago and *kau kau* provide a basic if poor quality diet [in Papua].

‖ **kavadi** (kā·vădi). [ad. Tamil *kāvaṭi.*] A decorated arch carried on the shoulders as an act of penance, esp. by Hindus in Malaysia.

1954 V. BARTLETT *Rep. from Malaya* ii. 27 A 'kavadi'.. is a gaily-decorated but heavy wooden harness normally supported on one shoulder. **1961** *Times* 8 Mar. 14/6 [Ceylon] On their shoulders the traditional kāvadis. **1963** J. KIRKUP *Tropic Temper* 254 Blocks of pure camphor for burning..before the holy men and penitents carrying kavadis. **1966** S. WAVELL et al. *Trances* 148 Many are poor and walk long distances carrying upon their shoulders a heavy superstructure known as *kavadi* bearing flowers and fruit and peacock feathers to place before the image of Subramaniam. **1970** S. ARASARATNAM *Indians in Malaysia & Singapore* vi. 171 Popular forms of devotion..as practised in South India have persisted...Among the most significant of these is the carrying of the *kavadi*, a large wooden decorated arch, as an act of penance. **1972** *Straits Times* (Malaysian ed.) 27 Nov. 26/1 (Advt.), Devotees of Lord Subramaniam carry penitent 'kavadis'. **1973** *Observer* 7 Oct. 36/6 The penitents..climb 272 steps to the place where the Lord's image is installed, their bodies enclosed in the kavadi, a wooden frame decorated with feathers and supported by long metal rods which are hooked into their flesh.

kavir (kăvīᵊ·ɹ). Also **kevir.** [Pers.] A salt-desert, or more rarely a saline swamp, in Persia; terrain of this type; also *spec.* (*the Kavir*), the great central salt-desert of Persia, more commonly called the Dasht-i-kavir.

1881 *Proc. R. Geogr. Soc.* III. 515 The road..across the Kavir or Great Salt Desert was very difficult. *Ibid.* 517 Soon after passing Illahabad a small piece of *kavir* or salt desert is passed. *Ibid.* 518 There are various sorts of kavir, depending upon the soil and the amount of salt. **1896** *Geogr. Jrnl.* VII. 34 These bushes grow..along the borders of the swampy part of the salt desert, which is

known as the Kavir or Dasht-i-Kavir. *Ibid.* 166 The greater portion of the tract consists of *kavir*, or sandy soil strongly impregnated with salt. **1902** P. M. SYKES *Ten Thousand Miles in Persia* iii. 33 And that *Kavir* is applied to every saline swamp in the whole blighted expanse. **1963** D. W. & E. E. HUMPHRIES tr. *Termier's Erosion & Sedimentation* v. 118 As a result of evaporation, some closed basins are floored by a saline crust which is called *sebkha* in North Africa.., *solonchak* in the region of the Caspian, and *kevirs* in Transcaspia.

Kavirondo (kā:virǫ·ndo). Also **Kaverond(a)**, **Kavirond.** [Native name, meaning 'cut around', 'circumcised'.] **a.** The name of two Kenyan peoples, one Nilotic, one Bantu (also called Wa-Kavirondo); a member of these peoples; any of the languages spoken by these peoples. Also *attrib.*

1870 *Jrnl. R. Geogr. Soc.* XL. 308 At Kaverond..there are villages. The people of this place are called Wa-Kaverond. They are the same as the Wa-Kosóva, only a different tribe or clan. The language is one. **1873** C. NEW *Life E. Afr.* xxiii. 468 Captain Speke gives only a few words of the Gani dialect..and these are the very words which are used by the Wakavirondo for the same things. *Ibid.* 526 A Table showing the variations in the dialects and languages spoken by some of the tribes... Kisuaheli..Masai, Kavirondo. **1882** *Proc. R. Geogr. Soc.* New Ser. IV. 743 The town of the Kavirondo chief Sendēge. *Ibid.* 744 Mr. Wakefield's vocabulary of the Kavirondo language clearly shows that this tribe does not belong to the Bantu family... Two islands lie off Kisumo... Both are cultivated by Kavirondo. **1885** J. THOMSON *Through Masái Land* (ed. 3) xi. 475 Their shields are of all shapes and sizes, though the characteristic Kavirondo form is enormous in dimensions and weight. *Ibid.* 478 We picked the bones of fat Kavirondo fowls. *Ibid.* 485 The Wa-kavirondo are apparently a homogeneous race... Yet..there were two totally distinct languages. The inhabitants of..Lower Kavirondo..speak a language resembling..that spoken by the Nile tribes, while those of Upper Kavirondo speak a Bantu dialect. **1902** C. W. HOBLEY *Eastern Uganda: Ethnol. Survey* i. 13 No Kavirondo marries in his own clan, and the degeneracy due to inbreeding is obviated. *Ibid.* vi. 88 There are many striking resemblances between the Nyamwezi language and the Bantu language of Kavirondo. **1921** *Manual on E. Afr.* (Church Missionary Soc.) 13 Leaving the coast.., we come to the Nilotic tribes—the Masai.. and Nilotic Kavirondo. The greatest tribe of all in point of numbers is the Kavirondo, of which there are about 9,000,000; but it is divided by language into two groups, Nilotic and Bantu. **1950** HUNTINGFORD & BELL *E. Afr. Background* (ed. 2) xiv. 111 *Kavirondo*, this is properly a name of the Nilotic Luo people in Kenya. According to one native explanation, it was applied by the people of one side of Kavirondo Gulf to the people of the other side as a term of abuse, derived from a Luo word *rondo* 'to deceive'... From this restricted area it has become applied to (1) The Nilotic Luo as a whole;..(3) the Bantu inhabitants of this area. **1956** *Linguistic Survey Northern Bantu Borderland* (Internat. Afr. Inst.) I. III. 129 The northern corner of the 'Bantu Kavirondo pocket'. *Ibid.* 130 A note on 'Bantu Kavirondo'. This name refers to a pocket of Bantu-speaking peoples between the..'Nilotic Kavirondo'..and the Jopadhola and speakers of Nandi dialects.

b. Kavirondo crane = *Kaffir crane* (*KAFFIR 4).

1928 *Daily Express* 31 July 4 The handsomest [bird] is the Kavirondo or golden-crested crane, kept as a pet by some native tribes in Kenya, a gorgeous stork-like bird plumaged in browns, blues, greys, and gold. **1938** F. J. JACKSON *Birds Kenya Colony* I. 317 The East African Crowned Crane, known locally as the Straw-crested, Golden-crested, and sometimes the Kavirondo crane, is found throughout Kenya colony... Why it ever became known as the Kavirondo crane is a mystery.

Kaw (kǭ). *U.S.* Also **Caw, Kah.** Another name for the *KANSA. Also *attrib.* or as *adj.*

1804 LEWIS & CLARK in R. G. Thwaites *Orig. Jrnls. Lewis & Clark Exped.* (1905) VI. 84 (*in list*) 3. Kanzas; Karsea; Kah. **1823** W. BECKNELL in *Missouri Intelligencer* 22 Apr. 2/5 We..shaped our course over the high land which separates the waters of that and the Caw rivers. Among the Caw Indians we were treated hospitably. **1844** J. GREGG *Commerce Prairies* I. 41 It was either a hoax.. or else a stratagem of the Kaws (or Kansas Indians). **1930** E. FERBER *Cimarron* xviii. 280 The Oklahoma Territory and the Indian Territory, with an Indian population of..various tribes..Kaws, Choctaws, Seminoles. **1942** *R.A.F. Jrnl.* 16 May 28 The festivities..were planned by Mose Bellmard, chief of the Kaw Indian tribe.

kawai, var. *KAHAWAI.

kawaka (kā·wăkă). *N.Z.* [Maori.] A New Zealand cedar, *Libocedrus plumosa.*

1832 G. BENNETT in *London Med. Gaz.* 7 Jan. 506/2 A tree of the Natural Family *Coniferæ*, collected without ..flower or fruit: it is named Káwaka by the natives of New Zealand, attaining the height of from 60 to 70 feet... The natives informed me that it derived the name Káwaka from the branches growing out regularly on each side of the tree. **1855** R. TAYLOR *Te Ika a Maui* 440 *Kawaka, koaka* (*dacrydium plumosum*). This tree grows in large quantities on the central plains; the wood is of a very dark red grain, and is said to be as durable as the *totara.* **1906** T. F. CHEESEMAN *Man. N.Z. Flora* 647 *Kawaka*; *New Zealand Arbor-vitæ.* Wood dark-red, beautifully grained, said to be durable, but on account of its scarcity little used. **1966** *Encycl. N.Z.* II. 208/2 Kawaka occurs in lowland forest from Northland to the centre of the North Island and again in the north-west tip of the South Island.

kawa-kawa[1] (ka·wăka·wă). [Maori.] **1.** A shrub or small tree, *Macropiper excelsum*, of the family Piperaceæ, native to New Zealand and neighbouring islands; also called pepper-tree.

1850 J. GREENWOOD *Journey to Taupo* 30 A most refreshing light beverage made from the leaves of the Kawa-kawa tree. **1910** L. COCKAYNE *N.Z. Plants* v. 80 On the Little Barrier, at the foot of the cliffs, it [*sc.* a member of the gourd family] is abundant, scrambling over the kawakawa. **1938** R. FINLAYSON *Brown Man's Burden* 47 The wreaths of bitter kawakawa around their heads were not more bitter than their tears of grief. **1949** P. BUCK *Coming of Maori* (1950) III. vi. 407 Hot infusions of leaves such as the *kawakawa.* **1966** *Encycl. N.Z.* II. 785/1 Numerous other berries were eaten raw, especially by children... Examples are kahikatea..and kawakawa.

2. *N.Z.* A variety of GREENSTONE 2.

1880 *Encycl. Brit.* XIII. 540/2 The green jade-like stones which are known to the Maories as *kawa-kawa* and *tangiwai* do not appear to be either jade or jadeite. **1909** *Q. Jrnl. Geol. Soc.* LXV. 368 The variety [of greenstone], however, which is almost exclusively used by the lapidary and jeweller, is the common green kawakawa. **1965** G. J. WILLIAMS *Econ. Geol. N.Z.* x. 156/2 *Kawakawa*.. was named from its resemblance to the leaf of a shrub; the colour is dark green in various shades including spinach-green, seaweed-green, and olive-green.

kawakawa[2] (ka:văka·vă). [Hawaiian.] The little tuna, *Euthynnus yaito.*

1887 H. H. GOWEN *Let.* in *Paradise of Pacific* (1892) xi. 130 The *kawakawa*, a large fish tasting somewhat like mackerel. **1915** W. A. BRYAN *Nat. Hist. Hawaii* xxvii. 363 The little tunny or kawakawa is at once recognized as a mackerel. **1944** S. W. TINKER *Hawaiian Fishes* 156 The kawakawa is dark blue in color above and almost silvery beneath.

kay (kēi), *int.* [Representation of the sound of the letter *K*.] = *O.K. used as *int.*

1959 I. JEFFERIES *Thirteen Days* v. 66 'How about a quick half-hour *now*?' I said. 'Kay.' **1968** S. CHALLIS *Death on Quiet Beach* v. 72 Kay. We'll check her out. **1972** J. WAINWRIGHT *Night is Time to Die* 189 'And sling him in the cells,' added the D.D.I... 'Kay.'

kaya (ka·ya). [Jap.] A Japanese evergreen tree, *Torreya nucifera*, of the family Taxaceæ, with large seeds which contain oil; also, the wood of this tree.

[**1727** J. G. SCHEUCHZER tr. *Kæmpfer's Hist. Japan* I. I. ix. 119 Of all the Oils express'd out of the seeds of these several plants, only that of the *Sesamum* and *Kai*, are made use of in the kitchen.] **1889** J. J. REIN *Industries Japan* I. iii. 157 Kaya-no-abura, Kaya-oil, is manufactured by the Japanese from the seeds of *Torreya nucifera*, S. and Z., the Kaya, which are like hazel-nuts or acorns... The Kaya resembles our yew. It is found in most cases as of underwood, scattered like brush in mountain forests; seldom as a tree. In autumn the plant is laden with nuts, which are good to eat, although having a resinous aftertaste. **1894** C. S. SARGENT *Notes Forest Flora Japan* 76 The Kaya should be cultivated wherever the climate permits it to display its beauty. **1923** DALLIMORE & JACKSON *Handbk. Coniferæ* 75 *Torreya nucifera*, Siebold & Zuccarini. Kaya... Wood lustrous yellow to pale brown, durable under water, used for chests, boxes, cabinets, furniture, water-pails, and for Japanese chessmen. **1965** J. OHWI *Flora Japan* 110/1 Kaya. Glabrous tree with spreading brownish branches. **1969** R. C. BELL *Board & Table Games* II. iii. 61 The best boards are made of a species of yew, called 'Kaya' (*Torreya Nucifera*).

kayak[1]. Add: **b.** Any canoe developed from the Eskimo kayak, used for touring or sport.

1936 A. R. ELLIS *Canoeing for Beginners* i. 10 Constructional plans of the British Scout Kayak... This craft is a very seaworthy little piece of work... It is about 15 feet in length. **1946** P. W. BLANDFORD *Canoeing To-Day* i. 4 It is common to refer to a folding craft as a canoe and a rigid craft as a kayak, although the latter is not built on Eskimo lines. *Ibid.* 62 *Kayak*, originally the Eskimo craft, but now generally applied to any rigid canvas-covered decked canoe. **1962** —— *Canoes & Canoeing* i. 15 What the European calls a canoe the American calls a *kayak*, and what the American calls a canoe the European usually qualifies as a *Canadian canoe*, keeping the word kayak for the special slim craft based on the Eskimo pattern. **1966** J. SAMSON in B. C. Skilling *Canoeing Complete* i. 24 About 1840 the first copies of Greenland kayaks appeared in Europe... After 1865 canoeing began to rise as a new kind of sport. The Scot, McGregor, made his sensational voyages in kayaks of his own design.

c. *attrib.* and *Comb.*

1963 *Internat. Jrnl. Social Psychiatry* IX. I. 19 Kayak-angst (kayak-phobia, kayak dizziness) is well known throughout all districts of West Greenland... Kayak-angst is scarcely mentioned in English written accounts, with the exception of brief references in Freuchen, Birket-Smith and a few others. **1963** B. C. SKILLING in *Canoe Venture* 20 In the kayak world it was accepted that to have complete control the canoe and man must become as one. **1964** *Slalom & White Water Course* (Ontario Voyageurs Kayak Club) i. 4 Modern kayak-paddling technique is a combination of the classical style and of elements adopted from the Canadian canoe. **1964** N. HUNT *Adventures in Canoeing* i. 13 He feels his individual make-up is in line with these exciting aspects of kayak sport. *Ibid.* ii. 24 A lightweight, strong and watertight hull, easy to make and no more expensive than a soft-skinned kayak kit. *Ibid.* iii. 37 Free your legs from the knee grips by pressing the thighs towards the kayak floor. *Ibid.* vii. 89 A broken kayak paddle.

Hence **kay·ak** *v. intr.*, to travel by kayak; **kayaker, kayaking** *vbl. sb.* (further examples); also *attrib.*; **kay·akist**, one who paddles a kayak.

1875 H. RINK *Tales & Trad. Eskimo* l. 294 Another day, when he was kayaking along the coast, he remarked some loose pieces of ice. *Ibid.* 295 His wife repeated the tale of his misfortunes to every kayaker on his return home. *Ibid.* lxii. 349 The following day the father kayaked the same way past the cape, and came in sight of the tents. **1960** *Spectator* 2 Sept. 340 She's training with the world's top kayakists. **1963** R. GEORGE in *Canoe Venture* 5 The Australian and American founders, who swore that they would never raise the status of kayak to canoe even though it was going to be a canoeing club of kayakists. *Ibid.* 21 The paddlers sat on their wickerwork seats and watched with disdain the gyratics of the new kayakers. **1964** *Slalom & White Water Course* (Ontario Voyageurs Kayak Club) v. 12 His name is probably not mentioned in Czech kayaking literature. *Ibid.* xii. 22 Slalom competitions are considered the 'matriculation' of the kayaking fraternity. **1966** B. C. SKILLING *Canoeing Complete* 11 The knowledge and experience which he and other members of his parties gained in kayaking with the Eskimos. *Ibid.* x. 176 It will be found that few kayakers can paddle with equal facility on both sides of their canoe using a single-bladed paddle stroke. **1967** *Nat. Geographic* Sept. 328/1 Halting for lunch, the kayakers beach their craft..then join youngsters splashing in the mole-protected harbor. **1969** *Pubn. Amer. Dial. Soc.* LI. 1 The sport of whitewater kayaking was developed in the United States... Kayak slalom, the most complex form of kayaking, is a competition in which the kayakist or paddler must pass through a series of gates in the rapids. **1973** *New Earth Catalog* 17/1 A kayak outfitter with kits and..instruction on the art of kayaking down some of Colorado's rivers.

kayak[2] (kəi·æk). *Canada.* Also **kia(c)k, kyack.** [Prob. f. Algonquian.] = ALE-WIFE[2].

1849 A. GESNER *Industr. Resources Nova Scotia* 121 Sometimes a hundred men, among whom is a sprinkling of Indians, are engaged in taking the 'kiacks' from the stream. **1878** C. HALLOCK *Sportsman's Gazetteer* (ed. 4) 271 Kyack.—*Pomolobus pseudoharengus.* **1965** *Canad. Geogr. Jrnl.* June 209/1 'Alewives' is the common name used in Britain and New Zealand, while the MicMac Indians called the fish 'kayaks', and in Latin it's *Pomolobus pseudoharengus.* **1965** E. RICHARDSON *Living Island* 109 To feast upon the sweet spring clams and the running kyack-cooks (we still call alewives 'kyacks').

Kayan (kəi·ăn). Also **Kyan.** [Native name.] The name of a people of Sarawak and Borneo, of a member of this people, and of their language. Also *attrib.* or as *adj.*

1846 C. D. BETHUNE in *Jrnl. R. Geogr. Soc.* XVI. 297 The indigenous population [of Borneo] is included under the names of Dayák, Kadáyan, Milanau, Káyan, Murút, Dusúr. *Ibid.* 299 The Káyan is the most numerous tribe. ..Their dialect is different from the Dayák. *Ibid.*, Hill tribes..much oppressed by the Káyans. **1848** H. LOW *Sarawak* iv. 97 The Dyaks, the Kyans, and other aboriginal tribes. *Ibid.* x. 331 The swords of the Kyan tribes are of very peculiar construction. **1858** S. ST. JOHN *Jrnl.* 1 Sept. in *Life Forests Far East* (1862) II. iii. 45, I then made Japer hail in the Kayan and also in the Murut languages. **1873** *Proc. R. Geogr. Soc.* XVII. 133 Their [*sc.* the Pakattans'] language is quite different to Malay, Dyak, or Kyan. **1886** in F. Hatton *N. Borneo* (ed. 2) vii. 322 No European blade is more finely tempered than these Kayan weapons. *Ibid.* 329 This Kayan instrument gives forth a soft and soothing kind of music. **1914** *Sat. Rev.* 31 Jan. 147/2 The Ranee carries her love for her people to the extent of even finding excuses for the head-hunting propensities of the Dyaks and Kayans. **1938** C. H. HARTLEY in T. Harrisson *Borneo Jungle* 149 The orators spoke in Kayan, but subsequently translated their remarks into Malay. **1960** K. F. WONG *Pagan Innocence* pl. 64 (*caption*) Her baby has been given a good start in life, from the Kayan point of view, by the acquisition of ear-rings to elongate the lobes. **1960** *Guardian* 9 Nov. 10/3 The population [of Sarawak] includes..Malays, Melanaus, Kayans..and others. **1964** T. HARRISSON in Wang Gungwu *Malaysia* III. xi. 170 A Kayan put down among Kelabits will not understand a word.

kayf (kēif). Representation of a slang or jocular pronunciation of CAFÉ. Cf. *CAFF.

1962 F. NORMAN *Guntz* i. 8, I had some eggs and bacon in a kayf just around the corner. **1964** *Spectator* 20 Mar. 380/1 This kayf-world follows every cool, snide and beat twist of Sixties fashion.

kaylong, var. *KELONG.

kayo (kēi·ōu), *a. slang* (orig. *U.S.*). [Reversal of the pronunc. of *O.K. under the influence of next (see *K. 4 b).] = *O.K. *a.*

1923 H. C. WITWER in *Cosmopolitan* Apr. 128/2 Anything you say is kayo with me, kid, unless you tell me good bye! **1928** WODEHOUSE *Money for Nothing* v. 103 If you think it's kayo, then it's all right by me. **1946** *Amer. Speech* XXI. 138 How these new speech forms [*sc.* abbreviations] in turn may be translated back into the written word is shown by *kayo*, [etc.]

kayo (kēi·ōu), *v.* and *sb. colloq.* (orig. *U.S.*). [Representation of the pronunc. of K.O. (*s.v.* *K. 4).] **A.** *v. trans.* = *KNOCK *v.* 12 a. **B.** *sb.* = KNOCK-OUT *sb.* 2.

1923 H. C. WITWER *Fighting Blood* 324 You never been knocked cold in your life—why go out of your way to get kayoed? **1932** J. T. FARRELL *Young Lonigan* iii. 112 He sat down, saying to himself that he was Young Studs

Lonigan..now in training for the bout when he would kayo Jess Willard for the title. **1933** *Amer. Speech* VIII. III. 39/1 The knockout blow or kayo itself is variously called kay,..K.O. **1939** WODEHOUSE *Uncle Fred in Springtime* xx. 303, I still don't see..why he should have slipped kayo drops in. **1968** *Globe & Mail* (Toronto) 3 Feb. 40/4 Quarry with 14 kayos in a 25–1–4 record is known as a stopper. **1972** *Times* 10 Nov. 14/6 There was ..the kayoing of the prop forward by a deliberate punch. **1975** *Cleveland* (Ohio) *Plain Dealer* 23 Mar. 2-C/2 Rademacher, who was kayoed by Patterson in the sixth round in 1957, won a gold medal in the 1956 Olympic Games for boxing.

kayser (kəi·zəɹ). *Physics.* [Name of J. H. G. *Kayser* (1853–1940), German spectroscopist.] A name proposed for the unit of wave number, cm^{-1}.

1951 W. F. MEGGERS in *Jrnl. Optical Soc. Amer.* XLI. 1064 Because H. Kayser first founded the correct procedure in determining spectroscopic wave numbers..I think it appropriate to propose that the name of the unit, hitherto called cm^{-1}, be Kayser, with *K* as the natural abbreviation. **1953** *Ibid.* XLIII. 411 The Joint Commission for Spectroscopy recommends that the unit of wave number hitherto designated as cm^{-1} be named kayser. **1968** HILL & DAY *Physical Methods Adv. Inorg. Chem.* iv. 112 The units of wave numbers are cm^{-1} or kayser (K) with 1000 kayser = 1 kilokayser (kK).

Kayser–Fleischer ring (kəi·zəɹ,fləiʃəɹ riŋ). *Path.* [f. the names of Bernhard *Kayser* (1869–1954) and Bruno *Fleischer* (b. 1874), German ophthalmologists.] A pigmented ring around the cornea of a variable orange, green, or brown colour, diagnostic of Wilson's disease.

1930 *Amer. Jrnl. Ophthalm.* XIII. 1049/2 We must rely to a great extent upon the presence of a Kayser-Fleischer ring for a differential diagnosis [of Wilson's disease]. **1948** *Amer. Jrnl. Med. Sci.* CCXV. 601/2 Both brothers present an unusually well developed orange-green Kayser-Fleischer ring. **1970** PASSMORE & ROBSON *Compan. Med. Stud.* II. xxv. 38 A characteristic brown ring sometimes visible in the outer cornea, the Kayser-Fleischer ring.

kaza, var. *CAZA.

1885 *Encycl. Dict.* IV. 468/3 *Kāz'-a*,..a district or subdivision of sandjak, marked out for administrative purposes. **1920** *Glasgow Herald* 27 Aug. 9 General Gouraud has arrived at Zableh, where he announced the reunion with the Lebanon of the four kazas of Baalbek, Bekoa, Ruchaya, and Hasbaya. **1972** D. DAKIN *Unification of Greece* xii. 162 A broad band of territory composed of the *kazas* (districts) of Monastir and Florina in the west; of Gevgeli, Vodena.., and Yanitsa in the central region; and Serres and Zihna in the east.

kazachoc (kæzătʃǫ·k). Also **kozatchok** and other forms repr. the acc. or pl. of the Russ. word. [Russ., dim. of *kazák* Cossack.] A Slavic, mainly Ukrainian, dance with a fast and usu. quickening tempo. Sometimes used erron. for a step of this dance, properly called the *prisiadka*, in which the male dancer squats on his heels and kicks out each leg alternately to the front.

1928 C. GARNETT tr. *Gogol's Mirgorod* 65 No-one could have watched without inner emotion how all danced that most free, most furious dance the world has ever seen, called from its mighty originators the Kozatchok. **1960** B. KEATON *Wonderful World of Slapstick* (1967) ii. 45 He couldn't walk straight because of the dense smoke, he couldn't bend down or even do a Russian Kazatsky. **1962** *Listener* 11 Jan. 71/1 He played Polish and Russian dances like the mazurka, the polka, and the Kozochka. **1966** K. GILES *Provenance of Death* iii. 78 She switched on the player and danced the *Kazachka*, mainly to spite Harry who invariably fell over when he tried.

Kazak (kăzā·k). [ad. *Kazakh*, name of a town in Azerbaijan.] A type of Caucasian wool rug, characterized by large geometric designs in striking colours, and a thick durable quality.

1900 J. K. MUMFORD *Oriental Rugs* (1901) ix. 107 The regulation rug of the Derbend variety..partakes of the character of the Kazak. **1954** I. MURDOCH *Under Net* vi. 90 An exquisitely golden yellow and midnight blue striped Kazak rug. *Ibid.* 102, I took a last..look at the Afghans and Kazaks. **1962** C. W. JACOBSEN *Oriental Rugs* 233 Kazaks and Karabaghs are thick piled Caucasian rugs. The Kazaks are geometric in design. **1973** *Times* 2 Apr. 6 (Advt.), A fascinating Royal Pakistani Kazak.

Kazakh (kăzā·k). Also **K(h)asa(c)k, Kazak, Qazaq.** Pl. **Kazakhi, Kazakhs.** [Russ.] One of a Turkic people of central Asia, forming the basic population of the Kazakh SSR (Kazakhstan); the language spoken by this people. Also *attrib.* or as *adj.*

1832 J. BELL *Syst. Geogr.* IV. 396 Amongst the names of tribes noticed..are: the *Kuthai Kipchaucks, Kuzzauks*, ..and *Kara Kalpaks*. **1886** R. N. CUST *Lang. as Illustr. by Bible-Translation* 32 The Túrki Branch [of Ural-Altaic], containing Chuvásh, Kazáni, Nogái..and Kirghíz in the Kazák Dialect. **1907** G. W. HUNTER in M. Broomhall *Chinese Empire* 296 There are large numbers of Kirghiz—Khasack tribes—here in the district of Urumchi. They are mostly wandering nomadic tribes, though some have farms and settled abodes. **1918** G. W. HUNTER *Examples Turki Dial.* Pref., Whilst doing some Qazaq Turki translation work we found it necessary to read some native Qazaq books. And we thought it might be useful to keep a record of our studies in Qazaq, and in the various other Turkish dialects... Much still requires to be done in Qazaq, Tartar and the Kirghese dialects. **1945** *Dairy Sci. Abstr.* VII. 3 Crossbred cows..gave an average milk yield ..39·2 per cent. more than Kazakh cows... Crossbreeding Kazakh and Schwyz cattle. **1948** D. DIRINGER *Alphabet* 568 Eastern or Altai-Kirghiz Turkish or Kazakh Turkish, spoken by several hundred thousand nomads in the Altai and T'ien Shan mountains. **1949** N. JASNY *Socialized Agric. USSR* III. xiv. 330 On the price paid by the Kazakhi for collectivization see the end of the preceding chapter. *Ibid.* III. xiii. 323 The Kazakhi, a Mongol pastoral tribe inhabiting mainly Kazakhstan... The Kazakhi should have numbered 4·6 million in 1939. **1957** *Chambers's World Gazetteer* (rev. ed.) 359/2 Kazakh SSR, or Kazakhstan... Kazakhs..constitute 60% of the total pop... The written Kazakh language has existed only since the revolution. **1968** BETHELL & BURG tr. *Solzhenitsyn's Cancer Ward* I. iv. 49 Next to him Egenberdiev, a middle-aged Kazakh shepherd, was not lying but sitting on his bed, legs crossed as though he was sitting on a rug at home. **1969** *Guardian* 21 June 9/5 The Russians have broadcast propaganda in the Kazakh language from Alma Ata. **1972** *Times* 11 Dec. 1/7 An 800-mile border with China. It crosses mountainous areas which provide pasture land used by Kazakh and other hill shepherds.

kazoo. For def. read: (See quot. 1938.) Now also made of plastic or metal and played as a jazz instrument. Also **kazoo·** *v.*, to make a sound like that of a kazoo; **kazoo·er, kazoo·ist,** one who plays the kazoo; **kazoo·ing** *vbl. sb.*

1895 *Montgomery Ward Catal.* 245/3 Kazoos, the great musical wonder,..anyone can play it; imitates fowls, animals, bagpipes, etc. **1909** R. A. WASON *Happy Hawkins* (1912) xxvi. 301 The storm that was presently kazooin' along was fierce an' horrible. **1926** *Daily Colonist* (Victoria, B.C.) 24 Jan. 9/3 There will be an abundance of paper hats, balloons, kazoos and other novelties. **1926** WHITEMAN & MCBRIDE *Jazz* ix. 201 Did you ever see a kazoo? Of course you must have—a small worthless-looking piece of tin. A kazoo stuck into a mute will give a buzzy sound that comes handy in certain pieces. **1938** *Oxf. Compan. Mus.* 583/2 *Mirliton*, the French name for what English children call (or used to call) 'Tommy Talker', or 'kazoo'. It is a tube with a membrane at each end and two holes in the side, near the two ends, into one of which holes one sings in one's natural voice, the tone issuing in a caricatural fashion. **1940** *Amer. Speech* XV. 125 George Gershwin's..'Blue Monday' has..*Kazoo Mutes* (to cornets). **1956** J. LATIMER *Sinners & Shrouds* ix. 83 'A neglected instrument, the kazoo,' he was saying. 'A cock's challenge in Red McKenzie's hands, raucous and lewd, a braggart, a bully, a flap-wing lover.' **1956** M. STEARNS *Story of Jazz* (1957) xv. 171 Jack Bland, Dick Sliven, and Red McKenzie played a banjo, a comb wrapped in tissue paper, and a kazoo (a toy horn with tissue paper that vibrates with humming). **1959** *Guardian* 26 Aug. 5/2 The kazooers' parents give tremendous support. *Ibid.*, One hears that there is..a new outbreak of kazooing in South Wales and Bootle. **1965** G. MELLY *Owning-Up* xi. 135 A kind of sub-jazz in which kazoos, tea-chest and broom-handle basses..and empty suitcases replaced the more conventional musical instruments. **1966** T. PYNCHON *Crying of Lot 49* i. 10 The Fort Wayne Settecento Ensemble's variorum recording of the Vivaldi Kazoo Concerto. **1968** *Blues Unlimited* Nov. 8 Dewey Corley..now plays kazoo and washtub bass. **1970** *Guardian Weekly* 14 Mar. 16/1 Running the gauntlet of a battalion of kazooists. **1970** *Peace News* 8 May 8/4, I think the time has come for us to make our own music. ..To beat on pots and pans, blow kazoos and our combs wrapped in wax paper. **1972** *Guardian* 29 May 5/5 The unusual cigar-shaped instrument, the kazoo—a cheap toy which makes a vibrant noise when blown—can help unmusical children to sing in tune. **1973** *Ibid.* 19 Feb. 8/4 A Kazoo will give out a sort of buzzing noise... As one of the 120 Kazooing members of the audience I found it fun.

Keating (kī·tiŋ). The name of Thomas *Keating*, a 19th-century chemist, used (usu. *attrib.* or in the possessive) as the proprietary name of an insect powder first manufactured by him.

1876 *Trade Marks Jrnl.* 11 Oct. 576/2 Keating's Persian insect destroying powder..Thomas Keating. **1886** B. POTTER *Jrnl.* Dec. (1966) 193 The little room above the saddle room was sprayed with Keatings powder and shut up. **1893** E. F. BENSON *Dodo* II. xviii. 378, I am in England... I shall sleep in a clean white bed, and I shall not have to use Keating. **1909** *Trade Marks Jrnl.* 24 Mar. 487 Keating's Powder... Insect Destroying Powder. Thomas Keating..Wholesale Chemists. **1915** A. D. GILLESPIE *Lett. from Flanders* (1916) 218, I have plenty of Keating's powder left. **1920** D. H. LAWRENCE *Touch & Go* III. ii. 84 And are you going to comb 'em out, or do you propose to use Keating's? **1926** A. HUXLEY *Let.* 10 Aug. (1969) 271 The typhoid is said to be very bad...be forearmed and take a lot of Keatings. **1928** F. STARK *Lett. from Syria* (1942) iv. 136 As for fleas, Keating's has succumbed to numbers. **1941** G. GREENE in *Spectator* 4 July 8/2 Keating's Powder has taken the place of the military escort.

keatite (kī·təit). *Min.* [f. the name of P. P. *Keat* (born 1923), U.S. chemist who first synthesized it + -ITE[1].] An artificial modification of silica produced at high pressures as tetragonal crystals.

1954 [see *COESITE]. **1955** *Trans. Brit. Ceramic Soc.* LIV. 665 The polymerized silicic acid now crystallizes.. to the crystalline tetragonal phase, keatite. **1959** *Zeitschr. für Kristallogr.* CXII. 410 The density of keatite (50 /gr·cm³) is intermediate to that of cristobalite..and quartz. **1962** C. FRONDEL *Dana's Syst. Min.* (ed. 7) III. 308 Keatite has been synthesized by heating commercial dried silica..in water containing an alkali.

Keatsian (kī·tsiăn), *a.* and *sb.* [f. the name of the English poet John *Keats* (1795–1821) + -IAN.] **A.** *adj.* Of, pertaining to, or characteristic of Keats or his poetry. **B.** *sb.* A student or admirer of Keats or his poetry.

1845 T. WADE *Let.* 26 May in H. E. Rollins *Keats Circle* (1948) II. 119 A Keats-ian poem. **1891** *Athenæum* 23 May 667/3 A little manuscript book..of some interest to Keatsians. **1901** H. B. FORMAN in Keats *Compl. Works* III. 112 He [*sc.* Woodhouse] opens with a Keatsian enough punctuation of the first four lines. **1910** H. WALKER *Lit. Victorian Era* II. ii. 299 A Keatsian worship of beauty.. is his [*sc.* Tennyson's] characteristic. **1934** F. L. & P. LUCAS *From Olympus to Styx* vi. 69 In spite of its Keatsian name, Lamia has little romance or even history. **1968** *Guardian* 22 Mar. 9/3 The kind of detail, immensely rewarding to Keatsians, with which Mr Gittings's biography swarms, is well exemplified by his suggestion about the authorship of the essay for 'The Indicator' which Leigh Hunt was composing extempore..while Keats..lay listening on a sofa. **1970** *Daily Tel.* 19 Sept. 9/6 The day.. beginning as a mist wherein the Keatsian 'mellow fruitfulness' lay wrapped in its own swaddling clothes.

So **Keatsia·na** (see ANA *suff.*, *-IANA).

1818 R. WOODHOUSE *Let.* Nov. in H. E. Rollins *Keats Circle* (1948) I. 66, I shod like to add that to my collection of 'Keatsiana'. **1898** [see *-IANA]. **1962** *Daily Tel.* 21 Mar. 17/5 (*heading*) Keatsiana... I have been commissioned to write a book on Keats [etc.].

kebab, keebaub, khubab, kibab, kibaub, qabab, varr. CABOB. (The usual form is *kebab.*) Pieces of meat roasted on a skewer (see also quot. 1970). Cf. *SHISH KEBAB.

1813 J. FORBES *Oriental Mem.* II. xvi. 12 A superb dinner of fifty covers, cooked in the Mogul taste..pilaurs, keb-abs, curries, and other savoury dishes. **1839** C. M. KIRKLAND *New Home* xiv. 87 She would have made out nobly on kibaubs. *a* **1861** T. WINTHROP *John Brent* (1883) xii. 105 Mr. Clitheroe was like a lamb whom the shepherd intends first to shear close..and at last to cut up into keebaubs. **1902** *Daily Chron.* 19 Nov. 8/4, I leave these, and press on past rows of animals, heaps of fodder, dealers and kibab sellers and market women. **1932** *Times Lit. Suppl.* 10 Nov. 836/4 A learned disquisition on skewer-cooking, of Eastern origin, leading to various kinds of *kebabs*. **1954** *Gd. Housek. Cookery Bk.* 450/2 The Muslims who gave the dish its name (which can also appear in such forms as khubab, kibbab and qabab) used their swords to impale the food. **1955** G. BAND *Road to Rakaposhi* viii. 100 The evening meal was preceded by a *kebab*. Beef liver and kidney sliced in small chunks was skewered on to long thin sticks and roasted over an open fire. **1963** R. CARRIER *Great Dishes of World* 139 If the weather is too cool for outdoor cookery, *kebabs* can be grilled indoors with ease. **1970** SIMON & HOWE *Dict. Gastron.* 234/1 Cubes of vegetables are also called kebabs; there are kebab ragoûts...There are also fish kebabs. **1973** *Times* 9 Nov. 14/4, I then bought some kebab skewers. **1974** *Times* 4 May 11/6 The Open Space in Tottenham Court Road..is within easy reach of..the kebab houses around Charlotte Street. The least frantic at lunchtime seem to be the Cypriana Kebab House..and the Venus Kebab House.

kebaya, var. KABAYA.

The spelling *kebaya* is now usual.

1909 R. O. WINSTEDT *Papers on Malay Subjects: Life & Customs* II. 40 The long, shapeless *kĕbaya*..[is] now universally worn by women. **1939** A. KEITH *Land below Wind* vi. 92 The *kebaya*, a short Malay blouse, was purchased, and Kuta..fastened it with one insecure brooch. **1958** H. FORSTER *Flowering Lotus* ii. 25 My eye was often disappointed by chromatic discords between the ladies' skirts and their *kebayas*, long-sleeved jackets for which they favoured brightly variegated flower patterns. **1963** *N.Z. Woman's Weekly* 17 June 21/2 For sheer glamour, Nancy's sarong kebaya (the Malayan dress) stole the day. This was a closely fitting skirt in a royal blue with a pleated panel in the front worn with an overblouse of lace in a paler shade of blue. **1966** D. FORBES *Heart of Malaya* iv. 52 He dressed her up in beautiful clothes—sometimes cheongsams, sometimes saris, sometimes sarong kebayas. **1972** *Guardian* 13 Jan. 5/3 Our beautiful M[alaysia] S[ingapore] A[irlines] hostesses in their sarong kebayas are dedicated to superb in-flight service.

kebla(h, kebleh, varr. KIBLAH (in Dict. and Suppl.).

Kechua, var. *QUECHUA.

keck-handed *a.*, var. *CACK-HANDED *a.*

Ked (ked), *sb.*[2] orig. *U.S.* [See quot. 1967.] Proprietary name of a soft-soled canvas shoe.

1917 *Trade Marks Jrnl.* 14 Nov. 1092 Keds...Rubber, Leather, and Fabric Footwear. United States Rubber Company..New York,..Manufacturers of Rubber Goods. **1961** *Encounter* Apr. 23/2, I am wearing Keds, and feel light on the foam rubber soles. **1966** B. H. DEAL *Fancy's Knell* (1967) i. 15 He found the Ked. He picked it up..reluctant to think beyond the small canvas shoe in his hand. **1967** L. J. HEALEY in R. L. Cohen *Footwear Industry* x. 93 We [*sc.* U.S. Rubber Co.] wanted to call it Peds, but..it came too close to..other brand names. So we batted it around for awhile and decided on the hardest-sounding letter in the alphabet, K, and called it Keds, that was in 1916. **1968** H. C. RAE *Few Small Bones* II. viii. 138 He dug a hole in the junk on the couch, tossing a track-suit and a pair of Keds..on to the floor.

kedgeree. Add: Also *transf.* and *fig.*

1909 in WEBSTER. **1928** R. CAMPBELL *Wayzgoose* ii. 48 English, art, music, vegetables, and song, All to the same consistency you mash. Your life—a Kedgeree! Your mind—a hash! **1938** *Archit. Rev.* LXXXIII. 3/1 Winstanley's Eddystone was a remarkable kedgeree of bits and pieces—its builder had previously been known chiefly for some remarkable waterworks in Hyde Park. **1968** R. WEST *Sk. Vietnam* ii. 65 Furniture, clothes, shrines.. were heaped on to the lorry in a gigantic kedgeree.

keebaub: see *KEBAB.

keel, *sb.*[1] Add: **3. b.** A longitudinal member or assembly of members running the length of a rigid or semi-rigid airship at the bottom of the envelope.

In quot. 1877, and perh. also 1888, *keel* has not acquired this specific sense.

[**1877** *Design & Work* 1 Dec. 602/2, I arrived at this principle [of propelling the air boat]:..that though the car must contain the weight of passengers, cargo, and machinery, even to do duty as the weighted keel or plummet, yet it is only in that character it can serve the navigation in aid of propulsion.] **1888** *Peel City Guardian* 22 Sept. 3/3 Connecting the balloon with the arrow-like rod beneath is a keel of the same material as that composing the body of the balloon. **1893** *Eng. Illustr. Mag.* July 746/2 From the outer gallery the [airship] *Attila* looks as if her bottom was gently curved, terminating in the customary orthodox keel... But three feet below the level at which we stand lies a flat projecting bottom. **1910** A. WILLIAMS *Engin. Wonders of World* III. 48/2 The distribution of the load over the gas holder in such a way as not to strain any part unduly is, in the case of a Zeppelin airship, simplified by the employment of a girder keel. **1929** E. F. SPANNER *About Airships* iii. 28 Throughout the length of the keel there is a more or less uniform lift, varying according to the size of the gasbags. **1955** *Oxford Jun. Encycl.* IV. 20/2 The semi-rigid type, in which a long rigid keel supports the passenger and engine-cars, has been developed mainly by the Italians. *Ibid.*, Keels running through the hull [of a rigid airship] add strength and provide access to various parts of the ship. **1974** J. B. COLLIER *Airship* 12/1 The distinction between these two types [*sc.* non-rigid and semi-rigid airships] is sometimes hard to draw, but 'semi-rigid' implies..that the airship in question has a rigid keel.

† **c.** In some early aeroplanes and kites, a vertical fin fixed towards the rear of the fuselage and parallel to it, and intended to give lateral stability. *Obs.*

1894 O. CHANUTE *Progress in Flying Machines* 184 Very good results with central keels have been obtained by M. Boynton with his various forms of 'Fin' kites. *Ibid.* 185 Keels have been frequently proposed for aeroplanes, in which they will produce less resistance to forward motion than obtains with other arrangements. **1907** C. DIENSTBACH in *Navigating the Air* (Aero Club Amer.) p. xxxix, A multiplicity of 'keels', which might be called 'barbarian' if compared to American moderation. **1910** R. W. A. BREWER *Art of Aviation* xvii. 230 The Antoinette machine has a smaller keel, but some of the monoplanes dispense with this surface altogether. **1911** G. C. LOENING *Monoplanes & Biplanes* xii. 255 In the old Voisin type use was made of several vertical keels, partitions, placed not only at the rear, but also between the main surfaces themselves. **1919** H. SHAW *Text-bk. Aeronaut.* vii. 97 The dihedral planes give rise to a greater righting moment, when tilted at a similar angle, than the keel, and so are more efficient.

d. A longitudinal member running along the centre of the bottom of the hull of a flying boat (or the float of a seaplane), or the fuselage of a landplane from one end to the other.

1920 *Flight* 23 Sept. 1019/2 The hull lines are somewhat unusual, the downward sweep of keel and chines in front of the rear step being rather more pronounced than usual. **1930** P. H. SUMNER *Marine Aircraft* vi. 164 The type of keel used in the flexible circular flying boat hull is that which is built up as a light girder, comprising a keel proper, keelson and rider piece. The keel proper..is rabbeted on its upper face and receives the vertical keelson. **1933** W. MUNRO *Marine Aircraft Design* iv. 58 The detail design of frames, bulkheads, stringers, keel, etc., is very definitely affected by the heat treatment and anodic treatment of the material. **1968** *Flight International* 12 Dec. 983/1 Because of the four-leg main undercarriage [of the Boeing 747]..a centre-line keel links the lower part of the forward and rear fuselage. **1969** *Jane's 100 Significant Aircraft* 81/1 Four-engined commercial flying-boat... Structure composed of deep keel, widely spaced transverse frames and heavy stringers.

4. In dogs, the sternum or breast-bone, esp. in the dachshund and other breeds in which it is a prominent feature.

1950 C. L. B. HUBBARD *Dachshund Handbk.* iv. 50 Chest oval, well let down between the forelegs, with the deepest point of the keel level with the wrist joints. **1962** R. H. SMYTHE *Anat. Dog Breeding* i. 19 Dachshunds possess an over-lengthy body and an over-developed sternum, the 'keel'. **1971** F. HAMILTON *World Encycl. Dogs* 344 The Standards [for dachshunds] require that the height at the shoulder should be half the length of the body..the lowest point of the keel being on a level with the wrist joint.

6. b. [Norw. *kjøl*.] The spinal ridge of mountains stretching down the centre of Norway.

1856 LD. DUFFERIN *Lett. High Latitudes* (1857) xii. 381 The back-bone, or *keel*, as the sea-faring population soon learnt to call the flat snow-capped ridge that runs down the centre of Norway. **1968** G. JONES *Hist. Vikings* II. i. 59 The upturned keel of mountains running south from Finnmark almost to Stavanger and Värmland. *Ibid.* 69 The mountain wildernesses of the Keel.

keel-boat. Add: **b.** *U.S.* (Earlier and later examples.)

1786 in *Mag. Amer. Hist.* (1877) I. 176 Great numbers of Kentucke and keel boats passing every day; some to the Falls, others to Post Vincent—Illinois Country. **1874** E. EGGLESTON *Circuit Rider* xxvii. 266 A stranger.. reported that he had seen such a man on a keel-boat. **1949** *Indiana Mag. of Hist.* June 147 The first keelboat on the St. Joseph River, the 'Fair Play', arrived at South Bend July 1, 1832.

Hence **keel-boater, -boatman.**

1839 *Knickerbocker* XIII. 344 A..keel-boatman..saw a steam-boat gallantly paddling up against the centre current of that 'Father of Rivers'. **1883** 'MARK TWAIN' *Life on Mississippi* iii. 41 The keelboatman became a deck hand, or a mate. **1912** I. S. COBB *Back Home* 296 [He was] the roughest of them all..rougher even than the keel-boaters and the trappers. **1941** F. L. DORSEY *Master of Mississippi* 129 Keelboatmen and 'broadhorn' pushers eyed it with suspicion. **1949** B. A. BOTKIN *Treas. S. Folklore* II. ii. 191 Besides madmen and devils the Mississippi River also bred giants—the keelboatmen whose acknowledged king was Mike Fink.

keeled, *a.* Add: **c. keeled scale,** in certain reptiles, a scale with a central ridge.

1870 A. R. WALLACE *Contrib. Theory Nat. Selection* iii. 99 The large caterpillar..startled him by its resemblance to a small snake... It resembled a poisonous viper, not a harmless species of snake, as was proved by the imitation of keeled scales on the crown produced by the recumbent feet, as the caterpillar threw itself backward! **1907** R. L. DITMARS *Reptile Bk.* xviii. 160 With most of the species [of plated lizard], the scales of the middle portion of the back are strongly keeled. **1970** *New Yorker* 19 Sept. 30/3 It [*sc.* DeKay's snake, *Storeria dekayi*] has keeled scales—a keeled scale is one with a ridge down its middle—which give it a smooth, unshiny appearance.

d. keeled scraper (F. *grattoir caréné*) Archæol., a form of prehistoric flint-tool.

1911 W. J. SOLLAS *Anc. Hunters* viii. 218 Carefully flaked like the snout of the keeled scraper. **1921** M. C. BURKITT *Prehistory* iv. 75 *Keeled scrapers.* This tool..is very common in Middle Aurignacian times. It has a flat under surface, from which the flakes on the upper surface are struck off in a fan-shaped manner. **1927** PEAKE & FLEURE *Hunters & Artists* iv. 46 Here [*sc.* at La Ferrassie etc.] we find keeled scrapers, of a massive form but carelessly made, and more rarely gravers trimmed obliquely. **1968** *Encycl. Brit.* IX. 448/1 Core scrapers were made on small blocks or were actual cores reutilized as scrapers. Keeled scrapers present a systematic and symmetric removal of tiny blades to form a thick, fluted scraper extremity.

keeler[2]. **1.** (Later examples.)

1854 *Househ. Words* 2 Sept. 54/2 They are pressed into keelers—tubs made of substantial oak, lessening in size to suit the lessening bulk of the cheese as it dries. **1895** *Montgomery Ward Catal.* 578/3 Indurated Wood Fibre Ware... Keelers..Diam. 20 in. **1909** E. I. DENNY *Blazing the Way* III. i. 393 A distracted grey-haired lum-e-i, his mother, came to our house to beg for a keeler of water.

keelie. 2. (Later examples.)

1909 *Athenæum* 1 May 528/2 Most people will..appreciate the sterling..character..of the Glasgow 'keelie' of twelve. **1937** *Times Lit. Suppl.* 13 Nov. 870/3 Wondering ..whether the rascally little Glasgow 'keelie'..will succeed in betraying both sides for pay. **1962** 'H. CALVIN' *System* ii. 31 A Glasgow keelie who had grown up in a two-roomed slum. **1969** I. & P. OPIE *Children's Games* iv. 155 'It has to be played in the dark,' remarks a keelie. **1973** *Times* 18 May (Glasgow Suppl.) p. iv/2 The archetypal Glasgow keelie is a gallus man.

Keemun (kī·mʊn). Also **Kee-Moon, Kee Mun, Kee-mun.** The name of a district in China used to describe a black tea grown there. Also *attrib.*

1892 J. M. WALSH *Tea* v. 85 Kee-mun..is another of the newest descriptions of China Congou teas... The dried leaf varies considerably in style and appearance, some lots having an evenly-curled and handsome leaf, while others again are brownish and irregular. **1907** *Yesterday's Shopping* (1969) 1 Finest China, Plain (Keemun) — lb. 3/2. **1935** W. STEVENS *Let.* 20 Dec. (1967) 303 This morning for breakfast I had some of the best Kee-Moon, and found it to be a delightful tea. **1958** *Catal. County Stores* (Taunton) June 18 A Blend of Pure China Keemun and Finest Formosan Oolong Teas. **1967** V. C. CLINTON-BADDELEY *Death's Bright Dart* 64 Neither Lapsang, nor Kee Mun, nor Oolong, nor Jasmine..and certainly not Earl Grey. He brewed a pot of Darjeeling.

keen, *a.* Add: **3. b.** Of prices: competitive. Cf. quot. 1862 in Dict., sense 6, and *KEENLY *adv.* 6.

1964 A. FIBER *Independent Retailer* v. 55 (*heading*) Mail order has grown rapidly in recent years... As warehouses and offices are situated in low-rent areas and there is no need of a sales staff, overheads are low. Prices, therefore, are often very keen. **1975** *Evening Herald* (Dublin) 8 May 13/3 (Advt.), Dennis Rent a Car. Keenest rates. New Street, Dublin 8.

4. d. Jolly good, very nice, splendid. *colloq.* (orig. *U.S.*).

1914 'HIGH JINKS, JR.' *Choice Slang* 14 *Keen*, excellent... 'A keen day.' 'A keen time.' **1925** *College Humor* Aug. 76/1 *Keen*, fine, attractive, splendid. **1940** *New Yorker* 16 Nov. 19/3 'My mother's going to buy me four new dresses.'..'That's keen.' **1948** *Hearst's International* Dec. 162/3 'What are you studying at school?' 'Journalism.' 'That sounds keen,' said Sally. **1964** *Punch* 8 July 38/1 It's fab, Henchcliffe, it's gear, moody, groovy, keen and withitly gogo. **1968** N. FLEMING *Counter Paradise* vi. 87 He slowed to a standstill beside the second flag. 'Keen,' he said.

6. b. *keen on* (earlier example). Also, sweet on, in love with.

1889 E. DOWSON *Let.* 15 May (1967) 78 Is there anything you are particularly keen on? **1936** R. LEHMANN *Weather in Streets* IV. iii. 418 She's attractive, intelligent, amusing—and obviously pretty keen on me, my dear. **1943** C. BAX *Time with Gift of Tears* xxxix. 226 Maxine urged Guinivere to take Buster Graham more seriously. 'He's frightfully keen,' she said, 'on *you*.'

C. a. *keen-bladed* (example), *-eared* (example), *-eyed* (later example), *-nosed* (later example), *-sighted* (example).

1906 *Macm. Mag.* Apr. 457 An escort of sturdy little Japanese armed with service rifles and the keen-bladed *katana*. **1908** E. WHARTON *Hermit* iv. 25 She was a light sleeper, and keen-eared. **1921** Keen-eyed [see *firm-lipped*]. **1952** C. DAY LEWIS tr. *Virgil's Aeneid* IV. 76 Massylian riders galloped behind a keen-nosed pack. **1862** BAGEHOT in *National Rev.* Jan. 214 If you place the most keen-sighted lady in the midst of the pure futilities..of an aristocracy, she will sink to the level of those elements.

Keene (kīn). [Name of Richard Wynn *Keene*, who patented the plaster in England in 1838.] *Keene's cement*: a plaster which sets to a very hard white finish and consists of gypsum that contains added alum (or another salt) and has been thoroughly calcined at a high temperature.

1869 J. RUST *Brit. Pat. 621* 2, I would prepare a slab of the required size in cement, by preference Keene's cement. **1917** E. A. DONCASTER in G. Martin *Industr. & Manuf. Chem.: Inorg.* II. lix. 117 Keene's cement is now the general name for a number of different plasters prepared by various manufacturers, the original patent having expired. **1947** J. C. RICH *Materials & Methods Sculpture* iv. 60 Dry, powdered mineral colors can be added to Keene's cement, which is occasionally used sculpturally as a casting material.

keener[2] (kī·nəɹ). *U.S.* [f. KEEN *a.* + -ER[1].] One who drives a hard bargain; also, a person or thing in some way superior.

1839 [see *FIX *sb.* 1]. **1860** BARTLETT *Dict. Amer.* (ed. 3), *Keener*, a very shrewd person, one sharp at a bargain, what in England would be called 'a keen hand'. Western. **1872** SCHELE DE VERE *Americanisms* 496 *Keener*, a noun made from the adjective, is a Western term for a sharp man. 'I tell you he is a keener, you can't get on his blind side.' **1942** BERREY & VAN DEN BARK *Amer. Thes. Slang* § 436/2 *Cheat*, keener. § 461/18 *Swindler*, keener. § 542/22 *Bargainer*, keener. § 743/2 *Cardsharp*, keener.

keenly, *adv.* Add: **6.** *Comm.* At a keen price, cheaply.

1928 *Daily Express* 28 Aug. 7 With advantages like this we can quote more keenly.

keeno, var. KENO (in Dict. and Suppl.).

keep, *v.* Add: **16. d.** *to keep wicket*: see WICKET 3. Also *absol.*, to act as wicket-keeper.

1862 *Baily's Monthly Mag.* Aug. 85 The Surrey people ..selecting..a John Walker to keep. **1920** P. F. WARNER *Cricket Reminisc.* 161 Lockyer 'kept' for the Players on and off between 1854 and 1866. **1931** *N. & Q.* 14 Feb. 121/2 Alfred [Lyttelton], of course, 'kept' for England. **1959** *Times* 29 June 11/4 One of Somerset's clerical wearers of the gloves..who, after 'keeping' to W.G...recorded that not a single ball had passed the bat.

29. e. Colloq. phr. *you* (etc.) *can keep* (something): it arouses no desire, envy, or interest in me; I am not interested in (it), I do not like (it).

1956 J. POPPLEWELL in *Plays of Year 1955* XIII. 335 *Robert.* My hobby's writing plays. *Tom.* You can keep it. **1962** M. DRABBLE *Summer Bird-Cage* i. 8 The reviews ..talk about his delicate perception and keen wit, but for me they can keep them. **1967** R. WILKINSON *Pressure Men* viii. 72, I felt better here. They could keep London. **1971** *Guardian* 11 Dec. 5/1 They're a miserable lot of sods. If that is an example of the spirit of the people of Windsor, they can keep it. **1973** *Ibid.* 12 Apr. 13/3 It makes me a bit sick actually and they can keep their mag as far as I am concerned.

35. (U.S. examples of *to keep school.*)

1847 *Knickerbocker* XXX. 511 A girl whose education does not qualify her for 'keeping school'. **1849** E. CHAMBERLAIN *Indiana Gazetteer* (ed. 3) 196 There are in the County..school houses in which schools are kept, a portion of the year, in most of the school districts. **1867** 'T. LACKLAND' *Homespun* II. 264 Mr. John Porringer.. 'kept' this school, and was in the way of keeping it so long as he lived and liked.

38. b. Of a school: to be held. *U.S.*

1845 *Knickerbocker* XXVI. 277 One afternoon, when 'school didn't keep', some one got into the house. **1867** 'T. LACKLAND' *Homespun* I. 123 The District School has not 'kept' since the week began. **1908** M. E. FREEMAN *Shoulders of Atlas* 68 School ain't going to keep today.

44. b. *to keep oneself to oneself* (examples).

1748 RICHARDSON *Clarissa* IV. 27, I was resolved to keep myself to myself till I knew the issue of it. **1846** *Swell's Night Guide* 45 The divil a rap but that had bin her own, if she'd bin after keeping hersilf to hersilf. **1848** J. H. NEWMAN *Loss & Gain* III. ix. 374 What might I have done better than keep myself to myself, go by my best reason, consult the friends whom I happened to find around me, as I have done, and wait in patience till I was sure of my convictions? **1905** H. G. WELLS *Kipps* I. i. 7

They 'kept themselves *to* themselves', according to the English ideal. **1960** 'H. Carmichael' *Seeds of Hate* iv. 37 My husband and I like to keep ourselves to ourselves. We haven't got many friends. **1960** D. Lessing *In Pursuit of English* iv. 158 She keeps herself to herself so much. **1973** J. Porter *It's Murder with Dover* ii. 17 Miss Marsh has always been one for keeping herself to herself.

48. a. *spec.* To retain (food, etc.) in one's stomach, without vomiting.

1955 'A. Gilbert' *Is she Dead Too?* vi. 119 Think you could keep some hot tea down? Well, have a try. **1968** 'S. Woods' *Past Praying For* ii. 71 Nothing had been given to Oliver without Dr. Noyes's consent; and, anyway, he couldn't keep anything down. **1969** A. E. Lindop *Sight Unseen* xxix. 246 He's best with his Eno's if I can get him to keep it down. **1973** 'A. York' *Captivator* iv. 62 'Aren't you going to eat?..' 'I don't think I could keep it down.'

50. c. *trans.* To avoid or stay away from; not to use; also as *attrib. phr.*; *keep off the grass*: see *GRASS *sb.*[1] 9.

1949 M. Mead *Male & Female* ii. 42 Tchamwole.. placed a keep-off sign on the coconut-palm-trees. **1968** *Listener* 12 Dec. 790/3 Girls at Amman University have been instructed..to keep off heavy make-up.

57. f. Esp. in phr. *keep it up*; *spec.* to prolong a party, drinking-spree, etc.; to 'live it up'. (Later examples.)

1752 J. Millward *Let.* in M. M. Verney *Verney Lett.* (1930) II. ii. xxxiv. 250 When they [*sc.* the Welsh] get in liquor they are very troublesome and noisy. They kept it up all night. **1788** Grose *Dict. Vulgar T.* (ed. 2), *To keep it up*, to prolong a debauch. We kept it up finely last night; metaphor drawn from the game at shuttlecock. **1801** C. Keith *Har'st Rig & Farmer's Ha'* (ed. 2) 62 Clear-blooded health..flees awa' frae *keeping 't up*, and midnight riot. **1810** M. Dwight *Journey to Ohio* (1912) 16 The men dress much better—they put on their best cloaths on sunday,..& 'keep it up' as they call it. **1837** Dickens *Pickw.* lii. 565 We were keeping it up pretty tolerably at the Stump last night, and I'm rather out of sorts this morning. **1874** L. Troubridge *Life amongst Troubridges* (1966) 76 There were forty-six people and we kept it up till one... I had several good valses. **1958** A. Huxley *Let.* 11 Jan. (1969) 842 Thank you for your long and very interesting letter—written, too, in the most wonderfully black ink... Keep it up!

j. Esp. in phr. *to keep up* (often *keeping up*) *with the Joneses* (or *Jones's*): to strive not to be outdone by one's neighbours; to emulate one's neighbours. Also *transf.* orig. *U.S.*

1913 A. R. Momand in *Globe* (N.Y.) 1 Apr. 16/3 (*Comic-strip title*) Keeping up with the Joneses—by Pop. **1926** *Amer. Speech* I. 281 Today most of us live in automobilia, where the automocracy is everlastingly trying to 'keep up with the Joneses'. **1927** Chase & Schlink *Your Money's Worth* i. 7 Certain things we buy.. to keep up with the Joneses, or happily, to surpass the Joneses. **1933** E. Weekley in *Trans. Philol. Soc.* 94 This tendency to personify by the use of a familiar name is due to the same psychology which describes the social ambitions of the suburbs as 'keeping up with the Joneses'. **1952** F. P. Keyes *Larry Vincent* (1953) xxi. 284 He could not be thankful enough that he did not have a nagging wife, one who insisted on making a show, on 'keeping up with the Joneses', as people were beginning to say. **1957** *Observer* 25 Aug. 7/3 Britain.., always wanting to keep up with the Joneses of the richer South, hankered all the time after white bread only and achieved it one hundred per cent. by the mid-nineteenth century. **1958** *Times* 8 Nov. 7/2 Keeping up atomically with the Joneses is precisely what the talks were supposed to prevent. **1963** [see *DOOR-STEP c]. **1970** *Times* 25 May 7/4 We like to keep up with the Joneses and are therefore well disposed to the new definition of democracy. **1971** *Times Lit. Suppl.* 1393/3 The lesser funerals, of Pooters with Joneses to keep up with, increased in cost, display and competitiveness.

l. To continue to maintain a friendship or acquaintance; to keep in touch. (Cf. 57 f.)

1903 C. Coleridge *C. M. Yonge* iv. 127 She did not seem to be able to keep in personal touch with them... She could not, as we say, 'keep up' with them. **1916** E. V. Lucas *Vermilion Box* xlii. 45, I heard this morning of the death..of two of my oldest friends—Jack Cazalet, who was at school with me, and Sandford Thrale, whom I knew at Oxford. Both went straight into the army, but we had kept up. **1947** 'N. Shute' *Chequer Board* 205 We were all in it together then. We ought to have kept up. **1971** 'L. Marshall' *Murder's just for Cops* xviii. 125 We always kept up—even after I got married. **1971** 'D. Shannon' *Ringer* (1972) i. 20 Mrs. Sneed had known Carolyn..before she got married, five years back, and they had 'kept up'.

58. keep-fit *a.*, denoting exercises, etc., designed to keep people fit and healthy; (occas.) a person who does such exercises; also *ellipt.* as *sb.*; **keep-left** *a.*, designating a sign, etc., directing traffic to the left of the road; **keep-out** *a.*, designating a sign that prohibits entry.

1938 M. Carter *Living Soul in Holloway* vi. 77 Gardening comes into their day's programme and 'keep fit' exercises. **1939** 'N. Blake' *Smiler with Knife* v. 88 A healthy, bouncing, Keep-Fit sort of girl. **1961** J. Stroud *Touch & Go* xii. 119 A Girls' Keep Fit class was in session. **1965** W. Lamb *Posture & Gesture* ii. 31 There could be a revolution in all physical behaviour pursuits,..including ..country dancing, ballet, and 'Keep Fit'. **1967** O. Norton *Now lying Dead* iii. 54 Monday he goes to his Keep Fit. Imagine him in his little black shorts! **1971** *Fremdsprachen* XV. 63 Women..going to 'Keep Fit' classes. **1974** H. R. F. Keating *Bats fly Up* vii. 78 The OSP's well-known mania for keep-fit. **1936** *Discovery* Nov. 359/1 Street lamps, traffic bollards, and 'keep left' signs are automatically lit. **1962** C. Watson *Hopjoy was Here* iv. 38 A pair of dogs..coupled on the road's crown and performed a six-legged waltz around a keep-left bollard. **1971** J. McClure *Steam Pig* v. 75 A deserted area surrounded by Keep Out signs. **1974** *Times* 9 May 6/5 To protect your garden a 'keep out' sign is not enough. You also need a tall fence.

keep, *sb.* Add: **6. c.** (Earlier and later examples.) Freq. in phr. *to earn one's keep* (also *fig.*).

1801 Jane Austen *Let.* 3 Jan. (1952) 101 The keep of two will be more than of one. **1815** M. Birkbeck *Notes Journey through France* (ed. 3) 21 M. Tessier hires the whole of the keep of this flock. He pays £62. 10s. sterling to the farmer for the sheep pasture... He buys Lucerne hay for four winter months..making the expense of keep £142. 10s. sterling. **1937** R. Macaulay *I would be Private* i. xv. 137 Now he can just earn his keep digging treasure on those cays. **1963** A. Ross *Australia 63* iv. 99 The four Test stars..whose appearance cost the Tasmanian authorities £A300, again individually and in bulk failed to earn their keep. **1971** *Country Life* 4 Nov. 1237/2 Under favourable growing conditions this will provide late autumn keep, really valuable spring feed, or both. **1972** *Accountant* 19 Oct. 497/3 'All assets must earn their keep,' declared Mr Shaw.

7. For *U.S. colloq.* read *colloq.* (orig. *U.S.*). Also in extended use: in deadly earnest. In *Cricket*, defensively, in order to remain at the wicket. (Add further examples.)

1861 *Ladies' Repository* Oct. 627/1 Pay him! Nothing. He and I played for 'keeps', and I was the best player and won all his. **1871** *Wright County Monitor* (Clarion, Iowa) 29 Nov., Winter has at last come 'for keeps'. **1893** S. R. Crockett *Stickit Minister* 79 She'll even set down the black bag to play for keeps wi' the boys at the bools. **1897** *National Police Gaz.* (U.S.) 26 May 3/1 He is in the business for 'keeps', as they say in America. **1905** *Westm. Gaz.* 19 Sept. 3/2 Any other batsman..would doubtless have played for 'keeps' and taken not the slightest risk. **1923** *Cricketer Ann. 1922–3* 90 To-day, the dominant feature of the game is the individual 'playing for keeps'. **1933** D. L. Sayers *Murder must Advertise* xv. 253 Ten to one 'e'll lose 'im for keeps, now. **1949** D. G. Smith *I capture Castle* iii. xii. 214 Maybe when I bring you back we shall find it's gone for keeps. **1970** G. E. Evans *Where Beards wag All* xix. 219 You played *for keeps* sometimes, in other words all the marbles you won became yours. **1972** D. Lees *Zodiac* 107 These bastards are playing for keeps. ..I'm in trouble. **1973** 'H. Howard' *Highway to Murder* ix. 108 Everybody belonged to the rat race where people played for keeps.

keepable, *a.* Add: Hence **keepabi·lity.**

1898 R. H. Wallace *Adulteration of Dairy Prod.* 12 The keepability was also tested. and Swedish butter proved to be on an average more keepable than butter from other countries. **1962** *Times* 3 July (Agric. Suppl.) p. vii/4 The keepability of these pig meat products.

keep-alive (kī·pǎləiv), *a. Electronics.* [f. *to keep alive* (Keep *v.* 24).] Applied to devices and phenomena in certain kinds of discharge tube which operate or occur continuously and serve to initiate an intermittent main discharge or facilitate its establishment. Also *ellipt.*, such a device or phenomenon.

1933 J. H. Morecroft *Electron Tubes* viii. 182 In large bulbs a 'keep-alive' circuit is used to maintain the ionization. **1947** A. E. Whitford in L. N. Ridenour *Radar Syst. Engin.* xi. 410 To insure rapid breakdown at the beginning of each pulse, a supply of ions in the gap is maintained by a continuous auxiliary discharge inside one of the cones. This requires an extra electrode, known as the 'keep-alive' electrode. **1947** Crowther & Whiddington *Science at War* i. 47 The final form was a cavity ..with a small pilot discharge or 'keep alive' to help the gas discharge to start. **1959** R. L. Shrader *Electronic Communication* xxix. 842 To make the TR tube more sensitive, a d-c keep-alive voltage is applied across it at all times. This voltage is not quite high enough to support ionization. **1965** Gewartowski & Watson *Princ. Electron Tubes* xv. 554 Tubes in which radioactive material has been placed for the purpose of obtaining short ionization times are said to have a radioactive keep-alive. *Ibid.*, In some tubes a low-current discharge between auxiliary electrodes is operated continuously as a keep-alive mechanism.

keeper, *sb.* Add: **1. f.** *Cricket.* A wicket-keeper.

1744 *Laws* [of Cricket] in *New Dict. Arts & Sci.* (1755) IV. 3459/2 When the ball has been in hand by one of the keepers or stoppers. **1868** J. Lillywhite *Cricketers' Compan.* 49 The best 'keeper' who ever stood behind a wicket. **1926** H. Strudwick *25 Yrs. behind Stumps* 244 There were very few, if any, better keepers than the Notts man. **1927** [see *AUNT 4 b]. **1975** *Cricketer* May 9/2 A tall 'keeper's rise from his crouch is less rapid than a smaller man's.

g. *Football.* A goal-keeper.

1957 J. Milburn *Golden Goals* 140 (*caption*) Milburn rates Ditchburn among the greatest 'keepers he has ever faced. **1974** *Oxf. Mail* 21 Aug. 16 (*caption*) Bicester's Phillip Pratt (10) heads the ball past Thame keeper Micky Taylor for his second goal.

4. (Later examples.)

c **1810** W. Hickey *Mem.* (1960) xviii. 291 He at that time was the professed keeper of Mrs. Cuyler, a great jack whore, without pretensions to manners. **1846** *Swell's Night Guide* 83 Keepers are the sinews of your trade.

6. d. A simple ring worn in the ears to keep a pierced hole open.

1960 *Woman's Realm* 2 Apr. 69/3 Pure gold keeper rings to keep the ear-piercing open, ready for the first real earrings. **1968** K. O'Hara *Bird-Cage* vii. 55, 1 pair gold keeper ear-rings.

keeper (kī·pəɹ), *v.* [f. the sb. or as a back-formation f. Keepering.] *trans.* To look after as a gamekeeper. So **kee·pered** *ppl. a.*

1921 *Chambers's Jrnl.* Sept. 388 An estate well-preserved and well-keepered. **1958** *Times* 13 Sept. 9/3 The full benefits of hand-rearing can be enjoyed only on ground which is adequately keepered. **1961** R. Jefferies *Evidence of Accused* i. 9 If the estate were keepered.. it would become a rattling good shoot. **1971** *Country Life* 23 Sept. 766/3 In recent years this chalk-stream water [*sc.* River Itchen] has been well keepered and only lightly fished by a maximum of three rods. **1972** *Times* 7 Aug. 22/3 (Advt.), Keepered partridge and pheasant shoot.

keepering. (Earlier and later examples.)

1861 *Baily's Monthly Mag.* Jan. 185 His keepering consisted..in an amiable crusade..against 'them darned rats'. **1963** P. MacTyre *Fish on Hook* iii. 48 Wynrame isn't much of a hand at the keepering. **1971** *Country Life* 12 Aug. 363/3 A shepherd..deplored the increase in the depredations of the fox, since, he said, 'keepering' had gone out of fashion.

keeping, *vbl. sb.* Add: **2. d.** *Cricket.* Wicket-keeping.

1868 in W. A. Bettesworth *Walkers of Southgate* (1900) 291 Stephenson's 'keeping' was also first-rate. **1920** P. F. Warner *Cricket Reminisc.* 156 His [*sc.* Blackham's] keeping to Mr. Spofforth with the 1878 Australian XI. was a revelation.

5. b. Delete † *Obs.* and add later examples.

1853 Mrs. Gaskell *Ruth* III. i. 29 She beguiled a young gentleman, who took her into keeping. **1932** J. M. S. Tompkins *Pop. Novel in England 1770–1800* v. 193 Women of the town flaunt at the races and are taken into keeping. **1964** *Listener* 12 Mar. 444/3 There is no stigma on 'keeping' or 'living', nor on illegitimacy.

keeping, *ppl. a.* Add: Esp. of fruit (cf. Keep *v.* 41).

1816 Jane Austen *Emma* II. ix. 187 There never was such a keeping apple any where as one of his trees. **1842** Hood *Let.* 12 Oct. in F. F. Broderip *Memorials Thomas Hood* (1860) II. iv. 140 Our gardener said they [*sc.* pears] were a *keeping* sort, and would be good at Christmas. **1963** *Times* 11 Feb. 13/5 The majority of pupils ate sandwiches and keeping-apples.

keepsake. b. (Earlier example.)

1839 Thackeray in *Corsair* (N.Y.) 26 Oct. 522/1 A book on Versailles with numerous engravings in the Keepsake fashion.

keertan, var. *KIRTAN.

keeshond (kē̆i·shǫnd). Also **-hound.** Pl. **-honden.** [Du.] A grey, long-coated dog, a variety of the spitz, of medium size, with a fox-like head, pointed ears, and tail curled over the back; originally a Dutch or German breed.

1926 *Westm. Gaz.* 10 Feb., Kesshonds [*sic*] will find many admirers on account of their showy wolf-coloured coats. Some have been exhibited recently as Dutch barge dogs. **1927** *Daily Express* 15 June 15 The Keeshounds, Dutch dogs,..were shown in this country for the first time. They are about the size of a Chow, grey black in colour, exceedingly strong. **1927** E. C. Ash *Dogs: their Hist. & Devel.* I. 159 The keeshond is the well-known Dutch dog, often seen on the barges. **1950** A. C. Smith *Dogs since 1900* 260 In 1926 the Kennel Club decided that ..all previously registered as Dutch Barge Dogs should be transferred to the Keeshond registers. **1971** F. Hamilton *World Encycl. Dogs* 596 Keeshonden were the dogs of the peasantry—living in villages and on farms as well as barges. *Ibid.* 598 The Keeshond's long coat requires special attention once a week with a stiff brush. **1972** *Country Life* 10 Feb. 328/3 Miss H. M. Loughrey..picked out a Dalmatian, a chow chow,..a keeshound.

keessel, var. *KISSEL.

keester, var. *KEISTER.

'keet (kīt). *Austral.* Colloquial shortened form of Lorikeet or Parakeet.

1936 A. Russell *Gone Nomad* x. 83 Snow-white cockatoos flashed in flocks across the stream, green 'keets screeched among the gums. **1959** S. H. Courtier *Death in Dream Time* iii. 27 That's where the 'keets come... They're a wonderful sight in the flame-trees..all green and gold.

Keewatin (kīwē̆i·tin). *Geol.* The name of a district in the Northwest Territories, Canada, used *attrib.* and *absol.* to denote the oldest division of the Archæan in North America and rocks representing it, found in the Canadian Shield region.

1886 A. C. Lawson in *Ann. Rep. Geol. Survey Canada 1885* I. 14cc, The most appropriate name for the series that suggests itself to me is 'Keewatin', the Indian name for the North-west, or the North-west wind, which has been applied to the district within which the rocks occur. *Ibid.* 19cc, The contact of the Laurentian gneiss and the Keewatin schists. **1925** *Bull. Geol. Soc. Amer.* XXXVI. 363 The Coutchiching beds pass down under the Keewatin. **1927** *Jrnl. Geol.* XXXV. 143 At present the general use of the term Keewatin in the United States and Canada is as the name of the oldest rock series of the region. *Ibid.*, The view that the Keewatin rocks are the oldest in Canada is moreover inconsistent with much recent geological work. **1970** Dorr & Eschman *Geol*

Michigan iv. 39/1 Nearly 3·5 billion years ago, during Keewatin time, streams from bordering highlands deposited sediments and lavas poured out on the surface of the earth in what is now the Upper Peninsula of Michigan. **1972** L. W. Mintz *Hist. Geol.* xiii. 388 Keewatin rocks, like all other very old sediments, appear to be oceanic in origin and consist chiefly of metamorphosed lavas and turbidites.

kef: see *kif.

‖ **keftedes** (kefte·ðīz), *sb. pl.* Also **keftedhes, keftethes, keph-.** [Gr. κεφτές, pl. κεφτέδες meat ball, f. Turk. *köfte*.] A Greek dish of small meat balls made with herbs and onions.

1912 E. Craies *Recipes from East & West* 82 Mix.. some grated Parmesan cheese, as it makes the keftedes much lighter. **1958** R. Liddell *Morea* ii. vii. 173 The pleasant young woman in charge of the children handed round *keftédhes* and hard-boiled eggs. **1966** *Observer* (Colour Suppl.) 2 Oct. 45/4 Keftethes..minced veal.. grated onion..breadcrumbs. **1970** *Times* 29 Apr. 18/4 You will get..keftedes (spiced meat balls).

Keftian (ke·ftiăn), *sb.* and *a.* Also **Keftiu** sing. and *coll.*; pl. **Caphtorim** (Heb. *Kaphtōrīm*). [Cf. *Caphtor*, Heb. *Kaphtōr*, name in O.T. for the place of origin of the Philistines.] **A.** *sb.* Name in Egyptian records of a people of the E. Mediterranean, identified by some authorities with the Cretans; a member of this people.

c **1000** Ælfric *Heptateuch* Gen. x. 14 Mesraim, Cames oþer sunu, gestrynde six suna; of þam comon þa Philistei & seo mægð Capturym. **1611** Bible *Gen.* x. 14 And Mizraim begat..Casluhim (out of whome came Philistiim) and Caphtorim. **1891** A. H. Sayce *Races Old Testament* iii. 53 The Caphtorim..were the natives of the coast-land Caphtor. **1903** H. R. Hall in *Ann. Brit. Sch. Athens 1901–1902* 164 The facial type of the Keftians..is definitely European. *Ibid.* 165 Apparently Müller regarded the Keftiu not as themselves genuine Mycenaeans, but as mere handers on of Mycenaean objects. **1913** R. A. S. Macalister *Philistines* i. 14 The Egyptians were brought into direct contact with the Keftians. **1931** *Times Lit. Suppl.* 13 Aug. 623/2 G. A. Wainwright in 'Keftiu: Crete or Cilicia?' publishes further evidence in support of his thesis that the Keftiuans of the Egyptian monuments are not Cretans..but Cilicians. **1961** C. F. Pfeiffer *Baker's Bible Atlas* (1962) iii. 41/2 The family of Mizraim had several branches: Ludim, Anamim, Lehabim,..and Caphtorim. **1967** H. E. L. Mellersh *Minoan Crete* v. 55 There can hardly be any doubt at all that the Keftiu were the Cretans.

B. *adj.* Belonging to or relating to this people or their language.

1903 H. R. Hall in *Ann. Brit. Sch. Athens 1901–1902* 175 A list of Keftian proper names on a writing-board and a list of words of the Keftian language on papyrus,..are the last records of the men of Keftiu. **1913** R. A. S. Macalister *Philistines* i. 13 It has been suggested that it might be a nominative suffix of the Keftian language. *Ibid.* iv. 115 The sign *a*, a man running, shows the simple waist-band which forms the sole body-covering of the Keftian envoys. **1929** J. Garstang *Hittite Empire* ii. 42 It was left to the Keftian traders to carry on commercial intercourse that brought to Egypt the wares of Crete and Mycenae.

keg, *sb.* Add: **1. d.** *spec.* A barrel of beer; beer. *Austral.* and *N.Z. slang.*

1945 E. G. Webber *Johnny Enzed in Middle East* 15/2, I thought it was the keg. **1957** 'N. Culotta' *They're a Weird Mob* (1958) viii. 110 We struggled with the kegs, and got them set up on the bench. **1959** M. Shadbolt *New Zealanders* 108 Wild proletarian parties, in slummy Freeman's Bay, where kegs flowed and fights flared. **1965** J. O'Grady *Aussie English* 16 Containers run from five-ounce glasses to eighteen-gallon kegs.

e. In full *keg ale, beer, bitter.* Ale, etc., from a keg (see quot. 1972).

1949 M. Weeks *Beer & Brewing in Amer.* 25 Keg (draught) beer is kept at low temperatures. **1961** *Brewers' Jrnl.* XCVII. 373/2 Mr. G. Dent drew attention to increased beer sales, and in particular a large increase in Keg beers. **1963** *Times* 12 Feb. 17/1 When demand for keg beer rose, they would seek to expand. **1967** C. Drummond *Death at Furlong Post* xii. 151 The brewery.. had rushed out twenty-four gallons of keg beer... 'The whole bleedin' world wants keg ale.' **1968** W. Garner *Deep, Deep Freeze* vi. 73 The Duke of York..stocked a good line in keg bitter. **1968** 'D. Rutherford' *Skin for Skin* ii. 18 Crispin ordered two pints of Keg and carried them to the dimmest corner of the Saloon. **1971** *Times* 12 June 14/5 The new drinkers who do like beer are willing to pay extra for keg. **1972** *Which?* Apr. 124/2 One way to think of 'keg' beer is as a 'bottled' beer, but in a five or 11 gallon sealed metal container. Keg is chilled, filtered and (usually) pasteurised beer which has had carbon dioxide added.

kegler (ke·glǝɹ, kē·glǝɹ). *N. Amer.* Also **keggler.** [G. *kegler* skittle-player.] One who plays tenpin bowling, skittles, ninepins, etc.

1932 *Lincoln* (Neb.) *State Jrnl.* 9 Mar., Floyd Olds.. began calling the pin topplers, keglers, and the folk in Cleveland began looking at him askance. **1943** Falcaro & Goodman *Bowling for All* vii. 28 The kegler who feels that he has a 300 game..will discover that every delivery gets tougher after that. **1956** *Wall St. Jrnl.* 22 Mar. 1/1 These sportsmen and women, known to each other as 'keglers', will spend about $250 million on their sport, 10 times as much as both major baseball leagues collected in a gate receipts last year. **1958** *Economist* 20 Dec. 1085/1 If the 'keggler' does not knock down all the pins with his two balls he is credited merely with the number of pins he does knock over. **1970** *Daily Colonist* (Victoria, B.C.) 5 Apr. 15/2 The Kokomo, Ind., kegler beat Dick Ritger, of Hartford, Wis., in the championship [bowling] match. **1974** *Plain Dealer* (Cleveland, Ohio) 27 Oct. 12-C/5 In match play, each kegler faces each other one time, with the winner of a contest receiving 30 bonus pins.

‖ **kehilla** (kǝhi·lă). Also **kehillah, kille.** Pl. **kehi(l)lot, kehilloth.** [ad. Heb. *qěhillāh* community.] The Jewish community in a town or village.

1882 tr. *L. Kompert's Scenes from Ghetto* 67 She grew up, became beautiful, and in all the *kille* people talked of nothing but Hendel, the daughter of Rebb Paltiel Wolf. **1892** I. Zangwill *Childr. Ghetto* I. 126 Every town which could muster the minimum of ten men for worship boasted its Kehillah. **1950** [see *Judenrat]. **1961** *Observer* 3 Dec. 10/6 The formal communities of Russian Jews, the *kehilot*, were abolished in 1919 and never restored. **1967** N. Cohn *Warrant for Genocide* vii. 163 The official New York Jewish community organization,.. under the name Kehilla (Yiddish for 'Kahal') was chiefly concerned with protecting and educating Jewish immigrants. **1971** *Jewish Communities of World* (Inst. Jewish Affairs) (ed. 3) 29 The Buenos Aires Community (*Kehillah*) is the largest. *Ibid.* 90 There are no organized local Communities (*Kehillot*) in France. **1973** *Jewish Chron.* 2 Feb. 7/2 We have no intention..of creating a separatist movement or a new *kehilla* or some political group.

kehoeite (kihōu·ǝit, ki·ho͵ǝit). *Min.* [f. the name of Henry *Kehoe*, who discovered it + -ite¹.] A hydrated hydroxide and phosphate of aluminium, zinc, and calcium, found as white, chalky, amorphous masses in South Dakota.

1893 W. P. Headden in *Amer. Jrnl. Sci.* CXLVI. 24, I propose the name Kehoeite as the name of this mineral, after Mr. Henry Kehoe, to whom I am indebted for the material and who was the first to observe its occurrence. **1964** *Mineral. Mag.* XXXIII. 799 The hardness of kehoeite cannot be determined because of its microcrystalline nature.

keister (kī·stǝɹ, kǝi·stǝɹ). *U.S. slang.* Also **keester, keyster.** [Etym. unknown.] **1. a.** A suitcase, satchel; a handbag; a burglar's tool-case; a salesman's sample-case, etc.

[**1881** *National Police Gaz.* (U.S.) 1 Oct. 10/1 Prominent among the small army of confidence operators in this city are: 'Grand Central Pete'..'The Guinea Pig'.. 'Keister Bob'.] **1882** G. W. Peck *Peck's Sunshine* 227 The boy took the knight's keister and went to the elevator. **1910** G. B. McCutcheon *Rose in Ring* 80 Ruby Noakes..was directing the contortionist in his efforts to construct a table out of three 'blue seats' and a couple of property trunks, or 'keesters', as they were called. **1926** *Flynn's* 16 Jan. 637/2 All this chatter 'bout keisters with false bottoms an' mushes is mostly pipe stuff an' hopchin. **1926** *Clues* Nov. 161/2 *Keyster*, handbag or suitcase. **1933** 'P. Cain' *Fast One* vi. 211 Hang on the front..until you see three big pig-skin keesters go in. **1935** Collier & Westrate *Reign Soapy Smith* i. 2 An open sample case of liberal dimensions..the typical 'keister' of the street hawker. **1935** *Jrnl. Abnormal Psychol.* XXX. iii. 363 *Keyster*, a suitcase. **1950** H. E. Goldin *Dict. Amer. Underworld Lingo* 114/2 Ditch that keister. It draws heat (attracts police attention).

b. A strong-box in a safe; a safe (see also quot. 1924).

1913 A. Stringer *Shadow* 36 He made a mental record of dips and yeggs and till-tappers and keister-crackers. **1921** P. & T. Casey in *Adventure* (U.S.) 18 July 22/2 They..breaks inter the keester o' the bank safes an' gits away with all the stored-up jack. **1924** G. C. Henderson *Keys to Crookdom* 409 *Keister*, bars on certain type of safe. A handbag that can be strapped and locked. **1931** *Amer. Speech* VII. 110 Can we use can-opener on this keister? **1950** H. E. Goldin *Dict. Amer. Underworld Lingo* 114/2 Easy on the soup (crude nitro-glycerine) with that keister or she'll jam.

2. The buttocks.

1931 *Amer. Speech* VI. 439 *Keister*, a satchel; also what one sits on. **1951** Wodehouse *Old Reliable* xi. 132 And then they'd leave me flat on my keister and go off and buy candy and orchids for the other girls. **1968** *McLean's Mag.* Dec. 1/1 His job at Christ the King was defined by Father Mooney as 'getting people off their keesters'. **1975** *New Yorker* 10 Mar. 90/2 Just put your keyster in the chair and shut your mouth.

Kekchi (ke·ktʃi), *sb.* and *a.* Also **Quecchi, Quekchi. A.** *sb.* Name of an ancient people belonging to the Maya Empire, the modern descendants of whom now live in Guatemala. Also, a member of this people (ancient or modern); their language. **B.** *adj.* Of or pertaining to the Kekchi or their language.

1823 J. Baily tr. *Juarros's Statistical & Commercial Hist. Guatemala* ii. vi. 198 No one of the kingdoms of the New World has so many different languages as Guatemala, the following 26 being peculiar to it, *viz.* Quiché.. Quecchi. **1888** *Encycl. Brit.* XXIV. 760/1 Poconchi Group ..*Quekchi*..Coban district, Guatemala. **1949** E. A. Nida *Morphol.* (ed. 2) ii. 6 In Kekchi, a Mayan language of Guatemala. **1960** R. C. Bell *Board & Table Games* I. ii. 89 This is another running-fight game played by the Kekchi Indians of Central America. **1964** E. A. Nida *Toward Sci. Transl.* iii. 46 In fact, at one time some Kekchis in Guatemala asked the missionary not to attempt to explain the 'truths of their faith', for if such matters could be explained and understood, they would then 'cease to be religion'.

Kekulé (ke·kiule). *Chem.* The name of Friedrich August *Kekulé* (1829–1896), German chemist, used *attrib.* and in the possessive with reference to a system of structural formulæ devised by him, the principal features of which are the quadrivalency of the carbon atom and the linking of carbon atoms to form chains, and esp. his conception of the benzene molecule as having a closed hexagonal ring of six carbon atoms with alternate double and single bonds between them (later extended to other conjugated cyclic carbon compounds).

1871 *Jrnl. Chem. Soc.* XXIV. 824 The author says that he acknowledges the value of Kekulé's ring formula. **1908** A. W. Stewart *Rec. Adv. Org. Chem.* i. 6 But as they actually existed in isomeric forms, the same was to be expected in benzene, if the Kekulé theory were correct. **1938** H. Gilman *Org. Chem.* I. ii. 57 A further, rather serious objection to the Kekulé formula arose from the difficulty of understanding why, if benzene contains three ordinary double bonds, it is so inferior to the ethylenic hydrocarbons in reactivity. **1951** I. L. Finar *Org. Chem.* I. xx. 408 The difficulty with the Kekulé formula is that it represents benzene with three double bonds, and the oscillation does not account for the difference in behaviour between these and olefinic bonds. *Ibid.* 409 The Kekulé structures contribute far more to resonance (about 80 per cent.) than do the Dewar structures (about 20 per cent.). **1961** L. F. & M. Fieser *Adv. Org. Chem.* i. 16 The Kekulé theory of structure performed valuable service for half a century before the nature of the Kekulé bond became understood. **1964** Cram & Hammond *Org. Chem.* (ed. 2) xxiii. 543 Two equivalent Kekulé structures may be drawn for this $C_{18}H_{18}$ hydrocarbon [*sc.* cyclo-octadecanonaene]. **1972** E. Clar *Aromatic Sextet* vi. 29 The VB theory assumes nine Kekulé structures for triphenylene which are supposed to contribute equally to the ground state.

kel: see *Kelly, kelly *sb.*² 2.

kelch (keltʃ). *slang.* Also **kelt, -tch, keltz.** [Etym. unknown.] A white person: only in depreciatory use.

1912 F. M. Hueffer *Panel* i. i. 14 'Do you mean to say that you haven't got a single book of James'?' 'Never heard the name,' the bookstall boy said. 'But there's plenty by Mrs. Kerr Howe.' 'That kelch!' Major Foster exclaimed. **1938** C. Himes *Black on Black* (1973) 173 Then he met a high-yellah gal, a three-quarter keltz, from down Harlem way. **1970** C. Major *Dict. Afro-Amer. Slang* 73 *Kelt, keltch*, white person; Negro passing for white.

‖ **kelebe** (ke·lĕbi). *Gr. Antiq.* [Gr.] (See quot. 1890.)

1858 S. Birch *Hist. Anc. Pott. & Porc.* I. ii. iv. 262 The Archaic *pyxis* or Apulian *stamnos*, the *kelebe*, or *crater*, with columnar handles, is seen for the first time. **1890** *Cent. Dict.*, *Kelebe*, in Greek Archæol., a large ovoid, wide-mouthed vase, with a broad flat rim and two handles connecting the rim and the body, and not extending above the rim. **1960** R. M. Cook *Greek Painted Pott.* 367 *Kelebe*, obsolete, a conventional name for a column krater.

K-electron: see *K 3 e.

kelep (kĕle·p). [Kekchi.] A Central American stinging ant, *Ectatomma tuberculatum*.

1904 W. M. Wheeler in *Science* 30 Sep. 439/1 There is little probability that the kelep can be successfully established in Texas. **1910** —— *Ants* i. 9 It [*sc.* United States Department of Agriculture] recently introduced a Guatemalan ant, the 'kelep' (*Ectatomma tuberculatum*) into Texas for the purpose of destroying the very injurious cotton-boll weevil. **1951** C. F. W. Muesebeck et al. *Hymenoptera of Amer. North of Mexico* 783 *Ectatomma.. tuberculatum...* This species, known as the kelep, was introduced into Texas in the early part of this century to combat the cotton boll weevil. It has apparently become extinct.

Kelim, var. *Kilim.

Kellaways (ke·lăwēiz). *Geol.* Also formerly **Kellaway, Kelloway(s).** The name of a village near Chippenham in Wiltshire, used *attrib.* to designate a group of clays and calcareous sandstones of Jurassic age lying below the Oxford clay and above the cornbrash, and found in a belt extending from Dorset to Yorkshire.

1813 J. Townsend *Character of Moses* I. vi. 103 Kelloway rock. The next calcareous stratum, first attracted our notice, at Kelloway Bridge. **1888** J. Prestwich *Geol.* II. xiv. 217 On the Continent the Kelloways Rock forms a division of almost equal importance with the Oxford Clay. **1913** *Q. Jrnl. Geol. Soc.* LXIX. 152 (*heading*) The 'Kelloway rock' of Scarborough. [*Note*] The appellation 'Kelloway' is here used for quotations from Leckenby [1859] or in reference to Yorkshire beds, and 'Kellaways' in relation to deposits in Wiltshire and elsewhere. **1933** W. J. Arkell *Jurassic Syst. Gt. Brit.* xii. 346 The thickest development of the Kellaways Rock exposed in the West of England was seen in a short cutting on the Midland and South-Western Junction Railway at South Cerney, near Cirencester. **1946** [see

*CALLOVIAN *a.*]. **1969** BENNISON & WRIGHT *Geol. Hist. Brit. Isles* xiii. 307 The sandy limestone with hard flaggy bands of the Upper Cornbrash has a fauna resembling that of the overlying Kellaways Beds.

‖**keller** (ke·lə̆ɹ). [G., = cellar.] A beer-cellar in Austria or Germany. Also *attrib.*

1927 *Sat. Rev. Lit.* 3 Dec. 382 Meetings of congenial colleagues in some Keller. **1968** *Guardian* 21 Sept. 10/2 The moonlit sleigh rides, and keller bars. **1969** A. GLYN *Dragon Variation* viii. 229 Drinking beer in a keller, singing German songs. **1969** *Guardian* 11 Oct. 10/5 Austria, with its..boisterous bars and kellers. **1973** *Daily Tel.* 3 Feb. 12/4 Ski-ing, they wear bright, crazy clothes; après-ski-ing, they whoop it up in the *kellerbars.*

Kellgren (ke·lgrĕn). The name of Henrik *Kellgren* (1837–1916), Swedish physician, used *attrib.* to denote a system of massage devised by him. Hence **Ke·llgrenite** *a.* and *sb.*, (one) that is a practitioner of this system.

1907 *Boston Med. & Surg. Jrnl.* CLVII. 493/1 In the Kellgren method, the fingers of the gymnast remain in contact with the skin, and thus they are enabled to really manipulate the parts beneath. **1918** G. B. SHAW in *Eng. Rev.* Jan. 14 Osteopathy, for instance, is, like Kellgren massage, a no-drug system. *Ibid.* 10 The Kellgrenites are not recognized by the Medical Gymnasts. *Ibid.*, Some time ago a Kellgrenite masseur..qualified himself for the British register. **1925** —— in *Times* 12 Nov. 10/2, I do not hold any brief for osteopathy, or Kellgren massage, or naturopathy or homœopathy. **1944** —— *Everybody's Pol. What's What?* xxiii. 205 A manipulative technique which, like Kellgren massage.., needed about two years training to acquire.

kellin, obs. var. *KHELLIN.

Kello·vian, *a. Geol. rare.* [ad. F. *kellovien* (A. d'Orbigny *Paléont. française. Terrains Jurassiques* (1842–9) I. 608), f. Kelloway(s), former name of *KELLAWAYS.] = *CALLOVIAN *a.*

1888 J. PRESTWICH *Geol.* II. i. 9 Kellovian Limestones and Marls.

Kelloway(s), varr. *KELLAWAYS.

Kelly, kelly (ke·li), *sb.*[2] [Prob. f. the name *Kelly*, a common Irish surname.] **1.** (With capital initial.) A type of pool (POOL *sb.*[3] 3) using fifteen balls (see quot. 1934). In full, *Kelly pool. U.S.*

1898 *Handbk. Rules of Billiards* (Brunswick-Balke-Collender Co.) (rev. ed.) 78 The game of Kelly pool is played with fifteen numbered balls, and one white ball not numbered. **1913** *Billiards Mag.* Oct. 25 (*caption*) A 'Nine' of billiard notables gathered from different states by Artist Carlson for a pictorial game at 'Kelly'. **1918** *Ibid.* Jan. 55/1 A new idea for the old game of Kelly. **1934** WEBSTER, *Kelly pool*, a variety of fifteen-ball pool in which each player draws a number and, while playing on the object balls in numerical order, aims to pocket the ball of the number corresponding to his own, thereby winning the game. **1948** MENJOU & MUSSELMAN *It took Nine Tailors* 29 The only sports I cared to indulge in personally were Kelly pool and bowling.

2. Rhyming slang for *belly*. Also *Derby* (or *Darby*) *kelly* or *kel.*

1906 E. DYSON *Fact'ry 'Ands* viii. 96 Er cold, proud man tumbles on his Darby Kel in the dirt. **1928** M. C. SHARPE *Chicago May* xxxi. 287/2 *Darby Kelly*, belly. **1942** T. RATTIGAN *Flare Path* II. ii. 138 Just that ride home. Cor, I still feel it down in the old darby kel. **1967** L. DEIGHTON *London Dossier* 40 The only places now making boiled beef available to your darby kellies, or bellies, are the Jewish salt-beef bars. **1970** A. DRAPER *Swansong for Rare Bird* vi. 41 My old kelly was rumbling and I fancied a pie and chips.

3. A man's hat; *spec.* a derby hat (cf. sense 2 above). *slang* (chiefly *U.S.*).

1915 *Recruiter's Bulletin* (U.S.) Dec. 33/2 Say, old top, when you go home tonight, Pull your old brown Kelly down real tight. **1922** *Collier's* 4 Mar. 8/2, I have got to wear a brass Kelly on my head which weighs at least ten pounds. **1927** E. HEMINGWAY in *Atlantic Monthly* July 11/1 John put his kelly down on the table. It was all wet. His coat was wet, too. **1948** LAIT & MORTIMER *New York: Confidential* xxxi. 276 Some of the larger clubs reap up to $50,000 a year for the privilege of checking your kellys.

4. *slang.* (See quots. 1942 and 1963.)

1934 H. N. ROSE *Thesaurus of Slang* viii. 57/1 Oilfield slang... Hole to set the 'Kelly' in when not in use..: *rat hole.* **1939** D. HAGER *Fund. Petroleum Industry* ix. 203 In older drilling methods where the kelly was not used, the drill pipe was badly cut by the gripping devices. **1942** BERREY & VAN DEN BARK *Amer. Thes. Slang* § 516/4 *Kelly*, a square joint on top of the drill stem passing through a square hole in the rotary table. **1946** *Mod. Petroleum Technol.* (Inst. Petroleum) 87 As drilling proceeds the square section of the kelley is lowered through the rotary table until its full length is below the table. The drilling string is then raised, the kelley removed, a fresh length of drill pipe is coupled up and the kelley is replaced. **1963** *Gloss. Mining Terms* (*B.S.I.*) III. 10 *Kelly*, the rod attached to the top of the drill column in rotary drilling. It passes through the rotary table and is turned by it, but is free to slide down through it as the borehole deepens. **1974** *Scotsman* 22 Apr. p. x, Only in oil can you break off kelly and set down on rams while keeping a straight face.

5. In full, *kelly green.* A light green colour. orig. *U.S.*

1936 *Mademoiselle* Sept. 13 (Advt.), A slipon with sleeveless sweater...rust with Churchill green, kelly with brown. *Ibid.* Nov. 49/1 (Advt.), Sweaters..in..yellow, kelly green, gray. *Ibid.* Dec. 3/2 (Advt.), Sweaters with an English pedigree..jockey red, Kelly green or natural. **1958** 'E. MCBAIN' *Killer's Choice* (1960) vi. 69 'What sort of green was it?' 'Almost a Kelly green...' **1966** G. BAXT *Queer Kind of Death* (1967) xvi. 223 Kelly green lanterns at the end of the garden. **1972** 'R. CRAWFORD' *Whip Hand* I. ix. 54 The kelly-green jungle was tangled; it hid a gunner.

6. *attrib.* and *Comb.* **kelly board, joint** (see quot. 1942); **Kelly's eye** *colloq.* (see quot. 1925).

1925 H. C. GEORGE in *Bull. U.S. Bureau of Mines* No. 224. 115 Means of escape from..the kelly board on every drilling and redrilling derrick shall be provided. **1942** BERREY & VAN DEN BARK *Amer. Thes. Slang* § 516/2 *Kelly-board*, a platform at the height of the 'kelly'. *Ibid.* § 516/4 *Kelly joint*, the first joint of pipe attached to the 'kelly'. **1925** FRASER & GIBBONS *Soldier & Sailor Words* 134 *Kelly's eye*, no. 1 in the game of 'House'. **1933** L. A. G. STRONG *Sea Wall* 256 A game of 'house' was in progress, and a voice monotonously droned the numbers: '..Kelly's eye.' **1945** E. WAUGH *Brideshead Revisited* II. i. 230 The voice of the officer in charge of tombola—'Kelly's eye—number one; legs, eleven; and we'll Shake the Bag.' **1962** *Daily Tel.* 25 June 11/4 Miss L. Brahmer ..began calling the numbers over the loudspeakers... 'Kelly's Eye, No. 1; and Legs Eleven' echoed throughout the ship.

Kelmscott (ke·lmzkǫt). The name of Kelmscott House, Hammersmith (named after Kelmscott Manor, Kelmscott, Oxfordshire), the home of William Morris (1834–1896), used in the name of the Kelmscott Press, which was founded there by him in 1891 and worked until 1898; also used *absol.* or *attrib.* to designate the books produced or their design.

1891 W. MORRIS *Story of Glittering Plain* 188 Here endeth the Glittering Plain, printed by William Morris at the Kelmscott Press, Upper Mall Hammersmith, in the County of Middlesex. **1896** G. B. SHAW in *Sat. Rev.* 10 Oct. 387/2 If he [*sc.* William Morris] had started a Kelmscott Theatre instead of the Kelmscott Press, I am quite confident that..he would have produced work that would within ten years have affected every theatre in Europe. **1920** A. SMELLIE in C. Jerdan *Scottish Clerical Stories* vii. 242, I had rather be the owner of its twenty-seven volumes than have all the Elzevirs and Kelmscotts in the world. **1938** *Times Lit. Suppl.* 12 Mar. 174/1 The book has somewhat of a Kelmscott air. **1963** *Listener* 21 Mar. 522/1 There is a vigour and vitality in his decorations that make Burne-Jones's Kelmscott borders rather tame. **1966** BERRY & POOLE *Ann. Printing* 262/1 The beauty of the Kelmscott books was due to harmony of type and decoration, the spacing of words and lines, the positioning of the text on the page, the careful choice of paper and ink, and the excellent presswork... Other private presses followed which served to increase the interest in fine book printing.

kelong (kĕ·lǫŋ). Also 9 **kaylong.** [Malay.] A large fish trap built with stakes, common along the coasts of the Malay Peninsula. Also *transf.*, a building erected over one.

1878 F. MCNAIR *Perak & Malays* ix. 93 The kaylongs are made of hurdles composed of strips of bamboo, some five feet long, fastened closely together with rattans. **1900** W. W. SKEAT *Malay Magic* v. 315 *Kelong* is the name given to one of the kinds of fishing-stakes (something like weirs) common on the coasts of the Peninsula. **1953** R. GRAHAM *War Damage Report* (Malaya War Damage Commission) xiv. 52 As one approaches the coast of Malaya one cannot fail to notice the large number of fish traps, or kelongs, built in some cases far out to sea. **1971** *Daily Tel.* 18 Sept. 11/3 At Ponggol Point on the north-east shore you can dine at the Sea Palace restaurant on a kelong or fish trap of stakes driven into the shallow sea bed, where fish are lured by lamps at night into a net. **1972** *Guardian* 6 Sept. 16/4 Fashionable now is a kelong visit. The kelongs are thatched huts over stakes driven into the seabed from which local fishermen cast their nets. Some of these have been 'improved' with bar, restaurant, and changing rooms for tourists to spend the day swimming and sunning and in the evening watch the fishermen bring in their haul.

kelp[1]. Add: **4. kelp crab,** a spider crab, *Pugettia producta,* found on the Pacific coast of North America.

1884 *Bull. U.S. Nat. Museum* No. 27. 112 The Kelp Crabs are used by the natives. **1939** RICKETTS & CALVIN *Between Pacific Tides* I. 80 A dark, olive-green, spider crab, *Pugettia producta*, occurs so frequently on strands of the seaweed *Egregia* and others that it is commonly called the kelp crab. The points on the carapace and the spines on the legs are sharp. **1954** S. F. LIGHT et al. *Intertidal Invertebr. Cent. Calif. Coast* 342 A few organisms (e.g. the kelp crab *Pugettia producta*..) graze directly on the larger attached algae.

†**kelp**[3] (kelp). *Obs. slang.* Also **kilp.** [Origin unknown.] A hat. Hence **kelp** *v. trans.* (see quot. 1812).

1736 J. COLE in *Ordinary of Newgate, his Account* I. 13/2, I and Thomas Campson..broke open a Hatters.. and robbed it of three Dozen of Kilps. **1753** J. POULTER *Discoveries* (ed. 2) 26 We jostle him up, and one knocks his Kelp off. **1812** J. H. VAUX *Vocab. Flash Lang.* in *Mem.* (1964) 247 *Kelp*, a hat; to *kelp* a person, is to move your hat to him.

Kelper (ke·lpəɹ), *sb.* and *a.* Also **kelper.** [f. KELP[1] + -ER[1].] **A.** *sb.* The name given locally to a native or inhabitant of the Falkland Islands, the shores of which abound in kelp. **B.** *adj.* Of or pertaining to a Kelper.

1960 M. B. R. CAWKELL et al. *Falkland Islands* viii. 93 Improved sanitation and street lighting, main drainage and a telephone exchange, were improvements the Kelper's business-like nature could readily appreciate. **1960** E. R. PETTINGILL *Penguin Summer* (1962) i. 7 Some of them were native Falklanders—'Kelpers', they called themselves. **1968** *Economist* 7 Dec. 33/2 More and more [Falkland Islands] young people are emigrating to New Zealand to escape the isolated monotony of kelper life. **1971** *Daily Tel.* 19 Jan. 10/4 Successive British Governments have laid it down firmly that the 'kelpers', all 2,000 of them, must decide their own destiny.

kelpie[2] (ke·lpi). *Austral.* [f. the name of an early specimen of the breed.] A smooth-coated, prick-eared, Australian sheep-dog, which may be black, black-and-tan, blue, or red; first bred from imported Scottish collies about 1870.

1907 R. LEIGHTON *New Bk. Dog* 472/2 The Kelpie.. is not perhaps an example of high, scientific breeding; but he is a useful, presentable dog. **1934** *Bulletin* (Sydney) 14 Feb. 40/2 Lassie was, like all kelpies, highly strung, with brains under her broad, thin-boned skull. **1946** [see *BARB *sb.*[3] 3]. **1971** F. HAMILTON *World Encycl. Dogs* 74 Kelpies were bred back in the early days of settlement from the Collie type dogs which came to Australia with the early farmers. **1972** *Southerly* XXXII. 9 A kelpie and a blue cattle dog had raced to meet them, barking frantically.

kelson, keelson. Add: **1. c.** (Spelt *keelson.*) A structure in the hull of a flying-boat (or the float of a seaplane) analogous to the keelson of a ship's hull.

1920 *Flight* 2 Sept. 948/1 Such members as keelson and chines are of rock elm. **1928** CHATFIELD & TAYLOR *Airplane & its Engine* xiii. 237 Since the loads on the bottom of the float in landing are large, additional longitudinal members called keelsons are provided to stiffen it. **1930** [see *KEEL *sb.*[1] 3 d]. **1942** R. H. LONGE in R. A. Beaumont *Aeronaut. Engin.* xviii. 486/1 The keelson..is the backbone of the hull [of a flying-boat], and runs the full length of the hull, from the stem or bow, to the stern-post. **1969** *Jane's 100 Significant Aircraft* 38/2 Twin-engined flying-boat... Floors notched out for two-thirds of depth to fit over solid keelson... Keelson is continuous member from stem to stern. **1974** *Flight International* 7 Nov. 646/2 The fuselage..is based on a twin-girder keelson running from nose to tail.

kelt[1]. Delete from def. 'Now only *Sc.*' and add later examples.

1937 *Evening News* 15 Feb. 8/5 A kelt—that is a fish which has paid its visit to the gravel beds—is a sad wreck and is in no form to put up a fight. An otter can deal with such salmon. **1963** *Times* 26 Jan. 11/4 If the fish has shed only a few eggs..it is still technically and in law a kelt.

kelt, keltch, varr. *KELCH.

kelter[2], **kilter.** (Earlier and later examples of *out of kilter.*)

1628 W. BRADFORD in *Mass. Hist. Soc. Coll.* (1856) 4th Ser. III. 235 Ye very sight of one [*sc.* a gun] (though out of kilter) was a terrour unto them. **1938** 'E. QUEEN' *Four of Hearts* (1939) xii. 173 Jack's death sort of knocked you out of kilter. **1960** M. PHILLIPS in *Analog Science Fact/Fiction* Nov. 16/1 We've had some reports that some of the government machines are out of kilter, and I'd like you to go over them for me. **1968** J. C. HOLMES *Nothing More to Declare* 77 A deeply traditional nature thrown out of kilter, and thus enormously sensitive to anything uprooted. **1973** *Times* 15 Oct. 17/3 There [*sc.* in N. Ireland], an allotment of 12 seats at Westminster is based upon electoral quotas wildly out of kilter with the quotas for England, Scotland, and Wales.

keltz, var. *KELCH.

Kelvin, kelvin (ke·lvin). [The title of Sir William Thomson, Lord *Kelvin* (1824–1907), British physicist and inventor.] † **1.** (With lower-case initial.) A name proposed (but little used) for the kilowatt-hour, the ordinary commercial unit of electric energy. *Obs.*

1892 *Electrician* 6 May 1/1 The President of the Board of Trade having cordially approved and Lord Kelvin having acquiesced; after the word 'unit' in the Provisional Orders of this year, the words 'hereinafter called a kelvin' will be introduced. **1911** *Encycl. Brit.* XXVII. 740/1 The corresponding energy unit being the kilowatt-second, and 3600 kilowatt-seconds or 1 kilowatt-hour called a 'Board of Trade unit' or a 'kelvin'.

2. (With capital initial.) Used *attrib.* and in the possessive to designate instruments and concepts devised by Lord Kelvin, as **Kelvin balance,** an electrical measuring instrument having a set of horizontal coils arranged in the form of a balance with a sliding weight, which is used to balance the electromagnetic forces produced by a current passed through the coils and so to measure its strength; **Kelvin (double) bridge,** a modification of the Wheatstone bridge used for measuring low

resistances and having two pairs of variable ratio resistors, an adjustable standard resistor, and the unknown one; **Kelvin's law,** the law that the most economical cross-sectional area of a conductor used as a transmission line is that for which the cost of the energy dissipated in any period is equal to the charges during the same period on the capital cost of the line.

1896 *Proc. Physical Soc.* XIV. 166 A convenient method for determining low resistances, such as..a Kelvin bridge. **1903** F. A. C. PERRINE *Conductors for Electr. Distribution* viii. 160 (*heading*) Kelvin's law of economy in conductors. **1904** SWENSON & FRANKENFIELD *Testing Electro-Magn. Machinery* I. 122 The Kelvin Balance is recognized as a standard instrument. **1906** *Rep. Brit. Assoc. Adv. Sci.* 119 The current leads of standard resistances intended for measurement on the Kelvin double bridge should have a resistance not greater than the standard itself. **1933** E. W. GOLDING *Electr. Measurements* ii. 14 Kelvin balances are manufactured with ten different ranges up to 2,500 amp. **1957** W. J. JOHN *Mod. Electr. Engin.* III. x. 301/2 Kelvin's law is usually expressed in terms of annual costs, though it is equally true of capitalized costs. **1967** H. COTTON *Adv. Electr. Technol.* iii. 92 Calculate the current flowing in the galvanometer of the Kelvin double-bridge circuit.

3. (With capital initial.) Used *attrib.* to designate an absolute scale of temperature (defined thermodynamically in terms of the operation of an ideal heat engine) in which the zero is identified with absolute zero and values are assigned to one or more fixed points so as to make the degrees correspond in size to those of the centigrade (Celsius) scale. So *Kelvin temperature,* a temperature expressed in terms of this scale.

As the scale was orig. defined, the temperature interval between two fixed points (the freezing point and the boiling point of water) was made to be exactly 100 degrees, so that the value of each point was a matter of experiment (which produced values of about 273° and 373° respectively); in 1954 the scale was redefined in terms of a single fixed point, the triple point of water, to which was assigned the value 273·16° exactly (giving a figure of approximately 273·15° for the ice point).

[**1871** J. C. MAXWELL *Theory of Heat* viii. 155 (*heading*) Thomson's absolute scale of temperature. **1899** W. WATSON *Text-bk. Physics* vi. 334 The temperatures..are 283°, 293°,..on Lord Kelvin's absolute scale.] **1908** *Amer. Jrnl. Sci.* CLXXVI. 421 The derivation of the Kelvin thermodynamic scale from the expansion of nitrogen. **1922** GLAZEBROOK *Dict. Appl. Physics* I. 270/2 If the same size of degree be adopted for the Kelvin scale, then..the readings, on either scale, will be identical. **1937** M. W. ZEMANSKY *Heat & Thermodynamics* ix. 140 Two temperatures on the Kelvin scale are to each other as the heats absorbed and rejected respectively by a Carnot engine operating between reservoirs at these temperatures. *Ibid.* 144 The Kelvin temperature is therefore numerically equal to the absolute temperature and may be measured with a gas thermometer. **1958** CONDON & ODISHAW *Handbk. Physics* v. iii. 30/2 This new absolute thermodynamic scale, called the Kelvin scale, does not differ from the thermodynamic 'centigrade' scale by an amount which can be determined experimentally at the present time. **1962** *Units & Standards of Measurement: Temperature* (Nat. Physical Lab.) 3 The thermodynamic Kelvin scale..is recognized as the fundamental scale to which all temperature measurements should ultimately be referred.

b. *degree Kelvin* (or *Kelvin degree*): a degree of the Kelvin scale (in size equal to the degree centigrade), symbol °K (see *K 4 f); now formally called a *kelvin* (symbol K) and incorporated into the International System of Units as a basic unit.

1911 *Physical Rev.* XXXIII. 220 The writer has assumed that the degree Kelvin and the degree centigrade were equal. **1930** *Engineering* 9 May 595/3 A perfect gas of one free electron per atom would necessarily contribute three calories per gram-atom per degree Kelvin to the specific heat of the metal. **1941** *Temperature* (Amer. Inst. Physics) 11 When using the Thermodynamic Centigrade Scale one is simply expressing the number of Kelvin degrees that a particular thermal state is above or below the ice point. **1945** G. R. NOAKES *Text-bk. Heat* i. 26 The name 'degrees Kelvin' (°K.) is used for the true absolute scale temperature, and 'degrees absolute' (°A., or °abs.) for temperatures measured by other means on any other scale numbered up from absolute zero. **1962** CORSON & LORRAIN *Introd. Electromagn. Fields* iii. 108, *T* is the absolute temperature in degrees Kelvin. **1968** *Nature* 16 Nov. 651/2 Resolution No. 3 [of the thirteenth General Conference of Weights and Measures] changes the name of the 'degree Kelvin' (symbol °K) simply to 'kelvin', with symbol K... The terms of the revised definition of the unit of thermodynamic temperature are (resolution No. 4): 'the kelvin..is the fraction 1/273·16 of the thermodynamic temperature of the triple point of water'. **1971** *Physics Bull.* Mar. 144/1 The inversion transitions.. indicate that the ammonia molecules are at a temperature of several tens of kelvin. **1973** *Sci. Amer.* Aug. 84/3 Only liquid hydrogen will serve, and it must be stored at an extremely low temperature (22 degrees Kelvin, or 22 degrees Celsius above absolute zero).

Kelvinside (ke·lvinsəid). The name of a residential district of Glasgow, used *attrib.* or *absol.* to designate the supposedly affected and refined accent with which its residents are said to speak.

1903 J. H. MILLAR *Lit. Hist. Scotl.* 317 A mincing and quasi-genteel lingo of their own (the sort of English known in some quarters as 'Princes Street' or 'Kelvinside'). **1928** I. C. WARD *Phonetics of English* x. 76 Some types of Scottish town speech—sometimes called 'Kelvinside' or 'High English'. **1932** N. M. GUNN *Lost Glen* II. ii. 117 A thin..woman.., fair and full of merriment and a Kelvinside-English accent. **1935** *Trans. Philol. Soc.* 8 The artificial variety of speech which has been called Kelvinside English. **1969** G. PAYTON *Proper Names* 243 *Kelvinside,* the north-western area of Glasgow around the University and Kelvingrove Park, where the..residents were supposed to speak with a mincing ('Kelvinside').. accent.

Kemalism (ke·maliz'm). [f. the name of *Kemal* Atatürk (*c* 1880–1938), Turkish soldier and statesman + -ISM.] The political, social, and economic policies advocated by Kemal Atatürk, which aimed to create a modern republican secular Turkish state out of a part of the Ottoman empire. So **Ke·malist,** one who advocates or believes in the theory of Kemalism; an adherent or supporter of Kemalism; also as *adj.*

1920 *N.Y. Times* 3 Dec., Greek troops have dispersed the Kemalists in the district of Nicee. **1921** *Manch. Guardian Weekly* 29 July 65 The Kemalists are evacuating Angora. **1925** *Ibid.* 11 Dec. 476 The anti-Kemalist revolt ..has as its centre the town of Erzerum, where, curiously enough, Kemalism was born. **1927** *Observer* 18 Sept. 7 In Turkey an utter victory for the Kemalists over the Greeks supplied the opportunity for a comprehensive scrapping of Turkey's Ottoman habits... Quite the most striking of these post-war metamorphoses has been accomplished by Kemalist Turkey, the leader among Oriental nations in the race for 'Westernisation'. **1947** A. KOESTLER in *Partisan Rev.* XIV. 344 Under a de Gaulle regime of the Kemalist type you could after all go on publishing your stuff within limits. **1959** *Encounter* Sept. 36/1 The theoretical justification of Kemalism. **1963** *Times* 23 Apr. 11/3 The pamphlets were said to have been signed 'the Army of Young Kemalists'. **1966** *Tablet* 12 Mar. 299/2 The Kemalist revolution was often brutal.

kempas (ke·mpăs). Also 9 **kompas, koompass.** [Malay.] A hardwood timber tree, *Koompassia malaccensis,* native to Malaya, Sumatra, and Borneo; also, the wood of this tree.

1839 T. J. NEWBOLD *Pol. & Statistical Acct. Straits of Malacca* II. viii. 100 The ore and charcoal, (of the Kompas, Kamoui, or other hard woods,) are gradually heaped up. *a* **1869** A. C. MAINGAY in *Kew Bull.* (1890) 122 Koompass...Wood yellowish white...Used for shipbuilding. **1935** I. H. BURKILL *Dict. Econ. Products Malay Peninsula* II. 1286 Kempas sheds all its leaves every year. **1940** E. J. H. CORNER *Wayside Trees Malaya* I. 397 The *Kempas* occurs throughout the lowland forest in swampy ground or on hillsides. **1956** *Handbk. Hardwoods* (Forest Prod. Res. Lab.) 127 Kempas normally seasons fairly well. **1959** 'M. DERBY' *Tigress* ii. 98 He waited in the fork of the kempas tree. **1965** C. SHUTTLEWORTH *Malayan Safari* i. 16 There are..medium hardwoods such as kapur, kempas and keruing. **1972** T. C. WHITMORE *Tree Flora of Malaya* I. 266/2 Kempas is a smaller tree than tualang, it is more often cut for timber.

‖ **Kempeitai** (ke·mpē̆itai). Also **Kempetai.** [Jap.] The Japanese Secret Service in the period 1931–1945.

1947 J. BERTRAM *Shadow of War* 197 A single communication..to the *kempeitai* revealing my identity would be more than enough. **1953** J. TRENCH *Docken Dead* xiv. 217 Docken had betrayed Richard to the Kempetei. **1961** R. SETH *Anat. Spying* viii. 148 The Kempeitai, like the Nazi Gestapo, was the most powerful and most hated of all Japanese institutions. It derived its power for the most part from the semi-independent position which it held within the army. *Ibid.* 149 Wherever the Kempeitai was, its most important function was counter-espionage. **1965** B. SWEET-ESCOTT *Baker St. Irregular* v. 127 If the Gestapo or the Kempetai had kept track of his movements, they would have had a good idea of what was likely to happen. **1965** *This is Japan 1966* 107 A tough *kempeitai gendarme,* with the customary red armband, two holstered revolvers, gold-and-black teeth, and foul *daikon* breath. **1969** J. M. GULLICK *Malaysia* ii. 97 The teachers..played a leading part in maintaining the underground resistance in the towns despite torture and other reprisals by the Japanese Security Police (the Kempeitai).

kempite (ke·mpəit). *Min.* [f. the name of J. F. *Kemp* (1859–1926), American geologist + -ITE[1].] An emerald-green basic chloride of manganese, $Mn_2(OH)_3Cl$, found in California.

1924 A. F. ROGERS in *Amer. Jrnl. Sci.* VIII. 150 The name kempite is given in honor of Professor James Furman Kemp. **1949** *Bull. Geol. Soc. Amer.* LX. 1944 It seems likely that the formula of kempite is $MnCl_2.3MnO.3H_2O$. **1968** I. KOSTOV *Mineral.* 195 Kempite is orthorhombic-dipyramidal, occurring as a weathering product of a manganese deposit.

kempt, *ppl. a.* Delete '*arch.*' and add later examples. Also *transf.*

1905 *Daily Chron.* 15 June 4/4 The little girls wear clean pinafores; their hair is neatly kempt. **1929** R. ALDINGTON *Death of Hero* III. xii. 398 The street paving was badly worn, but looked marvellously smooth and kempt to Winterbourne. **1946** S. SPENDER *European Witness* I. i. 9 Gardens as well kempt as a short hair-cut. **1951** W. SANSOM *Face of Innocence* i. 1 The kempt yellow gravel of drives. *a* **1954** F. B. YOUNG *Wistanslow* (1956) 113 A spacious expanse of greensward, smooth and kempt as the ancient turf of an Oxford college. **1975** *Times* 21 July 10/7 Artificially beautified people looking kempt and highly coloured for the hairdressers' and beauticians' trade fair.

‖ **ken** (ken), *sb.*[3] Also 8–9 **kin.** Pl. **ken,** occas. **kens.** [Jap.] A Japanese unit of length equal to six *shaku*; equivalent to approximately 71·5 inches (1·82 metres).

1727 J. G. SCHEUCHZER tr. *Kæmpfer's Hist. Japan* II. 405 The *Tsjo* contains sixty *Kin,* or Mats, according to their way of measuring, or about as many European fathoms. *Ibid.* 407 This bridge is supported, in the middle, by a small island, and consequently consists of two parts, the first whereof hath 36 *kins,* or fathoms, in length, and the second 96. **1845** *Encycl. Metrop.* XX. 486/2, 1 kin = 1 fathom. **1884** SATOW & HAWES *Handbk. for Travellers Cent. & N. Japan* (ed. 2) 17 The *chō* is further subdivided into 60 *ken* and the *ken* again into 6 *shaku,* the *shaku* being about 11·9 English inches. **1956** K. TOMIKI *Judo* i. 22 The floor space for a contest shall be 5 *ken* (30 feet) square of 50 *tatami.*

‖ **ken** (ken), *sb.*[4] [Jap.] A prefecture; one of the territorial divisions of Japan.

1882 *Encycl. Brit.* XIV. 490/2 His [*sc.* Sho-tai's] territory was declared first a *han* or feudal dependency and afterwards a *ken* or province of the Japanese monarchy. **1890** B. H. CHAMBERLAIN *Things Japanese* 134 There are two current divisions of the soil of the Empire—an older and more popular one into provinces (*kuni*)..and a recent, purely administrative one into prefectures (*ken*) of which at the present moment..there are forty-three. **1899** KIPLING *From Sea to Sea* I. xviii. 378 Away in the western *kens*—districts, as you call them. **1947** E. O. REISCHAUER *Japan Past & Present* ix. 119 Two years later, in 1871, the fiefs were entirely abolished, and the land was divided into a number of new political divisions called *ken* or 'prefectures'. **1965** J. W. HALL et al. *Twelve Doors to Japan* i. 16 Today..they [*sc.* the *kuni*] have been merged into the larger prefectures (to, dō, fu, and ken, of which there are forty-six) and have lost much of their contemporary meaning.

‖ **ken** (ken), *sb.*[5] [Jap.] A Japanese game of forfeits played with the hands and with gestures.

1890 B. H. CHAMBERLAIN *Things Japanese* 125 The Japanese play various games of forfeits, which they call *Ken,* sitting in a little circle and flinging out their fingers, after the manner of the Italian *mora.* **1898** A. DIÓSY *New Far East* v. 236 Dignified and sedate as if *ken,* and other rollicking games of forfeits, were frivolities far beneath her notice. **1958** *Japan* (Jap. Nat. Commission for Unesco) xxix. 1030 *Ken* is a game introduced from ancient China with many variations... The game was held at banquets and feasts in the Edo Period when *ken* meets were also held.

kenaf (kĕnæ·f). Also **kanaff.** [Persian.] = *AMBARI.

1891 *Kew Bull.* 204 Recently an announcement has been made of the discovery of a new textile plant on the shores of the Caspian. The plant known as Kanaff by the natives is said to yield a soft elastic and silky fibre... It is supposed that Kanaff fibre..will successfully compete with any other textile for sacking, ropes, and packthread. **1945** *Bot. Gaz.* CVI. 349/1 The identity of the plant [introduced into Cuba] has been established as kenaf (*Hibiscus cannabinus,* L.) which..is capable of producing more than a ton of dry fiber per acre. **1952** A. E. HAARER *Jute Substitute Fibres* i. 2 Kenaf is the name used principally in Russia, America and Cuba..and the word is derived from the local names Kanaff, Kanap or Kanaph, given to the plant where it grows on the Persian shore of the Caspian sea. *Ibid.* i. 8 No one seems to know why this fibre plant was given the name Kenaf in the Western Hemisphere. **1967** *New Scientist* 14 Dec. 660/1 The kenaf plant which is already a leading substitute for jute fibres..is now being seriously considered..as a substitute for the hardwoods used in papermaking. **1974** *Times* 12 Jan. (Ghana Suppl.) p. iv, Achievements [in the production of raw materials] were sparse except in some agricultural sectors like cotton and kenaf.

‖ **kendo** (ke·ndo). [Jap.] The Japanese sport of fencing with bamboo swords.

1921 S. K. UYENISHI *Text-bk. Ju-Jutsu* i. 14 *Kendo* or *Ken-jutsu,* 'the hard way' and 'the hard art'..is the elaboration of the old two-sword play of the *samurai* or 'two-sworded men'. **1933** *Official Guide to Japan* (Jap. Imperial Govt. Railways) p. clxxxvi, *Kenjutsu* or *Kendō* (also called *Gekken*), the art of handling a sword, corresponds to European fencing and is as old as Japanese history. **1939** R. KAJI *Japan* facing p. 56 (*caption*) *Kendō,* Japanese fencing, in which the participants use bamboo swords. **1958** *Economist* 1 Nov. 422/1 The government has reintroduced the forbidden *kendo* or military fencing in schools. **1964** R. A. LIDSTONE *Introd. Kendō* 15 Quite understandably Kendō, with its militant background, lost favour after the last war. **1966** J. BALL *Cool Cottontail* (1967) iv. 37 He had become interested in the basic Oriental martial arts: judo, kendo, aikido, and karate. **1974** *Publishers Weekly* 28 Jan. 100/1 (Advt.), Kendo, or Japanese sword fighting, is an ancient method of training body and mind that now is becoming popular throughout the world.

keneme (kenī·m). *Linguistics.* Also **ceneme.** [f. Gr. κενός empty: see *-EME.] (See quot. 1966.) Cf. *empty word* (*EMPTY *a.* and *sb.* C). Hence **kenema·tics, kene·tics,** the aspect of language concerned with kenemes; **kenema·tic, kene·mic, kene·tic** *adjs.*

The forms with initial *c*- predominate over the etymological forms with *k*-.

1939 L. HJELMSLEV in *Proc. Third Internat. Congr. Phonetic Sci.* 271 A language is a category of two members. ..One of these planes, the plerematic plane, gives form to the content..; the other, the cenematic plane, forms the expression. *Ibid.* 272 The constituents—in plerematics: the pleremes, in cenematics: the cenemes—are usually of two types: central and marginal constituents. **1950** S. POTTER *Our Lang.* vii. 86 Beginning with the phoneme, philologists pass on to speak about *morphemes*, *taxemes* or *tagmemes*, *sememes* (including *pleremes* and *kenemes*).., as if *-eme* were a brand-new suffix meaning 'linguistic agent'. **1958** C. F. HOCKETT *Course in Mod. Ling.* lxiv. 575 Phonemes are linguistic *cenemes*; morphemes are linguistic *pleremes*. *Ibid.*, It will be better to introduce two new terms for general applicability: *cenematic* and *plerematic*. The cenematic structure of language is phonology; the plerematic structure of language is grammar. **1966** M. PEI *Gloss. Ling. Terminol.* 35 *Ceneme*, 1. Linguistically, a phoneme, or anything pertaining to phonology (Hockett). 2. The smallest unit of expression without corresponding content, differing from a phoneme in that it does not necessarily consist of sound, but may include letters and other semantic indicators (Hjelmslev). **1967** [see *FUNCTOR 2]. **1967** *Word* XXIII. 469 My observations apparently support the structuralist separation of cenetics and pleremetics. *Ibid.* 471 In addition to their two cenetic and two plerematic systems, bilingual children naturally have to master two sets of form-to-meaning relationships. **1969** *English Studies* L. 432 The tradition from Saussure and Hjelmslev brought about a phonemic—or cenemic—analysis based on pure relations.

Kenite (kī·nəit), *sb.* and *a.* [f. Heb. *ḳênî* a gentilic adjective associated with Heb. *ḳayin* a weapon made of metal, Arab. *ḳayn* an iron-smith, maker of iron weapons and tools, Aram. *ḳênay*, *kaynāyā* smith, metal-worker, Nabatæan *ḳynw*, Old South Arabian *'ḳnw*: see -ITE[1].] **A.** *sb.* A member of an ancient nomadic people from S. Palestine, freq. mentioned in the Old Testament. **B.** *adj.* Of or pertaining to the Kenites.

From the etymology it has been conjectured that the Kenites were chiefly metal-smiths.

[*c* **1000** ÆLFRIC *Heptateuch* Gen. xv. 19 Cynei & Cenezei; Cetmonei. **1382** WYCLIF *Num.* xxxii. 12 Caleph, the sone of Jephone, Ceneze, and Josue, the sone of Nun.] **1535** COVERDALE *Gen.* xv. 19 The Kenytes, the Kenizites, the Kydmonites. —— *Judg.* iv. 11 Heber the Kenyte. *a* **1679** M. POOLE *Annotations Holy Bible* (1688) I. *Judg.* iv. 11 Which removal is here mentioned, lest any should wonder to find the Kenites in this place. **1710** M. HENRY *Exposition Five Bks. Moses Num.* xxiv, The Kenites were now the securest of the Nations. **1876** *Encycl. Brit.* IV. 763/1 The aboriginal Rephaim and three Arab tribes, the Kenites, Kenizzites, and Kadmonites. **1911** *Ibid.* XV. 729/2 Moses himself married into a Kenite family (Judges i. 16). **1962** G. A. BUTTRICK *Interpreter's Dict. Bible* III. 7/1 The last mention of the Kenites in connection with the history of Israel is during the time of David before he became king over all Israel (ca. 1000). **1968** *Encycl. Brit.* XIII. 281/1 *Kenites*, a clan closely related to the Midianites and Amalekites, frequently mentioned in the biblical narratives about the early history of Israel. The name was derived from Cain, whose descendants they were believed to be (Gen. iv).

† **kennedy** (ke·nĕdi). *Obs. slang.* [Said to be f. the name of a man who was killed by being struck on the head with a poker.] **a.** A poker. **b.** A blow inflicted by a poker, freq. in the phr. *to give* (someone) *kennedy*. Also **kennedy** *v. trans.*, to strike with a poker.

1823 *Morning Herald* in *Spirit of Public Jrnls. for M.DCCC.XXIII* (1825) 77 Mr. Davis bore these irregularities as long as he could, but at last..he ventured to tell *Mykle* that he could bear it no longer! When, what does *Mykle* do but seize the *poker*, and threaten to '*Kennedy* him' (beat him with a poker). **1859** HOTTEN *Dict. Slang* 55 *Kennedy*, to strike or kill with a poker. A St Giles' term, so given from a man of that name being killed by a poker. Frequently shortened to *Neddy*. **1864** *Athenæum* 29 Oct. 559 St Giles's perpetuates the memory of a..man..who was killed by a poker by calling that instrument a kennedy.

kennel, *sb.*[1] Add: **1. a.** Also (usu. *pl.*), an establishment where dogs are bred, or where they are cared for in the absence of their owners.

1887 G. STABLES *Practical Kennel Guide* (ed. 3) xv. 145, I know some kennels..which are a disgrace to civilised society—dirty and beastly in the extreme. **1896** *Notable Dogs of Yr.* (Advt.), Borzoi kennels and sanatorium for dogs and cats. Patients treated at the kennels. **1925** J. LUCAS *Pedigree Dog Breeding* 61 Those intending to board their dogs for more than a week or two should try and visit one or two kennels before making their selection. .. Many kennels..make a speciality of whelping cases. **1931** N. W. LEWIS *Your Dog* iii. 173 Good bitches can be bought..from big kennels that have become overstocked. **1969** [see *boarding kennel* s.v. *BOARDING *vbl. sb.* 7]. **1974** R. RENDELL *Face of Trespass* ii. 27 I've never left her since she was a puppy... I couldn't put her in kennels. She'd fret.

3. *kennel-maid, -man* (further examples), *-work*; **Kennel Club**, an organization, founded in 1873, which establishes dog breeds, records pedigrees, issues the rules for dog shows and trials, etc.; also, a branch of this organization; **kennel lameness**, a rheumatic disease in dogs, freq. affecting the forelegs.

1874 F. C. S. PEARCE *Kennel Club Stud Bk.* p. v, The Club shall be called the Kennel Club, it shall endeavour in every way to promote the general improvement of dogs, dog shows, and dog trials. **1935** *Discovery* Oct. 310/2 The breed has been taken up by kennel clubs and the dogs are now officially called Illyrian Sheepdogs. **1959** *Listener* 12 Mar. 447/1 These details were vouched and signed for by the chief of the local kennel club. **1971** F. HAMILTON *World Encycl. Dogs* 620 Registration of a pedigree dog at the Kennel Club is a simple matter; it is usually completed by the breeder, the fee of 5s...registers the dog for life. **1841** R. T. VYNER *Notitia Venatica* 45 Kennel-lameness, or shoulder-lameness, as it is sometimes called. **1885** BEAUFORT & MORRIS *Hunting* 112 That mortal scourge which among men is known as rheumatism, and among hounds as kennel lameness. **1930** C. FREDERICK et al. *Fox-Hunting* viii. 108 Through this cause they appear to stiffen up, which is mistaken for kennel lameness. **1948** H. KIRK *Index of Treatm. in Small-Animal Pract.* II. 445 *Kennel lameness.* This layman's term is meant to indicate a condition brought about by a diet deficient in calcium which affects mainly full-grown animals kept for some weeks or months in kennels and fed chiefly on dog biscuit. **1907** *Westm. Gaz.* 5 July 9/1 In the lady's service was the prisoner, who occupied the position of kennel-maid. **1929** *Daily Express* 16 Jan. 5/2 The showing of dogs is skilled work for a kennelmaid. **1970** *Daily Tel.* 14 Apr. 17/2 He had bought substantial quantities of veterinary preparations for the mange and had left the treatment to a young kennelmaid. **1954** C. L. B. HUBBARD *Compl. Dog Breeders' Manual* x. 103 With reliable staffing the kennel runs smoothly enough, therefore it is essential that he selects his kennelmen and kennelmaids with care. **1972** *Shooting Times & Country Mag.* 27 May 18/3 To manage such a large kennel Sheppard has two kennel-men in addition to four girls. **1929** *Daily Express* 16 Jan. 5/2 Kennelwork as a career for educated girls. **1971** DANGERFIELD & HOWELL *Internat. Encycl. Dogs* 268 Kennel work cannot be classed as an effeminate career for a male or an overly masculine job for a woman.

kennel, *v.* Add: **1. b.** With *up*. To return to one's kennel (also *fig.*); to keep quiet, to shut up. *colloq.*

1913 GALSWORTHY *Fugitive* III. i. 63 You've run her to earth; your job's done. Kennel up, hounds! **1919** W. H. DOWNING *Digger Dial.* 30 *Kennel-up*, stop talking. **1929** GALSWORTHY *Roof* ii. 37 Kennel up, Reggie! You've had too much and you know it. **1972** *Shooting Times & Country Mag.* 4 Mar. 37/3 After clean straw had been put on their benches, the order 'kennel up!' was given, though not immediately obeyed.

Kennelly (ke·nĕli). [Name of Arthur Edwin *Kennelly* (1861–1939), U.S. electrical engineer, who in 1902 suggested (as did Heaviside independently) that such a layer existed.] *Kennelly(–Heaviside) layer* or *region*: = *E-layer* (*E II. 9), **Heaviside layer*.

1925 *Science* 22 May 540/1 (*heading*) The Kennelly–Heaviside layer. **1925** *Nature* 24 Oct. 609/2 The hypothesis of an electrically conducting stratum in the upper air was clearly enunciated in an article by Prof. A. E. Kennelly..published in the *Electrical World and Engineer* of New York on March 15, 1902. The official date of Heaviside's disclosure of his hypothesis is December 19, 1902. ..If names are to be attached to the hypothetical layer it should be called, in equity, the 'Kennelly–Heaviside' layer, a name which is beginning to be used in America. **1932** *Discovery* Oct. 308/1 The Kennelly–Heaviside layer ..is responsible for the reflection of long and medium wireless wavelengths. **1933** *Ibid.* Oct. 306/1 Professor Appleton..observed that there was yet another layer beyond the Kennelly layer. **1963** G. M. B. DOBSON *Exploring Atmosphere* viii. 142 These different ionized regions are usually known by the letters which have been placed alongside them in the diagram, but the *E* region is also known as the 'Kennelly–Heaviside' region, and the *F* region as the 'Appleton' region, after their discoverers. **1972** *Science* 5 May 463/2 It was not until 1926 that the existence of this 'Kennelly–Heaviside layer' was established beyond all doubt.

kennetic (kene·tik), *a.* [f. KEN *v.*[1] 11 after KINETIC *a.*] (See quot. 1955.) Usu. in phr. *kennetic inquiry*.

1950 A. F. BENTLEY in *Science* CXII. 775/1 Kennetic inquiry is a name proposed for organized investigation into the problem of human knowings and knowns, where this is so conducted that the full range of subject matters—all the knowings and all the knowns—form a common field. *Ibid.* 775/2 To form the name 'kennetic', the Scottish 'ken' or 'kenning' has been preferred to any word in the groups centering around 'cognition'. **1955** M. REIFER *Dict. New Words* 116/1 *Kennetic adj.*, pertaining to the study of the acquisition of knowledge viewed as a transaction between the learner and the entire matter to be learned. **1960** H. C. SHANDS *Thinking & Psychotherapy* ii. 40 It is important for an understanding of the processes of kennetic inquiry to remember always the shifting nature of means and ends. **1970** —— *Semiotic Approaches to Psychiatry* 8 Natural philosophy must be primarily oriented toward the understanding of communicative process, and..toward 'kennetic inquiry'.

‖ **kennetjie** (ke·nəkʸi). *S. Afr.* Also **kennetje**. [Afrikaans.] = TIP-CAT.

1947 *Cape Times Weekend Mag.* 21 June 22 Whether they were climbing in hedges..or playing kennetjie or marbles, the youthful Miss H—— and her companions were like all healthy children. **1953** *Cape Argus* 28 Feb. 3/6 On these grassy squares we played 'rounders' and on the paths marbles, tops, hop-scotch, and kennetje. **1959** *Cape Times* 2 May 9/1 A South African in England tells me that what they call *kennetjie* in the Boland is sweeping Lancashire, where it is known as tip-cat. **1971** *Standard Encycl. S. Afr.* III. 190/2 In his delightful memoirs P. B. Borcherds mentions the games of 'kennetjie' (tip-cat) in which he took part..at the close of the 18th century... The kennetjie itself was a piece of wood about 5 inches..long and 1½ inch..in diameter, tapered off at both ends.

keno. (This spelling is now usual.) Also 9 **keeno, quino.** For etym. read: [ad. F. *quine* set of five winning numbers in a lottery, f. L. *quīnī* distributive of *quinque* five.] Add earlier and later examples.

1814 B. F. PALMER *Diary* 30 May (1914) 70, I employ'd in washing & mending my messmate playing keeno. **1843** J. F. COOPER *Ned Myers* 93, I commenced operations by purchasing shares in a dice-board, a *vingt-et-un* table, and a quino table. **1870** A. S. EVANS *Our Sister Republic* xx. 462 A great shed capable of seating one thousand or fifteen hundred people, which is devoted exclusively to *quino*, played for money. The cards or tickets are pasted down upon the tables and must number at least one thousand all told. Each player is provided with a handful of corn with which to keep the game as the numbers drawn out by the dealer are called... One game..takes about three minutes. **1871** *Figaro* 15 Apr., The police pulled every Keno establishment in the city. **1873** J. H. BEADLE *Undevel. West* iv. 95 This game, like keno, has less of the 'cutthroat' about it than the others. **1875** E. KING *Southern States N. Amer.* xx. 206 A man..tried to shoot the keno-dealer in the back. **1889** K. MUNROE *Golden Days of '49* iv. 40 We'll have a drawin' over in Slim Jim's keno ranch. **1904** W. N. HARBEN *Georgians* xxiii. 218 The town's got what they call the 'White Elephant'—a gamblin', keno shebang on a giant scale. **1907** C. E. MULFORD *Bar-20* (1914) ix. 108 I'd shore look nice loping around a keno lay-out without my guns, in th' same town with some cuss huntin' me, wouldn't I? **1951** E. KEFAUVER *Crime in Amer.* (1952) xii. 144 Another huge gambling casino..ran dice, keno and card games. **1968** R. F. ADAMS *Western Words* (ed. 2) 169 Keno..is played with a large globe, called the keno goose.

b. *int.* An exclamation (expressing encouragement or approval).

1868 *Terr. Enterprise* (Virginia, Nevada) 30 Sept. 3/2 When they thus got three beans in a row they were to call out 'Keno!' and rake in the pot. **1884** [in Dict.]. **1907** C. E. MULFORD *Bar-20* (1914) xix. 193 He wants to know where th' cards are stacked an' why he can't holler 'Keno'. **1920** in J. M. Hunter *Trail Drivers of Texas* I. 205 Shake yer spurs an' make 'em rattle! Keno! Promenade to seats.

kenotron (ke·nŏtrǫn). *Electr.* [f. Gr. κενό-ς empty + *-TRON.] A kind of highly evacuated thermionic diode designed for rectification at high voltages.

Kenotron was formerly a proprietary name in the U.S.

1915 S. DUSHMAN in *Gen. Electric Rev.* Mar. 159/2 In the case of a rectifier containing a hot filament as cathode and exhausted to as high a degree of vacuum as possible, there is no conduction except by electrons. In order to distinguish the latter type of hot cathode rectifier from other forms..the designation, kenotron, has been specially coined. **1915** *Electrician* 21 May 242/1 A kenotron has been built capable of rectifying 250 milliamperes at 180,000 volts. **1918** *Official Gaz.* (U.S. Patent Office) 1 Jan. 291/1 General Electric Company... Kenotron... Rectifying apparatus. Claims use since about May, 1916. **1946** W. T. SPROULL *X-Rays in Pract.* vii. 120 Kenotrons are widely used in the electric circuits that are provided to supply the high voltage for x-ray tubes. *Ibid.* 121 In an x-ray tube, the space current is said to be 'emission limited', while in a kenotron the current is 'space charge limited', as in most radio vacuum tubes.

kenozooid (ke:nozōᵘ·oid). [f. Gr. κενό-ς empty + ZOOID *sb.*] In a colonial bryozoan of the phylum Ectoprocta, an individual consisting of the body wall or ZOŒCIUM alone, without tentacles or an alimentary canal. Also called † **kenozoœ·cium** [f. Gr. κενό-ς empty + ZOŒCIUM].

1909 G. M. R. LEVINSEN *Cheilostomatous Bryozoa* 46 We can distinguish between four main forms of individuals (Bryozooids)...*Kenozoœcia* (*Kenozooids*), which not only have no polypide, but as a rule no aperture and always no operculum. *Ibid.*, The Kenozoœcia must be regarded as supporting, fastening and connecting individuals. **1959** L. H. HYMAN *Invertebrates* V. xx. 331 Kenozooid is the name applied to heterozooids that lack zooidal differentiation and consist simply of body wall enclosing strands of tissue.

Kensal Green (kensăl grī·n). The site of a large cemetery in London, used allusively as the type of a cemetery or as a symbol of death and burial. Also *fig.*

1842 DICKENS *Let.* 26 Apr. (1974) III. 211 What would I give if the dear girl whose ashes lie in Kensal-Green, had lived. *c* **1885** A. W. PINERO in M. R. Booth *Eng. Plays of 19th Cent.* (1973) IV. 332 In less than that, unless I am lucky enough to fall in some foreign set-to, I shall be in Kensal Green. **1903** KIPLING *Five Nations* 122 That Kensall-Green of greatness called the files. **1914** G. K. CHESTERTON *Flying Inn* xxi. 252 Before we go to Paradise by way of Kensal Green. **1967** O. LANCASTER *Eye to Future* I. 24 My mother was wholly free from the lachrymose necrophilia of the Victorians; not for her the

pious outings to Kensal Green. **1975** P. Somerville-Large *Couch of Earth* iv. 73 The necropolis was huge... We wandered about this devastated Kensal Green, Ismael..kicking at the piles of bones.

Kensington (ke·nziŋtǝn). The name of a borough of London (now part of the Royal Borough of Kensington and Chelsea), used *attrib.* or quasi-*adj.* to designate speech supposedly characteristic of people living in Kensington (cf. next).

1968 J. Lock *Lady Policeman* viii. 62 'Haymarket!' the manner is brusque and the voice exaggerated Kensington. **1971** *Guardian* 22 Oct. 10/3 One spectator exclaimed, 'all the peasants speak Baliganj Bengali!' (read: 'Kensington English').

b. *Kensington* (*outline*) *stitch*, a needlework stitch which is formed by putting the needle into the material from the front and returning it some way back whilst splitting the thread.

1881 C. C. Harrison *Woman's Handiwork* i. 33 Feather stitch..is often incorrectly termed 'Kensington' or 'crewel' stitch. **1883** *Century Mag.* Sept. 787/1 They know little of Kensington stitch or of Eastern-woven portières. **1909** *Cent. Dict.* Suppl. s.v. *stitch*, *Kensington stitch*, in *embroidery*, a long and a short outline-stitch, appearing alternately. **1934** M. Thomas *Dict. Embroidery Stitches* 186 Split Stitch... Also known as Kensington Outline Stitch.

Kensingtonian (kenziŋtōu·niǎn), *sb.* and *a.* [f. *Kensington* (see prec.) + -ian.] **A.** *sb.* An inhabitant of Kensington.

1889 G. B. Shaw in *Star* 6 Dec. 2/5 The Kensingtonians are asses to neglect these concerts. **1951** R. Campbell *Light on Dark Horse* 45 Zulus are far more important.. than dogs to Kensingtonians. **1965** G. McInnes *Road to Gundagai* xv. 267 The whole of this great grey sun-baked continent [*sc.* Australia] she regarded much as if it were Hornsey or Tooting Bec, and she a Kensingtonian of high degree. **1968** *Listener* 6 June 733/1 Hot or cool jazz would have been just too much and might have driven out the dreary West Kensingtonians with their dim uniformed escorts. **1974** *Times* 23 May 16/7 A Kensingtonian in her eighties..missed the style and elegance of the old shop.

b. A supposedly refined or affected manner of speech typical of people living in Kensington. *rare.*

1911 A. Bennett *Hilda Lessways* i. x. 91 Hilda..had been deprived of her Five Towns accent at Chetwynd's School, where the purest Kensingtonian was inculcated.

B. *adj.* Of, pertaining to, or characteristic of Kensington; *spec.* denoting refined or affected speech.

1902 A. Bennett *Anna of Five Towns* xi. 290 His broad Five Towns speech contrasting with the Kensingtonian accents of the coroner. **1936** *Times Lit. Suppl.* 27 June 541/1 Superior Margery Seymour, with her Kensingtonian 'mothah and brothah'. **1958** *Listener* 2 Oct. 537/1 A truly Kensingtonian drawing-room. **1960** *Times* 24 Feb. 15/3 Miss Maggie Smith and Miss Moyra Fraser at times vocally suggested mere Kensingtonian refinement. **1961** Wodehouse *Service with Smile* (1962) v. 73 Somehow it seemed worse and more wounding coming from those Kensingtonian lips. **1971** *Listener* 28 Oct. 596/3 Kensingtonian shrieks, with fiddle, indicated Gypsies relaxing.

Kensitite (ke·nzitəit). [f. the surname *Kensit* (see below): see -ite¹.] A follower of John Kensit (1853–1902), a Low Church extremist who objected to alleged Romanizing aspects of the Anglican Church.

1898 *Tablet* 6 Aug. 207/1 It was disloyalty, with which Mr. Drummond and his brethren were charged by an irate and portly Kensitite with a Hyde Park voice. **1904** *Daily Chron.* 5 Mar. 6/6 The cheering of the 'Kensitites' brought a crowd quickly to the scene. **1907** *Ibid.* 14 May 5/4 Some of the audience endeavoured to expel the Kensitites. **1927** W. E. Collinson *Contemp. Eng.* 50 The Ritualists, strongly opposed by the Kensitites or followers of John Kensit. **1928** *Daily Express* 1 Dec. 11 (*heading*) Kensitite protests at the new Archbishop's election. **1936** A. Huxley *Eyeless in Gaza* iv. 29 The Ritualists and the Kensitites were at it again.

kenspeckle, *a.* (Later examples.)

1916 J. Buchan *Greenmantle* xx. 259 The immediate front of a battle is a bit too public for any one to lie hidden in by day, especially when two or three feet of snow make everything kenspeckle. **1930** H. S. Walpole *Rogue Herries* ii. 392 He..wondered what it must be for such a boy to be in charge of so wild and tumultuous and kenspeckle an army. **1971** *Lancet* 6 Nov. 1028/2 He [*sc.* a cockerel] was..a kenspeckle figure in the neighbourhood [*sc.* in Scotland]. **1973** *Perthshire Advertiser* 8 Aug. 13/2 There have been others..who, if not as kenspeckle and dynamic in the public eye, have given of their time, talents and means.

kent, *sb.*² Add: (Earlier examples.) Also *attrib.*

1820 W. Scoresby *Acct. Arctic Regions* II. 296 The fat of the neck, or what corresponds in other animals with the neck, is called the Kent. **1837** R. Hamilton *Nat. Hist. Whales* 106 A band of blubber two or three feet in width, encircling the fish's body at what is the neck in other animals, is called the *kent*, because by means of it the fish is turned over or *kented*. To this band is fixed the lower extremity of a combination of powerful blocks, called the *kent-purchase*, by means of which, the whole circumference of the animal is, section by section, brought to the surface.

Kent (kent), *sb.*³ [Name of a county in England.] In full, *Kent sheep*. (See quot. 1957.)

1809 D. Price *Syst. Sheep-Grazing Romney Marsh* iv. 186 The New Leicester breed..were ripe for the slaughter-house in April, whereas the South Down and the Kents would not be so till the latter end of the summer. *Ibid.* 201 The Kent sheep being 65 lb. lighter than the Leicesters ..makes the gainings of the Kent sheep in the whole 152 lb. of mutton. **1891** R. Wallace *Rural Econ. Austral. & N.Z.* Plate lxix (*caption*) Romney Marsh or Kent Sheep. **1894** *Country Gentlemen's Catal.* 52/1 Sheep—Kent or Romney Marsh. Bred by owner. **1957** *Encycl. Brit.* XX. 476/1 The *Romney* is a long-coarse-wool, white-face, hardy, polled sheep that originated in Kent, Eng. It is sometimes called the Kent or the Romney Marsh. **1960** *Farmer & Stockbreeder* 8 Mar. 15/1 Grassland types [of sheep] include ..Greyface and Kent. **1972** *Country Life* 16 Mar. 607/1 The sheep..can break down organo-phosphates by blood enzymes. Among Dorset Downs 3 per cent could do this efficiently..and among Kent 37 per cent.

kent, *v.*² (Earlier example.)

1820 W. Scoresby *Acct. Arctic Regions* II. 296 By means of it, the fish is turned over or kented.

kentallenite (kentæ·lėnəit). *Petrogr.* [f. *Kentallen*, name of a village in Strathclyde (formerly in Argyllshire) + -ite¹.] An olivine-bearing monzonite.

1900 Hill & Kynaston in *Q. Jrnl. Geol. Soc.* LVI. 532 Taking..the Kentallen rock as our type, we propose that the term kentallenite should be substituted for olivine-monzonite. Kentallenite may be briefly defined as a coarse or medium-grained holocrystalline rock, consisting of olivine and augite, with orthoclase, plagioclase, and biotite in varying proportions. **1960** E. B. Bailey et al. *Geol. Ben Nevis & Glen Coe* (ed. 2) xv. 192 The handsome black kentallenite, once worked as an ornamental stone, is pierced by a few white felspathic segregations. **1969** *Scottish Jrnl. Geol.* V. 11 Kentallenite is a pyroxenic member of the dominantly hornblendic Appinite Suite..of the British Caledonian calc-alkaline igneous province.

kente (ke·ntə). Also **Kente.** [Twi, = cloth.] In full, *kente cloth*. In Ghana, a banded material; also, a long garment made from this material, loosely draped on or worn around the shoulders and waist.

[**1881** J. G. Christaller *Dict. Asante & Fante Lang.* 228 *Kente*, country cloth, a home-made negro-dress, consisting of a number of narrow stripes of cotton-cloth sewed together.] **1957** M. Banton *W. Afr. City* xii. 218 They may forsake western dress for Kente cloth. **1959** A. Abbs *Ashanti Boy* i. 38 The Chief was dressed in a gorgeous silk Kente... He was accompanied by some elders and friends, all wearing colourful Kentes.. with quick, characteristic swings of the right arm, each man re-arranged his cloth. *Ibid.* 255 *Kente*, cloth woven on native loom, usually in narrow strips that are sewn together. The designs are geometrical and each one has a distinctive name. **1962** *Times* 23 Nov. 4/2 The Ghanaian girls came past in their Kente dresses of gold, dark blue or deep pink and mauve. **1963** *Economist* 1 June 894/1 The confident swirling of Ghanaian *kente* robes. **1964** *Ibid.* 8 Feb. 488/2 Dr Nkrumah..intends to clutch his people by the lapels (or kente cloths). **1969** *Times* 22 Oct. (Ghana Suppl.) p. viii/4 Not even the..King of the Ashanti, knows much more than six weeks in advance when he is going to hold his durbah..when the Golden Stool of the Ashanti is paraded before a crowd robed in its gaudiest *kente* cloth.

kentia (ke·ntiǎ). [mod.L. (C. L. Blume 1836, in *Rumphia* II. xvii. 94), f. the name of William *Kent* (d. *c* 1828), botanical collector + -ia¹.] A palm with pinnate leaves of the genus so called, native to Australia and some Pacific islands, or one formerly included in this genus.

1870 B. S. Williams *Choice Stove & Greenhouse Ornamental-leaved Plants* 223 The *Kentias* are handsome robust plants, with pinnate leaves. **1909** *Westm. Gaz.* 8 Jan. 9/2 Over 1,000 Kentia palms from the South Sea Islands. **1937** M. James *Family Garden* i. 46 *Kentias* are sometimes called curly palms. **1951** *Dict. Gardening* (R. Hort. Soc.) II. 1015/2 The Howeas (usually called Kentias in the market) are the most popular of Palms for general decorative work. **1966** E. J. H. Corner *Nat. Hist. Palms* vii. 172 They [*sc.* pigeons] have been thought responsible..for the wide distribution of *Areca* and *Kentia* in the South Pacific.

Kenticism. Restrict *rare* to sense in Dict. and add: **b.** A word, idiom, or expression peculiar to the OE. or ME. Kentish dialect; language characteristic of such dialect.

1933 *Amer. Jrnl. Philol.* LIV. 307 They show traces of the Kentish dialect, which is not surprising as there is Kenticism in the inked glosses in the manuscript. **1965** H. Kökeritz in Bessinger & Creed *Medieval & Ling. Stud.* 294 We can discern in his [*sc.* Wyatt's]..poems the survival of certain Kenticisms.

Kentish, *a.* **3. b. Kentish glory** (examples).

1775 M. Harris *Eng. Lepidoptera* 27 (*heading*) Glory, Kentish. **1869** E. Newman *Illustr. Nat. Hist. Brit. Moths* 47 The Kentish Glory.—Fore wings of the male brown; hind wings orange-colour: all the wings of the female alike, pale smoky-brown. **1899** D. Sharp *Cambr. Nat. Hist.* VI. vi. 406 The 'Kentish glory', *Endromis versicolor*, ..is a large and strong moth, and flies wildly in the daytime in birch-woods. **1971** *Times* 28 Jan. 12/6 The birch which provides the last English home of the Kentish glory moth.

kentrogon (ke·ntrǒgǫn). *Zool.* [ad. Fr. *kentrogone* (Y. Delage 1884, in *Arch. Zool. Expér. & Gén.* 2 Sér. II. 606), f. Gr. κέντρον sharp point + γόν-ος offspring.] A larval form of parasitic barnacles of the order Rhizocephala, in which state the barnacle first attaches itself to the host.

1909 A. Sedgwick *Student's Text-bk. Zool.* III. v. 430 At this stage the young Cirripede is known as the Kentrogon larva. **1909** W. T. Calman in E. R. Lankester *Treat. Zool.* VII. v. 134 (*caption*) *Kentrogon*-stage, after the *Cypris* shell has been cast off and the 'dart' has been formed. **1940** *Chambers's Techn. Dict.* 473/1 Kentrogon (*Zool.*). A stage in the life-history of certain parasitic *Cirripedia* (e.g. *Sacculina*) which succeeds the Cypris stage and precedes the entry of the parasite into the body of the host.

Kentuck (ke·ntɒk), *a.* and *sb.* *U.S.* Also Kaintuck. [Abbrev. of *Kentucky.] = next.

1826 T. Flint *Recoll.* 15 A 'Kentuck' is the best man at a pole. **1831** *Constellation* (N.Y.) 143/2 Placing a huge lump of his favorite 'Kentuck' [tobacco] in his mouth. **1834** W. A. Caruthers *Kentuckian in N.Y.* I. 24, I gets a quid of the real Kentuck twist into my mouth. *Ibid.* 25 When we Kentuck boys get at it, it won't all end like a log rollin'. **1842** *Amer. Pioneer* I. 157, I then entered a Kentuck boat and descended the river. **1852** B. Casseday *Hist. Louisville* ii. 69 'And you waded in like a raal Kaintuck,' rejoined Nine-Eyes. **1872** W. J. Flagg *Good Investment* 544/1 You must expect me to defend myself *Kaintuck* fashion. **1941** L. D. Baldwin *Keelboat Age* 61 The Americans..considered a 'Kentuck' best at the setting poles. **1942** in H. Wentworth *Amer. Dial. Dict.* (1944) 338/2 The Kaintucks were spared a feud with the N.Y.C. police.

Kentuckian (kentɒ·kiǎn), *a.* and *sb.* *U.S.* Also 8–9 **Kentuckyan.** [f. next: see -ian.] **A.** *adj.* Of or pertaining to Kentucky. **B.** *sb.* A native or inhabitant of Kentucky.

1779 G. R. Clark *Campaign in Illinois* (1869) 85 If not deceived by the Kentuckyans, I should still be able to compleat my design. **1784** [see *Indianian]. **1804** C. B. Brown tr. *Volney's View Soil & Climate U.S.A.* 71, I have observed the Kentuckian bank of the river to be formed of similar ridges. **1831** [see *bead *sb.* 5 d]. **1886** F. C. Baylor *On Both Sides* 145 A handsome carriage.. drawn by a beautiful pair of Kentuckian thoroughbreds. **1949** B. A. Botkin *Treas. S. Folklore* p. xix, The pioneer saga of planting colonies..and creating names, legends, and ballads in that wild and wonderful country that the first Englishmen found in Virginia, the first Virginians in Kentucky, and the first Kentuckians and Virginians in Texas. **1969** I. Kemp *Brit. G.I. in Vietnam* iii. 43 Staff Sergeant Howell was..a paunchy, cheerful, easy-going Kentuckian.

Kentucky (kentɒ·ki). Chiefly *U.S.* Also **Kentucke.** [From the name of the river; the original meaning of this is uncertain.] One of the south-eastern United States, lying south of the Ohio River and east of the Mississippi; used *attrib.* to designate things originating in, or connected with, this state.

Only a selection of collocations is given here: see D.A.E. and D.A. for fuller lists.

1785 E. Denny *Mil. Jrnl.* (1859) 57 Our fleet now consists of..batteaux, besides two large flats called Kentucky boats. **1785** [see *coffee-tree 2]. **1811** A. Wilson *Amer. Ornith.* III. 85 [The] Kentucky Warbler, *Sylvia Formosa*,..inhabits the country whose name it bears. **1832** in A. Nicoll *Hist. Eng. Drama 1660–1900* (1959) VI. 487 (*title of play*) The Kentucky Rifle; or, the horse and the murderer. **1835** J. H. Ingraham *South-West* II. 175 The young Mississippian..dresses plainly,..often in pantaloons of Kentucky jean. **1849** E. Emmons *Agric. N.Y.* II. 68 An earlier kind of grass than timothy, is the Spear grass, Meadow grass, or Kentucky blue grass. **1872** Schele de Vere *Americanisms* 416 The Coffee-tree (*Gymnocladus canadensis*), often called Kentucky Coffee-tree, or Kentucky Locust, derives its name from the fact that in the days of early settlements the seeds were frequently used as a substitute for coffee. **1875** *Courier-Jrnl.* (Louisville, Ky.) 18 May 4/3 The Kentucky Derby, a dash of 1½ miles for three-year olds. **1901** *Jrnl. Chem. Soc.* LXXIX. i. 984 Several kilograms of Western Kentucky leaf, used mainly as 'fillers'. **1943** J. S. Huxley *TVA* vi. 49 The famous Kentucky blue grass (which won't grow without plenty of phosphorus). **1962** R. B. Fuller *Epic Poem on Industrialization* 40 Lawyer vice-presidents were fast being substituted For the Kentucky colonels As executive heads of industry. **1966** [see *burgoo 2]. **1968** *Canad. Antiques Collector* Aug. 11/1 Their gunsmiths developed and perfected the 'Kentucky' rifle, the accuracy and superiority of which was proven. **1972** E. Thorpe *Night I caught Santa Fé Chief* xiv. 183, I went into the drug store and ordered Kentucky fried chicken.

kentum, var. *centum.

Kenya (ke·nyǎ, kī·nyǎ). The name of an E. African state used *attrib.*, as **Kenya Asian** = **Kenyan Asian*; **Kenya coffee,** a mild coffee grown in Kenya.

1968 *Times* 22 Feb. 1/7 The unrestricted right of entry to Britain of some Kenya Asians must be respected, insisted Mr. Heath. *Ibid.* 1/7 Some Kenya Asians were allowed to opt for British passports. **1971** *Guardian* 27 Feb. 5/1 A Kenya-Asian teacher..said that the Walsall Education Authority refused her a job because of her accent. **1926–7** *Army & Navy Stores Catal.* 3/2 Coffee. Kenya. Roasted, whole—lb. 2/5. **1937** *Discovery* Oct.

p. xciii/1 Finest Kenya Coffee. **1970** *E. Afr. Standard* 2 Jan. 5/3 In 1965 some 20,000 bags of Kenya coffee were sold locally, consumption per head being around 130 grams per year.

Kenyah (ke·nyă). Also **Kenniah, Kenya.** [Native name.] A member of one of the aboriginal peoples inhabiting parts of Borneo and Sarawak.

1866 C. Brooke *Ten Yrs. Sarawak* I. ii. 73 The branches [of the Malanans] inhabiting the inland and up-rivers.. are Kanowit..Kenniah, Bakatan..and numerous others. **1901** Hose & McDougall in *Jrnl. Anthropol. Inst.* XXXI. 174 The Kenyahs inhabit a district far inland among the head-waters of the Baram river. *Ibid.* 175 Of the many animals that the Kenyahs dare not eat or kill..the common white-headed carrion-hawk..is by far the most important. **1911** J. G. Frazer *Golden Bough: Magic Art* (ed. 3) II. xxi. 385 In the interior of Borneo the Kenyahs generally place before the main entrance of their houses the wooden image of Balli Atap, that is, the Spirit or God (*Balli*) of the Roof. **1957** *Encycl. Brit.* XIII. 346/1 Kenyah economy is based on the cultivation of dry rice in jungle clearings. **1960** *Guardian* 9 Nov. 10/3 The population [of Sarawak] includes..Kelebits, Kenyas, Muruts, and others.

Kenyan (ke·nyăn, kī·nyăn), *sb.* and *a.* [f. *Keny(a + -an.] **A.** *sb.* A native or inhabitant of Kenya.

1938 T. W. Wallbank in *Jrnl. R. Afr. Soc.* Suppl. Apr. 20 Perhaps a more immediate and vital problem concerns the character of the young, native-born Kenyan. **1960** *Daily Tel.* 21 Jan. 10/3 Moderate Kenyans can regard the claims of the African group only with distrust. **1969** *Listener* 8 May 634/3 This week a number of Asian Kenyans, holders of British passports, are due to arrive in Britain without work permits. **1971** *Sunday Nation* (Nairobi) 11 Apr. 8/5 We must, as Wa Kataka says, try to encourage self-analysis as part of our national political ethic, and the best people, nay the people best qualified to do this, are Kenyans themselves. **1972** *Daily Tel.* 29 Dec. 2/8 The bank clerk, Rajendrakumar Thakrar, a Kenyan, who lived in Clovelly Road, Southampton, was said to be a 'happy man' until a month ago.

B. *adj.* Of, pertaining to, or characteristic of Kenya or its people. *Kenyan Asian*, an Asian, esp. one from India or Pakistan, resident, or formerly resident, in Kenya.

1946 R. Capell *Simiomata* I. 14 Kenyan gossip in the Aegean. **1960** *Guardian* 22 Apr. 6/5 Ex-Mau-Mau members..padded through the Kenyan forests. **1962** *Times* 23 Aug. 11/1 Tony, the epitome of all the New Kenyan morality must destroy. **1968** *Times* 13 Feb. 9/1 That so many Kenyan Asians are now claiming their legal right of entry to Britain is embarrassing. **1968** *Guardian* 5 Sept. 18/8 The settler farmers who opted for Kenyan citizenship. **1970** *Ibid.* 24 Mar. 11/3 Europe's airport lounges are still littered with passportless Kenyan Asians. **1972** *Ibid.* 26 June 6/5 What have Ulster Catholics, Russian Jews and Kenyan Asians in common? They are all members of underprivileged minorities.

Ke:nyaniza·tion. [f. *Kenyan *a.* + -ization.] In Kenya, the replacement of settlers and Asians by Kenyan Africans in government posts, the civil service, and other occupations. So **Ke·nyanize** *v. trans.*, to make Kenyan in character, organization, etc.

1963 *Times* 17 May 13/7 Nowhere will Europeans be required more than in administration, since the pace of Africanization—or Kenyanization, to use the locally preferred term—has been until recently far too slow to produce adequate numbers of trained and experienced African civil servants. **1970** *Guardian* 25 Nov. 11/6 The Kenyanisation and Ugandanisation law. **1971** *Inside Kenya Today* Mar. 7/1 The target of Kenyanizing the top management personnel will be reached sooner than later. **1973** *Daily Tel.* 11 Jan. 1/1 Kenya is to order 418 non-citizen Asian traders to shut their businesses and quit the country by June 1 under its Kenyanisation policy.

Kenyapithecus (ke:nyăpi·þīkǝs). [mod.L., f. *Kenya + Gr. πίθηκος ape.] A fossil hominid of the genus so called, first discovered in Kenya in 1961 by L. S. B. Leakey; sometimes included in the genus *Ramapithecus*.

[**1961** L. S. B. Leakey in *Ann. & Mag. Nat. Hist.* IV. 690 The following is a diagnosis and preliminary description of this new Kenya Lower Pliocene primate. Super-Family Hominoidea. Family Incertae sedis. Genus *Kenyapithecus* gen. nov... The type of the genus is the new species *Kenyapithecus wickeri* described below. Species *Kenyapithecus wickeri* sp. nov.] **1963** *Times* 1 June 6/1 The pelvis of *Oreopithecus*..is probably farther removed from human ancestry than its East African contemporary, *Kenyapithecus*. **1967** *Observer* 15 Jan. 9/6 Dr. Leakey..endeavours to show..that his *Kenyapithecus* hominids are quite distinct from the ancestors of apes living at the same time. **1971** J. Z. Young *Introd. Study Man* xxxi. 440 The fossils of *Ramapithecus* are less ape-like and more human. They were first named from specimens from the late Miocene of India, but the form known as *Kenyapithecus* from East Africa..is similar.

kenyte (ke·nəit, kī·nəit). *Petrogr.* [f. the name of Mount *Kenya*, Kenya: see -ite[1].] A light red to pale brown rock consisting of olivine-bearing phonolitic trachyte.

1900 J. W. Gregory in *Q. Jrnl. Geol. Soc.* LVI. 209 It is unadvisable to include the Mount Kenya lavas among the pantellerites, and the name of kenytes is accordingly proposed for them. **1921** H. G. Ponting *Gt. White South* xi. 103 One of the most grotesque of these shapes was a monolith of kenyte... The geologists were much interested in this curiosity, and, as kenyte lava is very brittle, exhorted all not to injure it. **1954** W. C. Smith in *Brit. Antarctic 'Terra Nova' Expedition 1910, Nat. Hist. Rep.: Geol.* II. iii. 41 It is now known that there is an important difference between the rocks of Mount Kenya named kenyte by J. W. Gregory and the lavas of Mount Erebus to which Prior extended the name. The kenytes of Mount Kenya actually contain large insets of nepheline. **1968** *Mineral. Abstr.* XIX. 323/1 A K/Ar date determined from anorthoclase indicates an age of 0·68(±0·14) m.y. for the Antarctic kenyte of the Cape Royds area.

kephalin. Now usu. spelt *cephalin* (see *cephalin[2]).

Kepler (ke·plər). The name of Johann *Kepler* (1571–1630), German astronomer, used, chiefly in the possessive, to designate things and concepts discovered or investigated by him, as **Kepler's equation**, the equation $\theta = \phi - e \sin \phi$ relating the mean anomaly θ of a planet to the eccentric anomaly ϕ and the eccentricity e of the orbit; **Kepler's laws** (see Law *sb.*[1] 17 c (*a*)); **Kepler's nova** or **star**, a supernova which appeared in 1604 in the constellation Ophiuchus and disappeared in 1606; **Kepler('s) problem**, the problem of solving Kepler's equation for the eccentric anomaly of a planet in a known orbit given the mean anomaly, which is effectively that of finding the position of the planet at any given time.

[**1714** *Phil. Trans. R. Soc.* XXVIII. 1 (*heading*) Problematis Kepleriani, de inveniendo vero motu planetarum, areas tempori proportionales in orbibus ellipticis circa focorum alterum describentium, solutio Newtoniana.] **1721** J. Keill *Introd. Astron.* xxiii. 287 (*heading*) Kepler's problem. **1883** *Encycl. Brit.* XV. 709/1 By far the most important problem is to find the values of θ and r as functions of t, so that the direction and length of a planet's radius-vector may be determined for any given time. This generally goes by the name of Kepler's Problem. **1890** A. M. Clerke *Syst. Stars* vii. 97, 1604, Kepler's star. **1902** F. R. Moulton *Introd. Celestial Mech.* v. 148 (*heading*) Geometrical derivation of Kepler's equation. **1954** C. Payne-Gaposchkin *Introd. Astron.* (1956) xiv. 392 Attempts to identify the remains of Tycho's and Kepler's novae with stars have failed. **1958** Condon & Odishaw *Handbk. Physics* II. iv. 32/2 Kepler's equation defines ϕ as a function of nt.., which functional relation is the subject of a large mathematical literature. **1964** *Yearbook Astron. 1965* 49 The most brilliant 'new star' of which we have an accurate record was Tycho's Star of 1572, which was, of course, a supernova, and which became equal to Venus... Its only subsequent rival has been Kepler's Star of 1604, which also seems to have been a supernova. **1970** G. K. Woodgate *Elem. Atomic Struct.* ii. 28 This is called an accidental degeneracy. It occurs likewise in the equivalent classical problem—the Kepler problem of planetary motion under an inverse square law of force.

Keplerian (keplīə·riăn), *a.* [f. prec. + -ian.] Of or pertaining to *Kepler or his discoveries and investigations; applied *spec.* to (*a*) motion, orbits, and trajectories such as occur when one body moves freely in the gravitational field of another (much more massive) body, viz. an ellipse (in accordance with Kepler's laws) or some other conic section; (*b*) a refracting telescope that has a positive objective and a positive eyepiece and gives an inverted image.

1851 Mill *Logic* (ed. 3) I. iii. ii. 313 If the Keplerian operation, as a logical process, be really identical with what takes place in acknowledged induction, the definition of induction ought to be so widened as to take it in. **1909** Webster, Keplerian telescope. **1922** A. D. Udden tr. *Bohr's Theory of Spectra* ii. 37 The orbit of the electron deviates a little from a simple ellipse and is no longer exactly periodic. This deviation from a Keplerian motion is, however, very small compared with the perturbations due to the presence of external forces. **1935** E. A. Milne *Relativity, Gravitation & World-Struct.* xiv. 267 Newton ..determined the nature of the possible motions of the particle and showed that it consisted of Keplerian orbits, or parabolas or hyperbolas with Keplerian properties. *Ibid.*, Newton's solution of the Keplerian problem. **1958** *Listener* 20 Nov. 839/1 The Keplerian universe, which did away with the epicycles, was systematically ignored by Galileo. **1959** K. A. Ehricke in H. S. Seifert *Space Technol.* viii. 92 Figure 8–50 presents a survey of possible Keplerian (in distinction to powered) mission profiles for the inner and outer solar system. **1966** *McGraw-Hill Encycl. Sci. & Technol.* VII. 452/2 If the second lens has a positive power, the telescope is called a..Keplerian telescope and the separation of the two parts is equal to the sum of the focal lengths. **1966** *Daily Tel.* 31 Oct. 9/8 True weightlessness..can best be simulated in an aircraft flying in a so-called Keplerian trajectory. **1968** R. A. Lyttleton *Mysteries Solar Syst.* iv. 124 It is to be remembered that in computing an orbit, the aim is to obtain a Keplerian path about the sun—an ellipse, parabola, or hyperbola—that fits the observation.

kept, *ppl. a.* Add: **1. a.** Also of a man or boy maintained or supported in a homosexual relationship.

1963 *Economist* 27 Apr. 304/1 The complete failure to translate his off-beat characteristics into homosexual or kept-man terms. **1966** 'R. Standish' *Widow Hack* xi. 121 The appalling indignities endured by kept men pass belief. **1969** *Jeremy* I. iii. 25/1 At the upper-end of the scene is the kept-boy who has little or nothing in common with the humbler 'rent-boy'.

ker-. Add: Also **che-, co-.** (Further examples.)

1836 *Public Ledger* (Philadelphia) 27 July (Th.), Down I came chewallop..and overset the chair. **1844** 'J. Slick' *High Life N.Y.* II. 88 We drew up co-wallop right afore Jase's house. *Ibid.* 154 Ca-smash went the chair. **1854** M. J. Holmes *Tempest & Sunshine* 2 Then, again, you'll go in co-slush. **1855** *Spirit of Times* 29 Sept. 387/1 And the fust thing you knows he falls and down he comes kerflumix. **1858** S. P. Avery *Harp of Thousand Strings* 44 He fell 'kerslap' upon the hot goose of the pressman! **1884** 'Mark Twain' *Huck. Finn* xxiii. 234 Jes' den, 'long come de wind en slam it to, behine de chile, ker-*blam!* **1903** *Outing* XLIII. 83/1 The sound made by the water when the frog dives, we used to express when we were boys, by the word 'kerplunk'. **1908** *Magnet* I. 1, 'Ker-woosh!' ejaculated the junior, as he sprawled on the floor over Harry Wharton's legs. 'What's that in the way?' **1923** *Public Opinion* 15 June 565/1 With both feet set down kerplunk he closed the interview. **1926** F. M. Ford *Man could stand Up* ii. iv. 164 Kerumph—the wagons of coal would fly over until we recalled our planes. **1935** H. G. Wells *Things to Come* xi. 96 Can I go when I grow up? And see the other side of the moon! And plump back *ker-splosh!* into the sea! **1937** *New Masses* 26 Oct. 18/1 Their [*sc.* Hollywood journalists'] vernacular divides the failures into three subdivisions: flop, flopperoo, and ker-plunk. **1939** T. S. Eliot *Old Possum's Pract. Cats* 17 Growltiger to his vast surprise was forced to walk the plank. He who a hundred victims had driven to that drop, At the end of all his crimes was forced to go ker-flip, ker-flop. **1939** J. Cary *Mr. Johnson* 41, I go trow him.. In de river Thames, kersplash. **1942** Z. N. Hurston in A. Dundes *Mother Wit* (1973) 26/2 Ker-blam-er-lam-er-lam! And dat was de last of Brer Engine-driving Monk. **1959** M. Gilbert *Blood & Judgment* vi. 59 The boat hit the surface with a solid ker-splash. **1963** *Punch* 30 Jan. 178/2 The boot..kerplonked to the carpet as straight and true as Newton's apple. **1963** *New Yorker* 29 June 26 That's why I nearly went kerplunk when you walked out of here with him. **1970** *Observer* (Colour Suppl.) 15 Feb. 36/4 They wear..extraordinary bathing costumes with Mighty Mouse zigzags across their chests, so that one half-expects them to rush about the beach shouting 'Pow!' and 'Zap!' and 'Kerrump!'

kera, var. *kra.

keramat, var. *kramat.

kerasin (ke·răsin). *Biochem.* Also **cer-, -ine.** [irreg. f. Gr. κέρας horn + -in[1].] A cerebroside, $C_{48}H_{93}NO_8$, which gives lignoceric acid, D-galactose, and sphingosine on hydrolysis and is a white amorphous powder.

1878 Kerasine [see Phrenosin]. **1884** J. L. W. Thudichum *Treat. Chem. Constitution Brain* iv. 178 Kerasin.. is a cerebroside, namely a body which contains the sugar cerebrose, combined with at least two other radicles. **1933** Cameron & Gilmour *Biochem. of Med.* v. 78 In kerasin or cerasin it [*sc.* the fatty acid] is lignoceric acid, $C_{24}H_{48}O_2$. **1951** *Arch. Path.* LI. 338 A lipoprotein fraction containing 62 per cent kerasin has been isolated from two spleens removed surgically from patients with Gaucher's disease.

keratinize, *v.* Add: (Further example.)

1973 *Nature* 9 Feb. 398/1 Ambivalent cells of the vaginal squamous epithelium keratinize under oestrogenic action.

2. *trans.* To make horny, to subject to keratinization.

1909 in Webster. **1924** *Q. Jrnl. Microsc. Sci.* LXIX. 33 The centre [of the tumour] is completely keratinized. **1971** J. Z. Young *Introd. Study Man* xi. 146 The products of the epidermal line are ultimately keratinized.

Hence **ke·ratinized, ke·ratinizing** *ppl. adjs.*

1896 Keratinising [in Dict.]. **1904** *Trans. Ophthalm. Soc.* XXIV. 13 Meibomian secretion organisms, etc., will become adherent to the keratinised plaques. **1912** A. S. Grünbaum *Essent. Morbid Histol.* ii. 11 In epithelial cancer, the result is the formation of somewhat typical cell nests, which are composed of concentric groups of keratinised cells. **1924** *Q. Jrnl. Microsc. Sci.* LXVIII. 105 Keratinized epidermis, e.g. a finger-nail, can be resolved after treatment with sulphuric acid. **1924** *Ibid.* LXIX. 49 In the keratinizing cells the volume of the cytoplasm becomes only slightly greater. **1952** *Brit. Jrnl. Dermatol.* LXIV. 424 The diagnosis of well-differentiated keratinizing squamous carcinoma. **1964** G. H. Haggis et al. *Introd. Molecular Biol.* i. 6 When sufficient vitamin A is present, the cells [in the tissue culture] fail to form a keratinized squamous epithelium as they usually do. **1966** *Lancet* 31 Dec. 1457/2 There is thus gradually built up a picture of increasing epidermal hyperplasia which at length becomes heaped up into a papilloma composed of the keratinising remnants of former follicles.

keratino- (ke·rătino), used as combining form of Keratin, as **kerati·nocyte**, an epidermal cell which produces keratin; **keratino·lysis**, lysis or destruction of keratin; so **ke:ratinoly·tic** *a.*, bringing about keratinolysis; **ke:ratinophi·lic** *a. Bot.*, growing on keratinous material such as hair, feathers, etc.

1956 D. M. Pillsbury et al. *Dermatol.* ii. 7 The epidermis..contains two distinct cell types... The most numerous and important of these are the keratin synthesizing cells (Malpighian cells or keratinocytes) which make up 95 per cent of the epidermis. **1964** *Progress Biol. Sci. Rel. Dermatol.* II. 415 The keratinocytes are derived

from the surface ectoderm. **1972** *Amer. Zoologist* XII. 35/1 Melanin pigmentation of mammalian epidermis results from the interaction of melanocytes and keratinocytes in the synthesis, transfer, transport, and ultimate disposition of melanosomes. **1956** *Experientia* XII. 309/1 Enamel minerals stimulate keratinolysis, and keratinolysis contributes to dissolution of enamel apatite. **1905** *Jrnl. Investigative Dermatol.* XLIV. 308/2 True keratinolysis is within the capability of the dermatophytes. **1952** *Mycologia* XLIV. 177 The keratinolytic power of the fungus is reduced. **1970** *Biol. Abstr.* LI. 9627/1 (*heading*) Keratinolytic and keratinophilic fungi in the immediate surroundings of cattle. **1946** J. S. Karling in *Amer. Jrnl. Bot.* XXXIII. 751/1 Inasmuch as these species appear to be limited in occurrence and growth to tissues which contain keratin they will be described as keratinophilic chytrids. **1971** *Indian Jrnl. Med. Res.* LIX. 1699 Three hundred and thirty-one domestic animals ..were examined for the presence of dermatophytes and other keratinophilic fungi.

kerato-. Add: **keratecta·sia** *Ophthalm.* [Ectasia], protrusion of the cornea; **kera·tic** *a. Ophthalm.*, occurring on the cornea; **ke:rato-acantho·ma** (pl. -omas, -omata) *Path.* [Acanth(o- + *-oma], a tumour-like overgrowth of the skin, resembling a squamous carcinoma with a keratinized centre, but usually healing spontaneously; molluscum sebaceum; **ke:rato-conjuncti·val** *a.*, of or pertaining to the cornea and the conjunctiva, or keratoconjunctivitis; **ke:ratoconjunctivi·tis** *Path.*, inflammation of the cornea and conjunctiva; any disorder so characterized; **keratode·rma, -ia** *Med.*, a local or general thickening of the horny layer of the epidermis; **keratoge·nic, kerato·genous** *adjs.*, producing, or promoting the production of, keratinous material; **keratohy·alin(e** *Biochem.* [ad. G. *keratohyalin* (W. Waldeyer in *Beiträge zur Anat. und Embryol. als Festgabe Jacob Henle* (1882) 149], the substance which makes up the granules in the granular layer of the epidermis; **kerato·ma** *Path.* [*-oma], a hard patch of thickened epidermis, due either to hypertrophy of the horny layer or to friction or pressure; a callus; **keratomala·cia** *Path.* [Malacia], a disorder in which the cornea becomes soft and opaque, associated with vitamin A deficiency; **kerato·meter** *Ophthalm.*, an instrument for measuring the radii of curvature of the front surface of the cornea by observing images reflected in it; an ophthalmometer; so **keratome·tric** *a.*, obtained by using a keratometer; **kerato·metry**, measurement of the radii of curvature of the cornea; **ke:ratomyco·sis** *Path.*, fungal infection of the cornea; **kerato·pathy** *Ophthalm.* [-pathy], any of various disorders of the cornea; **keratopla·stic** *a.*, promoting keratinization, and hence restoration, of the epidermis; **keratoplasty**, add: [ad. G. *keratoplastik* (F. Reisinger 1824, in *Baiersche Ann. f. Abhandl.*, etc., *aus d. Gebiete d. Chir.*, etc. I. 215)] (examples); **keratoscope**, add: [ad. Sp. *keratoscopio* (Placido 1880, in *Periódico de Oftalm. Prát.* Sept.–Nov. 44)] (examples); **kerato·scopy**, add: [ad. F. *kératoscopie* (Cuignet 1873, in *Rec. d'Ophthalm.* I. 14)] (examples); **kera·to·sis** (pl. -oses) *Path.* [-osis], (*a*) any of various disorders characterized by circumscribed hyperkeratosis; (*b*) a keratotic lesion; hence **kerato·tic** *a.*, of or pertaining to keratosis.

1887 *Syd. Soc. Lex.*, Keratectasia. **1904** L. W. Fox *Dis. Eye* vi. 172 *Keratectasia.* The term applied to the undue protrusion of an opaque cornea as the result of some inflammatory condition. **1918** J. H. Parsons *Dis. Eye* (ed. 3) xi. 198 As the cicatrix becomes consolidated the bulging may disappear, or it may remain permanently as an ectatic cicatrix (keratectasia from ulcer). **1972** *Biol. Abstr.* LIV. 6213/2 Differential diagnosis is discussed for keratoconus, keratectasia,..and corneal transplant marginal degeneration. **1907** J. H. Parsons *Dis. Eye* xiii. 301 The keratic precipitates..consist of leucocytes which are deposited from the aqueous upon the back of the cornea and stick there. **1955** P. D. Trevor-Roper *Ophthalm.* xxiii. 415 The endothelial cells become distended and tacky, so that any corpuscles that have been exuded into the aqueous from the iris and ciliary vessels are liable to adhere, forming keratic precipitates. **1950** A. Rook in *Proc. R. Soc. Med.* XLIII. 839 MacCormac and Scarff (1936, *Brit. J. Derm.*, **48**, 624), in the first published account of the condition, proposed to name it molluscum sebaceum, but as this term has been employed as synonymous with molluscum contagiosum, we prefer the name kerato-acanthoma which was suggested some years ago by Dr. Freudenthal. **1950** *Q. Cumulative Index Medicus* XLVIII. 1201/2 Kerato-acanthoma (molluscum sebaceum). **1952** *Brit. Jrnl. Dermatol.* LXIV. 425, I wonder if Dr. Ferguson Smith's cases of multiple self-healing epitheliomata..are really very different from these kerato-acanthomata. **1954** *Jrnl. Amer. Med. Assoc.* 5 June 562/2 Keratoacanthoma enlarges rapidly to maximum size (1 to 2 cm.) in four to eight weeks. **1972** *Cancer* XXIX. 1387 Histopathologic study of 108 keratoacanthomas and 14 squamous cell carcinomas failed to reveal any consistent single feature allowing for their distinction. **1941** *Amer. Jrnl. Ophthalm.* XXIV. 900 (*heading*) Keratoconjunctival lesions observed at high altitudes in Bolivia. **1965** *Biol. Abstr.* XLVI. 4694/1 Diagnostic value of the keratoconjunctival test in dysentery. **1887** *Syd. Soc. Lex.*, Keratoconjunctivitis. **1892** *Arch. Ophthalm.* XXI. 445 On kerato-conjunctivitis of rhino-pharyngeal origin. **1954** S. Duke-Elder *Parsons' Dis. Eye* (ed. 12) xxxiii. 554 Kerato-conjunctivitis sicca (Sjögren's syndrome), a general systemic disturbance of unknown origin usually occurring in women after the menopause.., is characterized by deficiency of the lacrimal secretion leading to dryness of the eyes. **1960** *Jrnl. Infectious Dis.* CVI. 162/1 Keratoconjunctivitis in sheep of an infectious character is prevalent in many sheep-breeding districts in Norway. **1972** *Biol. Abstr.* LIV. 325/2 An outbreak suspected to be infectious bovine keratoconjunctivitis in Zebu cattle was reported in Khartoum, Sudan. **1933** *Arch. Dermatol. & Syphilol.* XXVII. 87 In man a diffuse keratoderma is the result of a different mutation than that causing papular keratoderma. **1967** H. Montgomery *Dermatopath.* I. v. 68/2 Recently a 34-year-old woman was seen who had had diffuse keratoderma of the palms and soles all of her life. **1972** C. B. S. Schofield *Sexually Transmitted Dis.* xvi. 183 Skin lesions..are found in about 10 per cent of patients with Reiter's disease... These fully developed lesions are known as keratoderma blenorrhagica, and histologically are indistinguishable from pustular psoriasis. **1902** H. W. Stelwagon *Treat. Dis. Skin* iv. 502 Besnier divides the cases into four classes:..(2) the symmetric keratodermia developing in childhood, of an erythematous and irritable character..; (3) symmetric keratodermia, especially of the feet, developing primarily in isolate foci..; (4) accidental keratodermias. **1970** *Dermatologica* CXLI. 321 Localized congenital erythrokeratodermias are a separate entity of keratodermias among erythrodermias and hyperkeratoses. **1923** Keratogenic [see *encephalitogenic *a.*]. **1959** *Science* 26 June 1744/2 The presence of CO_2 at concentrations higher than atmospheric concentrations restricts the ability of the chorion to undergo keratogenic changes. **1971** *Dermatologica* CXLII. 14 The follicular-keratogenic properties of several fatty acids were investigated. **1887** *Syd. Soc. Lex.*, Keratogenous. **1907** *Practitioner* Dec. 849 The keratogenous and analgesic properties of picric acid, as exhibited in the treatment of burns. **1951** *Ann. N.Y. Acad. Sci.* LIII. 474 In the hair, the fibrils..are most pronounced in the keratogenous zone. **1962** *Jrnl. Investigative Dermatol.* XXXVIII. 237/1 Keratohyalin granules occur in abundance in epidermal cells located next to the keratogenous zone. **1887** *Syd. Soc. Lex.*, Keratohyaline. **1889** *Brit. Jrnl. Dermatol.* I. 235 Waldeyer held that they [*sc.* granules] were composed of a solid hyalin-like substance, which he called Keratohyalin. **1937** E. Wolff *Dis. Eye* i. 13 In the cells of the deeper layers are found numerous granules of keratohyaline. **1972** *Biochim. & Biophys. Acta* CCLXI. 416 The three most common amino acid residues in the keratohyalin material ..are glutamic acid, glycine and alanine. **1887** *Syd. Soc. Lex.*, Keratoma. **1902** H. W. Stelwagon *Treat. Dis. Skin* iv. 498 Callositas. Synonyms—Tyloma; Tylosis; Keratoma; Callus. **1931** L. McCarthy *Histopath. Skin Dis.* ix. 438 Keratoma senilis is one of the factors that make up the clinical condition known as old-age atrophy of the skin. **1972** *Biol. Abstr.* LIV. 374/1 (*heading*) A case of senile keratoma on the eyelid. **1876** Dunglison *Dict. Med. Sci.* (rev. ed.) 565/1 Keratomalacia. **1886** C. M. Culver tr. *Landolt's Refraction & Accommodation of Eye* v. 413 Certain affections of the cornea, as keratomalacia, or central corneal ulcers, may bring about a notable flattening of this membrane. **1920** *Biochem. Jrnl.* XIV. 519 The histological and bacteriological evidence shows that keratomalacia among rats consists in a breakdown of the corneal tissue, caused by bacterial invasion. **1969** *New Scientist* 30 Jan. 227/1 Keratomalacia, scurvy and beriberi are also frequent aftermaths of infection in people living on diets deficient in vitamin A, ascorbic acid, and thiamine respectively. **1886** C. M. Culver tr. *Landolt's Refraction & Accommodation of Eye* iv. 330 Javal and Schiötz have adapted a similar disc to their keratometer. **1927** *Amer. Jrnl. Ophthalm.* X. 683/2 In the measurement of irregular astigmatism in the center of the cornea, the keratometer is usually extremely valuable. **1972** Stone & Phillips *Contact Lenses* iv. 105 Since the optic radii of a contact lens are similar to those of the cornea, a keratometer may be used to check them. **1885** *Arch. Ophthalm.* XIV. 175 The hyperbolic lenses..can be manufactured to order to suit each particular case from data furnished by the keratometric measurements. **1927** *Amer. Jrnl. Ophthalm.* X. 678/1 The accuracy of a keratometric record..depends primarily on having a good modern instrument. **1973** W. G. Sampson in *Symposium Contact Lenses* (New Orleans Acad. Ophthalm.) ii. 22 Javal's rule was used in the past to estimate the predicted spectacle cylinder from keratometric measurements. **1891** *Ophthalmic Rev.* X. 250 (*heading*) Contributions to keratometry. **1972** Stone & Phillips *Contact Lenses* iv. 105 The central radius is determined by 'classical' keratometry. **1883** *Ophthalmic Rev.* II. 369 (*heading*) Keratomycosis. **1951** H. L. Birge in A. Sorsby *Syst. Ophthalm.* ix. 305 Keratomycosis (moniliasis) is rarely seen in the cold climates, and usually follows some sort of trauma to the eye with an earthy substance. **1971** *Amer. Jrnl. Ophthalm.* LXXI. 1191/2 A fifth case of keratomycosis due to Allescheria boydii is reported. **1948** D. G. Cogan et al. in *Arch. Ophthalm.* XL. 625 The corneal changes are those generally called band keratitis, but, for obvious reasons, are more properly designated as band keratopathy. **1958** *Circulation* XVIII. 524/2 Lipid keratopathy..consists clinically of a fatty plaque in an area of the cornea that has been previously vascularized. **1972** H. M. Leibowitz in Gasset & Kaufman *Soft Contact Lenses* xxv. 202 Hydrophilic contact lenses have been found to be extremely useful in the therapy of bullous keratopathy. **1887** *Syd. Soc. Lex.*, Keratoplastic. **1907** W. A. Pusey *Princ. & Pract. Dermatol.* i. 126 The keratoplastic action that is noted from the application of various powders upon raw epithelial surfaces may be due partly to their drying action. **1951** A. Grollman *Pharmacol. & Therapeutics* xxv. 522 Chrysarobin is used in skin diseases, especially in psoriasis... In a strength of 10 to 20 per cent it has a keratolytic action while in more dilute form (5 per cent) it exercises a keratoplastic action. **1857** Dunglison *Dict. Med. Sci.* (rev. ed.) 518/1 Keratoplasty. **1888** *Arch. Ophthalm.* XVII. 524 In making his experiments on keratoplasty Wagenmann..first took flaps from the cornea of rabbits which were left in partial communication with it. **1939** E. B. Spaeth *Princ. & Pract. Ophthalmic Surg.* xvi. 489 Circumscribed or partial penetrating keratoplasty has offered up to the present day the best permanent results. **1948** *Sci. News* VIII. 31 This problem has been resolved by keratoplasty, or corneal transplantation. **1972** *Arch. Ophthalm.* LXXXVII. 538/1 Corneas more than 50 hours old and from elderly donors are dependable for use in penetrating keratoplasties. **1886** C. M. Culver tr. *Landolt's Refraction & Accommodation of Eye* iv. 329 This author [*sc.* Placido] uses, as a 'keratoscope', a disc of card-board, wood or zinc, 23 centimetres in diameter. On one side is drawn a series of concentric circles, alternately black and white. **1910** H. C. Parker *Handbk. Dis. Eye* 81 The cone is observed by inspection..with an instrument known as the keratoscope. **1972** *Jrnl. Optical Soc. Amer.* LXII. 169/1 In a conventional keratoscope, light from a flat or curved target subtending about 150° at the eye is specularly reflected by the anterior surface of the cornea. **1882** C. Macnamara *Man. Dis. Eye* (ed. 4) ii. 40 Keratoscopy may assist us in forming a diagnosis. **1902** E. H. Lendon *Method of Cuignet* 5 The word 'Keratoscopy' has now come..to be equivalent to 'Shadow Test'. **1972** Feldman & Carney in Gasset & Kaufman *Soft Contact Lenses* xxxiii. 269 By using photoelectric keratoscopy and lenses designed by computer to fit the measured eye, we were able to resolve these problems. **1885** *Buck's Handbk. Med. Sci.* I. 419/2 (*heading*) Laminated epithelial plugs (*Keratosis obturans*, Wreden, Burnett). **1888** *Trans. Path. Soc. London* XXXIX. 357 That the keratoses were in their turn due to arsenic no one will, I think, doubt. **1939** *Arch. Dermatol. & Syphilol.* XXXIX. 235 A unique case of tumor-like keratoses developing on the dorsum of the hands after severe sunburn is reported. **1966** Wright & Symmers *Systemic Path.* II. xxiv. 1487/2 The type of keratosis that is caused by arsenic has a microscopical picture much less complex than that of senile and solar keratosis. **1972** *Daily Colonist* (Victoria, B.C.) 26 Jan. 2/1 These brown spots..can be generally called senile keratoses, although they are not all of the same type. **1934** *Brit. Jrnl. Dermatol.* XLVI. 162 Keratotic lesions..were observed with this distribution in nine of the ten cases. **1972** *Arch. Dermatol.* CV. 249/3 An 18-year-old daughter of the patient..began developing firm keratotic papules on her thighs at the age of 13. **1972** C. B. S. Schofield *Sexually Transmitted Dis.* xvi. 183 The lesions tend.., if dry, to develop keratotic crusts.

keratolysis (kerătǫ·lisis). *Med.* [f. Kerato- + *-lysis.] **1.** (In Dict. s.v. Kerato-.)

2. A condition in which parts of the epidermis (esp. on the palms and soles) peel off periodically.

1895 *Brit. Jrnl. Dermatol.* VII. 37 (*heading*) A case of congenital exfoliation of the skin—(keratolysis exfoliativa?). **1902** J. W. Ballantyne *Man. Antenatal Path. & Hygiene: Foetus* xviii. 320, I place fœtal keratolysis here among the idiopathic maladies..simply to emphasise the fact that sometimes no such pathogenesis is possible. **1939** Lewis & Hopper *Introd. Med. Mycol.* ix. 102 In keratolysis exfoliativa the lesions consist of superficial scaly macules, which may coalesce and are localised to the palms and/or soles.

b. Loosening or removal of the horny layer of the epidermis through the action of chemical or mechanical agents.

1936 C. W. Dodge *Med. Mycol.* xx. 736 The infection ..extends to the thick palmar or plantar surface as a gyrate area of keratolysis. **1956** D. M. Pillsbury et al. *Dermatol.* iv. 22 The chemical disorganization of keratin is called keratolysis. It may be brought about chiefly by two classes of chemical agents: (1) strong alkalies and (2) reducing agents. **1969** *Arch. Dermatol.* C. 10/2 Pitted keratolysis is quite common in our military patients who have spent at least several days in wet conditions.

keratolytic (kerătoli·tik), *a.* and *sb. Med.* [f. Kerato- + *-lytic.] **A.** *adj.* Able to destroy keratinous material, esp. the horny layer of the epidermis.

1893 P. H. Pye-Smith *Introd. Study Dis. Skin* xi. 244 The hardened skin may be covered with salicylic acid... The best method of applying this valuable keratolytic agent is probably..as a plaister. **1917** M. B. Hartzell *Dis. Skin* vi. 47 (*heading*) Keratolytic agents (those which soften the horny cells of the epidermis and cause its exfoliation). **1956** D. M. Pillsbury et al. *Dermatol.* iv. 22 Common examples of this type of keratolytic agent are the thioglycate salts (reducing agents) which are the principal ingredients of home sets for the permanent (cold) waving of hair. **1961** *Sabouraudia* I. 87 Keratolytic enzymes have not yet been isolated from dermatophytes.

B. *sb.* A keratolytic agent.

1932 A. C. Roxburgh *Common Skin Dis.* iii. 25 Keratolytics. For removal of horny thickening. **1940** Becker & Obermayer *Mod. Dermatol. & Syphilol.* iv. 36/1 Resorcin. This drug is somewhat similar in action to salicylic acid, and the two are the only drugs we use as keratolytics. **1971** *Brit. Jrnl. Dermatol.* LXXXIV. 311 Keratolytics and other topical agents have proved unhelpful.

keratophyre (ke·rătǒfəiəɹ). *Petrogr.* [ad. G. *keratophyr* (C. W. Gümbel *Die paläolith. Eruptivgesteine des Fichtelgebirges* (1874) 44), f. Kerato-: see *-phyre.] (See quot. 1972.)

1889 *Geol. Mag.* Feb. 71 Microscopical examination and chemical analysis show that these rocks consist, in part at least, of soda-felsites or keratophyres. The keratophyres (so named from their resemblance to hornstone) were first described by Gümbel. **1937** A. Johannsen *Descr. Petrogr. Igneous Rocks* III. 49 The keratophyres

are similar in appearance [to normal trachytes] but usually are much weathered and show brown or green tones. **1956** E. W. HEINRICH *Microscopic Petrogr.* iii. 51 Trachytes occur as volcanic rocks and minor hypabyssal intrusives. ..Albitized types (keratophyres) occur with spillites. **1972** *Gloss. Geol.* (Amer. Geol. Inst.) 385/2 *Keratophyre*, a name originally applied by Gümbel..to trachytic rocks containing highly sodic feldspars, but now more generally applied to all salic extrusive and hypabyssal rocks characterized by the presence of albite or albite-oligoclase and chlorite, epidote, and calcite, generally of secondary origin. Originally the term was restricted to lavas of pre-Tertiary age but this distinction is not recognized in current usage.

keratosulphate (kerătosʌ·lfēit). *Biochem.* Also (*U.S.*) **-sulfate.** [f. KERATO- + SULPHATE *sb.*] A mucopolysaccharide composed of galactose and sulphated acetylglucosamine units which is found in the cornea and in costal cartilage.

1953 K. MEYER et al. in *Jrnl. Biol. Chem.* CCV. 611 A polymer composed of *N*-acetylglucosamine, galactose, and sulfate in equimolar portions.., a novel type of sulfated mucopolysaccharide, we propose to name keratosulfate. **1960** G. K. SMELSER in Duke-Elder & Perkins *Transparency of Cornea* 33 Loss of metachromatic staining, following digestion of the sections with testicular hyaluronidase, suggests that keratosulphate appears late in development. **1972** *Jrnl. Pediatrics* LXXXI. 108/2 Keratosulfate was clearly visible on the chromatograms [of the urine] of three patients with Morquio's disease, whereas none of the normal subjects or patients with other mucopolysaccharidoses tested had any visible keratosulfate.

kerb, *sb.* Add: **2. b.** *kerb-edge, -side; kerb market, stocks* (see *on the kerb* in 2 a and *CURB *sb.* 15); **kerb crawling** *vbl. sb.*, = *gutter crawling* vbl. sb. (*GUTTER *sb.*[1] 8); also as *ppl. a.*; also **kerb-crawl** *v. intr.* [as a back-formation]; **kerb-crawler; kerb drill,** the exercise of standing on the kerb and looking right, then left, then right again before crossing the road; **kerb service,** see *curb service* (*CURB *sb.* 15); **kerb weight** (see quot. 1967).

1971 *Daily Tel.* 13 Jan. 11/1 A man who kerb-crawls is not committing an offence. **1972** *Ibid.* 16 Oct. 3 A campaign against motorists who 'kerb crawl' in search of prostitutes. **1955** 'C. H. ROLPH' *Women of Streets* ii. 43 The solicitation of respectable women in the streets by 'kerb-crawlers'..is causing much disquiet. **1969** *Sunday Tel.* (Brisbane) 20 Apr. 3/6 Women who complain of kerb-crawlers who pester them are often hypocritical to sex. **1949** in PARTRIDGE *Dict. Slang* 1091/2 Kerb-crawling vbl. sb. and ppl. a. **1971** *Times* 10 Aug. 2/1 The Rev. Peter Hawkins..complaining of kerb-crawling by men looking for girls. *Ibid.* 2/2 Respectable women had complained of being importuned by kerb-crawling motorists. **1948** R. BAILEY *Safety Way* iii. 17 In some schools the children practise Kerb Drill with their teachers and learn to judge speeds. **1969** *Highway Code* 5 *Kerb drill.* Before you cross, stop at the kerb, look right, look left, look right again. **1970** R. RENDELL *Guilty Thing Surprised* ix. 105 They poured through the gates.., paying no attention to the kerb drill. **1930** D. H. LAWRENCE *Nettles* 11 Idle we stand at the kerb-edge, Auntie, Dangling our useless hands. **1955** W. FAULKNER *Fable* 306 On through the gate into an alley, a blank wall opposite and at the kerb-edge [curb-edge, 1954 U.S. ed.] a big..car. **1905** *Daily Chron.* 28 Apr. 4/4 The kerb market in New York reflects in a general way the tone of the stock market. **1956** P. HIGHSMITH *Blunderer* viii. 69 Walter..bought her chocolate sodas at the kerb-service drugstore. **1905** *Daily Chron.* 11 Nov. 4/7 Fruit from the kerbside barrow is marvellously cheap nowadays. **1923** *Daily Mail* 21 July 3 The growing tendency of motorists to avail themselves of kerb-side pumps. **1959** *Times* 8 Dec. 5/6 The all-day parker has become so accustomed to free kerbside accommodation that the very idea of having to pay a parking charge seems to him an outrage. **1969** *Daily Tel.* 19 Aug. 15/1 A kerbside cafe. **1971** SLAUGHTER & GOODMAN *Every Man should have One* ii. 18 If they succeed in looking like a model girl..it is meant as a compliment to you, not an expectation of ritzy treatment with champagne flowing and nothing less than an Aston Martin at the kerbside. **1923** *Daily Express* 30 July 2/6 Kerb Stocks. **1958** *Economist* 25 Oct. (Suppl.) 10/1 With a kerb weight of 26 cwt and 240 BHP of power from the 3.7-litre engine, the maximum speed will equal that of any four-seater car in the world, close to 150 mph. **1967** E. RUDINGER *Consumer's Car Gloss.* (ed. 2) 64 *Kerb weight*, weight of a car without occupants or luggage but with oil and water and some petrol.

ker-blam: see *KER-.

Kerch (kəɪtʃ). Also **Kertch.** The name of a town in the Crimea used *attrib.* to designate a type of ancient red-figured Greek pottery found there.

1936 G. M. A. RICHTER *Red-Figured Athenian Vases* I. vii. 213 (*heading*) Kerch style... With the Kerch period we reach the last phase of Athenian red-figured pottery. *Ibid.* 214 Kerch vases have been found at Alexandria. **1960** R. G. HAGGAR *Conc. Encycl. Cont. Pott. & Porc.* 412/2 In the Greek decadence, popular vases of so-called 'Kertch' ware, from the name of the town where they have been found, were exported to South Russia. **1965** J. V. NOBLE *Techniques Painted Attic Pott.* (1966) iii. 64 Attic chous in the Kerch style, mid fourth century B.C., in the Metropolitan Museum of Art.

kerel (ke·rəl). *S. Afr.* Also **kêrel.** [Afrikaans, f. Du. = CARL *sb.*[1]] A fellow, chap, young man.

1873 *Cape Monthly Mag.* Oct. 215, I have always known you to be a *slimme kerel.* **1896** H. A. BRYDEN *Tales S. Afr.* 214 *Kerel* (my boy) you have never by chance heard the story of the vrouw there and her Frenchman? **1902** J. H. M. ABBOTT *Tommy Cornstalk* 81 It is that 'kerel' French who is coming. **1939** S. CLOETE *Watch for Dawn* 41, I want no more than justice, kerels. **1974** *Cape Times* 11 Nov. 9/2 Willem Prinsloo..served his lekker peach brandy on the stoep as the kêrles gathered to bid good afternoon to the setting sun.

kereru (ke·rĕru). [Maori.] The New Zealand pigeon, *Hemiphaga novæseelandiæ.*

1873 W. L. BULLER *Hist. Birds N.Z.* 157 *Carpophaga Novæ Zealandiæ* (New-Zealand Pigeon)..*Native names.* Kuku, Kukupa, and Kereru. **1905, 1949** [see *KUKU 1]. **1955** W. R. B. OLIVER *N.Z. Birds* (ed. 2) 440/1 New Zealand Pigeon. Kereru..was noticed and recorded by all the early explorers.

Keres (kēi·rēis). Also **Queres.** [American Indian.] **a.** A Pueblo Indian people inhabiting parts of New Mexico. **b.** The language of the Keres, forming the Keresan group. Also *attrib.* or as *adj.*

1893 T. DONALDSON *Moqui Pueblo Indians* 91 The Queres group (Keresan stock) are the Pueblos of Santa Ana, San Felipe, Cochiti, San Domingo, Acoma, Zia, and Laguna. **1925** *Amer. Indian Life* 397 The Pueblo Indians..number about 10,000. They are usually classified according to language into four or five stocks, the Hopi of Arizona, the Ashiwi or people of Zuñi, the Keres of Acoma and Laguna to the west and, to the east, of five towns on the Rio Grande, and, also in the east, the Tanoans including the Tewa and the people of Jemez. **1957** *Encycl. Brit.* XVIII. 753/2 At the discovery in 1540 the Hopi, Zuñi and Keres may have been twice.. as numerous as to-day. **1965** *Canad. Jrnl. Linguistics* Spring 99 Hokan-Siouan in Sapir's arrangement includes six major units...The six units are: ..Keres (Powell's Keresan)..and an 'Eastern Group'.

Keresan (ke·rəsăn). [f. prec. + -AN.] A linguistic group consisting of Keres only. Also *attrib.* or as *adj.*

1893 [see *KERES]. **1939** L. H. GRAY *Found. Lang.* xii. 408 In North America, twenty-five linguistic families are listed..*Algonkin... Iroquois... Keresan* with two dialects. **1950** F. EGGAN *Social Organiz. Western Pueblos* 2 The more western Keresan-speaking villages. *Ibid.* 223 The Keresan villages of the Rio Grande. **1968** A. M. JOSEPHY *Indian Heritage Amer.* xvi. 149 Keresan-speaking people of Acoma and Laguna in western New Mexico [are] considered western Pueblos. **1969** H. E. DRIVER *Indians N. Amer.* (ed. 2) xxvii. 517 As one proceeds eastward, to Zuñi, Acoma, Laguna, and other Keresan pueblos, the system [of matriarchy] becomes more bilocal and bilateral.

ker-flip, -flop, -flumix: see KER- (in Dict. and Suppl.).

kerfuffle (kəɪfʌ·f'l). = CURFUFFLE *sb.*, *GEFUFFLE.

1959 J. FLEMING *Miss Bones* xiv. 150 The kerfuffle over the stolen jewels last week. **1960** E. W. HILDICK *Jim Starling & Colonel* viii. 62 Butcher said he didn't know what all the kerfuffle was about. **1965** *New Statesman* 30 Apr. 693/3 After..some abortive backstage kerfuffles at the National Theatre, Wedekind's *Spring Awakening* has scraped past the Lord Chamberlain. **1968** 'B. MATHER' *Springers* xii. 130 In the kerfuffle of the last half hour I had forgotten the poor soul's personal needs. **1973** K. AMIS *Riverside Villas Murder* ii. 40 A lot of our readers are going to think all this kerfuffle over an old skeleton being snatched is..a bit of a joke.

Kerguelen (kəɪge·lən, kō·ɪgələn). The name of a group of islands in the southern Indian Ocean, used *attrib.* in **Kerguelen cabbage,** a cabbage-like plant, *Pringlea antiscorbutica,* of the family Cruciferæ, which is confined to several islands in this region.

1847 J. D. HOOKER *Bot. Antarctic Voy.: Flora Antarctica* II. 240 The illustrious Cook first discovered and drew attention to the 'Kerguelen's Land cabbage' during his first voyage, when accompanied by Mr. Anderson as surgeon and naturalist. The latter gentleman drew up an account of some of the more remarkable plants which he collected there and in other islands, which are preserved in the Banksian library. *Ibid.* 241 The Kerguelen's Land cabbage, cabbage though it be, [is] a cherished object in the recollection of the mariner. **1879** H. N. MOSELEY *Notes by Naturalist on 'Challenger'* viii. 191 The feature which distinguishes the general appearance of the vegetation of Christmas Harbour..is the presence of the Kerguelen Cabbage in large quantities. The plant grows on the slopes and bases of the cliffs in thick beds. The cabbage is in appearance like a small garden cabbage, but often with a long trailing stalk. **1952** J. A. KING in F. A. Simpson *Antarctic Today* xv. 305 The Kerguelen cabbage (*Pringlea antiscorbutica*) is not as abundant [in the Prince Edward Islands] as at Kerguelen. **1960** *Times* 20 Apr. 14/7 There are no trees or shrubs and only some 17 species of other vascular plants, the largest being the so-called Kerguelen cabbage.

Kerman, var. *KIRMAN.

Kermanji (kəɪmā·ndʒi). [Kurdish.] A language of the Iranian group spoken by the Kurds of Kurdistan.

1882 *Encycl. Brit.* XIV. 157/2 The present Kurdish language which is called Kermánjí..is an old Persian patois, intermixed to the north with Chaldæan words and to the south with a certain Turanian element which may not improbably have come down from Babylonian times. **1914** T. E. LAWRENCE *Home Lett.* (1954) 295 A grammar of Kermanji (Kurdish). **1959** *Chambers's Encycl.* VIII. 274/1 They [*sc.* the Kurds] speak Kermanji, derived from an old Persian dialect.

Kermanshah, var. *KIRMANSHAH.

kermesse (kəɪme·s). *Cycling.* [Fr.: see KERMIS.] A circuit race.

1963 *Times* 13 June 3/5 They stopped..to put on a.. 26-mile, 10-lap kermesse (circuit race). **1965** *Times* 31 May 4/5 *Kermesse* is a Continental term which British cycling uses to describe a circuit race. It originates from Belgium and is the Flemish for the carnival which usually includes such a race. **1971** D. ARMSTRONG in N. G. Henderson *Cycling Year Bk.* xii. 101 Any rider who has ever won some little local kermesse would label it a classic event if he thought anyone would listen to him.

kern, *sb.*[2] Restrict *rare* to senses in Dict. and add: **3.** *Meteorol.* [abstracted from G. *kernzähler* kern (nucleus) counter (A. Wigand 1913, in *Meteorol. Zeitschr.* XXX. 13).] A particle which acts as a condensation nucleus in a **kern counter,** a device in which a sample of air is supersaturated and condensation nuclei made visible and collected for counting: orig. intended to measure the concentration of condensation nuclei in the air, but now known to respond to particles too small to act as such under atmospheric conditions.

1941 *Jrnl. R. Aeronaut. Soc.* XLV. 72 The Aitken nucleus or 'kern' counter determines the number of nuclei in an air sample by subjecting it to a rapid expansion. This causes a considerable degree of supersaturation, and the drops which form around each nucleus fall on to a ruled slide where they may be counted. **1951** H. G. HOUGHTON in T. F. Malone *Compendium Meteorol.* 165/2 The sweeping action of the dust particles on the kerns. **1954** J. C. JOHNSON *Physical Meteorol.* vii. 206 These dusts, or kerns, as they are called, which make up most of the suspensoids in the atmosphere and are important for their light scattering effects on visibility, contribute little or nothing to the condensation process. *Ibid.* 207 Dust counts made by instruments such as the Aitken kern counter have little correlation with the number of active condensation nuclei in the atmosphere. **1967** R. W. FAIRBRIDGE *Encycl. Atmospheric Sci.* 84/2 Such nuclei counters (or kern counters..) have some distinct advantages.

kernel, *sb.*[1] Add: **7. d.** *Chem.* = *CORE *sb.*[1] 7 f.

1916 G. N. LEWIS in *Jrnl. Amer. Chem. Soc.* XXXVIII. 768 In every atom is an essential kernel which remains unaltered in all ordinary chemical changes. *Ibid.* 769 It must not be assumed..that the distinction between kernel and shell is absolutely hard and fast. **1927** E. N. DA C. ANDRADE *Struct. Atom* (ed. 3) xv. 552 The interaction of the outer electrons with one another is large compared to the interaction of the single electrons with the core. We may refer to it as the kernel scheme. **1927** [see *CORE *sb.*[1] 7 f]. **1957** SIENKO & PLANE *Chem.* iii. 64 The letters represent the entire core, or kernel, of the atom.

8. b. *Linguistics.* (i) The stem or common basis of a set of inflectional forms, such as *lach-* in the German verb *lachen*; (ii) in full *kernel sentence* (in an early version of transformational grammar), a relatively simple sentence that results from the application of only a few (obligatory) transformations, and to which other sentences may be related by further transformations; a set of such sentences.

1894 O. JESPERSEN *Progress in Language* vi. 143, I shall have to separate word and case-ending, as far as this is feasible... We want a special term for this distinction; and I propose to call the substantial part of the word, felt as such by the instinct of each generation as something apart from the ending (*eag* in the example chosen [*sc.* O.E. *eage*]), the *kernel* of the word, while *eagan* is the historic 'stem'. **1918** *Amer. Jrnl. Philol.* XXXIX. 91, I think it unfortunate that the author feels it necessary to use the term *kernel* in place of the now generally used name *root.* **1933** L. BLOOMFIELD *Lang.* xiii. 225 This *lach-*, strictly speaking, is a bound form; it is called the kernel or stem of the paradigm.

1957 N. CHOMSKY *Syntactic Structures* v. 45 We define the kernel of the language (in terms of the grammar G) as the set of sentences that are produced when we apply obligatory transformations to the terminal strings. **1961** R. B. LONG *Sentence & its Parts* 494 'Kernels'. This term is applied to stripped-down nucleuses. **1963** J. LYONS *Structural Semantics* ii. 14 It appears that the kernel for English consists of simple, active, declarative sentences. **1969** *Canad. Jrnl. Linguistics* XV. 25 Sentences of the form *she is eager to please* demand that the subject, but no other nominal, of their embedded kernels be deleted. **1969** *Neuphilol. Mitt.* LXX. 204 The oft-repeated claim that all 'well-formed' sentences of a language are derivable from a single syntactic kernel is clearly unfounded.

c. *Math.* [tr. G. *kern* (D. Hilbert 1904, in *Nachrichten von d. Königl. Ges. d. Wissensch. zu Göttingen* (Math.-physik. Kl.) 49).] A function of two or more variables which, multiplied by one or more functions each of just one of the variables, constitutes the integrand of an integral with respect to these latter variables. (Orig. defined for integral

equations in which the kernel is known and the other function(s) unknown, but now used in other situations also.)

1909 M. Bôcher *Introd. Study Integral Equations* 13 Comparing Abel's equation..with Liouville's equation.. we see that they come respectively under the following types: $f(x) = \int_a^x K(x, \xi)u(\xi)d\xi$ [and] $u(x) = f(x) + \int_a^x K(x, \xi)u(\xi)d\xi$ in which $f(x)$ and $K(x, \xi)$ are to be regarded as known functions and $u(x)$ is the function to be determined... K is called the kernel of these equations. **1924** W. V. Lovitt *Linear Integral Equations* i. 6 An integral equation is also said to be singular if the kernel becomes infinite for one or more points of the interval under discussion. **1962** *Newnes Conc. Encycl. Nucl. Energy* 762/2 The function $P(\mathbf{r}, \mathbf{r}_0, E, E_0)$ is called the slowing-down kernel of the moderator. It cannot, in general, be calculated exactly, but various approximations have been developed. **1971** J. W. Miles *Integral Transforms in Appl. Math.* i. 1 We define $F(p) = \int_a^b K(p, x)f(x)\,dx$ to be an integral transform of the function $f(x)$; $K(p, x)$, a prescribed function of p and x, is the kernel of the transform.

d. *Math.* The set of all the elements that are mapped by a given homomorphism into the identity element (for the group operation in the case of groups, for addition in the case of rings).

1946 E. Lehmer tr. *Pontrjagin's Topological Groups* i. 11 The set of all the elements of the group G which go into the identity of the group G^* under the homomorphism g is called the kernel of this homomorphism. **1959** G. & R. C. James *Math. Dict.* 224/2 If a homomorphism maps a ring R onto a ring R^*, then the kernel of the homomorphism is the set I of elements which map onto the zero element of R^*. **1971** G. Glauberman in Powell & Higman *Finite Simple Groups* i. 9 Since ϕ maps G into an abelian group, (G' is contained in the kernel of ϕ.

9. (sense *8 b (ii)) *kernel string, word*; **kernel sentence**: see quot. 1968 and 8 b (ii) above.

1957 N. Chomsky *Syntactic Structures* viii. 89 Both 'the hunters shoot' and 'they shoot the hunters' are kernel sentences. **1968** J. Lyons *Introd. Theoret. Ling.* vi. 256 A kernel sentence..is any sentence which is generated from a single kernel string without the application of any *optional* transformations. **1972** *Science* 23 June 1304/1 The basic units of information in language are the 'kernel sentences'—primitive nondecomposable sentences that can be modified and combined in various ways..to produce a very large number of different messages. **1957** N. Chomsky *Syntactic Structures* viii. 88 Alternative transformational developments from the same kernel strings. **1965** *Language* XLI. 392 Variants occurring under unique operators or kernel-words.

kernicterus (kə̄ɹni·ktĕrŏs). *Path.* Formerly also **kern-, Kernikterus.** [ad. G. *kernikterus* (G. Schmorl 1903, in *Verhandl. d. Deut. Path. Ges.* VI. 112), f. *kern* nucleus + *ikterus* Icterus, jaundice.] The staining of nuclei of the brain cells with bilirubin, which sometimes occurs, usu. associated with rhesus incompatibility, in neonatal jaundice, and which causes permanent brain damage; the disease or condition characterized by or associated with such staining.

1912 *Brain* XXXIV. 488 An important analogy may be drawn from the occurrence of 'Kernikterus' in certain cases of familial icterus gravis neonatorum. **1933** *Amer. Jrnl. Dis. Children* XLV. 757 Opinion is almost unanimous on the subject of the pathogenesis of kernikterus, namely, that following some injury, the nerve cells are subsequently stained with the bile pigments carried to them by the blood stream. **1950** *Jrnl. Laryngol. & Otol.* LXIV. 505 Sixteen cases of perceptive deafness associated with kernicterus are reported. In fourteen of these cases the jaundice was due to Rh iso-immunization. **1953** *Lancet* 28 Mar. 613/1 Kernicterus is never found apart from jaundice. **1965** *Amer. Jrnl. Path.* XLVI. 336 Yellow ganglion and glial cells, characteristic features of human kernicterus, were demonstrated in 23 rabbits.

Hence **kerni·cteric** *a.*, afflicted or associated with kernicterus.

1956 *Jrnl. Speech & Hearing Disorders* XXI. 407 (*heading*) Clinical pathologic aspects of kernicteric nuclear 'deafness'. **1967** *Jrnl. Neurochem.* XIV. 192 The kernicteric animals are known to have pathologic lesions in the CNS comparable to those found in brain tissue of infants dying with kernicterus.

Kernig's sign (kə̄·ɹnigz səin). *Med.* [f. the name of V. M. *Kernig* (1840–1917), Russian physician.] The inability of a patient to straighten his leg at the knee when lying on his back with the hips fully flexed, an indication of meningitis.

1901 *Brit. Med. Jrnl.* 16 Feb. 396/2 'Kernig's sign' was well marked. **1924** *Ibid.* 20 Dec. 1159/1 The angle at which Kernig's sign begins to be positive is clearly very different for a baby who can suck his own toe and a stocky middle-aged man. **1950** T. R. Harrison *Princ. Internal Med.* viii. 94/2 If the head cannot be so flexed and Kernig's sign is positive, it is likely that the patient has either meningitis or subarachnoid hemorrhage. **1969** I. J. T. Davies *Postgrad. Med.* vi. 201 The cardinal signs of inflammation of the meninges are neck stiffness..and Kernig's sign which is spasm of the hamstring muscles when the knee is extended with the hips fully flexed.

kernite (kə̄·ɹnəit). *Min.* [f. *Kern*, name of the county in California where it was discovered + -ite[1].] A hydrated form of sodium borate, $Na_2B_4O_7.4H_2O$, that occurs as large transparent crystals and is used as a source of borax.

1927 W. T. Schaller in *Amer. Mineralogist* XII. 24 The new mineral kernite, $Na_2B_4O_7.4H_2O$, was received through Hoyt S. Gale..and is reported to occur in quantity in the southeast corner of Kern County, California... The name kernite is proposed. **1930** *Prof. Papers U.S. Geol. Survey* No. 158. 1. 146/1 The extreme abundance of kernite, its large crystals, its perfect cleavage, and its clearness and transparency render the occurrence one of almost unique character as well as of striking beauty. **1951** C. Palache et al. *Dana's Syst. Min.* (ed. 7) II. xv. 337 The material had earlier been called rasorite..but the name kernite has published priority. **1972** M. H. Battey *Mineral. for Students* 235 Borax and the related mineral kernite, $Na_2B_4O_6(OH)_2.3H_2O$, are the principal sources of borax and of boron.

kernos (kə̄·ɹnǫs). *Archæol.* Pl. **kernoi.** [Gr.] An ancient Mediterranean and Near Eastern earthen vessel with small cups around the rim or fixed in a circle to a central stem.

1903 J. E. Harrison *Proleg. Study of Gk. Relig.* iv. 158 *Kernos*, a vessel made of earthenware, having in it many little cups fastened to it, in which are white poppies, wheat, barley..; and he who carries it..tastes of these things. **1955** L. Woolley *Alalakh* xii. 344 Three black impressed sherds, one from a beaker and one from a *kernos*. **1960** T. Burton-Brown *Early Mediterranean Migrations* ii. 35 The kernos shape..is known in Azarbaijan, for there is an unpublished example from there exhibited in the Tehran Museum. **1967** A. D. Lacy *Greek Pott. Bronze Age* v. 260 The kernos or cluster vase..is a composite vessel in which one or more rings of small cups are mounted upon a central stem. Kernoi have been found at Phylakopi in Milo, and in Crete. **1971** *Ashmolean Mus. Rep. Visitors 1970* 16 Purchased:..a Proto-White Painted kernos, Late Cypriot IIIB. **1972** Y. Yadin *Hazor* ii. vii. 101 The cultic aspect of the whole area is further attested by the enormous nests of vessels, which included incense-stands, 'cups and saucers', kernoi, and 'rattles'.

kero (ke·ro). Austral. and N.Z. colloq. abbrev. of Kerosene *sb.*

1930 *Bulletin* (Sydney) 10 Sept. 22/3 Never feed in troughs. With little stalls and cut-down kero.-tins.. calves can be fed quickly enough for anybody. **1938** X. Herbert *Capricornia* ix. 129 Take it and buy some tucker and kero. **1957** 'N. Culotta' *They're a Weird Mob* (1958) vi. 78 Pat threw in ..a 'kero tin' of water. **1961** P. White *Riders in Chariot* xi. 411 The rusted kero stove. **1968** *N.Z. Listener* 15 Mar. 6/2 Just picture us flicking on lights (no candles and kero to mess with). **1970** M. Kelly *Spinifex* xv. 214 The fire's all right. I put out a quart of kero and there's stacks of green stuff.

kerogen (ke·rŏdʒĕn). *Petrogr.* [f. Gr. κηρό-ς wax + -gen.] Orig., the carbonaceous material in oil shale that gives rise to crude oil on distillation; in later use extended to denote any organic material in sedimentary rock which, like the oil-yielding kind, is insoluble in the usual organic solvents.

1906 D. R. Steuart in H. M. Cadell et al. *Oil-Shales of Lothians* iii. 142 We are indebted to Professor Crum Brown, F.R.S., for suggesting the term Kerogen to express the carbonaceous matter in shale that gives rise to crude oil in distillation. **1923** P. E. Spielmann *Genesis of Petroleum* ii. 17 In some cases it may have been that kerogen consisting of unicellular algae and of spores like those of the lycopods, had actually been distilled. **1941** *Jrnl. Inst. Petroleum* XXVII. 426 The term 'kerogen'.. is merely a convenient name for the organic matter from which oil is obtained when rocks containing it are heated; hence the kerogens of different deposits may be chemically different. *Ibid.* 427 The insolubility of kerogen in organic solvents is a characteristic property which serves to distinguish true kerogen rocks from such materials as oil- or tar-sands, bituminous limestones, etc. **1958** *Habitat of Oil* (Amer. Assoc. Petroleum Geol.) 758 Kerogens isolated from the marine rocks were obtained as very fine, amorphous, soft powders that varied from dark brown to jet black... When the samples were heated in an open test tube only small amounts of an oily distillate were formed. **1961** *Fuel* XL. 387 Colorado oil-shale kerogen is predominantly a cyclic material, highly saturated with hydrogen, and contains oxygen, nitrogen and sulphur atoms associated with ring structures. **1963** J. P. Forsman in I. A. Breger *Org. Geochem.* v. 148 The term 'kerogen'..may be defined as the insoluble organic matter occurring in sedimentary rocks. *Ibid.*, Since the dividing line between oil shales and other rocks is rather arbitrary, there appears to be no logical reason for restricting the name 'kerogen' to a certain rock type. **1968** *Times* 16 Nov. 9/6 The most ancient kerogen yet known comes from the Fig Tree System of rocks in Swaziland, thought to be 3,100 million years old.

kerosene, *sb.* Add: Also **kerosine** (see note below). Now important as a fuel for some kinds of internal-combustion engines, esp. jet engines.

Kerosene, -ine is now the usual name for paraffin in much of the U.S. (see quot. 1961[1]) and in Australia and New Zealand; in Britain its currency is largely restricted to technical contexts. The spelling *kerosine* was adopted in 1925 by the Amer. Soc. for Testing Materials and (in Britain) by the Institute of Petroleum; the *-ene* form remains the usual one in general usage and still occurs in technical contexts.

1864 Kerosine [in Dict.]. **1925** *Proc. Amer. Soc. Testing Materials* XXV. 287 The sub-committee [on nomenclature] wishes to call particular attention to the spelling of the word 'kerosine'. This matter was brought to our attention by the Executive Committee of the Standardization Committee of the Institution of Petroleum Technologists, it being pointed out that the ending 'ene' is very generally applied to pure hydrocarbons. The suffix 'ine' already applied to gasoline is therefore also applied to kerosine. **1933** *Industr. Chemist* IX. 227/2 High sulphur, low quality, off-colour kerosene distillates..may be hydrogenated. **1949** *Thorpe's Dict. Appl. Chem.* (ed. 4) IX. 389/2 The word 'kerosene'..is an alternative name with paraffin oil (British) and coal oil (American). **1950** *Inst. Petroleum Rev.* IV. 9/1 The American Society for Testing Materials and the Institute of Petroleum..desire to reiterate their strong recommendation for international recognition of the spelling *kerosine.* **1951** C. R. Noller *Textbk. Org. Chem.* iv. 53 Previous to 1910, kerosene was the most important product derived from petroleum. *Ibid.*, The demand for the kerosene fraction is increasing again, since it is being used as the fuel for gas turbines and jet engines. **1954** *Chem. & Engin. News* 5 Apr. 1386/3 'Kerosene' is commoner than 'kerosine'. The ASTM [*sc.* American Society for Testing Materials] and ASA [*sc.* American Standards Association] have preferred 'kerosine', probably in order to make it consistent with 'gasoline', and *CA* [*sc. Chemical Abstracts*] has adopted 'kerosine' as the choice of an authoritative group in the petroleum field. **1957** Frazer & Eshelman *Tractors & Crawlers* i. 14 Kerosene and distillate..will burn satisfactorily in engines which are designed for low-grade fuels. **1960** *B.S.I. News* Dec. 25 (*heading*) Kerosine (paraffin) unflued space heaters. **1961** *Amer. Speech* XXXVI. 27 Fuel for lamps: Kurath found *kerosene* in general use through the North. The Atlas field interviewer, on the other hand, encountered *coal oil* in all three Cleveland interviews. Both terms are in widespread use today. 1. The commercial *kerosene*..increases in frequency with the youth and the cultivation of the informant. 2. *Coal oil*.. appears to find its chief strength among the old and the uncultivated. **1961** D. Petrie *Petroleum* xi. 62 The heavier products condense on the lower trays, and the lighter ones like kerosine and petrol near the top. **1966** C. Orr *Particulate Technol.* ix. 439 Organic liquids like benzene, toluene, kerosine. **1966** G. W. Turner *Eng. Lang. Austral. & N.Z.* i. 22 Trade has given currency to such words as *kerosene*: an English lady surprised a New Zealand chemist by asking for four gallons of 'paraffin' and he surprised her by supplying four gallons of 'liquid paraffin'. **1967** W. A. Gruse *Motor Fuels* i. 6 The next higher-boiling fraction, kerosene, will cover the range about 180 to 290°C. **1970** *Sci. Jrnl.* Mar. 44/1 Aviation kerosine has a strong and unpleasant odour.

b. *kerosene box, bucket, case, engine, flare, lamp* (earlier and later examples), *stove, tax, tin*; *kerosene-lit, -soaked* adjs.

1948 V. Palmer *Golconda* x. 76 There was a bookcase made of kerosene-boxes nailed together. **1929** K. S. Prichard *Coonardoo* xxiv. 235 Coonardoo had kerosene buckets of water boiling. **1905** W. B. *Where White Man Treads* 304 He invited me to his whare, and seated me in the seat of honour—the slab bunk—while he made shift with the ubiquitous kerosene case store-all. **1909** *Westm. Gaz.* 3 Feb. 2/2 A gasolene- or kerosene-engine. **1920** D. H. Lawrence *Women in Love* ix. 125 The market-place was hot with kerosene flares. **1869** *Bradshaw's Railway Manual* XXI. p. xii (Advt.), Dietz & Co., petroleum and kerozene lamp manufacturers. **1945** *Coast to Coast 1944* 75 It was a dingy hole all right, with a feeble kerosene-lamp trying to soak up some of the shadows. **1974** 'I. Drummond' *Power of Bug* viii. 113 The smell of gasoline could not have come from..kerosene lamps. **1932** W. Faulkner *Light in August* v. 107 He saw himself enclosed by cabinshapes, vague, kerosenelit. **1908** *Westm. Gaz.* 3 June 12/1 No sooner had the speeches concluded than..a light was set to the stack of kerosene-soaked pipes. **1946** *Coast to Coast 1945* 175 In the shed that had been fitted up with taps and shelves, a sink and an old smoky kerosene stove, Bennie was always happy. **1928** *Manch. Guardian Weekly* 10 Aug. 113/4 Mr. Churchill was deeply chagrined by being compelled to withdraw his proposed kerosene tax. **1891** C. Roberts *Adrift Amer.* xii. 211 There was no difficulty in cooking it as an old kerosine tin furnished a pot, and..I soon had it boiling away. **1908** E. J. Banfield *Confessions of Beachcomber* i. i. 48 All convenient vessels available, even to the never-to-be despised kerosene tins, were utilised to store the nectar. **1937** *Discovery* June 169/2 Dozens of boys and girls..came along with calabashes, bags and kerosene tins full of locusts. **1969** *Coast to Coast 1967–68* 18 Kate had been boiling clothes in kerosene tins on the kitchen stove and carrying them outside to be rinsed in big tubs on the back veranda.

ker-plonk, -plunk: see Ker- (in Dict. and Suppl.).

Kerr (kēəɹ, kāɹ, kə̄ɹ). The name of John *Kerr* (1824–1907), Scottish physicist, used *attrib.* to designate certain devices, phenomena, and concepts discovered by him or arising out of his work, as **Kerr cell,** a transparent cell containing two plate electrodes in a substance exhibiting a strong Kerr (electro-optical) effect, by means of which an applied voltage may be made to vary the plane of polarization of plane-polarized light and hence (when the cell is placed between crossed nicols) the intensity of a beam; **Kerr constant,** a number expressing the degree to which a substance exhibits the electro-optical Kerr effect, equal to the difference between the extraordinary and ordinary indices of refraction of the substance divided by the wavelength of the monochromatic light used and by the square of the electric field strength; **Kerr effect,** (*a*) the rotation of the plane of

polarization of light when it is reflected from a magnetized surface; (*b*) the production of birefringence in a substance by the application of an electric field.

[**1893** J. J. THOMSON *Notes Rec. Res. Electr. & Magn.* v. 501 There is..no reason to expect that the order of the metals with respect to Kerr's effect should be the same as that with respect to Hall's.] **1909** *Chem. Abstr.* III. 2084 The theory of the Kerr effect shows that..the effect of the mirror of ferromagnetic metal placed in the magnetic field is the same as would be the face of a naturally active crystal without the magnetic field. **1910** *Hawkins' Electr. Dict.* 232/2 *Kerr effect*, the effect produced in dielectrics when subjected to electro-static stresses, so that they become double refracting. **1927** *Proc. Nat. Acad. Sci.* XIII. 506 These experiments involved measuring the differences in the lag of the Kerr effect behind the electric field for the liquids in two Kerr cells. **1927** *Phil. Mag.* III. 715 All the substances which possess a large Kerr constant have molecules which are electrically polar. **1937** G. S. MONK *Light* xvi. 318 Gases exhibit a Kerr electric effect which is about 1/1000 that for ordinary liquids. **1953** J. R. PARTINGTON *Adv. Treat. Physical Chem.* IV. x. 279 Kerr cells containing this liquid [*sc.* nitrobenzene]..are used in television and cinema apparatus as instantaneous switches or relays. **1953** J. MORGAN *Introd. Geom. & Physical Optics* xvi. 361 The Kerr effect depends on the difference in the dipole moments produced by the electric field along different axes of the molecule, and such measurements give information about the molecular structure of the liquid. **1969** MCGUIRE & FLANDERS in Berkowitz & Kneller *Magnetism & Metall.* I. iv. 145 The Kerr magnetooptical effect refers to polarized light reflected from a magnetized surface. The reflected light is elliptically polarized with the major axis of the ellipse rotated with respect to the original axis of the light. **1972** J. R. MEYER-ARENDT *Introd. Classical & Mod. Optics* III. i. 297 Kerr cells are used most often as ultra-fast shutters.

kerria (ke·riă). [mod.L. (A. P. de Candolle 1817, in *Trans. Linn. Soc.* XII. 154), f. the name of William *Ker* or *Kerr* (d. 1814), English botanical collector.] A deciduous shrub of the monotypic genus so called, native to China and Japan, belonging to the family Rosaceæ, and bearing single or double yellow flowers; = CORCHORUS 2; *white kerria*, a closely related shrub, *Rhodotypos kerrioides*, which bears white flowers.

1823 J. LINDLEY *Donn's Hortus Cantabrigiensis* (ed. 10) 200 *Kerria japonica*, Kerria. Japan... 1804. **1829** J. C. LOUDON *Encycl. Plants* 455 *Kerria*. So named after Mr. William Ker, a botanical collector, who was sent some years since to China, whence he sent many curious plants. The plant named after him is the common Corchorus japonica of the gardens. **1836** *Edward's Bot. Reg.* XXII. 1873 (*heading*) Japan Kerria. **1896** J. H. VEITCH *Traveller's Notes* VII. 112 Some lovely flowering bushes of double Kerria are..to be seen. **1900** M. THORN in W. D. Drury *Bk. Gardening* xi. 407 *Rhodotypos kerrioides* (White Kerria) is a charming and easily-grown shrub. *Ibid.* 465 The double-flowered Kerria (*K. japonica florepleno*) is a favourite wall-shrub. **1939** W. J. BEAN *Wall Shrubs & Hardy Climbers* II. 100 The typical, single-flowered kerria is a spreading, twiggy shrub. **1951** *Dict. Gardening* (R. Hort. Soc.) 1103/1 Kerria, White. See *Rhodotypos kerrioides*. **1970** C. LLOYD *Well-Tempered Garden* iv. 356 Japanese quinces, weigelas, kerrias, mahonias..are all stripped by birds at various times.

kerrie. (Examples of *kierie*, now the more usual form.)

1939 A. W. WELLS *S. Afr.: Planned Tour* 410/1 Some Afrikaans words are used in English conversation, e.g.: ..*kerie*, walking-stick. **1953** *Cape Times* 5 Jan. 1/7 There were about 1,000 fighting with kieries. **1959** *Ibid.* 10 Nov. 1/1 Two other Europeans had been discharged after being treated for kierie wounds. **1970** *Cape Herald* 15 May 3/3 He found..a kierie, a two-piece pink costume, a night gown... The costume and gown had blood spots on them.

Kerry. Add: **2.** (Earlier and later examples.) Also, *Kerry cow*.

1829 G. GRIFFIN *Collegians* (ed. 2) I. xi. 233 Her little cow was a kind Kerry, and had the best of grazing. **1907** *Macm. Mag.* May 514 We saw a cattle-boat bringing Kerries to Scariff. **1929** E. BOWEN *Last September* III. xxiii. 294 Look at those little teeny black cows. Those are Kerry cows. **1975** *Irish Times* 9 May 4/6 Kerries, Ayrshires, Herefords, Charolais, and the Jerseys, the nicest of all.

3. *Comb.* **Kerry blue terrier**, a breed of Irish terrier, of medium size, with a long, silky, blue coat, found in Kerry and neighbouring counties and introduced elsewhere during the nineteen-twenties; also *Kerry, Kerry blue*.

1922 D. MATHESON *Terriers* 145 The Kerry (Blue) Terrier. Since the close of the Great War we have had this variety of Irish Terrier introduced to us under its present title. **1930** E. C. ASH *Pract. Dog Bk.* 150 The history of the Kerry Blue is not easy to obtain. **1955** N. FITZGERALD *House is Falling* x. 169 She had firmly attached herself to the big Kerry Blue. **1971** F. HAMILTON *World Encycl. Dogs* 455 Kerry pups are born black. The blue color comes later, showing at any time after six or seven months. **1973** *Country Life* 15 Feb. 384/3 The terriers replaced the gundogs..the eventual winner the Kerry Blue terrier.

Kerry[2] (ke·ri). The name of a town and neighbouring range of hills in the county of Powys, on the Welsh borders, used *attrib.* in **Kerry Hill sheep** to designate a breed of sheep developed there, distinguished by a thick fleece and black markings near the muzzle and feet. Also *absol.*

1908 *Daily Chron.* 1 May 4/6 Many people are under the impression that the famous Kerry Hill sheep come from Ireland. As a matter of fact, they come from Kerry in Montgomeryshire. **1937** F. B. YOUNG *Portrait of Village* v. 102 By the time he had finished stocking it with Wessex Saddleback pigs, Kerry Hill sheep, short-horn cows, runner ducks and Rhode Island Red poultry,..he had made another big hole in his dwindling capital. **1945** J. F. H. THOMAS et al. *Sheep* ii. 33 The Kerry Hill (Wales) ..is a polled breed of medium size which carries a dense fleece. **1960** [see *DEVON]. **1971** *Farmers Weekly* 19 Mar. 83/1 For many years we kept Kerrys at Downton, now we have commercial Cluns—with some Welsh blood.

kerseymere. 2. (Earlier example.)

1808 JANE AUSTEN *Let.* 30 June (1952) 204 My kerseymere Spencer is quite the comfort of our Even[g] walks.

ker-slap, splash, -splosh: see KER- (in Dict. and Suppl.).

kerstenite (kə̄·ɹstĕnəit). *Min.* [f. the name of K. M. *Kersten* (1803–1850), German chemist, who first reported it + -ITE[1].] A yellow selenite or selenate of lead, of uncertain composition, with a greasy to vitreous lustre.

1868 J. D. DANA *Syst. Min.* (ed. 5) 669 Kerstenite *Dana*. **1930** J. W. MELLOR *Comprehensive Treat. Inorg. & Theoret. Chem.* X. lviii. 833 C. M. Kersten reported normal lead selenite... J. D. Dana called the mineral kerstenite—*cf.* cobalt arsenide. The data do not distinguish whether the mineral is a selenite or selenate. **1951** C. PALACHE et al. *Dana's Syst. Min.* (ed. 7) II. 640 Kerstenite was found as botryoidal masses with a fibrous fracture as an alteration of zorgite at the Friedrichsglück mine near Hildburghausen, Thuringia, Germany. **1962** W. A. DEER et al. *Rock-Forming Min.* V. 188 Several other minerals and compounds have the 'barytes structure'; among them are: $BaSeO_4$, $PbSeO_4$ (kerstenite)..and (K, Cs)BF_4.

kertch, var. CURCH.

1900 A. CARMICHAEL *Carmina Gadelica* I. p. xxv, On the morning after the marriage the mother of the bride.. placed the 'breid tri chearnach', three-cornered kertch, on the head of the bride before she rose from her bed. *Ibid.*, The feast of the 'bord breid', kertch table, was almost as great as the feast of the marriage table.

Kertch, var. *KERCH.

keruing (ke·ru,iŋ). Also **kruin.** [Malay *kĕruing*.] The light or dark brown hardwood timber of several trees of the genus *Dipterocarpus*, found in Malaysia, Sabah, and Indonesia.

1921 F. W. FOXWORTHY in *Malayan Sci. Bull.* I. 36 Meranti and Keruing, because of their contained resinous substances, are better firewoods than some of the heavier woods. **1934** A. L. HOWARD *Man. Timbers of World* (rev. ed.) 152 In the Malay Peninsula there are many species of Dipterocarpaceæ which produce timber known as keruing. **1948** *Ibid.* (ed. 3) 282 Keruing. See Kruin. *Ibid.* 291 Kruin.—This is produced by 15 to 20 species of the genus Dipterocarpus. **1950** C. W. BOND *Colonial Timbers* 54 Keruing is not unpleasant to handle at the bench. **1966** P. F. BURGESS *Timbers of Sabah* 102 Keruing is remarkable among tropical timbers for its generally straight grain. **1970** *Timber Trades Jrnl.* 21 Mar. 54/1 There have been few 'spot' offers of keruing circulating, and this timber has been hard to buy in the popular specifications.

kerumph, ker-woosh: see *KER-.

kerygma. Add: Pl. **kerygmata.** (Further examples.)

1936, etc. [see *DIDACHE 2]. **1949** *Scottish Jrnl. Theol.* II. 316 And the miracle of the *kerygma* is just this that through it the once and for all event in Jesus Christ becomes event all over again in the faith of the hearer. **1953** *Ibid.* VI. 314 The essential difference from Christianity, however, lies in the place occupied by such speculations about the kosmos, its beginnings and end, its hierarchies and denizens, in the respective *kerygmata*. **1955** *Ibid.* VIII. 158 Usage in direct speech may also be due to the editor, but the ruling presumption is against that, especially in the *kerygmata*. **1958** *Times Lit. Suppl.* 23 May p. vii/1 And what he writes, without a word of justification, about the unity of the mind of the apostles with that of Christ, and of the apostolic *kerygma* with the activity of Christ, could be used by the Pope himself and welcomed by him as coming from a Protestant source. **1962** *Ibid.* 17 Aug. 628/2 It is also true that historical facts become objects of religious faith only when they belong to salvation-history and are part of the *kerygma*, the proclamation of the gospel, which presents them as sources and types of the redemption offered to mankind. **1970** WEST & FRANCIS *Scandal in Assembly* xxviii. 151 Without the *Kerygma*, the *didache* reduces itself to a system of ethics as unstable as the customs of men.

Hence **kerygma·tic** *a.*, belonging to or of the nature of preaching; **kerygma·tically** *adv.*

1929 *Church Times* 18 Jan. 82/1 Our ministry..before all else..is 'kerygmatic', the proclamation of a Kingdom and a King. **1949** *Scottish Jrnl. Theol.* II. 88 They hold that the Scriptures of the New Testament witness to Jesus Christ Himself *kerygmatically*, that is in such a way that He Himself, by the power of His Spirit, speaks to men through them. **1955** *Ibid.* VIII. 346 The present Hexateuch represents the elaboration and the heaping up of traditions around the simple kerygmatic theme, the chief premonarchial elements of which can be discerned in old confessions. **1969** E. SIMONS in *Sacramentum Mundi: Encycl. Theol.* III. 246/1 This dialectic of mediation..which may be termed dialogal, is a kerygmatic event. **1970** J. DONCEEL tr. *Rahner's Trinity* II. 57 Some new word..may be more precisely and easily understood, hence kerygmatically more useful than the word 'person'.

‖ **kesa-gatame** (ke:sa,gatā·me). *Judo.* [Jap.] The 'scarf' hold, a way of holding the opponent by the edge (the so-called 'scarf') of his jacket in an attempt to immobilize him.

1932 E. J. HARRISON *Art of Ju-Jitsu* v. 68 (*heading*) 'Locking in the form of a scarf' (kesagatame; otherwise hongesa, or 'regular scarf'). **1957** TAKAGAKI & SHARP *Techniques Judo* III. viii. 112 *Kesa gatame* is one of the simplest holds to secure. **1968** P. & K. BUTLER *Judo & Self-Defence for Women & Girls* 141 (*heading*) Kesa-gatame—scarf hold. T applies kesa-gatame, U struggles then submits.

Keshan, var. *KASHAN.

keskeedie, keskidee, varr. *KISKADEE.

kest (kest), *v. dial.* var. of CAST *v.* esp. in senses 'cast aside, throw away' and (*fig.*) 'do down, outdo'.

1590 SPENSER *Faerie Queene* I. xi. 163 That infernall Monster, hauing kest His wearie foe into that liuing well. **1862** C. C. ROBINSON *Dial. Leeds* 334 A man who has been abroad in bad weather, ill-clad, says,—'Ah sal nivver kest what I've gotten to neet I knawah.' **1892** J. WRIGHT *Gram. Dial. of Windhill, W. Riding* iii. 29 In the following words we have *e* which in many of the examples is no doubt the *i*-umlaut of *a*:..*kest* (ME. *kesten*) to cast. **1893–4** R. O. HESLOP *Northumb. Words* II. I. 421 He kest his claes ower syun an' gat caad. **1913** D. H. LAWRENCE *Sons & Lovers* II. vii. 164 At seven o'clock the family heard him buy threepennyworth of hot-cross buns... He turned away several boys who came with more buns, telling them they had been 'kested' by a little lass. *Ibid.* viii. 200 Just then Wesson entered... 'I see you've kested me,' he said, smiling rather vapidly. 'Yes,' replied Barker.

kësterite (ke·stĕrəit). *Min.* Also **kesterite.** [ad. Russ. *kësterit* (Z. V. Orlova, 1956), f. *Këster*, name of its locality in Yakutia, Siberia: see -ITE[1].] A black sulphide of copper, tin, zinc, and iron, $Cu_2(Zn,Fe)SnS_4$.

1958 *Mineral. Mag.* XXXI. 963 *Kësterite*...(Cu,Sn,Zn) S, containing Cu 30·56, Sn 25·25, Zn 11·16, S 23·40%. **1968** I. KOSTOV *Mineral.* ii. 147 Sakuraiite..is considered an indium analogue of kesterite.

Keswick (ke·zik). The name of a town in Cumbria, used to designate a variety of cooking apple, in full **Keswick codlin(g)**, which has a greenish skin tinged with red and was first introduced by John Sander, who lived in the town.

1814 *Mem. Caledonian Hort. Soc.* I. 374 (*title*) Information regarding the Carlisle and Keswick Codlin Apples. *Ibid.* 376 The Keswick Codlin tree has never failed to bear a crop since it was planted..twenty years ago. **1831** H. RONALDS *Pyrus Malus Brentfordiensis* 5 Keswick Codlin. A favourite sauce apple from the North of England. **1912** MULFORD & CLAY *Buck Peters* xxii. 198 It's Buck as sure as little apples Kesicks. **1936** H. V. TAYLOR *Apples Eng.* vii. 74 Those [apples] that became soft and frothy, even on coddling (i.e. parboiling), were known as coddlings—the Keswick Codling, English Codling. **1973** *Countryman* LXXVIII. IV. 42, I could watch the sheets billowing, and the clothes flapping and being confettied by blossom from the crabs, keswicks and white heart cherries.

ket-: see *KETO-.

keta (kī·tă). Also † **keth.** [Russ.] = *CHUM *sb.*[4]

1824 S. BLACK *Jrnl. Voy. from Rocky Mountain Portage* (1955) 52 In Bears River near the Lake they speared a kind of salmon he names Keth in the Rapids. **1901** A. M. B. MEAKIN *Ribbon of Iron* xviii. 263 At Nikolaevsk upwards of a hundred and ninety-three thousand pnds of a salmon called 'keta'—*salmo lagocephalus*—are salted annually. **1905** D. S. JORDAN *Guide to Study of Fishes* II. iv. 73 In Japan *keta* is by far the most abundant species of salmon. **1933** A. W. SHIELS *Seward's Ice Box* 83 Chums or keta are plentiful in all districts. **1962** *Co-op Grocery News Bull.* (Saskatoon) 1 Aug. 1 Formerly known as dog salmon, the chum, with the scientific name Oncorhynchus Keta, has also been called the qualla, keta and calico salmon. It is caught all along the coast of British Columbia.

ketal, ketamine, etc.: see *KETO- a.

ketch (ketʃ), *v.*[2] *dial.* var. (pa.t. **ketched**) of CATCH *v.*

1815 D. HUMPHREYS *Yankey in England* I. 21, I guess, he is trying to ketch me—but it won't du. I'm tu old a bird to be ketch'd with chaff. **1865** DICKENS *Mut. Fr.* II. IV. xv. 287 Wot is it, lambs, as they ketches in seas, rivers, lakes, and ponds? *a* **1883** [see *KNUCK 2]. **1911** E. WHARTON *Ethan Frome* ii. 60 You'll ketch your death. The fire's out long ago. **1916** W. O. BRADLEY *Stories & Speeches* 18 You'll never ketch me hollerin' at no Republican gatherin'. **1929** H. W. ODUM in A. Dundes *Mother Wit* (1973) 184 If so you gonna ketch hell. **1967**

Atlantic Monthly Apr. 103/1 You heard about that joke a dollar down and a dollar when you ketch me? **1968** S. STUCKEY in A. Chapman *New Black Voices* (1972) 445 Run, nigger, run, de patrollers will ketch you.

ketchak, var. *KETJAK.

kete, kête, varr. *KIT *sb.*[11]

ketene (kī·tīn). *Chem.* Also **-en.** [ad. G. *keten* (H. Staudinger 1905, in *Ber. d. Deut. Chem. Ges.* XXXVIII. 1735): see KETONE and -ENE.] **a.** Any compound containing an ethylenic double bond adjacent to a carbonyl group, i.e. the structure $>C{=}C{=}O$.

[**1905** *Jrnl. Chem. Soc.* LXXXVIII. 444 Diphenylketen $CPh_2{:}CO$, the first representative of a new type of compound, is prepared by the action of zinc on an ethereal solution of diphenylchloroacetyl chloride.] **1907** *Ibid.* XCI. 1941 There can..be no doubt that the new substance is a keten, having the formula $CH_2{:}CO$. **1942** FUSON & SNYDER *Org. Chem.* xxi. 296 Carbonyl compounds which contain the grouping $>C{=}C{=}O$ are known as ketenes... Ketenes fall into two classes, aldoketenes and ketoketenes. **1971** *Jrnl. Chem. Soc.* (C) 3645 The addition of ketenes to conjugated dienes generally yields 1,2-adducts.

b. The simplest of the ketenes, $CH_2{:}C{:}O$, a pungent colourless gas which dimerizes on liquefaction and has wide applications in synthesis owing to its high reactivity.

1907 *Jrnl. Chem. Soc.* XCI. 1941 Keten has a peculiar penetrating smell. **1946** [see *ACETYLATION]. **1964** N. G. CLARK *Mod. Org. Chem.* xi. 211 On heating acetic acid vapour at 700° to 800° under reduced pressure, it loses the elements of water to form keten. **1972** *Guardian* 16 Oct. 15/2 Although keten and its organic relations have been known and used for generations, no one had realised that they could produce salts.

kethubah, var. *KETUBAH.

‖ **Kethubim** (keþūvī·m, ket-), *sb. pl.* Also 7 **Chetoubim,** 20 **Ketubim, K'tubhim, -vim.** [Heb. *k'thūbīm* writings.] = HAGIOGRAPHA *sb. pl.*

1690 tr. *J. Le Clerc's Five Lett.* ii. 102 Others..they call Chetoubim, or simply Writings; that is to say, the Psalms [etc.]. **1892** H. E. RYLE *Canon of Old Testament* vi. 127 The *Psalter* is the most important book of the 'Kethubim'. *Ibid.* 132 The Book of Job..had no fitting place in the Canon save in the mixed group of 'the Kethubim'. **1904** *Jewish Encycl.* VI. 151/1 It can not now be ascertained when the name 'Ketubim' and the Greek designation 'Hagiographa' were first given to the collection. **1961** *Jrnl. Biblical Lit.* LXXX. 106 Tanak..stems from the abbreviations of the three divisions, *T*orah, *N*ebhi'im, and *K*'tubhim, of the Hebrew Scriptures. **1967** D. T. KAUFFMAN *Dict. Relig. Terms* 274 *Ketuvim* or *Kethubim,* third section of the Jewish Scriptures: the Sacred Writings beginning with the Psalms and ending with the Chronicles.

‖ **ketjak** (ke·tʃæk). Also **ketchak, 'tjak.** [Balinese, f. *'tjak-a-tjak'*, the sound of the chanted refrain accompanying the dance.] A Balinese dance, with a male chorus. Also *attrib.*

1937 M. COVARRUBIAS *Island of Bali* (1972) viii. 219 *Ketjak*, large groups of men singing in chorus, moving and dancing to the rhythm of the music. **1938** DE ZOETE & SPIES *Dance & Drama in Bali* ii. 85 The *ketjak* dance is primarily a dance of exorcism. **1942** C. BARRETT *On Wallaby* ix. 176 The Monkey Dance or Ketchak Ceremonies impressed me more than all other dances and dramas... A Ketchak was held solely for our entertainment. **1954** J. COAST *Dancing out of Bali* viii. 161, I had suggested the gamelan club forming a 'Tjak, or Monkey Dance chorus. **1972** C. SIMPSON *Bali & Beyond* 26 *Ketjak* is the name of the male chorus in the *sanghyang* and this dance extends the role of that chorus to a *Ramayana*-story presentation in which the number of men is increased to about 150. **1972** *Times* 11 Nov. 13/4 The dancers you see performing the *Barong* or the *Ketchak* ..are not professionals.

keto- (kī·to), comb. form of KETONE. **a.** (Before a vowel also **ket-.**) As an inseparable formative element of terms in *Chem.* and *Med.*: **ketal** (kī·tæl) [after ACETAL], any compound of the type $R^1R^2C(OR^3)OR^4$, where neither R^1 nor R^2 is a hydrogen atom (see quot. 1926); **ke·tamine,** a crystalline anæsthetic and analgesic substance, $C_{13}H_{16}NOCl$; 2-*o*-chlorophenyl-2-methylaminocyclohexanone; **ke·tazine** [ad. G. *ketazin* (Curtius & Thun 1891, in *Jrnl. f. prakt. Chem.* XLIV. 162)], any compound of the type RR′C:N·N:CR″R‴, made by reacting one molecule of hydrazine with two molecules of (identical or different) ketones; **ke·timine,** any compound containing the grouping $>C{=}NH$, formed e.g. by the action of ammonia on a ketone; **ke:toacido·sis,** acidosis due to enhanced production of ketone bodies; hence **ke:toacido·tic** *a.*, of or pertaining to ketoacidosis; **ke:tobe·midone** [perh. f. car*be*thoxy- + M(ETHYL + -ID[4] + -ONE], an analgesic, $(C_6H_4OH)(CO{-}C_2H_5)C_5H_8N{\cdot}CH_3$, with action similar to that of morphine; **ketoge·nesis,** production of ketone bodies; **ketoge·nic,** † **-gene·tic** *adjs.*, producing ketone bodies; applied *spec.* to a diet that is rich in fats and low in carbohydrates and has been used therapeutically to produce ketosis; *(17-)ketogenic steroid,* any steroid which yields a (17-)ketosteroid on oxidation with a bismuthate; **α-ketogluta·ric acid,** a dibasic keto-acid, $HOOC{\cdot}CO{\cdot}CH_2{\cdot}CH_2{\cdot}COOH$, which is formed by oxidation and decarboxylation of isocitric acid in the Krebs cycle; hence **α-ketoglu·tarate,** a salt or ester, or the anion, of α-ketoglutaric acid; **keto-he·xose,** any ketose with six carbon atoms; **α-ke:toi:sovale·ric acid,** a crystalline carboxylic acid, $(CH_3)_2CH{\cdot}CO{\cdot}COOH$, from which valine is synthesized by transamination in fungi; hence **α-ke:toi:sova·lerate,** a salt or ester, or the anion, of α-ketoisovaleric acid; **ketoke·ten(e)** [a. G. *ketoketen* (Staudinger & Klever 1908, in *Ber. d. Deut. Chem. Ges.* XLI. 909)], any ketene of the type RR′C:C:O; **keto·lysis,** decomposition of ketone bodies; hence **ketoly·tic** *a.*, causing or pertaining to ketolysis; **ketoly·tically** *adv.*; **ketoste·roid,** any steroid whose molecules contain a ketone group; *17-ketosteroid* (see quot. 1964); **keto·xime,** an oxime of a ketone (i.e. any compound containing the group $>C{:}NOH$), formed by the action of hydroxylamine on a ketone; **ke·tyl** [-YL], any salt containing a free-radical anion of the type $RR'{\cdot}\dot{C}{\cdot}O^-$, formed by dissolving a metal in a ketone.

1924 *Chem. Abstr.* XVIII. 3518 (*heading*) Velocity of hydrolysis of acetals and ketals. **1926** *Ibid.* XX. 2937 The saponification of ketals (acetals of ketones) was studied in the presence of mineral acid catalyzers. They are liquids of disagreeable odor, insol. in water, sol. in alc., ether, etc., stable towards dil. alkali, rapidly hydrolyzed by dil. acid. **1933** *Jrnl. Amer. Chem. Soc.* LV. 3744 The method described in this paper..furnishes a simple approach to cyclic ketals which are difficult or impossible to make by the usual method. **1965** *Nomencl. Org. Chem.* (I.U.P.A.C.) C. 104 Compounds containing the group $>C<^{OR^1}_{OR^2}$ are termed acetals. [*Note*] The name 'ketal' is abandoned. **1967** I. L. FINAR *Org. Chem.* (ed. 5) I. viii. 189 Ketones do not readily form ketals when treated with alcohols in the presence of hydrogen chloride... Ketals may, however, be prepared by treating the ketone with ethyl orthoformate. **1966** *Approved Names* (Brit. Pharmacopœia Comm.) 23 Ketamine. **1967** *Martindale's Extra Pharmacopoeia* (ed. 25) 1530/2 Ketamine hydrochloride is a potent analgesic and anaesthetic with actions similar to those of phencyclidine hydrochloride.., to which it is chemically related. **1968** *Anesthesia & Analgesia Current Res.* XLVII. 775/2 Ketamine has both a stimulatory and a depressive effect on the cardiovascular system. The stimulation predominates with small doses. **1972** *Anesthesiology* XXXVI. 311 With the increased medical and veterinary use of ketamine, it will probably become a popular hallucinogenic street drug. **1894** *Jrnl. Chem. Soc.* LXVI. 348 (*heading*) Transformation of ketazines into pyrazolines. **1911** *Ibid.* C. I. 571 The ketazines from the following ketones have been prepared and examined: benzophenone, fluorenone, and tetramethyldiaminobenzophenone. All the compounds are stable..and when hydrolysed by hot mineral acids yield hydrazine and ketone. **1943** H. GILMAN *Org. Chem.* (ed. 2) I. ix. 812 Hydrazones and ketazines have also been hydrogenated by means of platinum..catalysts. **1909** J. F. THORPE in *Proc. Chem. Soc.* XXV. 309 It is suggested that as the compounds containing the group C:NH are in many respects analogous to the ketones, the general name ketimine should be applied to them, leaving the name imine to be applied to the secondary amines. **1938** ALLEN & BLATT in H. Gilman *Org. Chem.* I. vi. 568 Monomolecular ketimines..have been prepared; they too are readily hydrolyzed and reduced. **1971** N. L. ALLINGER et al. *Org. Chem.* xxi. 586 Grignard reagents add to the cyano group of most nitriles to give salts of ketimines. **1958** *Diabetes* VII. 230 (*heading*) The nature and correction of diabetic ketoacidosis. **1961** *Endocrinology* LXVIII. 815 Rather marked insulin insufficiency is necessary for the development of uncontrolled diabetic ketoacidosis. **1969** *Nature* 20 Dec. 1155/1 All the children suffered from vomiting, lethargy and ketoacidosis, and did not grow. **1966** DUNLOP & ALSTEAD *Textbk. Med. Treatm.* (ed. 10) 353 The patient in ketoacidotic coma must be sent without delay to hospital. **1972** *Jrnl. Clin. Invest.* LI. 493/2 Intensive therapy for 72–96 hr with parenteral glucose and alkali were necessary before he recovered from his ketoacidotic episodes. **1949** *Jrnl. Pharmacol. & Exper. Therap.* XCVII. 188 Keto-bemidone appears to be one of the most addictive drugs yet discovered. **1958** *A.M.A. Arch. Internal Med.* CI. 745 Comparison of ketobemidone with other common analgesics shows that it is one of the safest drugs to use for analgesia because of the great difference between its analgesic and euphoria-producing doses. **1972** J. BALL *Five Pieces Jade* vi. 73 Have you heard of keto-bedmidone [*sic*]? Or Claradon, that's another name for it... It is extremely addictive. Considerably more than heroin. **1915** *Arch. Internal Med.* XV. 65 Feeding of pancreas may augment ketogenesis by determining increased absorption of fat. **1933** CAMERON & GILMOUR *Biochem. of Med.* v. 77, 1 gram by weight of glucose can be oxidized in the body along with 4·8 grams of fat, without ketogenesis. **1972** *Diabetes* XXI. 50/2 Ketogenesis from fatty acid is thus tied into the liver cell's energy metabolism. **1915** *Arch. Internal Med.* XV. 63 It seems probable that it falls in the same category as that increased sensitiveness of the diabetic organism to ketogenetic factors after repeated pancreatic opotherapy. **1911** STEDMAN *Med. Dict.* 452/1 Ketogenic. **1921** *Jrnl. Biol. Chem.* XLIX. 162 A method is described by which the ratio of ketogenic to antiketogenic molecules in the metabolic mixture of a subject may be calculated from the respiratory quotient. **1930** *Sci. Amer.* Nov. 391 This is called a ketogenic diet, because it tends to produce an excessive amount of ketones and their derivatives in the blood. **1952** J. K. NORYMBERSKI in *Nature* 20 Dec. 1075/1 The difference between 17-ketosteroids found before and after oxidation of urine affords a measure of '17-ketogenic steroids' which represent an important group of corticosteroids. **1968** R. F. STEINER *Life Chem.* ix. 168 Four amino acids—leucine, isoleucine, phenylanine [*sic*] and tyrosine—can give rise to ketone bodies... The..group of amino acids are termed ketogenic. **1972** *Jrnl. Clin. Endocrinol. & Metabolism* XXXIV. 580/1 Routine urine steroid analysis showed normal excretion of 17-ketosteroids and 17-ketogenic steroids. **1973** *Nature* 2 Mar. 74/1 He was interested in the mechanism of action of ketogenic diets which were then used for the treatment of urinary tract infections. **1911** *Jrnl. Chem. Soc.* C. I. 520 Ethyl α-ketoglutarate, b.p. 114°/13 mm., obtained by esterification of the acid in a closed tube at 120°, is a colourless liquid. **1940** *Jrnl. Biol. Chem.* CXXXVI. 302 Carbon dioxide combines directly with pyruvic acid to yield oxaloacetic acid, the latter then combining with an additional molecule of pyruvate to form α-ketoglutarate. **1971** *Scand. Jrnl. Clin. & Lab. Invest.* XXVIII. 365/1 The known ammonia-detoxifying processes..involve amination of α-ketoglutarate to glutamate and amidation of glutamate to glutamine. **1908** *Jrnl. Chem. Soc.* XCIV. I. 713 When ethyl oxalosuccinate is treated with hydrogen chloride in the cold and the solution boiled, hydrolysis takes place and α-ketoglutaric acid..is formed. **1937** *Biochem. Jrnl.* XXXI. 300, α-Ketoglutaric acid thus appears to arise in the course of pyruvic acid oxidation. **1938** *Ibid.* XXXII. 112 Ten human urines contained between 10 and 40 mg. α-ketoglutaric acid per 24 hr. specimen. **1968** R. F. STEINER *Life Chem.* xii. 219 α-Ketoglutaric acid represents an important junction between the metabolic pathways of carbohydrates and amino acids. **1899** *Jrnl. Chem. Soc.* LXXV. 423 With ketohexoses (lævulose, sorbose), the purple colour appears after a few minutes. **1938** M. L. WOLFRAM in H. Gilman *Org. Chem.* I. xvi. 1442 The French scientist, Pelouze, described the isolation of a new ketohexose from the juice of the berries of the mountain ash. **1971** N. L. ALLINGER et al. *Org. Chem.* xxvii. 698 Fructose, another common hexose, has a ketone group at C-2 and is called a ketohexose. **1953** *Jrnl. Biol. Chem.* CCV. 480 Conversely, α-ketoisovalerate accumulation is depressed whenever the supply of valine is sufficient to permit maximal growth rate. **1966** *Biochemistry* V. 409/1 A soil microorganism, *Pseudomonas* P-2, growing on pantothenate as sole carbon source, converts this in part to β-alanine, α-ketoisovalerate, and valine. **1953** *Jrnl. Biol. Chem.* CCV. 475 (*heading*) Isoleucine and valine metabolism in Escherichia coli. V. α-Ketoisovaleric acid accumulation. **1971** *Jrnl. Nutrition* CI. 1165/1 The effect of substituting α-ketoisovaleric acid for L-valine upon the nitrogen balance of a young female was evaluated. **1908** *Jrnl. Chem. Soc.* XCIV. I. 318 The first groups are termed aldo-ketens and the second, keto-ketens. **1937** F. C. WHITMORE *Org. Chem.* 281 The ketoketenes are colored, are easily auto-oxidized to give peroxides, and form addition cpds. with cyclic tertiary amines. **1951** I. L. FINAR *Org. Chem.* I. xii. 230 If the compound is of the type R·CH:C:O, it is known as an aldoketen; and if $R_2C{:}C{:}O$, then a ketoketen. **1937** *Amer. Jrnl. Physiol.* CXIX. 734 Any reduction in the ketosis consequent to carbohydrate administration must be due to either a decrease in the rate of the former ('antiketogenesis') or to an increase in the rate of the latter ('ketolysis'). **1938** *Jrnl. Biol. Chem.* CXXVI. 106 Liver slices from a well fed monkey have a very low rate of ketolysis as compared with liver slices from well fed rats, rabbits, and guinea pigs. **1921** *Ibid.* XLVII. 435 Glucose thus exhibits, in alkaline solution *in vitro*, a 'ketolytic' action in hastening the oxidation of acetoacetic acid which would appear to be analogous to its 'antiketogenic' action in the body. **1936** *Jrnl. Nutrition* XII. 646 That aspect of the quantitative relationship of ketolytic to ketogenic factors which has interested us especially.., is the relation of carbohydrate combustion to the reduction of ketogenesis. **1938** *Jrnl. Biol. Chem.* CXXVI. 106 The large amount of work..showing the extrahepatic tissues..to be much more active ketolytically than the liver is very convincing. **1939** *Biochem. Jrnl.* XXXIII. 931 (*heading*) The isolation of 17-ketosteroids from the urine of normal women. **1959** *Austral. Jrnl. Exper. Biol. & Med. Sci.* XXXVII. 147 It was decided to employ enzymatic hydrolysis and separation of the individual ketosteroids in an attempt to identify and estimate them individually. **1964** A. WHITE et al. *Princ. Biochem.* (ed. 3) xlviii. 856 Since each of the various urinary metabolites of testosterone has a ketone group at C-17, these substances are referred to as 17-ketosteroids, and their concentration in the urine is a useful index of endogenous production of androgenic hormones. **1888** *Jrnl. Chem. Soc.* LIV. 443 (*heading*) Conversion of ketoximes into pseudonitroles. **1938** C. D. HURD in H. Gilman *Org. Chem.* vii. 636 The reaction of bromine with ketoximes yields bromonitrosoparaffins. **1971** N. L. ALLINGER et al. *Org. Chem.* xxii. 605 The oximes of ketones (ketoximes) undergo an overall rearrangement to amides when heated with certain inorganic reagents, followed by treatment with water. **1914** *Chem. Abstr.* VIII. 113 (*heading*) Metal ketyls, a large class of compounds with trivalent carbon. **1934** *Trans. Faraday Soc.* XXX. 23 By using dioxan as solvent high concentrations of the ketyls were obtained and their paramagnetism placed beyond doubt. **1971** N. L. ALLINGER et al. *Org. Chem.* xix. 493 If benzophenone is converted to the ketyl with sodium, for example, the ketyl concentration is sufficient to give the solution a beautiful blue color.

b. In Combs. in which *keto* may be used *attrib.* (without a hyphen) as an independent

word or joined by a hyphen to the second element, as *keto-acid, -compound, -ester, -form,* etc. (in which *keto-* denotes the presence of a ketone group); also **keto-e·nol** *attrib. phrase,* **-eno·lic** *a.*, applied to the tautomerism between the ketonic and enolic forms of certain compounds.

1911 *Chem. Abstr.* V. 3686 (*heading*) Preparation of amino acids from keto acid phenylhydrazones and aluminium amalgam. **1968** R. O. C. Norman *Princ. Org. Synthesis* vii. 237 A dibasic acid which, as a β-keto-acid, is readily decarboxylated by heat. **1891** *Proc. Chem. Soc.* VII. 91 The resinous matters often formed in large amount on nitrating many phenols are, doubtless, products of the interaction of several molecules of the addition compounds, or of the keto-compounds formed from them in the first instance. **1927** *Jrnl. Amer. Chem. Soc.* XLIX. 849 Acetylacetone may undergo keto-enol tautomerism in the following way.

$$CH_3COCH_2COCH_3 \rightleftharpoons CH_3COCH{:}C(OH)CH_3.$$

1971 N. L. Allinger et al. *Org. Chem.* viii. 172 Keto-enol interconversion is subject to catalysis by acid or base. **1909** *Proc. Chem. Soc.* XXV. 309 It is advisable to apply some general term to this form of isomerism, similar to the phrase keto-enolic isomerism in use with the oxygen derivatives. **1936** *Biochem. Jrnl.* XXX. 745 The present paper contains some observations..on certain substances ..which under similar conditions yield colours with this reagent [*sc.* diazotized sulphanilic acid]. The group has the common character that all its members are capable of keto-enolic tautomerism. **1937** F. C. Whitmore *Org. Chem.* 444 Diacetosuccinic ester, as a beta keto ester gives reactions like those of acetoacetic ester itself. **1958** *Oxf. Univ. Gaz.* 23 Apr. 882 Grignard reactions of keto-esters. **1927** *Jrnl. Amer. Chem. Soc.* XLIX. 856 Acetylacetone in 95% alcohol solution is an equilibrium mixture of the keto and enol forms. **1968** R. O. C. Norman *Princ. Org. Synthesis* i. 18 For ethyl acetoacetate..two factors increase the bonding..of the enol form relative to the keto form.

ketolic (kīto̜·lik), *a. Chem.* [f. Ketol + -ic.] Having the functional groups of a ketol.

1960 *Biochem. Jrnl.* LXXVII. 400/1 A method for the quantitative fractionation of..ring D α-ketolic oestrogens. **1971** *Folia Histochem. & Cytochem.* IX. 391 (*heading*) Oxidative enzymes and α-ketolic steroids in the interrenal cells of the South African clawed toad.

ketonæmia (kītŏnī·miă). *Med.* Also (chiefly *U.S.*) **-nemia.** [f. Keton(e + Gr. αἷμα blood: see -ia[1].] An abnormally high concentration of ketone bodies in the blood.

1917 *Amer. Jrnl. Med. Sci.* CLIII. 343 Marriott demonstrated ketonemia in such animals. **1941** *Jrnl. Biol. Chem.* CXXXVIII. 128 Ketonemia develops within 39 hours in man, as compared to 2 to 3 days in the dog. **1962** *Lancet* 29 Dec. 1350/2 The diabetic syndrome in this patient was unusual in that he had severe hyperglycæmia, insulin resistance, and no ketonæmia. **1965** Lee & Knowles *Animal Hormones* vii. 112 The effect of removal or destruction of the islet tissue varies in different animals... Ketonaemia does not occur in rabbits and it is slight in calves; in pigs ketonaemia may be severe, yet coma does not occur.

ketone. Add: **2.** Special combs.: **ketone body,** any of the three related compounds acetone, acetoacetic acid, and β-hydroxybutyric acid, which are produced in the body in fatty- and amino-acid metabolism; an 'acetone body'.

1915 *Arch. Internal Med.* XV. 40 There are in the literature only casual references to the influence of organotherapy on the formation and excretion of ketone bodies. **1936** *Jrnl. Nutrition* XII. 647 The term 'rate of ketogenesis'...takes into account both the ketonemia, or level of ketone bodies in the blood, and the ketonuria, or the rate of ketone body excretion in the urine. **1959** A. White et al. *Princ. Biochem.* (ed. 2) xix. 479 The total ketone body concentration in blood, expressed as β-hydroxybutyrate, is normally below 1 mg. per 100 ml., and the average total daily excretion in the urine is approximately 20 mg. **1974** *Nature* 18 Jan. 161/2 Urine samples were tested for 'ketone bodies' with a commercial preparation that contains sodium nitroprusside.

ketonic acid (earlier example); **ketol, ketose** (examples).

1876 *Jrnl. Chem. Soc.* XXIX. 926 The ketonic acids are converted by nascent hydrogen into oxy-acids. **1891** *Ibid.* LX. 1176 Ketoses. **1892** E. F. Smith tr. *V. von Richter's Chem. Carbon Compounds* (ed. 2) 498 Bromine water..oxidises the aldoses to their corresponding monocarboxylic acids..whereas the ketoses (fructose and sorbinose) are not attacked. **1894** G. McGowan tr. *Bernthsen's Text-bk. Org. Chem.* (ed. 2) 237 (*heading*) Ketone-alcohols (ketols). **1938** M. L. Wolfram in H. Gilman *Org. Chem.* I. xvi. 1442 The Lobry de Bruyn dilute alkali interconversion reaction was used..in obtaining the crystalline ketose of lactose (lactulose). **1968** R. O. C. Norman *Princ. Org. Synthesis* xvi. 501 Treatment [of an epoxide] with dimethyl sulphoxide gives an α-ketol. **1972** *New Phytologist* LXXI. 475 The phenomenon of ketose formation in polyol media is much better documented for bacteria where, for example, fructose may be formed from mannitol in yields of up to..95%.

ketonize (kī·tŏnəiz), *v. Chem.* [f. Keton(e + -ize.] *intr.* Of a compound which undergoes keto–enol tautomerism: to change into the keto-form.

1937 F. C. Whitmore *Org. Chem.* 345 The free enediol is unstable and ketonizes to the acyloin at once. **1938** L. F. Fieser in H. Gilman *Org. Chem.* I. ii. 55 The hydroxyl derivatives of benzene show much less tendency to ketonize than do the aliphatic enols. **1962** E. L. Eliel *Stereochem. Carbon Compounds* viii. 242 The enolate..ketonizes in such a way that the proton approaches equatorially.

Hence **ketoniza·tion,** the process of changing into a keto-form.

1931 *Canad. Jrnl. Res.* V. 26 The suggested formation of the lignosulphonic acids by ketonization of a phenolic nucleus is most unlikely. **1937** F. C. Whitmore *Org. Chem.* 280 Ketonization gives acetic acid, esters, acid amides, acid chloride, etc. **1968** R. O. C. Norman *Princ. Org. Synthesis* i. 19 Compared with the ketonization of phenol.., the ketonization of β-naphthol is more favourable by about 11 kcal per mole. **1972** *Jrnl. Chem. Soc. Perkin Trans. I* 987/1 Kinetic control of enolisation and ketonisation is replaced by thermodynamic control at higher temperatures.

ketonuria (kītŏniūə·riă). *Med.* [f. Keton(e + -uria.] The excretion of abnormally large amounts of ketone bodies in the urine.

1913 *Jrnl. Amer. Med. Assoc.* 13 Dec. 2161/1 No one is justified at present in concluding that the liver is the sole organ concerned in the phenomena of ketonuria. **1923** *Glasgow Herald* 25 July 7 Daily injections of insulin ..removed entirely the ketonuria for a period of some days. **1939** *Nature* 29 Apr. 728/1 During rest after work there is a reduction in the glucose tolerance,..associated with a low respiratory quotient and ketonuria. **1972** *Drugs of Choice 1972–73* xxxi. 468/2 One of the more pernicious consequences of hypoglycemia is the hyperglycemia and ketonuria that may follow.

ketosis (kĭtōu·sis). *Med.* [f. *ket(o- + -osis.] A condition characterized by an increased production of ketone bodies, which is associated with a predominance of fat metabolism and with diabetes.

1917 F. M. Allen in *Amer. Jrnl. Med. Sci.* CLIII. 335 No other name but acidosis exists for the metabolic process which it denotes. Ketonuria and ketonemia have their accurate place but do not cover the ground. Possibly the word ketosis might be suggested and used for special purposes, but the change of established usage would be difficult and seems unnecessary. **1925** *Biochem. Jrnl.* XIX. 948 In man after a relatively short period of starvation..a considerable ketosis appears. **1951** A. Grollman *Pharmacol. & Therapeutics* vii. 151 The paroxysmal cerebral dysrhythmia characteristic of epilepsy may be altered by inducing ketosis by a low carbohydrate, high fat diet. **1960** *Farmer & Stockbreeder* 22 Mar. 136/1 There does appear to be a connection between the heavy feeding of kale, and the incidence of ketosis (acetonæmia), but in rather a roundabout way. **1961** [see *acetone]. **1970** R. W. McGilvery *Biochem.* xxii. 530 However, the meat-fat diet does cause the appearance of an asymptomatic ketosis.

Hence **keto·tic** *a.*, suffering from or associated with ketosis.

1943 *Jrnl. Amer. Med. Assoc.* 2 Jan. 52/2 During episodes of ketotic acidosis it was necessary to give 2,360, 2,500 and 2,795 units of insulin in twenty-four hours before adequate control was accomplished. **1959** *Jrnl. Appl. Physiol.* XIV. 1028/1 The turnover time was increased also by about $\frac{1}{5}$ in the ketotic cows. **1961** L. Martin *Clin. Endocrinol.* (ed. 3) ii. 52 Uncontrolled diabetics with high blood sugar levels do not as a rule suffer from anorexia unless they are also ketotic. **1972** *Jrnl. Clin. Invest.* LI. 1440/1 The cause of ketotic hypoglycemia, the commonest form of hypoglycemia in childhood, is not known.

kettle. Add: **1. b.** A bowl- or saucer-shaped vessel in which operations are carried out on low-melting metals, glass, plastics, etc., in the liquid state.

a **1817** [see *potash kettle* (Potash *sb.* 4)]. **1892** P. Benjamin *Mod. Mechanism* 803 A rendering and refining kettle for making..fancy toilet soap. **1895** E. L. Rhead *Metall.* xv. 214 The ore is ground to a pulp in the mill, or arastra, and transferred to kettles with bottoms made of copper. **1929** *Industr. Chemist* V. 487/1 A Pfaudler, all cast-iron, glass-lined, 300-gallon, reaction kettle or chemical still. **1940** H. L. Hind *Brewing* II. xxiv. 576 The vessel[s] in which the mash is boiled..are usually known as kettles in America. **1952** M. R. Mills *Introd. Drying Oil Technol.* iii. 48 Oleo-resinous varnishes are commonly produced in portable kettles of 450–3,000 lb...capacity. **1953** *Archit. Rev.* CXIV. 187/1 The raw materials used in the former process [*sc.* the manufacture of synthetic resins] are highly inflammable, and it was desirable that the 'kettles' in which this process is carried out should be in a separate building. **1955** Kirk & Othmer *Encycl. Chem. Technol.* XIV. 653 Stationary open kettles are used to polymerize large batches of oil. **1967** J. D. Gilchrist *Extraction Metall.* x. 259 Softening—at 750°C, in a wide, open hearth furnace or in the open saucer-shaped lead 'kettle' which presents a very large surface for oxidation, Sb, Sn and As are slowly oxidized out with air or litharge.

2. b. Also, *a different* or *another kettle of fish*: a different state of affairs, a different matter altogether.

1937 *Discovery* Nov. 353/1 H. S. Thompson's 'Garnet in Flight' is another kettle of fish. **1938** R. Warner *Professor* vi. 141 Professor..you're very good at thinking out schemes—brainwork, I mean..if you understand what I mean; but that's only half the battle you know, in fact a different kettle of fish altogether. **1942** E. Waugh *Put out More Flags* iii. 172 Until now the word 'Colonel' for Basil had connoted an elderly rock-gardener on Barbara's G.P.O. list. This formidable man of his own age was another kettle of fish. **1959** J. L. Austin *Sense & Sensibilia* (1962) ii. 14 Looking..at a distant village on a very clear day across a valley, is a very different kettle of fish from seeing a ghost.

4. c. (Earlier and later examples.) Also (now the usual meaning in *Geomorphol.*), a *kettle hole* (see sense *6 b).

1866 *Smithsonian Contrib. Knowl.* No. 197. 3 To form an idea of the appearance of the 'potash kettle' country, we may imagine a region of drift moraines inverted, and.. occupied by cavities of irregular size and depth. *Ibid.* 4 On the north of the Peshattego river..the 'kettles' are very numerous. **1877** T. C. Chamberlin *Geol. Wisconsin: Survey of 1873–79* II. ii. v. 206 The peculiar feature of this range..consists of numerous depressions in the drift variously known as 'Potash Kettles', 'Kettles', 'Potholes', 'Pots and Kettles', 'Sinks', etc. Those which have most arrested popular attention are circular in outline, and symmetrical in form...Large numbers of these depressions are not perfectly circular, but rudely oval, oblong or elliptical, or are extended into trough-like, or even winding hollows. *Ibid.* 214 If masses of the ice became incorporated within the drift, ..their subsequent melting would give rise to a depression constituting one form of the kettles. **1896** T. G. Bonney *Ice-Work* i. i. 34 These 'kettles', when first discovered, were filled with débris, and still contained the large rounded boulders by which they had been mainly excavated. **1926** *Jrnl. Geol.* XXXIV. 315 The ice blocks that formed the kettles in pitted outwash varied in size from a few yards to several miles in diameter. **1942** C. A. Cotton *Climatic Accidents* xxiv. 328 Both bowl-like round pits and elongated trench-like kettles are common. **1970** R. J. Small *Study of Landforms* xi. 384 A bare tract of boulders, gravels and sand separates the two glacier snouts, and is pitted by numerous circular water-filled hollows ('kettles') marking small masses of ice that calved from the glaciers, became trapped in the debris, and subsequently melted.

d. A watch. *slang* (chiefly *Criminals'*).

1889 Barrère & Leland *Dict. Slang* I. 516/2 *Kettle* (thieves), a watch; *red kettle,* gold watch. **1931** [see *groin *sb.*[2] 3*]. **1935** G. Ingram *Cockney Cavalcade* xiv. 234, I pinched his 'kettle' what those two blunderers left behind. **1936** J. Curtis *Gilt Kid* xxv. 244 Next buckshee kettle that comes my way I'll just stick to it. **1960** 'A. Burgess' *Doctor is Sick* xvi. 122 Edwin, student of philology, knew what kettles were, cheap smuggled watches guaranteed to go for a day or two. **1970** *Brewer's Dict. Phrase & Fable* (rev. ed.) 603/2 A tin kettle is a silver watch and a red kettle a gold one.

6. a. *kettle-lid, -scrubber, -stand.* **b. kettle-bail** *U.S.*, a dredge used in taking scallops; **kettle-holder** (earlier example); **kettle hole,** a depression in the ground thought to have been formed by the melting of an ice block trapped in glacial deposits, esp. one that is circular and deep; freq. *attrib.* in *kettle-hole lake* = **kettle lake*; **kettle lake,** a lake in a kettle hole; **kettleman,** restrict † to sense in Dict. and add: (*b*) (also **kettle man**) one who attends to a kettle in various industries; **kettle moraine** *Geomorphol.* [orig. applied as a proper name to such a moraine in Wisconsin], moraine characterized by the presence of numerous kettle holes.

1881 E. Ingersoll *Oyster-Industry* 245 *Kettle bail,* a dredge used in catching scallops, which has the blade adjusted to swing in the eyes of the arms, in order to prevent its sinking into the mud of the soft bottom on which it is used. **1887** G. B. Goode *Fisheries U.S.: Hist. & Methods* II. 571 The dredge for a soft bottom differs from the other in having the 'blade' adjusted to swing in the 'eyes' of the arms in order to prevent its sinking into the mud. This is called the 'kettle-bail' style of dredge. **1813** M. Edgeworth *Let.* 1 May (1971) 32 After having admired..a picture of Cromwell and Fanny's kettle-holder we sallied forth. **1882** *Proc. Amer. Assoc. Adv. Sci.* XXXI. 395 The kames of Cherry Valley..are composed of stratified water-worn gravel, ..and, as a series of conical hills and reticulated ridges, enclosing 'kettle holes', form conspicuous objects in the centre of the valley. **1895** J. D. Dana *Man. Geol.* (ed. 4) 970 Kettle-holes are bowl-shaped depressions, usually 30 to 50 feet deep and 100 to 500 feet in larger diameter. Each depression..was the resting-place, and often the burial-place, of a huge mass of ice that became detached during the melting. **1902** Gilbert & Brigham *Introd. Physical Geogr.* vi. 143 Many lakes with steep rims in the midst of much glacial waste are known as Kettle-hole Lakes. **1930** *Q. Jrnl. Geol. Soc.* LXXXVI. 112 Numerous lakes and pools lying in kettle-holes dot the surface of the moraine. **1957** G. E. Hutchinson *Treat. Limnol.* I. i. 90 The exact nature of such basins depends largely on the details of the process of deglaciation..producing an extraordinary number of kettle-hole lakes in North America. **1970** Dorr & Eschman *Geol. Michigan* vii. 151/2 Most of the smaller inland lakes of Michigan occupy kettle-holes. **1914** *Prof. Papers U.S. Geol. Survey* No. 82. 163 Till or similar impervious material appears to be present in considerable amounts, as indicated by the numerous springs, kettle lakes, and similar features. **1968** R. W. Fairbridge *Encycl. Geomorphol.* 587/2 The hollow is frequently water filled, so that it forms a kettle lake, kettle pond or swamp. **1920** 'K. Mansfield' *Bliss* 44 They spent half their time ..dosing him with various awful mixtures concocted by Pip, and kept secretly by him in a broken jug covered with an old kettle lid. **1833** B. Silliman *Man. Sugar Cane* 15 The manner in which the hands are distributed during the cutting season is the following..forty hands with knives..six kettle men. **1960** *Classification of Occupations* (General Register Office) 51/2 Kettleman—gelatin, glue, size mfr... metal mfr... oil seed crushing. **1963** *Lebende Sprachen* VIII. 130/2 Kettleman. [**1883** T. C. Chamberlin *Geol. Wisconsin: Survey of 1873–79* I. i. xv. 275 That portion of the moraine which..was formed by the joint action of the Green Bay and Lake Michigan glaciers, constitutes a succession of irregular hills and ridges, locally known as the Kettle Range, from the peculiar depressions which characterize it... As this moraine will need a specific name to distinguish it from other similar

accumulations, the term Kettle Moraine may fittingly be applied to it.] **1889** G. F. WRIGHT *Ice Age N. Amer.* vii. 120 Attention was first directed..by President T. C. Chamberlin to the character and connection of the kettle-moraine in Wisconsin. **1897** W. B. SCOTT *Introd. Geol.* viii. 155 When such masses melt they form depressions in the mound and give rise to the 'kettle moraines'. **1937** WOOLDRIDGE & MORGAN *Physical Basis Geogr.* xxii. 387 Mounds and ridges of gravelly drift are referred to in British glacial literature as eskers and kames, or, generally, as kettle-drift or kettle-moraine. **1970** B. B. LUCKMAN in C. A. Lewis *Glaciations Wales* viii. 176 (*heading*) The Kington–Orleton kettle moraine. **1843** THACKERAY *Irish Sk.-Bk.* II. 278 Thus it was I drew her Scouring of a kettle. .. That sweet kettle-scrubber! **1881** C. SCHREIBER *Jrnl.* 1 Nov. (1911) II. 367 Found a fine old kettle stand..and a few minutes after had the good luck to find the kettle to fit. **1960** H. HAYWARD *Antique Coll.* 157/1 *Kettle-stand*, a special stand which was introduced with tea-drinking in the later 17th-cent., of two main kinds. (a) A small table ..with a gallery or raised edge round the top... (b) A box-like arrangement set on four legs. **1970** D. ASH *Dict. Eng. Antique Furniture* 92/2 Kettle-stands were lower than contemporary tripod tables so that the kettle, mounted on its lamp-stand, would be at a convenient height.

kettler. Restrict † to sense in Dict. and add: **2.** A colour-mixer's assistant who attends to the boiling of dyestuffs.

1921 in *Dict. Occup. Terms* (1927) § 381. **1960** *Classification of Occupations* (General Register Office) 51/2 Kettler..106 [dyers of textiles].

kettle-stitch. (Earlier and later examples.)

1818 H. PARRY *Art of Bookbinding* 2 *Kettle-stitch*, the stitch at head and foot of the book, independent of the bands, to tack or fasten the sheets together. **1846, 1906** [see *catch-stitch* (*CATCH- 3 a)]. **1973** *Islander* (Victoria, B.C.) 30 Sept. 11/1 Dick shewed me some of the stitches used in book binding. Among them, the kettle stitch, used in hand sewing during the early days of book binding.

kettling, var. CHITLING.

1869 *Overland Monthly* III. 130 Then there are the delusive 'kettlings', among the 'low-down' people... I will simply say that it is fried sausages, minus all the unhealthy and absurd meat which most people insist on stuffing into the intestinal integuments.

‖ **ketubah** (ketūvā·). Also **kethubah, ketuba.** [Heb. *kethūbhāh* written statement.] A formal Jewish marriage contract which includes financial provisions for the wife in the event of the husband's death or of divorce.

1841 BORROW *Zincali* I. II. vii. 344 The walking of the bride..to the house of her betrothed..the reading of the Ketubah. **1891** M. FRIEDLÄNDER *Jewish Relig.* II. vii. 487 The fulfilment of the conditions agreed upon in the *kethubah*..tended to render divorce a rare event. **1960** *Commentary* June 500/1 The Rabbinical Assembly has modified the *Ketubah* (marriage contract). **1960** [see *GET *sb.*[3]]. **1962** B. ABRAHAMS tr. *Life Glückel of Hameln* iv. 79 When we stood all together under the *chuppah* with the bride and bridegroom, we found that..the Ketuba had not been drawn up! **1974** H. KEMELMAN *Tuesday Rabbi saw Red* 7, I read the *Ketubah*, that is the marriage contract, which the groom has signed previously.

keurboom (kūe·ɹbum). Also **keur.** [Afrikaans, f. *keur* choice + *boom* tree.] A small South African tree of the genus *Virgilia* (*V. oroboides* or *V. divaricata*) of the family Leguminosæ, having pinnate leaves and racemes of white, pink, mauve, or red, scented flowers.

1731 G. MEDLEY tr. *Kolb's Present State of Cape of Good-Hope* II. 258 The Amaquas Tree. This Tree the Cape-Europeans call *Keur-boom*. It grows so quick, that in Two Years Time it becomes, from a Small Plant, a Tree of Eight or Nine Foot in Height. **1854** L. PAPPE *Silva Capensis* 13 *Virgilia Capensis.* Lamk. (*Keurboom*)... Wood rather light and soft. Looks well when polished. **1907** T. R. SIM *Forests & Forest Flora Cape Good Hope* 204 Keur is often cultivated for its ornamental evergreen foliage and sweetly scented flowers. **1925** R. MARLOTH *Flora S. Afr.* II. I. 72 *Virgilia capensis.* Keurboom... In favourable localities it reaches a height of 40 feet with trunks three feet in diameter. Such trees form a beautiful sight when covered with their pale rose or lilac coloured, sweet-scented flowers. **1955** J. PACKER *Valley of Vines* iv. 58 The *keurbome* toss fragrant pale-pink plumes in the wind. **1973** PALMER & PITMAN *Trees S. Afr.* II. 903 Botanists, foresters, and gardeners have not yet decided to their mutual satisfaction whether the genus *Virgilia* is composed of one, two, or three different species of keurboom.

kevir, var. *KAVIR.

kew. Short for THANK YOU.

1939 G. B. SHAW *Geneva* II. 30 Sit down. *Begonia* [complying]: Kew. **1961** *Times* 14 Aug. 9/4 Of 20 recipients of sitting space, five said 'Thank you' or 'Thanks'; three said 'Kew'.

Keweenawan (kiwi·nǭăn), *a.* Also † **Keweenawian.** [f. the name of *Keweenaw* Peninsula, Michigan + -AN, -IAN.] Of, pertaining to, or designating the most recent division of the Proterozoic in North America, as represented by rocks in the region of the Great Lakes. Also *absol.*, the Keweenawan period or rocks.

1876 T. B. BROOKS in *Amer. Jrnl. Sci.* CXI. 210 We are therefore justified, I think, in regarding the Copper-bearing rocks of Lake Superior as a distinct and independent series, marking a definite geological period which separates the Silurian from the Huronian ages... Since Keweenaw Peninsula forms one of the most striking geographical features in Lake Superior.., I suggest the name Keweenawian for this period. **1883** R. D. IRVING *Copper-Bearing Rocks Lake Superior* ii. 25 The Keweenawan rocks form the larger part of Keweenaw Point. **1893** *Jrnl. Geol.* I. 126 The source of the lavas of the Keweenawan. **1930** *Econ. Geol.* XXV. 252 Erosion had peneplained the original folds of the Keewatin and Timiskaming rocks before Keweenawan time. *Ibid.* 262 They are distinctly younger than the Algoman and older than the Keweenawan. **1935** *Bull. Geol. Soc. Amer.* XLVI. 504 The Keweenawan lavas of the Lake Superior district form the inner border of the Lake Superior syncline. They crop out over an area of several thousand square miles, and in one section on Keweenaw Point, Michigan, form a series with a minimum thickness of 15,000 feet. **1970** DORR & ESCHMAN *Geol. Michigan* iv. 56/1 Keweenawan lavas were derived from molten magmas of the 'basic' or ferromagnesian type.

kewpie (kiū·pi). orig. *U.S.* Also **cupie.** [A dim. form of CUPID.] In full, *kewpie doll.* A chubby doll with a curl or topknot on its head, from a design by R. C. O'Neill (1874–1944). Also *transf.*, of a person.

1909 R. O'NEILL in *Ladies Home Jrnl.* Dec. 28/1 The Kewpie wights stay up at nights, All gayly singing rum-te-tum. *Ibid.*, The reason why these funny, roly-poly creatures are called Kewpies..is because they look like little Cupids. **1912** *Ibid.* Oct. 109 The kewpies were invented by Rose O'Neill. They are always doing good, helping Dotty Darling and her Baby Brother to have a good time... So Rose O'Neill has made the Kewpie Kutouts. **1913** *Official Gaz.* (U.S. Patent Office) 13 May 536/1 Rose O'Neill Wilson... Kewpie. Particular description of goods.—Dolls. **1922** A. HADDON *Green Room Gossip* 176 The floor is strewn with at least fifty toys—teddy bears, golliwogs, bunnies, and woolly mascots galore. Kewpies, too, on the dressing-table. **1926** G. S. CHAPPELL *Younger Married Set* iv. 48, I have here..a magnificent kewpie doll. **1929** T. WOLFE *Look Homeward Angel* (1930) xxii. 324 Over the screened hearth, on a low mantel, there was a Kewpie doll, sashed with pink ribbon. **1937** *Official Gaz.* (U.S. Patent Office) 15 June 543/2 Rose O'Neill Wilson. The Kewpies. For Cartoons in Periodical Publications. Claims use since Dec. 21, 1912. **1937** J. STEINBECK *Of Mice & Men* iii. 93 They got a rag rug on the floor and a kewpie doll lamp on the phonograph. **1943** K. TENNANT *Ride on Stranger* vii. 60 Outside the turnstiles, vendors vie for custom, waving gilded cupie dolls on canes. **1946** I. L. IDRIESS *In Crocodile Land* xxvi. 180 With the little black kewpie of a piccanin aboard her tiny canoe, Wagis paddled downstream towards the river mouth. **1947** *Archit. Rev.* CI. 206/3 There are dolls for sale on the pier, too, Kewpie or cuddly or fashionable. **1952** M. MCCARTHY *Groves of Academe* (1953) ii. 18 Decorated with the same rag-dolls and teddy-bears, pink kewpies won at shooting-ranges. **1954** *Encounter* Feb. 52/1 Art Young, a white-haired little kewpie, sitting in a corner, was pointed out to me. **1957** M. MILLAR *Soft Talkers* 62 A kewpie doll. One of those tiny celluloid kewpie dolls you can buy in the dime store. **1960** *Birmingham Mail* 13 June 3/4 Each year Roo..has brought his woman..a cupie-doll. **1960** *Official Gaz.* (U.S. Patent Office) 30 Aug. TM 174/1 Cameo Doll Products Co., Inc., Port Allegany, Pa... Kewpie. For Dolls. **1961** A. CHRISTIE *Pale Horse* v. 67 A most terrible Kewpie doll from the hoop-la. **1969** N. COHN *A WopBopaLooBop* (1970) viii. 81 She'd be like some kewpie doll, all sheen and varnish and eyes that really roll. **1972** M. J. BOSSE *Incident at Naha* iii. 126 Kewpie dolls..staring at you stupidly and insanely from their glass eyes.

b. A sweet made in the form of a kewpie doll.

1916 *Daily Colonist* (Victoria, B.C.) 28 July 12/6 (Advt.), Kewpie Dolls, made of pure barley sugar, a box 10¢. **1918** *T. Eaton & Co. Catal.* Fall & Winter 385/3 Kewpie Kandy Dolls are made from the pure cane sugar. ..Twelve little kewpie dolls in each package.

key, *sb.*[1] Add: **6. c.** *Chess.* (*a*) In full *key move.* The first move in the solution of a set problem, upon which depends the style of the whole solution. Also *attrib.* or as *adj.* (*b*) The whole solution of a set problem.

1827 W. LEWIS *Chess Probl.* Pref., I defer for the present publishing the Solutions, that the reader may solve the Problems without being tempted to refer to the Key. **1846** *Chess Player's Chron.* VI. 65 Amateurs wanting either time or perseverance to undertake the solution themselves, ..may obtain the key by addressing a note to the Editor. **1878** S. LOYD *Chess Strategy* 60 Key-moves which threaten an easy mate. *Ibid.* 201 There is always a great deal of chance in solving a problem, such as hitting upon the key by accident. **1923** B. G. LAWS *Artistry of Chess Probl.* 5 Key, continuations and principal mates are all of the first order... The key abandoning an important protective Pawn..is little short of being superb. **1938** C. S. KIPPING *Chess Probl. Sci.* I. 51 This was followed by six dis. checks..with a check key, and J. L. Millins showed that it could be done with a quiet key... Ua Tane, using White King diagonal battery and Pawn promotion key showed that six were possible. *Ibid.* 56 Petrovic's astounding triple task has not a key which will appeal to everyone. **1945** *Chess in Schools* (Chess Educ. Soc.) 27 *Problems*, composed positions in which a key move is to be found, after which mate is forced in a specified number of moves. **1958** MANSFIELD & HARLEY *Mod. Two-Move Chess Probl.* 19 The solver's attention is drawn to it, and Key possibilities are limited. *Ibid.*, Such a Key is thematic and good.

d. The device used to 'key' an advertisement (see *KEY *v.* 5). orig. *U.S.*

1905 CALKINS & HOLDEN *Art of Mod. Advertising* xi. 266 A variation of the 'key' in advertising is the coupon. **1915** H. W. HESS *Productive Advertising* xiii. 199 Accounts may be opened charging up to each key not only (1) number of inquiries, but (2) amount spent on that particular key, [etc.]. **1957** CLARK & GOTTFRIED *University Dict. Business & Finance* (1967) 201/1 The key may be a special street or box number, or a department to which the reply is to be addressed, or it may be a number or letter code included in the reply coupon if one is used.

8. b. Phr. *in key* (*with*): in harmony (with); in a style that matches; *out of key* (*with*): out of harmony (with); not matching; unsuitable.

1919 B. RUCK *Disturbing Charm* II. xiv. 287 Everything in that drawing-room was in key with that mantelpiece. **1920** E. POUND *Hugh Selwyn Mauberley* I. 9 For three years, out of key with his time, He strove to resuscitate the dead art Of poetry. **1931** E. WILSON *Axel's Castle* ii. 34 We shall be thrown fatally out of key with reality. **1934** H. G. WELLS *Exper. Autobiogr.* II. vii. 489 That was entirely out of key with James's assumptions.

15*. [Respelling of *ki* in *kilo.*] A kilogramme of a drug. *U.S. slang.*

1968–70 *Current Slang* (Univ. S. Dakota) III–IV. 76 *Key*, kilo of any narcotic; a measurement for marijuana, 215 lbs, $300.00+. **1970** *Time* 13 Apr. 36 A $10 or $20 'key' of Lebanese hash can fetch $1,500 or more in the U.S. **1972** J. WAMBAUGH *Blue Knight* (1973) iv. 45 On her coffee table she had at least half a key and that's a pound of pot and that's trouble.

16. (sense 7) *key-centre, -change, -system.*

1940 *Scrutiny* Sept. 122 Without establishing a key-centre the fluctuating basses eventually soar..into another homophonic passage. **1931** G. JACOB *Orchestral Technique* iii. 24 The choice..should..rest entirely on simplicity of key—the piece as a whole with all its modulations and sectional key-changes being taken into consideration. **1959** 'F. NEWTON' *Jazz Scene* 115 The free and continual key changes. **1973** J. WAINWRIGHT *Pride of Pigs* 175 He rippled through a key-change bridge passage, then moved into the beat. **1934** C. LAMBERT *Music Ho!* I. 28 His [*sc.* Debussy's] destruction of the key-system. **1959** D. COOKE *Lang. Mus.* ii. 44 All the modes eventually became major and minor scales..; and so arose our key-system.

b. Passing into *adj.* in the sense of 'dominant', 'controlling', 'chief', 'essential'; esp. designating some person or thing that is of crucial importance to others. See also *key man* (sense 17 below).

1913 E. C. BENTLEY *Trent's Last Case* xi. 207 When chance or effort puts one in possession of the key-fact in any system of baffling circumstances, one's ideas seem to rush to group themselves anew in relation to that fact. **1916** *Economic Jrnl.* XXVI. 24 We are asked to learn one essential lesson from the war, and that is, not to be caught short of any 'Key' industry. **1926** D. L. COLVIN *Prohibition in U.S.* 509 Occupants of key offices such as the Presidency or the Attorney-Generalship. **1927** W. E. COLLINSON *Contemp. Eng.* 94 Greek was said to occupy a key-position. **1928** J. BOON *Victorians, Edwardians & Georgians* I. 203 There had been considerable difficulty in getting hold of a key witness. **1931** C. A. LEJEUNE *Cinema* 4 A study of these key-names, unobscured by any commercial considerations of box-office value. **1934** C. LAMBERT *Music Ho!* II. 110 It is Stravinsky who is the key-figure of our times. **1941** *Hutchinson's Pict. Hist. War* 19 Mar.–13 May 103 German airmen..were ensconced in key positions. **1945** K. R. POPPER *Open Soc.* I. viii. 135 The key-passage of the philosopher king. **1946** *Sun* (Baltimore) 6 Mar. 1/6 The news was spread all over front pages with photographs of the key figures. **1955** *Ann. Reg. 1954* 256 Investments in the key industries were to be gradually reduced. **1959** *Times Rev. Industry* June (London & Cambridge Econ. Bull.) p. i/1 The key factor in an assessment of the economic position and prospects of the country is Mr. Amory's Budget. **1963** *Times* 12 Feb. 7/4 A small number of key-workers among the affected men stayed away from work. **1964** *English Studies* XLV. 243 One wonders..how many of their key-questions will in fact gain in coherence. **1966** *Illustr. London News* 30 July 27/2 Australia and North America are key areas. **1969** *Times* 16 July 5/8 Key abbreviations used by mission control and the astronauts. **1970** J. ARDAGH *New France* xi. 529 It was in 1943 that Sartre brought out his key philosophical work. **1970** *Physics Bull.* Nov. 493/1 Two ideas were key in the discovery of the kinoform. **1971** *Black Scholar* Dec. 55/2, I viewed myself as assisting everything that was done, and you must recognise that this is what's key in the liberation of women.

17. key-block, (*a*) a block, usu. of wood, also of metal or, in lithography, stone, used in the printing of chiaroscuro and colour pictures to give the outline, and to provide a guide for the accurate registration of the tint or colour blocks; (*b*) in limestone and marble quarrying, the first block or blocks to be removed from a new layer of stone; **key-chain,** a chain to which a key or keys may be attached; **key-drawing,** (*a*) in lithography and colour printing, an outline drawing which is transferred on to the key-plate and used as a guide to printing the colours; (*b*) *Cinematogr.* (see quot. 1940); **key-holder,** (*a*) 'an electric-lamp holder or socket containing a switch' (Webster 1909); (*b*) a person who keeps the key or keys of a workshop, factory, etc.; **key-**

log *Logging*, a log which is so caught or wedged that a jam is formed and held by it; **key man, key-man,** (*a*) *Logging*, a man who finds and dislodges the key-logs in a jam (*Obs. U.S.*); (*b*) an operator of telegraph keys (*Obs. U.S.*); (*c*) one who plays a leading or important role in a group, an industry, etc.; **key-money** (further examples); **key move** (see sense 6 c above); **key-plate,** (*a*) a key-hole escutcheon; (*b*) in colour-printing from a metal surface, the outline plate answering to a keystone in lithography; **key-ring** (examples); **key-word,** (*a*) a word serving as a key to a cipher or the like; (*b*) a word or thing that is of great importance or significance; *spec.* in information-retrieval systems, any informative word in the title or text of a document, etc., chosen as indicating the main content of the document; so **key-word-in-context,** used *attrib.* of an index or concordance in which key-words are listed alphabetically, preceded and followed by a fixed amount of the immediate context.

c **1870** A. Ashley in *Jrnl. Printing Hist. Soc.* (1969) V. 73 Key blocks. **1910** R. M. Burch *Colour Printing* v. 126 Baxter's process was simply the colouring of an impression from an outline or key block, which could be either a copper, zinc or steel plate, or a litho stone..by successive impressions from colour blocks of wood or metal, one for each tint used. **1934** O. Bowles *Stone Industries* II. ix. 212 In opening up a new floor the first blocks to be removed are known as 'key blocks'. **1937** *Discovery* Mar. 77/1 In order to get the colours fitting accurately, prints are taken from the first or key-block and pasted on to each successive block. **1966** Berry & Poole *Ann. Printing* 241/1 They vary in quality, many being spoiled by the heavy impression from the wood key block. **1967** *Amer. Speech* XLII. 290 Once this first troublesome block, called the *key block*, is out, further quarrying becomes much easier. **1895** *Montgomery Ward Catal.* 86/2 Polished steel key chains, 18 inches long. **1950** F. P. Walkup *Dressing the Part* (rev. ed.) 368 A ridiculous fad..was the 'zoot suit'..adorned with a keychain that swept the ground. **1973** K. Giles *File on Death* ii. 42 He locked the door... He had a housekeeper-like key chain attached to the top button of his fly. **1937** *Discovery* Oct. 300/1 The use of several colours, flat or stippled, combined with a black or dark-coloured key drawing. **1940** *Chambers's Techn. Dict.* 475/2 *Key drawing* (*Cinema*). In animated cartoon production, *key drawings* indicate situations at special instants, such as at beats in the bar of music, after which the in-between drawings are made to fit with the timing. **1951** D. Bland *Illustration of Bks.* ix. 133 The artist first makes his key drawing in black, regardless of whether it is intended finally to print in black. From this non-actinic prints are prepared, one for each colour, showing the key drawing in a pale blue colour that will not photograph. **1928** *Daily Tel.* 11 May 5/6 Workmen were waiting outside ready to begin work for the day... The key-holder had not arrived. **1970** P. Laurie *Scotland Yard* iii. 66 The Inspector calls the nick to check the keyholder's register and see who can let us in. *Ibid.*, The keyholder is the caretaker of the flats. **1851** J. S. Springer *Forest Life & Forest Trees* 166 It may be thought best to cut off the key-log, or that which appears to be the principal barrier. **1902** S. E. White *Blazed Trail* xxxii. 211 By pulling out or chopping through certain 'key' logs which locked the whole mass. *a* **1951** B. Cronin in *Austral. Short Stories* (1951) 173 Half-way up the kiln a key-log had swung loose. **1851** in C. M. Wilson *Aroostook* (1937) 104 The key man then commences prying while they are pulling. **1907** *Washington Star* 30 Sept. 9 Some of the leading keymen are sounding as their shibboleth the cry of 'government ownership of the telegraph systems'. **1921** *Daily Colonist* (Victoria, B.C.) 15 Oct. 1/1 Following the conference of 'Key' men of the G.W.V.A. last July, arrangements were advanced to have in attendance at the convention the foremost leaders of the navies and armies of the allied nations in the Great War. **1949** I. Deutscher *Stalin* 143 The 'handful' of Bolsheviks consisted of well-organized and disciplined 'key-men'. **1963** *Times* 18 Feb. 8/3 One of the key men in this new method of assessing needs and opportunities is the local prefect. **1906** *Westm. Gaz.* 28 Mar. 5/2 Some house-agents would still extort 'key-money' from tenants. **1963** *Times* 21 Feb. 5/2 A former property manager was alleged at Southend-on-Sea Magistrates' Court today to have exploited the housing shortage to extort key money. **1969** R. Rendell *Best Man to Die* iii. 26 They'd had to find the key money for the flat themselves. **1903** T. A. Strange *Hist. Guide French Interiors* 326 The key plate is formed as a vase-shaped burning lamp. **1909** R. E. Le Blond *Let.* in H. G. Clarke *Baxter Colour Prints* (1919) 103 These prints were first engraved on a steel plate, a key-plate, or, as I should call, a master-plate. **1969** J. Gloag *Short Dict. Furnit.* (rev. ed.) 317 (*caption*) The simplest type of escutcheon, pivoted to cover the key-plate. **1970** *Jrnl. Printing Hist. Soc.* VI. 73 A key plate of the design was printed in black or brown, usually from an..engraved steel or copper plate. **1889** *Cent. Dict.* III. 3280/2 *Key-ring.* 1. A finger-ring from which projects a tongue or blade which is either fixed or movable on a hinge, and serves as the key to a lock. Such key-rings were formerly common, and were often of rich design. 2. A ring used for keeping a number of keys together by being passed through their bows. **1906** E. Nesbit *Story of Amulet* xi. 261 Jane added a key-ring. **1967** *Economist* 11 Feb. 512 An advertising firm..has now been hired to show that gaullism washes whiter. It has begun to do so in American fashion with badges, key-rings, drum-majorettes and all. **1859, 1885** Key-word [in Dict., sense 16]. **1922** J. C. H. Macbeth tr. *Langie's Cryptogr.* iv. 166 Suppose the key-word to be 'bankruptcy'. **1926** *Encycl. Brit.* II. 822/1 As to shop detail, the keyword to mass production is simplicity. **1948** Blunden *Shakespeare to Hardy* (1964) 211 The key-word is the 116th of the Sonnets. **1956** E. W. F. Tomlin in A. Pryce-Jones *New Outl. Mod. Knowl.* 91 Let us take the keyword 'science'. **1967** Cox & Grose *Organiz. Bibliogr. Rec. by Computer* iv. 82 The system can process documents represented by a set of keywords. **1971** *New Scientist* 1 Apr. 32/2 'Keywords'..are supposed to describe the content of the document as concisely and exactly as possible. **1959** Key-word-in-context [see *KWIC* (*K 4 f)]. **1969** *Computers & Humanities* IV. 23 Current book catalogs of John Wiley and Sons..among many others, already contain all the elements of data proposed for the data bank except a key-word-in-context index. **1971** *Ibid.* VI. 32 Indices and concordances..can be unlemmatized, like the key-word in context concordance to Livy. **1975** *Studies in Eng. Lit.: Eng. Number* (Tokyo) 121 The concordance employs the KWIC (key-word-in-context) principle: Each index word appears, separated by appropriate spacing, in the middle of a line, with its context extending to the left and right.

key, *sb.*³ Add: Also, **key deer,** a subspecies of the North American white-tailed deer, *Odocoileus virginianus clavium*, found in the Florida keys.

1955 *Sci. News Let.* 29 Oct. 277/2 The Key deer is the smallest of all North American deer, only about 26 to 29 inches tall, 38 inches from nose to tail, and averaging only about 30 pounds. **1964** L. S. Crandall *Managem. Wild Mammals in Captivity* 590 Size seems to decrease from north to south, ranging..down to tiny creatures such as the Florida key deer.

key, *v.* Add: **2. c.** To cause (glued surfaces, pigments, etc.) to adhere.

1922 *Encycl. Brit.* XXX. 34/2 Roughing of the surfaces to be glued was adopted to secure keying. **1963** R. R. A. Higham *Handbk. Papermaking* ix. 226 Adhesives are used in coating to 'key' the pigment to the surface of the paper.

3. a. *to key up* (further examples); also, to render (someone) nervous or tense, freq. as *keyed-up* ppl. adj.; so *to key down*: to lower in pitch or intensity.

1889 *Cent. Dict.* s.v., *Keyed up*, high-strung; excited. **1904** Ade *True Bills* 35 He was all keyed up for Matrimony, and the next thing to do was to choose the Lucky Bride. **1922** R. S. Woodworth *Psychol.* vii. 126 It is the state of *excitement*, or of being 'all keyed up'. **1923** D. H. Lawrence *Phoenix II* (1968) 251 Everything that everybody feels is keyed down, and muted, so as not to impinge on anybody else's feelings. **1926** H. Crane *Let.* 5 Jan. (1965) 231 One really has to keep one's self in such a keyed-up mood for the thing. **1927** *Daily Tel.* 16 Aug. 12/5 He has keyed down his playing to such a pitch that we get no impression at all of his character as a man. **1961** C. McCullers *Clock without Hands* ix. 187 Although he was emotionally keyed up, Sherman yawned.

5. To distinguish (an advertisement) by some device which will identify responses to it. orig. *U.S.*

1905 Calkins & Holden *Art of Mod. Advertising* xi. 264 The advertiser likes to know which particular mediums pull best. To accomplish this the advertising is 'keyed'. Some form of address is used which can be varied in each magazine. **1927** *Daily News* 7 June 5/5 Advertisers who key their advertisements report their best results from the 'Daily News'. **1943** C. S. Forester *Ship* 56 How often had he devised ingenious methods by which to 'key' advertisements to discover which had the greatest pulling power. **1952** *Economist* 20 Sept. 718/1 This 'coupon sales' technique in a limited area..has the virtue in terms of publicity of being elaborately 'keyed'; the sales technicians can follow the success of their advertising and promotion schemes round by round. **1967** *Times Rev. Industry* Oct. 82/2 One keys advertisements and measures returns.

6. *Electronics.* **a.** To switch on or off, or from one state to another, by means of a key or relay, as in telegraphic transmission. **b.** To provide (electronic equipment) with means by which it may be switched abruptly from one state to another. Cf. *keying *vbl. sb.* 1.

1929 K. Henney *Princ. Radio* xvii. 443 (*heading*) Keying a transmitter. **1930** *Proc. IRE* XVIII. 1691 The transmitters are started or stopped and keyed locally or from Burnham. **1933** K. Henney *Radio Engin. Handbk.* xviii. 460 Keying the output is accomplished by means of a magnetic modulator. **1943** F. E. Terman *Radio Engineers' Handbk.* ix. 629 Unless the oscillator is keyed, the low-power portions of the transmitter operate continuously. **1954** E. Molloy *Radio & Television Engineers' Ref. Bk.* ix. 16 Means must be found ..to minimize any 'thumps' in the receiver when the transmitter is keyed. **1961** Gray & Graham *Radio Transmitters* vi. 137 Where 'break-in' is needed it may be necessary to key the transmitter oscillator to avoid generating an interfering signal ..in the receiver. **1966** M. Schwartz et al. *Communication Syst. & Techniques* vii. 280 The carrier is 'keyed' on and off to describe the two telegraph states.

7. To cause (something) to fit *in* with something else or *into* a group, pattern, etc. Also *intr.*

1947 *Sun* (Baltimore) 13 Nov. 18/2 (*heading*) Mr. Reuther's victory keys into a world-wide pattern. *Ibid.*, The Socialist Premier..went so far as to speak of an invisible 'orchestra leader' keying these strikes into a symphonic program whose purpose seemed clear. **1949** *Ibid.* 14 Feb. 8/4 (*heading*) Keying labor law into the facts of life. **1958** *Times Lit. Suppl.* 14 Mar. 133/3 It [*sc.* the Book of Mormon] is much longer than the New Testament. Moreover, it is elaborately 'keyed-in' to the Bible. **1960** E. Bowen *Time in Rome* i. 14 Lean young skyscrapers..key in with Rome's general virtuosity. **1969** *Guardian* 21 July 1/4 A carefully planned schedule which keys into the two-hourly orbit of their mother craft.

8. *trans.* To operate on (esp. to transfer (data) or to set (copy)), or to produce, by manipulating the keys of a keyboard. Also with various advbs.

1963 Gregory & Van Horn *Automatic Data-Processing Syst.* (ed. 2) v. 145 The user makes an inquiry by keying in an address in high-speed or bulk storage. **1964** C. Dent *Quantity Surveying by Computer* vii. 100 Checking can be done using a comparator machine or by reading over the print-out against the dimensions; this last method has the advantage of requiring the data to be keyed only once, instead of twice. **1967** Cox & Grose *Organiz. Bibliogr. Rec. by Computer* iv. 101 Messages requesting search information are printed out directly on the console typewriter. The search criteria are then keyed back through the console and the keyword file is searched. **1972** *Physics Bull.* Sept. 531/3 Instead of manually selecting individual type slugs from a case..the compositor keys in the copy at a specially laid out keyboard.

‖ **keyaki** (keˌa·ki). Also **kiaki.** [Jap.] An important Japanese timber tree, *Zelkova serrata*, or its pale, elm-like wood.

1904 [see *hinoki]. **1907** *Yesterday's Shopping* (1969) 203/1 Japanese Trays..Kiaki..Inlaid Wood..Polished. **1948** A. L. Howard *Man. Timbers of World* (ed. 3) 653 While there is some resemblance to the keyaki of Japan (*Z*[*elkova*] *serrata*), there is an entire absence of that beautiful sheen or lustre which the Japanese wood possesses in a high degree. **1965** J. Ohwi *Flora Japan* 381/1 *Zelkova serrata*... Keyaki. Tall trees with gray-brown smooth bark.

keyboard, *sb.* Add: **1. b.** *pl.* Musical instruments that have keyboards. *colloq.*

1971 *Ink* 12 June 19/2 Toni Brown wrote most of the songs..and plays keyboards. **1971** *Melody Maker* 13 Nov. 40/6 Rod's been playing keyboards since he was six. **1974** *Ibid.* 30 Nov. 46 The other four are the originals: Darryl Way on violin, Francis Monkman on keyboards and guitar, [etc.].

2. Also, a similar set in other kinds of machine. (Further examples.)

1846 H. Highton *Brit. Pat. 11,070* 3 Feb., Each terminus of telegraphic communication..is provided with..one of the key boards in use in single magnetic needle electric telegraphs. **1859** *Abridgments of Specifications relating to Printing* (Patent Office) 594 By depressing any one of the several keys on a key-board a lever is acted on,..thus giving motion to certain guide pulleys and cords which work the pistons by which the type is thrust out on to the guide plate. **1892** A. Powell *Southward's Pract. Printing* (ed. 4) xxxii. 310 *Hattersley's Composing Machine.* The type..is contained in the upper part of an iron framework about 3 feet square and 5 feet high. In the lower part of this framework is the key board. **1893** *Times* 25 Sept. 2/6 A machine..possessing remarkable capabilities for printing and adding up figures has recently reached this country from the United States... The keyboard has a number of buttons or keys, each representing a figure, and these are actuated for pounds, shillings, and pence just in the same way as a typewriter. **1911** *Encycl. Brit.* XXVII. 545/1 Composing machines in which the compositor put together types in the required order..by operating a keyboard which liberated them from magazines and assembled them in the order in which the keys had been struck. **1958** Gotlieb & Hume *High-Speed Data Processing* iii. 57 A keyboard transcriber for preparing magnetic tapes offers the advantage of eliminating records intermediate to the source document and the tape. **1970** O. Dopping *Computers & Data Processing* xix. 321 The programmer sits at an electric typewriter connected to the computer, and keys in his program with the keyboard.

keyboard (kī·bōᵊɹd), *v.* [f. the sb.] *trans.* = *key *v.* 8. Also *absol.* or *intr.*

1961 H. W. Larken *Compositor's Work in Printing* xii. 166 Concentration on the task of keyboarding the copy to the exclusion of any concern over the performance of the operations of matrix assembly, casting and distribution, gives a remarkably clean proof with a high setting speed. **1965** *Rep. Proc. Computer Typesetting Conf. London Univ. 1964* v. 153 She is now keyboarding at a rate of 120 to 150 words a minute. **1967** Cox & Grose *Organiz. Bibliogr. Rec. by Computer* ii. 43 Let me now digress..to illustrate some keyboards and photocomposing machines, for the more conventional way of generating character codes is to keyboard them. **1967** Karch & Buber *Offset Processes* ii. 40 The RCA-301 computer accepts punched paper tape and produces a new tape, adding justification (otherwise keyboarded by the Teletypesetter operator). **1969** *Sci. Amer.* May 68 After the encyclopedia..has been keyboarded into the computer. **1973** *Ann. N.Y. Acad. Sci.* CCXI. 284 It is now possible..to keyboard matter on an ordinary IBM Selectric typewriter..and feed it into an OCR machine where the characters are read automatically ..and then transcribed onto magnetic tape.

Hence **key·boarded** *ppl. a.*; **key·boarding** *vbl. sb.*, the action or process of keyboarding something; manipulation of the keys of a keyboard.

1965 *Rep. Proc. Computer Typesetting Conf. London Univ. 1964* iv. 143 Due to the rather inferior setting in the first hand keyboarded material counted, we probably opened up the computer parameters a little too widely. **1965** *Practical Printing & Binding* (ed. 3) iii. 41/1 An attachment to speed up the keyboarding of lines which require to be letter-spaced. **1967** V. Strauss *Printing Industry* ii. 96/2 The product of keyboarding is a punched tape which is used to assemble lines of justified type images on composing machines equipped for tape operation. **1970** *Brit. Printer* Mar. 67/3 No operator with less

than five years' keyboarding experience scored higher than 87 per cent in the test.

keyed, *a.* Add: **4.** *keyed-up*: see *KEY *v.* 3 a. **5.** *Electronics.* **a.** Of electronic equipment or devices: provided with a means by which it may be rapidly switched on or off, or 'keyed' (see *KEY *v.* 6). **b.** Of a signal: intermittent, abruptly stopped and started, as in telegraphic transmissions.

1942 *Proc. IRE* XXX. 15/1 Among the novel features of the design [of the television camera] are..keyed diodes for black-level setting. **1943** *Gloss. Terms Telecomm.* (*B.S.I.*) 65 *Type A1 waves* (*keyed continuous waves*), continuous waves which are keyed according to a telegraphic code. **1943** F. E. TERMAN *Radio Engineers' Handbk.* IX. 630 Keying causes the load placed on a power-supply system by the keyed stages to change abruptly. **1961** GRAY & GRAHAM *Radio Transmitters* vi. 138 Frequency variation of a keyed oscillator..can be reduced by making the oscillator frequency independent of supply voltages.

keyer (kī·əɹ). *Electronics.* [f. KEY *v.* + -ER[1].] A device for switching the signal supply to electronic equipment on and off.

1933 K. HENNEY *Radio Engin. Handbk.* XVIII. 466 (*heading*) Tube keyer for transmitter. **1965** L. E. FOSTER *Telemetry Syst.* iv. 195 The signals are passed through a keyer which converts them from varying-amplitude to constant-amplitude signals of varying pulse width, or pulse duration. **1967** *Electronics* 6 Mar. 346/2 (Advt.), Electronic musical instrument engineer. Should have knowledge of transistor and diode keyers, wave shapers, [etc.].

keyhole, *sb.* Add: **1. b.** (See quots.) *slang.*

1896 FARMER & HENLEY *Slang* IV. 95/1 *Keyhole*, the female *pudendum.* **1927** *Jrnl. Abnormal & Social Psychol.* XXII. 14 Another term for the female organs is *cabbage*... Other symbols are *keyhole* and *bread.* The former is found infrequently.

c. *Astronautics.* A comparatively narrow area through which a spacecraft must pass to reach its objective. *colloq.*

1962 *Times* 21 Feb. 10/1 He swept towards the so-called 'keyhole in the sky', through which he had to pass if orbit was to be achieved. **1968** *Daily Tel.* 27 Dec. 1/2 It must hit a corridor only 35 miles wide. If it dips below this tiny 'keyhole in space', Apollo 8 and its crew will be burned up.

4. key-hole urchin, a flattened North American sea-urchin, with openings in the test, belonging to the genus *Mellita* or closely related genera.

1897 in WEBSTER, Key-hole urchin. **1904** H. L. CLARK in *Bull. U.S. Fish. Comm. 1902* XXXII. 565 *Mellita pentapora* (Gmelin). Key-hole Urchin. **1962** D. NICHOLS *Echinoderms* v. 76 Among the gnathostomes the clypeasteroid sand-dollars achieve probably the greatest specialization, some, such as the Key-hole Urchin, *Rotula*, becoming remarkably flat and possessing holes through the test.

keyhole, *v.* For *trans.* read *intr.*, and add further examples.

1905 *Kynoch Jrnl.* Oct.–Dec. 172 Some of these weapons ..shot wildly, the bullet invariably keyholing. **1910** KIPLING *Land & Sea Tales* (1923) 190 The bullet must have ricochetted short of the butt, and it has key-holed, as we say. **1957** *Amer. Speech* XXXII. 194 *Keyhole*, of a bullet: to enter the target with the side foremost so that a rectangular or oblong hole is cut; of a handgun: to shoot bullets that keyhole.

keying, *vbl. sb.* **1.** (Examples corresponding to *KEY *v.* 6.)

1918 W. H. ECCLES *Wireless Telegr.* (ed. 2) 247 When the high voltage in the repeat side does not exceed 100 or 200 volts it is easy to interrupt that circuit by aid of a morse key. Other suggestions for keying will be found in the section on Wireless Telegraphy. **1931** L. B. TURNER *Wireless* v. 131 To start a Poulsen arc it must be struck... In keying, therefore, the oscillation cannot be started and stopped as in a spark transmitter. Instead, the Morse key—or..the set of relay contacts controlled by the key—is made to alter the wavelength slightly. **1966** S. STEIN in M. Schwartz et al. *Communication Syst. & Techniques* vii. 280 With rectangular modulation, the states are described by which of a pair of possible frequencies is transmitted. The system is commonly known as frequency-shift keying (FSK). Phase-shift keying (PSK) is the analog of phase modulation.

Keynesian (kēi·nziăn), *a.* and *sb.* [f. the name of J. M. *Keynes* + -IAN.] **A.** *adj.* Of or pertaining to the English economist John Maynard Keynes (1883–1946) or his economic theories, esp. regarding State control of the economy through money and taxes. **B.** *sb.* An adherent of these theories. Hence **Key·nesianism.**

1937 *Economic Jrnl.* XLVII. 153 The latest Keynesian analysis does indeed justify..such policies as redistribution of income. **1942** *Fortune* May 61 Mr. Keynes is now a Director of the Bank of England, and he is not the only Keynesian on the Board. **1946** *Ann. Amer. Acad. Pol. & Soc. Sci.* Nov. 284 The distinctive feature of this textbook ..is Keynesianism. **1947** A. P. LERNER in S. E. Harris *New Economics* (1948) IX. xlv. 654 The very simplified form of the Keynesian system..speaks as if there were only one kind of asset. *Ibid.* 655, I say, as a Keynesian, that the rate of interest is determined by the supply and demand for cash. **1951** R. F. HARROD *Life J. M. Keynes* x. 414 Not prepared to accept Keynesian doctrine. **1960** *Commentary* June 463/2 The war left a legacy of wild Keynesianism that continues in a new war economy to sustain prosperity. **1965** *New Statesman* 9 Apr. 560/1 Devious and vulgarised Keynesian calculations of the 'inflationary gap'. **1974** *Times Lit. Suppl.* 20 Sept. 1022/4 The notion of Keynesianism as a system might have been attractive to his vanity but it would have been repellent to his intelligence.

key-note, *sb.* Add: Also **keynote.**

2. b. *attrib.*, as **keynote address** or **speech** orig. *U.S.*, a speech, usu. an opening address, designed to state the main concerns or to set the prevailing tone for a conference or the like; often used at political rallies merely to arouse enthusiasm or promote unity; so **keynote speaker,** one who gives a keynote speech.

1905 *Milwaukee Jrnl.* 28 July 8/1 His address tonight will undoubtedly be a keynote speech. *c* **1908** *Great Issues & National Leaders of 1908* 54 He..began his 'keynote' address. *Ibid.* 133 The 'Keynote' Speech of Democracy. **1948** *Times* 21 June 5 The first two days [of the Republican Convention] will be taken up with..the 'keynote' speech. To heighten suspense and increase the mystery, the 'keynoter' is Governor Green. **1957** *Observer* 13 Oct. 2/5 Mr. Eugene Black, president of the International Bank for Reconstruction and Development, will deliver the 'keynote address' to-morrow. **1967** *Economist* 23 Sept. 1072/2 Mr Thorpe decided to set the tone for the week with a short keynote speech. **1968** *Globe & Mail* (Toronto) 3 Feb. 3/6 A first-rate keynote speaker from the party. **1973** *Observer* 14 Jan. 44/3 Roy Jenkins, MP, will give the keynote speech. **1973** *Black World* Mar. 49 A number of speakers are scheduled for each panel following keynote addresses.

keynote (kī·nōut), *v. colloq.* (orig. *U.S.*). [f. the sb.] *trans.* To express the prevailing tone or idea of (something); to address (a meeting) as a keynote speaker. Hence **key·noting** *vbl. sb.*

1934 in WEBSTER. **1945** *News Review* 10 May 14 Keynoting the surface atmosphere, a Daily Express cartoon showed strap-hanging travellers reading splash-headlined newspapers. **1955** E. LOWRY in Sperber & Trittschuh *Amer. Pol. Terms* (1962) 226/1 Keynoting implies the ability to make melodic noises and give the impression of passionately and torrentially moving onward and upward while warily standing still. **1963** *Amer. Mineralogist* XLVIII. 959 Dr. Ira Cram..will keynote the meeting [of the Society of Exploration Geophysicists]. **1965** *Daily Tel.* 9 June 21/6 Keynoting the meeting, Dr. —— highlighted the need for [etc.]. **1974** *State* (Columbia, S. Carolina) 5 Mar. 9-B/2 Judge George N. Leighton, Howard University and Harvard Law School graduate, will keynote the symposium.

keynoter (kī·nōutəɹ). *colloq.* (orig. *U.S.*). [f. KEY-NOTE *sb.* + -ER[1].] A keynote speaker.

1926 *S.P.E. Tract* XXIV. 123 *Keynoter*, one who outlines the policy of a campaign, sounds the key note. **1948** [see *KEY-NOTE *sb.* 2 b]. **1962** *Economist* 3 Nov. 462/1 The same evangelistic style he displayed as keynoter of the 1960 Republican convention.

keypunch (kī·pʌntʃ), *sb.* Also **key-punch, key punch.** [f. KEY *sb.*[1] + PUNCH *sb.*[1]] A device for punching holes or notches in cards or paper tape in which one of a set of keys is pressed to produce the hole or holes corresponding to a particular character.

1933 L. J. COMRIE *Hollerith & Powers Tabulating Machines* 7 The Powers automatic key punch..has automatic feeding and ejection. **1948** *Math. Tables & Other Aids to Computation* III. 127 Data, transferred by keypunch operators onto teletype tapes. **1970** O. DOPPING *Computers & Data Processing* iii. 57 Tape can be punched in keypunches. **1970** *Honey* June 18/2 (Advt.), A keypunch operator..prepares the cards that tell computers what to do.

keypunch (kī·pʌntʃ), *v.* Also **key-punch.** [f. prec. sb.] **1.** *trans.* **a.** To produce holes or notches in (a card or paper tape) by means of a keypunch.

1947 *Jrnl. Chem. Education* XXIV. 62/1 A master table of cards, bearing *x* and *f*(*x*), is key-punched from printed tables. **1959** *Science* 16 Oct. 958/1 A number of other items were then added from cards which had been especially key-punched for the purpose.

b. To put into the form of punched cards or paper tape by means of a keypunch.

1959 *Jrnl. Assoc. Computing Machinery* VI. 13 The completed output definition form is..keypunched directly into cards. **1960** E. DELAVENAY *Introd. Machine Transl.* 119 The text of the foreword was given in French typescript to Mr Brown...He proceeded to the I.B.M. headquarters where he keypunched it. **1971** *Computers & Humanities* V. 304 The computer phase of the project consists of key-punching an Old Church Slavonic–English composite glossary. **1973** *Ann. N.Y. Acad. Sci.* CCXI. 319 There have been thousands of lines of poetry.. keypunched in order to produce concordances.

2. *intr.* To operate or use a keypunch.

1970 O. DOPPING *Computers & Data Processing* iii. 59 In keypunching for automatic data processing, checking methods other than verification punching are normally used.

So **key·punching** *vbl. sb.* Also **key·punchable** *a.*, capable of being represented on punched cards or paper tape.

1954 *Jrnl. Assoc. Computing Machinery* I. 155/1 The punched-card input makes it possible to use keypunching and verifying techniques. **1965** L. E. FOSTER *Telemetry Syst.* iv. 221 Card-handling equipment provides keypunching, verifying, sorting..and listing services. **1969** P. B. JORDAIN *Condensed Computer Encycl.* 395 Programming..may end with coding (writing in keypunchable form). **1970** *Computers & Humanities* IV. 210 Gould adapted the *Plaine and Easie* keypunchable notation of 48 characters to a code specifically for the uniquely-written chant.

keypuncher (kī·pʌntʃəɹ). Also **key puncher.** [Partly f. KEY *sb.*[1] + PUNCHER, partly f. *KEY-PUNCH *v.* + -ER[1].] **a.** = *KEYPUNCH *sb.*

1965 L. E. FOSTER *Telemetry Syst.* iv. 224 The semiautomatic area consists of..two oscillograph readers with six associated card punchers, 13 key punchers, four verifiers, three *X-Y* plotters, [etc.].

b. One who operates or uses a keypunch.

1967 COX & GROSE *Organiz. Bibliogr. Rec. by Computer* 144 The keypuncher should transcribe this.

keysender (kī·sendəɹ). *Teleph.* [f. KEY *sb.*[1] + SENDER.] A device for applying electric impulses representing a telephone number to a circuit by means of a set of keys (numbered 0 to 9), in place of a dial.

1929 *Telegraph & Telephone Jrnl.* XVI. 34/1 The light, airy switchroom, the tap-tap of the keysenders and the humming of the dials, this is my introduction into the subscribers' Paradise—an Automatic Exchange. **1934** *Post Office Electr. Engineers' Jrnl.* XXVII. 32/1 It has recently been decided..to provide mechanical keysenders both for P.B.X. operators and, if desired, for individual telephones. **1948** J. ATKINSON *Herbert & Procter's Telephony* (new ed.) I. xi. 216/2 The keysender..is a device introduced as an alternative to the dial on large type private branch exchange switchboards to reduce the time expended by a P.B.X. operator when dialling numbers from the switchboard. By its use, the P.B.X. operator is free to attend to other calls whilst the keysender is still transmitting the digits which have been keyed up. **1970** *New Scientist* 5 Nov. 275/1 Tests at the St Albans exchange showed that the keysender was markedly quieter than the rotary dial and saved an average of 2–3 seconds on each call.

So **key·sending,** the use or operation of a keysender.

1928 C. W. BROWN *Automatic Telephony Simplified* viii. 143 Key sending, and not dial sending, would, of course, be provided at manual exchanges when necessary. **1930** *Gloss. Terms Telegraphs & Telephones* (*B.S.I.*) 26 *Keysending B-position*, a B-position equipped with digit keys for the purpose of making calls direct to an automatic exchange. **1938** HERBERT & PROCTER *Telephony* II. ix. 393 Each manual exchange adopting direct 7-digit keysending utilizes a suitable automatic exchange as a routing centre for the whole of its indirectly routed traffic. **1950** J. ATKINSON *Herbert & Procter's Telephony* (new ed.) II. xvii. 558/2 There are three alternative arrangements of the keysending equipment.

keyster, var. *KEISTER.

keystone, *sb.* Add: **1. d.** *ellipt.* = *Keystone State* (in Dict., sense 5). Also *attrib. U.S.*

[**1803** in H. M. Jenkins *Pennsylvania* (1903) II. xii. 316 Pennsylvania is the Keystone of the democratic arch.] **1844** *Congress. Globe* 4 June 662/3 The old Key-stone has never furnished the Union with either President or Vice President. **1948** *Time* 21 June 22/3 The control of keystone Pennsylvania was one of the big question marks of the convention.

5. keystone effect, in *Cinemat.*, the formation of a trapezial projected image as a result of the line of projection not being normal to the screen; a similar distortion of a television picture in which a rectangular object gives a trapezial image; **Keystone State** (examples).

1914 J. B. RATHBUN *Motion Picture Making* vi. 135 With the projector installed at one side of the screen, the keystone effect will be horizontal instead of vertical. **1940** D. G. FINK *Princ. Television Engin.* iv. 142 When such a scanned image is reproduced in the receiver, all the picture elements in the lower lines are spread out too far relative to those in the top line. This is the so-called keystone effect. **1967** *Electronics* 6 Mar. 79/1 (Advt.), The electron gun is set at an angle to the phosphor and the deflection system compensates for keystone effects. **1836** *Southern Lit. Messenger* II. 277 The little German farmer..in the Key Stone State. **1948** *Daily Ardmoreite* (Ardmore, Okla.) 27 Apr. 6/2 Republican aspirants matched strength in the politically important keystone state.

b. Used *attrib.* (with capital initial) in allusion to the slapstick comedy films produced by the Keystone film company, formed by 'Mack Sennett' in 1912; esp. of films featuring the 'Keystone Cops', a group of bumbling policemen. Hence *Keystones*, slang for 'police'.

1913 *Writer's Mag.* Nov. 188/2 If you have never written burlesque or vaudeville material..you will do well to watch a dozen of the Keystone comedies. **1918** R. H. KNYVETT *Over There* 54 We received at this time the nickname 'Keystone soldiers', some genial ass conceiving that we looked as funny as the Keystone police. **1935** A. J. POLLOCK *Underworld Speaks* 66/2 *Keystone*, a special, uniformed police officer. **1964** W. MARKFIELD *To Early Grave* x. 168 He was straddling the running board like a Keystone cop. **1967** [see *JAMES BOND]. **1969** J. WAINWRIGHT *Big Tickle* 162 Get the keystones in the act. They watch. We perform. **1971** A. HUNTER *Gently at Gallop* i. 6 The local Keystones move in demanding

alibis. **1974** N. FREELING *Dressing of Diamond* 107 The extreme infantilism of mentalities unable to distinguish between the Keystone Kops and a shattered child.

keystone (kī·stōun), *v. Television.* [f. the sb.] *trans.* To subject to a keystone effect (see *KEYSTONE 5). Hence **key·stoning** *vbl. sb.*

1940 ZWORYKIN & MORTON *Television* xv. 473 If the complete sawtooth..is a modulation, the shape will be keystoned. **1940** D. G. FINK *Princ. Television Engin.* iv. 142 (*caption*) Trapezoidal distortion ('keystoning') of scanning pattern in the iconoscope. **1951** S. DEUTSCH *Theory & Design Television Receivers* xv. 495 This characteristic is counteracted by keystoning the CRT picture in the opposite sense by means of two permanent magnets. **1972** R. G. MIDDLETON *Transistor Television Servicing Guide* (rev. ed.) vii. 86 A thermistor in the vertical-deflection coil circuit will occasionally..develop an abnormal resistance characteristic that will produce keystoning.

keystroke (kī·strōuk), *sb.* Also **key-stroke, key stroke.** [f. KEY *sb.*[1] + STROKE *sb.*[1]] A depression of a key on a keyboard, esp. as a measure of work.

c **1910** *Comptometer* (Felt & Tarrant Manufacturing Co.) 4 Because a simple key-stroke does it all, the Comptometer saves 60% of time on addition. **1914** E. M. HORSBURGH *Mod. Instruments & Methods of Calculation* 101 A beginner..might by a slurred or partial key-stroke make it add a wrong amount. **1921** J. A. V. TURCK *Origin Mod. Calculating Machines* 160 Felt was interested in the solution of the problem for detection and correction of the errors in key-strokes. **1966** E. J. & J. A. MCCARTHY *Integrated Data Processing Syst.* v. 122 Most work is figured on the basis of 100 key strokes a minute. **1972** *Sci. Amer.* May 14/1 (Advt.), Although it's only 3 by 6 inches and weighs 9 ounces..it computes transcendental functions with a single keystroke in less than a second.

Hence **key·stroke** *v. trans.* = *KEY *v.* 8; **key·stroking** *vbl. sb.* Also **key·stroker,** one who operates the keys of a keyboard, esp. of a keypunch.

1966 *Ann. Rev. Information Sci.* I. 192 One of the impediments to greater use of automation in library and information center operations is the formidable prospect of keystroking an existing corpus of text. **1967** *Library Jrnl.* 1 Mar. 975 *All* publications..have to be key-stroked at some stage in their life-cycle. **1971** J. B. CARROLL et al. *Word Frequency Bk.* p. xix. The samples [of text] were keystroked freeform onto IBM cards using IBM 029 keypunch equipment. **1971** *Computers & Humanities* VI. 40 If key-stroking plays a part in data entry, the key-stroker's own deviations will be added to those already in the text.

‖ **kgotla** (kgǫ·tlă). Also 9 **cotla, kotla.** [Tswana.] An assembly of tribal elders among some Bantu peoples; also, the place of such assembly (see also quot. 1857). Cf. *KUTA.

1840 B. SHAW *Memorials of S. Afr.* xx. 303 Morokos Kotla had no attractions yesterday; we went and sat down in it, but we could not bear to remain. **1846** H. H. METHUEN *Life in Wilderness* viii. 253 We threaded our way between the wattle hedges..and reached the cotla, or place of assembly, set apart in all native tribes for the purpose of holding public meetings. **1857** D. LIVINGSTONE *Missionary Trav. & Res. S. Afr.* i. 15 Near the centre of each circle of huts there is a spot called a 'kotla', with a fireplace; here they work, eat, or sit and gossip over the news of the day. **1896** H. A. BRYDEN *Tales S. Afr.* 192 They reached the large *kotla*, or enclosure, in the centre of the town, where Tapinyani's own residence stood. **1949** *Cape Times* 10 Nov. 2/8 Chief Bathoen, of the Bangwaketse tribe, gave evidence about the June *kgotla*, saying that the Assistant Government Secretary had told the tribesmen that they were gathered to discuss the right of succession of chieftainship. **1966** *New Statesman* 15 Apr. 531/2 The *kgotla*..until recently the arena of decision in Bechuanaland. **1972** *Times* 11 Sept. (Botswana, Lesotho & Swaziland Suppl.) p. iii/4 Until now, the traditional place for dealing with such matters has been the *kgotla*.

khad, var. KHUD.

1925 *Dollar Mag.* Mar. 35 Our bungalow is situated on a little knoll with steep khads on three sides down to the river about 150 feet below. **1961** L. D. STAMP *Gloss. Geogr. Terms* 279/2 *Khad*, a torrent in the hills.

‖ **khadar** (kā·dəɪ). *India.* Also **kadir, khádar, khaddar, khâder, khadir,** and with capital K. [Hindi.] **a.** A flood-plain; land susceptible to flooding.

1832 G. C. MUNDY *Pen & Pencil Sk.* I. v. 269 The road continued partly along the khâder of the river. **1879** MEDLICOTT & BLANFORD *Man. Geol. India* I. xvii. 404 The alluvial plain itself..is composed of *bhángar*, or high land..and *khádar*, or low land, the low plain through which each river flows. **1882** W. THEOBALD *Mason's Burma* I. 4 The delta..of the Ganges, the richest land of Lower Bengal, being composed of *Khadir* land. **1887** J. M. BROWN *Shikar Sk.* 247 Pig-sticking in the Kadir, or old bed of the Ganges. **1887** *Encycl. Brit.* XXII. 98/2 Eastward of the khádar lies the sandy central tableland. **1904** A. KNOX *Gloss. Geogr. & Topogr. Terms* 193 *Khadar* (Hind.), low lands fit for rice-growing. **1929** *Blackw. Mag.* Oct. 526/2 There is more game and greater variety of game in a kadir country than in any other kind. **1955** BROWN & DEY *India's Mineral Wealth* (ed. 3) xix. 691 In the Brahmaputra valley, and the whole of the Assam plain is one great *khadar* or strath.

b. Recently deposited alluvium.

1919 D. N. WADIA *Geol. India* xxii. 251 The Khadar deposits are, as a rule, confined to the vicinity of the present channels. **1945** H. L. CHHIBBER *India* I. xiv. 187 The Newer Alluvium is confined to the river channels and their flood plains and is locally termed as *Khaddar*. **1949** M. S. KRISHNAN *Geol. India & Burma* xx. 519 The Newer Alluvium (called *Khadar* in the Punjab) is light coloured and poor in calcareous matter.

khaddar (kæ·dăɪ). Also **khadder, khadi.** [Hindi.] Indian home-spun cotton cloth.

1921 *Glasgow Herald* 27 Dec. 7 This tent will be made of hand-spun 'khadder'. **1922** *Ibid.* 22 Dec. 9 Delegates are already pouring into Neaya for the session of Congress that opens on December 26, and a huge marquee of khaddar (homespun) material has been erected. **1923** *Daily Mail* 23 Feb. 8 No person wearing clothes other than those made from 'Khadder'—Mr. Gandhi's own favourite brand of hand-woven cloth—is tolerated in the 'presence'. **1924** C. D. GROTH tr. *Rolland's Mahatma Gandhi* 72 Tagore, too, praised this *khaddar*, or *khadi*. **1925** E. S. JONES *Christ of Indian Road* v. 116 The whole city was dressed in white home-spun khaddar, the sign of the Nationalist. **1936** J. NEHRU *Autobiogr.* xv. 106 Khadi clothes and third-class railway travelling demand little money. **1960** KOESTLER *Lotus & Robot* 278 The produce of the cotton mills is cheaper than homespun *khadi*. **1971** *Illustr. Weekly India* 18 Apr. 6 He alighted, this huge khadder-clad mountain of a man, his eyes alert and smiling. **1974** *New Yorker* 3 June 28/2 Gandhi called on all Indians..to raise cotton and to spin and weave it, so that there would be no shortage of *khadi*, or homespun cloth. **1975** *Bangladesh Times* 22 July 5/2 There may be easily manageable industries such as handloom, Khadi, village industries, handicrafts, [etc.].

khaki, *a.* and *sb.* Add: **B.** *sb.* Also (usu. *pl.*), a uniform or garment made from this fabric.

1936 *Amer. Speech* XI. 50 Unless he learns..to restrict the use of *khaki* to cotton uniforms of that shade..he is still a *John* [*viz.* a recruit]. **1956** *Ibid.* XXXI. 192 A marine's uniform wardrobe consists of *greens, blues, khakis.* **1956** H. GOLD *Man who was not with It* (1965) xviii. 157 Once I sat wearing nothing but a pair of shiny starched new khakis. **1961** *Harper's Mag.* Oct. 43/2 The only clothing I owned was four pairs of khakis, three sweat shirts, a tweed jacket. **1970** 'T. COE' *Wax Apple* (1973) i. 8 He was short and wiry, dressed in khakis and T-shirt.

C. *khaki election* (examples); also used of the general elections of 1918 and 1931. So *khaki vote.*

1913 *Everyday Phrases Explained* 164 *The Khaki Election.* This was the General Election of 1900, when the Government appealed successfully to the country for its approval of the South African War. **1917** G. B. SHAW *What I really wrote about War* (1930) x. 273 You may look forward with exultation to a century of triumphant khaki elections. **1918** *Times* 23 Aug. 8/4 Parliament clearly contemplated a khaki election in the best sense, with every soldier, sailor,..and Red Cross worker voting on the sole but splendid qualification of national service. *Ibid.*, Above all, in 1900 there was no khaki vote. That is the great dividing line which the Reform Act has drawn between 1900 and 1918. **1958** *Times* 15 Feb. 8/4 In November, 1918, she was adopted..as a candidate for Parliament. At the 'khaki election' she stood as a Coalition candidate. **1963** *Times* 6 Feb. 15/1 The 'khaki election' of 1900, when the Conservatives swept the country. **1968** A. MARWICK *Brit. in Cent. of Total War* iii. 94 The election of 14 December 1918..was a 'Khaki' election in which the dominant element was patriotic hysteria. **1971** D. AYERST *Guardian* xxx. 472 Sir Warren Fisher..remained at the Treasury..and Ramsay Macdonald at 10 Downing St. He decided to hold a khaki election.

D. khaki bos, bush *S. Afr.*, (*a*) one of several herbs of the family Compositæ, *Tagetes minuta, Inula graveolens,* or *Schkuhria pinnata*; (*b*) = **khaki weed*; **khaki weed,** *Alternanthera repens,* a member of the family Amaranthaceæ which has spread from South America to South Africa and Australia.

1907 R. W. THORNTON in *Agric. Jrnl. Cape of Good Hope* 7 Jan. 76 The Khaki Bush is a species of *Aplopappus*... The plant is an annual shrub, rising on a straight main stem to a height of about from two to three feet, with fine pointed leaves and light yellow flowers, which yield an enormous quantity of fine seed. **1913** C. PETTMAN *Africanderisms* 258 Khakibush. A species of *Aplopappus.* The name has reference to the dull fawn colour the withered leaves assume... The name is also applied to *Alternanthera Achyrantha*, R. Br., a troublesome weed now spread widely throughout South Africa, the seeds having been introduced from the Argentine Republic with imported fodder. The name was given to this plant because it made its appearance in military camps during the late war in places where it was previously unknown. **1932** R. MARLOTH *Flora S. Afr.* III. II. 239 Species [of *Schkuhria*] 12, one as a weed in S.A., *S. bonariensis,* Tr., *khaki bush.* **1932** WATT & BREYER-BRANDWIJK *Medicinal & Poisonous Plants S. Afr.* 192 *Inula graveolens* Desf., Khaki bush, Khaki weed, Stinkweed (Australia) is an introduced species. *Ibid.* 195 *Tagetes minuta* L., an introduced weed, known as Khaki bush, Mexican marigold, and Kakiebos, is frequently referred to in the daily Press as an excellent parasiticide for cattle. **1947** H. C. BOSMAN *Mafeking Road* xix. 108 He seemed to have picked out all the useless bits for his pictures—a krantz and a few stones and some clumps of khaki-bos. **1956** A. G. MCRAE *Hill called Grazing* ii. 15, I had never in all my life seen such a profusion of cockle burr, Scotch thistle and 'khaki bush'. **1907** H. G. MUNDY in *Transvaal Agricultural Jrnl.* V. 939 Khaki-weed or Amaranthus weed (*Alternanthera echinata*). **1932** R. MARLOTH *Flora S. Afr.* III. II. 239 Species [of *Tagetes*] about 40, Amer., one as a weed in S.A., *T. minuta* (*khaki weed*). **1953** P. LANHAM *Blanket Boy's Moon* II. vi. 131 *Matekoane* is a weed resembling the khaki weed. **1958** N. GORDIMER *World of Strangers* xiv. 212 Khaki-weed, the growth of neglect and desolation, standing dead and high. **1965** *Austral. Encycl.* I. 167/2 The South American annual needle burr (*Amaranthus spinosus*) and khaki weed (*Alternanthera repens*) have become serious pests in Queensland.

Hence (often with capital initial) **kha·kied** (kā·kid) *pa. pple.*, dressed in khaki; *fig.* possessed by a militant spirit; **kha·kiism,** militant spirit or policy; **kha·kiite,** an enthusiast for a war policy; **kha·kiness** = **khakiism.* (All *temporary.*)

1900 *Westm. Gaz.* 4 May 2/2 The Portsmouth electors..did not allow themselves to be persuaded..into khakiness. **1900** *Daily Express* 26 June 5 (Cassell's Suppl.), The departure of khakied troops for the front. **1900** *National Rev.* June 535 There is no reason to suppose that Lord Salisbury has, so far, surrendered to Khakiism. *Ibid.*, The Khakiites are strenuous and determined. **1904** *Westm. Gaz.* 19 Nov. 2/1 The last election, when certainly the confidence-trick was indeed played on a Khakied nation. **1945** *Brit. Jrnl. Psychol.* Jan. 34 These millions of Khakied citizens run the whole gamut of traditional military gradation.

‖ **khal** (kāl). *India.* [Bengali.] (See quot. 1958[2].)

1903 *Jrnl. Trop. Med.* VI. 200/2 This [*sc.* the anahar plant] is steeped in the big khal at Ishapur, and during the fermenting stage mosquitoes are generated very plentifully. **1904** A. KNOX *Gloss. Geogr. & Topogr. Terms* 193 *Khal* (Bengali), a creek. **1958** N. AHMAD *Econ. Geogr. E. Pakistan* I. i. 15 The upper part of the plain between the Garai-Madhumati and the Padma,..is full of rivers, streams, and *khals* of various sizes. *Ibid.* 338 *Khāl*, narrow natural channel of water.

khalasi (kălæ·si). Also **calassie, kalashi, -y** (-ʃ-), **kalas(s)i, khalishee, khelasse,** etc. [Hind.] A native servant or labourer, esp. one employed as a seaman. Also *attrib.* in **khalasi watch** (see quot. 1911).

1800 F. GLADWIN tr. *Ayeen Akbery* I. II. 232 The tundeil is the chief of the khelasses, or sailors. **1848** *Alfred in India* 44 Alfred saw the *calassies*, or tent-pitchers, beginning to take down the tent to pack it on the cart. **1848** J. H. STOCQUELER *Oriental Interpreter* 115/1 *Kalashy*, an Indian menial. His business is, properly speaking, confined either to what relates to camp equipage, or to the management of the sails and rigging on board a budjrow or river boat. *a* **1865** SMYTH *Sailor's Word-bk.* (1867) 421 *Khalishees*, native Indian sailors. **1907** M. ROBERTS *Flying Cloud* 22 He had sailed with Khalasi crews for ten years. **1911** *Coast Seamen's Jrnl.* 9 Aug. 1/2 There is growing up a system, mostly in steamers, sometimes called Kalashi watches. This means that certain men are kept on the regular watch-and-watch while the other members of the crew are what is called 'day men'. The 'day men' work all day and are supposed to sleep all night. **1917** *Yachting Monthly* XXII. 197/1 Nothing loth the Kalassis [*sc.* bunder boat crews at Karachi] obeyed. **1931** W. H. PARKER *Leaves from Unwritten Log-Bk.* xi. 95 All hands were kept on deck (or keeping Kalasi watches) for two days and nights. **1957** D. G. O. BAILLIE *Sea Affair* 237 The Lascars, known as *khalassies*, belong to the Deck Department. They are Moslems. **1963** P. J. ABRAHAM *Last Hours* 9, I noticed some of the seamen, or Khalassis, in their blue dungaree uniforms. **1973** *Times of India* 16 Oct. 4/5 Those on strike include..winch operators, khallasis, tindals and other workmen.

Khaldian (kæ·ldiăn). [f. *Khaldis* or *Khaldi* the name of the supreme god in Urartu + -AN, -IAN.] **a.** Also **Khaldæi, Khaldean.** Orig. the divine offspring of Khaldi; more usually, a native or inhabitant of the ancient Armenian kingdom of Urartu. **b.** Also **Khaldic.** The language spoken by this people. Also as *adj.*

1882 A. H. SAYCE in *Jrnl. R. Asiatic Soc.* XIV. 412 Khaldis..was also the father of other gods who were called 'the Khaldians' after him. **1898** —— in J. Hastings *Dict. Bible* I. 140/1 The supreme god of Armenia was Khaldis..from whom the inhabitants of the country took the name of 'people of Khaldis'. From this was derived the name of Khaldæi or Khaldeans. **1901** *Westm. Gaz.* 29 July 5/2 The Khaldians..are to be identified with the Chaldaioi of the Greek writers, who figure prominently in Xenophon. **1908** A. H. SAYCE in *Encycl. Relig. & Ethics* I. 793/1 The present article deals with Proto-Armenian religion as revealed in the Vannic or 'Khaldian' cuneiform inscriptions. **1925** —— in *Cambr. Anc. Hist.* III. viii. 170 If another title is wanted in place of Vannic, Alarodian would be preferable to Khaldian. **1939** L. H. GRAY *Foundations of Lang.* xii. 381 *Khaldic* (also called *Urartaean* or *Vannic*), the language of a kingdom which flourished between 900 and 600 B.C...is known from nearly two hundred inscriptions in Akkadian cuneiform. **1952** O. R. GURNEY *Hittites* vi. 124 A direct descendant of Hurrian is the language of the kingdom of Urartu, sometimes called Vannic or Khaldian. **1959** *Chambers's Encycl.* XIV. 243/1 The people were called Khaldis, they worshipped a sun-god and an air-god. **1966** *Ibid.* XIV. 179/1 Urartu was an ancient kingdom in the highlands of Armenia...The people called themselves 'children of Khaldi' (their national god) and so have sometimes been called Khaldians by modern historians.

khalifa. Add: **2.** *S. Afr.* Also **califa, chalifah, kalifa.** A Malay sword-dance which originally had religious significance. Also *attrib.*

1856 *Cape Monitor* 16 Jan. 2/3 (*heading*) Checking the Malay 'Califa'. *Ibid.*, Several Malay priests have been examined..and it would seem from their evidence that the Califa is by no means part of the Mahomedan religion, and..ought only to be played on a certain night in each year. **1861** *Cape Monthly Mag.* Dec. 356 The most characteristic of their customs is the 'Khalifa', a religious

ceremonial of the highest solemnity. **1867** M. Kollisch *Mussulman Population Cape Good Hope* 59 The feats which the 'Khalifa' involved were highly amusing. **1900** *Diamond Fields Advertiser* (Kimberley) 31 May 2/3 Town Hall, Kimberley. Khalifa Representation in aid of the fund for the relief of the sick and wounded in the Transvaal war. **1950** M. Masson *Birds of Passage* xv. 142 But the *pièce de résistance* of the whole affair was a kalifa dance by two hundred Malays. **1953** Du Plessis & Lückhoff *Malay Quarter* iii. 62 During the previous century..there were many bands of Chalifah-players. *Ibid.*, The chief priest..is designated by the term *Chalifah*, which has now, through common usage, come to be applied to the performance itself. **1972** *Standard Encycl. S. Afr.* VII. 147/1 The most spectacular custom of the Cape Malays is the performance of the Chalifah.

Khalkha, Khalka (ka·lkă), *sb.* and *a.* [Native name.] **A.** *sb.* **a.** One of a Mongol people in Outer Mongolia; the people themselves. **b.** The language spoken by them. **B.** *adj.* Of or pertaining to this people, their language, or the territory they inhabit.

1873 *Jrnl. R. Geogr. Soc.* XLIII. 122 The *K* of *Kuren* being pronounced *H* by the Kalkas,..would leave a word having..a much greater affinity than many Chinese names have to those in use amongst the natives of the soil. **1876** H. H. Howorth *Hist. Mongols* I. viii. 468 Lamaism had spread very greatly among the Mongols, and it was a subject of pride among the Khalkha chiefs to have a..regenerate Buddha among them. **1926** A. N. J. Whymant *Mongolian Gram.* i. 1 The Khalka (or as it is generally spelt according to Russian orthography, Khalkha) Mongolian possesses seven vowels and twenty consonants. *Ibid.* 4 The Kalmuck presents consonantal difficulties over the Khalkha. *Ibid.* 5 A common word in all dialects of Mongolian is one mostly heard as *chichik* (a flower) among the Khalkhas. **1948** D. Diringer *Alphabet* 318 The three principal [Mongolian] dialects, Khalkha, Kalmuck and Buriat. **1967** D. S. Parlett *Short Dict. Lang.* 87 Modern literature based mainly on Khalkha dialect in an alphabet based on Cyrillic. **1970** H. Elvin *Incredible Mile* xlviii. 132 If Bernard Shaw..had known as much about Mongolian costume as about English dialects..he could have told me..that blue and brown meant a Khalka,..that if a woman's sleeves had horizontal pleats they would be of a Khalka.

‖ **khalukah** (halu·kă). Also **chalukah, haluka, halukkah, haluqqah.** [Talmudic Heb. *ḥ°luqqāh* distribution, f. Heb. *ḥālaq* to distribute.] The distribution of contributions or donations sent by the Jews of the diaspora to support the Jews in Palestine. Now *Hist.*

1880 *Encycl. Brit.* XIII. 686/2 Annual contributions (*haluka*) amounting to about £50,000 a year. **1920** *19th Cent.* Oct. 627 Fear has been expressed that Jewry in Palestine..will degenerate into a new form of 'Chalukah'. **1923** W. P. Livingstone *Galilee Doctor* 48 The Jew who followed his native genius, engaged in commerce, and made a success of it, was independent of the khalukah. **1927** *Scots Observer* 9 Apr. 8/3 This class has not increased owing to the failure of the Haluka by which it was supported. **1941** *Universal Jewish Encycl.* V. 188/2 In..the 1930's and 1940's, the collections dwindled away... The Halukkah had been replaced..by contributions through Zionist organizations. **1944** M. Hadas tr. *Elbogen's Cent. Jewish Life* III. i. 246 A system of distributing alms to the various national groups (*kolelim*)..was elaborated and given the name *Halukkah*. *Ibid.* 250 He also worked for the education of girls and for freeing the Jewish population from the scourge of the *Halukkah*. *Ibid.* 251 The *Halukkah* used its power to penalize parents who sent their children to the modern schools and to hinder any progress in making them productive. **1957** S. W. Baron *Social & Relig. Hist. Jews* (ed. 2) V. xxiii. 37 The..'Babylonian' congregation..demanded independent control over the distribution of charitable funds..for the poor of the Holy Land. It thus adumbrated the nineteenth-century struggles over the distribution of *ḥaluqqah* funds raised in the various countries of the dispersion. **1962** *New Jewish Encycl.* 185/2 Halukkah..began in olden times and continued until replaced by modern fund-raising. **1970** *New Stand. Jewish Encycl.* 831/1 *Halukkah*, the distribution of collections made abroad for the support of the poor in Palestine. 'H. Jews' were those living on such contributions.

Khamba (ka·mbă). Also **Kamba, K(h)ampa.** [f. Tibetan *Kham* East Tibet + suffixal element *-ba* or *-pa*.] **a.** A Tibetan people from Kham; one of this people. **b.** The language spoken by this people. Also *attrib.* or as *adj.*

1928 C. Bell *People of Tibet* i. 4 Eastern Tibet...This area is known as Kam, the people as Kam-pa. *Ibid.* vi. 59 The Lhasa men, they used to say, were fonder of talking than of working; the Kam-pas (eastern Tibetans), irritable and quarrelsome. **1955** G. T. Bull *When Iron Gates Yield* iv. 58 The soldiers..were looking forward to a good scrap, for such is the Tibetan Khamba's temperament. *Ibid.* v. 67 A Kamba Tibetan..would rather his blood be spilt in the snow..than to be found alive and defamed. **1957** R. Ford *Captured in Tibet* i. 22, I had picked up enough words of the Khamba dialect to be able to talk to the local inhabitants. *Ibid.* iii. 47 When Radio Peking switched its Tibetan broadcasts to a more suitable hour, it still had no audience, for the news-reader spoke with a Khamba accent. **1960** 'S. Harvester' *Chinese Hammer* ii. 31 The only fighting in the country is in the east and restricted to Khambas. **1962** H. E. Richardson *Tibet & its Hist.* i. 11 The Khampas..live between the upper Yangtse and the Chinese border. *Ibid.* xii. 201 The Chinese..exploited the traditional mistrust of Lhasa officialdom existing among the Khampa and Amdowa tribes to the east of the upper Yangtse. **1973** *Times* 20 Oct. 3/2 The fourteenth Dalai Lama is..now 38 and has lived in exile in the Indian Himalayas since 1959, when Khamba rebels persuaded him to flee from Lhasa with them after their abortive uprising against the Chinese occupation.

Khamitic, var. Hamitic *a.*

1880 A. H. Sayce *Introd. Sci. of Lang.* II. vii. 181 A number of dialects..are classed together as Ethiopian or Khamitic.

khan². (Later examples.)

1947 *Archit. Rev.* CII. 99 (*caption*) The nearest building, with a row of small domes, is the khan or shopping centre. **1951** A. Christie *They came to Baghdad* i. 8 Captain Crosbie..turned down a small alleyway into a large Khan or Court. **1958** R. Liddell *Morea* II. vii. 165 The buses going to Arcadia pull up at a khan near the village of Alepochori.

‖ **khana** (kā·nă). *India.* [Hind. *khānā* food, dinner.] Food, a meal.

1859 G. F. Atkinson *Curry & Rice* Plate 23 (*caption*) There, now, an invitation to dinner!—to a 'Burra Khanah', literally a grand feed. **1888** Kipling *Phantom 'Rickshaw* 33 The *khansamah* went to get me food. He did not go through the pretence of calling it '*khana*'—man's victuals. **1933** *Discovery* Nov. 349/1 Vital ingredients for the preparation of the *khana* for the Sahib. **1953** E. M. Forster *Hill of Devi* 73 The cooking of our Indian khana. **1953** L. Iremonger in *Caribbean Anthol. Short Stories* 19 At noon they would be eating their *khana*, sitting over the open fire.

‖ **khanda,** var. Khanjar.

1888 Kipling *From Sea to Sea* (1899) I. vii. 53 'And what do you make in Udaipur?' 'Swords,' said the man.. throwing down an armful of..*kuttars*, and *khandas*. **1957** *Encycl. Brit.* XX. 647/2 In that rite, with a two-edged dagger (*khanda*) sugar is stirred up in water. **1971** *Daily Tel.* 11 June 3 (*caption*) An alternative to the kirpan is the khanda, a small dagger.

‖ **khanga** (ka·ŋgă). Also **kanga.** [Swahili.] In East Africa, a fabric printed in various colours and designs with borders, used esp. for women's clothing.

1967 *Sunday Times* 15 Jan. 31/5 *Kangas*..are the most riotous with words and even jokes printed on them. **1969** *Flamingo* (E. Afr.) x. 18/2 They often wear the two-piece dress, kanga, and this allows the smoke to pass everywhere. **1970** [see *kitenge]. **1971** *Daily Nation* (Nairobi) 10 Apr. 5/1 (Advt.), Kitenge Khanga Kikoy..at African Drapering. **1975** *Daily Tel.* 7 July 9 Khangas..come from Kenya, and are fine soft cotton rectangles about 60 in by 44 in, printed in literally hundreds of the most fabulous colours and designs... Wear them as a stunning beach dress or sarong type skirt knotted dead front.

‖ **khansu** (kanzu·). Also **khanzu.** [Swahili *kanzu* shirt, f. Arab. *kasā* to clothe.] A loose outer garment worn in East Africa.

1969 M. Hastings *Killing in Black & White* i. 5 Steel watched the Africans in the street below. Only the older men..wore loose-fitting khanzus; the young favoured European dress. **1971** D. Creed *Trial of Lobo Icheka* I. ii. 23 Salim..went away, his white khansu swishing agitatedly about his legs. **1973** *Daily Tel.* (Colour Suppl.) 30 Nov. 63/1 A servant at a club was going to be wearing a *khanzu*, somewhat resembling a nightshirt.

‖ **khanum** (kā·nŏm). Also **caño, canum, hanim, hanum.** [Turk. *khānim*, fem. of *khān* Khan¹.] In the near East, a lady of rank, the wife of a khan. Also = Mrs., madam, as a title or term of address.

1824 J. Morier *Adventures Hajji Baba* I. xxiv. 256 My situation is that of hand-maid to the *khanum*, so my mistress is called. **1826** Leyden & Erskine tr. *Mem. Zehir-Ed-Din* 12 The second daughter [of Shir Haji Beg], Kullûk Nigâr Khanum, was my mother. **1834** [see *khatun]. **1848** J. H. Stocqueler *Oriental Interpreter* 125/2 *Khanum*, the feminine of Khan, 'Lord', and signifies Lady, the wife of a Khan. **1859** C. R. Markham tr. *Gonzalez de Clavijo's Narr. Embassy to Court of Timour* vi. 145 The first wall and tents were for the use of the chief wife of the lord, who was called *Caño*. **1900** *Daily News* 9 Jan. 7/2 The Queen of Greece..won the hearts of the Moslem feminine world by returning in person all the visits of the harem ladies..and was smothered with gifts from these enthusiastic hanums. **1929** *Spectator* 21 Aug. 276/1 Closely-veiled figures of Turkish *Khanums*. **1950** I. Orga *Portrait of Turkish Family* xi. 123 Hasan.. peered at my mother..and said uncertainly: 'I went to your house first... I did not know it was like that, hanim efendi...'

khapra (kā·pră). [ad. Hindi *khaprā* destroyer, f. *khapna* to destroy.] In full, *khapra beetle*. A small, brownish-black beetle, *Trogoderma granarium*, of the family Dermestidæ, native to India but widely found elsewhere as a pest of stored grain.

1896 E. C. Cotes in *Indian Museum Notes* III. 119 It [*sc.* a dermestid beetle] is known as *Kapra* in the Delhi bazaar, where it is said sometimes to destroy as much as six or seven per cent. of wheat stored in godowns. **1928** *Bull. Entomol. Res.* XVIII. 251 (*title*) Investigations on the control of the Khapra beetle. **1955** *Hilgardia* XXIV. 1 The khapra beetle, *Trogoderma granarium* Everts, was first identified in the United States in stored wheat and barley..in October, 1953. **1959** *Jrnl. Econ. Entomol.* LII. 313/1 Each food sample was placed in a plastic cell with a single khapra-beetle egg. **1971** *New Scientist* 27 May 503/2 Khapra beetles may be baited by merely suspending large pieces of jute fabric on top of the infested grain.

kharif (karī·f). [(Hind. a.) Arab. *kharīf* gathered, autumn, harvest, autumnal rain.] **1.** In India, the autumn crop, sown at the beginning of the summer rains.

1845 *Encycl. Metrop.* XXIII. 785/1 [Hindustan's] harvests..are equally profitable both in Spring (rabí) and Autumn (kharíf). **1882** W. W. Hunter *Indian Empire* 385 The *kharif* or autumn harvest. **1886** A. H. Church *Food-Grains India* 99 Where indigo is grown in the kharif, barley is its usual accompaniment in the rabi. **1911** *Encycl. Brit.* XXVII. 610/2 The *kharif*, or autumn crops, sown in June and reaped in October or November. **1969** *Pioneer* (Lucknow) 13 Aug. 2/3 There has been no kharif sowing in about 2,000 villages in Western Rajasthan due to failure of monsoon this year, according to official sources here. **1975** *Bangladesh Observer* 22 July 5/4 In spite of improved irrigation facilities most areas of India are dependent on rainfall for cultivation. Timely and adequate rainfall is essential for good kharif crops.

2. Also **khareef.** The rainy season in the Sudan.

1920 *Blackw. Mag.* Nov. 668/1 The gazelle here do not drink from khareef to khareef, a period of very nearly ten months. **1951** R. A. Hodgkin *Sudan Geogr.* ii. 10 If we plant a grass seed and a tree seed at the beginning of the *kharif* in a semi-desert they will both start to grow during the months of rain. *Ibid.* vi. 61 If there is..enough rain during..the *kharif*, there will be a good crop. **1961** L. D. Stamp *Gloss. Geogr. Terms* 280/1 *Kharif*, applied to the rainy season in the northern Sudan.

Kharoshti (kărǫ·ʃti). Also **Kharoshthi, Kharosthi, Kharosti.** [Skr. *kharoṣṭī*.] The name of one of the two oldest alphabets in India, derived from Aramaic and used for about seven centuries from *c* 300 B.C. in north-western India. Cf. *Brahmi.

1891 A. Cunningham *Coins Anc. India* 36 A script named *Kharosti*, which was read from right to left, is said to have been one of the forms taught to the youthful Buddha. *Ibid.* 37 As the name was derived from the inventor of the writing, I think it probable that the name of Zoroaster, or *Zardusht* himself, may have been preserved in the term *Kharosti*, as the inventor or introducer of that particular form of writing. The *Kharosti* alphabet, under this view of its origin, would naturally have penetrated into every country under Akhæmenian rule. **1902** [see *Brahmi]. **1934** A. Toynbee *Study of Hist.* III. 130 In India, the Kharoshti script is certainly derived from the Aramaic alphabet. **1948** D. Diringer *Alphabet* II. v. 301 Many Indian scripts..exist to-day used for tongues belonging to various linguistic groups... All these scripts seem to have descended from two prototypes, the *Kharoshthi* and the *Brahmi*. **1958** L. Woolley *Hist. Unearthed* 123 The documents..were in strangely different scripts and languages... Many were in Kharoshthi, a script known from..inscriptions of north-west India. *Ibid.* 129 Most of the Kharoshthi documents were written on wooden tablets. **1972** W. B. Lockwood *Panorama Indo-Europ. Lang.* 193 Two alphabetic scripts were in use in ancient India. One of these, the Kharosthi,..is found only from the middle of the third century B.C. to the third century A.D... It seems certain that the Brahmi script, like Kharosthi, also goes back to a Semitic model.

Khasi (kā·si). Also †**Cossyah, Khas, Khasia(n), Khasiya.** [f. the name *Khasi* (see below).] **a.** Name of a Mongoloid people found in the Khasi and Jaintia Hills in north-eastern India; also, an Indo-Aryan people inhabiting the hills of Kumaon and Garhwal; a member of one of these peoples. **b.** A language of the Mon-Khmer group spoken by them. Also *attrib.* or as *adj.*

1789 in Seton-Karr & Sandeman *Selections from Calcutta Gaz.* (1865) II. 218 We understand the Cossyahs, who inhabit the hills to the north-westward of Sylhet, have committed some very daring acts of violence. **1824** R. Heber *Narr. Journey Upper Provinces India* (1828) I. xvii. 479 The Khasiyah nation pretend to be all Rajpoots of the highest caste. **1855** W. Pryse *Introd. Khasia Lang.* p. iii, The Khasia or Cossyah is the dialect of a small tribe, reckoning..somewhat under 200,000 souls. *Ibid.* p. vi, It is hoped that the majority of the Khasia words..will be found in the Vocabulary. **1882** *Encycl. Brit.* XIV. 295/1 The true Khas can be distinguished from the Laos only by the lobe of the ear. **1907** P. R. T. Gurdon *Khasis* 11 We can..suppose that the Khasis are an offshoot of the Mon people of Further India. **1911** *Encycl. Brit.* VIII. 830/2 In language 27,272,895 of the inhabitants [of Eastern Bengal and Assam] speak Bengali, 1,349,784 speak Assamese, and the remainder Hindi and various hill dialects, Manipuri, Bodo, Khasi and Garo. **1918** *Trans. Scottish Ecclesiol. Soc.* V. 230 A barbaric tribe of the Khasias burn their dead and raise to their honour menhirs... If a Khasian is in distress of any kind, he prays to some deceased ancestor. **1926** *Other Lands* July 151/2 There are six Khasis, five Nepalis, and two Lepchas from the Darjeeling Hills. **1936** *Discovery* July 205/2 The Khasis and Syntengs are an isolated group of the great Mon-Khmer family. **1937** H. W. Tilman *Ascent Nanda Devi* i. 7 The..Khasiyas, a race of a caste lower than the Brahmans or Rajputs..yet generally allowed to be also immigrants from an Aryan source, adore ..the mountain god Siva. **1967** D. S. Parlett *Short Dict. Lang.* 73 *Khasi*,..a dialect apparently transitional between Mon-Khmer and Munda language types.

Khaskura (kāskū·ră). Also **Khaskra.** [Native name.] An Indic dialect spoken in Nepal.

1911 [see *Gurkhali]. **1928** R. L. Turner in Northey & Morris *Gurkhas* iv. 70 The Indo-Aryan dialect,..variously called Khaskurā, Parbatiyā, Gorkhālī, or officially

and preferably, Nepāli. **1943** E. Shipton *Upon that Mountain* vi. 112 We had two main occupations on the voyage out. One was to learn Khaskra, a language spoken by the Sherpas. **1950** T. Longstaff *This my Voyage* v. 93 Besides speaking Khaskura, the common tongue of Nepal. **1971** J. Pemble *Invasion of Nepal* i. 10 Nepali is but one dialect among a number of related tongues known generically as *Khas kura* (Khas speech) or *Parbatiya* (relating to the hills). Modern Nepali is often referred to by either of these names.

khassadar (kæ·sădāɹ). Also **kassidar.** [Native name.] In the border region of north-western India and Afghanistan, a local militiaman (see quots. 1930 and 1950).

1901 T. H. Holdich *Indian Borderland* xii. 273 An Afghan force of about 1,000 men, half of whom were Kassidars (irregulars)... The Kassidars were but half-trained troops. **1909** *Daily Chron.* 13 Apr. 3/5 The Khyber Pass will be closed to caravans..due to the aggressive attitude of the Khassadars, or Militia, on the Afghan border. **1923** *Glasgow Herald* 16 July 6 The object of the murder is to discredit the Khassadar movement. **1930** *Aberdeen Press & Jrnl.* 22 Apr. 5/2 The khassadar is an extremely irregular soldier, performing a sort of police duty on caravan routes on the North-West Frontier. **1950** W. K. Fraser-Tytler *Afghanistan* xiii. 260 Khassadars were tribal police responsible for the general safety of the roads running through the areas of their respective tribes. **1965** K. P. S. Menon *Many Worlds* 94 These outposts are manned by Khassadars, a kind of irregular tribal police, formed for the purpose of enforcing the security of the road.

khat, var. Kat.

1858 [see Kat]. **1932** E. Waugh *Black Mischief* iv. 119 Mahmud el Khali bin Sai'ud..sat among his kinsmen, moodily browsing over his lapful of khat. **1960** A. Waugh *Foxglove Saga* vi. 107 The standard British Pig, the very mention of whose name was said to make distant sheikhs and rebellious tribesmen in savage areas of the Empire drop their weapons and chew khat with a renewed vigour. **1969** Verdcourt & Trump *Common Poisonous Plants E. Afr.* 98 Khat is a narcotic drug well-known to Arabs and Somalis. *Ibid.*, If khat-eating is accepted as less harmful than some have supposed, then a very profitable native local industry could be properly controlled.

‖ **khatak** (katā·k). Also **khata, khatag.** [Tibetan *k'a-btágs* a scarf of salutation.] In Tibet, a scarf presented to visitors.

[**1863** E. Schlagintweit *Buddhism in Tibet* xiii. 190 The silken scarfs inscribed with sentences which Tibetan politeness requires should be offered by visitors or enclosed in letters..are called in Tibetan Khatak, or Tashi Khatak, 'scarf of benediction'.] **1902** *Daily Chron.* 23 Oct. 3/1 Having presented his *khatag*, and placed in the lap of the Dalai Lama a piece of gold..he took his seat..about ten feet distant from the Grand Lama. **1960** 'S. Harvester' *Chinese Hammer* vii. 70 The traditional ceremony of exchanging white silk *khatas*, scarf tokens of goodwill usually decorated with swastikas.

khatib (katī·b). Also **khateb.** [ad. Arab. *kaṭīb*.] A Muslim preacher; one who recites the khutbah.

1625 Purchas *Pilgrimes* II. ix. xix. 1661 These Atollons are subdiuided into many Ilands, in each of which..is a Doctor called Catibe, superior in the Religion of that Ile, who hath vnder him the particular Priests of the Moschees. **1821** J. Leyden tr. *Malay Annals* v. 50 The letter was read by the khateb. **1839** T. J. Newbold *Pol. & Statistical Acct. Straits of Malacca* I. v. 249 The Khatib..recites the khatbeh, an oration or sermon, in praise of God..on Friday, in the mosque. **1875** T. P. Hughes *Notes Muhammadanism* 131 The Khatib or preacher then seats himself on the *Mimbar* (pulpit). **1971** R. Lewis *Everyday Life in Ottoman Turkey* 43 The khatib, who delivered the Friday sermon and led the invocation of God's protection on the Sultan and his family.

Khatti, var. *Kheta.

‖ **khatun** (kā·tūn). Also **kadun.** [Pers.] A lady. Also used as a title of courtesy.

1834 J. Morier *Ayesha* I. iv. 80 She once made the sign of the cross..but now she is a kadûn—a khanûm, a head of a harem. **1927** *Blackw. Mag.* Nov. 687/2 My wife and other senior *khatuns*. **1959** P. N. Bazaz *Daughters of Vitasta* vi. 144 The next queen to be noticed by contemporary historians is Gul Khatun. *Ibid.* vii. 153 The last of the Muslim queens to achieve renown was Habba Khatun.

khaya (kəi·yă, kē·yă). [mod.L. (A. de Jussieu 1830, in *Mém. Mus. Hist. Nat.* XIX. 249), ad. Wolof *khaye*.] A tropical African tree of the genus so called, belonging to the family Meliaceæ; the timber of a tree of this kind, better known as African mahogany.

1910 H. Thompson *Gold Coast: Rep. Forests* 38 in *Parl. Papers* (Cd. 4993) LXV. 201 *Khayas* and *Pseudocedrelas* were frequently met with in this direction [*sc.* to the east of N'kwansia]. **1916** C. E. Lane-Poole *List of Trees Sierra Leone* 53 The Khayas yield the African Mahogany so esteemed in Europe. **1936** J. D. Kennedy *Forest Flora S. Nigeria* 157 A characteristic of *Khaya* seedlings is the very long drip-tip on the primary leaves. **1956** *Handbk. Hardwoods* (Forest Prod. Res. Lab.) 138 Mahogany, African... Other names..khaya (United States). **1962** Watt & Breyer-Brandwijk *Medicinal & Poisonous Plants S. & E. Afr.* (ed. 2) 1406/3 *Khaya grandifoliola*... African mahogany, Big-leaf mahogany (Uganda), Khaya mahogany. *Ibid.*, *Khaya nyasica*... Khaya mahogany. **1964** R. W. J. Keay et al. *Nigerian Trees* II. 259 Although known to the trade as 'Benin Mahogany', this species [sc. *Khaya grandifolia*] is not the typical Khaya of the southern Benin forests.

Khazar (kăzā·ɹ). Also **Chazar, Chozar, Khozar.** [Heb.] A member of a people of Turkish origin who from the 8th to the 10th or 11th century occupied a large part of southern Russia. Also *attrib.*

1854 J. H. Newman *Lect. Hist. Turks* II. i. 63 The horde of Chozars, as this Turkish tribe was called,..transported their tents..into Georgia. **1854** R. G. Latham *Native Races Russ. Empire* x. 143 The Khazars poured themselves over eastern Europe in the 7th, 8th, 9th, 10th, and 11th centuries. **1863** [see Turkic *a.*]. **1878** R. G. Latham *Russian & Turk* viii. 210 The Khazars seem to play the same part in the history of Eastern Russia that the Avars played in that of Southern Bavaria... We meet the term *Chazaria* as the land of the *Khazars*. **1882** *Encycl. Brit.* XIV. 60/1 Merchants from every nation found protection ..in the Khazar cities. **1903** *Jewish Encycl.* IV. 1/1 The Chazars..established themselves in the territory bounded by the Sea of Azov, the Don and the lower Volga. **1930** C. A. Macartney *Magyars in 9th Cent.* 62 From a short time after the arrival of the Khazars, the Cuban Bulgars disappear from history. **1934** A. G. Chater tr. *Undset's Stages on Road* i. 29 The Khozars of the Crimea..were Tartars who had been converted to Judaism and were ruled by a Jewish king. **1952** E. Hyams *Soil & Civilization* 171 The Jewish religion was adopted by the Chazar princes. **1965** [see *Bulgar *sb.*].

khellin (ke·lin). Also † **kellin.** [Orig. coined as F. *kelline* (I. Mustapha 1879, in *Compt. Rend.* LXXXIX. 442), f. *kell*, given as the Arabic name of *Ammi visnaga*; the *h* originated with Samaan (1931), who gave the Arabic name as *khella*: see -in[1].] A tricyclic crystalline compound, $C_{14}H_{12}O_5$, obtained from the fruit of the North African umbelliferous plant *Ammi visnaga* and formerly used in the treatment of angina pectoris.

The name was orig. given to the glucoside of this compound.

1879 *Jrnl. Chem. Soc.* XXXVI. 1041 The author proposes for this glucoside the name *kellin*, from the Arabic name of the Ammi Visnaga. **1931** K. Samaan in *Q. Jrnl. Pharmacy* IV. 14 Ibrahim Mostapha described a crystalline principle which he named Khellin. **1938** *Chem. Abstr.* XXXII. 2120 Fantl and Salem..obtained from the fruits of *Ammi visnaga* a compd., kellin, $C_{14}H_{12}O_5$. **1947** *Lancet* 26 Apr. 557/2 Khellin causes a conspicuous and long relaxation of all the visceral smooth muscle—the intestines, uterus, bile-ducts, bronchi, and especially ureters. *Ibid.*, In 1945 a fresh interest in khellin arose as the result of the discovery that it acts as an extremely potent coronary vasodilator which, in doses used, has no effect on the general blood-pressure and does not increase the oxygen requirements of the heart. **1957** M. Plotz *Coronary Heart Dis.* xvii. 301/2 Favorable results with khellin therapy in man have been reported by many investigators. *Ibid.*, The most important factor limiting the use of khellin orally has been the high incidence of toxic reactions. **1964** *To-Day's Drugs* (B.M.A.) 132 Khellin had a brief period of popularity about ten years ago, but when the drug was evaluated by controlled clinical trials and by objective methods it was found that it was no better than a placebo.

‖ **khet** (kēt). [Hind., Hindi.] In India, a tract of cultivated land.

1878 P. Robinson *In my Indian Garden* 176 In the still air could be heard..from the scattered *khets*, the bark of the prowling fox. **1886** —— *Valley of Teetotum Trees* 63 In all the swampy jheels and crop-grown khets. **1922** *19th Cent.* Oct. 589 The land is divided by one broad distinction into the khet and the jungle—that is to say, into the cultivated and the wild.

Kheta (ke·tă, χe·tă). Also **Khatti, Khita.** [Egyptian name.] Name of an ancient people and kingdom in the Near East: now usually equated with the Hittites. See *Hittite *sb.* and *a.*

1884 W. Wright *Empire of Hittites* ii. 19 The war between Egypt and Kheta was brought to a close by a treaty of peace concluded between Rameses I. and Saplel the Hittite king. **1890** T. Ely *Man. Archæol.* v. 76 On the monuments [of the Hittites] the name *Khita, Kheta*, or *Khatti*..frequently occurs. **1948** D. Diringer *Alphabet* 89 Egyptian inscriptions mention the powerful Kheta-empire. **1952** O. R. Gurney *Hittites* 2 Who could doubt that the Kheta-folk of the Egyptian texts and the Hittites of the Old Testament were one and the same? **1957** *Encycl. Brit.* XI. 599/1 Egyptian evidence shows that in the time of the 18th to the 20th dynasties, between the years 1500–1190 b.c., a powerful northern kingdom *Kheta* sought perpetually to obtain political influence over Syria and therefore often fought with Egypt. Already the Pharaoh Thutmosis III. (1501–1447), who had conquered Syria as far as the Upper Euphrates, received presents from the prince of Kheta. **1970** Bray & Trump *Dict. Archaeol.* 104 *Hittites, Hatti* or (to the Egyptians) *Kheta*, a people who infiltrated Anatolia and in smaller numbers the Levant from the north *c* 2000 b c, but the details of their origin are more than somewhat obscure.

Khilafat (kilā·făt). [ad. Arab. *kilāfat* caliphate, office or rule of a caliph.] The spiritual headship of Islam, residing in the person of the Turkish Sultan; used *attrib.* to designate the Muslim anti-British movement in India after the treaty of Sèvres in 1920. Hence **Khila·fatist**, a supporter of this agitation.

1921 [see *extremist]. **1923** *Edin. Rev.* Jan. 182 The *Khilâfat*..is the Vice-gerency of the Prophet. **1925** *Contemp. Rev.* Apr. 430 An influential section of the Moslem community, dissociating itself from the Khilafatist section. **1926** *Encycl. Brit.* Suppl. II. 429/2 The 'Khilāfat' agitation. **1950** R. C. Majumdar et al. *Adv. Hist. India* (ed. 2) 985 The two brothers Muhammad Ali and Shaukat Ali, and Maulana Abul Kalam Azad organized a mass movement of the Muslims known as the Khilafat movement. **1957** M. D. Kennedy *Short Hist. Communism in Asia* vi. 58 The movement thus launched for creating disaffection among Moslems in India was known as the Khilafat movement. **1964** A. Swinson *Six Minutes to Sunset* ix. 163 Nair and many others considered that it had been Gandhi's espousal of the Khilafat cause which had triggered off the rebellion. **1972** P. Hardy *Muslims of Brit. India* 190 The philosophy of the *Khilafat* movement was not that of territorial nationalism, but of community federalism, and of a federalism wherein one party, the Muslim, looked outside the common habitat, India, for the *raison d'être* of the federal relationship.

Khilim, var. *Kilim.

Khirbet Kerak (kə̄·ɹbĕt ke·răk). *Archæol.* Name of a town on the south-west edge of Lake Tiberias in Syria, used *attrib.* to designate a type of early Bronze Age pottery first found there in the 1940s, which is red and black in colour with highly burnished finish and fluted decorations.

1949 W. F. Albright *Archaeol. of Palestine* iv. 76 The most interesting new pottery of this age is the lustrous red and black burnished 'Khirbet Kerak' ware, which first became known at the site which bore this name, ancient Beth-Yerah, at the south-west corner of the Sea of Galilee. **1952** V. G. Childe *New Light Most Anc. East* xi. 219 The pottery includes wheel-made red-slipped and lattice-burnished vases and—but only in the last phase of a long occupation—hand-made particoloured black and red vases of 'Khirbet Kerak ware'. **1960** K. M. Kenyon *Archaeol. in Holy Land* v. 124 Side by side with the native wares are vessels of Khirbet Kerak ware. ..This type of pottery is also found in northern Syria. **1968** *Encycl. Brit.* II. 610/2 This Khirbet Kerak ware is characteristically Anatolian, but is distinguished by its ornament of ribs and flutings and of raised geometrical patterns, especially spirals.

Khirgese, var. *Kirghiz *sb.* and *a.*

Khita, var. *Kheta.

khiva, var. *kiva.

Khlist (χlist). Also **Chlist, Khlyst.** Pl. **Chlists, Khlisti, Khlysts, Khlysty.** [Russ., lit. a whip.] A member of a sect of ascetic Russian Christians, formed in the 17th century, who believed that Christ could be re-incarnated in human beings through their suffering.

1856 R. Farie tr. *A. von Haxthausen's Russ. Empire* I. viii. 254 On Easter night the Skoptzi and Khlisti all assemble for a great solemnity, the worship of the Mother of God. **1874** J. H. Blunt *Dict. Sects* 250/1 *Khlisti*, a name signifying 'Flagellants' given to a Russian sect..formed about 1645 by a deserter from the army named Daniel Philipitch. **1920** A. Paget tr. *Nekludoff's Diplomatic Reminisc.* vii. 71 Rasputin was in fact a *Khlyst*, *i.e.* half 'Shaker', half Flagellant—a strange sect which from time to time rises in Russia from the common depths to the upper classes of society. **1929** A. Huxley *Do what you Will* 152 None but heretics have preached it [*sc.* humility]. The Russian Khlyst, for example. *Ibid.* 153 Rasputin practised what he preached, and sinned—most conspicuously, as was the custom of the Khlysty, in relation to the seventh commandment. **1967** D. T. Kauffman *Dict. Relig. Terms* 274 *Khlysts, Chlists*, or *Klysty flagellants*, Russian ascetics originating in the seventeenth century.

Khmer (k'mēəɹ), *sb.* and *a.* [Native name.] **A.** *sb.* **a.** A native or inhabitant of the ancient kingdom of Khmer in south-east Asia, which reached the peak of its power in the 11th century and was destroyed by Siamese conquests in the 12th and 14th centuries; also (from 1863) such a person in Cambodia; now, a native or inhabitant of the Khmer Republic (established 1970). **b.** The monosyllabic language of this people, belonging to the Mon-Khmer group of the Austro-Asiatic family. **B.** *adj.* Of or pertaining to the Khmers or their language.

1876 *Encycl. Brit.* IV. 723/2 The name given by the people of Camboja to their own race is *Khmér*. **1881** C. J. F. S. Forbes *Compar. Gram. Lang. Further India* I. iv. 48 The Cambodians acknowledge..the Kouys, as the most ancient stock, and style them the 'Khmerdom', or ancient Khmers. **1921** *Edin. Rev.* July 172 If the Khmers were the ancient people of Cambodia, here we have an important land mark in common between them and the Khasis. **1921** E. Sapir *Lang.* iv. 71 The use of prefixed elements to the complete exclusion of suffixes, is far less common. A good example is Khmer (or Cambodgian). **1932** W. L. Graff *Lang.* 417 Mon-Khmer comprises the three civilized languages Mon, Khmer, and Cham. **1943** *Burlington Mag.* Aug. 198/1 Of imitations of Khmer bronzes, on the other hand, a number have passed through my hands. **1959** *Chambers's Encycl.* VII. 499/2 What the Khmer and Indians called this state is not known. **1966** *Listener* 22 Sept. 409/1 The Khmers, as the people of Cambodia are known, have a maturity about their nationalism. **1967** *Economist* 23 Sept. 1088/1 Prince Sihanouk has been at odds with the Chinese since April, when he accused the *Khmers rouges*, his local communists, and their foreign friends of launching a guerrilla campaign

in north-western Cambodia. **1970** *Guardian* 5 May 9/5 The men were being lectured, in both French and Khmer, on tactical formations. **1970** M. Pereira *Pigeon's Blood* iv. 48 The closest resemblance..was the medieval Khmer craftsmanship of Cambodia. **1971** *Nat. Geographic* Mar. 316/1 When the Khmer people were docile, the Vietnamese would withdraw all but a token force. **1972** M. Sheppard *Taman Indera* 6 Funan was eventually conquered by a Khmer prince of Kambuja,..in the middle of the sixth century. **1973** *Times* 10 Apr. 6/7 Khmer Rouge and Vietcong guerrillas have launched several rocket attacks.

Khoikhoi (koi·koi). *S. Afr.* Also **Khoi Khoi, Khoi Khoin,** † **Quaiquae,** etc. [Hottentot, lit. 'men of men'.] The Hottentots' name for themselves; also used by others in the sense 'Hottentots'; the language which they speak. Also *attrib.* or as *adj.*

1791 tr. *Le Vaillant's Travels into Interior Parts of Africa* II. 154 A Hottentot man..Khoé-Khoep. **1801** J. Barrow *Acct. Trav. S. Afr.* I. iii. 151 [The name] by which the whole nation was distinguished, and which at this moment they bear among themselves in every part of the country, is *Quaiquae*. **1880** *Encycl. Brit.* XII. 309/2 The common denomination adopted by themselves was Khoi-Khoin (men of men). **1881** T. Hahn *Tsuni-‖Goam* i. 1 These Khoikhoi generally go by the name of *Hottentots. Ibid.* 5 The Khoikhoi language is entirely void of prefixes. **1897** A. J. Butler tr. *Ratzel's Hist. Mankind* II. 247 The Khoi-Khoi (Bushmen and Hottentot) group of languages. **1910** G. M. Theal *Yellow & Dark-Skinned People of Afr.* iv. 79 Those destitute Hottentots..had more Bushman than pure Khoikhoi blood in their veins. **1930** I. Schapera *Khoisan Peoples of S. Afr.* i. 5 The term [*sc.* Khoisan] is compounded of the names *Khoi-Khoin*, by which the Hottentots call themselves, and *San*, applied by the Hottentots to the Bushmen. **1969** *Oxf. Hist. S. Afr.* I. i. 10 Blood group studies suggest, however, that certain Khoikhoi speakers are closely allied in their blood-group patterns to African negroids. *Ibid.* ii. 43 There were also groups of herders, most of whom spoke Khoikhoi. *Ibid.* 56 The Khoikhoi may have been shepherds before they were cattle-men.

Khoja. Add: **2.** A member of a Muslim sect of converts from Hinduism, found mainly in western India and retaining some Hindu customs. Also *attrib.*

1882 *Encycl. Brit.* XIV. 64/1 Only the military class, the priesthood, and the khodjas are exempt from the payment of taxes. The khodjas consider themselves descendants of the prophet. **1921** C. Eliot *Hinduism & Buddhism* III. lviii. 455 The sects known as Khojas and Bohras owe their conversion to the zeal of Arab and Persian missionaries who preached in the eleventh century. **1931** G. MacMunn *Relig. & Hidden Cults India* 97 A portion of the Assassins escaped to India where they have developed into a wealthy trading fraternity known generally as the Khojas or 'worthy men'. **1937** L. Bromfield *Rains Came* I. vi. 41 The prospect of putting over a sharp deal in Bombay on the Khojas and Parsees. **1970** D. G. Mandelbaum *Soc. in India* II. vii. xxix. 555 There are several Isma'ili jatis, the Bohras and Khojas of Gujarat being the major groups among them...Khoja doctrine held..that the Aga Khan was an incarnation of the 'glorious Tenth Avatar'.

khoker, var. *Koker.

Khond (kǫnd). Also **Kandh, Kond, Kondh.** [Native name.] **a.** A Dravidian people inhabiting Orissa in eastern India; one of this people. **b.** The language spoken by the Khonds. Also *attrib.* or as *adj.*

1852 S. C. Macpherson in *Jrnl. R. Asiatic Soc.* XIII. 217 The ancient state of Orissa was formed chiefly from the territories of..the Khonds, the Koles, and the Sourahs. *Ibid.* 221 The Khond religion exists in oral traditions alone. **1867** [see *Gond *sb.* and *a.*]. **1881** *Encycl. Brit.* XII. 778/2 Bishop Caldwell recognizes twelve distinct Dravidian languages:— (1) Tamil,.. (10) Khond. **1909** E. Thurston *Castes & Tribes S. India* III. 398 A Kondh funeral dance in the Ganjam Māliahs. **1937** H. G. Rawlinson *India* viii. 128 Among the Khonds, one of the primitive tribes, a human victim known as the *meriah* was until recently sacrificed in order to secure fertility for the fields. **1946** R. C. Majumdar et al. *Adv. Hist. India* 826 To the first Lord Hardinge's Government belongs the credit of taking steps to stop the human sacrifices practised by the Khonds in Orissa. **1959** *Chambers's Encycl.* VII. 480/2 The most eastern member of the Central group [of Dravidian languages] is the language of the Khonds or Kandhs. *Ibid.* X. 244/2 The most interesting of the aboriginal races are the Konds. **1970** D. G. Mandelbaum *Soc. in India* II. xxii. 422 His trade is carried on with men of the Kond tribe who are rated as a clean jati by the neighbouring Oriyas.

Khorassan (korăsā·n). Also **-asan, Khurasan.** Name of a province in north-east Iran, used *attrib.* and *ellipt.* to designate a carpet or rug made there, usu. with vivid colouring and fine silky texture.

1900 J. K. Mumford *Oriental Rugs* xi. 218 The realism which marks certain carpets of the Feraghan group is fairly outdone in many of the proper Khorassans. **1904** M. B. Langton *How to know Oriental Rugs* ii. 68 The Khorasan is a most satisfactory rug, beautiful in colour, durable, and pliable. **1931** A. U. Dilley *Oriental Rugs & Carpets* Pl. 25 (*caption*) Khorassan Prayer Rug. Characteristic minute floral pattern, Herati, with border of narrow bands. **1931** C. Tattersall *Carpets of Persia* 39 Mashhad. Much like Khorasans, but with shorter and closer pile. **1962** C. W. Jacobsen *Oriental Rugs* 238 No rugs have been imported as Khurasans in the past 20 years. **1971** K. Watson tr. *Hubel's Bk. Carpets* 213 Another peculiarity of the ground-weave of the Khorassan carpet is the weft: the thick straight weft is covered by the thin sinuous weft threads accompanying it.

Khotan (kǫtā·n). Also **Khoten.** Name of a city and district on the south of the Takla Makan desert in Chinese Turkestan, used *attrib.* and *ellipt.* to designate a carpet or rug made there, usu. with Chinese geometrical patterns or stylized natural designs.

1871 R. B. Shaw *Visits to High Tartary* xii. 259 There is a large covered reception-place with a verandah in front of all. Here an immense Khoten carpet is spread with rugs along the back. **1899** Kipling *From Sea to Sea* I. xvi. 362 The English can only be artistic in spots and by way of the art of other nations—Sicilian tapestries, Persian saddle-bags, Khoten carpets. **1904** M. B. Langton *How to know Oriental Rugs* viii. 228 Bayard Taylor, in his Travels, speaks of the beautiful Khotan carpets which were spread on divans in the 'royal rest' rooms near Yarkand. **1920** E. & P. Sykes *Through Deserts & Oases Cent. Asia* iv. 82 The old Khotan carpets, their colours made from vegetable dyes, were attractive, and the silk carpets are highly prized and very difficult to obtain. **1931** A. U. Dilley *Oriental Rugs & Carpets* x. 224 Khotan rugs of the ancient vintage, with geometric blocked design, numerous borders, half-Chinese and half-Persian,..are the outstanding jewels of the Chinese Turkestan family. **1960** G. & C. W. Digby tr. *Haack's Oriental Rugs* vii. 56 Kashgar and Khotan are the names by which these carpets are more properly known; they show a strong Chinese influence in their design. **1967** *Times* 21 Feb. 21/4 (Advt.), An extremely rare and beautiful 18th century Khotan carpet, 12 ft. 7 in. × 7 ft. 4 in.

Khotanese (kōᵘtănī·z), *sb.* and *a.* [f. *Khotan* (see prec.) + -ese.] **A.** *sb.* The people of Khotan; one of this people; the Middle Iranian language of Khotan. **B.** *adj.* Of or pertaining to Khotan.

1882 *Encycl. Brit.* XIV. 67/2 The Khotanese keep camels, horses..and fowls. **1907** A. Stein *Anc. Khotan* I. 141 It is a point of special interest that dancing..is a pastime freely indulged in by Khotanese of both sexes and of all classes. *Ibid.* 144 In the case of the Khotanese there has been, besides a slight admixture of Turkī blood, an admixture also of Tibetan. **1939** C. H. Gray *Foundations of Lang.* 320 Besides Middle Persian proper, we have a fair amount of material in some other Middle Iranian dialects, notably Middle Parthian..and Khotanese or Middle Sakian..in the southern part of East Turkistān. **1948** D. Diringer *Alphabet* ii. vi. 350 The material contained in Khotanese manuscripts is of great variety; there are official and business documents, translations of Indian tales, [etc.]. *Ibid.*, There are some indications to show that Khotanese began to be used in writing in the second century A.D. **1957** *Archivum Linguisticum* IX. ii. 128 The most likely source would seem to be Khotanese. **1961** H. W. Bailey *Khotanese Texts* IV. 14 The Buddhist literature of which complete or partial translations existed in Khotanese is of large extent. *Ibid.* 17 A celebrated Khotanese painter of Buddhist subjects.

Khowar (kōᵘ·wāɹ). A Dardic language spoken in Chitral in north-west Pakistan. Also *attrib.* or as *adj.*

1882 *Encycl. Brit.* XIV. 9/2 Their [*sc.* inhabitants of Chitral's] language, *Khowâr*, is closely allied to the dialects of the Kafir tribes. **1950** T. Longstaff *This my Voyage* x. 199 The singing must be in Khowar, the tongue of Chitral, which sounds like Romany. **1964** *Language* XL. 304 A native Khowar speaker. **1967** D. S. Parlett *Short Dict. Lang.* 73 *Khowar*.., 7 th[ousand] speakers of a dialect in N.W. India related to Kalash and probably (less closely) to Kafir. **1974** 'S. Harvester' *Forgotten Road* i. 11 He had a working acquaintance with dialects of most Kafir valley tribes, even Khowar and the almost extinct Domali language.

Khozar, var. *Khazar.

Khrushchevism (kru·stʃǭfiz'm). [f. the name of Nikita Sergevich *Khrushchev* (1894–1971), Soviet statesman + -ism.] The practice or principles of Khrushchev, notable for his denunciation of Stalin and his advocacy of peaceful coexistence with the Western powers. So **Khrushche·vian** *a.*, of, pertaining to, or characteristic of Khrushchev or his policies.

1957 *Amer. Speech* XXXII. 294 The party has switched from Stalinism to Khrushchevism. **1961** *Listener* 28 Dec. 1107/2 The world of romance and fairy tale is never far away from the Khrushchevian Utopia. **1962** *Ibid.* 18 Jan. 112/1 There are several kinds of communism in the world—Titoism, Khrushchevism, Maoism in China. **1963** *Economist* 3 Aug. 418/2 Khrushchevism is..to be preferred by the West to Maoism. **1964** *New Statesman* 17 Apr. 592/2 What strikes one in the record of Krushchevism is the great number of vital issues which Krushchev and his men have posed but not tackled. **1973** *Daily Tel.* 22 Nov. 10/6 We know now that 'Ivan Denisovich' was not the harbinger of better things, but the high point of Khruschevian 'liberalism' from which there has since been a steady retreat.

khubab: see *kebab.

khud. *attrib.* Add: *khud-climbing, -stick.*

1906 *Westm. Gaz.* 13 Aug. 7/1 Killed..in India while khud-climbing. **1925** A. G. Arbuthnot in G. Burrard *Big Game Hunting* 118 Take your telescope, rest it on a rock or on your 'khud stick'. **1928** *Blackw. Mag.* Jan. 25/2 He jabbed his khudstick into the ground.

khurta, var. *kurta.

khyal (ki̯ā·l). Also **kheal.** [Skr.] A traditional type of song in northern India, with instrumental accompaniment, usually containing two main themes.

1882 N. A. Willard in R. S. M. Tagore *Hindu Mus.* (ed. 2) i. 102 In the *Kheal* the subject generally is a love tale, and the person supposed to utter it, a female. **1914** A. H. F. Strangways *Mus. Hindostan* vi. 165 Both are *Khyāls*, and by Rabindranath Tagore. **1921** H. A. Popley *Mus. India* vi. 89 The *Khyāl* was introduced later than the Dhrupad, in order to find a place for the graces which are not allowed in the former. *Ibid.*, Khyal singers and Dhrupad singers are usually different. **1971** *Shankar's Weekly* (Delhi) 4 Apr. 24/4 Lines of a khyal are ordinarily made to sprawl over several matras each of a long duration.

Khyber Pass (kəi·bəɹ pɑs). [The chief pass in the Hindu Kush mountains between Afghanistan and north-west Pakistan.] *Rhyming slang* = Arse *sb.* 1. Also *ellipt.* **Khyber.**

1943 M. Harrison *Reported Safe Arrival* 32 Not knowin' wevver they wz on their 'eads or their Kybers [*sic*]. **1960** J. Franklyn *Dict. Rhyming Slang* 88 *Khyber Pass*, arse, not the buttocks but the anus. Usually 'He can (you can) (they can) stick it up his (your) (their) Khyber!' It is an expression of disapproval. **1966** *New Statesman* 16 Sept. 408/3 Can it really be..that 'Khyber' is genuine rhyming slang for the posterior? **1968** *Crescendo* Jan. 6/3 If we sit on our Khybers, we will miss out on all the things that make our lives the richer.

kia, var. *kya.

kiaat (kiʸā·t). *S. Afr.* Also **coyatte hout** (*hout* = wood), **kajat, kajatenhout, kiatt, kijaat.** [Afrikaans, f. Du., f. Malay *ki djati, kajoe djati* good wood.] The tree *Pterocarpus angolensis*, belonging to the family Leguminosæ, and found in southern Africa; the timber of this tree.

1801 J. Barrow *Acct. Trav. S. Afr.* I. v. 339 Catalogue of Useful Woods... Coyatte hout... Tough. [Uses:] Staves for butter firkins. **1862** L. Pappe *Silva Capensis* (ed. 2) 29 *Atherstonea Decussata* (Cape Teak, or Kajatenhout)... This tree grows 20–25 feet high. **1921** D. E. Hutchins in T. R. Sim *Native Timbers S. Afr.* 108 The stem of Kajatenhout is not wanting in thickness. **1947** *Cape Times* 8 Nov. 12/3 Desks: Large selection in imbuia, kijaat, African mahogany and teak. **1956** *Handbk. Hardwoods* (Forest Prod. Res. Lab.) 159 Muninga—*Pterocarpus angolensis.* Other names..kajat, kajatenhout, kiatt (Union of South Africa). **1957** *Cape Times* 3 Sept. 3/3 There was not a scrap of wool in sight in the theatre-like, kiaat-panelled hall. **1973** Palmer & Pitman *Trees S. Afr.* II. 937 The kiaat is a medium-sized deciduous tree.

kiaki, var. *keyaki.

kian, early form of Cayenne. (Examples.)

1794 A. Thomas *Newfoundland Jrnl.* 13 May (1968) 39 The Cook was holding, at an unseasonable moment, the Saucepan of Mock Turtle to season it higher with Kian. **1845** B. Upton *Let.* 10 Sept. in *Amer. Hist.* (1966) XVII. iv. 87/2 Cayenne pepper (kian) grows wild here on the prairies.

kiang. The more usual spelling of Kyang.

1882, 1885 [see Kyang]. **1906** [see **desert-frequenting* adj.]. **1934** *Times Educ. Suppl.* 22 Sept. p. iv/3 The father is a very old Kiang, a true wild donkey from Tibet. **1970** *Guardian* 26 Mar. 3/1 Tibet's wild donkeys..known as kiangs. **1973** *Times* 20 Feb. (India Suppl.) p. xi/3 The plateau of Ladakh in the high Himalayas harbours forms related to those in Tibet such as the wild yak, the kiang, and the chiru.

‖ **kia ora** (ki̯ă ōᵊ·ră). *N.Z.* [Maori.] An exclamation of good will: good health! be well!

1896 in E. E. Morris *Austral Eng.* (1898) 247 You will hear any day at a Melbourne bar the first man say *Keora ta-u*, while the other says *Keora tatu*... These expressions are corruptions of the Maori, *Kia ora taua*, 'Health to us too!' and *Kia ora tatou*, 'Health to all of us!' **1905** W. B. *Where White Man Treads* 273 Kia ora, oh coloured brother! **1914** A. A. Grace *Tale of Timber Town* v. 32 The digger put his pint to his hairy lips, [and] said, '*Kia ora.* Here's fun.' **1933** 'E. Milton' *Waimana* ii. iii. 82 Good-byeee, and kia-ora! **1938** R. Finlayson *Brown Man's Burden* 66 They smiled sweetly and said 'Kia ora', as they bought bunches of the bitter cherries. **1966** G. W. Turner *Eng. Lang. Austral. & N.Z.* viii. 169 Some of these [*sc.* Maori terms] seem to have been commoner in the past than they are now, e.g. *Kia ora* 'good health', more often seen in England (as a brand name for soft drinks) than in New Zealand now. **1970** *N.Z. Listener* 12 Oct. 12/5, I heard her soft, sad voice: 'This is the kia ora, Dave.'

‖ **kiap** (ki·ăp). [Native name.] In New Guinea, a European patrol officer or policeman.

1923 W. R. Humphries *Patrolling in Papua* xv. 162 They had been told by their 'Kiap' to make a road. **1943** S. W. Reed *Making of Mod. New Guinea* v. 174 Fear and respect for the *kiap* seem to be mingled in the native mind: fear of punishment..at the *kiap's* command, and respect..for the authority of the officer. **1969** *New Guinea & Austral.* IV. iii. 9/1 Those who are subservient to Kiap doctrine. *Ibid.*, We cannot be expected to remain

within the fence of racial integration whose fencing materials—the persuasiveness of the Kiap, the teaching of the church, and the legislation of a colonial administration—show distinct signs of weathering. *Ibid.* 10/1 His motion was defeated in a council whose views were predictably Kiap-dominated. **1970** *Times* 31 Mar. (Austral. Suppl.) p. ii/4 Australia was content to provide an underpaid administration whose *kiaps* (patrol officers) were largely concerned with exploration of one of the world's wildest countries.

kiawe (kiˌa·ve). [Hawaiian.] = ALGARROBA.
1915 W. A. BRYAN *Nat. Hist. Hawaii* xvii. 241 (*caption*) A fine Algaroba tree (Kiawe) (*Prosopis juliflora*). **1917** *Nature* 20 Sept. 57/2 One of the introduced trees of great economic importance is the algaroba tree (*Prosopis juliflora*) or kiawe, as the Hawaiians call it. It is found in a belt on the lowlands along the shores of all the islands, and occupies the soil almost to the exclusion of other plants. The pods are very nutritious, and are eagerly eaten by all kinds of stock. Its flowers furnish an excellent quality of honey. **1937** D. & H. TEILHET *Feather Cloak Murders* v. 102 The feathery boughs of a Kiawe tree. **1965** M. C. NEAL *Gardens of Hawaii* 413 The kiawe, a fairly large tree, seldom reaching a height of 60 feet... is the commonest and most valuable tree introduced to Hawaii.

kibab, kibaub: see *KEBAB.

kibble, *sb.*³ (Further examples.)
1834 *Chambers's Jrnl.* 9 Aug. 223/2 He had been a kibble-boy in the mine. **1843** *Ainsworth's Mag.* IV. 507 Huge quantities of iron, boiler and kibble plates. **1881** *Instructions to Census Clerks* (1885) 84 Copper Miner... Kibble Filler. **1901** G. L. KERR *Pract. Coal Mining* iii. 35 The centre of the cradle contains an opening which provides space for two buckets or 'kibbles' passing each other. **1924** *Hist. Rev. Coal Mining* (Mining Assoc. Gt. Brit.) iii. 38 The advantages of running two kibbles simultaneously are generally more than overbalanced by the increased complications of guides and shaft fittings required. **1967** *Gloss. Mining Terms* (*B.S.I.*) IX. 10 *Kibble*, a large steel bucket used to remove debris and to transport men and materials in a shaft sinking.

kibbler (ki·bləɹ). [f. KIBBL(E *v.*¹ + -ER¹.] A machine which kibbles or grinds coarsely; also, one who operates or tends such a machine. So **ki·bblerman.**
1882 OGILVIE *Imp. Dict.*, *Kibbler*, one who or that which kibbles or cuts, especially a machine for cutting beans and peas for cattle. **1921** *Dict. Occup. Terms* (1927) § 159 *Kibbler, kibblerman*;..attends and feeds machine in which he breaks up oil cake into nodular pieces before grinding into meal. **1922** *Glasgow Herald* 21 Feb. 3 Chaff and root cutters, grinding mills, or kibblers. **1945** J. F. LOCKWOOD *Flour Milling* i. 42 Wheat should always be ground into a coarse meal before testing... A small hand kibbler, such as a coffee grinder, is suitable for this purpose. **1968** *Encycl. Brit.* VI. 804/2 *Crushers or kibblers* are used mainly for oats, corn and linseed, which are bruised, broken or flattened without being ground into a meal.

‖ **kibbutz** (kibu·ts). Pl. **kibbutzi·m** (-īm) (occas. **kibbutzes**). [ad. mod.Heb. *ḳibbūṣ* gathering.] A collective settlement in Israel, owned communally by its members, and organized on co-operative principles. Also *attrib.*
1931 tr. *Ann. Rep. Central Tenuvah Federation* (Palestine) *1930* i. 3 'Tenuvah' is a co-operative marketing association... Its members are the kvutzoth (collective farms), moshavim (smallholders' settlements), and kibbutzim (large farm training groups). **1944** H. F. INFIELD *Co-operative Living in Palestine* 22 The term Kvutza is used alternately with Kibbutz, which has practically the same meaning... The present study uses Kvutza only for the rural settlements and Kibbutz for the superior co-ordinating organization. *Ibid.* viii. 119 (*heading*) Kibbutzim—the roof-organizations. **1957** *Observer* 29 Sept. 13/2 Miss Helga Pilarczyk ..danced the Dance of the Seven Veils..with sturdy acrobatics that suggested rather more of the kibbutz than the necrophile. *Ibid.* 1 Dec. 5/2 We saw..people in *kibbutzim*, the voluntary collective farms—some of the serenest people I have ever met. **1958** *Times Lit. Suppl.* 20 June 341/4 It describes how a London-bred girl, with a carping and snobbish mama, ups and joins a *kibbutz* in Israel. **1960** *Times* 15 Oct. 7/6 The kibbutz movement, whose jubilee occurs tomorrow, has been slumping. **1962** L. R. BANKS *End to Running* I. iv. 57 Kibbutzes, I remembered from somewhere, were some kind of communistic settlements in Israel, where children were raised away from their parents and nobody owned anything. **1964** M. ARGYLE *Psychol. & Social Probl.* xvi. 204 Some communities have arranged for children to be brought up in groups... The best-known example of this is the *kibbutz* system in Israel. **1968** C. A. DOXIADIS *Between Dystopia & Utopia* ii. 46 Alfonso Reyas, who states that even 'America is a Utopia' ..and the Kibbutzim in Israel are the results of utopian theories. **1972** *Sci. Amer.* Dec. 43/2 Children in the kibbutz are cared for from infancy in small, one-age peer groups by trained personnel. They live apart from their parents for most of the day and in most kibbutzes during the night as well. **1973** *Jewish Chron.* 6 July 3/1 (*heading*) Kibbutzim back land appeal by sheikh.

‖ **kibbutznik** (kibu·tsnik). [Yiddish, f. prec. + *-NIK, Pol. and Russ. noun suffix denoting person connected with (something).] A member of a *kibbutz.*
1949 KOESTLER *Promise & Fulfilment* II. ii. 221 We.. had the treat of an hour's moonlight journey across the Sea of Galilee, with *kibbutzniks* from Ein Geb sprawling all over the deck and singing Hebrew songs. **1950** G. MIKES *Milk and Honey* III. 129 The main characteristics of *Kibbutz*-life are:— (*a*) *Kibbutzniks* have no money at all;.. (*c*) *Kibbutzniks* eat their soup at the end of their meals. **1959** F. M. WILSON *They came as Strangers* III. iii. 203 The kibbutzniks believed that by redeeming the soil of the Holy Land..they were..redeeming..the Jewish people. **1965** *New Statesman* 3 Sept. 314/2 Kibbutzniks played chess in the shade. **1967** *Listener* 13 July 62/1, I wandered along the tranquil shores of Galilee, stepping over trenches and talking to armed *kibbutzniks.* **1973** *Jewish Chron.* 6 July 10/2 (*caption*) Ehud Adiv, kibbutznik and paratrooper.

kibitz (ki·bits), *v. slang* (orig. *U.S.*). Also **kibbitz.** [Yiddish, f. G. *kiebitzen* to look on at cards, f. *kiebitz* lapwing, pewit; interfering onlooker at cards.] *intr.* To look on at cards, or some other activity, esp. in an interfering manner (e.g. by standing close to the shoulders of the players); to offer gratuitous advice to a player; to act as a kibitzer. Also *trans.*, to watch (a game, person, etc.), esp. in an officious or meddling way. Hence **ki·bitzing** *vbl. sb.* and *ppl. a.*
1927 in *Amer. Speech* (1928) IV. 159 The trade journal.. devotes an editorial..to the 'kibbitzer'. It defines 'kibbitzing' as a slang expression used to indicate the act of offering gratuitous advice by an outsider. **1951** M. MCLUHAN *Mech. Bride* 67/1 The children..have retired to a philosophic knoll to do a little uneasy kibitzing. **1955** I. FLEMING *Moonraker* iv. 43 Drax..[sorted] his cards.. only into reds and blacks, ungraded, making his hand very difficult to kibitz. **1957** R. STOUT *If Death ever Slept* (1958) viii. 106 Corey Brigham stood behind them, kibitzing. **1961** A. SMITH *East-Enders* vi. 96 Do you remember the café proprietor with whom I kibbitzed on the soarers? **1966** P. J. NICHOLSON *Rat Race* I. iii. 66 Harry moved about, kibitzing on conversations here and there. **1967** *Sci. Amer.* Sept. 64/2 (Advt.), Reilly—with one shipmate posing and two others kibitzing—is finishing off a watercolor. **1972** *New Yorker* 26 Aug. 51/1 Even when the equipment is operating smoothly, the temptation is all but irresistible to gather around the polygraph and kibitz.

kibitzer (ki·bitsəɹ, kibi·tsəɹ). *slang* (orig. *U.S.*). Also **kibbitzer.** [Yiddish *kibitser*; cf. prec.] An onlooker at cards, etc., esp. one who offers unwanted advice; a busybody, an officious meddler.
1927 Kibbitzer [see *KIBITZ *v.*]. **1935** A. J. POLLOCK *Underworld Speaks* 66/2 *Kibitzer*, an onlooker of a card game who seldom plays but frequently criticizes the play of the contestants, and offers advice freely. **1936** WODEHOUSE *Laughing Gas* xii. 135 The fiend leaped on to the porch and immediately dispelled any notion that might have been lurking in the minds of the checker players that here was a mere kibitzer who had come to breathe down the backs of their necks and offer advice. **1948** *Chess Rev.* Sept. 1, I tried to outline several plans of attack, but, in the excitement, with many kibitzers moving the pieces, I was unable to concentrate. **1950** J. DEMPSEY *Championship Fighting* x. 52 Keep your eyes closed to the kibitzers or wise guys. **1966** H. YOXALL *Fashion of Life* ix. 85 A member of the club was sitting watching... I went one down and the kibitzer added, 'If I'd known how you played I'd have bet..you wouldn't make it.' **1970** *Globe & Mail* (Toronto) 25 Sept. 30/6 The spectators held their breaths like kibitzers watching a pinball player try to coax the ball into a pocket. **1970** L. M. FEINSILVER *Taste of Yiddish* iii. 294 It was not until the growth of radio and films that Yiddishisms like *Kibitzer*, [etc.],.. began to achieve wider circulation.

kiblah. Add: Also **kebla, keblah, kebleh, kibla, qibla(h.** Also *transf.* (Further examples.)
1740 W. STUKELEY *Stonehenge* v. 24 A *kebla*, or a place towards which we are to address the Deity. **1825** SCOTT *Talisman* in *Tales Crusaders* III. iii. 91 The Moslem turned towards his *kebla*, the point to which the prayer of each follower of the prophet was to be addressed. **1876** R. D. OSBORN *Islam under Arabs* I. iii. 82 There have been few incidents more disastrous in their consequences to the human race than this decree of Muhammad changing the *kibla* from Jerusalem to Mekka. **1883** *Encycl. Brit.* XVI. 553/2 Mohammed..altered the direction of prayer (ḳibla)..towards Mecca. **1883** E. O'DONOVAN *Merv* xi. 106 Other pilgrims were standing on their little carpets with their faces towards the *keblah*..commencing their evening devotions. **1902** M. ROBERTS *Immortal Youth* i. 1 Ah, yes, to be in London, at the centre of things,..at the kebleh of the universe. **1911** *Encycl. Brit.* XVII. 420/2 In prayer the worshipper faces the *qibla*. **1973** *Times Lit. Suppl.* 28 Dec. 1590/1 A concatenation of aisles on one side of the building indicated the qiblah. *Ibid.* 1590/5 Attested early associations with 'David's Sanctuary' and the first Qiblah.

kiboko (kibōᵘ·ko). *Africa.* [Swahili, = hippopotamus.] A strong, heavy whip made of hippopotamus hide. Cf. SJAMBOK *sb.*
1921 *Chambers's Jrnl.* 118/1 One of those who had long ruled them with the *kiboko* (sjambok) in times gone by. **1922** C. T. CAMPION tr. *Schweitzer's On Edge Primeval Forest* iv. 67 A kiboko (or sjambok) of hippopotamus hide. **1947** J. STEVENSON-HAMILTON *Wild Life S. Afr.* vii. 62 The whips made of the skin of the hippopotamus, variously known in Africa as sjamboks, kibokos, kourbashes, and so on, have considerable value. **1969** *Tanzania Notes & Records* July 11 There were also many references to the 25 or 30 strokes of the *kiboko* used as a punishment in German days.

kibosh, *v.* Add: (Earlier and later examples.) Cf. *KYBOSH.
1884 'CRUCK-A-LEAGHAN' & 'SLIEVE GALLION' *Lays & Legends N. of Ireland* 87 The Rector pull'd out an' oul' fourpinny-bit..An' handed the pill that wid kibosh the fun. **1890** *Punch* 16 Aug. 74/3 Wy, they'd queer the best pitches in life, if they kiboshed the Power of the Quid! **1969** *Listener* 27 Feb. 264/2 What a pity that the stipend has not kept pace..with the fall in the value of money (and it even comes to you less PAYE, thus kiboshing manoeuvrability in the field of expenses!).

Kichua, var. *QUECHUA.

kick, *sb.*¹ **1. a.** *free kick*, substitute for def.: (see quots. 1961.) Add earlier and later examples.
1882 in Charles-Edwards & Richardson *They saw it Happen* (1958) 299 A free kick awarded for a handling of the ball enabled Suter to place it well to the right wing forwards. **1961** F. C. AVIS *Sportsman's Gloss.* 26/1 *Free kick*, an uninterrupted kick allowed to a team for an infringement against it, the opposing players having to stand ten yards away. *Ibid.* 268/2 *Free kick*, in Rugby Union football, an optional drop-kick, place-kick, or punt, taken as the result of a fair catch, the player free-kicking from the mark. **1972** *Guardian* 16 Mar. 23/3 From a free kick on the right, Foggo chipped on and the net bulged with relief.

fig. (Further examples.) Esp. in phr. *a kick in the pants*: a grave or humbling set-back; an expression of severe criticism or disapproval; similarly, *a kick in the teeth.*
[**1836** D. CROCKETT *Exploits & Adv. Texas* i. 14 If a man is only determined to go ahead, the more kicks he receives in his breech the faster he will get on his journey.] **1925** D. H. LAWRENCE *Refl. Death Porcupine* 105 The novel itself gives Vronsky a kick in the behind. **1933** E. O'NEILL *Ah, Wilderness!* (1934) IV. ii. 134 Aw, you deserved a kick in the pants..making such a darned slob of yourself. **1937** PARTRIDGE *Dict. Slang* 881/1 It's better than a kick in the pants. **1940** R. A. J. WALLING *Why did Trethewy Die?* i. 25 Giving the Methusalahs a kick in the pants. **1963** *Listener* 24 Jan. 152/2 General de Gaulle's statement on the Common Market was described by the East German Deutschlandsender as 'a kick in the pants' for Britain. **1970** *Globe & Mail* (Toronto) 25 Sept. 41/4 As some philosopher once noted, the only difference between a pat on the back and a kick in the pants is about eight inches. **1972** *Guardian* 28 Oct. 12/1 The Liberals' proud victory at Rochdale..has given the two major parties the kick in the teeth that each of them deserves.

d. (Earlier and later U.S. examples.)
1839 *Chemung* (N.Y.) *Democrat* 25 Dec. (Th.), Take the hint without a kick, and shut the open door. **1904** F. LYNDE *Grafters* xii. 155 To-day he came around and gave me back my opinion, clause for clause as his own. But I have no kick coming. **1910** C. E. MULFORD *Hopalong Cassidy* viii. 57 'We ain't got no kick, have we?' retorted Cavalry. **1948** *Gainesville* (Texas) *Daily Reg.* 3 July 6/2 The admission price will be upped to six-bits, which shouldn't draw any kicks from fans.

2. b. (Further examples.) Hence, a pulse or surge of electricity capable of producing a jerk in a detecting or measuring instrument. *B kick* Telegr. (see quot. 1928¹).
1910 *Hawkins's Electr. Dict.* 233/1 *Kick.* 1. In general, a recoil. 2. Any impulsive movement imparted in telegraphy to delicate instrument parts by a discharge from the line. *Ibid.*, *Kick of coil*, a discharge taking place from an electromagnet coil. **1928** A. E. STONE *Text Bk. Telegr.* xiii. 191 With the non-polarised relays a different method has had to be adopted, in order to eliminate the effects of what is known as the B kick. This term is applied to the break in the continuity of signals received on the non-polarised relays, due to the momentary demagnetisation of their cores when the current in the line is reversed. *Ibid.* 194 The 'kick' observed on the galvanometer. **1930** *Proc. R. Soc.* A. CXXIX. 214 An ambiguity arises in determining the residual range of an α-particle from the magnitude of the 'kick' recorded by the counter. *Ibid.* 216 The third record..shows the kicks smaller and more uniform in size. **1957** [see *KICKSORTER]. **1959** J. W. FREEBODY *Telegr.* vii. 200/2 Another difficulty found in the operation of diplex and quadruplex circuits was known as the B-kick which occurred when the B-side relay was operated by a marking current and the current was then reversed by the operation of the A-side key.

c. A strong or sharp stimulant effect, esp. that of liquor or drugs; *spec.* something that makes a drink potent; a thrill, excitement, pleasure; a feeling of marked enjoyment or the cause of such enjoyment; esp. in phr. *to get a kick out of* (something), to be excited or pleased by, to enjoy; *for kicks*, purely for pleasure or excitement, freq. recklessly or irresponsibly.
1844 *Bentley's Misc.* XVI. 597, I then demanded a common cocktail. 'With the kick in it?' said he. 'Oh, by all means,' I replied... It was..somewhat strong; but then that was my fault, for having ordered it 'with the kick in it'. **1899** R. WHITEING *No. 5 John St.* xxi. 216 'My Gawd! won't them chaps from the Collynies 'ave the kick!' he observes, in allusion to their entertainment at the public expense. **1903** *Daily Chron.* 16 Jan. 5/1 With cayenne and mustard (to give their food the missing 'kick' [of alcohol]). **1924** P. MARKS *Plastic Age* xi. 101 'Who wrote "La Belle Dame sans Merci"?'..'I think Jawn Keats wrote it. It's one of those bedtime stories with a kick.' **1927** W. E. COLLINSON *Contemp. Eng.* 81 Home-brew with a kick in it. **1928** *Daily Express* 4 Dec. 10/3, I was determined to get a kick out of that journey—and I certainly did. **1929** *Evening News* 18 Nov. 15/6 A cocktail basis with a real kick (42 deg. proof spirit). **1933** D. L. SAYERS *Murder must Advertise* ix. 159 There's a kick in being afraid. **1935** S. SPENDER *Destructive Element* 82 Strether accepts even the fact that he is living with Madame de Vionnet; in fact, he gets a kick

out of it. **1941** *Jazz Information* Nov. 22/2 A man who.. worked hard and got his kicks and saved a little money. **1942** *R.A.F. Jrnl.* 2 May 35 We get a great kick out of wearing it. **1946** Mezzrow & Wolfe *Really Blues* (1957) 373 *For kicks*, for pleasure's sake. **1951** *Manch. Guardian Weekly* 28 June 2 To seek a heftier 'kick' from real narcotics. **1956** [see *cramp *v.* 5 c]. **1961** Wodehouse *Service with Smile* (1962) x. 155 He added that the beverage had a kick, and Lord Ickenham agreed that its kick was considerable. **1963** *Listener* 17 Jan. 133/1 Anti-social, sexually ruthless, stealing cars for kicks. **1967** M. M. Glatt et al. *Drug Scene* iii. 39 He no longer got a 'kick' or 'flash' from taking drugs. **1974** *Advocate News* (Barbados) 5 Mar. 3/2 The pusher can more easily persuade him to try something with a bit more kick to it.

d. An interest or enthusiasm, esp. one that is temporary; a fashion, fad (cf. sense 4 in Dict.); a subject, line of thought, or manner of behaving; = *bag *sb.* 1 d; esp. in phr. *on the —— kick* = doing, or enthusiastic about, the thing specified by the prefixed word or words. orig. *U.S. slang*.

[**1942** Berrey & Van den Bark *Amer. Thes. Slang* § 233/2 The fashion; rage,.. *the kick*.] **1946** *Jazz Record* July 8 The whole jazz world was on a Hawkins kick. **1955** M. McCarthy *Charmed Life* ii. 34 He had been..a magazine editor. He was on that kick, as he called it, when he met Martha. **1955** B. Bailey in Shapiro & Hentoff *Hear Me Talkin' to Ya* xviii. 298 When I was starting up, they used to say the two races couldn't get along playing. They used to say stuff like they were afraid we'd go after their women. All that's been proved false, and everything else on that prejudice kick has been proved false. **1957** M. Millar *Soft Talkers* ii. 20 'He's rather sensitive about being caught by the cops in bed with another man's wife.' 'For Pete's sake, Esther, get off that kick, will you?' **1959** C. MacInnes *Absolute Beginners* 88 Mannie wasn't in on the Angries kick. *Ibid.* 93 They didn't like it when little Emmanuel got on the writing kick? **1963** B. S. Johnson *Travelling People* iv. 66 The star of the production is Maurice Bunde,..fifty-ish but on a tremendous Back-to-Youth kick. **1970** *Globe Mag.* (Toronto) 26 Sept. 8/3 We must get off this kick that every job is a career—it isn't. **1971** *Times Lit. Suppl.* 12 Nov. 1409/1 Somewhere behind the cumulative high, the peace-kick, the good vibes, efficient entrepreneurs.. were smiling their mean smiles all the way to the bank.

e. *Athletics*. A sharp burst of speed, esp. towards the end of a middle-distance race.

1955 F. Stampfl *On Running* vii. 108 By making his final burst of 300 yards from home Bannister could hope to draw the sting of Nielsen's powerful kick and late finish. **1966** R. Clarke *Unforgiving Minute* xvi. 143, I was obviously holding his finishing 'kick' with no effort whatever and I certainly ran faster when I did sprint. **1972** *N.Y. Times* 4 June 4/5 Instead, Wottle overtook Bob Wheeler of Duke starting the stretch run and turned back a belated kick by Jerome Howe of Kansas State, who finished second in 3:39.8.

6. b. *pl.* Shoes. orig. *U.S.*

1904 'No. 1500' *Life in Sing Sing* 250/1 *Kicks*, shoes. **1936** K. Mackenzie *Living Rough* xi. 160 My new kicks, every time I took a step, made a sound like the back of a bird store. **1937** Partridge *Dict. Slang* 601/1 *Pair o(f) kicks*, boots, shoes: tramps' c[ant]. **1964** L. Hairston in J. H. Clarke *Harlem* 285 After I brushed my kicks, I looked my wig over in the mirror. **1973** *Black World* Apr. 63 My terrible blue-and-white kicks.

7. (Further examples.)

1938 Wodehouse *Summer Moonshine* i. 18 'She slung your brother Joe out.' 'And with only ten dollars in his kick, mind you.' **1962** R. Cook *Crust on its Uppers* (1964) iii. 27 I'm about to stuff my pony in my kick. **1968** *Sunday Truth* (Brisbane) 22 Sept. 22/8 One of Luke's jobs was to see that the money was banked every week. Luke put it in his own kick.

8. *Comb.*, as **kick-pleat** (or plait), a pleat in a narrow skirt to allow freedom of movement; **kick-stand**, 'a device for holding up a bicycle or motorcycle when not in use consisting of a metal bar or rod that is attached by a swivel device to the frame and may be kicked to a vertical position as a prop' (Webster, 1961); **kick-start, -starter**, a device for starting an internal combustion engine, esp. on a motor-cycle, by a downward thrust on a pedal; hence **kick-start** *v. trans.* and *intr.*, to start (an engine) thus; **kick-turn** *Skiing*, a form of standing turn; **kick-wheel**, a potter's wheel worked by a foot pedal.

1934 Webster s.v. *plait*, A kick plait is a variation of the latter [*sc.* box plait] used to give breadth to a narrow skirt. **1960** *Sunday Express* 20 Nov. 14/2 Pencil skirt with back 'kick' pleat. **1947** *Cycling Handbk.* (League of Amer. Wheelmen, Inc.) 23 Heavyweights are generally equipped with coaster brakes,..kickstands, and other accoutrements dear to the hearts of juvenile Americans. **1963** D. Broun *Subject of Harry Egypt* i. 8 There was a metered space..and he eased the cycle into it and over onto the kickstand. **1914** *Motor Cycle* 2 Apr. 138/1, 1912 P. and M., free engine, 2-speed, kick start. **1928** *Manch. Guardian Weekly* 15 June 474/2 The biggest boy is demonstrating..how to kick-start an engine. **1959** I. Jefferies *Thirteen Days* i. 17, I..turned my bike down the slope to save kick-starting. *Ibid.* xi. 188, I kick-started and zoomed up the rock-slope. **1962** 'D. Wilson' *Search for Geoffrey Goring* viii. 170 He kickstarted the motor and rode on. **1916** *Motor Cyclists' A.B.C.* 107 A kick starter is fitted to a machine for the purpose of allowing the engine to be started whilst the rider is in the saddle by a downward kick of a pedal. **1919** C. P. Thompson *Cocktails* 235 She mounted on the kickstarter and stamped on it with resolute vigour. **1961** *Engineering* 13 Oct. 486 The clutch, gearbox, kickstarter, transmission and rear stub axle are combined with the engine into a single unit. **1910** W. R. Rickmers *Ski-ing* 27 People with stiff or short legs should take short ski, as otherwise certain necessary movements (*i.e.*, the kick-turn) become difficult or impossible. **1960** *Sunday Express* 18 Dec. 15/4 Kick-turns, in which you stand on one ski on a slope, lift the other and turn it right round, and then bring the second ski round too so that you are facing in the opposite direction. **1893** E. A. Barber *Pott. & Porc. U.S.* xii. 250 Such wares..were produced in large quantities by negro men and boys, who employed the old-fashioned 'kick-wheel' in their manufacture. **1949** K. S. Woods *Rural Crafts Eng.* v. xvi. 233 A kick-wheel is driven by a horizontal movement of one foot on a treadle. **1968** J. Arnold *Shell Bk. Country Crafts* 15 With the employment of an improved kick-wheel for 'throwing', they were able to make tremendous advances. **1972** *Islander* (Victoria, B.C.) 30 July 5/1 The pottery produced is hand built. However, the group does work with a kick-wheel, as well as an electric-wheel.

kick, *v.*[1] Add: **I. 3. b.** Said also of the ball, and of the bowler. Also with *up*. (Further examples.)

1866 'Captain Crawley' *Cricket* 25 You will most likely get a run whether the ball shoots or kicks. **1877** C. Box *Eng. Game Cricket* 453 The ground is said to kick when the ball, after being pitched, rises almost perpendicularly. **1888** Steel & Lyttelton *Cricket* 152 Spofforth was bowling rather more than medium pace, bringing the ball back a foot or more very quickly from the pitch, sometimes kicking to the height of the batsman's head and at others shooting. **1904** P. F. Warner *How we recovered Ashes* xiii. 246 The ball was always turning, and one or two deliveries kicked up rather awkwardly. **1963** A. Ross *Australia 63* i. 33 McKenzie got one to kick in the next over.

c. *Telegr.* Of a relay: to break contact momentarily.

1928 A. E. Stone *Text Bk. Telegr.* xiii. 192 If during this period the tongue of the relay 'kicks', the local circuit is momentarily broken. **1959** J. W. Freebody *Telegr.* vii. 195/2 In a duplex circuit this surge flows through the line coil of the relay and would cause the relay to 'kick' if a similar balancing surge were not also allowed to pass through the relay balance coil.

4. e. *refl.* To reproach or be angry with (oneself); to be annoyed at something one has done or omitted to do.

1891 *Voice* (N.Y.) 29 Jan., In the absence of any of the committee to kick I went home kicking myself. **1892** W. S. Walsh *Handy-bk. Lit. Curiosities* 584 To kick one's self, often used with an infinite variety of adjuncts,—*i.e.*, to kick one's self 'all over the house', 'all over the place', etc.,—means to feel or express violent dissatisfaction with one's self. **1903** *Independent* (N.Y.) 15 Jan. 148/2 He goes away kicking himself. **1907** A. Bennett *Let.* 5 May (1966) I. 90 Those who persuade themselves to act on this assumption from the start will have least cause to kick themselves in the distant future. **1955** L. P. Hartley *Perfect Woman* xxi. 188 All the way to Tilecotes he could have kicked himself for not having made the engagement for next week. **1966** B. Kimenye *Kalasanda Revisited* 48 Mrs. Mulindwa could have kicked herself for making the suggestion in the first place. **1973** *Times* 27 Dec. 13/4 Rangers were rightly kicking themselves afterwards.

f. *trans.* To give up or overcome (a habit, esp. drug-taking). Also *intr. colloq.* (orig. *U.S. slang*).

1936 *Amer. Speech* XI. 123/2 *To kick the habit*, to stop using drugs. **1951** *Nat. Educ. Assoc. U.S. Jrnl.* May 342/2 Later on they find themselves hooked and can't kick the habit unless they receive medical and psychiatric help. **1956** B. Holiday *Lady sings Blues* (1973) xiv. 121 Along about the end of the war I went to Joe Glaser's office and told him I wanted to kick and I'd need help. **1958** *Oxford Mail* 29 July 6/5 Harmony would again be restored if Johnny could 'kick' his craving. **1964** S. Bellow *Herzog* (1965) 334 Between his false teeth (to help him kick the smoking habit, as he had once explained to Herzog) he kept a plastic toothpick. **1971** *Black World* Mar. 56/1 I'll help you, man, cuz I know you want to kick. *Ibid.* Apr. 22/1 Let's kick that habit, let's use soul music. **1972** *Times* 3 Jan. 8/3 In a moment of weakness, I watched an episode of this [television serial] after having kicked the habit for more than 12 months.

5. b. *to be kicked upstairs* (earlier and later examples); also, *to kick* (someone) *upstairs*.

c **1697** [see Upstairs *adv.* 1 b]. **1750** C'tess of Shaftesbury *Let.* 28 Nov. in Earl of Malmesbury *Lett.* (1870) I. 78 The Bedfordian set will be honourably kicked up or down stairs. **1952** 'W. Cooper' *Struggles of Albert Woods* III. v. 197 The plot was devastatingly simple—Dibdin was to be kicked upstairs and Albert was to take his place. **1962** R. B. Fuller *Epic Poem on Industrialization* 27 Kicking the bosses upstairs—high out of the way. **1967** G. F. Fiennes *I Tried to run a Railway* vii. 78, I got eventually kicked upstairs to Paddington. **1970** *Guardian* 11 Nov. 20/6 Which party has kicked more people upstairs?

II. kick about or **around.**

a. *intr.* To walk or wander about; to go from place to place, esp. aimlessly. *colloq.* (orig. *U.S.*).

1839 C. M. Kirkland *New Home* xxv. 195 We heard that he was better, and would be able to 'kick around' pretty soon. **1846** B. Upton *Let.* 12 Dec. in *Amer. Heritage* (1966) June 93/2, I have been kicking about with scarcely leisure enough to take my meals. **1946** F. Sargeson *That Summer* 56 We're going to have a good time just kicking around.

b. *to be kicking about* or *around*: to lie scattered around, esp. in a casual or untidy fashion; to be available, unused, or unwanted.

1867 'T. Lackland' *Homespun* I. 80 The..doctor, whose instruments..lie kicking about like ordinary household trumpery. **1877** E. Peacock *Gloss. Words Manley & Corringham, Lincolnshire* 148/2 When I went ower to Rotterdam, bacca was that cheap, it was kickin' aboot i' th' streets. **1906** J. F. Kelly *Man with Grip* 99 Now kindly remove that old radiation, It's been kicking around for a week. **1955** W. Gaddis *Recognitions* II. viii. 658 Too much gold, that was their difficulty, gold kicking around all over the place. **1967** 'V. Siller' *Biltmore Call* 128 'Is there a sandwich kicking around?' 'Oh, sure, and I just made a fresh pot of coffee.'

c. *trans.* To kick in all directions; also *fig.*, to treat (someone) harshly, unfairly, or contemptuously. Chiefly *U.S.*

1938 C. Porter *Most Gentlemen don't like Love*, Most gentlemen don't like love,—They just like to kick it around. **1939** J. Steinbeck *Grapes of Wrath* ii. 8 A good guy and also he was not one whom any rich bastard could kick around. *a* **1940** F. Scott Fitzgerald *Last Tycoon* (1949) i. 25 You seem to take things so personally... You just ask to be kicked around.

d. To discuss or examine (a subject, idea, etc.); to try out. *colloq.* (orig. *U.S.*).

1939 *Esquire* May 75 Speaking again of Swing: few tunes deserve its name till they've been 'kicked around' by good performers. **1947** F. Wakeman *Saxon Charm* vi. 118 He agreed to write the scene experimentally. 'Maybe I'll get excited about it when I start kicking it around.' **1966** 'D. Shannon' *With a Vengeance* (1968) iii. 42 They ..drifted over by the other side of the big room to kick it around a little. **1971** 'G. Douglas' *Time to Die* xv. 159 They kicked the details around for a few more minutes and then left them to stew.

kick back.

a. *intr.* (See quot. 1909.)

1909 Webster, *To kick back, Mech.*, to start backwards; —said of an internal-combustion engine in starting with the crank when the spark is advanced and a too early ignition is effected. **1935** T. E. Lawrence *Let.* 13 Feb. (1938) 855 We launched the Dinghy: the quietest and sweetest tick-over of any Dinghy yet! It kicked back, when cold. So we put the ignition back a trifle.

b. *trans.* and *intr.* To return (money, stolen goods, etc.) to the person from whom they were obtained; to pay (money), esp. as a kick-back (see *kick-back). *colloq.* (orig. *U.S.*).

1926 Maines & Grant *Wise-Crack Dict.* 10/2 *Kick-back*, have to return a sucker's money. **1930** *Amer. Mercury* Dec. 456/2 Kick back with that hooch or we give you the works. **1934** *Atlantic Monthly* Aug. 139 The kick-back operates in the following manner. A wage scale is set either by law, as in government contracts, or by agreement between capital and labor. The worker assumes that he is to get so much per day or per hour for his work. At the end of the week, he is required to return or kick-back part of his wages to a designated person, often a foreman or a bookkeeper. **1970** 'B. Mather' *Break in Line* v. 59 The luggage coolies..kicked back half of their take to the Pathan hall porter.

kick down. *trans.* and *intr.* To operate a kick-down device (see *kick-down).

1909 *Cent. Dict.* Suppl. s.v., *To kick down*, to bore (a well) by a drill worked as follows: A wooden casing is sunk in the ground or rock for a few feet and the boring-tool works inside of and is guided by this casing... The tool is moved or kicked down by the pressure of the operators' feet. **1959** *Observer* 1 Mar. 21/5 Second can be obtained by kicking down the accelerator. **1963** *Which?* Oct. (Car Suppl.) 116/2 More effort was needed to 'kick-down' on the Zephyr 6.

kick in.

a. *trans.* To break down (a door, etc.) by kicking against the outer side; *spec.* (*U.S. slang*), to break into (a building).

1881 R. L. Stevenson *Treas. Isl.* (1883) v. 39 Then there followed a great to-do.., furniture thrown over, doors kicked in. **1926** J. Black *You can't Win* vii. 78 I'll kick in the first private house that looks good. We'll surely find a coat and maybe a few dollars. **1931** *Detective Fiction Weekly* 17 Jan. 23/1 Harold G. Slater's big jewelry store safe had been 'kicked in' and robbed of twelve thousand dollars.

b. *trans.* and *intr.* To contribute (money, etc.); to pay (one's share). *slang* (orig. *U.S.*).

1908 K. McGaffey *Sorrows of Show-Girl* 45 The lawyer guy kicked in with the balance of the ten thousand. **1908** H. Green *Maison de Shine* 282 If somebody else will get 'em to kick in I'll play the show. **1928** [see *chin *sb.*[1] 1 d]. **1936** Wodehouse *Laughing Gas* xxiv. 254 To encourage the Christmas spirit in whoever was supposed to kick in with my ransom. **1948** *Lawton* (Okla.) *Constitution* 2 July 8/1 The spectators 'kicked in' with a little cash. **1972** *Fortune* Jan. 112/2 Hillard Elkins, producer of *Oh! Calcutta!*, asked him to help back his productions of two Ibsen plays; Lufkin kicked in $10,000.

kick off.

b. Also *fig.*, to start, begin. Freq. const. *with*.

1911 R. Brooke *Let.* 25 Apr. (1968) 300 'Are you ready to kick off?' he said... I *gathered* it merely meant was she ready to go out to San Lorenzo. **1942** F. Sargeson in *N.Z. New Writing* I. 5 To kick off with we'd fool about in the water. **1954** L. Durrell *Let.* 14 Mar. in *Spirit of Place* (1969) 124, I will kick off with Freya Stark and Sir Harry Luke. **1968** *Blues Unlimited* Nov. 17 It kicked off with Bob Hite..ranged through Dave Kelly's bottleneck playing. **1969** G. E. Evans *Farm & Village* xii. 131 The old bo's would come in, and my father and I used to go down to the bar to *kick off with*.

c. To die. *slang* (orig. *U.S.*).

1921 J. Dos Passos *Three Soldiers* II. i. 61 Another kid's kicked off with that—what d'they call it?—menegitis. **1948** E. Waugh *Loved One* 22 'It belonged to some old Britisher who's just kicked off.' 'I am that Britisher and I have not kicked off.' **1969** C. Burke *God is Beautiful*,

Man (1970) 29 If he don't come back his old man will get sick and kick off too. **1970** R. Lowell *Notebk.* 122 The old bitches Live into their hundreds, while I'll kick off tomorrow.

8. kick out.

d. *Surfing.* (See quots.)

1962 T. Masters *Surfing Made Easy* 64 *Kicking out*, turning up and over the wave to end a ride. **1965** J. Pollard *Surfrider* ii. 20 First let's 'kick out'—shift the weight to the rear of the board and pull it over the top of the wave.

10. kick-and-rush, used *attrib.* to describe football played with more vigour than art; **kick-ball,** for *Sc.* read orig. *Sc.*, and add further examples; **kick-out,** (*b*) *Surfing* (see quots. and cf. sense 8 d above); **kick-the-can** (or -tin, etc.), a children's game in which a tin can is kicked (fully described in I. & P. Opie *Children's Games* (1969) 164–6).

1906 *Daily Chron.* 26 Nov. 9/2 It was a kick-and-rush game, played badly. **1930** *Daily Express* 9 Sept. 12/5 The football they played was of the kick-and-rush order. **1971** E. Shorris *Great Spirit* i. 17 You played kickball in the streets. **1972** J. E. Franklin in W. King *Black Short Story Anthol.* 354 During recess the children played kick-ball, tag, and other games. **1967** J. Severson *Great Surfing* Gloss. *s.v.*, A kick-out is a last-ditch effort to keep from losing your board. **1970** *Studies in English* (Univ. Cape Town) I. 32 The *kick-out*..involves stepping on the rear of the surfboard with considerable force and, at the same time, raising the lead foot, lifting the nose of the surfboard out of the water, and making it possible to pivot the board on its tail. **1971** *Ibid.* II. 27 The *kick-out* is an act of desperation. The surfer turns his board violently from the tail and as he leaves the board kicks it—so he hopes—over the top of the wave. **1909** *N. & Q.* 5 June 445/2 Children's games in Orkney... Kick the tinnie. **1959** I. & P. Opie *Lore & Lang. Schoolch.* xviii. 377 Orthodox games like 'Kick the Can' and 'Jacky Shine a Light'. **1959** B. Sutton-Smith *Games N.Z. Children* ii. 58 More popular were those games in which the players helped one another to fight the He, and of these the most widespread was the game known as *Kick the Tin.* **1966** 'L. Lane' *ABZ of Scouse* 59 *Kick-ther-can*, a form of street football, using old tin cans. **1971** *Stornoway Gaz.* 10 July 1/8 Children are inventive folk, They make their own best ploys. Smooring, leevo, kick the can, Sufficed when we were boys. **1973** B. Broadfoot *Ten Lost Years* viii. 86 My father called me in from outside, kick the can or one of those games we used to play.

Kickapoo (ki·kăpū). *U.S.* [Amer. Indian.] **a.** One of a tribe of North American Indians of the Algonquian family, now resident in reservations in Kansas, Oklahoma, and Mexico. **b.** The language of this people. Also *attrib.* or as *adj.*

1722 D. Coxe *Descr. Carolana* 50 Nations to the West of this Lake, besides the beforemention'd, are Part of the Outogamis, Mascoutens, and Kikpouz. **1835** C. F. Hoffman *Winter in West* I. 276 The Indians that frequent the neighbourhood of Chicago..are chiefly Pottawattamies and Ottawas, with a few Chippewas.., and a straggling Kickapoo. **1933** L. Bloomfield *Lang.* 72 The languages of..the Great Lakes region (Ojibwa,..Kickapoo,..and so on). **1960** B. Keaton *Wonderful World of Slapstick* (1967) 19 He had a Kickapoo squaw on one side of him, a Kickapoo brave on the other.

kick-back, kickback (ki·kbæk). orig. *U.S. colloq.* [f. phr. *to kick back* (*kick *v.*[1] II).] **a.** A. refund, a rebate; the return of money, goods, etc.; a payment (usu. illegal) made to a person who has made possible or facilitated a transaction, appointment, etc. Also *attrib.*

1932 *Editor* 6 Feb. 112/2 *Kick-back*, a return of money. **1934** [see *kick back* s.v. *kick *v.*[1] II]. **1934** *Sun* (Baltimore) 24 Jan. 1/3 The 'kick-back' system of cutting PWA workers' pay. *Ibid.* 1 Feb. 1/5 These 'kickbacks' were described as levies amounting to from $15 to $25 a week on the musician's salary. **1935** N. Ersine *Underworld & Prison Slang* 49 *Kickback*, loot that must be returned to avoid arrest. 'They took a grand off the hoosiers, but they had to make a kickback when the marks beefed.' **1939** *Ibid.* 13 Feb. 16/5, 150,000 persons and companies throughout nation get 'kickback'... Several hundred Maryland Corporations and individuals received tax refunds during the last fiscal year. **1940** F. Riesenberg *Golden Gate* 308 Longshoremen were finding it tougher than ever to get jobs, even through kick-backs of pay, bottles of liquor, and cigars. **1958** M. Dickens *Man Overboard* xiv. 218 With Mr Pearse and his little kick-backs out of the picture, the food budget was reduced. **1959** *Listener* 3 Dec. 960/1 A number of employers were prepared to offer bribes, pay 'kickbacks'. **1971** *Courier Mail* (Brisbane) 8 Mar. 4/7 The [U.S. official tax] guide says: 'Bribes and kickbacks (a form of bribe) to non-government officials are deductible.' **1972** *Daily Tel.* 19 June 10/5 The promoter claims that another member of the committee approached him demanding a kick-back on the profits and, after he had refused this proposal, the permit was somehow no longer forthcoming.

b. A strong reaction or repercussion; an undesirable result.

1935 M. M. Atwater *Murder in Midsummer* xxii. 210 His bluster was the kick-back of his strained nerves. **1940** *Amer. Speech* XV. 64 This kickback of the idea into the word, wherein..the word is..vested with unusual suggestive power. **1953** Wodehouse *Performing Flea* 177 The feeling that he showed a lack of public spirit in getting away and leaving us to receive the kick-back. **1954** R. Knox *Retreat for Lay People* xiv. 140 Even as a matter of psychology, isn't it probable that all this negative business has a kick-back which is bad for us? **1965** *Listener* 6 May 658/1 We can over-mechanize it [*sc.* education]. One of the kick-backs of this is the University of California situation, over-planning, the over-administering of education.

c. *Railways.* A device whereby the direction of wagons, etc., can be reversed.

1947 *Richmond* (Virginia) *Times Dispatch* 1 Apr. 6/1 The empty [coal] car is then kicked off the dumper by the next loaded car, rolls by gravity to a high 'kickback' at the outshore end of the pier and thence by gravity to the yard for empty cars. **1962** *Times* 26 Oct. (Spencer Steelworks Suppl.) p. xviii/2 The gravity operated kick-back which reverses the wagon's direction.

d. In timber preservation (see quots.).

1947 *N.Z. Timber Jrnl.* Sept. 61/2 *Kick back* (wood preservative), surplus antiseptic released from the wood when pressure is withdrawn after impregnation. **1968** *Gloss. Terms Timber Preservation (B.S.I.)* 21 *Kickback*, the amount of preservative forced out of the timber when pressure is released.

kick-down (ki·kˌdaun). [f. Kick *v.*[1] + Down *adv.*] A device that is operated by the foot; *spec.*, on a motor vehicle, a device whereby one can change to a lower gear, esp. by pressing right down on the accelerator pedal in a vehicle with automatic transmission; also, the act of thus changing to a lower gear. Freq. *attrib.*

1909 *Cent. Dict.* Suppl., *Kick-down*, the apparatus used in kicking down. See *to kick down*. **1954** *New Automotive Encycl.* 35e/1 A valve operated by a solenoid magnet, which is connected to a governor and kickdown switch. **1958** *Times* 15 July 7/6 The unduly light pressure required for the kick-down. *Ibid.*, The ease with which the kick-down change occurred. **1959** *Times* 17 Mar. 14/7 The accelerator kick-down is an over-riding control that can be brought into play for maximum acceleration at any speed up to about 65 m.p.h. **1971** *Daily Tel.* 24 Mar. 11/4 The kick-down switch on the accelerator was unusually light and pleasant to use.

kicker. Add: **5.** *Poker.* A high third card retained in the hand with a pair at the draw.

1892 W. J. Florence *Handbk. Poker* 91 To keep two small cards and an ace is called holding up 'a kicker'. This draw is made by the player, hopeful of getting two pairs, with the additional ace or king. **1895** 'Templar' *Poker Manual* 57 Sometimes a player raises on a single pair and a kicker, *i.e.* a high card. **1946** Morehead & Mott-Smith *Penguin Hoyle* 127 To keep an ace or other high card as a 'kicker' seriously decreases the chances of improving.

6. An outboard motor, or a boat driven by one. Also *attrib. N. Amer. colloq.*

1928 L. R. Freeman *Nearing North* ii. i. 132 The kicker is hung in a hole cut at a proper height in the long overhang of the stern. **1937** *Times* 13 Oct. 15/6 At Fort Simpson..four of us went upstream to a creek in a 'kicker' (which is a canoe powered by an out-board motor) and swam luxuriously. **1942** L. Rich *We took to Woods* (1944) ii. 33, I want to cut the stern off square, when I get the price of an outboard motor, and make a kicker-boat out of it. **1953** Berrey & Van den Bark *Amer. Thes. Slang* (1954) § 82a/1 *Kicker*, an auxiliary motor on a boat. **1963** R. D. Symons *Many Trails* xvi. 165 Travelling downstream with a good 'kicker' (outboard motor) pushing the canoe at a good speed is easy. **1967** E. B. Nickerson *Kayaks to Arctic* iv. 30 Soon we learned to..differentiate outboard motors, or 'kickers' as they are universally called here.

7. *Printing.* (See quots.)

1930 K. E. Olson *Typogr. & Mechanics of Newspaper* xiii. 421 Every fiftieth or one-hundredth paper is turned slightly askew by an automatic 'kicker' in order to facilitate the making up of bundles of given content. **1967** V. Strauss *Printing Industry* vi. 384/1 Counting of newspapers is made easier by the 'kicker', a metal arm which pushes, say, every 25th or every 50th paper out of line, thereby dividing the flow of papers into smaller batches.

kick-in (ki·kin), *sb. Football.* [f. Kick *v.*[1] + In *adv.*] Practice goal-shooting before the start of a match.

1961 *Times* 10 Feb. 19/7 Previously the British method had demanded a general kick-in before the toss-up. **1972** G. Green *Great Moments in Sport: Soccer* ii. 33 The moment the Hungarians..began their 'kick-in' before the start one got the distinct feeling that something unusual was in store. **1973** *Shoot!* 1 Dec. 15/1 The home team's goalkeeper is injured during the pre-match kick-in.

kicking, *vbl. sb.* Add: **b. kicking plate,** a metal plate fixed to the lower part of a door, etc., to prevent damage or wear; **kicking-strap,** (*b*) *Naut.* a rope lanyard fixed to the boom to prevent it from rising.

1940 *Chambers's Techn. Dict.* 476/1 *Kicking plate* (Join.), a plate fixed on the face of the bottom rail of a door, to prevent the damage caused by persons kicking the door to open it. **1959** *Engineering* 16 Jan. 94/3 At the base of each frame is a kicking plate of porcelain-enamelled sheet steel. **1951** G. Pennant *Young Sailor* v. 70 It is to prevent the boom from lifting that a kicking strap is fitted. **1961** R. M. Tetley *Sailing* ii. 47 It is in a gybe that a kicking-strap proves its worth, since it holds down the after end of the boom thereby allowing complete control to be maintained over the sail at all stages of the manœuvre.

kicking, *ppl. a.* Phr. *alive and kicking*, add def.: indubitably alive; very lively and active. (Earlier and later examples.)

c **1831** J. R. Planché *Olympic Devils* in *Extravaganzas* (1879) I. 71 *Plu.* Alive? *Char.* And kicking. **1840** *New Monthly Mag.* LVIII. 497 He is (as the Irishman says), 'alive and kicking'. **1930** R. Lehmann *Note in Music* 130 He seemed to imply with amusement how particularly alive they were. 'Father, mother, two young brothers, and sister Clare, all alive and kicking.' **1966** L. Southworth *Felon in Disguise* xi. 158 I'd feel happier if I knew Donaldson was alive and kicking.

b. *Cricket.* Of the ground, a bowler, or his bowling: causing the ball to 'kick' (see Kick *v.*[1] 3 b in Dict. and Suppl.). Also of a lawn-tennis service.

1885 J. Lillywhite *Cricketers' Compan.* 53 The Gloucestershire batsmen found Palmer unplayable on a 'kicking' wicket. **1888** [in Dict.]. **1891** W. G. Grace *Cricket* iii. 67 My brother was the faster [bowler], and on a rough kicking wicket met with great success. **1924** F. G. Lowe *Lawn Tennis* 12 The only way to take a fast kicking service.

kickininee, var. *kokanee.

kick-off. Add: **b.** *fig.* The start, beginning; an inaugural or opening event.

1875 [in Dict.]. **1919** Wodehouse *My Man Jeeves* 200 The kick-off was scheduled for one o'clock in the morning, when the household might be expected to be..asleep. **1969** *New Yorker* 11 Oct. 43/2 The kickoff starts tonight, with a dinner for the living benefactors of the Museum. **1973** M. Truman *Harry S. Truman* i. 20 The first major crisis came on Labor Day, when we went to Detroit to make the traditional kickoff speech in Cadillac Square.

kicksorter (ki·ksǭɹtəɹ). *colloq.* Also **kick sorter.** [f. Kick *sb.*[1] + Sorter.] An instrument that classifies electrical pulses according to their amplitude and registers the number received in each amplitude range; a pulse-height analyser.

1947 *Rev. Sci. Instruments* XVIII. 90/2 Five instruments, which have been named Pulse Analysers, Pulse Amplitude Analysers, or 'Kicksorters', have been developed in England and Canada. **1957** *Economist* 7 Sept. 767/2 (Advt.), But why 'kick sorter'? Because it sorts out electrical 'kicks' or impulses according to their amplitude—more than 16,000 of them in each of 100 channels and at speeds up to 1,250 pulses per second. **1968** *Brit. Med. Bull.* XXIV. 259/1 The same equipment can also be used to generate a histogram of spike amplitude, comparable to the pulse-height analyser or 'kick sorter' used by the nuclear physicist.

kickster (ki·kstəɹ). [f. *kick *sb.*[1] 2 c + -ster.] One whose behaviour is governed principally or solely by the desire for 'kicks'.

1963 *Guardian* 4 Oct. 20/6 Christine is a kickster... She will go with 15 or 18 men at a time. **1967** J. G. Morgan *Involved* 57 'He looked a real kink, you know, a regular kickster.' 'Educate me,' Frankie said, 'I want to be with you.' 'A nut,' Janet explained, 'a kink who likes going to a scene but won't participate, he gets his kicks out of watching everyone else knocking themselves out.' **1972** *New Society* 9 Nov. 346/3 Apart from the bovver-boy type, there are some girl gangs..and middle class kickster groups... There's a theory it's best to have something to steal, rather than nothing, but this is no help with kicksters.

kick-up. Add: **2. b.** A dance or party. *colloq.* (orig. *U.S.*).

1778 W. Beatty *Jrnl.* 1 Dec. in *Maryland Hist. Mag.* (1908) III. 116 We Collected the Girls in the neighbourhood and had a kick up in the Evening. **1796** Grose *Dict. Vulgar T.* (ed. 3) s.v. *kicks*, A kick up; a disturbance, also a hop or dance. **1899** R. Whiteing *No. 5 John St.* x. 100 There's a little bit of a kick-up to-night with a few of us—sort of sing-song. **1910** 'G. B. Lancaster' *Jim of Ranges* vi. 126 'What d'yer do at a kick-up, Jim?' 'Oh, hide-an'-seek..an' kiss-in-the-ring,' explained Jim.

4. (See quots.)

1883 W. S. Gresley *Gloss. Terms Coal Mining* 147 *Kick-up*, see *tipper*. **1893–4** R. O. Heslop *Northumberland Words* II. 423 *Kick-up*, an apparatus at a pit bank, made like an iron cradle, by which a tram is turned upside down and emptied on to the screen. **1909** H. Louis *Dressing of Minerals* 451 In larger mines it is more usual to use cars with fixed sides and to use some form of 'Tippler' or 'Tumbler' for turning the car over and thus emptying out its contents. Tipplers are of two kinds: end tipplers or 'Kick-ups' and side tipplers.

5. = Kick *sb.*[2] 1.

1901 in *Oxf. Eng. Dict.* s.v. *Kick sb.*[2] 1. **1923** H. J. Powell *Glass-Making in Eng.* ii. 22 Feet of goblets, showing hem and kick-up. *Ibid.* v. 74 Stability had been given by pushing upwards and inwards the base of the bulb to form the familiar 'kick-up' of modern wine-bottles.

kicky (ki·ki), *a.* [f. Kick *v.*[1] + -y[1].] **1.** *Sc.* (See quot. 1808.) Also, clever, lively; provoking, teasing, annoying.

1790 A. Shirrefs *Poems* 213 Auld Meg hersel' began the play, Clad in a bran-new hudden gray, And in't, I wat, she look'd fu' gay, And spruce and kicky. **1806** G. S. in J. Cock *Simple Strains* 93 Fu' mony a witty touch, and kicky line, Wad won the praise o' langer heads than mine. **1808** Jamieson, *Kicky.* 1. Showy, gaudy... 2. High-minded, aiming at what is above one's station. **1910** in *Sc. Nat. Dict.* (1960) V. 395/1 Isna' that kicky 'at I canna min' fat comes neest.

2. *Cricket.* Causing the ball to 'kick' (see Kick *v.*[1] 3 b in Dict. and Suppl.).

1888 STEEL & LYTTELTON *Cricket* iii. 150 It is a slow easy wicket he has to bat on, and not a 'caked', kicky one. **1903** *Windsor Mag.* Sept. 393/2 A very kicky wicket generally averages matters somewhat by supplying one dead shooter.

3. Providing 'kicks', exciting, lively. *N. Amer. colloq.*

1968 *N.Y. Times* 15 Aug. 42 It brought out some kicky styles to preview its new fur boutique. **1969** *New Yorker* 20 Dec. 79 (Advt.), One of our kids said it would be 'kicky' to have one of those 'blow-up' chairs. **1970** J. G. VERMANDEL *Dine with Devil* i. 5 Yes, all right, let's do the kicky stuff first and then try some high fashion. **1972** M. J. BOSSE *Incident at Naha* i. 60 At first impressed, she seemed doubtful after I had unloaded our theories. 'It's kicky and all..but where's it lead to?' **1973** *Time* (Canada ed.) 25 June 8/1 The designs are variously casual, racy, sporty—or kicky, trendy and funky.

kid, *sb.*[1] Add: **5. d.** A young man or woman. *colloq.* (orig. *U.S.*).

1884 *Cheyenne* (Wyoming) *Sun* 3 Nov. 3/1 There were some strange pranks played by the Cheyenne 'Kids' on the occasion of the 'Halloween'. **1896** *Emporia* (Kansas) *Gaz.* 15 Aug. 15 We have discovered a kid without a law practice and have decided to run him for attorney general. **1926** J. BLACK *You can't Win* iv. 26 I'll tell you what I'll do with you, kid. **1949** *N.Y. Times* 9 Oct. 50/3 A kid [*sc.* a college freshman] from anywhere immediately feels that he belongs to a great family. **1955** J. D. MACDONALD *Brass Cupcake* v. 46 Kathy came into my office... I spoke out of the corner of my mouth. 'We can't talk here, kid.' **1974** N. FREELING *Dressing of Diamond* 127 You got to learn. That's a kid's job. Make yourself useful.

6. kid brother orig. *U.S.*, one's younger brother; **kid-brush**, a soft brush used in the process of finishing goatskins; **kid sister** orig. *U.S.*, one's younger sister; **kid** (also **kid's, kids'**) **stuff** *colloq.* (orig. *U.S.*), something suitable for children; a very simple or trivial task, etc.

1895 J. L. WILLIAMS *Princeton Stories* 143 The evenings would pass pleasantly enough in fighting with Helen, his married sister, across the table, and in guying his kid brother. **1941** *Penguin New Writing* IX. 106 She.. lived with her parents and kid brother in Kennington. **1971** B. COBB *I fell among Thieves* iii. 39 He was the kid-brother whom I helped as far as I could, seeing that we had no mother. **1885** C. T. DAVIS *Manuf. Leather* xxxii. 532 The skins..are then wet over with gum-water and brushed with a very soft brush, called a 'kid-brush'. **1920** F. SCOTT FITZGERALD *This Side of Paradise* (1921) I. i. 36, I let people impose on me..entertain their kid sisters. **1939** 'N. BLAKE' *Smiler with Knife* xi. 159 His manner towards them was affectionate, teasing, whimsical... They might have been his kid sisters just out of the schoolroom. **1962** 'M. INNES' *Connoisseur's Case* xiv. 172, I don't sound a very nice kid sister. But I'm quite fond of him. **1929** F. D. BROOKS *Psychol. Adolescence* xviii. 605 The little fellow looked at the book a minute,..and in a very caustic, critical manner sneered, 'Kid stuff.' **1959** J. BRAINE *Vodi* ii. 39 He only had to say, 'Bloody nonsense' or 'Kid's stuff, Coverack' and close his ears to Tom. **1962** L. DEIGHTON *Ipcress File* xxi. 141 Communists..won't be using kids' stuff like this bomb. **1967** *Spectator* 7 July 9/3 One addiction specialist described it [*sc.* marijuana] to me contemptuously as 'kid-stuff'. **1974** M. BABSON *Stalking Lamb* viii. 50 I've taught you the only system that makes real money... Anything else is just kids' stuff.

kid, *sb.*[5] Add: In colloq. phr. *no kid*, no kidding, I am not kidding.

1873 [in Dict.]. **1880** *Punch* Dec., *'Arry.* My gloves was the cheese no kid. **1899** R. WHITEING *No. 5 John St.* xxiii. 234 He do seem to enjoy hisself, no kid! **1916** J. B. COOPER *Coo-oo-ee* i. 14, I tell you, Nelly, she's a woman as will blaze a track right enough, no kid. **1922** JOYCE *Ulysses* 418 Got a prime pair of mincepies, no kid. **1964** *Amer. Folk Music Occasional* 1. 91 True story, no kid.

kid, *v.*[4] Add: Also, to joke with, tease. Also *intr.* or *absol.*, and const. *along* or *on*; freq. in phr. *no kidding*, I am not kidding; that is the truth.

1839 H. BRANDON in W. A. Miles *Poverty, Mendicity & Crime* 163/2 *Kidding on*, to entice one on. **1879** [in Dict.]. **1901** [see *DOWN AND OUT *adj. phr.*]. **1903** G. B. SHAW *Man & Superman* II. 70 Garn! youre kiddin. **1906** S. FORD *Shorty McCabe* xiii. 273 I'll stand for all the private kidding you can hand out. **1914** E. E. CUMMINGS Let. 27 July (1969) 9 There's a dead monkey-fish hard by the boat club... No kidding! **1916** C. J. DENNIS *Moods of Ginger Mick* 89, I can see ole Ginger..Grinnin' a bit to kid 'is wound don't pain. **1920** S. LEWIS in *Sat. Even. Post* 11 Dec. 11/2 The boss ain't such a bad pill if you know how to kid him along. **1928** D. L. SAYERS *Lord Peter views Body* 287 Really? No kidding? **1932** J. T. FARRELL *Young Lonigan* iv. 154 'You wouldn't fool us, Gov'nor, would you?' kidded Johnny. Studs thought it wasn't every guy who could kid with his old man, like Johnny could. **1936** J. L. HODSON *Our Two Englands* vi. 103 'No, we don't even get kidded (chaffed) for doin' the housework any more,' a man of thirty told me. **1947** W. STEVENS *Let.* 20 Aug. (1967) 565 Next to the passion flower I love fuchsias, and no kidding. **1952** 'J. TEY' *Singing Sands* xii. 205 'I'm a policeman.' 'No kidding!' **1959** *Times* 27 June 7/7 If the Australian had not.. 'kidded himself along',..then his heart might have broken. **1969** *Listener* 9 Jan. 34/3 Mrs O'Hare has, of course, come in for a lot of kidding and wry jokes. **1969** *New Yorker* 30 Jan. 18/3 We asked some reclining youths where the Festival was, and they pointed across a vast valley to some tiny lights... 'You're kidding!'.. We sank to the grass. **1974** *Titbits* 30 May 22/4, I have always known I was impotent but kidded myself that if I could find the right wife everything would miraculously become O.K.

kidang. Now usually **kijang.** Substitute for def.: The Malay name for the Indian muntjac or barking deer, *Muntiacus muntjak.* Add earlier and later examples.

1783 W. MARSDEN *Hist. Sumatra* 94 Deer: *rooso*: *keejang*. These are variety [*sic*] of the deer species. **1824** T. HORSFIELD *Zool. Res. Java* s.v. *Cervus muntjak*. In the Javanese language..the name is Kĭdang, which with a slight modification—Kijang—is also employed in the Malayan language. **1839** T. J. NEWBOLD *Pol. & Statistical Acct. Straits of Malacca* I. vii. 436 Of the genus Cervus, are the Kijang or Cervus Muntjac, the Rûsa etc. **1880** *Encycl. Brit.* XIII. 602/2 The kidang or mintjac (*Cervulus muntjac*) and the rusa (*Rusa hippelaphus*) are the chief representatives of the deer kind [in Java]. **1900** W. W. SKEAT *Malay Magic* v. 251 The Gold spirit being supposed to take the shape of a *kijang* or roe-deer. **1958** J. SLIMMING *Temiar Jungle* ii. 28 They'll eat *Rusa*, *Pelandok*, and *Kijang*. **1965** C. SHUTTLEWORTH *Malayan Safari* iii. 38 The first visitor to the salt-lick was a *kijang* or barking deer.

kidder[1]. Add: (Examples.) Also, one who jokes or teases.

1888 *Sporting Life* 15 Dec. 3/2 The champion kidder. **1891** J. NEWMAN *Scamping Tricks* xi. 88 [He] was a beautiful kidder and could patter sweet and pretty. **1899** ADE *Fables in Slang* 84 They wanted a..Name.., so the Side-Show-Announcer, who was something of a Kidder.. gave them Zoroaster. **1922** WODEHOUSE *Clicking of Cuthbert* ix. 223 'Mr Winklethorpe told me I was very good with the wooden clubs,' she said defiantly. 'He's a great kidder,' said Ramsden. **1963** J. N. HARRIS *Weird World Wes Beattie* (1964) xvii. 196 Mr. Herbert Jackson was known as a real salesman, a man with personality, a great kidder, a hot sport and a number of other things.

kiddie, var. KIDDY *sb.* in Dict. and Suppl.

kiddleywink (ki·dliwiŋk). *dial.* Also **kiddle-a-wink, kiddle-e-wink, kiddleliwink, kiddle-wink, kiddley wenk, kiddlywink, kidley-wink.** [Origin unknown; cf. TIDDLYWINK 1.] An ale-house, esp. in the West Country; a low or unlicensed public house (see also quot. 1859).

1830 *Royal Cornwall Gaz.* 25 Dec. 4/6 One hundred and forty public-houses..opened..are called 'Kidley Winks'. *Ibid.*, A gentleman..suggested to the late Chancellor of the Exchequer the idea of retail-breweries. His name is Kidley Wink—hence the term 'Kidley Wink', as applied to the new beer shops. **1859** HOTTEN *Dict. Slang* 56 *Kiddleliwink*, a small shop where they retail the commodities of a village store. **1864** 'F. DERRICK' *Kiddle-a-Wink* ii. 92 The dreary little chamber allotted to him..bad as it was,.. was better than many a Kiddle-a-wink could boast of. **1865** R. HUNT *Pop. Romances W. of Eng.* 2nd Ser. 109 A drunken frolic..at a low beer shop or 'Kiddle-e-Wink'. **1890** *N. & Q.* 18 Jan. 48/2 Can any of your correspondents inform me what is the derivation of the word 'kiddlewink', or 'tiddley winks'? A friend tells me in the Midland Counties it denotes a house where beer is sold without a licence. **1964** C. DAVEY *Cornish Holiday* ii. 20 The potency of the drink sold in the innumerable public houses in Downlong, and in the 'kiddleywinks' or ale-houses near the mines. *Ibid.* x. 140 A tin-miner, laced with courage from the 'kiddley-wink', saw lights amongst the rocks.

kiddo (ki·do). *colloq.* [f. KID *sb.*[1] + *-O.] = KID *sb.*[1] 5 a, b, and *d; freq. as a familiar form of address.

1896 A. MORRISON *Child of Jago* xiii. 135 Josh was up almost before Kiddo Cook reached him. **1905** *Dialect Notes* III. 85 Say, kiddo, what are you going to do this evening? **1916** [see *GUESS *v.* 6]. **1938** M. ALLINGHAM *Fashion in Shrouds* xix. 340 'Have I ever let you down, kiddo?' The pseudo-American accent was slick. **1959** [see *BAT *v.*[1] 4]. **1961** *John o' London's* 9 Nov. 517/3 When it comes to choosing between the balance of power and unborn babies, I'm for the kiddos, every time. **1974** N. FREELING *Dressing of Diamond* 128 'How long do I have to stay?'.. 'Just as long as we thinks right, kiddo.'

kiddush (ki·duʃ). Also **K-.** [Heb. *qiddūš*, sanctification.] A ceremony of prayer and blessing over bread and wine, performed by the head of a Jewish household at the meal ushering in the Sabbath or a holy day. Also *attrib.*

1753 *Jewish Ritual* 34 All together with him in Concert, say the *Keedush*, i.e. the Sanctification. **1891** M. FRIEDLÄNDER *Jewish Relig.* 254 On Friday evening, before the meal, we praise God for sanctifying the Sabbath by a prayer called *Kiddush*, 'sanctification'. **1932** A. Z. IDELSOHN *Jewish Liturgy* II. x. 133 The text of the *Kiddush* consists of Gen. 1:31 and 2:1–3. Then there follows the blessing over wine and the closing paragraph... In the home, the benediction over bread follows. **1945** G. DIX *Shape of Liturgy* iv. 88 On festivals there was another common cup blessed and partaken of, besides the cup of blessing, both at a *chabûrah* meeting and at the ordinary family meal of a pious Jewish household. This was the *kiddûsh*-cup. **1960** *Commentary* June 500/1 Perhaps only one out of every two families begin the meal with the *kiddush*. **1973** *Jewish Chron.* 18 May 50/2 A service was conducted..at the Friern Hospital Synagogue and a kiddush was provided for the patients.

kiddushin (kidū·ʃīn). Also **K-.** [Aramaic *qiddūshīn*, pl. of *KIDDUSH.] The section of the Jewish Mishnah treating of betrothal and marriage; also the ceremony of betrothal, and the money or article given by the groom to effect the betrothal.

1883 *Encycl. Brit.* XVI. 505/2 Kiddushin (betrothal and marriage), in four chapters. **1904** *Jewish Encycl.* VII. 485/2 'Kiddushin' is the rabbinical term for betrothal, because the wife becomes thereby the sacrosanct possession of the husband... In the Mishnah, Kiddushin is divided into four chapters and comprises..forty-seven paragraphs. **1936** H. FREEDMAN in I. Epstein *Babylonian Talmud* VIII. p. xi, The Hebrew name Ḳiddushin ('Consecration') for betrothal, is worthy of note. The Talmud defines it as an act whereby the bride is rendered sacrosanct. *Ibid.* 51 There it was given her as a deposit... But here he gave it to her as *ḳiddushin*: if she did not want it [as such], she should have thrown it away. *Ibid.* 218 Her father [alone can accept *kiddushin* on her behalf] but not she herself. **1971** *Encycl. Judaica* X. 986 *Kiddushin*.., the last tractate in the order *Nashim*... It deals with matrimonial matters... There is no corresponding word for *kiddushin* in English. It is more than an 'engagement'.., as it can be dissolved only by divorce, and moreover the law of adultery..applies from the moment of *kiddushin*.

kiddy, *sb.* For 'Also 6 kiddie' read 'Also kiddie'. Add: **4. b.** *Comb.*, as **kiddy brother** = **kid brother*; **kiddy car** orig. *U.S.*, (*a*) a small toy car for a child; (*b*) a perambulator; **kiddy sister** = **kid sister*.

1963 C. MACKENZIE *My Life & Times* II. 82 That was my kiddy brother. He's a new boy. **1918** *Sears, Roebuck Catal.* Index, Kiddy car. **1951** I. SHAW *Troubled Air* xx. 331 There wasn't enough left of the cab to make a kiddie car. **1953** WODEHOUSE *Performing Flea* 58 You'll hear them call for Mr. Warner's bicycle, Mr. Lasky's kiddie car and Mr. Louis B. Mayer's roller-skates. **1959** *Times* 24 Feb. 13/4 A toy making factory..for the manufacture of fibreglass toys, kiddy cars, and rocking horses. **1973** *Sci. Amer.* Jan. 10/2 The invention by her [*sc.* Fräulein Gretel Steiff] of the 'Teddy Bear Doll' will go down in history with the kiddie car and other things that make life happy for children. **1913** C. MACKENZIE *Sinister St.* I. I. vii. 103 He also learnt to speak..of..'my people' and 'my kiddy sister'. **1915** A. BENNETT *Those Twain* (1916) I. ix. 159 'He's taken a terrific fancy to Maud, my kiddie sister,' said Daisy. **1963** C. MACKENZIE *My Life & Times* II. 60 Still laughing uncontrollably..in a fresh recollection of the face of our kiddy sister and the tone of her voice.

kiddy-wink, kiddywink (ki·diwiŋk). *colloq.* Also **kiddiewinkie, kiddywinkle, kiddywinky.** [Familiar extension of KIDDY *sb.*] = KIDDY *sb.* 2 (usu. jocular or affected). Also *attrib.*

1957 P. WILDEBLOOD *Main Chance* 201 Delicious milky-boo for the kiddy-winks. **1959** P. BULL *I know Face* x. 183 My performance..was pretty macabre, and must have frightened the bejesus out of the kiddy-winks. **1962** *Spectator* 22 June 827/2 Morality plays for the kiddie-winkies. **1968** L. BERG *Risinghill* 250 The approach was fine. None of this kiddywinky stuff. They became grown-up emotionally and mentally well in advance of their years. **1970** M. TRIPP *Man without Friends* xiii. 142 He's at Bognor with his kiddiewinkie. **1974** *Times* 13 Aug. 8/8 Dad Robinson..puts off the average incompetent father. Still, the kiddywinkles aren't to know.

kidlet (ki·dlĕt). [f. KID *sb.*[1] + -LET.] A young child. Also *fig.*

1899 'J. FLYNT' *Tramping with Tramps* ii. 31 The other 'kidlets', as they were nicknamed, were as deformed morally as was the adopted girl physically. **1903** J. DEWEY *Let.* Mar. in R. B. Perry *Tht. & Char. W. James* (1935) II. lxxxi. 521 We won't attempt to father you with all the weak kidlets which are crying in the volume to be born. **1959** C. MACINNES *Absolute Beginners* 165 A lot of kidlets helping him to do so.

kidley-wink, var. *KIDDLEYWINK.

kidnap (ki·dnæp), *sb.* [f. the vb.] The act of kidnapping. Also *attrib.*

1961 WEBSTER *s.v.*, A kidnap plot. The kidnap car. **1973** 'I. DRUMMOND' *Jaws of Watchdog* xv. 204 There was no money in killing you, but maybe a lot in a kidnap. **1973** *Observer* 12 Aug. 1/2 (*heading*) Jet kidnap was attempt to capture top guerrilla. **1974** N. FREELING *Dressing of Diamond* 201 A kidnap case—yes..we had it on our telex last night.

kidnapper. Add: Also (*U.S.*) **kidnaper.**

1909 O. JESPERSEN *Mod. Eng. Gram.* I. 149 Americans write *kidnaper*, which to an Englishman would suggest [kidneipə] or [-nəpə]. **1969** *Eugene* (Oregon) *Register-Guard* 3 Dec. 3A/2 The two men..freed themselves moments after the kidnaper abducted Miss Birdsong and called police. **1973** *Philadelphia Inquirer* 7 Oct. 19 The kidnapers agreed to call the Millers back several hours later.

kidney. Add: **5. c. kidney dressing-table,** a dressing-table with a kidney-shaped top; **kidney fern** *N.Z.*, a fern, *Cardiomanes reniforme*, with kidney-shaped leaves; **kidney graft,** the operation of transplanting a kidney from one person to another (see GRAFT *sb.*[1] 3); **kidney machine,** a machine for effecting hæmodialysis; = *artificial kidney* (*ARTIFICIAL *a.* 5), *HAEMODIALYSER; **kidney-pie,** (*a*) a pie containing kidneys; (*b*) *Austral.* and *N.Z. slang*, flattery, humbug, deceit; **kidney punch** (see quot. 1954); **kidney-rotter** *Austral.* and *N.Z. slang* (see quot. 1958); **kidney worm,**

either of two parasitic nematodes, *Stephanurus dentatus*, which attacks pigs, or *Dioctophyma* (or *Dioctophyme*) *renale*, which attacks man, dogs, and other mammals.

1932 *Times Lit. Suppl.* 9 June 420/3 A walnut suite with a kidney dressing-table. **1965** D. TORR *Diplomatic Cover* iii. 46 She leant over her frilly kidney dressing-table. **1867** E. SAUTER tr. *F. von Hochstetter's New Zealand* vi. 133 The singular form of the Kidney-fern (*Trichomanes reniforme*). **1926** J. DEVANNY *Lenore Divine* xx. 185 The kidney-fern was everywhere, sprawling over ground and trees. **1951** J. FRAME *Lagoon* 7 My..grandmother..could find kidney fern. **1966** *Encycl. N.Z.* I. 645/2 The kidney fern, *Cardiomanes reniforme*, with undivided leaves fringed with prominent sori, is common throughout the country. **1962** *Daily Tel.* 26 Nov. 1/3 (*headline*) Kidney graft doctor worse. **1970** Kidney graft [see *GRAFT *sb.*[1] 3]. **1966** *Daily Tel.* 28 Sept. 19/4 Kidney patients would be able to use an artificial kidney machine in their own homes. **1972** *Guardian* 9 Feb. 20/2 Patients who rely on electrical machinery (such as kidney machines) in their homes. **1836–9** Kidney-pie [see KIDNEY 5]. **1937** PARTRIDGE *Dict. Slang* 455/1 *Kidney-pie*, insincere praise. **1896** ADE *Artie* i. 3 Artie..gave him a friendly blow, known to ringside patrons as a 'kidney-punch'. **1954** F. C. AVIS *Boxing Reference Dict.* 61 *Kidney punch*, a blow falling at the kidneys—a foul punch liable to result in disqualification. **1964** Kidney punch [see *CAPER *sb.*[2] 1 c]. **1958** *Tararua* XII. 27 The frameless pack..being more familiarly known by that elegant term, *kidney-rotter*. **1971** *N.Z. Listener* 22 Feb. 51/2 Twenty-odd years ago..we slogged along in hobnailed boots, carried 'kidney-rotter' packs, [etc.]. **1893** W. B. E. MILLER et al. *Dis. Live Stock* vi. 410 Various symptoms are popularly attributed to 'kidney worms', especially a weakness or partial palsy of the hinder limbs, inclination to lie down, and awkwardness in the gait. **1905** MOUSSU & DOLLAR *Dis. Cattle* iii. 539 This so-called kidney worm of hogs (*Sclerostoma pinguicola*) should not be confounded with the kidney worm (*Dioctophyme viscerale*) of dogs and man. **1934** H. O. MÖNNIG *Vet. Helminthol. & Entomol.* III. 170 The 'kidney-worm' of swine occurs in the perirenal fat. **1963** JUBB & KENNEDY *Path. Domestic Animals* II. vi. 272/1 *Dioctophyma renale* is the giant kidney worm, the largest of parasitic nematodes... It is usually found in dogs, mink, and other fish-eating mammals, but is recorded in ox and horse.

kid-stakes, kidstakes (ki·dstēiks). *Austral.* and *N.Z. slang.* Also **kidsteaks.** [Cf. KID *sb.*[5]] Humbug, pretence.

1916 C. J. DENNIS *Songs Sentimental Bloke* 124 *Kid stakes*, pretence. **1919** W. H. DOWNING *Digger Dial.* 30 *Kid-stakes*, insincere flattery; inveiglement; a wheedling or deceitful speech or action. **1922** A. WRIGHT *Colt from Country* 201 'It was no kid stakes,' declared Bucks. 'The old man had the roll ready.' **1945** G. CASEY *Downhill is Easier* 138 All his kidstakes during the afternoon had probably been caused by his jealousy of Peter South. **1949** F. SARGESON *I saw in Dream* II. xiv. 154 But it looked as if it was all kidsteaks. **1960** A. KIMMINS *Lugs O'Leary* ii. 17 This isn't kid-stakes... This is deadly serious.

kief, var. KEF 2. Also **kieff.**

1878 [see KEF 2]. **1907** *Daily Chron.* 7 Dec. 3/5 What opium is in China, Kieff (Indian hemp) is threatening to become in Morocco. **1925** *Blackw. Mag.* Nov. 621/2 The sentry..lays down his rifle to accept the pipe of kieff from this same officer. **1971** *Frendz* 21 May 13 Dope... Turkish... Commonly cut with Honey, earth, kief glue & boot polish to make it black.

Kieffer (kī·fəɹ). The name of Peter *Kieffer* (d. 1890), American gardener, used *attrib.* in **Kieffer pear** to designate a variety of yellow-skinned pear (*Pyrus pyrifolia* var. *culta* × *P. communis*) developed by him. Also *absol.*

[**1879** *Amer. Agriculturist* Jan. 21/1 (*heading*) A New Pear—Kieffer's Hybrid. *Ibid.*, Mr. Parry secured the original tree, and has called the new variety 'Kieffer's Hybrid'.] **1880** *Gardener's Monthly* Feb. 49/1 The Kieffer Pear.—A contemporary asks what evidence there is that this is a hybrid between the Chinese Sand Pear, and the ordinary garden variety? **1901** L. H. BAILEY *Cycl. Amer. Hort.* III. 1242/2 The Kieffer Pear originated with Peter Kieffer, of Roxborough, Philadelphia, an Alsatian gardener. *Ibid.*, The Kieffer Pear is now very popular in many parts of the country because of its great vigor, healthfulness, productiveness, and the keeping qualities of the fruit. *Ibid.*, 1243/1 Such varieties as Kieffer and Bartlett are usually classed as self-sterile kinds. **1916** —— *Pruning-Manual* v. 116 Young pear trees, particularly of the Kieffer type, make very long and erect growths. **1948** W. STEVENS *Let.* 19 Aug. (1967) 610, I..asked him to try to find Kieffer pears for me this autumn. **1961** M. W. BLACK in Hyams & Jackson *Orchard & Fruit Garden* xxix. 160/1 Each of the other export varieties [of pear] (Beurré Hardy,..Winter Nelis, Kieffer, Josephine de Malines, Doyenné du Comice, etc.) are tested individually.

kie-kie. (Earlier and later examples.)

1847 *N.Z. Jrnl.* No. 191. 106/1 Passed..through a wet wood of supplejack and kiekie. **1905** W. B. *Where White Man Treads* 16 Aye, and kie kie also, with its two kinds of sweet-meats, both on the same vine. **1966** *Encycl. N.Z.* II. 785/1 The only non-berry fruit of significance was that of kiekie (*Freycinetia banksii*), the flavour of which has been likened to that of a pear.

|| **kielbasa** (kīlbæ·să, ki-). Also **kolbasa, -i.** [Pol. *kielbasa* sausage, Russ. *kolbasa* sausage.] (See quot. 1965.)

1953 S. BELLOW *Adventures of Augie March* xx. 435 All these poor punks..with immigrant blood and washday smells and kielbasa and home-brew beer. **1958** 'RYSIA' *Old Warsaw Cook Bk.* 2 (*heading*) Kielbasa, Polish sausage cut in small pieces and served on tooth-picks with a drink of vodka. *Ibid.* 49 Until the sixteenth century..the preferred meat was..Polish sausage—'kielbasa', or 'bigos'. **1959** *Times* 23 Jan. 12/6 Attaché cases—which must surely contain the innermost secrets of the Kremlin, but which usually turned out to harbour a lump of black bread and a petrified portion of kolbasa. **1965** *House & Garden* Jan. 60 *Kielbasa* or *kolbasi* (Polish sausage), a highly seasoned garlicky sausage. It comes fresh, smoked, uncooked and cooked, but usually must be poached before it is eaten. **1969** R. & D. DESOLA *Dict. Cooking* 133/2 *Kielbasa*, red-cased Polish sausage..often served with sauerkraut.

kierie: see *KERRIE.

kiering (kīə·riŋ), *vbl. sb.* [f. KIER + -ING[1].] Boiling in a kier or vat.

1922 *Encycl. Brit.* XXX. 590/2 A uniform process of 'kiering' (boiling under pressure with a lye of caustic soda) was introduced. **1954** *Textile Terms & Definitions* (Textile Inst.) 22 *Kier boil* (*Kiering*), the process of prolonged boiling of cotton or flax materials with alkaline liquors in a..Kier. **1963** A. J. HALL *Textile Sci.* iv. 162 Kiering and bleaching. In the first [bleaching stage] the textile material is boiled..within a..kier.

Kierkegaardian (kīəɹkĕgā·ɹdiăn, -gōə·ɹd-), *a.* and *sb.* [f. the name of Sören *Kierkegaard* (1813–55), a Danish philosopher + -IAN.] **A.** *adj.* Of or pertaining to Kierkegaard or his philosophy. **B.** *sb.* An adherent or admirer of Kierkegaard's philosophy.

1943 *Horizon* Oct. 260 The great psychological crisis has now been given its actual material content, and one of the most important keys..to the inner Kierkegaardian room, has been found. **1947** *Partisan Rev.* Mar.–Apr. 187 The terminology of the neo-Kierkegaardian, Karl Barth. **1950** *Mind* LIX. 415 What possible appeal..could a Kierkegaardian Christianity have for children? **1963** AUDEN *Dyer's Hand* 444 In some of Brand's speeches, however, there is an emphasis on the human will which is Nietzschean rather than Kierkegaardian. **1964** *English Studies* XLV. Suppl. 243 A kierkegaardian must be struck by the radical and extreme position taken by Pater. **1971** G. STEINER *In Bluebeard's Castle* III. 57 The Kierkegaardian concept of 'total possibility', of a fabric of reality open at all points to the rift of absurdity and disaster, has become a commonplace.

Kievan (ki,e·făn, ki,e·văn), *a.* Also **Kievian.** [f. *Kiev*, a city in Russia + -AN.] Of or pertaining to the city of Kiev, esp. with reference to the historical period (*c* 900–*c* 1150) when it dominated European Russia.

1927 D. S. MIRSKY *Hist. Russia* ii. 8 The golden age of the Kievian political power occurred in the reigns of Vladimir and of his son Yaroslav (1019–1054). **1957** K. A. WITTFOGEL *Oriental Despotism* x. 418 In Medieval Sweden and Kievan Russia the decisive social relations.. never seem to have matured... We may view them as..'marginal' feudal society. **1959** *Listener* 26 Mar. 564/1 The rise of the Kievan State in the tenth and eleventh centuries. **1965** *Language* XLI. 140 A recent study..includes some [foreign] loanwords as borrowed in the..Kievan period.

kieve, var. KEEVE, KIVE 1.

1875 [in Dict.]. **1887** R. HUNT *Brit. Mining* (ed. 2) 910/2 *Kieve*, a vat or large iron-bound tub for washing ores. **1959** *Times* 10 Nov. p. iii/5 Large mashing vessels called kieves from which the wort is drawn off leaving the grains behind. **1967** *New Scientist* 6 July 23/1 The mash is cooked up with water in mash tuns, or kieves.

kiewiet (kī·vit). *S. Afr.* Also **kievietjie, kiewietjie, kiewit, kiewitje, kivit.** [Echoic.] The crowned lapwing, *Vanellus* (or *Stephanibyx*) *coronatus*.

1785 G. FORSTER tr. *Sparrman's Voy. Cape Good Hope* I. iv. 153 Flocks of *keuvitts*..towards the dusk of the evening, screamed out a disagreeable sound resembling that of the name they bear. **1818** C. I. LATROBE *Jrnl. Visit S. Afr.* vi. 131 Some kivits, or plovers, were the only birds.. we saw, during several hours' ride. **1867** E. L. LAYARD *Birds S. Afr.* 294 The 'Kiewit' makes known its presence by its loud plaintive call. **1896** H. A. BRYDEN *Tales S. Afr.* 121 The cry of one or two night birds may be heard—the dikkop and kiewitje plovers. **1936** E. L. GILL *First Guide S. Afr. Birds* 139 Crowned Lapwing, Kiewiet; *Stephanibyx coronatus*. The commonest and most generally distributed of the dry-land plovers in South Africa. **1939** [see *DIKKOP 1]. **1957** MCLACHLAN & LIVERSIDGE *Roberts's Birds S. Afr.* 131 Crowned plover. Kiewietjie... Widespread but local all over South Africa to north-eastern Africa. **1964** P. A. CLANCEY *Birds Natal & Zululand* 156 *Vanellus coronatus*... Not normally shy, but extremely vociferous, uttering a harsh cry which has given rise to its local name of 'kiewit'. **1974** *Eastern Province Herald* (S. Afr.) 7 Nov. 5 The wide-eyed appearance of this 'kiewietjie' yesterday, nesting on a lawn.., is understandable after it had to sit through the surrounding Guy Fawkes celebrations this week.

kif, var. KEF 2. Cf. *KIEF.

1880 BENTLEY & TRIMEN *Medicinal Plants* IV. § 231 In Algeria the Hemp is cultivated under the name of Kif. **1938** *Mr.* (N.Y.) Dec. 117/1 In one corner two Arabs were sitting quietly smoking, and the smell of *kif* (hashish) was in the air. **1960** *Spectator* 29 July 176 He lived longest in Tangier, in a room in the Medina where he cooked hashish candy..crouched in a Reich orgone box smoking kif. **1962** *Ibid.* 3 Aug. 165 The triumphs of various kif (hashish) smokers over their persecutors. **1963** T. TULLETT *Inside Interpol* iv. 45 Hashish..is generally smoked in a 'kif' pipe. **1969** [see *DAGGA[1]].

kijaat, var. *KIAAT.

kijang: see *KIDANG.

kike (kəik). *slang* (orig. *U.S.*). [Said to be an alteration of *-ki* (or *-ky*), a common ending of the personal names of Eastern European Jews who emigrated to the U.S. at the turn of the 20th c.] A vulgarly offensive name for a Jew. Also *attrib.* or as *adj.*

1904 R. L. MCCARDELL *Show Girl & her Friends* 49 And what do you think? He had the impudence to tell me that Louie Zinsheimer was a kike! **1912** *McClure's Mag.* XXXIX. 230/2 'It's a mascot, be-dad! Jam it, ye kike!' screeched Tracy. **1919** F. HURST *Humoresque* 211 A little red-haired kike like her! **1919** MENCKEN *Amer. Lang.* 115 An Englishman..knows nothing of our common terms of disparagement, such as *kike*..and *rube*. **1924** P. MARKS *Plastic Age* xviii. 201 You go chasing around with kikes and micks. **1932** J. DOS PASSOS *1919* 164 The little kike behind the desk had never been to sea. **1940** R. STOUT *Over my Dead Body* vi. 84, I don't care if the background is wop or mick or kike..so long as it's American. **1956** D. KARP *All Honorable Men* 74 If you repeat that lie, I'll wring that skinny kike neck of yours with my own hands! **1963** V. NABOKOV *Gift* iii. 179 My better half..was for twenty years the wife of a kike and got mixed up with a whole rabble of Jew in-laws. **1963** *Spectator* 21 June 815 He knocks down Stern's wife, calls her a kike. **1972** *National Observer* (U.S.) 27 May 17/3 When kikes are shrewd and dagos or wops are sly and murderous, it is only one step from the epithet to contempt.

|| **kikoi** (kikoi·). [Swahili.] In East Africa, a striped cloth of distinctive design with an end fringe, worn round the waist. Also *attrib.*

1942 *E. Afr. Ann. 1941–2* 27/1 His loin-cloth, 'kikoi', was edged with stripes of red, black and yellow, and showed below his shirt. **1970** *Vogue* Jan. 96/4 Mwembe Tayari is a lively, open free-for-all, with *kikois* (Arab-style sarongs), beaded jackets..and handicrafts. **1971** *Daily Nation* (Nairobi) 10 Apr. 5/1 (Advt.), Kikoy Shirts and Dresses.

Kikuchi (kiku·tʃi). *Physics.* [Name of Seishi *Kikuchi* (b. 1902), Japanese physicist, who first observed the lines.] *Kikuchi line*: each of a series of lines in electron diffraction patterns which are attributed to the elastic scattering of previously inelastically scattered electrons and may be used to determine the orientation of crystalline specimens; so *Kikuchi pattern*.

1934 *Physical Rev.* XLV. 43/1 The [electron scattering] patterns from stibnite consist of spots, Kikuchi lines, bands, circles and parabolas. **1948** *Proc. Physical Soc.* LX. 343 The elementary diffraction theory for single scattering also leads to a Kikuchi-line breadth proportional to the corresponding plane spacing *d*/*n*. **1966** D. G. BRANDON *Mod. Techniques Metallogr.* ii. 113 Kikuchi line patterns can be used to give a more accurate estimate of the specimen orientation than can be determined from the normal spot pattern. **1968** *Mineral. Abstr.* XIX. 83/2 A simplified stereographic projection from a Kikuchi pattern is used to determine the orientation of a crystal. **1970** *New Scientist* 23 July 176/2 Kikuchi patterns, well known to users of the transmission electron microscope.

Kikuyu (kikū·yū). [Native name.] **a.** The name of an agricultural Negro people, the largest Bantu-speaking group in Kenya; a member of this people; the language they speak. Also *attrib.* or as *adj.*

1894 N. BELL tr. *L. von Höhnel's Discovery Lakes Rudolf & Stefanie* II. vi. 298 Our attention was called to another party of about forty natives approaching us... Whether they were Masai or Kikuyu neither we nor our guide could tell, so the Count went off with one or two of our Kikuyu friends to ascertain. **1904** H. HINDE *Vocab. Kamba & Kikuyu Lang.* p. v, Both the Kamba and Kikuyu languages belong to the Bantu group and their construction is precisely similar to that of Swahili. *Ibid.* p. xviii, It is not unfrequent, in general conversation, both in Kamba and Kikuyu, to ignore the conjugated forms of the verb. **1911** J. G. FRAZER *Golden Bough: Magic Art* (ed. 3) I. iii. 76 This curious pretence of being born again regularly formed part of the initiatory rites through which every Kikuyu lad and every Kikuyu girl had to pass before he or she was recognised as a full-grown member of the tribe. **1920** *New Statesman* 10 July 391/1 The Kikuyu, bending over their cultivated plots. **1935** E. HEMINGWAY *Green Hills Afr.* (1936) III. i. 173 Kamau, the driver, was a Kikuyu. **1936** *Discovery* June 195/1 Brought up to speak Kikuyu from childhood. **1950** D. JONES *Phoneme* 20 In one form of the Kikuyu language of Kenya the sounds ϕ, β and b appear to be..constituting a single phoneme. **1955** *Times* 7 June 6/5 The weakening of the Mau Mau is most noticeable to the east of Mount Kenya, where its Meru and Embu supporters are less determined than the Kikuyus. **1958** *Times* 8 Jan. 6/7 After warnings in Kikuyu had been given over a loudhailer and ignored, the staff opened fire on the rioters' barricade. **1967** M. J. COE *Ecol. Alpine Zone Mt. Kenya* 1 Kikuyu folk-lore tells how, when the earth was formed, a man named Mogai made a great mountain. **1973** *Nature* 11 May 107/1 At Cambridge he studied Modern French, Medieval French and Kikuyu for Part 1 of the Tripos.

b. Kikuyu grass, a creeping perennial grass, *Pennisetum clandestinum*, native to the highlands of Kenya, and cultivated elsewhere as a lawn and fodder grass.

1913 *Rep. Dept. Agric. Union S. Afr. 1910–11* 241 Kikuyu grass...We received in good condition a rooted plant of the Kikuyu-grass of British East Africa. This has been planted out and has made vigorous growth; it has not yet flowered, and I am therefore unable to name it. **1921** *Kew Bull.* 85 (*heading*) Kikuyu grass. *Ibid.* 93 Kikuyu grass in the presence of water will put on top-growth. **1934** *Bulletin* (Sydney) 31 Oct. 22/2 Now is the time in N.S.W. to plant Kikuyu grass, which is suitable to any class of soil that is not binding. **1951** Edwards & Bogdan *Important Grassland Plants of Kenya* II. 62 In the Highland Forest regions Kikuyu grass occupies the land for a period following clearance of the forest climax. **1970** W. Smith *Gold Mine* xxviii. 67 Rod escorted the Steyners down across the vivid green lawns of Kikuyu grass.

c. A controversy in the Anglican Church, which first arose at the Kikuyu Conference of 1913, regarding the admissibility to Holy Communion of the members of other Christian churches. Also *attrib.*

1914 H. Henson (*title*) The issue of Kikuyu. **1915** C. Kelway *Story of Kikuyu* 8 The mission field is, in fact, full of potential 'Kikuyus'..the vital questions which emerge from the Kikuyu Conference. **1915** L. Pullan *Missionary Princ. & Primate on Kikuyu* 31 This pronouncement on the Kikuyu question is considered official. **1965** S. Neill *Anglicanism* (ed. 3) xiii. 366 The years after the First World War introduced a new period of more dramatic possibilities and intenser strains. The trouble started with the Kikuyu controversy.

‖ **kikyo** (kī·kyo). Also **kikiyo, kikuyo.** [Jap.] A local name for *Platycodon grandiflorum*, a herbaceous perennial of the family Campanulaceæ, native to China and Japan; the Chinese bell-flower.

1884 tr. *J. J. Rein's Japan* I. vii. 145 The splendid blue-flowered Kikiyo (Platycodon grandiflorum DC.)..appear in numbers only at a height of about 1,000 metres. **1899** L. Hearn *In Ghostly Japan* ii. 15 The crest upon the robe was the *kikyō*-flower. **1911** *Encycl. Brit.* XV. 162/1 If some familiar European flowers are absent, they are replaced by others strange to Western eyes..the *kikyo* (*Platycodon grandiflorum*). **1965** J. Ohwi *Flora Japan* 853/1 *Platycodon grandiflorum*... Kikyō... Frequently planted as an ornamental and for medicine.

kilch (kilʃ). [Swiss German *kilch.*] The Swiss name for a small whitefish, *Coregonus pidschian*, found in northern Europe, Asia, and Canada.

1881 K. Semper *Nat. Conditions of Existence* 320 The little fish of the Lake of Constance known as the Kilch. **1931** J. R. Norman *Hist. Fishes* ix. 175 One of the White-fishes (*Coregonus*), an important food-fish of Lake Constance, known locally as the Kilch. **1962** D. W. Tucker tr. *Sterba's Freshwater Fishes of World* 56 The following may be kept successfully...the Blaufelchen or Grosse Schweberenke (*Coregonus wartmanni* Bloch) from the lakes of the Voralpen, and even the very rare Kleine Schweberenke or Kilch (*Coregonus acronius* Rapp).

kilchoanite (kilχōu·ănəit). *Min.* [f. *Kilchoan*, the name of the village in Strathclyde near which it was first found + -ITE[1].] A colourless, orthorhombic polymorph of a calcium silicate, $Ca_3Si_2O_7$, of which rankinite is another polymorph.

1961 Agrell & Gay in *Nature* 4 Mar. 743/1 A mineral corresponding to phase *Z* has been found in limestones thermally metamorphosed by gabbro at Ardnamurchan, Scotland, and Carlingford, Eire. It has been named kilchoanite after the village in Ardnamurchan near where it was first found. *Ibid.*, Kilchoanite has always been found as a replacement of rankinite and no crystal form has been observed. **1969** *Mineral. Mag.* XXXVII. 517 Two polymorphs of tricalcium disilicate, rankinite and kilchoanite, have been discovered near Tokatoka, New Zealand. **1969** *Trans. Brit. Ceramic Soc.* LXVIII. 225/1 The morphology of synthetic kilchoanite made at ~200°C, as revealed by transmission electron microscopy, is platy with a characteristic lozenge shape.

kiley. *Austral.* [var. KYLIE.] = *BAT *sb.*[2] 3 e.

1945 [see *BAT *sb.*[2] 3 e].

kilhig (ki·lhig). *U.S. Logging.* Also **killig.** [Origin unknown.] A short stout pole used as a lever or brace to direct the fall of a tree.

1905 *Terms Forestry & Logging* (U.S. Dept. Agric. Bureau Forestry) *Kilhig*, a short stout pole used as a lever or brace to direct the fall of a tree (N.W.). **1913** R. C. Bryant *Logging* 83 Kilhig or sampson...It consists of a pole..either sharpened or armed on one end with a spike. **1971** F. C. Ford-Robertson *Terminol. Forest Sci.* 148/2 *Killig* (USA), *Pushpole* (Cw), a stout pole, sometimes notched into the tree stem at one end and braced against the base of a peavey handle at the other, used to push a small tree manually in the desired direction of fall.

kilian (ki·liăn). *Ice-dancing.* Also **killian.** [Origin unknown.] A fast ice-dance executed by a pair of skaters side by side.

1935 *Skating* Dec. 34 The Killian is one of the new English dances and has been described by Mrs. Willie Frick. It is a fast tenstep, done side by side. **1936** *Skating Rev.* III. 13 The lady's mohawk is an ordinary.. mohawk, right foot crossed behind, and not as done in the Kilian, crossed in front. **1938** T. D. Richardson *Ice Rink Skating* vii. 50 The Kilian is a delightful dance, but is strictly more of a pair skating step. **1941** *U.S. Figure Skating Assoc. Rulebk. 1940–41* 76 The Killian is of Austrian origin. It analyzes as a snappy side by side Man's Fourteenstep—using a choctaw in place of a spread eagle turn. **1962** *Times* 3 Mar. 3/5 A fine tango by the British champions..enabled them to make up ground which they had lost on the kilian. **1968** *Daily Tel.* 29 Feb. 13/8 Skating both the kilian and blues with advanced techniques and deportment too impeccable to criticise, Ford and Miss Towler look well set for a third successive victory in tomorrow's free style.

Kilim (kilī·m). Also **Kelim, Khilim.** [Turk., f. Pers. *kilīm.*] In full *Kilim carpet, rug*, etc. A pileless woven carpet, rug, etc., made in Turkey, Kurdistan, and neighbouring areas.

1881 C. C. Harrison *Woman's Handiwork* III. 139 A Kelim rug..may be bought at a reasonable price..to lay before the fire. **1884** J. R. G. Griffitt *Turkey Carpets & their Manufacture* 12 Carpets without a pile, known as Kilims. *Ibid.*, The Oushak Kilims..differ from the many varieties of Kilims made by the Nomad tribes throughout Asia-Minor. **1895** *Brit. Warehouseman* Feb. 25/2 Arabian 'Kelims' or hand-woven woollen tent hangings. **1900** J. K. Mumford *Oriental Rugs* (1901) Pl. XXIII (*caption*), The real color value of Khilims must become very clear to everyone who sees this plate. **1923** *Daily Mail* 27 June 14 The heavier Kurdish Kelim rugs make the best floor covering. **1926** T. E. Lawrence *Seven Pillars* (1935) II. xix. 124 Feisal would buckle on his ceremonial dagger and walk across to the reception tent, which was floored with two horrible kilims. **1931** A. U. Dilley *Oriental Rugs & Carpets* i. 4 Theoretically, the product of this weaving was flat-surfaced, and would be classified by us as khilim or tapestry. **1960** S. Foot *Emergency Exit* xiv. 113 The front hall, with its gay Kelims. **1967** [see **goat hair*]. **1972** *Vogue* Jan. 10/2 Kurdish Kelim rugs from £22. **1972** *Country Life* 3 Feb. 258/3 A fine collection of woven goods and felts: carpets, Kilims, tent bands.

Kilkenny (kilke·ni). Name of a county and city in Leinster in the Republic of Ireland, used *attrib.*, as in **Kilkenny cat,** one of a pair of cats fabled to have fought until only their tails remained; *transf.*, of combatants who fight until they annihilate each other; so *Kilkenny fight.* Also **Kilkenny coal,** an Irish name for anthracite; **Kilkenny marble** (see quot. 1959).

1822 *Hive* I. II. 32/2 (*heading*) Kilkenny cats. *Ibid.*, One gentleman stated his opinion, that a *Kilkenny* cat was, of all other animals, the most ferocious;..'..I once,' said he, 'saw two of these animals fighting..and..drove them into a deep saw-pit, and..left them to their amusement. Next morning,..what d'ye think I saw?..there was nothing left in the pit *but the two tails and a bit of flue*.' **1849** *Pict. Guide Birmingham* 162 Whatever may be the ultimate fate of the combatants—and it once seemed likely to be that of the Kilkenny cats. **1861** Mrs. Beeton *Bk. Househ. Managem.* 33 Of *coal* there are various species: as, pit, culm, slate, cannel, Kilkenny, sulphurous, bovey, jet, &c. **1900** J. London *Let.* 2 May (1966) 105 If Russia and England played the Kilkenny cat act, there would be peace in the world. **1901** *Graphic* LXIV. 288/1 The fate of the Kilkenny cats will meanwhile have overtaken the villains. **1910** *Encycl. Brit.* II. 105/2 Other terms [for anthracite]..are ..'blind coal' in Scotland, and 'Kilkenny coal' in Ireland. **1930** F. J. North *Limestones* 145 Black Kilkenny Marble is widely used. **1931** *Sun* (Baltimore) 7 Mar. 8/2 He has been in the center of a good old-fashioned Democratic kilkenny fight. **1931** *Times Lit. Suppl.* 23 July 578/2 All these excitable disputants have disappeared like the Kilkenny cats through the excess of their own zeal. **1959** *Chambers's Encycl.* VIII. 217/1 The Kilkenny marbles are greyish crystalline limestones which become deep blue or black on polishing. **1970** I. Origo *Images & Shadows* ii. 40 The home of my mother's Anglo-Irish parents..was an Italianate house built towards the end of the eighteenth century of the grey local limestone known as 'Kilkenny marble'. **1972** *Guardian* 10 Mar. 1/3 Mr Heath and Mr Wilson..guard the rival despatch boxes with the mutual respect and tolerance of a pair of Kilkenny cats.

kill, *sb.*[1] Add: **2. b.** Phr. *in at the kill*: present at the killing of an animal; also *transf.* and *fig.*

1814 Prince William *Let.* 18 Feb. in P. Ziegler *King William IV* (1971) ix. 115 The game is up with Bonaparte and I shall be in at the kill. **1969** *Amer. Heritage Dict.* s.v., *In at the kill*, present at the moment of triumph.

c. *Lawn Tennis* and *Rackets.* The striking of a ball in such a way that it cannot be returned. Cf. Kill *v.* 7 a.

1903 *Westm. Gaz.* 31 Aug. 8/1 Grant put in some mighty 'kills' from the service line. **1908** *Baily's Mag.* June 483/1 They both of them fairly bombarded the wall, often.. bringing off beautifully low 'kills'. **1920** W. T. Tilden *Lawn Tennis* 87 The server covers and strives for a kill at once. **1969** *New Yorker* 14 June 68/2 Graebner delivers a Wagnerian kill. The ball digs a hole in the turf near Ashe's left foot.

d. The destruction or putting out of action of an enemy aircraft, submarine, etc.; the aircraft, etc., so destroyed. *colloq.*

1944 *Times* 7 Mar. 2/3 The men of this station..can show plenty of evidence of 'kills'. **1951** N. Monsarrat *Cruel Sea* v. vi. 360 But this was to be no swift kill: perhaps, indeed, it was to be no kill at all. **1962** *Daily Tel.* 20 July 1 (*headline*) Atlas rocket 'kill' by anti-missile. **1969** G. Macbeth *War Quartet* 60 We had sailed five weeks Without a kill. **1971** *Daily Tel.* 22 Nov. 7 (*caption*) Mr H. M. Stephen..examining..parts of a Messerschmitt 109 fighter which, as a pilot officer, he shot down on Nov. 30, 1940, while operating from Biggin Hill. It was the war-time base's 600th 'kill'.

e. *Boxing.* (See quots.) *colloq.*

1950 J. Dempsey *Championship Fighting* xxv. 200 His opponent will be after him quickly for 'the kill'—for the knockout. **1954** F. C. Avis *Boxing Reference Dict.* 61 *Kill*, a knock out.

4. kill ratio *U.S.*, the proportion of casualties on each side in a military action.

1968 *N.Y. Times* 11 Aug. 1. 3 Those Nigerians who had escaped the cross-fire had fled northward into the forest, leaving behind 41 dead, the Biafrans said. They put their own losses at three killed and a dozen wounded. The lieutenant was pleased with the kill ratio. **1973** *New Yorker* 17 Feb. 89/1 Our military..can produce sickeningly effective 'kill ratios'.

kill, *v.* Add: **2. b.** *kill out* (later examples).

1966 R. M. Lockley *Grey Seal, Common Seal* x. 147 In New Zealand I saw how the red deer are killing out the young native forest trees in the South Island Alps. **1970** *New Scientist* 31 Dec. 576/1 Broilers are 'killed out' at eight weeks. **1972** *Country Life* 30 Nov. 1504/2 These small birds [*sc.* turkeys]..are killed out at 10–12 weeks of age.

e. Also, *to kill out.*

1950 *N.Z. Jrnl. Agric.* Apr. 364/1 The Southdown has the advantage over the Leicester in that its progeny are quicker maturing and kill out at prime weight and at an earlier age (3 to 4 months). **1971** *Country Life* 30 Dec. 1857/3 Limousin-sired fat cattle killed out at 68 per cent; far above our national average for our native breeds.

3. d. To consume; to eat or drink; *spec.* to empty (a bottle of liquor). *colloq.* (orig. *U.S.*).

1833 *Sk. & Eccentr. D. Crockett* xi. 145, I can kill more lickur..and cool out more men than any man you can find in all Kentucky. **1887** *Lantern* (New Orleans) 20 Aug. 2/2 The lady had killed a dozen [oysters]. **1934** J. T. Farrell *Young Manhood* xviii. 291 'We'll drink to that,' said Fat. They killed the bottle. **1967** N. Fitzgerald *Affairs of Death* vii. 125 We drank with maudlin solemnity to Stella's memory, killing the bottle in the process.

e. In printing or journalism, to cancel or delete (matter) before publication; to discard (type); to suppress or deny (a story, etc.). *colloq.* (orig. *U.S.*).

1865 *Wilkes' Spirit of Times* 16 Dec. 256/1 Two galleys of equal length, one being marked 'Must', the other 'Kill this'. **1887** *Courier-Journal* (Louisville, Ky.) 29 Jan. 5/4 Please kill the deer story sent by Associated Press this morning. **1903** E. L. Shuman *Pract. Journalism* 62 The editor can make room by killing the last paragraphs of the other stories. **1929** [see *copy-desk* s.v. *copy *sb.* C]. **1938** E. Waugh *Scoop* II. i. 133 We're killing this story... Go round to the Press Bureau and have Benito issue an official *dementi*. **1967** Karch & Buber *Offset Processes* ii. 40 'Dead' ads are killed. **1972** *Human World* May 75 This is a dull and confused book. (We killed our review of it as not worth the space.)

f. To turn off or stop (an engine, esp. the motor of a car). *colloq.* (orig. *U.S.*).

1886 *Philadelphia Even. Tel.* 20 Mar., The hose was cut ..and engines killed so that it will take days to bring them to life again. **1907** E. S. Field *Six-Cylinder Courtship* 9, I lost no time in starting. What a blessing that I hadn't killed my engine! **1935** M. M. Atwater *Murder in Midsummer* iv. 41 Jim killed the engine and switched off the lights. **1971** D. MacKenzie *Sleep is for Rich* vi. 196, I moved the hired car into the cobbled courtyard... I killed the motor.

g. *Metallurgy.* To treat (steel when molten) so as to prevent the evolution of oxygen on solidification (now done by adding a reducing agent: cf. *killed *ppl. a.* 2 b); to remove (iron oxides) from the molten metal by this means.

1906 W. Macfarlane *Princ. & Pract. Iron & Steel Manufacture* iv. 46 Higher class steel requires 'killing'—that is, it requires to be kept in the furnace for about half an hour..after it has become fluid and it must be poured at a proper temperature. **1918** A. W. & H. Brearley *Ingots & Ingot Moulds* x. 172 When cast steel was made by the crucible process..it was necessary to continue the heating, and..increase the temperature as far as possible, in order to 'kill' the steel. **1926** *Jrnl. Iron & Steel Inst.* CXIV. 407 On account of the titanium alloy being of only 17 per cent. strength, it is not practicable to kill a heat of steel with titanium only. **1940** Simons & Gregory *Steel Manuf.* vi. 31 There are several ways of killing steel. One ..is the addition in the ingot mould before teeming of about 0·02 per cent of metallic aluminium (Al) to the melt. **1969** R. Stephen *Iron & Steel for Operatives* xii. 56/1 All the iron oxide has been removed, or killed by de-oxidation, and has entered the slag in the ladle.

h. To extinguish or obscure (a light); also, to extinguish (a cigarette). *colloq.*

1934 *Tit-Bits* 31 Mar. 12/1 'Niggers' are not men of colour, but blackboards used to 'kill' unwanted reflections from the powerful lights. **1939** *Evening News* 7 Nov. 4/5 'Kill that baby and put a nigger in its place.' ('Put out that small spotlight and substitute a black screen'). **1940** *Chambers's Techn. Dict.* 476/2 *Kill* (Cinema), colloquialism for extinguish lights. **1942** R. Chandler *High Window* (1943) xix. 135 She killed her cigarette in Morny's copper goldfish bowl, speared the crushed stub absently with the letter opener and dropped it into the

waste-basket. **1959** M. PUGH *Chancer* 153 Could you kill that cigarette..? It's smouldering somewhere. **1967** J. WAINWRIGHT *Worms must Wait* lxxvii. 200 The window shattered and the lights were killed almost simultaneously.

4. c. *Theatr. colloq.* (See quot. 1952.)

1933 [see *COMEDY¹ 2 c]. **1952** GRANVILLE *Dict. Theatr. Terms* 106 *Kill a laugh*, to start a fresh line before the laugh evoked by the preceding one has died down.

d. *Athletics.* To put (a rival runner) out of contention in a race by setting a fast pace, or suddenly accelerating. Also with *off*.

1962 B. HEWSON *Flying Feet* xi. 132 Derek..slowed the pace to a crawl, obviously hoping to use his finishing kick to kill off Mike and myself. **1968** G. GRETTON *Out in Front* v. 74 He set a fast pace which 'killed' Heino, who collapsed and retired.

6. a. Also, to convulse (someone) with laughter; to excite, thrill, delight.

[**1856** C. M. YONGE *Daisy Chain* II. viii. 414 Ethel saw Meta in fits of laughing... 'Ethel! you will kill me!' said Meta, sinking back on the sofa.] **1938** C. CALLOWAY *Hi De Ho* 16 *Kill me*, show me a good time, send me. **1942** BERREY & VAN DEN BARK *Amer. Thes. Slang* § 591/5 Delight the audience,..*kill 'em.* **1951** J. D. SALINGER *Catcher in Rye* x. 82, I took her to see this French movie... It killed her. *Ibid.* 83 She killed Allie, too. I mean he liked her, too. **1960** C. DALE *Spring of Love* ix. 176 He kills me sometimes, the things he says. **1971** *Melody Maker* 13 Nov. 31/6 During the Elton John tour in the States, which was a gas, man, we killed them night after night.

b. Delete '(An Irishism.)' and add further examples.

1816 JANE AUSTEN *Emma* III. vi. 106 Nothing killed him like heat—he could bear any degree of cold. **1899** G. W. PECK *Uncle Ike* (1903) xix. 172 'Now wouldn't that kill you,' said the boy... 'That breaks up my scheme to fight the French.' *a* **1953** E. O'NEILL *Long Day's Journey* (1956) II. i. 53 No wonder my feet kill me each night. **1962** J. CANNAN *All is Discovered* i. 19 My feet are killing me anyway and this dam' strapless bra is rubbing me raw. *Ibid.* vi. 140 The 'middy'-heeled shoes which after the long walk along the hot roads had been 'killing' her. **1965** J. PORTER *Dover Two* v. 61 The long cold walk..did nothing to lighten Dover's mood. His feet were killing him.

c. Used in the infinitive form after another verb with adverbial force = 'to a great or impressive degree'; esp. in phr. *dressed* (*got up*, etc.) *to kill*, dressed showily or impressively. *colloq.*

1818 KEATS *Let.* 23 Jan. (1958) I. 216 One chap was dressed to kill for the King in Bombastes. **1845** *N.Y. Even. Express* 5 Mar. 2/4 Mrs. Polk..dresses 'to kill'. **1848** BARTLETT *Dict. Amer.* 194 To do anything *to kill*, is a common vulgarism, and means to do it to the uttermost; to carry it to the fullest extent; as, 'He drives to kill'; 'she dances to kill'. **1862** J. R. LOWELL *Biglow Papers* 2nd Ser. 36 'T was Concord Bridge a-talkin' off to kill With the Stone Spike thet's druv thru Bunker Hill. **1922** JOYCE *Ulysses* 280 Got up to kill: on eighteen bob a week. **1957** N. MITFORD *Voltaire in Love* xviii. 218 Mme du Châtelet..always took the part of the leading lady, dressed up to kill and covered with diamonds. **1970** G. W. BARRAX in S. Henderson *Understanding New Black Poetry* (1973) III. 358 Dress to kill Shoot to kill Love to kill If you will But write to bring back the dead.

7. d. (Earlier and further examples.)

c **1558** *Enterlude of Welth, & Helth* sig. Dᴵᵛ, With kindnes my her ye do kyll. **1582** G. WHETSTONE *Heptameron of Civil Discourses* sig. T4ᵛ, You will kill her with kindnesse. **1607** T. HEYWOOD (*title*) A woman kilde with kindnesse. **1761** G. COLMAN *Jealous Wife* IV. i. 67 You absolutely kill Him with Kindness. **1842** F. A. KEMBLE *Let.* 31 Mar. in *Rec. Later Life* (1882) II. 189 Lord Morpeth..has a..mother and sisters, and really should not, on their account, be killed with kindness. **1898** F. P. DUNNE *Mr. Dooley in Peace & War* 38 'They'll kill him with kindness if he don't look out,' said Mr. Hennessy. **1925** A. HUXLEY *Along Road* 61 The country..has not been killed by the deadly kindness of those who, like myself, are nature's townsmen. **1935** I. BROWN *Heart of England* viii. 84 Now we purge by persuasion that new Beelzebub, the complex, or kill it by kindness.

f. *to kill two birds with one stone*: see STONE *sb.* 16 b.

g. Ironical phr. *it won't* (etc.) *kill you* (or *him*, *us*, etc.): that would not be too much to endure.

1858 TROLLOPE *Three Clerks* I. vii. 130 'We are both used to that, I fancy,' said Tudor, 'so it won't kill us.' **1913** J. VAIZEY *College Girl* vi. 83 Suppose I ask them? Twopence three farthings each would not kill them! **1945** A. KOBER *Parm Me* 123 Even if your father's gonna lay out a few dollars, O.K., so it's not gonna kill him! **1967** 'G. NORTH' *Sgt. Cluff & Day of Reckoning* ii. 16 'You could have stopped in bed...' 'Lie there awake?' 'It wouldn't have killed you.' 'Getting my own breakfast didn't either.'

h. *to kill the goods*: in soap-making, to emulsify the melted fat by a partial saponification.

1885 W. L. CARPENTER *Treat. Manuf. Soap* 167 The boiling, and the addition of fat and lye, must be continued until a small sample..has a tolerably firm consistence... Practice alone will enable the operator to judge of the completion of this first operation, called 'pasting'. In English phraseology, it is called 'killing the goods' or raw material. **1888** J. CAMERON *Soaps & Candles* 82 Saponification, pasting, or killing the goods. **1894** C. R. A. WRIGHT *Animal & Veg. Fixed Oils* 468 The effect of the action of the hot ley on the melted fatty matter is to 'kill the goods'—*i.e.*, to emulsify the whole, so that no distinct layer of melted fat swims up on taking a sample.

Killarney (kilā·ɹni). The name of a town in Co. Kerry, Ireland, used *attrib.* in **Killarney fern**, the bristle fern, *Trichomanes radicans*, which was formerly abundant in the neighbourhood of Killarney.

[**1844** E. NEWMAN *Hist. Brit. Ferns* 313 It has lately been supposed by many excellent botanists, that there are two Irish species of *Trichomanes*,—the Killarney and the Glouin Caragh plants.] **1863** *Fern Manual* 160 It is not only a native of Ireland, as the popular name (Killarney Fern) would lead us to believe, but is found also in many other parts of the world. **1888** C. T. DRUERY *Choice Brit. Ferns* vi. 59 We have been very successful in the culture of the Killarney Fern. **1891** L. T. MEADE *Sweet Girl Graduate* x. 89 I'll take you into our fern-house... We have got such exquisite maidenhairs, and such a splendid Killarney fern. **1910** C. T. DRUERY *Brit. Ferns* 257 In Ireland it has been found so frequently as to have acquired the popular name of the Killarney Fern. **1960** P. TAYLOR *Brit. Ferns & Mosses* 88 The Killarney Fern has a most unusual distribution, being found chiefly in the tropics of the Old and New Worlds, with an extension northwards in Europe to the Pyrenees and Ireland. **1973** *Times* 17 Dec. 2/7 Picking wild plants prohibited in peer's Bill... The 20 flowers are..in danger of extinction... The plants are:..Killarney fern,..Snowdon lily, spiked speedwell, spring gentian, Teesdale sandwort.

kill-crazy (ki·l krēi·zi), *a. colloq.* (orig. *U.S.*). [f. KILL *v.* + CRAZY *a.* 4.] Insanely desirous of killing; murderous.

1942 BERREY & VAN DEN BARK *Amer. Thes. Slang* § 184/14 *Kill Crazy Dillinger*.., John Dillinger, Midwest outlaw. **1949** *Sun* (Baltimore) 1 Dec. 3/4 All the prior plans to kill me have been made by the same man—a kill-crazy man. **1959** G. JENKINS *Twist of Sand* xiii. 280 Scientists don't go kill crazy..just for the sake of one lost species. *Ibid.* xiv. 306, I had no plan. I was as kill-crazy as he. **1972** 'J. RIPLEY' *My Word you should have seen Us* 179, I was pure animal, and kill-crazy.

kill-devil, *sb.* (*a.*). **2.** Substitute for def.: A colloq. name for rum (see also quot. 1846). *Obs.* exc. *Hist.* (Add earlier and later examples.)

1639 J. JOSSELYN *Jrnl.* 24 Sept. in *Acct. Two Voy.* (1674) 26 Captain Thomas Wannerton..drank to me a pint of kill-devil *alias* Rhum at a draught. **1846** *Swell's Night Guide* 123/2 *Kill-devil*, new rum, from its pernicious quality. **1885** *Century Mag.* Apr. 884/2 Rum, or 'kill-devil', as it was everywhere called, was rendered plentiful by the trade with the West Indies and by the New England stills. **1970** M. SLATER *Caribbean Cooking* 7 From sugar came rum, 'kill-devil', the spirit of cane.

killed, *ppl. a.* Add: **1. c.** *Med.* Applied to bacteria and viruses that have been killed or rendered non-infectious, and hence to preparations containing them.

1919 *Med. Ann.* XXXVII. 493 A special series of vaccines have been prepared... They are standardized emulsions in normal saline of killed bacteria. **1925** J. W. BIGGER *Handbk. Bacteriol.* xiii. 152 Workers have found it possible to immunize monkeys against experimental pneumonia by the intratracheal inoculation of killed cultures. **1930** *Syst. Bacteriol.* (Med. Res. Council) VII. vii. 117 There remains a considerable doubt whether immunity..can be produced by the use of killed virus. **1964** M. HYNES *Med. Bacteriol.* (ed. 8) xxv. 385 The killed vaccine [of poliomyelitis] does not necessarily prevent subsequent intestinal infection, but it evokes sufficient neutralizing antibodies to prevent the viræmia which precedes central nervous system involvement. **1964** H. JOLLY *Dis. Children* xvi. 343 Salk vaccine is a killed preparation containing all three types of virus. **1971** BEESON & MCDERMOT *Cecil-Loeb Text-bk. Med.* (ed. 13) 416/2 Killed poliomyelitis vaccine is now used very infrequently.

2. b. *Metallurgy.* Of steel: treated when molten so as to prevent the evolution of oxygen on solidification and the consequent formation of blow-holes (now done by adding a reducing agent).

1884 W. H. GREENWOOD *Steel & Iron* xviii. 425 When the metal throws out sparks or teems fiery, it is said not to be 'killed', and it is indicative of the metal not having been sufficiently long in the fire after fusion, and such steel will yield unsound or honey-combed ingots. **1926** *Jrnl. Iron & Steel Inst.* CXIV. 406 In the application of titanium to killed steel the conditions are entirely different, and a complete absence of gas evolution as well as the maximum degree of deoxidation are generally desired. **1935** *Jrnl. R. Aeronaut. Soc.* XXXIX. 1121 Scientific metallurgists would like to see all steels fully killed,..but economic considerations at present compel the manufacture of rimming and partly-killed steel. **1970** A. CIBULA in O. Kubaschewski et al. *Gases & Metals* ii. 31 Small amounts of hydrogen and nitrogen are detected, and in killed ingots these gases predominate over carbon dioxide.

killer. Add: **2.** In full, *killer whale.* For '*Orca gladiator*' substitute '*Orcinus orca*'. (Later examples.) Also *fig.*

1884 G. B. GOODE *Fisheries U.S.: Nat. Hist. Aquatic Animals* 17 The Killer Whales are known the world over by their destructive and savage habits. **1931** W. G. CARR *By Guess & by God* 89 The British had been developing the mechanical killer-whales since 1904, when, unescorted, a flotilla of A-boats engaged in fleet manœuvres. **1937** NORMAN & FRASER *Giant Fishes, Whales, & Dolphins* xiii. 290 The colour of the Killer is well marked and is distinctive for the species. The back is black and the belly white. *Ibid.* 291 A feature unusual in cetaceans is the great discrepancy in size between the male and female Killer Whale. **1973** R. BURTON *Life & Death Whales* i. 23 Killer whales live in small groups and feed mainly on fish but they also kill seals and other whales.

4. b. A contrivance for killing a large ferocious animal (e.g. a wolf, a shark); also, an explosive implement for the painless killing of cattle, horses, etc. Cf. *HUMANE *a.* 1 d.

1892 *9th Ann. Rep. U.S. Bureau Amer. Ethnol. 1887–88* 259 (*heading*) Whalebone wolf-killers. **1901** *Amer. Anthropologist* Apr.–June 391 Eskimo and Samoan 'Killers'. **1901** *Morning Leader* 18 Dec. 3/7 The deadly instrument known as 'Greener's Killer',..for the painless destruction of old and incapacitated horses, is the invention of the well-known gun manufacturer, Mr. W. W. Greener... The 'killer' consists of a noiseless explosive apparatus resembling a short rifled barrel, which contains a small cartridge with steel-pointed bullet. **1919** T. HARDY *Let.* 7 Nov. in *One Rare Fair Woman* (1972) 187, I am a strange member of the Wessex Pig Society. I accepted the nomination entirely in the hope of helping to popularize the 'killer'. **1968** A. WILSON *Pract. Meat Inspection* i. 1 Cattle are usually stunned by a captive-bolt pistol (Humane Killer). The types usually employed are..3. Schermer mechanical killer.

6. A cow, sheep, etc., that is killed or destined to be killed for food. Usu. *pl. colloq.* (chiefly *Austral.* and *N.Z.*).

1897 I. SCOTT *How I stole over 10,000 Sheep in Austral. & N.Z.* 9 'You know the killers, don't you?'..i.e. the sheep the boss used for his own mutton at the house. **1907** W. H. KOEBEL *Return of Joe* 294 We were to be treated to a portion of a valuable stud ram for supper in place of the ordinary 'killer'. **1931** V. PALMER *Separate Lives* 124 He had put it [*sc.* the bullock] among the herd of killers in the home paddock in the hope that the new overseer might use it for beef in mistake. **1937** *Amer. Speech* XII. 104 As killing cattle or killers (cattle ready for killing) they are inferior to corn-fed stock. **1952** *Coast to Coast 1951–52* 210 One afternoon they had brought in some killers to the yards, and Murray went over to the kitchen for the bucket and the knives. **1972** P. NEWTON *Sheep Thief* iii. 27 The yarding of the killers..was regarded as a tryout for new dogs—with the stench of blood sheep are loth to approach the yard.

7. An impressive, formidable, or excellent person or thing; one who 'kills' people (see KILL *v.* 6 a in Dict. and Suppl.). Cf. *lady-killer* (LADY *sb.* 16). *slang* (orig. *U.S.*).

[**1900** *Dialect Notes* II. 44 *Killer.* 1. One who does things easily. 2. One who recites perfectly.] **1937** *Metronome* Apr. 55 That Zutie drummer-man is really a killer! **1940** *Swing* Jan. 26 *Farewell Blues* is another of those very fast killers. *Ibid.* May 10/3 I'm a killer with my new shepherd plaid suit. **1968** *Blues Unlimited* Sept. 6 'They were going to put out some records, and Luther went to see about it' said Percy, 'his "Dust my broom" was sure a killer.' **1970** *Melody Maker* 19 Sept. 28/6 George Khan has a solo on the up-tempo passage of the same track which is an absolute killer.

8. *attrib.* and *Comb.*, as *killer instinct*; **killer submarine** (see quot. 1955); **killer whale** (see 2 above).

1931 VISCT. KNEBWORTH *Boxing* 78 He [*sc.* Dempsey] had more fighting spirit and more of the sheer killer instinct in him than was in all four of them rolled together. **1960** J. FINGLETON *Four Chukkas to Austral.* vi. 64 Unless Peter May can instil into his men the killer-instinct they so plainly lack, the next two Tests..will be lost. **1973** *Times* 20 Feb. 12/2 Already he has given Oxford a lift with his drive, enthusiasm, attack and killer instinct. **1955** M. REIFER *Dict. New Words* 116/2 *Killer submarine*, a small submarine designed for hunting down and sinking enemy submarines. **1960** *Economist* 31 Dec. 1378/2 The other kind of vessel that the Navy wants to build in larger numbers is the 'killer' submarine driven by atomic power and equipped with vastly improved sonar devices to seek out and destroy enemy submarines under water.

killer-diller (ki·ləɹ,di·ləɹ). *slang* (orig. *U.S.*). [Rhyming reduplication of *KILLER 7.] = *KILLER 7. Also *attrib.* or as *adj.*

1938 *Life* 8 Aug. 56 The hot musician..shudders when he hears Benny Goodman announce his next radio number as a 'killer-diller'. **1939** R. P. DODGE in Ramsey & Smith *Jazzmen* xv. 341 The fast 'killer-diller' arrangement. **1957** W. C. HANDY *Father of Blues* x. 147 My old friend Wilbur Sweatman—a killer-diller and jazz pioneer. **1970** *Melody Maker* 3 Oct. 15/6 The inevitable concessions to the gallery made by the band in some of the more 'killer-diller' specialities.

killian, var. *KILIAN.

killick, killock. Add: **b.** A leading seaman's badge, bearing the symbol of an anchor; hence, a leading seaman. Also *attrib.* or as *adj.*, leading, chief. *colloq.*

1915 'BARTIMEUS' *Tall Ship* iii. 62 He paid for the misplaced generosity of his well-wisher with his 'Killick'. (*footnote*) Anchor. The distinctive badge of a leading rating. **1920** —— *Unreality* II. iii. 115 Picked up my killick. *Ibid.* iv. 126 The sight-setter raised his brows at the red worsted anchor adorning Bill's sleeve. 'Killick, eh!' he ejaculated. **1925** FRASER & GIBBONS *Soldier & Sailor Words* 135 *Killick*.., the lower deck term for the Petty Officers' Anchor arm badge. **1930** G. WELLS *Naval Customs* 91 *Killick*,..a slang term for a 'leading seaman'. **1945** 'TACKLINE' *Holiday Sailor* xiv. 143 Been in barracks for a matter of six months. Killick then, o' course. **1949** PARTRIDGE *Dict. Slang* Add. 1092/2 *Killick-scribe*, a Leading Writer.

killing, *vbl. sb.* Add: **b. killing bottle,** a bottle containing a poison for killing captured insects, etc.; **killing-circle,** the area within which, at a certain range, the charge of shot from a gun is sufficiently compact to kill the game; cf. PATTERN *sb.* 11.

1877 *Encycl. Brit.* VI. 134/2 Beetles when caught may ..be dropped..into what is known as the 'killing bottle', the bottom of which contains cyanide of potassium covered over with a layer of gypsum. **1960** B. K. WILSON *Lovely Summer* ii. 21 He could not understand how his mild-mannered father could trap the butterflies in his killing-bottle with such enthusiasm. **1974** *Guardian* 20 Sept. 17/8 Insects hitting a panel dangling below the tent will fly up into the dome, where they will be anaesthetised by fumes being given off by a killing bottle. **1886** WALSINGHAM & PAYNE-GALLWEY *Shooting: Field & Covert* vi. 94 The charge of a 20-bore is smaller, lighter, and has a less killing circle than has a 12-bore. **1892** W. W. GREENER *Breech-Loader* 148 For ordinary sporting purposes a gun which shall give its largest killing circle at 30 yards with the first barrel, and at 40 with the second, will be found the most convenient of good shots.

2. A large profit; a quick and profitable success in business, etc. *slang* (orig. *U.S.*).

1888 *Texas Siftings* 24 Mar. 13/2 Fred Jarvis..getting $15,000 in The Louisiana State Lottery drawing... Many.. would like to know something relative to the man who was fortunate enough to 'make a killing'. **1912** T. DREISER *Financier* xxx. 340 Railroad securities..were considered weak under the present circumstances, and a great killing was expected. **1938** 'N. SHUTE' *Ruined City* i. 11 I'm a banker, of course. I don't take tips, and I don't make any great killings, but in my quiet way I get along all right. **1959** F. HOBSON *Death on Back-Bench* x. 136 Instead of making a financial killing which would have made him far wealthier and more powerful than ever before, he was going to be worse off than he had ever been. **1967** M. MCCARTHY in *Observer* 30 Apr. 12 Their personal..aim..was to make a killing..in Vietnamese real estate. **1972** WODEHOUSE *Pearls, Girls & Monty Bodkin* iv. 52 If Soapy Molloy made a killing nobody could be more eager to celebrate than Dolly. **1972** *Times Lit. Suppl.* 12 May 544/2 Authors hold on in the hope of making a killing on film rights.

killing, *ppl. a.* **2. e.** (Examples.)

1844 'J. SLICK' *High Life N.Y.* I. xvi. 255 Then the tall man in whiskers would begin to look as if he raly had been a killing critter with the women folk. **1874** L. TROUBRIDGE *Life amongst Troubridges* (1966) 83 She was in her dressing-gown and looked too killing, exactly like those fat chinamen flying kites on Amy's Japanese screen. **1889** 'MARK TWAIN' *Connecticut Yankee* 111 A lecturer.. flooded an audience with the killingest jokes for an hour. **1923** [see *DINE *v.* 1 b]. **1960** M. SPARK *Bachelors* iii. 47 'That's exactly what I expected you to say,' Marlene said. 'I think you're killing.'

Kilmarnock (kilmā·ɹnǫk). **1.** The name of a town in Ayrshire (now Strathclyde), used (freq. *attrib.*) to designate various articles made there, or practices characteristic of its inhabitants; *spec.* **Kilmarnock bonnet, cowl,** a cap resembling a tam-o'-shanter.

1643 *Edinburgh Testaments* (MS.) LX. 292b (D.O.S.T.), Sextene pair of Kilmarnock stokinges estimat ale to fyftie pundis. **1681** S. COLVIL *Mock Poem, or, Whiggs Supplication* 15 He used to take lives With Whingers, and Kilmarnock Knives. **1713** R. WODROW *Analecta* (1842) II. 262 Ther ar some of your Kilmarnock whittles, that, though they look not soe fair on it as your English knives, yet have a better edge. **1789** D. DAVIDSON *Thoughts on Seasons* 84 An honest wabster..Whase haffet a Kilmarnock hood Kept warm an' snug. **1790** A. WILSON *Poems* 72 His fearsome blue Kilmarnock cowl. **1806** J. PATTERSON in J. Greenshields *Ann. Lesmahagow* (1864) App. 46 And some..with subtle wrist, Give to their stane, the true 'Kilmarnock twist'. **1822** H. AINSLIE *Pilgrimage to Land of Burns* 6 The manner in which the whole man was so properly roofed in with the ancient Kilmarnock bonnet. *Ibid.* 31 Flourishing..their 'Kilmarnocks' manfully round their heads. **1828** *Blackw. Mag.* Jan. 40 Kilmarnock bonnets, pixie caps, and mittens. **1833** CARLYLE *Sart. Res.* in *Fraser's Mag.* Dec. 670/1 Even the Kilmarnock nightcap is not forgotten. **1877** J. M. NEILSON *Poems* 49 He..cover'd the bald pow o' Willie Shakspeare Wi's big blue Kilmarnock. **1902** *Daily Chron.* 20 Dec. 5/2 The Scottish team of curlers who have departed for Canada wanted to be rigged out with old-style Kilmarnocks. **1946** *Glasgow Herald* 24 Aug., Having recently taken up bowling, I have heard players saying, 'That's a Kilmarnock one' when a shot has shown evidence that the player was determined to run no risks in disturbing the head. **1949** J. DRUMMOND *Behind Dark Shutters* i. 21 They agreed to pipe a water line from Townhead and put in a 'Kilmarnock well' in the Row. **1951** J. MASTERS *Nightrunners Bengal* ix. 94 The two infantry regiments tried to get the new white Kilmarnock caps to replace their heavy shakos. **1953** J. E. SHAW *Ayrshire* 32 The Kilmarnock bonnet manufacturers strike a specially sentimental note in the hearts of all Scotsmen... It was at one time a national headwear. **1960** H. HAYWARD *Antique Coll.* 157/2 *Kilmarnock carpets*, double-cloth carpeting was made in Kilmarnock from 1778 and three-ply was perfected in 1824.

2. Kilmarnock willow, a pendulous form of the goat willow, *Salix caprea* forma *pendula*, first discovered by James Smith (*c* 1760–1840), a Scottish botanist, and subsequently distributed by Thomas Lang, a Kilmarnock nurseryman.

1854 *Gardeners' Chronicle* 17 June 392/1 The name Kilmarnock Willow was bestowed upon it to distinguish it from the common Weeping Willow. **1869** *Rep. Comm. Agric. 1868* (U.S. Dept. Agric.) 202 Kilmarnock willow (*Salix caprea* var. *pendula*)..becomes one of the most distinct of the hardy weeping plants which we possess. **1892** A. C. APGAR *Trees Northern U.S.* 166 The Goat-willow is the one generally used for the stock of the artificial umbrella-formed 'Kilmarnock Willow'. **1913** ELWES & HENRY *Trees Gt. Brit. & Ireland* VII. 1746 [*Salix caprea*] Var. *pendula*... Pendulous in habit, usually grafted on a stock about 4 ft. high, and forming a weeping shrub, which is known as the Kilmarnock Willow. This was discovered in 1840 on the banks of the river Ayr, and was propagated by Lang, nurseryman at Kilmarnock. **1972** S. C. WARREN-WREN *Willows* iii. 61 It [*sc.* a pendulous variety] is *S*[*alix*] *caprea* forma *pendula* Th. Lang, and is commonly referred to as the Kilmarnock willow. Its branches are stiffly pendulous.

Kilner jar (ki·lnəɹ dʒā·ɹ). The proprietary name of a type of preserving jar. Also *Kilner preserving jar*.

1930 *Trade Marks Jrnl.* 19 Nov. 1777 The 'Kilner' jar... Glass fruit preserving jars. Kilner Brothers, Limited,.. London,..manufacturers. **1972** 'S. WOODS' *They love not Poison* vi. 82 Jenny came through from the kitchen with a Kilner jar about one third full of cream which she proposed to shake until it separated. **1973** *Listener* 25 Jan. 117/2 The old-fashioned Kilner preserving jar lent itself to both wet and dry methods of bottling. **1974** *Times* 16 Nov. 11/1 Old-fashioned vinegar crocks can be things of beauty... You can otherwise simply use a Kilner jar.

kilo[2] (ki·lo). Abbrev. of KILOMETRE, -METER.

1888 E. DOWSON *Let.* 13 Nov. (1967) 17, I hope..that you are now ..laying in a stock of hygiene many kilos from this foggy, pestilent metrop. **1948** G. H. JOHNSTON *Death takes Small Bites* viii. 195 They drove five kilos in silence. **1973** *Evening Standard* 11 Oct. 1/2 After bogging down in the sand by a wrecked tank, we dug ourselves out and hastily retreated a few kilos until we reached a tank laager.

kilo-. Add: **b.** *kilo-ampere, -bar* [*BAR *sb.*[6] 1, 2], *-bit* [*BIT *sb.*[4]], *-byte, -curie, -electron volt, -gauss, -hertz, -joule, -parsec.* Also *kilobuck* (joc.) [*BUCK *sb.*[8]], a thousand dollars.

1901 J. A. FLEMING *Handbk. for Electr. Laboratory* I. i. 68 The standard kilo-ampere balance. **1972** *Physics Bull.* Mar. 152/3 A few calculations, taking into account material and engineering limitations show that the voltage produced is low, say up to 10 V, but currents of kiloampères are readily achieved. **1928** N. SHAW *Man. Meteorol.* II. p. xxxii, *Kilobar*, a name which it is proposed to substitute for the word 'millibar' to express a pressure of 1000 dynes per square centimetre, on the ground that the word 'bar' had been used in Physical Chemistry to denote the C.G.S. unit of pressure (1 dyne per square centimetre) before it was employed in meteorology to express a million dynes per square centimetre. **1971** I. G. GASS et al. *Understanding Earth* iii. 60/2 Olivine Mg_2SiO_4 can recrystallize at pressures of over 150 kilobars to a new polymorphic form called a spinel structure. **1961** GRAY & GRAHAM *Radio Transmitters* i. 3 In the case of the transmission of business-machine or telemetered data, it is more usual to express the speed in bits or kilobits (1,000 bits) per second. **1972** *Sci. Amer.* Sept. 126/3 High-speed leased lines provide a data speed of 48 to 240 kilobits per second. **1951** *N.Y. Times Mag.* 22 Apr. 35 'Kilobuck'..is a scientist's idea of a short way to say 'a thousand dollars'. **1955** *Sci. Amer.* June 126/2 This instrument became the prototype of a commercial spectroscope which sells for about a kilobuck. **1970** *Times* 30 June 22/7 Its storage capacity could be 2,048 kilobytes compared with a maximum of 512 kilobytes for the 360/50. **1973** *Physics Bull.* Oct. 626/1 It has a 64 kilobyte store with 4·8 megabytes of exchangeable disc storage. **1946** *Science* 2 Aug. 92/1 We came to the Project thinking in terms of millicuries and found that we had to face problems of curies and sometimes..even kilocuries. **1968** *Listener* 27 June 828/1 This power package contained as its energy source 17 kilocuries of Plutonium 238. **1950** GLASSTONE *Sourcebk. Atomic Energy* iii. 82/1 One [*sc.* energy unit], equal to a thousand electron volts, called the kilo-electron volt, is represented by Kev. **1971** D. W. SCIAMA *Mod. Cosmol.* ii. 31 The distinction between X- and γ-rays is a somewhat arbitrary one, but..we may take the dividing line to be an energy of 100 keV (kilo-electron volts). **1895** F. C. BAILY in *Rep. Brit. Assoc. Adv. Sci.* 206 Gaussage would be about 50 in small transformers, up to 40,000 in large dynamos. The latter could be conveniently reckoned in kilogausses. **1973** *Sci. Amer.* Oct. 21/1 If the magnetic field at the surface of a continuous-sheet guideway is 20 kilogauss (about the field strength at the pole face of a good magnet), the lift force is 60 pounds per square inch. **1929** *Daily Express* 11 Jan. 3/6 A national common frequency of 1,040 kilohertz (288·5 metres). **1935** TURNER & BANNER *Electr. Measurements* i. 4 Cycle per second. [*Note*] For radio purposes this is sometimes termed the 'Hertz' and a practical unit called the 'Kilohertz' or 1000 cycles per second used. **1967** *Electronics* 6 Mar. 183/1 Since the power is limited, the bandwidth has to be restricted to 500 kilohertz. **1893** T. O' C. SLOANE *Stand. Electr. Dict.* 317 Kilojoule. **1938** *Jrnl. R. Aeronaut. Soc.* XLII. 885 Formation of frost on the wing is accompanied by a rise in temperature which raises the deposit to 0°C. A curve is given showing the energy in kilojoules necessary to remove ice. **1974** *Times* 20 Feb. 12 Each of the colourfully illustrated cards shows a different food, together with its value in carbohydrate, calories and kilo-joules (the measurement that will be used instead of calories when Britain goes metric). **1922** *Encycl. Brit.* XXX. 301/2 The most remote cluster known is distant 67 kiloparsecs or 200,000 light years. **1970** *Sci. Jrnl.* Mar. 71/3 The solar system is located on the mid-plane of the disc 10 kiloparsecs from the galactic centre.

kilocalorie (ki·lǒkæ:lǒri). Also **-calory** (*rare*). [f. KILO- + CALORIE.] = *CALORIE a.

1894 J. H. RAYMOND *Human Physiol.* ii. 166 It is estimated that an average man produces daily 2500 kilo-calories, which is about 100 kilo-calories per hour. **1909** *Cent. Dict.* Suppl., *Kilocalory.* **1923** H. MOORE *Textbk. Intermediate Physics* xxii. 202 The Continental Engineers' Unit is..the kilogram-calorie or kilocalorie. **1969** *Listener* 16 Jan. 67/3 The food intake was very low, 1,600 kilo-calories per head per day, but the population was healthy and apparently active. **1971** *Nature* 12 Nov. 112/3 Moreover, SI units are nowhere mentioned, the traditional Torr and kilocalories being preferred. **1974** *Sci. Amer.* Sept. 162/3 The 'calorie' of nutritional parlance is actually a kilocalorie.

kilocycle (ki·lǒsəik'l). [f. KILO- + CYCLE *sb.*] **a.** One thousand cycles (of an oscillation or other periodic phenomenon). **b.** *ellipt.* One thousand cycles per second: = **kilohertz*.

1921 *Wireless Board List Radio Telegr. Waves* 3 Frequency is expressed in 'Kilo-cycles' (K.C.). **1926** E. B. MOULLIN *Theory & Pract. Radio Frequency Measurements* iii. 73 (*heading*) Interpolated frequency in kilocycles per sec. **1927** *Daily Tel.* 14 June 5/3 The decision of the B.B.C. to adopt forthwith the kilocycle method of stating frequencies instead of the wave-length method. **1950** *Engineering* 7 Apr. 379/2 The high-velocity sound-level recorder...is designed for inputs with frequencies between 50 cycles and 15 kilocycles per second. **1959** R. L. SHRADER *Electronic Communication* iv. 86 A frequency of 3,500,000 cycles can be expressed as 3,500 kilocycles (3,500 kc), or 3·5 megacycles (3·5 Mc).

kilogramme, -gram. Substitute for def.: A unit of mass (formerly also taken as a unit of weight) that was introduced as a fundamental unit of the metric system and is now one of the base units of the International System of Units, being equivalent to approximately 2·205 lb.; it was intended to be the mass (or weight) of a cubic decimetre of distilled water, but in practice has been defined almost from its inception as the mass of a unique physical standard (orig. the 'Kilogramme des Archives', and since 1889 the International Prototype of the Kilogramme). (Earlier and later examples.)

1797 *Jrnl. Nat. Philos.* I. 197 The kilogramme [is] equal to 2 pounds 5 gros 49 grains. **1946** *Proc. R. Soc.* A. CLXXXVI. 171 The kilogram was originally defined by reference to a 'natural' standard, i.e. the mass of the cubic decimetre of water. The material representation of this standard was the Kilogramme des Archives, a simple cylindrical piece of platinum which was constructed in the latter part of the eighteenth century. **1964** H. S. HVISTENDAHL *Engin. Units* iii. 20 Study of the archives of the BIPM [*sc.* the Bureau International des Poids et Mesures] has shown that whilst due to the lack of precision in scientific terminology at that time, the word 'poids' (weight) was improperly used as a synonym of 'mass', the kilogramme étalon was definitely intended to represent the unit of what we now always call mass, and not the force by which that mass unit was attracted to the earth. **1969** *Changing to Metric Syst.* (Nat. Physical Lab.) (ed. 3) 5 The spellings of the units of length (metre) and mass (kilogramme) given above are those used by the General Conference of Weights and Measures. In North America the spellings are meter and kilogram. **1969** *Symbols, Signs, & Abbreviations* (R. Soc.) 22 Kilogramme. **1971** *Quantities, Units, & Symbols* (R. Soc.) 22 Kilogram. **1971** *Nature* 8 Jan. 80/1 A thousand kilogrammes of ice. **1972** *N.Z. News* 26 Jan. 1/5 The prices for all classes of fleece wool showed an improvement of from 10c to 16c per kilogram. **1973** *SI Units* (Internat. Stand. ISO 1000) 20 The kilogram is the unit of mass; it is equal to the mass of the international prototype of the kilogram.

b. An object having a mass of one kilogramme and made as a standard of mass or weight.

1831 *Jrnl. R. Inst. Gt. Brit.* II. 65 The rather unsightly appearance of the standard kilogramme of Monsieur Fortin's making. **1856** *Phil. Trans. R. Soc.* CXLVI. 875 Permission was obtained from the French Government to compare the pound with the standard kilogramme of platinum deposited in the Archives on the 22nd of June, 1799, known as the 'kilogramme des Archives'. *Ibid.* 878 The kilogramme, after having been washed with alcohol, was suspended from the right-hand pan of the balance. **1922** *Nature* 19 Oct. 622 During the nineteenth century.. serious doubt arose as to whether the accepted standard kilogramme [*sc.* the 'Kilogramme des Archives' made by Lefèvre-Gineau and Fabbroni in 1799] actually did comply with the original definition of the kilogramme... A proposal to construct a new standard kilogramme brought the whole subject under review in 1872, and the Commission Internationale du Mètre..decided that the international kilogramme should be a copy of the 'Kilogramme des Archives'. **1936** *Rep. Board of Trade Standards Dept. Comparisons Imperial Standards* 3 The opportunity was..taken to undertake..the comparison of the national copy of the kilogram with the principal standard kilograms of the Board of Trade. **1946** *Proc. R. Soc.* A. CLXXXVI. 172 Some forty or more copies of the international kilogram were constructed. The principal copies ..are preserved at the International Bureau of Weights and Measures, Sèvres, Paris... One such copy, No. 18, designated the British Copy of the Kilogram, is kept in this country. **1962** *Brit. Jrnl. Appl. Physics* XIII. 456/1 The international kilogramme, which is a platinum-iridium weight at the head of an extensive hierarchy of similar kilogrammes, was known to be extremely stable.

2. *attrib.* and *Comb.*, as **kilogramme calorie** = *CALORIE a; **kilogramme-force** (pl. *kilogrammes-force*), a unit of force equal to the

weight of a mass of 1 kilogramme, esp. under standard gravity.

1900 E. BUCKINGHAM *Outl. Theoret. Thermodynamics* ii. 12 The small or gram calorie, in distinction from the large or kilogram calorie, which is one thousand times as large. **1930** *Engineering* 21 Nov. 640/1 Curve I shows the maximum liberation of heat in kilogram-calories per cubic metre per hour. **1951** B. L. GOODLET *Basic Electrotechnics* i. 4 Heat energy is measured in kilogram-calories, one of which equals 4186 joules. **1960** *McGraw-Hill Encycl. Sci. & Technol.* VII. 347/1 The kilogram is also sometimes defined as a unit of force, that is, the weight of a 1-kilogram mass, hence the expression kilogram-force. **1972** *Physics Bull.* May 285/1 The addition of small weight pieces by hand to the scalepan system permits forces in newtons and kilograms-force to be obtained readily.

kilometre, -meter. Also with pronunc. (kilǫ·mītəɹ), prob. under the influence of such words as *speedometer, thermometer*.

kilometric, *a.* Add: (Further examples.) *kilometric guarantee*, a guarantee of gross receipts per kilometre of line conceded by the Turkish government in the late 19th and early 20th centuries to (foreign) companies constructing railways within the then Empire.

1902 *Daily Chron.* 24 Jan. 3/3 The revenues to be assigned for the service of the kilometric guarantee have not yet been specified. **1909** *Westm. Gaz.* 16 Dec. 2/1 The Bagdad Railway (with the iniquitous kilometric guarantee). **1909** D. FRASER *Short Cut to India* iii. 39 A heavy kilometric guarantee was provided. *Ibid.* 45 When the kilometric receipts exceed..4500 francs, the whole of the surplus goes to the government. **1943** *Gloss. Terms Telecomm.* (*B.S.I.*) 64 Radio-waves are classified as follows: A. According to wavelength, in metres... Kilometric 10 000 to 1 000. **1973** *Nature* 21 Sept. 144/2 Urey assumes that the..heart-and-soul of a comet is a solid nucleus of kilometric size.

kilo-stone (ki·lŏ-, kī·lo,stōun). Also **kilostone.** [f. *KILO[2] + STONE *sb.*] = *kilometre-stone.*

1925 *Brit. Weekly* 1 Jan. 342/2 Down the road..a woman was crying with maternal, anxious voice, 'Louise! Louise!' The cry was wafted up to the kilostone. **1936** *Discovery* Feb. 63/2 We dispute the author's recollection of the kilo-stones on the Seres Road [in Macedonia].

kiloton (ki·lŏtʋn). [f. KILO- + TON[1].] **a.** One thousand tons. Somewhat *rare*. **b.** A unit of explosive power, equal to that of one thousand tons of T.N.T. Freq. *attrib.*

1950 J. O. HIRSCHFELDER et al. *Effects of Atomic Weapons* i. 14 It is necessary for about 3 × 10^{24} atoms to suffer fission to release the energy equivalent to 20 kilotons of TNT. **1952** *Birmingham* (Alabama) *News* 24 Apr. 14/5 According to informed forecasts, the new bomb will have an explosive power of between 200 and 300 kilotons. **1956** A. H. COMPTON *Atomic Quest* v. 303 A 20 kiloton explosion (i.e., energy released equivalent to 20,000 tons of conventional explosives). **1959** *Times Lit. Suppl.* 22 May 306/4 The atomic strategy..relies on technology rather than on men and reckons fire-power in terms of kilotons of explosive. **1971** I. G. GASS et al. *Understanding Earth* xxiv. 333/1 The difficulties of discriminating between minor 'background' Earth tremors and the effects of [nuclear] tests of a few kilotons were seen to be formidable. **1973** *Sci. Amer.* Oct. 47/3 One of the aerial bombs, a comparatively low-yield weapon, had an explosive force equal to 'a few hundred kilotons' of TNT.

kilovolt (ki·lŏvōult). [f. KILO- + VOLT *sb.*] **a.** One thousand volts.

In quot. 1861 the sense is 'a milliohm'.

1861 *Electrician* 9 Nov. 3/2, 1 Farad per second = 1 Volt, or unit of resistance. 1/1000 Volt = 1 Kilovolt. **1905** *Nature* 7 Dec. 142/1 The disruptive voltage is V kilovolts. **1927** *Glasgow Herald* 8 Dec. 13 Kilovolt transformers. **1938** R. W. LAWSON tr. *Hevesy & Paneth's Man. Radioactivity* (ed. 2) v. 65 The hardest characteristic radiation known, viz. the *K*-radiation of uranium, has a wavelength of 101 X.U. and requires an excitation potential of 115 kilovolts. **1948** *Sci. News* VII. 103 The thickness of metal which can be penetrated is directly related to the kilovoltage of the X-ray set, and a modern portable industrial unit employing 400 kilovolts will penetrate up to 5 inches of steel. **1973** *Sci. Amer.* Nov. 133/1 Bigger sizes are foreseen, but 10 kilovolts at low current is not attractive.

b. *attrib.* and *Comb.*, as **kilovolt-ampere**, a unit of apparent electric power, used when an alternating current is not in phase with the voltage, equal to the product of an r.m.s. voltage of 1000 volts and an r.m.s. current of 1 amp; **kilovoltmeter**, a voltmeter for measuring thousands of volts.

1909 *Cent. Dict.* Suppl., Kilovolt-ampere. **1933** EDGCUMBE & OCKENDEN *Industr. Electr. Measuring Instruments* xxii. 443 These quantities..are directly proportional to the kilo-watts and the reactive kilo-volt-amperes, respectively. **1950** *Engineering* 6 Oct. 281/3 Automatic control is provided to enable either the power factor or the reactive kilovolt-amperes to be maintained constant. **1923** R. KNOX *Radiogr. & Radio-Therapeutics* (ed. 4) I. i. 45 The kilovoltmeter for measuring the high-tension current. **1971** STERN & LEWIS *X-Rays* xiii. 232 The kilovoltmeter is connected across the primary of the high-voltage transformer.

Hence **ki·lovoltage**, voltage expressed in, or of the order of, thousands of volts.

1933 *Proc. R. Soc.* B. CXII. 366 A kilovoltage of 78 was used..to ensure the production of the characteristic K radiation of tungsten. **1948** [see *KILOVOLT a above]. **1971** STERN & LEWIS *X-Rays* xiii. 233 The quality and quantity of x-ray output for a tube are..not described uniquely in terms of the kilovoltage and milliampere meter readings.

kilowatt. Add: **a.** (Earlier example.)

1884 *Engineering* 17 Oct. 358/1 Professor Koyle thought the term kilowatt sufficiently explicit.

b. *Comb.* **kilowatt-hour**, a unit of energy equal to that produced in one hour by a power of one kilowatt, viz. 3·6 million joules.

1892 [in Dict.]. **1905** *Daily Chron.* 20 July 6/4 If he uses this 300 kilowatts for every minute he is working throughout the quarter, say..720 hours, he will use 300 × 720 kilowatt hours or 'units'. **1951** B. L. GOODLET *Basic Electrotechnics* i. 11 Electrical energy is sold commercially by the kilowatt-hour—1000 watts acting for 1 hour. **1965** OWENS & SANBORN *Fund. Electr.* vii. 366 If a lighting circuit uses 2000 watts for a period of one hour, the amount of electric energy consumed is 2 kilowatt-hours.

Hence **ki·lowattage**, power expressed in kilowatts; also *fig.*

1935 *Daily Express* 5 Apr. 8 A human dynamo of enormous kilowattage. **1971** *Sci. Amer.* Sept. 212/1 (Advt.), There was a time when 'the more, the better' was a national attitude—when a surging yearly increase in kilowattage scored prestige points.

kilp, var. *KELP[3].

Kilroy (ki·lroi). The name of a mythical person, popularized by American servicemen in the war of 1939–45, who left such inscriptions as 'Kilroy was here' on walls, etc., all over the world.

The explanation in quot. 1946 is one of numerous unverifiable accounts of the origin of the name.

1945 *Sat. Even. Post* 20 Oct. 6/2 On the crib hung a hand-lettered sign which asserted: 'Kilroy Slept Here'... Wherever he was, Kilroy had been there and left his mark behind: 'Kilroy Was Here', or 'Kilroy Passed Through' or 'You're in the Footsteps of Kilroy'. **1946** *N.Y. Times* 24 Dec. 18/4 As far as the American Transit Association is concerned, the identity of the elusive Kilroy of 'Kilroy Was Here' fame has been established, and in token of this recognition a street car was shipped today to James J. Kilroy of Halifax, Mass. *Ibid.* 18/5 In brief, Mr. Kilroy's claim is based on the following: During the war he was employed at the Bethlehem Steel Company's Quincy shipyard, inspecting tanks, double bottoms and other parts of warships under construction. To satisfy superiors that he was performing his duties, Mr. Kilroy scribbled in yellow crayon 'Kilroy was here' on inspected work. Soon the phrase began to appear in various unrelated places, and Mr. Kilroy believes the 14,000 shipyard workers who entered the armed services were responsible for its subsequent world-wide use. **1951** *Here & Now* (N.Z.) May 10/1 United Nations forces wonder what the jolly rodger they're doing [*sic*] to do when they reach the northernmost point. Mark 'Kilroy' in the snow and come back again perhaps. **1952** P. ATKEY *Juniper Rock* xvii. 149 Such English as was possessed by the C.Q.M.S. was of a somewhat dated military character... 'Kilroy was 'eah,' said the C.Q.M.S. helpfully. **1962** *Guardian* 27 Nov. 7/5 For a long time Kilroy was the exclusive possession of the American forces. **1966** *Sunday Times* (Colour Suppl.) 4 Dec. 73/2 GI Jargon '*Kilroy was here*', standard graffito. **1968** M. ALLINGHAM *Cargo of Eagles* iii. 48 'A lot of people would like to know where he is just now. I wonder why he left that little pointer behind?' 'A "Kilroy was here" sign..?' **1969** L. DURRELL *Spirit of Place* 162 When I am rich I shall have a memorial plaque placed..on Inverness station..reading 'Kilroy was here—but oh so briefly'!

‖ **kilta** (ki·ltă). Also **kilter.** [Origin unknown.] In India, a kind of wicker basket. Also *attrib.* = made of wicker.

1876 C. F. G. CUMMING *From Hebrides to Himalayas* II. v. 134 Our provisions were packed..in long native baskets, called *kilters*. **1896** S. J. STONE *In & beyond Himalayas* 39 The provisions and cooking apparatus were carried in kiltas (wicker baskets covered with leather). **1901** KIPLING *Kim* xiii. 338 He skipped nimbly from one *kilta* to the next, making pretence to adjust each conical basket. **1927** *Blackw. Mag.* Mar. 312/1 A *kilta* carrying-chair, carried on the back of one man.

kilter (ki·ltəɹ). *Poker.* [prob. var. of dial. KELTER[4].] A hand consisting only of cards of little or no value.

1895 'TEMPLAR' *Poker Manual* 55 Suppose you have an utterly valueless hand dealt you, say for example, deuce, four of hearts, six of clubs, seven of spades and nine of diamonds; this sort of hand is termed a 'kilter'. **1904** R. F. FOSTER *Pract. Poker* 126 The Southern custom of raising the ante on a kilter, and then standing pat. **1948** O. JACOBY *On Poker* xii. 144 There are any number of additional combinations of cards which are given rank in various localities. Some of these are the Dog, the Tiger, the Skeet, the Kilter, [etc.].

kilter, var. *KILTA. See also *KELTER[2].

kilty (ki·lti). *colloq.* Also **-ie.** [f. KILT *sb.* + -Y[6].] One who wears a kilt; esp. a nickname for a Highland soldier. Also, *attrib.* and as *adj.*

1842 D. VEDDER *Poems* 112 In double quick time did the kilties career. **1900** S. R. CROCKETT *Little Anna Mark* xii. 103 Yon's nae lassie! Yon's a kiltie lad. **1902** J. MILNE *Epistles of Atkins* xi. 208 A second Gordon communicates the views of a second Boer also upon the Gordon men. 'The "kilties" are devils to fight.' **1906** *Daily Chron.* 6 Aug. 3/6 A picturesque touch..is given to the town by the presence of the 'kilties' and other regiments of soldiers. **1921** *Daily Colonist* (Victoria, B.C.) 18 Oct. 3/7 (Advt.), St. Margaret Kiltie Dresses for girls 2 to 10 years, in navy, brown, saxe and green, [etc.]. **1927** *Scots Observer* 14 May 16/4 The Kilty piping for money. **1927** H. A. VACHELL *Dew of Sea* 261 She..assured him..that he was the 'kiltiest' boy she had ever met.

kimchi (ki·mtʃi). Also **kimchee, kimch'i.** [Korean.] A raw strongly-flavoured vegetable pickle, the Korean national dish.

1898 I. L. BISHOP *Korea & her Neighbours* I. vii. 98 Wine, soup, eggs, and *kimchi*..were produced, and had to be partaken of. **1898** J. S. GALE *Korean Sk.* iii. 100 We found a Korean hut and, to our delight, dined on rice and *kimch'i* (pickle) once more. **1905** J. LONDON *Jacket* (1915) xvi. 210, I know *kimchi*. It is a sort of sauerkraut. **1925** *Blackw. Mag.* Mar. 320/1 Then five different sorts of *Kimchee*, a horrible dish made out of vegetables which have become rotten. **1951** C. OSGOOD *Koreans & their Culture* v. 85 The women prepare cucumber kimch'i by washing the vegetables, then cutting small pieces off their ends, and slitting the sides in three or four places. **1966** S. MCCUNE *Korea* iv. 33 A unique part of the diet and important for its vitamin content is *kimchi*, an unbelievably 'hot' pickle. **1972** P. M. BARTZ *S. Korea* 40/2 Korea emphasizes pickled cabbage (*kimchi*), hot peppers, and other seasonings. **1972** *Korea Times* 19 Nov. 6/3 With the onset of the kimchi-making season, housewives are concerned about preparing jars in which the pickled vegetables are stocked.

Kimeridge, var. KIMMERIDGE (in Dict. and Suppl.).

Kimmerian, var. CIMMERIAN *a.* and *sb.* in Dict. and Suppl.

1917 E. POUND in *Poetry* (Chicago) Aug. 251 To the Kimmerian lands and peopled cities..came we. **1950** H. L. LORIMER *Homer & Monuments* ii. 52 The description of the country of the Kimmerians..would suit their settlements on the north coast of the Black Sea. *Ibid.* v. 286 The conflict between Kimmerian and Scyth in South Russia. *Ibid.* 306 The result of Kimmerian and Scythian invasions.

Kimmeridge. Add: Also **Kimeridge.** (Earlier and additional examples.)

Although the village name is now spelt *Kimmeridge*, the form *Kimeridge* is current in geological usage, reflecting the former spelling of the name; cf.:— **1933** W. J. ARKELL *Jurassic Syst. Gt. Brit.* xiv. 441 The spelling *Kimeridge* was used by H. B. Woodward.., by Damon.., and by most earlier authorities. The new form *Kimmeridge* was not heard of before Webster and Buckland introduced it in the [early] nineteenth century and seems to have no justification. **1947** —— *Geol. Country around Weymouth* (Mem. Geol. Survey Gt. Brit.) v. 68 Inland towards Kimmeridge village. [*Note*] The name of this village was Cameric in Domesday Book and Kymerich by 1293; by the time of Hutchins' great work on Dorset it had become Kimeridge... The Ordnance map of 1811 (Sheet 16, Old Series) retained one 'm', and so did Damon in his *Geology of Weymouth* (1860 and 1884–8) and H. B. Woodward in '*The Jurassic Rocks of Britain*', (vol. v, 1895), *Mem. Geol. Survey.* In the resurvey of 1892 (Sheet 342, New Series), two 'm's' were adopted and the Geological Survey followed suit in 1898.

1760 *Phil. Trans. R. Soc.* LI. 549 The Kimeridge [*printed* Kimendge] coal..appears in most of the cliffs of the isle of Purbeck. **1774** J. HUTCHINS *Hist. & Antiquities Dorset* I. 194/1 He says the Kimeridge coal, of which I sent him some pieces, is very much like, but not so large as, the Bovey coal. **1814** T. WEBSTER in *Trans. Geol. Soc.* II. 167 Clay with limestone and bituminous shale, containing the Kimeridge coal. **1816** —— in H. C. Englefield *Descr. Isle of Wight* 187 The whole of the Kimmeridge strata, consisting of a series of argillaceous and calcareous layers, are situated below the Portland oolite. **1818** W. PHILLIPS *Selection of Facts Geol. Eng. & Wales* 61 The shale is so bituminous as to form a coaly matter of considerable extent near Kimmeridge, whence it is termed the Kimmeridge coal. **1830** *Phil. Mag.* VII. 198 The manner in which the fossils are disposed in the Kimmeridge clay at Havre. **1855** *Q. Jrnl. Geol. Soc.* XI. 125 The present example from the Kimmeridge shales appears to be a distinct species. **1860** R. DAMON *Handbk. Geol. Weymouth* 54 From the coast of Dorsetshire the Kimeridge clay extends inland, with little interruption, to the coast of Norfolk. **1923** L. D. STAMP *Introd. Stratigr.* xiv. 230 In the upper part is a band of oil-shale ('Kimmeridge Coal'). **1931** GREGORY & BARRETT *Gen. Stratigr.* x. 155 The Kimmeridge Clay varies in thickness from 100 ft. in the Midlands to 1250 ft. in the Wealden bore near Hastings. **1946** L. D. STAMP *Britain's Struct.* xii. 135 Almost everywhere the Kimeridge Clay coincides with low ground. **1967** D. H. RAYNER *Stratigr. Brit. Isles* ix. 303 The thickest sequences of Kimeridge Clay come from Wessex and the Weald;..near the type locality of Kimeridge Bay in east Dorset 1,650 feet are known. **1970** *Oxford Times* 12 June 14 This field was mostly Kimmeridge clay, with some sand at the bottom, and not so intractable as the Oxford clay.

Kimmeridgian, *a.* (s.v. KIMMERIDGE). Add: Also **Kimeridgian.** [ad. F. *kimméridgien* (A. d'Orbigny *Paléont. française. Terrains Jurassiques* (1842–9) I. 610), replacing earlier *kimméridien* (J. Thurmann *Essai sur les Soulèvemens jur. du Porrentruy* (1832) I. 11).] Hence, of or pertaining to this subdivision (which is a stage of the Upper Jurassic next below the Portlandian). Also *absol.* (Earlier and later examples.)

1851 *Q. Jrnl. Geol. Soc.* VII. II. 75 The characteristic condition of most of the Jurassic formations (Sequanian, Kimmeridgian, and Portlandian). **1931** GREGORY & BARRETT *Gen. Stratigr.* x. 155 In places the Kimeridgian becomes sandy towards the top before passing into the Portlandian. **1967** D. H. RAYNER *Stratigr. Brit. Isles* ix. 303 The onset of marine muds at the beginning of Kimeridgian times brought in a period of exceptionally uniform sedimentation in the Jurassic shelf seas of Great Britain. **1969** *Proc. Geol. Soc. London* Aug. 153 It is recommended that the beginning/base of the Age-Standard Stage Kimmeridgian be taken at the base of the Baylei Chronozone at the bottom of bed 26 of Arkell (1947) in Ringstead Bay, Dorset, England.

‖ **ki-mon** (kī·mǫn). [Jap., f. *ki* demon, devil + *mon* gate.] In Japanese tradition, the name given to the north-east, supposed to be the source of evil.

1871 A. B. MITFORD *Tales Old Japan* II. 57 The Temple Tô-yei-zan..faces the Ki-mon, or Devil's Gate, of the castle. **1901** F. BRINKLEY *Oriental Series: Japan* III. iii. 111 Prominent among the ancient superstitions of Japan was a belief that all evil influences had their abode in the northeast, the Demons' Gate (Kimon). **1904** L. HEARN *Japan: Attempt at Interpretation* vii. 144 In almost every garden, on the north side, there is a little Shintō shrine, facing what is called the *Ki-Mon*, or 'Demon-Gate',—that is to say, the direction from which, according to Chinese teaching, all evils come... The belief in the Ki-Mon is obviously a Chinese importation. **1972** *Nat. Geographic* May 689/2 The avoidance of *kimon*, the devil's gate..not a single doorway faced in a north-easterly direction.

kimono. Add: (Earlier and further examples.) Now freq. applied to a similar loose, wide-sleeved garment, fastened with a sash, and worn as a dressing gown, coat, etc., in Western countries. Also *attrib.*, as *kimono blouse, coat, gown, shirt, sleeve.*

The spelling *kimona* is occasionally found.

1886 W. CONN *Japanese Life, Love, & Legend* xii. 134 There were no unwieldy articles difficult to carry, no useless luxury; the *tatami*, the *kimono*, a few musical instruments, a collection of cooking and household utensils constituted the bulk. **1891** A. M. BACON *Jap. Girls & Women* vii. 188 The old-fashioned embroidered *kimonos* which are now entirely out of style in Japan. **1902** *Daily Chron.* 11 Jan. 8/3 Over a soft skirt a silken kimono makes a new looking tea-gown. **1903** *Ibid.* 11 July 8/4 Lightweight canvas cloths..are used for kimono coats. **1908** *Westm. Gaz.* 9 May 13/2 Tailors are trying to get their clientèle away from the kimono line of bodice or of coat. They are weary of it; and no wonder, when one comes to think of the hundreds they must have turned out—kimono blouses, kimono bodices, kimono coats. **1919–20** *T. Eaton & Co. Catal.* Fall & Winter 153 Slip-over night-gown.., short kimona sleeves. *a* **1922** T. S. ELIOT *Waste Land Drafts* (1971) 33 line 137 A bright Kimono wraps her as she sprawls In nerveless torpor on the window seat. **1922** JOYCE *Ulysses* 554 Under the umbrella appears Mrs Cunningham in Merry Widow hat and kimono gown. **1949** WODEHOUSE *Uncle Dynamite* viii. 127 When a housemaid in curling pins and a kimono finds herself in a drawing-room..with her employer.., she should as soon as possible make a decorous exit. **1960** B. LEACH *Potter in Japan* ii. 51 She wiped the bowls..and folded and replaced the napkin in the breast of her kimono. **1968** *Guardian* 13 June 10/2 Kenneth Tynan, in a kimono shirt. **1968** J. IRONSIDE *Fashion Alphabet* 57 *Kimono* [*sleeve*], a sleeve cut in one with the body of the garment and hanging loose. **1970** *Times* 9 Mar. 7/7 The Japanese bride has always worn the traditional wedding kimono. **1971** *Guardian* 28 Dec. 9/3 Japanese influenced dresses with kimona sleeves. **1972** V. C. CLINTON-BADDELEY *To study Long Silence* i. 15 The green kimono wrapped across her bosom.

Kim's game (kimz gēɪm). Also **Kim game.** [Developed from the 'Jewel Game' in ch. ix of Kipling's *Kim* (1901); as *Kim's Game* introduced by R. S. S. Baden-Powell in the Scouting movement.] A memory-testing game (see quots.).

1908 BADEN-POWELL *Scouting for Boys* I. i. 54 *Kim's Game.* Place about twenty or thirty small articles on a tray..and cover them over... Then uncover the articles for one minute... The boy who remembers the greatest numbers wins the game. **1948** 'J. TEY' *Franchise Affair* vii. 73 She has a photographic memory... When we played the Kim game—you know? the objects on the tray—we had to put Betty out of the game because she invariably won... She would remember what she saw. **1972** 'M. INNES' *Open House* II. viii. 74 Kim's Game consists in enumerating as many as possible of a miscellaneous assemblage of objects briefly glimpsed shortly before. **1973** *Times* 1 Oct. 13/1 We can, for example, play Kim's game, looking at a collection of objects on a table for 30 seconds before covering them up.

kimzeyite (ki·mzi,əit). *Min.* [f. the name of the *Kimzey* family (see quot. 1958) + -ITE[1].] A dark brown zirconian garnet.

1958 MILTON & BLADE in *Science* 6 June 1343/3 This mineral..is here named 'kimzeyite'. The Kimzey family has been actively associated with mineralogical developments in Magnet Cove for almost a century... Notably William J. Kimzey, his son Joe Kimzey, former state geologist of Arkansas, and Lawton D. and John Kimzey. **1960** *Bull. Geol. Soc. Amer.* LXXI. 1930 Kimzeyite, $Ca_3(Zr, Ti, Mg, Fe'', Nb)_2 (Al, Fe''', Si)_3 O_{12}$, is a new type of garnet occurring as dodecahedrons modified by trapezohedron [*sic*] at Magnet Cove, Arkansas. **1967** *Amer. Mineralogist* LII. 773 The garnet compositions synthesized include the end-compositions..$Ca_3Zr_2Fe_2SiO_{12}$ (kimzeyite).

kin, *sb.*[1] Add: **9.** *attrib.* and *Comb.* **kinfolk** chiefly *U.S.*, = KINSFOLK, -FOLKS; **kin group,** a group of people related by blood or marriage.

1873 'MARK TWAIN' & WARNER *Gilded Age* ii. 33 No father, no mother, no kin folks of no kind. **1947** S. J. PERELMAN *Westward Ha!* (1949) xii. 153 We managed to unsnarl our respective kinfolk. **1959** *Listener* 24 Dec. 1128/1 They [*sc.* the Bwamba] were organized into self-contained patrilineal villages, consisting of a group of male kinfolk with their wives and children. **1964** MRS. L. B. JOHNSON *White House Diary* 8 Apr. (1970) 103, I had asked Mrs. MacArthur and her son, and the Ambassador and all the kinfolks, to stop by the White House to warm up and have a cup of tea. **1970** *Daily Progress* (Charlottesville, Virginia) 21 Mar. c 2/1 Two willing young women have started 'The Bride's Workshoppe' to cope with everything from choosing a gown to picking up kinfolk at the airport. **1973** *Publishers Weekly* 20 Aug. 75/3 He was always surrounded by affectionate and eccentric kinfolk. **1942** A. R. JOHNSON *One & Many in Israelite Conception God* 25 The conception of the individual may not be dissociated from that of his kin-group (conceived in ever-widening circles of relationship). **1951** R. FIRTH *Elem. Social Organiz.* ii. 55 Differential family growth..affects the control of wealth by kin groups. **1957** E. BOTT *Family & Social Network* v. 117 Bilateral descent cannot give rise to enduring corporate kin groups. **1970** G. A. & A. G. THEODORSON *Mod. Dict. Sociol.* 220 *Kin group*, a group united by ties of blood or marriage.

kin (kin), var. CAN *v.*[1] A. I. Common in written Black English.

Also in many representations of regional English.

1875 *Independent* (N.Y.) 2 Sept. 25/4 I'll bet you I kin ride um. **1880** J. C. HARRIS *Uncle Remus* i. 20, I speck de ole 'oman en de chilluns kin..git up sump'n fer ter stay yo' stummuck. **1880** [see *LALLYGAG *v.*]. **1894** F. D. BANKS in *Jrnl. Amer. Folklore* VII. 148 Ef she can look him squar in de face when she talks to him, den she kin be trusted. **1936** M. MITCHELL *Gone with Wind* v. 77 You kin allus tell a lady by dat she eat lak a bird. **1952** V. WILKINS *King Reluctant* I. iii. 46, I kin 'spicion wat Miz Fell gwine ter say. **1964** J. H. CLARKE *Harlem* 263 Don' sent fer m'gal 'n Alabama, So she kin marry me. **1967** in A. Dundes *Mother Wit* (1973) 272/1 She kin throw 'em out the window. **1973** *Black World* Oct. 58/2 How much kin you like Boston when you used to the Bayou?

kin, var. *KEN *sb.*[3]

kinæsthesis. Add: Also **kinesthesis.** Add to def.: Also, the sense or faculty by which such sensations are perceived; **kinæsthetic** *a.*, also, involving or utilizing kinæsthesis. (Further examples.) Hence **kinæsthe·tically** *adv.*

1939 [see *HAPTIC *a.* (and *sb.*)]. **1942** E. G. BORING *Sensation & Perception* xiv. 532 The fact that such small angular displacements can be sensed at such relatively slow speeds did much to direct attention upon the importance of kinesthesis. **1952** *Dance Observer* Jan. 9 A happy gang of young people being kinesthetically hypnotized by a clarinetist. **1953** H. HABER *Man in Space* 149 Whenever we move a limb or perform more complex physical tasks we rely on the delicate co-ordination of these three senses, and the so-called 'kinesthetic' sensations we derive from them serve as a very effective means of control. **1953** *Jrnl. Psychol.* XXXVI. 51 (*heading*) Kinesthetically guided movements of head and arm. **1955** *Sci. News Let.* 26 Mar. 200/2 Although these children initially learn best kinesthetically, their visual perception eventually develops so that they then learn readily by visual methods. **1958** S. H. BARTLEY *Princ. Perception* xiv. 321 This being the case, kinesthesis is responsible for more than appreciation of muscle position, movement and tension. It is the mediator of general well-being or general discomfort and malaise. **1960** *Aeroplane* XCIX. 804/2 Control is kinesthetic (body leaning) and top speed approximately 20 m.p.h. **1968** F. LEUKEL *Introd. Physiol. Psychol.* vii. 128/2 The general senses are somesthesis (pressure, pain, warmth, and cold), and kinesthesis. The special senses are olfaction, vision, gustation, audition, and vestibular sensitivity. **1970** *Nature* 20 June 1173/2 A species endowed with vision as the chief distance-sense and kinaesthesia (the muscle-and-joint sense commonly confused with touch) as the sense that chiefly guides his movements. **1970** *Motoring Which?* July 111/1 The steering was 'kinesthetic' (..it means that you have to lean over and move your weight to make the craft go round corners).

‖ **kinaki** (kina·ki). *N.Z.* [Maori.] A relish; a tasty or savoury addition to a meal.

1820 *Gram. & Vocab. Lang. N.Z.* (Church Missionary Soc.) 164 *Kinaki*, victuals, added for variety's sake. **1873** T. CHAPMAN in W. L. Buller *Hist. Birds N.Z.* 93 Norway rats..by diving for these freshwater pipis, provide a *kinaki* (relish) for their vegetable suppers. **1878** *Trans. N.Z. Inst.* XI. 76 Fifty years back it would have been a poor *hapu* that could not afford a slave or two as a *kinaki*, or relish, on such an occasion. **1905** W. B. *Where White Man Treads* 17 If his kinaki (relish) were fish, his predatory instincts invented the means to catch them. **1921** H. GUTHRIE-SMITH *Tutira* x. 70 This man's body..was eaten as a relish—*kinaki*—with the fern-root. **1949** P. BUCK *Coming of Maori* (1950) II. i. 110 Less difficulty was experienced in providing the meat complement, or *kinaki*, to go with the vegetable foods.

kinase (kəi·nēɪz, -s). *Biochem.* [f. Gr. κιν-εῖν to move + *-ASE.] **a.** Any substance which converts an inactive precursor (a zymogen) into an active enzyme.

1902 W. H. THOMPSON tr. *Pawlow's Work of Digestive Glands* ix. 160 When a tube was introduced into the fistula, and the succus entericus afterwards collected in separate portions, the amount of kinase in the secretion became steadily less and less. **1903** *Jrnl. Chem. Soc.* LXXXIV. II. 497 When kinase is mixed with inactive pancreatic juice, it forms a powerful proteolytic mixture. **1923** [see *enterokinase* (*ENTERO-)]. **1956** I. L. FINAR *Org. Chem.* II. xiii. 502 Many enzymes are inactive unless an activator is present. The inactive enzyme is known as a zymogen, and the activator as a kinase (if this is inorganic), *e.g.*, trypsinogen (the zymogen) together with enterokinase (the kinase) forms the enzyme trypsin.

b. Any enzyme capable of catalysing the transfer of a phosphate group from adenosine triphosphate (or other nucleoside triphosphate) to another molecule; also used with preceding sb. or prefix indicating the accepting molecule, as in *HEXOKINASE (from which this use derives).

1953 *Jrnl. Biol. Chem.* CC. 187 The enzyme myokinase, or adenylate kinase, which catalyses the establishment of an equilibrium between the three nucleotides, adenosine-triphosphate (ATP), adenosinediphosphate (ADP), and adenylic acid (AMP). **1962** P. D. BOYER et al. *Enzymes* (ed. 2) VI. i. 7 Enzymes transferring phosphoryl groups from ATP to acceptors have been termed kinases, phosphokinases, [etc.]... The term kinase stems from Meyerhof's designation of the enzyme that activates glucose as hexokinase. **1964** FLORKIN & STOTZ *Comprehensive Biochem.* (ed. 2) XIII. 34 A number of special words are used to indicate reaction types, e.g. 'kinase' to indicate a phosphate transfer from ATP to the named substrate (not 'phosphokinase'). **1970** *New Scientist* 29 Jan. 196/1 Elegant methods of joining large oligonucleotide sequences of DNA to one another using the enzymes polynucleotide kinase and ligase have, in fact, been worked out.

kind, *sb.* Add: **8. b.** *the worst kind* used advb. = severely, extremely, very badly. *U.S. colloq.* ? *Obs.*

1839 F. MARRYAT *Diary Amer.* II. 227 He loves Sal, the worst kind. **1877** BARTLETT *Dict. Amer.* (ed. 4) *Worst Kind.* Used in such phrases as..'I licked him the worst kind', *i.e.*, in the worst manner possible, most severely. **1892** *Harper's Mag.* Feb. 437/2, I want something to read the worst kind. **1901** M. E. RYAN *That Girl Montana* xvii. 221 Now that you have got here, I'd hate the worst kind to lose you. **1904** *N.Y. Tribune* 26 June, 'So you want to go to Cuba, do you?'..'I do, worst kind.'

13. c. A literary genre.

1667 DRYDEN *Annus Mirabilis 1666* Pref., Those who write correctly in this kind [*sc.* quatrains] must needs acknowledge, that the last line of the Stanza is to be consider'd in the composition of the first. **1908** H. JAMES *Awkward Age* Pref. p. xvii, 'Kinds' are the very liie of literature, and truth and strength come from the complete recognition of them. **1943** J. T. SHIPLEY *Dict. World Lit.* (1945) 346 *Kind*, term used esp. in 17th and 18th c. Eng. for genre or class of work, *e.g.* epic, tragedy. **1966** G. HOUGH *Ess. on Crit.* xiii. 83 The impetus to the theory of kinds was initially given by Aristotle, who discussed tragedy, comedy and epic as separate genres.

14. d. (Further examples.) Also *kind of sort of, kinder sorter* (see SORT *sb.*[2] 8 c).

1804 T. G. FESSENDEN *Orig. Poems* 100, I kind of love you, Sal—I vow. **1830** *Massachusetts Spy* 6 Jan. 1/5, I was kind of provoked at the way you came up. **1834** C. A. DAVIS *Lett. Jack Downing* 90 This kinder corner'd me, and made me a little wrathy. **1855** T. C. HALIBURTON *Nat. & Hum. Nat.* I. vi. 190, I rather kinder sorter guess so, than kinder sorter not so. **1901** F. NORRIS *Octopus* I. iii. 102 Makes it go down kind of sort of slick. **1963** J. N. HARRIS *Weird World Wes Beattie* iii. 28 He was one of these handsome guys with a kind of ugly expression. **1967** *Boston Sunday Herald Mag.* 30 Apr. 34/3, I kind of want to choose my war since it's my life. **1973** *Washington Post* 5 Apr. B.2 Introducing him as 'my old man' and adding, 'We're kind of a middle-aged Sonny and Cher.'

kinda (kəi·ndă), colloq. shortening of *kind of* (see KIND *sb.* 14).

1912 *Collier's* 12 Oct. 18/2 He..started whistling to himself kinda soft. **1925** T. DREISER *Amer. Trag.* (1926) I. xii. 83 He's kinda soft on me, you know. **1935** 'R. WEST' *Harsh Voice* ii. 132, I kinda like being way out beyond everywhere. **1945** A. KOBER *Parm Me* 17, I feel kinda stuffed up. **1953** A. BARON *Human Kind* 185 Movies, shows, do you get a lot of that kinda thing? **1966** L. COHEN *Beautiful Losers* (1970) I. 72 Thank you, my friend, I guess you kinda saved my life. **1972** *Punch* 1 Mar. 278/2 This some new kinda gimmick? **1973** *Black World* July 56/1 Bop ain't goan bless me no kinda way.

kindergarten. Add: **1.** (Earlier and later examples.) Also *attrib.* and *fig.*

The word was coined by Froebel in German in 1840: 'Entwurf..eines Kinder-Gartens' 1 May 1840 in *Kinder-garten-Briefe* (1887) 132.

1869 *Macm. Mag.* July 221/1 Singing a few Kinder Garten songs with movements in unison. **1874** H. HOFFMANN *Kindergarten Toys* 31 Having become well acquainted with the first Six Gifts of the Kindergarten, children will be fitted to proceed to the more advanced Kindergarten Amusements. **1890** W. JAMES *Princ. Psychol.* I. xi. 443 In kindergarten instruction one of the exercises is to make the children see how many features they can point out in such an object as a flower or a stuffed bird. **1926** T. E. LAWRENCE *Seven Pillars* xxxiv. 195 We kindergarten soldiers were beginning our art of war in the atmosphere of the twentieth century. *Ibid.* lxxxiii. 442 They refused to learn from me..and I could not be bothered to set up a kindergarten of the imagination for their benefit. **1942** *Tee Emm* (Air Ministry) II. 148 We can still do with a few more chaps..but be fit, because this ain't no kindergarten. **1945** E. WAUGH *Brideshead Revisited* II. i. 207 The painted panels of the walls were like kindergarten work in flat, drab colours. **1961** *Facts about Korea* (Pyongyang, N. Korea) 156 For the working women and their children, a great number of creches and

kindergartens are established in factories. **1968** *Harrods Christmas Catal.* 22/1 A kindergarten toy which is lots of fun.

kindergartener, also, a pupil at a kindergarten.

1919 G. A. MILLER *Prowling about Panama* ix. 129 (*caption*) Happy kindergartners, Panama. **1937** D. ALDIS *Time at her Heels* v. 103 The procession would end with the kindergarteners, looking very bustling and important as they hurried towards the little red chairs reserved for them. **1967** *Boston Sunday Herald* 26 Mar. I. 35/7 There will be no school sessions for currently enrolled kindergarteners on that day. **1973** *Jrnl. Genetic Psychol.* CXXII. 255 Eighty children, 40 kindergarteners and 40 third-graders.

2. *transf.* The nickname given to a group of young men with imperialist ideals who were recruited by Alfred, Lord Milner (1854–1925), High Commissioner of South Africa, to aid with reconstruction work after the South African war of 1899–1902. Freq. *Milner's kindergarten.*

1902 *Cape Times* 12 Sept. 6/10 Lord Milner described the nature of the government that was to be set up, which was a Council. He (Mr. Merriman) wondered what sort of rag-tag and bob-tail they would have got to sit on that Council... What did he expect to set up? A sort of kindergarten of young Balliol men—laughter—to govern this great country. **1913** W. B. WORSFOLD *Reconstruction New Colonies* I. x. 259 Mr Curtis was one of the most flagrant examples of Lord Milner's 'kindergarten'. **1958** *Spectator* 22 Aug. 244/3 The ideas of Milner and his dedicated 'kindergarten' about the treatment of the African. **1958** *Listener* 6 Nov. 739/3 Those were the days when the group of Englishmen who helped to bring order out of chaos and to prepare the way for the future came to be nicknamed Lord Milner's 'kindergarten'. **1971** *Oxf. Hist. S. Afr.* II. vii. 331 Locally he appointed young Oxford graduates—'Milner's kindergarten'—to the administrative positions. *Ibid.* 346 To Selborne and the members of the Kindergarten..unification was desirable.

‖ **kinder, kirche, küche** (ki·ndəɹ, ki·rχʸə, kü·χʸə). Also in different order. [G.] 'Children, church, kitchen'; a phrase, freq. used ironically, to denote the interests and preoccupations of a housewife.

1935 D. L. SAYERS *Gaudy Night* xxii. 453 The Nazi doctrine that woman's place in the State should be confined to the 'womanly' occupations of *Kinder, Kirche, Kuche.* **1953** E. SIMON *Past Masters* III. iii. 155 Good heavens! *Kinder, Kirche, Küche,* however you pronounce it. Still..at least you haven't given up smoking. **1963** *Economist* 10 Aug. 519/2 Her countrywomen are unhappy housewives trapped in the home by an ideal of *Kinder, Küche, Kirche* which is vigorously pressed by American educators,..and husbands. **1965** R. RENDELL *To fear Painted Devil* x. 124 He was an awfully *kinder, küche, kirche* sort of person, house-proud, passionately neat and tidy. **1968** R. HARRIS *Nice Girl's Story* xv. 112 As a wife, I should expect you to make it [*sc.* the bed]—*kinder, kirche, küche,* you know. **1970** W. GARNER *Puppet-Masters* v. 40 He subscribed wholeheartedly to Hitler's womanly ideal of *Kinder, Küche, Kirche.* **1970** G. GREER *Female Eunuch* 303 The women students..had not yet formed any clear idea of the disabilities which increasingly encumber women as they move..towards *kinder* and *küche.*

kinderspiel (ki·ndəɹʃpīl). [G.] A dramatic piece performed by children.

1902 *Daily Chron.* 19 Dec. 5/2 An opera..and a kinderspiel are being rehearsed. **1930** *Aberdeen Press & Jrnl.* 28 Feb. 3/2 'Blossom Time', a pretty kinderspiel, was part of a delightful entertainment given..by the Sunday School children.

kindhea·rtedly, *adv.* [-LY[2].] In a kind-hearted manner.

1900 H. C. BEECHING in *Monthly Rev.* Nov. 91 The brass lectern, which the good sister..kindheartedly uncovered for him. **1957** B. SPOCK *Common Sense Bk. Baby & Child Care* (new ed.) 148 Whenever her child has a crying spell in the daytime or wakes at night, she kind-heartedly makes another bottle for him. **1972** A. W. READ in *Current Trends in Linguistics* X. 588 Wentworth (1931) complained that *kindheartedly* was missing from all dictionaries, though he knew it from all sources; it was thereupon inserted into the Merriam–Webster of 1934.

kindred, *sb.* and *a.* Add: **B. 2.** Esp. in phr. *kindred spirit* (see quot. 1950).

1849 GEO. ELIOT *Let.* 13 Sept. (1954) I. 307 She says, 'You won't find any kindred spirits at Plongeon, my dear.' **1898** E. HOWARD *To-Morrow* viii. 83 They can see their way to join with a sufficient number of kindred spirits. **1950** PARTRIDGE *Dict. Clichés* (ed. 4) 124 *Kindred spirit, a,* a person like another in character and temperament.

kindy (ki·ndi). Austral. and N.Z. colloq. abbrev. of KINDERGARTEN.

1966 G. W. TURNER *Eng. Lang. Austral. & N.Z.* viii. 173 If a child eats his vegies as he should, he is soon ready for kindy. **1968** *Wanganui* (N.Z.) *Photo News* 8 June 78 (*caption*) Kindy Ball. Guests of honour at the recent Wanganui Free Kindergarten Ball. **1973** *Courier-Mail* (Brisbane) 4 June 15/6 (*heading*) Off to kindy..at home. A new scheme under consideration by the State Education Department will provide children in isolated areas with a pre-school education... A scheme for 'kindy by correspondence' would be available by the start of 1974. **1975** *Telegraph* (Brisbane) 28 Feb. 12 Self-help is basis for special kindy.

kine (kəin), *sb.*[2] *Linguistics.* [Back-formation from *KINE(SICS.] An isolable element of body movement or gesture made in non-vocal communication. Also *attrib.*

1952 R. L. BIRDWHISTELL *Introd. Kinesics* (U.S. Dept. State, Foreign Service Inst.) 15 Most users of kinesic material will not be able to record and analyze every kine played by the actor in any given situation. **1955** *Etc.: Rev. Gen. Semantics* XIII. I. 13 The least isolated particle with discriminational meaning we call a *kine.* **1965** OSGOOD & SEBEOK *Psycholinguistics* iv. 84 A particular motion or posture of a given part of the organism (facial or bodily) is called a *kine* (equivalent to *phone*). *Ibid.* 85 Various 'minimal pairs' of kine patterns (for example, variations in eyebrow position with the rest of the facial pattern constant).

kine-. Most words of Greek etymology beginning with *kine-* are now commonly pronounced with (i).

kine-[2] (ki·ni), var. *CINE (reverting to the Gr. initial κ).

1899 *Daily Chron.* 31 Aug. 3/2 The British Museum authorities have made arrangements for the safe custody of kinenegatives dealing with events of national importance. **1923** *Chambers's Jrnl.* 603/2 The kinegraph registers the short intake of the breath marking his embarrassment. **1927** *Bulletin* 12 Aug. 14/2 An enthusiast for the kine camera. **1928** *Daily Express* 28 Mar. 13 He has turned the music-hall into a home of kine-variety. **1959** *Listener* 3 Sept. 356/2 Kine-recordings are used in large numbers to help distribution.

kinema (ki·nĭmă, kəinī·mă). Variant of *CINEMA with initial *k* from the Greek original. Now *rare.*

1914 *Evening News* 29 Sept. 4/5 It was my first step in the path of the kinema actor. **1921** *19th Cent.* Apr. 672 Properly handled, the Kinema could be made to endear the two races to one another. **1928** *Western Morning News* 28 Dec., The new kinema on the site of the old Post Office at Totnes. **1942** *Electronic Engin.* XIV. 708/1 The commercialisation of the sound film in the kinema over twelve years ago. **1954** A. CORNWELL-CLYNE *3-D Kinematogr.* 8 Commercial kinemas had only exhibited coloured short films which had to be viewed through spectacles. **1974** *Listener* 22 Aug. 252/1 A period's grandest buildings..indicate a community's current concern: medieval castles..1920s Kinemas.

b. *attrib.* and *Comb.,* as *kinema-camera, drama, film, producer, projection, theatre;* **Ki·nemacolo(u)r,** proprietary name of a method of producing motion pictures in the natural colours by means of revolving colour screens.

1927 *Manch. Guardian Weekly* (Suppl.) 2 Dec. p. xvi/2 The kinema-camera. **1909** *Trade Marks Jrnl.* 19 May 830 Kinema Color... Kinematographic apparatus and photographic films bearing finished pictures in natural colours for use therewith. Charles Urban,..Wardour Street, London; manufacturer. **1909** *Daily Chron.* 3 June 7/2 'Kinema-color', or animated scenes in nature's actual tints. **1914** *Times* 29 Jan. 4/3 These lectures might perhaps be illustrated by kinemacolour photographs. **1918** H. CROY *How Motion Pictures are Made* 288 By the Kinemacolor process colored motion pictures were made of the Coronation. **1949** R. LOW *Hist. Brit. Film 1906–14* iii. 101 As the sheer novelty of colours wore thin the company perforce became more ambitious and in September 1910 it was announced that the first drama in Kinemacolor was being filmed. **1916** A. BAKSHY *Path Mod. Russ. Stage* 221 The kinema-drama raises some of the most fundamental problems of art. **1915** *Truth* 6 Oct. 567/1 A levy of 1d. per foot on all imported kinema film. **1929** *Melody Maker* Apr. 418/2 A mixed programme of kinema films and variety acts. **1921** *19th Cent.* Apr. 672 The Kinema-producers in California. **1916** *Chambers's Jrnl.* 26 Feb. 207/1 [The lamp's] suitability for kinema projection. **1929** *Melody Maker* Apr. 418/2 In nearly all kinema theatres which have been converted from Music Halls. **1932** B. B. HAMPTON *Hist. Movies* xii. 257 Tally..sold his Kinema Theater and First National franchise to Gore Brothers and Lesser.

kinematic, *a.* Add: **b.** *spec.* in *Mech.* Applied to a set of mechanical elements so disposed in relation to each other that the relative position and motion of each is uniquely determined by the relative position and motion of the other(s).

1876 A. B. W. KENNEDY tr. *Reuleaux's Kinematics of Machinery* i. 43 A machine consists solely of bodies which thus correspond, pair-wise, reciprocally. These form the kinematic or mechanismal elements of the machine. *Ibid.,* If a kinematic pair of elements be given, a definite motion can be obtained by means of them if one of the two be held fast or fixed in position. *Ibid.* 46 The whole now forms a linkage returning upon itself... A combination of pairs of elements in this way we shall call a chain, or more fully a kinematic chain. **1915** R. F. MCKAY *Theory of Machines* viii. 92 When one of the links of the kinematic chain is fixed, the chain is called a mechanism. When the mechanism transmits force..it is called a machine. **1957** R. M. PHELAN *Fund. Mech. Design* i. 1 A chain..in which with one link fixed every point in every other link must move in a definite path is called a constrained or kinematic chain.

2. *kinematic viscosity*: see *VISCOSITY.

kinematically (kinĭmæ·tikăli), *adv.* [f. KINEMATIC, -ICAL *adjs.*: see -ICALLY.] From the point of view of kinematics.

1876 A. B. W. KENNEDY tr. *Reuleaux's Kinematics of Machinery* vi. 234 Thus..the force-closed beam-chains became the imperfect but still kinematically far more complete 'parallel motion'. **1915** R. F. MCKAY *Theory of Machines* viii. 93 A direct-acting steam engine and a quick-return motion are kinematically identical, though their general appearance would not suggest such a connection. **1955** J. S. BEGGS *Mechanism* vi. 194 The kinematically equivalent chain thus obtained has all lower pairs, and Eq. (6–5) may be applied. **1971** D. W. SCIAMA *Mod. Cosmol.* xvi. 198 The rotation of the Galaxy can be detected not only dynamically from its flattened shape but also kinematically by observing the motions of stars ..far out from the centre.

kinematics. Add: **b.** The kinematic features or properties of something. Const. as *sing.* or *pl.*

1955 J. S. BEGGS *Mechanism* ix. 273 The kinematics of the area wheel is shown in Fig. 9–11. **1973** *Sci. Amer.* Aug. 33/1 The kinematics of the decay required that the mass of the particle be very small, perhaps even zero.

kinematograph. Add: (Further examples.) Hence **kinema·tograph** *v. trans.,* **ki:nemato·grapher, ki:nematogra·phical** *a.,* **ki:nematogra·phically** *adv.,* **ki:nemato·graphy.** (Variants of the corresponding *cine-* forms.)

1896 *19th Cent.* July 135 The Kinematograph is already at more than one of them [*sc.* the music-halls], showing a stormy sea, the Thames at Waterloo Bridge, the race for the Derby. **1900** *Nature* 15 Feb. 384/2 Prof. R. W. Wood will exhibit..the Kinematographical Demonstration of the Evolutions of Reflected Wave-fronts. **1907** *Westm. Gaz.* 24 Aug. 6/3 Acting, Sir, is mere kinematography. What we require is something more static, reposeful, and intellectual. **1908** *Daily Chron.* 26 Sept. 7/2 Mr. Charles Urban during the past five months has enjoyed facilities to kinematograph the efforts made during this period to salve the Gladiator. **1911** *Chambers's Jrnl.* 412/1 Here, however, the scientific kinematographer has gone farther. **1925** *Daily Mail* 13 Apr. 6/5 One..important thing..is to get into the hiding-place unobserved by the birds which he happens to be kinematographically on the track of. **1954** A. CORNWELL-CLYNE *3-D Kinematogr.* 7 Colour kinematography and synchronized sound. **1969** T. H. GUBACK *Internat. Film Industry* v. 102 The Kinematograph Renters Society..brought action against the two Maltese films. **1971** (*title*) British kinematography sound and television.

kinematoscope. = *CINEMATOSCOPE. (*Disused.*)

1898 *Windsor Mag.* VIII. 113/1, I knew that conjurors were to be obtained there,..and the kinematoscope. **1926** *Encycl. Brit.* Suppl. II. 960/2 This machine was patented in the United States as the Kinematoscope Feb. 5 1861.

kineme (kəi·nīm). *Linguistics.* [f. Gr. κίνη(σις movement + *-EME.] A meaningful unit of body movement or gesture made in non-vocal communication.

1952 R. L. BIRDWHISTELL *Introd. Kinesics* (U.S. Dept. State, Foreign Service Inst.) 22 Phone: Allophone Phoneme. Kine: Allokine (? Kineme?). **1955** *Etc.: Rev. Gen. Semantics* XIII. I. 13 Each of these *classes* of allokines or variants within a range, we define as *kinemes.* **1965** OSGOOD & SEBEOK *Psycholinguistics* iv. 85 The second step in analysing any gestural 'language'—again, in parallel with linguistics—would be to determine what movements are significant in the code, i.e., what classes of kines constitute *kinemes* (equivalent to *phonemes*) by virtue of having the same significance. **1972** B. G. COOKE in T. Kochman *Rappin' & Stylin' Out* 34 In this paper the gestures of giving and getting skin shall be considered as *kinemes* according to Birdwhistell's classification.

kinemics (kəinī·miks). [f. *KINEM(E + -ICS.] (See quot. 1954.)

1953 J. B. CARROLL *Study of Lang.* 279 Kinemics. **1954** PEI & GAYNOR *Dict. Ling.* 115 *Kinemics,* the study of units of gestural expression.

kinescope (ki·nĭskōᵘp). *Television.* [f. Gr. κίνη(σις movement + -SCOPE.] **1.** A cathode-ray tube specially constructed for use in a television set. Chiefly *U.S.*

The registration as a proprietary name was cancelled in 1950.

1932 *Official Gaz.* (U.S. Patent Office) 17 May 568/1 RCA Victor Company, Inc., Camden, N.J. Filed Feb. 6, 1931. *Kinescope* for Cathode Ray Tubes and Thermionic Tubes. **1933** V. K. ZWORYKIN in *Proc. IRE* XXI. 1656 The name 'kinescope' has been applied to the cathode ray tube used in the television receiver to distinguish it from ordinary cathode ray oscilloscopes because it has several important points of difference. **1949** B. GROB *Basic Television* ix. 144 The picture tube, or kinescope, has the funnel-shaped form and internal structure of a conventional cathode-ray tube. **1971** H. E. ENNES *Television Broadcasting* viii. 357 The kinescope upon which the image to be recorded is displayed is a special type of tube employing a flat face, with phosphor and brightness characteristics that allow use of inexpensive film.

2. A film recording made from a television broadcast.

1949 *Richmond* (Va.) *News Leader* 25 Oct. 30/1 Kinescope or television recording, the process of filming a television show off the receiving tube. **1953** *Manch. Guardian Weekly* 2 July 15/1 On June 2 a United States television network transmitted a kinescope version of the B.B.C.'s television of the Abbey Coronation service. **1957** *Economist* 19 Oct. 226/1 It buys a programme or series of programmes from, say, station KETC in St Louis, and

then makes it available to all the other ETV outlets on kinescope. **1957** P. FRANK *Seven Days to Never* ii. 20 He took a course in American television and radio. Every Tuesday afternoon he listened to recordings, and watched kinescopes, of the most popular programs. **1964** L. A. WORTMAN *Closed-Circuit Television Handbk.* v. 93 The major advantage in kinescope recording is that the final film can be shown wherever there is a 16-mm projector.

Hence **ki·nescope** *v. trans.*, to make a kinescope of; **ki·nescoped** *ppl. a.*, reproduced from a kinescope recording; **ki·nescoping** *vbl. sb.*

1949 *Life* 17 Oct. 75 Each show is kinescoped (filmed and sound-tracked) and re-telecast from stations in the rest of the country. **1961** P. LEWIS *Educ. Television Guidebk.* iv. 70 (*heading*) Kinescoping possibilities. **1964** L. A. WORTMAN *Closed-Circuit Television Handbk.* v. 93 One can usually recognize a kinescoped telecast by virtue of its visual quality. **1967** *Telegraph* (Brisbane) 3 Mar. 12/1 The only way then to record a show was by a film technique called 'kinescoping'... At that time the quality was diabolical.

kinesic (kəinī·sik), *a. Linguistics.* [f. Gr. κίνησις movement + -IC.] Of or pertaining to communication effected non-vocally through movements or gestures. Hence **kine·sically** *adv.*

1952 R. L. BIRDWHISTELL *Introd. Kinesics* (U.S. Dept. State, Foreign Service Inst.) 15 It is suggested that any student beginning kinesic recording work on but one part of the body at a time. **1952** *Rep. 3rd Ann. Round Table Meeting Ling. & Lang. Teaching* (Georgetown Univ. Inst. Lang.) 66 A rather thorough preliminary study of *kinesics* has indicated that the kinesic system can be analyzed and described. **1955** *Etc.: Rev. Gen. Semantics* XIII. I. 18 He was kinesically more 'mature' than the other boys. **1959** *College English* XX. IV. 172 Kinesic and paralinguistic phenomena constitute separate patterned systems, which differ in their structure from culture to culture. **1964** CRYSTAL & QUIRK *Prosodic & Paralinguistic Features Eng.* ii. 18 Those kinesic phenomena which are unintended by the individual. **1965** L. PEDERSON in *Lang. Programs for Disadvantaged* (U.S. Nat. Council Teachers of English) 247 Most speech occurs in the form of dialogue with two or more participants actively cooperating at the structural, paralinguistic, kinesic, proxemic, and haptic level. **1967** L. THAYER *Communication* 61 Inspection of the working transcript of the linguistically and kinesically recorded data revealed repetitive and apparently systematic body behaviors. **1968** *Amer. Speech* XLIII. 202 There are many conventionalized kinesic systems, each with its own hierarchy. **1972** J. L. DILLARD *Black English* v. 203 It is quite believable..that gestural and kinesic cues might 'give away' a member of the Negro subculture to people who knew that culture.

kinesics (kəinī·siks). *Linguistics.* [f. Gr. κίνησις movement + -ICS.] The study of those body movements and gestures by which, as well as by speech, communication is made; body movements and gestures which convey meaning non-vocally.

1952 R. L. BIRDWHISTELL (*title*) Introduction to kinesics: an annotation system for analysis of body motion and gesture. **1955** *Etc.: Rev. Gen. Semantics* XIII. I. 12 Kinesics may be defined as the systematic study of the visually sensible aspects of non-verbal interpersonal communication. **1957** *Psychiatry* XX. 74 Kinesics, or gestures and motions, are not instinctive human nature but are learned systems. **1958** A. A. HILL *Introd. Ling. Struct.* xxi. 409 The vocal qualifiers together with kinesics make up the paralinguistic system. **1970** J. FAST *Body Lang.* (1971) i. 11 To understand this unspoken body language, kinesics experts often have to take into consideration cultural differences and environmental differences. **1972** W. M. AUSTIN in A. L. Davis *Culture, Class, & Lang. Variety* viii. 152 Kinesics is the study of body posture, tonus, and movement in man and the other animals.

kinesimeter (kəinĭsi·mĭtəɪ). [f. KINESI- + -METER.] An instrument for investigating the properties of different areas of the skin, by which a movable point whose position can be measured may be applied to the surface with a known force.

1885 H. H. DONALDSON in *Mind* X. 402 This machine was devised by Prof. [G.] Stanley Hall, and will be described in a forthcoming paper, under the name of the 'Kinesimeter'. **1901** E. B. TITCHENER *Exper. Psychol.* I. II. 145 (*caption*) Arm-rest, designed for use with kinesimeter.

kinesiology (kəinĭsi,ǫ·lŏdʒi). [f. KINESI- + -OLOGY.] The field of study concerned with the mechanics of (human) bodily movement.

1894 N. POSSE *Special Kinesiology* p. v, I have deemed it desirable to change the title into *Special Kinesiology*,—it being a treatise on the mechanics, effects, and classification of special exercises. **1936** *Nature* 14 Mar. 438/2 This book [sc. *Mechanics of Normal and Pathological Locomotion in Man*] should take a prominent place in the literature of kinesiology. **1941** *Res. Q. Amer. Assoc. Health & Physical Educ.* XII. 163 While kinesiology borders on the field of several sciences, its greatest practical interest is in the field of physical education. **1963** M. G. SCOTT (*title*) Analysis of human motion: a textbook in kinesiology.

Hence **kinesiolo·gic, -lo·gical** *adjs.*, **kinesio·logist**, a person who studies kinesiology or kinesics.

1941 *Res. Q. Amer. Assoc. Health & Physical Educ.* XII. 167 He presents a concise kinesiological analysis. *Ibid.* 165 The importance of the part he [*sc.* Aristotle] played as a founder of the study of the mechanics of movement is hardly realized by many contemporary kinesiologists. **1950** K. F. WELLS *Kinesiology* xvi. 350 (*heading*) The kinesiologic analysis of a movement. **1952** R. L. BIRDWHISTELL *Introd. Kinesics* (U.S. Dept. State, Foreign Service Inst.) 3 The term *social* kinesiologist has been selected as the term for one attempting to analyze systematically the data covered by kinesic investigation. *Ibid.* 15 This is particularly difficult for the average American mover when working with the kinesiological systems of other Americans. **1965** OSGOOD & SEBEOK *Psycholinguistics* iv. 85 Kinesiologists require training in objective looking—the untrained observer will be likely to perceive only those movements which are significant in his own 'language'.

kinesis (kəi-, kĭnī·sis). Pl. kineses. [mod.L., f. Gr. κίνησις motion.] † **1.** *Cytology.* Karyokinesis, mitosis. *Obs. rare.* (Cf. *KINETIC *a.* 4.)

1904 *Jrnl. R. Microsc. Soc.* 529 At the first metaphase there is a second division (? longitudinal) which appears preparatory to the second kinesis. **1906** *Ibid.* 282 The two constitutive branches of the definitive chromosomes ..separate from one another in each chromosome at the first kinesis.

2. *Biol.* [Adopted (in G.) by W. Rothert 1901, in *Flora* LXXXVIII. 374, after its use as a suffix in *photokinesis*.] An undirected movement of an organism that occurs in response to a particular kind of stimulus.

1905 *Jrnl. Compar. Neurol.* XV. 139 Kinesis is a term which seems to have been first used by Engelmann for the increase or decrease of activity produced by certain agencies. The fact that certain bacteria increase or decrease movement in the light he called photokinesis. Rothert accepted the term kinesis for such changes in the amount of activity produced by chemicals, calling this chemokinesis. **1940** FRAENKEL & GUNN *Orientation of Animals* i. 10 The term *taxis* is to-day used for directed orientation reactions... Undirected locomotory reactions, in which the speed of movement or the frequency of turning depend on the intensity of stimulation, we call kineses. **1955** STORER & USINGER *Elem. Zool.* xxiii. 394 Taxes and kineses..enable insects and many other animals to find and inhabit the small environmental niche or microclimate in which each kind is most successful. **1960** L. PICKEN *Organization of Cells* x. 450 The formation of cell aggregates is undoubtedly favoured by a non-directional movement of the cells, by a kinesis, with thigmotaxis taking over once contact is established.

kinetheodolite (kinĭþiǫ·dŏləit). Also (with hyphen) **kine-theodolite.** [f. Gr. κίνησις movement + THEODOLITE.] A telescope used to follow the path of a projectile, aircraft, or the like, and mounted so that its elevation and azimuth angles are indicated.

1941 *Illustr. London News* CXCVIII. 380/2 The girls work with two kine-theodolites set far apart and connected at the firing position by a central control post which photographs the shell-bursts. **1946** *Jrnl. R. Aeronaut. Soc.* L. 925/1 Bombs of differing weights were dropped... They were followed visually by kine-theodolites, which gave the flight path. **1958** *New Scientist* 21 Aug. 655/1 The contributions..on the tracking of the Russian satellites..were quite outstanding. Thus the data obtained using kine-theodolites by scientists of the Ministry of Supply were the most accurate optical observations reported. **1961** *Engineering* 26 May 750/3 Woomera has a number of double kinetheodolite sites, one instrument tracking the missile, the other the target aircraft. **1965** K. J. TURNER in M. A. Perry *Flight Test Instrumentation* III. 229 The model trajectories are recorded by..kinetheodolites.

kinetic, *a.* Add: **2.** *kinetic heating*, heat generated by the compression and acceleration of air by a fast-moving body.

1954 *Aircraft Engineering* XXVI. 138/3 Kinetic heating is caused by two related phenomena; first the adiabatic compression of the air as it is brought up to the velocity of the leading edge or nose of the body and second the frictional heating which takes place in the boundary layer as the air adjacent to the surface tends to accelerate the air, through which the plane is passing, up to the flying speed. **1959** L. BROGLIO in *Adv. Aeronaut. Sci.* I. 216 The design of an aircraft or missile is often ruled by the transient-temperatures of its external surface, due to kinetic heating and radiation. **1970** *Progr. Aerospace Sci.* XI. 64 Another effect which occurs in flight..concerns the influence of kinetic heating.

b. *Biol.* Of or pertaining to a kinesis (sense *2).

1905 *Amer. Naturalist* XXXIX. 167 It has been found convenient to distinguish between two factors in the effect of light on Drosophila, a kinetic effect and a directive one. **1914** *Jrnl. Exper. Zool.* XVII. 273 Animals, such as the blowfly larva, which respond phototactically to horizontal light show a simple kinetic response when subjected to uniform illumination from above. **1941** S. O. MAST in Calkins & Summers *Protozoa Biol. Res.* v. 277 Kinetic responses.—If an amoeba is kept for some time in very weak light it becomes inactive; if the light is then increased, the organism gradually becomes active again.

c. *transf.* and *fig.*, esp. active, dynamic, full of energy.

1931 H. G. WELLS *Work, Wealth & Happiness of Mankind* (1932) ix. 382 In every preceding phase where there has been a concentration of wealth it has been far less easily converted into kinetic purchasing power. **1934** —— *Exper. Autobiogr.* II. ix. 658 For the purposes of the state I proposed a division into four types of character, the poietic, the kinetic, the dull and the base. A primary problem of government was to vest all the executive and administrative work in the kinetic class. **1939** —— *Holy Terror* III. i. 218 They were at least kinetic, they wanted to make things happen even if they did not quite know what or how. **1956** N. CARDUS *Close of Play* 89 His life was short and kinetic. **1957** L. DURRELL *Justine* II. 134 It was these very defects of character—these vulgarities of the psyche—which constituted for me the greatest attraction of this weird kinetic personage. **1961** *Listener* 20 Apr. 707/3 His was an aural and kinetic imagination, not a visual one.

3. *Chem.* Of, pertaining to, or governed by the kinetics of a reaction.

1882 *Nature* 21 Dec. 183/2 What may perhaps be called the kinetic theory of chemical actions, the theory, namely, that the direction and amount of any chemical change is conditioned not only by the affinities, but also by the masses of the reacting substances, by the temperature, pressure, [etc.]. **1926** C. N. HINSHELWOOD *Kinetics Chem. Change Gaseous Syst.* ii. 48 We are concerned now with the kinetic measurements only. **1964** ROBERTS & CASERIO *Basic Princ. Org. Chem.* xiii. 402 Carbon–deuterium bonds are normally broken more slowly than carbon–hydrogen bonds and this so-called kinetic isotope effect provides a very general method for determining whether or not particular carbon–hydrogen bonds are broken in slow reaction steps. **1968** G. E. COATES et al. *Princ. Organometallic Chem.* i. 11 The 'kinetic stability' of carbon compounds has a variety of causes. **1968** R. O. C. NORMAN *Princ. Org. Synthesis* xiv. 458 The *para*-derivative is formed the faster (kinetic control).

4. *Cytology.* Pertaining to or involved in mitotic division; undergoing division. (Cf. *KINESIS 1.)

1894 *Jrnl. R. Microsc. Soc.* 581 Nuclear division takes place under the control of the kinetic centres. **1910** G. N. CALKINS *Protozoöl.* i. 29 Definite, active, kinetic bodies closely associated with the mechanism of nuclear division and of locomotion. **1931** J. GRAY *Text-bk. Exper. Cytol.* viii. 141 The chromatic constituents of the kinetic nucleus. **1940** G. S. CARTER *Gen. Zool. Invertebr.* iii. 43 The centrosome seems to control the kinetic activities of the cell at division. **1960** L. PICKEN *Organization of Cells* iv. 150 Navashin (1933)..suggested that the number of kinetic bodies (centromeres) is primary and conditions the number of chromosomes. **1965** C. D. DARLINGTON *Cytology* II. i. 657 *Holomastigotoides tusitala*, whose giant chromosomes ..are always attached to the kinetic body or centriole [during mitosis].

5. *Phonetics.* Of consonants, vowels, etc.: changing in quality during utterance as opposed to being held constant.

1931 *Programme for Vacation Course for Foreign Students Cambridge* 3 Static and kinetic vowels. **1939** L. H. GRAY *Foundations of Lang.* iii. 53 Consonants can be..static (or continuant), i.e. can be held continuously without changing quality..; or are kinetic, i.e., cannot be so held (plosives, affricates, and flaps). **1956** *English Studies* XXXVII. 68 The rise can be continued until the next kinetic tone is reached. **1961** Y. OLSSON *On Syntax Eng. Verb* ii. 21 Kingdon distinguishes between two types of intonation, static, with pitch kept level, and kinetic, with pitch changed in the course of the same note.

6. Of, pertaining to, or producing an artistic construction which depends upon movement for its effect. Esp. in phr. *kinetic art*.

1957 J. LYNCH *Metal Sculpture* v. 105 It might be easier to define constructions, stabiles, mobiles and kinetic sculpture by what they are *not*. **1964** *Times Lit. Suppl.* 3 Sept. 775/3 The 'kinetic art' which is occupying so many of the younger artists today..is largely based on a quasi-mathematical analysis of variation and motion. **1966** *Cambr. Rev.* 28 May 449/1 Schöffer..claims that kinetic works of art are 'man's biological and psychological extension'. **1967** *Listener* 30 Mar. 434/1 At the Indica Gallery there is a kinetic exhibition. **1968** S. BANN tr. *Popper's Orig. & Devel. Kinetic Art* vii. 156 The majority of kinetic works composed on plane surfaces bring white or coloured light into play. **1969** *Listener* 16 Jan. 93/1 Modern developments fall more or less exactly into two groups which might roughly be called kinetic and psychedelic. **1971** J. WILLETT in A. Bullock *20th Century* x. 244/2 Serialism in every art owed an obvious debt to Schönberg and Webern; the kinetic artists to Calder and Moholy-Nagy. **1973** *Times* 27 Nov. 12/6 A good deal of European kinetic art was mere flashy mechanics (the light machines of Nicolas Schöffer, for example) but one of the best kinetic artists has been the German, Gerhard von Graevenitz, who now works in Amsterdam. **1974** *Evening News* (Edinburgh) 10 Apr. 1/8 The kinetic sculpture—the first of its kind in Scotland—was erected by Edinburgh Corporation and the Scottish Arts Council at a cost of £11,000. The structure blends perfectly with the rows of scaffolding masking the north side of Picardy Place.

kinetically (kəine·tikăli), *adv.* [f. KINETIC *a.*: see -ICALLY.] By kinetics; from the point of view of kinetics.

1909 in *Cent. Dict.* Suppl. **1926** C. N. HINSHELWOOD *Kinetics Chem. Change Gaseous Syst.* ii. 42 The thermal decomposition of nitrous oxide is kinetically bimolecular. **1941** [see *CONTOUR *sb.* 1 e]. **1964** J. W. LINNETT *Electronic Struct. Molecules* vi. 101 This would mean that 1:2 addition would be favoured kinetically relative to 1:4 addition. **1967** *Oceanogr. & Marine Biol.* V. 198 An enzyme reaction that can readily be studied kinetically and the results analysed using the theory of absolute reaction rates. **1968** R. O. C. NORMAN *Princ. Org. Synthesis* iii. 92 In most reactions which can proceed by two or more pathways each of which gives a different set of products, the products isolated are those derived from the pathway of lowest free energy of activation... These reactions are described as being kinetically controlled.

kineticism (kəine·tisiz'm). [f. KINETIC *a.* + -ISM.] = **kinetic art*; also, in *Music*, a mechanical and inexpressive style.

1939 B. FLES tr. *Křenek's Music Here & Now* iii. 84 A modern trend..which, through its misinterpretation of neoclassicism, fell in with a streamlined kineticism. **1966** *Time* 28 Jan. 44 Manhattan's avant-garde Jewish Museum is currently showing 102 works by kineticism's established practitioners, Jean Tinguely and Nicolas Schöffer. **1972** *Daily Tel.* 28 Nov. 12/7 Dada was fostered by its nihilist aspects and from there we can trace the seeds of multi-media kineticism, underground cinema, and even the liquid theatre.

kineticist (kəine·tisist). [f. KINETIC(S + -IST 2.] **1.** An expert in or student of kinetics (sense *2) or gas kinetics.

1960 S. W. BENSON *Found. Chem. Kinetics* p. ix, I should like to acknowledge my most profound indebtedness to the many kineticists whose work has served as guide and inspiration. **1972** J. C. POLANYI *Chem. Kinetics* p. ix, The earliest concern of the kineticist was the overall rate of chemical reactions. **1972** *Nature* 17 Mar. 99/2 It is also very likely that the stem cells of a tumour..are not estimated by the averaged measurements easily available to the kineticist. **1973** *Ibid.* 16 Feb. p. xv (Advt.), Applicants should be either gas kineticists, with an interest in photochemistry and spectroscopy, or have experience in mass spectroscopy.

2. A kinetic artist. Cf. *KINETIC *a.* 6.

1970 *Guardian* 10 Feb. 8/4 Like a lot of the kineticists, she went on record..with some dauntingly pretentious statements..[about] the need to create constellations in her 'Perspex' and liquid reflections. **1971** *Guardian* 24 June 10/3 In the late fifties..many kineticists..were enraged by the élitism of the gallery system. **1971** J. WILLETT in A. Bullock *20th Century* x. 245/1 The Swiss kineticist Jean Tinguely's prodigally ingenious self-destructive machines.

kinetics. Add: **2. a.** A field of study concerned with the mechanisms and rates of chemical reactions or other kinds of process; see also **gas kinetics*.

1884 M. M. P. MUIR *Treat. Princ. Chem.* p. ix, The second part of the book is devoted to the subjects of dissociation, chemical change and equilibrium, chemical affinity, and the relations between chemical action and the distribution of the energy of the changing system. These, and cognate questions, I have ventured to summarise in the expression Chemical Kinetics. **1898** C. L. SPEYERS *Text-bk. Physical Chem.* vi. 125 Chemical kinetics.—Sometimes called chemical dynamics. It treats of the velocity of chemical reactions. **1910** *Encycl. Brit.* VI. 28/2 The law of chemical mass-action not only defines the conditions for chemical equilibrium, but contains at the same time the principles of chemical kinetics. **1953** FROST & PEARSON *Kinetics & Mechanism* i. 1 Kinetics deals with the rate of chemical reaction, with all factors which influence the rate of reaction, and with the explanation of the rate in terms of the reaction mechanism. **1956** G. R. KEEPIN *Physics Nucl. Kinetics* i. 2 The fields of fission physics and reactor kinetics have developed in the main as quite distinct and separate disciplines. **1972** CAPELLOS & BIELSKI *Kinetic Syst.* i. 1 The raw data of chemical kinetics are the measurements of the rates of reactions.

b. Those aspects of a particular process that relate to the rate at which it occurs; the details of the way a process occurs, esp. as regards its rate. Const. as *sing.* or *pl.*

1907 *Chem. Abstr.* I. 2763 (*heading*) The kinetics of nitration. **1924** *Jrnl. Gen. Physiol.* VII. 280 Studies on the kinetics of growth. **1926** C. N. HINSHELWOOD *Kinetics Chem. Change Gaseous Syst.* vii. 193 The kinetics of a reaction taking place on such a surface would be almost the same as on a surface of uniform structure. **1931** J. GRAY *Text-bk. Exper. Cytol.* xiii. 337 (*heading*) The kinetics of osmotic equilibria. **1939** *Chem. Abstr.* XXXIII. 4851 The kinetics of evaporation of droplets, and surfaces of pure liquids and of solns. of surface-inactive and surface-active substances..are treated mathematically. **1946** *Proc. R. Soc.* A. CLXXXVII. 129 The kinetics of these reactions are not well understood. **1961** *Federation Proc.* XX. 437/2 The kinetics of infection by the virus of foot-and-mouth disease was determined as a function of virus cell concentration. **1968** *Brit. Med. Bull.* XXIV. 245/2 The techniques of investigating cell kinetics include gross measurement of increase in size, of a tumour cell colony for instance. **1968** R. O. C. NORMAN *Princ. Org. Synthesis* iii. 75 We have assumed the mechanism of the reaction in order to show how it leads to the observed kinetics. *Ibid.* 76 Although the complete kinetics are complex, they are given approximately by

$$-d[CH_3CHO]/dt = k[CH_3CHO][OH^-].$$

kinetin (kəi·nĕtin). *Biochem.* [f. KINET(O- + -IN[1].] 6-Furfurylaminopurine, $C_{10}H_9N_5O$, a compound that is a decomposition product of the deoxyadenosine present in DNA and promotes cell division in plants.

1955 C. MILLER et al. in *Jrnl. Amer. Chem. Soc.* LXXVII. 1392/1 The name *kinetin* is proposed for this substance. *Ibid.* 2662/2 It was concluded that kinetin most probably is 6-furfurylaminopurine... The correctness of this structure has now been verified by synthesis. **1957** *Times* 11 Sept. 6/2 The practical uses of such substances as gibberellic acid and kinetin could not be forecast until further experiments were completed. **1971** I. D. J. PHILLIPS *Introd. Biochem. & Physiol. Plant Growth Hormones* i. 32 Kinetin does not occur naturally in plants. **1973** *McGraw-Hill Yearbk. Sci. & Technol.* 277/1 Enlargement of [cambial] rays, both in height and width, was also obtained in pine plants by the application of a mixture of kinetin and auxin.

kinetite (kəi·nĭtəit). [f. KINET(O- + -ITE[1].] A disused kind of explosive (see quot. 1918).

1887 *Jrnl. Soc. Chem. Industry* 29 Jan. 3/1 The so-called kinetite is virtually one of what Dr. Sprengel terms his 'safety explosives'. **1918** E. DE W. S. COLVIN *High Explosives* 142 Kinetite, an explosive which was considerably used from about 1885 to 1900, consisted of potassium chlorate incorporated with nitrobenzene and gelatinised with collodion cotton and sulphur.

kineto-. Add: **kine·tochore** (-kōᵊɹ) *Cytology* [Gr. χῶρ-ος place] = *centromere* (*b*) (s.v. *CENTRO-); **kinetode·sma** (pl. **-desmas, -desmata**) *Biol.* [ad. F. *cinétodesme* (Chatton & Lwoff 1935, in *Compt. Rend. hebd. d. Séances et Mém. de la Soc. de Biol.* CXVIII. 1069), f. Gr. δεσμ-ός band, bond], in ciliates and flagellates, a thin fibre situated to one side of a row of kinetosomes and composed of a number of fibrils each of which terminates in one of them; hence **kinetode·smal** *a.*; **kine·togram**, a motion picture taken by a kinetograph; **kine·tograph** *v. trans.*, to make a cinematographic record of; **kineto·grapher** = *CINEMATOGRAPHER; **kineto·graphy** = *CINEMATOGRAPHY; **kine:tonu·cleus** *Biol.* = *KINETOPLAST a; **kine·tophone**, an apparatus combining the functions of a kinetoscope (*b*) and a phonograph.

1934 L. W. SHARP *Introd. Cytol.* (ed. 3) ix. 116 The region..has been variously called the 'fiber-attachment point', 'insertion region', 'primary constriction', 'kinetic constriction', 'attachment constriction', and 'Trennungstelle'... The convenient term kinetochore (= movement place) has been suggested to the author by J. A. Moore. The use of the term is recommended. **1936** *Biol. Bull.* LXX. 484 The mitotic movement of chromosomes is closely associated or perhaps even dependent on the activities of the kinetochore. **1961** WILSON & MORRISON *Cytol.* iv. 90 In many chromosomes, segments near or adjacent to the kinetochore are covered by this definition [of heterochromatin] and are also frequently heteropycnotic in the purely cytological sense. **1970** AMBROSE & EASTY *Cell Biol.* ix. 296 Each chromosome carries a distinct region known as a centromere or kinetochore which plays a fundamental role in chromosome movements during mitosis. **1949** Kinetodesma [see *KINETY]. **1953** *Biol. Bull.* CIV. 419 The kinetodesmas on the right ventral side of the animal. **1967** E. J. W. BARRINGTON *Invertebr. Struct. & Function* iii. 49 One special problem..is presented by the existence in ciliate Protozoa of patterns of fibres, called kinetodesmata, which lie in the ectoplasm and which are closely associated with the basal bodies of the cilia. *Ibid.*, The kinetodesma is visible as a fibre with the light microscope,..but electron microscopy is needed to elucidate fully its complex relationships. **1950** A. LWOFF *Probl. Morphogenesis Ciliates* vii. 54 Kinetodesmal fibers. **1953** Kinetodesmal [see *KINETOSOMAL *a.*]. **1897** *Knowledge* Sept. 217/2 When making the original kinetograms. *Ibid.* 218/1 Slow movements may be kinetographed. *Ibid.* 217/2 Reproduced through the labours of 'special' kinetographers. *Ibid.* 217/1 Kinetography is based upon the principle of the well-known zoetrope. **1906** H. M. WOODCOCK in *Q. Jrnl. Microsc. Sci.* L. 182 The resulting body, which may be termed the kinetonucleus, passes into the now rounded trophonucleus. **1920** W. E. AGAR *Cytol.* vi. 193 This view was founded partly on analogy with certain Protista; for example Trypanosomes, where a darkly staining body ('kinetonucleus') which is in close anatomical relation to the flagellum and therefore apparently concerned with the function of locomotion, is supposed by many to have been derived from the nucleus. **1938** [see *KINETOPLAST]. **1960** L. PICKEN *Organization of Cells* vi. 240 The kinetonucleus of trypanosomes and of the bodonids normally multiplies by division. **1896** *19th Cent.* July 135 The Kinetophone is not at the [music-] halls yet, perhaps; but is probably on the way to them.

kinetoplast (kəinī·toplɑst). *Biol.* [ad. F. *kinétoplaste* (A. Alexeieff 1917, in *Compt. Rend. hebd. d. Séances et Mém. de la Soc. de Biol.* LXXX. 512): see KINETO- and -PLAST.] **a.** A structure lying close to a kinetosome in some protozoa, esp. trypanosomes. **b.** This structure together with the kinetosome; now *rare* or *Obs.*

1925 *Manson's Trop. Dis.* (ed. 8) 636 This composite body is known as the kinetoplast, and is composed of a minute blepharoplast, or basal body, and a parabasal body. **1938** *Trans. R. Soc. Trop. Med. & Hygiene* XXXII. 333 In referring to the prominent dark-staining structure at the base of the flagellum in trypanosomes I have at one time used the term *parabasal*, later changing to *kinetonucleus*, while the name *kinetoplast* has been employed to denote the complex kinetonucleus (or parabasal) + blepharoplast (or basal granule)... While the conception of the nuclear nature of this element (hence 'kinetonucleus') has been discarded long ago, considerable doubt has also been thrown on its interpretation as a parabasal body... In the present paper the term *kinetoplast* has accordingly been employed in its original sense, to denote the kinetonucleus alone (without the blepharoplast). **1961** MACKINNON & HAWES *Introd. Study Protozoa* II. 101 In the Trypanosomidae and some other protomonads..there is a body lying near the blepharoplast which..is generally well preserved by acetic acid fixatives like Bouin; it is F +; it is self-perpetuating, divides when the blepharoplast divides, and one of its daughters goes to each product of fission... To it the name kinetoplast is applied... The term parabasal body (unfortunately applied at times to the structure just defined as a kinetoplast) is here reserved for an organelle best seen in the Trichomonadida... It is more complex than the kinetoplast, usually compound, F –, and rarely if ever completely preserved except by 'cytological' fixatives. It is not self-reproducing. **1971** *New Scientist* 13 May 370 Certain single-celled organisms are propelled forwards in the water by flagellae, which draw their power from a single huge mitochondrion called a kinetoplast.

kinetosome (kəinī·tosōᵘm). *Biol.* [f. KINETO- + *-SOME[4].] A cytoplasmic structure which forms the base of a cilium or flagellum.

1912 C. E. ALLEN in *Archiv für Zellforschung* VIII. 134 It seems plain..that the plates and the groups of smaller bodies—which will be referred to as kinetosomes—are mutually equivalent. **1934** L. W. SHARP *Introd. Cytol.* (ed. 3) xiv. 203 The granules and plates in the earlier spermatogenous cells [of bryophytes] were called 'kinetosomes' and 'kinoplasmic plates' by Allen (1912). **1949** *Growth* XIII. Suppl. 61 In all animals or plants, as well as in flagellates or ciliates, at the basis of each flagellum or cilium, a spherical corpuscle is to be seen: the kinetosome. **1960** L. PICKEN *Organization of Cells* vii. 273 In molluscan, amphibian, and ciliate kinetosomes, but not in those in mammalian ciliated tissues, there is a prolongation of the kinetosome base as a single or double, striated fibre. *Ibid.*, In the ciliates, kinetosomes appear to generate not only cilia but (and alternatively, only) trichocysts and a variety of types of fibril. **1961** MACKINNON & HAWES *Introd. Study Protozoa* II. 71 Asexual reproduction is universal [among the Mastigophora]... The basal granule (blepharoplast or kinetosome) of the flagellum divides, and it frequently acts as a centriole. **1974** BROWN & BERTKE *Textbk. Cytol.* (ed. 2) xiii. 273/2 At the base of the shaft of a cilium or flagellum but within the cell itself is the basal body... This structure is called the kinetosome by protozoologists or the blepharoplast by some phycologists.

Hence **kinetoso·mal** *a.*

1949 *Growth* XIII. Suppl. 77 (*heading*) Genetic continuity of kineties. Organization of kinetosomal populations. **1953** *Biol. Bull.* CIV. 418 The kinetodesmal bundles lie to one side of the kinetosomes and..the individual fibrils curve laterally from their kinetosomal origins to join the main bundle.

kinety (kəi·nĕti). *Biol.* [ad. F. *cinétie* (Chatton & Lwoff 1935, in *Compt. Rend. hebd. d. Séances et Mém. de la Soc. de Biol.* CXVIII. 1069), f. Gr. κινητ-ικός for putting in motion: see -Y[3].] In ciliates and flagellates, a kinetodesma together with its row of associated kinetosomes.

1949 *Growth* XIII. Suppl. 62 Consider..a classical and simple ciliate of the *Leucophrys* type... The cilia are organized in 29 somatic rows. These rows, or kineties, are complex structures. You see: 1) a fiber: the kinetodesma; 2) a line of kinetosomes. **1953** *Biol. Bull.* CIV. 408 The primary fibrillar apparatus of ciliates consists of a number of parallel structural units, the kineties. **1967** J. H. WILMOTH *Biol. Invertebr.* ii. 19 The connecting kinetosomes and kinetodesma form a functional and structural unit called a kinety.., but are not connected to other kineties. *Ibid.*, It is of extreme significance that flagellates at cell division cleave parallel to the kineties, while among ciliates the cleavage plane crosses kineties.

kinfolk: see *KIN *sb.*[1] 9.

king, *sb.* Add: **1. b.** *king and country*: the objects of allegiance for a patriot in a monarchy.

1625 BACON *Ess.* xxiii. 135 Be so true to thy Selfe, as thou be not false to Others; Specially to thy King, and Country. **1773** C. JENNENS *Saul* III. 204 O Jonathan! how nobly didst thou die, for thy King and Country Slain! **1803** M. WILMOT *Russ. Jrnls.* (1934) 11 Tis pleasant to see how true the Britons are to their King & Country. **1814** SCOTT *Waverley* III. v. 60 Colonel Talbot was in every point the English soldier. His whole soul was devoted to the service of his king and country. **1913** BARRIE *Quality St.* I. 15 If..death or glory was the call, you would take the shilling, ma'am... For King and Country. **1933** *Times* 11 Feb. 8/4 After a debate at the Oxford Union Society on Thursday, a motion 'that this House will in no circumstances fight for its King and country' was carried by 275 votes to 153. **1941** 'G. ORWELL' in *Partisan Rev.* Mar.–Apr. 109 There does not effectively exist any policy between being patriotic in the 'King and Country' style and being pro-Hitler. **1965** A. NICOL *Truly Married Woman* 48 Kill for food, kill dangerous things, kill for King and country.

2. c. *King Charles* (earlier examples).

1808 M. WILMOT *Russ. Jrnls.* (1934) III. 352 One of Princess D's great passions..is that for Dogs of the King Charles's breed. **1848** THACKERAY *Van. Fair* lxiv. 589 A King Charles in her lap, a white parasol swaying over her head. **1858** GEO. ELIOT *Scenes Clerical Life* I. 56 A little 'King Charles', with a crimson ribbon round his neck..is jumping on the sofa.

5. *King Cæsar*, a children's game (see quot. 1849).

1849 *Boy's Own Bk.* 36 *King Cæsar*,..the ground is divided into three parts... The spaces at the end, called bases, being much smaller than the middle one. The.. players..all go into one of the bases, except 'the King'..; he places himself..between the two bases, and the others run from base to base... Should the King..succeed in intercepting one of them, he claps him on the head with his hand three times, and each time repeats the words, 'I crown thee, King Cæsar'...This game is sometimes called 'Rushing Bases'. **1969** I. & P. OPIE *Children's Games* iii. 140 The Victorian schoolboys' excuse for a rough-house called 'King Caesar' or 'Rushing Bases'.

6. a. (Further examples of 'recent use'.)

1846 J. G. SAXE *Progress* (1847) 28 How would she [*sc.* the Muse] strive, in fitting verse, to sing The wondrous Progress of the Printing King! **1847** E. D. BANCROFT *Lett. from England* (1904) 113 We both went to a concert at Mr. Hudson's, the great railway 'king', who has just made an immense fortune from railway stocks. **1919** F. HURST *Humoresque* 194 You've never met Mr. Feist, have you, the film king? You two ought to get acquainted—one makes the films and the other makes them famous. **1927** WODEHOUSE *Small Bachelor* ii. 25 She had also been the relict of the late P. Homer Horlick, the Cheese King, and he had left her several million dollars. **1966** 'J. HACKSTON' *Father clears Out* 83 He began to tell me what the sheep kings had to put up with. *Ibid.* 123 The young sheep king.

b. *King Willow*, the game of cricket. Cf. quot. 1876 s.v. WILLOW *sb.* 5.

1933 A. G. MACDONELL *England, their England* xvii. 285 The evening papers were already beginning to talk of the Advent of King Willow. **1936** S. R. JONES *Eng. Village Homes* iii. 36 Football thrives lustily, and King Willow reigns on the old turf of the greens in summer. **1972** P. DICKINSON *Lizard in Cup* vi. 92 Loyalty to..the imagined spirit of King Willow.

7. a. *King of Six*, the male of certain polygamous South African birds.

1913 C. PETTMAN *Africanderisms* 260 *King of six*, a King Williamstown name for the Rooibekje...The reference is to the number of females by which the male is generally accompanied during the breeding season. **1931** R. C. BOLSTER *Land & Sea Birds S.-W. Cape* 133 Of the two Bishop Birds, the Black and Yellow one is said to be polygamous, whence the name 'King of Six' in the vicinity of Cape Town.

11. c. (Usu. with capital initial.) The British national anthem, 'God Save the King'.

1932 *Week-end Rev.* 30 Apr. 554/2 Programme to-night as follows:—British Movietone News. Sunshine Susie. Mickey Mouse. The King. **1959** I. JEFFERIES *Thirteen Days* vii. 95 The band played the King and we all stood up. **1967** R. HARRIS *All my Enemies* iii. 34 We applauded, stood for 'The King'.

12. a. *King-Emperor, -Sovereign.*

1902 *Westm. Gaz.* 27 Feb. 11 The King-Emperor is honoured among us [*sc.* Americans] because he stands for the great people whom he rules. **1971** R. RUSSELL tr. *Ahmad's Shore & Wave* xv. 159 'Have you ever attended the King-Emperor's levée?' asked the Diwan Bahadur. **1908** H. H. JOHNSTON *George Grenfell & Congo* I. xx. 448 The Governors-General or heads of departments representing the King-Sovereign in Africa.

13. a. king-carp, a variety of the common carp, *Cyprinus carpio*; **King Country** *N.Z.*, an extensive region in the North Island of New Zealand formerly allotted to the Maoris under a king; so *King Movement, Party*, etc., referring to the followers of this king; **king-hit** *Austral. slang*, (*a*) a knock-out blow; a hard punch; (*b*) a fighter or bully; a leader; hence as *v. trans.*, to punch hard or knock out; **king-list**, a list of the names of kings; **king mackerel**, a game fish of the eastern U.S. coast, *Scomberomorus cavalla*, also called Spanish mackerel or king-fish; **king salmon** *N. Amer.*, the Chinook or quinnat salmon, *Oncorhynchus tshawytscha* (earlier and later examples); **king-side** *a. Chess*, made or done on the king's side of the board; also applied to men situated on that side; **king-size** *a.*, of an extra large size; of larger size than normal; *spec.* designating an extra large cigarette; hence *ellipt.* as *sb.*, a king-size cigarette; also *king-sized* adj.

1908 *Westm. Gaz.* 7 Aug. 10/3 Yesterday a king carp was hooked. **1930** E. PARKER et al. *Fine Angling for Coarse Fish* 162 A very heavy king-carp..weighed 18½ lb. This fish is rarer than the common carp. **1971** B. J. MUUS *Freshwater Fish Brit. & Europe* 136/1 Scaled carps (often known as king carps) are covered by small uniform scales. **1884** J. H. KERRY-NICHOLLS (*title*) The King Country; or, explorations in New Zealand, a narrative of 600 miles of travel through Maoriland. **1910** J. COWAN *Maoris of N.Z.* xxvii. 294 The men..finally faced death..in the famous redoubt at Orakau, on the borders of what afterwards came to be known as the King Country. **1917** G. H. SCHOLEFIELD *New Zealand* iii. 19 A railway ran from Auckland..until it touched..the boundary of the native preserve known as the 'King Country', which stretched like a neutral zone across the island. **1944** A. MULGAN *From Track to Highway* ii. 58 In the end he took refuge in the King country, below the military frontier in the Waikato, where the defeated Kingites had been left unmolested. **1966** *Encycl. N.Z.* II. 223/2 The King Country, or Rohe Potae, was originally a large tract of the western central North Island... Europeans called the area 'the King Country' because it was here that Tawhiao sought refuge following the Maori Wars. **1923** G. COLLINS *Valley of Eyes Unseen* i. 29 Neither blow was a true king hit, however, and neither Chink was anything near knocked out. **1941** BAKER *Dict. Austral. Slang* 41 *King hit*, a knock-out blow. (2) As for 'king dick' [= a leader, boss]. **1944** L. GLASSOP *We were Rats* xiii. 76 'Do this galah over,' he whispered in my ear. 'He's a king-hit merchant.' **1945** BAKER *Austral. Lang.* vi. 120 To bump, comb down,..king hit. **1962** S. GORE *Down Golden Mile* 277 'King-hit me, the bastard,' he muttered. 'With me own gun.' **1970** *Sunday Truth* (Brisbane) 16 Aug. 32/6 You king-hit him with what appears to be savage brutality. **1974** *Sunday Mail* (Brisbane) 29 Sept. 28 D/2 A piece of legislation that has been described as..a king-hit to human rights. **1914** E. A. W. BUDGE *Short Hist. Egyptian People* iii. 27 The famous King-List drawn up for Seti I, and cut upon a wall in a temple built by him at Abydos. **1962** J. GRAY *Archaeol. & Old Testament World* ii. 34 In the king-lists the 'Flood' demarcates between historical dynasties and the early ages. **1939** J. O. LA GORCE *Bk. Fishes* (ed. 2) 338/2 King mackerel serves as Spanish, and bonito may be served as either Spanish or King mackerel. **1953** F. ROBB *Sea Hunters* vii. 104 Old Drum Watts says these aren't barracouta at all—says they're king-mackerel or something. **1965** A. J. MCCLANE *Standard Fishing Encycl.* 449/2 King mackerel reach a much larger size than any other American Spanish mackerel. **1970** M. SLATER *Caribbean Cooking* 11 *Kingfish*, a game fish, sometimes called King Mackerel which can weigh up to 100 lb. **1858** King movement [see *HUI]. **1860** T. BUDDLE *Maori King Movement* 3 This chief..initiated a Maori King movement in the South. **1884** J. H. KERRY-NICHOLLS *King Country* 6 In 1854,.. Te Heuheu ..summoned a native council at Taupo, when the King movement began in earnest. **1959** K. SINCLAIR in J. E. Gorst *Maori King* p. xxiii, The King movement survives today, though its followers are less numerous than a century ago. **1860** T. BUDDLE *Maori King Movement* 72 It becomes..the duty of those entrusted with native interests..to enter promptly into negociations with the King party. **1944** A. MULGAN *From Track to Highway* ii. 55 The King party wanted to keep their king and their flag. **1881** *Amer. Naturalist* XV. 177 These species [in the North Pacific] may be called the quinnat or king salmon. **1959** *Vancouver Sun* 28 Aug. 5/1 Fall is also in the return of the salmon to their rivers—not in the early king salmon runs that come to a few rivers in May. **1941** F. REINFELD *Keres' Best Games of Chess* 86/1 Not only winning a Pawn, but devaluating the remaining Black King-side Pawns. **1954** H. GOLOMBEK *Game of Chess* 12 In the case of King side castling, the King is moved two squares to the right. **1973** *Times* 13 Aug. 12/7 Hartston won quickly with a strong king-side attack against Mestel. [**1825** J. CONSTABLE *Let.* 10 Dec. in *Corr.* (1964) II. 419 Sir Thomas has done 4 pictures in Paris—the two of the King & Dolphin are very large King size, & fine—the others, are the Dolphiness and Duchess of Berry head size.] **1942** *Time* 7 Sept. 18/1 (Advt.), Regent Cigarettes, King Size. *Ibid.*, King Size Regent's the cigarette for *moderns* like you. **1949** *Sun* (Baltimore) 1 July 2/1 He..allowed Stryker to read the king-size question summarizing the life of Whittaker Chambers. **1957** H. ROOSENBERG *Walls came tumbling Down* iv. 88 We..had a king-size meal. **1957** P. WILDEBLOOD *Main Chance* 159 'Have you got a cigarette?' 'King-size,' said Mrs. Tull. 'Oh, I can't stand them big ones.' **1966** King size [see *ECONOMY 9]. **1971** *New Scientist* 17 June 707/2 It's a pity that Rudolph de Salis..never had the advantage of his king-size burgers. **1971** WODEHOUSE *Much Obliged, Jeeves* xiii. 133 The snag which had raised its ugly head was one of formidable—you might say king-size—dimensions. **1943** in *Amer. Speech* (1944) XIX. 111/2 So that's it for king-sized beauties. **1953** *Manch. Guardian Weekly* 24 Apr. 7 A kingsized defence programme.

c. King Edward (VII potato), an oval variety of potato with a white skin mottled with red, introduced in 1902 by J. Butler; **king fern**, (*b*) *N.Z.*, a large fern, *Marattia salicina*, with a swollen, starchy rhizome; (*c*) *Todea barbara*, a fern closely related to the royal fern, *Osmunda regalis*, found in Australia, New Zealand, and South Africa.

1926 R. N. SALAMAN *Potato Varieties* xxvi. 274 (*heading*) King Edward VII. *Ibid.* 275 King Edward, whose parentage is unknown, was raised by a gardener in Northumberland... This variety is today the most popular in England. **1949** —— *Hist. & Social Influence Potato* x. 170 The 'King Edward' became a favourite in the kitchen. **1963** *Times* 22 Apr. 2/6 The three most popular potato varieties grown in England and Wales are all relatively old. Arran Pilot..was introduced just over 40 years ago. Majestic..was introduced in 1912 and King Edward VII, with about 25 per cent [of the maincrop acreage], in 1902. **1911** W. R. GUILFOYLE *Austral. Plants* 354 *Todea barbara*. 'King Fern' or 'Swamp Sponge Fern'. **1921** H. B. DOBBIE *N.Z. Ferns* (ed. 2) xxix. 374 *M[arattia] fraxinea* (like an ash leaf). 'Para', 'King Fern', 'Horseshoe Fern'. The largest herbaceous fern in New Zealand; plentiful in the early days, now becoming scarce. **1962** J. H. WILLIS *Handbk. Plants Victoria* I. 10 *T[odea] barbara*...Austral King-Fern (King Fern)..all States except W.A. (but very localized in S.A.), N.Z., S. Afr. **1963** B. PEARSON *Coal Flat* xxii. 379 The three of them huddled under a king fern.

14. king's blue, a shade of blue (see quots.); a substance giving that colour; **King's messenger**: see MESSENGER 3; **king's peg**, a drink consisting of brandy and champagne; **King's (National) Roll**, a roll of employers pledged to employ at least a fixed proportion of disabled ex-service men after the war of 1914–18.

1908 C. MAYER tr. *Zerr & Rübencamp's Treat. Colour Manuf.* II. 200 The blue cobalt compounds known in commerce as smalt, king's blue, cobalt blue, [etc.]. **1951** R. MAYER *Artist's Handbk.* ii. 52 *King's blue*, cobalt blue; formerly smalt. **1970** *Canad. Antiques Collector* Oct. 17/1 Very little, if any, Bristol-blue glass was made between about 1800 and about 1820, when it again came into vogue under the name of king's blue. This was a loyal gesture to George IV. **1890** King's peg [see *HEIDSIECK]. **1899** C. J. C. HYNE *Further Adv. Capt. Kettle* xi. 265 Cranze kept up a steady soak on king's peg—putting in a good three fingers of the liqueur brandy before filling up the tumbler with champagne. **1958** M. PROCTER *Man in Ambush* xiii. 148 This was the shy man who drank champagne laced with brandy, a millionaire's drink... It was called King's Peg. **1919** HAIG in *Times* 11 Nov. 10/5, I..appeal to employers..to give a pledge of their sympathy by enrolling their names on the King's National Roll under the national scheme for the employment of disabled men. **1920** *Times* 16 Feb. 9/4 The King's Roll. First edition, with 9,500 firms, now in the press.

15. King Charles's head [with reference to Mr. Dick in Dickens's *David Copperfield* xiv], an obsession or fixed idea; **King James('s) translation** or **version**, the Authorized Version of the Bible (1611); also *King James*.

1882 W. How *Let.* in H. Barnett *Canon Barnett* (1918) I. xxii. 275 Like King Charles's head, there was no keeping you out. **1889** G. B. SHAW *London Music 1888–89* (1937) 124, I am afraid I shall have to drag in the subject of music rather often in this column. I know that it is my King Charles's head. **1929** C. MACKENZIE *Gallipoli Memories* xii. 198 And then, of course, he produced his King Charles's head, which was the landing at Bulair. **1972** F. M. LÓPEZ-MORILLAS in R. Highfield *Spain in 15th Cent.* xiv. 441 His King Charles' head was the role played on the first voyage by Martín Alonso Pinzón. **1973** *Times* 30 June 13/5 My own King Charles's head is the use of 'nerve-wracking' for 'nerve-racking'. **1835** *Penny Cycl.* IV. 374/2 The period of King James's translation. **1931** *Sunday School Times* (Philadelphia) 22 Aug. 458/1 A good English translation should be in good English idiom, and the old King James was that at least. **1932** *Jrnl. R. Anthrop. Inst.* LXII. 283 He made 'a serpent of brass', as the King James version says. **1973** *Sci. Amer.* Aug. 98/3 Add the number on the top of *A* to the number on the bottom of *B*, then find the chapter of Genesis (in a King James Bible) that corresponds to the sum.

king-bird. 1. For '*Paradisea regia*' substitute '*Cicinnurus regius*'. (Later example.)

1958 G. DURRELL *Encounters with Animals* II. 47 Here [*sc.* in a Brazilian zoo]..three king birds of paradise were living... The male is about the size of a blackbird, with a velvety orange head contrasting vividly with a snow-white breast and a brilliant scarlet back.

2. (Later example.)

1926 D. H. LAWRENCE *David* viii. 65 *Jonathan*:..Shall not the leader shine forth? *Saul*: Even so. And the young King-bird shall moult his feathers in the same hour.

3. Substitute for def.: One of several North American tyrant fly-catchers of the genus *Tyrannus*. (Earlier and later examples.)

1778 J. CARVER *Trav. N. Amer.* 475 The King Bird is like a swallow, and seems to be of the same species as the black martin or swift. **1801** *Massachusetts Spy* 25 Nov. 1/2 Just as a parcel of King-birds will pick at a Crow. **1959** VAN TYNE & BERGER *Fund. Ornith.* vii. 205 The Gray Kingbird (*Tyrannus dominicensis*) and the Black-whiskered Vireo (*Vireo altiloquus*)..leave Cuba to winter in South America.

kingdom, *sb.* Add: **4. d.** *to come* (*in*)*to one's kingdom*: to acquire authority, power, attractiveness, or the like. Cf. *Luke* xxiii. 42.

1892 KIPLING & BALESTIER *Naulahka* xviii. 211 Now we are come to our Kingdom..Little it profits us. **1930** L. G. MOBERLY *Eternal Dustbin* xiv. 194 That woman has come into her kingdom. **1973** R. RENDELL *Some lie & Some Die* iii. 30 Good luck. Remember me when thou comest into thy kingdom.

king-fish. Add: **2.** A leader, chief, boss; freq. used as a nickname for a particular person, notably for Huey Long (1893–1935), Governor and Senator from Louisiana. *U.S. slang.*

1933 HUEY P. LONG *Every Man a King* xxvii. 277 We from time to time termed various of our political enemies the 'Kingfish', most prominent of which was..a certain corporation lawyer. *Ibid.*, I am participating here anyway, gentlemen. For the present you can just call me the Kingfish. **1934** *Sun* (Baltimore) 21 Aug. 10/2 The Kingfish [*sc.* Huey Long] is ideally equipped for a dictator's rôle. **1939** *Ibid.* 17 July 11/1 King Levinsky, the Kingfish, who earned a fortune..during four spectacular years in the ring. **1946** *Richmond* (Va.) *Times Dispatch* 26 Dec. 1/5 Mr. Brown..is sometimes referred to as the 'kingfish' of City Council. **1968** *Word Study* Dec. 4/1 The term *kingfish* may be applied to an undisputed leader or master. It has been used as a personal appellation, self-applied I believe, to Huey Long, and to a character in the enduring radio show of Amos 'n' Andy.

kingfisher. Add: **3.** In full, *kingfisher blue*. A brilliant blue colour.

1922 *Daily Mail* 11 Dec. 1 (Advt.), All the leading colours including Ivory, Apricot, Jade, Kingfisher, [etc.]. **1956** G. DURRELL *My Family* v. 58 The sea smooth and opalescent, kingfisher-blue. **1970** *Observer* 18 Jan. 1/8 (Advt.), Both dresses in navy, deep oatmeal or kingfisher. **1971** R. RENDELL *One Across* vi. 55 A wool dress of brilliant kingfisher blue.

Kingite (ki·ŋəit). *N.Z.* [f. KING *sb.* + -ITE[1] 1 b.] A follower of the Maori king (see *King Country* s.v. *KING *sb.* 13 a). Also *attrib.* or as *adj.*

1860 T. BUDDLE *Maori King Movement* 60 On this point the kingites carry with them the sympathies of the majority. **1884** J. H. KERRY-NICHOLLS *King Country* 6 In 1857 Kingite meetings were held in Paetai. *Ibid.* 9 Sir George Grey..opened up communication with the chiefs of the Kingites. **1910** J. COWAN *Maoris of N.Z.* xxvii. 286 This Kingite war-song..is still on the lips of the Waikato people. *Ibid.* 289 All might have gone well had the Kingites been able to restrain their more turbulent spirits. **1959** K. SINCLAIR in J. E. Gorst *Maori King* p. xiv, He was driven out by the Kingites on 18 April, 1863. *Ibid.* 263 There were no large Kingite meetings, at which he could have been formally 'installed'.

kingklip (ki·ŋklip). In full, **kingklipfish** (**-visch**). [Afrikaans, f. Du. *koningklipvisch*: see *KLIPFISH.] One of several South African marine food fishes, esp. *Epinephelus andersoni*, of the family Serranidæ.

[**1843** J. C. CHASE *Cape of Good Hope* 169 Koning Klip Fish, King Rock Fish. Scarcer than the preceding, very considerably larger, and less delicate, but in much repute.] **1876** H. BROOKS *Natal* iv. 141 Klipvisch, king-klip fish..are held in very high estimation. **1878** K. JOHNSTON *Africa* xxiii. 393 Not fewer than forty-four varieties of edible fishes have been enumerated, including ..'King Klip'. **1893** H. A. BRYDEN *Gun & Camera S. Afr.* xx. 449 Many of the fish in Cape waters furnish excellent eating; the Roman, kingklipvisch, stomneus, steenbras, and klipvisch being among the choicest. **1923** *Nature* 24 Feb. 271/1 The kingklip (in appearance like a ling). **1930** C. L. BIDEN *Sea-Angling Fishes of Cape* 2 Angling for..kabeljou, stockfish, and king klipfish. **1950** M. MASSON *Birds of Passage* xii. 121 Vendor and buyer alike haggled over the merits of..Kingclipfish. **1971** *Rand Daily Mail* 4 Sept. 1/3 Kingklip, soles and Cape salmon were almost unobtainable.

King Kong (ki·ŋ,kǫ·ŋ). [Name of the ape-like monster featured in the film *King Kong* (1933).] **a.** Used as a nickname for anyone of outstanding size or strength. (In quot. 1966 used ironically.)

1955 E. WAUGH *Officers & Gentlemen* I. vi. 62 He looks like a gorilla. They..sent him here to teach us to climb. We call him King Kong. **1966** 'L. LANE' *ABZ of Scouse* 59 *King Kong*, derisory name for a weedy, undersized individual. **1970** M. KELLY *Spinifex* vi. 103 'What about King Kong?'..'He's just an honest murderer.' **1970** K. PLATT *Pushbutton Butterfly* (1971) xi. 123 'He looked like a big ape.'.. 'Make it a gorilla...That way we can pin it on King Kong.' **1974** *Guardian* 23 Aug. 8/4 Finn MacCool was a legendary Irish giant, a King Kong with a generous heart.

b. Cheap alcohol. *slang.*

1946 MEZZROW & WOLFE *Really Blues* 357/2 *King Kong*, cheap moonshine, corn whisky. **1950** H. E. GOLDIN *Dict. Amer. Underworld Lingo* 117/1 *King Kong*, (South) a potent drink made from the skimmings of boiling sugar cane.

king-maker. Add: Also *transf.* and *fig.*

1899 E. WHARTON *Greater Inclination* 162 John Oberville? I'll tell you what he is—the power behind the throne, the black Pope, the King-maker. **1949** *Sun* (Baltimore) 10 Aug. 1/6 Hunt boasted of responsibility for getting so many Government officials their jobs that he was known 'socially' as 'the kingmaker'. **1959** *Manch. Guardian* 4 Aug. 4/2 Governor Ribicoff, of Connecticut.. has launched his career as a kingmaker by taking command of the Kennedy forces. **1968** 'G. BAGBY' *Another Day* iv. 76 This was a young man who was clearly destined to make his mark... The kingmakers had their eye on him. He was going to go places. **1972** *Times* 27 Dec. 5/8 This was a sad example of a politician still trying to play the kingmaker long after his influence had waned.

king-pin. Add: **2.** (Earlier and later examples.) Also, the most important or outstanding person in a party, organization, etc.

1867 *Harper's Weekly* 14 Sept. 590/2 His best position was as a batter. He was a 'King-pin' there. **1914** *Chambers's Jrnl.* Jan. 62/1 The cars are mounted on bogie trucks, the connection being by means of a central or 'king-pin'. **1915** C. J. DENNIS *Songs of Sentimental Bloke* 102 But 'struth! 'E is king-pin! The 'ead serang! **1926** K. S. PRICHARD *Working Bullocks* (1956) 206 'My!' Mary Ann gasped incredulously, 'and you was the king pin last week.' **1957** J. WATEN *Shares in Murder* 99 Then he must be the biggest fence of the lot. The kingpin. The daddy of all fences. **1957** *Economist* 5 Oct. 22/1 The balloting for the seven seats filled by the constituency parties revealed that, with the kingpin removed, the former Bevanite machine is showing signs of disintegration. **1958** *Engineering* 28 Feb. 265/3 Another remarkable feature of the design is a front suspension which uses telescopic dampers as the king pins and steering swivels. **1970** *Daily Tel.* 30 Oct. 2/6 The owner of three shops was the kingpin behind a wholesale shoplifting plot. **1971** M. TAK *Truck Talk* 96 *Kingpin*, the bolt on the underside of the front of a trailer that fits into the tractor's fifth wheel to couple the tractor and the trailer together.

king-post. Add: **2.** On a ship (see quots.).

1927 G. BRADFORD *Gloss. Sea Terms* 95/2 *King post*, a short derrick mast to support the smaller cargo booms. **1948** R. DE KERCHOVE *Internat. Maritime Dict.* 385/1 *King post.* 1. A short heavy mast which serves to support a boom. 2. The centerline pillars in a ship's hold. **1961** F. H. BURGESS *Dict. Sailing* 127 *Kingpost*, a vertical post, sometimes resembling a mast, erected near the hatches, to support and top a derrick boom.

king's man, kingsman. Add: **1. b.** *the King's men*: a name for the dramatic company otherwise known as 'the King's Majesty's Servants' under James I.

1613 R. DABORNE *Let.* 29 Oct. in P. Henslowe *Henslowe Papers* (1907) 76 They shall have the play or noe, they rale upon me I hear bycause the kingsmen hav given out they shall hav it. *Ibid.* 77 Eight pound besyds my rent which J will fully satisfy y^u^ eather by them or the kings men as y^u^ please. **1886** *Dict. Nat. Biogr.* VII. 286/1 Burbage's position justifies the conjecture..that he had been connected with the lord chamberlain's men, subsequently called the king's men, and originally called Lord Strange's company. **1923** E. K. CHAMBERS *Eliz. Stage* II. 218 The King's men gave eight plays at Court..during the winter of 1614–15. **1951** M. CHUTE *Shakespeare of London* xi. 233 The King's Men gave a Sunday production of *The Merry Wives of Windsor* and then followed it on St. Stephen's night with *Measure for Measure.*

c. *U.S.* One who supported the British cause at the time of the American Revolution. *Obs.* exc. *Hist.*

1809 P. FRENEAU *Poems* II. 11 Whate'er some angry king's-men say, You play a game that must be won. **1857** *Ladies' Repository* XVII. 83/1, I never feed kingsmen if I can help it. **1949** *Sat. Even. Post* 2 Apr. 98/4, I am neither king's man nor rebel.

4. A member of King's College, Cambridge.

1803 C. SMART in *Gradus ad Cantabrigiam* 81 Ev'n gloomiest Kings-men, pleas'd awhile, Grin horribly a ghastly smile. **1852** C. A. BRISTED *Five Yrs. in Eng. Univ.* (ed. 2) 127 He came out the winner, with the Kingsman and one of our three close at his heels. **1968** *Tablet* 17 Aug. 820/1 He was anxious, like many Kingsmen, to be recognised as a Fabian. **1973** *Observer* 1 July 32/3 He was a fellow of King's College, Cambridge..and immediately after his death he received what must have been regarded by most Kingsmen as the ultimate accolade. **1974** *Times Lit. Suppl.* 29 Nov. 1346/3 Basileon. A Magazine of King's College, Cambridge... The founder-editors believed that facility in writing resulted from early practice, and their rather solemn purpose was to give Kingsmen a chance of trying their hand... To a Kingsman of between the wars they still give off that faint but delightful savour.

Kingston² (ki·ŋstən). *Naut.* The name of John *Kingston*, 19th-century British dockyard foreman, used *attrib.* and *absol.* († and in the possessive) to designate a kind of conical valve he invented for use in the sides of ships below the water-line which opens outwards with a screwing action.

1846 J. BOURNE *Treat. Steam Engine* xi. 223/1 In modern steam vessels Kingston's valves are..used, which consist of a spindle or plate valve fitted to the exterior of the ship, so that if the internal pipe or cock breaks, the external valve will still be operative. **1859** *Reed's New Guide Bk. Local Marine Board Exam.* 62 (*heading*) Boiler valves and cocks... Kingston valves. **1883** A. E. SEATON *Man. Marine Engin.* xvi. 301 For all large inlets the Kingston valve is preferable, as it acts as a non-return valve in case of the spindle breaking, and can then always be worked by simply forcing it outwards. *Ibid.* 303 A valve may be fitted in lieu of a cock to even the smallest Kingston. *Ibid.*, In the Navy, Kingston valves are fitted to all inlets and blow-off pipes. **1905** E. M. & B. DONKIN tr. *Bauer's Marine Engines & Boilers* 418 Most of the valves in merchant ships consist of ordinary valves opening inwards, but on warships the old so-called 'Kingston' valves are still frequently met with. **1933** 'L. LUARD' *All Hands* 124 Drop of air in three main. Open three Kingston. Close air. Open three vent. **1966** P. E. SEGDITSAS *Elsevier's Naut. Dict.* 111 Kingston valve; sea cock.

King Street (ki·ŋ strīt). [Name of the street near Covent Garden, London, in which the headquarters of the Communist Party of Great Britain Executive Committee has been situated since 1920.] Used *transf.* to designate the Communist Party of Great Britain, its members, or its leaders. Also *attrib.*

1958 C. COCKBURN *Crossing Line* iii. 49 The place did good business in those days..because the *Daily Worker* staff and the people from King Street..used it. *Ibid.* v. 83 This was a situation which gave many people at King Street nightmares. **1961** *Guardian* 5 June 8/4 The Labour party..shunning the support of King Street. **1964** C. DRIVER *Disarmers* iii. 72 If the King Street commissars were not so invincibly stupid, they would have insisted that the movement be left severely alone. **1970** *Times Lit. Suppl.* 18 Sept. 1016/3 Even if not a card-carrying member of the Communist Party, Strachey was at this time the grey eminence of King Street. **1972** *Observer* 8 Oct. 29/2 One version of events is that 'King Street' had decided the miners wouldn't end the strike unless they were given 25 per cent. King Street means the headquarters of the Communist Party.

kingy (ki·ŋi). [f. KING *sb.* + -Y⁶.] A children's game resembling 'He' but played with a ball; the winner is declared King.

[**1916** N. DOUGLAS *London Street Games* 5 There are other ball-games, such as hot rice..and king and missings out.] **1959** B. SUTTON-SMITH *Games N.Z. Children* II. 150 Kingy. In this game the players begin by standing round in a circle with their arms on one another's shoulders. The ball is dropped in the middle of the circle. When it touches someone's foot that person is He. **1969** I. & P. OPIE *Children's Games* ii. 95 'Kingy' is a ball game in which those who are not He have the ball hurled at them, without means of retaliation. **1972** *Where* Apr. 102/2 Transferred to playground or playing field, such games as 'kingy' can lose much of their colour and point, since the existence of natural and human obstacles and hazards are of their essence.

kinin (kəi·nin). [f. Gr. *κιν-εῖν* to set in motion + -IN¹; in sense 1 abstracted from *bradykinin* (s.v. *BRADY-).] **1.** *Biochem.* Any of a group of polypeptides of low molecular weight which are formed in tissue (from inactive precursors in the blood) in response to injury and have local effects that typically include pain and the dilatation of blood vessels.

1954 SCHACHTER & THAIN in *Brit. Jrnl. Pharmacol.* IX. 352/1 Since this substance in wasp venom cannot as yet be identified with any substance hitherto described, it is tentatively designated as wasp (or venom) kinin, or simply as kinin. **1962** *New Scientist* 4 Oct. 35/2 If the kinins get into the general circulation they are destroyed before they can produce general effects throughout the body. **1963** *Listener* 7 Nov. 741/2 An important factor in rheumatism may be an accelerated formation and release of certain compounds known as kinins, which are formed from amino-acids. The kinins may cause many of the painful symptoms, such as the swollen joints that are a prominent part of the disease. **1970** PASSMORE & ROBSON *Compan. Med. Stud.* II. xvii. 1/2 In addition to the above kinins, bradykinin homologues..are found in many parts of the animal kingdom, e.g. in wasp and scorpion venoms ..and in the plasma of reptiles and birds.

2. *Plant Physiol.* = *CYTOKININ.

1956 C. O. MILLER et al. in *Jrnl. Amer. Chem. Soc.* LXXVIII. 1375 A substance which markedly promotes cell division in various plant tissue cultures..has been shown..to be 6-furfurylaminopurine. The specific name *kinetin* has been applied to this substance, and the generic term *kinin* is suggested for any substance which similarly stimulates cytokinesis. **1965** *New Scientist* 25 Mar. 788/3 The third and most recently investigated group of plant growth substances is that of the kinins. **1971** F. C. STEWARD *Plant Physiol.* VIA. iii. 356 The photoperiodic responses to red light may also involve kinin effects.

kininogen (kəini·nŏdʒĕn). *Biochem.* [f. *KININ + *-OGEN.] Any biologically inactive precursor of a kinin (sense *1).

1963 *Jrnl. Physiol.* CLXIX. 45P The plasmin preparation..did not form kinin from purified kininogen. **1970** PASSMORE & ROBSON *Compan. Med. Stud.* II. xvii. 2/1 Although plasma and tissues contain readily activated kinin-forming enzymes and kininogens, free active kinin is rarely detected in biological fluids.

kinjal (kindʒā·l). [Native name in the Caucasus (= Russ. *kinzhál*), a. Pers. (Arab., Turk., Urdū) KHANJAR.] (Among Caucasians and Kurds) = HANDJAR, HANJAR, KHANJAR.

1862 *Harper's Mag.* XXVI. 803/1, I laid aside revolver and kindshall. **1889** J. ABERCROMBY *Trip E. Caucasus* 130 At his waist hung a *kinjal* and a long native sabre. **1897** R. D. BLACKMORE *Dariel* viii. 86 His hand was playing with his *kinjal* all the time, for so they call those deadly bits of steel, without which they never think their attire complete. **1924** *Blackw. Mag.* Feb. 149/1 The scar of a Kurdish kinjal.

kink, *sb.*¹ Add: **1.** (Examples of use with reference to hair; also earlier and later *transf.* examples.)

1848 *Yale Lit. Mag.* XIV. 82 (Th.), Come! wake up, and shake the kinks out of your land legs. **1857** MAYNE REID *War Trail* xiii. 67 Yes, there was the same negress with.. the little well-oiled kinks hanging like corkscrews over her temples! **1930** [see *CRONK *a.*]. **1962** *Kenyon Rev.* XXIV. 94 Don't worry about Saturday night. Play around. Work the kinks out. **1970** G. F. NEWMAN *Sir, You Bastard* 259 There existed kinks in the man's career; it was only a question of drawing on the right one.

b. A sudden bend in a line, course, or the like that is otherwise straight or smoothly curved.

1899 S. BARING-GOULD *Furze Bloom* 27 That [wall] on the left makes a kink to respect 'The Brothers' Grave'. **1928** L. S. PALMER *Wireless Princ. & Pract.* v. 132 The curve sometimes exhibits a sudden 'kink' or discontinuity. **1965** G. MCINNES *Road to Gundagai* v. 74 Below the kink the street degenerates rapidly. **1971** *Sunday Express* (Johannesburg) 28 Mar. 7/1 A new grandstand for 2,000 spectators at the kink on the main straight.

2. a. (Earlier U.S. and later examples.) In recent use also = a state of madness; an instance of, the practice of, or suffering resulting from sexual abnormality.

1803 T. JEFFERSON *Let.* 24 Nov. in *Writings* (1897) VIII. 280 Should the judges take a kink in their heads. **1915** F. M. HUEFFER *Good Soldier* IV. ii. 229 By a kink, that I could not at the time understand, Miss Hurlbird insisted that I ought to keep the money all to myself. **1924** [see *ENSNARL *v.*¹]. **1950** T. S. ELIOT *Cocktail Party* II. 120 And so you suppose you have what you call a 'kink'? **1959** *Encounter* Mar. 22 Hates kissing. Undertakes most kinks..but no buggery. **1959** M. GEE in C. K. Stead *N.Z. Short Stories* (1966) 279 He's got a kink I reckon. He'll end up in the nuthouse. **1965** *Movie* Summer 44/4 The result is the story of the sexual hallucinations of a young girl..played for flat-out kink.

3. *U.S.* A human being in various slang applications. **a.** A Negro. *Obs.*

1865 J. H. BROWNE *Four Yrs. in Secessia* xxxix. 288 'Coming the kink' was to steal a negro from the country, and dispose of him in town. **1944** *Amer. Speech* XIX. 173 *Kink* shows an obvious allusion to the Negro's hair.

b. A criminal.

1914 JACKSON & HELLYER *Vocab. Criminal Slang* 52 *Kink*, a crook; a larcenous criminal. Also used by yeggs to designate a non-criminal tramp, or one who is not initiated into the particular craft of the speaker. **1950** H. E. GOLDIN *Dict. Amer. Underworld Lingo* 117/2 *Kink* (scattered areas of East and near South), a thief, especially an expert in stealing automobiles.

c. A sexually abnormal person; one who practises sexual perversions; loosely, an eccentric, a person wearing noticeably unusual clothes, behaving in a startling manner, etc.

1965 *Harper's Bazaar* Jan. 54/1 His phone is ex-directory because of all the kinks who used to phone at 2 a.m. **1967** [see *KICKSTER]. **1968** B. TURNER *Sex Trap* xv. 149, I believe the psychiatrists have other ideas about what makes a kink kinky. **1972** 'J. RIPLEY' *My Word you should have seen Us* 35, I have known queers. I have known kinks.

kinked, *ppl. a.* [s.v. KINK *v.*² in Dict.] (Later examples in extended uses.)

1966 *Punch* 5 Oct. 521/1 Others were delighted by the elegance of the language and the sinister kinked logic governing the behaviour of the characters. **1967** A.

Hunter *Gently Continental* viii. 127, I *am* scared. I can't protect Trudi. Frieda is kinked. **1969** D. C. Hague *Managerial Econ.* iv. 92 The kinked demand curve is derived from the..curves we have already been using in our analysis of trade association pricing. **1970** D. Uhnak *Ledger* (1971) vii. 97 Stoner Martin massaged the back of his neck. 'This kind of work can sure leave you kinked up.'

kinker (ki·ŋkəɹ). [f. Kink *sb.*[1] + -er[1].] An acrobat, a contortionist (see also quot. 1948).

1926 *Amer. Speech* I. 282/2 *Kinker*, a performer or acrobat. **1931** *Amer. Mercury* Nov. 353/1 *Kinkers*, circus performers. **1948** Mencken *Amer. Lang.* Suppl. II. 684 A contortionist is a *frog*, *bender* or *Limber Jim*, a freak or snake-charmer is a *geek*, and all performers are *kinkers*.

kinkiness (ki·ŋkinės). [f. Kinky *a.* + -ness.] The quality or habit of being kinky (in the senses of Dict. and Suppl.); a kinky state.

1924 W. Deeping *Three Rooms* ii. 15 His black hair was wavy even to kinkiness. **1951** G. C. Shattuck *Dis. Tropics* lvii. 694 The hair loses its luster... The natural kinkiness disappears. **1959** C. MacInnes *Absolute Beginners* 22 'What kind of print might you be needing?' I went on, not sure yet what kinkiness I had to cater for. **1966** *Punch* 28 Sept. 483/1 Normally he [*sc.* a cat] prefers to bite men and scratch women, which seems to point to some kinkiness in his make-up. **1968** R. V. Beste *Repeat Instructions* x. 104 What's wrong with her? Or is a certain kinkiness in spelling now evidence of a security risk? **1971** S. Jepson *Let. to Dead Girl* iii. 23 If black vinyl thigh boots under a slit midi skirt..wasn't kinky on purpose, he'd be glad someone else would tell him what it was... Trust Fatty to look for kinkiness. **1972** *Daily Tel.* 27 Apr. 9/2 His book..is too smuttily concerned with 'kinkiness' to justify its sub-title.

kinkless (ki·ŋklės), *a.* [f. Kink *sb.*[1] + -less.] Without a kink: applied in *Electronics* to a kind of tetrode designed so as to eliminate the irregularity of the current–voltage characteristic of an ordinary tetrode (which shows up as kinks in the characteristic curve).

1943 C. L. Boltz *Basic Radio* x. 164 The second method of suppressing the secondary emission is to align the control grid and screen very carefully so that the wires are opposite... Such a valve is a kinkless tetrode. **1953** F. Langford-Smith *Radio Designer's Handbk.* (ed. 4) i. i. 8 Some 'kinkless' tetrodes are also used as v-f and i-f amplifiers. **1958** W. F. Lovering *Radio Communication* viii. 170 To avoid the kink in the E_a–I_a characteristic it is necessary to return the secondary electrons to the anode even when the screen is positive to anode... The first solution to this problem was the pentode... A later solution was the kinkless tetrode (or Beam tube).

kinky, *a.* Add: Also **kinkey. 1.** Also *Comb.*, as *kinky-bearded, -haired, -headed, -tailed* adjs.

1844 *Congress. Globe* 6 Jan. App. 42/3 [The Negro's] skull is as thick, his hair is as kinkey, his nose as flat..as they were the day he was first introduced. **1848** W. T. Thompson *Major Jones's Sk. Trav.* 146, I happened to call one of the nigger waiters 'boy'. The kinky-headed cuss looked at me sideways, and rolled the whites of his eyes at me. **1861** in *Rebellion Rec.* (1862) I. iii. 137 A marked distinction is laid Between the rights of the mistress, And those of the kinky-haired maid. **1865** Kinky-haired [in Dict.]. **1925** W. Deeping *Sorrell & Son* xxix. 290 The hard-bitten, kinky-haired casualty-sister assisting him with critical and voiceless composure. **1937** *Time* 16 Aug. 58/2 Ill lay kinky-bearded, 64-year-old Thorvald Stauning, Premier of Denmark, after breaking a leg. **1956** C. Auerbach *Genetics in Atomic Age* 93 When a female mouse is irradiated during the second week of pregnancy, some of her young may be born with kinky tails. Unlike true mutations to kinky tail, these deformities are not inherited. If, later on, visible mutants should turn up in the progeny of such a kinky-tailed mouse, they are not more likely to affect the tail than the eyes or the ears or the coat.

2. For (*U.S. colloq.*) read (*colloq.*). (Later examples.)

1889 *Sportsman* 2 Jan. (Farmer), The kinky ones and the worthy ones who play hole-and-corner with society. **1907** E. M. Forster *Longest Journey* viii. 100 This jaundiced young philosopher, with his kinky view of life, was too much for him. **1929** W. J. Locke *Ancestor Jorico* xix. 263 A fellow ought to know something about the funny kinky ways of ordinary men and women. **1950** T. S. Eliot *Cocktail Party* ii. 120 But when everything's bad form, or mental kinks, You either become bad form, and cease to care, Or else, if you care, you must be kinky.

b. Lively, spry, energetic. *U.S. local.*

1903 G. S. Wasson *Cap'n Simeon's Store* vi. 107 'He ain't over and above kinky, though, I s'pose likely?' 'No, ..nothin' very antic about him...there must be some buckram left into him, too, the way he keeps a-going.' **1914** *Dialect Notes* IV. 4 *Kinky*, in high spirits. 'You seem to be feeling pretty kinky to-day.'

c. *Criminals' slang.* Of things: dishonestly come by (see also quot. 1954). Cf. Crooked *a.* 3 b, *bent *ppl. a.* 5 a, b.

1927 *Collier's* 23 July 15/1 'Why, you can't tell me that you didn't know those five big cars were kinky.' 'Kinky?' ..'Those cars were bent.' **1931** G. Irwin *Amer. Tramp & Underworld Slang* 117 *Kinky*, criminal; crooked; unlawful. Said of stolen goods, or of an individual known to be without the law. **1942** Berrey & Van den Bark *Amer. Thes. Slang* § 470/1 *Booty*,..killing, kinky goods, lift. **1954** W. R. & F. K. Simpson *Hockshop* 275 Canfield..was never accused..of having 'kinky' gambling paraphernalia. By that I mean dice and cards and roulette wheels that gave the house an unfair advantage.

d. In senses corresponding to *kink *sb.*[1] 3 c. Of persons: perverted, esp. sexually; *spec.* homosexual. Of things or situations: suggestive of sexual perversion, as of certain items or styles of dress (e.g. *kinky boots*); in weakened sense, bizarre.

1959 C. MacInnes *Absolute Beginners* 16 Suze..meets lots of kinky characters..and acts as agent for me getting orders from them for my pornographic photos. **1960** 'A. Burgess' *Doctor is Sick* xviii. 145 'If you think I'm perverted you're completely mistaken. I'm quite normal.' 'Normal? You? That's a laugh. You're kinky, the same as what I am.' **1960** F. Norman *Fings ain't wot they used t'Be* ii. i. 52 Fancy anyone being so kinkey about a brown teapot. **1963** *Daily Tel.* 11 Dec. 19/2 The phrase 'kinky advert'..meant that she acted as an advertisement for irregular sexual practices. **1964** *Ann. Reg. 1963* 1 It [*sc.* 1963] was the year..that women adopted the fashionable long 'kinky' boot. **1964** J. Burke *Hard Day's Night* i. 11 She was dead kinky for sweetbreads. **1964** *Times Lit. Suppl.* 8 Oct. 925/1 Zoo men receive a constant stream of kinky letters. **1966** *Listener* 6 Jan. 23/1 One of the girls—a buxom specimen in kinky patent leathers. **1966** J. Porter *Sour Cream* ix. 117 On the one hand I had to trust Zinaida, on the other I knew she was perfectly capable of fabricating the whole scheme just to get rid of Katia whom she loathed. It was like something out of Greek tragedy, only kinkier. **1967** A. Diment *Dolly Dolly Spy* ii. 19 He produced a pack of Black Russian cigarettes, dead kinky, and tossed me one. **1968** [see *kink *sb.*[1] 3 c]. **1971** *Daily Tel.* 16 July 11/4 In a moment of excessively kinky passion a husband strangles his mistress. **1972** F. Warner *Lying Figures* iii. 36 Kinky sex makes them feel inadequate.

B. *sb.* **a.** A person with 'kinky' hair. **b.** An object dishonestly obtained. **c.** A sexually abnormal or perverted person. **d.** *pl.* Kinky boots.

1926 J. F. Dobie *Rainbow in Morning* 4 One considers the negro as a shining apostle of sweetness and light, another as a jolly old darkey, and still another as a 'phallic kinky'. G. Thomas *Ibid.* 154 The Fayette County and other South Texas 'kinkies' whose songs I have been noting. **1927** *Collier's* 23 July 14/1 *A kinky*, any stolen car. **1941** *Amer. Mercury* Mar. 349/2 The titles of every car Joe sold could be searched clear back to the factory... Yet the cars were strictly kinkies. **1942** Berrey & Van den Bark *Amer. Thes. Slang* § 430/2 *Curly-headed person*, curly, curly-locks, curly-pate, kinks, kinky. **1950** 'N. Bell' *I am Legion* vii. 216 O Good Lord... Quite half of them *are* kinkies. **1959** *Encounter* July 83/1 No prostitutes, no queers, no kinkies. **1965** *Punch* 19 May 755/1 Palm memory of the agreeable feel of the two-in-hand will come back, and if snakeboots replace kinkies, the thrill of the double slalom round the sprigs above the eyelet-holes. **1967** A. Diment *Dolly Dolly Spy* vi. 82 Porny photos, various drugs and birds for kinkies at Oxford.

kinnikinic. The more usual forms are now **kinnikinnick, kinnikinnik.** Also many other varr. **1.** (Earlier, *attrib.*, and later examples.)

1805 J. Ordway in Lewis & Ordway *Jrnls. Western Explor.* (1916) 199 Some Indians had hung up..a Scraper a paint bag.., kinikaneck bags, flints, [etc.]. **1827** T. L. McKenney *Sk. Tour to Lakes* 181 The pipe of an Indian.. and a pouch made of the skin of some animal, in which he carries his *kinnikanic*, a kind of fragrant weed that has a leaf like our box wood. **1839** C. A. Murray *Trav. N. Amer.* II. 22 We took out our kinnekinik-bag. **1844** —— *Prairie-bird* II. 179 Volumes of *kinnekenik* smoke. **1860** H. Y. Hind *Narr. Canad. Red River Expedition* I. 315 A sandy ridge..was covered with the bear-berry from which kinnikinnik is made. **1867** 'Mark Twain' *Amer. Drolleries* (1875) 41 The most popular..smoking tobacco is.. Killikinick. **1889** K. Munroe *Golden Days* xxvi. 284 Put that in your pipe and smoke it, along with your killikinick. **1890** E. Custer *Following Guidon* viii. 101 Kinnikinnic.. is a mixture of willow bark, sumach leaves, sage leaf, and tobacco, and is thoroughly mingled with marrow from buffalo bones. **1920** *Chambers's Jrnl.* 31 Jan. 136/1 The curling wisps of *kinickinick* smoke. **1969** *Islander* (Victoria, B.C.) 23 Nov. 13/2 Since their canoe had been swamped, the two pipe-smoking canoeists had been without tobacco. They used kinnikinik..which the Indians smoke.

2. (Earlier, *attrib.*, and later examples.)

1822 A. Eaton *Man. Bot.* (ed. 3) 178 *Arbutus uva-ursi*, bear berry, kinnikinnick... Dry, barren sand plains. **1853** J. W. Bond *Minnesota & its Resources* 303 Some dry Kinne-kin-nick bark is generally carried along, cut very fine for the purpose of smoking. **1910** *Anthropos* V. 420 Nor should we forget to mention the fruit of the *kinnikinik* or bearberry bush (*Arctostaphylos uva-ursi*), which, though insipid enough to a white man, is of such importance in the eyes of some tribes, as the Chilcotins, that it gives its name to one of their minor seasons. **1938** M. Thompson *High Trails of Glacier Nat. Park* 86 As we climb into the Hudsonian zone we find extensive carpets of kinnikinnick. **1956** V. Fisher *Pemmican* xxviii. 259 They went another day, and another, eating nothing but rose hips, leaves, kinnikinnik bark, moss, water cress. **1963** *Vancouver Sun* 23 Nov. 21/1 The rolling hills..are park-like with their copses of fir, tamarack, poplar and willow, dotted through open stretches of bitterbrush and kinnikinnik.

kino- (kəi·no), comb. form of Gr. κινεῖν to set in motion, as in **kinoci·lium** (pl. **-cilia**) *Biol.*, a cilium which is capable of moving (in contrast to an immobile cilium, called a stereocilium), *spec.* such a cilium borne singly on each hair cell of the maculæ of the inner ear amid a group of about a hundred stereocilia; **ki·noform** *Physics*, a transparent plate with a contoured surface so made as to introduce phase differences into an incident parallel beam in such a way as to form a single three-dimensional image of the particular object for which the calculation of the surface was made; **ki·noplasm** *Cytology* [ad. G. *kinoplasma* (E. Strasburger *Histol. Beiträge* (1892) IV. 60)], a supposed special kind of cytoplasm which was formerly held to be fibrillar in nature and to give rise to the active parts of a cell (such as the membrane and the mitotic apparatus); hence **kinopla·smic** *a.*

1933 M. Fernán-Núñez tr. *Ramón y Cajal's Histol.* x. 148 These cilia [of ciliated epithelium] are completely free and carry out spontaneous vibratory and whip-like movements, both of flexion and extension in the greater number of cases (kinocilia); in other cases, as in the epididymis, they appear immobile (stereocilia). **1956** *Acta Oto-Laryngol. Suppl.* No. 126. 46 The kinocilium in each cell is closely consistent in structure with the kinocilia that have been observed in the trachea, the fallopian tube, and in a number of unicellular organisms. **1971** *New Scientist* 29 July 283/1 The kinocilium, an apparently active hair among the passive hairs of each hair cell on the basilar membrane of the ear. **1968** P. M. Hirsch et al. *Digital Holograms & Kinoforms* in *IBM Technical Symposium on Laser Applic., Sept. 1968* (typescript) 244 Our efforts have been in making digital holograms and a new kind of imaging element, which we call a kinoform. **1969** L. B. Lesem et al. in *IBM Jrnl. Res. & Devel.* XIII. 150/1 The kinoform is a new, computer-generated wavefront reconstruction device which, like the hologram, provides the display of a three-dimensional image. In contrast, however, the illuminated kinoform yields a single diffraction order and, ideally, all the incident light is used to reconstruct this one image. *Ibid.* 151/2 Unlike the making of holograms, which can be physical recordings of actual wavefront interference patterns.., it does not appear possible to create a kinoform using completely optical techniques. **1970** *Physics Bull.* Nov. 493/1 Kinoforms, like digital holograms, are also made by calculating the wavefront scattered from the numerically defined object, but instead of adding in a reference beam, the amplitude of the scattered wavefront is assumed constant. A photographic plot of the phase distribution (mod 2π) is made, and translated into a phase plate. *Ibid.* 495/2 Kinoforms can be used as arbitrarily shaped phase plates in lens applications. **1894** *Jrnl. R. Microsc. Soc.* 581 Prof. E. Strasburger concludes that in the cytoplasm two constituents are contrasted in their activity. To one of these, the kinoplasm, the radiations round the centrospheres, the spindle-fibres, and the combining filaments.. owe their origin... The other constituent..is the trophoplasm. **1910** G. M. Calkins *Protozoöl.* i. 29 Some [observers]..have endeavored to show that archoplasm, or, in a larger sense, kinoplasm, is not only specific, but a kind of 'superior' protoplasm, self-perpetuating and distinct. **1934** L. W. Sharp *Introd. Cytol.* (ed. 3) ii. 45 It appears to be the kinoplasm that is responsible for protoplasmic streaming; it flows through the relatively stationary trophoplasm, carrying with it the plastids and chondriosomes. **1965** K. Esau *Plant Anat.* (ed. 2) iii. 57 The old concept of the existence of a special kind of active, fibrous cytoplasm, the kinoplasm. **1900** E. B. Wilson *Cell* (ed. 2) vi. 322 Beyond this the two forms of protoplasm show a difference of staining-reaction, the kinoplasmic fibrillæ staining deeply with gentian-violet and iron-hæmatoxylin, while the trophoplasm is but slightly stained. **1905** *Rep. Brit. Assoc. Adv. Sci.* 577 Strasburger considers them [*sc.* blepharoplasts] as kinoplasmic in nature, and thus brings them into relation with his other kinoplasmic structures, the centrosome and spindle. **1927** *Protoplasma* II. 201 The kinoplasmic spheres from which the contractile vacuoles arise in *Spirogyra*.

-kins, *suffix.* Variant of -kin, as in *babykins, boykins*, etc., and formerly in certain oath-words, as *bodikins, lakens* (see Lakin[2]), *maskins, pit(t)ikins.*

kinship. Add: **1. b.** *Anthropology.* The recognized ties of relationship, by descent, marriage, or ritual, that form the basis of social organization. So *attrib.* and *Comb.*, as *kinship category, group, structure, term*; **kinship system,** the system of relationships traditionally accepted in a culture and the rights and obligations which they involve.

1866 J. F. M'Lennan in *Fortn. Rev.* 15 Apr. 580 Kinship through the mother had been in Homer's time undisputed among the Greeks. **1910** J. G. Frazer *Totemism & Exogamy* I. 20 The Psylli, a Snake clan in Africa, had a similar test of kinship. **1914** W. H. R. Rivers (*title*) Kinship and social organization. *Ibid.* 1 The aim of these lectures is to demonstrate the close connection which exists between methods of denoting relationship or kinship and forms of social organisation. **1937** R. H. Lowie *Hist. Ethnol. Theory* x. 171 In 1909 Kroeber, while fruitfully paving the way for work on the linguistic categories embodied in kinship systems, denied any social determinants. **1945** G. & M. Wilson *Analysis of Social Change* vi. 162 Any attempt to bolster up a legal system based on kinship is doomed to failure in an expanding society. **1949** E. E. Evans-Pritchard in M. Fortes *Social Struct.* 101 Nuer themselves..see that it is undesirable to obliterate.. the boundaries between kinship categories. **1949** F. Eggan in *Ibid.* 121 One of the most significant advances in the study of kinship systems in modern times has been Professor A. R. Radcliffe-Brown's method of structural or sociological analysis. **1951** R. Firth *Elem. Social Organiz.* i. 32 Other basic relations..are due to position in a kinship system. **1955** M. Gluckman *Custom & Conflict in Afr.*

iv. 99 Children are desired by a Zulu kinship-group because they strengthen it. **1957** V. W. TURNER *Schism & Continuity in Afr. Soc.* iii. 77 In most primitive societies social control at the local level is associated with position in the kinship structure. **1958** A. R. RADCLIFFE-BROWN *Method in Social Anthropol.* II. iv. 171 The kin of any given person were classified into a limited number of categories, each denoted by one kinship term. **1969** M. FORTES *Kinship & Social Order* (1970) p. vii, My thesis is that the structuralist theory and method of analysis in the study of kinship and social organization..stems directly from Morgan's work. **1970** E. LEACH *Lévi-Strauss* vi. 99 Ties of filiation and..ties of siblingship..provide the basic bricks out of which kinship systems are built up. **1971** *World Archaeol.* III. 217 Ethnographic evidence therefore focuses on metalworking as a kinship or descent group-organized activity.

kinzigite (ki·ntsigəit). *Petrogr.* [ad. G. *kinzigit* (H. Fischer 1860, in *Neues Jahrb. f. Min.* 797), f. the name of the *Kinzig* valley, W. Germany: see -ITE^1.] A metamorphic schistose rock containing garnet, biotite, and varying amounts of quartz, plagioclase, sillimanite, and cordierite. Hence **kinzigi·tic** *a.*, containing kinzigite.

1878 *Jrnl. Chem. Soc.* XXXIV. 208 Garnet-graphite-gneiss was hitherto unknown [in the Black Forest],..being formerly known by the name of Kinzigite. **1947** *Bull. Geol. Soc. Amer.* LVIII. 1024 The kinzigites of the Askainen-Lemu zone are fine- to medium-grained and contain garnet as well as cordierite. **1965** *Mineral. Abstr.* XVII. 227/2 A kinzigitic formation..occurs in the district of Miglierina (Catanzaro). This formation is composed of kinzigites, kinzigitic gneiss, and amphibolic kinzigites.

Kioko (ki*ōu*·ko). Pl. **Kioko, -os.** [Native name.] The name of an African people inhabiting Zaïre and Angola, and their language; a member of this people. Also *attrib.* or as *adj.*

1884 *Encycl. Brit.* XVII. 319/1 *Equatorial Group*:.. Wa-Lunda, Kioko, Wa-Shinsh, [etc.]. **1897** A. J. BUTLER tr. *Ratzel's Hist. Mankind* II. 376 It is otherwise with the Songos and Kiokos, who let you deal with them in the usual way. *Ibid.* 404 Here, Lunda will be spoken; there, perhaps only half a mile away, Kioko. **1908** H. H. JOHNSTON *George Grenfell & Congo* I. xi. 194 Round him [*sc.* a person of Hima descent] a community would group itself... Thus..the kingdoms..of the Luba, Lunda, Kioko, and other Bantu countries came into existence. **1948** M. GUTHRIE *Classification Bantu Lang.* Index 86/1 Kioko (A[ngola]). **1966** *Chambers's Encycl.* III. 50/1 Among the African Kioko, however, it is the availability of criminals for food that seems paramount.

kiore (kiō·re). *N.Z.* [Maori.] In full, *kiore rat.* A small vegetarian rat, *Rattus exulans*, native to New Zealand. Also *transf.*

1838 J. S. POLACK *New Zealand* I. ix. 314 The *kiore*, or rat, has been introduced at an early period by European vessels. **1840** —— *Manners & Customs New Zealanders* II. xiii. 125 A thin person [is termed] Kioré or rat. **1843** E. DIEFFENBACH *Trav. N.Z.* II. I. vii. 114 The fat of the native rats (Kiore) killed on such lands should be given to the principal proprietor. **1883** in A. R. Wallace *Australasia* (ed. 3) xxvi. 559 The native rat, called Kiore, has been destroyed by the imported European rat. **1949** P. BUCK *Coming of Maori* (1950) II. i. 102 The Polynesian rat (*kiore, Mus exulans*) arrived in the voyaging canoes... They were probably stowaways. **1959** TINDALE & LINDSAY *Rangatira* 203 The kiore rat, taken to New Zealand by the ancestors of the Maori..was a small vegetarian animal..now extinct..except on a small island off the coast. **1966** *Encycl. N.Z.* III. 50/1 By the early 1920s it was believed that the kiore had become extinct. Today it is known to have survived in a few localities in widely separated areas.

kiosk. Add: (Now usu. with pronunc. kī·ǫsk.) **2.** No longer restricted to France and Belgium.

1933 P. MACDONALD *Mystery of Dead Police* xvii. 186 His quarry was at the change kiosk. **1963** V. NABOKOV *Gift* iii. 156 There was..a triangular island with a kiosk, at which tram conductors regaled themselves with milk. **1964** G. JOHNSTON *My Brother Jack* 36 Somehow we were able to get to the big kiosk-restaurant behind the point. *Ibid.* 37 The kiosk had been very late Victorian, with imitation turrets and spires. **1966** *South Australian Yearbk.* No. 1, 169 There are refreshment kiosk facilities. **1966** *Listener* 18 Aug. 227/2 Breaking into a tobacco kiosk. **1971** *E. Afr. Standard* (Nairobi) 10 Apr. 7/8 Most of the food sold in the kiosks is approved by medical officers.

3. = **telephone kiosk.*

1928 *Daily Mail* 25 July 19/4 It is expected that nearly 500,000 new lines will be laid, several thousand new kiosks erected, and several hundred telephones fixed at rural railway stations. **1972** H. BUCKMASTER *Walking Trip* 197 'I'd better call Norman..he has a right to know.' 'Here's a kiosk. Have you enough change?' **1974** M. BABSON *Stalking Lamb* xxiv. 179 He broke off the connection, swung open the door and stepped out of the kiosk.

Kiowa (kəi·ŏwă, kəi·ŏwǭ), *sb.* and *a.* Also **Kiawa, Kyaway,** etc. [Native name.] **A.** *sb.* **a.** An Indian people of the south-western U.S.; a member of this people. **b.** The language of this people.

1810 Z. M. PIKE *Acct. Expeditions Sources Mississippi* App. II. 16 The only nations with whom the Pawnees are now at war, are the Tetaus, Utahs, and Kyaways. **1849** G. A. F. RUXTON *Life in Far West* vii, The Kioway loves the pale-face, and gives him warning. **1856** W. W. WHIPPLE in *Rep. Explor. Route to Pacific* (U.S. War Dept.) III. v. 80 Some resemblances are likewise to be observed between the Kioway and the languages of the southern and western tribes of the Sioux or Dakota stock. **1874** [see *COMANCHE *sb.* 2]. **1928** *U.S. Bureau Amer. Ethnol. Bull.* No. 84. 2 Six vowel qualities and twenty-two consonants are found in Kiowa. **1959** E. TUNIS *Indians* 106/1 The fingers of one hand, held up and moved in a shaking circle, was the Kiowa—rattlebrained. **1965** *Canad. Jrnl. Linguistics* Spring 78 Kiowa (Powell's 'Kiowan'), a language of the western Plains, seems now to have been reasonably well established as a part of the Aztecan-Tanoan phylum. **1969** *Observer* (Colour Suppl.) 18 May 25/4 When the son of a wealthy Kiowa achieved an exploit, everyone heard about it.

B. *adj.* Of or pertaining to any of the above; *Kiowa Apache*, an Athapascan people associated with the Kiowa; a member of this people; also, their language.

1821 J. FOWLER *Jrnl.* (1898) 64 The Kiowa cheef with his nation had stoped and intended we shold stop with them. **1865** J. PIKE *Scout & Ranger* iv. 64 Houston's design was to carry the war into the Comanche and Kiowa country. **1885** W. P. CLARK *Indian Sign Lang.* 33 This gesture refers to the Apaches living with the Kiowas at the Wichita Agency, Indian Territory..frequently called Kiowa Apaches. **1928** *U.S. Bureau Amer. Ethnol. Bull.* No. 84. 2 (*heading*) Vocabulary of the Kiowa language. **1937** J. G. MCALLISTER in F. Eggan *Social Anthropol. N. Amer. Tribes* iii. 100 Communication was carried on by means of the sign language, and most of the old Kiowa-Apache knew a little Kiowa, though very few of the Kiowa had any knowledge of the Kiowa Apache tongue. **1963** *Univ. Calif. Publ. Linguistics* XXIX. 102 Western Apache..is one of the Apachean languages. Others are Chiricahua, Mescalero, Jicarilla, Kiowa Apache, Navaho, and Lipan. **1969** *Observer* (Colour Suppl.) 18 May 25/4 A Kiowa warrior was forced by custom to give away some of his wealth.

kip, *sb.*^{2} Add: **3.** *Gymnastics.* (See quot. 1972^1.) *U.S.*

1909 in WEBSTER. **1967** [see *KIP *v.*^{3}]. **1972** W. VINCENT *Gymnastic Routines for Men* 123 A kip is a vigorous and rapid extension of the hip joint for the purpose of developing momentum to raise the center of gravity of the body. It may be performed on all the events in gymnastics in one form or another. *Ibid.*, Kips may be performed forward (clockwise) or backward (counter-clockwise) with either the legs or the upper body as the moving part and the other as the stabilizing part. **1972** B. TAYLOR et al. *Olympic Gymnastics for Men & Women* v. 108/2 The movement begins with the gymnast jumping to a glide swing on the low bar and continuing into a glide kip position.

kip, *sb.*^{3} **1.** Delete † *Obs.* and add later *Comb.* examples.

1922 JOYCE *Ulysses* 541, I saw him, kipkeeper! Pox and gleet vendor! **1965** BROPHY & PARTRIDGE *Long Trail* 140 *Kip-shop*, a brothel.

2. Also (*rare*) **kipp**, and *Comb.* as *kip-house, -shop.* Also, a sleep, the action of sleeping.

1889 BARRÈRE & LELAND *Dict. Slang* I. 521/2 *Kip house*, a tramps' or vagrants' lodging-house. **1893** *Sessions Papers Cent. Criminal Court* 16 Nov. 39 He said, 'I only came here for a *kip*.'..*Kip* means sleep, I believe. **1908** J. M. SULLIVAN *Criminal Slang* 14 *Kipp*, a lodging house. **1925** FRASER & GIBBONS *Soldier & Sailor Words* 136 *Kip*: A sleep. Rest. A bed. A hammock, *e.g.*, 'To do a kip—to have a sleep.' **1932** *Fortn. Rev.* Mar. 325 The jake drinker's..earning capacity is nil, and if he has no lair of his own there is the 'doss house' or 'kip shop'. **1936** J. CURTIS *Gilt Kid* i. 12 He had spent a few nights in kip-shops. **1938** —— *They drive by Night* ix. 103, I got to have a rest. I ain't had no kip. **1943** M. HARRISON *Reported Safe Arrival* 18 Like the Professor, Harry was 'partial to a kip'. **1946** *Penguin New Writing* XXVIII. 123 Conditions under which the transport drivers work, of their cafés and kip-houses. **1962** *Observer* 11 Mar. 34/3 (*caption*) Dossers at a London kip-house. **1971** B. W. ALDISS *Soldier Erect* 78, I had to stay with the captain..while the other lucky sods settled down for a brief kip.

kip (kip), *sb.*^{6} *Austral.* and *N.Z.* [Origin unknown.] A small piece of wood from which pennies are spun in the game of two-up.

1898 *Bulletin* (Sydney) 17 Dec. Red Page/2 The *kip* is the piece of wood used in 'two-up', otherwise pitch and toss. **1933** *Ibid.* 5 July 20/1, I see the pennies in the air, The outstretched hand that holds the kip. **1945** [see *BAT *sb.*^{2} 3 e]. **1948** V. PALMER *Golconda* xxx. 250 He [was].. becoming more convinced every day that his whole future lay in winning the [Parliamentary] seat. At first the idea had been hardly more than a toss of the kip to him; now it was woven into his daily fantasies. **1964** A. WYKES *Gambling* iii. 62 In this game [*sc.* two-up], two pennies are placed on a flat stick (called the 'kip') and are thrown into the air by the 'spinner'.

kip (kip), *sb.*^{7} *Engin.* orig. *U.S.* [Prob. f. KI(LO- + P(OUND *sb.*^{1}] A unit of force equal to the weight of 1,000 lb., used in expressing loads.

1915 H. R. THAYER *Struct. Design* II. vi. 87 Shear in kips. [*Note*] 1 Kip = 1000 lbs. *Ibid.* 250 Maximum shear 110 kips. **1949** S. BUTTERWORTH *Struct. Analysis* ii. 30 The actual sway force is 3 kips. **1959** L. C. URQUHART *Civil Engin. Handbk.* (ed. 4) v. 45 The panel load on the upper lateral system is $25 \times 150 = 3{,}750$ lb = 3·75 kips. **1962** *Engineering* 8 June 746/3 Each of these pavement designs could be expected to carry a million applications of the 18 kip axle load..before serviceability dropped to 2·5.

kip (kip), *sb.*^{8} [Thai.] The basic monetary unit of Laos.

1955 *Britannica Bk. Year* 265/1 The Laotian unit of currency had its name changed from *piastre* to *kip*, without any effect on its purchasing power. **1959** *Economist* 24 Jan. 305/2 The *kip* has been devalued. **1965** *Ibid.* 20 Nov. p. xxxvi/1 An indelible public impression of foreign exchange dealers..inhabiting a rarefied world of eight-ball arbitrage and private jokes about the baht, the kip and the won.

kip (kip), *v.*^{2} *slang.* [f. KIP *sb.*^{3}] *intr.* To go to bed, sleep. Also, to lie *down*. So **ki·pping** *vbl. sb.*; also *attrib.*, as **kipping-house**, a lodging-house.

1889 BARRÈRE & LELAND *Dict. Slang* I. 522/1 *Kip, to* (popular and thieves), to sleep or lodge. **1899** C. ROOK *Hooligan Nights* i. 10 Next door..that's where me and my muvver kipped when I was a nipper. **1919** *Athenæum* 1 Aug. 695/2 'To kip' is to go to bed—or what serves for a bed. **1925** E. JERVIS *25 Yrs. in Six Prisons* xix. 243, I used to conduct services in the 'kippin'-'aases', or common lodging-houses. **1929** J. B. PRIESTLEY *Good Companions* I. iv. 116 Yes, we'll have to kip down for an hour or two, Annie. **1938** J. CURTIS *They drive by Night* iv. 46 I'm kipping here tonight and all. **1939** *Airman's Gaz.* Dec., This will be very useful if you forced-land and have to kip out in a field. **1961** *New Statesman* 26 May 830/3 Nancy..set her persuasive charms to work to get Billy, Bob and Nick a free sky-sheltered bench to kip on. **1973** *Weekly News* (Glasgow) 11 Aug. 14/4 A driver whose van broke down near Bristol, decided to kip down in the driver's seat.

kip (kip), *v.*^{3} *Gymnastics. U.S.* [f. *KIP *sb.*^{2} 3.] *intr.* To perform a kip.

1909 in WEBSTER. **1967** LOKEN & WILLOUGHBY *Compl. Bk. Gymnastics* (ed. 2) ii. 12 Go to the bridge from the kip position on back of the shoulders using the kipping action.

Kipchak (kiptʃā·k). Also **Qipchak.** [Russ., f. Jagatai.] **A.** *sb.* **a.** A member of a Mongolian people of central Asia. **b.** The language of this people, a Turkic dialect. **B.** *adj.* Of or pertaining to this people, or their language.

1865 J. & R. MICHELL tr. *Valikhanof's Russians Cent. Asia* iii. 62 The towns of Almalyk..were chief stations on the high road traversed by the Genoese traders..as well as by the Kipchak ambassadors on their..missions to the great Khan. **1879** *Encycl. Brit.* IX. 85/2 The nomads are mainly Kipchaks and Kara Kirghiz or Buruts. **1898** A. J. BUTLER tr. *Ratzel's Hist. Mankind* III. 319 The Kiptchaks, whose fame for extraordinary valour is known throughout Central Asia. *Ibid.* 348 The Kiptchaks are only a clan of the Kara-Kirghis. **1953** O. CAROE *Soviet Empire* I. iii. 37 The migrations of the Oghuz may have been prompted by Kipchak pressure. *Ibid.* 38 The Kipchak language was of the Turkic family. **1959** *Chambers's Encycl.* VI. 426/2 *Golden Horde*, or West Kipchak Horde, the name given to the western division of the great Mogul empire..after.. 1241... The neighbouring East Kipchak Horde was known as 'White'. **1970** D. M. LANG *Armenia* xi. 273 Other Armenian communities of the diaspora adopted the Mkhitar Code as their own, so that it was translated into Latin, Polish, Georgian, Russian and even Qipchak. **1972** G. CLAUSON *Etym. Dict. pre-13th-Cent. Turkish* p. xix, In XI the Kıpçak were west of the Oğuz in southern Russia.

Kiplingese (kipliŋī·z). [-ESE.] The literary style and characteristics of the writer Rudyard Kipling (1865–1936). Also **Kiplinge·sque** *a.* [see -ESQUE], resembling Kipling in style; so **Kiplinge·squely** *adv.*; **Ki·plingish** *a.*, typical of Kipling or his works; **Ki·plingite** [see -ITE^1 1 b], an admirer of Kipling; as *adj.*, characteristic of Kipling; **Ki·plingize** *v.* [see -IZE] *trans.*, to make Kipling-like.

1894 *'Sunlight' Year Bk. 1895* 77 A glance at the adaptation is enough to reveal its Kiplingesque roll and emphasis. **1898** *Windsor Mag.* Dec. 131/1 True Kiplingites. **1899** 'G. F. MONKSHOOD' *Kipling* 188 Perhaps the most distinctly Kiplingite piece of prose in the whole book. **1899** *Westm. Gaz.* 28 June 3/1 Thorpe..is, merely, the primitive Kiplingesque type of man transferred from the battle-field or the plains of India to the Stock Exchange. **1899** *Daily News* 1 Dec. 8/2 The account of the making of the first axe..is told quite in the heroic style of Kingsley and Morris, flavoured here and there with more than a dash of 'Kiplingese'. **1903** *Times Lit. Suppl.* 2 Oct. 277/3 The whole poem..has another claim upon the attention of the reader as an example of Kiplingized Longfellow. **1905** CHESTERTON *Heretics* iii. 45 The modern army is not a miracle of courage; it has not enough opportunities, owing to the cowardice of everybody else. But it is really a miracle of organization, and that is the truly Kiplingite ideal. *Ibid.* xx. 292 No man has any business to be a Kiplingite without being a politician, and an Imperialist politician. **1909** H. G. WELLS *Tono-Bungay* IV. iii. 492 They served me up to the public in turgid degenerate Kiplingese. **1921** G. B. SHAW *Back to Methuselah* IV. i. 170 You have actually Kiplingized me... He is said to have invented the electric hedge. I consider that in using it on me you have taken a very great liberty. **1928** *Weekly Dispatch* 24 June 15/3 The road to home these days lies across the 49th degree of latitude between Bishops Rock and Nantucket. It is a sad, un-Kiplingish thought. **1931** *Times Lit. Suppl.* 17 Sept. 692/3 It contains also quite a number of amusing and quite Kiplingesque 'Just So' stories. **1966** *Punch* 8 June 826/1 Nor am I sure that the anonymous genius who originally picked 'East of Suez' to describe the sphere of our Asian involvement chose wisely. It's so emotively Kiplingesque, so redolent of imperial splendours and miseries. **1969** *Guardian* 27 Nov. 14/6 No one ran Kiplingesquely amuck; no shot was fired in anger. **1972** J. WAINWRIGHT *Night is Time to Die* 53 *The Green Eye of the Yellow God*... It's Kiplingish... But

it was written by J. Milton Hayes. **1973** *Daily Tel.* 24 Nov. 16 Kiplingites will be interested to learn that Kipling Terrace, a Victorian development at Westward Ho!, North Devon, is to be auctioned next month.

Kiplingism (ki·pliŋiz'm). [-ISM.] †**1.** *Cambridge Univ. slang.* A sarcastic term for the errors and solecisms alleged to occur in the edition of the 'Codex Bezæ' (1793) by Thomas Kipling (d. 1822), afterwards Dean of Peterborough.

1803 *Gradus ad Cantabrigiam* 81 A *Kiplingism*; a blunder-*bus* levelled at poor Priscian's head by the *learned* Dr. Kipling. The opposition wits at Cambridge have composed an epigram of *Kiplingisms*. **1899** 'G. F. MONKSHOOD' *Kipling* 15 A 'Kiplingism' was long an expression for a Latin blunder. **1950** M. MARPLES *University Slang* 110 An anthology of *Kiplingisms*, somewhat on the lines of modern collections of *howlers*, is said to have been current in Cambridge for some years.

2. Views or opinions or style of expression characteristic of Rudyard Kipling (see *KIPLINGESE).

1898 *Daily News* 7 Oct. 6/3 The manner otherwise may degenerate into sheer mannerism, a Kiplingism of Kipling. **1901** *Speaker* 26 Jan. 469/1 Sportsmen may be divided into two classes—those who care more for the chase than the killing and those who merely make 'bags' and break records. But the latter are not sportsmen..and their method is nothing but Kiplingism out of place. **1920** H. G. WELLS *Outl. Hist.* 524/1 The crude Darwinism and the Kiplingism of the later Victorian years.

Kipp (kip). *Chem.* The name of Petrus Jacobus *Kipp* (1808–64), German chemist, used in the possessive (less commonly *absol.* or *attrib.*) to denote an apparatus for the generation of gas by the action of a liquid on a solid as and when gas is required.

The apparatus consists essentially of three glass bulbs, of which the upper and lower ones are connected and contain the liquid and the middle one is connected with the lower one and contains the solid; while a tap in the middle bulb is open, liquid rises into the bulb and gas is evolved, whilst closing the tap causes the pressure of the gas to increase until the liquid is forced out of the middle bulb into the lower and upper ones, out of contact with the solid.

1879 *Proc. Cambr. Philos. Soc.* III. 160 A gentle current of hydrogen from the Kipp's apparatus *A*..was led into *D*. **1901** F. G. BENEDICT *Chem. Lect. Exper.* 3 The Kipp generator, or one of its various modifications, remains today the only portable gas generator for the lecture table... The simpler and less expensive the form of Kipp used, the better. **1912** J. W. MELLOR *Mod. Inorg. Chem.* iii. 45 Kipp's apparatus is very convenient when a steady current of hydrogen is needed for some time. **1921** J. R. PARTINGTON *Text-bk. Inorg. Chem.* xi. 185 Instead of a flask, a Kipp's apparatus may be used, the metal being placed in the central globe *B* and acid poured in the top funnel until the lower bulb *A* is full and the metal covered with acid. **1965** D. ABBOTT *Inorg. Chem.* xi. 535 It [*sc.* hydrogen sulphide] is most conveniently prepared for laboratory use in a Kipp's apparatus by the action of dilute hydrochloric acid on ferrous sulphide.

kipper, *sb.* and *a.* Add: **A.** *sb.* **3. a.** A person, esp. a young or small person, a child. *slang.*

1905 *Daily Chron.* 30 Mar. 4/7 The expression 'giddy kipper', which Mr. Charles Brookfield has introduced to Mr. Justice Darling's notice. **1907** *Punch* 10 Apr. 254/2 Half-a-dozen dreadfully common young bicyclists were commenting on her discomfiture with delighted exclamations of 'Giddy old Kipper', 'Sweet Seventeen', 'Cheero, Maudie—you'll win!' **1923** M. M. GIBB *Hetherington's Affinity* xx. 175 If you're enterprizing enough to climb one of the trees christened by usage 'The Kipper's Tree', which hardly needs to be translated into plainer terms. **1959** I. & P. OPIE *Lore & Lang. Schoolch.* ix. 170 A chap who has got duck's disease is most often labelled 'Tich'... Alternatively: ankle biter,..kipper, microbe, midge, [etc.].

b. An Englishman, an English immigrant in Australia. *Austral. slang.*

1946 R. RIVETT *Behind Bamboo* 397/1 *Kipper*, Englishman. **1946** *Sunday Sun* (Sydney) 8 Aug. Suppl. 15 An able seaman on a kipper warship called the Eagle. **1963** *Times Lit. Suppl.* 24 May 370/2 Quite often they [*sc.* English immigrants in Australia] are referred to as Kippers. **1967** K. GILES *Death & Mr Prettyman* ii. 57 You kippers—no guts and two faces—are only strong under the armpits... What about the east of Suez caper, eh?

4. *Naut. slang.* A torpedo. Cf. *FISH *sb.*^{1} 1 h.

1953 A. MARS *Unbroken* iii. 74 As she was only crawling along I aimed my first 'kipper' just a fraction ahead of her bows. **1959** G. JENKINS *Twist of Sand* v. 86, I evaluate its firing power at eighteen torpedoes—I think kipper is a distressing piece of naval slang—in thirty minutes.

C. kipper kite *R.A.F. slang* (see quot. 1943); **kipper tie** [see quot. 1969], a gaudy and very wide neck-tie.

[**1941** L. WALMSLEY *Fishermen at War* ix. 138 Kipper, I discovered, was airman's slang for a fishing boat. The chief function of this particular station was the escorting of convoys and fishing fleets, and the section which had the latter duty to perform was known as the 'Kipper Patrol'.] **1942** *Gen* 1 Sept. 14/1 A Coastal Command plane is a 'kipper kite'. **1943** HUNT & PRINGLE *Service Slang* 42 *Kipper-kites*, aircraft engaged on convoy escort duties over the North Sea and usually giving protection to the fishing-vessels. **1966** *Daily Tel.* 20 Jan. 15/6 Neckties are slightly wider and pointed, though not yet as floppy as London's Carnaby Street kipper ties. **1969** *Guardian* 16 Sept. 9/4 Michael Fish [*sc.* a London designer of menswear]..can..take credit for popularising the wide tie, named 'kipper' after him. **1973** *Times* 30 May 18/3 He had come from his Suffolk home wearing a kipper tie and black and white patterned shirt, full of energy and ideas.

ki·pper, *sb.*^{2} *Austral.* [Native name.] A young Aboriginal who has been initiated and is admitted to the rights of manhood.

1841 C. EIPPER *Statement German Mission to Aborigines* 8 With these weapons the natives invest their young men at the age of from fourteen to sixteen years... These young men are then called *kippers*, and for the first time enjoy the privilege of taking an active part in the fight. **1853** H. B. JONES *Adventures Austral.* 126 Around us sat 'Kippers', i.e. 'hobbledehoy blacks'. **1885** R. C. PRAED *Austral. Life* i. 24 A ceremony at which the young men.. receive the rank of warriors and are henceforth called *Kippers*. **1966** W. S. RAMSON *Austral. Eng.* vi. 129 *Bora*, 'a rite of initiation', *kipper*, used of a youth who has passed through such a rite, and *boyla* and *koradji*, 'an aboriginal medicine-man or witchdoctor', are used only in their original and specific senses.

kipper, *v.* Add: Also *intr.*, *transf.*, and *fig.*

1894 KIPLING *Seven Seas* (1896) 36 The Leevin' God, That does not kipper souls for sport or break a life in jest. **1909** R. BEACH *Silver Horde* 129 He's an awful spender. I'm half kippered [= drunk] myself. **1924** *Glasgow Herald* 28 Jan. 10 Oily cotton-waste was picked up at the gates of yards and factories, and our hands were duly kippered over smoking lumps of this stuff. **1930** R. CAMPBELL *Adamastor* 20 Hang him up to kipper in the sun. **1963** *Times* 14 May p. ii/3 (Advt.), Central heating designed to prevent the average household from being kippered on one side and frozen on the other. **1969** *Daily Tel.* 30 Dec. 6/5 On the last day of addiction, smoke twice or thrice as many cigarettes as normal. The next morning you should feel sufficiently kippered as to see the sense of your new plan.

ki·pperer. [-ER^1.] One who kippers herrings.

1902 *Nature* 4 Sept. 435/2 The 'kipperer' and the 'gutter' have their peculiar troubles. **1920** *Glasgow Herald* 10 July 6 Joint meetings of fishermen, curers, salesmen, freshers, and kipperers were held at both places. **1930** *Aberdeen Press & Jrnl.* 21 Mar. 6/5 A shed..standing alongside a kippering kiln.., occupied by Mr. David Mackenzie, kipperer. **1955** *Times* 3 May 6/3 Merchants and kipperers refused to pay the new minimum price of 91s. a cran.

kippersol (ki·pəɹsǫl). *S. Afr.* Also **kiepersol.** [Corrupt f. KITTISOL.] A small evergreen African tree of the genus *Cussonia*, belonging to the family Araliaceæ.

1893 'R. IRON' *Dream Life* 26 A kippersol tree. *Ibid.* 29 She..cut at the root of a kippersol, and got out a large piece..and sat down to chew it. Kippersol is like raw quince. *Ibid.* 34 When one has had no food but kippersol juice for two days. **1921** T. R. SIM *Native Timbers S. Afr.* 194 Kipperkol [*sic*]. *Cussonia*, all species. **1954** K. COWIN *Bushveld, Bananas & Bounty* v. 78 According to legend the [*Cussonia*] *umbellifera*, with its broad flat leaves, was first called Kiepersol by the Cape Malays, whose word for monkey is *kie* and for umbrella is the Afrikaans word *persols* and the combination results in the picturesque name of Monkey's Umbrella. **1973** PALMER & PITMAN *Trees S. Afr.* III. 1691 Most of the species [of *Cussonia*] are known as 'kiepersol'... The name travelled to the Cape where it was first used for the *Cussonia* species common around Cape Town, *Cussonia thyrsiflora* Thunb., and is now a general name for all the cussonias with their parasol-like mops of leaves at the ends of the branches.

kipsie, kipsy (ki·psi). *Austral.* [f. KIP *sb.*^{3} + -Y^6, -IE.] A house (see also quot. 1919).

1916 C. J. DENNIS *Songs Sentimental Bloke* 124 *Kipsie*, a house, the home. **1919** W. H. DOWNING *Digger Dial.* 31 *Kippsie*—lean-to; shelter; house; dugout. **1943** *Coast to Coast 1942* 91 He turned and looked our little weather-beaten kipsie over. **1946** *Coast to Coast 1945* 236 Our little kipsy breathed a heavy stillness like that leaden hush that hangs over tree and earth before a storm breaks. **1969** *Courier-Mail* (Brisbane) 29 Nov. 13/1 Our kipsy was an aloof-looking little place.

Kipsigis (ki·psigis). [Native name.] The name of a people inhabiting western Kenya, and their Nilotic language; a member of this people. Also *attrib.* or as *adj.*

1931 *Africa* IV. 467 The Kipsigis and the other tribes speaking an almost identical language..are really pastoral in custom and thought, though they have ceased to be truly nomadic, like the Masai. **1939** E. E. EVANS-PRITCHARD in J. G. Peristiany *Social Inst. Kipsigis* p. xx, The Kipsigis are Nandi-speaking. *Ibid.* p. xxxi, The Kipsigis clan (*oret*) is a totemic non-exogamous group of persons. **1939** J. G. PERISTIANY *Ibid.* i. 1 The Kipsigis, also called Kipsigi or Kipsigisiek, are better known to the European as Lumbwa, a misnomer of unknown origin, as none of the neighbouring tribes seems to be responsible for this name. *Ibid.* xii. 231 The Kipsigis text accompanies the translation for the better understanding of Kipsigis thought. **1947** *E. Afr. Ann. 1946–7* 43/1 Nilo-Hamitic tribes such as the Nandi, Suk and Kipsigis. **1964** A. N. TUCKER in D. Abercrombie et al. *Daniel Jones* 445 The Kalenjin languages are spoken by two groups of non-Bantu speakers in the Rift Valley Province..the Nandi Group, comprising Nandi, Kipsigis, Keyo ('Elgeyo'), Tugen ('Kamasia'), Kony ('Elgon'), Sabiny ('Sabei'), and others. *Ibid.*, The languages chosen here as representative are Nandi (with occasional reference to Kipsigis) and Western Päkot. **1971** *E. Afr. Standard* (Nairobi) 10 Apr. 7/4 A fight..broke out between Kipsigis and Kisii tribesmen.

kir (kīr). Also **Kir.** [The name of Canon Felix *Kir* (1876–1968), mayor of Dijon, who is said to have invented the recipe.] A drink made from dry white wine and crème de cassis.

1966 *Times Lit. Suppl.* 19 May 456/5 M. Follain's work should be read with a kir, a benedictine or a calvados. **1967** *Sat. Rev.* (U.S.) 22 Apr. 50/2 In 1967 the drink..is *Kir*, which the pros call *blanc Cassis*, or if they are *really* switched on, a *blancass*. **1967** L. DEIGHTON *Expensive Place* x. 74 'Waiter,' he called. 'Four kirs.'..The white wine and cassis came. **1967** A. LICHINE *Encycl. Wines* 172 Around Dijon it [*sc.* Cassis] is used as a popular aperitif, a little Cassis being put in a glass that is then filled with a fairly neutral, dry white wine...Also called kir. **1968** M. TRIPP *One is One* xvii. 159 You couldn't get Kir, his customary drink, anywhere. **1974** *Guardian* 22 Aug. 11/6 The summer aperitif 'Kir'.

kiradjee, var. *KORADJI.

Kirby (kɔ̄·ɹbi). The name of Charles *Kirby*, 17th-c. English fish-hook maker, used *attrib.* and *absol.* († and in the possessive) to denote a design of fish-hook originated by him.

[**1655** WALTON *Compleat Angler* (ed. 2) xvii. 313 But if you will buy choice hooks, I wil one day walk with you to Charles Kerbyes in Harp Alley in Shooe-lane, who is the most exact and best Hook-maker that the Nation affords.] **1804** T. BEST *Conc. Treat. Art of Angling* (ed. 6) ii. 23 Ford and Kirby's hooks are excellent ones. **1823** T. F. SALTER *Angler's Guide* (ed. 5) xvi. 140 In choosing Eel hooks, prefer the single ones whose shank is similar to the Kirby hook, to those which have a loop shank. **1870** H. CHOLMONDELEY-PENNELL *Mod. Pract. Angler* i. 9 The round and Kirby bends are very deficient in penetrating power, and disproportionately short in the shank as compared to their breadth of bend, either for appearance or use, more particularly in the matter of flies. **1967** B. KNOX *Blacklight* ii. 32 The box held a collection of wickedly barbed Kirby hooks.

kirby-grip (kɔ̄·ɹbi grip). Also **Kirbigrip** (proprietary name), **kirbigrip.** A type of sprung hair-grip.

1926 *Trade Marks Jrnl.* 6 Jan. 12 Kirbigrip...Hair-pins of ordinary Metal. Kirby, Beard & Co., Limited,.. Birmingham; Manufacturers. **1945** 'A. GILBERT' *Don't open Door* xi. 95 Two plain brown combs and a kirbigrip. **1949** 'J. TEY' *Brat Farrar* xxiii. 214 The aged kirby-grip that kept Jane's hair off her face. *a* **1953** DYLAN THOMAS *Adventures Skin Trade* (1955) I. 18 Mrs. Probert next door, ..butting the air with her kirby-grips. **1955** [see *hair-grip* s.v. *HAIR *sb.* 9 b]. **1959** *Woman's Own* 12 Dec. 21/3 Ribbon bows fixed to kirby-grips or combs. **1960** C. STORR *Marianne & Mark* i. 20 Marianne bought a card of kirbigrips. **1973** B. BAINBRIDGE *Dressmaker* i. 20 Nellie, when put out, could appear to be suffering, her white hair plastered to her head in waves and a kirby grip to keep it neat.

Kirchhoff (kīə·ɹtʃǫf, ‖ ki·rχhof). Also (erron.) **Kirchoff.** The name of Gustav Robert *Kirchhoff* (1824–87), Ger. physicist, used in *Kirchhoff's law*: **a.** *Electr.* Either of two laws concerning electric networks in which steady currents are flowing: (*a*) (the first law) the algebraic sum of the currents in all the conductors that meet in a point is zero; (*b*) (the second law) the algebraic sum of the products of current and resistance in each part of any closed path in a network is equal to the algebraic sum of the e.m.f.s in the path.

1869 R. MAIN *Rudimentary Astron.* (new ed.) 164 (*heading*) Kirchhoff's law. *Ibid.* p. xx (*heading*) Application of Kirchhoff's law. **1876** H. R. KEMPE *Handbk. Electr. Testing* v. 45 Kirchoff's laws.., though exceedingly simple.., are not so well known as they ought to be. **1905** W. C. D. WHETHAM *Theory Exper. Electr.* v. 117 The principles of continuous current-flow which we have now established may conveniently be applied to complex circuits and networks of conductors in the form of two statements known as Kirchhoff's laws. **1970** M. NELKON *Electr.* v. 130 Kirchhoff's first law is a mathematical statement of the fact that the charges do not accumulate at any junction of an electrical circuit. *Ibid.* 132 We need to apply Kirchhoff's second law to two complete circuits as there are two unknowns.

b. *Physics.* The law that the absorptivity of a body for radiant energy of any particular wavelength is equal to its emissivity at the same temperature for the same wavelength.

1901 G. K. BURGESS tr. *Le Chatelier & Boudouard's High-Temperature Measurements* viii. 140 (*heading*) Kirchhoff's law. **1945** F. A. BERRY et al. *Handbk. Meteorol.* IV. 288 It is an immediate consequence of Kirchhoff's law that the intensity emitted by a body can never exceed the black-body intensity and can equal it only in the spectral regions where the body is opaque. **1967** R. W. FAIRBRIDGE *Encycl. Atmospheric Sci.* 793/1 We assume black-body radiation which is that of a body that is characterized by maximum possible absorption at all incident wavelengths, insuring maximum emissivity according to Kirchhoff's Law.

Kirghiz (kīəɹgī·z), *sb.* and *a.* Also **Khirgese, Kirghis, Kirgiz.** [ad. Russ. *Kirgiz.*] **A.** *sb.* A widespread Mongolian people of west central Asia, now chiefly inhabiting the Kirghiz Soviet Socialist Republic; a member of this people; their Turkic language. **B.** *adj.* Of or

pertaining to the Kirghiz; *spec.* **Kirghiz pheasant** = *Mongolian pheasant* (*MONGOLIAN *a.* 4). Also **Kirghi·zian** *a.* and *sb.*

1652 P. HEYLYN *Cosmographie* III. 190 These again subdivided into severall Tribes, which they call their Hordes, of which the most considerable are, 1. the Nagaian Tartars, 2. the Zavolhenses, 3. the Thumenenses, 4. the Kirgessi. **1837** DE QUINCEY in *Blackw. Mag.* July 109/2 The murderous attacks of their cruel enemies the Bashkirs and the Kirghises. **1888** *Encycl. Brit.* XXIII. 661/2 Tatar dialects (Kirghizian, Bashkiri, Nogai). **1898** A. J. BUTLER tr. *Ratzel's Hist. Mankind* III. 326 The Kirghiz women adorn their plaits with beads, shells, and copper buttons. **1908** T. G. TUCKER *Introd. Nat. Hist. Lang.* 134 *Kirghiz*, comprising the speeches of the Black Kirghiz (or *Buruts*) in the part of Turkestan bordering on China, and of the Cossack Kirghiz to the north of the Caspian, the sea of Aral and Lake Balkash. **1921** *19th Cent.* May 871 Kirghizes, Lesghiens, Mingrelians. **1922** C. W. BEEBE *Monogr. Pheasants* III. 96 On the south-east the enormous Tian-Shan serve as the boundary between the Kirghiz Pheasant and both *shawi* and *tarimensis*. **1922** *Contemp. Rev.* Sept. 342 The Kirgisian population has retained its nomadic habits. **1924** *Blackw. Mag.* Aug. 256/1 The Russians, who were conscripting young Khirgese men for use on the railway. **1931** A. U. DILLEY *Oriental Rugs & Carpets* x. 226 Kirghiz rugs..are country-bred, vigorous and coarse. **1932** R. JOHN tr. *Popoff's City of Red Plague* iii. 46 One could not help being struck by the large number of Mongolian types—torn by their Muscovite masters from the remote steppes and forests of Siberia and Asiatic Russia;..Kalmucks, Kirghiz, Yakuts, and similar obscure, semi-barbaric tribes. **1935** HUXLEY & HADDON *We Europeans* vii. 212 Ethnologists use the word [*sc.* Turki] loosely and in several different senses:—..(*b*) To designate a certain ethnic group of which the Turks, the Kirghis and the Tatars are best known. **1946** G. MILLAR *Horned Pigeon* i. 12 A dashing White Russian officer..spoke frequently of the Kirghesian sheep that drag their fat-containing tails behind them on little sleighs. **1955** V. CRONIN *Wise Man from West* xiii. 243 In this country of chasms and precipices roamed the Kirghiz, a predatory tribe. **1961** L. F. BROSNAHAN *Sounds of Lang.* viii. 177 A palatalisation of syllables..occurs in most of the Turco-Tartar languages of..Kirghiz, Turkmenian, etc. **1963** [see *Mongolian pheasant* s.v. *MONGOLIAN *a.* 4]. **1967** D. S. PARLETT *Short Dict. Languages* 73 *Kirgiz*.., apparently one of the oldest (or oldest attested) Turkic tribes. **1971** *Whitaker's Almanack 1972* 966 The Kirghiz S.S.R. occupies the north-eastern part of Soviet Central Asia and borders in the south-east on China.

‖ **kiri** (kīə·ri). [Jap.] = PAULOWNIA.

1727 J. G. SCHEUCHZER tr. *Kæmpfer's Hist. Japan* I. I. ix. 119 *Kiri*, is a very large but scarce Tree. **1822** F. SHOBERL tr. *Titsingh's Illustr. Japan* 255 Sometimes this cane is made of the wood of the *kiri*-tree. **1877** *Trans. Asiatic Soc. Japan* V. I. 9 The second of the Imperial badges is a representation of the leaf and flower of the *kiri*, or *Paulownia Japonica*. **1893** A. M. BACON *Jap. Interior* xiv. 237 The blossoms and leaves of the kiri-tree, (paulownia imperialis), which is the sign of the imperial family. **1928** BLUNDEN *Jap. Garland* 22 The broad-leaved *kiri*. **1972** *Nat. Geographic* Sept. 374 Miss Hori still goes into the forests to select the best *kiri*, or Paulownia wood.

‖ **kirin** (kīə·rin). Also **Kirin.** [Jap., f. Chinese (see KYLIN).] A fabulous beast of composite form, freq. portrayed in Japanese pottery and art (see quots.); = KYLIN.

1727 J. G. SCHEUCHZER tr. *Kæmpfer's Hist. Japan* I. I. x. 123 *Kirin*, according to the description and figure, which the Japanese give of it, is a winged Quadruped, of incredible swiftness, with two soft horns standing before the breast, and bent backwards, with the body of a Horse, and claws of a Deer, and a head which comes nearest to that of a Dragon. **1875–80** AUDSLEY & BOWES *Keramic Art Japan* I. p. xxxviii, The Japanese have described the *kirin* as a supernatural animal, requiring for its creation the concurrence of a certain constellation in the heavens. **1900** F. LITCHFIELD *Pott. & Porc.* vii. 172 Figure subjects are not common in this kind of china, but one finds representations of..the *Kirin*.., a monster with the body and hoofs of a deer, the tail of a bull, and a horn on his forehead. **1908** H. L. JOLY *Legend in Jap. Art* 148 The Chinese *Shang Huen Fujen*, female Sennin, shown riding upon a Kirin. **1963** [see *HO-HO]. **1971** L. A. BOGER *Dict. World Pott. & Porc.* 170/2 Included among other popular [porcelain] motifs were..the five fabulous creatures:..Kirin (Japanese unicorn), [etc.].

Kiriwinian (kirivi·niăn), *sb.* and *a.* [f. *Kiriwin(a*, the name of the largest of the Trobriand Islands + -IAN.] **A.** *sb.* A native or inhabitant of Kiriwina; the Austronesian language spoken there. **B.** *adj.* Of or pertaining to Kiriwina.

1916 *Jrnl. R. Anthrop. Inst.* XLVI. 356 There is very little of the universally reported native's dread of darkness among the Kiriwinians. *Ibid.* 354 He..acquired sufficient knowledge of the Kiriwinian language to be able to dispense with the services of an interpreter. *Ibid.* 391 Archaic expressions..the natives only partially understand, and..it is extremely difficult to make them translate the meaning correctly into modern Kiriwinian. **1922** B. MALINOWSKI *Argonauts W. Pacific* xx. 480 The Kiriwinians have to go inland to the industrial districts of Kuboma..to acquire the articles needed. **1964** *Language* XL. 308 These Kiriwinian and English sentences.

Kirlian (kīə·ɹliăn). The name of S. D. and V. K. *Kirlian*, 20th-cent. Russian electricians, used *attrib.* with reference to the process invented by them of directly recording corona discharges from the surfaces of objects on photographic material.

1970 OSTRANDER & SCHROEDER *Psi Psychic Discoveries behind Iron Curtain* xvi. 218 In the color Kirlian pictures of plant leaves we saw the same basic colors: blue and reddish-yellow. **1973** *Popular Photogr.* LXXII. 90 Examples of Kirlian photographs—that is, images obtained on film without camera or lens by direct recording of an electric charge transmitted by the given object, to which a high-frequency charge has been applied. **1974** *Sciences* Jan.–Feb. 19/2 Kirlian photographs may also offer a measure of interpersonal relations.

Kirman (kirmā·n, kəɹmā·n). Also **Karman, Kerman.** The name of a province and town in south-east Iran, used (freq. *attrib.*) to designate a carpet or rug made there, usu. having soft delicate colouring and naturalistic designs.

1876 O. B. ST. JOHN in F. J. Goldsmid *Eastern Persia* I. vi. 101 Not only flowers and trees, but birds, beasts, landscapes, and even human figures are found on the Karmán carpets. **1900** J. K. MUMFORD *Oriental Rugs* xi. 187 It has been customary, until very lately, among the rug dealers of the West and Constantinople as well, to attribute the Kirman rugs to Kermanshah. **1931** A. U. DILLEY *Oriental Rugs & Carpets* iv. 94 Of all the villages weaving Kerman rugs, Rawar only has general rug fame. **1953** A. C. EDWARDES *Persian Carpets* xiii. 208/2 The new styles were dictated by America, which is by far the largest consumer of Kermān carpets. **1953** R. GODDEN *Kingfishers catch Fire* xv. 184 It was a Kirman rug: a Kirman is the only Persian carpet that looks feminine. **1957** R. STOUT *If Death ever Slept* (1958) iii. 30 Through the reception room, across a Kirman twice as big as my room at home. **1967** S. REED *Oriental Rugs & Carpets* v. 69 By the turn of the century some very good Tabriz and Kirman pieces were being made. **1969** C. W. JACOBSEN *Check Points How to buy Oriental Rugs* vii. 132 Take the name Kirman, which is one of the highest priced and best of new rugs being woven today... Many people bought these as Kirmanshah (also spelled Kermanshah). **1970** *Canad. Antiques Collector* Dec. 22/2 On the floor is a fine pile pink Persian Kerman rug [etc.].

Kirmanshah (kiɹmānʃā·, kəɹ-). Also **Kermanshah.** The name of a city in west Iran, used confusedly (freq. *attrib.*) to designate a carpet made in Kirman, usu. one with white field and flowered medallion and borders. See prec. word.

The confusion with *Kirman* seems to have arisen because of the similarity of the two names and the great importance of Kirmanshah as a wool-trading town.

1900 J. K. MUMFORD *Oriental Rugs* xi. 188 In design, the best of the Kermanshahs affect the floral treatment. **1904** M. B. LANGTON *How to know Oriental Rugs* ii. 78 There are a few antiques in this country; but the modern Kirman or Kermanshah rug, made throughout the district, rivals the old. **1931** A. U. DILLEY *Oriental Rugs & Carpets* Pl. 20 (*caption*), Kerman, Southeast Persia (mistakenly called Kermanshah). *Ibid.* iv. 94 Some fifty years ago, large flower-strewn medallion patterns with graceful pendants and floriated corners were devised and applied to large carpets by weavers working for Tabriz rug-merchants who saw in the fine Kerman workmanship opportunity for commercial enterprise. These rugs and carpets were called Kermanshah, to permanent confusion with the rug-weavings of the city of that name located miles to the west. **1969** C. W. JACOBSEN *Check Points How to buy Oriental Rugs* vii. 133 The Kirmanshah was never a correct name for these rugs because they were woven in and around Kirman, while the town of Kirmanshah was 1,000 miles to the west.

kirombo (kirǫ·mbo). [Malagasy.] The cuckoo-roller, *Leptosomus discolor*, a large grey or black and brown bird found only in Madagascar and the Comoro Islands.

1891 *Ibis* Apr. 224 The natives of the north-west of Madagascar give this bird the name of *Kiròmbo*. It has the curious habit of hovering in the air and uttering a very loud note, striking its wings against the body as it calls. **1915** J. SIBREE *Naturalist in Madagascar* x. 138 The *Vorondreo*, or Kiròmbo roller. **1964** A. L. THOMSON *New Dict. Birds* 172/1 Cuckoo-roller: *Leptosomus discolor*, sole member of the Leptosomatidae (Coraciiformes, suborder Coracii). This monotypic family is restricted to Madagascar and the nearby Comoro Islands; the bird is called 'Courol' in some works, and less frequently 'Kirombo'.

‖ **kirpan** (kiɹpā·n). [ad. Panjabi and Hindi *kirpān*, f. Skr. *kṛpaṇa* sword.] The sword or dagger worn by Sikhs as a religious symbol.

1904 J. J. H. GORDON *Sikhs* iv. 41 Every true Sikh must always have five things with him, their names all commencing with the letter *k*—namely,..*kard* (knife), and *kirpan* (sword). **1923** *Contemp. Rev.* Sept. 293 Guru Govind Singh..prescribed for his Singhs five symbols, of which it is sufficient to note here..the *kirpan*, a weapon which is sometimes a miniature carried in the hair, sometimes a dagger not more than a foot in length, sometimes a sword. **1952** J. MASTERS *Deceivers* v. 45 He whipped a twelve-inch dagger, the Sikh kirpan, from his belt. **1964** A. SWINSON *Six Minutes to Sunset* vi. 120 It is possible that many people, especially the Sikhs, were armed with their *kirpans* or short swords. **1969** H. R. F. KEATING *Inspector Ghote plays Joker* vii. 99 At his side there hung a kirpan, traditional knife of the Sikhs. **1971** *Daily Tel.* 11 June 3 (*caption*) Sant Mann Singh,..a visiting Sikh religious leader who has agreed not to carry his kirpan, a sword, in public.

Kirschner (kīə·ɹʃnəɹ). [Name of Aage *Kirschner* (fl. 1905), Da. chemist.] *Kirschner value*, a number expressing the proportion of certain fatty acids (esp. butyric acid) in a fat (see quot. 1961).

1911 *Analyst* XXXVI. 337 The Kirschner value is practically a measure of the butyric acid content of the mixture. **1928** E. R. BOLTON *Oils, Fats & Fatty Foods* iv. 83 Although in general practice the Kirschner value is a measure of the amount of butter fat present, yet there are a few vegetable oils that give large Kirschner and Reichert-Meissl, and low Polenske values. **1961** *Methods for Chem. Analysis of Butter* (*B.S.I.*) 8 The Kirschner value is the number of millilitres of 0·1N aqueous alkali solution required to neutralize the water-soluble volatile fatty acids which form water-soluble silver salts distilled from 5g of the fat under the precise conditions specified in the method. **1973** D. PEARSON *Laboratory Techniques Food Analysis* vi. 156 Genuine butter fat gives Kirschner values from 20·5 to 26·4.

kirschsteinite (kīə·ɹʃstəinəit). *Min.* [f. the name of Egon *Kirschstein* (see quot. 1957) + -ITE[1].] Iron-monticellite, esp. as a naturally occurring mineral.

1957 SAHAMA & HYTÖNEN in *Mineral. Mag.* XXXI. 698 For this natural $CaFeSiO_4$ the name kirschsteinite is proposed, in honour of the German geologist, the late Dr. Egon Kirschstein, who died in the events of the World War I in East Africa. *Ibid.*, The analysis corresponds to the following molecular composition: $CaFeSiO_4$ 69·4 mol. %, $CaMnSiO_4$ 4·3, $CaMgSiO_4$ 22·6, excess Fe_2SiO_4 3·7. Accordingly, the mineral is to be called magnesian kirschsteinite. **1962** W. A. DEER et al. *Rock-Forming Min.* I. 1 The iron analogue of monticellite, kirschsteinite, $CaFeSiO_4$, is known from slags, but has not been reported from a natural occurrence, and a magnesium-rich kirschsteinite containing 69 per cent. $CaFeSiO_4$ is the most iron-rich mineral of the Fe_2SiO_4—$CaFeSiO_4$ series yet reported. **1966** *Amer. Mineralogist* LI. 1192 Mineralogical studies on the debris formed during the underground Gnome nuclear explosion in a salt horizon of the Salado formation near Carlsbad, New Mexico have shown that significant quantities of olivine and kirschsteinite are present in the water insoluble fraction.

Kir-Shehr (kə̄·ɹʃīəɹ). Also **Kirshehir.** The name of a town in Central Turkey, used *attrib.* and *ellipt.* to designate the brightly coloured prayer rugs made there.

1900 J. K. MUMFORD *Oriental Rugs* x. 139 Border medallions,..are found in Kir-Shehrs of old date. *Ibid.*, Some of the small Kir-Shehr mats have several particolored tufts at each end. **1931** A. U. DILLEY *Oriental Rugs & Carpets* vi. 165 Kir-Shehr..prayer rugs [are distinguished] by central panels covered by 'flight of stairs roofs'. **1967** *Times* 21 Feb. 21/4 (Advt.), Several fine prayer rugs: *Ladik, Mudjur, Kirshehir*, [etc.]. **1971** K. WATSON tr. *Hubel's Bk. Carpets* 86 Cherry red and grass green are noticeable in the colour scheme of Kirshehirs.

kirtan (kī·ɹtan). Also **keertan, kirtana.** [Skr.] (See quots.)

1898 B. A. PINGLE *Indian Mus.* (ed. 2) vii. 313 The *Kirtana* or *Hari-kirtana* is a musical performance, vocal and instrumental, of a sacred character, the theme of which is always a moral...The *Kirtana* is a beautiful combination of *rhetoric, rhyme* and *rhythm*. **1960** KOESTLER *Lotus & Robot* I. i. 65 During Kirtans her body got stiff and benumbed. **1967** SINGHA & MASSEY *Indian Dances* xv. 129 The poet Jayadeva, author of the *Gita Govinda* who composed numerous keertans or devotional songs, and whose wife expressed them through dance. **1966** J. & R. GODDEN *Two under Indian Sun* iii. 82 Indian singing too was usually about the gods, kirtans or sacred poems that told these epics of Krishna, or Rama and his love Sita. **1970** *Listener* 24 Sept. 404/3 The Kirtan..is the traditional song that seems to be always about spiritual love and pain. **1971** *Illustr. Weekly India* 18 Apr. 10/2 *Tamashas*..consisted of long-drawn recitations from mythology and legend, interspersed with *bhajans, keertans* and folk songs.

kirving, *vbl. sb.* (s.v. KIRVE *v.* 2). Add: **b.** *pl.* Coal dust or small pieces of coal produced during mining operations.

1956 [see *GUMMING *vbl. sb.*[2] b].

‖ **kisaeng** (kī·saŋ, -eŋ). Also **gesang, ki-saing, kisang.** [Korean.] In Korea, a trained female entertainer, the Korean equivalent of the geisha girl.

1895 L. J. MILN *Quaint Korea* vi. 155 The Korean word for the class of women of whom I am writing is ki-saing; but they are generally called geisha. **1904** C. J. D. TAYLER *Koreans at Home* ix. 50 The favourite entertainment for those who can afford it is the dancing of 'gesang'. **1905** J. LONDON *Jacket* (1915) 212 Tell us more about the *kisang* and the curries. **1908** H. N. ALLEN *Things Korean* viii. 125 The best performances..consist of dances by the class of public dancing girls or gesang. **1951** C. OSGOOD *Koreans & their Culture* xiv. 259 The kisaeng entertainments seem to have started as a court institution. **1953** D. PORTWAY *Korea* vi. 107 The Korean married woman is much too home-bound to be expected to sit down at a public dinner, and the kisaeng girl takes her place...The kisaeng girl is definitely not a prostitute, though probably the height of her ambition is to become the concubine of some wealthy man. **1973** *Guardian* 31 Jan. 4/6 In South Korea they [*sc.* Japanese tourists] are herded to mock 'kisaeng' parties designed to camouflage courtesans as trained 'kisaeng' (traditionally skilful, geisha-like entertainers).

kisan (kisā·n). [Hindi *kisān*, f. Skr. *kṛṣāṇa* one who ploughs.] In India, a peasant, an agricultural worker.

1935 *Ann. Reg. 1934* 152 The Communist Party of India..had through a *kisan* (peasant) organisation in the

Punjab sought to make propagandist capital out of economic discontent. **1936** J. Nehru *Autobiogr.* ix. 62 The Indian *kisans* have little staying power, little energy to resist for long. *Ibid.* x. 63 Agrarian troubles are frequently taking place in various parts of India..and the *kisan* agitation in certain parts of Oudh in 1920 and 1921 was but one of them. **1959** M. Brecher *Nehru* iii. 69 Jawaharlal's discovery of the *kisans* (peasants) spurred him to action on their behalf. *Ibid.* 70 His [*sc.* Nehru's] reputation as a friend of the *kisan* spread into the interior. **1969** *Hindu* (Madras) 28 July 9/8 Eleven Communist kisans were arrested yesterday by the Kilayur Police when they obstructed the ploughing with tractor of some fields in Kazhakkarai village. **1969** *Pioneer* (Lucknow) 13 Aug. 5/2 The whole legal system should be overhauled to make dispensation of justice speedy and cheap, specially to the poor kisans.

kishke (ki·ʃkə). Also **kishka, kishkeh, kishker.** [Yiddish.] **a.** Beef intestine casing stuffed with a sausage-like savoury filling. **b.** In *sing.* and *pl.* The guts. *slang.*

1936 Mencken *Amer. Lang.* (ed. 4) 217 In New York City the high density of Eastern Jews in the population has made almost every New Yorker familiar with a long list of Yiddish words *e.g.*, ..*kishkes, kittl,*[etc.]. **1951** L. W. Leonard *Jewish Cookery* xiv. 190 Stuffed kishke may be roasted with chicken, duck, goose or turkey. **1959** B. Kops *Hamlet of Stepney Green* I. 12 You sweat your *kishkers* out to give them a good education. **1964** *Amer. N. & Q.* Jan. 72/1 Ishka, pishka, Hit him in the *kishka*. **1967** G. Sims *Last Best Friend* vi. 53 They had..dined at Bloom's in Whitechapel High Street on beetroot bortsch and stuffed kishka. **1968** *Guardian* 8 Oct. 2/6 It is not every city where you go into a café and find yourself offered 'knishes, blintzes, kishka, [etc.]'. **1968** L. Rosten *Joys of Yiddish* 181, I laughed until my *kishkas* were sore. **1970** L. M. Feinsilver *Taste of Yiddish* iii. 293 Gentiles are learning to enjoy and pronounce such typical dishes as *kishke* and *tsimmes*. **1972** *Listener* 16 Mar. 341/3 Kishkeh vaguely resembles a kosher haggis..stuffed with a mixture of flour meal, grated onion and fat.

Kisii (ki·si,i). [Name of a district on the east side of Lake Victoria, Kenya.] A Bantu people from Kisii; a member of this people. Also *attrib.* or as *adj.*

1905 C. Eliot *E. Afr. Protectorate* vii. 131 The Kisii people are practically unknown to Europeans. *Ibid.*, Igizzi (the language of the Kisii) would appear from these vocabularies to have some resemblance to the Kikuyu tongue. **1934** N. K. Strange *Kenya To-Day* vi. 82 The ornamental bead belts.., and Kisii ware, various shaped vases and bowls made from soapstone..are amongst the attractive curios to be bought throughout Kenya. **1939** J. G. Peristiany *Social Inst. Kipsigis* p. xxi, The traditional enemies of the Kipsigis are the Masai to the south and the Kisii and Luo to the west. **1963** *Times* 31 May 10/2 Mr. Sagini is a Kisii. **1971** *E. Afr. Standard* (Nairobi) 10 Apr. 7/4 Kisii farmer killed in fight after stock theft.

kiskadee (kiskădī·). Also **keskeedie, keskidee.** [Echoic, f. the call of the bird.] A tyrant flycatcher, *Pitangus sulphuratus*, found in Central and South America; also used for related birds of the family Tyrannidæ.

1891 *Timehri* V. 61 One of the most common of birds.. is a brown and yellow Tyrant-shrike called the keskeedie (*Pitangus sulphuratus*). *Ibid.* 88 The large kiskadee (*Pitangus sulphuratus*)..whose loud, harsh and fierce cry of kis-kis-kiskadee is to be heard at all times of the day. **1922** *Blackw. Mag.* July 16/1 Glorious clumps of bamboo with kiskadees clinging like yellow blossoms to the bending plumes. **1941** *Penguin New Writing* VI. 75 Some keskidees were singing in the mango tree. **1953** E. R. Blake *Birds Mexico* 347 While mainly insectivorous like their relatives, Kiskadees also commonly catch small fish. **1958** J. Carew *Wild Coast* i. 7 Hector watched the birds and remembered..a pair of kiskadees. **1964** A. L. Thomson *New Dict. Birds* 316/1 Some larger species with shrike-like or terrestrial habits, such as the Kiskadee Flycatcher (or Great Kiskadee) *Pitangus sulphuratus*..take lizards, frogs, mice, and small birds.

kiskitomas. *U.S.* (Earlier and later examples.)

1809 A. Ritson *Poetical Pict. Amer.* 161 Their nuts, black walnuts, persimins, Kiscatoma nuts, and Chinquapins. [**1810** F. A. Michaux *Histoire des arbres forestiers* I. 20 *Shell bark hickery* [*sic*]..nom le plus en usage dans tous les Etats-Unis... *Kiskythomas*, par les Hollandois du New-Jersey.] **1832** D. J. Browne *Sylva Americana* 184 The Dutch settlers..near the city of New York, call it Kisky Thomas Nut. **1836** W. Dunlap *Mem. Water Drinker* (1837) I. 48 While the rustic jest, or the tale of..wars.. mingle with the cracking of the kisskatomasses..and walnuts. **1894** *Jrnl. Amer. Folk-Lore* VII. 98 *Carya alba*, kiskytom, Otsego Co., N.Y.

Kislev (ki·slef, -liŭ). Also 4–7 **Casleu**, 6–7 **Chisleu**, 8– **Kislew.** [Heb.] The third month of the Jewish civil year and the ninth of the ecclesiastical year, corresponding to parts of November and December.

1382 Wyclif *Zech.* vii. 1 The word of the Lord is maad to Zacharie, in the fourthe day of the nynthe monethe, that is Casleu [*later version* Caslew; **1535** Coverdale Casleu]. **1388** —— *Neh.* i. 1 It was doon in the monethe Casleu [**1535** Coverdale Chisleu], in the twentithe ȝeer. **1611** *Bible* 1 Macc. i. 54 The fifteenth day of the moneth Casleu. **1838, 1876** [see *Hesvan]. **1880** *Encycl. Brit.* XIII. 421/2 Upon the great altar of burnt offering a small altar to Jupiter Capitolinus was erected, on which the first offering was made on 25th Kislev 168. **1904** *Jewish Encycl.* VII. 515 On the twenty-fifth of Kislew the *Hanukkah* festival..commences. **1940** *Universal Jewish Encycl.* II. 632/2 If the day is subtracted, it is taken from the month of Kislev, and the year is termed *haserah*. **1962** D. Bridger *New Jewish Encycl.* 269 *Kislev*, the third month of the Jewish calendar, corresponding to November–December, and consisting of 30, and sometimes 29 days.

kiss, *sb.* Add: **6.** Also *attrib.* **kiss impression** *Printing* (see quot. 1960); **kissproof** *a.*, of lipstick, that will not smudge, come off, etc., if its wearer kisses or is kissed; also *fig.*

1946 B. Dalgin *Advertising Production* 89 If a highlight dot carries little ink, only contact ('kiss impression', we call it) would be required. **1960** G. A. Glaister *Gloss. Bk.* 208 *Kiss impression*, one in which the ink is deposited on the paper by the lightest possible surface contact and is not impressed into it. This technique is required when printing on coated papers. **1962** F. T. Day *Introd. to Paper* ix. 98 The letterpress process employs various machines all of which operate on the same principle, that of bringing inked type surfaces together in a 'kiss impression' with the paper. **1967** Karch & Buber *Offset Processes* ix. 446 Long press runs with a single plate are possible because the offset plate does not touch the paper but contacts the blanket with a very light 'kiss' impression. **1967** V. Strauss *Printing Industry* vii. 448/2 The inking cylinder should be set for a 'kiss impression', a term indicating that the least pressure compatible with proper image transfer is to be used. **1934** Dylan Thomas *18 Poems* 26 Happy Cadaver's hunger as you take The kissproof world. **1937** M. Sharp *Nutmeg Tree* iii. 40 She exchanged her more subdued..lipstick for a new Kiss-proof in flamingo red. **1940** 'N. Shute' *Landfall* ii. 37 'You don't use lipstick.' 'That's all you know. They told me it was kissproof in the shop.' **1959** *Punch* 19 Aug. 39/2 Eight refills of genuine English kissproof lipstick, in the new, passionate tangerine shade. **1962** *New Scientist* 27 Sept. 686/3 Kissproof lipstick was among the most profitable inventions of the present century. **1974** V. Canning *Painted Tent* ix. 194 You can give me a kiss. It's all right —don't fret—the stuff's kiss-proof.

b. Phr. *the kiss of death* [f. the association with the kiss of betrayal given to Jesus by Judas in the Garden of Gethsemane (Matthew xxvi. 48–50)], a seemingly kind or well-intentioned action, look, association, etc., which brings disastrous consequences; *the kiss of life*, the mouth-to-mouth method of artificial respiration; also *attrib.* and *fig.*

1948 'N. Shute' *No Highway* iv. 113, I told you that he'd put the kiss of death on it. **1952** H. Waugh *Last seen Wearing* (1953) 141 I'm starting to take a liking to that guy... The kiss of death. **1960** *Times* 20 July 13/3 Military assistance from Rhodesia would be the kiss of death to Mr. Tshombe. **1960** *Guardian* 10 Dec. 5/1 Let us hope that the critics' approval does not, at the box-office, prove a kiss of death. **1970** *New Scientist* 27 Aug. 405/1 In some countries state participation is essential for a scientific programme, in others it often seems the kiss of death. **1961** *Daily Mail* 22 Sept. 1/7 Mrs. Alice Lowe..used the 'kiss-of-life' to save her 19-month-old nephew Geoffrey Ahmed at Oldham yesterday. **1962** *Guardian* 25 June 4/4 Two children..were given the 'kiss of life' artificial respiration treatment. **1964** *Ibid.* 21 Apr. 18/4 Here was Mr Houghton giving the debate the kiss of life, and Mr Boyd-Carpenter responding to treatment. **1969** P. Dickinson *Pride of Heroes* I. 28, I cut the rope..and lowered him to the floor to administer the kiss of life, a technique in which I have taken instruction. **1969** *Private Eye* 5 Dec. 17/2 Finding her six years old goldfish 'Bubbles' on the carpet beside its tank, a Nottinghamshire woman gave it the kiss of life. **1972** *Daily Tel.* 6 Jan. 15/6 Firemen rescued them from their first-floor flat..and tried to revive them on the footpath with the kiss of life and oxygen.

kiss, *v.* Add: **6. e.** *to kiss the hand* (*hands*) (later examples). **k.** *to kiss and be friends, to kiss and make up*: to become reconciled; also as a substantival phr. **l.** *to kiss* (a person's) *arse, behind, bum*: to behave obsequiously towards (a person). As *imp.*, esp. in phr. *kiss my arse*: a vulgar rejoinder, stronger than 'go to hell'. **m.** *to kiss and tell*: to recount one's sexual exploits. **n.** *to kiss better* (or *well*): to comfort (a sick or injured person, esp. a child) by kissing him, esp. by kissing the sore or injured part of the body; also *fig.* **o.** *to kiss goodbye*: to bid farewell with a kiss; freq. used *fig.* and ironically. **p.** *to kiss off, slang,* (*a*) *trans.* to dismiss, get rid of, kill (see also quot. 1935²); (*b*) *intr.* to go away, die.

e. 1955 H. Nicolson *Diary* 6 Apr. (1968) 281 Anthony [Eden] drives to the Palace and kisses hands on his appointment as Prime Minister. **1963** *Times* 31 Jan. 14/2 Mr. F. J. Blakeney was received in audience by The Queen this morning and kissed hands upon his appointment as Her Majesty's Ambassador Extraordinary and Plenipotentiary for the Commonwealth of Australia at Bonn. **1974** *Guardian* 7 Mar. 26/4 Mr Foot..started work to settle the miners [*sic*] dispute even before kissing hands with the Queen.

k. *a* **1654** J. Selden *Table-Talk* (1689) 36 The People and the Prince kist and were Friends, and so things were quiet for a while. **1657** W. Denton *Let.* 5 Feb. in M. M. Verney *Mem.* (1894) III. ix. 301 Go, kisse and be friends, which is the advice of Wm. D. **1834** G. Cornish *Let.* 8 Feb. in G. Battiscombe *John Keble* (1963) x. 191 After knocking each other down half-a-dozen times, kiss and be friends. **1942** Berrey & Van den Bark *Amer. Thes. Slang* § 334/3 *Become reconciled; make up*.., kiss and make up. **1958** *Listener* 2 Oct. 508/1 The party to which I had invited myself was a sort of Kiss-and-make-up. **1969** M. Pugh *Last Place Left* xviii. 128 Play the argument bit again..and then play the kiss-and-make-up bit.

l. 1705 in *N. & Q.* (1971) Feb. 46/1 You can father it.. just as you did another man's philosophical essay upon the wind..when you made bold with several pages from the learned Dr. Bohun, without saying so much to the Dr. for his assistance as kiss my a–se. **1749** Fielding *Tom Jones* I. vi. ix. 288 The Wit..lies in desiring another to kiss your A— for having just before threatened to kick his. **1934** H. Miller *Tropic of Cancer* (1948) 207 If it weren't that I had learned how to kiss the boss's ass, I would have been fired. **1937** 'G. Orwell' *Road to Wigan Pier* x. 196 You 'get on'..by..kissing the bums of verminous little lions. **1938** L. MacNeice *Earth Compels* 34 Let us thank God for valour in abstraction For those who go their own way, will not kiss The arse of law and order. **1956** B. Holiday *Lady sings Blues* (1973) vi. 60 You've got to kiss everybody's behind to get ten minutes to do eight sides in. *Ibid.* vii. 66, I threw the money at him and told him to kiss my ass and tell Miss Waters to do the same. **1963** *Amer. Speech* XXXVIII. 169 To curry favor with a professor... There are three occurrences of *kiss ass*. **1972** *Fairbanks* (Alaska) *Daily News-Miner* 3 Nov. 1/5 McGovern had told an airport antagonist to 'kiss my a..'. The candidate's national political director ..joked that the remark had been rather natural for a Democratic nominee. 'After all,' Mankiewicz said, 'he can't say kiss my elephant.'

m. 1695 Congreve *Love for Love* II. 30 Oh fie Miss, you must not kiss and tell. **1846** *Swell's Night Guide* 88 Let those who wish to know her qualifications as *une coucheuse*, try her; for we will not, on all occasions, *kiss* and *tell*. **1921** G. B. Shaw *Let.* 30 Dec. in *B. Shaw & Mrs. Campbell* (1952) 235 A gentleman does not kiss and tell.

n. 1808 A. Taylor *Original Poems for Infant Minds* (1814) 72 Who ran to help me when I fell, And would.. kiss the place to make it well? My Mother. **1929** E. Bowen *Last September* xvi. 207 She kept..feeling the bump: David must 'kiss it better' for her. **1966** *New Society* 23 June 19/1 Mothers..welcome the opportunity of being able to 'kiss their baby better'. They find it easier to have the sick child at home. **1972** *Guardian* 6 May 9/1 I've got this old pain back. 'You must go to the doctor's,' Maggie said, when she'd failed to kiss it better.

o. 1935 C. Day Lewis *Time to Dance* 33 On January 8, 1920, their curveting wheels kissed England goodbye. **1944** 'N. Shute' *Pastoral* ix. 209 I'll tell Proctor he can kiss his truck good-bye for the rest of the day. **1959** *Listener* 8 Jan. 50/1 It would be exaggerating the trend to say that the Chinese are almost ready to kiss the Soviet experts goodbye. **1970** V. Gielgud *Candle-Holders* v. 45 If she chooses one of the Eltham team for a partner, poor George can kiss the trophy goodbye.

p. 1935 *Amer. Speech* X. 22/1 *To throw* (*someone*) *down*. ..Modern *to kiss* (*someone*) *off* (usually restricted in use to a person of the opposite sex). **1935** A. J. Pollock *Underworld Speaks* 68/1 *Kissed off*, defrauded of share of loot or plunder. **1945** L. Shelly *Jive Talk Dict.* 28/1 *Kiss off*, to die. **1946** 'J. Evans' *Halo in Blood* xi. 134 I'm a private eye and I've got a customer who wants to know who kissed off Marlin..and why. **1948** —— *Halo for Satan* (1949) vi. 83 The man who..had kissed off all raps except..the one ..for income tax evasion. **1967** D. Skirrow *I was following this Girl* xxxvi. 219 'Kiss off,' he said... 'I told you, the girl's not here.' **1970** C. Major *Dict. Afro-Amer. Slang* 73 *Kiss-off*,..to die. **1973** M. & G. Gordon *Informant* xviii. 74 The same FBI agents..getting tough. Well, kiss them off. **1973** W. McCarthy *Detail* iii. 216 'I thought you had stopped smoking.' 'Kiss off, I just started again.'

7. Used in various collocations to denote the comparative ease of an action, etc.; as in (*as easy as*) *kiss my* (or *your*, etc.) *hand, finger*, etc.

1891 [see Thumb *sb.* 5 i]. **1909** P. Webling *Story of Virginia Perfect* xxv. 249 It isn't so easy to make respectable friends, and so Miss Malet will find out, though she finds it as easy as kiss-your-'and to drop them! **1924** Kipling *Debits & Credits* (1926) 167 The 'ole Somme front washed out as clean as kiss-me-'and! **1926** F. M. Ford *Man could stand Up* I. ii. 21 The prospect had seemed as near—as near as kiss your finger! **1949** J. Symons *Bland Beginning* 187 He wanted us to do a little job for him. It was as easy as kiss your hand. **1961** *Sunday Express* 12 Feb. 9/4 The cars have to be insured and that's as easy as kiss your hand. **1968** *Punch* 4 Sept. 330/3 The furs.. dropped down like kiss-your-arm into net provided. **1973** V. Canning *Flight of Grey Goose* v. 92 You might be on to a bit of all right here. Yes... Sweet and easy as kiss your hand.

kiss-. Add: **kiss-curl,** a small flat curl worn on the forehead, in front of the ear, or at the nape of the neck.

1856 *Punch* 29 Nov. 219/1 Those pastry-cook's girl's ornaments called kiss-curls. **1867** H. Spicer *Bound to Please* II. 15 Bob Jessamy..was nursing a kiss curl, though it hung limperer than what it usually did do. **1930** *Daily Express* 8 Sept. 3/6 Any kind of curls from Nell Gwynn ringlets to kiss curls. **1966** *Punch* 21 Dec. 933/3 'It's the little touches,' he murmurs.., faintly disordering his kisscurl before pretending to be laid low by a heart attack. **1968** J. Ironside *Fashion Alphabet* 194 Although a kiss curl is usually regarded as being on the cheek, like a 'confidante', sometimes it can hang in the middle of the forehead. **1974** *Guardian* 27 Mar. 12/6 Haley..came on looking much the same as ever, the kiss curl immaculately in place.

kissage (ki·sĕdʒ). [f. Kiss *v.* + -age.] Kissing.

1886 Kipling *Departmental Ditties* (ed. 2) 1 Ere they hewed the Sphinx's visage Favouritism governed kissage Even as it does in this age. **1898** G. B. Shaw *Let.* 5 Jan. in *Ellen Terry & Shaw* (1931) 287 The best thing for the knee is kissage; for the heart, careful wrapping round by the arms of a rather tall man, with, if possible, a red beard. **1960** F. Frankfurter *Felix Frankfurter Reminisces* iii. 28 This system, the objectivity of the marking, and the other considerations—no kissage by favors has always

been the slogan there—creates an atmosphere and habits of objectivity and disinterestedness..and a zest for being very good at this business which is law.

kissar (ki·sāɹ). [ad. colloq. Arab. *ḳīsār*.] (See quot. 1964.) Also *attrib.*

1864 C. ENGEL *Music Most Anc. Nations* ii. 41 A kissar from Abyssinia..is so far different from the common Nubian kissar, that its body is square, without sounding-holes. *Ibid.* iv. 158 The songs with the kissar accompaniment..are called by the Nubians ghouna. **1941** J. PULVER tr. *Panum's Stringed Instruments Middle Ages* 12 Engel..points to the striking likeness existing between the type of lyre depicted here and the lyre which, under the name of *Kissar*, is still used by several North African peoples. **1964** S. MARCUSE *Mus. Instruments* 291/1 *Kissar* (Gk. *kithara*), bowl lyre of E. Africa, a survival of the ancient Gk. lyra, still found in Ethiopia, Sudan, and Uganda. The body is shallow, of wood, covered with a sheepskin membrane laced to the back of the body.

‖ **kissel** (ki·səl, *ki*sye·l). Also **keessel.** [ad. Russ. *kiséľ*.] A sweet dish made from fruit juice mixed with sugar and water, which is boiled and thickened with potato or cornflour.

1924 A. GAGARINE *Russ. Cook Bk.* x. 191 When eaten hot, the keessel should be thick as honey; when cold, like custard. **1943** E. M. ALMEDINGEN *Frossia* vii. 266 A hut odorous of freshly baked rye loaves, singed chicken feathers, and cranberry jelly, '*kissel*', and pickled cucumbers lying in a wooden bowl. **1952** M. MCCARTHY *Groves of Academe* (1953) iii. 34 The small presents she was in the habit of bringing them—a dish of Russian kissel with a white napkin over it. **1969** *Guardian* 15 Aug. 7/4 *Blackberry kissel*... Blend the cornflour with a little cold water, and with the brandy, stir into the blackberry puree. **1971** *Times* 9 Aug. 5/8 Moscow housewives are buying up huge amounts of berries just now—mostly blackcurrants, redcurrants and cranberries—to preserve them as jam or make a thin jelly (*kissel*).

kisser. Add: **2.** The mouth; the face. orig. *Boxing slang.*

1860 *Chambers's Jrnl.* XIII. 348/1 His mouth is his 'potato-trap'..or 'kisser'. **1892** P. H. EMERSON *Son of Fens* iv. 43 'Oh,' he say, and dabbed the wet mittens across my kisser kind of smart. **1927** W. E. COLLINSON *Contemp. Eng.* 27 In speaking of parts of the body we might use..the boxer's term claret-jug or conk, but we did not..use 'I'll hit you on the kisser (*mouth*)'. **1938** D. RUNYON *Furthermore* v. 81 He is a tall skinny guy with a long, sad, mean-looking kisser, and a mournful voice. **1953** R. CHANDLER *Let.* 15 Mar. in *R. Chandler Speaking* (1966) 28 Chandler..consumed three double gimlets and fell flat on his kisser. **1973** J. WAINWRIGHT *High-class Kill* 156 Open that sweet little, lying little, kisser of yours, and start saying something that makes sense.

Kissi (ki·si), *sb.* and *a.* [Native name.] **A.** *sb.* An agricultural people inhabiting the regions of Guinea, Sierra Leone, and Liberia near the headwaters of the Niger; one of this people; also, their language. **B.** *adj.* Of or pertaining to the Kissi.

1884 *Encycl. Brit.* XVII. 319/1 *Felup Group*,..Kissi. **1916** [see *KONO[2]]. **1949** E. A. NIDA *Morphol.* (ed. 2) v. 107 In Kissi, a language of French Guinea,..the distinction between monosyllabic and polysyllabic verbs is pertinent. **1957** M. BANTON *W. Afr. City* ii. 36 The Army had ..recruited a high proportion of its soldiers among the Koranko, Kono, and Kissi tribes in the farthest corners of the Protectorate. *Ibid.* vii. 122 The Kissi, who speak a separate language similar to that of the Bulom but now much influenced by Mandinka, live far inland in the high ground where the French, British, and Liberian frontiers meet. **1970** *Western Folklore* XXIX. 241 Among some of the Liberian Kissi of the frontier regions the musical bow accompanies tribal initiation rites in the forest, being utilized in place of the wooden drum.

kissing, *vbl. sb.* Add: **1. b.** Phr. (*when*) *the kissing had* (or *has*) *to stop*: (when) the 'honeymoon' period finished (or finishes); (when) one is forced to recognize harsh realities.

1855 BROWNING *Toccata of Galuppi's* xiv, in *Men & Women* I. 61 What of soul was left, I wonder, when the kissing had to stop? **1960** C. FITZGIBBON (*title*) When the kissing had to stop. **1965** *Guardian* 20 Aug. 12/3 In the past 15 years more than 190,000 adult Jamaicans have come to settle in this country... Now the kissing has to stop. **1973** *Times* 28 Dec. 8/3 If left wing extremists continue to exploit..grievances..we should not have to wait long for the emergence of extremists of the right... It is then a few short steps to the place where the kissing has to stop.

2. kissing-ball, -bough, -bunch, -bush, a Christmas wreath or ball of evergreens, freq. arranged with fruit and ribbons, which is hung from the ceiling and under which a kiss may be taken; **kissing time,** the time to kiss, freq. used as a joc. reply to children who ask the time.

1970 *Canad. Antiques Collector* Dec. 10/1 A kissing ball, consisting of evergreen, wrapped round a cluster of apples, provides the 'mistletoe'. **1956** B. CHUTE *Green Willow* viii. 91 In some houses..kissing-boughs hung over doorways. **1969** E. WILKINS *Rose-Garden Game* viii. 191 The old English Christmas globe, called a kissing-bough, which was made up of three interlocking hoops of greenery, hung from the ceiling and lit up with candles. **1857** T. WRIGHT *Dict. Obsolete & Provincial English* II. 614/2 *Kissing-bunch*, a bush of evergreens sometimes substituted for mistletoe at Christmas. **1913** D. H. LAWRENCE *Sons & Lovers* vi. 116 It [*sc.* the kitchen] was small and curious to her, with its glittering kissing-bunch. **1859** C. W. WILSON *Mapping the Frontier* (1970) i. 77 It will be a hard matter if we cannot get something wherewith to drink success to the 'kissing bush'. **1879–81** G. F. JACKSON *Shropshire Word-Bk.* 237 *Kissing-bush*, a bunch of evergreens or mistletoe garnished with ribands and fruit, which is hung in the kitchen, or hall, at Christmas-tide. **1875** W. ALEXANDER *Sk. Life among my Ain Folk* v. ii. 245 When the leading fiddler pushes his fourth finger far up his first string..this is 'kissing time'; and, after an attempt more or less successful on the part of each male dancer to kiss his partner's cheek, at it they go! **1916** F. NORTON (*song-title*) Any time is kissing time. **1922** JOYCE *Ulysses* 354 Edy asked her the time and Miss Cissy..said it was half past kissing time, time to kiss again. **1935** T. S. ELIOT *Murder in Cath.* i. 25 If you will remember me, my Lord, at your prayers, I'll remember you at kissing-time below the stairs. **1947** W. DE LA MARE *Coll. Stories for Children* 165 Nobody ever wasted *any* time (except kissing-time). **1959** I. & P. OPIE *Lore & Lang. Schoolch.* xii. 247 It is kissing time after four o'clock. If the girls trip you up they say you have got to kiss them after four o'clock.

kissing, *ppl. a.* Add: **b. kissing bug** *U.S.*, a blood-sucking bug of the family Reduviidæ; **kissing cousin,** a relative or friend with whom one is on close enough terms to greet with a kiss; also *transf.*; **kissing gourami,** a small Malaysian freshwater fish, *Helostoma temmineki*, often kept in aquaria; **kissing trap** *slang*, the mouth.

1899 *Pop. Sci. Monthly* Nov. 33 Several persons suffering from swollen faces visited the Emergency Hospital in Washington and complained that they had been bitten by some insect while asleep... Thus began the 'kissing bug' scare. **1904** *N.Y. Even. Post* 4 Aug. 1 The doctors were unable to decide whether he had been bitten by a mosquito or a kissing bug. **1932** METCALF & FLINT *Fund. Insect Life* viii. 222 Family Reduviidæ. The Assassin or Kissing Bugs.—This is a very large family of mostly flattened, oval bugs... The assassin bugs catch small insects and suck their blood as food. Some species, when handled, inflict painful bites on man. **1973** L. E. CHADWICK tr. *Linsenmaier's Insects of World* 120/1 The bite of many reduviids is very painful, even to man; in warm countries certain species even enter homes on occasion at night and suck the blood of people. In North America this may be done by the black 'kissing bug' (*Melanolestes picipes*). About 0·6 inch long, this bug prefers to bite the face, especially in the region of the mouth. **1974** A. DILLARD *Pilgrim at Tinker Creek* xiii. 232 The cone-nose bug, or kissing bug, bites the lips of sleeping people, sucking blood and injecting an excruciating toxin. **1951** in Wentworth & Flexner *Dict. Amer. Slang* (1960) 306/2 You guys talk like kissing cousins. **1961** *John o' London's* 20 Apr. 436/3 Marianne Spottiswoode, who is also a kissing cousin of the publishing Spottiswoodes. **1961** *Economist* 18 Nov. 676/2 The relationship will be more on the order of 'kissing cousins'—the experience gained will be valuable for later and more serious efforts. **1970** *Guardian* 31 Aug. 7/4 We resemble the Dutch more than we resemble the people of any other country—we are truly kissing cousins. **1973** *Publishers Weekly* 25 June 33/2 (Advt.), From cream pies to their kissing cousins, soufflés. **1935** W. T. INNES *Exotic Aquarium Fishes* 360 *Helostoma temmineki*... Popular name, Kissing Gourami. **1952** H. R. AXELROD *Tropical Fish* iii. 59 The Kissing Gourami [is]..so named for the unusual shape of its mouth when eating or sucking debris from the sides of the tank. **1962** D. W. TUCKER tr. *Sterba's Freshwater Fishes of World* 794 There is an unpigmented variety of the Kissing Gourami which is a uniform dull pink. **1854** 'C. BEDE' *Further Adventures Verdant Green* iv. 31 To one gentleman he would pleasantly observe..in the still more elegant imagery of the Ring,..'How about the kissing-trap?' **1887** G. D. ATKIN *House Scraps* 54 The 'offside' of his 'kissing-trap' Displays an ugly mark! **1942** BERREY & VAN DEN BARK *Amer. Thes. Slang* § 121/66 *Mouth*,..kissing trap, loud-speaker, maw, [etc.].

kiss-in-the-ring. (Earlier and later examples.)

1801 J. STRUTT *Sports & Pastimes* IV. iv. 285 A boy must touch a girl, and a girl a boy, and when either of them be caught they go into the middle of the ring and salute each other; hence is derived the name of *kiss in the ring*. **1925** W. DE LA MARE *Broomsticks* 26 There were quantities of things to eat and lots to see, and Kiss-in-the-Ring. **1936** 'R. CROMPTON' *Sweet William* vii. 171 The games were to be Kiss in the Ring, Postman's Knock, Turn the Trencher, ..and others of similar kind. **1957** J. MASTERS *Far, Far the Mountain Peak* i. 5 Why don't I suggest a game of ring-a-ring-a-roses or kiss-in-the-ring? **1969** I. & P. OPIE *Children's Games* vi. 201 Throughout the nineteenth century 'Kiss in the Ring' was a favourite game at Christmas time and midsummer.

kiss-me-quick. Add: **4.** *kiss-me-quick hat*: a hat bearing the words 'kiss me quick' (or some other, usu. jocular, phrase) on the front.

1963 *Guardian* 12 July 9/6 Mature matrons..now.. wear kiss-me-quick hats. **1974** J. WAINWRIGHT *Evidence I shall Give* xxiv. 120 Whitby... Genuine Olde Worlde charm, wearing a Kiss-Me-Quick hat. A fishing community, taken over by day-trippers.

kist, *sb.*[1] Add: **1. a.** (S. Afr. examples.)

1958 *Personality* 4 Dec. 27/3 Ancient brass-bound *kists* of teak help to furnish the back stoep. **1959** *Star* (Johannesburg) 22 Jan. 7/4 (Advt.), Heavy bowfronted *kists* price cut to £15:19:6. **1971** *Cape Times* 13 Feb. 21/3 (Advt.), Furniture and effects..walnut bedroom suite, easy chairs..several large teak glass fronted cupboards, 2 carved Zanzibar camphor-wood kists. **1971** *Leader* (Durban) 7 May 15 (Advt.), Imbuia Kist..R29.00.

c. *kist o' whistles, whustles*, an organ (ORGAN *sb.*[1] 2). *Now rare.*

1772 A. RAMSAY *New Misc. Scots Sangs* [*Tea-Table Misc.*] 141 The Kist fou of Whistles, That make sic a Cleiro. **1828** J. RUDDIMAN *Tales & Sk.* 60 To cram down our craigs, will we, nill we, their kists o' whistles. **1866** [in Dict., sense 1]. **1889** G. B. SHAW *London Music in 1888–89* (1937) 116 M. Gigout, who was performing on the 'Kist o' whustles'. **1891** R. FORD *Thistledown* vi. 106 There was no such thing as an organ, or 'kist o' whustles', in any Presbyterian kirk in the land. **1936** *Discovery* July 223/2 The normal 'kist of whistles' would spoil the architectural effect. **1947** 'H. MACDIARMID' (*title*) A kist of whistles. **1969** C. GEESON *Northumberland & Durham Word Bk.* 118 *Kist o' whistles*, an organ in Scotland and Northumberland.

Kiswa (ki·swa). Also **Kiswah.** [Arab.] The black cloth which covers the Kaaba.

1599 HAKLUYT *Voyages* II. I. 203 Moreouer he deliuereth vnto him ye *Chisua Talnabi*, which signifieth in the Arabian tongue, The garment of the Prophet. *a* **1817** J. L. BURCKHARDT *Trav. Arabia* (1829) I. 254 The four sides of the Kaaba are covered with a black silk stuff, hanging down, and leaving the roof bare. This curtain..is called *kesoua*. **1855** R. F. BURTON *Pilgrimage* II. xvi. 82 The Kiswa is a black, purple, or green brocade, embroidered with white or with silver letters. **1912** A. J. B. WAVELL *Mod. Pilgrim in Mecca* viii. 152 The 'Ihram'..remains till the day of the festival, when the 'Kiswah', that is the covering itself, is changed. **1928** E. RUTTER *Holy Cities Arabia* I. xiii. 178 The beautiful silk and wool kiswa with its gold-embroidered band..not having been sent this year, Ibn Sa'ûd had supplied a covering of black Bedouin hair cloth. **1959** *Chambers's Encycl.* IX. 192/2 Each old Kiswa is cut up and sold to pilgrims. **1963** *Ann. Reg. 1962* 375 Saudi refusal to accept the *kiswa*, the traditional holy cloth for the Kaaba shrine in Mecca sent annually from Cairo.

Kiswahili (kiswahī·li). [Native word, f. *ki-* prefix designating an abstract or inanimate object + SWAHILI.] A major language of the Bantu family, spoken widely in Kenya, Tanzania, and elsewhere in East Africa, where it serves as a lingua franca.

1864 J. A. GRANT *Walk across Afr.* p. xvi, *Kisuahili*, the dialect of the Wasuahili on the east coast of Africa. **1936** *Discovery* June 196/1 A record of certain Bena customs, written in Kiswahili. **1966** C. SWEENEY *Scurrying Bush* ii. 23 He could read Swahili... He knew little English, but this was an advantage as it forced me to learn Kiswahili. **1967** C. W. RECHENBACH *Swahili-Eng. Dict.* p. v, The Swahili language (*Kiswahili*) is a Bantu language spoken by perhaps as many as forty million people throughout a large part of East and Central Africa. **1969** *Nationalist* (Dar Es Salaam) 25 Jan. 6/2 (Advt.), Candidates must be Tanzanian Citizens fluent in both Kiswahili and English. **1971** *Inside Kenya Today* Mar. 39/1 The School..manages to arrange the course for Kiswahili speakers from time to time. **1972** G. WIGG *George Wigg* v. 110 Facilities for learning Kiswahili were made available in Chinyanja speaking units.

kit, *sb.*[1] Add: **1. b.** (Later examples; also in extended use, and, by metonymy, the contents of a kit, used as a measure of weight.)

1906 *Daily Chron.* 12 Apr. 6/3 One vessel alone brought in a thousand kits of fish. **1934** 'TAFFRAIL' *Seventy North* ix. 185, 20,000 to 25,000 'kits' of fish, each weighing ten stone might be landed from the trawlers—say 125 to 150 tons. **1935** 'L. LUARD' *Conquering Seas* ii. 20 Within two hours of berthing, with a full two thousand kit aboard.. over a hundred tons of fish. **1961** *Guardian* 18 Jan. 9/2 He was pushing a barrow on the fish dock, wheeling aluminium 'kits' which, when full, each contain 10 stone of fish.

2. d. A set or outfit of tools, equipment, etc.; *spec.*, a collection of parts sold for the buyer to assemble. Also *fig.* and *attrib.*

1859 G. W. MATSELL *Vocabulum* 48 *Kit*..the implements of a burglar. **1907** *Yesterday's Shopping* (1969) 277/2 The Army & Navy Boot Kit contains 3 shoe brushes,..1 tin of boot polish, complete in leather case. **1935** A. J. POLLOCK *Underworld Speaks* 68/1 *Kit*, a safe-cracker's tools. **1955** *Amer. Speech* XXX. 226 Kit, all the necessary parts to assemble one section of the plane. **1955** A. HUXLEY *Genius & Goddess* 51 A make-up kit and a bottle of cheap perfume. **1961** PARTRIDGE *Dict. Slang* Suppl. 1160/1 *Kit*, paint-kettle and -brushes: house-painters' coll. **1967** *Listener* 3 Aug. 148/2 Beckett forces upon you a do-it-yourself Tantalus-kit. He requires you to seek and not to find. **1970** *House & Garden* Mar. 77/2 'Cena' chair...Comes in kit form (see components below).. from £14 19s. plus tool kit. **1970** *Times* 26 Sept. 18/1 Make your own sausages... Kit includes hand-filler, recipes and full instructions, also herbs, spices, skins. **1970** D. MARLOWE *Echoes of Celandine* i. 12, I have also a penchant for vintage-car kits... I have constructed the 1929 Mercedes Benz SSK three times.

e. An outfit of drums, cymbals, and other percussion devices and accessories used by a drummer in a dance-band, jazz-group, or the like.

1929 *Melody Maker* Mar. 259/3 Lyman plays the drums in the band—at least he sits behind a nice kit. **1934, 1965** [see *drum kit* s.v. *DRUM *sb.*[1] 12 a]. **1971** *Melody Maker* 27 Nov. 47/3 It's more important to think about the music than the colour of your kit. A good drummer is going to sound good even if he plays on the table top.

f. A quantity of printed matter on a specified topic for students, etc.

1968 *Globe & Mail* (Toronto) 17 Feb. 36 (Advt.), Savannah's full of colonial names... Why not add your name to an illustrious list? Write for our free travel kit. **1971** J. B. CARROLL et al. *Word Frequency Bk.* p. vi, The materials themselves include text-books, periodicals, encyclopedias, novels, student workbooks, kits, and so on,

all of which contain vocabulary to which students are exposed. **1971** *Guardian* 7 June 6/7 The SACK—School and Community Kit—is made up of information and ideas on community projects for schools, together with reference material. **1974** *Catholic Herald* 4 Oct. 4/2 The study kits come in colourful folders and contain pictures, taped songs, fact sheets and quotations from Church leaders.

3. Also, *the whole kit and boiling* (*boodle, caboodle, cargo*). (Cf. *CABOODLE.) *U.S.*

a **1852** F. M. WHITCHER *Widow Bedott Papers* (1856) xxiii. 257 The hull kit and cargo on 'em had conspired together. **1859** BARTLETT *Dict. Amer.* (ed. 2) 32 *Biling*, a vulgar pronunciation of *boiling*. The phrase *the whole* (or more commonly *hull*) *kit and bilin*, means the whole lot, applied to persons and things. *a* **1861** T. WINTHROP *John Brent* (1883) xxviii. 237, I motioned we shove the hul kit an boodle of the gamblers ashore on logs. 'Twas kerried. **1888** *Boston Globe* 5 Feb. 1/3 If any 'railroad lobbyist' cast reflections on his character he would wipe out the whole kit and caboodle of them. **1908** *Dialect Notes* III. 327 (East Alabama) *Kit an*(*d*) *bilin*, the crowd. Usually in the expression 'the whole kit and bilin'. Cf. *kit and cargo* of the middle west. **1920** S. LEWIS *Main St.* 50 The whole kit and bilin' of 'em are nothing in God's world but socialism in disguise. **1946** *Newsweek* 16 Sept. 32/2 It gave the farm and the whole kit and boodle to Stanley. **1969** *Listener* 22 May 707/3 The whole kit and caboodle of us were then investigated by the FBI to see how many subversives there were among us.

4. b. kit-car, a motor car sold in parts for assembly by the owner; a build-it-yourself car; **kitset** *N.Z.*, the components and aids for assembling an article (radio, furniture, etc.) or model (aeroplane, etc.).

1953 G. DURRELL *Overloaded Ark* xiii. 216, I..set off early one morning in the back of the Schiblers' kit-car. **1964** *Sunday Times* (Colour Suppl.) 29 Nov. 53/3 The modern kit car... All you need is practical application, a few hand tools. **1970** *Sunday Truth* (Brisbane) 18 Jan. 60/3 Here we loaded the kit-car..and travelled south to Biafra. **1963** *Weekly News* (Auckland) 8 May 56/5 *Transistor radio kitsets.* New low prices. Easy-to-build range from crystal set, £1, to 7T portables, £9/19/6. **1966** *Ibid.* 26 Jan. 6/6 Many other clubs throughout the Auckland province assist the young yachtsman with kitsets and drawings for home building [of yachts].

kit, *sb.*[3] Also = KITTEN *sb.* 1 b.

1957 Kitt [see *KITTEN *sb.* 1 b]. **1970** *Times* 8 Sept. 11/3 The kits [*sc.* young mink] are fully grown at six months. **1974** A. DILLARD *Pilgrim at Tinker Creek* ii. 15 You crouch motionless on a bank..and are rewarded by the sight of a muskrat kit paddling from its den.

kit (kit), *sb.*[11] *N.Z.* Also **kete, kête.** [ad. Maori *kete.*] A basket plaited from flax. Hence **ki·tful.**

1834 E. MARKHAM *N.Z. or Recollections of It* (MS.) 44 They make Baskets or Kits as we call them for potatoes. **1841** W. COLENSO *Jrnl.* (typescript) I. 120 Opening his *kete* and taking out his Blanket. **1856** E. B. FITTON *New Zealand* 68 Neatly made baskets, plaited from flax, and known by the name of 'Maori kits'. **1877** W. T. PRATT *Colonial Experiences* 31 Potatoes were procurable from the Maories [*sic*] in flax kits, at from one to five shillings the kit. **1882** W. D. HAY *Brighter Britain!* I. ii. 38 [The well-to-do Maori] stops and..examines the kitful of fruit. **1884** LADY MARTIN *Our Maoris* 44 My heart is like an old kête (*i.e.*, a coarsely-woven basket). **1902** W. SATCHELL *Land of Lost* xviii. 161, I will give you a kitful when you go away. **1936** 'R. HYDE' *Check to your King* xiii. 156 Great flax-kits of *Kumaras*..were left outside the door. **1938** R. FINLAYSON *Brown Man's Burden* 75 So the three men got enough kitfuls [of shellfish] long before Hira came back. **1941** BAKER *N.Z. Slang* vi. 55 We have also put into wide use the term *kit* for a shopping basket. **1958** S. ASHTON-WARNER *Spinster* 41 When I comes to this word 'basket' in my book I never says 'basket'... I always says 'kit'. **1969** F. SARGESON *Joy of Worm* iii. 105 Between the two of them they carried a flax kit of food.

kit, *v.*[1] Add: **2.** To equip (someone or something) with a uniform, an outfit, personal effects, equipment, etc. Freq. with *out, up.* So **kitted (out, up)**, provided with clothing, accessories, etc.; **kitting (up)** *vbl. sb.*

1919 W. LANG *Sea-Lawyer's Log* ii. 13 It is pleasant to march down to the kitting-up store and have garments thrown at you..without price. *Ibid.* 16 Now we have been 'kitted up', as the nautical expression has it. **1925** T. E. LAWRENCE *Let.* 25 Aug. (1938) 481 Sergeant take this man to the Q.M. Stores, kit him at once, and put him into the first train for Cranwell. **1945** *Times* 25 May 2/2 In a day or so these men would be kitted up in smart new uniform and go on leave. **1948** 'N. SHUTE' *No Highway* ii. 50 I'll get a letter through to Ottawa asking them to kit you up for the trip. **1958** *Technology* May 68/3 Some firms may wish to give students a 'kitting up allowance'. **1960** K. AMIS *New Maps of Hell* (1961) iv. 95 There are cases on record of writers having to kit out contemporary narratives with aliens and space-ships in order to make a sale. **1962** *Guardian* 7 Aug. 5/1 A child can have ten days skiing for under £25 and be kitted out by Moss Brothers into the bargain. **1963** *Times* 18 Jan. 3/6 The cars—numbered, polished and kitted with every conceivable gadget to compete against time and the elements—will set course for the Côte d'Azur. *Ibid.* 20 Apr. 3/4 Probably the business locality this weekend will be Bristol, where the England players for the short Antipodean tour will foregather to be kitted and generally vetted. **1970** *New Society* 5 Mar. 384/1 Voluntary labour repaired and kitted out about 20 houses in three months. **1973** *Daily Tel.* 21 Nov. 14/3 The 1500 TC offers good value at £1,295 for a well kitted-out four-door 1½-litre.

Kitab (kitā·b). [Arab. *kitāb*, lit. writing, book.] The Koran; also, a sacred book of certain other revealed religions, e.g. the Bible.

[**1652** J. NOTSTOCK tr. *Andrés's Confusion Muhamed's Sect* ii. 53 O Moore,..what thinkest thou of the Scripture which you so much reverence, that..ye..keep it like a God, and call it *Alkitib Alhazim*, (i.e.) a glorious book and *Alcoran alhadin*, (i.e.) the Mighty *Alcoran.*] **1885** T. P. HUGHES *Dict. Islam* 280/2 *Al-Kitāb*.., 'the Book', a term used for the Qur'ān, and extended to all inspired books of the Jews and Christians, who are called *Ahlu'l-Kitāb*, or believers in the book. *Ibid.* 484/1 The Muhammadan Scriptures..are usually appealed to and quoted from as..*al-Kitāb*, 'the Book'. **1912** *Moslem World* II. 168 Mohammed..knew of the existence of the Holy Scriptures of both Testaments, and..fully intended to refer to them... In the first place, *Al Kitāb*, 'the Book', is a clear reference to 'the Bible'. **1927** *Encycl. Islam* II. 1044/2 The 'Book' par excellence is..the Ḳur'ān itself; it is the revelation of God... As the Kitāb is the word of God it has also the meaning in the Ḳur'ān of 'a decree of God' or it becomes the 'impression' which God stamps upon the hearts of man. **1959** S. & N. RONART *Conc. Encycl. Arabic Civilization* 297 *Al-Kitāb* as a specifically Moslem term denotes the Holy Book, i.e. the Koran, but is also extended to the Scriptures of..Christianity and Judaism, whose adherents are called *Ahl al-Kitab* (People of the Book). *Ibid.* 298 (*heading*) Koran,..the Holy Book of Islam, frequently spoken of by Moslems simply as The Book (*al-kitāb*).

kitchen, *sb.* Add: **1. b.** *hell's kitchen*, an area or place that is regarded as very disreputable or unpleasant; *spec.* a district of New York City once regarded as the haunt of criminals; *thieves' kitchen*, a place inhabited by thieves or other criminals; also *transf.*

1838 N. HAWTHORNE *Amer. Notebks.* (1932) 15 He..swore fervently in favor of driving the British 'into Hell's kitchen' by main force. **1868** A. J. MUNBY *Diary* 29 Jan. in D. Hudson *Munby* (1972) 248 We went to see the Thieves' Kitchen,..a large long antique cellar,..men and lads, perhaps 15 in all, lounging on benches. All thieves. **1894** *Harper's Mag.* July 223/2 Her father had moved into..a ramshackle old barrack just at the edge of Hell's Kitchen. **1894** W. J. LOCKE *At Gate of Samaria* (1895) xxvii. 319 They went together to East End music halls, bank holiday gatherings, thieves' kitchens, night clubs in the West End. **1900** 'FLYNT' & WALTON *Powers that Prey* 98 'Think Hell's Kitchen 'ud learn him?' Hell's Kitchen, in the speech of people who do not know what it means to work there, is the foundry. **1909** J. R. WARE *Passing Eng.* 243/2 *Thieves' kitchen* (London Street, 1882), the name satirically given to the then new Law Courts. **1941** C. O. SKINNER *Soap behind Ears* 168 She asked me a few routine questions..in the manner of someone questioning a welfare worker concerning life in Hell's Kitchen. **1949** *Sat. Even. Post* 15 Jan. 39/1 It stands between a greasy garage and a tawdry row of brownstone tenements on the edge of Hell's Kitchen, west of Eighth Avenue on 49th Street. **1960** *Observer* 24 Jan. 5/5 Where did I think the biggest thieves' kitchen was to-day? **1973** P. GEDDES *Ottawa Allegation* iii. 32 A Whitehall trusty, too, once away from the thieves' kitchen of intelligence and admitted to the counsels of the mandarins. **1974** D. RAMSAY *No Cause to Kill* II. 141 A bar on the East Side, almost the width of Manhattan Island away from Hell's Kitchen. **1974** 'M. INNES' *Mysterious Commission* xviii. 162 The place was certainly no thieves' kitchen. Honeybath..became aware of its respectable opulence.

f. Phr. *to go into* (or *to take tea in*) *the kitchen*: see quots. ?*Obs.*

1889 BARRÈRE & LELAND *Dict. Slang* I. 415/2 *To go into the kitchen* (popular), to drink one's tea out of the saucer; an allusion to the vulgar method of drinking very common among servants. **1894** G. F. NORTHALL *Folk-Phrases* 30 To take tea in the kitchen = To pour tea from the cup into the saucer, and drink it from this.

g. A part of a casino at Monte Carlo where gamblers place smaller bets than in the *salles privées.*

1931 W. HOLTBY *Poor Caroline* i. 25 In the kitchen the whirring of wheels, the jangle of voices..had grown intolerable. **1932** WODEHOUSE *Louder & Funnier* 255 It may be that your neighbours at the Le Touquet tables have a winsomeness lacking in those who congest the 'kitchen' at Monte Carlo. **1964** A. WYKES *Gambling* xii. 288 The old Winter Casino has 11 rooms. The smallest (i.e., the ones where the stakes are smallest) are known collectively as 'the Kitchen'. This is where the majority of Monte Carlo's 'amateur' gamblers play.

h. The percussion section of an orchestra or band. *slang.*

1931 G. JACOB *Orchestral Technique* vii. 68 We now come to a consideration of the percussion group (commonly known as 'the kitchen'), chief among which stand the *Timpani* (or kettledrums). **1934** S. R. NELSON *All about Jazz* ii. 49 Next in the rhythm section we will have a look at the 'gentlemen of the kitchen'.

5. a. *kitchen-folk, -girl* (later examples), *-man* (later examples), *-mechanic.*

1901 M. FRANKLIN *My Brilliant Career* iii. 13 The dashing snake yarns told by our kitchen-folk at Bruggabrong. **1912** W. OWEN *Let.* 1 Feb. (1967) 114, I..must unpack a Crate of *China*... Fit occupation for me, who have far more knowledge of these matters than the kitchen-folk. **1835** J. H. INGRAHAM *South-West* II. 253 There are some Yankee 'kitchen girls',..who can do more house work..than three or four negro servants. **1957** M. SPARK *Comforters* ii. 33 The kitchen girls grumble about the work. **1910** *Granta* 11 June 10 His door was sported, but on a covered dish left outside by a kitchen-man I observed three slices of cold beef. **1930** Kitchen man [see *BED *sb.* 1 f]. **1887** *Lantern* (New Orleans) 23 July 2/2 A..dirty looking kitchen mechanic called Maggie Howard. **1931** 'D. STIFF' *Milk & Honey Route* 215 A hobo camp cook, a kitchen mechanic. **1942** Z. N. HURSTON in A. Dundes *Mother Wit* (1973) 224/2 Best you can do is to confidence some kitchen-mechanic out of a dime or two. **1969** L. G. SORDEN *Lumberjack Lingo* 67 *Kitchen mechanic*, a dishwasher in a logging camp. Cookee.

b. *kitchen-stair.*

1844 C. M. YONGE *Abbeychurch* ix. 188 Katherine, seeing Elizabeth go towards the kitchen stairs. **1902** *Granta* 3 May 287 It was the Fancy Dress Ball of the season, and the Duchess of Billingsgate was waiting at the head of the kitchen-stair to receive her guests.

c. *kitchen cupboard, -furniture* (example), *-knife, -range* (earlier example), *scissors, stool, unit, -ware* (later examples).

1865 *Trans. Illinois Agric. Soc. 1862* V. 161 The warm kitchen cupboard. **1916** *Daily Colonist* (Victoria, B.C.) 4 July 12/2 (Advt.), Kitchen cupboard with closed cupboard and drawers in base, separate open shelving on top. **1785** *Daily Universal Reg.* 1 Jan. 2/2 Two waggons, loaded with his Majesty's kitchen furniture. **1969** M. PUGH *Last Place Left* xi. 68 She turned with a kitchen knife in her hand. **1785** *Daily Universal Reg.* 1 Jan. 3/2 Perpetual ovens, in Kitchen Ranges..upon an entirely new construction, heated without the assistance of any flue. **1907** *Yesterday's Shopping* (1969) 214/2 Scissors, kitchen—6½ in., 0/11½. **1966** *Olney Amsden & Sons Ltd. Price List* 33 Kitchen Scissors..10/6. **1926–7** *Army & Navy Stores Catal.* 140/2 *Kitchen stools*..Made of Deal..height 14 in—3/9. **1968** A. LASKI *Keeper* ii. 15 'Now, tell me all about it,' she commanded, perched..on the kitchen stool. **1937** *N.Y. Times* 21 Mar. III. 9/2 The demand for electrical kitchen units is greatest in the Midwest. **1958** *House & Garden* Mar. 120 (Advt.), You can start with an EZEE Sink Unit and gradually build your dream kitchen around it... EZEE are the only kitchen units you can buy in a complete range. **1930** H. CRANE *Bridge*, I ran a donkey engine..In Panama..Then Yucatan selling kitchenware. **1967** *Times* 11 Nov. 13/8 It was common ground that 'kitchen-ware' meant 'ware' of such a class as to be appropriate to use in a kitchen, but that consumer goods and mere packaging were excluded. **1974** J. DRUMMOND *Boon Companions* xxv. 78 The display windows were still lit. He looked past kitchen-ware and crockery.

d. *kitchen foil, match, paper.*

1958 *Observer* 21 Sept. 8/5 Stud the joint with a few cloves..before wrapping it up generously in kitchen foil. **1961** *Guardian* 24 Mar. 12/6 Wrapping the fish in well-buttered kitchen foil. **1955** J. D. MACDONALD *Brass Cupcake* iii. 29 Chief Powy stood nibbling on a kitchen match. **1973** R. THOMAS *If you can't be Good* (1974) xix. 165 He would stick a cigarette between his lips and light it with a kitchen match. **1846** *Jewish Manual, or Pract. Information Jewish & Mod. Cookery* 186 Tie with pack-thread white kitchen paper, so as to prevent the paste coming off. **1962** F. T. DAY *Introd. to Paper* viii. 87 Household rolls, plain or with printed designs, tile and kitchen papers..are a few of the varieties which are rewound on the winding machine from the larger diameter rolls. **1974** D. FLETCHER *Lovable Man* i. 37 A wad of absorbent kitchen paper.

f. *Comb.*, as *kitchen-bed-sittingroom, -diner, -dining-room, -living-room.* A room serving both as a kitchen and as a room of the type designated in the second (or further) element.

1951 KOESTLER *Age of Longing* ix. 152 The 'study' had at first been a corner of their kitchen-bed-sittingroom, partitioned off by a sheet. **1961** *Times* 11 Dec. 13/7 The kitchen-diner is much favoured and consequently catered for. **1974** *Country Life* 28 Feb. (Suppl.) 30/2 Bathroom, lounge, kitchen/diner, cloakroom. **1963** N. MARSH *Dead Water* (1964) vi. 161 Nobody had visited the kitchen-dining-room while she drank her coffee. **1974** *Times* 3 May 11/3 The kitchen-dining room..is 19 ft. by 8 ft. **1904** *Westm. Gaz.* 13 Dec. 8/1 Three bedrooms, kitchen-living room, scullery, and out-houses. **1955** D. CHAPMAN *Home & Social Status* ii. 32 Houses built in pairs or small rows, with a kitchen or kitchen-living-room..bedrooms and bathroom. **1963** N. MARSH *Dead Water* (1964) v. 121 The old kitchen..had been converted into a kitchen-living-room.

7. kitchen Dutch [tr. Du. *kombuis-Hollands*], now *rare*, the dialect of Afrikaans spoken by Cape Coloured people in the Western Province of S. Africa; later, used by English speakers as a contemptuous term for Afrikaans; **kitchen evening** *Austral.* and *N.Z.*, a party to which guests bring gifts of kitchenware for a bride-to-be; **kitchen Kaffir**, now *rare*, a *lingua franca* of southern Africa; = *FANAGALO; **kitchen police**, in the U.S. army, enlisted men detailed to help the cook, wash dishes, etc.; the work of these men; **kitchen shower** *U.S.*, = **kitchen evening*; **kitchen tea** *Austral.* and *N.Z.*, = **kitchen evening.*

1894 F. A. BARKLY *Boers & Basutos* (ed. 2) vii. 109 By this time they [*sc.* our two children] could both speak Sesuto and 'Low' or 'Kitchen Dutch' (as it is called in those parts) well. **1899** W. S. LOGEMAN *How to speak Dutch* (ed. 2) Pref., My friend J. F. van Oordt, who has tried to strike the happy medium between 'High Dutch', not often understood by the people, and the 'Kombuis-Hollands' (Kitchen-Dutch) of the uneducated coloured servants. **1959** *Chambers's Encycl.* XII 763/2 By 1875, when the spoken language was firmly established, S. J. du Toit founded a 'Society of True Afrikaners' to propagate the written language; this met at first with violent opposition from the peasant and the politician—both English and Dutch—and Afrikaans was called kitchen Dutch, as the Greek of the Bible was once supposed to be 'bad' Greek. **1964** V. POHL *Dawn & After* 102 What delighted us most was the originality of Gashep's speech. To us he spoke a kind of kitchen Dutch into which he introduced English and Sesuto words. **1931** *Auckland Star* 22 Mar. 7/2 A kitchen evening was given by Mr. and Mrs. A. R.

Gillett at their residence..in honour of Miss Sabina Gardner, whose marriage..to Mr. P. Richardson takes place shortly. **1862** G. H. MASON *Zululand* iv. 38 In adopting [the official dialect]..no doubt, the Bishop has been guided by one of the chief clerks in the native department; who was born and reared amongst the Cape Colony Caffres, and, consequently, prefers it to learning Zulu proper; which, of course, is held in contempt by all officials, and sneeringly called 'Kitchen Kaffir'. **1924** *Cape Argus Mag.* 2 Feb. 5 A wonderful language is kitchen Kafir, a weird medley of dialects, interspersed with English words. **1936** [see *BAROTSE]. **1962** 'D. WILSON' *Search for Geoffrey Goring* vii. 144 He speaks a bit of English and some Kitchen Kaffir as well as Swahili. **1971** T. SHARPE *Riotous Assembly* (1973) ii. 15 She had spoken to him in Kitchen Kaffir, a pidgin Zulu reserved only for the most menial and mentally retarded black servants. **1917** Kitchen police [see *K.P.* s.v. *K 4 f]. **1918** *Wells Fargo Messenger* Jan. 87/3 My present position does not require me to perform any of the so-called dreaded duties, such as guard duty, kitchen police, stable orderly. **1918** FARROW *Dict. Mil. Terms* 330 *Kitchen police*, those charged with the scullery work of the kitchen. **1929** F. A. POTTLE *Stretchers* (1930) 33 Before first call, six or more unfortunates crept out of bed and went on kitchen police...'K.P.' is for good reason the most hated detail in the army. **1936** *Amer. Speech* XI. 51 When you have reached the stage where you know that an M.P. is not a Member of Parliament and that kitchen police do not carry clubs, no one can send you to the warehouse to bring back a skirmish line. **1924** H. CROY *R.F.D. No. 3* 89 It was a 'kitchen shower'. The glittering array was piled high, like a special sale in a racket store—dishpans, saucepans, pie pans,..and so on. **1974** *News & Reporter* (Chester, S. Carolina) 22 Apr. 2-A/5 Mrs. J. J. Key and Miss Mary Smyre were joint hostesses last Wednesday evening when they honored Miss Marilyn Hicks, bride-elect of the season, with a kitchen shower at the Key home on Columbia Street. **1948** N. SCANLAN *Rusty Road* xvii. 195 A 'linen tea' for the bride-elect, and a 'kitchen tea' and a 'China tea' followed. **1965** *Sunday Mail* (Brisbane) 28 Nov. 26 Michelle Bowes and Patricia Donovan.. gave the bride a kitchen tea on Friday. **1970** G. GREER *Female Eunuch* 116 The more class the families can pretend to the more they can exact in the way of presents at showers, kitchen teas and the like.

kitchenable (ki·tʃěnăb'l), *a.* [f. KITCHEN *sb.* or *v.* + -ABLE.] Suitable for cooking and serving at table.

1905 *Chambers's Jrnl.* Feb. 193/2 There is probably no bird upon our game-list which is more eagerly sought after than the wood-cock..for his kitchenable qualities. **1913** G. BOLAM *Wild Life Wales* vi. 50 In judging of the probable kitchenable qualities of a bird.

kitchen cabinet. orig. *U.S.* [f. KITCHEN *sb.* + CABINET.] **1.** *Politics.* A group of unofficial advisers (orig. of the President of the U.S.A.), popularly believed to have greater influence than the actual Cabinet (or the elected representatives, etc.). Hence, a private or unofficial group of advisers to the holder of an elected office.

1832 W. S. ARCHER *Let.* 8 July in A. C. Cole *Whig Party in South* (1913) 13 If there be no other mode of preventing its being given to the most despicable of all the Protegees of the Kitchen Cabinet. **1842** *Ainsworth's Mag.* Dec. 554 We will hurl the kitchen cabinet tyrants from their stools. **1860** J. PARTON *Life A. Jackson* III. xvi. 183 These were the gentlemen—Lewis, Green, Hill and Kendall—who, at the beginning of the new administration, were supposed to have most of the President's ear and confidence, and were stigmatized by the opposition as the Kitchen Cabinet. **1893** 'MARK TWAIN' in *Century Mag.* Dec. 237 Her master left a couple of dollars lying unprotected on his desk... She covered the tempter with a book, and another member of the kitchen cabinet got it. **1904** *N.Y. Herald* 14 Sept. 5 The kitchen cabinet is a development of the ascendency of Governor Odell in republican affairs. It consists of the body guard of his closest friends and advisers. **1952** *Manch. Guardian Weekly* 27 Nov. 3 Mr. Brownell is part of the Dewey 'kitchen cabinet'. **1969** *Guardian* 21 Mar. 1/1 Key policy decisions were being taken by the Prime Minister and a kind of 'Kitchen Cabinet' of intimates. **1975** *Times Lit. Suppl.* 23 May 576/4 Every ruler operates on two levels, the personal and the official, that is, he has a kitchen cabinet and a body of ministers.

2. A cabinet for domestic and culinary utensils, etc., in a kitchen.

1895 *Montgomery Ward Catal.* 607/1 Kitchen Cabinets. Very useful about a house where a 'shortage' of closets or cupboards is felt. *Ibid.* 612/1 Kitchen Cabinet Table... Has a molding board, spice and cutlery drawer, sugar and groceries drawer, flour drawer..and a cupboard for cooking utensils. **1911** *Daily Colonist* (Victoria, B.C.) 29 Apr. 4/4 (Advt.), These Kitchen Cabinets have revolutionized labor-saving in the kitchen of today. **1922** S. LEWIS *Babbitt* vi. 68 Babbitt picked up his partner..at his kitchen-cabinet works. **1933** *Discovery* July 219/2 Most houses and flats are fitted as a matter of course with kitchen cabinets and refrigerators, hanging cupboards in bedrooms and so on. **1972** M. J. BOSSE *Incident at Naha* 14 The sugar bowl would have gone back into a kitchen cabinet.

Kitchener^{2} (ki·tʃěnəɹ). The name of Herbert Horatio *Kitchener*, first Earl Kitchener of Khartoum and of Broome (1850–1916), British soldier, used *absol.*, *attrib.*, or in the possessive to denote a man of his imposing and taciturn personality, soldiers recruited while he was Secretary of State for War (1914–16), or aspects of appearance or of dress characteristic of him or of these troops. Also allusively. So **Ki·tchenerism,** a quality characteristic of Kitchener.

1903 *Westm. Gaz.* 31 Aug. 1/2 The outer man of this 'Kitchener of Russian finance'..is in keeping with his personality. **1916** J. N. HALL *Kitchener's Mob* i. 1 'Kitchener's Mob' they were called in the early days of August, 1914, when London hoardings were clamorous with the first calls for volunteers. *Ibid.* iii. 23 'Kitchener's Rag-Time Army I calls it!' growls the veteran of South African fame. *Ibid.* viii. 125 It was not until the arrival on active service of Kitchener's armies that the construction of the double line of reserve or support trenches was undertaken. **1916** H. G. WELLS *Mr. Britling* I. iii. 74 He was presented as a monster of energy and self-discipline; as the determined foe of every form of looseness, slackness, and easy-goingness... 'It's Kitchenerism.'.. 'It's the army side of the efficiency stunt.' **1925** FRASER & GIBBONS *Soldier & Sailor Words* 136 *Kitchener's blue*, a name given to the blue serge uniform served out to recruits in the autumn of 1914 in consequence of the shortage of khaki. **1928** BLUNDEN *Undertones of War* 43 The first Kitchener battalion, they said, to hold the sector. **1929** *Papers Mich. Acad. Sci. Arts & Lett.* X. 304/1 *Kitcheners*, a name given by the Regulars to soldiers enlisting for the emergency. **1930** C. D. BAKER-CARR *From Chauffeur to Brigadier* ix. 127 The new Kitchener Divisions were now beginning to arrive. **1937** PARTRIDGE *Dict. Slang* 458/1 *Kitchener wants you!* A military c.p. to a man selected for filthy, arduous or perilous work. **1965** BROPHY & PARTRIDGE *Long Trail* 139 *K1* (*K One*), the first 100,000 of the the New (Kitchener's) Army of 1914 volunteers. **1969** A. CADE *Turn up Stone* i. 20 A large European wearing a pink shirt, baggy grey trousers and a drooping Kitchener moustache. **1971** D. MEIRING *Wall of Glass* viii. 62 He wore summer khaki drill, with Kitchener helmet and Sam Browne.

kitchenette (kitʃěne·t). orig. *U.S.* [See -ETTE.] A small room or alcove in a house, flat, etc., combining kitchen and pantry. Also *attrib.*

1910 *Variety* 7 May 10/4 Mr. and Mrs. Nellie are going to have a swell apart. and they call the 'cook house' in a swell apart. a kitchenette. **1919** *Ladies' Home Jrnl.* Oct. 117 Ovenette and kitchenette cookery. **1921** *Daily Colonist* (Victoria, B.C.) 2 Oct. 26/7 Kitchenettes and bathrooms are also installed. **1922** *Hotel World* 25 Mar. 10/2 Kitchenette suites of 2 rooms. **1922** *Glasgow Herald* 28 Apr. 5 The New York business woman..wants her kitchenette and her home cooking, be it ever so simple. **1929** F. KILBOURNE *Dot & Will* 188 They had a little kitchenette apartment on the North Side. **1930** J. CANNAN *No Walls of Jasper* iii. 56 She had never thought it..too much trouble to..bustle away into the kitchenette to make up something nice and tasty for her George. **1934** [see *drying-rack*]. **1955** [see *DINETTE]. **1960** *Times* 25 Feb. 1/3 Bed-sitter, with kitchenette, in private house Kensington. **1974** *Country Life* 30 May (Suppl.) 20 Granny annexe comprising: living room, kitchenette, bedroom and shower room.

Kitchen rudder. [Named after J. G. A. *Kitchen*, Englishman, who patented the device in 1914.] A steering device for small craft consisting of a pair of curved deflectors either side of the propeller whose position is altered to change the course or speed of the vessel or to cause it to go backwards.

1920 *Engineer* 6 Feb. 149/1 The essential parts of the Kitchen rudders consist of two curved deflectors generally formed as parts of a circular cylinder, partly enclosing the propeller. **1920** *Shipbuilding & Shipping Rec.* 12 Feb. 200/2 (*caption*) Admiralty pinnace with Kitchen rudder. **1923** *Man. Seamanship* (Admiralty) II. 200 Boats are fitted with a clutch and reverse gear, clutch and reversing propellers, or clutch and Kitchen rudder. **1961** F. H. BURGESS *Dict. Sailing* 127 *Kitchen rudder*, one comprising two curved blades that may completely enclose the propeller; they are rotated by a wheel on the tiller to open or close for going either ahead or astern; the direction and speed are thus controlled from the tiller, while the engine runs unattended at one speed.

kitchen sink. [f. KITCHEN *sb.* + SINK *sb.*^{1} 1 c.] **a.** A sink in which dirty dishes, vegetables, etc., are washed. Freq. used as a symbol of women's enslavement to the kitchen.

1873 *Young Englishwoman* May 259/3 Unwholesome smells—which I found all proceeded from (what Miss Nightingale calls) that abomination, the kitchen sink. **1930** *Archit. Rec.* Jan. 13/1 Until a few years ago, the kitchen sink would have been made of sheet zinc fitted over a box made by the carpenter. **1969** *Guardian* 6 Nov. 9/5 A situation in which married women find it impossible to return to work and have to return once more to the kitchen sink. **1973** J. CLEARY *Ransom* iii. 67 It was the housewives' hour... Perry Como..sang of the past; housewives dreamed with him over their kitchen sinks and unmade beds. **1973** *Guardian* 14 Feb. 11/2 Women stayed right where they were: for the most part at the kitchen sink, or in low-paid clerical or light manual work.

b. *fig.*

1888 KIPLING *Under Deodars* (1889) 5 All his ideas and powers of conversation..are taken from him by this—this kitchen-sink of a Government.

c. *everything but the kitchen sink* and similar phr.: everything imaginable.

1948 PARTRIDGE *Dict. Forces' Slang* 106 *Kitchen sink*, used only in the phrase indicating intense bombardment—'They chucked everything they'd got at us except, or including, the kitchen sink.' 'The kitchen stove' was also used. **1958** *Wall St. Jrnl.* 23 Oct. 4/4 Gen. Trudeau said the military services often slow down development of new weapons 'because we are such perfectionists that we want everything but the kitchen sink in a weapon'. **1965** 'E. MCBAIN' *Doll* x. 128 Brown began searching. 'Everything in here but the kitchen sink,' he said. **1966** —— *Eighty Million Eyes* xi. 189 We'll throw everything but the goddamn kitchen sink at you. **1967** L. WHITE *Crimshaw Memo.* (1968) iii. 61 He goes out and buys himself an XKE Jaguar..it had everything but the kitchen sink on it.

d. Used (with hyphen) *attrib.*, or *absol.*, to designate a group of English realistic painters of the 1950s and later, or their type of art, or a group of English realistic authors (chiefly playwrights) of the same period or their plays or publications.

1954 D. SYLVESTER in *Encounter* Dec. 61 (*title*) The kitchen sink. *Ibid.* 62/1 The post-war generation takes us back from the studio to the kitchen... The kitchen sink too. *Ibid.* 62/2 It is evident that neither objectivity nor abstraction is the aim of the young painters of the kitchen-sink school. **1956** L. MCINTOSH *Oxford Folly* 69 On the walls were several drawings and paintings of the 'Kitchen Sink' school of modern English painters, whose sordid subject matter contrasted with their luxurious setting. The one above the mantelpiece depicted a lavatory. **1959** *Listener* 19 Feb. 340/3 'Kitchen sink' painting is not an exclusive English phenomenon: it originated in France, with Rebeyrolle and Minaux. **1960** *Times* 15 Mar. 13/6 Mr. Ronald Duncan is reported as saying that the English Stage Company..presents only left wing 'kitchen sink' drama. **1960** *Guardian* 28 Oct. 9/5 The day of the social-realist, kitchen sink advertisement has dawned. **1963** *Times* 16 Feb. 9/3 If the British new wave were interested only in easy money they would stick to the slag-heap and the kitchen sink. **1965** *Punch* 26 May 762/1 The 'Kitchen-Sink' tag..began as descriptive heading for a post-war school of painters (nudity, violence, squalor, blasphemy, subversiveness and distortion are somehow morally OK qualities in the visual arts) and only later became a pejorative title for a school of playwrights. **1973** *Black World* Apr. 41, I wasn't going to write any more Black 'kitchen sink' dramas.

So **ki:tchen-si·nkery.**

1964 *Listener* 16 Apr. 624/1 We've been attacked for too much pessimism, sordidness, and kitchen-sinkery. **1969** B. TURNER *Circle of Squares* i. 7 The longest-ever season of kitchen-sinkery on our stages.

kitchen stove. [f. KITCHEN *sb.* + STOVE *sb.*^{1} 5 a.] **a.** A stove in a kitchen.

1845 *Knickerbocker* XXV. 106 He wished her in the south of France or the kitchen stove, rather than there. **1925** F. AYSCOUGH *Chinese Mirror* 386 Ts'ao Chün, Lord of the Kitchen-Stove. **1959** P. H. JOHNSON *Humbler Creation* xvi. 108 'Mrs. Fisher is a most awful stick,' Lucy said. 'One might as well say one's lines to the kitchen stove.' **1974** *Times* 21 Sept. 7/2 The kitchen stove, a low stout Rayburn of chipped yellow enamel.

b. *everything but the kitchen stove* and similar phr. = *KITCHEN SINK c.

1927 E. WALLACE *Feathered Serpent* i. 9 'Got everything on except the kitchen stove,' said Mr. Crewe pleasantly... 'You're a fool to go out with all that stuff on you.' **1928** [see *BOB *v.*^{3} 2 b]. **1948** [see *KITCHEN SINK c]. **1959** *Listener* 8 Jan. 63/2 The assumption that, since Christmas is the only time children go to the theatre, they must therefore be given everything, including the kitchen-stove. **1960** M. CECIL *Something in Common* xxi. 235 'I suppose you haven't an ulcer?' Colin said that—apart from the kitchen stove—it was the one item he'd forgotten to bring. **1964** C. DALE *Other People* x. 178 There's Mum, hair tinted, face done up, everything on bar the kitchen stove.

kitcheny, *a.* Delete *rare* and add later examples.

1926 KIPLING *Debits & Credits* 328 We eat kitcheny food. **1971** P. DICKINSON *Sleep & his Brother* vi. 137 Doll had left the room..and was making kitcheny noises beyond. **1973** *Times* 16 Nov. 15 (*caption*) Most of the things are decidedly kitcheny.

kite, *sb.* Add: **3.** (Examples referring to modifications of the toy kite designed to support a man in the air or to form part of an unpowered flying machine (cf. *AEROPLANE 1).)

1826 VINEY & POCOCK *Brit. Pat. 5420*, This Patent is obtained for an Invention by which kites are made to act as..sails, for the purpose of navigating or drawing vessels .., for the purpose of raising weights or persons in the air, .. or for the hoisting of flags. The peculiarities of these kites are:—..they have four lines by which their power is controlled or their course directed. **1875** A. M. CLARK *Brit. Pat. 169*, This Invention relates to a kind of kite or ærial apparatus to be used for military and other purposes, its chief object being to raise to the desired height in the air, and to support in a sufficiently tranquil position for reconnoitring a scout, look out man, or sentry. **1889** H. S. MAXIM *Brit. Pat. 16,883*, My invention is chiefly designed..to provide for the construction of an aëronautic machine which can, while moving forward in the air, be caused to rise or descend at any desired velocity or to travel at any predetermined height above the ground... I provide an adjustable covered framework or kite of very large dimensions... For convenience of description I will hereinafter term this covered framework or kite an 'aëroplane'. **1893** *23rd Rep. Aeronaut. Soc.* 17 What we have to do is to make the wings, whether fixed or flapping, in the requisite form, and add aëroplanes or kites, and find the necessary power to drive them along at their proper angles. **1894** *Proc. Internat. Conf. Aerial Navigation, Chicago, 1893* 253 Among the different free-flying models which I exhibited..in the large hall of the Engineering Society in Vienna there was a model of my gliding aeroplane or kite, which illustrated the support to be obtained from the air.

b. A proposal or suggestion offered or 'thrown out' tentatively in order to 'see how the wind blows'. (Cf. *BALLON D'ESSAI.) See also FLY *v.*[1] 5 a in Dict. and Suppl.

1902 *Nature* 14 Aug. 380/2 A few suggestions have been thrown out by various students which must be regarded more as trial hypotheses than as definite conclusions, indeed they should be looked upon rather as 'Kites'. **1904** *Westm. Gaz.* 5 Aug. 2/2 The new Army scheme..is to be debated on Monday, but whether as a Government proposal or the private kite of the Minister for War remains wholly obscure. **1973** A. MACVICAR *Painted Doll Affair* ii. 29 'I'm sorry ye're lumbered wi' me,' he said, sounding anything but sorry. I ignored this blatant kite.

c. An aeroplane. *slang*, esp. *Services'*.

The popular use of *kite* in this sense prob. originated with the 'box-kite' aeroplane (see *BOX *sb.*[2] 24); but the uses in quots. 1838, 1909 are direct applications of *kite* in sense 3.

[**1838** J. H. PENNINGTON *Aerostation*, (*caption*) Steam-kite, or inclined plane, for navigating the air.] **1909** S. F. CODY in *Aeronaut. Jrnl.* XIII. 15/2, I had to turn my hobby into manufacturing a kite in order to raise money to build a flying machine, or to put 'power' into my kite, consequently the term 'Power Kite'. *Ibid.* 19/1 This is the finished power kite ready to start. The screws are not really propellers. You may call them tractors or propellers, which you like. **1917** in A. J. L. Scott *Hist. Sixty Squadron R.A.F.* (1920) 100 He told me that he had managed to fly his kite back with great difficulty. **1934** T. E. LAWRENCE *Let.* 19 Mar. (1938) 793 The German kites will be new and formidable. **1942** T. RATTIGAN *Flare Path* I. 33 A kite from the Polish squadron. **1952** M. TRIPP *Faith is Windsock* xii. 183 The Squadron hasn't lost a single kite in the last three raids. **1969** [see *HARRY *sb.*[2] 8 b].

d. Phr. *high as a kite*: see *HIGH *a.* 16 b.

4. b. *Criminals' slang.* A communication (esp. one that is illicit or surreptitious); *spec.* a letter or verbal message smuggled into, out of, or within a prison.

1859 G. W. MATSELL *Vocabulum* 49 *Kite*, a letter; fancy stocks. **1923** J. F. FISHMAN *Crucibles of Crime* ix. 203 Sometimes..prisoners manage to plant notes in various parts of the prison which are to be picked up by the intended recipient. This practice of 'shooting' contraband notes is known among the prisoners as 'flying a kite'. **1925** *Flynn's* 3 Jan. 665/2 *Kite*, a message per lip. *Kite*, a letter or note. **1927** [see sense *4 c]. **1953** H. BRYAN *Inside* (1954) xvii. 279 Having settled on the girl, one would send her a 'kite', or love letter. **1960** WENTWORTH & FLEXNER *Dict. Amer. Slang* 194/2 *Fly a kite.* 1. To write a letter; esp. to smuggle a letter into or out of prison. *Underworld use.* 2. To send an airmail letter, often requesting money or assistance. *Modern use, mainly underworld but gaining some popularity.* **1971** *N.Y. Times* 21 Oct. 52/2 *Kite*, a complaint to the police about an illegal operation, often originating with a disgruntled gambler.

c. *slang.* A cheque (sense 3), *esp.* a blank cheque or a cheque drawn on insufficient funds or forged from a stolen cheque-book.

1927 *Dialect Notes* V. 446 *Fly a kite*, v. (1) To pass a bad cheque. (2) To sell worthless stocks and bonds. (3) To write mournful letters, as of prisoners, to sympathetic old women and charitable institutions. **1928** E. WALLACE *Gunner* xxx. 243 He had spent the afternoon searching London for the right 'kites'. There is quite a brisk trade in blank cheque forms. **1936** J. CURTIS *Gilt Kid* iv. 45 Used to say that he'd been done for kites, but everyone reckoned it was for poncing. **1962** R. COOK *Crust on its Uppers* i. 21 The real morries..flying dodgy kites with each other at bent spielers till the punter..outs his kiting-book too and scribbles a straight one. **1969** T. PARKER *Twisting Lane* 41 He's in for what they call 'kites', dud cheques, you know.

5. b. On a minesweeper, a device attached to a sweep-wire submerging it to the requisite depth when it is towed over a minefield.

1915 *Chambers's Jrnl.* June 386/1 Between the vessels of each pair is the sweep-wire, sunk to the necessary depth in the water by means of towed 'kites', wooden arrangements acting on the same principle as the ordinary air-kites. **1923** *Man. Seamanship* (Admiralty) II. 172 The present form of kite consists of a specially shaped metal plate which has a tendency to dive when towed. This is towed over the stern by a kite wire.

9. a. *kite-like* adj.; **kite bar**, a bar or stripe of an undesirable colour in the plumage of a fancy pigeon. **b.** *kite-line, -maker, -string*; *kite-faced, -like* adjs.; **Kite mark, Kitemark,** a quality mark, similar in shape to a kite, granted for use on goods approved by the British Standards Institution; also *transf.*; hence **kite-mark** *v. trans.*, to use the Kite mark on; **kite-marked** *ppl. a.*, bearing the Kite mark; **kite-tail** (earlier non-attrib. U.S. example). **c.** in sense 4, **kite-man**, a person who obtains money against bills of exchange or cheques that will not be honoured; *spec.* (see quot. 1967).

1876 R. FULTON *Illustr. Bk. Pigeons* 108 A softer shade of blue, with brown, or what are called by Pouter fanciers 'kite' bars. **1922** JOYCE *Ulysses* 537 Alone on deck,.. yellow kitefaced, his hand in his waistcoat opening, declaims. **1901** KIPLING *Kim* xiv. 365 From the edge of the sheep-pasture floated a shrill, kite-like trill. **1909** *Daily Graphic* 26 July 10/1 When floating on an up-draught they [*sc.* the planes] will be expanded as a fan expands, and will present a larger kite-like surface. **1828** *Kaleidoscope* 12 Aug. 48/2 There is no obstacle to interfere with the kite-lines. **1876** 'MARK TWAIN' *Tom Sawyer* xxx. 304 He took a kite-line from his pocket. **1926** M. LEINSTER *Dew on Leaf* v. 211 The kite-makers were busy making fantastic objects in bamboo and paper. **1928** E. WALLACE *Double* v. 64 This was a favourite rendezvous of the swell mob, the 'kite' men, the confidence artists. **1967** J. PHELAN *Nine Murderers & Me* 162 *Kite-man*, one who passes forged cheques. **1952** *B.S.I. Monthly Information Sheet* Oct. 16 (*heading*) The 'Kite' mark on consumer goods. *Ibid.*, In March, 1952, when the Utility schemes for textiles and clothing were brought to an end, most of the industries concerned undertook to co-operate with the B.S.I. in preparing voluntary standards..to ensure that at least the same levels of quality could be maintained. It was also agreed that wherever possible the B.S.I. 'Kite' mark would replace the former Utility mark as a guarantee to consumers that the goods bearing the mark were, in fact, 'up to standard'. **1956** *Observer* 12 Feb. 6/4 It is hoped that eventually the B.S. Kite-Mark will certify the quality of many..consumer goods. **1957** *Times* 23 Sept. 11/4 The first fireguards bearing the kite mark of the British Standards Institution will be in the shops this autumn. **1957** *Economist* 12 Oct. 157/1 'Shoppers' Guide' discusses articles against the measure of the BSI Kite-mark, which is a guarantee only of minimum satisfactory performance. **1958** *B.S.I. News* Nov. 3 Buyers, particularly large-scale purchasers, can do much to safeguard their workpeople from injury by insisting, wherever possible, that the safety equipment which they buy should be Kite-marked. *Ibid.* 17/1 We hear from Kirk and Company (Tubes) Ltd., that they have recently been granted a licence to Kite-mark their malleable cast iron and cast copper alloy pipe fittings under B.S. 1256. **1960** *Ibid.* Apr. 5/2 (*heading*) Kitemarking should be extended. **1966** *New Scientist* 12 May 338/3 The findings will be used by the British Standards Institution when it publishes the 'rules' for 'kite-marked' toothpastes later this year. **1971** *Brit. Standards Yearbk.* p. xvi, The British Standards Mark (known as the Kitemark) is a registered certification trade mark owned by BSI. Manufacturers may apply to BSI to use the mark on their products when their quality control arrangements are considered satisfactory and they have agreed to comply with a Scheme of Supervision and Control involving..inspection, sampling and testing. **1971** *Daily Tel.* 24 Nov. 11/5 The annual Civic Trust Awards,..emphasising architectural and design excellence in a total lived-in environment, have become sought-after kitemarks for planners..and architects. **1972** *Ibid.* 12 June 2/6 It will be illegal for shops to sell crash helmets which do not have the BSI's 'kitemark' seal of approval. **1972** *Which?* June 192 So far, no cabinets with mirrors have been given the Kitemark... If we hear of any Kite-marked cabinets, we will mention them. **1841** THOREAU *Jrnl.* 6 Aug. in *Writings* (1906) VII. 266 Like pasteboards on a kite string. **1971** *N.Z. Listener* 22 Mar. 13/1 Get seen around with a good woman on your kite-string and no-one bothers you regardless. **1869** L. M. ALCOTT *Little Women* II. x. 150 The others are torn up to..bandage cut fingers, or make kite-tails.

kite, *v.* **1. a.** Add to def.: To move quickly, to rush; to rise quickly. Const. *around, off, up, etc.*

1854 'O. OPTIC' *In Doors & Out* (1876) 92 You did not use to be fond of 'kiting' round in this manner. **1864** L. N. BOUDRYE *Jrnl.* 21 Aug. in *Hist. Rec. Fifth N.Y. Cavalry* (1865) 165 A well directed shell..sent them 'kiting' to the woods again. **1870** W. W. FOWLER *Ten Yrs. Wall St.* 504 Would seem to be enough to start a panic, or send the market 'kiting' up among the tall figures. **1908** KIPLING *Lett. to Family* viii. 72 We have seen a financial panic.. send whole army corps of aliens kiting back to the lands whose allegiance they forswore. **1931** WODEHOUSE *Big Money* viii. 181 The stock kited sixty points the first day. **1935** C. S. FORESTER *Afr. Queen* vi. 116 Bet they were surprised to see the old *African Queen* come kiting past. **1965** J. POTTS *Only Good Secretary* i. 13 Yes, and her too, kiting off to Long Island when she ought to be here.

3. b. (Earlier U.S. example.) Now usually, to write or cash a dud or temporarily unbacked cheque. Hence **ki·ting** *vbl. sb.*, the raising of money on credit; the passing of forged or unbacked cheques. Cf. *KITE-FLYING *vbl. sb.* 2.

1839 C. F. BRIGGS *Adventures H. Franco* II. iv. 35 He stuffed half a dozen blank checks into his hat, and said he must go out and kite it to save his credit. **1866** *Congress. Globe* 29 June 3482/1 Every kiting charter like this one—I speak of the National Telegraph Company. **1872** *Ibid.* 3 Apr. 2128/2 (Th.), They may hold the bonds, as has often been done in kiting corporations, and then take the property they have thus swindled the public out of. **1934** H. N. ROSE *Thesaurus of Slang* iii. a. 21/1 Issue a check which hasn't sufficient backing: *to kite.* **1942** BERREY & VAN DEN BARK *Amer. Thes. Slang* § 556/1 Kiting, kite flying, extending credit or sustaining a balance in the bank by means of 'kites'. **1950** H. E. GOLDIN *Dict. Amer. Underworld Lingo* 118/1 *Kite*, v. 1. To issue or pass, as a forged check or bond; (more accurately) to issue or pass a check against insufficient funds... *Kite checks* (New England States). 1. To issue forged checks. 2. To write checks, usually post-dated, against insufficient funds. 3. To raise illegally the face value of otherwise good checks. **1959** N. MAILER *Advts. for Myself* (1961) 438 Her ideas about.. those investors with some credit rating whom an exurban bank, proud of its personal touch, might allow to kite a cheque for twenty-four hours..intrigued the banker. **1960** F. GIBNEY *Operators* vi. 158 Check kiting..is a different and more complex process than forging...Few up-and-coming businessmen..can claim to have resisted the temptation to write a pressing check just a day or two before some money is due, in the prayerful expectation that their deposit will get into the bank's ledgers before the check they have cashed comes home to roost. **1962** R. COOK *Crust on its Uppers* x. 90 We'll kite 'em at the airport! **1963** J. N. HARRIS *Weird World Wes Beattie* (1964) xv. 184 He was up to his ears in debt—always kiting checks before payday. **1969** 'E. LATHEN' *Murder to Go* (1970) xvii. 173 If it had been a question of..kiting a cheque—well, that wouldn't surprise you at all. Clyde cut corners all his life. **1970** R. LEWIS *Wolf by Ears* iii. 137 The technical terms..are 'kiting' and 'lapping'. Money is transferred between two accounts, recording the receipt prior to the balancing date and the payment after the balancing date. That's 'kiting'.

c. To send a communication; *spec.* to smuggle a letter into, out of, or within a prison. (Cf. *KITE *sb.* 4 b.)

1925 *Flynn's* 3 Jan. 665/2 *Kite*, to send a signal; to send a message. **1936** *Detective Fiction Weekly* 4 Jan. 116 A letter which I had 'kited' out of the prison. **1945** L. SHELLY *Jive Talk Dict.* 13/2 *Kite*, to air mail or exchange.

kite-flying, *vbl. sb.* [KITE *sb.* 9 b.] **1.** *lit.* The flying of a kite on a string. Also *attrib.*

1804 T. A. WARD *Diary* 5–6 Oct. in *Peeps into Past* (1909) viii. 51/1 He went away..to renew the sport of kite-flying. **1827** [in Dict. s.v. KITE *sb.* 9]. **1849** DICKENS *Dav. Copp.* (1850) zvii. 179 He never took an active part in any game but kite-flying. **1926** M. LEINSTER *Dew on Leaf* v. 199 Towards the end of the kite-flying season, numerous Chinese had made their way to various pieces of rising ground with these toys. **1962** W. O. MITCHELL *Kite* ii. 14 Kite-flying would be a lot like taking a drive on Sunday or going on a picnic.

2. *slang.* The raising of money (*a*) by persons collusively exchanging accommodation bills or cheques on different banks, in none of which they possess sufficient funds; (*b*) by one person transferring accounts between banks and creating an illusory balance against which he cashes cheques; (*c*) by a person passing forged, stolen, or unbacked cheques.

1834 [in Dict. s.v. KITE *sb.* 9]. **1848** BARTLETT *Dict. Amer.* 195 *Kite flying*,..a combination between two persons, neither of whom has any funds in bank, to exchange each other's checks, which may be deposited in lieu of money, taking good care to make their bank accounts good before their checks are presented for payment. *Kite flying* is also practised by mercantile houses... A house in Boston draws on a house in New York at 60 days or more, and gets its bill discounted. The New York house, in return, meets its acceptance by re-drawing on the Boston house. **1850** THACKERAY *Pendennis* II. xxiv. 244 That kite-flying, you know, Mr. M., always takes two or three on 'em to set the paper going. Altamont put the pot on at the Derby, and won a good bit of money. **1951** 'H. CECIL' *Painswick Line* vi. 55 'Kite flying' is a method of borrowing money from a bank, which is not prepared to lend it to you. **1964** Z. PROGL *Woman of Underworld* xix. 178 Passing dud cheques (kite-flying) calls for unwavering nerve and audacity. **1970** M. KENYON *100,000 Welcomes* iv. 23 Forgery? Fraudulent conversion? Kite-flying?

3. Sending up a 'kite' or *ballon d'essai*. Also *attrib.*

1898 'A. HOPE' in *Daily News* 4 Apr. 7/1 Principally it [*sc.* the press interview] was said to be used as a means of what might be called kite-flying. **1899** *Ibid.* 29 June 5/4 The object of Boer diplomacy is to prolong the kite-flying stage indefinitely until commercial interests..urge England to accept anything. **1927** *Daily Tel.* 30 Aug. 8/6 These suggestions are dismissed in British circles as mere 'kite-flying'. **1958** *Economist* 20 Dec. 1058/2 The Belgrade newspaper, *Borba*, which is often the government's mouthpiece, has emphasised..that if other countries would accept immigrants from Jugoslavia these would be allowed to leave... If this was kite-flying, the kite has been allowed to drop to the ground with a thud. **1969** *Courier-Mail* (Brisbane) 2 May 3/8 State D.L.P. secretary (Mr. J. Judge), said: 'This is nothing but kite-flying. The D.L.P. will be making no decision on preferences until the Central Council meets mext Tuesday.'

So (as a back-formation) **ki·te-fly** *v. trans.* and *intr.*; **ki·te-flyer.**

1844 *Knickerbocker* XXIV. 258 The most persevering kite-flyers that I know of, are the Reformers. **1860** BARTLETT *Dict. Amer.* (ed. 3) 231 *Kite-flier*, a financier who practises the operation of '*kite-flying*'. **1876** *Monthly Packet* June 577 Heavy bets are laid on the best kite-flyers. **1896** Kite-flyer [in Dict. s.v. KITE *sb.* 9]. **1935** 'D. HUME' *Gaol Gates are Open* 8 Higher in the hierarchy of crime come the 'kite flyers', who cash worthless cheques. **1965** *Listener* 22 July 111/2 The irrelevance of his office to foreign affairs..stressed that he was merely kite-flying. **1968** 'L. EGAN' *Serious Investigation* (1969) iii. 34 Right now we've got a con man operating on the pensioners, and a kite flyer passing all the rubber checks. **1972** *Daily Colonist* (Victoria, B.C.) 16 Jan. 2/7 Sarasota, Fla... Some 89 contestants jammed Lido Beach for the Association's 4th Annual International Flyoff, held in honor of America's foremost kiteflyer Ben Franklin.

‖ **kitenge** (kite·ŋgi). Pl. **kitenges, vitenge(s.** [Swahili.] In East Africa, a fabric, usu. of cotton and printed in various colours and designs with distinctive borders, used esp. for women's clothing.

1969 *Daily Nation* (Nairobi) 31 Oct. 5/1 Betty was taking a good look at the lovely things on sale, but had almost made up her mind to wear traditional kitenge on the 'Big Day'. **1970** *Sunday News Mag.* (Tanzania) 30 Aug. 8 Take the case of a polygamous peasant whose wives have been turned into working machines to bring wealth to him while all they get in return are pieces of kitenge or khanga. **1971** *Inside Kenya Today* Mar. 42/1 Local fabrics such as Kitenges and Kangas are also used to make clothes at the Institute. **1971** *Standard* (Tanzania) 7 Apr. 1/8 UWT members have been urged to reflect the African culture in their dress and other items that convey our intrinsic values. May Day vitenges will be on sale at 19/20.

kite's-foot, kitefoot. **2.** (Earlier and later U.S. examples.)

1788 *Mass. Centinel* 4 June 94/2 Crowley & Clark Have just received a quantity of Kitefoot Tobacco, of a *superior*

quality for smoking. **1835** H. C. Todd *Notes Canada & U.S.A.* 50 Maryland produces..the Bright Kite's Foot Tobacco.

kitful: see *kit *sb.*[11]

kiting: see *kite *v.* 3 b.

ki·tless, *a.* [f. Kit *sb.*[1] + -less.] Having no kit (Kit *sb.*[1] 2 b); without (adequate, suitable) clothing.

The definitions in the work cited in quot. 1846 are often unsatisfactory; it nevertheless seems to provide a genuine example of the sense defined above.

1846 *Swell's Night Guide* 123/2 *Kitless*, a bare, naked fellow. **1936** J. Buchan *Island of Sheep* ix. 160 [He] went off with the women..to look after her wardrobe, for she also was kit-less.

‖ **kitsch** (kitʃ). Also **Kitsch.** [G.] Art or *objets d'art* characterized by worthless pretentiousness; the qualities associated with such art or artifacts. Also *attrib.*, *Comb.*, and *transf.*

1926 B. Howard *Let.* in M. J. Lancaster *Brian Howard* (1968) ix. 166 A healthy week..riding, chasing dogs and listening to 'Kitsch' on his wireless. **1939** *Partisan Rev.* VI. 40 Kitsch is mechanical and operates by formulas. Kitsch is vicarious experience and faked sensations. Kitsch changes according to style, but remains always the same. Kitsch is the epitome of all that is spurious in the life of our times. **1941** Auden *New Year Let.* iii. 59 Reason's depravity that takes The useful concepts that she makes As universals, as the kitsch. **1949** Koestler *Insight & Outlook* 410 The more romantic a work of art, or a landscape, the quicker its repetitions are perceived as *kitsch* or 'slush'. **1955** *20th Cent.* June 541 In a time of crassness and stridency perhaps unique in history, a time when an alternative civilization of *kitsch* is not only available to all but clamantly thrust upon them, it is imperative to strive for agreement, order, and coherence in the ranks of the cultivated. **1958** *Observer* 23 Feb. 14/1 What is so extraordinary about some of these *kitsch* masterpieces is the way they can be enjoyed on two planes, both as themselves and as their own parodies. **1958** *Times* 4 July 13/4 Few attempts are made in England to mount productions of plays of the *commedia dell' arte* tradition; and such attempts are in danger of being dismissed as 'art theatre *kitsch*'. **1961** *Times* 11 May 10/4 There are the same highbrows as in England, who consider that the quality of the pure entertainment as such is generally *kitsch* or trash. **1962** *Times* 6 Apr. 17/3 Their attitude to this *kitsch*-culture is highly equivocal. **1965** *Spectator* 22 Jan. 108/1 If leaders of the state choose their job..they must choose to be the victims of the kitsch and whitewash and balderdash. **1967** *Ibid.* 29 Dec. 812/2, I have never seen such kitsch, not even in French provincial towns or Irish church bazaars. **1972** *Listener* 24 Aug. 236/1 A galloping fancy for Victoriana, a sophisticated and uncritical taste for Kitsch and the cute. **1972** *New Yorker* 30 Sept. 24/3 This is one of the liveliest and most popular of their *kitschfests.*

So **kitsch** *v. trans.* (*rare*), to render worthless, to affect with sentimentality and vulgarity; **ki·tschy** *a.*, possessing the characteristics of kitsch.

1951 W. Sansom *Face of Innocence* ii. 16 Situations that have for many become unendurably hackneyed, spoiled by bad artists or kitsched by politics. **1967** *Time* 17 Feb. 104 The kitschy existential slogan: 'Things just happen. No reason, no reason, just a happening.' **1969** R. Petrie *Despatch of Dove* i. 19 Her family owned a furniture factory. 'We make..mostly kitschy bits fit to furnish Grimm's fairy tales.' **1973** *Times* 27 Aug. 5/6 Costumed in a distressingly 'kitschy' manner.

kittel (ki·t'l). [Yiddish (G., overall, smock), ad. MHG. *kitel, kietel* cotton or hempen outer garment, prob. ad. Arab. *quṭn* cotton.] A white cotton or linen robe worn by orthodox Jews on certain holy days; also used as a shroud.

1891 M. Friedländer *Jewish Relig.* 492 The *kittel* or *sargenes* is part of the raiment in which the dead are clothed... In some countries..the bride presents the bridegroom with this article on the wedding-day: and it is worn by the husband on New-Year's Day and on the Day of Atonement and on the *Seder*-evening during the service. **1972** C. Raphael *Feast of Hist.* i. 11/2 A Yemenite Seder... The celebrants are wearing their traditional festive clothes, the men in white '*kittels*'. **1973** *Synagogue Light* Sept. 46/2 Garbed in the white Kittel, head wrapped in a Tallitli, he who blows stands near the Rabbi.

kitten, *sb.* Add: **1. b.** (Later examples.)

1957 J. H. F. Stevenson *Mink in Britain* (ed. 2) v. 18 Once the kittens, or kits as they are called, are able to fend for themselves, they do so. **1964** R. M. Lockley *Private Life Rabbit* iv. 54 It was possible to handle and weigh week-old kittens without causing their desertion by the doe. **1972** R. Adams *Watership Down* xliii. 356 Clover's had her litter. All good, healthy kittens. Three bucks and three does.

c. In extended use: a girl-friend; a young woman; often as a form of address.

1870 D. J. Kirwan *Palace & Hovel* xliii. 612 The 'Kitten' is a blonde, with black eyes, a pretty, babyish face,..a profusion of golden hair. **1908** W. De Morgan *Somehow Good* xii. 119 'Kitten,' said Sally's mother to her suddenly, 'I think I shall go away to bed.' **1938** W. G. Hardy *Turn back River* iii. 28 'You'll have to go, kitten,' Clodia whispered hurriedly... For an instant she held her sister close. **1961** 'E. Lathen' *Banking on Death* (1962) vii. 59 He..accepted a sherry from June with a somewhat absent, 'Thanks, Kitten.' **1970** G. Greer *Female Eunuch* 266 There are the cute animal terms like.. *kitten* and *lamb* [to signify a woman].

4. Slang phr. (orig. *U.S.*), *to have kittens*: to lose one's composure; to get into a 'flap'.

1900 *Dialect Notes* II. 44 *Kitten.* In phrases 'get kittens', 'have kittens'. 1. To get angry. 2. To be in great anxiety, or to be afraid. **1937** *Times* 15 Feb. 13/4 Mr. Partridge allows 'jitters'..but not 'having kittens'. **1940** K. M. Knight *Rendezvous with Past* xx. 141 If he knew what I know about you he'd have kittens. **1943** Hunt & Pringle *Service Slang* 38 *Having kittens*, perturbed. 'The Colonel is having kittens'—the Colonel is upset and he is very, very angry. **1950** M. Kennedy *Feast* ii. ix. 42 She's been having kittens all day because Mrs. Siddal says she's got to empty slops. **1952** W. Plomer *Museum Pieces* xxv. 210 My doctor nearly had kittens when I suggested my being dropped to the *maquis* by parachute. **1959** 'A. Gilbert' *Third Crime Lucky* ii. 28 Gertrude was going to have kittens when she discovered that extravagance. **1967** N. Freeling *Strike Out* 76 When one of the horses has something wrong with it—then everybody has kittens.

ki·ttenishness. [-ness.] Kittenish characteristics or behaviour.

1905 *Smart Set* Sept. 15/1 Monsieur de Latour felt, as well as saw, that Madame de Beauregard, for all her kittenishness, was really a very great lady. **1926** *Chambers's Jrnl.* Aug. 610/1 Ages back the American girl abjured all that was in the nature of kittenishness. **1974** F. Nolan *Oshawa Project* xv. 99 'What do you mean..?' she said, every trace of the kittenishness falling away.

Kittitian (kiti·ʃăn), *sb.* and *a.* Also **Kittician.** [f. *St. Kitt(s* + *-itian* as in *Haitian.*] **A.** *sb.* A native or inhabitant of the island of St. Kitts, in the West Indies; also, the form of regional English spoken in St. Kitts. **B.** *adj.* Of or pertaining to St. Kitts or its inhabitants.

1966 *Listener* 26 May 754/2 The factors which drew Kitticians to this particular area. **1970** J. Brown *Unmelting Pot* vii. 104 They also came as islanders: Jamaicans, Barbadians, Kittitians, or Grenadans. **1973** *Observer* (Colour Suppl.) 16 Dec. 25/1 Carol Browne's brother will not speak Kittitian..but he will speak the Jamaican dialect. **1973** *Country Life* 31 May 1544/1 Rodney Lad.. carried off a considerable amount of Kittitian property, leaving the local whites in an unpatriotic mood. **1974** *Advocate-News* (Barbados) 19 Feb. 9 By rescuing sugar the Government was in fact rescuing Kittitians.

kittle cattle (ki·t'l kæt'l). orig. *Sc.* [f. Kittle *a.* + Cattle *sb.*] Used to denote people or animals that are capricious, rash, or erratic in behaviour; also *transf.*, objects, concepts, etc., that are difficult to use, sort out, or comprehend.

Initially in phr. (*kings are*) *kittle cattle to shoe behind*, an elaboration of *kittle to shoe behind* (1600 in Dict. s.v. Kittle *a.*).

1818 Scott *Heart Midl.* in *Tales my Landlord* 2nd Ser. IV. i. 5 Kings are kittle cattle to shoe behind, as we say in the north. **1876** [see Kittle *a.*]. **1881** H. Shanks *Peasant Poets Scott., & Musings* 342 Now, women are (compared wi' men), More contumacious; and when Their 'birse' is up,—my certy! then They're kittle cattle. **1888** *Trans. Highland Soc.* 197 Even as machines are easily deranged so sheep are 'kittle cattle'; no more delicate animal breathes. **1900** E. T. Fowler *Farringdons* i. 15 She knew a great portion of the Methodist hymn-book by heart, and pondered long over the interesting preface to that work, wondering much what 'doggerel' and 'botches' could be—she inclined to the supposition that the former were animals and the latter were diseases; but even her vivid imagination failed to form a satisfactory representation of such queer kittle-cattle as 'feeble expletives'. **1926** Fowler *Mod. Eng. Usage* 717/1 It is well known that *and which & but which* are kittle cattle, so well known that the more timid writers avoid the dangers associated with them. **1935** *Times Educ. Suppl.* 28 Dec. p. iv/1 It helps to discount the general impression that, as a race, they [*sc.* lilies] are kittle-kattle. **1942** F. Smythe *Alpine Ways* 14 The 'he man' mountaineer who scorns tourists as mere kittle kattle, the tourists who jeer at the mountaineer as mad, have yet to gain that fuller understanding which abhors intolerance. **1966** *Sunday Express* 13 Mar. 16/7 Princesses in love..are at times Kittle Cattle.

kitty[4]. Add: **2.** (Earlier examples.) Also, the money (freq. placed in the centre of the table) taken by the winner of a game or round (the usual sense). So *transf.*, earnings, liquid capital, a reserve fund; a sum of money made up of contributions by people involved in a common activity.

1887 J. W. Keller *Game of Draw Poker* 12 Widow, or *Kitty*—A percentage taken out of the pool to defray the expenses of the game or the cost of refreshments. **1891** E. Dowson *Let.* 1 July (1967) 206, I shall..refuse to associate myself with penny nap & an unlimited Kittie. **1903** 'J. Flynt' *Rise of Ruderick Clowd* iii. 106 'Forty [cents] out of every dollar you cop out—understand?'—'Who gets the rest?'—'The mob an' the kitty. The kitty is the fall-money reserve. A mob like ours ought to carry a $3000 kitty all the time. It's drawn on when one of us gets arrested an' has to hire lawyers an' get bail. If you get a tumble, for instance, the rest of us'll have to stand by you—see?' **1905** *Daily Chron.* 12 Sept. 4/7 'Kitty wins everything,' is the bookmakers' plaint. **1909** 'O. Henry' *Roads of Destiny* xiii. 213 Your thousand dollars is gone into the kitty of this corrupt country on that last bluff you made. **1924** T. Rohan *Confessions of Dealer* iv. 51 The King of the Knock-Out..counts out banknotes to the tune of £1,000, and places these notes in the bowl or kitty which occupies the centre of the table. The first man to help himself from the kitty is the dealer who did £100 at the sale. **1929** [see *full house 2]. **1935** A. J. Pollock *Underworld Speaks* 68/1 *Kitty*, money taken from virtually every gambling pot for purpose of profits or expenses, or whangdoodles at the end of a friendly home game. **1969** *Listener* 17 July 77/1 In 1949, the authorities at the hall had enough money in the kitty to install a new aluminium roof. **1971** *Ink* 12 June 14/1 Bernie's salesmen kept bringing in the lolly..until by 1970 they had $2·4 billion in their management kitty.

3. *Bowls.* The jack.

1898 D. Willox *Poems & Sk.* 174 Now, in throwing up the 'Kitty', Oor first player's quite a card, But in playing tae't he seldom Ever gangs within a yard. **1909** *Westm. Gaz.* 6 Sept. 4/1 When the bowl goes near the kitty. **1926** H. Hendry *Poems* 98 Kitty, that licht and lively quean, Wha links athort the bowling-green. **1959** *Chambers's Encycl.* II. 476/1 The small white earthenware ball, known as the jack or 'kitty', at which the bowls are aimed, must not be more than 8 in. in circumference or 10 oz in weight.

kittydid, var. Katydid.

kiva (kī·vă). Also **khiva, kiver.** [Hopi.] A chamber, built wholly or partly underground, used by the male Pueblo Indians for religious rites, etc.; Estufa. Also *attrib.* and *transf.*

1871 in *Utah Hist. Q.* (1939) VII. 54 Found pieces of pottery and arrowheads... Also saw a 'kiver' or underground 'clan room'. **1875** *Scribner's Monthly* Dec. 205/2 This kiva, as it is called in their own tongue, is called '*Estufa*' by the Spaniards, and is spoken of by writers in English as the 'Sweat House'. **1898** *17th Ann. Rep. U.S. Bureau Amer. Ethnol. 1895–6* 611 A pueblo of the size of Awatobi..would no doubt have ceremonial chambers or kivas. **1927** W. Cather *Death comes for Archbishop* iv. ii. 132 It was a smothered fire in a clay oven, and had been burning in one of the kivas ever since the pueblo was founded. **1931** *Discovery* Sept. 279/2 The 'khiva' as they are called by the present Hopi Indians... It seems clear that their purpose was to provide a meeting place for councils and ceremonies for the men of the clan. **1950** F. Eggan *Social Organiz. Western Pueblos* ii. 28 Between the members of the kiva groups there are no special kinship ties. **1958** J. Cleugh tr. *Jungk's Brighter than Thousand Suns* xviii. 295 The mechanism used took the form of a 'critical assembly' under remote control. Processes going on inside the 'Kivas'—the buildings had been called after the sacred ceremonial chambers of the Pueblo Indians, which could only be approached, with the greatest awe, by their priests—were to be observed solely on television screens. **1964** E. A. Nida *Toward Sci. Transl.* viii. 169 For the Zuñis, uttering *melika* in a kiva ceremony would be as out of place as bringing a radio into such a meeting.

Kiwanis (kiwā·nis). [Origin obscure.] In full, *Kiwanis Club.* A society of business and professional men formed in Detroit in 1915 for the maintenance of commercial ethics, and as a social and charitable organization; any similar society formed later elsewhere in the U.S.A. or in Canada. Also **Kiwa·nian,** a member of a Kiwanis Club.

1921 *Daily Colonist* (Victoria, B.C.) 16 Mar. 5/4 An initiation ceremony for the purpose of welcoming into the organization three new members took place at the weekly luncheon of the Kiwanis Club yesterday. *Ibid.* 30 Mar. 7/5 As Kiwanians and citizens, Mr Smith claimed, it was a duty to look after the children. **1922** *Collier's* 29 Apr. 5/2 It had a civic association, and Rotary, Kiwanis, and Lion Clubs. **1926** *Glasgow Herald* 18 Sept. 4 Take Galveston, for example... A newspaper describes how the local Kiwanians and their lady friends..rounded off an evening's delight by indulging in a hand-shaking competition. **1948** *Daily Ardmoreite* (Ardmore, Okla.) 30 Mar. 3/1 A class of older girls recently entertained the local Kiwanis club. **1949** *Amer. Speech* XXIV. 29 Virginians..show little of the exuberant affability of a Midwestern Rotarian or Kiwanian. **1964** Mrs. L. B. Johnson *White House Diary* (1970) 5 Jan. 30 We drove to the little house in Johnson City.., which we are having restored as a Community Center, where, hopefully, 4-H youngsters or the PTA, or Kiwanis, or Lions, or ladies' groups, or whatever can hold their meetings. **1972** *Fairbanks* (Alaska) *Daily News-Miner* 3 Nov. 1/2 Alaska Attorney General John Havelock analyzed and approved the moral basis of Alaska's Oil Legislation in an address before a joint Kiwanis banquet here last night.

kiwi. Add: **2.** (With capital initial.) A New Zealander, esp. a New Zealand soldier; also, a New Zealand sportsman. Also *attrib.*

1918 *N.Z.E.F. Chrons.* 24 May 179/1 In the evening the 'Kiwis' gave a performance to a crowded hall. *Ibid.* 21 June 225/1 The New Zealand boys..will find the 'Kiwi' A.D.S. as reasonably safe as is possible. **1945** Baker *Austral. Lang.* ix. 178 New Zealand football representatives acquired the names *All Blacks, Fernleaves*, and *Kiwis.* **1947** B. Mason in D. M. Davin *N.Z. Short Stories* (1953) 333 We were Kiwis, and a long way from home. **1958** R. France *Race* 12 Laurie was not a real Kiwi, or hard-bitten New Zealander. **1960** B. Crump *Good Keen Man* 58, I suspect she was a real Kiwi mum, with a soft spot for her little Harry. **1961** in J. Reid *Kiwi Laughs* 10 Told in a homely Kiwi idiom. **1963** N. Hilliard *Piece of Land* 35 They fill the place with immigrants... A Kiwi 'd never look at the prices some of them want. **1974** *Times* 17 June 12/7 It is hurtful to many Australians to see the Kiwis take all the credit for Antipodean anti-Pom feelings.

3. Also **Kiwi.** A non-flying member of an air force (see also quot. 1938). *slang.*

1918 B. Hall *Diary* 22 Jan. in Hall & Niles *One Man's War* (1929) xxxii. 289 Visited the Avenue Montaigne Headquarters. It is full of non-flying aviators. The American pilots call them Kiwis. **1925** Fraser & Gibbons *Soldier & Sailor Words* 137 *Kiwi*, Air Force slang for a man on ground duty and not qualified for flying service. **1931** *Vanity Fair* (N.Y.) Nov. 78/3 There are terms with which to plaster the green pilot and the non-flyer. *Quirks* or *kiwis* are beginners—sometimes the terms are broadened

to include the layman. The origin of *quirk* is somewhat obscure..but *kiwi* is a derogatory reference to the Australian [*sic*] kiwi-bird, which, having only stub wings, is unable to fly. **1938** *Amer. Speech* XIII. 156/2 *Kiwi*,..a person with no practical flying experience; often used as a term of disparagement toward one who speaks with authority concerning flying but whose knowledge is entirely theoretical. **1943** HUNT & PRINGLE *Service Slang* 43 *Kiwi*, a word brought over by the New Zealand airmen with a new meaning: men who do not belong to air crews. **1960** WENTWORTH & FLEXNER *Dict. Amer. Slang* 307/1 *Kiwi*, an air force man, esp. an officer who cannot, does not, or does not like to fly.

4. = **kiwi berry, fruit.*

1972 *Daily Colonist* (Victoria, B.C.) 2 Aug. 19/1 Have you noticed a small brown fruit called kiwi in local markets lately?.. Sometimes called a Chinese gooseberry. **1973** *Sat. Rev. Soc.* (U.S.) Mar. 53/1 Twenty-six different crops, most of them fruit—almonds, apples..kiwis, nectarines, olives.

5. *attrib.* and *Comb.*, as *kiwi feather, -hunter, -preserve;* **kiwi berry, fruit** = *Chinese gooseberry* (*CHINESE *a.* 2).

1968 *N.Z. News* 23 Oct. 2/4 New Zealand exports of chinese gooseberries will enter the United States—where they are called 'giant Kiwi-berries'—almost duty-free from next season. **1905** *Daily Chron.* 7 July 6/5 The presents included..a rug of kiwi feathers from New Zealand, and three rare engravings. **1938** R. D. FINLAYSON *Brown Man's Burden* 47 They had covered his shrunken body with fine kiwi-feather cloaks. **1966** *N.Y. Times* 13 Aug. 12 Chinese gooseberries, also known as kiwi fruit, are in metropolitan markets for the third season in increased quantities. **1970** *N.Z. News* 7 Jan. 4/4 A storage technique first developed for bananas has been tested on Chinese gooseberries, now renamed 'Kiwi fruit'. *Ibid.* 4/5 A 20 lb. pack of Kiwi fruit. **1973** *Massey Ferguson Rev.* (N.Z.) Mar./Apr. 3/4 Chinese gooseberries or 'kiwi fruit', bear extravagantly. **1873** Kiwi-hunter, -preserve [in Dict.].

ki-yi, *sb.* Add: **2.** A dog.

1895 *Harper's Mag.* Nov. 962/1 I'm not really a ki-yi, and while I don't like bicyclists,..I won't bite you. **1904** *Buffalo* (N.Y.) *Express* 20 June 4 A butcher in Brussels made sausage of the carcass of a zoo elephant which had been killed. Doubtless the Brussels kiyis yelped for joy. **1913** J. LONDON *Valley of Moon* I. x, But them sickenin', sap-headed stiffs, with the grit of rabbits and the silk of mangy ki-yi's, a-cheerin' me—*me!*

Kizil (kizi·l), *a.* and *sb.* Also **Kyzyl.** [ad. Turk. *kızıl* red.] **A.** *adj.* Of or pertaining to a Turkic Tartar people of southern Siberia. **B.** *sb.* A member of this people.

1898 A. J. BUTLER tr. *Ratzel's Hist. Mankind* III. v. xiii. 336 The Kizil Tartars on the Upper Chulym. *Ibid.* 342 The Kizil tribe of the Tomsk Kirghises. **1909** WEBSTER, Kizil *n.* **1964** tr. *Levin & Potapov's Peoples of Siberia* 358 The Kyzyls belonged to a large Turkic-speaking group living in the Chulym Basin. *Ibid.* 360 The language of the present-day Kyzyls is identical with Kachin.

Kizilbash (ki·zilbāʃ). (Also used as *pl.*) Also 8 **-bac,** 9– **Kizzil-, -bashi.** [ad. Turk. *kızılbaş,* f. *kızıl* red + *baş* head.] **a.** A Persianized Turk of Afghanistan. **b.** A member of any of several cultural or religious minorities in Asian Turkey.

1727 J. G. SCHEUCHZER tr. *Kæmpfer's Hist. Japan* I. I. vi. 88 The *Kizilbacs*, or Noblemen, and great Families, in Persia value themselves mightily upon their being of Turcoman extraction. **1815** [see TURK[1] 1]. **1875** *Encycl. Brit.* I. 235/1 The *Kizilbâshes* may be regarded as modern Persians, but more strictly they are Persianised Turks. **1898** A. J. BUTLER tr. *Ratzel's Hist. Mankind* III. v. xv. 365 In Persia and Afghanistan the Turks, Kizilbashes, Usbeks, Turcomans, are even more sharply distinguished from the Persians. **1902** *Encycl. Brit.* XXV. 120/1 The Kizzilbashes of Kabul. **1920** *Blackw. Mag.* Jan. 121/2 Hosts of Tartar, and Afghan, Persian and Kizilbash. **1960** *Guardian* 28 June 8/5 Mingled with the Pathans of the south [of Afghanistan]..are..Turkomans, Kizilbashes, Kirghis. **1960** *Spectator* 2 Dec. 889/3 Religious sects living apart like the Kizil Bashis, Shiah, Tartars and Kára Papachs [in Turkey, *c* 1912].

Kjeldahl (ke·ldāl). *Biochem.* The name of Johann *Kjeldahl* (1849–1900), Danish brewing chemist, used *attrib.* and in the possessive to denote a method of estimation of nitrogen invented by him, in which the organic substance to be analysed is treated with concentrated sulphuric acid and the ammonium sulphate so formed is converted by excess alkali to ammonia, which is then titrated; **Kjeldahl flask,** a glass flask having a round bottom and a long wide neck, used in the Kjeldahl method.

1885 *Jrnl. Chem. Soc.* XLVIII. 688 (*heading*) Nitrogen determinations by Kjeldahl's method. **1909** P. B. HAWK *Pract. Physiol. Chem.* (ed. 2) xxii. 382 Place 5 c.c. of urine in a 500 c.c. long-necked Jena glass Kjeldahl flask. **1964** [see *COLORIMETRICALLY *adv.*]. **1970** R. W. MCGILVERY *Biochem.* xxviii. 704 The Kjeldahl method has the advantage of being applicable to insoluble materials, such as most foodstuffs, and the disadvantage of not distinguishing proteins from other sources of nitrogen, such as nucleic acids, urea, and the like.

Klá, var. *KULLAH.

Klaas (klās). The name of a servant who travelled with the French explorer, François Le Vaillant (1753–1824), used in the possessive in **Klaas's cuckoo,** a bronze and green cuckoo, *Chrysococcyx klaas,* found in the southern part of Africa.

1867 E. L. LAYARD *Birds S. Afr.* 250 Klaas's cuckoo is not uncommon in most wooded parts of the colony. **1903** A. C. STARK *Birds S. Afr.* III. 188 This cuckoo was first obtained by Levaillant and named by him after his faithful Hottentot servant Klaas... Klaas' Cuckoo frequents both bush and thorn lands. **1936** E. L. GILL *First Guide S. Afr. Birds* 108 Among the birds parasitized by Klaas's Cuckoo are various sunbirds, warblers and kingfishers. **1951** R. CAMPBELL *Light on Dark Horse* x. 143 The bird known to this day as Klaas's Cuckoo..is the ruby cuckoo. **1964** P. A. CLANCEY *Birds Natal & Zululand* 222 The young Klaas' cuckoo ejects the nestlings of the foster parent a few days after hatching.

klaberjass, var. *KLOBBIYOS.

Klamath (klæ·mǎþ). Also †**Clamet.** [f. Chinook *łámał* Klamath.] **A.** *sb.* A Penutian Indian people of the Oregon–California border; a member of this people; also, their language. **B.** *adj.* Of or pertaining to this people.

1826 J. MCLOUGHLIN *Lett.* (1941) I. 33 Mr. Ogden [goes]..thence towards Lac Sale makes a Circuit West and comes Out above the Clamet tribe. **1853** H. R. SCHOOLCRAFT *Hist. & Stat. Information Indian Tribes* III. 133 The goods destined for the Klamath Indians had been sent to Trinidad. **1881** *Encycl. Brit.* XII. 826/2 The *Klamath* family,..comprises the Lutuami or Klamaths proper. *Ibid., Californian Races.*—This is mainly a geographical grouping, but with three large ethnical and linguistic families—the Klamath, Pomo, and Runsien. **1890** A. S. GATSCHET *Klamath Indians* I. 209 Triphthongs are not infrequent, since Klamath has a greater tendency to accumulate consonants than vowels. **1923** [see *DAKOTA *sb.* 2]. **1965** *Canad. Jrnl. Linguistics* Spring 123 The last family represented in Oregon is Klamath-Modoc. Klamath speakers are found in fairly large numbers... Modoc is represented by only about seven or eight speakers.

C. Klamath weed, the local name of a species of St. John's wort, *Hypericum perforatum.*

1922 F. J. SMILEY *Weeds Calif.* 54 (Hypericum perforatum L.) English names:..Common St. John's-wort.. Klamath weed. **1949** *Sunday World-Herald Mag.* (Omaha) 1 May 10/1 Klamath weed probably can be controlled or destroyed chemically. **1971** DEBACH & HUFFAKER in C. B. Huffaker *Biol. Control* v. 118 Figure 1.. shows the degree of biological control achieved in California of the formerly serious Klamath weed, *Hypericum perforatum* L., by colonization of an imported exotic beetle which feeds upon it.

Klan, short for KU-KLUX-KLAN. Also *Klansman,* occas. *Clansman.*

1867 [see *KU-KLUX 1]. **1868** *Century Mag.* XXVIII. 409/1 The Klan now, as in the past, is prohibited from doing such things. **1884** [see INVISIBLE *a.* 1 c]. **1905** T. DIXON (*title*) The Clansman. **1924** J. M. MECKLIN *Ku Klux Klan* i. 3 The modern Klan was organized by William J. Simmons in 1915. *Ibid.* 5 Masked men leaped from their cars clad in Klan regalia. *Ibid.* 6 Public sentiment..seems to have supported the Klansmen. **1953** *Manch. Guardian Weekly* 31 Dec. 11 A klansman from Georgia. **1973** *Freedomways* XIII. 31 The..killings and the Attica prison slaughter are remindful of the post-Civil War Klan days. **1973** *Guardian* 23 Mar. 15/2 A former member of the Klan, Senator Byrd has a dismal voting record on social and civil rights issues. **1973** *Black Panther* 1 Sept. 8/3 The Assistant District Attorney tossed out the charges saying that although the law prohibits Klansmen from appearing in public, the faces of the 24 were visible.

‖ **klang** (klaŋ, klæŋ). [G., = sound.] A musical tone composed of fundamental and overtones; = CLANG *sb.* 3. Hence **kla·ngfarbe** (-fa·rbə) [G. *farbe,* colour], musical quality of a note, timbre, 'clang-tint' (see CLANG *sb.* 4); **klangfarbenmelodie,** melody of timbres.

1867 [see CLANG *sb.* 3]. **1890** J. KLAUSER *Septonate* i. 37 (Funk), In music a tone or a *klang* is thought, heard, and treated as a unit. **1959** *Listener* 12 Nov. 834/2 It is possible that some of the mannerisms—disjointed rhythms, 'Klangfarbenmelodie' (the playing of notes that have no connection with each other one by one), etc., may fall by the wayside. **1966** *Ibid.* 19 May 736/3 No. 3..is systematically subjected to *klangfarbenmelodie,* emphasis of instrumental timbre.

klapper (klæ·pəɹ). *S. Afr.* [perh. ad. Malay *kĕlapa* coconut or Afrikaans *klapper* rattle.] = *Kaffir orange* (*KAFFIR 4); also used for other shrubs or trees with similar fruit.

1863 W. C. BALDWIN *Afr. Hunting* vi. 199 We had a capital lunch from some wild fruit about three times the size of an orange, called a clapper. It has a hard shell outside, which one must batter against a tree to crack or break. **1921** T. R. SIM *Native Timbers S. Afr.* 120 *Strychnos pungens*... Klopper [*sic*], Wild Orange. **1932** WATT & BREYER-BRANDWIJK *Medicinal & Poisonous Plants S. Afr.* 140 The pulp of the fruit of *Strychnos pungens* Solered., Wild orange, Kaffir orange, Klapper..*Strychnos spinosa* Lam. (*Brehmia spinosa* Harv.), Kaffir orange, Klapper..and *Strychnos gerrardi* N.E. Br...is acidulous from the presence of citric acid, and is very refreshing. **1939** tr. *E. N. Marais's My Friends the Baboons* iii. 29 Wild peaches, sour klappers (unknown in the south), medlers, moepels, and various other kinds of fruit made our wilderness a veritable orchard. **1966** E. PALMER *Plains of Camdeboo* x. 177 The spekboom, the wild plum and the klapper, now bright with colour. **1973** PALMER & PITMAN *Trees S. Afr.* III. 1857 The monkey orange, or klapper as it is often known,..is an evergreen tree.

‖ **klatsch** (klatʃ). Also **klatch.** [G., tittle-tattle, gossip.] A visit; a coffee-party. Cf. **coffee-klatsch,* *KAFFEEKLAT(S)CH.

1953 A. MILLER *Crucible* (1956) I. 34 There are accounts of similar *klatches* in Europe, where the daughters of the towns would assemble at night and..give themselves to love. **1967** E. B. NICKERSON *Kayaks to Arctic* xvi. 155 So later, when the men returned and set up their camp we had them over for a klatch.

klaxon (klæ·ksən), *sb.* orig. *U.S.* Also **Klaxon.** [Name of the manufacturing company.] An (electric) horn or warning hooter, orig. one on a motor vehicle. Also *klaxon-horn.*

1910 *Sat. Even. Post* 17 Sept. 48 The Klaxon has never taken a life; it has saved thousands. **1911** *N.Y. Times* 16 Oct. 12/7 Speedometer, slip covers, pigskin upholstery and klaxon. **1917** 'CONTACT' *Airman's Outings* 66 A signal rocket streaked from the first Boche biplane, and the trio dived almost vertically, honking the while on Klaxon horns. **1918** R. H. KNYVETT *Over There with Australians* IV. xx. 199 These noises were made chiefly with klaxon horns. **1920** *Motor Manual* (ed. 23) xv. 150 The electrically-operated Klaxon horn. **1924** B. GILBERT *Bly Market* 343 Emery Stamp sounded his klaxon. **1949** *Reader's Digest* Apr. 140/2 It was a gray Pierce Arrow, equipped with two bulb horns and an electric Klaxon. **1965** 'J. LE CARRÉ' *Looking-Glass War* 8 He heard the klaxons,.. moaning out over that godforsaken airfield like the howl of starving animals. **1973** P. EVANS *Bodyguard Man* i. 14 The evening traffic was thick, shrill with sudden braking and klaxon noise.

Hence **kla·xon** *v. intr.,* to sound a klaxon; also *trans.;* **kla·xoning** *vbl. sb.*

1922 E. V. LUCAS *Genevra's Money* vi. 38 The almost constant clatter and Klaxoning of motor-cars and lorries on the high-roads. **1924** G. FRANKAU *Gerald Cranston's Lady* iv. 48 Lees, Klaxoning furiously, slackened pace round the dangerous stone-wall turning. **1971** *Daily Tel.* 15 Sept. 12 There are two sides to every situation, once the Press, television and radio have 'klaxoned' the story to the general public. **1973** G. BEARE *Snake on Grave* vii. 35 A little white Fiat klaxoning shrilly.

Kleagle (klī·g'l). [f. *KL(AN + EAGLE *sb.*] A title given to an officer of the KU-KLUX-KLAN.

1924 J. M. MECKLIN *Ku Klux Klan* i. 8 The head of the promotion department as a whole was Imperial Kleagle E.Y. Clarke... The head of the 'realm', or state, was called a King Kleagle, and the house-to-house solicitors, or legwork men, were called Kleagles. **1924** E. T. BYNUM *Personal Recoll.* 8 The Kleagle showed considerable irritation in the conversation which followed. **1929** *Sun* (Baltimore) 31 Jan. 1/2 There was a time when Johnston could have called the roll of the kleagles and merely waited for donations to roll in. **1949** *Time* 13 June 24/1 Samuel Green, the Grand Dragon of the Ku Klux Klan, was frantically exhorting his Kleagles and Cyclops to mass for a big night of cross-burning and hate-spieling.

klebsiella (klebzi,e·lă). [mod.L. (V. Trevisan 1885, in *Atti Accad. Fisio-Medico-Statistica Milano* 4th Ser. III. 105), f. the name of *Klebs* (see next) + L. *-ella* (see -EL[2]).] A coliform bacterium of the ill-defined genus so called, which includes Friedländer's bacillus, *Klebsiella pneumoniæ,* and others associated with respiratory, urinary, and wound infections and occas. with hospital epidemics.

1928 W. GILTNER *Elem. Text Bk. Gen. Microbology* [sic] xxv. 337 (*heading*) Klebsiella infections. **1948** H. F. DOWLING *Acute Bacterial Dis.* xx. 364 Cholecystitis and cholangitis are frequently the site of klebsiella infections. **1957** R. Y. STANIER et al. *Microbial World* xvi. 341 The members of the *Klebsiella* group are encapsulated. **1962** *Lancet* 12 May 989/1 In 1 patient with a urinary-tract infection a klebsiella strain was isolated. **1973** A. L. SMITH *Princ. Microbiol.* (ed. 7) xxiii. 351 *Klebsiella* are non-motile, gram-negative, aerobic organisms.

Klebs–Löffler (klebz,lö·flər). The names of T. A. E. *Klebs* (1834–1913) and F. A. J. *Löffler* (1852–1915), German bacteriologists, used *attrib.* to designate the bacterium (*Corynebacterium diphtheriæ*) which is the cause of diphtheria in man and similar diseases in other animals.

1895 *Lancet* 21 Dec. 1577/1 The differences between it and the Klebs-Löffler bacillus [were] pointed out. **1897** *Ibid.* 5 June 1533/1 We might now fitly speak of conjunctival inflammations as due to gonococci, to trachomacocci, to Weeks bacilli, to streptococci, to Klebs–Löffler bacilli, or to pneumococci. **1897** MUIR & RITCHIE *Man. Bacteriol.* xv. 329 The organism is..known as the Klebs–Löffler bacillus, or simply as Löffler's bacillus. **1935** *Discovery* XVI. 244/1 An enormous number of cases, mostly drain throats, are rushed off to hospital because the Klebs–Loeffler (diphtheria) bacillus has been found. **1972** PELCZAR & REID *Microbiol.* (ed. 3) xxix. 567 Diphtheria is an acute febrile infection caused by *Corynebacterium diphtheriae,* also known as the Klebs–Löffler bacillus.

Kleenex (klī·neks). orig. *U.S.* The proprietary name of an absorbent disposable cleansing paper tissue. Also *attrib.*

1925 *Picture-Play Mag.* Apr. 107/2 (Advt.), This secret of famous stage beauties... is simply the use of Kleenex in removing cold cream and cosmetics... This soft velvety absorbent is made of Cellucotton... Use it once, throw it away. **1925** *Trade Marks Jrnl.* 15 July 1545 Kleenex... Absorbent pads or sheets (not medicated) for surgical or curative purposes or in relation to the health. Cellucotton Products Company.., City of Neenah,.. Winnebago, State of Wisconsin, United States of America; Manufacturers. **1936** N. COWARD *Play Parade* (1954) IV. 90 They stuff wads of Kleenex paper in between their collars and their necks to prevent the make-up soiling their ties. **1942** M. MCCARTHY *Company She Keeps* (1943) 197 The tears streamed from her eyes... He took a box of Kleenex from a drawer and handed it to her. **1956** E. AMBLER *Night-Comers* iv. 84 She had a box of Kleenex... She began to wipe off the grease. **1957** 'GYPSY ROSE LEE' *Gypsy* xxiv. 315 She dabbed at her eyes with a tattered Kleenex, then shoved it back in her purse. **1967** *Listener* 16 Mar. 368/3 The Master himself fulminates in California against some of his more conservative juniors, in an essay not yet reprinted in England (it dismisses Britten's War Requiem as *Kleenex Music*). **1969** G. GREENE *Trav. with my Aunt* xvii. 179 She wiped her fingers on the Kleenex and opened the yellow envelope. **1971** *Trade Marks Jrnl.* 12 May 910/1 Kleenex... Babies' disposable napkins, diapers and lining sheets for all such goods... Kimberly-Clark Corporation.., Neenah, State of Wisconsin, United States of America; Manufacturers. **1974** *Listener* 11 July 61/3 The almost unpopulated wilderness of Maine, where TV dinners and Kleenex are in short supply.

kleig, Kleig, varr. *KLIEG.

Klein bottle (klaɪn-). [Named after Felix *Klein* (1849–1925), Ger. mathematician.] A closed non-orientable surface that can be represented in three dimensions by passing the neck of a bottle through its side and joining its end to a hole in the base.

1941 COURANT & ROBBINS *What is Math.?* v. 262 Another interesting one-sided surface is the 'Klein bottle'. **1950** *Astounding Sci. Fiction* Dec. 75/2 'The Möbius band', Turpelo said, 'has unusual properties because it has a singularity. The Klein bottle, with two singularities, manages to be inside of itself.' **1965** H. EVES *Survey of Geom.* II. xv. 357 The surface is homeomorphic to a sphere with two crosscaps, and is called a Klein bottle, after Felix Klein who first called attention to it in 1882. *Ibid.*, Show that a Klein bottle can, by one cut, be converted into a disc and a Möbius strip.

‖ **kleindeutsch** (klaɪ·ndoitʃ), *a.* [G.] Referring to or favouring a United Germany, excluding Austria. Also as *sb.*, a supporter of such a policy. Cf. *GROSSDEUTSCH *a.*

1916 A. W. WARD *Germany 1815–90* I. vi. 484 The Austrian members..formed a faction..coalescing..on the question of the exclusion of Austria..under the attractive name *Grossdeutsche*, and designating their opponents (who..included E. M. Arndt) as *Kleindeutsche*. **1945** F. DARMSTAEDTER *Germany & Europe* iv. 53 In the Frankfurt Assembly the adherents of the 'kleindeutsche' solution (exclusion of Austria) gained the upper hand over those of the 'grossdeutsche' (inclusion of Austria). **1946** [see *GROSSDEUTSCH *a.*]. **1968** F. EYCK *Frankfurt Parl. 1848–9* vii. 255 The exclusion of Austria from Germany (which was to become the programme of the *Kleindeutsche* who proposed the King of Prussia as hereditary German Emperor). *Ibid.* viii. 363 The antithesis of *Kleindeutsch* (Lesser German) and *Grossdeutsch* (Greater German) is not sufficiently subtle to describe the real difference between the parties.

Kleinian (klaɪ·niăn), *a.* and *sb. Psychol.* **A.** *adj.* Of or pertaining to Melanie *Klein* (1882–1960) or her theories which, though basically Freudian, differed particularly in the field of child psychoanalysis. **B.** *sb.* A follower of the theories of Melanie Klein.

1955 R. L. MUNROE *Schools of Psychoanal. Thought* 663/1 Introjection,..in Kleinian theory. **1959** *Encounter* Apr. 41/1 A..comprehensive interpretation of various aspects of art in terms of Kleinian theory. **1960** R. WAELDER *Basic Theory Psychoanal.* xi. 233 Analysts of the Kleinian school of thought have made different claims. **1961** J. A. C. BROWN *Freud & Post-Freudians* iv. 79 The biological emphasis further stressed by the Kleinians, who are now regarded by many as the main movement in orthodox psychoanalysis. **1963** *Times Lit. Suppl.* 15 Feb. 111/2 It has become almost impossible to write even a lyric poem without being diagnosed as a Freudian, a Kleinian, [etc.]. **1972** *Guardian* 6 July 15/3 The Kleinian examination of infantile development.

kleinite (klaɪ·naɪt). *Min.* [ad. G. *kleinit* (A. Sachs 1905, in *Sitzungsber. d. preuss. Akad. d. Wissensch.* 1094), f. the name of J. F. C. *Klein* (1842–1907), German geologist: see -ITE[1].] A hydrous chloride and sulphate of mercury and ammonia, occurring as transparent or translucent crystals of a yellow to orange colour.

1907 *Chem. Abstr.* I. 2454 Kleinite may be a mixture of a mercury-ammonium chloride..in great preponderance, with an oxychloride and sulphate or oxysulphate of mercury. **1932** *Amer. Mineralogist* XVII. 547 Specimens of kleinite, terlinguaite, montroydite, and mosesite from the Texas locality were then prepared for *x*-ray examination. **1954** *Mineral. Abstr.* XII. 433 Comparison of the data for kleinite..with those of mosesite..suggests that the former has a three-dimensional structure of $[Hg_2N]^{1+}$..with a formula $[Hg_2N](Cl,SO_4)xH_2O$, where *x* is about ½.

klementite (klĕme·ntaɪt). *Min.* [ad. G. *klementit* (G. Tschermak 1891, in *Sitzungsber. d. kaiserl. Akad. d. Wissensch.* (*Math.-nat. Cl.*) Abt. I. C. 40), f. the name of Constantin *Klement* (b. 1856), curator of the Natural History Museum, Brussels: see -ITE[1].] A variety of thuringite containing more magnesium than iron.

1892 E. S. DANA *Dana's Syst. Min.* (ed. 6) 656 *Klementite.* In thin scales in quartz veins at Vielsalm in Belgium. Probably monoclinic... Color dark olive-green. **1954** *Mineral. Mag.* XXX. 279 It may be found convenient to retain the name klementite as a variety of thuringite with Mg>(Fe″+Fe‴); the original klementite analysis falls in this field. **1968** *Ibid.* XXXVI. 753 This chlorite has been identified as klementite, a variety of thuringite... In thin flakes the mineral is light green but deeper coloured in aggregates... The composition approximates to $Mg_{3\cdot3}Fe_{1\cdot8}Al_{2\cdot8}Si_{2\cdot3}(O,OH)_{18}$.

klendusity (klendiū·sĭti). *Bot.* [f. Gr. κλ·είς bar, bolt + ἔνδυσις entry: see -ITY.] The resistance of a plant to disease, through the presence of some characteristic that inhibits infection. So **klendu·sic** *a.*, showing resistance of this kind.

1940 J. I. WOOD et al. in *Phytopathology* XXX. 362 The ..continued misuse of such words as *immunity, resistance, tolerance* and *klendusity* (with *resistance* as a catch-all) tends definitely to confuse readers. *Ibid.* 364 Klendusity: Ability of a susceptible variety to escape infection because of possession of some quality preventing or hindering successful inoculation under conditions conducive to infection in other varieties. **1943** *Phytopathology* XXXIII. 19 A few seedlings in subsequent generations that were derived indirectly from the almost sterile hybrid were about as capable of escaping infection as *L[ycopersicon] chilense* itself, thus showing heritability of klendusity. *Ibid.* 692 This klendusic seedling did not fruit for some time. **1950** *Trans. Brit. Mycol. Soc.* XXXIII. 156 On this side of the Atlantic 'klendusity' and 'suscept' were each thrown out without a hearing, because they are the very opposite of comfortable words. **1958** *Virology* VI. 303 The nature and inheritance of the tendency to escape infection (klendusity) was investigated. **1967** R. K. S. WOOD *Physiol. Plant Path.* xii. 400 Before these different forms of resistance are dealt with in detail, it is as well to refer to what some pathologists regard as a form of resistance, and which is usually referred to as 'disease escape'. Less frequently the term 'klendusity' is used for the same thing. **1973** *Guide Use Terms Plant Path.* (Federation Brit. Plant Pathologists) 22 Klendusity: the failure of a susceptible host to become infected, in the presence of the pathogen, because of qualities preventing or hindering the operation of a vector or other inoculating agent... Klendusity may be considered a form of disease escape.

klep (klep), *sb.* Slang abbrev. of KLEPTOMANIAC. Hence as *v. intr.*, to steal.

1889 BARRÈRE & LELAND *Dict. Slang* 523/1 *Klep*, a thief; to *klep*, to steal. **1896** FARMER & HENLEY *Slang* IV. 117/2 *Klep* (popular), a thief. Short for kleptomaniac. **1949** 'N. R. NASH' *Young & Fair* 20 The kleps have started!

klepto (kle·pto). Slang abbrev. of KLEPTOMANIAC.

1958 *New Yorker* 25 Jan. 29 Some befuddled guest (or klepto, more likely) abstracted a hat. **1962** *Punch* 4 July 24/1 Playwrights of the imminent Klepto school. **1964** 'E. V. CUNNINGHAM' *Lydia* (1965) xii. 178 You got it.. right out of Helen Sarbine's purse... What are you—some kind of nut or klepto?

kleptobiosis (kle:ptobaɪ,ōu·sis). *Zool.* In quots. **clepto-**. [f. Gr. κλέπτης thief, κλέπτειν to steal + βίωσις way of life.] Among ants and certain other social insects, an association in which a small species feeds on the refuse of a neighbouring nest inhabited by a larger species, or robs returning workers of the host species of the food they are carrying. Hence **kle:ptobio·tic** *a.*

1901 W. M. WHEELER in *Amer. Naturalist* XXXV. 516, I have therefore adopted the following headings... Cleptobiosis. Wasmann's 'Diebsameisen'; first regular form of compound nest. *Ibid.* 529 All the known cleptobiotic ants are of minute size and of subterranean habits. **1927** H. ST. J. K. DONISTHORPE *Guests of Brit. Ants* iii. 78 Ants exhibit a variety of associations, symbiotic, mutualistic, and parasitic... Such associations consist of—Cleptobiosis (originally used to denote thievery, now applied to brigandage by Wheeler); Lestobiosis [etc.]. **1971** E. O. WILSON *Insect Societies* xix. 377/2 As a rule, cleptobiotic aculeates prey on only one or a very few species of other aculeates. *Ibid.* 381/2 Members of the melipomine genus *Lestrimelitta* do engage in nest robbing, or 'cleptobiosis'.

kleptocracy. Add: Also, government by thieves; a nation ruled by this kind of government. (Further examples.)

1968 S. L. ANDRESKI *African Predicament* vii. 109 The essence of kleptocracy is that the functioning of the organs of authority is determined by the mechanisms of supply and demand rather than the laws and regulations. **1971** *Guardian Weekly* 10 July 18 The Federal Republic of Cameroon, which he [*sc.* Leonard Barnes] seems to regard as one of the less wicked kleptocracies. **1975** *Times Lit. Suppl.* 4 July 740/4 The role of corruption within the [Franco] regime..and the growth of a virtual kleptocracy within the administration.

kleptolagnia (kleptolæ·gniă). [mod.L., f. Gr. κλεπτο-, combining form of κλέπτης thief + λαγνεία lust; formed by analogy with *ALGOLAGNIA.] A morbid desire, associated with fetishism, to achieve sexual gratification through theft.

1917 J. C. KIERNAN in *Urologic & Cutaneous Rev.* **1928** H. ELLIS *Stud. Psychol. Sex* VII. viii. 491 Kleptolagnia.. is an effort to attain the direct gratification of the sexual impulse by the aid of emotional energy generated by the excitement of the theft. **1960** HINSIE & CAMPBELL *Psychiatric Dict.* (ed. 3) 414/1 *Kleptolagnia*, a morbid desire to steal. **1969** E. M. BRECHER *Sex Researchers* (1970) ii. 55 *Psychopathia Sexualis* presents cases of satyriasis and nymphomania,..kleptolagnia (sexual arousal through stealing), [etc.]. **1972** *Cumulated Index Medicus* XIII. 7662/2 A case of kleptolagnia.

‖ **kletterschuh** (kle·təɪʃū). Pl. **-schuhe.** [G.] A cloth- or felt-soled light boot worn esp. for rock-climbing; usu. in *pl.* Sometimes colloquially abbrev. to *klets.* Also *attrib.*

1920 J. P. FARRAR in G. W. Young *Mountain Craft* ii. 96 Kletterschuhe are much used in the Dolomites, and..they can be used..not only on dry rocks but also in great climbs... A good kind is the so-called Sexten pattern, the soles of which are built up of layers of cloth. **1950** tr. *Mountaineering Handbk.* (Assoc. Brit. Members Swiss Alpine Club) ii. 23 Kletterschuhe (cloth soled boots) are an advantage for difficult rock climbs because they hold and do not slip. **1951** C. D. MILNER *Dolomites* 88 The usual wear in the Dolomites for many years has been felt-soled *kletterschuhe*... Today *kletterschuhe* and rubber tennis shoes are both used... An interesting compromise..is to have Vibram soles, over a thin leather undersole, on *kletterschuhe* soft uppers. **1963** *Climber* Aug. 11/1 Beginners come to climbing without being aware that there is any kind of mountain footwear other than 'vibs'—barring..the P.A.'s or kletterschuhe to which they eventually hope to aspire. *Ibid.* 12/2 If you're a rock climber rather than an all-round mountaineer..then Vibrams, P.A.'s or 'klets' are the wear for you.

kleywang (klēi·wæŋ). Also † **calewang; kelewang.** [ad. Malay *kĕlewang.*] A single-edged Indonesian sword.

1783 W. MARSDEN *Hist. Sumatra* 277 There are.. weapons of a make between that of a scimitar, and a knife ..as..the calewang. **1839** T. J. NEWBOLD *Pol. & Statistical Acct. Straits of Malacca* I. i. 39 The crew are armed with ..swords (the parang and kleywang). **1900** W. W. SKEAT *Malay Magic* 24 The articles of Malay regalia usually consist of a *silasila*..and a few weapons, generally a *kris, kleywang*, or spear. **1936** G. B. GARDNER *Keris & Other Malay Weapons* 73 *Golok jambu* or the Kĕlantan *kĕlewang*. This is short and curved. *Ibid.* 75 The *sulu kĕlewang*. A single edge sword that gets wider and heavier towards the point.

klieg (klīg). *Cinemat.* Also **kleig** and with capital initial. [f. the name of two brothers, A. T. and J. H. *Kliegl*, who invented it in the U.S.] In full, *klieg light.* **a.** Orig., a kind of arc lamp invented for use as a studio light; hence, any powerful electric light used in film-making, or in television.

1925 *Movie Mag.* Nov. 57/1 The scene in a motion picture studio is eternally the same. It doesn't matter what difference there is in the set which raises its skeleton wings towards the Kleigs. **1927** U. SINCLAIR *Oil!* xiv. 355 The kleigs glare upon them, and a dozen moving picture cameras grind. **1931** A. NADELL *Projecting Sound Pict.* xiv. 250 Klieg (arc) lights are passé; they made too much noise; 1,000-watt incandescents are used. **1932** S. GIBBONS *Cold Comfort Farm* xvii. 237 The sunshine, vivid as a Kleig light, revealed every wrinkle in his melancholy ..face. **1947** AUDEN *Age of Anxiety* II. 39 The polychrome Oval With its kleig lights and crowd engineers. **1951** 'J. WYNDHAM' *Day of Triffids* viii. 141 At the first blink it was as dazzling as a klieg light. **1957** *New Yorker* 13 July 21/1 My brother and I [*sc.* Mr. John H. Kliegl] invented the klieg light around 1911—the first practical light for taking motion pictures indoors. It projected a beam, by means of carbons, that emitted a light of high actinic power. **1967** *Economist* 7 Jan. 40/2 Inaugurated in a blaze of familiar kleig lights. **1969** *Rolling Stone* 28 June 13 The kleig lights shine for a mercifully brief moment upon an aging cosmetic face.

b. klieg eyes, an eye condition caused by exposure to very bright light, characterized by watering and conjunctivitis. Hence *klieg-eyed* adj.

1923 *Sci. Amer.* Oct. 243/1 The burning of the eyeball by the ultra-violet rays... This malady appears so freely among motion-picture actors..that a name, 'Kleig eyes', has been coined for it. **1941** *Amer. Cinematographer* Dec. 589 The ultra-violet glare from those unshielded arcs.. literally sunburned the actors' eyeballs and created the dread malady, 'kleig eye'. **1973** *Rolling Stone* 30 Aug. 38 Most folks got back to San Clemente sated, klieg-eyed and tired.

Kline (klaɪn). *Med.* The name of Benjamin S. *Kline* (b. 1886), U.S. pathologist, used *attrib.* to designate a diagnostic test for syphilis devised by him in which serum, blood, or spinal fluid is mixed on a slide with a lipid antigen and examined under a microscope for precipitation.

1929 *Amer. Jrnl. Syphilis* XIII. 583 (*heading*) The Kline slide precipitation test for syphilis..with a clinical evaluation in syphilitic and non-syphilitic cases. **1944** J. H. STOKES et al. *Mod. Clin. Syphilol.* (ed. 3) x. 471 The Kline finger-puncture blood test procedure avoids the objection of donors to a double venipuncture. **1963** *Amer. Jrnl. Clin. Path.* XL. 551/2 The Kline test with cardiolipin–synthetic lecithin antigen yielded more accurate results in terms of TPI–reactivity than did the tests with cardiolipin–natural lecithin antigens.

Klinefelter (klǝi·nfeltǝɹ). *Med.* The name of Harry Fitch *Klinefelter* (b. 1912), U.S. physician, used in the possessive (less commonly *attrib.*) to designate a syndrome he described (with others) in 1942 which affects males and becomes evident at puberty or after, being characterized by small testes, eunuchoidism, gynæcomastia, and infertility, usu. now restricted to those cases in which the cells have an extra X sex chromosome (most commonly in an XXY constitution, in contrast to the XY of normal males and the XX of normal females).

[**1946** *Med. Jrnl. Austral.* 28 Sept. 446/1 (*heading*) The Klinefelter–Reifenstein–Albright syndrome.] **1950** *Jrnl. Clin. Endocrinol. & Metabolism* X. 630 (*heading*) Dystrophia myotonica, with special reference to endocrine function (Klinefelter's syndrome). *Ibid.* 635 In the 2 male patients the diagnostic criteria for the so-called Klinefelter syndrome were satisfied. **1958** H. J. ROBERTS *Difficult Diagn.* I. i. 37 The evolution of the belief that micro-orchidism with gynecomastia (the Klinefelter syndrome) probably represents a genetic defect in the sex chromosomes. **1964** L. MARTIN *Clin. Endocrinol.* (ed. 4) vi. 209 Apart from these two main XXY and XY types, Klinefelter's syndrome has also been described in variants possessing the chromosomal constitutions of XXXY, XXXXY, and XXYY. **1969** *Nature* 16 Aug. 680/2 Züblin and Pasqualini noted a childishness, shyness, lack of drive and a degree of intellectual impairment in patients with Klinefelter's syndrome. **1970** PASSMORE & ROBSON *Compan. Med. Stud.* II. xxxi. 15/2 The most important findings were that abnormal females with Turner's syndrome were sex chromatin negative like normal males, and that abnormal males with Klinefelter's syndrome were sex chromatin positive like normal females. **1971** *Daily Tel.* (Colour Suppl.) 10 Dec. 20/1 One of the most common physical intersex conditions affecting a minimum of 2·65 males out of every 1,000 is the Klinefelter syndrome.

b. *ellipt.*

1961 DAVIDSON & ROBERTSON SMITH *Proc. Conf. Human Chromosomal Abnormalities* ii. 23 In 5 of the Klinefelter cases our observations were consistent with the belief that the chromosome number was regularly 47. **1967** BARTALOS & BARAMKI *Med. Cytogenetics* x. 155 In Hornstein's experience, only a few of the Klinefelter patients were free from some form of psychopathological traits. **1971** *Daily Tel.* (Colour Suppl.) 10 Dec. 20/1 In Klinefelter there is an extra X chromosome added to the male XY.

Kling (kliŋ). [Malay *Keling* Tamil, ad. *Kalinga* an old name for a strip of coast along the Bay of Bengal.] A disparaging term applied to Indian settlers in Malaysia.

1606 E. SCOTT *Exact Discourse E. Indians* sig. F4 If it were not for the Sabyndar, the Admirall, and one or twoe more, which are Clyn men borne, there were noe liuing for a Christian amongst them. **1625** PURCHAS *Pilgrimes* I. IV. ii. 385 The fifteenth of Iune, heere arriued Nockhoda Tingall a Cling-man from Banda, in a Iaua Iuncke. **1839** T. J. NEWBOLD *Pol. & Statistical Acct. Straits of Malacca* I. i. 8 The Chinese, and the natives from India (Chuliahs and Klings,) are by far the most useful class. **1868** C. COLLINGWOOD *Rambles of Naturalist on Shores & Waters China Sea* xv. 245 The Klings are, indeed, the only people who can contest the field with the Chinese. **1869** A. R. WALLACE *Malay Archipelago* I. ii. 31 The Klings of Western India are a numerous body of Mahometans, and, with many Arabs, are petty merchants and shopkeepers. **1890** KIPLING *Barrack-Room Ballads* (1892) 135 The frigate-bird shall carry my word to the Kling and the Orang-Laut. **1968** *Encycl. Brit.* XIII. 400/1 In Malay usage 'Kling' carried associations of disparagement from the start. It..was replaced by 'Tamil' early in the 20th century.

kling-kling (kli·ŋkliŋ). Also **cling-cling, clinkling, klinkling.** [Echoic.] A Jamaican name for a grackle, *Quiscalus niger.*

1847 GOSSE & HILL *Birds Jamaica* 219 It is to the first of these notes that the bird before us owes his local names of Tinkling, Tintin, Clinkling. **1949** *Caribbean Q.* I. IV. 42 What to Miss Bottome is a tropical bird, is to Vic Reid a pechary or a klinkling. **1955** R. G. TAYLOR *Introd. Birds Jamaica* 11 Kling-kling, a bird of medium size with shining black plumage, pointed beak, a pale yellow eye and long boat-shaped tail. **1960** J. BOND *Birds W. Indies* 217 Greater Antillean Grackle *Quiscalus niger.* Local names: Tinkling; Cling-cling; Ting-ting (Jamaica). **1965** I. FLEMING *Man with Golden Gun* v. 75 Two large black birds.. whirled in... She said, 'We call them kling-klings but learned folk call them Jamaican grackles.'

klino-. Add: **klinokine·sis** [*KINESIS 2], a kinesis in which the movement is one of turning; hence **klinokine·tic** *a.*, **klinokine·tically** *adv.*; similarly **klinota·xis** [TAXIS 6], a taxis in which the movement is one of turning.

1937 D. L. GUNN et al. in *Nature* 18 Dec. 1064/2 We propose to divide kineses into (*a*) ortho-kineses..and (*b*) klino-kineses..—variations in angular velocity. **1954** *New Biol.* XVII. 49 A klino-kinesis (a higher rate of turning in dry than in moist air) is also present [in woodlice]. **1970** R. A. & B. M. MAIER *Compar. Animal Behavior* v. 81 A second category of kinetic response—klinokinesis—involves changes in the rate of turning associated with shifts in the intensity of stimulation. **1940** FRAENKEL & GUNN *Orientation of Animals* v. 45 In some animals there is a klino-kinetic response in which the rate of random turning, or angular velocity, depends on the intensity of stimulation. **1964** *Oceanogr. & Marine Biol.* II. 478 Unoriented klinokinetic movements occur [in two species of Erycinidæ] under uniform overhead light. **1946** *Nature* 13 July 58/2 When behaving photopositively *Hydra* orientates itself klinokinetically. **1940** FRAENKEL & GUNN *Orientation of Animals* vi. 59 The kind of reaction in which these regular deviations are a necessary part of the orientation mechanism is here named klino-taxis. *Ibid.* 75 Klino-taxis is an uncommon type of reaction to light. **1958** *New Biol.* XXVII. 72 A fly larva with a single median eye moves away from a single source of light... The movement involves swinging from side to side; as the eye is illuminated from one side so the swing is away from that side... This swinging motion is a klinotaxis. **1970** R. A. & B. M. MAIER *Compar. Animal Behavior* v. 81 The first type [of taxis]—klinotaxis—involves a series of successive comparisons of the intensity of stimulation.

klip (klip), *sb. S. Afr.* Also dim. **klippie.** [Afrikaans, a. Du. *klip* cliff, rock, stone.] **1.** Also, *blink klip* [Afrikaans *blink* shining]. A diamond; † micaceous iron ore (quot. 1835).

1835 A. SMITH *Diary* 22 Jan. (1939) I. 225 [The Bechuana] mix fat with the blink klip and rub it over the body in moderate quantities, but in great quantities upon the head. **1887** J. W. MATTHEWS *Incwadi Yami, or Twenty Yrs. S. Afr.* xiii. 186 The natives had not yet acquired a knowledge of the value of diamonds or *klips* as they were then termed. **1892** J. R. COUPER *Mixed Humanity* vi. 48 Flogged to death for stealing a 'klip' (as the Dutch and many of the Kaffirs call a diamond). **1893** T. REUNERT *Diamonds & Gold S. Afr.* I. 6 By this time the attention of every one in that neighbourhood was turned to seeking *blink klippe*..and during the following year several diamonds were picked up. **1897** *Pearson's Mag.* July 67/1 Fifteen years on that blathted breakwater, just for being found with a few little klips on you. **1911** L. COHEN *Remin. Kimberley* 35 'I'll show you the klip. Here it is.' With that he pulled out his snuffbox..; inside was a fairly sized beautiful octahedron diamond. **1967** L. G. GREEN *Like Diamond Blazing* xiii. 144, I met old Hottentots who remembered Luderitz; they said he had two little boxes of *blink klippies*..and that he carried these diamonds with him.

2. A stone, pebble.

1852 C. BARTER *Dorp & Veld* vi. 50 Stooping to set large *klips* (stones) behind the wheel, to prevent the wagon from slipping back. **1899** A. WERNER *Captain of Locusts* 63 She left me when we were on the trek over into Basutoland..and the boys and I could only cut a cross on the thorn-tree..and put a heap of klippies to mark the spot.

Hence **klip** *v. trans.*, to place a stone behind (a wheel) in order to prevent a vehicle from rolling backwards.

1878 H. A. ROCHE *On Trek in Transvaal* iv. 91 We crawling into the wagon, the wheels of which were 'klipped', to keep us from running down the hill, trying to nap at intervals.

klipbok (kli·pbǫk). Also **klipbokkie, klipbuck.** [Afrikaans, f. Du. *klip* rock + *bok* buck.] = *KLIPSPRINGER.

1886 G. A. FARINI *Through Kalahari Desert* i. 4 Not even the beasts of the desert, the klip-bok (rock buck), or stein-bok (stone buck)..are to be seen. **1895** J. G. MILLAIS *Breath from Veldt* 92 The most curious thing about the klipbuck is the shape of its feet and the manner in which it uses them in springing up and down its native rocks. **1939** tr. *E. N. Marais's My Friends the Baboons* v. 59 The troop must often have had the chance of catching little klipbuck, dassies, and red hares. **1947** *Cape Argus* (Magazine Section) 23 Oct. 1/9 The dog..brought down a klipbok. **1953** J. R. ELLERMAN et al. *S. Afr. Mammals* 188 *Oreotragus oreotragus* Zimmerman, 1783. Klipspringer. Klipbokkie.

klipdas (kli·pdas). [Afrikaans, f. Du. *klip* rock + *das* badger.] = *DASSIE 1.

1853 *Edin. New Philos. Jrnl.* LV. 214 Basking themselves on the sunny side of the krantzes..may generally be seen several of the Klipdas, Cony, Rock Rabbit, or Cape Hyrax (*H. capensis*). **1886** P. GILLMORE *Hunter's Arcadia* xxvi. 248 From this descendant of Holland..I bought..the skins of some rock rabbits, the *klip das* of the Dutch. **1953** J. R. ELLERMAN et al. *S. Afr. Mammals* 157 *Procavia capensis* Pallas, 1766. Dassie; Hyrax. Klipdas. Distribution: one of the commonest mammals in the Union.

klipfish (kli·pfiʃ). Also **clipfish, klepvis, klippfish, -fisch, klipvissie.** [ad. Du. *klipvisch* (f. *klip* rock) and Da. *klipfisk* (f. *klippe* rock).] **1.** *S. Afr.* A viviparous, brightly-coloured, marine fish of the family Clinidæ, living in shallow water or rock pools.

[**1731** G. MEDLEY tr. *Kolb's Present State Cape Good-Hope* I. xx. 256 The Hottentots frequently take Abundance of a Sort of Fish, call'd Rock-fish. These are Fish without Scales.] **1790** E. HELME tr. *Le Vaillant's Trav. Afr.* I. ii. 22 The *klepvis*..is without scales, and taken among the rocks on the sea shore. **1806** J. BARROW *Trav. S. Afr.* (ed. 2) II. i. 38 The *Klip* or rock-fish, the *Blennius viviparus*, makes no bad fry. **1838** J. E. ALEXANDER *Expedition Interior Afr.* I. iv. 88 Abundance of excellent fish are to be procured here; such as the delicious Roman fish, Hottentot, 'Jacob Fever', mullet, stump nose, and clip fish. **1876, 1893** [see *KINGKLIP]. **1902** *Trans. S. Afr. Philos. Soc.* XI. 224 Several names, or parts of names, are derived from the localities in which the fish are found. Thus we have..Klip Visch, Steen Klip Visch (a peculiar redundancy). **1953** U. KRIGE *Dream & Desert* i. 14 They had..gazed into rockpools full of starfish, slowly waving sea plants and green-and-gold *klipvissies* drifting lazily from crevice to crevice. **1969** *Nature* 8 Nov. 540/1 The shores of South Africa are enlivened by a group of typically littoral viviparous fishes known locally as klipfishes (but as clinids to the academic). **1973** *Farmer's Weekly* (S. Afr.) 18 Apr. 102 The klipfish is fried in butter and carefully filleted on the plate with knife and fork.

2. A codfish split open, boned, salted, and dried.

1835 *Penny Cycl.* IV. 273/2 The klip-fish is cut along the back, and the back-bone taken out, after which it is salted down in the bottom of the vessel. **1881** S. WALPOLE in *20th Ann. Rep. Salmon Fisheries 1880* 23 in *Parl. Papers* (C 2901) XXIII. 299 Cod are either cured as stock fisch or as klipp fisch... The klipp fish are split and boned before they are salted. **1925** J. T. JENKINS *Fishes Brit. Isles* 136 The bulk of the cod caught in the northern fisheries is split open, washed, and salted in pickle and then dried on rocks (Klippen). This is the so-called Klipp-fish. **1961** H. ANGERMAN et al. in Borgstrom & Heighway *Atlantic Ocean Fisheries* 80/2 The klipfish is subjected to more complicated treatment than the stockfish.

klipkous (kli·pkōus). *S. Afr.* Also **klipkoes, klipkos.** [Afrikaans, f. Du. *klip* rock + *kous* stocking.] = SEA-EAR 1; *ABALONE.

1731 G. MEDLEY tr. *Kolb's Present State Cape Good-Hope* II. 209 The *Klip-Kousen* are sometimes call'd, by the Virtuosi, *Nabel*-Snails. **1785** G. FORSTER tr. *Sparrman's Voy. Cape Good Hope* I. ii. 26 A sort of snail or cockle, *klipkous* (*Haliotis*, Linn.) from half a foot to a foot and a half diameter, is usually stewed, but makes in my opinion a very unsavoury dish. **1843** J. C. CHASE *Cape of Good Hope* vii. 168 Klip Kous... A shell fish, most delicious, but requiring much trouble in the preparation. **1910** D. FAIRBRIDGE *That which hath Been* xxv. 303 The first muscadel grapes and the finest klip-kous from the rocks had invariably found their way across the sands to Meerlust. **1930** C. L. BIDEN *Sea-Angling Fishes of Cape* xviii. 260 The crushed remains of klipkoes or venus ear—a shellfish, *Haliotis*. **1947** L. G. GREEN *Tavern of Seas* viii. 66 The perlemoen or klipkous, largest and most beautiful of Cape shellfish. **1950** M. MASSON *Birds of Passage* iii. 41 Souvenirs, among which was a Venus ear or klipkos whose brown crust had been scraped away to reveal the iridescent shell. **1966** H. J. DUCKITT *Bk. Recipes* 73 The Perlemoen, or Klipkous (stone-stocking) a species of shellfish found on many parts of the South African coast, adhering to the rocks.

klippe (kli·pǝ). *Geol.* Also **Klippe.** Pl. **klippes, ‖-en.** [a. G. *klippe* partly or totally submerged rock.] A part of a nappe which has become detached from its parent mass by sliding or by erosion of intervening parts.

1902 *Encycl. Brit.* XXV. 333/2 These [structures], called Klippen, are abrupt pyramidal masses, the beds in the upper part being not only older than those in the lower, but also 'contorted, fractured, crushed, and mixed up', while the newer are comparatively undisturbed. **1912** *Smithsonian Misc. Coll.* LVI. No. 31. 12 It is well known that some of these isolated masses, those of the Klippes, are 'exotic'; that is to say, no strata of the same facies have ever been found in place. **1942** O. D. VON ENGELN *Geomorphol.* xv. 332 Klippen are peculiar in that, unlike the outliers which persist beyond the main front of a weathering escarpment, and which have younger beds capping older strata, they have older beds over younger beds. **1954** W. D. THORNBURY *Princ. Geomorphol.* x. 273 Chief Mountain, Montana, is a well-known example of a klippe, in which an isolated mass of Pre-Cambrian rock rests upon Cretaceous beds. **1969** M. G. RUTTEN *Geol. W. Europe* xi. 239 Further southwest, these isolated klippen ..merge into a continuous nappe.

klippie: see *KLIP *sb.*

klipspringer. Substitute for def.: A small African antelope, *Oreotragus oreotragus.* Add later examples.

1907 P. FITZPATRICK *Jock of Bushveld* 245 The dainty little klipspringers led them many a crazy dance along the crags and ledges of the mountain face, jumping from rock to rock. **1936** R. CAMPBELL *Mithraic Emblems* 68, I always thought to be A klipspringer or chamois. **1947** J. STEVENSON-HAMILTON *Wild Life S. Afr.* xvi. 115 The klipspringer (*Oreotragus oreotragus*). *Ibid.*, The ubiquitous klipspringer, truly the chamois of Ethiopia. **1960** *Times* 29 Sept. (Nigeria Suppl.) p. xxi/5 But two other local races special to Nigeria, of that curious little pithy-haired antelope, the Klipspringer,..seem doomed. **1972** L. VAN DER POST *Story Like Wind* vi. 180 This man in front of him wore nothing except a loin-cloth of soft yellow klipspringer leather.

Klischograph (kli·ʃograf). *Printing.* [f. G. *klischee* stereotype or electrotype plate: see -GRAPH.] The proprietary name of a type of electronic engraving plate (see quots. 1955 and 1963).

1955 *Trade Marks Jrnl.* 16 Mar. 288/1 Klischograph... Machines for making printers' blocks, printers' cliches and printers' formes; and plain and engraved printers' plates. Dr. Ing. Rudolf Hell.., Kiel-Dietrichsdorf, Germany; Manufacturer. **1963** *Times* 17 July 6/7 In the field of electronic engraving a German firm, Dr. Ing. Rudolf Hell,

are demonstrating their latest type of klischograph. This consists of an electronic scanning instrument, capable of dealing with both black and white and multi-colour reproductions, which operates an engraving stylus to produce a gravure cylinder. Preparation of gravure cylinders can be a lengthy business, and this process, it is claimed, can reduce the time taken from several days to a matter of hours. **1967** KARCH & BUBER *Offset Processes* ii. 20 These machines [*sc.* electronic platemakers] include the models of..Klischograph, Photo-lathe and Elgramma.

klister (kli·stəɹ). *Skiing.* [Norw. *klister* paste.] A soft wax for applying to the running surface of skis to facilitate movement, used esp. in warm weather.

1936 B. LUNN tr. *Hallberg & Mückenbrünn's Compl. Bk. Ski-ing* iv. 39 We specially recommend the following waxes: Ostbye (Medium..Klister); Bratlie (Nysnö.. Klister). **1948** —— *Ski-ing Primer* xix. 95 Klister..is generally sold in tubes. There are many brands. **1951** EUGEN & ATWATER *Ski with Sverre* xi. 94 For wet snow, well above freezing, use a soft klister type wax.

klob: see next.

klobbiyos (klǫ·biyǫs). *Cards.* Also **klaberjass, klobbyosh, klobiosk,** etc. [ad. G. *klaberjass,* f. Du. *klaverjas* a type of piquet.] A type of piquet, esp. popular with eastern European Jews. Also in shortened form **klob.**

1892 I. ZANGWILL *Childr. Ghetto* I. 124 They played loo, 'klobbiyos', napoleon, vingt-et-un. **1928** *Daily Tel.* 6 Nov. 9/2 Dice, nap, and klobiosk were played... The Magistrate: What is klobiosk? Inspector Dyer: It is similar to the English game known as 'Five hundred'. **1937** D. RUNYON *More than Somewhat* 10, I find Little Isadore playing klob with a guy. **1946** MOREHEAD & MOTT-SMITH *Penguin Hoyle* 94 Klaberjass, a game for two players, is better-known under corrupted names—Clobber, Clob, and the like and particularly under the name Kalabrias, which is a popular Hungarian game. **1946** MEZZROW & WOLFE *Really Blues* ii. 20 Easygoing guys who spent half their lives playing klabiasch, pinochle, and tarok. **1961** A. SMITH *East-Enders* ix. 159 They will create a few private gambling hells... There will be klobby-osh and strip poker.

klockmannite (klǫ·kmænəit). *Min.* [ad. G. **klockmannit** (P. Ramdohr 1928, in *Centralbl. f. Mineral.* A. 226), f. the name of F. F. H. *Klockmann* (1858–1937), Ger. mineralogist: see -ITE[1].] A slate-grey selenide of copper, CuSe, found impure as granular aggregates and synthesized as crystal plates.

1939 *Mineral. Mag.* XXV. 295 Another copper selenide from the same locality [*sc.* Sierra de Umango, Argentina] has since been named klockmannite. **1969** *Acta Crystallogr.* XV B.2420 (*heading*) Twinning in the superlattice structure of CuSe, synthetic klockmannite.

‖ **klomp** (klǫmp). *S. Afr.* Also **clompie, clumpjie, klompie, klompje, klumpjie.** [Afrikaans, f. Du. *klomp*: see CLUMP *sb.*] A group, esp. of animals.

1853 W. R. KING *Campaigning in Kaffirland* 215 Even at three quarters of a mile, we were able to disperse small 'clumpjies' of Kaffirs and cattle. **1861** T. BAINES *Jrnl.* 25 Nov. in *Explor. S.-W. Afr.* (1864) ix. 241 Snyman also saw nothing except one 'klumpjie' of kameels. **1896** H. A. BRYDEN *Tales S. Afr.* 70 Rather suddenly we came upon a *klompje* of giraffe. **1920** F. C. CORNELL *Glamour of Prospecting* xi. 170 Next day we were off well before sun-up, anxious to shoot something for the pot, but it was not till late in the afternoon that Pouley spotted a *klomp* of springbok. **1937** S. CLOETE *Turning Wheels* xxviii. 434 We saw some of them [*sc.* cattle]..a big clompie of a thousand head or more. **1963** —— *Rags of Glory* v. 44 Great *klompies* of them [*sc.* stallions] could live together with hardly a serious quarrel till a female came along.

klompie (klǫ·mpi). *S. Afr.* Also **klompje.** [Afrikaans, f. Du. *klomp* a small blue brick + Afrikaans *-ie* a dim. ending.] A type of brick.

1926 S. G. MILLIN *South Africans* IV. ii. 111 Open hearths outlined in stone or in the small bricks called *klompjes.* **1949** L. G. GREEN *In Land of Afternoon* xv. 199 When you step on to the klompie brick stoep and into the low cool rooms..you are in a more leisurely world. **1950** *Cape Times* 4 Mar. 11/8 (Advt.), Golden Brown Klompies 9 in. × 4 in. × 1¾ in. and 2,500 face bricks.

Klondike (klǫ·ndəik), *sb.* Also **Klondyke.** [f. the Kutchin name *tron-duik* hammer river, a tributary of the Yukon River.] **1.** The name of a region (and river) in the Yukon, NW. Canada, the scene of a gold-rush in the years following 1896. Hence many *attrib.* uses, as *Klondyke fever,* (*gold*) *rush,* etc., applied to this period and to the life lived during it. **b.** *ellipt.* as *sb.,* a mine or quarry of valuable material.

1897 *Slocan* (B.C.) *Pioneer* 31 July 4/2 The Klondike fever has struck Slocan City in a mild form. **1897** *Athenæum* 9 Oct. 483/3 The rich Klondyke of Malory and Geoffrey of Monmouth had not escaped the eyes of previous prospectors. **1898** *Century Mag.* Mar. 697/2 These men made their way home, as best they could, out of the wreckage of the first Klondike rush. **1898** *T. Eaton & Co. Catal.* Spring & Summer 124 Men's Klondike mining coats... Men's Klondike sleeping bag... Men's Klondike shirts. **1912** H. FOOTNER *New Rivers of North* 192 We guessed that we were upon the spot where our last white predecessors had made camp in the year of the Klondike rush. **1948** *Life* 2 Feb. 49/3, 78-year-old Emil J. N. Ott,.. a veteran of the Klondike Rush, who smelts rough gold into ingots. **1958** *Encycl. Canadiana* VI. 15 (*caption*) Hundreds watch as the *Australia*..leaves Seattle for the North at the height of the Klondike fever. **1961** *Tamarack Rev.* XIX. 4 For a long time, before the Klondike days, there was a feud and a battle between them two logging camps. **1964** *Edmonton* (Alberta) *Jrnl.* 11 July 3/6 The past 60 years have obscured or distorted the extraordinary strength and endurance, and the Klondike wealth of the erstwhile sourdough who became a legendary character during his own lifetime. **1965** *Star Weekly* (Toronto) 2 Jan. 37/2 Mrs. MacCleave was a young girl at the height of the Klondike gold rush. **1973** *Times* 1 Feb. 12/8 He combed the reports of Congressional committees rarely read or reported by others. It was a new Klondike.

2. A card-game played with a single pack of fifty-two, the object being to see how many cards can be built up in sequence and suit on a row of aces. *N. Amer.*

1902 L. MCKEE *Land of Nome* 163 All the games were going—roulette, vingt-et-un,.. Klondike, and craps. **1908** U. SINCLAIR *Metropolis* vi. 91 The smoking-room, where the stout little Major had gotten a group of young bloods about him to play 'Klondike'. **1910** R. SERVICE *Trail of '98* 183 There were crap-tables,..the Klondike game, Keno, stud poker, roulette and faro outfits. **1946** MOREHEAD & MOTT-SMITH *Penguin Hoyle* 174 Klondike is probably the most widely known solitaire game. **1953** J. WALKER *Pardon my Parka* (1958) 127 We sat around.. and we played a vicious gambling patience called Klondike..which cost me a vast amount of money. **1968** *Encycl. Brit.* XX. 875/2 Many solitaires can be played by two, but Klondike is by far the favourite for this purpose.

3. The name given to a herring fishery off the W. coast of Scotland. (Cf. *KLONDIKE *v.*)

1929 W. KEIR *Herring Trade on Continent 1928* 16 In the early part of the season the trawlers fished mostly on the 'Klondyke' grounds off the West Coast of Scotland.

Klo·ndike, *v.* Also **Klondyke,** and with small initial. [See prec., sense 3.] *trans.* To export (fresh herring) (as opp. to pickled herring).

1923 *Glasgow Herald* 25 Oct. 6 A regular fleet of steamers 'Klondyking' or running the fresh fish direct from the various landing ports to Germany. **1930** *Aberdeen Press & Jrnl.* 30 Jan. 8 If a boycott was attempted, they would klondyke their supplies into the Dutch and other markets. **1930** *Morning Post* 2 Aug., Reference is made to the quantities of herrings 'klondyked'—which means despatched fresh to the Continent. **1945** [see *BISMARCK 3].

Klondiker (klǫ·ndəikəɹ). Also **Klondyker.** [f. *KLONDIKE *sb.* + -ER[1].] **1.** A prospector in the Klondike. Also *transf.*

1897 *Brit. Columbia Mining Jrnl.* (Ashcroft, B.C.) 9 Oct. 1/6 The venturesome Klondiker who may select this valley as his road to the diggings may rest assured that his daily bill of fare will not only be ample but of good variety. **1901** *Daily Colonist* (Victoria, B.C.) 5 Nov. 3/2 Steamer Amur arrived from Skagway and way ports early this morning, with gold, salmon, and many Klondikers, among her 78 passengers. **1904** BURGESS & IRWIN *Picaroons* 102 The Story of the Returned Klondyker. **1917** *Dialect Notes* IV. 420 Terms from New Orleans. *Klondiker,* an heiress-hunter. **1954** A. M. BEZANSON *Sodbusters invade Peace* 4 There's an old trail that some Klondikers tried to take their outfits over.

2. An exporter of or dealer in fresh herring from the Scottish fisheries; a ship used for this.

1926 *Glasgow Herald* 19 Dec. 8 The 'Klondykers' are.. the German boats which buy the herring and transport them for sale in Germany. **1938** L. MACNEICE *I crossed Minch* II. xii. 166 The herring fishing was nothing here now. He remembered when the German Klondikers used to come into Loch Seaforth and buy [herrings] from the natives on the spot. **1953** *Press & Jrnl.* (Aberdeen) 17 June, The klondykers, however, sent only about one-third of the 1951 quantity of fresh herring to Western Germany. **1971** *Stornoway Gaz.* 7 Aug. 3/3 The first Klondyker of the season, from Norway, arrived at Stornoway during the week-end for a cargo of herring.

Klondiking (klǫ·ndəikiŋ), *vbl. sb.* Also **Klondyking,** and with small initial. [f. *KLONDIKE *v.* + -ING[1].] **1.** Prospecting in the Klondike during the gold-rush period.

1900 J. LONDON *Let.* 31 Jan. (1966) 87, I spoke at length in previous letter concerning my tramping and Klondiking.

2. Dealing in or exporting fresh herring from the Scottish fisheries.

1927 J. T. JENKINS *Herring* 146 While trawled herring are unsuitable for pickling, they are well adapted for 'Klondyking'—a method of preparing herring for export practically fresh by sprinkling them with salt and ice. **1930** P. F. ANSON *Fishing Boats & Fisher Folk E. Coast Scotl.* 20 On an average about 12 per cent [of the herring catch] is exported fresh to Germany. This freshing export trade is known as 'klondyking'. **1973** *Stornoway Gaz.* 27 Jan. 1/1 The herring was disposed of as follows: Freshing and kippering—27 crans; klondyking—3,565 crans. **1973** *Courier & Advertiser* (Dundee) 21 Feb. 9/1 Ullapool.—Herring 3420 crans—1430 crans for home market, £5·50 to £6·70; 220 for freezing, £4·60 to £5; 120 for canning, £4·50 to £5; 1650 for klondyking.

klong (klǫŋ). Also **khlong.** [Thai.] In Thailand, a canal. Also *attrib.*

1898 E. YOUNG *Kingdom Yellow Robe* ii. 26 When agricultural enterprise led to the formation of inland settlements, no roads were made..but canals or 'khlongs' were cut instead. **1928** *Daily Express* 13 Mar. 12/4 A broad flat field..beribboned with klongs (canals). *Ibid.,* Millions of happy frogs sing in high shrill voices, perched on the banks of the klongs. **1967** *Nat. Geographic* July 81 Where were the *klongs* of yesteryear, all those colorful canals, crisscrossing the city, that had made travel agents abroad burble about Bangkok as the Venice of the East? **1970** M. PEREIRA *Pigeon's Blood* i. 10 A wooden jetty on the banks of one of the numerous klongs, or canals, which intersected the city. **1972** *Nation* (Bangkok) 22 Nov. 4/4 He had made a survey of the plant and found that the water released from the ponds into the nearby klongs and later to the Chao Phya river needed to be medically treated.

‖ **klonkie** (klǫ·ŋki). *S. Afr.* [Afrikaans, a blending of *klein* small and *jong* small boy + dim. suff. *-kie.*] A coloured boy; occas., an African boy; a coloured man.

[**1913** PETTMAN *Africanderisms* 268 *Klong*..is in common use in various parts of South Africa, and is applied to coloured males without reference to age, much as the word 'boy' is among the English colonists.] **1953** A. PATON *Too Late the Phalarope* viii. 58 The small *klonkies* from the black people's location..liked to hang around the store. **1955** D. JACOBSON *Trap* i. 32 Strained and shy, the boy's voice came: 'Good night, baas. Thank you, baas.' 'Good night, *klonkie*,' Van Schoor replied. **1960** D. LYTTON *Goddam White Man* iv. 102 But don't tell me the coloured klonkie living in those huts on the farm feels shame at his failure to provide better for his kids.

klooch (klūtʃ). *NW. Amer.* Also **klootch.** [Chinook Jargon (from Nootka) *klootchman* woman.] An Indian woman, a squaw. Also (variously spelt) **kloo·chman.**

Quot. 1861 illustrates the erroneous form *kloochwoman.* **1837** H. BEAVER *Let.* 10 Mar. (1959) 38 'Klout-che-man' is the term used to express the whole female sex, in whatever degree of relationship, whether rational or irrational. **1860** *Brit. Colonist* (Victoria, B.C.) 24 Mar. 2/3 About 75 Cape Flattery Indians arrived in canoes yesterday..on a visit to the Songish tribe, for the purpose of buying a *clootchman* for their chief. **1861** in C. Maiden *Lighted Journey: Story of B.C. Electric* (1948) 1, I perceived two clootch-vimmen a' standin' outside of a 'ouse, and they was a-laughing at me. **1865** G. STUART *Montana as it Is* 83 Oregon is the place to hear the 'Chinnook' in all its glory; it has 'played' the English language 'square out' in that land of..'cloockmans' and camus. **1897** M. H. E. HAYNE *Pioneers of Klondyke* 25 The klūtch (short for klūtchman, the local name for squaws) dress exactly like the men. **1901** *Daily Colonist* (Victoria, B.C.) 8 Oct. 3/1 Old klootchmen were to be seen with their arms filled with all kinds of goods. **1907** R. DUNN *Shameless Diary of Explorer* iv. 28 Starved dogs, half-naked children, shawled klootches, bucks in prospectors' old clothes, all gathered, stared, shook hands, clucked questions. **1945** R. W. SERVICE *Ploughman of Moon* 176 In the old days he had taken up with a klootchman, and had written home, saying he was married to an Indian Princess. *Ibid.,* On one side of me I had a klootch with a papoose tied to her back. **1956** *Beaver* Summer 44 The Indians had respected the promises of the Great White Queen—or as she was known—'King George's Klootchman'—and they relied upon the word of the Hudson's Bay Company. **1966** H. MARRIOTT *Cariboo Cowboy* vi. 58 An Indian 'klootch' with three kids playing around the tent. **1969** *Islander* (Victoria, B.C.) 31 Aug. 10/2 Jenny, a Klootchman as Indian women were called, washed, ironed, sewed on buttons and mended.

klops (klǫps). [Ger.] A type of meat-ball or meat-loaf.

1936 I. S. ROMBAUER *Joy of Cooking* (ed. 2) 89/2 German meat balls. (Koenigsberger Klops). **1966** L. DAVIDSON *Long Way to Shiloh* ix. 132 The proprietor was eating a plate of klops at the next table. **1972** N. FROUD *Some of our Best Recipes are Jewish* 75 Klops is an East European improved version of a meat loaf.

Klucker, var. *KLUXER.

† **klumene** (klū·mīn). *Chem. Obs.* [f. mod.L. *kalium* potassium (see quot. 1900) + -ENE.] = ACETYLENE.

1853 H. WATTS tr. *Gmelin's Hand-bk. Chem.* VIII. 150 A carbide of potassium..gives off, when immersed in water, a peculiar combustible gas, which is klumene gas. **1900** V. B. LEWES *Acetylene* iii. 63 Edmund Davy, in 1836, named the newly-discovered gas bicarburet of hydrogen..; whilst later the name 'klumene' was bestowed upon it, because it had been derived from a kalium compound—potassium carbide. **1901** *Oxf. Univ. Gaz.* 3 Dec. 204 Olefine and Klumene Compounds. **1902** *Encycl. Brit.* XXV. 35/1 *Acetylene,* klumene or ethine, is one of the gaseous compounds of hydrogen and carbon.

klunk (klɒŋk). *U.S. slang.* Also **clunk.** [Of unknown origin.] A derogatory designation for a person.

1942 BERREY & VAN DEN BARK *Amer. Thes. Slang* § 396 Klunk [in list of terms of disparagement for a person]. **1959** N. MAILER *Advts. for Myself* (1961) 399 What was unique about Jones was that he had come out of nowhere, self-taught, a clunk in his lacks. **1964** S. BELLOW *Herzog* (1965) 78 He sat there, in her own words, like a clunk, bored, resentful. **1964** *N.Y. Herald-Tribune* 2 Jan. 8/1 Mr. Wagner has been a remarkably good mayor, and the klunks who don't realize this, they add, understand neither the Mayor himself nor the nature of his responsibilities.

klutz (klɒts). *U.S. slang.* Also **klotz, kluhtz.** [Yiddish, f. G. *klotz,* lit. = wooden block. Cf. CLOT *sb.*] A clumsy, awkward person, esp. one considered socially inept; a fool. Also as *v.* So **klu·tzy** *a.,* awkward, foolish.

1965 *Sat. Rev.* (U.S.) 28 Aug. 51/2 The dancers look good and the artists look a little *klutzy*. **1968** F. MULLALLY *Munich Involvement* i. 10 Look, I feel a bit of a klutz in this crumpled day suit. **1968** L. ROSTEN *Joys of Yiddish* 185 Two *klutzes* were discussing their wives. **1970** L. M. FEINSILVER *Taste of Yiddish* 276 Recent bilingual jokes about Christmas, like 'Santa *Kluhtz*'. *Ibid.* 303 Choreographer Kenneth MacMillan has attempted a compromise between dancing and acting that too often leaves Nureyev..with nothing to do but klutz around the stage. **1970** *New Yorker* 17 Jan. 72 The sad, klutzy ballerinas of the Music Hall pollute children's first live experience of dance. **1970** *Time* 2 Nov. 83 Basically I'm the klutz who makes a terrific entrance to the party and then trips and falls and walks around with food in her hair. **1973** E.-J. BAHR *Nice Neighbourhood* ix. 99 Janet is an utter klotz.

Kluxer (klɒ·ksəɹ). *U.S.* Also **Klucker.** [f. (KU-)KLUX (KLAN) + -ER[1].] A member of the Ku-Klux Klan. Also *attrib.*

1879 A. W. TOURGÉE *Fool's Errand* xxvii. 141 Ef dere's any mo' Kluckers raidin' roun' Burke's Corners, dar'll be some funerals tu. **1923** *Nation* (N.Y.) 21 Nov. 570 We are not much impressed with the desireability of organizations specially formed to fight the 'Kluxers'. **1929** *Sun* (Baltimore) 31 Jan. 1/2 Johnston is disowned by the kluxers or whatever is left of them in Oklahoma. **1944** J. S. PENNELL *Hist. Rome Hanks* 176 Are you a Klucker, Mr. Ocamb? **1948** *Daily Ardmoreite* (Ardmore, Okla.) 25 July 20/4 Some 20 more noted Kluxers..and similar ragtag and bobtail were on hand. **1963** D. B. HUGHES *Expendable Man* (1964) v. 146 There's not going to be any color business in this case. I'm not going to have it messed up with Kluxers or with bleeding hearts. **1965** C. COLTER in A. Chapman *New Black Voices* (1972) 72 Jus' ask her t' pull up that Kluxer sheet and show you her arm.

Hence **Klu·xery,** conduct or behaviour characteristic of members of the Ku-Klux Klan; **Klu·xism,** the principles and practice of the Ku-Klux Klan or of similar organizations.

1929 *Sun* (Baltimore) 31 Jan. 2/2 When Henry Johnston announced for Governor, carrying the flambeau of kluxism, Mrs. Hammonds became his Joan of Arc. **1949** *Richmond* (Virginia) *Times-Dispatch* 23 Jan. IV. 2-D/2 There have been too many episodes in the Old Dominion of late which reflect the spirit of kluxery.

klydonograph (kləidōu·nogrɑf). *Electr. Engin.* [f. Gr. κλύδων wave, billow + -O + -GRAPH.] An instrument for making a photographic record from which the voltage and polarity of a surge can be inferred, consisting of a point electrode resting (in darkness) on a stationary or moving film behind which is a plate electrode.

1924 J. F. PETERS in *Electr. World* 19 Apr. 769 (*heading*) The Klydonograph. An instrument for accurately measuring and recording voltage surges. *Ibid.* 769/1 The word 'klydonograph' was coined by Dr. Roscoe M. Ihrig of the Carnegie Institute of Technology. **1940** *Nature* 22 June 982/1 Three klydonographs were coupled to the line by means of concentric-cylinder type capacitance 'potential-dividers'. **1963** D. J. MALAN *Physics of Lightning* xi. 92 Since the Klydonograph indicates voltage, it is necessary to know the surge impedance of the system of conductors in order to calculate the peak current.

klystron (kləi·strɒn). *Electronics.* Also **Klystron** (now *rare*). [f. Gr. κλύζειν (stem κλυσ-) to wash or break over + *-TRON.] An electron tube for amplifying or generating microwave signals in which a beam of electrons from a thermionic cathode is passed through a gap in a cavity resonator across which is applied a high-frequency voltage, so that the electrons collect into bunches and on reaching a second gap induce a (larger) high-frequency voltage across it. Freq. *attrib.*, as *klystron oscillator, tube.*

1939 R. H. & S. F. VARIAN in *Jrnl. Appl. Physics* X. 324/1 Such an apparatus we call a 'klystron', from the Greek verb 'klyzo', expressing the breaking of waves on a beach. **1945** H. D. SMYTH *Gen. Acct. Devel. Atomic Energy Mil. Purposes* xi. 118 The varying electric field.. introduces small, periodic variations in ion velocity, and has the effect of causing the ions to 'bunch' at a certain distance down the tube. (This same principle is used in the klystron high-frequency oscillator...) **1959** G. TROUP *Masers* i. 1 In conventional microwave amplifiers and oscillators such as the Klystron, an alternating electromagnetic field interacts with elementary particles, electrons, by virtue of their charge. **1959** *New Scientist* 19 Nov. 982/3 The Jodrell radar pulses originated in a big ultra-high-frequency valve of the type known as a klystron. **1964** *Listener* 16 Apr. 626 (Advt.), EEV 25 kW klystrons are being supplied to the British Broadcasting Corporation for use in the new UHF television transmitters. **1973** *Sci. Amer.* Sept. 74/3 The microwaves are produced by a pair of 30-kilowatt klystron tubes powered by a diesel generator.

K(-)meson. Also (*rare*) **k meson.** *Nuclear Physics.* [f. *K* (in *K(-)PARTICLE) + *MESON[3].] = *KAON.

1954 *Phil. Mag.* XLV. 1219 The mass of the K-meson, measured by ionization-range is $970 \pm 100\ m_e$. **1954** *Physical Rev.* XCIV. 1794/2 All the *K* mesons observed lived at least 2×10^{-9} sec before coming to rest in the emulsion. **1964** *Listener* 30 Apr. 711/1 Usually the beams consist of particles called pi-mesons which have 270 times the mass of the electron, or the more exotic K-mesons with about 1,000 electron masses. K-meson beams have been particularly valuable recently in the production of further new particles. **1968** M. S. LIVINGSTON *Particle Physics* iv. 81 The new particles were of two basic types: *k* mesons with mass values less than nucleon mass, now called kaons; and hyperons, with masses greater than the nucleon mass. **1973** L. J. TASSIE *Physics Elem. Particles* ix. 84 There are two kinds of neutral *K*-mesons, the K^0 and the $\overline{K^0}$.

Hence **K-me·sic** *a.* = *KAONIC *a.*

1958 *Phil. Mag.* III. 33 Negative K-mesons captured by the heavy nuclei in nuclear emulsion form K-mesic atoms. **1967** *Comments Nucl. & Particle Physics* I. 112 *K*-mesic x-rays from Li, Be, B, and C.

knacker, *sb.*[1] Add: **3.** *pl.* The testicles. *slang.*

1866 T. EDMONDSTON *Etym. Gloss. Shetland & Orkney Dial.* 76 *Nackers*, testes, S. **1877** in E. PEACOCK *Gloss. Words Manley & Corringham, Lincolnshire* 150/2. **1889** BARRÈRE & LELAND *Dict. Slang* I. 523/2 *Knackers*... (Butchers, &c.), the testicles, also 'knuckers'. **1922** JOYCE *Ulysses* 576 Eh, Harry, give him a kick in the knackers. **1940** J. CARY *Charley is my Darling* xlv. 261 I'll murder the bastards... I'll take the knackers offen them. **1951** *Landfall* Sept. 177 Sling your hook out of this dump before it gets you by the knackers. **1969** G. GREENE *Travels with my Aunt* I. v. 42, I may regret him for a while tonight. His knackers were superb.

knacker, *sb.*[3] Add: **2.** *knacker's yard*: Also *transf.* and *fig.*

1961 F. H. BURGESS *Dict. Sailing* 128 *Knacker's yard*, the shipbreaker's yard. **1966** 'L. LANE' *ABZ of Scouse* 59 *Knacker's yard*: said of a place that looks a complete mess. **1967** T. GUNN *Touch* 42 The graveyard is the sea...They have all come who sought distinction hard To this universal knacker's yard.

knacker (næ·kəɹ), *v. slang.* [f. KNACKER[3] 2 or *KNACKER *sb.*[1] 3.] *trans.* To kill; to castrate; usu. in weakened sense, to exhaust, to wear out. So as an imprecation. Freq. as *pa. pple.* or *ppl. a.*

1886 H. BAUMANN *Londinismen* 90/2 *Knacker*, umbringen; he's knackered, er ist abgemurkst worden. **1936** B. PENTON *Inheritors* ix. 72 Coons is cheap. They'd knacker us white bushmen if they got the chance and let them Chows and Jimmy Tannas breed like rabbits. **1946** *Penguin New Writing* XXVII. 79 His eyes narrowed but he knew I had him knackered. **1959** M. PUGH *Chancer* vi. 86 'Wasn't it Major Fleming with the Bren-gun?' 'Major Fleming be knackered. It was Ramsay.' **1963** *New Society* 22 Aug. 5/1 Other adoptions are 'get knotted' and 'knackered' which have come to mean innocently enough, 'go to hell', and '*kaput*'. **1971** B. W. ALDISS *Soldier Erect* 258 Gor-Blimey came up, panting like a dog. 'I'm knackered,' he said. Blood was streaming down his face from a cut on his temple. **1971** *Times* 21 May 8/7, I kept thinking I should whip up the pace and then I'd think 'I'm knackered, I'll leave it for another lap.' **1973** C. BONINGTON *Next Horizon* xxi. 283 We've been above Base Camp for twenty-eight days. If we had to go back to carrying now we'd have to go all the way back down for a rest. We're just too knackered to carry. **1975** *Sunday Times* (Colour Suppl.) 23 Feb. 25/2 Oot a' mornin' daein' thae miracles. I'm *knackered*! Gie's a glass o' that wine. Nae kiddin' son, I'm knackered.

knackwurst (na·kvūɹst). Also **knockwurst.** [Ger.] A type of German sausage.

1939 M. BRINIG *Anne Minton's Life* (1940) 241 This very second, with us full of beer and knackwurst and sauerkraut.., there's nothing to worry about. **1965** *House & Garden* Jan. 60 *Knockwurst, knackwurst*, a sausage similar to but larger than the frankfurter, and more highly seasoned. **1968** *Washington Post* 5 July A 19/3 (Advt.), Foremost knockwurst, kosher style. **1968** A. WHITNEY *Every Man has his Price* xvii. 147 The waiter came, and they ordered—Knackwurst for Deb, and a dish improbably called Kalbshaxe for Robin. **1970** 'E. LATHEN' *Pick up Sticks* (1971) x. 86 Beer and knockwurst. **1971** *Sunday Times* (Colour Suppl.) 27 June 50/2 *Knackwurst*: not unlike a thicker Frankfurter lightly flavoured with garlic, and also best served hot.

knaidel (knēi·dəl). Also **knaydl.** Usu. in pl. **knaidlach** (knēi·dlaχy), **kneidlach.** [f. Yiddish *kneydel*, ad. MHG. (and mod.G.) *knödel* *KNÖDEL.] A type of dumpling eaten esp. in Jewish households during Passover. Also *transf.*

1951 L. W. LEONARD *Jewish Cookery* i. 6 The *Seder* is a home festival, and every part of it, from *Haggada* to *Knaidlach*, has been enriched with traditions that are passed along to the children from generation to generation. **1955** —— *Jewish Holiday Cook Bk.* 87 Drop..into rapidly boiling clear soup..and cook..till Knaidlach rise to the top. **1960** S. H. RIVKIN *Mama's Meichulim: Trad. Jewish Cooking* 150 Looking down at our faces after the long prayers, Papa would say perceptively, 'Children! They are not so hungry for religion as they are for knaidlach.' **1968** L. ROSTEN *Joys of Yiddish* 185 *Knaydl* is used affectionately for a child..or to describe a round, fat, chubby woman. **1973** *Times* 3 Feb. 13/4 You can try the kneidlach soup (with matzo-meal dumplings).

knall-gas (knæ·lˌgæs). *Chem.* Also **knallgas** and with capital initial. [a. G. *knallgas*, f. *knall* bang, detonation + *gas* gas.] Any explosive mixture of gases, esp. one of two volumes of hydrogen with one of oxygen.

1899 R. E. BAYNES tr. *Meyer's Kinetic Theory of Gases* iii. 86 (*table*) Knallgas. [*Note*] This is the mixture of hydrogen and oxygen produced by electrically decomposing water. **1923** *Jrnl. Chem. Soc.* CXXIII. 1026 Berthelot measured the *initial* rates of the flame in hydrogen and in carbon monoxide Knall-gas..; he also made a similar series with hydrogen and with ethylene Knall-gas. **1924** *Nature* 8 Mar. 373/2 The explosion of an undiluted $2\,CO + O_2$ 'knall-gas'. **1927** BONE & TOWNEND *Flame & Combustion in Gases* xxxiv. 432 In cases where excess of either hydrogen or oxygen was present in the system, the observed rate was still..proportional to the partial pressure of the '*knall-gas*' present. **1969** OTTAWAY & IRVINE tr. *Netter's Theoret. Biochem.* iii. 72 The reverse reaction (the Knall-gas reaction) $2H_2 + O_2 = 2H_2O$ releases the same energy [as is absorbed in the forward reaction].

knapsack. Add: **b. knapsack pump** = **knapsack sprayer*; **knapsack sprayer** (or **spray**), a sprayer consisting of a hand-held nozzle supplied from a pressurized reservoir that is carried on the back like a knapsack.

1894 *Country Gentlemen's Catal.* 302/2 Vermorel's knapsack pumps. **1944** *Living off Land* vii. 153 Firefighting weapons are many and varied...The knapsack pump—a 4-gallon container with shoulder straps, brass hand pump and nozzle—is most effective. **1897** *Sears Roebuck Catal.* 162/3 The Celebrated Myers Knapsack Spray Pump. **1909** *Cent. Dict.* Suppl. s.v. *sprayer, Knapsack sprayer.* **1950** *N.Z. Jrnl. Agric.* Feb. 177/2 Obtaining complete coverage of tall [orchard] trees with a knapsack sprayer is most difficult. **1971** *Community* (E. Afr. Community) Apr. 8/1 The new method could well replace the present widespread use of knapsack sprayers which was considered inefficient in insecticide application.

knapsacked (næ·psækt), *a.* [f. KNAPSACK + -ED[2].] Equipped with a knapsack.

1905 *Westm. Gaz.* 26 Aug. 3/1 The knapsacked mountaineers come and go. **1908** HARDY *Dynasts* III. II. ii. 76 The sunset slants an ochreous shine Upon the English knapsacked line. **1926** R. MACAULAY *Crewe Train* I. i. 5 Knapsacked British walkers.

knarr, var. *KNORR.

knaydl, var. *KNAIDEL.

knead, *v.* Add: **3. b.** *trans.* and *intr.* To manipulate or paw repetitively with or as with the action of (the claws of) a cat.

1954 G. DURRELL *Bafut Beagles* iii. 69 The cloud seemed to move,..padding and kneading the mountain crests like a cat on the arm of a gigantic chair. **1967** 'T. WELLS' *Dead by Light of Moon* (1968) ii. 27 He..began to purr and knead at the blanket. **1968** V. CANNING *Melting Man* vi. 144 The cat woke me by kneading determinedly on my chest. **1968** R. SAWKINS *Snow along Border* xii. 102 It began kneading dough, claws exposed.

knee, *sb.* Add: **1. b.** A damaged condition of the knee. Cf. *housemaid's knee* (HOUSEMAID c in Dict. and Suppl.), *tennis-knee* (TENNIS *sb.* 3 b).

1921 J. C. JENKINS in E. H. D. Sewell *Rugby Football* ix. 195 Unfortunately developed a 'knee' and had to retire in his prime. **1922** JOYCE *Ulysses* 127 'Are you hurt? I'm in a hurry.' 'Knee,' Lenehan said. He made a comic face and whined, rubbing his knee. **1971** I. PEEBLES *Denis Compton* x. 97 Denis, handicapped by his knee, was no longer able to get down the pitch to the slower bowlers.

2. d. *across one's knee*, (of someone, esp. a child) placed face-down on the knee(s) to be spanked.

1866 [see WHIPPING *vbl. sb.* 1 a]. **1916** 'TAFFRAIL' *Pincher Martin* ix. 154 If yer don't stop it I'll put yer across my knee an' give yer wot for. **1936** 'N. BLAKE' *Thou Shell of Death* xiii. 230 Manny's the time I've had him across me knee—and Miss Judith, too—and belted them with a slipper. **1959** I. FLEMING *Goldfinger* ix. 126 This one has got to go dead or I'll put you across my knee.

11*. An abrupt obtuse or approximately right-angled bend in a graph between parts where the slope varies smoothly.

1880 *Proc. R. Soc.* XXX. 513 An interval of constant stress of even five seconds produces a perceptible 'knee' in the curve. *Ibid.* 514 We get a stepped curve, having a number of 'knees' upon it. **1904** *Physical Rev.* XIX. 114 On the rising curve there is seen to be a more or less well defined 'knee' where the relation of stress to strain undergoes a marked change. This 'knee' might be said to mark the elastic limit. **1926** R. W. HUTCHINSON *First Course Wireless* viii. 144 Consider now the parts of the curve where the bending is greatest, i.e. the 'knees'. **1957** G. E. HUTCHINSON *Treat. Limnol.* I. vii. 429 From the upper plane of maximum curvature, termed by Munk and Anderson the knee of the thermocline, to the lower plane of maximum (inverse) curvature. **1967** L. G. LAWRENCE *Electronics in Oceanogr.* iii. 56 The arrangement makes special use of the knowledge that the saturation 'knee' of a *B-H* loop of a given material can be modified by allowing the magnetism of the earth to contribute to the effective operating point of this knee.

12. *knee-buckle* (earlier Amer. example), *-grip, -pad, -pants, -room, -sock, -trousers* (U.S.); *kneewards* adv.

1754 *South Carolina Gaz.* 1–8 Jan. 4/3 To be sold...shoe and knee buckles, snuffers, gun hammers. **1903** *Westm. Gaz.* 12 Feb. 2/4 The bridle-rein light in the hand, The knee-grip steady and sure. **1925** E. T. BROWN *Compl. Moter-Cyclist* 126 The non-essential accessories include a luggage grid, speedometer, leg-shields.., knee-grips, handle-bar gloves. **1858** J. A. WARDER *Hedges & Evergreens* 71 As it is easier to work on your knees, you will provide thick knee-pads for them. **1955** E. POUND *Classic Anthol.* I. 71 Saw I white knee-pads decent misery I'd know one man still feels and thinks as I. **1972** P. DRISCOLL *Wilby Conspiracy* (1973) xi. 145 September, on all fours

with a pair of rubber knee-pads on, was vigorously polishing the slate floor. **1869** *Atlantic Monthly* July 74/2, I made my initial bow before the foot-lights, in my small Canton flannel knee-pants. **1916** *Daily Colonist* (Victoria, B.C.) 1 July 12/4 (Advt.), Boys' Straight Knee Pants, of good quality English tweeds. **1942** *Short Guide Gr. Brit.* (U.S. War Dept.) 20 There are..youngsters in knee pants ..who have lived through more high explosives..than many soldiers saw..in the last war. **1969** WIDDOWSON & HALPERT in Halpert & Story *Christmas Mumming in Newfoundland* 162 More modern costumes reported alongside the older disguises include service uniforms, ice-hockey clothing (presumably with padded shoulders and knee pants), [etc.]. **1958** *Times* 19 Aug. 11/6 The headroom is only just sufficient, and the same reservation applies to the kneeroom in the back when the driver's seat is pushed back for a fairly tall driver. **1970** *Times* 16 Apr. 18 More front headroom and rear kneeroom could be devised by reducing the bulk of their cushions and backrests. **1964** *Punch* 19 Aug. 284/3 Green plaid knee-socks end in sling-back shoes. **1966** T. PYNCHON *Crying of Lot 49* ii. 41 A long-leg girdle and a couple pairs of knee socks. **1899** T. HALL *Tales* 162 Since she was a little girl in short dresses and he a boy in knee trousers. **1926** *Brit. Weekly* 24 June 250/5 On the patterned skirt the design grew larger as it reached kneewards. **1968** G. JONES *Hist. Vikings* III. iv. 255 Ibn Rustah notes the full baggy trousers gathered kneewards vouched for by Scandinavian picture stones.

13. **knee-action,** (*a*) in a horse, the action or coordination of movement of the knee joint; (*b*) exaggerated raising of the knee by an athlete; (*c*) in motor vehicles, a form of independent front-wheel suspension; **knee-bend,** the action of bending the (human) knee, esp. used of a physical exercise in which the body is raised and lowered without use of the hands; so **knee-bend** *v. intr.*; **knee-board,** (*b*) in a cotton-yarn winding-machine (see quot.); **knee-brace** *Engin.*, a strut fixed diagonally between the lower chord of a truss and one of its supporting columns; hence **knee-braced** *ppl. a.*, **-bracing** *vbl. sb.*; **knee-breech,** sing. of *knee-breeches*; **kneecap** *v. trans.*, to shoot a person in the knee (or leg) as a form of punishment; so **kneecapping** *vbl. sb.*; **knee-chest position,** a position adopted by some women in sexual intercourse (see quot. 1936); **knee-hobbling** *vbl. sb.*, fastening an animal's knees with a hobble; **knee-jerk,** also *attrib.*, and *fig.*, predictable, automatic, stereotyped; **knee-length** *attrib.*, reaching down (or up) to the knee; also *ellipt.*, (a garment of) such a length; **knee-plate,** (*b*) *Shipbuilding*, an angled metal plate used as a knee (sense 7 a); **knee-slapper** *U.S.*, an uproariously funny joke; **knee-sprung** *a. Farriery* (see quot. 1905); **knee-stake** *v. trans.*, in *Leather manuf.*, to soften (a skin) by aid of the knee; **knee-trembler** *slang*, an act of sexual intercourse between persons in a standing position (so **knee-tremble**).

1868 H. W. WOODRUFF *Trotting Horse* iv. 62 [The colt] continually hit himself in the elbows, by reason of excessive knee-action as it appeared. **1903** A. ADAMS *Log of Cowboy* xv. 100 They will discuss how to shoe that filly so as to give her certain knee action which she seems to need. **1908** *Westm. Gaz.* 22 July 2/1 My action is low and sweeping, mainly from the hips, but many men..have a lot of what may be called 'knee-action'. **1935** A. C. BAUGH *Hist. Eng. Lang.* x. 370 Of late we have heard a good bit about *free-wheeling, safety-glass, knee-action*, while *service stations* and *tourist camps* are everywhere along the road. **1963** R. F. WEBB *Motorists' Dict.* 144 *Knee-action suspension*... The front wheels are supported on upper and lower radius arms, the upper of which has an action like the human knee joint where it joins the king pin link support. **1941** *Penguin New Writing* IX. 62, I practise the knee-bend, the stare, and the slow roll. **1961** A. MILLER *Misfits* xi. 119 Guido half knee-bends with his rope over his thighs and pulls. **1963** I. FLEMING *On H.M. Secret Service* xi. 117 He proceeded to a quarter of an hour of knee-bends and press-ups. **1972** *Village Voice* (N.Y.) 1 June 26/2 La Lanne moves from knee bends and neck stretches to pitching his mattresses and reducing aids without the slightest break in his pace or enthusiasm. **1895** R. MARSDEN *Cotton Weaving* 257 The board.. generally called the knee-board, an incorrect name if regard be had to its function. This board is usually covered with flannel, and forms a check upon the too easy delivery of the yarn to the draught of the spindle, thereby securing uniformity of tension in the winding. **1912** A. MORLEY *Theory of Struct.* xv. 423 The kneebraces meeting the stanchions 4·75 feet below the caps. **1959** L. C. URQUHART *Civil Engin. Handbk.* (ed. 4) v. 3 Frequently.. trusses are stiffened in their own vertical planes by inserting knee braces at both ends between the bottom chord and supporting columns. **1915** H. R. THAYER *Struct. Design* II. xii. 448 (*heading*) The knee-braced steel frame. **1940** *Archit. Rev.* Mar. 102/2 The roof unit and ceiling members..in the 27 ft. wide blocks [form] a knee-braced truss. **1950** *Engineering* 31 Mar. 366/1 By using a knee-braced portal structure, broad-flange beams may be employed for spans up to about 70 ft. **1912** H. R. THAYER *Struct. Design* I. iii. 53 It is sometimes necessary to use knee bracing..but it is not as strong as the X bracing.. and it introduces large bending stresses. **1904** *Daily Chron.* 11 Oct. 3/5 Men do not dress now, they merely clothe themselves, and they will not alter this fact by adopting the knee-breech. **1927** *Observer* 22 May 12 (*heading*) A blow to the knee-breech crusade. **1975** *Daily Tel.* 12 Aug. 2/7 Man 'kneecapped' in Carrickfergus. **1975** *Observer* 8 June 4/3 Ulster's gunmen have found they can get hold of Government cash by giving victims a 'knee-capping'—their grim colloquialism for a bullet in the legs. .. Kneecapping..has replaced tarring and feathering as the province's most common form of terrorist punishment... 'This so-called kneecapping is really a misnomer, because the kneecap itself is rarely touched.' **1936** H. M. & A. STONE *Marriage Manual* vii. 249 The woman in the so-called 'knee-chest' position, that is kneeling face downward. **1968** R. KYLE *Love Lab.* ix. 127 The arm can be set for only two positions, the supine and knee-chest. **1908** *Animal Managem.* 150 Grazing should be afforded at every opportunity, and for this purpose knee-hobbling is the best plan to adopt. **1951** J. HOLLOWAY *Lang. & Intelligence* v. 79 The knee-jerk reflex may be more or less rapid. **1963** *N.Y. Times* 7 Oct. 30 The place has always been full of liberals... In Washington, we call them crackpots, knee-jerks, do-gooders. **1969** *Time* 30 May 22/3 'What you have here,' he said, 'is the opposite of the knee-jerk liberal—the knee-jerk conservative.' **1970** *Daily Tel.* 2 June 19 In spite of knee-jerk reactions speculating on a Swiss franc revaluation, the Swiss franc never reached its 'ceiling' against the dollar. **1973** *Washington Post* 5 Apr. B.2 There is also some tired business about 'educating abroad' and a knee-jerk Mafia joke because Candoli is Italian. **1895** *Montgomery Ward Catal.* 483/3 Horsehide leggings, either 'knee' or 'thigh' lengths. **1897** *Sears, Roebuck Catal.* 240/1 Ladies'..Union suit..shaped form fitting waist, knee length. **1909** *Daily Chron.* 6 Jan. 7/1 Both sexes wear deerskin breeches and knee-length coats. **1922** JOYCE *Ulysses* 517 To lace up crisscrossed to knee-length the dressy kid footwear. **1958** B. NICHOLS *Sweet & Twenties* xvi. 206 The taste of the twenties was not entirely represented by knee-length frocks and bobbed fringes. **1966** *Guardian* 25 July 6/2 A hovering knee-length is generally expected to be the winter norm. **1967** *Punch* 4 Jan. 1/1 The lengths of female laid bare by minis are apt to be covered anew by costly knee- and thigh-length boots, thick tights and miscellaneous 'warms'. **1858** J. GRANTHAM *Iron Ship-Building* 217 Bulkheads to be five in number;.. to have brackets, or knee plates, riveted horizontally against the ship's side. **1969** *Jrnl. Abstr. Brit. Ship. Res. Assoc.* XXIV. 218 (*heading*) Determination of the effectiveness of a knee plate by plastic theory. **1966** *New Yorker* 5 Nov. 128 'How's the World Treating You', an English comedy at the Music Box, is full of knee-slappers like that one. **1970** W. BURROUGHS, JR. *Speed* 84, I needed a phone book which the guard thought a real knee slapper. **1875** *Scribner's Monthly* June 208/1 Particularly when that animal's foundered and knee-sprung. **1905** J. W. AXE *Horse* I. 74 When the knee is displaced forward in advance of the vertical line it is said to be 'bowed', or the horse 'stands over', 'knee sprung'. **1903** L. A. FLEMMING *Pract. Tanning* 51 When in just the right condition, the skins are knee-staked for the purpose of softening them to get rid of the stretch. **1896** FARMER & HENLEY *Slang* IV. 119/1 *Knee-trembler*, a standing embrace; a fast-fuck; a perpendicular. **1965** G. MELLY *Owning-Up* vi. 67 A member of the band..gave her a knee tremble at the back of the building. **1966** F. SHAW et al. *Lern Yerself Scouse* 62 *We wen up der jigger fera kneetrembler*, we went courting in lovers' lane. **1971** B. W. ALDISS *Soldier Erect* 18 They would be going to the pub for a pint and afterwards Nelson would get her against our back wall for a knee-trembler... He claimed that knee-tremblers were the most exhausting way of having sex.

knee, *v.* Add: **3.** *spec.*, to strike a person (esp. in the groin) deliberately with the knee. Also *fig.*, implying foul play.

1953 *Time* 20 July 13/1 Like most successful rough and tumble fighters, Senator Joe McCarthy always presses in, and is adept at forensic kneeing, gouging and butting. **1955** [see *BUTT-END *v.* 2]. **1967** K. GILES *Death in Diamonds* ix. 176 He belted the P.C., kneed another in the stomach and tried to bolt. **1968** 'R. RAINE' *Night of Hawk* xxxvi. 174, I..knee'd him in the groin. **1972** J. MOSEDALE *Football* ix. 122 Guyon..spun round and kneed Halas, breaking three of his ribs. **1973** *N.Y. Times* 6 Oct. 4/5 One plainclothesman repeatedly kneeing Mr Ogden in the back.

b. To urge (a horse) on by pressing the knees against its flanks. *U.S.*

1924 C. E. MULFORD *Rustlers' Valley* iii. 33 Then he.. turned his own animal southward and kneed it forward. **1926** —— *Cassidy's Protégé* x. 133 The herder,..kneeing his horse, rode swiftly back and forth several times for a hundred feet each way.

7. To renew the knees of (a garment). *U.S.* and *dial.*

1847 H. HOWE *Hist. Coll. Ohio* 348 After wearing out their woollen pantaloons, [they] were obliged to have them seated and kneed with buckskin. **1891** R. KERR *Maggie o' Moss* 36 Corduroys! and them sae clouted, Backside, foreside, knee'd an a'.

kneed, *a.* **1.** Also, *feeble-kneed.*

1904 E. M. FORSTER in *Independent Rev.* Mar. 280 They are so weak-chested and anæmic and feeble-kneed.

knee-halter, *v.* Add: (Earlier and later examples.) So **knee-haltering** *vbl. sb.*

1835 A. STEEDMAN *Wanderings S. Afr.* I. vii. 215 While the servants knee-haltered and watched the horses, we returned on foot to where the corpse lay. **1908** *Animal Managem.* 126 The practice of grazing may be taken advantage of to accustom horses to knee haltering. **1926** T. E. LAWRENCE *Seven Pillars* (1935) xi. 85, I was rolled up in my cloak and asleep in a most comfortable little sand-grave before Tafas had done knee-haltering my camel. **1939** S. CLOETE *Watch for Dawn* ii. 23 Dismounting, he off-saddled, knee-haltered his horse.

knee-high, *a.* Reaching as high as the knees. Freq. in jocular phrase (orig. U.S.) *knee-high to a grasshopper* (and varr.), i.e. very short.

1743 W. ELLIS *Mod. Husbandman* Aug. xvi. 64 By Michaelmas following they were Knee high. **1799** C. B. BROWN *Arthur Mervyn* I. xv. 141, I never cried in my life, since I was knee-high. **1814** *Portsmouth* (New Hampsh.) *Oracle* 2 Apr. 3/2 One..who, as farmer Joe would say, is 'about knee high to a toad'. **1824** *Microscope* (Albany, N.Y.) 12 June 55/1 (Th.), He has lived with me ever since he was 'knee high to a musquitoe'. **1833** *Louisville Herald* 20 Mar., It is really the best version of an old story we have heard 'ever since we were knee-high to a frog'. **1833** J. NEAL *Down-Easters* I. 78 A bit of a rogue he was too, when he wa'n't more'n knee high to a bumbly-bee. **1841** W. G. SIMMS *Kinsmen* II. 63 (Th.), Ever since I was knee high to a splinter. **1843** [in Dict. s.v. KNEE *sb.* 12]. **1851** *Democratic Rev.* XXVIII. 301 You pretend to be my daddies; some of you who are not knee-high to a grasshopper! **1887** *Harper's Mag.* Oct. 754/2 Their myriads of gray trunks stood knee-high in water. **1892** *Dialect Notes* I. 230 Knee high to a duck. **1925** R. GRAVES *Welchman's Hose* 25 He gibed at modern poets, 'Show me one Knee-high in stature to a Tennyson.' **1937** *Discovery* June 170/2 The grass grows in thick tufts and is knee high. **1942** *R.A.F. Jrnl.* 18 Apr. 2 Air gunners..envisage him [*sc.* a gremlin] as something fairly big—say, knee-high to an air-gunner. **1957** I. CROSS *God Boy* (1958) xxii. 187 Sister Theresa, who is not much more than knee-high to a grasshopper. **1973** H. CARVIC *Miss Seeton Sings* (1974) 35 A little Italian cock sparrow about knee-high to a grasshopper.

kneeler. Add: **4.** (Later examples.) Also *attrib.* in *kneeler chair.*

1909 M. B. SAUNDERS *Litany Lane* I. xi, She would follow the Stations of the Cross with a slow dreaminess, and lean longer over her kneeler chair when the services had finished. **1969** E. H. PINTO *Treen* 94 The traditional U-shaped elm kneeling mat or 'kneeler'..had many uses on the farm. It was also used until early in this century in the house. **1972** S. BURNFORD *One Woman's Arctic* (1973) iii. 70 Some beautiful inset work sewn in to the sealskin kneelers.

kneeling, *vbl. sb.* Add: **3.** *kneeling-desk* (earlier Amer. example), *-mat*, *-stool* (earlier and later examples).

1647 in *Archives of Maryland* (1887) IV. 321 A kneeling desk, & a picture of Paules. **1907** *Yesterday's Shopping* (1969) 231/4, 2 Housemaid's Kneeling Mats—0 2 [s] 6 [d]. **1969** Kneeling mat [see *KNEELER 4]. **1844** C. M. YONGE *Abbeychurch* v. 64 Do you not remember how much trouble Rupert took to find a pattern for the kneeling-stools? **1954** W. HANNAH *Christian by Degrees* xii. 167 To the west of the Sepulchre is a kneeling-stool.

knees up, Mother Brown. A light-hearted popular song beginning thus; a popular dance in which the knees are vigorously raised to the accompaniment of the song. So *ellipt.*, as **knees-up** *sb.*, *spec.* a lively party or gathering. Also occas. in extended uses.

1939 WESTON & LEE *Knees up Mother Brown!* 3 Ooh! Knees up Mother Brown! Well! Knees up Mother Brown!..knees up, knees up! Don't get the breeze up Knees up Mother Brown. **1945** *Daily Mirror* 8 May 1/2 We are dancing the Conga and the jig and 'Knees up, Mother Brown'. **1958** *Times* 15 Aug. 9/4 'Knees up, Mother Brown' is an injunction to apprehend nothing but jollity. **1961** A. WILSON *Old Men at Zoo* iv. 213 Matthew ..was involved with a circle of old women out on the spree who were doing 'Knees up Mother Brown'. **1963** P. WILLMOTT *Evolution of Community* vii. 75 We went to another house on the banjo for a 'knees-up'. **1966** K. MARTIN *Father Figures* iv. 88, I happened to get leave on Armistice Day and crossed to London in time to witness the glorification in Trafalgar Square. We danced round and round all night long, singing 'Knees up, Mother Brown' and other fragments from English folklore. **1966** A. PRIOR *Operators* xvi. 259 He..turned to see Emmie doing a knees-up, her skirt held high. **1967** L. DEIGHTON *London Dossier* 54 As indigenous to London as a Saturday-night knees-up in the boozer. **1969** *Guardian* 31 Jan. 22/3 An irrepressible bunch of girls chanted 'Knees up Barbara Castle'. **1971** *Ibid.* 18 Sept. 8/5 He and Mr [Harold] Wilson finished up doing Knees Up Mother Brown together. **1974** *New Scientist* 3 Oct. 39/1 Two new video discs were demonstrated last month during the annual video industry knees-up at Cannes. **1975** *Oxford Times* 3 Jan. 16/5 (Advt.), Saturday January 4th. 8 pm. (New Year's Knees-Up).

kneesy, -ie (nī·zi). *colloq.* [Jocular dim. of *knees*: see -Y⁶.] Amorous play with the knees; the relationship implied by such activity. Also redupl.

1951 'M. SPILLANE' *Big Kill* v. 102 We got back to the table and played kneesies while we talked. **1954** A. MELVILLE *Simon & Laura* in *Plays of Year* XI. 83 Ramming Le Touquet down *my* throat, as though you'd never heard of kneesy-kneesy under a table at the Café de Paris. **1970** *New Yorker* 26 Sept. 36/3 Ha! No kneesies, no invitations to a midtown matinée?

kneidlach: see *KNAIDEL.

‖ **Kneipe** (knəi·pə). Also *erron.* **Kneip, Knipe.** Pl. **-en, -es.** [G.] A convivial meeting of German university students (and the like) at a tavern or restaurant. So **kneip** *v. intr.* [after G. *kneipen*], to indulge in this conviviality.

1854 I. ALDRIDGE *Diary* 9 June in Marshall & Stock *Ira Aldridge* (1958) 189 Visited a Knipe or a Society of German Students. **1864** H. MAYHEW *German Life & Manners* II. 243 Youths whose lives are apparently given up to the mere conviviality of '*Kneiping*' or beer-drinking.

1874 J. M. Hart *German Univ.* ix. 139 In whatever other respects the German student may be irregular, he always *kneips* according to rule. **1880** 'Mark Twain' *Tramp Abroad* iv. 43 Kneips are held, now and then [at the University of Heidelberg], to celebrate great occasions,—like the election of a beer king. **1911** R. Brooke *Let.* 31 Jan. (1968) 275 Last night he took me to a '*Kneipe*'. The students who are working at some special subject band together to form a club... Every Monday evening this Verein has a 'Kneipe', a meeting. **1924** A. Geikie *Long Life's Work* vii. 217 After the meetings during the day, every night a 'Kneipe' at which Zirkel, Lossen, Reusch.. and a host of younger men took part.

Kneipp (nəip). The name of Sebastian *Kneipp* (1821–97), Bavarian priest, used *attrib.* to designate (a system of) hydropathic treatments advocated by him, a special feature of which was walking barefoot through dewy grass. Hence **Knei·ppism.**

[**1891** A. de F. tr. *Kneipp's My Water-Cure* p. xviii, It is evident that in Germany, at least, Pfarrer Kneipp's cure is going to influence the present state of medicine to a considerable extent.] **1895** *N.Y. Med. Jrnl.* LXII. 523/2 Is the Kneipp cure injurious? **1900** Dorland *Med. Dict.* 341/1 Kneippism. **1901** J. H. Kellogg *Rational Hydrotherapy* i. 28 The leading features of the so-called 'Kneippism' are simply a revival of these rude practices of ignorant peasants a century and a half ago. **1911** Stedman *Med. Dict.* 454/2 *Kneipp method*, the treatment of disease by hydrotherapy in various forms—douches, wet packs, full and local baths, compresses, vapor baths, walking barefoot in the dew of early morning, etc. **1933** H. F. Wolf et al. *Textbk. Physical Therapy* xxiii. 268 Such headaches are promptly relieved..by walking barefooted in wet grass (Kneipp cure). **1966** *Punch* 2 Feb. 161/2 Bavaria also offers a range of Kneipp cures. The good Father Kneipp..knew that walking barefoot on wet stone floors would cure constipation.

Knesset (kne·sĕt). [Heb., lit. gathering.] The parliament of the State of Israel. Also *attrib.*

1949 *Jewish Chron.* 11 Feb. 1/2 On Monday next Israel's newly elected Constituent Assembly, to be known as the Knesset Gedola, will hold its first meeting in Jerusalem. **1956** *Ann. Reg. 1955* 283 The General Election for the Knesset. **1959** *New Statesman* 14 Nov. 648/1 At the other political pole, the Communists slumped heavily, losing three of their six Knesset seats. **1972** *Guardian* 27 Mar. 4/4 Arab propagandists are wrong in claiming that a map hangs in the Knesset building showing the land from the Nile to the Euphrates.

knick (nik), *sb.*² *Geomorphol.* Also **nick.** [a. G. *knick* bend, kink, break.] **a.** = *knickpoint.

1932 *Bull. Geol. Soc. Amer.* XLIII. 416 If one convex nick can not be produced in the profile of a stream that is eroding its valley in an enlarging dome of continuously accelerated upheaval, all the less can a series of nicks be produced. **1941** C. A. Cotton *Landscape* xx. 233 Even where nicks occur at resistant outcrops, this is quite commonly a result merely of retardation at such points of headward erosion due to rejuvenation. The most widely accepted explanation of nicks in valley profiles is that they are the effects of successive lowerings of base-level. **1970** I. Cornwall *Ice Ages* i. 35 At the point where renewed erosion begins there will be a sharp increase in rate of fall, showing a 'knick', or downward break in gradient.

b. The angle formed by a pediment and the adjacent mountain slope.

1936 *Zeitschr. für Geomorphol.* IX. 132 Massive rocks, on weathering, produce steep mountain slopes because of their widely spaced joints. They are also characterized by a relatively sharp 'Knick', whereas in the same area more closely jointed rocks have lower slopes and there is a more gradual transition into the pediment at the base. **1952** *Ann. Assoc. Amer. Geogr.* XLII. 305 Johnson..pointed to the sharp angle (knick) between pediment and inselberg as an indication that lateral corrosion and not weathering-retreat is the cause of destruction of the feature. **1963** D. W. & E. E. Humphries tr. *Termier's Erosion & Sedimentation* ii. 36 Pediments are surfaces cut into hard rocks at the foot of mountains which they continue to erode. At their highest point, they join the mountain side at a break of slope called a 'knick'.

knicker². Add: **1. b.** *attrib.* and *Comb.* *knicker fabric, hose, skirt; knicker-pink* adj.; **knicker yarn,** = *knickerbocker yarn* (*knickerbocker 3 c).

1974 *News of World* 22 Sept. 14/4 Faiman's in Southampton sold us a skirt in nasty 'knicker' fabric. **1899** *Northern Times* (Golspie, Sutherland) 22 June 1/2 (Advt.), In the Gents. Department..Hand-Knitted knicker hose a speciality. **1973** *Sunday Times* 7 Oct. 36/5 Alive and well in a spanking new knicker-pink emporium at 100 Mount Street. **1912** *Woman's Weekly* 27 Jan. p. iii/2 (Advt.), Knicker Skirts, Nightdresses, Pyjamas, &c. **1929** *Encycl. Brit.* XXIII. 879/2 'Knicker yarns' are produced by throwing little bits of highly coloured material into the last cylinders of the card so that instead of being broken up by carding they are carried forward as 'knickers' into the spun thread. **1951** *Good Housek. Home Encycl.* 327/2 'Knicker' yarns may be produced by including bits of coloured material in the final cording.

2. Usu. in pl. A short-legged (orig. knee-length), freq. loose-fitting, pair of pants worn by women and children as an undergarment. In extended use, the shorts worn by boxers, footballers, etc. (the application of the term to men's garments is now almost exclusively *U.S.*). Cf. *Directoire *a.* 1, *knicks *sb. pl.*

1882 *Queen* 7 Oct. 328/3, I recommend..flannel knickers in preference to flannel petticoat. **1895** *Home Chat* 2 Nov. 301/2 Serge knickers..for girls from twelve to sixteen. **1926** *Ibid.* 22 May 507 French Knicker made in Grafton's Voile and Grafton's Chiffonelle. Trimmed with lace. Elastic waistband. **1926** *Vogue* Late Nov. p. xxiii, An Original Directoire Knicker of milanese. **1928** G. B. Shaw *Intelligent Woman's Guide Socialism* i. 2 Laws..are amended and amended and amended like a child's knickers until there is hardly a shred of the first stuff left. **1938** Dylan Thomas *Let.* 16 June (1966) 201, I find a tripper's knicker in the gully. **1951** *Good Housek. Home Encycl.* 156/1 Iron knickers lengthwise, one leg at a time. **1954** F. C. Avis *Boxing Reference Dict.* 62 *Knickers*, boxing shorts. **1966** F. Shaw et al. *Lern Yerself Scouse* 49 *Ee's got both legs in one knicker*, he is not playing [football] well. **1968** 'C. Saint-Laurent' *Hist. Ladies Underwear* x. 145 (*caption*) Little girls wore short knickers before women did. **1974** *Guardian* 19 Feb. 1/5 Women workers in a lingerie factory..waved yellow knickers at Mr Thorpe as a gesture of support.

b. *pl.* as *int.* An expression of exasperation, surprise, contempt, etc.

1971 *TV Times* 23 Sept. 6/1 When things go wrong then I'll say: 'Knickers. I'll have another go.' **1974** *Pacifist* June 20/2 This is where the revolution's happening, man, and knickers to the metropolis! **1974** *Daily Tel.* 5 Oct. 5/3 Asked whether she would tell them more about the man.., she said: 'Knickers. I have told you all I know.'

knickerbocker. Add: **3. a.** (Later examples.)

1962 *Times* 14 Apr. 9/4 Plus-fours, or knickerbockers, as the Americans prefer to call them. **1967** *Daily Tel.* 26 Aug. 7/2 Boots were all around Paris and so were tweed.. knickerbockers as the logical successor to the now-almost-boring trouser suits. **1969** J. Laver *Concise Hist. Costume* ix. 251 The new baggy knickerbockers were known as 'plus-fours'.

b. = *knicker² 2.

1872 *Young Englishwoman* Oct. 554/2 *Lady's longcloth knickerbockers.* These drawers fasten behind. **1887** *Lady's World* Oct. 403 It [*sc.* a peasant's blouse] is girdled at the waist by a leather belt, and falls over the short woollen skirt, which just reaches the knees, where it meets the linen knickerbockers. **1895** *Home Chat* 20 Apr. 176 We spoke of satin knickerbockers in connection with this trousseau. **1913** B. L. Blackmore *ABC of Cutting Garments* 140 In girls' knickerbockers, the back band is sometimes buttoned to the front band, instead of the whole garment being attached to the under-bodice or to stays. **1969** R. T. Wilcox *Dict. Costume* (1970) 234 (*caption*) Muslin knickerbockers—girl's 6 to 8—buttoned at sides—pleated cambric frill.

c. *Comb.* **knickerbocker suit** (see sense 3 in Dict.); **knickerbocker yarn,** a yarn flecked with different colours.

1868 C. L. Eastlake *Hints Household Taste* xi. 264 The knickerbocker suit..has been adopted for wear in many country gentlemen's houses. **1879** C. M. Yonge *Burnt Out* iii. 52 A knickerbocker suit, just Charlie's size, had been turned over to his cousin Ada. **1911** *Encycl. Brit.* XXVIII. 906/2 *Flaked Yarn* has a cloudy appearance imparted to it..as in *Knickerbocker Yarn*, by dropping small quantities of dyed fibres into two..rovings at the spinning machine. **1932** E. Midgley *Technical Terms Textile Trade* II. 81 True 'knickerbocker' yarn is obtained by flecking the spotting material during carding. **1950** '*Mercury*' *Dict. Textile Terms* 303 *Knickerbocker tweeds*, rough-faced wool and cotton mixture dress goods made with nub yarns, in mixed colours. The yarn is known as knickerbocker yarn.

d. Knickerbocker Glory, a quantity of ice cream served with other ingredients in a tall glass.

1936 G. Greene *Gun for Sale* i. 11 Have a *parfait*... They do a very good Maiden's Dream. Not to speak of Alpine Glow. Or the Knickerbocker Glory. **1941** M. Treadgold *We couldn't leave Dinah* xvi. 256 'Lyons' Corner House,' capped Caroline, envisaging the increasing possibilities of Knickerbocker Glories. **1963** *Times* 25 Feb. 11/4 Knickerbocker Glory oddly has become the name of a specially luscious mixture of ice-creams and the 'plus fours' deserved a similar grandeur of title. **1973** *Times* 20 Oct. 12/7 At five in the morning it must have had all the charm of a pre-breakfast Knickerbocker Glory.

knickpoint (ni·kpoint). *Geomorphol.* Also **nickpoint** and as two words. [Partial tr. G. *knickpunkt*, f. *knick* (see *knick *sb.*²) + *punkt* point.] A break of slope in a river profile, esp. one where a new curve of erosion arising from rejuvenation intersects an earlier curve.

1924 *Bull. Geol. Soc. Amer.* XXXV. 638 Since erosion progresses headward when a region is uplifted by a uniform tilting movement.., the longitudinal profiles of those streams will record a knickpoint at the headward limit of quickened erosion. **1937** Wooldridge & Morgan *Physical Basis Geogr.* xv. 220 The rate of upstream recession of knickpoints will evidently vary with the character of rocks eroded. **1954** W. D. Thornbury *Princ. Geomorphol.* v. 110 Along some streams..nickpoints are found which do not seem to be related to more resistant rock. **1967** J. Challinor *Dict. Geol.* (ed. 3) 142/2 To the present writer it seems that nearly all knick points are due to some commoner and more compelling cause [than rejuvenation], such as the outcropping of a hard bed or glacial erosion. **1968** C. R. Twidale *Geomorphol.* vi. 190 Not all falls and rapids indicate nick points, for hard-rock strata crossing the river's path may well produce a break of slope. **1973** *Nature* 9 Nov. 75/1 Recession of valley nickpoints inland from the coastal margin was followed by valley widening, scarp retreat and pedimentation.

knicks, *sb. pl.* Colloq. shortening of *knickers* or *knickerbockers.*

1895 *Punch* 15 June 285/2 One young piece in grey knicks and cream cloth.. took my fancy perdigious, dear boy. **1923** J. Manchon *Le Slang* 173 Knicks..s. pl., un pantalon de femme. **1937, 1952** [see *cami-]. **1972** J. Wilson *Hide & Seek* vi. 105 Mary, if you'd just stand up I could take your wet knicks off.

knife, *sb.* Add: **1. e.** (Earlier and later examples.) Also *while (one) would say knife.*

1874 M. Clarke *His Natural Life* II. iii. viii. 170 He was over the wall before you could say 'knife'. **1922** Joyce *Ulysses* 158 Toss off a glass of brandy neat while you'd say knife. **1954** A. Macrae *Both Ends Meet* in *Plays of Year* X. 509 With a couple like that you'll be in a lawsuit before you can say 'knife'. **1973** M. Muggeridge *Infernal Grove* i. 71 Like alcoholics after taking the cure—never another drop; well, just a taste perhaps, and then, before you could say knife, back on the meths.

f. *the knife*: used as typical of surgical operations. Also *attrib.*

1880 Tennyson *Ballads* 88 But they said too of him He was happier using the knife than in trying to save the limb. *Ibid.* 95 My sleep was broken besides with dreams of the dreadful knife. **1932** Kipling *Limits & Renewals* 350 And leave you knife-*wallahs* to kill our patients? **1961** *Woman* 18 Mar. 10/4 Had she seen the new nurse on women's surgical? The knife men always had the luck.

g. *to get* or *have one's knife into* (a person): to exhibit a malicious or vindictive spirit towards; to persecute unrelentingly.

1890 D. C. Murray *John Vale's Guardian* III. xxxvi. 173, I reckon you've got your knife into Mr. Jousserau. **1911** H. S. Walpole *Mr. Perrin & Mr. Traill* vi. 116 This was to be the beginning of persecution. The Reverend Moy-Thompson had got his knife into him. **1930** J. B. Priestley *Angel Pavement* ix. 440 You got your knife into him the first time he came here, and after that of course he had to be blamed for everything. **1963** N. Marsh *Dead Water* (1964) i. 26, I don't know what's got into you. Why've you got your knife into this reporter chap?

h. *night of the long knives*: see *long knife 2.

i. *you* (or *one*) *could cut* (something) *with a knife*: colloq. phr. used to describe an atmosphere(lit. or fig.) so thick that it seems capable of being cut with a knife.

1892 A. W. Pinero *Magistrate* i. 18 There's a fog on the line—you could cut it with a knife. **1954** M. Sharp *Gipsy in Parlour* (1955) xiii. 111 The smell was chiefly cabbage ..and one could have cut it with a knife. **1973** G. Moffat *Deviant Death* v. 68 You could have cut the atmosphere with a knife.

2. a. *knife-back* used *attrib.*; *knife-case* (examples); *knife-thrust* used *fig.*; *knife-tray* (examples); *knife-throwing*; *knife-featured* (example); *knife-happy, -sharp, -skewed* adjs.

1886 *Harper's Mag.* June 119/2 Between these knife-back ledges are plots of sea-green grass. **1966** *Listener* 2 June 789/1 Miniature trains of rubber-tyred, electrically-driven cars (with knife-back seats or flat decks for standing passengers) would run on set routes. **1790** *Pennsylvania Packet* 6 Jan. 1/4 Steel and gilt hat buckles, and A few inlaid mahogany knife cases. *c* **1807** Jane Austen *Watsons* (1954) 344 Nanny..was beginning to bustle into the parlour with the Tray & the Knife-case. **1971** *Canad. Antiques Collector* May 3 (Advt.), Rare and elegant pair of circular inlaid mahogany Knife Cases of the highest quality. English. Circa 1800. **1895** *Century Mag.* Aug. 638/2 A tall, lanky, sharp-boned, knife-featured fellow. **1961** *Amer. Speech* XXXVI. 147 *Knife happy*, overeager to resort to operation, said of a surgeon. **1964** *New Statesman* 21 Feb. 306/3 Sacha Pitoeff scowls away as a canapé-ferrying, knife-happy villain. **1955** E. Pound *Classic Anthol.* i. 73 Down from the spring the knife-sharp waters run. **1973** J. Wainwright *Devil you Don't* 145 The wind came in, knife-sharp, from the North Sea. **1974** H. R. F. Keating *Bats fly Up* ix. 95 Ghote felt a knife-sharp happiness. *a* **1918** W. Owen *Coll. Poems* (1963) 41 Your slender attitude Trembles not exquisite like limbs knife-skewed. **1923** G. Collins *Valley of Eyes Unseen* i. 28 If there's shooting or knife-throwing. **1959** *Times* 24 June 13/1 The knife-thrusts of Ibsen's dialogue. **1967** *Coast to Coast 1965–6* 228 The first knife-thrusts of hunger had developed into a permanent ache of emptiness. **1851** C. Cist *Cincinnati* xiii. 215 Among the principal articles are..knife trays. **1939–40** *Army & Navy Stores Catal.* 168/1 Knife trays. Japanned and filleted.

b. knife-bar (earlier U.S. example); **knife-blade,** (*a*) the blade of a knife; (*b*) something sharp or pointed; (*c*) in *Mountaineering*, a kind of piton (see quot. 1968); also *attrib.* and *Comb.*; **knife-cleaner** (earlier U.S. example); **knife-money** (example); **knife-pleat,** a narrow sharply creased pleat (in a garment, esp. a skirt); so **knife-pleated** *a.* (see also Pleated *ppl. a.*), **knife-pleating** *vbl. sb.*; **knife-rest,** (*b*) *Mil. slang*, a barrier or obstruction composed of barbed wire and timber; **knife switch** *Electr. Engin.*, a switch consisting of a conducting blade or set of blades hinged at one end so that it may be swung out of or into a fixed contact or set of contacts at the other end; **knife-thrower,** one who throws knives (*spec.* as a form of entertainment); also *U.S. slang* (see quot. 1905); **knife-work,** the use of knives as weapons or instruments; also *fig.*

1867 *Trans. Illinois Agric. Soc.* VII. 312 By the arrangement of its parts the knife-bar is placed further forward than in most machines. **1799** Knife-blade [in Dict., sense

2 a]. **1902** *Daily Chron.* 12 Sept. 3/2 The snowy knife-blade *arête*. **1911** J. A. Thomson *Biol. Seasons* I. 44 The knife-blade-like larvæ of the eel. **1950** J. Dempsey *Championship Fighting* x. 49 All fingers, including the thumb, pressing tightly against each other to form a 'knife blade'. **1955** E. Pound *Classic Anthol.* II. 106 A shallow basin gives the fish no shade, Dive as they will, there's flash of fin's knife-blade. **1968** P. Crew *Encycl. Dict. Mountaineering* 75/2 *Knife-blade*, a long thin piton. The name is mainly applied to chrome-molly pitons of this type. **1971** D. Haston in C. Bonington *Annapurna South Face* xvii. 206 It was a long and tortuous pitch done in one run-out on one of our big ropes. Firstly knee-deep mushy snow, then hard ice to exit, with one miserable knife-blade for protection. **1869** L. M. Alcott *Little Women* II. i. 12 A knife-cleaner that spoilt all the knives. **1901** *Chambers's Jrnl.* Apr. 255/2 Between 1122 and 224 B.C. a very curious knife-money was used in the state of Tsi. This coin was of copper, shaped like a bill-hook, and about seven inches long, with the handle terminating in a ring, doubtless for the purpose of stringing the coins together. **1891** *Cassell's Family Mag.* Nov. 753/2 'Knife-pleats'—as the Americans call them, to distinguish the single from the box-pleat—are turned towards the centre of the back [of the mantle]. **1928** *Daily Mail* 31 July 1/2 Well made with smart knife pleats at sides. **1964** *McCall's Sewing* ii. 30/1 *Knife pleats*, series of pleats that turn in the same direction, are usually equal in width and are pressed straight to the hem. **1905** Knife-pleated [see Pleated *ppl. a.*]. **1937** *Times* 27 Sept. 19/2 A knife-pleated vermilion dinner gown. **1965** *Punch* 12 May p. xvii, Knife-pleated travel skirts. **1895** *Montgomery Ward Catal.* 37/1 Fast Black Sateen Waists... 2 rows knife pleating from shoulder to belt. **1937** *Times* 27 Sept. 19/2 Knife pleating was used in several graceful gowns. **1919** *Athenæum* 15 Aug. 759/1 Knife-rests, *chevaux de frise*. **1921** F. W. Bewsher *Hist. 51st Div.* vii. 114 Stooks of cut strands of wire and overturned knife-rests lay everywhere. **1958** P. Kemp *No Colours or Crest* iv. 54 The entrance to the courtyard was blocked by a heavy 'knife-rest' barbed wire entanglement. **1964** A. H. Farrar-Hockley *Somme* ii. 83 Gaps had been filled with wired knife-rests and concertina rolls pegged down with iron pickets. **1907** H. H. Norris *Introd. Study Electr. Engin.* ix. 225 Open knife switches as described are not commonly used for circuit-breaking purposes above 500 volts and a few hundred amperes. **1962** *Newnes Conc. Encycl. Electr. Engin.* 726/2 Air-break isolators are made in a large variety of forms and range from the simple knife switch to those suitable for the highest transmission voltages. **1905** *Smart Set* Oct. 3/1 'They got a new knife-thrower up to the hotel,' he announced... (A 'knife-thrower', be it known, is parlance for waitress.) **1953** Wodehouse *Performing Flea* 190 He would shoot all round you till you felt like a knife-thrower's assistant, but you were really quite safe. **1973** *Listener* 19 July 80/1 Electrons are fired at an object, and they trace its outline like a knife-thrower at a fair. **1845** W. G. Simms *Wigwam & Cabin* 2nd Ser. 143 But none of your knife-work, le'me tell you. **1931** D. L. Sayers *Five Red Herrings* xxii. 255 Copying a canvas isn't the same thing as painting direct... It's the technique that's a nuisance... I don't feel handy with so much knife-work. **1954** J. R. R. Tolkien *Two Towers* 141 It has been knife-work up there. **1955** J. Morrison in *Austral. Short Stories* (1963) 2nd Ser. 147 Collins the overseer did all the knife-work—castrating, ear-marking, and tailing. **1965** J. Lawlor in J. Gibb *Light on C. S. Lewis* 76 Then proceed to the knife-work of murdering to dissect, in order to sweep the vile body aside to make room for the certified masterpieces.

knife, *v.* Add: **3.** *intr.* To move as with the action of a knife cutting or passing through.

1920 W. Camp *Football without a Coach* 107 If any of these three center men lunges through—'knifes' through, as it is called—he opens the door on either side of him. **1950** J. Dempsey *Championship Fighting* xx. 120 Deflection of the blow by..knifing with the forearm. **1958** *Times* 25 Sept. 3/2 The principal advantage of the American yacht seemed to be her ability to sail closer to the wind and knife more smoothly through the water than Sceptre. **1965** *Harper's Bazaar* June 68/2 If you come across a Salon 1959..knife on to it. **1971** *Flying* (N.Y.) Apr. 30/3 Skirting the coast for awhile before knifing northwest to Bordeaux.

knife and fork. 1. b. (Further examples.)

1838 *Manch. Guardian* 26 Sept. 3/2 This question of universal suffrage is a knife-and-fork question, a bread-and-cheese question, after all. **1909** J. R. Ware *Passing Eng.* 163/2 *Knife and fork tea* (middle class, 1874). Vulgarisation of high tea. **1929** J. B. Priestley *Good Companions* III. vi. 624 A sound specimen of their knife-and-fork tea. **1963** Bird & Hutton-Stott *Veteran Motor Car* 150 The first model of Lutzmann was a knife-and-fork copy of the Benz.

knife-board. Add: **1.** (Earlier example.)

1829 in A. Mathews *Mem. Charles Mathews* (1839) IV. ii. 26 *Joe Merriman*,—formerly imp of the ring, slave of the knife-board, and footman to Mr. Jenkins.

2. Also *attrib.* and *transf.*

1931 *Times Lit. Suppl.* 24 Dec. 1043/2 The photograph ..is delightful..of a very primitive 'knifeboard' omnibus with its top-hatted travellers. **1963** *Times* 6 Feb. 11/4 Those devoted to seeing Shakespeare on his home-ground and taking the full treatment will no doubt be thankful that the Stratford Theatre is not of the old and austere style with hard benches in the pit and knife-board seats in the gallery.

knife-edge. Add: **1.** (Further examples.)

a **1930** D. H. Lawrence *Last Poems* (1932) 39 The sudden dripping down of the knife-edge cleavage of the lightning. *a* **1935** T. E. Lawrence *Mint* (1955) II. xii. 132 He creases everybody's trousers with the knife-edge that Stiffy demands. **1969** *Sci. Jrnl.* Nov. 35/2 Steel wheels or even solid rubber tyres..give a knife-edge response which would render driving at speeds over 80 km/h impossibly dangerous.

2. b. (Further examples.) *Esp.* a sharp crest of rock, ice, sand, or the like. Also *attrib.*, as *knife-edge ridge*.

1907 *Westm. Gaz.* 26 Nov. 3/2 The road thereto lies along a 'knife-edge'. **1925** W. J. Miller *Introd. Physical Geol.* viii. 252 A knife-edge ridge may also develop where glaciers in two parallel valleys erode and steepen the valley sides until only a very sharp divide separates the valleys. **1925** E. F. Norton *Fight for Everest, 1924* I. ii. 31 A ridge which begins in a knife-edge of rock worthy of the Chamounix Aiguilles. **1945** Baker *Austral. Lang.* iii. 58 Knife edges, as certain razor-back sandhills are known. **1963** *Times* 24 Jan. 10/3 Mr. John Brass, chairman of the West Midlands Division of the N.C.B., said yesterday that west Midland coal supplies were poised 'on a knife edge' at the present. **1964** C. Willock *Enormous Zoo* v. 74 The immediate foreground beneath the sandstone cliff..was eroded into a series of gullies and knife-edges like row upon row of yellowed shark's teeth. **1969** C. R. Longwell et al. *Physical Geol.* xii. 266/2 An arête is a jagged, knife-edge ridge created where two groups of cirque glaciers have eaten into the ridge from both sides. **1971** *Country Life* 25 Feb. 408/3 The ridge goes easily at first on firm snow..and finally ends in a snow knife-edge. **1972** *Guardian* 18 Feb. 24/5 The Government's knife-edge victory for the European Communities Bill in the Commons last night. **1974** *Times* 12 Oct. 1/1 A government with a knife-edge majority. *Ibid.* 1/2 Mr Wilson intends to govern on a parliamentary knife-edge for at least two or three years.

3. *Diamond-cutting.* (See quot.)

1909 J. Wodiska *Bk. Precious Stones* 349 *Knife-edge*. The girdle of a brilliant cut to a sharp edge and polished.

knifeless, *a.* (Later example.)

1916 H. G. Wells *Mr. Britling* III. ii. 412 Knifeless and forkless meals.

kni·fe-man. One who uses a knife as an instrument, a tool, or a weapon; *spec.* † (*a*) in the parlance of N. American Indians, an Englishman *Obs.*; (*b*) *slang*, a surgeon.

1643, 1852 [see Knife *sb.* 2 a]. **1901–2** *Ann. Brit. Sch. Athens* VIII. 294 The few picked 'knife-men' who lay or crouched in the trenches cutting through the compost of bones and pottery inch by inch. **1923** *Dialect Notes* V. 235 *Knifeman*, a man who fights with a knife... Not common. **1956** J. Masters *Bugles & Tiger* i. 19 There was always the sense-sharpening chance of a sudden storm of bullets, a rush of knifemen. **1961** [see *knife *sb.* 1 f]. **1964** *Amer. Speech* XXXIX. 271 *Cutter man, knife man*, a worker who operates the cutter. **1973** 'R. MacLeod' *Burial in Portugal* v. 110 A third man..was coming in at a rush with a knife... Gaunt..felt the jar as his heel took the knife-man low in the stomach.

knifer. Add: **2.** One who carries or uses a knife as a weapon.

1870 Dickens *E. Drood* xxiii. 188 Jacks. And Chayner men. And hother Knifers. **1905** *Times* 11 Dec. 5/2 This is a new move of the hooligans and knifers, who lately committed attacks on enlightened working men.

knifey, knifie (nəi·fi), *sb.* Chiefly *Sc.* [f. Knife *sb.* + -y[6], -ie.] Either of two games played by boys with knives: (*a*) = Mumble-the-peg; (*b*) (see quot. 1969).

1896 E. Turner *Little Larrikin* iv. 40 An angel in little blue knickerbockers playing knifey on a heap of builders' sand. **1901** *Scottish Antiquary* XVI. 49 'Bonnety' and 'Knify'..are the 'Hatty' and 'Knifey' which..the Edinburgh Academy once knew so well. **1934** G. M. Martin *Dundee Worthies* 179 'Knifie'..[was] played with a knife with open blade on any grass plot. **1939** F. L. Combs *Harrowed Toad* 90 Another fieldsman who may have seen the ball but had been indulging spasmodically in 'knifey'. **1951** *Banffshire Advertiser* 16 Aug., I eest tae be the best knifey player in the toonie squeel. **1969** I. & P. Opie *Children's Games* vii. 221 The first boy throws a knife..so that it sticks in the ground not more than twelve inches to the left or right of one of his opponent's feet. The other boy..plucks the knife out of the ground, and moves his nearest foot to the place where the knife went in... Throughout Scotland..it is 'Knifie'. **1973** 'J. Patrick' *Glasgow Gang Observed* xii. 113 A game of 'knifey' began with Rose's front door as target. Bayonets and commando knives..sank into the woodwork.

knifey (nəi·fi), *a.* [f. Knife *sb.* + -y[1].] Resembling the edge of a knife in narrowness or sharpness; also *fig.* (see quot. 1937).

1906 G. A. B. Dewar *Faery Year* 258 Hovering, he presents to the wind but a knifey edge of wing. **1937** Partridge *Dict. Slang* 459/2 *Knifey*, (of a person, esp. a customer) that cuts things painfully fine when dealing in the money-market: stockbrokers'. **1955** H. Smith *Horseman through Six Reigns* xix. 192 Withers that are neither rounded nor knifey.

knight, *sb.* Add: **4. e.** Fig. phr. *knight in shining armour*: in informal or ironic use, a person regarded as a medieval knight in respect of his chivalrous spirit, especially towards women.

1965 V. Canning *Whip Hand* xv. 188 A man..didn't have to be a knight in shining armour. **1967** M. Summerton *Memory of Darkness* x. 124 Most people regard him as a crank. I'm afraid, so far as Dilys is concerned, he makes a very ineffectual knight in shining armour. **1968** A. Diment *Gt. Spy Race* i. 8, I was one of the new knights in shining PVC armour. Come to rescue the lower-middle class maiden from the dragon of boredom. **1973** *Ottawa Jrnl.* 16 Aug. 1/6 'Throughout his whole brief, Mr. Cassidy has attempted to portray himself as a knight in shining armor but on close examination it portrays our whole judicial system as something less than perfect,' said Chief Seguin.

7. a. fig. *knight's move*, an indirect or devious move.

1958 P. Shore in N. Mackenzie *Conviction* 37 The favoured entrant moves, to quote the current jargon, by a series of 'knight's moves' over the management board. **1959** *Listener* 29 Jan. 219/2 Mankind does move forward, even if it is often by the Knight's move. **1963** V. Nabokov *Gift* iv. 228 Any genuinely new trend is a knight's move, a change of shadows, a shift that displaces the mirror. **1967** G. Sims *Last Best Friend* xviii. 168 We took a kind of Knight's move, one step forward and a jump to the side. **1972** W. McGivern *Caprifoil* (1973) ii. 37 You've made a knight's move in thought.

12. c. *knight of the pencil*, a bookmaker; *knight of the road*, (*b*) a commercial traveller; (*c*) a tramp; (*d*) the driver of a lorry, taxicab, etc.

1885 *Punch* 7 Mar. 109 The Knights of the Pencil, Sir, hold that backers, like pike, are more ravenous in keen weather, and consequently easier to land. **1927** *Daily Express* 11 June 7/3 We have mentioned the knights of the pencil. Bookmakers are not permitted to take up positions at will on racecourses under Greyhound Racing Association jurisdiction. **1889** J. Burnley *Romance Mod. Industry* 317 Customers used to come out miles upon summer evenings to meet the 'knights of the road',..and the old travellers on their part would spend two or three days with some of their clients. **1928** *Sunday Express* 12 Feb. 11/4 Secrets of the Commercial Traveller's Bag. By John S. Banks, for twenty years a 'Knight of the Road'. **1928** *Daily Express* 8 Aug. 3/5 If something of this spirit could be instilled into the regular 'knights of the road', if they could be inspired with some notion of the dignity of work and the shame of alms-taking. **1971** R. Reisner *Graffiti* vi. 82 Truck drivers are notorious for their..loudly expressed admiration for women. They are true knights of the road. **1974** L. Deighton *Spy Story* ii. 20 Finally some knight of the road deigned to do a Gloucester Road to Fulham.

d. *Knights of Columbus*, a society of Roman Catholic men founded at New Haven, Connecticut, in 1882.

1901 *N.Y. Tribune* 22 July 3/4 Wednesday the Knights of Columbus of Columbus and Utah people will unite their forces; on Thursday another double-header. **1929** F. A. Pottle *Stretchers* (1930) iv. 66 Besides the enormous structures of the Y.M.C.A. and..Knights of Columbus,.. the general public had provided at Merritt many other agencies of relaxation and amusement quite peculiar to the camp. **1948** *Green Bay* (Wisconsin) *Press-Gaz.* 12 July 16/7 Members of the Green Bay lodge Knights of Columbus were reminded today that the annual Fish Fry will be held at the Shorewood Country club next Tuesday. **1974** *Listener* 21 Nov. 683 The Knights of Columbus are associated with lodge meetings and bingo.

Knipe, var. *Kneipe.

kniphofia (niphōu·fiă). [mod.L. (C. Moench *Methodus Plantas Horti Botanici et Agri Marburgensis* (1794) 631), f. the name of Johann Hieronymus *Kniphof* (1704–63), German physician and botanist + -ia[1].] A perennial herb of the genus so called, native to southern or eastern Africa, belonging to the family Liliaceæ, and bearing spikes of red, yellow, or orange flowers; also called red-hot poker, torch lily, and formerly Tritoma, a synonymous generic name.

1854 *Curtis's Bot. Mag.* LXXX. 4816 Serrulated-leaved Kniphofia... Of late years visitors to the Royal Gardens of Kew have been much struck with the beauty of the flower-spikes of a *Kniphofia* (*Tritoma* of most authors), planted in several of the beds. **1900** W. D. Drury *Bk. Gardening* x. 336 Kniphofias may be accommodated in shrubberies and wide borders. **1935** A. G. L. Hellyer *Pract. Gardening* x. 81 Delphiniums, kniphofias, and ordinary lupins may be planted from 2 feet to 2 feet 6 inches apart. **1971** *Country Life* 2 Sept. 567/2 You will probably put your emphasis..on delphiniums, kniphofias, [etc.].

knish (kniʃ). [Yiddish, f. Russ. *knish*, *knysh* a kind of cake.] A dumpling of flaky dough filled with chopped liver, potato, or cheese, and baked or fried.

1930 A. Gross *Kibitzer's Dict.* 47 Knishes—Dyspepsia. **1932** L. Golding *Magnolia St.* III. vii. 560 There would be *knishehs* to eat. **1960** *New Yorker* 29 Oct. 36/3 Have a canapé. The knishes are especially delicious. **1965** 'E. Queen' *Fourth Side of Triangle* iv. 164 We take one of these thin little pancakes, or knishes—almost like tortillas, aren't they? **1973** *Times* 12 Apr. 18/7 Arthur Goldberg, the Democratic candidate, was running a gauntlet of knishes, pizza and egg-roll wherever he went. **1973** *Daily Colonist* (Victoria, B.C.) 27 May 2/4 He consumed three meat knishes, two blueberry knishes, four potato knishes and two cream-filled knishes.

knit, *v.* Add: **2. c.** *spec.* To do knitting in plain stitch as opposed to purl.

c **1890** tr. *T. de Dillmont's Encycl. Needlewk.* 196 Piqué pattern..1st and 2nd row—purl 7, knit 1, purl 1, knit 1, [etc.]. **1902** [see Purl *v.*[1] 4]. **1944** A. Thirkell *Headmistress* iii. 61 She was well settled into knit two, purl two. **1972** 'B. Graeme' *Tomorrow's Yesterday* xiv. 142 She would have to undo three rows of knitting. Knit two, purl two, the pattern called for, but she had knitted one and purled three.

knit, *sb.* **1.** Delete † *Obs.* and add later examples. Also, a knitted fabric. **knit stitch,** the plainest stitch in knitting.

1897 *Sears, Roebuck Catal.* 217/3 Turtle Neck Sweater. Extra heavy knit. All wool. **1932** D. C. MINTER *Mod. Needlecraft* 68/2 (*caption*) Rows of plain knitting... Smooth knit stitch;..rough purl stitch. **1960** *Guardian* 19 Feb. 8/6 Dress and jacket of corded cotton knit. **1960** *News Chron.* 22 Mar. 11/3 Textured nylon is making news with new chunky knits, and fur fabrics. **1963** *New Yorker* 29 June 44 It looks like sharkskin, but it's really a knit. **1964** *Guardian* 22 Jan. 8/4 Knits are used for dresses, coats, suits.., so that it is possible to dress in knitwear from dawn to dark. **1964** *McCall's Sewing* iv. 53/1 When buying a knit, remember that it is a resilient fabric.

b. The action or process of knitting.

1926 E. K. MIDDLETON *New Knitting* Pref., Left hand knit and left hand purl are simpler and quicker than the old right hand knit.

c. A knitted garment. Freq. in *pl.*

1938 D. BAKER *Young Man with Horn* I. iv. 38 His brother Henry..was selling jersey knits. **1965** *Harper's Bazaar* June 66 Sportive, can't-wait-for-winter knits. **1972** *Daily Tel.* 30 Oct. 13/1 Glitter knits are one of the top fashions for winter.

knit, *ppl. a.* Add: **2.** [Or a use of *KNIT *sb.* I.] (Further examples.)

1895 *Montgomery Ward Catal.* 283/1 Children's Knit Undershirts. Ladies' Jersey Knit Ribbed Vests. **1897** *Sears, Roebuck Catal.* 203/1 Lumberman's Knit Socks. **1922** E. E. CUMMINGS *Enormous Room* vii. 155 A knit sweater of a strangely ugly red hue. **1962** F. I. ORDWAY et al. *Basic Astronautics* xiii. 517 The inner liner of the suit is of neoprene-coated fabric with knit stretch sections. **1970** *Catal. L. L. Bean* (Freeport, Maine) Fall 32 Deluxe insulated coverall... Knit cuffs at wrists. **1970** *Women's Wear Daily* 23 Nov. 31/2 So many knit pants in the market are dumb, missy looks.

knitted, *ppl. a.* Add: Also as *sb.*, a knitted garment. Freq. in *pl.*

1958 *Woman* 9 Aug. 31/4 Briony is going to Ardoaghy to buy more knitteds. **1960** *Woman's Own* 19 Mar. 34/2 Two elegant knitteds from one set of instructions. **1963** *Harper's Bazaar* Feb. 41 The knitteds we can't do without.

knitting, *vbl. sb.* Add: **1. c.** A girl or girls. *slang.*

1943 C. H. WARD-JACKSON *Piece of Cake* 39 *Knitting*, girl or girls. **1946** J. IRVING *Royal Navalese* 104 *Knitting*, girls in the plural. The singular of this is '*A Piece of Knitting*'. **1962** GRANVILLE *Dict. Sailors' Slang* 68/2 *Knitting*, girl friend or girls collectively.

3. *knitting bag, bee, book, frolic, machine, pattern, silk* (example), *wire, wool*; **knitting-pin** (earlier example); **knitting sheath** (later U.S. example).

1789 W. COWPER *Let.* 31 Jan. in *Corr.* (1904) III. 347 A basket..[which] contained..a Knitting bag, and a piece of plumcake. **1939** J. CARY *Mister Johnson* 209 The accomplished..traveller..sets up her household, complete with family and knitting bag, even in trains and tram shelters. **1971** A. CHRISTIE *Nemesis* ii. 20 Taking her knitting out of its embroidered knitting bag. **1855** *Chicago Times* 19 Mar. 2/6 This girl had been at a knitting bee, at the house of a friend. **1880** *Harper's Mag.* Sept. 508/1 In winter they sometimes had knitting bees. **1843** A. LAMBERT (*title*) My knitting-book. **1873** *Young Englishwoman* June 311/3 We must refer you to Madame Goubaud's Knitting and Netting Book. **1973** HORNE & BOWDEN *Bk. Knitting & Crochet* i. 10 The contents of the knitting books of the 1840s differed greatly from those of today. **1818** H. B. FEARON *Sk. Amer.* 223 They are invited to the preacher's house, to partake of a supper... This is termed a knitting frolic. **1858** P. L. SIMMONDS *Dict. Trade Products* 216/2 *Knitting machine*, a machine for weaving and making knitted work. **1927** M. OSTENSO *Mad Carews* (1929) iv. 44 Her mother had sent to the city for a knitting machine in the hope that she might be able to supply her neighbours with woollen socks. **1974** *Times* 12 Feb. 11/5 He started..with a couple of hand frame knitting machines. **1885** C. M. YONGE *Nuttie's Father* II. i. 7, I couldn't get a knitting pattern Miss Headworth was to send Lady Ronnisglen. **1961** M. STEWART *Ivy Tree* iii. 46 The colourless voice..might have been discussing a knitting pattern. **1973** 'J. ASHFORD' *Double Run* xi. 85 Nina, at a critical point in the intricate knitting pattern, ..dropped a stitch. **1857** C. M. YONGE *Dynevor Terrace* I. iv. 49 He had in the other pocket..wools..the long knitting-pins under his arm like a riding-whip. **1867** T. LACKLAND' *Homespun* I. 23 A great tear trembles on her cheek as she adjusts her needle in the knitting sheath she wears. **1897** *Sears, Roebuck Catal.* 321/2 Knitting and Crochet Silk..is used for knitting mittens, stockings and other articles which require washing. **1850** *Rep. Comm. Patents 1849* (U.S.) 491 The needle itself, and thimble will be exhibited in museums with distaffs, spinning-wheels, knitting-wires, [etc.]. **1860** GEO. ELIOT *Mill on Floss* III. VI. vi. 87 Maggie's ball of knitting-wool rolled along the ground. **1965** A. CHRISTIE *At Bertram's Hotel* xii. 114 She had a splendid time rounding up knitting patterns, new varieties of knitting wool, and suchlike delights.

knitwear (ni·twēəɹ). [f. KNIT *ppl. a.* + WEAR *sb.*] Knitted articles of clothing.

1925–6 *Army & Navy Co-op. Soc. Price List* 698 'Braemar' Knitwear for Gentlemen. **1928** *Daily Express* 7 May 4 Two-piece suits, knitwear, leather coats and raincoats. **1957** L. F. R. WILLIAMS *State of Israel* 111 There is already some considerable export of cotton goods, as well as of knitwear. **1966** *Illustr. London News* 26 Feb. 5 The knitwear is made of Shetland wool and is fully fashioned with raglan sleeves. **1973** J. THOMSON *Death Cap* vi. 91 He was in Bradford, seeing some knitwear manufacturers on business.

knob, *sb.* Add: **1. e.** *with knobs on*: jocular slang phr. = 'that and more' (indicating ironic or emphatic agreement, or in retort to an insult, etc.).

1930 M. KENNEDY *Fool of Family* xiii. 129 'I'm waiting for the Marchese Ferdinando Emanuele Maria Bonaventura Donzati.' 'With knobs on,' agreed Gemma airily. 'Who's he?' **1931** J. J. FARJEON *House Opposite* ii, 'You are nothing,' said the Indian. 'And so are you, with knobs on!' barked Ben, and slammed the door. **1938** WODEHOUSE *Code of Woosters* viii. 196 '"Ha jolly ha!" to you, young Stiffy, with knobs on,' I retorted with quiet dignity. **1941** M. TREADGOLD *We couldn't leave Dinah* xv. 232 '*Schweinhund*,' screamed Nannerl. '*Schweinhund* yourself with knobs on,' returned Petit-Jean tartly. **1959** I. & P. OPIE *Lore & Lang. Schoolch.* iii. 45 Same to you with knobs on. **1969** *Guardian* 22 Feb. 9/6 They shouted something... 'The same to you with knobs on,' Jim shouted back. **1970** A. PRICE *Labyrinth Makers* xiv. 179 If the A.S. 12 was the answer to Egypt's Russian missile boats, the A.S. 15 was the answer with knobs on.

2. (Later U.S. example.)

1895 *Century Mag.* Aug. 621/2 One of the many knobs from which Daniel Boone is said to have looked first over the Blue Grass land.

4. b. *Austral.* and *N.Z. slang.* A double-headed penny. Also *nob*.

1928 J. DEVANNY *Dawn Beloved* xv. 163 Sometimes two pennies are filed down to half their thickness and then joined together. A double-tailer is called a 'grey'; a double-header a 'nob'. Of course, anyone caught cheating is liable to get bashed about a bit. **1941** BAKER *Dict. Austral. Slang* 41 *Knob*, a double-headed penny.

8. *knob-twiddling, -twister, -twisting*; **knob-cone pine,** *Pinus attenuata*, a species native to California; **knob-nose** *S. Afr.*, name applied to a member or to a tribe of 'Kaffirs' having this distinguishing feature; also *attrib.* (or as *adj.*); **knob-nosed** *a.*, having a knob-shaped nose; *spec.* = **knob-nose*.

[**1882** A. KELLOGG *Forest Trees of California* in *Rep. State Mineralogist California* Appendix II. 51 Knobby-cone Pine... The Knobby Pine is a lofty tree of much beauty.] **1884** C. S. SARGENT *Rep. Forests N. Amer.* 196 *Pinus tuberculata*...Knobcone pine. **1905** —— *Man. Trees N. Amer.* 22 *Pinus attenuata*, Lemm. Knob-cone pine... Fruit..becoming light chestnut-brown, with thin flat scales rounded at the apex, those on the outer side being enlarged into prominent transversely flattened knobs. **1932** W. DALLIMORE in *Conifers in Cultivation* (R. Hort. Soc.) 28 *Pinus.. attenuata* Lemm. (*P. tuberculata* Gord.)—Knob-cone Pine—Oregon to California. **1967** N. T. MIROV *Genus Pinus* iii. 170 *Pinus attenuata* is known as 'knobcone pine'. Its area is chiefly in California, although..it extends northward to the mountains of southwestern Oregon. **1900** A. H. KEANE *Boer States* vii. 99 Hence the extraordinary differences that are observed between..the degraded Magwamba ('demons' or 'devils'), called 'Knobnoses' by the Transvaal Boers, and the Basutos. **1943** D. REITZ *No Outspan* iv. 59 We went up along the Sami river to Sibasa's country and then to the chief of the knob-nose kaffirs. **1839** W. C. HARRIS *Wild Sports S. Afr.* xxxix. 350 A friendly tribe of natives, whom, from a peculiarity in the nasal prominence, they dignified with the appellation of 'knob-nosed Kafirs'. **1864** J. A. GRANT *Walk across Afr.* 93 A knob-nosed duck. **1887** Knob-nosed [in Dict.]. **1905** *Westm. Gaz.* 2 Oct. 8/2 The knob-nosed lizard (*Lyriocephalus scutatus*) from Ceylon. **1968** *Times* 29 Nov. 1/1 Some are hi-fi maniacs, knob-twiddling perfectionists. **1973** *Times* 7 June 18/6 He thinks commercial competition could benefit the BBC..by encouraging them to do more knob-twiddling, instead of staying tuned to one programme all day. **1940** *Chambers's Techn. Dict.* 478/2 *Knob-twister*. A casual reference to monitor man or recordist in motion-picture production. **1950** *People* (Austral.) 7 June 50/2 He believes that 90 per cent of the 'knob-twisters', as they are called, favor the abolition of the [betting] boards. **1929** *Radio Times* 8 Nov. 450/2 'Earth's End' stations can be received..if you..find your fun in knob twisting. **1958** *Listener* 13 Nov. 799/2 Audiences for a number of these [programmes] have dropped considerably since they were transferred from their old places in the Light Programme. This might be blamed on mass inertia, as applied to knob-twisting.

knobbler. 1. (Later example.)

1971 *Country Life* 19 Aug. 431/2 They were all dead, six of them: five hinds and calves and a small knobbler.

knobbly, *a.* Add: Esp. of knees; *knobbly-knees competition*, a competition in which a prize is awarded to the competitor with the 'knobbliest' knees.

1958 *Times* 15 Aug. 9/4 These knees are..knobbly and ..unsightly. **1968** *Listener* 12 Sept. 349/3 When I witness a theatrical 'happening' and 'audience participation' is urged upon me, I generally feel that I would sooner enter for a knobbly-knees competition at Butlin's.

knobby, *a.* Add: **3.** Full of rounded knolls or hills; hilly. *U.S.*

1869 'MARK TWAIN' *Innoc. Abr.* liii. 558 It is as knobby with countless little domes as a prison door is with bolt-heads.

knobby (nǫ·bi), *sb. Austral.* [f. the adj.] An opal.

1921 K. S. PRICHARD *Black Opal* I. i. 8 'Look at this.. and this!' he cried eagerly, going over the two or three small knobbies in his hand... 'I'm going in now,' he said, thrusting the opals into the bag. *Ibid.* iii. 23 Paul was holding up a good-looking knobby so that red, green, and gold lights glittered through its shining potch as he moved it. **1971** J. S. GUNN *Opal Terminol.* 24 *Knobby*, opal which is found as a solid lump..rather than in a seam formation.

knobkerrie. Add: (Earlier and later examples.) Also **knob-kerri, knobkier(r)ie, knobkirrie, knob-kurrie, knopkierie.**

1844 *United Service Mag.* July 337 With the precious book..in one hand, and his knob-kurrie in the other, away he trudged. **1926** T. E. LAWRENCE *Seven Pillars* (1935) VI. lxix. 384 Spattering the brains of a cornered mob of Germans one by one with his African knob-kerri. **1940** BAUMANN & BRIGHT *Lost Republic* 220 When a Basuto beats his wife, he does it with a knopkierie. **1949** *Cape Argus* 10 Nov. 1/6 Motibeli was struck on the head with a knobkierie. **1961** *Reader's Digest* Feb. 142/1 On the river-bed lay the weapon—an African knopkierie. **1973** *Times* 8 Feb. 1/5 The chanting Africans, waving knobkerries, were cordoned off by police. **1974** *Eastern Province Herald* 2 Sept. 1 Miners attacked each other with knobkerries.

knock, *v.* Add: **2.** Also, *to knock a hole, gap,* etc.; *to knock daylight into* (cf. DAYLIGHT I c).

1881 *Punch* 17 Sept. 124/1 Ready at the call of duty to frame a new programme or knock daylight into an old one. **1890** A. CONAN DOYLE *Sign of Four* iv. 68 He knocked a hole..in the lath and plaster ceiling. **1906** SOMERVILLE & 'ROSS' *Some Irish Yesterdays* 85 You may see him skilfully 'knocking a gap' (*i.e.* unbuilding a wall).

c. (Later examples.)

1898 A. BENNETT *Man from North* xi. 95 Two guineas the suit, my boy! Won't I knock 'em in the Wal-worth Road! **1910** WODEHOUSE *Psmith in City* xix. 167 He told him that he had knocked them at the Bedford the week before. **1947** K. TENNANT *Lost Haven* vii. 97 The skirt was flared with cunning little tucks at the waist, so that it fitted her like a glove... 'That ought to knock them,' Mark's granddaughter said aloud. **1954** 'N. BLAKE' *Whisper in Gloom* I. vi. 83 Wasn't she in pantomime?.. Bet she knocked them.

d. To copulate with; also, to make pregnant. So in phr. *to knock a child* (or *an apple*) *out* (*of*).

1598 FLORIO *Worlde of Wordes* 94/1 *Cunnuta*, a woman nocked. **1604** MARSTON *Malcontent* III. iii. sig. E2v Haue beate my Shoomaker, knockt my Sempstres, cuckold my Pottecary, and vndone my Taylor. **1785** GROSE *Dict. Vulgar T.*, *Knock*, to knock a woman, to have carnal knowledge of her. **1818** KEATS *Let.* 5 Jan. (1931) I. 80 They call good Wine a pretty tipple, and call getting a Child knocking out an apple. **1922** JOYCE *Ulysses* 401, I cannot but extol the virile potency of the old bucko that could still knock another child out of her. **1936** J. STEINBECK *In Dubious Battle* iv. 45 Sooner or later some girl'd get knocked higher than a kite. **1963** T. PARKER *Unknown Citizen* v. 120 You give your missus so much money a week, you knock a few kids out of her, and that's about it, really. **1967** D. PINNER *Ritual* ix. 96 I've knocked some girls in my time but I've never had such a rabbiter as you. The cruder it is, the more you like it.

e. To rob (esp. a safe or till). *Underworld slang.*

1767 *Sessions Papers* IV. 151/2, I heard him say he got twelve shillings once by *knocking the lobb*... What is that?.. That is breaking open a place. **1924** G. C. HENDERSON *Keys to Crookdom* App. B. 397 Blowing a peter. Blowing a safe open with explosives. Also called knocking a peter, blowing a pete, getting a box. **1963** *Times* 25 May 12/2 The appellant had been asked if he had told someone in the 'Norfolk' that he got the money by safe breaking. The appellant had replied: 'Aye but you will never prove that I got it by knocking a safe.'

f. To speak ill or slightingly of, disparage, find fault with, criticize captiously. Also *intr.* and *absol. colloq.* (orig. *U.S.*).

1892 'J. MILLER' *Workingman's Paradise* 85 Admit it's a business concern and that everybody growls at it, it's the only paper that dares knock things. **1896** ADE *Artie* xii. 106 There's a lot o' people in the ward that's got their hammers out and they're knockin' him all they can. *Ibid.* 110 He's got to make good with 'em to keep 'em from knockin. **1901** 'H. MCHUGH' *John Henry* 54 I'm not knocking, remember; I'm only saying what I think. I hate a knocker. **1904** *Sun* (N.Y.) 4 Aug. 5 'Of course there'll be plenty of cranks to knock this scheme,' said he. **1906** *Daily Colonist* (Victoria, B.C.) 16 Jan. 4/3, I refer to the practice of allowing any kicker in the city to avail himself of newspaper space to knock some public man or some public institution. **1919** 'IAN HAY' *Last Million* iii. 36 A certain licence is permitted to professional grouchers; but 'knocking' the Cause is the one thing that the New Crusaders will not permit. **1926** *Spectator* 3 Apr. 635/2 A reputation for 'knocking' is enough to ensure being blackballed from some of the best clubs. **1930** WODEHOUSE *Very Good, Jeeves!* ii. 44 Where does a valet get off, censoring vases? Does it fall within his province to knock the young master's chinaware? **1958** K. AMIS *I like it Here* xvi. 205, I shouldn't like you to get the idea I'm trying to knock Portugal and the Portuguese. **1958** *Spectator* 12 Dec. 865/1 On the last page he protests about 'the growing tendency in some newspapers today to write only "knocking" stories about stars as big as Tommy'. But..almost any publicity is good publicity: you can knock around the clock and the moon-faced masses will only hear applause. **1970** *New Scientist* 5 Mar. 478/2 They're knocking Concorde again, the cads. **1974** *Observer* 22 Sept. 14/5 It's fashionable nowadays to 'knock' England for its shortcomings.

5. b. (Further examples.) Also, (i) of an internal-combustion engine, to suffer from knock caused by faulty combustion (see *KNOCK $sb.^{1}$ I c). (ii) Of fuel for an internal-combustion engine: to give rise to knock when burnt in an engine.

1905 *Daily Chron.* 5 May 3/5 You advance your spark.. to the point at which your engine does not knock. **1909** *Motor Cycling* 22 Nov. 32/1 If the engine begins to 'knock', a few vigorous thrusts at the pedals should be given immediately. **1916** Eighinger & Hutton *Steam Traction Engineering* v. 156 The main shaft boxes..will often knock. **1925** R. J. B. Sellar *Sporting Yarns* 186, I shall have to pull up, old chap. Cylinder's knocking! **1927** *Industr. & Engin. Chem.* Jan. 145/1 There is at present no satisfactory method of expressing the tendency of a fuel to 'knock', or detonate. **1937** Wodehouse *Lord Emsworth & Others* ix. 299, I became aware that the engine was not humming so smoothly. It had begun to knock. **1960** V. B. Guthrie *Petroleum Products Handbk.* iv. 21 Engine designers..have done a great deal to minimize the tendency of engines to knock. **1966** *McGraw-Hill Encycl. Sci. & Technol.* III. 309/2 Hydrocarbon fuels with compact molecular structures are less likely to knock.

6. b. *to knock the end in* or *off*: to spoil the whole affair. *slang.* ? *Obs.*

1919 *Athenæum* 8 Aug. 727/2 To 'knock the end in' is to spoil the whole show. **1925** Fraser & Gibbons *Soldier & Sailor Words* 138 *Knock the end off, to*, to spoil anything.

e. Also *to knock all of a* *heap, *down with a* *feather, *for a* *loop, *for* *six; *to knock* silly, *cold, *endways, *rotten, *sideways; *to knock the nonsense*, etc., *out of*.

1856 C. M. Yonge *Daisy Chain* i. v. 48 The girlishness and timidity will be knocked out of him by the boys. **1892** 'Mark Twain' *Amer. Claimant* v. 63 'When I came to breakfast Miss Gwendolen—well, she knocked everything out of me, you know—.' 'Wonderful girl, wonderful.' **1931** *Times Lit. Suppl.* 15 Oct. 787/1 The boy returned to Turin, where his royal relatives did their best to get his revolutionary notions knocked out of him. **1935** L. & A. Maude tr. *Tolstoy's Iván Ilých & Hadji Murád* 273 They'd have knocked the nonsense out of you in the army, and he was worth five of such as you at home!

7. knock about. a. (Earlier and later examples.)

a **1817** Jane Austen *Persuasion* (1818) III. iii. 44 They [*sc.* sailors] are all knocked about, and exposed to every climate, and every weather, till they are not fit to be seen. **1926** T. E. Lawrence *Seven Pillars* (1935) lxxvi. 424 Young Mustafa refused to cook rice; Farraj and Daud knocked him about until he cried. **1969** *Listener* 24 July 103/2 After being knocked about to an appalling extent in the first week of the war, the Poles were rallying until the Russians came in on the other side.

b. (Earlier and later examples.)

1833 *Sk. & Eccentr. D. Crockett* i. 31 David, collecting his clothes,..began to knock about. **1834** W. G. Simms *Guy Rivers* II. viii. 98 I've been a matter of some fifteen or twenty years knocking about..in one way or another. **1929** C. Mackenzie *Gallipoli Memories* iii. 21 He had knocked about all over the Pacific and would have been a splendid companion. **1937** M. Sharp *Nutmeg Tree* xx. 265 You're older, and you've knocked about a bit.

c. *to knock the balls about*: to strike a (billiard, croquet, etc.) ball idly; to play (such a ball game) in a casual fashion.

1864 C. M. Yonge *Trial* II. vi. 123 Tom..had seen the Andersons knocking about the balls in the new gardens.. and proposed to..try to get up a match. **1872** Trollope *Golden Lion* xviii. 305 He knocked the balls about with his cue. **1907** F. E. E. Bell *At Works* vi. 130, I have seen a club with two free tables, where men..have been happily knocking the balls about from 9 a.m. onwards. **1916** A. Bennett *These Twain* ii. xiv. 271 'Shall we knock the balls about a bit?' They began a mild game of croquet.

d. To lie around, to be available or in the vicinity; to impend.

1866 F. Hunt *25 Yrs. Experience N.Z.* ix. 45 My carpet bag I left knocking about amongst them with utmost carelessness. **1870** R. P. Whitworth *Martin's Bay Settlement* 23/1, I have commenced to make a dingy..out of old boards that are knocking about. **1889** G. B. Shaw *London Music 1888–89* (1937) 116 There is plenty of musical talent knocking about misused or misdirected. **1897** P. A. Philips *Memories of Past* 21 When we did have them they were pretty severe [fires], such as..W. S. Grahame's in Fort Street (any amount of drink knocking about), the fire in High Street. **1902** Conrad *Typhoon* ii. 22 Observing the steady fall of the barometer, Captain MacWhirr thought, 'There's some dirty weather knocking about.' **1908** W. H. Koebel *Anchorage* ii. 45 Do you know of a billet knockin' about anywhere that'ud suit him, boss? **1916** A. Bennett *These Twain* i. v. 60 'There are one or two ordinaries knocking about the place,' said Edwin, 'but we haven't got a proper bicycle-house.' **1939** [see *eye *sb.*[1] 3 b]. **1948** R. Finlayson *Tidal Creek* i. 17 I'll just see about a box that ought to be knocking about.

e. *to knock about with*: to be a habitual companion of.

1915 T. Burke *Nights in Town* 323 We talked of Love, Wines, Dinners, Music-halls, of the men we had knocked about with, the girls we had loved. **1924** M. Kennedy *Constant Nymph* viii. 122 Look at the sort of people the poor child has knocked about with.

7*. knock around, round = *knock about* (sense 7 b). Also *fig.*

1848 W. T. Thompson *Major Jones's Sk. Travel* 8 I'm gwine..to New York,..and Boston and all about thar, and spend the summer until pickin time, nockin round in them big cities, mong them peeple what's so monstrous smart. **1856** C. E. Delong in *Calif. Hist. Soc. Q.* (1930) IX. 65 Got up late knocked around. **1874** V. Pyke *Adventures G. W. Pratt* (1890) i. vi. 27 Seems there's a joke knocking around somewhere. **1884** [in Dict., sense 5 d]. **1924** C. Mackenzie *Heavenly Ladder* iii. 55 Not that I'm against your style of services myself. But most of the people round here haven't knocked around like I have. **1938** G. Greene *19 Stories* (1947) 76 He's knocking around somewhere. **1959** P. McCutchan *Storm South* xiii. 198 Mrs. van Neyland's been a married woman, and she's knocked around.

7. knock back. a.** *trans.* To refuse, to rebuff. *Austral.* and *N.Z. colloq.*

1930 V. Palmer in *Bulletin* (Sydney) 19 Feb. 51/1 Not the sort of man we want... I knocked him back. **1939** K. Tennant *Foveaux* iv. ii. 368 Why, she knocks back the boss where she works, if he gets gay. **1944** L. Glassop *We were Rats* xviii. 104 Still goin' to keep knockin' back the sheilas? **1948** V. Palmer *Golconda* xi. 85 Most of them knocked his appeals back lightly and watched the proceedings with tolerant amusement. **1952** J. Cleary *Sundowners* ii. 108 He wouldn't knock it [*sc.* money] back if you offered it to him. **1957** 'N. Culotta' *They're a Weird Mob* (1958) vi. 86 Never knock back O.P's [*sc.* other people's smokes]. **1969** *Private Eye* 12 Sept. 14 (*caption*) Knocking back a free night at the *flea-pit* too. **1973** *Nation Rev.* (Melbourne) 24–30 Aug. 1398/6 Never knock back a dollar, I guess.

b. *trans.* To drink (esp. intoxicants) or eat heartily or heavily; to swallow a drink at a gulp. Also in phr. *to knock it back. colloq.*

1931 Brophy & Partridge *Songs & Slang 1914–18* (ed. 3) 326 *Knock it back.*—To eat; sometimes, to drink. **1939** *Eastbourne Herald* 6 May 13/2 Thirsty Eastbourne really does 'knock back' thousands of gallons in the course of a year. **1947** 'A. P. Gaskell' *Big Game* 8 'Boy oh boy oh boy,' he chanted, 'won't I knock back those handles tonight.' **1951** J. B. Priestley *Festival at Farbridge* iii. ii. 476 That's why he knocked a few back—and he doesn't as a rule. **1951** 'J. Wyndham' *Day of Triffids* i. 26, I knocked back the last of my brandy, and went out. **1953** X. Fielding *Stronghold* iii. iv. 221, I hear you knock it back a bit. Well, so do I. **1957** C. MacInnes *City of Spades* i. ix. 69 My two friends knocked back their gins. **1957** 'N. Culotta' *They're a Weird Mob* (1958) iii. 42 'What is this pin one on, Joe?' 'Knock one back. Gunna 'ave a drink?' **1961** M. Kelly *Spoilt Kill* ii. 71 When you were fourteen you knocked back a whole jar..at one sitting. **1968** M. Richler in R. Weaver *Canad. Short Stories* 2nd Ser. 194 Hod was knocking back large snifters of brandy.

c. *trans.* To retard, to check. *Austral.* and *N.Z.*

1945 J. Pascoe in *N.Z. Geographer* I. 27 An early winter will knock his flock back. **1946** F. Sargeson *That Summer* 85 The two sprees had knocked me back considerably [financially].

8. knock down. a. Also, to bring down by a shot, or by artillery, etc., fire.

1733 W. Byrd *Journey Land of Eden* in *Writings* (1901) 311 We pursued our Journey thro' uneven and perplexed Woods, and in the thickest of them had the Fortune to knock down a young Buffalo, 2 Years old. **1809** M. L. Weems *Life F. Marion* xi. 98 Many a family goes without dinner unless the father can knock down a squirrel in the woods. **1940** *War Illustr.* 12 Apr. 366/3 But before the Germans had managed to recover from their surprise that only three British 'planes dared to attack them, the young flight leader had knocked down two of them.

f. (Further examples. Cf. Knock-down *a.* 3 (in Dict. and Suppl.), *knocked-down* s.v. *knocked *ppl. a.* 2.)

1945 B. Macdonald *Egg & I* (1946) xix. 194 The six-hundred-gallon water tank arrived, knocked down and looking disappointingly like a bundle of faggots. **1958** *Times Rev. Industry* Dec. 65/3 Motor-car body shells.. knocked down for export. **1973** *Amer. Speech 1969* XLIV. 206 *Knock down*, disassemble freight or merchandise.

h. (Earlier and later examples.) Also *N.Z. slang.* Hence **knocking down** *vbl. sb.*

1852 in *Occasional Papers Univ. Sydney Austral. Lang. Res. Centre* (1966) No. 9. 15 They then go 'upon the burst' as they call it, and drink until all their earnings are 'knocked down'. **1861** H. W. Harper *Lett. from N.Z.* (1914) 65 [Station hands] proceed to 'knock down their cheque', giving it to the landlord and bidding him treat all comers as long as it lasts. **1866** *Bk. Canterbury Rhymes* 19, I knock my earnings down [at the Royal Hotel]. **1874** A. Bathgate *Colonial Experiences* xi. 142 He would get amongst a bad lot and knock down every penny of our hard-earned cash. **1879** J. Grey *His Island Home* iii. 32/1 They were 'knocking down' their cheques and living at the rate of ten thousand a year. *Ibid.*, They appeared to derive intense satisfaction from the knocking down process until their resources were exhausted. **1904** M. Cradock *Sport in N.Z.* i. i. 10 Their rabbit cheques generally find their way to the nearest public house, to be 'knocked down' as soon as received. **1965** J. S. Gunn *Terminol. Shearing Industry* i *Knock down*, to spend a cheque, usually in one quick celebration.

i. (Earlier examples.) Also, to embezzle generally.

a **1854** J. F. Kelley *Humors of Falconbridge* (1856) 86 No knocking down, sir! **1864** T. L. Nichols *40 Yrs. Amer. Life* I. 89 The omnibus-drivers were expected to 'knock down' a certain proportion of the receipts. **1872** J. D. McCabe *Lights & Shadows N.Y. Life* xi. 214 In order to make up the deficiency between their actual wages and their necessities, the conductors and drivers have fallen into the habit of appropriating a part of the money received from passengers to their own use...This practice of 'knocking down', or appropriating money, begins with the conductor, as he alone receives the money paid for fares. **1949** 'J. Evans' *Halo in Brass* xx. 172 Some..clerk who was knocking down on the till.

k. *pass.* Of a ship (see quots. 1891 and 1948). *U.S.*

1873 G. H. Procter *Fisherman's Memorial* 128 A severe gale, which knocked the vessel down and nearly swamped her. **1891** H. Patterson *Illustr. Naut. Dict.* 104 *Knocked down*, said of a vessel when, by the force of the wind acting upon her sails and spars, she is careened to such an extent that she does not recover herself. **1948** R. de Kerchove *Internat. Maritime Dict.* 387/1 *Knocked-down*, the situation of a vessel listed over by wind to such an extent that it does not recover.

l. To earn, get paid. *U.S.*

1929 M. Lief *Hangover* vi. 100 She and Humphrey rented a cottage in Westport..where authors who knocked down $3,000 for knocking out a short story of 5,000 words, built such magnificent houses. **1949** *New Yorker* 5 Nov. 76/2 You wanna know hommuch that animal knocks down a week?

10. knock off. b. (Later example.) Also, to discharge or dismiss from employment, to 'lay off'.

1881 A. Bathgate *Waitaruna* xii. 172 [The boss] would growl at the offending shearer and make use of some vague threat of 'knocking him off'. **1896** 'M. Rutherford' *Clara Hopgood* xxvi. 256 As reg'lar as winter comes Longwood is knocked off—no work. **1955** *Times* 9 June 8/3 The Cunard company put the main restaurant at his service and the staff captain 'knocked off all the men from their duties'.

c. (Earlier and later examples in sense 'to desist from one's work or occupation'.)

1842 *Spirit of Times* 4 June 158/2 My tackle being very light I had to humor him, and 'twas full half an hour before I killed him. Knocked off, and set Joe to work to boil rock [i.e. fish]. **1851** H. Melville *Moby Dick* II. xii. 95 Do you want to sink the ship, by knocking off at a time like this? **1916** 'Boyd Cable' *Doing their Bit* iii. 49 The factory was knocking off for dinner as we came away. **1969** M. Crouch *Essex* ii. 28 One who has just knocked off for his tea-break.

d. (Earlier Amer. example.)

1767 'A. Barton' *Disappointment* i. i. 10 As for McSnip, he intends to knock off business, home to England and purchase a title.

e. *spec.* To write, paint, etc., in a hurried and perfunctory fashion.

1886 in *Amer. Speech* (1950) XXV. 35/1 When he knocked off a few stanzas of poetry. **1925** R. Fry *Let.* 11 Nov. (1972) II. 584 Derain..lets 'em [*sc.* dealers] have any old thing, or rather, what's much worse, any new thing which he's knocked off. **1970** W. Garner *Puppet-Masters* xv. 124 Look, you could knock off a few hundred words on Baxx without so much as scratching the surface of your *magnum opus*.

f. (Earlier and later examples.)

1811 Jane Austen *Let.* 6 June (1952) 288 As *you* knock off a week from the end of her visit, & *Martha* rather more from the beginning, the thing is out of the question. *a* **1817** —— *Persuasion* (1818) III. ii. 26 Every comfort of life knocked off! Journeys, London, servants, horses, table. **1869** *Bradshaw's Railway Manual* XXI. 384 A great deal is knocked off from our claim against the Grand Trunk. **1926** J. Buchan *Dancing Floor* i. i. 11 First string of the 'Varsity mile. Believed..to be going to knock five seconds off his last year's time. **1966** *Melody Maker* 15 Oct. 19 (Advt.), Quality instruments at knocked-off prices. **1972** *Daily Tel.* 30 Mar. 19/2 The gloomy assessment..knocked 12p off ICI's share price in London.

g. *Cricket.* Of batsmen, to score the runs requisite for victory, or to oblige (a bowler) to be taken off by scoring heavily from his bowling.

1851 J. Pycroft *Cricket Field* ii. 30 If in the field..and trying hard to prevent these few runs being knocked off by the last wickets, I know of no excitement so intense. **1860** *Baily's Monthly Mag.* Mar. 34 These two gentlemen scored 123 runs between them, knocking off Caffyn, Jackson, Parr, [etc.]. **1963** A. Ross *Australia 63* 18 Pullar and Cowdrey knocked off the 49 required to win without actually being separated.

h. [*imp.* use of 10 c.] *knock it off!*: leave off! stop it!

1902 *N.Z. Illustr. Mag.* V. 488 Knock it off, boys. **1945** D. Dempsey *It ain't Brooklyn* in *Best One-Act Plays 1944* 28 Will you knock it off, please? **1961** J. Heller *Catch-22* (1962) xxvii. 294 'Hey, knock it off down there,' a voice rang out from the far end of the ward. 'Can't you see we're trying to nap?'

i. *slang.* To steal, to rob. Also *transf.*

1919 *Athenæum* 8 Aug. 729/1 A curious term used by a Tommy, in 'explaining' his deficiencies of kit, is 'Someone knocked it off' for 'Someone pinched (or made away with) it'. **1925** E. Wallace *Mind of Mr. J. G. Reeder* vi. 224 A big-shouldered man whose speciality was the 'knocking-off' of unattended motor-cars. **1938** F. D. Sharpe *Sharpe of Flying Squad* i. 14 They learn to 'knock things off'. **1956** C. Willock *Death at Flight* iv. 42 Mr. Goss had shown himself willing to knock off a pheasant himself. **1959** *New Statesman* 26 Sept. 404/2 After quietly knocking off a couple of retail shoe chains at the end of 1958, he entered the public takeover lists and won control of a Connoisseur's gobbet—Temperance Billiard Halls. **1960** *Observer* 24 Jan. 5/2 The boys either knocked off a hut where they knew gelly was kept or straightened a quarry man. **1963** J. Prescot *Case for Hearing* i. 16 Always dropping in on me..with search-warrants..and turning over that place of mine as if they expected to find some knocked-off gear there. **1969** *Sunday Truth* (Brisbane) 20 July 30/5 Only a few weeks after he finished up at St. Laurence's Christian Brothers College, Luzzcek knocked the place off. **1973** A. Hunter *Gently French* iii. 24 Just met a bloke..in the nick... Him what was in there for knocking-off cars.

j. *slang* (orig. *U.S.*). To kill; to murder.

1919 E. Streeter *Same Old Bill* 28 Im goin to rite just as much as I can. Thats partly sos you wont worry an partly so that if I get knocked off you will have something to amuse you in case you go into a convent. **1929** *Papers Mich. Acad. Sci., Arts & Lett.* X. 304 *Knocked off*, killed. **1942** E. Paul *Narrow St.* xxiv. 217 Hitler..ordered the blood purge which knocked off Roehm, Von Schleicher, and others among his former pals. **1943** P. Cheyney *You can always Duck* iv. 75 A United States Army officer was knocked off in a joint of his off Mount Street. **1948** Partridge *Dict. Forces' Slang* 107 *Knock off*, to kill. **1959** H. Hobson *Mission House Murder* xxii. 145 One of my boys..got knocked off—an' nobody does a damn' thing

about who knocked him off. **1973** C. MULLARD *Black Britain* I. ii. 24 In one village a white launched a murder campaign because 'he liked knocking off blacks'.

k. *Underworld slang.* To arrest (a person); to raid (an establishment).

1926 F. D. WILKINSON in *Flynn's* 6 Feb. 58/1 'Willie of Detroit is here and is knocking everybody off.' (Meaning, arresting them.) **1930** *Amer. Mercury* Dec. 456/2 *Knock off*, to raid; to arrest. 'The feds knock off the scatter.' **1930** G. SMITHSON *Raffles in Real Life* xix. 256 About ten days or so after being 'knocked off'..the Chief Warder came to my cell. **1939** 'D. HUME' *Heads you Live* ii. 24 You..acted as a so-called hostess at the Angel Club in Dean Street for a year before it was knocked off. **1960** J. STROUD *Shorn Lamb* iii. 33 There was two other boys wiv Egg when you knocked him off, why ain't they 'ere? **1969** R. V. BESTE *Next Time I'll Pay* xi. 157 You're the sort who'd knock off his mother because she hadn't got a lamp on her bike five minutes after lighting up time.

l. *slang.* To copulate with, to seduce (a woman).

1952 S. KAUFFMANN *Philanderer* (1953) viii. 134 Hell, she isn't much,..but she's all there is around here. And if you don't want her, I don't mind knocking her off. **1965** A. PRIOR *Interrogators* v. 69 Do you think that young twit Wilkinson is knocking her off? **1970** G. GREER *Female Eunuch* 265 The vocabulary of impersonal sex is peculiarly desolating. Who wants to..'knock off a bit? of belly? of crumpet?' **1974** *Times Lit. Suppl.* 11 Oct. 1109/4 Knocking off his best friend's busty wife during boozy sprees on leave in Soho.

12. knock out. a. Also, to stun or kill by a blow.

1903 *Sun* (N.Y.) 2 Dec. 1 Scott's reputation is excellent, and the managers fear that he has been knocked out and robbed. *a* **1918** W. OWEN *Coll. Poems* (1963) 7 Ye get knocked out; else wounded—bad or cushy; Scuppered; or nowt except yer feelin' mushy.

d. *to knock out of time*: also in extended use.

1874 TROLLOPE *Phineas Redux* II. xxviii. 228 You'll come all right after a few weeks. You've been knocked out of time;—that's the truth of it. **1891** *Young Man* Apr. 140/2 A [bicycle] ride of ten miles within the hour may mean comfort and the capability of doing another twenty easily; a ride of eleven miles in the hour may just mean knocking a man out of time. **1970** *Brewer's Dict. Phr. & Fable* (ed. 12) 613/2 *To knock out of time*, to settle one's hash, to double him up.

h. *trans.* To earn. *Austral.*, *N.Z.*, and *U.S. slang.*

[**1871** C. L. MONEY *Knocking about in N.Z.* ii. 18 They knocked out in this day as much gold as sufficed to make them afterwards two rings.] **1873** V. PYKE *Story Wild Will Enderby* (ed. 4) I. xiv. 62 Two industrious young men who worked very hard for a bare living—'just knocking out tucker', as the phrase went. **1874** —— *Adventures G. W. Pratt* 12/2, I can knock out tucker enough for the pair of us. **1920** *Sat. Even. Post* 27 Mar. 3/2 At that I was knocking out about eighteen hundred dollars per annum selling cigars out of South Bend. **1959** BAKER *Drum* (1960) II. 123 *Knock out*, to earn (a sum of money).

i. *trans.* To eliminate, remove forcibly, get rid of, destroy. orig. *U.S.*

1883 'MARK TWAIN' *Life on Mississippi* 465 The religious feature has been pretty well knocked out of it [i.e., Mardi-Gras at New Orleans]. **1889** *Kansas City* (Missouri) *Times & Star* 17 May, By a vote of 11 to 9 the Missouri senate knocked out the legislative reduction of tolls here by the Bell Telephone Company. **1904** *Sun* (N.Y.) 5 Aug. 4 In power, the Democrats wouldn't knock out protection if they could. **1927** J. N. MCILWRAITH *Kinsmen at War* xvii. 170, I will have to knock that idea out of Lucy's head too, straightway. **1933** F. BALDWIN *Innocent Bystander* (1935) ii. 30, I got a good deal of it knocked out of me. **1944** *Return to Attack* (Army Board, N.Z.) 15/1 In the Bir el Gubi area the 22nd Armoured Brigade..knocked out forty-five enemy tanks. **1955** *Times* 28 June 4/4 It is now believed that even if all the major ports of the United Kingdom were knocked out by atomic attack sufficient food for the population could still be passed through minor ports. **1971** *Daily Tel.* 17 Dec. 1 India claimed to have knocked out forty tanks in a major battle on the Kashmir front.

j. *trans.* (*Founding.*) To separate (a flask) from a casting contained inside it, or (a casting) from a flask containing it.

1906 *Jrnl. Iron & Steel Inst.* LXX. 174 The castings were all made in green sand, and were allowed to cool before being 'knocked out', *i.e.* taken from the sand. **1942** *Engineering* 6 Mar. 195/2 One difficulty was to get cool sand after the castings had been knocked out. **1955** H. E. CRIVAN in W. C. Newell *Casting of Steel* vi. 227 Heavier, dry sand work can be knocked out over a grid using hammers to loosen the sand.

k. *to knock oneself out*: to make a considerable effort, to apply oneself energetically (to the point of exhaustion).

1936 *Mademoiselle* Mar. 43/2 All the fancier lassies.. are practically knocking themselves out in an effort to get to Hollywood. **1951** GREEN & LAURIE *Show Biz* p. xxi, They like 'knocking themselves out' for *Variety*.

l. To give (a person) enjoyment, to excite. Often *refl.* and in *pass. slang* (orig. *U.S.*).

1942 *Amer. Mercury* July 95 *Knock yourself out*: have a good time. **1944** *New Yorker* 8 July 27/1 There are times when Duke laughs naturally and exuberantly; for example, when the boys..are competing to see who can whistle the lowest note. 'I knock myself out,' he says. **1947** *Band Leaders & Record Rev.* Feb. 20 'When I heard it,' Ella Mae says, 'it knocked me out.' **1953** D. WALLOP *Night Light* xix. 236 It's pretty hard to be knocked out with a baby when you know its old man is bored with the whole idea. **1956** B. HOLIDAY *Lady sings Blues* (1973) ii. 26, I used to make them crazy dishes... This used to knock him out. When my time was running out, he made me an offer to stay on and cook for him. **1957** J. KEROUAC *On Road* (1958) III. iv. 202 A man who knocked himself out every evening and let the others put the quietus to him in the night. **1966** *Melody Maker* 7 May, I only heard half an hour of Ornette but I wasn't knocked out at all.

13. knock over. a. (Further examples.)

1852 DICKENS *Bleak Ho.* (1853) xxix. 285 Such a resemblance..that it completely knocked me over. **1882** W. D. HAY *Brighter Britain!* I. vii. 184 If a single bushman could not have knocked that tree over before dinner time, he would not have been worth wages.

c. *trans.* In warp knitting: to cause (a stitch) to pass *over* the head of the needle on which it was held.

a **1877** KNIGHT *Dict. Mech.* II. 1238/1 *Knocking-over bar*, the bar against which the loops and fabric are drawn as the needles retreat, so that the loops shall be thrown or knocked over the heads of the needles. **1885** W. T. ROWLETT tr. *Willkomm's Technol. Framework Knitting* II. iii. 145 These sinkers..must move up and down, and backwards and forwards, so as to sink the thread into loops, bring them forward under the needle beards, land and knock over the old stitches, and..lock in the new stitches, and take them to the back of the needles. **1952** D. F. PALING *Warp Knitting Technol.* i. 6 The presser is now withdrawn and the needle bar continues its downward motion, thus causing the fabric loops to pass further up the needle beards until finally they are knocked-over the needle heads as the latter pass below the level of the sinkers. **1964** H. WIGNALL *Knitting* ii. 28 The old loop is now cast-off or knocked over.

d. *trans.* (*Underworld slang.*) To rob (a person), to burgle (a building); to steal (from).

1928 *Detective Fiction Weekly* 7 July 52/2, I just got knocked over for that wad we jest lifted... My pocket was picked... I was tapped, touched, if that's any plainer. **1932** *Ibid.* 6 Feb. 129/2, I ain't knocked nothin' over for some little time now. **1937** C. R. COOPER *Here's to Crime* iv. 89 There's the real fun of bank-robbing—running the roads. Old Harve used to love it. I've seen him run roads when he had no intention of ever knocking over a can. **1940** *Illustr. London News* 26 Oct. 548/2 The job looks easy enough—a big hotel at Tropico Springs that any fool could 'knock over'. **1941** K. TENNANT *Battlers* i. 9 Life 'on the track' was not so bad, with good places to camp and 'cockies' sheep to knock over.

16. knock up. a. *Bootmaking.* To cut or flatten the edges of the upper after its attachment to the insole.

1905 *Westm. Gaz.* 30 Oct. 7/3 A mechanical device for trimming off the surplus material from the lasted boot before it is 'knocked up', and a machine for the 'knocking-up' process itself, the latter guaranteed to 'knock up' between 400 and 500 pairs of boots per week.

d. (Later examples.) Also, to prepare (food) quickly. *U.S.*

1869 L. M. ALCOTT *Little Women* II. v. 61 Don't cry, dear, but just exert yourself a bit, and knock us up something to eat. **1890** *Harper's Mag.* May 894/2, I jest killed a chicken, and knocked up a few biscuit. **1931** H. NICOLSON *Diary* 14 Aug. (1966) 87 He has got out several tenders for printing... He and Joseph have..knocked up a dummy lay-out. **1967** *Official Jrnl. Patents, Trade Marks & Designs* (Austral.) XXXVII. 1538/2 Plumbing means can be purchased ready made by factories whereas they once might have to be 'knocked up'..from basic materials. **1972** *Shooting Times & Country Mag.* 4 Mar. 21/2 They will knock you up a meal to hold you through the coldest day's fishing or wildfowling.

e. (Further examples.)

1860 *Baily's Monthly Mag.* Oct. 41 Tinley in a trice knocked up 8. **1955** *Publ. Amer. Dial. Soc.* xxiv. 37 This adds up to over $1500 per week which must be *knocked up*—just to meet operating expenses.

f. (This sense is not current in the U.S.)

1973 *National Observer* (U.S.) 3 Feb., Fielding's guidebook considerately explains that a male host may quite casually tell a female American house guest that he will 'knock you up at 7:30 tomorrow morning'. The term, of course, conveys nothing more than a rapping at the door until one is awakened.

h. (Later examples.)

1897 A. BEARDSLEY *Let.* 25 Feb. (1971) 259, I am aghast at the amount of travelling she [*sc.* his sister Mabel] has to get through before the tour comes to an end. I do hope she won't 'knock up' while she is over there. **1941** I. L. IDRIESS *Great Boomerang* x. 78 They travelled fast then, taking the chance. But their horses knocked up.

j. To make (a woman) pregnant; (*less commonly*) to have sexual intercourse with (a woman). *slang* (orig. *U.S.*).

1813 C. EARLE *Diary* 12 Apr. in J. McPhee *Pine Barrens* (1971) ii. 33 William Mick's widow arrived here in pursuit of J. Mick, who she says has knocked her up. **1836** D. CROCKETT *Exploits & Adv. Texas* vii. 97 Nigger women are knocked down by the auctioneer, and knocked up by the purchaser. **1860** HOTTEN *Dict. Slang* (ed. 2) 166 *Knocked up.* In the United States, amongst females, the phrase is equivalent to being *enceinte*, so that Englishmen often unconsciously commit themselves when amongst our Yankee cousins. **1925** E. HEMINGWAY *In Our Time* (1926) 165 Hell, no girls get married around here till they're knocked up. **1934** H. MILLER *Tropic of Cancer* 241 Nearly all the co-eds had been knocked up some time or other. **1952** B. MALAMUD *Natural* 133 You haven't knocked up a dame maybe? **1971** H. C. RAE *Marksman* I. vi. 51 He screwed her, knocked her up first go and.. married her..before she could even contemplate abortion. **1973** E. BULLINS *Theme is Blackness* 170 The girls all got knocked-up and set up homes, got married, went on the block or on welfare or turned into booze hounds.

knock, *sb.*[1] Add: **1.** (Earlier and later examples of *double knock*.)

1819 KEATS *Let.* 13 Mar. (1958) II. 46 The variations of single and double knocks. **1883** C. J. MATHEWS *Patter versus Clatter* ii. 10 (*Double knock*, L.H.) There, someone come to call. Polly, go and see who it is; stop, child, take off your apron, it's a double knock.

b. A misfortune, a rebuff, a blow; adverse criticism. Freq. in phr. *to take the knock*: to sustain a severe financial or emotional blow, to suffer a setback.

The *fig.* examples in Dict. belong here.

1890 *Globe* 21 Apr. 6/1 A broken backer of horses who has taken, what is known in the language of the turf, as the knock. **1900** E. WELLS *Chestnuts* xxiii. 226 When a prominent backer takes the knock racing, he sometimes has the greatest difficulty to avoid his creditors. **1905** 'H. MCHUGH' *You can search Me* iii. 50 There are only four people in New York city who can write criticisms—the rest of the bunch are slush-dealers, and a knock from any one of them is a boost. **1906** GALSWORTHY *Man of Property* III. iv. 322 Here's a poor devil whose mistress has just been telling him a pretty little story of her husband... He's taken the knock, you see. **1929** D. RUNYON in *Hearst's International* Nov. 73/1 It will be a knock to his reputation. **1930** V. PALMER in *Bulletin* (Sydney) 30 Apr. 38/3 [McCurdie] lay there... 'He's taken the knock,' said a cattle-buyer... In a moment a change came into the atmosphere around the sleeping man. **1930** D. RUNYON in *Collier's* 13 Sept. 7/1 They are always doing something which is considered a knock to the community, such as robbing people. **1936** A. HUXLEY *Eyeless in Gaza* vi. 54 'One's had a pretty bad knock,' he added self-consciously, in that queer jargon which he imagined to be colloquial English... That 'bad knock' was a metaphor drawn from the boxing contests he had never witnessed. **1948** V. PALMER *Golconda* xiv. 111 He saw himself..ready to stand up and take the knock if they got into trouble with the john. **1955** *Times* 19 Aug. 2/5 In a dress suit much too large for him, he is on top of the world by submitting with such cheerful readiness to its knocks. **1959** *Encounter* Aug. 7/1 Like other institutions of the Establishment, it has taken a knock or two in recent years. **1962** *B.S.I. News* June 9/1 Advertising has had some hard knocks from its critics recently. **1973** A. BEHREND *Samarai Affair* ii. 24 The pilot..in the event of an accident will.. [be] summoned to appear before the Pilotage Committee to explain his actions and take the knock if held to blame.

c. A knocking noise, or knocking noises, in an engine; *spec.* in a reciprocating internal-combustion engine, noise caused by a very abrupt rise in pressure in the cylinder as a result of too rapid combustion (in spark-ignition engines, the sudden spontaneous ignition of all the unburnt portion of the mixture before the flame from the sparking plug reaches it); faulty combustion of this character. Cf. *KNOCK *v.* 5 b.

1899 J. PERRY *Steam Engine* v. 115 In double-acting engines we can often utilise the inertia forces to alter the point in the crank pin path at which the knock occurs, so that it shall not produce such serious effects. **1903** M. P. BALE *Gas & Oil Engine Managem.* iv. 61 Knocking in the Cylinder.—This often arises from premature firing of the charge before the end of the compression stroke is reached, thus throwing a greater pressure than usual on the piston before it commences the power stroke, and causing a jar or knock as the crank turns the dead centre. **1903** *Cassell's Cycl. Mech.* 3rd Ser. 264/1 Locating 'Knock' in Steam Engine. **1908** *Motor Cycle* 15 Jan. 46/1, I have had a number of letters lately referring to the existence of 'knock' in engines that have run a year or two in private hands. **1920** *Cornh. Mag.* Sept. 314 The carbon knock, the ignition knock, and the bearing knock are fairly simple propositions. **1927** W. DEEPING *Doomsday* xxv. 265 Half-way up the long hill..'Cherry's' engine developed a sudden and rather fearsome 'knock'. **1933** [see *compression-ignition]. **1939** CROFT & TANGERMAN *Steam-Engine Princ.* (ed. 2) xiii. 410 By far the commonest causes of knocks are water in the cylinder and loose bearings. **1956** MOLLOY & LANCHESTER *Automobile Engineer's Ref. Bk.* v. 5 The well-known effect of ignition timing on knock is due to the fact that the relative timing of the piston and the spark-ignited flame controls the pressure in the end-gas. **1963** C. CAMPBELL *Sports Car Engine* ix. 181 During knock more heat is transferred to the cylinder walls. **1973** A. PARRISH *Mech. Engineer's Ref. Bk.* II. 17 Correct choice of mixture strength, ignition timing, fuel (octane number) and good combustion chamber design will allow smooth combustion without knock which occurs if the end gas reaches the condition where self-ignition causes an explosion of all the mixture remaining in the chamber.

3. *Cricket.* An innings; a spell at batting (in a match or at practice).

1889 J. LILLYWHITE *Cricketers' Ann.* 72 Surrey were fortunate to get first 'knock', and..were able to just reach the second hundred. **1898** G. GIFFEN *With Bat & Ball* i. 2 At last..I would..bowl for a little while; and then they began to give me an occasional knock. **1900** *Captain* III. 200/1 'You play cricket yourself, then?' 'Oh, I have an occasional knock.' *Ibid.* 210/1 'W.G.' advises every batsman to have a knock..before going in. An over or two at the nets loosens your muscles. **1909** *Pearson's Mag.* Aug. 180/1 Crofton's had won the toss and taken first 'knock'. **1927** *Observer* 27 Nov. 28 His knock..included eight boundaries. **1958** 'N. BLAKE' *Penknife in my Heart* iii. 50 I'm taking first knock. I've got to be sure you'll go in when it's your turn. **1970** *Times* 26 Aug. 11/8 A fine knock by Mushtaq, who batted for two hours and hit ten fours.

4. *knock for knock*: applied to an agreement between insurers that each will pay his own policy-holders without regard to the question of liability.

1906 *Daily Chron.* 26 July 6/6 Mr. Fairbank said that the 'knock for knock' agreement had never paid with the horse vehicles. **1927** B. C. HOSKINS *Insurance Lexicon* 127

Knock for knock agreement.—An arrangement made between Companies..for dealing automatically with collisions between vehicles owned by their respective insureds; each Company undertakes to pay for the damage to its own insured's vehicle irrespective of the question of liability as between the parties in collision. **1958** *Manch. Guardian* 11 June 9/6 The knock-for-knock agreement is an arrangement whereby when two insured vehicles have been in collision each insurance company pays for the damage to the car it has insured,..without regard to the degree of blame, if any, of the driver. **1972** *Mod. Law Rev.* XXXV. 1. 18 Some types of cases which are handled by small claims courts in other jurisdictions are dealt with in England in ways which obviate the necessity for a claim. Perhaps the most significant example is knock-for-knock agreements among motor-vehicle insurers.

5. a. (An act of) copulation; so *on the knock*, engaged in prostitution. **b.** *Austral.* Phr. *to do a knock with*: (see quot. 1941).

1933 N. Lindsay *Saturdee* 138 Supposin' I was to do a knock with girls, what 'ud I say to them? **1937** Partridge *Dict. Slang* 460/2 *Knock*, a copulation. **1941** Baker *Dict. Austral. Slang* 23 *Do a knock* (*line*) *with*: to take an amorous interest in a member of the opposite sex. **1969** D. Bagley *Spoilers* i. 11 Maybe she was on the knock.

6. Special Comb.: **knockmeter**, an instrument for measuring the intensity of knock in the cylinder of an internal-combustion engine; **knock rating**, (the determination of) the insusceptibility of a fuel to knock.

1934 *Jrnl. R. Aeronaut. Soc.* XXXVIII. 353 Knock intensity is measured by a bouncing pin, in conjunction with either a knockmeter or a gas-evolution burette. **1960** V. B. Guthrie *Petroleum Products Handbk.* iv. 17 The test engine is equipped with a pressure-sensitive pickup mounted in the cylinder head in direct contact with the combustion chamber. A knockmeter is used in conjunction with this pressure-sensitive element to indicate on a scale the intensity of the engine knock... A fuel that is to be tested is brought up to a standard knock intensity, as indicated on the knockmeter, by adjustment of the engine compression ratio. **1932** *Engineering* 8 July 45/3 The marked effect of cylinder temperature upon the relative knock ratings of fuels was observed by Heron in 1928. **1933** *Aircraft Engineering* Aug. 177/1 To have an agreed scale of knock-rating for aviation fuels is no less important. **1959** *B.S.I. News* Aug. 14 Two draft ISO recommendations covering the motor and research methods of determining knock rating.

knock-. Add: **knock-knock** *sb.*, *v.*, and *int.* in various senses (see quots.); **knock-toe**, a galley-punt; **knock-u·pable** *a.* (*nonce-wd.*), likely to be 'knocked up' or weak; **knocku·pedness** (*nonce-wd.*), the state of being 'knocked up' or weak.

1904 *Daily Chron.* 2 July 8/1 The knock-knocking at the door sending a thrill through the pulse. **1936** *Variety* 19 Aug. 25/5 Manager Russell Bovim, of Loew's Broad, Columbus, cashed in handsomely on the 'Knock Knock' craze now sweeping the country. **1941** C. Graves *Life Line* 179 Certain trawlers have the job of sweeping for magnetic mines (known as 'Maggies') and the latest acoustic mines (known as 'knock-knocks'). **1957** O. Nash *You can't get there from Here* 151 Who, rapped Mr. Webster, escapes an escapee? That, knock-knocked Mr. Merriam, is what puzzles me. **1959** I. & P. Opie *Lore & Lang. Schoolch.* v. 82 A craze for Wellerisms is apt to develop in a school in the same way that there are still sometimes crazes for limericks, Little Audrey jokes, Knock-knocks, and Shaggy-dog stories. **1961** Partridge *Dict. Slang* Suppl. 1161/1 *Knock! knock!* A c.p., dating from the middle of Nov. 1936... Orig. ex U.S. It is used, esp. among busmen, by a person about to tell a dirty story or, esp., to make a pun, gen. in doubtful taste. **1974** *Radio Times* 19–25 Oct. 59 'Knock, knock.' 'Who's there?' 'Richard Milhous.' 'Richard Milhous who?' 'Ah...how quickly people forget.' **1903** W. C. Russell *Overdue* vi. 104 It is the Deal galley-punt too, called in the parts she belongs to 'knocktoe'. **1929** F. C. Bowen *Sea Slang* 80 Knock-toe, an old name for the Deal lugger-rigged galley punt, in which there was little room for the feet. **1857** Geo. Eliot *Let.* 5 Apr. (1954) ii. 314 For some time I have been unusually weak and knock-upable. **1855** D. G. Rossetti *Let.* 19 Sept. (1965) I. 271, I am very sorry indeed to hear of your knockupedness but I warned you about that window.

knock-about, knockabout, *a.* (*sb.*) Add: **A.** *adj.* **1. b.** Also *transf.*

1914 A. Huxley *Let.* Feb. (1969) 57 The whole city is permeated with the Mission to Undergraduates—the Bp of Oxford being heard twice nightly in a knock-about sermon at St. Mary's. **1924** J. Buchan *Three Hostages* xiii. 183 He liked plays with shooting in them, and knockabout farce. **1969** *New Yorker* 31 May 110/2 His strong colloquial flavour and knock-about verbiage cannot be conveyed in French. **1974** *Daily Tel.* 5 Oct. 16/1 One would have expected the argument in the Election campaign to have been conducted with a high level of rigour and seriousness, which would not be incompatible with some of the traditional knockabout fun.

3. Designating a class of sloop-rigged sailing-yacht (see quots. 1894, 1897); also, designating a sailing-yacht without a bowsprit. Also as *sb. N. Amer.*

1894 in *Forest & Stream* (1895) 12 Jan. 35/2 A knockabout boat is a seaworthy keel boat (not to include finkeels) decked or half-decked, of fair accommodations, rigged simply, without bowsprit, and with only mainsail and one head sail. **1897** *Outing* (U.S.) Dec. 235/1 The knockabout class, which originated in Boston a few seasons ago, has much to recommend it... It is free from all freakiness. It has no fin-keel... With a moderate sail area it is under control at all times... This class is limited to five hundred square feet of sail. All are keel-boats, and all must be under twenty-one feet on the load water-line. **1919** *Canad. Fisherman* 695/1 The fine new knockabout schooner, General Haig, the first of her kind ever built here. **1927** G. Bradford *Gloss. Sea Terms* 96/1 *Knockabout*, a sloop or schooner without a bowsprit and whose jib sets from a stay at the stern. **1970** *Amer. Neptune* XXX. 196 The term knockabout soon was restricted to the type lacking a bowsprit and was further used attributively to designate any rig in which a long fore overhang took the place of a bowsprit. *Ibid.* 197 The single knockabout yawl was *Arapahoe*, built in 1893.

b. More generally, descriptive of small yachts or dinghies. Also as *sb.*

1904 *N.Y. Even. Post* 21 May 6 There are numerous knockabouts and other small yachts in the Pawcatuck River. **1921** *Yachting Monthly* XXXII. 105/2 The usual lug and mizen clinker built 'knockabout' boats, common to seaside watering places. **1970** *Motor Boat & Yachting* 16 Oct. 39/2 It [*sc.* the balanced lug] is a powerful sail and very well suited to knockabout dinghies.

B. *sb.* **1.** (Examples of sense 'knockabout performance'; also *transf.*)

1899 Ade *Fables in Slang* (1900) 83 These two Troupers began their Professional Career with a Road Circus.. doing a Refined Knockabout in the Grand Concert or Afterpiece. **1930** *Observer* 2 Mar. 15/3 The actors attack both the recitative and knockabout delightfully. **1955** *Times* 9 Aug. 2/5 One called The Cold War, in which Mr. Wisdom, suffering from a fever, tries out different miraculous cures evincing immediately their different after-effects, is the most intricate piece of knockabout seen on the London stage for some time. **1959** *Ann. Reg. 1958* 50 The proceedings were wound up by a forcible speech from the leader of the party, Mr Grimond, in a style of party-political knockabout in which he demonstrated that it was easier to abuse the other parties than to explain the purposes of one's own. **1970** *New Society* 5 Mar. 406/3 For while there is some knockabout..most of the pieces here are technically of a high order.

4. A small motor vehicle for casual use.

1956 W. H. Whyte *Organization Man* (1957) vi. 71 A little knock-about for the wife to run down to the station in.

knock-back, knockback, *sb. dial.*, *Austral.* and *N.Z. colloq.* [Phr. *to knock back* (see *knock *v.* 7** a) used as sb.] A refusal, a rebuff.

1898 *Evesham Jrnl.* 21 May 7/1 He..objected to the powers of the guardians being relegated to the officers. It was a knock-back. **1902** *Eng. Dial. Dict.* III. 478/2 It was a nasty reply—a complete knock-back. **1919** W. H. Downing *Digger Dial.* 31 *Knock-back*, a refusal. **1933** *Bulletin* (Sydney) 18 Jan. 17, I sought casual work... Result, six flat knockbacks. **1941** K. Tennant *Battlers* xvii. 182 She could take a 'knock-back' as though it didn't matter. **1943** F. Sargeson in *Penguin New Writing* XVII. 56 And I said to myself, well, a knock-back from one of yous isn't going to make me lose any sleep. **1960** N. Hilliard *Maori Girl* ii. xiv. 161 She had mentioned the knock-back from the Tallahassee Milk Bar. **1962** [see *daddy 2]. **1972** *Sunday Mail* (Brisbane) 9 Jan. 5/2 When he lead[s] the conversation..on to Jesus and Christianity we don't get any knockbacks.

knock-down, *a.* and *sb.* Add: **A.** *adj.* **1.** (Earlier and later lit. examples.)

1794 *Sporting Mag.* IV. 78/2 After the first knock-down blow, Johnson attempted to shift. **1971** *Nature* 15 Oct. 441/1 They are used against houseflies, mosquitoes and cockroaches..; their great advantage is that pyrethrin I has a high kill rate and pyrethrin II a high knock down rate.

2. Also, *knock-down book, fee. U.S.*

1888 *Harper's Mag.* Nov. 934/2 Bills for knock-down fees are presented for payment to auctioneers every month. *Ibid.* 937/2 The knock-down book records the price, buyer, and all particulars of every sale in the Auction-room.

3. Add to def.: sold as, or in the form of, a number of separate parts that require to be assembled. (Earlier and later examples.)

1795 W. Winterbotham *Hist. View Amer. U.S.* III. 305 Articles of exportation [were]..231,776 Barrels of dried and pickled fish..48,860 Shook or knock-down casks. **1952** *Archit. Rev.* CXI. 241/1 Swedish 'knock-down' furniture. *Ibid.*, The production of 'packaged' furniture (an adjective which is preferable to either knock-down or demountable, since it not only sounds better, but is more definitive). **1969** *Sunday Mail* (Brisbane) 2 Feb. 26/6 Cars imported in the complete knockdown form. **1971** *Rand Daily Mail* 4 Sept. 10/3 The boat is imported in a knock-down form and is assembled here. **1972** 'E. Lathen' *Murder without Icing* (1973) vii. 65 Millions of Americans..had stayed up late Christmas Eve to struggle with knockdown toys.

B. *sb.* **2.** Also *knock-down* (*and*) *drag-out*: a free-for-all, a rough-and-tumble fight; also *transf.* and *attrib. U.S. colloq.*

1827 J. F. Cooper *Prairie* I. iv. 93 Making it a real knock-down and drag-out! **1834** *Amer. Railroad Jrnl.* III. 304/1 He was one of our careless unconcerned knock down and drag out looking sort of fellows. **1932** *Tulsa* (Okla.) *World* 13 Mar. v. 2/3 A knock-down-and-drag-out battle between Roosevelt and Smith forces. **1941** Auden *New Year Let.* ii. 34 The hard self-conscious particles Collide, divide like numerals In knock-down drag-out laissez-faire. **1949** B. A. Botkin *Treas. S. Folklore* ii. iii. 251 When it comes to knock-down-and-drag-out..political bickering..well, as Donald Davidson's typical Middle Georgia country gentleman, 'Cousin Roderick', puts it, 'Politics is for lawyers.' **1952** B. Ulanov *Hist. Jazz in Amer.* (1958) viii. 89 Whole choruses..and ensemble sections..are delightful..in knockdown and dragout choruses. **1968** *Punch* 1 May 624/1 An elderly bum who's just sold him the Lincoln Centre at the knock-down drag-out price of fourteen bucks.

4. The heeling of a ship by the force of the wind.

1888 *Scribner's Mag.* May 526/1 Every bit of that water came in through the hatch at the time of the knock-down. **1926** H. Howard *Yacht 'Alice'* 13 Raised deck amidships which gives excellent room below, increases the structural strength and adds greatly to her stability and righting moment in case of a knockdown. **1951** H. I. Chapelle *Amer. Small Sailing Craft* 242 Such a maneuver takes room and also might lead to a knockdown when the boa pays off, as she has no way on. **1973** J. R. L. Anderson *Death on Rocks* xi. 201 Anthea had seen our knockdown... They stood by us until it was clear that we were not going to sink.

5. An introduction. *U.S.*, *Austral.*, and *N.Z. slang.*

1865 'D. Rattlehead' *Adventures of Fudge Fumble* v. 61, I asked the young man if he would go down some night and give me a 'knock down' to the family, and Miss Kate, more especially. **1885** 'Phudge Phumble' *Adventures Greenhorn in Gotham* 39 He loved Lucy at first sight and couldn't help it. So he managed to get a knock down to her. **1896** Ade *Artie* iii. 24 Take me over and gi' me a knock down to the queen in the corner. **1916** C. J. Dennis *Songs Sentimental Bloke* 125 *Knock-down*, a formal introduction. **1930** *National Education* (N.Z.) May 197/2, I heard one young fellow ask another to 'give him a knockdown to that tart in the green skirt'. I gathered that he was asking for an introduction to a young lady!! **1937** J. Weidman *I can get it for you Wholesale* xvi. 156 'Meet the stable,' he said, waving his hand to take in the girls... 'You want a knockdown to something?' **1945** *Chicago Daily News* 7 Sept. 31/3, I know her well! I'll sell you a knockdown to her for two-bits. **1946** F. Sargeson *That Summer* 66 He called me over and gave me a knock-down, and she was certainly the goods. **1974** *Telegraph* (Brisbane) 28 May 24/1, I think you should meet Fred. And maybe Bert, too. So here's for the knock-down.

knocked, *ppl. a.* Add: **2. knocked-down.** In the form of a number of separate parts that require to be assembled.

1776 [in Dict.]. **1908** *Sears, Roebuck Catal.* 371/1 The patent knocked down construction..give [*sic*] this splendid rocker additional strength and rigidity and permit its shipment in a package 33 inches long. **1950** *Engineering* 3 Feb. 139/2 For carriage in merchant vessels all vehicles..should possess a 'knocked-down' height of less than 7 ft. 9 in. **1960** *Times Rev. Industry* July 74/1 Cars..imported..in completely knocked down packs. **1971** *Timber Trades Jrnl.* 14 Aug. 58/1 Filters in a new 'knocked down' kit form.

knocker. Add: **1. e.** A fault-finder, one who is addicted to captious criticism. (Cf. *knock *v.* 2 f.) *colloq.* (orig. *U.S.*).

1898 in Wentworth & Flexner *Dict. Amer. Slang* (1960) 308/2 That pack of knockers and snapping curs. **1901** [see *knock *v.* 2 f]. **1911** *Daily Colonist* (Victoria, B.C.) 22 Apr. 4/2 The Cranbrook Herald says that the 'pestilential knocker' has been doing his best to injure the Southeast Kootenay by misrepresenting the condition of a party of English settlers. **1923** J. Moses *Beyond City Gates* 154 The 'knocker' of his home town is, on this line of deduction, a 'knocker' of his Empire, a destroyer of thought, labour, and enterprise. **1928** *Sunday Express* 18 Mar. 5/2 All the knockers were there,..yearning to find fault. **1956** W. H. Whyte *Organization Man* (1957) ix. 124 This system virtually ensures that the over-zealous or the 'knocker' type of man will not get ahead. **1958** *Times Lit. Suppl.* 24 Jan. 37/3 Today it would be difficult to get together such a team of 'knockers' as Harold Stearns did for his *Civilization in the United States*. Cheerfulness has been creeping in among the intelligentsia. **1962** M. Harris in P. Coleman *Austral. Civilization* 57 It is said that Australians are 'knockers'; that is, they gain pleasure from seeing superiority in talent, intellect or energy reduced to the scale of average mediocrity. **1969** *Telegraph* (Brisbane) 5 Dec. 3/2 Knockers are people who identify the ordinary Australian bloke as an easy-going, irresponsible oaf who spends more time drinking and arguing with his mates than working. **1972** *Shooting Times & Country Mag.* 1 July 26/3 Today the 'knockers' seem to delight in slamming anything British.

2. d. *Austral.* and *N.Z.* (See quots.)

1933 L. G. D. Acland in *Press* (Christchurch, N.Z.) 4 Nov. 15/7 *Knocker*, a small leather pad fixed near the heel of shears to keep the blades from closing too far. **1938** R. M. Burdon *High Country* viii. 84 A piece of rawhide known as a knocker is now used to prevent the shears clashing when closed, but before this was introduced the clack and snap of steel meeting steel was a noise inseparable from any busy shearing shed. **1941** Baker *Dict. Austral. Slang* 42 *Knocker*, a leather pad fixed near the heel of a pair of hand shears to prevent the blades closing too deeply. **1959** H. P. Tritton *Time means Tucker* 31/1 Shears do not click. The gullets of the blades are filled with soft wood, or sometimes with cork. These are called 'knockers', and they stop the heels of the blade from meeting. **1965** J. S. Gunn *Terminol. Shearing Industry* i. 34 *Knockers*, small pads, usually of leather or softwood, inset near the heel of hand shears. These stopped jarring and prevented the blades from closing too far and cutting the shearer's hand... It is likely that the name developed because they knocked together, but it could be a misspelling of 'nock'.

e. One who buys from, or sells to, persons at their residences; a door-to-door salesman; also, the action of selling (etc.) from door to door. Phr. *on the knocker* (and varr.), (engaged in

buying from, selling to, or canvassing) from door to door; also, (obtained) on credit.

1934 P. Allingham *Cheapjack* xiii. 166 A 'knocker-worker' is one who sells things at people's front doors. *Ibid.* xv. 186 'The knocker's the only game in the winter' said London Joe. **1936** *Evening News* 11 Dec. 11/1 A valued and regular lady customer drives up..and.. orders petrol..finds she has left her handbag at home... The hand..yells out: 'Oi, there's a lidy 'ere wants some juice on the knocker!' **1959** *Listener* 7 May 802/2 That record of progress in Blackpool shows what can be done if we work, in the first place, as our canvassers say, on the knocker. **1959** G. Savage *Antique Collector's Handbk.* 156 'Knockers' are jewellery and antique dealers who operate by calling from door to door in search of something to buy, and their purchases are sold to larger dealers. **1960** A. Prior in *Pick of Today's Short Stories* XI. 185 If I kept getting as much jewellery for him on the knocker then perhaps he wouldn't have to sell. **1963** J. F. Straker *Final Witness* viii. 81 Once she got a whole pile of stuff on the knocker, and then the firm came and took it back. **1967** *Sun* 17 July 7/2 The 'knocker boys'..trick old ladies into parting with family heirlooms for a fraction of their value. **1968** M. Allingham *Cargo of Eagles* ix. 116 I've worked the knocker if you know what that means—the door-to-door selling racket. **1970** *Sunday Times* 18 Jan. 37 A knocker was a specially trained salesman working, not under the authority and generally not in the pay of a district sales agent, but for the company itself, out of the Dayton executive offices.

f. Pl. The female breasts. *vulgar.*

1941 J. Smiley *Hash House Lingo* 25 Fix the knockers—look at the nice breasts on that woman. **1948** N. Mailer *Naked & Dead* (1949) iii. ii. 484 Look at the knockers on her, Murray says. **1967** J. Kennaway *Some Gorgeous Accident* i. 15 She was slight..but with great little knockers—breasts being for mothers. **1970** *Private Eye* 11 Sept. 16 Hello, luv! Phew, look at them knockers!! **1972** M. J. Bosse *Incident at Naha* 24 I'm jealous. She has those big knockers, and I'm afraid you like them.

5. *knocker-off*, (*b*) *Underworld slang*, a thief.

1926 E. Wallace *Door with Seven Locks* iii. 28 Tommy Cawler had been a notorious 'knocker-off' of motor-cars. **1952** 'J. Henry' *Who lie in Gaol* iv. 61 They are mostly house-breakers and petty thieves, or 'knockers-off' in prison parlance.

knockered (nǫ·kəɹd), *a.* [See -ed².] Of a house door: fitted with a knocker.

1921 *United Free Ch. Miss. Rec.* May 137/1 We entered by those massive brass-studded and knockered doors. **1928** *Daily Tel.* 24 Apr. 12/7 Knockered front doors and curtained windows.

knocking, *vbl. sb.* Add: **1.** (Examples, some corresponding to *knock *v.* 5 b.)

1899 J. Perry *Steam Engine* ii. 30 Knocking or Back-lash.—It will be noticed that however good may be the fit of a brass to a pin, when the forces between them are suddenly reversed, there is a blow. **1903** M. P. Bale *Gas & Oil Engine Managem.* iv. 61 Knocking may also arise from the key of the flywheel becoming loose. **1928** [see *decoke *v.*]. **1946** *Mod. Petroleum Technol.* (Inst. Petroleum) 245 All reciprocating petrol engines, if run on unsuitable fuel, will produce a characteristic noise known as knocking, the quality of the sound varying from a sharp pink to a low thud according to the design of the engine and the composition of the fuel. **1971** *Guardian* 13 Dec. 1/4 Steam injection could eliminate 'knocking' on unleaded fuel even in high compression engines.

b. (Earlier and later examples with *about*; also with *up*.)

1840 *N.Z. Jrnl.* 1 Aug. 183/1 Any one coming out must expect to have a good knocking about. **1897** *Organ Voicing & Tuning* 9 A knocking-up cup, similar in form to the cone... It is of great substance, and, therefore, heavy, that it may the more readily effect its mission, namely, that of 'knocking up' or reducing the wind-hole of the pipe. **1905** *Westm. Gaz.* 19 Aug. 15/2 It is always the brim that matters in one's knocking-about hat. **1922** A. E. Crawley *Lawn Tennis Do's & Don'ts* 42 As in many other games, it is not normal to get into your stroke at once; hence the need of a few minutes' knocking-up before a game. **1924** F. G. Lowe *Lawn Tennis* 10 When a new stroke has been learnt..it is an excellent idea to practise it against a wall until it becomes perfect. This 'knocking up' will also materially improve footwork and quicken up the player. **1970** *Country Life* 20 Aug. 469/3 (*caption*) 'Knocking-up' slate in front of a miner's house.. Co. Durham. **1973** *Oxf. Mag.* 4 May 9/2 *Knocking-up* is notoriously not done in America, even by tennis players trying to warm up their partners before a match.

c. knocking-off: (i) = *knock-off *sb.* 2; also (in full *knocking-off time*), the time laid down for the end of a spell of work.

1886 in *Amer. Speech* (1950) XXV. 35/1 The entire mill is kept on operation long after knocking off..to make up for time lost during the day. **1887** in *Ibid.*, Saturday evening last, just about knocking off time. **1894** in *Leeds Mercury Weekly Suppl.* 11 Aug. (E.D.D.). **1922** C. E. Montague *Disenchantment* ix. 123 He..knocked off work for the day. There was no knocking off for the army. **1944** *R.A.F. Jrnl.* Aug. 292 At knocking-off time..the hooter sounds and everyone climbs thankfully out of their overalls. **1958** *Times* 14 Apr. 6/1 It is not all *that* difficult to control tea-breaks, knocking-off times or shift changes without upsetting your employees. **1974** N. Freeling *Dressing of Diamond* 45 Another cubic metre to shift before knocking-off time.

(ii) *Spinning.* Automatic stopping of the bobbin and flyer frames when a sufficient length of yarn has been wound on to the bobbin.

1883 H. E. Walmsley *Cotton Spinning* 15 See that the saddles and weights are accurate, and that both front and back knocking-off motions are in perfect working order. **1901** —— *Cotton Spinning* II. iii. 67 It is still more difficult to invent a motion that will prevent tenters from doffing bobbins before knocking-off does take place. **1908** H. Priestman *Princ. Woollen Spinning* x. 282 If a mule were empty, and were run with the knocking-off gear out of action,..the rollers would revolve at all kinds of varying speeds. **1927** T. Thornley *Cotton Spinning* (ed. 4) iii. 61 This completes the knocking-off motion and the lap may now be doffed.

(iii) *Weaving.* Automatic stopping of the loom when the shuttle fails to reach the box.

1912 T. Roberts *Tappet & Dobby Looms* ix. 198 In order to reduce the vibration and strain on the various parts of the loom when knocking-off takes place, strong springs..are employed which serve as cushions for the frogs. **1935** J. W. Hutchinson *Mod. Looms* xxix. 265 The sudden knocking-off of the loom may crack the cast iron brushes on the sword pin.

d. knocking over. *Machine Knitting.* = *knock-over.

a **1877** Knight *Dict. Mech.* II. 1237/1 The stripping or knocking-over wheel..then throws the old loops entirely over the tops of the needles. **1964** H. Wignall *Knitting* ii. 28 The needle now moves to its lowest position drawing the new loop through the fabric loop which is now cast off. On the original Lee knitting frame this called for physical effort and this action was called knocking over.

e. Phr. *the last knockings*, the last earnings; so *to be on the last knockings*, to approach the end of one's employment or earnings.

1939 H. Hodge *Cab, Sir?* iii. 31, I..have left it late, and come in 'at the last knockings'. **1958** F. Norman *Bang to Rights* iii. 137 When I was on the last knockings I tried to get my bird out earning again.

knocking, *ppl. a.* Add: **b.** *knocking copy*, advertising which claims that the product of another manufacturer is inferior to one's own. (Cf. *knock *v.* 2 f.)

1958 *Times* 1 July 11/5 Certain types of announcement covering such things as..politically and religiously controversial statements, 'knocking' copy, and so on. **1960** *Guardian* 19 Dec. 3/2 In advertising, the pamphlet advocates the ending of the 'no knocking copy rule', which restricts competition by preventing one advertiser from 'fairly disparaging' another's product. **1966** G. N. Leech *Eng. in Advertising* iv. 37 'Knocking copy', designed to discredit competing products, offends against the principle of 'positiveness' mentioned earlier, and is besides considered bad form. **1969** *Listener* 23 Jan. 127/3 Knocking copy means advertisements which point out clearly that one brand is better than another brand.

kno·cking-shop. *slang.* [Cf. *knock *v.* 2 d; Eng. Dial. Dict. s.v. *knocking-house*.] A brothel.

1860 Hotten *Dict. Slang* (ed. 2) 166 *Knocking-shop*, a brothel, or disreputable house frequented by prostitutes. **1938** 'J. Spenser' *Crime against Soc.* xiii. 126 She might wonder if you hadn't been gettin' scragged in a knockin' shop for not payin' yer dues. **1945** E. Waugh *Brideshead Revisited* 300 This eye-sore..always reminds me of one of the costlier knocking-shops. **1959** 'O. Mills' *Stairway to Murder* xiv. 149 I'm a clean-living man... I wouldn't go to any back-street knocking shop. **1969** L. Kennedy *Very Lovely People* ii. 111 Yes, it seems that some of the girls are running a knocking-shop on the side. **1971** B. W. Aldiss *Soldier Erect* 115 Somewhere there must be a woman whose longings corresponded to mine. Perhaps she could be found, that unknown She, even within the confines of a knocking shop.

knock-kneed, *a.* Add: **a.** (Earlier Amer. example.)

1774 in *Maryland Hist. Mag.* (1911) VI. 41 Charles Blundell, an Englishman,..a very slender made fellow much knock-kneed, with light brown hair very short.

knock-knock: see *knock-.

kno·ckless, *a.* [See -less.] **a.** *Nonce-wd.* That enters without knocking on a door. **b.** Of an engine: free from knock (*knock *sb.*¹ 1 c).

1907 W. de Morgan *Alice-for-Short* xlvii. 500 Alice was interrupted by the advent of the doctor, knockless but with musical boots. **1928** *Daily Chron.* 9 Aug. 11 (Advt.), A 'knockless', livelier engine; reduced vibration and less wear and tear of engine parts.

knock-me-down, *a.* and *sb.* **A.** *adj.* (Later *fig.* examples.)

1922 Joyce *Ulysses* 300 And Bloom, of course, with his knockmedown cigar putting on swank with his lardy face. **1944** Dylan Thomas *Let.* 31 Dec. (1966) 270, I haven't read more than a scattered few of the poems..stopping with delight..at many knock-me-down lines. **1958** *Times Lit. Suppl.* 26 Dec. 757/1 Its current number deals with the very subject..and it does so in a brisk, knock-me-down way which is extremely refreshing. **1967** *Listener* 16 Feb. 235/1 It was not yet fashionable for poets to present themselves as knock-me-down sales representatives of verse.

knock-off, *sb.* and *a.* Add: **A.** *sb.* **2.** The act of leaving off one's work or occupation; the signal for doing this. Also *attrib.*, as *knock-off signal, time, whistle.*

1899 'Knock-off' time [in Dict., sense B]. **1902** *Daily Chron.* 13 June 6/3 Just at that moment the officer in charge gave what is technically known as the 'knock-off', or the signal to discontinue the play of water on the building. *Ibid.*, After the 'knock-off' signal had been given. **1947** K. Tennant *Lost Haven* xvi. 249 The knock-off whistle blew at the mill. **1948** D. Ballantyne *Cunninghams* (1963) i. 13 From early morning to morning smoko, to lunch, to afternoon smoko, then to knockoff.

3. *slang.* A robbery; *concr.* (see quot. 1963); phr. *on the knock-off*, engaged in stealing.

1936 J. Curtis *Gilt Kid* x. 100 They [*sc.* gloves]..gave away the fact that he was still on the knock-off. **1963** *Austral. T.V. Times* 18 Apr. 10/2 *Knock-off*, loot or illegally found goods. **1969** J. Gardner *Complete State of Death* vi. 94 The really profitable knock-offs, like the Train Robbery.

4. A copy or reproduction of a design, e.g. of a textile, china, etc. *U.S.*

1966 *N.Y. Times* 25 Jan. 44 Copying designs to sell for less has a name in the industry. It is called the 'knockoff'. **1970** *Washington Post* 30 Sept. B. 14/1 People who appreciate genuine pate de foie gras..might like to serve it on a decently designed plate, and not on a knock off..of 18th Century English china. **1971** *Time* 25 Jan. 38 [Coco] Chanel had long since refused to join the cabal of Paris designers who tried to prevent style piracy... Private customers paid $700 for the original; buyers, intent on knockoffs, paid close to $1,500.

B. *adj.* **2. a.** Machine Knitting. *knock-off lap* (see quot. 1957).

1884 W. T. Rowlett tr. *Willkomm's Technol. Framework Knitting* I. ii. 102 In the second lap..the loops are simply taken back into the throats of the sinkers with the old stitches. This second lap is called a 'knock off lap', because it does not form stitches. *Ibid.*, The purpose of such knock off laps is manifestly to bring as much thread as possible into the fabric, which thus becomes thick and soft, and suitable for underclothing or linings for shoes, &c. **1926** J. Chamberlain *Hosiery, Yarns & Fabrics* vii. 173 As a lap is formed without pressing and clearing the knock-off lap it is in every sense a parallel to the tuck-stitch of ordinary knitting. **1952** D. F. Paling *Warp Knitting Technol.* viii. 106 Knock-off laps can be used in conjunction with striped warps to produce purely vertical stripes on the face of the fabric without any overlap between adjacent colours. **1957** *Textile Terms & Definitions* (Textile Inst.) (ed. 3) 55 *Knock-off lap* (*warp knitting*), a length (or lengths) of yarn received by a needle and not pulled through the loop of the previous course.

b. Designating a mechanical part (e.g. of a vehicle) that may be removed or disengaged by knocking.

1896 W. E. Hipkins *Wire Rope* 47 They are connected and disconnected..by means of suitable couplings. When the rope is under considerable tension 'knock-off' hooks have to be used. **1905** C. Hurst *Valves & Valve-Gearing* (ed. 4) vii. 130 In high-class Corliss engines it is often necessary to fit an automatic knock-off gear in connection with the governer, so that should the speed of the engine exceed or fall below certain limits the trips will be thrown into such a position that will prevent engagement of the catches,..the engine thus [being] brought to rest. **1958** *Sunday Times* 26 Jan. 27/1, I would recommend that knock-off hubs are fitted in future; they can be changed in thirty seconds. **1963** A. F. W. Coulson et al. *Man. Cotton Spinning* II. ii. v. 122 The doffing cycle commences when the desired length of lap has been made; the measuring plate..on the measuring motion releases the spring-loaded knock-off lever, which..disengages the brake on the rack-shaft. **1967** *Guardian* 12 Sept. 3/4 Knock-off wheels with proper splined hub and graduated spokes.

c. *Spinning.* Associated with or bringing about knocking off (*knocking *vbl. sb.* 1 c (ii)).

1927 T. Thornley *Cotton Spinning* (ed. 4) iii. 56 It is customary to apply a full lap automatic stop motion..to automatically stop the feed and delivery parts every time a lap is sufficiently full... The favourite..knock-off motion is worked from one of the calenders on the Hunter cog principle.

knock-o·n, *sb.* and *a.* **A.** *sb.* In *Rugby Football* (see Knock-).

1845, 1881 [see Punt *sb.*³ 1]. **1888** [in Dict. s.v. Knock-]. **1905** *Daily Chron.* 29 Dec. 9/5 The alleged incident of the referee in the New Zealanders–Newport match sounding the whistle when a knock-on by an All Black proved to the advantage of the Welsh team was..contrary to law. **1960** *Times* 11 Jan. 17/1 A body of dedicated Scots thought that France's last [try] followed a knock-on. **1974** *Sunday Tel.* 23 June 35/7 The referee did not see the knock-on.

B. *adj.* **1.** *Physics.* Ejected, produced, or caused as a result of the collision of an atomic or sub-atomic particle with an atom.

1940 *Nature* 13 July 65/2 A few particles of energy greater than 10^8 ev...were therefore considered to be mesons responsible for the production of 'knock on' showers. **1953** *Jrnl. Brit. Interplanetary Soc.* XII. 203 These [*sc.* nuclear fragments] may be accompanied by knock-on particles (or shower particles) which also move with velocities comparable to the original particle. **1967** A. H. Cottrell *Introd. Metall.* ii. 14 There are three main types of radiation damage... (3) Knock-on damage in which atoms inside the material are knocked from their sites by the impacts of nuclear particles. **1971** *Nature* 6 Aug. 422/2 Knock-on protons produced by 3MeV neutrons would not..produce visible flashes.

2. Designating a mechanical part (e.g. of a vehicle) that may be attached or fastened by knocking. Also *absol.*

1952 *Motor Manual* (ed. 34) vii. 150 There are two principal types of wheel fastening. The less common, known as the knock-on, has at its centre a large nut with two lugs or projections. *Ibid.* p. x, Knock on wheel fastening. **1959** *Times* 12 Sept. 3/3 Moss's car has knock-on wheels. **1965** *Punch* 20 Oct. 567/2 The imitation knock-on hubs had been knocked off by genuine thieves. **1967**

I. HAMILTON *Man with Brown Paper Face* ii. 24 The strengthened knock-on wire wheels were original M.G.

knock-out, *a.* and *sb.* Add: **A.** *adj.* **b.** Also *fig.*

1938 *Ann. Reg. 1937* 90 The task of the Government.. was to make impossible the greatest danger to civilisation—the knock-out blow. **1955** *Times* 9 May 19/1 A new fashion has, however, arisen—the cry for knock-out competition in private enterprise.

c. Designating (a system used in) a competition or tournament in which the defeated competitors in each round are eliminated.

1896 W. BROADFOOT et al. *Billiards* i. 40 Scarcely a dozen really important handicaps on the old 'knock-out' principle have been played in the last twenty years. **1897** K. S. RANJITSINHJI *Jubilee Bk. Cricket* 281 The first elevens meet in a series of matches, played on the 'knock-out' system. **1920** *Motor Cycle* 22 July 114/1 Competitors in the motor cycle events were run off in pairs on the knock-out principle. **1921** E. B. TURNER in E. H. D. Sewell *Rugby Football* xiv. 244 The competition was run on 'knock-out' lines as it is at the present time, the teams which entered being drawn in ties, and those left in after each round being again paired by lot until only two were left in the final. **1928** *Daily Mail* 25 July 16/4 The singles championship held by the Ayton Tennis Club..was played on the knock-out principle. **1953** E. SMITH *Guide Eng. Traditions* 94 Besides the League there is also a 'knock-out' competition for the English Cup. **1955** *Times* 18 Aug. 4/3 Leeds, Huddersfield, Halifax, and Hull will be expected to go a long way in the various knock-out competitions again. **1966** *Listener* 30 June 936/1 The British Isles are to be invaded by football fans from all over the world bent on seeing the knock-out international competition known as the World Cup. **1974** *Country Life* 2 May 1070/2 By mid-summer we are left with 32 [cricket] clubs who fight it out on a knockout basis.

d. *knock-out drops* (also occas. *sing.*), a liquid drug of which drops are put into liquor to render a person unconscious or stupefied (e.g. in order to rob him). Also *fig. colloq.* (orig. *U.S.*).

1895 J. S. WOOD *Yale Yarns* 152 Our dandy team played a logy, tired sort of game, as if each man had been given knock-out drops, and we all felt blue! **1904** Ex-INSPECTOR ELLIOTT *Tracking Glasgow Criminals* 23 The use of drugs..or what is more familiarly known in criminal circles as 'knock-out' drops is common enough in most cities. What is known as 'knock-out' drops is chloral hydrate, and from fifteen to thirty grains of it produces a sleep that lasts three hours. **1926** J. BLACK *You can't Win* xii. 152 Here I learned to beware the crafty shanghaier with his knockout drops. **1955** 'N. SHUTE' *Requiem for Wren* viii. 242 About midnight..I took one of Aunt Ellen's things. It was a knock-out drop all right because I didn't wake up till half past nine. **1958** *Sunday Times* 10 Aug. 8/3 The first [film] was a typical knock-out drop—a study of 'inter-specific interdependence'.

e. *Mech.* Designating or pertaining to a knock-out (see *B. 5 a, b).

1907 *Installation News* Nov. 6/2 The 'knock-out' principle as applied to junction boxes. **1925** HODKIN & COUSEN *Textbk. Glass Technol.* xxxii. 439 The knock-out arm moves outwards, so that the bottle falls off the mould base into the trough. **1946** DU BOIS & PRIBBLE *Plastics Mold Engin.* iii. 104 As the press continues to open, the pin attached to the knockout bar rises and pushes the wedge, with molded piece attached, up out of the cavity. **1955** *Die Design Handbk.* (Amer. Soc. Tool Engineers) v. 23 Knockout slugs should be readily removable from the outside of the box; so care should be exercised to see that the material is pierced from the proper side. *Ibid.*, Knockout dies. **1963** H. R. CLAUSER *Encycl. Engin. Materials* 104/1 If necessary knockout pins are cast into the mold.

f. *Founding.* Used in or pertaining to the knocking out of castings and flasks (see *KNOCK *v.* 12 j).

1942 *Engineering* 6 Mar. 195/2 With continuous casting with a mould conveyor, there was great difficulty in adjusting the whole conveyor for uniform speed, so that, when the castings came to the knock-out grid, they would be cool enough for knocking out. **1958** *Ann. Rep. Chief Inspector of Factories on Industr. Health 1957* 15 in *Parl. Papers 1958–9* (Cmnd. 558) XIII. 183 Various types of exhaust systems used to control dust and fumes at central knock-out positions..have been examined. **1973** *Steel Castings Abstr.* XXII. 24 (*heading*) Improving the knock-out properties of silicate bonded sands.

g. *colloq.* Of a person or thing: of overwhelming or surpassing quality. Cf. *B. 4.

1966 *Crescendo* Aug. 41 (Advt.), Chasing a real knockout sound? You'll find the most rewarding instrument..is the Hammond organ. **1968** *Listener* 5 Sept. 307/2 The wit and repartee of the DJ... 'Hi there—it's great to be with you and welcome to another knock-out show.'

B. *sb.* **2.** (Earlier and *transf.* examples.)

1887 in *Amer. Speech* (1950) XXV. 35/1 A knock-out was no more possible with these youngsters. **1891** *Sporting Life* 25 Mar. 7/3 The Barrier man was nearly helpless, and Choynski tried frantically to pull himself together for one good knock out. **1895** G. B. SHAW *Let.* 17 Sept. (1965) 560 Got up [after cycling smash] within the prescribed ten seconds, but had subsequently to admit knock-out. *a* **1918** W. OWEN *Coll. Poems* (1963) 71 One of us got the knock-out, blown to chops. **1944** *Return to Attack* (Army Board, N.Z.) 23/2 The tanks, which had suffered three knockouts from 88-millimetre guns.

4. *colloq.* A person or thing of overwhelming or surpassing quality. Cf. *A. g.

1892 *Idler* June 549 'E's a knockout! **1898** J. D. BRAYSHAW *Slum Silhouettes* 28 Got a rippin' good voice, ain't he? It's a knock-out. **1908** *London Mag.* June 473/2 The tent is a knock-out. **1918** A. QUILLER-COUCH *Foe-Farrell* xi. 163 The view from the top is a knock-out. **1920** WODEHOUSE *Jill the Reckless* (1922) xiv. 213 He had a respect for Wally's opinion, for Wally had written 'Follow the Girl' and look what a knock-out that had been. **1935** A. HUXLEY *Let. c* May (1969) 394 The greatest knockout is the 'Assumption' at S. Vincente, where there are also some small pictures of absolutely staggering beauty. **1953** R. LEHMANN *Echoing Grove* 190 A *whizzing* beauty! Really but really a knock-out. **1958** *Daily Mail* 1 Sept. 10/8 The clever, wicked face of Emlyn Williams expressing the words of Dylan Thomas was once again a knock-out. **1970** A. CAMERON et al. *Computers & O.E. Concordances* 24 I've got a version of *Paradise Lost* that is a knock-out. **1971** *Daily Colonist* (Victoria, B.C.) 11 June 2/1 I'm sick to death of women's liberation. I don't see any real knockouts running around with those placards, just a bunch of unhappy uggas. Nobody would want to spend an evening—much less a lifetime—with them.

5. a. *Mech.* A device for 'knocking out' or ejecting something, esp. from a mould or die.

1893 *Funk's Stand. Dict.*, *Knock-out*, a device for throwing out finished work from a punching- or stamping-machine. **1896** O. SMITH *Press-Working of Metals* xii. 243 There is a distinct class of ejecting press- or die-attachments known by the general name of 'knockouts', or sometimes and if limited to the lower die, as 'knockups'. **1915** F. D. JONES *Diemaking & Die Design* vii. 282 The mechanically operated knockout..applied to a punch press..operates more satisfactorily than a rubber bumper. **1919** F. A. STANLEY *Punches & Dies* vii. 152 The die is made..with a knock-out which ejects the work after the trimming operation. **1946** DU BOIS & PRIBBLE *Plastics Mold Engin.* ix. 371 The knockout pins may be made as sleeve knockouts working over a core pin. **1960** EARY & REED *Techniques Pressworking Sheet Metal* xviii. 377 Basically, there are two main types of knockouts: the spring knockout and the solid knockout.

b. A part of a box or other article designed to be forced out to form a hole.

[**1907**: implied in A. e above.] **1939** H. P. RICHTER *Pract. Electr. Wiring* x. 124 Around the sides [of the outlet box] and in the bottom are found 'knockouts'—sections of metal that can be easily knocked out to form openings for wire to enter. The metal is completely severed around these sections except at one small point. **1955** *Die Design Handbk.* (Amer. Soc. Tool Engineers) v. 23 Typical single and double dies for producing knockouts in conduit boxes, enclosing boxes, and similar products. **1962** *Gloss. Terms Glass Industry* (*B.S.I.*) 36 *Button* (cap, knockout), a portion of a piece of pressed ware so designed that it can be knocked out or off to make a hole.

c. *Founding.* The process of separating a casting from the flask and sand in which it was made (cf. *KNOCK *v.* 12 j); the place where, or equipment with which, this is carried out.

1942 *Engineering* 6 Mar. 195/3 The method of dealing with mould-making, closing and knock-out must depend upon the nature of the product. *Ibid.*, The cooling of the sand on its way from the knock-out to the reconditioning mill presented some difficulty. **1955** H. E. CRIVAN in W. C. Newell *Casting of Steel* vi. 227 Mechanical jolt knock-outs are in operation. **1972** P. R. BEELEY *Foundry Technol.* viii. 417 The interval before knockout is important from the points of view of moulding box utilisation and of the temperature of the sand in the system. **1973** *Steel Castings Abstr.* XXII. 11 The redesign of castings.. and alterations to the plant layout, including the knock-out, have reduced the labour required.

6. A 'knock-out' competition: see *A. c.

1928 *Observer* 4 Mar. 22 Pembroke..have won the finals ..of both the football 'knock-outs'. **1959** A. WESKER *Roots* III. 66 The fireman's whist drive. Won seven'n six in the knockout.

kno·ck-over. *Machine Knitting.* [f. vbl. phr. *to knock over* (*KNOCK *v.* 13 c).] The act or process of causing a stitch to pass over the head of the needle on which it was held. Also *attrib.*

1952 D. F. PALING *Warp Knitting Technol.* i. 6 A forward movement of the sinker bar combined with a further downward movement of the needle bar ensures a gradual knock-over. **1964** H. WIGNALL *Knitting* ii. 29 The frame needle goes down to its first knock-over. *Ibid.* 39 When the needle and point are locked together below the top of the knock-over bit they rise and the needle passes through the transferred loop.

kno·ck-up, *sb.* and *a.* **A.** *sb.* A practice or casual game at lawn tennis, squash rackets, etc.

1884 E. W. HAMILTON *Diary* 4 May (1972) II. 609 In the afternoon had a little 'knock up' at lawn tennis. **1922** F. HAMILTON *P.J.: Secret Service Boy* iii. 89 Shall we have a little knock-up against the wall of the stables? It doesn't make half a bad squash court. **1930** W. S. MAUGHAM *Breadwinner* II. 73 Why don't you and Dinah go and have a knock-up? **1946** *Penguin New Writing* XXVIII. 29 Expecting to find the three of them having a knock-up while they waited for him. **1973** G. MITCHELL *Murder of Busy Lizzie* xiv. 159 'I think I *will* go to bed.'.. 'All right, unless you'd like a knock-up at table tennis first.'

B. *adj.* Designating a knock-up: see above.

1928 *Weekly Dispatch* 24 June 21/7 Many of the world-famous players engaged in final 'knock-up' games at Wimbledon yesterday.

knockwurst, var. *KNACKWURST.

knödel (knö·dəl). Also **knoedel**. Pl. **-s,** ‖ **-n.** [G.] In Germany, a type of dumpling. Cf. *KNAIDEL.

1827 M. WILMOT *Jrnl.* 23 July in *More Lett.* (1935) 276 [H]oltzknecht Knödel—Woodcutter's dumpling, a sort of rice moistened with butter..fried..in little round balls. **1873** *German Nat. Cookery for Eng. Kitchens* x. 176 'Klösse' or 'Knödeln'... The bread used for them must be light, and without crust, either grated, crumbled, or soaked in cold milk or water. **1948** R. SYSONBY *Cook Bk.* (ed. 2) 144 Mariller Knoedel... Wrap some peeled fresh apricots each in a square of the paste... Drop the dumplings into..boiling water. **1968** L. DEIGHTON *Continental Dossier* §45 Baden-Württemberg... 'Knödel' ('dumplings') are famous. **1971** A. R. DANIEL *Baker's Dict.* (ed. 2) 108/2 *Knödel*, Bavarian name for a special kind of small dumpling.

Knoevenagel (knö·vĕnāgĕl). *Chem.* The name of Emil *Knoevenagel* (1865–1921), German chemist, used *attrib.* and occas. in the possessive to designate various reactions in organic chemistry, *esp.* the reaction between an aldehyde or ketone and malonic acid or a related compound containing active hydrogen, catalysed by ammonia or an amine, to yield an acid with the group —CH·CH·COOH.

1907 J. B. COHEN *Org. Chem. Adv. Students* I. vii. 285 (*heading*) Knoevenagel's reaction. **1931** *Jrnl. Chem. Soc.* 745 Catalytic action..effected by the salts of bases with mineral acids in the malonic acid condensation and the Knoevenagel reaction generally. **1938** G. H. RICHTER *Textbk. Org. Chem.* xvi. 289 The Knoevenagel reaction is the condensation of the carbonyl group of aldehydes and ketones with *active methylene* hydrogens; the reaction takes place in the presence of primary and secondary amines, especially diethylamine or piperidine. Knoevenagel was the first to point out the great catalytic power of ammonia and amines for this type of condensation. **1967** *Organic Reactions* XV. 204 (*heading*) The Knoevenagel condensation. **1969** R. C. DENNEY *Named Org. Reactions* 52 An interesting development has been the use of the Knoevenagel condensation to increase the chain length of sugars.

Knole sofa (nōᵘl sōᵘ·fă). [f. the name of the prototype at *Knole* Park, Kent, *c* 1605–20.] A sofa designed in the style of an early 17th-century model, having adjustable sides that may be lowered to make it into a day-bed. So *Knole couch, settee.*

[**1868** C. L. EASTLAKE *Hints Household Taste* vi. 142 The sofa at Knole..is an example of thoroughly good design... The sides can be raised or lowered..thus enabling the sofa to be used as a couch or a settee, at pleasure.] **1942** R. KING *Design in Evil* xxi. 207 A Knole sofa sheened with lemon-colored damask. **1943** D. WELCH *Maiden Voy.* xv. 122 Two fringed and tasselled Knole settees. **1945** *Burlington Mag.* LXXXVI. 114/1 The famous Knole couch..is the first comfortable type of couch that was made in England. **1951** A. CHRISTIE *They came to Baghdad* ii. 17 That Knole settee..in electric blue satin.

knoop[1] (nūp), *dial.* var. KNOP *sb.*[1] 2.

1871 G. M. HOPKINS *Jrnls. & Papers* (1959) 209 Then the knot or 'knoop' of buds some shut, some just gaping.

Knoop[2] (nūp, knūp). The name of Frederick *Knoop* (1878–1943), U.S. instrument-maker, used *attrib.* with reference to an indentation test devised by him, in which hardness is measured by the size of the indentation produced in a substance by a pyramidal diamond indenter of specified shape under a known load.

The pronunc. (knūp) is used by members of the Knoop family.

1940 *Metals & Alloys* Sept. 292/1 The article is a description of the Knoop Indenter, a new instrument for determining the micro-hardness of thin layers of metals. **1945** *Amer. Mineralogist* XXX. 595 The Knoop hardness of gypsum is approximately 32 to 45 or more, depending on orientation. **1961** E. CAMERON *Ore Microsc.* iv. 75 The Knoop hardness (*KV*) is given by the formula KV (in kg/mm²) $= 14230 \times P/l^2$ where P is the test load in grams, and l is the long diagonal of the indentation in 0·001 mm. **1971** *Nature* 14 Nov. 661/1 A study..on anisotropy in the hardness of crystals using the Knoop indenter. **1971** *Brit. Jrnl. Nutrition* XXVI. 234 The Knoop test of hardness..was applied to human nails.

knop, *sb.*[1] Add: **1. b.** A loop or tuft (often of different colour) formed in a strand of yarn for ornament. Also *attrib.* in *knop yarn.* (See quots.)

1904 GOODCHILD & TWENEY *Technol. & Sci. Dict.*, Knop yarn. **1914** BARKER & MIDGLEY *Analysis Woven Fabrics* 272 *Knop yarn.*—A yarn upon which knops or lumps of yarn of one or more colours appear at intervals. **1929** *Encycl. Brit.* XXIII. 879/2 The knop yarn—in which knops are formed at any required intervals on an otherwise level thread by holding one thread tightly and allowing the second thread to run in slackly to form knops of the required size. **1964** *Which?* Sept. 284/2 *Knop or nub*, a compound yarn with lumps or balls of yarn at regular or irregular intervals. **1968** E. GALE *From Fibres to Fabrics* iv. 44 *Knop yarn.* Two threads are twisted together, with one at regular intervals being given in very rapidly so that it is wound round and round the first thread in the form of a hard knop or lump.

knopite (nǫ·pəit, knǫ·pəit). *Min.* [ad. Sw. *knopit* (P. J. Holmquist 1894, in *Geol. För.*

Förh. XVI. 73), f. the name of Adolf *Knop* (1828–93), Ger. mineralogist: see -ITE[1].] A variety of perofskite occurring in lead-grey crystals, in which calcium is partly replaced by cerium.

1896 *Mineral. Mag.* XI. 158 Minerals at first thought to be perofskite and dysanalyte are here described under the new name knopite. **1927** *Mineral. Abstr.* III. 412 Knopite, a mineral new to Canada, occurs sparingly in small bunches in a basic pegmatite. **1947** *Ibid.* X. 138 Knopite is here a rock-forming mineral of primary magmatic origin, in contrast to its other occurrences as a contact mineral or in pegmatite. **1962** W. A. DEER et al. *Rock-forming Min.* V. 50 A variety [of perovskite] rich in rare earths, chiefly cerium, has been called knopite... In addition to rare earths of the cerium group, the lanthanum group is usually present.

knopkierie: see *KNOBKERRIE.

knopped, *a.* Restrict ? *Obs.* to sense a in Dict. and add: **b.** (Further example); *spec.* of the stem of a glass.

1869 G. M. HOPKINS *Jrnls. & Papers* (1959) 193 A fine sunset..; along the earth-line a train of dark clouds of knopped or clustery make. **1960** H. HAYWARD *Antique Coll.* 158/2 Knopped stem, a type of stem found on 18th cent. drinking glasses composed of a varying number of knops. **1963** *Times* 30 Apr. 14/4 C. Davis bought..a cylinder-knopped wine glass for £155. **1973** *Times Lit. Suppl.* 6 Apr. 374/5 There are knopped and wrythen wine glasses.

c. *knopped yarn,* yarn ornamented with knops or tufts. See *KNOP *sb.*[1] 1 b.

1911 *Encycl. Brit.* XXVIII. 906/2 *Knopped Yarn* is formed by twisting together several strands, one of which is at intervals delivered in greater lengths than the others, in order to allow a loop to be made.

knopper (nǫ·pəɹ). Pl. **knoppern, knoppers.** [G., = gall-nut.] A kind of oak-gall caused by an insect of the genus *Cynips,* formerly used in tanning and dyeing.

1879 *Encycl. Brit.* X. 44/1 The 'knoppern' galls of *Cynips polycera,* Gir., are cones having the broad, slightly convex, upper surface surrounded with a toothed ridge. **1903** H. R. PROCTER *Princ. Leather Manuf.* xviii. 262 *Knoppern* are galls produced on the immature acorns of various species of oaks, principally *Q[uercus] Cerris* in Hungary... They..have been largely replaced by valonia. **1908** E. T. CONNOLD *Brit. Oak Galls* 143 *Cynips calicis...* 'The Knopper Gall'... It occurs principally on *Quercus pedunculata,* but also on *Q. sessiliflora.* **1953** F. N. HOWES *Vegetable Tanning Materials* xxxvii. 260 The best known European galls are those obtained from eastern Europe (the Balkans and adjoining regions), which are commonly known as 'knoppers' or 'knoppern' or 'acorn galls'... There are various kinds of knoppern recognized, such as those formerly obtained from Hungary, Bohemia, Dalmatia and Serbia.

knopple (nǫ·p'l), *v. rare*[−1]. [?f. KNOBBLE *sb.* or KNOP *sb.*[1]] *trans.* = KNOB *v.* 1.

1870 G. M. HOPKINS *Jrnls. & Papers* (1959) 201 Herds of towering pillow clouds, one great stack..was knoppled all over in fine snowy tufts and pencilled with bloom-shadow.

knorr (nǭr). Also **knarr, knörr.** [ad. ON. *knörr* ship, merchant ship.] A mediæval type of ship of Northern Europe, having a single sail (see quots.).

1889 P. B. DU CHAILLU *Viking Age* II. xiii. 212 We find them [*sc.* trading ships] mentioned under their different names—viz., Knörr, Kugg, Byrding (ship of burden), Vistabyrding, [etc.]. **1932** C. M. SMITH *Northmen of Adventure* xiv. 320 The round ships went under a variety of names. The largest class was the *knorr.* **1967** H. HARRISON *Technicolor Time Machine* xi. 114 Where the dragon-prowed Viking ship was long and narrow, this *knorr* was wide and stood high out of the water—and was at least a hundred feet long. **1968** G. JONES *Hist. Vikings* III. ii. 188 Captain Folgar..in 1932 took a replica of a 60-foot knörr across the Atlantic. **1971** S. E. MORISON *European Discovery Amer., Northern Voys.* iii. 35 The Norse discoverers of Greenland and Vinland did not use a long Viking ship... There is ample evidence that they used the *knarr,* a beamy type propelled principally by one big square sail made of a coarse woolen cloth called 'wadmal', rigged with an additional sprit to set well close-hauled. **1973** *Country Life* 17 May 1373/2 A Knarr, the cargo ship in which the great [Viking] voyages to Greenland and North America were made.

Knossian (knǫ·siăn, knōᵘ·-), *a.* Also **Cnossian.** [f. Gr. *Κνωσσός* Knossos or Cnossos + -IAN.] Of or pertaining to Knossos, a city in ancient Crete, where, according to classical tradition, King Minos ruled and kept the Minotaur in a labyrinth; historically, the centre of the Minoan civilization as revealed by the ruins of a vast labyrinthine palace (18th–14th centuries B.C.). Also as *sb.*

1894 A. J. EVANS in *Jrnl. Hellenic Stud.* XIV. 283 The incised marks on the slabs of the Knôsian building do not..stand alone. **1895** H. S. JONES tr. *Sel. Passages Anc. Writers* I. i. 4 The Knossians also possess the dance of Ariadne a relief in white marble. **1900** A. J. EVANS in *Ann. Brit. Sch. Athens* VI. 16 An artistic advance which ..was not reached till the fifth century before our era, some eight or nine centuries later than the date of this Knossian fresco. *Ibid.* 59 Out of about 25 distinct signs..near parallels to about 6 occur in the Knossian linear series. **1909** —— *Scripta Minoa* I. I. iii. 21 A perfect clay bar of the same general class as some of those from the Knossian deposit..had been acquired... The first stage represented by the existing West Wing of the Knossian palace goes far back into the Second Middle Minoan Age. **1939** J. D. S. PENDLEBURY *Archaeol. Crete* iv. 180 L.M. II vases of Knossian fabric in L.M. I deposits at Pseira. **1950** G. E. DANIEL *100 Yrs. Archaeol.* vi. 192 To the great Bronze Age civilisation which he discovered in Crete, Sir Arthur Evans gave the name Minoan... Other names were suggested, such as Knossian, Cretan, or Aegean. **1962** *Times* 21 Apr. 9/6 Deposits are 'telescoped', material of several Knossian periods being represented in a single layer of rubbish... It cannot be assigned..to any particular subdivision of the Knossian system. **1963** *Listener* 21 Mar. 495/1 The Cnossian ruler's contemporaries in Egypt.

knot, *sb.*[1] Add: **3. c.** *at the rate of knots,* very fast, quickly. *colloq.*

1892 R. WARDON *Macpherson's Gully* vi. 40 When she's [*sc.* the Teremakau river has] got her back up, travellin' in a hurry, like—tearin' along at the rate o' knots like she is to-day—..she's got to be treated with all doo respeck. **1921** 'T. COLLINS' *Rigby's Romance* xxxii. 222, I went for it at the rate of knots, with the fire lathering along behind me roaring like fury. **1932** KIPLING *Limits & Renewals* 80 A natty little grey and black self-driven coupé came from Brighton way at the rate of knots. **1941** BAKER *N.Z. Slang* vi. 53 To travel at the rate of knots.

10. a. *to tie* (a person) (*up*) *in(to) knots* (or *a knot*): to confuse or nonplus (someone).

1860 *Baily's Mag.* Aug. 368 Never before..were bowlers or fielders so 'tied up in a knot'. **1888** A. G. STEEL in Steel & Lyttelton *Cricket* iii. 167 The team was beginning to get tied up into a knot. **1957** D. ROBINS *Noble One* (1960) xx. 191 He is tied up in knots. He's fighting himself as well as me. **1974** I. MURDOCH *Sacred & Profane Love Machine* 154, I could tie you into such knots, but I won't bother... You won't tell me the truth even now.

19. knot-catcher (see quot.); **knot-gall,** a species of oak-gall produced by the cynipid *Andricus noduli*; **knot-head** *N. Amer.,* a stupid person (see also quot. 1940); a stupid horse; **knot-hole,** (*b*) (example); (*c*) a hole formed by the excavation of clay; **knot-horn** = *knot-horn moth*; **knot-stitch** (examples); **knot-writing,** a mnemonic aid consisting of strings in which a number of knots are made.

1927 T. WOODHOUSE *Artificial Silk* 100 The threads or yarn from the cone cheeses are first led up through coils in wires termed knot catchers. **1894** C. R. STRATON tr. *Adler's Alternating Generations* 34 The knot gall is found in June on *Q[uercus] pedunculata, Q. sessiliflora,* and *Q. pubescens.* **1908** E. T. CONNOLD *Brit. Oak Galls* 65 The Knot Gall. **1940** *Amer. Speech* XV. 447/2 *Knot head,* low intelligence. **1961** WEBSTER, *Knothead,* a dull-witted blunderer. **1961** R. P. HOBSON *Rancher takes Wife* i. 21 Harold called in a loud voice to the horse. 'Step up there, you old knothead.' **1962** A. FRY *Ranch on Cariboo* xv. 160 I'd the repertoire of a mule skinner, developed behind a wide variety of knothead horses. **1972** J. AIKEN *Butterfly Picnic* ix. 163 Why hadn't he *said* he was going to, the silly knothead? **1903** *Westm. Gaz.* 31 Dec. 3/2 The little coons..climbed up to the knot-hole, and scrambled down inside. **1964** E. HUXLEY *Back Street New Worlds* x. 98 There are craters..called knot-holes, and from them clay has been scooped and loaded into tub-like steel wagons to proceed..to the kilns. **1967** M. CHANDLER *Ceramics in Mod. World* i. 29 The underlying Lower Oxford clay.. is taken from the claypit or 'knot-hole' by a mechanical excavator. **1899** D. SHARP in *Cambr. Nat. Hist.* VI. 424 The males frequently have the basal-joint of the antennæ swollen; hence the term 'Knot-horns' applied by collectors to these moths. **1881** C. C. HARRISON *Woman's Handiwork* I. 84 Beginning with the hemstitch of our grandmothers, we may add..lace stitches, herring-bone, buttonhole..darning and knot stitch. **1964** *McCall's Sewing* ii. 30/1 *Knot-stitch,* stitch used to secure thread at beginning and end of stitching. **1896** A. J. BUTLER tr. *Ratzel's Hist. Mankind* I. 344 In West Australia,..a network of reed serves for a messenger's credentials,—a reminiscence of the once more widely-developed knot-writing.

knotted, *a.* Add: **1. c.** Colloq. phr. *to get knotted,* to 'go to hell'. Usu. in *imp.,* stop annoying me!

1963 *New Society* 22 Aug. 5/1 Other adoptions are 'get knotted' and 'knackered' which have come to mean innocently enough, 'go to hell', and '*kaput*'. **1964** B. W. ALDISS *Dark Light Years* iii. 39 Get knotted, Duffield, you ruddy trouble-maker. **1965** M. FORSTER *Bogeyman* viii. 144 'You are to behave properly.' 'Get knotted,' said Natalie, deliberately. **1968** 'H. CALVIN' *Miranda must Die* ii. 19, I don't know why the hell you didn't tell him to get knotted and be done with it. **1969** O. BLAKESTON *For crying out Shroud* v. 46 'That boy in Rome said we looked like a hero.'.. 'Get knotted. We might as well be dead.' **1972** G. LYALL *Blame the Dead* xii. 80 'I'll lend you a good book about security.' 'Get knotted, Major.'

knottedness (nǫ·tĕdnĕs). [f. KNOTTED *a.* + -NESS.] The character or manner of being formed into a knot.

1909 in WEBSTER. **1962** C. S. OGILVY *Tomorrow's Math* vi. 109 Does the system of lines of magnetic force in space surrounding the knot reflect topologically the knottedness of the curve?

knotter. Add: **3.** With prefixed numeral: a boat or ship that makes (so many) knots an hour.

1908 *Pall Mall Gaz.* 20 Apr. 6/1 Not many of the so-called '30-knotters' could steam at this speed. **1929** 'SEAMARK' *Down River* i, Essex noted the stolid little ten knotter ahead.

know, *v.* Add: **1. b.** Phrases: *not to know one's arse from one's elbow* (and similar phrases): a coarse expression suggestive of complete ignorance or innocence; (*not*) *to know from nothing* (*U.S.*): to be totally ignorant (about something).

1930 R. BLAKER *Medal without Bar* xiii. 69 'But nor 'an 'un' (this phrase was his masterpiece of thoughtful emphasis), 'nor 'an 'un of us knows 'is ears from 'is elbow when it comes to learning—learning like you officers have got up your sleeves.' **1936** *Mademoiselle* Mar. 43/1, I find I belong to the wrong gender to take part in such confabulations, and know from nothing. **1942** BERREY & VAN DEN BARK *Amer. Thes. Slang* §150/3 *Be ignorant,* know from nothing. **1944** 'N. SHUTE' *Pastoral* iv. 75, I wish I'd had a crowd like that for my first crew. We none of us knew arse from elbow when they pushed me off. **1945** 'F. FEIKEMA' *Boy Almighty* (1950) xvii. 162 Them San dietitians, they don't know from nuthin'. **1945** T. SHOR in Mencken *Amer. Lang.* (1948) Suppl. II. 695 A *square* don't know from nothin' and a *creep* is worse'n a jerk. **1966** 'L. LANE' *ABZ of Scouse* 29 Don't know Thairsday from brekfuss-time. *Ibid.,* Don't know 'is arse from 'is elbow. **1968** *Encounter* Sept. 22/1 He knows from nothin'.

5. *to know like a book* (see *LIKE *adv.* 1 c). **b.** (Earlier and later examples of *know thyself.*)

c **1527** tr. *Erasmus's Dicta Sapientium* sig. A3v *Nosce te ipsum,* know thy selfe. **1849** LYTTON *Caxtons* III. XVI. x. 183 'Know thyself,' said the old philosophy. 'Improve thyself,' saith the new. **1905** A. MACLAREN *Gospel St. Matthew* I. 43 The proud old saying of the Greeks, 'Know thyself'..would result in this profound abnegation of all claims, in this poverty of spirit. **1929** A. HUXLEY *Let.* 7 Jan. (1969) 306 'Know thyself' was probably one of the stupidest pieces of advice ever given. *a* **1930** D. H. LAWRENCE *Last Poems* (1932) 266 When at last we escape the barbed wire enclosure Of *Know Thyself,* knowing we can never know. **1941** *N. & Q.* Feb. 138 The folly of that impossible precept 'Know thyself'.

9. e. *to know one's* ——: to be well acquainted with something, to be well up in something. E.g. *to know one's business, onions* (see *ONION *sb.*), *stuff* (see *STUFF *sb.*[1]).

11. b. *not to know what hit one*: see *HIT *v.* 8 e. Also, *you know*: a phrase used with aposiopesis (the implication to be imagined) or const. *what, whom,* etc. (as a means of avoiding naming the person, etc., referred to).

1867 TROLLOPE *Phineas Finn* (1869) I. x. 84 She told me once..it would lead to my being everlastingly—you know what. She isn't so squeamish as I am, and said it out. **1875** GEO. ELIOT *Let.* 13 Jan. (1956) VI. 116, I had a letter from 'you know whom' last night. **1911** D. H. LAWRENCE *White Peacock* II. i. 219 It's the way she swings her body—an' the curves as she stands. It's when you look at her—you feel—you know. **1925** *New Yorker* 7 Mar. 19/1 Of course there's no use me asking you if you took in all the revues where the girls come out—you know. **1937** C. DAY LEWIS *Starting Point* iii. 44 Never mind, kick him in the you know where—he's used to it. **1948** D. BALLANTYNE *Cunninghams* ii. 12 She is you know [*sc.* in the family way] to a Maori. **1949** D. M. DAVIN *Roads from Home* 99 Too much you know what last night, eh? **1970** *Harrap's French-Eng. Dict. Slang* 201 *Qui-vous-savez,* (said of person one does not wish to name) you know who.

e. *you know*: now freq. as a mere conversational filler. Also, *don't you know?,* a variant of *you know* (cf. *DONCHER).

1880 'MARK TWAIN' *Tramp Abroad* App. D. 611 Nothing gives such an air of grace and elegance and unconstraint to a German or an English conversation as to scatter it full of 'Also's' or 'You-knows'. **1885** A. EDWARDES *Girton Girl* II. iii. 40 Attack me? Why that was only a foolish joke, don't you know? **1896** F. C. PHILIPS *Undeserving Woman* 104 'When?' said George. 'I'd like to put the thing right at once, don't you know.' **1924** D. H. LAWRENCE *Phoenix II* (1968) 304 Little smart man of the shabby world, very much on the spot, don't you know. **1926** G. HUNTING *Vicarion* iv. 63 This represents some years of study, you know, this little exhibition I have given you. **1930** 'SAPPER' *Finger of Fate* 225 My wife is such a nervous woman, don't you know. **1947** [see *BOUDIN]. **1965** *Listener* 2 Dec. 914/1 A. They're supposed to be, you know, sexy. B. That's all right, but all men are the same, after one thing, but sometimes, you know, it can be wonderful. **1968** *Ibid.* 16 May 626/2 Too often one hears people on the wireless beginning an elaborate sentence—they flounder about for a bit and then break off with: 'you know'. **1969** WIDDOWSON & HALPERT in Halpert & Story *Christmas Mumming in Newfoundland* 151 You could buy them in St. John's, you know, the false faces. **1974** *Sunday Times* (Colour Suppl.) 3 Feb. 66/4 People get the wrong idea, thinking we might be, you know, glamorous or brilliant or something.

f. *not if I know it* (earlier example).

1865 TROLLOPE *Miss Mackenzie* I. ii. 33 'Tom,' said I, when he asked me to go down to Drunder Street, 'not if I know it.'

Also (the phrases are arranged in the chronological order of their first recorded use in English as far as this is determinable):

to know little (or *nothing*) *and care less*: to be unconcerned *about*; to be studiously ignorant of.

1814 JANE AUSTEN *Mansf. Park* II. xi. 251 'I know nothing of the Miss Owens,' said Fanny calmly. 'You know nothing and you care less, as people, say Never did

tone express indifference plainer.' **1853** LYTTON *My Novel* II. VIII. iv. 322 'Ah!' said Egerton, who, as it has been before said, knew little, and cared less, about the Hazeldean pedigree, 'I..had forgotten it.' **1893** R. L. STEVENSON *Catriona* xxii. 267, I tell ye I ken naething and care less either for him or his breed. **1924** R. H. MOTTRAM *Spanish Farm* I. 71 Madeleine knew little and cared less as to what this might mean, except as it affected the work of the farm. **1925** F. HARRIS *My Life & Loves* III. xii. 183 The great London doctors knew nothing about leprosy and cared less. **1925** O. W. HOLMES in *Holmes–Laski Lett.* (1953) I. 741, I think he generally was kind in his judgment of me, except when Roosevelt was so angry at my dissent in the *Northern Securities* case (about which you probably know little and care less). **1931** F. L. ALLEN *Only Yesterday* v. 88 The shock troops of the rebellion were not alien agitators, but the sons and daughters of well-to-do American families, who knew little about Bolshevism and cared distinctly less. **1937** N. COWARD *Present Indicative* VIII. v. 321 Even at the time we realised in our hearts that the bulk of the public knew nothing about *Sirocco* and cared less.

to know the reason why: to demand (and get) an explanation. Cf. REASON *sb.*[1] 5.

1825 R. S. HAWKER *Cornish Ballads* (1869) 1 And shall Trelawney die? Here's twenty thousand Cornish men Will know the reason why! **1894** SOMERVILLE & 'ROSS' *Real Charlotte* III. xxxix. 87 She had laid out a good deal of money on the house and farm, but she was going to get a good return for it, or know the reason why. **1934** G. B. SHAW *On Rocks* II. 68 My Union Jack men would keep order, or theyd know the reason why. **1941** *Punch* 20 Aug. 155/2 Two months ago Herr Hitler said his armies would sweep through Russia or he would know the reason why. **1942** *Ibid.* 11 Feb. 113/2, I caught him in the wash-house for an explanation or I'd know the reason why, and it appeared I'd ruined his life.

and knows (or *knew*, etc.) *it*: is clearly aware of (what has been stated).

1848 MRS. GASKELL *Mary Barton* I. vi. 103 The son was strikingly handsome and knew it. **1898** G. B. SHAW *Mrs. Warren's Profession* III. 208 I'm not a young man, and I know it. **1930** J. B. PRIESTLEY *Angel Pavement* v. 248 Well, she's pretty enough, and knows it, the little monkey. **1932** E. V. LUCAS *Reading, Writing & Remembering* xi. 182 Meredith was very handsome, and he knew it.

to know what one likes: a phrase used to imply that the speaker knows which works of art, poems, etc., he likes without necessarily having an informed opinion to support his view.

1873 H. JAMES *Compl. Tales* (1962) III. 72, I went with Harold a great deal to the Louvre, where he was a very profitable companion. He had the history of the schools at his fingers' ends, and, as the phrase is, he knew what he liked. **1881** —— *Portrait of Lady* II. v. 67, I don't care anything about reasons, but I know what I like. **1959** *Listener* 9 July 75/3 In reality, she was just a wealthy collector. She knew what she liked. **1974** R. HILL *Very Good Hater* xi. 93 'Are you interested in art?' asked Mrs Housman politely. 'I know what I like,' he answered.

don't I know it: I am well aware of it, you need not tell me.

1874 M. CLARKE *His Natural Life* (1875) II. iii. 192 The old trick. Ha! ha! don't I know it? **1899** KIPLING *Stalky & Co.* 151 'We didn't always knock him about, though!' 'You did when you could catch him... Don't I know it!' **1936** 'R. WEST' *Thinking Reed* xii. 419 'I hate it,' she said. 'I hate it.'..'Don't I know it,' said Alan. **1964** J. CREASEY *Look Three Ways* x. 96 'He's in a mess that poor devil is.' 'And don't I know it?' **1970** B. COBB *Catch Me* i. 13 'They've only been married a few months. She's still starry-eyed.' 'Don't I know it!'

before you know where you are (and similar phrases): very soon, very quickly.

1916 A. HUXLEY *Let.* 30 June (1969) 104 Steps must quickly be taken, or we shall find the place full of effigies and all the money spent before we know where we are. **1930** W. S. MAUGHAM *Bread-Winner* ii. 102 Almost before you know where you are, they're young men and women with characters of their own. **1936** WODEHOUSE *Laughing Gas* i. 9 And little by little and bit by bit, before you know where you are—why, there you are, don't you know. **1956** A. WILSON *Anglo-Saxon Att.* II. ii. 341 Gerald said at the end of her story, 'Yes, that's certainly jolly sad,' and, before he knew where he was, he had given her a cheque for the dispensing of charity. **1970** C. WHITMAN *Death out of Focus* xii. 183 You're a clever devil... You'll be an Inspector before you know where you are.

not to know whether one is coming or going (see *COME *v.* 26 e).

to know too much: used in a context of murder, or of a threat to kill, because the victim knows too much to be allowed to live.

1922 CHESTERTON (*title*) The man who knew too much. **1953** A. CHRISTIE *After Funeral* xxi. 163 'And why should anyone want to kill you, beautiful Rosamund?'.. 'Because I know too much, of course.' **1966** 'S. WOODS' *Enter Certain Murderers* xii. 191 At the risk of being melodramatic..you know too much.

to know where one stands (or *is*) *with* (someone): to know how one is regarded by (someone); to know a person's views (on an issue).

1950 J. CANNAN *Murder Included* ii. 33 'Those blunt, downright people are never irritating—you know where you are with them.' 'They're irritating to some people.' **1951** E. PAUL *Springtime in Paris* iv. 90 An honest whore knew where she stood. **1954** L. P. HARTLEY *White Wand* 37 One never quite knew where one was with her. **1966** *Oxf. Univ. Gaz.* 23 Dec. 433/2 If the majority now rise and say they support Council's paragraph (*a*), we shall know where we stand—we shall all be standing! **1972** F. WARNER *Lying Figures* II. 9, I wasn't a pushover. All I wanted was to know where I stood.

(*do*) *you know something?*: shall I tell you this surprising fact?, I am going to tell you something.

1965 I. FLEMING *Man with Golden Gun* viii. 113 Mr. Paradise..said softly 'You know something?' **1971** J. BRUNNER *Honky in Woodpile* v. 37 'You know something?' We looked expectant. **1972** P. DICKINSON *Lizard in Cup* x. 159 You know something? She was reared in a home. **1972** J. WILSON *Hide & Seek* ii. 29 Do you know something, Mary? Mr Harris is the nicest man I know, except for my father.

g. Misc. phrases in which *know* is used *intr.* or *absol.* (usually with something implied and sometimes with specific idiomatic force):

I want to know: well, well! *U.S. colloq.*

1833 J. NEAL *Down-Easters* I. 45, I *want* to know! exclaimed the other down-easter. Well, you *do* know, replied the southerner. **1840** *Knickerbocker* XVI. 20 'I want to know!' said the lady; 'precious soul!' **1888** *Harper's Mag.* Sept. 530/1 'Why, Jered Hopkins!' she said, looking up at him; 'I want to know!' **1904** J. C. LINCOLN *Cap'n Eri* iii. 39 'I want to know!' exclaimed Captain Perez. 'You don't tell me!' said Captain Jerry. **1911** —— *Cap'n Warren's Wards* x. 154 'She said she would be delighted!' 'I want to know!' **1923** R. D. PAINE *Comrades of Rolling Ocean* 169 And you come from North Dakoty! I want to know.

that's all you know: you do not know the facts, you do not understand (used censoriously of the person to whom the phrase is addressed). Also, *that's all you know about it.*

1876 TROLLOPE *Prime Minister* III. xi. 183 'They may do foolish things, dear; and yet..not interfere with politics.' 'That's all you know about it, Plantagenet.' **1879** C. M. YONGE *Magnum Bonum* III. xxxiv. 723 'She thought you a catch in the old days.' 'That's all you know about it!' **1930** E. H. YOUNG *Miss Mole* ii. 20 'And breakfast in bed is not what you want, Hannah.' 'That's all you know about it,' Hannah said. **1961** I. FLEMING *Thunderball* ii. 19 'I wouldn't have thought these people would be interested.'..The young man snorted, 'That's all you know.' **1973** 'S. WOODS' *Enter the Corpse* 165 '*He* hasn't been near them,' said Boney Nelson confidently... 'That's all you know,' Meg retorted.

what do you know?: used as an expression of mild surprise = 'Isn't that amazing?' 'Well I never!' 'Just fancy!' Also, *What do you know about that?*

1914 [see *GET *v.* 21 d]. **1916** 'B. M. BOWER' *Phantom Herd* ii. 33 Now what do you know about that, Mig? **1933** E. E. CUMMINGS *eimi* 245 What do you know—out of every 50 chances to make a mistake, those greedy tovariches took advantage of 4 (versus 1 mistake out of 10,000 chances in America). **1943** K. TENNANT *Ride on Stranger* vii. 72 Why, the louse!..He's glad to get rid of us. What do you know about that? **1947** 'N. SHUTE' *Chequer Board* iii. 63 Say, what do you know? They ain't got no sewer here. **1952** 'C. BRAND' *London Particular* xvi. 216 Well, what do you know, boys?—let's call it a day. **1957** J. KEROUAC *On Road* (1958) xii. 80 And that thousand dollars was..right there on top of the safe, what do you know about that? **1959** 'M. NEVILLE' *Sweet Night for Murder* xxi. 200 'Yeah... That's right... I'll say! What do you know!' Which crescendo of surprise was a clear..statement of agreement. **1968** 'A. GILBERT' *Night Encounter* v. 80 'Well,' marvelled Frankie, 'what do you know?' **1971** R. DENTRY *Encounter at Kharmel* (1973) v. 89 Well! What do you know? So the Company has been getting off its well-padded bum at last.

wouldn't you (or *he*, etc.) *like to know?*: I have no intention of telling you.

1923 G. ATHERTON *Black Oxen* xx. 105 'Look here!' he said. 'How far do you go?' 'Wouldn't you like to know?' 'I should. Not for personal reasons, for girls..bore me.' **1941** I. BAIRD *He rides Sky* 123 The old crumpet fires off a lot of bilge like..'What do you do in your spare time?' (wouldn't *he* like to know?)... And so on and on. **1942** BERREY & VAN DEN BARK *Amer. Thes. Slang* § 205/6 *I won't tell you*, don't you wish you knew?..wouldn't you like to know?, you'd like to know? **1963** M. BORRELLI *Street Lamp & Stars* xiv. 127 'And what did *you* do, Naso Stuorto?' 'Wouldn't you like to know.' 'I can guess.'

you never know or *one never knows*: something unexpected or surprising may occur.

1924 G. B. SHAW *St. Joan* vi. 94 A flaw in the procedure may be useful later on: one never knows. **1926** F. W. CROFTS *Inspector French & Cheyne Mystery* viii. 103 'I don't see that we should gain much by looking at the outside of the house.' 'You never know... If we see nothing no harm is done.' **1948** 'J. TEY' *Franchise Affair* xiv. 147 It would be too great luck that he should be staying at the Midland, but one never knows. **1972** E. BERCKMAN *Fourth Man on Rope* iii. 38 Among the most unpromising debris there might lurk..some jewel as yet undiscovered. *You never know*, faithfully she invoked the formula that spurred the weariest..*you never know*. **1974** J. MANN *Sticking Place* viii. 129 'I'll come with you,' Edward said...He added in a low, ominous voice..'You never know.'

for all I know (or *he knows*, etc.): as far as I am aware, since I know nothing to the contrary.

1930 E. WAUGH *Vile Bodies* viii. 143 But these young people have got hold of another end of the stick, and for all we know it may be the right one. **1934** F. W. CROFTS *12.30 from Croydon* xxi. 292 They stood to gain by Mr. Andrew Crowther's death, and though they didn't stand to gain so much as the other two, for all we know to the contrary any one of them may have been in greater need. **1937** D. RUNYON *More Than Somewhat* v. 104 Leaving the wop yelling very loud, and maybe cussing us in wop for all I know. **1954** W. S. MAUGHAM *Ten Novels* i. 3 Everybody skips, but to skip without loss is not easy. It may be, for all I know, a gift of nature, or it may be something that has to be acquired by experience. **1954** E. CALDWELL *Love & Money* (1955) xiii. 171 How do I know you're telling the truth? For all I know, this might be some more scheming between you and Tess. **1955** D. GARNETT *Aspects of Love* IV. 119 Well, if you believe in mermaids I might be one, for all you know.

I wouldn't know: I cannot be expected to know, that is outside the range of my knowledge. Also, *I wouldn't know about that.*

1939 W. M. RAINE *River Bend Feud* x. 72 Faint wrinkles creased the forehead of the engineer. 'Has he fixed up an alliance with the outside ranchmen?' he asked. 'I wouldn't know about that,' Raleigh answered. 'But if he hasn't, he will.' **1950** J. CANNAN *Murder Included* iii. 44 'The bedroom..was only locked by the deceased during her ablutions.' 'As you say nowadays—I wouldn't know,' said Sir Charles. **1952** M. R. RINEHART *Swimming Pool* xii. 110, I wouldn't know. I've never had one. **1960** L. P. HARTLEY *Facial Justice* xvi. 133 'Every man has his type, of course—.' 'I wouldn't know about that.' **1961** J. B. PRIESTLEY *Saturn Over Water* v. 64, I wouldn't know... I'm just a painter. **1968** B. FOSTER *Changing Eng. Lang.* i. 42 As an avowal of ignorance, British English has long used 'I couldn't say', but this is often replaced now by the *I wouldn't know*... In Britain it started making headway in the 'thirties, and in a British serial film (*Pimpernel Smith*) of 1940 the late Leslie Howard remarked 'In the deplorable argot of the modern generation, "I wouldn't know".' **1969** M. PUGH *Last Place Left* vii. 45 'That's why married people get so complicated in bed, isn't it?' 'Do they? I wouldn't know.'

wouldn't you (*just*) *know?*: 'just fancy!' 'imagine that!'; as one might have foreseen. orig. *U.S.*

1946 H. P. M. BROWN *Sound of Hunting* I. 52 Wouldn't you know? Of all the days to get stuck out there, he has to pick this one. **1966** *Listener* 3 Mar. 325/2 George Scott is an English professor (wouldn't you know?) who's engaged in the *bellum sexuale* with his wife. **1973** *Washington Post* 13 Jan. B.8/7 Wouldn't you just know. Lorne Greene, also known as Ben Cartwright, has gone right out and gotten himself another steady job; this time with the ABC network.

I don't (or *he*, etc., *doesn't*) *want to know*: I am not interested. Occas. const. with person as object.

1948 'N. SHUTE' *No Highway* iii. 79, I was trying to tell her what to do if things look bad. But if she doesn't want to know, I can't do more. **1967** *Listener* 14 Sept. 326/1 After doing a hard week's work I had nothing in my pocket..nothing at all and that went on for four years... After that I said: 'Well, that's it. I don't want to know. I can get a living a lot easier than going to work.' **1969** *Focus* Feb. 16/2 But if you are paying it all in on a Friday, and taking it all out again on Saturday, do not be surprised if the building society does not want to know you. **1973** *Observer* 14 Jan. 7/3 It remains to add that all this, and much more, was well enough known at the time. But the fellow-travellers didn't want to know. **1973** *Times* 19 Sept. 13/4 (Advt.), Graduates you have a problem. If you wanted the summer following graduation free, you missed out on the 'milk round'. Many employers don't want to know by the autumn.

15. *to know a thing or two* (later examples); *to know it all*: not to be aware of one's deficiencies, to be deaf to advice or instruction; also *to think one* (or *he, she*, etc.) *knows it all.* Cf. *know-all, know-it-all* s.v. KNOW- in Dict. and Suppl.

to know the ropes (see Dict. and ROPE *sb.*[1] 4 c); *to know all the answers* (see *ANSWER *sb.* 6 b); *not to know beans* (see *BEAN *sb.* 6 e).

1870 E. G. WHITE *Testimonies for Church* No. 19. 73 You have so long thought, with the peculiar class I have mentioned, that you knew it all, that you will not see your deficiencies when they are presented before you. **1929** J. B. PRIESTLEY *Good Companions* I. iii. 24 Ted..admitted that he knocked about a bit and knew a thing or two. **1944** E. CALDWELL *Tragic Ground* (1947) iii. 31 Jim Howard Vance is a pretty smart fellow. He was talking in there just a while ago like he knows a thing or two. **1972** G. DURRELL *Catch me a Colobus* vi. 111 As I had warned Long John, there comes a time on every collecting trip when you begin to think that you know it all. This is a moment of great danger, for you *never* know it all, however hard you try. *Ibid.*, I made a mistake once by thinking I knew it all, and got bitten by a snake. **1973** WODEHOUSE *Bachelor Anonymous* iv. 33 The serfs and vassals now know a thing or two and prefer to make their living elsewhere. **1973** *Black World* Sept. 97/1 To my once respected student who has taken over the pompous entitlement as chief white critic of inferior Black literature, let me say..: 'Stop knowing it all.'

know-. Add: **know-all, know-it-all**: also *attrib.* or as *adj.*, full of knowledge; esp., deaf to advice or instruction.

1881 TENNYSON *Tiresias* (1885) 49 *We* have knelt in your know-all chapel. **1906** *Daily Chron.* 30 Aug. 3/4 He..maintains in his know-all manner that the two counties of Wigtown and Kirkcudbright..were integral parts always of the kingdom of Scotland. **1923** D. H. LAWRENCE *Birds, Beasts & Flowers* 185 Fool, in spite of your pretty ways, and quaint, know-all, wrinkled old aunty's face. **1935** WODEHOUSE *Blandings Castle* ix. 225 These know-it-all directors make me tired. **1956** H. GOLD *Man who was not with It* (1965) ii. 16 He looked over the apprehensive afternoon crowd with its know-it-all faces. **1959** *Encounter* XIII. II. 57 All big smart know-it-all Marxists. **1974** *Times* 23 Jan. 1/8 We didn't realize, until it was too late, how our know-it-all attitude was undermining the self-assurance of parents.

knowed. Widespread dial. pa. t. of KNOW *v.*

Numerous examples in *E.D.D.* (q.v.). The examples that follow are *U.S.*

1848 J. R. LOWELL *Poet. Wks.* (1873) 252/1 My! when he made Ole Hunderd ring, She *knowed* the Lord was

nigher. **1872** W. COLEMAN in *Rep. 42nd U.S. Congress 2 Sess. Joint Select. Comm. Condition of Affairs Late Insurrectionary States* XI. 484 Of course I knowed him. **1929** *Amer. Mercury* Sept. 50/1 Got in trouble one time... Knowed officers couldn't 'rest me. **1942** *Ibid.* July 87, I knowed you'd back up. **1949** in B. A. Botkin *Treas. S. Folklore* III. i. 434, I knowed dad-blamed well they wa'n't no fox in that sourwood.

know-how (nōu·hau). orig. *U.S.* [f. vbl. phr. *to know how* (KNOW *v.* 12).] Knowledge of how to do some particular thing; technical expertness, practical knowledge.

1838 *New Yorker* 14 July 260/2, I promise, 1st. To do the duties of the office to the best of my know-how, and have a stouter man than myself to help me. **1857** *Spirit of Times* 26 Dec. 270/3 'No, no, Massa,' replied the gentleman from Africa, 'charge fifty cents for killing, and fifty for the know how.' **1899** KIPLING *From Sea to Sea* II. 95 He has the money. We have the know-how. He comes in winter to play poker... When he's lost his money we make him drunk and let him go. **1936** J. Dos PASSOS *Big Money* 282 Charley Anderson, the boy with the knowhow. **1944** H. A. WALLACE *Century of Common Man* 52 We have the 'know how' to help many of the poverty-stricken peoples to set their feet on the path of education, manual dexterity, and economic literacy. **1946** *Times* 10 Dec. 2/6 With regard to American investments in this country the Government welcomed such applications if they brought to this country real industrial knowledge, the 'know how', which otherwise we should be without. **1947** AUDEN *Age of Anxiety* (1948) i. 26 A modern product Of nerve and know-how with a new thrill. **1949** *Listener* 15 Sept. 451/3 A manager may have knowledge of a process in his charge, but not the know-how possessed by the foreman who controls it. **1952** R. M. HARE *Lang. Morals* x. 159 Everything that we are taught how to do must..be reducible to principles, though these may be 'know-hows' hard to formulate in language and more easily taught by example. **1953** *Encounter* Oct. 68/2 There were some who were persuaded that technical knowledge—that intangible but wonderful thing called American 'know-how'—could somehow be made a substitute for capital in the poor countries. **1967** L. B. ARCHER in Wills & Yearsley *Handbk. Managem. Technol.* 129 It takes special talent and know-how on the part of a properly trained designer to create a successful house style. **1972** P. M. HUBBARD *Whisper in Glen* ix. 91 She hasn't got the mere social know-how to carry it off.

knowing, *ppl. a.* Add: **3.** Comb. *knowing-looking* ppl. a.

a **1817** JANE AUSTEN *Northanger Abbey* (1818) I. vii. 81 A gig, driven along on bad pavement by a most knowing-looking coachman. **1927** H. V. MORTON *In Search of England* i. 9 [Newbury, in Berkshire] is, like all towns which have any traffic with race-horses, a knowing-looking, bandy-legged town.

5. Restrict ?*Obs.* to 'Const. *of, in*' and add later U.S. examples of *knowing to.*

1905 *Springfield* (Mass.) *Weekly Republ.* 29 Dec. 16 Some of the neighbors were knowing to the event. **1906** *Dialect Notes* III. 144 I'm knowing to that; you're wrong. **1913** *Ibid.* IV. 2 You are knowing to that. **1913** H. KEPHART *Our Southern Highlanders* xiii. 297 Reckon Pete was knowin' to the sarcumstance?

knowledge, *sb.* Add: **8. c.** Philos. *knowledge about, knowledge by description*: knowledge of a person, thing, or perception gained through information of facts about it rather than by direct experience (opp. *knowledge by* (or *of*) *acquaintance*, see *ACQUAINTANCE I b).

1885, etc. [see *ACQUAINTANCE I b]. **1945** E. MAYO *Social Probl. Industr. Civilization* (1949) I. i. 15 The student is required to relate his logical *knowledge-about* to his own direct acquaintance with the facts. **1952** B. MAYO *Logic of Personality* iii. 30 Knowledge *about* something is called knowledge by *description*. **1954** [see *ACQUAINTANCE I b]. **1967** *Encycl. Philos.* IV. 350/1 Parallel to this on the side of knowledge of things is the distinction between knowledge by acquaintance and knowledge by description. **1968** A. J. AYER *Origins Pragmatism* II. iii. 293 The mind has 'knowledge about' an object not immediately there.

16. knowledge factory, term applied pejoratively to a university or college, etc., which places undue emphasis on vocational training; **knowledge industry,** term applied fancifully or pejoratively to the development and use of knowledge, *spec.* in universities, polytechnics, etc.

1928 *World's Work* May 55 Next day we visited the knowledge factory, and..the head teacher asked if I had ever been sent to school. **1968** *Listener* 4 July 6/2 Some students who rioted on British campuses (like some in France and Italy) have been protesting at having found themselves in a knowledge factory when they thought they were headed for something else. They find themselves being trained for the managerial and technocratic élites, whereas what they demand is the right to question the structure of society which makes such élites necessary. **1969** C. DAVIDSON in Cockburn & Blackburn *Student Power* 341 The production of an increase in socially useful and necessary labour power is the new historic function of our educational institutions that enables us to name them, quite accurately, knowledge factories. **1962** F. MACHLUP *Production & Distribution of Knowledge in U.S.* iii. 45 If the phrase 'knowledge industry' were to be given an unambiguous meaning, it would be a collection of industries producing knowledge or rather a collection of occupations producing knowledge in whatever industries they are employed. **1963** C. KERR *Uses of University* iii. 87 Basic to this transformation is the growth of the 'knowledge industry', which is coming to permeate government and business. **1968** *Economist* 28 Feb. 51/3 This is a book for the serious investor who..wants to learn something about the operations of the New York Stock Exchange and the 'knowledge industry', with its analysts, theorists..and numerous other 'ists'. **1970** *Globe & Mail* (Toronto) 25 Sept. B2/2 The report notes the emergence of the knowledge industry, growing emphasis on people values.

knowledgeable, *a.* Add: Also **knowledgable. 2.** Delete *colloq.* and add earlier and later examples. Also, cognisant *of.*

1829 G. GRIFFIN *Collegians* (ed. 2) I. xi. 233 She went.. to Shaun Lauther, the knowledgeable man, and put a half-a-crown into his hand, and asked his advice. **1901** *Academy* 21 Sept. 240/2 The review..is not only able and knowledgeable; it is also..fair. **1903** *Daily Chron.* 4 Aug. 3/2 His manner is so knowledgable and convincing that they will question nothing of his theories. **1905** *Westm. Gaz.* 2 Feb. 2/1 If any official English politician has a knowledgable opinion of how these Powers are likely to combine or to clash..he should be sought. **1908** *Daily Chron.* 13 Feb. 5/7 All 'knowledgable opinion'..is against the Bill. **1945** MENCKEN *Amer. Lang.* Suppl. I. 423 The English have many counter-words that fail to make the Atlantic journey, *e.g., knowledgeable.* **1955** *Sci. Amer.* June 102/2 It will be a great day for mankind when we become equally knowledgeable about the lives of microbes. **1973** *Times* 31 July 6/7 Mr Dean drew the erroneous conclusion that the President was fully knowledgeable of the cover-up at the time of the March 13 meeting.

Hence **knowledgeabi·lity.**

1946 *Time* 19 Aug. 98 His portrait shows Caesar to be a man as far beyond mere knowledgeability as a Hitler or a Stalin. **1957** N. FRYE *Anat. Criticism* 263 This has a truth that the myopia of knowledgeability is more apt to overlook. **1965** F. SARGESON *Mem. Peon* iv. 62, I had impressed my host by my..knowledgeability.

know·ledgefully, *adv. rare.* [f. KNOWLEDGE *sb.* + -FUL + -LY². Cf. *knowledge-full* adj. s.v. KNOWLEDGE *sb.* 16.] In the manner of one who is fully informed.

1906 *Harper's Mag.* Feb. 474/2 He has written of this very knowledgefully, of course, and very justly.

known, *ppl. a.* Add: **1. c.** *known to the police*: applied to a person with a criminal record. Also ellipt. *known* (itself occas. used as *sb.*).

1909 GALSWORTHY *Silver Box* III. 75 Is she known here? ..No, your Worship, they're neither of them known, we've nothing against them at all. **1924** A. CHRISTIE *Poirot Investigates* ix. 255 Billy Kellett?.. He's known to the police! **1938** F. D. SHARPE *Sharpe of Flying Squad* ix. 112 A long communication telling us that Mrs. Cousins was not 'known to the police'. **1971** E. MCGIRR *No Better Fiend* 69 The late Mantel had been 'known' since 1928. It was a dismal dirty story. **1973** K. GILES *File on Death* vi. 149 A lot of Irish boys in Granchester... I spotted a couple of 'knowns'.

know-nothing, *sb.* and *a.* Add: **A.** *sb.* **1.** (Earlier example.)

1827 J. F. COOPER *Red Rover* I. ii. 42 The fellow is a know-nothing!

2. (Earlier example.)

1854 *Harper's Mag.* Aug. 400/1 A secret combination designated as 'Know-Nothings'..have operated with much success in local elections in many of the larger places.

B. *attrib.* or *adj.* **1.** (Later examples.)

1959 *Encounter* XII. II. 32 He..sounds most like a know-nothing native writer. **1972** *Computers & Humanities* VII. 13 Robert Wachal has offered a humorous account of the problems encountered by the know-nothing humanist who wishes to learn about computing.

2. (Earlier example.)

1854 *Southern Lit. Messenger* XX. 540/1 This Know Nothing movement will prove to be..a giant evil.

know-nothingism. 2. (Earlier example.)

1854 W. G. SIMMS *Southward Ho!* 252 Know-Nothingism had not then become a fixed fact in the political atmosphere.

Knoxian (nǫ·ksiăn), *sb.* and *a.* [f. the proper name *Knox* (see below) + -IAN.] **A.** *sb.* An adherent or follower of John *Knox* (*c* 1505–72), the Scottish Reformer who was mainly responsible for establishing the Presbyterian Church. **B.** *adj.* Of or pertaining to John Knox.

1714 J. COLLIER *Eccl. Hist. Gt. Brit.* II. v. 394/2 In this Abstract, the Knoxians make a scandalous Representation of some Part of the Litany. **1905** *Westm. Gaz.* 4 Mar. 12/3 His Knoxian project was dropped in favour of his works on Cromwell. **1906** *Daily Chron.* 22 May 3/3 Buchanan, in fact, never was a Reformer in the Knoxian sense. **1933** *Times Lit. Suppl.* 30 Nov. 848/2 In Scotland —after the Knoxian supremacy was established—'not one single adherent of the Roman Communion was martyred because of his faith'. **1937** E. PERCY *John Knox* IV. xv. 253 A strong anti-clerical party..who would have nothing to do either with Knoxians or with sectaries. **1961** C. H. & K. GEORGE *Protestant Mind of Eng. Reformation* II. v. 177 Knoxian precepts from Geneva had altered the entire course of Scottish history.

knubbly, *a.* (Later examples.)

1910 W. DE LA MARE *Three Mulla-Mulgars* iv. 55 Three big knubbly cudgels. **1917** W. J. LOCKE *Red Planet* xxi. 277 He held out his hand, a dirty, knubbly, ragged-nailed hand. **1939** 'A. BRIDGE' *Four-Part Setting* vii. 79 Two loose knubbly little cushions.

knuck (nʌk). Also occas. **nuck.** [Shortening of KNUCKLE *sb.*, KNUCKLER.] **1.** *slang.* A thief, a pickpocket. Cf. *KNUCKLE *sb.* 2 c, KNUCKLER I. ? *Obs.*

1812 J. H. VAUX *Vocab. Flash Lang.* in *Mem.* (1819) II. 184 *Knuck, knuckler,* or *knuckling-cove,* a pickpocket, or person professed in the knuckling art. **1848** 'N. BUNTLINE' *Mysteries & Miseries N.Y.* I. 33 There is a house in Cherry street..[that] has been known to the 'crossmen' and 'knucks' of the town as 'Jack Circle's Watering place' and 'fence'. **1903** A. H. LEWIS *Boss* 168 But knucks, dips, sneaks,..an' strong-arm men have got to quit. **1904** 'NO. 1500' *Life in Sing Sing* 251/1 *Nuck,* a thief. **1935** A. J. POLLOCK *Underworld Speaks* 68/2 *Knuck,* a thief.

2. *pl.* 'A game of marbles in which the winner shoots at his adversary's knuckles' (Clapin). *U.S.*

1840 *Southern Lit. Messenger* VI. 385 To the game of marbles he devotes much of his leisure time, and is counted a proficient particularly in knucks and five in the ring. *a* **1883** G. W. BAGBY *Sel. Misc. Writings* (1885) II. 20 He tries to keep somebody's country store, but will close the doors whenever the weather is fine to 'ketch chub' or play knucks. **1886** *Harper's Mag.* Dec 41/2 They were playing 'knucks' together. **1935** *Amer. Speech* X. 159/1 More on Marble Names and Games... Knucks Down. A variant of *knuckle down.*

3. Shortening of KNUCKLE-DUSTER.

1897 *Sears, Roebuck Catal.* 593/1 Knucks, heavy nickel plated and polished. $0.30 per pair. **1918** C. SANDBURG *Cornhuskers* 88, I slipped my fingers into a set of knucks. **1966** WODEHOUSE *Plum Pie* i. 48 To reason successfully with that king of the twisters one would need brass knucks and a stocking full of sand. **1973** D. WESTHEIMER *Going Public* ix. 130 He produced a two foot length of stout nylon cord with brass knucks at either end. 'You can hit or strangle with it..' he explained.

knuckle, *sb.* Add: **2. b.** *near the knuckle*: near the permitted limit (esp. in regard to decency); *to go the knuckle* (*Austral. slang*), to punch, to fight.

1895 W. P. RIDGE *Minor Dialogues* vii. 72, I can stand a joke as well as anyone, but whispering's a bit *too* near the knuckle. If you've got anything to say, say it. **1909** *Westm. Gaz.* 4 May 2/2 A series of articles entitled 'Crimes of Passion', full of abominable details 'as near the knuckle' as the police would allow. *Ibid.* 6 Sept. 1/3 If a play shows that its author has..a sincere respect for his art, it must be stopped if it goes at all 'near the knuckle'. **1930** W. S. MAUGHAM *Cakes & Ale* 147 What I like about 'er is that she gives you a good laugh. She goes pretty near the knuckle sometimes, but she never jumps over the fence. **1944** J. DEVANNY *By Tropic Sea & Jungle* xviii. 160, I always got on well with the blacks, because I never went the knuckle on them, and never interfered with their women. **1945** L. A. G. STRONG *Othello's Occupation* iv. 89 Did you notice how she stiffened, when I slipped in that bit about remembering what she was looking at—what was on the table? I got a bit near the knuckle there. **1962** S. GORE *Down Golden Mile* i. 26 Then he said: 'Want to watch out for them quiet snoozers. Sometimes they can go the knuckle a bit themselves!' **1973** D. JORDAN *Nile Green* xiii. 58 He ho-ho'd jovially to show he was joking. It was a little close to the knuckle for my taste.

†**c.** = PICKPOCKET *sb.* I. Cf. *KNUCK I. *Obs.*

1781 G. PARKER *View of Soc.* II. i. 73 *Knuckle,* in the flash language, signifies those who hang about the Lobbies of both Houses of Parliament, the Opera-House and both Play-Houses, and in general wherever a great crowd assemble. They steal watches, snuff-boxes, &c. **1785** GROSE *Dict. Vulgar T., Knuckles,* pickpockets who attend the avenues to public places, to steal pocket books, watches, &c., a superior kind of pickpockets. **1846** *Swell's Night Guide* 124/1 *Knuckles,* pickpockets.

6. *knuckle-length, -rapper, -rapping* vbl. sb. and ppl. adj.; **knuckle ball, knuckleball** *Baseball* (see quots.); **knuckle-head,** a slow-witted or stupid person; **knuckle sandwich** *slang,* a punch in the mouth.

1927 *Secrets of Baseball* iii. 37 If you're worrying about when to use a 'knuckle ball'. **1929** *Encycl. Brit.* III. 163/1 There is what is known as the knuckle ball, in which the knuckles of the pitcher's hand play a prominent part in giving the ball erratic motion. **1970** *New Yorker* 24 Oct. 39/2 The knuckleball is thrown not with the knuckles but with the fingertips. **1972** *N.Y. Times* 4 June v. 2/5 Phil Niekro baffled the Mets with his celebrated knuckleball, allowing them only three hits. **1975** *Cleveland* (Ohio) *Plain Dealer* 6 Apr. 13–C/3 Oakland, aiming for a fourth straight world championship, opens at home with Vida Blue pitching against Chicago's veteran knuckleball specialist, Wilbur Wood. **1944** in WENTWORTH & FLEXNER *Dict. Amer. Slang* (1960) 310/2 You knuckle-heads. **1948** *Amer. Speech* XXIII. 249/1 Knucklehead, a slow or stupid person. **1971** R. PARKES *Line of Fire* xvii. 158 What I'm trying to get across to you knuckleheads is that it was *not* murder! **1973** J. CLEARY *Ransom* i. 25 He's a knuckle-head, he knows nothing and doesn't want to know. **1906** *Daily Chron.* 29 Mar. 6/4 A man..proceeded to measure it with the knuckle-length of his closed fist. **1938** *Times* 9 Mar. 19/4 The knuckle-length coat is in stripes of various sizes. **1910** H. G. WELLS *Hist. Mr. Polly* iv. 56 The aunt..was..a knuckle-rapper and sharp silencer: no friend for a slovenly little boy. **1944** R. LEHMANN *Ballad & Source* 243 'No,' he said shortly, but not in the knuckle-rapping way I had half feared. **1968** *Globe & Mail Mag.* (Toronto) 13 Jan. 3/1 Anti-Dow demonstrations at U of T drew just polite knuckle-rapping. **1968** *Listener* 18 July 75/1 Did you ever suggest to him..how a field commander might feel when he got one of these knuckle-rappings? **1974** *Farm & Country* 26 Mar. 4/2 Your knuckle-rapping will teach him to think before he is carried away on a flow of words. **1973** A. BUZO *Norm & Ahmed* 12 He tried to hang one on me at Leichhardt Oval

once, so I administered a knuckle sandwich to him. **1973** *Ottawa Jrnl.* 17 July 23/3 Give the guy a knuckle sandwich and let the teeth fall where they may.

knuckle, *v.* Add: **2.** (Later examples.)

1955 *Times* 19 May 15/4 He replied that there was no power on earth to make a local party accept a candidate. He was rather sorry they knuckled under to Transport House in this division. **1964** *Ann. Reg. 1963* 10 Britain, he said, had 'knuckled under' to threats of African violence, but there was little he could constitutionally do about it. **1973** *Nation Rev.* (Melbourne) III. 31 Aug. 1444/1 Now the last group of any size..has knuckled under following a series of splits and coups.

3. b. To dig (one's hand) into a specified position, knuckles first.

1890 Hall Caine *Bondman* I. i. 10 Thrusting his head beneath his chin, he knuckled his left hand under the islander's rib.

6. *Farriery.* With *over,* of the knee or fetlock: ? to project through weakness of the ligaments. Also with *forwards.* (Cf. *knuckle-kneed* adj. s.v. Knuckle *sb.* 6.)

1877 A. Sewell *Black Beauty* (c 1878, ed. 5) xl. 198 The knees knuckled over, and the forelegs were very unsteady. **1877** M. H. Hayes *Vet. Notes for Horse Owners* i. 30 'Knuckling over', as a result of hard work, appears to be due to relaxation of the capsular and lateral ligaments [of the fetlock joint]. **1906** J. W. Axe *Horse* IV. 53 The animal knuckles over at the joints. **1907** *Ibid.* V. 298 The movements of the hind-limbs are for a time weak, and the fetlocks knuckle over now and again during progression. **1907** *Ibid.* VI. 347 In young horses it is common to meet with a knuckling forwards of the hind fetlocks.

7. *Golf.* To bend (the knee) inward. Also *absol.*

1909 *Times* 23 Apr. 16/2 An elaborate knuckling of the right knee in putting. *Ibid.,* The 'knuckling' habit in putting has long been exposed as fallacious. **1909** *Westm. Gaz.* 11 May 12/3 You may 'knuckle' if knuckling conduces to comfort, provided that..you get the process over before beginning the actual stroke.

knu·ckle-dust, *v.* [Back-formation from Knuckle-duster.] *trans.* To strike with a knuckle-duster. So **knu·ckle-dusting** *vbl. sb.*

1909 *Daily Chron.* 29 Dec. 1/7 One boy..got the robber's head under his arm and gave it a knuckle-dusting. **1962** V. Nabokov *Pale Fire* 151 The brief affray during which two of the attackers were knuckledusted and knocked out by the brave Lorrainer.

knuckler. Add: **3.** *Baseball.* A knuckle ball (see *knuckle *sb.* 6).

1928 G. H. Ruth *Babe Ruth's Own Bk. Baseball* vi. 79 Eddie used to toss 'knucklers' until he had the hitters blue in the face. **1972** *N.Y. Times* 4 June v. 2/5 The Mets, meanwhile, were subdued by Niekro's knuckler.

knucklesome (nʌ·k'lsəm), *a. rare.* [See -some[1].] Having prominent knuckles. Also *transf.*

1919 W. De Morgan *Old Madhouse* xx. 306 That young woman was bony and knucklesome. **1922** C. E. Montague *Disenchantment* xii. 170 The twisty valley and knucklesome banks of the Somme.

knu·ckle-walker. [f. Knuckle *sb.* + Walker *sb.*[1]] Any monkey, such as the gorilla or chimpanzee, which has a quadrupedal gait involving the backs of the knuckles (rather than the tips of the fingers or flat of the palm) making contact with the ground. So **knu·ckle-walk** *v.*, **knu·ckle-walking** *vbl. sb.*

1859 R. Owen *On Classification & Geographical Distribution of Mammalia* 75 Of the broad-breasted quadrumana, are the knuckle-walkers or the brachiators, i.e. the long-armed gibbons, most nearly and essentially related to the human subject? **1967** R. H. Tuttle in *Amer. Jrnl. Physical Anthropol.* XXVI. 171 (*title*) Knuckle-walking and the evolution of Hominoid hands. *Ibid.,* Most orang-utans assume one of a variety of flexed hand postures, but they cannot knuckle-walk. *Ibid.* 171/2 The knuckle-walking posture of chimpanzees and gorillas is unique among primates. **1967** S. L. Washburn in *Proc. R. Anthrop. Inst.* 23/1 Both chimpanzees and gorillas are knuckle walkers. *Ibid.,* It appears that our ancestors were arboreal apes for many millions of years, that they then shared a common knuckle-walking stage with the ancestors of the chimpanzee and gorilla, and that only later they became bipeds. **1969** A. H. Schultz *Life of Primates* v. 56 In the orang-utan the mode of using the hands in walking..is more in the form of a clenched fist, rather awkwardly twisted sideways, and rarely like real knuckle-walking. **1972** O. J. Lewis in R. H. Tuttle *Functional & Evolutionary Biol. Primates* ix. 212 Thick palmar radio-carpal ligaments are not the exclusive property of knuckle-walkers... It thus seems that knuckle-walking requires no especially striking modifications of the wrist joint. **1973** *Nature* 10 Aug. 373/2 The first component separates quadrupedal cercopithecoids from both knuckle-walkers (*Pan* and *Gorilla*) and the quadrupedal arm-swinger.. *Ateles.*

Knudsen (knu·dsən). The name of Martin H. C. *Knudsen* (1871–1949), Danish physicist, used *attrib.* (or occas. in the possessive) to designate apparatus, phenomena, and concepts connected with his work.

a. *Physics.* **Knudsen cell,** a vessel in which a substance is heated in equilibrium with its vapour, which is allowed to diffuse out of a small orifice; **Knudsen effect, flow,** the effusion from an orifice (also called *Knudsen effusion*) or the flow through a tube of a gas with a high Knudsen number, so that the resistance to flow arises principally from collisions of the molecules with the walls rather than with one another; **Knudsen gas,** any gas in a state characterized by a Knudsen number much greater than one; **Knudsen gauge** or **manometer,** an instrument for measuring the absolute pressure of a rarefied gas by means of the transfer of momentum by the gas molecules between two fixed plates at different temperatures and a suspended vane, which undergoes a rotation dependent on the pressure; **Knudsen number,** the ratio of the mean free path of the molecules of a gas to a length derived from the dimensions of the apparatus in which or past which it is flowing.

1954 *Jrnl. Chem. Physics* XXII. 1414/2 The vapor pressure was determined by collecting a known fraction of the vapor effusing from a Knudsen cell. **1960** *Ibid.* XXXIII. 530/1 The equilibrium vapor from a Knudsen cell was collimated into a molecular beam and allowed to pass through the ionizing region of a mass spectrometer. **1953** *Physical Rev.* LXXXIX. 796/1 The Knudsen effect occurs when two portions of a gas are separated by a very fine capillary or a porous plate with openings so small that collisions between the gas molecules in the capillary or the pores are infrequent compared with the collisions of the gas molecules with the walls. **1954** *Jrnl. Chem. Physics* XXII. 1414/1 The vapor pressure has been redetermined over a temperature range from 1630 to 1970°K. As in the previous measurements the Knudsen effusion method was used. **1937** *Bull. Chem. Soc. Japan* XII. 199 If the mean free path is large in comparison with the diameter the flowing quantity is independent of the viscosity but inversely proportional to the square root of the molecular weight of the gas, and such flow is called Knudsen's or the molecular flow. **1958** R. D. Present *Kinetic Theory of Gases* iv. 61 Effusion through a circular orifice can be considered as a special case of Knudsen flow in which the length of tube is small compared to its diameter. **1958** *Encycl. Physics* XII. 212 Another example which is more intuitive is afforded by a Knudsen gas. This is a gas which is sufficiently rarefied so that intermolecular forces can be completely ignored. **1972** *Chem. Abstr.* LXXVI. 87851 A collision-free Knudsen gas was considered between 2 parallel plates with a time-dependent temp. gradient. **1918** *Physical Rev.* XII. 452 Delicate equilibria at low pressures in this way make it possible to measure exceedingly small quantities of emission products even with the use of a less sensitive form of Knudsen gauge. **1925** F. H. Newman *Production & Measurement Low Pressure* viii. 155 These investigators have also constructed Knudsen gauges capable of measuring pressures as high as 10^{-2} mm. **1959** *Chambers's Encycl.* XI. 188/1 Knudsen gauges can be constructed to cover ranges from 10^{-3} to 10^{-7} mm Hg. **1961** J. Thewlis et al. *Encycl. Dict. Physics* IV. 185/2 The functions of the Knudsen manometer essentially depend on the variation of the thermal conductivity of a gas with pressure, provided the pressure is low enough, i.e. the mean free path is sufficiently great. **1956** G. N. Patterson *Molecular Flow of Gases* v. 159 In both high-vacuum systems and high-altitude flight, the Knudsen number becomes large. **1957** Liepmann & Roshko *Elem. Gas Dynamics* xiv. 353 For flow similar to Couette flow, i.e., flow that is confined between walls, one can easily define these two limiting cases by the ratio of mean free path Λ to channel diameter d. Λ/d is often called the Knudsen number; if $\Lambda/d \ll 1$, intermolecular collisions dominate; if $\Lambda/d \gg 1$, collisions with the boundaries dominate.

b. *Oceanogr.* **Knudsen burette, pipette,** special types of burette and pipette for use in Knudsen titrations; **Knudsen method, titration,** a method for determining the chlorinity and hence salinity of sea-water by titration against silver nitrate solution and reference to a set of tables, *Knudsen's tables,* first published by Knudsen in 1901.

1959 H. Barnes *Apparatus & Methods Oceanogr.* I. iv. 86 *The Knudsen burette.* The silver nitrate solution contained in a reservoir is delivered from a special burette, with an automatic zero. **1966** B. B. Baker et al. *Gloss. Oceanogr. Terms* (ed. 2) 32/1 By using normal water as a comparison standard, Knudsen burettes and pipettes for the analysis, and Knudsen's Tables to compute the results, determinations as accurate as those of a time-consuming gravimetric analysis can be made with a rapid titration of the sea water against silver nitrate solution, employing potassium chromate or other suitable indicator for the end-point. **1954** *Jrnl. Marine Res.* XIII. 246 The keystone of the Knudsen method is the adjustment of the silver nitrate concentration so that at the end of the titration the number representing the burette reading is approximately equal to the chlorinity in per mille. [**1923** Glazebrook *Dict. Appl. Physics* III. 677/2 The pipette.. generally used is of the Knudsen pattern, with a three-way tap instead of a mark.] **1951** *Jrnl. du Conseil Internat. Explor. de la Mer* XVII. 223 By means of a Knudsen pipette 15 ml. were taken out of a number of sea-water samples. **1966** Knudsen pipette [see *Knudsen burette* above]. **1923** Glazebrook *Dict. Appl. Physics* III. 677/2 The salinity and density can, of course, be determined from the 'chlorine' content by Knudsen's Tables. **1966** Knudsen's Tables [see *Knudsen burette* above]. **1962** *Nature* 10 Feb. 520/1 The precision of measuring conductivity on a good salinometer is at least five times better than that of the standard Knudsen titration.

knur. 3. (Later examples.)

1967 *Antique Finder* Aug. 11/3 Knur and Spell. This Georgian tavern game must really be a forerunner of darts. **1972** *Daily Tel.* (Colour Suppl.) 14 Jan. 22/3 In fact Knur and Spell is simply a formalisation of something that every male person in the world must have done at some time—throwing a ball or stone in the air and giving it a tremendous clout with a stick. How maddening when you miss! What a marvellous eye you feel you have when you do it fair and square! The Spell is the device that throws the ball (the Knur) into the air. It is an iron contraption that lies on the ground looking a bit like a rat trap; the framework holds a flat horizontal spring, held down by a catch. On the releasable end of the spring is a little cup containing the knur, a tiny white ball (porcelain, of all things), one inch across and weighing half an ounce. You stand about four feet away from the spell, armed with a 'stick', rather like a billiard cue with a hammer head (called the 'pommel'). You tap the catch on the spell, the knur jumps up about four feet; the object is to hit it farther, over a fixed number of goes, than anyone else.

knut, jocular variant, often pronounced (kənʌ·t), of *nut *sb.*[1] 8* (a fashionable or showy young man). Hence **knu·tty** *a.*

1911 *Granta* 25 Nov. 136/2 He, Timothy Gray, bhoy, lad, knut. **1913** L. A. Harker *Ffolliots of Redmarley* v. 57 He was..a 'knut' of the nuttiest flavour. **1914** *Scotsman* 5 Oct. 8/1 It is clear that he has once been a 'knut' in spite of his oil-stained khaki service jacket and trousers. **1915** A. Wimperis *Gilbert the Filbert* (*song*), I'm Gilbert, the Filbert, The Colonel of the Knuts. **1916** E. V. Lucas *Vermilion Box* 52 Among the people staying here is a knut. He must be almost the last of the tribe; but here he is, just as knutty as though the Algies and Berties were still ruling the roast, and not Mars at all. **1919** C. Orr *Glorious Thing* xvii. 212 He was trying to be knutty, he said. **1929** G. Stowell *Hist. Button Hill* 183 The Knut was an urban and suburban phenomenon of the years 1912 to 1914 inclusive. **1973** *Listener* 6 Sept. 320 The 'silly asses', the 'knuts' who were wiped out on the Somme.

‖ **ko**[1] (kōu). *N.Z.* [Maori.] A digging-stick.

1843 E. Dieffenbach *Trav. N.Z.* II. iii. 367 *Ko*—a tool with which the natives plant their sweet potatoes. **1868** W. Colenso in *Trans. N.Z. Inst.* I. Essay 15 A *ko*, a rude kind of narrow and pointed spade with a very long handle, to which, at about 18 inches or more from the point, they [*sc.* Maoris] fitted a small crooked bit of carved wood, as a rest for the foot. **1905** W. B. *Where White Man Treads* 2 Plantations of kumara..which the Maori with his primitive ko (native wooden spade) had brought under tillage with much labour. **1941** Alley & Hall *Farmer in N.Z.* i. 3 His [*sc.* the Maori's] instant casting aside of his poor crude *ko* and *timo* (or grubbing stick) in favour of European spades and hoes. **1955** W. J. Phillipps *Maori Carving Illustr.* 16 Designs carved on the upper ends of ko or digging sticks.

‖ **Ko**[2] (kōu). *Ceramics.* [Chinese, = elder brother. See quot. 1954.] In full, *Ko iú* or *yao* [Chinese, = ware], *Ko ware.* A crackled Sung ware closely related to Southern Kuan; also, a name for other crackled porcelains.

1882 *China Rev.* X. v. 310/1 Speaking of porcelain ware.., it is absolutely necessary to distinguish the kinds called Ch'ái porcelain.., Ü porcelain.., Government porcelain.., Ko porcelain. **1882** *Ibid.* XI. iii. 176/2 Ko-iú (Ko porcelain) has, on its ground, hidden lines like spawn. **1904** E. Dillon *Porcelain* v. 63 The word Ko yao is used as a general name for many kinds of [Sung] crackle ware... In a more restricted sense it includes only the early pieces with a greyish white glaze and well-marked crackles. **1954** G. Savage *Porcelain* i. i. 67 *Ko yao* was, by tradition, made by the elder of two brothers Chang...The type has a very dark stoneware body. **1972** *Collector's Guide* June 95/3 Traditionally there is Northern Kuan, Southern Kuan, Altar Kuan and the related Ko ware.

koa. (Later examples.)

1954 J. Sheridan in J. Macdonald *Lethal Sex* (1962) 181 Four men carried the pigs on huge *koa* platters carved with supporting feet. **1965** *N.Z. Listener* 17 Dec. 4/2 The commoners [in Hawaii] were permitted only the heavier and less buoyant Koa boards.

koaftah, var. *kofta.

koala (ko,ā·lă). Now the usual spelling of Koolah. In full, *koala bear.* (Examples.)

1808, 1859 [in Dict. s.v. Koolah]. **1902** *Daily Chron.* 3 July 3/4 The koala of Australia, has also a very big cæcum. **1937** C. Kearton *I visit Antipodes* x. 132 The Koala Bear was first seen by a young explorer who journeyed to the Blue Mountains in 1798. **1944** A. Russell *Bush Ways* xix. 95 There was..scarce a gum tree but that sheltered an opossum or a koala. **1966** G. Durrell *Two in Bush* v. 173 Fortunately, before it became too late, the Government stepped in and passed laws strictly protecting the Koalas, and slowly over the years their numbers have built up again.

‖ **koan** (kōu·ān). [Jap., f. *kō* public + *an* matter, material for thought.] In Zen Buddhism, a paradox put to a student to stimulate his mind.

1946 R. Benedict *Chrysanthemum & Sword* (1947) xi. 246 The significance of the koan does not lie in the truths these seekers after truth discover. **1957** *Time* 4 Feb. 66/2 A less physical shock technique is the *koan,* a problem designed to shock the mind beyond mere thinking. **1958** A. Huxley *Let.* 11 Jan. (1969) 844 They might act as Zen koans and cause sudden openings into hitherto unglimpsed regions. **1960** Koestler *Lotus & Robot* ii. x. 236 The koan—the logically insoluble riddle which

the pupil must try to solve. *Ibid.* 237 There are said to exist some one thousand seven hundred koans, divided into various categories... The oldest-known koans are the 'Three Barriers of Hung-Lun', an eleventh-century Zen master. **1972** *Times Lit. Suppl.* 28 Jan. 85/1 What he comes up with—his runes and enigmas and impromptu koans—builds gradually into a supplementary creation.

koatuku, obs. var. *KOTUKU.

kob[1]**.** Add: Esp. the species *Kobus kob*. In full, *kob antelope*. (Later examples.)

1897 SCLATER & THOMAS *Bk. Antelopes* II. VII. 139 The first specimen of the Kob Antelope that reached Europe alive, so far as we know, was that presented to the Zoological Society of London by Mr. John Foster in 1836. *Ibid.* 140 From Senegal and the Gambia the Kob extends through the interior of West Africa to Togoland. **1964** C. WILLOCK *Enormous Zoo* iv. 40 The kob... To look at, this lovely creature with the back-raked horns is a little like a larger version of the impala... In fact its nearest relative is the large, shaggy, big-horned waterbuck. **1964** G. B. SCHALLER *Year of Gorilla* (1965) iii. 75 Rwindi, near the southern end of Lake Edward,..is the central location from which to see the herds of buffalo, elephant, hippopotamus, waterbuck, kob antelope. **1967** *Listener* 6 Apr. 459/2 Among the Ugandan kob males may defend small territories... By tradition a certain number of kob are associated with each breeding ground. **1974** *Nature* 29 Nov. 345/3 In the Uganda kob antelope there exists a system of social behaviour designed to prevent clandestine matings.

kob[2] (kǫb). *S. Afr.* = *KABELJOU.

1906 *East London* (Cape Province) *Dispatch* 26 June 3/7 Our well-known and very common kabeljaauw, called for briefness 'cob' or 'kob'. **1913** W. W. THOMPSON *Sea Fisheries Cape Colony* 155 Kabeljaauw..; Cob or Kob (East London). **1930** C. L. BIDEN *Sea-Angling Fishes of Cape* v. 108 Kabeljou; Kob (abbreviated name). **1950** *Cape Times* 17 Nov. 13/8 Kob are well worth a try from the usual spots around the sandy sweep of the bay. **1959** *Ibid.* 16 Nov. 2/5 Visitor Lands Big Kob. **1974** *South-Western Herald* (S. Afr.) 2 July 5 'I am now after kob,' said Mr. Thomson.

2. kob water, disturbed, discoloured water in which the kob is often found.

1930 C. L. BIDEN *Sea-Angling Fishes of Cape* v. 113 On the south-east coast particularly they keep a watchful eye on what is known as 'kob-water'—a discoloration of the sea, either milky, dirty yellow, or what one would liken to pea soup. **1957** S. SCHOEMAN *Strike!* iii. 71 Kob-water usually results from a disturbance of the seabed. **1974** *Argus* (Cape Town) 31 Dec. 4/2 The familiar, ginger-beer coloured water known to anglers as 'kob water' is moving in along parts of the Strandfontein coast-line.

kobeite (kōᵘ·bi͵əit). *Min.* [Partial tr. Jap. *kobeishi* (J. Takubo et al. 1950, in *Jrnl. Geol. Soc. Japan* LVI. 512), f. *Kobe*, name of a locality in Kyoto prefecture, Japan + *ishi* mineral (formative suffix of names of minerals): see -ITE[1].] A black, prismatic, hydrated multiple oxide of formula close to $AB_2(O,OH)_6$ (where A represents mainly yttrium, iron, and uranium and B represents mainly titanium, zirconium, hafnium, niobium, and tantalum), but with much less $(Nb,Ta)_2O_5$ than minerals of the euxenite-polycrase series and more TiO_2.

1950 J. TAKUBO et al. in *Jrnl. Geol. Soc. Japan* LVI. 513 [Eng. abstr. of article in Jap.] The content of TiO_2 is.. exceedingly high compared with that of polycrase or blomstrandite. So the writers propose here to call this mineral 'Kobeite' after the name of the locality. **1957** *Amer. Mineralogist* XLII. 342 The kobeite-bearing cobble ..was collected while panning sands and gravels in the Paringa River, South Westland, New Zealand. **1961** *Mineral. Jrnl.* III. 146 The writers are inclined to recognize kobeite as a distinct mineral species belonging to multiple oxides rich in titanium, zirconium and yttrium group rare earths.

kobo (kōᵘ·bo). Pl. **kobo.** [See quot. 1972[1].] A unit of currency in the Federal Republic of Nigeria, equal to $\frac{1}{100}$ naira.

1972 *N.Y. Times* 9 Aug. 14 Kobo..is a corruption of the word 'copper' and the popular term here [*sc.* Nigeria] for a penny, a copper coin... The kobo, symbolized by a lower-case k, will be produced in coins of one-half kobo, 1, 5, 10 and 25 kobo. **1972** *Times* 9 Oct. (Nigeria Suppl.) p. viii/4 The new currency being introduced by the Central Bank of Nigeria consists of naira and kobo... Kobo was the popular name for the old penny pieces... The new kobo is the same size as the old Nigerian shilling and carries a depiction of cocoa seeds. **1973** *Whitaker's Almanack 1974* 985 Nigeria (Federal Republic of)... Naira = 100 Kobo.

Koch (kǫχ, kǫk). The name of Robert *Koch* (1843–1910), Ger. bacteriologist, used in the possessive (less commonly *attrib.*) to designate certain things related to his work on tuberculosis, as **Koch's bacillus,** *Mycobacterium tuberculosis*, which causes tuberculosis in man, and was first isolated by Koch; **Koch's laws** = **Koch('s) postulates*; **Koch('s) phenomenon,** the altered reaction to an inoculation of (living or dead) tubercle bacilli of an animal already infected with tuberculosis from that of a healthy animal, the infected animal showing a reaction which is quicker and locally more severe but which is not followed by a general infection; (now regarded as a classic example of delayed hypersensitivity); **Koch('s) postulates,** a set of four criteria which should be satisfied before a given disease is attributed with certainty to any particular micro-organism, viz. (*a*) the organism concerned is present in each case of the disease; (*b*) it is possible to isolate it from the diseased animal in a pure culture; (*c*) the introduction of such a culture into a suitable healthy animal produces the disease in it; and (*d*) the organism is recoverable from the animal so infected; **Koch's tuberculin,** either of two kinds of tuberculin (*Koch's old* and *new tuberculin*) orig. devised by Koch; formerly also called *Koch's fluid, liquid, lymph,* and now usually just *tuberculin*.

1885 *Jrnl. R. Microsc. Soc.* 557 (*heading*) Staining of Koch's bacillus. **1890** *Lancet* 22 Nov. 1119/2 He drew attention to the advantage of being able, by the injection of Koch's fluid, to diagnose whether a serious laryngeal affection was carcinomatous..or tubercular. *Ibid.* 1120/1 Experiments with Koch's lymph. *Ibid.* 1121/1 He was inoculated with Koch's liquid for distinct facial lupus, and at the same time for pulmonary tuberculosis. **1891** Dr. Koch's lymph [see TUBERCULIN]. **1897** MUIR & RITCHIE *Man. Bacteriol.* ix. 229 (*heading*) Koch's tubercu-lin. **1898** R. T. HEWLETT *Man. Bacteriol.* ii. 31 With regard to the pathogenic organisms..Koch has laid down the following conditions, which have been termed Koch's Postulates, which must be complied with before the relation of an organism to a disease process can be said to be completely demonstrated. **1899** Koch's lymph [see TUBERCULIN]. **1910** MUIR & RITCHIE *Man. Bacteriol.* (ed. 5) x. 284 (*heading*) Koch's old tuberculin. *Ibid.* 288 Another preparation has..been introduced, known as 'Koch's new tuberculin'. **1911** *Encycl. Brit.* XX. 783/1 Koch's tuberculin has been of inestimable value in the early diagnosis of tuberculosis, especially in animals. **1929** TOPLEY & WILSON *Princ. Bacteriol. & Immunity* II. xlix. 729 There are two classical examples, which provide striking illustrations of this double aspect of the allergic reaction. One of these is the well-known Koch's phenomenon (Koch 1891). **1939** K. L. BURDON *Med. Microbiol.* ii. 20 These principles have become known as 'Koch's laws' or 'Koch's postulates'. **1944** L. E. H. WHITBY *Med. Bacteriol.* (ed. 4) i. 2 Very few organisms pathogenic to man fulfil Koch's postulates rigidly. **1955** *Sci. Amer.* June 103/1 Koch found the bacillus in body tissues, in sputum and in urine. He was able to grow the microbe in an artificial culture, to reproduce tuberculosis by injecting it into new animals and to recover it again from the infected tissue—a procedure which has become standard for connecting a given disease with a germ and is known by the name Koch's Laws. **1963** HUMPHREY & WHITE *Immunol. for Students of Med.* x. 322 The injection into a normal guinea-pig of as much as 2 ml of Koch's old tuberculin has little effect. But the injection of 0·1 [*printed* 0·0] ml into a guinea-pig, in the eighth or tenth week of tuberculous infection, may kill it within a few hours. **1964** WHEELER & VOLK *Basic Microbiol.* xxiii. 263/2 *Mycobacterium tuberculosis* (more commonly called the tubercle bacillus and sometimes Koch's bacillus) was shown by Robert Koch to be the causative agent of tuberculosis. **1970** PASSMORE & ROBSON *Compan. Med. Stud.* II. xxi. 17/1 This Koch phenomenon is a specific example of cellular immune response. **1973** *Sci. Amer.* Oct. 28/1 Thus the famous 'Koch postulates' have been satisfied, and the tumor is firmly placed among those transmitted by an infectious agent.

kochubeïte (kǫtʃū·bi͵əit). *Min.* Also **kotschubeite.** [ad. G. *kotschubeit* (N. von Kokscharow 1863, in *Bull. de l'Acad. Imp. des Sci. de St.-Pétersbourg* V. 369), f. the name of Count P. A. *Kochubei*, 19th-century Russian mineralogist: see -ITE[1].] A mineral of the chlorite group that is a chromiferous variety of clinochlore and occurs as rose-red rhombohedral crystals.

1868 J. D. DANA *Syst. Min.* (ed. 5) 500 *Kotschubeite*.. in the district of Ufaleisk, Southern Ural. **1910** *Encycl. Brit.* VI. 256 Alumina may also be partly replaced by chromic oxide, as in the rose-red varieties [of chlorite] kämmererite and kotschubeite. **1954** *Mineral. Mag.* XXX. 280 The chromiferous chlorites include three varieties: kämmererite..; chrome-clinochlore, with less than 4% Cr_2O_3; and kochubeïte, a variety of clinochlore with more than 4% Cr_2O_3. **1958** [see *KÄMMERERITE].

Koch–Weeks bacillus. *Med.* [f. the names of Robert *Koch* (see *KOCH) and J. E. *Weeks* (1853–1949), American ophthalmologist: see BACILLUS.] The bacterium, *Hæmophilus ægyptius*, which is a common cause of infectious conjunctivitis.

[**1897** *Arch. Ophthalmol.* XXVI. 102 Peters and Fuchs claimed never to have been able to find the Koch–Weeks's bacillus.] **1898** R. T. HEWLETT *Man. Bacteriol.* xx. 359 Conjunctivitis is usually of three kinds—viz. the acute, caused by the Koch–Weeks bacillus; the gonorrhœal; and the chronic. **1974** PASSMORE & ROBSON *Compan. Med. Studies* III. II. xxxiii. 8/1 Conjunctivitis may occur in epidemic form in schools, offices, etc., the classical epidemic pink-eye, being caused by *H. aegyptius* (the Koch-Weeks bacillus).

Kodachrome (kōᵘ·dăkrōᵘm). [f. KODA(K *sb.* + *-chrome* (Gr. χρῶμα colour).] The registered trade name of a method of colour photography used by Kodak Ltd. Also, a colour film manufactured by this method; a photograph or slide produced from a Kodachrome film. Also *attrib.*

The spellings in quots. 1915 and 1966 are *erron.*

1915 *Chambers's Jrnl.* 25 Sept. 687/2 The kodachchrome process offers a means of enabling the former [*sc.* the amateur] to realise his ambition. **1926** *Trade Marks Jrnl.* 22 Sept. 2158 Kodachrome... All Goods included in Class 8 [*sc.* philosophical instruments, scientific instruments, apparatus for useful purposes, etc.]. Kodak, Limited,..London, W.C.2; Manufacturers and Dealers. **1930** C. W. ACKERMAN *George Eastman* viii. 285 Ever since the advent of the Kodak system, Eastman had dreamed of photographs in natural colors and the research workers..had just succeeded in a color process for portraiture, which was called Kodachrome. **1935** *Discovery* July 190/2 Recently Kodak have introduced a very interesting three-colour subtractive film for sub-standard cinematography which is to be known as 'Kodachrome'. **1936** *Times* 10 Jan. 7/5 Among other short films shown was one which illustrated the results obtained by the new Kodachrome process. **1951** L. Z. HOBSON *Celebrity* (1953) ii. 22 Each grandchild, whether in the flesh or on Kodachrome, was Beauty and Goodness personified. **1960** A. COREN in *Introduction: Stories by New Writers* 102 Brash teased-up Kodachrome lupins and a postcard sky. **1961** G. SMITH *Business of Loving* xv. 271 The air had a tint of Kodachrome blue in it. **1966** *Guardian* 28 Dec. 4/6 Pope Pius, in Kodakchrome, smiled at stacks of institutional china. **1969** *Focal Encycl. Photogr.* 815/2 *Kodachrome*, pioneer subtractive process of colour photography worked out by L. D. Mannes and L. Godorosky and introduced by Kodak... It makes use of an integral tripack in which the emulsions contain no colour formers but are subjected to individual dye development. **1970** *Daily Tel.* (Colour Suppl.) 7 Aug. 7 A vivid Kodachrome of the coach roaring down a hillside became the background for the new cheques. **1971** R. DENTRY *Encounter at Kharmel* (1973) ix. 148 Bloody marvellous country... I've got a box of Kodachromes to prove it.

Kodak, *sb.* For def. read: The proprietary name of a range of cameras produced by Kodak Ltd. Add earlier and later (including *attrib.*) examples.

1888 *Official Gaz.* (U.S. Patent Off.) XLIV. 1072/1 Photographic Cameras and Sensitized Plates and Film Therefor.—The Eastman Dry Plate and Film Company... 'The word "Kodak".' **1899** MERWIN & WEBSTER *Short Line War* v. 62 Near the box was a kodak picture of Miss Porter. **1907** W. JAMES *Pragmatism* viii. 290 We want a Kodak-picture and we press a button. **1913** F. A. TALBOT *Pract. Cinematogr.* 22 Contrary to general belief, taking the 'movies' is quite as simple as snapshot photography with a Kodak. **1933** R. L. SUTTON *Arctic Safari* 43 We had to exercise considerable self-restraint in the matter of kodak portraiture... I think that we did not use up more than three packs of film. **1966** J. BETJEMAN *High & Low* 47 These are the walls adorned with portraits, Camera studies and Kodak snaps. **1974** *Times* 26 Jan. 8/3 Americans walk the length of the street market in the Portobello Road snapping it with Kodaks.

b. (Later examples.)

1898 *N.Y. Observer* 3 Mar. 258/1 Some of the rest took kodaks of us. **1901** E. HORNBY *Jrnl.* 22 Mar. in *Sinai & Petra* (1907) 180 M. at once took two kodaks of it. **1930** B. WILLIS *Living Afr.* vii. 98 After I had taken a couple of kodaks.

Kodak, *v.* Add: (Later examples of senses a and b.) Now *rare*. The derivatives *Kodaker, Kodakist,* and *Kodakry* seem to be obsolete.

1924 *New Republic* 24 Dec. 120 Our Main Street is the happy-hunting ground of the ill-willed camera. Picture ahead, Kodak as you go. **1928** *Ibid.* 12 Dec. 90 The young cook who had been one of the last to leave the ship, Kodaking as he went. **1934** J. COLLIER *Defy Foul Fiend* 318 Willoughby's eye had kodaked the attitude of a beaten child, sulking in tears. **1936** *Time* 14 Dec. 21 A French actress who recognizes Mrs. Simpson and tries to Kodak her gets a blow from the British bodyguard knocking her camera from her hand. **1948** H. M. GLOSTER *Negro Voices Amer. Fiction* 165 McKay's second novel, *Banjo* (1929), an impressionistic kodaking of life among the colored boys of the Marseilles breakwater. **1954** *Life* 26 Apr. 155 Kodaked by friend as he himself aimed a Kodak, Eastman was photographed on a ship in 1890 by early model which took round pictures.

Kodiak (kǫ·dyæ̆k). Also **Kadiak** (kæ·dyæ̆k). The name of an island off Alaska, used *attrib.* to designate the large brown bear, *Ursus arctos middendorffi*, found there, as well as in Alaska itself and on other islands off the coast. Also *absol.*

1899 R. WARD *Rec. Big Game* (ed. 3) 474 Even more gigantic is the Kadiak bear..of Kadiak Island, Alaska. **1904** C. R. E. RADCLYFFE *Big Game Shooting in Alaska* 268 The Kodiak brown bear (*Ursus middendorffi*). **1930** *Sat. Even. Post* 13 Dec. 11/2 A Kodiak bear looks as big as an elephant as he ambles..through vegetation that comes only to his stomach. **1955** *Arctic Terms* 47/1 Kodiak bear. The world's largest carnivore, *Ursus middendorfi*, occasionally weighs 1,500 pounds, yellowish to dark brown in color, ranging from the Alaska Peninsula southeast on coasts and adjacent islands to British Columbia. Also called the 'big brown bear', 'brownie', 'Alaskan brown bear', 'Kadiak bear'. **1966** R. PERRY *World of Polar Bear* ix. 111 In both size and weight polar bears approximate to the giant Alaskan and Kodiak bears. **1974** 'R. B. DOMINIC' *Epitaph for Lobbyist* xx. 173 He was going to

walk..into the Zoo... Kodiaks and Himalayas, the tourist booklet said.

koechlinite (kō·χʸlinəit). *Min.* [f. the name of Rudolf *Koechlin* (1862–1939), curator of the mineral collection, Hof-Museum, Vienna + -ITE[1].] A molybdate of bismuth, Bi_2MoO_6, found as minute, greenish-yellow plates, and in soft white to yellow masses.

1914 W. T. SCHALLER in *Jrnl. Washington Acad. Sci.* IV. 354 Koechlinite (bismuth molybdate), a new mineral from Schneeberg, Saxony. **1943** *Amer. Mineralogist* XXVIII. 537 Koechlinite also was found as soft white to yellow masses associated with bismoclite on specimens from Bygoo, New South Wales. Here, too, the mineral has formed by the alteration of a pre-existing bismuth mineral. **1966** *Jrnl. Inorg. & Nucl. Chem.* XXVIII. 1125 The lattice parameters were equal to those of natural koechlinite within the experimental error.

koedoe: see *KUDU.

koek(oe)makranka, varr. *KUKUMAKRANKA.

‖ **koeksister** (kū·sistəɪ). *S. Afr.* Also **koeksuster, koesijster, koesister.** [Afrikaans *koe(k)-sister.*] A kind of sugared doughnut popular in South Africa.

1904 *Hilda's Where is it? of Recipes* (Pettman) 128 *Koesisters* (Batavian or old Dutch sweetmeat recipe). **1913** C. PETTMAN *Africanderisms* 272 *Koesijsters,*—a confection or sweetmeat which has been boiled in fat and dipped in powdered sugar. **1947** L. G. GREEN *Tavern of Seas* viii. 72 There was a koesister (doughnut) specialist. **1953** *Cape Times* 24 Mar. 16/1 Tea and coffee, *boerebeskuit, koeksusters, melktart,* and scores of other platteland delicacies. **1959** H. GERBER *Trad. Cookery Cape Malays* 9 Some of them [*sc.* Malay housewives] turn out lighter pastries, spongier *koesisters* than others. **1967** E. M. SLATTER *My Leaves are Green* 9 The coffee was hot and strong and the flaky koeksisters melted in my mouth. **1974** *Sunday Times* (Johannesburg) (Colour Suppl.) 3 Mar. 7 Those delicious onions with a sour sauce, melk snysels, koeksisters.

koelie: see *COOLIE, COOLY 2 b.

koelreuteria (kōlroitiᵊ·riă). [mod.L. (E. Laxmann 1772, in *Nov. Comm. Acad. Sci. Imp. Petrop.* XVI. 561), f. the name of Joseph G. *Koelreuter* (1733–1806), German naturalist + -IA[1].] A deciduous tree of the east Asian genus so called, belonging to the family Sapindaceæ, esp. *K. paniculata,* from northern China, which has large panicles of yellow flowers and pinnate leaves which turn bright yellow in autumn.

1789 W. AITON *Hortus Kewensis* II. 7 Panicled Kœlreuteria. Nat[ive] of China. **1818** *Bot. Reg.* IV. 330 (*heading*) Panicled Koelreuteria. **1914** W. J. BEAN *Trees & Shrubs Hardy in Brit. Isles* II. 687 Mr Wilson introduced from China, in 1900, a rather distinct Koelreuteria with very large and often quite bipinnate leaves. **1920** A. D. WEBSTER *London Trees* 71 The Koelreuteria is readily propagated by cuttings of either root or branch. **1946** L. J. F. BRIMBLE *Trees in Brit.* xxvii. 209 *Koelreuteria* is a native of northern China, but it is sometimes cultivated in Britain for ornamental purposes since its yellow flowers and autumnal foliage are so attractive.

koembang, var. *KUMBANG.

koenenite (kō-, kō·nĕnəit). *Min.* [ad. G. *koenenit* (F. Rinne 1902, in *Centralblatt f. Mineral.* 493), f. the name of Adolph von *Koenen* (1837–1915), German geologist who first found it: see -ITE[1].] A hydroxide and chloride of magnesium, aluminium, and sodium (formerly thought to be an impurity), which forms pale yellow scales when pure, but is normally red owing to enclosed hæmatite.

1902 *Jrnl. Chem. Soc.* LXXXII. II. 611 Koenenite. This new mineral was found..in crevices in the clay of the salt deposits at Volpriehausen, in the Sollinger Wald, Hanover. It is red in colour. **1952** *Mineral. Abstr.* XI. 459 Koenenite is widely distributed in the German salt deposits, occurring in salt-clay with blue halite, in anhydrite 'Hartsalz', and carnallite. **1968** *Zeitschr. für Kristallogr.* CXXVI. 7 Koenenite, $4NaCl.4(Mg,Ca)Cl_2.5Mg(OH)_2.4Al(OH)_3$, is built up of two trigonal substructures: $[Na_4(Ca,Mg)_2Cl_{12}]^{4-}$ and $[Mg_7Al_4(OH)_{22}]^{4+}$. **1968** I. KOSTOV *Mineral.* II. iii. 195 Koenenite is trigonal with perfect {0001} cleavage.

koesijster, koesister, varr. *KOEKSISTER.

‖ **kofta** (kǫ·ftă). Also **koaftah, kooftah.** [Hind. *kofta* pounded meat.] A rissole, made of meat or fish, popular in the East. Also *attrib.*

1888 W. H. DAWE *Wife's Help to Indian Cookery* 71 *Koftá kabáb.* [Recipe given.] **1932** M. R. ANAND *Curries* 49 In Kofta Curry..all the tomatoes should be put in at once to form the gravy. **1936** E. P. VEERASAWMY *Indian Cookery* 51 Kooftahs..are usually balls of minced mutton or beef, blended with onions, garlic, ginger and certain spices, and cooked in a curry sauce. **1955** H. DAY *Curries of India* iii. 27 Koaftah curry is quite simple to make and is a universal favourite all over India and Pakistan. **1971** *Femina* (Bombay) 16 Apr. 57/2 Put *koftas* in it [*sc.* the water] and cook till soft enough.

‖ **kogai** (kōᵘ·gai). [Jap.] Environmental pollution in Japan.

1970 *New Yorker* 23 May 94 Although *kogai* is one of the most controversial and thoroughly covered topics in the Tokyo press, the daily seminars [on pollution] were closed to Japanese reporters. **1971** *Peace News* 17 Sept. 1 (*heading*) Basic theory of Kogai. *Ibid.*, 'Kogai' is the Japanese word which is used to identify the pollution problem. It cannot be literally translated, for it is also used to refer to environmental problems above and beyond simple pollution: factory noise, vibration, obstruction of sunlight, traffic congestion, water shortage, etc.

kohekohe (kō·ikō:i). *N.Z.* [Maori.] A deciduous tree, *Dysoxylum spectabile,* of the family Meliaceæ, which has pinnate leaves and panicles of fragrant white flowers.

1835 W. YATE *Acct. N.Z.* (ed. 2) ii. 48 Kohekohe (*Laurus kohekohe*).—A fine handsome tree, with a trunk free of branches to a height of forty feet. **1855** H. R. RICHMOND *Let.* 11 Aug. in *Richmond–Atkinson Papers* (1960) I. iv. 173 There is a beautiful view of the splendid kohekohe bush on your ridge. **1910** L. COCKAYNE *N.Z. Plants* iii. 29 In some few cases the flowers of a tree are produced on the thick branches, as in the kohekohe (*Dysoxylum spectabile*), and not, as usual, from amongst the leaves. **1950** *N.Z. Jrnl. Agric.* Sept. 215/3 The main-range forest, consisting of tawa, beech, rimu..kohekohe. **1966** *Encycl. N.Z.* II. 234/2 Kohekohe is a medium-sized tree usually 30–40 ft in height, with a trunk 1–3 ft in diameter.

kohl[1]. Add: Hence **kohl** *v. trans.*, to darken with kohl. So **kohled** *ppl. a.*

1947 *Penguin New Writing* XXIX. 10 Altogether the face..of an actor roughed and kohled. **1964** *Punch* 26 Feb. 298/2 She had appeared..in her most glamorous *sari*..eyelids kohl-ed. **1971** R. DENTRY *Encounter at Kharmel* (1973) x. 183 Ten-year-old boy sopranos with kohl-ed eyes.

Kohlrausch (kōᵘ·lrauʃ). *Physical Chem.* [The name of Friedrich Wilhelm *Kohlrausch* (1840–1910), German physicist.] *Kohlrausch's law*: that the equivalent electrical conductivity of an electrolyte at infinite dilution may be represented as the sum of two constants, viz. the ionic mobilities of the cation and the anion respectively.

1888 *Jrnl. Chem. Soc.* LIV. 331 Kohlrausch's law that the conductivity of a neutral salt may be represented as a sum of two constants, one of which depends on the nature of the acid and the other on that of the base. **1924** H. J. CREIGHTON *Princ. & Applications Electrochem.* v. 91 This additive relationship..is called Kohlrausch's law or 'the law of the independent migration of ions'. **1964** G. I. BROWN *Introd. Physical Chem.* xxxiii. 369 The immediate usefulness of Kohlrausch's law is that it provides a method for finding the Λ_∞ [*sc.* the equivalent conductivity at infinite dilution] value for weak electrolytes from Λ_∞ measurements on strong electrolytes. **1969** R. A. HORNE *Marine Chem.* iii. 117 Kohlrausch's law..of the additivity of conductivities..is valid only in the limiting case. Solutions of finite concentration exhibit an appreciable departure from the law.

Kohs block (kōᵘz blǫk). *Psychol.* Also **Kohs' block.** [f. the name of Samuel *Kohs* (b. 1890), U.S. psychologist.] One of a set of coloured cubes used in psychiatric testing with which the subject is required to reproduce patterns presented to him.

1930 *Child Development* I. 341/2 The Kohs block design test was given to 29 children in the Child Institute of Johns Hopkins University. **1941** *Jrnl. Appl. Psychol.* XXV. 420 The Kohs Block Designs test..has found extensive application in clinical psychological work. **1954** A. ANASTASI *Psychol. Testing* x. 245 In the Kohs Block Design.., the subject is presented with a set of identical one-inch cubes, whose six sides are painted red, blue, yellow, white, yellow-and-blue, and red-and-white, respectively. Colored designs are presented on each of 17 test cards, the subject being required to reproduce each design by assembling the proper blocks. **1964** M. CRITCHLEY *Developmental Dyslexia* ix. 57 Constructional tasks.. include the assembling of jig-saw puzzles, a game which may not be easy for some of these dyslexics. This difficulty is readily assessed by the test of Kohs' blocks, where some dyslexics fare badly.

‖ **kohua** (kōᵘ·ˌhuă). *N.Z.* [Maori *kōhua.*] **a.** A Maori oven. **b.** A three-legged iron pot or kettle. Cf. *go-ashore* (c) (Go *v.* VIII).

1843 E. DIEFFENBACH *Trav. N.Z.* II. iv. 43 The native oven, *hangi* or *kohua*, made in the well-known manner with heated stones. **1901** A. A. GRACE in D. M. Davin *N.Z. Short Stories* (1953) 53 Soon the *kohua* was sizzling over a bright fire. **1905** W. B. *Where White Man Treads* 72 The last day of all he [*sc.* Captain Cook] gave Toia another pot, and..with much pointing at it, said: 'Now go ashore.' So we took that to be its name; for do we not call it at this distant day a 'kohua'? (corruption of 'go ashore'). **1949** P. BUCK *Coming of Maori* (1950) II. i. 112 The early trade goods included three-legged iron pots which from their function were also termed *kohua.*

koi (koi). [Jap.] A local name in Japan for the common carp, *Cyprinus carpio.*

1727 J. G. SCHEUCHZER tr. *Kæmpfer's Hist. Japan* I. I. 136 *Koi* is another sort of it [*sc.* Steenbrass], which also resembles a Carp. **1875** H. W. BATES *Illustr. Trav.* VI. 140/2 Some *koi*, a coarse-tasted fish of the carp species. **1884** tr. *J. J. Rein's Japan* I. viii. 197 The most conspicuous [of the Cyprinodontidæ] in size and importance are the Carp or Koi (Cyprinus carpio L.) and the Japanese Crucian or Funa. *Ibid.* II. ii. 440 In every house in which during the previous year a boy has been born, a flag waves on a long bamboo staff, consisting of a large painted koi (carp) of paper. **1896** L. HEARN *Kokoro* vi. 89 The real koi, the great Japanese carp, ascends swift rivers against the stream. **1971** S. ELIOVSON *Gardening Jap. Way* 86 The carp (*koi*) is a symbol of strength and perseverance.

‖ **koi-cha** (koi·tʃă). Also **koi cha, koicha.** [Jap.] In Japan, powdered tea mixed to a thick brew and drunk ceremonially.

1727 J. G. SCHEUCHZER tr. *Kæmpfer's Hist. Japan* II. App. I. 15 This powder is mix'd with hot water into a thin pulp, which is afterwards sip'd. This Tea is call'd *Koitsjaa*, that is, thick Tea, by way of distinction from the thinner Tea, made only by infusion, and it is that which all the rich people and great men in Japan daily drink. **1890** B. H. CHAMBERLAIN *Things Japanese* 338 The resulting beverage resembles pea-soup in colour and consistency. There is a thicker kind called *koi-cha*, and a thinner kind called *usu-cha.* **1960** B. LEACH *Potter in Japan* iii. 66 That was the first time I have had 'Koi Cha'. It is a variant of the Tea Ceremony in which the powdered tea is mixed to a thick brew and the bowl is passed from hand to hand. **1965** W. SWAAN *Jap. Lantern* xvi. 182 It is *koi-cha*, or thick tea, made from leaves which have been ground to a powder. **1970** J. KIRKUP *Japan behind Fan* 206 The host is ready to serve his guests with the *koi-cha*, or thick tea.

‖ **koi hai,** var. QUI-HY.

1960 M. MALGONKAR *Distant Drum* II. xxiii. 162 The very senior officers, right close to the top and steeped in the tradition of the old *koi-hais.* **1962** *Listener* 8 Nov. 776/1 There was dry knowing laughter among the *Koi Hais* in the shuttered clubs. **1967** *Ibid.* 11 May 610/1 It is..almost a generation since the last of the *koi hais* packed up..and the ghosts of Poona are now faint indeed. **1971** *Illustr. Weekly India* 4 Apr. 22/3 On the boat, coming out to rejoin Maurice, I had learnt quite a lot of Hindustani, unfortunately from a very charming British army officer who had an atrociously *koi hai* accent which I never quite managed to shed. **1973** *Times* 19 Feb. (India Suppl.) p. ix/2 The *Koi Hais* and 'bottoms up, old boy', are confined, in Britain, to the personal column of *The Times*, and in India, to a brittle crust of individuals who seem to prefer the caricature to the real thing.

koilonychia (koiloni·kiă). *Path.* [a. G. *koilonychia* (J. Heller 1897, in *Dermatol. Zeitschr.* IV. 490), f. Gr. κοῖλ-ος hollow + ὄνυξ, -υχος nail + -IA[1].] A condition of the finger-nails in which the outer surfaces are concave instead of convex; spoon-nail.

1902 *Trans. Med. Assoc. Missouri* XLV. 157 The disease..is known technically as koilonychia and ordinarily as 'spoon' nails... Koilonychia may be observed in one or more of the nails of the fingers of one or both hands. **1934** J. M. VAUGHAN *Anaemias* iii. 43 Koilonychia is not found in 'splenic anaemia', while some degree is extremely common in idiopathic hypochromic anaemia. **1970** *Jrnl. Pediatrics* LXXVII. 1057/2 There is a significant correlation between koilonychia and iron deficiency in infants 9 to 13 months of age.

koine (koi·ni). [Gr. κοινή, fem. sing. of κοινός common, ordinary.] **a.** Originally the common literary dialect of the Greeks (ἡ κοινὴ διάλεκτος) from the close of classical Attic to the Byzantine era. Now extended to include any language or dialect in regular use over a wide area in which different languages or dialects are, or were, in use locally.

[**1886** *Encycl. Brit.* XXI. 653/1 As might be expected, this κοινή, like the κοινή of the Greeks, has a comparatively limited vocabulary.] **1913** D. B. DURHAM *Vocab. Menander* 8 The year 600 A.D. is a convenient date at which to divide the Koine from the Greek of the middle ages. **1926** *Germanic Rev.* I. IV. 297 Assuming that all our dialects had given way to a High German *koiné*, we should still recognize the characteristic distinctions of the former dialects. **1927** A. H. MCNEILE *Introd. New Testament* 278 Such [constructions] as were rapidly making their way into the *Koine* Greek. **1933** *Amer. Speech* VIII. Oct. 5/1 The American *koiné* in eliminating the extreme variations in English dialects nevertheless absorbed enough of their peculiarities to make it a highly varied unity. **1956** A. TOYNBEE *Historian's Approach to Relig.* xix. 270 In the first century of the Christian Era the dissemination of the books of the New Testament in the Attic *koinê*—the 'standard Greek' of the day—ensured their finding readers as far afield..as Britain..and India. **1958** D. WHITELOCK *Changing Currents Anglo-Saxon Stud.* 6 The general use of the West Saxon literary *koine* in the tenth and eleventh centuries. **1964** S. M. ERVIN-TRIPP in J. A. Fishman *Readings Sociol. of Lang.* (1968) 197 Superposed varieties [of speech] include many types, from occupational argots to koines used for trade and regional communication, such as Melanesian Pidgin and Swahili. **1965** *Times Lit. Suppl.* 22 Apr. 317/2 A 'disc-jockey' found himself saying 'take time *out*', in accordance with the conventional mid-Atlantic koine these people have to use. **1966** K. H. ALBROW in C. E. Bazell *In Memory of J. R. Firth* 2 F. Roberts is in the habit of speaking standard Welsh with a Northern accent as his Welsh koine except at home.

b. A set of cultural or other attributes common to various groups. Also *attrib.*

1924 A. J. B. WACE in *Cambr. Anc. Hist.* II. xvi. 466 During the last two centuries, at least, of the Mycenaean dominion in Greece and the Aegean, there was a cultural *koiné*, and it is at least likely that there was a linguistic *koiné* as well. **1939** J. D. S. PENDLEBURY *Archaeol. Crete*

vi. 358 Crete had entered the Hellenistic *koine* and its individuality is nearly lost. **1962** *Economist* 28 Apr. 340/3 The Mauretanian and Numidian kingdoms..were centres of an Afro-European 'koiné'.

‖ **koinonia** (koinōᵘ·nia). *Theol.* [Gr. κοινωνία communion, fellowship.] Christian fellowship or communion, either with God or, more commonly, with fellow Christians.

1907 W. P. Du Bose *Gospel according to St. Paul* xvii. 243 As the first two truths of our faith in Christ might be called those of the Father and the Son, so the third may be designated that of the Spirit. Or, to put it in the other way, as the first two may be called those of the divine love and the divine grace, so the third may be named that of the divine *koinonia*. **1920** 'W. S. Palmer' *Christianity & Christ* 177 Thinking of the Church I am reminded of the 'Koinonia', the fellowship of early Christians which came of the Pentecostal inflowing of the Spirit of God. **1938** *Theology* XXXVI. 211 The Church's tradition of social and economic justice; the primitive koinonia, the medieval just price and condemnation of usury. **1949** *Scottish Jrnl. Theol.* II. 67 We exist in the Image of the Living God who Himself confronts Himself to become one God in the *koinonia* of the Holy Spirit. **1967** J. Macquarrie *Dict. Christian Ethics* 73/1 The point of departure for Christian thinking about ethics is the concrete reality in the world of a community, a *koinonia*, called into being and action by Jesus of Nazareth.

‖ **koji** (kōᵘ·dʒi). [Jap.] An enzyme preparation derived from various moulds, esp. *Aspergillus oryzæ* and closely related species, and used to bring about the fermentation involved in the production of saké, soy sauce, etc.

1878 R. W. Atkinson in *Nature* 12 Sept. 522/2 The rice-grains are found to be covered with large quantities of fine hair-like threads, the mycelium of the fungus added. In this state it is called 'kōji'. **1926** Thom & Church *Aspergilli* vi. 64 Koji in its various forms is used in several fermentations. **1953** J. Ramsbottom *Mushrooms & Toadstools* xxiii. 275 The Koji for the enormous fermentation industries of Japan is *Aspergillus Oryzae*, or closely allied species. **1960** A. E. Bender *Dict. Nutrition* 122/1 Takadiastase. Or Koji, an enzyme preparation produced by growing the fungus, *Aspergillus oryzae*, on bran, leaching the culture mass with water and precipitating with alcohol. **1965** Raper & Fennell *Genus Aspergillus* xviii. 358 *A. flavus*..had been encountered frequently among cultures received from Japanese workers as isolates from commercial inoculum, or 'koji', for fermentation industries. *Ibid.* 391 The manufacture of saké is dependent upon the use of *A. oryzae* for the preparation of the koji used to digest rice starch and protein.

kojic (kōᵘ·dʒik), *a. Chem.* [f. *koji: see -ic.] *kojic acid*: 5-hydroxy-2-hydroxymethyl-γ-pyrone, $HO \cdot C_5H_2O_2 \cdot CH_2OH$, a crystalline pyrone derivative produced from dextrose by some fungi of the genus *Aspergillus* and having mild antibacterial properties.

[**1912** T. Yabuta in *Orig. Communications 8th Internat. Congr. Appl. Chem.* XXV. 455, I have given the name 'Koji acid' to this substance.] **1913** *Jrnl. Chem. Soc.* CIV. i. 180 Kojic acid..obtained from finely powdered *Aspergillus oryzae* forms colourless needles or prisms. **1947** *New Biol.* II. 88 Kojic acid is a mild disinfectant of the same order of activity as phenol. **1971** *Jrnl. Trop. Med. & Hygiene* LXXIV. 164/1 Kojic acid production which is supposed to be a constant property of *A[spergillus] flavus*.

kokama, var. *kukama.

kokanee (ko·kani). Also **kickininee**. [ad. Salish *kikinee*.] A landlocked dwarf subspecies, *Oncorhynchus nerka kennerlyi*, of the sockeye salmon.

1875 in *Okanagan Hist. Soc. Rep.* (1953) 17 There we would fill our basket with the shining kik-e-ninnies. **1937** *Kootenay & City of Nelson, B.C.* 62 The Kokanee or 'Silver Trout', which is in reality a landlocked Sockeye salmon abounds in the larger lakes of the district. **1940** *Nature* 3 Aug. 172/1 Attempts to explain the origin of kokanee (a variety of sockeye salmon) were made. **1963** *New Scientist* 31 Jan. 228/2 The kokanee, *Oncorhynchus nerka kennerlyi*, might increase overall production when cultured with trout. **1963** *Globe & Mail* (Toronto) 2 Mar. 8/6 The kokanee (or kickininee) is a sockeye salmon that does not migrate to the ocean. Its life span is similar to that of the sockeye in that it returns to the nursery stream after three or four years, at which time it weighs about a pound. **1965** A. J. McClane *Standard Fishing Encycl.* 457/2 The kokanee was originally found in Oregon, Idaho, Washington, British Columbia, and northward into Alaska... In Japan it is found in Lake Akan in northern Hokkaido... Morphologically the kokanee and sockeye are identical. **1970** D. Waterfield *Continental Waterboy* i. 2 Enabling the silver trout or kokanee..to reach the formerly inaccessible river.

‖ **koker** (kōᵘ·kəɹ). *Guyana.* Also **khoker**. [Du.] A sluice-gate, a lock-gate; the narrow stretch of water between such gates.

1851 J. A. Tinne *Rep. Outfall Drainage Brit. Guiana* 11 By means of a koker or sluice near the sea, the drains are emptied at low tide and the sluices are shut when the tide rises higher than the water in the drains. **1893** J. Rodway *Hand-bk. Brit. Guiana* 9 Through openings in the front dams, closed at high water by marine gates called kokers, the canals empty themselves into the sea. **1944** *Drainage & Irrigation Schemes* (Brit. Guiana Bureau of Publicity) 3 Investigations have to be made concerning..Capacity of sluices and kokers. *Ibid.* 5 The surplus water being discharged through..kokers when the tide is sufficiently low. **1951** E. A. Mittelholzer *Shadows move among Them* ii. ix. 240 The ditch was wide and..where it entered the stream stood what seemed to be a sluice-gate. 'That's the *koker*... It's a Dutch word... The *koker* is left open so that the tide can rise and fill the ditch... Then at high tide the *koker* is shut.' **1958** J. Carew *Black Midas* iv. 61 The procession moved out of sight down the path by the khoker and towards the river. **1965** 'Lauchmonen' *Old Thom's Harvest* iii. 34 The dereck of the first koker from the sea toppled over.

kokerboom (kū·kəɪbūm). *S. Afr.* [Afrikaans, f. Du. *koker* quiver + *boom* tree.] A large aloe, *Aloe dichotoma*, the size of a small tree, whose branches were formerly used to make quivers for arrows; = *quiver-tree* (Quiver *sb.*¹ 2).

1774 F. Masson *Jrnl.* 2 Nov. in *Phil. Trans. R. Soc.* (1776) LXVI. 309 We found a new species of aloe here, called by the Dutch Koker Boom, of which the Hottentots make quivers to hold their arrows. **1812** W. J. Burchell *Jrnl.* 14 May in *Trav. S. Afr.* (1824) II. vii. 199 The natives more towards the western coast, frequently use the branches of the *Aloë dichotoma*, which is therefore called by the Hottentots and Colonists, *kokerboom* or quiver tree. **1920** F. C. Cornell *Glamour of Prospecting* 116 We outspanned about sunset on an open plateau covered with vegetation and studded with many of the queer looking aloes known as *koker boomen*, or 'quiver trees'. **1950** *Cape Argus* 5 Aug. 7/5 As you drive northwards through the mountains to Springbok you may see that weird tree-aloe, the kokerboom, flowering beside the road. **1959** J. D. Clark *Prehist. S. Afr.* ix. 226 The arrows were usually kept in a quiver made from leather..or bark, in particular the bark of the 'Kokerboom' tree which is a species of aloe. **1974** *Eastern Province Herald* (S. Afr.) 28 Jan. 11 Those who lived in houses built of Kokerboom trunks stood back and watched as..the flames leapt and crackled through the wooden structures.

‖ **kokeshi** (kōᵘ·keʃi). [Jap.] A kind of wooden Japanese doll.

1959 R. Kirkbride *Tamiko* xxii. 172 He bought Tamiko a kokeshi doll. **1970** J. Kirkup *Japan behind Fan* 63 Some stalls were selling celluloid masks and *kokeshi*. **1973** R. Littell *Defection of A. J. Lewinter* iv. 19 Sarah's 'things'—sea shells..Japanese *kokeshi* dolls, paperweights.

kokila. (Later example.)

1931 L. H. Myers *Prince Jali* iii. 37 A kokila-bird was sounding its single, inexpressive note.

kokkewiet (kǫkĕvī·t). *S. Afr.* Also **cock-o-veet, kook-a-vic**. [Afrikaans, echoic.] = *bokmakierie.

1896 E. Clairmonte *Africander* vii. 126 The kook-a-vic was piping his shrill note in a bush hard by. 'Kook-a-vic, kook-a-vic, kook-a-vic.' **1926** O. Schreiner *From Man to Man* 49 A cock-o-veet came flying up to her. *Ibid.*, Kokkewiet: The Bush-shrike, a very handsome bird with resonant call notes of great beauty. **1936** E. L. Gill *First Guide S. Afr. Birds* 49 Bokmakierie, Bacbakiri, Kokkewiet... The calls are duets by the inseparable pair. **1970** *Standard Encycl. S. Afr.* II. 401/1 Bokmakierie..is sometimes locally referred to as bakbakiri, kokkewiet, janpierewiet or bush-shrike.

kokko, var. *koko².

koklas(s (kōᵘ·klăs). Also **cocklass, kuklass**. [Nepalese, var. of *pokras, pukras*.] The pheasant, *Pucrasia macrolopha*, several subspecies of which are found in the Himalayas and China and have been introduced elsewhere.

1864 T. C. Jerdon *Birds India* III. 525 The Cocklass is of a rather retired and solitary disposition. *Ibid.* 524 *Koklas* or *Kokla*, in various hill dialects. **1898** *Ibis* Jan. 39 The Koklass was not uncommon in the forest above Gund. **1922** *Blackw. Mag.* Mar. 323/2 In the woods below a kuklass crowed hoarsely. **1952** Bates & Lowther *Breeding Birds Kashmir* 278 The Koklas is the commonest pheasant in Kashmir. **1965** P. Wayre *Wind in Reeds* xv. 219, I recognised them at once as Koklass Pheasants. *Ibid.*, Koklass are high mountain birds and come from the western Himalayas and North Eastern Tibet across to Eastern and Northern China. **1974** *Country Life* 25 July 244/3 From a dealer's shop in London, came a pair of Koklass pheasants..[which] the Trust succeeded in breeding..in captivity.

koko¹. Add: = *cocoyam. (Later example.)

1938 *Jrnl. R. Anthrop. Inst.* LXVIII. 125 These [*sc.* cultivated crops] are..koko yams (*Colocasia antiquorum*), maize, [etc.].

koko² (kōᵘ·ko). Also **kokoh, kokko**. [Burmese name for the tree.] The brown hardwood obtained from *Albizia lebbeck*, a tropical, deciduous tree of the family Leguminosæ, or the tree itself.

1862 E. Balfour *Timber Trees of India* (ed. 2) 30/2 In the Prome district a special tax was levied on the felling of 'Kokoh' and 'Padouk' under the Burmese rule. **1881** J. S. Gamble *Man. Indian Timbers* 157 *A[lbizzia] Lebbek*... The Siris Tree. Vern[acular]... Kokoh, Burm. **1911** J. H. Holland *Useful Plants Nigeria* II. 299 *Albizzia Lebbek*... East Indian Walnut, Kokoh or Kokka (Rangoon). Wild in Tropical Asia..; distributed to Tropical Africa. **1930** *Observer* 29 June 18/2 In respect of woods the building itself is an exhibition: every piece of joinery..has come from India... Most of the floors are of a pleasant brown wood called koko. **1937** J. M. Dalziel *Useful Plants W. Trop. Afr.* 211 *Albizzia Lebbek*... The timber is sometimes called East Indian Walnut, and is marketed as Kokko or Koko. **1947** J. C. Rich *Materials & Methods Sculpture* x. 290 *Koko* or East Indian Walnut is a hard, dense, close-grained tropical wood imported from Burma. It is dark brown and is usually available in log form. **1956** *Handbk. Hardwoods* (Forest Prod. Res. Lab.) 128 Kokko varies considerably in size according to locality. *Ibid.* 129 Kokko is said to be used for sliced veneers and in the furniture industry.

kokopan, var. *cocopan.

‖ **kokopu** (kǫ·kŏpu). *N.Z.* [Maori.] A small freshwater fish, *Galaxias fasciatus*.

1886 R. A. Sherrin *Handbk. Fishes N.Z.* 138 'Kokopu', Dr Hector says, is the general Maori name for several very common fishes in the New Zealand streams and lakes, belonging to the family of *Galaxiidæ*. **1929** W. Martin *N.Z. Nature Bk.* I. xix. 175 The Kokopu or 'Native Trout' (*Galaxias fasciatus*) is known from all parts of New Zealand south of the Bay of Islands. **1949** P. Buck *Coming of Maori* (1950) ii. viii. 236 The *kokopu* do not run until March. **1962** *Post-Primary School Bull.* (Wellington, N.Z.) XV. i. 27 Kokopu, *Galaxias fasciatus*, live in most of our streams and smaller rivers. **1966** *Encycl. N.Z.* I. 675/2 *Galaxias fasciatus*, the kokopu or banded galaxias, is found throughout the country.

‖ **kokowai** (kōᵘ·kowai). *N.Z.* [Maori.] Red ochre, burnt red clay (see quot. 1949).

1836 J. A. Wilson *Jrnl.* July in *Missionary Life & Work N.Z.* (1889) iii. 43 Two large totara posts..daubed with *kokowai*. **1840** J. S. Polack *Manners & Customs New Zealanders* I. xix. 210 The *powáka* is kept neatly painted red with *kokowai*. **1845** E. J. Wakefield *Adventure N.Z.* I. 124 A carved post which was painted with *kokowai*, or red ochre. *Ibid.* II. 87 The *kokowai*-painted monuments which I have mentioned. **1878** *Trans. N.Z. Inst.* XI. 75 *Kokowai* is a kind of pigment, burnt, dried, and mixed with shark-liver oil. **1905** W. B. *Where White Man Treads* 7 The rafters painted with kokowai (iron-ore rust), for a ground colour in red, and adorned with intricate volutes in pipe-clay for white. **1949** P. Buck *Coming of Maori* (1950) ii. xiii. 319 The decorative painting of woodwork did not advance very far in Polynesia. In New Zealand, red ochre, or haematite, was termed *karamea* and after it was burnt and powdered it became *kokowai* or *horu*. The *kokowai* was mixed with shark oil to form a red paint. **1963** T. Barrow *Life & Work Maori Carver* 28 The red clay or haematite used by the Maori for paint was first burnt, then powdered, when it became *kokowai*.

kok-saghyz (kǫksagi·z). [ad. Russ. *kok-sagýz*, of Turkic origin.] A kind of dandelion, *Taraxacum koksaghyz*, whose roots contain a latex used for making rubber.

1932 *Bull. Rubber Growers' Assoc.* Sept. 534 The Kak-Saugyiz, gave a material with even more resilience, but it has a lower content of caoutchouc. **1945** K. E. Knorr *World Rubber* x. 182 Experiments with *kok-saghyz*, the Russian dandelion, and *Cryptostegia* were soon abandoned. **1954** H. J. Stern *Rubber* i. 18 Kok saghyz (*Taraxacum kok saghyz*. Rodin). This plant was discovered in 1931... The roots contain about 90 per cent. of the total rubber in the plant. *Ibid.*, The amount of information [about Krim Saghyz] available is less than in the case of Kok Saghyz. **1959** J. C. T. Uphof *Dict. Econ. Plants* 354/2 *Taraxacum kok-saghyz* Rodin., Kok-saghyz. (Compositae).—Herbaceous perennial. Turkestan. Roots are a source of rubber. Cultivated in some parts of Russia. **1971** Roff & Scott *Fibres, Films, Plastics & Rubbers* 681/2 (*index*) Kok-saghyz.

koktaite (kǫ·ktă,əit). *Min.* [ad. Czech *koktait* (J. Sekanina 1948, in *Acta Acad. Sci. Nat. Moravo-Silesiacae* XX. i. 1), f. the name of Jaroslav *Kokta*, Czech mineralogist (see quot. 1948): see -ite¹.] Hydrated calcium ammonium sulphate, $(NH_4)_2Ca(SO_4)_2.H_2O$, occurring in acicular monoclinic crystals and identical with artificial ammonium syngenite.

1948 *Mineral. Abstr.* X. 352 Artificial ammonium-syngenite..has the composition $(NH_4)_2Ca(SO_4)_2.H_2O$ (analysis by J. Kokta..), and agrees in the optical data with the mineral, named koktaite, from Žeravice. **1968** I. Kostov *Mineral.* ii. ix. 504 Syngenite and koktaite are isotypic.

‖ **koku** (kōᵘ·ku). [Jap.] **a.** A Japanese unit of capacity equal to ten *to*, used for liquids and solids (esp. of rice as a monetary measure); equivalent to approximately 39·7 gallons (180 litres) or 4·96 bushels. **b.** A Japanese unit of capacity equal to ten cubic *shaku*, used for vessels; equivalent to approximately 9·8 cubic feet (0·278 cubic metres).

1727 J. G. Scheuchzer tr. *Kæmpfer's Hist. Japan* I. ii. v. 199 The Emperor..order'd, that three *koku's* of rice should be given, or lent to any family, that stood in need of it. **1871** A. B. Mitford *Tales Old Japan* I. 96 His revenue of eight million kokus reverted to the Government. *Ibid.*, The koku of rice, in which all revenue is calculated, is of varying value. **1892** Kipling *Lett. of Travel* (1920) 42 Five Japanese dollars (fifteen shillings) per *koku* of 330 lbs. **1896** L. Hearn *Kokoro* x. 170 The seat of a daimyō of three hundred thousand koku. **1904** *Daily Chron.* 30 Mar. 4/5 Jeyas..reduced the civil list to 9,000 kokus, or 44,500 bushels of rice, which was the way then that revenue was paid. **1911** *Encycl. Brit.* XV. 193/1 Any vessel having a capacity of more than 500 *koku* (150 tons). **1931** G. B. Sansom *Japan* ii. viii. 168 Any who could produce from the new fields one thousand *koku* of rice were promised lifelong immunity to tax.

1938 D. T. Suzuki *Zen Buddhism & its Influence on Jap. Culture* I. vii. 153 Hideyoshi gave him three thousand *koku* of rice for his service to him as tea-master.

Kol (kōᵘl). *India.* Also **Col(e), Kole.** [Of disputed origin.] Mundu-speaking tribes of Chota Nagpur and Bengal in India (see also quot. 1896); a member of any of these tribes. Also *attrib.* or as *adj.*, of or relating to any of these tribes or their languages.

1795 J. T. Blunt Jrnl. 2 Feb. in *Asiatick Res.* (1803) III. 61 Not wishing to injure the *Coles* by encamping on the little spots, which, with much care and toil, they had cleared..we took up our abode..in the jungle. **1827** R. Jenkins *Rep. Territories Rajah of Nagpore* ii. 30 The Koorkoo dialect is found to resemble that spoken by the Lurka Koles, on the frontier of Singbhoom. **1847** B. H. Hodgson *On Aborigines India* p. ii, The Kól or Dhánger race. *Ibid.* iii. 149 The Kóls are, indeed, as enterprising as industrious. *Ibid.* iii. 150 Kól is an old and classical name, and the best I think for the great mass of aborigines intervening between the Bhils, the Gonds, and the Ganges—at least till we know them better. **1866** *Jrnl. Asiatic Soc. Bengal* XXXV. II. 154 The present population..are of the race best known to us by the name of 'Kol'. **1871** [see *Dravidian *adj.*]. **1872** E. T. Dalton *Descr. Ethnol. Bengal* v. i. 125 The Kols rejecting all change adhered to their impurity of life. **1896** W. Crooke *Tribes & Castes N.W. Provinces & Oudh* III. 294 *Kol*, a Dravidian tribe found in considerable numbers along the Vindhya Kaimûr plateau. **1903** Risley & Gait *Rep. Census India 1901* I. 282 The Kol language has..two main dialects, Mundari and Ho. **1931** E. A. H. Blunt *Caste System N. India* xiv. 287 The Kol is a tribe of aboriginal jungle folk, akin to the Bengal Mundas. **1957** C. B. Mamoria *Tribal Demogr. India* iv. 62 In the iron-ore industry..the labour force..consists of largely Santhals and Kols.

kola¹. Now the usual spelling of Cola, used to refer to two trees of the genus *Cola*, *C. acuminata* or *C. nitida*, or their seeds, also called kola nuts.

1830 [see Cola]. **1868** *Curtis's Bot. Mag.* XCIV. 5699 (*heading*) Kola-nut tree. *Ibid.*, The Kola has been introduced into the Royal Gardens, Kew. **1890** *Kew Bull.* 255 Kola nuts contain some constituent analogous to caffeine. **1932** J. Cary *Aissa Saved* xv. 82 A family of kola-nut traders, father, mother, sister, and two children, hurrying to Kolu to sell at good prices. **1937** J. M. Dalziel *Useful Plants W. Trop. Afr.* 101 Elephants eat the fruits of kola and damage the tree. *Ibid.* 103 Kola is generally supposed to contain about equal quantities of caffeine and theobromine. *Ibid.* 104 Amongst some peoples a kola tree is planted to commemorate a joyful event. **1957** M. Banton *W. Afr. City* ix. 170 That afternoon he will 'pin flour'—a small ceremony for which he will invite an *alfa* and some respected local Muslims to pray for the deceased; after praying they will eat kola and balls of rice flour mixed with sugar and water. **1964** E. Huxley *Back Street New Worlds* xiv. 141 Had I been a Nigerian, he'd have offered me a kola nut, symbol of hospitality among his people.

Kola² (kōᵘ·lă). *India.* (See quot. 1873.)

1873 E. Balfour *Cycl. India* (ed. 2) III. 255/1 *Kola*, Beng. A class of hindoos whose principal avocations are basket and mat-making. **1916** [see *Kolam]. **1937** L. Bromfield *Rains Came* III. xxvii. 412 There were Kathis and Kolas.

kolach (kǫ·lātʃ). Also **kolache, kolachi, kolachy.** Pl. **kolache** (kǫ·lātʃi), **kolaches.** [ad. Czech *koláč*, f. *kolo* wheel, circle.] A small tart or pie popular in Czechoslovakia, topped or filled with a sweet mixture, preserve, etc.

1918 W. Cather *My Antonia* (1926) v. i. 381 'Show him the spiced plums, mother. Americans don't have those,' said one of the older boys. 'Mother uses them to make *kolaches*,' he added. **1947** M. Given *Mod. Encycl. Cooking* I. 528 (*heading*) Fillings for kolachy. **1953** A. Heath *Internat. Cookery Bk.* 187 Cover the kolach with it [*sc.* pastry]..and bake in a hot oven. **1961** H. Watney tr. *Břízová's Cooking Czech Way* 143 Kolache (flat fruit buns) and filled rolls made from yeast dough are typically Czech. **1967** Mrs. L. B. Johnson *White House Diary* 7 July (1970) 545 For dessert a typical specialty of the area—'kolaches', a rich pastry that has a center of dried apricots or prunes. **1969** O. Hesky *Sequin Syndicate* xviii. 169 Mamma's sent you some of her *kolachis*. I don't know if they'll let you eat them?

Kolam (kōᵘ·lām). Also **Kolamb.** [Origin unknown.] In India, a group of people (whose name for themselves is *Kōlavar*) speaking a Dravidian language similar to that of the Parji of Bastar.

a **1863** S. Hislop *Papers Aboriginal Tribes Cent. Provinces* (1866) I. 10 The Kolâms and the common Gonds do not intermarry... Their dress is similar; but the Kolâm women wear fewer ornaments. **1885** E. Balfour *Cycl. India* (ed. 3) II. 593 *Kolam* or *Kolamb*, a Gond tribe, along the Kandi Konda or Pindi Hills, on the south of the Wardha, and along the table-land stretching east and north of Manikgarh, and thence south to Dantanpilly, running parallel to the right bank of the Pranhita... The Kolam race are found also in the Amraoti, Wun, and Maiker districts as a wild race. **1916** Russell & Lal *Tribes & Castes Cent. Provinces India* III. 521 Mr. Hīra Lāl suggests that the Kolāms may be connected with the Kolas, ..who regard the Kolamallai hills as their original home. He further notes that the name of the era by which the calendar is reckoned on the Malabar coast is Kolamba.

Hence **Ko·lami,** the language spoken by these people.

a **1863** R. Temple in S. Hislop *Papers Aboriginal Tribes Cent. Provinces* (1866) II. p. i, The English words having been..classified, the design was to ascertain and record ..the equivalents in..Gondi, Gayeti,..Kolami. **1916** Russell & Lal *Tribes & Castes Cent. Provinces India* III. 520 The Kolāms..have a language of their own, called after them Kolāmi. **1968** *Encycl. Brit.* VII. 655/1 Five of the Central Dravidian languages..form a closely related group—Kolami, Naiki, Parji, Ollari and Poya Gadaba.

Kolarian (kolēᵊ·riăn). [f. *Kolar* (see quot. 1869) + -ian.] A non-Aryan linguistic stock of India, the Munda group. Also as *adj.*, of or pertaining to this stock.

1866 G. Campbell in *Jrnl. Asiatic Soc. Bengal* XXXV. II. 28, I propose then to call the northern tribes Kolarian or Coolee Aborigines. **1869** —— in *Jrnl. Ethnol. Soc. London* I. 130, I designate these tribes 'Kolarian' (as distinguished from the Dravidians), from the name Kol, Kolee or Coolee, applied to many of them, and the old name 'Kolar' by which India was known in very ancient times. **1915** Risley & Crooke *People of India* (ed. 2) i. 48 The hypothesis of the north-eastern origin of the Kolarians depends on the fancied recognition of Mongolian characteristics among the people of Chutia Nāgpur. **1923** A. L. Kroeber *Anthropol.* iii. 46 Typical representatives [of Indo-Australian people] are the Vedda of Ceylon; the Irula and some of the Kolarian tribes of India. **1928** V. G. Childe *Most Anc. East* iii. 52 Early Indian races, particularly the Dravidians, the Kolarians, and even the Veddahs of Ceylon. **1957** G. S. Ghurye *Mahadev Kolis* i. 6 Kolis of Bombay..do not show the slightest trace of Kolarian tongue in their languages. **1972** W. B. Lockwood *Panorama Indo-Europ. Lang.* 226 Munda or Kolarian are names given to a group of languages spoken today in the central part of India.

kolbasa, kolbasi, varr. *kielbasa.

Kolbe (kǫ·lbə). *Chem.* The name of A. W. H. *Kolbe* (1818–84), German chemist, used *attrib.* and in the possessive to designate two syntheses devised by him: (*a*) the electrolysis of a salt of a carboxylic acid, R·COOH, to yield a (substituted) paraffin R_2; and (*b*) the reaction between sodium phenoxide and carbon dioxide to yield sodium salicylate.

1885 *Jrnl. Chem. Soc.* XLVIII. 982 The successive reactions in Kolbe's process are then (1) the formation of sodium phenyl carbonate..; (2) the conversion of this substance into sodium salicylate..; and (3) the formation of disodium salicylate and phenol. **1915** *Chem. Abstr.* IX. 294 The K and NH_4 salts, on electrolysis, give first an alk. and later an acid reaction, the electrolysis probably proceeding in accordance with Kolbe's..reaction. **1926** J. Read *Text-bk. Org. Chem.* xxvi. 570 Kolbe's reaction is also given by other phenols. **1942** Fuson & Snyder *Org. Chem.* xi. 133 Still higher members [of the dibasic acid series] may be made by the Kolbe electrolysis of the potassium salt of an acid ester. **1951** I. L. Finar *Org. Chem.* I. xxviii. 557 The original industrial method of preparing salicylic acid was Kolbe's synthesis (1859)... The method now used is a modification of the Kolbe synthesis..known as the Kolbe–Schmidt method. It is carried out by heating sodium phenoxide with carbon dioxide at 120–140° under pressure. **1969** R. C. Denney *Named Org. Reactions* xxiii. 76 Woolford has used the Kolbe reaction to prepare long-chain ω,ω′-dibromohydrocarbons which can only be obtained with considerable difficulties by other methods.

kolbeckite (kǫ·lbekəit). *Min.* [ad. G. *kolbeckit* (F. Edelmann 1926, in *Jahrb. f. d. Berg- u. Hüttenwesen in Sachsen* C. A74), f. the name of Friedrich *Kolbeck* (1860–1943), German mineralogist: see -ite¹.] A blue hydrated silicate-phosphate of beryllium, calcium, and scandium (and possibly aluminium).

1928 *Mineral. Mag.* XXI. 568 *Kolbeckite.* Beryllium phosphate or silicophosphate as cyan-blue monoclinic crystals from Saxony. **1959** *Bull. Geol. Soc. Amer.* LXX. 1649 Sterrettite and kolbeckite are the first known scandium-bearing phosphates. **1966** Z. Lerman tr. *Vlasov's Geochem. & Mineral. Rare Elements* II. vi. 219 Kolbeckite is distinguished by its marked pleochroism. It is a very rare mineral.

kolea (kolē·ă). [Hawaiian.] A local name for the Pacific golden plover, *Pluvialis dominica fulva*, which is native to the northern parts of North America and eastern Siberia, but winters in Hawaii and other parts of the Pacific.

1887 *Proc. U.S. Nat. Mus.* X. 80 *Charadrius dominicus fulvus* (Gmel.) Pacific Golden Plover, Kolea. **1933** E. H. Bryan *Hawaiian Nature Notes* 256 The golden plover, called kolea by the Hawaiians, is a little larger than the mynah bird but longer in the leg. **1944** G. C. Munro *Birds Hawaii* 56 The kolea is a valuable bird to Hawaii as a destroyer of insects... Yet it has so long been considered a game bird and table delicacy that efforts to obtain the protection it deserves have not been very successful.

Koli: see *Kori².

kolinsky (kǫli·nski). Also **kolinski.** [f. Russ. *Kola*, name of a port in north-west Russia.] A name for the fur of a *Mustela sibirica*, the Japanese mink. Also *attrib.*

1851 *Illustr. Catal. Gt. Exhib.* III. 803 Skins and Furs... Kolinski. **1892** H. Poland *Fur-Bearing Animals in Commerce* p. li, Kolinski, undressed. **1919** *Queen* 5 July 21 (Advt.), Kolinsky coat in the fashionable Sable Colour. **1923** J. C. Sachs *Furs & Fur Trade* 62 The 'sable' brushes, which are in such request by artists, are generally made of kolinski tails. **1928** *Strand Mag.* Aug. 183/2 A Persian lamb coat with a collar of kolinsky. **1968** J. Ironside *Fashion Alphabet* 155 The Siberian China mink is known as Kolinsky.

‖ **kolkhoz** (kǫ·lkǫz). Also **kolhoz, kolkhos,** etc. Pl. **kolkhozes, kolkhozes, kolkhozy.** [Russ., f. *kol(lektívnoe khoz(yáĭstvo* collective farm.] A collective farm in the U.S.S.R. Also *transf.*

1921 *Russian Economist* I. II. 389 The 'Kolkhoses' are the means of a guerilla war with the peasants... The measure in which..support is given depends on the degree to which a particular kind of 'Kolkhose' approximates to the ideals of Communism. **1931** *Ann. Reg. 1930* 190 There was a real rush of the peasants to enter the *Kolchosy* (the abbreviated Russian denomination of the collectivised farms). *Ibid.* 191 A sensational article by Stalin entitled, 'Intoxicated by Success'. It dealt with the Kolchos movement, and in it the dictator strongly condemned the forcible methods of collectivisation hitherto used. **1931** H. G. Wells *Work, Wealth & Happiness of Mankind* (1932) iv. 184 The Kolkhoz seems to be the old Tsarist Mir in a state of emotion. *Ibid.* x. 508 The great fields of the Kolkhozy. **1943** E. M. Almedingen *Frossia* viii. 285 He knows Russia... He has seen Sovhozes and Kolhozes. **1946** [see *ejido]. **1949** F. Maclean *Eastern Approaches* I. viii. 133 The eating-house..seemed to be monopolized by the higher *kolkhoz* officials whom I found engaged in preparations for the forthcoming elections to the Supreme Council of the Kazakh S.S.R. **1951, 1952** [see *agrogorod]. **1957** *Ann. Reg. 1956* 256 The villages [in Hungary] seem quietly to have dissolved most of their local *kolkhoz* and then returned to work. **1958** *New Statesman* 5 Apr. 423/3 The *kolkhozes*..will now be in a position to introduce certain measures hitherto found only on state farms, including a guaranteed minimum wage. **1968** C. A. Doxiadis *Between Dystopia & Utopia* 46 The Kolkhozes in Russia..are the results of utopian theories. **1972** *Guardian* 4 Aug. 4/4 A kolkhoz, or collective farm, is a symbol of the crude rustic for city dwellers.

Hence **ko·lkhoznik** (pl. **-niki**), a member of a *kolkhoz*.

1955 H. Hodgkinson *Doubletalk* 27 Each worker, or *kolkhoznik*, has to give between 100 and 150 work days on the common land. **1964** *Economist* 18 July 255/1 With their dependants the *kolkhozniki* amounted to about 56 million persons.

kolladie, var. *korari.

kollergang (kǫ·ləɪgæŋ). [G., = crushing action.] A crushing machine used in milling paper-pulp.

1890 A. Watt *Art of Paper-Making* 82 For the purpose of crushing the knots of the straw, and other hard particles ..a machine termed the 'kollergang' or 'edge-runner' is sometimes employed. **1907** G. Clapperton *Pract. Paper-Making* (ed. 2) iv. 38 The ability of the Scandinavian makers to allow a considerable time for milling the pulp in kollergangs or beaters. **1963** [see *edge-runner* s.v. *edge *sb.* 12 b].

kolm (kǫlm). *Petrogr.* [Sw.] (See quot. 1954.)

1930 *Jrnl. Amer. Chem. Soc.* LII. 4848 The ash of the kolm constitutes from 20 to 40% of the original, and contains a few hundredths of a per cent. of lead. **1954** S. I. Tomkeieff *Coals & Bitumens* 61/1 *Kolm*, variety of cannel coal occurring locally as lenticles in Swedish alum shales, and containing 30% of ash rich in rare metals, including uranium and radium. **1969** M. G. Rutten *Geol. W. Europe* iii. 44 Within these black shales lenses may occur of a sort of coal, the 'kolm'. Both shales and kolm have in recent times acquired importance for their uranium content.

Kolmer (kǫ·lməɪ). *Med.* The name of John *Kolmer* (1886–1962), U.S. pathologist, used *attrib.* and *absol.* to denote a modification proposed by him of the Wassermann complement fixation test for syphilis using beef heart cardiolipin as the antigen. Also **Kolmer–Wassermann.**

1921 *Med. Clinics N. Amer.* V. 670 We have studied the results of the Kolmer method of performing the Wassermann test in over 2000 tests. **1925** *Jrnl. Laboratory & Clin. Med.* X. 315 (*heading*) Red corpuscle suspension for the Kolmer–Wassermann reaction. **1932** Schamberg & Wright *Treatm. Syphilis* xxxiii. 591 The Kolmer–Wassermann test is not usually positive until the primary lesion has been present for eight days. **1971** S. M. Brooks *V.D. Story* iv. 60 A positive Kolmer or vdrl..practically always indicates nervous system involvement. **1971** *Amer. Jrnl. Clin. Path.* LV. 735 The automated Kolmer test appeared less satisfactory than the manual Kolmer test.

Kol Nidre (kǫl ni·dre). Also **Kol Nidry.** [Aramaic *kol nidhrē*, all the vows.] A mournful Aramaic prayer, opening with the words *Kol nidhrē*, sung by Jews at the beginning of the service on the eve of Yom Kippur: it asks for annulment of vows made in the previous year and for forgiveness of sins. Also, the service itself or the melody to which the prayer is sung.

1881 M. Keizer in I. L. Mombach *Sacred Mus. Compositions* p. viii, (*heading*) New Year & Atonement... Ki Vayoum Hazeh..Kol Nidry..Mechalkyl. **1891** M. Friedländer *Jewish Relig.* ii. 408 Transgressors..desirous to

pray in the Synagogue on the Day of Atonement, were admitted... Such was the original object of *Kol-nidre.* **1893** I. ZANGWILL *Ghetto Tragedies* 47 It was *Kol Nidré* night, the commencement of..the Day of Atonement. **1908** *Daily Chron.* 5 Oct. 5/2 All this time services are held wherever a few of the children of the Ghetto are gathered together. The first, held at 6 o'clock on Sunday evening, at the opening of the fast, is called 'Kol-Nidré'. **1922** JOYCE *Ulysses* 470 A..band is heard..playing the Kol Nidre. **1932** C. ROTH *Hist. Marranos* 379 The famous ceremony of the Annulment of Vows on the eve of the Day of Atonement, the Kol Nidre service. **1966** H. KEMELMAN *Saturday the Rabbi went Hungry* (1967) i. 7 The chanting of Kol Nidre ushered in the Holy Day. **1973** *Synagogue Light* Sept. 12/1 On Tish B'Av..we take off our shoes. On Yom Kippur also, commencing before Kol Nidre.

kolo (kōu·lo). [Serbo-Croatian, = wheel.] A Yugoslav dance performed in a circle.

1911 E. L. URLIN *Dancing Anc. & Mod.* iii. 45 The Kollo Dance (or Kolo) is seen depicted on very ancient tombs of the Bogomiles in Dalmatia, archaic in type; it must therefore have been of ancient religious origin. **1941** 'R. WEST' *Black Lamb* I. 398 They had our men and women brought in to dance the kolo to them. **1952** L. & D. JANKOVIĆ *Dances Yugoslavia* 21 The kolo usually has many phases and very often works up from a gentle swaying motion to more animated movement, which dies down to a moderate level according to the directions of the musician and the leader. **1963** *Daily Mail* 24 Aug. 2/2 A frolicking Mr. Kruschev... With his holiday host, President Tito, he joined the girls in the kolo, a popular dance performed in a circle to the accompaniment of singing. **1969** *Daily Tel.* 5 Nov. 13/6 The dancers launched themselves on an old Bosnian dance, a silent kolo from Glamotch.

kolong, var. *KULANG.

kolovratite (kǫlǒvrā·təit). *Min.* [ad. Russ. *kolovratit* (V. I. Vernadsky 1922, in *Compt. Rend. de l'Acad. d. Sci. de Russie* A. 37), f. the name of L. S. *Kolovrat*-Chervinsky (1884–1921), Russian radiochemist: see -ITE[1].] A greenish-yellow amorphous or finely crystalline mineral that is probably a hydrous vanadate of nickel and zinc.

1925 *Mineral. Mag.* XX. 290 A new mineral, named kolovratite by V. I. Vernadsky, which..appears to be widely distributed in Fergana... The mineral is a vanadate of nickel. **1927** *Mineral. Abstr.* III. 234 Kolovratite.. from Kara-Chagyr occurs as a fine powder disseminated in carbonaceous quartz-schist. **1962** *Canad. Mineralogist* VII. 314 Our evidence suggests, however, that kolovratite is a hydrous zinc-nickel vanadate, or possibly a silico-vanadate, rather than a nickel vanadate as inferred in the original description.

komatik (kǫ·mătik). Also **kamotik, kamootik**, etc. [Eskimo.] A dog-sledge used by the people of Labrador. Also as *v. intr.*, to travel on a komatik.

1824 W. E. PARRY *Jrnl. Second Voy.* 567/1 *Sledge, a,* ka-mōō-tik. **1853** *Trans. Lit. & Hist. Soc. Quebec* IV. 337 They..are so hardy that six or eight of them tackled to a heavily laden sledge or 'commettek' will travel as much as twenty leagues in a day. **1905** N. DUNCAN *Dr. Grenfell's Parish* xi. 133 The sick and starving are sought out by dog-team and komatik. **1919** W. T. GRENFELL *Labrador Doctor* (1920) xi. 199 Sails can sometimes be used with advantage on the komatik as an adjunct. **1921** *Beaver* Jan. 16/1 We had the ordinary length of sled or 'komatik', which is about twelve feet long and weighs about a hundred pounds. We carried a load of about six hundred pounds, which..is considered light. **1934** G. M. SUTTON *Eskimo Year* xxxvi. 233 Jack and I decided we would *komatik* to the head of the bay to set traps and locate some fox-dens. **1936** *Discovery* Sept. 274/2 An Eskimo *komatik* (sledge) complete with driver and several dogs neatly harnessed. **1940** R. FINNIE *Lure of North* 117 In the dead of winter, however, the native komatik reigns supreme, gliding easily where a basket sled would drag. **1965** *Globe & Mail* (Toronto) 6 Jan. 1/3 The dog sled, or komatik, has replaced the bicycle for northern Cubs. **1973** C. BONINGTON *Next Horizon* xvii. 235 The komatic or sledge... Now I was sitting on the back of a komatic, near the head of Cumberland Sound in Baffin Island.

kombaars (kǫ·mbaɹs). *S. Afr.* Also **kombers(e.** [Du. *kombaars* coverlet, rug.] A blanket, coverlet, or rug.

1812 W. J. BURCHELL *Jrnl.* 1 May in *Trav. S. Afr.* (1824) II. 175 This *kombaars,* or coverlet, is a genuine South-African manufacture, being nothing more than a Hottentot *karóss* of large dimensions. **1840** B. SHAW *Memorials S. Afr.* i. 28 His *kombaars* tied with leathern strings. **1850** R. G. CUMMING *Five Yrs. Hunter's Life S. Afr.* I. ix. 186 In the evening I took my pillow and 'komberse', or skin blanket, to the margin of a neighbouring vley. **1913** C. PETTMAN *Africanderisms* 274 *Komberse,* a rug, blanket; sometimes a kaross is so styled.

‖ **kombé** (kǫ·mbi). [Mang'anja.] The juice obtained from the seeds of *Strophanthus kombe,* a Central African climbing plant of the family Apocynaceæ, which is one of the sources of the drug strophanthin.

1859 J. KIRK *Zambesi Jrnl. & Lett.* (1965) I. 171, I take a walk in the neighbourhood, find the plant used to poison the arrows. It is an arborescent twiner, getting quite to the top of the trees. The juice of the fruit is used... They call it *Kombe.* **1888** *Buck's Handbk. Med. Sci.* VI. 663/1 Strophanthus (Kombé, Arrow Poison). **1934** G. E. TREASE et al. *Text-bk. Pharmacognosy* xx. 512 One of these [species of *Strophanthus*], known to the natives of the Shiré River as *kombi,* was noted by Livingstone in 1861... In 1885 Fraser isolated strophanthin and recommended the use of the seeds in medicine. **1952** *Ibid.* (ed. 6) xviii. 479 The glycosides of *kombé* contain cymarose. **1967** *Martindale's Extra Pharmacopoeia* (ed. 25) 541/2 Strophanthin-K (B.P.C. 1954). Strophanthin; Kombé Strophanthin.

kombu (kǫ·mbu). [Jap.] A brown seaweed, one of the local species of *Laminaria,* used as food, esp. as a base for stock.

1884 SATOW & HAWES *Handbk. for Travellers Cent. & N. Japan* (ed. 2) 519 *Kombu,* a broad, thick, and very long species of seaweed, most of which is exported to China. **1905** *Nat. Geogr. Mag.* May 218 Kombu is one of the staple foods of the country [*sc.* Japan], entering into the dietary of almost every family. **1949** *New Biol.* VII. 96 The various preparations of 'kombu' are said to have quite distinctive flavours. **1958** G. MIKES *East is East* 67 *Kombu* (a kind of seaweed) is not less delicious than boiled cabbage. **1969** G. W. PRESCOTT *Algae* x. 350 In Japan, laminarian food (from stipes) is called *kombu*; food from *Alaria* is called *sarumen.* Stipes of some of the larger brown algae are cut, washed in fresh water, boiled and seasoned with preserving fluids.

komfoor (kǫmfōə·ɹ). *S. Afr.* Also **komvoor, konfoor.** [Afrikaans, f. Picard form of OFr. *chaufoire* kettle for hot water.] A small brazier; a chafing-dish; a foot-stove.

1841 *Cape of Good Hope Almanac* (Advt.), Tools of all descriptions... Brushes, kettles and komfores. **1844** J. BACKHOUSE *Narr. Visit Mauritius & S. Afr.* v. 84 To preserve warmth, the Dutch women use an apparatus to set their feet upon, called a Komfoor. **1940** 'B. KNIGHT' *Walking the Whirlwind* vii. 144 She signalled to the slave near the door to hand round charcoal from the komfoor to relight some of the pipes. **1951** *Cape Times* 6 Sept. 16/1 Samovars are almost as common in Cape Town as komvoors and spittoons used to be in the salesrooms. **1965** A. GORDON-BROWN *S. Afr. Heritage* II. 21 Brass Coffee Pot under which is the original Konfoor to contain burning charcoal for keeping the coffee hot. **1972** A. A. TELFORD *Yesterday's Dress* 81 She sits drinking coffee with her bare feet upon a 'komfoor' which as its name implies was a wooden 'chaufette' containing a pan of charcoal, a comfortable footwarmer.

Komi (kōu·mi). [Native name (see quots. 1800 and 1888).] **a.** A people of northern central U.S.S.R.; a member of this people. **b.** The language of the Komi. Also *attrib.*

[**1800** W. TOOKE *Hist. Russia* I. i. 13 *Komanes.* They were neighbours of the Madshares or Ugres, and migrated in conjunction with them at the close of the eighth century to Pannonia. They dwelt upon the river Kuma, from which they also had their name. On the other side of the Terek is still a people named Kumuiks; perhaps remains of the old Kumanians. *Ibid.* 42 One part of these were called Kumani or Komani, from the river Kuma.] **1888** *Encycl. Brit.* XXIV. 283/1 The Zyrians..constitute the bulk of the population on the Ural slopes. They formerly inhabited the Kama and Vyatha basins, and call themselves Komi-yurt, or Komi-yas. **1911** *Ibid.* XXVI. 317/2 They [*sc.* the Syrenians] call themselves Komi. **1933** H. KOHN *Nationalism in Soviet Union* 62 These Finnish peoples, the Komi, the Mari, and the Mordvins, were steadily pushed back by the Russians into less fruitful areas with severe climates. **1942** K. W. DEUTSCH in J. A. Fishman *Readings Sociol. of Lang.* (1968) 600 Syryen (Komi). **1959** *Chambers's Encycl.* XIV. 121/1 (table) Komi. **1964** *Language* XL. 906 Komi is today represented by two literary languages, Komi(-Zyryan) and Komi-Permyak. *Ibid.* 98 The semantic functions of the Komi and Udmurt forms.

komita(d)ji, var. *COMITADJI.

‖ **Kommandatura** (kǫma:ndătūə·ră). Also **-antur, -atur.** [ad. G. *Kommandantur* commandant's headquarters, command post.] The centre of operation of a military government.

1937 BLUNDEN *Elegy* II. 31 We met the walls the Roman host Used for their *Kommandantur* post. **1949** *Ann. Reg. 1948* 238 The machinery of four-Power rule set up under the Potsdam Agreement, the Allied Control Council and the Berlin *Kommandatura,* had become more and more an instrument for political propaganda. **1957** H. ROOSENBERG *Walls came Tumbling Down* iii. 65 We saw several people lugging shot-guns and rifles to the new *Kommandatura.* **1958** P. KEMP *No Colours or Crest* x. 220 The miserable Eles..had been a frequent visitor to the German *Kommandatur* in Peć. **1969** *Listener* 9 Jan. 35/3 The Soviet Kommandatura in the centre of Prague. **1975** *New Yorker* 22 Sept. 78/2 The site of the Russian Kommandatura in Leipzig had been shown on the map of the city.

‖ **Kommers** (komẹ̄·rs). Also **commerce, -se, -s.** [G., ad. Fr. *commerce,* L. *commercium* COMMERCE *sb.*] = COMMERS.

1839 LONGFELLOW *Hyperion* I. II. iv. 120 Come in; come in. You shall see some sport. A Fox-Commerce is on foot, and a regular Beer-Scandal. **1841** W. HOWITT *Student-Life Germany* xvi. 315 For these Commerses, the rule is to drink beer, and this is called a Commers in beer. **1908** C. SIDGWICK *Home Life Germany* vi. 56 A *Kommers* is a students' festival in which the professors and other senior members of a university take part. **1960** *Times* 17 Sept. 9/7 One may be fortunate enough to be invited to a *Kommers,* a meeting in which the students settle round tables for the evening, quaffing beer..and singing.

Komodo (komōu·do). The name of an Indonesian island, used *attrib.* in **Komodo dragon, monitor** to designate a large monitor lizard, *Varanus komodoensis,* native to this island and neighbouring ones.

1927 *Daily Express* 15 June 15 The curator of the reptiles..introduced me to her latest novelty, a Komodo dragon, seven feet long and as ugly as a bad dream. **1927** *Proc. Zool. Soc.* 256 Lord Rothschild exhibited a mounted specimen of *Varanus komodensis* [*sic*], the so-called 'Dragon' of Komodo Island... The interesting feature of the Komodo Monitor, apart from its bulk, lies in its relationship. **1928** *Ibid.* 1017 (*title*) On a living Komodo Dragon. **1941** J. S. HUXLEY *Uniqueness of Man* viii. 184 The gorilla, the orang-utang, the Komodo dragon, and other creatures are on the margin of this category [of creatures kept from extinction only by rigorous protection]. **1969** A. BELLAIRS *Life of Reptiles* II. xi. 468 The Komodo dragon (*Varanus komodoensis*) has been generally regarded as the largest existing lizard and reaches a length of at least 3 metres (10 ft.) and a weight of 163 kg. (360 lb.). It is found only on the small island of Komodo to the east of Java and on one or two neighbouring islands. **1973** *Nature* 7 Sept. 52/1 There is evidence that the Komodo monitor can take prey as heavy as itself.

kompas, var. *KEMPAS.

Komsomol (kǫ·msǒmǫl). Also **Comsomol.** [Russ. *komsomól,* short f. *Kommunistícheskiĭ Soyúz Molodëzhi* Communist Union of Youth.] An organization of Communist youth in Russia; a member of this organization. Also *attrib.*

1934 T. S. ELIOT *Rock* i. 39 That's what they do in Russia. Ever 'ear o' the Comsomol? We'll turn all the churches into workers' clubs. **1944** G. B. SHAW *Everybody's Pol. What's What?* x. 82 Comsomols, Ballillas, Leagues of Youth and cognate bodies and movements which are sprouting everywhere. **1948** J. TOWSTER *Political Power in U.S.S.R.* 137 The closest auxiliary of the Party is the Komsomol or Young Communist League. **1949** *Ann. Reg. 1948* 211 Communists and Komsomols had helped to build mosques. **1958** *Listener* 5 June 934/1 Why should Chekhov's characters proclaim prophetic and optimistic truths about a better future which sounds [*sic*] as if they were gleaned from a Komsomol textbook? **1959** *Ibid.* 3 Dec. 964/2 A Komsomol branch secretary. **1973** *Nat. Geographic* May 606/2 The Komsomol (Communist youth organization) in her district had advertised openings at Togliatti stating that a modern low-rent apartment was part of the employment contract.

komvoor, var. *KOMFOOR.

kona (kōu·nă). [Hawaiian; orig. the name of the leeward areas of the Hawaiian Islands.] A stormy south-west wind in the Hawaiian Islands.

1864 R. ANDERSON *Hawaiian Islands* i. 28 Occasionally a prolonged gale comes from the south, called a Souther, or 'Kona'. **1866** 'MARK TWAIN' *Lett. from Hawaii* (1967) 23 In the stormy season—in the season of the terrible kona. **1892** STEVENSON & OSBOURNE *Wrecker* 9 It was blowing a kona, hard. **1934** M. D. FREAR *Lowell & Abigail* p. xiv, But by night..how the Kona wind moaned and drove the rain up from the sea. **1967** J. SEVERSON *Great Surfing* Gloss., *Kona wind,* a south wind in the Hawaiian Islands, generally onshore at most of the southern exposure beaches. Occasionally offshore or glassy on the north shore.

konak (konā·k). [ad. Turk. *qonaq* halting-place, inn.] A large house, palace, or official residence, in Turkey, or in the (former) Ottoman Empire.

[**1675** J. COVEL *Diary* (1893) 175 We..had a man who alwayes went before to every *Conáck,* or stage, and brought in muttons, beafes, veales, and the like.] **1852** C. T. NEWTON *Let.* 30 Sept. in *Trav. & Discov. Levant* (1865) I. vii. 87 We asked for the konak, or official residence of the Aga. **1878** S. L. POOLE *People of Turkey* I. ix. 221 When in the interior I had the opportunity of visiting some Konaks worthy of note. **1897** E. A. BARTLETT *Battlefields Thessaly* iv. 88 The Konak was deserted by all except the Mushir's valet. **1908** tr. *P. Draganof's Macedonia & Reforms* ii. 23 The latter drove them from the konak. **1926** *Spectator* 17 July 88/2 The delicate 'konak' or palace of Prince Milosh Obrenovitch. **1957** L. DURRELL *Bitter Lemons* 163 There is also a wretched Konak and prison.

‖ **konaki** (kǫ·naki). *N.Z.* Also **koneka.** [Corruption of Maori *kōneke* sledge.] A horse-drawn wooden sledge.

1914 M. HALL *Woman in Antipodes* I. 86, I also got some insight into up-country life..noting..the primitive Maori 'koneka' or sledge. **1953** J. W. BRIMBLECOMBE in J. Reid *Kiwi Laughs* (1961) 179 He had to go and haul lime tomorrow with the konaki. **1959** M. SHADBOLT *New Zealanders* 15 The trunks were lashed to a konaki, which Mother discovered was the Maori word for a horse-drawn wooden sled. **1961** B. CRUMP *Hang on Minute* 109 Uncle Wally lifted the [cream-]can..out to the old konaki.

Kond, Kondh, varr. *KHOND.

‖ **konditorei** (kǫ:ndĭtǒrəi·). Pl. **konditorei, konditoreien.** [Ger., f. *konditor* confectioner.] Confectionery; a confectioner's shop, a shop where pastries are sold.

1935 J. BUCHAN *House of Four Winds* iii. 69 He was in the habit of sampling..whatever Unnutz produced in the way of café and konditorei. **1963** N. FREELING *Because of Cats* ii. 35 When she went to a concert it would be to satisfy a need, like women who went to konditoreien to stuff themselves with wonderful cream cakes. **1973** *Times* 30 May (Austria Suppl.) p. iv/6 *Konditorei* abound, and you will find it hard to resist those delectable Viennese pastries bulging with cream.

‖ **konfyt** (kǫnfēi·t). *S. Afr.* Also † **comfaat, conf(e)yt.** [Afrikaans, = Du. *konfijt* COMFIT *sb.*] Fruit preserved in sugar; preserve.
1862 LADY DUFF-GORDON *Let.* 15 Apr. (1927) 144, I have bought some Cape 'confeyt'; apricots, salted and then sugared, called 'mebos'—delicious! **1871** *Cape Monthly Mag.* II. 25 Coffee and cakes, tea and '*comfäät*'. **1929** *Daily Tel.* 15 Jan. 9/4 Now that Cape fruits are being sent over to this country in ever-increasing quantities, the word 'konfyt' has come into our vocabulary. 'Konfyts' are delicious preserves made from these exotic fruits. **1939** S. CLOETE *Watch for Dawn* 39 He had konfyt of melon and little oranges. **1947** L. G. GREEN *Tavern of Seas* ix. 87 Malay families sometimes sell these fine eighteenth century saucepans, kettles and konfyt pots. **1950** *Cape Argus* 8 May 4/4 She became particularly famous for her konfyts and jams. **1955** L. G. GREEN *Karoo* xi. 140 White housewives made *konfyt* of it. **1974** D. ROOKE *Margaretha de la Porte* 229 'Konfyt and meerbos, what a typical Dutch spread,' Fanny commented with a patronizing smile; but she was quick enough to help herself to the glazed watermelon and sugary apricots.

kongkang: see *KUKANG.

kongoni (kǫŋgōu·ni). [Swahili.] An alternative name for Coke's hartebeest, *Alcelaphus buselaphus cokei*, found in the plains of East Africa.
[**1889** J. C. WILLOUGHBY *E. Afr. & its Big Game* 54 These hartebeest (*swahili Kongoni*) are of the species known as *Cokii*, and..are very plentiful here. **1905** H. A. BRYDEN in H. G. Hutchinson *Big Game Shooting* II. vi. 114 Coke's hartebeest (*Bubalis cokei*) (*Kongoni* of the Swahilis) is the commonest..of this group in East Africa.] **1908** W. S. CHURCHILL *My Afr. Journey* i. 9 Herds of red kongoni—the hartebeeste of South Africa. **1921** *Outward Bound* June 40 Within the noonday shade Of mushroom-headed thorn trees, the great 'Kongoni' wade. **1942** *E. Afr. Ann. 1941–2* 127/2 Zebra, kongoni, steinbuck, Thomson's gazelle, and ostrich are numerous on the plains. **1971** *Nature* 24 Dec. 483/2 Eland..and boran ..cattle were equal in water demands, while kongoni (*Alcelaphus buselaphus*) and wildebeest..are comparable with sheep.

‖ **kongsi** (kǫ·ŋsi). [ad. Chin. *kung-ssu* (as pronounced in Hokkien) company, corporation.] In Malaysia, an association or partnership, esp. an association of Chinese people.
1839 T. J. NEWBOLD *Pol. & Statistical Acct. Straits of Malacca* I. i. 14 Their interior affairs..are arranged by the heads of their respective kongsis or fraternities. **1900** W. W. SKEAT *Malay Magic* v. 255 The men of a rival *kongsi* had brought limes. **1964** D. K. BASSETT in Wang Gungwu *Malaysia* II. vii. 122 A *kongsi* is an association of Chinese based on regional, occupational or dialect ties. **1966** D. FORBES *Heart of Malaya* x. 116 Three or four hundred jammed together in a junk chartered by a merchant combine, called a *kongsi*. **1969** J. M. GULLICK *Malaysia* ii. 48 In its primary sense 'kongsi' denotes a Chinese association or secret society. **1972** *Straits Times* (Malaysian ed.) 23 Nov. 11/3 The tin mine kongsi house in which I found her was occupied by the accused's brother.

koniak, koniaku (kǫ·nyak, kǫnya·ku). Also **konjak, konnyaku.** [ad. Jap. *ko-n-nya-ku, konya-ku.*] A local name for *Amorphophallus rivieri*, a large herb of the family Araceæ, cultivated in Japan for the flour obtained from its roots.
1884 tr. *A. de Candolle's Orig. Cultivated Plants* II. i. 76 The konjak is a tuberous plant of the family Araceæ, extensively cultivated by the Japanese. **1954** J. M. MORRIS *Wise Bamboo* iv. 54 Anything edible can be put into *sukiyaki*. That night we had leeks, *tofu* (beancurd), *konnyaku* (a gelatine-like vegetable which I could not identify), onions and bamboo sprouts. **1965** *This is Japan 1966* 80/3 All the balloons were fashioned of Japanese rice paper and *konnyaku* (devil's-tongue root) which is a chief ingredient in the popular Japanese dish *sukiyaki*. **1970** J. KIRKUP *Japan behind Fan* 4 Lumps of *tofu* (white beancurd) and *konyaku* (devil's tongue jelly). **1972** Y. LOVELOCK *Vegetable Bk.* II. 269 The related giant arum or devil's tongue..known to the Japanese as *koniaku*, is often cultivated for food... Their [*sc.* the tubers'] taste and smell is [*sic*] strong and disagreeable, but this is lost after they have been soaked in whitewash (i.e. milk of lime), crushed and cooked. The resulting flour is used for making a kind of pasta and other dishes.

konimeter (kǒni·mĭtəɹ). [f. Gr. κόνις dust: see -METER.] A kind of impinger in which a known volume of air is directed on to a slide coated with a substance to which any dust particles will adhere.
1918 *Jrnl. Chem., Metall. & Mining Soc. S. Afr.* XVIII. 200/1 We are indebted to the perseverance and ingenuity of Mr. R. N. Kotzé, the Union Government Mining Engineer, for a simple solution by means of an instrument he has devised and called a Konimeter. **1937** DRINKER & HATCH *Industr. Dust* vi. 99 The dust-collecting efficiency of the konimeter is admittedly low and is selective with respect to size. **1958** *Ann. Rep. Chief Inspector of Factories on Industr. Health 1957* 17 in *Parl. Papers 1958–9* (Cmnd. 558) XIII. 183 A team..travels to particular factories and takes samples, using..a Kotzé konimeter... Dust samples..are analysed..and the particle size and particle counts recorded. **1965** *Guide to Prevention & Suppression of Dust in Mining* (Internat. Labour Office) xvi. 306 Side-by-side sampling with a thermal precipitator and a konimeter was performed on the dust created by a series of different underground operations.

konini (kōu·nini). *N.Z.* [Maori.] A native shrub or small tree, *Fuchsia excorticata*, or its berries.
1867 J. D. HOOKER *Handbk. N.Z. Flora* II. 765/2 Konine. *Fuchsia excorticata.* **1869** T. H. POTTS in *Trans. N.Z. Inst.* II. 48 Beneath, Bell-birds..seek the konini, clinging to its brittle sprays. **1889** T. KIRK *Forest Flora N.Z.* 53 The settlers sometimes term it Kotukutuku or Konini, but more generally fuchsia. **1949** P. BUCK *Coming of Maori* (1950) II. i. 88 The berries of the..konini..are transient and were not important as food. **1960** B. CRUMP *Good Keen Man* 12 When a pigeon shirred up out of a konini I almost dropped my rifle. **1968** M. JOHNSON *N.Z. Flowering Plants* 57 One seldom sees now a rich display of the purple black berries, konini, that delicacy of the Maori palate of former times.

koniscope (kǫ·niskōup). [f. Gr. κόνις dust + -SCOPE.] An instrument for estimating the concentration of dust in the air by observing the depth of colour in a sample of the air when it is expanded into a tube with glass ends and containing moist paper to saturate it with water vapour.
1892 J. AITKEN in *Proc. R. Soc.* LI. 435 This new instrument we intend to call a Koniscope. In its present form this instrument consists of an air-pump and a metal tube with glass ends. **1905** *Westm. Gaz.* 26 Aug. 13/1 Dr. Aitken has invented a very simple instrument for this purpose, which he calls the koniscope, or dust detective. **1925** SHAW & OWENS *Smoke Probl. Gt. Cities* viii. 145 Condensation of water on the dust particles is utilised in Aitken's..koniscope; a fog is produced and compared with a standard.

konjak, var. *KONIAK, KONIAKU.

konk, var. CONK, the nose.
1846 *United Services Mag.* May 13 Indignant at the liberty thus taken with his konk.

konk, var. *CONK *v.*[2]
1917 E. MIDDLETON *Glorious Exploits of Air* 20 The latter [*sc.* the engine] 'konked'. Down went the aeroplane. **1919** 'RAFBIRD' *Zooms & Spins* 19 I'm flapping from Puddlemarsh..—came down there with a konking engine. **1919** *Air Pie* 93 What would you do if your engine 'konked' out at 20,000 feet? **1925** FRASER & GIBBONS *Soldier & Sailor Words* 138 *Konked* (*konked out*), an Air Force term used of an aeroplane engine stopped working, failed, or broken down. Also a general expression, meaning 'knocked out', dead. **1942** C. S. LEWIS *Broadcast Talks* II. iii. 49 Some fatal flaw always brings the selfish and cruel people to the top and it all slides back in misery and ruin. In fact, the machine konks. It seems to start up all right and runs a few yards, and then it breaks down.

Konkani (kǫ·ŋkăni). [Marathi *Koṅkaṇī*, f. *Koṅkaṇ* Konkan, a coastal region of western India.] **a.** A native or inhabitant of the Konkan. **b.** The Indic language of the Konkani. Also *attrib.* or as *adj.*
1873 *Cycl. India* (ed. 2) III. s.v. *Konkan*, The mixed Konkani tongue, appears to be only Marathi with a large infusion of Tulu and Canarese words... Mr. H. Mogling however mentions that the Konkani-speaking brahmins of Mangalore, consider it quite distinct from, though cognate with, Marathi. **1885** G. C. WHITWORTH *Anglo-Indian Dict.* 169/2 The southern Konkanis..are much more in the habit of seeking their living abroad than other natives. **1905** G. A. GRIERSON *Ling. Survey India* VII. 1 The dialectic differences within the Marāṭhī area are comparatively small, and there is only one real dialect, *viz.*, Kōṅkaṇī. *Ibid.* 17 A Kōṅkaṇī translation of the Bible appeared at Serampore in 1819. **1948** D. DIRINGER *Alphabet* 372 Konkani, one of the most important Marathi forms of speech. **1959** *Chambers's Encycl.* VIII. 354/2 There is a western group composed of Kashmiri, Lahnda.., Sindhi.., Rajasthani,..and Konkani. **1969** *Eve's Weekly* (Bombay) 20 Dec. 55/2 Boy-carollers.. singing Christmas carols in Konkani. **1971** *Hindustan Times Weekly Rev.* (New Delhi) 4 Apr. p. iv/5 Konkani has no script, no grammar, no rules.

Konno(h), varr. *KONO[2].

konnyaku, var. *KONIAK, KONIAKU.

kono[1] (kōu·no). Also **ko-no, Ko-No.** [Korean.] A Korean board game.
1895 S. CULIN *Korean Games* 100 The games played on diagrams, like our game of Merrells, receive the name of *Ko-no* in Korea, a term my informant could not further define. *Ibid.* 101 In all games of *Kono*, as in Pa-tok, the black men move first. **1960** R. C. BELL *Board & Table Games* I. iii. 98 Five Field Kono... The object of the game is to move the pieces across to the other side of the board to occupy the places vacated by the opponent, and the first player to do so wins the game. **1970** *Nature* 19 Sept. 1206/1 Ko-No (Fig. 1) is probably the simplest fully determined board game known.

Kono[2] (kōu·no). Also **Konno(h).** [Native name.] **a.** A Mandingo-speaking people of Sierra Leone; a member of this people. **b.** The language of the Kono people, having affinities with Vai. Also *attrib.* or as *adj.*
1909 R. H. K. WILLANS in *Jrnl. R. Afr. Soc.* XXX. 130 The history of the Konnoh people is of great interest... The Konnohs at the present day have degenerated into an almost insignificant tribe. *Ibid.* 145 *Soa*..in Mendi and Konnoh means three. **1916** N. W. THOMAS *Specimens Lang. Sierra Leone* Introd., Kono, Susu and Kisi were recorded from informants with a very moderate knowledge of English. **1925** T. N. GODDARD *Handbk. Sierra Leone* 55 The *Konnos* and *Korankos* are closely connected with the Mandingos. **1925** H. C. LUKE *Bibliogr. Sierra Leone* (ed. 2) 148 Kono Hymns. **1926** F. W. BUTT-THOMPSON *Sierra Leone* vi. 44 The present border of the Kono lands. **1951** K. L. LITTLE *Mende of Sierra Leone* iii. 70 The Kono men, who are mostly labourers in the town, wear European shorts and shirt outside the trousers. *Ibid.* vii. 147 The Mende tend to look down on certain peoples, such as the Kono. **1964** C. FYFE *Sierra Leone Inheritance* 250 During the march to Weeima we were attacked on all sides by the Konnos and several of our people were wounded.

konze (kǫ·nzi). Also **konzi, nkonze.** [Swahili.] A local name for Lichtenstein's hartebeest, *Alcelaphus lichtensteini*, an antelope found in the plains of central and southern Africa.
1877 F. C. SELOUS *Jrnl.* 20 Dec. in *Hunter's Wanderings Afr.* (1881) 303 In the afternoon I went out with my rifle, and shot a konze antelope... The black mark down the front of the face of the hartebeest is..wanting in the konze. **1908** R. LYDEKKER *Game Animals Afr.* 111 The konzi, or Lichtenstein's hartebeest. **1964** E. P. WALKER et al. *Mammals of World* II. 1446/1 Hartebeests; Ngondo, Nkonze, Kondikondi, Sig (native names).

kooftah, var. *KOFTA.

kook (kūk). *slang.* [prob. abbrev. of *CUCKOO *a.* or CUCKOO *sb.* 3.] **1.** A cranky, crazy, or eccentric person. Freq. *attrib.* or as *adj.*
1960 *Daily Mail* 22 Aug. 4/5 A kook, Daddy-O, is a screwball who is 'gone' farther than most. **1963** *Time* 4 Oct. 37 'Don't think that just because he talked about those way-out rockets he's a kook,' cautioned a fellow officer. **1964** *Economist* 28 Nov. 969/2 Thousands of 'beatniks, kooks and crackpots'. **1965** J. POTTS *Only Good Secretary* (1966) ii. 26 Max is kind of a kook. He paints these kooky pictures. **1968** MRS. L. B. JOHNSON *White House Diary* 18 Jan. (1970) 623 Mrs. Hughes..said ..'I think that anybody who takes pot because there is a war on is a kook.' **1968** *N.Y. Times* 26 Mar. 32 'Has it ever occurred to you that the kook market has grown?' said a United States auto executive when asked to explain the growing sales of foreign cars. **1970** E. R. JOHNSON *God Keepers* (1971) xv. 166 It's a kook clique all right. It's ..a happy place. That's kooks to you cops. **1971** *Black World* June 67/1 These marchers were all probably a bunch of kooks like Harry always said. **1973** *Publishers Weekly* 25 June 68/1 A bona fide kook who is never quite able to get in gear till he finally dies paddling his canoe across the Atlantic.
2. orig. *U.S.* A novice, or one who is inexpert, in surf-riding. Also *attrib.*
1961 in *Amer. Speech* (1962) XXXVII. 150. **1966** *Surfer* VII. 9 This letter is to protest about dumb kook girls out in the water. *Ibid.* 17 All most of [these surfers] are is a bunch of loud-mouthed kooks who come down here and clutter up the beach. *Ibid.* 39 Malibu..was also the birthplace of the 'kook box', that monstrosity known as the poor man's paddle board. **1971** *Studies in English* (Univ. of Cape Town) II. 25 The reason for this reticence is that surfers wish to differentiate themselves from kooks, who surf badly.

kooka (ku·kă). *Austral. slang.* = KOOKABURRA.
1933 *Bulletin* (Sydney) 13 Sept. 21/4 An article on upsetting the balance of nature in which one Shepstone quotes the sad case of the kooka. **1949** *Geogr. Mag.* Feb. 374/1 Hence such names for the Kookaburra as.. *breakfast bird, kooka* and *ha ha pigeon*. **1964** P. CARLON *Price of Orphan* iv. 44 He was going to be grabbed like a kooka sighting a snake.

kookaburra. Substitute for def.: A large, arboreal, brown kingfisher, *Dacelo novæguineæ*, distinguished by its peculiar laughing cry; formerly called the GOBURRA and also called the laughing jackass. (Later examples.)
1906 *Westm. Gaz.* 13 Oct. 16/3 Just before the hour of sunrise the echoes of the Australian bush are awakened by the extraordinary cackling laughter of the great brown kingfisher, or kookaburra, as the aboriginals call it. **1934** *Bulletin* (Sydney) 3 Jan. 31/3 An assembly of kookaburras in the trees close at hand burst into a chorus of derisive laughter. **1936** F. CLUNE *Roaming round Darling* ii. 13 A kookaburra laughed sardonically as we passed the Assembly Hall. **1959** *Guardian* 28 Nov. 5/2 The chortled comments of the kookaburra bird. **1966** G. DURRELL *Two in Bush* iv. 132 The first of these were three fat young Kookaburras, or Laughing Jackasses as these giant kingfishers are called in Australia.

kook-a-vic, var. *KOKKEWIET.

kooky (kū·ki), *a. slang.* Also **kookie.** [f. *KOOK + -Y[1].] Cranky, crazy, eccentric.
1959 *Motion Pictures* Aug. 32/1 Get set for some far-out talk on teen-age romance by the kookiest cat in town—Edd Byrnes. **1961** *Spectator* 15 Sept. 360 I've got this kooky Aunt who reads novels. **1961** *John o' London's* 30 Nov. 615/4 The dialogue is conscientiously kookie. **1962** *Sunday Express* 21 Jan. 17/1 A Hollywood comedienne noted for her 'kookie' performances. **1963** E. L. WALLANT *Tenants of Moonbloom* (1964) iv. 48, I feel like dropping the Muse and this kooky life and marrying a nice tired businessman. **1965** [see *KOOK 1]. **1971** *Daily Tel.* 21 Aug. 16/1 A 'kooky' young American woman: enthusiastic, energetic, enterprising and 'a bit nuts'. **1973** *Nation Rev.* (Melbourne) 31 Aug. 1452/3 (Advt.), 'No Sex Please, We're British!' The funniest, kookiest night of your life.

So **koo·kily** *adv.*, in a kooky manner; **koo·kiness**, the state of being kooky.

1962 *Sunday Express* 21 Jan. 17/3 Kookiness doesn't go with a kimono. **1968** *Punch* 19 June 899/1 This study of a kooky girl is also..kookily narrated. **1970** *Sudbury* (Ontario) *Daily Star* 26 Feb. 18/4 There's nothing you can do, so accept your mother's kookiness gracefully. Her antics in no way diminish you in the eyes of your friends. **1974** *Observer* 21 Apr. 37/1 'Isadora' kookily takes off on a Freudian odyssey round Europe.

koolack, obs. var. *KULAK.

Kooleen, var. *KULIN.

kooliman, var. *COOLAMON.

koolookamba (kūlūkæ·mbă). Also **kulu-kamba** and shortened form **kulu.** [Native name in Gabon.] A West African variety of the chimpanzee, *Pan troglodytes.*

1860 P. B. Du Chaillu in *Proc. Boston Soc. Nat. Hist.* VII. 360 The cry of the Kooloo-Kamba is very different from that of the *Troglodytes calvus* and chimpanzee. **1896** R. L. Garner *Gorillas & Chimpanzees* 176 The kulu-kamba is..by far the finest representative of his genus. *Ibid.*, A young female kulu. **1929** R. M. & A. W. Yerkes *Great Apes* xxiv. 302 This observer [*sc.* Du Chaillu] means to imply that the three types of chimpanzee called by him Kooloo-Kamba, *Troglodytes calvus*, and chimpanzee, have distinctive calls or cries.

koompass, var. *KEMPAS.

Koonbee, var. *KUNBI.

Kooranko, var. *KORANKO.

koorn kriek, var. *KORINGKRIEK.

kootchar (kū·tʃaɹ). *Austral.* Also **koochee.** [Aboriginal name.] A small, stingless bee, *Trigona australis.*

1884 H. J. Hockings in *Trans. Entomol. Soc. London* 149 The second species [of stingless bee] ('Kootchar') is also black in colour but has a fine yellow streak across the upper part of the thorax. *Ibid.* 154 'Kootchar' are only to be found where a sandy soil is present. **1932** Koochee [see *KARBI]. **1961** *Amer. Mus. Novitates* No. 2026. 5 It was perhaps by error that Hockings attributes this species (under the aboriginal name of *kootchar*) to the coast.

Kootenai, var. *KUTENAI, KUTENAY.

kootie, var. *COOTIE *sb.*[2]

‖ **kop** (kǫp). [Afrikaans, f. Du. *kop* head, Cop *sb.*[2]] **1.** *S. Afr.* A hill. Cf. Kopje.

1835 C. L. Stretch *Jrnl.* 1 Apr., The troops..advanced in the direction of T'Slambies Kop, a high point visible from the heights near Graham's Town. **1878** H. A. Roche *On Trek in Transvaal* xiv. 303 One fine Kop or Kopje we passed upon which grazed an immense herd of fine oxen and heifers. **1900** A. H. Keane *Boer States* p. xvii, *Kop*, a crest, an eminence. **1901** L. James in J. Ralph *War's Brighter Side* 347 The three field batteries then came into action against a high tableland *kop* which formed the right of the held position. **1932** C. Fuller *Louis Trigardt's Trek* ii. 26 It is east by north of Taikundo Kop. **1939** tr. *E. N. Marais's My Friends the Baboons* i. 74 On one side the kloof was bordered by a krans, two to three hundred feet high, and on the other by a kop so steep that it could almost be called a krans too. **1971** *Rand Daily Mail* (Home Owner Suppl.) 26 June 5 Two of Johannesburg's most famous 'kops'—Langermann's Kop..and Pullinger Kop.

2. *Assoc. Football.* (With capital initial.) In full, but now less usu., **Spion Kop** (spəi·ǒn kǫp). [f. *Spion Kop*, Afrikaans name of a hill near Ladysmith in S. Afr., scene of a battle in the Boer War (1899–1902).] A high bank of terracing for standing spectators, orig. and especially the one at Anfield, home ground of Liverpool Football Club, but now of more general U.K. application (see quot. 1974[2]). Also, the spectators themselves, massed on such terracing, and *attrib.*

1926 *Liverpool Daily Post* 29 May 9/3 At last night's meeting of the Liverpool Football Club an important step was made known... The club had decided to..concentrate upon improving Spion Kop at the back of the Oakfield-road goal. **1960** B. Liddell *My Soccer Story* vi. 43 All they [*sc.* the spectators] wanted was the final whistle, so that they could come swarming over the ground from the Kop..and carry us off the field. *Ibid.* viii. 54 Kicking into our favourite goal, at the Spion Kop end. **1966** P. Moloney *Plea for Mersey* 56 There is in Liverpool a school of indigenous verse—known as the Kop choir, which produces, as it were spontaneously, verses to suit every situation that might occur within the game of football. **1966** *Liverpool Echo* (Football ed.) 30 Apr. 1/3 Liverpool went into the lead again in 69 minutes... This set the Kop off again and they gave us pretty well their whole repertoire [of songs and chants]. **1973** B. Shankly in *News of the World Football Ann. 1973–74* 4 For a time it seemed as if the Kop would never stop singing. **1973** *Liverpool Echo* (Football ed.) 22 Dec. 1/5 Liverpool immediately resumed the first half pattern of constant attack, this time towards the Kop goal. **1974** *Times* 18 Mar. 10/8 A match of electric energy..ended with the heaving Kop awash with red banners and scarves. **1974** *Sunday Times* 14 Apr. 26/2 What Anfield sings today, other Kops will be singing tomorrow.

So **Ko·pite, Ko·ppite,** a spectator who frequents the Kop terracing.

1960 B. Liddell *My Soccer Story* viii. 53 He got a tremendous ovation from the generous Koppites at the finish. **1966** P. Moloney *Plea for Mersey* 58 'You'll never walk alone,' the Koppites sing. **1974** *Liverpool Echo* (Football ed.) 6 Apr. 16/9 The president of the Cambridge University Boat Club who comes from Birkenhead is also a loyal Kopite. **1974** *Sunday Times* 14 Apr. 26/2 It makes Liverpool Kopites smile..to hear other fans singing their songs.

kopasetic, var. *COPACETIC *a.*

‖ **kopdoek** (kǫ·pduk). *S. Afr.* [Afrikaans, f. *kop* head, Cop *sb.*[2] + *DOEK cloth.] A head-cloth.

1911 *State* (Cape Town) Dec. 642/2 He deposited his shapeless hat on the floor, tapped his red kopdoek with a clawlike forefinger, and waited for an inspiration. **1957** *Cape Times Week-end Mag.* 6 Apr. 3/5 The Swazis barter the bones for food and clothing..; half a monkey means a new kopdoek. **1974** *S. Afr. Panorama* Feb. 10 In their bright blue-and-pink 'kopdoeks' (headscarves), they lend a colourful note to an already colourful scene.

‖ **kopi** (kōᵘ·pi). [Austral. Aboriginal word.] Gypsum- or selenite-bearing rock or mud.

1898 D. W. Carnegie *Spinifex & Sand* ii. ii. 42 We came on a small tract of 'kopi country' (powdered gypsum). *Ibid.* 43 This kopi is peculiar soil to walk over. *Ibid.* iii. iii. 91 A sort of powdery gypsum, called 'Kopi' by the natives. **1936** A. Russell *Gone Nomad* ix. 71 The drying bed of the lake was composed of a clinging kopi mud that would have enmeshed a duck. **1957** D. Niland *Call me when Cross turns Over* i. 8 The lie of all that barren land he knew, the shelves, the pits, the mullock dumps of kopi, every mound and every rise and fall. **1971** J. S. Gunn *Opal Terminol.* 24 *Kopi*, gypsum which sometimes carries good opal. In L. Ridge the kopi is different, being flattish crystals of silenite, rather than the gypsum clay of S. Aust. and Qld.

kopje: see *KOPPIE.

Koplik (kǫ·plik). *Med.* [The name of Henry *Koplik* (1858–1927), U.S. pædiatrician.] *Koplik('s) spot*: a small greyish-yellow spot, usually with a red halo, occurring on the buccal mucosa (or sometimes on the intestinal mucosa) in the early stages of measles.

1899 *Med. News* (N.Y.) LXXIV. 734/2 Koplik's spots were seen on the inner surface of the cheeks and under lip. **1939** Duval & Schattenberg *Textbk. Path.* ix. 284 Microscopically the macule or Koplik spot is a dense central collection of lymphocytes surrounded by tissue that is edematous and hyperemic. **1948** H. Pinkerton in W. A. D. Anderson *Path.* xv. 359 Koplik spots have been described in fatal cases in the intestinal mucosa. **1970** Hornstein & Gorlin in Gorlin & Goldman *Thoma's Oral Path.* (ed. 6) II. xvii. 756/2 Koplik's spots result from superficial necrosis of the mucosa and disappear after two to six days.

koppa (kǫ·pă). A letter (ϙ) standing between π and ρ in the early Greek alphabet (= Heb. *koph* ק, Lat. *q*). It was later displaced by κ, but survived as a numeral = 90.

1870 W. W. Goodwin *Elem. Greek Gram.* i. 2 Two obsolete letters—*Vau* or *Digamma*..equivalent to F or W, and *Koppa* (ϙ), equivalent to Q..are used as numerals. **1883** I. Taylor *Alphabet* II. 138 The letters *vau* and *koppa*, which were discarded in the Eastern alphabets, except as numerals, were retained in Latin. **1888** King & Cookson *Princ. Sounds & Inflexion Gr. & Latin* iii. 52 The Phoenician ϙ, *Koppa*, fell into disuse; it survived longest in the alphabet of Chalcis, whence it passed into the Roman alphabet as Q. **1933** C. D. Buck *Compar. Gram. Gr. & Latin* 73 The *wau*, *koppa*, and *san*, which disappeared from the alphabet, were maintained as numeral signs. **1970** *Oxf. Class. Dict.* (ed. 2) 48/1 K was used originally before *a*, C before *e* and *i*, ϙ (Greek Koppa) before *o* and *u.*

koppel (kǫ·pĕl). Also **capel, coppel.** [Yiddish.] A skull-cap worn by male Jews.

1892 I. Zangwill *Childr. Ghetto* I. 118 Old Hyams..had been sitting quiet with brow corrugated under his black velvet *Koppel.* **1972** *Jewish Chron.* 1 Sept. 22/1 (Advt.), For the high festivals: Machsorim—Tallisim—Kittles—Coppels. Unrivalled selection of New Year cards. **1973** *Ibid.* 9 Feb. 22/5 Some pious Jews..make a point of wearing a hat and not a 'capel' for prayer and some Chasidim wear both a hat and 'capel' underneath it.

koppie (kǫ·pi). Now the usual spelling of Kopje.

1848 R. Gray *Jrnl.* 14 Nov. (1849) 76 Large dreary plains interrupted by rocky koppies, abounding with the springbok and the gnu. **1850** N. J. Merriman *Cape Jrnls.* (1957) 136 This will account for our retiring behind a koppie to pitch our tent. **1853** *Edin. New Philos. Jrnl.* LV. 79 The bush..covers over all inequalities of ground..and makes almost every kloof and koppie exactly resemble each other. **1881** [see Kopje]. **1884** E. P. Mathers *Trip to Moodie's* 143 He was prospecting about and tried the quartz at the bottom of the koppie... The koppie dips into a gully on each side of it. **1926** O. Schreiner *From Man to Man* viii. 290 You will creep on hands and knees over rough koppies. **1957** *Times* 19 Nov. 12/7 In the course of my afternoon walk over the koppies one day I came upon two of my pupils engaged in a strange game. **1966** E. Palmer *Plains of Camdeboo* v. 74 The low ridge of koppies overlooking the gap. **1971** *Rand Daily Mail* (Home Owner) 27 Mar. 9/2 It is a hilly area and there are the Melville koppies to add something extra to the area. **1971** *World Archaeol.* III. 182 With few exceptions, however, smelting sites are not found on the koppies themselves.

Comb. **koppie** (also **kopje**) **walloper,** a diamond-buyer. *Hist.*

1886 G. A. Farini *Through Kalahari Desert* ii. 21 The wily Jew was a 'partner' in a 'company' of ten 'Koppje wallopers'. **1897** H. Raymond *B. I. Barnato* i. 14 The slang camp term..for this [*sc.* diamond-buyer] was 'kopje walloper', derived from the circumstance that in the earliest days the diamonds were obtained from a number of kopjes or small hills in the neighbourhood of the camp, and the dealers travelled on foot from one to the other purchasing the finds as they were turned out at the sorting tables. **1947** *Cape Argus* 20 Dec. 2/5 A 'koppie walloper' was a diamond buyer who went from claim to claim buying stones. The name was used in Kimberley in the early days. **1949** K. L. Simms *Sun-Drenched Veld* viii. 70 Profits dwindled quickly, especially as native workmen stole many diamonds, which they sold to unscrupulous 'kopje wallopers' who made enormous profits without having done any hard work. **1955** E. Rosenthal in Saron & Hotz *Jews in S. Afr.* vi. 114 A 'koppie-walloper', that is one who went from claim to claim buying diamonds as the diggers produced them. **1967** E. M. Slatter *My Leaves are Green* 38 Now don't sell it to any of these kopje-wallopers.

kora[1] (kōᵊ·ră). Also **cora, korro.** [Native name.] A West African stringed instrument resembling a harp.

1799 M. Park *Trav. Afr.* xxi. 278, I have now to add a list of their musical instruments, the principal of which are,—the *koonting*, a sort of guitar..; the *korro*, a large harp, with eighteen strings; [etc.]. **1874** C. Engel *Descr. Catal. Musical Instruments S. Kensington Museum* (ed. 2) 151 Mungo Park enumerates, among the popular instruments which he saw in Senegambia, the *e-korro.* **1935** G. Gorer *Africa Dances* iv. 305 The drums are sometimes supplemented and occasionally supplanted by..the cora, a six-stringed instrument somewhere between a guitar and a harp. **1965** *Economist* 16 Jan. 229/3 The Senegal national anthem..begins..'Strum your koras, strike the balafous'. **1970** P. Oliver *Savannah Syncopators* 47 The great harp-lute, called the *kora.*

Kora[2] (kōᵊ·ră). Also **Coranna, Koran(n)a,** occas. **Koraqua.** [Of disputed origin.] **a.** Any of a group of Hottentot peoples in southern Africa; also, a member of any of these groups. **b.** The language spoken by them. Also *attrib.* or as *adj.*

1801 J. Barrow *Acct. Trav. S. Afr.* I. vi. 403 The country to the eastward of the Roggeveld, is inhabited by different hordes of Bosjesmans. One of these, called the *Koranas*, dwelling on the right bank of the Orange river, directly east from the Roggeveld, is represented as a very formidable tribe of people. **1806** —— *Voy. Cochinchina* 373 The native inhabitants which are settled on the banks of the Orange river..are a variety of the Hottentot race..called the *Koras.* *Ibid.*, What the Gonaquas were on the eastern coast the *Koras* seem to be to the northward, a mixed breed between the Hottentot and the Kaffer. **1824** W. J. Burchell *Trav. S. Afr.* ii. 251 The following specimen of the Kora, or Koraqua, dialect, was obtained. **1831** *Graham's Town Jrnl.* 30 Dec. 3 At a Koranna kraal.., the first cases of Small Pox presented themselves. **1871** J. Mackenzie *Ten Yrs. North of Orange River* 493 A certain word in Koranna, if pronounced in a loud key, means *handkerchief.* *Ibid.* 501 The insecure villages of the pastoral Korannas. **1881** *Encycl. Brit.* XII. 312/2 The Kora dialect, spoken by the Korannas, or Koraquas, dwelling about the middle and upper part of the Orange, Vaal, and Modder Rivers. **1936** J. A. Engelbrecht *Korana* i. 2 The history of the origin of the Korana can only be approximately arrived at. *Ibid.* ii. 83 Kora tribes..left the Cape to seek new pastures. *Ibid.* iii. 197 A complete linguistic survey of all the areas in which Kora..is still spoken at the present day could not be undertaken. **1955** J. H. Wellington *S. Afr.* II. xvi. 234 The tribes occupying the Cape Peninsula and adjacent areas at the time of Van Riebeeck's arrival were the Goringhaiqua and the Kora (later known as the Koranna). **1961** *Encycl. S. Afr.* 278/1 Today pure Koranas are almost extinct. **1968** *Encycl. Brit.* XI. 751/1 Hottentot is the European name for the Nama, Kora and other languages comprising 14 or 15 subdivisions of the main Hottentot speech. **1974** [see *HOTTENTOT 1].

kora, var. *KOURA.

koraddy, koradi, varr. *KORARI.

‖ **koradji** (kǫ·rădʒi). *Austral.* Also 8 **carradygan, carrahdy,** 9 **coradge(e, karaji, kiradjee, korradgee.** [Austral. Aboriginal word.] Amongst the Australian Aborigines, a medicine-man.

1793 J. Hunter *Hist. Jrnl.* xxi. 523 Having taken leave of their new friends the *Car-ra-dy-gans* (doctors), our party set off. **1798** D. Collins *Acct. Eng. Colony New South Wales* I. 594, I think I may term the car-rah-dy their high priest of superstition. **1845** J. O. Balfour *Sk. New South Wales* 14 The coradgees, who are their wise men, have, they suppose, the power of healing and foretelling. Each tribe possesses one of these learned pundits, and if their wisdom were in proportion to their age, they would indeed be Solons. **1865** W. Howitt *Hist. Discovery in Austral.* I. 287 One who seemed a coradge, or priest, went through a strange ceremony of singing, and touching his eyebrows, nose and breast, crossing himself, and pointing to the sky like an old Druid. **1867** S. Bennett

Hist. Austral. Discovery 250 *Kiradjee*, a doctor. **1885** R. M. PRAED *Austral. Life* 23 The korradgees, or medicine men, are the chief repositories (of the secrets of their religion). **1892** J. FRASER *Aborigines New South Wales* 63 For some diseases, the karáji, or native doctor when he is called in, makes passes with his hand over the sick man, much in the same way as a mesmerist will do. **1966** [see *BOYLA].

Koranko (kǒræ·ŋko). Also **Kooranko.** [Native name.] **a.** Name of a West African people; also, a member of this people. **b.** The language of this people.

1825 A. G. LAING *Trav. W. Afr.* iv. 200 The manner of courtship among the Korankos is exactly the same as among the Timannees. *Ibid.* 208 Dancing is a prominent feature among the amusements of the Koorankos. **1883** R. N. CUST *Sk. Mod. Lang. Afr.* I. xi. 184 There appear to be Dialects [of Temne], the Quiah,..and the Koranko. **1957** M. BANTON *W. Afr. City* vii. 127 Koranko is a closely related dialect [to Mandinka]... The Koranko and Kono inhabit the high lands to the north-east and east. **1962** *Times* 3 Mar. 10/6 The man is a Koranko of west Africa.

Koran(n)a, Koraqua: see *KORA².

korari (kōᵘ·rari). *N.Z.* Also **coorraddie, kauradi, kolladie, koraddy, koradi, kraddy.** [Maori.] The flower stalks of the New Zealand flax, *Phormium tenax*; also occasionally used for the plant itself.

1832 G. BENNETT in *London Med. Gaz.* 18 Feb. 750/2 *Phormium Tenax*, or flax plant. *Koradi* of the natives of New Zealand... This valuable plant is indigenous to New Zealand. **1834** E. MARKHAM *N.Z. or Recollections of It* (MS.) 44 Koraddy or Flax undrest split green and worked up. **1840** J. S. POLACK *Manners & Customs New Zealanders* I. xvi. 175 The flax (*Korari*)..is of two or three kinds. **1843** *N.Z. Jrnl.* No. 92 177/2 With a piece of kauradi or flax. **1845** E. J. WAKEFIELD *Adventure N.Z.* I. iii. 63 The plant is called *phormium tenax* by naturalists. The general native name for the plant..was *korari*. **1873** V. PYKE *Story Wild Will Enderby* (ed. 4) III. iii. 115 A 'mohiki' is constructed of 'koradies'—*Anglice*, the flowering stalks of the flax. **1879** J. BARR *Old Identities* 53 A 'kolladie' (the flower-stalk of the flax, about 7 ft long) was carried by each as a balancing pole or staff. **1888** A. H. DUNCAN *Wakatipians* ii. 12 We collected all the dried *coorraddies* (flower stalks of the flax-bush). **1933** *Press* (Christchurch, N.Z.) 19 Oct. 15/7 The individual plants are called *flax bushes* and the dried reed stalks (which Maoris and children tied into bundles to make rafts) are called *flax-sticks, koradi sticks*, or *kraddy sticks*. **1949** P. BUCK *Coming of Maori* (1950) II. ix. 238 Children armed with a flax flower stalk (*korari*) were taught to spar by their parents.

Kore (kōᵊ·re). Also 9 **Cora, Core.** [Gr. κόρη, = maiden.] **1.** In Greek mythology, the daughter of Zeus and Demeter, known as Persephone when she married Hades.

1844 L. SCHMITZ in W. Smith *Dict. Gr. & Roman Biogr. & Mythol.* I. 852/1 Core..the maiden, a name by which Persephone is often called. **1849** *Ibid.* III. 204/2 In the mysteries of Eleusis, the return of Cora from the lower world was regarded as the symbol of immortality. **1885** *Encycl. Brit.* XIX. 824/1 Proserpine herself was commonly known as the daughter (Core). **1916** E. POUND *Lustra* 18 Korè is seen in the North Skirting the blue-gray sea. **1930** —— *XXX Cantos* xvii. 79 Koré through the bright meadow, with green-gray dust in the grass. **1968** *Encycl. Brit.* XVII. 644/2 One of the variants of the name Persephone is..a form with a pre-Hellenic suffix that suggests that she was a pre-Hellenic deity..a goddess of the dead. If this is so, her connection with Demeter came later, when she was identified with Kore (the Greek word for 'maiden')..daughter of Demeter; Demeter and Kore were the leading goddesses in the Eleusinian mysteries.

2. *Gr. Sculpture.* (Often with lower-case initial.) A statue of a draped maiden.

1920 *Q. Rev.* July 28 There are, in our Archaic Room, good examples both of the *Kore* and her male companion the *Kouros*. **1934** *Burlington Mag.* Jan. 46/1 The archaic bronzes include..an Ionian kore..and a warrior. **1950** H. L. LORIMER *Homer & Monuments* vi. 356 This arrangement can be plainly seen on a Kore from the Acropolis. **1971** *Ashmolean Mus. Rep. of Visitors 1970* 18 A terracotta scent vase in the form of a standing kore, Rhodian, late 6th century B.C.

Korean (kǒrī·ăn), *a.* and *sb.* Also 7–9 **Corean.** [f. *Korea* country in Eastern Asia + -AN.] **A.** *adj.* Of or pertaining to Korea, since 1954 divided into the *Republic of Korea* (capital, Seoul) in South Korea and the (Communist) *Korean People's Republic* (capital, Pyongyang) in North Korea (respectively S. and N. of the 38th parallel). **B.** *sb.* **a.** A native or inhabitant of Korea. **b.** The agglutinative language of Korea, which is related to Japanese.

1614 R. COCKS *Let.* 25 Nov. in *Diary* (1883) II. 270 He was prevented by a Corean Noble-man. **1727** J. G. SCHEUCHZER tr. *Kæmpfer's Hist. Japan* I. 63 The Coreans had been subdued. *Ibid.* 76 Encompass'd by the Corean sea. **1813** *Q. Rev.* Oct. 256 Classes and Families of Languages... Tartarian... Corean. **1822** F. SHOBERL tr. *Titsingh's Illustr. Japan* 323 A Corean Fisherman and his Wife. **1885** E. W. HAMILTON *Diary* 11 Apr. (1972) II. 834 The idea was broached in the Cabinet of endeavouring to make arrangements with the Chinese and Japanese Governments for our occupying Port Hamilton in Korean territory in the event of war with Russia. **1899** A. H. KEANE *Man Past & Present* viii. 307 An adaptation of the Chinese symbols to the phonetic expression of the Korean syllables. **1921** [see *ANNAMITE *a.* and *sb.*]. **1966** *Listener* 24 Mar. 423/2 The Korean people..are genuine Tartars. *Ibid.*, Korea proves that it is possible for a poor Asian country to hope for both bread and freedom. The Koreans value that freedom. **1967** D. S. PARLETT *Short Dict. Lang.* 70 Agglutinative structure, like Korean, unlike Chinese. **1972** *Korea Times* 19 Nov. 1/6 Written tests in English, Korean and general knowledge will be held.

C. Korean chrysanthemum, a late-flowering hybrid chrysanthemum first developed from *Chrysanthemum coreanum* by A. Cumming, American nurseryman, about 1930; also *ellipt.*; **Korean pine,** a slow-growing pine with dark green leaves, *Pinus koraiensis.*

1931 *Horticulture* 15 Sept. 392/1 No list of Fall flowering perennials would be complete if the Korean chrysanthemum were omitted. When the flowers of this splendid novelty open, they are a pure white color with a chrysanthemum gold center, but as the flowers mature they assume a claret pink shade. **1936** K. LUXFORD *Culture of Chrysanthemum* 72 The hardy hybrid Korean chrysanthemum is one of the most notable acquisitions to the border of recent years. **1938** A. E. WRIGHT *Outdoor Chrysanthemums* ix. 87 The Koreans have made a tremendous impression in America. **1961** *Amat. Gardening* 30 Sept. 9/2 Some of the later flowering pompon chrysanthemums and Koreans I am lifting and putting into pots. **1866** 'SENILIS' *Pinaceæ* 115 Pinus Koraiensis: The Corean Pine. **1914** W. J. BEAN *Trees & Shrubs Hardy in Brit. Isles* II. 182 *P[inus] koraiensis*, Siebold. Corean Pine..introduced by J. G. Veitch in 1861. **1969** T. H. EVERETT *Living Trees of World* 55/1 The Korean pine (*P. koraiensis*) occurs both in Korea and Japan, and under favorable circumstances it may grow to 150 feet high.

Hence **Kore·anize** *v. trans.*, to give a Korean character to.

1930 W. F. SANDS *Undiplomatic Memories* (1931) 70 Emily, Koreanized as Lady Om, was now reigning sweetly in Seoul. **1972** *Korea Times* 16 Nov. 1/7 A new turning-point in the realization of a 'Koreanized democracy'.

Koreish (kǒrəi·ʃ). Also 7–9 **Coreis(h),** 9– **Koreisch, -eysh, Ḳoraish, -aysh, Ḳur-, Quraysh,** etc. [Arab. *ḳuraiš* Koreish, *qurašī* Koreishite.] An Arabic tribe living around Mecca, to which Muhammad belonged; also, a member of this tribe. Also *attrib.* or as *adj.*

1649 A. ROSS tr. *Alcoran* Introd., He declaimeth against such as worship Idols, particularly against the Inhabitants of the City of Mecca, and against the Coreis, who were enemies to his designe. **1734** G. SALE tr. *Koran* Prelim. Disc. i. 25 There were several dialects of it [*sc.* the Arabic language], very different from each other: the most remarkable were that spoken by the tribe of Hamyar and the other genuine Arabs, and that of the Koreish... The dialect of the Koreish is usually termed the pure Arabic. **1856** R. F. BURTON *Personal Narr. Pilgrimage to El-Medinah* III. xxvi. 157 It was closed by the Kuraysh when they rebuilt the house in Mohammed's day. **1858** W. MUIR *Life of Mahomet* I. I. iii. 197 The likeliest is the meaning '*noble*'; but it is also possible that the Coreish..may have conferred upon the word that meaning... Again, it is derived from a metaphorical resemblance to *Coreish*, the name of a fish which eats up all others; or to *cursh*, a high-bred camel. Others refer it to a root which signifies *to trade*. **1861** J. M. RODWELL tr. *Koran* p. viii, Othman.. entrusted the redaction to..Zaid.., with whom he associated as colleagues, three, according to others, twelve of the Koreisch, in order to secure the purity of that Meccan idiom in which Muhammad had spoken. **1871** C. M. YONGE *Pioneers & Founders* iv. 81 Sabat was an Arab of the tribe of Koreish, the same which gave birth to Mahomet himself. **1880** E. H. PALMER in *Sacred Bks. East* VI. p. lix, Zâid..with three men of the Qurâis (Mohammed's own tribe),..to fix the reading definitely according to the pure Qurâis idiom. **1907** D. S. MARGOLIOUTH tr. *J. Zaydan's Umayyads & ᶜAbbásids* 11 The poet Ibn Harmah..was an adoptive member of the clan Khalj which was itself adoptive in the tribe Kuraish. *Ibid.* 14 The Ḳuraish dealt in slaves as they did in other merchandise. **1916** J. BUCHAN *Greenmantle* ii. 23 To capture all Islam..the man must be of the Koreish, the tribe of the Prophet himself... There are families..that claim Koreish blood. **1957** *Encycl. Brit.* XV. 646/2 A member of the tribe Koreish.., Muhammad is said to have been a posthumous child. **1959** T. B. IRVING in Kritzeck & Winder *World of Islam* II. 189 The Quraysh, centring around Makkah, used the purest Arabic of all; the ratio of any tribe's distance from the Quraysh was a good index for ascertaining the purity or corruption of any Arab dialect.

So **Korei·shite, Qurayshite,** etc., a member of the Koreish tribe.

1708 S. OCKLEY *Conquest Syria, Persia & Ægypt by Saracens* I. sign. DD5 verso, Koreishæ, or Korashites, a noble Tribe among the Arabs, of which Mahomet was. **1734** G. SALE tr. *Koran* Prelim. Disc. vi. 145 The spoil.. he bestowed..on the Meccans only.., highly distinguishing the principal Korashites, that he might ingratiate himself with them. **1871** C. M. YONGE *Pioneers & Founders* iv. 81 He formed a close friendship with his colleague, Abdallah, likewise a Koreishite Arab. **1903** D. B. MACDONALD *Devel. Muslim Theol.* App. i. 305 The unlettered Qurayshite prophet, Muhammad. **1968** *New Larousse Encycl. Mythol.* (new ed.) 323/1 The goddess El-ᶜOzza was also held in high honour among the Koreishites.

koreke (kore·ke). *N.Z.* [Maori.] An extinct native quail, *Coturnix novæzealandiæ.*

1871 F. W. HUTTON *Catal. Birds N.Z.* 22 Native Quail. Koreke. Black, streaked with white, and varied with reddish brown on the back. **1882** W. D. HAY *Brighter Britain!* II. 223 The Koreke..the native quail. **1930** W. R. B. OLIVER *N.Z. Birds* 374 New Zealand Quail. Koreke. **1966** R. A. FALLA et al. *Field Guide Birds N.Z.* 100 Galliformes. The only indigenous member of this order, *Coturnix novæzealandiæ*, Koreke of the Maoris, became extinct about 1870.

‖ **korero** (kōᵘ·reᵊro). *N.Z.* Also 9 **corero,** etc. [Maori.] Talk, conversation, discussion; a conference.

1807 J. SAVAGE *Some Acct. N.Z.* xi. 75 Corero..Speaking. **1834** E. MARKHAM *N.Z. or Recollections of It* (MS.) 4 A grand Corrirow or talk. **1845** E. J. WAKEFIELD *Adventure N.Z.* I. 78 There were about sixty men assembled, and they proceeded to hold a *korero* or 'talk' on the all-important subject. **1855** C. W. RICHMOND *Jrnl.* 20 Aug. in *Richmond–Atkinson Papers* (1960) I. 176 They had a long korero about New Zealand and the Bay, where the Doctor has been quartered for 5 years. **1863** T. MOSER *Mahoe Leaves* 30 He had to pass several pahs on the road, at all of which there would be 'koreros'. **1883** J. P. WARD *Wanderings with Maori Prophets* ii. 13 He was brim full of talk, or *korero*. **1930** B. GUTHRIE *N.Z. Memories* 54 After some *korero* and polite speeches the Maoris stood aside. **1936** 'R. HYDE' *Check to your King* xx. 236 The old and conspicuous means of the *korero* as a call to arms. **1938** R. D. FINLAYSON *Brown Man's Burden* 13 There was to be a korero on politics and the revival of Maori art. **1966** *Weekly News* (Auckland) 22 June 58/3 After New Zealand's first test defeat in South Africa in 1960 by 13–0 all members of the touring team had a korero the next morning. **1971** *N.Z. Listener* 22 Mar. 7/2 The *korero*..would let the Maoris tell the pakehas what they couldn't so easily tell them in a setting shaped by European conventions.

Korewah, var. *KORWA.

korfball (kǭ·ɹfbǭl). Also **korfbal.** [Du. *korfbal*, f. *korf* basket + *bal* ball.] A game of Dutch origin, resembling basketball and netball. Also *attrib.*

1915 J. FEITH *Sport in Netherlands* 27 '*Korfbal*', a game not known in England... The ball, which is as big as that used for football, is thrown.., and the place of the goal is taken by a bottomless basket attached to a pole. **1960** *Sunday Times* 5 June 40/6 Holland beat England 10–8 in a korfball international at Mitcham, Surrey, yesterday, after leading 7–3 at half-time. **1965** J. B. PICK *Phoenix Dict. Games* (rev. ed.) 89 *Korfball* (24 players)..is a net-ball-basketball game of Dutch origin..usually played by teams of six ladies and six gentlemen. Starting humbly in 1902..in the Netherlands.., the game was introduced into Britain..in 1946. *Ibid.* 90 There are now ten British korfball clubs. **1969** D. C. JOYNSON *Guide for Games* (ed. 2) vi. 157 Korfball Netball. The court is marked as for Netball. Team—5 players. *Ibid.* viii. 211 *Indoor Korfball.* Two teams of 6 players. The pitch may be (a) a basket-ball court; (b) a netball court; (c) a rectangular court 60 to 80 ft. by 30 to 40 ft. **1973** *Observer* 7 Oct. 26/1 There is only one mixed team sport in the world: korfball, and the first of its summarised rules is that you can only hinder someone of the same sex.

korhaan (korhā·n, kǒrā·n, kurā·n). *S. Afr.* Also **knorhaan, knoraan, koerhaan, koorhaan, korhaen,** etc. = KORAN². (For 'genus *Eupodotes*, esp. *E. afra*' in definition, substitute 'the family Otididæ'.)

1731 G. MEDLEY tr. *Kolb's Present State Cape of Good-Hope* II. 139 The Knorhan. Among the Wild Fowls at the Cape, there is a Sort of Birds, a Male of which the Europeans there call Knor-Cock: a Female they call Knor-Hen. **1775** [see KORAN²]. **1785** G. FORSTER tr. *Sparrman's Voy. Cape Good Hope* I. iv. 153 *Knorrhane* is the name of a kind of *Otis*. **1786** *Ibid.* (ed. 2) I. iv. 153 *Korr-haen* is the name of a kind of *Otis*. **1801** J. BARROW *Acct. Trav. S. Afr.* I. iv. 264 A new species of Korhaen or bustard was seen here. **1819** [see KORAN²]. **1867** E. L. LAYARD *Birds S. Afr.* 287 The Knorhaan (lit. Scolding Cock) is abundant throughout the whole colony, frequenting the open country. **1876** H. BROOKS *Natal* 137 The koraan or knoraan of the Dutch settlers (*Eupodotis scolopacea*). **1896** H. A. BRYDEN *Tales S. Afr.* 250 The bush *koorhaan*..are playing their strange aerial pranks. **1906** W. L. SCLATER *Birds S. Afr.* IV. 291 The Red-crested Knorhaan is found singly or in pairs. **1936** *Blackw. Mag.* Mar. 296/2 The country was still rolling grass, with little game except koerhaan, which were plentiful everywhere. **1955** E. L. GILL *First Guide S. Afr. Birds* 150 The 'Korhaans' are the smaller-sized Bustards. **1964** P. A. CLANCEY *Birds Natal & Zululand* 143 The blue korhaan occurs sparingly in the interior of Natal. **1972** L. G. GREEN *When Journey's Over* (1973) xii. 143 Casserole of guinea fowl, stewed *korhaan* and pigeon and Namaqua partridges were as familiar at Klipfontein as grouse in the Savoy Grill.

kori¹ (kōᵊ·ri). *S. Afr.* [Sechuana.] In full, *kori bustard* = *GOMPAAUW.

1811 W. J. BURCHELL *Jrnl.* 27 Oct. in *Trav. S. Afr.* (1822) I. xvi. 393 We shot a large bird of the bustard kind... The present species, which is called *Kori* in the Sichuana language, measured, in extent of wing, not less than seven feet. *Ibid.*, A representation of the head of the Kori Bustard..is given at the end of this chapter. **1872** L. LLOYD tr. *Andersson's Notes Birds of Damara Land* 258 Kori Bustard... This splendid bird is found throughout the year in Damara. **1889** H. A. BRYDEN *Kloof & Karroo* xvii. 306 Among the bustards stands pre-eminent the great Kori bustard—the gom paauw of the Dutch colonists. **1962** [see *GOMPAAUW]. **1966** E. PALMER *Plains of Camdeboo* xii. 209 The Kori bustard, a dweller of the desert or semi-desert, a gigantic creature weighing up to fifty pounds or more, heavier than the great bustard of Eurasia which is usually held to be the heaviest bird of the air. It has a wing span of up to eight feet, and it stands nearly five feet high.

Kori² (kōᵊ·ri). Also **Koiri, Koli, Koree.** Name of a tribe of low-caste Hindu weavers of northern India; also, a member of this tribe.

1839 J. Tod *Travels in W. India* vii. 143 The chief fragment of this once superb monument is enclosed and half-hidden by the huts of Koli weavers. *Ibid.* xvii. 361 The rest is made up of the agricultural and artizan classes, as Aheers, Kolis, &c. &c. **1868** *Rep. Ethnol. Comm. Specimens Aborig. Tribes Jubbulpore Exhib. 1866–67* I. 11 The Mahars, Korees, and other weaving clans. **1873** *Cycl. India* (ed. 2) III. s.v. *Kori*, All the weaver caste throughout Hindoostan are stated by Colonel Tod to be Koli. They call themselves Julai, but are sometimes styled Kori. **1885** J. C. Nesfield *Brief View Caste Syst. N.-W. Prov. & Oudh* xi. 106 The weaver caste is better known to this day by the tribal name of Kori than by the functional names of Bunkar or Joria. **1896** J. N. Bhattacharya *Hindu Castes & Sects* xi. ii. 233 The Kori and Koli of Northern India are weavers professing the Hindu faith; but they are very low castes. **1896** W. Crooke *Tribes & Castes N.-W. Prov. & Oudh* III. 316 Kori, the Hindu weaver caste. *Ibid.* 318 The Koris are all Hindus... The status of the Kori is very low. **1916** R. V. Russell *Tribes & Castes Cent. Prov. India* IV. II. 133 Bodies of the Kori and Katia weaving castes of northern India have been amalgamated with the Mahārs. **1957** G. S. Ghurye *Mahadev Kolis* i. 6 Koris or Koiris are known over a large part of Northern India. I do not know that any responsible student of Indian ethnography has suggested an ethnic connection between Kori and Koli.

Koriac(k), Koriak, varr. *Koryak.

korimako (kǫrimā·ko). *N.Z.* [Maori.] A New Zealand honey-eater, the bell-bird, *Anthornis melanura*.

1855 R. Taylor *Te Ika a Maui* 75 In the first oven a korimako was cooked. **1863** A. S. Atkinson *Jrnl.* 29 Sept. in *Richmond–Atkinson Papers* (1960) II. 63, I lay on my back..listening dreamily to the birds, just waked up. The Korimakos in full chorus in the bush and the larks and matatas in the open land about us. **1873** W. Buller *Hist. Birds N.Z.* 94 Certain forest-ranges were famed as Korimako preserves. **1888** *Trans. N.Z. Inst.* XXI. 213 In fine weather the bush along the south shores of Lake Brunner re-echoes with the rich notes of the tui and korimako. **1930** W. R. B. Oliver *N.Z. Birds* 487 Bell Bird. Korimako. *Anthornis melanura.* **1966** *Encycl. N.Z.* I. 193/2 Common Maori names for the species [*sc.* the bell-bird] are korimako or makomako.

korin¹ (kōᵊ·rin). [Local name.] A small West African gazelle, *Gazella rufifrons*.

[**1846** J. E. Gray in *Ann. & Mag. Nat. Hist.* XVIII. 214 Senegal Gazelle. *Gazella rufifrons...* The Corinne, F. Cuv[ier]..not of Buffon.] **1852** *Catal. Mammalia Brit. Mus.* III. 60 *Gazella rufifrons.* The Korin. **1893** R. Lydekker *Horns & Hoofs* v. 232 The korin (*G. rufifrons*), from Senegal, is a species of fully 24 in. in height, distinguished by the uniformly sandy yellow colour of the central streak on the face, and the absence of any tufts of hair on the knees. *Ibid.* 407/2 (*index*) Korin gazelle. **1962** M. Burton *Syst. Dict. Mammals of World* 255 Common Gazelles of E. Africa include..Korin or Red-fronted Gazelle (*G. rufifrons*), Senegal to Sudan.

Kōrin² (kōᵊ·rin). The name of the Japanese artist Ogata *Kōrin* (1658–1716), used *attrib.* in *Kōrin school, style*, to denote a school of Japanese painting, founded in the Edo period and associated chiefly with Kyoto, of which Kōrin was the greatest exponent.

[**1884** Satow & Hawes *Handbk. for Travellers Cent. & N. Japan* (ed. 2) 96 The only new school that appeared in the seventeenth century was that of Kōrin, a famous lacquer painter, who appears to have been originally a pupil of the Tosa school.] **1898** M. Tomkinson *Jap. Collection* II. 113 The Kōrin style was a late offshoot of the Yamato-Tosa school..stamped by a bold flowing line and vigorous composition, and usually by a supreme contempt for naturalistic rules. **1909** L. Binyon *Jap. Art* v. 34 Here we have the first attempts at a fusion of the two styles, Chinese and Japanese, which reached its final development in the Korin school. **1912** E. F. Fenollosa *Epochs Chinese & Jap. Art* II. xiv. 129 We can call the chief masters of this Korin school the greatest painters of tree and flower forms that the world has ever seen. **1970** *Oxf. Compan. Art* 632/2 The Kōrin style represented a reversion to classical Japanese tradition.

koringkriek (kōᵊ·riŋkrīk). *S. Afr.* Also **koorn kriek.** [Afrikaans, f. Du. *koren* corn + *kriek(en* to chirp.] One of several long-horned grasshoppers of the family Tettigoniidæ.

1913 C. Pettman *Africanderisms* 277 *Koorn kriek*,..an insect belonging to the *Locustidæ*; it is very destructive to pumpkins, mealie cobs, etc., and does at times great damage to crops. **1954** S. H. Skaife *Afr. Insect Life* ii. 30 Many people in South Africa fear the koringkrieks because they have the reputation of being poisonous. **1955** D. Jacobson *Trap* iii. 73 The only sound was the shrill call of the koringkrieks, rasping frenziedly in one dry scream. **1966** E. Palmer *Plains of Camdeboo* i. 13 The koringkrieks lurching on immense and crooked legs.

Korku (kǭ·ɹku). Also **Korkoo, Kurku. a.** Name of a Kolarian tribe of the Central Provinces of India; also, a member of this tribe. **b.** Their language. Also *attrib.* or as *adj.*

a **1863** S. Hislop *Papers Aborig. Tribes Cent. Provinces* (1866) App. p. xi, All Kurkus are of one caste. They eat from the hands of Hindus, but not from Gonds or Mahars. **1868** *Rep. Ethnol. Comm. Specimens Aborig. Tribes Jubbulpore Exhib. 1866–67* III. 17 Vocabulary of Korkoo words. **1874** Watson & Kaye *People of India* VII. 404 Korkoos are more migratory than Gonds. **1906** G. A. Grierson *Ling. Survey India* IV. 167 There is onlyone sub-dialect of Kūrkū, the so-called Muwāsī... It does not differ much from ordinary Kūrkū. **1908** H. H. Risley *People of India* ii. 100 Totems found among sixteen castes and tribes, including..the primitive Gonds, Korkus, and Orāons. **1950** N. S. Saigal in A. V. Thakkar *Tribes India* 74 Among Korkus, 3% are Christian converts and 1·5% are Muslim converts. **1961** *Amer. Speech* XXXVI. 223 Korku phonology and morphophonemics... (Analysis of Korku with particular emphasis on low tone-*cum*-aspiration and stress..). **1962** J. J. Gumperz in J. A. Fishman *Readings Sociol. of Lang.* (1968) 468 Similarly in India the North Dravidian tribal languages and Munda languages such as Korku are found deep in the Indo-Aryan territory.

kornelite (kǭ·ɹnĕləit). *Min.* [ad. Hung. *kornelit* (J. Krenner 1888, in *Magyar tudomānyos akad. értes.* XXII. 131), f. the name of *Kornel* Hlavacsek, who found the original specimen: see -ite¹.] A violet to pale pink hydrated ferric sulphate, $Fe_2(SO_4)_3.7H_2O$.

1892 E. S. Dana *Dana's Syst. Min.* (ed. 6) 957 Kornelite... Stated to be a hydrous ferric sulphate. **1910** *Mineral. Mag.* XV. 429 Rhomboclase..occurring together with szomolnokite..and other iron sulphates (kornelite, copiapite, coquimbite, &c.) at Szomolnok, Hungary. **1937** *Amer. Mineralogist* XXII. 569 The mineral designated as kornelite is a lower hydrate of normal ferric sulphate than coquimbite. **1965** *Mineral. Abstr.* XVII. 180/2 The minerals kornelite..from Tintic Standard mine, Utah.., coquimbite.., and quenstedite.., have been re-examined.

‖ **koro** (kōᵊ·ro). Also **kora.** [Jap. *kōro* incense-pot, censer.] An elaborate Japanese vase, usu. of bronze, jade, or porcelain, in which incense is burned.

1822 F. Shoberl tr. *Titsingh's Illustr. Japan* II. 234 *Koro*, a fire-terrine. *Ibid.* 228 A..chafing-dish, with its *koro*, or stand, for burning..incense. **1889** M. B. Huish *Japan & its Art* vii. 89 No notice of the contents of a Japanese house would be complete without some reference to the incense-burners (*ko-ro*) which find a place there, and also in the Buddhist temples. These afforded employment for a large number of artists in bronze. **1891** Chamberlain & Mason *Handbk. Travellers Japan* (ed. 3) 13 The *Kōro*, or incense-burner, generally in bronze or porcelain. **1959** *Times* 28 Apr. 20/6 A spinach green jade koro and cover. **1974** *Daily Tel.* 4 June 16/6 The koro is carved in archaic style, has large horned dragon handles and is surmounted by a Buddhistic lion and a cub.

koromiko. For '*Veronica salicifolia*' substitute '*Hebe salicifolia*'. Add later examples.

1921 H. Guthrie-Smith *Tutira* iv. 26 Flourished green tutu..and Koromiko (*Veronica salicifolia*). **1933** *Bulletin* (Sydney) 9 Aug. 21/2 The shoots of the koromiko were chewed and swallowed for dysentery. **1963** S. Ashton-Warner *Teacher* 76 The idea has its duplicate often enough outdoors—in the right-angled leafing arrangements and the pairs of leaves set exactly opposite each other as in the Koromiko.

koroplast, var. *coroplast.

1888 *Amer. Jrnl. Archæol.* IV. 417 The independence and capriciousness which characterize the work of Greek koroplasts. **1950** H. L. Lorimer *Homer & Monuments* v. 163 Greek soldiers of fortune would now and again drift to Cyprus and furnish a subject for local koroplasts. **1952** *Antiquity* XXVI. 104 The Tarsus koroplasts were more closely allied..with those of Alexandria than with the more sophisticated craftsmen of Myrina and Tanagra.

korora (ko·rora). *N.Z.* [Maori.] The southern blue penguin, *Eudyptula minor*.

1871 F. W. Hutton *Catal. Birds N.Z.* 53 *Eudyptula minor*... Blue Penguin. Korora. **1905** W. B. *Where White Man Treads* 62 A smaller canoe and men..crowding into it..like 'korora' (penguins) awaiting the tide. **1966** R. A. Falla et al. *Field Guide Birds N.Z.* 22 Southern Blue Penguin. Maori name: Korora.

‖ **korowai** (kǫ·rowai). *N.Z.* [Maori.] A cloak or mat made of flax, ornamented with black twisted thrums. Also *attrib.*

1820 *Gram. & Vocab. Lang. N.Z.* (Church Missionary Soc.) 168 *Kōro ai*, a certain garment. **1845** E. J. Wakefield *Adventure N.Z.* I. 244 The *korowai*..is woven of *muka*, or scraped flax, and ornamented with bunches of twisted tags of the same, dyed black. *Ibid.* 245 A great many varieties of the *korowai* are made. **1900** A. Hamilton *Maori Art* (1901) v. 285 The ground-work of a feather cloak is the same as that for a *korowai* mat. *Ibid.* 326 A plain *korowai* mat with the strings arranged in bands. **1921** H. Guthrie-Smith *Tutira* xi. 92 The foe can be seen cloaked in their *korowai* mats. **1938** R. Finlayson *Brown Man's Burden* 10 In the clear space by the flagpole old Tamarua is delivering a speech of welcome, mere in hand, korowai cloak swishing. **1955** W. J. Phillipps *Carved Maori Houses* p. xii, *Korowai*, cloak ornamented with twisted black thrums.

korradgee, var. *koradji.

korrigan (kǫ·rigăn). Also **corrigan,** and with capital initial. [f. Breton (Vannes dial.), fem. of *korrig* gnome, dim. of *korr* dwarf. Cf. Cornish *coryk*.] The name of a fairy or witch in Breton folklore, noted esp. for stealing children.

1855 C. M. Yonge *Hist. Sir Thomas Thumb* 106 She has lost her dear little Louis; the Korrigan has taken him. **1865** T. Taylor tr. *Hersart de la Villemarqué's Ballads & Songs Brittany* p. xiv, Vannes is the home of the legends of gnomes and spirits, of dwarfs and fairies that haunt rocks and woods, streams and fountains, of the *dus* and *mary-morgan*, the *poulpican*, and the *korrigan*. **1883** J. S. Stallybrass tr. *J. Grimm's Teutonic Mythol.* II. xvii. 447 In Bretagne the *korr*, pl. *korred* answers to our elf, the *korrigan* to our elfin. *Ibid.* 469 A Breton story of the *korrigan* changing a child is in Villemarqué. **1949** *Funk's Stand. Dict. Folklore* I. 253/2 *Corrigan*, in the folklore of Brittany, a female fairy: said to have been one of the ancient druidesses, and therefore malicious towards Christian priests. She is fond of pretty human children, and usually gets the blame for all changeling substitutions. **1969** V. Rowe *Loire* i. 43 The sea-cave of the korrigans, a reminder that this is still very much a part of Brittany. The korrigans, in its [*sc.* Brittany's] Celtic folklore, are the pigwidgeons or leprechauns, or hobgoblins, with which most Celtic lands seem always to have been infested.

korrigum (kǫ·rigə̆m). [f. Kanuri *kargum*.] A West African antelope, *Damaliscus korrigum*; also called the topi.

1826 Denham & Clapperton *Narr. Trav. N. & Cent. Afr.* 192 Senegal Antelope..was found on the plains of central Africa. The natives call this species *Korrigum*. **1836** *Proc. Zool. Soc.* IV. 103 The Korrigum of Denham and Clapperton's Travels..was a very distinct animal from the Koba. **1895** Sclater & Thomas *Bk. Antelopes* I. II. 61 About the year 1840 Whitfield, a collector employed by Lord Derby..obtained specimens of the korrigum from the vicinity of Macarthy's Island on the River Gambia. **1964** L. S. Crandall *Managem. Wild Mammals in Captivity* 669 The korrigum or Senegal hartebeest (*Damaliscus k. korrigum*), found from Lake Chad to Senegal, was described from an animal living in the Zoological Gardens of London.

korro, var. *kora¹.

Korsakoff (kōᵊ·ɹsăkǫf). Also **Korsakow, -ov.** The name of S. S. *Korsakoff* (1854–1900), Russian physician, used *attrib.* or in the possessive to denote a type of psychosis, namely a syndrome, often the result of chronic alcoholism, which is characterized by disorientation, memory loss for recent events, and consequent confabulation.

1900 Dorland *Med. Dict.* 546/1 *Korsakoff's psychosis*, delirium or insanity associated with polyneuritis. **1903** *Jrnl. Mental Sci.* XLIX. 673 (*heading*) Twelve cases of 'Korsakow's disease' in women. **1924** [see *confabulation 2]. **1938** *Arch. Neurol. & Psychiatry* (Chicago) XXXIX. 483 We decided..to study the forces of organization in perception and memory in cases of the Korsakoff syndrome. **1941** *Brit. Jrnl. Psychol.* XXXI. 230 The object of this paper is to describe a variety of paramnesia recently observed in..Korsakow's psychosis. **1967** *Brit. Jrnl. Psychiatry* CXIII. 619 (*heading*) A case of craniopharyngioma presenting as Korsakov's syndrome. **1968** G. A. Talland *Disorders of Memory & Learning* iii. 63 A Korsakoff patient who, when asked to draw a woman.. accurately reproduced the style..current ten years earlier. **1970** R. M. Suinn *Fund. Behavior Path.* xi. 288/1 The characteristic signs of Korsakoff's psychosis are disorientation of time and place, anterograde amnesia.., and a marked tendency to fabricate answers to fill in the past.

‖ **koru** (kǫ·ru). *N.Z.* [Maori.] A common motif in Maori carving and tattooing, consisting of a spiral pattern terminating in a bulb.

1938 W. J. Phillipps in *Art in N.Z.* X. 205 The *koru*, or *pikopiko*, which today rarely appears in carving, but is used in the construction of composite patterns for rafters. **1946** —— in *Dominion Mus.* (N.Z.) *Rec. Ethnol.* I. 16 In tattoo it was also customary to incise a koru type of design on the centre of the forehead. *Ibid.* 21 Two pairs of koru, large and small. **1964** T. Barrow *Decorative Arts N.Z. Maori* iv. 64 Painted patterns appear on the underside of rafters in ceremonial meeting-houses and superior dwellings. Their elaborate curvilinear designs are usually based on a small bulb-like motif (*koru*) shaped like the looped top of an uncurling fern frond. **1970** *Dominion Mus.* (N.Z.) *Rec. Ethnol.* II. 31 An example of a carved *koru* design in its simplest form. *Ibid.* 34 The *koru* motifs (the curved stalk-like forms that terminate in a bulb).

koruna (kǫ·rună). Also *erron.* **korona.** Pl. **korunas, koruny.** [Czech, lit. crown.] The basic monetary unit of Czechoslovakia, introduced as the Czech crown after the 1914–18 war (abbrev. *Kč*), and replaced and revalued after the 1939–45 war as the crown of the Czech and Slovak State (abbrev. *Kčs*); 1 Kčs = 100 hellers (*haléř*, pl. *haléře*). Also, a coin corresponding to this unit. Also *attrib.*

The forms *KC* and *KCS* (for Czech *Kč* and *Kčs*) in quot. 1947 are erroneous.

1920 *Czecho-Slovak Trade Jrnl.* Apr. 9/1 Prices..between 1100 and 1500 Kč per cwt... Already 3000 to 3200 Kč are being asked for small quantities. **1930** G. Druce *Wanderings Czechoslovakia* i. 29 It may..be taken that 1 crown (*koruna*, abbreviated to Kč, which signifies the Czechoslovak crown) is worth 1½d... These coins are in denominations of 1 and 5 crowns, and also 20 and 50 hellers (halíř, plural haléřů; 100 h. make 1 kč.). **1947** *Whitaker's Almanack* 891/2 Pre-war revenue (1938) in the currency then in use Czechoslovak *Koruna* (Crown) of 100 *heller* was *KC*10,120,000... In October, 1945, currency reform was introduced and a new coinage *KCS* (*Koruna* of Czechs and Slovaks) adopted. **1962** R. A. G. Carson *Coins*

387 The new coinage system took as its unit the korona struck in cupro-nickel. **1967** *Economist* 19 Aug. p. xxvi/3 An annual turnover in the region of 6,000 million koruna (just under £900 million).

|| **korupe** (ko·rupe). *N.Z.* Also **korurupe.** [Maori *kōrupe, kororupe.*] The outer facing of the lintel of a door, often richly carved.

[**1844** W. WILLIAMS *Dict. N.Z. Lang.* 36/2 *Karupe,*.. lintel of a door.] **1897** A. HAMILTON *Maori Art* (1901) II. 84 The front of the doorway was finished off by a carved slab, the *korupe*, or *korurupe*, which rested on the carved edges of the *whakawai*. The *korupe* was not put in its place until the spaces in the walls had been filled in with *raupo*. **1927** T. E. DONNE *Maori, Past & Present* xix. 160 The *paré* or *korupe*, which was placed over the outside of the doorway to a house. **1949** P. BUCK *Coming of Maori* (1950) II. ii. 128 A carved lintel (*korupe, pare*) was rested on the upper ends of the forward flanges of the jambs and so completed a doorway that was unique in Polynesian art.

|| **koruru** (ko·ruru). *N.Z.* [Maori.] **1.** A wooden carving of a man's head, esp. one placed on the gable of a house.

[**1871** W. WILLIAMS *Dict. N.Z. Lang.* (ed. 3) 64/2 *Kōrŭrŭ,*..figure placed on the gable of a house.] **1897** A. HAMILTON *Maori Art* (1901) II. 85 The junction of the barge-boards was covered by a carved flat face, the *koruru*, which was adorned with feathers, and sometimes surmounted by a full-length figure, the *tekoteko*. The *koruru* was kept in place by a boss at the back. **1916** E. BEST *Maori Storehouses* i. 3 The carvings thereof were of the *koruru*..type. *Ibid.* 25 Such minor adornments as a carved head (*koruru*) on the gable. **1949** P. BUCK *Coming of Maori* (1950) II. ii. 129 Sometimes a complete human figure (*tekoteko*) was used instead of the *koruru* type and sometimes a combination took place in which the *tekoteko* stood on the head of the *koruru*. **1966** W. J. PHILLIPPS *Maori Life & Custom* xvii. 123 A group of carved heads, koruru, illustrating a variety of presentation.

2. A Maori version of knuckle-bones (see also quot. 1897).

1897 A. HAMILTON *Maori Art* (1901) II. 106 *Koruru,*.. 2. A toy with two strings, which when played with makes a whizzing or roaring noise. **1924** E. BEST *Maori* II. xi. 92 The game of jackstones, or knucklebones..is known as *ruru, koruru*..and *tutukai*.

korvort, repr. an ignorant pronunc. of CAVORT *v.*

1909 H. G. WELLS *Tono-Bungay* III. iii. 356 She described the knights of the age of chivalry as 'korvorting about on the off-chance of a dragon'.

Korwa (kǭ·ɹwă). Also **Korewah. a.** A Kolarian tribe of the Chota Nagpur area of India; also, a member of this tribe. **b.** Their language. Also *attrib.* or as *adj.*

1865 E. T. DALTON in *Jrnl. Asiatic Soc. Bengal* XXXIV. II. 29 The Khairwars.., Korewahs and Coles number from 5000 to 7000 each. *Ibid.* 18 The Korewah iron..is greatly prized. **1872** —— *Descr. Ethnol. Bengal* v. 125 Not one of them would acknowledge that he could speak a word of Korwa. **1875** WATSON & KAYE *People of India* VIII. 424 Korwas..are basket makers by profession... Korwas are evidently descended from an aboriginal stock, and are hardly recognised as Hindoos... Korwa dacoits do not intermarry with Korwa burglars. **1906** G. A. GRIERSON *Ling. Survey India* IV. 148 The most idiomatic Korwā is spoken in Jashpur and Sarguja, in the south of Palamau, and in Mirzapur. *Ibid.* 149 Remarks on Korwā grammar which follow. **1908** H. H. RISLEY *People of India* i. 44 Among the large groups..the Korwa (74·4) are just included in the long-headed division. **1923** R. B. DIXON *Racial Hist. Man* III. i. 259 Groups of 'casteless' aboriginal peoples, such as the Munda, Korwa, Malé. **1950** R. K. DESHPANDE in A. V. Thakkar *Tribes India* 112 The Korwa Language has much affinity with that of the Korkus of the Mahadoo hills. **1957** G. S. GHURYE *Mahadev Kolis* i. 6 The Korwas and the Korkus..have a better claim to relationship with the Koris. But the Korwa,..and the Korku are..assigned to the Kol or the Kolarian ethnic stock. **1972** W. B. LOCKWOOD *Panorama Indo-Europ. Lang.* 227 The languages in question are.. Koda (35,000) and Korwa (25,000).

Koryak (kǫ·ryak). Also **Korak, Koriac(k), Koriak.** [Russ. *Koryáki* (pl.), the Koryak people.] **a.** A people inhabiting the northern part of the Kamchatka peninsula; also, a member of this people. **b.** The Palæo-Asiatic language of this people. Also *attrib.* or as *adj.*

1780 W. COXE *Acct. Russ. Discoveries* I. i. 3 The first expedition..was made in 1696, by sixteen Cossacs, under the command of Lucas Semænoff Morosko, who was sent against the Koriacks of the river Opooka. *Ibid.* 5 The peninsula of Kamtchatka..is bounded..on the North by the country of the Koriacs. *Ibid.* iv. 49 In the autumn of 1754 they were joined by a Kamtchadal, and a Koriac. **1790** tr. *J. B. B. de Lesseps's Trav. in Kamtschatka* II. 105 The idiom of the Koriacs has no affinity to that of the Kamtschadales. *Ibid.* 117, I recognized in his features a Koriac prince... I have long owed the reader a description of a Koriac sledge. **1832** J. BELL *Syst. Geogr.* IV. vi. 74 The Koriaks inhabit the country between the Anadyr and the peninsula of Kamtschatka. **1893** *Funk's Stand. Dict.* I. 989/1 *Koriak,*..a member of a race inhabiting northeast Siberia; also, their language, related to Kamchatkan. *Koryak.* **1898** J. Y. SIMPSON *Side-Lights on Siberia* i. 12 Of the sub-Arctic races that inhabit the north-east of Siberia, it is sufficient to recall the names of the.. Tchuktchi,..the wild Koryaks..and Yukaghirs, all differing in speech and appearance, but still related. **1907** W. JOCHELSON in *Internat. Congr. Americanists* XV. 121 The subterranean Koryak house is still in use among the maritime Koryak, who are not Russianised. **1910** G. KENNAN *Tent Life in Siberia* xx. 203 The Korak numerals are:—Innín, One... Meen-ye-geet-kᵒhin, Ten. *Ibid.* 204 It would be a hard day's work for a boy to explain in Korak one of the..problems in Ray's Higher Arithmetic. **1917** W. BOGORAS *Koryak Texts* 2 The Koryak dialects may be divided into two large groups,—the western branch, which includes the Maritime Koryak of Penshina Bay and also the Reindeer Koryak; and the eastern branch, which includes the Maritime Koryak of Kamchatka. *Ibid.* 3 The Koryak language, in contrast to the Chukchee,..is furthermore divided into several local dialects. **1928** W. JOCHELSON *Peoples of Asiatic Russ.* ii. 49 The northern Kamchadal dialect..contains a considerable number of Koryak words. **1953** J. RAMSBOTTOM *Mushrooms & Toadstools* v. 45 The Fly Agaric is among the objects believed by the Koryak to be endowed with particular power. **1954** PEI & GAYNOR *Dict. Ling.* 116 *Koryak*, a language, spoken by about 1,000 persons in north-eastern Asia; a member of the Chukchi-Kamchadal family of languages, classified in the *Hyperborean* or *Palaeo-Asiatic* group.

kosh, var. *COSH *sb.*³

Koshare (kōᵘʃā·ɹi). [f. a Keresan language.] A member of a Pueblo Indian clown society representing ancestral spirits in rain and fertility ceremonies.

1890 A. F. BANDELIER *Delight Makers* 8 Shyuote, what have you heard about the Koshare? **1924** D. H. LAWRENCE *Mornings in Mexico* (1927) 123 The intermittent black-and-white fantasy of the hopping Koshare, the jesters, the Delight-Makers. *a* **1956** F. LAWRENCE *Mem. & Corr.* (1961) 4 These Koshares wore big Spanish hats with plumes. **1959** E. TUNIS *Indians* 129/1 Clowns, called Koshare, were provided to lighten the solemnity of the ceremonials.

kosher, *a.* (*sb.*) Delete || and add further examples.

1934 J. BROPHY *Waterfront* i. 23 To cook food in the prescribed kosher manner. **1959** *Hotel Managem. & Restaurant Trade Jrnl.* Feb. 28/2 Only kosher meals are served on El Al aircraft. **1971** *Guardian* 14 Oct. 11/2 The artificial meat business has a very good-going trade already in Kosher bacon made from soya beans. **1973** *Jewish Chron.* 19 Jan. 1/5 The Kissingers will also be given kosher food.

b. Also *kosher butcher*.

1932 KIPLING *Limits & Renewals* 359, I had a whole tin of salmon once from a kosher butcher. **1973** *Guardian* 16 June 3/6 The last kosher butcher left for Israel.

c. Correct, genuine, legitimate. *colloq.*

1896 FARMER & HENLEY *Slang* IV. 135/1 *Kosh* (or *Kosher*)... Adj. (common).—Fair; square. **1924** *Cosmopolitan* Nov. 104/2 It don't sound kosher to *me!* **1930** D. RUNYON in *Sat. Even. Post* 13 Sept. 7/3 'Everything is very Kosher,' Harry the Horse says. 'You need not be afraid of anything whatever. We have a business proposition.' **1930** *Amer. Mercury* Dec. 456/2 Listen shamus, you got me wrong. I'm strictly kosher. **1953** H. MILLER *Plexus* iv. 164, I made little or no effort to keep up with the others, it being no concern of mine what went on in this realm of make believe. All I felt called upon to do was to keep a straight face and pretend that everything was Kosher. **1959** C. MACINNES *Absolute Beginners* 80 It's so as to play down the queer thing in our country, and hide it behind the kosher game. *Ibid.* 157 It's all very well sneering at universities..but really and truly, it would be wonderful to have a bit of kosher education. **1961** L. GRIBBLE *Wantons die Hard* iv. 48 'No financial irregularities?' 'Strictly kosher... It's so good it stinks.' **1966** T. PYNCHON *Crying of Lot 49* iii. 60 They got the contracts. All drawn up in most kosher fashion, Manfred. **1973** *Jewish Chron.* 8 June 22/5 As for the children of a couple married in a register office, these are quite kosher.

B. Also, *to keep kosher*, to observe the Jewish law regarding diet.

1963 'R. L. PIKE' *Mute Witness* vii. 119, I wouldn't go on the stand and state that my mother kept kosher without a chance to check.

Also **ko·sherness.**

1949 KOESTLER *Promise & Fulfilment* III. iii. 317 Kosherness..is only one of the relatively minor rabbinical plagues in the young state. **1950** G. MIKES *Milk & Honey* 117 The Kosherness of a meal depends just as much on the way of cooking as on the raw material bought in the shop.

kosher, *v.* Add: (Earlier and later examples.) Hence **ko·shering** *vbl. sb.*

1871 E. LEVY *Jewish Cookery Bk.* 40 Take a fresh tongue, porge and..cosher it. **1960** *Commentary* June 499/2 *Kashrut* has survived in a mangled form... Scarcely anyone *kashered* the meat. **1974** *Times Lit. Suppl.* 31 May 592/3 What Mrs Wahlhaus has tried to do is to bring a new and more interesting approach to many traditional recipes, but without enough style or detail; she does not even explain how to kosher. **1974** W. FOLEY *Child in Forest* II. 218 Meat was meat (until all that Koshering business of soaking it in water and salt had emasculated it).

kosin (kōᵘ·sin). *Chem.* Also † **koussin.** [ad. It. *koussino* (C. Pavesi 1858, in *Giornale di Farm., di Chim.* VII. 49), f. *kouss-o* KOUSSO + *-ino* -IN¹.] Either of two related bicyclic phenols (not orig. differentiated), $C_{25}H_{32}O_8$, which are responsible for the anthelmintic property of kousso and are isolated as pale yellow crystals.

1875 *Pharmaceutical Jrnl. & Trans.* V. 562/2 From the aqueous residue of the alcoholic extract the koussin of Bendall, existing as a calcium compound, is precipitated as a more or less crystalline whitish powder. **1875** *Jrnl. Chem. Soc.* XXVIII. 468 The koso flowers yield about 3 per cent. of kosin. **1911** *Encycl. Brit.* XV. 921/1 *Kousso*... The active principle is koussin or kosin,..which is soluble in alcohol and alkalis, and may be given in doses of thirty grains. **1937** *Jrnl. Chem. Soc.* 563 The pale yellow product was identical with Merck's kosin... By fractional crystallisation we were able to separate this material into two distinct compounds, α-kosin, m.p. 158° (yellow needles), and β-kosin, m.p. 120° (yellow prisms). **1952** *Ibid.* 3103 Extracts of the flowers [sc. *Hagenia abyssinica*] contained large amounts of amorphous material, some of which could be converted into kosins by the action of alkali.

kos-kos, var. *KAS-KAS.

|| **koss, kos.** = Coss, cos *sb.*²

1826 LEYDEN & ERSKINE tr. *Mem. Zehir-Ed-Din* 393, I directed Chikmâk Beg..to measure the distance from Agra to Kâbul; that at every nine kos he should raise a minâr, or turret, twelve gez in height. **1884** [see Coss, cos *sb.*²]. **1893** KIPLING *Many Inventions* 193 He may have gone to the next hut... It is only four *koss*. **1901** —— *Kim* ii. 50 Think how far thou art on the road—an hundred *kos* from Lahore already. **1912** —— *Divers. Creatures* (1917) 227, I stood in the line..one *koss*, two *koss* distant.

Kossæan: see *KASSITE *sb.* and *a.*

Kossak, var. COSSACK (see *COSSACK 2 d). Also, *Canad.*, a sealskin or deerskin jacket.

1845 W. D. COOLEY tr. *Parrot's World Surveyed* I. i. 10 This portion of the empire is traversed by a line of Kossak posts. **1919** W. T. GRENFELL *Labrador Doctor* (1920) vii. 155 He wore it over a deerskin kossak, which is not the custom of cavalrymen.

kosso (kǫ·so). = KOUSSO.

1936 E. WAUGH *Waugh in Abyssinia* i. 13 His mother lived by selling *kosso*, a specific against tapeworm, in the streets of Gondar.

koswite (kǫ·zwəit). *Petrogr.* Also **kosvite.** [a. F. *koswite* (Duparc & Pearce 1901, in *Compt. Rend.* CXXXII. 892), f. the name of the *Kosw-inski* Mountains, Pawda, in the Middle Urals: see -ITE¹.] A coarse-grained peridotite consisting mainly of diopside, olivine, and magnetite. Hence **koswi·tic (kosvitic)** *a.*

1901 *Jrnl. Chem. Soc.* LXXX. II. 398 Associated with olivine-gabbros in the Solimask district, near the source of the Kosswa river, is a new type of basic eruptive rock to which the name koswite is given... As the magnetite decreases in amount and becomes idiomorphic, there is a passage from koswite to ordinary pyroxenite. **1922** *Mineral. Abstr.* I. 327 The mining district around Nikolae-Pavdinsk on the eastern slopes of the northern Urals.. consists largely of basic igneous rocks (dunite.., &c., and the local types koswite, tilaite, [etc.]). **1964** *Doklady Earth Sci.* CLIV. 149/2 The exceptionally high contents of volatile components in kosvites (mainly apatite-ore pyroxenites) increase the acidity of the melt. *Ibid.*, In the case of a kosvitic melt, which itself contains a considerable quantity of volatile components.

kotare (kōᵘ·tare). *N.Z.* [Maori *kōtare.*] The native kingfisher, *Halcyon sancta.*

1873 W. L. BULLER *Hist. Birds N.Z.* 69 *Halcyon vagans.* (New-Zealand Kingfisher.)..Native names. Kotare and Kotaretare; 'Kingfisher' of the colonists. **1882** W. D. HAY *Brighter Britain!* II. 221 The Kotare..is a kingfisher. **1930** W. R. B. OLIVER *N.Z. Birds* 430 Sacred Kingfisher. Kotare. *Halcyon sanctus.* **1968** *Landfall* XXII. 249 Like worm in kotare's beak my old maori lies limp.

|| **kotatsu** (kota·tsu). [Jap.] A wooden frame which is placed over the hearth in Japanese houses and covered with a thick quilt to give an enclosed area within which people can warm their hands and feet. Also applied to the hearth and the cover together. Also *attrib.*

1876 W. E. GRIFFIS *Mikado's Empire* II. vii. 416, I got up, entered the best room in the house, and curled up under a kotatsŭ. **1880** I. L. BIRD *Unbeaten Tracks Japan* II. lv. 254 The *kotatsu*..consists of a square, wooden frame, standing over a basin of lighted charcoal, and supporting a large wadded quilt or *futon*, under which you creep... The invitation to creep under the *kotatsu* is as welcome as the 'sit in' of the Scotch Highlands or the 'put your feet in the stove' of Colorado. **1889** M. B. HUISH *Japan & its Art* vii. 86 The only other articles of furniture will be the kotatsu, a square wooden frame, which in winter is placed over the hibachi or stove, and is covered with a large wadded quilt or *futon* (under this the whole family huddle for warmth). **1970** J. KIRKUP *Japan behind Fan* 126 A limited life of kitchen and *kotatsu* gossip in some narrow-minded village.

kotla, var. *KGOTLA.

|| **koto.** Add: (Earlier and later examples.) Also † **kotto.**

1795 tr. *C. P. Thunberg's Trav. Europe, Afr. & Asia* IV. 58 The *koto* bears a strong resemblance to our dulcimers, having a number of strings, which are struck with sticks. **1822** F. SHOBERL tr. *Titsingh's Illustr. Japan* 234 *Kotto*, a kind of harp. **1891** A. M. BACON *Jap. Girls & Women* ii. 42 The *koto* is an embryo piano, a horizontal sounding board, some six feet long, upon which are stretched strings supported by ivory bridges. **1893** F. T. PIGGOTT *Mus. Japan* III. 135 The Koto is the chief of modern Japanese instruments. **1932** F. L. WRIGHT

Autobiogr. II. 210 A fine lady plays the Koto, its graceful length laid upon the expanse of matting. **1961** A. BAINES *Mus. Instrum.* 208 The *koto*, the national instrument of pre-Westernized Japan. Its six-foot long soundbox is placed on the floor... Along it run thirteen waxed silk strings of equal length and played open, each tuned by its own movable bridge to contribute to a pentatonic scale of the 'major third' type..over two and a half octaves. **1965** W. SWAAN *Jap. Lantern* i. 10 The chief item is a concerto for *koto*, the traditional Japanese harp. **1973** E. T. SITHOLE in T. Kochman *Rappin' & Stylin' Out* 69 You would have expected me to write about the music of Bach..and not about Koto music (Japan).

kotschubeite, var. *KOCHUBEÏTE.

kotuku (kōu·tuku). *N.Z.* Also † **koatuku.** [Maori.] The white heron, *Egretta alba.*

1846 C. HEAPHY *Jrnl.* 23 Apr. in N. M. Taylor *Early Travellers N.Z.* (1959) 218 Shot a very fine *koatuku*, or white heron. **1882** W. L. BULLER *Man. Birds N.Z.* 52 The White Heron occurs so sparingly in most parts of New Zealand that 'rare as the Kotuku' has passed into a proverb among the Maoris. **1949** P. BUCK *Coming of Maori* (1950) II. xii. 284 Feathers of the..heron (*kotuku*) were also valued. **1963** *Evening Post* (Wellington, N.Z.) 26 Oct., In the..action shots..are the..kaka and spectacular kotuku or white heron.

kotwalee. Add: Also **kotwali.**

1964 A. SWINSON *Six Minutes to Sunset* ii. 34 Major MacDonald marched a company of troops down Hall Gate as far as the Kotwali. **1969** *Pioneer* (Lucknow) 13 Aug. 6/7 The kotwali police claim to have arrested last night three of the inter-district gang of burglars operating for several years in Pratapgarh, Sultanpur and Allahabad districts.

kotyle. = COTYLE I.

1926 C. DAY LEWIS in *Oxf. Poetry* 18 (*title*) Naked woman with kotyle. **1948** A. LANE *Greek Pott.* iv. 26 Kotyle, painted in brown-black on greenish buff clay.

kou (kōu). [Hawaiian.] A Hawaiian tree, *Cordia subcordata*, of the family Boraginaceæ, or its dark brown wood.

1825 W. ELLIS *Jrnl. Tour Hawaii* i. 27 The houses, which are neat, are generally built on the sea-shore, shaded with cocoanut and *kou* trees. **1866** 'MARK TWAIN' *Lett. from Hawaii* (1967) 128 It [*sc.* the coffin] is made of those two superb species of native wood, kou and koa. The former is nearly as dark as ebony. *Ibid.* 207 Among the varied and handsome foliage of the kou, koa, kukui.. its [*sc.* the orange's] dark, rich green cone was sure to arrest the eye. **1913** J. F. ROCK *Indigenous Trees Hawaiian Islands* 415 The Kou, which is indigenous in the Hawaiian Islands,..can only be found along the sea-shore here and there... The wood of the Kou was much sought for. **1969** T. H. EVERETT *Living Trees of World* 292/2 A native of sandy shores of the Indian and the western Pacific oceans, the kou or sea trumpet (*C*[*ordia*] *subcordata*) is an evergreen tree that grows up to 50 feet in height and has a dense, spreading crown.

koukou, var. *KUKU I.

Koula(h), varr. *KULAH[1].

koulak, var. *KULAK.

kouprey (kū·pre). [Cambodian native name.] A large wild ox, *Novibos* (or *Bos*) *sauveli*, first discovered in Cambodia in 1937.

1940 *Mem. Mus. Compar. Zool. Harvard* LIV. 421 On comparing the measurements of the skull and skeleton of the kouprey with those of a gaur and a bantin, the kouprey revealed important differences. **1955** F. BOURLIÈRE *Mammals of World* iii. 131 Mention should also be made here of the curious Kouprey or Cambodian Forest Ox, whose taxonomic status is still rather uncertain. **1970** *New Scientist* 23 July 177/1 The kouprey (*Novibos sauveli*) was..a large blackish-brown animal, with prominent white legs and a chestnut facial pattern, the bull stands over 6 feet tall. **1971** *Ibid.* 11 Feb. 342/1 The American invasion of Cambodia last year probably put paid to the kouprey *Bos sauveli*, a primitive wild cow.

‖ **koura** (ku·ră). *N.Z.* Also **gorau, kora.** [Maori.] A small freshwater crayfish, *Paranephrops planifrons.*

1847 J. JOHNSON *Jrnl.* 5 Jan. in N. M. Taylor *Early Travellers N.Z.* (1959) 152 A small settlement, occupied in the summer for the purpose of catching *gorau*, a species of cray-fish, or rather fresh water lobster. **1867** E. SAUTER tr. *F. von Hochstetter's New Zealand* viii. 171 Of the Macrura I may mention especially *Paranephrops tenuicomis Dana...* The natives call it Koura. **1873** J. H. H. ST. JOHN *Pakeha Rambles through Maori Lands* viii. 151 Rotorua has its *kora*, a large prawn, or a diminutive freshwater lobster. **1945** F. SARGESON *When Wind Blows* 92 In the creek they saw the crayfish and Mr Jones said he called them crawlers, but the Maoris called them koura. **1974** *N.Z. Listener* 20 July 13/1 Here we were fed koura and kouras are a real luxury in the North Island.

‖ **kouros** (kū·rǫs). *Gr. Antiq.* Pl. **kouroi.** [Gr. (Ionic form of κόρος boy).] A sculptured representation of a youth.

1920 [see *KORE 2]. **1932** BEAZLEY & ASHMOLE *Greek Sculpture & Painting* vi. 27 For all the beauty and variety of the late archaic kouroi and korai, it is not in these that late archaic sculpture finds its most perfect expression, but in the action-figures—men not being but doing. **1939** *Ann. Brit. Sch. Athens* XXXVI. 2 The Anarysos Kouros is of Parian marble. It has a reddish tint; but in many places..the surface has perished to some extent. **1963** *Listener* 21 Mar. 511/1 The great *Kouroi* at the National Museum in Athens. **1965** D. E. STRONG *Classical World* 58 In figure-sculpture the ideal schemes of the nude *kouros* and the draped female (*kore*) hold the field until the early years of the 5th century.

koutekite (kū·tėkəit). *Min.* [f. the name of J. *Koutek* (see quot. 1958) + -ITE[1].] An arsenide of copper, Cu_5As_2, found as bluish-grey microscopic grains with a metallic lustre.

1958 Z. JOHAN in *Nature* 31 May 1554/1 While studying specimens from Černý Důl in Krkonose (Giant Mountains), Bohemia, a new mineral of composition Cu_2As has been found in the bicarbonate gangue... The new mineral has been named koutekite in honour of Academician J. Koutek, professor of economic geology, Charles University, Prague. **1967** *Mineral. Abstr.* XVIII. 281/2 Koutekite, Cu_5As_2.., has been recognized at Daluis in the upper Var Valley, where it occurs with domeykite.

kovsh (kǫvʃ). Pl. **kovshi.** [Russ.] A ladle or container for drink.

1884 A. MASKELL *Russ. Art* vi. 134 The bowls or ladles termed kovsh. **1935** *Burlington Mag.* June 298/1 The large kovsh, or ladle..follows an interesting evolution. **1949** H. C. BAINBRIDGE *Peter Carl Fabergé* vii. 133 Objects in..painted enamels in the way of ikons, kovshi, tea sets, [etc.]. **1960** *Harper's Bazaar* Aug. 11/1 A silver-gilt kovsh: used in Russia for drinking vodka. **1966** *Daily Tel.* 18 Oct. 16/5 At Sothebys... A Russian silver and enamel kovsh, a squat wine jug, went to G. Lawrence for £210.

kowdie, obs. var. KAURI.

1899 T. KIRK *Forest Flora N.Z.* 143 When the timber was first introduced into Britain it was termed 'cowrie' or 'kowdie-pine'.

kowhai. Substitute for def.: An evergreen shrub or small tree, *Sophora tetraptera*, of the family Leguminosæ, native to New Zealand and bearing racemes of yellow flowers. Add earlier and later examples.

1831 G. BENNETT in *London Med. Gaz.* 12 Nov. 182/1 *Sophora tetraptera...* This tree is the Kowhy, or Kongia, of the natives, and attains the height of from forty to fifty feet. **1897** D. MCK. WRIGHT *Station Ballads* 123 There are dreams in the gold of the kowhai. **1926** *Trans. N.Z. Inst.* LVI. 670 'Kowhai' went through many stages —'goa', 'gohi', etc., before settling to the two forms 'kowhai' in the North and 'gowhai' or 'gowai' in the South. **1947** O. RUHEN in *Coast to Coast 1946* 1 Old gold blossom freckled the untidy lattice of brown boughs that the kowhais threw up on the top of the bank. **1952** 'J. GUTHRIE' *Paradise Bay* i. 12 In a kowhai bush, among the yellow beak-shaped blossom. **1966** *New Statesman* 16 Dec. 915/3 The beach itself is sheltered by..bush patched with yellow and gold kowhai bloom and white clematis.

kow-tow. Now the usual form of KOTOW *sb.* and *v.* (with pronunc. kautau·). So **kow-tow·er.**

1863 *Fraser's Mag.* Dec. 709/2 With one dash of the brush a clever artist at once hits off all the characteristics of his subject, whether it be a bat or moth in the gloaming, or a humble cricket *kow-towing* to a lordly mantis perched on a blade of grass. **1864** [see KOTOW *v.*] **1874** A. C. MACLAY *Let.* 1 May (1886) 47 Then followed a tempest of *kow-towing* that beggared description. **1883** [see KOTOW *v.* b]. **1898** W. G. GULLAND *Chinese Porc.* I. p. xxiv, Lord Amherst..would not perform the *kow-tow* (kneeling) before the emperor. **1905** [see *HEWGAG]. **1907** *Westm. Gaz.* 12 Nov. 14/1 The degrading custom of high native Ministers of the Crown kowtowing. **1920** *Blackw. Mag.* Aug. 225/1 The conventional bowing or kow-tow position. **1961** *Spectator* 8 Sept. 313 They regard the Russians as..kow-towers to the West. **1966** D. FORBES *Heart of Malaya* xi. 129 Miss Khan kowtowed to the laughing monk. **1966** *Listener* 29 Sept. 443/2 Not even the emissaries of the Pope could escape the Great Kow-tow—the ceremony involving the three kneelings and nine prostrations before the throne of the Chinese Emperor. *Ibid.* 444/1 An envoy of the Tsar who arrived in Peking in the sixteen-seventies to discuss Russo-Chinese differences refused to kow-tow to the Emperor. **1972** *Times* 21 Oct. (Hongkong Suppl.) p. i/6 Peking has referred officially to Hongkong's shameful colonial status only once since President Nixon's dignified *kowtow* and the belated entry of the people's republic into the United Nations.

‖ **koyan** (koya·n). Also 9 **coyan.** [Mal. *koyan.*] In Malaysia, a unit of weight equal to 40 *piculs*, equivalent to approximately 5,330 lb. (2·42 tonnes).

1783 W. MARSDEN *Hist. Sumatra* 157 The *coolah* or bamboo, containing very nearly a gallon, is the general standard of measure among the Rejangs: of these eight hundred make a *coyan.* **1820** J. CRAWFURD *Hist. Indian Archipelago* I. III. i. 273 Thirty pikuls [make] one *koyan.* **1839** T. J. NEWBOLD *Pol. & Statistical Acct. Straits of Malacca* I. i. 26 Salt, and..rice, etc. are sold by measure, generally by that of the coyan. **1900** W. W. SKEAT *Malay Magic* v. 228 A field which..produces a *koyan* of rice a year will fetch a rent of about two hundred gallons more or less. **1947** R. O. WINSTEDT *Malays* 125 The produce of rice formerly exceeded the internal consumption by about the annual average of 2,500 *koyan.* **1957** *Federation of Malaya Ann. Rep.* II. iv. 519 The *koyan* (40 *piculs*)..—5,333⅓ lbs.

K(-)particle. *Nuclear Physics.* Also † **k-particle.** = *KAON.

1949 *Nature* 15 Jan. 85/2 The agreement between the sets of values for mesons..gives strong support for the assumption of a spontaneous decay of the *k*-particle. **1954** *Proc. R. Soc.* A. CCXXI. 293 Those charged particles more massive than the π-meson which, at the end of their range in the emulsion, transmute with the emission of a singly-charged particle, are referred to as *K*-particles... The charged particles are in some cases μ-mesons, and others π-mesons. **1955** *Sci. News Let.* 19 Feb. 117/2 K particles are mesons of mass intermediate between electrons and protons. **1966** D. L. LIVESEY *Atomic & Nucl. Physics* x. 468 The neutral *K* particle must therefore possess a rest mass greater than 550 *me*, the measured energy release being such that the calculated mass is about 1000 *me.*

kra (krā). Also **kera.** [Mal. *kera.*] The long-tailed or crab-eating macaque, *Macaca fascicularis* (= *M. irus*), native to southern and south-eastern Asia.

1821 T. S. RAFFLES in *Trans. Linnean Soc.* XIII. 247 The Malay name has frequently a close resemblance to the cry of the animal it designates; and this is remarkably the case in the present instance... The Kra is not easily domesticated. **1839** T. J. NEWBOLD *Pol. & Statistical Acct. Straits of Malacca* I. vii. 432 Of the genus Semnopithecus are..the Lotong,..the Kra, or Simia fascicularis. **1911** *Encycl. Brit.* XVII. 472/2 The *lotong*, *kra*, and at least twenty other kinds of monkey. **1932** S. ZUCKERMAN *Social Life Monkeys* ix. 143 No periodicity has been noted in the rarely observed sexual response of bonnet monkeys and adult female kra monkeys (common macaques). **1969** LD. MEDWAY *Wild Mammals Malaya* 50/2 Long-tailed or Crab-eating Macaque. Kera. *Macaca fascicularis.*

‖ **kraak porselein, kraakporselein** (krāk pōə·rsĭlēin). Also (with partial tr.) **kraak porcelain.** [Du.; see quot. 1954.] Blue-and-white Chinese porcelain of the Wan-li period (1573–1619) or later in the seventeenth century, or a European imitation of this.

1954 H. GARNER *Oriental Blue & White* v. 37 This type of porcelain is known as *Kraak porselein*, from the Dutch term for the type of Portuguese ship from which the porcelain was first captured in 1603. The ship, the carrack *Catherina*..was..taken to Amsterdam. *Ibid.*, Kraak porcelain had a great influence on the development of European pottery, being extensively copied at Delft. **1956** J. A. POPE *Chinese Porc. Ardebil Shrine* II. 137 In terms of general shape the most noticeable difference between these *kraakporseleins* and other sixteenth-century wares is to be found in the dishes. **1961** M. SULLIVAN *Introd. Chinese Art* ix. 185 Soon after 1600 a particular type of thin, brittle Wan-li export blue-and-white began to reach Europe. This ware, called *kraak* porcelain.. caused a sensation when it appeared. **1969** *Times* 25 Mar. 15/5 (Advt.), Kraak porselain [*sic*] dishes.

kraal, *sb.* Add: **2. b.** In Sri Lanka, an enclosure into which wild elephants are driven; also, the process of capturing elephants in this way. Also *attrib.* So **kraal-town,** a town formed to accommodate the company assembled to view a kraaling of elephants.

1891 *Outing* (U.S.) Dec. 171/1 An elephant kraal is no simple matter, the drive taking possibly a couple of months to accomplish. *Ibid.*, Gradually, slowly but surely, the herds..are driven toward the kraal. *Ibid.* 174/1 In less than a week's time a town springs into existence. 'Kraaltown!' with its clubs, hotels, saloons, cafés, and 'chummeries', to say nothing of suburban villas, etc. **1933** D. E. BLUNT *Elephant* ii. 103 Great difficulty was experienced in finding the best way of capturing the young African elephants, the *keddah* or *kraal* method used in Ceylon proving impossible in the Congo. **1956** R. PIERIS *Sinhalese Social Organization* v. ii. 185 The *pannikalē* assisted in driving the elephants into the *kraal* or enclosure.

c. An enclosure in water for holding live sponges or turtles.

1939 *Nature* 13 May (Suppl.) 807/2 Inshore waters in close proximity to sponge kraals. **1961** *Encounter* Apr. 18/2 The turtles swim in dense kraals.

kraal, *v.* Add: Also of elephants.

1891 *Outing* (U.S.) Dec. 174/2 Hurrying them to the kraal we lowered the huge bars and kraaled our first elephant.

krab (kræb), colloq. abbrev. *KARABINER.

1963 *Oxf. Mountaineering* 8 To add to my worries I found that I was down to my last krab. **1970** *Sunday Mail* (Brisbane) 3 May 7/6 On the way up, the leader puts pitons in the rock, and runs his rope through krabs behind him so he cannot fall far.

kraddy, var. *KORARI.

Kraft (krāft). Also **kraft.** [Sw., = strength, in *kraftpapper* kraft paper.] A strong smooth brown paper made from unbleached soda pulp. Also *attrib.* In full, *kraft paper, kraft brown.*

1907 G. CLAPPERTON *Pract. Paper-Making* (ed. 2) 37 'Kraft' brown papers. *Ibid.*, No Kraft yet produced in this country combines the crispness and elasticity which form so distinctive a feature of the Kraft papers produced by the best Scandinavian mills. **1914** E. A. DAWE *Paper* 56 Kraft browns may be described as glazed browns, as they are sometimes finished with a glazed surface both sides. A special kind of pulp is used for krafts. **1920** *Glasgow Herald* 12 June 5 In the case of sulphite and kraft processes the pulp is prepared by cooking chips of

wood under pressure with different liquor solutions. **1930** *Economist* 8 Feb. 303/1 The market for kraft paper must be regarded as declining, but the Swedish newsprint mills are well supplied with orders. **1959** *Gloss. Packaging Terms (B.S.I.)* 67 *Kraft liner*, a kraft paper used as the outer or inner facing in the manufacture of solid and corrugated fibreboard, and in the manufacture of fibreboard drums and tubes. **1968** *Economist* 3 Feb. 63/2 Swedish pulps are mainly for kraft, including sack paper, and newsprint. **1969** T. C. Thorstensen *Pract. Leather Technol.* ix. 143 In the manufacture of paper, lignin of the logs of the wood chips is released by cooking the chips with bisulfite in accordance with the Kraft process.

‖ **kragdadig** (kraχdā·diχ), *a. S. Afr.* Also **kragdadige.** [Afrikaans, = Du. *krachtdadig.*] Resolute, firm, vigorous. Hence **kragda·digheid** (-hēit), resoluteness, spirit of determination.

1949 *Cape Times* 21 Sept. 8 Where any evidence can be found in this rigmarole of tentativeness for the *kragdadigheid* which is supposed to distinguish Nationalist Ministers we fail to see. **1952** *Ibid.* 21 May 5/3 The Government wanted to make scapegoats of himself and Mr. Carneson so that it could claim *kragdadige* (strong) steps against communism. **1957** *Cape Argus* 11 Feb. 8/8 Signs of that kragdadigheid of which Cabinet spokesmen claim a monopoly. **1958** *Cape Times* 18 Feb. 8/5 Mr. Sauer's answer was that the inquiry was merely United Party propaganda and he was not going to answer it... That is at least a nice *kragdadige* answer. **1963** *Time* 10 May 30/2 Helen Suzman warned that black nationalism as well as white nationalism feeds 'on this type of *kragdadigheid* (toughness)'. **1973** *Sunday Times* (Johannesburg) 15 Apr. 17 Even the Minister of Sport..could not restrain himself from issuing one of those kragdadige statements that get no one anywhere. **1974** *Daily Despatch* (East London) 4 Feb. 8 The new Parliamentary session has barely started and already there are distressingly clear pointers that it will be the season for kragdadigheid.

Krag–Jørgensen (kræg,yō·ɹgənsən). The names of O. H. *Krag* (1837–1912) and E. *Jørgensen*, Norwegian firearm designers, used to designate a type of rifle (and carbine) introduced in Denmark and Norway in the late nineteenth century and adopted in U.S.A. Abbrev. (colloq.) Krag.

1899 *Scribner's Mag.* XXV. 20/1 Our arms were the regular cavalry carbine, the 'Krag', a splendid weapon, and the revolver. **1901** *Kynoch Jrnl.* Aug.–Sept. 133/2 He has also the latest pattern..Ross straight pull Krag–Jorgensen. **1902** *Encycl. Brit.* XXV. 658/1 The cavalry is armed with the Krag–Jorgensen carbine. *Ibid.*, The infantry and coast artillery have the Krag–Jorgensen rifle. **1910** *Harper's Weekly* 5 Mar. 16/3 Krag–Jorgensen rifles were cracking merrily in their users' pursuit of the wily amigo... Damn, damn, damn the Filipinos, cross-eyed kakiak ladrones. Underneath our starry flag civilize 'em with a Krag, And return us to our own beloved homes. **1964** H. L. Peterson *Encycl. Firearms* 186/1 The bolt-action Krag–Jørgensen..was developed during the 1880's. *Ibid.* 186/2 The loading gate on the Danish Krag pivots forward, while those of the Norwegian and American Krags pivot horizontally.

krai, var. *Kray.

Krakowiak (krăkōᵘ·vi,æk). Also **-wyak.** [Polish, f. *Kraków* (Eng. Cracow), a city and region in southern Poland.] = Cracovienne.

1888 F. Niecks *Frederick Chopin* II. xxx. 233 Chopin has only once been inspired by the krakowiak—namely, in his Op. 14, entitled *Krakowiak, Grand Rondeau de Concert.* **1958** P. Kemp *No Colours or Crest* xii. 278 Waltzes and foxtrots were abandoned for the whirling, stamping folk dances of Poland—the Krakowiak, Oberek, and Kujawiak. **1966** *New Statesman* 1 Apr. 465/2 A yellowing piece of paper testifying that in 1952 its bearer danced the Krakowyak satisfactorily before an audience of experts.

Krama, var. *Kromo.

kramat (kramā·t, krā·măt). Also 8 **crammat;** 9 **grammat, kramet; karamat, keramat.** [ad. Mal. *keramat* adj., numinous, sacred, holy, unusual, having supernatural qualities; sb., holy place, holy person; ad. Arab. *karāmāt*, pl. of *karāma* miracle worked by a saint other than a prophet.] A Muslim holy place or place of pilgrimage (see also quot. 1833). Also as *adj.*, sacred.

1783 W. Marsden *Hist. Sumatra* 203 The place of greatest solemnity for administering an oath, is the *crammat* or burying ground of their ancestors. **1833** G. Greig *S. Afr. Almanac & Directory* 156 A tomb of a celebrated Malay Priest, near the farm Zandvliet, is frequently visited by the Mahomedans, and where they perform Divine Service, or what is called Grammat. **1839** T. J. Newbold *Pol. & Statistical Acct. Straits of Malacca* I. v. 252 In every part of the country are found tombs of men famed for piety... They call such tombs Kramets. **1900** W. W. Skeat *Malay Magic* 61 There is usually in every small district a holy place known as the *kramat.* **1910** D. Fairbridge *That which hath Been* xxiii. 283 Near the sand hills and the sea lies the kopje on the summit of which is the white mosque, the kramat, which marks to this day the resting place of Sheik Joseph. **1944** I. D. Du Plessis *Cape Malays* iii. 31 From the tomb of Sjech Yussuf a series of *Karamats* stretches in a rough circle round the Peninsula. **1947** L. G. Green *Tavern of Seas* xiv. 136 Followers of the Prophet listening to the reading of the Koran within the 'kramat'. **1947** R. O. Winstedt *Malays* 24 Many sacred (*Keramat*) places are the graves of by-gone shamans. **1964** R. Perry *World of Tiger* xiv. 221 The *kramat* tiger of Malaya..is protected by a guardian spirit and can be driven away from a cattle-fold by a child. **1965** R. McKie *Company of Animals* v. 84 He was *kramat* which is as near as any animal can come to being regarded as sacred. **1970** *Straits Times Ann.* 68 Here are three Malay Tombs. They are *keramat*, a sacred or respected place. **1971** *Drum* July 55 As the street fills, there'll be Coons and a band and a jam session, the scene fading out into a shot on Signal Hill, where the Karamat singers will chant the sacred Islamic music.

kran (krān). [ad. Pers. *qrān.*] A Persian coin and monetary unit.

1882 E. O'Donovan *Merv Oasis* I. 249 The Turcomans ..will accept only the old-fashioned *kran* and *toman.* **1902** *Encycl. Brit.* XXXIII. 513/2 The Indian rupee and the Persian kran are widely circulated through Mesopotamia. **1920** *Brit. Mus. Return* 75 in *Parl. Papers* XXXVI. 673 A silver kran of Muzaffar al-Din, Shah of Persia. **1922** *Blackw. Mag.* Mar. 393/1 For two krans an Arab will swear a false oath. **1933** V. Sackville-West *Coll. Poems* 178, I bought these beads in Isfahan; I bought a handful for a kran,—That's sixpence—at the motley stall. **1934** F. Stark *Valleys of Assassins* ii. 130 He allowed me to give him two krans with which he wandered off to buy our horses' dinner. **1958** F. Maclean *Person from England* v. 246 O'Donovan had with him a silver casket,..for which he had paid about six hundred *krans*, or twenty-five pounds sterling.

krans(e. *S. Afr.* = Krantz, kranz.

1785 G. Forster tr. *Sparrman's Voy. Cape Good Hope* II. xi. 48 He looked out for a *klipkrans* (so they generally call a rocky place level and plain at top, and having a perpendicular precipice on one side of it). **1852** C. Barter *Dorp & Veld* 93 We had been directed to look out for a white krans in the mountain. **1927** W. Plomer *I Speak of Afr.* i. 37 Eddies of sound reaching the nervous leaf-like ears of the krans-coloured sheep in the stones overhead cause them to lift their heads. **1939** tr. *E. N. Marais's My Friends the Baboons* iii. 32 The leopard was still ahead of us in the kloof and unless he had fled up the kranses, it was probable that we would meet him again. **1961** L. van der Post *Heart of Hunter* xiv. 189 All day long she [*sc.* the rock-rabbit] darts in and out of the shadows and clefts of our Kranses and rocky hill-tops.

krantz, kranz. Add: Pl. krantze, krantzes. (Later examples.)

1903 Kipling *Five Nations* 196 But 'e wasn't takin' chances in them 'igh an' 'ostile kranzes. **1916** J. Buchan *Greenmantle* xxi. 283 A little hill split the valley, and on its top was a *kranz* of rocks. **1924** R. Campbell *Flaming Terrapin* iv. 72 Her pitchy crows..cling with gnarly toes To their steep krantzes. **1952** *Cape Times Mag.* 19 July 6/5 Inquisitive baboons often watch the bathers from the krantze above. **1959** G. Jenkins *Twist of Sand* xiv. 301 Peaks and valleys, fretted with razor-like kranzes and unscaleable cliffs. **1966** E. Palmer *Plains of Camdeboo* v. 89 Koeltas, our guide, led us round the side of a krantz by a pathway as narrow as a bit of string.

‖ **krapfen** (kra·pfĕn). [G.] In Germany and other German-speaking areas: a doughnut (see also quot. 1845).

1845 E. Acton *Mod. Cookery* (ed. 4) App. 581 *Appel krapfen*... Boil..apples..mix them with..almonds, beaten to a paste,..raisins..cinnamon..roll out some butter-crust..cut into four-inch squares,..fill them.. lay another square on each,..bake them. **1877** E. S. Dallas *Kettner's Bk. of Table* 156 Beignets à la Dauphine. .. Throughout Germany they are known as Berliner Pfannkuchen; throughout Austria as Wiener Krapfen. **1966** P. V. Price *France: Food & Wine Guide* 151 *Krapfen* (rather like little light doughnuts).

krater, var. Crater 1.

1857 [see Crater 1]. **1935** *Antiquity* IX. 414 The low stems..are more difficult to place, but they resemble the stems of the kraters in the contemporary group from Lakkéthra in Cephallenia. **1950** H. L. Lorimer *Homer & Monuments* ii. 73 Argive Geometric krater of early type from Amathus. **1969** R. Tashkent *Ambiguous Man* viii. 80 The great swords, the daggers, pins, cups, kraters, spears. **1974** *Times* 8 Mar. 9/3 Mr Hecht bought fragments from Mr Sarrafian as a cover for selling fragments of a krater unearthed in Italy and smuggled out for sale to the Metropolitan.

kratogen (kræ·tŏdʒen). *Geol.* [a. G. *kratogen* (L. Kober *Der Bau der Erde* (1921) i. 21), f. Gr. κράτο-ς strength: see -gen.] An area of a continent that has resisted deformation over a (geologically) long period of time. Hence **kratoge·nic** *a.*

1923 *Bull. Geol. Soc. Amer.* XXXIV. 210 The 'Kratogens', once the area of the most ancient geosynclines, may, after they are peneplained, be widely flooded by epeiric seas. **1934** *Geogr. Jrnl.* LXXXIII. 515 After a few preliminary chapters dealing with the evolution of orogenic and kratogenic (continental) areas, he sets forth his views on..mountain-building. **1939** R. Ruedemann in Ruedemann & Balk *Geol. N. Amer.* I. 48 The geosynclines appear to be the compensating areas of subcrustal flowage between the subsiding oceans and the unmoved or horst-like neutral areas or 'kratogens' of the positive elements. **1969** Bennison & Wright *Geol. Hist. Brit. Isles* v. 91 Certainly, the Midlands of England formed a kratogen which persisted throughout the Ordovician and Silurian. *Ibid.* vi. 129 The marginal facies of south Shropshire and the English Midlands, which were similarly laid down on the margins of the (Midlands) kratogenic block and by shallow seas spreading across it.

kraurosis (krǭrōᵘ·sis). *Path.* [mod.L. (A. Breisky 1885, in *Zeitschr. f. Heilkunde* VI. 75), f. Gr. κραῦρ-ος brittle, dry + -osis.] Atrophy of the skin of the vulva, by some regarded as a distinct disease.

1888 *Trans. Amer. Dermatol. Assoc.* 64 Under the name 'Kraurosis' Professor Breisky, in his book on gynaecology, describes a disease of the vulva, which he considers a hitherto unknown form... The same disease has been described, fourteen years ago, by Robert F. Weir, of New York, as 'Ichthyosis of the Vulva'. **1901** C. H. Roberts *Outl. Gynæcol. Path.* i. 14 In Kraurosis, the tissues of the vulva are smooth and pale, with irritable tender red patches along the margins of the hymen and in the vestibule. **1948** W. Schiller in W. A. D. Anderson *Path.* xl. 1167 Kraurosis rarely follows the artificial menopause produced by operative removal of the ovaries. **1973** A. S. Woodcock in Fox & Langley *Postgrad. Obstetr. & Gynaecol. Path.* iv. 57 Kraurosis and senile atrophy are generally accepted as synonymous.

Hence **krauro·tic** *a.*, affected with kraurosis.

1894 *Brit. Med. Jrnl.* 7 Apr. Suppl. 63/1 Carcinomatous nodules were detected in the kraurotic tissue.

Krause (krau·zə). The name of Wilhelm *Krause* (1833–1909), Ger. anatomist and histologist, used in the possessive and with *of*-adjunct to designate structures in the body which he investigated, as: **a.** A kind of encapsulated plexus of sensory nerve endings found in mucous membranes, the dermis, the conjunctiva, and elsewhere. **b.** (A transverse membrane appearing as) a thin dark line separating adjacent sarcomeres in a striated muscle fibril. **c.** Each of the numerous small accessory lacrimal glands situated under the conjunctiva close to where it joins the eyeball.

a. 1872 H. Power tr. *Stricker's Man. Human & Compar. Histol.* II. xxix. 317 The nerves of the glans [penis] are very numerous and..end within the papillae in Krause's terminal bulbs. **1875** A. Gamgee tr. *Hermann's Elem. Human Physiol.* x. 457 Terminal nerve bodies (Krause's corpuscles) are oval, or more or less rounded vesicles of 0·03–0·06 mm, consisting of an areolar sheath, with nuclei and soft homogeneous contents, in which the nerve-fibre runs, terminating in a point. **1888** A. Flint *Text-bk. Human Physiol.* (ed. 4) xvi. 516 In certain membranes the nerves terminate in end-bulbs, or corpuscles of Krause. **1953** C. E. Osgood *Method & Theory Exper. Psychol.* i. 7 Pain is attributed to free nerve endings; cold to Krause's end bulbs. **1960** R. A. Weale *Eye & its Function* ii. 30 Their shape is reminiscent of one type of pressure receptor, namely Krause's corpuscle. **1972** M. L. Barr *Human Nervous Syst.* iii. 35/2 It was thought at one time that end-bulbs of Krause were receptors for coolness and end-bulbs of Ruffini for warmth, but the evidence that these are special temperature sensors is no longer regarded as conclusive.

b. 1873 *Phil. Trans. R. Soc.* CLXIII. 442 The transverse membrane of Krause and the narrow disk of intermediate substance..of Heppner would seem to be referable to the heads of two contiguous series of muscle-rods, which..often meet in the middle of the clear stripe. **1887** *Buck's Handbk. Med. Sci.* V. 65/2 Krause's membrane or intermediate disk. **1939** W. E. Le Gros Clark *Tissues of Body* v. 99 Cutting through the isotropic disc is a thin dark line which is believed by some histologists to mark the position of a membrane (Krause's membrane) separating the length of the fibril into a series of partially isolated segments. **1970** Fallis & Ashworth *Textbk. Human Histol.* viii. 58 The major cross bands of the myofibrils are the A and I bands... In the center of the I band is a thin dark line known as the Z (Zwischenscheibe) band, or intermediate line of Krause; the Z band attaches to the sarcolemma at the periphery of the cell.

c. 1905 *Trans. Ophthalm. Soc.* XXV. 1 (*heading*) Cyst of Krause's gland. **1933** E. Wolff *Anat. Eye & Orbit* iii. 113 The glands of Krause are accessory lacrimal glands occurring under the conjunctiva from the fornix to the convex border of the tarsus. **1960** R. A. Weale *Eye & its Function* xii. 185 Accessory lacrimal apparatus is provided by Krause's glands.

krausite (krau·sait). *Min.* [f. the name of Edward Henry *Kraus* (1875–1973), U.S. mineralogist + -ite[1].] A pale yellow hydrated sulphate of potassium and iron, $KFe(SO_4)_2 \cdot H_2O$.

1931 W. F. Foshag in *Amer. Mineralogist* XVI. 352 In the Calico Hills, San Bernardino County, California, a small deposit of sulfates of iron [was found]. This deposit was found to contain a fair abundance of a new sulfate of iron and potash... For this new mineral species the writer proposes the name *krausite.* *Ibid.*, Krausite occurs in several different forms. That found in the alunite forms comparatively large but rough crystals... The krausite of the transition zone is in lemon yellow crystals, often clear and with brilliant luster. **1935** J. W. Mellor *Comprehensive Treat. Inorg. & Theoret. Chem.* XIV. 340 Krausite is insoluble in water; and is slowly hydrolyzed when left in contact with water. **1965** *Amer. Mineralogist* L. 1929 This spatial arrangement of the coordination polyhedra accounts for the perfect (001) and good (100) cleavages in krausite.

kraut (kraut). [a. G. *kraut* herb, vegetable, cabbage.] **1.** = Sauerkraut, sourcrout. Also *attrib.* and *Comb.*

[**1845** *Punch* IX. 94/1 Happy midst his native *kraut* [*sc.* cabbage] My princely Albert wanders.] **1855** Geo. Eliot in *Fraser's Mag.* June 311/1 *Kraut* and *wurst* may be

called the solid prose of Thuringian diet. **1895** *Montgomery Ward Catal.* 574/1 Kraut Forks..Combined Clothes Pounder and Kraut Stamper. *Ibid.* 576/2 Kraut Cutters, 8×26 inches. 3 cast steel knives. **1937** D. Runyon in *Collier's* 16 Jan. 47/2 Nicely-Nicely now observes that the very choicest spareribs are on Jake's plate, and also the most kraut. **1950** *Amer. Speech* XXV. 315/1 The recipe for krautfurters..under the title 'Kraut and Frankfurters Team in Delightful Casserole Dishes'. **1961** *John o' London's* 13 July 88/3 Such words as..turkeyfurter and krautfurter: the last-named being made from *sauerkraut.*

2. (Often with capital initial.) A German, esp. a German soldier. Also *attrib.* and *Comb. slang* (orig. *U.S.*).

1918 G. E. Griffin *Ballads of Regiment* 34 But he always loved a soldier, be he..'Krout' or 'Mick'. **1919** C. B. Hoyt *Heroes of Argonne* 41 The Frogs and Krauts got it fixed up between 'em. **1926** *Sat. Even. Post* 12 June 148/3 'Wait a while, fellers,' he said. 'The krauts are sockin' the crossroads.' **1929** W. T. Scanlon *God have Mercy on Us!* 4 What gives me a pain in the neck is all the time we wasted up at Verdun in the old trenches when we might have been killing Krautheads. **1936** *Our Army* Feb. 14 We and the kraut-eaters were mixing it up to make the world safe for bigger and better wars. **1938** Johnson & Pratt *Lost Battalion* 17 There were 'kraut' machine guns barking at them in the dark. **1945** *Daily Herald* 8 May 4/4 The men just said things like, 'Well, the Krauts are done for.' **1946** J. M. Scott *Other Side of Moon* ii. 32 It is the only building left standing in the village. The Krauts blew up the rest. *Ibid.* v. 86 The Kraut will soon have to fall back. **1954** W. Faulkner *Fable* 376 He's got to be killed from in front, by a Kraut bullet—see? **1957** M. K. Joseph *I'll soldier no More* (1958) xiii. 291 I'll fix you, you kraut bastard. **1962** R. Cook *Crust on its Uppers* i. 24 We were doing some biz near Munich.. back to this day in krautland. **1966** T. Pynchon *Crying of Lot 49* i. 15 Maybe..he should have been in a war, Japs in trees, Krauts in Tiger tanks. **1971** J. Osborne *West of Suez* i. 27 An odd Kraut or two, bellowing at their Fraus. **1974** *New Society* 21 Feb. 435/2 The Hitler stuff, together with the usual illustrations of inflated multi-million mark notes..looks more like what is inelegantly called 'Kraut-bashing'. **1974** L. Deighton *Spy Story* xviii. 195 'That goddamn Kraut sub,' said the Conning Officer.

kray (krai). Also **krai.** [Russ.] In the U.S.S.R., a second-order administrative division, a region, a territory.

1938 N. de Basily *Russ. under Soviet Rule* iv. 153 Practically each republic is administratively divided into provinces or regions (*oblast* or *kraĭ*). These provinces and regions are in turn divided into districts (*rayon*), towns, and villages. **1951** T. Shabad *Geogr. U.S.S.R.* ii. 46 An oblast or kray is usually organized in such a manner as to include..a well-coordinated economic region centering on an important industrial and commercial center and specializing in the production of some particular commodity, while striving for regional self-sufficiency in the greatest possible degree. *Ibid.* 47 Krays, which occur only in the Russian SFSR, are identical to the oblasts, but are usually larger in area—the term 'kray' is given to those divisions which contain autonomous oblasts. **1967** J. P. Cole *Geogr. U.S.S.R.* vi. 101 In Siberia some krays and oblasts are enormous, and extend from the Trans-Siberian Railway as far as the Arctic Coast.

Krebs (krebz). *Biochem.* The name of Sir Hans Adolf *Krebs* (b. 1900), German-born British biochemist, used *attrib.* (or occas. in the possessive) to designate a circular sequence of enzyme-catalysed reactions occurring in mitochondria as part of cell respiration in aerobic organisms, in which an acetyl group (bound to a coenzyme and produced by glycolysis or other catabolic processes) is combined with oxaloacetic acid and then oxidized by a succession of reactions which produces carbon dioxide, serves to convert adenosine diphosphate to the energy-rich triphosphate (by means of the cytochrome system), and regenerates oxaloacetic acid.

1941 *Jrnl. Biol. Chem.* CXXXIX. 483 Oxidation of pyruvate by the Krebs cycle involves its union with oxalacetate. **1950** *Chem. Abstr.* XLIV. 1552 (*heading*) Final stage in biological oxidation processes: Krebs' tricarboxylic acid cycle. **1955** *New Biol.* XIX. 85 The Krebs cycle is a mechanism through which the various synthetic activities of the cell mutually affect each other. **1969** *New Scientist* 9 Oct. 64/3 Because some of the intermediate compounds in the Krebs cycle need to be bled off for other purposes, the bacillus has a special mechanism for stoking up its level from glucose. **1971** *Sci. Amer.* May 128/2 Next are the tens or hundreds of mitochondria, the enclosures where the complicated biochemical machinery of the Krebs cycle is mounted, producing most of the cell's ATP fuel by the oxidation of small organic molecules. **1971** Yudkin & Offord *Harrison's Guidebk. Biochem.* (new ed.) xi. 101 The Krebs cycle is responsible for the oxidation of the acetyl group of acetyl coenzyme A.

kredemnon. (Later examples.)

1865 E. Rimmel *Bk. Perfumes* v. 94 There were many other modes of wearing the hair, such as the *strophos*, the *nimbo*, the *kredemnon*. **1940** *Times* 19 Mar. 6/3 The captains of two East Coast colliers exchanging views..on the merits of their kredemnons. **1959** E. Pound *Thrones* xcvi. 3 Κρήδεμνον..κρήδεμνον..and the wave concealed her, dark mass of water.

kreef (krīf, krēf). *S. Afr.* [Afrikaans, f. Du. *kreeft* lobster.] = *crawfish *sb.* 1 b.

1863 *Queenstown Free Press* 30 June (Pettman), A new theological schism has sprung up amongst the Malays touching the important question whether *Kreef* or crawfish is to be considered ceremonially unclean or not. **1902** [see *Cape lobster* (*Cape *sb.*[2] 4)]. **1936** *Nature* 11 Jan. 74/1 (*heading*) The natural history and utilisation of the Cape crawfish, kreef or spiny lobster, *Jasus* (*Palinurus*) *lalandii.* **1959** *Cape Argus* 7 Nov. 11/7 The three month open season for kreef fishing..opened last Sunday. **1970** *Cape Times* 28 Oct. (S.A. Fishing Rev.) 5/4 Previously the Government had allowed producers to export 6·9 m. tailweight pounds of kreef. **1970** G. Croudace *Scarlet Bikini* vi. 73 'And no *kreef*,' Tony said, referring to the rock lobster.

KREEP (krīp). [f. *K*, chem. symbol for potassium + *REE*, abbrev. for *r*are-*e*arth *e*lement + *P*, chem. symbol for phosphorus (in allusion to its unusual composition).] A substance found on the moon as glassy fragments and as a constituent of fines and breccias, characterized by a high content of potassium, phosphorus, and rare-earth elements and unusually little iron.

1971 *Sci. News Let.* 23 Jan. 62 Another Apollo 12 find ..was that of an exotic component called KREEP by some—for high content of potassium, rare earth elements and phosphorus—found in rock 13. **1971** N. J. Hubbard et al. in *Earth & Planetary Sci. Lett.* X. 343/1 We will refer to this distinctive glass as KREEP glass (from its distinctive potassium, rare-earth element, and phosphorus content). **1971** *Geochim. & Cosmochim. Acta Suppl.* 2 I. 393 Hubbard et al. (1971a) designated this class of material as the KREEP component. *Ibid.* 398 Breccias with glass matrices..are the most abundant form of KREEP in the soil samples. **1973** *McGraw-Hill Yearbk. Sci. & Technol.* 284/2 The activity fell off smoothly in the adjacent regions to the east and west, including the other near-side maria. ..The localization of the high U-Th regions indicates a restricted distribution of KREEP (a potassium, rare-earth, phosphate-bearing phase), with which the high U-Th component is associated in returned lunar samples.

Kremlin. Add: *The Kremlin* (in Moscow): (used for) the government of the U.S.S.R. Also *transf.* (in trivial use).

1933 H. G. Wells *Shape of Things to Come* II. § 9.211 The Kremlin was content to consolidate the kindred Slav Soviets. **1943** *Sun* (Baltimore) 28 Sept. 12/2 Moscow itself has taken pains to assure us that Mr. Browder has no direct pipeline into the secret councils of the Kremlin. **1961** *Evening Bull.* (Philadelphia) 5 Mar., The Kremlin is the only world capital powerfully arrayed against crossing the new frontier. **1966** [see *Elysée]. **1966** H. Sheppard *Dict. Railway Slang* (ed. 2) 7 *Kremlin*, British Rail Headquarters. **1973** *Times* 19 Feb. 18/7 People who referred to their head offices as 'the Kremlin'..were somehow lacking in motivation. **1974** *Times* 10 Apr. 18/2 Kremlin-watchers study the pages of *Pravda* for the slight shift in nuance.

So **Kremlino·logy**, the study and analysis of the Soviet Government and its policies; **Kremlinolo·gical** *a.*; **Kremlino·logist**, such an analyst; also *transf.*

1958 *Oxf. Mag.* 13 Feb. 289/1 For all his interest in Kremlinology..the author is not really very good at it. **1960** *Daily Tel.* 7 Dec. 12/2 Kremlinologists, versed in the mysteries of Marx and Lenin, Mao Tse-tung and Mr Khruschev, tell us that the signs are that Mr Khruschev has won yet another battle, at least on points. **1961** *Spectator* 2 June 806 The approach commonly nicknamed 'Kremlinological'. *Ibid.*, Exaggerated claims on behalf of this method by some of its practitioners..who..equate Kremlinology with Soviet studies as a whole. **1968** *Guardian* 2 Apr. 11/5 The 'Kremlinological' expertise which enabled the White House to play the Kremlin power game. **1970** *Ibid.* 1 Oct. 15/4 The question now teasing Labour Kremlinologists is how long Denis [Healey] will be satisfied to remain a mere member of the NEC. **1971** *Times* 22 Jan. 8/8 Kremlinology gone wild. **1972** A. Ulam *Fall of Amer. University* i. 35 The budding Kremlinologists were put in their place, which often and quite properly turned out to be the C.I.A.

Kremnitz, var. *Cremnitz.

Krems (kremz). [f. *Krems*, the name of a town of northern Austria.] Used *attrib.* to designate a white lead pigment used as a paint base; the same as Cremnitz white.

1854 F. W. Fairholt *Dict. Terms Art* 256/2 Krems White. A carbonate of lead;..it takes its name from the city where it is manufactured, Krems or Crems, in Austria, and is sometimes termed Vienna white. **1940** *Chambers's Techn. Dict.* 479/2 Krems white.

‖ **kreplach** (kre·plaχ), *sb. pl.* Also **creplach, -lich.** [Yiddish *kreplech*, pl. of *krepel*, ad. dial. G. *kräppel* fritter, cogn. w. G. *krapfen.] Triangular noodles filled with chopped meat or cheese and served with soup.

1892 I. Zangwill *Childr. Ghetto* I. 114 *Creplich*, which are triangular meat pasties. **1932** L. Golding *Magnolia St.* iii. vii. 555 She will also make *knishehs*, *varennikas*, *creplach* and *blintsies* for the old-fashioned Jewish people. **1954** *Amer. Speech* XXIX. 104 Though partial to gefilte fish, They scorn the kreplach and the knish, They list pastrami, but evince A total apathy to blintz. **1957** L. Stern *Midas Touch* viii. 66 The thought of *kreplach* and *matzoth* dumplings made his mouth water. **1965** *New Statesman* 20 Aug. 250/1 Kreplach (sing. krepl) are a kind of Jewish dumpling served in hot chicken soup on festive occasions... Chinese serve remarkably good kreplach in.. soup... Other close cousins of kreplach are ravioli and especially tortellini. **1972** F. B. Maynard *Raisins & Almonds* 89 My mother was making *kreplach.* She placed a dab of cheese on the dough and pinched it in carefully... The *kreplach* dropped into the boiling pot with a sharp plopping noise.

‖ **kretek** (kre·tek). [Indonesian *kerétèk.*] In Java, a cigarette containing cloves.

1958 H. Forster *Flowering Lotus* i. 6 These were the famous *kretek* cigarettes, in which the tobacco is mixed with cloves; their crackling gives the cigarettes their name. **1966** *Economist* 16 Apr. 235/2 A packet of *kretek*, the clove cigarette smoked by most people, costs almost as much. **1973** *Times* 27 Dec. 10 It also turns out that although Kawung smoking is in general associated with low socio-economic status, and that low status itself affects development of the disease, the relatively small numbers of patients with higher socio-economic status who smoke these cigarettes are also adversely affected, compared with patients of the same status who smoke Kretek or Western cigarettes.

kriegie (krī·gi). *slang.* [Abbrev. of G. *kriegsgefangener* prisoner of war: see -ie.] An Allied prisoner of war in Germany during the war of 1939–45 (see also quot. 1948).

1944 *World's Press News* 31 Aug. 17/1 The *Yorkshire Post* reports receipt of a remarkable publication from Yorkshire prisoners of war in Germany. This takes the form of a special volume called the 'Kriegie Edition' of the *Yorkshire Post. Ibid.* 17/2 Kriegie..is an abbreviation of the German for prisoner of war. **1946** Brickhill & Norton *Escape to Danger* 11 The worn track..which kriegies 'pounded' or 'bashed' (walked) for hours at a time. **1948** *Amer. Speech* XXIII. 217 (*heading*) Kriegie talk. *Ibid.* 218 Ex-prisoners from the E.T.O. speak of Jap kriegies, or, 'If there is another war I'll probably be a Russian kriegie,' and my personal usage would apply it to any prisoner of war from now on. **1956** D. M. Davin *Sullen Bell* ii. vii. 153 But there I was, a bloody kriegie for the rest of the war.

kriegspiel. Add: **2.** A form of chess invented about 1900 by M. H. Temple. Two players at separate boards play without seeing or being told each other's moves, though they may ask some strictly limited questions of an umpire who conducts the game at a third board.

1903 *Brit. Chess Mag.* Sept. 370 Kriegsspiel..may have merits, but it is not a war game. **1906** H. Cayley in *Chess Amat.* Nov. 46 (*heading*) Kriegspiel or the Chess War Game. **1922** *Brit. Chess Mag.* Oct. 375 As a chess-player he..preferred Kriegspiel, at which he was always the life and soul of the table. **1961** *Times Lit. Suppl.* 1 Dec. 870/5 Kriegspiel itself together with further variations. **1969** A. Glyn *Dragon Variation* viii. 237 There'd be simuls, rapid-transit, five-minute chess, kriegspiels, lectures in the evenings.

So **krie·gspieler, krie·gsspieler,** one who plays kriegspiel (in the senses of Dict. and Suppl.).

1891 *19th Cent.* Feb. 299 Keen Volunteers..are enthusiastic Kriegsspielers. **1916** *Brit. Chess Mag. Chess Ann. 1915* 58 The chartered libertine among P.E.'s, kriegspielers, and chess-players in general.

Krilium (kri·liŏm). [f. *kril-*, altered form of *-cryl-* of *polyacrylonitrile* + *-ium.*] A proprietary name of various mixtures of polyacrylate salts and other carboxylated polymers manufactured as soil conditioners for improving the texture of soil and its ability to resist erosion.

1952 *Sci. News Let.* 5 Jan. 8/2 The soil improvement chemical will come on the market soon under the name of Krilium. **1952** *Official Gaz.* (U.S. Patent Off.) 8 July 226/2 *Krilium* for synthetic resin materials in the form of powders, granules, emulsions, dispersions, and solutions. **1958** Teakle & Boyle *Fertilizers* iv. 116 Krilium is the name given to several compounds selected from over seven hundred chemical synthetics tested by Monsanto. Two of these, VAMA 6—Krilium (6 vinylacetate: maleic acid complex) and HPAN 9—Krilium (9 polyacrylonitrile) have earned good reports. **1967** G. W. Cooke *Control of Soil Fertility* xxix. 458 'Krilium' produced an improvement in the percentage of soil aggregates which were stable in water.

krill (kril). Also **kril.** [ad. Norw. *kril* very small fry of fish.] A small, shrimp-like crustacean of the order Euphausiacea, or a large group of these animals, forming food for fishes and whales.

1907 J. G. Millais *Newfoundland* viii. 164 In June.. whales suddenly become extremely scarce, owing..to the trend seawards of the stream of 'kril' or red shrimp, on which the great *Balænoptera* subsist. **1912** *Rep. Brit. Assoc. Adv. Sci.* 178 A small red crustacean...forms the 'krill' of the whalers. **1928** Russell & Yonge *Seas* v. 117 Euphausiids, or 'krill', as they are called by the Norwegians..are about an inch and a half in length, but are so abundant that they form a large part of the food of many of the northern fishes, and are the chief food of nearly all of the whalebone whales. **1931** *Discovery* XII. 317/1 The catches of plankton show that the shrimp-like crustaceans, or 'kril', on which the whales feed are not.. to be found only in local concentrations, but are spread over immense areas in the open ocean. **1959** A. Hardy *Fish & Fisheries* i. 10 The largest of these whales, the rorquals,..specialise in feeding upon the krill (euphausiacean shrimps) which, though large for plankton animals, are but an inch or so in length. **1970** *Sci. Amer.* Dec. 20/3 Perhaps a crop of suitably large zooplankton such

as krill—the shrimplike animals that are the principal food of the baleen whales in the Antarctic—could be raised in a fertilized lagoon.

krimmer (kri·məɹ). Also **crimmel, crimmer, krimma.** [G., f. *Krim* (Russ. *Krym*) Crimea (see *CRIMEAN *a.*).] A grey or black fur made from the wool of young lambs in or near the Crimea; an imitation of this. Cf. *ASTRAKHAN b, *KARAKUL b.

1834 *Penny Cycl.* II. 519/2 The lamb yields a fine and beautiful fleece, which the dealers call a 'crimmel', the bulk of them being imported from the Crimea. **1892–3** *T. Eaton & Co. Catal.* Fall & Winter 10/2 The same styles of garments trimmed in a hundred different ways with krimmer, imitation lamb, persian-lamb, beaver, otter, nutria, sable, [etc.]. **1904** *Westm. Gaz.* 28 Jan. 4/2 Chinchilla or krimmer. **1906** *Ibid.* 3 Nov. 13/1 Grey krimmer. **1923** *Ibid.* 26 Jan. 11/1 A definition of 'crimmer lamb', as a commodity in the fur trade, was agreed upon at Marlborough-street yesterday. **1929** [see *KARAKUL]. **1930** *Economist* 1 Nov. (Russian Suppl.) 37/2 Hare-Peschanik, Persian Lamb, Persian Lamb-Broadtail, Crimmer Lamb. **1949** *Amer. Speech* XXIV. 96 Another common type of Persian lamb is the krimmer... It is characterized by heavier fur and looser curl. Other strains of lamb can be dyed to simulate krimmer.

Krio (krī·,o). [Native name.] An English-based Creole language in Sierra Leone. Also *attrib.* or as *adj.*

1955 P. STREVENS *Papers in Lang.* (1965) ix. 116 There is the Freetown Krio, an English-based language, containing many borrowings from Yoruba. **1957** M. BANTON *W. Afr. City* i. 6 The Creoles..developed a distinctive dialect version of the English language, known as Krio, which incorporates Portuguese, African, and other loan words, has an African rather than a European syntax, and is incomprehensible to the untrained English ear. Krio is to be distinguished from the native pidgin. *Ibid.* ix. 166 *Geda* is the Krio form of the English 'together'. **1961** *Guardian* 16 Feb. 6/4 Krio, the special Creole patois spoken in Sierra Leone. **1963** *Ann. Reg. 1962* 452 The threat of a collapse into a dialect deriving from English but not easily understood, a dialect less accessible than the base but genuine *lingua franca* of 'Pidgin': Krio, the language spoken at Freetown, was an example. **1972** W. B. LOCKWOOD *Panorama Indo-Europ. Lang.* 119 Creole English has also developed in West Africa. Krio 'Creole', centred on Freetown, Sierra Leone, is of complex origin.

kris, kriss. Now the usual forms of CREESE *sb.*

1883 [see CREESE *sb.*]. **1895** CONRAD *Almayer's Folly* xi. 220 With a shout and a leap he would be in the midst of them, kriss in hand, killing, killing, killing. **1927** R. J. H. SIDNEY *In Brit. Malaya To-Day* 62 She will give Raja Besi a *kris* by means of which he will be able to kill the Jin. **1935** WODEHOUSE *Blandings Castle* iv. 107 Malays, when pushed past this point, take down the old *kris* from its hook and go out and start carving up the neighbours. **1948** W. S. MAUGHAM *Here & There* 315 He awakened just as he thought a kriss was being drawn across his throat. **1953** *News Chron.* 2 June 7/1 In the first carriage is the Sultan of Kelantan... He carries a kris (a dagger) made from an elephant tusk. **1964** R. PERRY *World of Tiger* vii. 106 The bull succumbed to stabs from poisoned *krises* tied to poles. **1965** R. MCKIE *Company of Animals* i. 16 An ancient Malay kris with ivory scabbard and garuda hilt. **1972** M. SHEPPARD *Taman Indera* 127 A short beak and a pair of folded arms can be recognized on many Malay kris-hilts to this day.

Krishna (kri·ʃnă). The name of a Hindu deity or hero (see KRISHNAISM), used *attrib.* to designate Krishnaism or followers of this cult. Cf. *HARE KRISHNA.

1875 MONIER WILLIAMS *Indian Wisdom* xii. 332 Kṛishṇa-worship is comparatively modern. **1895** E. W. HOPKINS *Religions of India* xv. 405 One may represent the attitude of a Krishna-worshipper in the epic somewhat in this way. *Ibid.* 411 The regular Vishnuite laudation affected by the Krishna sect. *Ibid.* xvi. 469 The parallels between the latest Krishna cult and the Biblical narrative are found..in the Puranas. **1958** GERTH & MARTINDALE tr. *Weber's Religion of India* (1960) iv. 138 Vishnu..is honored..as patron of the dance drama and erotic orgies of the Krishna-cult. *Ibid.* v. 188 The ardent love of the redeemer of the later Krishna religion. **1970** J. NEEDLEMAN *New Religions* (1972) x. 212 Who has walked the streets of any American..cities without encountering the young followers of the Krishna Consciousness movement? **1971** [see *HARE KRISHNA]. **1973** R. THOMAS *If You can't be Good* (1974) vi. 44 A fairly old town house..a couple of doors or so down from the Krishna kids.

Kriss Kringle (kri:s kri·ŋg'l). *U.S.* ?*Obs.* Also **Christ-kinkle, Kriskringel, Krisking'l, Kris Kringle.** [See quot. 1919.] = SANTA CLAUS.

1830 J. F. WATSON *Annals of Philadelphia* 242 Every father in his turn remembers the excitements of his youth in Belsh-nichel and Christ-kinkle nights. **1849** J. REES *Myst. City Life* 93 Do you think Kris Kringle will come down the chimney to-night? **1864** *Sacramento Union* 7 Jan. 5/2, I do not know whether the good Saint Nicholas.. answers in those regions to the musical title of Kriss Kringle, as in the Queen City. **1919** H. L. MENCKEN *Amer. Lang.* iii. 89 Another example of debased German is offered by the American *Kriss Kringle.* It is from *Christkindlein*, or *Christkind'l*, and properly designates, of course, not the patron saint of Christmas, but the child in the manger. A German friend tells me that the form *Kriss Kringle*, which is that given in the Standard Dictionary, and the form *Krisking'l*, which is that most commonly used in the United States, are both quite unknown in Germany. **1928** G. ADE *Let.* 9 Oct. (1973) 136 We really believed that Kris Kringle could..go down chimneys which were not large enough to take care of a nest of barn swallows in the summer time. **1947** *Chicago Tribune* 20 July IV. 3/1 It is the story of an old man whose name was Kris Kringle and who believed he really was Santa Claus.

kriti (kri·ti). Also **krithi.** [Skr. *kṛti* the act of composing.] In the music of southern India, a song, often devotional in character, which is deliberately composed and not an improvisation on a set theme.

1914 A. H. F. STRANGWAYS *Mus. Hindostan* iii. 84 In Mudaliar Chinnaswami's *Oriental Music* sixty of his [*sc.* Tyagarāja's] songs (*Kritis*) are printed in staff notation. **1957** O. GOSVAMI *Story Indian Mus.* xix. 211 The *Kriti* is the most developed type of musical composition in the South. **1969** *Indian Express* (Bombay) 28 July 3/2 The krithi 'Naradamuni' in this raga was extremely pleasing. **1972** P. HOLROYDE *Indian Mus.* iii. 107 Kritis are sung in all tempos but without the long monosyllabic passages of the alamkaras or ornamentations.

Kromayer lamp (krōᵘ·məi,əɹ læmp). *Med.* [f. the name of Ernst *Kromayer* (1862–1933), German dermatologist.] A water-cooled mercury-vapour lamp used therapeutically for local ultra-violet irradiation.

1911 *Allbutt's Syst. Med.* (ed. 2) IX. 480 The comparative value of the Finsen-Reyn and Kromayer lamps has been studied by Maar. **1927** *Observer* 18 Dec. 9/2 We [*sc.* Bermondsey Council] have eight large mercury vapour lamps, two carbon arcs, and one water-cooled Kromayer lamp. **1949** E. B. CLAYTON *Electrotherapy & Actinotherapy* xx. 342 The Kromayer lamp is designed for local irradiation only. It has the advantages that, being water-cooled, it can be held in contact with the skin [etc.].

kromesky, -eski (krome·ski, krǫ·meski). Also **crom-, -esque, -esqui.** [ad. Polish *kroméczka*, little slice.] A croquette made of meat or fish minced, rolled in bacon or calf's udder and fried.

1846 C. E. FRANCATELLI *Mod. Cook* 309 Croquettes of Fowl and Mushrooms. The mince for these is prepared in the same way as for *Kromeskys.* **1861** —— *Cook's Guide* 120 Kromeskys are made with all kinds of croquet preparations, whether of meat, fish, or shell-fish. **1884** *Girl's Own Paper* May 428/1 A dozen oysters will make a moderate sized dish of kromeskies. **1892** *Encycl. Pract. Cookery* I. 478/2 Some authorities spell it Cromesquis, some Kromesquis, and others Kromeskies. **1920** E. SILVESTER *Sensible Cookery* 54 Kromesques of veal. **1928** *Evening News* 28 Dec. 4/5 Kromeskies of Turkey. **1951** *Good Housek. Home Encycl.* 348/2 A coating batter is used for making fritters, kromeskies, etc.

kromnek disease (krǫ·mnek). *S. Afr.* [Afrikaans, f. Du. *krom* crooked + *nek* neck.] A local name for the spotted wilt virus disease of tomato; also, a similar disease of tobacco.

1932 *Grocott's Mail* (S. Afr.) 2 Apr. 4 'Kromnek' or Kat River Wilt of tobacco is a disease which is not known anywhere in the world outside the Cape Province. **1933** E. S. MOORE in *Sci. Bull. Dept. Agric. Union S. Afr.* No. 123. 1 The disease known locally as 'Kromnek' or 'Kat River Wilt' is by far the most serious of the diseases of tobacco in the Stockviström division. *Ibid.* 15 The evidence indicated not only that the tomato disease is of virus nature but that probably it is caused by the same virus which is responsible for the tobacco kromnek. **1941** *Nature* 19 Apr. 480/2 Control of the Kromnek (Spotted Wilt) Disease of Tomatoes. **1957** K. M. SMITH *Textbk. Plant Virus Dis.* (ed. 2) 572 Tomato Spotted Wilt Virus... Synonyms: T.S.W. Virus; Kromnek or Kat River Disease Virus.

Kromo (krōᵘ·mo). *Indonesia.* Also **Krama.** [ad. Javanese *krama*, Indonesian *keromo.*] The polite form of Javanese, used by those of lower status when addressing social superiors.

1817 T. S. RAFFLES *Hist. Java* I. viii. 366 Nearly one half of the words in the vernacular language have their corresponding term in the *Bása Kráma* or polite language, without a knowledge of which no one dare address a superior. **1893** W. B. WORSFOLD *Visit to Java* xiii. 228 Two forms of modern Javanese are employed in everyday speech. First, the language of ceremony, called Krama; and secondly, the common speech, or Ngoko (meaning literally the thou-ing speech). **1925** P. RADIN tr. *Vendryès's Lang.* IV. ii. 257 Among the natives of Java, a superior speaks to his inferior in Ngoko, but the inferior answers in Kromo. **1932** W. L. GRAFF *Lang.* xi. 423 Official Javanese is called *kromo.* **1948** D. DIRINGER *Alphabet* II. vii. 424 Modern Javanese gradually breaks up into.. Krama Inggil, a form of speech used in addressing gods and the aristocracy, [etc.].

kromogram (krōᵘ·mŏgræm). *Photogr. Obs.* exc. *Hist.* Also **Kromogram.** [Altered form of *CHROMOGRAM.] = *CHROMOGRAM.

1897 *Brit. Jrnl. Photogr.* 8 Jan. 18/1 We understand that kromskops and sets of kromograms will shortly be obtainable from the Photo-chromoscope Syndicate Limited. **1898** [see *KROMSKOP]. **1969** H. & A. GERNSHEIM *Hist. Photogr.* (ed. 2) xliii. 523 In his Photochromoscope camera (1893) three separation negatives were taken in succession on one plate by means of a repeating back containing red, green and blue-violet filters. From these, diapositives were made by contact printing. When cut into the three separate pictures and laid on the Kromskop viewing instrument (1892) containing filters of the same colour and mirrors, the optically superimposed Kromograms appear in perfect colour.

kromskop (krōᵘ·mskōᵘp). *Photogr. Obs.* exc. *Hist.* Also **Kromskop.** [f. *krom-*, Ives's altered form of CHROMO- + *-skop*, altered form of -SCOPE.] A viewer for the three positives of a chromogram, enabling them to be visually combined and seen as a single coloured picture. Freq. *attrib.* (in Ives's use).

1897 *Brit. Jrnl. Photogr.* 8 Jan. 17/2 The Kromskop is the name finally chosen for Mr. Fred. E. Ives's perfected stereo-photo-chromoscope. **1898** F. E. IVES *Krōmskōp Color Photogr.* i. 6 The Kromogram must be placed in the Krōmskōp in order to visually reproduce the object photographed. *Ibid.* xi. 36 It is absolutely necessary to use in any of the Krōmskōp cameras the kind of orthochromatic sensitive plates for which that particular camera has been adjusted. **1928** O. WHEELER *Colour Photogr.* iii. 14 Almost equally obsolete, though still of considerable interest and comparatively practical from the amateur standpoint, is the additive arrangement adopted in an instrument..variously designated a photo-chromoscope, chromoscope or kromskop. **1968** E. DE MARÉ *Colour Photogr.* ii. 43 Ives also produced the Lantern Photochromoscope which projected the three pictures first through red, green and blue filters and then through three lenses directed to form a single image on a screen. He improved his camera and a viewer, which in a new form he called the Kromscope [*sic*]. It revealed stereoscopic pictures in full colour and this he demonstrated in 1896.

króna (krōᵘ·nă). Also **krona.** Pl. **krónur.** [Icel.; cf. KRONE.] The basic monetary unit of Iceland; also a coin representing one króna.

1886 R. SENF *Illustr. Postage Stamp Album* 47 Iceland ..Coinage:..100 öre (= aur) = 1 krona. **1922** P. A. ÓLAFSSON *Iceland* 24/2 The coinage is the same as elsewhere in Scandinavia, i.e. 1 króna (pl. krónur) = 100 aurar. **1938** *Encycl. Brit. Bk. of Year* 321/2 Currency unit: *króna* (exchange 22·15 krónur = £1). **1946** K. TRYGGVASON in T. Thorsteinsson *Iceland* (ed. 4) 164 Up to the end of the [1914–18] war there was little or no difficulty in keeping the Icelandic króna at par with the Danish Krone. **1958** *Spectator* 6 June 726/3 The Communists in the Icelandic Government are playing the fishing dispute for all they're worth, and trying to evade collective responsibility for economic measures which will drastically devalue the Kronur. **1970** D. BAGLEY *Running Blind* i. 28 A 100-kronur banknote.

Kronecker delta (krōᵘ·nekəɹ de·ltă). *Math.* [f. the name of Leopold *Kronecker* (1823–91), Ger. mathematician + DELTA.] A function of two integers defined as equal to one if the integers have the same value and zero otherwise; symbol δ_{ij} or $\delta_j^{\,i}$. Also (the *generalized Kronecker delta*), a function of $2k$ integers that takes the values 0 or ±1 (see quot. 1927[2]) (*rare*).

1927 O. VEBLEN *Invariants Quadratic Differential Forms* i. 3 The theory of determinants and allied expressions is essentially a theory of alternating sets of quantities, and can be made to depend on certain fundamental alternating sets of quantities which have only the values 0 and +1 and −1. These sets of quantities are known as generalized Kronecker deltas because of their analogy with the Kronecker delta which is already well known. *Ibid.*, The generalized Kronecker delta has *k* superscripts and *k* subscripts, each running from 1 to *n*... If the superscripts are distinct from each other and the subscripts are the same set of numbers as the superscripts, the value of the symbol is +1 or −1 according as an even or an odd permutation is required to arrange the superscripts in the same order as the subscripts; in all other cases its value is 0. **1937** A. A. ALBERT *Mod. Higher Algebra* (1938) x. 228 Our rule for multiplying matrices implies that $E_{ij}E_{kl} = \delta_{jk}E_{il}$ $(i, j, k, l = 1, \ldots, s)$ where δ_{jk} is the Kronecker delta. **1961** P. E. PFEIFFER *Linear Systems Analysis* ii. 30 The value Δ of a determinant whose elements are δ_{ik} is unity, where δ_{ik} is the Kronecker delta.

Kru: now the more usu. spelling of KROO.

1884, 1897 [see KROO]. **1957** M. BANTON *W. Afr. City* i. 5 Another important group was that of the Kru. They are members of a sea-faring tribe inhabiting part of what is now the Liberian coast. **1970** P. OLIVER *Savannah Syncopators* 41 The Kru speaking peoples of Liberia. **1973** *Times* 17 Apr. (Liberia Suppl.) p. vi/5 Elizabeth Tonkin has recently been from Birmingham on a study of Kru linguistics.

krug[1] (krug). [Ger.] A beer-mug or tankard.

1866 C. M. YONGE *Dove in Eagle's Nest* II. xii. 235 He has..excused himself from aiding his two gentlemen-squires in consuming their krug of beer. **1963** T. PYNCHON *V.* viii. 203 They seemed to seek some Hofbrauhaus of the spirit like a grail, hold a krug of Munich beer like a chalice.

Krug[2] (krug). The proprietary name of a champagne made by the firm of Krug et Cie. of Reims.

1876 *Trade Marks Jrnl.* 6 Sept. 455/1 Krug & Co. Reims. .. Paul Krug, of and on behalf of the firm of Krug and Co., Reims, France; champagne wine merchants. **1891** in C. Ray *Compleat Imbiber* (1967) IX. 122 All Brands of Champagne in stock..Pol Roger, Krug, Moët et Chandon. **1920** G. SAINTSBURY *Notes on Cellar-Bk.* v. 71 Taking

well-known brands..I do not know that I was more faithful to any than to Krug. **1967** G. SMITH in L. Deighton *London Dossier* 125 The best game pies..ideal for demolishing with a bottle of Krug in the car park before the Oxford and Cambridge game at Twickenham. **1974** D. MACKENZIE *Zaleski's Percentage* xv. 222 'Champagne for my friend, Inspector-Detective.' It was vintage Krug and perfectly chilled.

Krugerism (krū·gəriz'm). *Hist.* [f. the name of Stephanus Johannes Paulus *Kruger* (1825–1904), president of the Transvaal 1883–1901.] The nationalist (pro-Boer) policy of President Kruger. So **Krugerite** (krū·gərəit) *sb.* and *a.*, an adherent of, adhering to President Kruger or his policy.

1896 *Westm. Gaz.* 3 Dec. 5/1 Those who have effusively championed Mr. Chamberlain for what they imagined was his agreement with their Krugerite sympathies. **1897** *Daily News* 25 Jan. 5/6 Krugerites we know, and Rhodesites, but the Schreinerites (politically) all seem to live in London. **1897** *Times* 4 Feb. 3 Pure and unadulterated Krugerism. **1897** *Daily News* 24 Mar. 7/1 The conflict between the two ideals—the Rhodesian or British, and the Krugerite or non-British. **1900** *Pall Mall Gaz.* 29 Mar. 8/1 There are those who suggest that, perhaps, if the scrutineers had not been Krugerites, Joubert would have been found at the head. *Ibid.* 11 June 2/3 In the spring of last year he denounced the corruption of the Krugerite gang. **1902** KIPLING *Traffics & Discov.* (1904) 33 Van Zyl wasn't any Krugerite. **1923** B. RONAN *Forty S. Afr. Yrs.* 183 Rhodes..was recognised as the only leader capable of checking the spread of Krugerism in South Africa. **1972** *Sunday Times* (Johannesburg) Colour Suppl. 11 June 9 My father was not a Krugerite, he was a follower of Joubert, who would be called a Progressive today, I suppose.

Kruger rand (krū·gəɹ rænd, rant). Also **Kruger Rand, Krugerrand.** [f. *Kruger* (see prec.) + *RAND *sb.*] A South African gold coin bearing a portrait of President Kruger.

1967 *S. Afr. Digest* 14 July 3/3 The first gold Krugerrand coin was struck at the South African Mint in Pretoria last week by the Minister of Finance, Dr. N. Diederichs. *Ibid.*, The Krugerrand is to be minted in limited numbers and is intended for overseas issue. **1971** *Standard Encycl. S. Afr.* III. 313/2 The Krugerrand, a gold coin of 32·7 mm diameter containing 1 troy oz. of fine gold, was first struck in 1967. The obverse shows the bust of Paul Kruger. **1974** *Harpers & Queen* Sept. 33/2 Keep some Kruger rands under your mattress. **1974** *Daily Tel.* 14 Dec. 18/3 The South Africans are quickly taking advantage of the price rise by minting Krugerrands (made legal tender to avoid capital gains tax) and Britons have been flocking to buy the coins.

Krukenberg (kru·kĕnbəɹg). *Med.* The name of Friedrich Ernst *Krukenberg* (1871–1946), Ger. scientist, used *attrib.* to designate a kind of metastatic ovarian carcinoma that is usually secondary to a carcinoma of the stomach or colon (described by Krukenberg in 1896).

1911 *Amer. Jrnl. Obstetr.* LXIV. 930 Among a series of metastatic ovarian carcinomata two.. showed the picture of a Krukenberg tumor. **1934** R. A. WILLIS *Spread of Tumours* xxiii. 312 Gastric carcinomas which yield Krukenberg ovarian growths seldom yield metastases in other tissues. **1961** R. D. BAKER *Essent. Path.* xvii. 464 The most characteristic of the metastatic tumors [of the ovary] comes from the stomach, produces mucous, signet-ring cells, and is called Krukenberg tumor.

krummholz (krʊ·mhǫlts). [G. *krummholz* crooked wood, the popular name of a dwarf pine, *Pinus mugo* var. *pumilio*, adopted as the name for a particular type of vegetation by A. Grisebach in *Vegetation der Erde* (1872) II. xxiii. 488.] = *elfin-wood* (*ELFIN *sb.* 4).

[**1903** [see *ELFIN *sb.* 4].] **1908** *Bot. Gaz.* XLV. 334 The *Krummholz* is composed of two trees only... In its *Krummholz* form it [sc. *Pinus flexilis*] assumes the most fantastic shapes. **1942** R. PEATTIE *Friendly Mountains* 162 The upper part of the spruce slope dwindles to a 'scrub' forest, or 'krummholz'. **1964** GLEASON & CRONQUIST *Nat. Geogr. Plants* ix. 101 (*caption*) Dense, stunted growth of the sort here shown is known as Krummholz. **1967** *Jrnl. Glaciol.* VI. 820 Shading by krummholz spruce and fir, blueberry and willow.

krummhorn. Add: Also *CRUMHORN, **krumhorn, krum horn. a.** Delete 'obsolete' and add later examples.

1864 Krumhorn [in Dict.]. **1883** J. W. MOLLETT *Illustr. Dict. Art & Archæol.* 186/2 *Krumhorn*, an old musical instrument of the cornet kind. **1955** AUDEN *Shield of Achilles* iii. 76 There I stand in Eden again, welcomed back By the krumhorns, doppions, sordumes of jolly miners. **1969** *Daily Colonist* (Victoria, B.C.) 6 July 23/1 That's if you call 14th, 15th and 16th century harpsichords, clavichords, recorders, krum horns, citterns, lutes and oboes up to date.

Krupp (krʊp, ‖krup). [Name of Alfred *Krupp* (1812–87), German metallurgist, founder of steel and armament works at Essen in Germany.] A gun made at a Krupp factory.

1883 *Whitaker's Almanack* 445/1 She is a casemate ship ..armed with four 10-in. steel Krupps and one 12-in. Krupp. **1887** *Times* (Weekly ed.) 26 Aug. 8/1 The Krupps ..are mounted on Vavasseur carriages. **1900** *Daily News* 23 July 5/4 The Bogue Forts are being re-armed by the Chinese with quick-firing Krupps. **1916** 'BOYD CABLE' *Action Front* 264 One solitary Krupp dropping in here, and we'd have a pretty-looking mess. **1926** T. E. LAWRENCE *Seven Pillars* (1935) I. xiii. 95 The Arabs rejoiced when they came, and believed they were now equals of the Turk; but the four guns were twenty-year-old Krupps, with a range of only three thousand yards.

Hence **Krupped** (krʊpt), **Kru·ppized** *ppl. adjs.*, made or carried out in a manner originated by Krupps.

1899 *Army & Navy Register* (U.S.) 3 June 361/3 The great severity of the ballistic tests..necessitates the employment of a Kruppized process. **1902** *Encycl. Brit.* XXXI. 355/2 An A.P. shot should perforate two calibres of wrought iron, one calibre of Harveyed steel, or $\frac{6}{7}$ calibre of Krupped armour.

Kruschen (krū·ʃən). *Kruschen salts*, a proprietary aperient; also *ellipt.* As an advertising catch phr. *that Kruschen feeling*, a feeling of vigorous health.

1925 R. W. G. HINGSTON in E. F. Norton *Fight for Everest, 1924* 350 Kruschen salts, 2 bottles. **1925** R. MACAULAY *Casual Commentary* 131 The happy spring when..we are full of that Kruschen feeling. **1928** L. C. DUNSTERVILLE *Stalky's Reminisc.* xv. 226 He was very liverish in the early morning and had none of that 'Kruschen feeling' about him. **1936** C. DAY LEWIS *Friendly Tree* xii. 174 That Crane girl acts like a dose of Kruschen on the staff.

kryo-. Delete the def. of **kryokonite** (see *KRYOKONITE below).

kryokonite (krəiˌokōᵘ·nəit). Now usu. **cryoconite.** [f. KRYO- + Gr. *κόν-ις* dust + -ITE¹.] A grey powder found in layers at the bottom of holes in glaciers, at one time thought to be meteoric in origin but now thought to consist of dust blown by wind from areas beyond the ice margin. Also *attrib.* in *kryokonite hole.*

1872 A. E. NORDENSKIÖLD in *Geol. Mag.* IX. 356 In the bottom of them [*sc.* holes in the ice filled with water] we found everywhere..a layer..of grey powder, often conglomerated... The substance is not a clay, but a sandy trachytic mineral... I propose for this substance the name Kryokonite. **1889, 1891** Kryokonite [in Dict. s.v. KRYO-]. **1925** N. E. ODELL in E. F. Norton *Fight for Everest, 1924* 311 On the East Rongbuk Glacier were some rather beautiful examples of the so-called 'cryoconite holes' or 'dust holes', in which small particles of morainic material had melted their way down into the surface of the ice, as is so often to be seen on arctic glaciers especially. **1957** *Gloss. Geol.* (Amer. Geol. Inst.) 69/2 Absorption of radiation by the cryoconite causes ablation and formation of cryoconite holes or Dust wells. **1963** J. L. DYSON *World of Ice* xii. 138 In the bottom of every pit is a fine-grained gelatinous material called cryoconite, consisting partly of dust blown by the wind from areas beyond the ice margin. But cryoconite contains a considerable amount of organic material in the form of several kinds of blue-green algae and fungi. **1967** HAMELIN & COOK *Illustr. Gloss. Periglacial Phenom.* iii. 87 (*caption*) Cryoconite holes.

kryzhanovskite (kriʒǎnǫ·vskəit). *Min.* [ad. Russ. *krўzhanovskit* (A. I. Ginzburg 1950, in *Doklady Akad. nauk SSSR* LXXII. 763), f. the name of V. I. *Krўzhanovskiĭ* (1881–1947), Russ. mineralogist: see -ITE¹.] A greenish-brown hydrated basic phosphate of manganese and ferric iron, $MnFe_2(PO_4)_2(OH)_2.H_2O$, found in Kazakhstan, U.S.S.R.

1951 *Mineral. Abstr.* XI. 189 Kryzhanovskite, a new mineral in the group of phosphates... Rough crystals (2–3 cm.) of prismatic habit occur..in the oxidation zone of pegmatite. **1971** *Amer. Mineralogist* LVI. 5 Since kryzhanovskite is predominantly the ferric equivalent of the phosphoferrite group, the species has valid status and the name is to apply to all members of the phosphoferrite group containing an excess of 50 mol percent Fe^{3+} in the octahedral sites.

K-shell: see *K 3 e.

ktypeite (ti·pĕˌəit). *Min.* Also -ïte. [ad. F. *ktypéite* (A. Lacroix 1898, in *Compt. Rend.* CXXVI. 605), f. Gr. *κτυπέ-ω* crash, resound: see -ITE¹.] A form of aragonite, occurring as pisolites under strain, which decrepitates.

1898 *Jrnl. Chem. Soc.* LXXIV. 604 The violent decrepitation, on account of which the name ktypeite is given. **1902** *Ibid.* LXXXII. II. 89 Conchite..is identical with aragonite, and the same is probably also true of ktypeite. **1951** C. PALACHE et al. *Dana's Syst. Min.* (ed. 7) II. 191 Ktypeïte..is a name given to the substance of certain fibrous pisolites in the belief that it represented a new polymorph but which is very probably identical with aragonite. **1962** W. A. DEER et al. *Rock-Forming Min.* V. 312 'Ktypeite', from hot spring pisolites, is almost certainly aragonite.

kuaka (kwa·kă). *N.Z.* [Maori.] The bar-tailed godwit, *Limosa lapponica.*

1873 W. L. BULLER *Hist. Birds N.Z.* 198 *Limosa baueri.* (Barred-rumped godwit.) ... Native name.—Kuaka. **1882** W. D. HAY *Brighter Britain!* II. 222 The Kuaka..is the bird spoken of as 'curlew' and 'grey snipe' by colonists. **1905** W. B. *Where White Man Treads* 252 These thoughts flow through my brain like a covey of kuaka (snipe). **1966** *Encycl. N.Z.* I. 819/1 In New Zealand the great majority of our migrant birds are waders, and the best known and most abundant of these is the eastern race of the bar-tailed godwit, the kuaka of the Maori (*Limosa lapponica*).

Kuan, Kwan (kuān). [f. Chinese *guān, kuān* official.] Used to denote imperial patronage or official usage in China, as:

1. *Kuan Hua* (hwā) [language, speech] = MANDARIN¹ 2.

1814 J. MARSHMAN *Clavis Sinica* II. 559 The most correct and extensive colloquial dialect is termed..Kwan-hwà. **1845** *Encycl. Metrop.* XVI. 583/2 The learned language of the present day (*Kwan-hwa*) or dialect of the Mandarins. **1848** [see *mandarin dialect* (MANDARIN¹ 4)]. **1889** L. C. HOPKINS (*title*) Guide to Kuan Hua. **1932** W. L. GRAFF *Lang.* xi. 421 The modern Chinese of Pekin, the Mandarin, Kuan Hua, or Guoryu..has become the language of officialdom. **1968** *Encycl. Brit.* V. 634/1 Mandarin... Formerly called variously *kuan-hua* 'official speech', whence the term 'Mandarin', or *p'u-t'ung-hua* 'general (*v.* local) speech'.

2. *Kuan Yin* (yin) [Lord of Mercy], a goddess of Chinese Buddhism, to whom intercession for aid or protection is made; a representation in sculpture of this deity.

1845 *Encycl. Metrop.* XX. 490/2 The Kwan-yin, or merciful Goddess of the Chinese. **1871** S. BEAL *Catena of Buddhist Scriptures* 121 The work known as the Po-kien ..says:..The spirit..gazing on Kwan-Yin, a covenant saviour (a sworn friend). **1906** S. W. BUSHELL *Chinese Art* II. viii. 7 Large images of Kuan-Yin enamelled with turquoise blue and other soft colours. **1922** E. T. C. WERNER *Myths & Legends China* x. 251 As Mary is the guiding spirit of Rome, so is Kuan Yin of the Buddhist faith. **1930** O. SIRÉN *Hist. Early Chinese Art* III. iv. 47 In the tall eleven-headed Kuan-yins..a suggestion of movement may be observed. **1943** *Burlington Mag.* Dec. 311/2 Kuan yin figures of the Ming and Ch'ing period are represented in great numbers and show the eagerness of the artist to excel in decorative variations and in manual skilfulness. **1963** P. C. SWANN *Art of China, Korea & Japan* vi. 142 The best known of Sung Buddhist sculptures are the indolent *Kuan-yin* 'Goddess of Compassion' (the Sanskrit Avalokitésvara) figures with their full, fleshy bodies seated in the *maharaja-lila* or position of royal ease. **1969** R. QUEST *Cerberus Murders* v. 35 Some benign deity —Kuan Yin, perhaps.

3. In full, *Kuan ware, yao* (yau) [jade]. A type of thickly glazed celadon made in predominantly greyish colours at Hangchow during the Sung dynasty; similar pottery (as the *Kuan jar*) produced elsewhere in China in later centuries.

1888 F. HIRTH *Anc. Porc.* 19 Kuan-yao, or Mandarin Porcelain, is the produce of certain Government factories. **1915** R. L. HOBSON *Chinese Pott. & Porc.* I. iv. 48 One of the puzzling features in the study of the Sung wares is the interrelation of the various makes, such as the Ju, Kuan, [etc.]. *Ibid.* v. 59 A new pottery..copied the forms of the older Kuan ware. **1938** *Burlington Mag.* July 37/1 A *Kuan yao* saucer of a delicate bluish grey glaze. **1944** W. E. COX *Bk. Pott. & Porc.* I. xviii. 426 Neither of the Kuan yao factories so far as we know survived the Mongolian conquest. *Ibid.* II. xx. 592 (*caption*) Bottle vase with glaze of Kuan type of pale blue-green. **1960** *Times* 21 June 22/6 A..blue and white Kuan or wine jar. **1961** M. SULLIVAN *Introd. Chinese Art* viii. 158 As soon as Southern Sung had established themselves at Hangchow they naturally sought for factories which could produce a ware fine enough to be classed as *kuan.* **1971** P. DAVID *Chinese Connoisseurship* 139 *Kuan Ware.* This was made on the orders of the Palace Works Department.

Kuba (kūbā·). [The name of a town in north-east Azerbaijan, U.S.S.R.] = *KABISTAN.

1900 J. K. MUMFORD *Oriental Rugs* viii. 100 *Caucasian.* ..'Kabistan' or 'Kuba'. **1931** A. U. DILLEY *Oriental Rugs & Carpets* vii. 178 The name Kuba is applied both to the old weavings, allied to dragon rugs, and to semi-antique rugs of a Kabistan character. **1963** *Times* 23 Feb. 4/7 A small Kuba carpet, woven in a pattern of dragons and flowers, fetched £2,000. **1972** P. L. PHILLIPS tr. *Formenton's Oriental Rugs & Carpets* 242 *Kuba or Kabistan*, Caucasian carpets of the Shirvan family. The most common decoration is made up of lines of rectangles or squares one above the other along the central part of the field.

kubong (kū·bǫŋ). Also **kubung.** [Malay.] The flying lemur, *Cynocephalus variegatus*, a small, south-east Asian mammal of the order Dermoptera, which glides by means of stretching the membranes linking its limbs and tail; also called the colugo.

1821 T. S. RAFFLES in *Trans. Linn. Soc.* XIII. 248 *Lemur volans* Linn. Kubung of the Malays. **1929** S. S. FLOWER *List Vertebrated Animals in Gardens Zool. Soc. Lond. 1828–1927* I. 68 The 'Flying Lemurs', 'Kubong' or 'Colugo' of Malaya and the Philippines..not yet alive in the Gardens, 31 Dec. 1927. **1961** *Listener* 2 Nov. 740/1 The flying Kubong as seen in 'Wings in the Malayan Forest'. **1965** C. SHUTTLEWORTH *Malayan Safari* vi. 84, I was anxious to trap kubong (flying lemur). **1969** LD. MEDWAY *Wild Mammals Malaya* 6/1 Malayan Flying-lemur, Kubong... *Cynocephalus variegatus.*

Kuchaean, Kuchean (kutʃī·ăn). [ad. F. *koutchéen* (S. Lévi 1913, in *Jrnl. Asiatique* II. 315), f. *Kucha*, the name of a town in Sinkiang,

China: see -AN.] The western dialect of *TOCHARIAN, Tocharian B. Also *attrib.* or as *adj.*

1939 *Cambr. Anc. Hist.* XII. iii. 97 A..language formerly known as Tocharish but now more correctly called the Kuchean or Turfanese language. **1939** L. H. GRAY *Foundations of Lang.* 101 Kuchaean *ñäkte* 'god'. *Ibid.* 322 Relatively little of Kuchaean is yet accessible. **1948** D. DIRINGER *Alphabet* vi. 348 There is..a general agreement to call 'Dialect B' [of Tocharian] *Kuchean.* **1965** *Language* XLI. 108 The Kuchean 3 pl. preterite of *käm* 'come' is *kameṃ.* **1972** W. B. LOCKWOOD *Panorama Indo-Europ. Lang.* 254 It was subsequently established that Tocharian B was the language proper to Kucha and may therefore be called Kuchean.

‖ **Kuchen** (ku·χěn). Also **kuchen.** Pl. **Kuchen, Küchen.** [G., lit. 'cake'.] (In Germany or among people speaking German or Yiddish) a cake; now freq. a coffee cake.

1854 GEO. ELIOT *Let.* 12 Nov. (1954) II. 185 The Germans eat their Bratwurst and Küchen from house to house in gladness of heart. **1855** —— in *Fraser's Mag.* June 706/1 Kuchen (generally a heavy kind of fruit tart). **1858** MRS. GASKELL *Let.* 1 Oct. (1966) 894 M. Mohl treated us to coffee & kuchen. **1861** —— *Grey Woman* I. in *All Year Round* 5 Jan. 300/1 We had nearly finished our coffee, and our '*kucken*' [sic], and our cinnamon cake. **1894** G. DU MAURIER *Trilby* I. II. 164 They will..bring him tea and gin and *küchen* [in *Harper's Mag.* Feb. 348/2 printed kuchen] and *marrons glacés.* **1907** I. ZANGWILL *Ghetto Comedies* 316 Home-made Kuchen and other dainties. **1972** L. P. BACHMANN *Ultimate Act* xxiii. 208 We sat at the kitchen table having coffee and *Kuchen.*

kudos. Add: (Further examples.) Now general *slang* and *colloq.* ¶ Sometimes *erron.* treated as *pl.* (kiū·dōᵘz); so **ku·do** (back-formation) *sing.*, honourable mention, praise for an achievement (see also quot. 1941).

1941 J. SMILEY *Hash House Lingo* 34 *Kudo*, good standing with the management. **1950** F. ALLEN in G. Marx *Groucho Lett.* (1967) 73 A man sitting on a toilet bowl swung open the men's room door and added his kudo to the acclaim. **1961** *Wall Street Jrnl.* (Eastern ed.) 18 Oct. 12/2 This did not win Mr. Eisenhower many kudos in the press. **1963** *Life* 19 Apr. 29/2 A kudo to *Life* for a fine story on baseball's spring training. **1970** G. F. NEWMAN *Sir, You Bastard* vii. 196 News services buzzed, but George Doodie sought no kudos; his name was mentioned only once. **1972** *Sunday Mirror* 17 Sept. 47/1 This below-strength Chelsea side captured the few kudos that were going. **1972** J. CREASEY *Splinter of Glass* vii. 55 He wanted Roger to take the kicks if this failed but was prepared to give him the kudos if the use of the newspapers succeeded. **1972** *Homes & Gardens* Nov. 60 It seems almost a kudos to have a lady pilot. **1972** *Bankers' Mag.* Winter 23/2 Kudos are expressed to Messrs. Gene Jackson, Joel Anderson, and John Tolford for their aid.

kudu. Now the most common spelling of KOODOO, although *koedoe* is also used in S. Afr. Substitute for first part of def.: Either of two African antelopes, *Tragelephas strepsiceros*, the greater kudu, or *T. imberbis*, the lesser kudu, which is confined to East Africa. (Later examples.) Also *attrib.*

1901 *Knowledge* July 150/2 The horns take the form of upwardly directed corkscrews, mimicking in fact to a certain degree those of the beautiful African kudu antelope. **1903** J. Y. F. BLAKE *West Pointer with Boers* xxvii. 367 Where the duiker, spring-bok and koedoe roam. **1931** *Discovery* XII. 61/2, I doubt if the black rhinoceros will long survive, or the sable or the eland or the kudu. **1947** L. HASTINGS *Dragons are Extra* viii. 176 A Kudu bull with his great spiral horns a good sixty inches long. **1957** *Cape Times* 6 Apr. 5/7 A variety of rhinos, nyalas, koedoe, blou wildebees and other game. **1961** *Guardian* 9 June 9/3 He roused the boys..with a kudu horn he had captured in Matabeleland. **1964** C. WILLOCK *Enormous Zoo* i. 20 Greater kudu..are antelope of scrub-covered mountains. **1971** *Inside Kenya Today* Mar. 52/1 Other craters in Marsabit Forest are frequented by Greater Kudu. **1973** *Nature* 12 Jan. 106/1 The most obvious change has been a decline in woodland-associated species such as lesser kudu, baboon, vervet-monkey, leopard and impala.

kudzu (ku·dzu). [Jap. *kuzu.*] In full, *kudzu vine.* A perennial climbing plant, *Pueraria thunbergiana* (or *P. lobata*), of the family Leguminosæ, native to China and Japan, and cultivated elsewhere as a fodder plant, an ornamental, or an aid in the prevention of soil erosion.

1893 *Garden & Forest* VI. 504/2 In Japan the Kudzu.. has some economic value. **1901** L. H. BAILEY *Cycl. Amer. Hort.* III. 1465/2 Kudzu Vine. Perennial with large tuberous starchy roots..fl[ower]s pea-shaped, purple, in axillary spikes late in the season, not showy: pod large and flat. **1948** *Atlantic Monthly* Nov. 60/1 Kudzu, a coarse, rapidly growing legume of incredible efficiency in checking gullies, restoring drainage, and storing nitrogen, came from Japan. **1951** *Dict. Gardening* (Roy. Hort. Soc.) IV. 1713/2 P[ueraria] *lobata.* Kudzu Vine. Climber with twining, scarcely woody stems growing many feet long in a season; roots thick, fleshy, starchy. **1973** *Daily Colonist* (Victoria, B.C.) 1 Apr. 24/5 The Kudzu vine..is probably the fastest growing of all the perennial vines, making as much as ten feet the first year from seed, and capable of making annual growth of 30 feet or more. **1974** A. DILLARD *Pilgrim at Tinker Creek* xii. 212 In summer that path is wrapped past finding in saplings, bushes, kudzu, and poison oak.

‖ **kuei** (kū͡ēi). [Chin.] A Chinese bronze food-vessel.

1935 A. J. KOOP in L. Ashton *Chinese Art* 77 The *fu* is an oblong tray with straight, steeply sloping sides, a dragon-head loop handle at each end, and a spreading hollow foot cut away in the centre of each side... The *kuei* is somewhat similar but has a more rounded form. **1954** H. MUNSTERBERG *Short Hist. Chinese Art* iii. 60 New shapes ..appear, while others like the kuei and the chung, or bell, become very common. **1963** *Times* 23 Jan. 12/7 Aberdeen University paid £580 for a massive bronze *kuei* (food vessel), decorated with vertical ribs between borders of dragon and monster masks. **1963** P. C. SWANN *Art of China, Korea & Japan* i. 26 *(caption)* Chinese ritual bronze food vessel (*kuei*) of about 1000 BC, with dragon-headed handles. **1973** *Oxf. Univ. Gaz.* CIII. Suppl. 5. 55 Two-handled bowl of *Kuei* shape, moulded decoration derived from bronze.

Kufic. Now the more usual form of CUFIC *a.*

1792 R. HERON tr. *Niebuhr's Trav. Arabia* I. VIII. vi. 270, I copied here [*sc.* at Beit el Fakih] an ancient *Kusic* [sic] inscription. **1906** *Harmsworth Encycl.* VI. 422/3 The Kufic script was in use for coins from the end of the 7th to the 13th century. **1913** H. J. R. MURRAY *Hist. Chess* 171 The titles being in the Kufic character upon a blue ground. **1931** A. U. DILLEY *Oriental Rugs & Carpets* Pl. 40 *(caption)* Turkish Rug of Arabesque Design and Kufic Border. **1968** G. JONES *Hist. Vikings* III. i. 157 Arabic, German, and Anglo-Saxon coins on Gotland; kufic silver, Arabic and Rhenish glassware..at Birka. **1971** R. RUSSELL tr. *Ahmad's Shore & Wave* i. 10 He had the name of the house..written in Kufic script.

kufuffle, var. CURFUFFLE *sb.*

1960 A. WYKES *Snake Man* iii. 38 After this kufuffle was over and we were on our way again.

‖ **Kuge** (kū·ge). Also † **Cangue; kuge, Kugé.** [Jap.] In feudal Japan, the name of the nobility attached to the Imperial Court at Kyoto; a court noble.

1577 R. WILLES in Eden & Willes tr. *Hist. Trauayle W. & E. Indies* f. 255 The heads and beards of his ministers are shauen, they haue name Cangues. **1727** J. G. SCHEUCHZER tr. *Kæmpfer's Hist. Japan* I. II. ii. 152 The whole Ecclesiastical Court in general assumes the title of *Kuge*, which signifies as much as Ecclesiastical Lords, and this they do by way of distinction from the *Gege.* **1871** A. B. MITFORD *Tales Old Japan* I. 71 The cap and robes worn by the Kugé, or nobles of the Mikado's court. **1880** F. V. DICKINS tr. *Chiushingura* (new ed.) 159 They were noble ladies, daughters of *Kugé*, who were peers of the Mikado's creation. **1904** L. HEARN *Japan: Attempt at Interpretation* xii. 265 Next to him stood the kugé, or ancient nobility,—descendants of emperors and of gods. **1957** *Times Lit. Suppl.* 11 Oct. 607/2 The court nobles, almost as useless and cut off from real life by the habits of the Court, of '*ce pays-ci*', as Mme. de Grignan called it, as so many Kuge nobles of old Japan. **1970** [see *HININ].

kugel (kiū·gěl). Also **coogle, kuggol.** [Yiddish, lit. ball, f. MHG. *kugel, kugele* ball, globe.] In Jewish cookery, a kind of pudding served as a main course or as a side-dish.

1846 *Jewish Manual, or Pract. Information Jewish & Mod. Cookery* iv. 55 *Kugel and commean.* Soak..Spanish peas and..Spanish beans..take..fine gravy-beef [etc.]. **1871** E. LEVY *Jewish Cookery Bk.* 58 Coogle, or pudding, and peas and beans. **1892** I. ZANGWILL *Childr. Ghetto* I. 114 Other delicious things there are in Jewish cookery... *Kuggol*, to which pudding has a far-away resemblance. **1914** N. NEWNHAM-DAVIS *Gourmet's Guide to London* 149 In the great earthenware jar which holds the soup is cooked the 'kugel', a kind of pease-pudding. **1958** J. GROSSINGER *Art Jewish Cooking* 115 Vegetables are comparatively unimportant in most Jewish homes. In their place, *kugels* and *charlottes*, resembling puddings or pudding-soufflés, were substituted. They may be served as separate courses, as accompaniments to meat or poultry, or even as dessert if they are sweet. **1972** *Listener* 16 Mar. 341/3 It [*sc.* chollant] was a mélange of meat, potatoes, butter-beans, onions, kishkeh, kugel and hope... The kugel (German for bullet) looked like an anaemic cannon-ball... The basic formula included fat, flour, grebenes or fried onion.

kugelhupf: see *GUGELHUPF. Also **kugelhopf.**

1886 [see *CENTRE *v.* 4]. **1906** *Mrs. Beeton's Bk. Househ. Managem.* lxii. 1656 *Kugelhopf*, a German cake; a kind of rich dough cake. **1961** J. HELLER *Catch-22* (1962) xxiv. 249 Napoleons and *petits fours* from Paris, Reims and Grenoble, *Kugelhopf*, pumpernickel and *Pfefferkuchen* from Berlin. **1966** P. V. PRICE *France: Food & Wine Guide* 148 The traditional *kugelhopf* (a light yeast cake, usually with a hole in the centre).

kuhn-kan, var. *COON-CAN.

1936 G. GREENE *Journey without Maps* I. iii. 42 They.. played Kuhn-Kan for very small stakes. **1951** —— *Lost Childhood* 14 The mild nursery game of Kuhn Kan.

kuka (kū·kă). [Native name.] A name used in Ghana for *Khaya senegalensis*; also *kuka-tree*; see *KHAYA.

1882 *Encycl. Brit.* XIV. 153/2 Kuka [a Central African town]..received its name from a kuka or monkey bread tree (*Adansonia digitata*), which attracted the attention of the settlers as a rare thing in the district. **1924** *Blackw. Mag.* Sept. 351/1 A kuka-tree is a stumpy smooth, grey-barked thing of enormous girth. **1932** J. CARY *Aissa Saved* xliii. 230 We should go there by the kuka tree. **1961** F. R. IRVINE *Woody Plants of Ghana* 523 *Khaya senegalensis*... Kuka (local name).

kukama (*kukā·mă*). Also **kokama, kookaam.** [Sechuana.] The southern African antelope, *Oryx gazella*; see ORYX b.

1852 *Catal. Mammalia Brit. Mus.* III. 105 *Oryx gazella.* The Kookaam or Gemsboc. Horns straight, shelving backwards. **1857** D. LIVINGSTONE *Missionary Trav. & Res. S. Afr.* iii. 56 The gemsbuck or kukama. **1888** J. S. KINGSLEY *Riverside Nat. Hist.* V. 326 The *Oryx capensis* of South Africa, or Gemsbok of the Dutch colonists, Kokama of the Bechuanas, is even more striking in its coloring. **1971** R. H. N. SMITHERS *Mammals Botswana* 238/2 *Oryx gazella.* Kukama. Gemsbok.

kukang. Add: Also **kongkang.** Substitute for def.: The slow loris, *Nycticebus coucang*, found in south-east Asia. (Earlier and later examples.)

1821 T. S. RAFFLES in *Trans. Linn. Soc.* XIII. 247 *Lemur tardigradus* Linn. Kukang (Malay)... Of this the natives distinguish a large and a small variety. **1900** *Proc. Zool. Soc.* 321 The Slow Loris... 'Kúkang', 'Kong-kang', and 'Kongka' of the Malays. *Ibid.*, At one time I used to sleep in a hammock slung in a veranda close to a cage of Kongkangs. **1969** LD. MEDWAY *Wild Mammals Malaya* 47/1 Slow Loris. Kongkang, Kera duku. *Nycticebus coucang.*

Kuki[1] (ku·ki). [Native name.] Any one of several peoples inhabiting the hills of Manipur and Mizoram, on the Indo-Burmese border; a member of one of these peoples; also, their language. Also *attrib.* and *Comb.*, as *Kuki-Chin* [*CHIN *sb.*[2]] (see quot. 1954).

1799 *Asiatick Researches* II. 188 If a *Cúcí* assail the house of an enemy..he acquires honour and celebrity in his tribe. *Ibid.* 193 A party of *Cúcìs* visited the late Charles Croftes..at Jáfarābád, in the spring of 1776, and entertained him with a dance. **1803** *Ibid.* VII. 186 The *Kookies* choose the steepest and most inaccessible hills to build their villages..which..are called..in the *Kookie* language, *K'hooah.* **1871** E. B. TYLOR *Primitive Culture* I. xi. 424 The Kukis of Assam think that the ghost of every animal a Kuki kills in the chase or for the feast will belong to him in the next life. **1872** E. T. DALTON *Descr. Ethnol. Bengal* 75 English..one..Kuki khut. **1885** E. BALFOUR *Cycl. India* (ed. 3) II. 618/2 The new Kuki clans are presided over by rajas and muntris. **1927** *Blackw. Mag.* June 816/1 The Kuki alone of all these hill tribes understands the value of combination. *Ibid.* 817/1 Roaring and retaliation keep alive a warlike and truculent spirit among the Kukis. **1939** L. H. GRAY *Found. Lang.* 389 Arakan-Burmese, comprising Kuki-Chin.., Old Kuki (Rānkhōl, Shō or Khyang, Khami, etc.), and Burmese. **1948** D. DIRINGER *Alphabet* vi. 367 Manipuri or Meithei, a Kuki-chin speech. **1954** PEI & GAYNOR *Dict. Ling.* 116 *Kuki-Chin*, a group of dialects (Lai, Lushei, Meithei, Tashon, etc.), constituting a subdivision of the Arakan-Burmese branch of the Tibeto-Burmese sub-family of the Sino-Tibetan family of languages. **1971** B. W. ALDISS *Soldier Erect* 219 But the Assam Battalion kept coming across the road, Kukis, Karsis, and all the other tribesmen. **1972** *Language* XLVIII. 476 The crucially important and ramified group of Tibeto-Burman languages known variously as Kukish, Kuki-Chin, or Kuki-Chin-Naga, spoken in Assam and Western Burma.

‖ **kuki**[2] (ku·ki). *N.Z. Hist.* Also **kooky.** [Maori, ad. COOK *sb.*] A slave of a Maori chieftain.

1832 A. EARLE *Narr. Residence N.Z.* (1966) 60 A chief had set one of his kookies (or slaves) to watch a piece of ground planted with the koomera, or sweet potato. **1845** E. J. WAKEFIELD *Adventure N.Z.* I. 230 The alarm had been caused by some *kuki*, or slaves. **1882** W. D. HAY *Brighter Britain!* I. x. 283 Her father and mother were only kukis.

kuklass, var. *KOKLAS(S.

Ku-Klux. Add: **1.** (Earlier and later examples.) This society was revived in 1915 and spread outside the Southern States, terrorizing various ethnic and religious minorities, and acting violently against white Protestants whom they judged to be opposed to their cause. Later the society fragmented into several State organizations. The Ku-Klux Klan regained strength in the Southern States of the U.S. in the 1950s in opposition to the Civil Rights movement of American Blacks. Cf. *KLAN, *KLUXER.

1867 *Citizen* (Pulaski, Tenn.) 29 Mar. 3/1 The Kuklux Klan will assemble at their usual place of rendezvous.., exactly at the hour of midnight, in costume and bearing the arms of the Klan. **1868** *N.Y. Herald* 1 July 6/4 If the Democratic Convention can only be induced..at the dictation of the Knights of the Golden Circle and the Ku Klux Klan, to place upon their ticket some copperhead opponent of the war, the radicals will have a clear track next November. **1915** *Atlanta* (Ga.) *Jrnl.* 6 Dec. 2/4 (*heading*) Charter is granted for the Ku Klux Klan. *Ibid.*, Secretary of State Philip Cook Monday issued a charter to the Knights of the Ku Klux Klan, a fraternal insurance order which was organized on Stone Mountain a few nights ago with weird and mystic ceremony. **1920** *N.Y. Times* 11 Oct. 1/2 The old Ku Klux Klan has been re-organized and is regularly chartered under the laws of Georgia. **1924** *Imperial Night-Hawk* 10 Sept. 6 The district meeting of the Ku Klux Klan held recently at Twin Lakes, Realm of Iowa, was a huge success. **1944** *Atlanta* (Ga.) *Jrnl.* 4 June 1/1 The Knights of the Ku Klux Klan, Inc. has officially ceased to exist. **1945** *N.Y. Times*

21 Oct. 33/3 The Ku Klux Klan, claiming a membership of more than 20,000 in Georgia, is burning its fiery cross again. **1958** *News & Observer* (Raleigh, N. Carolina) 19 Jan. 1/5 A shouting horde of Robeson County Indians tonight routed the Ku Klux Klan here. **1962** A. S. RICE *Ku Klux Klan in Amer. Politics* ix. 114 [In 1949] the secret order splintered into many rival groups, each considering itself..the direct spiritual heir of the Invisible Empire, Knights of the Ku Klux Klan founded in 1915. **1970** in J. F. Kirkham et al. *Assassination & Political Violence* iv. A. § 3. 216 The first Ku Klux Klan, which lasted from 1865 to 1876, was a principal means of administering this violence in the South. *Ibid.* § 4. 218 White Capping seems to have been an important link between the first and second Ku Klux Klans. White Cap methods of punishment and costume seem to have been influenced by the first Klan. *Ibid.* App. D. § 1. 364 It was not until 1956 when the efforts..failed to stem the trend toward integration in the South that the Ku Klux Klans revived... In San Antonio, Tex., a cross was burned..to 'let the niggers, Jews, and Catholics know we're back in operation'.

b. In extended use, of other vigilante groups. Also *transf.* and *fig.*

1930 W. & E. MUIR tr. *Feuchtwanger's Success* IV. xvi. 539 The Munich Ku Klux Klan..evidently consisted of young men who did not understand that a match, once it is decided, can't be fought all over again. **1944** A. HUXLEY *Let.* 28 July (1969) 511 You might pass on to your agent these simple talking points, with which to allay the studios' fears of the medical Ku Klux Klan. **1966** A. SACHS *Jail Diary* xxiv. 215 Then he asks me what I know about the local Ku Klux Klan.

2. (Earlier examples.)

1868 in T. D. CLARK *Pills, Petticoats & Plows* (1944) 62 We are inclined to think he is somewhat disloyal, and may be in sympathy with the Ku Kluxes. **1877** J. M. BEARD *K.K.K. Sk.* 40 The Ku-Klux themselves were about as intangible examples of ghostliness as were ever wrapped in loose-fitting bombazine.

Hence **Ku-Klux Kla·n(n)er, Kla·nism, Kla·nsman.**

1868 in S. F. Horn *Invisible Empire* (1939) 335 Let every Ku Klux Klansman heed The General Order of General Meade. **1923** *Nation* (N.Y.) 11 July 35 He will help his fellow Ku Klux Klaners. **1924** H. CRANE *Let.* 5 Mar. (1965) 177 O'Neill's new play..in which a white woman marries a Negro... He..receives terrible threats and insults through the mail from the *Ku Klux* Klanners. **1924** J. M. MECKLIN *Ku Klux Klan* 98, I have yet to come in contact with the first trace of Ku Klux Klanism. **1933** H. G. WELLS *Shape of Things to Come* II. § 1. 141 They became Ku Klux Klansmen, Nationalists, Nazis. **1948** *Time* 15 Mar. 29/2 Last week Georgia's Grand Dragon Samuel Green carefully explained that Ku Klux Klansmen wore masks to protect themselves against the prejudice of Jews, Catholics and foreigners.

kuku (kū·kū). *N.Z.* [Maori.] **1.** Also **koukou, kukupa.** = *KERERU.

1835 W. YATE *Acct. N.Z.* iii. 53 *Kou-kou*—The bird so-called is a small owl, a native of New Zealand. **1873** [see *KERERU]. **1881** J. L. CAMPBELL *Poenamo* vii. 115 The *kukupa*..was just the bird created expressly for the true cockney sportsman. **1905** W. B. *Where White Man Treads* 19 For food..in his [*sc.* the Maori's] catalogue, for flavour and bulk, the plentiful kereru, or kuku (pigeon) headed the list. **1936** 'R. HYDE' *Check to your King* xiii. 157 Your wild pigeon (*kuku*)..beds itself on the fern. **1949** P. BUCK *Coming of Maori* (1950) II. i. 93 The principal forest birds sought for food were the wood pigeon (*kereru, kukupa, kuku*), [etc.].

2. Either of two common mussels, *Perna canaliculus* or *Mytilus edulis aoteanus.*

1905 W. B. *Where White Man Treads* 2 White seashore sandhills, representing the accumulated deaths of ages of pipi, pupu, kuku, and other molluscs. **1949** P. BUCK *Coming of Maori* (1950) II. i. 106 Shellfish such as..sea mussels (*kuku*)..were cooked..and dried also as reserve food. **1960** N. HILLIARD *Maori Girl* 153 Shellfish—*paua, kuku, kina.*

kukui (*kuku·*ˌi). [Hawaiian.] An evergreen tree, *Aleurites moluccana,* of the family Euphorbiaceæ, native to the Moluccas and south Pacific islands; its large seeds yield an oil used for lighting and other purposes, and the tree is also called the candlenut or candleberry tree.

1825 W. ELLIS *Jrnl. Tour Hawaii* vii. 167 Along the narrow and verdant border of the lake at the bottom, the bread-fruit, the *kukui,* and the *ohia* trees, appeared. **1866** 'MARK TWAIN' *Lett. from Hawaii* (1967) 98 These trees were principally of two kinds—the koa and the kukui—the one with a very light green leaf and the other with a dark green. **1890** *Ibis* II. 175 The delicately-indented foliage of the kukui has..a lovely silvery appearance in certain lights. **1913** J. F. ROCK *Indigenous Trees Hawaiian Islands* 257 The Kukui is one of the most common of Hawaiian forest trees... The nuts contain 50 per cent of oil, which is known as Kekuna in India and Ceylon, and Kukui in Hawaii. **1937** D. & H. TEILHET *Feather Cloak Murders* viii. 143 Silvery Kukui trees draped their clustered pink flowers over old walls. **1967** *Economist* 9 Sept. 892/1 The luau lights outside nearly every [Hawaii] hotel and restaurant may now consist of a concealed gas jet instead of kukui nut-meat burning gently in a shell.

kukumakranka (*kukumakra·ŋkă*). *S. Afr.* Also **koekmakranka, koekoemakranka.** [Afrikaans, prob. f. Hottentot name for the plant.] A small, bulbous, perennial plant of the genus *Gethyllis,* belonging to the family Amaryllidaceæ, and bearing fragrant white flowers and an underground fruit.

1793 tr. *C. P. Thunberg's Trav. Europe, Afr. & Asia* I. 116 Kukumakranka (*gethyllis*) is the name given to the legumen or pod of a plant, that grew at this time among the sand-hills near the town, without either leaves or flowers. This pod was of the length of one's finger, somewhat wider at top than at bottom, had a pleasant smell, and was held in great esteem by the ladies. The smell of it resembled in some measure that of strawberries, and filled the whole room. **1811** W. J. BURCHELL *Jrnl.* 31 Jan. in *Trav. S. Afr.* (1822) I. ii. 55 On Green Point on the Flats in the neighbourhood of Cape Town, grows a celebrated little plant, which still preserves its original Hottentot name, being known by no other than that of *Kukumakranki.* **1857** L. PAPPE *Floræ Capensis Medicæ Prodromus* (ed. 2) 39 The elongated, club-shaped, orange-coloured fruit of this plant has a peculiar fragrance, and still preserves its old Hottentot name of *Kukumakranka.* **1932** WATT & BREYER-BRANDWIJK *Medicinal & Poisonous Plants S. Afr.* 28 An alcoholic infusion of the fruit of *Gethyllis spiralis* L.f. (*Gytheilia spiralis*), Koekoemakranka (Bramakranka), Koekmakranka, was taken by the early Cape colonists for the relief of colic and flatulence. **1950** *Cape Times* 15 May 14 Before I found a palate for mushrooms, it was the kukumakranka we used to go seeking in the veld. *Ibid.* 18 May 12/3 Two explanations of how the koekmakranka got its name have reached me. **1973** Y. BURGESS *Life to Live* 179 When the drug did not help she asked the old women to gather 'kukumakranka' leaves for her, and she asked Magriet for brandy to steep them in.

kukupa: see *KUKU 1.

‖ **kula** (*kū·*lă). Also **Kula.** [Melanesian.] In some Pacific communities, esp. in the Trobriand Islands, an inter-island system of ceremonial exchange of items as a prelude to or concomitant of regular trading.

1920 B. MALINOWSKI in *Man* XX. 97 (*heading*) Kula; the circulating exchange of valuables in the archipelagoes of eastern New Guinea. *Ibid.* 101 Glancing at the map we see a number of circles, each of which represents a certain sociological unit which we shall call a *Kula* community. **1927** —— *Sex & Repression Savage Soc.* II. iii. 93 Those in charge of the overseas expeditions called *Kula* are often supposed to have dreams about the success of their ceremonial trading. **1951** R. FIRTH *Elem. Social Organiz.* i. 3 The Trobriand islanders of New Guinea exchange in the kula. **1970** *Nature* 12 Dec. 1064/2 The best known exchange mechanism of this kind of recent times is the kula trade of the Trobriand islanders of the western Pacific.

Hence **kula** *v.*, to exchange ceremonial gifts in this manner.

1922 B. MALINOWSKI *Argonauts W. Pacific* iii. 101 Several villages do not kula. *Ibid.* xi. 281 Bokuyoba..gave the pair..to Kadamwasila..her son..*kula'd* it on to some of his southern partners.

Kula, var. *KULLAH. See also next word.

Kulah[1] (*kū·*lă). Also **Koula(h), Kula.** The name of a town in W. Turkey used *attrib.* or *ellipt.* to denote a rug using the Ghiordes knot made there.

c **1882** *Cardinal & Harford's Price List Oriental Carpets & Rugs* 13 *Koula rugs and mats.* Various qualities, bright colours, Red usually predominant. **1899** *Northern Times* (Golspie, Sutherland) 22 June 1/5 (Advt.), About 600 to 800 Oriental and other Rugs, from 4s 9d upwards, including..Koula. **1900** J. K. MUMFORD *Oriental Rugs* x. 150 The narrow stripe with undulating pattern, referred to as a characteristic of all Ghiordes, antique and modern, is rarely found in pure Kulahs. *Ibid.*, In design the modern Kulahs have nothing characteristic. **1904** M. B. LANGTON *How to Know Oriental Rugs* v. 165 The antique Koulah prayer-rug differs from the Ghiordes in various ways. **1931** A. U. DILLEY *Oriental Rugs & Carpets* vi. 164 Ghiordes and Kula prayer rugs were made in adjacent cities. **1962** C. W. JACOBSEN *Oriental Rugs* 248 With their close neighbours, Ghiordes, Kulahs share the position of being one of the rarest and most sought after of all Oriental Rugs. **1972** P. L. PHILLIPS tr. *Formenton's Oriental Rugs & Carpets* 94 Kula rugs, like most Anatolian rugs..have no special distinguishing motif and so are difficult to identify.

kulah[2] (*kū·*lă). Also **kulla, kullah.** [Pers. *kulah* a cap.] (See quot. 1969.)

1920 *Chambers's Jrnl.* 29 May 408/1 Dark-blue *pugris,* with red and white silk stripes, tied round a *kulla* or conical skull-cap of scarlet. **1952** J. MASTERS *Deceivers* xi. 125 The prisoner second from the left wore a Mohammedan kulla under his turban. **1969** R. T. WILCOX *Dict. Costume* (1970) 189/1 *Kulah,* a conical cap of felt or lambskin, the headgear of Middle Eastern monks and dervishes. **1971** R. DENTRY *Encounter at Kharmel* iii. 45 The men wore round kullah caps, ragged chogas over long grey tunics, and scarves.

kulak (*kū·*læk). Also † **koolack, koulak.** [Russ. *kulák* fist, tight-fisted person, pl. *kulaki,* f. Turki *ḳul* hand.] In pre-Revolution Russia, a well-to-do farmer or trader; in the Soviet Union, a peasant-proprietor working for his own profit. Also *transf.*

1877 D. M. WALLACE *Russia* (ed. 2) I. vii. 159 Not a few industrial villages have thus fallen under the power of the *Kulaki*—literally Fists—as these monopolists are called. **1886** *Encycl. Brit.* XXI. 84/1 The enrichment of a few 'kulaks'. **1921** *Contemp. Rev.* Jan. 26 'Kulaks'..a nickname for the close-fisted village traders, usurers, and rich peasants. **1925** P. GIBBS *Unchanging Quest* xiv. 109 These peasants think the Duma will..kill all the Koulaks, or Jewish moneylenders. **1929** [see *COLLECTIVE A. 2 f]. **1931** M. HINDUS *Red Bread* iv. 66 Legally, a *koolack* is a man who indulges in some form of exploitation, employs hired help or derives an income from rent or interest or the operation of an agricultural or industrial machine. Actually, however, a *koolack* is a successful farmer as success is measured in Russia. **1934** G. B. SHAW *On Rocks* 164 They [*sc.* the Soviet government] also proscribed the kulak, the able, hardheaded, hardfisted farmer who was richer than his neighbors. **1951** G. MIKES *Down with Everybody* 48 He was a kulak, a spy and an enemy agent, but now he had realised his mistake—namely that it *was* a mistake to be a kulak, a spy and an enemy agent. **1952** R. CAMPBELL *Lorca* 7 Lorca was by birth a landowning 'kulak'. **1957** *Observer* 10 Nov. 5/8 The peasants [in China] have been 'voluntarily' collectivised..but there has been no Russian-style campaign for the 'elimination of the *kulak* as a class'. **1970** *New Scientist* 1 Jan. 15/1 The improved grain husbandry..may favour the rise of 'kulaks' or 'improving landlord' groups.

kulang (*kū·*læŋ). Also **kolong, kulan, kullung.** = *COOLUNG.

1838 [see *COOLUNG]. **1887** [see *DHANDH]. **1910** *Blackw. Mag.* Feb. 285/2 The kulan, too, or demoiselle cranes, are lovely birds..and are found in great numbers all up the river Jumna. **1915** [see *COOLUNG]. **1949** N. B. KINNEAR *Whistler's Pop. Handbk. Indian Birds* (ed. 4) 444 The Common Crane and the Demoiselle Crane are not usually distinguished from each other in India and are well known collectively under the names of Kunj and Kulung.

kulchur. ¶ With distortion of spelling to indicate an affected or vulgar pronunciation of CULTURE *sb.* Cf. *CULTURE *sb.* after sense 5 a.

1940 E. POUND *Cantos* liv. 43 The 10th a charter of labour And the last on keepin' up kulchur. **1959** *Listener* 4 June 997/3 The famous six essential books, Pound's guide to Kulchur. **1971** *Frenzy* 21 May 3/4 There is a spirit of freedom, solidarity and struggle; an intensity of life worth all the ephemeral fantasies to be offered so far by the Rock/alternative Kulchur.

Kulin (*kū*lī·n). Also **Kooleen, Kulina.** [ad. Skr. *kulīna,* f. *kulin* well-born.] In Bengal, a Brahman of the highest class. Also *attrib.* or as *adj.*

1866 *Atlantic Monthly* Dec. 733/1 The privilege of maintaining a plurality of wives is restricted to a very few.. except in the case of *Kooleen* Brahmins, that superlative aristocracy of caste. **1873** E. BALFOUR *Cycl. India* (ed. 2) III. 312/1 *Kulin,* a class of brahmans in Bengal, who are deemed by other brahmans to be of very pure descent and in consequence many are anxious to wed their daughters to them. **1911** *Encycl. Brit.* XIII. 511/2 Only an extreme section—the so-called *Kaulas* or *Kulinas*..persist in carrying on the mystic and licentious rites taught in many of the Tantras. **1911** G. B. SHAW *Getting Married* 139 Kulin polygyny, though unlimited, is not really a popular institution. **1932** [see *Kulinism* below]. **1970** N. B. BONARJEE *Under Two Masters* 3 The Kulins became an integral and important part of Bengal's life and culture.

Hence **Ku·linism,** the polygamous system of the Kulins.

1890 in *Cent. Dict.* **1891** H. H. RISLEY *Tribes & Castes of Bengal: Ethnogr. Gloss.* I. 146 The Bansajas are those Kulins who lost their distinction on account of..their want of charity, discipline, and due observance of marriage law, three qualities which in later times constituted Kulinism. **1932** L. S. S. O'MALLEY *Indian Caste Customs* i. 10 A Kulin Brahman who had an embarrassing number of female relatives is known to have had eighteen of them..married in a batch to a boy ten years old—.. Kulinism, as the practice is called, has nearly died out. **1968** B. WALKER *Hindu World* II. 229 In Bengal.. polygamous relationships..were common among certain brāhmin sub-castes, notably the *Kulin,* 'noble',..and the custom is called kulīnism.

Kullah (kŭlā·). Also **Kalá, Klá, Kula.** [Pegu *Goḷa* Indian Buddhist immigrant, f. Skr. *Gauḍa* ancient name of N. Bengal (Yule and Burnell).] (See quot. 1886.)

1800 M. SYMES *Acct. Embassy to Kingdom of Ava* xii. 290 On being informed that I was 'a Colar', or stranger,.. they were reconciled. **1858** H. YULE *Narr. Mission to Court of Ava* i. 5 His private dwelling was a small place on one side of the court, from which the women peeped out at the *Kalás.* **1886** YULE & BURNELL *Hobson-Jobson* 378/1 *Kulá* or *Klá,* n.p. Burmese name of a native of Continental India; and hence misapplied also to the English and other Westerns who have come to Burma from India; in fact used generally for a Western foreigner. **1890** KIPLING *Departmental Ditties* (ed. 4) 82 For the Burmans said That a kullah's head Must be paid for with heads five score. **1929** F. T. JESSE *Lacquer Lady* I. iii. 21 All foreigners are kalās to the Burmans.

kulla(h), varr. *KULAH[2].

kullum, var. *COOLUNG.

kullung, var. *COOLUNG, *KULANG.

kultur (kultū·r). Also **Kultur.** [G., ad. L. *cultūra,* or F. *culture* CULTURE *sb.*] Civilization as conceived by the Germans; esp. used in a derogatory sense during the 1914–18 and 1939–45 wars, as involving notions of racial and cultural arrogance, militarism, and imperialism. Also *attrib.* and *transf.*

1914 *Punch* 16 Sept. 239/1 (*heading*) The Imperial Prussian College of Culture. *Telegrams*: 'Kultur, Berlin'. **1914** *Spectator* 31 Oct. 589/1 The idea that the extension of the *Kultur* of a nation can be effected by the extension

by arms of its Empire. **1915** *Times* 30 Mar. 6/4 *Kultur*, in fact, has become the exact opposite of 'culture'. **1915** A. Huxley *Let.* Oct. (1969) 84 We have founded a club, chiefly for the purpose of self protection against Queen's and for the propagation of Kultur. **1916** J. B. Cooper *Coo-oo-ee* xii. 170 People have no time for Germans after their kultur demonstration in Belgium. **1917** A. G. Empey *Over Top* 305 A British rat resembles a bull-dog, while a German one, through a course of Kultur, resembles a dachshund. **1918** Kipling *Kipling's Message*, It is the peculiar essence of German Kultur, which is the German religion, that it is Germany's moral duty to break every tie, every restriction that binds man to fellow-man, if she thinks it will pay. **1926** C. H. Herford *Mind of Post-War Germany* v. 22 The stabilizing forces which post-war Germany derived from her inherited Kultur. **1939** tr. *C. Leiser's Nazi Nuggets* 82 Since the Nazis and the Japanese have been getting cozy and have signed a pact to foster their Kultur. **1973** L. Snelling *Heresy* i. i. 4 How ignorant I am of contemporary Kultur.

Also (with varying degrees of naturalization) **ku·lturbild** [G. *bild* picture, image], a description of the culture (of a period, etc.); **ku·lturgeschi·chte** [G. *geschichte* history], the history of the cultural development (of a country, etc.); history of civilization; **ku·lturgut** [G. *gut* possession], a cultural asset; **ku·lturhund** [G. *hund* dog], **kultur-hound** = **culture vulture*; **ku·lturkampf** [G. *kampf* conflict], the conflict between the German government and the Papacy for the control of schools and church appointments (1872–87); also *transf.*; **ku·lturkreis** [G. *kreis* circle], a cultural group; a cultural complex (the term is associated esp. with the German anthropologists F. Graebner and W. Schmidt); **ku·lturstaat** [G. *staat* state], a civilized country; **ku·lturträger** [G. *träger* carrier], an upholder or defender of civilization.

All usu. with capital initial in Eng. as in German.

1961 *Times* 23 Nov. 16/4 This book had to be a *Kulturbild* rather than a biography. **1964** *English Studies* XLV. 91 Professor Schirmer in his *Kulturbild* attempts to relate John Lydgate to his age by means of his poetry. **1876** *Mind* I. 447 The novel facts and attractive generalisations of *Culturgeschichte* are insensibly casting discredit upon the thoughtful introspection of one's own adult experience. **1938** *Year's Work Eng. Stud. 1936* XVII. 29 Brandenstein's little monograph on the first Indo-European migration is a return to the study of comparative vocabulary as a means for re-imagining some aspects of *Kulturgeschichte*. **1968** *Listener* 4 Apr. 448/1 English music historians have, on the whole, concentrated on the chronicling of technical matters and have avoided *Kulturgeschichte*, as it is practised elsewhere. **1952** *Man* June 83 A member of a lower caste tends to imitate the '*kulturgut*' of higher-caste people... At the same time he is attached to his own *kulturgut*. **1966** *Amer. N. & Q.* June 158/1 No effort was made to segregate the demonstrably regional *Kulturgut* from that which is literary, and even worldwide. **1969** *Language* XLV. 235 The later association of the term with the very poor may represent a sort of..Kulturgut. **1946** Mezzrow & Wolfe *Really Blues* (1957) xi. 196 That Kultur-hound didn't know..that underneath the phony label was a genuine Victor one. **1963** *Listener* 17 Jan. 138/3 So our provincial *Kulturhunde* had thirty minutes of that Vassar-educated Mona Lisa, Miss Mary McCarthy. **1879** *Dublin Rev.* Oct. 350 History of the Prussian 'Kulturkampf'. **1896** W. Miller *Balkans* ii. v. 205 A regular *Culturkampf* raged for nearly twenty years, in which the Turkish officials were far less adverse than the Greek clergy to the Bulgarian demands. **1902** *Encycl. Brit.* XXXII. 271/2 In Germany, when the Pontificate of Leo XIII. began, a disastrous conflict between the Imperial Government and the Church was in progress. It was called the Kulturkampf, as professing to be undertaken on behalf of civilization and culture. **1926** C. H. Herford *Mind of Post-War Germany* i. 6 The Rhinelands, fervently Catholic, and still acutely mindful of Bismarck's *Kulturkampf*. **1936** H. G. Wells *Anat. Frustration* xiii. 150 A vast Kultur-Kampf lies between mankind and peace. **1966** *New Statesman* 18 Feb. 218/3 The *kulturkampf* between Flemish and Walloon French has now reached the Catholic University of Louvain. [**1897** L. Frobenius in *Petermann's Mitteilungen* XLIII. 225 (*title*) Der westafrikanische Kulturkreis. *Ibid.* 225/2 Es mag deshalb die Bezeichnung 'Westafrikanischer Kulturkreis' zunächst beibehalten werden.] **1948** A. L. Kroeber *Anthropol.* (rev. ed.) xvii. 770 Part of a wider theory advanced by the *Kulturkreis* (culture-sphere) movement or school of ethnology in continental Europe is that the Indonesian–Melanesian cultures are also characterized by the same block of culture traits that includes those enumerated for West Africa. **1971** *English Studies* LII. 256 It will have important implications..for the whole theoretical question of genre study in literature and the whole historical one of Anglo-Irish relations in the early middle ages, indeed of all of the early Christian *Kulturkreis*, which included the British Isles, Iceland, Scandinavia, and parts of Germanic Europe. **1925** *Manch. Guardian Weekly* 16 Oct. 311 There is no 'Kulturstaat' (civilised State) that would not punish political crimes. **1936** *Mind* XLV. 295 A state must at least preserve its existence, as a condition of becoming a *Kulturstaat*. **1948** J. Towster *Political Power in U.S.S.R.* i. i. 6 Such conceptions of the state as *Rechtstaat* or *Kulturstaat*. **1920** D. H. Lawrence *Women in Love* i. 13 She was a *Kulturträger*, a medium for the culture of ideas. **1962** *N. & Q.* May 190/2 Two types of borrowing situation are envisaged, the bilingual community with oral/aural mediation, and the unilingual community with *Kulturträger* and written mediation.

‖ **kulturny** (kultu·rni), *a.* [Russ. *kul'túrnyĭ* civilized.] In the Soviet Union: cultured, civilized.

1955 H. Hodgkinson *Doubletalk* 39 Cultured, or *kulturny* behaviour, is highly esteemed in the Soviet Union. **1959** *New Statesman* 23 May 711/3 Aesthetic considerations never played a part in the previous drives for a more *kulturny* mode of life, which were more concerned with manners than with the cultivation of good taste. **1973** J. Shub *Moscow by Nightmare* ix. 97 She let the porter take her one small suitcase—it wouldn't be '*kulturny*' to carry it herself.

kulu, kulukamba: see *koolookamba.

kumara. Now the usual spelling of Kumera. For '*Ipomœa edulis*' in def., substitute '*Ipomœa batatas*'. Add further examples.

1851 H. R. Richmond *Jrnl.* 23 Feb. in *Richmond–Atkinson Papers* (1960) I. ii. 88 There was nothing else to help ourselves to except kumara or sweet potato, in appearance like long thin potatoes, in taste like boiled chesnuts. **1905** W. B. *Where White Man Treads* 2 Park-lands, blurred and dotted with plantations of kumara. **1934** *Bulletin* (Sydney) 26 Sept. 20/1 The supplies of pig, eel, shark and kumara were unlimited. **1936** [see *kit *sb.*[11]]. **1905** *N.Z. Jrnl. Agric.* July 55/1 Most home gardeners purchase their kumara plants from seedsmen. **1971** *N.Z. Listener* 16 Aug. 54/4 Be careful with the kumara... Its energy value is twice that of the potato.

kumbang (ku·mbæŋ). Also **koembang.** [local Javanese *koembang.*] A föhn wind which blows in Java.

1931 A. A. Miller *Climatol.* v. 83 These winds have a foehn-like nature, their dry heat doing considerable damage to the more sensitive crops, especially tobacco. Such a wind is the 'Koembang' of Java. **1954** E. D. Laborde tr. *Robequain's Malaya, Indonesia, Borneo & Philippines* ix. 187 At that time,..the lowlands between Cheribon and Tegal fairly often experience the drying effort of the south-east wind which, after crossing the Pembarisan Hills, becomes a foehn known as the *kumbang*. **1969** M. Sukanto in H. Arakawa *Climates N. & E. Asia* iv. 222 Tjirebon and Tegal (Central Djawa) are also exposed to such a wind during the dry season. In this case, the wind flows down from the western part of Mount Slamet and blows in a northern and northeastern direction. This wind is called the Kumbang.

‖ **kumbuk** (kʊ·mbʊk, ku·mbuk). [Sinhala.] A name used in Sri Lanka (Ceylon) for the arjun, *Terminalia arjuna*, an Indian evergreen tree of the family Combretaceæ.

1869 R. H. Beddome *Flora Sylvatica* I. 17 It [sc. *Terminalia tomentosa*] is called..Koombook in Ceylon. **1894** H. Trimen *Hand-bk. Flora Ceylon* II. 160 *T*[*erminalia*] *glabra*...Kumbuk. **1923** *Blackw. Mag.* Dec. 860/2 A lovely clear purling stream with the most beautiful Kumbuk trees fringing it on either side. **1971** *Ceylon Observer* (Mag. ed.) 19 Sept. 3/3 She had heard the beast sigh loudly behind the great big *kumbuk* tree.

‖ **kumkum** (ku·mkum). Also **kum-kum, kunku.** [Hindi *kuṅkum* saffron.] A red powder used ceremonially, and by Hindu women to make a small distinctive spot on the forehead; the spot so made. Also *attrib.*

1938 K. van A. Gates tr. *Ramabai Ranade's Himself* vii. 57 A pleasant custom..allows a hostess at a ladies' party to apply a dot of red powder (*kunku*) to the forehead of each guest. *Ibid.* xv. 133 Don't you have the custom of wearing..*kunku* marks, and such things? **1943** Moraes & Stimson *Introd. India* (ed. 3) 113 Hindu women wear on the forehead a red dot (called *kumkum*, which is also the name of the powder from which it is made). An orthodox Hindu widow does not wear a *kumkum*. **1958** *Times* 15 Oct. 24/5 Mrs. Usha Rajwade, who earlier..rubbed on Kum-Kum powder. **1969** *Commerce* (Bombay) 26 July 149/3 Sometime back there was understandable furore in the city of Bombay when some missionary school asked the girls not to apply *kumkum* which is a sign of good fortune for an Indian girl. **1973** *Guardian* 14 Apr. 11/3 God needs offerings—garlands, coconuts, kum-kum powder, incense.

kümmel. (Earlier examples.)

1864 P. Marié *Tribute to Fair* p. x, Our friend here sipping Kümmel. *c* **1870** in H. W. Allen *Number Three St. James Street* (1950) 186/1 Liqueurs. Bottle... Kummel..9/-. **1877** E. S. Dallas *Kettner's Bk. of Table* 269 Caraways in palpable form have now disappeared from our tables, but only to return in the spirit—in Russian bottles labelled Kümmel.

Kümmell's disease (kü·mělz dizī·z). *Path.* [f. the name of Hermann *Kümmell* (1852–1937), German surgeon.] Delayed collapse of a vertebra after an injury.

1903 *Index-Catal. Library Surg.-General's Office U.S. Army* 2nd Ser. VIII. 874/2 (*heading*) Kümmel's [*sic*] disease. **1923** *Jrnl. Amer. Med. Assoc.* 1 Dec. 1866/1 Kümmell's disease is a distinct clinical entity, having as its basic origin a traumatism to the spine, which may be mild or severe. **1951** *Amer. Jrnl. Surg.* LXXXI. 166/2 The diagnosis of Kümmell's disease is not justified without negative lateral roentgenograms taken in the early postinjury period, with later films showing positive findings of collapse.

‖ **kumpit** (ku·mpit). [Native name.] A trading-vessel of the Philippine Islands.

1951 *People* (Austral.) 17 Jan. 48/3 They were finally got away by a Filipino..who paddled over from the Philippines in a 'kumpit' and took them back under a small cargo of rice. **1968** *Economist* 12 Oct. 81/3 There's many a fast kumpit no doubt leaving Sabah bound for the Sulu shores. **1969** R. Thomas *Singapore Wink* xiii. 138 '..the *Wilfreda Maria*.' 'What's that?' 'A *kumpit*.' 'And a *kumpit* is a what?' 'It's an eight-ton ship. I bought it from a Moro pirate. I'm a smuggler.' **1972** *Sunday Times* (Singapore) 24 Sept. 7/3 Strict watch is maintained on all kumpits (Filipino boats) arriving in Sabah.

kumquat (kʊ·mˌkwǫt). [See Cumquat.] **1.** A small, orange-like citrus fruit from a tree of the genus *Fortunella*, native to southern China and Malaysia; now the usual spelling of Cumquat.

1870 *Jrnl. R. Hort. Soc.* II. 46 (*title*) Observations on the kumquat. **1882** [see Cumquat]. **1913** E. H. Wilson *Naturalist in W. China* II. iii. 25 The Kumquat (*C. Japonica*) is sparingly cultivated for its fruits, which, preserved with sugar, are an esteemed delicacy. **1968** *Punch* 13 Mar. 402/2 Mr. Adams is..occasionally affected (a face like 'a hybrid kumquat'). But he's written a master thriller.

2. *Austral.* A very small native citrus fruit, *Eremocitrus glauca*, or the tree producing it.

1889 J. H. Maiden *Useful Native Plants of Austral.* 8 *Atalantia glauca*..'Native Kumquat', 'Desert Lemon'... New South Wales and Queensland. **1955** P. White *Tree of Man* (1956) 400 Boys should eat kumquats, the syrup running from the corners of their mouths. **1965** *Austral. Encycl.* IV. 227/2 *Eremocitrus glauca*, native kumquat or wild lime (Rutaceæ): small spiny tree of western New South Wales and Queensland; the globular ½ inch fruits are pleasantly acidic and suitable for preserves, also cool drinks.

‖ **kumri** (ku·mri). [Native term.] A system of shifting cultivation practised in Kanara, western India (see quot. 1938). Freq. *attrib.*

1904 W. Schlich *Man. Forestry* (ed. 3) II. i. iv. 106 The system is still extensively practised in India under a variety of names, as jhooming, dhya, kumri, taungya cultivation, etc. **1938** *Jrnl. Madras Geogr. Assoc.* XIII. 272 These people started what is known as 'Kumri' or 'Podu' cultivation. This is simply clearing the virgin forest, burning the felled trees and sowing rice, ragi, dhall etc., after the fire has died out, without any previous preparation of the soil. As the quantity of the ashes available was considerable, agricultural crop flourished and all that the 'Kumridar' had to do was a little weeding and protection of the crop from wild animals. He then left that area and selected another virgin forest close by. **1954** O. H. K. Spate *India & Pakistan* xxii. 624 The jungle is largely occupied by tribal remnants practising shifting *kumri* cultivation.

Kumyk (kū̆·mik). Also 8 **Coumyk**; 20 **Kumik, Kumuk.** [f. *Kumyk* name of a plateau in the Caucasus.] **a.** A Turkish people from the Kumyk plateau; also, a member of this people. **b.** Their language.

1788 G. Ellis *Mem. Map Countries between Black Sea & Caucasus* 15 The Tartars are of three tribes, viz. 1. Terekemens, Turcomans, or Trukhmenians... 2. Coumyks. These live to the northward of the former, about the lower parts of the rivers Sundsha, Koisu, and Axai. **1902** *Encycl. Brit.* XXX. 81/2 Having long been more civilized than the surrounding Caucasian mountaineers, the Kumyks have always enjoyed some respect among them. **1948** D. Diringer *Alphabet* 568 Kumuk Turkish. **1970** *Encycl. Brit.* V. 102/2 Feudal relations developed..in the northern Caucasus among the Kabardians and Kumyk. *Ibid.* XXII. 399/2 Kumyk is also spoken in the Dagestan A.S.S.R.

kunai (ku·nəi). [Native name in New Guinea.] A large coarse grass, *Imperata cylindrica*, found in tropical Asia, Australia, and the Pacific region; also called *blady grass* (*blady *a.*) and *lalang. Also *attrib.*

1933 *Bulletin* (Sydney) 6 Sept. 39/4 Soon the weeds will have overrun the scar by the river bank, and a field of lush *kunai* will grow. **1945** *Coast to Coast 1944* 102 A gale ..set the tall kunai grass swaying. **1958** *Times* 27 Nov. 12/6 On the waterfront, the buildings were..of native design, thatched with kunai grass. **1962** *Coast to Coast 1961–62* 53 Beyond him was the fantasy of New Guinea green:..in front the kunai plain which reached for five miles to the Finisterre Ranges. **1965** *Austral. Encycl.* IV. 367/1 *Imperata cylindrica* var. *major* (blady grass) is widely spread over eastern and northern Australia, chiefly in coastal districts, and extends through Polynesia and Malaysia to tropical Asia where it is popularly known by other names (kunai, lalang, and kogon).

Kunbi (kū̆·nbi). Also 6 **Corumbijn**, 9 **Coombie, Koonbee, Kunbee.** [ad. Hindi *kurmī*.] A member of an Indian agricultural caste.

1598 W. Phillip tr. *J. H. van Linschoten's Discours Voy. E. & W. Indies* i. xxxix. 73/2 The Canarijns & Corumbijns [*sic*] are the Countrimen. **1808** R. Drummond *Illustr. Gram. Parts Guzerattee, Mahratta & Eng. Lang.*, *Kunbee, Koonbee* or *Koolumbee*. (Guz. and Mah.) *Koonbee* is a term, which is given, whatever be his profession or occupation, to the pure *Sooder* or first of the fourth class, who are, in Guzerat for the most part, Cultivators of the Land. This title, in the Deccan distinguishes the Cultivator, from him, who wears arms, and prefers to be called a Mahratta. **1826** W. B. Hockley *Pandurang Hari* I. x. 230, I begged the coombie, or cultivator, to give me some bread and rice. **1845** *Encycl. Metrop.* XX. 33/1 The Kunbí is a pure Súdra. **1875** *Encycl. Brit.* I. 423/2 The bulk of the population [of

Ahmadnagar] consists of Marhattás and Kunbís, the latter being the agriculturists. **1923** *United Free Ch. Miss. Rec.* June 250/2 Patils of villages, the kunbi, the cartman, the man on the road with whom I passed the time of day, ..all of them were kindly polite and courteous.

Kung-fu, kung-fu (kuŋˌfū·, kɒŋ-). Also without hyphen. [Chinese.] The Chinese form of *KARATE. Also *attrib.*

1966 *Punch* 14 Sept. 388/3 Kung-fu is here. **1968** *Clarendonian* XXII. 270 Chinese Kung-fu is still taught today—but only as a Martial Art to a very select, carefully chosen few. **1970** K. Platt *Pushbutton Butterfly* i. 9 The Chinese now call their form of karate *Kung Fu*... It's mostly leg-fighting. **1971** 'A. Hall' *Warsaw Document* xvii. 213 It was probably *kaminari*, a bastardized form of *kung fu*. **1974** *Listener* 17 Jan. 93/3 The plot.. hinges on Lee wiping out an ex-monk, Kung-fu (martial arts) vice chief. **1974** *Bookseller* 13 Apr. 1961/1 There has been a great upsurge of popular interest recently in kung fu, the ancient Chinese art of self-defence, encouraged by the films of Bruce Lee...and the television series Kung Fu.

kungu (kɒ·ŋgu). Also **kungo.** [Nyanja *nkungu.*] A small East African gnat, *Chaoborus edulis.* Hence **kungu cake**, the bodies of large numbers of these gnats, compressed to form a cake.

1865 D. & C. Livingstone *Narr. Expedition Zambesi* 373 A kungo cake, an inch thick..was offered to us. **1897** H. H. Johnston *Brit. Cent. Afr.* 436 The 'Kungu' fly of Lake Nyasa. **1899** D. Sharp in *Cambr. Nat. Hist.* VI. vii. 467 The kungu cake mentioned by Livingstone as used on Lake Nyassa is made from an Insect which occurs in profusion there, and is compressed into biscuit form. **1902** H. H. Johnston *Uganda Protectorate* I. 413 The kungu fly has a soft little body, scarcely as large as that of a flea, with gauzy wings. **1964** H. Oldroyd *Nat. Hist. Flies* pl. 30 (a) (*caption*) A piece of 'kungu-cake', made up entirely from the bodies of small midges, *Chaoborus edulis*, from an East African lake.

kunku, var. *KUMKUM.

‖ **Kunst** (kunst). [G., = art.] The G. word in Comb. (which are in varying degrees naturalized in Eng. scholarly writings), as **Kunstforscher** (ku·nstfǫrʃər), practitioner of *Kunstforschung*, art historian; also **Ku·nstforschung**, (scientific) study of fine art, art history; **Kunstgeschichte** (ku·nstgəːʃi·χʏtə), the history of art, art history; **Kunsthistoriker** (ku·nsthistǭːrikər), an art-historian; **Kunstlied** (ku·nstlīt) = *art song* (see *ART *sb.* 18 b); **Kunstprosa** (ku·nstprōᵘză), literary prose, stylized or highly wrought prose.

1899 R. Fry *Let.* 15 Nov. (1972) I. 175 We are in the thick of a *Kunstforscher* fight. **1923** A. Huxley *Antic Hay* vii. 104 As a connoisseur and *kunstforscher*, Mr. Clew was much esteemed. **1933** *Burlington Mag.* Oct. 145/1 It would almost seem as though the Government had never recognized the existence of such a being as the 'Kunstforscher', perhaps because we have no better name for him in English than the clumsy and not altogether accurate 'art historian'. **1959** *Times Lit. Suppl.* 17 July 420/3 The editor, an industrious and knowledgeable *Kunstforscher*, supplies interesting scraps of information concerning the artist and his pictures, his models, his friends, and his methods. **1966** *Punch* 2 Nov. 683/2 There being no formal *Kunstforschung* in his student days. **1892** W. James *Let.* 7 Oct. (1920) I. 328, I have mapped out a profitable course of winter reading, *Naturphilosophie* and *Kunstgeschichte*. **1936** *Mind* XLV. 515 The range of questions that it opens out is exemplified by the two essays in *Kunstgeschichte*. **1937** H. Nicolson *Diary* 31 Dec. (1966) 315 Ben has been..in Florence preparing himself as a *Kunsthistoriker*. **1971** 'M. Innes' *Awkward Lie* iii. 64 All the professors and judges, the *Kunsthistoriker*, the Ministers of the Crown. **1880** Grove *Dict. Mus.* II. 133/1 The Volkslied has gradually disappeared, giving place to the Kunstlied, of which the accompaniment is an important feature. **1936** C. S. Lewis *Allegory of Love* 223 Usk is trying to write prose which shall have wings like verse—coloured and tunable prose—*Kunstprosa* in a word. **1960** K. J. Dover *Greek Word Order* i. 11, I cannot swear that the decrees of the Ozolian Locrians do not betray the hand of a mute inglorious Gorgias, but I may be allowed to doubt that and to believe that in early documents from the Peloponnese, the North-West and Crete the influence of *Kunstprosa* is minimal. **1965** *Listener* 19 Aug. 281/1 That gigantic waste-paper basket, the Short Story... Straight tales, character-sketches,.. experimental *Kunstprosa*, automatic writing, [etc.].

‖ **Künstlerroman** (kü·nstlərˌromaːn). [G.] A *BILDUNGSROMAN about an artist.

1941 H. Levin *James Joyce* 41 The novel of development..becomes a novel of the artist, a *Künstlerroman*. **1957** N. Frye *Anat. Criticism* 307 The confession flows into the novel, and the mixture produces the fictional autobiography, the *Künstler-roman*, and kindred types. **1969** J. Gross *Rise & Fall Man of Lett.* i. 20 *Pendennis* can be seen as a first faltering step towards the *Künstlerroman*, the novel about the making of a novelist.

kunzite (kɒ·ntsəit, kɒ·nz-). *Min.* [f. the name of George F. *Kunz* (1856–1932), U.S. gemmologist; see -ITE¹.] A lilac-coloured variety of spodumene which is valued as a gem and becomes phosphorescent or changes colour when irradiated (see quot. 1962); a gemstone of this mineral.

1903 C. Baskerville in *Science* 4 Sept. 304/2 On account of this unusual and characteristic phosphorescence, as well as the other properties, I propose the name *Kunzite*. **1905** *Westm. Gaz.* 18 Jan. 12/1 To those who love some new thing the latest discovery in precious stones, Kunzite, will..be extremely welcome. **1949** *Rocks & Minerals* Mar.–Apr. 177 Kunzite. A perfect pear shaped stone of good color, 4·70 carats, $50.00. **1962** R. Webster *Gems* I. vii. 129 Kunzite shows a golden-pink or orange glow under long-wave ultra-violet light, and a similar but much weaker effect is seen under the short-wave ultra-violet lamp. Under an x-ray beam kunzite shows a very strong orange fluorescence with a strong and persistent afterglow. When the phosphorescence has died away the stone is found to have changed its colour to a bluish-green; this remains stable provided that the stone is kept away from a strong light. **1973** *Fortnum & Mason Ltd. Christmas Catal.* 23/1 Openwork ring, in 18 ct. gold set with diamonds and one freeform kunzite, £265·00.

Kuomintang (kuomintæ·ŋ, -tā·ŋ). [Chin., lit. 'national people's party'.] A nationalist radical party founded in China under Sun Yat-Sen in 1912, and led, after his death in 1925, by Chiang Kai-Shek, constituting the government before the Communist Party took power in October 1949, and subsequently forming the central administration of Taiwan.

1912 J. O. P. Bland *Recent Events & Present Policies China* iv. 107 In the beginning of September, an arrangement was effected, by the leaders of the T'ung-Meng-hui, to amalgamate with five minor political groups 'for the sake of harmony' under a new name, the Kuo-Min-tang, or Nationalist party. **1913** W. H. Hosking *Great Squeeze* iii. 36 The *Kuomintang* is a coalition of parties and is the only one that counts just now. **1928** T. F. Millard *China* 39, I remember the assassination of one Sung, a Kuomintang leader. **1941** E. Hemingway *Let.* 30 July in *Morgenthau Diary* (*China*) (U.S. Senate Committee on Judiciary) (1965) I. 458 The bitterness between the Communists and most of the Kuomintang leaders I talked to including the Generalissimo, can hardly be exaggerated. **1948** J. K. Fairbank *U.S. & China* ix. 193 The National Government of China at Nanking in the decade from 1927 to 1937 was the most modern and effective that China had known. It was led by Chiang Kai-shek and controlled by the Kuomintang on the basis of party dictatorship. **1952** C. P. Fitzgerald *Revolution in China* ix. 229 It will be argued that the Kuomintang remnants in Formosa are 'White Chinese', and much Right Wing American misconception of the Chinese Revolution is due to this belief. But..the Nationalists are failed revolutionaires. **1957** *Times Lit. Suppl.* 27 Dec. 782/3 This bitter struggle between Kuomintang and Communists. **1971** K. Hopkins *Hong Kong* 216 For the present the fifty-year-old struggle between the Communists and the Kuomintang continues, muted, with the British administration holding the ring. **1972** S. L. Appleton in *Asian Survey* Jan. 35 Kuomintang and government leaders, summoned to an emergency meeting following the U.N. vote, themselves cited the need for political reforms.

‖ **Kuo-yü** (kuoˌyü). Also **Guoryu, Kuoyu.** [Chin., lit. 'national language'.] The name given to the Chinese 'national tongue', a form of Mandarin adopted for official use.

1932 Guoryu [see *KUAN, KWAN 1]. **1934** in Webster. **1954** Pei & Gaynor *Dict. Ling.* 116 *Kuo-yü*, the new 'national tongue' of China, based on the Peiping dialect of North Mandarin; now estimated to be used by about 300,000,000 persons. **1957** *B.B.C. Handbook* 132 There were large audiences to the relays by Radio Hong Kong of BBC programmes in Cantonese, English, and Kuoyü. **1964** *New Statesman* 10 Apr. 581/4 (Advt.), Applicants must be native Kuoyu speakers. **1968** D. Torr *Treason Line* 45 He remembered just enough of the *Kuo-yü* he had learnt in Chungking. **1969** J. M. Gullick *Malaysia* i. 29 The universal teaching in Chinese schools of the national Kuo-Yu dialect should in time provide a *lingua franca*.

Kupferschiefer (ku·pfəɹʃīfəɹ). *Petrogr.* Also 9 **Kupfer-schiefer**; and with small **k.** [a. G. *kupferschiefer*, f. *kupfer* COPPER *sb.*¹ + *schiefer* shale, slate.] A bituminous brown or black shale of the Permian series, which is worked in Germany for copper; = *copper schist, -slate* (COPPER *sb.*¹ 11).

1830 H. T. De la Beche *Sections & Views* 47 Professor Sedgwick..considers that he can trace the equivalents of the copper slate (kupfer-schiefer)..of the Thuringerwald, in the magnesian limestone of England. **1831** *Phil. Mag.* X. 46 Those sandstones and conglomerates which surmount the carboniferous series, and separate it from the *kupfer-schiefer* and magnesian limestone. **1879** *Encycl. Brit.* X. 352/1 The Kupfer-schiefer contains numerous fish.. and remains of plants. **1886** J. Geikie *Outl. Geol.* xxi. 298 The Kupferschiefer (2 feet thick) has long been famous for its ores of copper and other metals. **1921** A. W. Grabau *Textbk. Geol.* II. xxxviii. 506 At the base of this limestone series lies the important black copper-bearing shale, the Kupferschiefer, which rests upon the red sandstone. **1967** D. H. Rayner *Stratigr. Brit. Isles* viii. 253 The Hilton Plant Bed..consists of dolomitic sands and silts whose flora includes some species common to the Marl Slate and Kupferschiefer.

Kupffer (ku·pfəɹ). *Histology.* The name of Karl Wilhelm von *Kupffer* (1829–1902), Bavarian anatomist and embryologist, used in **Kupffer('s) cell** (also *cell of Kupffer*), a phagocytic cell that occurs in the lining of the sinusoids of the liver and has long radiating processes of cytoplasm (described by Kupffer in 1876).

1901 tr. *H. Dürck's Atlas & Epitome Special Path. Histol.* II. 18 The so-called stellate cells, or Kupffer's cells, ..are faintly visible. **1924** H. E. Roaf *Text-bk. Physiol.* xx. 262 Kupffer cells have been seen containing remnants of red blood corpuscles and they may be instrumental in collecting the hæmoglobin for the formation of bile pigment. **1956** *Nature* 24 Mar. 575/2 Blocking of Kupffer cells interferes with the storage of vitamin A ester in the liver of the rat. **1966** C. R. & T. S. Leeson *Histol.* xiv. 314/1 It is probable..that the stellate cells of Kupffer are increased in number in time of need by differentiation of the more primitive, endothelial cells.

‖ **Kur** (kūr). [G.] A cure, a taking of the waters (in Germany or another German-speaking country, as at a KURSAAL); a spa.

1885 Geo. Eliot *Let.* 25 June in J. W. Cross *George Eliot's Life* (1885) II. xiii. 369 It would have marred the Kur for me if I had every day to undergo a *table d'hôte*. **1892** C. M. Yonge *That Stick* I. xx. 238 The end of Constance's holidays was in view, the limit that had been intended for the Kur at Ratzes. **1915** F. M. Hueffer *Good Soldier* i. 10 The music of the Kur orchestra. **1974** *Country Life* 24 Oct. 1212/1 The Kur park and its monuments are still as the Edwardians knew them.

‖ **kura** (ku·ră). [Jap.] In Japan, a fire-proof store-house.

1880 I. L. Bird *Unbeaten Tracks Japan* I. x. 106 There is a *kura*, or fire proof storehouse, with a tiled roof on the right of the house. **1906** R. A. Cram *Impressions Jap. Archit.* iii. 63 Every house of any pretension possesses its 'kura', or storehouse, built of wood and bamboo, but covered two feet thick with clay... After a big fire in a Japanese city, nothing is left but fine ashes and the scorched but reliable kura. **1936** K. Nohara *True Face of Japan* iii. 44 Between the houses of wood, paper and thin plaster, tower the white-washed massive buildings of the kura. **1965** W. Swaan *Jap. Lantern* v. 58 The works of art may be brought in still packed in the special boxes in which they are stored in the *kura*.

kurakkan (ku·răkˌkān). Also 7 **coracan.** The Sinhala name for a type of cereal grass, *Eleusine coracana* (Indian *raggee*), which is extensively grown in chenas in Sri Lanka (Ceylon) where flour from its grain forms a staple food of the poorer villagers.

1681 R. Knox *Hist. Relation Ceylon* I. iii. 11 There are divers other sorts of Corn, which serve the People for food in the absence of Rice... There is *Coracan*, which is a small seed like Mustard-seed. This they grind to meal or beat in a Mortar, and so make cakes of it. **1824** A. Moon *Catal. Indigenous & Exotic Plants Ceylon* 9 Eleusine... 1 coracana, common,..Kurakkan,..Ceylon, *cult.* **1864** G. H. K. Thwaites *Enumeratio Plantarum Zeylaniæ* v. 371 *E. Coracana*, Gærtn. (nom. vulg. 'Koorakkan'), is extensively cultivated by the Cinghalese as a food grain. **1900** J. D. Hooker in H. Trimen *Hand-bk. Flora Ceylon* V. 277 The Sinhalese 'Kurrakan'..is a very stout prolific form of this, with the spikelets crowded in many series, and a globose rugose seed. It is extensively cultivated for its grain in Ceylon. **1913** L. Woolf *Village in Jungle* i. 10 When the rains fall in November the ground is sown broadcast with millet or kurakkan. **1971** *Ceylon Daily News* 18 Sept. 4/6 In the villages around here the traditional food has been kurakkan and curd.

kurchatovium (kɒ̄ɹtʃătōᵘ·viɒm). *Chem.* [ad. Russ. *kurchátovii* (Flerov & Kuznetsov 1967, in *Priroda* Nov. 35), f. the name of Igor *Kurchatov* (1903–60), Russ. nuclear physicist: see -IUM.] (A name proposed for) an artificially produced transuranic element, atomic number 104. Symbol Ku. Cf. *RUTHERFORDIUM.

1967 I. Zvára et al. *Joint Inst. Nucl. Res.* (Dubna, U.S.S.R.) *Preprint D6–3281* (*title*) Experiments on chemistry of element 104—kurchatovium. **1968** *New Scientist* 11 Jan. 85/1 Scientists working..at Dubna..were last year awarded the Lenin Prize for their work on the synthesis of transuranium elements, in particular element 104. This latter element was named Kurchatovium by the Russians. **1970** *Soviet Radiochem.* XII. 536 It was confirmed..that kurchatovium forms a chloride $KuCl_4$, with properties close to those of the chloride $HfCl_4$, and, consequently, is an analog of hafnium and zirconium, i.e., a member of sub-group IVb. **1971** *Inorg. & Nucl. Chem. Lett.* VII. 1115 The present work shows once again that the doubts expressed by the Berkeley group..concerning the chemical identification of kurchatovium are completely unfounded. *Ibid.* 1119 [*Reply of the 'Berkeley group'*.] We believe that these comments raise some valid questions as to whether or not 'element 104 (kurchatovium—Ku) was chemically isolated and identified'.

Kurd (kɒ̄ɹd). Also 7 **Coord,** 8–9 **Curd.** [Native name.] One of a pastoral and agricultural people of Aryan stock, found in northern Iran and Iraq and eastern Turkey, with the adjacent regions of the U.S.S.R. (the area being collectively known as *Kurdistan*). Also *attrib.* or as *adj.* So **Ku·rdish** *a.*, of or pertaining to the Kurds or their language, a dialect belonging to the Iranian group; as *sb.*, the language itself; **Kurdista·n** *a.* and *sb.*, (of) a Kurdish rug.

1616 T. ROE *Let.* 30 Oct. in *Embassy to Court of Gt. Mogul* (1899) II. 310 The King..tooke occasion to take in by force a reuolted Nation to the East of Babilon. The People are Called Coords. **1776** GIBBON *Decl. & F.* I. xiii. 381 The arrows of the Carduchians... Their posterity, the Curds,..acknowledge the nominal sovereignty of the Turkish sultan. **1813** *Q. Rev.* Oct. 257 Languages and Dialects... Median. Zendish. Pehlvish. Persian. Kurdish. *Ibid.* 267 The Kurds speak a corrupt Persian. **1823** BYRON *Don Juan* VI. lxxxvi. 29 Asia, where Kaff looks down upon the Kurds. **1836** T. SKINNER *Adventures Journey Overland to India* II. v. 69 The wife of the Kurdish traveller. **1854** J. H. NEWMAN *Lect. Hist. Turks* IV. iii. 265 Saladin was a Curd. **1868** W. D. WHITNEY *Lang. & Study of Lang.* (ed. 2) v. 192 The Persian..with its outliers on the north-west and on the east—as the Armenian, the Kurdish, the Ossetic, and the Afghan. **1882** E. O'DONOVAN *Merv Oasis* I. 325 A Kurd encampment. **1899** MRS. L. M. ELTON tr. *Nazarbek's Through the Storm* 204 About thirty Kurdish brigands rushed out of the forest. **1920** *Glasgow Herald* 12 May 9 Turkey accepts..a scheme of local autonomy for the predominantly Kurdish areas east of the Euphrates, south of the southern frontier of Armenia. *Ibid.*, The Kurds inhabiting that part of Kurdistan which has hitherto been included in the Mosul vilayet are to be allowed..to adhere to the independent Kurdish State. **1924** *Blackw. Mag.* Nov. 583/2 Pursued by a volley of oaths in English, Scots, and Kurdish. **1926** T. E. LAWRENCE *Seven Pillars* (1935) II. xix. 124 It was an ordinary bell tent, furnished with..a fairly good Kurd rug, a poor Shirazi, and the delightful old Baluch prayer-carpet on which he prayed. **1931** A. U. DILLEY *Oriental Rugs & Carpets* Pl. 22 (*caption*) Kurdistan, Mina Khani Design. **1955** *Times* 21 May 9/6 The Kurds of Iraq live along the frontiers of Turkey and Persia, among the mountains that form Iraq's natural boundaries. They are a hill people, and recognizably related to the Alpine Swiss, the Sherpas, and other mountaineers. **1963** *Times* 12 June 11/1 Kurdish would be the first language in elementary education in Sulaymaniya. **1970** D. M. LANG *Armenia* i. 39 Many of the neighbours of the Armenians in antiquity have vanished from the map, like the Hittites..; relapsed into barbarism, like the Kurds, descendants of the proud Medes; [etc.]. **1970** L. SANDERS *Anderson Tapes* lxv. 174 The brothers had taken a very nice Kurdistan [rug] down to the truck. **1971** *Guardian* 3 Dec. 4/4 An unfortunate Pesh Merga (Kurdish soldier). **1973** *Times* 9 Aug. 5/1 Mr Baluk told the court that he was a member of the Kurdish minority in Turkey. **1974** *Evening Standard* 12 Feb. 48/5 (Advt.), Superb oriental carpets & rugs. Including:..outstanding Kurdistan rugs in fascinating geometric designs.

kurdaitcha (kuɹdəi·tʃă). *Austral.* Also 9 **kooditcha.** [Austral. Aboriginal.] (See quot. 1909.) Also, a malignant supernatural being. Also *attrib.*

1886 E. M. CURR *Austral. Race* I. v. 148 It was discovered in 1882..that the Blacks..wear a sort of shoe when they attack their enemies by stealth at night. Some of the tribes call these shoes Kooditcha, their name for an invisible spirit... The soles were made of the feathers of the emu, stuck together with a little human blood... The uppers were nets made of human hair. **1896** *Proc. R. Soc. Victoria* VIII. 66 The wearing of the Urtathurta and going Kūrdaitcha lūma appears to have been the medium for a form of vendetta. **1909** *Cent. Dict.* Suppl. I. 693 *Kurdaitcha.* 1. Among the tribes of central Australia, a man chosen to avenge the death of one who had died, every death being supposed to be due to the magic influence of some enemy. 2. A kind of shoe, made of emu-feathers matted together with human blood, worn by the kurdaitcha when on his errand. **1932** *Times Lit. Suppl.* 28 Jan. 52/2 The *Kurdaitcha* among the tribes of Central Australia goes forth against his enemy with a medicine-man skilled in this sinister art. **1940** A. UPFIELD *Bushranger of Skies* (1963) xvi. 156 You ought to make us Kurdaitcha shoes. *Ibid.* xix. 183 A Kurdaitcha man is an evil spirit—always wandering about the poor blackfellows' camp at night. **1953** —— *Murder must Wait* xxii. 146 All good aborigines should be fast asleep..safe from the dread Kurdaitcha. **1959** S. H. COURTIER *Death in Dream Time* ii. 19 The bewildering display of aboriginal weapons and implements... death-bones and kurdaitcha shoes. **1962** A. UPFIELD *Will of Tribe* vi. 57 The fear of the Kurdaitcha Man and the Great Snake.

kurfuffle, var. CURFUFFLE *sb.*

1955 C. S. LEWIS *Surprised by Joy* vii. 114, I could put up with any amount of monotony far more patiently than even the smallest disturbance, bother, bustle, or what the Scotch call *kurfuffle.*

‖ **Kurhaus** (kū·rˌhaus). [G.] A building at a German health resort where the medicinal water is dispensed for drinking and external use; a pump-room; hence, sometimes, a similar building at a watering-place outside Germany.

1855 GEO. ELIOT in *Fraser's Mag.* July 61/2 The white *Kurhaus* glittering on a grassy slope. **1857** C. KINGSLEY *Two Yrs. Ago* III. ix. 269 He drives up to the handsome old Kurhaus. **1935** J. BUCHAN *House of Four Winds* 12 Mr McCunn..accepted the consultant's prescription, and rooms were taken for him at the Rosensee *kurhaus.* **1962** N. FREELING *Love in Amsterdam* I. 38 Tuesday night he was at the Kurhaus in Scheveningen.

‖ **kuri** (ku·ri). *N.Z.* [Maori *kurī.*] A Maori dog, long extinct: now usu. = *GOORIE, GOORY.

1838 J. S. POLACK *New Zealand* I. ix. 308 The karáráhé, or dog (Canis Australis), which, when young, is known as *kuri*, has been an inhabitant some two or three centuries. **1843** E. DIEFFENBACH *Trav. N.Z.* II. iv. 46 The New Zealand dog is different from the Australian dingo;..the native name is kuri. **1900** J. SCOTT *Tales Colonial Turf* 180 It was a sort of poodle..no one would think of asking who owned the kuri. **1930** J. COWAN in J. Reid *Kiwi Laughs* (1961) 97, I wish you'd give it to them hot and strong about the blasted 'kuris' worrying my sheep. **1949** P. BUCK *Coming of Maori* (1950) I. iv. 64 The dog (*kuri*) figures a good deal in tradition. **1959** TINDALE & LINDSAY *Rangatira* 195 *Kuri dog.* The Maori dog was small... It was kept as a pet, it gave some aid in hunting, and it provided..fresh meat... It appears to be a domesticated strain of the feral dog of India..now extinct in New Zealand.

Kurile (kiū·rīl), *sb.* and *a.* [f. the *Kurile islands*, a chain of small islands stretching northwards from Japan to Kamchatka, since 1945 held by the U.S.S.R.] **A.** *sb.* A native or inhabitant of the Kurile islands. **B.** *adj.* Of or pertaining to these islands or this people. Hence **Kuri·lian** *a.* and *sb.*

1764 J. GRIEVE tr. *Krasheninnikov's Hist. Kamtschatka* I. i. 19 When the ice is carried thither with the beavers on it, then the Kuriles, who follow the ice along the shore, assemble here in great multitudes. **1819, 1843** [see *AINU]. **1845** *Encycl. Metrop.* XXV. 866/2 A small portion of the continent..opposite to the Isle of Sakhalyin..is occupied by the Aïnos or Kurīls, whose Isles extend from Japan to the Southern extremity of Kamchatka. **1875** *Encycl. Brit.* I. 426/2 The Ainos..are distinguished by an exuberance of hair on the head and body, a circumstance which has given rise to their name of 'Hairy Kuriles'.

Kurku, var. *KORKU.

kurl-a-mo, kurl-the-mo: see *CURL *v.*[1] 1 c.

Kurnai (ku·ɹnəi). [Austral. Aboriginal.] **A.** *adj.* Of or pertaining to an Aboriginal tribe of south-eastern Australia. **B.** *sb.* This tribe; a member of this tribe; their language.

1911 J. G. FRAZER *Golden Bough: Magic Art* (ed. 3) I. v. 324 The Kurnai tribe of Gippsland in Victoria. **1965** *Austral. Encycl.* I. 72/2 The Kurnai of Gippsland used to cut one or both hands from a corpse. The hand was wrapped in grass and dried, and a possum-fur string attached so that it could be worn about the neck of a near relative. By pushing or pinching the wearer, it was said to give warning of an approaching enemy. **1965** W. E. H. STANNER in R. M. & C. H. Berndt *Aboriginal Man in Austral.* viii. 230 Much mischief has resulted from the supposition that all Aborigines in all important respects resemble the Aranda, Kamilaroi, Kurnai, and Murngin. **1972** *Talanya* I. 29 In Kurnai..he gives the following phrases.

kurnakovite (kɒ̄ɹnăkǫ·vəit). *Min.* [f. the name of N. S. *Kurnakov* (1860–1941), Russian mineralogist: see -ITE[1].] A hydrated borate of magnesium, $Mg_2B_6O_{11}·13H_2O$, found as colourless granular aggregates with a vitreous lustre at Inder, Kazakhstan, U.S.S.R.

1940 M. N. GODLEVSKY in *Compt. Rend.* (*Doklady*) *de l'Acad. des Sci. de l'URSS* XXVIII. 638 During my visit to the Inder deposit in 1938, I found in the dump of one of the pits..a solid colourless mineral which proved to be a borate, of the composition $2MgO.3B_2O_3.13H_2O$. The new mineral was named kurnakovite. **1962** *Amer. Mineralogist* XLVII. 402 In the monoclinic and triclinic dimorphs..inderite and kurnakovite respectively, the asymmetric unit has been found to contain three chemically different boron sites. **1970** *Soviet Physics: Doklady* XIV. 1141/2 In kurnakovite an isolated H_2O particle is bonded to four boroxy rings by a single Mg octahedron.

‖ **Kurort** (kū·rˌōᵊrt). Also 9 **curort; kurort.** [G.] In Germany or other German-speaking countries, a health-resort, a watering-place; also *fig.*

1868 GEO. ELIOT *Let.* 27 June (1955) IV. 454 We..daily rejoice that we have found such a Cur-ort, suiting both mind and body. **1926** *Spectator* 21 Aug. 276/1 A company is being formed..to erect a modern thermal *Kurort*, and build an up-to-date hotel. **1930** *Discovery* June 171/2, I had no troubles, except a longing for the mountains.. and even the attractions of Prague, the Riesengebirge, and several magnetic *kurorts* failed to hold me back. **1941** V. NABOKOV *Real Life S. Knight* xv. 146 She loved inventing some rare illness and going to some famous kurort. **1949** KOESTLER *Promise & Fulfilment* III. iv. 325 Others, like Naharia, are German Kurorts grafted on by plastic landscape surgery.

Kuroshiwo. Add: Also **Kuroshio, Kurosiwo,** and as two words (with or without a hyphen). (Further examples.)

1928 RUSSELL & YONGE *Seas* x. 231 In the Pacific.. there is a system of oceanic currents much after the manner of that in the Atlantic, the Japan Current or 'Kuro Shiwo' corresponding to our Gulf Stream. **1967** *Oceanogr. & Marine Biol.* V. 57 Often compared with the Gulf Stream and Kuroshio, the East Australian Current is essentially different because it does not, as do the other two, make up an eddy system extending towards the east across the ocean. **1969** *Sci. Jrnl.* Jan. 16/1 The Kuroshio ..is a swift current that runs along the western edge of the Pacific just as the Gulf Stream does in the North Atlantic.

kurper (kɒ̄·rpəɹ). *S. Afr.* Also **karper, kerper, kurpur.** [Afrikaans, f. Du. *karper* carp.] A name used for several fresh-water fishes resembling carp, esp. *Sandelia capensis.*

1831 *S. Afr. Q. Jrnl.* Oct. 19 Kurper... Inhabits most of the rivers towards the Southern extremity of Africa. **1902** *Trans. S. Afr. Philos. Soc.* XI. 213 In an expedition to the interior, led by Surgeon Pieter van Meerhoff, we are told by him that in the space of 1½ hours they caught 'beautiful Carp (Karper)'... This is undoubtedly the fish (*Spirobranchus capensis*) still called Karper in the Colony by the Dutch. **1913** C. PETTMAN *Africanderisms* 285 Kurper or Kerper... *Spirobranchus capensis*, a well-known freshwater fish. See Karper. **1947** K. H. BARNARD *Pict. Guide S. Afr. Fishes* 80 The Cape Kurper (*Sandelia capensis*) is a very well-known fish in the rivers and vleis of the southwest Cape... In the Eastern Province a closely allied species known as the Rockey or Bain's Kurper (*Sandelia bainsii*) occurs. **1952** *Cape Times* 31 Jan. 9/8 The casualties include yellow fish..mudfish, carp and kurpur. **1971** *Sunday Times* (Johannesburg) *News Mag.* 28 Mar. 8/5 The big kurper are found much deeper than usual.

Kurrichane (kɒritʃa·ne). The name of a place in the western Transvaal, South Africa, used *attrib.* in **Kurrichane thrush** to designate a thrush, several races of which are found in Africa south of the Sahara.

1924 *Ibis* 770 *Turdus libonianus.* Kurrichane Thrush. This thrush is common in Nyasaland. **1936** D. A. BANNERMAN *Birds Trop. W. Afr.* IV. 314 The Kurrichane Thrush is not unlike a female European Blackbird. **1960** G. DURRELL *Zoo in my Luggage* i. 32 A kurrichane thrush treated us to a waterfall of sweet song.

‖ **kurta** (kɒ̄·ɹtă). *India.* Also **khurta, kurtha.** [Hind.] A loose shirt or tunic worn by men and women.

1913 W. G. LAWRENCE in T. E. Lawrence *Home Lett.* (1954) 485 Me in a dhoti and khurta, white Indian clothes. **1920** *Chambers's Jrnl.* 29 May 408/1 A guard of honour in scarlet *kurtas* (blouse-tunics). **1966** *New Statesman* 2 Sept. 316/3 A painfully thin youth—very Hindu, whose kurtha was always clean. **1968** *Observer* 25 Feb. 3/4 Beatle George Harrison..dresses in the flowing pyjamas and *kurta* worn by people in North India. **1969** *Femina* (Bombay) 26 Dec. 8/4 Allambana of Delhi, run by Mohini Tandon, held an exhibition of embroidered saris and kurtas at Calcutta's Park Hotel. **1972** *Vogue* May 137 Atlantic and Othello Khanh..in Indian cotton kurtas and tie-dyed turbans.

kurtosis (kɒ̄ɹtōᵘ·sis). *Statistics.* [mod.L., f. Gr. κύρτωσις a bulging, convexity, f. κυρτός bulging, convex.] A shape-characteristic of a frequency distribution that reflects the sharpness of the peak (for a unimodal distribution) and the shortness of the tails, and is generally measured by the quantity μ_4/μ_2^2 or its excess over 3 (μ_4 and μ_2 being the fourth and the second moments about the mean of the distribution).

1905 K. PEARSON in *Biometrika* IV. 181, I have already called $\beta_2 - 3 = \eta$ the degree of kurtosis. **1931** L. H. C. TIPPETT *Methods of Statistics* ii. 28 There are several curves having the same standard deviation but varying kurtosis. **1952** W. L. GORE *Statistical Methods for Chem. Exper.* ii. 16 The kurtosis is useful in determining if a frequency distribution differs from the normal error curve. The kurtosis of a normal distribution is equal to 3; smaller values than 3 indicate a flatter distribution than the normal (a platykurtic distribution), while values above 3 indicate a more sharply peaked distribution than the normal (a leptokurtic distribution). **1968** P. A. P. MORAN *Introd. Probability Theory* vii. 317 Tables of..the coefficient of kurtosis $\mu_4\mu_2^{-2} - 3$. **1972** P. LASLETT *Household & Family in Past Time* iv. 129 These variables were then summed and averaged: measures of skewness and kurtosis were computed.

kuru (ku·ru). [Native name.] A progressive and fatal degenerative disease of the brain which is endemic in an area of the Eastern Highlands of New Guinea and is characterized by ataxia and tremor.

1957 *New Eng. Jrnl. Med.* 14 Nov. 974/1 The current report of our preliminary findings is based on the careful study of 114 cases of this new disease, which the local populace know by the name of 'kuru'. **1958** *Times* 9 Jan. 10/1 It is estimated that about 1 per cent. of the population is affected with *kuru.* **1965** *Sunday Mail* (Brisbane) 10 Oct. 2 Outside the Fore region only the adjacent areas where inter-marriage has certainly occurred show cases of kuru. **1967** *New Scientist* 26 Jan. 190/2 A brain disease known as *kuru*..appeared about 45 years ago in a tribe of cannibals in New Guinea and is now the tribe's most common cause of death. **1971** *Nature* 30 Apr. 589/1 Kuru ..has so far been transmitted from eleven different human patients to eighteen chimpanzees with incubation periods of 14–39 months after intracerebral inoculation. **1973** *Sci. Amer.* Jan. 126/3 The prototype of the slow virus [disease] is probably kuru, that remarkable affliction of the people of the South Fore River of New Guinea, apparently spread by ritual cannibalism of the brain tissue.

‖ **kuruma** (kurū·mă). [Jap.] A rickshaw. So **kuruma·ya,** one who pulls a rickshaw.

1727 J. G. SCHEUCHZER tr. *Kæmpfer's Hist. Japan* I. II. iv. 180 Sai Sin first obtain'd leave of the Emperor to be carried about in a *khuruma*, or cover'd Chariot, drawn by two Oxen. **1880** I. L. BIRD *Unbeaten Tracks* I. i. 18 From *kuruma* naturally comes *kurumaya* for the *kuruma* runner. **1889** E. ARNOLD *Seas & Lands* (1891) xiv. 188 The Kurumas are wheeled sharply round and brought up with a general shout of arrival in front of a Japanese inn. **1892** —— *Japonica* 44 The *Kuruma*-men can trot in safety round every corner. *Ibid.* 62 The Tokio citizens call their little cab *kuruma*, which means 'a wheel', and the coolie who pulls it is termed *kurumaya.* **1894** L. HEARN *Glimpses Unfamiliar Japan* I. i. 2 The..charm of Japan.. began for me with my first kuruma-ride... The jinrikisha,

or kuruma, is the most cozy little vehicle imaginable. **1898** I. L. BISHOP *Korea & her Neighbours* II. xxiv. 79 Warm winter clothing, a Japanese *kurumaya's* hat..and Korean string shoes completed my outfit. **1904** R. J. FARRER *Garden of Asia* ii. 12 At dangerous corners the kurumaya howls dolefully to make the people avoid the path. *Ibid.* xxiii. 234 Mr. Desire,..taking us up in the kuruma, proceeds to whirl us home to our friends. **1909** *Daily Chron.* 21 Oct. 7/2 A couple of stalwart kuruma-ya who do their eight miles an hour with ease.

Kurume (*kuru·me*). The name of a Japanese town on the island of Kyushu, used *absol.*, or *attrib.* in **Kurume azalea,** to designate one of a group of small, evergreen azaleas developed there from a variety of *Rhododendron obtusum* early in the nineteenth century and introduced to America and Europe by Ernest Henry Wilson (1876–1930) in 1919.

1920 E. H. WILSON in *Garden Mag.* Mar. 38/1 It was during the Arnold Arboretum expedition to Japan in 1914 that I first became acquainted with these Kurume Azaleas. **1924** E. H. M. COX *Rhododendrons for Amat.* v. 98 Kurume azaleas should be consistently fed to ensure good flowers. **1949** *Jrnl. R. Hort. Soc.* LXXIV. 145 When first introduced the Kurumes were given an undeserved reputation for tenderness. **1964** J. BERRISFORD *Rhododendrons & Azaleas* iii. 41 In the eighteen-twenties a cult arose among the feudal gentlemen of Japan and the dwarf evergreen azaleas were bred privately... Thus arose the two-hundred-and-fifty-odd varieties of Kurume azaleas, so called from the town of Kurume where they were later discovered. **1965** 'M. NEVILLE' *Ladies in Dark* x. 101 I'd taken up two Kurumes that she'd ordered. **1970** S. B. SUTTON *Charles Sprague Sargent & Arnold Arboretum* x. 258 The pilgrimage to the Kurume Azaleas came at the latter part of an expedition which was, as one expected from Wilson, a success both botanically and horticulturally.

‖ **kurus** (kŭrū·ʃ). Also formerly **ghrush, ghurush, grouch, grush, gurush.** [Turkish *kuruş*.] A Turkish piastre, $\frac{1}{100}$ of the value of a lira; a coin of this value.

1882 *Numismatic Chron.* 3rd Ser. II. 175 Suleyman II. issued his own large silver pieces in 1099, and gave them the name of *ghrúsh*, which recalls the grossi, groschen, and groat of the Western States... Without entering deeply into the question of the exchange value of this Turkish ghrúsh, or piastre, as it was called by travellers—not, however, to be confounded with the small modern piastre—it is interesting to notice that the ghrúsh and the akcheh, which was its lowest 'divisionnaire', were constantly altering their relations. **1906** *N.E.D.* s.v. *Piastre* 2, The English (French, German, etc.) name..of a small Turkish coin, called in Turkish *ghūrūsh*, $\frac{1}{100}$ of a Turkish pound, having in Turkey, in 1900, a circulating value of about 2*d*. **1917** A. R. FREY *Dict. Numismatic Names* 93/1 *Ghrush*,..The name of the coin is variously written Grush, Gurush,..etc. **1927** *Weekly Dispatch* 6 Nov. 18 Turkish stamps have a perpetual 'grouch'... There are eleven stamps, values 1, 2, 2½, 3, 5, 6, 10, 15, 25, 50 and 100 *grouch*, which is the current coinage. **1959** E. POUND *Thrones* xcvii. 24 The olde double-ducat, The olde turkish grouch. **1960** M. CASE tr. *Boulanger's Turkey* (Hachette World Guides) p. lxxvi, The monetary unit of Turkey is the Turkish pound (lira), which is made up of 100 kuruş. There are metal coins for 1 K.; 2 1/2 K.; 5 K.; 10 K.; 25 K.; 50 K.; 1 T.L. **1971** *Whitaker's Almanack 1972* 954/1 The Turkish *Lira*..is divided into 100 *Kurus*.

kurvey (kɒɪvē¹·), *v. S. Afr.* Also **karwey.** [f. Du. *karwei* hard work, big job (ad. F. *corvée*): see KURVEYOR.] *intr.* To carry goods in an ox wagon. Hence **kurvey·ing** *vbl. sb.*

1873 *Queenstown Free Press* 8 Aug. (Pettman), For various reasons not a farmer kurveys between either Concordia or Springbok and Port Nolloth. **1876** T. STUBBS *Reminiscences* I. 49, I tryed a trip at Kerveying, I took a load to Fort Wiltshire. **1884** M. A. CAREY-HOBSON *At Home in Transvaal* I. iii. 29 'There will be an end to those visits one of those days,' said the merchant, 'and then good-bye to your karweying, Walters.' **1902** *Encycl. Brit.* XXXI. 81/2 'Kurveying' (the conducting of transport by bullock-waggon) in itself constituted a great industry.

Kushan (ku·ʃān), *sb.* and *a.* Also **Kushana. A.** *sb.* A people originating in central Asia who invaded India and established a powerful dynasty (1st–3rd centuries A.D.) in the North-West; also, a member of this people. **B.** *adj.* Of or pertaining to this people, esp. to the dynasty.

1872 *Numismatic Chron.* New Ser. XII. 182 Some time before the Christian era, the chief of the *Kuei-shwang* tribe of the great *Yuchi*..subjected the other four tribes of the nation, and assuming the title of King of the *Kuei-shwang*, or *Kushân*, conquered..Ophiana, Kophene, and Parthia. *Ibid.* 183 The *Asiani* are evidently the *Kushân* tribe. **1935** [see *fire-altar* (*FIRE *sb.* B. 5)]. **1935** [see *HAN¹]. **1948** D. DIRINGER *Alphabet* vi. 343 More important in the development of Indian writing were the inscriptions of the Kushana kings. **1966** F. STARK *Rome on Euphrates* xi. 261 The Kushans had entered history in the first half of the first century A.D. with their king, Kujula Kadphises. *Ibid.* 262 This expansion of the young Kushan kingdom occurred while the vigorous policy of Nero and his advisers was making itself felt. **1971** *Fashion Panorama* (Ceylon) July–Sept. 25 On the coins of the Kushanas are depicted the portraits of monarchs like Kaniksha, Huvishka, Kadphises etc. The Kushan rulers are depicted in these portraits as wearing trousers and a coat. **1972** *Times* 25 Oct. 21/7 The shrine emerged as a Mazdaean fire-temple dedicated to the memory of Kanishka, legendary emperor of the Kushan dynasty.

kus-kus, var. *KAS-KAS.

kuta (ku·tă). = *KGOTLA.

1943 M. GLUCKMAN *Admin. Organization Barotse Native Authorities* 7 *Kuta* (*khotla*),..council, court, Native Authority. *Ibid.* 12, I think the kuta would be made more efficient if its numbers were reduced; but this..can only be discussed after the kuta organisation has been made regular, instead of muddled. **1955** —— *Judicial Process among Barotse* i. 9 Since the council is not only a court, I use the native term *kuta*... Usually the ruler does not attend the hearings of cases, though the kuta's judgment is referred to him for confirmation. Even if the ruler chooses to sit in the kuta while a case is being tried, it proceeds as if he were not there. **1959** G. D. MITCHELL *Sociol.* 83 The council, known as the *kuta*, is both a political and a judicial body.

Kutani (kutā·ni). [f. the name of the village of *Kutani-mura* in the former province of Kaga, Japan.] Used esp. *attrib.*, as *Kutani ware*, a kind of gold and dark red Japanese porcelain.

[**1875–80** AUDSLEY & BOWES *Keramic Art Japan* I. 43 Almost all the good and important pieces of Kaga ware which we have seen are marked with the two characters signifying Kutani.] **1880** A. W. FRANKS *Jap. Pott.* 80 The amateur prefers the original Kutani ware of dark-red and greyish-white colour. **1890** B. H. CHAMBERLAIN *Things Japanese* 283 There were two principal varieties of the ware: *Ao-Kutani*, so called because of a green (*ao*) enamel of great brilliancy and beauty..used in its decoration, and Kutani with painted and enamelled *pâte* varying from hard porcelain to pottery. **1960** B. LEACH *Potter in Japan* vii. 170 Contemporary and old examples of Kutani wares. **1967** *N.Y. Times* 22 Oct. 1. 10 The dramatic bronze castings were discovered in Hong Kong, the hand-decorated Kutani porcelains in Japan.

Kutenai, Kutenay (kū·tĕnē¹, -ni). Also **Kootenai** and many other variants. [Native, name, *Kútonâqa*.] **A.** *sb.* **a.** An Indian people of the Rocky Mountains; also, a member of this people. **b.** Their language. **B.** *adj.* Of or pertaining to this people or their language.

1801 A. MACKENZIE *Voy. from Montreal* (map following pref.) Cattanhowes. **1809** D. THOMPSON *Jrnl.* 9 Sept. in *Washington Hist. Q.* (1920) XI. 99 They all smoked, say 54 Flat Heads, 23 Pointed Hearts & 4 Kootenaes, in all about 80 men. **1831** R. COX *Adventures Columbia River* II. vii. 152 The Cootonais are the remnants of a once brave and powerful tribe. **1838** S. PARKER *Jrnl. Exploring Tour beyond Rocky Mts.* xxiii. 304 The Cootanies inhabit a section of the country to the north of the Ponderas along M'Gillivray's River... They speak a language distinct from all tribes about them, open and sonorous, and free from gutturals. **1846** H. HALE in *U.S. Exploring Expedition 1838–42* VI. 204 (*heading*) Kitunaha, or Coutanies, or Flat Bows. **1877** A. S. GATSCHET in *Mag. Amer. Hist.* I. III. 170 The Kootenai, Kitunaha, or Flatbow language. **1891** *7th Ann. Rep. U.S. Bureau Amer. Ethnol. 1885–86* 85 (*heading*) Kitunahan Koluschan Families. **1893** *Rep. Brit. Assoc. Adv. Sci.* 575 The Kootenays believe that they came from the East, and one of their myths ascribes to them an origin from a hole in the ground east of the Rocky Mountains. **1894** *Amer. Anthropologist* Jan. 69 The tomtit, the owl, the robin, and a few other birds are believed [by the Kootenays] to speak Kootenay. **1929** *Amer. Speech* V. 116 Indian tribal names..were usually transcribed by persons whose ears were unaccustomed to any but European languages... We inherited..corruptions..*Kutenai* from *Kutonaqua*. **1932** D. JENNESS *Indians of Canada* ii. 20 Kootenayan, Siouan, Iroquoian, and Algonkian, are spoken also in the United States. *Ibid.* xxii. 360 In the firm conviction that the dead would one day return to life at lake Pend-d'Oreille, all the Kootenay bands assembled at that lake in certain winters to hold a religious festival. **1955** P. E. BAKER *Forgotten Kutenai* i. 8 The word Kutenai is spelled..Kootenai, Kootenay, Kootenae, Cootanie, and Cootenai as well as Kutenai. **1959** E. TUNIS *Indians* viii. 112/2 One tribe, the Kutenai, made bark canoes with exaggerated back-slanting bows, like the ram bows of 1898 battleships. **1965** *Canad. Jrnl. Linguistics* Spring 78 Kutenai (Powell's 'Kitunahan'), spoken in the eastern Plateau area bordering on the north-western Plains, stands in lonely isolation among a variety of languages of sure affiliation. **1969** O. W. JOHNSON *Flathead & Kootenay* 16 The Kutenais sowed and harvested sacred plants for ceremonial smoking before they ever heard of White men.

kutnahorite (kutnăhō·rəit). *Min.* Also **kutno-.** [ad. G. *kutnohorit* (A. Bukowsky, 1901 (see *Neues Jahrbuch f. Min., Geol. u. Pal.* (1903) II. 338)), f. *Kutná Hora*, name of the town in Czechoslovakia where it was first found: see -ITE¹.] A reddish-white rhombohedral carbonate of calcium, manganese, magnesium, and sometimes iron, belonging to the dolomite group of minerals.

1907 *Mineral. Mag.* XIV. 402 *Kutnohorite*... A rhombohedral carbonate with the atomic ratios Ca:Mn:Fe: Mg = 7:5:1:2 occurring as reddish-white cleavage-masses. **1955** *Amer. Mineralogist* XL. 751 Kutnahorite occurs at Franklin as anhedral masses with curved cleavage surfaces up to three centimeters in size in a small veinlet cutting the normal franklinite ore. It is translucent, with a pale pink color. **1962** W. A. DEER et al. *Rock-Forming Min.* V. 267 Kutnohorites from Franklin containing approximately 10 per cent. excess $CaCO_3$ show some degree of order in their structure. **1967** *Amer. Mineralogist* LII. 1751 Occurrences of kutnahorite have been recorded from Franklin, New Jersey.., Kutná Hora, Czechoslovakia.., Chvaletice, Czechoslovakia..and Providencia, Mexico.

kuvasz (kū·vaʃ, kū·vas). Pl. **kuvaszok.** [Hungarian, fr. Turkish *kavas* guard.] A large white long-coated Hungarian breed of dog, used as a guard dog in its native country.

1935 *Working Dogs* (Amer. Kennel Club) 103 Being a working dog of the larger size, the Kuvasz should be sturdily built and impress the eye with its strength and activity. **1947** C. L. B. HUBBARD *Working Dogs of World* II. 100 The Kuvasz is the best-known Hungarian breed of dog... Kuvaszok on 'sentry-go' are most unpleasant if met by strangers. **1971** F. HAMILTON *World Encycl. Dogs* 75 The Kuvasz is spirited, intelligent and courageous.

Kuwaiti (kuwē¹·ti). [Arab. *kuwaytī*, f. *Kuwayt* Kuwait.] A native or inhabitant of Kuwait, a principality on the Persian Gulf; the dialect of Arabic spoken there. Also *attrib.* or as *adj.*, of or pertaining to this country or its inhabitants.

1928 A. RIHANI *Ibn Sa'oud of Arabia* xxviii. 352 The Ikhwan marched on Jahrah, slaughtered five hundred of the *mushrekin*, the infidel Kuwaitis. **1930** —— *Around Coasts Arabia* III. i. 242 The sail—in its shadow and from its bounties, the Kuwaitis live. **1947** *R. Cent. Asian Jrnl.* 271 The Kuwaitis..had invariably used the Turkish flag. **1950** *Middle East Jrnl.* IV. 18 All know the majesty of the Kuwaiti *boom* entering their harbors to exchange cargoes. **1961** *Daily Tel.* 8 July 16/6 The field commander of the Kuwaiti army. **1967** T. M. JOHNSTONE *Eastern Arabian Dial. Studies* 29 The consonant system in Kuwaiti is the same as for the dialect group as a whole. **1970** *Times* 3 Apr. (Arab League Suppl.) p. iii/3 In the field of social affairs and labour, the Public Assistance Law has been issued with special regard to the stipulations of our religion about social welfare as well as the traditions of the Kuwaiti society and in accordance with the constitution. **1971** *Guardian* 30 Aug. 3/2 Kuwaitis can afford a summer-long holiday. Kuwait is the richest country on earth in terms of income per capita. **1972** H. OSBORNE *Pay-Day* I. i. 11 A young Kuwaiti called Rifai. **1975** *Times* 20 Jan. 61/2 Even after the recent Arab purchase by Kuwaiti interests of 14% of Daimler-Benz AG, there seems to be little chance of a change in the laws.

‖ **kuzushi** (kuzu·ʃi). [Jap.] In Judo, a method of unbalancing one's opponent.

1950 E. J. HARRISON *Judo* 103 *Kuzushi*, breaking opponent's posture or balance. **1957** TAKAGAKI & SHARP *Techniques Judo* I. ii. 18 *Kuzushi*, methods of unbalancing the opponent. **1968** P. & K. BUTLER *Judo & Self-Defence for Women & Girls* ii. 36 Do, please, remember that you can break your opponent's balance to *any* angle you wish... *Tsukuri* is the action you take to break your opponent's posture, *kuzushi* is the effect that it has on her.

kvell (kvel), *v. U.S. slang.* [ad. Yiddish *kveln*, ad. G. *quellen* to gush, well up.] *intr.* To boast; to feel proud or happy; to gloat.

1967 *Listener* 28 Dec. 849/3 *The New York Spy* is a useful and terribly bright guide to New York, conscientiously *kvelling* through 'the city's pleasures', charmed alike by brutal manners, as chronicled by Tom Wolfe, and the Jewish takeover (London swings but Jewish New York *kvells*). **1968** L. ROSTEN *Joys of Yiddish* 199 Only from your children can anyone *shep* (derive) such *naches* (prideful pleasure) as makes you *kvell*. **1970** L. M. FEINSILVER *Taste of Yiddish* 364 'You've got reason to kvell'; 'is he kvelling!'

kvetch (kvetʃ). *U.S. slang.* Also **kvetsch.** [Yiddish *kvetsh*, ad. G. *quetsche* crusher, presser.] A term of personal abuse: *spec.* a person who complains a great deal, a fault-finder. Also **kve·tcher.**

1964 S. BELLOW *Herzog* (1965) 61 She's got a disgusting father and a *kvetsch* of a mother. **1964** W. MARKFIELD *To Early Grave* (1965) xi. 187 There was Ozzie Waldman, Ozzie the *kvetch*. For his favor you could die. He gave away nothing. **1966** *New Society* 12 May 9/2 The idiom of the New Yorker—Gentile or Jew—..has a lot of Yiddish words, like schlepp..shiksa and kvetsch. **1968** L. ROSTEN *Joys of Yiddish* 200 What a congenital kvetcher! *Ibid.*, It will take forever, he's such a kvetch. **1970** S. ELLIN *Man from Nowhere* xix. 94 A bagger [*i.e.* investigator] should not dress so conspicuous that even these old *kvetchers* around here turn and look.

Hence as *v. intr.* [ad. Yiddish *kvetshn*], to complain, to whine; so **kve·tching** *vbl. sb.*

1965 *Holiday* July 98 The Beatles..came along in the middle of a wave of *kvetching*—songs constantly stressing the negative. **1968** *Atlantic Monthly* Oct. 70 He is an amiable one, not given to angry kvetching. **1971** *Harper's Mag.* Feb. 111 After listening to Kashouk *kvetch* for a couple of hours, Sol Hurok..put the question direct. 'Tell me, Kashouk,' Hurok wanted to know. 'If you always lose so much money, why do you stay in business?'

kvutza (kvu·tsā). Also **kvutzah, kwuza.** Pl. **kvutzot, -oth.** [mod.Heb. *qĕbhūṣāh*, f. Heb., group.] In Israel, a communal and cooperative settlement, which, with others, may form a kibbutz.

1921 H. M. KALLEN *Zionism & World Pol.* xvii. 255 *Kwuzoth* or coöperative workmen's colonies were outfitted. **1929** J. H. HOLMES *Palestine To-Day & To-Morrow* iv. 188 (*heading*) The 'Kvutzoth', or communal colonies. *Ibid.* 195 Most of the settlers in Nahalal, for example, had originally been members of a *Kvutzah*. **1934** *Cook's Traveller's Handbk. Palestine, Syria & Iraq* (ed. 6) 48 The post-war settlements of the Zionist Organisation are all based on co-operative principles, and belong to two classes:—(a) The *Moshav*... (b) The *Kvutzah*, which is more or less

communal in character. The entire assets and produce of the village are owned in common... Several of these *kvutzoth* are organised into groups (*kibbutzim*) based on the principle of mutual assistance and exchange of man power. **1944** H. F. INFIELD *Co-operative Living in Palestine* (1946) 6 The Kvutza is well established. The first of these settlements was founded in 1908... A recent census.. shows seventy-six Kvutzot. **1967** *Encycl. Brit.* VI. 456 The 'Kibbutz' and 'Kvutza', where all property is collectively owned. **1973** *Times Lit. Suppl.* 23 Feb. 212/5 The burning of the Degania B kvutza by the Arabs.

Kwa (kwā). Also **Kwo, Qua.** [Native name.] A branch of a Niger-Congo language family, including Akan, Ewe, Ibo, and Yoruba. Also applied to a native speaker of one of the languages in this family. Also *attrib.* or as *adj.*

1857 H. GOLDIE *Princ. Efik Gram.* p. viii, If we take Creek Town..as a centre, and describe a circle of one hundred miles radius, we shall either include or touch upon the tribes of Usahadet..Efut..Aqua (Qua), [etc.]. **1883** R. N. CUST *Sk. Mod. Lang. Afr.* xi. 238 Kwa or Qua. Is different from the Efik and is spoken to the South of that Language... It is stated that the Efik are immigrants from the Interior, and that the Qua are the indigenous inhabitants. **1919** [see *IBIBIO *sb.* and *a.*]. **1930** A. WERNER *Struct. & Relationship Afr. Lang.* II. 33 Along the coast of the Gulf of Guinea—say from Cape Mount to the Niger mouth—we have what Westermann calls the Kwa group. **1955** [see *FANTI *sb.* and *a.*]. **1970** P. OLIVER *Savannah Syncopators* 39 The Kwa group [of tribes] which stretches from Liberia east to Ibo territory in Nigeria. *Ibid.* 42 The Kwa-speaking peoples of the coastal rain forest. **1971** A. KIRK-GREENE in J. Spencer *Eng. Lang. W. Afr.* 128 The Kwa group of languages, of which Yoruba is one.

kwacha (kwa·tʃā). [Chibemba *kwacha* dawn.] **a.** Used as a Zambian nationalist slogan. **b.** The basic currency unit in Zambia and Malawi. Also, a banknote of this value.

1962 K. KAUNDA *Zambia shall be Free* xvii. 160 For a long time I have led my people in their shouts of *Kwacha* (the dawn). We have been shouting it in the darkness; now there is the grey light of dawn on the horizon and I know that Zambia will be free. **1966** *Times* 10 Mar. 8/7 Mr. Arthur Wina, Finance Minister, told Parliament today that in 1968 Zambia will have its own decimal currency. The new unit will be the 'Kwacha', worth 10s. and meaning 'Dawn of Freedom'. **1967** D. C. MULFORD *Zambia* v. 198 Speaking to the Conference's 4,000 delegates amid shouts of 'Action Now' and 'Kwacha', Kaunda launched into an impassioned attack. **1971** *Whitaker's Almanack 1972* 757 Malawi. Decimal currency was introduced on Feb. 15, 1971. The unit is the *kwacha* (= 50p. sterling). *Ibid.* 775/1 Zambia adopted decimal currency on Jan. 16, 1968, the unit being the *Kwacha*, equivalent to 10 s. of the former currency. The *kwacha* = 58 p. sterling. **1972** *Daily Tel.* 18 Sept. 18/8 The company has a fully paid up capital of 2·7 million kwacha, which is to be purchased by Indeco from Unilever of Britain over seven years. **1973** *Guardian* 23 Mar. 14/5 The exchange rate is given as ·7143 kwachas per US dollar.

‖ **kwai-lo** (kwai,lo). Also **kwai-tze** (kwai,tse). [Chinese (Cantonese dial.).] 'Foreign devil', a name given by the Chinese to foreigners.

[**1878** H. A. GILES *Gloss. Far East* 76 *Kwei-tsze* or *Kuei-tzŭ*, devils. A Chinese term for foreigners. **1910** J. S. THOMSON *Chinese* i. 70 Now and then an urchin spits at a foreigner's chair and shouts, *Fan kwei lai* (See, here's a foreign devil). **1944** H. B. RATTENBURY *China, my China* i. 9 On the streets they cursed me for..a '*yang kuei-tze*'—'a foreign devil'.] **1969** *Times* 9 Dec. (Taiwan Suppl.) p. viii/6 To the *kwai-lo's* innocent suggestion that the Foochow or coastal school might be classified under the generic label 'shanghai', Master Wei responded with a sour oath. **1972** *South China Morning Post* (Hong Kong) 4 Dec., *Kwai Lo*, a foreigner (or literally devil man). **1972** *Times* 21 Oct. (Hongkong Suppl.) p. i/4 A discreet variety of Mao-style padded-coat is admirable wear for young and elderly *kwai-lo* (foreign devils) in the Hongkong winter.

Kwakiutl (kwā·kiut'l). Also 9 **Kwahkewlth**, etc. [Native place-name, *Kwa'gul.*] **a.** An Indian people of the north-west coast of N. America; also, a member of this people. **b.** Their language. Also *attrib.* or as *adj.*

1848 *Jrnl. Ethnol. Soc. London* I. 233 (*in list*) 7. Quagheuil. Inhabiting Broughton's Archipelago. **1874** *Rep. Indian Branch, Canada Dept. Minister of Interior 1873* 33 Quackewelths, with sub-tribes 2,000. **1897** F. BOAS in *Rep. U.S. Nat. Mus. 1895* 311 (*title*) Social organisation and secret societies of the Kwakiutl Indians. *Ibid.* 321 Kwakiutl, Salishan, and Chemakum..show certain similarities in form. **1921** E. SAPIR *Lang.* iv. 81 Causative duplications..as in Kwakiutl *metmat* 'to eat clams' (radical element *met-* 'clam'). **1933** L. BLOOMFIELD *Lang.* xxvi. 470 Thus, Quilleute, Kwakiutl, and Tsimshian all have different articles for common nouns and for names, and distinguish between visibility and invisibility in demonstrative pronouns. **1937** R. H. LOWIE *Hist. Ethnol. Theory* ix. 133 A blue-blood in the caste-ridden Kwakiutl society. **1944** [see *DEVIANT *ppl. a.* 1]. **1951** R. FIRTH *Elem. Social Organiz.* i. 3 The Kwakiutl Indians of British Columbia compete in the potlach. **1955** W. GADDIS *Recognitions* I. i. 23 With the loss of Camilla he returned to the times before he had known her, among the Zuñi and Mojave, the Plains Indians and the Kwakiutl. **1959** E. TUNIS *Indians* 136/1 The Kwakiutl and Nootka languages were similar to one another but unlike any other known tongue. **1965** W. P. ALSTON in M. Black *Philos. in Amer.* 24 What in our culture would be a look of contempt would be a look of affection among the Kwakiutl. **1969** *Times* 22 Sept. 14/3 A Kwakiutl door post from Cape Commerell is sculptured in the form of a gigantic bear—a forest spirit—its lips rounded in a mysterious hooting cry.

‖ **kwanga** (kwa·ŋgă). [Native name.] In Zaïre (formerly the Congo), a kind of bread made of manioc.

1907 *Daily Chron.* 28 Oct. 7/3 With the exception of a few people..who supply the State with 'kwanga' (native bread)..all the people I saw are taxed with rubber. **1908** H. H. JOHNSTON *George Grenfell & Congo* II. xxviii. 796 In those happy days ten cakes of kwanga..could be bought for one brass rod. **1971** *Guardian* 31 July 10/6 Kwanga..looks..like..candlewax.

kwashiorkor (kwǫʃi,ǭ·ɹkǭɹ). [Native name in Ghana (formerly the Gold Coast).] A wasting disease that is caused by an insufficient intake of protein by the body and chiefly affects young children in tropical countries, producing apathy, oedema of the extremities, desquamation, and partial loss of pigmentation (and is generally associated with diarrhoea and stunted growth), and leading in severe cases to death.

1935 C. D. WILLIAMS in *Lancet* 16 Nov. 1151/1 The name 'kwashiorkor' indicates the disease the deposed baby gets when the next one is born, and is the local name in the Gold Coast for a nutritional disease of children, associated with a maize diet. **1951** G. C. SHATTUCK *Dis. Tropics* lvii. 695 The early stage of kwashiorkor is difficult to recognize. Probably there are many mild cases which never develop the typical syndrome. **1954** *New Biol.* XVII. 20 One of the commonest diseases, called Kwashiorkor, is associated with protein deficiency in the diet when young and especially at the stage when breast-feeding ceases and no very suitable foods to replace it are available. **1959** *Times* 2 Dec. 10/5 Another hospital doctor described the incidence of kwashiorkor as 'needless slaughter' which could easily be prevented by funds for milk and other proper nourishment. **1968** *Observer* (Colour Suppl.) 29 Dec. 18/3 We saw a fretful baby with the unmistakable signs of early *kwashiorkor*, the disease of protein starvation that ravages Africa. **1970** D. B. JELLIFFE *Dis. Children Subtropics & Tropics* (ed. 2) vii. 172 The 'sugar baby' type of child..which conserves his subcutaneous fat, may even be obese and recovers very rapidly on a high-protein diet, is the typical example of kwashiorkor without previous malnutrition. **1971** *Progress* (Cape Town) May 9/1 One of the unit's major achievements was to prove that the cure of kwashiorkor.. could be initiated by the administering of a synthetic skimmed milk.

‖ **kwedini** (kwidi·ni). *S. Afr.* Also **khwedini, khwidini, kweding, kweedini.** [ad. Kaffir *kwenkwendini* vocative form of *kwenkwe* boy (Pettman).] A native boy.

1912 *Queenstown Representative* 27 Jan. 5/1 This '*kween dine*' was walking behind the pole driving the bullocks on. **1946** *Spotlight* (Johannesburg) 23 Aug. 6/1 A twelve-year-old *kwedini* asleep across some sacks. **1949** *Cape Argus Mag.* 12 Nov. 7/5 Uneducated, 'raw' Native kwedinis, aged 15 and upwards. **1955** J. B. SHEPHARD *Land of Tikoloshe* v. 37 A Khwidini is 'not old enough for a man, nor young enough for a boy'. *Ibid.* viii. 59 Abakhweta.. do not mix with the younger Khwedinis. **1970** *Daily News* (Durban) 18 Dec. 13 One White trader complained that kwedings (boys) had destroyed more than 1000 white telephone cups.

kweek (kwē¹k). *S. Afr.* [Afrikaans, f. Du. *kweek* couch grass.] In full, *kweek grass.* A local name for several creeping grasses, esp. *Cynodon dactylon.*

1904 *Transvaal Agric. Jrnl.* Oct. 185 The Transvaal kweekgras is shorter and more of a surface grass than the Bermuda grass. **1929** J. W. BEWS *World's Grasses* v. 184 It [sc. *Cynodon dactylon*] is commonly known as 'Bermuda grass' and in S. Africa as 'Kweek grass', though that name is applied to other species of creeping grasses as well. **1937** S. CLOETE *Turning Wheels* xviii. 294 The dark-green rings of kweek grass marking the site of his kraals. **1947** *Cape Times* 2 May 9 Only 342 acres were planted to marram grass and kweek. **1954** C. E. HUBBARD *Grasses* 335 Like other well-known grasses it [sc. *Cynodon dactylon*] has numerous common names, being known as 'Kweek' in S. Africa, 'Doob' in India, 'Couch' in Australia, 'Bermuda Grass' in the United States, and in the British Isles sometimes as 'Creeping Dog's-tooth-grass' or 'Creeping Finger-grass'. **1970** A. FULTON *I swear to Apollo* 4 The redgrass gave way to kweekgrass and steekgrass that grew not in a soft thick carpet but in sparse little tufts dotted here and there amongst the boulders.

kwela (kwē¹·lă). [Afrikaans, ? ad. Zulu *khwela* climb, mount.] A popular dance, or its accompanying jazz-like music, of mid- and southern Africa.

1958 *Time* 16 June 37/1 The haunting sound of penny-whistle jazz has become the favorite music of South Africa's slum-caged blacks—and of a great many white hipsters. In the dusty streets, urchins rock to the penny-whistle's fast *kwela* beat; in shabby speakeasies, women shuffle to its slower *marabi* rhythm. **1958** *Gramophone* Dec. 328/2 Those addicted to the shrill squawking of the Kwela flute will have to hear..*Something New From Africa.* **1960** *Guardian* 1 Apr. 10/7 When night falls, she can dance the kwela, mambo, or high-life with any or all of them [*sc.* Nigerians]. **1961** *Sunday Times* 12 Mar. 15/7 One of the tin whistle bands that make kwela music at street corners in Johannesburg. **1969** J. BRUNNER *Plague on Both your Causes* xiii. 96 The music—all local stuff halfway between *kwela* and the long Arab-influenced melodic lines of the Sudan—rose to a pitch of frenzy. **1974** *Sunday Times* (Johannesburg) 13 Oct. 15, I would..listen to kwela music and dance with gouty feet.

kya (kəi·ă). Also **kaia, kia.** [ad. Zulu *-khaya* place of abode.] In South Africa and Rhodesia, an African's hut; also, quarters of an African servant.

1909 K. FAIRBRIDGE *Veld Verse* 85 Where the high-veld breaks to valley..Stands a kaia looking Northward through the mountains to the plain. **1910** J. BUCHAN *Prester John* xvi. 257 Inanda's Kraal was a cluster of kyas and rondavels. **1911** *East London* (Cape Province) *Dispatch* 24 Nov. (Pettman), A native living in a kraal at Lydenberg quarrelled with another native, whom he accused of having fired his *kya.* **1935** L. G. GREEN *Great Afr. Mysteries* (1937) xvi. 192 Each house has a separate *kya* in the back garden for the servant. **1950** *Cape Argus* 4 Mar. 9/5 Fowl-pens, temporary tin Native kias and big heaps of rubble. **1956** N. GORDIMER *Six Feet of Country* iii. 38 These two white-washed servants' rooms (some white people called them kyas,..wanting to keep in their minds the now vanished mud huts which the word indicated). **1971** *Guardian* 29 Sept. 19/3 The houseboys' Kias (usually one small room) at the bottom of the garden.

kyack (kəi·æk). *U.S.* [Orig. unknown.] 'A form of packsack consisting of two hollow containers swung on either side of a pack-saddle' (*Dict. Americanisms*).

1901 *Sunset* Mar. 138/1 Our camp now lay in perfect chaos—blankets, kyacks, saddle-bags, and cooking utensils in a jumble. **1904** *Outing* (U.S.) Oct. 98/2 Exactly the same bitter partisanship obtains in the choice of saddle, in the choice of alforjas or kyacks. **1944** R. F. ADAMS *Western Words* (1945) 88/2 Kyacks might be described as hollow containers, one on each side of the horse, each of sufficient capacity to hold the equal of two five-gallon oil cans placed side by side. **1948** *Sierra Club Bull.* (San Francisco) Dec. 2/2 Stock that..don't mind getting wet up to the kyacks at a stream crossing.

kyack, var *KAYAK².

Kyan, var. *KAYAN.

kyang. (Earlier and later examples.)

1869 A. A. A. KINLOCH *Large Game Shooting* I. iv. 13 Kyang are found all over the elevated plateaux and valleys of Thibet. **1960** 'S. HARVESTER' *Chinese Hammer* xii. 118 The risk of being reincarnated as a female *kyang*, the wild asses who roamed the *tangs* and high plateaux.

‖ **kyat** (kī,ā·t). [Burmese.] The basic monetary unit of Burma since 1952.

1952 *Times* 17 June 10/3 It has been announced in Rangoon that the Union Bank of Burma Act, 1952, will become effective on July 1 next, when the new standard unit of monetary value, the *kyat*, comes into force. The kyat will be the exact equivalent of the present Burma rupee and will be divided into 100 units, each of which will be called a *pya.* **1955** E. MANNIN *Land of Crested Lion* xi. 155 We..buy baskets of strawberries from Ghurkas..at half a *kyat* a basket. **1971** *Nat. Geographic* Mar. 361/1 Working seven days a week for nine months of every year, the couple extract an average of 120 pounds of sap from each tree, earning about 7½ *kyats* ($1.56) a day. **1972** *Guardian* 15 Aug. 3/4 Burma's foreign reserves are currently down to..£12 millions... The local currency, the kyat..is worth less than a third its official rate of 14 to the pound sterling.

kyathos. = CYATHUS 1 a.

1889 in *Cent. Dict.* **1935** RICHTER & MILNE *Shapes & Names Athenian Vases* 30 *Kyathos*... Ladle in the form of a cup with foot and long upward curving handle. **1948** A. LANE *Greek Pott.* ii. 9 The *kyathos* or ladle for dipping the mixture off into jugs. **1960** R. G. HAGGAR *Conc. Encycl. Cont. Pott. & Porc.* 211/1 *Kyathos*—ladle;.. *Oenochoe*—jug for wine; *Kylix*—shallow stem cup.

kybosh. Add: **1.** = KIBOSH 1.

1846 *Swell's Night Guide* 124 *Kybosh on, to put the*, to turn the tables on any person, to put out of countenance. **1896** H. G. WELLS *Wheels of Chance* xli, 'I put the kybosh on *his* little game,' he remarks. **1924** *Chambers's Jrnl.* May 296/2 Standofer's fairly put the kybosh on us this time. **1952** J. CLEARY *Sundowners* iii. 122 Well, that puts the kybosh on it. **1956** H. G. DE LISSER *Cup & Lip* xxii. 246 Good for you... You have put the kybosh on them. **1971** *Times Lit. Suppl.* 7 May 531/2 Not only did the First World War liquidate the Edwardian douceur de vivre. It also put the kybosh on the rationalist's faith in progressive social evolution. **1975** *Sunday Post* (Glasgow) 10 Aug. 7/3 She'd been looking forward to some salmon fishing, but the heatwave's put the kybosh on that.

2. (See quots.)

1845 G. W. M. REYNOLDS *Mysteries of London* I. xxiii. 60/1 The Thieves' Alphabet... *K* was a kye-bosh [*f.n.* 1s. 6d.], that paid for his treat. **1968** *Gloss. Brit. Argot, Kybosh*, one and a half shillings.

As *vb.* (var. KIBOSH *v.*).

1933 J. CARY *Amer. Visitor* iv. 41 The question is, can I kybosh the whole scheme at the same time?

kye (kəi). *Naut. slang.* [Origin unknown; but cf. E.D.D. *kyish* dirty.] **1.** (See quots.)

1929 F. C. BOWEN *Sea Slang* 80 A kye. A rating who is mean with his money. **1946** J. IRVING *Royal Navalese* 105 *Kye*, a mean, unworthy sort of fellow.

2. Cocoa or chocolate.

1943 HUNT & PRINGLE *Service Slang* 42 *Kie*, seaman's slang for cocoa. **1943** BAKER *Dict. Austral. Slang* (ed. 3) 46 *Kye*, chocolate. (R.A.N. slang.) **1962** GRANVILLE *Dict. Sailors' Slang* 68/2 *Kye*, ship's cocoa which used to be issued in slabs, already sweetened, cut as needed and dissolved in boiling water to the desired consistency. The origin of the word is dialectal, from the adjective *kyish*,

muddy-looking, brown. **1968** *Times* 17 Apr. 6/6 Kye, as the service names drinking chocolate, is to end.

kylindrite, var. *CYLINDRITE.

kylix. Add: (Examples.) Pl. **kylikes, kylixes.**

1892 *Times* 7 Feb. 20/1 An Athenian kylix by Sotades. *Ibid.*, These three beautiful kylixes have the ground a pale cream-colour. **1905** H. B. WALTERS *Hist. Anc. Pott.* I. 417 The kylikes of the Epictetan cycle. **1922** *Encycl. Brit.* XXX. 183/2 An Attic *kylix* signed by Pamphaios. **1935** *Antiquity* IX. 508 In the dromoi many kylix fragments were found. **1948** A. LANE *Greek Pott.* iv. 31 About the middle of the sixth century, the pedestal-cup (kylix) became common in East Greece. **1960** [see *KYATHOS].

kymogram (kəi·mogræm). [f. KYMO(GRAPH + -GRAM.] A recording made with a kymograph (sense 1 or *2). **a.** *Radiology.* (Corresponding to *KYMOGRAPH 2.) Also (and orig.) called a *ROENTGENKYMOGRAM.

1923 *Proc. R. Soc. Med.* XVI. (Electro-Therapeutics Section) 21 For taking the kymogram a Polyphos universal inductor with a rapid switch was used. **1941** *Jrnl. Amer. Med. Assoc.* 11 Jan. 117/1 Such a paradoxical movement [of the heart] may be recorded in some instances by kymogram, but this affords help only as a permanent record of what can be seen much more satisfactorily by the fluoroscope. **1959** BOONE & NOBLE in A. A. Luisada *Cardiol.* II. IV. viii. 205/1 Roentgen kymography has not become thoroughly established as a mandatory procedure in the examination of the heart. It seems that this is due to the analytical difficulties inherent in the fuzziness, smallness, and brevity of the recorded waves to be examined on the roentgen kymogram, ..and the difficulties of simultaneously recording, on the kymogram, curves of other cardiac events.

b. (Corresponding to KYMOGRAPH 1 in Dict. and Suppl.) *Esp.* in *Phonetics*, a recording of pressure variations produced during articulation.

1934 *Amer. Speech* IX. 229/1 Kymograms are obtained from discs by means of an electromagnetic inscriber. **1950** [see *CENTISECOND]. **1964** N. C. SCOTT in D. Abercrombie et al. *Daniel Jones* 434 Kymograms for such a word.. show wave-forms between the sections for the stops on the mouth tracings.

kymograph. Add: [ad. G. *kymographion*, the name given by A. W. Volkmann (in *Die Hämodynamik* (1850) iv. 120) to the instrument invented by K. F. W. Ludwig.] Later used more widely; the instrument consists of a cylinder rotated by a clockwork or electric motor, together with a stylus designed to trace on a roll of paper wrapped around the cylinder a curve representing pressure variations or motion communicated to the stylus. (Further examples.)

1901 E. B. TITCHENER *Exper. Psychol.* I. I. viii. 112 O fixates the outermost grey ring of the disc... As the grey fades or drops out of view, he presses the bulb... As (or when) the grey returns, he relaxes the pressure. The curve of fluctuation is thus written, above the time line, upon the smoked paper of the kymograph. **1918** A. L. F. SNELL *Pause* 1 The results in this investigation are based upon speech records made with an apparatus such as is used in experimental phonetics... The kymograph used in all the work was the complete Zimmerman pattern, with Herring slide and writing plane. **1928** *Science* 20 July 62/1 When such phenomena as the speed of a nerve impulse or reaction time are to be recorded, a very fast kymograph drum is an absolute necessity. **1938** *Trans. Philol. Soc.* 76 The apparatus used is the physiological kymograph, fitted with three appropriate Marey tambours. The upper bold tracing is that of jaw movement; the second supplies a record of sound obtained..; the third the time-marking inscribed by a tuning-fork. **1949** B. J. UNDERWOOD *Exper. Psychol.* vi. 163 These markers write on a kymograph, a slowly rotating drum covered with waxed or smoked paper. The rat..bounces the cage on the tambours, thus changing the air pressure which in turn activates the markers which record the animal's activity. **1959** E. PULGRAM *Introd. Spectrogr. of Speech* vi. 52 The kymograph produces registrations representing variations in the total amount of pressure during articulation. **1970** REESE & LIPSITT *Exper. Child Psychol.* iii. 83 Head-turning responses were recorded by means of a head harness mechanically attached to a kymograph.

2. *Radiology.* An apparatus for recording the movement of the heart or other internal organs by moving an X-ray plate or film past one or more slits in a screen placed between it and the subject, so that movement of the organ in a direction parallel to a slit is recorded as a curve separating differently exposed portions of the radiograph; = *ROENTGENKYMOGRAPH.

1936 P. KERLEY *Rec. Adv. Radiol.* (ed. 2) iv. 69 In its simplest form the X ray kymograph consists of a metal grid with a row of transverse slits of equal width and equidistant from each other. **1938** *Q. Jrnl. Med.* XXXI. 463 In cardiac aneurysm..a paradoxical pulsation—expansion of the sac during ventricular systole—has been recorded by kymograph. **1959** P. CIGNOLINI in A. A. Luisada *Cardiol.* II. IV. viii. 199/1 The RK's of Gott and Rosenthal were recorded through a single slit. Later, Crane (1916) used a kymograph with two overlapping slits.

kymographic *a.* (further examples); hence **kymogra·phically** *adv.*, by means of a kymograph.

1930 J. R. FIRTH *Speech* ii. 16 Kymographic speech tracings are invaluable in the study of the length and pitch of vowels..and other characteristic elements of speech. **1936** P. KERLEY *Rec. Adv. Radiol.* (ed. 2) iv. 70 The kymographic appearance of the right border of the heart is more complicated than that of the left border. **1942** *Biol. Abstr.* XVI. 496/1 The temp. and the specific gravity of the inner soln. were kymographically recorded. **1948** J. W. MCLAREN *Mod. Trends Diagn. Radiol.* xiv. 183 Kymographic exposures require much higher loading on an x-ray tube than does ordinary radiography. *Ibid.* 190 Systolic contraction of the ventricle..recorded kymographically. **1963** *Amer. Speech* XXXVIII. 72 Considerable sampling of Hungarian unstressed vowels recorded in natural situations submitted to kymographic analysis. **1964** L. KAISER in D. Abercrombie et al. *Daniel Jones* 106 Rousselot..showed kymographically the large differences in the activity of articulation muscles in stressed and unstressed syllables.

kymography (kəimǫ·grăfi). [f. KYMOGRAPH: see -GRAPHY.] The technique or process of using a kymograph (in either sense). (In *Radiology* also known by its orig. name of *ROENTGENKYMOGRAPHY.)

1930 J. R. FIRTH *Speech* iii. 24 Phonetic kymography measures phone length to within 0·005 of a second. **1933** H. A. JARRE in O. Glasser *Sci. of Radiol.* xi. 202 We should record here..a publication by T. Gött and J. Rosenthal..concerning the original method of 'kymography'... It probably will not become very popular anywhere, as it is limited in its application and its evaluation is quite tedious. **1938** *Q. Jrnl. Med.* XXXI. 463 Kymography has been applied to the study of the localized cardiac infarct. **1957** *Times Lit. Suppl.* 8 Nov. 677/1 Some of the papers..are in the first instance 'School' material, being technical in an equipmental, laboratory sort of way like those on Word-palatograms and on Palatology and Kymography. **1959** P. CIGNOLINI in A. A. Luisada *Cardiol.* II. IV. viii. 201/2 In Stumpf's method of kymography, there is a regular movement of the film or of the grid in the space between two slits (12 mm.).

kynurenic (ki-, kəiniure·nik), *a. Biochem.* Also † **cyn-.** [tr. G. *kynuren-säure* kynurenic acid (J. Liebig 1853, in *Ann. d. Chem.* LXXXVI. 125), f. Gr. κυν-, κύων dog + *-uren-*, irreg. f. οὖρον URINE *sb.*[1]: see -IC 1.] *kynurenic acid*: a crystalline carboxylic acid, $C_{10}H_7NO_3$, that results from the metabolism of tryptophan and is excreted in the urine of man and various animals; 4-hydroxyquinoline-2-carboxylic acid.

1872 *Jrnl. Chem. Soc.* XXV. 1028 When heated by 265° kynurenic acid evolves pure carbon dioxide and melts to a brown liquid. **1889** ROSCOE & SCHORLEMMER *Treat. Chem.* III. v. 226 When..cynurenic acid is heated with zinc dust in a current of hydrogen, it is reduced to quinoline. **1946** W. R. FEARON *Introd. Biochem.* (ed. 3) xvii. 351 Surplus dietary tryptophane is excreted in the urine as kynurenine (in rabbits), and as kynurenic acid (in dogs, rats, foxes and wolves). **1971** *Pediatrics* XLVII. 47/1 This study measured urinary excretion of kynurenic acid ..and xanthurenic acid.., two tryptophan metabolites via the kynurenine pathway, in 26 hospitalized children.

kynurenine (ki-, kəiniure·nīn). *Biochem.* [ad. G. *kynurenin* (Kotake & Iwao 1931, in *Zeitschr. f. physiol. Chem.* CXCV. 140), f. *kynuren-säure*, *kynurenic acid*: see -INE[5].] A crystalline amino-acid, $H_2N{\cdot}C_6H_4{\cdot}COCH_2CH(NH_2)COOH$, that results from the metabolism of tryptophan and is a precursor of kynurenic acid in man and various animals; *β-o*-aminobenzoylalanine.

1931 *Chem. Abstr.* XXV. 2444 When tryptophan is injected subcutaneously into rabbits whose metabolism has been lowered by a regime of polished rice, a product intermediate between tryptophan and kynurenic acid is excreted in the urine. The name *kynurenine* is proposed for this substance. **1938** H. GILMAN *Org. Chem.* II. 943 An amino acid, kynurenine, in which the pyrrole ring of tryptophan has ruptured. **1946, 1971** [see *KYNURENIC *a.*]. **1972** *Chem. Abstr.* LXXVII. 16364 L-Kynurenine, colorless needles from EtOH, m. 194°, was obtained in a yield of 120 mg from 30 g of rat hair by extn. with hot water and sepn. on a Sephadex column.

kyogen (kyōᵘ·gen). Also **kiogen, kiyogen, kyōgen.** [Jap.] In the Noh theatre of Japan, a comic interlude presented between performances of Noh plays.

1871 A. B. MITFORD *Tales Old Japan* I. 164 The classical severity of the Nô is relieved by the introduction between the pieces of light farces called Kiyôgen. **1899** W. G. ASTON *Hist. Jap. Lit.* V. iii. 213 The Kiōgen (mad-words) are to the Nō what farce is to the regular drama. They are performed on the same stage in the intervals between the more serious pieces. **1911** *Encycl. Brit.* XV. 170 The Kyōgen needs no elaborate description; it is pure farce, never immodest or vulgar. **1951** *Oxf. Compan. Theatre* 411/2 The language of the *kyōgen* or comic interludes which accompany their performance is the vernacular of the second half of the sixteenth century. **1958** *Spectator* 3 Jan. 24/3 The typical *No* juxtaposition of bleak tragedy and witty comedy (which in the traditional *No* is split into separate but consecutively performed plays—the *No* play proper followed by the *kyogen*). **1964** [see *KATSURAMONO]. **1970** *Daily Tel.* 16 May 9/4 The two No pieces were separated by a kyogen (farce) about a melon thief, acted and danced with delightful joviality. **1973** *Times* 5 June 8/8 Following the usual custom, the two main pieces are sandwiched round a kyogen farce; this one about two lords who unload their swords on to a passer-by who then puts them through some undignified games before making off with their weapons and their clothes.

kyoodle (kəi·ūd'l), *v. U.S. dial.* and *colloq.* [Imit.] *intr.* To make a loud noise; to bark, to yap. So **kyoo·dling** *vbl. sb.*

1922 S. LEWIS *Babbitt* vii. 99 Now I guess the folks in this man's town will quit listening to all this kyoodling from behind the fence. **1935** J. STEINBECK *Tortilla Flat* xv. 263 The dogs..sought out a rabbit and went kyoodling after it.

kyped (kəipt), *ppl. a. Sc.* [f. KIP *sb.*[2] + -ED[2].] = KIPPER *sb.* and *a.* B 1.

1948 *Scots Mag.* Oct. 44 Presently he was lifting the net under a mate for his catch, a deep-bodied kyped male to match his female [sea-trout]. **1963** *Times* 9 Mar. 11/5 A spring salmon, long before it grows black and ugly and kyped in the autumn of its fortunes.

kyrine (kəiə·rin). *Biochem.* [a. G. *kyrin* (M. Siegfried 1902, in *Ber. ü. d. Verh. d. k. Sächs. Ges. d. Wissensch. zu Leipzig* (*Math.-phys. Kl.*) LV. 70) f. Gr. κῦρ-ος authority, validity: see -INE[5].] Any of various basic substances or mixtures obtained by partial hydrolysis of proteins and thought at one time to be the kernel or nucleus of the proteins from which they were derived; also used with prefix indicating the protein, as *glutokyrine*.

1903 *Jrnl. Chem. Soc.* LXXXIV. I. 587 The protamines of fish spermatozoa are possibly formed by the polymerisation or condensation of kyrine or similar decomposition products of the proteids. **1928** *Physiol. Rev.* VIII. 408 The close resemb[l]ance of these preparations to each other in properties and composition led him [*sc.* Siegfried] to suggest the generic name kyrine for them with the implication that they were the kernel, or nucleus, of the molecular structure of the proteins from which they were derived. This view was founded upon the resistance to hydrolysis of the kyrines under the conditions employed in their preparation. **1953** *Chem. Abstr.* XLVII. 12474 Gelatin was..hydrolyzed with acid by Grassman's method..to kyrine sulfate.

Kyrle (kɔ̄ɪl). The name of John *Kyrle* (1637–1724), English philanthropist, used *attrib.* in *Kyrle Society*, the title of a charitable society concerned with horticulture founded in 1877.

1877 O. HILL *Our Common Land* vi. 142 My sister has founded a society, called, after the Man of Ross, the Kyrle Society, which has for its object to bring beauty into the haunts of the poor. **1888** G. B. SHAW *Let.* 14 Sept. (1965) 195 The books distributed..by the Kyrle Society. **1913** C. E. MAURICE *Life Octavia Hill* vii. 317 Octavia..took an active share in the work of the Commons Preservation Society; but she felt that the Kyrle Society had a different function. **1964** D. OWEN *Eng. Philanthropy* III. xvii. 496 The Kyrle Society, of which Octavia Hill's sister Miranda was the principal architect.

‖ **kyu** (kiū). [Jap.] In Judo or Karate, the Japanese name for the grade given to the less proficient; such a pupil.

The sixth *kyu* is the lowest grade.

1937 J. KANO *Judo (Jujutsu)* iii. 38 The course of Jūdō is divided into two grades or ranks called 'Dan' and 'Kyū'. In the Dan grades, the numbers increase to indicate the higher grade, but in the Kyū grades it is different: thus the first Kyū grade follows the first Dan grade. **1941** M. FELDENKRAIS *Judo* 166 There are two different ranks: Dan and Kyu. A white belt is worn by beginners, corresponding to the sixth kyu. **1954** [see *DAN[5]]. **1960** *Oxf. Mail* 10 Mar. 8/2 Roger Young (Jesus), an American and 3rd kyu (learner grade), beat the Cambridge captain,..a..1st dan (teacher grade) by two and a half points to nil. **1972** *Austin Morris Express* (Oxford) July 8/2 Under the skilful guidance of Maurice King, who is a 2nd Kyu in karate.

Kyzyl, var. *KIZIL *a.* and *sb.*

L

L. Add: **I. 2.** (Earlier examples. See also *ELL².)

1843 'R. CARLTON' *New Purchase* I. xi. 80 On the first floor were two rooms, and connected with a Lilliputian half-story kitchen forming an L—as near as possible. **1873** T. B. ALDRICH *Marj. Daw* etc. 167 Mr. Jaffrey's bedroom was in an L of the building. **1874** *Rep. Vermont Board Agric.* II. 510 To save expense, it is apt to be the case that no cellar is put under the L part of the house.

3. L-head, -headed *adjs.*, applied to (a reciprocating internal-combustion engine having) L-shaped combustion chambers, in which the valves are situated in a side arm.

1916 L. MANTELL *Man. Motor Mech.* iii. 17 One of the most frequent errors made by designers is in attempting to obtain high compression in an L-headed engine with a short stroke. **1920** *Sci. Amer.* 3 Jan. 6/3 The intake manifold of several power plants, both on overhead-valve and L-head types of engine, is cast entirely within the detachable cylinder head. **1922** *Encycl. Brit.* XXX. 37/2 The.. Vee Renault of 1912,..the..Vee RAF of 1913–14, and the..Vee RAF 4a, all of which had cast-iron L-headed cylinders. **1946** R. F. KUNS in Kuns & Plumridge *Automobile Engines* iv. 60 L-head engines are quiet in operation and are long lived. *Ibid.*, The L-head or, as the English call it, the side-valve engine. **1963** BIRD & HUTTON-STOTT *Veteran Motor Car* 98 Their cylinders were L-headed and cast in pairs.

II. 6*. Other symbolic uses in science.

a. In *Physics L* is used to designate the series of X-ray emission lines of longer wavelength than the *K*-series obtained by exciting the atoms of any particular element (cf. *K 3 e); these arise from electron transitions to the atomic orbit of second-lowest energy, with principal quantum number 2, which is thus termed the *L-shell*, and electrons in this shell *L-electrons*. **L-capture**, the capture by an atomic nucleus of one of the *L*-electrons.

1911, 1923 [see *K 3 e]. **1930** PAULING & GOUDSMIT *Struct. Line Spectra* x. 172 There are three absorption edges corresponding to the removal of an electron from the L shell. **1930** *Phil. Mag.* IX. 205 The K electron distribution in carbon will be determined mainly by the central nucleus, and the influence of the L electrons will be comparatively small. **1934** H. E. WHITE *Introd. Atomic Spectra* xvi. 326 When a *K* electron is missing,.. the binding energy of the *L* electron is approximately that for the corresponding electron in the element with the next higher atomic number. **1956** *Nucl. Sci. Abstr.* X. 1123/2 (*heading*) Effect of the correlations existing between the electron positions on the ratio ρ of the probability of L capture to that of K capture. **1968** *Physical Rev.* CLXVI. 945/1 The exchange correction..in the case of Be^7 increases the *L*-capture probability by a factor of almost 4. **1970** E. P. BERTIN *Princ. & Pract. X-Ray Spectrometric Analysis* vi. 182 Elements having atomic number 57 (lanthanum) or higher..are usually determined by measurement of their *L* lines with gas-flow proportional counters. **1972** R. BOLTON *Org. Mechanisms* i. 14 The K-shell is now filled... A third electron must..be placed in the higher-energy L-shell.

b. In *Physics l* and *L* denote the quantum numbers of the orbital angular momentum of one electron or a group of electrons, respectively (superseding the k ($= l+1$) of the old quantum theory).

The use of *l* as a quantum number, and the values assigned to it, varied until shortly after the publication (in 1926) of Schrödinger's theory of the atom.

LS-coupling, an approximation used in the quantum theory of the atom when the spin–orbit interaction of individual electrons is small compared with the remaining electrostatic interaction between one electron and another, so that the orbital angular momenta of the electrons may be coupled to give a resultant L, their spins coupled to give a resultant S, and these resultants coupled in turn to give the total angular momentum J of the electrons. Also called *Russell–Saunders coupling*. Cf. *jj-coupling* (*J II. 6 c).

[**1925** RUSSELL & SAUNDERS in *Astrophysical Jrnl.* LXI. 61 Their remaining properties may be explained on the assumption that the two displaced electrons have fixed orbital momenta, L_1, L_2, of the amount indicated by Landé, but that the inclination of their planes is quantized, so that the resultant angular momentum *K* may have any geometrically permissible value in the series 1/2, 3/2, [etc.]. **1926** *Proc. R. Soc.* A. CXI. 84 The spectroscopic nature of each term..is specified by a quantum number *l* which relates to the whole set of electrons not in complete groups. It..is taken to be $\frac{1}{2}, \frac{3}{2}, \frac{5}{2}$...for S, P, D terms, so that $l = k_1$ [$\equiv k - \frac{1}{2}$] when there is only one electron in an incomplete group. It may perhaps be thought of as the resultant angular momentum of the incomplete group. **1926** *Ibid.* CXII. 81 Spectral terms are to be designated in the usual way as follows:—S, P, D, F, G,...corresponding to the values 1, 2, 3, 4, 5,...for a spectral term quantum number denoted by '*l*'.] **1928** H. S. ALLEN *Quantum* iv. 66 The quantum number j_a is now denoted by *l*, which is called the 'group quantum number'... Its value in this case [*sc.* of a single electron] is $l = k - 1$. *Ibid.*, The inner quantum number *j* is compounded vectorially from *s* and *l*. **1934** H. E. WHITE *Introd. Atomic Spectra* xii. 190 These cases are known as *LS*-, or Russell–Saunders, coupling, on the one hand, and *jj*-coupling, on the other. **1934** [see *K 3 f]. **1970** G. K. WOODGATE *Elem. Atomic Struct.* vii. 140 Along the sequence $np(n+1)s$ from light to heavy elements, for example $C(2p3s)$, $Si(3p4s)$, $Ge(4p5s)$, $Sn(5p6s)$, there is a progression from *LS* to *j-j* coupling. $Ge(4p5s)$ is an example of intermediate coupling for which neither *L*, *S* nor j_1, j_2 are even approximately good quantum numbers.

c. *Bacteriol.* [*L* said to be f. the *L*ister Institute, where Klieneberger worked.] The designation (now usu. as *L-form*) of an atypical form of certain bacteria which arises from and usually reverts to the normal form but is sometimes stable, and which lacks a cell wall, exhibits a very variable shape, and somewhat resembles a mycoplasma.

1935 E. KLIENEBERGER in *Jrnl. Path. & Bacteriol.* XL. 93 These swollen elements [among the bacillary chains of *Streptobacillus moniliformis*], with an associated fine mycelial system resembling that of pleuropneumonia and agalactia, constitute an independent colonial system containing all strains of *S. moniliformis* so far examined. A delicate streptococcus has also been recovered..from the nasopharynx of healthy guinea-pigs harbouring a similar pleuropneumonia-like symbiont. These two pleuropneumonia-like organisms in association respectively with *S. moniliformis* and a streptococcus..will be referred to..simply as L1 and L2 pending the coining of appropriate generic names. **1950** C. E. CLIFTON *Introd. Bacteria* vi. 132 *Streptobacillus moniliformis*..resembles the actinomyces in many respects but gives rise after several days' incubation to highly pleomorphic forms characteristic of the pleuropneumonia group... Present evidence indicates that there is but one organism involved and that the actinomyces-like form and the L_1 form represent different stages of growth of one organism characterized by a complex reproductive cycle. **1968** *Zinsser Microbiol.* (ed. 14) lii. 794/2 Some L phase mutants revert back to normal size organisms as soon as the penicillin is removed from the medium. Others are stable in the L phase on solid media but revert back when subcultured in broth. **1973** J. LEVY et al. *Introd. Microbiol.* ii. 39 Because they did not have a wall, they were not affected by penicillin or other antibiotics that interfere with cell wall synthesis. The mutation to an L-form is therefore troublesome if the bacterium is a pathogen.

d. *L-band*: a frequency band of electromagnetic waves used for radar, extending from 390 to 1550 megahertz.

1947 J. S. HALL *Radar Aids to Navigation* vii. 223 A cross-band airborne interrogator-responser recently developed consists of an L-band (about 25 cm) transmitter operating on a number of preselected frequency channels and a 10-cm receiver. **1967** *Electronics* 6 Mar. 52/1 Tradex, an adaptation of the radar developed for the ballistic missile early warning system, operates at uhf and L band.

7. Abbreviations.

L, learner; Liberal (in politics); low (on the selector mechanism in a car with automatic transmission).

L.A., local authority; LA, L.A., Los Angeles; L.A.F.T.A., Latin-American Free Trade Association; L.C. (A., I., M., T., etc.), landing craft (assault, infantry, mechanized, tank, etc.); *l.c.* (*Printing*) (examples); L.C.C., London County Council; LD, lethal dose: used with following numeral, as LD50, LD_{50}, indicating the percentage of a large group of similar animals that is killed by such a dose; LD or L-D (process), in steel-making, the Linz-Düsenverfahren (process) or Linz-Donawitz-Verfahren (process); L.D.C., less developed country; L.D.V., Local Defence Volunteers; L.E., LE (*Med.*), lupus erythematosus; usu. *attrib.*; L.E.A., Local Education Authority; L.E.M., lunar excursion module; see also *LEM; L.F., low frequency; LH (*Biochem.*), luteinizing hormone; L.M., lunar module; LMF, lack of moral fibre; L.M.S., London, Midland, and Scottish (Railway); L.N.E.R. (earlier L.N.E.), London and North-Eastern Railway; LNG, liquefied natural gas; LOI, lunar orbit insertion; LOS, loss of signal; L.P., long-playing (record); LPG, liquefied petroleum gas; LRL, Lunar Receiving Laboratory (building where astronauts and lunar samples are quarantined for a period after returning from the moon); LRV, lunar roving vehicle; L.s., letter (not autograph) signed; cf. *A.L.(S.)* s.v. *A III; L.S. (*Cinemat.*), long shot; L.S.E. (occas. L.S. of E.), London School of Economics; LSI, large-scale integration (of electronic microcircuits); L.S.T., landing ship, tank(s); LTH (*Biochem.*), luteotrop(h)ic hormone; L.V., luncheon voucher.

See also *LOX *sb.*¹, *LSD² (as main entries).

1936 *Motor Manual* (ed. 29) xiii. 193 'L' plates must be carried at the front and rear of the car. **1936** *Punch* 26 Feb. 248/1 Ermyntrude, inspired by blind jealousy (and aided by some rather L driving by Rachel), emerged from the garage. **1959** *Manch. Guardian* 27 Aug. 6/3 There are still an unknown number of drivers..who may have used L-plates for years without even applying for a test. **1963** P. ROBERTS *Know the Law Handbk.* vi. 154 (*caption*) An L driver involved in an accident. **1970** G. S. WILKINSON *Road Traffic Offences* (ed. 6) v. 472 On and from 1st January, 1961, he may drive only as a learner-driver, i.e., with L plates. **1869** *Whitaker's Almanack* 83/1 *Andover*—Hon. D. F. Fortescue, *L.* **1908** *Daily Chron.* 16 Dec. 1/2 Mr. Mackarness (L, Newbury) asked whether [etc.]. **1974** *Times* 11 Oct. 4/1 Accrington... Total vote 42,259 (83·8%)—Lab 20,050 (47·4%), C 15,018 (35·5%), L 7,191 (17·0%). **1951** TOBOLDT et al. *Automatic Transmissions* i. 15 The selector may be set in any one of five positions, namely, parking (P), neutral (N), low (L), drive (D), and reverse (R). **1932** J. L. P. W. HEWISON *Local Expenditure: Address E. Sussex Ratepayers' Assoc.* 4 Let every L.A. be rationed as to the percentage of its income which it may spend on loan charges. **1967** *Punch* 1 Mar. 292/2 The LAs spend between them on nursery schools 0·281 per cent of their total educational expenditure. **1949** H. G. ALSBERG et al. *American Guide* 1199 Los Angeles... Airports: Union Air Terminal, & L. A. Mun. Airport. **1953** *Amer. Speech* XXVIII. 54 If you're confused—its still L.A... (Native votes on pronunciation of 'Los Angeles'.) **1969** *Daily Tel.* 12 Nov. 20/3 The centre of California is LA, a concrete and glass *mélange* embracing 102 incorporated cities and spread over 4,851 square miles. **1972** B. RODGERS *Queens' Vernacular* 109, I can't walk around LA without gettin' the horns—there's so many pretties. **1973** *Black World* Apr. 96 On a junket to L.A. and New York. **1960** *Times Rev. Industry* July 73/1 In February this year Argentina, Brazil, Mexico, Paraguay, Peru, and Uruguay signed the Montevideo Treaty, setting up the Latin American Free Trade Association... The L.A.F.T.A. aims at removing customs duties to fellow members in 12 years. **1966** *Economist* 19 Nov. 826/1 As a member of LAFTA, Venezuela hopes not only to increase exports but also to reap economies of scale, especially in the heavier industries. **1972** *Buenos Aires Herald* 2 Feb. 3/3 A large share of the disequilibrium stemmed from trade with LAFTA (Latin American Free Trade Association) nations. **1833** *Penny Mag.* Monthly Suppl. Oct.–Nov. 468 *l.c.*,..to have words or letters printed in 'lower case', or small letters. **1892** A. POWELL *Southward's Pract. Printing* (ed. 4) xvii. 129 *l.c.*, set the word in lower case letters. **1911** A. E. HOUSMAN *Let.* 28 Aug. (1971) 119 The type-written text contains the letters: J (cap.) j (l.c.). **1973** *Collins's Authors & Printers Dict.* (ed. 11) 244/2 *l.c.*,..(typ.) lower case, that is *not* caps. **1961** B. FERGUSSON *Watery Maze* i. 42 The mahogany boat..became the standard Landing Craft Assault, or LCA. **1967** *Jane's Surface Skimmer Systems 1967–68* 97/2 Current amphibious vehicle programmes being conducted for the Bureau of Ships are: Landing Craft Assault (LCA), [etc.]. **1898** L.C.C. [see *BETTER-TO-DO *adj. phr.*]. **1907** *Daily Chron.* 3 Sept. 4/7 This is one of the little matters that the L.C.C...might well look into. **1970** RUCK & RHODES *Govt. Greater London* iii. 45 The Labour Party Opposition were convinced that a scheme of reform was unnecessary and particularly a scheme which involved the abolition of the L.C.C. **1943** *Time* 22 Nov. 24/3 The broad wake of a PT, plus the outline of the LCI, must have looked like bigger game. **1944** *Hutchinson's Pict. Hist. War* 12 Apr.–26 Sept. 344/1 One company of Pioneers, some of whom had spent two hours in the sea, after their L.C.I. had been torpedoed. **1943** *Time* 4 Oct. 63/2 As early as 1936 the Navy experimented with tank lighters, and from these tests emerged the LCM (Landing Craft, Mechanized), a 50-footer which carries a crew of four and a medium tank. **1943** *Newsweek* 27 Sept. 23/2 The row of LCT's on the beach belching vehicles looks like a long line of stranded, gasping whales. **1955** 'N. SHUTE' *Requiem for Wren* iii. 79 This was the L.C.T. Mark 4, the standard tank landing craft, British built and the most common of the lot. **1927** J. W. TREVAN in *Proc. R. Soc.* B. CI. 483 Toxicity should be stated primarily in terms of the 'median lethal dose', that is the dose which kills 50 per cent. of a large group of animals. As a convenient abbreviation I would suggest the symbol LD50... For doses which kill other proportions of large groups of animals it is convenient to use the analogous symbols LD75, LD25, for doses which kill 75 per cent., and 25 per cent., and similarly for doses killing other proportions. **1950** *Proc. Soc. Exper. Biol. & Med.* LXXIII. 497/2 Only 400r of X-irradiation was used. This dose corresponds to LD_{85-30} for swine. **1958** THOMSON & STRAUBE in W. D. Claus *Radiation Biol. & Med.* iv. 101 Two-thirds of an LD_{50} dose will probably kill less than 1 percent of the animals exposed. **1968** *Observer* 16 June 9/1 Sarin is 30 times more toxic than phosgene, and the amount necessary to achieve what the experts know as 'LD50'..is 40 drops on the skin. **1954** H. A. TRENKLER in *One Year LD-Oxygen Refining Process* 11/1 Our method of steel refining with pure oxygen by blowing downwards into a bath of metal..is called 'LD-process' (Linzer Düsenverfahren). **1965** *New Statesman* 7 May 709/3 The building of modern plants, LD converters, bigger blast-furnaces, wider sinter plants, automated soaking pits and rolling mills. **1973** *Times* 30 May (Austria Suppl.) p. iii/7 The Japanese have the highest production of LD steel, and by 1972 51 per cent of world steel production was based on the LD process. **1967** *Times* 25 Sept. p. xiv, There is no doubt that the speedy economic advancement of the less developed countries (L.D.C.s) would benefit the whole world economy. **1973** *Advocate-News* (Barbados) 19 Feb. 9/1 The assembled CARIFTA leadership prepared a package for progress,

and the LDCs emerged apparently satisfied that their future was assured. **1940** H. Nicolson *Diary* 20 July (1967) 104 Opinion slides off into..rage that the L.D.V. are not better equipped. **1967** G. F. Fiennes *I tried to run a Railway* iii. 21, I fired this shot without first putting on my L.D.V. armlet. **1948** *Proc. Mayo Clinic* XXIII. 26 The..cell..has been called an 'L.E.' cell in our laboratory because of its frequent appearance in bone marrow cases of acute disseminated lupus erythematosus. **1961** R. D. Baker *Essent. Path.* x. 263 Systemic (disseminated) lupus erythematosus... In the blood are L.E. cells (lupus erythematosus cells), consisting of damaged polymorphonuclear cells or lymphocytes which are surrounded by viable polymorphonuclear leukocytes. **1970** Passmore & Robson *Compan. Med. Stud.* II. xxv. 26/1 The serum of patients suffering from lupus erythematosus..contains an abnormal globulin (LE factor) which can exert a uniquely harmful action on nuclei. *a* **1912** W. T. Rogers *Dict. Abbrev.* (1913) 113/1 *L.E.A.*, (educ.). Local Educational Authority. **1945** [see *Burnham]. **1966** P. H. J. H. Gosden *Devel. Educ. Admin. Eng. & Wales* x. 213 The Inner London Education Area, has a special committee of the G.L.C. to exercise the powers of an L.E.A. **1963** M. Caidin *Man-in-Space Dict.* 26 Two astronauts will transfer to the LEM and descend to the moon. **1969** *Listener* 6 Feb. 162/2 The weakest link is likely to be the LEM or Lunar Excursion Module, which will be the craft used in the actual touch-down of two astronauts. **1969** *Guardian* 22 July 6/1 Armstrong: Going to step off the LEM now... That's one small step for man, one giant leap for mankind. **1922** *Wireless World* 18 Nov. 233 (*heading*) The switching of L.F. valves. **1923** *Ibid.* 6 Jan. 463/1 Methods of intervalve coupling, namely, 'high frequency transformer',..and 'low frequency transformer'.. 'H.F. transformer' and 'L.F. transformer'. **1941** *Electronic Engin.* XIV. 404 The L.F. input to the amplifier must be kept at the same voltage for all frequencies. **1971** *Wireless World* Apr. 184/2 It follows that the difference frequency produced when h.f. noise is sampled at a high rate will be l.f. noise. **1936** *Anatomical Rec.* LXV. 267 The LH produced..enlargement of the testicles. **1957** [see *Gonadotrophin, -tropin]. **1970** *New Scientist* 29 Jan. 200/2 An important cause of infertility in women is the failure to ovulate because of a lack of FSH or LH (or both). **1969** L.M. [see *command service module* (*command sb.* 10)]. **1970** R. Turnill *Lang. of Space* 73 Because it is not used for re-entry, and the moon has no atmosphere, the LM does not need to be heat-shielded. **1952** M. Tripp *Faith is Windsock* i. 19 They whose nerves snapped with the prolonged tension of operational flying, who refused to go on with it, were grounded, with the terrible initials LMF (Lack of Moral Fibre) against their names. **1971** *New Society* 22 July 150 When the second world war began..the term LMF ('lack of moral fibre') was coined as a pejorative for those pilots who would today be diagnosed and treated as having psychiatric illness. **1923** *Times* 28 Dec. 15/7 (*heading*) L.M.S. railway's dock charges. **1934** *Discovery* Nov. 314/2 Many expresses on the L.M.S. and G.W.R. now load up to 500 tons or over..and loads exceeding 600 tons are not unknown on the L.N.E.R. **1967** J. Joyce *Story Passenger Transport in Brit.* vii. 173 The LMS..locomotive was also a streamliner,..of the same wheel arrangement as its LNER counterpart. **1972** 'G. North' *Sgt. Cluff rings True* iv. 30 'You travel much?' 'Not since they did away with the LMS.' **1923** *Times* 6 Dec. 9/4 Alternative routes are wholly within the L.N.E. system. **1934, 1967** L.N.E.R. [see *L.M.S.]. **1967** N.Y. *Times* 13 Jan. 22 Technology is currently being developed for the use of liquefied natural gas, LNG, as a motor fuel. **1970** *Sci. Jrnl.* Mar. 39/1 LNG is already widely used wherever natural gas is transported or piped on a large scale. **1972** *Sunday Times* 17 Dec. 55/2 There is still uncertainty about what would happen if an LNG carrier were holed in a collision. **1969** *Radio Times* 10 July 31/4 *LOI*, Lunar orbit insertion. **1970** N. Armstrong et al. *First on Moon* ix. 204 On the first LOI the crew had burned two seconds less than the flight plan called for. **1969** *Times* 22 July (Moon Rep.) p. i/1 Neil Armstrong on the porch of the Eagle at 109 hours 19 minutes and 30 seconds to L.O.S., all systems go. **1970** N. Armstrong et al. *First on Moon* x. 222 Got about two minutes to LOS here, Mike. **1948** *Musical Amer.* July 19/3 The new disc, called LP (long playing) Microgroove, requires a new pickup. **1958** *Times* 20 Jan. 10/4 Stereo records will give almost as much playing time as present LPs. **1958** *Spectator* 15 Aug. 220/2 That barbarous invention, the LP song recital. **1967** LP [see *Anthology 2]. **1961** *New Scientist* 23 Mar. 730/2 The gas used, butane or propane, becomes available as a by-product of oil refining, and is commonly known as LPG (liquefied petroleum gas). **1974** *BP Shield Internat.* Oct. 26/4 The natural choice for cooking and heating is butane or LPG. **1969** *New Yorker* 12 Apr. 88/2 The L.R.L. is the building to which the astronauts, the spaceship, and the samples will be brought when the trip is over. **1970** N. Armstrong et al. *First on Moon* xiii. 330 The manager of the LRL, thought the chance of anything harmful coming back with the astronauts was 'probably one in a hundred billion'. **1971** *New Scientist* 3 June 574/1 Design requirements for the LRV were such that a pneumatic tyre would not be practical. **1894** *Ellis & Elvey's Gen. Catal. Rare Bks. & MSS.* 38 George I. King of England. L.S. 'George R.', dated St. James, le 1er Octobre, 1715, to Madame de Kameke, congratulating her on the birth of a son. **1971** *Sotheby & Co. Catal. Bks., Autogr. Lett., Hist. Documents* 20 July 104 (*heading*) Tennyson:..L.s. (text in his wife's hand), acknowledging a gift of *Misunderstood*. **1953** K. Reisz *Technique Film Editing* iii. 71 *Shooting up* subway steps. The blind man stands helpless at the top... L.S. Blind man. A small boy is helping him. **1960** C. Morris in D. Wilson *Television Playwright* 447 L.S. of a drive in summer along which, walking towards the Camera, are a woman..and a boy. **1896** B. Webb *Diary* 16 Sept. in J. Dunbar *Mrs. G. B. S.* (1963) ix. 116 We, knowing she was wealthy, and hearing she was socialistic, interested her in the LS of E. She subscribed £1,000 to the Library. **1942** Partridge *Dict. Abbrev.* 58/2 *L.S.E.*, London School of Economics. **1969** G. S. Jones in Cockburn & Blackburn *Student Power* 45 Then, in 1967, mass demonstrations against the raising of overseas student fees and the explosion at the LSE suddenly signalled the beginnings of change. **1973** G. Sims *Hunters Point* xv. 136, I..did a course of Political Science at the L.S.E. **1966, 1967** LSI [see *large-scale adj.* (*Large

a. 15 a)]. **1968** *New Scientist* 7 Mar. 521/2 The very high circuit density possible with LSI means that the time-delays inevitable in the cabled interconnections of present day computers will be greatly reduced. **1971** *Illustr. Weekly India* 18 Apr. 19/1 In 1958, integrated circuits were invented. Since then they have been joined by LSI—large scale integration. **1943** F. D. Roosevelt *Let.* 6 Nov. in W. S. Churchill *Second World War* (1952) V. xiv. 222 The Combined Chiefs of Staff to-day authorised Eisenhower to retain until December 15 sixty-eight L.S.T.s now scheduled for an early departure for the United Kingdom. **1946** T. Blore *Commissioned Bargees* ii. 21 And by the time victory arrived there had grown..a great fleet of weird craft, some of American origin, ranging from those quaint sea monsters, the L.S.T., or Landing Ship–Tank, to the Landing Barge. **1973** *Philadelphia Inquirer* 7 Oct. 17/4 The Defense Department..provides..elderly LST's. **1961** *Recent Progress Hormone Res.* XVII. 119 The demonstration that a luteotropic hormone (LTH) causes the maintenance of corpora lutea in rats..established the concept that the pituitary glands of all mammalian females secrete a luteotropic substance. *Ibid.*, The term 'LTH' will be used in this review (for animals other than rats) with the understanding that it could be an as yet unidentifiable substance, or that it could be LH. **1965** Lee & Knowles *Animal Hormones* ii. 20 After ovulation blood levels of LH increase which induce the development of a corpus luteum, but it may be that this will only secrete progesterone if sufficient LTH reaches it. **1955** *Evening Standard* 28 Oct. 15/3 (*heading*) Copy typist with some experience of statement work, required by City firm. Commencing salary..according to age & ability plus L.V's. **1966** *New Statesman* 4 Mar. 317/1 (Advt.), 32½-hour week (no Sats) LV's and superannuation scheme. **1974** *Times* 2 Oct. 27/1 (Advt.), American law firm..seeks ..secretary... Own office, IBM Golfball, excellent salary and L.V.s.

b. Alphabetic abbreviation of *elevated*, = Elevated Railroad. Also *attrib.* U.S. (Cf. *El, el.)

1881 [see *Elevated *ppl. a.* 1]. **1899** J. L. Williams *Stolen Story* 23 He was making for the Seventy-second Street 'L' Station. *Ibid.* 189 He took the L train for Cortlandt Street. **1904** *Sun* (N.Y.) 4 Sept. 7 The owners of express wagons are praying that the L strike will come off. **1929** E. L. Rice *Street Scene* i. 5 The noises of the city rise, fall, intermingle: the distant roar of 'L' trains, automobile sirens and the whistles of boats on the river.

c. *Chem.* (i) *l* = lævorotatory.

[**1891** *Jrnl. Chem. Soc.* LX. 1175 Arabinose can be converted into l.-glucose, whilst xylose, under the same conditions, yields l.-gulose.] **1894** *Ibid.* LXVI. 1. 487 The cultures have no action on *l*-mannose, *l*-gulose, *l*-arabinose,..or α-glucooctose. **1926** J. Read *Text-bk. Org. Chem.* xvii. 353 Most of the essential oils of plants are also optically active, owing to the presence of such constituents as *d*- and *l*-pinene, *l*-menthone, *l*-menthol, *d*-camphor. **1939** *Jrnl. Amer. Chem. Soc.* LXI. 3201/1 *l*-Propylenediamine was prepared by resolving commercial propylenediamine with tartaric acid. **1971** J. D. Roberts et al. *Org. Chem.* xiv. 392 The sign of rotation of an enantiomer, (+) or *d*, (−) or *l*, reveals neither the molecule's absolute configuration nor its configuration relative to some other compound. **1971** L. S. Harris in D. H. Clouet *Narcotic Drugs* iii. 93 With pentazocine the *l*-isomer is 20 times more potent than the *d*-isomer.

† (ii) *l* was formerly used to denote configuration (now superseded by L: see (iii)). *Obs.*

1890 *Jrnl. Chem. Soc.* LVIII. 1. 466 In view of the fact that the rotation of derivatives of each isomeride is not always in the same direction..it is necessary to adopt some method of indicating the optical activity of the parent glucose, and the author [*sc.* E. Fischer] proposes to distinguish the derivatives of dextro- and lævo-rotatory, and of inactive mannose, irrespective of their own peculiar rotation, as derivatives of d-, l-, and i.-mannose respectively. *Ibid.* 469 The l.-levulose (that is, the dextrorotatory modification) could not be isolated. **1906** *Jrnl. Amer. Chem. Soc.* XXVIII. 114 The chemical relationships are indicated by the letters *d* and *l* prefixed to the names of compounds. Thus, ordinary glucose and its corresponding fructose (levulose) are designated, respectively, *d*-glucose and *d*-fructose, notwithstanding the levo-rotation of the latter. **1937** F. C. Whitmore *Org. Chem.* 481 When the cinchonine salts of racemic acid are crystallized, the *l*-tartrate separates first. **1947** *Jrnl. Biol. Chem.* CLXVIII. 443 *d*-Alanine of previous experiments..is *l*-alanine according to the nomenclature used in the present paper.

(iii) As a small capital L: applied to (a compound having) a configuration about an asymmetric atom analogous to that of an arbitrarily chosen standard compound (now L-glyceraldehyde for organic compounds). When there is more than one asymmetric carbon atom: (*a*) for sugars, the L refers to the configuration about the asymmetric carbon atom most remote from the aldehyde group (in aldoses) or the ketone group (in ketoses); (*b*) for amino-acids, the L refers to the configuration about the carbon atom adjacent to the —COOH group.

When it is desired to indicate the direction of optical rotation in addition to configuration, a + or − (for dextro- and lævo-rotation respectively) are added in parentheses, as D(−).

1947 *Jrnl. Biol. Chem.* CLXIX. 237 Distinction between the stereoisomers of the amino acids is made by a prefixed small capital letter D or L to denote the configurational family to which the α-carbon atom belongs. **1951** I. L. Finar *Org. Chem.* I. xvii. 333 D(−)Ascorbic acid (vitamin C) is more efficient than L(+)-. **1964** *Jrnl. Chem. Soc.* 1370 The most stable isomer of the tris-(−)-*trans*-cyclohexane-1,2-diamineiridium (III) cation will have the L-configuration. **1968** R. F. Steiner *Life Chem.* ii. 26 Only amino acids of the L-configuration occur in natural proteins. **1970** R. W. McGilvery *Biochemistry* xxviii. 699

Some L-amino acids cause a rotation of plane polarized light to the left, others to the right.

La, la (la). [Fr. or It., fem. def. art., ad. L. *illa* fem., *ille* that.] Prefixed to a woman's name, ironically as if to that of a prima donna.

In quot. 1869 the reference is to a singer.

1869 [see *Blood *sb.* 3 e]. **1919** A. Huxley *Let.* 5 Jan. (1969) 174 A poem by myself with an outgush of la Whilcox [*i.e.* Ella Wheeler Wilcox]. **1943** N. Balchin *Small Back Room* x. 121 What's the time? Four o'clock? Let's go and see if La Susan has rustled up any tea. **1961** *New Statesman* 10 Feb. 210/3 It all began with La Starkie clutching her brandy in front of the Tavern at Lord's with her back to the cricket. **1967** Wodehouse *Company for Henry* xi. 197 You can't avoid encountering La Simmons. **1974** E. McGirr *Murderous Journey* 78 La Siskin had another woman with her.

laager, *sb.* Add: **b.** *transf.* A defensive position in a country other than S. Africa, esp. one protected by armoured vehicles. Also *fig.*, an entrenched policy, viewpoint, etc., under attack from opponents.

1896 G. Meredith *Let.* 7 Dec. (1970) III. 1253, I have lowered my health by writing at night..and am now in laager against a host of Matabely assailants. **1901** *Daily Tel.* 9 Mar. 11/5 It has been the custom of the Secretary of State to lie in laager, surrounded by his civilian secretaries. **1941** *Illustr. London News* CXCIX. 719 According to the dictionary, a *zareba* or *laager* is 'an enclosure against enemies', but now the term is used to describe the protective dispositions of armed and mechanised forces at night. **1946** G. Millar *Horned Pigeon* ii. 19 Our close night's formation (called either a 'leaguer' or a 'laager'). **1958** *Times Lit. Suppl.* 14 Feb. 87/4 That the leaders of the Nationalist Party have created a 'laager' mentality and hate all opponents of *apartheid* is a fact. **1960** *Economist* 15 Oct. 216/2 Whether to take Southern Rhodesia into the South African laager for whatever period of time this may buy them. **1968** *Ibid.* 14 Dec. 12/2 It would be disastrous if it showed that members of both faiths [in N. Ireland] have been driven by the atmosphere of crisis back into their laagers. **1971** *Rand Daily Mail* 27 Mar. 12/3 A confrontation which would only drive White South Africa deeper into its laager. **1973** *Times* 1 Oct. (Nigeria Suppl.) p. viii/7 These real or imagined anti-Ibo factors translate themselves inside the state into a kind of laager mentality, 'them' against 'us'. **1975** *Guardian* 11 Jan. 11 What's happening there will only make the Afrikaners withdraw further into their laager.

laager, *v.* Add: Also *fig.*

1895 *Westm. Gaz.* 28 Aug. 1/2 What, then, can be more absurd, to adopt Mr. Healy's picturesque phrase, than 'to laager the Postmaster-General in the Lords'? **1949** *Cape Times* 27 Apr. 10/5 Are we really going to keep ourselves laagered when other countries in Africa get together on economic expansion projects?

laagte (lä·χtə). *S. Afr.* Also **leegte.** [Afrikaans, a. Du. *laagte* a valley.] A valley or shallow dip in the veld.

1868 J. Chapman *Trav. S. Afr.* I. 25 We emerged on a sandy elevation or 'buet' [?bult] overlooking an extensive undulation or *leegte*. **1897** Schulz & Hammar *New Afr.* xv. 188 As far as I could see up the open laagte the ground was teeming with heavy game. **1932** C. Fuller *Louis Trigardt's Trek* 136 Tall grass on the *bults*—not so thick as near the mountain—with the *laagtes* in between, for the most part, wet and boggy. **1944** V. Pohl *Adventures Boer Family* 68 Dudley decided that..they should turn left.. and take shelter in a *laagte* where they might easily shake off their pursuers in the dark. **1949** M. Leigh *Cross of Fire* v. 89 On the laagte between ourselves and the main encampment other dim figures moved evenly. **1971** H. C. Bosman *Jurie Steyn's Post Office* 155 He emerged from his cottage in the leegte that was all grown about with the thorniest kind of cactus.

laavenite, var. Lavenite (in Dict. and Suppl.).

lab (læb), *sb.*[2] *colloq.* [Shortened from Laboratory.] A laboratory. Also *attrib.* and *Comb.*, as *lab assistant, boy, coat*, etc.

1895 W. C. Gore in *Inlander* Nov. 64 *Lab*, laboratory. **1900** *Captain* III. 312/1 Permission to footle in the lab. on half-holidays. **1912** *Chums* 5 Oct. 69/3 They walked along the corridor towards the chemistry lab. **1918** P. Maubyn *Wartime Ballad* 26 Be sure they say the lab's the place For bold experiment. **1937** Auden & MacNeice *Lett. from Iceland* v. 57 A Prince must be anonymous, observant, a kind of lab-boy, or a civil servant. **1949** R. Chandler *Let.* 10 Apr. in *R. Chandler Speaking* (1966) 206 There might be excellent reasons for picking up a letter with a handkerchief:..to avoid putting more prints on it and thus making more work for the lab men. **1951** 'J. Wyndham' *Day of Triffids* ii. 50 He..lacked the qualifications for lab work. **1955** *Times* 26 July 10/5 Everyone who did even elementary 'stinks' at school remembers the name of Bunsen and his burner—even if nothing else remains in memory from those hours in the 'labs'. **1957** E. Hyams *Into Dream* 114 In no time at all he'd be furnace-man, lab-boy. **1961** A. Wilson *Old Men at Zoo* ii. 87, I must also give preliminary seeding out interviews for Beard's four new lab assistants. **1962** L. Deighton *Ipcress File* xviii. 108 Practically all the little countries have got their labs working on this. **1962** 'E. McBain' *Like Love* (1964) xvi. 214 We just got a lab report... I'm talking about your fingerprints on the glass. **1964** R. Petrie *Murder by Precedent* iii. 63 Pollard, covered by a white lab coat. **1967** 'E. Peters' *Black is Colour* v. 92, I hope to have some specimens for the lab. boys. **1972** *Listener* 6 Apr. 467/1 An honest lab assistant loses his job

for refusing to work on a poison gas project. **1972** *Lebende Sprachen* XVII. 72/2 Every hospital approved by the American College of Surgeons has all tissues lab-examined right after their surgical removal.

Laban (lēi·băn). The name of Rudolph *Laban* (1879–1958), Hungarian-born choreographer, used *attrib.* to describe a system of dance notation invented by him. Hence **La:banota·tion,** this system.

1954 R. LABAN *Princ. Dance & Movement Notation* 11/1, I have lived to see several excellent dance creations of our time preserved for coming generations by being written down in my Laban notation. *Ibid.* 19/2 The most active American stage dancers have taken up our notation ..and this is largely due to the work of Ann Hutchinson. It may be mentioned here that the American group calls our system 'Labanotation'. **1954** A. HUTCHINSON *Labanotation* 5 Labanotation is a means of recording movement by means of symbols. **1958** *Times* 3 July 14/2 'Labanotation' is now the most widely used of all the notations that have been attempted to set down in score the steps, movements and patterns of the choreographer. **1961** WEBSTER s.v. *Icosahedron*. An imaginary polyhedron in the Laban system of dance notation representing the 20 principal movement directions of a dancer in its center. **1974** *Home & Store News* (Ramsey, New Jersey) 2 Jan. 39 The new typing element, developed by IBM and the Dance Notation Bureau, brings the speed and facility of the electric typewriter to Labanotation, a universally used system of notating movement.

labaria (labā·riă). Also **labarri, labarria.** [Amer. Sp., prob. f. native name.] A name used in Guyana for any of several poisonous coral snakes or pit vipers, esp. the fer-de-lance, *Trimeresurus* (or *Bothrops*) *atrox*, and the bushmaster, *Lachesis muta*.

1825 C. WATERTON *Wanderings* I. 12 The Labarri snake is speckled, of a dirty brown colour. *Ibid.* III. 185 One day..I caught a Labarri alive. **1889** J. RODWAY *In Guiana Wilds* 76 It was a snake, and as its colour could be distinguished, he perceived that it must be the deadly labarria. **1903** *Sci. Amer.* 7 Mar. 176 The Labarri is usually found coiled on the stump of a tree. **1918** W. BEEBE *Jungle Peace* (1919) viii. 188 'Huge labaria, yards long! Big as leg!' The flight of queen bees and their swarms, the call to arms in a sleeping camp creates somewhat the commotion that the news of the bush-master aroused with us. **1956** D. ATTENBOROUGH *Zoo Quest to Guiana* x. 145 Labaria is the local name for the fer-de-lance, one of the most dangerous and venomous of all the South American snakes. **1958** J. CAREW *Wild Coast* vi. 78 Only the small poisonous snakes like the labaria were really dangerous. **1968** *Daily Tel.* 24 July 20/4 The terrain is..full of dangerous snakes including the lethal labaria.

Labarraque (labara·k). The name of Antoine Germain *Labarraque* (1777–1850), Fr. pharmacist, used in the possessive and with *of*-adjunct (also in *eau de Labarraque*) to denote an aqueous solution of sodium hypochlorite used as a bleach and disinfectant, also known as *eau de Javelle* (see *JAVELLE).

1827 *Q. Jrnl. Sci., Lit. & Art* I. 381 Since the notice which has been taken in this country of Labarraque's liquid, through the public journals, a person has actually forwarded to London the pretended chloride of oxide of sodium in a dry state, so cheap as to undersell the metropolitan chemists. **1863** RICHARDSON & WATTS *Chem. Technol.* (ed. 2) I. III. 393 Chloride of Soda, or Liquid of Labarraque. This solution may be prepared from liquid chloride of lime by double decomposition with carbonate or sulphate of soda, or by passing chlorine into a solution of caustic soda..or into a solution of carbonate of soda. **1875** Labarraque's Liquor [see *JAVELLE]. **1886** *Buck's Handbk. Med. Sci.* II. 406/1 In the sick-room, a solution of chloride of lime..is to be recommended, both as a deodorant and as a disinfectant; or Labarraque's solution of hypochlorite of soda..may be substituted for the cheaper preparation. **1939** *Thorpe's Dict. Appl. Chem.* (ed. 4) III. 64/2 Sodium hypochlorite solution (Eau de Labarraque, usually called Eau de Javelle). **1949** KIRK & OTHMER *Encycl. Chem. Technol.* III. 683 Sodium hypochlorite solution U.S.P. 'contains not less than 4 per cent and not more than 6 per cent of NaClO'. This has replaced the former more dilute solution called Labarraque's solution. **1951** Labarraque's solution [see *JAVELLE].

label, *sb.*^{1} Add: **7. c.** A circular piece of paper on the centre of a gramophone record on which descriptive details of the record are printed; a recording company, or a section of one, producing records under a distinctive name; a record thus produced.

1907 *Yesterday's Shopping* (1969) 1037/1 Not more than one old 7 in. record will be allowed for against each New Concert Red Label, or 12 in. record. **1929** *Melody Maker* Apr. 369/1 A very fine example of this 'Scat Singing' is in 'Candy Lips' by Louis Armstrong's Washboard Beaters.., the label rightly describing it as 'Scat' chorus by Clarence Williams. **1939** S. W. SMITH in Ramsey & Smith *Jazzmen* 289 There are those who will have nothing but the original label. **1952** B. ULANOV *Hist. Jazz in Amer.* (1958) xviii. 216 The QRS Piano Roll Company was taking a flier in the record business and they invited Earl to record for their new label. **1957** G. EVANS in D. Cerulli et al. *Jazz Word* (1962) 174 A friend of mine.. was told by an a&r man at a relatively new major label that if he insisted on charging scale, he'd never be used there again. **1964** *Amer. Folk Music Occasional* I. 16 *R.* A recording company heard of us and wanted to record us. *Q.* What label was that? *R.* That was United. A fellow by the name of Allen was the president of that label. **1970** *Melody Maker* 20 June 27/1 The above could well be the theme song for most record companies today who have finally realised that jazz is a good seller for budget price labels. **1971** *Daily Tel.* 16 Aug. 6/3 Are there precedents for a primadonna appearing on three different labels virtually at the same time?

d. *Biol.* and *Chem.* A substance (as a distinctive isotope, or a dye) used to label another substance (see *LABEL *v.* 2).

1935 [see *LABEL *v.* 2]. **1939** *Jrnl. Biol. Chem.* CXXVII. 287 The use of two independent isotopic labels (D and N^{15}) in the same amino acid molecule may reveal a more complete picture of its metabolism. **1962** R. C. NAIRN *Fluorescent Protein Tracing* i. 1 The choice of a tracing method with fluorescent rather than radioactive labels is governed by the type of information sought. **1971** *Nature* 23 July 225/3 By allowing the 'toluenized' cells to incorporate the density label bromodeoxyuridine triphosphate and then isolating and characterizing the newly made DNA they have been able to prove that synthesis is semiconservative. **1972** *Science* 13 Oct. 185/1 Frogs injected with labeled (radioactive) Na^+ rapidly lose the 'label' to bathing medium containing Na^+.

e. *Computers.* A character or set of characters used as an arbitrary name for a statement in a program so as to facilitate reference to it elsewhere in the program.

1958 *Communications Assoc. Computing Machinery* Dec. 14 A statement may be made identifiable by attaching to it a label L, which is an identifier I, or an integer G (with the meaning of identifier). The label precedes the statement labeled, and is separated from it by the separator colon (:). **1962** B. A. GALLER *Lang. Computers* iii. 27 To indicate a transfer to another part of the program, we must be able to label the place to which the transfer is to be made. In other words, we need a way to attach a label such as START to a statement. Let us specify that statement labels must have the same form as names of variables, i.e., up to six letters or digits, the first of which must be a letter. **1969** P. B. JORDAIN *Condensed Computer Encycl.* 272 The use of labels makes it easier to write programs, for mnemonic names may be used for labels..and the programmer is relieved of the detail of maintaining the layout of locations assigned in the computer memory. **1970** O. DOPPING *Computers & Data Processing* xix. 308 In automatic coding..each data item receives a name, or symbolic address... Not only data cells need names, but also certain instructions, for example, instructions to which the program has to branch. Names of instructions are often called labels.

f. *Computers.* A set of data recorded on a reel of magnetic tape that is descriptive of its contents and serves for identification by a computer.

1961 L. W. HEIN *Introd. Electronic Data Processing* ix. 170 To prevent the incorrect use of tape files, internal labels should be incorporated into every tape. *Ibid.* 171 Wherever possible, the checking of the tape label should be done without operator intervention. **1967** MCLACHLAN & MOLSOM *Data Processing* xiii. 187 One item usually written in the label is known as a retention period, or purge date... This is to provide on the tape information from which a program can detect whether the data recorded on the tape is out of date and can be overwritten. In addition the name of the file and its generation number are also written in the label... Tape reels are, of course, also labelled externally for visual identification by computer operators.

label, *v.* Add: **2.** *Biol.* and *Chem.* To make (a substance, a molecule, or a constituent atom) experimentally recognizable but essentially unaltered in behaviour, so that its path may be followed (e.g. through chemical reactions) or its distribution ascertained: esp. by replacing an atom in a proportion of the molecules by an atom of another isotope of the same element, identifiable by its radioactivity or its different mass, or by causing a (usu. fluorescent) dye to become attached to a proportion of the molecules. Cf. *LABEL *sb.*^{1} 7 d.

1935 *Jrnl. Biol. Chem.* CXI. 164 In order successfully to label a physiological substance, it is essential that the chemical and physical properties of the labeled substance be so similar to the unlabeled one that the animal organism will not be able to differentiate between them. The chemist, on the other hand, must be able to distinguish and to estimate them in small quantities and at high dilutions. A possibility for such a label is the use of an isotope. **1949** *Ann. Rep. Progr. Chem.* XLV. 251 Feeding $CH_2{\cdot}^{13}CO_2H$ [to rats] labels the 2 and the 8 carbon atoms of uric acid, but not the 4 carbon atom. $NH_2{\cdot}CH_2{\cdot}{}^{13}CO_2H$, however, labels carbon atom 4, but not carbon atom 2 or 8. **1951** C. P. LEBLOND in G. E. W. Wolstenholme *Ciba Foundation Conf. Isotopes in Biochem.* (Ciba Foundation symposia) 5 A number of radioactive steroids have been synthesized: progesterone labelled with ^{14}C in positions 21 or 3; œstrone labelled in position 16; [etc.]. **1951** *Sci. News* XXII. 76 It can be shown that all oxygen evolved by the illuminated chloroplasts comes from water. If some of the molecules of the water in which the chloroplasts are suspended is [*sic*] 'labelled' with isotopic oxygen, i.e. if the water is made to contain an excess of H_2O^*, where O* is an isotope of oxygen, then the evolved oxygen contains O^*_2, in precisely the same concentration at which H_2O^* is present in the water. **1962** R. C. NAIRN *Fluorescent Protein Tracing* i. 1 Proteins, including serum antibodies, can be labelled by chemical combination with fluorescent dyes, without material effect on the biological or immunological properties of the proteins. **1971** J. Z. YOUNG *Introd. Study Man* v. 82 These isotopes can be introduced into the body and used to 'label' a particular compound and discover for how long it remains in the tissues. The isotope differs in nuclear mass from the normally occurring form..but this does not, in general, make it behave chemically in any markedly different way.

labelled, *a.* Add: **d.** *Biol.* and *Chem.* Of an atom: of a different isotope (of the element normally present). Of a molecule or substance: made recognizable by labelling (see prec.).

1935 [see *LABEL *v.* 2]. **1949** *Ann. Rep. Progr. Chem.* XLV. 244 In the acetate, both carbon atoms were derived from the labelled atom in glycine. **1953** *Sci. News* XXIX. 35 If we take a thin sheet of a metal and deposit upon its upper surface a very thin layer of its radioactive isotope.. and heat the sheet to a sufficiently high temperature, self-diffusion will occur, and the labelled atoms will move into, and about, the lattice of atoms in the sheet. **1961** *Lancet* 29 July 258/1 [They] gave ^{131}I-labelled insulin to pregnant rats to study the role of the placenta in the metabolism of carbohydrate. **1962** R. C. NAIRN *Fluorescent Protein Tracing* i. 3 Less commonly used is direct fluorescent tracing..in which labelled proteins are injected into animals and their distribution in the body determined by subsequent microscopy of tissue sections. **1970** *Sci. Amer.* Mar. 92/1 After the hens had been fed the radioactive calcium for a week the skeleton became intensely labeled.

labiality (lēibiæ·lĭti). *Phonetics.* [f. LABIAL *a.* 2 + -ITY.] The quality of being labial; an instance of this.

1893 *Funk's Stand. Dict.* 991/1 Labiality, the quality of being labial. **1952** [see *ALVEOLARITY]. **1973** *Word 1970* XXVI. 140 A language is modified toward an ideal system, as was Sanskrit in developing voiceless aspirates and losing concomitant labiality.

labially, *adv.* (s.v. LABIAL *a.* and *sb.*). Add: **2.** Toward the lips.

1905 in GOULD *Dict. New Med. Terms* 325/1. **1908** G. V. BLACK *Work on Operative Dentistry* I. 241 The broad cutting edge of the central incisor is that which most frequently pushes the root of the deciduous tooth labially. **1963** C. R. COWELL et al. *Inlays, Crowns & Bridges* iv. 38 The slice is inclined towards the lingual aspect and only extends far enough labially for the margin to reach the embrasure. **1971** *Nature* 30 July 311/1 At the incisor sockets the alveolar margin seems to be preserved lingually but is broken labially.

labile, *a.* Add: Now usu. pronounced (lēi·bil, -əil). **3.** (Further examples in scientific use.)

1947 *New Biol.* VII. 66 In both spring and winter rye the first seven initials to be developed at the growing point give rise to leaves under any combination of environmental factors so far tried. These are followed by about 18 'labile' initials which may give rise either to leaves or flowers according to treatment. **1951** I. L. FINAR *Org. Chem.* I. x. 170 When one tautomer is more stable than the other under ordinary conditions, the former is known as the stable form, and the latter as the labile form. **1970** *Nature* 4 Apr. 25/2 The other component of nitrogenase from the two bacteria has a molecular weight of about 40,000, two iron and two labile sulphide groups.

lability. Add: (Earlier and later examples.) Now chiefly in scientific use.

1557 R. EDGEWORTH *Sermons* Pref. sig. ✠3, I euer fearinge the labilitie of my remembraunce, vsed to pen my sermons. **1810** COLERIDGE *Lit. Remains* (1838) III. 353 To the species water continuity and lability are essential. **1903** A. R. WALLACE *Man's Place in Universe* xi. 207 Those peculiarities which are essential to life—extreme sensitiveness and lability. **1904** *Jrnl. R. Microsc. Soc.* 188 By combining these two methods there is induced a 'nuclear lability', which renders these eggs susceptible to the influence of carbon dioxide as a provocative of cleavage. **1924** J. G. A. SKERL tr. *Wegener's Orig. Continents & Oceans* 154 The frequently described 'lability' of the geosynclinals. **1942** *Jrnl. Immunol.* XLV. 164 The lability in formalin of any antigen studied must thus be determined. **1970** H. C. SHANDS *Semiotic Approaches to Psychiatry* xxiii. 395 Clinical observation often suggests that the emotional lability of the 'schizophrenic' is not only often less than, it is also sometimes greater than, that of the normal. **1973** J. M. ANDERSON *Structural Aspects of Language Change* 143 The holes in the phonological paradigm are characterized by a general condition of lability.

labilize (lēi·biləiz), *v.* *Chem.* and *Biochem.* [f. LABIL(E *a.* + -IZE.] *trans.* To render labile (esp. a chemical bond). So **la·bilizing** *ppl. a.* and *vbl. sb.*

1903 *Nature* 26 Feb. 385/2 The *rôle* of the oxygen must have been that of a labilising agent. **1938** *Jrnl. Biol. Chem.* CXXV. 1 These and other polar groups..may conceivably labilize adjacent carbon-bound hydrogen atoms. **1957** *New Biol.* XXIII. 77 Proteins could also have become radioactive by an exchange reaction in which two peptide bonds in the chain of a protein are labilized, allowing an amino acid held at this point to be exchanged with another molecule of the same amino acid present in the surrounding medium. **1962** *Biochem. Pharmacol.* IX. 113 Stabilization disappears and is replaced by a labilizing influence. **1972** *European Jrnl. Biochem.* XXVI. 540/1 Free lysosome enzymes can labilize lysosomal membrane. **1973** *Chem. Soc. Rev.* II. 177 The factor responsible for a high labilizing ability depends on this mechanism.

Hence **la:biliza·tion,** the process of rendering or becoming labile; **la·bilizer,** a labilizing agent.

1938 *Jrnl. Biol. Chem.* CXXV. 19 Stekol and Hamill.. have claimed that proteolytic enzymes can carry out such

a labilization. **1956** *Radiation Res.* V. 263 The increased susceptibility of X-irradiated DNP to the action of trypsin is not inconsistent with the concept of a labilization of the DNA-to-protein salt-like secondary linkages. **1965** *Dissertation Abstr.* XXV. 4355/2 It is concluded that the labilization of the carboxyl carbon of glycine is a discrete reaction which can be measured independently of reactions related to further metabolism of the α-carbon. **1967** Pike & Brown *Nutrition* vii. 145 Other labilizers of the lysosomal membrane are ultraviolet light and ionizing radiation. **1974** *Nature* 13 Dec. 579/1 The labilisation of the ligand *trans* to an oxo group is a well known effect.

labio-. Add: (*a*) **labiovelar** adj. (later example); also as *sb.*; hence **labiove·larize** *v.*, to pronounce with labiovelar articulation; **la:biovelariza·tion.** (*b*) **labio-lingual** *a.*, pertaining to the lips and the tongue; existing or occurring along a line from the lips to the tongue; hence **la:bioli·ngually** *adv.*, in the labio-lingual direction.

1908 G. V. Black *Work on Operative Dentistry* II. 15 The axio-bucco-lingual plane, or the bucco-lingual plane, ..passes through the tooth bucco-lingually parallel with its long axis. In the incisors and cuspids this is the labio-lingual plane. **1940** O. A. Oliver et al. *Labio-Lingual Technic* 10 Used jointly, labial and lingual appliances represent the labio-lingual technic. **1972** *Nature* 24 Nov. 236/2 The labiolingual compression of the tooth in hominids. **1949** V. H. Sears *Princ. & Technics for Compl. Dent. Constr.* xxiii. 284 The upper incising occlusal unit should be narrow labio-lingually in order to cut through the food with application of little force. **1963** C. R. Cowell et al. *Inlays, Crowns & Bridges* iv. 30 Some anterior teeth are exceptionally thin labiolingually and gold on the lingual aspect may cause the crown..to lose its natural translucence. **1971** *Nature* 23 Apr. 514 The right lateral incisor is represented only by the broken root which measures 4·5 mm mediodistally and 6·0 mm labiolingually. **1895** W. M. Lindsay *Short Hist. Latin Gram.* x. 156 We must distinguish..Labiovelars,..which become Labials in some languages. **1939** E. Prokosch *Compar. Germanic Gram.* 72 The treatment of the labiovelars in Germanic is similar to that in Latin. **1952** A. Cohen *Phonemes of English* 31 *bail*-[beil] v. *wail*-[weil] dist[inguished] by labial v. labiovelar art[iculation]; plosion v. glide. **1968** Chomsky & Halle *Sound Pattern Eng.* 311 An interesting pattern arises with regard to the labiovelars. We may ask whether these are labials with extreme velarization or velars with extreme rounding. **1937** J. R. Firth *Papers in Linguistics* (1957) vii. 80 The tonal diacritica and possibly also what we have called yotization and labio-velarization may be considered as syllabic features. **1953** K. Jackson *Lang. & Hist. Early Brit.* 440 Some degree of labiovelarisation of the ʒ caused by the *u*. **1933** L. Bloomfield *Lang.* 118 These two modifications appear together in labiovelarized consonants. **1964** E. Palmer tr. *Martinet's Elem. Gen. Ling.* ii. 51 Consonants..which possess the timbre of [u] are called labiovelarized.

labium. 1. b. Add to def.: Now usu. called in full *labia majora*, and formerly † *labia externa* (or *external labia*). Also (in full *labia minora*, † *smaller labia*, † *labia interna*, *inner labia*), the two smaller folds of skin situated within the labia majora and extending downwards and backwards from the clitoris: the nymphæ. (Further examples.)

The sing. forms *labium majus*, *minus* occas. occur.

1634 A. Read *Man. Anat.* I. vi. 85 In the externall part ..first appeare labia, the lippes which are parted by the magna rima or fossa, the large chinke. **1826** J. Lizars *Syst. Anat. Plates* xi. 82 The mucous surface of the labia externa is the seat of syphilitic ulcers. *Ibid.* 84 The nymphæ, or labia interna. [*Note*] Syn. Labia pudendi minores: Alæ minores. **1838** R. Hunter *Text Bk. Human Anat.* (ed. 2) ix. 208 Female organs of generation... 1st, the mons veneris—2d, the two labia majora, or labia pudendi —3d, the clitoris, with its prepuce—4th, the two labia minora, or nymphæ—[etc.]. **1845** *Encycl. Metrop.* VII. 493/1 The external or proper labia are thick folds of integument which bound the vulva on either side; and within these are the nymphæ or smaller labia. **1906** H. Ellis *Stud. Psychol. Sex* V. 134 The inner lips, the nymphæ or labia minora, running parallel with the greater lips which enclose them, embrace the clitoris anteriorly. **1907** W. N. Parker tr. *R. Wiedersheim's Compar. Anat. Vertebr.* (ed. 3) 483 'Labia majora' also occur in certain other Primates, but in most Monkeys 'labia minora' are alone present bounding the vulva, and these belong morphologically to the clitoris and not to the scrotal folds. **1936** H. M. & A. Stone *Marriage Manual* iii. 89, I have often seen labia barely a quarter of an inch wide and I have examined women whose inner labia measured two and a half inches in width. **1953** A. C. Kinsey et al. *Sexual Behav. Human Female* xiv. 577 As sources of erotic arousal, the labia minora seem to be fully as important as the clitoris. *Ibid.* 578 Sometimes the labia [minora] are rhythmically pulled in masturbation. *Ibid.*, We do not yet have evidence that the labia majora contribute in any important way to the erotic responses of the female. **1962** *Gray's Anat.* (ed. 33) 1547 Anteriorly, each labium minus divides into two portions. **1965** Masters & Johnson in J. Money *Sex Research* iv. 67 During the excitement phase of the human sexual response cycle, the labia minora (sex-skin) turn bright pink in color and..engorge to approximately twice their previously normal size.

laboratory. Add: Also with pronunc. (lăbǫ·rătəri). **4. laboratory animal,** any animal (e.g. rat, monkey, mouse) commonly used for experiments in a laboratory; **laboratory frame (of reference)** *Nuclear Physics*, the frame of reference in which a laboratory is stationary, and with respect to which measurements of particle energy, velocity, etc., are generally made (see quot. 1958); **laboratory system** *Nuclear Physics* = **laboratory frame*.

1899 *Allbutt's Syst. Med.* VI. 517 The so-called 'irritation contracture' observable in the monkey (but not in other laboratory animals). **1937** *Nature* 24 July 155/1 Among those using this fish as a 'laboratory animal'. **1958** O. R. Frisch *Nucl. Handbk.* xix. 22 From a theoretical standpoint it is most convenient to calculate in a frame of reference in which the total linear momentum is zero (centre of mass frame, or..centre of momentum frame..). Experimentally the target particle is usually at rest in the laboratory frame of reference. **1971** *Sci. Amer.* June 76/3 The theoretical analysis of events in the rapidly moving frame can be made with some degree of confidence and transformed back to the laboratory frame. In this way theory can be compared with experiment. **1951** D. Bohm *Quantum Theory* xxi. 525 Collisions usually involve firing particles at other particles that are at rest in the laboratory system.

labour, labor, *sb.* Add: **2. b.** (Earlier and later examples.)

1839 J. F. Bray (*title*) Labour's wrongs and labour's remedy; or, The age of might and the age of right. **1848** *Punch* XV. 261 Thither [*sc.* to Australia] should Labour repair to seek Demand. **1916** A. Richardson *Man-Power of Nation* 55 The time is..opportune for trade unions to recognise their responsibility for the encouragement of the flow of capital for the benefit of industry... This subject of the relationship of labour to economy of output may be said to be hackneyed. **1940** W. Temple *Hope of New World* 61 If there is to be tension at all, let it be between the financial interests of Shareholders and the productive interests of Management and Labour in co-operation. **1970** *Encycl. Brit.* XXII. 652/2 Until after the turn of the century organized labour seldom gained any measure of public sympathy.

c. (With capital initial.) Short for 'the Labour Party'. Also *attrib.* (see sense *8). Quasi-*adv.* in phr. *to vote Labour*.

1906 *Times* 19 Jan. 4/3 (*heading*) The Liberals and the Labour men. *Ibid.* 10/1 Just before going to press the news arrived that Lord Stanley..had been defeated..by Mr. W. T. Wilson (Labour). **1918** A. Huxley *Let.* 25 Nov. (1969) 171 Tell Brett also to remember to vote, and to vote Labour, our only hope. **1920** *Manch. Guardian* 5 Jan. 6/2 Could any conceivable Labour Government have made blunders so gross? **1924** *Ibid.* 2 May 9/1 The Labour party and Labour leaders have always been divided upon the subject of P.R. [Proportional Representation]. **1932** J. Buchan *Gap in Curtain* iii. 149 The younger Tories as a whole were enthusiastic, and, what is more significant, the Left Wing of Labour blessed it cordially. *Ibid.*, Collinson, a young Labour member from the Midlands, declared that Geraldine was the best Socialist of them all. **1945** *Let us face the Future* (Labour Party) x. 10 Labour led the fight against the mean and shabby treatment which was the lot of millions while Conservative Governments were in power. **1949** Lewis & Maude *Eng. Middle Classes* I. iv. 81 Both Conservatives and Labour competed for the middle-class vote. *Ibid.* 82 The new Labour formula was nicely expressed by Philip Snowden. **1956** C. Cockburn *In Time of Trouble* xix. 244 The Labour people, the 'progressive intellectuals'. **1966** M. Edelman *The 'Mirror'* viii. 151 Its brilliance was that at no time did the *Mirror* specifically urge its voters to vote Labour. **1971** B. Hindess *Decline Working-Class Politics* viii. 173 The teenagers of the 1960s..missed the political experience of their parents, the long identification with and support for Labour.

d. Short for *Labour Exchange 2.

1935 M. Harrison *Spring in Tartarus* I. 105 You see, mister, I can't go on the Labour, cause I'aven't been stood off. I'm on'y ill. **1963** T. Parker *Unknown Citizen* iii. 88 I'll ring you up Monday to tell you how I went on at the Labour. **1971** R. Rendell *One Across* iv. 37 Work's not easy to come by when you've no qualifications... Can't they find you anything down at the Labour? **1972** L. Henderson *Cage until Tame* vi. 45 I'm going for a job the Labour picked out for me.

8. *labour bank* (earlier example); also (in senses 2, 2 b, and *2 c), *labour-bill, bureau, candidate, colony, content, cost, government, law, leader* (later examples), *master, movement, permit, power, song, union*. **b.** instrumental, as *labour-dominated* adj. Also **labour camp,** a penal settlement where the prisoners are obliged to undertake labouring work; **Labour Day** *U.S.*, a legal holiday observed on the first Monday of September; a similar holiday observed in Australia, New Zealand, and elsewhere; **labour force,** (*a*) = **labour power*; (*b*) [cf. *force *sb.*[1] 4 d] a body of workmen; workers, as opposed to employers, considered as a single body; **labour-intensive** *a.* (see *intensive *a.* (*sb.*) 5 b); **Labour-Liberal** *a.* and *sb.*, (a Member of Parliament) combining Labour and Liberal ideas (in early use a Labour M.P. who accepted the Liberal whip); **labour market** (earlier and later examples); **labour note,** a note indicating value in terms of work; **labour-only** *a.*, denoting a sub-contractor who, or sub-contracting which, supplies only the labour for a particular piece of work; **Labour Party,** a political party specially supporting the interests of labour; in the United Kingdom, the organized party formed in 1906 by a federation of trade unions and advanced political bodies to secure the representation of labour in Parliament; **labour relations,** the relations between management and labour; **labour-saving** *a.*, designed to ease or eliminate work (later examples); so **labour-saver; labour ward** (sense 6 in Dict.), a room in a hospital set aside for childbirth.

1832 *Crisis* 28 Apr. 16/1 In Poland-street they had established a Labour Bank. **1898** *Engineering Mag.* XVI. 26 Every improvement in labour-saving machinery diminishes the proportion which the labour-bill bears to the cost of the product. **1832** *Crisis* 11 Aug. 90/3 Perhaps the best preliminary mode..will be by the establishment of Equitable Exchange Labour Bureaus. **1893** *Rep. Agencies & Methods Unemployed* 6 in *Parl. Papers 1893–4* (C. 7182) LXXXII. 377 A detailed account of..labour bureaux and of various organisations dealing with distress. **1908** *New Encycl. Social Reform* 998/2 The recent establishment of a system of public employment bureaux called labor bureaux. **1900** *Jrnl. Soc. Arts* 11 May 510/1 Prisoners.. might serve their time in..quarries, which would be turned into labour camps. **1931** J. S. Huxley *What dare I Think?* iii. 88 Infringement of this order could probably be met by a short period of segregation, say in a labour camp. **1958** *Spectator* 6 June 723/3 Recsk, one of the most abominable labour camps in the world. **1974** *Times* 18 Feb. 14/7 Perhaps the conference helped to save Mr Solzhenitsyn from a labour camp. **1893** H. F. McLelland *Jack & Beanstalk* 16 You'd make a good Labour Candidate. **1921** F. W. P. Lawrence *Labour Party* 3 For nearly every seat there is a Labour candidate. **1948** M. Phillips in H. Tracey *Brit. Labour Party* I. 9 Labour candidates are selected by the Constituency Parties in co-operation with the National Executive Council. **1963** J. Blondel *Voters, Parties, & Leaders* v. 136 Labour candidates are mainly drawn from the middle and lower middle classes. **1888,** etc. Labour colony [see *colony *sb.* 5 c]. **1948** *Spectator* 9 Jan. 38/2 Fine worsteds..have a high 'labour content', and raw material is a low item in the cost of their production. **1896** J. A. Hobson *Probl. Unemployed* 69 The labour cost of distributing a given quantity of goods. **1903** *Westm. Gaz.* 9 July 2/1 The imposition of such duties as will equalise our labour-costs with the labour-costs of our foreign competitors. **1914** [see *assembly line* s.v. *assembly 1 c *attrib.*]. **1966** A. Gilpin *Dict. Econ. Terms* 117 *Labour-costs per unit of output*, the cost of the labour in real terms involved in making each unit of output from a factory. **1886** *N.Y. Times* 7 Sept. 8/1 (*heading*) How Labor Day was observed by all classes of workmen. **1887** *Westm. Gaz.* 6 Sept. 7/1 An Act passed last winter by the State Legislature, making the first Monday in September a legal holiday, to be called 'Labor Day'. **1910** *World Almanac* (N.Y.) 30 An act [of 1893–4] making Labor Day a public holiday in the District of Columbia. **1931** *Daily Express* 2 Sept. 1/5 The governing committee of the New York Stock Exchange, in response to requests of members, decided to close on Saturday, and also to close on Monday, on account of Labour Day, and to resume on Tuesday. **1963** *Times* 26 Feb. 9/1 The city's [*sc.* Melbourne's] big retail stores invented this affair, which has taken over the traditional public holiday called Labour Day, now in any case a quaint anachronism in a country of trade union strength. **1974** *Anderson* (S. Carolina) *Independent* 23 Apr. 1B/1 This is a drastic change from present and past school calendars which start several days prior to Labor Day and finish earlier in the spring. **1959** *Daily Tel.* 19 Aug. 9/2 Nottingham Conservative leaders last night denounced as 'full of inaccuracies and false inferences' a report prepared on behalf of the local Labour party... [The] Conservative vice-Chairman of the Labour-dominated Watch Committee, said: 'The entire report is..full of inaccuracies and false inferences.' **1974** *Listener* 23 May 650/3 The finished film was shown to the Labour-dominated committee. **1885** J. L. Joynes tr. *Marx's Wage-Labour & Capital* (1886) 8 Capital necessarily pre-supposes the existence of a class which possesses nothing but labour-force. **1909** B. Webb et al. *Socialism & National Minimum* 1. 38 The parasitic trades, where the employers are able to exact from their workers more labour-force than they replace. **1911** F. T. Carlton *Hist. & Probl. Organized Labor* xvi. 431 In times of depression there are unemployed land and capital as well as an unemployed labor force. **1940** *Economist* 11 May 849/2 Men are being tempted away and the labour force is being shifted round without any consideration of the relative urgency or importance or even skill of different jobs. **1969** *Times* 12 Feb. 9/2 They have run a computer model of an underdeveloped country's economy which relates the growth of g.n.p. to the labour force, capital stock and other factors. **1926** *Encycl. Brit.* II. 653/2 In Jan. 1924.. the first Labour Govt. in this country was formed. **1945** *Let us face the Future* (Labour Party) x. 10 A Labour Government will press on rapidly with legislation extending social insurance..to all. **1971** *New Statesman* 9 July 34/2 Aneurin Bevan had a very simple rule about the role of a Foreign Secretary under a Labour Government. **1897** J. Bryce *Impressions S. Afr.* xxi. 447 There are also certain 'labour laws', applying to natives only, and particularly to those on agricultural locations. **1902** *Ann. Amer. Acad. Pol. & Social Sci.* XX. 240 When a state legislature passes a new labor law, or revises an old one. *Ibid.* 241 Labor laws, however good, cannot enforce themselves. **1967** A. Hepple *Verwoerd* ix. 122 With the intensification of race and labour laws, the Non-whites began to resist. **1920** S. Lewis *Main St.* xvi. 202 You socialists make me sick! I'm an individualist. I ain't going to be nagged by no bureaus and take orders off labor-leaders. **1972** *N.Y. Times* 3 Nov. 21/8 He is scheduled to meet..labor leaders. **1973** *Times* 16 Nov. 20/8 Labour leaders have been appointed to the boards of nationalized industries..in a personal capacity and not in their own industries. **1902** *Westm. Gaz.* 26 Feb. 6/3 If he could do that when he was returned as a Labour Liberal member. **1904** *Daily Chron.* 7 Jan. 5/4 Two English Liberal Members (one Liberal and one Labour-Liberal). **1834** Mill in *Monthly Repos.* New Ser. VIII. 320 We have to lessen the pressure on the

labour-market. **1946** *R.A.F. Jrnl.* May 160 There must be many a man..awaiting his release with some trepidation on account of uncertainty about his future in the labour market. **1965** SELDON & PENNANCE *Everyman's Dict. Econ.* 152 It [*sc.* the employment exchange] thus helps to make the labour market work by acting as a clearing-house of information about employment. **1974** *Guardian* 24 Jan. 13/3 Parents are not going to stay at home, and the labour market needs them. **1901** *Daily News* 10 Jan. 9/3 The labour master..certified him able to do the work. **1921** *Dict. Occup. Terms* (1927) § 731 *Labour master*, engages and discharges casual labour..employed by dock or harbour authority [etc.]. **1870** *Scribner's Monthly* I. 71 The preacher..beats about..in a dissertation on..the 'labor movement'. **1893** L. T. HOBHOUSE (*title*) The Labour Movement. **1944** M. LASKI *Love on Supertax* ix. 88 Her ignorance of Party matters, Labour Movements, working-class life. **1969** A. PLATER *Close Coalhouse Door* III. 66 The Labour movement that was made by the miners out of blood, sweat and tears. **1832** *Crisis* 28 Apr. 12/1 Money was not necessary. Labour-notes were sufficient. **1894** B. JONES *Co-operative Production* I. 89 These labour notes were to supersede the use of metallic coins and ordinary bank notes, and were to become a superior kind of money. **1967** *Times Rev. Industry* Apr. 64/2 It is partly the search for regular and reasonably high earnings that makes men hire themselves to labour-only sub-contractors. **1969** M. GAGG in R. Fraser *Work* II. 132 A third system is labour-only sub-contracting in which a bricklayer or a group of bricklayers will undertake to do the brickwork on a job for so much per yard super (98 bricks). *Ibid.* 133 For the past seven years I have been a labour only sub-contractor. **1974** *Shelter News* Easter 3/2 From the trade union point of view, the labour-only sub-contracting practice gives rise to many problems. **1886** Labour party [in Dict.]. **1892** ROYDHOUSE & TAPERELL (*title*) The Labour Party in New South Wales. **1896** *Labour Annual* 39 This [of 1895] was the first General Election in which an organized Labour party, independent of either Liberal or Tory, and opposing either or both, has taken part in the United Kingdom. **1905** J. R. MACDONALD in W. T. Stead *Coming Men* 222 The Labour Party..will represent trades; it will represent the working class; it will represent a coherent body of fundamental Labour opinion. **1922** *Encycl. Brit.* XXXII. 507/1 The Labour party..included the Independent Labour party and the Fabian Society and one or two smaller Socialist bodies. Locally it was organized in several hundred Local Labour parties. *Ibid.* 884/2 For many years there was a Labor or Socialist Labor national party, which regularly nominated a candidate for the [U.S.] presidency. **1926** *Daily Chron.* 13 May 2/3 What are we to say of the Trade Union and Labour Party leaders who on Saturday, May 1, agreed to the sending out of the strike instructions? **1945** W. K. RICHMOND *Educ. in England* vi. 116 The generous programme for free secondary education issued..by the Labour Party. **1971** *New Statesman* 9 July 37/1 You could lift almost any quote from the Labour Party's guide for women's sections to illustrate the patronising view they take of us. **1971** *Sunday Australian* 8 Aug. 3/4 The Federal President of the Australian Labor Party..yesterday called on his party to dissociate itself from extremist students. **1927** *Melody Maker* Aug. 777/1 Al Payne should have been leader, but the necessary labour permits could not be obtained, and the band remains in America. **1943** E. M. ALMEDINGEN *Frossia* ii. 107, I have no right to employ anyone..without a proper labour permit. **1866** *Leisure Hour* 17 Mar. 171/1 The competition of labourers with each other for employment, which, in a country like ours, where there is always a vast reserve of labour-power, must far more than counterbalance any good to the labourer arising from the competition of the masters for his services. **1896** J. A. HOBSON *Probl. Unemployed* 2 Off-time..implies waste of labour-power. **1959** B. WOOTTON *Social Sci. & Social Path.* ix. 280 He matters in himself, and not merely as a unit of cannon-fodder, labour-power or population. **1943** J. S. HUXLEY *TVA* 116 The TVA's work in making a comparative survey of rates and conditions in all the fertilizer plants of the region, which helped materially in promoting better labour relations. **1973** *Guardian* 12 Mar. 11/7 Leyland's personnel manager declined to comment. ..'I personally am anti-press. I have had too much trouble with you lot buggering up labour relations.' **1902** *Chambers's Jrnl.* Dec. 830/2 The machine appears to be a real labour and time saver, and is moderate in price. **1929** A. HUXLEY *Do what you Will* 86 The machine..is..a labour-saver. **1904** *Sci. Amer.* 21 May 404/2 The present enormous industry..was rendered possible only by the introduction of labor-saving machinery. **1932** *Discovery* Jan. 10 Many remarkable labour-saving machines have been evolved in recent years. **1957** *Observer* 11 Aug. 8/4 The old owners have dwindled, departed, and found labour-saving bungalows in quieter spots. **1964** M. MCLUHAN *Understanding Media* xvi. 161 The American farmer, confronted with new tasks and opportunities, and at the same time with a great shortage of human assistance, was goaded into a frenzy of creation of labor-saving devices. **1971** *Engineering* Apr. 92/2 With its time and labour-saving features. **1888** L. A. SMITH *Music of Waters* 275 Isaac D'Israeli, in his 'Curiosities of Literature', mentions the numerous labour-songs used by the ancient Greeks. **1921** Labour song [see *BLUES]. **1974** *Times* 25 Sept. 14/8 She..sang a labour song about joining the union. **1866** in *Documentary Hist. Amer. Industr. Society* (1910) IX. 133 Each member belonging to the National Labor Union. **1884** J. HAY *Bread-Winners* xi. 183 The labor unions have ordered a general strike. **1944** H. A. WALLACE *Century of Common Man* 25 July 84 The people of America know that the second step towards Nazism is the destruction of labour unions. **1973** *Times* 16 Nov. 20/7 Nationalism has had an important effect on labour union attitudes in Canada. **1933** A. W. BOURNE et al. *Queen Charlotte's Text-bk. Obstetr.* (ed. 3) xiv. 266 No person is allowed in the hospital labour ward without a mask, which covers both the mouth and nose. **1953** E. SIMON *Past Masters* IV. vi. 260 That first time the baby had been born..at home... Now..I was taken straight to the Labour Ward. **1968** S. BENDER *Obstetr. for Pupil Midwives* xi. 147 The woman admitted to the labour ward and her accompanying relative or friend are greeted cheerfully.

labour, *v.* **9.** For *Obs.* read *Obs.* exc. *poet.*, and add later example.

1872 TENNYSON *Gareth & Lynette* 31 But Kay the seneschal who loved him not Would hustle and harry him, and labour him Beyond his comrade of the hearth.

laboured, *ppl. a.* Add: **3.** Also *laboured-at.*

1876 G. M. HOPKINS *Poems* (1918) 9 And lily-coloured clothes provided Your spouse not laboured-at nor spun.

Hence **la·bouredly** *adv.*, **la·bouredness.**

1882 *Daily Tel.* 24 Feb. (Cass.), He spoke labouredly and with hesitation. **1930** J. W. MACKAIL *Largeness in Lit.* 6 Largeness is..the opposite..of thinness, of tightness, of labouredness.

Labour Exchange. Also with lower-case initials. [LABOUR *sb.* 2 + EXCHANGE *sb.*] **1.** An establishment for the exchange of the products of labour without the use of money. Also *attrib.* Now only *Hist.*

1832 *Crisis* 28 Apr. 16/1 Mr. B. Warden..stated that they had erected a new school, called a Labour Exchange School. *Ibid.* 25 Aug. 97/3 To investigate the Principles upon which the proposed Equitable Labour Exchange was to be founded. *Ibid.* 6 Oct. 122/1 Labour Exchange notes. ..Labour Exchange banks. **1894** B. JONES *Co-operative Production* I. 90 The exchange was opened on September 3, 1832, under the title of 'The Equitable Labour Exchange'. **1906** G. J. HOLYOAKE *Hist. Co-operation in Eng.* (rev. ed.) I. 65 The Labour Exchange was not Mr. Owen's idea, but he adopted it.

2. An office serving as a means of connection between workers and employers, esp. one forming part of an organization to assist in the finding of employment. Also *attrib.*

1869 C. L. BRACE *New West* v. 53 One of the remarkable instances of the intelligence and humanity of this new community was the establishment, in 1868, of the 'Labor Exchange'. **1893** *Rep. Agencies & Methods Unemployed* 15 in *Parl. Papers 1893–4* (C. 7182) LXXXII. 377 Registry offices..for shore labourers having the title of the 'British Labour Exchange'. **1896** J. A. HOBSON *Probl. Unemployed* 130 If the Bureaux are to perform effectively the work of Labour Exchanges. **1911** R. BROOKE *Let.* 20 Apr. (1968) 299, I share the Old Vicarage with the Labour Exchange man. **1958** *New Statesman* 22 Feb. 224/3 It hankers after the seaplane factory, the oil refinery, the atomic power station—'better a line of pylons than a line outside the labour exchange'. **1973** [see *job centre* s.v. *JOB *sb.*[2] 7].

3. The finding of employment for workers.

1896 J. A. HOBSON *Probl. Unemployed* 128 No system of mere labour-exchange, however well-conducted, would increase the total quantity of employment over a long area of time.

Labourism (lēⁱ·bəriz'm). [f. LABOUR *sb.* 2 b + -ISM.] The principles or tenets of the Labour Party in politics; the holding or advocacy of these principles.

1903 *Rep. 3rd Ann. Conf. Labour Representative Comm.* 30/1 in *Labour Party Foundation Conf. & Ann. Conf. Rep. 1900–05* (1967) 109 Let them have done with Liberalism and Toryism and every other 'ism' that was not Labourism. **1905** *Westm. Gaz.* 13 May 2/2 Mr. Haldane has plied him with Imperialism, Mr. Keir Hardie with Labourism. **1908** *Ibid.* 4 May 9/2 Two years ago many Liberals coquetted with Labourism, and the result gave them a fright. **1924** J. R. MACDONALD in *Public Opinion* 14 Mar. 248/3 Their Toryisms, Liberalisms and Labourisms. **1975** *Time Out* 8 Aug. 21/1 The play becomes a neat exposition of Labourism over the last 50 years.

Labourist (lēⁱ·bərist). [f. LABOUR *sb.* 2 b + -IST.] A supporter of the interests of Labour in politics; an advocate of Labourism.

1903 *Handy Notes for Unionist Workers* Aug. 3 The Labourists in Parliament..number over a dozen. **1910** *Daily Chron.* 2 Feb. 1/7 Liberals, Labourists and Nationalists are solid against the veto of the Lords and against Food-Taxes. **1927** *Observer* 5 June 12/3 Six months ago the five seats concerned were represented by two Conservatives, two Labourists, and one Liberal. **1969** *Guardian* 23 June 4/2 An ideological struggle [in the U.S.] between the Labourists, who favour Maoism..and the new Leftists.

Labourite (lēⁱ·bərəit). [f. LABOUR *sb.* 2 b + -ITE[1].] = *LABOURIST, often used of members of Parliament representing the Labour Party in Britain, Australia, or other countries.

1903 *Daily Chron.* 19 Dec. 5/5 Free Traders and Free Trade Labourites—40. **1909** T. HODGKIN *Let.* 15 Nov. in L. Creighton *Life & Lett. T. Hodgkin* (1917) xiii. 326 It is this abominable selfishness of men whether Capitalists or Labourites which seems to wreck all forms of government. **1920** *Blackw. Mag.* June 830/1 The moderate Labourites have reason to remember this. **1923** *National Rev.* Jan. 646 The Labourites were led by Mr. Ramsay Macdonald before the war. **1927** [see *ANGLO-SAXON IV. A. *adj.*]. **1955** [see *DE GAULLIST *a.* and *sb.*]. **1960** *20th Cent.* May 452 He [*sc.* Michael Young] was the first of those Labourites who renounced the tired phrases of inherited socialist doctrine.

Labrador. Add: **Labrador (dog, retriever)**, a medium-sized, black or yellow, short-coated retriever belonging to a breed originally developed in Newfoundland and Labrador; **Labrador pine**, the grey or jack pine, *Pinus banksiana*, native to the northern parts of North America.

[**1829** G. HEAD *Forest Scenes* 41 The dog was of the Labrador breed, extremely powerful, and of enormous stature.] **1842** R. H. BONNYCASTLE *Newfoundland in 1842* II. ix. 24 They [*sc.* water-dogs] are of two kinds; the short, wiry-haired Labrador dog, and the long, curly-haired Newfoundland species. **1910** *Kennel Encycl.* III. III. 1099 Labrador Retrievers..were originally imported from Labrador. **1921** *Blackw. Mag.* Dec. 794/1 All the guns had dogs—beautifully trained Labradors. **1963** A. SMITH *Throw out Two Hands* xix. 195 John arrived..with a remarkable collection of people, plus a black labrador who loathed nettles, and a rifle. **1971** C. FICK *Danziger Transcript* (1973) 155 Finding out..whether he liked Brahms, silk pajamas, Labrador retrievers and such. **1973** *Country Life* 8 Feb. 325/1, I have just chosen a new labrador puppy. **1803** A. B. LAMBERT *Descr. Genus Pinus* I. 7 Labradore Pine ... Habitat in Americâ Septentrionali. **1921** H. KEPHART *Camping & Woodcraft* (new ed.) I. 239 The gray (Labrador) pine or jack pine is considered good fuel in the far North.

labradorescence (læ:brădǭre·sĕns). *Min.* [f. LABRADOR(ITE + *-ESCENCE.] The brilliant play of colours exhibited by some specimens of feldspars, esp. labradorite.

1911 *Encycl. Brit.* XVI. 30/1 This optical effect, known sometimes as 'labradorescence', seems due in some cases to the presence of minute laminæ of certain minerals.. arranged parallel to the surface which reflects the colour. **1962** W. A. DEER et al. *Rock-Forming Min.* V. 143 The phenomenon of labradorescence, however, has not been conclusively explained. **1966** J. SINKANKAS *Mineral.* viii. 235 Vivid colors also arise from within labradorite feldspar, the effect being known as labradorescence.

Labradorian (læ:brădōᵊ·riăn), *sb.* and *a.* Also **-ean.** [f. LABRADOR + IAN.] **A.** *sb.* A native or inhabitant of Labrador. **B.** *adj.* Of or pertaining to Labrador.

In quot. 1947 the Labradoreans are Eskimos.

1863 H. Y. HIND *Explor. Labrador Peninsula* II. 135 The residents on the coast, or Labradorians as they may well be termed, frequent the St. Augustine in the winter and travel towards its source. **1888** J. PRESTWICH *Geol.* II. 20 Labradorian or Norian group. **1895** J. D. DANA *Man. Geol.* (ed. 4) 446 C. H. Hitchcock..adopts the subdivisions, beginning below: Laurentian, Montalban.., Labradorian, and Huronian. **1907** L. MOTT *To Credit of Sea* ii. 43 'An' you a Labradorian!' Johnson said. *Ibid.* iii. 111 The Labradorian..caught it cleverly. **1909** P. W. BROWNE *Where Fishers Go* 146 Off *Cape Charles* the coast again becomes broken and rugged—'hummocky', as it is termed by Labradorians. **1910** C. W. TOWNSEND *Labrador Spring* 68 Dr. Grenfell's hardest work is to teach the Labradorians the value of fresh air inside their houses. **1947** V. TANNER *Outl. Geogr., Life & Customs Newfoundland-Labrador* II. 527 The heavy, clumsy *tupek* of the Labradoreans, the skin tent, is said to have never given complete protection from rain or wind. **1962** *Encycl. Brit.* XVIII. 74A During the Illinoian, the third glacial age, the Labradorean area of radiation was preponderant and the Keewatin played a minor role. **1973** *Town Crier* (St. John's, Newfoundland) May 43/3 The purpose of the club is to provide..assistance in a practical way to Labradorians living here.

labretifery (lēⁱ:brĕti·fĕri). [f. LABRET + L. *fer-*, carrying + -Y[3].] The practice of wearing labrets.

1884 *Science* 3 Oct. 345/1 Dr. W. H. Dall then read a paper on the use of labrets, its title being 'The geographical distribution of labretifery'. **1905** C. DAVENPORT *Jewellery* v. 89 In Mexico there was a very remarkable civilisation, and labretifery..was practised.

‖ **labrys** (læ·bris). [a. Gr. λάβρυς, double-headed axe.] The double-headed axe of ancient Crete.

1901 *Jrnl. Hellenic Stud.* XXI. 108 It seems natural to interpret names of Carian sanctuaries like Labranda in the most literal sense as the place of the sacred *labrys*, which was the Lydian (or Carian) name for the Greek πέλεκυς, or double-edged axe. *Ibid.* 109 On Carian coins indeed of quite late date the *labrys*, set up on its long pillar-like handle, with two dependent fillets, has much the appearance of a cult image. **1928** C. DAWSON *Age of Gods* viii. 188 Especially remarkable is the word for the sacred Double Axe—Labrys—which forms the root, not only of the Cretan Labyrinthos..but also appears in the title of the god of the Double Axe, Zeus Labrandeus, at Mylasa on the mainland of Asia Minor. **1957** A. MACNAB *Bulls of Iberia* i. 6 The emblem which appears on French coins of the Pétain régime..is precisely the *labrys*, or sacred double-headed axe of Minoan Crete.

labyrinthitis (læbĭrinþəi·tis). *Med.* [f. LABYRINTH 3 + -ITIS.] Inflammation of a labyrinth of the internal ear.

1912 ADAMI & MCCRAE *Text-bk. Path.* viii. 519 Extension of the disease [*sc.* inflammation of the middle ear].. tends to involve the bone in the direction of least resistance, which may lead to extradural inflammation, labyrinthitis, or infection of the lateral sinus. **1934** *Times Lit. Suppl.* 25 Jan. 56/2 Although..the labyrinthitis from which Swift suffered..can create an anxiety-complex, it is almost certainly true that any recurrent disability.. will induce a similar neurosis. **1939** *Anatomical Rec.* LXXIV. 221 Sporadic cases of labyrinthitis appear at times in strains of rats in which no form of ear disease is commonly found. **1972** *Audiology* XI. 322 Variations occur in..viral labyrinthitis.

laburnum. Add to etym. [Adopted as a generic name by P. K. Fabricius (*Enum. Meth. Plant. Hort. Med. Helmstadiensis* (1759) 228).] Substitute for def.: A small tree of the genus so

called, esp. *L. anagyroides* or *L. alpinum* and their hybrids, belonging to the family Leguminosæ and bearing long pendulous racemes of bright yellow flowers followed by pods of poisonous seeds; also, the dark wood of a tree of this kind. (Further examples.)

1812 E. SANG *Nicol's Planter's Kalendar* v. 91 The Laburnum timber which brought so high a price was of the variety called the Tree Laburnum. **1838** J. C. LOUDON *Arboretum et Fruticetum Britannicum* II. xli. 592 Hop-poles..are said, when formed of laburnum, to be more durable than those of almost any other kind of wood. **1914** W. J. BEAN *Trees & Shrubs Hardy in Brit. Is.* II. 1 Few trees..are so beautiful as the two common laburnums. **1947** A. L. HOWARD *Trees in Britain* 134 In earlier times ..British-grown laburnum was greatly prized for inlay, turnery and cabinet work... Cut in cross section in the round, it was known by the term 'oyster work'. **1974** W. CONDRY *Woodlands* xiv. 154 There are long stretches of hedge that are almost purely laburnum which make a marvellous show in June when they are hung with golden chains of blossom. **1975** *Times* 15 Jan. 17/6 An early eighteenth-century oyster walnut and laburnum cabinet.

lac[2]. See also *LAKH.

lac[3] (læk). *Biol.* An abbrev. of LAC(TOSE used (usu. *attrib.*) as a symbol or name (and printed in italics): orig. used to denote the ability (of normal individuals) or inability (of mutants) of the bacterium *Escherichia coli* to metabolize lactose (see quot. 1947), and later to designate (the parts of) the genetic system involved in this ability; as ***lac* operon**, a group of adjacent genes in the chromosome of *E. coli* which, in the presence of lactose, cause the bacterium to synthesize the enzymes that enable it to metabolize lactose. Also as *sb.*, the (in)ability to metabolize lactose; a lac^+ bacterium; the *lac* operon.

1947 J. LEDERBERG in *Genetics* XXXII. 505 Particular attention was paid to the isolation of 'lactose-negative' or 'Lac^-' mutants [of *E. coli*]. *Ibid.* 506 (Table), Symbols used for various loci... 'Sugar' fermentation. The ability to ferment is designated '+'; the inability '−'. *Lac* lactose. *Gly* glycerol. **1952** *Nature* 24 May 882/2 The number of papillæ forming on surface colonies of lac^- bacteria, grown on agar containing lactose and another carbon source, is a reflexion of the number of mutations to the lac^+ condition. **1961** SAGER & RYAN *Cell Heredity* v. 136 If a cell [of *E. coli*] heterozygous for lac^+ and lac^- is isolated, it produces some progeny still heterozygous and others in which the lac^- has segregated from the lac^+. **1961** JACOB & MONOD in *Cold Spring Harbor Symp. Quant. Biol.* XXVI. 197 (*caption*) Genetic map of the *Lac* region of *E. coli*... The lower line represents an enlargement of the *Lac* region, with the two structural genes *z* and *y* and the regulator gene *i*. **1961** S. E. LURIA in *Ibid.* 210/1 An altered sensitivity of phage-carried *lac* genes to the specific repressor of the *lac* operon. **1970** J. R. BECKWITH in Beckwith & Zipser *Lactose Operon* ii. 5 (*heading*) *Lac*: the genetic system. *Ibid.*, Strains in which the *lac* genes are fused to other bacterial operons, such as the *trp* operon and *purE* operon... Since, in such strains, the *lac* genes are now part of the other operon, nearly all the methodology used for analysis of *lac* can be used for that operon. *Ibid.*, Most of the major concepts of operon structure, expression and regulation have come out of the work on the *lac* operon of *E. coli*. **1971** *Times Lit. Suppl.* 13 Aug. 958/4 Dr Beckwith..[is] the centre of a political storm-in-a-scientific-teacup following his isolation of the lac operon gene.

laccase (læ·kēiz, -s). *Biochem.* [a. F. *laccase* (G. Bertrand 1894, in *Compt. Rend.* CXVIII. 1217), f. mod.L. *lacc-a* LAC[1]: see *-ASE.] A copper-containing enzyme which effects the oxidation of hydroquinones to quinones, involved in the setting of lac.

1895 *Jrnl. R. Microsc. Soc.* 649 Laccase resembles the diastatic ferments in its properties, except that, instead of hydrolysing, it incites direct oxidation. **1899** J. R. GREEN *Soluble Ferments* xix. 296 The fungus which yields laccase most readily is *Russula fœtens* Pers., one of the Basidiomycetes, which is fairly common in woods during the summer. **1961** *Jrnl. Biochem.* (Tokyo) L. 264/1 In the present investigation laccases of Japanese and Indo-Chinese lacquer trees have been purified..and their properties compared. **1966** L. I. INGRAHAM in Florkin & Stotz *Comprehensive Biochem.* XIV. 440 Laccase catalyzes the aerobic oxidation of hydroquinones to *p*-quinone. It contains four copper atoms per mole which react with one mole of oxygen. **1971** *European Jrnl. Biochem.* XXIII. 487/2 Whether the unequal load of laccase II with carbohydrate is associated with a fixation of this enzyme to the cell walls, or whether it plays any role in the postulated aggregation of the low molecular weight laccases II and III to the high molecular weight laccase I..must be elucidated by further experiments.

laccolite. For 'mass' read 'concordant mass'. Add further examples.

1937 WOOLDRIDGE & MORGAN *Physical Basis Geogr.* viii. 110 Laccolites are closely related in manner of origin to the stratiform intrusions of igneous rock..termed 'sills'. **1946** L. D. STAMP *Britain's Struct.* ix. 80 A special type of sill is one where the lava swells out to form a lens-shaped mass—which according to its particular form is known as a laccolite (with a flat base) or a phacolite (with a curved base).

laccolith. Add: Now commoner in use than *laccolite*. (Further examples.)

1944 A. HOLMES *Princ. Physical Geol.* vi. 86 There are few good examples of laccoliths in Britain, though many stocks have been wrongly called laccoliths. Stocks are discordant intrusions, whereas laccoliths, like sills, are concordant. **1960** B. W. SPARKS *Geomorphol.* vii. 151 Laccoliths, which are closely related to sills but which were formed from a magma too viscous to spread far, may form local dome-like features when exposed by erosion.

Hence **laccoli·thic** *a.*, of, pertaining to, or characteristic of a laccolith.

1896 *Jrnl. Geol.* IV. 741 The hypothesis..that the granites are batholithic, not laccolithic. **1898** *Ibid.* VI. 705 When vertical displacement with faulting is one of the chief characteristics of the intrusion, a distinction from normal laccolithic intrusion should be recognized. **1933** [see *BYSMALITHIC *a.*]. **1968** R. W. FAIRBRIDGE *Encycl. Geomorphol.* 281/2 The Devil's Tower of Wyoming is sometimes claimed to be an eroded laccolithic dome.

lace, *sb.* Add: **8. a.** *lace-box*, *-curtain* (examples; also *fig.* and *attrib.*, middle- or upper-class, 'respectable', having social pretensions), *-stitch*. **c.** *lace-trimmed* adj. (earlier examples). Also *laceless* adj.

1904 Lace box [see **Bible-box*]. **1969** E. H. PINTO *Treen* 370 Lace boxes, to stand on chests of drawers..enjoyed their greatest popularity during the second half of the 17th century and during Queen Anne's reign. **1895** *Montgomery Ward Catal.* 347/3 Lace curtains and lambrequins. **1934** J. T. FARRELL *Young Manhood* xviii. 282 They were all trying to put on the dog, show that they were lace-curtain Irish, and lived in steam-heat. **1949** *Sat. Rev. Lit.* (U.S.) 25 June 33/1 Mrs. Ruskay's folks were lace-curtain Jews; they had a piano and a Polish maid. **1960** *Guardian* 8 July 8/4 The Kennedy millions..were..wrested by a lace-curtain Irishman from..the Boston Brahmins. **1964** *Publ. Amer. Dial. Soc.* XLII. 35 The most common-place of these is the distinction between *shanty-* and *lace-curtain Irish*, i.e., those who remain in the lower-class communities near the center of the city..and those who move into lowermiddle-class communities and work hard to approximate the ideals of vulgar respectability. **1965** 'E. QUEEN' *Fourth Side of Triangle* iii. 122 Also, I have the misfortune to be Irish. And not lace-curtain Irish, either! **1970** *Guardian* 5 June 10/2 Britain has a long tradition of what might be called lace-curtain racialism. **1974** J. STUBBS *Painted Face* iii. 56 Every house in the square was veiled in lace curtains. **1901** *Daily News* 4 June 2/6 The shoes, low and laceless, slip on easily. **1968** R. CLAPPERTON *No News on Monday* xi. 129 His feet were thrust into a pair of laceless tennis shoes. **1872** *Young Englishwoman* Dec. 658/2 These medallions are worked in appliqué of muslin or net, in satin stitch, knotted-stitch etc. Lace stitches fill the centre of the flower. **1961** A. LILEY *Craft of Embroidery* i. 28 (*heading*) Lace stitch filling... This is also a buttonhole stitch variation giving the laciest effect of all the buttonhole fillings. **1835** DICKENS *Sk. Boz* (1836) 1st Ser. I. i. 4 Her previous admiration of 'the board'..fades into nothing before her respect for her lace-trimmed conductor [*i.e.* the beadle]. **1861** GEO. ELIOT *Silas Marner* xii. 217 A lace-trimmed cradle.

9. lace-bark, (*b*) substitute for def.: any of several small New Zealand trees of the family Malvaceæ, including *Plagianthus betulinus* and several species of *Hoheria* (cf. *HOUHERE), with toothed leaves and clusters of white flowers; also *attrib.*; add examples; **lace-bug**, an insect of the family Tingidæ, including many species of bugs that feed on plants and sometimes become pests; **lacecap**, a hydrangea whose corymbs are made up of small fertile flowers or a mixture of these with larger sterile ones, giving the effect of lace; also used *attrib.* or as *adj.* to describe flower-heads of this type belonging to hydrangeas or other plants; **lace-wood**, (*a*) *Austral.* = **lace-bark* (*b*); (*b*) the wood of a plane tree, *Platanus occidentalis* or *P. acerifolia*.

1868 *Trans. N.Z. Inst.* Essays 33 Ribbon Wood, or Lace-bark tree (*Plagianthus Lyalli*). A very ornamental shrub tree, with large leaves and flowers. **1906**, etc. [see *HOUHERE]. **1957** *Landfall* XI. 234, I lay in a patch, Of bush—giant manuka, some lace-bark. **1958** S. ASHTON-WARNER *Spinster* 189 Flaring out above the long grass and from beneath the lace-bark tree. **1966** *Weekly News* (Auckland) 6 Apr. 40 The lacebark which is also known as mountain ribbonwood (Hoheria glabrata), grows on the western side of the Southern Alps. **1895** J. H. & A. COMSTOCK *Man. Study Insects* xiv. 139 The Lace-bugs. Dainty as fairy brides are these tiny, lace-draped insects. One glance at the fine white meshes that cover the wings and spined thorax is sufficient to distinguish them from all other insects, for these are the only ones that are clothed from head to foot in fine white Brussels net. **1923** E. A. BUTLER *Biol. Brit. Hemiptera–Heteroptera* 196 In the *Tingidae*, or Lace Bugs, we are not rich, for we have but twenty-four in our fauna. **1932** METCALF & FLINT *Fund. Insect Life* viii. 225 Lace bugs look as though they were cut out of fine gauze. **1967** K. M. SMITH *Insect Virol.* xi. 225 The vector in both cases is somewhat unusual, it is not a leafhopper but a 'lace bug'. **1972** SWAN & PAPP *Common Insects N. Amer.* xii. 123 The Tingidæ, or lace bugs, are..small, oval or rectangular in outline, and lacelike in appearance owing to reticulated pattern on the head, thorax, and wings. **1950** W. E. SHEWELL-COOPER *Compl. Gardener* iv. 339 Besides the hortensia type there is another type of *H*[*ydrangea*] *macrophylla*, the Lacecaps, which have a flat head with small fertile flowers in the centre and a ring round the outside formed by the larger sterile flowers. **1966** J. BERRISFORD *Wild Garden* ii. 29 Hydrangeas will grow extremely well in woodland... Grow the lacecaps too. Their flower-pattern is exquisite... The nearly related *Schizophragma hydrangeoides* is a climbing version of the hydrangea family... Its lacecap flower-heads have a solitary large bract-like sepal. **1967** *Sunday Times* 21 May 14/5 The lovely lacecap hydrangea 'Blue Wave'. **1971** *Guardian* 17 Apr. 7/7 The lacecap-flowered Viburnum mariesii. **1898** MORRIS *Austral Eng.* 258/1 Lace-bark, Lacey-bark, or Lacewood. **1902** G. S. BOULGER *Wood* v. 101 Very choice ornamental woods are employed mainly as veneers. Such are..those of Walnut; and the beautiful Lacewood or Honeysuckle wood of North America (*Platanus occidentalis*). **1930** *Morning Post* 2 Aug. 12/2 The anomaly that Queensland silky oak should be purchased by the United States..and then shipped to this country where it is sold as lace-wood. **1962** J. C. S. BROUGH *Timbers for Woodwork* (rev. ed.) xvi. 168 Cut upon the quarter, plane-wood shows an exceedingly handsome figure, and American grown wood converted in this fashion was sent over in fairly large quantities some years ago under the name of Lace-wood.

lace, *v.* Add: **4. b.** *spec.* in Bookbinding, to attach the boards to a volume sewn on cords by passing the slips through holes pierced in them. Also with *in*.

1818 H. PARRY *Art of Bookbinding* 15 Put the pasteboards on each side of the book..and mark on them, with a bodkin, the places where the bands are to be drawn or laced in. **1835** J. HANNETT *Bibliopegia* 30 One board is then placed on each side of the volume, even at the head, and marked with a bodkin opposite to the slips intended to be laced in. **1871** *Amer. Encycl. Printing* 74 When the boards are affixed to the volume by means of the bands being passed through holes made in the boards, they are said to be laced in. **1946** A. J. VAUGHAN in H. Whetton *Pract. Printing & Binding* xxxi. 382/1 The boards are held to the book by three or more cords. These are the cords upon which the sections have been sewn and the boards are said to be 'laced on'. Should these cords not have been laced through the boards the binding is what is known as a cased book, a cheaper style. **1961** [see *LACING *vbl. sb.* 3 e].

e. *intr.* Of structures that resemble or suggest lacing: to pass *across* a gap or *about* an object. Also *fig.*, to become entwined.

a **1889** G. M. HOPKINS *Poems* (1918) 76 Her dearness.. more and more times laces round and round my heart. **1899** H. G. WELLS *When Sleeper Wakes* x. 103 The cables and bridges that laced across the aisles were empty. *Ibid.* xxii. 288 A flimsy seeming scaffolding that laced about the great mass of the Council House.

f. *trans.* To pass (film or tape) between the guides and other parts of a projector, tape recorder, or the like so that it occupies the path taken from one spool to the other when the machine is running. Usu. with *up*.

1948 C. A. HILL *Cine-Film Projection* v. 54 Unless the film is your own, you must put its care before everything else, even if you have to stop the show, but this should never be necessary if you always lace the film correctly. **1966** G. SINSTADT *Whisper in Lonely Place* vi. 106 A facia panel opened to reveal a tape deck. He removed a spool from the metal container and laced up the tape. **1968** C. N. G. MATTHEWS *Tape Recording* ix. 80 Press the stop button almost at once or you will come to the end of the tape and have the trouble of lacing it up again. **1974** *Some Technical Terms & Slang* (Granada Television), *Lace up*, to thread film through a machine for projection or transmission.

6. (Later examples.)

1923 H. G. WELLS *Men like Gods* I. vi. 89 'Tell me', that engaging phrase, laced his conversation. **1971** *Nature* 2 July 70/2 That work led to two by-products: a Beilby award in 1948 and a fund of sea stories with which to lace his general conversation.

laced, *ppl. a.*[1] Add: **8*.** *laced valley* (Building): a valley between the slopes of two adjoining roofs in which the end tile of each row abuts against a tile-and-a-half tile laid diagonally on the valley board.

1931 C. G. DOBSON *Roof Tiling* iii. 39 No lead is required in a laced valley. **1947** R. GREENHALGH *Mod. Building Construction* II. 582/2 Other methods..give swept and laced valleys.

‖ **lacet**[2] (lase). [Fr., 'lace, hairpin bend'.] A hairpin bend in a road.

1895 S. WEYMAN *Red Cockade* vi. 84 The road there descends not in *lacets*, but straight. **1922** *Glasgow Herald* 18 July 9 A series of lacets brings one to the bleak crest of the Col de Cavolles. **1932** KIPLING *Limits & Renewals* 342 The Massif in Spring, the multiplied lacets Hampered by slips or drifts. **1970** 'S. TROY' *Blind Man's Garden* ix. 116 The Route Napoléon with its frequent *corniche* and *lacet*.

lace-up (lēi·sʌp), *a.* (and *sb.*). [LACE *v.* 10.] Of boots or shoes: that are fastened with laces. Also *ellipt.* as *sb.*, a lace-up boot or shoe.

1836, etc. [see LACE *v.* 10]. **1889** J. K. JEROME *Three Men in Boat* xi. 170 He would have his lace-up boots. **1951** [see *button-up* s.v. *BUTTON *v.* 4]. **1964** *Observer* 15 Nov. 14/4 Girls' shoes are much worse for the feet than the usual boys' lace-up. **1972** R. QUILTY *Tenth Session* 20 Her funny old-fashioned lace-up shoes. **1973** *Times* 7 Nov. 18/3 A..quantity surveyor was clumping along in tan three-inch lace-ups.

Lach, L'ach, varr. *LECH, LEKH *sb.*[5] and *a.*

lachenalia (laʃənēi·liă). [mod.L. (N. J. Jacquin 1787, in *Nova Acta Helvetica* I. 39),

f. the name of Werner de *la Chenal* (1736–1800), Swiss botanist + -IA¹.] A small, bulbous plant of the genus so called, belonging to the family Liliaceæ, native to South Africa, and bearing thick, often spotted leaves, and spikes or racemes of tubular or bell-shaped flowers; also called *Cape cowslip*.

1789 *Curtis's Bot. Mag.* III. 82 Like most of the Cape plants, the *Lachenalia* requires to be sheltered in the winter. **1900** L. H. BAILEY *Cycl. Amer. Hort.* II. 866/1 Lachenalias are Cape bulbs that are easily flowered in a cool greenhouse in early spring or even in winter. **1923** *Chambers's Jrnl.* Dec. 786/2 A host of delightful, and to us strange, things—..sombre-hued babianas, and the lachenalias with their weird-spotted foliage. **1961** P. WHITE *Riders in Chariot* viii. 236 A plaster pixie..out on the front lawn, beside the golden cypresses, amongst the lachenalia. **1970** *Guardian* 9 May 9/2 It is more than 200 years since the Cape cowslip was first introduced to England... Lachenalias flower in midwinter.

Lachmann (la·χman). [The name of Karl *Lachmann* (1793–1851), German philologist.] *Lachmann's law*: the rule that in Latin, a short root-vowel in the present-tense stem of a verb is lengthened in the past participle if the present-tense stem ends in a voiced plosive.

[**1850** C. LACHMANN *In T. Lucretii Cari De Rerum Natura Libros Commentarius* 54 Participia passiva ea quorum in praesenti consonans est aut liquida aut *s* semivocalis, quantitatem praesentis secuntur..contra ubi in praesenti media est, participia producuntur.] **1913** *Classical Rev.* XXVII. 122 It is true that 'Lachmann's Law'.., admittedly impossible as originally stated, was revived in a much modified form by Pedersen. **1928** *Language* IV. 181 (*title*) Lachmann's law of vowel lengthening. **1965** W. S. ALLEN *Vox Latina* 70 The same evidence indicates that Lachmann's Law also applies before *s* in the subjunctive *adāxim*..as against *effēxim*. **1970** *Harvard Stud. Classical Philol.* LXXIV. 58 Kuryłowicz therefore saw correctly..that a morphophonemic solution was indicated; that Lachmann's law was not a phonetic rule. **1973** W. S. ALLEN *Accent & Rhythm* 18 Thus, referring to the Latin phenomenon of 'Lachmann's Law' (whereby e.g. *făcio* forms a past participle *fāctus*, but *ăgo* forms *āctus*), Kiparsky..suggests that it can be accounted for by introducing the presumed Latin vowel-lengthening rule V→long/—*g* before, rather than after, the Indo-European consonant-assimilating rule C→voiceless/—*t*.

lachrymal, *a.* and *sb.* Add: The etymologically correct form **lacrimal** is now usual in scientific use. (Further examples of sense 2 of the adj.)

1913 *Gray's Anat.* (ed. 18) 960 The lacrimal [*ed. 17* (*1909*): lachrymal] ducts or canals..commence at minute orifices, termed *puncta lacrimalia*. **1913** *Cunningham's Text-bk. Anat.* (ed. 4) 824 The lacrimal gland..is supplied by the sympathetic and lacrimal nerves. [*Ed. 3* (*1909*): lachrymal.] **1919** *Lancet* 10 May 792/2 During the stage of surgical anæsthesia the lacrymal glands cease to secrete. **1919** *Physiol. Abstr.* IV. 183 [*From abstract of article containing the prec. quot.*] The lacrimal gland in anæsthesia. **1950** D. B. KIRBY *Surg. Cataract* xii. 276/1 Care must be exercised to prevent the solution from going through the lacrimal duct to the nose. **1954** S. DUKE-ELDER *Parsons' Dis. Eye* (ed. 12) xxxiii. 543 The lacrimal apparatus consists of the lacrimal glands and the lacrimal passages. [*Edd. 1* (*1907*)–*11* (*1948*): lacrymal.] **1968** PASSMORE & ROBSON *Compan. Med. Stud.* I. xxiv. 54/2 The cornea is continually bathed by the secretion of the lacrimal glands.

B. *sb.* **2.** *pl.* (Later example.)

1931 M. SUMMERS *Supernatural Omnibus* 31 What an event [in Dickens] was a funeral from a house! The way to all these sadly sentimental lachrymals had been paved before by the lugubrious cortèges of the time of Anne.

lachrymate, *v.* Delete *Obs.*$^{-0}$ and add pronunc. (læ·krimēit). Now current chiefly in scientific use (freq. as **lacrimate**: cf. *LACHRYMAL *a.* and *sb.*), with the sense: to discharge moisture from the eyes. (Examples.) Hence **la·chrymating** *vbl. sb.* and *ppl. a.*

1922 *Encycl. Brit.* XXXII. 110/2 If a sufficient number of lachrymating grenades could be thrown. **1944** *Brit. Jrnl. Ophthalm.* XXVIII. 330 The patient lacrimates when he salivates. **1962** W. K. MCEWEN in H. Davson *Eye* III. x. 272 In man there is the added ability to weep, or lacrimate, which is an excessive outpouring of the lacrimal gland. **1964** *Amer. Jrnl. Ophthalm.* LVIII. 1056/1 Tension in lacrimating patients is more easily measured with the Schiøtz tonometer.

lachrymator (læ·krimēitǫ̆ɹ). Also **lacrimator.** [f. *lachrymat-, lacrimat-* (in LACHRYMATORY *a.* and *sb.*, etc.) + -OR.] Any substance which causes irritation and copious watering of the eyes when it comes into contact with them (in the form of a gas, spray, dust, or the like).

1918 *Jrnl. Amer. Med. Assoc.* 30 Nov. 1823/1 Lacrimators (acetone, xylene or benzene bromid). **1922** *Encycl. Brit.* XXXII. 111/2 Lachrymators, on account of the extreme sensitiveness of the eye, can produce an effect in extraordinarily weak concentrations. **1948** *Biochem. Jrnl.* XLII. p. xxvi, The '—SH' theory provides an explanation for the existence of two main groups of lachrymators: (a) substances containing a halogen atom in some such group as —CH_2Cl together with a neighbouring keto or other group which makes the halogen 'positive', (b) substances containing a —CH=CH— group, also with a neighbouring keto or other group which polarizes the double bond. **1963** *Times* 25 Apr. 6/4 Chloracetophenone, a lacrimator in adequate concentrations, had toxic effects.

lachrymatory, *a.* and *sb.* **A.** *adj.* (Further examples.)

1916 *Yorks. Post* 21 July 5/5 A violent artillery preparation with asphyxiating and lachrymatory shells. **1935** *Brit. Med. Jrnl.* 20 July 133/1 Lachrymatory gases were here and off again unless there was a continual rain of tear-gas shells. **1971** *Agric. & Biol. Chem.* (Tokyo) XXXV. 1831 The lachrymatory character and the pungent flavor [of onions] had been decreased by γ-irradiation.

lachrymogenic (læ:krimodʒe·nik), *a.* [f. LACHRYM(ATION + -O + *-GENIC.] Giving rise to lachrymation.

1921 *Chem. Abstr.* XV. 398 (*heading*) Estimation of the lachrymogenic power of irradiating substances by the threshold method. **1971** *Jrnl. Agric. & Food Chem.* XIX. 269/2 Thioethanol, thioacetone, thiobutanal, and thiohexanal *S*-oxides were also synthesized and their lachrymogenic properties were evaluated.

‖ **lachsschinken** (la·χsʃiŋkĕn). Also erron. **lachschinken.** [G., f. *lachs* salmon + *schinken* ham.] Cured and smoked loin of pork.

1923 A. WARD *Encycl. Food* 463 *Lachsschinken*, two trimmed, boneless pork-loins, mild sweet-cured, faced and pushed into large beef casings, sixteen inches or so in length, pressed, tied with strings, dried, and lightly smoked. **1937** *Atlantic Monthly* Mar. 267, I burst into enthusiasm on the subject of *Lachs-schinken* (which, as the name indicates, is a sort of ham that both looks and tastes like salmon). **1958** *Catal. County Stores, Taunton* June 5 Continental sausages... Lachsschinken, eaten cold, finely sliced—4 ozs. 2/7. **1965** *New Statesman* 11 June 914/2 'Sausages of all kinds not in airtight containers'—which include the mortadella and the salami, the krakauer and lachsschinken. **1971** *Sunday Times* (Colour Suppl.) 27 June 50/3 *Lachschinken*: pork fillet, cured, smoked and rolled in a thin casing of pork back fat. Serve with fresh fruit as an alternative to *prosciutto*.

laciness (lēi·sinės). [f. LACY *a.* + -NESS.] Lace-like quality or effect.

1903 *Westm. Gaz.* 9 July 4/2 Flowered silk, or embroideries, or chiffon, and laciness.

lacing, *vbl. sb.* Add: **3. e.** *Bookbinding* (see quot. and *LACE *v.* 4 b).

a **1877** KNIGHT *Dict. Mech.* II. 1244/1 *Lacing*,..securing the book to the sides by carrying the bands or slips through perforations in the boards. **1961** T. LANDAU *Encycl. Librarianship* (ed. 2) 189/1 *Lacing-in*, in hand-binding, in the 'extra' style, the method of attaching boards to the sewing cords, which are laced through holes in the boards.

4. lacing course *Building*, a special course built into an arch or wall in order to bond different parts together and give added strength.

1886 H. C. SEDDON *Builder's Work* i. 66 It is better..to build the arch in half-brick rings, with a few bonding or lacing courses built in at intervals, to tie the separate rings together. **1899** *Notes on Building Construction* (rev. ed.) I. iii. 46 Walls such as those built with flints, or other small stones,..are frequently strengthened by building in with them lacing courses, consisting of horizontal bands either of ashlar, coursed rubble, or brickwork. **1947** R. GREENHALGH *Mod. Building Construction* I. 229/1 In arches of very wide span, the different rings are sometimes bonded to each other by inserting courses of stretchers in the depth of the arch at intervals. These courses are termed lacing courses.

lacis (la·si). [Fr.] A kind of lace made by darning patterns on net.

1865 F. B. PALLISER *Hist. Lace* ii. 14 The volume..is that of the Venetian Vinciolo..dating from 1587... The work is in two books. The first of Point coupé... The second of Lacis, or subjects in squares, Fig. 3, with counted stitches, like the patterns for worsted-work of the present day. **1875** *Encycl. Brit.* XIV. 183/2 The productions of this art, which has some analogy to weaving, in the early part of the 16th century came to be known as.. 'lacis' in France... With the development of the renaissance of art, free flowing patterns and figure subjects were introduced and worked in lacis. **1953** [see *FILET 1]. **1963** *Times* 1 June 11/6 One development was the introduction of all-white lacis, such as was recorded in the bed furnishings of Mary Queen of Scots with ornament built up in darning stitches on a basis of open-mesh net.

lack, *v.*¹ Add: **4.** Also with *for*.

1892 'MARK TWAIN' *Amer. Claimant* 40 Here's hoping he'll never lack for friends. **1898** SKEEL & BREARLEY *King Washington* (1899) 170 He was one of the many who had lacked for partners. **1906** E. PHILLPOTTS *Portreeve* II. iv. 154 The outward signs that she had marked upon him did not lack for inner causes.

lackadaisy, *int.* (Earlier examples.)

1748 SMOLLETT *R. Random* I. viii. 56 She exclaimed, 'Good lack-a-daisy! the rogue is fled!' **1796** M. EDGEWORTH *Parent's Assistant* (ed. 2) I. 164 The carpenter.. said '*lack-a-daisy!*' when he saw that the old theatre was pulled down.

lackey, *sb.* Add: **1. c.** *spec.* As a term of political abuse: a servile follower.

1939 G. E. R. GEDYE *Fallen Bastions* ii. 37 The Communists did not hesitate to condemn them [*sc.* the Austrian Socialist leaders], as 'Social Fascists' who did 'lackey service' to capitalist reaction. **1941** *Amer. Mercury* Apr. 417/2 American bankers..have already stepped into the role of lackeys of British Imperialism. **1957** C. HUNT *Guide to Communist Jargon* p. xiv, The Soviet Union stands for peace, and the imperialists for war, in which they are once again supported by their socialist 'lackeys'. **1969** *Listener* 27 Apr. 429/3 Whatever else went under the name of socialism was either 'wilful deception by lackeys of the bourgeoisie' or the self-deception of those who hesitated 'between life-and-death struggle and the role of assistants to the expiring bourgeoisie'. **1972** *Sat. Rev.* (U.S.) 24 June 30/2 As any good Maoist..can tell you, Hussein is nothing more than a Western lackey. **1973** *Black Panther* 21 July 10/2 The U.S. government or its lackeys. **1974** A. ROSS *Bradford Business* 129 Bloody fascist lackeys!

lack-wit, lackwit (læ·kwit). [LACK *v.*¹ 7.] A witless or stupid person.

1667, 1809 [see LACK *v.*¹ 7]. **1911** H. S. HARRISON *Queed* iv. 42 West..abused himself for a shiftless lackwit who was slated for an unwept grave. **1936** F. CLUNE *Roaming round Darling* xxi. 210, I was embarrassed exceedingly by an inarticulate lack-wit, while I filled the petrol tank.

Laconian, *a.* and *sb.* Add: **B.** *sb.* **2.** The dialect of ancient Greek spoken in Laconia (Sparta).

1830 TUFNELL & LEWIS tr. *Müller's Hist. & Antiq. Doric Race* II. App. viii. 502 We have considered the Doric dialect in general, as spoken by the whole race, only marking out the Laconian as its purest variety. **1875** *Encycl. Brit.* XI. 133/2 Three changes characteristic of Laconian came in at a comparatively late date. **1954** PEI & GAYNOR *Dict. Ling.* 118 *Laconian*, one of the Doric dialects of ancient Greek.

‖ **lacrimæ rerum** (læ·krimǝi reᵊrŏm). [L.] With reference to Virgil, *Aeneid* I. 462: the sadness of life; tears shed for the sorrows of men.

[**1841** CARLYLE *Let.* 19 July in R. K. Webb *H. Martineau* (1960) vi. 196 Poor Harriet! She was..almost sublime to me there. *Sunt lachrymae rerum.*] **1929** A. HUXLEY *Do what you Will* 195 Hellenic lovers..may have wept the *lacrimae rerum*. **1951** AUDEN *Nones* (1952) 71 Only the young and the rich Have the nerve or the figure to strike The lacrimae rerum note. **1959** *Times* 19 Mar. 4/1 He [*sc.* Mahler] told in his music truths of humanity, of the *lacrimae rerum*, and of alleviating beauty. **1969** G. SMITH in A. Huxley *Lett.* (1969) 1 Though often tinged with a profound instinct to weep for life, it—and by no means the sadness of *lacrimæ rerum*—is Huxley's hallmark.

lacrimal, lacrimate, -or, see *LACHRYMAL *a.* and *sb.*, etc.

lacsamana, var. *LAKSAMANA.

lactalbumin (læktæ·lbiŭmin). *Biochem.* [ad. F. *lactalbumine* (A. Commaille 1866, in *Rec. de Mém. de Méd.* XVII. 155), f. *lact(o-* LACTO- + *albumine* ALBUMIN.] **a.** The fraction of milk proteins which is obtained after the removal of casein and which is soluble in a salt solution such as saturated magnesium sulphate or ammonium sulphate.

1885 [see *LACTOGLOBULIN 1]. **1936** *Biochem. Jrnl.* XXX. 956 Probably the so-called lactalbumin is a mixture of the two molecules α and β and the molecule usually referred to as lactoglobulin is γ. **1970** [see *b].

b. (Usu. *α-lactalbumin.*) A protein or mixture of closely similar proteins occurring in the lactalbumin fraction of milk and having a molecular weight of about 17,400.

1937 *Nature* 19 Jun. (Suppl.) 1058/2 In cow's milk there are two albumins, the α-lactalbumin, of molecular weight 17,600 and sedimentation constant $1{\cdot}9 \times 10^{-13}$ and β-lactalbumin (also called Palmer's lactoglobulin) with $M = 39{,}000$ and $s = 3{\cdot}12 \times 10^{-13}$. **1948** [see *LACTOGLOBULIN 2]. **1953** *Jrnl. Amer. Chem. Soc.* LXXV. 329/1 It is proposed, therefore, that the protein isolated by the Sørensens also be called α-lactalbumin even though the isoelectric protein is only slightly soluble in water. **1962** *Biochem. Jrnl.* LXXXIII. 271/1 The lactalbumin was prepared from human-milk whey. **1970** R. JENNESS in H. A. McKenzie *Milk Proteins* I. ii. 22 When later the proteins β-lactoglobulin and α-lactalbumin were crystallised from the 'lactalbumin' fraction, the Greek letters used by Pedersen were incorporated into the names... The β-protein was named as a globulin because of its insolubility near the isoelectric point in the absence of salt and the α-protein as an albumin because of its source in the 'lactalbumin' fraction of whey... Two α-lactalbumins, A and B, have been found.

lactam (læ·ktæm). *Chem.* [a. G. *lactam* (Baeyer & Oekonomides 1882, in *Ber. d. Deut. Chem. Ges.* XV. 2102), f. *lact-on* LACTONE + *am-id* AMIDE.] Any of the class of cyclic amides analogous to the lactones, characterized by the group —NH·CO— as part of a ring (*lactam ring*) and formed by the elimination of a molecule of water from an amino and a carboxyl group of an acid; freq. with prefixed Gr. letter (see *LACTONE 2).

1883 *Jrnl. Chem. Soc.* XLIV. 202 The authors propose the name *lactam* for bodies formed like acetylisatin, and *lactim* for those formed like isatin. **1910** *Encycl. Brit.* VI. 59/1 The internal anhydrides of aminocarboxylic acids (lactams, betaines). **1936** L. J. DESHA *Org. Chem.* xxvi. 522 Lactam–lactim tautomerism involves the shift of a hydrogen atom from nitrogen to oxygen and vice versa. **1949** E. P. ABRAHAM et al. in H. W. Florey et al. *Antibiotics* II. xv. 669 The four-membered lactam ring which was present in this structure [of penicillin] had not previously been found in natural compounds, and the ease with which it could be broken was responsible for the instability of penicillin under a variety of conditions. **1964** ROBERTS & CASERIO *Basic Princ. Org. Chem.* xx. 712 Formation of α- and β-lactams is expected to generate considerable ring strain, and other more favorable reactions usually intervene. **1966** *McGraw-Hill Encycl. Sci. & Technol.* VII. 377/1 Although γ- and δ-amino acids are nontoxic themselves, the corresponding lactams show pronounced strychnine-type toxicity.

lactamase (læ·ktămēiz, -s). *Biochem.* [f. *LACTAM + *-ASE.] *β-lactamase*: any of the enzymes (produced by certain bacteria) which cause the breaking of the carbon–nitrogen bond in the lactam ring of penicillins and cephalosporins (so rendering them ineffective as antibiotics).

1964 *Jrnl. Gen. Microbiol.* XXXVI. 206 Amidase-forming coliform organisms did not attack the 6-APA nucleus, whereas β-lactamase-forming coliform organisms opened the lactam ring. **1971** N. CITRI in P. D. Boyer et al. *Enzymes* (ed. 3) IV. ii. 24 The role of penicillinase and other β-lactamases in conferring resistance to penicillins and the closely related cephalosporins has been amply demonstrated.

lactase (læ·ktēiz, -s). *Biochem.* [a. F. *lactase* (M. W. Beijerinck 1889, in *Arch. néerl. d. Sci. exactes et nat.* XXIII. 434), f. *lact-ose* LACTOSE: see *-ASE.] Any enzyme which catalyses the hydrolysis of lactose to glucose and galactose.

1891 *Jrnl. R. Microsc. Soc.* 374 The fermentation [of milk sugar] is effected by a diastase distinct from invertin, which he calls lactase. **1906** *Jrnl. Physiol.* XXXV. 28 The conclusion is from these experiments that lactase is distributed fairly equally through the whole of the mucous membrane of the intestine. **1959** JENNESS & PATTON *Princ. Dairy Chem.* iii. 80 There are at least three significant origins of lactase enzymes which may be used for the hydrolysis of lactose. These are: (a) certain species of yeasts..; (b) the intestinal mucosa of mammals..; and (c) β-galactosidase from almonds.

lactate (læktēi·t), *v.* [f. L. *lactāt-*, ppl. stem of *lactāre* to suckle.] *intr.* To secrete or discharge milk. Chiefly as **lacta·ting** *ppl. a.*

1889 in *Cent. Dict.* **1908** *Arch. Middlesex Hosp.* XIII. 59 In the lactating breast the number of acini is very large. **1913** *17th Internat. Congr. Med.* III. II. 173 The pregnant and lactating animals survived the extirpation of the adrenal glands much longer than normal, non-pregnant, or male animals. **1948** *New Biol.* IV. 127 Purified preparations of prolactin were found inferior to more crude pituitary preparations..in their power to increase the milk yield of cows already lactating. **1953** E. GELLHORN *Physiol. Found. Neurol. & Psychiatry* xiii. 305 There is still another function of oxytocin..: the ejection of milk from the lactating mammillary gland. **1956** J. S. FOLLEY *Physiol. & Biochem. Lactation* ii. 28 Mammary tissue from lactating rats..exhibits much greater respiratory activity *in vitro*. **1956** *Jrnl. Pediatrics* XLIX. 550/2 She had suckled all her daughter's children and lactated freely each time. **1971** J. Z. YOUNG *Introd. Study Man* xxiv. 319 To estimate reliably the number of children born to a group of women under the conditions that their husbands are freely available and that they are not using contraceptives or lactating is nearly impossible.

lacta·ted, *a.* [f. as prec. f. L. *lact-*, *lac* milk.] Combined with a milk-product.

1889 *Buck's Handbk. Med. Sci.* VIII. 100/2 In Horlick's and Mellin's there is said to be no unconverted starch. Hawley's contains eleven per cent.,..as does also the Lactated Food. **1896** *Rep. Vermont Board Agric.* XV. 25 This is used in making..lactated food for infants and invalids. **1907** *Yesterday's Shopping* (1969) 500/2 Lactated Pepsin Tablets.

lactational (læktēi·ʃənăl), *a.* [f. LACTATION + -AL.] Of or pertaining to lactation.

1903 *Med. Rec.* (N.Y.) 28 Feb. 337/2 Both suicidal and infanticidal promptings are more common in lactational than puerperal cases—that is, in cases in which insanity commenced more than six weeks after confinement. **1970** *Nature* 19 Dec. 1222/2 It has been found that cows excrete less DDT in lactational fluids than human females.

lactim (læ·ktim). *Chem.* [a. G. *lactim* (Baeyer & Oekonomides 1882, in *Ber. d. Deut. Chem. Ges.* XV. 2102), f. *lact-on* LACTONE + *im-id* IMIDE.] Any of the class of cyclic imines which are isomers of the lactams and characterized by the group —N:C(OH)— as part of a ring.

1883, 1936 [see *LACTAM]. **1951** I. L. FINAR *Org. Chem.* I. xxx. 619 Isatin exists in two forms, the term ψ-isatin being applied to the lactam form I, and isatin to the lactim form II. **1971** *Canad. Jrnl. Chem.* XLIX. 2612 Investigation showed the free lactim ether to be a probable intermediate in this reaction.

lacto-. Add: **la·ctochrome** *Biochem.*, a yellow-orange pigment orig. extracted from milk and now identified with riboflavin; **lactofla·vin** *Biochem.* [a. G. *lactoflavin* (Ellinger & Koschara 1933, in *Ber. d. Deut. Chem. Ges.* LXVI. B. 808)] = *RIBOFLAVIN; **la·ctogen** *Physiol.*, any lactogenic hormone; *spec.* = *PROLACTIN; **lactoge·nesis** *Physiol.*, the initiation of milk secretion; **lactoge·nic** *Physiol.* [*-GENIC], pertaining to or having the ability to initiate the secretion of milk; hence **lactoge·nically** *adv.*; **lacto-vegeta·rian** *a.*, consisting of milk and vegetables; so **lacto-vegeta·rianism.**

1879 A. W. BLYTH in *Jrnl. Chem. Soc.* XXXV. 532 After the liquid from which the galactin has been removed had been freed from the excess of lead by hydrogen sulphide, an alkaloïdal colouring matter, for which I propose the name of 'lactochrome', may be separated by the addition of nitrate of mercury solution. **1914** *Jrnl. Biol. Chem.* XVII. 261 The facts brought out by this investigation point very clearly to a very close relationship existing between the yellow lactochrome of milk whey and the urochrome of urine. **1936** W. L. DAVIES *Chem. Milk* xi. 218 Milk from other species of mammals also contains lactochrome. It is present in human milk. **1953** FRUTON & SIMMONDS *Gen. Biochem.* xiii. 319 In 1879 Blyth described the isolation from milk of a yellow pigment (named lactochrome) which showed a striking green fluorescence... By 1936 the chemical nature of the yellow pigment of egg yolk and of milk had been established..; it was shown that this pigment, named riboflavin, is identical with vitamin B_2. **1933** *Brit. Chem. Abstr.* A. 847/2 (*heading*) Lactoflavin, the pigment of milk. **1938** *Encycl. Brit. Bk. of Year* 651/1 Recently it has been found that vitamin B_2 consists of three components, lactoflavin, vitamin B_6..and pellagrous preventing or p.p. factor. **1943** SUMNER & SOMERS *Chem. & Methods of Enzymes* xiii. 244 Various flavins were described, *e.g.*, lactoflavin of milk, hepatoflavin of liver... The flavin of these workers was the same substance which is called today 'riboflavin', or sometimes, 'lactoflavin'. **1946** J. F. FULTON *Howell's Textbk. Physiol.* (ed. 15) liv. 1209 Both the onset and maintenance of lactation require lactogen. **1952** S. J. FOLLEY in A. S. Parkes *Marshall's Physiol. Reproduction* (ed. 3) II. xx. 558 When first discovered it [*sc.* an anterior-pituitary protein hormone] was variously named prolactin (Riddle), galactin (Turner) and mammotropin (Lyons). Recent American practice tends to favour the terms lactogen or lactogenic hormone; the name prolactin is adopted in this chapter in accordance with English usage. **1962** *Endocrinology* LXXI. 218/2 The Raben preparation.., although quite potent as a lactogen in the pseudopregnant rabbit,.. has little activity in the local intradermal pigeon crop assay. **1967** *Proc. Nat. Acad. Sci.* LVIII. 2307 The recent identification of human placental lactogen (HPL), a polypeptide hormone which shares both biological and immunological properties with pituitary growth hormone (HGH). **1939** RIDDLE & BATES in E. Allen *Sex & Internal Secretions* xx. 1089 Lactogenesis is a *response* to this hormone which excites also—in both sexes—additional responses more ancient phylogenetically and perhaps more significant generally. **1948** Lactogenesis [see *galactopoiesis* (*GALACTO-)]. **1969** S. R. WELLINGS in Reynolds & Folley *Lactogenesis* 5 Lactogenesis may be defined as the process by which full lactation is initiated in an already prepared mammary gland. **1933** *Proc. Soc. Exper. Biol. & Med.* XXI. 300 We have never observed milk secretion in normal or ovariectomized virgin guinea pigs uninjected with the lactogenic hormone. **1946** J. F. FULTON *Howell's Textbk. Physiol.* (ed. 15) liv. 1209 The lactogenic activity of pituitary extracts was first shown by Stricker and Grüter in 1928. **1952** Lactogenic [see *lactogen* above]. **1969** A. T. COWIE in Reynolds & Folley *Lactogenesis* 159, I now turn to the rabbit, the species in which the lactogenic role of the anterior pituitary was first discovered. **1969** R. DENAMUR in *Ibid.* 60 Thus, lactogenically prolactin modifies the polyribosomes by increasing their number in the cell. **1907** *Practitioner* June 845 The lacto-vegetarian diet..lessens auto-intoxication. **1929** *Encycl. Brit.* VII. 359/1 A lacto-vegetarian diet which permits the free use of milk and eggs. **1940** *Nature* 7 Dec. 726/2 It..looks as if the Briton's dietary will gradually shift, at least during the war years, towards lactovegetarianism. **1951** *News Chron.* 13 Dec. 3/2 Man was not designed for a purely vegetable diet. There was no objection whatever to lacto-vegetarian diet (this includes milk and eggs).

2. Used as comb. form of LACTIC *acid* or LACTOSE: as in **lactobio·nic** *a.*, in *lactobionic acid* [tr. G. *lactobionsäure* (Fischer & Meyer 1889, in *Ber. d. Deut. Chem. Ges.* XXII. 362)], 4-(β-D-galactosido)-D-gluconic acid, $C_{12}H_{22}O_{11}$: a syrup produced by oxidation of lactose; hence **lactobi·onate,** a salt of lactobionic acid; **lactoni·trile,** a yellow liquid, $CH_3 \cdot CH(OH) \cdot CN$, that is the nitrile of lactic acid and is used in a method of manufacturing acrylonitrile; acetaldehyde cyanohydrin; **lactophe·nol,** a mixture of approximately equal weights of phenol and lactic acid dissolved in glycerol and distilled water, used for mounting biological specimens.

1927 *Jrnl. Chem. Soc.* 546 Barium lactobionate was methylated in a manner similar to that already mentioned. **1964** *Chem. Abstr.* LXI. 16697 Ca lactobionate.. may be used under the Federal Food, Drug, and Cosmetic Act as a firming agent in dry pudding mixes. **1889** *Jrnl. Chem. Soc.* LVI. 485 Lactobionic acid, $C_{12}H_{22}O_{12}$, is obtained when milk-sugar (1 part) dissolved in water (7 parts) is treated with bromine (1 part). *Ibid.* 486 Lactobionic acid is decomposed into galactose and gluconic acid when warmed with dilute mineral acids. **1967** KIRK & OTHMER *Encycl. Chem. Technol.* (ed. 2) XIII. 571 The sequestrant and emulsifying properties of lactobionic acid suggest a commercial potential, especially in the food industry, for this product. **1898** *Jrnl. Chem. Soc.* LXXIV. II. 509 When silicon tetrachloride is heated with mandelonitrile or lactonitrile, silicic acid and complex tarry products are formed. **1935** *Chem. Abstr.* XXIX. 814 For prepg. an aliphatic cyanohydrin such as lactonitrile, reaction is effected between HCN and an aliphatic aldehyde or ketone such as acetaldehyde. **1961** *Ibid.* LV. 8268 The alkyl and aralkyl α-hydroxy nitriles, i.e. lactonitrile, [etc.].., are effective reagents for the extn. of Au and Ag by cyanidation... Crude lactonitrile which is a by-product from the manuf. of acrylonitrile is inexpensive and very efficient. **1896** *Jrnl. R. Microsc. Soc.* 481 M. J. Amann recommends the following fluids for preserving and imbedding mosses..(1) Lactophenol. **1929** W. R. TAYLOR in C. E. McClung *Handbk. Microsc. Technique* iv. 139 A solution (Lactophenol) composed of lactic acid [etc.]..is very serviceable and may be used for mounting various materials, softening dried material (especially algæ) or decalcifying specimens. **1970** *Watsonia* VIII. 140 Pollen grains stained with cotton blue in lactophenol.

lactobacillus (læ:ktobăsi·lŭs). *Biol.* Pl. **-bacilli.** [mod.L. (M. W. Beijerinck 1901, in *Arch. néerl. d. Sci. exactes et nat.* VI. 213), f. LACTO- + BACILLUS.] Any bacterium of the genus *Lactobacillus* (family Lactobacillaceæ), which includes microaerophilic or anaerobic, non-motile, Gram-positive rods which convert glucose and related carbohydrates to lactic acid and are found in the intestinal tract and in fermenting plant and animal (esp. dairy) products.

1924 *Jrnl. Bacteriol.* IX. 375 A study of lactobacilli from the intestines. **1928** B. W. HAMMER *Dairy Bacteriol.* xv. 410 The lactobacilli constitute another type of organism bringing about changes that are important in the ripening of cheddar cheese. **1958** W. C. FRAZIER *Food Microbiol.* iii. 51 Characteristics that make the lactobacilli important in foods are (1) their ability to ferment sugars with the production of considerable amounts of lactic acid, enabling their use in the production of fermented plant and dairy products, or the manufacture of industrial lactic acid, but resulting in the deterioration of some products, e.g. wine or beer; (2) production of gas and other volatile products..; (3) their inability to synthesize most of the vitamins they require,..making them useful in assays for the vitamin content of foods; and (4) the heat resistance..of most of the high-temperature lactobacilli. **1961** R. D. BAKER *Essent. Path.* ix. 190 Although many microorganisms are observed in association with caries,..most investigations have centered around the parasitic lactobacilli. These organisms may have a role in the initiation of the process.

lactoglobulin (læktoglǫ·biŭlin). *Biochem.* [a. Da. *lactoglobulin* (J. Sebelien 1885, in *Oversigt o. d. K. Danske Viedensk. Selskabs Forhand.* 4), f. *globulin* GLOBULIN: see LACTO-.] † **1.** The fraction of milk proteins which is obtained after the removal of casein and is precipitated by a salt such as magnesium sulphate or ammonium sulphate. *Obs.*

1885 *Jrnl. Chem. Soc.* XLVIII. 1000 The author has isolated from milk two albuminoïd substances distinct from caseïn. Lactoglobulin, the first of these, is present in minute quantity only... Lactalbumin, the second albuminoïd, is precipitated by acetic acid in the filtrate from the preceding compound. **1936** [see *LACTALBUMIN a].

2. (Usu. *β-lactoglobulin.*) A protein or mixture of closely similar proteins occurring in the lactalbumin fraction of milk, insoluble near the isoelectric point in the absence of salt and having a molecular weight of about 40,000.

1936 *Biochem. Jrnl.* XXX. 968 This investigation shows that the lactoglobulin prepared according to the method of Palmer from the lactalbumin fraction of cow's milk is a monodisperse protein. **1945** *Jrnl. Amer. Chem. Soc.* LXVII. 1531/2 β-Lactoglobulin consists of 370 amino acid residues with 366 peptide bonds, arranged in 4 sub-units (polypeptide chains). **1948** *New Biol.* IV. 133 The typical milk proteins, casein, lactalbumin and lactoglobulin, are believed to be mainly products of the serum globulin of the blood. **1955** *Nature* 30 July 218/2 Individual cows produce either a mixture of two electrophoretically distinct β-lactoglobulins or only one or the other of these. *Ibid.* 219/2 β_1-Lactoglobulin forms rectangular plates indistinguishable from the well-known crystals hitherto prepared from mixed milk..whereas β_2-lactoglobulin forms diamond-shaped plates. **1961** *Biochim. & Biophys. Acta* XLIX. 591 In cow's milk β-lactoglobulin constitutes approx. half of the whey proteins and 7–12% of the total proteins.

lactol (læ·ktǫl). *Chem.* [a. G. *lactol* (Helferich & Fries 1925, in *Ber. d. Deut. Chem. Ges.* LVIIIB. 1246), f. *lact-on* *LACTONE 2 + *-ol* -OL.] Any cyclic compound that is formed by the oxygen atom in a —C(OH)— group (esp. one in a sugar) becoming linked to the carbon atom of a carbonyl group in the same molecule (with the transfer of the hydrogen atom of the former group to the oxygen atom of the latter).

1925 *Chem. Abstr.* XIX. 2931 The name lactol (aldo-lactol, ketolactol) is proposed for the cyclo-form of hydroxyaldehydes and ketones, the length of the O-bridge being indicated by Greek letters (as for the lactones) or by nos. in brackets (as for the sugars). **1967** [see *GLUCOSIDE].

lactone. Add: **2.** *Chem.* [ad. G. *lacton* (R. Fittig 1880, in *Ann. d. Chem.* CC. 62).] Any of the class of cyclic esters formed (in theory) by the elimination of a molecule of water from a hydroxyl and a carboxyl group of an organic acid, and characterized by the group —O·CO— as part of a ring; freq. with preceding Gr. letter corresponding to the size of the ring (an α-lactone having a three-membered ring, a β-lactone a four-membered one, etc.).

1880 *Jrnl. Chem. Soc.* XXXVIII. 378 Pyroterebic acid ..is the internal anhydride of hydroxyisocaproic acid... It is the first representative of its class in the lactic series. For this class of anhydrides the author proposes the name 'lactones'. **1929** *Jrnl. Pharmacol. & Exper. Therap.* XXXVI. 355 The pharmacological study of a series of lactones with a view to their possible usefulness as anthelmintics pointed towards beta angelica lactone and the dilactone of the diacetone diacetic acid as the most promising. **1936** L. J. DESHA *Org. Chem.* xxi. 414 All hydroxy acids lose water when heated..: α-Hydroxy acids yield lactides; β-hydroxy acids are converted into unsaturated acids; γ- and δ-hydroxy acids form lactones. **1971** G. A. TAYLOR *Org. Chem. for Students Biol. & Med.* xiii. 188 α- and β-hydroxy-acids cannot be converted directly into the corresponding α- and β-lactones (three- and four-membered rings).

lactonic (læktǫ·nik), *a. Chem.* [f. LACTO- (in chem. names: see below).] **1.** *lactonic acid*: [tr. G. *lactonsäure* (Hlasiwetz & Habermann 1870, in *Ann. d. Chem. u. Pharm.* CLV. 139), f. *lact-ose* LACTOSE + *-on* -ONE: see -IC.] **a.** = *galactonic acid.*

1871 *Jrnl. Chem. Soc.* XXIV. 547 Lactonic acid, which, according to Fittig's views, must also be monobasic..is found to be really a bibasic acid. **1886** E. F. SMITH tr. *V. von Richter's Chem. Carbon Compounds* 378 Lactonic acid, $C_6H_{10}O_6$, is produced from milk sugar and galactose by the action of bromine water and silver oxide. It is a deliquescent, crystalline mass, melting at 100°.

b. = *lactobionic acid* s.v. *LACTO- 2.

1957 *Chem. Abstr.* LI. Subject Index 1358/1 Lactonic acid, calcium salt, calcium gluconate solubilization with. **1964** N. G. CLARK *Mod. Org. Chem.* xvi. 328 Hydrolysis of lactonic acid yields galactose and gluconic acid.

2. [f. LACTON(E + -IC.] Containing the characteristic ring structure of lactones (sense *2).

1885 *Jrnl. Chem. Soc.* XLVIII. 963 (*heading*) Conversion of lactonic acids into lactones. **1888** *Ibid.* LIV. 251 When the lactonic acids, $CHX\left\langle\begin{matrix}CH(COOH)\\ O\cdot CO\cdot CH_2\end{matrix}\right\rangle$, obtained by the union of aldehydes with succinic acid, are boiled..the greater portion decomposes yielding..the monobasic unsaturated acids..together with the lactones. **1924** *Ibid.* CXXVI. I. 45 When it [*sc. iso*campholactone] is oxidised by means of nitric acid, there are formed nitro-*iso*campholactone and a lactonic acid. **1968** *Jrnl. Agric. & Food Chem.* XVI. 252 (*heading*) Lactonic compounds of apricot. **1970** *Acta Chem. Scand.* XXIV. 3428/1 (*heading*) Investigation of lactonic acids in the latex of *Euphorbium canariensis* L. **1971** *Agric. & Biol. Chem.* (Tokyo) XXXV. 27 (*heading*) Studies on the new seventeen member lactonic antibiotics.

lactonization (læ:ktǒnəizē¹·ʃən). *Chem.* [f. LACTON(E + -IZATION.] Conversion into a lactone.

1909 *Jrnl. Chem. Soc.* XCVI. I. 551 (*heading*) Lactonisation of acid alcohols. **1939** *Jrnl. Amer. Chem. Soc.* LXI. 3198/1 Of the three possible points of lactonization two, C–9 and C–10, should yield secondary hydroxyl groups when the lactone is opened. **1968** R. O. C. NORMAN *Princ. Org. Synthesis* i. 24 Consider the lactonization of ω-hydroxybutyric acid in comparison with the esterification of acetic acid by methanol.

lactonize (læ·ktǒnəiz), *v. Chem.* [f. LACTON(E + -IZE.] *trans.* and *intr.* To change into a lactone. Hence **la·ctonized, -izing** *ppl. adjs.*

1912 *Chem. Abstr.* VI. 1133 The HCl seems to lactonize the Et pyruvate, while on pyruvic acid it acts in 2 ways, either esterifying and then lactonizing, or *vice versa.* **1939** *Jrnl. Amer. Chem. Soc.* LXI. 3198/1 The strong tendency of tetrahydrohydroxyabietic acid..to lactonize further complicated the oxidation experiments. **1939** *Ibid.* 3199/2 A rapid method for hydrolysis of lactonized dihydroabietic acid by caustic fusion has been developed. **1967** *Jrnl. Bacteriol.* XCIV. 1975/1 The mutation affects the activity of the lactonizing enzyme in one of two possible ways.

lad, *sb.*¹ **2. b.** Delete † and add later examples; used esp. in phrs. *a bit of a lad, quite a lad.* Also (*colloq.*), a spirited girl.

1913 [see *BIT *sb.*² 4 c]. **1926** T. E. LAWRENCE *Seven Pillars* (1935) v. lxi. 346 He, Rahail, was quite a lad: a free-built, sturdy fellow, too fleshy for the life we were to lead. **1935** G. INGRAM *Cockney Cavalcade* iv. 54 'That matcher of ours is a lad, Mum!'.. 'Oh, what's she been up to now?' **1935** *Punch* 13 Mar. 294/1 Women..Describe him freely to my face As quite a lad. **1960** 'H. CARMICHAEL' *Seeds of Hate* xiii. 117 Bit of a lad is Mr. Alan Clark..running round fancy-free for years. **1969** A. CADE *Turn up Stone* iii. 76 Oh dear! The late Clive Neilson was certainly a bit of a lad, wasn't he?

c. A stable-groom of any age; also, a female one.

1848 *Sporting Life* 8 Jan. 242/1 The more important a groom is, the more mysterious, conceited, pedantic he is... The first thing a lad does now-a-days is to set up a watch, after which, if his mind incline towards horses, he buys what he calls a 'printed book' about them. **1862** *Once a Week* 1 Nov. 512/1 Judging..from the quarter in which these betting operations were carried on, they were led to think that the lad who attended to the horse Gosport,..conveyed intelligence to his master. **1894** *Strand Mag.* May 554/1 He was a good lad, tinged with the archaic stable-slang of Thessaly. **1968** D. FRANCIS *Forfeit* iv. 49, I..called on the trainer, whom I saw almost every time I went racing... 'Did you find Sandy Willes?.. She's one of my best lads.' **1971** *Daily Tel.* 5 Apr. 11 (*caption*) A celebration snack for Specify, winner of the Grand National... Celebrating with him are Mr John E. Sutcliffe (left), his trainer, Mr Richard Bullen, his 'lad', and Mrs Sutcliffe. **1971** D. FRANCIS *Bonecrack* 17 The elderly lad who looked after him was standing at the door. *Ibid.* 19 There had been quite a stir in Newmarket when my father had promoted her to head lad. **1972** *Guardian* 6 May 11/3 A famous owner..was watching his horse on the gallops... 'Who's that lad on 'im?' he said to the trainer. 'Oh,' came the reply, 'that's Cynthia.' **1973** *Daily Tel.* 30 Oct. 9/2 Lads and girls serving their five-year apprenticeship get pocket money..with clothing and keep paid for by the trainer.

Ladakhi (ladā·ki). Also **Ladaki.** [Native name.] **a.** A native or inhabitant of Ladakh, a district of eastern Kashmir. **b.** The language spoken in Ladakh, a dialect of Tibetan. Also *attrib.* or as *adj.*

1893 E. F. KNIGHT *Where Three Empires Meet* viii. 123 A good-natured Ladaki, with a stolid face like that of a Chinese idol, puckered up into an inscrutable and perpetual smile. **1896** *Geogr. Jrnl.* VII. 476 Our Ladakis informed us that this man's predecessor..was promptly put in jail by the Wazir for having defrauded some Ladakis who had been trading in Tibet. **1899** A. H. FRANCKE *Ladakhi Songs* 1st Ser. 2 The Ladakhi rhyme is, as many examples prove, a rhyme of sentence. *Ibid.* 4 The orthography of the Ladakhi and Purig dialects has always kept as near to that of the book-language as possible. *Ibid.* 5 Silent prefixed letters..are written with the Ladakhi verb. **1911** *Encycl. Brit.* XVI. 59/1 It [*sc.* Ladakh] was, however, conquered and annexed in 1834–1841 by Gulab Singh of Jammu—the unwarlike Ladakhis, even with nature fighting on their side, and against indifferent generalship, being no match for the Dogra troops. **1939** L. PETECH *Study Chron. Ladakh* 6 There is urgent need of collecting and publishing the most important Ladakhi inscriptions. **1959** *News Chron.* 28 Nov. 4/2 He's a Ladakhi, really. An Indian national, like us. He became a Christian.

‖ **ladang** (ladā·ŋ). Also 8 **laddang.** [Malay.] A piece of land under dry cultivation, often a jungle clearing. Also *attrib.*

1783 W. MARSDEN *Hist. Sumatra* 60 *Paddee*, on Sumatra and the Malay islands, is distinguished into two sorts, *Laddang* or up-land paddee, and *Sawoor* or low-land. **1839** T. J. NEWBOLD *Pol. & Statistical Acct. Straits of Malacca* I. iv. 119 A small quantity only is grown on the ladangs, or dry-land plantations. *Ibid.* v. 263 The ladang rice, however, is affirmed by some to be sweeter and whiter, and to keep better than the produce of the sawah. **1906** SKEAT & BLAGDEN *Pagan Races Malay Peninsula* I. i. 119 A blackberry..grows amongst the underwood ('blukar') on the old Sakai clearings ('ladang'). **1935** *Discovery* Sept. 263/1 Nomads of long habit, they [*sc.* the Sakai and the Semang] roam through their territory but no longer from one 'ladang' to another but rather from the borders of kampong to kampong as they lose their..fear of the Malay. **1954** E. D. LABORDE tr. *Robequain's Malaya, Indonesia, Borneo & Philippines* vi. 94 In Indonesia most of the cultivation is done on the *ladang* system. **1958** *Times Lit. Suppl.* 19 Sept. 531/3 Nomads of the deep jungle, they clear and cultivate patches of a few acres, known as *ladangs*..; but in a year or two they move on, clearing new *ladangs* in other parts of the jungle. **1965** C. SHUTTLEWORTH *Malayan Safari* ii. 32 In a number of ladangs..they had planted hill rice.

ladder, *sb.* Add: **1. c.** (Further examples.)

1847 DE SMET *Oregon Missions* 31 It was on this occasion he conceived the idea of the Catholic ladder—'a form of instruction which represents on paper the various truths and mysteries of religion in their chronological order'. **1910** *Daily Chron.* 24 Jan. 8/3 Some kind of ladder of subjects..would be a great gain. **1942** *R.A.F. Jrnl.* 18 Apr. 15 Knowledge that would serve as a ladder to further research. **1951** R. FIRTH *Elem. Social Organiz.* i. 29 Special attention was..given to such important matters as the breadth of the educational ladder. **1974** 'W. HAGGARD' *Kinsmen* x. 98 When he'd made a great fortune Duncan Gregg had gone up the ladder a little. But not very much, he was still in trade.

3. b. In knitted garments or stockings: a longitudinal strip of unravelled fabric, so called from the appearance of the threads.

1838 A. MATHEWS *Mem. Charles Mathews* II. xi. 246 He had been diverted by observing a fracture (or what a sempstress would term a *ladder*) in the back part of His Majesty's black-silk stockings. **1875** [in Dict., sense 3]. **1908** *Daily Chron.* 31 Dec. 4/6 Silk tights are fragile things, sadly given to 'ladders' on the least provocation. **1919** 'C. DANE' *Legend* 128 Someone ought to see that his socks were mended properly, for there was a great ladder down one ankle. **1957** M. SPARK *Comforters* iv. 76 There was a ladder in her stocking. **1973** J. CLEARY *Ransom* vii. 158 Sylvia looked up from examining the ladders in her stockings.

c. *Naval gunnery.* A series of range-finding shots up to or back from the target.

1922 *Grand Fleet Gunnery & Torpedo Memoranda on Naval Actions 1914–18* (Admiralty) vii. 57 The procedure generally found best by the control officers when the shot should have been straddling but nothing could be seen was to ladder down with a 200 ladder till shorts were clearly seen, and then ladder up till shorts were not seen, when the process was repeated... Although this blind ladder is extravagant in ammunition, it appears that no other course is open under similar conditions of visibility.

6. ladder-back (chair), a chair in which the back is formed of horizontal pieces of wood, suggestive of a ladder; **ladder-back(ed) woodpecker** *U.S.*, one of several North American species of woodpecker with black and white, barred markings, esp. *Dendrocopos scalaris*; **ladder fern,** a fern of the genus *Nephrolepis*, which spreads by creeping rhizomes, producing new crowns; **ladder network** *Electr.*, a network having two pairs of terminals and consisting of impedances that are alternately in series and in parallel, so that the circuit diagram has the form of a ladder; **ladder polymer,** a polymer in which pairs of long straight-chain molecules are joined by recurring cross-links; **ladder-proof** *a.*, of fabrics: not liable to ladder; **ladder-stop,** at the top and toe of a stocking, a band of open-work designed to prevent a ladder; **ladder woodpecker** = **ladder-back(ed) woodpecker.*

1908 *Daily Report* 24 Aug. 8/3 Three ladder-back chairs, with cherubs and a crown, brought £46. **1923** *Daily Mail* 11 Jan. 11 Let the table be of the gate-leg variety and the chairs of the style known as ladder-backs. **1966** A. W. LEWIS *Gloss. Woodworking Terms* 51 *Ladder back*, chairs made at the end of the seventeenth century with horizontal slats across the back like a ladder. **1973** J. BURROWS *Like an Evening Gone* i. 14 Greta was sitting on a ladderback chair by the kitchen table. **1884** E. COUES *Key to N. Amer. Birds* (ed. 2) 485 *Picoïdes americanus*.. Ladder-backed Three-toed Woodpecker. **1917** T. G. PEARSON *Birds Amer.* II. 149/1 The Ladder-back Woodpeckers are divisible into three regional varieties, the American, the Alaska.., and the Alpine. **1964** A. WETMORE et al. *Song & Garden Birds N. Amer.* 92/1 Ladder-backed woodpecker. *Dendrocopos scalaris.* Vast stretches of hot, treeless desert seem a curious habitat for a woodpecker. Yet to the ladderback such country is home. **1884** W. MILLER *Dict. Eng. Names Plants* 222/2 *Nephrolepis cordifolia*, Ladder Fern, of New Zealand. **1893** G. SCHNEIDER *Bk. Choice Ferns* II. xliii. 583 Nephrolepis... Ladder Ferns... This genus..belts the world in the Tropics, passing a little beyond them both north and south. **1951** *Dict. Gardening* (R. Hort. Soc.) III. 1365/2 *Nephrolepis*,.. Ladder fern. A genus of about 35 species of handsome ferns, widely dispersed over the tropics. **1969** *Coast to Coast 1967–68* 49 Beyond that was the swamp—tea-trees, paperbarks, huge ladder ferns. **1930** A. C. BARTLETT *Theory Electr. Artificial Lines* iii. 41 The theory of a general ladder network, in which all the elements may have arbitrary values, will first be considered, and..from it will be derived a class of symmetrical ladder artificial lines, of which the T and Π section lines are but simple cases. **1966** H. J. REICH et al. *Theory & Applications Active Devices* xviii. 543 Ladder-network oscillators ..consist of a voltage-inverting amplifier and a ladder-type resistance–capacitance feedback network that usually has three or more similar sections. **1971** *New Scientist* 24 June 761/2 The use of conventional straight-chain polymers seems to be restricted by an upper temperature limit of about 550°C, but the ladder polymers (so-called because of their integral cross-linked structure) offer more exciting possibilities. **1974** *Sci. Amer.* Mar. 66/3 Ladder polymers, or double chains, are found in amphibole minerals, such as one form of asbestos. **1927** *Observer* 3 Apr. 25 Celanese cami-bockers... In Ladder-proof Self Stripe. **1962** *Economist* 2 June 897/1 The new answers to feminine prayer [*sc.* a new type of seamless stockings] are said..to be ladderproof, although not hole-proof. **1931** *Daily Express* 15 Oct. 12/7 (*caption*) Pair of Lady's Artificial Silk Hose with ladder-stop tops. **1962** *Which?* Apr. 114/1 Most of the leading firms sell a style with a band of open-work knitting at the welt, known as a ladder-stop. **1870** *Amer. Naturalist* III. 474 The resident species not found westward [of the Colorado Valley] were the Ladder Woodpecker (*Picus scalaris*), the White-bellied Wren, [etc.].

ladder, *v.* Delete ? *Obs.* and add later examples. Also, to furnish with a fish ladder.

1901 J. BLACK *Illustr. Carpenter & Builder Ser.: Scaffolding* 67 The stack was laddered from the bottom to the top with a series of ladders. **1901** *Chambers's Jrnl.* Sept. 585/2 When Mr. Grant..laddered the Moriston falls.., the Crown claimed and gained the new fishings. **1923** *Daily Mail* 22 June 5 Having just laddered the spire of Truro Cathedral, he found every crevice crammed with jackdaws' nests.

2. *intr.* Of garments, esp. stockings: to develop ladders as the result of the breaking of a thread or threads. Also *trans.* Hence **la·ddering** *vbl. sb.*

1922 *Daily Mail* 14 Nov. 12 (Advt.), Your stockings cannot ladder. Laddering and damage to stockings..are entirely obviated. **1927** W. DEEPING *Doomsday* viii. 78 At the last moment a stocking had 'laddered'. **1963** A. J. HALL *Textile Sci.* iii. 152 The demand for excessive sheerness and transparency in ladies' stockings is the root cause of the tendency to ladder. **1973** 'S. WOODS' *Enter Corpse*

171 Her dress [was] crumpled, and both her stockings were laddered.

3. *Naval gunnery.* To fire shots in a ladder (sense *3 c).

1922 [see *LADDER *sb.* 3 c]. **1959** *Chambers's Encycl.* VI. 662/2 In the case of surface vessels, finding the accurate gun range, which is done by 'laddering' i.e. increasing or decreasing the range of successive salvoes until the target is crossed, is not difficult if the enemy maintains his course and speed.

laddic (læ·dik). *Electronics.* [f. *ladd(er-log)ic.*] A ladder-like device consisting of a rectangular block of a magnetic ferrite containing a line of rectangular apertures, the cross pieces and side pieces being of the same cross-sectional area and having wires passing round them in such a way that the device may be used as a logic element.

1959 GIANOLA & CROWLEY in *Bell Syst. Techn. Jrnl.* XXXVIII. 45 The Laddic is a ladder-like structure cut out of a rectangular hysteresis-loop ferrite. *Ibid.* 46 Any Boolean function can be realized as the output of a single Laddic of suitable length. *Ibid.* 50 The operation of the Laddic as an AND gate. **1963** *Engineering* 25 Jan. 170/3 Logical circuit applications of both toroidal cores and multi-apertured elements—the transfluxor and laddic—are discussed.

laddie. (Examples in wider use.)

1919 WODEHOUSE *Damsel in Distress* xv. 171 'I've got a headache.' 'I thought you would have, laddie, when I saw you getting away with the liquid last night.' **1962** *Coast to Coast 1961–62* 66 'Now get yourself a beer,' he said. 'Pour a couple of beers, laddie.' **1973** J. PORTER *It's Murder with Dover* iii. 22 I've been ready for the last bleeding half-hour, laddie!

la·ddish, *a.* [f. LAD *sb.*[1] + -ISH[1].] Of or pertaining to a lad or lads; like a lad. Also **la·ddishness.**

1841 S. BAMFORD *Passages in Life of Radical* I. xiv. 91 A young officer..very laddish, and with limbs long enough for windmill arms. **1886** *Wesleyan-Methodist Mag.* 63 Want of sympathy with..the laddishness of lads. **1907** *Daily Chron.* 24 Oct. 8/3 Missing the laddish laugh, the boisterous gaiety, which they had known aforetime.

laddo (læ·do). *colloq.* (orig. *Ir.*). Also **lado.** [f. LAD *sb.*[1]] Lad, boy.

1870 [see *BOYO]. **1939** JOYCE *Finnegans Wake* 404 Sure, he's lightseyes, the laddo! **1968** J. WAINWRIGHT *Edge of Extinction* 57 She's..out of range. The laddoes at the Kremlin'll know that. **1970** R. HILL *Clubbable Woman* v. 140 Your intruders'll all turn out to be like that laddo last night. **1973** —— *Ruling Passion* II. vi. 125 You're not seriously suggesting that Lewis wasn't killed by laddo, but by someone else.

la-di-da, *v.* Also **lah-de-dah.** [Cf. the sb.] *intr.* To use affected manners or speech.

1901 *N. & Q.* 6 July 20/2, I like to la-di-da with the ladies. **1930** *John o' London's* 15 Mar. 907/3 There is perhaps too much 'lah-de-dahing about' when royalty is concerned.

Ladik (ladi·k). The name of a village in Turkey, formerly Laodicea, used *attrib.* to describe a type of prayer rug made in the district. Also *ellipt.*

1900 J. K. MUMFORD *Oriental Rugs* x. 155 Ladik rugs resemble..those of Kulah... The Kulah small stripes, however, are not often found in the Ladiks. **1931** A. U. DILLEY *Oriental Rugs & Carpets* vi. 165 Among later weavings Ladik prayer rugs display a versatile art that ranges in architectural pattern from impressive columns to dwarf apexes. **1972** *Country Life* 23 Nov. 1412/2 Antique Turkish Ghiordes and Ladik prayer rugs.

Ladin (lădī·n). [L. *Latīn-us, -um.*] The Rhæto-Romanic dialect spoken in the Engadine in Switzerland, closely related to Romansh.

1877 A. H. KEANE tr. *Hovelacque's Sci. of Lang.* v. 238 Known also as the language of the Grisons, the Rheto-Romance, the Rumonsh, and Rumansh. But it seems best to call it simply *Ladin*, with Ascoli, who has recently devoted an important work to its elucidation. **1879** *Encycl. Brit.* VIII. 213/2 The language [in the Engadine] is a dialect known as 'Ladin'. **1880** *Ibid.* XI. 205/1 The remainder [of the inhabitants of the Grisons] use the Romansch or the Ladin dialect. **1969** *Daily Tel.* 29 Jan. 16/5 The first book to be translated into English from Ladin, one of the Romansh group of languages which is spoken in the canton of Grisons, Switzerland, will be published..tomorrow.

ladino[1] (ladī·no). [Sp.] **1.** A vicious or unmanageable horse, steer, etc.; a stray animal. Also as *adj.*, wild, vicious, cunning.

1863 H. W. BATES *Naturalist on River Amazons* II. iv. 265 The old Indians told us..the turtles were 'ladino' (cunning), and would take no notice of the beating a second day. **1891** *Dialect Notes* I. 191 *Ladino*, in Spanish, learned, knowing Latin; then crafty, cunning. In Texas as a noun, a vicious, unmanageable horse, full of cunning and tricks. **1929** J. F. DOBIE *Vaquero of Brush Country* ii. 14 They were all outlaws, *ladinos*, wild as bucks, cunning and ready to fight anything that got in front of them... Among them were wrinkled-necked maverick cows and bulls that had never had a loop tossed over their heads. **1942** BERREY & VAN DEN BARK *Amer. Thes. Slang* § 916/2 *Ladinos, outlaw cattle*, unbranded strays.

2. In Central America, a mestizo or a white person. Also *attrib.* or as *adj.*

1877 *Encycl. Brit.* VI. 682/2 The inhabitants of Cuba are divided into four classes..; those under servitude, constituting the fourth class, divided into the *bozales*, those recently brought from Africa,—the *ladinos*, those imported before the law of 1821 prohibiting the slave trade,—and the *criollos*, those born on the island. **1902** *Ibid.* XXXII. 395/1 The number of Ladinos (whites and persons of mixed blood) [in Salvador in 1887] was returned at 772,200, and of Indians at 234,648. **1934** A. HUXLEY *Beyond Mexique Bay* 69 Whites and *ladinos* were conspicuously absent from the ranks. *Ibid.*, These Quichés and Cakchiquels from the hills are as foreign in the white and *ladino* capital as Nepalese in the Punjab. *Ibid.* 70 *Ladino* housewives stood bargaining at the stalls. **1959** *Times* 17 Jan. 7/7 The basic division in Chiapas is that between Indian and *ladino*, the *ladino* being a white or a *mestizo*, who follows the customs of the *patrón* and of western civilization. **1973** 'F. CLIFFORD' *Amigo, Amigo* v. 46 She was dressed *ladino* style, blouse and skirt, and was lighter skinned than pure Indian.

3. (Usu. with capital initial.) A language based on Old Spanish and written in modified Hebrew characters, used by some Sephardic Jews, esp. in Mediterranean countries. Also *attrib.* and *Comb.*

1889 in *Cent. Dict.* **1932** C. ROTH *Hist. Marranos* xiii. 324 A few works..were printed..in Ladino (or Spanish in Hebrew characters) in the Levant, at Smyrna or at Salonica. **1948** [see *JUDÆO-]. **1949** *Spectator* 4 Nov. 595/2 A dialect of Hebrew-cum-Spanish called Ladino is still spoken by many Sephardic Jews everywhere; it is common at the Holland Park synagogue in London..whose members mostly come from the Middle East. **1959** *Israel Digest* 23 Jan. 6/3 Another important project..is the preparation of a Ladino dictionary. **1965** *Listener* 30 Sept. 490/2 He records a meeting with three Ladino-speaking Jews in the railway station in Sofia. **1972** O. SELA *Bearer Plot* xvi. 101 Ashraf and I are both Sephardic. We both speak Ladino which is very close to Spanish.

ladino[2] (lădī·no). [It.] In full, *ladino clover.* A large fast-growing variety of white clover (*Trifolium repens*), native to northern Italy and cultivated elsewhere, esp. in the U.S.A., as a fodder crop.

1924 A. G. ERITH *White Clover* xii. 139 In Italy white clover is named Trifoglio ladino or Ladino clover. **1931** *N.Z. Jrnl. Agric.* XLII. 83 In many ways the Italian Ladino type seems to be related to the large-leaved New Zealand Wild White No. 1... The New Zealand form is..altogether the more valuable pasture type. **1937** COX & JACKSON *Crop Managem. & Soil Conservation* xxiv. 385 *Ladino* is a large-growing type of white clover that provides much more pasture per acre and is of value for hay. Ladino is a native of northern Italy and is established in importance in Idaho, Oregon, and Washington and is gaining in importance in New England. **1950** CARROLL & KRIDER *Swine Production* xviii. 367 Ladino clover hay contains 19 per cent protein. **1956** GILLESPIE & HATHAWAY *Textbk. Gen. Agric.* viii. 151 *Ladino* or *Giant White Clover*, also called Lodi, is Italian in origin and has all the appearance of a giant form of the other white clovers... Its demerit is that it is not frost-hardy and so cannot stand British winters. **1969** J. JANICK et al. *Plant Sci.* xix. 381/1 White clover..includes the robust ladino variety from Italy.

ladle, *sb.* Add: **1. b.** In Scottish churches: a similar instrument consisting of a wooden box at the end of a long wooden handle used for taking up the collection and communion tokens.

1813 W. LESLIE *Gen. View Agric. Nairn & Moray* 412 The elders make these collections by going round to each with a ladle or small box with a handle to it, when the public worship is concluded. **1830** *2nd Rep. Evidence Sel. Comm. State of Poor in Ireland* § 3369 in *Parl. Papers* VII. 459 The elders carrying about what they call a ladle. **1871** W. ALEXANDER *Johnny Gibb* xi. 81 The elders seized the ladles..and perambulated the kirk. **1929** *Life & Work* Oct. 232/2 A ladle preserved in the parish church of Foulis Easter. **1960** *Press & Jrnl.* (Aberdeen) 26 Apr., Long may they continue to use the ladle and metal communion tokens.

ladle, *v.* Add: *Fig.* examples with *out.* Also const. *up.*

1851 H. MELVILLE *Moby Dick* III. xlviii. 287 Stubb was lustily singing out for some one to ladle him up. **1872** W. H. G. KINGSTON *On Banks Amazon* iii. 93 Wooden spoons were served to enable us to ladle up the soup. **1913** R. BROOKE *Let.* 8 Sept. (1968) 508 But it's absurd to ladle out indiscriminate praise, as most people do. **1969** *Listener* 27 Feb. 278/2, I..was concerned at the way the present system..ladles out routine scientific and technological qualifications which one in five graduates later find are not useful to them.

ladro·nism. *Hist.* [f. Sp. *ladrón* (see LADRONE), a hostile Filipino, an insurgent + -ISM.] In the Philippine Islands, organized resistance to law or authority among the native population.

1902 *Outlook* (N.Y.) LXXII. 298/1 A local police and an insular constabulary system have been created, and ladronism, or organized robbery and brigandage,..has almost disappeared. **1903** *Daily Chron.* 26 Dec. 5/6 Ladronism had also been successfully treated by the Courts.

lady, *sb.* **4. b.** (*a*) Delete 'now confined to poetic and rhetorical use', and add further examples.

1914 G. B. SHAW *Pygmalion* (1916) I. 107 *The Flower Girl.* Thank you kindly, lady. **1924** I. GERSHWIN (*song title*) Lady, be good. **1953** *Manch. Guardian Weekly* 10 Sept. 7 Why, lady, take route 128. **1972** P. RUELL *Red Christmas* xiv. 148 'Lady,' he said, 'you talk sense. Just remember, it's guns that count.' **1974** M. BABSON *Stalking Lamb* xxiii. 176, I *know* it can, lady. It won't be the first time.

e. *Lady Bountiful* (see BOUNTIFUL *a.* 1); *a lady in the case*, indicating that the key to the problem is a lady (cf. *CHERCHEZ LA FEMME); *the Old Lady* (*in* or) *of Threadneedle Street*, the Bank of England; *the lady of the house*, the mistress of a household; a housewife.

1727 J. GAY *Fables* I. l. 172 And when a lady's in the case, You know, all other things give place. *c* **1793** JANE AUSTEN *Volume Second* in *Minor Works* (1954) 136 We had scarcely paid our Compliments to the Lady of the House. **1797** J. GILLRAY *Caricature* 22 May, Political Ravishment, or The Old Lady of Threadneedle-Street in danger! **1816** JANE AUSTEN *Emma* III. xiv. 254 It was with difficulty that she could summon enough of her usual self to be the attentive lady of the house, or even the attentive daughter. **1820** *Black Dwarf* IV. 36 Van went to wheedle—the street of Threadneedle, To get him, poor dog, a loan;..He ask'd the old lady to cash him a bill. **1821** BYRON *Don Juan* v. xix. 243 'Ay,' quoth his friend, 'I thought it would appear That there had been a lady in the case.' **1850** *Househ. Words* 6 July 337 (*heading*) The Old Lady of Threadneedle Street. **1861** MRS. BEETON *Bk. Househ. Managem.* 9 The more usual plan is for the lady of the house to have the joint brought to her table, and afterwards carried to the nursery. **1863** A. TROLLOPE *Rachel Ray* I. xiii. 260 Luke, is there no young lady in the case? **1884** *Peel City Guardian* No. 26. 2/1 The rest of the 'Old Lady in Threadneedle-street' remained unbroken. **1909** W. S. GILBERT *Fallen Fairies* II. 37 In all the woes that curse our race There is a lady in the case. **1958** R. GENDERS *Pansies, Violas & Violets* x. 100 Those who have retired will be able to give the plants their full attention, whilst those who have to go out to work each day may have to entrust the care of the plants to the lady of the house. **1971** *Guardian* 19 Aug. 9/3 Door-to-door sales people were asked why the opening question is always, 'Is the lady of the house home?' **1974** G. VAIZEY *Tangled Web* ii. 26 He..is highly respected by the Old Lady of Threadneedle Street.

f. *pl.* Designation of a public convenience for females. Freq. *ladies'*, and with capital initial.

1918 'K. MANSFIELD' *Jrnl.* (1954) 140 Also, when she goes to the 'Ladies', for some obscure reason she wears a little shawl. **1936** R. CAMPBELL *Mithraic Emblems* 120 No 'Ladies' here or 'Gentlemens' are seen For most of you to hesitate between. **1938** G. GREENE *Brighton Rock* III. i. 98 The white steps down to the ladies'. **1939** C. MORLEY *Kitty Foyle* 36 How to get undressed in a Pullman berth, how to find the Ladies. **1944** T. RATTIGAN *While Sun Shines* I. 190, I lost the plans of the Station Defence...We found them again all right. I'd only left them in the Ladies. **1965** G. MELLY *Owning-Up* vi. 64 'They're no good,' he'd tell us as two of them swayed past on their way to the ladies. **1974** D. MEIRING *President Plan* vi. 42 Comunicado Number Two..was found, as anonymously advised, in the Ladies' of a San Agustín restaurant.

6. b. *Lady Luck* = FORTUNE *sb.* 1.

1932 M. SHORT (*title*) Lady Luck in 1941. **1936** C. SANDBURG *People, Yes* 165 Yes, get Lady Luck with you and you're made. **1961** T. HENROT *Belgium* 119 A thousand ways of flirting with Lady Luck.

d. *lady wife.* (*Arch.* or *genteel.*)

1840 DICKENS *Lett.* (1969) II. 7, I wish I could send you some autographs..but I find..that my lady wife has been bestowing them upon her friends. **1895** C. M. YONGE *Long Vacation* xxviii. 292 Mr. White, in his joy at possessing his graceful lady wife, had spared no expense. **1969** *Listener* 27 Mar. 417/3 We don't think you've laid enough emphasis on the colonel's foresight, courage, and heroic lady wife. **1971** 'A. GILBERT' *Tenant for Tomb* viii. 142, I don't know how far your lady wife's in your confidence.

e. *Lady Macbeth*, with allusion to the character in Shakespeare's play *Macbeth*: a remorseless or melodramatic woman, usu. leading or assisting a weak man.

1876 TROLLOPE *Prime Minister* I. xi. 169, I feel myself to be a Lady Macbeth, prepared for the murder of any Duncan or any Daubeny who may stand in my lord's way. **1919** KIPLING *Years Between* 92 A boy drowning kittens Winced at the business; whereupon his sister (Lady Macbeth aged seven) thrust 'em under. **1969** M. PUGH *Last Place Left* iv. 26 'I know you're up to something,' Nell repeated. 'You're taking all this far too calmly.' 'All right, Lady Macbeth.' **1974** J. MANN *Sticking Place* x. 153 Hasn't there been enough killing? I am no Lady Macbeth.

13*. *N. Amer.* A female harlequin duck, *Histrionicus histrionicus.* See *lord and lady* (*duck*) (*LORD *sb.* 16).

1792 G. CARTWRIGHT *Jrnl.* I. p. xii, *Lady*, a water-fowl of the duck genus, and the hen of the lord.

14. a. *lady doctor* (earlier and later examples), *friend* (later examples), *novelist.*

1858 *English Woman's Jrnl.* I. 90 As she went through the streets,..rude cries of 'Come on, Bill! let's have a good look at the lady-doctor!' would meet her ears. **1873** C. M. YONGE *Pillars of House* IV. xlii. 219 To be a lady-doctor was surely her vocation! **1879** GEO. ELIOT *Let.* 18 Mar. (1956) VII. 117 This week for the first time I am going to see a lady friend. **1895** HARDY *Jude* v. iii. 343, I couldn't very well tell it to your lady friend. **1912** A. BRAZIL *New Girl at St. Chad's* iv. 69 'We have a lady doc-

tor, you see,' said Ruth, 'and she's so jolly.' **1923** Lady-novelist [see *APOLLINE *a.*]. **1928** R. CAMPBELL *Wayzgoose* ii. 35 And still new-comers to the Wayzgoose throng And lady-novelists a thousand strong. **1931** *Weekend Rev.* 17 Oct. 496/1 The night-watchman, after taunting Larry with his inexperience in affairs of the heart, is obliged to stand by and see the youngster making rapid headway in the affections of his own lady-friend. **1961** *Listener* 30 Mar. 574/3 If 'women novelists' are to become 'lady novelists' as a matter of course, I give notice..that in future, when reviewing the novels of male writers of fiction, I shall make a point of referring to these writers as 'gentlemen novelists'. **1975** C. AIRD *Slight Mourning* vi. 58 The lady doctor had arrived.

15. c. *lady-laden* (earlier example).

1870 TENNYSON *Holy Grail* 54 Where the long Rich galleries, lady-laden, weigh'd the necks Of dragons clinging to the crazy walls.

16. b. lady-of-the-night, an evergreen shrub, *Brunfelsia americana*, native to the West Indies and bearing white and yellow flowers which are particularly fragrant at night; **lady orchid, orchis,** *Orchis purpurea*, a European and Western Asian orchid with white and reddish-purple flowers.

1924 L. H. BAILEY *Man. Cultivated Plants* 667 *B[runfelsia] americana*, L. Lady-of-the-Night. **1959** M. M. KAYE *House of Shade* xiii. 167 Lash..had taken her down into the garden—ostensibly to look at the nocturnal flowering Lady-of-the-Night which grew in profusion in a bed some distance from the house. **1960** *Harper's Bazaar* July 80/2 The scent of frangipane and lady of the night. **1855** A. PRATT *Flowering Plants & Ferns Gt. Brit.* V. 208 Kentish country people call it [sc. *O. fusca*] the Lady Orchis; and..though its form is not very suggestive of its name, yet..there exists some slight similarity in each blossom to a lady attired in wide-spread gown and close bonnet. **1933** M. J. GODFERY *Monogr. & Iconogr. Native Brit. Orchidaceæ* 171 *Orchis purpurea* Huds. Brown-winged Orchid, Maids of Kent, Lady Orchid. **1951** V. S. SUMMERHAYES *Wild Orchids Brit.* xiii. 251 (*heading*) Brown-winged or lady orchid (*Orchis purpurea*). *Ibid.* 252 The lady orchid belongs to the Southern Eurasian Element of the British orchid flora.

17. a. Ladies' Aid (Society), † (*a*) *U.S.* (*Obs.*) during the American Civil War, a women's organization devoted to sending garments, bandages, etc., to the soldiers; (*b*) *N. Amer.*, an organization of women who support the work of a church by fund-raising, arranging social activities, etc.; **ladies' cabin, car, carriage,** on public transport, a compartment, etc., reserved for ladies; **ladies' cloakroom,** a cloakroom or lavatory for ladies; **lady's horse,** a horse trained to carry a lady riding side-saddle; similarly **lady's hunter; ladies' night,** a function at a men's club, etc., to which ladies are invited; **ladies' room** = **ladies' cloakroom*; **lady's waist** *Austral. colloq.*, a small gracefully-shaped glass; a drink served in such a glass.

1866 F. MOORE *Women of War* 214 Mrs. Wittenmeyer, as president of the Ladies' Aid Society of Iowa. **1873** *Sentinel* (Woodstock, Ont.) 5 Dec. 3/1 The Ladies' Aid Society in connection with the Baptist Church in this Town will hold a social this evening. **1893** 'O. THANET' *Stories Western Town* 185 The furnishing of the church.. is in charge of the Ladies' Aid Society. **1895** *Times* (Niagara-on-the-Lake, Ont.) 4 Apr. 1/2 The Social [was] under the auspices of the Ladies Aid of the Methodist Church. **1908** L. M. MONTGOMERY *Anne of Green Gables* xiv. 143 She had taken it off..when returning from the Ladies' Aid. **1913** E. H. PORTER *Pollyanna* iii. 21 Part of the Ladies' Aid wanted to buy me a black dress and hat, but the other part thought the money ought to go toward the red carpet they're trying to get,—for the church, you know. **1964** *Calgary Herald Mag.* 21 Mar. 8/9 The 'Apron Social' and tea given in the basement of the Knox Church last evening under the auspices of the Ladies' Aid Society of the congregation. **1832** E. GROSVENOR *Diary* July in G. Huxley *Lady Elizabeth & Grosvenors* (1965) vi. 124 There were 20 fellow-passengers, so that the Lady's cabin was utterly untenable. **1925** E. H. YOUNG *William* iv. 42 She sat down on a velvet-covered couch in the ladies' cabin. **1842** DICKENS *Amer. Notes* I. iv. 145 There are no first and second class carriages..but there is a gentlemen's car and a ladies' car. **1847** F. A. KEMBLE *Let.* 29 May in *Rec. Later Life* (1882) III. 183 From Liverpool to Crewe I had companions in the ladies' carriage in which I was. **1860** E. HALL *Diary* 30 July in O. A. Sherrard *Two Victorian Girls* (1966) 263, I am thankful today that 'Ladies' carriages have been given up in *our* country! **1922** E. H. YOUNG *Bridge Dividing* III. ix. 289 'I have to catch a train.'.. 'Be careful to get into a ladies' carriage, Henrietta.' **1918** A. BENNETT *Pretty Lady* xxiii. 157 She hurried..to the ladies' cloakroom, got her wraps. **1814** JANE AUSTEN *Mansf. Park* I. iv. 71 Fanny should have a regular lady's horse of her own. **1894** KIPLING *Day's Work* (1898) 46 An absolutely steady lady's horse—proof against steam-rollers, grade-crossings, and street processions. **1938** D. A. HOUBLON *Side-Saddle* vii. 64 In Victorian days and even later a lady's horse to be perfect had always to canter with the off fore leading. **1948** *Horseman's Year* 172 (*heading*) Royal Welsh Agricultural Society show... Hunters... Ladies' Hunters. To be ridden side-saddle. **1955** *Horse & Pony Ann. Illustr. 1954–55* iii. 101 The leading ladies' hunters were Cufflink, Earmark,..Mighty Grand. **1889** G. B. SHAW *London Music 1888–89* (1937) 266 An invitation from the Grosvenor Club to their 'ladies' night' at the Grosvenor Gallery. **1970** K. GILES *Death in Church* i. 18 The atmosphere of a Masonic ladies' night. **1970** G. GREER *Female Eunuch* 142 On ladies' nights..men embrace and fool about. **1880** 'E. LEATHES' *Actor Abroad* xviii. 226 Many of them retire to the ladies' room, and changing their costume for evening dress reappear in the ball-room. **1927** D. L. SAYERS *Unnatural Death* xi. 120 The attendant in the Ladies' Room. **1948** G. VIDAL *City & Pillar* (1949) iii. 64 'I think,' said Emily, when she came back from the ladies' room, 'I think that we should go over to that room on the left and get a drink.' **1971** D. EDEN *Afternoon Walk* ix. 124 I'll go to the ladies' room while you do. **1934** *Bulletin* (Sydney) 4 Apr. 20/1 But a daintier goblet I never fingered than the hourglass shape of a lady's waist. **1963** A. LUBBOCK *Austral. Roundabout* 59 A pony is drunk out of a small glass called a lady's waist.

b. lady's delight (earlier example); **lady's ear-drop,** the common fuchsia.

1843 L. M. CHILD *Lett. from N.Y.* i. 2, I am like the Lady's Delight, ever prone to take root. **1829** A. H. LINCOLN *Familiar Lect. Bot.* xxv. 145 The Ladies'-ear-drop (*Fuschia,*) is a beautiful exotic. It has a funnel-form calyx of a brilliant red colour... This plant is a native of Mexico, except one species brought from the island of New Zealand. Ten species are said by horticulturists to be cultivated. **1882** H. FRIEND *Gloss. Devon. Plant Names* 33 Lady's Eardrops. The common garden Fuchsia. Still employed by the older people, but not so commonly as of yore. **1887** M. E. WILKINS *Humble Romance* 195 He cut lavishly sprays of dioletra, or lady's ear-drop, snowballs, daffodils. **1908** L. M. MONTGOMERY *Anne of Green Gables* i. 1 A little hollow, fringed with alders and ladies' eardrops. **1967** D. G. HESSAYON *Be your own House Plant Expert* (ed. 2) 18/2 Fuchsia (Lady's Eardrops). Spring and summer flowering plant with pendant blooms.

lady-bird. Add: **3.** The pintail duck, *Anas acuta.*

1885 C. SWAINSON *Provincial Names & Folklore Brit. Birds* 155 Pintail (*Dafila acuta*)... Also called Cracker, Winter duck, Lady bird (Dublin Bay). From its grace of form. **1917** T. G. PEARSON *Birds Amer.* I. 128 Pintail. *Dafila acuta*... Winter Duck; Lady-bird; Long-necked Cracker. **1968** C. E. JACKSON *Brit. Names of Birds* 61 Pintail..lady bird Ire[land].

lady-bug. *dial.* and *U.S.* = LADY-BIRD.

1699 *Phil. Trans. R. Soc.* XXI. 50, I have happened upon..three or four sorts of Lady-Bugs. **1787** [see LADY *sb.* 16]. **1844** 'J. SLICK' *High Life N.Y.* II. 30 Like lady bugs round a full blown rose. **1886** *Harper's Mag.* June 45/2 We may discover lady-bugs—small red or yellow and black beetles—among our vines. **1889** M. E. BAMFORD *Up & Down Brooks* 49 Very frequently one will find a lady-bug with the spider. **1910** *N.Y. Even. Post* 4 Apr. (Th.), Los Angeles, April 1.—Millions of ladybugs are receiving free transportation..to the melon fields of the Imperial valley. **1972** SWAN & PAPP *Common Insects N. Amer.* xx. 403 Lady Beetles (Coccinellidae). The common British name for these beetles, 'ladybird', is still used to some extent in America; 'ladybug' is probably the most familiar name.

lady's finger. 2. a. Delete ? *Obs.* and add later examples.

1864 'MARK TWAIN' in Harte & 'Twain' *Sk. Sixties* (1926) 138 'Lady-fingers'..suggestive of..soft dalliance with pastry, ices, and sparkling Moselle. **1906** *Westm. Gaz.* 30 Apr. 10/1 Lady-fingers and ice-cream. *a* **1938** T. WOLFE *Web & Rock* (1939) I. ii. 22 Was..President Taft the easy prey of lady fingers? **1942** C. BARRETT *On Wallaby* iii. 39 'Nana' nibbled at a sponge 'lady's finger'. **1974** H. MCCLOY *Sleepwalker* vi. 108 We adjourned for tea and ladyfingers at quarter of six.

c. (Example of *c.*)

1876 J. BURROUGHS *Winter Sunshine* VII. 154 Others are indeed lady apples..like the egg-drop and lady-finger.

d. = *OKRA.

1905 W. R. BEATTIE in *U.S. Dept. Agric. Farmers' Bull.* no. 232. 12 There are three general types of okra, viz., tall green, dwarf green, and lady finger. **1935** M. MORPHY *Recipes of all Nations* 771 Chicken with 'Ladysfingers'... Put in..a few *bamies*, or 'ladysfingers'. This vegetable.. is a variety of okra, or *gombo* [*sic*], but smaller than the okra of the Southern United States. **1972** Y. LOVELOCK *Vegetable Bk.* 147 Indians call it [*sc.* okra] *bhindi* and, in their restaurants, *ladies' fingers*, although this is a name applied to many other plants, including grapes, bananas and a kidney vetch.

lady's-maid, *v.* [See LADY *sb.* 17.] *trans.* To wait on (one) as a lady's maid. Also **lady's-maiding** *vbl. sb.*

1914 W. DE MORGAN *When Ghost meets Ghost* I. xxxii. 392 Maggie goes with her, to lady's-maid her. **1923** U. L. SILBERRAD *Lett. J. Armiter* v. 115 It prevents her suffering under his lady's maiding.

lady's slipper. 2. (Earlier examples.)

1836 A. H. LINCOLN *Familiar Lect. Bot.* (ed. 5) xv. 101 The Impatiens of the garden is sometimes called Ladies'-slipper, sometimes Balsamine. **1874** B. F. TAYLOR *World on Wheels* II. iv. 220 The lady-slippers dance upon the air, while wild Sweet Williams stand admiring by.

Lætare (lītēᵊ·rī, ləitā·rī). [L., imper. sing. of *lætārī* to rejoice: see quot. 1921.] *attrib.* (with *Sunday*) or *ellipt.* Mid-Lent Sunday.

1870 BREWER *Dict. Phr. & Fable* 491/1 *Lætare Sunday.* The fourth Sunday in Lent is so called from the first word of the Introit. **1886** E. L. DORSEY *Midshipman Bob* 6 We would notify the Catholic neighbours the day before 'Lætare-Sunday' (as we called our Mass-day). **1921** *Spectator* 19 Feb. 243/2 The Fourth Sunday of Lent or Mothering Sunday, called 'Laetare' from the opening word of the Introit. **1951** R. KNOX *Stimuli* III. vi. 100 The Church gives us Laetare Sunday in the middle of Lent. **1974** *Oxf. Dict. Chr. Ch.* (ed. 2) 792/2 Laetare Sunday..is also known as Mothering Sunday and Refreshment Sunday.

lævodopa, var. *LEVODOPA.

lævulosan, levulosan (lī·viŭlŏsæn). *Chem.* Also **-ane** (see next). [ad. F. *lévulosane* (A. Gélis 1860, in *Compt. Rend.* LI. 333), f. *lévulose* LÆVULOSE, LEVULOSE.] **a.** An anhydride, $C_6H_{10}O_5$, of lævulose. ? *Obs.*

1862 H. WATTS tr. *Gmelin's Hand-bk. Chem.* XV. 338 Cane-sugar quickly heated to 160°, and kept in the melted state at that temperature for a moderate time, is converted into..lævulosan and dextro-glucose. **1887** *Encycl. Brit.* XXII. 624/1 It [*sc.* lævulose] fuses at 95° C.; at 170° it passes into lævulosan, $C_6H_{10}O_5$, analogous to glucosan.

b. Any polysaccharide composed chiefly of lævulose residues. Cf. *LEVAN.

1913 *Chem. Abstr.* VII. 3511 (*heading*) Hydrolysis of levulosans and application to vegetable analysis. **1931** [see *FRUCTOSAN]. **1966** NOWAKOWSKI & CLARKE tr. *Kretovich's Princ. Plant Biochem.* ix. 295 Higher plants also contain enzymes which catalyse the conversion of sucrose into a variety of polyglucosides and polyfructosides. In some plants (members of the Gramineae and Liliaceae) levulosans..function as transport carbohydrates.

lævulosane (in Dict. s.v. LÆVULOSE, LEVULOSE). For '(see quot.)' substitute: obs. var. *LÆVULOSAN, LEVULOSAN a.

lævulose, levulose. For 'fruit-sugar' substitute: The naturally occurring (lævorotatory) form of fructose, D(−)-fructose. Add further examples.

Lævulose is not a form of glucose as the latter word is now used.

1902 *Encycl. Brit.* XXII. 721/1 Glucose and fructose (lævulose)—the two isomeric hexases of the formula $C_6H_{12}O_6$ which are formed on hydrolysing cane sugar. **1948** W. PIGMAN *Chem. Carbohydrates* xv. 605 Hydrolysis of inulin by enzymes leads to a practically quantitative yield of levulose (D-fructose). **1974** *Nature* 10 May 194/3 Although it is true that some bacteriologists are extremely conservative in the names they use for carbohydrates, surely nobody now uses 'levulose'..in preference to 'fructose' these days.

Lafite (lafī·t). Also (now considered erron.) **Lafitte.** [Fr., place-name.] Used as the designation of the claret produced and bottled at Château Lafite, in the Médoc district of the Gironde, France.

1707 [see CLARET *sb.*² (*a.*) 1 b]. **1792** [see *HAUT-BRION]. *a* **1845** BARHAM *Ingol. Leg.* (1847) 3rd Ser. 186 Chambertin, Chateau Margaux, La Rose, and Lafitte. **1871** M. COLLINS *Marquis & Merchant* II. viii. 237 We'll have some Lafitte. **1888** *Athenæum* 21 Apr. 499/1 Your noble magnum of *Lafitte* E'en Rothschild would have deem'd a treat. **1920** G. SAINTSBURY *Notes on Cellar-Bk.* iv. 48 A '71 Lafite which hailed from Pall Mall. **1931** S. JAMESON *Richer Dust* iv. 77 His glass about to be filled for the third time with an excellent Lafitte. **1963** A. L. SIMON *Guide Good Food & Wines* 732/1 The spelling of *Lafite* with two *f's* and two *t's* instead of one occurs in old records and even on old labels, but all forms are now obsolete other than *Lafite*. There are other Châteaux in the Gironde, however, bearing the same name with different spelling. **1973** *Country Life* 19 Apr. 1052/2 Similar bottles of '66 of Lafite and Latour brought £360 and £300 respectively.

La France (la frañs). [Fr.] An early type of hybrid tea rose, introduced in 1867, and bearing large, pink, scented flowers. Also *attrib.*

1868 *Floral Mag.* VII. 399 La France has evidently a mixture of Tea and Bourbon blood in it. **1906** *Westm. Gaz.* 11 Aug. 2/3 Roses red, roses yellow, roses white, roses of all known shades and varieties—fragrant La Frances, flaunting Jacqueminots, stately American Beauties. **1928** [see *GLOIRE DE DIJON]. **1937** F. B. YOUNG *Portrait of Village* vi. 119 Its flowers are all old-fashioned and mostly sweet-scented:..moss-roses and silvery-pink *La France*. **1952** 'M. COST' *Hour Awaits* 78 Fanchon, lovely as a La France rose, but English as Mayfair, was also leaning from her window. **1969** V. C. CLINTON-BADDELEY *Only Matter of Time* 48 He wished so many of the old roses had not disappeared. When did you last see La France? **1973** [see *HYBRID B. 1 b].

lag, *sb.*¹ Add: **4. b.** (Further examples.) More widely in general use: a period of time separating any phenomenon or event from an earlier one to which it is related (causally or in some other way); = *time-lag* (TIME *sb.* 52); *angle of lag* (Electr.), the fraction of a complete cycle, multiplied by 360° or 2π radians, by which a sinusoidal current lags behind the associated sinusoidal voltage. See also *jet lag* (*JET *sb.*³ 11).

1886 S. P. THOMPSON *Dynamo-Electr. Machinery* (ed. 2) xviii. 330, φ is called the retardation or angle of lag. *Ibid.* 331 The retardation will increase with increased speed... There will be less lag therefore if the machine is so designed that it can be driven at a slow speed. **1902** *Encycl. Brit.* XXVIII. 42/1 [His] method consisted in measuring the interval which elapses between the application of a potential difference..and the passage of the spark. This lag of the spark, as we may call it, is a very important quantity. **1909** *Jrnl. Hygiene* IX. 240 He found that there is an initial period after inoculation during which growth is almost absent: the length of time of this 'lag' varies with the age of the culture used for inoculation and with the species of the bacillus. **1923** *Glasgow Herald*

2 Nov. 12/4 The operation of the 'lag' of two months between the period of ascertainment and the months when the wages based on such ascertainment are paid. **1934** L. T. AGGER *Alternating Currents* iii. 38 The current goes through all the events in its cycle one-quarter of a period, or 90°, later than the P.D. For this reason it is said to lag behind the P.D. by 90°; or, expressed in another way, the angle of lag of the current is 90°. **1934** Cultural lag [see *CULTURAL *a.* 3]. **1940** *Economist* 7 Dec. 707/1 It must not be forgotten that a very considerable lag must occur between the dates when insured losses are incurred and compensation is paid. In the case of certain shipping losses,..this lag may extend for the duration of the war. **1962** J. THEWLIS et al. *Encycl. Dict. Physics* VII. 190/1 Lag in a control system may be defined briefly as delayed response of the output to changes of input. **1966** *McGraw-Hill Encycl. Sci. & Technol.* VII. 153/2 No instrument responds instantaneously to a change in the measurand; the lag is dependent on the natural frequency of the instrument system and its degree of damping.

c. *Comb.* **lag fault** *Geol.*, a type of overthrust formed when the uppermost of a series of rocks moves more slowly than the lower ones; **lag phase** *Biol.*, the period elapsing between the introduction of an inoculum of bacteria into a culture medium (or other new environment) and the commencement of its exponential growth; **lag time**, the period of time elapsing between one event and a later, related, event, esp. between a cause and its effect; (the extent of) a lag.

1900 J. E. MARR in *Proc. Geologists' Assoc.* XVI. 461 These fissures..would have an outcrop similar to those of thrust-planes or over-faults which approached the horizontal; but they would differ from these, inasmuch as no inversion on a large scale would accompany them. We shall speak of them here as 'lag' faults. **1947** *Q. Jrnl. Geol. Soc.* CIII. 100 There are several lag-faults in the district, but..only in the case of the Tirbach lag-faults is the evidence considered to be conclusive. **1963** E. S. HILLS *Elem. Struct. Geol.* vii. 191 Lag faults.—These are low angle faults with normal fault displacement, that originate from the upward movement of the footwall block in a region of general thrusting. The hanging-wall block appears to have lagged behind in the regional movements. **1914** *Jrnl. Hygiene* XIV. 260 A seeding taken during the lag-phase grows with diminished lag. **1944** L. E. H. WHITBY *Med. Bacteriol.* (ed. 4) i. 6 Multiplication [of bacteria] passes through four phases: (1) Lag phase—lasting from half an hour to eight hours, during which time there is no increase in numbers..; during this time the organism adjusts itself to its new environment. **1972** *Biochim. & Biophys. Acta* CCLXX. 41 When *E. coli* cells are exposed to low temperatures, they enter a prolonged lag phase. **1956** *Nature* 24 Mar. 579/1 Fragments of chorioallantoic membrane..support the growth of hæmagglutinating particles, but there is a lag-time of about ten hours. **1962** F. I. ORDWAY et al. *Basic Astronautics* xiii. 530 (*table*) Equipment lagtime before response. **1972** *Times* 26 June 12/4 The typical lag times for technological and cultural change. **1973** *Nature* 7 Dec. 327/1 The lag time of four years has been reduced to two at the behest of the governing council.

lag, *v.*[2] Add: **4.** *trans.* To lag behind.

1930 M. G. MALTI *Electr. Circuit Analysis* iii. 26 A curve lags the origin if its zero value..occurs after the point $x = 0$. **1966** L. A. MANNING *Electr. Circuits* iv. 56 The current function lags the voltage by 90 degrees; that is, the current rises to a maximum value a quarter of a cycle later than does the voltage. **1973** *Nature* 21/28 Dec. 444/1 After the time step, Atomic Time will lag UT by 0·7 s.

lager (lā·gəɹ), *v.* [ad. G. *lagern* to store.] To store (beer) (see quots.). Hence **la·gering** *vbl. sb.*

1946 A. SIMON *Conc. Encycl. Gastron.* VIII. 98/2 *Lager beer*, a light type of beer which is brewed from malt, with hops and water, fermented, and then stored (*lagered*). **1962** *Economist* 10 Feb. 543/1 A continuous fermentation process can eliminate the 'lagering' time. **1965** O. A. MENDELSOHN *Dict. Drink* 193 *Lagering*, the almost obsolete process of aging beer by holding it in large tanks, where it clarifies naturally.

lagetta. (Later example.)

1871 C. KINGSLEY *At Last* II. xiii. 196 A bit of veritable natural lace, similar to..the famous lace-bark of the Lagetta-tree.

‖ **lagg** (læg). [a. Sw. dial. *lagg* edge of a bog or marshland, bank of a stream or river (see LAG *sb.*[2]).] A natural ditch along the edge of a raised bog.

1939 A. G. TANSLEY *Brit. Islands & their Vegetation* xxxiv. 675 The marginal watercourses from the *lagg* (a Swedish term) of raised bog. **1968** R. F. DAUBENMIRE *Plant Communities* iii. 149 Raised bog..is a type confined to the area of a wet basin... The surface becomes convex so that the feeble drainage channels (*lagg*) that run across the basin are pushed to one or both sides of the peat dome.

lagniappe (lanyæ·p). *U.S.* Also **lagnappe, lanyap, -yappe.** [Louisiana Fr., ad. Sp. *la ñapa*, in the same sense.] Something given over and above what is purchased, earned, etc., to make good measure or by way of gratuity.

1849 *Knickerbocker* XXXIV. 407/1 Ime sum pumkins in that line; but he's a huckleberry above my persimmon, and right smart lanyope too, as them creole darkies say. **1883** 'MARK TWAIN' *Life on Mississippi* xliv. 402 We picked up one excellent word—a word worth travelling to New Orleans to get; a nice limber, expressive, handy word—'lagniappe'. They pronounce it lanny-*yap*. It is Spanish—so they said. **1884** G. W. CABLE *Creoles of Louisiana* xvi. (1885) 114 The pleasant institution of *ñapa*—the petty gratuity added, by the retailer, to anything bought—grew the pleasanter, drawn out into Gallicized *lagnappe*. **1936** W. FAULKNER *Absalom, Absalom!* viii. 338 As lagniappe to the revenge as it were. **1947** S. J. PERELMAN *Westward Ha!* (1949) vii. 84 Since the ship was calling there anyway, the trip would be pure lagniappe, an extra dash of stardust unforeseen in our program. **1958** M. MAYER *Madison Ave.* xiv. 217 Finally, as lagniappe, Nielsen told the company the extent of 'dealer push'. **1966** *New Yorker* 1 Oct. 186 This amusing architectural lagniappe. **1971** *N.Y. Times Bk. Rev.* 7/4 And, as lagniappe, they threw in a list of 'spurious words' the scholars had come upon in dictionaries. **1972** *New Yorker* 7 Oct. 15/2 (Advt.), 64 pieces of exquisite Limoges porcelain sculpture..with superb porcelain tiles to play on as lagniappe.

lagoon[1]. Add: **1.** After 'sand-banks' insert 'or a similar barrier'. (Further examples.)

1877 A. GEIKIE *Elem. Lessons Physical Geogr.* iv. 271 Lagoons along the sea-margin are for the most part shallow and narrow, running parallel with the coast, from which they are separated by a strip of low land formed of sand, gravel, or other loose material. **1939** W. H. TWENHOFEL *Princ. Sedimentation* xii. 455 The barrier separating a lagoon from its parent body may result from many causes, but under most conditions it is thrown up by the waves. **1952** W. SHEPHERD *Living Landscape Brit.* iii. 50 Two bays have been cut off from the sea by shingle. These now form a salt-water lagoon, and may slowly silt up to form a marsh. *Ibid.* 53 A line of rocks across the bay encloses a 'lagoon'. **1968** R. W. FAIRBRIDGE *Encycl. Geomorphol.* 590/2 The entrance of a lagoon is restricted by the narrow tidal inlets through the barrier islands and the complex of sand bars which form on both the lagoonal and seaward side of the inlet.

2. (Further examples.) Also, the stretch of water inside a barrier reef.

1848 M. SOMERVILLE *Physical Geogr.* I. xiv. 215 Encircling reefs differ in no respect from atoll reefs except that they have one or more islands in their lagoon. **1863** J. B. JUKES *School Man. Geol.* vi. 67 There are..many islands in tropical seas in front of which coral reefs are found at a distance of many miles from the beach of the dry land, their outer edge being nearly dry at low tide, but plunging steeply down into fathomless water, while a broad navigable channel or lagoon..extends between this outer edge and the shore. These are called Barrier reefs. **1928** W. M. DAVIS *Coral Reef Probl.* xi. 271, I made a circuit of the island on trading steamers, following the lagoon for the greater part of the way. **1959** *Chambers's Encycl.* IV. 121/1 Barrier reefs surround islands or lie off the mainland, with an intervening navigable channel or lagoon, the width of which may be many miles.

2*. *Austral.* and *N.Z.* (See quots. 1849 and 1933.)

Adopted from Amer. Eng.: 1766—examples in *D.A.E.* in sense 'a shallow, fresh-water pond or lake, sometimes artificially formed and usually located near or connected with a lake, river, etc.'

1838 W. C. SYMONDS in *Jrnl. R. Geogr. Soc.* VIII. 422 On the S.E. coast at this island [*sc.* South Island] are several immense lagoons, into which flow rivers. **1844** *Nelson* (N.Z.) *Examiner* 7 Sept. 108/1 A lagoon..quite a lake in fact. **1849** F. WAKEFIELD *Colonial Surveying* II. 59 Lagoons differ from lakes in being generally formed by surface water gathering in low grounds during the winter, from which there is no outlet. **1927** M. M. BENNETT *Christison* iii. 37 At the back was a shallow lagoon. **1933** *Press* (Christchurch, N.Z.) 4 Nov. 15/7 *Lagoon*, any tarn, pond, or open water too small to be called a lake.

2.** An artificial shallow pool used in the treatment and concentration of sewage and slurry.

1909 E. C. S. MOORE *Sanitary Engin.* (ed. 3) II. xviii. 691 Drying in lagoons is the system which is often adopted at works where sufficient land is available, and it is without doubt the least satisfactory method. **1926** G. M. FLOOD *Sewage Treatment & Disposal* x. 106 The sludge produced by any method of treatment may be pumped into lagoons in almost every case. **1975** *Daily Tel.* 9 Jan. 16/6 Sometimes 7,000 or 8,000 wading birds came..to the ash lagoons of West Thurrock power station.

lagoon (lăgū·n), *v.* [f. the sb.] *trans.* To treat (by oxidation) in lagoons. So **lagoo·ning** *vbl. sb.*

1911 G. B. KERSHAW *Mod. Methods Sewage Purification* xi. 155 (*heading*) Lagooning. **1922** H. E. BABBITT *Sewerage & Sewage Treatment* xx. 495 The results of lagooning at Philadelphia are given in Table 103. **1935** METCALF & EDDY *Amer. Sewerage Pract.* (ed. 3) III. ii. 23 Odors from sludge lagooned at Houston were so objectionable that another method of sludge disposal was required. **1969** J. G. BRENNAN et al. *Food Engineering Operations* xvii. 380 Lagooning is extensively used for the treatment of cannery wastes. **1972** J. SKITT *Disposal of Refuse & Other Wastes* iii. 36 Do not lagoon the top layer.

lagoonal (lăgū·năl), *a.* [f. LAGOON[1] + -AL.] Of or characteristic of a lagoon or lagoons.

1910 *Encycl. Brit.* IX. 663/2 Of the Gasteropod genera *Cerithium* with its estuarine and lagoonal forms *Potamides, Potamidopsis*, &c., is very characteristic. **1950** *New Biol.* VIII. 92 The earliest known birds were quite small, about the size of a crow, and are known from only two specimens..; even these were preserved in an unique lagoonal environment. **1956** *Nature* 31 Mar. 607/2 The coral reef was not bottomed, the strata penetrated consisting entirely of fine detrital limestones..originally deposited in lagoonal waters not less than 30 fathoms in depth. **1963** D. W. & E. E. HUMPHRIES tr. *Termier's Erosion & Sedimentation* ix. 192 The marine and lagoonal faunas of the Cretaceous in the Gulf of Guinea. **1971** I. G. GASS et al. *Understanding Earth* xii. 158/2 The reefs and lagoonal sediments which flourished during the Mesozoic and Tertiary periods. *Ibid.* 159/1 For the past 50 million years reefs have been very efficient structures leading to the formation of vast lagoonal areas.

Lagrange (lăgrā·ṅʒ). The name of Joseph Louis *Lagrange* (1736–1813), Italian-born mathematician who worked in Prussia and France, used *attrib.* and in the possessive to designate various concepts introduced by him or arising out of his work, as **Lagrange('s) equation**, each of a set of equations of motion in classical dynamics relating the total kinetic energy T of a system to a set of generalized co-ordinates q_r and forces Q_r, and to the time t, and having the form $d(\partial T/\partial \dot{q}_r)/dt - \partial T/\partial q_r = Q_r$. (In many contexts interchangeable with *Lagrangian.*)

1858 *Rep. Brit. Assoc. Adv. Sci. 1857* I. 12 The force function U is independent of the differential coefficients η',..and, consequently, of the variables ω,.., hence, writing H = T − U, the equations take the form $d\eta/dt = d\mathrm{H}/d\omega$, $d\omega/dt = -d\mathrm{H}/d\eta$,..which correspond to the condensed form obtained by writing T − V = R in Lagrange's equations. **1902** *Encycl. Brit.* XXVII. 568/1 Hence the typical Lagrange's equation may be now written in the form $d(\partial\mathrm{T}/\partial\dot{q}_r)/dt - \partial\mathrm{T}/\partial q_r = -\partial\mathrm{V}/\partial q_r$, or, again, $\dot{p}_r = -\partial(\mathrm{V}-\mathrm{T})/\partial q_r$. *Ibid.*, A classical example of the application of Lagrange's equations is to the motion of a top. **1942** SYNGE & GRIFFITH *Princ. Mech.* xv. 453 Two features of Lagrange's equations should be emphasized. First, there is no unique set of generalized coordinates; however we choose them, the equations of motion always have the form (15.215). Secondly, since only working forces contribute to δW, reactions of constraint are automatically eliminated. [*Note*] Except where forces of friction do work. **1958** CONDON & ODISHAW *Handbk. Physics* v. ii. 18/1 If the total number of systems is N, $\Sigma n_j = N$ $\Sigma n_j E_j = E$... Using the method of Lagrange multipliers, introduce multipliers β and λ and find the set of n_j's which make $\delta[\log P - \lambda(N - \Sigma n_j) + \beta(E - \Sigma n_j E_j)] = 0$. **1962** J. RIORDAN *Stochastic Service Syst.* iv. 66, $g(y)e^{-g(y)} = y$. The solution of this, obtained by Lagrange expansion, is $g(y) = \sum_{n=1} (n^{n-1}y^n)/n!$ **1967** M. G. SMITH *Introd. Theory Partial Differential Equations* i. 3 Comparing (1.2.8) and (1.2.9) we have the Lagrange equations $\dot{p}_k = \partial L/\partial q_k$ and $p_k = \partial L/\partial \dot{q}_k$.

Lagrangian (lăgrā·ṅʒiăn), *a.* and *sb. Math.* Also **lagrangian, Lagrangean.** [f. prec. + -IAN, -AN.] **A.** *adj.* Of or pertaining to the work of J. L. Lagrange (see prec.); of the kind introduced by Lagrange or associated with his work; *spec.* applied to (*a*) **Lagrange('s) equation*; (*b*) the difference between the kinetic energy and the potential energy of a system expressed as a function of generalized co-ordinates, their time derivatives, and time. (In many contexts interchangeable with *Lagrange('s)*.)

1858 A. CAYLEY in *Rep. Brit. Assoc. Adv. Sci. 1857* I. 2 The above-mentioned form is *par excellence* the Lagrangian form of the equations of motion, and the one which has given rise to almost all the ulterior developments of the theory. *Ibid.* 15 When there is no force function..the forms corresponding to the untransformed forms in T and U are as follows, viz. the Lagrangian form is $dq/dt = q'$, $d(d\mathrm{T}/dq')/dt - d\mathrm{T}/dq = \mathrm{Q}$, and the Hamiltonian form is $dq/dt = d\mathrm{T}/dp$, $dp/dt = -d\mathrm{T}/dq + \mathrm{Q}$. **1870** *Rep. Brit. Assoc. Adv. Sci. 1869* II. 10 Equations of motion in the Lagrangean form. **1882** Lagrangian method [see EULERIAN *a.*]. **1904** E. T. WHITTAKER *Treat. Analytical Dynamics* ii. 38 If we introduce a new function L of the variables $q_1, q_2, \ldots q_n, \dot{q}_1, \ldots \dot{q}_n, t$, defined by the equation $L = T - V$, then Lagrange's equations can be written $d(\partial L/\partial \dot{q}_{ir})/dt - \partial L/\partial q_r = 0$ ($r = 1, 2, \ldots n$). The function L is called the Kinetic Potential, or Lagrangian function; this single function completely specifies, so far as dynamical investigations are concerned, a holonomic system for which the forces are conservative. **1908** J. H. JEANS *Math. Theory Electr. & Magn.* xvi. 484 The Lagrangian equation corresponding to the coordinate r is found to be..$d(\partial T/\partial \dot{r})/dt - \partial(T - w)/\partial r = R$. *Ibid.* 486 Let Q be the charge on the positive plate at any instant, and let this be taken as a Lagrangian coordinate. **1949** *Math. Tables & Other Aids to Computation* III. 466 Tables of 4-point and 6-point Lagrangean interpolation coefficients. **1954** D. TER HAAR *Elem. Statistical Mech.* 445 The values of the x_i for which f is [an] extremum while equations (MA4.01) are satisfied can be determined from the equations

$$\frac{\partial f}{\partial x_i} + \sum_{j=1}^{p} \lambda_i \frac{\partial g_j}{\partial x_i} = 0, \qquad i = 1, \ldots, n.$$

The x_i are now functions of the λ_j, but these quantities, which are called the undetermined multipliers or the Lagrangian multipliers, can be eliminated by substituting for the x_i into equations (MA4.01) and solving for the λ_j. **1957** L. FOX *Numerical Solution Two-Point Boundary Probl.* ii. 31 Lagrangian [interpolation] formulae..may be defined as formulae in which all significant differences have been replaced by pivotal values. **1964** *Oceanogr. & Marine Biol.* II. 14 The velocity along a particular trajectory varied more slowly than one would expect from the variability between one trajectory and another, suggesting that the Lagrangian scale of motion was noticeably larger than the Eulerian scale.

B. *sb.* The Lagrangian function (see (*b*) above).

1938 R. C. TOLMAN *Princ. Statistical Mech.* ii. 22 For more complicated mechanical systems, or even non-mechanical ones, suitable choices of the Lagrangian may be possible which will make Hamilton's principle still applicable. **1961** J. THEWLIS et al. *Encycl. Dict. Physics* II. 99/2 This function, called the Lagrangian of the given mechanical system, contains everything for the unique determination of the motion of the system, provided that we know its initial position and velocity. **1964** E. A. POWER *Introd. Quantum Electrodynamics* ix. 129 Then for the interaction with the electromagnetic field the substitution $\mathbf{p} \rightarrow \mathbf{p} - (e/c)\mathbf{A}$, $i\hbar\partial/\partial t \rightarrow i\hbar\partial/\partial t - e\phi$ is made in the Lagrangian of the free electron according to the principle of minimal electromagnetic coupling. **1973** *Physics Bull.* Mar. 183/3 Nonlinear lagrangians.

lagting (la·gtiŋ). Also **lagthing.** [Norw. Cf. LAWTING.] **1.** A functional division of the Norwegian Parliament, operating primarily for law-making purposes.

1836 S. LAING *Jrnl. Residence Norway* xi. 456 The Storthing then proceeds to elect what is equivalent to our House of Peers, the Lagthing, or division in which the deliberative functions of the legislative body are invested. *Ibid.*, The functions of the Lagthing are not exactly the same as those of our House of Lords... It can only receive bills from the other house, the Odelsthing; deliberate.. and approve or reject. **1927** *Glasgow Herald* 21 Mar. 13 The Bill is now going up to the Lagting. **1957** *Encycl. Brit.* XVI. 556/1 After the opening, parliament divides itself into two sections, the *lagting* consisting of 38 members and the *odelsting* of the remainder. **1974** *Whitaker's Almanack 1975* 918/1 The *Storting* (Parliament) itself elects one-quarter of its members to constitute the *Lagting* (Upper Chamber).

2. Also **Løgting.** [Faroese *Løgting.*] The Provincial Parliament of the Faeröe Isles.

1948 K. WILLIAMSON *Atlantic Islands* iv. 104 The Løgting imposes a small money tax on every whale.. caught. **1961** *Denmark* (Danish Ministry for Foreign Affairs) 136 Under the Home Rule Act of March 27, 1948, the publicly elected Faroese assembly, the Lagting or Løgting, has legislative powers in various fields. **1972** J. F. WEST *Faroe* x. 199 The members of the government may address the Løgting, but they may not vote unless they are elected members.

lahar (lā·hāɹ). [Javanese.] A mud-flow of volcanic ash mixed with water.

1929 *Geol. Mag.* LXVI. 433 (*heading*) The mudstreams ('lahars') of Gunong Keloet in Java. **1944** C. A. COTTON *Volcanoes* xiii. 247 Lahars follow mainly channels already existing, filling them temporarily to the brim with rushing torrents but leaving them empty again and eventually depositing their loads of debris on low ground many miles beyond. **1954** W. D. THORNBURY *Princ. Geomorphol.* xix. 497 A lahar that accompanied an eruption of the volcano Galunggung, in Java, in 1822, spread over 114 villages. **1972** *Science* 9 June 1119/1 The site of the eastern spillway is now covered by lahar deposits.

Hence **laharic** (lāhā·rik) *a.*, of or pertaining to a lahar.

1968 *Mem. Geol. Soc. Amer.* CXVI. 472 Approximately 300 cubic miles of laharic debris came from the source areas.

Lahnda (lā·ndă). Also **Lahndi.** [Punjabi, 'western' (see quot. 1907).] An Indo-Aryan language spoken in the western Punjab. Also *attrib.* or as *adj.*

1903 RISLEY & GAIT *Rep. Census India 1901* I. 311 Lahndā is a language the existence of which has long been recognized, but under many names. In the last Census Report it was called Jatkī... I therefore think it best to give it the name which is indicated by the natives of the Punjab themselves, i.e. Lahndā or the Language of the West (Panjabi *Lahndē-di Bōli*). **1907** G. A. GRIERSON in *Imperial Gazetteer India* I. vii. 371 Lahndā or Western Panjābī is a language which appears under many names, such as Pothwārī, Chibhālī, Jatkī, Mūltānī, or Hindko... Lahndā, i.e. 'Western', has been lately suggested, and has been tentatively adopted, although it..is far from satisfactory. **1911** *Encycl. Brit.* XVI. 80/2 *Lahnda* (properly *Lahndā* or *Lahindā*, western, or *Lahndē-dī bōlī*, the language of the West), an Indo-Aryan language spoken in the western Punjab... Lahnda is also known as Western Panjabi and as Jatki, or the language of the Jats, who form the bulk of the population whose mother-tongue it is. **1948** D. DIRINGER *Alphabet* vi. 376 Kashtawari, which is a dialect of Kashmiri.., but is much influenced by the Pahari and Lahnda languages, spoken by its southern and south-eastern neighbours. **1967** D. S. PARLETT *Short Dict. Lang.* 76 *Lahnda*... Closely related to Punjabi proper, with some features associated with the contiguous Dardic dialects.

lai[1] (lē̆i). [OFr. (see LAY *sb.*[4]).] **a.** One of a number of short narrative poems written either in French or in English in England between the twelfth and the fifteenth centuries, of a Celtic type and concerned with love, magic, and music. Often called *Breton lais.* **b.** A medieval French lyric associated with the *trouvères* of Northern France.

1774 T. WARTON *Hist. Eng. Poetry* I. Diss. I. sig. a2 At the conclusion of most of the tales it is said that these Lais were made by the poets of Bretaigne. **1824** R. PRICE in T. Warton *Hist. Eng. Poetry* II. 430 But Marie's was not the only Collection of British Lais, in French. **1838** E. GUEST *Hist. Eng. Rhythms* II. 103 The 'short measures' of Skelton..may perhaps be looked upon as the *direct* descendants of the Anglo-Saxon rhythms, though it must be confessed they much resemble, in their flow, the *lais* and *virelais* of the fifteenth century. **1855** H. H. MILMAN *Hist. Latin Christianity* VI. vii. 547 Slighter pieces which may call to mind the Lais and Serventes of the South. **1865** T. TAYLOR tr. *Hersart de la Villemarqué's Ballads & Songs of Brittany* 125 A *lai* by a northern *trouvère* on the same subject was discovered by M. de Fréminville, in the Bibliothèque du Roi. **1883** H. KENNEDY tr. *B. ten Brink's Hist. Eng. Lit.* I. II. 179 The Breton *lais* retain most fully their native fragrance. They are usually romantic even when the topic is comic... The poem is often pervaded by a tone of elegiac longing. **1905** E. RICKERT in *Mod. Philol.* II. 376 The fresh literary impulse that came with the Normans found little to do with the old Saxon heroes. A few tales were transformed into the *lai* or *chanson de geste* or *roman d'aventure—Havelock, Horn, Guy of Warwick, Bevis of Hampton.* **1906** [see *CONTE b]. **1907** ST. J. LUCAS in *Oxf. Bk. French Verse* p. vii, Various other kinds of lyric poetry begin to appear at the end of the twelfth century, *motets,..rondeaux, lais, ballettes* and *virelais.* **1923** J. VISING *Anglo-Norman Lang. & Lit.* 47 Breton lais in England are mentioned in *Roman de Renard.* **1925** A. BELL *Le Lai d'Haveloc* 26 There is, however, not only a general connection with the 'lais' but also a special one with those of Marie. **1929** [see *CONTE b]. **1932** *Oxf. Hist. Music* (ed. 2) II. II. v. 285 The initial stanzas of two trouvères *lais* are written on the melody of 'Ave gloriosa virginum regina'. *Ibid.* 286 On the other side the *lai* is related to the *chanson de geste* and to the other popular songs of the time, to which many of the anonymous *lais* show some resemblance. **1940** *Grove's Dict. Mus.* (ed. 4) III. 269/1 The *lais* (long lyrical poems written in twelve pairs of stanzas, each pair having a different metrical form and a different melody from the rest, except the last pair, which repeats metre and melody of the first) are all set to one musical part only. **1954** [see *CONTE b]. **1965** R. S. LOOMIS in Bessinger & Creed *Medieval & Ling. Stud.* 237 We possess three Breton *lais*: *Doon, Desiré,* and *Gurun*..which evince some knowledge of Scottish geography.

Lai[2] (ləi). [Local name.] A Mongoloid people living in the Chin hills of Burma; a member of this people; also, the language spoken by this people. Also *attrib.* or as *adj.*

1896 CAREY & TUCK *Chin Hills* I. I. i. 3 The Northern Chins call themselves Yo, the Tashons, Haka, and more southern tribes Lai. *Ibid.* iii. 23 The Hakas call themselves Lai, and Yo is the general name by which the Chins call their race. *Ibid.* xiv. 152 The clans which claim the title of Lais are the Hakas, Klang-klangs, Yokwas... The first two are universally acknowledged as Lais, and refuse to admit that the others belong to their race. **1897** A. G. E. NEWLAND *Pract. Hand-bk. Lang. Lais* 1 The *Lais* are the great tribe and its offshoots that occupy the Chin Hills... The language of these people is the *Lai* language, called by the Burmese *Baungshè*, by which term we have hitherto known it. Dialects of it are spoken by all the surrounding tribes, but nearly all understand the *Lai* tongue. *Ibid.* 3 Unlike the Southern Chin language, it will be found that the consonants 'f' and 'r' are both used in the *Lai* speech. **1906** J. G. SCOTT *Burma* I. 106 The Tashôn tribe is..the most numerous, and next to them come the Hakas, also called the Lai... Lai is said to be likely to become the *lingua franca* of the Chin Hills. **1924** C. M. ENRIQUEZ *Races Burma* iii. 15 The Haka (a group of about ten villages including the parent village) claim to be the only true Lai. *Ibid.* vii. 43 The Lai tribes are controlled..by Chiefs. **1963** F. K. LEHMAN *Struct. Chin Soc.* i. 30 The Haka villagers call themselves *lai*, thinking of themselves as better than their cultural near relations to the South.

laicism (s.v. LAICIZE *v.*). (Later examples.)

1931 *Economist* 4 July 13/1 The political antagonisms which the Spanish Revolution has let loose: the issues of Republicanism versus Monarchism, Syndicalism versus Capitalism, and Laicism versus Clericalism. **1966** *Ibid.* 11 June 1178/2 Their priests, many of whom equate laicism with socialism, have been outraged by its [*sc.* the government's] plans to modify the present confessional structure of education.

laicity (lēi·sĭti). [f. LAIC *a.* and *sb.* + -ITY.] The principles of the laity; the rule or influence of the laity; the fact of being lay; also *attrib.*

1909 WEBSTER, *Laicity*, laicality. **1925** *Brit. Weekly* 19 Mar. 587/3 The text of the document, which is directed against the 'laicity laws', lies before us. **1928** *Daily Tel.* 30 Oct. 12/3 Accused by his own hotheads of betraying the cause of 'laicity' by acquiescing in these details of the Budget. **1939** A. TOYNBEE *Study of Hist.* VI. 20 This laicity of the Gods was taken so much in earnest that in a Mahayanian sutra a chapter..is formally addressed to the Gods, as a hint that it is an *œuvre de vulgarisation.*

laid, *ppl. a.* Add: **a.** (Further examples.)

1634 J. TAYLOR *Needles Excellency* (ed. 10) sig. A2 For Tent-worke, Raisd-worke, Laid-worke, Frost-worke. **1860** GEO. ELIOT *Let.* 27–28 Aug. (1954) III. 337 It is piteous to see the laid corn, and then hear the rain pouring in the still night! **1865** F. B. PALLISER *Hist. Lace* xxiii. 275 Then there is..true stitch, laid-work,..and cut-work. **1960** [see *brick-stitch* (*BRICK *sb.*[1] 10)]. **1971** *Country Life* 10 June 1440/2 Reaping a small field of badly laid corn with sickles and reaping hooks.

c. Also, *laid-back, -by* (cf. *LAY *v.*[1] 50 f), *-off* (cf. LAY *v.*[1] 54 f), *-on.*

1868 Laid-off [see LAY *v.*[1] 54 f]. *a* **1877** KNIGHT *Dict. Mech.* II. 1246/1 *Laid-on* (Joinery), a term applied to moldings which are got out in strips and nailed on to the surface of the object. **1906** *Westm. Gaz.* 9 June 16/3 The Valenciennes running around the laid-on tucks surrounding the skirt. **1908** *Ibid.* 23 Dec. 4/1 To get in under the ball you must have a shallow head..or else a very much laid-back face. **1909** *Ibid.* 30 Apr. 4/2 You can take a laid-back club and loft right over it. **1932** W. FAULKNER *Light in August* xviii. 394 Any man could look at him and perhaps recognise him: Byron Bunch, that weeded another man's laidby crop, without any halvers. **1934** *Archit. Rev.* LXXVI. 13 Central heating, lighting, cooking, vacuum cleaning, laid-on water and drainage. **1943** HUNT & PRINGLE *Service Slang* 43 *Laid on*, confirming that transport and supplies are available, that men are on the spot, and, in short, that everything is ready for action. **1955** *Times* 31 May 5/3 The union proposed that the guaranteed level of pay for 'laid off', meaning temporarily unemployed, workers, should be 80 per cent. of gross pay rather than 100 per cent. of take-home pay as originally proposed. **1960** *Farmer & Stockbreeder* 15 Mar. 75/3 The appeal of zero-grazing is that it requires no fencing, no laid-on water, but maintains fertility. **1967** *Guardian* 26 July 10/7 A group of laid-on Turkish peasants in costume, dancing a jig. **1970** *Daily Tel.* 11 Sept. 6/2 Laid-off workers at Coventry are receiving..£5 unemployment benefit. **1973** *Melody Maker* 28 July 36/2 This hit-writer of the early 60s came out with a highly contemporary style which fitted the fashionable term 'laid-back', and her 'Tapestry' album zoomed up to become one of the three biggest-selling LPs of all time. **1974** *New Society* 7 Mar. 589/3 It's all cheerfully grotty and relaxed in the usual laid-back Montreal style.

laika (lai·kă). Pl. **laiki.** [Russ. *laĭka*, f. *laĭ* bark.] A dog belonging to a group of Asiatic breeds of the spitz type, characterized by a pointed muzzle, pricked ears, a stocky body with a thick, rough, grey, fawn, white, or black coat and a tail curled over the back.

1905 H. DE BYLANDT *Dogs All Nations* I. 576 Samoyed dog. (Laika or Siberian dog)... Dog of medium size, well built and cobby, covered with a thick fur. **1928** *Daily Sketch* 7 Aug. 4/3 The Elkhound is of similar type to the Russian Laïka (barking) dog, so-called because, unlike others of the lupine group, its tongue is a bark and not a howl. **1948** C. L. B. HUBBARD in B. Vesey-Fitzgerald *Bk. Dog* II. 517 The Spitz of the Asiatic sphere shew considerable variation, and are consequently divided into many well-defined breeds. These are collectively known as Laiki, and each Laika is called (in most cases) after its province or its people. **1971** F. HAMILTON *World Encycl. Dogs* 599 Laiki are seen all over Northern Russia... When a Laika, out hunting, sees a bird in a tree or bush, it barks ceaselessly.

Laingian (læ·ŋiăn), *a.* [-IAN.] Of or pertaining to the theories of the British psychologist R. D. *Laing* (1927–), esp. that a disintegrative mental illness such as schizophrenia is due to 'normal' social or family pressures which are intolerable to the self, and that re-integrative therapy is therefore possible only when such conventionally accepted pressures are removed. Hence as *sb.*, one who adheres to Laing's theories or practises his method of therapy.

1971 *New Statesman* 16 Apr. 535/1 A Laingian stereotype has blossomed. **1972** *Listener* 20 Jan. 95/3 Her psychiatrist..a 'Laingian' who wants to treat the underlying cause..and not the symptoms. **1973** E. Z. FRIEDENBERG *Laing* (1974) i. 27 Edward Chamberlayne, an archetypical victim..of a Laingian entrapment. **1973** *Listener* 10 May 623/2 The now-familiar Laingian argument that language is the first and strongest of the prison-houses with which our civilisation enslaves the free self.

lair (lēəɹ), *sb.*[4] *Austral. slang.* Also **lare.** [Back-formation from *LAIRY *a.*[2]] A flashily dressed man, one who 'shows off'. Also (*rare*) **lai·rize** *v. intr.*, to act like a lair, to show off.

1935 K. TENNANT *Tiburon* ix. 106 He was also considered something of a lare among the girls. **1941** BAKER *Dict. Austral. Slang* 42 *Lair*, a flashily-dressed man. **1941** K. TENNANT *Battlers* iii. 29 But a brainy young lare called 'the mob' together on the pavement outside the shop. 'This can be worked, can't it?' he asked, displaying his slip. **1953** —— *Joyful Condemned* iii. 22 You came lairizing round at our place like you owned it. **1955** H. DRAKE-BROCKMAN *Men without Wives* 83 A flash young man. What they call on the goldfields 'a regular lare'. Hair much slicked, double-breasted coat, patent leather shoes. **1956** J. WRIGHT in *Coast to Coast 1955–56* 168 But he was what they called a bit of a lair; he couldn't keep a job and had run through three already. **1956** K. TENNANT *Honey Flow* xvi. 188 When they dressed in their best, they looked cheap lares, the type you see leaning against the hotel or the general store. **1973** A. BROINOWSKI *Take One Ambassador* iii. 31 Two young lairs from the surf club carried their boards down..and tossed them onto the sea. With insolent grace they hopped on.

lair (lēəɹ), *v. Austral. slang.* Also **lare.** [f. *LAIR *sb.*[4] or *LAIRY *a.*[2]] To dress flashily, to dress *up*; to act in a lairy manner. Freq. in pa. pple. (*all*) *laired up.*

1941 BAKER *Dict. Austral. Slang* 42 *Lair up*, to dress, esp. to don one's best clothes for a festive occasion. **1945** —— *Austral. Lang.* vi. 119 *All laired up* and its synonym *all mockered up* may also be noted. **1955** H. DRAKE-BROCKMAN *Men without Wives* 83 It's that Rienzi. He's a trimmer. Always laring round. No good to girls. **1962** S. GORE *Down Golden Mile* 64 He climbs out of the cockpit, all laired up in this red rig-out.

lairy (lēə·ri), *a.*[2] Also **lary.** [ad. LEERY *a.*[2]] **1.** *Cockney slang.* Knowing, 'fly', conceited.

1846 *Swell's Night Guide* 78 Lairy and cautious to the green ones, never too fast. **1933** J. MASEFIELD *Conway* 211 *Lairy*, slow, slack; also cunning. **1945** B. NAUGHTON in C. Madge *Pilot Papers* 99 We'll have to keep an eye on

him. Spivs are lary perishers. Anything goes wrong they'll never risk their own skin. *Ibid.* 108 They appear to be mentally quicker than most young men: ('Lary' is the word they use for it). **1958** *News Chron.* 23 May 4/7 If someone..is conceited he's lairy. **1967** *Spectator* 4 Aug. 130/3 What I was getting at—before that lairy loon butted in about his thumb—was this. Down the East End we're overcrowded an' we're bleedin' poor.

2. Also **leary, leery.** Flashily dressed; vulgar. *Austral. slang.*

In quot. 1906 used as quasi-*adv.*

1906 E. DYSON *Fact'ry 'Ands* xii. 160 Found drownded with a bloke what done-up 'is 'air dead leary. **1916** C. J. DENNIS *Songs Sentimental Bloke* 125 *Leery*, vulgar; low. **1936** F. CLUNE *Roaming round Darling* xxiv. 258 Then climbed..Jack the Ripper on to Tugboat Annie, his hat at a leery angle, and the pommel leerier still. **1941** BAKER *Dict. Austral. Slang* 42 *Lairy*, vulgar, flashily or showily dressed. **1966** B. BEAVER *You can't come Back* (1968) 146, I just stood still under the big lairy neon, chuckling a bit and trying to roll a smoke.

‖ **laisse** (lęs). [Fr.] In Old French verse, = TIRADE *sb.* 2.

1872 [see *CHANSON 2]. **1879** [see TIRADE *sb.* 2]. **1929** *Encycl. Brit.* II. 567/2 All the lines in a *laisse* or stanza close with the same vowel-sound. **1955** J. T. SHIPLEY *Dict. World Lit. Terms* 246/1 *Laisse*; tirade. Fr. Pros. Running lines (of 8 or 10 syllables) assonanced; later, rhymed; the verse form of the *chanson de geste*.

laissez-aller. (Later *attrib.* examples.)

1871 [see **fatigue man*]. **1923** [see *DOZY *a.*[1] 2].

laissez-faire. Add: Hence **laissez-fai·r(e)ist,** one who believes in a doctrine of *laissez-faire*.

1932 G. B. SHAW *Platform & Pulpit* (1962) 252 A Cabinet of talkers and Laisser-fairists. **1944** A. JONES *Right & Left* 16 The Conservative is neither a planner nor a laisser-faire-ist. **1966** *Guardian* 1 Dec. 8/6 Professor Peacock..isn't too keen on being cast as a 'relentless laisser-fairist'.

‖ **laissez-passer** (lęse pase). Also **laisser-passer.** [Fr., lit. 'allow to pass'.] A permit, a pass.

1914 T. A. BAGGS *Back from Front* xx. 94 You must first pass grim Charon and his watchdogs at the entrance, where your passports, laisser-passers, sauf-conduits, are inspected. **1928** *Sunday Express* 1 July 5 The Ballet was given a laissez-passer and were allowed to come to England through Paris. **1936** E. WAUGH *Waugh in Abyssinia* 77 Many writers have left accounts of the intricate system of tolls and hospitality by which the traveller was passed on from one chief to another and of the indifference with which the Emperor's *laissez-passer* was treated within a few miles of the capital. **1951** J. B. PRIESTLEY *Festival at Farbridge* I. i. 34 He handed over an Order to View as if it were a *laissez-passer* for the captain of the Swiss Guard at Versailles. **1955** *Times* 28 July 8/4 He has been granted by the Greek Foreign Ministry a laisser-passer to the Greek military zone of the Greek-Bulgarian frontier. **1970** R. G. FELTHAM *Diplomatic Handbk.* 178 *Laissez-passer*, a permit to travel or to enter a particular area.

laitakarite (ləităkā·rəit). *Min.* [ad. Finn. *laitakariittii* (A. Vorma 1959, in *Geologi* (Helsinki) III. XI. 11), f. the name of Aarne *Laitakari* (b. 1890), director of the Geological Survey of Finland (see quot. 1959): see -ITE[1].] A white rhombohedral selenide and sulphide of bismuth, Bi_4Se_2S.

1959 *Mineral. Abstr.* XIV. 139/2 The new mineral was named, in the honour of the discoverer of the material from which it was disclosed, laitakarite, and it is supposed to be isomorphous with joseite. **1963** *Canad. Mineralogist* VII. 678 The data given in Table 1 show the probable identity of laitakarite and selenjoseite. **1968** I. KOSTOV *Mineral.* II. ii. 164 Additional minerals are laitakarite (Bi_4Se_2S) and paraguanajuatite ($Bi_2(Se,S)_3$), which are isostructural with the minerals of the tetradymite group.

laitance (lē̆i·tăns). Also (*erron.*) **laitence.** [Fr.] A milky scum appearing on the surface of freshly laid cement.

1909 TAYLOR & THOMPSON *Treat. Concrete* (ed. 2) xv. 303 The milky laitance which appears on concrete laid under water represents an actual loss of cement. **1930** *Engineering* 23 May 677/3 The value of carefully providing for the adequate junction between successive layers and the elimination of laitance. **1939** *Archit. Rev.* LXXXV. 267 First is the way in which the tile is fixed to its backing, due to insufficient soaking of both the tile and the rendering, robbing the cement of the water necessary for proper hydration; 'killing' the cement by re-mixing new and old compo that has already started to set; 'laitence', a white scum of water and cement which forms on the surface of the bed of floor tiles, if it is pressed up and down too much while the tiles are being levelled. **1968** D. C. TIBBETTS in E. G. Swenson *Performance of Concrete* (1969) x. 168 Laitance was removed and necessary holes cut in the sides of the cylinders for the setting of the low water ends of the concrete braces.

lak (læk). Repr. *U.S. dial.* (esp. *Black English*) pronunc. of LIKE *a.*, *adv.*, and *v.*[1]

1881 J. C. HARRIS *Nights with Uncle Remus* (1884) xvi. 80 He'd skuze hisse'f, he would, en gallop down de big road a piece, en paw up de san' same lak dat ar ball-faced steer w'at tuck'n tuck off yo' pa' coat-tail las' Feberwary. **1901** F. L. STANTON (*song-title*) Mighty lak' a rose. **1936** M. MITCHELL *Gone with Wind* v. 78 Ain' nobody got a wais' lak mah lamb. **1949** *Crisis* (N.Y.) Nov. 303/1 Would you lak t'go t' the sto'..lak a darlin' li'l boy. **1973** B. GATES in S. Henderson *Understanding New Black Poetry* 310 Now, you gon' stop Yo ackin lak a fool!

Lak (læk). The name of a Caucasian language (see quot. 1954).

1954 PEI & GAYNOR *Dict. Ling.* 118 *Lak*, a language.. spoken in the Caucasus; a member of the Eastern Caucasian group of the North Caucasian family of languages. **1971** *Language* XLVII. 233 The West Caucasian languages, where..Lak has forty cases and Tabassaran forty-eight. **1972** *Ibid.* XLVIII. 845 Hockett exemplifies 3a with 'Arunta..Lak and Wishram'.

‖ **lakatoi** (læ·kătoi). [Papuan.] In New Guinea, a native dug-out canoe, with two or more hulls.

1885 W. W. GILL in Chalmers & Gill *Work & Adventures New Guinea* II. i. 258 We were fortunate in seeing two *lakatoi* or Gulf-going crafts; the larger one consisted of fourteen immense canoes lashed firmly together and decked. *Ibid.* 259 Each *lakatoi* starting for the Gulf is filled with earthenware pots. **1911** *Encycl. Brit.* XX. 742/2 The Papuans build excellent canoes and other boats... The most remarkable of their vessels is the 'lakatoi', composed of several capacious dug-outs, each nearly 50 ft. long, which are strongly lashed together. **1926** *Mariner's Mirror* XII. 216/2 Fig. 2 is a *lakatoi* of Port Moresby, S.E. New Guinea. **1964** *Sunday Truth* (Brisbane) 9 Aug. 20/5 Some of them have purchased £400 outboard motors which they fit to lakatois—generally two hollowed out logs with a connecting wooden decking. **1964** *Punch* 26 Aug. 319/2 How will the *lakatoi* run before the wind of change? **1968** *Mariner's Mirror* LIV. 348 Today the sails used on lakatoi are rectangular, with the peak held by a sprit.

lake, *sb.*[4] Add: **1. b.** (Further *fig.* examples.)

1974 *Daily Tel.* 30 July 17/1 The Common Market has a 'wine lake' estimated at 8 million litres..—and yesterday a Labour MP called for some of it to be brought to Britain. **1975** *Times* 9 Apr. 15/3 Butter mountains and wine lakes are part of the price which Europe pays for a common agricultural policy.

c. *the Great Lakes* (examples).

In earlier use freq. without the adjective.

c **1665** P. E. RADISSON *Voyages* (1885) 187 Those great lakes had not so soone comed to our knowledge if it had not ben for those brutish people. **1748** H. ELLIS *Voyage to Hudson's-Bay* 151 A Communication with the great Lakes behind Canada. **1759** P. COLLINSON in W. Darlington *Memorials J. Bartram & H. Marshall* (1849) 217, I don't remember ever reading of any [goats] in the country about the lakes. **1803** W. B. GROVE *Let.* 25 Feb. in J. Steele *Papers* (1924) I. 367 The Ocean, the Mexican Gulf, the Mississippi & the Lakes must be our boundaries. **1813** *Niles' Reg.* V. 65/1 The position of the great lakes is..well known to the people of the United States. **1840** J. F. COOPER *Pathfinder* I. p. v, Incidents that might be supposed characteristic of the Great Lakes. **1902** *Encycl. Brit.* XXXII. 551/1 Plan of Great Lake steamer. **1904** N. S. SHALER *Citizen* 77 Where the territory borders on the sea or the Great Lakes, the authorities have charge of such harbours as are not in the control of the federal authority. **1966** *Canadian Geogr. Jrnl.* Apr. 113/2 The abnormally low water levels on the Great Lakes.

d. *to jump* (or *go* (*and*) *jump*) *in the lake*: see *JUMP *v.* 1 d.

5. a. *lake-bass, -bed, -front, -herring* (examples), *-island, -isle, -shore* (earlier and later examples), *-steamer, -water*.

1795 J. SCOTT *U.S. Gazetteer* s.v. *Vermont*, A species of fish called lake bass. **1884** G. B. GOODE *Fisheries U.S.: Nat. Hist. Aquatic Animals* 424 The White Bass or Striped Lake Bass, *Roccus chrysops*. **1973** R. LOCKRIDGE *Not I, said the Sparrow* (1974) vi. 87 There was only one right way to cook lake bass. **1906** *Yorks. N. & Q.* July 100 Their position on the edge of the old lake-bed. **1937** *Discovery* Jan. 24/1 The bones [of the shovel-tusked Mastodon] lay embedded in the hardened mud deposit of an ancient lake-bed in Mongolia. **1880** 'MARK TWAIN' *Tramp Abroad* 245 The lake-front is walled with masonry like a pier. **1968** *Economist* 13 July 38/3 A lakefront site that would be better as a park. **1842** J. E. DEKAY *Zool. N.Y.* IV. 267 The Lake Moon-eye, *Hyodon clodalis*,..is common in Lake Erie. At Buffalo and Barcelona, it is called Moon-eye, Shiner, and Lake Herring. **1875** *Amer. Naturalist* IX. 135, I received..a collection of deep water 'Siscoes'... Compared with Coregonus most of the species have a more slender form; hence their popular name of 'lake herrings', although their resemblance to the sea herring is quite superficial. **1955** *Arctic Terms* 48/1 *Lake herring*, any of various whitefish of the genus *Leucichthys*, caught in great numbers in circumpolar fresh waters. Also called 'cisco'. **1893** W. B. YEATS in *Bookman* May 43/1 It is said that an enchanted tree once grew on the little lake-island of Innisfree. **1890** —— *Countess Kathleen* (1892) 121 (*title*) The Lake Isle of Innisfree. **1917** E. POUND *Lustra* 61 (*title*) The lake isle. **1798** I. ALLEN *Nat. & Pol. Hist. Vermont* 61 The two Frenchmen were landed..with instructions to follow the lake shore. **1813** *Niles' Reg.* IV. 159/1 Previous to this period, a great deal of prejudice existed against the lake *shore*, as unhealthy. **1849** *Ex. Doc. 31st U.S. Congress 1 Sess. House* No. 5. II. 731 The sandstone on the lake-shore is..covered by fifteen.. feet of sand and clay. **1851** C. CIST *Sk. Cincinnati in 1851* 319 Hence [arise] their efforts to reach Chicago, by way of the Erie lake shore. **1973** *Tucson* (Arizona) *Daily Citizen* 22 Aug. 1/1 The 15½-foot-deep lake gives Tucson the appearance of being a major lakeshore metropolis. **1847** *Knickerbocker* XXX. 456 He has been inspired by looking down through the iron foot-grating of a great lake-steamer. **1888** C. D. FERGUSON *Experiences Forty-Niner* i. 11 It was in the month of September, 1849, when..I embarked on the lake-steamer, A. D. Patchen for Chicago. **1890** W. B. YEATS *Countess Kathleen* (1892) 121, I hear lake water lapping with low sounds. **1906** *Westm. Gaz.* Oct. 6 6/2 And far below the blue lake-waters shine. **1920** JOYCE *Let.* 5 June (1966) II. 469 It should be read in the evening when the lakewater is lapping.

b. *lake-girt* adj.

1878 H. M. STANLEY *Through Dark Continent* I. x. 222 From the summit of this lake-girt isle. **1908** *Daily Chron.* 4 Aug. 3/1 The *noche triste* when the Spaniards found themselves surrounded in the lake-girt capital of the Aztecs.

6. a. lake-basin (further examples); also, the area drained by all the streams entering a lake; **lake country** (earlier example); **Lake District** = LAKE-LAND; **Lakehead** *Canad.*, (*a*) *Hist.*, the western end of Lake Ontario (quot. 1827); (*b*) the cities of Port Arthur and Fort William, Ontario, and the surrounding region on the north-west shore of Lake Superior; **lake rampart, ridge** = *ice-rampart* (*ICE *sb.* 8).

1865 D. PAGE *Handbk. Geol. Terms* (ed. 2) 272 *Lake-basin*, in geography, the depressed area which contains the waters of a lake; also the entire area drained by the streams that fall into a lake. In geology, the concavity.. in which the waters of a lake rest. **1882** *Proc. Boston Soc. Nat. Hist.* XXI. 326 In the Himalaya, the valleys of Nepal and Kashmir are old orographic lake basins. **1965** W. D. THORNBURY *Regional Geomorphol. U.S.* xxiv. 494/2 Fish can be carried by birds from one lake basin into another. **1967** JENNINGS & MABBUTT *Landform Stud. Austral. & New Guinea* vi. 111 Such an argument would explain why well formed alluvial fans survive outside the catchment of Lake Torrens and why they are absent or present in only a degraded form within the lake basin. **1842** *Amer. Pioneer* I. 211 No where was the pressure or want of money more sensibly felt than in the lake country. **1835** WORDSWORTH *Yarrow Revisited* 241 *Force* is the word used in the Lake District for Water-fall. **1851** *Art Jrnl.* 1 May 132/2 The scale upon which the scenery of the English Lake district is laid out. **1886** J. PRESTWICH *Geol.* I. 267 In the Lake District the planes of cleavage also usually strike about E.N.E. **1936** *Discovery* May 150/2 Lovers of the Lake District..feel that the peculiar wild beauty of the innermost fells will be destroyed by the introduction of large acreages of larch and spruce planted in small rows on the hillsides. **1957** G. E. HUTCHINSON *Treat. Limnol.* I. i. 1 Lakes therefore tend to be grouped together in *lake districts*. *Ibid.*, The whole group of lakes of a given lake district may be compared with another group. **1827** *Gore Gaz.* (Ancaster, Ont.) 25 May 50/4 It appeared, that a person at the Lake Head, had furnished the York Garrison with 800 bbls. of Flour last year. **1955** *Beaver* Summer 37 From the deck of the loaded freighter, bound for the Sault and Welland Canals, the grain strongholds of the lakehead stand like castles against the sunset. **1968** *Globe & Mail* (Toronto) 13 Feb. B7/2 One of the world's largest multiple-line insurance companies requires a sales oriented management man to establish a sales force in the lakehead. **1860** C. H. HITCHCOCK in *Proc. Amer. Assoc. Adv. Sci.* XIII. 335 We have discovered similar walls of stone in Vermont, and venture to describe this form of drift under the name of Lake Ramparts. **1870** *Amer. Naturalist* IV. 199 Above all these Drift deposits..are the 'lake ridges'—embankments of sand, gravel, sticks, leaves, etc., which run imperfectly parallel with the present outlines of the lake margins.

b. Lake poets (earlier examples), **school** (earlier example).

1816 *Edin. Rev.* XXVII. 278 His [*sc.* Byron's] views fell more in with those of the Lake poets, than of any other party in the poetical commonwealth. **1824** MILL in *Westm. Rev.* I. 516 Mr. Southey..and the other Lake poets..commenced writing with higher objects. **1816** *Edin. Rev.* XXVII. 66 Other productions of the Lake School.

lake, *v.*[3] Add to def.: *spec.* by causing the hæmoglobin in red blood cells to pass out into the plasma. Hence **laked** *ppl. a.* (Further examples.)

1903 *Science* 6 Mar. 369 For the preparation of hæmoglobin the blood was collected in ammonium oxalate, washed, laked with distilled water [etc.]. **1912** GULLAND & GOODALL *Blood* vi. 48 Dilution of the plasma causes the corpuscles to swell up and become rounded, and if the dilution be carried too far the corpuscle ruptures and the hæmoglobin passes into solution. The blood is then said to be 'laked'. **1925** C. H. BROWNING *Bacteriol.* vi. 122 If now tetanus toxin is added the suspension soon becomes transparent, *i.e.* it is laked or lysed, owing to the hæmoglobin diffusing out of the red cells. **1946** *Nature* 28 Dec. 953/1 This is..far from reaching the refractive index level of the red cells (which would have resulted in producing 'laked blood' without hæmolysis).

lake-land, lakeland. Add: **2. Lakeland terrier,** a rough-coated, red or black and tan terrier with a stocky body and a broad muzzle, belonging to a breed developed in Lakeland; also *ellipt.*

1928 *Kennel Gaz.* Dec. 1294/1 (*heading*) Any other breed or variety of British, Colonial or foreign dogs not classified... Lakeland terriers. **1931** *Times Lit. Suppl.* 13 Aug. 620/4 Others [*sc.* terriers] in favour are the Border, the Lakeland, the Fox, the Sealyham. **1960** *Guardian* 18 Nov. 12/6 Two Lakeland Terriers were lost for four days in a disused mine. **1971** F. HAMILTON *World Encycl. Dogs* 457 It is doubtful if anyone knows exactly how the Lakeland Terrier was developed but it is generally thought the Border Terrier, the Bedlington and the Fox Terrier were used in its formation. *Ibid.* 458 The trimming of the Lakeland for the show ring has reached a high peak of perfection.

laker[1]**.** Add: **2.** (Earlier example.)

1814 *Edin. Rev.* XXIV. 1 Imitations of Cowper, and even of Milton.., engrafted on the natural drawl of the Lakers.

3. (Earlier example.)
1823 J. F. Cooper *Pioneers* II. xxiv. 261, I see a laker there, that has run out of the school. It's seldom one finds such a creater in the shallow waters.

4. (Later examples.)
1945 *Seafarers' Log* 27 Apr. 6/3 She is a small laker but generally has more beefs than would the SS Queen Elizabeth. **1961** *Guardian* 15 June 1/2 Until the Seaway opened in April, 1959, the 'freshwater' trade was carried in specially-designed lakers and smaller canallers... New 20,000-ton lakers..are coming into service. **1970** *Daily Colonist* (Victoria, B.C.) 23 Sept. 26/1 The 5,300-ton laker Orefax ran aground..off Battery Island in the St. Lawrence River. **1974** *Globe & Mail* (Toronto) 11 Sept. 8/9 The Canadian pilots will continue to serve ocean vessels downbound through the canal and take U.S. lakers westbound.

5. One accustomed to sailing on a lake.
1838 J. F. Cooper *Home as Found* II. 75 After fishing a few hours, the old laker [*sc.* Captain Truck] pulled the skiff up to the Point. **1910** *Blackw. Mag.* Aug. 173/1 He was an experienced 'Laker', but the scene..had completely unmanned him. **1936** K. Mackenzie *Living Rough* 274 When the deep-water sailor goes on the lakes, he has a tendency to..refer to the lakers as farmers, niggerhead sailors, and other salt-water jokes.

lakh. Now the more usual spelling of Lac^{2}.
a. Of things or persons in general.
1964 E. Huxley *Back Street New Worlds* x. 100 Plenty of Pakistanis are here already—the High Commissioner's estimate is one *lakh*, or 100,000. **1969** *National Herald* (New Delhi) 29 July 6/5 The labour acts which relate to factories, mines, plantation, transport, shops and establishments, wages, safety and welfare, industrial relations and protection of children are expected to benefit lakhs of workers and wage-earners in the state. **1969** *Hindu* (Madras) 3 Aug. 6/4 The area worst hit by the recent floods in the Brahmaputra Valley is the Sibsagar district where about two lakhs of people have been affected, with thousands rendered homeless.

b. *spec.* Of coins or sums of money.
1859 [see Lac^{2} b]. **1955** *Times* 3 Aug. 2/6 Detailed prospecting, which has so far cost 19·80 lakhs of rupees, led to the location of iron ore in Kalabagh and its suburbs in the Punjab. **1971** *Weekend* (Ceylon) 12 Sept. 3/2 The project would cost four lakhs of rupees. **1972** *Times of India* 28 Nov. 5/3 The parcel actually contained 900 Japanese-made wrist watches worth Rs. 2 lakhs. **1975** *Bangladesh Times* 18 July 1/3 The Finance Minister said that the Government had already increased the ceiling of private investment for setting up industries from Tk 25 lakh to Taka three crore.

la·kish, *a. rare.* [f. Lake *sb.*^{4} + -ish^{1}.] **a.** Like a lake. **b.** Characteristic of the Lake poets.
1872 G. M. Hopkins *Jrnls. & Papers* (1959) 222 The broad smooth fall of a lakish apron of water. **1946** *Mod. Lang. Q.* Dec. 497 Bitterly as he attacked Southey for his faults, Jeffrey did not accuse him of the 'Lakish' fault of 'mysticism'.

Lakoda (lakōᵘ·dă). [Name of an area in the Pribilof Islands in the Bering Sea.] Used *attrib.* or *absol.*: a type of sealskin used as a material for coats.
1969 *New Yorker* 8 Nov. 179 A midicoat of Lakoda in its natural caramel uses black beaver for the collar and cuffs. **1975** *Ibid.* 7 Apr. 118/2 On the Atlanta trip, he wore a Lakoda-sealskin coat.

lala, var. *ilala.

‖ **laksamana** (la:ksămā·nă). Also 7 **laxaman,** 9 **lacsamana.** [Malay, ad. Skr. *lakshmaṇa* 'having fortunate tokens' (the name of a mythical hero, Rama's half-brother).] The title formerly given to a high dignitary or admiral in Malaya.
1615 in Danvers & Foster *Lett. received by E. India Co.* (1900) IV. 6 On the morrow I went to take my leave of Laxaman, to whom all strangers' business are resigned. **1821** J. Leyden tr. *Malay Annals* xi. 96 Whoever bears the title of sangcuan may succeed to the rank of lacsamana. **1839** T. J. Newbold *Pol. & Statistical Acct. Straits of Malacca* II. iii. 46 Paul de Gama attacked Johore, but was defeated and slain by the Lacsamana. **1969** J. M. Gullick *Malaysia* ii. 40 Command of the navy rested with the Laksamana.

la-la (lā·lā·), *v.* [Redupl. La *int.*] *intr.* To sing or say the syllable *la* repeatedly, esp. in place of the words or notes of a tune. Also *trans.*, to sing (a song) in this way.
1906 *Daily Chron.* 19 Sept. 9/6 Miss Neale..'la la'-ed a simple tune. **1908** *Ibid.* 18 Aug. 7/1 They search out the secret places of past grandeur, la-la-ing as they issue from court and passage. **1974** *Listener* 17 Jan. 84/1 Those boys who couldn't sing didn't just 'la-la': they said the words, and they were called 'Talking Josephs'. The boys who really could sing were called 'Canaries'.

lalang (lā·lăŋ). Also **lallang.** [Malay.] A local name for *Imperata cylindrica,* a large coarse grass, widespread in tropical countries.
1779 T. Forrest *Voy. New Guinea* II. iii. 192 The country hereabouts is now covered with long grass, called lalang. **1887** H. W. Daly *Digging, Squatting, & Pioneering Life S. Austral.* 158 A shake-down..made up of dried lallang—the thick strong grass of the country. **1887** *Encycl. Brit.* XXII. 93/1 There are waste spaces..covered with coarse lalang grass. **1912** *Chambers's Jrnl.* Feb. 98/1 As I stood in the lalang patch..there passed over my head..all the turmoil of a great city. **1918** [see *blady *a.*]. **1925** *Chambers's Jrnl.* June 408/2 The manager..contracted with a Chinese to eradicate some four hundred acres of lalang grass on his estate. **1933** L. Ainsworth *Confessions Planter in Malaya* 190 It was decided to tackle all 'lallang' land (areas that in the past had been cleared of virgin jungle by the Chinese, but which subsequently had been..allowed to become overgrown with lallang weed). **1969** J. M. Gullick *Malaysia* ii. 67 Lallang is the Malay name for *Imperata cylindrica,* a coarse grass which grows freely on untended land in Malaya. **1972** *Malay Mail* (Kuala Lumpur) 25 May 6/3 Poisons to kill weeds and lallang..could have been absorbed by the jering tree.

-lalia, a terminal element repr. Gr. λαλιά speech, chatter, used in forming words denoting various disorders or unusual faculties of speech; as in *dyslalia* (s.v. Dys-), *echolalia, Glossolalia, *idiolalia* (s.v. *idio-).

Lalique (lalī·k). [f. the name of René *Lalique* (1860–1945), French designer of jewels and glassware.] Used *attrib.* and *ellipt.* to designate jewellery and decorative glassware by or after the manner of Lalique.
1902 *Daily Chron.* 31 May 2/3 Any jewel of uncommon design is modish, but prominently a Lalique, strung upon an imperceptible platinum chain. **1927** *Daily Express* 28 Oct. 5/3 Both tray and stopper are decorated in the Lalique manner. **1936** O. Lancaster *Progress at Pelvis Bay* 67 Its modernistic sofas, lalique panels and cleverly concealed lighting. **1939** A. Keith *Land below Wind* xiii. 224 Like figures on a Lalique vase. **1970** G. Savage *Dict. Antiques* 232/2 A good deal of Lalique glass deserves to be classified as 'antiques of the future'. **1972** *Vogue* 15 Mar. (*inside front cover*) Pair of 'Lalique' glass doves—£65·00.

Lallan. Add: **B.** *sb.* (Now usu. *Lallans.*) Esp., in modern use, a revived and modified form of the spoken dialect as a literary language.
1946 M. Lindsay *Mod. Scottish Poetry* 18 It is largely under MacDiarmid's influence..that the younger poets, especially those who use Gaelic and Scots (or Lallans, as I prefer to call their Scots, drawing more, as it does, upon middle Scots) have developed. **1947** D. Young *Plastic Scots* 3 As it is convenient to have some term of distinction for that part of Scottish literature which is written in Braid Scots or Anglic, to refer to it separately from Scots literature written in Gaelic, English, Latin, or any other tongue, I suggest '*Lallans*', adopting the term of Robert Burns. **1959** *Glasgow Herald* 29 May 8 Lallans is an artificial plaything of frustrated xenophobes. **1974** *Encycl. Brit. Macropædia* XVI. 410/1 Hugh MacDiarmid,..the most prominent exponent of Lallans, achieved an international reputation, but the Lallans revival has faded.

lallang, var. *lalang.

lallapaloosa (læ:lăpălū·să, -ză). *U.S. slang.* Also **lala-, lolla-, -palooser, -paloozer,** etc. [Fanciful formation.] Something outstandingly good of its kind.
1904 'H. McHugh' *I'm from Missouri* vi. 89 Saturday night we had our final parade with the fireworks finish, and it was a lallapalootza! **1909** F. B. Calhoun *Miss Minerva* xxvi. 204 You sho' is genoowine corn-fed, sterlin' silver, all-wool-an'-a-yard-wide, pure-leaf, Green-River Lollapaloosas. **1911** *Dialect Notes* III. 545 A second word-list from Nebraska... *Lallapaloosa,* something fine or grand; a term of approbation. 'You have a lallapaloosa of a hat', 'That's a lallapaloosa.' **1926** Wodehouse *Heart of Goof* i. 40 To-day he had been so preoccupied with his broken heart that he had made his shots absently, almost carelessly, with the result that at least one in every three had been a lallapaloosa. **1933** A. Merritt *Burn Witch Burn!* (1934) x. 135 She thinks this doll woman a lallapaloozer. Yeah, a lallapaloozer, a corker! **1947** W. Stevens *Let.* 28 Feb. (1967) 547, I think that the book, as a book, is a lollapalooza. **1951** *New Yorker* 20 Oct. 28/3 Though I had long ago forgotten the background, characters, and plot, I distinctly remembered it as a lollapaloosa. **1966** *Listener* 2 June 811/1 What is the tone of lalapalooza, since Hector was a pup, bumbershoot, hornswoggle, Milwaukee tumour, benzine buggy—or lalapalooza's equivalent, époustouflante? **1970** S. J. Perelman *Baby, it's Cold Inside* 172 All agreed that Luba Pneumatiç was a lollapaloosa, the Eighth Wonder of the World.

lallygag (læ·ligæg), *v. U.S. slang.* Also **lollygag.** [Origin unknown.] *intr.* To fool around; to 'neck'; to dawdle, to dally. Also as *sb.*, fooling around. Hence **la·llygagging** *vbl. sb.* and *ppl. a.*
1862 *Harper's Mag.* Aug. 324/1 Mr. Biggs paused and turned the flesh of the succulent lobster over with his finger. The gentleman inside addressed him: '..Try er lobstaw, bossy?' 'Ain't got no money,' said Mr. Biggs, still fingering the morsels. 'Oh, come now, none o' that ere lallygag,' responded the gentleman. **1868** *Northern Vindicator* (Estherville, Iowa) 30 Dec., The lascivious lolly-gagging lumps of licentiousness who disgrace the common decencies of life by their love-sick fawnings at our public dances. **1869** *Tidal Wave* (Silver City, Idaho) 15 Jan. 3/2 They are too pious to encourage dicing, and the feature of their entertainments may be what the boys call 'lally-gagging'. **1870** *Northern Vindicator* (Estherville, Iowa) 19 Feb., The weather once more is 'salubrious' and balmy, and indicates that winter will not lollygag in the lap of spring. **1880** E. L. Wheeler *Boss Bob, King of Bootblacks* vii. 9/1, I kin get lots o' jobs, if I'd take my pay in friendship an' all sech lollygag. **1910** *Sat. Even. Post* 30 July 19/1 Frank lally-gagged through the first term and came back for the second. **1927** D. Runyon *Trials & Other Tribulations* (1947) 112 When your correspondent was a 'necker' of no mean standing back in the dim and misty past, they called it 'lally-gagging'. **1949** *Jrnl. Amer. Folk-Lore* Jan.–Mar. 63 'Lally-gaggin' was Grandmother's word for love-making. **1965** 'E. Queen' *Fourth Side of Triangle* i. 2 Lallygagging around under the awning away from the gassy streets. **1969** S. Greenlee *Spook who sat by Door* xi. 95 We lolly-gag, maybe turn on, or cook up some soul food. **1971** D. Bagley *Freedom Trap* iii. 20, I said there was to be no lally-gagging around with the staff, Rearden; you just stick to doing your job. **1973** *Springfield* (Mass.) *Union* 25 Sept. 14/1 The Dow Jones average of 30 industrials, which lollygagged most of the day, gained strongly in afternoon trading.

lam (læm), *sb.*^{3} *U.S. slang.* [f. *lam *v.* 3.] Escape, flight. Esp. in phr. *on the lam,* on the run; *take it on the* (or *a*) *lam* (see quot. 1935).
1897 *Appleton's Pop. Sci. Monthly* Apr. 832 *To do a lam,* meaning to run. **1904** 'No. 1500' *Life in Sing Sing* xiii. 263 He plugged the main guy for keeps and I took it on a lam for mine. **1931** [see *area-way* s.v. *area 2 b]. **1935** A. J. Pollock *Underworld Speaks* 118/2 *Take it on the lam,* to run away; escape. **1953** W. R. Burnett *Vanity Row* xiii. 94 The dolly was on the lam. **1959** *John o' London's* 10 Dec. 322/3 A young man stops the car, points a gun at them, and orders them to drive him to the border. He is a juvenile delinquent, 'on the lam' after a robbery. **1968** *Washington Post* 5 July A20/1 What useful public purpose is served by making it easy for convicts on the lam from a state penitentiary to acquire an arsenal? **1972** G. Baxt *Burning Sappho* ix. 158 Were you stalling for time while your Brunhilde takes it on the lam?

lam, *v.* Add: **3.** *intr.* To run off, to escape, to 'beat it'. *U.S. slang.*
1886 A. Pinkerton *Thirty Yrs. a Detective* 41 After he [*sc.* a pickpocket] has secured the wallet he will..utter the word 'lam!' This means to let the man go, and to get out of the way as soon as possible. **1901** *Smart Set* Oct. 3/2 Well, when he [*sc.* Uncle Remus] was just driven to desperation he 'lammed aloose', and so shall I. **1932** *Evening Sun* (Baltimore) 9 Dec. 31/5 *Lam,* run away from the police. **1935** R. E. Sherwood *Petrified Forest* II. 124 Say, boss—we better lam out of here. *Ibid.* 158, I hear a car coming, boss. We better lam. *Ibid.* 162 When they get around there, we'll lam. **1946** 'P. Quentin' *Puzzle for Fiends* (1947) xvi. 111 When I get my share, I'll lam out of this place so fast you won't see me for dust. **1959** P. Townend *Died o' Wednesday* iv. 61 What was it they always did in any self-respecting cowboy film?—lammed out..and took to the hills. **1973** M. Mackintosh *King & Two Queens* xii. 171 The time of death..[was] four days before Fisher lammed out.

Hence **la·mster, la·mmister,** a fugitive, a person on the run.
1904 'No. 1500' *Life in Sing Sing* 250 *Lamaster,* fugitive from justice; one who forfeits bail-bonds. **1926** *Clues* Nov. 161/2 *Lamster,* fugitive. Also a member of a pickpocket gang that leaves with the loot. **1948** E. L. Irey *Tax Dodgers* (1949) 47 'My line,' he said, 'is keeping quiet.' With that he had told Kelly that he was a lammister, in other words fleeing justice. **1953** W. Burroughs *Junkie* (1972) ix. 81 Gamblers, perverts, drifters, and lamsters from every state in the Union. **1962** K. Orvis *Damned & Destroyed* xii. 81 Smuggling American lamsters into Canada.

Lamarckian. A. *adj.* (Later examples.) **B.** *sb.* (Examples.)
1928 G. H. Carpenter *Biol. Insects* xii. 365 To sum up this brief discussion on the Lamarckian factor in evolution, it must be admitted that belief in it is encouraged on account of the simple manner in which it explains—if it be a true cause—many observed facts of life. **1953** E. Mayr et al. *Methods & Princ. Syst. Zool.* i. 11 Most of them [*sc.* late nineteenth-century taxonomists]..were Lamarckians. **1972** *Science* 12 May 623/1 The Lamarckian postulate that characters acquired by parents during their own lives can be passed on to their offspring. **1972** *National Observer* (U.S.) 27 May 21/3 The controversy between Darwinians and Lamarckians has raged for nearly a century.

Lamarque (lamā·ɹk). [Prob. a. the name of Comte Maximilien *Lamarque* (1770–1832), French general and politician.] A variety of noisette rose first introduced in 1830, bearing large, fragrant, white flowers with a yellow centre. Also *attrib.*
1837 T. Rivers *Rose Amateur's Guide* II. 82 Lamarque is another hybrid Noisette, approaching to the tea-scented rose, in the size and fragrance of its flowers. **1869** S. R. Hole *Bk. about Roses* viii. 122 Lamarque, the parent of Cloth-of-gold, well deserves a place on some sunny wall.. with its refined and graceful flowers. These are large and full, the outer petals of a soft pure white, the inner of a pale straw colour. **1885** C. M. Yonge *Nuttie's Father* II. viii. 101 She came in leading her little son..carrying a little bouquet for the guest of one La Marque rosebud and three lilies of the valley. **1965** G. S. Thomas *Climbing Roses* vi. 99 'Lamarque'..is a plant only for the warmer west outdoors.

lamb, *sb.* Add: **6.** *lamb-chop* [Chop *sb.*^{1} 2 b] (also *fig.*).
c **1838** C. Mathews in M. R. Booth *Eng. Plays of 19th Cent.* (1973) IV. 136 He ate three pounds and a half of lamb chops. **1865** Mrs. Stowe *House & Home Papers* 248 All the edible matters..would form those delicate dishes of lamb-chop. **1962** E. Lucia *Klondike Kate* ii. 40 Mrs Bettis was persistent and her daughter was quite a lamb chop, so he finally agreed. **1963** R. Carrier *Great Dishes of World* 145 Place lamb chops in a flat dish just large enough to hold them and pour marinade mixture over them. **1974** 'E. Lathen' *Sweet & Low* xvii. 165 Deep in a choice between lamb chops and pork chops.

7. **lamb's fry** (in U.S. also **lamb fries**) [cf. FRY *sb.*² 2 b] (further examples); in the U.K., lamb's offal, esp. testicles; in Austral. and N.Z., lamb's liver.

1822 W. KITCHINER *Cook's Oracle* (ed. 4) 492 *Lamb's fry.* Fry it plain..garnish with crisp parsley. **1861** MRS. BEETON *Bk. Househ. Managem.* 353, 1 lb. of lamb's fry. **1894** [see FRY *sb.*² 2 b]. **1936** S. E. NASH *Cooking Craft* (ed. 3) xii. 106 Lamb's fry consists of the liver, sweet-bread, heart, and some of the inside fat. **1944** H. WENTWORTH *Amer. Dial. Dict.* 345 *Lamb fries*, lamb's testicles. **1951** *Good Housek. Home Encycl.* 530 *Lamb's fry*, sliced lamb's offal, cooked as a rich stew. **1963** ROMBAUER & BECKER *Joy of Cooking* (ed. 4) 449/1 Skin, cut into quarters: 4 medium lamb fries. **1966** BAKER *Austral. Lang.* (ed. 2) iv. 83 We could pause to consider *lambs' fry*, as a euphemism for testicles from *marked* or castrated lambs... Our later use of *lamb's fry* for lamb liver is one of our most 'refined' additions. **1969** R. & D. DE SOLA *Dict. Cooking* 138 *Lamb fries*, lamb testicles.

Lamba (læ·mbă), *sb.* and *a.* Also **Ilamba.** [African name.] **A.** *sb.* **a.** An African of a Bantu people in Northern Zambia and Zaïre; also used as collect. sing. = this people. **b.** The language of this people. **B.** *adj.* Of or pertaining to this people or their language.

1908 A. C. MADAN *Lala–Lamba Handbk.* p. iii, The Lala and Lamba dialects are so nearly identical, and both so closely allied to the Wisa, that knowledge of either is a sufficient introduction to the other. **1919** H. H. JOHNSTON *Compar. Study Bantu & Semi-Bantu Lang.* I. iii. 207 Lala-Lamba is spoken..east and north of the Kafue watershed. **1937** I. SCHAPERA *Bantu-Speaking Tribes S. Afr.* xiv. 314 In Lamba (Central Bantu) the word is *umusi*. **1948** M. GUTHRIE *Classification Bantu Lang.* 78 Njlamba, iki—(Ilamba). **1949** E. A. NIDA *Morphol.* (ed. 2) 51 Ilamba, a language of Tanganyika. **1950** RADCLIFFE-BROWN & FORDE *Afr. Syst. Kinship & Marriage* 221 The Lamba on the Kafue river seem to have a very similar family system. **1956** W. V. BRELSFORD *Tribes N. Rhodesia* vi. 46 Lamba area as a whole, because of its proximity to the copperbelt, is the most mixed area in the territory. **1956** J. LOTZ in Saporta & Bastian *Psycholinguistics* (1961) 9/2 In certain languages the whole sentence is constructed in a single syntactic key..as in Ilamba of Northern Rhodesia. **1957** W. M. HAILEY *Afr. Survey* (rev. ed.) iii. 113 Studies made..of the Zulu, Shona, and Lamba languages. **1957** V. W. TURNER *Schism & Continuity in Afr. Soc.* viii. 255 Among the Lamba of the Ndola District of Northern Rhodesia..traceable cross-cousin marriages formed an extremely low proportion of the total marriages recorded.

Lambadar, Lambardar, varr. LUMBERDAR.

1855 [see LUMBERDAR]. **1908** *New Reformer* (Madras) II. 68 Securing the co-operation of the literate among them and the Lambardars to bring about sanitary reforms, etc. **1920** *Glasgow Herald* 12 Jan. 9/6 At one village the Lambardar was obstructive, would give no information, and refused to accompany him. **1960** J. MASTERS *Venus of Konpara* xxiii. 177 Our lambardar thinks she [*sc.* a tigress] has not started to eat yet. **1971** R. DENTRY *Encounter at Kharmel* iii. 46, I am not the Wazir... I am only the Lambadar, Raza Khan. *Ibid.* 48 Lambadar is honorific. I am Mayor, you see?

lambaste, *v.* Delete *slang* and *dial.* Add: Also **lambast.** **b.** *fig.* To scold, castigate.

1886 *Harper's Mag.* July 321/2 With an avalanche of facts, sarcasm and ridicule..a more complete lambasting and more vigorous and thorough roasting than Wise gave Bontelle was never known. **1891** KIPLING *Light that Failed* viii. 151, I only gave him his riding-orders to—to lambast you on general principles for not producing work that will last. **1930** *Times* 13 Jan. 14/4 Mr. Maxton was heard to say, 'Mr. Chairman... It has been said that you were going to "lambast" me at this conference.' **1938** J. RICE *Somers Inheritance* I. iv. 29 His sermons got down to the bed-rock..even if they..failed to lambaste wickedness with quite the fury it deserved. **1947** *People* 22 June 4/2 So he has castigated America for daring to interfere in Palestine, and now he lambasts Russia for meddling in the affairs of the little countries. **1951** *Oxf. Dict. Nursery Rhymes* 28 Halliwell struck a saner note (1842) but greedily copied down as facts any theories related to him, and though he lambasted Ker, he was not above speculation himself. **1956** *Jrnl. Educ.* July 304 Having myself been lambasted more than once by the Italicists because I dared to qualify my praise of their handwriting. **1958** *Times* 16 Oct. 8/5 To this lambasting Dr. Rowse was all smiles and soothing words. **1967** *Boston Globe* 20 May 2/2 He lambasted teaching techniques, saying they have become 'a disciplinary practice'. **1969** N. HARE in A. Chapman *New Black Voices* (1972) 428 They lambasted the ultradevotion of many black intellectuals to jazz music. **1972** *Newsweek* 10 Jan. 19/1 If the economy should stay sour, the alternative script called for Mr. Nixon to lambaste the labour bosses.

lambda. Add: **4.** *Physics.* **lambda point,** the temperature (approximately 2·18 K) below which liquid helium in equilibrium with its vapour exhibits superfluidity, and at which there is a sharp maximum and apparent discontinuity in its specific heat; *transf.*, any temperature at which the specific heat of a substance exhibits similar behaviour, increasing at an increasing rate as the temperature is raised to this value and then dropping abruptly; hence *lambda curve, line* (on a phase diagram), *transition.* Freq. written as *λ point*, etc.

1932 W. H. & A. P. KEESOM in *Proc. Sect. Sci. Kon. Akad. Wetensch. Amsterdam* XXXV. 742 The specific heat of liquid helium at about 2·19° K falls from a value of 3·0 to a value of about 1·1 certainly within 0·02 degree... For convenience sake it is desirable to introduce a name for the point at which this jump occurs. According to a suggestion made by Prof. Ehrenfest we propose to call that point, considering the resemblance of the specific heat curve with the Greek letter *λ*, the lambda-point. **1933** W. H. KEESOM in *Ibid.* XXXVI. 149 It is in this sense that..we speak of the lambda-point..and of the lambda-curve. **1940** *Physical Rev.* LVII. 417 Measurements of the temperature variation of the adiabatic and isothermal Young's and rigidity moduli and of the coefficient of thermal expansion of pressed specimens of ammonium chloride in the neighbourhood of the λ-point transition at 242·8° K are reported. **1952** J. F. ALLEN in F. E. Simon et al. *Low Temperature Physics* iii. 73 The phase diagram of liquid helium..is crossed by a line which has been called the λ-line. **1958** CONDON & ODISHAW *Handbk. Physics* v. xi. 159/2 The λ transition involves no detectable change in spatial structure. **1964** *Physical Rev.* CXXXV. A1696/1 One would expect that the elastic properties of *β* brass near its lambda point should strongly resemble those of other solids which undergo cooperative order–disorder transitions. **1966** K. MENDELSSOHN *Quest for Absolute Zero* x. 234 The characteristic feature of superflow..was transport completely free of friction, taking place at a 'critical velocity' which only depended on temperature and vanished at the lambda-point.

5. *Chem.* A millionth of a litre; usu. denoted by λ.

1934 P. L. KIRK in *Mikrochemie* XIV. 13 It seems logical to use the designations mm³ = μl = λ. Such a procedure could simplify discussion considerably if the letter lambda were used with this significance, and we shall in future adhere to this usage. *Ibid.*, Since 1 l. of normal solution contains 1 equivalent..1 λ contains 1 micro-equivalent. **1939** *Mikrochemie* XXVI. 32 All the drops should have the same volume, 1 λ. **1939** E. J. CONWAY *Micro-diffusion Anal.* i. 4 For the actual designation of the minute quantities or volumes..we have the milligramme (mg.), and the gamma (γ or 0·001 mg.), also termed the microgramme (μg) and the lambda (λ or 0·001 ml.—introduced by Kirk). **1961** A. STEYERMARK *Quantitative Org. Microanalysis* (ed. 2) i. 2 The terms gamma (γ), and lambda (λ) are to be substituted with microgram (μg.) and microliter (μl.) respectively. **1974** *Nature* 15 Nov. p. xi (Advt.), Corning disposable micro-sampling pipettes are made from 'Pyrex' brand borosilicate glass... The accuracy of the graduated 5 Lambda (λ) is ± 1%.

b. *Nuclear Physics.* Used, usu. *attrib.*, to denote a neutral hyperon (and its anti-particle) which has a mass 2183 times that of the electron, a spin of ½, and zero isospin, and on decaying usually produces a nucleon and a pion; † orig. applied to other hyperons also. Freq. written as *Λ*.

1954 *Physical Rev.* XCIII. 861/1 We have reported two examples of $Λ^0$ particles produced in hydrogen by negative pions ($π^-$) of 1·5-Bev kinetic energy. *Ibid.*, We are using here the nomenclature suggested for *V* events at the International Congress on Cosmic Radiation, Bagnères-de-Bigorre, France. Accordingly $Λ^{0,+,-}$ → nucleon + pion + $Q_Λ$. *Ibid.* XCVI. 543/1 The known hyperons, $Λ^-$, $Ω^-$, have masses equivalent to 1200 and 1320 Mev, respectively. **1963** *Sci. Amer.* Jan. 40/2 When a $\bar{K}^-$ meson struck a proton (p), a small fraction of the collisions produced a neutral lambda particle ($Λ^0$) and a negative and a positive pi meson. **1963** K. W. FORD *World of Elem. Particles* vi. 179 The sigma particle lives too short a time to move a measurable distance.., decaying almost at once into a lambda and a photon ($Σ^0 \to Λ^0 + γ$). **1968** M. S. LIVINGSTON *Particle Physics* iv. 80 This evidence was the observation of V tracks consisting of two charged-particle tracks coming from a common origin, of which one was identified as a proton and the other as a negative pion. The neutral particle which decayed to give these products, now called the lambda-zero, ($Λ^0$), must have had a mass greater than the sum of proton and pion masses.

Lambeg (læ·mbeg). The name of a village near Belfast, N. Ireland, used *attrib.* of the large drums traditionally beaten there on ceremonial occasions; also *absol.* Hence **La·mbegger,** one who beats such a drum.

1932 *Sun* (Baltimore) 18 Nov. 3/6 The booming 'lamlegs' [*sic*], huge goatskin drums which are an important part of this kind of celebration. **1938** R. HAYWARD *In Praise of Ulster* 23 Of all the bands the Lambeggers alone are of the real vintage. *Ibid.* 24 Nothing in the world is quite like a Lambeg Band... The combination is usually composed of four or six gigantic drums. **1949** H. SHEARMAN *Ulster* xxxiii. 299 Not far from Lisburn, on the Belfast side, is Lambeg, a place traditionally famous for drums, for it used to be a great centre for..the drumming parties which used to be so characteristic of the Orange organization. The largest type of Orange drum used to be referred to as a Lambeg drum, and when one beat a tattoo on it one was said to beat Lambeg. **1952** D. O'D. HANNA *Face of Ulster* x. 112 Slowly and inexorably the drumming parties creep past, for the Lambeggars do not march. **1966** S. HEANEY in *Listener* 29 Sept. 475/3 Orange drums, Tyrone 1966. The lambeg balloons at his belly, weighs Him back on his haunches. **1970** *Guardian* 8 Aug. 1/5 The Lambeg drums, the noisiest and most fervent symbol of Protestant supremacy in Northern Ireland, will not be beaten in Londonderry next Wednesday.

Lambert (læ·mbəɹt). [The name of Johann Heinrich *Lambert* (1728–77), German mathematician.] **1.** **a.** In *Cartography* used *attrib.* and in the possessive to designate certain map projections devised by Lambert, *spec.* a conical conformal projection having two standard parallels along which the scale is true. Also *ellipt.* as *Lambert.*

1879 *Encycl. Brit.* X. 207/2 A translation of this essay [of Gauss's] is to be found in the Philosophical Magazine for 1828.., where Lambert's projection comes out as a particular solution of the general problem. **1912** A. R. HINKS *Map Projections* ii. 18 When the conical orthomorphic projection is used, it is always that with two standard parallels, which is Lambert's second, or Gauss'. **1953** A. H. ROBINSON *Elem. Cartogr.* iii. 43 The Lambert conic projection..has concentric parallels and equally spaced straight meridians that meet the parallels at right angles... It has two standard parallels, but the spacing of the other parallels on the Lambert increases away from the standard parallels. *Ibid.* iv. 74 The Lambert azimuthal equal-area projection is most useful when centered in the area of interest. **1971** I. G. GASS et al. *Understanding Earth* xv. 224 (*caption*) A possible geometrical fit of the southern continents at the 500-fathom..contour... Lambert equal area projection.

b. In *Physics* used in the possessive to designate two laws enunciated by Lambert: (*a*) the intensity of the light emitted by an element of area of a perfectly diffusing surface is proportional to the cosine of the angle between the direction of emission and the normal to the surface; (*b*) (see quots. 1911, 1966).

1895 *Electrician* 20 Sept. 672/2 The diffused reflection practically follows Lambert's cosine law. **1911** R. W. WOOD *Physical Optics* (rev. ed.) xv. 437 Lambert's law states that each layer of equal thickness absorbs an equal fraction of the light which traverses it. **1952** R. W. DITCHBURN *Light* xv. 441 Experimental observations on the transmission in a homogeneous medium which absorbs, but does not scatter, the light are summarized in Lambert's law, which may be written $L(z) = L_0 e^{-2αz}$. The constant 2*α* is called the absorption coefficient. **1966** D. G. BRANDON *Mod. Techniques Metallogr.* ii. 65 The fraction of the incident intensity transmitted through a thin slice, of thickness *t*, can be calculated from Lambert's law: $I/I_0 = \exp(-μt)$, where *μ* is the absorption coefficient.

2. (Written **lambert.**) A unit of luminance equal to one lumen per square centimetre (equivalent to approximately 3180 candelas per square metre).

1915 P. G. NUTTING in *Electr. World* 6 Feb. 333/1, I prefer to speak of a brightness of so many 'lamberts'. This term is now well understood in our laboratory. Where required it is easily translated into lumens and any desired units of area. **1915** H. E. IVES in *Ibid.* 20 Feb. 460/1 Dr. Nutting..comes forward with an excellent name,..the 'lambert'. But he applies it, in my opinion, to the wrong unit... Let us say that a surface has a brightness of one 'lambert' if it is as bright as a 'Lambert's law' white surface under unit illumination. **1923** L. C. MARTIN *Colour* 178 The normal radiation corresponds to 1/π candles per square centimetre when the brightness is 1 lambert. **1953** AMOS & BIRKINSHAW *Television Engin.* I. 280, 1 lambert = 1 lumen per square centimetre = 0·3183 candle per square centimetre = 2·054 candles per square inch = 929 foot-lamberts. **1962** F. I. ORDWAY et al. *Basic Astronautics* iii. 37 (*table*) Sun... Surface brightness, lamberts... $6{\cdot}24 \times 10^5$. **1966** D. G. BRANDON *Mod. Techniques Metallogr.* i. 58 Haine gives the minimum practical screen brightness [of an electron microscope] as 3×10^{-4} lamberts.

Lambeth (læ·mbĕþ). [The name of a South London borough.] **1.** Used allusively (chiefly *attrib.*) to refer to the Archbishop of Canterbury, whose palace is at Lambeth, or to the Church of England; esp. in **Lambeth Conference,** an assembly of the Anglican bishops, usu. held decennially at Lambeth Palace; **Lambeth degree,** a degree *honoris causa* conferred by the Archbishop of Canterbury.

1859 W. F. HOOK *Church Dict.* (ed. 8) 429/2 *Lambeth degrees*, the popular designation given to degrees conferred by the Archbishop of Canterbury, who has the power of giving degrees in any of the faculties. **1867** *Times* 10 Dec. 7/3 The Bishops..complain that the necessary work of their dioceses is too much for them, and demand an addition to their numbers. That demand is not likely to be listened to while they can find time and thought for a Lambeth Conference. **1875** *Encycl. Brit.* II. 369/2 The archbishop also continues to grant degrees in the faculties of theology and law, which are known as Lambeth Degrees. *Ibid.* 654/2 In 1595,..the Primate, Whitgift, accepted a series of articles proposed by Dr Whitaker of Cambridge. These, generally known as the Lambeth Articles, were strongly Calvinistic in tone. **1902** *Ibid.* XXX. 120/2 The resolutions of the Lambeth Conferences have never been regarded as synodical decrees, but their weight has increased with each conference; and in particular the 'Lambeth Quadrilateral' of 1888 has already had a great effect as a plan of reunion. **1941** W. TEMPLE *Citizen & Churchman* iv. 70 It is the duty of Lambeth to remind Westminster of its responsibility to God; but this does not mean that Westminster is responsible to Lambeth. **1958** E. L. MASCALL *Recovery of Unity* vii. 153 The often-quoted statement of the Lambeth Conference Committee. **1974** J. MELVILLE *Nun's Castle* iii. 62 She kept to a set of religious observances which.. would have caused raised eyebrows in both the Vatican and Lambeth Palace.

2. Used *attrib.* or *absol.* to designate a kind of glazed and painted earthenware manufactured in Lambeth from the 17th to the 19th century.

[**1863** W. CHAFFERS *Marks Pott. & Porc.* 131 *Lambeth.* About 1640 some Dutch potters established themselves here, and by degrees the manufacture of earthenware became important... The ware made here was a sort of

Delft, with landscapes and figures painted in blue.] **1884** C. Schreiber *Jrnl.* 23 Sept. (1911) II. 440 One of the Lambeth Wine bottles. *Ibid.* 17 Nov. 456 A cat..which he pronounced to be Lambeth (dated 1676). **1900** [see *Doulton]. **1948** F. H. Garner *Eng. Delftware* iv. 29 A Lambeth brick is illustrated. **1961** L. G. G. Ramsey *Connoisseur New Guide Antique Eng. Pott., Porc. & Glass* 27 'Lambeth' and 'Bristol' polychrome 'delftwares' of the second half of the seventeenth century. **1974** *Times* 26 Oct. 13/3 Immigrant Dutch potters had come to set up there [*sc.* in Lambeth], bringing with them the techniques for tin-plating earthenware which had been associated with Delft. The English products of these potters and their successors are called English Delftware, and that made in Lambeth is called Lambeth Delftware.

3. Lambeth Walk, the name of a street in Lambeth, used as the title of a Cockney song and dance first performed by Lupino Lane in the revue *Me and my Gal* in 1937.

1937 Furber & Gay (*song-title*) Lambeth Walk. **1939** *Times* 23 Mar. 14/4 The 'Lambeth Walk' and its successors have destroyed the tyranny of the foxtrot which for 20 years has made the ball-room an unsociable place. **1942** J. W. Drawbell *Dorothy Thompson's Eng. Journey* ix. 83 She can hardly pull herself away from that cheerful, excited London throng—from the people who have fought fires while the bombs fell and can still sing and dance the Lambeth Walk. **1962** *Guardian* 31 Dec. 5/1 The Lambeth Walk, invented in the thirties..to publicize 'Me and My Girl'.

‖ **Lambic** (lañbik). Also **Lambick.** [Fr.; cf. *alambic* a still.] A strong beer brewed in Belgium.

1889 *Cent. Dict., Lambick,* a kind of strong beer made in Belgium by the process called the self-fermentation of worts. **1908** *Daily Chron.* 2 Mar. 5/6 On being offered a glass of champagne he refused it, asking for some 'Lambic', a popular beverage in Belgium. **1952** G. Gordon in E. Fodor *Benelux in 1952* 69 The high-density drink..is *Geuze* (so called when it is bottled, and *Lambic* when it is on tap). **1956** A. Campbell *Bk. Beer* vi. 95 In Belgium there is a beer known as *Lambic,*..left to stand and mature for about two years in granaries, fermenting slowly in wooden casks. **1960** [see *Faro[2]]. **1964** L. Brewer *A to Z of Holidays Abroad* 107 A wheat-and-barley based beer is made, draught called *Lambic,* bottled *Geuze.*

lambie. (Later examples.)

1879 C. M. Yonge *Burnt Out* ix. 149 Is he hurt? Is my little lambie hurt? **1935** N. Mitchison *We have been Warned* iv. 357 Oh, Lilias, what have you got, Lambie—oh, a *lovely* stone.

la·mbkill. *N. Amer.* (See Lamb *sb.* 7 b.)

1790 L. Castiglioni *Viaggio negli Stati Uniti dell'America* II. 271 *K[almia] Angustifolia...* Sheep poison, Ivy, Dwarf-Laurell, Lamb-kill. **1814** J. Bigelow *Florula Bostoniensis* 103 *Kalmia angustifolia,*..a low shrub with rose coloured flowers, very common in low grounds, and known by the names *sheep poison, lambkill, low laurel,* &c. **1851** [see Lamb *sb.* 7 b]. **1898** C. A. Creevey *Flowers of Field* 515 Lambkill..is a low shrub.. with narrow, evergreen leaves in whorls of three. **1939** *Nat. Geogr. Mag.* Aug. 255/1 Other poisonous members of the heath family are the kalmias, frequently called 'lambkill' from the effect they have on grazing animals. **1954** C. J. Hylander *Macmillan Wild Flower Bk.* 281 Sheep laurel..is also known as lambkill because of the severely toxic substance in the leaves. **1965** E. Richardson *Living Island* 120 Not yet completely grown up in lambkill, wild-roses and blueberry bushes. **1974** A. Huxley *Plant & Planet* xxv. 283 In North America species of *Kalmia*.. are known as Sheep-kill or Lamb-kill.

Lamb shift (læm ʃift). *Physics.* [f. the name of Willis E. *Lamb* (b. 1913), U.S. physicist (who with R. C. Retherford demonstrated the effect in 1947) + Shift *sb.*] A displacement of energy levels in hydrogen and hydrogen-like atoms such that those with the same values of the quantum numbers *n* and *j* but different values of *l* are not coincident, as predicted by Dirac's theory, but separated by a very small amount (the level with the lower value of *l* being the higher).

1948 *Physical Rev.* LXXIV. 1157 The effects treated are the Lamb shift, the correction of the *g*-factor..and the correction of the Compton scattering cross section. **1950** *Ibid.* LXXVII. 745 (*heading*) Departure of the Lamb shift from the h^{-3} law in He+. **1958** Condon & Odishaw *Handbk. Physics* vii. 63/1 The Lamb shift has been interpreted..as resulting from changes in the electron self-energy which results from its interactions with the electromagnetic and electron–positron fields. **1964** E. A. Power *Introd. Quantum Electrodynamics* i. 7 The modern versions of quantum electrodynamics have enabled a very accurate comparison to be made between theory and experiment. Well-known examples are the Lamb shift energy splitting of the $2S_{\frac{1}{2}}$ and $2P_{\frac{1}{2}}$ levels in hydrogen and the radiative corrections to the magnetic moment of the electron. **1970** G. K. Woodgate *Elem. Atomic Struct.* iv. 69 Figure 4.3 shows the fine structure of the $n=2$ and $n=3$ levels of hydrogen, modified to take account of the Lamb shift. **1973** *McGraw-Hill Yearbk. Sci. & Technol.* 111/1 Experimental programs to measure heavy-ion Lamb shifts are now in progress.

‖ **lamdan** (læmdā·n). [Heb. *lamdān,* lit. one who has learned, f. *lāmadh* to learn.] A person learned in Jewish law; a Talmudic scholar.

1907 I. Zangwill *Ghetto Comedies* 124, I am enough of a *Lamdan* (pundit) to answer it. **1925** 'R. Learsi' *Kasriel the Watchman* 98 Some asserted that Getzel was a learned man, a *lamdan.* **1948** M. Samuel *Prince of Ghetto* xvii. 251 In Radziwiil there lived a *lamdan,* a scholarly Jew... All day long he studied, while his wife attended to the shop. **1970** *New Stand. Jewish Encycl.* 1174/1 *Lamdan,*..a person steeped in talmudic learning. **1973** *Jewish Chron.* 16 Mar. 18/3 He lives in the ideal Jewish world, where the rabbi is the lamdan.

lame, *sb.*[2] Restrict †*Obs.* to sense in Dict. and add: **2.** *U.S. slang.* A socially unsophisticated person; one who is not skilled in the behaviour patterns of a particular group.

Freq. in Black English.

1959 *Esquire* Nov. 70J *A lame,* one who doesn't know what's happening. A square. **1967** *Trans-action: Social Sci. & Community* Apr. 5/2 One either knows 'what's happening' on the street, or he is a 'lame'... Negroes..have contributed much to the street tongue... Such expressions as 'a lame', 'taking care of righteous business'..and 'soul' can be retraced to Negro street life. **1968** in A. Dundes *Mother Wit* (1973) 331/1 Who's the lame who says he knows the game And where did he learn to play? **1971** *Black Scholar* Sept. 39/2 'You owe me some buns, lame!' teased a tall, lanky, yellow young man. **1972** J. Wambaugh *Blue Knight* (1973) vi. 93 They're a couple of lames trying to groove with the Kids. They're nothing.

lame, *a.* **3.** *lame duck,* substitute for def.: (*a*) (see Duck *sb.*[1] 9); (*b*) *U.S. Politics,* an office-holder who is not, or cannot be, re-elected; *spec.* (before 1933), a defeated member in the short session of Congress after a November election; also *attrib.*; (*c*) a ship that is damaged, esp. one left without a means of propulsion; (*d*) an industry, commercial firm, etc., that cannot survive without financial help, esp. by means of a government subsidy. Hence as *v. trans.* (*rare*), to help (a disabled person); *to lame-duck it*: to travel with difficulty..

1761, etc. [see Duck *sb.*[1] 9]. **1863** *Congress. Globe* 14 Jan. 307/1 In no event..could it [*sc.* the Court of Claims] be justly obnoxious to the charge of being a receptacle of 'lame ducks' or broken down politicians. **1876** C. Chapman *First Ten Yrs. Sailor's Life at Sea* x. 411 A lame duck on the sea means a ship which has been more or less damaged while crossing the perilous ocean. **1910** *N.Y. Even. Post* 8 Dec. 8 'Lame Duck Alley'..is the name they [*sc.* reporters] have given to a screened-off corridor in the White House offices, where statesmen who went down in the recent electoral combat may meet. **1922** *N.Y. Times* 6 Dec. 18/2 Senator Norris is all for the plan 'to have the convening of Congress moved up to avoid lame-duck Congresses'. **1925** *Independent* (Boston, Mass.) 21 Feb. 213/1 The proposed Constitutional amendment..has been usually designated as the 'lame-duck' amendment. **1932** *Times* 14 Dec. 13/2 A 'lame duck' Administration was in power, and a 'lame duck' Congress still in being. **1933** P. A. Eaddy *Hull Down* xiv. 256 Our old 'lame duck' had not done so badly after all. **1943** N. Balchin *Small Back Room* 70 It's so bloody *dangerous* lame-ducking it home by yourself. **1963** J. Fowles *Collector* ii. 213, I want to be his friend and lameduck him in London. **1970** *New Yorker* 14 Nov. 175/3 My father, with his predilection for lame ducks, was the natural person to try to rescue it. **1972** *Economist* 26 Aug. 8 The *Economist* calls lame ducks those industries whose survival is claimed to depend on government subsidy. In the United States a lame duck is a politician whose current term is his last, owing to defeat in a primary or general election, or other reasons. **1973** *Times* 5 June 22/6 The Government, being at that stage still keen on its lame duck policy, refused to help, and the board went away to have a further think. **1973** *Listener* 29 Nov. 741/1 It is now the Congress..which will be disposing what a lame duck President may propose.

lamé (la·me). [Fr., f. *lame* Lame *sb.*[1]] A material consisting of silk or other yarns interwoven with metallic threads.

1922 *Daily Mail* 16 Dec. 15/3 Fur panels trim evening gowns of lamé. **1930** *Times* 13 Mar. 11/6 The collection included some beautiful Court gowns, one in pink marquisette embroidered in silk for a débutante had a silver lamé train. **1950** P. Bottome *Under Skin* xii. 106 The Paris doll, splendid in turquoise-blue taffeta under a golden lamé coatee, was poised within reach of Henriette's hand. **1968** J. Ironside *Fashion Alphabet* 235 Synthetic metal yarns are now used in lamés. **1973** *Fortnum & Mason Christmas Catal.* 41/1 Gold..light-weight lamé jersey turban. Also available in silver. £27.50.

la·me-brain. *colloq.* [f. Lame *a.* + Brain *sb.*] A dull-witted or stupid person. Also **la·me-brained** *a.*

1929 Wodehouse *Mr. Mulliner Speaking* i. 16 A girl with an aunt who knew all about Shakespeare and Bacon must of necessity live in a mental atmosphere into which a lame-brained bird like himself could scarcely hope to soar. **1945** S. J. Perelman *Crazy like Fox* 82 'Well, Miss "Lame Brain",' he retorted sardonically, 'maybe you had better stop galvanizing around nights and pay attention!' **1948** G. H. Johnston *Death takes Small Bites* vii. 163 But it's the same bunch of lame-brains kiddin' themselves they're master minds of crime. **1962** K. Orvis *Damned & Destroyed* xix. 142 Not like the usual lame-brained addict. **1968** *New Yorker* 14 Sept. 58 None of your lame-brain philosophers ever cut any ice with me. **1972** *Times Lit. Suppl.* 24 Nov. 1426/3 We have finished feeling indulgent towards the disaffected lamebrains who turn this kind of stuff out.

lamellar, *a.* Add: **2.** *Physics.* = *laminar *a.* 2 (in the broader sense).

1931 W. Wilson *Theoret. Physics* I. viii. 190 Problems of lamellar flow in an incompressible fluid are mathematically identical with electrostatic problems in regions free from electric charges. **1942** M. P. Billings *Struct. Geol.* xvi. 299 In lamellar flow..the individual particles move in parallel sheets which slide over one another like the cards in a sheared playing pack. In such a viscous substance as magma beneath the surface of the earth, the flow is lamellar. **1966** *McGraw-Hill Encycl. Sci. & Technol.* XIII. 175/1 In some instances, streamline flow can best be depicted as formed from thin layers of fluid which slip past each other (lamellar flow).

lamelloid (lăme·l-, læ·mĕloid), *a. rare.* [f. Lamell(a + -oid.] Resembling a lamella.

1866 *Mem. Boston Soc. Nat. Hist.* I. 141 These transverse processes..possess regular lamelloid walls, so as to form rather canals than simple foramina for the artery.

lament, *v.* Add: **2.** Also with *over.*

1831 T. L. Peacock *Crotchet Castle* v. 85 He laments bitterly over the inventions of gunpowder, steam, and gas. **1853** C. Kingsley *Hypatia* I. xiii. 271 Why should they lament over other things?

lamented, *ppl. a.* Add: Also *absol.* or as *sb.*, esp. in phr. *the late lamented,* someone recently dead.

1864 C. M. Yonge *Trial* I. ix. 172 Depend upon it, the late lamented will remain in the ascendant till there are no breakers ahead. **1908** *Daily Chron.* 28 Sept. 4/7 An alternative in the Greek language was 'the blessed', but English can get no farther in the way of euphemism than 'the late lamented'. **1952** D. Ames *Murder, Maestro, Please* xvi. 111 You're the one whose husband identified the late lamented, aren't you? **1972** A. Hunter *Vivienne* ix. 113 He wouldn't happen to be the late lamented's husband?

‖ **lamentoso** (lamentōu·so). *Mus.* [It.] A direction indicating that a passage is to be played in a mournful style.

1876 Stainer & Barrett *Dict. Mus. Terms* 251/1 *Lamentoso,*..mournfully, plaintively. **1959** D. Cooke *Lang. Mus.* iii. 137 The *lamentoso* opening of the finale of Tchaikovsky's *Pathétique* Symphony. **1967** *Listener* 2 Feb. 177/3 This serene opening is followed by a striking fugue, in five parts, marked *lamentoso.*

laminagraph (læ·minăgrɑf). *Radiology.* Also **lamino-.** [f. Lamina + -graph.] = *tomograph. (Originally a particular design of tomograph.)

1938 J. Kieffer in *Amer. Jrnl. Roentgenol.* XXXIX. 497/1 The laminagraph is a device embodying the principle of roentgenographic body sectioning, or planigraphy... It was built at the instigation of, and in cooperation with, the director, Dr. Sherwood Moore, who named it (lamina: a thin layer). **1942** *Surg., Gynecol. & Obstetr.* LXXV. 508/2 The last case..demonstrates the increase of bone detail by laminagraph as compared to the usual x-ray examination. **1960** *Jrnl. Speech & Hearing Disorders* XXV. 137/2 With a multilayer laminagraph cassette or film-holder, it is possible to record simultaneously a number of adjacent planes or body sections with a single exposure.

Hence **la:minagra·phic** *a.*, of or pertaining to laminagraphy; **la·minagram,** a radiograph taken using a laminagraph; **lamina·graphy** = *tomography.

1938 *Amer. Jrnl. Roentgenol.* XXXIX. 507/2 The extent of the layer sharply rendered during laminagraphic motion is limited only by the size of the object roentgenographed and by the size of the film used. *Ibid.* 503/2 Satisfactory chest laminagrams can be made in one second. **1939** *Radiology* XXXIII. 560/1 The last method has also been spelled 'laminography' by various authors. *Ibid.* 560/2 Laminagraphy—a method whereby body-section roentgenography is accomplished by motion of the tube and film in planes parallel to one another and at any angle to the film surface. **1942** *Urologic & Cutaneous Rev.* XLVI. 706/1 Laminography permits the roentgenographic delineation of structures at different levels... Laminograms are made by synchronously moving the X-ray film and the tube carrier in opposite directions. **1960** *Jrnl. Speech & Hearing Disorders* XXV. 137/2 Laminagraphy is used most advantageously when skeletal structures are not clearly visualized with standard techniques. **1966** *Amer. Speech* XLI. 229 Clear images of vocal fold cross-sections during actual phonation by laminagraphic X-ray photographs. **1968** H. O. Anger in Gottschalk & Beck *Fund. Probl. in Scanning* xiv. 195 A tomographic or laminographic series will be obtained from a single rectilinear scan. **1969** R. & E. Brecher *Rays* xix. 258 The modern technique, known generally as body-section radiography but also as laminography, stratigraphy, tomography, and planigraphy, depends upon imparting a reciprocal motion to the X-ray tube and film. **1971** *Jrnl. Amer. Med. Assoc.* 16 Aug. 927/2 The ability to record both dynamic studies and 'thick' laminagrams.. reduces the time necessary for the physician to view the films. **1971** *Radiology* CI. 617/1 A rounded soft-tissue mass was seen near the canal of the infraorbital nerve at laminagraphy.

laminal, *a.* Add: **b.** *Phonetics.* Produced by the blade of the tongue.

1956 C. F. Hockett in *Internat. Jrnl. Amer. Ling.* XXII. 202/1 In all the Central Algonquian dialects.. there is..an apical or laminal affricate /c/. The affricate is laminal, with hushing offglide, in those languages.. which distinguish two spirants. **1964** P. Ladefoged *Phonetic Study W. Afr. Lang.* iv. 19 There are clear differences in the formant transitions which are due to using the blade as opposed to the tip of the tongue in the (laminal) denti-alveolar as opposed to the apical alveolar articulations. **1966** M. Pei *Gloss. Ling. Terminol.* 141

Laminal, pertaining to the blade (upper front surface) of the tongue; sometimes applied to palatal phonemes ([ʃ], [ʒ], [č] or [tʃ], [ǧ] or [dʒ], [j]). **1968** CHOMSKY & HALLE *Sound Pattern Eng.* vii. 313 The difference characterized by distributed versus nondistributed does not correspond precisely to the distinction between laminal and apical.

laminar, *a.* Add: **2.** *Physics.* Of the flow of a fluid: smooth and regular, the direction of motion at any point remaining constant as if the fluid were moving in a series of layers sliding over one another without mixing; *occas.* restricted to the case in which the layers are plane (cf. *LAMELLAR *a.* 2).

1895 H. LAMB *Hydrodynamics* iii. 34 This analysis may be illustrated by the so-called 'laminar' motion of a liquid. **1949** H. F. P. PURDAY *Streamline Flow* i. 6 In laminar flow in the strict use of the term, the fluid moves in a system of parallel planes, the velocity having everywhere the same direction, but the magnitude of the velocity is a function of the distance from some fixed plane of the system. The motion is not necessarily steady; it may, for instance, be periodic. **1965** D. A. GILBRECH *Fluid Mech.* (1966) vi. 265 In general, laminar flow occurs at low velocities, between close boundaries, when the fluid is very viscous, and when the fluid is of low density. **1968** PASSMORE & ROBSON *Compan. Med. Stud.* I. xxix. 8/2 Flow of gas through tubes is laminar at slow speeds, but at faster rates of flow molecular collisions set up eddies and the flow is then turbulent.

b. *transf.* Applied to a body whose shape is such as to produce a laminar flow of fluid in the boundary layer round it (at normal speeds).

1955 J. KESTIN tr. *Schlichting's Boundary Layer Theory* xiii. 229 The prevention of transition on laminar aerofoils. **1963** *Ann. Reg. 1962* 390 Handley Page continued the development of their laminar wing project, in which hundreds of small slits in an aircraft wing were used to suck air away from the so-called boundary layer around the wing and thus to reduce friction and hence fuel costs.

laminaria (læminēə·riă). [mod.L. (J. V. F. Lamouroux *Essai sur les genres de la famille des Thalassiophytes non articulées* (1813) 20), f. L. *lamina* thin plate or leaf.] A thin, flat, brown seaweed of the genus so called; also known as oar-weed or kelp. Also *attrib.*

1848 A. HENFREY tr. *Schleiden's Plant* xiv. 399 For its [*sc.* the sea's] trees stand the Laminarias, often 30 feet long, waving their broad bands. **1857** GEO. ELIOT *Jrnl.* 28 June in *Lett.* (1954) II. 356 A long stretch of fine pale sand where the large roots of the *laminaria* were thrown up in abundance. **1883** [see LAMINARIAN *a.*]. **1935** J. E. TILDEN *Algae* vi. 269 Yendo, a Japanese phycologist, gives a recipe for making *kombu-mati*, or '*Laminaria* roll'. **1963** C. I. DICKINSON *Brit. Seaweeds* 82 The Laminarias are closely related to *Macrocystis* and *Lessonia*.

laminarize (læ·minărəiz), *v. Aeronaut.* [f. LAMINAR *a.* + -IZE.] *trans.* To design (an aircraft surface) so as to maximize the area over which the flow in the boundary layer is laminar. So **la·minarized** *ppl. a.*

1960 *Times* 2 Sept. 6/3 Handley Page are about to test in flight a complete laminarized wing. **1961** *Aeroplane* CI. 428/1 This has been achieved by 'laminarizing' nearly half the metal skin of the airframe, including the fuselage forward of the cabin, and the leading-edges back to half-chord on the tailplane and fin. These surfaces are free from protruding rivet heads or skin overlap. **1966** D. STINTON *Anat. Aeroplane* 265 The most promising technique is to laminarize a large part of the surface of an aeroplane—70 per cent or more—to bring about greatly improved lift/drag ratios.

Also **la:minariza·tion**, the design or use of laminarized surfaces.

1960 *Times* 2 Sept. 6/3 The airliner would cruise at high subsonic speed, although laminarization was still effective above sonic speed. **1964** *New Scientist* 6 Feb. 329/3 Beyond the first generation supersonic airliner, which is already half-way towards being an all-lifting surface, the next step might be laminarisation..in combination with an all-wing design. **1966** D. STINTON *Anat. Aeroplane* 265 The conclusion is that laminarization leads to huge savings in fuel weight.

laminate, *v.* Add: **5.** *trans.* To unite so as to form a laminated material.

1945 H. BARRON *Mod. Plastics* xi. 238 Latterly there has been a trend to use plastic fibres for weaving into fabrics which are then laminated in the usual way. **1949** B. L. DAVIES *Technol. Plastics* xiii. 238 The technique of laminating wood veneers using synthetic adhesives was developed to the stage when the very high strength bonds were sufficiently good for the manufacture of airscrews. **1955** KIRK & OTHMER *Encycl. Chem. Technol.* XIV. 696 These adhesives are much used for laminating metal foils to paper. **1973** *Daily Tel.* 6 Nov. 3/6 It [*sc.* the glue] is used in laminating and veneering wood.

laminating *vbl. sb.* (examples other than in comb.).

1939 H. R. SIMONDS *Industr. Plastics* (1940) v. 115 The paper or other laminating material is impregnated with the varnish. **1965** *Guardian* 31 Mar. 16/2 The British laminating trade is respected even as far away as North America for the severity of its standards.

laminate (læ·minĕt), *sb.* [Substantival use of the adj.] **1.** A manufactured laminated structure or material, as: **a.** = **laminated plastic*; **b.** a fabric or a flexible packaging material consisting of two or more layers held together by an adhesive.

1939 H. R. SIMONDS *Industr. Plastics* (1940) v. 118 Care must be taken to keep the steel platens free from scratches and dents, for even the most minute defect on the platen will repeat itself on the surface of the laminate. **1952** KIRK & OTHMER *Encycl. Chem. Technol.* VIII. 189 Paper- and fabric-base laminates have now been generally accepted as an engineering material. **1964** *McCall's Sewing* iv. 57/2 *Laminate*, a layer of fabric which has been fused with a layer of foam; currently the term is widely used for fabrics fused with foam rubber. **1967** *Times Rev. Industry* May 84/3 A host of combinations of film, foil and paper can provide the correct balance of product resistance, strength and light, vapour and moisture barrier. Such combinations, or laminates, are made possible by the availability of modern two-part adhesives. **1969** W. R. R. PARK *Plastics Film Technol.* vi. 148 For purposes of clarity, a laminate is defined as any combination of distinctly different plastic film materials or plastic plus nonplastic materials. **1970** *Financial Times* 13 Apr. 13/8 A layer of plastic is sandwiched between thin strips of steel. This has advantages in weight and strength and can compete with other types of laminates in office partitions, gearbox casings and building cladding. **1970** O. DOPPING *Computers & Data Processing* x. 138 Another static magnetic memory is the laminated ferrite memory which consists of a laminate of a number of thin sheets. **1973** *Sci. Amer.* July 39/1 Sandwich materials (such as plasterboard) and metal laminates (such as the active element of a thermostat) are constructed entirely of laminae, or layers, which taken together give the composite its form.

2. = *LAMINATION 3.

1968 W. E. WILLIS *Timber* v. 100 Laminated timber can be made with the laminates either vertical or horizontal.

laminated, *ppl. a.* Add: (Earlier and later examples.) Now common as a designation of various manufactured materials made by lamination, as *laminated glass*, a material consisting of two outer layers of plate or sheet glass attached to an inner layer of transparent plastic; *laminated plastic*, a more or less rigid material made by bonding together, usu. by means of heat and pressure, layers of cloth, paper, or the like that have been impregnated or coated with a synthetic resin; *laminated wood*, layers of wood bonded together with the grain in adjacent layers parallel (in contrast to plywood); also *laminated spring*, a leaf spring.

1665 HOOKE *Microgr.* 209 Each of them consisting of an infinite number of very thin shells or laminated orbiculations. **1888** *Lockwood's Dict. Mech. Engin.* 202 *Laminated spring*, a curved spring composed of thin plates superimposed one over the other, as distinguished from helical and coiled springs. **1912** *Automobile Engineer* Feb. 63/3 The main laminated springs are lighter than usual. **1930** *Engineering* 3 Jan. 26/1 The experience of the war showed unexpected weakness in the laminated springs of motor vehicles. **1930** *Canad. Patent Office Rec.* 12 Aug. 2145/1 (*title*) Laminated glass. **1931** *Official Gaz.* (U.S. Patent Office) 1 Dec. 270/2 The process of making a low moisture absorption laminated wood product which comprises.. impregnating the dried wood under pressure with a phenolic resin,..covering a plurality of laminations of the impregnated wood with a surface coating of powdered phenolic resin and molding the laminations into a homogeneous solid mass. **1933** *Product Engineering* Dec. 456/2 Laminated plastics, for example, can be given any of the usual machining operations. **1936** Laminated board [see *block-board* (*BLOCK *sb.* 23)]. **1937** R. S. MORRELL et al. *Synthetic Resins* iv. 125 Laminated material can also be made in the form of blocks, bars, rods, and tubes, by rolling the paper in special machines to the cross-section required, and then moulding them in the hydraulic press. **1938** *Encycl. Brit. Bk. of Year* 147/2 Translucent laminated plastic..made its appearance for use in instrument dials and lighting fixtures. **1939** *Chem. Abstr.* XXXIII. 3209 A pressed board consisting of 2 layers of asbestos stone bound together under pressure by a layer of resin-impregnated hard paper board has outstanding chem. resistance... This laminated board is especially well suited as the top for lab. benches. **1947** W. J. BROWN in P. I. Smith *Pract. Plastics* xxi. 281/2 Modern laminated plywoods can also be considered as belonging to the plastics group of materials because the plies are bonded together by means of synthetic resins. **1953** KIRK & OTHMER *Encycl. Chem. Technol.* X. 860 If the direction of the grain in adjacent layers is parallel, the product is called laminated wood and is not considered to be a type of plywood. **1957** *N. Z. Timber Jrnl.* Sept. 61/2 *Laminated board*, a number of veneers about ½in. thick placed edge on between an upper and a lower sheet of veneer or ply. **1958** BROWN & BETHEL *Lumber* (ed. 2) x. 293 Glued laminated timber structures are prepared by gluing together relatively small pieces of wood into a large timber member or structure..in such a manner that the grain of each of the small pieces or laminations is parallel to the length of the member. *Ibid.*, Laminated arches have been erected that provide buildings with clear spans up to 170 feet. **1962** *Which? Car Suppl.* Oct. 131/1 The windscreens in the Fiat 1500, Ford Taunus and Riley 4/72 were made of laminated glass. The windscreens in the other cars were made of toughened glass. **1965** R. B. ORAM *Cargo Handling* v. 84 Parcels of plywood, laminated boards, block boards, boxboards. **1965** *Guardian* 31 Mar. 16/1 Quantities of laminated fabric were imported from the United States to bridge the temporary gap between fashion demand and the setting up of domestic facilities. **1968** J. IRONSIDE *Fashion Alphabet* 235 Laminated fabric is one where two or more layers have been fused together by the use of an adhesive... Originally the idea was to provide the fabric either with a built-in lining or to make it reversible, but developments have proved that almost any two fabrics can be bonded together, and the desirable characteristics of both are retained. **1974** *Daily Tel.* 12 Jan. 5 (Advt.), Non-shrinking laminated curtains with the look of velvet.

lamination. Add: **1. c.** The process of uniting two or more layers of material so as to form a laminated material or object; the manufacture of laminates.

1945 H. BARRON *Mod. Plastics* xii. 259 Low pressure lamination is now a very popular technique. *Ibid.* 269 The continuous lamination of veneers into tubing and ducts by the winding method. **1952** J. P. CASEY *Pulp & Paper* II. xx. 1211 The lamination of metal foil to sulfite paper in the manufacture of candy or gum wrappers. **1967** *Times Rev. Industry* May 84/3 No plastic film is outstanding for all requirements but the lamination of, say, cellulose film and polypropylene provides a combination of properties not otherwise attainable. **1968** J. ARNOLD *Shell Bk. Country Crafts* xvii. 219 As far back as the sixteenth century..a Manchester bowyer, one Kelsall, laid a strip of ash along the belly of his bows and so became a pioneer of lamination.

2. Delete 'Also *concr.* in pl. laminæ' (see sense *3).

3. Any of the layers of a laminated material or object.

1858 [in Dict., sense 2]. **1905** S. P. THOMPSON *Dynamo-Electr. Machinery* (ed. 7) II. iii. 173 A laminated ring core built up of segmental laminations. **1920** *Whittaker's Electr. Engineer's Pocket-Bk.* (ed. 4) 241 Many [transformer] makers prefer laminating the conductor, and, of course, insulating each lamination. **1940** 'PLASTES' *Plastics in Industry* v. 59 Another form of laminated product, that made up of laminations of wood, should be especially attractive to the engineering world. **1968** J. ARNOLD *Shell Bk. Country Crafts* xvii. 218 The bows are built up with laminations of various woods and glass-fibre. **1971** I. G. GASS et al. *Understanding Earth* xiii. 171/1 [Sedimentary] laminations are defined as layers less than 1 cm in thickness.

laminator (læ·minēitəɹ). [f. LAMINAT(E *v.* + -OR.] A person or organization that makes laminates, esp. plastic laminates.

1941 *Modern Plastics* Oct. 31 (Advt.), Complete lists of molders, fabricators, laminators, material manufacturers, press and equipment manufacturers. **1952** KIRK & OTHMER *Encycl. Chem. Technol.* VIII. 185 With the advent of World War II, a tremendous amount of development and testing work was instituted and carried on, not only by laminators, but by suppliers, fabricators, [etc.]. **1965** *Guardian* 31 Mar. 16/1 Some laminators tried to help manufacturers to move fabrics which had been gathering dust on warehouse shelves, producing laminated fabrics entirely unsuited for the applications they were used for.

laminboard (læ·minbōəɹd). [f. *lamin(ated) board.*] (A) composite board consisting of numerous thin strips of wood glued face to face between two facing sheets of wood (or laminated plastic).

1927 S. B. WAINWRIGHT *Mod. Plywood* iii. 15 The newer forms of laminated wood,..generally known as laminboards. *Ibid.* vi. 24 Laminboards, ⅝″ thick or more, may be used..for ceilings or walls. *Ibid.* viii. 44 There is no risk of the joints opening, as the laminboards cannot shrink. **1938** *Archit. Rev.* LXXXIV. 219 (*caption*) Veneered laminboard doors. **1965** MALLINSON & LEIGH *Timber Trade Pract.* (ed. 3) xxi. 286 In 1961 out of the total import of all these materials, plywood counted for 80%, blockboard, laminboard and battenboard accounted for 20% and of this the bulk was blockboard. **1971** *Cabinet Maker & Retail Furnisher* 24 Sept. 531/2 Worktops are of laminboard which is bought in faced with Warerite.

laminectomy (læmine·ktŏmi). *Surg.* [f. LAMIN(A + *-ECTOMY.] Excision of one or more of the posterior arches of the vertebræ (each arch being formed by the junction of two laminæ), esp. as a method of access to the spinal canal.

1892 *Med. Ann.* 458 Formerly the operation was called 'trephining'.., but the trephine is now seldom used, and the term 'laminectomy' has been substituted. **1921** J. S. HORSLEY *Operative Surg.* xvi. 290 The operation by which tumors or other lesions of the spinal cord are approached is laminectomy. **1962** *Punch* 24 Oct. 598/1 That was the worst laminectomy I've seen for months! **1971** *Canad. Jrnl. Surg.* XIV. 229 The spinal cord was decompressed by laminectomy from T3 to T6.

lamington (læ·miŋtən). *Austral.* and *N.Z.* [app. f. name of Lord *Lamington*, Governor of Queensland, 1895–1901.] A square of sponge cake dipped in melted chocolate and grated coconut.

1929 *Kookaburra Cookery Bk.* (ed. 2) 242 (*heading*) Lamington cake. **1944** J. K. EWERS in *Coast to Coast 1943* 61 Mrs. Whiskers making scones; even Filthy Kate enlisted to turn out lamingtons by the score, because they were her specialty. **1952** *P.W.M.U. Cookery Bk.* (9th impr.) 132 Lamingtons..spread icing on all sides of cake.. roll cakes in desiccated coconut. **1969** *Southerly* XXIX. 4 They had the innocence of oatmeal porridge, the sweetness of lamingtons.

la·mino-. Combining form of *LAMINAL *a.* b used in *Phonetics*, as **lamino-dental** *a.*, produced by pressing the blade of the tongue against the front upper teeth; **lamino-palatal**

a., produced by pressing the blade of the tongue against the palate.

1968 P. M. POSTAL *Aspects Phonol. Theory* iv. 82 Hence there are few languages with lamino-dental consonants. **1966** *Publ. Amer. Dial. Soc.* XLVI. 34 Aspirated, voiceless, lamino-palatal stop. **1968** P. M. POSTAL *Aspects Phonol. Theory* iv. 82 But apico-dental and lamino-palatal segments are found almost everywhere.

laminograph, -graphic, etc.: varr. *LAMINAGRAPH, etc.

Lammas, *sb.* Add: **4. lammas growth, shoot** *Forestry* [Equivalent of G. *Johannestrieb* St. John's shoot, in allusion to St. John the Baptist's day, 24 June], a shoot produced by a tree in summer, after a pause in growth.

1929 T. THOMSON tr. *Büsgen's Struct. & Life Forest Trees* i. 10 The part of the annual shoot formed after the pause..appears as a new growth to which the name of Lammas Shoot has been given in view of the approximate date of its appearance... The lammas shoots of the oak are very vigorous. **1950** F. S. BAKER *Princ. Silviculture* xv. 302 So-called 'lammas growth' is common in some species... In vigorous young oak trees the lammas shoot formation may be repeated three or four times a season. **1971** T. T. KOZLOWSKI *Growth & Devel. Trees* I. v. 202 Lammas shoots often form in response to abundance of available water. *Ibid.* 204 Lammas growth often causes profuse branching and knotty lumber.

‖ **lammervanger** (la·məɹfaŋəɹ). *S. Afr.* Also **laemer-vanger, lamvanger.** [Afrikaans, f. *lam* lamb + *vanger* catcher.] The martial eagle, *Polemaetus bellicosus*, or the African lammergeyer or bearded vulture, *Gypaetus barbatus meridionalis*.

1830 *S. Afr. Q. Jrnl.* Jan./Apr. 105 *Gypaetus Barbatus*, Cuv.—Arend and Lammervanger of the Colonists. **1835** A. STEEDMAN *Wanderings S. Afr.* II. i. 7 Others [*sc.* jackals] had been destroyed by the *Læmer-vanger*, or bearded vulture. **1846** J. C. BROWN tr. *Arbousset & Daumas's Narr. Tour N.-E. of Cape Good Hope* xxi. 220 The English of the Cape call it the *golden eagle*.., and the Dutch farmers, *lamvanger*, or *lamb seizer*, because it is accustomed to seize, and carry off to its aerie, a lamb or kid. **1920** F. C. CORNELL *Glamour of Prospecting* xii. 205, I had wasted a shot on a splendid *lammer-vanger*, a fine specimen of an eagle. **1944** V. POHL *Adventures Boer Family* xiii. 79 The *lammervanger* is one of the wariest, shyest and most keen-eyed of all birds. **1959** *Cape Times* 20 June 2/3 Mr. Sonny Waks..saw an eagle—commonly known as a *lammervanger*—catching one of his young lambs. **1970** *Daily News* (Durban) 4 June 21 A 13-year-old White youth captured a long taloned golden eagle (lammervanger) with his bare hands.

lammie, lammy. Add: (Examples.) Also *lammy coat, suit*.

Sometimes written as *lamby*.

1886 Lammy suit [in Dict.]. **1903** G. S. BOWLES *Stretch off Land* 268 The 'lammy-suit' known aboard Torpedo-Boats and Destroyers. **1915** KIPLING *Fringes of Fleet* 64, I loathe destroyers,..the smell of the wet 'lammies' and damp wardroom cushions. **1916** 'TAFFRAIL' *Pincher Martin* xi. 191 He undid the toggles of his lammy coat, and gave the muffler another turn round his neck. **1920** *Blackw. Mag.* Jan. 7/2 North Sea fishermen, fully accoutred in their thick 'lamby' suits. **1931** 'TAFFRAIL' *Endless Story* xxiii. 357, I arrayed myself in a tolerably dry 'lammy coat'. **1948** PARTRIDGE *Dict. Forces' Slang* 108 *Lammies*, hooded coats of lamb's wool worn by officers and men in severe weather. Also known as 'duffle coats'.

lammister: see *LAM *v.*

lamnoid. Substitute for def. of **A.** *adj.*: Resembling a mackerel-shark of the genus *Lamna*. (Add examples.)

1898 D. S. JORDAN *Descr. Species of Fish from Japan* title-page, The Type of a Distinct Family of Lamnoid Sharks. *Ibid.* 199 A remarkably distinct new genus of lamnoid affinities. **1925** —— *Fishes* (rev. ed.) xiv. 190 The most active and most ferocious of the sharks, as well as the largest and some of the most sluggish, belong to a group of families known collectively as Lamnoid, because of a general resemblance to the mackerel-shark or *Lamna*.

Lamoot, Lamout, varr. *LAMUT.

lamp, *sb.*[1] Add: **2. b.** (Later examples.)

1899 C. ROOK *Hooligan Nights* iv. 63 Ole ruby boko put 'is lamps over me, wiv no error, an' he says, 'Why you're the youngster as come in 'ere afore.' **1901** 'H. MCHUGH' *John Henry* 90 The old hen with the languishing lamps was still on my trail. **1928** *Daily Express* 29 Aug. 7/4 Woman in an assault case at Weymouth: I said I would fill her lamps for her. Clerk: What does that mean? Woman: Blacken her eyes. **1938** F. D. SHARPE *Sharpe of Flying Squad* 331 He had his lamps on the copper.

4. a. *lamp-bulb, -chimney* (examples), *-flame, -glass* (later examples), *-glow, -house* (earlier example), *-shine, -stand* (examples), *-worm.*

1911 *Chambers's Jrnl.* Jan. 78/1 If a thin gold film is deposited on the lower half of the lamp-bulb. **1847** *Rep. Comm. Patents 1846* (U.S.) 276, I also claim the lamp chimney, formed of glass, with two contractions. **1870** A. S. STEPHENS *Married in Haste* xv. 85 She unscrewed the lamp-chimney..and polished off a stain of black smoke. **1906** JOYCE *Let.* 6 Nov. (1966) II. 186 A lamp chimney here costs one lira! **1904** *Westm. Gaz.* 13 Aug. 6/2 Not a single lamp-flame stirs or quivers. **1920** J. MASEFIELD *Enslaved* 52 The lamp-flame purred from want of oil. **1914** D. H. LAWRENCE *Widowing of Mrs. Holroyd* I. i. 7 She has been lighting the lamp and holds the lamp-glass. **1974** G. JENKINS *Bridge of Magpies* vii. 99 The condensation dripped from the lamp-glass. **1922** JOYCE *Ulysses* 423 Their tunics bloodbright in a lampglow. **1849** F. B. HEAD *Stokers & Pokers* vii. 63 The driver.. then takes his lamps to the lamp-house to be cleaned and trimmed by workmen solely employed to do so. **1913** C. MACKENZIE *Sinister St.* II. xviii. 449 The uneasy warmth of the overarching trees would draw them very close, while hushed endearments took them slowly into lamp-shine. **1938** W. DE LA MARE *Memory* 90 He shook his rascal head, Its curls by the lamp-shine gilt. **1893** *Funk's Stand. Dict.*, Lamp-stand. **1909** H. G. WELLS *Tono-Bungay* II. iv. 235, I found her in our drawing-room, standing beside the tall lamp-stand that half filled the bay. **1961** NEW ENG. BIBLE *Hebr.* ix. 2 For a tent was prepared—the first tent—in which was the lamp-stand, and the table with the bread of the Presence. **1965** M. SPARK *Mandelbaum Gate* vii. 223 He then unscrewed the base of the mosaic lampstand. **1917** HARDY *Moments of Vision* 61 As delicate as lamp-worm's lucency.

b. *lamp-locking* (see quots.).

1894 *Gloss. Terms Evidence R. Comm. Labour* 51/2 in *Parl. Papers 1893–4* (C.7063) XXXVIII. 411 *Lamp-locking station*, the place in a mine where the safety-lamps of all the miners are examined and locked by an official. **1905** *Westm. Gaz.* 12 July 7/1, I was in the lamp-locking cabin, which is a short distance from the bottom of the shaft.

c. *lamp-like* adj. (later example).

1913 D. H. LAWRENCE *Love Poems* 17 But the Moon.. unfurled Her white, her lamp-like shape.

5. lamp-cap, the base of an electric light bulb or lamp into which are sealed the terminals and the neck of the glass globe; **lamp-house,** the part of a photographic enlarger or projector which houses the light-source; **lamp-mat,** a mat on which a table-lamp is placed; **lamp-socket,** = *LAMP-HOLDER; **lamp-standard,** a post or other strong support for a lamp; **lamp-wick** (earlier example); **lamp-worker** (see quot. 1962).

1899 W. P. MAYCOCK *Electr. Wiring* iii. 324 The lamp caps are fitted with a central plunger contact. **1971** L. E. VRENKEN in W. Elenbaas *Fluorescent Lamps* (ed. 2) v. 60 To connect a lamp to the electrical circuit a number of different lamp caps have been designed. **1912** J. F. HODGES *Opening & Operating Motion Pict. Theatre* 49 (*caption*) Lamp house. **1916** R. E. WELSH *A-B-C of Motion Pict.* 17 In the first place, there is a 'lamp-house', a small cabinet which contains the light. **1933** *Discovery* Mar. 90/1 The illuminant itself [is] enclosed in a lamp house which is glazed with a filter of the same type as that used in the camera. **1971** L. B. HAPPÉ *Basic Motion Pict. Technol.* x. 306 A xenon arc lamp can be substituted for a carbon arc in an existing lamphouse optical system but it is preferable to have a complete lamphouse designed around the new source. **1842** *Spirit of Times* 15 Oct. 389/2 (Weingarten), Also to Miss Waterman..[a diploma] for various specimens of her exquisite work of lamp mats. **1856** *Trans. Mich. Agric. Soc.* VII. 700 Some beautiful lamp-mats and other worsted and crochet work. **1873** *Young Englishwoman* June 302/1 Embroidered border for lamp-mat. **1883** 'MARK TWAIN' *Life on Mississippi* xxxviii. 400 Lamp..standing on a gridiron, so to speak, made of high-colored yarns, by the young ladies of the house, and called a lamp-mat. **1908** *Westm. Gaz.* 27 Oct. 6/1 A small transformer can be placed in the lamp-socket. **1968** *Lighting Equipment News* Mar. 23/1 The adaptor fits into the existing lamp socket. **1908** *Daily Chron.* 5 Aug. 3/5 A motor fire engine..collided with a lamp standard. **1967** *Lighting Equipment News* Jan. 26/3 The complete lamps and lamp standard are constructed on zinc coated sheet metal and painted. **1845** C. M. KIRKLAND *Western Clearings* 135 Miss Teeny had picked up the lamp-wick with a pin several times. **1665** HOOKE *Micrographia* 209 The blowing of Glass into exceeding thin shells, and then breaking them into scales, which any lamp-worker will presently do. **1962** *Gloss. Terms Glass Industry* (*B.S.I.*) 46 *Lamp worker*, a worker who forms glassware from tubing or rod by heating in an oxy-gas or air-gas flame at a work bench. **1970** *Canad. Antiques Collector* Apr. 26/2 He may..watch a lampworker forming ornaments from glass softened over a gas torch.

lamp, *v.*[1] Add: **4.** *slang* (orig. *U.S.*). To see, look at, recognize, watch. Cf. LAMP *sb.*[1] 2 b.

1916 H. L. WILSON *Somewhere in Red Gap* v. 198 Stella ..was standing on the centre table by now, so she could lamp herself in the glass over the mantel. **1921** *Adventure* (U.S.) 18 July 42/2 But she lamps me auburn mug all to oncet an' draws back sudden, like I was a rattler. **1923** L. J. VANCE *Baroque* viii. 50 Nobody even lamped its number. **1928** E. WALLACE *Again Sanders* x. 259 These niggers have lamped the gats. **1938** G. GREENE *Brighton Rock* III. ii. 113 Afraid we'd lamp you if you didn't change your mug? *Ibid.* v. i. 190 Come an' lamp the bathing belles. **1953** K. TENNANT *Joyful Condemned* xi. 96 One of the fellows from Central has only to lamp you coming in here, and we all go up. **1962** R. COOK *Crust on its Uppers* ii. 34 We were dying to have a butchers and lamp all the new bird. **1969** R. BUSBY *Robbery Blue* iii. 26 I'd like to know how the coppers got on to us. They couldn't have lamped us on the road.

lampbrush (læ·mpbrʌʃ). *Cytology.* Also (with hyphen) **lamp-brush.** [repr. G. *lampencylinderputzer* lit. 'lamp-glass cleaner', to which lampbrush chromosomes were likened by J. Rückert (in *Anat. Anzeiger* (1892) VII. 115): see LAMP *sb.*[1] and BRUSH *sb.*[2]] Used *attrib.* to designate chromosomes having numerous paired lateral projections or loops, which loops are usu. apparent only during diplotene in a few groups of animals and give the whole chromosome the appearance of a bottle-brush.

[**1901** *Jrnl. R. Microsc. Soc.* 135 This large nucleoslu then breaks up..with the production of 'bottle-brush' and plumose figures in the caryoplasm.] **1911** *Ibid.* 456 The formation of the curious 'lamp-brush' chromosomes. **1925** E. B. WILSON *Cell* (ed. 3) iv. 350 Thus are the very loose so-called 'lamp-brush' chromosomes.., characteristic of the middle growth-period in large, yolk-bearing eggs. **1940** *Proc. Nat. Acad. Sci.* XXVI. 344 The typical lamp-brush chromosomes of the ovocytes of lower vertebrates. **1965** PEACOCKE & DRYSDALE *Molecular Basis Heredity* vii. 72 In the newt, *Triturus cristatus*, large diplotene chromosomes may be isolated from oocytes and maintained for several days in buffer. These 'lampbrush chromosomes' are sufficiently large for the action of enzymes on the chromosomes to be studied microscopically. Evidence obtained from this material supports the conclusion that chromosomes contain protein, RNA and DNA.

lamp-holder. Also **lampholder.** [LAMP *sb.*[1] 4 b.] A device for securing an electric lamp, a lamp-socket.

1885 *Electrician* XIV. 416/1 Fig. 1 is the lamp-holder as fitted at the Royal Courts of Justice. **1907** *Installation News* Sept. 14/2 In wiring Electroliers..it is generally found to be impracticable to group wires into the lamp-holders. **1935** *Discovery* June 183/2 An operation which is typical of a vast number of manipulative jobs in industry —the assembly of an ordinary electric lampholder consisting of eighteen parts. **1963** *Times* 6 May p. vii/5 Similarly, when in the interests of safety the traditional brass lampholder was replaced by its plastics successor, this was more or less a slavish imitation of the metal one.

lamplighter. Add: **4.** A North American freshwater sunfish of the genus *Pomoxis*, esp. the white crappie, *P. annularis*.

1877 *1st Ann. Rep. Ohio State Fish Comm.* 77 *P*[*omoxys*] *hexacanthus*... Strawberry Bass;..Lamp-lighter, of Portsmouth. **1892** C. F. LUMMIS *Tramp across Continent* 33 For three years I had been fairly starving for a bout with these beauties—a hunger which the catfish and 'lamplighters' of Ohio had utterly failed to satisfy. **1947** B. W. DALRYMPLE *Panfish* 84 Here, my friend, are the various names by which you would address that little gamester, the Crappie, depending on where you happened to be at the moment: Bachelor,..Lake Bass, Lake Erie Bass, Lamplighter.

lamprey. b. **lamprey-eel** (earlier and later examples).

1726 S. PENHALLOW in *Coll. New Hampsh. Hist. Soc.* (1824) I. 31 Next day, they kill'd Edward Taylor near Lamprey-Eel River. **1831** R. COX *Adventures Columbia River* I. vii. 149 We got plenty of salmon while we remained here, and some lamprey eels, the latter of which were oily and very strong. **1885** *Amer. Naturalist* XIX. 922 The lamprey eel of Kansas..proves to be usually the *chestnut* lamprey.

lampro-. Add: **lamprophy·llite** *Min.* [ad. G. *lamprophyllit* (V. Hackman 1894, in *Fennia* XI. 119): see PHYLLO-], a silicate of sodium, strontium, and titanium, $Na_2SrTiSi_2O_8$, found as golden-brown prisms; **lamprophyre,** add: [a. G. *lamprophyr* (C. W. Gümbel *Die paläolith. Eruptivgesteine des Fichtelgebirges* (1874) 36] (examples); **lamprophyric** *a.* (examples).

1899 E. S. DANA *Dana's Syst. Min.* (ed. 6) 1st App. 40 *Lamprophyllite*... A mineral related to astrophyllite in form and cleavage. **1942** *Amer. Mineralogist* XXVII. 416 The Bearpaw and Kola lamprophyllite are almost identical in refringence, habit, and orientation. **1965** *Scientia Sinica* (Peking) XIV. 1839 The lamprophyllite in general belongs to the monoclinic system and the orthorhombic lamprophyllite exists as a submicroscopic crystallite in the polysynthetic twin of monoclinic lamprophyllite. **1890** *Mineral. Mag.* IX. 43 The rock..is most closely paralleled by the olivine-bearing lamprophyres. **1923** *Geol. Mag.* LX. 553 The potash series of lamprophyres, in which orthoclase and abundance of biotite form the expression of excess of potash over soda, is not so complex a group as that of the soda-lamprophyres. **1959** W. W. MOORHOUSE *Study of Rocks in Thin Section* xvii. 325 Lamprophyres..are for the most part melanocratic to mesotype rocks... Nearly all..of the true lamprophyres are characterized by a definitely alkaline aspect, indicated by the presence of abundant biotite, alkali feldspar, soda pyriboles, nepheline, or analcite, combined with a low silica content. **1966** *Jrnl. & Proc. R. Soc. New South Wales* XCIX. 38/1 Many of the common lamprophyres, such as minettes, vogesites, kersantites and spessartites are almost chemically identical. **1892** *Geol. Mag.* IX. 201 An intermixture of the acid and lamprophyric magmas took place during the injection. **1965** G. J. WILLIAMS *Econ. Geol. N.Z.* xiii. 205/1 Narrow lamprophyric dykes and sills cut granite, Ohika beds and the Breccia.

lamp-shade, lampshade. [LAMP *sb.*[1] 4 a.] A shade placed over a lamp to diffuse or direct the light. Also *attrib.* and *fig.*

1850 GEO. ELIOT *Let.* 30 Nov. (1954) I. 337, I have bought the Lucifers and done my duty about the Lamp shade. *a* **1877** KNIGHT *Dict. Mech.* II. 1248/1 *Lamp-shade*, a screen placed above the light to intercept or mellow it. It may have a dark exterior and reflecting interior surface. **1899** A. WERNER *Captain of Locusts* 212 He removed the burnt matches, set the lamp-shade straight. **1908** *Stratford-upon-Avon Herald* 24 July 7/2 Lamp-shade-like protectors are obtainable cheaply. **1908** *Daily Chron.* 2 Oct. 4/4 There were the young ladies of gay Bohemia in Directoire dresses and lamp-shade hats. **1953** R. MACAULAY *Last Lett. to Friend* (1962) 107 It didn't really *destroy* very much, except some pictures (which I

mourn) and curtains and covers and a few books and lamp-shades, etc. **1960** J. Brophy *Front Door Key* 179 She had compromised with the present, babyish neo-1920's fashion, refusing to wear, along with bows and tiers and lampshade hems, very short and very tight skirts. **1967** E. Short *Embroidery & Fabric Collage* iii. 83 Care should be taken with lampshades to avoid fancy shapes and over-fussy trimmings. **1971** *Shankar's Weekly* (Delhi) 18 Apr. 18/4 He pointed to two burly figures who came out of the nearby tea-shop, one of them wiping his lampshade moustaches.

lampuki (læ·mpuki). Also **lampuca, lampuka.** [Maltese.] A large marine food fish, *Coryphæna hippurus* or *C. equisetis*; = Dolphin 2.

1925 J. A. Hammerton *Countries of World* IV. 2673/1 The lampuca, a migratory fish which comes to the islands in autumn, is caught in considerable quantities and is eaten by all classes of the people. **1958** G. G. Lanfranco *Compl. Guide Fishes Malta* 28 *Coryphaena hippurus*, Linn. ..Lampuka; easily distinguished..much valued as food. **1964** G. Butler *Coffin in Malta* iii. 80 The smell of *calamai* and *lampuki* mingling beautifully with onion and tomato grew stronger. **1969** *Vogue* Nov. 68/2 Lampuki is a delicious fish. **1975** *Times* 11 Jan. 11/6 The greatest [Maltese] delicacy is *lampuki*, which is a fish similar in size to seabass..usually grilled.

lampyrid (læ·mpĭrid). [f. mod.L. family name Lampyridæ: see Lampyrine *a.* and *sb.*] An insect belonging to the Lampyridæ, a family of Coleoptera which includes the glow-worms and fire-flies.

[**1841** E. Newman *Familiar Introd. Hist. Insects* v. 249 Glow-worms or *Lampyrites*.] **1895** J. H. & A. B. Comstock *Man. Study Insects* xxi. 550 (*heading*) The Firefly Family or Lampyrids. *Ibid.* 551 Another common diurnal Lampyrid is *Calopteron reticulatum*. **1899** D. Sharp in *Cambr. Nat. Hist.* VI. ii. v. 248 The Lampyrides, or glow-worms, are of special interest, as most of their members give off a phosphorescent light when alive. **1916** *Jrnl. Morphol.* XXVIII. 145 (*title*) Photogenic organs and embryology of Lampyrids. **1961** *New Scientist* 16 Nov. 664/1 They [*sc.* the Cantharids] include..the photogenic Lampyrids.

lamsiekte (la·msi:ktə). *S. Afr.* Also **lamziekte.** [Afrikaans, f. *lam* lame, paralysed + *siekte* disease.] A cattle disease, usually fatal, found on land deficient in phosphorus, caused by the bacterium *Clostridium botulinum* and characterized by paralysis or muscular weakness; bovine botulism. Also *attrib.*

1790 E. Helme tr. *Le Vaillant's Trav. Afr.* II. v. 92 The first [disease], called at the Cape *Lam-Sikte*, is a sudden paralitic stroke. **1798** S. H. Wilcocke tr. *Stavorinus's Voy. E. Indies* II. 64 The *lamziekte*, is when the cattle are not able to stand; it comes on gradually, and is slow in its progress. **1896** R. Wallace *Farming Industries Cape Colony* xiv. 286 Stiff-sickness or 'stijf-ziekte' and 'lam-ziekte' or paralysis, would appear to be two forms of the same disease. **1946** *Nature* 17 Aug. 239/1 In practice, 0·5–1 unit of circulating antitoxin adequately protects a bovine against natural botulism (lamsiekte). **1948** *Cape Argus* 6 Nov. 1/9 The Division of Veterinary Services ..will shortly make available a new, improved and concentrated lamsiekte vaccine. **1974** *Eastern Province Herald* (S. Afr.) 15 Nov. 15 A young couple..who lost about 70 per cent. of their income when 34 of their dairy cows died of botulism (lamsiekte), have been given three cows and lent four.

lamster: see *lam *v.*

Lamut (lamū·t). Also **Lamoot, Lamout. a.** A branch of the Tungus people living on the shores of the Sea of Okhotsk. **b.** The language spoken by this people, belonging to the Tunguso-Manchurian group of the Altaic language family. Also *attrib.* or as *adj.* Also **Lamu·tic** *sb.*

1764 J. Grieve tr. *Krasheninnikov's Hist. Kamtschatka* iii. xxi. 223 The people that they [*sc.* the Koreki] border upon are the Kamtschadales, the Tchukotskoi,..and the Tungusi or Lamuti. **1790** tr. *J. B. B. de Lesseps's Trav. Kamtschatka* II. 383 Vocabulary of the Kamtschadale, Koriac, Tchouktchi, and Lamout languages. *Ibid.*, (*heading*) Koriac... Tchouktchi... Lamout. **1830** P. Dobell *Trav. Kamtchatka & Siberia* I. ix. 189 Lamoots are the Wild Reindeer Tongusees, who seldom inhabit one spot more than a month or two at a time. **1880** A. H. Sayce *Introd. Sci. of Lang.* II. viii. 201 To find them we must look to the ruder Lamutic and Tungusian. **1888** *Encycl. Brit.* XXIII. 608/2 On the Pacific the chief subdivisions of the race are the Lamuts, or 'sea people', grouped in small isolated hunting communities round the west coast of the Sea of Okhotsk. **1927** F. Whyte tr. *Bergman's Through Kamchatka* xii. 196 One of the older men..was..chanting monotonous Lamut melodies... The Lamuts..are nominally Christians. *Ibid.* xiii. 215 So ended the Lamut winter festival. **1957** G. Clark *Archaeol. & Soc.* (ed. 3) iii. 94 The best preserved..of the Siberian mammoths was found at Beresovka by a Lamut tribesman. **1964** tr. *Levin & Potapov's Peoples of Siberia* 670 The Evens, who were formerly known as Lamuts,..border in the north and northeast with the Yukagirs, Koryaks and Chukchi.

lanai (‖ lana·*i*, lănəi·). Also 9 **ranai.** [Hawaiian.] In Hawaii (and by imitation elsewhere), a porch or veranda; a roofed structure with open sides near a house. Also *attrib.*

1823 C. S. Stewart *Jrnl.* 28 Apr. (1828) v. 97 The chiefs were all under one *ranai*, or rude bower. **1826** W. Ellis *Narr. Tour Hawaii* xiv. 387 At half-past ten, the bell rung for public worship, and about 800 people..assembled under a large *ranai* (a place sheltered from the sun) formed by two large canvass awnings, and a number of platted cocoa-nut leaves, spread over the place from posts fixed in the fence which enclosed the court-yard around the house of the governor's wife. *a* **1869** L. Smith in M. D. Frear *Lowell & Abigail* (1934) 124 We soon found that the school house did not accomodate one half of the congregation; and we built a large *lanai* in the front yard and covered it with rushes for them to sit upon, a la Hawaii. **1897** 'Mark Twain' *Following Equator* iii. 61 Nearly every house [in Honolulu] has what is called a *lanai*. It is a large apartment, roofed, floored, open on three sides, with a door or a draped archway opening into the drawing-room. **1898** M. H. Krout *Hawaii* v. 93 On these verandahs or in the *lanai* the family practically lives. **1937** D. & H. Teilhet *Feather Cloak Murders* x. 174 The wide windows opening upon an immense lanai, or porch, with cool overhanging eaves. **1945** L. Mumford *City Devel.* (1946) 81 Without it, adequate gardens are impossible and the private lanai, even when provided, is stuffy. **1947** M. Lowry *Under Volcano* ix. 272 He sat on the lanai sipping okoolihao and singing plaintive Hawaiian songs. **1963** D. B. Hughes *Expendable Man* (1964) ii. 31 Sliding glass lanai doors opened to a vast expanse of close-cropped green. **1964** D. Teilhet *Big Runaround* ii. 30 She hadn't ever seen a couch this wide, she said; and I explained that it was called a lanai-couch. **1969** *New Yorker* 31 May 95/2 (Advt.), 1000 air-conditioned rooms, tower suites and lanais surrounding the..swimming pool.

Lancashire. Add: *Lancashire cheese*, a white semi-hard cheese made in Lancashire. Also *ellipt.*

1896 J. T. Law *Grocer's Manual* 811/1 The peculiarity and distinctive mark of Lancashire, as distinct from Cheshire and Cheddar, is that it is a softer cheese, a good toaster, mellower, and very palatable when ripe. **1910** *Encycl. Brit.* VII. 749/2 Lancashire cheese, when well made and ripe, is loose in texture and is mellow; it has a piquant flavour. As a rule it ripens early and does not keep long. **1937** 'G. Orwell' *Road to Wigan Pier* i. 15 For supper there was the pale flabby Lancashire cheese and biscuits. **1955** J. G. Davis *Dict. Dairying* (ed. 2) 195 *Lancashire cheese.* Although not well known outside the county of its origin, it is in great demand in Lancashire, especially in the industrial areas of the south, and is reckoned an excellent cheese for toasting. **1960** S. Fraser *Cheeses Old Eng.* 29 It was dark when I arrived in Preston in search of Lancashire cheese. **1971** *Sunday Times* (Colour Suppl.) 28 Mar. 36/1 *Lancashire.* When young it is slightly sharp and soft enough to spread, but it mellows with age.

Lancaster[2] (læ·ŋkǣstəɹ). [Name of the county town of Lancashire.] Used *attrib.* in *Lancaster cloth* (see quot. 1950). Cf. *American cloth* (*American *a.* 3).

1939 *Archit. Rev.* LXXXVI. 258/1 *Lancaster cloth.* This is a muslin base impregnated with a linseed oil compound. **1950** '*Mercury*' *Dict. Textile Terms* 312/2 *Lancaster cloth*, a light, washable oilcloth used on shelves, tables, round wash basins, etc. Made with a cotton back and with a face dressing of linseed oil, etc. compound. **1951** *Good Housek. Home Encycl.* 166/2 A less expensive covering is provided..by Lancaster (or American) cloth. **1960** *Design* Sept. 71/2 The indicator boards..are faced with Lancaster cloth in red, grey-green and yellow.

lance, *sb.*[1] Add: **6*.** = *lance-corporal* (Lance *sb.*[1] 8). *colloq.*

1888 Kipling *Wee Willie Winkie* (1889) 74 The reg'ment don't go 'ome for another seven years. I'll be a Lance then or near to. **1961** Partridge *Dict. Slang* Suppl. 1164/1 *Lance*, lance-corporal: coll. late C. 19–20.

6.** In full, *oxygen lance.* **a.** A thin metal pipe through which oxygen under pressure may be passed in order to burn away metal, concrete, or the like using heat generated by the burning of either the metal to be cut or the pipe itself.

1925 *Iron Trade Rev.* 24 Sept. 749/1 The oxygen lance is a means of burning a hole quickly through steel, slag or brick. Essentially it is nothing but a stream of pure oxygen flowing through a small iron pipe. If the oxygen strikes hot iron or steel, the metal burns rapidly... If the oxygen strikes non-metallic substances, like firebrick or slag, the lance pipe itself burns, produces the necessary heat and flux to melt the way through. **1926** *Blast Furnace & Steel Plant* XIV. 19/1 If a layer of slag is encountered, the lance pipe itself burns. **1944** *Ibid.* XXXII. 1077/1 The oxygen lance..has been used..for opening tap holes in blast furnaces and open-hearth furnaces, for tapping slag from soaking pits, for cutting up spills and skulls, and for..piercing or severing..heavy masses of iron and steel. **1945** *Machinery* (N.Y.) Nov. 156/1 Since the oxygen lance can sever metal of practically any thickness, it is an effective 'trouble-shooter' for metal-disposal problems.

b. A metal pipe, often water-cooled, through which oxygen under pressure may be injected into molten metal or directed on to its surface.

1948 *Jrnl. Iron & Steel Inst.* CLX. 221/1 Oxygen can be used in the basic electric-arc furnace for decarburization, either by means of the 'oxygen lance' or by direction of a strong blast of the gas through the slag cover. **1950** *Ibid.* CLXV. 411/1 The use of the oxygen lance for refining a high-chromium steel..enables the heat to be worked at a temperature some 200°C higher than normal. **1959** *New Scientist* 30 Apr. 965/2 Oxygen for the refining action is injected into the through metal water-cooled jets or 'lances'. **1971** *Engineering Index 1970* 3426/2 Effect of blowing practices in the LD converter on oxygen content of steel. ..Statistical methods were employed to study this influence, with particular reference to the effect of..the height of the lance on the bath.

8. lance-bombardier, the rank in the Royal Artillery corresponding to lance-corporal in the infantry; **lance-jack** *Army slang*, lance-corporal, lance-bombardier.

1935 A. H. Burne *Royal Artillery Mess, Woolwich* xi. 230 In 1901 Driver Homewood was appointed kennel-huntsman. He has since received well merited, if not exactly rapid, promotion to the rank of Lance-Bombardier. **1943** Hunt & Pringle *Service Slang* 43 *Lancejack.* Army for Lance-Corporal or Lance-Bombardier. **1960** D. A. Campbell *Dress R. Artillery* ix. 47 In 1920 the rank of bombardier was upgraded to replace that of corporal, the latter rank being abolished in the Regiment... In the same year the appointment of acting bombardier was changed to that of lance bombardier, both these appointments wear a single chevron. **1968** *Listener* 22 Aug. 252/3 Tempting to identify with the lance-bombardier in charge of this guard squad. **1912** H. Wyndham *Following the Drum* vii. 80 A junior corporal is a 'lance-jack'. **1937** D. Jones *In Parenthesis* iii. 28 Tin soldiers, toy soldiers, militarymen in rows—you somehow suffer the pain of loss —it's an ungracious way of life—buttocked lance-jacks crawling for the second chevron. **1953** A. Baron *Human Kind* ix. 68 Foller the Salvation Corporal an' 'is Saintly Lance-Jack. **1971** L. Deighton *Declarations of War* 11 Lance-jack at the time, actually. *Ibid.*, You're not looking too good, Colonel, if you don't mind an ex-lance-jack saying so.

lance, *v.* Add: **8.** *trans.* To cut (a hole) or inject (oxygen) by means of an oxygen lance.

1945 *Machinery* (N.Y.) Nov. 156/1 After a hole had been lanced completely through, the cut was continued to the bottom of the casting. **1946** *Steel* 11 Feb. 114/2 It was planned..to drain the salamander..by drilling and lancing a hole below the taphole in the base of the furnace. **1963** *Times* 22 Apr. p. viii/6 Oxygen is lanced into the furnace as it is being tapped. This causes the slag and lead to run.

lanceolated, *a.* (Later example.)

1901 *Chambers's Jrnl.* May 348/2 The under side [of the *phiale*] is occupied by narrow lanceolated leaves.

lancet. Add: **4.** *lancet-pointed* (cf. 4 b).

1888 *Century Mag.* Aug. 585/1 These parts..are all in the Lancet-Pointed (Early English) style. **1956** *Nature* 10 Mar. 484/1 This is then crushed to a very fine paste by means of a lancet-pointed dissecting needle.

lancewood. Add: **2.** = *horoeka.

1910 L. Cockayne *N.Z. Plants* viii. 120 The lancewood is neither *Pseudopanax crassifolium* nor *P. ferox*—it is *P. chathamica*. **1966** *Encycl. N.Z.* II. 258/2 Lancewood, Horoeka (*Pseudopanax crassifolium*). *Ibid.* 259/1 *P. ferox*, a rather rare and local tree occurring from about latitude 35° southwards, has the same juvenile form as that of lancewood.

lancing, *vbl. sb.* (Examples corresponding to *lance *v.* 8.)

1945 *Machinery* (N.Y.) Nov. 156/1 It was decided that oxygen lancing was the only feasible means of cutting the huge piece. **1955** *Jrnl. Iron & Steel Inst.* CLXXX. 74/1 A new development is the small-scale intermittent process to convert iron in the ladle directly into steel by oxygen lancing.

land, *sb.*[1] Add: **3. e.** Also, (*for the*) *land's sake, land sakes, my land*(*s*).

1846 *Knickerbocker* XXVII. 18 (Th.), Jedediah, for the land's sake, does my mouth blaze? **1848** J. F. Cooper *Oak Openings* I. v. 82 Land's sake! I've forgotten all about them barrels! **1854** M. J. Holmes *Tempest & Sunshine* xvi. 223 For land's sake dont tell Tempest. **1863** A. D. Whitney *Faith Gartney's Girlhood* ii. 12 Land sakes, Miss Faith! I don't know what you mean. **1894** 'Mark Twain' in *Century Mag.* XLVII. 337/2 My lan', what de reason 't ain't enough? **1908** L. M. Montgomery *Anne of Green Gables* xiv. 141 'For the land's sake!' gasped Marilla. ..'I believe the child is crazy.' **1913** A. Huxley *Let.* 30 July (1969) 51 The Americans..say Gee, whiz, bully, my lands, my soul, [etc.]. **1916** A. Bennett *Lion's Share* xlv. 350 'My land!' exclaimed Nick. 'If he sees me here he'll think I've come on purpose to talk about him.' **1930** J. Dos Passos *42nd Parallel* 50 Land sakes, it gives me the creeps to think of it. **1952** V. Wilkins *King Reluctant* i. iii. 45 But land's sake, how did he get into dat ole lonesome graveyard? **1974** K. Benton *Craig & Tunisian Tangle* xiii. 180 We've only got another week, for land's sake.

4. d. *S. Afr.* An area of ground under cultivation; = Field *sb.* 4 a. Freq. in *pl.*

1731 G. Medley tr. *Kolb's Present State Cape Good-Hope* I. xxviii. 357 The Value of the Tenth of the Produce of Lands is computed at 14000 Florins yearly. *Ibid.* 358 The Colonies are encreasing daily, and daily taking in new Lands for Tillage. **1806** J. Barrow *Trav. S. Afr.* (ed. 2) I. i. 5 At the feet of the hills..are several pleasant farms, having gardens well stored with vegetables for the table, vineyards, and extensive corn lands. **1896** H. A. Bryden *Tales S. Afr.* 248 She had..some good tobacco 'lands', which yielded no mean profit each year. **1926** O. Schreiner *From Man to Man* 23 They burnt harpuis bushes on the lands. **1939** tr. *E. N. Marais's My Friends the Baboons* ix. 112 If he raids a land..he will..hand over to her a share of the mealies or fruit. **1941** S. Cloete *Hill of Doves* (1942) xxviii. 398 They were riding through a mealie land. **1966** E. Palmer *Plains of Camdeboo* xviii. 297 Dust enveloped the world. Maurice and Sita could not even see where the lands had been.

9. a, b. In wider use, esp. in *Engin.*: an area left between adjacent grooves, holes, or the like in any surface; e.g. that between the flutes of a twist drill or the grooves of a gramophone record, or the top of a tooth on various metal-cutting tools immediately behind the cutting edge. (Further examples.)

1907 J. V. Woodworth *Grinding & Lapping* ii. 62 The flutes [of the reamers] were milled sharp—without land. *Ibid.* 63 Cutting the reamer sharp with no lands on the teeth. **1935** H. C. Bryson *Gramophone Record* iv. 81 The engineer has a table showing the widths and depths of the grooves and the amount of land for various cuts per inch. **1949** Baker & Kozacka *Carbide Cutting Tools* x. 213 The land is that portion of the tooth which is just behind the cutting edge. **1958** *Proc. IRE* XLVI. 1063/2 The diffusion regions in the lands of the grooved surface [of the silicon] are then removed in a second step of lapping. **1962** A. Nisbett *Technique Sound Studio* 255 The groove normally used for 78 rpm recordings... About 4 mils land between grooves, and a pitch of the order of 100–150 grooves per inch. **1964** S. Crawford *Basic Engin. Processes* ix. 228 The lands run along the leading edge of the flutes and act as a guide in the hole already drilled. **1971** B. Scharf *Engin. & its Lang.* xi. 97 Studs. These are very useful headless fastening devices which are threaded on both ends, with an unthreaded section (land) in the middle.

10. a. *land certificate, claim, classification, deal, distribution, improvement, market, question, reclamation, reform, room, speculation, taxation, title, use, utilization, work.*

1838 in *Indiana Mag. Hist.* (1926) XXII. 451 Gentle had settled that he was to pay in land and made an assignment on a land certificate. **1967** E. Rudinger *Wills & Probate* 97 A week or so later he receives from the registry the land certificate, which is substantially the same as the charge certificate, but with the very important difference of having had the details of the mortgage removed from it. **1812** J. McDonogh *Papers* (1898) 12 They therefore, sir, look forward to you, knowing..your knowledge of their land claims, to have those claims before Congress. **1949** *Minnesota Hist.* Mar. 30 The Sioux disputed the German colonists' right to establish land claims on the site. **1930** *U.S. Dept. Agric. Yearbk. 1929* 39 These considerations point to the need for a public policy of economic land classification. **1970** *Toronto Daily Star* 24 Sept. 27/7 The report's principal authors were Angus Hill, a specialist in land classification, Professor David Love and Professor Douglas Lacate. **1974** *Guardian* 11 Apr. 1 Mrs Marcia Williams, Mr Wilson's private secretary, said last night she would not resign over the land deals affair. **1965** L. Chevalier in Glass & Eversley *Population in Hist.* iii. 75, I have myself tried to study the evolution of the population in three cantons of Vendée..in terms of land-distribution and the social and religious structure. **1968** R. A. Lyttleton *Mysteries Solar Syst.* vi. 213 The configuration of the land-distribution could also have been somewhat different at the time of fall. **1849** *Hansard Commons* 4 May 1266 An advance of money..under the Land Improvement Act. **1902** *Encycl. Brit.* XXIX. 554/2 The number and amount of loans..under the Land Improvement Acts from 1847 to 1900. **1909** *Daily Chron.* 14 Sept. 5/6 The other kind of banks are rent charge and land-improvement banks. **1845** C. M. Kirkland *Western Clearings* 5 *Standing round*; i.e., watching the land market for values. **1962** H. R. Loyn *Anglo-Saxon Eng.* iv. 171 There is evidence indeed for something approaching a land-market in late Anglo-Saxon England. **1830** *Deb. Congress U.S.* 26 Feb. 210/1 The final adjustment of the land question. **1962** H. R. Loyn *Anglo-Saxon Eng.* viii. 329 In connection with the land-question, the situation is more complicated. **1881** W. D. Seymour (*title*) Waste land reclamation and peasant proprietorship with practical suggestions for the establishment of a land bank in Ireland. **1939** *U.S. Dept. Agric. Yearbk. 1938* 1171 *Land reclamation*, making land capable of more intensive use by changing its character, environment, or both through operations requiring collective effort. **1955** Land reclamation [see *con amore]. **1940** *Economist* 6 July 12/2 The land reform [in Transylvania] which had aroused such bitter protest was admittedly more severe..than in the Old Kingdom. **1955** *Times* 4 July 8/4 His post in the Tokyo Embassy as an expert on land reform. **1871** *Leisure Hour* 8 Apr. 223/1 An aeronaut cannot get far enough from the sea in England, and requires all the land-room of a continent to make his voyage. **1960** *Tamarack Rev.* xiv. 6 The rough half-moon of islands on the western periphery of the North Atlantic contains under 8,000 square miles of landroom for three and a half million people. **1807** *Deb. Congress U.S.* 6 Oct. (1852) 605 We made a purchase of a single tract of land together. Perhaps you call that land speculations. **1848** 'D. Knickerbocker' *Hist. N.Y.* (1850) ii. vii. 121 He was soon permitted to land, and a great land-speculation ensued. **1885** W. D. Howells *Rise S. Lapham* xx. 366 He's been dabbling in..patent-rights, land speculations. **1974** D. Francis *Knock Down* xiv. 172 It was like property development and land speculation. You could make a great deal of money without breaking the law. **1794** D. Robertson *Tour through Isle of Man* v. 37 Here the oppression of game-laws, land-taxation, and excise-establishment are utterly unknown. **1883** *Peel City Guardian* 8 Dec. 4/1 Land Taxation. **1909** *Westm. Gaz.* 19 May 2/1 The land-taxation proposals of the Budget would affect them. **1812** J. McDonogh *Papers* (1898) 11 The people.. of Florida are..in a dissatisfied state, arising from this uncertainty in which their land titles are placed. **1936** *Discovery* May 131/2 Land titles have taken nearly 20 years or more to prepare. **1935** *Ibid.* Aug. 223/1 A careful land use survey. **1961** *Listener* 7 Sept. 347/2 Recent scientific advance in land-use policy in Africa. **1971** *New Scientist* 21 Jan. 134/2 We are ahead of most countries in democratic land-use planning. **1935** *Discovery* Aug. 220/1 Land Utilisation is the problem of the moment. **1936** *Archit. Rev.* LXXX. 1 (*title*) The Land Utilization Survey of Britain: the first part of the report. **1945** F. M. Lockley *Islands round Brit.* 47 Much of the landwork is done by hand with rude implements. **1971** *Daily Tel.* 19 Nov. 13/1 By 1942, the NUS had 1,000 students in its summer landwork camps.

b. *land-locator, -seeker, -speculator, -worker; land-planning.*

1816 U. Brown *Jrnl.* in *Maryland Hist. Mag.* (1915) X. 364 Those present Land Locaters Surveys will hold good until the former can be Established. **1971** *Islander* (Victoria, B.C.) 30 May 5/1 The tragedy..occurred.. when two land locators..came to grief on the Bear River glacier. **1936** *Discovery* Feb. 49/1 There has been a certain amount of 'land-planning', though not on the scale undertaken in the United States. **1961** E. A. Powdrill *Vocab. Land Planning* ii. 22 Thus, in administering the same aims of land planning, the instrument used for expressing them differs in the fundamental aspect of policymaking. **1845** J. J. Hooper *Some Adventures Simon Suggs* iii. 37 By the time he had ridden half a mile, he overtook the land-seeker. **1946** C. McWilliams *Southern California Country* 126 They sold prospective settlers so-called 'land-seekers' tickets', under an arrangement whereby the fare could later be applied on the purchase of railroad land. **1798** I. Allen *Nat. & Pol. Hist. Vermont* 24 Lawyers and land speculators called on Mr. Allen. **1873** 'Mark Twain' & Warner *Gilded Age* l. 456 He might have been a 'railroad man', or a politician, or a land-speculator. **1948** *Reader's Digest* May 124/1 He was ill-educated, selfmade, an incurable land speculator. **1887** *Andover* (Mass.) *Rev.* VIII. 154 Only the tradesworkers and the landworkers are specially considered. **1960** *Farmer & Stockbreeder* 15 Mar. 72/3 Land-workers in the Thirsk and Easingwold districts of Yorkshire.

11. *land-power.*

1928 *Observer* 1 Apr. 14/3 Sea-power took the place of land-power in the sixteenth century. **1957** [see *geostrategy* (*geo-)]. **1962** *Listener* 29 Mar. 543/1 A world which, seen from Moscow, is divided into three or four land masses, and a number of similar areas which can be dominated by land power.

b. land moccasin (see Moccasin 3) (example); **land otter** (examples); **land pike** (*a*) (earlier example); (*b*) an inferior type of pig.

1836 M. Holley *Texas* v. 104 Land and water moccasin..are the only venomous snakes, besides the rattlers, found in Texas. **1844** Lee & Frost *Ten Yrs. in Oregon* vi. 71 Beaver was valued at two dollars per skin,..land otter at fifty cents. **1947** V. H. Cahalane *Mammals N. Amer.* 200 The river or land otter has the outline of a small seal or a very big weasel. **1687** R. Blome *Present State Isles & Territories in Amer.* 56 A Land-Pike is another strange Reptile, so called from its likeness to that Fish; but instead of Fins, it hath four Feet. **1841** *Cultivator* VIII. 152, I am anxious that he should soon get rid of his land-pikes and alligators. **1842** *Ibid.* X. 37 Hogs, landpike variety, are so cheap. **1856** *Trans. Mich. Agric. Soc.* VII. 716 The Suffolk swine..are of the same descent as the long-nosed, slabsided land pike, so often seen in the highways. **1890** *Amer. N. & Q.* V. 21/2, I think the term *land-pike* more frequently designates a thin, lank, half-wild swine.

12. land army, (*a*) (see sense 11 a in Dict.); (*b*) a corps of women established in 1917 for work on the land in wartime (in full *Women's Land Army*); also *attrib.*; **land-base, -based** *a.*, operating from a base on land, as opp. to one on a ship or water; **land-borne** *a.*, carried by land, effected over land; **land-bridge,** (*a*) a connection (usu. prehistoric) between two land masses; (*b*) an overland route linking countries more directly than previously, esp. one used by containerized freight; **land company** (earlier examples); **land-connection** = **land-bridge* (*a*); **land cress,** a biennial herb of the family Cruciferæ, *Barbarea verna*; also, occasionally used for *B. vulgaris*; **land district** *U.S.*, one of the districts into which a state or territory is divided for matters connected with land; **land-drain** (see quot. 1967); also as *vb.*; hence **land-draining** *vbl. sb.*, **land-drainage; landfast** *a.*, firmly attached to the shore; **land fever** *N. Amer.*, eager desire for, or excitement about, securing land (cf. *gold-fever*); **landfill** orig. *U.S.*, the disposal of refuse by burying it under layers of earth; the refuse so disposed of; also *fig.*; **land-floe,** a sheet of sea-ice extending from the land; **land-gift** = *Bhoodan; **land girl,** a member of the Women's Land Army (see *land army* (*b*) above); **land grant,** a grant of land; *spec.* attrib. in **land-grant college** *U.S.*, a college set up orig. under the Morrill Land Grant Act of 1862, which donated public lands to certain States for the establishment of colleges of agriculture, etc.; **land-jobbing** (examples); **land legs** [cf. Sea legs *pl.*], used to designate the ability to walk comfortably on land after being at sea, in a train, etc.; **land-looker** (earlier and later examples); also (*obs.*), a person claiming to have appraised the land in a given area; **land-mine,** (*a*) an explosive mine used on land; (*b*) a bomb dropped by parachute from an aircraft; ‖**landnám** [ON. *land-nám* f. *land* land, territory + *nám*, f. *nema* to take] = **land-take*; **land-office,** hence **land-office business,** a thriving business, like that done in a land-office in boom times; a 'roaring trade'; **landplane,** an aircraft which can only operate from land (opp. *seaplane); **land-poor** *a.* (*U.S.*), poor through owning much land and being unable easily to support the burden of taxation; **Land-Rover, Landrover** [trade name], a sturdy, four-wheel-drive motor vehicle designed esp. for work in rough or agricultural country; **land-scrip** (examples); **land-sealing,** hunting seals on land; **land-shark** (*b*) (further examples); † **land-sharking** *vbl. sb. N.Z.* (see quot. 1840) *Obs.*; **land-sick** *a.*, (*c*) sick of being on the land; (*d*) sick as a result of being on land again after a long sea voyage; **land-slide,** delete *U.S.* and add further *fig.* examples, esp. with reference to a sweeping electoral victory; **land-speed,** (*a*) speed (of an aircraft) relative to the ground; (*b*) speed on the ground (e.g. in a motor vehicle); **land-take** [ON. *land-taka*], the action of taking land; *spec.* with reference to the Norse colonization of Iceland, the land taken by a chief as his province; **land-taxer,** one who believes in, or advocates, the taxing of land-values; **land-value,** the economic value of land in all respects, especially as a basis for rating or taxation; hence *land-valuation*; **land wheel,** the wheel of a plough that runs on the unploughed land; **land wire** = Land-line 2 (in Dict. and Suppl.); **land-yacht,** a land vehicle similar to a yacht. Also *land form, *landship.

1917 *Times* 4 Aug. 5/4 The work of appealing for the Women's Land Army will be carried on by the Board of Agriculture. **1918** *Times* 6 Feb. 3/5 The conditions under which the land army women are recruited have recently been changed. **1940** *Punch* 19 June 660/1 As soon as you join the Land Army you will find..that you are in the thick of a whole lot of live stock. **1943** K. Tennant *Ride on Stranger* xxv. 275, I could always sack you, George,.. and get some of these land army girls. **1974** *Country Life* 26 Sept. 829/1 One looks..at a model wearing Land Army uniform, or stoops..to peer into an Anderson shelter. **1962** *Listener* 29 Mar. 540/1 Land-base missiles and sea-going missiles. **1933** Land-based [see *based *pa. pple.*]. **1941** *Air News* May 9 The intrinsic disparity between carrier- and land-based planes. **1960** *Times* 11 Feb. 11/6 Though land-based missiles can be 'hardened'.. they are still vulnerable to a fairly accurate nuclear attack. **1973** *Sci. Amer.* May 42/3, 2,500 [nuclear warheads] in land-based missiles. **1888** *Pall Mall Gaz.* 30 Oct. 12/1 Another class of coal—best selected brights—which are landborne, fetch at the pit mouth 10s. **1934** J. L. Myres in E. Eyre *European Civilization* I. 156 The profoundly different qualities of sea-borne and land-borne cultures. **1957** *Economist* 5 Oct. 19/2 Few [Arab states] fear Russian imperialism because, unlike Turkey or Iran, they have never felt the dead-weight of landborne pressure. **1897** W. B. Scott *Introd. Geol.* xx. 353 Fossils of land animals may demonstrate the former existence of land bridges between regions which have long been separated by water. **1898** W. Turner in *Nature* 13 Jan. 259/1 A 'Neolithic land bridge' was produced..and a free immigration of Neolithic man with his domestic animals became possible. **1911** J. L. Myres *Dawn of Hist.* vii. 138 Some think..that the Hyksos conquest of Egypt may have been a further adventure along this southern land-bridge. **1941** *Manch. Guardian Weekly* 26 Sept. 194/4 There is now also a land bridge to Russia through Iran, and the Government is certain to consider whether and when we can give any military aid to Russia by that route. **1950** A. L. Rowse *England of Elizabeth* ii. 39 He cites the opinion of Master Twyne that a land-bridge once existed between Dover and Calais. **1969** *Jane's Freight Containers 1968–69* 28/1 The Port of Vancouver..put into operation the concept of the 'Land-Bridge'. *Ibid.* 32/2 The land bridge concept which foresees Canada being used as a rail-link for containers moving between Europe and the Orient. **1970** *Times* 2 June (Container Suppl.) p. ii/2 What is this concept, land-bridge? The term refers to the part of a movement from one place to another..consisting of an overland haul between ports. **1973** A. Quinton *Nature of Things* x. 301 It is generally believed that Britain was connected to the continent of Europe by a land-bridge at some time in the fairly remote past. **1805** *Deb. Congress U.S.* 30 Jan. (1852) 1044 Having never thought of purchasing any land from the Georgia land companies. **1833** *Knickerbocker* I. 283 'Look,' said an old man..to the agent of the land company. **1876** A. R. Wallace *Geogr. Distribution Animals* I. iii. xiii. 402 There is no evidence of a former land-connection between the Australian and Neotropical regions. **1924** J. G. A. Skerl tr. *Wegener's Orig. Continents & Oceans* ii. 19 The former existence of broad land connections between continents which are widely separated at the present day can scarcely be doubted. **1957** J. K. Charlesworth *Quaternary Era* II. xxxii. 696 Glaciation seems irreconcilable with a land-connexion, so often suggested, between Australia and South America during Tertiary time. **1856** W. A. Bromfield *Flora Vectensis* 33 Mr R. Loe of Newchurch tells me it [sc. *Barbarea verna*] is often substituted by the people of this island [*sc.* the Isle of Wight] for the common Water Cress, being known by the opposite cognomen of Land Cress. **1878** Britten & Holland *Dict. Eng. Plant-Names* 129 Cress, Land. (1) *Barbarea præcox*, Br... (2) *Cardamine hirsuta*, L. **1944** W. J. Stokoe *Caterpillars Brit. Butterflies* 179 Wintercress *Barbarea vulgaris*..is also known as Yellow Rocket and Land Cress, to distinguish it from Watercress, which, in general appearance, it closely resembles. **1946** *Nature* 21 Dec. 920/1 Investigations under the Dairy Research Institute have included landcress

taint in cream and butter. 1969 Oxf. Bk. Food Plants 152/2 Winter Cress or Land Cress (Barbarea verna), is a useful but rarely-grown salad plant. 1812 Deb. Congress U.S. 9 Dec. (1853) 28 The Board of Commissioners for the western land district, in the State of Louisiana. 1831 J. M. Peck Guide for Emigrants 257 The State is divided into land districts, which are designated by Congress. 1883 Rep. Indian Affairs (U.S.) 187 An Act to create three additional land districts in the territory of Dakota. 1767 A. Young Farmer's Lett. 245 When the ditching is done, the next work is to land-drain the whole fields in such a manner that every part of them may be laid dry. Ibid. 251 In some fields..it is very difficult to tell exactly where to make the land-drains. 1841 J. F. Burke On Land-Drainage 4 Remains have been found of some very ancient land-drains. 1932 Blunden Fall in, Ghosts 9 The trickling land-drain under the culvert did not report the imminence of an enemy. 1967 Gloss. Sanitation Terms (B.S.I.) 6 Land drain, a drain, composed of porous or perforated pipes, laid in a trench filled with gravel, broken stone, or the like, for sub-soil drainage. 1841 J. F. Burke (title) On land-drainage, subsoil-ploughing and irrigation. 1950 Engineering CLXIX. 143/3 The book should be of great value also to designers of..land-drainage, irrigation and water-supply works. 1841 J. F. Burke On Land-Drainage 35 Land-draining..should never be undertaken but with a determination to do it effectually. 1926 Daily Colonist (Victoria, B.C.) 24 Jan. 6/4 Amundsen's experience in the Arctic has been on shipboard, on land, and on landfast polar ice. 1973 Nat. Geographic Mar. 350 Anchoring block and tackle to land-fast ice, all strain together to haul the bowhead out of the water. 1839 Picayune (New Orleans) 23 Apr. 2/2 Then came the land fever, which swept over the country like a pestilence. 1845 C. M. Kirkland Western Clearings 4 In the days of the land-fever. 1900 E. B. Osborn Greater Canada 60 Many years passed before the North-West recovered from the commercial lethargy which followed this attack of land-fever. 1946 E. Hodgins Mr. Blandings builds his Dream House 16 Then, suddenly the land fever seized them. 1972 J. Minifie Homesteader vi. 40 Many of the harvesters were bitten by the land fever, and filed on land for themselves once the harvest was over. 1942 in Sun (Baltimore) (1944) 10 Feb. 8/1 The so-called sanitary or land fill [system]. 1953 Richmond (Va.) News Leader 2 Sept. 21 A bulldozer struck water in the landfill dump area. 1967 Boston Sunday Globe 23 Apr. 20/3 By 1970, it is expected that the majority of the area's dumps and landfill sites will be filled to capacity. 1969 New Yorker 17 May 131/2 We intend to put a lot of landfill in the Credibility Gap. 1971 Pollution: a Review (Greater London Council) 8 The Greater London Council..operates a code of practice for good management of landfill sites under its own control. 1971 Guardian 11 Oct. 3/6 Landfill is considered one of the most economical ways to dispose of refuse. 1823 W. Scoresby Jrnl. Voy. Northern Whale-Fishery iv. 101 The drift of the ice towards the south-west,..for three weeks preceding our entrance amid the land floes, had averaged seven or eight miles a-day. 1866 C. E. Smith Diary 20 July in Listener (1969) 17 Apr. 525/2 We are unable to stir, with a tremendous land-floe on one side of us and, on the other side, a body of ice extending as far as we can see from the mast-head. 1939 Beaver June 31 By May literally hundreds of thousands [of eider ducks] have arrived to feed in the sea and rest idly on the edge of land-floe and ice-pan. 1953 Land-gift [see *Bhoodan]. 1957 Listener 30 May 889/3 The Land Gifts Movement..aims at persuading landowners large and small to surrender voluntarily a sixth of their land for distribution to the poor. 1964 T. Zinkin India vi. 125 Vinoba Bhave..managed to create such a response for his 'Bhoodan'—land-gift—that the bitterness on which the communists had thrived in Telengana vanished. 1918 Times 20 Mar. 9/4 The land girls [had] little felt hats and smocks and their red badges of service. 1919 'I. Hay' Last Million 81 We have consorted with..Farmers, Hedgers, and Land Girls. 1928 'R. Crompton' William—the Good iv. 103 He found his sister Ethel wearing a neat land girl's costume and weeding a bed. 1940 Manch. Guardian Weekly 8 Nov. 325 One German pilot even turned his guns against land girls working in the fields. 1958 Times Lit. Suppl. 11 July 399/5 A young Tunisian land-girl and youth leader. 1974 M. Cecil Heroines in Love vii. 175 Down on the farm the Land Girl was swept off her feet by the farmer. 1862 N.Y. Tribune 21 Mar., Some years since, the movement for a Pacific Railroad, attended by an enormous land-grant, assumed proportions that indicated the probable success of the movement. 1869 Bradshaw's Railway Manual XXI. 431 Expended..Land grant expenses—$7,205. 1889 Century Mag. Jan. 404/2 The land-grant colleges graduate men fitted to superintend farms and workshops. 1900 Daily Chron. 28 Aug. 5/1 At the present time no land-grants to emigrants are being made by the Natal Government. 1943 J. S. Huxley TVA vi. 30 In 1862..Land Grant Colleges were established—so called because in every State lands were granted from the public domain to endow a College for the teaching of 'Agriculture and the Mechanic Arts'. 1944 F. Clune Red Heart 5 He was..a hander-out of liberal land-grants to sycophantic favourites. 1962 H. R. Loyn Anglo-Saxon Eng. iv. 158 If arable is at the centre of the land-grant, connected rights in meadow, pasture..and wood were closely associated with it. 1967 Mrs. L. B. Johnson White House Diary 14 Mar. (1970) 498 Federal participation in education is not exactly new, going back as far as 1785 in the Land Ordinance, the land grant colleges of the 1860's, [etc.]. 1781 in Mass. Hist. Soc. Coll. (1814) 2nd. Ser. I. 186 Toryism, British interest, and Land-jobbing views, combine numbers without and within doors. 1885 Century Mag. Apr. 826 When the bill to establish a State park at Niagara was on its passage,..the great majority of the country members were opposed to it, fearing that it might conceal some land-jobbing scheme. 1871 City-Road Mag. I. 242/1 If Mr. Goschen has had to get his sea-legs on, Jack finds it as difficult to put on his land-legs. 1927 Sunday Times 6 Mar. 23/4 The tourists will disembark..and proceed to Teignmouth to spend eighteen days recovering their 'land legs' and developing combination. 1938 H. Nicolson Let. 17 Apr. (1966) 337 Have you..recovered your landlegs as yet? After three days in the train one feels the room rocking like after three days at sea. 1840 Knickerbocker XVI. 206 Another class of operators..became popularly known as 'land-lookers'. These met you at every turn, ready to furnish 'water power', 'pine-lots', 'choice farming tracts' or any thing else, at a moment's notice. 1845 C. M. Kirkland Western Clearings 6 These blunders called into action another class of operators, who became popularly known as 'land-lookers'. 1893, 1900 Landlooker [see *cruiser 3]. 1902 S. E. White Blazed Trail xvi. 116 This is the usual method of procedure adopted by land-lookers everywhere. 1890 Electrician 16 Mar. 502/1 Land Mines. These mines..are intended to be placed a few inches below the surface of the ground, and are so constructed that they..fire themselves electrically or mechanically when the measure of the weight of a man is brought to bear upon them. 1915 R. W. Campbell Private Spud Tamson xix. 288 A terrific explosion of land mines, which burst beneath the feet of the enemy. a 1917 E. A. Mackintosh War, the Liberator (1918) 134 Two sappers brought up land mines and laid them. 1940 N. & Q. 21 Dec. 440/2 Up to September of this year a land-mine..signified a receptacle filled with explosive and concealed immediately below the surface of the ground... In popular parlance it has come to mean a mine, that is to say a thin metal container holding a large quantity of explosive, dropped from an enemy aeroplane upon the land. 1959 Chambers's Encyl. II. 413/1 The effectiveness of the 'land-mines' dropped by the Luftwaffe on Britain. 1968 M. Richler in R. Weaver Canad. Short Stories 2nd Ser. 183 Had a little disagreement with a land mine, son. 1973 'R. MacLeod' Nest of Vultures vi. 129 British anti-personnel Claymore land-mines. 1858 G. W. Dasent in Oxford Ess. 185 Chief after chief coming out [to Iceland]..settling himself on some great chief's lot or landnám, who allotted him a portion on condition of the acknowledgement of his supremacy. 1877 C. A. V. Conybeare Place of Iceland in Hist. European Inst. 28 The Goðorð was no doubt intimately connected with the landnám of the most powerful of the immigrants. 1915 K. Gjerset Hist. Norwegian People (1932) xxv. 140 The chieftains..claimed large tracts of land by right of settlement and occupation..while the freemen..with their consent, settled in their landnám. 1839 Picayune (New Orleans) 2 Apr. 2/3 A practical printer..could do a land-office business here. 1877 'Mark Twain' in Atlantic Monthly Nov. 590/1 Naturally, the prophets of Baal took all the trade. Isaac..went a-prophesying around, letting on to be doing a land-office business, but 't wa'n't any use. 1882 Land-office business [in Dict.]. 1935 M. M. Atwater Murder in Midsummer v. 51 He was doing a land-office business in gas and pop and candy. 1951 E. Paul Springtime in Paris xi. 203 American students..used to do a land-office business in contraband cigarettes. 1972 New York 12 June 35/2 Allen & Co...was doing a land-office business touting Planet Oil. 1923 Daily Mail 23 June 5 Among landplanes there are huge new troop-carriers. 1932 19th Cent. Feb. 205 One squadron of flying-boats and one of torpedo-bomber landplanes. 1941 E. C. Shepherd Military Aeroplane 27 The Coastal Command..has..landplane reconnaissance craft which can also carry bombs. 1942 Tee Emm (Air Ministry) II. 61 Land planes are not designed for alighting on the sea. 1969 K. Munson Pioneer Aircraft 1903–14 152/2 Unlike Fabre's seaplane, however, this was both a landplane and a biplane, with a twin-girder 'fuselage' on which was lightly attached an aluminium nacelle encompassing side-by-side seats for pilot and passenger. 1873 J. H. Beadle Undevel. West 781 In the country, the old settlers are 'land-poor'—so rich that they can not pay their taxes. 1914 Collier's Mag. 31 Jan. 22/2 The land-poor farmer is a well-known institution in the Middle West. a 1953 E. O'Neill Long Day's Journey (1956) iv. 125 All I told them was I couldn't afford any millionaire's sanatorium because I was land poor. 1948 Trade Marks Jrnl. 29 Sept. 786/2 Land-rover... Land motor-vehicles and parts thereof... The Rover Company Limited. 1948 Motor 3 Nov. 381/1 Also exhibited is the Land Rover, as a closed estate car with seven-seat capacity, a go-anywhere, four-wheel-drive model powered by the '60' engine. 1953 New Statesman 13 June 696/3 Commuting barristers and stockbrokers in their shooting brakes and land-rovers. 1959 Times Lit. Suppl. 24 Apr. 243/4 It is one of the few recent books about the Sahara desert in which there is no mention of a Land-Rover. 1960 Times 5 July (Agric. Suppl.) p. iv/1 The Land-Rover is as much part of the farming scene as the cattle or the sheep. 1971 Country Life 25 Feb. 436/2 Then came the Landrover, also a multi-purpose, cross-country vehicle. 1834 A. Jackson in Messages & Papers of Presidents (1896) III. 52 Mr. St. Clair..had permitted the clerk in his office to be the agent of speculations in land scrip. 1848 Indiana Gen. Assembly Doc. (1849) I. 181 Such land Scrip as had been issued on the Wabash and Erie Canal. 1862 Congress. Globe 10 June 2628/1 There is no railroad company..that has the right to locate land scrip. 1943 L. V. Hamner Short Grass 174 Surveyors..bought up a lot of land scrip for almost nothing. 1921 Chambers's Jrnl. July 475/2 In the land-sealing..thousands of fur-seals are driven and forced onwards. 1829 in Ohio Archaeol. & Hist. Q. (1939) XLVIII. 331 The Counsel is sure to be supported by the presiding Judges..& thus the Property of Society is Confiscated Legally between these Land Sharks. 1839 J. D. Lang N.Z. in 1839 i. 14 A class of persons in that Colony [sc. New South Wales] who were known by the name of Land Sharks..have turned their eyes all at once to New Zealand. 1865 C. F. Hursthouse Lett. on N.Z. Subjects 89 'Land Sharks', twenty years ago this was a term rife in Australia and New Zealand. a 1910 'O. Henry' Rolling Stones (1915) 218 A class of land speculators commonly called land sharks, unscrupulous and greedy. 1935 A. Sullivan Great Divide 342 The Metis are being stirred up by the land sharks to demand their scrip, then the sharks will swallow them. 1839 Colonial Gaz. 28 Aug. 627/2 Land-sharking means pretending to purchase, but really obtaining somehow, land from the natives. 1840 N.Z. Company Rep. I. 31 The practice of land-sharking, or the acquisition of land from the barbarous natives by private persons, without any reserves for the use of the natives, or indeed any sort of regard for their just rights. 1855 C. W. Richmond Let. 28 Apr. in Richmond–Atkinson Papers (1960) I. 162 Such agreements favor landsharking and tend to produce strife and contention. 1888 L. A. Smith Music of Waters 219, I could understand any land-sick lad longing for a sea-life if he once heard this ballast-throwing song. 1908 Westm. Gaz. 13 Feb. 2/1 The joy of the land-sick sailors who cried, 'The sea, the sea!' 1908 Daily Chron. 10 June 4/4 It was very curious, that first step ashore... I was thoroughly land-sick. 1922 D. H. Lawrence Let. 5 Sept. (1962) II. 714 We were twenty-five days at sea and are still landsick—the floor ought to go up and down, the room ought to tremble from the engines, the water ought to swish around but doesn't, so one is landsick. The solid ground almost hurts. 1924 —— & Skinner Boy in Bush 19 Jack was a little tired and a little land-sick, after the long voyage. 1888 N.Y. Times 4 Nov. 5/1 A veritable landslide in Mr. Hewitt's favor. 1896 Westm. Gaz. 6 Nov. 7/1 We were justified in urging our readers yesterday to accept with caution the earlier views of the extent of McKinley's majority. It is not a 'landslide'. 1936 Punch 23 Sept. 362/1 The first volume of the long expected biography of Arthur James Balfour (which takes us as far as the Conservative landslide in 1906). 1946 Ann. Reg. 1945 239 Another undoubted shock was the Labour landslide in the British general elections. 1955 Times 9 May 11/4 The electoral landslide which swept into power the hastily organized Labour Front. 1974 Times 27 Feb. 18/5 Modern Toryism..wants a land-slide victory. 1910 R. Ferris How it Flies xx. 464 Land-speed, the speed of aircraft as related to objects on the ground. 1935 Eyston & Lyndon Motor Racing & Record Breaking vi. 56 Record breaking can be somewhat grim, as is shown by the land-speed attempts at Daytona. 1963 Times 2 May 11/2 Donald Campbell reached 110 miles an hour on the salt flats here today when his turbo-jet car Bluebird made a first trial run for his world landspeed record bid. 1971 Guinness Bk. Records (ed. 18) xi. 160 The highest land speed recorded by a woman is 335·070 m.p.h. by Mrs. Lee Ann Breedlove. 1906 Ann. Rep. Board of Regents Smithsonian Inst. 287 Until a Parliament for Iceland was established in 930 these chieftains were the rulers of the island, each in his district or land-take (landnám), as it was called. 1908 W. G. Collingwood Scandinavian Brit. 193 In each landtake the bóndi fixed his homestead, neither on the exposed hill-top, nor on the marshy flat. 1927 E. V. Gordon Introd. Old Norse 235 The method of land-take used by settlers in Iceland; they carried fire through the land they were to occupy, and around its limits. 1905 Westm. Gaz. 13 Apr. 4/1 The land taxers have an idea that valuable sites are being held back by grasping ground landlords. 1909 Daily Chron. 30 Apr. 1/6 As land-taxers, we are thoroughly satisfied that we have got a complete system of land valuation. 1928 Daily Express 6 June 2/4 Colonel Wedgwood, the famous Socialist land-taxer. 1851 Fraser's Mag. XLIII. 117 Luckily..for railway companies,..land-valuation is a remarkably elastic art. 1908 Daily Chron. 6 Aug. 8/3 The land-valuation proposals of the Government. 1880 H. George Progress & Poverty viii. ii. 365 To abolish all taxation save that upon land values. 1900 W. Smart Taxation of Land Values 38 Of late years we have heard much of a proposal called the taxation of land values. 1908 Westm. Gaz. 20 Feb. 2/2 The rates charged on the land-value basis. 1962 H. R. Loyn Anglo-Saxon Eng. viii. 319 Considerable variation in land-values..occurred between 1066 and 1086. 1743 W. Ellis Mod. Husbandman Sept. iv. 27 The Land Wheel being obliged to go on the Turf its Share is kept too high. 1960 Farmer & Stock-breeder 15 Mar. 102/3 For a one-man unit the spreader should be land-wheel-driven for ease of hitching on and off. 1970 G. E. Evans Where Beards wag All ii. 46 A two-horse iron plough with round coulter,..land and furrow wheel. 1972 Country Life 10 Feb. 321/3 It [sc. a plough] had no land wheel, so that depth had to be kept by bearing on the stilts. 1876 Preece & Sivewright Telegraphy v. 128 Between London and Amsterdam there are 130 miles of land wire over the Great Eastern Railway, then a cable 120 miles long, and then 20 more miles of land wire. 1908 Westm. Gaz. 24 Feb. 4/1 The..cable from Ascension touches land in Cornwall.., whence a land-wire passed the signals on to Greenwich. 1930 Aberdeen Press & Jrnl. 23 Jan. 7/6 A microphone was installed at 10 Downing Street, and the Premier's words were carried by land wire to Chelmsford. 1928 Daily Express 26 May 9/3 There was shown at Olympia last year a 'land-yacht' that was palatial in its appointments. 1967 Times 23 Jan. 9 A school that has its own land yacht, wind tunnel, go-kart and canoeing clubs.

‖ **Land** (lant), *sb.*[2] Pl. Länder (le·ndər), Laender, Lands. [G.] A semi-autonomous unit of local government in Germany and Austria.

[1920 G. Young New Germany 321 The transformation of this Constitution from a centralised republic..back to a federation has been reviewed already. The word 'lander' is literally translated for this and other reasons.] 1920 H. W. V. Temperley Hist. Peace Conf. Paris III. 347 The word Länder..has been deliberately used instead of the word Staaten... The word States for the members of a federal Constitution seems therefore to be misleading as expressly repudiated and 'Lands' is used, a new word coined by Professor Young. Ibid. 348 Article 5. Constitutional power is exercised..in matters pertaining to the Lands, by the Constitutional bodies of those Lands within the lines laid down by the constitutions of those Lands. 1950 Theimer & Campbell Encycl. World Politics 42 Austria became a federal republic, consisting of eight Lands. 1955 Times 26 Aug. 7/2 Many wage agreements are settled on a Land and not a federal basis. 1958 Listener 9 Oct. 571/1 In the Laender under its sway..it [sc. Austria] produced the nearest approach to the Welfare State that existed before its establishment in the United Kingdom. 1966 Economist 13 Aug. 633/1 The ambitious and consequently hard-pressed Länder are demanding that..Bonn's share of the tax-collectors' booty should be no more than 35 per cent. 1969 Nature 15 Nov. 633/2 The German universities are at present the responsibility of the Länder. 1973 Times 30 Jan. 4/6 The four Länder—Hamburg, Bremen, Lower Saxony and Schleswig-Holstein—have asked the Bonn Government to sanction a boycott.

land, *v.* Add: **1. c.** *pass.* In Canada, to be given the status of a landed immigrant (see *landed *ppl. a.* 3).

1910 [see *LANDED *ppl. a.* 3]. **1962** *Canada Month* Aug. 16/3 They arrived from an Italian refugee camp in three groups around mid-month, were duly 'landed' by immigration officials. **1974** *Globe & Mail* (Toronto) 16 May 3/3 So far 22,905 have actually been 'landed'—given legal status as landed immigrants—and it's just a matter of time before most of the others achieve the same goal.

2. e. (Earlier and later examples.) Also *intr.* with *out.*

1886 H. Baumann *Londinismen* 93/1 He landed him a little one on his left ogle. **1898** J. D. Brayshaw *Slum Silhouettes* 2 That on'y made Bill madder 'n ever, an' 'e lands aht wiv 'is right, but the Gent. jest ketched 'is arm. **1912** *Chambers's Jrnl.* June 395/2 After sparring for five minutes, and frustrating every attempt you made to 'land' on him, he would sit down. **1928** *Manch. Guardian Weekly* 5 Oct. 274/3 Why didn't his man 'land out' at the insulting blighter?

g. *Machine knitting.* To secure (a loop) on the closed beard of a needle.

1885 [see *KNOCK *v.* 13 c]. **1926** J. Chamberlain *Knitting Math. & Mech.* v. 98 Using different lengths of beards in the same machine may result in certain loops not being landed, and consequently not cast off. **1952** D. F. Paling *Warp Knitting Technol.* i. 6 The old fabric loops on their upward movement pass over the tips of the beards which are embedded in the needle eyes, and the old loops are landed on to the closed beards.

h. To bring (an aircraft) to earth from the air; to place (an aircraft or spacecraft, or its contents) on the ground or some other surface after a flight.

1916 H. Barber *Aeroplane Speaks* 49 I'll guarantee to safely land the fastest machine in a five-acre field. **1926** *Encycl. Brit.* I. 65/2 Attempts were later made to land machines on this forward deck [of the aircraft carrier]. **1931** *Times* 19 Feb. 17/2 There was a difference of opinion as to who should land the flying boat?—Very definitely. **1932** W. E. Johns *Camels are Coming* ii. 35 Agents..are usually taken over by aircraft; sometimes they drop by parachute and sometimes we land them. **1948** Gregory & Allan *Helicopter* xvi. 190 There are a lot of things that we have to do to this machine before you can take off and land it. **1952** K. W. Gatland *Devel. Guided Missile* vi. 103 (*caption*) Instead of landing the entire space-ship, a secondary rocket will descend to the surface. **1962** *Times* 30 Apr. 12/7 Russia's latest earth satellite has been successfully landed in a predetermined area. **1967** J. Rowland *Jet Man* vi. 59 Now Whittle's experience of aerobatics came in useful, for he had to 'land' the machine in the water. **1968** *Ann. Reg. 1967* 178 The two accidents were a severe setback to American plans to land a man on the moon before 1970. **1972** *Nature* 3 Mar. 3/1 It is simply too dangerous to attempt to land a manned spacecraft in the lunar mountains.

3. b. Also, to obtain (employment). Also *absol.*

1926 Whiteman & McBride *Jazz* viii. 167 That is another reason why the outsider fails to land. He doesn't know about these rogues. **1946** E. O'Neill *Iceman Cometh* (1947) III. 152 I'll bet you tink yuh're goin' out and land a job, too. **1952** Granville *Dict. Theatr. Terms* 108 *Land a spot*, obtain an engagement.

8. a. (Later examples.) Also with *up.*

1927 H. Crane *Let.* 19 Mar. (1965) 291, I had just landed in town after three months with the bossy cows. **1958** *Listener* 30 Oct. 694/3 They [*sc.* migrants] land up, exhausted, on islands and headlands. **1965** *Ibid.* 2 Sept. 351/2 After unspecified work in a map shop he landed up, furnished with a testimonial from Charles Graves, in the publishing house of Novello.

b. (Further examples.) Esp. of an aircraft or spacecraft, or a person in one: to alight upon or reach the ground, or some other surface, after a flight.

1784 V. Lunardi *Acct. First Aërial Voy. in Eng.* 37 My principal care was to avoid a violent concussion at landing, and in this my good fortune was my friend. At twenty minutes past four I descended in a spacious meadow. **1899** H. G. Wells *When Sleeper Wakes* xxiv. 326 On Blackheath no aëroplane had landed. **1908** —— *War in Air* ii. 60 The balloon was bumping as though its occupants were trying to land. **1911** W. Kaempffert *New Art of Flying* xiv. 238 Ely's remarkable feat in landing on the deck of a warship in the harbour of San Francisco. **1917** [see *FLATTEN *v.* 2 b]. **1917** 'Contact' *Airman's Outings* ii. 45 The machine in question was probably hit, however, for it did not return, and I saw it begin a glide as though the pilot meant to land. **1930** *Times* 11 Nov. 16/4 She [*sc.* a flying boat] circled the station and then landed in comparatively calm water. **1952** *Oxf. Jun. Encycl.* X. 7/2 When landing, the pilot is guided on to the deck by the Deck Control Officer who signals with 'bats'. **1953** Leslie & Adamski (*title*) Flying saucers have landed. **1969** *Times* 21 July 1/1 The first word from man on the moon came from Aldrin: 'Tranquillity base. The Eagle has landed.' **1973** *Sci. Amer.* Dec. 102/1 If the birds are pursued, they take off, but they do not fly far before they land again.

d. With *on.* Of an aircraft: to land on the deck of an aircraft carrier. Hence **landing-on** *vbl. sb.*

1937 *Aeroplane* 9 June 691/1 The ship was headed into wind and permission to land-on was given to the first Nimrod. *Ibid.* 16 June 724/1 The landing-on is organised similarly to the flying-off. **1939** *Nature* CXLIII. 592/2 'Landing on' had proved safer than driving a car on an English road. **1954** P. K. Kemp *Fleet Air Arm* 95 They took off and landed on without difficulty, completely independent of the sea.

landaulet. Add: **b.** In form *landaulette.* A type of motor car with a leather hood above the rear seats. Also *attrib.*

1901 *Autocar* 17 Aug. 153 (*heading*) The Peugeot landaulette. *Ibid.*, Mr. C. Friswell's Peugeot landaulette... The vehicle may be stated to be of the standard Peugeot type, but with only such alterations made as are necessary for the accommodation of the landau body. **1905** *Daily Chron.* 17 Nov. 8/4 Now the 'landaulette' is the popular car of the moment. **1906** *Ibid.* 15 Sept. 6/2 The cabs would be of the landaulette type. **1922** A. Haddon *Green Room Gossip* viii. 172 The other evening I rolled up to the Palladium in a big landaulette that carries seven persons. The chauffeur and I had it to ourselves. **1968** G. N. Georgano *Complete Encycl. Motorcars* 175 (*caption*) 1912 *Dennis* 24 hp landaulette. **1973** *Country Life* 18 Oct. 1190/3 It was not until 1909 that..I hired a cumbersome Astor landaulette from the Oxford garage. **1974** *Daily Tel.* 19 Oct. 17/2 Rolls-Royce's most expensive current car is the open landaulette, made in very limited numbers for heads of State at a cost of about £36,000.

landdrost. Add to def.: Under British administration, the office was abolished. (Further examples.)

1801, etc. [see *HEEMRAD]. **1947** L. Hastings *Dragons are Extra* ii. 35 Any old leader or *landrost* of the Free State or Transvaal had just Botha's sort of serenity. **1952** E. H. Burrows *Overberg Outspan* i. 16 Outwardly the old Dutch form persisted until 1827 when the *Collegies* were abolished, and the *landdrosts* replaced by Resident Magistrates and Civil Commissioners.

landed, *ppl. a.* Add: **2.** Caught, stuck, encumbered *with.*

In some of the examples a use of the pa. pple. of *land* v. rather than a ppl. adj.

1866 W. Gregor *Dial. Banffshire* 100 A'm fairly lantit wee the aul' coo. **1900** G. B. Shaw *Press Cuttings* 34 Sometimes..they get an idea of their own; and then of course youre landed. **1910** A. Bennett *Clayhanger* iv. vi. 508 The right sort of women don't get landed as the wives of convicts. **1943** J. B. Priestley *Daylight on Saturday* xxii. 171 One thing leads to another..an' then, before you know where you are, you're landed. **1947** 'G. Orwell' *Let.* 23 Oct. in *Coll. Ess.* (1968) IV. 382 I've been landed with another long article which I can't dodge out of. **1960** 'N. Shute' *Trustee from Toolroom* i. 7 You'll be landed with a cat for the rest of your lives. **1974** K. Royce *Trap Spider* i. 27, I told you that I'd speak to your son and I'm landed with it.

3. *landed immigrant*: an immigrant to Canada, admitted for permanent residence; so *landed (immigrant) status.*

1910 *Statutes of Canada* c. 27, s. 2 (p), 'Land', 'landed' or 'landing', as applied to passengers or immigrants, means their lawful admission into Canada by an officer under this Act, otherwise than for inspection or treatment or other temporary purpose provided for by this Act. **1963** *Maclean's Mag.* 20 Apr. 18/3 The only black people freely admitted to Canada as landed immigrants are a limited number of women. **1964** *Calgary Herald* 4 May 25/3 If he is to see his child, he will have to..be accepted as a landed immigrant. **1968** *Globe & Mail* (Toronto) 2 May 2/4 Brooks..was granted landed immigrant status but Stonehill was refused. *Ibid.*, Stonehill's bid to obtain landed status had strong political repercussions in Ottawa. **1973** *Ibid.* 27 Dec. 2/2 Most Canadians don't realize it but any visitor or landed immigrant with less than five years residence can be deported, together with his entire family, for any criminal code offence, including impaired driving or shoplifting. **1975** *Canadian Mag.* (Toronto) 8 Mar. 6/4 [Some] East Indians who have obtained citizenship or landed immigrant status have been involved in illegal immigration rackets.

Landenian (lænde·niăn), *a. Geol.* [a. F. *Landenien* (A. Dumont 1839, in *Bull. de l'Acad. R. des Sci.*, etc., *de Bruxelles* VI. II. 466), f. *Landen*, name of a town near Liège in Belgium: see -IAN.] Of, pertaining to, or designating a stratigraphic stage at the top of the Palæocene series (or the bottom of the Eocene), lying above the Montian. Also *absol.*

1852 *Q. Jrnl. Geol. Soc.* VIII. 254 In his visit to this country..he [sc. Dumont] pointed out to me the many characters common to these Thanet sands and his 'Landenian System', which occupies the same position in the Belgian series. **1902** A. J. Jukes-Browne *Student's Handbk. Stratigr. Geol.* xvi. 485 In Belgium the Montian limestone..is overlain by glauconitic sands which are known as the Lower Landenian and unquestionably correspond to our Thanet Beds. **1923** L. D. Stamp *Introd. Stratigr.* xvi. 274 Upper or Continental Landenian strata succeed [the lower or Marine Landenian] conformably, and are known as the Woolwich and Reading Beds. **1955** G. G. Woodford tr. *M. Gignoux's Stratigraphic Geol.* ix. 485 The English Tertiary begins with the transgressive Landenian. **1969** Bennison & Wright *Geol. Hist. Brit. Isles* xv. 336 Sedimentation commenced with the inundation by the sea of the eastern part of the London Basin in Landenian times, depositing the Thanet Beds. *Ibid.*, The marine facies may not have persisted throughout the Landenian even in the east of the London Basin.

lander. Add: **1. b.** A spacecraft, or a part of one, which is designed to land on the surface of a planet or of the moon.

1961 *Astronautica Acta* VII. 130 The rotary drill..is designed to penetrate 1·5 ft or more into the lunar surface and bring samples into the lander for chemical analysis. **1962** F. I. Ordway et al. *Basic Astronautics* v. 176 Hard landers contain retrorockets to reduce the terminal velocity to between 100 and 300 m.p.h... Soft landers.. are built to descend gently onto the surface. **1967** *Technology Week* 23 Jan. 61/1 (Advt.), This calls for a varied series of probes, orbiters and hard and soft landers. **1971** *Listener* 7 Oct. 476/3 Each vehicle consists of two main parts: an orbiter and a lander.

landesite (læ·ndizəit). *Min.* [f. the name of K. K. *Landes* (b. 1899), American geologist + -ITE[1].] A brown hydrated phosphate of manganese and ferric iron, occurring as an alteration product of reddingite at Berry Quarry, Poland, Maine, U.S.A.

1930 Berman & Gonyer in *Amer. Mineralogist* XV. 385 This mineral seems to represent a new species for which the name landesite is here proposed in honor of Professor Kenneth K. Landes who has done much work on the pegmatites of Maine. **1964** *Ibid.* XLIX. 1123 The landesite formula is better expressed in the following manner...

$$[Mn^{2+}_{1-x}(Fe^{3+}OH)_x]_3[(3-3x)H_2O](PO_4)_2$$

in which, for type landesite, *x* is approximately 0·25.

landfall. Add: **1. c.** Arrival at land after a flight over the sea; also, = *LANDING *vbl. sb.* 1 d.

1908 H. G. Wells *War in Air* vi. 194 New York had risen out of the blue indistinctness of the landfall. **1909** —— *Tono-Bungay* IV. i. 449, I remember our prolonged dragging landfall. **1928** C. F. S. Gamble *Story N. Sea Air Station* ix. 121 The airship L.3..made her 'landfall' off Ingham. **1942** *R.A.F. Jrnl.* 3 Oct. 31 You get a feeling of warming pride as a good landfall is made. Once round the beacon and down you come. **1954** 'J. Christopher' *22nd Cent.* 86 They check you each landfall. Hans got his final warning at Luna City. **1959** *Listener* 22 Jan. 160/1 The average drift-migrants [*sc.* birds] that make a landfall are not necessarily lost.

d. The place where an undersea pipeline reaches land.

1974 *People's Jrnl.* (Inverness & Northern Counties ed.) 7 Sept. 2/6 Burmah and British Petroleum..have.. approached Zetland County Council about the possibility of a pipeline landfall in Shetland. **1975** *Petroleum Rev.* XXIX. 387/2 It took twelve months..to select Flotta.. as the landfall for the oil pipeline from the Piper field.

la·nd form. Also **land-form, landform.** [LAND *sb.* 10 a.] **1. a.** A physical feature of the earth's surface such as a hill, plain, cirque, or alluvial fan.

1893 Land form [see *GEOMORPHOLOGY]. **1910** *Encycl. Brit.* XI. 633/2 Thus new land forms are created—valleys of curious complexity, for example—by the 'capture' and diversion of the water of one river by another. **1938** L. D. Stamp *Physical Geogr. & Geol.* ix. 142 The land forms in deserts developed in sedimentary rocks are similar to those in damper temperate climates except that slopes are usually sharper and steeper. **1970** R. J. Small *Study of Landforms* i. 8 Classification can be attempted not only of individual kinds of landform (such as slopes, cliffs, terraces, beaches, lakes, volcanoes, planation surfaces and so on) or types of process.., but of landform assemblages.

† **b.** A landscape of any particular kind. *Obs.*

1893 W. M. Davis in *Nat. Geogr. Mag.* 10 July 73 Every land-form passes through a systematic series of changes from its youth, when its form is defined chiefly by constructional processes, past its maturity, when the processes of sub-aerial sculpture have carved a variety of mouldings and channellings, to its old age in which..denudation reduces the mass to base-level. **1899** —— in *Geogr. Jrnl.* XIV. 485 Where the forces of uplift or deformation have lately..initiated a cycle of changes, the destructive forces can have accomplished but little work, and the land-form is 'young'.

2. A kind (of living organism) found on land.

1897 Land form [in Dict. s.v. LAND *sb.* 11]. **1926** J. S. Huxley *Ess. Pop. Sci.* 93 There are three or four other species of animals, such as Proteus,..which..are not known in a land-form at all.

landing, *vbl. sb.* Add: **1. d.** The (or an) action of approaching and alighting on the ground or some other surface after a flight. *happy landings!*: see *HAPPY *a.* 3.

1784 [see *LAND *v.* 8 b]. **1909** *Flight* 13 Feb. 93/1 (*heading*) Flight 'landings'. **1912** *Aeroplane* 19 Dec. 621/2 Major Cameron and Capt. Salmon with Mr. Barnwell and, later, Mr. Knight up behind, put in large number [*sic*] of straights each making very good flights and landings. **1916** H. Barber *Aeroplane Speaks* 49 You can..imagine what a difference that would make where forced landings are concerned! **1923** H. G. Wells *Men like Gods* I. iii. 37 The aeroplanes made an easy landing. **1927** G. Aston *Navy of To-Day* v. 31 The airman, and the airman's home, the aircraft carrier, must steam head to wind..when the airmen want to accomplish 'landings' on her deck. **1936** *Discovery* Aug. 238/1 The camera is raised during takeoffs and landings. **1956** [see *EMERGENCY 5]. **1967** D. P. Davies *Handling Big Jets* iii. 30 For take-off and landing the weight should be known to within 5,000 lb. **1969** *Times* 21 July 1/1 The landing, in the Sea of Tranquillity, was near perfect and the two astronauts on board Eagle reported that it had not tilted too far to prevent take-off. **1974** *Daily Tel.* 21 Feb. 17/7 He [*sc.* a balloonist] has food and water for 10 days and the gondola is equipped with floatation devices to keep it upright if he is forced to make a water landing.

5. (Later U.S. examples.)

1832 S. Cumings *Western Pilot* 49 There is a pretty good landing at the upper end of the town. **1867** J. N. Edwards *Shelby* xx. 366 The next day the brigade moved to the river near Gaines Landing. **1895** M. A. Jackson *Mem. Stonewall Jackson* (ed. 2) xii. 211 Just before reaching the landing I stopped to look back.

8. *landing area, fee, field, ground, -leg, site, -tower, vehicle;* **landing beam** *Aeronaut.,* a radio beam to guide aircraft when landing; **landing card,** a card issued to a passenger on an international flight or voyage, which is surrendered on arrival; **landing craft,** a naval vessel with a shallow draught designed for landing troops, tanks, etc., in an amphibious assault; hence *transf.* in *Astronaut.,* the section of a spacecraft which is used for the final descent to the surface of a planet or moon; **landing flap** *Aeronaut.,* a flap that can be lowered to increase the lift and the drag and so make possible lower speeds for take-off and landing; **landing gear,** (*a*) *Aeronaut.,* the structure underneath an aircraft that is designed to support it on the ground and to absorb the shock of landing (in modern aircraft made to be retracted in flight); (*b*) the retractable support at the front of a semi-trailer that supports it when not attached to the tractor; **landing light,** (*a*) a light on the runway of an aerodrome to guide an aircraft in a night landing; (*b*) a light attached to an aircraft to illuminate the ground for a night landing; **landing pad,** (*a*) a small area of an aerodrome or heliport, used for the landing and taking off of helicopters; (*b*) a cushioned or strengthened foot which supports a hovercraft, spacecraft, or the like when stationary on the ground; **landing ship (tank(s))**, a large landing craft for the transport of tanks and other vehicles; **landing speed,** the speed at which an aircraft lands (see also quot. 1911); **landing strip** = *air-strip* (*AIR *sb.* [1] B. III. 7); **landing ticket** = *landing card;* **landing wire,** *Aeronaut.,* a wire on a biplane or light monoplane that is designed to take the weight of a wing when the aircraft is on the ground.

1910 R. FERRIS *How it Flies* xx. 464 *Landing area,* a piece of land specially prepared for the alighting of aeroplanes without risk of injury. 1951 *Gloss. Aeronaut. Terms (B.S.I.)* iii. 23 *Landing area,* the part of the movement area primarily intended for the take-off and landing of aircraft. 1974 G. MITCHELL *Javelin for Jonah* ix. 115 You may go ahead with the new landing-areas for jump and pole. 1929 Landing beam [see *BEAM *sb.* [1] 24 b]. 1933 *Flight* 1 June 524 A pointer on a simple instrument showed him any deviation from the landing beam. 1945 *Aeronautics* Feb. 30 (*heading*) Diagram showing the aircraft..entering the landing beam. 1932 G. GREENE *Stamboul Train* I. i. 3 The purser took the last landing card..and watched the passengers cross the grey wet quay. 1950 P. BOTTOME *Under Skin* ii. 18 Got your landing card ready, and your passport? 1966 'W. HAGGARD' *Power House* vi. 58 He could be asked for a landing card and as a through-booking he didn't have one. 1973 *Times* 13 Dec. 11/2 He included landing cards among the paraphernalia of controls. 1940 W. S. CHURCHILL *Second World War* (1949) II. 593 Great efforts should be made to produce the landing-craft as soon as possible. 1942 *R.A.F. Jrnl.* 18 Apr. 32 Two landing craft were sent ashore with reconnaissance parties. 1943 Landing craft [see *ASSAULT *sb.* 8]. 1953 *Jrnl. Brit. Interplanetary Soc.* XII. 275 The landing craft (a small supplementary vehicle designed for vertical descent with rocket braking, carried to the destination by the parent spaceship). 1957 P. WORSLEY *Trumpet shall Sound* vii. 144 Landing-craft of all kinds poured out their cargo upon the beaches. 1966 D. HOLBROOK *Flesh Wounds* 93 Three thousand landing craft were ready to move out of all the ports all along the coast, from Falmouth to Harwich. 1969 *Times* 21 July 8/2 At 1,500 ft., the astronauts slowed the landing craft and brought it gently down four miles off the scheduled target in the Sea of Tranquillity. 1922 *Flight* XIV. 660/1 No extra landing fee will be charged in respect of test flights before departure. 1972 *Times* 11 Feb. 1/1 Strong opposition has come from the airlines to a new system of landing fees which is to be introduced at Heathrow. 1921 *Aeronautics* 13 Jan. 26/1 The improvement of landing fields and equipment. 1959 *Chambers's Encycl.* I. 97 The emergency landing fields, which were set aside by the Royal Air Force for special purposes, were usually grass covered. 1936 *Technical Rep. Aeronaut. Res. Comm. 1934–35* I. 30 Now that so many aeroplanes are being fitted with landing flaps it is important to permit the flap to extend along the whole span. 1940 *War Illustr.* 19 Jan. 620 With wheels and landing flaps lowered, the pilot makes his approach. 1966 *McGraw-Hill Encycl. Sci. & Technol.* XIV. 517/1 Structurally, the aileron is similar to the landing flap. 1911 *Rep. & Mem. Advisory Comm. Aeronaut.* No. 59. Nov. 103 The efficiency of landing gear on various sorts of ground may be tried. 1931 *Flight* 9 Jan. 30/1 The landing gear is designed to give very smooth landing and taxiing characteristics. 1931 J. E. YOUNGER *Airplane Construction & Repair* iii. 48 Some airplanes are designed with landing gears which fold up into the fuselage and hence offer no dirt wind resistance. 1951 *Amer. Speech* XXVI. 308/2 *Landing gear,* a strong support that holds up the front end of a semi-trailer when it is not attached to a tractor. 1971 M. TAK *Truck Talk* 97 *Landing gear,* the retractable supports on a trailer that prop up the front end when the trailer is unhitched from the tractor. 1971 *Physics Bull.* Apr. 217/1 Steels with improved fracture properties needed in nuclear submarines and aircraft landing gear are also under development. 1912 *Aeroplane* 12 Dec. 584/1 The great deterrent at present is the lack of proper landing grounds. 1920 Landing ground [see *flying school* (*FLYING *vbl.* sb.* 3)]. 1943 T. S. ELIOT in

Ld. Sempill et al. *Friendship, Progress, Civilisation* 20 To descend from this flight into generalities on to the particular landing-ground of the present occasion. 1961 L. VAN DER POST *Heart of Hunter* I. v. 80 The great pan..had a floor so wide, level and firm that..the biggest aircraft could land on it. I myself had used it as a landing-ground many times. 1951 *Jrnl. Brit. Interplanetary Soc.* X. 101 In the case of a Moonflight..this means a vertical descent using reverse rocket braking in conjunction with a radar-altimeter and landing-legs. 1969 *Sun* 22 July 1/2 The Eagle, leaving its spidery landing-legs behind, soared away. 1917 *Flight* 4 Jan. 18/1 A new system, called 'Triplex glass landing lights', proved to be inferior to petrol flares. 1920 *Proc. Air Conf., London* 11 Aerodromes will be equipped..as night flying is practicable. Permanent electric landing lights..are being installed. 1922 *Flight* XIV. 519/2 Lighting Set (including navigation lights, landing lights and illumination of instruments). 1937 *Times* 16 Apr. 9/3 They see no reason why they should confuse coloured Véry lights or landing lights in the air. 1942 *R.A.F. Jrnl.* 3 Oct. 7 From beneath him a landing light groped downwards. 1969 I. KEMP *Brit. G.I. in Vietnam* iii. 69 He..switched on his landing light, illuminating three paratroopers standing on the landing zone signalling us in. 1973 *Times* 11 Apr. 3/7 They used landing lights to make three trips and everyone on board was winched to safety. 1958 *World Helicopter* Apr. 6/1 Our cover picture shows one of Sabena's fleet of 12-passenger Sikorsky S.58's making a landing at the heliport on the strip between the two 80 ft. diameter landing pads. 1961 *New Scientist* 2 Mar. 528/3 The actual landing pad need still be no more than 150 ft square. 1967 *Gloss. Terms Air-Cushion Vehicles (B.S.I.)* 6 *Landing pads,* strong points, protruding below the rigid bottom of an ACV, which support the vehicle when at rest on land. 1969 *Islander* (Victoria, B.C.) 23 Mar. 10/1 The first landing pad for the young [helicopter] company was a patch of open land way down Shelbourne Street, at that time the outskirts of Victoria. 1969 *Times* 17 May 8/5 Its landing pads are 37 in. across, each of them fitted with a probe which can sense the surface. 1943 *Life* 11 Oct. 34/2 The first is the LST (Landing Ship, Tank), 327 ft. long and displacing 5,500 tons. 1944 *Hutchinson's Pict. Hist. War* 27 Oct. 1943–11 Apr. 1944. 166 (*caption*) Landing Ship Tanks. These two landing ships tanks close inshore at Bougainville are unloading supplies and equipment for the U.S. Marines and army troops. 1944 *Daily Tel.* 11 July, It [*sc.* the port of Cherbourg] will be open shortly for craft of the L.S.T. type (landing ship tanks). 1945 T. BLORE *Turning Point—1943* vi. 51 Cedric and I put off in a motor fishing vessel to find our Tank Landing Ship. 1951 W. S. CHURCHILL *Second World War* (1952) V. ii. 26 The 'landing-ship, tank'..had first been conceived and developed in Britain in 1940. 1961 B. FERGUSSON *Watery Maze* iv. 106 Rear-Admiral Burrough, with the cruiser *Kenya* and four destroyers, was to escort the two landing ships. 1966 D. HOLBROOK *Flesh Wounds* 93 Paul's Squadron embarked on its Landing Ship Tank late on the 3rd June. 1969 *Times* 4 Feb. 13/4 The eastern end of the planned Apollo landing site. 1972 *Nature* 3 Mar. 3/1 The landing site of Luna 20 was some 120 km north of the region from which Luna 16 recovered specimens. 1911 R. M. PIERCE *Dict. Aviation* 144 *Landing-speed..,* the speed with which a landing or descent to the earth is made, as by a man falling from a height. 1937 *New Republic* 19 May 35/1 The modern air liner's landing speed has gone up as designers have boosted its top speed by refining line and form. 1951 P. W. BROOKS *Mod. Airliner* iii. 75 Wheel brakes..now became a necessity because of the increased take-off and landing speeds of the more heavily loaded monoplanes. 1930 *Aircraft Engineering* Jan. 16/1 The standard intermediate field in low altitudes provides two landing strips or runways. 1944 *Times* 1 July 4/3 Squadrons flying from landing strips in Normandy are taking advantage of every break in the clouds. 1956 W. GRAHAM *Sleeping Partner* 62 Llanveryan had been an aerodrome—a glorified landing strip—in the first place. 1973 G. GREENE *Honorary Consul* IV. iii. 218 Señor Escobar has a landing strip on his *estancia.* 1925 E. GELLIBRAND *Travelling Do's & Don'ts* v. 19 While the cool, collected person gets things done without unnecessary waste of energy, the flustered one..not having his landing ticket ready..is hustled by the impatient ones. 1930 A. BENNETT *Imperial Palace* li. 382 The hand of the official at the bottom of the gangway was full of landing tickets. 1912 KIPLING *Divers. Creatures* (1917) 23 They began turning out traffic-lights and locking up landing-towers. 1967 *Jane's Surface Skimmer Systems 1967–68* 97/2 Landing Vehicle Hydrofoil. 1969 *Observer* 20 July 7/1 The astronauts crawl into the landing vehicle..and spend three hours checking it. 1917 'CONTACT' *Airman's Outings* 46 Something sang to the right, and I found that part of a landing-wire was dangling helplessly from its socket. 1942 C. C. REDMAN in R. A. Beaumont *Aeronaut. Engin.* xvii. 482/1 Landing wires support the wings on the ground, but when the aircraft becomes airborne, the stresses are transferred to the flying wires, as the wings tend to lift upwards. 1952 A. Y. BRAMBLE *Air-Plane Flight* vii. 100 Those above [the wings of the glider] are obviously supporting the weight of the wings when the machine is on the ground. They are called 'landing wires'. Those below the wing..are called the 'flying wires'.

landing-place. Add: **1. c.** A place where a bird, insect, aircraft, etc., can or does land.

1776 T. PENNANT *Tour in Scotl. & Voy. Hebrides 1772* II. 24 Woodcocks... Their first landing-places are in the eastern counties. 1889 *Leisure Hour* 642/2 Insect 'landing-places' would thus, according to the theory, acquire considerable importance in affecting the structure of the flower. 1899 *Strand Mag.* Aug. 183/1 Captain Spelterini's sharp eye had quickly chosen an advantageous landing-place, and the anchor was thrown [from the balloon]. 1909 *Flying: the Why & Wherefore* v. 33 Another advantage of flying high is that in case of an engine stoppage the aeronaut will have time to look round and choose a landing place. 1935 C. DAY LEWIS *Time to Dance* 35 The oil ran out and cursing they turned about Losing a hundred miles to find a landing-place. 1962 K. W. GATLAND *Astronautics in Sixties* xi. 338 After reconnaissance spacecraft and soft-landing probes had given information concerning

a suitable landing place, a Surveyor-type probe would be put down close to the desired landing point.

‖ **ländler** (le·ndlər). Also *erron.* **landler.** [G.] An Austrian peasant dance, similar to a slow waltz; the music for such a dance.

1876 STAINER & BARRETT *Dict. Mus. Terms* 251 *Ländler,* the name given to a dance popular among the Styrian peasants. 1934 C. LAMBERT *Music Ho!* I. 58 The romantic orchestration, the solid hymn-tune harmonies, the *Landler* rhythms, [etc.]. 1961 *Times* 21 Oct. 11/3 The humorous ländler that forms the second movement. 1964 *Listener* 6 Feb. 250/2 If the trio-section is taken at the same speed, it may sound unnaturally hurried, since its *Ländler*-like characteristics justify a more leisurely pace.

land-line. Add: Also **landline** and as two words. **2.** (Earlier and later examples.) Also, an overland (or underground) line for tele-communication by other means.

1865 *Phil. Mag.* XXIX. 409 (*heading*) On the retardation of electrical signals on land lines. 1869 *Bradshaw's Railway Manual* XXI. 454 Telegraph to India... A provisional agreement entered into for leasing the land line in Egypt to the proposed British-Indian Submarine. 1927 *Observer* 12 June 20 Last Sunday I had the curiosity to listen to the Eastbourne programme... There were obvious defects in the landline, which made the general effect thin and poor. 1930 *Bell Syst. Techn. Jrnl.* IX. 408 The linking of ships at sea with the land line telephone network. 1962 *B.B.C. Handbook* 109 A separate receiving station where broadcasts are intercepted and fed to the monitors by land line. 1970 'J. EARL' *Tuners & Amplifiers* iv. 77 It sometimes 'filters' the signal so as to rid it of certain shortcomings that could have been picked up during its transmission through the ether (radio waves) and studio landlines.

Hence **la·ndline** *v. trans.,* to transmit over a land-line.

1966 *Times Lit. Suppl.* 24 Mar. 248 This Crusade is going to be landlined to most major cities in the United Kingdom. 1969 J. BENNETT *Dragon* iii. 43 That at least means no radio pictures to Peking... They'll probably take us ashore tomorrow and landline our pictures to Canton. 1974 J. DRUMMOND *Boon Companions* xxxi. 98 That first story's been land-lined and it's going to hit nine o'clock television all over the country.

landlord, *sb.* Add: **4.** *attrib.* and *Comb.*

1845 *Douglas Jerrold's Shilling Mag.* I. 515 Judge-made law may be bad, but landlord-made law is worse. 1880 'MARK TWAIN' *Tramp Abroad* 586 The landlord-apprentice serves as call-boy, then as under-waiter. 1908 *Daily Chron.* 26 June 5/7 With an air of detachment, as though he were not addressing a landlord-ridden assembly. 1924 R. GRAVES *Mock Beggar Hall* 72 Waiting the landlord-absentee's return. 1959 *Good Food Guide* 383 Both landlord-chef and waiter are Spanish. 1963 *Times Lit. Suppl.* 17 May 350/5 The parasitic landlord-usurers had to be destroyed as a class.

land-lubbing, *a.* [Irreg. f. LAND-LUBBER.] Land-lubberly.

1885 *Punch* 29 Aug. 100/2 The Judge, a land-lubbing chap in a wig. 1927 *Daily Express* 4 Oct. 3/3 We land-lubbing civilians know less about the Navy than our maiden aunts might be expected to know about alimony. 1960 *House & Garden* Aug. 31/2 Judged by sea-going or land-lubbing standards. 1966 *Economist* 21 May 799/2 Many..seamen are obeying their union's strike call with more enthusiasm than some landlubbing trade unionists would. 1974 *Sci. Amer.* June 132/2 The line-of-sight land-lubbing microwave relay networks are too expensive. What can the engineers do in orbit?

landmark, *v.* [f. the *sb.*] *trans.* To be or act as a landmark to; to provide with a landmark.

1921 J. F. PORTE *Sir E. Elgar* 8 It is not necessary here to landmark further successes. 1928 *Sunday Dispatch* 9 Dec. 2/2 Her mother, perhaps the only disinterested figure of all the many who landmarked those ten years, had died.

landolphia (lændọ·lfiä). [mod.L. (A. M. F. J. Palisot de Beauvois *Flore d'Oware* (1804) I. 55), f. the name of M. *Landolphe* (1765–1825), commander of the expedition on which the genus was first discovered + -IA[1].] A tropical African climbing plant of the genus so called, belonging to the family Apocynaceæ and yielding a latex formerly used as a source of rubber.

1887 *Curtis's Bot. Mag.* CXIII. 6963 The first notice of the *Landolphia* yielding India-rubber..is by Col. now Sir J. A. Grant, in the appendix to Speke's Journal. 1910 *Westm. Gaz.* 20 Apr. 4/1 Landolphias, woody climbers,.. yield the African rubbers. 1951 *Dict. Gardening* (R. Hort. Soc.) III. 1125/1 Landolphias are an important source of caoutchouc.

landrace (læ·ndrēis). [Da.] A large white pig of the variety so called, originally developed in Denmark, now used elsewhere to produce bacon. Also *attrib.*

1935 LAYLEY & MALDEN *Evolution Brit. Pig* 98 (*heading*) Landrace. The modern model. *Ibid.,* The Danish Landrace..is the model set up to which it is the ambition of our state to mould all British pigs. 1937 G. R. H. BISHOP *Improvement of Bacon Pigs* ii. 27 The contented Landrace sows were hardy and prolific. 1948 H. R. DAVIDSON *Production & Marketing Pigs* ix. 126 There [*sc.* in Denmark], in 1895, were set up the first breeding

centres to maintain and improve the breed type of the native Landrace. **1958** 'R. Crompton' *William's Television Show* viii. 253 'A Landrace pedigree, that pig is,' said the farmer. **1971** *Country Life* 2 Dec. 1588/1 Our breeders [of pigs]..readily accept Large White, Landrace, or crosses of these breeds.

Landsborough (læ·ndzbərə). *Austral.* The name of a small town in Queensland, used *attrib.* in **Landsborough grass**, a pasture grass, *Iseilema membranaceum*, found in the area, and better known as small Flinders grass.

1883 F. M. Bailey *Synopsis Queensland Flora* 646 The Landsborough grass. A weak, very leafy, brittle grass of a reddish color, one of the most valuable for fodder. **1889** [see *Barcoo]. **1891** R. Wallace *Rural Econ. Austral. & N.Z.* xxii. 294 *Anthistiria membranacea*, Lindl.—Barcoo grass of Queensland; also called Landsborough grass. West and South Australia, New South Wales and Queensland. **1927** M. M. Bennett *Christison* v. 55 Landsborough grass..shimmered gold and silver. **1929** J. W. Bews *World's Grasses* vi. 253 'Barcoo', 'Landsborough' or 'Red Gulf grass', covers large tracts of the north and interior of Australia.

landscape, *sb.* Add: **1. c.** = Oblong *a.* 1 c. Also as *adv.*

1932 Sayers & Smart in W. Atkins *Art & Pract. Printing* I. xii. 139 The frontispiece..may be printed either upright (termed portrait) or broad way (termed landscape). If a full-page illustration be printed landscape, the inscription or caption beneath must read from foot to head. **1951** D. Bland *Illustration of Books* ix. 146 The landscape plate is always a problem. It is unfortunate that the tall narrow format which is so suitable for a page of type does not lend itself to the average photograph. **1956** H. Williamson *Methods Bk. Design* iii. 16 The same formats can..be used for landscape or oblong books. **1966** G. Hamilton-Edwards *In Search Ancestry* ii. 24 This can be done by buying the full quarto size exercise book..and asking a printer to cut it in half, wide-ways, or 'landscape'. ..This gives you two booklets of 8″ × 5″.

2. b. A tract of land with its distinguishing characteristics and features, esp. considered as a product of modifying or shaping processes and agents (usually natural).

1886 A. Geikie *Class-Bk. Geol.* i. 2 The surface of a country is not now exactly as it used to be. We notice various changes of its topography going on now,..the accumulated effect of which may ultimately transform altogether the character of landscapes. **1896** *Rep. 6th Internat. Geogr. Congr. 1895* 749 We thus have six ranks of units: (1) The form-element. (2) The fundamental form [*sc.* land form]. (3) The group of forms or landscape. [Etc.]. **1922** L. Mumford in H. E. Stearns *Civilisation in U.S.* 4 West of the Alleghanies, the common, with its church and school, was not destined to dominate the urban landscape. **1925** *Univ. Calif. Geogr.* II. 37 The works of man express themselves in the cultural landscape. There may be a succession of these landscapes with a succession of cultures. They are derived in each case from the natural landscape, man expressing his place in nature as a distinct agent of modification. **1937** Wooldridge & Morgan *Physical Basis Geogr.* p. ix, Geography cannot dispense with geomorphology, for a real understanding of the characters and development of the physical landscape is an indispensable preliminary to the study of the cultural landscape and of regions. **1944** A. Holmes *Princ. Physical Geol.* xi. 191 In the Grampian Highlands an old peneplain, now dissected into a landscape of late youth or early maturity (though modified by glaciation), is easily recognised by the even skyline. **1954** W. D. Thornbury *Princ. Geomorphol.* xiv. 364 Two contrasting ideas have developed regarding the ability of glaciers to modify by erosion the landscapes over which they move. **1971** I. G. Gass et al. *Understanding Earth* vii. 100/1 (*caption*) Two photographs of the lunar crater Tycho.., whose ramparts rise 5 400 m above the level of its floor, though only 1 600 m above the level of the surrounding landscape. **1974** H. F. Garner (*title*) The origin of landscapes: a synthesis of geomorphology.

4. h. Later *transf.* and *fig.* uses.

1952 G. Sarton *Hist. Sci.* I. x. 256 Let us return again to Athens and try to consider the intellectual landscape from the point of view of a well-educated man. **1953** A. Huxley *Let.* 31 Oct. (1969) 687 The jewelled palaces.. may..be actual *choses vues*—items in the ordinary landscape of certain kinds of people. **1963** *Listener* 7 Mar. 405/1 The landscape of international politics is now very different from what it was only two or three years ago.

5. *landscape-garden* vb.; *landscape-gardener* (earlier examples); **landscape architect**, a practitioner of landscape architecture; **landscape architecture**, the planning of parks or gardens to form an attractive landscape, often in association with the design of buildings, roads, etc.; **landscape-gardening** (earlier and later examples); **landscape-painter** (earlier and later examples).

1863 *6th Ann. Rep. Board of Commissioners Central Park* (N.Y.) *1862* between pp. 60–61 (Map), Olmsted and Vaux, Landscape Architects. **1879** *Chicago Tribune* 3 May 1/3 (Advt.), H. W. S. Cleveland, Landscape Architect. **1890** C. Eliot *Let.* 3 Dec. in *C. Eliot: Landscape Architect* (1924) xv. 273 Landscape gardening is that part of the landscape architect's labor which is directed to the development of formal or natural beauty by means of removing or setting out plants. **1927** T. H. Mawson *Life & Work Eng. Landscape Architect* xiv. 160 A young and able landscape architect..had heard me lecture in England. **1967** G. Collens in A. E. Weddle *Techniques Landscape Archit.* ii. 33/1 The employer should start by setting out his requirements as a basis for discussion with the landscape architect. **1972** *Times* 15 Sept. 2/1 For decades.. landscape architects' services were not sufficiently appreciated. **1840** J. C. Loudon in H. Repton *Landscape Gardening & Landscape Archit. of H. Repton* (new ed.) p. vii, These writings [*sc.* of Gilpin and Price] are full of the most valuable instruction for the gardener, relative to the general composition of landscape scenery, and landscape architecture. **1865** F. L. Olmsted *Let.* 1 Aug. in *F. L. Olmsted: Landscape Architect* (1928) II. vi. 74, I am all the time bothered with the miserable nomenclature of L.A. *Landscape* is not a good word, *Architecture* is not; the combination is not—*Gardening* is worse. **1891** C. Eliot in *C. Eliot: Landscape Architect* (1924) xx. 366 We cannot avoid seeing behind the fair figures of Gardening and Building a third figure of still nobler aspect..the art which, for want of a better name, is sometimes called Landscape Architecture. **1915** S. Parsons *Art of Landscape Archit.* p. vi, The study of nature assisted by the best examples is the proper field for the study of landscape architecture. **1967** A. E. Weddle (*title*) Techniques in landscape architecture. **1836** F. A. Kemble *Let.* 1 Mar. in *Rec. Later Life* (1882) I. 45 Adam and Eve landscape-gardened in Paradise, you know. **1891** W. Morris *News from Nowhere* iii. 17 The other day we heard that the philistines were going to landscape-garden it [*sc.* the place]. **1941** E. Wilson *Wound & Bow* ii. 119 When the transfer [of the land] had been effected, Mrs. Kipling set out to landscape-garden it. **1974** 'M. Innes' *Appleby's Other Story* i. 5 You don't care, Tommy, for wild nature tamed and landscape-gardened? *a* **1763** W. Shenstone *Works* (1764) II. 139, I have used the word landskip-gardiners; because in pursuance of our present taste in gardening, every good painter of landskip appears to me the most proper designer. **1788** A. Seward *Let.* 14 Oct. (1811) II. 172, I should suppose nobody has ever been so well qualified as yourself [*sc.* H. Repton] for the profession you purpose to assume, that of landscape gardener. *a* **1763** W. Shenstone *Works* (1764) II. 125 Gardening may be divided into three species—kitchen-gardening—parterre gardening—and landskip, or picturesque-gardening: which latter..consists in pleasing the imagination by scenes of grandeur, beauty, or variety. **1788** H. Repton in D. Stroud *Humphry Repton* (1962) ii. 37, I mean in this place to keep an account of the time employed and expenses incurr'd in this service at the same rate as if employ'd in my profession of Landscape Gardening. **1938** *New Statesman* 8 Jan. 56/2 In Andrew Young there are touches of a lesser, a more landscape-gardening Frost. **1946** R. Macaulay *They went to Portugal* 137 Landscape gardening always showed him [*sc.* William Beckford] at his most likeable. **1975** *Garden History* III. ii. 1 Mavis Batey's essay on Goldsmith, 'An Indictment of Landscape Gardening', is the clearest and best exposition we have had of that frequent eighteenth-century occurrence, the destruction of villages and hamlets to further the creation of landscape gardens. *a* **1763** W. Shenstone *Works* (1764) II. 129 The landskip painter is the gardiner's best designer. **1779** T. Blaikie *Diary Scotch Gardener* (1931) 159 Those Gardens are Layd out under the Derections of Mr Robert one of the first Landskape painters in France. **1937** *Discovery* July 211 The greatest of English landscape painters. **1974** B. Massingham *Turn on Fountains* iv. 65 They met a landscape painter..who confessed that he 'could do nothing with Connemara'.

landscape, *v.* (See at end of sb. in Dict.) Add: **2.** To lay out (a garden, etc.) as a landscape; to conceal or embellish (a building, road, etc.) by making it part of a continuous and harmonious landscape. Also *transf.* So **la·ndscaping** *vbl. sb.*

1927 [implied by *landscaped *ppl. a.*]. **1930** *N.Y. Times* 9 Feb. xi. 2/1 Suburban developers and home owners are paying more attention to landscaping today. **1930** *Publishers' Weekly* 15 Feb. 858/2 Landscaping is about to become the topic of smart conversation, with the result that garden books should sell as never before. **1943** Forshaw & Abercrombie *County of London Plan* vii. 103 Landscaping must play an important part in the layout of these open spaces particularly those which provide a setting for the houses and blocks of flats. **1957** *Listener* 13 June 949 The planners intend to plant trees round the perimeter and generally landscape the whole area. **1959** *Motor* 22 Apr. 410/1 New roads..are 'landscaped into the countryside and not stuck on it'. **1962** *Daily Tel.* 23 May 21/1 Some aspects of road landscaping were still not fully accepted in Britain. **1966** Mrs. L. B. Johnson *White House Diary* 11 Jan. (1970) 350 The check would be given to landscape the new automobile entrance of the National Zoo. **1974** *Country Life* 17 Oct. 1095/1 The National Trust has landscaped the island.

landscaped (læ·ndskēɪpt), *ppl. a.* [f. prec.] Laid out as a landscape; embellished by landscaping. Also *transf.*, of an office.

1927 *Brit. Weekly* 15 Dec. 283/2 Even factories..frequently have lovely landscaped grounds. **1957** V. Nabokov *Pnin* 9 An artificial lake in the middle of a landscaped campus. **1959** A. Harrington *Life in 'Crystal Palace'* (1960) viii. 112 Our landscaped grounds..will flower. **1968** *Guardian* 17 June 8/3 The open 'landscaped' office, or *burolandschaft* as it is called by its German inventors. **1968** *Daily Tel.* (Colour Suppl.) 29 Nov. 56/2 The American reaction now is for open-plan 'landscaped' offices where all workers, regardless of status, are visually connected in one low horizontal block. **1970** *Times* 9 Feb. 13/2 It will be an eight-storey block with about 60,000 sq. ft. in a landscaped site. **1974** *Daily Tel.* (Colour Suppl.) 8 Mar. 18/2 The initial impression one gets of a landscaped office is often one of irregularity and informality.

landscapist. Add: **2.** A landscape-gardener; one skilled in landscaping roads, offices, etc. Also **la·ndscaper.**

1936 T. Sharp *Eng. Panorama* iii. 48 The activities of the landscapists became founded on a realization and acceptance of natural informality. **1963** *Times* 4 June 12/5 Whereas seventeenth-century landscapers might have moved a tree across an estate, we now move them 30–50 miles. **1963** *New Society* 20 June 26/1 The British method of inviting a landscape committee (few of them landscapists) to study the landscaping of the road. **1965** I. Fleming *Man with Golden Gun* vii. 101 He soon came to the end of the young shrubs and guinea grass the landscaper had laid on. **1967** *House & Garden* Mar. 68/1 Several famous landscapists, including Bridgeman. **1974** *Daily Tel.* (Colour Suppl.) 8 Mar. 18/1 Open plan, say many landscapers, was..only too often a mere space-saving exercise.

Landseer (læ·ndsɪəɹ). The name of the English painter Sir Edwin *Landseer* (1802–73) used *attrib.* in **Landseer Newfoundland** to designate a black and white Newfoundland dog of a type once painted by him. Also *absol.*

1877 G. Stables *Pract. Kennel Guide* ix. 98 The black-and-white, or Landseer Newfoundland. This is quite a distinct breed, not as yet properly recognised at shows. *Ibid.* x. 113 A white chest in a Newfoundland or Retriever, indicates a cross with the Landseer or Setter. **1927** W. A. Wetwan in C. C. Sanderson *Pedigree Dogs* 281 In 1836 Sir Edwin Landseer painted a white and black Newfoundland ..imbuing the mind of the great British public with the idea that black and white was the only correct Newfoundland wear... 'Landseers', which are true to type, are a very beautiful dog. **1971** F. Hamilton *World Encycl. Dogs* 164 In 1779 a well-known English naturalist described a very fine specimen in Northumberland, England, and this dog was later identified as a Landseer. *Ibid.* 165 (*caption*) Taaran Taru..is a typical example of the Landseer Newfoundland.

land-ship. [Land *sb.* 11.] **a.** A wagon or other vehicle serving the same purpose on land as a ship on the sea; *spec.* = *tank *sb.*[7] **b.** A ship erected and kept on land for training purposes.

[**1627** J. Taylor *Armado* sig. B1v, (*heading*) A Navy of Land Ships.] **1837** *Penny Mag.* 22 July 276/1 The ox-carts of the Pampas..are quaintly termed by the natives, *barcos de tierra*, i.e., 'land-ships'. **1869** *Cassell's Mag.* Jan. 156/2 In some of the best schools of France and Belgium, it has long been a custom to erect a dry land-ship in the playground. **1907** L. Osbourne *Adventurer* xiii. 159 The land-ship..was hardly more than an aluminium shell.. requiring weeks of labor, possibly months, to make her habitable and ready. Ready? For what? To sail those vast and billowy plains? **1916** *Daily News* 19 Sept. 1/2 The new land-ships or tanks did invaluable work. **1916** *Daily Mirror* 22 Nov. 1/1 (*caption*) To-day we are able to publish the first photograph of one of his Majesty's land ships which have been making such successful cruises on the sea of mud on the Somme. **1934** W. S. Churchill *Gt War* II. xxxv. 519/1 The next day, the 20th [February 1915], I sent for Mr. Tennyson-d'Eyncourt..and convened a conference... As the result of it the Landships Committee of the Admiralty was formed. **1972** *Times Lit. Suppl.* 4 Feb. 113/4 The original initiative in tank development, the so-called 'landships', was naval rather than military.

‖**Landsmål** (la·ntsmǭl). Also **Landsmaal.** [Norw., f. *land* country + *mål* language.] A literary form of Norwegian devised by the Norwegian philologist Ivar Aasen (1813–1896) from the country dialects most closely descended from Old Norse, and considered to be a 'purer' form of the Norwegian language than the official Riksmål or Dano-Norwegian.

The *Landsmål* controversy followed the appearance of Aasen's grammar and dictionary (1848 and 1850); in 1885 *Landsmål* was given equal status with Dano-Norwegian.

1886 *Encycl. Brit.* XXI. 374/1 By the study of the Modern Norwegian dialects and the mother language, Old Norwegian, the eminent philologist J. Aasen was led to undertake the bold project of constructing..a Norwegian–Norwegian..language, the so-called 'Landsmål'. **1906** *Westm. Gaz.* 10 Aug. 2/3 The party programmes are said to lack definiteness, but that of the Liberals comprises.. the official recognition of the 'Landsmal', or Norwegian of Norway as against the Dano-Norwegian, which is at present the language of the Government. **1911** [see *Dano-]. **1924** *Glasgow Herald* 14 Nov. 7 Let him perpend the circumstances of the Czech revival or of the Norwegian landsmaal movement. **1927** *Observer* 6 Nov. 12 Now Norway has a linguistic national movement, called the Landsmaal or Real Norwegian Language-movement, which holds that the language generally used in Norway is not Norwegian but a Danish dialect, and their aim is to root out that dialect and make the Landsmaal compulsory. **1933** [see *Dano-]. **1957** T. K. Derry *Short Hist. Norway* ix. 190 For the peasantry, in the west at least, *landsmaal* had become a shibboleth by which to distinguish the true democrat from the adherents of the language of foreign snobbery. **1961** L. F. Brosnahan *Sounds of Lang.* ix. 205 The Landsmål, a somewhat more artificial creation based on the main dialects of the west of the country.

landsman. 1. b. Delete *rare* and add later examples.

1950 B. Malamud in *Partisan Rev.* Sept.–Oct. 664 With, after all, a *landsman*, he would have less to fear than with a complete stranger. **1971** *Islander* (Victoria, B.C.) 3 Jan. 10/3, I found out the mate was a landsman of mine who came from Helsingfors. **1973** *Listener* 20 Sept. 377/1 You put on your Shabbat suit..and descended on a near-by relative or *landsman.*

landswoman. [After Landsman.] A woman accustomed to live mainly or entirely on the land; one skilled in land-work.

1837 *Penny Mag.* 14 Oct. 398/1 The scene is presented exactly as it appeared to the eye and imagination of a landswoman. **1891** [see after Landsman]. **1923** *Weekly*

Dispatch 1 Apr. 7 Miss Ford might be described as 'the complete landswoman'. She can milk, do anything with horses, and do field tasks.

lane, *sb.* Add: **2.** (Further examples.) Also, a route prescribed for aircraft.

1911 [see *air lane* s.v. *AIR *sb.*[1] III. 8]. **1929** *Encycl. Brit.* I. 231/1 Neon lighting is particularly suitable for landing in fog owing to its distinctive colour, and to the fact that long 'lanes' of illumination can be provided. **1941** A. O. POLLARD *Bombers over Reich* 105 The clouds parted a little, and the approaching raiders found enemy fighters collected in the open 'lanes' like soldiers guarding breaches in a fortification. **1956** J. C. SWAYNE *Conc. Gloss. Geogr. Terms* 86 *Lane*, a much used ocean or air route. **1971** E. C. B. & K. LEE *Safety & Survival at Sea* i. 8 Safety sea-lanes, consisting of a series of two-way lanes with a safety buffer zone separating the inward and outward bound traffic, are used in the approaches to New York harbour and other seaports. **1971** *Sci. Amer.* July 1/1 [An automatic weather information station] was moored in the middle of the Gulf Stream, off the Florida Coast, in a hurricane lane. **1974** L. DEIGHTON *Spy Story* xv. 146 The pilot..climbed again, now that he was no longer forced down under the lanes.

c. In *Athletics*, a course for a runner marked out by broad chalk-lines (orig. strings). Hence also in *Swimming*, such a course marked out by ropes buoyed up by cork floats.

1909 in *Cent. Dict.* Suppl. **1911** *Encycl. Brit.* XXIII. 853/2 The course for sprinting races..is marked off in lanes for the individual runners by means of cords stretched upon short iron rods. **1927** *Daily Express* 23 Mar. 13/5 Sprint-racing in 'lanes' instead of in strings will be in force at the next Olympic Games... The 'lanes' are marked by chalk lines, and have been used in America for some time. **1955** R. BANNISTER *First Four Minutes* 21, I moved out into the second lane so that I could..avoid the danger of being boxed in. **1960** J. GRINHAM *Water Babe* xiv. 158 Suddenly the roar in the pool turned to a gasp—Di swam on to the lane ropes. **1970** MCGREGOR & STILL *Bobby McGregor Story* ix. 77, I stepped on to the poolside of the magnificent Olympic swimming stadium. I took up my position behind lane 2, officially the position for the fifth fastest qualifier. **1971** D. EMERY *Lillian* vii. 75 The bends were tighter on the inside lane and therefore harder to round at full speed.

d. A part of a road, wide enough for one file of vehicles, which is marked out by painted lines and is used to segregate traffic according to speed, intended direction, etc. Also *attrib.* and *Comb.*

1926 *Amer. City* Apr. 358/1 One of the most recent developments in highway design is the so-called super-highway where eight or more traffic lanes are provided for on the same right of way. **1933** *Evening Standard* 19 Apr. 7/2 Roads..would carry any volume of traffic, divided into slow, medium and fast 'lanes'. **1951** *Economist* 22 Sept. 685/3 Super-highways; with at least four lanes. **1959** *Times* 31 Mar. 15/6 The motorist who elects to park his car on a main road reduces the width of the road for a complete traffic lane for what may be hundreds of yards. **1960** *Guardian* 21 Nov. 2/4 Where there is good lane discipline, traffic should be able to pass on the near side. **1962** *Economist* 27 Jan. 327/1 Mr Barnes is a great believer in lane-painting to increase the capacity of streets. **1966** [see *fast lane* s.v. *FAST *a.* 11]. **1968** *Autocar* 7 Mar. 61/3 The first week's working of the London experiments with bus lanes in Park Lane and on Vauxhall Bridge. **1970** *Guardian* 4 Aug. 15/2 Lane-changing, the constant pressure to keep up speeds. **1971** *Daily Tel.* (Colour Suppl.) 22 Oct. 25/4 In town traffic, lane discipline is more a matter of cunning than of boldness. **1972** *Police Rev.* 8 Dec. 1597/2 Failure to judge distance at speed and bad lane drill accounted for most of the accidents. **1973** D. WESTHEIMER *Going Public* ix. 127 Drivers on the inbound lane slowed to a crawl.

e. In ten-pin bowling, etc.: = ALLEY 4.

1960 D. TAYLOR *Secret of Bowling Strikes* 125 Most old-fashioned lanes have a center peg in the center of the alley. **1964** F. BRUNDLE *Tenpin Bowling Tips* 79 In some localities a lane which allows the ball to take a wide hook is termed fast... Some authorities..speak of lanes as either 'holding' or 'running'. **1970** C. SCHUNK *Bowling* i. 4 When alleys were first built in the Southern United States, three-fourths of the lanes were constructed for duck pins. **1974** *Plain Dealer* (Cleveland, Ohio) 26 Oct. 5–D/5 Likewise, the lanes can also be too slick or too dry.

4. b. (Earlier and later examples.) Also *Chancery Lane, Mincing Lane.*

1831 P. EGAN *Show Folks* 29 The *swell* performers.. who proudly observe, 'I am engaged at the Lane.'.. But the 'Lane', alluded to in this instance, is Horsemonger Lane; where a number of engagements are suffered to *expire*. **1865** *Chambers's Jrnl.* 18 Feb. 106/1 The 'Lane' (as Chancery Lane is familiarly called). **1872** B. JERROLD *London* viii. 77 When on a certain Sunday we turned into Petticoat Lane, we had the key to the activity of the clothes market of Lazarus. The Lane clothes thousands at Epsom. **1909** *Westm. Gaz.* 6 Aug. 11/4 'The Lane', as that of Mincing is fondly known among the wholesale grocery crowd. **1926** F. M. FORD *Man could Stand Up* II. iii. 138 He had lately promised [them] tickets for Drury Lane... The Lane was the *locus classicus* of the race. **1959** B. KOPS *Hamlet of Stepney Green* I. 24, I also stand down the Lane [*sc.* Petticoat Lane] on Sundays now and again. I'm what you might call a purveyor of bad taste. **1974** M. BIRMINGHAM *You can help Me* i. 11 Wentworth Street, down which the stalls of Petticoat Lane market spill... We never say 'Wentworth Street'; it's 'The Lane' to us. Ibid. ii. 29 Friday is the day for buying flowers in the Lane.

5*. *Astr.* A narrow band or strip in the sky that differs markedly from its immediate surroundings (e.g. in containing no observable stars or in emitting strong radio signals).

1899 *Astrophysical Jrnl.* IX. 157 The wonderful nebulous region about Rho Ophiuchi..and..the great vacant lanes near that star. **1917** *Proc. Nat. Acad. Sci.* III. 678 A study of the negatives of spiral nebulae obtained with the Crossley Reflector has shown that the phenomenon of dark lanes caused by occulting or absorbing matter is much more frequent than had..been supposed. **1964** R. H. BAKER *Astron.* (ed. 8) xvii. 506 The hydrogen lanes traced by Dutch radio observers..in longitudes available to them are shown in Fig. 17·22... In a direction 80° from the sun we note three hydrogen lanes, which trace three spiral arms. **1970** *Nature* 12 Dec. 1077/1 This is identified with NGC 1579 which is a small, irregular, diffuse nebulosity..with a prominent dark lane. **1971** *Ibid.* 21 May 197/3 The underlying common feature of spiral galaxies is the existence of elongated spiral arms traced out by gaseous material (neutral hydrogen lanes; ionized HII regions and dust).

6. *lane-side* (later examples), *-way* (later examples); **lane-route** (examples).

1895 *Funk's Stand. Dict.* 1000/1 *Lane-route*, or *ocean-l. route*, one of the routes prescribed for transatlantic steamers in Northern waters, being different for eastward- and westward-bound vessels, to avoid collisions. **1950** *Ocean Passages for World* (Admiralty, Hydrographic Dept.) (ed. 2) B. I. ii. 41/1 The large number of steam vessels crossing the Atlantic..has necessitated the adoption of clearly defined separate routes to be followed by outward and homeward bound ships... These are known as the *North Atlantic Lane Routes*. *Ibid.*, Masters of all ships..who do not..make use of the 'lane routes', should make themselves acquainted with them, for their own safety. **1899** H. T. TIMMINS *Nooks & Corners Shropshire* ix. 167 An old country woman tending her cow by the laneside. **1923** *Daily Mail* 2 Apr. 6 To see the lanesides in this delicate livery of verdure and bloom. **1914** JOYCE *Dubliners* 185 A crowd which had followed him down the laneway collected outside the door. **1933** L. A. G. STRONG *Sea Wall* 258 He charged like a bull across the open space and disappeared into the human laneway.

Lane, *sb.*[2] The name of John *Lane*, 19th-c. English horticulturalist, used in the possessive in **Lane's Prince Albert** to designate a large, green cooking apple of a variety introduced by him in 1857.

1875 *Florist & Pomologist* 233 Lane's Prince Albert..is remarkable both for its excellent quality as a culinary apple and for its prodigious bearing qualities. **1902** [see *BRAMLEY]. **1933** HALL & CRANE *Apple* xii. 200 Lane's Prince Albert..is a mid-Victorian introduction. **1962** *Listener* 27 Sept. 495/1, I am thinking of cooking apples like Bramleys and Lane's Prince Albert.

Lang (læŋ). Also **lang.** The name of John *Lang*, used *attrib.* and in the possessive (esp. in *Lang('s) lay*) to designate a lay (LAY *sb.*[7] 7 b) used for wire ropes and patented by him in 1879, in which the strands forming the rope are twisted in the same direction as the wires forming each strand.

1883 *Engineering* 14 Dec. 537/1 In the Lang method the strands and the rope are laid in the same direction. **1887** J. B. SMITH *Treat. Cable or Rope Traction* viii. 156 (*heading*) The 'Lang lay', or construction of wire ropes. **1896** W. E. HIPKINS *Wire Rope* 52 Ropes on the lang principle. **1930** *Engineering* 1 Aug. 135/1 The hauling rope is of the Lang-lay type, built up of six three-cornered strands and a hemp core. **1959** *B.S. Handbk. No. 4: Lifting Tackle (B.S.I.)* I. 90 Ropes made Lang's lay require careful handling to ensure that the rope's end does not twist, and so allow 'turn' to come out of the rope. **1966** *McGraw-Hill Encycl. Sci. & Technol.* XI. 627/1 In lang lay, wires in the strand and the strands themselves are laid in the same direction. This type rope wears better, is more flexible, and lasts longer.

langbanite. Substitute for entry:

långbanite (lǭ·ŋbănəit). *Min.* [ad. G. *långbanit* (G. Flink 1887, in *Zeitschr. f. Kryst. und Min.* XIII. 1), f. *Långban*, the name of its original locality in Wermland, Sweden + *-it* -ITE[1].] A black silicate and oxide of antimony, iron, and manganese, near $(Mn^{II}, Sb)_4(Mn^{IV}, Fe^{III})_9SiO_{12}$, with a brilliant metallic lustre.

1887 *Jrnl. Chem. Soc.* LII. 782 (*heading*) Långbanite, a new Swedish mineral. **1949** *Mineral. Abstr.* X. 542 Tetragonal braunite with a cubic pseudo-cell can be fitted into the hexagonal structure of långbanite. **1968** *Arkiv för Mineral. & Geol.* IV. 456 Since the original discovery of långbanite, so many specimens have been identified that it may be considered a moderately abundant mineral.

langbeinite (læ·ŋbəinəit). *Min.* [ad. G. *langbeinit* (S. Zuckschwerdt 1891, in *Zeitschr. f. angew. Chem.* 356/2), f. the name of A. *Langbein*, 19th-cent. German chemist + *-it* -ITE[1].] A sulphate of potassium and magnesium, $K_2Mg_2(SO_4)_3$, colourless when pure, which is known only in salt deposits of marine origin and as a synthetic product, and is used in the production of fertilizers.

1898 *Jrnl. Chem. Soc.* LXXIV. II. 169 The crystals of langbeinite are optically inactive. **1932** *Bull. U.S. Geol. Survey* No. 833. 41 Most of the langbeinite..has a distinctive pink color. It is the 'hardest looking' of the saline minerals and has a conchoidal or irregular fracture with no cleavage. **1951** *Mineral. Abstr.* XI. 247 Langbeinite.. on exposure to air falls to powder consisting of picromerite..and epsomite. **1960** R. A. MACDONALD in V. Sauchelli *Chem. & Technol. Fertilizers* xv. 387 Langbeinite..is mined and processed by International Mineral & Chemical Corporation in the Carlsbad basin... The product is marketed at a purity in excess of 95 per cent langbeinite.

‖ **langeleik** (la·ŋĕləik). Also **langleik.** [Norw.] An early Norwegian stringed instrument, resembling the zither.

1907 *Westm. Gaz.* 10/1 Ancient music of the Vikings was played..on the 'langleik', the crude guitar of the Norsemen, by an aged minstrel..who is a direct descendant of King Harald Haarfager. **1938** *Oxf. Compan. Mus.* 839/2 Norway possesses several distinctive instruments. The Langleik.., used until near the end of the eighteenth century, was a sort of developed monochord. **1961** A. BAINES *Mus. Instruments* 210 A tuning given by Panum for the slightly more advanced Norwegian langeleik. **1970** *Daily Tel.* (Colour Suppl.) 13 Nov. 47 The fjord-loving fiddle is the offspring of a local zither-like instrument called the *langeleik*, whose strings were struck with a plectrum.

Langerhans (læ·ŋəɹhanz). *Histology.* The name of Paul *Langerhans* (1847–88), German anatomist, used *attrib.*, in the possessive, and with *of*-adjunct to designate a kind of dendritic or stellate cell found in the epidermis and characterized by the presence of cytoplasmic granules (*Langerhans granules*). (See also *islet of Langerhans* s.v. *ISLET 2 b).

1890 BILLINGS *Med. Dict.* II. 32/1 *Langerhans' cells*, stellate cells found in deeper layers of epidermis, apparently related to nerve terminations. **1934** E. V. COWDRY *Textbk. Histol.* xxix. 449 Cells of the third category are called melanoblasts (Langerhans, stellate or dendritic cells) because they are supposed to form melanin. **1953** *Phil. Trans. R. Soc.* B. CCXXXVII. 162 This technique ..led to the erroneous conclusion that the cells of Langerhans occur in the basal layer. *Ibid.*, Langerhans' cells are invariably unpigmented. **1965** *Jrnl. Investigative Dermatol.* XLIV. 202/2 The characteristic granules within the Langerhans cell are shaped like a tennis racket... The number, as well as the size, of the Langerhans granules is ..variable. **1965** *Ibid.* XLV. 403/1 The capability of Langerhans cells to synthesize melanin remains to be proven. **1969** S. BRADBURY *Hewer's Textbk. Histol.* (ed. 9) xvii. 237 It was at one time thought that the Langerhans cells were effete melanocytes, but they have been shown to be active in the uptake of tritiated thymidine and their E/M appearance suggests also that they are active cells. Their function is still unknown.

Langhans (la·ŋhanz). *Histology.* The name of Theodor *Langhans* (1839–1915), German pathologist, used *attrib.*, in the possessive, and with *of*-adjunct to designate: (*a*) (a cell of) an inner layer of large cuboidal cells, one cell thick, that covers chorionic villi and lies beneath the syncytial layer; (*b*) a distinctive kind of giant cell which has many nuclei, arranged in a ring around the periphery or clustered together at one end of the cell, and is observed esp. in tuberculosis and related granulomatous conditions.

1886 *Buck's Handbk. Med. Sci.* II. 146/2 (*heading*) Langhans' cellular layer. **1900** DUNGLISON *Dict. Med. Sci.* (ed. 22) App. 1276/2 *Langhans's giant cell*, giant-cell of tubercular granulation-tumor. **1906** *Practitioner* Nov. 663 A teratoma is defined as a growth that consists of elements represented in the developing ovum, whether at an early (e.g. syncytia, Langhans' cells, large mono-nuclear cells), or, at a later date (e.g. neuro-epithelial cutaneous, or other elements). **1937** E. E. HEWER *Textbk. Histol.* xxxii. 280 (*heading*) Layer of Langhans. *Ibid.*, The villi during early pregnancy are covered by an inner layer of cubical cells (Langhans' layer) and an outer syncytial layer. **1939** G. G. KAYNE et al. *Pulmonary Tuberculosis* I. iii. 38 Granulomata consisting of epithelioid and Langhans giant cells may be seen as early as the third to sixth day. **1968** H. HARRIS *Nucleus & Cytoplasm* v. 97 This peripheral distribution of nuclei in certain types of multinucleate cell was first discussed by Langhans, and when such cells are found in pathological conditions they are commonly referred to as 'Langhans' giant cells. **1972** EBE & KOBAYASHI *Fine Struct. Human Cells & Tissues* 226 Cytotrophoblasts or Langhans cells of the chorionic villus are thought to be the site of production of a proteinic hormone, chorionic gonadotrophin.

‖ **langlauf** (la·ŋlauf). [G.] Cross-country ski-ing; a cross-country skiing race. Hence **la·nglaufer**, a competitor in such a race.

1927 A. LUNN *Hist. Ski-ing* xvii. 223 The *Langlauf* was the logical development of Norwegian ski-ing. **1929** *Times* 6 Dec. 6/4 They [*sc.* the British] could not hope to compete against foreign Langlaufers and jumpers. **1963** I. FLEMING *On H.M. Secret Service* xvii. 191 Bond..somehow stayed upright on the two miles of treacherous Langlauf down the gentle slope to Samaden. **1968** *Punch* 28 Feb. 293/2 And not only did he win the jumping, but also the downhill, the slalom, and the langlauf. It was a great day for Britain! **1970** *Country Life* 17–24 Dec. 1214/3 The young and energetic have turned ski-loping into a competitive sport. The 30 and 50 km langlauf races are included in the Winter Olympics.

Lang lay: see *LANG.

langley (læ·ŋli). *Meteorol.* [f. the name of Samuel P. *Langley* (1834–1906), U.S. astronomer. Orig. proposed (in G.) by F. Linke 1942, in *Handbuch d. Geophysik* VIII. 30, as a unit of solar energy flux, equal to one gramme-calorie per sq. cm. per minute.] A unit of

solar energy per unit area, equal to one gramme-calorie per square centimetre (approximately 41,900 joules per square metre).

1947 *Nature* 6 Sept. 327/1 It is herewith proposed that the 'langley' be defined as the gm. cal./cm.^{2}, where 'gm. cal.' denotes the 15°C. gm. cal. It is also proposed that the written abbreviation of 'langley' be 'ly'. **1954** J. C. JOHNSON *Physical Meteorol.* iv. 108 $\sigma = ..8{\cdot}22 \times 10^{-11}$ langley minute^{-1}. σ is called the Stefan-Boltzmann constant. **1970** DAY & STERNES *Climate & Weather* v. 145 The solar constant..is alternatively expressed as nearly 2·0 langleys per minute. **1974** *Nature* 15 Nov. 217/1 For the point of equilibrium I take 17 langley per day (1 langley = 1 calorie cm^{-2}) above the 1950 value of 847 langley per day.

Langobard (læ·ŋgŏbāɹd). Also **Longobard.** [see LOMBARD *sb.*[1] and *a.*] = LOMBARD *sb.*[1] 1 a. Also as *adj.* Hence **Langoba·rdian** *a.*

1788 GIBBON *Decl. & F.* IV. xlii. 216 The original name of Langobards is expressive only of the peculiar length and fashion of their beards. **1902** L. VILLARI tr. *P. Villari's Barbarian Invasions Italy* II. III. i. 279 As usual the Longobard host comprised a motley throng of Bavarians, Bulgarians, Gepidæ,..and more especially Saxons. *Ibid.* 280 The beginning of the Longobard rule may be said to date from this event. **1925** *Contemp. Rev.* Aug. 212 The people are of Langobardian, French, or even Gothic origin. **1952** E. HYAMS *Soil & Civilization* iv. 30 The first we hear of the buffalo, as a domestic animal, in Europe, is as a gift to the Langobard Court, in Italy, about A.D. 600. **1974** R. A. HALL *External Hist. of Romance Lang.* v. 86 The Langobards' linguistic influence was exerted chiefly in Italy.

Langobardic, *a.* (Later examples.)

1839 K. H. DIGBY *Mores Catholici* IX. viii. 260 These fragments of Langobardic inscriptions. **1895** T. HODGKIN *Italy & her Invaders* V. iii. 140 Vast stores of wealth, taken from the Gepid dwellings, enriched the Langobardic homes. **1960** W. D. ELCOCK *Romance Lang.* iii. 228 Words of Langobardic origin having undergone certain sound-shifts characteristic of High German. *Ibid.* 259 A Langobardic king, Liutprand,..saw the possibility of exploiting the political situation.

‖ **langostino** (laŋgŏstī·no). [Sp.] = *Dublin (Bay) prawn* (*DUBLIN). Cf. *LANGOUSTINE.

1915 E. R. LANKESTER *Diversions of Naturalist* xii. 100 A very large Mediterranean prawn..is called 'Barcelona prawn' and 'Langostino'. **1967** [see *CAMARON]. **1970** 'D. HALLIDAY' *Dolly & Cookie Bird* ii. 20 A plate of fat pink *langostinas* [sic].

‖ **langouste** (laṅgu·st). [Fr.] A crawfish, *Palinurus vulgaris*, and related species; = CRAYFISH B. 3 b.

1832 W. MACGILLIVRAY *Trav. & Res. A. von Humboldt* xxi. 306 The sailors had been searching for *langoustes*. [**1835** W. KIRBY *On Power of God in Creation of Animals* II. xv. 49 There is one of a most ferocious aspect..called in the London market the *Thorny lobster*..: it is also called..by the French, who esteem it highly, the *Langouste*.] **1917** N. DOUGLAS *South Wind* xix. 232 Those succulent *langoustes* for which the coastal waters of the island are renowned. **1924** *Blackw. Mag.* Sept. 409/1 The fishwives..spread out before them all varieties of fish and shell-fish from langoustes to cockles. **1942** 'R. WEST' *Black Lamb* I. 23 In Nice, as I sat eating langouste outside a little restaurant down by the harbour. **1949** A. WILSON *Wrong Set* 171 The champagne, the langouste, the pine-scented air..were making of this dinner one of those ..never to be forgotten hours of happiness. **1951** E. DAVID *French Country Cooking* 53 Put in the cut-up pieces of *langouste* and let the pan simmer. **1960** I. FLEMING *For your Eyes Only* 230 The blue and yellow langouste came a few steps out from under the rock.

‖ **langoustine** (laṅgustī·n). [Fr.] = *Dublin (Bay) prawn* (*DUBLIN). Cf. *LANGOSTINO.

1946 G. MILLAR *Horned Pigeon* xiv. 192 *Langoustines* in the Union Bar at Alexandria. **1949** [see *DUBLIN]. **1951** E. DAVID *French Country Cooking* 35 *Langoustines* are the small..shell fish about three inches long, delicate pink, with a very thin shell, resembling Dublin Bay Prawns. **1965** M. WALLENSTEIN *Merlin's Forest* vii. 86 He began to plan their dinner; beginning with crab or *langoustine*. **1966** P. V. PRICE *France: Food & Wine Guide* 41 The *langoustine* is like a giant prawn or little langouste. **1974** J. STUBBS *Painted Face* xi. 151 You must try the *langoustine*. It is very good.

langsat (la·ŋsat). Also **langseh, lansat,** etc. [Malay.] The edible fruit of *Lansium domesticum*, a tree of the family Meliaceæ, native to Indonesia and Malaysia; also, the tree itself.

1783 W. MARSDEN *Hist. Sumatra* 83 *Lansai.* The tree which bears this fruit is large; the leaves are of a lightish green and somewhat pointed. [**1795** tr. *C. P. Thunberg's Trav. Europe, Afr. & Asia* (ed. 2) II. 276 *Boa lansay* is the Malay name for the fruit of a tree..which is yet unknown to botanists.] **1839** T. J. NEWBOLD *Pol. & Statistical Acct. Straits of Malacca* I. ii. 53 In the valley grow various fruit-trees, such as..the langseh. **1869** A. R. WALLACE *Malay Archipelago* I. v. 132 The Dyaks brought us daily heaped-up baskets of Mangustans and Lansats, two of the most delicious of the subacid tropical fruits. **1911** *Encycl. Brit.* XVII. 472/2 The principal fruit trees are the.. *langsat, rambai*, jack-fruit, etc. **1920** W. POPENOE *Man. Tropical & Subtropical Fruits* xvi. 427 The langsat has not yet become generally cultivated outside of the Asiatic tropics. **1938** *Nature* 14 May 866/2 Many of the fruits and vegetables..have been but names, if that, to dwellers in the temperate zones so far;..the mangosteen and the langsat are still awaited. **1940** E. J. H. CORNER *Wayside Trees Malaya* I. 463 The Langsat has an oblong fruit (about 1½ × 1″) with thin, pale greyish-buff rind containing much white latex. **1963** J. KIRKUP *Tropic Temper* 115, I had some chicken..followed by sour-sweet langsat fruit.

langsuir (læ·ŋsiūᵊɹ). Also **langsuyar.** [Malay.] A female vampire with a whinnying cry, that preys on newborn children. Cf. *PENANGGALAN.

1881 *Jrnl. R. Asiatic Soc., Straits Branch* June 28 If a woman dies in child-birth..she is popularly supposed to become a *langsuyar*, a flying demon of the nature of the 'white lady' or '*banshee*'. **1900** W. W. SKEAT *Malay Magic* vi. 320 The Langsuir..takes the form of an owl. **1972** *Daily Tel.* (Colour Suppl.) 12 May 58/3 The Malayan vampire family includes..the Langsuir, the spirit of a woman who died after hearing that her child was stillborn, known by her green robe, her tapering nails of amazing length and her long black hair which conceals a hole in the back of her neck through which she sucks the blood of children.

language, *sb.* Add: **1.** *first language*: one's native language. *second language*: a language spoken in addition to one's native language; the first foreign language one learns.

1875 W. D. WHITNEY *Life & Growth of Language* ii. 25 We realize better in the case of a second or 'foreign', than in that of a first or 'native' language, that the process of acquisition is a never-ending one. **1876** C. M. YONGE *Womankind* vi. 40 The second language has been really and grammatically learnt. **1943** I. A. RICHARDS *Basic Eng. & its Uses* 14 The history of the nationalist movement in India is an instructive instance. Its leaders and its chief supporters are speakers of English and sometimes use it rather as their first than as their second language. **1962** R. QUIRK *Use of English* i. 6 Something like 250 million people for whom English is the mother-tongue or 'first language'. **1971** *Guardian* 23 June 7/3 Indians and Pakistanis..using a second language at school and their first language for many home activities.

b. *language of flowers* (examples).

1834 tr. *C. de la Tour's Lang. Flowers* 95 It is more especially by..modifications that the Language of Flowers becomes the interpretation of our thoughts. **1847** THACKERAY *Van. Fair* (1848) iv. 31 Perhaps she just looked first into the bouquet, to see whether there was a *billet-doux* hidden... 'Do they talk the language of flowers at Boggley Wollah, Sedley?' asked Osborne, laughing. **1949** *Enquire within upon Everything* (ed. 122) 462 *Language of Flowers.* The symbolism of flowers has always possessed a certain fascination, especially for the young person of either sex.

d. *Computers.* Any of numerous systems of precisely defined symbols and rules for using them that have been devised for writing programs or representing instructions and data.

1949 E. C. BERKELEY *Giant Brains* iii. 29 We must translate into machine language, in this case punched holes in the program tape. **1956** *Jrnl. Assoc. Computing Machinery* III. 272 In the development of an automatic coding system, two major problems arise. The first is to develop a coding language which permits a programmer to specify the computation he wants the machine to perform. Once this has been done, there remains the task of coding a compiler for a particular high speed calculator which will translate the language into actual machine instructions... The language described here is the one translated by the PACT I Compiling Routine into instructions for the IBM Type 701. **1959** E. M. GRABBE et al. *Handbk. Automation, Computation, & Control* II. ii. 186 The purpose of these activities has been to..set up a class of languages that will be easily translatable by machine from one to another, and also easily recognizable to the ordinary human user... Such languages form the input to a class of automatic computer programs called translators, which perform a translation..into a second or target language. The latter may be either (1) an assembly language such as SOAP, SAP, or MAGIC.., or (2) a straight machine language, in pure decimal, binary (or in some cases such as the Univac I and II), alphanumeric. **1961** LEEDS & WEINBERG *Computer Programming Fund.* ii. 46 The best way of writing down operations is to write them in alphabetical format. A format used for writing down these alphabetical instructions is called the programming language or paper language, to distinguish it from the machine language..acceptable to the machine circuitry. **1964** F. L. WESTWATER *Electronic Computers* ix. 145 As the benefits of these codes were realised, each manufacturer produced different 'languages'. **1966** A. BATTERSBY *Math. in Managem.* viii. 206 If each manufacturer prepares a compiler routine which will translate instructions in some universal 'language' into a program in his own code, then programs written in the universal language can be run on any machine. **1967** A. HASSITT *Computer Programming* i. 1 An efficient way of learning to use a computing machine utilizes one of the problem oriented languages such as Fortran, Algol, or PL/1. **1970** A. CAMERON et al. *Computers & Old Eng. Concordances* 27 If we program in so-called higher-languages, like Fortran, conceivably PL1,..I myself will be very surprised if the next generation of machines will not accept Fortran programming and probably Cobol, Algol, and PL1 programming.

3. *bad language* (example); *strong language* (examples).

[**1759** BURKE *Philos. Enquiry Sublime & Beautiful* (ed. 2) v. vii. 338 We do not sufficiently distinguish, in our observations upon language, between a clear expression, and a strong expression.] *c* **1863** T. TAYLOR in M. R. Booth *Eng. Plays of 19th Cent.* (1969) II. 109 Come, cheeky! Don't you use bad language. *a* **1910** 'MARK TWAIN' *Autobiogr.* (1924) II. 88 She made a guarded remark which censured strong language. **1934** R. MACAULAY *Milton* vi. 100 Milton's familiarity with the tradition [of scurrility] may account for much of his strong language, even when reviling in English.

e. (Earlier and later examples.)

1860 DICKENS *Uncomm. Trav.* (1861) v. 65 Mr. Victualler's assurance that he 'never allowed any language, and never suffered any disturbance'. **1865** —— *Dr. Marigold's Prescriptions* i, in *All Year Round* Extra Christmas No., 7 Dec. 4/1 But have a temper in the cart, flinging language and the hardest goods in stock at you, and where are you then? **1929** C. C. MARTINDALE *Risen Sun* 173, I have heard more 'language' in a 'gentleman's' club in ten minutes than in all that evening in the Melbourne Stadium. **1974** 'M. INNES' *Mysterious Commission* vii. 75 'You behave like bloody fools.' 'Language, now, Mr Honeybath, language.'

f. Phr. *to speak* (*talk*) *someone's language, to speak* (*talk*) *the same language*: to have an understanding with someone through similarity of outlook and expression, to get on well with someone; *to speak a different language* (*from someone*): to have little in common (with someone).

1893 'S. GRAND' *Heavenly Twins* I. II. vi. 256 What could Evadne have in common with these flippant people..? They did not even speak the same language. (To their insidious slang she opposed a smooth current of perfect English.) **1904** H. JAMES *Golden Bowl* I. xvii. 297 They hung together, they passed each other the word, they spoke each other's language, they did each other 'turns'. **1915** CONRAD *Victory* IV. xi. 391 You seem to be a morbid, senseless sort of bandit. We don't speak the same language. **1923** H. CRANE *Let.* 13 Apr. (1965) 131 The older poets and writers down here..don't talk the same language as we do. **1930** A. HUXLEY *Brief Candles* viii. 284 You'll perceive that he speaks your language, that he inhabits your world of thought and feeling. **1938** F. SCOTT FITZGERALD *Let.* 7 July (1964) 33, I want my energies and my earnings for people who talk my language. **1957** J. OSBORNE *Look Back in Anger* II. ii. 64 As for Jimmy—he just speaks a different language from any of us. **1961** A. WILSON *Old Men at Zoo* i. 25 Bobby..had presumed that since he and I 'spoke the same language', I should naturally dislike the Director as much as he did. **1971** R. RENDELL *No More Dying Then* xix. 166 She really didn't understand him at all, his need to be respectable... They didn't speak the same language.

6. a. *language acquisition, change, course, description, engineering, event, -form, -group, -pattern, sign, structure, -study, -system, -use.* **b.** *language-learner, -learning, -maker* (later examples), *-teacher* (later example), *-teaching, -user, -using*; **language area,** (*a*) an area of the cerebral cortex regarded as especially concerned with the use of language; (*b*) a region where a particular language is spoken; **language barrier,** a barrier to communication between people which results from their speaking or writing different languages; **language-contact** *Linguistics* (see quot. 1964); **language-game** *Philos.*, a speech-activity or limited system of communication and action, complete in itself, which may or may not form a part of our existing use of language; **language laboratory** (*colloq.* **language lab**), a classroom, equipped with tape recorders, etc., where foreign languages are learnt by means of repeated oral practice; **language-particular** *a.*, = **language-specific* adj.; **language-specific** *a. Linguistics*, distinctive to a specified language.

1921 H. E. PALMER *Princ. Lang.-Study* 14 In addition to certain *spontaneous* capacities, we possess what we may term 'studial' capacities for language-acquisition. **1965** N. CHOMSKY *Aspects of Theory of Syntax* i. 52 The innate structure of a language-acquisition device. **1971** D. CRYSTAL *Ling.* 257 Alternative theories of language acquisition are much needed. **1937** *Bull. Los Angeles Neurol. Soc.* II. 36 (*heading*) Case illustrating capacity for use of symbols after destruction of the major (left) language area. **1939** L. H. GRAY *Foundations of Lang.* ii. 25 One may frequently say that such-and-such an individual is from such-and-such a district within the language-area. **1961** *Lancet* 12 Aug. 361/2 The insistence that the degree of disability—e.g., in aphasia—was proportional to the amount of 'language area' destroyed. **1933** *Discovery* Sept. 281/2 Science itself..might go forward with greatly increased efficiency if the language barrier were removed by the adoption of Basic for Abstracts and Congresses. **1961** *Guardian* 18 May 8/2 A German girl tries to talk to him, but the language barrier is impenetrable. **1971** *Physics Bull.* Sept. 514/2 Important work in a number of countries may be missed because of the language barrier. **1912** L. BLOOMFIELD in C. F. Hockett *Leonard Bloomfield Anthol.* (1970) 37 A suggestion of 'concerted effort to shape usage' is..hitched on to a discussion of the universal unconscious processes of language-change. **1968** J. LYONS *Introd. Theoret. Ling.* i. 22 To have developed a general theory of language change and linguistic relationship was the most significant achievement of nineteenth-century linguistic scholarship. **1954** U. WEINREICH in Saporta & Bastian *Psycholinguistics* (1961) 378/1 A full account of interference in a language-contact situation ..is possible only if the extra-linguistic factors are considered. **1964** M. A. K. HALLIDAY et al. *Ling. Sci.* 77 Situations in which one language community impinges on another have been called 'language contact' situations. **1966** *Amer. Speech* XLI. 39 A name in a language-contact situation is sometimes the only element which survives the impact of another language. **1921** H. E. PALMER *Princ. Lang.-Study* 54 Most language-courses must necessarily be *corrective courses*. **1973** A. PRICE *October Men* xi. 155 [He] had been sent on a language course at a provincial English university. **1963** J. LYONS *Structural Semantics* ii. 36 The distinction between language-operation and language-description. **1971** D. CRYSTAL *Ling.* 54 It proved necessary to..redefine many of the categories,.. to make them applicable to the task of language description. **1953** J. B. CARROLL *Study of Lang.* iv. 113 Linguistics

may play a part in the solution of certain social problems. If so, a new kind of applied science—'language engineering' as it has recently been termed—may come into being. 1957 *Economist* 7 Sept. 851/2 An electronic data-processing machine..is breaking new ground in 'language engineering' by providing words—as many as five consecutive ones—which are missing from the Dead Sea Scrolls. 1964 *English Studies* XLV. 21 This admits under the label of 'English' a great range of different kinds of 'language event'. 1965 R. M. W. Dixon *What is Lang.?* 93 The data to be accounted for are observed language events. 1901 H. Oertel *Lect. Study of Lang.* ii. 102 The results of all higher classification beyond these, such as language-forms, are ideal types. 1932 A. H. Gardiner *Theory of Speech & Lang.* iv. 207 Jespersen..points out that particular phrases used in this way have become so stereotyped as to be real language-forms, e.g. *Well, I never! I must say!* Most curious of all is *I say!* with nothing following. 1934 R. Benedict *Patterns of Culture* (1935) iii. 48 When we describe the process [of the evolution of Gothic architecture] historically, we inevitably use animistic forms of expression as if there were choice and purpose in the growth of this great art-form. But this is due to the difficulty in our language-forms. 1971 D. Crystal *Ling.* 71 The philosophical search for laws of thought underlying language forms. 1921 H. E. Palmer *Princ. Lang.-Study* 145 Language-games may not further the student sufficiently in the habit-forming process. 1933–4 Wittgenstein *Blue & Brown Bks.* (1958) 17, I shall in the future again and again draw your attention to what I shall call language games. These are ways of using signs simpler than those in which we use the signs of our highly complicated everyday language. Language games are the forms of language with which a child begins to make use of words. 1970 A. MacIntyre *Marcuse* vii. 80 Wittgenstein tries to construct language games. 1970 *Times Lit. Suppl.* 23 July 787/1 In this country it was a dominant caste of philosophers..who seemed to be most gainfully preoccupied with the verbal manifestations of mind, having been coached at 'language-games' by Wittgenstein. 1927 Peake & Fleure *Peasants & Potters* 121 A group with common speech, that is to say a language-group. 1964 *English Studies* XLV. Suppl. 11 His systematic sub-division of the principal language-groups ..represents an astonishing linguistic perception. 1963 *Guardian* 4 Oct. 4/3 In a 'language lab' each student has his own booth and a tape-recorder which guides his speaking in French, Russian, or in any other language. 1968 A. Diment *Bang Bang Birds* ii. 18 There was my speech training. Usually a couple of hours a day down in the language labs. 1931 R. H. Waltz in *Mod. Lang. Jrnl.* XVI. 217 (*title*) Language laboratory administration. 1946 *French Rev.* XX. 19 A large Language Laboratory was installed... Phonographs and records were available at all times of the day. 1963 *Listener* 14 Nov. 791/1 In 1942.. my ideas were referred to as the 'language laboratory', a name that has stuck..to this day. 1969 *Ibid.* 3 July 8/2 I've done most through the Language Laboratory. I think it's a marvellous idea to start off a language by listening to what people say in the language. 1973 *Jrnl. Genetic Psychol.* CXXIII. 7 The *S*s were brought in groups of 20 to 30 students each, to a language laboratory where they were seated at individual carrels. 1921 H. E. Palmer *Princ. Lang.-Study* 14 Most language-learners at the present day are found to make an almost exclusive use of their studial capacities. 1965 N. Chomsky *Aspects of Theory of Syntax* i. 43 Cyclic regularities..are much more difficult for the language-learner to construct. 1697 J. Sergeant *Solid Philos. Asserted* Pref. § 10 Perhaps there is not one Evident Truth in it..but only such a way of Plausible Discourse or Language-Learning, as may serve equally and indifferently to maintain either side of the Contradiction? 1964 *Language* XL. 134 Chomsky's hypothesis is that the child is innately equipped with a language-learning device. 1867 W. D. Whitney *Lang. & Study of Lang.* v. 197 Language-makers in different parts of the earth. 1952 H. Read in B. Hepworth *Carvings & Drawings* p. ix/1 In this situation the artists of a period are the language-makers, inventing visual symbols. 1968 P. M. Postal *Aspects Phonol. Theory* viii. 164 The function of morpheme structure rules was to represent those language-particular predictable constraints on the possible combinations of feature specifications both within a segment and sequentially. 1970 *Language* XLVI. 377 It is a possible language-particular constraint on pronominalization in complex structures that a pronoun and its antecedent must lie within the same 'chain of command'. 1935 G. K. Zipf *Psycho-Biol. of Lang.* (1936) 19 Conditions present in all speech-elements or language-patterns. 1961 J. B. Wilson *Reason & Morals* iii. 178 Accepted language-patterns..act primarily as conservative forces both in the individual and in society. 1946 C. Morris *Signs, Lang. & Behavior* 350 In this book 'language sign' is often used in place of 'lansign'. 1970 Language sign [see *lansign]. 1972 *Language* XLVIII. 431 The post-Saussurean debate on the arbitrary nature of the language sign. 1965 N. Chomsky *Aspects of Theory of Syntax* iv. 166 However, there are also many language-specific redundancies. 1969 *Computers & Humanities* III. 258 Studies of..relative frequencies of language-specific syllabic patterns. 1970 *Language* XLVI. 784 It is non-language-specific in that it is empirically based on studies in English, some ten Meso-American languages, some twenty-four Philippine languages, and a few scattered languages from other areas. 1933 L. Bloomfield *Lang.* i. 18 H. Steinthal..published in 1861 a treatise on the principal types of language structure. 1971 D. Crystal *Ling.* 59 Areas of language structure other than grammar were disregarded in most traditional accounts. 1921 H. E. Palmer (*title*) The principles of language-study. 1933 L. Bloomfield *Lang.* i. 1 Many people have difficulty at the beginning of language study. 1964 C. Barber *Ling. Change Present-Day Eng.* vii. 149 Your own speech..is always the right place to begin language-study. 1940 A. H. Gardiner *Theory of Proper Names* 67 Regardless of the language-system as a whole. 1946 *Mind* LV. 339 This task should be approached by construction of consistent language-systems. 1966 *English Studies* XLVII. 193 An item in a highly personal language-system. 1921 H. E. Palmer *Princ. Lang.-Study* 58 The language-teacher must possess a considerable knowledge of phonetic theory. *Ibid.* 15 The language-teaching forces of nature. 1964 W. R. Lee in D. Abercrombie et al. *Daniel Jones* 291 The clear purpose is to see in what manner aids can subserve language-teaching. 1956 J. Holloway in A. Pryce-Jones *New Outl. Mod. Knowl.* viii. 42 Discoveries about language-use which are in themselves not necessarily connected at all with metaphysics. 1963 J. Lyons *Structural Semantics* i. 7 The known or apparent facts of language-learning and language-use. 1965 N. Chomsky *Aspects of Theory of Syntax* 6 The grammar of a particular language..is to be supplemented by a universal grammar that accommodates the creative aspect of language use. 1953 *Mind* LXII. 332 The sentence..mentions neither linguistic expressions nor language users. 1959 *Brno Studies in English* I. 29 The consciousness in language-users of the existing quasi-ideographic trends of the written norm. 1961 *Encounter* Mar. 60/1 Intentional action is characteristic of human beings ..as language-users. 1971 D. Crystal *Ling.* 85 We must ..start with the study of individual language users. 1921 H. E. Palmer *Princ. Lang.-Study* 96 These then are the chief things to be done once we have decided to enlist on our behalf the universal and natural powers of language-using. 1954 U. Weinreich in Saporta & Bastian *Psycholinguistics* (1961) 376/1 The language-using individuals are thus the locus of the contact.

langue. Add: **3.** *Linguistics.* A language viewed as an abstract system, accepted universally within a speech-community, in contrast to the actual linguistic behaviour of individuals (opp. *parole *sb.*).

1924 L. Bloomfield in *Mod. Lang. Jrnl.* VIII. 318 This rigid system, the subject-matter of 'descriptive linguistics', as we should say, is *la langue*, the language. 1947 *Word* III. 16 Langue, tho described as a repository, is not to be thought of simply as a pile of words. 1953 W. J. Entwistle *Aspects of Lang.* i. 26 One may..treat language (*langue*) as a generalization which becomes concrete and individual in speech (*parole*). 1957 [see *diachronistically* adv. s.v. *diachronism]. 1964 *Language* XL. 214 Current theorizing about the acquisition and functioning of the speaker's langue. 1965 N. Chomsky *Aspects of Theory of Syntax* i. 4 The distinction..is related to the *langue–parole* distinction of Saussure; but it is necessary to reject his concept of *langue* as merely a systematic inventory of items. 1968 *Word* XXIV. 56 Accent, viewed dynamically, constitutes the *parole* which manifests the pattern or *langue*.

‖ **langue de chat** (lãŋ də ʃa). [Fr., lit. cat's tongue.] A long thin piece of chocolate; a crisp biscuit of the same shape.

1907 *Yesterday's Shopping* (1969) 48/2 Chocolate for dessert... Langues de Chat. 1926–7 *Army & Navy Stores Catal.* 54/1 Chocolate... Langues de Chat—box 2/6. 1931 R. H. Heaton *Perfect Hostess* 111 Hand round any Biscuits you prefer. Langue de Chat are popular. 1945 A. Huxley *Time must have a Stop* i. 2 It was French chocolate... Those delicious *langues de chat*. 1964 J. Fleming *The Chill & the Kill* ii. 26 The Christmas Hamper..included..Elvas plums, Turkish Delight,..Cape gooseberries, and Langues de Chat. 1970 Simon & Howe *Dict. Gastron.* 239/1 *Langue de chat*, a type of biscuit (cookie) which derives its name from its shape; thin, long and flat like a cat's tongue.

Languedoc. Add: **2. langue d'oc**, the language spoken in mediæval France in areas roughly south of the Loire, where the use of *oc* [f. L. *hoc*] for *yes* was characteristic of many phonetic variations; opp. **langue d'oïl, d'oui**, the language spoken in areas north of the Loire, where *oïl* [f. L. *hoc ille*] (mod. Fr. *oui*) was used for *yes*, and which has developed into standard modern French.

1703 *Acct. Theatre of War in France, being a Geogr. & Hist. Descr. Languedoc* 3, I more approve of the Etymology of those who observe, that, time out of mind, the French have been distinguish'd into *Langue d'Ouy*, and *Langue d'Oc*, that is, into such as say *Ouy*, and such as say *Oc* for *Yes*; the first living on this, and the other on that side the River Loire. [1819 Scott *Ivanhoe* II. iii. 42 The knight..asked..whether he would choose a *sirvente* in the language of *oc*, or a *lai* in the language of *oui*... 'A ballad, a ballad,' said the hermit, 'against all the *ocs* and *ouis* of France.'] 1854 C. M. Yonge *Little Duke* i. 8 The Normans ..had taken up what was then called the Languéd'oui, a language between German and Latin, which was the beginning of French. 1866 —— *Prince & Page* iv. 53 My own children..scarce knew whether they spoke English, Languédoc, or Languéd'oui. 1885 H. James *Little Tour in France* xx. 134 Meetings at which poems in the fine old *langue d'oc* are declaimed. 1903 G. E. C. Casey *Riviera Nature Notes* (ed. 2) liii. 377 The various *Provençal Dialects* are..remnants of the old 'Langue d'Oc'... The 'Langue d'Oïl', or northern French was spoken by men more warlike and more barbarous. 1931 G. J. Renier *The English* viii. 156 The Kings of France did what they could to extirpate the *Langue d'Oc* as soon as they had conquered the southern half of France. 1934 M. K. Pope *From Latin to Mod. French* ii. 17 In the twelfth century the vernaculars of the south and the north (the *Langue d'Oc* and the *Langue d'Oïl*, as they were called after their particles of affirmation) were held to be distinct languages. 1961 P. Green tr. *Oldenbourg's Massacre at Montségur* i. 8 The great barons of the North, the land of the *langue d'oïl*,..were by no means all loyal to the French King.

Languedocian (læːŋgədōu·ʃiăn), *a.* and *sb.* [f. *Languedoc* (see Languedoc).] **A.** *adj.* Of or pertaining to Languedoc, its inhabitants, or their language. **B.** *sb.* **a.** An inhabitant of Languedoc. **b.** The language spoken there, a dialect of Provençal.

1736 [see Unstained *ppl. a.* 1]. 1765 Sterne *Tr. Shandy* VII. xliv. 154 That sprightly frankness which at once unpins every plait of a Languedocian's dress. 1771 C. Burney *Present State of Mus. France & Italy* 391 Agreeable Provençale and Languedocian melodies. 1792 A. Young *Trav. France* I. 32 Languedocian bishops are certainly not English ones. 1823 A. Thiers *Pyrenees* v. 66 The old Romance language, which mixed with..the Spanish in Languedoc, forms..the Languedocian. 1908 *Daily Chron.* 25 May 6/4 He has..found time to write poems in the Languedocian language. 1927 A. L. Maycock *Inquisition* 178 The records of the Languedocian tribunals. 1936 A. W. Clapham *Romanesque Archit.* iv. 100 A series of apostles..typical of later Languedocian sculpture. 1960 *20th Cent.* Sept. 209 We have used the words *Languedoc* and *Languedocian* in some places where *land of Oc* and *occitanian* would be the literal translation. 1972 J. Avias in Herak & Stringfield *Karst* v. 131 Epeirogenic movements (on the Languedocian coast for example) together with climatic changes caused variations in the relative basal marine or oceanic level.

langue d'oïl, d'oui: see *Languedoc 2.

languent, *a.* Add: **2.** Languid. *poet. rare*$^{-1}$.

1862 G. M. Hopkins *Vision of Mermaids* (1929), Some would plash The languent smooth with dimpling drops.

languisher. (Later example.)

1896 *Godey's Mag.* Feb. 193/2 A few silly languishers flutter and simper, 'How nice! how lovely!'

languor, *v.* Delete † *Obs.* and add later examples.

1891 A. Beardsley *Let.* July (1971) 24 'I should like,' he [*sc.* Burne-Jones] says, 'to see your work from time to time... I know you will not fear work, nor let disheartenment languor you.' 1969 *Harper's Mag.* June 37 America languors with an illness of euphoria brought on by our leaders. 1975 *N.Y. Times* 11 May 73/2 It embraces contemporary English aristocracy at upper-crust social functions,..hedonistic Romans languoring in ancient cities, [etc.].

la·nikin, *a. rare*$^{-1}$. [Cf. Cheshire dial. *lankin* and *lanniky*.] Lanky.

1862 Borrow *Wild Wales* II. xxvi. 295 He was a tall lanikin figure with a pair of..staring eyes.

lank, *a.* Add: **4.** *lank-legged* adj.

1906 E. Dyson *Fact'ry 'Ands* xiii. 172 Levi Goss..a lank-legged, ungainly object. 1921 W. de la Mare *Veil* 56 Like lank-legged grasshoppers in June-tide meadows. 1937 —— *This Year, Next Year*, And out of window gaze At lank-legged Peggy.

la·nkily, *adv.* [f. Lanky *a.*] In a lanky fashion.

1903 Conrad & Hueffer *Romance* i. 37 The second mate was lankily stalking the deck. 1926 A. Bennett *Lord Raingo* I. xlviii. 215 'Yes, Raingo,' said the tall, gaunt old man, striding lankily into the presence [of the minister]. 1937 A. Waugh *Eight Short Stories* viii. 253 He was lankily over-grown, with a sallow complexion and a pimply chin.

lankly, *adv.* (See under Lank *a.* (*sb.*).) Delete † and add later example.

1924 C. Mackenzie *Old Men of Sea* xi. 182 Mrs. Ringshaw used to stand beside him, her grey hair wet with spray and lankly waving.

lanky, *a.* Add: **b.** *lanky-legged, -looking* adjs.

1932 Auden *Orators* iii. 90 Lanky-legged Lloyd, and Morgan from Aberdovey, Peacock and long-skulled Cornish Davy. 1922 Joyce *Ulysses* 108 Now who is that lankylooking galoot over there.

2. Used as *sb.*, as a nickname or form of address for a lanky person.

c 1863 T. Taylor in M. R. Booth *Eng. Plays of 19th Cent.* (1969) II. 109 Just you try it, lanky! Yah! Hit one of your own size—do. 1942 Berrey & Van den Bark *Amer. Thes. Slang* § 184/7 Nicknames for a tall, lanky person... Harry Longlegs, Lanky, Legs, Lengthy. 1948 D. Ballantyne *Cunninghams* 212 Hiya, Lanky! 1959 I. & P. Opie *Lore & Lang. Schoolch.* ix. 169 *Lankies.* Inevitably there is a fusion of terms between those for the thin and lanky lad and those for the overgrown.

lanosterol (lǣnǫ·stĕrǫl). *Biochem.* [f. L. *lān-a* wool + -o + *-sterol.] An unsaturated sterol, $C_{30}H_{50}O$, which occurs in wool fat.

1929 Drummond & Baker in *Jrnl. Soc. Chem. Industry* 9 Aug. 238T/2 We recommend that the misleading name *iso*cholesterol be replaced by the less committal lanosterol. 1955 *Soap, Perfumery & Cosmetics* XXVIII. 1262/2 Lanosterol. This lanolin derivative is the newest to arouse interest in the cosmetic and related fields... Pure lanosterol is a light-coloured, free-flowing amorphous powder. 1964 *New Scientist* 22 Oct. 220/1 No fewer than thirteen distinct enzymic reactions are required to build up the sterol prototype, lanosterol, from acetic acid, and about as many to modify lanosterol into cholesterol, the characteristic animal sterol.

lansign (læ·nsəin). Short for **language sign*.

1946 C. Morris *Signs, Lang. & Behavior* 36 We propose therefore to call sign-sets of the kind in question lansign-systems, and the individual members of these systems lansigns. 1970 *Sci. Jrnl.* Jan. 57 In the 1930s C. K. Ogden, I. A. Richards and A. Korzybski, and more recently C. E. Osgood, D. H. Mowrer and others, tried to show how language symbols and signs (lansigns, as they are sometimes called) are associated with their referents in much the same way as conditioned stimulus becomes associated with an unconditioned stimulus, as in the classical conditioning theory of Pavlov.

lansquenet. Add to forms: (sense 1) **lands-knecht** now usual; (sense 2) **lambskinnet. 1.** For '17th and 18th centuries' read '16th and 17th centuries'. Add later examples.

1911 *Encycl. Brit.* XIV. 521/1 The Landsknecht was the prototype of the infantryman of the 16th and 17th centuries. **1936** *Burlington Mag.* June 294/1 Among the daggers is an elaborate landsknecht one in its sheath. **1944** AUDEN *Sea & Mirror* in *For Time Being* iii. 56 Our moth-eaten..stock costumes which with only a change of hat and re-arrangement of safety-pins, had to do for the *landsknecht* and the Parisian art-student. **1959** *Chambers's Encycl.* I. 610 (*caption*) Landsknecht sword, first half 16th century.

2. (Later example.)

1917 'H. H. RICHARDSON' *Fortunes Richard Mahony* 9 Even the 'shepherds' beguiled the time with euchre and 'lambskinnet'.

lantana (læntā·nă). Substitute for def.: [mod. L. (Linnæus *Hortus Cliffortianus* (1737) 349), f. an earlier Latin name for *Viburnum*, to which its foliage bears a slight resemblance.] An evergreen herb or shrub of the genus so called, belonging to the family Verbenaceæ, often a native of sub-tropical America, and bearing heads of red, yellow, or white flowers. (Add later examples.)

1917 *Nature* 20 Sept. 57/2 Two introduced shrubs, Guava and Lantana, now occupy extensive areas [of Hawaii], and have become great pests. **1933** *Times Lit. Suppl.* 9 Nov. 776/4 The scene is the Tweed River district of New South Wales, where banana plantations compete with the lantana creeper for a foothold. **1947** K. TENNANT *Lost Haven* (1968) Prologue 3 The loveliness of the place is a faint, sweet corruption; old, grey, wooden wharves..heaps of coal overgrown with wild convolvulus and lantana. **1961** *Amat. Gardening* 21 Oct. Suppl. 31/1 Most of the lantanas form small shrub-like plants with roundish heads of small flowers. **1969** *New Scientist* 20 Feb. 385/1 The world's worst weeds..include purple nut-sedge, Bermuda grass..cogon grass, and lantana.

lanterloo. Restrict † *Obs.* to sense in Dict. and add: **2.** Used as a meaningless refrain (cf. etym. in Dict.).

1951 AUDEN & KALLMAN *Rake's Progress* I. 17 The sun is bright, the grass is green: *Lanterloo, lanterloo.* The King is courting his young Queen. *Lanterloo, my lady.* **1951** AUDEN *Nones* (1952) 54 Turning his barrel-organ, playing *Lanterloo, my lovely*, my *First-of-May.*

lantern, *sb.* Add: **8. a.** *lantern fruitage, lecture, roof* (later examples), *slide* (earlier and later examples). **c.** *lantern-fruited, -lighted* adjs.

1920 A. HUXLEY *Leda* 7 Moons of many-coloured light That swing their lantern-fruitage in the night. **1912** W. DE LA MARE *Listeners* 53 She rested her old eyes From the lantern-fruited yew trees. **1912** W. OWEN *Let.* 6 Feb. (1967) 114 Miss Lingley, brother, & friend, who are giving a Lantern Lecture on their tour among Korean Missions. **1938** L. MACNEICE *I crossed Minch* II. viii. 119 At the end of the service a lantern lecture was announced, which reminded me pleasantly of my childhood. **1871** M. S. JEUNE *My School Days in Paris* vii. 92 At midnight a procession, lantern-lighted, wound slowly through the garden-walks. **1906** *Westm. Gaz.* 14 July 2/3 And to our fog-bound window came A lantern-lighted ancient dame. **1942** *R.A.F. Jrnl.* 13 June 3 In caves and cellars,.. lantern-lighted, a multitude of people endure. **1967** *Gloss. Caravan Terms* (*B.S.I.*) 2 *Lantern roof*, a roof with raised centre portion usually throughout its length, the side walls of which are provided with windows and ventilators. **1969** *Canad. Antiques Collector* May 16/2 The Great Kitchen..has a lantern roof supported on four cast-iron columns. **1871** G. FOX in *English Mechanic* 13 Jan. 405/3 (*heading*) Lantern slides. **1909** W. OWEN *Let.* 4 Jan. (1967) 49 There was a Church Army Mission with lantern slides. *a* **1930** D. H. LAWRENCE *Phoenix II* (1968) 115 Gilbert's lectures..with lantern-slides, thrilled Woodhouse to the marrow.

9. lantern bug = *lantern-fly*; also *fig.* (see quot. 1774); **lantern clock,** a 17th-century bracket clock worked by weights and surmounted by a bell in a frame; **lantern test** *Ophthalm.*, a test for colour-blindness in which the subject is asked to name or match colours shown by a lantern.

1774 J. BURGOYNE *Maid of Oaks* I. ii. 14, I would have put out Mr. Lanternbug's stars with one dash of my pincil. **1847** G. A. F. RUXTON *Adventures Mexico & Rocky Mts.* xix. 156 Of bugs and beetles there is endless variety—including the cocuyo or lantern-bug, and the tarantula. **1927** HALDANE & HUXLEY *Animal Biol.* xi. 228 Many lantern bugs have this anterior prolongation of the head. **1913** L. V. LOCKWOOD *Furnit. Collectors' Gloss.* 18/1 Clock..Chamber... These clocks are intended to hang high on the wall on brackets. Called also Lantern and Bird Cage clocks. **1960** H. HAYWARD *Antique Coll.* 161/2 *Lantern clock*: a clock of typically English design evolved in the early part of the 17th cent., and persisting, especially in the provinces, until well into the 18th cent... All original lantern clocks are weight driven. **1970** *Canad. Antiques Collector* Dec. 12/1 Lantern clocks..were designed to hang on the wall, and were weight driven and regulated by a balance wheel. **1890** *Brit. Med. Jrnl.* 11 Jan. 73/2 The Lantern Test is the one which I recommend for the testing of sailors and railway *employés.* **1966** K. WYBAR *Ophthalm.* ii. 26 The Ishihara or Stilling Test... The tests are more subtle than the lantern tests and are of value in identifying the anomalous trichromats (of the protanomalous or deuteranomalous types) who are often able to pass the lantern tests successfully.

lanthana (læ·nþănă). *Chem.* [f. LANTHAN(UM + *-a*, after *alumina, magnesia, thoria*, etc.] Lanthanum oxide, La_2O_3, a white powder.

1887 *Chem. News* 12 Aug. 62/1 A specimen of white lanthana prepared by myself some years ago..on being strongly calcined, became of a fawn colour. **1917** H. F. V. LITTLE in J. N. Friend *Text-bk. Inorg. Chem.* IV. 406 Lanthanum sesquioxide or lanthana, La_2O_3, is obtained as a white powder by the ignition of the hydroxide, carbonate, nitrate, oxalate, etc. **1961** W. K. ANDERSON in Spedding & Daane *Rare Earths* xxii. 565 Use of ceria, yttria, and lanthana as diluents for oxide fuel bodies is a promising developmental area.

† **lanthanate** (læ·nþănēit). *Chem. Obs.* [f. LANTHAN(UM + -ATE[1].] = *LANTHANIDE.

1946 *Nature* 27 July 134/2 Actually, however, samarium has an abnormally large atomic volume, a peculiarity which it shares with the other two lanthanates having bivalent properties. **1953** [see *LANTHANOID].

lanthanide (læ·nþănəid). *Chem.* [ad. G. *lanthanid* (V. M. Goldschmidt et al. 1925, in *Skrifter Norske Vidensk-Akad.* (*Mat.-nat. Kl.*) v. 6), f. *lanthan* LANTHANUM: see *-IDE 2.] **1.** Any of the series of elements with an atomic number between 57 (lanthanum) and 71 (lutetium) inclusive, or (following the later definition by Goldschmidt et al., on the suggestion of A. Sommerfeld, in *loc. cit.* VII. 10), between 58 (cerium) and 71; all these elements occupy a single position in group IIIA of the periodic table, are predominantly trivalent electropositive metals with similar chemical properties, and occur together in monazite, gadolinite, and certain other minerals. Cf. **rare earth.*

1926 *Chem. Abstr.* XX. 1969 (*heading*) Synthetic pyromorphites, vanadinites and mimetites in which lead is partially substituted by lanthanides. **1937** *Jrnl. Chem. Soc.* 662 A large rather coherent group is furnished by the rare-earth elements, comprising the lanthanide family (elements of atomic number from 57 to 71) and yttrium. **1946** J. R. PARTINGTON *Gen. & Inorg. Chem.* x. 262 The rare-earth elements in this period (sometimes called lanthanides, to distinguish them from the total number of rare-earth elements which includes scandium and yttrium in earlier periods). **1950** N. V. SIDGWICK *Chem. Elements* I. 444 Two of the lanthanides, samarium and lutecium, have been found to be radioactive. **1957** *Sci. News* XLV. 95 In the conventional periodic table..the pigeon-hole allotted to the element lanthanum..contains fourteen additional elements, formerly called the 'Rare Earths', but now usually called the 'Lanthanons' or 'Lanthanides'. **1965** [see *F III. 1 j]. **1973** J. J. LAGOWSKI *Mod. Inorg. Chem.* xvi. 616 The trivalent lanthanide cations also exhibit striking colors in their crystalline salts and in aqueous solution. **1973** *Chem. Soc. Rev.* II. 49 The most common practice is to successively add known amounts of the lanthanide shift reagent..to the compound under study ..and record the n.m.r. spectrum after each addition.

2. *Comb.*: **lanthanide contraction** [tr. G. *lanthanidenkontraktion* (V. M. Goldschmidt et al. 1925, in *Skrifter Norske Vidensk.-Akad.* (*Mat.-nat. Kl.*) VII. 13)], the decrease in atomic and ionic radii with increasing atomic number observed in the lanthanide series; **lanthanide series,** the series of elements from lanthanum (or cerium) to lutetium.

1926 *Chem. Abstr.* XX. 131 'Lanthanide contraction' is the term applied to the volume contraction of the atoms in the rare earth series Ce–Cu [*sic*]. This contraction opposes the progressive increase of at. vol. in each vertical column of the periodic table. **1945** A. F. WELLS *Structural Inorg. Chem.* iii. 94 As a result of this 'lanthanide contraction', so called because it is observed in the elements following lanthanum, certain pairs of elements in the same Periodic Group have practically identical ionic (and atomic) radii. **1971** *Jrnl. Inorg. & Nucl. Chem.* XXXIII. 385 The lanthanide contraction as reflected in certain properties of the lanthanide compounds is not a smooth function of *Z.* **1945, 1958** Lanthanide series [see *ACTINIDE]. **1965** B. G. WYBOURNE *Spectroscopic Properties Rare Earths* i. 2 As we proceed through the lanthanide series, the nuclear charge, together with the number of 4*f*-electrons, increases by one at each step.

lanthanoid (læ·nþănoid). *Chem.* [f. *LANTHA-N(IDE + -OID.] Any element of the lanthanide series (including lanthanum).

1953 BARNETT & WILSON *Inorg. Chem.* xii. 135 In modern nomenclature the term 'lanthanons', with variations such as 'lanthanides', 'lanthanates', 'lanthanoids' and 'lanthans' is replacing 'rare earths'. **1969** H. T. EVANS tr. *Hägg's Gen. & Inorg. Chem.* xxviii. 681 The colored lanthanoid ions are used in many ways in the glass industry. **1971** *Nomencl. Inorg. Chem.* (I.U.P.A.C.) (ed. 2) 11 The name lanthanoids for the elements 57–71 (La to Lu inclusive) is recommended.

lanthanon (læ·nþănǫn). *Chem.* [f. *LANTHA-N(IDE + *-on*, prob. to avoid confusion with the systematic use of *-ide* (-IDE).] (See quot. 1947.)

1947 J. K. MARSH in *Q. Rev. Chem. Soc.* I. 126 The term 'lanthanon' (Ln) is proposed to denote any element of the group from lanthanum to lutecium inclusive and to replace such objectionable terms as 'lanthanate' or 'lanthanide' which have recently had some currency. **1951** *Nature* 31 Mar. 526/1 An analysis of the lanthanon (rare earth) fraction from davidite..has revealed an unusual variation in the abundance of the lanthanons. **1961** W. K. ANDERSON in Spedding & Daane *Rare Earths* xxii. 522 Advances in the technology and availability of the lanthanons..have brought about an upsurge of interest among nuclear technologists. **1973** *Jrnl. Chromatogr.* LXXVI. 459 *Sym.*-EDDA was studied..as a complexant for the trivalent lanthanons and yttrium.

Lao (lɑu), *sb.* and *a.* [Native name.] **A.** *sb.* **a.** A branch of the Thai people (see quot. 1949) in South-East Asia; also, a member of this people.

1882 *Encycl. Brit.* XIV. 294/2 The Laos are closely related in physique and speech to the Siamese proper. **1885** T. DE LACOUPERIE in A. R. Colquhoun *Amongst Shans* p. lii, We know more of the original seat of the *Lao* or *Ngai Lao*, than of the others. **1915** W. W. COCHRANE *Shans* I. 198 The teaching that God is more powerful than all the hosts of evil spirits..ought to be attractive..particularly to the Laos among whom the demons seem to be uncommonly active. **1949** *Jrnl. Amer. Oriental Soc.* LXIX. 63/1 The use of *Lao* is confusing because, while it is now specifically applied to a specific Tai people—called Laotians by the French—another branch, not especially close to the Laotian, has been called Ngai-lao, or Ai lao; while the name has also been sometimes used as synonymous with *Tai.* **1961** P. KEMP *Alms for Oblivion* ii. 22 The majority of Laos stood by the French, whereas the Annamites detested them. **1969** I. KEMP *Brit. G.I. in Vietnam* iv. 78 The Lao also look down on them [*sc.* montagnards], calling them *kha*, meaning 'slaves'.

b. A group of dialects (see quot. 1954) spoken in Laos and neighbouring areas.

1939 L. H. GRAY *Found. Lang.* 390 To the south-eastern division belong Siamese, Lao, Lü, and Khün. **1948** D. DIRINGER *Alphabet* 414 Lao is nowadays widely spoken in northern Siam. **1954** PEI & GAYNOR *Dict. Ling.* 120 *Lao*, a group of vernaculars spoken in Siam and in parts of Burma, classified as Shan dialects. **1961** *Times* 23 Jan. 13/6 One of the Lao-speaking provinces. **1966** *Economist* 6 Aug. 536/1 The Americans are beginning to bring in a flood of school textbooks in Lao.

B. *adj.* Of, concerning, or pertaining to the Lao or their language.

1882 *Encycl. Brit.* XIV. 294/2 The last surviving descendant of the ancient Lao dynasty. **1915** W. W. COCHRANE *Shans* I. 155 The Lao alphabet..has 45 consonants. **1970** *Times* 26 Feb. 11/2 Somehow a Laos for the Lao people will have to be conserved.

Laocoön (lēi̯ǫ·kǫ,ǫn). Also **Lacoon, Laocoon, Laokoon.** [ad. Gr. Λαοκόων.] The name of a legendary Trojan priest who, with his two sons, was crushed to death by two sea-serpents (Virgil *Aeneid* II. 40–56, 199–231), used allusively, esp. with reference to statues representing him and his sons in their death-struggle. Freq. *attrib.*

1601 P. HOLLAND tr. *Pliny's Hist. World* XXXVI. v. 569 This may bee seene in the image of Laocoon..a peece of worke to be preferred..before all pictures or cast images. *a* **1666** EVELYN *Diary* an. 1644 (1955) II. 107 Above all that fountaine of the Laocoon..is a most glorious & surprizing object. **1699** M. LISTER *Journey to Paris* 143 The Atteliers or Work-houses of Two of the famous Sculptures Tuby; in which was a Lacoon Copied in White Marble. **1811** B. R. HAYDON *Jrnl.* 12 Jan. in *Autobiogr.* (1853) I. ix. 150 Went to the Academy in the evening, and saw the Laocoon placed out as it was four years ago. **1843** DICKENS *Christmas Carol* v. 153 Scrooge..making a perfect Laocoön of himself with his stockings. **1910** H. G. WELLS *Hist. Mr. Polly* i. 11 If Mr. Polly..had been transparent..he might have realized, from the Laocoon struggle he would have glimpsed, that..he was not so much a human being as a civil war. *a* **1930** D. H. LAWRENCE *Last Poems* (1932) 172 Leave the fearful Laocoön of his fellow-man entangled in iron To its fearful fate. *Ibid.* 282 We have become..fatally entangled in the Laocoön coils of our conceit. **1938** L. MACNEICE *I crossed Minch* II. viii. 108 The usual Chirico nightmare of marble Fathers of the City and laocoons in plaster. **1967** I. MARDER *Paris Bit* 84 She was draped like a female Laocoön in yards of inky black silk. **1970** *Sunday Times* 18 Jan. 56/4 The old flexibility and flair may become Laocöon to the computers.

Laotian (lɑu·ʃən, la,ōu·ʃən), *a.* and *sb.* Also **Laosian.** [f. *Laos*, name of a country in South-East Asia: see -IAN, *LAO.] **A.** *adj.* Of or pertaining to the country of Laos. **B.** *sb.* A native or inhabitant of Laos; also the language of the Laotian people.

a **1861** H. MOUHOT *Trav. Indo-China* (1864) II. xviii. 154 The Laotian priests..make a frightful noise, chanting from morning to night. **1890** J. G. FRAZER *Golden Bough* I. i. 42 Before beginning to work at the salt-pans in a Laosian village, the workmen offer sacrifice to a local divinity. **1911** *Encycl. Brit.* XVI. 190/2 Laos is inhabited by a mixed population falling into three main groups—the Thais (including the Laotians..); various aboriginal peoples classed as Khas; and the inhabitants of neighbouring countries. **1931** *Times Lit. Suppl.* 12 Nov. 880/4 A Laotian festival. **1949** *Jrnl. Amer. Oriental Soc.* LXIX. 63/2 The Southern group of Tai in Indo-China includes the Siamese and the Laotians. **1954** PEI & GAYNOR *Dict. Ling.* 120 Thai Lao or Eastern Laotian..and Tai Yüan or Western Laotian. **1967** D. S. PARLETT *Short Dict. Lang.* 122 Siamese and Laotian boast literature from comparatively ancient times. **1968** *Guardian* 1 May 9/1 The American..was having an argument with four Laotian officials... Suddenly the American threw the contents of his glass at one of the Laotians. **1971** *Ibid.* 8 Apr. 2/1 The writer is an American freelance who speaks fluent Laotian. **1972** *Mainichi Daily News* (Japan) 6 Nov. 19/4 (*caption*)

Japanese 'peace corps' members..teach Laotian farmers how to operate a tractor.

lap, *sb.*[1] Add: **4. c.** A form of loin-cloth worn by Indians in Guyana.

1769 E. BANCROFT *Ess. Nat. Hist. Guiana* 273 This is called a lap, and is the ordinary covering of the Negroes also. **1876** C. B. BROWN *Canoe & Camp Life Brit. Guiana* 34 There were two Indians,..dressed in nature's garb, barring the 'lap'. **1899** J. RODWAY *In Guiana Wilds* 254 A party of Indians in nothing but their laps. **1924** *38th Ann. Rep. U.S. Bureau Amer. Ethnol.* xxi. 439 To this belt or girdle..the apron or lap may be attached. *Ibid.* 443 Among the Wapishana, the length of the bark 'lap' (tururi) was..a guide to the importance of the wearer. **1958** M. SWAN *Marches of El Dorado* I. 56 An Indian in these parts would be ashamed to wear the bead apron or the red cotton lap of his parents; he cleans his teeth and brilliantines his hair.

5. c. (Later examples.)

1920 'SAPPER' *Bull-Dog Drummond* 23 Perhaps a year —perhaps six months... It is in the lap of the gods. **1965** *New Statesman* 30 Apr. 674/3 Almost all power lies in the laps of the different Laender [in Germany]. **1971** *Guardian* 27 Feb. 5/5 Lord Justice Davies said it was in the 'lap of the gods' what would be the effect on the younger children if they were ordered to go to their mother's home.

6. Restrict † to senses in Dict. and add: *to drop, throw*, etc., (something) *in someone's lap*, to shift a burden to (someone). Also (intr.) *to drop into the lap of.*

1962 B. KNOX *Little Drops of Blood* ii. 35 'And Sammy Bell's gear?' 'We'll dump that one in the lap of the Scientific boys.' **1964** MRS. L. B. JOHNSON *White House Diary* 7 May (1970) 134, I showed Mr. Fosburgh the Winslow Homer painting and I think he was as amazed as I am that it should have so precipitously and happily dropped into our laps. **1970** 'M. HEBDEN' *Mask of Violence* (1971) xx. 187 I'll throw this into Pinow's lap. It's German and high-level, and I don't want to be mixed up in it. **1972** V. CANNING *Rainbird Pattern* ii. 33 Quite simply—and this is for you, Bush, because I'm dropping it in your lap—Trader has got to be scotched. **1973** M. WOODHOUSE *Blue Bone* ii. 12, I went..to meet some people who had a development problem they wanted to drop in our laps.

7. lap belt, a safety belt across the lap; **lap-board** (earlier examples); **lap-iron,** a piece of iron used as a lapstone; **lap-robe,** a rug or cloth to cover the lap of a person seated in a vehicle; **lap strap,** a safety strap across the lap.

1952 *Los Angeles Examiner* 21 Mar., Wider 'lap belts' than those now used. **1959** *Sunday Graphic* 25 Jan. 4/5 The easy-to-fit and unobtrusive 'lap-belts' which give 65 per cent of the protection afforded by the full harness. **1961** *B.S.I. News* Mar. 7/1 Car safety belts,..three types.. lap belt, diagonal strap and full harness. **1962** A. SHEPARD in *Into Orbit* 114, I took off my lap belt and loosened my helmet. **1973** *Sci. Amer.* Feb. 81/3 In the Utah statistics (from 1969) only 16.5 percent were wearing the seat belts; the estimate at present is that, notwithstanding all the urgings by authorities, only about 25 to 35 percent use the lap belt and only about 5 percent the lap-and-shoulder combination. **1974** *Country Life* 31 Jan. 191/2 The cab.. has a bench seat with diagonal belts for two and a further lap belt for a third occupant. **1840** *Picayune* (New Orleans) 18 Sept. 2/3 Ashamed! why, I feel as flat as my own lapboard. **1867** A. D. WHITNEY *Summer in L. Goldthwaite's Life* vi. 125 On the lap-board across her knees lies her work. **1962** *Westm. Gaz.* 8 Oct. 6/2 The lapstone and the lap-iron have gone out of existence. **1875** MRS. STOWE *We & Neighbors* xxxix. 373 He took her to ride in such a stylish carriage, white lynx lap-robe, and all! **1914** G. ATHERTON *Perch of Devil* I. 121 He smiled..into her.. eyes and tucked the lap-robe about her. **1948** *Chicago Tribune* 15 Jan. 3/2, I loved the sleighrides too—snuggled under great buffalo hide lap robes. **1955** W. GADDIS *Recognitions* III. iv. 846 Engulfed in the flow of a tartan lap robe..he stared fixedly at an open book. **1974** 'I. DRUMMOND' *Power of Bug* xvi. 220 The thin cotton lap-robe which protected the passenger's legs and feet from the dust. **1960** *Guardian* 22 July 20/2 For rear seat passengers a lap strap is probably sufficient. **1961** *Times* 10 Jan. 6/6 If the ordinary lap strap..is used, an occupant of the car will tend to 'jack knife' forward. **1968** A. DIMENT *Gt. Spy Race* ix. 165, I did up the lap strap [on a seat in a passenger aircraft] and went straight to sleep.

lap, *sb.*[3] Add: **2. e.** *Metallurgy.* A kind of defect that results when a projecting part is folded over against the surface of the metal and pressed in (e.g. during rolling or forging), so that a seam is produced on the surface.

1914 W. ROSENHAIN *Introd. Study Physical Metall.* xiv. 324 'Laps', 'rokes', etc.,..result from the partial welding up of fissures or of portions of metal which have become accidentally overlapped. **1939** E. C. ROLLASON *Metall. for Engineers* iv. 55 A defect, somewhat similar to a roke, is caused by poor roll design or by rolling at too low a temperature. The metal spreads to an extent greater than the designed pass and forms fins on opposite sides of the bar, which in subsequent passes are lapped over to give the lap illustrated. **1967** E. BISHOP tr. *M. van Lancker's Metall. Aluminium Alloys* viii. 238 Working may scratch the metal and result in corrosion damage.., or form laps..tears..and excessive work-hardening.

4. b. *Warp Knitting.* A loop of yarn on a needle.

1884 W. T. ROWLETT tr. *Willkomm's Technol. Framework Knitting* I. i. 41 Each warp thread is also laid *over* a needle and forms the 'lap' over one. **1884**, etc. [see *KNOCK-OFF *sb.* and *a.* B. 2 a]. **1926** J. CHAMBERLAIN *Hosiery, Yarns & Fabrics* vii. 173 The knock-off stitch is often used to produce pure longitudinal stripes on warp knitted fabrics in which case the pressed lap is always made on the same needle and only the knock-off lap..is traversed to effect a lateral joining. **1952** D. F. PALING *Warp Knitting Technol.* i. 5 Assuming that two fully threaded guide bars are used, then each needle will be provided with two threads across its beard. These laps may be in similar directions or in opposite directions according to the relative directions of the overlaps. **1964** H. WIGNALL *Knitting* ii. 44 The needles are then raised to move the laps below the beards.

6. (sense 2) *lap-boarded; lap-seam;* (sense 4) *lap-drum, -roller* (example), *-tenter;* (sense 5 b) *lap time.* Also **lap-dissolve** *v.*, = *DISSOLVE *v.* 7 b; **lap-join** *v. trans.*, to join by means of a lap joint; **lap-system** (see quot.); **lap winding** *Electr. Engin.*, a kind of armature winding in which the two ends of each coil are connected to adjacent commutator segments, so that each coil overlaps the next.

1927 *Chambers's Jrnl.* Sept. 597/2 Lap-boarded houses which overhang the sea. **1927** *Observer* 17 Apr. 3 No sooner has it [*sc.* the title] been read than it lap-dissolves into the director's name... It should be lap-dissolved in for a mere flash. [**1934** H. M. HARWOOD *Old Folks at Home* I. i. 21 Sometimes the next picture's on before the last one's gone... lap... dissolve... isn't it?] **1962** *Sunday Times* 5 Aug. 20/4 *The Stranger*: All right, pardon me for living, it's just you looked so much like this very attractive party I met down here last year. (*Lap dissolve to what may be the following day.*) **1902** T. THORNLEY *Cotton Combing Machines* 17 The six webs are..drawn by frequent pairs of press rollers to the lap-head, consisting of two pairs of heavily weighted press rollers..and of the lap drums. **1968** J. ARNOLD *Shell Bk. Country Crafts* vi. 116 The arrangement is to have a 'V' on one side and an inverted 'V' on the other, the apex of which is lap-joined flush with the top rail. **1850** *Rep. Comm. Patents 1850* (U.S.) 160, I also claim the combination of burring apparatus..with the calender and lap rollers. **1905** *Westm. Gaz.* 21 Mar. 5/1 He says the explosion was caused by a crack in the lap-seam [of the boiler]. **1964** H. HODGES *Artifacts* iv. 77 Bronze vessels of (riveted) sheet metal could be made perfectly watertight, even when the edges were joined by a simple lap seam. **1894** *Gloss. Terms Evidence R. Comm. Labour* 51/2 in *Parl. Papers 1893–4* (C. 7063) XXXVIII. 411 *Lap System*, also called 'trip system', is a system (in the carter's industry) of piece-work, *e.g.*, a driver taking loads of coal a given distance for a stated sum, works under the lap system. **1881** *Instructions to Census Clerks* (1885) 68 Lap Tenter. **1921** *Dict. Occup. Terms* (1927) 164/2 Lap tenter (cotton). **1909** *Westm. Gaz.* 7 Dec. 5/1 The net lap times of the Auvergne races of 1905. **1973** *Times* 28 Apr. 7/2 Both he and his team-mate, François Cevert, were later able to equal Regazzoni's lap time. **1892** S. P. THOMPSON *Dynamo-Electr. Machinery* (ed. 4) xii. 311 When we go on to those cases in which the winding is entirely exterior to the core, as for drum armatures, or to those in which there is no core at all, namely for disk armatures, we find that there are two distinct modes of procedure, which we may respectively denote as lap-winding and wave-winding. **1937** A. S. LANGSDORF *Theory Alternating-Current Machinery* v. 295 The end connections of a distributed winding may be arranged in several ways, all electrically identical... The order of grouping and the resultant shape of the coils give rise to the respective designations of spiral, lap, and wave windings. **1966** *McGraw-Hill Encycl. Sci. & Technol.* XIV. 505/2 Lap windings are adapted to high-current machines because they may have more than two parallel paths, whereas the wave windings are adapted to small-capacity machines and high-voltage machines because of the series connection of the coils.

lap, *sb.*[4] **b.** Delete '*Gun-making*' and add def.: A polishing tool of some relatively soft material (as lead or cast iron) made to a special shape for use in lapping (see LAP *v.*[4] in Dict. and Suppl.). Add further examples.

1905 W. S. LEONARD *Machine-Shop Tools & Methods* (ed. 3) xxxi. 506 The laps described above are of the simplest and cheapest forms, namely, a plain shaft for the internal, and a collar for the external, lap. **1920** OBERG & JONES *Gage Design* vii. 191 Laps for Ring Gages.—Three laps are shown in Fig. 15 for lapping ring gages... They are made of cast iron and are ground to fit the ring gage to be lapped. Grinding the thread on a lap will insure accuracy. **1932** HARDY & PERRIN *Princ. Optics* xvi. 338 The exposed surface of the blank is then ground by holding it against another tool, called a lap, which has previously been given the proper radius of curvature. The lap is rotated at a moderate speed on a vertical shaft and is fed with a mixture of coarse emery and water. **1942** A. F. COLLINS *Greatest Eye in World* ii. 43 A concave iron lap is then placed over the lenses on the head and the spindle is rotated by an electric motor.

lap, *v.*[1] Add: **2. b.** *U.S.* Of a bear: to gather and eat fruits or nuts. Hence *lapping-season.*

1868 *Amer. Naturalist* May 122 They climb in order to 'lap', as the hunter says. *Ibid.*, When mast is not plenty, they lap black-gum berries. **1881** *Scribner's Mag.* Oct. 858/2 This is called the lapping season, as he ensconces himself in a tree lap and breaks the limbs to pieces, in gathering nuts and fruits.

c. *to lap up*: (*fig.*) to receive (praise, news, etc.) eagerly.

1890 A. JAMES *Diary* 20 May (1964) 119 Where do you suppose they have discovered Self-Sacrifice now? In the heroic bosom of Stanley! who on his own showing laps up the *agréments* of African travel as I do my afternoon tea. **1922** S. LEWIS *Babbitt* xxx. 359, I was simply astonished, the way those women lapped it up! **1930** D. H. LAWRENCE *Phoenix II* (1968) 493 People wallow in emotion: counterfeit emotion. They lap it up: they live in it and on it. **1931** G. ATHERTON *Sophisticates* II. xix. 210 'Polly, of all women, to start such a thing!' muttered Emerey. 'Or Toddles, for that matter. I've found out it was she who fed Polly with the idea of doing something new and strange. Of course she lapped it up.' **1958** *Listener* 20 Nov. 815/1 The Indian Embassy in Bonn will lap up information about Eastern Germany. **1972** *Times* 20 Apr. 25/1 Americans have lapped the book up, already getting through Dell's first order of 100,000.

lap, *v.*[2] Add: **9. b.** (Earlier and later examples.) Also in *Motor Racing.* Also *fig.*

1847 W. T. PORTER *Quarter Race Kentucky* 50, I told you the brown horse was a mighty fast one... But soon I lapped him. **1857** *Lawrence* (Kansas) *Republ.* 11 June 3 This..was a killing pace, but Mahen lapped him inside the first quarter. **1961** J. S. SALAK *Dict. Amer. Sports* 259 *Lap*, pass another car for the second or third time. **1966** *Publ. Amer. Dial. Soc. 1964* XLII. 6 'To be lapped', to be passed by a car the race distance for which already exceeds the car being overtaken by the length of a complete lap. **1969** 'D. RUTHERFORD' *Gilt-Edged Cockpit* i. 18 The leading Ferrari..was in fourth place and about to be lapped by the Mascot. **1973** *Times* 9 Feb. 15/5 We are constantly being lapped in the wages race.

c. *trans.* and *intr.* Of persons engaged in a race, or their vehicles: to travel over (a distance) as a lap; also simply, to traverse.

1923 *Daily Mail* 24 May 10 The course, 37⅝ miles in length, has to be lapped six times. *Ibid.* 4 June 13 The Leyland expert put up the highest speed of the day when he lapped the 2¾ miles at an average of 117 miles an hour. **1927** *Daily Express* 2 June 12/4 Major Segrave hopes..to lap the course at a fair speed. **1928** *Ibid.* 26 May 9/2 There are many machines entered which could lap all day at sixty-five miles an hour. **1973** P. EVANS *Bodyguard Man* xiii. 93 Just lapping the track gently. Nothing too strenuous.

lap, *v.*[4] Add to def.: To rub or abrade so as to make a surface smooth (and often correctly shaped) to a high degree of precision, usually by the use of a rotating lap of suitable shape coated or impregnated with an abrasive dust, paste, or liquid. Add further examples.

1905 W. S. LEONARD *Machine-Shop Tools & Methods* (ed. 3) xxxi. 506 We sometimes lap a machine-shaft which is required to run at an extremely high speed... Other machine details may be lapped when an exceptionally high degree of refinement is required, but the process is more commonly applied to measuring-tools, such as the collar- and plug-gages, etc. **1928** E. BUCKINGHAM *Spur Gears* xii. 444 Hardened gears are sometimes run together under load with some form of abrasive introduced with the lubricant..to smooth the surfaces and correct some of the errors. This process, however, does more grinding or crushing of the abrasive than it does to polish or lap the gear-tooth profiles. **1958** *Proc. IRE* XLVI. 1063/1 Wafers, of dimensions 1 × ½ inch, of this material are lapped to a thickness of 10 mils. **1973** *Physics Bull.* July 427/2 The techniques devised for lapping and polishing x ray reflectors have been modified to allow the same basic principles to be employed in lapping and polishing surfaces more complex than the plane, sphere or cylinder.

lapageria (læpădʒīə·riă). [mod.L. (Ruiz & Pavon *Flora Peruviana* (1802) III. 64), f. the name of Joséphine Tascher de *la Pagerie* (1763–1814), Empress of France + -IA[1].] A climbing shrub of the monotypic genus so named, belonging to the family Liliaceæ, native to Chile, and bearing large, bell-shaped, pendulous, red or white flowers.

1849 *Curtis's Bot. Mag.* LXXV. 4447 (*heading*) Rose-coloured Lapageria. **1886** G. NICHOLSON *Dict. Gardening* II. 234/2 Lapagerias rank amongst the most beautiful greenhouse climbing plants in existence. **1929** *Times* 1 Nov. 19/6 A tiny, pillared stone temple of exquisite proportions bowered in clematis, lapageria, and a climbing yellow rose. **1971** *Country Life* 8 Apr. 820/2 This is one of the finest outdoor specimens of lapageria I have seen in the British Isles.

laparoscope (læ·părŏskōᵘp). *Med.* [f. LAPARO- + -SCOPE.] Any instrument used in examining the abdomen; now *spec.* one in the form of a tube for insertion into the peritoneal cavity in laparoscopy, having a source of light at the inserted end and an optical system for forming at the other end an image of the illuminated region.

1855 R. G. MAYNE *Expos. Lex. Med. Sci.* (1860) 571/2 *Laparoscopium*, name of an instrument for ascertaining the condition of the abdomen under disease; applicable to the stethoscope and the plessimeter: a laparoscope. **1941** DORLAND & MILLER *Med. Dict.* (ed. 19) 776/2 *Laparoscope*, a special form of trocar bearing a light by means of which the peritoneal cavity, especially the surface of the liver and the peritoneum, can be inspected. **1967** P. C. STEPTOE *Laparoscopy in Gynaecol.* ii. 11 A cold-light projector..is used with a fibre glass cable for transmission of light to a quartz rod incorporated in the laparoscope. *Ibid.* iii. 22 The laparoscope is introduced through the vaginal fornix into the pouch of Douglas. **1970** *Sci. Jrnl.* June 57/1 Human ovaries may be inspected by inserting a tube (laparoscope) through to body wall which both illuminates the internal organs and transmits an image back to the observer.

laparoscopy (læpărǫ·skŏpi). *Med.* [f. LAPARO- + *-SCOPY.] Examination of the loins or abdomen; now *spec.* [ad. G. *laparoskopie* (H. C. Jacobaeus 1910, in *Münchener Med. Wochenschr.* 4 Oct. 2091/1)], visual examination of the interior of the peritoneal cavity by means

of a laparoscope inserted into it through the abdominal wall or the vagina.

1855 R. G. MAYNE *Expos. Lex. Med. Sci.* (1860) 571/2 *Laparoscopia*, a term for the examination of the loins, by means of the stethoscope, plessimeter, etc.: laparoscopy. **1890** BILLINGS *Med. Dict.* II. 33/1 *Laparoscopy*, examination of the abdomen. **1916** *Jrnl. Amer. Med. Assoc.* 23 Sept. 982/2 Laparoscopy and Thoroscopy.—Johnsson has been applying the cystoscope in investigation of the interior of the abdomen and thorax. **1937** *Surg., Gynecol. & Obstetr.* LXIV. Internat. Abstr. Surg. Suppl. 560/1 By means of laparoscopy almost the same observations may be made as when the anterior wall of the abdominal cavity of a cadaver is removed. **1967** P. C. STEPTOE *Laparoscopy in Gynaecol.* viii. 42 An ovarian cyst is readily recognised by laparoscopy. **1969** *Nature* 15 Feb. 635/2 Work using laparoscopy has shown that oocytes can be recovered from ovaries by puncturing ripening follicles *in vivo.* **1970** M. R. COHEN *Laparoscopy, Culdoscopy & Gynecogr.* i. 3 By means of laparoscopy the gynecologist can obtain the same view of the pelvic organs as is seen in laparotomy.

Hence **laparosco·pic** *a.*, pertaining to or obtained by laparoscopy; **laparo·scopist**, one who uses the laparoscope.

1967 P. C. STEPTOE *Laparoscopy in Gynaecol.* iii. 25 It is..possible to present laparoscopic views direct to a large audience. *Ibid.* vi. 30 The experienced laparoscopist can offer sound advice about the technical errors. **1969** *Proc. R. Soc. Med.* LXII. 440/1 Interpretation of laparoscopic findings depends on..examination of the site, size and development of the ovary, the appearance of the surface and the presence of follicles or corpora lutea. *Ibid.* 441/2 The proper use of laparoscopic techniques is one of the most valuable advances..in gynæcology in the last twenty years. **1970** M. R. COHEN *Laparoscopy, Culdoscopy & Gynecogr.* xvii. 111 It is possible for the gynecologic laparoscopist to view upper abdominal organs as well.

lap-dog. (Later *attrib.* examples.)

1905 *Dial* (Chicago) 16 Feb. 114/2 Lap-dog poets. **1963** *Times Lit. Suppl.* 22 Feb. 132/4 A lap-dog lover.

lapel. (Later *attrib.* examples.)

1895 *Montgomery Ward Catal.* 180 Lapel Buttons, Enameled. **1940** *Chambers's Techn. Dict.* 486/2 *Lapel microphone*, a small microphone, worn on the lapel; suitable for use when the speaker is addressing an audience, or when he cannot remain in a stable position. **1967** *Observer* 26 Mar. 9 The hippies themselves do not need to pin on the lapel buttons they sell. **1969** *New Scientist* 16 Oct. 109/2 The indignity of wearing a lapel badge displaying their name, rank and work-place to the world at large. **1972** *Times* 7 Feb. 1/3 They were issued with lapel badges depicting a black coffin on a white background. **1973** *Country Life* 31 May 56/1 For the sportsman's wife... Lapel brooches in three colours of gold.

lapidarist. Delete † *Obs. rare* and add later examples. For '= LAPIDARY B 1 b' read '= LAPIDARY B. 1 a, b; also *fig.*'

1886 *Sci. Amer.* 7 Aug. 84/2 The stone called sapphire by Pliny is now known to lapidarists as lapis lazuli. **1926** C. L. WARR *Principal Caird* iv. 135 He was a slow-working lapidarist, polishing every literary pebble. **1967** *Sat. Rev.* 13 May 31 Limited editions presses are the lapidarists of the publishing world.

lapidicolous (læpidi·kŏləs), *a.* [f. L. *lapid-*, *lapis* stone + *-col-us* inhabiting + -OUS.] Of beetles: living under stones or similar objects. Hence **lapi·dicole** *sb.*, a beetle living in this kind of habitat.

1899 D. SHARP in *Cambr. Nat. Hist.* VI. II. v. 205 These blind lapidicolous Carabidæ are of extremely minute size, and of most sluggish habits. **1948** J. R. DIBB *Field Bk. Beetles* p. xiii, Habitat-group 4. Under Stones. Logs, timber, sacking, old metal objects and discarded material which has been thrown down in the open. Lapidicoles. **1959** E. F. LINSSEN *Beetles Brit. Isles* I. 57 Beetles found under stones are Lapidicoles. **1965** B. E. FREEMAN tr. *Vandel's Biospeleol.* ii. 20 Thousands of..lapidicoles..have been recorded.

lapiés (læ·pyez, læ·piez), *sb. pl. Geomorphol.* Also **lapiaz, lapies, lapiez.** [a. F. dial. *lapiaz*, *lapiés* pl. (used in the Jura), f. pop.L. **lapida* f. L. *lapis* stone.] **a.** (Const. as *pl.*) = *KARREN, KARREN *sb. pl.*; also (const. as *sing.*), a *karrenfeld.*

1902, etc. [see *KARREN, KARREN]. **1903** *Geogr. Jrnl.* XXI. 328 The surface formation met with most commonly in limestone districts, which is usually known by the German term *Karren*, or the French *Lapiaz.* **1921** *Geogr. Rev.* XI. 594 The identification of 'karren' and 'lapiez' is taken from Eugène Renevier's 'Monographie des Hautes Alpes Vaudoises' (Matériaux pour la carte géol. Suisse), p. 499. *Ibid.* 598 The name adopted by Professor Cvijić is 'lapiez', which is the term used in the French Jura. **1924** J. CVIJIĆ in *Geogr. Rev.* XIV. 27 Lapiés are found at all altitudes from sea level to lofty mountain summits. They were first observed and described in the limestone alps of Switzerland, where in the cantons of German speech they are called *Karren* or *Schratten* and in districts of French speech *lapiéz* or *lapiaz* or *lapiés. Ibid.* 40 Lapiés are formed principally by chemical erosion of limestone surfaces by meteoric water. *Ibid.* 44 Typical lapiés occur chiefly on moderately steep slopes. *Ibid.*, Scattered limestone monoliths are rapidly formed out of the lapiés ridges. **1954** W. D. THORNBURY *Princ. Geomorphol.* xiii. 319 Where relief is considerable, limestone surfaces are bare of terra rossa and there is exposed an etched, pitted, grooved, fluted and otherwise rugged surface to which the name *lapiés* is most commonly applied. Cvijić (1924) has described..the amazing diversity of surface and form which lapiés exhibits in the Dalmatian karst region. He maintained that lapiés is found chiefly on outcrops of naked rock. **1968** R. W. FAIRBRIDGE *Encycl. Geomorphol.* 645/1 Well developed lapiés with pinnacles standing up to 5 meters high are common in emerged limestone reefs, particularly in the South Pacific. **1972** BAUER & ZÖTL in Herak & Stringfield *Karst* vii. 236 At these altitudes [in Austria] lapies are dominant karst phenomena, covering wide areas. *Ibid.* 237 Where the surface of limestones is exposed by recent soil erosion, irregularly shaped, more or less rounded rills and lapies of different depth are found.

b. Used in the *sing.* form **lapié.** *rare.*

1968 R. W. FAIRBRIDGE *Encycl. Geomorphol.* 644/2 (*caption*) Lapiés formed in limestone covered by residual clay. .. When the lapié ridges are destroyed, a dolina will be formed, filled with clay.

Lapith (læ·piþ). *Gr. Mythol.* Pl. **Lapithæ, Lapiths.** [f. L. *Lapithæ*, ad. Gr. Λαπίθαι.] One of the Lapithæ, a people of Thessaly, celebrated for their wars with the Centaurs.

1607 TOPSELL *Foure-f. Beasts* 504 The fight betwixt the Lapithæ and the Centaurs. **1611** CORYAT *Crudities* sig. C8 Amongst the woers of Penelope themselues, amongst the huge bolles of the Lapithæ. *a* **1846** [see *HELLENIAN *sb.*]. **1874** *Guide Græco-Roman Sculptures Dept. Greek & Roman Antiquities Brit. Mus.* I. 57 One of the Centaurs.. attacked by Lapiths while carrying off Greek women. **1883** A. S. MURRAY *Hist. Greek Sculpture* II. 55 The Lapiths are youthful, beardless, slim, but firmly knit. **1886** *Guide Exhib. Galleries Brit. Mus.* 77 Sepulchral urn. On the front a Centaur carrying off a female Lapith. **1949** *Oxf. Classical Dict.* 179/2 The fight [*sc.* of the Centaurs] with the Lapiths occurs on the famous François vase and in sculpture on the pediment of the temple of Zeus in Olympia. **1968** *New Larousse Encycl. Mythol.* (new ed.) 169/2 (*caption*) A Centaur struggles with a Lapith at the wedding feast of King Peirithous.

Laplace (lăpla·s). **a.** The name of Pierre Simon, Marquis de *Laplace* (1749–1827), French astronomer and mathematician, used *attrib.* and in the possessive to designate various concepts and mathematical expressions devised by him or arising out of his work, as † **Laplace's coefficient**, a Legendre polynomial; **Laplace's equation**, the equation $\nabla^2 V = 0$, esp. its representation in Cartesian co-ordinates,

$$\frac{\partial^2 V}{\partial x^2} + \frac{\partial^2 V}{\partial y^2} + \frac{\partial^2 V}{\partial z^2} = 0,$$

where V is a function of x, y, and z; **Laplace('s) operator** = *LAPLACIAN *sb.*; **Laplace transform**, a function $f(x)$ related to a given function $g(t)$ by the equation $f(x) = \int_0^\infty \exp(-xt)\, g(t)\,dt$; so **Laplace transformation**, the transformation by which $f(x)$ is obtained from $g(t)$.

1845 F. LUNN in *Encycl. Metrop.* IV. 144 If f be the distance of the differential particle dm from the attracted particle $V = \int dm/f$. We have now to find the quantity V; this we shall do by expanding it into a series, the coefficients of which have peculiar properties, depending upon a partial differential equation to which they are subject... We shall..distinguish them by that [*sc.* name] of their illustrious inventor, calling the differential equation and the coefficients..Laplace's equation, and Laplace's coefficients. **1873** J. C. MAXWELL *Treat. Electr. & Magn.* II. I. ix. 162 The theory of spherical harmonics was first given by Laplace in the third book of his *Mécanique Celeste.* The harmonics themselves are therefore often called Laplace's Coefficients. *Ibid.* 164 It is shewn in treatises on Laplace's Coefficients that Q_i is the coefficient of h^i in the expansion of $(1 - 2\mu h + h^2)^{-1/2}$. **1812** *Phil. Trans. R. Soc.* CII. 31 It is exclusively confined to that class of spheroids which, while they differ from spheres, likewise have their radii expressed by rational and integral functions of a point in the surface of a sphere: in this hypothesis Laplace's equation has been rigorously demonstrated. **1813** *Phil. Mag.* XLI. 9 In Laplace's equation $(d^2V/dx^2) + (d^2V/dy^2) + (d^2V/dz^2) = 0$, ..V is a function of x, y, and z. **1962** CORSON & LORRAIN *Introd. Electromagn. Fields* ii. 36 If we introduce into Eq. 2–23 the electrostatic potential V,.. $\nabla^2 V = -\rho/\epsilon_0$. This is Poisson's equation. In a region of the field where the charge density ρ is zero, $\nabla^2 V = 0$, which is Laplace's equation. *Ibid.* iv. 154 Certain cases of symmetry are best treated in spherical polar coordinates. Laplace's equation then takes the form

$$\nabla^2 V = \frac{1}{r^2}\frac{\partial}{\partial r}\left(r^2 \frac{\partial V}{\partial r}\right) + \frac{1}{r^2 \sin\theta}\frac{\partial}{\partial \theta}\left(\sin\theta \frac{\partial V}{\partial \theta}\right) + \frac{1}{r^2 \sin\theta}\frac{\partial^2 V}{\partial \phi^2} = 0.$$

1873 J. C. MAXWELL *Treat. Electr. & Magn.* I. 29 One of the most remarkable properties of the operator ∇ is that when repeated it becomes $\nabla^2 = -(d^2/dx^2 + d^2/dy^2 + d^2/dz^2)$, an operator occurring in all parts of Physics, which we may refer to as Laplace's Operator. **1935, 1936** Laplace operator [see *LAPLACIAN *sb.*]. **1944** T. H. TURNEY *Heaviside's Operational Calculus made Easy* vii. 84 (*heading*) The Laplace transform method of circuit analysis. **1962** D. R. COX *Renewal Theory* i. 3 One of the main mathematical tools used in renewal theory is the Laplace transform. **1949** S. GOLDMAN *Transformation Calculus* iii. 57 The Laplace transformation transforms $f(t)$, a function of t, into $F(s)$, a function of some new variable s. **1956** *Nature* 21 Jan. 106/2 The approach is mathematical and based throughout on the use of the Laplace transformation. The book is..intended..as a supplement to introductory text-books on feedback systems and on the functions of a complex variable.

b. *Philos.* The name of Laplace (see a above), used in the possessive to designate an imaginary intelligence described by him which, given the values at any instant of certain physical quantities for all the particles in the universe, could predict in detail the whole of the future from the laws of physics.

1911 J. WARD *Realm of Ends* i. 17 The omniscience of Laplace's imaginary spirit with its completed world-formula. **1947** H. REICHENBACH *Elem. Symbolic Logic* viii. 390 Such verification may be technically impossible, although in principle it should be possible to foretell the results of a throw of a die from the initial conditions, given the position of the die, the physiological status of the person considered, and other factors. Let us say that Laplace's superman could do it. **1965** P. CAWS *Philos. of Sci.* xxxix. 300 This intelligence has been called 'Laplace's demon', and it has become the patron saint of determinism.

Laplacian, *a.* Add: Also **Laplacean** (*rare* in the physical sciences). (Earlier and later examples: cf. *LAPLACE.)

1836 *Rep. Brit. Assoc. Adv. Sci. 1835* 27 M. Poisson, indeed, carries much further than Laplace himself the Laplacian views of molecular action. **1852** *Cambr. & Dublin Math. Jrnl.* VII. 127 The class of partial differential equations to which the Laplacian equation belongs. **1908** *Westm. Gaz.* 21 Feb. 2/1 According to the Laplacian hypothesis no 'month' can be shorter than the corresponding day [of the parent planet]. **1911** J. WARD *Realm of Ends* i. 15 Laplace, brushing aside freewill as a palpable illusion, proclaimed the implicit omniscience of the mechanical theory. [*Note*] It was reserved for Clerk Maxwell to point out clearly the inevitable limitation of the Laplacean data. **1920** S. ALEXANDER *Space, Time, & Deity* II. 328 The famous puzzle of the Laplacean calculator is full of confusions but contains a truth. A person who knows the whole state of the universe at any moment can calculate, so it urges, the whole future. **1929** V. BUSH *Operational Circuit Analysis* x. 184

$$f(\omega)/\omega = \int_0^\infty e^{-\omega\lambda} A(\lambda)\,d\lambda.$$

..In an expression of this sort $f(\omega)/\omega$ is called the Laplacian transform of A. **1936** P. M. MORSE *Vibration & Sound* v. 136 Writing the wave equation as $\nabla^2\eta = (\partial^2\eta/\partial t^2)/c^2$ where the symbol ∇^2 is called the Laplacian operator, or simply the Laplacian. It stands for the operation of finding the bulginess of the surface at some point. **1962** SIMPSON & RICHARDS *Physical Princ. Junction Transistors* 468 In these [equations] ∇, $\nabla\cdot$, and ∇^2 are symbols for the gradient, divergence, and Laplacian operators. **1971** I. G. GASS et al. *Understanding Earth* iii. 64/2 The planets have only 0·1% of the mass of the solar system, but 98% of..the energy of angular momentum. From the Laplacian hypothesis [of their origin] the Sun would be expected to have much more angular momentum. **1972** J. RAWLS *Theory of Justice* § 28. 171 They must follow what some may have called the Laplacean rule for choice under uncertainty. The possibilities are identified in some natural way and each assigned the same likelihood.

B. *sb.* The Laplacian operator, i.e. the differential operator ∇^2 ('del squared') that occurs in Laplace's equation.

1935 PAULING & WILSON *Introd. Quantum Mech.* iv. 85 This [Schrödinger] equation is often written as

$$\frac{-h^2}{8\pi^2}\sum_{i=1}^{N}\frac{1}{m_i}\nabla_i^2\Psi + V\Psi = -\frac{h}{2\pi i}\frac{\partial\Psi}{\partial t},$$

in which ∇_i^2 is the Laplace operator or Laplacian for the ith particle. **1936** P. M. MORSE *Vibration & Sound* vii. 232 We can write the wave equation as $\nabla^2 p = (\partial^2 p/\partial t^2)/c^2$... The operator ∇^2 is called the Laplace operator, or the Laplacian: it measures the concentration of a quantity (or, rather, the negative of the concentration). The value of $\nabla^2 p$ at a point is proportional to the difference between the average pressure near a point and the pressure right at the point. **1962** CORSON & LORRAIN *Introd. Electromagn. Fields* i. 17 The product $\nabla.\nabla f$ is commonly abbreviated to $\nabla^2 f$, and the operator ∇^2 is called the Laplacian.

Lapland. Add: **2. Lapland bunting,** a northern species of bunting, *Calcarius lapponicus.*

1862 [see LARK *sb.*[1] 2]. **1912** W. E. CLARKE *Stud. Bird Migration* II. xxiv. 268 Lapland bunting, *Calcarius lapponicus.*—Since our discovery of this species, Eilean Mor has been visited annually. **1953** D. A. BANNERMAN *Birds Brit. Isles* I. 313 The Lapland bunting was added to the British list in 1826, when Selby described an example sent from Cambridgeshire to Leadenhall Market. **1971** *Country Life* 9 Sept. 616/2 Rare visitors [in Yorkshire].. such as..Lapland Bunting.

‖ **laplap, lap-lap** (læ·pˌlæp), *sb.*[2] [Local word.] In New Guinea, a loin-cloth.

1930 M. MEAD *Growing up in New Guinea* xi. 191 A gorgeous new *laplap* proclaims his special state. **1957** O. RUHEN in B. James *Austral. Short Stories* (1963) 197 They were not bush natives, because all three wore cloth laplaps. **1967** 'E. LINDALL' *Time too Soon* i. 3 A couple of policemen, militarily smart in their new uniforms... Earlier they had worn dark blue *laplaps.* **1973** *Sunday Times* (Colour Suppl.) 10 June 51/3 When Michael Somare walked through the bar of a Bougainville motel.. he heard himself described as a 'bush kanaka in a lap-lap'.

‖ **lappa** (læ·pă). *W. Afr.* [Hausa.] A woman's shawl or skirt.

1954 E. WARNER *Trial by Sasswood* (1955) iv. 68 Gloriously decked out from the waist down in a bright new

golden wrap-around *lappa*. **1957** M. BANTON *W. Afr. City* ix. 173 A woman may dance with two or three trilby hats on her head and a man with a woman's *lappa* or shawl, round his shoulders. **1966** C. ACHEBE *Man of People* ix. 100 She rubbed her eyes with a corner of her lappa and blew her nose into it.

lapped, *ppl. a.* **c.** (Later examples.)
1894 J. E. DAVIS *Elem. Mod. Dressmaking* iv. 83 Where the back basque of the bodice is box-pleated, full in any way, or has a lapped centre seam, and is not sewn together much below the waist. **1964** *McCall's Sewing* ix. 130/2 *Single lapped seam.* This seam is used for joining seams in interfacings and interlinings because it gives the least possible bulk.

lappet, *sb.* Add: **5*.** *Weaving.* **a.** A figure produced on cloth during lappet-weaving; also, cloth bearing such figures, lappet-cloth.
1863 J. WATSON *Theory & Pract. Art of Weaving* vi. 207 The framing of a power-loom for weaving Lappets is nearly the same as the framing of one for plain cloth. *Ibid.* 227 In working lappets with the jacquard machine, the length of the figure will depend upon the number of cards used. **1884** *Encycl. Brit.* XVII. 109/2 For window-curtains, hangings, &c., there are manufactured harness and book muslins, lenos, sprigs, spots, and lappets. **1920** R. BEAUMONT *Union Textile Fabrication* ix. 304 Combinations of Lappet and Gauze.—Pattern origination in gauze, lappet, and plain or straight weaving, provides for additional changes in the materials of which the yarns are spun. The lappet (dark sections in Fig. 187) being a surface warp yarn is quite a supplementary element. **1957** *Encycl. Brit.* XXIII. 460/2 Crossed Weaving.—This group includes all fabrics, such as gauzes, in which the warp threads intertwist amongst themselves to give intermediate effects between ordinary weaving and lace. Also those, such as Lappets, in which some warp threads are laid transversely..to imitate embroidery.
b. A mechanism for producing the figures in lappet-weaving.
1894 T. W. FOX *Mechanism of Weaving* IX. 250 Elaborate figures are beyond the range of lappets, still there are many small effects that can be economically woven by them. **1924** W. P. CRANKSHAW *Weaving* xi. 121 Lappets, Swivels, Smallwares and Warp Piles... Lappet and swivel mechanisms are used to produce effects which resemble those obtained by embroidery. **1927** T. THORNLEY *Cotton Spinning* (ed. 4) ix. 311 *(heading)* The lappets or thread boards and wires. *Ibid.*, During recent years metal thread lappets have become very largely used, being much less likely to warp, become damaged or to lose concentricity with the spindles although the first cost of metal lappets is greater than wood ones.

lappie (læ·pi). *S. Afr.* Also formerly **lapje.** [Afrikaans *lappie* (formerly *lapje*).] A dish-cloth, a small rag.
1892 J. WIDDICOMBE *Fourteen Yrs. in Basutoland* vi. 106, I kept them rolled up in a *lappie* (old piece of rag). **1900** B. M. HICKS *Cape as I found It* x. 179 The dish-cloth is a great institution in the Boer household. A dirty bit of 'lapje' (rag) it is. **1926** E. LEWIS *Mantis* IV. xiv. 208 Pouring out a saucerful of water and using his handkerchief for a 'lappie' as he called it, he cleaned the cup. **1939** S. CLOETE *Watch for Dawn* 325 It was a beautiful little dress..and Kaspar never gave back the lappie in which it was wrapped. **1970** *Cape Times* 16 Sept. 7/6 There had been 'dramatic evidence about the finding of the *lappie* and the hair stuck in the middle'.

lapping, *vbl. sb.*[3] Add: (Further examples.) Also *attrib.*, as *lapping machine, plate.*
1907 J. V. WOODWORTH *Grinding & Lapping* II. 65 *(caption)* Flat cast iron lapping plate. *Ibid.* 68 For lapping small thread gages a lapping machine was constructed. **1935** H. J. DAVIES *Precision Workshop Methods* xiii. 242 The general effect produced by lapping is to remove the crests of a ground surface down to the bases of the intervening hollows. **1950** C. R. HINE *Machine Tools for Engineers* xii. 241 Rough lapping may remove as much as 0·003 in., and finish-lapping as little as 0·0001 in... Commercial lapping operations can produce parts to limits of 0·000025 in. **1950** W. COOPER in A. W. Judge *Grinding, Lapping & Polishing* II. vi. 201 The Newall 10U Universal Lapping Machine..is a type employed..for lapping anvils and parts of gauges and the locating rollers of their jig-borers and measuring machines. **1971** B. SCHARF *Engin. & its Lang.* x. 94 Lapping is regularly used in order to finish gear teeth, plug gauges,..straight surfaces, etc.
b. lapping in, the action of grinding in a valve (see *GRIND *v.*[1] 5 b).
1921 *Daily Colonist* (Victoria, B.C.) 12 Oct. 6/1 (Advt.), The quick-seating feature of 'Burd's' Piston Rings enables them to be perfectly and quickly fitted to the engine wall. No slow, laborious 'lapping-in' is necessary. **1950** W. COOPER in A. W. Judge *Grinding, Lapping & Polishing* II. vi. 188 It has long been recognized by bearing and lubrication engineers that the 'lapping-in' method of bearing conditioning, by abrasive means, is the only sure and certain way to obtain best bearing performance and life.

Lapponoid (læ·pŏnoid), *a.* [ad. med.L. *Lap(p)ōn-em* (see LAPP *sb.* and *a.*) + -OID.] Descriptive of racial, particularly cranial, features associated with the early Lapp peoples.
[**1882** QUATREFAGES & HAMY *Crania Ethnica* I. iv. 142 Ce type *Laponoïde*, si l'on peut s'exprimer ainsi,..se confond, suivant nous, avec celui qu'Eschricht, Masch et Nilsson ont les premiers fait connaître.] **1939** C. S. COON *Races of Europe* viii. 288 Czekanowski defines his Lapponoid in such a way as to include the Alpine of Ripley, as well as the Lapps proper. **1948** A. L. KROEBER *Anthropol.* (rev. ed.) iv. § 71. 151 *Yellow Race.* Lapponoid: Enters into several European crossed races. **1957** V. G. CHILDE *Dawn European Civilization* (ed. 6) xi. 209 Most of the skulls from sites in North and Central Russia are described as Lapponoid.

Lapsang Souchong (la·psaŋ sūʃǫ·ŋ). [Cf. SOUCHONG.] A variety of Souchong China tea with a smoky flavour. Also *ellipt.* **Lapsang.**
Lapsang is a 'market name'. In quot. 1942 the spelling *Lapseng* is erron.
1883 *Junior Army & Navy Stores* 71 China Lapsang Souchong. **1935** M. MORPHY *Recipes of all Nations* 726 Among the most popular for exportation are the different grades of Lapsang Souchong. **1938** S. BECKETT *Murphy* v. 68 'I hope you like the aroma,' said Miss Carridge. 'Choicest Lapsang Souchong.' **1942** G. MITCHELL *Laurels are Poison* xvii. 184 Jonathan..took the lid off the teapot, sniffed, said: 'Lapseng? All right, I'll have some.' **1946** *Aristotelian Soc. Suppl. Vol.* XX. 167 X may *think*, without much confidence, that it tastes to him like Lapsang. **1947** A. HUXLEY *Let.* 8 Jan. (1969) 562 We have taken to drinking maté, to which a smoky flavour as of Lapsang Soochong has been imparted. **1962** I. MURDOCH *Unofficial Rose* vii. 69 He took a sip of the sweet Lapsang Suchong. **1966** *Punch* 28 Sept. 476/1 Both knees free for the Lapsang and seedcake. **1973** G. BUTLER *Coffin for Pandora* ii. 71, I drank my favourite Lapsang Souchong tea.

lapsarian (læpsē³·riăn), *sb.* and *a.* [f. L. *laps-us* fall + *-ARIAN, or as back-formation from *infralapsarian*, etc.] **A.** *sb.* (See quot. 1928.) **B.** *adj.* Of or pertaining to the fall of man. Also *transf.*
1928 *Funk's Stand. Dict.*, *Lapsarian*, one who believes in the doctrine of the fall of man from innocence. **1954** DILLENBERGER & WELCH *Protestant Christianity* 91 The holders of lapsarian theories..attempted to safeguard the priority of God's activity by ascribing all events and all happenings to him. **1969** A. RICHARDSON *Dict. Chr. Theol.* 189/2 *(heading)* Lapsarian controversy. **1970** K. MILLETT *Sexual Politics* (1971) 181 The awesome lapsarian moment when the female discovers her inferiority.

lapse, *sb.* Add: **8.** Special Comb. **lapse rate** *Meteorol.*, the rate of fall of temperature with height; also *transf.*
1918 *Meteorol. Gloss.* (Meteorol. Office) 183 *Lapse*,..a word suggested for use instead of gradient..to denote the loss of temperature or pressure of the atmosphere with height. So that *lapse-rate*, or *lapse-ratio*, for temperature will be the fall of temperature per kilometre of height. **1928** D. BRUNT *Meteorol.* vi. 46 The average conditions in the troposphere are specified by a lapse-rate of 3°F. per 1,000 feet. **1957** HALTINER & MARTIN *Dynamical & Physical Meteorol.* xiii. 210 The local increase in lapse rate was due to a combination of low-level warming and high-level cooling by horizontal advection. **1972** *Biol. Abstr.* LIV. 1081/2 The lapse rate of soil temperature indicates a large value in summer and a small one in winter.

lapse, *v.* Add: **1.** Also with *out.*
1920 D. H. LAWRENCE *Women in Love* xxiii. 351 She possessed him so utterly and intolerably that she herself lapsed out. **1928** —— *Phoenix II* (1968) 525 If I could dance all day as well, I might keep going. It's this leaving off that does me in.—And she lapsed out.

lap-streak. Add: Also **lapstrake.** (Earlier U.S. and later examples.) Hence **la·pstraked** *a.* = LAPSTREAKED *a.*
1771 *Boston Gaz.* 11 Mar. (Advt.) (Th.), Whale-boats and all sorts of Lapstreak Boats. **1959** *Times Lit. Suppl.* 9 Jan. 22/4 How to fit clinker (or lapstrake) planking on a hull. **1961** F. H. BURGESS *Dict. Sailing* 130 *Lap jointed, lap straked.* Describes the system of planking as used in clinker-built boats. **1971** *Islander* (Victoria, B.C.) 10 Oct. 2/1 His 25-foot lapstrake boat was built by Vancouver shipbuilders.

laquearia (lækwi,ē³·riă). *rare*[−1]. [L., pl. of *laqueāre* a panelled ceiling.] A ceiling, roof. Cf. LAQUEAR, LAQUEARY.
1922 T. S. ELIOT *Waste Land* ii. 18 Odours..ascended In fattening the prolonged candle-flames, Fling their smoke into the laquearia.

larboarder, *sb. rare.* [f. LARBOARD *sb.*] One who is on the larboard side of a boat.
1846 H. MELVILLE *Typee* vi. 44 The poor larboarders shipped their oars, and commenced pulling us ashore.

larch. Add: **3. larch blister, canker,** a disease caused by the fungus *Trichoscyphella willkommii*, which causes cankers on the bark of larch trees; **larch needle cast,** a disease caused by the fungus *Meria laricis*, which attacks and kills the foliage of larch trees.
1895 W. R. FISHER *Schlich's Man. Forestry* IV. 402 The larch-blister or canker..is most prevalent in damp places with moist air and in frosty and cloudy localities. [**1891** *Jrnl. R. Agric. Soc.* II. 300 In the course of last summer's visit of inspection..the Consulting Botanist found cases of canker in larch plantations all over England and Wales.] **1895** Larch canker [see *larch blister*, above]. **1919** W. E. HILEY *Fungal Dis. Common Larch* ii. 19 At present larch canker is prevalent only in Europe. **1968** F. G. BROWNE *Pests & Dis. Forest Plantation Trees* II. 990 *Trichoscyphella willkommii* (Hartig) Nannf. Fungi, Ascomycotina Helotiales. Synonym: *Dasyscypha willkommii* (Hartig) Rehm. Larch canker. Europe, including Britain and Northern Ireland, and also in the north-eastern United States of America. **1921** *Q. Jrnl. Forestry* XV. 61 The larch needle-cast appears to be very widespread in Britain. **1968** F. G. BROWNE *Pests & Dis. Forest Plantation Trees* II. 877 Larch leaf blight, Larch needle cast. Widely distributed in north western Asia and northern Europe..and also recorded in New Zealand and the United States of America.

lard, *sb.* **2.** Add to def.: Also, in mod. use, any edible pig-fat, and (in commercial use) a fatty preparation containing or resembling lard. (Further examples.)
1881 *Analyst* VI. 233 Watered lard being now used extensively, owing to the high price of the pure quality, we are giving our special attention to its manufacture. **1887** *Buck's Hand-bk. Med. Sci.* IV. 380/2 Commercial lard is so universally impure, either being mixed with water or salt, or having a portion of its liquid oil removed, that it is in general unfit for medicinal use. **1906** L. L. LAMBORN *Mod. Soaps* iii. 44 Two grades of neutral lard are made—one from the leaf, the other from the back fat of the hog. **1913** BOLTON & REVIS *Fatty Foods* iv. 100 Lard is often adulterated with a judicious mixture of beef fat and vegetable oils. **1944** H. G. KIRSCHENBAUER *Fats & Oils* vi. 63 After a Congressional investigation the compounded products which up to then had been sold as 'pure lard', 'refined lard', etc., were required to be labelled 'lard compounds'. **1974** *Guardian* 27 Dec. 9/2 Rub 4 oz butter and 2½ oz lard into 10 oz flour sifted with a pinch of salt.
3. *lard-cake, -pail;* **lard-bladder** *colloq.*, a fat person; **lard compound,** a substitute for lard made from lard stearin, oleostearin, or esp. cottonseed oil; **lard oil** (examples); **lard stearin(e,** the solid residue left after the expression of lard oil from lard, used for stiffening soft lard, as an ingredient of some lard substitutes and margarines, and in the manufacture of some soaps.
1891 KIPLING *Life's Handicap* 195 Mulcahy confused the causes of things, and when a very muzzy Maverick smote a sergeant on the nose or called his commanding officer a bald-headed old lard-bladder..he fancied that rebellion and not liquor was at the bottom of the outbreak. **1928** W. GIBSON *Between Fairs* 19 Ay, but I'd have you know there is offence, when an old lard-bladder of a circus-clown, the likes of you, tries to teach her own business to Nanny Ragtag. **1858** C. M. YONGE *Christmas Mummers* v. 59 Mrs. Harper was..preparing a lard cake for tea. **1861** GEO. ELIOT *Silas Marner* x. 160 Some small lard-cakes, flat paste-like articles. **1904** L. L. LAMBORN *Cottonseed Products* ix. 172 The ingredients of lard-compound are summer white cottonseed-oil and oleo-stearin. **1913** BOLTON & REVIS *Fatty Foods* iv. 103 We have found products described as 'lard compounds' in which no lard was present at all. **1946** *Thorpe's Dict. Appl. Chem.* (ed. 4) VII. 189/1 Under pressure of reformative legislation..the term 'refined lard' was replaced by the expressions 'compound lard' or 'lard compound'..; later the term 'lard compound' was still further restricted to products containing more than 50% of genuine lard. **1843** *Rep. Comm. Patents 1842* (U.S.) 82 The article of lard offered for sale in the market for domestic use, and now about to be so much in demand as material for the manufacture of lard oil and candles, is prepared from the adipose matter of the omentum and mesentery of the hog. **1920** OBERG & JONES *Gage Design* vii. 198 When a very slow cutting abrasive is required and the amount to be removed by lapping is small, rouge and lard oil may be used. **1957** *Encycl. Brit.* XIII. 723/2 Lard oil is the limpid, clear, colourless oil expressed by hydraulic pressure from pure lard after it has been 'grained' by storage at a temperature of 45°F. **1891** *Fur, Fin & Feather* Mar. 195 Two empty lard pails with their covers..will complete the culinary outfit. **1968** R. M. PATTERSON *Finlay's River* 178 Soon the tea-pail—an old lard-pail, smoked and blackened by hundreds of camp fires—was singing, swaying a little over the flames. **1885** W. L. CARPENTER *Treat. Manuf. Soap* ii. 26 The so-called 'lard-stearin' left in the presses is frequently used as a substitute for tallow in the soap-pan, when the price of it is suitable. **1906** L. L. LAMBORN *Mod. Soaps* iii. 46 Lard-stearin of non-edible quality is a soap-stock for certain grades of soap. **1944** H. G. KIRSCHENBAUER *Fats & Oils* vii. 109 Lard stearine and lard oil for edible purposes are obtained from lard by graining and pressing.

larder[1]. Add: **1. c.** The collection of prey formed by a butcher-bird or shrike.
1919 H. F. WITHERBY *Pract. Handbk. Brit. Birds* (1920) I. 277 J. H. Gurnsey also records a shrew impaled in a 'larder' and Oldham a young bank-vole. **1964** A. L. THOMSON *New Dict. Birds* 733/1 Many species [of shrike] have the habit of impaling their prey on thorns..or of hanging it from the fork of a branch... This provision of a 'larder' is responsible for the English popular name 'butcher bird'.
3. larder beetle (examples); **larder bird** = BUTCHER-BIRD.
1895 J. H. & A. COMSTOCK *Man. Study Insects* xxi. 539 The Larder Beetle, *Dermestes lardarius*..is the most common of the larger members of this family. **1942** E. O. ESSIG *College Entomol.* xxxii. 559 Small convex scaly beetles usually feeding on dead or dry animal matter. (Skin or Larder Beetles.) Dermestidæ. **1974** *Times* 16 Apr. 12/7 The larder beetle has been left on the shelf, but a related species..is piling up its numbers. **1948** *Brit. Birds* XLI. 200 Because of the habit of pinning up spare food on thorns the Red-backed Shrike (*Lanius c. collurio*) was far better known in Essex when I lived there, as the Larder Bird.

la·rder, *v. rare.* [f. LARDER[1].] *trans.* To store up as in a larder.
1904 RIDER HAGGARD *Gardener's Year* (1905) July 251 The first wasp which came into being must have paralysed caterpillars and lardered them in key-holes. **1948** *Brit. Birds* XLI. 200 The male bird..is much more given to lardering than the hen.

larding, *vbl. sb.* **c. larding-needle** (earlier and later examples).

1675 S. FELL *Let.* 4 Mar. in *Househ. Acct. Bk. 1673–78* (1920) p. xvii, Two larding needles. **1855** E. ACTON *Mod. Cookery* (rev. ed.) ix. 181 Secure one end of the bacon in a slight larding-needle. **1958** *House & Garden* Feb. 85/1 A larding needle... With this,.. you can thread strips of bacon fat through the breast of a chicken. **1970** SIMON & HOWE *Dict. Gastron.* 239/1 *Larding needle,* a long steel needle with a large eye into which narrow strips of pork fat or larding bacon are threaded.

lardy, *a.* *lardy cake* (earlier and later examples).

1879 C. M. YONGE *Magnum Bonum* I. xiv. 261 Hot tea and 'lardy cake' tendered for his refreshment. **1933** W. DE LA MARE *Lord Fish* 64 She had brought Griselda not only a pitcher of new milk..but some lardy-cakes and a jar of honey. **1970** SIMON & HOWE *Dict. Gastron.* 239/2 *Lardy cake,* country-style bread-dough cakes which appear in several English counties: Sussex, Wiltshire, Oxfordshire and Cambridgeshire.

lare, var. *LAIR *sb.*[4]

lares: see LAR.

larf. ¶. Jocular spelling of LAUGH *sb.* and *v.*, esp. representing Cockney speech.

1847 *Punch* XII. 2/1 She is so innocent..a half-larfin, and a half-poutin. **1851** MRS. STOWE *Uncle Tom's Cabin* (1852) I. iv. 45 'And what did mother say?' said George. 'Say?—why, she kinder larfed in her eyes—dem great handsome eyes o' hern...' **1894** KIPLING *Day's Work* (1898) 62 The folks..larfed—why, they all but lay down themselves with larfin'. **1901** M. FRANKLIN *My Brilliant Career* (1966) xxxi. 196 A sorrowful lookin' delicate creetur', that couldn't larf to save her life. **1965** L. DEIGHTON *Horse under Water* iii. 19 'I'll larf, sir, that's what I will do; larf.' The Chief gave no sign of laughing either now or at any future time: I thought for a moment that LARF was some strange nautical verb. **1968** —— (*title*) Only when I larf. **1971** *Guardian* 8 Apr. 10/2 Give us a larf, pass the time.

‖ **larga** (lā·ɹgă). [Sp.] In bull-fighting, a pass using the cape (see quots.).

1932 E. HEMINGWAY *Death in Afternoon* xv. 170 Quites were made..by the use of largas. In these the cape was fully extended and one end offered to the bull who was drawn away following the extended cape and then turned on himself to fix him in place by a movement made by the matador who would swing the cape over his shoulder and walk away. **1957** A. MACNAB *Bulls of Iberia* v. 52 It is now the job of the peones to 'run' it, *correr al toro.* That means, to wave capes at it, get it to charge the capes, and give it long-distance passes. These are called *largas,* the big cape being held by one tip and sent flying out at full length. **1967** MCCORMICK & MASCAREÑAS *Compl. Aficionado* ii. 61 He works the toro with *largas. Ibid.*, In the larga, the cape is trailed in the sand with one hand as the torero runs (bregar) the toro.

Largactil (lā·ɹgæ·ktil). *Pharm.* Also **largactil.** A proprietary name of chlorpromazine hydrochloride, $C_{17}H_{19}ClN_2S{\cdot}HCl$, the form in which chlorpromazine is usually administered.

1953 *Trade Marks Jrnl.* 20 May 430/1 Largactil... May & Baker Limited, Dagenham, Essex; manufacturing chemists. **1965** J. POLLITT *Depression & its Treatment* iv. 56 In uncomplicated cases, the intramuscular injection of chlorpromazine (Largactil) 100 mg. is helpful. **1966** *New Statesman* 4 Feb. 168/1 Others might use a quarter grain of Largactil to take the edge off life in London or the Midlands. **1970** G. GREER *Female Eunuch* 90 If all else fails largactil..and other forms of 'therapy' will buttress the claim of society.

‖ **largamente** (lā:ɹgăme·nte), *adv. Mus.* [It.] (See quots.)

1876 STAINER & BARRETT *Dict. Mus. Terms* 252/1 *Largamente* (*It.*), slowly, widely, freely, fully. **1880** GROVE *Dict. Mus.* II. 92/1 (s.v. *largo*), The term *Largamente* has recently come into use to denote breadth of style without change of *tempo.* **1958** *Times* 27 Nov. 6/6 He did cause just one raised eyebrow with the very much slower tempo he adopted for the *largamente* second subject tune in the finale.

‖ **largando** (lāɹgæ·ndo), *adv. Mus.* [It.] = *ALLARGANDO.

1893 J. S. SHEDLOCK tr. *Riemann's Dict. Mus.* 429/1 *Largando* (*slargando, allargando*) Ital., 'broadening'; as a rule it is united with *crescendo.* **1972** *Harper's Dict. Mus.* 178/1 *Largando*..Italian, another spelling of *allargando.*

large, *a.*, *adv.*, and *sb.* Add: **A.** *adj.* **8. b.** Further examples of use, esp. in names of plants and animals.

The compar. *larger* and superl. *largest* are also used in specific names, as *larger cabinet beetle, larger red-crested woodpecker, largest red oak.*

Large Black (pig), a pig belonging to the variety so called, developed late in the 19th century and formerly called the Devonshire Black; **Large White** (pig), a heavy bacon pig of the variety so called, first introduced in Yorkshire about 1850 and formerly called the Yorkshire pig.

1787 W. SARGENT in *Mem. Amer. Acad. Arts & Sci.* 1793) II. 159 Large Laurel. **1810** F. A. MICHAUX *Hist. Arbres Forestiers de l'Amérique Septentrionale* I. 39 American large aspen..nom donné par moi. **1813** H. MUHLENBERG *Catal. Plant.* 92 Large aspen (*Populus trepida* or *grandidentata*). **1832** D. J. BROWNE *Sylva Amer.* 255 As it surpasses the aspen in height, we have given it the name of Large Aspen. **1832** J. RENNIE *Conspectus Butterflies & Moths Brit.* 259/1 Large Blue..Large Copper. **1832** T. BROWN *Bk. Butterflies, Sphinxes & Moths* I. 18 (*heading*) The large white cabbage butterfly. **1837** *Southern Lit. Messenger* III. 660 There are for sale hats, boots and shoes, India rubber articles,..large bread,..everything on earth. **1845** C. M. KIRKLAND *Western Clearings* 154 'You'd ought to begin with large-hand, Joshuay,' said Master Horner to this youth [instructing him in penmanship]. **1857** H. T. STAINTON *Man. Brit. Butterflies & Moths* I. 11 The Swallow-tail and the Large Copper are only to be obtained in the fens of Cambridgeshire and Huntingdonshire. **1859** BAGEHOT *Coll. Works* (1965) II. 190 A large-hand copy of life. **1867** *Jrnl. R. Agric. Soc.* III. 633 Some of the classes, the large white breed and those not qualified for the specified classes were only scantily filled. **1876** H. E. SCUDDER *Dwellers in Five-Sisters Court* i. 7 There was a large-bread bakery at Skōlas. **1896** W. J. MALDEN *Pig Keeping for Profit* i. 12 The Large White started with a strong frame. **1906** J. LONG *Bk. Pig* (ed. 2) xii. 156 The Large Blacks are regarded as being of gentle disposition... The chief counties in which the Large Black pig is bred are Cornwall and Devon. **1947** J. STEVENSON-HAMILTON *Wild Life S. Afr.* xxv. 205 The large grey mongoose (*Herpestes caffer*).—Colour, grizzled grey, limbs darker. A black brush at the end of the tail. Length over all, about 45 inches. This animal is spread throughout the Ethiopian region. **1961** J. FITZHUGH *Pig Breeding* xiv. 160 The National Pig Breeders' Association caters for the Large Blacks, Large Whites, [etc.]. **1966** E. PALMER *Plains of Camdeboo* x. 181 The large grey mongoose is nocturnal and rarely seen. **1970** *Times* 19 Aug. 9/7 There are five or six species (e.g. the Large Blue or Glanville Fritillary) which ought to be protected. **1971** *Farmers Weekly* (Extra) 19 Mar. 37/2 The Farnsworths fatten all progeny from a herd of 60 Welsh sows, put to the Large White boar. **1973** T. G. HOWARTH *South's Brit. Butterflies* 51 The tiny parasitic wasp, *Apanteles glomeratus* Linnaeus..normally acts as a control to the common Large White caterpillar.

i. *law of large numbers* [tr. F. *loi des grands nombres* (S. D. Poisson 1835, in *Compt. Rend.* I. 478)]: a statistical law which states that if a series of independent trials or observations is made, in each of which there is the same probability of a particular outcome, then as the number of trials is made larger the chance that the observed proportion of such outcomes differs from the probability by less than any given number, however small, approaches a certainty (or, in stronger terms, the observed proportion approaches the probability).

[**1921** J. M. KEYNES *Treat. Probability* xxviii. 336 The 'Law of Great Numbers' is not at all a good name for the principle which underlies Statistical Induction. The 'Stability of Statistical Frequencies' would be a much better name for it. The former suggests, as perhaps Poisson intended..., what is certainly false, that every class of event shows statistical regularity of occurrence if only one takes a sufficient number of instances of it. It..encourages the method..by which it is thought legitimate to take an observed degree of frequency or association, which is shown in a fairly numerous set of statistics, and to assume..that, because the statistics are numerous, the observed degree of frequency is therefore stable.] **1937** J. V. USPENSKY *Introd. Math. Probability* x. 182 A far reaching generalization of Bernoulli's theorem, known under the name of the 'law of large numbers'. **1949** W. KNEALE *Probability & Induction* III. 139 Many people who have heard of it under the name of the law of large numbers..suppose it to be a mysterious law of nature which guarantees that in a sufficiently large number of trials a probability will be 'realized as a frequency'. *Ibid.* 141 As an illustration of the importance of the law of large numbers in practical affairs it will be sufficient to mention the business of insurance... The greater the number of persons insuring with the company, the greater the probability that the company's finances will remain sound. **1960** S. GOLDBERG *Probability* iv. 227 The law of large numbers can be used to supply a theoretical counterpart to our intuitive feeling that if an event *A* occurs *f* times in *n* identical trials and if *n* is large, then *f/n*, the proportion of times *A* occurs, should be near the probability *P*(*A*) of the event *A*.

j. larger-than-life *attrib. phr.* Cf. LIFE *sb.* 7 a.

1950 *New Yorker* 23 Dec. 42 Inviting Mr. Churchill..as the living, larger-than-life embodiment of the British people's opposition to appeasement. **1967** *Sunday Times* 23 Apr. 49 The larger-than-life political figures thunder their dogmas through the act. **1972** D. FRANCIS *Smokescreen* ii. 27, I had very little in common with the sort of larger-than-life action man I played in film after film. **1972** *Jazz & Blues* Oct. 22/1 For many years Mezzrow was an almost larger than life personality.

15. a. *large-berried, -billed, -featured, -flowered, -framed* (earlier example), *-fruited, -leaved, -mouthed, -scaled* adjs.; *large-angle, -aperture, -denomination, -signal, -size* adjs. **c. large calorie** = *CALORIE a; **large-lung** *a. Path.* = *large-lunged* adj.; **large-mouth (bass)** (earlier and later examples); also **large-mouthed bass; large-scale** *a.*, drawn to a large scale, on a large scale, extensive, widespread, relating to large numbers; so **large-scale integration** *Electronics*, the development or use of integrated circuits that each contain a large number of components.

1956 *Nature* 3 Mar. 413/1 Large-angle scatters of cosmic-ray particles. **1966** D. G. BRANDON *Mod. Techniques Metallogr.* iii. 138 Few electrons are backscattered out of the target, and those which do escape do so principally by large-angle Rutherford collisions. **1935** *Discovery* Jan. 25/1 The picture was taken on sensitised paper, probably with a small short-focus camera having a large-aperture lens. **1966** D. G. BRANDON *Mod. Techniques Metallogr.* i. 10 Using a large-aperture reflecting surface to give good resolution and a reflecting plate to project the reflected image into the microscope column. **1785** G. WASHINGTON *Diary* 2 Mar. (1925) II. 346 Planted..all the large berried thorns. **1835** J. J. AUDUBON *Ornith. Biogr.* III. 599 The birds observed were Large-billed Puffins. **1908** E. J. BANFIELD *Confessions of Beachcomber* I. iii. 123 Many of the birds are..named in accordance with their notes...'Piln-piln' the large-billed shore plover. **1954** FISHER & LOCKLEY *Sea-Birds* 294 *Phaëtusa simplex,* large-billed tern. **1927** HALDANE & HUXLEY *Animal Biol.* iii. 88 The kilocalorie of 1,000 calories is the unit of energy which is most useful in human physiology. It is sometimes called the 'Large calorie'. **1973** P. EVANS *Bodyguard Man* ii. 19 A wallet thick with large-denomination banknotes. **1974** J. CLEARY *Peter's Pence* viii. 237 The large-denomination notes would be distributed by those banks. **1847** THOREAU *Let.* 29 Dec. in *Corr.* (1958) 200 He is large featured. **1963** J. FOUNTAIN in B. James *Austral. Short Stories* 269 His face, large-featured, serious and brown. **1813** H. MUHLENBERG *Catal. Plant.* 53 Large-flowered Custard Apple. **1846** D. J. BROWNE *Trees Amer.* 2 The Large-flowered Magnolia is most remarkable. **1952** A. G. L. HELLYER *Sanders' Encycl. Gardening* (ed. 22) 142 There are many large-flowered hybrid strains [of cyclamen] in cultivation. **1971** J. RAVEN *Botanist's Garden* iv. 84 Our native large-flowered Geraniums.. afford excellent illustrations..of the second type of plant distribution. **1869** *Rep. Comm. Agric. 1868* (U.S. Dept. Agric.) 438 Large-framed, wide and straight-backed, and deep-bodied, short-horn cows. **1813** H. MUHLENBERG *Catal. Plant.* 48 Large fruited Hawthorn. *Ibid.* 88 Large-fruited Shellbark hickory. **1952** A. G. L. HELLYER *Sanders' Encycl. Gardening* (ed. 22) 198 Large-fruited varieties [of strawberry] now in cultivation are all hybrids. **1785** H. MARSHALL *Arbustrum Americanum* 93 Large-leaved Virginian Mulberry Tree. **1832** D. J. BROWNE *Sylva Amer.* 212 We have given it the specific name of Large-Leaved Umbrella Tree. **1957** M. HADFIELD *Brit. Trees* 399 Large-leaved Lime-tree... This species varies a good deal, and has for long been extensively planted as an ornamental tree. **1974** *Country Life* 28 Nov. 1639/3 The large-leaved rhododendrons..will grow only on acid soils. **1961** R. D. BAKER *Essent. Path.* xv. 372 Hypertrophic, or 'large lung' emphysema, is seen at autopsy as voluminous lungs which do not collapse when the pleural cavities are opened. **1884** G. B. GOODE *Fisheries U.S.: Nat. Hist. Aquatic Animals* 401 The Large-mouth is known in the Great Lake region..as the 'Oswego Bass'. **1973** *Sat. Rev. World* (U.S.) 4 Dec. 47/3 Fresh-water fishermen..can try for..large-mouth bass. **1878** C. HALLOCK *Sportsman's Gazetteer* 679 Large mouthed bass. **1883** 'MARK TWAIN' *Life on Mississippi* 264 Every detail of the pilot-house was familiar to me, with one exception—a large-mouthed tube under the breast-board. **1883** *Century Mag.* July 376/2 There are but two well-defined species, the large-mouthed bass and the small-mouthed bass. **1919** E. POUND *Quia Pauper Amavi* 39 Oh august Pierides! Now for a large-mouthed product. **1956** *Nature* 3 Mar. 413/2 The fish is related to the freshwater large-mouthed bass of the eastern United States. **1887** Large scale [see SCALE *sb.*[3] 11 a]. **1897** [in Dict., sense 15 a]. **1907** *Daily Chron.* 9 Dec. 3/3 Schumann is a minor poet among musicians. We remember his lesser things..and remain cold to his large-scale pieces. **1920** T. P. NUNN *Education* ix. 114 This large-scale experiment. **1934** *Discovery* Oct. 303/2 We do not all realise that the first large-scale (6-inch) survey of these islands was made in Ireland. *a* **1942** B. MALINOWSKI *Sci. Theory of Culture* (1944) vii. 72 Every army must get along on its stomach and..also most large-scale organizations. **1952** V. A. DEMANT *Relig. & the Decline of Capitalism* i. 21 A period which preceded the appearance of large-scale manufacturing industry. **1957** L. F. R. WILLIAMS *State of Israel* 33 The Security Council's action brought large-scale fighting in Palestine to an end. **1966** *AFIPS Conference Proceedings* XXIX. (1966 Fall Jt. Computer Conf.) 65/1 We are now entering another phase of the expansion of materials technology, in which complete equipment components will be processed on slices of semiconductor... This phase has already been given several names, some of which are 'large-scale integration' (LSI), 'computer on a slice', and 'array technology'. The term 'large-scale integration' is close to being the most descriptive, although at times the syntax is awkward. A somewhat more precise term is 'large-scale integrated electronics'. We will use LSI to abbreviate both 'large-scale integrated electronics' and 'large-scale integration'. **1967** *Proc. IEEE* LV. 1988/2 Large scale integration (LSI) presents an opportunity to exploit many of the concepts of design automation. **1968** *Times* 24 Oct. 7/7 The permissible number of large-scale accidents in nuclear reactors should be about one every 100 million years. **1970** *Sci. Amer.* Feb. 22/1 The technology that produces such high-density electronic circuits is called large-scale integration, or LSI. Although the term has no precise definition, it is usually reserved for integrated circuits that comprise 100 or more 'gates', or individual circuit functions, laid down with a density of 50,000 to 100,000 components per square inch. **1973** A. BEHREND *Samarai Affair* iii. 30 The large-scale model which occupied the centre of the big oval table..was made of painted wood and represented the approaches to the Port of Liverpool. **1869** Large-scaled [see *brown-banded snake]. **1936** J. T. JENKINS *Fishes Brit. Isles* (ed. 2) 157 The Hake is a large-scaled member of the cod family. **1955** COBLENZ & OWENS *Transistors* xi. 146 No truly large-signal theory for transistors exists today that can be applied directly by the design engineer. **1962** SIMPSON & RICHARDS *Physical Princ. Junction Transistors* vii. 139 Other applications in which transistors are used to a considerable extent include the following: 1. Large-signal steady-state amplification. [Etc.] **1904** *Westm. Gaz.* 30 Mar. 2/1 A reason for utilising the gas-engine as a large-size power unit for central engine work. **1960** E. DELAVENAY *Introd. Machine Transl.* 93 A large-size dictionary.

B. *adv.* **3.** Delete † *Obs.* and add later U.S. examples.

1834 S. Smith *Sel. Lett. J. Downing* 149 Other folks may talk larger and bluster more. **1872** in A. W. Tourgée *Fool's Errand* (1880) II. v. 411 He had just talked large about the Ku-Klux.

C. *sb.* **5. f.** *gentleman-at-large*: see Gentleman 2 c.

k. *verdict at large*: see Verdict *sb.* 1 c.

8. b. *in the large*: also, in general, as a whole.

1943 *Sun* (Baltimore) 24 Aug. 2/6 In the large, there is something else to be said for this recent destruction of more than one hundred of the enemy's fighter planes. **1961** A. J. Deutsch in 'E. Crispin' *Best SF Four* 75 The missing persons did not return. In the large, they were no longer missed. **1968** *Times* 15 Oct. 16/7 Much of the information needed to produce a uniformly precise map therefore will be missing. However, it is only the picture in the large that will suffer.

larghetto (lāɹge·to). *Mus.* [It., dim. of Largo.] A term indicating that a passage is to be played slowly; also, a movement or passage played in this way.

1724 *Short Explication Foreign Words in Musick Bks.* 40 *Largetto, or Larghetto* denotes a Movement a little quicker than *Largo.* **1801** Busby *Dict. Mus., Larghetto*... A word specifying a time not quite so slow as that denoted by *Largo*, of which word it is the diminutive. **1877** G. B. Shaw *How to become Mus. Critic.* (1960) 28 The overture was taken too rapidly at the *larghetto.* **1958** *Listener* 4 Dec. 964/3 The beautiful *larghetto* from the E minor *sinfonia.* **1959** *Times* 2 Feb. 12/4 In Haydn's F major sonata..there was finesse in his phrasing of its central larghetto. **1970** *Oxf. Compan. Mus.* (ed. 10) 566/1 *Larghetto*,..slow and dignified.

lark, *sb.*[1] Add: **3.** *lark-note, -pie, pudding; lark-charmed, -crested, -high* adjs.; **lark bunting,** the prairie bobolink, *Calamospiza melanocorys*, a bird found on the plains of central North America.

1869 *Amer. Naturalist* III. 296 That pretty and musical bird of the high plains, the Lark Bunting (*Calamospiza bicolor*), also occurred [along the Upper Missouri River]. **1963** R. D. Symons *Many Trails* iii. 30 Small black ones [*sc.* birds] with white wing patches, which the children at once called white wings, not knowing that they were lark buntings. **1879** G. M. Hopkins *Poems* (1918) 41 Cuckoo-echoing, bell-swarmèd, lark-charmèd. **1848** E. S. Dixon *Ornamental & Domestic Poultry* 319 Lark-crested Fowls are of various colours; pure snow-white, brown with yellow hackles, and black. **1909** *Westm. Gaz.* 29 Dec. 8/3 Sometimes he wings straight up, lark-high, into the blue. **1946** Dylan Thomas *Deaths & Entrances* 22 A stone lies lost and locked in the lark-high hill. **1866** R. Leighton in *Westm. Gaz.* (1909) 6 Mar. 6/3 Deep in my soul the throbbing lark-notes lie. **1906** *Westm. Gaz.* 14 Apr. 6/2 Yet hear the lark-note piercing the grey morn. **1723** J. Nott *Cook's & Confectioner's Dict.* sig. R6 (*heading*) To make a Lark Pye. **1861** Mrs. Beeton *Bk. Househ. Managem.* 479 (*heading*) Lark Pie (an Entree). **1910** W. de la Mare *Three Mulla-Mulgars* xii. 166 What's lark-pie to a hungry sailor? **1963** T. Fitzgibbon *Game Cooking* 96 Lark pie. **1863** G. Meredith *Let.* 1 Feb. (1970) I. 189 A new Receipt:—I try it at Orridge's tonight. '*Lark Pood'n*'. **1877** E. S. Dallas *Kettner's Bk. of Table* 272 *Lark Pudding or Pie.*—For the perfection of a lark pudding, go to the Cheshire Cheese, in Fleet Street. **1934** J. J. Williams *Seasonal Cook. Bk.* 263 Lark pudding... Grease a pudding basin... Clean and bone the larks.

lark, *sb.*[2] Add: **2.** An affair, line of business, etc. *colloq.*

1934 P. Allingham *Cheapjack* xiii. 167 There are many Jews among the grafters, but they usually stick to the chocolate 'lark'—or auction. **1936** [see *con c]. **1961** *New Statesman* 22 Sept. 376/3 Exhibitionists they may be but they mean business. This wet sitting for hours on end is not my lark. **1964** J. Porter *Dover One* i. 11 There's an outbreak of fowl pest..or something and, naturally, that's far more up his street than one of these vanishing-lady larks. **1967** G. F. Fiennes *I tried to run a Railway* iii. 28 Jeremy came in one day while this lark was going on. *Ibid.* vii. 86, I am up to my ears in this bloody diesel lark.

lark, *v.*[2] Etym. note, last line, read: 'which is found a few years earlier (1809)'.

larked (lāɹkt), *a. poet. nonce-wd.* [f. Lark *sb.*[1] + -ed[2].] With larks overhead, noisy with the song of larks.

1952 Dylan Thomas *Coll. Poems* 173, I hear the bouncing hills Grow larked.

larkiness (lā·ɹkinės). [f. Larky *a.* + -ness.] The quality of being larky; sportiveness.

1896 *Columbus* (Ohio) *Dispatch* 22 Aug., In reality he [*sc.* a choirboy] is the incarnation of all that is mischievous; and..if he sings at a cathedral or important church, the more 'larkiness' is found in his composition. **1905** Chesterton *Heretics* 90 It is hard to see at first sight why so human a thing as leisure and larkiness should always have a religious origin. **1924** R. Hichens *After Verdict* II. xx. 303 The ball-boys stood ready, looking alert and full of suppressed larkiness. **1928** *Observer* 26 Feb. 15/3 Miss Helen Gilliland..has great quality.., but she needs the supreme gift for this work, of larkiness. **1973** *Times Lit. Suppl.* 30 Nov. 1466/4 Wastage or mere larkiness is fatal both to its intention and execution.

larkish, *a.* (Earlier and later examples.)

1823 *Spirit of Public Jrnls. M.DCCC.XXIII* (1825) I. 75 She went to see the lamplighter's burying, and the folks were all very merry 'and quite *larkish*, in a manner'. **1926** F. M. Ford *Man could stand Up* I. ii. 32 The larkish freak of a school-girl.

larkspur. Add: **b.** The blue colour characteristic of the larkspur.

1927 *Sunday Express* 27 Feb., Newest Season's colours including..Grey, Cocoa, Larkspur, Fawn. **1927** *Daily Express* 12 Mar. 3/5 Larkspur, a pastel blue slightly inclining to the mauve.

larky, *a.* Add: (Earlier and later examples.)

1841 *Punch* 25 Dec. 278/2 The old girl has her two nieces home for the holidays—devilish handsome, larky girls. **1909** [see *buck *v.*[7] 2 a]. **1911** E. M. Clowes *On Wallaby* ii. 35 The young people..are loud and larky and irreverent. **1912** D. H. Lawrence *Lett.* (1932) 28 Every blessed place was full of men, in the larkiest of spirits. **1958** *Vogue* July 57 Osborne has shocked the stage with a real-life genus of larky lower-middle class humanists and given them the heroic status of being worried. **1967** *Listener* 8 June 747/2 A character in whom humility and submissiveness are combined with a larky humour. **1974** *Ibid.* 21 Nov. 673/1 The only disk jockey who sounds genuinely happy... Larky, insouciant and very funny.

b. *transf.*

1925 *Blackw. Mag.* July 80/2 (*Rugby School*) The 'swells' were allowed to wear 'larky' waistcoats, *i.e.*, waistcoats of various hues often with flowery designs embroidered on them.

Larmor (lā·ɹməɹ). *Physics.* The name of Sir Joseph *Larmor* (1857–1942), Irish-born physicist, used *attrib.* and in the possessive with reference to a theorem enunciated by him in 1897, according to which the effect of a uniform magnetic field on a rotating particle is (to a first approximation) to cause the frame of reference in which the particle is rotating to rotate in turn about the direction of the magnetic flux with a frequency $\gamma B/2\pi$ (where γ is the magnetomechanical ratio and B the magnetic induction), which for an orbital electron in a monatomic molecule represents a precessional frequency of $eB/4\pi m$ (e and m being the charge and mass of the electron); so *Larmor frequency, precession; Larmor's theorem*; also **Larmor radius,** the radius of the helical path of a free charged particle spiralling about magnetic field lines.

1923 Larmor's theorem [see *Coriolis]. **1926** E. C. Stoner *Magnetism & Atomic Struct.* iv. 68 The Larmor precession is of great importance in the treatment of the Zeeman effect, this and diamagnetism being different aspects of the same phenomenon. **1951** *Physical Rev.* LXXXIII. 1000/2 The Larmor frequency, $\omega_p = 2\mu_p H/\hbar$, of a sample of protons in the magnetic field is measured by the resonance absorption method. **1957** B. I. & B. Bleaney *Electr. & Magn.* viii. 186 As a consequence of the Larmor precession, each electron acquires a component of angular momentum about the direction of [the magnetic induction] **B**. **1962** W. B. Thompson *Introd. Plasma Physics* vii. 151 In a magnetic field a second length becomes important, the Larmor radius, r_L, i.e. the radius of the circle formed by the particle orbit about the magnetic field lines. **1971** D. W. Sciama *Mod. Cosmol.* ii. 36 The galactic magnetic field thus has an important effect on the motion of cosmic rays if their Larmor radius is substantially less than the size of the Galaxy.

larn (lāɹn), *v. colloq.* [f. dial. form of Learn *v.* 4; see *E.D.D.* for further examples.] *trans.* To teach; to give (a person) a lesson; freq. used ironically as a threat of punishment.

1790 T. Wilkinson *Mem.* I. 117 You are unfit for the stage, Muster Whittington, and I won't larn you—you may go, Muster Whittington. **1851** [see *jes, jes']. **1899** *Manch. Guardian* 13 Mar. 10/1 Said Mr. Dooley, '..we'll larn thim a lesson.' **1902** E. Nesbit *Five Children & It* viii. 204 I'll larn you, you young varmint! **1928** 'Brent of Bin Bin' *Up Country* xiii. 228 The taller ruffian put a bullet in the wall above his head just to larn him, and his companions advised him to be still. **1931** W. Holtby *Poor Caroline* v. 180 'I'll larn her,' swore he to himself. **1949** 'J. Tey' *Brat Farrar* xvii. 183 Bee took him to call on the tenants... 'Gates last; just to larn him,' Bee said. **1956** C. Blackstock *Dewey Death* ix. 216 That'll larn you, you so-and-sos.

larnax (lā·ɹnæks). *Gr. Antiq.* Pl. **larnakes** (lā·ɹnăkīz). [Gr. λάρναξ chest, urn.] A chest, ossuary, urn, or coffin, usually of terra cotta, frequently ornamented with designs.

1870 *Catal. Greek & Etruscan Vases Brit. Mus.* II. 191 In the centre Aphroditê seated on a chest, *larnax*, and looking back at a youthful male figure. **1901** A. J. Evans *Mycenaean Tree & Pillar Cult* 77 In a chambered tomb at Milato..was a painted clay ossuary chest or larnax of the usual Cretan type. **1901** *Rep. Brit. Assoc. Adv. Sci.* 444 The one [tomb], a square chamber with a dromos, yielded parts of two painted *larnakes*, thoroughly Mycenean in design. **1904** *Westm. Gaz.* 24 Aug. 7/3 A later cemetery, containing larnax burials, yielded bronze implements, beads, and vases like those in the palace magazines. **1910** *Encycl. Brit.* I. 248/2 The Cretan 'larnax' coffins..have no parallels outside the Aegean. **1939** V. G. Childe *Dawn European Civilization* (ed. 3) ii. 24 Individual burial..in clay coffins (larnakes). *Ibid.* 27 Larnax burials.

larnite (lā·ɹnəit). *Min.* [f. *Larne*, the name of a town in Co. Antrim, N. Ireland + -ite[1].] A mineral consisting of a metastable monoclinic phase of dicalcium silicate, Ca_2SiO_4.

1929 C. E. Tilley in *Mineral. Mag.* XXII. 79 Next in importance to spurrite comes a mineral consisting of calcium orthosilicate. As this is the first recorded natural occurrence of this compound it is proposed to designate it as larnite, from Larne, in the vicinity of which these contact minerals occur. **1950** *Ibid.* XXIX. 182 Both the nagelschmidtite and larnite phases have been seen in slags. **1957** *Amer. Mineralogist* XLII. 384 The larnite zone is very prominent, forming a band about thirty inches thick, dark grey to almost black in color, hard, flinty, and very tough. The dark color is..due to..the presence of a small amount of very fine-grained magnetite. Pure larnite is presumably white. **1966** [see *bredigite].

Larose (laro·z). [Name of some vineyards in the Bordeaux area of France.] A type of claret; the vineyard or area itself.

1841 Thackeray in *Fraser's Mag.* June 720/1 It is my firm opinion that a third-rate Burgundy, and a third-rate claret—Beaune and Larose for instance, are *better* than the best. **1863** G. Meredith *Let.* 3 Feb. (1970) I. 190 Vins..Claret—Larose. **1920** G. Saintsbury *Notes on Cellar-Bk.* iv. 66 It is true that some of the very best vineyards (Léoville, Larose, Ducru-Beau-Caillou..) are situated there [*sc.* at Saint-Julien]. **1958** A. L. Simon *Dict. Wines* 99/2 Larose, Château. There are several wine-producing estates in the Gironde bearing this name, mostly hyphenated with the name or names of present or past owners.

larrigan (læ·rigăn). *N. Amer.* Also 9 **larigan, larrigin.** [Of unknown origin.] A long boot made of undressed leather.

1886 *Engineering News* XVI. 99/1 And the ordinary foot-gear is a pair of cow-hide moccasins (called shoe-packs or larrigans). **1889** *Amer. N. & Q.* III. 308 A *larigan*, or *larrigin*, in Maine and New Brunswick, is a kind of boot or moccasin of yellow leather, having a long leg reaching above the knee. It is worn by lumbermen in the deep snows of winter. **1915** *Outing* (U.S.) Oct. 27/2 A 'shoe-pac' or 'larrigan' is a beef-hide moccasin with eight to ten-inch top, and with or without a light, flexible sole. **1922** *Short Stories* (U.S.) Feb. 128/2 Over six feet in his larrigans. **1931** 'Grey Owl' *Men of Last Frontier* 180, I was much hampered by a pair of still hard-soled larrigans which I had donned. **1961** *Saturday Night* (Toronto) 23 Dec. 18/1 After breakfast that day I rode to school.. wearing a pair of cowhide larrigans greasy with linseed oil. **1968** E. R. Buckler *Ox Bells & Fireflies* ii. 25 Little Tim was six foot seven..who could yet sew a larrigan together with the waxed end neater than a woman could hemstitch.

Hence **la·rriganed** *a.*, wearing larrigans.

1904 C. G. D. Roberts *Watchers of Trails* 287 Then turning on his larriganed heels, he strode up the trail. **1922** *Short Stories* Feb. 129/1 [The dogs] clipped fangs at Cherriman's larriganed legs.

larrikin. Add: [Wright, Suppl. to *E.D.D.*, cites *larrikin* 'a mischievous or frolicsome youth' from informants in Warwickshire and Worcestershire; see also quot. 1882. Cf. *E.D.D.*, *Larack* (*larack about*, to 'lark' about), cited from C. C. Robinson's *Dial. of Leeds* (1861).] (Further examples.) Also *transf.* and *attrib.*

1868 H. W. Harper *Lett. from N.Z.* (1914) vii. 123 We are beset with larrikins, who lurk about in the darkness and deliver every sort of attack on the walls and roof with stones and sticks. **1871** *Evening Post* (Wellington, N.Z.) 27 Apr. 2/4 Such rowdyism I never saw before, even in Melbourne and San Francisco, the hotbeds of larrikins. **1882** F. W. P. Jago *Anc. Lang. & Dial. Cornwall* 205 *Larrikins*, mischievous young fellows, larkers. 'Mischievous larrikins who pull the young trees down.' *The Cornishman.* **1901** *Daily Tel.* 8 Mar. 8/7 The larrikins of the Legislature..could not be visited retrospectively with an adequate punishment. **1925** E. Wallace *King by Night* xlix. 224 The desire of the larrikin for closer association with his social superiors. **1943** D. Stewart in *Coast to Coast 1942* 204 For all his larrikin assurance, Les was afraid to put his feeling for Leila into words. **1966** 'J. Hackston' *Father clears Out* 26 It had headed straight for the sturdiest, roughest, most larrikin-looking mob of cattle. **1972** *Southerly* XXXII. 199 He had come around a corner in a corridor to find her confronting a larrikin from 2D.

larrikinism (further examples).

1871 *Evening Post* (Wellington, N.Z.) 27 Apr. 2/4 (*heading*) Larrikinism v. Public Entertainments. **1879** C. L. Innes *Canterbury Sk.* v. 39 We had not then [*sc.* in 1852–3] the pestilential element of 'larrikinism' which is so rife now, and which makes many public meetings so objectionable. **1927** M. M. Bennett *Christison* xxviii. 264 This last piece of larrikinism took Mimi so completely by surprise that she could not think of anything to say.

larrup, *v.* Add: (Later examples.) Also *intr.*

1922 Joyce *Ulysses* 498, I let him larrup it into me for the fun of it. **1939** C. Fry *Boy with Cart* 26 Heard the first spatter of drops, the outriders Larruping on the road. **1953** Dylan Thomas *Under Milk Wood* (1954) 81 From the larrupped waves the lights of the lamps in the windows call back the day. **1970** [see *cruelty 1 b].

Larry (læ·ri), *sb.*[3] [Etym. uncertain.] Phr. *happy as Larry*, extremely happy.

1905 T. Collins in *Barrier Truth* (Broken Hill) 29 Dec. 1 Now that the adventure was drawing to an end, I found

a peace of mind that all the old fogies on the river couldn't disturb. I was as happy as Larry. **1915** L. STONE *Betty Wayside* xix. 254 If it hadn't been for that busybody we'd have been as happy as Larry. **1934** T. WOOD *Cobbers* iii. 25 He said he was as happy as Larry to see a fresh face. **1938** S. BECKETT *Murphy* ix. 180 Kept in peace they would have been as happy as Larry, short for Lazarus. **1946** F. SARGESON *That Summer* 32 Then he'd hop round happy as Larry. **1966** BAKER *Austral. Lang.* (ed. 2) xii. 271 *Happy as Larry*, extremely happy. Possibly but not certainly commemorating the noted Australian pugilist Larry Foley (1847–1917). **1966** B. KENNELLY *Collection One: Getting Up Early* 26 The Knockanore woman was happy as Larry. **1967** *Daily Mail* 18 Jan. 12/3 The tobacco and pipe trade..are as happy as Larry that Dr. Cameron..has won the award.

larva. Add: **2. c.** *larva-case, -stage.*

1855 J. PHILLIPS *Man. Geol.* 459 Thin tufaceous limestones, sometimes full of the larva-cases of phryganidae. **1893** J. TUCKEY tr. *Hatschek's Amphioxus* 159 Those stages which form the transition from the development of the embryo..to the larvae stages which are self-nourishing.

larvikite (lā·ɹvikəit). *Petrogr.* Also **laurvikite**, † **-vigite** (lau̇ə·ɹ-). [ad. G. *laurvikit* (W. C. Brögger 1890, in *Zeitschr. f. Kryst.* XVI. 29), f. *Laurvik* (now *Larvik*), name of a Norwegian seaport: see -ITE[1].] A kind of syenite that has a characteristic coarse texture dominated by rhombs of soda or soda-lime feldspar, with augite as the chief mafic mineral, and is used as a decorative stone.

1895 A. HARKER *Petrol.* 304 (Index), Laurvikite. **1911** *Encycl. Brit.* XVI. 30/1 The ornamental stone from south Norway, now largely used as a decorative material in architecture, owes its beauty to a felspar with a blue opalescence..which Professor W. C. Brögger has termed cryptoperthite, whilst the rock in which it occurs is an augite-syenite called by him laurvigite, from its chief locality, Laurvik in Norway. **1962** R. WEBSTER *Gems* I. ix. 157 The Norwegian rock known as laurvikite..is a material extensively used for building façades. **1965** *Norsk Geol. Tidsskr.* XLV. 69 The two monsonitic syenites from the Oslo area, larvikite and tönsbergite, differ mainly in the colour of the feldspar minerals. The blue schiller which is so predominant in the larvikite varieties is normally completely masked by the red colour of the tönsbergite varieties. **1971** *Country Life* 16 Sept. 683/1 By the date of the opening of Highgate [Cemetery]..the Victorians had become eclectic in their choice, employing all manner of stones, often of distant source, simply on account of their pleasing colour or texture. So we find the iridescent Larvikite from Norway together with all colour tones of granite-type rock from Finland or Sweden.

laryngal, *a.* Add: (Later examples.) Also *absol.*

1922 D. JONES *Outl. Eng. Phonetics* (ed. 2) vi. 14 Glottal or laryngal sounds, viz. sounds articulated in the glottis. **1933** L. BLOOMFIELD *Lang.* vii. 99 A glottal or laryngal stop is produced by bringing the vocal chords tightly together and then letting them spring apart under the pressure of the breath. **1939** L. H. GRAY *Foundations of Lang.* iii. 49 Two other glottal (or laryngal) sounds of importance are represented by the *h*'s of English *how, ahoy*.., unvoiced and voiced respectively. **1958** PRIEBSCH & COLLINSON *German Lang.* (ed. 4) 6 It [*sc.* Hittite] has 'laryngeal' sounds—not identical with the Semitic 'laryngals'.

laryngeal, *a.* and *sb.* Add: **A.** *adj.* **2.** Of a sound: produced in or modified by the larynx; = prec. Also *absol.*

1921 E. SAPIR *Lang.* 249 Articulations, laryngeal. **1927** R. BRIDGES in *S.P.E. Tract* xxvi. 177 The method is that in singing the mouth is fixed in the position that gives the required vowel resonance..and that the laringeal note is as it were forced through it. **1932** W. L. GRAFF *Lang.* 28 *Laryngeals* or *glottals*, produced by a narrowing or closure of the vocal cords.

3. Corresponding to sense B. 2 below.

1952 *Bull. Board Celtic Stud.* XIV. 296, I reconstruct in terms of the so-called 'laryngeal theory', here, however, without committing myself to the number of laryngeals necessarily to be assumed at a given time. **1958** [see *LARYNGAL *a.*]. **1958** A. S. C. ROSS *Etym.* 7 It is certainly quite impossible for anyone to understand Laryngeal Theory without being thoroughly familiar with junggrammatisch Ablaut.

B. *sb.* **2.** *Philol.* A hypothetical phonetic element with a laryngeal quality supposed to have existed, spec. in Proto-Indo-European, and to have left traces in the vocalic features of extant Indo-European languages.

1942 E. H. STURTEVANT *Indo-Hittite Laryngeals* 15 In this book the word *laryngeals* designates certain consonants of Proto-Indo-Hittite. The name is historically a translation of German *Laryngale*, which term was borrowed from Semitic grammar by Hermann Möller to designate five phonemes of his Proto-Indo-European-Semitic. **1951** *Trans. Philol. Soc.* 88 (*title*) A reconsideration of the Hittite evidence for the existence of 'Laryngeals' in Primitive Indo-European. **1963** *Language* XXXIX. 252 It is intrinsically implausible that a presumably nonsyllabic laryngeal next to a syllabic resonant should vocalize. **1969** *Ibid.* XLV. 260 Plain stops immediately followed by a laryngeal became aspirated stops in Indo-Iranian. **1971** F. R. ADRADOS in *Archivum Linguisticum* II. 95, I refer particularly to those stems in which the presence of laryngeals gives rise to diverging interpretations.

So **lary·ngealist**, an adherent of a laryngeal theory; also *attrib.* or as *adj.*; **lary:ngealiza·tion**, the action or fact of being laryngealized; **lary·ngealized** *a.*, of a sound produced in or affected by the larynx.

1943 K. L. PIKE *Phonetics* vii. 127 Laryngealization may conveniently be said to be trillization with superimposed voice. *Ibid.*, In English one often hears laryngealized vowels. **1964** O'CONNOR & TOOLEY in D. Abercrombie et al. *Daniel Jones* 176 Glottal stop and laryngealization before word-initial vowel were accepted. **1964** *Language* XL. 138 The laryngealist will retort that another..problem..is also solved by applying a laryngeal solution. *Ibid.* 140 A typical phonemic analysis of the PIE vowels in laryngealist terms. **1968** *Ibid.* XLIV. 529 Much is made of the fact that only one laryngealized stop (i.e. glottalized or aspirated) occurs per word in Quechua. **1968** CHOMSKY & HALLE *Sound Pattern Eng.* 315 Several African and Caucasian languages exhibit the so-called laryngealized or 'creaky' voice. **1971** *Canad. Jrnl. Ling.* Fall 70 He rejects phonemic /ə/..thus discomfiting the more elderly laryngealists.

laryngo-. Add: **laryngo-pharynx**, substitute for def.: = *HYPOPHARYNX 2; (earlier and later examples); **lary·ngophone**, a microphone designed to be placed or attached to the throat so as to pick up the voice directly with little intrusion of other sounds; **lary:ngotra:cheobronchi·tis** *Path.*, inflammation of the larynx, trachea, and bronchi; *spec.* an acute febrile disease (a form of croup) that exhibits these symptoms and occurs chiefly in young children, in which excessive secretion of mucus causes obstruction of the larynx and sometimes the bronchi.

1893 A. W. MACCOY in C. H. Burnett *Syst. Dis. Ear, Nose, & Throat* II. 195 The laryngo-pharynx..is chiefly interesting because of its relationship to the epiglottis and the superior margin of the larynx, which is situated in front of it. **1960** Laryngopharynx [see *INLET *sb.* 4*]. **1927** *Observer* 6 Nov. 19/3 We have a special instrument, the laryngophone, by means of which we can speak to each other in flight. **1941** *Jrnl. R. Aeronaut. Soc.* XLV. 402 The picking up of the throat vibrations is done with a laryngophone. **1932** DORLAND & MILLER *Med. Dict.* (ed. 16) 685/2 Laryngotracheobronchitis. **1956** HINSHAW & GARLAND *Dis. Chest* xi. 183 Among the most serious and difficult ailments affecting small children are a group of diseases variously called acute laryngotracheobronchitis, bronchiolitis, fibrinous bronchitis or 'croup'. These are characterized by violent cough, often associated with laryngospasm and bronchospasm and appear to be of infectious origin. **1972** *Daily Tel.* 2 Feb. 13/5 Two American pathologists have been claiming that laryngotracheobronchitis is frequently responsible for cot deaths, since they have found signs of inflammation in the larynxes, windpipes and bronchial tubes of babies who died.

lasagne (lasā·nye). In sing. **lasagna.** [It.] An Italian dish: a variety of pasta cut in long wide strips.

[**1760** BARETTI *Dict. Eng. & Ital. Lang.* I, *Lasagna*, a kind of thin paste cut into slices and dry'd, boiled in water or broth, [etc.].] **1846** E. ACTON *Mod. Cookery* (ed. 5) 579 The ribbon maccaroni (or lasagnes). **1849** BROWNING *Englishman in Italy* in *Poems* II. 333 We shall feast our grape-gleaners..With lasagne so tempting to swallow In slippery ropes. **1960** *News Chron.* 17 Feb. 6/2 Excellent ravioli and lasagne (soft ribbon noodles)..at 2s. 6d. a pound. **1961** *Listener* 20 Apr. 719/1 To make *lasagne verdi* (green *lasagne*)..you will need [etc.]. **1966** T. PYNCHON *Crying of Lot 49* i. 10 The layering of a lasagna, garlicking of a bread. **1972** *Guardian* 18 Aug. 11/3 Lasagne..perhaps the finest of all pasta dishes. **1974** *Times* 7 Feb. 16/7 To assemble the lasagne, spoon a little of the meat sauce into the base of a large shallow baking dish. Cover with a layer of lasagne, spoon over a layer of cottage cheese and sprinkle with Parmesan.

lase (lēiz), *v.* [Back-formation from next, the ending *-er* being treated as the ending -ER[1] of agent nouns.] *intr.* Of a substance, or an atom or molecule: to undergo the physical processes (of excitation and stimulated emission) employed in the laser; to function as the working substance of a laser. Of a device: to operate as a laser.

1962 *New Scientist* 1 Feb. 270/3 This is well illustrated by the uses now being made of the entirely novel verb 'to lase'.. It is common currency among those..whose lives are given to the search for materials that will emit light in coherent and narrow-pencilled beams. **1963** *Ibid.* 10 Jan. 65/3 Hitherto, only certain ionic crystals (notably ruby), some gas mixtures and..one or two liquids, had been persuaded to 'lase'; that is, to emit coherent infrared or visible light of a single wavelength. **1963** *Ibid.* 7 Feb. 293/2 Scientists at Standard Telecommunications Laboratories..last week persuaded their version of the gallium arsenide laser to 'lase'. **1963** *Monsanto Mag.* Mar. 10/2 Calculations..indicated that gallium arsenide would 'lase', or amplify light, if suitably stimulated. **1967** *Guardian* 11 Feb. 1/1 Can X-ray lasers be made? There is no problem in getting substances to lase at the right frequency. **1969** *Sci. Jrnl.* Apr. 55/2 The term 'dye laser' is generally used. Different dyes lase at different wavelengths and..it has been possible to span without a break the range 700–1000 nm by using some 20 different dyes. **1970** *Daily Tel.* (Colour Suppl.) 28 Aug. 16/2 Not all atoms can be made to 'lase'. **1971** *Sci. Amer.* July 37/2 When the injection current becomes high enough so that the light in the crystal making a round trip along the junction plane is amplified enough to offset losses due to absorption, to scattering, to leakage out of the mirrors and so on, the diode is said to be lasing.

Hence **la·sing** *ppl. a.* and *vbl. sb.*

1963 *Monsanto Mag.* Mar. 9/3 Many variations have been produced since then, employing other solids, as well as gases and liquids, as 'lasing' materials. **1966** SMITH & SOROKIN *Laser* vii. 369 The characteristics of these lasing diodes..differ considerably from those of other lasers. **1973** *Physics Bull.* Dec. 723/1 Lasing at 145 nm in high pressure krypton has also been achieved..with intense electron beam pumping.

laser[2] (lēi·zəɹ). [f. the initial letters of '*l*ight *a*mplification by the *s*timulated *e*mission of *r*adiation', after the earlier *MASER.] **1.** Any device that is capable of emitting a very intense, narrow, parallel beam of highly monochromatic and coherent light (or other electromagnetic radiation), either continuously or in pulses, and operates by using light to stimulate the emission of more light of the same wavelength and phase by atoms or molecules that have been excited by some means.

Orig. treated as the name of a particular kind of maser (*optical maser*) emitting visible light, *laser* is now the general term for all devices of this kind, whatever the wavelength of the emitted radiation.

1960 *N.Y. Times* 8 July 7/6 The Hughes device is an optical maser, or 'laser', (the 'l' standing for 'light'). **1960** *Aviation Week* 18 July 97/2 The optical Maser is also referred to by the term Laser. **1960** *Daily Tel.* 29 Dec. 9/4 The laser, a device for amplifying light which could conceivably be developed to produce a searchlight beam that would reach the moon, is still a paper project as far as British scientists are concerned. **1961** *Jrnl. Appl. Physics* XXXII. 178 [*Paper received 13 June 1960.*] The Fabry–Perot interferometer has been suggested for use as a high-mode LASER (light amplification by stimulated emission of radiation) resonator. **1961** *Observer* 19 Feb. 5/2 The new 'laser', as it is called, uses a mixture of helium and neon gas to produce a continuous beam of infra-red radiation... Previous devices have produced only brief pulses of light. **1962** *Science Survey* III. 27 The principle of the maser has been extended also to solid materials and, in addition, it has been found possible to make a light maser (or 'laser') that produces, not microwaves, but visible light. **1963** *Electronics Weekly* 2 Jan. 1/4 The new high-power laser uses a six-inch by half-inch ruby. **1963** *Monsanto Mag.* Mar. 9/2 Early lasers absorbed energy from a strong burst of ordinary white light, organized it, then expelled a powerful beam of a different kind of light. **1963** *Daily Tel.* 24 Oct. 19/4 Already in metal working the term 'Gillette power' is used as a measure of the laser's metal-vaporising capabilities. It represents the number of stacked razor blades through which a beam can bore its way. **1964, 1966** [see *HOLOGRAM]. **1969** *Sci. Jrnl.* Apr. 53/1 Lasers have been operated which produce visible radiation, ultraviolet, infrared and even submillimetre radiation. **1970** [see *HOLOGRAPH *v.*]. **1971** *Sci. Amer.* June 21/3 A laser is a device for generating or amplifying a beam of light whose waves are both monochromatic (all the same wavelength) and coherent (all in step). The light beam emitted by a laser can be made almost perfectly parallel, its divergence angle being theoretically limited only by diffraction effects. **1972** *McGraw-Hill Yearbk. Sci. & Technol.* 266/2 The first purely chemical lasers requiring no external source of energy to initiate or sustain laser excitation have been operated successfully.

2. *attrib.* and *Comb.*, as *laser beam, bomb, light, reflector*; *laser-guided, -ignited* ppl. adjs.; *laser-heat* vb.

1963 *Monsanto Mag.* Mar. 10/3 A laser beam can generate intense heat—10,000°F. or higher—in a small area. **1970** *Daily Tel.* (Colour Suppl.) 28 Aug. 17/1 A laser beam, focused through the lens of the eye, can weld a detached retina back into place by creating scar tissue. **1970** *Daily Tel.* 31 Jan. 4/2 Scientists..maintain that the laser bomb..is a theoretical possibility. **1972** *Guardian* 29 June 4/3 The drawback to the laser bomb is that the plane producing the beam must keep it on target until the bomb's impact. **1967** *New Scientist* 11 May 326/2 With the laser-guided bomb, the large bombers might be able to drop their loads over the target area from high altitudes with greater assurance of putting them on target. **1972** *Science* 9 June 1108/3 The laser-guided bombs now being used are mostly in the 2000 to 3000-pound range. **1971** *Sci. Amer.* June 27/1 The second question—regarding the feasibility of laser-heating a small dense plasma to thermonuclear conditions without the necessity of a confining magnetic field—is receiving increased attention. *Ibid.* 29/1 A method for converting the fusion energy from laser-ignited deuterium-tritium pellets into electrical power was evolved..early in 1969. **1966** *Listener* 28 July 129/3 The editor..will brandish a laser-light pen to indicate alterations which a computer will make. **1971** B. DE FERRANTI *Living with Computer* ix. 83 In laser light the waves are all in the same plane and in phase. **1969** *New Scientist* 9 Oct. 81/1 The first men on the Moon have..already placed one laser-reflector on the lunar surface.

lash, *sb.*[1] Add: **4.** An attempt; esp. in phr. *to have a lash (at)*, to make an attempt, to 'have a go at'. *Austral.* and *N.Z.*

1941 BAKER *Dict. Austral. Slang* 42 *Lash at, have a*, to make an attempt at (something). **1945** J. PASCOE *Canterbury High Country* 28 A few may spend their cheque in a glorious lash at the beer. **1948** D. BALLANTYNE *Cunninghams* (1963) vii. 38 Hoping to get a lash at the Huns. **1949** R. PARK *Poor Man's Orange* (1950) 193 The blithe pipings of old men who, safe [from the fight] up on their balconies, leaned over rails and exhorted everyone to 'ave a lash. **1971** *Sunday Sun* (Brisbane) 17 Oct. 14/2, I am a natural sportsman. Only last week I donkey licked the local kindy kids at drop the hankie. So I went out to Surfers Paradise course to have a lash.

5. (sense 3) *lash-tender* adj.; **lash rope** *N. Amer.*, a rope used for lashing a pack or load on a horse or vehicle.

1806 LEWIS & CLARK *Orig. Jrnls. Lewis & Clark Expedition* (1905) V. 114 Sergt. Gass, McNeal, Whitehouse and Goodrich accompanyed them [*sc.* Indians] with a view to procure some pack or lash ropes. **1822** J. FOWLER *Jrnl.* 18 June (1898) 159 We then took the lash Roaps and tyed up the Horses. **1843** *Amer. Pioneer* II. 162 Each horse was provided with..a lash rope to secure the load. **1888** LEES & CLUTTERBUCK *Ramble in Brit. Columbia* 229 The lash rope is from thirty to forty feet long. **1929** *Collier's* 5 Jan. 33/3 'Wait until I get my lash rope' (i.e., the rope with which he bound his load on his sledge). **1963** R. SYMONS *Many Trails* vii. 77 Lash ropes were tightened till the pack animals grunted. *a* **1889** G. M. HOPKINS *Poems* (1918) 74 Whether..furled Fast or they [*sc.* ash-boughs] in clammyish lashtender combs creep Apart wide.

LASH, Lash, lash (læʃ). The initials of *l*ighter *a*board *sh*ip, used, freq. *attrib.*, to denote a ship, or system of shipping, in which loaded barges are placed directly on board the ship.

1965 *Maritime Reporter* 1 Nov. 21 (Advt.), The LASH System combines an ultra-simple, fast, automated ship with a large number of low-cost lighters. **1967** *Economist* 7 Jan. 51/2 This is the LASH shipping system (Lighter Aboard Ship Inc.) which both the Americans and Germans are now building. A LASH ship is designed to pick up and carry 250-ton lighters, which are towed to and from the ship regardless of tides or port labour schedules. **1969** *Jane's Freight Containers 1968–69* 378/2 No container ships, but 5 Lash vessels..are under construction. **1970** *Times* 12 Aug. 18 Shipowners also hastened the introduction of..lash vessels in which laden barges are floated directly into a large hull.

lash, *v.*¹ Add: **4.** (Later example.)

1922 JOYCE *Ulysses* 736 You cant get on in this world without style all going in food and rent when I get it Ill lash it around I tell you in fine style.

5. (Later examples.)

1959 G. FREEMAN *Jack would be Gent.* i. 10 He'd never had the money to lash out properly. **1973** 'M. YORKE' *Grave Matters* i. vi. 35 He must have paid plenty for the place, besides what they're going to lash out in alterations.

6. *absol.* (Later examples.)

1876 G. M. HOPKINS *Wreck of Deutschland* viii, in *Poems* (1967) 54 Oh, We lash with the best or worst Word last! **1877** A. SEWELL *Black Beauty* (c 1878, ed. 5) xx. 93 The man, fiercely pulling at the head of the forehorse, swore and lashed most brutally. **1892** A. CONAN DOYLE *Adventures Sherlock Holmes* viii. 205 The sudden glare.. made it impossible for me to tell what it was at which my friend lashed so savagely.

lash, *v.*² Add: **3.** *Comb.* **lash-up,** (*a*) a makeshift or hastily contrived improvisation; also *attrib.*; (*b*) (see quot. 1925). Hence **lashed-up** *a.*, improvised.

1898 W. P. DRURY *Tadpole of an Archangel* 86 Such a godforsaken lash-up of a bridge you never clapped eyes on! **1907** J. MASEFIELD *Tarpaulin Muster* viii. 102 And down they all go—ship, and tea, and mate, and bishop, and general, and Jimmy and the whole lash-up. **1920** *Blackw. Mag.* Feb. 154/1 By 'lashed up' means—(that is to say, 'improvised')—and with a makeshift staff of assistants, a tolerable chart was produced. *Ibid.* 158/1 We..had been obliged to make 'lash-up' (*i.e.*, makeshift) arrangements. **1924** P. P. ECKERSLEY *Captain Eckersley Explains* i. 5 A 'lash-up' or experimental station was erected at the Marconi Works. **1925** FRASER & GIBBONS *Soldier & Sailor Words* 140 *Lash-up*, a failure. A fiasco. The break-down of anything. **1929** O. HARLAND *Golden Plough* iv. 97 Until we come to the present Imbroglio, the Glorious Lash-up of this very age. **1936** 'TAFFRAIL' *Mystery at Milford Haven* 281 The boat..was what a blue-jacket would have called a 'lash-up', a thing of bits and pieces. **1958** *Economist* 13 Sept. 869/2 Black Knight is essentially a lash-up on which to test various designs of nose cone for the 2,500 mile ballistic weapon Blue Streak that should be ready for test in the early 1960s. **1962** W. SCHIRRA in *Into Orbit* 46 It [*sc.* the couch] was a simple bit of furniture compared to the lashup of tubing, fans, filters and tanks which was built around it. **1966** M. WOODHOUSE *Tree Frog* xxv. 182 We didn't have time for an instrument check. It's just a lash-up really. **1974** *Exchange & Mart* (South) 27 June 53M/3 Rebuilt motor, not a lash-up.

lashing, *vbl. sb.*¹ **1. b.** Delete (*Anglo-Irish*): this sense is now in general use. Add later examples.

1901 E. W. HORNUNG *Black Mask* v. 74 There were lashings of sound wine for one and all. **1927** D. L. SAYERS *Unnatural Death* xxiii. 278 Nice little dinner—lashings of champagne. **1942** *R.A.F. Jrnl.* 3 Oct. 30 We fought through lashings of rain and mud to our billets. **1962** J. WAIN *Strike Father Dead* 164 Real comfort. And plenty of money. Lashings! She earned a good solid packet at this job. **1966** *Lancet* 2 Apr. 765/1 The crusty wholemeal bread..eaten with lashings of butter. **1975** *Country Life* 6 Feb. 336/3 Chicory..requires lashings of water.

lashkar. b. Substitute for def.: A body of Afridi soldiers. (Add further examples.)

1897 *Times* 6 Oct. 3/1 The lashkar is prepared to offer terms on behalf of the Afridi, Mamund, and Malakand tribesmen. **1908** *Daily Chron.* 27 Apr. 1/7 General Willcock's columns yesterday searched out the enemy's lashkars. **1924** *Glasgow Her.* 14 May 8 The rebel lashkars are melting away. **1955** *Times* 31 May 7/6 Inside this frame, lashkars, or tribal columns, are still raised occasionally. **1973** *Times* 22 Mar. (Pakistan Suppl.) p. ii/3 Baluchistan..is led largely by tribes amenable only to the jurisdiction of their own *sardars*..who often command sizeable *lashkars*, or private levies.

lash-up: see *LASH *v.*² 3.

lasiocampid (lēɪsɪokæ·mpid), *sb.* and *a.* [f. mod.L. family name *Lasiocampidæ*, f. the generic name *Lasiocampa* (N. Contarini *Catal. Uccelli e Insetti Padova* (1843) 37), f. Gk. λάσιος hairy, shaggy + κάμπη caterpillar.] A member of the family Lasiocampidæ, a group of large moths also known as eggars or lappet-moths, including some species whose larvae are called tent-caterpillars; of or pertaining to an insect of this kind.

1895 J. H. & A. B. COMSTOCK *Man. Study Insects* 360 The larvæ of the Lasiocampids feed upon the foliage of trees, and are frequently very destructive. **1912** *Proc. Entomol. Soc. London* p. iv, Prof. Poulton exhibited specimens of the Lasiocampid moth *Mimopacha gerstaeckeri*, Dewitz. **1934** *Discovery* XVII. 98/1 Sometimes the hairs and spines are..exhibited in an ostentatious manner whenever an enemy appears. This is well illustrated in Lasiocampids. **1964** V. B. WIGGLESWORTH *Life of Insects* vii. 112 The male..may be specially modified for the recognition and location of these scents. That is most evident in the Saturniid, Bombycid, and Lasiocampid moths, in most of which the female is sluggish and sedentary.

lass. Add: **1. d.** A female member of the Salvation Army.

1886 *War Cry* 9 Oct. 9/4 Cadets to be grouped together in Brigades..Lads or Lasses, as the case may be. **1890** W. BOOTH *In Darkest Eng.* I. vi. 55 Our two lasses go unharmed and loved at all hours. **1907** G. B. SHAW *Major Barbara* Pref. 171 Bill Walker,..having assaulted the Salvation Lass,..finds himself overwhelmed with an intolerable conviction of sin. **1967** W. S. SMITH *London Heretics* III. v. 238 In 1879 two of General Booth's lasses arrived in the Quaker stronghold of Darlington.

Lassa (læ·să). The name of a village near Mubi in NE. Nigeria, used *attrib.* in **Lassa fever**, an acute febrile virus disease that occurs in tropical Africa with a high mortality rate (first reported at Lassa in 1969); similarly *Lassa virus*.

1970 *Times* 11 Feb. 7/3 Lassa fever infection can involve almost all the body's organs; symptoms may vary. The virus produces a fever as high as 107°F, mouth ulcers, a skin rash with small haemorrhages, pneumonia, infection of the heart leading to cardiac failure, kidney damage, and severe muscle aches. **1970** *Amer. Jrnl. Trop. Med. & Hygiene* XIX. 690/1 There is no epidemiologic evidence to indicate that Lassa virus is an arthropod-borne virus. **1973** *Nature* 12 Jan. 92/1 Man-to-man spread of Lassa virus undoubtedly takes place through contact with blood or infectious secretions, but a reservoir of infection has yet to be identified. **1975** *Ibid.* 15 May 185/1 Lassa fever..seems to be one of the most virulent virus diseases yet discovered.

'lasses, colloq. abbreviation of MOLASSES. *U.S.*

1775 in O. E. Winslow *Amer. Broadside Verse* (1930) 141/1 The 'lasses they eat every day, Would keep an house a winter. **1807** *Salmagundi* 16 May 205 This manufacture is called by the Bostonians *lasses candy*. **1854** M. J. HOLMES *Tempest & Sunshine* xxii. 317 Get along Jack, pokin' your fingers into the 'lasses cup. **1909** F. B. CALHOUN *Miss Minerva* 174 Aunt Minerva's in the kitchen right now makin' me a 'lasses custard. **1948** *Chicago Tribune* 14 Mar. VII. 17/2 Now, come spring, it's ''lasses time' right over the border and 'sap 's a-bilin''.

lassie. Add: **1. b.** = *LASS 1 d.

1906 'O. HENRY' *Four Million* 84 A Salvation lassie shook her contribution receptacle. **1970** *Guardian* 12 May 10/5 Such items as whether Army lassies should wear lipstick in uniform.

lasso, *sb.* Now usu. with pronunc. (lăsū·).

Fowler remarked (*Mod. Eng. Usage*, 1926, p. 315) '*lasso* is pronounced lasōō' by those who use it; but the English pronunciation is lă'sō.' In ed. 2 (1965) Sir E. Gowers changed this to '*lasso* is pronounced lăsōō' by those who use it, and by most English people too'.

1. (Further examples.)

1824 W. BULLOCK *Six Months' Residence Mexico* 179 It requires the use of a lasso to catch them. This is thrown with great dexterity by every hostler or servant. **1837** W. IRVING *Capt. Bonneville* III. vi. 86 The California horsemen seldom ride out without the laso; that is to say, a long coil of cord, with a slip noose, with which they are expert, almost to a miracle. **1940** H. L. MENCKEN *Happy Days* 284 They lay in wait in dark Greene street with their ..lassos, and knives. **1966** H. MARRIOTT *Cariboo Cowboy* v. 53 Al was sure a good man with a lasso rope.

fig. **1922** JOYCE *Ulysses* 50 In long lassoes..the water flowed full. **1924** R. CAMPBELL *Flaming Terrapin* i. 15 He..hurled Lassoes of dismal smoke around the world.

3. *lasso-throw, -throwing.*

1841 G. CATLIN *Lett. on N. Amer. Indians* II. 152 A line, with a sort of 'laso throw', came from an awkward hand on the deck. *a* **1861** T. WINTHROP *John Brent* (1883) ii. 11 Man to them was power, and nothing else,—a lasso-throwing machine.

lasso, *v.* Add: Now usu. with pronunc. (lăsū·). Also *fig.*

1965 V. BONHAM CARTER *Winston Churchill* xviii. 253 Fisher happened to be at Naples and it seemed a heaven-sent opportunity for lassoing him there and roping him in again.

lassoer, lassoing. Add: (Earlier examples.) Also **lasso·ist.**

1838 'TEXIAN' *Mexico v. Texas* 48 The men were collecting the mules, and when these were driven together, the lassoing began. **1883** SWEET & KNOX *On Mexican Mustang through Texas* xli. 584 Juan Gonzales..is said to be the champion lassoer in the world. **1884** W. SHEPHERD *Prairie Experiences* 40 The lassoer picks out the unbranded calves, and drags them off to the fire. **1906** *Daily Chron.* 16 May 5/7 There have been lassoists before, but never, perhaps, such a master of the art as Will Rogers.

lassu (lā·ʃū). [Hung. *lassú.*] The slow part of a Hungarian csardas (opp. *friss*).

1880 GROVE *Dict. Mus.* II. 198/2 Every Csárdás consists of two movements,—a 'Lassu', or slow movement, andante maestoso, and a 'Friss', or 'quickstep', allegro vivace. **1944** [see *CSARDAS]. **1961** *Times* 13 May 5/1 A Haydnish *lassu*.

last, *a., adv.*, and *sb.*⁶ Add: **A.** *adj.* **1.** *spec.* in Cricket, (*the*) *last man* (*in*): the batsman who is not out at the end of an innings; the man who goes in to bat last. Hence *the last pair, wicket.*

1773 *Kentish Gaz.* 24 July, Surry. Yaldin, Last man in, 17. Kent. Mr. Hussey, Last man in, 0. **1833** J. NYREN *Young Cricketer's Tutor* 113 Small went in the last man for fourteen runs, and fetched them. **1870** *Times* 20 July 10/3 Southerton appeared as 'last man'. **1897** H. NEWBOLT *Vitai Lampada* in *Admirals All* 21 An hour to play and the last man in. **1953** R. WEBBER *Australians in Eng.* 155 Oldfield (123) and Mailey (46 not out) added 124 for the last wicket in only 40 minutes. **1957** R. CAMPBELL *Coll. Poems* II. 101 No last-man-in has ever batted With a more desperate intent. **1963** A. ROSS *Australia 63* iii. 88 The last pair, perched not uncomfortably for forty-nine minutes, had put on 20 runs.

b. Also preceded by an ordinal number, to denote how many places from the end of a series an object, name of a person, etc., occurs.

1880 W. F. SKENE *Celtic Scotl.* III. 122 Dathi the second last of the pagan monarchs of Ireland. **1938** I. GOLDBERG *Wonder of Words* ix. 186 There are technical names for words having accented last, second-last, and third-last syllables. **1963** J. LUSBY in B. James *Austral. Short Stories* 235 Before breakfast on our second-last day the Eccentric stood facing Mooney on the sand.

d. Delete † *Obs.* and add later examples in N. Amer. use. Also, the final portion of a period of time, esp. in *the last of pea-time*; also *fig.*

1834 W. A. CARUTHERS *Kentuckian in N.Y.* I. 190 Our parson whines it out like an old woman in the last of pea-time. **1883** *Century Mag.* Oct. 921/2 The snipe usually makes its appearance in New Jersey and New York about the last of March or the first of April. **1904** E. ROBINS *Magnetic North* I. 63 Things looked pretty much like the last of pea time. **1908** L. M. MONTGOMERY *Anne of Green Gables* xxxvi. 405 There is a distinguished oculist coming to the Island the last of June. **1931** A. E. MARTIN *Hist. U.S.* II. ii. 24 By the last of May he had formulated his plan and on the twenty-ninth he issued two proclamations.

f. *last across* (*the road*): a children's game in which each tries to be the last to cross a road (or railway) safely in front of an approaching vehicle (or train). Also *fig.*

1904 A. B. F. YOUNG *Compl. Motorist* ix. 230 If it seems good to them [*sc.* children] to play at 'last across', you had better go very gingerly in their neighbourhood. **1914** 'I. HAY' *Knight on Wheels* xi. 108 A frisky calf, encountered by the way, almost wrecked its own prospects of ever becoming veal by an untimely indulgence in the game of 'Come to Mother, or Last Across the Road'. **1928** *Sunday Dispatch* 15 July 11/3 Socialist back-benchers are playing a dangerous game of 'last across' with Mr. Speaker—just seeing how far they can go at question time without being 'named'. **1957** *Times* 12 Mar. 4/6 Engine drivers are threatening to refuse to drive trains over a section of track ..because children are using it for a game of 'last across'. **1958** R. LIDDELL *Morea* II. iv. 103 Chickens seemed to be playing 'last across the road';..dogs tried to meet us head on. **1969** 'A. HALL' *Striker Portfolio* v. 45 We finished up playing 'Last Across' and he cut it too fine.

2. *the four last things* (further examples); also with omission of *four*; *last words*, a person's dying words.

1522 MORE *De Quat. Noviss.* in *Works* (1557) 76/2 The busi minding of thy .iiii. last things, and the depe consideracion therof, is the thyng that shal kepe thee fro synne. **1606** (*title*) Foure-fould Meditation, of the foure last things: viz...of the Houre of Death. Day of Iudgement. Paines of Hell. Ioyes of Heauen. **1734** J. TRAPP (*title*) Thoughts upon the four last things... A poem in four parts. **1808** SCOTT *Marmion* VI. xxxiii. 366 'Charge, Chester, charge! On, Stanley, on!'..Were the last words of Marmion. **1845** G. BUSH *Anastasis* p.v, The great scheme of Scriptural Eschatology, or the doctrine of the last things. **1864** C. M. YONGE *Trial* II. xi. 189 Come, come,..there must be some last words. **1897** J. A. BEET *Last Things* xix. 231 This vision of glory..will be the closing scene of our study of the Last Things. *a* **1916** H. JAMES *Middle Years* (1917) iv. 49 Those 'last words' of the *raffiné* that were chanted and crooned in the damask-hung temple of the Grosvenor Gallery. **1945** E. WAUGH *Brideshead Revisited* I. vii. 173, I can't remember all he told me..plenary indulgences, four last things. **1948**, etc. [see *FAMOUS *a.* 1 c]. **1975** J. AIKEN *Voices in Empty House* viii. 190 The four last things are death, judgement,

heaven and hell. **1975** R. PLAYER *Let's talk of graves* i. 31 Languishing in the Condemned Cell, contemplating the Last Things.

d. Phr. *if it's the last thing I* (etc.) *do*: used to indicate a very strong desire to do something.

1921 E. O'NEILL *Emperor Jones* 180, I kills you, you white debil, if it's de last thing I evah does! **1938** M. ALLINGHAM *Fashion in Shrouds* ix. 146 He's got to go on that plane. If it's the last thing he does he's got to go back today. **1971** D. CORY *Sunburst* iii. 44, I want to kill him if it's the last thing I do. **1972** P. NEWTON *Sheep Thief* xv. 119 I'll get that bloke if it's the last thing I do.

5. Also *last lap* [LAP *sb.*³ 5 b]: the final circuit of a track, course, etc.; also *fig.*

1885 *Daily News* 1 Sept. 2/5 At half-distance the positions remained unaltered, and, as they began the last lap, it appeared to be any one's race. **1908** *Daily Chron.* 7 Mar. 7/5 Such an event [*sc.* a cycling race]..is declared to have been won on the last-lap sprint. **1922** JOYCE *Ulysses* 234 Bang of the lastlap bell spurred the halfmile wheelmen to their sprint. **1926** O. BARFIELD *Hist. in Eng. Words* 56 There is a..tendency to transmute.. [modern sports] terms into lively idiom. In this way we can use..the *last lap*. **1932** *Discovery* Dec. 393/1 We learned that weather conditions there had improved and that, for the last lap, we might expect better flying conditions.

b. (Further examples.)

1751 FIELDING *Amelia* IV. x. vii. 74 This was indeed almost the last man in the World, whose company he wished for. **1840** H. REEVE tr. *A. de Tocqueville's Democracy in Amer.* IV. IV. iii. 269, I am the last man to contend that these propensities are unconquerable. **1967** *Listener* 28 Sept. 395/3 Degas was the last man to believe in untutored brilliance.

6. *last word* (later examples).

1933 *Punch* 17 May 543/3 Although to my mind the Inverness alterations are absolutely the last word [in modernity], opinions are bound to differ. **1936** *Discovery* Apr. 130/1 The book cannot be the last word on M. Coué. **1966** *Listener* 6 Jan. 12/2 The Trombay establishment is the last word in nuclear sophistication. **1973** *Archivum Linguisticum* IV. 12 Perhaps it is most reasonable to leave the last word to Pidgin.

7. Also *last cry* [tr. Fr. *le dernier cri*]: something in the newest fashion. Cf. *DERNIER *a.* c.

1916 W. J. LOCKE *Wonderful Year* x. 133 A morning coat (last cry of Bond Street).

9. c. Delete † *Obs.* and add later examples.

1918 GALSWORTHY *Five Tales* 308 The last of daylight from without mingled with faint intrusion from the lamp within. **1943** K. O'BRIEN (*title*) The last of summer.

h. (Further examples.)

1816 SCOTT *Old Mortality* in *Tales my Landlord* 1st Ser. II. x. 241 'Ye hae seen the last o' me, and o' this bonny dye too,' said Jenny, holding between her finger and thumb a silver dollar. **1862** MRS. H. WOOD *Mrs. Halliburton's Troubles* III. xvii. 218 Dick little thought the manufactory had seen the last of him [*sc.* Cyril]. **1889** 'MARK TWAIN' *Connecticut Yankee* 280 That is the last you are going to see of him till he emerges on the other side. **1910** 'M. RUTHERFORD' *More Pages from Jrnl.* 22, I shall be thankful to see the last of you! **1924** G. B. SHAW *St. Joan* VI. 97 Her heart would not burn, my lord; but everything that was left is at the bottom of the river. You have heard the last of her.

10. b. Delete 'Now *rare*' and add later examples. Now always without *the*.

1923 W. DE LA MARE *Private View* (1953) 244 And at long last the acquisition of a technical mastery in any art ..is by no means nothing but a gain. **1926** *Manch. Guardian Weekly* Feb. 104/1 The Government followed up the references to agriculture..by launching at long last its land policy. **1936** KING EDWARD VIII in *Times* 12 Dec. 14/4 (*abdication speech*) At long last I am able to say a few words of my own. *a* **1936** KIPLING *Something of Myself* (1937) vi. 159 At long last we were left apologising to a deeply-indignant people. **1971** J. AIKEN *Nightly Deadshade* ii. 21 Someone answers the phone at long last, making me jump.

C. *Comb.* **2.** *last-chance, -gasp, -resort, -war, -wicket*; **last-minute**, (given, done, made, etc.) at the latest possible time.

1962 *Aeroplane* CIV. 18/1 Carbon deposits had clogged the 'last chance' filter, causing the oil starvation of No. 2 bearing in the JT3D-1 turbofan. **1963** J. LUSBY in B. James *Austral. Short Stories* 234 He was giving the Eccentric a last-chance test in individual combat. **1974** G. JENKINS *Bridge of Magpies* xvi. 239 It was a desperate last-chance throw. **1921** D. H. LAWRENCE *Let.* 2 Mar. (1962) II. 643 K.—who is doing the last-gasp touch. **1971** R. THOMAS *Backup Men* xxii. 191 All last-gasp businesses with no need for much of a front. **1972** *Sat. Rev.* (U.S.) 6 May 34/3 Our strategists have spoken too often of 'last-gasp' offensives for us to believe that this one will be any different. **1920** *Ladies' Home Jrnl.* May 140/2 Last-minute sketches from Paris. **1929** J. B. PRIESTLEY *Good Companions* II. iii. 329 Jimmy had a last-minute inspiration. **1931** E. LINKLATER *Juan in Amer.* III. i. 204 I've been doing some last-minute Christmas shopping. **1948** 'J. TEY' *Franchise Affair* xix. 227 A last-minute reprieve with the rope round the hero's neck? **1974** M. YORKE *Mortal Remains* II. i. 39 People were trying to buy last-minute tickets for the day's excursions. **1950** J. DEMPSEY *Championship Fighting* 170 The pull-away should only be used as a last-resort defence. **1965** H. KAHN *On Escalation* i. 10 The threat of a strike or a lockout is ever present as a last-resort pressure for compromise. **1942** S. SPENDER *Ruins & Visions* 42 The ghastly last-war voices. **1959** *Encounter* July 29/2 The plan..envisaged the defence of Western Europe almost completely in last-war terms. **1909** *Westm. Gaz.* 1 June 12/2 A great last-wicket stand might once in a way occur. **1975** *Times* 6. Jan. 7/7 A last-wicket partnership of 37 between Mallett and Thomson.

last, *v.*¹ Add: **3.** Also with *out*.

1881 MRS. J. H. RIDDELL *Senior Partner* III. 56 What would hinder him lasting out to ninety [years] or a hundred even? **1921** G. B. SHAW *Back to Methuselah* IV. II. 194 You people lived on the assumption that you were going to last out for ever and ever and ever.

last-ditch, *a.* [See DITCH *sb.*¹ 5.] Of opposition, resistance, etc.: maintained to the end. Of an effort, etc.: made at the last minute in an attempt to avert disaster. Also **last-di·tcher**, one who fights to the last ditch; **last-di·tchery**.

1909 *Westm. Gaz.* 30 Jan. 2/1 The only part he is likely to take in the Social Revolution is to be what may be called a last-ditcher in the attempt to resist it. **1927** *Daily Express* 19 Nov. 3/1 A constituency which is to be congratulated on a true last ditcher. **1928** *Daily Tel.* 17 July 18/3 There are few performers who have decided not to broadcast. Almost the 'last-ditcher' is perhaps Harry Tate. **1932** *Mind* XLI. 53 Formal Logic dies hard. It still commands the services of numbers of 'last ditchers'. **1936** 'J. TEY' *Shilling for Candles* i. 6 'Might have walked into the water till she drowned,' said Bill, who was a last-ditcher by nature. *Ibid.*, 'Might have died of an overdose of bulls-eyes,' said Potticary, who approved of last ditchery in Arabia but found it boring to live with. **1951** KOESTLER *Age of Longing* II. i. 205, I would rather have been one of the last-ditchers at Thermopylae. **1951** M. MCLUHAN *Mech. Bride* 44/1 A last-ditch stand of denuded minds. **1955** *Bull. Atomic Sci.* Feb. 54/2 If the French in their last ditch stand at Dien Bien Phu had appealed for U.S. nuclear aid, there would have been similar reactions. **1961** W. VAUGHAN-THOMAS *Anzio* viii. 171 Some got as far as the Loyals manning their last-ditch line on the Lateral Road. **1961** M. BEADLE *These Ruins are Inhabited* (1963) vi. 76 All that defeated them was a last-ditch appeal. **1971** *Times* 27 Apr. 9/5 Charlton himself surely was offside before McNab made his last ditch effort to recover the situation. **1973** *Times* 27 Aug. 3/1 Colonel Gaddafi, the Libyan leader, today began a last-ditch attempt to forge a full union with Egypt after his unexpected arrival in Cairo.

Lastex (læ·steks). Also **lastex**. The proprietary name of an elastic yarn formed from a combination of rubber (see also quot. 1968) with silk, cotton, or rayon, used in the manufacture of corsetry, etc.

1934 *Trade Marks Jrnl.* 17 Jan. 70/1 *Lastex.* Yarns and threads composed of a mixture of india-rubber and silk, the silk predominating. Dunlop-Revere Thread Co., Ltd., ..Birmingham. **1935** *Times* 12 June 15/6 Bathing suits are of woollen fabrics woven with lastex yarn. **1946** 'G. ORWELL' in *Tribune* 8 Nov. 12/2 Someone has just sent me a copy of an American fashion magazine...Here are a few sample sentences..'Gentle discipline for curves in lacy lastex pantie-girdle'. **1951** J. D. SALINGER *Catcher in Rye* xviii. 161 He wore those white lastex kind of swimming trunks. **1955** *Punch* 16 Mar. 348/3 Beautifully less! The ideal is now achieved with a caress of nylon, lastex, and lace. **1968** J. IRONSIDE *Fashion Alphabet* 236 Lastex yarns... The rubber is now being replaced by synthetic elastomeric fibres, which are easier to wash and quicker to dry.

lasting, *vbl. sb.*³ (Further examples, not in *attrib.* use.)

1880 *Encycl. Brit.* XXI. 830/2 Lasting is a crucial operation, for, unless the upper is drawn smoothly and equally over the last, leaving neither crease nor wrinkle, the form of the boot will be bad. **1907** *Westm. Gaz.* 4 Nov. 8/4 This method of 'lasting' is new. **1968** J. IRONSIDE *Fashion Alphabet* 126 The lasting, i.e. the making of the upper on the last.

lastness. (Further examples.)

a **1665** J. GOODWIN *Filled with Spirit* (1867) 92 Lastness or worstness in estate or condition. **1927** 'E. BRAMAH' *Max Carrados Myst.* 72 Your account..is entirely based on the fact that you were the last... There stands the man we want,..only you and your lastness get between.

lasya (lā·sya). [Skr. *lāsya*.] A graceful style of female dancing in India.

1937 SUBRAHMAṆYA ŚĀSTRĪ & ŚRĪNIVĀSA AYYAṄGĀR in Śaṅkara Āchārya *Saundarya-Lahari* 160 The Lāsya or female-dance and the Tāndava or male-dance, both being types of the same Nṛtya. **1967** SINGHA & MASSEY *Indian Dances* 23 Lasya is that element of the dance which is graceful and delicate and expresses emotions on a gentle level... Krishna's dance with the *gopees* (milkmaids) is in lasya. **1973** *Daily Tel.* 28 Mar. 15/1 What was most striking was her combination of the tandava (masculine) and lasya (feminine) in a way unique to her.

lat². [f. the first syllable of *Latvija* Latvia.] A unit of gold currency established by the state of Latvia in August 1922, with a par value of about 25 to the pound sterling, and discontinued in 1941.

1923 *Glasgow Herald* 23 June 10 The last Budget year was closed with a surplus of over 18,000,000 lats gold. **1928** *Daily Express* 29 Aug. 2/5 The Latvian Ministry of Finance has decided to place an order for five-lat silver pieces..with the Royal Mint, London. **1942** *Statesman's Year-Bk.* 1261 Latvia... The U.S.S.R. authorities abolished the lat currency on April 10, 1941.

lat³. (Usu. in pl. *lats*.) Slang abbrev. of LATRINE.

1927 W. E. COLLINSON *Contemp. Eng.* 92 At Salisbury Plain and Camberley in 1909/10 I learnt a number of camping expressions like..lats (*latrines*). **1940** M. MARPLES *Public School Slang* 112 Other synonyms [for lavatories] are rears, lats..and dubs. **1957** J. I. M. STEWART *Use of Riches* I. ii. 25 Turk says that conscientious objectors have to clean out the lats in lunatic asylums.

latania (lătēⁱ·niă, lăta·niă). **1.** *U.S.* [Amer. Sp.] = *LATANIER 1.

1799 in F. Cuming *Sk. Tour Western Country* (1810) 336 Some..cabins [were] covered over with a shrub like a large fan, called latania. **1819** E. DANA *Geogr. Sk. Western Country* 238 On the..outer margin of the cane, the palmetto, or latania, fill the slope between the cane and the inundated lands.

2. [mod.L. (P. Commerson in A. L. de Jussieu *Genera Plantarum* (1789) 39), f. F. *latanier* the name used in Mauritius.] A fan palm of the genus so called, native to Mauritius and neighbouring islands.

1856 B. SEEMANN *Pop. Hist. Palms* 229 The Latanias are middle-sized trees. **1900** L. H. BAILEY *Cycl. Amer. Hort.* II. 887/1 Latanias are tall, spineless palms. *Ibid.* 887/2 Latanias are essentially warmhouse palms. **1910** [see *GEONOMA]. **1966** E. J. H. CORNER *Nat. Hist. Palms* vii. 162 (*caption*) The Borassoid *Latania*; male inflorescence.

latanier (‖latanʸe, lătæ·niəɹ). [Fr.] **1.** *U.S.* [See quot. 1939.] One of several fan palms found in the southern United States and central America, esp. the cabbage palmetto, *Sabal palmetto*.

[**1719** tr. *H. Joutel's Jrnl. Voy. Mexico* 14, I could see from the Ships..[an] Abundance of that Sort of Palm-Trees, in French call'd *Lataniers*.] **1827** *Western Monthly Rev.* I. 315 Palmetto, or latanier, peet, and long moss, add an aspect of novelty to the view. **1868** *Putnam's Mag.* I. 594/1 Here and there..is a 'latanier-hut' with adobe walls and a roof thatched with..palmetto. [**1939** W. A. READ in *Zeitschrift für franz. Sprache* LXIII. I–II. 46 The usual term in Louisiana-French for this palmetto is *latanier*, m., a derivative of Carib *alāttani*, a name recorded by Breton for a West Indian palm with fan-shaped leaves.]

2. The Mauritian name for several fan palms, esp. = *LATANIA 2.

1929 *Encycl. Brit.* XV. 108/1 The coco-nut palm, an importation [to Mauritius], the palmiste (*Palma dactylifera latifolia*), the latanier (*Corypha umbraculifera*) and the date-palm.

latch, *sb.*¹ Add: **3. b.** *Electronics.* A logic circuit which retains whatever output state results from a momentary input signal until the application of a different signal to the same input point or the same signal to a different point. Also *latch circuit*.

1959 E. M. GRABBE et al. *Handbk. Automation, Computation, & Control* II. xvii. 6 A delay element is provided with external gating which enables it to hold information provided on the 'set' input until a 'reset' input of 1 occurs. This configuration..is sometimes referred to as a latch. **1962** SIMPSON & RICHARDS *Physical Princ. Junction Transistors* xvi. 403 A variant of it [*sc.* the 'flip-flop'], known as the latch, is an asymmetric bistable multivibrator. **1971** J. H. SMITH *Digital Logic* iv. 54 A push button might be pressed and at a certain time in a machine sequence the fact that the button was pressed may be needed to change the sequence. The latch circuit is therefore used to 'remember' that a push button has been pressed. *Ibid.*, A *1* signal applied momentarily to the set input of NOR 1 will make O/P_1 a *o* signal... To reset the latch a *1* signal is fed to the reset input which makes O/P_2 fall to *o*. As NOR 1 no longer has a *1* input, O/P_1 changes to *1*, thereby holding O/P_2 at the *o* level.

5. latch bolt (see quots.).

1909 *Cent. Dict.* Suppl., *Latch-bolt*, any latch or door-bolt, controlled by a spring and having a beveled head which, when the door is closed, is pressed back by meeting the strike and is thrown out again when the door is shut: the common form of self-locking bolt. **1958** *Encycl. Locks* (J. Parkes & Sons Ltd.) 247 A spring bolt, called also a latch bolt, of a lock or latch is one which having been drawn in shoots out automatically as soon as the handle or key is released.

latch, *v.*¹ **1.** Delete † *Obs.* and add later examples (senses 1 and 1 b) with *on*.

1937 *Esquire* Jan. 146/2 Dar's uh green sedan up front, uh fo' do' job. Latch on it 'n earn dis dime. **1940** *Sat. Even. Post* 13 Jan. 17/3, I latched onto a shark and killed it. **1946** B. TREADWELL *Big. Bk. of Swing* 125/1 *Latch on*, grab on to. **1951** I. SHAW *Troubled Air* viii. 144 They're out for something of their own and they latch on to us. **1954** D. RIESMAN *Individualism Reconsidered* xiv. 220 [He] has latched on to American consumption know-how at its most garish. **1957** *New Yorker* 29 June 68/2 Mr. Kelly has latched on to a sound (indeed, indestructible) idea for keeping a film in motion. **1959** C. MACINNES *Absolute Beginners* 58 Hundreds of pure pink numbers.. who've latched on to the Welfare thing, but don't belong here. **1962** J. WAIN *Strike Father Dead* 107 It was a long time before I could latch on to what was happening. Then I got it. **1968** *Listener* 27 June 837/1 When the doctor said, 'You're going to die, you'd better come back into hospital,' I said: 'Thanks for telling me. I'm going to latch on to life and I'm not coming back to hospital.' **1971** *Engineering* Apr. 41/3 The astute entrepreneurs are latching on to the idea. **1972** C. DRUMMOND *Death at Bar* i. 36 Jarvis soon latched on to two portly dowagers—relatives of his hostess.

latch, *sb.*³, var. LETCH *sb.*¹

latch-key. Add to def.: Now usu. the key of a spring door-lock. Freq. allusive and *attrib.*, with reference to the use of a latch-key by a

younger member of a household (esp. one who comes home from school when his parents are still at work) or a lodger. (Earlier and later examples.)

1825 C. MATHEWS *Memorandum-Bk.* (ed. 2) 19 At last he recollected he had a latch key in his pocket. **1836** DICKENS *Pickw.* (1837) xx. 199, I couldn't find the place where the latch-key went in. **1902** *Daily Chron.* 22 Aug. 3/6 At the beginning of the latchkey life everything looks delightful. **1905** *Ibid.* 17 Nov. 1/7 The names of 2,596 workmen in Devonport, known as latch-key voters,.. were restored to the occupiers' list. **1944** in *Amer. Speech* (1965) XL. 145 Latchkey children. **1945** BAKER *Austral. Lang.* 158 The arrival of American servicemen in Australia produced..*latch-key kids* for children left at home on their own by mothers engaged in war industry. **1946** *Life* 8 Apr. 90/2 His was a latchkey existence. **1950** T. S. ELIOT *Cocktail Party* I. iii. 70 Lavinia lets herself in with a latch-key. **1960** *Guardian* 23 Nov. 8/5 What happens to the 'latch-key children' in Germany? **1974** *Courier-Mail* (Brisbane) 14 June 11/5 One in every four school children was a latch-key child.

Also as *v.*, to open with a latch-key; to let oneself into (a house, etc.) by means of a latch-key.

1939 E. S. GARDNER *Case of Rolling Bones* (1940) v. 60 Mason latch-keyed the office door to find Gertrude down on hands and knees scrubbing at the charred carpet. **1961** WODEHOUSE *Ice in Bedroom* xv. 119 As he latchkeyed himself into Peacehaven..there was a song on his lips.

latch-string. (Earlier and later examples.)

1791 in W. R. Jillson *Tales Dark & Bloody Ground* (1930) 109 The doors and the window shutters are..secured by stout bars on the inside with a latch-string of leather hanging out. **1859** *Trans. Illinois Agric. Soc.* III. 342 It is but another proof of the well known characteristics of the people of the west, that they are always to be found with 'their latch strings out'. **1937** V. D. SCUDDER *On Journey* III. ii. 298 Especially at Commencement time, when the latch-string hangs out for returning alumnae.

late, *a.*[1] Add: **2. d.** *late developer*: see *DEVELOPER e.

e. *late cut* (see CUT *sb.*[2] 10 a and CUT *v.* 31 a), in Cricket, a cut, but with the actual stroke delayed until after the usual moment. Hence also as vb.

1887 F. GALE *Game of Cricket* 263 A splendid bat, back player, and great at a late 'cut'. **1906** [see *square-cut* s.v. SQUARE *a.* 14]. **1912** J. B. HOBBS *Recovering the Ashes* 124 An off ball gave Mr. Trumper a chance to late cut one nicely to the cycle path. **1960** *Times* 3 June 21/2 He will..late cut another in a way possible to few. **1963** *Times* 7 June 4/5 Padgett, after a delicate late cut for four.., was bowled off his pads. **1974** *Observer* 9 June 24/7 When Underwood came on, Gavaskar danced out to drive him straight, then lay back to late cut through the slips.

f. *late-tackle* v. trans. in Rugby and Association Football, to tackle (an opponent) illegally, when he is no longer in possession of the ball. Also as *sb.* So *late-tackling* vbl. sb.

1957 Late-tackling [see *BLATANT *a.* 2 c]. **1960** T. MCLEAN *Kings of Rugby* xi. 198 Raureti for the second time in the match palpably late-tackled Young. **1962** *Times* 26 June 3/6 People who have seen the film are now satisfied that he was not late-tackled at Pretoria. **1971** J. B. G. THOMAS *Roaring Lions* vi. 117 McNaughton swung him round to the ground without malice, but it was a late tackle, and Referee Pring..had no alternative but to award a penalty. **1974** *Times* 22 Nov. 11/1 England got bogged down..against a defence..in which a combination of offside tactics, obstruction and the cynical late tackle played a major role. This is what has come to be expected from visitors to Wembley.

g. Applied to a woman whose menstrual period has failed to occur at the expected time. *colloq.*

1962 J. LUDWIG in R. Weaver *Canad. Short Stories* (1968) 2nd Ser. 255 Shirley, maybe you're late this month, eh, dollie? **1969** 'V. PACKER' *Don't rely on Gemini* (1970) xiv. 119 Penny was two weeks late... There was a very good possibility that she was carrying Neal Dana's child. **1974** D. FLETCHER *Lovable Man* i. 21 Linda realised that she was late... It was impossible to consult her family doctor.

3. Hence *late-afternoon, late-night*, used attrib. Also *late-late* (*show*, etc.). Also, further examples referring to persons, esp. in *late bird*. Further examples of fig. phr. *late in the day*.

1816 JANE AUSTEN *Emma* I. xvii. 303 It was rather too late in the day to set about being simple-minded and ignorant. **1861** C. J. LEVER *Day's Ride* xlvii. in *All Year Round* 23 Mar. 568/1 Rather late in the day, I take it, to ask who Bob Rogers is! **1885** 'MARK TWAIN' in *Century Mag.* Dec. 202/2 The damp, earthy, late-night smells. **1888** E. BELLAMY *Looking Backward* v. 64 If I was inclined to wakefulness nothing would please him better than to bear me company. 'I am a late bird, myself,' he said. **1898** *Daily News* 30 June 6/3 His friend was what might be called a late man. The Duke [of Wellington], as everybody knew, was quite the reverse. The appointment was for eight o'clock in the morning... 'How can you manage to keep it?' 'Oh,' he replied, 'it's the easiest thing in the world. I shall take it the last thing before going to bed.' **1912** A. HUXLEY *Let.* 16 June (1969) 44 They are also on the point of putting up a war memorial, though none of the people who were in the war want it and it is now a little late in the day. **1944** D. EDWARDS in *Austral. Short Stories* (1951) 338 The street that glows with late-afternoon sun. **1956** B. HOLIDAY *Lady sings Blues* (1973) xv. 124 If you're an American citizen and unless you go to bed early these nights, you're liable to see me on the late-late show. **1957** J. OSBORNE *Entertainer* iii. 31 He plays the piano in one of these late-night drinking places. **1965** *Listener* 16 Dec. 1012/1 Just when the smoke..has cleared ..Mr Roger Pemberton [tells]..why he hates the views of Miss Laski... Surely this is a bit late in the day? **1968** *Ibid.* 5 Sept. 306/2 For thousands of young people Peel has the only late-night show worth turning on. **1969** V. C. CLINTON-BADDELEY *Only Matter of Time* 9 He had never been a late bird... He was seldom out after twelve. **1971** *Black Scholar* Apr.–May 47/1 Some are sleeping because they're the late late TV show viewers. **1971** P. PURSER *Holy Father's Navy* xxii. 109 We got them on to the late-afternoon plane to Zagreb. **1972** P. A. WHITNEY *Listen for Whisperer* ii. 22. 'I've brought her something from my father.'.. 'It's a bit late in the day for such a message.' **1973** *Amer. Speech 1969* XLIV. 277 An unusual example evolved on a late-night television talk show.

b. *late dinner*: esp. in Victorian society, the main evening meal, held later than the children's dinner.

1838 MRS. GASKELL *Let.* 2 Dec. (1966) 38 Mr Bradford coming home to late dinner and so agreeable. **1873** L. TROUBRIDGE *Life amongst Troubridges* (1966) 11 Mrs Quick is the cook... She makes very good things for late dinner but not for our [*sc.* the children's] dinner. **1885** A. EDWARDES *Girton Girl* I. vi. 136 The dinner-hour at Tintajeux was five, the 'late dinner' of Andros Bartrand's youth. **1941** MRS. BELLOC LOWNDES *I, too, have lived in Arcadia* xviii. 350 Even now the presence of a child at late dinner would certainly occasion surprise, to almost any guest of that child's parents.

4. spec. *late-Victorian* adj.; **late blight,** a disease of potatoes caused by the fungus *Phytophthora infestans*; = *potato blight* (POTATO *sb.* 7); **late wood,** a denser section of the annual ring of a tree, formed late in the growing season.

1905 *28th Ann. Rep. Connecticut Agric. Exper. Station* 379 Spraying will be of greater value, especially if early blight has been injurious or the late blight appears before the end of their season. **1909** B. M. DUGGAR *Fungous Diseases of Plants* x. 165 The late blight and rot of the potato is so generally known that frequently this malady is simply called the 'potato disease'. **1913** W. J. LOCKE *Stella Maris* iii. 26 Risca's room was transformed from late-Victorian solidity into early-Georgian elegance. **1918** E. J. BUTLER *Fungi & Dis. in Plants* viii. 277 The potato disease known as 'blight', 'late blight' or 'Irish blight' first attracted general attention in Europe in 1845. **1920** BEERBOHM *And Even Now* 3 A tired suit of Late Victorian pattern. **1929** T. THOMSON tr. *Büsgen's Struct. & Life Forest Trees* vi. 178 The difference between early and late wood consists in the former appearing more porous and open than the latter and often differently coloured. **1933** F. D. HEALD *Man. Plant Dis.* (ed. 2) xvi. 419 The late-blight attacks and kills the tops of the potato plant and invades the tubers, causing either a *dry* or a *wet rot.* **1955** *Sci. News Let.* 11 June 381/1 In an effort to find clues that might help clear up the mystery surrounding late blight.. plant pathologists..have surveyed the world. **1969** J. MANDER *Static Soc.* vi. 175 Teasingly sexless in the late-Victorian manner. **1972** *Sci. Amer.* May 92/1 Effect of smog on a Jeffrey pine that was growing in a forest near Los Angeles may be indicated by the narrowed rings and a reduced amount of latewood in the last nine years of the tree's life. **1975** *Nature* 10 Apr. 507/1 Whatever the cause, there is no indication that the width of the subsequent latewood was significantly altered.

6. *late model*, a recent model of a motor vehicle (usu., with hyphen, *attrib.*); *the late unpleasantness* (U.S.), the Civil War (see *UNPLEASANTNESS).

1917 G. ADE *Let.* 26 Apr. (1973) 63 Our own majestic work of art..has more late-model cars parked around it. **1973** R. BUSBY *Pattern of Violence* i. 15 They had found a late-model Ford Cortina XL unmistakably tooled up for violent crime.

late, *adv.* Add: **2.** *Proverb.* (Later examples.)

1852 C. M. YONGE *Two Guardians* xviii. 364 She obtained from Agnes some admiration for Caroline's conduct, though in somewhat of the 'better late than never style'. **1876** G. H. LEWES *Let.* 10 Jan. in Geo. Eliot *Lett.* VI. (1956) 211, I think that in the next number at any rate a bill might be inserted with effect—better late than never! **1950** G. GREENE *Third Man* ix. 77 Oh, Mr. Dexter, we have been so anxious, but better late than never. **1954** A. HUXLEY *Let.* 16 Sept. (1969) 711, I am sorry your holiday will have to be postponed so long; but better late than never.

7. *late-acquired, -departing, -discovered, -enfranchised, -gone, -hatched, -houred, -learnt, -maturing* adjs.

1933 *Mind* XLII. 279 The physiological and psychological processes which *cause* it to be given may be as complex and as late-acquired as you please. **1923** BLUNDEN *To Nature* 10 Late-departing yelps the fox. **1932** —— *Halfway House* 72, I have contrived that some most secret treasures Shall lie an age untouched, and late-discovered Shall be the source of hope and peace. **1923** D. H. LAWRENCE *Birds, Beasts & Flowers* 57 About your feet spontaneous aconite..and purple husband-tyranny Enveloping your late-enfranchised plains. **1937** BLUNDEN *Elegy* 30 Child of late-gone gale. **1906** *Westm. Gaz.* 16 Oct. 10/1 Only a few stragglers—most of them birds with their late-hatched broods—are left. **1908** *Daily Chron.* 10 Jan. 4/6 The pantomime crowd is a very good crowd after all, late-houred and not without failings, perhaps, but generous..to a fault. **1865** G. M. HOPKINS *Poems* (1948) 36 That yield That I may win with late-learnt skill uncouth. **1936** AUDEN *Look, Stranger!* 29 On their behalf guard all the more This late-maturing Northern shore.

lateener. (Earlier and later examples.)

1873 *Young Englishwoman* Oct. 515/2 'Here comes a lateener,' says the captain, as a light vessel rigged in the style familiar to mariners of the Mediterranean,..takes a flight up the Broad. **1953** C. S. FORESTER *Hornblower & Atropos* 245 The lateener's heading this way.

latency. Add: **b.** *Psycho-analysis.* (See quot. 1934.) Freq. *attrib.*, esp. in *latency period.*

1910 A. A. BRILL tr. *Freud's Three Contrib. to Sexual Theory* ii. 38 It is during this period of total or at least partial latency that the psychic forces develop which later act as inhibitions on the sexual life. *Ibid.* ii. 39 Sexual activity remains throughout the whole duration of the latency period until the reinforced breaking through of the sexual impulse in puberty. **1913** E. JONES *Papers on Psycho-Anal.* ii. 26 A period of latency follows, usually from the fifth to the tenth years, when the process of sublimation is at its highest activity. **1934** H. C. WARREN *Dict. Psychol.* 150/1 *Latency period*, the period of life between the ages of 4 or 5 and ca. 12 years, which separates the infantile or pregenital sexuality from the beginning of puberty or genital sexuality and in which the sexual manifestations are as a rule less prominent. **1949** J. STRACHEY tr. *Freud's Three Ess. Theory of Sexuality* ii. 57 It is from Fliess that I have borrowed the term 'period of sexual latency'. **1960** *Encounter* Jan. 80/2 The life of latency groups in Britain. *Ibid.* 81/1 These beliefs and customs are passed on entirely within the latency world without any intervention of adults. **1967** B. RUSSELL *Autobiogr.* I. ii. 38, I remember a very definite change when I reached what in modern child psychology is called the 'latency period'. **1968** E. ERIKSON *Identity: Youth & Crisis* iv. 156 In postulating a 'latency period' which precedes puberty, psychoanalysis has given recognition to some kind of psychosexual moratorium in human development.

2. a. Delay between a stimulus and a response, esp. in muscle; a latent period.

1882 *Proc. R. Soc.* XXXIII. 463 If, after a muscle has been powerfully extended, and while it is returning, by reason of its elasticity, towards its normal condition, a stimulation be applied, the latency may become as short as the 1/200–1/400 second. **1932** *Jrnl. Physiol.* LXXIV. 17 The general interest in the problem of latency increased when it was found, that while recording the action current of the muscle the latent period was absent, or seemed to be absent. **1951** H. DAVSON *Textbk. Gen. Physiol.* xvii. 483 The latency, as ordinarily recorded, is thus of the order of 3·5 msec. at 23°C; if, however, we take as a measure of the mechanical latent period the time between the stimulus and the moment when the tension [in the muscle] begins to rise from its minimum value, the period is 3·0 msec. **1963** *Jrnl. Pediatrics* LXII. 724 Cry latency is defined as the time which elapses between the moment of painful stimulation and the onset of crying. **1973** *Jrnl. Genetic Psychol.* CXXII. 177 The child was presented with a standard stimulus along with a number of comparison stimuli and told to point to the one that was the same as the standard... *E* recorded, to the nearest half-second, latency to the first response.

b. *Computers.* More fully *latency time.* The delay before a transfer of data begins following an instruction for its transfer, esp. to or from a rotating storage device.

1954 *First Gloss. Programming Terminol.* (Assoc. Computing Machinery) 11 *Latency*, in a serial storage system, the access time less the word time, e.g. the time spent waiting for the desired location to appear under the drum heads or at the end of an acoustic tank. **1961** P. SIEGEL *Understanding Digital Computers* xii. 258 The access time consists of the latency time plus the transfer time. The latency represents the amount of time it takes to find the chosen address. **1970** O. DOPPING *Computers & Data Processing* x. 145 If the drum makes 3,000 revolutions per minute, each revolution takes 20 milliseconds, and the average latency time becomes 10 milliseconds.

La Tène (latę̄·n). The name of a district at the east end of Lake Neuchâtel, Switzerland, where archæological finds were made, used esp. *attrib.* to denote a culture (fl. *c.* 3rd century B.C.) of the second Iron Age of central and west Europe, and objects found there.

[**1866** J. E. LEE tr. *Keller's Lake Dwellings* 239 A La Tène, Near Marin (Lake of Neuchâtel). This station was known and mentioned in my first report on the lake dwellings to the Society of Antiquaries at Zürich, in 1858. *Note.* The terms Tène (shallow) and Ténevière (submerged hillock) are provincialisms of the fishermen in the lake of Neuchâtel, and Professor Desor in his late work 'Les Palafittes', derives them from the Latin '*tenuis*'.] **1890** R. MUNRO *Lake-Dwellings of Europe* iv. 278 In making a section through the La Tène elevation there is first encountered a bed of water-worn gravel and sand. **1905** H. B. WALTERS *Hist. Anc. Pott.* II. xxiii. 502 It is interesting for its close relation to the older La Tène pottery. **1917** [see *BEADED *ppl. a.* 4 b]. **1932** *Antiquity* VI. 198 *La Tène.* A trading post on Lake Neuchâtel gives its name to certain cultures of the *Second Iron Age.* **1935** *Discovery* Apr. 102/1 The three tumuli..proved to be Early Iron Age in date, one of them yielding a small bone plaque with advanced La Tène ornament. **1943** J. & C. HAWKES *Prehist. Brit.* v. 94 Already when the first Hallstatt settlers were arriving in this country their kinsfolk in eastern France and south Germany were building up a new culture, that known as La Tène, which came to represent the height of early Celtic achievement. **1961** *Antiquaries Jrnl.* XLI. 44 Barrows, or burials, within square-ditched inclosures have recently been recognized as characteristic of the La Tène cultures both in the Rhineland and in France. **1962** *Times* 29 Mar. 15/5 The British Celts had evolved..their own superb, non-naturalistic late-La Tène art. **1970** BRAY & TRUMP *Dict. Archaeol.* 130/2 An art style with La Tène elements persisted into the Early Christian period.

latensification (lēⁱte:nsifikēⁱ·ʃən). *Photogr.* [f. LATEN(T *a.* + INTEN)SIFICATION.] Intensification of an existing latent image on a photographic film or plate by treatment with a chemical, prolonged exposure to light, or other means. Cf. *HYPERSENSITIZATION b.

1940 *Amer. Cinematographer* XXI. 499/2 With no more equipment than a panchromatic safelight, any photographer can increase the speed of a film from two to four times right in his own darkroom. 'Latensification', the name describing this new process, is an outgrowth of the research being done by Du Pont Film Manufacturing Corporation on high speed 35 mm. films. **1948** *PSA Jrnl.* XIV. 675 (*heading*) Latensification studies with sodium perborate. **1956** [see *HYPERSENSITIZATION b]. **1973** H. W. CLEVELAND in W. Thomas *SPSE Handbk. Photogr. Sci. & Engin.* vi. 417 Latensification is primarily an increase in the rate of development and therefore more effective with development well below γ_∞.

latent, *a.* Add: **a.** *latent partner,* one whose name does not appear as a member of a firm or company.

1913 *Act* 3 & 4 *Geo. V* c. 20 § 90 Any latent partner of a company whose estates have been sequestrated.

d. (Further examples in *Ophthalm.* and *Biol.*) *latent virus,* a virus causing no apparent disease in a plant or animal, but capable of producing disease in another to which it is transmitted.

1886 *N.Y. Med. Jrnl.* 4 Dec. 626/2 Heterophoria may, like hypermetropia, be partly or entirely latent. **1931** *Phytopathology* XXI. 593 A virus remaining latent or producing a mosaic in some varieties may cause a well-defined necrotic effect in others. **1937** *Science* 20 Aug. 179 (*title*) A latent virus of lily. **1950** K. M. SMITH *Introd. Study of Viruses* ii. 17 We have seen already a good example of the 'lighting up' of a latent virus when discussing swine influenza... The virus is latent in its intermediate host, the swine lungworm, and to induce infection in the pig it must be rendered active by the application of a provocative stimulus. **1951** *Nature* 30 June 1061/1 The presence of latent or 'silent' viruses in plants and other organisms is not, of course, new. **1954** S. DUKE-ELDER *Parsons' Dis. Eye* (ed. 12) xxix. 483 In all types [of squint] if the fusion mechanism is well-developed and the defect slight, visual alignment may be maintained in normal circumstances by a continued effort of fusion: the squint is then latent and can only be made manifest when fusion is impossible (as by covering up one eye). **1962** W. CARTER *Insects in Relation to Plant Dis.* viii. 329 Latent viruses are often important components of virus complexes.

h. Biol. *latent period*: a period between a stimulus and a response, esp. in a muscle or an irradiated individual. (See also sense d and *LATENCY 2 a.)

1877 M. FOSTER *Text Bk. Physiol.* I. ii. 37 A phase antecedent to any visible alteration in the muscle..during which invisible preparatory changes are taking place in the nerve and muscle, is often called the 'latent period'. **1926** L. HOGBEN *Compar. Physiol.* viii. 140 The rate of conduction can be determined directly by observing the difference in the latent period of muscular contraction, when a nerve-muscle preparation is stimulated at points along the nerve separated by a measured distance apart. **1933** O. GLASSER *Sci. of Radiol.* xviii. 319 Should the criterion be the first reaction which can be observed under the microscope in the living cell, the latent period will be very short. **1947** *Radiology* XLIX. 361/2 The incidence of bone tumors was approximately proportional to the dose administered, and the latent period—in no case less than about 200 days—increased gradually with decreasing dose. **1966** *McGraw-Hill Encycl. Sci. & Technol.* VIII. 638/1 Between the stimulus and the first tension development there is a brief latent period of a few thousandths of the twitch duration.

i. Math. *latent root*: a scalar quantity λ which, when subtracted from each of the elements in the principal diagonal of a square matrix A, makes the determinant of the resulting matrix equal to zero (and so is a solution of the equation $Ax=\lambda x$, where x is a column vector).

1883 J. J. SYLVESTER in *Phil. Mag.* XVI. 267 It will be convenient to introduce here a notion (which plays a conspicuous part in my new theory of multiple algebra), viz. that of the latent roots of a matrix—latent in a somewhat similar sense as vapour may be said to be latent in water or smoke in a tobacco-leaf. If from each term in the diagonal of a given matrix, λ be subtracted, the determinant to the matrix so modified will be a rational integer function of λ; the roots of that function are the latent roots of the matrix; and there results the important theorem that the latent roots of any function of a matrix are respectively the same functions of the latent roots of the matrix itself: *ex. gr.* the latent roots of the square of a matrix are the squares of its latent roots. **1958** R. V. ANDREE *Sel. Mod. Abstract Algebra* ix. 195 In quantum mechanics and elsewhere, the terms latent roots, proper value, eigenvalue, and eigenwerte are often used in place of characteristic root. **1968** E. T. COPSON *Metric Spaces* viii. 117 The condition..is known to imply that all the latent roots of A lie in $|z|<1$. Hence the latent roots of $I-A$ lie in $|z-1|<1$. Thus $z=0$ is not a latent root of $I-A$, so that $I-A$ is non-singular.

j. *latent (finger-)print* = *LATENT *sb.*

1923 J. A. LARSON *Single Fingerprint Syst.* i. 8 Take to your office all removable objects with visible or latent prints. *Ibid.* 9 Various powders, fumes, and solutions are recommended and have been used for the development and preservation of latent prints. **1937** *Discovery* Feb. 56/2 When a latent print is discovered, the area can receive a more liberal fuming to yield the maximum contrast. The amount of time required for fuming a single latent image is variable. **1956** 'E. MCBAIN' *Cop Hater* (1963) xix. 145 The tech crew dusted the latent fingerprints. **1962** M. PROCTOR *Devil in Moonlight* x. 102 'What's he expert on?' 'Latent fingerprints.' *Ibid.* xiv. 145 What they call latent prints, not visible to the human eye. **1974** G. F. NEWMAN *Price* viii. 242 Latent prints brought out on the non-absorbent surfaces with grey powder for photographing.

k. Psychol. *latent learning,* learning that has taken place without conscious purpose and that is not manifested until there is a goal to be achieved.

1929 H. C. BLODGETT in *Univ. Calif. Publ. Psychol.* IV. 122 Do these drops in errors which come after the introduction of reward indicate that something to be called a latent learning developed during the non-reward period—a latent learning which made itself manifest after the reward had been presented? *Ibid.* 133 During the non-reward period, the rats were developing a *latent* learning of the maze which they were able to utilize as soon as reward was introduced. **1938** R. S. WOODWORTH *Exper. Psychol.* vi. 137 'Latent learning', i.e., learning that is not revealed by the animal's path through the maze, until food has been found in the food box. **1957** *New Biol.* XXIV. 123 If rats, not deprived of any primary bodily needs, are put in a maze, they explore it... If such rats are later trained to run from one part of the maze to another to get food, they learn this task more quickly than similar rats which have not previously experienced the maze. This consequence of exploration is called latent learning. **1956** E. R. HILGARD *Theories of Learning* (ed. 2) vi. 214 This second phase demonstrates genuine latent learning of the true path. **1968** CHAPLIN & KRAWIEC *Syst. & Theories Psychol.* (ed. 2) vii. 277 Latent learning is hidden learning which goes on unobserved but which, under certain conditions, can be revealed in performance.

l. Sociol. *latent function,* a function which exists unrecognized within a social attitude or action and which will produce results that have not been foreseen.

1949 R. K. MERTON *Social Theory* i. 51 Latent functions..being those which are neither intended nor recognized. **1961** M. SPIRO in B. Kaplan *Studying Personality* ii. 108 Latent functions are those consequences which—whether intended or unintended—are not recognized by them [*sc.* members of a society].

m. *Sociol.* and *Statistics.* Applied to certain attributes, structures of relations, and the like (see quots. 1957).

1950 P. F. LAZARSFELD in S. A. Stouffer *Measurement & Prediction* x. 362 (*heading*) The logical and mathematical foundation of latent structure analysis. *Ibid.*, The latent structure approach to the treatment of itemized tests. **1952** GOODE & HATT *Methods in Social Res.* xvii. 286 One alternative..was to abandon the factorial approach and in doing so abandon the concept of a latent-attitude continuum. *Ibid.* 295 Another problem posed by latent-structure analysis..is the fact that its computations are both arduous and complex. **1957** KENDALL & BUCKLAND *Dict. Statistical Terms* 158 *Latent structure,*..a structure expressed in terms of variates or variables which are 'latent' in the sense of not being directly observable. Certain econometric relations (e.g. in terms of 'utility') are of this type. *Ibid., Latent variable,* a variable which is unobservable but is supposed to enter into the structure of a system under study, such as demand in economics or the 'general' factor in psychology. Unobservable quantities such as errors are not usually described as latent. **1961** J. ROTHENBERG *Measurement Social Welfare* IV. xi. 290 The spatial arrangement of alternatives is a uni-dimensional scale of some single 'latent attribute' calibrated by the particular alternatives. **1966** B. S. PHILLIPS *Social Res.* xi. 176 Latent structure analysis may prove to be of particular value in bringing to light a systematic set of assumptions or propositions about the probabilistic relationships between manifest data and latent structures. **1968** LAZARSFELD & HENRY *Latent Structure Analysis* ii. 15 It is necessary to make some assumptions about the nature of what we called the 'latent variable'. *Ibid.* iii. 47 Once a latent structure model has been specified, with accounting equations..relating the latent probabilities to the manifest probabilities, we must ask whether those equations can be solved uniquely.

latent (lēⁱ·tĕnt), *sb.* [f. the adj.] A kind of fingerprint, invisible to the naked eye.

1923 J. A. LARSON *Single Fingerprint Syst.* ix. 186 Several latents were left at the house which had been burglarized. **1937** *Discovery* 57/2 This method [of fingerprint detection] does not result in the destruction of the latent. **1939** E. S. GARDNER *D.A. draws Circle* (1940) iv. 48 'Any latents, Bob?' the sheriff asked. **1973** A. HUNTER *Gently French* iii. 23 The recognisable latents were either Quarles' or off-record, probably innocent.

later, *a.* and *adv.* Add: **B.** *adv.* Also used as a farewell, representing *I'll see you later.* (*U.S. slang.*)

1954 *Time* 8 Nov. 42 *Later,* catchall word for 'I'll be seeing you'; also used at the end of letters. **1955** L. FEATHER *Encycl. Jazz* x. 346 *Later,* parting phrase, short for 'I'll see you later'. **1972** J. MARYLAND in T. Kochman *Rappin' & Stylin' Out* 214 The players all started heading for the door, stating, 'Peace,' 'Later,' 'Hat Time,' 'I'm in the wind,' etc.

lateral, *a.* and *sb.* Add: **A.** *adj.* **1. b.** *lateral thinking*: a way of thinking which seeks the solution to intractable problems through unorthodox methods, or elements which would normally be ignored by logical thinking.

1966 *London Life* 22 Oct. 20/3 He [*sc.* Dr. Edward De Bono] divides thinking into two methods. One he calls 'vertical thinking'—that is, using the processes of logic, the traditional-historical method... The other type he calls 'lateral thinking', which involves disrupting an apparent sequence and arriving at the solution from another angle. **1967** E. DE BONO *Use of Lateral Thinking* 5 Some people are aware of another sort of thinking which..leads to those simple ideas that are obvious only after they have been thought of. This book is an attempt to look at this sort of thinking... For the sake of convenience, the term 'lateral thinking' has been coined to describe this other sort of thinking; 'vertical thinking' is used to denote the conventional logical process. **1972** *Observer* 5 Nov. 20/6 Don't trade on the argument that women have special qualities (intuition, perception, lateral thinking, or what have you) which are denied to men.

3. a. Also const. *to.* (Further examples.) Also, **lateral line,** in fishes and certain amphibia, a system of organs of sensory perception, arranged in a row along the sides of the body; also *attrib.*; **lateral plate,** in the early stages of vertebrate embryos, the ventral part of the mesoderm, from which certain internal organs develop.

1870 Lateral line [in Dict.]. **1874** FOSTER & BALFOUR *Elem. Embryol.* iii. 54 A transparent longitudinal line makes its appearance on either side of the notochord along the line of junction of the lateral with the vertical plate. **1913** *Gray's Anat.* (ed. 18) 242 Lateral to the foramen ovale is the foramen spinosum. **1914** W. E. KELLICOTT *Outl. Chordate Devel.* iv. 278 The lateral plate [of the chick] is separated into somatic and splanchnic layers by the extra-embryonic cœlom. **1926** J. S. HUXLEY *Ess. Pop. Sci.* xvii. 191 The special sense-organs for perceiving low-frequency vibrations in water which, like a herring or any other fish, it [*sc.* the tadpole] carries on a 'lateral line' along its flank. **1959** A. HARDY *Fish & Fisheries* ii. 24 We may not yet know all the functions of the lateral line system. **1964** H. W. MANNER *Elem. Compar. Vertebr. Embryol.* ix. 150 The mesoderm..was in three distinct, potentially different, portions: a medially located somite, an intermediate mesoderm, and a lateral plate mesoderm. **1968** C. OSBORNE tr. *Stenuit's Dolphin* (1969) v. 91 Fish perceive the variations in water pressure through a biological system known as the lateral line. **1972** *Nature* 31 Mar. 233/1 Electrodes..were placed at bilaterally symmetrical points over the left and right hemispheres,.. 2 mm lateral to the sagittal suture and 1 mm posterior to bregma.

i. *Phonetics.* Of a consonant: formed by partial closure of the air-passage by the tongue, which is so placed as to allow the breath to escape at one or both sides of the point of contact (e.g. English *l*). Also as *sb.*

1891 L. SOAMES *Introd. Phonetics* 34 Some persons..let the breath escape on one side only, so it seems better to call it [*l*] a *lateral* or *side* consonant. **1899** W. RIPPMANN *Elem. Phonetics* § 91. 72 For the *l* sounds the narrowing is between the side rim or rims of the tongue and the side teeth (*lateral* formation). **1903** SCHOLLE & SMITH *Elem. Phonetics* 75. § 148 In the articulation of 'l' both sides (or only one side) of the tongue form a narrow passage with the molars and side gums, hence the term *lateral* articulation. **1933** L. BLOOMFIELD *Lang.* vi. 97 In some of these the tongue actually touches the roof of the mouth, but leaves enough room at one or both sides for the breath to escape without serious friction-noise; such sounds are *laterals,* of the type of our [l]... In unvoiced laterals, which occur in Welsh and in many American languages, the friction-noise of the breath-stream is more audible than in unvoiced nasals. **1957** *Essays in Crit.* VII. 128 'Woolly' is composed of two vowels, a semi-vowel and a voiced lateral consonant.

j. Applied (orig. in *lateral cut*) to (the cutting of) gramophone records in which the undulations are cut in the plane of the record by the side-to-side movement of the recording stylus, and hence to equipment and techniques involved in this. Opp. *hill and dale* (*HILL *sb.* 1 b).

1917 *Sci. Amer.* 27 Oct. 307 While many of these patents are more in the nature of slight refinements, particularly means of twisting the mounting of the reproducer so that it can be used for hill-and-dale and for lateral cut records at will, a few of them represent a genuine effort to improve the tonal qualities of the conventional disk phonograph. **1934** *Amer. Speech* IX. 312/2 The records will be.. both of the ordinary lateral-cut type and of the new and superior hill-and-dale, long-playing, unbreakable kind. **1935** H. C. BRYSON *Gramophone Record* i. 16 From 1900 onwards there existed three types of record: (*a*) Discs with hill and dale cut... (*b*) Discs with a lateral cut... (*c*) Wax cylinders with hill and dale cut. **1942** *Proc. IRE* XXX. 356/2 (*heading*) Frequency characteristics for lateral recording. **1966** *McGraw-Hill Encycl. Sci. & Technol.* IV. 240/1 Modern lateral pickups are of the crystal, ceramic, magnetic, or dynamic type. *Ibid.* 241/2 A lateral disk record. **1968** *Times* 29 Nov. 11/5 A decade later Emil Berliner saw the advantages of a flat disc and also developed the technique of the lateral cut disc. **1975** *Hi-Fi Answers* Feb. 58/2 Test records used..were those by EMI..and Decca's own lateral cut record, LXT 5346. *Ibid.* 59/2 Modulation levels..which upset it at 8 kHz (for both vertical and lateral cuts) and 18 kHz (for lateral cuts only).

B. *sb.* **3.** *N. Amer. Football.* (See quot. 1971.) Also as vb., to make such a pass.

1934 WEBSTER, *Lateral,* a lateral pass. **1949** *Richmond* (Va.) *Times-Despatch* 10 Oct. 13/2 The last carried 27 yards as Quarterback Ben Raimondi threw a lateral to his left to End Cotton Howell. **1961** WEBSTER, *Lateral,* to throw a lateral pass. **1970** *Globe & Mail* (Toronto) 28 Sept. 18/4 He lateralled to Joe Hernandez, who ran the last 45 yards of a 59-yard touchdown play. **1971** L. KOPPETT *N.Y. Times Guide Spectator Sports* ii. 69 *Lateral,*

a pass to a teammate that does not travel forward. **1972** J. MOSEDALE *Football* iii. 40 The Bronk passed to Bill Hewitt who lateraled to Bill Karr for a 36-yard score. **1974** *Los Angeles Times* 13 Oct. III. 7/1 Greene ran 11 yards to the Badgers' 5-yard line and lateraled to Baschnagel, who sped into the end zone.

laterality. a. Delete † *Obs.* and add later examples of the sense: (right- or left-)sidedness; *spec.* the dominance of the right- or the left-hand member of a pair of bodily organs as regards a particular activity or function (such as the hands in writing, or the cerebral hemispheres in controlling speech).

1926 *Brit. Jrnl. Exper. Biol.* III. 317 The symmetry of right or left limbs will depend on the direction of growth.., and from a proximal cut surface an appendage of reversed laterality may thus originate. **1927** *Biometrika* XIX. 181 There is no evidence whatever of even a correlation between ocular and manual lateralities to say nothing of a master eye determining which is the master hand. **1937** S. T. ORTON *Reading, Writing & Speech Probl. in Children* i. 48 We have no guide..as to which is the dominant hemisphere except the 'laterality' of the individual, that is, his handedness, eyedness and footedness. **1950** *Brain* LXXIII. 168 In a systematic study of 100 cases of brain injury, these authors report varying degrees of deformation of the [visual] coordinates in patients with unilateral lesions of either hemisphere. They state that the direction and extent of deformation varied simply with the laterality of the lesion; deviations in right-sided cases were in an anti-clockwise direction..; in cases with left-sided lesions, they were in the opposite direction. **1964** *Dissertation Abstr.* XXIV. 3423/2 Predictions of laterality of cerebral hemisphere lesions can be made with a fairly high degree of confidence for those patients with well-lateralized, rapidly expanding lesions. **1964** M. CRITCHLEY *Developmental Dyslexia* viii. 51 Mixed laterality was then imagined to be a factor of special importance in dyslexics who might, for example, prove to be left-eyed, right-handed and left-footed. **1967** *Biol. Abstr.* XLVIII. 8522/2 (*heading*) Laterality in the use of the forepaws in cat. **1971** *Nature* 23 Apr. 524/1 Although usually used when speech dominance is questionable, amobarbital testing is also indicated in persons with apparently well established laterality when they are to undergo commissural section.

c. *Phonetics.* Lateral articulation (cf. *LATERAL *a.* 3 i).

1953 C. E. BAZELL *Ling. Form* 41 A voiced (or voiceless) character of *l* is not regarded as relevant even in languages in which voice is functionally discrete, on the grounds that it is not of functional relevance in combination with laterality.

lateralization (læ:tĕrălaizēⁱ·ʃən). [f. *LATERALIZ(E *v.* + -ATION (or LATERAL *a.* and *sb.* + -IZATION).] Laterality, esp. of cerebral activity; the property of being lateralized.

1950 PENFIELD & RASMUSSEN *Cerebral Cortex of Man* ii. 42 (*heading*) Table showing lateralization of sensory responses..in the face area. **1954** *Brain* LXXVII. 526 It is hardly possible to trace familial tendencies in the cerebral lateralization of language function. **1960** O. L. ZANGWILL *Cerebral Dominance* ii. 5 Conrad..regards left-handedness as in itself bound up with incomplete lateralization of higher cerebral function. **1964** *Dissertation Abstr.* XXIV. 3423/1 (*heading*) Lateralization of lesions of the cerebral hemispheres. **1971** *Nature* 23 Apr. 524/1 When brain surgery which may affect language mechanisms is being contemplated, lateralization of speech is sometimes ascertained before operation. **1973** *Sci. Amer.* Apr. 76/3 Although the relation between speech lateralization and hand preference is not perfect, the high incidence of both left-hemisphere control of speech and right-hand preference is probably not coincidental.

lateralize (læ·tĕrălaiz), *v.* [f. LATERAL *a.* + -IZE.] **1.** *trans.* To move or displace to the side; to render lateral. *rare*⁻¹.

1903 *Therapeutic Gaz.* 15 Feb. 74/2 The woven coudé catheter or soft-rubber catheter should be chosen to measure the urethral length,..since the bend..enables it more readily to surmount or pass projections on the floor,..providing the elbow tip is lateralized.

2. *pass.* To be largely under the control of the left- or the right-hand side of the brain.

1954 *Brain* LXXVII. 533 Milner reports visual-spatial defects consistently more severe in right temporal lobe excisions than left. She suggests that this is a function which is usually lateralized on the right. **1970** M. S. GAZZANIGA *Bisected Brain* vi. 116 The neural organization required for spoken language is usually lateralized to one cerebral hemisphere. *Ibid.* 85 Position sense is.. crisply lateralized.

lateralized, *ppl. a.* Add: **b.** Of consonants (cf. *LATERAL *a.* 3 i).

1968 P. M. POSTAL *Aspects Phonol. Theory* iv. 82 There are no languages with only Lateralized consonants, although languages with no Lateralized consonants are not uncommon. **1969** *Word* XXV. 19 It would seem to be a simple solution to interpret these Yakur sounds as lateralized plosives.

lateralward(s (læ·tĕrălwəɹd, -wəɹdz), *adv.* *Anat.* [f. LATERAL *a.* + -WARD, -WARDS.] Laterally; to or from the mesial plane of the body.

1913 *Gray's Anat.* (ed. 18) 236 Extending lateralwards ..on either side is the superior nuchal line. **1967** Lateralward [see *GENICULUM].

laterite. For 'rock' read 'clayey substance' and add to def.: and in other tropical and sub-tropical regions, which is soft when first dug but hardens irreversibly to the consistency of rock when exposed to the air. **b.** Applied *loosely* to various reddish or iron-rich surface materials in the tropics and sub-tropics. **c.** *Soil Science.* Any soil or soil horizon characterized by a high proportion of sesquioxides, esp. of aluminium and iron, and an unusually low proportion of alkali metals, alkaline earths, and combined silica, such as occurs as a product of chemical weathering in hot climates with periods of abundant rain; *esp.* one which hardens on exposure to air or is derived from one already exposed. (Add additional examples.)

The use and proper application of the word have been the subject of much debate.

1807 F. BUCHANAN *Journey from Madras* II. xii. 441 What I have called indurated clay is not the mineral so called by Mr. Kirwan. It..is one of the most valuable materials for building. It is diffused in immense masses, without any appearance of stratification, and is placed over the granite that forms the basis of Malayala... As it is usually cut into the form of bricks.., in several of the native dialects, it is called the brick-stone (*Itica cullu*). Where, however, by the washing away of the soil, part of it has been exposed to the air, and has hardened into a rock, its colour becomes black, and its pores and inequalities give it a kind of resemblance to the skin of a person affected with cutaneous disorders; hence in the Tamul language it is called *Shuri cull*, or itch-stone. The most proper English name would be *Laterite*. **1893** R. D. OLDHAM *Man. Geol. India* (ed. 2) xv. 385 The origin of laterite is still wrapt in obscurity. *Ibid.*, According to some geologists this laterite [of Buchanan] is in reality a soil and formed by the direct decomposition *in situ* of the underlying rock. **1898** *Agric. Ledger* (Calcutta) V. II. 34 If..it is difficult for the Geologist to decide what is 'laterite', it becomes practically impossible for the agriculturist to say what is a 'laterite soil'. Those 'laterite soils', that is, soils lying on or adjacent to what had every appearance of being laterite rock, which I have seen, had all a bright red appearance when dry; but as will be seen when discussing the analyses of the samples.., some at least of these are probably not true laterite. **1906** *Daily Chron.* 24 Aug. 6/5 The soil and the climate of Seychelles are evidently favourable to the growth of Para rubber, which thrives even in laterite soils where no other plants are at present growing. **1909** *Geol. Mag.* Decade V. VI. 431 The term 'laterite' has been used, in the Malay Peninsula at least, for many years by a large body of engineers for what are essentially masses of iron oxide replacing portions of weathered rock and filling fissures in such rocks near the surface. This (Malayan) laterite..is largely used for public works. **1910** *Ibid.* VII. 444 The foregoing representatives of the class of more or less ferruginous and aluminous deposits which in the Guianas..have been termed 'laterite' do not possess, except in the case of the concretionary ironstones, the property..of 'setting' or hardening on exposure to the atmosphere. Parts of them agree to some extent with what has been laid down as the modern scientific qualification for a rock to be termed 'laterite'—the fact that they are 'essentially characterized by the presence of free hydrate of alumina'. **1911** *Ibid.* VIII. 565 Laterite (or rather some varieties of it) is formed by a process..by which certain rocks undergo superficial decomposition, with the removal in solution of combined silica, lime, magnesia, soda, and potash, and with the residual accumulation..of a hydrated mixture of oxides of iron, aluminium, and titanium, with, more rarely, manganese. *Ibid.*, The property of hardening on exposure to the air is characteristic of many varieties of laterite, but it is not essential property. **1927** *Jrnl. Agric. Sci.* XVII. 546 It is..suggested that where the silica/alumina ratio in the clay fraction [of a soil] falls below 2·0 the soil should be described as 'lateritic', and where this ratio falls below 1·33 the soil should be described as laterite. **1932** G. W. ROBINSON *Soils* xiii. 279 Many of the descriptions of the supposed laterites merely relate to red soils... It is now generally agreed that the terms laterite and lateritic should be restricted to materials characterised by excess of sesquioxides. **1949** *Publ. Inst. Nat. pour l'Étude Agron. du Congo Belge* Sér. Sci. No. 46. 7 The word 'laterite' is used by us for the sesquioxide-rich, highly weathered clayey materials that change irreversibly to concretions, hardpans, or crusts, when dehydrated, and for the hardened relicts of such materials, more or less mixed with entrapped quartz and other materials. **1966** D. FORBES *Heart of Malaya* iii. 35 It [*sc.* a bungalow] was set on a hillside..at the end of a three-mile estate road of red laterite. **1967** *Nat. Geographic* July 110/2 [Thailand.] A foreman said this was laterite, a low-grade iron ore, good for making roads and filling land. **1970** E. M. BRIDGES *World Soils* ix. 72/1 Laterite..is formed by an accumulation in the soil of sesquioxidic material.

lateritic, *a.* Add: (Further examples.) Also, in *Soil Science*, applied to a soil that is not regarded as laterite but approaches it in composition.

1927, 1932 [see *LATERITE]. **1938** *U.S. Dept. Agric. Yearbk.* 974 Soils in which the laterization process has become markedly evident but has not reached completion are known as lateritic soils... They are very important in the West Indies... These soils are characterized by a colloidal fraction whose molecular ratio of silica to alumina is approximately 2. **1946** LUTZ & CHANDLER *Forest Soils* xi. 403 The laterization process, in conjunction with podzolization, has resulted in the development of six zonal soils in the forested warm-temperature and tropical regions: (1) laterites, (2) reddish-brown lateritic soils, (3) yellowish-brown lateritic soils, (4) red podzolic soils, (5) yellow podzolic soils, and (6) terra rossa. **1952** L. M. THOMPSON *Soils & Soil Fertility* xvii. 285 The clay soils which he studied..were lateritic in nature (high percentage of kaolinite or high in hydrated oxides of iron and aluminum), and it is now recognized that lateritic or kaolinitic materials are resistant to erosion. **1970** *Toronto Daily Star* 24 Sept. 14/7 He pointed to the lateritic, or oxide, ores of the tropics and subtropics as an area where future major expansion in the industry will occur.

lateritization (læ:tĕritəizēⁱ·ʃən). [f. LATERIT(E + -IZATION, rendering G. *lateritisirung* (now *-ierung*) (M. Bauer 1898, in *Neues Jahrb. f. Min., Geol. u. Paläont.* II. 203).] = *LATERIZATION.

1903 *Geol. Mag.* Decade IV. X. 62 That the formation of laterite is a mere question of average temperature seems unlikely, for lateritization is very prominent at elevations of 6,000–7,000 feet..in South India, where the temperature varies very little above or below 60° F. **1920** *Geol. Mag.* LVII. 212 The depth of lateritization was so great on the right bank of the Congo at a height of about 500 O.D. that [etc.]. **1934** *Discovery* July 202/1 Lateritization (silica leaching) may be considered as the reverse of podsolization (iron and aluminium leaching). **1966** *McGraw-Hill Encycl. Sci. & Technol.* VII. 406/2 The resulting concentrations of iron and aluminum oxides sharply differentiate lateritization from temperate-climate weathering in which the end product is largely clay minerals (hydrous aluminum silicates).

Hence (as a back-formation, or after G. *lateritisi(e)ren*) **la·teritize** *v. trans.*, to convert into laterite; **la·teritized** *ppl. a.*, **-itizing** *vbl. sb.*

1911 *Geol. Mag.* Decade V. VIII. 509 These five rocks.. were probably formed in situ under conditions in which the lateritizing processes were not pushed to a finish. **1920** *Geol. Mag.* LVII. 214 Certain inclined bands in the norite have been thoroughly lateritized for many yards along their outcrop, and seams of magnetite in them..run practically unaltered from norite into laterite. *Ibid.* 212 The lateritized portion was more readily removed by erosive agencies, and the masses of unaltered rock were left standing in relief. **1970** *Nature* 23 May 693/2 The southern half of Western Australia is an old, slightly dissected, lateritized land surface dating from the middle or late Tertiary. *Ibid.*, The Giles Complex of mafic and ultramafic igneous rocks..has been lateritized.

laterization (læ:tĕrəizēⁱ·ʃən). [f. LATER(ITE + -IZATION, rendering G. *lateritisirung* (see prec.).] The alteration of rock to laterite; the kind of weathering or soil-forming process that results in laterite and lateritic soils.

1903 A. GEIKIE *Text-bk. Geol.* (ed. 4) I. 169 Laterite... The peculiar kind of alteration exemplified by this rock and by Bauxite has been termed 'Laterisation' [by Bauer]. **1917** *Mining Mag.* XVII. 74/2 A very definite line must be drawn..between live laterite or that in process of formation, and dead laterite or that in which laterization is no longer actively operative. **1936** *U.S. Dept. Agric. Misc. Publ.* No. 229.22 The laterization process is, perhaps, more strictly a geological process than one of soil building. **1938** *U.S. Dept. Agric. Yearbk.* 973 The soil-forming process called laterization is essentially the progressive hydrolysis of rock minerals, and its full development results in their conversion to silicic acid, aluminum hydroxide, and iron hydroxide or their more or less complete dehydration products—the Laterites. **1952** P. W. RICHARDS *Trop. Rain Forest* ix. 209 This preferential leaching of silica from a soil is called laterization. **1967** M. J. COE *Ecol. Alpine Zone Mt. Kenya* 76 The clays show a certain number of darker stratifications but, due to the low temperatures, there are no signs of laterisation.

Hence (as back-formations) **la·terized** *ppl. a.*, converted into laterite; **la·terizing** *vbl. sb.* and *ppl. a.*

1917 *Mining Mag.* XVII. 67/2 Water from the laterizing zone when exposed to the air deposits ferric and aluminium hydrates with hydrous silicate of alumina. *Ibid.* 74/2 The upper portion of the laterite..is detrital, the lower part laterized and partly laterized schist merging gradually into altered schist. **1932** *Technical Communications Imperial Bureau Soil Sci.* No. 24. 19 Soils formed under laterising conditions. **1964** *Sci. Amer.* Nov. 97/2 Laterized soils occur most commonly in the tropical belt between the latitudes of 30 degrees North and 30 degrees South.

lates (lēⁱ·tīz). [mod.L. (Cuvier & Valenciennes *Histoire naturelle des Poissons* (1828) II. 88), f. Gr. λάτος Nile perch.] A large fish of the genus so called, esp. the *Nile perch* (*NILE), *Lates niloticus*; = LATUS².

1920 *Blackw. Mag.* May 655/1 Playing a giant lates is no joke. **1921** W. RADCLIFFE *Fishing from Earliest Times* xxv. 326 A picture of a bronze mummy-case containing remains of a small *Lates*.

latest, *a.*¹ Add: **2.** Also *ellipt.* as *sb.* in *the latest*: the most recent story, piece of news, fashion, etc.

1886 H. BAUMANN *Londinismen* 94/1 What's the latest: was gibt's Neues? **1889** *Kansas City* (Missouri) *Times & Star* 25 June, The latest the dear girls hereabouts are singing..is, Will he love you as today? **1911** A. BENNETT *Card* v. 128 This was Denry's 'latest', and it employed the conversation of the borough for I don't know how long. **1916** G. B. SHAW *Matter with Ireland* (1962) 95 If you want to dine in evening dress confronted with a bediamonded wife and flanked by daughters in the very latest,..you will be unhappy in Ireland. **1922** JOYCE *Ulysses* 319 Well, says the citizen, what's the latest from the scene of action? **1940** *War Illustr.* 19 Jan. 623 The newsvendor who still stands shivering at his wintry pitch, lustily shouting 'the latest' when you can only discern him dimly by the glow of his cigarette. **1961** WODEHOUSE *Service with Smile* (1962) iv. 58 'I say,' he said..'have you heard the latest?'

latex. Add: Pl. (see sense *3) **la·texes, latices** (lēi·tisīz). **2.** Also, *spec.* that of *Hevea brasiliensis* or other plants used to produce rubber. (Add further *attrib.* examples.)

1922 *Glasgow Herald* 4 Dec. 11 Rubber latex is a limpid liquid which is mixable with water. **1937** *Archit. Rev.* LXXXII. 57/3 The hearth-scene surround is constructed of re-inforced concrete, rendered in a mix of latex-rubber and *ciment fondu.* **1951** M. Abercrombie et al. *Dict. Biol.* 125 Latex of a number of species is collected and used in manufacture of several commercial products, most important being rubber. **1955** *Times* 14 June 11/1 Almost the entire production of the estates is in the form of latex..as distinct from sheet rubber. **1960** G. Lewis *Handbk. Crafts* 237 Latex Foam Cushion. In many of the modern suites of furniture latex foam or some other kind of rubber stuffing is used. **1966** L. Cohen *Beautiful Losers* (1970) II. 177 Several comfortable Latex cups assumed exciting holds here and there.

3. Any dispersion in water of particles of a polymer (originally synthetic rubber) that is formed in a polymerization process, such as is used as a binder in paints or for coating paper and leather.

1937 W. J. S. Naunton *Synthetic Rubber* viii. 140 'Rubber dispersions' should be divided into two groups: (1) Latices produced *in situ* by emulsion polymerisation... (2) Dispersed rubbers produced by the dispersion of preformed solid rubbers. *Ibid.* 150 This synthetic latex forms a good cement for assembling the numerous pieces of natural and artificial leather which constitute the modern mass-produced shoe. **1952** J. P. Casey *Pulp & Paper* II. xxi. 1247 Pulp treated with small amounts of elastomer latices has improved strength properties and increased wet strength. **1954** H. F. Payne *Organic Coating Technol.* I. ix. 372 During the past few years stabilized latexes of a variety of polymeric film-formers have been made available to the paint industry. **1969** T. C. Thorstensen *Pract. Leather Technol.* xiv. 226 In a latex system the binder is emulsified in water. When the latex is applied the water evaporates, or sinks into the leather, and eventually a phase inversion takes place.

4. Special Comb. **latex paint**, a paint having a latex as its binding medium.

1954 H. F. Payne *Organic Coating Technol.* I. ix. 372 Another advantage of latex paints is their very fast drying property. **1965** D. H. Parker *Princ. Surface Coating Technol.* xliv. 724 Exterior latex paints should not be applied directly to unpainted wood, for poor adhesion may result.

lath, *sb.* Add: **1. b. lath and plaster** *Rhyming slang*, master.

1857 'Ducange Anglicus' *Vulgar Tongue* 11 Lath-and-plaster, master.

2. b. (Later example.)

1922 A. Bennett *Lilian* II. iii, The entire office, thanks to that lath, Millicent, was disorganised.

c. *Min.* and *Petrol.* A mineral crystal that is thin, narrow, and elongated.

[**1908** L. V. Pirsson *Rocks & Rock Minerals* iv. 36 In some rocks, such..as the syenites, which are mainly composed of feldspar..they have more or less perfectly the shape of flat tables or rude laths.] **1916** A. Johannsen tr. *Weinschenk's Fund. Princ. Petrol.* x. 199 In this [intersertal] texture the interstices between the feldspar laths are filled with glass. **1941** *Proc. Prehist. Soc.* VII. 65 The rock is a strongly ophitic dolerite with..plates of fresh augite and laths of plagioclase. **1959** W. W. Moorhouse *Study of Rocks in Thin Section* v. 160 Intersertal includes diabasic and ophitic textures, in which the feldspar laths are enclosed with large grains of pyroxene.

4. a. *lath-hammer* (later examples). **b.** *lath-sword* (later example). **c.** *lath-cutting*. **d.** *lath-shaped* adj.

1827 *Western Monthly Rev.* I. 80 A lath-cutting machine..cuts them with great rapidity. **1847** *Rep. Comm. Patents 1846* (U.S.) 91 One patent has been granted for improvements in lath-cutting machines. **1901** J. Black *Illustr. Carpenter & Builder Ser.: Home Handicrafts* 35 The laths are nailed to each stud, or joist... For this purpose the best tool to employ is the..lath-hammer. **1964** J. S. Scott *Dict. Building* 188 *Lath hammer*.., a plasterer's hammer for nailing laths. **1888** J. J. H. Teall *Brit. Petrogr.* 435 This [interstitial] substance occurs in irregular masses wedged in between the lath-shaped felspathic constituent. **1973** *Nature* 9 Feb. 374/1 Lath-shaped crystals also occur and their size is about 0·15 × 0·05 mm². **1940** Blunden *Poems 1930–40* 250 While with a half-triumphant mind you crost Lath-swords of words on some uncertain matter.

lather, *sb.* Add: Also with pronunc. (lā·ðəɹ).

1926 Fowler *Mod. Eng. Usage* 315/2 Though lah'dher is often heard, *lather* apparently does not belong to the class of words in which ah & ă are merely southern & northern variants (*pass* &c.). **1968** *New Society* 22 Aug. 266/1 *Lather*: non-U to rhyme with 'father' (invariable in television advertisements) / U to rhyme with 'gather'.

1. *fig.* (Later example.)

1940 L. MacNeice *Last Ditch* 10 The sky is a lather of stars.

c. *transf.* A state of agitation, anxiety, irritation, or the like, such as induces sweat. (Cf. quot. 1660 in sense b.)

1839 F. Trollope *Fragment* in *Dom. Manners Amer.* (ed. 5) 271 Don't be in a lather, father, before you are shaved. I'll do your job, I expect, if you won't be in such a tarnation fuss. **1892** Kipling *Lett. of Travel* (1920) 99 Forced inaction frets the man to a lather. **1931** V. Woolf *Waves* 273, I arrived all in a lather at her house..but did not marry her, being..unripe for that intensity. **1948** 'J. Tey' *Franchise Affair* xvi. 181, I suppose Christina is in the usual lather of sentiment? **1945** E. S. Gardner *Case of Gold-Digger's Purse* (1949) v. 44 You're standing there in a lather of indecision. **1970** *Daily Tel.* 24 Sept. 4/8, I can't work myself up into a middle aged lather over long hair.

lather, *v.* Add: **1.** Also *fig.*

1917 P. Gibbs *Battles of Somme* 171 The enemy was 'lathering' the field of observation with every kind of 'crump' and shell.

lathering, *vbl. sb.* (Earlier and later examples in the sense of 'beating'.)

1835 J. P. Kennedy *Horse-Shoe Robinson* I. ii. 25 He shut that up..by giving Huger a most tremenjious lathering. **1843** 'R. Carlton' *New Purchase* I. xix. 169 Vain all pelting with clods and stones—all latherings with long bean poles! **1954** Weingarten *Amer. Dict. Slang* 222/2 *Lathering*, a scolding; a beating, a thrashing.

lathi. Now the more usual form of Lathee. Also *attrib.*

1850, 1895 [see Lathee]. **1920** *Glasgow Herald* 31 Dec. 7 Some disturbance..in which lathis were used. **1924** R. Graves *Mock Beggar Hall* 64 Then the new power, foreseeing grave events Calls out the lathi-wallahs to line the streets. **1930** *Daily Express* 6 Nov. 3/6 The police made a number of lathi charges to disperse the crowd. **1936** J. Nehru *Autobiogr.* 177 My body felt the baton and *lathi* blows of the police. **1972** *Times of India* 28 Nov. 11/2 A judicial inquiry was demanded into the lathi-charge at Gulbarga.

lati-. Add: **latise·ptate** *a.* = *latisept* adj.

1959 A. R. Clapham et al. *Excursion Flora Brit. Isles* 555 Latiseptate. Of a fr[uit] with the septum across the widest diameter.

latifundia. Add: (Later examples.) Hence **latifu·ndiarist** *a.* = Latifundian *a.* Also, the Italian form **latifo·ndi** (sing. *latifondo*). Also, later examples referring to large plantations in Latin America; so **latifundi·sta** [Sp.], the owner of a *latifundium* (Sp. *latifundio*) in Spain or Latin America; also in anglicized form **latifu·ndist**.

1902 *Encycl. Brit.* XXIX. 612/2 Special contracts..are applied to the *latifondi* or huge estates [in Italy]. **1930** C. F. Jones *S. Amer.* xxi. 310 The establishment of the *latifundia* first began on a large scale during Rosas' first campaign. *Ibid.* 447 The *latifundia* system. **1937** F. Borkenau *Spanish Cockpit* i. 48 Abolition of *de facto* serfdom, splitting up of the *latifundia* in the South and the Centre. **1954** Koestler *Invis. Writing* xxiv. 263 The ruin of farmers and the growth of large latifundia. **1961** *Listener* 24 Aug. 266/2 The actual state farms [in Cuba] have been set up on what were almost uncultivated latifundia. **1962** *Economist* 27 Jan. 333/2 There is no *latifundista* class [in the Dominican Republic] to prevent effective land reform. **1963** *Ibid.* 2 Nov. 461/2 The *latifundistas*, local dignitaries and conservative Catholics [in Spain]. **1964** Gould & Kolb *Dict. Social Sci.* 268/1 A polity dominated by the owners of large estates. As this type of society has been called latifundiarist, there is no point in wasting the word *feudal* on it. **1964** *Punch* 26 Aug. 291/1 The tired and near-forsaken *latifundia* in the main [W. Indies] sugar-producing islands. **1967** C. Seton-Watson *Italy from Liberalism to Fascism* viii. 312 Most of the proprietors of the *latifondi* were absentees. **1970** *Time* 2 Nov. 20 He is determined to expropriate the wealth of the big capitalists, the latifundists and the imperialists. **1974** *Times Lit. Suppl.* 8 Feb. 124/2 The 25,000 or so medium farmers [in Chile] whose holdings were below the minimum legally classified as *latifundia*.

‖**latigo** (la·tigo). *U.S.* [Sp.] A strap for tightening a cinch. Also *attrib.*, as *latigo strap*.

1873 A. S. Evans *À la California* 331 The wide band of woven horsehair, known as the cinch, is drawn up by the powerful purchase on the *latigo* strap until it deeply imbeds itself in the animal's belly. **1894** *Dialect Notes* I. vii. 325 Látigo: a thong... The two ends of the cinch terminate in long, narrow strips of leather—*látigos*—which connect the cinch with the saddle and are run through an iron ring called *larigo*. **1952** J. Steinbeck *East of Eden* 149 He was lacing the latigo through the cinch rings. **1962** W. Stegner *Wolf Willow* III. ii. 155 He picked at the latigo with one freezing unmittened hand. **1968** R. M. Patterson *Finlay's River* 237 The latigo laces are long, finely cut leather thongs, taken from a big hide.

latimeria (lætimīə·riă). [mod.L. (J. L. B. Smith 1939, in *Nature* 18 Mar. 456/2), f. name of Marjorie E. D. Courtenay-*Latimer* (b. 1907), director of the East London Museum at the time of the discovery + -ia[1].] A large marine fish of the genus so called, the only living representative of the order of crossopterygian fishes Actinistia, which was discovered in deep water off the south-east coast of Africa in 1938; = *cœlacanth.

1940 *Nature* 13 July 53/1 The exceptionally oily nature of Latimeria..is interesting geologically. **1953** J. S. Huxley *Evolution in Action* v. 128 Latimeria is the name of a rather primitive kind of fish, more nearly related to lung-fish than to modern Teleosts, one single specimen of which was recently brought up alive by a fishing vessel off the coast of South Africa. **1956** J. L. B. Smith *Old Fourlegs: Story of Coelacanth* 236 All [cœlacanths] have been large fishes..with fins like *Latimeria*. **1968** A. S. Romer *Procession of Life* viii. 166 (*caption*) *Latimeria*, about five feet long, is the last surviving coelacanth.

Latin, *a.* and *sb.* Add: **A.** *adj.* **2.** *Latin letter*, a letter of the Latin alphabet.

1535 [in Dict.]. **1953** K. Jackson *Lang. & Hist. Early Brit.* 179 Latin-letter inscriptions. **1965** *Language* XLI. 238 All Serbo-Croatian examples..are cited in conventional Latin-letter orthography.

4. b. *Latin-American* (adj.), of or belonging to those countries in Central and South America in which Spanish or Portuguese is the dominant language (and which are often referred to collectively as *Latin America*); also (sb.), an inhabitant of one of these countries. Also (ellipt.) *Latin*.

1893 *Funk's Stand. Dict.*, Latin American. **1903** *Westm. Gaz.* 22 June 11/1 Mexico..the richest district in the richest of the Latin-American countries. **1906** *Ibid.* 17 Apr. 9/1 Colombia..is taking her place with those Latin-American countries [etc.]. **1911** *Q. Rev.* Oct. 456 Serious competition for British merchants doing trade with the Latin-American States. **1912** *Chambers's Jrnl.* June 358/2 The amount of British capital invested in the countries of Latin-America is very great. *Ibid.* Nov. 720/2 An Englishman..soon wishes himself well rid of the..Latin-American. **1936** *Discovery* Dec. 365/1 An issue [of *Discovery*] devoted to Latin America. **1955** L. Feather *Encycl. Jazz* i. 30 The wedding of jazz with Latin-American rhythms. **1962** K. Orvis *Damned & Destroyed* iv. 30 The pianos segued smoothly into Latin rhythms. **1962** S. de Madariaga (*title*) Latin-America between the Eagle and the Bear. **1965** *Crescendo* Dec. 14/3 The arrangements are all in the Latin idiom and all of well-known tunes, getting off to a really swinging start with a L-A 'Peter Gunn' you *must* hear. **1966** *Ibid.* Nov. 6/1 All the side one tracks have this straight eight-to-the-bar or Latin feel about them. **1973** 'D. Jordan' *Nile Green* xxxi. 145 It's oil sheiks and Latin American generals and Lebanese rentiers who are going to buy your bonds. **1973** A. Mann *Tiara* i. 4 In the Philippines, some crazy Latin American got near enough to Paul VI to attack him with a knife. **1973** D. Robinson *Rotten with Honour* 8 He stood for a moment in the sunshine, snapping his fingers to a Latin beat. **1974** *Radio Times* 14 Sept. 26/3 Let's Go Latin..a fiesta of Latin-American music.

6. *Latin cross* (examples); *Latin square* [Named (as F. *quarré* (now *carré*) *latin*) by Euler 1782, in *Verh. uitgegeven door het Zeeuwsch Genootschap d. Wetensch. te Vlissingen* IX. 90, from the fact that letters of the Latin alphabet were used in forming it.] add: used as the basis of experimental procedures in which it is desired to control or allow for two sources of variability while investigating a third; hence used *attrib.* (also *absol.*) to designate such a procedure; (further examples).

1797 Latin cross [see Cross *sb.* 18]. **1936** A. W. Clapham *Romanesque Archit.* ii. 25 Although occasionally..the transept is of the T-form of the earlier ages, more generally the arrangement takes the Latin-cross form distinctive of the full Romanesque style. **1966** *Listener* 9 June 835/2 It is a Latin-cross church. *Ibid.*, A Latin cross is a more obviously Christian symbol than a regular geometric figure. **1925** R. A. Fisher *Statistical Methods Res. Workers* viii. 229 (*heading*) The Latin square. **1926** —— in *Jrnl. Ministry of Agric.* XXXIII. 510 For the purpose of variety trials, and of those simple types of manurial trial in which every possible comparison is of equal importance, the problem of designing economical and effective field experiments, reduces to two main principles..[of which the second is] the use of arrangements which eliminate a maximum fraction of the soil heterogeneity, and yet provide a valid estimate of the residual errors. Of these arrangements, by far the most efficient.. is that which the writer has named the Latin Square. *Ibid.*, The term Latin Square should only be applied to a process of randomization by which one is selected at random out of the total number of Latin Squares possible. **1935** —— *Design of Exper.* v. 80 The object of arranging plots in a Latin square is to eliminate from the experimental comparisons possible differences in fertility which may exist between whole rows of plots, and between whole columns of plots, as they stand in the field. **1960** D. J. Finney *Introd. Theory Exper. Design* iii. 30 Four different doses of insulin..were tested on rabbits and compared in terms of the subsequent sugar contents in the rabbits' blood... There is..a strong case for using rabbits as blocks and testing each dose, on different occasions on every rabbit. In addition, however, a block constraint based upon day of injection, so that on each day every dose is tested, is a useful precaution against the possibility that laboratory conditions on a particular day may tend to affect all animals in the same direction. A 4 × 4 Latin square with columns corresponding to different rabbits and rows corresponding to different days, enables both constraints to be incorporated. **1971** *Nature* 13 Aug. 499/1 On drug weeks each of six rats received one of six doses, each in a different order (latin-square design). *Ibid.*, An additional 6·0 mg/kg dose was administered to all subjects during the week after the completion of the latin-square.

B. *sb.* **3. c.** A member of any of the various communities in Europe (France, Italy, Spain, etc.) and Latin America whose language is derived from Latin.

1876 R. Brown *Races of Mankind* IV. xvii. 292 The Aryans of Europe are the Skipitar, Celts, Greeks, Latins, Germans of all branches, Lithuanians, or Letts and Slavs. **1908** Beerbohm *Lett. to R. Turner* (1964) 180 And then, of course, there is the pendant-fact that the Latins are born actors. **1936** J. Curtis *Gilt Kid* iii. 35 A kind of wooden..expression had come over her as it does over all Latins when they're scared of having to give something for nothing. **1949** H. van Zeller *We live with our Eyes*

Open 65 A Latin loves differently from a Saxon for instance. **1955** *Publ. Amer. Dial. Soc.* XXIV. 44 Most of these Latins [*sc.* immigrants from Cuba etc.] congregate on the East Coast. **1963** *Times* 2 Mar. 4/5 The Latins are said to be less susceptible to these emotions than we are.

5. *Latin-based, -derived* adjs.; **Latin–Greek,** of or pertaining to both Latin and Greek; **Latin Quarter** (F. *Quartier latin*; cf. QUARTER *sb.* 14), the district of Paris on the left or south bank of the Seine, where Latin was spoken in the Middle Ages, and where students and artists live and the principal university buildings are situated; also *transf.*; **Latin school** (also **Latin grammar school**) *U.S.*, a school offering Latin (and sometimes Greek) as part of the syllabus; cf. G. *Lateinschule*, Da. *Latinskole*, Du. *Latijnsche school.*

1964 M. A. K. HALLIDAY et al. *Ling. Sci.* I. 121 Old-fashioned Latin-based grammars. **1964** *Language* XL. 93 The inherited tradition of Latin- and Romance-based usage. **1946** H. JACOB *On Choice of Common Lang.* 38 A Latin-derived constructed language. **1965** W. S. ALLEN *Vox Latina* 109 As early as the fourteenth century one finds spellings with *ngn* for Latin-derived words. **1942** PARTRIDGE *Usage & Abusage* (1947) 290/2 Slang tends to be 'Saxon' rather than 'Latin–Greek'. **1960** *Amer. Speech* XXXV. 233 Unvoicing originated mainly in Latin–Greek bilingualism. **1869** 'MARK TWAIN' *Innocents Abroad* xv. 150 The *grisettes!*..so devoted to their poverty-stricken students of the Latin Quarter. **1878** R. L. STEVENSON *New Arabian Nights* (1882) I. 55 He had chosen to study the attractions of Paris from..a furnished hotel, in the Latin Quarter. **1904** J. T. GREIN *Dramatic Crit.* IV. 175 It was a generous mixture of the Latin Quarter and the various queer streets where London minor poetry flourishes. **1904** *Daily Chron.* 12 Dec. 4/4 They are good English garden-party hats, but they don't do for midi on an autumn day in the Latin Quarter. **1922** JOYCE *Ulysses* 18 And there's your Latin quarter hat, he said. **1930** E. B. CHANCELLOR (*title*) London's old Latin Quarter, being an account of Tottenham Court Road and its immediate surroundings. **1961** M. BEADLE *These Ruins are Inhabited* (1963) iv. 54 There is good reason now for wags to call the university 'the Latin Quarter of Oxford'. **1968** *Listener* 4 July 5/2, I left my friends in the Latin Quarter three weeks ago in a mood of exhausted elation. **1651** *Mass. Bay Rec.* (1854) III. 242 Whosoeuer shall..cause Schollers belonginge to the Colledge or any other Latine Schoole..to spend any of theire time [etc.]. **1680** in C. W. Manwaring *Digest of Early Connecticut Probate Rec.* (1904) I. 355, I give to the lattin Schoole in Hartford £50. **1685** *New Plymouth Laws* (1836) 300 That every County Town shall have and maintain a Latine School. **1781** S. PETERS *Gen. Hist. Connecticut* 185 Elms.. surround the center square, wherein are..the jail, and Latin school. **1856** B. H. HALL *Collection of College Words & Customs* (rev. ed.) 124 [A young man from the country] shall be examined and 'conditioned' in everything, and yet he shall come out far ahead of his city Latin-school classmate. **1959** C. V. GOOD *Dict. Educ.* (ed. 2) 311/2 *Latin grammar school*, a secondary school, emphasizing Latin and usually Greek, the purpose of which was to prepare youths for the universities. **1966** *Oxf. Compan. Amer. Hist.* 462/2 *Latin grammar schools*, the earliest type of college preparatory schools in the colonies, were established on the English model. The first, the Boston Latin School (1635), is still one of the principal schools in that city. *Ibid.* 463/1 By mid 18th century Latin schools were supplanted by academies.

latinate (læ·tinĕt), *a.* Also **Latinate.** [f. LATIN *a.* and *sb.* + -ATE² 2.] Of, pertaining to, or derived from Latin; having a Latin character. Also, occas., resembling an inhabitant of a Latin country.

1904 *Atlantic Monthly* Nov. 690/2 Cranmer transferred to the English..the rich sound and rhythm of the mediæval Latin; and that without the use of Latinate words. **1952** D. DAVIE *Purity of Diction in Eng. Verse* iv. 67 With intent Of being officious, grow impertinent... 'Officious' (in its Latinate sense, as in Johnson's 'Elegy on Robert Levett') defines and is defined by 'impertinent'. **1956** *Essays in Crit.* VI. 260 An anxious, questioning, excited passage, more latinate in diction. **1960** *Times* 16 Mar. 16/7 Miss Miranda, flamboyant and Latinate in temperament, is given..the part. **1962** W. NOWOTTNY *Lang. Poets Use* i. 23 Latinate syntax is important to Milton because it provides him with more ways..of devising contrasts. **1971** D. CRYSTAL *Ling.* 143 The distortions which..Latinate descriptions could impose.

Latinesque (lætine·sk), *a.* [f. LATIN *a.* and *sb.* + -ESQUE.] Resembling Latin; having a Latin character.

1887 E. C. STEDMAN *Victorian Poets* (ed. 13) 448 Its atmosphere, landscape, and notes of sympathy..are so unEnglish that one must possess the author's latinesque training to feel them adequately. **1903** *Westm. Gaz.* 8 Apr. 2/3 A new language, or a Latinesque language. **1960** *Times* 13 Jan. 6/4 Here the dances are lighter and predominantly Latinesque.

Latinical (lăti·nicăl), *a.* [f. LATINIC *a.* + -AL.] = LATINIC *a.*

1892 *Forum* (N.Y.) July 585 He [*sc.* Hardy] is, in point of diction, the most Latinical writer we have had since Dryden and Milton. **1919** [see *AUREATE *a.* 2].

Latining, *vbl. sb.* (Later example.)

1893 F. J. FURNIVALL in J. Capgrave *Life St. Katherine* p. xxiv, I don't think *Prata* above can be a latining of *Akker*, acre, field.

Latinish, *a.* (Later example.)

1920 H. G. WELLS *Outl. Hist.* 340/2 Neustria, the nucleus of France, speaking a Latinish speech.

Latinism. Add: The influence or authority of the Latin Church. (See LATIN *a.* 3.)

1920 *Contemp. Rev.* Oct. 495 The Spanish Court ladies were sheltered..under the vaulted roof of Latinism. **1970** H. BRAUN *Parish Churches* iii. 32 In Rome itself, Ravenna, and other towns of Latinism the basilican halls continued to be built out of the ruins of paganism.

Latinist. 2. (Later examples.)

1964 *Catholic Herald* 4 Dec. 13/2 (*heading*) The conversion of a convinced Latinist. **1965** *Ibid.* 29 Jan. 1/8 (*heading*) Latinists ask for prayers.

Latinity. Add: **3.** Latin character.

1915 M. C. FRASER *More Italian Yesterdays* x. 191 True to their Latinity, they gave their victim no chance of testing it [*sc.* their mistrust]. **1934** G. B. SHAW *Prefaces* 740/1 By the end of the nineteenth century the press and the theatre had lost all their Latinity.

Latinless, *a.* (Later examples.)

1906 *Athenæum* 21 July 71/3 The Latinless enthusiast who is curious to explore Propertius. **1958** *Duckett's Reg.* Apr. 44/2 The most Latinless lout cannot fail to understand what the monks are doing at Solesmes.

Latino (lătī·no). *U.S.* [Amer. Sp., f. *Latin-American* + Spanish ending *-o.*] A Latin-American inhabitant of the United States. Also *attrib.* or as *adj.*

1946 G. PEYTON *San Antonio* xxi. 232 The first program on the University's list is an exchange of students with Latin America. That in itself would be a fresh intellectual experience for Texas, where Latinos are usually looked on as sinister specimens of an inferior race. **1966** MRS L. B. JOHNSON *White House Diary* 2 Apr. (1970) 377 Six young girls, all Latinos, had encased themselves in cardboard boxes. **1972** *Listener* 9 Mar. 310/1 America..is meant to be a great melting-pot... Its racial components—Blacks, Latinos, Chinese, Japanese, [etc.]. **1973** *Black Panther* 17 Mar. 5/3 A program was drawn up..by an..action group composed of Blacks, Latinos, and Whites. **1974** *Ibid.* 19 Jan. 5/1 Mr. Rhodes' home was broken into..by a man who appeared to be of Latino origin.

Latino- (læ·tino), used as combining form of LATIN *a.* 2 and 4 b, as in *Latino-Faliscan, -Jazz, -Sabellian.* Also (with *Latino* = abl. of L. *Latīnus*) *Latino sine flexione*, the basis for the international language *Interlingua.*

1939 L. H. GRAY *Found. Lang.* 332 The Italic dialects fall into three groups: Latino-Faliscan, Osco-Umbrian, and Sabellian. **1954** PEI & GAYNOR *Dict. Ling.* 121 *Latino-Faliscan*, a branch of the Italic group of the Indo-European family of languages, consisting of the extinct languages Latin, Faliscan, Hernician and Praenestinian. **1958** P. GAMMOND *Decca Bk. Jazz* xxi. 265 It is worth remembering, when the history of the Latino-Jazz movement is written, that Kenton and the West Coast boys were years ahead of the boppers and the East Coast 'cool' men in hitching their wagon to the Latin star. **1880** A. H. SAYCE *Introd. Sci. of Lang.* II. vii. 110 We find in Italy two great stocks, the Iapygian and the Latino-Sabellian. **1928** O. JESPERSEN *Internat. Lang.* I. 45 In 1903 the famous Italian mathematician G. Peano started his *Latino sine flexione*... The idea is to take the ablative of each Latin noun and one simple form of each verb to be used practically everywhere. **1939** L. H. GRAY *Found. Lang.* 35 Esperanto, Ido, Latino sine flexione. **1946** H. JACOB *On Choice of Common Lang.* 16 *Latino sine flexione*, or Interlingua, as Peano called his system.

latitude. Add: **2. d.** *Photogr.* The range of exposures for which an emulsion, printing paper, etc., will give acceptable contrast; *spec.* the ratio (or its logarithm) of the exposures between which the characteristic curve is straight.

1889 E. J. WALL *Dict. Photogr.* 98 The extreme latitude of exposure which most plates possess. **1907** SHEPPARD & MEES *Investigations Theory Photogr. Process* III. i. 289 The latitude may be defined as the ratio of the exposure at which over-exposure commences to that at which under-exposure commences, and these two points must be arbitrarily defined. **1939** W. CLARK *Photogr. by Infrared* iv. 60 The range or latitude of printing papers is thus always less than that of negative materials. **1962** W. G. HYZER *Engin. & Scientific High-Speed Photogr.* v. 200 Actually the toe region of the curve is usable in recording shadow detail, which somewhat increases the effective latitude of the emulsion.

latitudinous, *a.* Add: **2.** = LATITUDINAL *a.*

1906 *Westm. Gaz.* 5 July 4/2 The race is not straight up to the limit of the earth's atmosphere and back again, but latitudinous.

lative (lēi·tiv), *a. Gram.* [f. L. *lāt-* ppl. stem of *ferre* to bring + -IVE.] Denoting the case used in some languages, e.g. of the Finno-Ugrian group, to express motion up to or as far as. Also *absol.* Cf. *ALLATIVE *a.*, *ELATIVE *a.*

1939 L. H. GRAY *Found. Lang.* vii. 194 The termination finds further analogues in..the Uralic lative and illative, the former indicating motion up to, and the latter motion to the interior of. *Ibid.* 195 The dative occasionally has, in Indo-Iranian, Latin, Teutonic, and Slavic, a lative force denoting the place toward which, in contrast to the illative force of the accusative. **1960** B. COLLINDER *Compar. Gram. Uralic Lang.* 239 The lative ending denoted that something is moving to the locality (or thing) expressed by the word stem. **1964** *Language* XL. 98 The same general discussion concerning the temporal function of the assumed Finno-Ugric lative case is presented twice.

‖ **latke** (lɒ·tkə). Also **lutka, lutke.** [Yiddish, a. Russ. *látka* a pastry.] In Jewish cookery, a pancake, esp. one made with grated potato.

1927 *Amer. Mercury* Feb. 206 Luscious potato *latkes*—pancakes made of grated, raw potatoes, [etc.]. **1958** J. GROSSINGER *Art Jewish Cookery* p. ix, A Jewish cookbook can be almost considered a history book... Just one instance—the *latke* (pancake), which the wives of the soldiers of..Judah Maccabee hurriedly cooked for their men. **1964** W. MARKFIELD *To Early Grave* (1965) iii. 50, I make a few *latkes*, I paint the kitchen chairs. **1967** A. BAILEY in L. Deighton *London Dossier* 55 If you hunger after gefillte fish or latkes when in Soho, try Grahame's Sea Fare restaurant. **1971** M. MASSON *Jewish Cookery* 44 Fry the *latkes* until a golden brown on both sides. **1974** *Times* 15 Oct. 13/8 He really does need a few more of my potato lutkas.

latosol (læ·tǒsǫl). *Soil Science.* [f. LAT(ERITE + -O + *-SOL.] (See quot. 1949.)

1949 C. E. KELLOGG in *Technical Communications Commonwealth Bureau Soil Sci.* No. 46. 79 We should like to suggest that some new term be adopted to comprehend all the zonal soils in tropical and equatorial regions having their dominant characteristics associated with low silica-sesquioxide ratios of clay fractions, low base-exchange capacities, low activities of the clay, low content of most primary minerals, low content of soluble constituents, a high degree of aggregate stability, and (perhaps) some red colour. The word 'Latosol' has been proposed as the name for this group at the categorical level of suborder... It is a collective term for those zonal soils previously called 'lateritic soils' where the characteristics just mentioned were dominant. **1955** K. LAWTON in F. E. Bear *Chem. of Soil* ii. 68 In the group of soils considered to be laterites or latosols, aluminum and iron may make up a large proportion of the soil mass... Some ferruginous latosols contain as much as 60 per cent Fe_2O_3 and thereby could be classified as low grade iron ore. **1965** B. T. BUNTING *Geogr. Soil* xvii. 199 In S. America, dark latosols occur in humid areas or on base-rich rocks; red latosols on acid materials and brown latosols on ash or basaltic terrain.

Latour (latū·ɹ). [Fr., ellipt. for *Château Latour*, the vineyard where it is produced.] A red Bordeaux wine from the Haut-Médoc district of France.

1833 [see *CHÂTEAU b]. **1920** G. SAINTSBURY *Notes on Cellar-Bk.* iv. 48, I think the best Latour rather better. **1931** S. JAMESON *Richer Dust* iv. 79 Nicholas watched his scout pouring claret into Hugh's glass... A Latour of '93. **1935** *Punch* 28 Aug. 238/2 Ah, the Old Latour and the Old Lafite, And the Old Yquem which was not too sweet. **1958** J. W. LAMBERT in C. Ray *Compleat Imbiber* II. 200 How, despite one's best endeavours, they echo in the mind, those great names—Lafite, Margaux, Latour, Mouton-Rothschild. **1967** A. LICHINE *Encycl. Wines* 321 Full-bodied and hard when young, Latour develops into something firm, rich, and noble. **1973** [see *LAFITE].

latrine. Add: **2.** *attrib.* and *Comb.* **latrine rumour** *Services' slang*, a baseless rumour believed to originate in gossip in the latrines; also *absol.*

1918 in *Amer. Speech* 1972 (1975) XLVII. 73 (*title of unofficial newspaper*) La Trine Rumor. **1925** in FRASER & GIBBONS *Soldier & Sailor Words* 140. **1929** F. A. POTTLE *Stretchers* (1930) i. 15 A 'latrine', we learned, was not only a building, but also the name for any particularly exciting but quite unfounded rumour emanating therefrom. **1929** A. W. WHEEN tr. *Remarque's All Quiet on W. Front* i. 15 Not for nothing was the word 'latrine rumour' invented; these places are the regimental gossip-shops and common-rooms. **1931** S. SOUTHWOLD in *Martial Medley* 105 This short essay..confines itself mainly to the rumours current among the fighting forces, and generally referred to as latrine-rumours and dump-rumours. **1950** PARTRIDGE *Here, There & Everywhere* 76 Late in the [First] War, tersely (*eine*) *Latrine*—the English term being *latrine-rumour.*

latrinogram (lătrī·nogræm). *Services' slang.* [f. LATRIN(E + -O + -GRAM.] = *latrine rumour* (*LATRINE 2).

1944 [see *DINKUM B. *adj.*]. **1946** [see *bush telegraph* s.v. *BUSH *sb.*¹ 11]. **1947** D. M. DAVIN *Gorse blooms Pale* 203 According to current latrino-gram we were going to be given a rest. **1966** *Sunday Times* (Colour Suppl.) 4 Dec. 73/2 GI Jargon. *Latrinogram*, latrine rumour.

lats: see *LAT³.

lattee, var. LATHEE.

1864 G. O. TREVELYAN *Competition Wallah* 170 Placing a lattee, which is the name for the quarter-staff carried by all Indian peasants, under the defaulter's knee.

latter, *a.* (*adv.*) Add: **A.** *adj.* **5. a.** and **b.** (Further examples.) Also used to denote the last of a group of more than two persons or things, or a person or thing that has been mentioned at or near the end of a preceding clause or sentence (see quots.).

1841 [see FORMER *a.* 2b]. **1853** [see *FILL-UP *sb.*]. **1903** G. B. SHAW *Man & Superman* 230 When a man teaches something he does not know to somebody else who has no aptitude for it, and gives him a certificate of proficiency,

the latter has completed the education of a gentleman. **1922** JOYCE *Ulysses* 616 'Eaten alive?' a third asked the sailor. 'Ay, ay,' sighed again the latter personage. *Ibid.* 680 The former returned to the latter..a sum of money.. advanced by the latter to the former. **1926** H. W. FOWLER *Mod. Eng. Usage* 316/2 *The latter* should not be used when more than a pair are in question, as in: The difficult problems involved in the early association of Thomas Girtin, Rooker, Dayes, & Turner are well illustrated..; & what was undoubtedly the best period of the latter artist is splendidly demonstrated... Neither should it be used when less than two are in question; the public and its shillings cannot be reasonably regarded as a pair of things on the same footing in: The mass of the picture-loving public, however, may be assured of good value for the shillings—whatever be the ultimate destination of the latter. **1928** [see *LENATE *v.*]. **1938** *Amer. Speech* XIII. 28 Faith, hope and charity are virtues, but few possess them, particularly the latter. **1957** B. & C. EVANS *Dict. Contemp. Amer. Usage* 267/2 *Latter* is the older of the two comparative forms... Its chief function is as a contrast to *former*. The contrast implies that some group has been separated into two parts, but more than two elements may be involved. We may say *the three latter events*. **1970** LOFTS & ADLEY *Saint* ii. 15 Another story..was written under the *nom de plume* of 'Leslie C. Bowyer'—the latter being his mother's maiden name. **1971** *Guardian* 24 Dec. 17/5 The Berlin Wall stands unbreached, passes are needed to get into Bethlehem and Father Christmas has been arrested in Oxford Street. It's the latter item that fascinates me. **1974** A. HUXLEY *Plant & Planet* xvi. 177 Light is also essential to the germination of many seeds such as tobacco, foxglove, many primulas and some lettuces. The dark-induced dormancy of the latter can be broken by quite low illumination.

lattice, *sb.* Add: **2. b.** *Her.* A charge representing lattice-work.

1828 W. BERRY *Encycl. Heraldica* I, *Lattice*, or *Lettice*, .. is formed of perpendicular and horizontal bars,.. and the lattice may be either interlaced, or not. **1889** C. N. ELVIN *Dict. Heraldry* 82/2 *Lattice*, *Tirlace*, or *Treilée*, consists of bars crossing one another at right angles, which do not interlace, but are nailed together at the crossings. **1969** FRANKLYN & TANNER *Encycl. Dict. Heraldry* 199 *Lattise*,.. alt. for 'trellis'.

c. In textile manufacture, a lattice-work apron or conveyer used to carry material into or out of a machine.

1884 W. S. B. MCLAREN *Spinning* x. 213 The wool is taken from it by a roller which combs it off, and passes it on to an endless lattice, marked 'upper lattice'. **1890** J. NASMITH *Mod. Cotton Spinning Machinery* iii. 19 In each case it is customary to attach lattices to the machine, by which the cotton is thoroughly broken up. **1967** SHAW & ECKERSLEY *Cotton* xi. 77 The machine employs a lattice and rollers to feed the thread waste to a revolving cylinder covered with steel spikes.

d. *Electr.* = *lattice network* (see *4).

1934 A. T. STARR *Electr. Circuits & Wave Filters* vi. 198 The lattice needs twice as many components as the bridged-T network. **1950** W. C. JOHNSON *Transmission Lines & Networks* xiv. 303 The filters most generally used are made up of T or π sections and L 'half sections' connected on an image basis to form a ladder network... A more general structure, called the lattice, is shown in Fig. 14.3. Not only can the performance of any T or π be duplicated at all frequencies by a lattice, but a lattice can be designed to provide characteristics unobtainable with the T or π. **1960** M. E. VAN VALKENBURG *Introd. Mod. Network Synthesis* xii. 339 If there is any symmetrical network realization for a set of specification functions at all, then there is a symmetrical lattice realization.

3*. a. Any regular arrangement of points or point-like entities that fills a space, area, or line; *spec.* a crystal lattice or a space lattice; **Bravais lattice** (bræ·ve) [named after Auguste *Bravais* (1811–63), French physicist], any lattice in which every point has exactly the same environment (as regards the distances and directions of other points of the lattice); *spec.* any of the fourteen different lattices of this kind in three dimensions (cf. **space lattice*); **crystal lattice,** the space lattice underlying the arrangement of atoms or molecules in a crystal; also, the arrangement of points occupied by the atoms or molecules or of the atoms or molecules themselves.

1895 W. J. POPE tr. *Fock's Introd. Chem. Crystallogr.* ii. 12 Frankenheim..found that fifteen different space-lattices are possible, and then, having deduced from the cleavage and general habit of the crystals that fifteen fundamental forms of crystals are possible, he showed that these latter in many respects correspond with the lattices. Frankenheim's views are not in all respects correct. **1917** *Physical Rev.* X. 441 Manganblende, MnS, is a simple cubic lattice like rock salt. **1926** [see *crystal lattice* s.v. *CRYSTAL B. 2 c]. **1927** T. VERSCHOYLE tr. *Haas's Atomic Theory* iii. 58 From the one-dimensional line-lattice, let us now pass to the two-dimensional plane-lattice, which will be formed by points with the coordinates $x = k_1 a$, $y = k_2 b$ constructed in a plane coordinate system, where *a* and *b* are two lattice constants, and k_1 and k_2 can assume every integral value. **1934** *Nature* 16 June 916/1 The electron extracted from the atom may only move through the periodic field of the lattice with certain discrete energies. **1935** *Discovery* May 132/2 The patterns in which the atoms or charged atoms are arranged are often called lattices. There are 'face-centred' lattices, and 'body-centred' lattices, hexagonal close-packed lattices, and so on. **1936** *Mineral. Abstr.* VI. 323 Recently structures have been suggested, e.g. for α-AgI, in which equivalent points are not completely filled or are occupied by different sorts of particles. These structures are said to have 'defect lattices'. **1938** W. A. WOOSTER *Text-bk. Crystal Physics* 280 A Bravais lattice is one of the fourteen possible arrangements of the points in space which have crystallographic symmetry. **1955** *Mineral. Mag.* XXX. 625 There are in all twenty types of lattices, as defined by their symmetry element[s]: one one-dimensional, five two-dimensional, and fourteen three-dimensional. *Ibid.* 626 All lattices are formed by translations, and all are characterized by inversion. **1958** W. K. MANSFIELD *Elem. Nucl. Physics* v. 39 These displacements distort solid lattices, producing effects similar to cold working, and decrease the electrical and thermal conductivity. **1966** C. R. TOTTLE *Sci. Engin. Materials* iii. 67 The crystal lattice of an ionic compound depends on the size of the ions and on their valency. **1969** A. P. CRACKNELL *Crystals* ii. 56 The mathematical condition to be satisfied in the definition of a lattice is quite stringent... In fact there are only five two-dimensional Bravais lattices. **1970** A. J. C. WILSON *Elem. X-Ray Crystallogr.* iv. 52 Thirteen of the fourteen Bravais lattices (all except the triclinic lattice) possess at least one reflexion plane passing through each point of the lattice. **1971** I. G. GASS et al. *Understanding Earth* i. 11/2 The halite lattice is built on a simple pattern in which sodium particles and chlorine particles occupy alternate corners of a continuously repeated set of cubes.

b. *Nuclear Engin.* An array of fuel and moderator in the core of a nuclear reactor.

1945 H. D. SMYTH *Gen. Acct. Devel. Atomic Energy Mil. Purposes* ii. 21 The steady production of atomic power requires a slow-neutron-induced fission chain reaction occurring in a mixture or lattice of uranium and moderator. **1959** H. JACOBOWITZ *Fund. Nucl. Energy & Power Reactors* iii. 50 The Bulk Shielding Reactor comprises little more than an assembly of enriched uranium fuel elements immersed in water. The height of the active lattice is 24 inches. **1960** S. E. LIVERHANT *Elem. Introd. Nucl. Reactor Physics* vii. 178 If the lattice or matrix arrangement (i.e., a heterogeneous system) is employed, a chain reaction becomes possible with natural uranium and graphite as moderator. **1973** *Jrnl. Nucl. Energy* XXVII. 458 For water-beryllium lattices, the band structure and Nelkin's expansion..is [*sic*] computed for various directions.

3.** *Math.* A partially ordered set in which every pair of elements has an infimum and a supremum.

1933 G. BIRKHOFF in *Proc. Cambr. Philos. Soc.* XXIX. 442 If we define a lattice to be any set of elements satisfying [axioms] I–VI, we can express our results as Theorem 3·1: The subalgebras of any algebra constitute a lattice. *Ibid.*, [F.] Klein calls a finite lattice a 'Verband'. **1951** N. JACOBSON *Lect. Abstr. Algebra* I. vii. 208 Boolean algebras were the first lattices to be studied. They were introduced by Boole in order to formalize the calculus of propositions. **1964** H. G. FLEGG *Boolean Algebra* iii. 18 The algebra of classes is frequently referred to as Boolean algebra. A rigorous treatment of the algebra has been made by Garrett Birkhoff and Saunders MacLane and of its generalizations, lattice theory, by Birkhoff alone. **1965** S. WARNER *Mod. Algebra* I. iii. 105 An ordered structure $(E, \leq)$ is a lattice and $\leq$ is a lattice ordering if for all $x, y \in E$, the subset $\{x, y\}$ of E admits a supremum and an infimum. **1966** *McGraw-Hill Encycl. Sci. & Technol.* VII. 409/2 Lattice theory deals with properties of order and inclusion, much as group theory treats symmetry. *Ibid.*, The real numbers form a lattice, if $x \leq y$ is given its usual meaning... Again, the set J of positive integers forms a lattice, if one lets $m \leq n$ mean 'm divides n'.

4. *lattice-box, -fence, -floor, -mast, -ornament, steel*; **lattice conductivity** *Physics*, the contribution to the thermal conductivity of a crystalline substance arising from transfer of energy between the vibrating atomic nuclei in the crystal lattice; so *lattice conduction*; **lattice constant** *Cryst.*, the length of a side, or the size of an angle, of the unit cell of a lattice; *spec.* the length of each of the sides of the unit cell of a cubic lattice; **lattice defect** *Cryst.*, an irregularity in a crystal lattice such as a missing atom or an interstitial one; **lattice energy** *Physics*, the energy required to separate the ions of a crystal to an infinite distance from one another; **lattice filter** *Electr.*, a filter consisting of components connected so as to form a lattice network; **lattice network** *Electr.*, a network having four impedances and two pairs of terminals, each terminal of one pair being connected by an impedance to each of the other pair; **lattice plane** *Physics*, any plane containing lattice points; a layer of atoms or molecules in a crystal; **lattice point,** for '(see quot.)' read: (*a*) a point on a graph or in space having integral coordinates (further examples); (*b*) any of the points of which a lattice, esp. a crystal lattice, is composed; **lattice-truss** (example); **lattice vibration** *Physics*, an oscillation of an atom or molecule about its equilibrium position in a crystal lattice; also, a lattice wave; **lattice wave** *Physics*, a displacement of atoms or molecules from their equilibrium position in a crystal which travels as a wave through the crystal.

1865 'MARK TWAIN' *Celebr. Jumping Frog* (1867) 16 Smiley kept the beast in a little lattice box. **1938** *Proc. Cambr. Philos. Soc.* XXXIV. 475 The lattice conduction is shown to be important in poor conductors. **1971** I. G. GASS et al. *Understanding Earth* v. 86/2 At moderate temperatures..heat transfer in rocks is almost entirely by 'lattice conduction'. **1938** *Proc. Cambr. Philos. Soc.* XXXIV. 474 In good conductors the lattice conductivity is unimportant. **1962** *Physical Rev.* CXXVII. 1888/2 The lattice conductivity was increased by high-temperature annealing. **1971** I. G. GASS et al. *Understanding Earth* v. 86/2 The lattice conductivity of the various rocks tends to converge with increasing temperatures to something like 2 to 3 W m^{-1} °K^{-1}. **1923** H. L. BROSE tr. *Sommerfeld's Atomic Struct. & Spectral Lines* iii. 154 The crystal of smallest known lattice constant, namely, diamond. **1927** Lattice constant [see sense 3* above]. **1944** *Ann. Reg. 1943* 363 Siegbahn's determination of the lattice-constant of calcite at 18°C. **1969** Lattice constant [see *LENGENBACHITE]. **1973** *Physical Rev.* B. VII. 674 Energy bands, Fermi surfaces, and densities of states of calcium as a function of lattice constant have been calculated. **1938** *Proc. Cambr. Philos. Soc.* XXXIV. 486 We define a free path L_t for scattering by impurities and lattice defects on an atomic scale. **1959** *Phil. Mag.* IV. 468 When a metal is strained, the lattice defects introduced cause scattering of the phonons and electrons. **1924** *Physical Rev.* XXIII. 497 (*caption*) Lattice energies, from compressibility data, in kg-cal/g-mol. **1942** C. E. K. MEES *Theory Photogr. Process* iv. 183 In the fifth column are given the differences between silver and sodium salts for the electrostatic lattice energy as another measure of deformation energy. **1965** *Geochem. Internat.* II. 416/1 The methods of calculations of lattice energy are based on the assumption that the crystal is ideally ionic, but such crystals do not exist, and results are always approximate. **1861** *Trans. Illinois Agric. Soc.* IV. 259 An octagon, for exhibition of fancy articles..with a good lattice fence to keep people from the exhibition tables. **1964** H. O. PERKINS *Espaliers & Vines* vi. 90 The lattice or Belgian fence types. **1935** E. A. GUILLEMIN *Communication Networks* II. x. 409 (*caption*) Behavior of the reactances (891 *a*) versus the frequency variable $x = \omega/\omega_1$ for the low-pass lattice filter whose index and characteristic impedance functions are given by eqs. (889 *a*) and (890 *a*). **1970** J. EARL *Tuners & Amplifiers* ii. 43 Another arrangement employs a pair of quartz elements within a transformer, the idea then being more representative of the ordinary quartz crystal filter. Such a filter, called a crystal lattice-filter, is shown in Fig. 2.18. **1916** BLUNDEN *Harbingers* 24 When the dryer in his oast Had loaded up his lattice-floors, He called a binman at the doors. **1924** *Harmsworth's Wireless Encycl.* II. 1274 *Lattice mast*, term used to describe a tall, composite structure for the support of a lofty aerial. This type of construction is carried out in both wood and metal... Such a mast is triangular in section, and comprises essentially three upright members held together by tie bars of metal and braced by diagonal bracing of stout timber. **1928** A. WILLIAMS *Telegr. & Telephony* xxi. 282 An aerial is carried by five 28-ton lattice masts, 287 feet high, each resting on four legs bolted to 20-ton concrete blocks. **1948** R. DE KERCHOVE *Internat. Maritime Dict.* 399/1 *Lattice mast*, steel mast constructed of riveted structural steel shapes or lattice work. **1931** H. W. BODE in *U.S. Pat. 1,828,454* 20 Oct. 1/1 An important general property of a symmetrical lattice network is that its propagation constant and its characteristic impedance are mutually independent. **1934** A. T. STARR *Electr. Circuits & Wave Filters* vi. 196 Such a lattice network has image impedance *R* at all frequencies, no attenuation at any frequency, and a phase shift which depends upon the reactance characteristic of Z_1. **1956** AMOS & BIRKINSHAW *Television Engin.* II. ix. 126 In general a lattice network has two series and two shunt elements as shown in Fig. 68; this particular network is a symmetrical one in which both series elements are equal to Z_1 and both shunt elements are equal to Z_2... For purposes of calculation it is often more convenient to redraw the network in the form of a bridge circuit. **1923** R. G. COLLINGWOOD *Roman Brit.* 75 Coarse ware with incised lattice-ornament. **1923** G. BARR tr. *Graetz's Recent Devel. Atomic Theory* iv. 96 We will call each such series of similar parallel planes a system of lattice planes. **1937** *Amer. Mineralogist* XXII. 449 Consider any two successive lattice planes perpendicular to a screw axis. **1973** K. W. ANDREWS *Physical Metall.* II. ii. 90 If the grating is actually composed of lattice planes, i.e. layers of atoms or molecules properly located in relation to the electron beam, then an image of these layers could be formed. **1926** *Encycl. Brit.* II. 832/2 A lattice point (*Gitterpunkt*) in space of any number of dimensions is a point with integral co-ordinates. **1936** A. H. WILSON *Theory of Metals* ii. 48 We assume as zero approximation that the electron is in the neighbourhood of one particular lattice point. **1955** *Sci. News* XV. 143 The gas is usually regarded as being accommodated on the lattice of the metal by occupying positions in its interstices, rather than replacing metal atoms at some of the lattice points. **1966** OGILVY & ANDERSON *Excursions in Number Theory* x. 120 The point (20, 47), having both its coordinates integers, is called a lattice point of the plane. It is a point of intersection of a horizontal and a vertical line of the coordinate grid, or lattice. **1967** A. H. COTTRELL *Introd. Metall.* xvii. 261 This array of lattice points is the space lattice of the crystal. It is important to notice that a lattice point is not an atomic site. In certain simple crystal structures..the pattern of atomic sites happens also to form a space lattice, but in many other structures..there is more than one atom in the motif. **1951** *Archit. Rev.* CIX. 389/2 The lattice-steel roof-trusses are supported on the inner leaf of the reinforced concrete walls and act as permanent shuttering for the concrete roof. **1942** R. H. NEWTON *Town & Davis: Architects* ii. 42 The few sources I have consulted say nothing significant..about Ithiel Town as the inventor of the lattice truss. **1936** A. H. WILSON *Theory of Metals* vi. 200 The coupling between the electrons and the lattice vibrations is due mainly to changes in the density of the solid. **1959** *Phil. Mag.* IV. 468 At low temperatures the dominant lattice vibrations are those of long wavelength which are not scattered by the impurity atoms. **1969** J. S. BLAKEMORE *Solid State Physics* ii. 114 The particle—or phonon—aspect of lattice vibrations is particularly appropriate when we are concerned with energy transformation. **1936** A. H. WILSON *Theory of Metals* vi. 201 We should then be compelled to take into account the dispersion of the lattice waves. **1955** H. B. G. CASIMIR in W. Pauli *Niels Bohr* 119 At temperatures well below the so-called Debye temperature Θ only lattice waves with a

wave-length of many atomic distances are excited. **1971** DONOVAN & ANGRESS *Lattice Vibrations* iv. 83 In the harmonic approximation the lattice waves travel independently, without hindrance, so that the mean free path is infinite and the thermal resistance is zero.

lattice, *v.* Add: **2.** *trans.* To form into a lattice, arrange as a lattice.

1950 *Amer. Speech* XXV. 24 'Homogeneous' piles and 'heterogeneous' piles, depending on whether the fissionable material is latticed with the moderating material.

‖ **latticinio** (lati·tʃī·nio), **latticino** (-ī·no). [It., f. L. *lacticinium* milk food.] An opaque white glass used in threads for decorative purposes in Venetian glass. Hence *attrib.*

1855 F. B. PALLISER tr. *Labarte's Handbk. Arts Middle Ages & Renaissance* ix. 348 The opaque white glass, the *latticinio* most usually employed in the filagree Venetian glasses, is only a glass coloured milk-white by oxide of tin or arsenic. **1881** C. C. HARRISON *Woman's Handiwork* III. 229 There are the *millefiori*,.. The *latticino*, with graceful milk-white spirals. The *avventurino*, with the lustre of pure gold. **1937** *Burlington Mag.* Nov. 218/2 Venetian *latticino* glass of the sixteenth and seventeenth centuries. **1969** *Canad. Antiques Collector* Sept. 26/2 Latticinio glass is produced by pouring clear glass around fine 'canes' or rods of white..glass to form a thick rod with thin white rods embedded in it. **1972** *Sunday Tel.* 21 May 10/7 Collectors..will be burying their visual senses in millefiori, butterflies, latticinio.

Latvian (læ·tviăn), *a.* and *sb.* [f. *Latvia*, Lett. and Lith. *Latvija*.] **A.** *adj.* Of or belonging to Latvia, since 1940 a constituent republic of the U.S.S.R., lying on the east coast of the Baltic Sea. **B.** *sb.* **a.** A native or inhabitant of Latvia. **b.** The language of Latvia; Lettish. Cf. LETT, LETTISH *a.* (*sb.*).

1920 *Contemp. Rev.* Aug. 283 Troops under German command on Latvian territory. **1924** J. M. MURRY *Voyage* ii. 28 All these new languages. Lithuanian, Latvian, Esthonian, Transcaucasian. **1926** *Spectator* 31 July 176/1 Latvian is certainly not so difficult to learn as Chinese. **1941** J. H. JACKSON *Estonia* ii. 38 A branch of the Estonian race, the Livs, waged endless warfare with the Letts or Latvians. **1955** *Times* 16 Aug. 9/6 The Lithuanians and Latvians, ethnologically Indo-European, are survivors of ancient peoples. **1964** G. BENNETT *Cowan's War* i. 22 The defences of Riga crumbled, which prevented the workers of all three Latvian ports from declaring for Bolshevism in November. **1973** *Listener* 15 Nov. 656/3 Those who have an ethnic or religious fellow-feeling, whether they be.. Latvians or Georgians, Kurds or Nagas.

‖ **lau** (lau). [Native word.] An African water monster supposed to live in the swamps of the Nile valley.

1923 H. C. JACKSON in *Sudan Notes & Rec.* VI. 187 There is also a third kind [of python] of which rumours have come to my ears... This serpent is called Lau by the Nuer and Dinka... It is reported to be of gigantic proportions. **1925** *Blackw. Mag.* Sept. 303/2 The *lau* is a composite beast; it is reputed to have a bit of the bird, snake and lizard in it, like the wyvern in coats-of-arms. **1937** *Discovery* Dec. 369/1 The *lau* and the *lukwata*, monstrous beasts whose hideous calls are heard booming through the grey night-mists of the lakes.

lauan (lawā·n). [Tagalog *lawaan*.] The Philippine name for the light hardwood timber produced by trees of the genus *Shorea* or closely related genera.

1894 H. M. WARD *Laslett's Timber & Timber Trees* (ed. 2) xxii. 226 The outside planks of the old Manilla and Acapulco galleons were of Lauan wood. **1936** *Nature* 26 Dec. 1090/2 The top and side clasps [of the tennis racket] are of Malayan lauan. **1971** N. E. HICKIN *Wood Preservation* 88 Shorea. A very extensive genus of hardwood trees found chiefly in Malaysia, Indonesia, Borneo and the Philippines, the principal timbers of which are generally known as meranti, seraya and lauan, suitably qualified.

laubmannite (lau·bmænəit). *Min.* [f. the name of Heinrich *Laubmann*, 20th-century German mineralogist + -ITE[1].] A basic phosphate of ferrous and ferric iron, $Fe^{II}_3Fe^{III}_6(PO_4)_4(OH)_{12}$, of yellow- to grey-green colour.

1949 C. FRONDEL in *Amer. Mineralogist* XXXIV. 536 The name laubmannite is proposed for the species. **1970** *Ibid.* LV. 138 A new locality was discovered, the laubmannite occurring as bright yellow-green aggregates and affording a powder pattern virtually identical with the Arkansas material. The location is Leveäniemi in the Svappavaara mining district, Norrbotten Province, Sweden.

‖ **laúd** (la,ū·d). [Sp.: see LUTE *sb.*[1]] A Spanish lute.

1876 STAINER & BARRETT *Dict. Mus. Terms* 276 The word [*sc.* lute]..is most probably from the Arabic *el'ood*, as the instruments came into Europe from the Moors through the Spaniards, who still call it *laud*. **1923** *Blackw. Mag.* July 38/1 The Spanish laud or lute Jo had bought in Murcia during the previous year. **1954** *Grove's Dict. Mus.* (ed. 5) I. 400/1 The instrument [*sc.* the bandurria] is in common use in the south of Spain, generally in conjunction with the *laud* and the *guitarra*.

laudanine. Add: [ad. G. *laudanin* (O. Hesse 1870, in *Ann. d. Chem. und Pharm.* CLIII. 49).] (Examples.)

1871 *Jrnl. Chem. Soc.* XXIV. 1064 White crystals are thereby obtained, from which the laudanine is separated by the action of hydriodic acid, with which it forms a difficultly soluble compound. Laudanine has the composition $C_{20}H_{25}NO_4$, instead of the formula $C_{20}H_{25}NO_3$, as formerly given. **1954** A. BURGER in Manske & Holmes *Alkaloids* IV. 57 Laudanine is optically inactive in spite of the presence of an asymmetric carbon atom in its formula.

laudanosine (lǫdæ·nosīn). *Chem.* [ad. G. *laudanosin* (O. Hesse 1871, in *Ber. d. Deut. Chem. Ges.* IV. 696): see LAUDANINE and -OSE[2].] Laudanine methyl ether, $C_{21}H_{27}NO_4$, the dextrorotatory form of which occurs in opium and is a strong tetanic poison.

1871 *Jrnl. Chem. Soc.* XXIV. 1065 Laudanosine..dissolves sparingly in cold, but easily in hot benzol; it forms colourless prisms which melt at 89°. **1900** *Chemist & Druggist* LVII. 846/1 It is therefore probable that laudanosine is *d-N*-methyl-tetra-hydro-papaverine. **1951** [see *GNOSCOPINE]. **1972** *Phytochemistry* XI. 461 The major alkaloids of the above-ground parts of *Argemone grandiflora*..were found to be berberine, α-allocryptopine and protopine; (+)-laudanosine..and chelerythine were identified as minor alkaloids.

‖ **laudator temporis acti** (lǫdēi·təɪ te·mpǒris æ·ktəi). [See LAUDATOR.] A Latin phrase, from Horace's *laudator temporis acti se puero* 'a praiser of time past when he himself was a boy' (*Ars Poetica* 173), used of one who looks back to the past as a better time.

1736 SWIFT *Let.* 2 Dec. in Pope *Works* (1757) IX. 209 Have you got a supply of new friends to make up for those who are gone?.. I am afraid it is with friends as with times; and that the *laudator temporis acti se puero*, is equally applicable to both. **1753** CHESTERFIELD in *World* 6 Dec. 293, I am neither sour nor silly enough yet, to be a snarling *laudator temporis acti*. **1814** *Edin. Rev.* XXIII. 316 The suspected praises of any of the *laudatores temporis acti*. **1870** A. C. EWALD *Guide Indian Civil Service* 13 Some old Indians—*laudatores temporis acti*—are wont to make the most doleful prophecies regarding the results of abolishing Haileybury and introducing the Civil Service Commissioners in its place. **1923** BEERBOHM *Peep into Past* 10 Not that he [*sc.* Wilde] is a mere *laudator temporis acti*. **1931** BLUNDEN *Votive Tablets* 360 We can hardly avoid being *laudatores temporis acti* when we think even of Oxford..as it has been, and as it now is. **1965** O. BARFIELD in J. Gibb *Light on C. S. Lewis* p. xv, He..ended his days..as a kind of..guilt-oppressed *laudator temporis acti*.

Laue[2] (lau·ə). *Cryst.* The name of Max von Laue (1879–1960), German physicist, used *attrib.* with reference to a method of X-ray diffraction developed by him in which a narrow parallel beam of polychromatic X-radiation is directed at a thin crystal and the resulting diffraction pattern is recorded on a photographic film placed either in front of the crystal (with a hole for the passage of the incident beam) or beyond it; as *Laue method, pattern, photograph*; also **Laue condition,** each of the three equations (one for each linear parameter of the unit cell) which must be satisfied for a diffracted beam to occur in a given direction for particular orientations of the crystal and the incident beam; **Laue spot,** a spot on a Laue photograph corresponding to a diffracted ray.

1915 W. H. & W. L. BRAGG *X Rays & Crystal Struct.* xii. 208 Each spot in a Laue photograph represents the reflection of the X-rays by a certain plane (*hkl*) of the crystal structure. **1935** *Jrnl. Chem. Physics* III. 421/1 Oscillation and Laue photographs were prepared with crystals of lepidocrocite from Eiserfeld, Westerfeld, Germany. **1940** *Physical Rev.* LVII. 448/1 Crystals that are naturally in a strained condition..show 'asterism' of Laue spots. **1940** *Nature* 7 Sept. 332/2 The diffuse spot pattern changes much more slowly than the Laue pattern on successive photographs. **1955** E. S. GOULD *Inorg. Reactions & Struct.* xx. 310 The Laue method, employing polychromatic radiation, is no longer important as a tool for structure determinations. Laue photographs are used chiefly for lining up crystals preliminary to examination by filtered radiation, for partial indications of symmetry, and for indicating imperfections and deformations in crystals. **1966** D. G. BRANDON *Mod. Techniques Metallogr.* 69 (*caption*) Derivation of Laue conditions for diffraction. **1973** P. WILKES *Solid State Theory in Metall.* viii. 197 For the three-dimensional case we require that for constructive interference all three Laue conditions..be satisfied simultaneously. **1973** *Soviet Physics: Crystallogr.* XVIII. 320/1 The symmetry of the Laue pattern allowed the mineral to belong to the hexagonal system.

Laufen (lau·fěn). The name of a place in W. Germany near Salzburg, adopted by A. Penck (in Penck & Brückner *Die Alpen im Eiszeitalter* (1909) I. ii. 157, 248) and used *attrib.* to designate a minor retreat and advance of glaciation which he believed followed the last major (Würm) glaciation in the Alps.

1927 PEAKE & FLEURE *Hunters & Artists* 4 After the maximum of the Würm glaciation came a shrinkage called the Laufen retreat, but only of relatively short duration. **1939** AUDEN & ISHERWOOD *Journey to War* 292 When we emerged from holes And blinked in the warm sunshine of the Laufen ice retreat. **1957** J. K. CHARLESWORTH *Quaternary Era* II. xlii. 1174 The Laufen oscillation is probably to be equated with the Aurignacian oscillation.

laugh, *sb.* Add: **3.** *to have the last laugh* (and similar phrs.): to be successful in the end; *to have*, or *get, the laugh on*, or *over*, (*someone*): to have (someone) at a disadvantage; so *the laugh is on* (someone).

1909 J. LONDON *Let.* 1 July (1966) 280 The laugh is on me. I confess to having been fooled by Mr. Harris's canard. **1925** *Times* 21 Mar. 12/4 *The Last Laugh*, the German film which was shown at the Capitol in the Haymarket for the first time on Thursday, is another example of the new school of film production, the basis of which is the recognition of imagination in the spectator. **1937** G. & I. GERSHWIN (song) *They All Laughed* 4 They laughed at us and how! But Ho, Ho, Ho! Who's got the last laugh now? **1942** E. PAUL *Narrow St.* v. 40 Guy was hauled up, put on the carpet, and when he learned that the uncle was willing to make a rather generous cash settlement, considered that he had the last laugh on his fellow workers. **1944** G. B. SHAW *Everybody's Pol. What's What?* xxx. 259 The laugh was on the mob, not on Fouquier. **1949** W. S. MAUGHAM *Writer's Notebook* 329 Sometimes we die sitting quietly in an armchair over a whisky and soda... Then, I suppose, we have the laugh over those who..never rested till the end. **1954** A. MARX *Groucho* xxiii. 200 If she happened to make an error..he would say, 'Well, who's got the last laaaaff now?' **1966** 'J. HACKSTON' *Father clears Out* 18 She's got the laugh on me this time, all right. **1968** D. GODFREY in R. Weaver *Canad. Short Stories* 2nd ser. 306 The Yankee came back about the end of August and we had to give him the last laugh. **1975** J. AIKEN *Voices in Empty House* iv. 121 The dead really have the last laugh on the living.

4. b. A cause of laughter; a joke. Freq. ironic, as in phr. *that's a laugh*, etc.

1895 G. B. SHAW *Our Theatres in Nineties* (1932) I. 51 The piece contained three or four 'laughs' which could not possibly have been explained or described at a dinner party. **1921** *Motion Picture Mag.* Oct. 21/2 There is unlimited room for the screen comedy of manners and for comedy that depends for its laughs upon the sheer power of clever situations. **1930** W. R. BURNETT *Iron Man* I. 3 Ain't that a laugh!.. That guy's been sleeping for the last half-hour, and he says we're a lot of company. **1960** J. WAIN *Nuncle* 165 'Your friends paid for it.' That was a laugh. My friends..were a one-way valve for drinks, cigarettes and loans. **1961** A. WILSON *Old Men at Zoo* i. 51 That's a laugh. When Leacock was head of the Aquarium, he did absolutely nothing. **1966** 'H. CALVIN' *Italian Gadget* ix. 149 Embellished or not, the story would be taken as a wild laugh. **1972** D. DEVINE *Three Green Bottles* III. 106 She fell for Dr Kendall and he chucked her too. It's a laugh when you think of it.

5. laugh-line, (*a*) in theatrical use, a comic line received with laughter; (*b*) = *laughter-line* (see *LAUGHTER *sb.* 3); **laugh track,** a recording of audience laughter added to a sound track.

1927 M. SULLIVAN *Our Times* II. 106 'Uncle Herbert's Speaker' gave text and minute directions for what modern comedians would call 'putting over the "laugh line"'. **1960** *20th Cent.* Nov. 470 The humour does not consist of laugh lines, but of moods and contrasts. **1967** 'T. WELLS' *Dead by Light of Moon* (1968) vi. 60 Bright green eyes and laugh lines around the mouth. **1969** W. GARNER *Us or Them War* i. 19 'It scared the living daylights out of me. Except it was dark,' he finished, but nobody played up to the laugh line. **1971** P. O'DONNELL *Impossible Virgin* xii. 252 The little laugh-lines at the corners of her eyes..had gone. **1962** *Variety* 22 Aug. 14 Universal is on the laugh-track for extended play. And the logic is unarguable, as witness the current 'Lover Come Back'. **1966** *N.Y. Times* 20 Nov. 19 Perhaps symptomatic of the quiet corrosion around 'The Jean Arthur Show' is the 'laugh track' or 'canned laughter' on the show. **1969** *Punch* 5 Feb. 193/3 The absence of a laugh track which would only foul up the pace. **1970** *Toronto Daily Star* 24 Sept. 30/3 (*caption*) Program's tired laugh-track..and tired non-plot.

laugh, *v.* Add: **1. b.** *don't make me laugh*: expostulatory phr. freq. used ironically; *to make a cat laugh*: see *CAT *sb.*[1] 13 j; *laugh! I thought I'd die*: exclamatory phr. to indicate excessive laughter; *to laugh like a drain*: see *DRAIN *sb.* 1 f; *to laugh on the other, wrong, side* (*of one's face*) (examples); *to laugh out of court*: see *COURT *sb.*[1] 12 c.

1837 CARLYLE *Diamond Necklace* iii, in *Fraser's Mag.* Jan. 7/1 By-and-by thou wilt laugh on the wrong side of thy face mainly. **1894** A. CHEVALIER *Humorous Songs*, Laugh! I thought I should 'ave died, Knock'd 'em in the Old Kent Road! **1898** J. D. BRAYSHAW *Slum Silhouettes* 246 'E does a bunk dahn the street, lookin' fer all the world like a hunder-done pancake. Laugh—I thought I should ha' died. *Ibid.*, An' as fer you, my lady, wait till I've got yer, I'll make yer laugh the uvver side o' yer face. **1925** D. H. LAWRENCE *Mornings in Mexico* (1927) 21 The monkey..mocks at you and gibes at you and imitates you. ..It's funny, and you laugh just a bit on the wrong side of your face. **1951** 'F. O'CONNOR' *Traveller's Samples* 43 'Who are ye laughing at?' I shouted, clenching my fists at them. 'I'll make ye laugh at the other side of yeer faces if ye don't let me pass.' **1958** *Spectator* 22 Aug. 241/3 The fact that a resolute Government (don't make me laugh) could stuff its fingers in its ears and carry on regardless makes no difference; nothing will in fact be done. **1966** *Observer* 20 Mar. 27/3 The jokes..tended to make one laugh on the other side of one's face. **1967** J. B. PRIESTLEY *It's an Old Country* xiii. 142 'Mind you, I'll never believe there was anything between him and Mum——' 'Don't make me laugh,' Vic said, giving Tom a wink. **1975** S.

JOHNSON *Urbane Guerilla* II. 70 Stanton will soon laugh on the other side of his face.

e. *to be laughing*: to be in a fortunate or successful position (see quot. 1930). *colloq.*

1930 BROPHY & PARTRIDGE *Songs & Slang Brit. Soldier* 136 *Laughing*, comfortable, safe, fortunate, especially in contrast with others or with normal circumstances. E.g. 'He's got a job at Brigade Head Quarters, so he's laughing'; 'Once I get to the C.C.S. I'm laughing'. **1968** *Listener* 19 Dec. 812/3 Oh, Ron, he's got a job—£30 a week he can get now, you know. Skilled motor mechanic, and not put-on like it used to be. Runs his own racket as well. Old Ron's laughing. **1975** M. STANIER *Singing Time* 255 So long as you're a jump ahead you're laughing.

7. *to laugh that off*: phrase used ironically (freq. in imperative) as an invitation to dismiss or get rid of (some accomplished fact) with a laugh; *to laugh* (someone) *out of it*: to persuade (someone) out of a depressed or serious, etc., mood with laughter.

1918 F. B. YOUNG *Crescent Moon* v. 96 Eva tried to laugh him out of it, to make him ashamed of being afraid. **1926** MAINES & GRANT *Wise-Crack Dict.* 11/1 *Laugh that off*, controversial triumph. **1936** 'N. BLAKE' *Thou Shell of Death* xii. 224 Why should he want them [*sc.* footprints] preserved if it wasn't he who originally made them?.. Laugh that one off! **1944** L. MACNEICE *Christopher Columbus* I. 57 They have given me all that I asked—Let Talavera laugh that off if he can. **1974** *Times* 15 Jan. 14/6, I claim to have a complete answer to the charge, so laugh *that* off, Sir Peter.

laugh-in (la·fin). [*-IN³.] A demonstration, event, or situation marked by laughter often staged for this purpose; *spec.* as the name of an American television comedy programme.

1968 *N.Y. Times* 23 Jan. 79/2 The increasing liberality and topicality of Hollywood variety comedy was further evidenced last night in the hour of Dan Rowan and Dick Martin, whose 'Laugh In' had a preseason tryout and now has deservedly won a niche as a regular series at 8 P.M. Mondays... Their hour is an extraordinary quick succession of sight laughs and sketches, many with a deft and good-natured satirical edge to give the show a contemporary pertinency. **1968** *Manch. Guardian Weekly* 21 Mar. 6 As part of their demonstration against the Defence Minister, Mr Healey,.. students at Cambridge proposed to organise a 'laugh-in'. **1968** *Listener* 26 Dec. 854/2 There's a kind of cathartic quality about Danny la Rue that is a tremendous relief after weeks of trying to admire the Rowan and Martin Laugh-In. **1969** *Time* 6 June 56 At an airport, Fielding's baggage check-in is a laugh-in. **1969** *Guardian* 10 Feb. 8/3 'Rowan and Martin's Laugh-in' is a proudly esoteric American comedy series shown late on Sunday night on BBC-2. **1974** HAWKEY & BINGHAM *Wild Card* ii. 26 It had not been Wallcroft's scene at all, and he'd had to eat a lot of dirt to stay in the [television] business through its *Laugh-in* phase.

laughing, *vbl. sb.* Add: **b.** **laughing death** = *KURU.

1958 *Times* 9 Jan. 10/1 The newly discovered illness in New Guinea..has become known as the 'laughing death'. ..The malady is comparable in some respects to paralysis agitans. **1967** *Acta Tropica* XXIV. 193 (*heading*) Kuru—the laughing death.

laughing, *ppl. a.* Add: **b.** **laughing dove**, the African dove, *Stigmatopelia senegalensis*; **laughing gull**, a North American gull, *Larus atricilla*; **laughing jackass** = JACKASS *sb.* 3 (q.v. for examples), *KOOKABURRA.

1881 E. E. FREWER tr. *Holub's Seven Yrs. S. Afr.* I. ii. 47 The most common birds in the Riet River valley are doves, and those almost exclusively of two sorts, the South African blue-grey turtle-dove, and the laughing dove. **1966** E. PALMER *Plains of Camdeboo* xii. 196 The thorn trees were full of laughing dove. **1789** J. MORSE *Amer. Geogr.* 59 American Birds [include].. Laughing Gull, Goose, Canada Goose [etc.]. **1884** *Bull. U.S. Nat. Museum* No. 27. 169 Laughing Gull... Atlantic coast, from Maine (casually) to mouth of the Amazon. **1968** *Times* 10 Oct. 8/8 The laughing gull could be a useful animal for studying colour perception.

c. *laughing-eyed* adj.

1851 H. MELVILLE *Moby Dick* cxxxii. 597 So have I seen little Miriam and Martha, laughing-eyed elves, heedlessly gambol around their old sire. **1896** H. BELLOC *Verses & Sonnets* 57 This is the laughing-eyed amongst them all: My lady's month **1909** *Westm. Gaz.* 7 Aug. 9/1 Pale-faced women were hugging to their hearts their rosy-cheeked, laughing-eyed children.

laughter, *sb.* Add: **3.** **laughter-line**, one of the small wrinkles at the corners of the eyes or mouth supposedly formed by years of intermittent laughter.

1938 M. ALLINGHAM *Fashion in Shrouds* xii. 180 His light grey eyes were entirely without humour in spite of the laughter-lines beside them. **1950** *Vogue Beauty Bk.* Autumn 26 You should watch for wrinkles—expression lines that run from nose to mouth, laughter lines round the eyes and frown lines on the forehead. **1971** R. FALKIRK *Chill Factor* iii. 35 Laughter-lines still cobwebbed the corners of his eyes.

laughy, *a.* (Later examples.)

1906 B. VON HUTTEN *What became of Pam* II. ix. 172, I suppose you felt teary, but now you must feel laughy. **1913** G. STRATTON-PORTER *Laddie* vii. 201 Then father, all laughy and criey, said: 'Thank God!' **1950** *Sunday Jrnl. & Star* (Lincoln, Nebraska) 29 Oct. (*headline*) Mister 880 is a charming laughy movie.

‖ **lauhala** (lauhā·lă). [Hawaiian *lau* leaf + *hala* pandanus.] A Polynesian screw pine, *Pandanus tectorius*; the dried leaves of the tree, or the material plaited from them.

1826 M. GRAHAM *Voy. H.M.S. Blonde to Sandwich Is.* II. 108 A church..has lately been erected here: its walls are of reeds, lined with the woven leaves of the lauhala. **1866** 'MARK TWAIN' *Lett. from Hawaii* (1967) 99 Shady groves of forest trees..the breadfruit, the lau hala, the orange, lime. **1875** I. L. BIRD *Hawaiian Archipelago* viii. 111 Then we come upon a whole cluster of grass houses under *lauhalas* and bananas. **1898** J. A. OWEN *Story Hawaii* iii. 87 Around the room are hung native mats woven from the long leaf of the 'lauhala' tree. **1933** E. H. BRYAN in *Ancient Hawaiian Civilization* 127 Much of the plaited work, such as baskets, mats, pillows, and fans, was made from *lauhala*, the leaf of the pandanus. **1954** J. SHERIDAN in J. Macdonald *Lethal Sex* (1962) 174 With *lauhala* mats and some reed furniture..it will be quite charming. **1957** P. H. BUCK *Arts & Crafts Hawaii* 250 Sandals.. were quickly woven of any tough fiber at hand: *lauhala*, ti, banana leaves.

‖ **laulau** (lau·lau). [Hawaiian, reduplicated form of *lau* leaf.] A portion of a Hawaiian dish of meat and fish wrapped in leaves and steamed or baked (see quots.). Also, this cover of leaves.

1940 K. BAZORE, *Hawaiian & Pacific Foods* i. 41 *Laulau*, an individual portion of fresh belly pork and of salted butterfish or salmon, wrapped in several taro leaves, then in ti leaves, and steamed or cooked in an imu. **1954** J. SHERIDAN in J. Macdonald *Lethal Sex* (1962) 162 We ate with the Hawaiian family..steamed *laulaus* (salt salmon, butterfish, and pork wrapped in *ti* leaves), *poi* and coconut pudding. **1957** P. H. BUCK *Arts & Crafts Hawaii* 18 Like fish, they might be wrapped in the ti-leaf cover called *laulau*. **1961** E. FODOR *Hawaii* 15 The Manoa campus is transformed..into a kind of miniature Pacific worlds fair where you can sample kim chee, laulaus, sukiyaki and other Pacific foods.

launch, *sb.*¹ Add: The usual pronunc. is now (lǭntʃ) (similarly with the vb. and its derivs.).

2. (Later example.)

1897 W. C. RUSSELL *Last Entry* 241 The schooner.. swept in long floating launches down upon the boat.

4. a. (Further *fig.* and *transf.* examples.)

1749 J. CLELAND *Mem. Woman Pleasure* I. 18, I soon came to a resolution of making this launch into the wide world, by repairing to London. **1857** *Trans. Mich. Agric. Soc.* VIII. 193, I have seen the commencement of railways, and witnessed the 'launch' of the first locomotive. **1969** J. ARGENTI *Managem. Techniques* v. 25 Anxiety that the launch date [of a product] will be missed. **1969** *Punch* 15 Jan. 96/2 The Ford Capri, a sort of shrunken Mustang, is being built in Britain and Germany and will be launched later this month. But, of course, 'the launch', as the trade calls it, is not as simple as that. **1971** *Sunday Express* (Johannesburg) 28 Mar. 5/1 Mr. Uys..vetoed the display of the same model's nipple when the launch advertisement was submitted.

c. The launching of a missile, spacecraft, glider, or the like. (See also sense 7 below.)

1935 C. H. LATIMER-NEEDHAM *Gliding & Soaring* x. 170 The wind velocity should be ascertained and allowed for in any method of mechanical launching or too vigorous a launch may be given unwittingly. **1952** F. GEEN *A.B.C. of Gliding* 95 The easiest launch is a full-height nose launch. **1963** *Ann. Reg. 1962* 397 The closely matched orbits of the two astronauts also required precise timing of their launches. **1966** *Economist* 18 June 1307/1 The first of three such launches which are to put a chain of 24 defence communications satellites in synchronous orbit round the earth. **1969** *Observer* 20 July 9/8 The astronauts ..sleep or doze for nearly five hours before preparing for the launch.

7. *attrib.* and *Comb.* (sense *4 c) *launch crew, date, site, vehicle*; **launch pad** = **launching pad*; **launch window**, a period outside which the planned launch of a spacecraft cannot take place if the journey is to be completed, owing to the changing positions of the planets.

1962 J. GLENN in *Into Orbit* 6 The most junior member of the launch crew. **1969** *Daily Mail* 15 Jan. 5/3 Then suddenly it was now—launch date just around the corner. **1960** *News Chron.* 29 Sept. 9/6 The 100-foot rocket sat immobile on its launch-pad. **1968** *Times* 23 Dec. 6/3 Captain Lovell and Major Anders..climbed into a van which took them to the launch pad. **1969** *Times* 3 June Suppl. p. iii/1 The world's largest tracked vehicle, 'the crawler',.. carried..Saturn 5..from its lofty assembly building to launchpad 39A. **1969** *Listener* 20 Feb. 233/2 When you fly over the Soviet Union, can you see their launch sites? **1965** *New Scientist* 18 Mar. 701/1 The Gemini spacecraft, launch vehicle and target vehicle are all derived from hardware and technology already in existence. **1966** *Sci. Amer.* Jan. 54 Because of various failures in the launch-vehicle guidance system..a lunar landing was not accomplished. **1965** *Newsweek* 29 Nov. 40/3 It is thought they may even try a third shot before the launch window closes in December. **1966** *Sci. News Let.* 3 Sept. 165 The 20-day period centered around the launch date allowing travel between planets on an orbit requiring the least amount of energy. This is the so-called 'launch window' used to hurl space vehicles from earth to the moon. **1968** *Radio Times* 19 Dec. 41/4 As to timing, they must choose a launch window several days long when the Moon is in the right position relative to the Earth, when the sun is in the right position relative to the lunar landing sites, and when Apollo 8 can return to a suitable landing on Earth.

launch, *sb.*² Add: **2.** *Comb.* **launchman**, a man who operates a launch.

1924 J. MASEFIELD *Sard Harker* 146 Everybody was very still, except for the launchman munching his onion. **1928** *Daily Mail* 13 Aug. 13/4 The complement consists of captain, first and second mate, two cooks, two stewards, boatswain, launchman, and able seamen. **1963** M. SHADBOLT in C. K. Stead *N.Z. Short Stories* (1966) 322 So my father produced the launchman and people from the township as witnesses.

3. Special Comb.: **launch-engine** (see quot. *a* 1877).

a **1877** KNIGHT *Dict. Mech.* II. 1266/2 Launch-engines generally consist of a boiler with engines attached thereto, and are used for propelling the launches of large ocean steamers in shallow harbors, etc. **1889** P. N. HASLUCK *Model Engineer's Handybk.* vi. 69 A double cylinder launch engine fitted with reversing motion. **1909** *Westm. Gaz.* 23 Mar. 4/3 A very fine launch-engine, fitted with.. reversing gear.

launch, *v.* Add: **2.** *spec.* To send off (a rocket, spacecraft, or the like, or an astronaut) on its (or his) course. (Cf. 4 b in Dict. and Suppl., from which this use may equally derive.)

1873 MERCIER & KING tr. *Verne's From Earth to Moon* 145 The gun destined to launch the projectile had to be fixed in a country situated between the 0 and 28th degrees of north or south latitude. *Ibid.*, Launched on the 1st of December,..it ought to reach the moon four days after its departure. **1922** *Encycl. Brit.* XXX. 50/1 A forecastle deck large enough to enable a seaplane to be launched therefrom on a light subsidiary carriage. **1952** *Oxf. Jun. Encycl.* X. 17/2 The German guided missiles.. launched against London from the French coast were driven by their own power and were automatically controlled. **1957** *Britannica Bk. of Year* 443 The first artificial earth satellite..was launched from a site in the U.S.S.R... on Oct. 4, 1957. **1960** J. N. BELL *Seven into Space* i. 15 He knows an excitement so intense that it seems he can no longer contain it. The first American has been launched into space. **1972** A. C. KERMODE *Mech. of Flight* (ed. 8) xii. 390 As with the X15 these [*sc.* lifting bodies] are launched from a mother craft. **1974** *Daily Tel.* 14 Feb. 1/3 Two more spaceships, Mars-6, and Mars-7, which were launched last August, were due to approach the planet next month.

4. b. *spec.* To release (a balloon or its contents) into the air at the beginning of a flight. (Cf. *2.)

1824 *Encycl. Brit.* Suppl. I. 83/1 It was soon found, that a balloon, launched into the atmosphere, is abandoned, without guidance or command, to the mercy of the winds. **1959** *Chambers's Encycl.* I. 103/2 On 19 Sept. 1783..they launched a sheep, a cock and a duck into the air, enclosed in a basket suspended beneath the balloon.

d. To publish (a book); to put (a product, etc.) on the market.

1870 'MARK TWAIN' *Lett. to Publishers* (1967) 45 We'll have someone standing ready to launch a book right on our big tidal wave and swim it into a success. **1919** J. QUINN *Let.* 3 Oct. in T. S. Eliot *Waste Land Drafts* (1971) p. xvii, My part in connection with launching your book is finished. **1926** H. CRANE *Let.* 5 Dec. (1965) 278 Once this first book is really launched and off my mind. **1966** *Listener* 17 Nov. 716/3 The complicated process of launching a new American car. **1969** J. ARGENTI *Managem. Techniques* v. 25 To launch a product is a complex project.

5. (Later example.)

1906 *Westm. Gaz.* 26 Nov. 6/2 The payment was refused on the ground that the Deal lifeboat launched to the same wreck.

launcher. Add: **2.** A device or structure that launches something or is used for launching; *spec.* (*a*) a structure that holds a rocket or missile during launching; (*b*) a rocket from which a satellite is released into orbit.

1911 T. O'B. HUBBARD et al. *Aeroplane* v. 61 There have been many..mechanical launchers invented, but none have met with any success..except the rail-and-falling-weight method originally used by the Wright biplanes. **1944** C. P. LENT *Rocket Research* 4 The photograph lower left is a German rocket launcher. **1945** *Aeroplane Spotter* 18 Oct. 250/2 Zero-type rocket-projectile launchers eliminated the drag of the earlier tube type to such an extent that the Lockheed P-38J and P-38L Lightning is able to carry seven under each wing. **1957** *Oxford Mail* 20 Aug. 1/4, I saw the 25 ft. long Bloodhound on its launcher, together with its special loading trolley, exactly as it would be on one of the coastal sites. **1958** *Times* 12 Aug. 7/3 Now that Britain can provide the launcher, she should certainly explore the field for partners in the actual launching of a satellite. **1959, 1969** [see *grenade launcher* s.v. *GRENADE *sb.*¹ 3]. **1970** *Daily Tel.* 28 Apr. 1/4 America was first to use a single launcher to put eight satellites into orbit, in June, 1966. **1971** *Nature* 2 Apr. 282/2 An extensive study of the propagation of Earth surface waves, including the design of launchers for such waves, is described. **1973** *Sci. Amer.* Aug. 105/2, I devised an apparatus for launching a continuous stream of water globules indoors... The launcher consists of a small nozzle that directs a jet of water upward at an angle of approximately 45 degrees. **1974** *Daily Tel.* 14 Feb. 4/8 The ship has been fitted with four missile launchers.

launching, *vbl. sb.* Add: (Later examples.)

1967 *Listener* 23 Feb. 263/3 Admittedly, the launchings will be carried out by American rockets from an American site, but the satellites themselves are purely British-built. **1971** *Nature* 6 Aug. 357/2 It is not safe to base a rocket development project on a single launching once a year.

b. *launching platform, site, station*; **launching pad**, the area on which a rocket stands for launching; also *fig.* and *transf.*

1951 COOKE & CAIDIN *Jets, Rockets & Guided Missiles* 138 Under a blazing afternoon sun, at 3.14 p.m., a modified V-2 rocket carrying a WAC-Corporal in its nose rose slowly from its concrete launching pad. **1958** *Daily Mail* 16 Aug. 1/4 The 88 ft. rocket stands poised on its concrete launching pad here tonight looking like a giant silver propelling pencil. **1959** *Encounter* Dec. 74/2 All this is by way of a launching-pad for the idea of the Non-Nuclear Club. **1963** A. HUXLEY *Let.* 17 Feb. (1969) 948 Julian tells me that your book is now definitely on the launching pad. **1973** *Guardian* 31 Jan. 13/7 The NUS sees the rent-strike movement as a launching pad for its main campaign. **1922** *Encycl. Brit.* XXX. 50/1 Ordinary aeroplanes were carried in fighting-ships with a launching-platform. **1957** *Jane's Fighting Ships 1957–58* 413 The missile is using jet-assisted rocket bottles to launch it from its zero-length launching platform. **1944** *Aeronautics* Aug. 27/1 The counter attack, by bombing the launching sites in the Pas de Calais, was intensified. **1958** *Listener* 13 Nov. 766/2 Israel had also agreed to launching-sites on her territory for United States atomic rockets and guided missiles. **1897** *Strand Mag.* June 712/1 We had better not make the launching station a place like the bank of the river, where it can go only one way. **1944** A. HUXLEY *Let.* 9 July (1969) 507 Five thousand launching stations, firing off twenty robots [*sc.* rockets] apiece—and that would be the end of any metropolis. **1958** C. C. ADAMS et al. *Space Flight* p. xi, A space station would serve as a 'launching station' for space ships to the moon, saving fabulous amounts of precious fuel.

launder, *sb.* For '4–9 **lander**' read '4– **lander**' and add: **2. d.** *Metallurgy.* A channel for conveying molten metal from a furnace or container to a ladle or mould.

1900 *Kynoch Jrnl.* Oct.–Nov. 20/1 The tapping hole is now cut through the bottom of the furnace, and a wrought iron channel—technically called a lander—fastened round it. **1906** W. MACFARLANE *Princ. & Pract. Iron & Steel Manuf.* x. 110 The Shoot or Launder, along which the steel and slag are conveyed from the taphole to the ladle, is a half-round gutter made of steel plates. **1929** W. LISTER *Pract. Steelmaking* x. 78 With all fixed furnaces the lander is necessarily 10 ft. to 15 ft. long, and sometimes up to 20 ft. long. **1967** P. MCGEOWN *Heat the Furnace* x. 97 We had her running down the lander as the twelve o'clock hooter sounded. **1971** W. K. V. GALE *Iron & Steel Industry: Dict. Terms* 195 The tapping spout of an open-hearth furnace is usually called a launder.

launder, *v.* Add: **1. b.** To transfer funds of dubious or illegal origin, usu. to a foreign country, and then later to recover them from what seem to be 'clean' (i.e. legitimate) sources. Also *transf.*

The use arose from the Watergate inquiry in the United States in 1973–4.

1973 *Guardian* 19 Apr. 14/2 Suitcases stuffed with 200,000 dollars of Republican campaign funds; money being 'laundered' in Mexico. **1973** *Publishers Weekly* 17 Sept. 54/2 A New York lawyer carrying $200,000 in his camera case to be 'laundered' in Switzerland. **1973** J. M. WHITE *Garden Game* 128 Phoenix is a city where the Mafia is well entrenched; its booming real-estate, building and service industries are ready-made havens for 'laundering' the extortion and gambling money from Nevada and California. **1974** *Globe & Mail* (Toronto) 3 Apr. 1 (*headline*) Kerr concedes U.S. criminals 'launder' money in Ontario.

3. *intr.* Of a fabric: to admit of being laundered; to bear laundering without damage to its texture, colour, etc. Used with adverbs.

1908 *Sears, Roebuck Catal.* 916 It will launder as well as a piece of linen. **1909** *Daily Chron.* 22 July 7/5 A single initial..done in satin stitch..is showy, quickly worked and launders well. **1923** *Daily Mail* 19 Feb. 1 (Advt.), This hard wearing fabric, which launders perfectly, can be obtained. **1951** *Good Housek. Home Encycl.* 252/1 Most silks launder well.

launderette (lǭndəre·t). Also **laundrette.** [f. LAUNDER *v.* + -ETTE.] An establishment providing automatic washing machines for the use of customers.

1949 *Vogue* Oct. 102/2 A new and interesting development in housekeeping—the advent of the self-service launderette. **1952** [see *BAGWASH]. **1955** PRIESTLEY & HAWKES *Journey down Rainbow* 117 Who does not understand the sudden success of our communal laundrettes? **1967** *Which?* July 216 Launderettes are shop-like premises, usually equipped with between 8 and 20 large automatic washing machines, supplied with hot water from a central source, and with about one tumbler drier for each three washing machines. **1968** *Listener* 7 Mar. 316/1 To me the world Strindberg created is like some enclosed launderette of the spirit—the underwear goes round and round but the water has been turned off. **1970** G. GREER *Female Eunuch* 227 Perhaps the failure of such community living could be avoided by including a pub and a laundrette in each block. **1973** E. BERCKMAN *Victorian Album* 113 The enemy lumbered into sight carrying two fat plastic bags: obviously bound for the launderette in the High Street.

lau·ndering, *vbl. sb.* [f. LAUNDER *v.*] The process or action of washing, drying, and ironing linen, etc. Also *fig.*

1894 *To-Day* 17 Mar. 182/2 French cambrics..are not to be starched in the laundering, but left soft. **1908** K. GRAHAME *Wind in Willows* x. 221 I'm in the washing and laundering line, you must know, ma'am. **1949** 'G. ORWELL' *Nineteen Eighty-Four* II. x. 221 Her life had been laundering, scrubbing, darning, cooking, sweeping, polishing, mending, scrubbing, laundering, first for children, then for grand-children. **1970** *Which?* Aug. 247/2 Many people were uninformed about certain aspects of laundering. **1974** *Globe & Mail* (Toronto) 3 Apr. 1/8 Mr. Kerr, who rose in the Legislature to answer Dr. Shulman's question last Friday about laundering of money in Ontario, began by saying, 'The washing or laundering of funds does occur in Toronto.' *Ibid.*, The laundering transaction itself is not illegal.

Launder-Ometer (lǭndərǫ·mītəɹ). orig. *U.S.* Also **Launderometer, launderometer.** [f. LAUNDER *v.* + -OMETER.] The proprietary name of a machine for making standard laundry tests, consisting of a number of jars clamped to a rotating shaft in which the washing is carried out.

1928 *Amer. Dyestuff Reporter* XVII. 731/2 We will now ..introduce to you this machine, which we have baptised the 'Launder-Ometer'... It was originally invented or devised by one of our fellow members, Hugh Christison. **1929** *Official Gaz.* (U.S. Patent Office) 21 May 591/1 Launder-Ometer. For laundry washing machines. Claims use since April 27, 1928. **1938** *Year Bk. Amer. Assoc. Textile Chemists & Colorists* XV. 138 The Launder-Ometer..consists of a heavily constructed copper tank.., supported upon a rigid angle-iron frame. Within this tank there is a brass and aluminum rotor that carries the twenty standard pint jars in which the tests are made. **1958** *Observer* 30 Mar. 11/5 Cotton and other coloured materials are tested in a launderometer, a machine which reproduces as many domestic washes as are considered necessary. **1961** K. DURHAM *Surface Activity & Detergency* ix. 229 The Launderometer..is merely a tank containing a simple mechanism for holding and rotating jars, each containing steel balls, into which the fabric and solution are placed; the jars are rotated and the steel balls provide agitation. The rate of rotation and the weight of the balls are both variable.

laundress, *v.* Add: **c.** To serve (a person) as a laundress.

1850 DICKENS *Dav. Copp.* xxvi. 281 'Sir,' said Mrs. Crupp, in a tone approaching to severity, 'I've laundressed other young gentlemen besides yourself.'

laundrette : see *LAUNDERETTE.

Laundromat (lǭ·ndrəmæt). orig. *U.S.* Also **laundromat.** [See *-MAT.] The proprietary name of a brand of automatic washing machines; also, by extension, a launderette.

1943 *Trade Marks Jrnl.* 14 July 300/1 Laundromat. Domestic electric washing (laundering) machines. Westinghouse Electric & Manufacturing Company..Pennsylvania. **1951** *Amer. Speech* XXVI. 166 The Westinghouse Company has a 'Laundramat', and there are also 'Laundromats'—often called 'Laundermats' and 'Laundry-mats'—open for public patronage. **1955** M. MCCARTHY *Charmed Life* (1956) i. 20 The village mind was still churning up the past, tossing the old dirty linen back and forth impersonally, like one of the washing machines in the new laundromat. **1956** A. HUXLEY *Adonis & Alphabet* 148 Junior colleges, jet-plane factories, Laundromats, six-lane highways. **1957** J. KEROUAC *On Road* (1958) III. ii. 187, I..found nothing but laundromats, cleaners, soda fountains. **1963** *Punch* 2 Jan. p. vi/2 Harrods' sale..includes..laundromats and dryers. **1964** *Economist* 30 May 1024/3 Coin operated Laundromats and dry cleaning machines. **1966** *New Scientist* 16 June 694/3 The 'local' is doomed, one day, to operate like a licensed laundromat. **1966** T. PYNCHON *Crying of Lot 49* v. 121 She found the symbol tacked to the bulletin board of a laundromat, among other scraps of paper offering cheap ironing and baby sitters. **1971** B. MALAMUD *Tenants* 219 They drag out of a laundromat, shoe store, [etc.], every Zionist they can find.

laundry. Add: **2. b.** Articles (linen, etc.) that need to be, or that have been, laundered.

1916 W. J. LOCKE *Wonderful Year* iii. 50 The proletariat hung laundry to dry over royal salamanders and proud escutcheons. *Ibid.* v. 67 Women below at the water's edge beat their laundry with lusty arms. **1965** *Which?* Mar. 80/1 What we have done is to see how much it would cost to wash three different amounts of laundry each week, by each of these methods. **1970** *Laundry & Cleaning Internat.* June/July 1/3 The traditional attitude—that the laundry is paid for from the housewife's weekly budget.

4. *laundry bag, list* (also *fig.*), *mark, room, soap, van, -work, -worker.*

1895 *Montgomery Ward Catal.* 23/2 Laundry Bag; size 14 × 25 inches; made from heavy figured drapery sateen, with white cotton drawing cord and tassels. **1971** P. PURSER *Holy Father's Navy* xi. 60, I shovelled my suit into a laundry bag to send to the cleaners. **1958** *Spectator* 4 July 24/2 Mr. Wardle makes a point of dissociating himself from the laundry-list species of biography-making. **1968** *Time* 10 May 22 The at-large ballot is a bewildering laundry list of 75 names. **1972** *Fortune* Jan. 3/1 As the archetype of U.S. corporations, General Motors is charged by its critics with primary responsibility for a laundry list of social ills, including air pollution, congestion in the cities, ugliness in the countryside, [etc.]. **1972** *Times Lit. Suppl.* 24 Mar. 333/1 A huge panorama of names and dates, as dull as a laundry-list. **1975** *Radio Times* 16 Jan. 5/4 Everybody knows..that there are exceptions to this laundry-list of woes, and that the author can be brilliantly served. **1924** G. S. DOUGHERTY *Criminal as a Human Being* 278 An important factor in this work is a collection of laundry marks. **1962** 'J. BELL' *Crime in our Time* II. i. 22 The..police.. overlooked a conspicuous laundry mark, 599, on some of the clothing. **1972** L. LAMB *Picture Frame* xviii. 155 Laundry mark on shirt and maker's name on hand-made shoes. **1967** J. REDGATE *Killing Season* (1968) II. vi. 102 There's a new laundry-room just behind the kitchen. **1971** *Country Life* 23 Dec. Suppl. 11/1 Unique single-story residence..kitchen, laundry room. **1937** *Discovery* Feb. 49/1 The Great Geyser had practically ceased activity, and could not be stimulated to life, even with a hundred-weight of laundry soap—the usual stimulant. **1958** M. DICKENS *Man Overboard* xii. 190 A homely smell compounded of many things, like roasting meat and leather and dogs and laundry soap. **1952** M. ALLINGHAM *Tiger in Smoke* xv. 217 He and two other boys stole a laundry van. **1972** *Guardian* 5 Oct. 28/2 The laundry van in which Sapper Stewart died. **1838** H. MARTINEAU *Retrospect of Western Travel* II. 185 The 10th was Sunday... There was no laundry-work going on. **1891** *Daily News* 15 Dec. 6/2 There was possibility of a good deal of family laundry work arising. **1930** *Times Educ. Suppl.* 16 Aug. 360/2 The teacher must hold full diploma in Cookery, Laundrywork and Housewifery. **1963** F. F. LAIDLER *Gloss. Terms Home Econ. Educ.* 52 *Laundrywork*, the washing and finishing of soiled fabrics. **1894** E. BANKS *Campaigns of Curiosity* 196 She did not consider me up to the mark for a laundry-worker. **1906** *Westm. Gaz.* 21 June 8/1 The attention of laundry-workers is drawn to this. **1975** *Times* 15 Feb. 3/3 Greater London Council..suggested that the post of..'laundry woman' should become 'laundry worker'.

laundry (lǭ·ndri), *v.* [f. the sb.] = LAUNDER *v.* Hence **lau·ndrying** *vbl. sb.*

1880 *American Mail Order Fashions* (1961) 14 The wires can be taken out..so that the entire bustle can be laundried with the greatest care. **1892** *Daily News* 15 Sept. 5/5 The great Chinese national industry is laundrying. **1901** D. SLADEN *In Sicily* I. 152 The ditch in which they did their laundrying. **1919** W. DEEPING *Second Youth* xxvi. 224 No, he can't ask you to laundry his man's clothes. **1957** B. & C. EVANS *Dict. Contemp. Amer. Usage* 268/2 The verb is *to launder*, not *to laundry*. Clothes are *laundered*, not *laundried*.

Laurasia (lǭrēi·ʃiă). *Geol.* [mod.L. (R. Staub *Der Bewegungsmech. der Erde* (1928) ii. 121), f. *Laur(entia*, name given to the ancient forerunner of N. America (from the Laurentian strata of the Canadian Shield by which it is represented today) + *Eur)asia* (see EURASIAN *a.* 1).] A vast continental area or supercontinent thought to have once existed in the northern hemisphere and to have broken up in Mesozoic or late Palæozoic times forming North America, Greenland, Europe, and most of Asia north of the Himalayas. Also, these land masses collectively as they exist today.

1931 *Trans. Geol. Soc. Glasgow* XVIII. 578 The long history of the Tethys girdling the continental shelf of the earth between Gondwanaland and Laurasia is a clear indication of the operation of some opposing force tending to pull the continents apart. **1937** A. L. DU TOIT *Our Wandering Continents* ii. 24 Through..alternating 'polar flight' and 'polar drift' Laurasia and Gondwana have successively impinged upon or else parted from one another. **1944** A. HOLMES *Princ. Physical Geol.* xvii. 367 The [earthquake] belts form two rings..: one enclosing North America and most of Asia and Europe (known collectively as Laurasia), and the other enclosing South America, Africa and Arabia, India, Australia, and Antarctica (known collectively as Gondwanaland). **1971** I. G. GASS et al. *Understanding Earth* xv. 229 Gondwanaland..probably formed about 500 million years ago, and Laurasia, west of the Urals, about 370 million years ago. **1974** *Daily Tel.* (Colour Suppl.) 10 Apr. 20/1 Whether Laurasia and Gondwanaland were themselves joined together into a supercontinent is a question still to be resolved.

Hence **Laura·sian** *a.*

1962 L. C. KING *Morphol. Earth* xii. 399 At the beginning of Cretaceous time virtually the whole of the vast continental interior had been reduced to a landscape of low relief—the Laurasian surface. **1973** *Nature* 1 June 278/2 The Atlantic and Indian Oceans originated from the break up of the Gondwanan and Laurasian continents.

laureate, *a.* and *sb.* Add: **B.** *sb.* **1. c.** *transf.*

1816 BYRON *Bards & Rev.* (ed. 5) 21 Laureat of the long-ear'd kind! *a* **1849** H. COLERIDGE *Ess. & Marginalia* (1851) II. 9 Herrick was the laureate of flowers and perfumes. **1930** R. CAMPBELL *Poems* 12 He..demonstrates, this laureate of the pubs, That 'all good poets have belonged to clubs'. **1941** *Scrutiny* IX. 384 According to their view he [*sc.* Proust] is the laureate of a dying society. **1954** G. W. KNIGHT (*title*) Laureate of peace. On the genius of Alexander Pope.

d. *Nobel laureate*, one who has been awarded a Nobel prize.

1947 CROWTHER & WHIDDINGTON *Science at War* 144 Professor W. N. Haworth of Birmingham, the famous organic chemist and Nobel laureate. **1965** *Listener* 2 Sept. 329/2 Three great physiologists, all Nobel laureates. **1975** *Sci. Amer.* May 53/2 (Advt.), Written by a Nobel Laureate in medicine, this is the first comprehensive treatment of DNA synthesis emphasizing its biochemical aspects and recent developments.

laurel, *sb.*[1] Add: **2. e.** As the name of a colour = **laurel-green.*

1923 *Daily Mail* 8 Oct. 5/1 (Advt.), Navy, Nigger,.. Amethyst, Laurel, Wine.

3. c. Versailles laurel (see quots.); **wood laurel**, spurge laurel, *Daphne laureola.*

1728 R. BRADLEY *Dictionarium Botanicum* II. s.v. *Laureola*, Laureola..in English, Spurge-Laurel and Bastard-Laurel, or Wood-Laurel, is a small Evergreen, frequent enough with us, blossoming about Christmas.

1873 W. B. HEMSLEY *Handbk. Hardy Trees* 394 *Daphne Laureola*, Wood Laurel. **1882** *Garden* 25 Feb. 134/3 The Versailles Laurel (*latifolia*) is a large, robust, and bold foliaged form. **1951** *Dict. Gardening* (R. Hort. Soc.) III. 1697/2 *P[runus] Laurocerasus*. Common, Versailles, or Cherry Laurel. Quick-growing shrub up to 15 or 20 ft.

5. *laurel-brake, -green, -leaf* (attrib.), *-leaved* (later example), *-thicket*.

1853 J. P. KENNEDY *Blackwater Chron.* vi. 73 A man could walk about for a week,..particularly if he got into a big laurel-brake. **1893** *Outing* (U.S.) Oct. 61/2 Only in the wilds of the backwoods,..or in the mountains where tracts of laurel brakes give refuge against men and dogs, do the Virginia deer hold their own. **1938** R. GRAVES *Coll. Poems* 92 Grass-green and aspen-green, Laurel-green and sea-green. **1927** PEAKE & FLEURE *Hunters & Artists* 49 The rude Proto-Solutrean examples of the 'laurel-leaf' blades. **1973** *Times* 26 July 18/3 More than 150 unfinished and broken axes lay on the surface, with hammerstones, anvils, laurel-leaf blades, and many thousands of waste flakes. **1855** A. B. GARROD *Essent. Materia Medica* 122 The bark of Canella alba or Laurel-leaved Canella..; growing in the West Indies. **1750** T. WALKER *Jrnl.* in J. S. Johnston *First Explor. Kentucky* (1898) 49 Just at the foot of the Hill is a Laurel Thicket. **1945** *Mass. Audubon Soc. Bull.* Jan. 274 It was June 25 when I sat on a log in a laurel thicket.

6. *U.S.* **laurel magnolia**, either of two species of *Magnolia*, the evergreen *M. grandiflora* or the sweet bay, *M. virginiana*; **laurel oak**, either of two species of oak, *Quercus laurifolia* or *Q. imbricata*.

1806 P. WAKEFIELD *Excursions N. Amer.* xiv. 93 The laurel magnolia reaches to the height of an hundred feet. **1831** J. M. PECK *Guide for Emigrants* II. 52 From the Walnut Hills to Baton Rouge..you begin to discover the ever verdant laurel magnolia, with its beautiful foliage, of the thickness and feeling of leather. **1850** S. F. COOPER *Rural Hours* 476 The small Laurel Magnolia, or Sweet Bay, is found as far north as New York, in swampy grounds. **1893** W. ROBINSON *Eng. Flower Garden* (ed. 3) 520/1 *M[agnolia] grandiflora*, the great Laurel Magnolia of the southern United States, is—in England—best treated as a wall-plant. **1903** *Flora & Sylva* I. 19/1 The Laurel Magnolia or Sweet Bay..is certainly a very handsome shrub. **1911** *Encycl. Brit.* XVII. 392/1 The most beautiful species of North America is *M. grandiflora*, the 'laurel magnolia'..introduced into England in 1734. **1810** F. A. MICHAUX *Hist. Arbres Forestiers de l'Amérique Septentrionale* I. 23 *Laurel oak*,..dénomination secondaire dans les Etats à l'ouest des monts Alléghanys. **1832** D. J. BROWNE *Sylva Amer.* 271 East of the Alleghanies this species..is called Jack Oak, Black Oak, and sometimes from the form of the leaves, Laurel Oak. **1901** C. T. MOHR *Plant Life Alabama* 131 Between Bon Secour and Perdido Bay low, sandy hills..support a high forest..of laurel oak and Cuban and long-leaf pine. **1947** COLLINGWOOD & BRUSH *Knowing your Trees* 201/1 Laurel oak has been widely used,e specially in the South, as an ornamental, particularly as a shade or street tree.

Laurentian (lǫre·nʃiăn), *a.*² [f. the name of Lorenzo (Laurentius) de' Medici, who founded a library in Florence in the 15th c.] Of or pertaining to the Laurentian Library in Florence or to manuscripts preserved there. Cf. MEDICEAN *a.*

1860 GEO. ELIOT *Jrnl.* in J. W. Gross *George Eliot's Life* (1885) II. x. 216 That unique Laurentian library, designed by Michael Angelo. **1875** *Encycl. Brit.* II. 438/2 His [*sc.* Michelangelo's] principal works are..the Laurentian Library at Florence. **1879** *Ibid.* IX. 332/1 There are three large and valuable libraries in the city [*sc.* Florence]... The Laurentian, founded by Lorenzo de' Medici, and attached to the convent of San Lorenzo. **1883** R. C. JEBB in *Sophocles, Plays & Fragments* I. p. liii, The manuscripts..used..are the following: In the Biblioteca Mediceo-Lorenziana, Florence, L, cod. 32.9, commonly known as the Laurentian MS. **1936** GREENHOOD & GENTRY *Chronol. Bks. & Printing* (rev. ed.) 14, 1437. A public library is founded at Florence on a bequest by Niccoli; becomes known later as Laurentian Library, and today is oldest existing library in Europe. **1960** G. A. GLAISTER *Gloss. Bk.* 214/2 *Laurentian Codex*, an 11th-century codex of the works of Sophocles, Apollonius Rhodius, and Aeschylus... It is now in the Biblioteca Mediceo-Laurenziana, Florence.

Laurentian: see *LAWRENTIAN *a.*

laurvigite, laurvikite, varr. *LARVIKITE.

lauryl (lǫ·r-, lǭ·ril). *Chem.* [f. LAUR(IC *a.* + -YL.] = *DODECYL; **lauryl alcohol**, $CH_3(CH_2)_{10}CH_2OH$, a crystalline, low-melting alcohol which is obtained by reduction of coconut oil and whose sulphate esters are used in detergents.

1915 P. E. SPIELMANN tr. *V. von Richter's Org. Chem.* I. iii. 227 Lauryl ketoxine, $(C_{11}H_{23})_2C{:}N.OH$, m.p. 39°. **1922** *Jrnl. Amer. Chem. Soc.* XLIV. 2649 By reducing 100 g. of ethyl laurate with 85 g. of sodium, 200 cc. of toluene and 600 cc. of absolute alcohol, there is obtained 53 to 57 g. (65–70%) of lauryl alcohol. **1960** E. L. DELMAR-MORGAN *Cruising Yacht Equipment & Navigation* xxiv. 231 Lauryl pentachlor phenol is..very effective [for rot-proofing canvas]. **1968** J. A. MONICK *Alcohols* iii. 174 A high-quality lauryl alcohol is currently produced by the same process used for *n*-decyl alcohol, namely, the catalytic reduction of coconut oil, coconut oil fatty acids, or their esters, under high pressure. *Ibid.* 175 Lauryl alcohol is also found in oils of lime and the flowers of *Furcraea gigantea*. **1972** *Sci. Amer.* Jan. 88/2 Experiments with lauryl sulfate, a common component of commercial detergents, showed that this substance would indeed break the mucosal barrier.

lausenite (lau·sĕnəit). *Min.* [f. the name of Carl *Lausen*, 20th-c. U.S. geologist + -ITE¹.] A hydrated ferrous sulphate, $Fe_2(SO_4)_3.6H_2O$, first found as aggregates of minute colourless fibres after a fire in a mine at Jerome, Arizona, U.S.A.

1928 *Amer. Mineralogist* XIII. 594 The name rogersite is already in use..so a new name will have to be assigned to the present mineral. Dr. G. M. Butler has suggested the name lausenite, after Carl Lausen the discoverer of the new mineral. **1968** I. KOSTOV *Mineral.* II. ix. 499 Lausenite and kornelite are monoclinic, found respectively in white and pale violet globular aggregates with radial-fibrous texture.

lautarite (lautā·rəit). *Min.* [ad. G. *lautarit* (A. Dietze 1891, in *Zeitschr. f. Kryst. und Min.* XIX. 447), f. Oficina *Lautar(o*, the name of the owners of the pampa where it was first found: see -ITE¹.] Calcium iodate, $Ca(IO_3)_2$, found as colourless or yellowish monoclinic crystals in Antofagasta Province, Chile.

1892 E. S. DANA *Dana's Syst. Min.* (ed. 6) 1040 (*heading*) Lautarite. **1943** R. D. GEORGE *Minerals & Rocks* vii. 198 Lautarite, calcium iodate,..is a colorless to pale yellow, easily fusible mineral having a specific gravity of 4·6 and a hardness of 4. **1968** K. A. JONES tr. *Kirsch's Appl. Mineral.* vi. 114 Lautarite $Ca(IO_3)_2$... Monoclinic, H: 3·0–4·0, D: 4·6.

lautite (lau·təit). *Min.* [ad. G. *lautit* (A. Frenzel 1881, in *Min. und Petr. Mittheil.* III. 516), f. *Laut-a*, the name of its original locality near Marienberg, E. Germany: see -ITE¹.] An orthorhombic, grey or black sulphide of copper and arsenic, CuAsS (possibly with silver replacing some copper), having a metallic lustre.

1883 *Encycl. Brit.* XVI. 392/1 Lautite (CuAg)As.S. **1940** *Mineral. Abstr.* VII. 489 Lautite associated with arsenic, tetrahedrite, [etc.].., is found in the Gabe Gottes mine at Sainte-Marie-aux-Mines (Haut-Rhin). It forms bunches of crystals up to 6 cm. × 6–7 mm., showing a brilliant (001) cleavage, enclosed in native arsenic. **1967** *Ibid.* XVIII. 97/1 Lautite was obtained by heating a mixture of realgar and electrolytic copper under 1000 kg/cm² to 315° C.

lav. (læv). A colloq. shortening of LAVATORY *sb.* 4.

1913 C. MACKENZIE *Sinister Street* I. vii. 99 Tell the army to line up behind the lav. at four o'clock. **1933** D. L. SAYERS *Murder must Advertise* i. 8 You've only got to warn him not to use the directors' lav., and not to tumble down the iron staircase. **1960** J. R. ACKERLEY *We think the World of You* 51, I asked instead if I could use the lav. **1961** [see *ELSAN]. **1973** J. THOMSON *Death Cap* iv. 64 Gilbert Leacock went out to the lav... I heard the chain being pulled.

lava. Add: **4. a.** *lava bed* (also *fig.*), *block, boulder, field* (also *fig.*), *-lake*; also **lava flow**, a mass of flowing or solidified lava.

1891 *Century Mag.* Mar. 645 The general direction [of march] was towards the lava beds of northern California. **1905** *Westm. Gaz.* 12 Aug. 13/1 She lived over a 'lava-bed of raw primeval passions'. **1937** *Discovery* Mar. 83/1 This arid lava bed. **1866** 'MARK TWAIN' *Lett. from Hawaii* (1967) 58 We climbed a hill a hundred and fifty feet high.. as full of rough lava blocks as it could stick. *Ibid.* 223 It had lava boulders piled around its base. **1902** *Athenæum* 30 Aug. 287/1 Where bed on bed of mountain-pinks Above the lava-boulders blow. **1866** 'MARK TWAIN' *Lett. from Hawaii* (1967) 222 We clambered over the surrounding lava field, through masses of weeds. **1899** *Geogr. Jrnl.* May 50 The most extensive lava-field in the island. **1906** *Daily Chron.* 21 May 7/3 The smoking lava fields of discussion. **1957** G. E. HUTCHINSON *Treat. Limnol.* I. i. 16 The lakes of the Modoc lava field are frequently regarded as lying on tilted block faults. **1866** 'MARK TWAIN' *Lett. from Hawaii* (1967) 222 Gathering up a fresh lot of specimens, having..discarded those he dug out of the old lava flows. **1888** Lava flow [in Dict.]. **1957** G. E. HUTCHINSON *Treat. Limnol.* I. i. 38 Not infrequently the surface of a newly formed lava flow may cool and produce a crust. **1974** *Country Life* 17 Jan. 66/1 The lava-flows on either side of the runway. **1895** Lava-lake [see *blowing-cone*]. **1902** *Nature* 4 Sept. 441/1 (*heading*) The lava-lake of Kilauea. *Ibid.* 441/2, I carefully observed the then existing lava-lake during six successive days.

c. (Later example.)

1878 SWINBURNE *Poems & Ballads* 2nd Ser. 182 All its lava-black Cones.

lavabo. Add: Now also (senses 2 b, *c) with pronunc. (læ·văbo).

2. b. (Example.)

1911 WEBSTER *Lavabo*, a wash basin with its necessary fittings, esp. one set in place and supplied with running water and a waste pipe.

c. = LAVATORY *sb.* 4.

1930 D. L. SAYERS *Strong Poison* xiv. 177 The little lavabo in the passage. **1934** H. MILLER *Tropic of Cancer* 83, I find a ticket in the *lavabo* for a concert. **1971** C. JOHNSTON *Mo* 58 The subject of each was unmistakeably the same—Belchamber's lavabos.

laval (lā·văl), *a.* [f. LAVA + -AL.] Of or resembling lava. Also *fig.*

1891 *11th Ann. Rep. U.S. Geol. Survey* II. 199 These great springs are the outlet of a system of under-laval channels and lakes. **1931** V. WOOLF *Waves* 84 It is the speed, the hot molten effect, the laval flow of sentence into sentence that I need. **1932** W. FRANK *America Hispana* I. v. 230 Volcanic earth has made these churches and these statues. Sometimes it is stone, black and yellow as in the north; sometimes, it is adobe. And sometimes, it is tezontli, the laval rock colour of clotted blood. **1963** A. SMITH *Throw out Two Hands* (1966) xxi. 205 We were 500 feet above that exceptionally laval and unpleasant-looking region.

lava-lava (lā·vă,lā·vă). [Samoan.] In Samoa and some other Pacific islands, a sort of skirt.

1891 R. L. STEVENSON *Vailima Lett.* (1895) xiii. 115 The weird figure of Faauma..in a black lavalava (kilt). **1900** *Fortn. Rev.* Jan. 49 New Zealanders, Chinese, East and West Indians, and half-castes who are more at home in lava-lavas than bifurcated garments. **1944** *Living off Land* viii. 159 He must produce..equipment consisting of a blanket, bowl, spoon, lava-lava. **1949** M. MEAD *Male & Female* 407 Clothes consisted of a short sarong—called a lavalava. **1957** M. B. PICKEN *Fashion Dict.* 207/2 *Lava-lava*, loincloth or waistcloth of printed calico worn by natives of Samoa and other islands in the Pacific. **1971** *Listener* 9 Sept. 334/3, I saw the famous lava-lava—the short, brightly-coloured skirt which they [*sc.* Samoans] wore below the naked torso. **1973** *Observer* (Colour Suppl.) 28 Oct. 53/1 Lavalavas (skirts made from a single length of cloth, originally introduced by the missionaries for reasons of modesty, often wrapped round the body from bosom to knee by Samoan women).

Lavallière (lavalyę̄r'). Also **Lavalière**, with lower-case initial, and without accent; **lavalier**. Name of Louise de *la Vallière*, French courtesan (1644–1710), used *absol.* or *attrib.* to designate certain styles in clothing and jewellery. Also *transf.*, a small microphone.

1873 *Young Englishwoman* July 350/1 (*heading*) White chip Lavalliere Hat. The crown is moderately high, with a rather broad brim, turned up in front and down at the back. **1916** *Daily Colonist* (Victoria, B.C.) 16 July 2/1 (Advt.), Our stock of moderately priced Necklets, Pendants and La Valieres is most attractive. **1942** *Horizon* Oct. 250 His collar and ready-made tie (a lavallière). **1951** E. PAUL *Springtime in Paris* vii. 136 Noel, with broad-brimmed felt hat, seersucker jacket and flowing *lavallière*, personified the artistic type. **1955** *Publ. Amer. Dial. Soc.* XXIV. 122 Any minor bauble such as a lavaliere..is a *dangler*. **1959** *Times* 28 Apr. 20/6 A diamond lavalliere. **1969** D. M. DISNEY *Fatal Choice* (1970) x. 80 Marcy was wearing John's farewell gift, a lavaliere set with an aquamarine..and seed pearls. **1970** *New Yorker* 12 Sept. 32/2 Mr. Siegel, whose clothes for public appearances are striking, running to vests and lavalieres, had a big grin on his face. **1972** R. HENDRICKSON *Human Words* 179 Today the small television microphone that hangs on a cord from the neck is also called a *lavaliere*, taking its name from the pendant necklace. **1974** *Amer. Speech 1971* XLVI. 55 A low impedance, unidirectional microphone is, I feel, better than a lavalier microphone.

‖ **lavandera** (lavănde·ră). [Sp.] In Spanish-speaking countries, a washerwoman; = LAVENDER *sb.*¹

1841 BORROW *Zincali* I. II. vi. 316 The lavanderas engaged in purifying the linen of the capital. **1918** W. H. HUDSON *Far Away & Long Ago* vii. 97 One of the most attractive spots to me was the congregating place of the *lavanderas*, south of my street.

lavatera (lavatīə·ră, lavā·tərā). [mod.L. (J. Pitton de Tournefort (1706), in *Hist. Acad. Roy. Sci. Mém.* 86), f. the name of the brothers *Lavater*, 17th- and 18th-c. Swiss physicians and naturalists.] A herb or shrub of the genus so called, belonging to the family Malvaceæ, and bearing pink, white, or purple flowers.

1731 P. MILLER *Gardeners Dict.* s.v. *Lavatera*, African Lavatera, with a most beautiful flower. **1790** *Curtis's Bot. Mag.* IV. 109 Annual Lavatera..flowers from July to September. **1916** G. JEKYLL *Annuals & Biennials* i. 4 Where a temporary filling is desired of plants of important aspect, there are the Tobacco plants,..Foxgloves, Solanums, and Lavatera. **1962** *Listener* 19 Apr. 708/3 Sow hollyhocks, lavatera, sweet peas.

lavatorial, *a.* Add: **2.** Of or pertaining to a style of architecture or decoration alleged to resemble that used for public lavatories.

1936 E. EATON *Summer Dust* I. vii. 42 The newer movement, which demands that every rising young lawyer should furnish an *appartement* in the neo-lavatorial style. **1957** *Sunday Times* 17 Nov. 3/3 The Examination Schools, that lavatorial building of awful omen. **1958** B. HAMILTON *Too Much of Water* ii. 42, I had to pull down an absolutely shattering piece of Victorian lavatorial Gothic. **1969** *Observer* 12 Jan. 25/3 A barber's, a lavatorial café, and nothing much else but grime and desolation. **1974** A. ROSS *Bradford Business* 63 Endless lavatorial town hall corridors.

3. Of or pertaining to lavatories; *spec.* of conversation, humour, etc.: making undue reference to lavatories and their use.

1967 *Daily Tel.* 15 Apr. 9/3 The average gent is of an aggressive disposition and a lavatorial sense of humour. **1969** *Daily Tel.* 17 Nov. 9/1 The words..are perfectly familiar, partly lavatorial, partly sexy, ranging in length from four to seven letters. **1969** C. DERRICK *Reader's Report* vii. 120 A great many poets, when talking about their art, drop instinctively and sub-consciously into the

use of obstetrical and even lavatorial imagery. **1974** *Times* 9 Nov. 10/4 The awful lavatorial embarrassment.

lavatory, *sb.* Add: **4.** In the 20th c. one of the more usual words for a W.C. (now giving way to more recent euphemisms: *lav., loo, toilet,* etc.).

In some examples ellipt. for the appliance itself.

1924 F. M. Ford *Some do Not* I. ii. 37 The hotel having been a former Grand Ducal hunting-box, freshened to suit the taste of the day with varnished pitch-pine, bathrooms, verandahs, and excessively modern but noisy lavatory arrangements. **1963** J. T. Story *Something for Nothing* iii. 106 Albert closed the door and sat down on the lavatory. **1965** *Listener* 2 Sept. 351/2 Flush Conscience down the lavatory. **1967** *Ibid.* 3 Aug. 144/3 Certain kinds of help are..needed... Lavatories a disabled person can get in and onto. *Ibid.* 21 Dec. 802/1 'Loo' is holding its own fairly well and most of 'Toilet's' gains have been at the expense of 'Lavatory'. **1973** A. S. Neill *Neill! Neill! Orange Peel!* (rev. ed.) II. 189 What did people use in the lavatory before the invention of paper?

8. *lavatory attendant, basin, brush, chain, cleanser, pan, paper, seat*; also **lavatory humour,** unsavoury or unwholesome humour making undue reference to lavatories (cf. *lavatorial *a.* 3); so *lavatory joke*; **lavatory period, style,** a period or style of architecture with 'lavatorial' characteristics (cf. *lavatorial *a.* 2).

1930 I. Low *His Master's Voice* xv. 217 A lavatory attendant might make a similar boast thought Nikulin. **1939** C. Isherwood *Goodbye to Berlin* 29 The little old lavatory attendant in his white jacket. **1964** R. Petrie *Murder by Precedent* i. 20 Lavatory attendants..aren't as likely to insure their lives as professional men. **1926–7** *Army & Navy Stores Catal.* 321 'Vitrella' should be used for cleaning all porcelain baths, lavatory basins, sinks. **1931** *Times* 16 Mar. 22/1 (Advt.), Lavatory basin in best bed room. **1963** *B.S.I. News* Apr. 33 Ceramic lavatory basins. **1939–40** *Army & Navy Stores Catal.* 167/2 Lavatory brush holder. **1962** *House & Garden* Dec. 51/1 Lavatory brush and container, 12 s. **1969** A. E. Lindop *Sight Unseen* xxix. 245 A bottle of bourbon..stood in the stand which usually held the lavatory brush. *c* **1932** Dylan Thomas *Lett.* (1966) 5 Give me..a book by Paul de Kock, and thou, thou old lavatory chain. **1964** V. S. Naipaul *Area of Darkness* iv. 94 At four..we heard him rise and get ready for his walk: lavatory chain, gargling, clattering, doors. **1926–7** *Army & Navy Stores Catal.* 469/3 Harpic Lavatory Cleanser. **1963** V. Nabokov *Gift* ii. 83 The lavatory humour and crude laughter. **1970** *Sunday Times* (Colour Suppl.) 15 Mar. 25/1 He was real blue, if you like. Some of his jokes. Lavatory humour, my Dan used to call it. **1954** N. Tomalin in *Granta* 6 Nov. 23/2 All in all the most amazing thing about the show is the preponderance of lavatory jokes. **1966** A. E. Lindop *I start Counting* xx. 256, I clutched my head over the lavatory pan. **1974** *Listener* 24 Jan. 100/1 After an atomic explosion, the last things to disintegrate would be articles made of vitreous porcelain—for example, wash-basins and lavatory pans. **1926–7** *Army & Navy Stores Catal.* 121/2 Lavatory Paper Holder. **1956** A. S. C. Ross in M. Black *Importance of Lang.* (1962) 103 Non-U *toilet-paper* / U *lavatory-paper*. **1974** *Times* 23 Jan. 14/4 The Americans..had their lavatory paper panic first. **1952** A. Christie *They do it with Mirrors* iii. 24 'It's pretty ghastly, really,' said Gina cheerfully. 'A sort of Gothic monstrosity. What Steve calls Best Victorian Lavatory period.' **1939** G. Household *Rogue Male* 255, I made him sit on the lavatory seat and read me the shipping news. **1973** *Country Life* 20 Sept. 784/2 Three industries of Derbyshire..[are] the manufacture of artificial flowers, lavatory seats and mint sauce. **1937** H. G. Wells *Camford Visitation* i. 5 That University affair they are building in London..is all made, they tell me, of a sort of mineral nougat, lavatory style. **1944** J. Agate *Red Letter Nights* 141 Liliom commits suicide, and is projected into a celestial police court, the architecture of which is copied from the Early Lavatory style of the National Liberal Club.

lave, *a.* **b.** *Comb.* **lave-eared** *a.* (later examples).

1926 *Blackw. Mag.* Sept. 431/1 If a poet..was lave-eared; if he had the eyes of a fawn, then you might be sure that he was a poet, and fear the worst. **1932** Auden *Orators* II. 44 The nasty lave-eared pop-eyed bitch.

lavender, *sb.*[2] and *a.* Add: **A.** *sb.* **1. c.** Phr. *lavender and old lace*: the title of a novel and play used to describe a gentle and 'old-fashioned' style.

The novel by Myrtle Reed was published in 1902 and the dramatized version by Rose Warner in 1938.

1966 *Guardian* 25 Nov. 14/7 Arthur Pollard..is largely concerned to dispel the notion that Mrs Gaskell is a writer of 'lavender and old lace'. **1966** M. Steen *Looking Glass* v. 88 E. V. Lucas..never wrote twaddle: the lavender and old lace of his titles masked erudition. **1968** Hocking & Healey *Murder cries Out* iv. 54 This astounded gentleman..had received a description of Miss Willoughby as all 'lavender and old lace'.

3*. *Cinemat.* Positive stock, or a positive print, used for producing duplicate negatives; also (quot. 1936), a print made from such a negative.

1936 C. B. DeMille in *Words* Oct. 6/1 A 'lavender' is something often spoken of in the industry... It is a print made from a negative on lavender stock, which is a weak print from a weak negative, because lavender negatives are only copies of the film originally exposed in the camera and are therefore not as sharp. **1959** W. S. Sharps *Dict. Cinematogr.* 106/1 *Lavender*, the name given to an obsolescent type of master positive stock with a lavender tinted base. The name remains in use to describe a master positive. **1973** D. A. Spencer *Focal Dict. Photogr. Technol.* 340 *Lavender*, fine grain motion picture film used for making duplicate black and white negatives..and coated on lavender tinted base to minimise halation and prevent confusion with ordinary positive stocks. Modern duplicating stock is on a grey tinted base and differs sufficiently in appearance from ordinary positive that the lavender tint is not necessary.

4. *lavender-blue* (later example), *-grey* (later example); *lavender-coloured, -hued* adjs.; *lavender-scented* (earlier and later examples); also **lavender bag,** a bag containing dried lavender; **lavender cream,** lavender-scented cream or furniture-polish; also *lavender furniture cream*; **lavender drawer,** a drawer containing or scented with lavender; **lavender drop,** a drop (sense 4) medicated with lavender; **lavender polish** = **lavender cream*; also *lavender floor polish*; **lavender sachet** = **lavender bag*; **lavender soap,** soap perfumed with lavender; also *lavender toilet soap*; **lavender wax** = **lavender cream*.

1865 Geo. Eliot *Let.* 6 Feb. in J. W. Cross *George Eliot's Life* (1885) II. xii. 396, I want to send my love, lest all the old messages shall have lost their scent, like old lavender bags. **1923** A. Huxley *Antic Hay* iv. 55 Give me..a lavender bag under every pillow. **1965** M. Sharp *Sun in Scorpio* III. xxv. 131 Elspet was peddling lavender-bags. **1936** *Burlington Mag.* Jan. 9/1 Vase with lavender-blue glaze splashed or suffused with purple. **1901** *Westm. Gaz.* 7 Sept. 1/3 Our lavender-coloured view of life. **1936** J. C. Powys *Maiden Castle* (1937) 40 A vision of lavender-coloured tights. **1926–7** *Army & Navy Stores Catal.* 1128/2 Hair and toilet preparations.. Lavender cream. *c* **1938** *Fortnum & Mason Price List* 36/1 Furniture polish..Lavender Cream..per jar 1/6. **1863** Dickens *Mrs. Lirriper's Lodgings* i, in *All Year Round* Extra Christmas No., 3 Dec. 9/1 An advertisement..which I mean always carefully to keep in my lavender drawer. **1811** Jane Austen *Sense & Sens.* II. vii. 126 Some lavender drops..which she was at length persuaded to take, were of use. **1969** A. E. Lindop *Sight Unseen* xix. 158 A clean smell of lavender floor polish. **1926–7** *Army & Navy Stores Catal.* 297/2 Lavender furniture cream. **1936** *Burlington Mag.* Jan. 4/1 Buff ware with a crackled lavender-grey glaze. **1901** *Westm. Gaz.* 7 Sept. 1/3, I speak from experience, having lately reached the lavender-hued period. **1961** J. Stroud *Touch & Go* v. 49 The aggressive lavender-polish aroma denoting the house-proud matriarch. **1966** L. Deighton *Billion-Dollar Brain* v. 51 There was a sweet smell of lavender polish as we walked through a couple of rooms. **1938** R. Field *All this, & Heaven Too* (1939) iv. 65 The lavender sachets in her bureau drawers. **1973** 'S. Harvester' *Corner of Playground* I. 49 Who can make tea with a bloody bag like a lavender sachet? **1855** Mrs. Gaskell *North & South* II. xxi. 283 Smoothing down the bed, and despatching Jenny for an armful of lavender-scented towels. **1938** O. Sitwell et al. *Trio* 124, I care for him [*sc.* de la Mare] less when he is in a melancholy mood, for the poems then have a tendency to become a little too lavender-scented. **1974** J. Wainwright *Evidence I shall Give* xv. 58 Lavender-scented handkerchiefs. **1875** E. Spon *Workshop Receipts* 385 *Lavender Soap.*—The basis of Windsor soap, scented with oil of lavender. **1949** D. Smith *I capture Castle* II. ix. 133 Rose was..varnishing her nails; the varnish had been her special treat... I had lavender soap. **1961** A. Wilson *Old Men at Zoo* I. 35 The Director caught up with me, all redolent with lavender soap to greet his lady wife, as he was apt to call her. **1890–91** *T. Eaton & Co. Catal.* Fall & Winter 42/1 Sweet lavender toilet soap. **1970** M. Kelly *Spinifex* vi. 97 A large bedroom scented with years of lavender wax.

B. *adj.* † **2.** Photogr. *lavender rays,* ultra-violet radiation. *Obs.*

1840 J. F. W. Herschel in *Phil. Trans. R. Soc.* CXXX. 20 As orange, indigo, and violet, vegetable tints, are used for those of the prismatic hues, I may be allowed to express by the epithet lavender the rays which produce the tint in question, rather for the purpose of abbreviating the uncouth appellation of *ultra-violet*..than for that of laying any undue stress on the observed fact. **1842** *Ibid.* CXXXII. 191 If the action of the spectrum be prolonged, a much feebler whitening becomes sensible in the red, and a trace of it also beyond the violet into the 'lavender' rays. **1858** Sutton & Worden *Dict. Photogr.* 248 The faintly luminous rays beyond the violet end of the spectrum are called 'lavender rays'. **1911** *Cassell's Cycl. Photogr.* 329/2 *Lavender rays*, a term (now practically obsolete) applied to the commencement of the ultra-violet rays just beyond the visible violet. [**1922** A. E. H. Tutton *Crystallogr.* II. li. 1139 This ultra-violet lamp is visible to the eye at close quarters owing to fluorescence of the retina of the eye itself; and the field of vision appears filled with a haze known as 'lavender fog', owing to fluorescence of the crystalline lens of the eye.]

lavendery (læ·vĕndəri), *a.* [f. Lavender *sb.*[2] + -y[1].] Perfumed with lavender; fragrant. Also *fig.*

1896 G. B. Shaw *Our Theatres in Nineties* (1932) II. 10 Mr Rose has often written pleasantly about these and other more remote and lavendery antiquities. **1968** P. Dickinson *Skin Deep* v. 107 Go now, the smile said, and I'll retain fond lavendery memories of you; stay and I'll bite. **1974** A. Price *Other Paths to Glory* I. v. 49 The lavendery smell of the strange room.

lavenite. Add: Also † **laavenite, låvenite.** (Further examples.)

1887 *Mineral. Mag.* VII. 234 The laavenite occurs as small honey-yellow crystalline grains. **1927** N. H. & A. N. Winchell *Elem. Optical Mineral.* (ed. 2) II. x. 245 Laavenite is a monoclinic zircono-silicate of Ca, Mn, Na with some Ti, Ta, F, OH. **1967** *Mineral. Abstr.* XVIII. 48/2 A new variety of låvenite occurs in a zone of veinlet nephelinization in massive quartz syenite in the alkalic massif of Burpala in northern Baikal [Siberia].

laventine. (Examples.)

1893 *Funk's Stand. Dict.*, *Laventine*, a thin silk: much used for sleeve-linings. **1921** *Daily Colonist* (Victoria, B.C.) 18 Oct. 19/7 (Advt.), Umbrellas at All Prices... Strong durable covers in mercerized cotton, gloria and laventine.

laver, *sb.*[1] Add: **2.** Also with pronunc. (lā·vəɹ). **laver bread** (also **lava bread**), a name in Wales for a food made from the fronds of *Porphyra umbilicalis,* which are boiled, dipped in oatmeal, and fried.

1701 W. Kennet *Cowell's Interpreter* (rev. ed.), *Laver-bread*, in Glamorganshire and some other parts of Wales, they make a sort of Food of a Sea plant, which seems to be the Oyster-green or Sea-Liver-wort. This they call Laver-bread. **1949** *New Biol.* VII. 94 In the days when butter was more plentiful, laver bread was heated with butter, lemon juice and pepper, and served with roast mutton. **1953** Dylan Thomas *Under Milk Wood* (1954) 5 Is there rum and laverbread? **1962** *Listener* 26 July 140/2 Lava bread..is the only truly Welsh food. It is made from seaweed. **1969** N. W. Pirie *Food Resources* v. 127 Welsh devotion to laverbread is an important factor which restrains the managers of nuclear installations from fouling the sea more than they do now.

Laverack (læ·vəræk). The name of Edward *Laverack* (d. 1877), English dog breeder, used *attrib.* in **Laverack setter** to designate the type of English setter (see Setter *sb.*[1] 11 a) developed by him, a large hunting dog having long white fur flecked with other colours. Also *absol.*

1878 C. Hallock *Sportsman's Gazetteer* (ed. 4) 689/2 Belton.—the ticked or spotted Laverack setter. **1904** *Daily Chron.* 15 Aug. 3/3 In America 'Laveracks' and 'Llewellins' are household words among sportsmen. **1971** F. Hamilton *World Encycl. Dogs* 245 These differing methods of breeding led in later years to the main division in the breed as we know it today, between show dogs and working dogs; although it must be remembered that both types originated with the Laveracks. *Ibid.*, (*caption*) An engraving of Mr. Purcell-Llewellyn's Laverack Setter, Countess.

Laves phase (lā·vəs fēiz). *Metallurgy.* [ad. G. *Laves-phase* (G. E. R. Schulze 1939, in *Zeitschr. f. Elektrochem.* XLV. 850/1), f. the name of Fritz-Henning *Laves* (b. 1906), German crystallographer + Phase *sb.*] Any of a group of intermetallic compounds of composition approximately AB_2 in which the relative sizes of the A and B atoms are such as to allow a stable packing arrangement with unusually high co-ordination numbers.

1940 *Chem. Abstr.* XXXIV. 1895 Laves phases are AB_2 intermetallic compds. whose structure and combination mechanism are detd. by the crystal lattice. **1956** Hume-Rothery & Raynor *Struct. Metals & Alloys* (ed. 3) v. 228 The Laves phases crystallize in one of three closely related structures, and are isomorphous with the compounds $MgCu_2$, $MgZn_2$, or $MgNi_2$. **1967** A. H. Cottrell *Introd. Metall.* xiv. 195 In a Laves phase AB_2, each A atom has 16 neighbours (4A and 12B) and each B atom has 12 neighbours.

lavvy (læ·vi). = *lav.

1961 Partridge *Dict. Slang* II. 1165/1 *Lavvy*, a Scottish, esp. children's, easing of lavatory. **1962** *John o' London's* 27 Dec. 588/1 An outside loo or 'lavvy'. **1971** *Guardian* 20 Jan. 8/2 A house where the lavvy is behind an arras.

law, *sb.*[1] Add: **1. b.** (Later example.) Also *colloq.* (orig. *U.S.*), a policeman, the police; a sheriff.

1929 M. A. Gill *Underworld Slang, Law*, police. **1935** A. J. Pollock *Underworld Speaks* 121/2 *The law*, a police officer. **1944** B. A. Botkin *Treas. Amer. Folklore* I. 131 There was plenty of precedent for Roy Bean in the usual Western 'Law' or sheriff. **1953** W. Burroughs *Junkie* (1972) x. 104 We were in the third precinct about three hours and then the laws put us in the wagon and took us to Parish Prison. *Ibid.* xii. 121 Whenever a law needs money for a quick beer, he goes over by Lupita and waits for someone to walk out on the chance he may be holding a paper [containing narcotic]. **1955** *Publ. Amer. Dial. Soc.* xxiv. 106 Some mobs have a strong prejudice against robbing any *law*, whatever he may be. **1958** F. Norman *Bang to Rights* 152 Two law..came up to me and grabbed hold of me. **1962** 'J. Bell' *Crime in our Time* I. 13 He had only one idea. To get rid of 'the law', clinging to his car. He drove from side to side of the road in an effort to force Meehan off. **1972** D. Lees *Zodiac* 5 Soon, car-loads of Maigret-type law would come screaming up the drive. **1972** *Times* 6 June 18/6, I inquired of the Law where I might cash a cheque, and was directed to the nearest travel agency. **1973** M. Woodhouse *Blue Bone* vi. 56 The Oxford law would know about this, I take it?

3. a. (Earlier and later examples of *law and order.*)

1598 Florio *Worlde of Wordes* 201/2 Legitimo..*according to law and order.* **1796** *Deb. Congress U.S.* 20 Dec. (1849) 1689 A military diploma, expressive of his patriotism and attachment to law and order. **1846** *Nat. Intelligencer* (Washington) 24 Mar. 3/4 The 'Law and Order'

party has clearly fulfilled.. its public mission. **1893** [see *COMFORTABLY *adv.* 5 a]. **1932** G. F.-H. BERKELEY *Italy in Making* I. iii. 42 This repression continued until..even his allies finally began to perceive that law-and-order can be bought at too dear a price. **1952** *N.Y. Times* 11 Mar. 11/1 (*heading*) Ex-sergeant rode to power on cry of 'Law and Order', seizing reins in 1933. **1962** S. WYNTER *Hills of Hebron* ix. 118 The Commissioner..had come to use words like 'duty', 'law and order' to cover up a lack of imagination. **1967** P. HENDERSON *William Morris* II. xii. 281 The SFD and the League..started a campaign for free speech, which suddenly brought Morris into conflict with the forces of Law and Order. **1968** *Economist* 5 Oct. 41/3 Mr Nixon and.. Mr Humphrey are both making concessions to this overriding concern about 'law and order'. **1970** *New Yorker* 26 Sept. 137/1 If it happens that rightists are successful in capturing most of the law-and-order vote, then, of course, the country will move to the right politically. **1972** *Daily Tel.* 24 May 15 The published motions cover a wider and more immediate political field than usual—from the economy and unemployment to the media, Ulster and law and order. **1973** *Black World* Dec. 19/1 A sense of determinism that is diametrically opposed to the ruler-class 'law-and-order' and individualism.

8. b. (Examples of *to take the law into one's own hands* (or, obs., *fists*).)

1847 E. BRONTË *Wuthering Heights* I. vii. 129 Next time, Master Edgar, take the law into your own fists. **1875** B. JOWETT tr. *Plato's Dialogues* (ed. 2) III. 63 Young men will take the law into their own hands. **1877** C. M. YONGE *Cameos from Eng. Hist.* 3rd ser. vii. 63 Cade took the law into his own hands. **1902** A. BENNETT *Grand Babylon Hotel* xxvii. 300, I have a few questions to put to you, and it will depend on how you answer them whether I give you up to the police or take the law into my own hands. **1942** A. BRYANT *Yrs. of Endurance* xiv. 333 The industrial workers and the starving peasants, deprived of their patrimony by enclosures, took the law into their own hands.

16. a. *a law unto* (or *to*) *himself* (or *themselves*, etc.) (later examples).

1878 R. H. DAVIS (*title*) A law unto herself. **1930** J. S. HUXLEY *Bird-Watching* iv. 75 Every male [ruff] is a law unto himself. Some grow black ruffs, others ruffs that are white, sandy, brown, grey, pepper-and-salt, and half a dozen other shades. **1942** PARTRIDGE *Usage and Abusage* (1947) 129/1 Certain idiosyncratic, law-unto-themselves writers fall into vagaries when..they depart from those rules. **1962** A. NISBETT *Technique Sound Studio* xii. 221 Electronic music is a law to itself... It really can be fundamentally different from conventional music. **1965** M. SPARK *Mandelbaum Gate* ii. 23 'What was your father's Law?'.. 'I'm afraid he was a law unto himself.' **1968** *Listener* 27 June 850/1 Hogarth is very much a law to himself.

c. Phr. *law of the jungle*, the code of survival in jungle life, now usu. with ref. to the superiority of brute force or self-interest in the struggle for survival.

1894 KIPLING *Jungle Bk.* 31 Baloo was teaching him the Law of the Jungle... Young wolves will only learn as much of the Law of the Jungle as applies to their own pack and tribe. *Ibid.* 34 A man's cub..must learn *all* the Law of the Jungle. **1895** —— *Second Jungle Bk.* 23 Now this is the Law of the Jungle—as old and as true as the sky; ..the strength of the Pack is the Wolf, and the strength of the Wolf is the Pack. **1927** C. A. & M. R. BEARD *Rise Amer. Civilization* I. ix. 403 So the law of the jungle prevailed; and in the frightful contest that followed, the rights of neutrals were as chaff before a hurricane. **1950** A. BRYANT *Age of Elegance* x. 329 In the manufacturing districts..the old framework of society..broke down completely. Here only the law of the jungle held. **1951** M. McLUHAN *Mech. Bride* 107/2 Mr. Queeny derives his 'law of the jungle' versus 'crusading idealist' from this later nineteenth-century phase of the older split. **1969** *New Yorker* 6 Sept. 33 (*caption*) May I remind you that here law and order means the law of the jungle. **1974** *Times* 4 Mar. 7/4 The Duke said that a purely materialistic society inevitably succumbed to the law of the jungle and political dictatorship.

17. b. *law of large numbers*: see *LARGE *a.* 8 i.

c. (*c*) (Earlier examples of *Grimm's law.*)

1838 W. B. WINNING *Man. Compar. Philol.* I. iii. 36 *Grimm's Law.*—I now proceed with the consideration of Grimm's important law..concerning the regular interchange of certain letters in different languages. *Ibid.* 47 On the principle of Grimm's law, we exclude the Perso-Grecians, High Germans, and Goths, from among the earliest colonists of Italy.

(*e*) *Meteorol.* **Buys-Ballot's law** (bīzbæ·lo) [enunciated by C. H. D. *Buys-Ballot* (1817–90), Dutch meteorologist, in 1857] (see quots.).

1875 *Encycl. Brit.* III. 29/1 Buys-Ballot's 'Law of the Winds'..may be thus expressed:—The wind neither blows round the space of lowest pressure in circles returning on themselves, nor does it blow directly towards that space; but it takes a direction intermediate, approaching, however, more nearly to the direction and course of circular curves than of radii to a centre. **1970** J. HULBERT *All about Weather* vi. 73 Buys Ballot's law..says that if a man stands with his back to the wind, the lower pressure will be to his left in the northern hemisphere, and to his right in the southern.

21. a. *law department, firm, language* (example), *reports* (examples), *school* (examples), *student* (earlier and later examples), *studies.*

1849 E. CHAMBERLAIN *Indiana Gazetteer* (ed. 3) 45 In the winter of 1838, the institution was chartered as an University, and in 1842, a law department was established. *c* **1876** 'MARK TWAIN' *Lett. to Publishers* (1967) 95, I suppose *our* law firm are [*sic*] above average. **1945** G. L. WILLIAMS *Learning the Law* xii. 130 There are law firms in the East, located in the great seaports, where young solicitors may often find good places. **1965** MRS. L. B. JOHNSON *White House Diary* 21 July (1970) 304 His greatest hope was to stabilize the law firm. **1973** *N.Y. Law Jrnl.* 31 Aug. 1/3 A New York attorney and a law firm have been found by Federal Judge Lloyd F. MacMahon of the Southern District of New York to have violated..the Code of Professional Responsibility. **1797** *Encycl. Brit.* IX. 725/1 (*heading*) Law-Language. *c* **1840** LADY WILTON *Art of Needlework* xviii. 298 No. 50 [of *The English Mercurie*], dated July 23, 1588, is the first now in existence... In it are no advertisements—no fashions—no law reports—no court circular. **1902** *Encycl. Brit.* XXXI. 181/2 The *Law Reports* (begun in 1884) are conducted by the large staff of *Times* law reporters, all of them barristers of at least five years' standing. **1972** *Mod. Law Rev.* XXXV. I. 22 The law reports, commonly regarded as our primary literature, tell us regularly and systematically how large claims are being determined. **1818** *North Amer. Rev.* Mar. 428 A Law School is established at the University. **1863** S. WARREN *Pop. & Pract. Introd. Law Stud.* (ed. 3) I. i. 89 In Ireland, there is a 'Law School' in the University of Dublin. **1893** W. K. POST *Harvard Stories* 128 'You couldn't do that if you were a biographee,' reasoned Dane Austin, the law-school man. **1966** G. WILSON in K. Boehm *University Choice* 242 It would be a rare law student who could do anything as straightforward as transfer his own house as a result of what he had learnt at law school. **1835** S. WARREN *Pop. & Pract. Introd. Law Stud.* iii. 102 Could the eye of the young law-student be brought to..see how heavily his bodily and mental energies will be taxed..how he would husband them! **1945** G. L. WILLIAMS *Learning the Law* iv. 36 A teacher must consider..the amount of time actually available to a law student for his studies. **1966** Law student [see *law school* above]. **1845** C. M. KIRKLAND *Western Clearings* 42 George Burnet had just come home after finishing what he called his 'law studies'.

c. *law-honest* (earlier example); also *law-honesty.*

1838 J. F. COOPER *Homeward Bound* III. xi. 333 Mr. Dodge belonged to a tolerably numerous class, that is quaintly described as being 'law honest', that is to say, he neither committed murder nor petty larceny. **1905** *Daily Chron.* 6 Dec. 7/7 What may be called law-honesty, the kind of honesty necessary in order to avoid falling into the clutches of the law.

22. b. *law-governed* adj.

1938 *Burlington Mag.* Mar. 148/1 The 'law-governed' development of the language of form. **1960** H. EDWARDS *Spirit Healing* iii. 25 Every change within our comprehension is the result of law-governed forces applied to the subject.

23. law enforcement, enforcement of the law; freq. *attrib.*; so *law-enforcer*; **law-lord,** (*a*) (later examples); **law-office** (earlier and later examples); **law station** *slang*, a police station; **law-writer,** (*c*) (example).

1936 L. HELLMAN *Days to Come* II. iii. 70 Dowel was found knifed, dead... That gives us a little job of law enforcement to do. **1955** D. W. MAURER in *Publ. Amer. Dialect Soc.* xxiv. 6 A problem which urgently demands the attention of the legislators, law-enforcement specialists, and the judiciary. **1956** 'E. McBAIN' *Cop Hater* (1963) xvii. 129 If they can do away with law enforcement, the rest will be easy... First the police, then the National Guard. **1960** *Times* 3 Oct. 13/6 Their functions as law-enforcement officers. **1972** A. ROUDYBUSH *Sybaritic Death* (1974) xiii. 119 His proposal..to help the overwhelmed police in their law-enforcement task. **1938** *Tablet* 1 Jan. 1/1 The world was pictured as consisting of the law-makers and law-enforcers. **1975** *Listener* 16 Jan. 67/1 The law enforcers themselves were bent. **1958** *Times* 24 July 8/7 The sons and daughters of law lords and life peers..shall be treated for their style, rank, dignity, and precedence in the same way as the wives..of hereditary barons. **1972** *Mod. Law Rev.* XXXV. I. 63 Two Law Lords with first instance experience in the Divorce Division. **1873** 'MARK TWAIN' & WARNER *Gilded Age* xii. 117 In the anteroom of the law-office where he was writing. **1973** *N.Y. Law Jrnl.* 2 Aug. 16/6 (Advt.), Political Science undergraduate seeks 4 years law study and clerkship in law office to gain credit to take Bar. **1958** F. NORMAN *Bang to Rights* 50 After a while we came to a law station. **1959** ANON. *Streetwalker* x. 180, I was in the law station. They got me early. **1852** DICKENS *Bleak Ho.* (1853) x. 94 Our law-writers, who live by job-work, are a queer lot.

Law: see *LAWD.

law-abiding, *a.* (Earlier and later examples.)

1839 *Congress. Globe* Dec., App. 14/2 Being a law-loving and law-abiding man, he had voted to preserve the laws. **1855** *Ibid.* 26 Jan. 416/2 The people of Oregon are a law-abiding, honest and gallant people. **1973** C. MULLARD *Black Brit.* II. vi. 68 A racist, however intelligent, will never accept that blacks are just like other average human beings, honest, industrious, clean, law-abiding, intelligent, etc.

Lawd (lǭd). Chiefly *U.S.* Also **Law, Lawdy.** Local (esp. Black English) variants of *Lord, Lordy*, usually as interjections or in humorous contexts.

1846 C. M. S. KIRKLAND *Bee-Tree* in *Amer. Short Stories* (1904) 204 Law sakes alive! **1851** MRS. STOWE *Uncle Tom's Cabin* (1852) II. xx. 49 Law, Missis, you must whip me; my old Missis allers whipped me. **1881** J. C. HARRIS *Nights with Uncle Remus* (1884) xii. 65 'Is dey anybody home?'.. 'Law, no, honey, folks all gone.' *Ibid.* xxxix. 183 Lawdy mussy, Brer Rabbit! Whar my vittles? **1898** 'J. KERR' *Cheery Bk.* 121 But, Lawdy! How dat coon can kiss! **1901** G. B. SHAW *Captain Brassbound's Conversion* I. 226 *Drinkwater.* Lawd,..wot jagginses them jurymen was! *Ibid.* II. 242 Git the plice ready for the British herristorcracy, Lawd Ellan and Lidy Wineflete? **1926** W. C. HANDY *Blues* 64 Feel so low down an' sad Lawd Lost ev'rything I ever had. *Ibid.* 91 Why did I go away? I used to be so gay There'll come a day! Oh Lawdy Lawd how happy I'll be Down home in Florida. **1928** R. BRADFORD in B. A. Botkin *Treas. S. Folklore* (1949) III. ii. 485 So about dat time de Lawd comed up on old man Noah. **1945** MENCKEN *Amer. Lang.* Suppl. I. 664 Euphemisms... For *Lord*: *land, law, lawks, lawdy, lawsy.* **1970** R. S. ABRAHAMS *Positively Black* vi. 142 Lawdy, lawdy, lawdy, lawd, I used to be your reg'lar, now I got to be your dog. **1971** *Black Scholar* Sept. 44/2 'Lawd!' he blurts out and begins to giggle. **1973** *Black World* Sept. 29 Hughes sometimes created short, vignette-type poems with the blues feeling..as he did in 'Bad Morning': Here I sit with my shoes mismated. Lawdy-mercy! I's frustrated!

lawful, *a.* **3.** (Later example.)

1890 M. C. FRASER *Let.* Nov. in *Diplomatist's Wife Japan* (1899) II. xxviii. 143 The Japanese are a profoundly lawful people (if I may use the word in its old sense).

6. Describable or governed by laws of nature.

1939 *Nature* 14 Jan. 64/1 Newton and others have found confirmation even for their religious beliefs in the lawful character of physical phenomena. **1958** M. ARGYLE *Relig. Behaviour* i. 2 It is commonly assumed that human behaviour is lawful and that it can be predicted by means of psychological laws and explained in terms of psychological processes. **1959** M. BUNGE *Causality* i. 22 The principle of universal lawfulness..may be taken to read thus: Every single event is lawful, i.e., is determined in accordance with a set of objective laws—whether we know the laws or not. **1975** *Nature* 3 Apr. 416/2 The results show that the tendency..can be brought under lawful control in such a way as to discriminate against the above hypotheses.

lawfully, *adv.* Add: **1. b.** In accordance with laws of nature.

1959 M. BUNGE *Causality* i. 22 The principle of universal lawfulness does not assert that facts are determined by laws, but in accordance with laws, or simply lawfully.

lawfulness. Add: (Later example of sense 'respect for law'.)

1924 B. WILLIAMS in *History* Jan. 273 The adventures of..the N.W. Mounted Police, in bringing half a continent to lawfulness and peace.

2. The quality of being describable by laws of nature, or of happening or behaving in accordance with certain general principles that always hold good.

1956 E. H. HUTTEN *Lang. Mod. Physics* vi. 210 To say that causality is the belief in the lawfulness of nature..is therefore quite meaningless. **1959** [see *LAWFUL *a.* 6]. **1972** *Science* 16 June 1208/3 Experiences..that do not show consistent patterns..will be distinguished from those phenomena which do show general lawfulness.

lawkamercy (lǭ:kămə·ɪsi), *int.* Var. of *lawk-a-mussy* (LAWK, LAWKS *int.*). (In quot. 1909 as quasi-*adj.*)

1909 J. MASEFIELD *Tragedy of Nan* I. 8 Idle lawkamercy girl. **1927** B. L. K. HENDERSON *Chats about our Mother Tongue* i. 54 Lawkamercy, lad, what's that?

lawless, *a.* **1.** (Later example.)

1956 E. H. HUTTEN *Lang. Mod. Physics* vi. 215 This confusion has prompted the view that chance events are lawless.

lawlessly, *adv.* (Later example.)

1972 *Daily Tel.* 4 Aug. 2/8 The council is insistent that it is not behaving lawlessly.

law-like, *a.* Add: **c.** *Philos.* Of a statement, explanation, etc.: resembling scientific laws in saying that some consequence would occur in any situation of a certain sort, though differing in containing reference to individuals; also, such as to be a law of nature if established as true.

1949 G. RYLE *Concept of Mind* iv. 89 How does the law-like general hypothetical proposition work? It says, roughly, that the glass, *if* sharply struck or twisted, etc. *would*..fly into fragments. **1961** E. NAGEL *Struct. of Sci.* ii. 21 The premises contain at least one 'lawlike' assumption. **1968** M. BLACK in R. Klibansky *Contemp. Philos.* II. 59 Scientific or 'lawlike' generalizations require, in Peirce's phrase, reference to a 'would-be'. **1973** *Nature* 27 July 241/1 Archaeological explanations should be very general, preferably of lawlike form.

lawman. Add: **4.** A law enforcement officer. *colloq.*

1959 P. COOK in *Granta* 6 June 33/1 Had he actually seen the rough law-men bundle the startled Widow into the Black Maria? **1962** R. BARKER *Clue for Murder* ix. 57 Some lawmen took a delight in seeing the criminal squirm. **1972** *Radio Times* 30 Mar. 14/4 A retired lawman, still sporting a tin star, demonstrated how he could kill with either hand. **1973** J. WAINWRIGHT *Devil you Don't* 65 He surely hated Davis... He also hated this goddam lawman.

lawn, *sb.*² Add: **2*.** *Bacteriology.* A layer of bacteria uniformly distributed over the surface of a culture medium.

1951 WHITBY & HYNES *Med. Bacteriol.* (ed. 5) xxiv. 433 Phage activity is readily observed on solid culture media. A plate is first thickly inoculated with susceptible bacteria to form a 'lawn' of growth. **1970** PASSMORE & ROBSON *Compan. Med. Stud.* II. xviii. 102/1 The routine test dilution (RTD) is determined by placing drops of tenfold dilutions of the phage suspension on a lawn of sensitive bacteria.

3. lawn billiards = TROCO; **lawn-cutter** = *lawn-mower*; **lawn-party** (later examples); **lawn sand,** a top-dressing of ammonium sulphate and iron sulphate mixed with sand, used as a fertilizer and weed-killer for lawns; **lawn-sprayer,** a sprayer for diffusing a fine spray of water over a lawn.

1873 *Young Englishwoman* Nov. 572/2 Jean would feel obliged if the Editor would tell her..if lawn billiards can be played on a croquet lawn?.. Is there a book of rules on lawn billiards? **1879** TROLLOPE *John Caldigate* I. xvi. 213 Hunting, shooting, fishing,.. lawn-billiards. **1882** [see TROCO]. **1910** *Encycl. Brit.* III. 934/2 The game [billiards] was at one time played on a lawn, like modern croquet... A later form of 'lawn billiards' again enjoyed a brief popularity during the latter half of the 19th century. **1897** S. HALE *Let.* 24 Mar. (1919) 315 Such a delicious drive,..and the lawn-cutters making hay smells. **1937** R. S. MORTON *Woman Surgeon* xxxi. 346 Many interesting people gather in our frequent outings, lawn parties and other expressions of comradeship. **1955** R. BLESH *Shining Trumpets* (ed. 3) viii. 181 Parades, picnics, funerals, Mardi Gras, lawn parties, dances—he and his band were in demand everywhere. **1973** *Lebende Sprachen* XVIII. 38/1 US lawn party—BE/US garden party—Gartenfest. **1907** *Yesterday's Shopping* (1969) p. xlii/4 Lawn sand. **1909** T. W. SANDERS *Lawns & Greens* vii. 68 Methods of exterminating daisies are to put a pinch of salt on the crown of each plant, or to sprinkle 'Watson's Lawn Sand' over the infested parts. **1939** R. B. DAWSON *Pract. Lawn Craft* xxi. 152 It may be found more convenient for owners of quite small areas of turf to buy a ready compounded lawn sand. **1968** *Punch* 20 Aug. 304/2 Add 1 oz of iron sulphate to 15 oz of dry sludge and you have a moss killing 'lawnsand'. **1943** WYNDHAM LEWIS *Let.* 15 Aug. (1963) 362 Watching the blue jays..having a shower-bath in a lawn-sprayer.

lawrencium (lǫre·nsiə̆m). *Chem.* [mod.L., f. the name of Ernest O. *Lawrence* (1901–58), U.S. physicist + -IUM.] An artificially produced transuranic element that concludes the actinide series, the longest-lived isotope of which has a half-life of a few minutes. Atomic number 103; symbol Lw.

1961 *Times* 15 Apr. 7/1 The isotope of element 103 was 'created' on February 14 by four nuclear scientists—Albert Ghiorso, Torbjorn Sikkeland, Almon Larsh, and Robert Latimer... The scientists intend to name the new element Lawrencium in honour of..the founder of the laboratory. **1972** K. M. & R. A. MACKAY *Introd. Mod. Inorg. Chem.* (ed. 2) xi. 151/1 Lawrencium behaves as expected for the $f^{14}d^1s^2$ configuration by forming only Lw(III)..and resisting oxidation or reduction. **1972** *Sunday Mail Mag.* (Brisbane) 23 Apr. 11/2 Until lawrencium was discovered, californium..was regarded as the world's most valuable metal.

Lawrentian (lǫre·nʃiăn), *a.* **1.** Also **Laure·ntian.** Of or pertaining to the military leader and author T. E. *Lawrence* ('Lawrence of Arabia') (1888–1935), or his deeds and writings.

1928 T. E. LAWRENCE *Let.* 20 Jan. (1938) 568 Laurentian, that sudden insult. I thought I'd sloughed off those manners with the names. **1949** KOESTLER *Promise & Fulfilment* i. 10 It would have necessitated a team of men with Byronic idealism and Lawrentian imagination. **1966** *Punch* 20 July 123/3 The great merit of Mr. Mousa's study is that while his mind is clearly weighted against the Lawrentian myth, he appears to be scrupulously fair to Lawrence.

2. Also **Laurentian, Lawrencian.** Of or pertaining to the English author D. H. *Lawrence* (1885–1930), or his work or style of writing. Hence **Lawrencia·na, Lawrentiana** [*-IANA], objects belonging to, literature about or characteristic of, D. H. Lawrence.

1930 L. P. HARTLEY in *Sat. Rev.* 15 Feb. 203/1 Morgan's description of the sisters has many Lawrentian echoes, especially in the use of the word 'dark'. **1931** R. ALDINGTON *Colonel's Daughter* v. 270 The good old Lawrentian dark abdomen. **1936** A. HUXLEY *Olive Tree* 211 A characteristically Lawrencian expression. **1938** *Times* 28 Jan. 367/3 It is..possible also to put her down as a mixture of the living and the merely Lawrentian. **1944** H. TREECE *Herbert Read* 92 Most of Read's 'Eclogues'..are filled with a dark passionate emotion, a Lawrentian impulse centred in the body. **1944** *Scrutiny* XII. 256 Levels at which the characteristic Laurentian contribution may well appear the reverse of helpful. **1948** H. T. MOORE in D. H. Lawrence *Lett. to Bertrand Russell* p. vi, Meanwhile, here is another contribution to Lawrence literature, one of the last important collections of Lawrenciana. **1959** *Listener* 16 Apr. 683/1 Dr. Leavis successfully established a Lawrentian enclave in Cambridge. **1959** *Times Lit. Suppl.* 30 Oct. 630/1 Mr. de Vries has nicely satirized.. Lawrencian and Bohemian 'free livers'. **1959** *N. & Q.* Mar. 120/1 There is an immense literature of 'Lawrentiana'. **1972** *Observer* 19 Nov. 4/2 There has been a 'tremendous revival' in Lawrentiana from a purely touristic point of view. **1973** *Daily Tel.* 7 Nov. 15/2 It has a Lawrentian turn of situation, too. There is a knight, Sir Tom, whose wife Margaret is ill-served—he comes home only for weekends and is too gentle anyway for her.

Lawson (lǭ·sən). The name of Peter *Lawson* (d. 1820) and his son Charles (1794–1873), partners in the firm of Lawson and Son, Edinburgh nurserymen, used *attrib.* or in the possessive in **Lawson('s) cypress** to designate *Chamæcyparis lawsoniana,* a conifer from Oregon first introduced to cultivation by them after seeds had been collected in 1854 by Andrew Murray (1812–78), Scottish botanist, who named the tree after the Lawsons.

1858 G. GORDON *Pinetum* 62 *Cupressus Lawsoniana,* Murray. Messrs Lawson's Cypress... A large graceful tree, growing 100 feet high, and two feet in diameter.. with the branches at first curved upwards..and towards the ends hanging down like an ostrich feather. **1866** *Curtis's Bot. Mag.* XCII. 5581 The Lawson Cypress..has for the last few years been a great favourite in our gardens and shrubberies. **1914** L. H. BAILEY *Stand. Cycl. Hort.* II. 730/2 Lawson's Cypress..is one of the most beautiful conifers and very variable, about 80 garden forms being cultivated in European nurseries. **1923** DALLIMORE & JACKSON *Handbk. Coniferæ* 200 The extraordinary variability of the Lawson cypress under cultivation has resulted in a large number of forms being given varietal names. **1957** M. HADFIELD *Brit. Trees* 120 The Lawson Cypress has a very limited natural distribution..restricted to a narrow belt on the Pacific coast of the United States. **1970** C. LLOYD *Well-Tempered Garden* iii. 215 One or other form of Lawson's cypress will give you a dense hedge. **1974** *Country Life* 12 Dec. 1855/2 A golden Lawson cypress..is a narrow column of bright gold.

lawsoniana (lǭsǭ^u^niˌā·nă). [a. the specific epithet of *Chamæcyparis lawsoniana.*] = **Lawson('s) cypress* (see prec.).

1959 R. E. HARRISON *Handbk. Trees & Shrubs S. Hemisphere* 89/1 The well-known golden Lawsoniana with stiff erect pyramidal habit, and lemon-golden foliage. **1965** F. SARGESON *Memoirs of Peon* ix. 270 We sat in the shade of a lawsoniana hedge.

lawsy, var. of *laws* (LAW *int.*).

1880 'MARK TWAIN' *Lett.* (1917) I. 383 A kind-hearted, well-meaning corpse was the Boston young man, but lawsy bless me, horribly dull company. **1884** —— *Huck. Finn* xvi. 142 But lawsy, how you did fool 'em, Huck. **1914** G. ATHERTON *Perch of Devil* I. 75 'Your room's pretty!'..'mine's pink—but lawsy!' **1945** [see *LAWD].

lawyer. Add: **6.** *lawyer-ridden* adj.; **lawyer cane** (examples).

1908 E. J. BANFIELD *Confessions of Beachcomber* I. vi. 209 The lawyer cane or vine (*Calamus*)..is a vegetable of tortuous ambitions. **1936** *Geogr. Jrnl.* LXXXVII. 229 They wore a band..made out of lawyer cane, around their middles as a protection against arrows. **1965** *Austral. Encycl.* V. 266/2 Lawyer Cane or Lawyer Vine, a name popularly if impolitely given to species of the rattan genus *Calamus*..and to *Flagellaria indica*. **1824** MILL in *Westm. Rev.* II. 376 Our lawyers, and lawyer-ridden legislators. **1907** *Daily Chron.* 29 Apr. 6/6 Land reform had been too long delayed, because they had been too frightened and lawyer-ridden.

law·yerish, *a.* [f. LAWYER.] Befitting a lawyer; like that of a lawyer.

1918 GALSWORTHY *Five Tales* 133 His lawyerish mind habitually put two and two together.

law·yerism. [f. LAWYER.] The influence, or principles, of lawyers.

1915 F. S. OLIVER *Ordeal by Battle* 221 To fall back on lawyerism was perhaps inevitable in the circumstances; but to think that it was possible to substitute lawyerism for leadership was absurd.

lax (læks), *sb.*³ Colloq. abbrev. of LACROSSE.

1951 E. TAYLOR *Game of Hide-and-Seek* II. i. 128 One late afternoon after lax-practice. **1966** J. GARDNER *Amber Nine* xii. 203 A far cry from the hockey and lax sticks of Roedean or Vassar. **1968** 'P. HOBSON' *Titty's Dead* viii. 86 Thank goodness Mummy doesn't know anything about LaX.

lax, *a.* Add: **5. c.** *Phonetics.* Of a speech-sound, esp. a vowel: produced with the speech organs relaxed.

1909 D. JONES *Pronunc. of Eng.* I. iii. 12 The difference in quality between a tense vowel and the corresponding lax vowel..is sometimes very considerable, especially in the case of closed vowels. **1933** WESTERMANN & WARD *Pract. Phonetics for Students Afr. Lang.* vi. 36 These two sounds occur in Bari as the 'lax' forms of *i* and *u*. **1949** R.-M. S. HEFFNER *Gen. Phonetics* v. 96 Later scholars have substituted the terms tense and lax for narrow and wide. **1964** JAKOBSON & HALLE in D. Abercrombie et al. *Daniel Jones* 97 A peculiar interplay of the lax-tense and compact-diffuse features underlies the vowel harmony. **1973** *Amer. Speech 1969* XLIV. 199 The diphthongizing of lax vowels..can be analyzed.

laxaman, var. *LAKSAMANA.

laxness. Add: **b.** (Later examples.)

1887 *Pall Mall Budget* 21 Apr. 2/2 This criminal laxness, so alarmingly on the increase, should be nipped in the bud. **1969** *Daily Tel.* 27 May 1/2 Mission Control has now been exonerated of any laxness in this respect, for it turns out that they were not required to remind the lunar module crew to operate this particular switch.

c. *Phonetics.* Of a speech-sound, esp. a vowel: the state of being lax (*LAX *a.* 5 c).

1909 D. JONES *Pronunc. of Eng.* I. iii. 13 The tenseness or laxness of a vowel can often be observed mechanically by placing the finger on the throat between the larynx and the chin. **1956** JAKOBSON & HALLE *Fund. of Lang.* I. iv. 43 In the opposition of tense and lax consonants, the laxness is frequently accompanied by voicing and the tenseness by voicelessness. **1967** D. STEIBLE *Conc. Handbk. Ling.* 71 *Laxness,* a distinctive acoustic feature of English characterized by relative relaxation of the tongue and jaw while in the act of articulation.

Laxton (læ·kstǫ̆n). The name of *Laxton* Brothers, a firm of English nurserymen, used in the possessive to designate several varieties of fruit bred and introduced by them, esp. the apple **Laxton's Superb,** a popular, late-ripening variety of red-skinned eating apple.

1920 *Jrnl. R. Hort. Soc.* XLV. p. xxxvii, Exhibit. Messrs. Laxton, Bedford: Apple 'Laxton's Superb'. **1926** A. J. MACSELF *Fruit Garden* vii. 98 Laxton's Superb.—One of the best of early Pears, ripening in August. **1933** HALL & CRANE *Apple* xii. 195 Laxton's Superb.—A comparatively new seedling introduced by Messrs. Laxton in 1921, which is now beginning to be generally planted. *Ibid.* 203 Laxton's Exquisite follows closely on James Grieve. **1937** A. H. HOARE *Commercial Apple Growing* ii. 50 Laxton's Epicure..received an Award of Merit from the Royal Horticultural Society in 1931. *Ibid.* 51 Laxton's Fortune, also a result of a Cox's Orange Pippin and Wealthy cross, is claiming attention as an early bright-coloured and attractive apple. **1966** C. R. THOMPSON *Pruning Apple Trees* II. 194 Other varieties..often crop profusely and yield small apples, e.g...Laxton's Fortune and Laxton's Superb. **1974** *Countryman* Summer 107/2 The Fire Blight Order of 1958..banished this bacterial disease of pears by prohibiting Laxton's Superb, the most susceptible variety.

lay, *sb.*⁷ **2.** Delete 'Now *rare*' and add: An oyster- or mussel-bed; = LAYING *vbl. sb.* 2 c, LAYER *sb.* 4 b.

1902 *Westm. Gaz.* 12 June 10/1 The oyster and mussel lays off the foreshore have hitherto been worked on the large scale. **1905** *Country Life* 25 Mar. 400/2 More than 200 fresh oyster 'lays' have now been staked out on the north side of the Witham.

7. c. *Printing.* Substitute for def.: The arrangement of type in the case from which a compositor takes it; in full, *lay of the case*; also = **lay gauge.* (Further examples.)

[**1683–4** MOXON *Mech. Exerc., Printing* (1962) 194 The manner how the several sorts of Letters are disposed in the several Boxes, is called, Laying of the Case.] **1884** J. GOULD *Letter-Press Printer* (ed. 3) 29, I give the following illustration of the upper-case as it is most commonly laid. In some offices, however, the 'lay' is quite different. **1915** *Southward's Mod. Printing* (ed. 3) I. xxvi. 150 A printed plan of the case..will also be useful to experienced compositors, for there are many variations of the lay to be found in printing offices. *Ibid.* II. iv. 45 The Feed or Laying-on Board is, in the Wharfedale machine, at the base of the cylinder... On the front of the board are the gauges, or 'lays', to which the sheet of paper is laid. **1946** A. MONKMAN in H. Whetton *Pract. Printing & Binding* ii. 20/1 There is no standardized lay in this country although the variations are in the main only concerned with such characters as the ligatures.., figures, and lower-case k and q. **1946** V. S. GANDERTON in *Ibid.* xi. 142/1 Lays, sheet-bands, grippers, and wheels shall be in identical positions on the sheet... If..the register is out along the grip edge, the fault may be due to the front lays lifting too early or too late. **1969** *Studies in Bibliogr.* XXII. 125 (*title*) The lay of the case. *Ibid.,* The single lay, as used for instance in Germany and Switzerland, employs one large case for a fount of type. **1970** E. A. D. HUTCHINGS *Survey of Printing Processes* 199 *Lays, machine,* the points against which a sheet is positioned on the machine prior to impression taking place. **1972** P. GASKELL *New Introd. Bibliogr.* 36 Lays for exotic founts were usually adaptations of those used for the Latin alphabet.

d. A woman who is readily available for sexual intercourse; an act of sexual intercourse. *slang* (orig. *U.S.*). Cf. *LAY *v.*¹ 2 b.

1932 J. T. FARRELL in *Story* Mar.–Apr. 46 A foursome passed homeward; two of the group were girls whom Jack and George agreed were swell lays. **1934** J. O'HARA *Appointment in Samarra* (1935) vi. 159 If there was ever an easy lay she was it. **1936** J. DOS PASSOS *Big Money* 254 There never been a girl got a spoken word by givin' that fourflusher a lay. **1955** W. GADDIS *Recognitions* II. i. 317 She's the girl you used to go around with in college? She's a good lay. **1955** G. GREENE *Quiet American* II. iii. 173 You'll just keep her as a comfortable lay until you leave. **1958** E. DUNDY *Dud Avocado* III. vi. 266 Roving photographer..blows into town on the lookout for a quick lay. **1962** *Listener* 9 Aug. 223/3 His characters are without perspective: engrossed completely in their own lives, hardly seeing..beyond the next drink, the next lay, the next five pounds. **1971** B. MALAMUD *Tenants* 16 Tonight an unexpected party, possibly a lay with a little luck.

11. lay-edge *Printing,* the edge of a sheet of paper which is used to determine the correct position of the sheet in a press; **lay gauge,** an attachment on a printing press that keeps the paper in the correct position.

1892 A. POWELL *Southward's Pract. Printing* (ed. 4) I. 444 Turn over the sheet..and place it upon the feeding or laying-on board, with the same lay-edge towards the grippers as before. **1946** V. S. GANDERTON in H. Whetton *Pract. Printing & Binding* xi. 143/2 An untrimmed lay edge is an unknown quantity, and no two sheets stand up to the lays in the same way if they have a feather edge. For exact work, paper should always be trimmed. **1892** A. POWELL *Southward's Pract. Printing* (ed. 4) xlix. 434 Now set the lay gauges on the machine, so that the paper when fed to these will..occupy the right position on the cylinder to receive the impression where it is intended to be. **1961** T. LANDAU *Encycl. Librarianship* (ed. 2) 190/1 Lay edges. The edges of a sheet of paper which are laid against the front and side lay gauges of a printing or folding machine.

lay, *a.* Add: **4. lay analysis,** psychoanalysis undertaken by an analyst who has not been medically trained; so **lay analyst, psychiatrist, psychoanalyst,** one who practises psychoanalysis without medical training; **lay preacher,** an unordained preacher, esp. among Methodists; **lay reader,** (*b*) a reader of a book, etc., on a subject of which he has no professional or specialist knowledge.

1927 *Internat. Jrnl. Psycho-Anal.* VIII. 174 The Central Executive of the International Psycho-Analytical Association informs us it is their intention to bring forward the question of 'Lay Analysis' at the next Congress, so that opinions may be heard and, so far as possible, decisions arrived at in the matter. **1928** A. P. Maerker-Branden tr. *Freud's Probl. Lay-Analyses* i. 25 Let me, therefore, state that the problem of Lay-Analyses expresses itself most succinctly in the question of whether medically untrained laymen should be permitted to practise psychoanalysis. *Ibid.* viii. 171 As soon as the physician has ascertained this, he may safely leave the treatment to the lay-analyst. **1955** M. McCarthy *Charmed Life* (1956) ii. 36 He had been..a lay analyst. **1747** Lay-preacher [in Dict., sense 1]. **1790** J. Wesley *Works* (1872) IV. 493 Joseph Humphrys; the first Lay Preacher that assisted me in England, in the year 1738. **1823** A. Clarke *Mem. Wesley Family* 34 From this conversation we learn..that he was a lay-preacher. **1906** 'Mark Twain' *What is Man?* (1917) iii. 31 In the Adirondack woods is a wage-earner and lay preacher in the lumber camps. **1962** H. Davies *Worship & Theol. in England* IV. ix. 258 John Nelson.. one of Wesley's most trusted lay preachers. **1975** R. Lewis *Double Take* ii. 58 He..was a Methodist lay preacher and a supporter of good causes. **1958** 'J. Bell' *Seeing Eye* xiv. 147 He has been more successful as a lay psychiatrist than he has as a general practitioner. **1933** *Harper's Mag.* Jan. 186/1 A lay psycho-analyst finds that the political philosophy of Thomas Jefferson was a product of Jefferson's infantile revolt against his father. **1885** W. James *Coll. Ess. & Rev.* (1920) 282 To the lay-reader, this absolute Idealism doubtless seems insubstantial and unreal enough. **1907** —— *Pragmatism* ii. 74 Farther than that the ordinary lay-reader in philosophy.. does not venture to sharpen his conceptions. **1912** *Motor* 17 Dec. 980/1 The subject matter is..written in a manner easily understood by the lay reader. **1947** *Mind* LVI. 156 This is done in so compressed and allusive a manner that..the lay reader could scarcely be expected to grasp it adequately.

5. *lay-minded* adj.

1898 S. Evans *Holy Graal* 134 We Englishmen of today, a lay-minded folk much misguided of philosophic historians.

lay, *v.*[1] Add: **2. b.** To have sexual intercourse with (a woman). Occas. *intr.*, const. *for*: (of a woman) to have sexual intercourse with (a man). Also *intr.*: (of a woman) to be willing to have (extramarital) sexual intercourse. *slang* (orig. *U.S.*). Cf. *Lay *sb.*[7] 7 d.

1934 J. O'Hara *Appointment in Samarra* ii. 38 I'm going to take Teddy out and get him laid tonight. *Ibid.* vii. 212 'You're wrong about one thing,' said Julian. ..'I didn't lay that girl.' **1936** J. Dos Passos *Big Money* 305 'Gosh,' he was saying at the back of his head, 'maybe I could lay Elsie Finnegan.' **1938** G. Greene *Brighton Rock* v. v. 214 I'm marrying her for your sake, but I'm laying her for my own. **1950** A. Wilson *Such Darling Dodos* 123 As soon as he laid a new wench..there was always a shift round of staff. **1955** 'H. Robbins' *Stone for Danny Fisher* i. vii. 55 'Does she lay, Danny?'.. His face was flushed as his eyes followed the girl on to the porch. **1956** H. Gold *Man who was not with It* (1965) xviii. 164 Whore! Babywhore! She been laying for you. **1960** J. Updike *Rabbit, Run* (1961) 184 You've laid for Harrison, haven't you? **1966** Auden *About House* 15 A great-great-grandmother who got laid By a sacred beast. **1969** P. Roth *Portnoy's Complaint* 182 All I know is I got laid, *twice*. **1973** B. Broadfoot *Ten Lost Years* viii. 83 The guy who knew her was one of our gang and he was laying her.

7. b. To place documents containing information on the table (see Table *sb.* 5 b) in order to present the information to the members.

[**1813** *Hansard Commons* 17 Mar. 142 Mr. Whitbread then moved, that the Petition be laid upon the table; which was ordered accordingly.] **1923** *Westm. Gaz.* 3 Aug., The Premier promised to lay all the correspondence, if M. Poincaré consents. **1924** *Hansard Commons* 10 Mar. 1931 His Majesty's Government have been willing to lay the complete records, but objections have been raised. **1964** *Erskine May's Law of Parl.* (ed. 17) xiii. 274 A similar order was made..in cases where a paper was laid under an Act that prescribed a period during which objection to it could be taken.

9. *to lay an egg*: fig. phr. used in various colloq. senses, *spec.*: (*a*) (of an aircraft) to drop a bomb; (*b*) orig. *U.S.* (of a performer or performance) to flop.

1918 [see *Egg *sb.* 3 d]. **1927** *Daily Express* 2 June 11/2 'Laying an egg' in Air Force slang means dropping a bomb. **1929** *Variety* 30 Oct. 1 (*headline*) Wall Street lays an egg... The most dramatic event in the financial history of America is the collapse of the New York Stock Market. **1940** J. O'Hara *Pal Joey* 38 You would just as well come wearing a shell if you ever took a job [singing] in a spot like this, that is how big an egg you would lay. **1947** [see *Egg *sb.* 3 d]. **1949** L. Feather *Inside Be-Bop* iii. 30 The singer had been laying eggs at the Zanzibar..and Shaw was undecided what to do with him. **1958** *Spectator* 6 June 730/2 The second gambit, when a joke is so drearily bad.. that even a studio audience can't laugh at it, is to admit, quite shamelessly, that one has, as they say, laid an egg. **1964** *People* (Austral.) 16 Dec. 45/1 A Stuka caught us in the town of Lamia. The plane duly laid an egg. I was crouched alongside a wall. The bomb landed on the other side of the wall.

12. c. To bet on (a horse).

1877 *Porcupine* 10 Mar. 790/1 Whether it is as immoral to 'bear the market' as to 'lay the favourite';.. all these are irrelevant issues. **1887** W. B. Gilpin *Set of Four Hunting & Racing Stories* vi. 68 They refused to lay him except at odds on. *Ibid.* x. 97 His..plans..'to lay the horse all he could without exciting too much suspicion'. **1891** N. Gould *Double Event* 6 The heaviest layers of odds ..had laid Caloola..for considerable amounts. **1901** *Daily Chron.* 24 July 3/2 For the Derby or other important races Davis would lay a horse to the extent of £100,000 in one bet.

43. *to lay low* (see Low *a.* 18 c).

An occas. use erroneously developed from *to lie low*.

a **1861** T. Winthrop *John Brent* (1883) viii. 70 They may..let their chances slide at cards, but my notion is they're layin' low for bigger hauls. **1894** W. T. Stead *If Christ came to Chicago!* 225 The Democrats laid low and said nothing, for reasons of their own. **1907** M. C. Harris *Tents of Wickedness* iv. iii. 359 He..laid low for the first passer-by, and slugged him.

49. lay away. c. *Tanning.* To place (hides) flat in a vat to steep in strong tan liquor for a long period, as the final stage in the process of tanning. Also *intr.* of the hides. Cf. *Lay-away 1.

1885 C. T. Davis *Manuf. Leather* xix. 368 In tanning heavy upper leather the practice..is to first handle the sides on sticks for ten or twelve days, and then lay them away twice in bark. **1901** F. T. Addyman tr. *Villon's Pract. Treat. Leather Industry* 139 Time required for Laying Away.—The hides are removed from the pit and put back three times so that the tan may be renewed. **1922** A. Rogers *Pract. Tanning* x. 302 The hides are sometimes rocked throughout the early stages up to the time when they are laid away. **1966** G. H. W. Humphreys *Manuf. Sole & Other Heavy Leathers* vii. 120 The goods may be laid away, but rarely these days with bark or other ground material as was the practice in former days when 'layers' were in general use.

50. lay by. f. To work (a crop or field) for the last time, before leaving it to grow without further husbandry. *U.S.*

1759 J. Gordon *Jrnl.* 12 July in *William & Mary College Q.* (1902) 1st Ser. XI. 106 Mowing oats & laying by corn. **1784** J. F. D. Smyth *Tour U.S.A.* II. 127, I was also accustomed to sow a quantity of faulty wheat..in my tobacco grounds, when I gave them the last ploughing, or *laid them by*. **1835** J. H. Ingraham *South-West* II. 285 The ploughing generally ceases and the crop is 'laid by' about the last of July. **1868** *Rep. Iowa Agric. Soc. 1867* 158 The ground should be thoroughly rolled;..then lay by with barshear plow. **1947** *Democrat* 25 Dec. 3/4 This year when the corn was 'laid-by' the crotalaria came up voluntarily.

51. lay down. q. Also of a paving material. Hence, to cover (a surface) *with* something.

1893 A. Conan Doyle *Mem. Sherlock Holmes* (1894) 225 The corridor..was laid down with a kind of creamy linoleum.

s. *intr.* To give up or submit; to break down or cease to act; to fail; to retire or withdraw. *U.S.*

1898 *Scribner's Mag.* XXIII. 453/2, I swear I hate to lay down to such a nincompoop. **1901** Merwin & Webster *Calumet 'K'* 64 You've never had to lay down yet, and you don't now. **1911** H. S. Harrison *Queed* vii. 87 Your body's got to carry your mind around, and if it lays down on you [etc.]. **1923** R. D. Paine *Comrades of Rolling Ocean* x. 193 'Any water leaking in?' 'A trickle under the floor, but the bilge pump will take care of it unless she lays down on me.' *Ibid.* xvii. 293 You stand by me and I won't lay down on you. **1927** *Cleveland Press* 4 Feb., Offered him a bribe to 'lay down' on the prosecution of George J. McKay, alleged arch-swindler.

t. To set up or establish (a certain beat). *Jazz slang.*

1950 Blesh & Janis *They all played Ragtime* viii. 149 The backwoods pianists 'laid down the beat' and 'stacked the blues'. *Ibid.* x. 194 He laid down a terrific stomp. **1959** 'F. Newton' *Jazz Scene* vi. 104 The 'rhythm section' laid down a rock-firm beat. **1968** *Melody Maker* 6 Apr. 8/4 The soloist can play anything he chooses to play on the time that I lay down for him. **1968** *Blues Unlimited* Sept. 23 Preston..takes a few vocals, and lays down some swinging rhythm guitar.

54. lay off. a. (Later U.S. example.)

1919 H. L. Wilson *Ma Pettengill* ii. 46 She took me up to her little bedroom to lay my things off and then down to the parlour.

f. For '*dial.* and *U.S.*' read: orig. *dial.* and *U.S.* (Further examples.)

1863 W. Whitman *Specimen Days* (1882–3) 41 Some of the men are cleaning their sabres.., some brushing boots; some laying off, reading, writing. **1886** H. James *Bostonians* I. iii. 26 She would expect him to be strenuous in return; but he couldn't—in private life, he couldn't; privacy for Basil Ransom consisted entirely in what he called 'laying off'. **1955** *Times* 6 June 7/2 But in the course of this week stocks in some factories will begin to run out. Workers will have to be laid off. **1970** G. Greer *Female Eunuch* 242 The lowest paid employees can be and are laid off. **1972** *Daily Tel.* 1 Feb. 2/7 A pay strike by 500 clerical workers..has caused the company to lay off 2,500 car assembly workers.

g. (See quot. 1901.)

1901 J. Black *Illustr. Carpenter & Builder Ser.: Home Handicrafts* 43 What painters term 'laying off', that is to say, going over the work with the brush uncharged with paint and with strokes all in one direction. **1945** C. H. Eaton in *Practical Painter & Decorator* iii. 90 The laying off should be vertical, that is, from ceiling to floor..on walls, and parallel with the main source of light on ceilings. **1951** *Good Housek. Home Encycl.* 65/1 Do not attempt to 'lay off' or brush out the distemper as with paint or varnish. **1963** W. Tee *Painting & Decorating* x. 77 Finally, you lay-off, which means brushing in the direction of the grain if you are painting wood, or in the longest direction if you are painting a metal gutter or pipe.

h. To desist from (doing something); to abstain from or stop using (something); to stop bothering or pestering (a person). Also *intr.*, freq. as *imp.*: cut it out! stop it!

1908 Kipling *Lett. to Family* ii. 17 The railways..had to find room somewhere..before Nature cried: 'Lay off!' **1919** *Amer. Mag.* May 42/2 If you guys don't lay off of me I'll bounce the two of you. **1919** *Saucy Stories* Aug. 107/2 She..resolved to 'lay off the bright lights in the future'. **1930** D. Hammett *Maltese Falcon* xviii. 221 Make him lay off me then. I'm going to fog him if he keeps it up. **1931** E. Linklater *Juan in America* iii. vii. 259 Lay off that ritzy laugh or I'll sock you. **1934** J. Agate *More First Nights* (1937) 59 You would think, wouldn't you, that Josephine, having done enough in the way of arousing suspicion, would lay off a little. **1934** Wodehouse *Right Ho, Jeeves* vi. 60 Lay off the sausages. Avoid the ham. **1936** —— *Laughing Gas* iv. 49 That's all she's after—the title. For heaven's sake, Reggie, lay off while there's still time. **1946** K. Tennant *Lost Haven* (1947) xix. 316 'For God's sake, shut up!..Lay off, Alec, lay off.' Alec laid off. **1947** 'N. Shute' *Chequer Board* 62 Aw, lay off, Jim.— You're not in the South now. **1953** J. Trench *Docken Dead* ii. 21 How does one set about telling one's senior officer to lay off one's friend's wife? **1968** M. Richler in R. Weaver *Canad. Short Stories* 2nd ser. 160 'Oh, lay off,' my father said. 'Give the man air.' **1974** D. Gray *Dead Give Away* vi. 65 I'd lay off stirring up trouble for a bit if I were you.

i. *Naut.* and *Aeronaut.* To indicate (on a chart, etc.), to work out (a course). Cf. Course *sb.* 12.

1942 *Tee Emm* (Air Ministry) II. 83 Always lay off Q.D.M.'s and Q.D.Y.'s as true bearings on your chart. **1943** 'T. Dudley-Gordon' *Coastal Command* 17 Drawing pencil lines which lay off courses of ships and aircraft, and indicate areas under patrol or to be searched. **1961** F. H. Burgess *Dict. Sailing* 131 *Lay off a course*, work out a proposed course on a chart.

j. Of a bookmaker: to insure against a substantial loss resulting from (a large bet) by placing a similar bet with another bookmaker.

1951 E. Kefauver *Crime in Amer.* (1952) xvi. 184 The Nevada bookies also protect themselves by laying off their biggest bets with out-of-state operators. **1974** *New Yorker* 25 Feb. 72 An outside man..runs along the line of bookies and keeps an eye on the odds and lays off some of the money.

55. lay on. i. *transf.* Delete 'in jocular use' and add further examples in sense: to provide, arrange.

Also influenced by sense 55 k in Dict.

1861 *Temple Bar* III. 23 Fifteen shillings an hour, to say nothing of refreshments laid on gratis and supplied at discretion. **1940** C. Gardner *A.A.S.F.* 84 Squadron Leader Dodds..said that he'd got my programme..laid on. 'Laid on' was the Army term for everything—and I found myself using it. **1944** N. Coward *Middle East Diary* 103, I was unable to give a concert as the piano..had not been 'laid on'. **1959** *Punch* 13 May 636/2 Universities do not exist to lay on degree courses to follow the idiosyncratic requirements of a particular employer. **1959** 'J. Welcome' *Stop at Nothing* ix. 139 As usual he had everything laid on and a car was waiting. **1964** E. O'Brien *Girls in Married Bliss* vi. 51 He'd have some hatchet-voiced secretary laid on to tell Kate some boring and familiar lie, like that he was in conference. **1971** B. W. Aldiss *Soldier Erect* 185 Pack your night things in a small pack and get weaving, while I lay on transport. **1973** E. Page *Fortnight by Sea* xvi. 177 Try and lay some coffee on. Plenty of it. Good and strong.

j. Also, to place (thread) on a material before couching it down with a separate thread.

1880 L. Higgin *Handbk. Embroidery* i. 8 '*Japanese gold thread*'..must..be laid on, and stitched down with a fine yellow silk. [**1906** A. G. I. Christie *Embroidery & Tapestry Weaving* viii. 166 A bunch of threads may be laid upon the material, and an open chain, buttonhole, or feather stitch worked over in order to fix it in place.] **1959** *Chambers's Encycl.* V. 155/2 Couching or laid work is a form in which the threads are 'laid' on material and couched down with matching or contrasting colour.

k. (Earlier and later examples.) Also, to provide (a telephone line).

1845 *Punch* 1 Mar. 100/1 Announcing that the water was going to be laid on when it wasn't. **1869** *St. Andrews Gaz.* 7 Aug., The special wires which the Scotch papers have 'laid on' between London and Edinburgh. **1870** Dickens *E. Drood* xxii. 170 There is two bedrooms..with gas laid on. **1885** *List of Subscribers, Classified* (United Telephone Co.) (ed. 6) 17 At 'The Clarendon' in Brighton ..they have a telephone laid on. **1909** *Chambers's Jrnl.* July 477/2 A large supply of hydrogen prepared by a new process is laid on for inflation.

l. To give (something) to (a person). *U.S. slang.*

1942 *Amer. Mercury* July 86 Lay de skin on me [shake hands], pal! **1952** G. Mandel *Flee Angry Strangers* 244 He lays some on his buddies 'n they get to like it; right, Buster? **1960** *Time & Tide* 24 Dec. 1599/3 I've fixed up a real wild basket of ribs and a bottle of juice, and I'd like you to fall by her joint and lay it on her. **1968** *New Yorker* 18 May 45/2 He..took out a copy of his newest album. He wrote something on the back of it and picked up one of the hotel bills. 'Let me just lay this album on the man downstairs. Maybe it'll keep him quiet for two or three

days.' **1970** *It* 9–24 Apr. 8/4 Of course you can't lay advice on someone.

56. lay out. b. (Further example.) Also, to knock (a person) unconscious; to kill.

1829 [see *COLD *a.* 1 c]. **1890** in Barrère & Leland *Dict. Slang* II. 9 Galletly was saying, 'I've laid one out' to the other prisoners... Witness also saw the knife, and there was blood on it. **1894** *Daily News* 26 May 8/6 If you strike me I will lay you out. **1896** *Wells Jrnl.* 3 Dec. 7/5 A disposition to 'injure, maim, and lay out an opponent, especially if he be a valuable element in the opposing team'. **1916** 'TAFFRAIL' *Pincher Martin* xviii. 337, I gits rated up ten days ago,.. death vacancy. Poor ole Byles got laid out, yer remember. **1929** J. B. PRIESTLEY *Good Companions* III. v. 589 'But do you mean to say he was laid out?' he demanded... 'On the jaw, I think you said?' **1973** *Scotsman* 21 Feb. 17/6 When they hit you with the word, cancer, it scares you to death. Boom! You're laid out. But I've learned a lot about cancer since then.

60. lay up. m. To assemble or stack (plies or layers) in the arrangement required for the manufacture of plywood or other laminated material (usu. prior to bonding into a single structure).

1927 KNIGHT & WULPI *Veneers & Plywood* xxvi. 286 Stock trucks..with suitable guides against which to jog layers of stock as the freshly glued plywood is laid up. **1942** WOOD & LINN *Plywoods* vii. 74 When working on thin 3-ply boards two panels are frequently 'laid up' between each caul. **1949** B. L. DAVIES *Technol. Plastics* xiii. 233 The dried, impregnated or coated material is cut to size..and the sheets are laid up, i.e. piled one upon the other to a predetermined number. **1962** *Newnes Conc. Encycl. Electr. Engin.* 115/2 Normally not less than three layers of tissue are laid up between the electrodes [of an industrial capacitor] for the lower voltages. **1965** *Plastics Tooling & Manuf. Handbk.* (Amer. Soc. Tool & Manuf. Engineers) vi. 114 Successive plies are laid up until the desired thickness is achieved; then the part is allowed to cure.

61. lay-down, (*b*) applied to a hand or contract at cards (esp. Bridge) which is such that success is possible against any defence, so that no harm would be done by exposing the player's cards on the table; also *ellipt.* as *sb.*, such a hand; also *fig.*

1906 *Westm. Gaz.* 8 Sept. 16/3 Enormous cards are held and we have a lay-down great or small slam. **1934** *Amer. Speech* IX. 10/2 A *cold* game is a sure game, and a *cold* contract is a *lay-down.* **1955** I. FLEMING *Moonraker* vii. 75 It was a laydown Grand Slam for Bond against any defence. **1959** *Listener* 12 Mar. 489/1 Seven Clubs, it will be seen, is a lay-down. **1961** *Times* 6 Dec. 8/3 A lay-down slam in Clubs. **1966** 'W. HAGGARD' *Power House* ix. 92 The interview had diverted him. He'd learnt a lot about Harry Fletcher; he'd held a crushing hand and had played it as a laydown. **1974** *Country Life* 17 Oct. 1139/3 The slam is a lay down.

layabout (lē̆ⁱ·ăbaut). [f. LAY *v.*¹ 43 + ABOUT *adv.* 8.] An habitual loafer, idler, or tramp. Also *attrib.* or as *adj.*

1932 G. S. MONCRIEFF *Café Bar* viii. 78 These layabouts were rotters. **1932** S. PEARSON *To Streets & Back* xxiv. 234 The 'down and outs' in Hyde Park are permanent 'layabouts'. **1959** *Punch* 19 Aug. 57/1 He simply uses any old-fashioned plot about layabout art-lecturers getting mixed up with funny spies. **1959** H. PINTER *Birthday Party* (1960) 81 Keep an eye open for low-lives [*sic*], for schnorrers and for layabouts. He didn't mention names. **1961** *John o' London's* 21 Sept. 327/1 A colourful tour of layabout London. **1968** *New Scientist* 2 May 217/2 Those of us gifted by nature with inertia but maligned by society as layabouts. **1972** D. HASTON *In High Places* ii. 35 There was another strong twosome..in the hut, otherwise only student layabouts left.

lay-away (lē̆ⁱ·ăwē̆ⁱ). Also **layaway.** [LAY *v.*¹ 49.] **1.** *Tanning.* A vat or pit in which hides are 'laid away'; = LAYER *sb.* 4 e. Freq. *attrib.*

1885 A. WATT *Art Leather Manuf.* xii. 145 The Layers.—In these pits, which are termed lay-aways by the Americans, the butts are stratified with ground oak-bark. **1885** C. T. DAVIS *Manuf. Leather* xix. 367 When heat is used on the head leaches the liquor sometimes enters the lay-away yard in a hot condition. **1901** F. T. ADDYMAN tr. *Villon's Pract. Treat. Leather Industry* 137 Tan-pits or lay-away pits are large vats, sometimes round, and made of oak, bound with iron. **1922** A. ROGERS *Pract. Tanning* x. 303 At this stage..the hides go to the layaways. These are vats large enough to permit the hide being spread out flat. *Ibid.* 304 All the layaway liquors are not so worked down and out, some being returned to the leach-house to be strengthened and freshened. **1957** *Encycl. Brit.* XIII. 848/1 The goods are moved from the strongest suspender vats to the layaway vats or floaters.

2. *N. Amer.* = *LAY-BY *sb.* 2 b.

1961 in WEBSTER. **1967** *Boston Sunday Herald* 26 Mar. I. 22/3 Her dress for Easter is on layaway... You can get it out. It only costs $5, but I don't own that much now. **1970** *Globe & Mail* (Toronto) 25 Sept. 32/7 (Advt.), No Dealers—All Sales Final—Christmas Lay-A-Ways... Sale at Toronto Warehouse. **1973** *Houston* (Texas) *Chron.* 21 Oct. 2/1 (Advt.), Use our layaway plan for Christmas!

lay-back. [f. vbl. phr. *to lay back.*] **1.** The receding position of the nose of certain breeds of dog, esp. the bulldog.

1894 R. B. LEE *Hist. & Descr. Mod. Dogs Gt. Brit. & Ireland* (*Non-Sporting Division*) 233 The bones of the lower jaw in specimens [of the bulldog] which have the desired appearance, known as 'upturn' and 'lay back' are found to have the contour of a segment of a circle. **1905** H. ST. J. COOPER *Bull-Dogs & Bull-Dog Breeding* 98 This well-known dog..has a grandly shaped head, with small well-carried ears, large under-jaw, turn-up and lay-back. **1909** *Ladies' Field* 28 Aug. 511/1 Bulldogs:..a brindle, good layback and under-jaw. **1968** H. HARMAR *Chihuahua Guide* 239 *Layback*, the receding nose found in some of the short-faced breeds.

2. a. *Mountaineering.* A method of climbing cracks in rocks (see quot. 1968).

1925 *Jrnl. Fell & Rock Climbing Club* VII. 17 The crack ..is then climbed, utilising the lefthand edge of the crack for a 'lay back'. **1957** CLARK & PYATT *Mountaineering in Brit.* xvi. 237 A layback is almost as tiring in descent as in ascent. If the leader's arms give out he cannot retreat, and has to fall off. **1968** P. CREW *Encycl. Dict. Mountaineering* 77 *Layback*, a method of climbing cracks and flakes by gripping the edge with the hands, leaning back and placing the feet flat on the rock at the side of the crack and slightly below the hands. As the climber pulls on the edge of the crack and presses his feet against the rock, the opposing pressures exerted can be sufficient to support the body. **1971** *N.Z. Listener* 19 Apr. 56/5 Pete had a dekko up a chimney. But there was a lay-back and too much exposure at the top. **1973** C. BONINGTON *Next Horizon* x. 145 Only the crack in its [*sc.* the rock's] back provided a mixture of hand-jamming and lay-back holds.

b. In various sports, the movement or position of leaning backwards or lying on one's back.

1948 R. F. HERRICK *Red Top: Reminisc. Harvard Rowing* 173 The chief differences between Washington and eastern rowing at that time were Washington's lack of layback, fast hands on the release and their tremendous emphasis on the catch. **1962** *Times* 6 Feb. 4/5 They [*sc.* the Cambridge crew] have a longer swing and a longer lay-back than recent crews. **1962** *Austral. Women's Weekly* Suppl. 24 Oct. 3/3 [Surfing] *Layback*, a supreme test of skill in trick riding. The rider lies flat on his back, with feet facing the way board is going. **1968** *Daily Tel.* 6 Dec. 15/6 As always, Miss Waghorn used her long legs to full advantage in the split jump, a majestic spreadeagle and well-timed lay-back and grab-parallel spins.

lay-by. Add: Also **lay-bye.**

A. *sb.* **1.** (Earlier example.)

1826 J. KAY *Let.* 7 July in *N. & Q.* (1960) Apr. 148/1, I have given permission for a Laybye to be formed in the bank of the Canal near Thornhill Bridge.

b. A railway siding.

1906 *Westm. Gaz.* 28 Sept. 7/1 A heavy goods train had left the up-line..and run into a short lay-by. **1955** L. T. C. ROLT *Red for Danger* x. 206 He therefore signalled the L.M.S. goods out of the lay-by, but the driver stopped in Charfield station for water.

c. An area adjoining a road where vehicles may park without interfering with the traffic.

1939 [see *draw-in* (*DRAW *sb.* 11 a)]. **1950** *Engineering* 17 Nov. 387/2 Stopping places off the carriageway in the form of lay-bys. **1959** *Manch. Guardian* 1 July 5/4 The emergence of a new type of picnic—the lay-by high tea.. On any arterial road you can see the family saloons.. heave into the lay-by. **1971** *Islander* (Victoria, B.C.) 8 Aug. 4/3 We enjoyed a Sunday picnic in a forest layby and then returned to Holland. **1972** *Daily Tel.* 13 Mar. 3/2 Caravanners who park in lay-bys causing litter and hygiene problems will face prosecution. **1973** *Times* 30 Apr. 14/1 My correspondent at the front owns a weekend cottage in Norfolk and was in the habit of collecting his empty wine bottles and baked bean cans and dumping them in the lay-by bins on the way home on Sundays. **1973** *People's Jrnl.* (Inverness & Northern Counties ed.) 4 Aug. 8/2 The holidaymakers had stopped in a lay-by at Oban and Miss Coldrick thinks she left the camera on the car boot.

2. b. A system of payment whereby a purchaser puts down a deposit on an article, which is then kept on one side for him until he has paid the full price. Also *transf.*, and as *vb.* Chiefly *Austral.* and *N.Z.*

1930 *Sydney Morning Herald* 16 Oct. 4 (Advt.), Avail yourself of our lay-by service. **1943** *Amer. Speech* XVIII. 95 [New Zealand] A few trade names have caught the public fancy, and become generalized .. A system of hire-purchase called the 'Lay-by' has resulted in the verb 'layby', pronounced and written as one word. **1944** W. E. HARNEY *Taboo* (ed. 3) 154 He did not complain, for it was to him a tribal law and custom—a lay-by system to protect him when he was old. **1957** *Rhodesia Herald* 16 Mar. (Advt.), Lay-Byes Accepted Now. **1960** *Times* 25 June 9/4 When in Australia..I was bewildered to find this expression 'Lay by' used widely in large shops, until I discovered that it meant that the management would put aside articles for customers. **1969** *Sydney Morning Herald* 24 May 26/8 (Advt.), Goldfish, tropical. Full range plants, access... Lay-by or terms. Get your discount card now.

layer, *sb.* Add: **I. 1. e.** (Further examples of *layer-out.*)

1895 HARDY *Jude* IV. ii. 248 In the afternoon, when everything was done, and the layers-out had finished their beer, and gone, he sat down in the silent place. **1928** *Observer* 10 June 7/4 Poetry, it is generally known, is dead... Our critics are a generation of layers-out. **1953** R. CAMPBELL tr. *E. de Queiroz's Cousin Bazilio* xiii. 264 The professional layer-out was a woman with a pocked face. **1958** L. DURRELL *Mountolive* xvi. 318 The dead man's clothes are the perquisites of the layer-out. **1974** W. FOLEY *Child in Forest* I. 51 His widowed mother.. acted midwife and washer-woman, or layer-out of the dead.

f. = *gun-layer* (*GUN *sb.* 15).

1896 *Daily News* 6 Aug. 7/2 Two gun detachments, including layers. **1898** G. S. ROBERTSON *Chitrál* xviii. 167 All the gunners, even the 'layers', wore bandages over their eyes. **1911** H. A. BETHELL *Mod. Artillery in Field* x. 147 If any officer or layer fails to locate the target correctly, the result is likely to be considerable waste of time and ammunition. **1971** D. A. LAMB *View from Bridge* ii. 16 On the twelfth of February three of the new artillerymen became first class layers.

II. 2. b. A formation of aircraft flying at the same height.

1940 N. MONKS *Squadrons Up!* iv. 113 One Hurricane, trying to get above the enemy aircraft, observed five layers of ten M.E. 110's each, between 10,000 and 15,000 feet. *Ibid.*, Another Hurricane spent about a quarter of an hour alternately dodging and flying in and out among the enemy layers. **1952** *Oxf. Jun. Encycl.* X. 52 The German fighters usually flew in formation well above the bomber formations... The R.A.F. replied by sending up layer formations, the upper layer to engage the fighters while a lower layer dealt with the bombers. **1959** R. COLLIER *City that wouldn't Die* v. 64 Since to-night was a 'fighter night' ..the guns could engage targets only at 12,000 feet and below—2000 feet below the bottom layer of fighters. *Ibid.* x. 167 As the youngest he had inevitably drawn the highest 'layer' on the Southend–Romford patrol line.

4. b. (Earlier example.)

1667 T. SPRAT *Hist. R. Soc.* II. 308 This Brood and other Oysters they carry to Creeks of the Sea..and there throw them into the Channel, which they call their Beds or Layers, where they grow and fatten.

g. *Cartography.* An area on a map depicted in a particular colour or tint chosen to represent all land between two specified heights. Cf. *layer system* in *5.

1918 BRYANT & HUGHES *Map Work* v. 84 Tints, or layers, of colour are used to denote all the land lying between any two named contours. **1932** J. W. CAMERON *Maps & Map-Work* iv. 45 Hill features are represented on the map by: 1. Contours. 2. Hachures. 3. Hill-shading. 4. Colour layers or layer-colouring. **1969** C. B. M. LOCK *Mod. Maps & Atlases* iii. 134 When the fifth (Relief) 'One inch' series was issued, relief was shown by contours in brown, hachures in orange and hill-shading in grey, with layers in buff tints.

5. layer-cake, a cake consisting of layers of sponge held together by a sweet filling, and usually iced; also *fig.*; **layer cloud** *Meteorol.*, a sheet-like cloud, having little vertical development but pronounced horizontal development; **layer colour** *Cartography*, a colour used in the layer system of showing relief on a map; so *layer colouring, -coloured* adj.; **layer lattice** *Cryst.* [tr. G. *schichtengitter* (F. Hund 1925, in *Zeitschr. f. Physik* XXXIV. 849)], a crystal lattice in which the atoms are arranged in layers a few atoms thick that are separated by a distance greater than the interatomic distance within the layers, so that the interlayer forces are relatively weak; **layer pit** or **vat** *Tanning* = *LAY-AWAY 1, LAYER *sb.* 4 e; **layer-pudding,** a steamed pudding, consisting of layers of suet crust pastry with a sweet filling; **layer shading** *Cartography*, the use of layer tints to show relief on a map; **layer system** *Cartography*, on a map, the representation of land between different heights or contours by different colours or tints that are graded so as to show relief at a glance; **layer tint** *Cartography*, a layer colour, or a tint of such a colour; so *layer tinting, -tinted* adj.

1881 F. OWENS *Cook Bk.* 265 *Lemon butter*, good to eat as sauce, or for layer cakes. **1895** *Montgomery Ward Catal.* 431/2 Tins for pies and layer cakes. **1902** *Daily Chron.* 3 May 8/4 Layer cakes can be made in great varieties according to the filling used. **1905** *N.Y. Even. Post* 16 Dec., In the mixing of this literary layer cake most of the humor rose to the top. **1933** 'R. CROMPTON' *William—the Rebel* iv. 94 He..began to eat the last piece of cream-layer cake. **1962** L. DEIGHTON *Ipcress File* xxi. 140 The sunset was a layer cake of mauve and gold. **1965** R. CARRIER *Cookbk.* xxii. 473 Mocha layer cake, a subtle blend of chocolate and coffee spiked with rum. [**1920** G. A. CLARKE *Clouds* iv. 73 The beautifully waved structure seen in nearly all of the layer-type of clouds from cirrus downward to stratocumulus is caused by the propagation upwards or downwards of the wave-motion that is produced by the flowing of air-currents of different velocities and directions over each other.] **1951** *Rep. Progress Physics* XIV. 192 Thick layer clouds often found over the oceans. **1956** *Nature* 18 Feb. 321/1 The great layer-cloud systems which are associated with cyclones and fronts. **1963** G. M. B. DOBSON *Exploring Atmosphere* iv. 78 The persistence of thick layer-clouds over a city in winter gives rise to a very dark, gloomy day. **1922** *Encycl. Brit.* XXX. 417/2 He extended and popularized the use of 'layer' colours exhibiting relief in land. **1969** C. B. M. LOCK *Mod. Maps & Atlases* iii. 135 A single-colour shadow tone in blue was printed in half-tone over the layer colours and the layer tints themselves were carefully chosen so as to reduce the 'step' effect of the layers. **1932** J. W. CAMERON *Maps & Map-Work* i. 12 There are two editions..: (*a*) In outline,..without contours. (*b*) Contoured and layer-coloured. **1924** *Catal. Maps Ordnance Survey* 4 Relief is indicated by..layer colouring in shades of brown and green. **1969** C. B. M. LOCK *Mod. Maps & Atlases* i. 40 For the best results of all, hill-shading is blended with layer-colouring. **1929** *Trans. Faraday Soc.* XXV. 265 Besides cadmium iodide there are known a number of other types of layer lattices. **1966** A. CAMERON *Princ. Lubrication* xxi. 21 The low friction of graphite may not..be directly related to its layer-lattice structure. **1901** F. T. ADDYMAN tr. *Villon's Pract. Treat. Leather Industry* 137 The object of handling is to give body to the plumped skin, so that it may be able

to support the weight which will press upon it in the layer-pit. **1949** D. Woodroffe *Stand. Handbk. Industr. Leathers* iii. 47 The butts or other leather, already completely penetrated in the previous stages of the tanning process, are placed singly in the layer pits, a layer of ground tanning material..is sprinkled over each butt, and the process continued with more pieces of leather until the pit is full. Finally, a very strong tan liquor..is run into the pit. **1909** *Daily Sketch* 14 Oct. 14/3 Layer pudding. **1951** *Good Housek. Home Encycl.* 489/2 Syrup is used..as a filling for tarts and layer puddings. **1952** Monkhouse & Wilkinson *Maps & Diagrams* ii. 61 (*heading*) Layer-shading and tinting. **1971** G. R. P. Lawrence *Cartogr. Methods* ii. 25 Information relating to the shapes of the floors of lakes and oceans can be presented in much the same way as relief information but in most cases only submarine contour lines are used, layer shading being found in some atlases. **1903** *Man. Field Sketching & Reconnaissance* (H.M.S.O.) vi. 28 There is also the layer system of showing hills. **1953** A. H. Robinson *Elem. Cartogr.* x. 215/2 The larger the scale, assuming a reasonable degree of contour simplification, the more useful the layer system. **1969** C. B. M. Lock *Mod. Maps & Atlases* iii. 135 The layer system was not used, but, instead, two printings in purple-grey tones on the shadow side of the hills and one printing in yellow on the illuminated side were added to the standard base map. **1918** Bryant & Hughes *Map Work* v. 84 In high country the layer tints become so dark as to obscure all detail. **1969** *Geography* LIV. 198 Relief is shown by contour and layer tint. **1934** J. Bygott *Introd. Mapwork & Pract. Geogr.* iv. 21 Certain layer-tinted Ordnance maps, especially the layered quarter-inch and half-inch maps. **1966** *McGraw-Hill Encycl. Sci. & Technol.* II. 534/2 On small-scale maps.. the intervals are frequently layer-tinted from green to brown. **1952** H. C. Brookfield in G. H. Dury *Map Interpretation* xvi. 184 The O.S. 1/63,360 Fifth (Relief) Edition, first published in 1929, employed contours at 50-ft. intervals... There was also layer tinting in buff, the tint changing at each 500 ft. **1971** G. R. P. Lawrence *Cartogr. Methods* ii. 24 Colour has been used in the depiction of relief for a number of years in the method known as 'layer tinting'. **1969** T. C. Thorstensen *Pract. Leather Technol.* v. 70 The bends lie in the layer vats for one or two weeks in a warm vegetable tan liquor, and again the liquor may be strengthened and heated to gain better penetration and fixation of the strong tanning liquors.

layer, *v.* Add: **3.** *trans.* To place or insert as a layer.

1906 *Times Lit. Suppl.* 12 Jan. 14/1 Mr. Lee has succeeded in neatly layering fallacies of argument. **1974** *Nature* 8 Mar. 110/2 Sample of 55 ml of a 110 ml linear density gradient..was layered into a 110 ml jacketed isoelectric focusing column. *Ibid.* 5 Apr. 519/2 Each incubation was then layered onto a 10–30% sucrose gradient in TKM.

layered, *a.* Add: *spec.* in *Cartography*, having relief shown by the layer system.

1922 *Encycl. Brit.* XXXI. 842/2 These remarks apply with special force to the 'layered' maps; changes in the tones of the layers will greatly alter their character. **1969** C. B. M. Lock *Mod. Maps & Atlases* i. 40 For reasons of economy, hachures were omitted from the fourth or 'popular' edition published after the 1914–18 war... Publication of layered or shaded maps of selected tourist areas followed.

layering (lē̆ⁱ·əriŋ). *Cartography.* [f. Layer *sb.* + -ing¹.] = *layer colouring, layer shading* (*layer *sb.* 5).

1922 *Encycl. Brit.* XXXII. 1174 (Index), Layering of maps. **1937** *Geogr. Jrnl.* LXXXIX. 52 It is possible that the ultimate solution will be a change in the ground tint of the map over areas of rock, though experiment may show that this gives a false impression of layering.

layette. 1. (Earlier and later examples.)

1839 F. A. Kemble *Jrnl. Residence Georgian Plantation* (1863) 158, I have worked my fingers nearly off with making..innumerable rolls of coarse little baby-clothes, layettes for the use of small new-born slaves. **1863** G. du Maurier *Let.* in *Young G. du Maurier* (1951) 212 She is now..making the layette and things for the son and heir, whom I am beginning to look forward to with a certain amount of curious expectation. **1939** [see *bajū]. **1974** *Selfridge Christmas Catal.* 47 Baby doll complete with layette.

laying, *vbl. sb.* Add: **1. b.** (Further examples.)

1900 *Daily News* 20 Sept. 6/2 The stoppage of coal traffic, and the consequent laying off of railway coal train crews. **1968** *Listener* 4 July 24/1 Nowadays in the US redundancy can mean displacement for good; then it was, at worst, a long laying-off. **1970** *Nature* 21 Nov. 709/2 Layings-off are, of course, nothing unusual in the volatile aerospace industry.

2. c. (Later example.)

1960 C. M. Yonge *Oysters* ix. 154 The Colchester and other natural oyster beds and the layings along the Essex coast flourished exceedingly during the eighteenth and much of the nineteenth centuries.

3. laying house (*b*), a building in which laying hens are kept; **laying mash, meal,** a special food for laying hens.

1913 H. R. Lewis *Productive Poultry Husbandry* vii. 128 (*heading*) Plans and specifications of laying houses. **1962** L. E. Card *Lippincott's Poultry Production* (ed. 9) vii. 179 (*caption*) Interior of..laying house, showing tiered roofs. **1926** *Daily Colonist* (Victoria, B.C.) 12 Jan. 2/1 (Advt.), Feed Prices..Laying Mash, sack $2.75. **1972** A. A. McArdle *Poultry Managem. & Production* (rev. ed.) xiv. 308 (*heading*) Quantity of laying mash and grain needed. **1908** *Illustr. Poultry Rec.* Oct. p. ix (Advt.), Laying Meal 12/6 Cwt. **1935** *Poultry Rec.* Jan. (Advt. inside cover), Alfalfa, Laying Meal, Grit, Shells etc.

lay·light. [f. Lay *v.*¹ + Light *sb.* 5 b.] A window or light made of glazed panels and set into a ceiling to provide natural or artificial light.

1932 H. Robertson *Mod. Archit. Design* vi. 174 The architect is well advised to make a critical study..of lighting through ceiling lay-lights, before determining his layout. **1934** *Archit. Rev.* LXXV. 31 The lay-light of the same type of glass is hung from the ceiling to provide day and artificial lighting. **1948** R. O. Ackerley *Introd. Sci. Artificial Lighting* iii. iv. 99 Laylights designed to provide alternatively natural and artificial light through the same glazing, like most dual-purpose devices, are liable to perform both functions badly unless great care is taken in the design. **1951** W. R. Stevens *Princ. Lighting* viii. 186 We find it difficult to provide high illumination..in interiors without discomfort glare unless we use very large sources, such as laylights or indirectly lighted ceilings. **1966** M. M. Pegler *Dict. Interior Design* (1967) 260 *Laylight*, a glass or translucent panel set flush into a ceiling to admit natural or artificial light.

lay-·off. [Lay *v.*¹ 54.] A rest, respite, spell of relaxation; a period during which a workman is temporarily dismissed or allowed to leave his work; a part or season of the year during which activity in a particular business or game is partly or completely suspended.

1889 *Gallup* (New Mexico) *Gleaner* 27 Mar. 1/3 Fred Diamond is taking a lay-off. **1904** *Minneapolis Daily Times* 8 June 8 The men who have been on for a year get a vacation of ten days. Those who have been working less than a year have to get along with only a five-day layoff. **1908** 'O. Henry' *Gentle Grafter* vii. 285 Me and my partner..tried to take a layoff from our professional and business duties; but..our work followed us wherever we went. **1909** R. A. Wason *Happy Hawkins* 148 Now take a lay-off if you want to,..then come back here. **1919** T. K. Holmes *Man from Tall Timber* vi. 58 At the lay-off,..he had given each man enough money on account to make their vacation..a very wet spell indeed. **1923** *Daily Mail* 10 Sept. 8/5 As a consequence of the 'lay-off' during the summer months it often happens that the muscles of the young player are not sufficiently supple for him to face the rigours of the game. **1926** J. Black *You can't Win* xix. 297, I decided to take a lay-off [from burgling]. **1927** *Sunday Express* 8 May 10/3 Although his salary on the speaking stage had fluctuated between £20 and £40 a week, there were..many lay-offs. **1928** *Sunday Dispatch* 8 July 22/2 His opponent will be a French boxer, Pierre Caillior. As nothing is known of the Frenchman here we shall be.. in the dark..as to what extent..Teddy's long lay-off has affected his form. **1952** B. Ulanov *Hist. Jazz in Amer.* (1958) xxii. 299 The Herman band took a layoff in Detroit in June 1945. **1956** B. Nankeville *Miracle of Mile* xii. 90 Chris Chataway..had only had ten days' training following a lay-off. **1969** *Daily Tel.* 12 Apr. 1/5 Workers protested at proposed factory lay-offs. **1972** *Guardian* 17 Feb. 6/1 Jaguar is one of the British Leyland groups where extensive lay-offs occurred. **1973** *Times* 17 Oct. 25/1 (*heading*) Lay offs threaten 28,000 workers at Vauxhall as car unrest grows.

lay-out. Add: **1.** Also, the plan or disposition of a house, factory, garden, etc. Also *fig.* and *transf.*

1852 *San Diego Herald* 10 Jan. 2/1 The new 'lay out', at the Wholesale Commission Warehouse and store..on California street, proves quite attractive. **1903** Kipling *Five Nations* 212 The day's lay-out—the mornin' sun Beneath your 'at-brim as you sight; The dinner-'ush from noon till one, And the full roar that lasts till night. **1905** W. Robinson *Eng. Flower Garden* (ed. 9) i. ii. 15 In many books on garden design the authors misuse words... One ..writes 'lay-out' for 'plan'. **1923** *Radio Times* 28 Sept. 28 (Advt.), The lay-out [of a radio set] is neat and compact; the cabinet work distinctive. **1930** *Oxford Times* 14 Mar. 13 A new 'lay-out' plan from the builders was before the meeting. **1931** H. G. Wells *Work, Wealth & Happiness of Mankind* (1932) 2 Almost all our political and administrative boundaries, the 'layout' of the human population, have become..misfits. **1937** *Discovery* Feb. 47/2 In the planning of new factories.., the engineer and the industrial psychologist should..ensure that, both in the general lay-out and in the smallest details, due regard is paid to the view-point of the men who will actually be doing the work. **1937** D. Runyon *More than Somewhat* i. 7, I go to see Mr. Tuesday at a Fifth Avenue hotel where he makes his home, and where he has a very swell layout of rooms. **1939** [see *ferry *sb.*¹ 3 e]. **1941** W. S. Churchill *Secret Session Speeches* (1946) 37, I am satisfied that up to the present a good lay-out of our available forces has been made. **1943** J. B. Priestley *Daylight on Saturday* xxv. 195 Both of 'em are up against a pretty tough problem on floor space and general lay-out. **1946** *R.A.F. Jrnl.* May 179 A layout was begun for a new medium bomber to replace the Hampden. **1960** *Observer* 24 Jan. 5/2 How they broke in in the first place depended on the layout. It could be through a lavatory window or by tunnelling laboriously from next door. **1962** *Which? Car Suppl.* Oct. 129/1 The pedal control layouts on the *Peugeot* 403B..were generally liked. **1964** *McCall's Sewing* ii. 30/1 *Layout*, the way the pattern pieces are placed on the fabric for cutting. **1974** J. Wainwright *Hard Hit* 131 The house—this 'Diasc Farm' place—tell me about it. The layout. The approach. The grounds.

b. Typographical specifications or rough designs for a piece of printing; in extended use, the design details of a cartoon film. Also *attrib.*

1910 *Brit. Printer* Feb.–Mar. p. lxv (Advt.), The Printer will be enabled to submit to his customer both original and artistic lay-outs. **1910** E. G. Gress *Art & Pract. Typogr.* 35/1 Every printshop should have a 'layout' man. **1913** *Technical World* XIX. 464 And the strange part of it is that from two to five good news picture layouts are made daily and enlarged in this small room. **1933** *Planning* I. vii. 2 A few years ago individualism in advertising would have rejected without hesitation the discipline of lay-out and design which has been accepted with such good effect this time. **1946** A. Monkman in H. Whetton *Pract. Printing & Binding* vii. 81/1 It is necessary also for the layout man to be expert in copying the numerous type faces. This is not so very important if the layout is for the compositor, because all he requires for his work is the general plan, indicating type sizes and faces and allocations of white space; but when the layout is for the client, markings showing type sizes and other particulars are not necessary. The sketch should be a clear indication of the appearance of the finished job. **1948** H. Missingham *Student's Guide Commercial Art* ii. 157 To see a first-class 'visualizer' romp through one with a flat-leaded layout pencil is a sight to stir the blood. **1955** M. Reifer *Dict. New Words* 119/2 *Layout*,..2. *Cartoon Animation*. The combined elements of the animation procedure which prescribe the relationship of characters and backgrounds to define a scene and its properties. **1958** *Clarendonian* XII. 198 Throughout his service at the Press he has shown great interest in the Layout Department and has been responsible for the design of many Oxford books. **1959** Halas & Manvell *Technique Film Animation* iii. 215 He [*sc.* the director] works closely with the lay-out artist, who in most studios is also the designer. **1967** Karch & Buber *Offset Processes* iii. 46 The layout man usually receives the reading matter in typewritten form, along with glossy photographs, line drawings or other artwork. **1968** J. R. Biggs *Basic Typogr.* 122/2 The layout which goes to the printer with the typographic instructions 'marked up'..should be quite accurate with nothing left to chance.

2. *spec.* The equipment used for smoking opium. *U.S. slang.*

1882 H. H. Kane *Opium-Smoking* iii. 32 (*heading*) Description of the 'lay-out', pipe, etc. **1887** in *Amer. Speech* (1948) XXIII. 247 A person that had a private layout in his room. **1891** H. Campbell *Darkness & Daylight* (1895) xxviii. 565 A small room at the rear of the temple contained an opium 'lay-out' for two persons. *Ibid.*, In the center of the platform was a tray which contained the smoker's 'lay-out'. **1946** Mezzrow & Wolfe *Really Blues* (1957) 376 *Layout*, set of instruments used to smoke opium.

b. A scheme, plan, or arrangement; a course of action. orig. and chiefly *U.S.*

1867 in *Amer. Speech* (1942) XVII. 71/1 A 'lay-out' is any proposed enterprise, from organizing a State to digging out a prairie-dog. **1901** S. E. White *Westerners* xxxi. 292 'I'm sorry that I have this to do, Billy,' said Lafond. 'I don't want to. It's none of my lay-out.' **1904** W. H. Smith *Promoters* ii. 53 There isn't a single move in this whole lay-out that we can't justify by history. **1928** *Sat. Even. Post* 4 Feb. 81/3 Here's the layout. The bonds bear 6 per cent. **1945** Baker *Austral. Lang.* vii. 142 *Layout, setup*, a trickster's plan of action.

c. A number of persons associated in some way; a set, party, gang (of persons); a family. (Often in a depreciatory sense.) *U.S. colloq.* or *dial.*

1869 *Overland Monthly* III. 128 Several persons in our 'lay-out' (*i.e.*, our company) in New Mexico 'swapped' good American horses for mustangs. **1884** 'C. E. Craddock' *In Tennessee Mts.* iii. 143 All them Peels, the whole lay-out, war gone down to the Settlement. **1903** A. Adams *Log of Cowboy* vii. 47 Surround this layout, lads, and let's examine them more closely. **1904** W. N. Harben *Georgians* 203 I'm a-goin' to close in on that Clegg lay-out to-night, an' locate the'r still. **1927** W. Rogers in C. M. Russell *Trails plowed Under* p. xiii, I tell you they was a pretty sad lookin outfit. They sho was a lonesome layout.

lay-·over. [Lay *v.*¹ 57.] **1.** An additional cloth laid over a table-cloth.

1777 *Monthly Rev.* LV. 108 Two servants appeared with a small table.., and laid a cloth and a lay-over upon it, in our English fashion, of the finest damask.

2. A stop or stay in a place, esp. overnight; a halt, rest, delay. *N. Amer.*

1873 J. H. Beadle *Undevel. West* xxxv. 756 Two invalids and myself..applied for a 'lay over', unable to go further. **1903** A. Adams *Log of Cowboy* viii. 53 Their cattle having grown restless during their enforced lay-over. **1911** *Daily Colonist* (Victoria, B.C.) 18 Apr. (Mag.) 7/4 The object of this [*sc.* an extra train]..is to allow those going through to Alberni to reach their destination the same day. This will do away with the present lay-over en route. **1968** *Listener* 27 June 841/2 Meanwhile, some principal themes of Beat mythology are being laid down:.. the pastoral theme of travelling on along the American highways with layovers for pot, mescalin. **1969** R. Stark *Blackbird* (1970) iii. 23 We have an airline ticket for this evening..with a change at New York. A four-hour layover there, I'm afraid. **1972** *National Observer* (U.S.) 27 May 13/5 Mrs. Bartels parks at Gateway for the three-hour layover.

layshaft (lē̆ⁱ·ʃɑft). Also **lay shaft, lay-shaft.** [Prob. f. Lay *v.*¹ 43.] A short secondary or intermediate shaft driven by gearing from the main shaft of an engine; *spec.* one inside a gear-box that transmits the drive from the input shaft to the output shaft.

1888 *Lockwood's Dict. Mech. Engin.* 205 *Lay shaft*, a small secondary shaft, which is placed beside, or at the end of a horizontal engine, for the purpose of actuating the valves. It is driven from the crank shaft by means of bevel or spur-wheels. **1908** *Westm. Gaz.* 7 May 4/2 The whole of the valve mechanism being contained in a neat, hinged lay-shaft on top of the cylinder heads. **1911** G. W. Hayter *Motor-Car Mech. for Beginners* (ed. 4) 45 For the next speed the gear wheel, B, is slid into mesh with the wheel marked C on the third or lay shaft, E. **1958** *Times Rev. Industry* Feb. 84/2 The engine, clutch, and layshaft are mounted on a light chassis and protected by a hinged

bonnet which allows easy access to the power unit. **1959** '*Motor' Manual* (ed. 36) iv. 73 Spaced along the layshaft are other gears, the total number being equal to the number of ratios which the gearbox can provide.

lay-up. [LAY *v.*[1] 60.] **1.** A period during which a person or thing is (temporarily) out of employment or use, as a ship in winter.

1927 *Daily Mail* 7 Apr. 3/6 During the winter lay-up of these vessels their passenger accommodation has been thoroughly overhauled. **1929** *Amer. Speech* V. 72 A compulsory stopping on the '[cattle-]drive' is a 'lay up'. **1955** *Times* 10 May 17/4 The winter demand brought tankers out of lay-up. **1959** C. OGBURN *Marauders* (1960) iii. 87 There were frequent lay-ups, and during one of these the men in a car down the train evidently spotted a couple of ducks beside the tracks. **1967** *Coast to Coast 1965–66* 160 The big hall where the Jap pearlfishers dossed during lay-up.

2. a. The operation of laying up in the manufacture of laminated material (see *LAY *v.*[1] 60 m). **b.** The assembly of layers ready for bonding so produced.

1942 T. D. PERRY *Mod. Plywood* vi. 169 The lay-up.. consists in assembling the layers of veneer and/or lumber with the adhesive. **1950** WEBSTER Add., *Lay-up*, an assembly of layers of veneers or cores for pressing. **1965** *Plastics Tooling & Manuf. Handbk.* (Amer. Soc. Tool & Manuf. Engineers) iii. 35 In wet layup, the workman saturates a piece of fabric in resin, and then may wring out the excess resin and drape the cloth on the laminate. **1972** *Physics Bull.* Nov. 665/2 *Layup*, a laminate that has been assembled, but not cured.

3. *Basketball.* In full, *lay-up shot.* (See quot. 1961.)

1948 A. F. RUPP *Championship Basketball* xv. 130 The drill gives the boys stamina and endurance and helps teach the lay-up shot when going in with the greatest speed. **1958** A. L. COLBECK *Mod. Basketball* iii. 59 In good-class basketball most plays are designed to get a player free for a lay-up shot. **1959** P. ROTH *Goodbye, Columbus* ii. 35, I took my set shot and, of course, missed. With the Lord's blessing and a soft breeze, I made the lay-up. **1961** J. S. SALAK *Dict. Amer. Sports* 260 *Layup shot*,..a shot taken from underneath or very close to the basket. On this type shot, the ball usually is banked off the backboard, but on occasion the player, on a straight run toward the basket, will 'lay' the ball up to the basket without using the backboard. **1967** *Boston Herald* 1 Apr. 16/4 There wasn't anyone in the Boston contingent who could recall him ever blowing three layups in a game before. **1969** Z. HOLLANDER *Mod. Encycl. Basketball* 121 He could also score on jumpers from the corner, driving lay-ups or tip-ins of rebounds. **1974** *Greenville* (S. Carolina) *News* 22 Apr. 13/3 Havlicek sank a layup with 26 seconds left, putting Boston safely ahead.

laywoman. (See after LAYMAN[1].) (Further example.)

1922 *Daily Mail* 11 Nov. 8 The success of this laywoman is a..cheerful omen of good luck for those women who.. will hold the position of practising members of the English Bar.

Laz (lāz). **a.** A group of Caucasian peoples giving its name to Lazistan in north-east Turkey. **b.** Usu. **Laze** (lā·zə) or **Lazi** (lā·zi). A member of any of these peoples. **c.** The south Caucasian language of the Laz people. Also (**Laz**) *attrib.* or as *adj.* Also **La·zic** *a.*

1836 *Jrnl. R. Geogr. Soc.* VI. 191, I embarked at Trebizond..in a galley, and kept along the shore to the Russian frontier..passing in succession the districts of Yomurah, Surmenah, O'f, Rizah, and Lázistán. All these..are known under the general name of Lázistán, and the people are called Láz. **1847** A. KERR tr. *L. von Ranke's Hist. Servia* xi. 219 The first step taken by Selim amongst the Lazes..excited open rebellion against him in his capital. **1897** *Daily News* 26 Feb. 5/4 These Lazes played an active part in the Armenian massacres. **1923** *Daily Mail* 21 Feb. 9 Travelling with Kemal is a bodyguard of 'Lazis'. Tall, robust dare-devils from the Black Sea coast..each carries an abundant supply of daggers and revolvers. **1934** *Geogr. Rev.* LXXXIV. 472 The ports and mouths of rivers have three names—Greek, Turkish, and Lazic. **1939** L. H. GRAY *Found. Lang.* 375 South Caucasian..consists of four languages: Georgian.., Mingrelian, Laz, and Svanian. **1948** D. DIRINGER *Alphabet* v. 322 According to Dr. O. N. Kazara, who is of Laz extraction, the physical type throughout Caucasia is remarkably uniform. *Ibid.*, There are various dialects, the principal of which are Kartlian, Mingrelian with Laz, and Svanian. **1950** [see *ERGATIVE *a.*]. **1954** PEI & GAYNOR *Dict. Ling.* 121 *Laz*, a language spoken in the Caucasus; a member of the South Caucasian family of languages. **1963** *Times* 12 Jan. 9/7 In fact it turned out his father was a Kurd from Elazig, his mother a Laze from Trabzon.

la·ze-off. *rare.* [f. LAZE *v.*] A rest from work.

1924 GALSWORTHY *White Monkey* I. xi. 93 Resenting regular work, enjoying a spurt, and a laze-off.

lazy, *a.* Add: **2. b.** Applied to an eye with poor vision which is consequently little used and tends to deteriorate further; *esp.* the unused eye in squint.

1939 R. B. SIMPKINS *Basic Mech. Human Vision* v. 62 Both exophoric and esophoric conditions are probably the most frequent causes of the development of a lazy eye. **1957** [see *heterophoria* (*HETERO-)]. **1971** E. RUDINGER *Eyes Right* 42 Up to the age of 5 years there is a fair chance of success by encouraging the child to use the lazy eye.

4. *lazy-minded* adj.; **lazy arm**, a type of boom from which a microphone may be slung; **lazy daisy (stitch)**, a petal-shaped embroidery stitch; **lazy dog** *U.S. Mil. slang*, a type of fragmentation bomb designed to explode in mid-air and scatter steel pellets at high velocity over the target area; **Lazy Susan, lazy susan** orig. *U.S.*, a revolving (wooden) stand on a table to hold condiments, etc.; a muffin stand.

1960 O. SKILBECK *ABC of Film & TV* 76 *Lazy arm*, a small, hand-held microphone Boom. **1962** A. NISBETT *Technique Sound Studio* 257 *Lazy arm*, simple form of boom consisting of an upright and a balanced cross-member from which a microphone may be slung. **1923** *Daily Mail* 10 Mar. 14 The way the 'lazy-daisy' stitch is worked is shown at the side of the sketch. **1948** J. CANNAN *Little I Understood* x. 133 Mildred completed six lazy daisies. **1963** N. MARSH *Dead Water* (1964) viii. 221 A rumpled nightgown embroidered with lazy daisies. **1965** *Times* 23 Mar. 12/7 Asked why something more deadly was not preferred—when such things as napalm and white phosphorus incendiary bombs and 'lazy dog' fragmentation bombs are frequently in use—the spokesmen said the gas was being used in situations where the Vietcong might be holding hostages. **1967** *N.Y. Times* 13 Jan. 8 The Lazy Dog is an advanced antipersonnel weapon introduced last spring. **1968** *Punch* 21 Feb. 258 Tomorrow, we'll get three divisions in here, four, we'll get two hundred B-52s, we'll get ground-to-grounds, and whole batteries of Lazy Dogs. **1879** C. M. YONGE *Burnt Out* xii. 192 George..had been getting more lazy-minded and stupid. **1929** V. WOOLF *Granite & Rainbow* (1958) 105 This lazy-minded man was quite capable..of filling a chapter or two..from a fountain of empty, journalistic phrases. **1917** *Vanity Fair* (N.Y.) Dec. 17 (Advt.), Revolving Server or Lazy Susan. **1966** B. ASKWITH *Step out of Time* ii. 35 The home-made jam on the Lazy Susan in the middle of the table. **1971** *Sunday Australian* 8 Aug. 10/1 The best china is used. Silver pots of steaming tea and coffee spin round with wheels of gateaux on a massive lazy susan.

lazy-tongs. Add: (Later example.) Also *attrib.*

1881 G. M. HOPKINS *Let.* 14 May (1938) 100 My only resource is to ask you if you..can suggest some fetch, some boomerang or lazytongs or round-the-corner means of having at him. **1912** *Proc. Amer. Philos. Soc.* LI. 558 A series of links of the 'lazy-tongs' pattern. **1942** 'M. INNES' *Daffodil Affair* II. 70 A lazy-tongs... It used to be quite a popular toy..something rather like a pair of scissors with a piece of lattice-work pivoted to the blades. **1955** *Archit. Rev.* CXVII. 356/3 The 'lazy-tongs' effect of every door being forced to open simultaneously.

lb. Add: **lbf**, the pound as a unit of force; **lbm**, the pound as a unit of mass.

1961 *B.S.I. News* Oct. 26/1 The B.S.I. committee which deals with units and symbols has accepted a form of notation in which a distinction is made between the two concepts 'mass' and 'force'. In this notation the pound has the abbreviation 'lb'; the unit called a pound-force has the abbreviation 'lbf' and is that force which, when acting on a body of mass one pound, gives it an acceleration equal to that of standard gravity. **1962** S. L. BRAGG *Rocket Engines* ix. 148 A jet velocity of 10^6 ft/s could be obtained, giving a thrust of 3 lbf for a flow of 0·0009 lbm/s. **1966** lbf [see **gravitational system*]. **1967** *Technology Week* 23 Jan. 104/1 (Advt.), Pictured from the top: 300 lbf monopropellant hydrazine rocket for orbit control. **1971** I. H. SHAMES *Introd. Statics* i. 12 (*table*) 1 slug ≡ 32·2 lbm.

l'chaim, l'chay(i)m, varr. *LECHAYIM.

L-dopa (eldōu·pă). *Chem.* and *Biochem.* Also **l-** (now *rare*), **L-, -DOPA.** [f. *L 7 c + *DOPA.] = *LEVODOPA.

1939 *Jrnl. Physiol.* XCVI. 51*P* Tyrosine given in the diet is partly excreted as *l*-dopa. **1942** *Ibid.* CI. 345 In tyrosinosis *l*(−)-dopa was found to be excreted in the urine after oral administration of *l*(−)-tyrosine. **1958** *Brit. Jrnl. Pharmacol.* XIII. 92/1 (*heading*) Effect of L-dopa and epinine. **1969** *3rd Symposium Parkinson's Dis.* (R. Coll. Surg. Edin.) 178 L-Dihydroxyphenylalanine (L-dopa) proved far less toxic and more effective than the racemic compound studied earlier. **1970** PASSMORE & ROBSON *Compan. Med. Stud.* II. v. 61/2 [In Parkinsonism] DOPA is given by mouth in doses up to 16 g/day of the racemic mixture or up to 8 g of L-DOPA. **1970** D. B. CALNE *Parkinsonism* x. 94 Disappointing results arise from unwanted effects of L-dopa, such as dyskinesia or psychiatric disturbances. **1970** *Times* 29 Apr. 2/3 L-Dopa, the drug used experimentally in treatment of Parkinson's Disease, has passed the clinical trial stage.

leach, *v.*[2] Add: **3. b.** Also used with reference to the action of water, esp. rain, on soil; also *absol.* (Earlier and later examples.)

1839 J. BUEL *Farmer's Compan.* ix. 74 The wind and the sun dissipate its virtues, and rains leach it and waste its fertilizing powers. **1917** *Mining Mag.* XVII. 75/2 The rocks..are altered and leached of iron. **1951** W. P. KELLEY *Alkali Soils* vii. 146 It should not be inferred that..all the farmer needs to do in order to reclaim any alkali soil is to drain and leach with water. **1954** W. D. THORNBURY *Princ. Geomorphol.* xvi. 420 Kansan and Nebraskan tills are leached to much greater depths. **1971** D. HILLEL *Soil & Water* v. 124 They suggested that leaching soils at a water content below saturation (e.g., under sprinkling irrigation or rainfall or under intermittent irrigation) could produce more efficient leaching and thereby reduce the amount of water required.

c. (Further examples.) Also, to percolate through and pass *out.*

1931 *Forestry* V. 143 In order to avoid any possible effect of some of the preservative leaching out into the medium, some workers raise the blocks above the surface of the medium. **1961** J. N. ANDERSON *Appl. Dental Materials* (ed. 2) xxiii. 240 Dentures should be kept in water after curing in order to allow as much residual monomer as possible to leach out. **1968** *Listener* 21 Mar. 376/2 Cacodylic acid is alleged to disappear very quickly, to leech down through the soil. **1974** A. HUXLEY *Plant & Planet* xviii. 198 Many [viruses] make use of materials which leach through the [leaf] skin.

4. (Further examples.) Also *fig.*

1964 *Listener* 13 Aug. 225/2 It [*sc.* a modern office block] has neither virtues nor vices; it just sits there like a graceless woman, leeching away a bit more of the city's vitality. **1971** *Nature* 13 Aug. 446/3 Insecticides are leached from soil by water. **1973** *Ibid.* 20 July 165/1 Particulate material was collected on fibreglass filters from which lead was leached with hot 70% nitric acid.

leached *ppl. a.* (earlier and later examples); add def.: (*a*) that has been subjected to the action of percolating liquid; (*b*) (also *leached-out*) that has been removed by percolating liquid.

1837 *Cultivator* Aug. 93/2 (*heading*) Leached ashes as manure. *Ibid.*, Leached or drawn ashes possess a highly beneficial effect, particularly when applied to lands deficient in calcareous matters. **1926** A. LOCKE (*title*) Leached outcrops as guides to copper ore. **1961** *Listener* 12 Oct. 559/1 So white are some leached layers [in a podsol] that they have entered archaeological literature as 'layers of ash'. **1963** D. W. & E. E. HUMPHRIES tr. *Termier's Erosion & Sedimentation* vi. 139 The lowest part is a zone of enrichment to which the leached-out soluble salts from the upper part of the soil are carried. **1972** J. G. CRUIKSHANK *Soil Geogr.* ii. 69 Part of the leached compounds are deposited in the lower zone of the soil, but some will be lost from the system through soil drainage and seepage.

leachable (lī·tʃăb'l), *a.* [f. LEACH *v.*[2] + -ABLE.] Capable of being leached out.

1944 *Experiment Station Rec.* Apr. 450 Potassium could be changed biologically from a leachable to a nonleachable state. **1955** *Sci. News Let.* 27 Aug. 132/2 Experiments indicate that an average of only about 25% of the thorium and uranium in granite rock is 'leachable'. **1972** *Ann. Rep. Freshwater Biol. Assoc.* XL. 40 This contrasts with dead leaves from which leachable substances are said to disappear in about a week. **1972** J. G. CRUIKSHANK *Soil Geogr.* ii. 46 Maximum mobilisation of leachable substances is related to both the volume and composition of the organic leachate. **1973** *Nature* 13 Apr. 452/2 The concentrations reported include the contribution of acid leachable mercury associated with particulate material.

leachate (lī·tʃēit). [f. LEACH *v.*[2] + *-ate*, after *filtrate, precipitate*, etc.] (A quantity of) liquid that has percolated through a solid and leached out some of the constituents.

1952 *Sci. Agric.* XXXII. 606 The pH of leachates from decomposing leaves rises as decomposition progresses. **1971** *Nature* 17 Sept. 211/1 The material was then filtered, washed several times and the leachates were combined. Both the residual material and the leachate were analysed for lead. **1972** [see *LEACHABLE *a.*].

leaching, *vbl. sb.*[2] Add: Also *leaching out.*

1906 E. W. HILGARD *Soils* ii. 24 A heavy depletion of the land by the leaching-out of this important plant food. **1938** R. W. LAWSON tr. *Hevesy & Paneth's Man. Radio-activity* (ed. 2) xxv. 265 In some minerals the ratio of lead to uranium has been altered by leaching-out processes in the course of the long periods of time involved. **1943** MILLAR & TURK *Fund. Soil Sci.* xv. 377 The leaching out of the alkali tends to leave the soil in an even worse physical condition. **1966** G. H. DURY *Ess. Geomorphol.* 56 It is the simple process of leaching out of contained salt, by groundwater, which rapidly reduces the shearing strength of the deposits.

lead, *sb.*[1] Add: **1. c.** (Later examples.)

1927 *Amer. Speech* Mar. 278/1 *Shake out the lead*, start action. **1942** BERREY & VAN DEN BARK *Amer. Thes. Slang* §578/26 Get the lead out of your pants, to play allegro. **1948** F. BROWN *Dead Ringer* i. 15 Quit asking.. questions and get the lead out. **1961** *Lebende Sprachen* VI. 101/1 He's as lazy as they come, he's got lead in his pants, shoes. **1964** WODEHOUSE *Frozen Assets* vi. 115 She knows I'm in imminent danger of dying of malnutrition unless she takes the lead out of her pants and gets a move on with that picture. **1967** —— *Company for Henry* xii. 207 Those wedding bells aren't going to ring if you don't take the lead out of your pants and get a move on.

3. (Earlier and later examples.) Phr. *lead in one's pencil*: implying (esp. sexual) vigour in a male.

1816 JANE AUSTEN *Emma* III. iv. 54 When he took out his pencil, there was so little lead that he soon cut it all away. **1922** S. LEWIS *Babbitt* i. 9 A silver pencil (always lacking a supply of new leads). **1941** BAKER *Dict. Austral. Slang* 43 (*This will*) *put some lead in your pencil*, this (esp. a drink of beer or spirits) will make you feel fighting fit. **1946** P. LARKIN *Jill* 190 'Well, ere's more lead in yer pencil.' He finished off his half-pint. **1969** [see *CURL *v.*[1] 1 c]. **1970** *Kay's Catal.* (Worcester) Autumn–Winter 947/3 Pencil both propels and retracts, contains twelve 3 inch leads. **1970** A. DRAPER *Swansong for Rare Bird* vii. 59 She came over with two glasses. 'If that doesn't put some lead in your pencil, Auk, I don't know what will.' **1972** D. LEES *Zodiac* 107 The couscous is supposed to put lead in your pencil but with Daria I needed neither a talking point nor an aphrodisiac.

4. (*cold*) *lead*, bullets.

1809 T. G. FESSENDEN *Pills Poetical* 32 Thus our sporting democrats,.. When they can't reason with a Fed, In logick substitute cold lead. **1837** W. H. WHARTON *Let.* in *Ann. Rep. Amer. Hist. Assoc. 1907* (1908) II. 190 We

would give Mexico nothing but lead. **1891** M. E. Ryan *Told in Hills* 332 [The message] belongs to the command, and I may get a dose of cold lead before I could deliver it. **1918** C. Sandburg *Cornhuskers* 50 Three riders emptied lead into him. **1964** F. O'Rourke *Mule for Marquesa* 146 Get 'em up or we'll pump you full of lead!

6. b. Phr. *to swing the lead*: to idle, to shirk; to malinger. *slang.* Hence in similar phrs. and in *Comb.*, as **lead-swing** *sb.* and *v. intr.*, **-swinger, -swinging** *vbl. sb.* and *ppl. a.*

1917 *To-Day* 6 Jan. 243/3 It is evident that he had 'swung the lead' (using Army phrase) until he got his discharge. **1918** B. K. Adams *Let.* 25 Jan. in *Amer. Spirit* 71 Lead-swingers are those that stall along, doing as little as they possibly can, hoping the war will be over before they finish. **1922** C. E. Montague *Disenchantment* iv. 56 Then grey hairs should be a lot of use to you..when you want to get swinging the lead. **1927** A. Brosnan *At Number 15* i. 30 'If they wanted a three-man job done they had to put forty on to it to make sure it was done.' 'And so they did. That's organisation, that is. Of course, there was some lead-swingers.' **1927** *Daily Express* 2 Mar. 3/4 He said he ..had been 'swinging the lead' for the purpose of getting a permanent pension. **1930** S. Beckett *Whoroscope* 1 The vile old Copernican lead-swinging son of a sutler! **1939** R. Campbell *Flowering Rifle* ii. 60 It was not we who lead-swung to the Pities, When half the loveliest of our ancient cities Were in the clouds rebuilt. **1940** J. B. Priestley *Postscripts* 70 A wary..old soldier, a lead-swinger, a dodger of the column. **1952** M. Allingham *Tiger in Smoke* iv. 77 He went sick... It was so hopeless, so damned silly and forlorn as a lead-swing that in the end he got away with it. **1957** A. Grimble *Return to Islands* ii. 32 Their number was not without its natural quota of cheerful leadswingers. **1968** *Manch. Guardian Weekly* 12 Sept. 9 Mr. Crossman..insisted that 'lead swinging' among the unemployed was confined to a very small minority. **1969** *Daily Tel.* 8 Jan. 26/1 Overall absenteeism in the coalfields is running slightly higher than last year... Out of this total, 4·66 per cent. is classified as voluntary absenteeism ('lead-swinging'). **1972** *Daily Colonist* (Victoria, B.C.) 12 Feb. 4/1 The mayor of Victoria accuses the four Greater Victoria members of the legislature of lead-swinging. **1973** *Daily Tel.* 29 Aug. 6/3 'It would soon put a stop to lead-swingers who take a few days off to paint the house or watch cricket,' the doctor added.

11. b. Also obj. genitive, as *lead-free* adj.

1946 [see *lead glass*, sense *12]. **1960** *Farmer & Stock-breeder* 16 Feb. Suppl. 36/2 Sow Feeder..painted [with] one coat lead-free paint. **1970** *Guardian* 13 Apr. 13/4 Lead-free petrol. **1973** *Country Life* 29 Mar. 854/1 Modifications were also made to the engine to enable it to run on lead-free fuels.

c. *lead-covered, -sheathed* (later example).

1891 Kipling *Light that Failed* xiii. 253 A hall at the foot of some lead-covered stairs. **1908** *Westm. Gaz.* 22 Apr. 8/3 Over twenty miles of lead-covered cables have been laid in the grounds. **1948** G. V. Galwey *Lift & Drop* vi. 137 The leads to the switchgear were buried. They were lead-sheathed.

12. lead accumulator, a lead-acid cell or battery; **lead-acid** *a.*, applied to a secondary cell or battery in which the anode is a plate or grid of lead (or lead alloy) coated with lead dioxide, the cathode is a similar plate coated with spongy lead, and both are immersed in dilute sulphuric acid; **lead balloon,** a failure, an unsuccessful venture; **lead bronze,** bronze containing lead, which is used in bearings; **lead bullion,** a mixture of lead and other heavy metals obtained as an intermediate product in the extraction of lead; **lead burning,** the welding of lead; so **lead-burn** *v. trans.*, to weld (pieces of lead); **lead cell,** a lead-acid cell; **lead chamber,** a large reaction vessel made of welded sheet lead which is used in the manufacture of sulphuric acid from sulphur dioxide, air, and steam using oxides of nitrogen as catalysts; so *lead chamber process*; **lead crystal** [Crystal *sb.* 5] = *lead glass* below; **lead-flat** (see quots.); **lead glass,** glass containing a substantial proportion of lead oxide; **lead-glaze** *Pottery,* a glaze containing lead oxide; so *lead-glazed* adj., *lead-glazier, lead-glazing* vbl. sb.; **lead-line,** (*d*) the narrow strip of lead between two pieces of stained glass; a came; so **lead-line** *v. trans.*, to put the lead-lines in (stained glass work); **lead-paper** (later examples); hence **lead-papered** *a.*, covered with or containing lead-paper; **lead-plant** (examples); **lead-poisoning** (earlier and later examples); **lead ratio,** the ratio, in a sample of rock, of the quantity of lead (or a lead isotope) to the quantity of its radioactive parents uranium and thorium (or an appropriate isotope of one of these elements), from which the age of the sample may be determined; **lead-tin** *a.*, containing lead and tin; also *ellipt.*, a lead-tin alloy; **lead wool,** lead in a fibrous state, used for caulking pipe joints.

1903 *Chem. News* 17 July 34/2 Dr. Lehfeldt's paper on 'The Total and Free Energy of the Lead Accumulator' was taken as read. **1928** Crennell & Lea *Alkaline Accumulators* i. 5 The lead accumulator suffers from certain inherent defects of which the most important are a rather large weight for a given capacity, [etc.]. **1971** G. F. Liptrot *Mod. Inorg. Chem.* xviii. 242 The voltage supplied by the lead accumulator is just in excess of 2 volts. **1926** W. S. Ibbetson *Accumulator Charging* iii. 26 Fig. 7 illustrates the actions and results of charging and discharging a simple lead acid cell. **1936** *Motor Manual* (ed. 29) iv. 78 The lead-acid type [of battery] is that most general as its cost is much lower. **1972** *Dry Cells, Batteries & Accumulators* iii. 36 Lead-acid accumulators have a good life in terms of charge/discharge cycles. **1974** *Railway Mag.* Apr. 176/2 The locomotive interior is taken up by no less than 160 lead-acid battery cells, giving a 300V supply. **1960** Wentworth & Flexner *Dict. Amer. Slang* 314/2 *Lead balloon,* a failure; a plan, joke, action or the like that elicits no favorable response; a flop; anything that lays an egg. **1962** L. Deighton *Ipcress File* xxv. 158 With this boy it went over like a lead balloon. **1970** *Sunday Times* 19 Apr. 31/3 *What the Dickens?* was a lead balloon literary quiz wherein the experts showed only how little they knew. **1937** H. N. Bassett *Bearing Metals & Alloys* viii. 296 Under the general title of lead bronzes are included.. the copper-tin-lead alloys..and the so-called 'tin-free' bronzes. **1951** *Engineering* 6 July 1/3 The main and big-end bearings are all fitted with steel shells, lined with lead-bronze. **1967** *Jane's Surface Skimmer Systems 1967–68* 123/2 Crankshaft... Lead-bronze bearings with steel cups. **1905** A. H. Low *Technical Methods Ore Analysis* viii. 56 The determination of bismuth in impure lead or lead bullion may be carried out on the same lines as described for refined lead. **1954** W. H. Dennis *Metall. Non-Ferrous Metals* iv. 242 The crude lead bullion may contain up to 4 per cent of these reduced metallics. **1963** *Times* 22 Apr. p. iv/4 This plant is producing about 40,000 tons of good ordinary brand zinc annually together with lead bullion and by-product cadmium and sulphuric acid. **1886** D. Salomons *Managem. Accumulators* 14 It is frequently necessary to perform the operation of soldering or lead burning. **1937** *Archit. Rev.* XXXI. 272/2 Leadburning is a variety of welding. As a process it has been known for centuries, but only since the invention of the gas welding flame have its possibilities been fully exploited. *Ibid.* 270 (*caption*) After casting the flat sheets [of lead] are bent round and the joint lead-burned to form the point. **1963** H. R. Clauser *Encycl. Engin. Materials* 368/2 Lead welding, commonly called lead burning, produces a true weld by fusing the parts together without the addition of any different material. **1897** *Physical Rev.* IV. 353 We owe the discovery of the lead cell to Planté. **1928** Crennell & Lea *Alkaline Accumulators* ix. 121 The energy, or watt-hour, efficiency of alkaline cells is about 50–55 per cent., as compared with 75 per cent. for lead cells. **1867** *Chem. News* 5 July 12/1 (*heading*) Lead-chamber process. *Ibid.*, This explains the loss of nitric acid in the manufacture of sulphuric acid, which always takes place when the sulphuric acid in the lead-chamber is below the normal strength. **1909** L. Kahlenberg *Outl. Chem.* xiii. 198 There are commonly three lead chambers, so connected that the gases enter the top of each and pass out at the bottom. **1946** J. R. Partington *Gen. & Inorg. Chem.* xxiv. 710 The lead chamber plant..consists of (i) pyrites (or sulphur) burners, (ii) a dust separator.., (iii) a nitre oven.., (iv) a Glover tower, (v) a series of lead chambers with arrangements for supplying steam or water spray, and (vi) a Gay-Lussac tower. **1969** H. T. Evans tr. *Hägg's Gen. & Inorg. Chem.* xxi. 529 The reaction takes place in reaction chambers, formerly lead chambers, that is, large lead-lined rooms, but now most often of other types. **1973** Thomas & Farago *Industr. Chem.* viii. 133 The lead-chamber process is by no means obsolete.., and is likely to remain in operation for the production of acid not exceeding 78 per cent in concentration..and where high purity is not essential. **1902** J. D. & A. Everett tr. *Hovestadt's Jena Glass* x. 364 Foerster recalls the fact that the resisting power of lead crystal glass to acids is increased by long-continued exposure to acids. Were it otherwise, the use of this material for wine glasses would long ago have been given up. **1968** *Canad. Antiques Collector* Dec. 19/2 When lead crystal came into fashion about 1800, it was possible to cut the glass in glittering facets. **1969** R. F. Lang tr. *Henglein's Chem. Technol.* 835 Lead crystal contains lead (instead of Ca) and potassium and has high light refraction; it is much used in colored glasses. *a* **1877** Knight *Dict. Mech.* II. 1270/1 *Lead-flat,* a level roof consisting of sheet-lead laid on boarding and joists. **1907** W. De Morgan *Alice-for-Short* xxv. 259 Charles remembers the lead-flat sunk in the roof. **1940** *Chambers's Techn. Dict.* 491/2 *Lead-flat,* a flat roof formed of sheet-lead laid on boarding and joists. [**1830** *Phil. Trans. R. Soc.* CXX. 43 The tri-borate of lead glass is almost as colourless as good flint glass.] **1856** W. A. Miller *Elem. Chem.* II. xi. 764 Lead glass has..the inconvenience of being readily scratched. **1946** *Nature* 26 Oct. 582/1 Colouring oxides such as iron, copper, etc., all produce more intense colours in heavy lead glasses than in ordinary lead-free glasses. **1965** Phillips & Williams *Inorg. Chem.* I. xiv. 546 Special glasses are made by adding other oxides: for example, lead glasses have a high refractive index and are used in crystal and flint glass. **1899** *Westm. Gaz.* 27 Mar. 6/2 There seems no reason..why.. the operatives should still continue to be exposed to the evils which the use of lead-glaze entails. **1969** *Canad. Antiques Collector* Jan. 28/3 Lead and lustre glazes came early from the Near East. **1901** *Daily News* 3 Dec. 3/7 He states that there is no difference now in price between the lead glazed and leadless glazed ware. **1968** J. Arnold *Shell Bk. Country Crafts* 231 Medieval pottery was mainly in the form of lead-glazed earthenware..and was known as faience or majolica. **1908** *Westm. Gaz.* 23 Nov. 9/3 The deceased came under his notice twelve years ago, when he was a lead-glazier. **1962** H. R. Loyn *Anglo-Saxon Eng.* iii. 110 The so-called Stamford ware, utilizing a type of lead-glazing that may have originated in the Netherlands, appears to have spread from East Anglia. **1907** W. De Morgan *Alice-for-Short* xxvii. 283 I'll lend you a hand over the lead-lines. *Ibid.* xii. 136 It was Pope's man, Buttivant, who lead-lines up all the windows. **1973** Harrison & Waters *Burne-Jones* iv. 50 All the designers had to supply were the cartoons, which were quite often bold drawings without indication of lead lines. **1922** Joyce *Ulysses* 659 A crinkled leadpaper bag. *Ibid.* 70 He..read the legends of leadpapered packets. **1952** M. Allingham *Tiger in Smoke* vi. 108 The final covering was a piece of lead paper off a tobacco package. **1833** A. Eaton *Man. Bot.* (ed. 6) 15 *Amorpha canescens,* lead plant... Somewhat woody... Galena. **1848** W. H. Emory *Notes Mil. Reconn.* 399 The lead plant, or tea plant..is in some places so abundant as to displace almost every other herb. **1939** *Nat. Geogr. Mag.* Aug. 220/1 Chief among the peas is a group of close relatives: lead plant,..prairie clovers, together with indigo plant. **1841–2** T. D. Mitchell in *Western & Southern Med. Recorder* (Lexington, Kentucky) I. 145 (*title*) Practical notes on lead poisoning. **1972** *National Observer* (U.S.) 27 May 10/1 The American Smelting and Refining Co. of New Jersey was accused in a civil suit of unduly polluting the air and environment with its huge smelters here and of causing lead poisoning in at least 135 children. **1920** *Discovery* Apr. 111/2 It is of course obvious that, if a mineral is altered, it has suffered chemical changes whereby the normal lead ratio is upset, for either introduction or elimination of lead may have taken place. *Ibid.* 112/1 In some cases the lead-ratio can be used..for determining the geological position of rocks which yield their age to no other method of investigation. **1946** F. E. Zeuner *Dating the Past* x. 325 In practice, the analyst measures the total amount of lead present, and the expression $Pb^{total}/(U + 0{\cdot}36\ Th)$, accounting for the presence of both uranium and thorium, is the one which has to be determined in every case. It is called the 'lead-ratio'. **1889** *Jrnl. Chem. Soc.* LV. 677 The first alloys experimented on were the lead-tin alloys. **1890** *Ibid.* LVIII. 336 The two alloys always correspond with two cognate points on the solubility curves of zinc in lead-tin, and of lead in zinc-tin. **1928** H. H. Cowley *Mod. Electr. Wiring* iv. 54 Either copper or lead-tin alloy is generally employed for ordinary wire fuses. **1931** G. O. Russell *Speech & Voice* viii. 67 The author has a lead-tin, round-walled open organ pipe. **1956** *Monogr. & Rep. Ser. Inst. Metals* No. 18. 73 In the lead-tin alloys, as in many other alloy systems, precipitation is accompanied by recrystallization. **1908** *Chambers's Jrnl.* Jan. 120/1 What is called 'lead wool', consisting of pure lead cut into fine strips by machinery. **1930** *Engineering* 10 Oct. 451/1 The end bracket structure on the ends of each tube formed the lateral forms for the joint concrete. The actual face joint was made with lead wool caulked.

b. lead tetraethyl = **tetraethyl lead.*

1924 *Jrnl. Inst. Petroleum Technologists* X. 337 Lead tetraethyl. **1926** *Encycl. Brit.* II. 127/2 The tendency to knocking is suppressed by adding to the motor spirit substances such as lead tetra-ethyl which, it is assumed, act by being adsorbed by the ferriferous carbon in the cylinder. **1971** *Daily Tel.* (Colour Suppl.) 28 May 16/2 The amounts of lead in the environment have increased dramatically since the introduction of lead tetraethyl as a petrol additive in the Twenties... By controlling the rate at which fuel burns, lead tetraethyl promotes smoother ignition.

lead, *sb.*[2] Add: **1. e.** (Further examples.) Also, a clue (to the solution of something).

1910 J. London *Let.* 19 Nov. (1966) 323 Again and again I have opened up leads of true life and found that it was wholly misunderstood by my reading public. **1959** *Times* 18 Feb. 8/3 The enquiry arose from a complaint.. that he had been given 'definite leads' to the questions in advance. **1971** *Daily Tel.* 17 Dec. 1/5 Three leads are being followed by detectives investigating the attempted assassination of the Jordanian Ambassador. They are a sub machine-gun.., an hotel bill..and fingerprints. **1973** *Times* 5 May 1/2 The French police have decided to shift their inquiry into the axe murder of Mr John Cartland, a Brighton schoolmaster, to Britain next week in search of new leads.

f. *Journalism.* A summary or outline of a newspaper story; a guide to a story that needs further development or exploration; the first (often the most important) item in an issue, bulletin, etc. Cf. *lead story,* etc., under sense 11 b below.

Quot. 1947 refers to a radio news broadcast.

1927 *Amer. Speech* II. 241 'Lead'..is used as a noun to refer to the initial summary of the story, or as a verb to instruct the printer what to put first. **1947** *Hansard, Commons* 19 Dec. 2113 There is what one calls the 'lead', which is..the first item. **1950** D. Hyde *I Believed* xvi. 189, I had several hundred accredited Worker Correspondents sending in regular reports and receiving regular 'leads' and directives from me. **1952** *Manch. Guardian Weekly* 20 Mar. 3 This discovery destroyed many a newsman's first confident 'lead'. **1961** 'B. Wells' *Day Earth caught Fire* viii. 119 Stenning's brought in a lead to something that could be big. **1973** A. Broinowski *Take one Ambassador* ix. 128 He's onto some lead about a mob of fanatical ratbags.

2. c. *Austral.* and *N.Z.* (See quot. 1933[1].)

1933 L. G. D. Acland in *Press* (Christchurch, N.Z.) 4 Nov. 15/7 *Lead,* the front part of a mob of sheep. *Ibid.* 2 Dec. 15/7 An injudicious turn with a dog in an abrupt gully may stop the lead and cause some sheep to be knocked over. **1946** F. D. Davison *Dusty* ix. 90 Tom.. sent [the sheepdog] Sapper to the flank [of the mob] and to turn the lead.

d. Finance. *leads and lags* (also attrib. phr. *lead-and-lag*): see quot. 1965[1]. Also *transf.*

1958 *Spectator* 31 Jan. 129/1 The 'leads and lags' are being replaced by a more natural pattern of commercial payments. **1959** *Economist* 14 Feb. 619/2 The customary 'leads and lags' are at work, postponing commercial demands for sterling and accelerating sales of sterling. **1962** S. E. Finer *Man on Horseback* xii. 220 Sometimes the demand for popular sovereignty has preceded nationalism, sometimes it has been the other way about; but the leads and lags were never very lengthy. **1964** A. Battersby *Network Analysis* iii. 37 The lead-and-lag (or ladder) system has the merit of simplicity, and it draws attention to the importance of planning the sequence of individual jobs within a departmental activity. **1965** J. L. Hanson *Dict. Econ.* 253/2 *Leads and Lags,* with reference to international payments and their effect on the balance of payments this term is used on the hastening or delaying of

payment, the former by residents and the latter to residents in order to take advantage of expectations of changes in the rate of exchange. **1965** *Listener* 13 May 692/2 Some foreigners, in the habit of acquiring sterling in advance of their commitments, refrained from doing so; that would be a mug's game, they thought, when sterling might be devalued before they had to pay. These are known as the 'leads and lags' in trade payments.

3. e. *N.Z.* (See quot.)

1878 E. S. Elwell *Boy Colonists* 214 They made a 'lead' in the stockyard for branding the cattle. This was something like a 'race' for drafting sheep, with a swing gate... It had a wide entrance gradually getting narrower till it became a lane only just wide enough for one beast at a time to squeeze through.

5. c. *Boxing.* The first punch thrown (of two or more) (see also quot. 1954).

1906 [see *cross *sb.* 22 d]. **1950** J. Dempsey *Championship Fighting* x. 50 The first punch thrown (by either) is a lead. **1954** F. C. Avis *Boxing Reference Dict., Lead,* a forward blow made at a fair distance from the opponent. **1970** *Times* 28 Sept. 13/5 Those sneak right leads I hit him with helped as well. **1971** *Black Scholar* Jan. 43/2 Man, this would make these fighters so mad they would forget about boxing and come out swinging wild. And that was all old Jack wanted. He'd step inside their leads and counter punch them to death!

6. a. Also *fig.*

1869 S. Bowles *Our New West* vii. 136 A quaint old miner of the valley, who, 'prospecting' for society that day, had struck a 'lead' in us.

7. a. and **b.** (Earlier and later examples.)

1831 J. Boaden *Life Mrs. Jordan* I. xi. 264 It gave him the lead in a successful play. **1865** *Punch* 7 Jan. 5/1 As a general rule an actor who plays the 'lead' ought to aim at becoming a general manager. **1937** *Daily Tel.* 14 Aug. 9/1 Many leading men and women (and some who are merely minor leads). **1939** [see *character part*]. **1953** [see *big stuff* (*big *a.* B. 2)]. **1973** *Listener* 21 June 844/2 The lead, Martin Thurley, must surely have studied the slovenly dialect of the area.

8. c. *Mus.* The most prominent part in a piece played by an orchestra, esp. a jazz band; the player or instrument that plays this; the leader of a section of an orchestra; also, the start of a passage played by a particular instrument. Freq. *attrib.* orig. *U.S.*

Further *attrib.* examples are given under sense 11 b below.

1934 S. R. Nelson *All about Jazz* v. 99 He evolved what he called a 'harmony chorus', the instruments all playing harmony, with a solo lead. **1937** *Amer. Speech* XII. 47 The lead melody is carried lower than the clarinet. **1952** B. Ulanov *Hist. Jazz in Amer.* (1958) xvii. 203 Hymie Schertzer's rich lead alto sounds. **1967** [see *attack *v.* 7]. **1968** *Blues Unlimited* Sept. 8 They played mostly Italian music and polkas, with Charlie McCoy on lead mandolin.

11. lead-bars (earlier U.S. example); **lead-net** = Leader[1] 15 b; **lead-rope,** a rope used as a lead for a horse or ox; also *fig.*; **lead sheet** *U.S. slang* (see quot. 1942); also *transf.*, an overcoat; **lead-time** orig. *U.S.*, the time taken to produce some manufactured article (see also quot. 1968); also *transf.*

1840 *Congress. Globe* 5 Mar. App. 227/2 The horse broke loose from the coach, taking with him a part of what are now called 'Lead bars'. **1910** *Chambers's Jrnl.* Mar. 192/2 The lead-net is about fifteen hundred feet long. The salmon strike this. **1846** R. B. Sage *Scenes Rocky Mts.* iii. 24 Holding in one hand the lead-rope of his horse. **1901** Kipling *Kim* vii. 169 'We be all on one lead-rope, then,' said Kim at last, 'the Colonel, Mahbub Ali, and I.' **1958** L. van der Post *Lost World of Kalahari* i. 15 Lifting the lead rope from the horns of the two guide-oxen. **1942** Berrey & Van den Bark *Amer. Thes. Slang* § 578/9 *Lead sheet,* a sheet of music containing the melodic line and lyric only. **1945** L. Shelly *Jive Talk Dict.* 28/2 *Lead sheet,* an overcoat. **1961** R. Russell *Sound* iii. 38 You never got around to writing out a lead sheet! **1945** *Birmingham* (Alabama) *News* 19 May 8/1 The 'lead-time' normally required to bring out new models. **1957** *Manch. Guardian* 4 May, The problem is..difficult, on account of the complex character of the equipment in question and the long lead-time involved. **1964** A. Battersby *Network Analysis* iii. 36 The chain-dotted arrows..represent *lead times* when they connect start events. **1968** J. F. Magee *Industr. Logistics* i. 19 'Lead time' is the response time lag of the system, the time that must be allowed at a stock point to replenish stock, including the time needed to process records, transmit information, and process and ship material. **1971** *Inside Kenya Today* Mar. 28/1 Because of the lead-time in switching the emphasis in the secondary schools, the University is under pressure to increase its Arts intake very rapidly. **1973** *Nature* 28 Sept. 179/1 The long lead time required for such a rendezvous or flyby mission makes it impossible to achieve a fruitful interception with Kohoutek.

b. Used in the sense of 'leading'.

1846 R. B. Sage *Scenes Rocky Mts.* xxxiii. 289 Bidding them adieu, with my lead pack-animal returned to the mountains. **1857** in *Ann. Wyoming* (1939) XI. 83 The carriage sustained no injury, but one of our lead Mules became detached from the wagon. **1869** *Overland Monthly* III. 127 With the Texan driver all oxen are 'steers', and he has his 'wheel-steers', his 'swing-steers', and his 'lead-steers'. **1888** Kipling *Barrack-Room Ballads* (1892) 117 Then the lead-cart stuck, though the coolies slaved, and the cartmen flogged. **1890** *Ibid.* 18 The rattle an' stamp o' the lead-mules. **1910** W. M. Raine *Bucky O'Connor* 189 It was as the man in charge circled round to head the lead cows in that a faint voice carried to him. **1929** *Randolph Enterprise* (Elkins, W. Virginia) 28 Mar. 1/2 Dick Collette played the lead violin and Bryan Gainer, second. **1942** Berrey & Van den Bark *Amer. Thes. Slang* § 523/3 Leader, lead story, a leading news item. **1959** J. Osborne *World of Paul Slickey* I. vi. 55 Congratulations..on today's lead story. **1962** *Amer. Speech* XXXVII. 87 A lead article satirizing American temperance groups. **1963** Mrs. L. B. Johnson *White House Diary* 22 Nov. (1970) 3 In the lead car were President and Mrs. Kennedy. **1967** *Time* 25 Aug. 38 The Group Image, one of the new, first-name-only hippie groups, of which Nancy is the den mother..and Artie the lead guitar. The tribe has about 25 musicians, artists and psychedelic experts in it. **1967** W. Soyinka *Kongi's Harvest* 3 Superintendent... Seizes the lead drummer by the wrist. **1973** 'F. Clifford' *Amigo, Amigo* xxi. 175 Ahead, the lead horse whinnied. **1973** *Listener* 6 Sept. 312/3 Carl Perkins..now playing lead guitar behind Johnny Cash. **1975** *Guardian* 7 Jan. 6/7 A mob of Hell's Angels set on members of the Troggs pop group in their dressing-room and during a fight the group's lead guitarist was stabbed five times in the back.

lead, *v.*[1] Add: **2. f.** To aim in advance of.

1892 W. W. Greener *Breech-Loader* 267 Theoretically it is correct to lead a quartering pigeon from five to seven feet. **1968** D. Hamilton *Menacers* xxii. 176, I led him by roughly two feet and pressed the trigger of the Luger.

g. Coll. phr. *lead me to* (something previously mentioned), expressing the ability to perform or a desire to comply, or merely expressing eager assent.

1929 W. E. Miller *To you I tell It* 107 'How wood you like to urn a piece of jack?' 'Leed me to it,' says Figgars. 'What's the propozishion?' **1934** D. L. Sayers *Nine Tailors* iv. 307 'Can you ride a motor-bike?' 'Lead me to it, guv'nor!' **1938** D. Smith *Dear Octopus* ii. iii. 90 Lead me to that whiskey.

h. *to lead with one's chin* (Boxing slang), to 'stick one's neck out', to leave oneself unprotected; *fig.*, to behave or speak incautiously.

1949 E. S. Gardner in *Argosy* Apr. 110/3 Let him lead with *his* chin. We'll work undercover. **1954** F. C. Avis *Boxing Reference Dict., Lead with chin,* to have a very bad stance or guard. **1968** *Listener* 18 Jan. 78/2, I thought it was a good idea to say that I was prejudiced to begin with, to lead with my chin. **1973** A. MacVicar *Painted Doll Affair* i. 19 Don't go leading with your chin, Bruce.

19. a. (Earlier examples.) **b.** Also with *to*.

1817 Jane Austen *Sanditon* vi in *Minor Works* (1954) 389 Sir Edw: Denham & Miss Denham, whose names might be said to lead off the Season. **1847** *Punch* 27 Mar. 126/2 To lead off a list of Expiring Acts with one that is to live till the National Debt is paid off..is a delusion. **1911** *Chambers's Jrnl.* July 463/2 From these [wagons] rubber tubes protected by encircling wire lead off to each of the streets.

21*. lead through. *Mountaineering.* Said of two climbers: to act alternately as leaders (see quots.). Hence **leading through** *vbl. sb.*

1945 G. W. Young *Mountain Craft* (ed. 4) v. 184 Nowadays, two such experts..make a practice of 'leading through': that is..the second man on reaching his leader climbs straight on past him and leads the next section. **1955** M. E. B. Banks *Commando Climber* ix. 177 We were leading through, that is to say, one of us would climb a pitch and belay himself to the rock, whereupon the other would climb up to him and then continue beyond to lead the next pitch. **1970** A. Blackshaw *Mountaineering* (rev. ed.) v. 143 For experienced climbers two is the best number since this is quick and allows them to 'lead through'. *Ibid.* xvii. 420 Leading through may not save as much time on alpine rock as it does on British rock.

lead, *v.*[2] **3.** (Later example.)

1842 C. J. Lever *Jack Hinton* (1843) xxv. 172, I..seated myself in the scale..and my saddle being leaded to the required weight, the operation took not a minute.

leadbeater[1] (le·dbītəɹ). The name of Benjamin *Leadbeater,* 19th-c. English naturalist, used *absol.* and in the possessive to designate a pink Australian cockatoo, *Kakatoe leadbeateri,* named after him in 1831 by N. A. Vigors (*Phil. Mag.* X. 55). In full, *Leadbeater's cockatoo.*

1848 J. Gould *Birds Austral.* V. 2 (*heading*) Leadbeater's Cockatoo. **1890** 'Lyth' *Golden South* xiv. 127 The birds are very beautiful—the Blue Mountain and Lowrie parrots,..lead-beater, and snow-white cockatoos. **1900** *Daily News* 10 Feb. 7/2 The foreign birds are many, and include Amazon and grey parrots, lead-beaters, rose cockatoos, [etc.]. **1973** A. H. Lendon *Cayley's Austral. Parrots* 89 Pink Cockatoo... Synonyms. Major Mitchell Cockatoo, Leadbeater's Cockatoo, [etc.].

Leadbeater[2]. The name of Mr. *Leadbeater,* taxidermist at the National Museum of Victoria, Melbourne, in 1867, used in the possessive to designate **Leadbeater's possum,** *Gymnobelideus leadbeateri,* a very rare Australian opossum named after him in 1867 by F. M'Coy (*Ann. Mag. Nat. Hist.*, 3rd Ser., XX. 287).

1937 *Discovery* XVIII. 364/1 The smaller gliding 'possums..whose ancestry is probably derived from the same stock as the extinct Leadbeater's 'Possum, feed on insects, nectar, fruit and sap. **1942** C. Barrett *On Wallaby* iii. 36 The rarest of all Australian animals—Leadbeater's possum. **1966** G. Durrell *Two in Bush* iv. 142 To the astonishment of incredulous naturalists, a tiny pocket of Leadbeater's Possum was discovered [in 1961] in the eucalyptus forest not far from Melbourne. **1968** *Times* 23 Jan. (Austral. Suppl.) p. xiii/3 Eric Wilkinson..saw something that made him stare in disbelief—clinging to the trunk of a wattle tree beside the road was a small, dainty animal which much resembled the Leadbeaters possum, presumed extinct.

leaded, *ppl. a.* Add: **d.** Affected by lead-poisoning.

1878 J. H. Beadle *Western Wilds* xxxv. 581 Great care must be taken by the workmen not to get 'leaded', that is, not to inhale the fumes from the melted lead, which are very poisonous. **1906** *Daily Chron.* 28 June 6/4 The children of 'leaded' mothers usually die, or if they live inherit the effects of the poison. **1914** *Dialect Notes* IV. 163 *Leaded,* among miners, ill from lead poisoning.

e. Containing added lead.

1936 *Blackw. Mag.* Mar. 359/2 It was said that Archie had obtained a special supply of leaded fuel, which would allow him to bring in the Kestrel supercharger near the ground. **1939** Carpenter & Robertson *Metals* II. xv. 1317 Alloys in the fifth group are those to which large amounts of lead are added to improve their suitability for certain types of bearings... These alloys are known as the 'plastic' or 'leaded' bronzes. **1963** H. R. Clauser *Encycl. Engin. Materials* 370/1 Sheet lead and sheets of leaded plastics are also being used to control noise. **1968** E. R. Petty *Physical Metall. Engin. Materials* xiii. 266 Operators must be shielded from this penetrating radiation and for this purpose..a foot of concrete or several feet of water (usually in a leaded-glass jacket) are necessary. **1972** *Lancet* 1 July 12/2 All the subjects had been simultaneously exposed to tetraethyl lead during the process of scaling a tank which had contained leaded petrol.

leaden, *a.* Add: **4.** *leaden-hearted* (later example), *-lidded, -locked* adjs.

1938 C. Day Lewis *Overtures to Death* 14 Infirm and grey This leaden-hearted day Drags its lank hours. **1946** W. de la Mare *Traveller* 18 His leaden-lidded eyes. **1963** *Listener* 7 Mar. 429/1 A man..Whiskered and leaden-locked.

5. leaden fly-catcher, a small grey-green Australian bird, *Myiagra rubecula,* of the family Muscicapidæ (see Fly-catcher 2).

1908 E. J. Banfield *Confessions of Beachcomber* i. iii. 95 Leaden Fly-catcher, *Myiagra rubecula* (*plumbea*). **1911** J. A. Leach *Austral. Bird Bk.* 125 Leaden Flycatcher... Upper wings, tail, breast leaden-gray glossed with green. **1965** *Austral. Encycl.* IV. 121/1 The best-known [tropical flycatchers] are the leaden flycatcher (*Myiagra rubecula*) which migrates south to Tasmania, and the black-faced flycatcher.

Leadenhall (le·dənhǭl). The name of an area in London, used *attrib.* in *Leadenhall Market,* a poultry market in London; *Leadenhall Street,* a street in London which from 1648 to 1861 contained the headquarters of the East India Company, hence designating the Company itself.

1587 J. Stow *Summarie Chron. Eng.* 407 The Northwest corner of Leaden Hall (the highest grounde of the Citie of London). **1720** Stow & Strype *Survey Cities London & Westminster* I. (*map facing p.* 1) Leaden Hall St. **1825** T. Moore *Mem. Life R. B. Sheridan* I. viii. 367 The people, by the unanimous outcry with which they rose, in defence of the monopoly of Leadenhall Street..proved how little of the '*vox Dei*' there may..be in such clamour. **1831** J. Boaden *Life Mrs. Jordan* II. i. 28 It showed, how the elegant mothers of Leadenhall Street, might, with the greatest gentleness, strain their young ones to bosoms equally *soft,* while they themselves were nourished by the *blood* and sweat of the unhappy peasant of Bengal. **1882** *Encycl. Brit.* XIV. 828/2 The principal markets..are Smithfield (central meat market and poultry market), Leadenhall (poultry and game), Billingsgate (fish), Covent Garden (fruit and vegetables). **1932** P. Spear *Nabobs* 28 Wellesley's remark about 'the cheesemongers of Leadenhall Street' would have horrified them. **1952** M. Bellasis *Honourable Company* p. viii, The factors and merchants, who first went out from Leadenhall Street to 'shake the pagoda tree', were transformed in the course of two or three generations into..self-effacing public servants. **1961** *Wonderful London* (Evening News) 56 Leadenhall market ..was rebuilt in 1881.

leader[1]. Add: **3.** *Leader of the House of Commons* (examples) (see also quot. 1964); freq. *ellipt.* as *Leader of the House*; so *Leader of the House of Lords* (or *of the Upper House*).

1835 *Ann. Reg. 1834* 335/2 It was requisite to find a new chancellor of the Exchequer, and a new leader of the House of Commons. **1852** Disraeli *Lord George Bentinck* xx. 397 The government abandoned this..project.. scarcely with decency, for the leader of the house of lords was eulogizing its virtues..at the moment it was cast away by the chancellor of the exchequer. **1852** Ld. Palmerston *Let.* 24 Dec. in J. Russell *Later Corr.* (1925) II. xx. 119 If the extensive duties of Leader of the House of Commons can be performed without salary why should any public officer have any? **1855** —— *Let.* 7 Feb. in Queen Victoria *Lett.* (1907) III. xxiv. 131 Proposed cabinet... Organ of the Government or Leader of the House of Lords. Marquis of Lansdowne. **1868** C. D. Yonge *Life 2nd Earl of Liverpool* I. iv. 145 According to the usage of that day, when the Prime Minister was a Commoner, the Home Secretary, if a peer, was the leader of the Upper House. **1869** A. Todd *On Parl. Govt. in Eng.* II. iv. 323 The leader of the House of Commons is at liberty to arrange the order of business appointed for government nights as he thinks fit. **1908** A. E. Steinthal tr. *Redlich's Procedure House of Commons* I. 120 The name and function of the chief member of the Government in the House of Commons, the Leader of the House. **1964** Abraham & Hawtrey *Parl. Dict.* (ed. 2) 111 The term 'Leader of the House' was originally applied to the chief spokesman for the Government in the House

of Commons when the Prime Minister was a member of the House of Lords. *Ibid.*, The Leader of the House receives no salary as such... His chief responsibility is for planning and supervising the Government's legislative programme, and in particular for the arrangement..of the business of the House. *Ibid.* 112 The Leader of the House of Lords is the chief spokesman for the Government in that House. **1974** *Guardian* 30 Apr. 1/4 A statement from Mr Short, Leader of the House, on the registration of interests is promised later this week, but there are deep differences between the parties over whether the register should be compulsory or voluntary. *Ibid.*, A promised personal statement by Mr Short, Deputy Leader of the Labour Party and Leader of the House of Commons, was delayed by several hours last night.

e. *spec.* as a rendering of G. *Führer*, It. *Duce*, or Sp. *Caudillo*: the head of an authoritarian state. Usu. with capital initial. Also *transf.* (in quot. 1934 applied to the leader of the British Fascists, Sir Oswald Mosley).

1918 [see *CAUDILLO]. **1934** H. G. WELLS *Exper. Autobiogr.* II. ix. 783 Quite a quantity of pleasant boys and nice young men..were acting as ushers, selling idiotic songs about their glorious Leader. **1937** A. HUXLEY *Ends & Means* i. 2 The twentieth [century] has already witnessed..the emergence of the sheep-like social man and the god-like Leader. **1939** S. SPENDER tr. *Toller's Pastor Hall* I. 48 I've never spoken a word against the Leader. **1952** A. BULLOCK *Hitler* iii. 123 There was persistent.. grumbling at the amount of money the Leader and his friends took out of Party funds for their own expenses. **1960** H. SETON-WATSON *Neither War nor Peace* viii. 226 The head of the government was the Chancellor, Adolf Hitler, who was also Leader (*Führer*) of the party, and on the death of President Hindenburg in 1934 replaced him as Head of State with the title of Leader of the German Nation.

8. c. For (?U.S.) read (orig. U.S.); cf. *loss leader* s.v. *LOSS *sb.*[1] 10. (Earlier and later examples.)

1851 C. CIST *Sk. Cincinnati in 1851* xv. 319 These articles [*sc.* sugar, molasses, coffee, etc.] are the leaders, as they are called, in commercial transactions, with the west. **1888** *Chicago Tribune* 29 Apr. 4/7 Goods advertised and sold below cost are technically known as 'leaders'. **1963** 'R. FINDLATER' *What are Writers Worth?* 14 Most [paperback] firms produce about a dozen titles every month..at the summit the 'leader'—the smash-hit novel on which the selling machine is focused. **1967** *Times Rev. Industry* Feb. 31/1 Establishing new products is both costly and hazardous..while old leaders tend to decline over the years. **1972** *Lebende Sprachen* XVII. 34/1 US leader—BE/US loss leader, BE leading article.

12. (Earlier examples.)

1837 *Southern Lit. Messenger* III. 418/2 The Editor thus commenceth his leader. **1838** DICKENS *Let.* 23 Dec. (1965) I. 475, I was very much obliged indeed to you for the paper. I..was greatly amused with the 'leader'.

19*. *Cinemat.* and *Tape Recording.* A short length of blank or uncoated film or tape attached at the beginning or end of a reel for purposes of threading or identification.

1917 C. N. BENNETT *Guide to Kinematogr.* xi. 185 Refrain from..cutting or punching holes in the film leaders. **1960** J. M. LLOYD *All-in-One Tape Recorder Bk.* (ed. 4) v. 63 The inside and outside leaders are usually of different colours. **1969** J. ELLIOT *Duel* III. ii. 233 She went to.. learn the mysteries of..opticals and leaders and parallel and printing sync. **1969** D. N. WOOD *On Tape* vii. 82 This brings me to the other main use of the leader tape—to act as a title... It is possible to use a chinagraph pencil on the tape itself, but it is much better to use leaders for this purpose.

19.** *Meteorol.* In full, *leader stroke.* A preliminary stroke of lightning that ionizes the path taken by the much brighter return stroke that follows.

1934 SCHONLAND & COLLENS in *Proc. R. Soc.* A. CXLIII. 657 These preliminary downward strokes will be referred to as leader strokes and the upward strokes which follow them will be called main strokes. *Ibid.*, Sometimes the leader is so faint that a portion only of the track can be seen. **1937** *Jrnl. Inst. Electr. Engin.* LXXXI. 6/2 Immediately the stepped leader stroke reaches the earth the ..return stroke begins to travel..from earth to cloud. *Ibid.*, The leaders to the second and subsequent strokes of a flash usually travel from cloud to ground in a single flight. **1963** *Meteorol. Gloss.* (Meteorol. Office) (ed. 4) 154 Leader strokes directed upwards from ground to cloud may predominate in the case of very high structures. **1966** *McGraw-Hill Encycl. Sci. & Technol.* VII. 510/1 Cloud-to-cloud strokes also involve a step leader and main return stroke.

20. *attrib.* and *Comb.*, as (sense *3 e) *leader-principle, -worship*; (sense 12) *leader-page, -writer* (earlier and later examples); **leader stroke** (see sense 19**); **leader tape**, uncoated tape intended for use as a leader on a reel of magnetic tape; a length of tape so used.

1932 J. BUCHAN *Gap in Curtain* i. 54 Each of us must concentrate on one particular part to which his special interest was pledged—Tavanger on the first City page, for example, Mayot on the leader page, [etc.]. **1938** *Observer* 9 Jan. 5/1 (Advt.), Eugene Lyons..Assignment in Utopia ..'A moving and truthful account..'—Malcolm Muggeridge (*D. Telegraph*, leader-page article). **1940** 'G. ORWELL' *Crit. Ess.* (1951) 80 The absence of the leader-principle. There is no central dominating character. **1960** J. M. LLOYD *All-in-One Tape Recorder Bk.* (ed. 4) v. 64 Leader tape is transparent and is shiny on both sides. **1962** A. NISBETT *Technique Sound Studio* vi. 107 A leader tape (giving summarized details of the contents) and a trailer (several feet of coloured tape to give a visual indication of the end) may be cut on to the recording. **1971** *Hi-Fi Sound* Feb. 42 (Advt.), We also carry a full range of Accessories, Leader Tape, Empty Spools, Splicing Tape etc. **1940** 'G. ORWELL' *Crit. Ess.* (1951) 83 More bloodshed, more leader-worship. **1882** C. PEBODY *Eng. Journalism* xix. 144 It is as a leader-writer and special correspondent that he will be best remembered. **1940** *Manch. Guardian Weekly* 22 Mar. 228 But now it is stated in Berlin that Mr. Kuusinen 'has been promoted to be a leader-writer on an obscure provincial paper'.

lea·dered, *pa. pple.* [f. LEADER[1] 12.] Treated in a leading article; made the subject of a leader.

1884 *Pall Mall Gaz.* 29 Nov. 3/2 If it [*sc.* an interview] had been a speech it would have been 'leadered' all round. **1897** *Westm. Gaz.* 25 Sept. 5/2 Seeing that the subject is 'leader-ed' in both papers.

lea·derly, *a.* [f. LEADER[1] 3 + -LY[1].] Having the character of a leader.

1918 H. G. WELLS *In Fourth Year* ii. 23 Very rarely has it [*sc.* the United States] failed to set up very leaderly and distinguished men [as Presidents]. **1922** —— *Short Hist. World* xix. 104 They distinguished certain families as leaderly and noble. **1973** *Daily Tel.* 24 Nov. 16 The engineering community..is entitled to a more leaderly and statesmanlike response.

leadership. (Earlier and later examples.) Add to def.: The position of a group of people leading or influencing others within a given context; the group itself; the action or influence necessary for the direction or organization of effort in a group undertaking. Also *attrib.*, as *leadership behaviour, school, skill.*

1821 C. W. WYNN *Let.* 11 Mar. in *Corr.* (1920) 268 Charles writes that Tierney has regularly resigned the Leadership of the Opposition. **1915** E. & C. PAUL tr. *Michels's Pol. Parties* iv. ii. 261 (*heading*) Analysis of the bourgeois elements in the socialist leadership. **1930** O. OESER tr. *Bühler's Mental Devel. Child* vii. 166 From the schoolgoing age onwards we find that some have the talent for leadership. **1933** M. S. VITELES *Industr. Psychol.* xxvii. 626 The substitution of morale for discipline and of integration for domination calls for a change in the quality of leadership in industry. **1939** J. D. BROWN in C. I. Barnard *Dilemmas of Leadership* 3 To treat the difficult problem of executive leadership. **1939** C. I. BARNARD *Ibid.* 24 If a system once accepted..destroys leadership or divides followers—then disorganization, schism, rebellion ..ensues. **1947** SHERIF & CANTRIL *Psychol. of Ego-Involvements* vii. 182 Leadership, then, was seen to be a function of the group and its activities. **1962** K. ORVIS *Damned & Destroyed* xiv. 95 He went to a communist leadership school. **1963** J. E. GERALD *Social Responsibility of Press* v. 100 Few of the editors of mass-circulation newspapers since 1830 have risked their careers to exert strong leadership in the community. **1964** GOULD & KOLB *Dict. Social Sci.* 380/2 The manifestation of leadership behaviour can be observed only in relation to other persons who act in response to the leader and who are collectively referred to as the *following*. **1964** MRS. L. B. JOHNSON *White House Diary* 16 Jan. (1970) 51 We had an early dinner this evening..for the heads of the Senate Committees..and the Leadership on both sides and their wives. **1964** *English Studies* XLV. 50 Administrative and leadership skill. **1972** *Jrnl. Social Psychol.* LXXXVI. 29 Investigations of the relationship between personality traits and leadership behavior have failed to reveal any consistent patterns. **1973** M. TRUMAN *Harry S. Truman* xv. 306 Dad once defined leadership as the art of persuading people to do what they should have done in the first place.

lea·d-in. [f. vbl. phr. *to lead in* (LEAD *v.*[1] 2); cf. *leading-in* adj. (*LEADING *ppl. a.* 1 c).] **1. a.** A wire that leads in from outside, *esp.* one connecting an outdoor aerial with an indoor receiver or transmitter. Freq. *attrib.*

1913 *Wireless World* Apr. p. xxxvii/2 The lead was taken from the mast in the garden down to the instruments, which were now moved to the ground floor. This gave me a lead-in wire of 65 ft. **1913** *Work* 14 June 217/3 Lead in, about 40 ft. insulated. **1924** *Wireless World* 10 Sept. 679/2 (*caption*) By fixing your lead-in in this way opening and closing the window is not interfered with. **1934** *Practical Wireless* V. 62/1 (*heading*) A weather-proof lead-in. *Ibid.*, About 6 in. from the end of the lead-in wire, bind round with a 3 in. length of..copper wire. **1950** *Jrnl. Sci. Instrum.* XXVII. 231 (*heading*) Insulated power lead-in for vacuum systems.

b. A wire in an electric lamp that carries the current between the cap and the filament or electrode. Freq. *attrib.*

1929 *Encycl. Brit.* VIII. 291/1 The lead-in wires which carry the current to the filament have to be sealed through the glass. **1962** N. H. CODLING in G. A. T. Burdett *Automatic Control Handbk.* viii. 6 Nickel-steel of 42 per cent composition, when copper-clad, is used for the lead-ins of lamps. **1970** A. BYERS *Home Lighting* ii. 45 (*heading*) Lead-in wires.

2. *transf.* and *fig.* An introduction, opening, etc.

1928 *Melody Maker* Feb. 188/2 It is electrifying to hear the solo instrumentalists rip in on some unexpected lead-in. **1952** W. R. BURNETT *Vanity Row* xiv. 118 Like a radio announcer with an embarrassingly far-fetched lead-in to the commercial. **1958** [see *LEAD-OUT 1]. **1958** *Economist* 15 Nov. 579/2 The fantasy life portrayed [*i.e.*, in certain children's comics] is simply a lead-in to the more elaborate and still more depressing dreamworld of the women's magazines. **1962** W. NOWOTTNY *Lang. Poets Use* iv. 90 That opening is seen to be not an embarrassed and forced lead-in to a technically necessary comparison but rather a first and major step in the development of the whole. **1963** P. MOYES *Murder à la Mode* i. 20 Helen Pankhurst finished her lead-in blurb to the Collections feature. **1963** D. OGILVY *Confessions Advertising Man* (1964) viii. 131 Don't mess about with irrelevant lead-ins. Start selling in your first frame. **1971** *Daily Tel.* 11 Feb. 30/6 Workers who agree in writing to operate incentive bonus schemes should get a 'lead-in' payment of £1 a week. **1972** D. HASTON *In High Places* xii. 155, I heard the full story about Harsh's death and began to get some lead-in to the political infighting that had been going on. **1973** *Listener* 30 Aug. 295/1 Keep the lead-in short; some [news]papers enforce a 14-word limit on opening sentences.

leading, *vbl. sb.*[1] Add: **5.** Also in the usage of other religious bodies, and in philosophy.

1821 *Congregational Mag.* Nov. 579 What is Christian experience, but this working in us, this leading of the spirit of God? **1859** GEO. ELIOT *Adam Bede* I. iii. 59, I thought it might be a leading of Providence for me to change my way of life. *Ibid.* 60 The strong love God has given me towards you was a leading for us both. **1969** *Listener* 23 Jan. 117/3 Hence their [*sc.* Peirce and James's] characteristic teaching that all thought exists in signs or in 'leadings' from one area of experience to another.

leading, *vbl. sb.*[2] Add: **d.** More widely, deposition of lead on a surface.

1946 *Happy Landings* (Air Ministry) July 3/2 Pilots can prevent leading of plugs by clearing engines..or by using higher r.p.m. when flying in cold conditions.

leading, *ppl. a.* Add: **1.** (Further example.)

1817 COLERIDGE *Biog. Lit.* II. xxi. 126 Suppose too all this done without a single leading principle established.

b. leading dog *Austral.* and *N.Z.* (see quot. 1933).

1897 I. SCOTT *How I stole over 10,000 Sheep in Austral. & N.Z.* ii. 9 We had no 'leading' dog. **1933** L. G. D. ACLAND in *Press* (Christchurch, N.Z.) 4 Nov. 15/7 *Leading-dog*, a dog trained to run ahead of a mob of sheep to keep them steady. **1934** *Bulletin* (Sydney) 16 May 38/3 Rock, the kelpie leading-dog..had never possessed any aspirations towards leadership.

c. *leading-in* adj.: applied to a lead-in wire (of either kind: see *LEAD-IN 1 a, b).

1876 PREECE & SIVEWRIGHT *Telegraphy* vii. 224 The leading-in wire from the terminal pole, consists of a copper conductor insulated with gutta-percha, and well protected by a coating of tarred tape. **1885** *Phil. Mag.* XX. 141 The envelope may have deposited upon it a metallic film, derived from the leading-in wires to which the carbon filament is clamped. **1891** F. C. ALLSOP *Telephones* viii. 131 The leading-in wire is joined to the line-wire close to the last shackle or insulator. **1914** S. C. BATSTONE *Electr.-Light Fitting* vii. 138 G is a long glass stem through which the leading-in wires pass for connexion to the filament F. **1924** *Wireless World* 13 Aug. 543/1 (*heading*) Doing away with the leading-in wire. **1936** ORR & FORREST *Introd. Neon Lighting* i. 2 A lighting tube consists of a length of glass tubing bent to the shape required and closed at both ends. Into each end is inserted an electrode, usually in the form of a hollow cylinder of metal, to which are attached leading-in wires, which are carried to the outside of the tube through a vacuum-tight seal.

2. *leading aircraftman, hand*; *leading lady* (in a film), *man* (earlier example; also, in a film).

1827 L. REDE *Road to Stage* 16 The salary is generally first-rate—at all events next to that of the leading man. **1900** *Daily News* 20 Jan. 6/4 'The leading hand in the teak trade', as Mr. Kipling, père, calls the elephant. **1918** Leading lady [see *DOUBLE *v.* 1 e]. **1921** Leading aircraftman [see *AIRCRAFTMAN]. **1939** I. BAIRD *Waste Heritage* vii. 88 He hated the way Bette's leading man looked, all slicked-up and Hollywood. **1955** T. H. PEAR *Eng. Social Differences* vi. 159 Leading-hand, charge-hand.

leading article. **2. a.** (Later example.)

1877 W. S. GILBERT *Sorcerer* I. 15 Sir, it is our leading article.

leading edge. [LEADING *ppl. a.*] **1.** The forward edge of a moving body; also *transf.*; *spec.* (*a*) that of a blade of a screw-propeller; (*b*) that of a wing, tailplane, or other part of an aircraft; (*c*) that of one of the plates of the earth's crust.

1877 W. H. WHITE *Man. Naval Archit.* xiv. 579 When the plane is moved obliquely, its leading edge, corresponding to the forward edge of a rudder, may be regarded as continually entering water which was comparatively little disturbed by the previous motion. **1888** *Lockwood's Dict. Mech. Engin.* 205 *Leading edge*, that edge of the blade of a screw propeller which cuts the water, as distinguished from the following edge. **1912** *Aeroplane* 12 Dec. 592/1 Looking over the leading edge of the wings from a constant position the ground disappeared regularly. **1922** GLAZEBROOK *Dict. Appl. Physics* I. 364/1 That part [of the surface]..over which the particles of fluid are being gradually retarded—i.e. the part in the neighbourhood of the leading edge of the surface such as, for example, the immersed surface of a ship. **1939** *Archit. Rev.* LXXXVI. 63/2 At the 'leading edge' of each wing-like roof, the wooden slats with which it is faced are slightly separated to allow for..ventilation. **1946** TAYLOR & ALLWARD *Spitfire* 99/2 Special wings were fitted, the leading edge portion of each being constructed as a fuel tank. **1959** H. BARNES *Oceanogr. & Marine Biol.* i. 49 On sand, where there is considerable resistance to the leading-edge of either the mud bucket or naturalist's oval dredge, only a small sample is usually brought up and deeper burrowing animals frequently avoid capture. **1967** M. CHANDLER *Ceramics in Mod. World* vi. 177 For very high-speed aircraft the sharp leading edges of engines and wings will also probably have to be made of ceramic materials.

1971 I. G. GASS et al. *Understanding Earth* xx. 289/2 A plate whose leading edge is of continental material will gradually increase in size; for new crust will be added where oceanic crust is generated at its trailing edge but little or no continental crust is being consumed at the leading edge. **1972** *Sci. Amer.* Mar. 33/3 The drifting of the continents is another theme; every continent must have a leading edge and a trailing edge.

2. *Electronics.* The part of a pulse in which the amplitude increases.

1945 *Nature* 15 Sept. 319/2 The beginning or 'leading edge' of the pulse marks a packet of energy which can be re-identified after the vicissitudes of travel, thus permitting accurate measurement of time of travel. **1962** SIMPSON & RICHARDS *Physical Princ. Junction Transistors* vii. 139 In the amplification of small pulses with sharp leading and trailing edges the frequency range may be very broad. **1972** *Radio Times* 6 Jan. 5/3 Listeners may have noticed a change in the Greenwich Time Signals broadcast since January 1... The exact time is signalled by the beginning or 'leading edge' of the long pip.

leadish, *a.* (Later example.)

1784 *Maryland Jrnl.* 27 July (Th.), There are two great-coats missing, one of which is a leadish-coloured country cloth.

lea·d-off. [f. vbl. phr. *to lead off* (LEAD *v.*¹ 19).] (See LEAD *sb.*² 11.) Also *attrib.*

1886 H. BAUMANN *Londinismen* 94/2 *Lead-off*, Journalisten-Slang: erste(r) (gew. von einem bekannten Schriftsteller herrührender) Artikel. **1892** [in Dict. s.v. LEAD *sb.*² 11]. **1922** *Ardmore* (Okla.) *Daily Press* 6 May 3/3 His ability to judge close ones..make[s] him an ideal leadoff man. **1938** D. BAKER *Young Man with Horn* (1939) iv. 264 For 'Sam, the Old Accordian Man', it was to be a lead-off by Jeff. **1963** MRS. L. B. JOHNSON *White House Diary* 27 Dec. (1970) 22 Our foreman, Dale Malechek, took the lead-off bus... I took the second bus and Lynda..the third. **1970** *Toronto Daily Star* 24 Sept. 17/1 Morton.. was greeted by a Willie Stargell leadoff single.

lea·d-out. [f. vbl. phr. *to lead out.*] **1.** A leading out (in various senses).

1906 *Dialect Notes* III. 158 *Stag lead-out*, a dance-number in which only men who have not brought women dance with the women present. **1958** *Spectator* 3 Jan. 13/2 In stark contrast to the Zilliacus broadcasts these received an implied disavowal in the lead-in and lead-out.

2. *attrib.* or as *adj. Electronics.* Applied to a conductor by which current may enter or leave an electronic device.

1939 *Amat. Radio Handbk.* iii. 45/2 These valves..are ordinary valve types mounted in a metal bulb, welded or brazed together, having the lead-out wires passed through eyelets..mounted in the metal bulb. **1962** F. E. DUFFIELD in G. A. T. Burdett *Automatic Control Handbk.* ix. 17 Fig. 18 illustrates a single inductance type of pressure transducer... The lead-out wires are connected to a pair of sealed terminals. **1967** F. LANGFORD-SMITH *Radio-Designer's Handbk.* (ed. 7) 1484 The lead-out groove is reduced in length due to the smaller ending diameters. **1970** J. EARL *Tuners & Amplifiers* ii. 29 There are other types [of IC] which represent a component 'block'..with leadout wires or tags. Transistors usually have three lead-out wires..with a possible fourth connecting to a screen or shield.

lead-pipe. [See LEAD *sb.*¹ 10.] Used *attrib.* with *cinch* to denote a complete certainty. *U.S. colloq.*

1898 'J. KERR' *Cheery Bk.* 71, I never had a 'lead pipe cinch'; I never had a 'pull'; I never had a 'straight' that was not beaten by a 'full'. **1911** H. QUICK *Yellowstone Nights* xi. 288 Oh its a cinch, a timelock, leadpipe cinch! **1926** *Punch* 7 July 17/1 The Office of Works does not borrow money even to back what Americans call a lead-pipe cinch. **1949** N. ALGREN *Man with Golden Arm* 23 Not early enough to move no tables, that's a lead-pipe cinch. **1973** *N.Y. Times* 25 Feb. IV. 2/6 To be sure, speculation in gold is not a lead-pipe cinch; its price can go down as well as up.

lea·d-up. [f. vbl. phr. *to lead up* (cf. LEAD *v.*¹ 22).] Something that leads up to something else.

1953 M. T. MONRO *Thinking about Genesis* I. i. 26 The lead-up is the ordinary one by which we establish, on rational grounds alone, the existence of God, His attributes, [etc.]. **1959** D. COOKE *Lang. Mus.* iii. 145 The Beethoven is the short, breathless lead-up to the final jubilant outburst of the finale of the Choral Symphony. **1959** D. D. C. P. MOULD *Peter's Boat* vi. 78, I had occasion to go into..that country's great mediaeval cathedrals now in Protestant hands... Here was a setting, a magnificent lead-up in stone..pointing to one thing and one thing only, the Mass and the Blessed Sacrament. **1972** *Lebende Sprachen* XVII. 73/1 During the vital lead-up to first flights, acceleration and deceleration tests were made during taxying trials.

leadwork² (lī·dwɒ̄ɹk). Also **lead work.** [Origin unknown.] (See quot. 1900.)

Not connected with *lead-work* s.v. LEAD *sb.*¹ 12.

1900 E. JACKSON *Hist. Hand-made Lace* 213 *Lead works or lerd works*, terms used to indicate Modes or Fillings. Fancy stitches employed to fill in enclosed spaces in needle-point and bobbin laces. **1919** T. WRIGHT *Romance of Lace Pillow* ix. 70 A Lille ground..sprinkled with *dots* (*plaits, leadworks* or *points d'esprit* as they are called). **1953** M. POWYS *Lace & Lace-Making* iv. 26 Maltese Lace. This specimen has the leaf or lead work used as an ornamental filling.

leaf, *sb.*¹ Add: **4. a.** Also, the leaves of other plants used for smoking.

1972 *Guardian* 29 Jan. 9/2 Mr Williams had three previous convictions for possession of cannabis... 'A man ..let me have some leaf for five shillings.'

9. Delete 'Now only *dial.*' and add further examples. Also *U.S.*

1886 *Harper's Mag.* July 206/2 Lard, 'made from hog round, say head, gut, leaf, and trimming', is..in demand. **1904** L. L. LAMBORN *Cottonseed Products* 166 Neutral lard is composed of the fat derived from the leaf of the slaughtered animal. **1911** *Encycl. Brit.* XVI. 214/2 The finest quality [of lard], used for making oleomargarine, is got from the leaf. **1934** F. ALLEN in *Meat Trade* II. iv. 100 The following parts [of a pig] are removed: the back bone, the blade bone,.. and the flair or leaf. *Ibid.* 113 The leaf, or flair, of the pig is generally regarded as producing the best lard. **1955** W. G. R. FRANCILLON *Good Cookery* iii. 53 The leaf or caul (a lining of fat taken from the inside of the animal)..should be placed over the joint before baking.

10. b. Also, a thin piece of soap or other detergent (larger than a 'flake').

1925 G. MARTIN *Mod. Soap & Detergent Industry* II. I. ii. 35 Soap Leaves are prepared by passing continuous paper sheets over rollers through a hot solution of soap, the excess of soap attached to the surface being scraped off. The paper is then passed over drying cylinders and from thence to a cutting machine. **1959** *Which?* Nov. 152/2 There were differences between these shampoos and some of the powder or leaf varieties. *Ibid.* 154 Packet of 6 leaves.

c. One of the metal strips of a leaf spring.

1905 R. T. SLOSS *Bk. Automobile* vi. 124 The friction of the leaves decreases with the tension of the spring. **1936** F. CLUNE *Roaming round Darling* ix. 78 We left the car to have a couple of extra leaves inserted in the springs. **1971** B. SCHARF *Engin. & its Lang.* xii. 147 The individual leaves are free to slide along each other and adequate grease lubrication must be provided to minimise friction.

15*. The external portion of the ear of a mammal or the nasal appendage of a leaf-nosed bat.

1851 H. MELVILLE *Moby Dick* II. xxxii. 225 The ear [of a whale] has no external leaf whatever; and into the hole itself you can hardly insert a quill. **1955** *Times* 16 July 12/1 (*caption*) A forest-living bat, with a very large nose leaf..caught by members of the expedition to British Guiana.

16. a. *leaf-base, -cell, -point, -rib, -shape; leaf-stalk* (later examples) = PETIOLE 1.

1865 P. H. GOSSE *Land & Sea* 26 This plant [*sc.* a grass] grows in large stools or tussocks formed of the densely-matted leaf-bases of successive seasons. **1894** *Pop. Sci. Monthly* XLIV. 488 The huge leaf-bases [of the banana tree]..tightly inclose each other. **1965** BELL & COOMBE tr. *Strasburger's Textbk. Bot.* 158 In many leaves..the leaf base is not specially developed. **1875** HUXLEY & MARTIN *Course Elem. Biol.* 49 The terminal leaf-cell soon attaining its full size and not dividing. **1974** A. HUXLEY *Plant & Planet* vii. 57 In which vein the xylem and phloem fit together, so that the sugars from the leaf cells can be passed into the remainder of the plant. **1871** C. KINGSLEY *At Last* II. x. 71 The curving leaf-points toss in the breeze. **1895** KIPLING *Second Jungle Bk.* 141 The lighting shows each littlest leaf-rib clear. **1909** GROOM & BALFOUR tr. *Warming's Oecol. Plants.* III. xxviii. 99 The properties of water bring forth leaf-shapes entirely different from those of land-plants. **1946** *Nature* 13 July 64/1 When a leaf-shape is transferred from a late to an early flowering species the action of the gene is accelerated. **1946** F. E. ZEUNER *Dating Past* xii. 381 If one compares this example of an aromorph with the evolution, for instance, of a highly specialized protective character, such as the leaf-shape of a leaf-insect.., one realizes the difference between an aromorph and an ordinary adaptational character. **1895** *Daily News* 27 Dec. 7/1 Both evergreens and deciduous plants are subject to this process of separation at the bottom of the leaf stalk. **1970** ROBERTSON & GOODING *Bot. for Caribbean* (ed. 2) iii. 27 The petiole or leaf-stalk varies somewhat in length and shape.

b. *leaf-boring* adj. See also *leaf-miner, -mining* (LEAF *sb.*¹ 17); LEAF-CUTTER; LEAF-CUTTING *ppl. a.*

a **1887** R. JEFFERIES *Field & Hedgerow* (1889) 115 The coils and turns upon this leaf..are the work of a leaf-boring larva.

c. *leaf-crowned, -encumbered, -hid, -hung, -lined, -roofed* (later examples), *-shadowed, -whelmed* adjs.

1891 W. B. YEATS *Countess Kathleen* (1892) 125 And no one any leaf-crowned dancer miss. **1925** V. WOOLF *Mrs. Dalloway* 21 That leaf-encumbered forest, the soul. **1869** J. R. LOWELL *Under Willows* 52 Our leaf-hid Sybaris. **1895** W. B. YEATS *Poems* 16 Down in a leaf-hid, hollow place. **1919** V. WOOLF *Night & Day* xi. 145 They swept together among the leaf-hung trees of an unknown world. **1921** W. DE LA MARE *The Veil* 7 The listening, leaf-hung creek. **1895** *Outing* XXVI. 394/2, I filled one of our leaf-lined pails with berries. **1844** J. TOMLIN *Missionary Jrnls.* v. 120 The capital of Siam is a large, but not very magnificent city..consisting mainly of leaf-roofed wooden cottages. **1906** *Westm. Gaz.* 10 Sept. 2/3 Where the much-loved birds in their leaf-roofed halls Will herald my morning in. **1845** E. COOK *Poems* 2nd Ser. 187 The leaf-shadow'd thicket. **1868** J. R. LOWELL *Under Willows* (1869) 22 So they in their leaf-shadowed microcosm Image the larger world. *a* **1889** G. M. HOPKINS *Poems* (1918) 89 We are leafwhelmed somewhere with the hood Of some branchy bunchy bushybowered wood.

d. *leaf-dark, -dry, -eyed, -light, -shaped* (of an arrowhead) adjs.

1936 E. SITWELL *Victoria of Eng.* xix. 227 Their leaf-dark hair smoothed into the Chinese style. **1946** W. DE LA MARE *Traveller* 20 He caught but leaf-dry whisper of what they said. **1949** S. SPENDER *Edge of Being* 20 Behind the hedge of leaf-eyed lovers. **1971** B. PATTEN *Irrelevant Song* 51 Into myth she faded, Leaf-eyed. *c* **1879** G. M. HOPKINS *Poems* (1918) 44 Low-latched in leaf-light housel his too huge godhead. **1921** V. WOOLF *Monday or Tuesday* 37 Flaunted, leaf-light, drifting at corners, blown across the wheels. **1872** J. EVANS *Anc. Stone Implements Gt. Brit.* xvi. 333 Of leaf-shaped arrow-heads..there are several minor varieties. **1923** C. FOX *Archaeol. Cambr. Region* i. 4 Both the leaf-shaped and the tanged types [of arrowhead] commonly occur in the district. **1940** C. F. C. HAWKES *Prehist. Found. Europe* iii. 78 Hollow-based and leaf-shaped arrowheads..appear in the flint industry.

17. leaf-arrowhead, an arrowhead shaped like a leaf, usu. of the Neolithic period and made of flint (cf. *leaf-shaped* adj. s.v. sense 16 d above); **leaf-bed,** a layer of leaves sometimes found in the upper stratum of the earth's surface; **leaf blight,** one of several plant diseases causing the death of foliage; **leaf blister,** (*a*) a disease of certain fruit trees caused by a parasitic mite; (*b*) a plant disease caused by a fungus of the genus *Taphrina*; **leaf blotch,** one of several plant diseases indicated by discoloured patches on foliage, esp. = *BLACK SPOT 1; **leaf brown,** the colour of (dead) leaves; **leaf-bud** (later examples); **leaf cast** = *larch needle cast* (*LARCH 3); **leaf-cup,** (*c*) a leaf folded and used as a cup; **leaf curl,** one of several plant diseases characterized by curling leaves, esp. (*a*) = **leaf-roll*; (*b*) a disease of peach, almond, and nectarine trees caused by the fungus *Taphrina deformans*; (*c*) a virus disease of cotton; **leaf-drift,** a place where fallen leaves have been blown together by the wind; **leaf-fall,** (*b*) *Bot.*, the shedding of leaves by a plant; **leaf-fat** (later examples); **leaf gelatine,** gelatine manufactured in sheet form for cooking purposes; **leaf-house, -hut,** a house or hut made of entwined leaves; **leaf-lard** (earlier and later examples); **leaf-mass,** a thick growth of leaves; **leafmeal** [-MEAL] *adv.* (*nonce-wd.*), with leaves fallen one by one; **leaf-monkey,** a monkey found in south or south-east Asia belonging to one of several species of the genus *Presbytis*; = LANGUR; **leaf-mould,** (*b*) a disease of tomatoes caused by the fungus *Cladosporium fulvum*; **leaf-nosed** (earlier and later examples); **leaf-plate, -platter,** a leaf or leaves used as a plate or dish for food; **leaf protein,** protein, or a protein, present in leaves, esp. when extracted for use as a possible dietary supplement; **leaf-roll,** a virus disease of potatoes shown by curled-up leaves; **leaf scald,** (*a*) = **leaf scorch*; (*b*) a disease of sugar-cane caused by the bacterial pathogen *Xanthomonas albilineans*; **leaf-scar** (later examples); **leaf scorch,** a plant disease caused by a deficiency of potassium, causing leaves to shrivel and turn brown; also, a virus disease causing similar effects; **leaf-shedding,** (*a*) a disease of pine trees caused by the fungus *Hendersonia acicola*; pine needle cast; (*b*) = **leaf-fall* (*b*); **leaf shelter,** a shelter made of leaves; **leaf-skin,** (*a*) the membrane enclosing the leaf-fat; (*b*) the epidermis of a leaf; **leaf-spot,** one of a large number of plant diseases caused by various fungi which mark the foliage; also *attrib.*; **leaf spring,** a spring consisting of a number of strips of metal curved slightly upwards and clamped together one above the other, each strip being longer than the one beneath; so *leaf springing, -sprung* adj.; **leaf warbler,** a small green or yellow bird of the genus *Phylloscopus*, living in bushes or trees; **leaf-work** (later examples).

1954 S. PIGGOTT *Neolithic Cultures* iii. 99 Leaf-arrowheads are a common feature in Belgium. **1963** L. F. CHITTY in Foster & Alcock *Culture & Environment* vii. 188 Flints found range from a microlith and a leaf-arrowhead to a gun-flint. **1873** *Archæologia* XLIV. 278 The upper surface of the leaf-bed was well marked and level, as was also..the upper surface of the moss. **1894** *Nature* 26 July 295/1 If we could only meet with some fairly representative leaf-beds, such as abound in newer formations, the Wealden would yield a flora, both varied, and of enormous interest. **1954** S. PIGGOTT *Neolithic Cultures* x. 295 'Leaf bed' with no large vegetable remains, 3–4 ft. thick. **1850** *Rep. Comm. Patents 1849* (U.S.) 440 During the last summer our seedling pears were for the first time badly affected with 'leaf-blight'. **1920** P. J. FRYER *Insect Pests & Fungus Dis. Fruit & Hops* 709 Cherry and Plum Leaf Blight..appears to be slightly on the increase. **1926** [see *frog eye*]. **1960** C. WESTCOTT *Plant Dis. Handbk.* (ed. 2) 125 *Mystrosporium adustum.* Leaf Blight, Ink Spot of bulbous iris. **1914** F. C. SEARS *Productive Orcharding* xi. 159 Leaf Blister Mite.—Another pest which is frequently troublesome on both pears and apples is the blister mite. **1960** C. WESTCOTT *Plant Dis. Handbk.* (ed. 2) 194 A single genus, Taphrina,

is responsible for most of the hyperplastic (over-growth) deformities known as leaf blister, leaf curl, or, occasionally, as pockets. **1906** M. C. Cooke *Fungoid Pests Cultivated Plants* 75 Iris Leaf-blotch. **1925** *Gardeners' Chron.* 31 Oct. 353/3 (*heading*) A leaf blotch of the Shasta daisy. **1928** *Daily Express* 7 July 4/2 See that none of your favourites [*sc.* roses] is attacked by leaf blotch. **1971** *Country Life* 18 Feb. 389/2 The diseases of mildew, rust and leaf blotch are prevalent throughout Britain. **1923** *Daily Mail* 19 Feb. 1 (Advt.), French Model Jumper made of..Crepe de Chine,..Jade..Leaf Brown, Navy and Black. **1932** W. Faulkner *Light in August* xx. 444 Patches of Confederate grey weathered leafbrown now. **1906** *Westm. Gaz.* 14 Apr. 8/1 The lilac and elder-bushes.. are beginning to unfold their leaf-buds. **1971** *Country Life* 10 June 1440/2 The ash..never makes the mistake of opening its leaf buds before the last night frost. **1933** *Oxford Forestry Mem.* XV. 7 *Meria laricis* Vuillemin, the leaf cast disease of larch, which was first described by Mer in 1895..is probably the most important fungal disease of European larch in nurseries in this country. **1952** E. Ramsden tr. *Gram & Weber's Plant Dis.* iv. 482/1 Leaf cast is the worst disease of young larch trees. **1901** Kipling *Kim* x. 263 He bought sweetmeats in a leaf-cup from a Hindu trader. **1899** G. Massee *Text-bk. Plant Dis.* 82 The disease [of peaches], which is very widespread, is popularly known as 'leaf curl', or simply as 'curl', owing to the fact that the diseased leaves become much curled, distorted, and thickened. *Ibid.* 323 The well-known disease of the foliage of potatoes known as 'leaf curl' attacks the stem..and gradually creeps up. **1926** W. H. Johnson *Cotton* viii. 259 Upland cotton appeared to be less affected by a peculiar leaf-curl disease. **1951** *Dict. Gardening* (R. Hort. Soc.) III. 1654/2 The most common and probably the most serious [virus disease of potatoes] is Leaf Curl (Leaf Roll). **1965** Ripper & George *Cotton Pests Sudan* i. 7 Leafcurl is transmitted from ratoon cotton and wild host plants to cotton by whitefly. **1967** *Punch* 18 Jan. 96/3 It [*sc.* Burgundy mixture] is a good fungicide to use on leafless trees and bushes, particularly against leafcurl in the peach family. **1905** E. Phillpotts *Secret Woman* I. i. 6 While death, not unlovely, appeared in leaf-drift and touch-wood, in acorn cups..and hollow hazel-nuts. **1958** C. Tomlinson *Seeing is Believing* (1960) 60 And it continues Falling flaking into the leaf-drift. **1914** M. Drummond tr. *Haberlandt's Physiol. Plant Anat.* iii. 143 The arrangements [for peeling bark scales] resemble those which occur in leaf-bases in connection with the autumnal leaf-fall. **1947** G. F. Wilson *Detection & Control Garden Pests* vi. 107 Premature leaf-fall is associated with several factors other than pest attack. **1971** *Homes & Gardens* Sept. 128/2 Most of the cornus family colour richly before leaf-fall. **1845** J. J. Hooper *Some Adventures Simon Suggs* v. 65 They've knocked the leaf fat outen him tonight, in wads as big as mattock handles. **1904** L. L. Lamborn *Cottonseed Products* 166 In the packing plants the leaf fat is taken from the animal immediately after killing. **1956** C. Spry *Cookery Bk.* xxx. 957 The incorporation of gelatine with various liquids is much easier now that powdered or very fine leaf gelatine is sold. **1957** E. Craig *Collins Family Cookery* 606 Ten perfect sheets of French leaf gelatine equals 1 oz. **1953** A. Moorehead *Rum Jungle* vii. 107 Green-ants that stitch their leaf-houses together by holding their babies in their arms and drawing out of the babies' mouths a sticky thread. **1958** *Listener* 14 Aug. 237/1 Johnny and Silas were my two servants and lived in a leaf house near mine. **1910** W. de la Mare *Three Mulla-Mulgars* i. 8 He taught them..to build leaf-huts and huddles against heat or rain. **1949** M. Mead *Male & Female* x. 220 A leaky leaf-hut on the side of a mountain. **1848** *Rep. Comm. Patents 1847* (U.S.) 538 The articles thus referred to are put up in these establishments, from the hams..leaf lard [etc.]. **1885** W. L. Carpenter *Treat. Manuf. Soap* ii. 25 The fat immediately surrounding the kidneys yields the best and purest lard. This, and that which is obtained in flaky layers between the flesh and the skin.., is known as 'leaf' lard. **1888** W. T. Brannt *Pract. Treat. Animal & Veg. Fats & Oils* ix. 344 The leaf lard is.. kept separate from the rest. **1908** G. Jekyll *Colour in Flower Garden* vii. 60 We gradually return to the grey-blues, whites and pale yellows, with..the splendid leaf-mass of a wide and high plant of *Euphorbia Wulfenii*, which.. rises to a height far above my head. **1958** C. Tomlinson *Seeing is Believing* (1960) 20 Light, swept perpendicular Into the leaf-mass Flickers out. *c* **1880** G. M. Hopkins *Poems* (1918) 51 Though worlds of wanwood leafmeal lie. **1888** W. T. Blanford *Fauna Brit. India: Mammalia* I. 41 Phayre's Leaf-Monkey is found in dense high forests. **1928** *Jrnl. Bombay Nat. Hist. Soc.* XXXII. 472 (*title*) The langurs or leaf-monkeys of British India. **1966** R. & D. Morris *Men & Apes* viii. 236 Various species of leaf monkeys..frequent salt licks and saline mineral springs in Borneo. **1913** M. T. Cook *Dis. Trop. Plants* vii. 217 Leaf Mould..spreads rapidly. **1931** *Times Lit. Suppl.* 24 Sept. 734/4 Leaf-mould (*Cladosporium*) is a source of much loss to growers of the tomato. **1971** T. F. Preece in J. H. Western *Dis. Crop Plants* ii. 12 *Cladosporium fulvum*. Tomato leaf mould. **1843** *List Mammalia Brit. Mus.* 21 Redman's Leaf-nosed Bat. **1850** A. White *Pop. Hist. Mammalia* 47 The bats are arranged by Mr. Gray in two great divisions—the Leaf-nosed bats and the Simple-nosed bats. **1960** G. Durrell *Zoo in Luggage* ii. 61 A handful of leaf-nosed bats with extraordinary gargoyle-like faces. **1965** R. & D. Morris *Men & Snakes* viii. 178 (*caption*) The leaf-nosed snake, showing an unusual form of serpentine camouflage. *a* **1843** Southey *Commonplace Bk.* (1849) 2nd Ser. 422/1 *Leaf-plates.* 'Their plates and dishes are generally formed from the leaf of the plaintain tree or the nymphæa lotos... These are never used a second time.' **1962** B. Harrisson *Orang-Utan* ii. 57 You bend slightly over and down for mouth and fingers to meet above your leaf-plate. **1901** Kipling *Kim* xi. 281 'And we,' said Kim, turning his back and heaping a leaf-platter for the lama, 'are beyond all castes.' **1937** *Rep. Brit. Assoc. Adv. Sci. 1937* 459 Man also eats leaves to some extent,..and these leaves are quite high in protein. In this case there has been no selection of the leaf proteins by animal or plant, and it is probable that this leaf protein is intermediate in value to man between animal and other vegetable protein. **1953** *Jrnl. Agric. Sci.* XLIII. 136/1 Work on laboratory-extracted leaf protein suggests that such material might provide valuable protein feed as it contains many of the amino-acids essential for poultry nutrition. **1971** N. W. Pirie *Leaf Protein* xvi. 157 People habituated to leaf protein accept its flavour so that a larger proportion can be added to a food. *Ibid.*, Freshly made slabs of leaf protein disperse in water to give a smooth paste but slabs stored in deep-freeze gradually become gritty and have to be passed through a mill. **1972** Goodwin & Mercer *Introd. Plant Biochem.* ix. 236 The major part of the leaf protein is in the chloroplast. **1926** *Sci. Proc. R. Dublin Soc.* XVIII. 177 Twenty-nine halves or thirds of tubers.. were infested with aphides from diseased sprouts... Only two..became infected (with leaf-roll, the aphides being *Myzus pseudosolani*). **1946** *Nature* 14 Dec. 885/2 Bismark is resistant to leafroll. **1960** *Times* 29 July 12/6 The telltale curl..shows a potato plant has leafroll. **1899** G. Massee *Textbk. Plant Dis.* 276 (*heading*) Leaf scald. **1924** *Phytopathology* XIV. 587 (*title*) Java gum disease of sugar cane identical to leaf scald of Australia. **1965** G. C. Stevenson *Genetics & Breeding Sugar Cane* v. 147 Resistance of sugar cane species and hybrids to leaf scald disease..is very much complicated by the presence, in various countries, of several different strains of the parasite. **1897** J. C. Willis *Man. Flowering Plants* I. iii. 167 This [*sc.* the absciss layer] splits down the middle and leaves one half upon the stem, where it forms the *leaf scar* covering the wound. **1965** Bell & Coombe tr. *Strasburger's Textbk. Bot.* 167 In almost all woody plants the leaves..are sooner or later shed, leaving leaf scars on the stem showing their former positions. **1921** *Ann. Rep. Agric. & Hort. Res. Station Univ. Bristol* 121 The correlation which has been noted between the amount of potash supply, root growth and the degree of leaf scorch, points very definitely towards the liberal application of potash manures as a remedial measure. **1929** *Misc. Publ. Ministry Agric. & Fisheries* no. 70. 27 Leaf Scorch..was common on Mangolds in Devon and Cornwall in 1927, and on Sugar Beet in the East Midland and Eastern Provinces in the same year. **1933** *Jrnl. R. Hort. Soc.* LVIII. 253 Leaf scorch of apples is a deficiency disease. **1943** *Bull. Ministry Agric. & Fisheries* no. 126. 30 Leaf Scorch..was formerly attributed to *Sporidesmium putrefaciens* Fuckel but is now regarded..as a later and secondary symptom of Yellows. **1952** E. Ramsden tr. *Gram & Weber's Plant Dis.* iii. 342/2 Leaf Scorch (Potassium Deficiency). Potatoes that lack potassium produce a low-growing, rather dark, open haulm. **1961** *Amat. Gardening* 21 Oct. Suppl. 31/2 Leaf scorch. A common disorder of grapevines under glass, in which the leaves take on a shrivelled appearance. **1891** W. Schlich *Man. Forestry* II. 302 In many cases a fungus (*Hysterium pinastre*) is present, and may occasion the disease, which is called 'leaf-shedding'. **1895** *Daily News* 27 Dec. 7/1 With most evergreens the process of leaf-shedding is exactly the same as in the case of deciduous trees. **1937** *Discovery* Sept. 274/2 Two dilapidated leaf shelters. **1816** 'A. Singleton' *Lett.* (1824) 75 (Th.), Being born smokers, [the Negroes] make pouches of the inner leafskin of a swine, peeled thin, which is soft, transparent, and tough. **1974** A. Huxley *Plant & Planet* xxv. 281 Alpine rhododendrons..have very thick leaf-skins reinforced with silica. **1901** H. M. Ward *Dis. in Plants* xii. 114 If the fungus becomes epidemic and myriads of leaf-spots are formed, the destruction of foliar tissue..may end in rapid defoliation. **1908** *Jrnl. South-Eastern Agric. College, Wye* XVII. 316 (*title*) Leaf-spot diseases of the apple. **1933** *Jrnl. R. Hort. Soc.* LVIII. 280 Infected seed as a source of the celery leaf-spot is discussed. **1951** *New Biol.* XI. 78 The leaf-spot disease of bananas..was not recorded in the western tropics until 1934. **1972** *Arable Farmer* Feb. 55/1 Latest list of approved products..includes: Benlate (systemic fungicide from Du Pont for control of Botrytis in green beans and leaf spot in celery). **1893** *Funk's Stand. Dict.*, Leaf-spring. **1896** R. Grimshaw *Shop Kinks* 123 In finishing leaf-springs by grinding care should be taken that the grinding-marks run lengthwise. **1905** R. T. Sloss *Bk. Automobile* vi. 123 Leaf-springs seem to give the best results in automobile construction. **1935** *Times* 22 Oct. 9/2 In applying independent front wheel suspension some designers use coil springs and others leaf springs. **1967** *Autocar* 5 Oct. 73/3 He built the car without dampers, having read somewhere that inter-leaf friction in leaf springs might be sufficient damping. It wasn't. **1958** *Times* 26 Sept. 6/4 Air suspension is confined mostly to passenger-carrying vehicles, for the normal leaf springing is considered satisfactory for goods vehicles. **1973** *Times* 4 Oct. 43/3 All the cars have a leaf sprung back axle. **1926** T. A. Coward *Birds Brit. Isles* 122 (*heading*) The Leaf-Warblers. **1929** W. E. Glegg *Hist. Birds Essex* 71 The Willow-Warbler is a very common summer resident, increasing, and the most numerous of the Leaf-Warblers. **1953** B. Campbell *Finding Nests* vii. 96 The off-nest call [of the wood-warbler]..is easier to pick up than similar notes of the other leaf-warblers. **1974** *Lady* 2 May 622/3 Linnaeus did not distinguish all three common leaf-warblers. **1880** J. L. Warren *Guide to Study of Book-Plates* ii. 10 Outside the inscription is some rather fine leaf-work. **1937** *Burlington Mag.* Aug. 69/1 Decorated with the famous leafwork.

leaf (līf), *sb.*² *Services' slang.* Also **leef.** [Var. Leave *sb.* 1 e.] Leave of absence, furlough; = Leave *sb.* 1 e.

1846 *Punch* 3 Jan. 10/2 The shabby Capting (who seames to git leaf from his ridgmint whenhever he likes). **1904** Kipling in *Windsor Mag.* Dec. 4/1 What a lot of 'ard work one misses on leaf! **1916** 'Taffrail' *Pincher Martin* viii. 124 Wot's the good o' seven days' leaf ter a bloke wot ain't got no money? **1919** *Athenæum* 8 Aug. 729/1 The soldier going on short leave speaks usually of 'going on pass'; sometimes, however, of 'going on leaf'. Why in this phrase (nowhere else) the voiceless *f* is substituted for voiced *v* in 'leave' is a mystery to me. **1929** *Papers Mich. Acad. Sci., Arts & Lett.* X. 306 *Leef*, leave, pass, furlough. **1946** J. Irving *Royal Navalese* 107 *Leaf*, a corruption of Leave—leave of absence... A sailor goes 'on leaf' and *never* on furlough.

leaf, *v.* Add: **3. a.** Also used *intr.* and *fig.* and with *through,* to go through (a book or papers) by turning the leaves, usu. in a casual manner.

1929 *Publishers' Weekly* 19 Oct. 1928/2 There are.. plenty of people who..like to leaf through a book before buying. **1936** J. G. Cozzens *Men & Brethren* II. 175 Ernest..leafed over the remaining letters. **1936** L. C. Douglas *White Banners* xi. 245 He found the book, opened it on the table and leafed to the pictures he had found most amusing. **1953** *Encounter* Nov. 34/1 So it is possible to leaf through the Essays, reading a few pages and turning away at pleasure, as Montaigne himself read. **1960** 'R. East' *Kingston Black* x. 98 She went on leafing through the transcript. **1960** 'S. Harvester' *Chinese Hammer* i. 16 [He] leafed through an old issue of the *New Yorker.* **1973** W. M. Duncan *Big Timer* xxi. 141 He.. picked up a paper and leafed through it idly.

leafit. (Later *poet.* example.)

1916 Blunden *Harbingers* 60 The lopped tree, be it but stub or stock, Thrives, and begems its leafits in a year.

leaflet, *sb.* Add: **2.** *spec.* the thin flap of a valve in the heart or a blood vessel. (Later examples.)

1936 G. R. Herrmann *Synopsis Dis. Heart & Arteries* xvii. 254 The degrees to which valvular lesions develop depend upon the extent of the allergic or inflammatory processes and the trauma to which these inflamed leaflets are subjected at the time and during the healing processes. **1961** R. D. Baker *Essent. Path.* xiv. 333 Uncomplicated insufficiency occurs when the valve leaflets are held against the wall of the heart or of the great vessels or when the ring of the valve is dilated.

3. b. *attrib.* and *Comb.*, as *leaflet literature, party, writer*; **leaflet raid,** a raid in which leaflets are dropped from an aircraft; also *transf.*; so *leaflet drop.*

1903 *Westm. Gaz.* 13 Aug. 2/3 Mr. C. A. Vince, M.A., chief leaflet-writer to Mr. Chamberlain. **1904** *Ibid.* 21 Jan. 2/1 Not even the profuse distribution of Birmingham leaflet literature can alter this fact. **1940** *Flight* 11 Apr. 337/1 This same officer commanded the Whitley which made the first leaflet raid over Berlin. **1940** Harrisson & Madge *War begins at Home* vii. 148 The first leaflet raid —in which the R.A.F. dropped 6,000,000 leaflets over Germany. **1943** Koestler *Arrival & Departure* III. 94 That is why I took part in those leaflet-parties, though it was not my job. **1961** *Guardian* 11 Nov. 1 (*caption*) Leaflet raid on Lisbon. **1969** *Listener* 31 July 145/2 We would send our lecturers out into the fringes of the jungle to soften people up, we would have special leaflet drops before the troops went in. **1974** *Times* 13 Nov. 2/6 Miners from the Nottinghamshire coalfield..made leaflet raids to pits in South Yorkshire.

leaflet (lī·flėt), *v.* [f. Leaflet 3.] *trans.* and *intr.* To distribute leaflets to (people or places). Hence **lea·fleting** *vbl. sb.*

1962 *Spectator* 24 Aug. 268/3 Thousands of campaigners will be putting this case..by leafletting and pamphleteering. **1968** *Peace News* 25 Oct. 5/3 Civilians who originally had tried to leaflet on bases were quickly kicked off. **1969** C. Davidson in Cockburn & Blackburn *Student Power* 361 We should make our presence felt everywhere —in the campus news media, leafletting and poster displays. **1969** *Oxf. Univ. Gaz.* XCIX. Suppl. VII. 156 The Proctors announced the withdrawal of the regulation prohibiting indiscriminate leafleting. **1972** *Listener* 27 Jan. 119/2 Tariq Ali..refers to the question whether factories should be leafleted. **1973** *Daily Tel.* 9 June 2/8 Our friends in Germany and elsewhere will be encouraged to leaflet British soldiers stationed there. **1973** C. Mullard *Black Brit.* I. iii. 33 The new group were people willing to leaflet, organize and demonstrate.

leafleteer (līflėtīə·ɹ). [f. Leaflet 3 + -eer.] A writer of leaflets; the author of a leaflet. (Often contemptuous.)

1892 *Sat. Rev.* 16 July 70/2 It..is written in clear, plain, simple English, the only 'leaf' we could wish our leafleteers to take from this example. **1903** *Westm. Gaz.* 6 Oct. 2/2 We do not in the least mind Professors becoming leafleteers if so they must. **1970** *Sunday Tel.* 14 June 8/2 The leafleteers have fairly polluted the streets this time.

league, *sb.*¹ Add: **b.** *league-wide* adj. (*poet.*).

1843 J. R. Lowell *Prometheus* in *Poems* (1844) 83 The vast Sarmatian plain, league-wide. **1848** —— *Columbus* in *Poems* 2nd Ser. 11 Some league-wide river. **1951** W. de la Mare *Winged Chariot* 56 Life's league-wide cornfields. **1957** R. Campbell *Coll. Poems* II. 254 Across a league-wide valley, white with sprays.

league, *sb.*² Add: **1. b.** *the League* = *League of Nations.

1917 H. N. Brailsford *League of Nations* 324 Without the firm resolve to make the League itself an article, and the first article, in the settlement, our need of security will drive us inevitably to other expedients. The settlement, unless the idea of the League penetrates it and inspires it, must draw its principle from the older state-craft of anarchy and force. **1919** J. M. O'Sullivan in *Studies* Dec. 577 Had not the basal idea of the League been thus early repudiated. **1936** A. Huxley *Let.* 2 Mar. (1969) 401 The..atmosphere wd be cleared and a chance given for the reconstruction of the League on a more satisfactory basis. **1944** J. S. Huxley *On Living in Revolution* iii. 32 The failure of the League merely served to underline the urgent need for *some* international political organization. **1950** Theimer & Campbell *Encycl. World Politics* 260/1 The Assembly did not meet again until April 1946, when it decided to dissolve the League, already replaced by the United Nations. **1952** *Oxf. Jun. Encycl.* X. 212/2 When the United States Congress repudiated President Wilson's proposals and failed to join the League, its hope of real success was small. **1971**

W. H. McNeill in A. Bullock *20th Cent.* 47/1 Should a government defy the League..all the League members would be obliged to..check aggression by imposing sanctions.

c. *Football League* (earlier and later examples). Similarly, *Baseball, Cricket League*. Also ellipt. *League*.

1879 *Chicago Tribune* 17 May 7/5 A misunderstanding has arisen as to the condition of the Cleveland Club, and its inability to play, which will end in an appeal to the League. **1891** *Amer. Cricket Annual* 10 The organisation of the Metropolitan District Cricket League was certainly a move in the right direction. **1892** *Athletic News Cricket Ann.* 51 Lancashire Cricket League... This organisation..has done for cricket what the League has done for football. **1892** J. A. Leighton (*title*) Leighton's North-Western Rugby Football League card. Season 1892–93. **1910** *Encycl. Brit.* IX. 622/1 In 1888 the Football League, a combination of professional clubs of the north and midlands of England, was formed. **1921** A. Huxley *Crome Yellow* ii. 13 All the players in all the teams of the League. **1930** J. Williamson *Amer. Hotel* 293 The Broadway Central has been the scene of several noteworthy episodes. It was there that the National League was organized in 1876. **1935** *Encycl. Sports* 187/2 A number of [cricket] clubs form themselves into a league; each plays all the others in turn, and the championship of the league falls to the one which wins the most matches. *Ibid.* 292/2 The first league, the Football League, was then formed [in 1888]. **1951** *Football Record* (Melbourne) 8 Sept. 12 Approximately 300 visiting schoolboys were recently entertained by the League at the Melbourne ground. **1957** *Encycl. Brit.* III. 159/2 The professional [baseball] clubs usually compete as members of leagues. **1960** B. Liddell *My Soccer Story* vii. 48 For years the Football Association and the Football League have been trying to help players to prepare for the new life ahead when they finish with football. **1969** *Listener* 20 Mar. 384/2, I cannot believe he would still maintain that Rugby League backs 'usually run across instead of straight'. **1973** *News of the World Football Ann. 1973–74* 78 (*heading*) Football League—Division One. *Ibid.* 100 Re-elected to Division [One] when League was extended after the war. **1974** *Daily Record* (Glasgow) 15 Apr. 27/2 Yesterday Stein admitted, 'The League is almost won. We know that!' **1974** *Guardian* 1 Aug. 22/8 It is not possible to be wrapped up in all the competitions and win them as the League exists at present.

e. *transf.* and *fig.* Cf. *big league* s.v. *big *a.* B. 2.

1935 J. T. Farrell *Judgment Day* viii. 185 You better go back and play in a grammar-school league. **1959** N. Mailer *Advts. for Myself* (1961) 389 You want to keep a girl who was born to travel in a big league. **1961** *Listener* 12 Oct. 547/1 At the Riga brewery..I saw a notice board with the photographs of the twelve workers who were topping the production league. **1965** *Listener* 23 Sept. 446/1 The English-speaking peoples are excellent at breakfasts, but after that they would scarcely claim to stand high in the gastronomic league. **1966** J. Chamier *Cannonball* xii. 115 She's out of your league, me lad, and you'll take a most almighty toss. **1970** *Washington Post* 30 Sept. B. 4/3 In such a league Paul Mellon has impeccable collections. **1971** *Austral. Seacraft* June 17/2 To join the big league [in speedboating]. **1971** *Where* Oct. 293/2 Neill has a lightness of touch, and a flair for comedy that were in the Wodehouse league. **1972** *New Society* 27 Jan. 187/1 Rory Gallagher, a minor league superstar blues guitarist. **1972** 'M. Yorke' *Silent Witness* v. 121 She was bored because he obviously wasn't in her league. **1973** *Times* 22 Feb. 5/3 The latest incident is not in the same league as the apparently endless series of espionage scandals in and around Bonn in 1968 and 1969.

3*. *Basket-making*. (See quots.)

1903 T. Okey in R. M. Jacot *Useful Cane Work* I. p. ix, When a single continuous cane is used as a combined bottom stick and stake it is termed a 'League'. **1910** *Encycl. Brit.* III. 482/2 When the 'bottom-stick' and 'stake' are formed of one and the same continuous rod, it is termed a 'league'.

4. (sense 1 c) *league championship, club, cricket, football* (hence *league footballer*), *match, player, star, system*; **league table**, a list of the members of a league in ranking order; also *transf.*, a systematic comparison of performance in any field of competitive activity.

1901 *Dundee Advertiser* 4 Jan. 6 That [*sc.* Guiseley] Club winning the League championship. **1969** *Official Baseball Rules* 16 The League is a group of clubs whose teams play each other in a pre-arranged schedule under these rules for the league championship. **1972** G. Green *Great Moments in Sport: Soccer* iv. 58 The previous season Chelsea had won the League Championship of the First Division. **1938** C. E. Sutcliffe et al. *Story of Football League* 14 A meeting of the League clubs was held on 8th February, 1909. **1973** *News of the World Football Ann. 1973–74* 163 (*heading*) Oldest League Clubs. **1961** F. C. Avis *Sportsman's Gloss.* 125/2 *League Cricket*, that organized, outside the county championship, etc., in competitive league groups, e.g. the Central Lancashire League. **1910** T. Charnley *Let.* 13 Jan. in C. E. Sutcliffe et al. *Story of Football League* (1938) 15 Reports are continually being received that the many unfair and unscrupulous tactics indulged in by some of the players engaged in League football are allowed to pass unpunished by the referees. **1959** I. & P. Opie *Lore & Lang. Schoolch.* xvi. 350 The mid-century schoolchild's sporting enthusiasms are more taken up with league football, [etc.]. **1951** *Football Record* (Melbourne) 8 Sept. 18 Congratulations to Ron Clegg, who won the..award for the best League footballer of 1951. **1909** A. Bennett *Matador* (1912) 30 Knype had yet five League matches to play. **1973** *Irish Times* 2 Mar. 3/2 Cup ties are very different to league matches. **1886** H. Chadwick *Art of Pitching & Fielding* 132 The following are the best fielding averages of the Eastern League players. **1938** C. E. Sutcliffe et al. *Story of Football League* 12 The forces outside the League were..ready to take away League players without paying anything for them. **1967** *Australian* 26 Apr. 12 Injuries to many League stars. **1902** *Encycl. Brit.* XXVIII. 425/2 An elaboration of this competition is the 'League system' of the Association game. This..has not been popular with Rugby players. Still it is prevalent in many districts... In the League system a certain number of clubs form a league to play one another twice each season; two points are counted for a win, and one for a draw. The club which at the end of the season comes out with most points wins the competition. **1912** *Football Chart* (G. F. Stirling, Liverpool), Note position of Club each week in League Table and mark the ups or downs. **1930** *Daily Express* 6 Oct. 16 (*heading*) Saturday's League results and tables. **1959** *Times* 19 Mar. 12/2 He also recited with telling effect a 'league table' of unemployment percentages in western countries, ending with Great Britain as the lowest of all. **1967** Coulthard & Smith in Wills & Yearsley *Handbk. Managem. Technol.* 205 Large and expensive personnel departments, which maintain extensive records, card indexes, files, annual appraisal systems, charts, league tables, and so on. **1970** F. C. Avis *Soccer Dict.* (ed. 3) 57 *League table*, the statement of teams in relation to each other during the season, [etc.]. **1972** *Human World* May 3 In 1971 they were half way up the 'league table' of wages instead of near the top. **1972** *Times* 11 July 2/7 A league table of tar and nicotine in most brands of cigarettes seems certain to be produced. **1973** C. Bonington *Next Horizon* ix. 131 Already a healthy element of competition was springing up between the big league climbers of the Alpine countries... This was a little like a League Table, which we all examined with care as we decided what to do next.

League of Nations. An association of self-governing states, dominions, and colonies created by a covenant forming part I of the Peace Treaty of 1919 'in order to promote international co-operation and to achieve international peace and security'. *League of Nations Society* (*later Union*): a society formed to promote the principles of the League of Nations.

1917 H. N. Brailsford (*title*) A League of Nations. *Ibid.* ii. 37 The programme of the British 'League of Nations Society' is as follows. **1917** A. Huxley *Let.* 30 Sept. (1969) 133, I have spent the morning in correcting.. essays on the possibility..of a League of Nations. **1919** *League of Nations Jrnl.* Jan. 1 The Union..Resulting.. from the amalgamation of the League of Nations Society and of the League of Free Nations Association,..includes members of a society which has been working since May, 1915, for the establishment of a League of Nations, and of a new and vigorous association which was inaugurated in the summer of 1918. **1919** *Treaty of Peace* (H.M.S.O.) xii. art. 376 Disputes which may arise..shall be settled as provided by the League of Nations. **1922** *Encycl. Brit.* XXII. 647/2 Perhaps the most important event which happened in Switzerland in 1920 was the first meeting of the League of Nations in Geneva. *a* **1930** D. H. Lawrence *Phoenix II* (1968) 442 He was the scourge of *God*: not the scourge of the League of Nations, hired and paid in cash. **1934** H. G. Wells *Exper. Autobiogr.* II. ix. 694 The term 'League of Nations' is of English origin and it seems to have been first used by a small group of people meeting in the house of Mr. Walter Rea... (E. M. Forster in his life of Lowes Dickinson (1934) gives reasons for ascribing the term to that writer, who may have used it for the two possible 'leagues' he sketched in the first fortnight of the war.) These people founded a League of Nations Society, with Lord Shaw as president, early in 1915. **1957** *Encycl. Brit.* XIII. 832/2 The League of Nations was legally inaugurated on Jan. 10, 1920. *Ibid.*, Pres. Woodrow Wilson espoused the cause of a league of nations in May 1916. **1971** W. H. McNeill in A. Bullock *20th Cent.* 47/2 Most of these lands were designated League of Nations 'mandates'.

leaguer, *sb.*[2] (Later examples.)

1943 M. Ward *G. K. Chesterton* (1944) xxvi. 435 Many leaguers..felt..that the spirit of criticism of others was too fully developed. **1949** M. L. Darling *At Freedom's Door* I. ii. 52 In this year's election he stood as a Unionist, and like most Unionists was defeated by a Leaguer. **1970** *Cape Times* 28 Oct. 26/2 There are few American major leaguers earning less than $30 000 a year.

leaguer, *sb.*[3] **b.** (Later S. Afr. examples.)

1881 F. R. Statham *Blacks, Boers, & British* iv. 61 You want to see what can be done with South African wine?.. Visit a great airy shed not far from the Cape Town docks, ..the rough and ready wine has become—what? Look at it and see it as it is drawn from the huge casks—leaguers they call them here. **1959** *Cape Times* 14 Mar. 2/6 Two lorries, one carrying a 5-leaguer tank of wine (some 800 gallons) collided here yesterday. **1970** *Ibid.* 28 Oct. 20/3 (Advt.), A wine quota of 320 leaguers.

leaguite (lī·gəit). Also **leagueite.** [f. League *sb.*[2] + -ite[1].] = Leagueist.

1841 *Times* 4 Feb. 5/4 The leagueites polled 9 dead men. **1892** E. Dowson *Let.* 22 Nov. (1967) 253 It seeming to be very much confined to the actual Leaguites themselves.

leak, *sb.* Add: **1. c.** *Electr.* A path or component of relatively high resistance through which a small current flows.

1896 T. E. Herbert *Electricity in Application to Telegr.* xvii. 81 B is connected to earth as is the end of our 40 ohm leak. **1919** [see *grid leak* (*grid 5 b)]. **1940** *Amat. Radio Handbk.* (ed. 2) ii. 33/2 The grid will take up a potential such that the current from grid to filament equals the current through the leak in either the positive or negative half cycle. **1966** [see *grid leak* (*grid 5 b)].

d. An improper or deliberate disclosure of information (e.g. for political purposes).

1950 H. D. Lasswell *National Security* ii. 34 Americans are accustomed to 'government by leak'. **1957** *Economist* 28 Sept. 1004/2 The allegation of a 'leak' about last Thursday's increase in Bank rate has brought forth understandable indignation from those City dealers whose fingers were burned, and an equally understandable demand by the Labour Party for a full inquiry. **1960** L. Cooper *Accomplices* I. ii. 17 Confidential stuff about a security leak from one of our research stations. **1960** *News Chron.* 30 Apr. 4/2 No agenda, no communiqué, no inspired leaks. **1965** H. Kahn *On Escalation* iii. 56 In.. 1964, the United States and the Chinese engaged in a series of such semiformal leaks and announcements about the war in Vietnam. **1967** *Punch* 4 Oct. 509/3 Long among the most skilled practitioners of leak journalism. **1973** *Guardian* 10 Apr. 15/3 The EEC Commission spent an hour and a half..discussing leaks and how to plug them (or so it is reliably leaked to Miscellany).

2. b. *Electr.* Leakage of electric charge or current (see *leakage 2 b).

1863 R. S. Culley *Handbk. Pract. Telegr.* iv. 65 Suppose..a fault to occur connecting the wire to the earth, and offering a resistance equal to that of 20 miles of the line. This 'leak' will lessen the total resistance of the circuit..as if a wire 20 miles long..were fixed to the line at the fault. **1893** [see *leakance]. **1895** [in Dict., sense 2]. **1906** *Phil. Mag.* XII. 403 With very thin paper..no discharge could be observed, whilst in the case of aluminium leaf 0·0005 mm. in thickness a difference in the rate of leak was observed. **1939** *Post Office Electr. Engineers' Jrnl.* XXXII. 138 (*heading*) The localization of small leaks in the underground transmission line system at Cooling Radio Station.

c. *slang.* An act of urination. Freq. in phr. *to take a leak*, to urinate. Cf. Leak *v.* 2 c.

1934 H. Miller *Tropic of Cancer* 182, I stood there taking a leak. **1968** K. Weatherly *Roo Shooter* 111, I saw Sam get out of the Rover... I thought he'd got out for a leak. **1969** G. Greene *Trav. with my Aunt* II. vi. 282 All these hours of standing without taking a leak. **1972** F. Raphael *April, June & Nov.* 283 'The guest toilets at the Palace aren't really all that marvellous.' '..Thanks for the tip, I'll remember to take a leak before I go next time.'

3. leak detector, any device for detecting leaks of fluid; **leak-proof** *a.*, not subject to leaks.

1921 *Chambers's Jrnl.* July 454/2 Each bag..is inflated with air and examined all over its surface with leak-detectors. **1968** *Non-Destructive Testing* I. 215/1 Shell have developed a portable hydrocarbon leak detector to facilitate the overhaul of [gas] mains. **1926** *Kitchen Kook* (Amer. Gas Mach. Co. Inc.) 3 The fuel..is contained in an electrically welded, leakproof, steel tank. **1929** *Daily Express* 8 Jan. 8/5 Waste heat in leak-proof pipes to towns near the coalfields. **1960** *Farmer & Stockbreeder* 15 Mar. 44/2 (*caption*) It's leakproof. **1971** *Engineering* Apr. 92/2 (Advt.), Instant..safe..leakproof joints... A pipeline which is flexible while remaining absolutely leak-proof.

leak, *v.* Add: **1.** (Examples relating to electric charge: cf. *leak *sb.* 2 b, *leakage 2 b.)

1863 R. S. Culley *Handbk. Pract. Telegr.* vii. 106 The dampness of the insulators enables part of the electricity to leak or escape from one wire to another, and to the earth. **1917** G. D. Shepardson *Telephone Apparatus* xiv. 224 Little talking current 'leaked' through the signaling equipment. **1959** *Which?* Winter 37/1 If there is a fault in an electrical appliance and current leaks to the exposed parts.

b. (Earlier U.S. examples.)

1832 Webster, *To leak out*,.. to escape privately from confinement or secresy; as a fact or report. **1834** S. Smith *Sel. Lett. J. Downing* 58 If it should leak out that I was going.

2. c. Delete *Obs.* and add later examples.

1957 J. Kerouac *On Road* (1958) 90 The prowl car came by and the cop got out to leak. **1971** D. E. Westlake *I gave at the Office* (1972) 173, I kept thinking he'd come back from the john—how long can one man leak?

4. c. To allow the disclosure of (secret or confidential information). (Cf. sense 1 b and *leak *sb.* 1 d.) Also *intr.* Hence **leaked** *ppl. a.*

1859 G. W. Matsell *Vocabulum* 50 *Leak*, to impart a secret. **1916** W. Owen *Let.* Aug. (1967) 402 Here I am beginning to 'Leak information', (when I have to read daily a solemn W.O. Letter, saying that no talk of the War is ever to be indulged in, even in private letters.) **1954** *Encounter* June 11/1 In practice [the dial number] was a secret in name only, since supervisors were instructed to 'leak' the number 'confidentially' to various employees. **1958** *Punch* 3 Nov. 10/3 It seemed pretty clear from what the F.O. had leaked to us that Bonaparte had crossed the Niemen. **1958** *Ann. Reg. 1957* 195 In a miscalculated effort to prepare the public and Congress for the new doctrine, it had been deliberately 'leaked' well beforehand. **1959** *John o' London's* 26 Nov. 265/3 A.. U.S. Air Force sergeant..promptly scares off the circling sharks by leaking information about her non-existent husband. **1962** *Listener* 25 Oct. 647/2 The Council Fathers are supposed to maintain complete discretion, though almost all of them 'leak' to the press. **1971** *Daily Tel.* 14 July 3/4 It was not sufficient for the tribunal merely to establish by whose hand information..was improperly leaked. **1972** *Times* 30 Sept. 3/1 Legislation covering 'leaked' information is proposed by the Franks Committee on Official Secrets. **1973** [see *leak *sb.* 1 d].

leakage. Add: **2.** (Later examples.) Add to def.: improper or deliberate disclosure of information from an office, etc.; unexplained continuous disappearance of something.

1859 'T. Titcomb' *Titcomb's Lett.* (ed. 12) ii. 185 It is entirely rational and right that your wife should understand the basis of all your requirements of her; and when

she does this, the chances are that she will not only be economical herself, but will point out leakages in your prosperity for which you are responsible. **1880** E. W. HAMILTON *Diary* 30 Nov. (1972) I. 83 There have of late curiously been some leakages. My own belief is that men like Chamberlain and Forster..are most unguarded in their language outside. **1890** *Daily News* 17 Oct. 7/2 It was discovered that there was a 'leakage' in the stamp transfer forms. **1894** *Westm. Gaz.* 19 Sept. 3/3 That leakage from the faith which is taking place among the poor Catholics. **1898** *Daily News* 17 Feb. 2/7 The prizes.. for three best essays on the cause of the leakage in the membership of the Methodist Church,.. have been awarded. **1898** *Ibid.* 20 Oct. 6/5 Some extracts..have found their way into the pages of the 'New York Critic'... I am unable..to account for this leakage. **1900** *Edin. Rev.* July 81 The tide of emigration has been stayed..the leakage is diminishing. **1904** A. B. F. YOUNG *Compl. Motorist* 347/2 Leakage of small moneys, during travel. **1908** H. G. WELLS *War in Air* i. 25 Mr. K. Butteridge.. intended to keep his secret safe from any further risk of leakage. **1945** E. WAUGH *Brideshead Revisited* 10 Our new commanding officer was making an unusual display of 'security'... 'If I find any of these female camp followers waiting for us the other end, I'll know there's been a leakage.' **1972** *Times* 30 Sept. 1/1 The [Franks] committee proposes an Official Information Act to cover leakage of information which would seriously injure the national interest. **1973** A. CHRISTIE *Postern of Fate* III. xvii. 248 There were leakages—as always there are leakages in time of war.

b. *Electr.* A gradual escape of charge or current, esp. as a result of imperfect insulation. Also, in *Magnetism*, an escape of flux from a magnetic circuit or device; flux which does not pass through the secondary of a transformer or induction coil, or through the armature of a motor or generator.

1863 R. S. CULLEY *Handbk. Pract. Telegr.* iv. 59 On a long line the leakage from wire to wire through damp air cannot be altogether without effect. **1902** *Encycl. Brit.* XXVII. 586/2 Since no substance is impermeable to the passage of magnetic flux, the only form of magnetic circuit free from leakage is one uniformly wound..over its whole length. **1922** GLAZEBROOK *Dict. Appl. Physics* II. 190/1 Allowance must be made for flux which leaks across the intervening space between the poles and does not actually enter the armature, and a magnetic circuit has to be designed so as to keep this leakage as small as possible. **1962** *Newnes Conc. Encycl. Electr. Engin.* 229/1 Danger from leakage may be prevented on metal pole lines by a continuous earth wire connected to the poles. **1962** D. F. SHAW *Introd. Electronics* i. 7 If the coil is long enough for the solenoid formula to apply there will be a considerable leakage of flux between the turns.

5. *attrib.*, as (sense *2 b) *leakage current, flux, path*; also **leakage conductance** *Electr.* = *LEAKANCE; **leakage detector**, (a) = *leak detector* (s.v. *LEAK sb. 3); (b) = *leakage indicator*; **leakage indicator** *Electr. Engin.*, any device for indicating or measuring leakage currents flowing to earth.

1887 *Electrician* 3 June 80/2 The attenuation factor is now $\epsilon^{-R/2Lv}.\epsilon^{-K/2Sv}$, if K be the leakage conductance, and S the permittance per unit length. **1880** *Jrnl. Soc. Telegr. Engin.* IX. 456 The additional term $(v/i)dx$ is the leakage current of dx, viz., the potential of dx divided by its insulation resistance. **1962** J. BELL in G. A. T. Burdett *Automatic Control Handbk.* iv. 3 The insulation to earth must be maintained in the megohms region otherwise the inaccuracy due to leakage currents will be significant. **1880** *English Mechanic* Oct. 107/3 Cowan's meters, and Mr. Young's..leakage-detector are prominent exhibits [at the Exhibition of Gas and Electrical Apparatus]. **1901** *Catal. Mech. Engin. Collection Sci. Div. V. & A. Mus.* (ed. 3) I. 220 Leakage detector... This is an instrument for rendering audible the slight sound made by water flowing in a pipe, so that if the noise continues, after certain valves are closed, the existence of a leak is indicated. **1923** MEARES & NEALE *Electr. Engin. Pract.* (ed. 4) I. xv. 499 In the Howard leakage detector a current transformer is connected in the earthing wire of, say, a switchboard frame, and the secondary of the current transformer is connected to a tripping relay. **1971** *Instruments & Exper. Techniques* XIV. 830 The leakage detector operates in stable fashion when the pickup is situated in a high vacuum. **1896** F. BEDELL *Princ. Transformer* xv. 302 The leakage flux varies inversely as the reluctance of the leakage path. **1962** CORSON & LORRAIN *Introd. Electromagn. Fields* vii. 291 Let us consider a toroid of magnetic material with a localized winding... The leakage flux, that is, the flux of **B** which leaves the core, produces poles on the surface..and these poles contribute an intensity **H** within the iron. **1920** *Whittaker's Electr. Engineer's Pocket-Bk.* (ed. 4) 276 The function of a leakage indicator is to provide information as to the insulation resistance of the whole of the electrical system ..to which it is connected. **1958** J. L. WATTS *Electr. Maintenance & Repairs* iii. 43 Where the supply is obtained from a three-wire d.c. system with earthed midpoint, a suitable differential ammeter connected across shunts in the positive and negative mains will serve as a leakage indicator. **1896** Leakage path [see *leakage flux* above]. **1909** *Installation News* III. 64/1 The leakage path to the conduit or earth is now very greatly reduced. **1962** *Newnes Conc. Encycl. Electr. Engin.* 437/1 It is usual to assume that those parts of a leakage path lying in ferromagnetic material will require a negligible proportion of the coil m.m.f.

leakance (lī·kăns). *Electr.* [f. LEAK v. + -ANCE as a shortening of *leakage conductance*.] Conductance attributable to leakage or imperfect insulation.

1893 O. HEAVISIDE *Electromagn. Theory* I. 453 A process..of representing a large number of separate leaks by

uniform leakance. *Ibid.*, Distribute the inductive leakance uniformly, in imagination, of course. **1928** BRADFIELD & JOHN *Telephone & Power Transmission* ii. 18 Since the insulation of the circuit..can never be perfect, there must be a certain leakance from wire to wire,..stated in 'mhos', or sometimes in 'micro-mhos' per mile of loop. *Ibid.* iv. 55 The leakance of aerial circuits varies irregularly between wide limits, owing to weather and other conditions. **1962** *Newnes Conc. Encycl. Electr. Engin.* 845/1 Leakance and capacitance effects are large [in telecommunication lines], so that the attenuation is much higher than could be tolerated in power transmission.

leaking, *vbl. sb.* (Later examples.)

1973 *Time* 16 Apr. 53/2 The leaking and publication of classified information has always been a murky area in criminal law. **1973** *Listener* 15 Nov. 658/1 There was.. some leaking to the Arabs from perhaps two EEC capitals, which had disclosed to them the line the Dutch had been taking in confidential Community discussions.

leaky, *a.* Add: **d.** *Electr.* Retaining electric charge only with gradual loss; connected to or having a high resistance that acts as a 'leak'; *leaky-grid detection*, detection in which the signal is applied to the grid of a valve through a series capacitor and a resistor (the latter being connected as a grid leak or in parallel with the capacitor).

1904 A. RUSSELL *Treat. Theory Alternating Currents* I. xvii. 384 (*heading*) Inductive coil and leaky condenser. **1922** J. SCOTT-TAGGART *Wireless Vacuum Tubes* (ed. 4) iv. 89 Leaky grid condenser rectification. *Ibid.* vii. 132 If we employ a leaky grid condenser we can obtain a suitable negative grid potential without..a battery. *Ibid.* viii. 167 A leaky grid condenser may be connected in the grid circuit. **1934** *Jrnl. Inst. Electr. Engin.* LXXV. 298/2 Leaky-grid detection is used in this receiver. **1962** D. F. SHAW *Introd. Electronics* ii. 35 A leaky capacitor..in which the leakage resistance is represented by a shunt. **1968** *Radio Communication Handbk.* (ed. 4) ii. 17/1 Any d.c. voltage developed across the grid leak by the rectification of a modulated or an unmodulated signal will thus constitute a negative bias for the grid and the anode current in the triode will fall... An excessively strong signal will tend to bias the valve beyond the cut-off point, and therefore a leaky-grid detector ceases to function satisfactorily when the input voltage is too great. **1969** R. G. MIDDLETON *Transistor Television Servicing Guide* ix. 105/1 A leaky transistor, such as 22..increases in temperature.

e. Of persons: lachrymose. Also as *sb.*

1905 H. A. VACHELL *Hill* vii. 151 'I ain't the leaky sort,' she added fiercely, still gasping. **1959** I. & P. OPIE *Lore & Lang. Schoolch.* x. 187 Croydon boys have twenty names for a cry-baby:..leaky, [etc.].

2. *Genetics.* Of a mutant: producing the protein specified by the mutated gene in a form with reduced activity compared with that produced by the wild type. Of a protein so produced: having reduced activity. Cf. *hypomorphic* adj. (s.v. *HYPO- II).

1955 *Proc. Nat. Acad. Sci.* XLI. 347 Under given conditions, however, the coefficient can be used as a comparative index of degree of phenotypic effect, a 'leaky' mutant having a high coefficient. **1959** *Ibid.* XLV. 204 This strain is a leaky derivative of strain 21863 [of *Neurospora crassa*]. **1961** *Nature* 30 Dec. 1227/2 Mutants produced by acridines are seldom 'leaky'; they are almost always completely lacking in the function of the gene. **1966** E. A. CARLSON *Gene* xiii. 112 The microbial geneticist today uses the term 'leaky mutant' for hypomorph. **1968** R. C. KING *Dict. Genetics* 141 Leaky protein, a mutant protein that has a subnormal degree of biological activity.

lean, *a.* and *sb.*² Add: **A.** *adj.* **4.** Delete 'Now somewhat *rare*' and substitute: Now *rare* except in various techn. senses, as: **a.** Of mortar or concrete: containing little of the binding material. **b.** Of clay: not very plastic. **c.** Of coal: of poor quality; *spec.* deficient in volatile material. **d.** Of ore: of low grade; containing little valuable mineral. **e.** Of fuel gas: of low calorific value. **f.** Of the mixture in an internal-combustion engine: containing a low proportion of fuel. **g.** Of an emulsion, painted surface, etc.: containing little oil.

a. **1726** J. LEONI tr. *Alberti's Archit.* I. 49/1 For small Stones, a thick lean Mortar is best; to a dry exhausted Stone, we should use a fat sort; tho' the Ancients were of the opinion that in all parts of the Walls the fattish sort is more tenacious than the lean. **1936** *Times Lit. Suppl.* 18 Apr. 325/4 Very rich concrete, one part cement with two-and-a-half sand and gravel (concrete so rich is seldom used), is hardly affected at all by sea water... But 'lean' concrete, one part cement to about ten of sand, gravel, or even pozzolani, disintegrates in a year. **1965** *Economist* 13 Nov. 745/3 Outside mining subsidence areas, one of the lower layers [in construction of 'black-top' roads] is often 'lean' (with little cement) concrete.

b. **1754** *New & Compl. Dict. Arts & Sci.* III. 2128/1 Mortar for furnaces, &c. is made with red clay wrought in water in which horse-dung and chimney-soot has been steeped..; this clay ought not to be too fat, lest it should be subject to crack; nor too lean and sandy, lest it should not bind enough. **1885** *Encycl. Brit.* XIX. 600/2 'Lean' clays—those that have a large proportion of free silica—shrink but little, and keep their form unaltered under the heat of the kiln. **1964** H. HODGES *Artifacts* i. 20 Such clays are sticky or greasy..and shrink seriously on drying... Equally a clay may be too aplastic to work, the material

being crumbly, also known as short, mealy, lean, or open.

c. **1883** W. S. GRESLEY *Gloss. Terms Coal Mining* 154 *Lean*, thin, poor; of inferior quality. **1960** *Gloss. Coal Terms (B.S.I.)* 9 *Lean coal*, term used in several European countries for coal with a low volatile matter.

d. **1901** *Daily Colonist* (Victoria, B.C.) 20 Oct. 10/3 There are..rumors..that lean ore has been struck in the lower workings. **1965** G. J. WILLIAMS *Econ. Geol. N.Z.* v. 57/1 Yields [of gold] ranging up to 0·75 oz. were reported but most of the quartz is very lean.

e. **1924** *Jrnl. Inst. Petroleum Technologists* X. 804 In handling lean [natural] gases of this type large throughputs are necessary if the operation of extraction is to be profitable. **1960** *Economist* 15 Oct. 271/3 A national high-pressure grid supplying industry direct and local systems with lean gas for enrichment to town gas.

f. **1932** F. J. CAMM *Bk. Motors* xxxii. 253 Misfiring may be due to incorrect petrol supply, too 'lean' or weak a mixture or an occasional short circuit. **1949** FRAZEE & BEDELL *Automotive Fundamentals* iii. 174 Too low a float level results in a slightly leaner mixture as too little fuel will leave the jets. **1973** *Physics Bull.* Apr. 241/2 The CVCC engine.. was designed with pollution control in mind. It operates on extremely lean air–fuel mixture from the carburettor which is varied according to the operating conditions.

g. **1934** H. HILER *Notes Technique Painting* iii. 171 The emulsions made from yolk of egg, some gum or resin, linseed oil and sometimes a little wax, are intimate mechanical but not chemical compounds... When egg-yolk is used..a somewhat yellowish tinted 'fat emulsion' results. If gum arabic is used, the result is a whitish 'lean emulsion'. **1961** M. LEVY *Studio Dict. Art Terms* 66 Lean Surface, the matt surface of a layer of pigment containing a minimum of oil. It is essential that an underpainting which is to be glazed should possess a lean surface. **1967** J. N. BARRON *Lang. of Painting* 75 For obtaining better permanence in paintings..the overlying or upper layers of paint are to be increasingly more 'fatty' and contain more oil than the layers they cover, or the 'leaner' ones.

7. *lean-faced* (later examples), -*ribbed* (earlier and later examples).

1892 W. B. YEATS *Countess Kathleen* ii. 34 A crowd of ugly lean-faced rogues. **1953** R. S. THOMAS *Song* 13 By a lean-faced people in black clothes. **1602** MARSTON *Antonio's Revenge* IV. i. sig. G1ᵛ, Whilst pale cheekt wisdome, and leane ribd arte Are kept in distance at the halberts point. **1925** E., O., & S. SITWELL *Poor Young People* 7 Neptune beat his lean-ribbed ass The braying sea uphill.

lean, *v.*¹ Add: **6. d.** *to lean on* (someone): to put pressure on (a person) in order to extract something from him or force him to do something against his will (see also quot. 1960).

1960 WENTWORTH & FLEXNER *Dict. Amer. Slang* 315/1 Lean against, lean on... 2. To beat up someone; to threaten to beat up someone or a member of one's family in order to get information, to persuade someone to suppress information, or to extort money; to act or be tough with someone; to coerce. **1965** J. PORTER *Dover Three* xv. 168 If you start leaning on her and you don't make the poison-pen business stick good and proper, she'll crucify you! **1967** K. GILES *Death in Diamonds* vii. 126 I'm going to lean on him until I get to know that contact. **1967** J. MORGAN *Involved* 51 You were too much tonight..the way you leaned on Tuttles, that was really something. **1972** J. BROWN *Chancer* vii. 101 Sandy Crump had been naughty, not telling me about Shag... I'd have to lean on him harder. **1975** *N.Y. Times* 3 Feb. 6/2 'An Attorney General would resign too if he thought he was being leaned on by the Prime Minister or senior ministers on a pending prosecution,' a former Attorney General said.

e. *to lean over backwards:* see *BACKWARDS adv.* A.

leangle, var. LEEANGLE.

1867 [see LEEANGLE.] **1945** BAKER *Austral. Lang.* xiii. 224 Those aboriginal words we have incorporated in our language... For example:..wurley, leangle, mulga, [etc.]. **1966** W. S. RAMSON *Austral. Eng.* vi. 132 Leangle, 'a club', and wirri, 'a throwing stick', are Victorian, both coming from the Gippsland area.

lean-over (lī·nōuvəɹ). [f. LEAN *v.*¹ + OVER *adv.*] An inclination down or forward; *concr.*, something over which one can lean.

a. **1885** G. M. HOPKINS *Poems* (1918) 79 So long to this sweet spot, this leafy lean-over. **1936** E. SITWELL *Victoria of Eng.* xiii. 163 For others, again, there is the twopenny lean-over. **1969** E. H. PINTO *Treen* 334 Early pipes had a very forward tilt, or 'lean over', on the bowl.

leap, *sb.*¹ Add: **1. c.** *a leap in the dark* (later examples); *by leaps and bounds* (earlier and later examples); *leap forward:* an advance of a marked or notable character.

1720 POPE tr. *Homer's Iliad* V. xxi. 1587 High o'er the surging Tide, by Leaps and Bounds, He wades, and mounts; the parted Wave resounds. **1891** GLADSTONE in *Star* 11 Dec. 2/5, I shall proceed by skips and jumps; or, as it is the fashion to say now, by leaps and bounds. **1915** Mrs. BELLOC LOWNDES *Let.* 10 Mar. (1971) 57 Everything is going up, in price, by leaps and bounds. **1940** By leaps and bounds [see *DOUBLE v.* 4 c]. **1947** By leaps and bounds [see *AFRIKANERIZING vbl. sb.* and *ppl. a.*]. **1954** T. S. ELIOT *Confid. Clerk* II. 63, I make decisions on the spur of the moment, But you'd never take a leap in the dark. **1961** *Ann. Reg. 1960* 170 The convention..would amount to a great 'leap forward' towards a virtual European federation. **1966** *Performing Right* Oct. 4 The leap forward of nearly 20 per cent in this revenue is a triumph for the skill and hard work of our administrative staff. **1973** *Times* 21 Mar. (China Trade Suppl.) p. xi/2 The backyard steel furnaces that sprang up during the Great Leap Forward (1958–60).

2. b. (Later example.)
1780 A. Young *Tour in Ireland* I. 126 All the fisheries are his to the leap at Colraine.

8. leap second [after *leap day*], a second which on a particular occasion is inserted into (or omitted from) a scale of reckoning time in order to bring it into correspondence with another scale.
1971 *Nature* 11 June 345/1 An adjustment will be made to all GMT time signal emissions on January 1, 1972, so that a GMT time of 0 h 0 m 0 s will correspond exactly to an IAT time of 0 h 0 m 10 s; thereafter 'leap seconds' will be inserted or omitted as necessary at the end of a particular GMT month... From then on, GMT will always be exactly 10 s slow compared with IAT. A so-called positive leap second will begin at 23 h 59 m 60 s on the last day of the month selected and end at 0 h 0 m 0 s on the first day of the next month; by contrast, if the leap second is negative, 23 h 59 m 58 s will be followed one second later by 0 h 0 m 0 s. **1972** *Daily Tel.* 28 Dec. 10/2 Shortly before 11 p.m. on Sunday (4 a.m. New Year's Day in Britain) technicians at the United States National Bureau of Standards in Boulder, Colorado, will add one leap second to America's atomic clock to correct it to match the Earth's rotation. **1973** *Nature* 21/28 Dec. 444/1 Currently, the Earth loses about 3 ms a day on Atomic Time, and the leap seconds are added where necessary..to keep UT and Atomic Time in close correspondence.

leap, *v.* Add: **6. c.** *Mus.* To pass from one note to another by an interval greater than a degree of the scale. Also *trans.* (Cf. Leap *sb.*[1] 7.)
1879 G. A. Macfarren *Counterpoint* iv. 10 After several consecutive 2nds, in melody, it is bad to leap, in the same direction, upward or downward to an accented note. **1889** E. Prout *Harmony* (ed. 3) xiii. 143 The third of the chord exceptionally leaping, instead of moving as usual by step. **1927** C. H. Kitson *Counterpoint for Beginners* 17 A part may not leap any interval greater than an octave.

leapable (lī·păb'l), *a.* [f. Leap *v.* + -able.] That can be leaped.
1925 A. S. Alexander *Tramps across Watersheds* 128 Some parts of the precipitous sides approach within leapable distance.

leap-frog, *sb.* Add: **3.** *Mil.* (See quot.)
1918 E. S. Farrow *Dict. Mil. Terms* 340 *Leapfrog*, a method of maintaining constant communication with a moving command by using two or more instruments with a single unit, keeping one in operation while another is moving past it to a position in front.

4. *transf.* Competing for higher wages by 'leap-frogging'. Cf. *leap-frog *v.* c.
1958 *Spectator* 31 Jan. 123/2 Nobody has much sympathy with the wage demands of busworkers, town or country; if you use dubious methods of wage bargaining, like the leap-frog, you must expect few tears to be shed if a leap lands you into a ditch. **1961** *Daily Tel.* 14 Oct. 16/6 'Leap-frog' in pay may be checked. **1974** *Times* 25 May 13/1 The wage 'leap frog'.. is the cause of a large part of our present tensions.

5. *attrib.* (in various *fig.* senses).
1904 *Daily Chron.* 13 July 6/5 Mr. Morley exposed what may be called the 'leap-frog' logic of the Protectionists. **1917** *Q. Rev.* July 190 The 'leap-frog' game of fleeting Ministries. **1952** L. Ross *Picture* i. 41 The 'leapfrog' director..whose job it would be to arrange things so that Huston would not have to wait between scenes. **1962** *Gloss. Terms Automatic Data Processing* (*B.S.I.*) 50 *Leapfrog test*, a test program stored in locations which are progressively changed by the program itself in order to test the store. **1972** *Times* 19 Dec. 14/1 An attempt to invoke the 'leap-frog' procedure under section 12 of the Administration of Justice Act, 1969, and go direct to the House of Lords from a decision of a judge of the High Court failed.

leap-frog, *v.* Add: **b.** *Mil.* Of detachments or units, esp. in an attack: to go in advance of each other by turns (see also quot. 1942).
1920 *National Rev.* Nov. 355 Behind them marched other divisions who, on the first momentum of the offensive slackening, were to 'leap-frog' over their comrades and continue the drive. **1922** C. E. Montague *Disenchantment* ix. 133 Leap-frogging waves of assault. **1927** *Daily Tel.* 30 Aug. 8/7 Two pairs of mobile picket groups, moving by long bounds and one pair 'leapfrogging' the other. **1942** *R.A.F. Jrnl.* 16 May 32 The Air Force followed on their heels..leap-frogging over huge stretches of desert... As the armies retreated, they leap-frogged back again. **1966** A. J. Barker *Eritrea* iv. 85 Due to the lack of transport it was possible only to lift two companies forward at any one time, the rest had to march. The two rear companies were picked up in turn and leap-frogged to the head of the main column.

c. *transf.* In wage negotiations: to pursue a policy of demanding higher wages every time a group or groups of comparable wage-earners have succeeded in pulling level or ahead. Chiefly as **leap-frogging** *vbl. sb.* and *ppl. a.*
1955 *Times* 6 June 7/2 And if the British Transport Commission and the Government were to give in now it could never again be fought with certainty, no matter how long the leap-frogging between the two unions went on. **1958** *Times* 30 Jan. 4/3 Sir Robert Grimston..said that there was much concern among the fare-paying public at the continual leap frogging in wages between London and the provinces. **1958** *Times Rev. Industry* June (London & Cambridge Bull.) p. x, Engineers..could not be well granted less than was granted to workers in prosperous industries. This seems to produce a threat of leap-frogging wages. **1959** *Listener* 2 July 6/1 The long-term contract relieves the strain of annual efforts to surpass the previous year's gains, or to leap-frog the advances won in another industry. **1967** *Times* 18 Jan. 16 There is leap-frogging in newspaper offices, such that when one department negotiates a rise the others follow regardless of justification. **1970** *Daily Tel.* 15 June 2/5 For the first time collective negotiations on new claims by all unions will replace individual 'leapfrogging' demands. **1973** *Times* 21 Dec. 1/7 To breach Phase Three..would lead to leap-frogging claims which would erode the miners' position in the league table.

d. Other *fig.* uses.
1935 J. C. Squire *Reflections & Memories* 6 It is a time before the jolly vulgarity of Earl's Court had leap-frogged westward to the White City, and then to Wembley. **1949** I. Deutscher *Stalin* xiii. 498 Only in 1943 did the newly built factories and those that had been 'leap-frogged' from the west to the Urals and beyond begin to pour out great quantities of tanks, planes, and guns. **1961** *Times* 28 Mar. 4/5 They [*sc.* Oxford] were accompanied by Imperial College, with whom they paddled in the familiar leap-frogging pattern to Chiswick Eyot. **1962** *Punch* 5 Sept. 330/2 The leap-frogged zones beyond [the Green Belts]. **1964** T. W. McRae *Impact of Computers on Accounting* vi. 175 In fact, they [*sc.* auditors] 'leapfrog' over the entire EDP system. **1971** P. Gresswell *Environment* 122 Development leap-frogs green belts. **1971** J. Wainwright *Last Buccaneer* III. 313 When a man leap-frogs me in the promotion stakes I'm human enough to feel narked. **1972** *Times* 23 Feb. 27/6 So soon as a case at first instance arose involving the ratio decidendi of *Rookes v Barnard* the parties concerned might use the 'leap-frogging' procedure now available. **1973** *Listener* 17 May 653/1 Haldeman..was put in charge of the advance men, leap-frogging ahead of the candidate and arranging for crowds.

learn, *v.* Add: **4.** (Later examples.)
Now regarded as a vulgarism.
1831 J. J. Strang *Diary* 31 Dec. in M. M. Quaife *Kingdom of St. James* (1930) 198, I have succeeded in regulating them and learning them what to do without punishing a single schollar. **1914** *Sat. Even. Post* 4 Apr. 10/3, I learned him that, yuh see. *a* **1935** T. E. Lawrence *Mint* (1955) II. iii. 107 We hear rumours that he..wants to make the Depot all drill, and will not permit other officers to learn the men, or men the officers. **1935** Wodehouse *Luck of Bodkins* xv. 181 The English public school system..isn't at all what an educational system should be... If you ask me, they don't learn the little perishers nothing. **1966** F. Shaw et al. (*title*) Lern yerself Scouse. **1974** *Times* 16 Dec. 12/8 We asked whether he had learned the instrument at school... 'No. He learned it himself and now he's learning me.'

¶ **e.** Phr. *I'll learn you*: used as a warning of impending punishment. *Non-standard.*
1822 J. Galt *Sir A. Wylie* III. xxxiii. 279 I'll learn you to fill yoursel fu'. **1873** C. D. Warner in 'Mark Twain' & Warner *Gilded Age* xxix. 266 The conductor..reached the bell rope, 'Damn you, I'll learn you,' stepped to the door. **1974** P. Wright *Lang. Brit. Industry* iv. 41 The common *I'll learn you*..when used ironically, has the unstandard meaning of 'I'll teach you never to do that again'.

learnability (lɜ̄:ɹnăbi·lĭti). [f. Learnable *a.* + -ity.] The quality or fact of being learnable.
1959 *Brno Studies in English* I. 16 The easiness or the difficulty with which it affects the person trying to acquire it (at the risk of coining another barbarous neologism one might term it 'learnability'). **1966** *Philos. Rev.* LXXV. 435 There are others of great importance: brevity, learnability, etc.

learned, *ppl. a.* Add: **2.** *learned society* (later examples).
1798 *Phil. Mag.* June 95 (*title*) Intelligence. Learned Societies. **1863** Hawthorne *Our Old Home* iv. 136 This bewildered enthusiast had recognized a depth in the man whom she decried, which scholars, critics, and learned societies, devoted to the elucidation of his unrivaled scenes, had never imagined to exist there. **1897** W. James *Will to Believe* 306 All our learned societies have begun in some such modest way. **1958** *Observer* 13 July 3/7 The battle of the learned societies with the Inland Revenue. **1973** *LSA Bull.* Mar. 28 He defined a learned society as one which publishes a journal and holds an annual meeting; a professional society as one which is involved in matters of concern to its members.

¶ **e.** (Earlier and later examples.)
1784 A. Seward *Let.* 29 Oct. in H. Pearson *Swan of Lichfield* (1936) 71 That amusing part of this conversation, which alluded to the learned Pig, and his demi-rational exhibitions, I shall transmit to you hereafter. **1785** W. Cowper *Let.* 22 Apr. in *Corr.* (1904) II. 314, I have a competitor for fame..in the Learned Pig. **1919** Conrad *Let.* 25 Jan. in G. Jean-Aubry *J. Conrad: Life & Lett.* (1927) II. 216 If the Alliances had been differently combined the Western Powers would have delivered Poland to the German learned pig.

3. d. Of publications: devoted to (esp. some branch of) scholarship.
1883 E. B. Bax tr. *Kant's Prolegomena & Metaphysical Found. Nat. Sci.* 128 There is a good deal to be done before a learned journal..can maintain its otherwise well-merited reputation, in the field of metaphysics as elsewhere. **1942** *Amer. Speech* XVII. 3 Since he [*sc.* the writer of detective stories] introduces characters from all walks of life, and since he usually avoids the more formal style, he is a better informant than..the writers for the learned journals. **1951** Auden *Nones* (1952) 61 Lone scholars, sniping from the walls Of learned periodicals, Our fact defend. **1954** E. E. Evans-Pritchard *Inst. Primitive Soc.* p. v, Monographs about primitive peoples and innumerable papers devoted to them in learned journals. **1961** A. Wilson *Old Men at Zoo* i. 50 Subscriptions to learned periodicals. **1969** M. Pugh *Last Place Left* xxii. 167 So you've just met him. And the rest you know..from the learned journals.

learner. Add: **3.** One who is learning to be competent but who does not yet have formal authorization as a driver of a motor vehicle, cycle, etc. Also *attrib.*, as **learner-driver.** (The abbrev. L is shown on the *learner plates* of the vehicle.)
1930 'A. Armstrong' *Taxi* viii. 103 Conversational freedom between..taximen and private 'learner drivers'. **1934** R. F. Broad et al. *Motor Driving made Easy* (ed. 5) ix. 140 A provisional licence will be issued to enable learners to receive instruction qualifying them for the official test. **1935** *Daily Tel.* 7 Mar. 9/4 New drivers..must start with a provisional or learner's licence. **1938** E. Waugh *Scoop* III. ii. 276 Bonnet and back bore battered learner plates. **1961** [see *book *v.* 2 c]. **1970** D. Marlowe *Echoes of Celandine* i. 15 A learner-car circling the block. **1973** *Times* 28 June 31/1 The learner driver holding up the traffic as he or she falters down the High Street is still part of the British motoring scene. *Ibid.* 21 Sept. 23/5 Although with its 1,000 cars and its 160 branches it is easy to get the impression that there are British School of Motoring learners everywhere..it still only has something like 2½ per cent of the learner-driver population training with it.

4. *Austral.* (See quot.)
1965 J. S. Gunn *Terminol. Shearing Industry* I. 35 A learner is not a shedhand or barrowner, but a budding shearer who has not yet shorn 5,000 sheep (10,000 in Queensland).

learning, *vbl. sb.* Add: **1. a.** spec. *Psychol.* A process which leads to the modification of behaviour or the acquisition of new abilities or responses, and which is additional to natural development by growth or maturation. Freq. opp. *insight*.
1897 Bryan & Harter in *Psychol. Rev.* IV. 29 While there are many exceptional cases of quickness and slowness in learning, it requires from two to two and a half years to become an expert operator. **1901** E. L. Thorndike in *Ibid.* VIII. 442 With the monkeys, however, the association is both more rapid and more permanent, and the approach to suddenness and definiteness in their learning simulates that of human beings. **1901** —— *Human Nature Club* iii. 38 This method of learning may be called the method of trial and error..or..the animal method of learning. **1922** R. S. Woodworth *Psychol.* xiii. 311 To compare human and animal learning..cannot but throw light on the whole problem of the process of learning. **1924** R. M. Ogden tr. *Koffka's Growth of Mind* ii. 41 Certain stages of development are attained only after learning has been added to growth and maturation. **1940** W. Köhler *Dynamics in Psychol.* (1942) iii. 114 If this is the case, retroactive inhibition..must also be a disturbance of the product of learning. **1948** E. R. Hilgard *Theories of Learning* xii. 353 It can be stated with reasonable confidence that there are changes in the nervous system accompanying learning. **1968** Gelernter & Rochester in Evans & Robertson *Cybernetics* 70 This is the learning involved when the machine uses results on one problem to improve its guesses about similar problems. **1970** M. H. Marx *Learning: Theories* p. v, It is no longer possible for one psychologist to be fully expert in all the areas of so broad and diversified a field as learning.

4. (sense *1 a) *learning process, programme, score, situation*; **learning curve,** a graph showing progress in learning; **learning machine,** a machine of the electronic computer type that can 'learn' by recording the results of attempts to solve a problem and giving preference to those which are successful; **learning resources** (also *attrib.*), collective materials for learning, e.g. microfilms, audio-visual aids, made accessible in a library, school, etc.; also *learning-resource* attrib. phr.; **learning theory,** theory attempting to account for the process of learning.
1922 R. S. Woodworth *Psychol.* xiii. 307 Learning curve for the rat in the maze. **1924** R. M. Ogden tr. *Koffka's Growth of Mind* iv. 168 All these facts..would naturally operate to shorten the learning-curve. **1967** M. Argyle *Psychol. Interpersonal Behaviour* x. 183 In fact some manual operatives also learn by doing, and learning curves can be plotted which show their rate of progress. **1968** Johannsen & Robertson *Managem. Gloss.* 74 Learning curves indicate how the rate of learning changes with increased practice and are used to predict labour productivity. **1950** A. M. Turing in *Mind* LIX. 458 The idea of a learning machine may appear paradoxical to some readers. *Ibid.* 459 It is probably wise to include a random element in a learning machine. **1954** *Oxf. Univ. Gaz.* 15 June 1035/2 Work..on the insightful learning machine was also continued. **1963** A. M. Andrew *Brains & Computers* 61 Future machines of this kind will certainly also be learning machines. **1967** R. Whitehead in Wills & Yearsley *Handbk. Management Technol.* 57 Brains, self-organizing systems, economic systems, learning machines, computers, and automated factories are among the many subjects examined by the cybernetician. **1922** R. S. Woodworth *Psychol.* xiii. 302 It makes the learning process easier to follow. **1947** A. W. Melton in *Harvard Educ. Rev.* XXIX. 96 Educators..must know how to manage the learning process. **1949** Shurr & Yocom *Mod. Dance* i. 13 Nothing can substitute for the physical activity which is necessary to the learning process. **1962** R. M. Gagné in *Psychol. Rev.* LXIX. 355/1 Autoinstructional devices and their component learning programs. **1969** *Library Jrnl.* 1 Apr. 1536/3 (Advt.), Student body of 5000 on two campuses; 300 teachers; new learning resources center. **1970** *Ibid.* 15 Feb. 800/3 (Advt.), Curriculum adviser to work..in planning..for new learning resource facility incorporating uses of all

learning materials. 1970 *Globe & Mail* (Toronto) 25 Sept. 39/1 (Advt.), The successful applicant..will be responsible for assisting the principal in organizing, equipping and stocking a 3-level Learning Resource Centre in an innovational secondary school. 1970 *Jrnl. Gen. Psychol.* LXXXIII. 46 The analysis of variance on learning scores. 1948 E. R. HILGARD *Theories of Learning* xii. 335 Many learning situations require the selection of one or another possible mode of action. 1947 *Harvard Educ. Rev.* XXIX. 84 (*heading*) The relation of learning theory to the technology of education. 1962 *Listener* 15 Nov. 793/2 The psycho-analysts..believe that learning theory..is doomed to give only an incomplete and sometimes misleading account of personality development. 1967 M. ARGYLE *Psychol. Interpersonal Behaviour* viii. 148 Various training techniques derived from learning theory have been developed for the removal of symptoms [of mental disorders]. 1968 E. LOVEJOY *Attention in Discrimination Learning* iii. 44 This selectivity is likely to be an important part of a learning theory.

lease (līz), *v.*⁴ [f. *leas*, pl. of LEA *sb.*⁴] *trans.* To divide (yarn or thread) into leas.

1884 W. S. B. MCLAREN *Spinning* 242 The length varies from one to twelve yards, and the forms of making up, leasing, and tying are endless. 1927 T. WOODHOUSE *Artificial Silk* 67 It is quite possible that all the remaining hanks have already been leased.

lea·se-back. [f. LEASE *sb.*³ or *v.*³ + BACK *adv.*] In full, *sale and lease-back.* The sale of a property, etc., to a purchaser on the understanding that the vendor may take out a lease on the property. Also *attrib.*

1947 J. W. KEARNS in *Amer. Bar Assoc. Proc., Section of Corporation, Banking & Mercantile Law* 46/1 The origin of the 'lease-back deal' is probably traced back to high taxes, high taxes coupled with the desire of almost any corporate manager to see a liquid balance sheet with very few fixed assets on it. The fewer the better. The lease-back deal is basically a transaction under which a corporation, which in the course of its business will use a considerable amount of real estate, sells that real estate to another entity which may be a university; it may be a charitable foundation; it may be any other type of organization which is tax free under the Internal Revenue Code. The real estate is usually sold at depreciated book value and simultaneously or concurrently a lease-back is granted to the industrial or merchandising concern that has sold the property. 1949 *Business Week* 22 Oct. 31/1 The device under attack is the sale-and-lease-back of real estate. 1964 *Financial Times* 12 Mar. 1/8 Excess cash produced by sale and lease-back arrangements. 1967 *Times Rev. Industry* July 33/2 The illusions of liquidity which can be created by..leaseback. 1970 *Daily Tel.* 30 Dec. 16 Factory-owners who sell their premises and take a lease-back of their accommodation. 1971 *Ibid.* 27 Apr. 21 (*heading*) Leaseback raises £5m for Grand Met. *Ibid.* 17 June 19 A £6 million plus sale and lease-back agreement. 1972 *Accountant* 26 Oct. 516/1 There is an increased use of real estate sale and lease-back and the non-cancellable leasing of capital equipment for a term approximating its economic life. 1974 *Country Life* 7 Mar. 506/1 It was arranged that immediately upon the transfer of the estate, the son would lease back the property to his father. The leaseback was for a term of five years.

leased, *ppl. a.* (Earlier example.)

1869 *Bradshaw's Railway Manual* XXI. 73 The gross earnings of the leased undertakings.

lease-lend. (Level stress.) Also **lease and lend** and *LEND-LEASE. [f. LEASE *v.*³ + LEND *v.*²] At first (in 1941) applied to an arrangement whereby sites in British overseas possessions were leased to the United States as bases in exchange for the loan of U.S. destroyers; later in extended uses. Also *attrib.* and as *vb.*

1941 *Economist* 1 Feb. 139/2 The great reduction in American payments under the 'Lease and Lend' Bill. 1941 *Hutchinson's Pict. Hist. of War* 9 July–30 Sept. 48 Mr Harry Hopkins..in charge of the administration of the Lease-Lend Act, arrives in England again. 1942 *Ann. Reg. 1941* 19 The signing of the Lease and Lend Bill in the United States on March 11..caused great rejoicing in England. 1942 *R.A.F. Jrnl.* 3 Oct. 24 The Canadians argued that by lease-lend the Old Man would get one [a Jeep]. 1943 *Daily Tel.* 23 Oct. 4 Britain's new aircraft-carrier Victorious was 'Lease-lent' to the United States. 1944 G. B. SHAW *Everybody's Pol. What's What?* xv. 120 Under the American Lease and Lend arrangements England and Russia are borrowing their war stores from the United States. 1945 *Reader's Digest* July 47/1 Hatch has been particularly successful in 'breeding up' the poultry and livestock of the country by lease-lending his pure-bred bulls. 1964 *Daily Tel.* 19 May 28/6 To-night 40 Eastbourne policemen were sent to Brighton. They formed part of a 'lease-lend' arrangement entered into by Brighton, Eastbourne and Hastings police forces to help each other out in case of riots.

lea·sing, *vbl. sb.*³ [f. LEASE *sb.*⁴ + -ING¹.] *Attrib.* in **leasing reed,** in weaving, a reed through which the warp threads pass as they come off the bobbins.

1927 T. WOODHOUSE *Artificial Silk* 108 The ends of the bobbins are threaded through a leasing reed. 1960 *Textile Terms & Definitions* (ed. 4) 90 (*caption*) Leasing.

least, *a.* (*sb.*) and *adv.* Add: **A.** *adj.* **1. c.** (Later examples.)

1870 *Amer. Naturalist* III. 234 The least Tern,..and the Roseate Tern, still breed on our coast. 1915 A. R. HORWOOD *Story Plant Life Brit. Isles* III. i. 105 Hooker recognises three divisions [of Gamopetalæ]: Chironieæ, including Yellow Wort, Least Yellow Gentian, [etc.]. 1946 T. M. STANWELL-FLETCHER *Driftwood Valley* 42 Sometimes he and the least chipmunks..play hide-and-seek round boxes and trees. 1955 E. B. FORD *Moths* xi. 166 This [*sc.* the Burren] is also the Irish locality for the Least Minor. 1960 M. BURTON *Wild Animals of Brit. Isles* 114 The Least weasel..has not so far been found in this country. 1975 *Country Life* 16 Jan. 131/1 Least tern nesting area.

e. *law* (or *principle*) *of least action* (Physics): the principle that an actual trajectory of a physical system is always such that, in comparison with any slightly different motion between the same end-points, the integral over the trajectory of the momentum with respect to distance (or more generally, of the sum of the generalized momenta with respect to generalized co-ordinates) has a minimum (or a maximum) value.

[1748 MOREAU DE MAUPERTUIS in *Hist. de l'Acad. R. des Sci. 1744* 423 Le chemin qu'elle [*sc.* la lumière] tient est celui par lequel la quantité d'action est le moindre. ..La quantité d'action..est proportionnelle à la somme des espaces multipliez chacun par la vitesse avec laquelle le corps les parcourt. 1748 —— in *Hist. de l'Acad. R. des Sci. et des Belles Lettres de Berlin 1746* 286 J'ai découvert le principe universel, sur lequel toutes ces loix sont fondées. ..C'est le principe de la moindre quantité d'action.] 1814 J. TOPLIS tr. *Laplace's Treat. Analytical Mech.* ii. 47 Maupertuis..asserted, that in all the changes which take place in the situation of a body, the product of the mass of the body by its velocity and the space which it has passed over is a minimum. This he called the principle of the least action, and it was applied by him to the discovery of the laws of the refraction and the reflection of light,.. the laws of equilibrium, &c. 1834 W. R. HAMILTON in *Phil. Trans. R. Soc.* CXXIV. 252 Although Lagrange and others, in treating of the motion of a system, have shown that the variation of this definite integral vanishes when the extreme coordinates and the constant H are given, they appear to have deduced from this result only the well known law of least action. 1920 A. S. EDDINGTON *Space, Time & Gravitation* ix. 149 The law of gravitation, the laws of mechanics, and the laws of the electromagnetic field have all been summed up in a single Principle of Least Action. For the most part this unification was accomplished before the advent of the relativity theory, and it is only the addition of gravitation to the scheme which is novel. 1966 J. L. MERIAM *Dynamics* viii. 349 Hamilton's principle and the principle of least action have found important but limited applications in engineering problems. Their use will undoubtedly grow with time as the complexity and generality of design situations increase. 1973 *Nature* 28 Sept. 223/1 The mechanics section begins with Hamilton's principle (here called the principle of least action) and gives a concise and elegant account of the relation between invariance and conservation laws.

4. (Earlier and later examples of *to say the least* (*of it*).)

1809 *Deb. Congress U.S.* 20 Feb. (1853) 422 To say the least of it, the people will perceive..an uncommon coincidence. 1811 *Ibid.* 17 Jan. 603 To say the least of such a measure, is to term it an experiment. 1928 R. CAMPBELL *Wayzgoose* i. 26 Muses Nine, Those strapping girls whose love, to say the least, Would make a rabid Mormon of a priest. 1974 D. SCANNELL *Mother knew Best* vi. 59 Mother said vanity was a besetting sin which Amy resented, to say the least of it.

leather, *sb.* Add: **2.** Also, a stirrup-leather.

1907 *Yesterday's Shopping* (1969) 300/2 Hunting saddle, ..complete with stirrup irons and leathers. 1928 D. BYRNE *Destiny Bay* vii. § 2. 314 The shorter your leathers, the less you know about your mount. 1936 J. CARY *Afr. Witch* vii. 137 'You ride too long... Take up your leathers.' Fisk obediently took up his stirrups a hole. 1952 M. ALLINGHAM *Tiger in Smoke* xiii. 197 Off you go! Shorten your leathers.

b. Also, a leather jacket or coat. Also *sing.*

1962 *John o' London's* 4 Jan. 20/1 A Banquo little more than an Oberon in his 'leather'. *Ibid.* 31 May 535/4 Two youths in leathers and crash-helmets. 1970 *Daily Tel.* 2 Mar. 14 Ankle-length, shiny, wet-look coats, suèdes and leathers were often trimmed with fur. 1972 ELLIS & NEWMAN in T. Kochman *Rappin' & Stylin' Out* 378 Wear 'black leathers'. 1973 P. DICKINSON *Gift* ix. 142 Ian got into his leathers, Davy put on two extra layers of clothing, the bike started first kick.

d. As the name of a colour.

1872 *Queen* 15 June 431/3 Costume cloth in all the new colours, including pink,..leather,..and all leading colours. 1923 *Daily Mail* 16 Jan. 1 (Advt.), Coat frock.. Grey, Mole, Leather,..New Brown. *Ibid.* 31 July 1/3 (Advt.), Grey, Smoke, Leather and Navy.

e. *slang.* Various articles made of, or clad in, leather, such as (*a*) a wallet or purse; (*b*) a leather-shod foot; hence a kick; (*c*) a boxing-glove; hence a punch or boxing.

(*a*) 1883 'MARK TWAIN' *Life on Mississippi* lii. 511, I pulled off an old woman's leather; (*robbed her of her pocket-book*). 1899 'J. FLYNT' *Tramping with Tramps* 395 'To reef a leather' means that the pickpocket pulls out the lining of a pocket containing the 'leather'. 1914 JACKSON & HELLYER *Vocab. Criminal Slang* 54 *Leather*,..Some general currency, but used chiefly by pickpockets. A pocketbook; a wallet; a billbook. 1938 F. D. SHARPE *Sharpe of Flying Squad* 331 *Leathers*, wallets. (An inveterate pickpocket is sometimes called 'A Leather Merchant'.) 1955 *Publ. Amer. Dial. Soc.* xxiv. 114 The ordinary billfold which men normally carry, folded double, in the hip pocket, is called a *leather*.

(*b*) 1931 D. RUNYON *Guys & Dolls* (1932) vi. 118 Dave walks over and starts to give Waldo Winchester the leather. 1936 J. CURTIS *Gilt Kid* vi. 61 Old boys never could stand the leather.

(*c*) 1936 'R. HYDE' *Passport to Hell* v. 86 It started off as a pretty little bout, though neither knew much about the leather. 1950 J. DEMPSEY *Championship Fighting* ii. 12 Meehan..threw so much leather and was so rugged that he and I broke even.

3. *spec.* The skin on the ear-flap of a dog.

1952 C. L. B. HUBBARD *Pembrokeshire Corgi Handbk.* 112 *Leather*, the skin on the ear flap. 1960 *Times* 2 Jan. 9/2 The ear leather of the workers [*sc.* spaniels] is shorter than in show specimens. 1968 H. HARMAR *Chihuahua Guide* 240 *Leather*, the skin of the earflap.

4. b. *leather goods.*

1902 *Westm. Gaz.* 14 June 8/3 A fire broke out in a leather goods manufactory. 1946 J. W. WATERER *Leather* xiii. 222 An..up-to-date manual of leather goods manufacture. 1971 D. MACKENZIE *Sleep is for the Rich* vi. 196 A leathergoods store downtown stayed open during the lunch hour.

5. a. *leather-work* (earlier and later examples); also *leather-hard* adj.

1960 H. POWELL *Beginner's Bk. Pott.* II. 64 Leather-hard, the condition of clay when it may be cut. Soap condition. 1967 M. CHANDLER *Ceramics in Mod. World* iv. 122 Each such blank, after partial drying to render it leather-hard, is turned on a semiautomatic lathe. 1971 *Islander* (Victoria, B.C.) 12 Dec. 7/1 The pot and the slip have reached a stage which is known as leather-hard. This means the pot may be handled safely without risk of damage, but is still capable of receiving the indented design. 1856 C. M. YONGE *Daisy Chain* I. xv. 143 Meta has been making a drawing for her papa, and is framing it in leather work. 1906 SANFORD & PHILLIPS *Art Crafts for Beginners* (rev. ed.) vi. 137 The great popularity of leather-work among amateurs is due..to the fact that a small and inexpensive equipment is all that is required. 1971 H. PLUCKROSE *Bk. of Crafts* 53/2 In the past amateur leatherwork meant punching and thonging.

b. *leather-sealer*; *leather-dressing* (example).

1850 *Rep. Comm. Patents 1849* (U.S.) 357, I claim the adjustable scraper..for the purposes and uses of leather dressing. 1662 *Public Rec. Colony of Connecticut* (1850) I. 377 The leathr sealers..shal haue allowed vnto them for each Dicker of Leather they seale, 18d. 1798 I. ALLEN *Nat. & Pol. Hist. Vermont* 272 Weights and measures, leather sealers &c. are regulated according to law.

c. *leather-bottomed, -coated, -faced, -jacketed, -lined* (also *fig.*), *-topped, -upholstered* adjs.

1783 in E. Parkman *Diary* (1899) 298, 9 black chairs.. five leather bottomed Do. 1854 J. E. COOKE *Virginia Comedians* I. xxii. 127 A rude oaken table and some leather-bottomed chairs. 1903 *To-Day* 4 Mar. 191/2 The implements consist of small leather-coated balls and wooden hockey sticks about seven inches long, which are held as one would hold a pencil. 1906 *Westm. Gaz.* 20 Nov. 4/2 Metal-to-metal clutches are..extending in favour at the expense of the old leather-faced bone type. 1908 *Ibid.* 29 Dec. 4/1 The three-speed gear-box.. to which the power is transmitted through the medium of a leatherfaced clutch. 1916 JOYCE *Portrait of Artist* ii. 81 There stood the stout leatherjacketed vaulting horse. 1846 W. H. EMORY in Frémont & Emory *Notes Trav. Calif.* (1849) 22/2 The first mouthful brought the tears trickling down my cheeks, very much to the amusement of the spectators with their leather-lined throats. It was red pepper, stuffed with minced meat. 1903 *Work* 18 July 382/1 The clutch..pulls the band (which.., is steel, leather-lined). 1913 W. OWEN *Let.* 13 Nov. (1967) 211, 2 shirts (leather-lined extra). 1911 O. ONIONS *Widdershins* 281 The large leather-topped table. 1936 E. E. EVANS-PRITCHARD in *Ess. Social Anthropol.* (1962) viii. 179 They were preceded in this romp through gardens and cultivations by a small boy beating on a leather-topped drum. 1965 G. MCINNES *Road to Gundagai* vii. 119 Soft..armchairs and sofas, a big leather-topped desk. 1923 F. L. PACKARD *Four Stragglers* II. v. 183 Polly Wickes rose hastily from the..big leather-upholstered Chesterfield.

d. *leather-coated, -faced* (also *-face*), *-jacketed* (cf. *LEATHER-JACKET 5) adjs.

1902 W. B. YEATS *In Seven Woods* (1903) 12 And leather-coated men, with slings. 1884 'MARK TWAIN' *Huck. Finn* xxviii. 287 You ain't one of these leather-face people. I don't want no better book than what your face is. 1919 W. DEEPING *Second Youth* xv. 128 She let this leather-faced old rascal flirt with her quite harmlessly. 1934 T. WILDER *Heaven's my Destination* 3 Brush.. chose a seat beside a tall leather-faced man. 1960 *Economist* 8 Oct 149/1 Among the cartoonists Herblock has drawn Mr Khrushchev as a leather-jacketed gang-leader. 1961 *Encounter* XVII. II. 17/2 The leather-jacketed 'Teddy Boy' gangs of Western Germany. 1969 *Daily Tel.* 2 Sept. 1/3 South and East coast resorts were invaded yesterday by hundreds of leather-jacketed Rockers and teenagers in jeans and steel-tipped boots. 1973 J. WAINWRIGHT *Pride of Pigs* 114 The leather-jacketed, stocking-feeted Hell's Angel.

6. leather-back, substitute for def.: a large marine soft-shelled turtle, *Dermochelys coriacea*; (later examples); **leather belting,** machine belting made of leather; also *attrib.*; **leather breeches (beans)** *U.S. dial.*, dried beans or dried bean-pods; beans that have been dried and then cooked in their shells; **leather-cloth** (also **leathercloth**), also, a synthetic product simulating leather; **leather-hunting,** esp. a *colloq.* term for fielding when the batsman is hitting out as freely as he likes; hence *leather-hunter*; **leather-leaf**: for '*Cassandra calyculata*' substitute '*Chamædaphne calyculata*'; (earlier examples); **leather medal** orig. *U.S.*, a medal made of leather instead of metal, sarcastically

suggested as an award; **Leather-Stocking**, a North American frontiersman [from a character portrayed by J. F. Cooper]; also *attrib.*

1965 R. McKie *Company of Animals* xii. 168 On the beaches of Trengganu..the leatherback turtles lay their eggs. **1969** A. Bellairs *Life of Reptiles* I. ii. 41 The tendency nowadays is to regard the leatherback as a specialised descendant of turtles of more 'ordinary' type. *a* **1877** Knight *Dict. Mech.* I. 273/1 Leather belting is ordinarily prepared in the following manner. **1877** *Design & Work* 9 June 23 (Advt.), Charles Churchill and Co., importers of American machinery and tools,..lathes, vices, planes,.. American leather belting. **1909** *Westm. Gaz.* 6 Apr. 2/1 The exposure of the graft..behind the duty on hides was made by tanners and shoe and leather-belting manufacturers. **1946** J. W. Waterer *Leather* 304 Included in its members are all the principal manufacturers of leather belting. *Ibid.*, Persons engaged in or intending to engage in the leather belting trade. **1913** H. Kephart *Our Southern Highlanders* 292 Beans dried in the pod, then boiled 'hull and all' are called leather-breeches (this is not slang, but the regular name). **1941** J. Smiley *Hash House Lingo* 35 *Leather breeches*, dried kidney beans. **1943** R. Chase in B. A. Botkin *Treas. S. Folklore* (1949) 470 Such communal tasks as stringing beans for canning, or threading them up to make the dried pods known as 'leather britches'. **1972** E. Wigginton *Foxfire Bk.* 15 He..dried leather britches beans. *Ibid.* 167 *Leather breeches beans...* Take a string of dried green beans down, remove the thread, and drop them in a pot of boiling water. **1929** *Publishers' Circular* 18 May 621/3 A revolution has taken place in the world of leather by the introduction of the synthetic product leathercloth. **1937** *Archit. Rev.* LXXXI. 291/1 The manufacturers of cheaper cars began to use leathercloth as a finish over the normal rigid type of body construction and the snob-appeal of purpose-made bodies was lost. **1961** *Times* 30 May (I.C.I. Suppl.) p. viii/1 The original amalgamation brought together..dyestuffs, leathercloth, paints and non-ferrous metals. **1973** *Daily Tel.* 21 Nov. 14/4 This test car was upholstered in a ventilated leathercloth. **1944** Blunden *Cricket Country* i. 19 The laugh at the unfortunate 'leather-hunter' on a hot chase. **1865** J. Pycroft *Cricketana* xiii. 224, I like science more than swiping, and enjoy 'fielding', but not leather hunting. **1905** H. A. Vachell *Hill* xii. 254 And then, when his 'eye' is in, he will give the Etonians such leather-hunting as they never had before. **1934** W. J. Lewis *Lang. Cricket* 143 *Leather-hunting*, a jocular term for the exertions of the fieldsmen when the ball is hit freely to all parts of the field. **1970** *Sunday Tel.* 20 Dec. 21/7 The voracious Richards was in action once more and M.C.C. are assured of more leather-hunting today. **1818** A. Eaton *Man. Bot.* (ed. 2) 173 *Andromeda calyculata*, leather leaf. **1870** *Amer. Naturalist* IV. 217 The Leather Leaf (*Cassandra calyculata*), and *Andromeda polifolia*, are both worthy of attention. **1831** J. Motte in A. H. Cole *Charleston goes to Harvard* (1940) 89 He must be a cute chap, and deserves to have a leather medal. **1837** *Harvardiana* III. 147 (Th.), A leather medal his reward should be, A leather medal and an LL.D. **1860** *Richmond* (Virginia) *Enquirer* 20 Apr. 2/5 (Th.), The individual who conceived the leather medal idea [for identifying dogs] deserves a leather medal himself. **1889** *Kansas City* (Missouri) *Times & Star* 5 Dec., A leather medal..awaits the first misguided person this season writing it 'Xmas'. **1922** Joyce *Ulysses* 750 He ought to get a leather medal with a putty rim for all the plans he invents. [**1823** J. F. Cooper *Pioneers* I. i. 18 His limbs were guarded with long leggings of the same material as the moccasins, which gartering over the knees of his tarnished buck-skin breeches, had obtained for him, among the settlers, the nick name of Leather-stocking.] *Ibid.* 11 The Leather-stocking has put his hounds into the hills this clear day. **1831** M. Holley *Texas* (1833) v. 43 The character of Leather Stocking, is not uncommon in Texas... The dress of these hunters is usually of deerskin. Hence the appropriate name *Leather Stocking*. Their generic name..is *Frontiers-men.* **1909** *Daily Chron.* 1 July 7/3 With most birds, you must make your approach with all the art of a leatherstocking. **1965** *English Studies* XLVI. 313 In this book Cooper draws repeated parallels between the Leather-stocking hero and Moses.

leathered, *ppl. a.* Add: **b.** Made into, or like, leather.

1797 in G. B. Goode *Fisheries U.S.: Hist. & Methods* (1887) II. 435 By walking it [seal-skin] becomes leathered and soft to the foot. **1869** S. Bowles *Our New West* 444 If you bring a liver not entirely leathered and lungs not over half consumed. **1970** L. Jeffers *My Blackness is Beauty of this Land* 9 His face was leathered, lean, and strong, Gashed with struggle scars.

leather-jacket. Add: **5.** A person, freq. a member of a gang or a delinquent group, dressed in a leather jacket.

1959 *New Statesman* 15 Aug. 180/1 All France has learnt about the bands of 'leather-jackets'... Why are these young rowdies called 'leather-jacket'?.. Certainly leather jackets seem to be the uniform for young American delinquents. **1960** *Britannica Bk. of Year* 557/2 The characteristic dress of juvenile delinquents in several countries produced the term *leather jackets*, meaning delinquents. **1963** V. Nabokov *Gift* v. 289 Not long before his deportation from Russia, when some revolvered leatherjackets had come to arrest him.

leathern, *a.* **2.** *Comb.* (Later example.)

1875 J. G. Holland *Sevenoaks* xii. 158 Blue-jays were screaming among leathern-leaved oaks.

lea·ther-neck, lea·therneck. *slang.* [f. Leather *sb.* + Neck *sb.*[1]] **1.** (See Leather *sb.* 6.)

1890 [see Leather *sb.* 6]. **1916** 'Taffrail' *Carry On!* 27 A Royal marine is a 'bullock', 'turkey', or 'Joey', while a soldier is a 'grabby' or 'leather-neck'.

b. A marine. *U.S.*

1914 *Dialect Notes* IV. 150 *Leatherneck*, a marine. **1919** *A Company, Eleventh Frapper* (U.S. Marines) 17 Apr. 1/2 We learn that between 700 and 800 warworn Leathernecks from the famous 5th and 6th Marines.. arrived at Camp Covington. **1926** *Amer. Speech* I. 354/2 'Leatherneck' for a Marine..is derived from the old custom of facing the stiff neck-band of the marine uniform with leather. **1931** *Punch* 3 June 606/1 I'd just passed the remark to the leather-neck on sentry that we was 'avin' a nice peaceful forenoon when the Admiral's buzzer goes, and I 'ops in to see what 'e wanted. **1955** W. Foster-Harris *Look of Old West* i. 11 Under this collar, the troopers were supposed to wear an atrocity of a stock, of black leather. This is where the name 'leather-neck' came from, since the Marines also had to wear these dog-collar affairs. **1968** R. West *Sk. Vietnam* ii. 37 The U.S. Marine Corps. These legendary troops, nicknamed 'leathernecks'.

2. = Rouseabout 2. *Austral.*

1898 *Bulletin* (Sydney) 1 Oct. 14/3 In a shearing shed: The boss is the 'finger', the shearers the 'brutes', the rouseabouts 'leathernecks'. **1899** W. T. Googe *Hits, Skits & Jingles* 155 And he 'pinked' him like a leatherneck when squatters paid a pound. **1945** Baker *Austral. Lang.* xvi. 286 *A leatherneck* is a marine in the U.S.; in Australia he is a station handyman.

leathery, *a.* Add: **b. leathery turtle** = *leatherback* (*Leather *sb.* 6).

1875 *Encycl. Brit.* III. 112/1 The 'leathery turtle'..is herbivorous, and yields abundance of oil. **1901** [see Luth]. **1963** J. Kirkup *Tropic Temper* 270 The 'leathery turtles' are among the world's largest and in Malaya they haunt the beaches of Trengganu. **1966** *Festival Malaysia 1966: Calendar of Events* 8 (*caption*) A giant leathery turtle of the East Coast of the Malay peninsula. **1969** A. Bellairs *Life of Reptiles* I. ii. 41 Some workers have believed that the huge leathery turtle (*Dermochelys*)..is more primitive than the rest.

leavable (lī·văb'l), *a.* [f. Leave *v.*[1] + -able.] Able to be left.

1923 H. G. Wells *Men like Gods* I. i. 10 The affairs of the *Liberal* were just then in a particularly leavable state. **1946** *N.Y. Herald Tribune* 2 June (Books) 5 Her rather rubbishy mother..had finally gone off with her artist, bringing despair to her 'leavable' husband, who could not help alienating the people he loved most.

leave, *sb.*[1] Add: **1. e.** Also *transf.*

1963 *Times* 28 Sept. 9/4 While not personally subscribing to the use of the term 'on leave' by office workers to describe their annual break(s), I can contribute reasons for their doing so. **1973** *Times* 17 Apr. 12/8 She will be on a six month leave-of-absence from the [National Theatre] company. **1974** P. De Vries *Glory of Hummingbird* xiv. 206 It'll only be a leave of absence... But..*if* there's a blowup, the firm will be able to say you were let go.

2. *to take leave*: used as a formula to draw attention, with a somewhat ponderous affectation of presumption, to a truth or state of affairs. Cf. Beg *v.* 3.

1611 [see Take *v.* 21]. **1814** T. S. Raffles *Substance of Minute on Java* 100, I take leave to observe, that the state of landed tenure here is very different from what it is reported to be in other parts of Java. **1820** [see Take *v.* 21]. **1834** M. Edgeworth *Helen* III. v. 93 We must take leave to pause one moment to remark..that the first little fib in which Lady Cecilia..indulged herself..occasioned her..a good deal of..trouble. **1928** *Sat. Rev.* 28 July 127/1 Stephen has many excellent qualities both of heart and head, though whether her sufferings would have cradled her into a first-rate novelist we take leave to doubt. **1938** 'M. Innes' *Lament for Maker* I. viii. 53 We may take leave to think the silly body stood there in the sleet and cursed the lure of the wanderer roundly.

b. (Later examples.)

1916 A. Bennett *Lion's Share* v. 40 'Mother!' cried Audrey. 'Have you taken leave of your senses?' **1942** 'M. Innes' *Daffodil Affair* II. iv. 58, I think you've taken leave of your senses. **1968** L. Goodman *Sun Signs* (1970) 325 You'll think I've taken leave of my senses, if you've just met that particular Pluto person. **1972** 'M. Innes' *Open House* II. xiii. 129 Nothing of the kind... You must have taken leave of your senses.

5. *leave camp, centre, list, period, permit, rota, -way*; **leave-boat,** a boat carrying troops on leave; **leave draft,** a detachment of troops on leave; **leave-out,** at certain schools, permission to go beyond the school precincts; cf. *leave-day, leave-out day* in Dict.; **leave party** *Mil.*, a group of servicemen on leave; **leave-taker,** one making his farewell; **leave-train,** a train carrying troops on leave.

1917 'Contact' *Airman's Outings* v. 118 Passengers on a Channel leave-boat are quieter than might be expected. **1922** Blunden *Bonadventure* iii. 21 To the Plate and back again, in a cargo ship!.. The voyage, no doubt, would be more arduous than that in the leave-boat from Boulogne to Folkestone. **1945** W. S. Churchill *Victory* (1946) 109 Eight new leave camps are under construction. **1961** *Reader's Digest* Feb. 24/1 Last March..the government was asked why African airmen in Her Majesty's service had been excluded from a Kenya leave centre. **1966** *New Statesman* 14 Oct. 537/3 The lavish structure of permanent installations, family homes, schools, leave centres and the like is enormously costly. **1920** *Blackw. Mag.* May 608/2 The sallow complexions..and leanness of a leave draft from the Palestine front. **1917** 'Contact' *Airman's Outings* v. 108 Only during the intervals of attack is the leave-list unpigeonholed. **1940** M. Marples *Public School Slang* 164 I've got leave-out. **1955** *Times* 18 Aug. 10/6 When I was in College at Winchester, one of our favourite pastimes used to be hitch-hiking on leave-out days. These were free days during term when we could do as we liked. **1916** W. Owen *Let.* 3 July (1967) 398, I had the Leave Party to conduct to the Station the other day. **1954** W. Faulkner *Fable* 128 During three of these two-week leave-periods..the entire squad had vanished from France.., and reappeared one morning two weeks later. **1906** *Daily Chron.* 14 May 5/2 The report..recommends.. that traffic in leave-permits be made illegal. **1940** 'Gun Buster' *Return via Dunkirk* I. x. 76 I've been looking at the leave rota, and see you're down for January 10. **1891** Kipling *Light that Failed* xv. 310 Bess found Dick his cabin in the wild turmoil of a ship full of leavetakers and weeping relatives. **1922** Joyce *Ulysses* 190 The quaker librarian came from the leavetakers. **1917** 'Contact' *Airman's Outings* v. 113 The train, true to the custom of leave trains, was very late. **1918** A. Bennett *Pretty Lady* xx. 132 Then I can't catch my train at Victoria..the leave-train. My leave is up to-night. **1913** T. E. Lawrence *Let.* 29 Sept. (1938) 157 They half suggested a royalty of a pound a head a day, as leave-way to dig.

leave (līv), *sb.*[2] [f. Leave *v.*[1] 3.] In Billiards, etc., the position in which the balls are left for the next player or stroke.

1896 W. Broadfoot et al. *Billiards* x. 319 Every leave was the result of accident rather than of design. **1903** W. Mitchell *Cue Tips* 6 The most interesting and not the least useful way to practise billiards..is..to place the balls in certain favourable positions upon the table and attempt to make as large a break as possible from the 'leave'. **1914** Ld. Tollemache *Croquet* xiv. 74 A well thought-out and finished Leave is one of the hall-marks of a first-class player. **1929** J. Davis *Billiards Up-to-Date* viii. 89 An exception..is seen when, at the commencement of a break, an opponent presents you with a leave which necessitates the use of side. **1936** —— *Improve Your Snooker* xii. 69, I cannot guarantee you will bring off this shot if you are presented with a similar leave. **1968** *Croquet* July 2/2 It is when we consider how to make leaves against good shots that the fun really begins.

leave, *v.*[1] Add: **3. e.** To allow, permit, let. *colloq.* (chiefly *U.S.*).

Cf. *to leave..be* s.v. sense 13 in Dict.

1840 *Southern Lit. Messenger* VI. 508/1 If you ha'nt a mind to go, you can leave it be, it's all one to me. **1863** T. D. Price *Diary* 14 Apr. (MS.), I left him have colt. **1910** J. Hart *Vigilante Girl* iv. 55 It's all right so long as you don't leave her get loose. **1916** 'Boyd Cable' *Action Front* 235 Prickles, me lad, it's deep enough we've dug to lave us get out to our German Gineral. **1935** Z. N. Hurston *Mules & Men* (1970) I. vi. 127 Leave the weeds go. Somebody 'll come chop 'em some day. **1940** J. O'Hara *Pal Joey* 103 But I said to him how can I pay you if you dont leave me wear it and I lose my job.

5. c. *to leave* (*something, much*, etc.) *to be desired* (*to wish*, etc.) (examples).

[**1769** F. Brooke *Hist. Emily Montague* IV. 189 Every anxiety is removed from my Emily's dear bosom: a father's sanction leaves her nothing to desire.] **1780** F. Burney *Diary & Lett.* (1842) I. viii. 335 Etty plays as if inspired, and in taste, expression, delicacy and feeling, leaves nothing to wish. **1835** *Athenæum* 16 May 371/1 Her style, too, leaves little to be desired. **1852** *Harper's Mag.* Aug. 422/2 This edition leaves nothing to be desired by the most fastidious book-fancier. **1876** F. Pollock *Pollock–Holmes Lett.* (1942) I. 6 Kent is a considerable advance, but leaves much to be desired. **1895** F. Espinasse *Life E. Renan* x. 185 Dean Stanley's French accent left much to be desired, but his volubility was indisputable. **1939** M. Allingham *Mr. Campion & Others* I. iii. 65 The staff still left much to be desired and the food..was certainly not cooked by a master. **1953** G. Durrell *Overloaded Ark* ix. 166 Apart from his face, which left much to be desired, his feet were swollen to twice normal size with elephantiasis. **1967** A. Bailey in L. Deighton *London Dossier* 52 The vegetables leave much to be desired, but the Stilton is worth having. **1974** *Times* 22 Jan. 2 When the clubs first applied for licences it was decided not to oppose them. 'Now that we know how they operate, we feel they leave a lot to be desired.'

7. d. (Earlier and later examples.)

1884 E. W. Nye *Baled Hay* 56 That is where we get left. **1908** *Daily Chron.* 16 Nov. 5/2 'Oh, never mind those,' says the admiral; 'what has the Navy got?' 'Got left, as usual,' replies the lieutenant. **1928** D. H. Lawrence *Lady Chatterley* vi. 73 It was no good being really good and getting left with it.

e. *Cricket.* Of the ball, to move away from (the batsman); used of a leg break delivery which turns away from the batsman.

1952 A. Bedser *Bowling* II. vii. 64 A type of leg-spin which, of course, makes the ball leave or go away from the batsman. **1956** R. Alston *Test Commentary* iii. 19 Both batsmen seemed especially fallible to the ball that left them.

13. *to leave... be* (later examples); *to leave* (a person) *cold*: see *Cold *a.* 7 e; *to leave it at that*: to proceed no further with a matter; to refrain from pressing a point; *to leave to* (*himself*, etc.): to let (a person, etc.) alone or without help or interference from another or others; *to leave* (a person) *to it*: to leave (someone) alone, esp. to allow him to proceed with a task in hand.

1833 *Chambers's Edin. Jrnl.* II. 145/1 The individual who writes the present paper was once 'so far left to himself' as to spend several months amidst the heartless frivolities which characterise a winter of fashionable life in the Scottish..capitals. **1902** *Captain* VII. 542/1 We'll leave it at that, then. **1910** 'Saki' *Reginald in Russia* 8 Left to themselves, Egbert and Lady Anne would unfailingly have called him Fluff. **1918** C. Mackenzie *Early Life Sylvia Scarlett* II. ii. 283 The petulant way in which she shook herself free from the embrace at last brought

Sylvia up to the point of leaving Lily to herself. **1928** GALSWORTHY *Swan Song* II. ii. 114 He had looked at her, and left it at that. **1943** J. B. PRIESTLEY *Daylight on Saturday* xvi. 114 'You never told her what she ought to do..,' said Freda to Jock. And then she left them to it. **1946** E. O'NEILL *Iceman Cometh* (1947) II. 102 Leave Hugo be!.. He's earned his dream! **1948** C. DAY LEWIS *Otterbury Incident* iv. 45 Ted and I left him to it. **1949** V. GROVE *Language Bar* viii. 114 If understanding and sense were not sought after, the ignorant would merely corrupt the 'meaningless' word, and leave it at that. **1958** L. A. G. STRONG *Light above Lake* xxi. 148 Toby..left him be for a while. **1966** *Oxf. Univ. Gaz.* 23 Dec. 445/2 If the House is content to leave it at that for the present,.. then I would ask if we might withdraw the resolution and leave it at that for today. **1967** SINGHA & MASSEY *Indian Dances* i. 34 South India had been more or less left to itself. **1970** D. STOREY *Contractor* I. 40 I'll leave you to it before the rest of 'em arrive. **1971** M. WEST *Summer of Red Wolf* 9 Leave me be for a moment, please. **1972** R. ADAMS *Watership Down* xxxiii. 258 They'll know which way we've gone and they won't leave it at that. **1974** W. T. BURLEY *Death in Stanley St.* vii. 127 Wycliffe stood up. 'Good. I'll leave you to it.'

b. (Earlier example of *leave go.*)

1776 in *Essex Inst. Hist. Coll.* (1907) XLIII. 118 Tis said we left go pieces of heavy cannon owing to the cowardice of a body of Connecticut troops.

14. e. Freq. in pa. pple. *left over*, remaining, not used up.

1892 'MARK TWAIN' *Amer. Claimant* xii. 107 Irish stew made of the potatoes and meat left over from a procession of previous meals. **1899** G. B. BURGIN *Bread of Tears* II. i. 138 The undigested fragments which were left over after the making of the world. **1907** *Smart Set* Mar. 72/1 You can go to the boss for your time—if there's anything left over from your breakage account. **1940** J. O'HARA *Pal Joey* 114 Choice meats like steak & chops etc. that was left over from the nite before. **1955** M. PATTEN *Learning to Cook* ii. 59 (*heading*) Foods that have been left over.

leave (līv), *adv.* Chiefly *U.S.* var. of *lieve* (LIEF *adv.*).

1840 *Southern Lit. Messenger* VI. 508/1 Never mind.. I'd as leave be here as anywheres else. **1898** M. DELAND *Old Chester Tales* 80, I would just as leave. **1902** A. D. MCFAUL *Ike Glidden* xviii. 144, I would 's leave git fired. **1921** D. H. LAWRENCE *Sea & Sardinia* 121 They would fetch you a bang over the head as leave as look at you. **1935** G. INGRAM *'Stir' Train* i. 16 'I've got a little instrument here,' Margot showed him a thin scalpel.., 'and.. I would as leave stick it into anyone's belly as any surgeon.'

leaver. Add: *spec.* a boy or girl who has just left or is about to leave school. See *school-leaver* (*SCHOOL *sb.*¹ 19).

1910 *Westm. Gaz.* 17 Jan. 5/1 Of the entrants and leavers examined, approximately 3 per cent. of the children.. suffered from..eye disease. **1930** *Times Educ. Suppl.* 28 June 289/3 One teacher..wearied to despair by the listlessness and lack of interest of his class of 'leavers', persuaded his head to allow him to hire an allotment. **1969** R. LAYARD et al. *Impact of Robbins* 121 The numbers of entrants to arts faculties are expressed as a percentage of leavers with arts A levels and similarly for science. **1972** *Guardian* 3 Aug. 6/6 Employers..were most favourably impressed with leavers' basic art and design skills.

Leavers: see *LEVERS.

leaves (līvz), var. *LIEVES.

1771 J. S. COPLEY *Let.* 17 Aug. in *Mass. Hist. Soc. Coll.* (1914) LXXI. 142 If Mr. Joy would as leaves wainscott the..Room as plaister,.. I should prefer it. *Ibid.* 20 Sept. 160, I had as leaves Miller should paper as any one, provided he does it as Cheep.

leaving, *vbl. sb.* Add: **3.** *leaving certificate* (later examples; and additional sense: see quot. 1923); *leaving scholarship*; **leaving-age**, the age at which a pupil is legally entitled to leave school; **leaving-off time**, the time of ceasing work.

1943 J. GRAVES *Policy & Progress Secondary Educ.* xix. 125 The curriculum would vary according to the normal leaving age and the different interests and abilities of the children. **1914** 'I. HAY' *Lighter Side School Life* i. 24 Oxford and Cambridge Locals..or, in Scotland, the Leaving Certificate. **1923** J. D. HACKETT in *Management Engineering* May, *Leaving Certificate*, a card given to laid-off employees, entitling them to consideration when work is resumed. **1963** J. FOUNTAIN in B. James *Austral. Short Stories* 275 Brilliant passes in the Intermediate and Leaving Certificate examinations. **1971** *Guardian* 2 July 7/4 With an examination reform which provides a leaving certificate..raising the school-leaving age to 16 would be a failure. **1907** *Westm. Gaz.* 26 Aug. 10/2 It is the usual practice at leaving-off time on Saturdays for the workmen ..to cease work at once. **1889** *Nation* (N.Y.) 7 June 464/1 This sum includes the 'leaving' scholarship given by the Clothworkers' Company.

Leavisian (lī·visiăn), *sb.* and *a.* [f. the name of the English literary critic, Frank Raymond *Leavis* (b. 1895) + -IAN.] **A.** *sb.* An admirer or follower of F. R. Leavis. **B.** *adj.* Of, pertaining to, or characteristic of F. R. Leavis or his writings.

1959 *Times Lit. Suppl.* 1 May 256/2 There are Leavisians, there are Empsonians, but, as an embattled band, preaching and practising the Master's doctrine, there are no Ricardians. **1963** *Ibid.* 17 May 357/1 The Arnoldian and Leavisian concern with 'high seriousness'. **1964** *Punch* 29 Apr. 624/2 The phrase 'quality of life'..is something of a Leavisian stock response. **1969** *Listener* 16 Oct. 508/2 Many speakers brought a Leavisian passion and concern to the study of popular culture. They kept, in other words, to a view of art as a humanising study. **1972** *Times Lit. Suppl.* 19 May 577/2 The Leavisian conceptual articulation is compact, powerful and cogent.

Leavisite (lī·visəit), *a.* and *sb.* = *LEAVISIAN *sb.* and *a.*

1958 *Times Lit. Suppl.* 17 Jan. 30/4 Mr Wain is still involved with Leavisite criticism. **1962** *Listener* 6 Sept. 364/2 The pages about which the Leavisite, or the general reader, may feel himself below G.C.E. 'O'-level on the Snow line are, happily, few. **1963** A. HARTLEY *State of England* ii. 50 Dr. Leavis seems to have been one of the rare contemporary examples of a teacher conveying a view of life to his pupils... The word 'Leavisite' is not an empty one. **1969** *Sunday Times* (Colour Suppl.) 21 Dec. 25/4 Arnoldians, Leavisites, Marxists, Fabians, Buberites were all free to get on with it. **1970** *Guardian* 16 Sept. 10/3 You can't go on writing Leavisite criticism when you've reviewed everything that relates to the great tradition.

Lebanese (lebănī·z), *sb.* and *a.* [f. *Leban-on* + -ESE.] **A.** *sb.* A native or inhabitant of Lebanon; also *collect.* **B.** *adj.* Of or pertaining to Lebanon or its inhabitants.

1920 *Glasgow Herald* 5 Apr. 6 The Lebanese..have.. dissociated themselves entirely from the action of the Syrian Congress. **1926** *Contemp. Rev.* Feb. 194 A distinguished Lebanese Druse. **1927** *Times* (Weekly ed.) 25 Aug. 208/3 Many..Lebanese residing in Egypt became French subjects. **1957** M. BANTON *W. Afr. City* v. 77 The Lebanese and Indians are not numerous. **1972** M. J. BOSSE *Incident at Naha* i. 39, I..accepted some authentic Lebanese hash. **1972** *Times* 27 June 9/1 Pressures within Lebanon to get them [*sc.* Palestine guerrilla forces] to leave Lebanese territory. **1973** *Guardian* 21 May 4/7 If the fighting had kept going, they would have been obliged to join in: Lebanese against Lebanese.

lebbek (le·bek). Also **labakh, lebba(c)k, lebbakh, lebbeck, lebek.** [ad. Arab. *labak*.] A large deciduous tree, *Albizia lebbeck*, of the family Leguminosæ, native to the tropics of north Africa and Asia and bearing heads of yellowish-white flowers; = SIRIS a.

1766 tr. *Hasselquist's Voyages & Travels in Levant* 249 Acacia of Upper Egypt... The Arabs call it Lebbeck. **1803** W. WITTMAN *Travels in Turkey* xiv. 346 In the vicinity of Cairo..a species of the cassia fistula grows to a considerable height, and affords a very agreeable shade... By the Arabs this tree is called lebback. **1916** J. B. COOPER *Coo-oo-ee* xvii. 253 The troops went past them, down the long avenue of lebbakhs. **1920** E. H. JONES *Road to En-Dor* (ed. 2) iv. 39 Along the long, straight road near Cairo..there was an avenue of lebbak trees. **1921** *Blackw. Mag.* Feb. 155/1 They drove out through the eight-mile tunnel of lebbek-trees. **1929** BROUN & MASSEY *Flora Sudan* 174 *A[lbizzia] Lebbek* Benth. Labakh, Lebbek. **1942** C. BARRETT *On Wallaby* vi. 134 The lebek trees were in bloom and delicate foliage rippled in the cool wind. **1965** ZAND & VIDEAN tr. *'Abd al-Latif al-Baghdādī's Eastern Key* 33 While the fruit of the labakh is green it has a styptic savour like a green date, but when it is ripe it becomes sweet and agreeable, and takes on a viscous quality.

‖**Lebensform** (lē·bənzfǭɹm). Pl. **Lebensformen.** [G., 'form of life'. Used notably by L. Wittgenstein in the German text of his *Philos. Investigations*.] Any type of human activity that involves values, e.g. the artistic or political or religious life; gen., a style or aspect of life.

1937 G. W. ALLPORT *Personality* viii. 231 These Lebensformen are at best only *categories* of value. **1959** *Times Lit. Suppl.* 11 Sept. 513/2 Mr. Stuart Hampshire in *Thought and Action* is aware of the scale of his undertaking. 'It is necessary first,' he says, 'to view the using of language as a particular form of human behaviour' (Wittgenstein called it *Lebensform*).

‖ **Lebenslust** (lē·bənzlust). [G., = joy of living.] = *JOIE DE VIVRE.

1890 W. JAMES *Let.* 22 Aug. in R. B. Perry *Tht. & Char. W. James* (1935) I. 414 Your last two letters..breathed a spirit of youth, a sort of *Lebenslust*. **1958** P. DE VRIES *Mackerel Plaza* 84 Security he could give her, yes, but not, I'm afraid, something else demanded by her *Lebenslust*. **1963** *Economist* 19 Oct. 228/2 As long as the *Lebenslust* continues to drive him regularly into Bonn.

‖ **lebensraum** (lē·bənzraum). Also **L-.** [G., f. genit. of *leben* life + *raum* space.] Territory which the Germans believed was needed for their natural development (now *Hist.*). Also *transf.*

1905 *Mind* XIV. 266 A universal activity..forms an all-comprehending *Lebensraum* in which the manifold may meet and enter into relation. **1935** [see *life-space* s.v. *LIFE *sb.* 16 a]. **1939** O. LANCASTER *Homes Sweet Homes* 46 These treasures were joined on..overcrowded ledges by a new wave of invaders..and..the problem of *lebensraum* had become acute. **1939** A. SALTER *Dual Policy* 25 *Lebensraum*, or a place in the sun, is the historic claim and ambition of Germany, as 'encirclement' is her historic anxiety. **1939** *War Illustr.* 9 Dec. 393/1 Moravia and Bohemia had been overrun by the Nazi armies and declared German Protectorates—part of the German people's 'lebensraum'. **1940** [see *APPEASEMENT 4]. **1951** S. VAN VALKENBURG in G. Taylor *Geogr. in 20th Cent.* iv. 109 Kurt Vohwinkel (..1939)..distinguishes three kinds of German *Lebensraum*. The first kind is the real area occupied solidly by Germans; the second the area where besides Germans there are other people but the German cultural influence prevails; and the third is the one in which Germans are outnumbered by others but still because of their racial and cultural superiority have a right to dominate. **1957** *Encycl. Brit.* VIII. 881/2 Hitler was convinced that..Germany..needed Russian territory for *Lebensraum*. **1959** *Listener* 25 June 1119/1 People, both white and black, either intent on gain or simply seeking *lebensraum* and resolved not to share it. **1960** *Guardian* 14 Mar. 6/6 Music, manuscripts, and her little daughter's toys compete amiably for *lebensraum*. **1960** *Times* 30 May 13/6 Lebensraum for the Japanese. **1972** W. A. PANTIN *Oxf. Life* iv. 49 The problem of *Lebensraum* for the developing natural sciences..was already beginning to appear in the early-nineteenth-century minutes of the Hebdomadal Council.

‖**lebensspur** (lē·bənzʃpūr). Also with capital initial. Usu. as *pl.* **lebensspuren.** [a. G. *lebensspur* (O. Abel *Grundzüge der Palaeobiol. der Wirbeltiere* (1912) 65), f. *leben* life + *spur* trace, track, remains (cogn. w. SPOOR *sb.*¹).] A small track, burrow, cast, or the like left in sediment by a living organism; *esp.* one preserved in fossil form in sedimentary rock.

1960 *Gloss. Geol.* (Amer. Geol. Inst.) Suppl. 37/2 Lebensspur. **1962** R. C. MOORE *Treat. Invertebr. Paleont.* W. 178/2 Lebensspuren are very transient structures as compared with shells, skeletons, or other hard parts, and in general they have little chance of being preserved as fossils. *Ibid.* 179/2 Many fossils..which have now been identified as Lebensspuren, were considered to be remains of marine algae. **1964** PETTIJOHN & POTTER *Atlas & Gloss. Primary Sedimentary Struct.* Plate 70A (*heading*) Lebensspuren on underside of sandstone. **1973** *Nature* 30 Mar. 323/2 In a recently completed series of laboratory studies, lebensspuren were produced by individual macrobenthic organisms on a variety of marine sand and mud substrates (freshly collected from..the Bristol Channel) from which all other macrofauna had been removed by passing it through a 1·0 mm mesh. But the resultant tracks, trails and burrows gradually disappeared when the aquarium tanks..were left undisturbed.

‖**Lebenswelt** (lē·bənzvelt). [Ger.] = *life-world* (see *LIFE *sb.* 17).

1962 A. W. LEVI *Lit., Philos. & Imagination* 138 What Husserl has called the *Lebenswelt*—the ongoing continuity of 'lived' experience. **1964** *Amer. Philos. Q.* I. 127/1 According to Wild the *Lebenswelt* is the world of direct, lived experience. **1966** *Philos. Rev.* LXXV. 394 Husserl's transcendental philosophy and..his concept of the *Lebenswelt*.

Leber (lēⁱ·bəɹ). *Ophthalm.* The name of Theodor *Leber* (1840–1917), German ophthalmologist, used in the possessive esp. in **Leber's disease**, hereditary optic atrophy, a rare hereditary disease in which partial blindness in both eyes sets in rapidly, typically affecting young men; also called *Leber's (hereditary optic) atrophy*.

1890 BILLINGS *Med. Dict.* II. 41/2 *Leber's disease*, hereditary optic atrophy. **1902** *Encycl. Medica* X. 358 Possibly the family cases known as Leber's atrophy may come under this heading. **1932** *Times Lit. Suppl.* 5 May 334/4 The theoretical analysis is applied to statistics of albinism, colour blindness, haemophilia and Leber's disease. **1952** C. P. BLACKER *Eugenics* x. 248 Among these genes [located on the human sex chromosomes] are those believed to determine:.. Leber's optic atrophy, a progressive form of blindness. **1971** DUKE-ELDER & SCOTT in S. Duke-Elder *Syst. Ophthalm.* XII. ii. 108 Leber's hereditary optic atrophy is a relatively rare condition of unknown ætiology. *Ibid.*, In the main Leber's disease is hereditary.

‖ **leberwurst** (lē·bəɹwŭɹst). [G.] = *liver sausage.

1855 GEO. ELIOT in *Fraser's Mag.* June 706/1 Goethe.. is enthusiastic about the delights of dining on blaukraut and leberwurst (blue cabbage and liver sausage). **1969** [see *BLUTWURST]. **1971** R. PETRIE *Thorne in Flesh* iii. 40 A packet of cane spaghetti and a jar of leberwurst.

‖ **lebes** (le·bīz). *Gr. Antiq.* [Gr. λέβης.] A deep round-bottomed bowl, usually set on a stand, for holding wine; often used as a wedding-gift (*lebes gamikos*).

1851 *Catal. Greek & Etruscan Vases Brit. Mus.* I. 34 Lebes..Clay ash-coloured; varnish black and maroon, [etc.]. **1885** *Encycl. Brit.* XIX. 614/1 (*caption*) On the left is a gilt pyxis with a tall lid, and an œnochoe on a low table; on the right two tall vases (lebes) on a plinth. **1935** RICHTER & MILNE *Shapes & Names Athenian Vases* 9 *Lebes* (Greek λέβης), deep bowl with round bottom, made to be set on a stand. *Ibid.* 11 *Lebes gamikos* (Greek λέβης γαμικός), 'marriage bowl'. High foot, double handles on the shoulder, the bowl in one piece with the foot. **1937** *Antiquity* XI. 246 The large nuptial lebes. **1974** SAVAGE & NEWMAN *Illustr. Dict. Ceramics* 177 Lebes (Greek), a type of bowl of Greek pottery used for mixing wine and water. It is ovoid in form and has a high shoulder, a low neck, and two vertical handles; it usually has a rounded bottom and rests on a stand.

Leblanc¹ (ləbla·ṅ). Also **LeBlanc.** The name of Nicolas *Leblanc* (1742–1806), French chemist, used *attrib.* to designate a (now obsolete) process for the manufacture of sodium carbonate in which sodium chloride is treated with hot concentrated sulphuric acid to form

the sulphate ('salt-cake'), which is then heated with limestone and coal and the resulting carbonate dissolved out with water.

[**1864** *Chem. News* 5 Mar. 111/1 (*heading*) Theoretical researches on the preparation of soda by Leblanc's process.] **1880** G. LUNGE *Theoret. & Pract. Treat. Manuf. Sulphuric Acid & Alkali* II. iv. 361 (*heading*) The manufacture of soda by the Leblanc process. **1930** J. A. TIMM *Introd. Chem.* xxxiii. 438 During the 75 years which followed, the LeBlanc process grew to be a great industry, spreading to Germany, Austria, and England. **1965** D. ABBOTT *Inorg. Chem.* iv. 157 Sodium sulphate is manufactured by the first stage of the Leblanc process.

Leblanc² (ləbla·ń). *Electr. Engin.* The name of Maurice *Leblanc* (1857–1923), French electrical engineer, used *attrib.* to designate apparatus invented by him, as **Leblanc connection,** a method of connecting three single-phase transformer windings to convert three-phase current to two-phase; **Leblanc exciter** or **phase advancer,** a device for advancing the phase of the rotor current of an induction motor, consisting of a direct-current armature and commutator, having three sets of brushes per pair of poles connected to the slip rings of the main motor, and driven somewhat faster than the main motor.

1924 M. WALKER *Control of Speed & Power Factor of Induction Motors* vii. 117 The Leblanc exciter, consisting of an armature built like a continuous current armature and excited by the rotor currents following either the armature itself or in a field magnet surrounding the armature. **1948** M. G. SAY *Performance & Design Alternating Current Machines* (ed. 2) v. 68 The Le Blanc connection has the advantage of using a standard three-phase transformer core. **1965** J. HINDMARSH *Electr. Machines* ix. 492 (*heading*) Leblanc phase advancer. **1966** BROSAN & HAYDEN *Adv. Electr. Power & Machines* vi. 243 In the Leblanc connexion there are three magnetic cores, and the primary windings may be connected in either star or delta. *Ibid.* x. 476 Another method of power factor control utilizes the Leblanc exciter. **1968** A. R. DANIELS *Performance Electr. Machines* v. 97 An alternative method of 3/2 phase conversion is the Leblanc connection.

leccer (le·kəɹ). Also **lecker, lekker.** [*-ER⁶.] Slang or colloquial alteration of LECTURE *sb.* (See also quot. 1900.)

1899 *Daily Tel.* 14 Aug., Leccers, lectures. **1900** FARMER *Public School Word-Bk.* 124 *Lecker*, 1. (Oxford). A lecture. 2. (Harrow). The electric light. **1904** [see *-ER *suffix*⁶]. **1907** 'B. BURKE' *Barbara goes to Oxf.* (1915) 115 I'm awfully sorry that I had to cut your leccer, my mother came up quite unexpectedly. **1911** W. ELMHIRST *Freshman's Diary* (1969) 10 Had 1st leccer from the Dean this morning. *Ibid.* 11 Had a caller, who..said good night saying we should meet in another sphere what one I don't know as he said he didn't row & he certainly doesn't come to P.Mods leccers. **1914** C. MACKENZIE *Sinister St.* II. III. viii. 455 And you won't come out..to watch people buying copies on their way to leckers? **1928** *Daily Express* 29 June 5/3 A..dilapidated basket filled with gay-coloured 'lekker' notebooks.

lech (letʃ), *sb.*⁴ Also **letch.** [Now regarded as a back-formation from LECHER *sb.*, but cf. LETCH *sb.*²] **a.** A strong desire or longing, esp. sexual. **b.** = LECHER *sb.*

1796 [see LETCH *sb.*²]. *c* **1830** *Venus School Mistress* Pref. in 'Pisanus Fraxi' *Index Librorum Prohibitorum* (1877) 399 It [*sc.* flagellation] is, however, a *lech*, which has existed from time immemorial. **1868** *Index expurgatorius of Martial* 39 There are various rumours as to the nature of your letch. *c* **1888–94** *My Secret Life* III. 147 Did they fuck with me for fun, for letch, or for money? **1934** G. GREENE *It's a Battlefield* 204 This is when a girl gets a baby; when she's got a lech like this. **1938** S. BECKETT *Murphy* vii. 126 A man could no more work a woman out of her position on her own ground of sentimental lech than he cd outsmell a dog. **1940** S. LEWIS *Bethel Merriday* xxxiii. 387 Your letch for power over everyone around you. **1941** 'R. WEST' *Black Lamb* II. 204 Those who had a lech for violence could gratify it. **1943** H. A. SMITH *Life in Putty Knife Factory* x. 157 If anybody noticed what I was doing, they'd think I was an old letch. **1956** E. POUND tr. *Sophocles' Women of Trachis* 17 All started when he had a letch for the girl. **1958** *Spectator* 10 Oct. 482/1 A post-war working-class family..—the grey letch of a father, his jolly rolypoly wife and their prissy daughter. **1959** J. BRAINE *Vodi* xix. 220, I don't mind admitting I always had a lech for her. **1960** *Times Lit. Suppl.* 27 May 333/4 Graves is 'a lech', whose current mistress is Purling's wife, Jo. **1964** [see *DROOL *v.*]. **1970** *Guardian* 13 Feb. 9/6 A rich man can have a beautiful young wife even if he is a gropy old letch! **1971** *Petticoat* 17 July 7/1 Out of ten girls who are invited back to men's flats for coffee, at least eight expect a cup of coffee and are quite shocked and horrified when they find themselves pinned to the bed, five seconds after walking into the lech's lair. **1972** *Sunday Times* 12 Nov. 40/3 Many so-called platonic friendships..are merely one-way leches.

Lech, Lekh (leχ), *sb.*⁵ and *a.* Also **Lach, L'ach** (lʸaχ). [ad. G. *Lech*, O.Russ. *lyakh*; f. O.Pol. *lęch.] **A.** *sb.* A member of an early Slavonic people once inhabiting the region around the upper Oder and Vistula, whose descendants are the Poles; also, the name of a legendary ancestor of this people. **B.** *adj.* Of or pertaining to the Lechs or their language. Cf. *LECHISH *sb.* and *a.*, *LECHITIC *sb.* and *a.*

1893 W. R. MORFILL *Poland* 23 In the sixth or seventh centuries some people settled on that river [*sc.* the Vistula] are called Lekhs, a word which has never been satisfactorily explained. The older form probably had a nasal: hence we get in the Latin chroniclers *Lenchitæ*, in Lithuanian, *Lenkas*, and in Magyar, *Lengyel*. **1911** *Encycl. Brit.* XXV. 236/2 In the north Polish is closely connected with Kašube, and this with Polab, making the group of L'ach dialects in which the nasals survived... The two Sorb dialects link the L'achs on to the Čechs and Slovaks, the whole making the N.W. group with its preference for *c, z, s* as against *č, ž, š*. **1929** *Ibid.* XVIII. 161/2 The nearest relative of Polish is Polabian, with which it forms the Lech group. **1939** G. SLOCOMBE *Hist. Poland* (new ed.) 12 The Western Slavs had become divided into three distinct sections: the Serbs..; the Czech group..; and the Lech group, in which were included the Obodrites, the Wiltzi, the Pomeranians.., and other tribes who were in the course of the succeeding centuries to form the Polish nation. **1950** A. P. GOUDY in *Cambr. Hist. Poland to 1696* i. 10 Besides the name Polanie, there existed another collective name—Lachy (Lechs). This term is used in the Chronicle of Nestor to indicate the Poles and came into frequent use by the old chroniclers.

lech (letʃ), *v.* Also **letch.** [Back-formation from LECHER *sb.*] *intr.* To behave lustfully, to feel or to be lecherous. Occas., to have a (non-sexual) desire.

1911 J. MASEFIELD *Everlasting Mercy* 68 And drunk and leched from day till morrow. **1940** E. POUND *Let.* 18 Jan. (1971) 334, I have now the text of Erigena, and *if* I could get hold of the recent publications about him, I could write quite a chunk. Not that I am letching to. **1948** PARTRIDGE *Dict. Forces' Slang* 110 *Letch*, to look at women, not necessarily in a lecherous way, in spite of its derivation. **1957** C. DAY LEWIS *Pegasus* 13 Unblest, Unchecked—what a serpent flame letched at her marrow! **1963** 'M. CORRIGAN' *Why do Women —?* xiii. 89, I..letch around looking for sex thrills. **1972** M. FARHI *Pleasure of your Death* vii. 173 He was still watching the..shapely ankles when Chastity pulled him to task. 'Don't lech!' **1973** *Guardian* 27 Feb. 10/1 A fortyish factory worker..lives with..an obsessively nubile sister whom he obviously leches after.

lechaim, var. *LECHAYIM.

Le Chatelier (ləʃäte·lye). [The name of Henry *Le Chatelier* (1850–1936), French chemist.] **a.** Used *attrib.* with reference to a test for the soundness (freedom from expansion) of cement using a small hollow brass cylinder split longitudinally and having pointers close to the split which indicate the extent of any expansion that occurs when the cylinder is filled with cement.

1904 *Specification for Portland Cement* (*B.S.I.*) 7 The cement shall be tested by the Le Chatelier method, and shall in no case show a greater expansion than 12 millimetres after 24 hours aeration and 6 millimetres after seven days aeration. The apparatus for conducting the Le Chatelier test..consists of a small split cylinder of brass. **1930** *Engineering* 18 July 62/1 Dry clay when adsorbing water increased in bulk and exerted..sufficient pressure to spring open the Le Chatelier gauge about 1 lb. per square inch. **1963** A. M. NEVILLE *Properties of Concrete* i. 50 The Le Chatelier test detects unsoundness due to free lime only.

b. Used *attrib.* and in the possessive († and in conjunction with the name of K. Ferdinand *Braun* (1850–1918), German physicist) to designate a principle enunciated by Le Chatelier, which states that if a constraint (such as a change in pressure or temperature) be applied to any system in equilibrium, the equilibrium will shift in such a way as to tend to counteract the effect of the constraint.

1910 *Chem. Abstr.* IV. 1600 (*heading*) New isomerization of benzopinacolins and Le Chatelier's law. **1911** *Ibid.* V. 3361 The author gives the following as the usual statement of the Le Chatelier–Braun principle. **1922** *Proc. Amer. Acad. Arts & Sci.* LVII. 25 The condition which must be satisfied in order that the Le Chatelier Principle may hold with regard to the effect of a change in the initial mass of *one* component, is that the addition of such component shall accelerate or retard the transformation (at equilibrium). **1943** *Thorpe's Dict. Appl. Chem.* (ed. 4) VI. 229/1 It would be expected from the Le Chatelier–Braun principle of mobile equilibrium that increase of pressure would exert a retarding effect upon the rate of a unimolecular reaction. **1954** A. R. BAILEY *Text-bk. Metall.* viii. 232 A reaction involving a gaseous reactant is favoured by increase in operating pressure, and one involving a gaseous product by decrease of pressure or by sweeping it away in a gas stream; these points also follow from Le Chatelier's Principle. **1961** A. HOLDERNESS *Inorg. & Physical Chem.* xviii. 258 If the temperature of an equilibrium system..is lowered, Le Chatelier's Principle requires the equilibrium to shift so as to tend to raise the temperature again; that is, to evolve heat. **1973** *Jrnl. Chem. Education* L. 124 Since stretching a rubber band is an exothermic process, Le Chatelier's principle predicts that heat applied to a stretched rubber band will contract it.

lechatelierite (ləʃäte·liərəit, ləʃätelīə·rəit). *Min.* Also † **-iérite.** [a. F. *lechateliérite* (A. Lacroix 1915, in *Bull. de la Soc. franç. de Min.* XXXVIII. 185), f. *LE CHATELIER + -ITE¹.] Naturally occurring vitreous silica, SiO_2, formed when siliceous material is intensely heated (as by lightning).

1916 *Mineral. Mag.* XVII. 353 *Lechatelierite*, naturally occurring fused (amorphous) silica. **1928** *Amer. Mineralogist* XIII. 77 Lechateliérite is unique in that it is the only naturally occurring glass that is definite enough to be considered a mineral. **1931** *Jrnl. R. Soc. W. Austral.* XVII. 146 Digging revealed a vertical core of lechatelierite in the soil. This core was hollow and very brittle, and extended downwards for about a metre. **1963** W. A. DEER et al. *Rock-Forming Min.* IV. 180 Silica glass (vitreous silica; lechatelierite): can exist at room temperatures and up to 1000°C... It is an unstable glass at all temperatures below 1713°C. **1964** *New Scientist* 16 Jan. 160/1 The invariable signs of flow and common presence of lechatelierite (pure silica glass) indicate that tektites were formed by rapid fusion at very high temperatures.

‖ **lechayim** (ləχəi·im). Also **l'chaim, l'cha-y(i)m, lechaim, lehayim.** [Heb., 'to life'.] A drinking toast: to life!

1932 L. GOLDING *Magnolia St.* III. ix. 582 'Here's mud in your eye!' says the Chicagoan. '*Lechayim!* To Life!' says Mr. Emmanuel. **1963** *Encounter* Apr. 35/1 The guests stood and raising their glasses honoured me, in Hebrew, with that most beautiful of toasts: *Lechaim!* To life! **1968** M. RICHLER in R. Weaver *Canad. Short Stories* 2nd Ser. 193 'I been here seven years ago and what we done since, it's remarkable. *L'chaym.*' '*L'chaym.*' **1968** P. DURST *Badge of Infamy* iii. 23 Chaim raised his glass. 'Good health.' '*L'chaim*,' Michael returned. **1968** L. ROSTEN *Joys of Yiddish* 205 *L'chayim*, pronounced *l-KHY-im*, with a resounding German *kh*, to rhyme with 'to fry 'em'. Hebrew: 'To life.' The toast offered, with raised glass, before sipping wine or liquor: 'To your health.' **1973** *Jewish Chron.* 2 Feb. 16/4 Miss Kitt raised her wine-glass. 'L'chayim,' she said.

Lecher² (le·χəɹ, le·tʃəɹ). *Physics.* Also **lecher.** The name of Ernst *Lecher* (1856–1926), Austrian physicist, used *attrib.* (esp. in *Lecher wires*) and † in the possessive to designate a pair of parallel wires in which the frequency of a high-frequency electric oscillation may be measured by means of a sliding detector or conductor placed so as to bridge the wires, positions of maximum response or absorption being separated by a distance equal to half the wavelength of the oscillation.

1897 *Phil. Mag.* XLIV. 202 In Lecher's arrangement.. the wires are of equal diameter. **1902** *Encycl. Brit.* XXVIII. 59/2 Many problems of electric waves along wires can readily be investigated by a method due to Lecher, and known as Lecher's bridge. **1929** J. A. RATCLIFFE *Physical Princ. Wireless* iii. 35 A pair of parallel wires is often used to guide the waves, instead of the single wire... This arrangement is known as the Lecher wire system. **1947** *Jrnl. Inst. Electr. Engin.* XCIV. 953/2 The tuned circuit consisted of a pair of lecher rods, the output being fed through a resonant line to a fixed end-fed half-wave vertical aerial. **1962** W. B. THOMPSON *Introd. Plasma Physics* ii. 12 In arc discharges the electron density is 10^{11}–10^{12} cm^{-3} and the plasma frequency ~100 Mc/s, so the high-frequency signals were picked up on resonant Lecher wires, rectified by a crystal and detected by a galvanometer. **1968** *Radio Communication Handbk.* (ed. 4) xix. 12/2 Lecher lines..comprise a pair of taut parallel wires, spaced an inch or so apart to form an open wire transmission line, and a bridge to short circuit the wires which can be moved along the line as required.

lecherously, *adv.* (Later example.)

1972 *Daily Tel.* 12 May 12/8 Amorous delusions concerning..a lecherously attentive neighbour and her kindly but pre-occupied husband.

Lechish (le·χiʃ), *sb.* and *a.* [ad. G. *lechisch*; cf. *LECH *sb.*⁵ and *a.*] = next.

1888 J. WRIGHT tr. *Brugmann's Elem. Compar. Gram. Indo-Germanic Lang.* I. 12 The Slavonic languages fall into a South-Eastern and a Western group... To the latter [belong] Czech.., Sorabian or Wendish..and Lechish (Polish and Polabian or Elbe-Slavonian). **1908** T. G. TUCKER *Introd. Natural Hist. Lang.* 224 The classification of the Slavonic tongues which appears to find most favour with students in that branch is as follows:—..(ii) West Group: e. Tzech. f. Sorbian. g. Lechish [Polish, Polabish (Elbe-Slavonic)]. **1936–7** *Slavonic & East European Rev.* XV. 477 The relationship of the present and past Baltic dialects of Slavonic to the other Lechish languages.

Lechitic (leχi·tik), *sb.* and *a.* Also **Lechite, Lekhite, Lekhitic.** [ad. G. *lechitisch*; cf. med.L. *Le(n)chitae* and *LECH *sb.*⁵ and *a.*] Name given by some linguists to certain West Slavonic languages (Polish, Kashubian, Slovincian, the extinct Polabian) showing characteristic features in common and sometimes held to have once formed a single subdialect within the Slavonic group. Also as *adj.*, of or pertaining to the Lechs or their language. Also comb. form **Lechito-, Lekhito-.** Cf. prec.

1934 G. C. ENGERRAND *So-called Wends of Germany* (Univ. of Texas Bull. No. 3417) 35 Its Western subgroup ..is composed of the Polish, Kashub-Slovince, former Polab, Wendish.., Czech, and Slovak languages. If we eliminate the three latter ones from that subgroup, we have a family, to which philologists give the name of Lechitic (L'Ach, Lekhite, etc.), that is characterized by the persistency of many old Slavic nasals. **1935** *Times Lit.*

Suppl. 15 Aug. 506/2 Like most of the Polish Slav philologists of the last two generations, he [*sc.* T. Lehr-Spławiński] holds the theory of a Lechitic linguistic community, that is to say, that all the Slav languages of the Baltic region from Polish in the east to Dravanian on the west bank of the Elbe constituted an unbroken chain of mutually related groups. **1939–40** *Slavonic & East European Rev.* XIX. 273 Schleicher states that Kashubian stands as a bridge between the West Lechite (Polabian) and East Lechite (Polish). **1946–7** *Ibid.* XXV. 493 Shakhmatov sees in this signs of an intermingling of certain Lechitic tribes with the Russians in North Russia. **1949–50** *Ibid.* XXVIII. 286 The Poles, as the most conservative and least mobile of the Western (Lechitic) tribes, stayed behind in the original habitat. **1950** A. P. Goudy in *Cambr. Hist. Poland to 1696* i. 9 From the linguistic point of view Slovinzish and Kashubish belong to the Polish group and it is usual to class these languages (or dialects) along with Polish and Polabian under the title Lechitic (grupa lechicka). **1964** M. Samilov *The Phoneme jat' in Slavic* 144 In Lekhitic the nasals have generally preserved their nasality. **1966** H. Birnbaum *Ancient Indo-European Dialects* 194 The dissociation of.. the West Slavs into a Lekhito-Sorbian group..and a Czechoslovak group. **1972** G. Stone *Smallest Slavonic Nation* 96 I. Taszycki's view that West Slavonic had first divided into two sub-groups—Lechito-Sorbian and Czecho-Slovak—was subsequently supported by Zdzisław Stieber.

lechwe (lī·tʃwī). Now the usual spelling of Leche. Also **lechwre, leshwe, letchwe, letshewe**; also *attrib.* (Examples.)

1881 E. E. Frewer tr. *Holub's Seven Yrs. S. Afr.* II. vi. 128 The letshewes were larger and the pukus smaller than blessbocks, and both, like all water bucks, had shaggy, light brown hair, and horns bent forward. **1907** *Westm. Gaz.* 6 Sept. 3/1 The haunts of the jacana, of the waders in general, and of the Lechwe and Situtunga. **1915** *Chambers's Jrnl.* Nov. 701/2 The lechwre is remarkable for its waterloving characteristics. **1920** *United Free Ch. Miss. Rec.* Aug. 138/1 The letchwe is an antelope much addicted to knee-deep water. **1936** P. M. Clark *Autobiogr. Old Drifter* x. 131 My first buck..was a large lechwe with beautiful curved horns. **1946** *Cape Times* 7 Aug., Herds of elephant up to 80 strong were seen, as well as.. the rare letchwe and puku buck. **1949** *Ibid.* 30 July 5/5 An expedition..has found many specimens in the Caprivi Strip, including..three genets, seven leshwe, one putu, [etc.]. **1969** *Times* 24 Oct. (Zambian Suppl.) p. xi/2 One of the rarest species of game in the world, the black lechwe antelope, is faced with extinction. **1972** *Nature* 7 Apr. 265/1 He further suggested that..the Okavango and Caprivi be set aside for species such as lechwe, puku and sitatungu.

-lecithal (le·sipăl), *suffix* [f. Gr. λέκιθ-ος yolk + -al], used to form adjs. describing egg cells with yolks of specified kinds, as *alecithal *a.*, *homolecithal* adj. (s.v. *homo-).

lecithin. Add to def.: In mod. use, any of a group of phospholipids found in plants and animals which are esters of a phosphatidic acid with choline and on hydrolysis yield choline, phosphoric acid, glycerol, and two fatty acids; also used as a generic name for these compounds. **b.** A commercial mixture of lecithin with other phosphatides and often other lipids obtained from natural products and used industrially, esp. that from soya beans. (Further examples.) [First formed as F. *lécithine* (N. T. Gobley 1850, in *Jrnl. de Pharm. et de Chim.* XVII. 411).]

1923 [see *lysolecithin* s.v. *lyso-]. **1926** G. D. Elsdon *Chem. & Exam. Edible Oils & Fats* iii. 15 Lecithin is a complex compound..and may be looked on as a triglyceride in which one of the fatty acid radicles has been replaced by a complex organic base containing phosphoric acid. *Ibid.* xii. 205 Maize oil contains 1·1 to 1·5 per cent. of lecithin. **1951** M. B. Jacobs *Chem. & Technol. Food & Food Products* (ed. 2) III. xlii. 2155 The addition of lecithin to chocolate results in a saving of cacao butter, counteracts moisture, and stabilizes the chocolate. **1951** K. S. Markley *Soybeans* II. xvi. 600 It has become customary in industrial circles to call the phosphatide residue obtained in the commercial manufacture of soybean oil soybean lecithin or simply lecithin. The commercial product contains roughly two-thirds phosphatides and one-third soybean oil. *Ibid.* 601 The term commercial lecithin or lecithin is applied almost exclusively to soybean lecithin, whereas 20 years ago it would have referred to egg lecithin. **1954** *Thorpe's Dict. Appl. Chem.* (ed. 4) XI. 47/2 Lecithins and cephalins, about 2%, are present in the oil [from soya beans] and have been widely used as emulsifiers in the food, textile, cosmetic, soap, and other industries. **1961** H. F. Payne *Organic Coating Technol.* II. xxiii. 970 Lecithin..is a balanced polar–non-polar compound and will concentrate at the interface between polar pigments and less polar oils and resins to reduce the interfacial tension and facilitate wetting. **1967** *Martindale's Extra Pharmacopoeia* (ed. 25) 293 Lecithins occur in all animal and vegetable cells and vary in composition according to the source from which they are obtained. The two chief commercial varieties are egg lecithin (ovolecithin).., and vegetable lecithin..from various vegetable sources, particularly leguminous seeds. **1970** Ambrose & Easty *Cell Biol.* viii. 272 The main lipid constituents of plasma membranes are phospholipids (in particular phosphatidylcholine or lecithin), and cholesterol, a steroid. **1973** *Sci. Amer.* Apr. 85/1 The alveolar fluid contains trace amounts of various large molecules; among them are the two principal lipids—lecithin and sphingomyelin—that represent the bulk of the pulmonary surfactant.

lecithinase (le·sipinēiz, -ēis). *Biochem.* [f. Lecithin + *-ase.] = *phospholipase.

1910 *Chem. Abstr.* IV. 2680 Lecithinase is itself almost or entirely free from toxicity, showing its independence from the neurotoxin of cobra venom. **1947** *Jrnl. Biol. Chem.* CLXIX. 704 Four types of lecithinases, each acting on a separate ester linkage of the lecithin molecule, were postulated by Contardi and Ercoli in 1932.., but the existence of only three of these has hitherto been demonstrated. These are (*a*) the enzyme found in cobra serum.. which splits off a single unsaturated fatty acid from the lecithin molecule; (*b*) the enzyme found in rice hulls..and *Aspergillus oryzae*..,which splits off both fatty acids; (*c*) the enzyme found in *Clostridium welchii*..,which separates the phospholipide molecule at its ester linkage between the glycerol and the phosphoric acid. **1959** *Biochem. Jrnl.* LXXI. 619/1 It may be of significance for the biological function of intestinal lecithinase that the optimum conditions for its activity are those which can be expected to prevail in the mucosal cells during absorption of fat. **1970** D. R. Dilley in A. C. Hulme *Biochem. Fruits* I. viii. 181 Proteases and lecithinase increase lysosomal permeability.

lecithotrophic (lesipotrǫ·fik, lekipo-), *a.* [f. Gk. λέκιθος yolk of egg + *-trophic.] Of the larvæ of certain marine invertebrates, feeding on the yolk of the egg from which they have emerged.

1950 G. Thorson in *Biol. Rev.* XXV. 10 The lecithotrophic pelagic larvae, mainly developing from fairly large yolky eggs, are of a clumsy shape, rather unfit for locomotion. **1962** D. Nichols *Echinoderms* x. 119 *Heliocidaris* has a lecithotrophic larva (feeding on stored yolk). **1967** *Oceanogr. & Marine Biol.* V. 360 Experiments refer to short-lived lecithotrophic larvae.

leck (lek), *v. rare* exc. *dial.* [Cf. E.D.D. *leck v.*] = Leak *v.* 2 c.

1922 Joyce *Ulysses* 749 Shes [a cat] as bad as a woman always licking and lecking.

lecker, var. *leccer.

Leclanché (ləklā·nʃe). The name of Georges *Leclanché* (1839–82), French chemist, used *attrib.* and *absol.* to denote a primary cell invented by him that has a zinc cathode in contact with zinc chloride, ammonium chloride (in solution or as a paste) as the electrolyte, and a carbon anode in contact with a mixture of manganese dioxide and carbon powder.

1871 *Chem. News* 6 Oct. 166/2, I find that what I said about the Leclanché battery..has led to a false impression. .. It is used only on circuits of considerable resistance, and not much work, for which it is found very suitable. **1878** *Encycl. Brit.* VIII. 93/1 Good instances of this kind of action are furnished by the bichromate battery of Bunsen and the Léchanché [*sic*] cell, which occupy a sort of middle position between one and two fluid batteries. **1891** E. M. Caillard *Electr.* iv. 264 A form of Daniell's cell has been chiefly adopted in England, but the Leclanché is also excellent for telegraphic purposes. **1907** M. K. Kassabian *Rontgen Rays & Electro-Therapeutics* iii. 64 The Leclanché cell consists of a porous cup and a carbon plate. **1946** J. R. Partington *Gen. & Inorg. Chem.* xxix. 827 Manganese dioxide is used..as a depolariser in the Leclanché cell. **1971** L. T. Agger *Introd. Electr.* xi. 171 The dry form of the Leclanché cell, which was introduced towards the end of the last century, has generally replaced the wet Leclanché and is now by far the most commonly used primary cell.

-lect, terminal element, f. L. *lect-*, *legere* to read, used to designate a regional or social variety within a language as in Dialect, *idiolect; also used in forming a number of technical terms in linguistics, as *acrolect, basilect, isolect, sociolect*, etc. (see quots.). Hence (without hyphen) as *sb.*, a social variety of a language or dialect.

1965 W. A. Stewart in R. W. Shuy *Social Dial. & Lang. Learning* 15, I will refer to this topmost dialect in the local sociolinguistic hierarchy as *acrolect* (from *acro-* 'apex' plus *-lect* as in *dialect*). In most cases what is meant by 'Standard' English is either acrolect or something close to it. At the other extreme is a kind of speech which I refer to hereafter as *basilect* (from *basi-* 'bottom'). **1969** *Florida FL Reporter* VII. 1. 48 Although acrolect differs also in sounds and words from basilect, grammatical differences between them create the real blocks to communication. **1971** C.-J. N. Bailey in *Working Papers in Ling.* (Univ. of Hawaii) III. v. 39 In this case, the creole becomes a satellite (*satellect* or *acoluthолect*) to the established language (*matrilect*). *Ibid.*, The matrilect serves as the *acrolect* in the continuum at one end, while the *basilect* ..will be separated from the acrolect by a graded (systematic) series of *mesolects*. *Ibid.*, An *isolect* has been defined by me elsewhere as a form of speech different from its isolectal correlate. *Ibid.* 41, I have suggested *paralect* to denote folk creations from the related systems (e.g. middle Arabic, Punti, Slavish). **1972** J. L. Dillard *Black English* iii. 107 Higginson recorded many clause and question forms which are much as they still are in Black English basilect today. *Ibid.* 300 Dialect refers to a set of features delimited geographically; sociolect to a socially distributed set. **1974** J. Nist *Handicapped Eng.* iii. 72 Any departure from that code..marks the speaker as confined to either the vernacular of mesilect or to the 'folk speech' of basilect. *Ibid.*, Geographical dialects in present-day British English automatically become social-class lects. **1975** *College Composition & Communication* XXVI. 1. 104/1 She is being primed to be the ideal teacher of basilect students in spite of her messy lect.

lectin (le·ktin). *Immunol.* [See quot. 1954 and -in[1].] A substance, usu. a protein of plant origin, which has the properties of an antibody but is not produced in response to an antigen.

1954 W. C. Boyd in Neurath & Bailey *Proteins* IIb. xxii. 789 It would appear to be a matter of semantics as to whether a substance not produced in response to an antigen should be called an antibody, even though it is a protein and combines specifically with certain antigens alone. It might be better to have a different word for these substances, and the present writer would like to propose the word *lectin*, from the Latin *lectus*, the past participle of *legere*, meaning to pick, choose, or select. **1971** *New Scientist* 8 Apr. 82/2 Over a dozen different agglutinins or lectins have now been isolated from a variety of plant materials, but most work has centred on just two of them—wheat germ agglutinin and concanavalin A. Both preferentially agglutinate several sorts of transformed cells, including those transformed by polyoma virus. **1971** *Nature* 30 July 299/2 During the past eighteen months plant agglutinins, or lectins.., have become a major topic of conversation in many cancer research laboratories.

lectio difficilior (le·ktio difiki·liǭɪ). *Textual Criticism.* Also **difficilior lectio.** [L., 'harder reading', from the maxim *difficilior lectio potior*.] Of two alternative manuscript readings, the one that is less obvious, and therefore less likely to be a copyist's error; also, the practice of giving preference to such a reading.

1901 F. G. Kenyon *Handbk. Textual Crit. New Testament* i. 13 One proposition is so often stated as a leading principle in textual criticism... It is..formulated by Bengel in the words, *Proclivi scriptioni praestat ardua*, or ..*Difficilior lectio potior*; the harder reading is to be preferred to the easier... The 'difficilior lectio' is preferable.. because a hard reading is likely to be altered into an easy one. **1901** W. Edie tr. *Nestle's Introd. Textual Crit. Greek New Testament* iii. 157 The principle laid down in the maxim, *lectio difficilior placet*..is perfectly sound. *a* **1955** B. Flower tr. *Maas's Textual Crit.* (1958) 13 It is right to prefer as a rule the '*lectio difficilior*'. **1962** E. J. Dobson in Davis & Wrenn *Eng. & Medieval Stud.* 130 A's is the *difficilior lectio* and somewhat better in sense. **1966** *English Studies* XLVII. 284 The 'lectio difficilior' can be the better or the worse reading as the case may be. **1968** Reynolds & Wilson *Scribes & Scholars* v. 150 Many references to the principle of *difficilior lectio* will be found in commentaries, and there is no doubt of its value. **1969** R. Renehan *Greek Textual Crit.* 27 As the rarer verb, it is a *lectio difficilior* and should be received into the text here.

lection, *sb.* **2.** Add: Also *attrib.*

1927 A. H. McNeile *Introd. New Testament* 383 It [*sc.* the Codex Bezae] contains certain lection marks which Brightman holds to be Byzantine.

lection (le·kʃən), *v. rare*[−1]. [f. the sb.] To read a lesson from.

1922 Hardy *Late Lyrics* 165, I went where my friend had lectioned The prophets in high declaim.

le·ctorship. [f. Lector + -ship.] The office or post of lector.

1605 H. Wotton *Let.* 18 Aug. in L. P. Smith *Life & Lett. Sir H. Wotton* (1907) I. xii. 331 He hath since been stayed with a Lectorship in Genua. **1906** *Westm. Gaz.* 24 Mar. 3/2 It is hereby expressly stated that the Lectorship cannot be held for life. **1911** A. Brennan *Life St. Lawrence of Brindisi* 42 The Lectorship was but the first step in his ascent to the highest dignities of the Order.

lectotype (le·ktotəip). *Taxonomy.* [f. Gk. λεκτός chosen + *type *sb.*[1]] A specimen from the original material serving as the basis for a description of a new species, selected as the type in the absence of a holotype.

1905 Schuchert & Buckman in *Ann. & Mag. Nat. Hist.* 7th Ser. XVI. 103 *Lectotype*, a syntype chosen, subsequently to the original description, to take the place which in other cases a holotype occupies. **1951** G. H. M. Lawrence *Taxon. Vascular Plants* ix. 204 A lectotype is a specimen or other element selected from the original material to serve as the nomenclatural type, when the holotype was not designated at the time of publication, or when the holotype is missing. **1953** E. Mayr et al. *Methods & Princ. Syst. Zool.* xii. 242 A selection of lectotypes should be undertaken only when it leads to the clarification of a taxonomic problem. **1963** Davis & Heywood *Princ. Angiosperm Taxon.* viii. 280 The lectotype should be chosen, if possible, from among the specimens actually seen by the author when he described the species. **1967** R. E. Blackwelder *Taxonomy* iv. 293 There can be no question that a type (at least holotype, lectotype, or neotype) belongs to the species it typifies. **1970** *Watsonia* VIII. 43 The lectotype of *E*[*uphrasia*] *rostkoviana* f. *borealis* was chosen by Mr. Sell and me [*sc.* P. F. Yeo] in 1968. **1975** *Trans. R. Entomol. Soc.* CXXVI. 615 This specimen..is here designated Lectotype and has been labelled accordingly.

lectrice. (Later example.)

1899 G. B. Shaw *Shaw on Theatre* (1958) 73 An attempt to force the Salvation Army to have their hymns licensed by the Archbishop of Canterbury, or the daily papers to

have their political leaders licensed by the Queen's Lectrice, would produce an overwhelming agitation at once.

lecturable (le·ktʃŭrăb'l), *a. rare.* [f. LECTURE *v.* + -ABLE.] That can be the subject of a lecture.

1828 DISRAELI *Voy. Capt. Popanilla* v. 48 The voices of boys lecturing upon every lecturable topic.

lecture, *sb.* Add: **1.** (Later examples.)

1904 CONRAD *Nostromo* I. vi. 47 In about a year he had evolved from the lecture of the letters a definite conviction. **1922** JOYCE *Ulysses* 708 What fractions of phrases did the lecture of those five whole words evoke? **1929** R. BRIDGES *Testament of Beauty* I. 24 If we read but of Europe since the birth of Christ, 'tis still incompetent disorder, all a lecture of irredeemable shame.

7. *lecture agency, agent, audience, circuit, course, -goer, -hall, list, note, -room* (earlier and later examples), *-theatre* (earlier and later examples), *-tour* (also as vb.); **lecture-day** (later U.S. examples); **lecture-recital,** a lecture illustrated by music.

1925 A. HUXLEY *Let.* 25 Jan. (1969) 240 You suggest lectures for lucre in the U.S.A.:—I have had several offers from various lecture agencies... The fatigue and the boredom of a lecture tour frighten me. **1949** DYLAN THOMAS *Let.* 1 Dec. (1966) 340 He said that the Lecture Agencies..have nowhere near his own acquaintanceship with the institutions. **1966** N. NICOLSON in H. Nicolson *Diaries & Lett.* (1966) 131 Colston Leigh Inc. was the lecture-agency. **1873** 'MARK TWAIN' & WARNER *Gilded Age* lviii. 527, I am a business man. I am a lecture-agent. **1949** DYLAN THOMAS *Let.* 1 Dec. (1966) 341 Surely a letter from Brinnin, acting as my secretary & Lecture-Agent,..would mean something to the Treasury. **1943** WYNDHAM LEWIS *Let.* 5 Dec. (1963) 372 Seeing the gas-shortage whittles down all lecture-audiences, I had quite a lot of people. **1974** M. FIDO *R. Kipling* 64/2 'Here's poetry at last!' he [*sc.* Professor Masson] burst out to his lecture audience on the day 'Danny Deever' appeared. **1965** *Times Lit. Suppl.* 25 Nov. 1057/3 Well-financed readings on large lecture-circuits..are staple. **1967** O. WYND *Walk Softly, Men Praying* v. 62 He sounded like the agent for a lecture circuit telling me that I was standing on the threshold of great things. **1890** H. FREDERIC *Lawton Girl* 150 It may take the form of.. a lecture course. **1956** *Nature* 10 Mar. 455/2 The American graduate student is usually forced to complete a relatively large number of lecture-courses. **1753** in *Essex Inst. Hist. Coll.* (1884) XXI. 153 The meeting adjourned to the next Lecture Day. **1779** E. PARKMAN *Diary* 94 Mr. Badcock has been with me to speak about ye Singing..on proposed Lecture day. **1897** Lecture-goer [see *class-attender* (*CLASS *sb.* 10)]. **1961** M. BEADLE *These Ruins are Inhabited* (1963) xii. 163 Oxford undergraduates aren't the inveterate lecture-goers and note-takers that American college students are. **1865** *Atlantic Monthly* XV. 369 The platform of the lecture-hall has been common ground for ..all our social..organizations. **1870** 'FANNY FERN' *Ginger-Snaps* 179, I get a comfortable seat in church,..or lecture-hall. **1961** NEW ENG. BIBLE *Acts* xix. 9 He..continued to hold discussions daily in the lecture-hall of Tyrannus. **1967** J. HAWGOOD in Cox & Grose *Organiz. Bibliogr. Rec. by Computer* III. 70 The number of minutes that..it takes him to walk there from college or lecture-hall. **1965** *Listener* 4 Nov. 700/2 It was the first time that either of these names had appeared on the Oxford lecture list. **1892** W. WALLACE tr. *Hegel's Logic* (ed. 2) 426 Cf. *Werke*, vii. I. 314 (lecture-note). **1920** G. SAINTSBURY *Notes on Cellar-Bk.* i. 2 An ordinary 'exercise book'.. devoted to base purposes of lecture-notes. **1944** *Mind* LIII. 269 Sometimes one gets the impression of a collection of lecture-notes. **1973** E. TAYLOR *Serpent under It* (1974) iv. 60 Could *you* continue to teach in a place where ..your students knew you had cribbed your lecture notes? **1961** *Observer* 26 Nov. 28/1 (Advt.), Lecture-Recitals..at Royal Academy of Music. **1817** COLERIDGE *Biog. Lit.* I. x. 219 Numerous and respectable audiences,..honored my lecture-rooms with their attendance. **1936** *Discovery* Oct. 301/2 The various buildings which housed the sectional lecture-rooms. **1849** W. ALLINGHAM *Diary* 30 June (1907) iii. 48 We..passed into the lecture-theatre. **1969** *Listener* 1 May 594/2 The ordinary university lecturer is no more exciting on film than he is in the lecture theatre. **1973** *Nature* 28 Sept. 225/1 Above the blackboards in the main physics lecture theatre of a Scottish university where I once worked there used to be written in large letters: 'Truth will in the end always flow in the direction of the greatest speculative reflection.' **1913** R. BROOKE *Let.* 24 July (1968) 486 The most unpopular person in Canada is Winston. Ever since his lecture-tour. **1921** R. FRY *Let.* 19 Dec. (1972) II. 519, I have just got back to London after my lecture tour in the north of England. **1952** 'J. TEY' *Singing Sands* ix. 138, I hope Mr. Brown doesn't go lecture-touring in the States. **1958** *Times Lit. Suppl.* 2 May 237/2 An actress whom he meets while on a lecture-tour in South America. **1973** R. LEWIS *Of Singular Purpose* i. 5 This lecture tour in America..is the first of many recognitions, I'm sure of it.

lecturee·. *rare.* [f. LECTURE *v.* + -EE[1].] One who attends lectures.

1900 J. H. WYLIE *Council of Constance* 191 To make lecturees independent of lecturers. **1939** W. ALLEN *Blind Man's Ditch* 15 There were the born lecturees; like Miss Wiggin, who had been attending classes for twenty years. **1972** *Listener* 9 Mar. 316/3 Poor American lecturees.

lecturing, *vbl. sb. attrib.* Add:

1897 'MARK TWAIN' *Following Equator* i. 25 The starting point of this lecturing-trip around the world was Paris. **1899** M. BEERBOHM *More* 140 His lecturing-tour through the States.

lecythid (le·siþid), *sb.* and *a.* [f. mod.L. family name *Lecythidaceæ*, f. the generic name *Lecythis* (P. Loefling *Iter Hispanicum* (1758) 189), f. Gk. λήκυθος a flask: see LECYTH.] **A.** *sb.* A tropical American tree of the order Lecythidaceæ. **B.** *adj.* Of or pertaining to a tree of this kind.

1871 C. KINGSLEY *At Last* II. xi. 113 The ground was strewn with large white flowers, whose peculiar shape told us at once of some other Lecythid tree high overhead. *Ibid.* 118 Some other Lecythids..go by the name of monkey-pots.

led, *ppl. a.* Add: **2.** *led lamp.*

1887 P. M'NEILL *Blawearie* 84 Will Hood had a 'led' lamp; it soon was kindled.

ledeburite (lē·dĕbiurəit). *Metallurgy.* [ad. G. *ledeburit* (F. Wüst 1909, in *Metallurgie* VI. 523), f. the name of Adolf *Ledebur* (1837–1906), German metallurgist + -ITE[1].] The eutectic of the iron/iron carbide system which is composed of austenite and cementite, contains about 4·3 per cent carbon, and occurs in cast iron.

1912 W. H. HATFIELD *Cast Iron* i. 16 This well-known structure, presented by the solidified eutectic, Wüst proposes to christen 'Ledeburite', after his distinguished compatriot. **1943** *Jrnl. R. Aeronaut. Soc.* XLVII. 218 A high carbon chromium steel in the cast condition..will have good sliding properties (ledeburite structure) and is widely employed in high pressure pump mechanism. **1972** G. A. CHADWICK *Metallogr. of Phase Transformations* iv. 140 The white iron eutectic, consisting of austenite and cementite, is often referred to as 'ledeburite'.

‖ **lederhosen** (lē·dəɹhōu:zən). [G.] Leather shorts, as worn in Alpine regions.

1937 *Night & Day* 8 July 8/2 The men, with any luck, will refuse to discard their grey flannels for lederhosen. **1953** *Time* 17 Aug. 27/2 The powerful Social Democratic Party is presided over by mild Erich Ollenhauer, a sort of chubby Clement Attlee in *Lederhosen.* **1956** WALLIS & BLAIR *Thunder Above* (1959) xv. 154 A boy in a checked sports shirt and *lederhosen.* **1973** *Listener* 25 Jan. 103/2 (*caption*) Hitler..in lederhosen.

ledge, *sb.* Add: **1. b.** *ledge(d) and brace(d) door* (see quots.).

1901 J. BLACK *Illustr. Carpenter & Builder Ser.: Home Handicrafts* ii. 19 (*caption*) Elevation and vertical section of what is termed a ledge and brace door. **1904** GOODCHILD & TWENEY *Technol. & Sci. Dict.* 352/1 *Ledged and braced door*, the same as a ledged door, with the addition of braces or pieces of wood running diagonally across between the opposite ends of two successive ledges. **1957** *N.Z. Timber Jrnl.* Oct. 73/1 *Ledged-and-braced door*, a door similar to a batten door, but framed diagonally with braces across the back, between the battens.

3. d. *Meteorol.* A layer in the ionosphere corresponding to a point of inflexion in a graph of ionization density against height, i.e. a layer in which the ionization increases less rapidly with height than in the regions immediately above and below it.

1949 *Gloss. Terms Radio Propagation* (*B.S.I.*) 5 Distributions in which the vertical gradient [of ionization] falls to a minimum value greater than zero are sometimes referred to as 'ledges'. **1960** RATCLIFFE & WEEKES in J. A. Ratcliffe *Physics Upper Atmosphere* ix. 437 The complicated loss process..stimulates recombination so that an F1 ledge is produced. **1967** *Proc. IEEE* LV. 17/1 Within the F region the main features of the vertical distribution of electrons are the F1 'ledge' at about 160 to 200 km.. and the F2 'peak' which generally lies between 250 and 400 km.

6. ledge-handle, a handle of distinctive shape found on Bronze Age ware.

1891 W. M. F. PETRIE *Tell el Hesy* vii. 42 The ledge-handles are very striking and quite unknown elsewhere. They belonged to large vessels with upright sides... The ledge is of various degrees... Sometimes it is very deeply and sharply waved..or else slightly curved,..or merely nicked,..or lastly a plain ledge.., without ornament or hollow. **1949** W. F. ALBRIGHT *Archæol. of Palestine* iv. 78 The envelope ledge-handle. This name, given it by P. L. O. Guy, is derived from the fact that the laps of the pushed-up ledge-handle,..are now folded over and fastened down as neatly as though each lap were the flap of an envelope. **1952** V. G. CHILDE *New Light Most Anc. East* (ed. 4) xi. 230 Four occupational layers are superimposed at Ghassul, and some rather suspicious ledge-handles are figured from the site. **1972** Y. YADIN *Hazor* III. x. 121 Large and deep bowls with ledge-handles.

ledger. Add: **A.** *sb.* **2. b.** In Thatching, a wooden rod laid across the thatch to hold it in place. Cf. *LEGGET.

1916 C. F. INNOCENT *Devel. Eng. Building Construction* xiii. 196 After the 'yelms' are laid, a ledger, that is, a pointed stick, is thrust into the straw, the length of it being carried across three or four 'yelms' and tied to the rafters at the opposite end. *Ibid.* 198 This method of securing thatch by rods laid across it is..that most generally used in England. The rods, or 'ledgers,' may be either tied or 'sewn' to the rafters, or they may be held down by 'broaches'. **1949** H. L. EDLIN *Woodland Crafts in Brit.* xi. 67 In most parts of Britain thatching materials are secured to the roofs of thatched houses or stacks by narrow pegs of wood, usually hazel. One common name for these is *spars*, but they have many others... *Withynecks, ledgers* and *roovers* have all been recorded. **1959** G. HOGG *Country Crafts* 123 The 'diamond' pattern which a thatcher produces by laying strips of cleft hazel or other thin wood, which he refers to as 'ledgers', criss-cross along the roof a little below the ridge on each side.

8. *ledger-account* (later examples), *-keeper, -scroll, -work*; **ledger-pole** = sense 2.

1902 G. H. LORIMER *Lett. Merchant* vi. 77 Some one who keeps separate ledger accounts for work and for fun. **1903** *Daily Chron.* 5 Jan. 5/5 It would be a bad day for loyalty when people considered loyalty as an item in the ledger account. **1906** *Ibid.* 18 Sept. 3/5 A female ledger-keeper and accountant in one office worked for 6*s.* a week. **1901** J. BLACK *Illustr. Carpenter & Builder Ser.: Scaffolding* 86 A combination of chains, clips, and screw bolts, used for securing a ledger-pole to standard. **1949** M. L. DARLING *At Freedom's Door* I. v. 116 Till two or three years ago..Hindu Bhats from Rajputana would come every year with their long ledger-scrolls to record in them any additions to the family. **1908** *Westm. Gaz.* 24 Mar. 6/3 He came to Paris, learnt ledger-work, and obtained a situation in a banking-house.

ledra (le·dra). *rare.* Also **ledrah.** [Cornish *ledr, ledra.*] A cliff, steep hill.

1942 A. L. ROWSE *Cornish Childhood* vii. 197 We picnicked all day on the ledrah. **1966** —— in *Listener* 9 June 845/3 When Devon was purple Cornwall was brown, With harvesting bracken On ledra and down.

lee, *sb.*[1] Add: **4.** *lee-rail* (later examples).

1913 J. LONDON *Let.* 20 Nov. (1966) 410 Sailing with lee-rail continually buried. **1961** F. H. BURGESS *Dict. Sailing* 132 *Lee rail awash, with,* heeled well over.

5. lee-helm, the helm when 'down' (cf. *down with the helm* s.v. HELM *sb.*[2] 1 c); **lee ho!, lee o!** (see quots.).

1883 *Man. Seamanship for Boys' Training Ships R. Navy* (Admiralty) (1886) 78 If carrying too much weather-helm, shift the weights further aft; if lee-helm, further forward. **1948** R. DE KERCHOVE *Internat. Maritime Dict.* 407/1 A sailing craft is said to carry lee helm when the helm has to be kept alee to counteract slackness and keep it on its course. **1962** A. G. COURSE *Dict. Naut. Terms* 120 *Lee helm*, a term used in sailing ships to indicate that the tiller is to leeward and the rudder and wheel to windward. **1927** G. BRADFORD *Gloss. Sea Terms* 99/2 *Lee ho!*, a command given by English yachtsmen preparatory to bringing a boat about; same as *hard a lee.* **1961** F. H. BURGESS *Dict. Sailing* 133 *Lee-o*, the helmsman's warning to a crew before going about.

lee·-boarded, *a.* [f. LEE-BOARD[2].] Fitted with a lee-board.

1897 KIPLING *Five Nations* (1903) 40 Do you know the shallow Baltic..Where the bluff, lee-boarded fishing-luggers ride?

leech, *sb.*[2] Add: **2.** *leech-like* adj.

1905 *Westm. Gaz.* 8 Jan. 3/2 He is prepared to stick to it with almost leech-like tenacity. **1908** *Ibid.* 6 Oct. 10/2 Parasitical and leech-like characteristics. **1963** R. P. DALES *Annelids* ix. 176 The parasitic leech-like branchiobdellids also belong to the Prosopora.

leech, *sb.*[3] For def. read: Either vertical edge of a square sail; the aft edge of a fore-and-aft sail. (Add later example.)

1948 R. DE KERCHOVE *Internat. Maritime Dict.* 407/1 *Leech*, the side of a square sail, or the afteredge of a fore-and-aft sail. Also called skirt when referring to square sails.

b. leech-lining (see quot.).

1883 *Man. Seamanship for Boys' Training Ships R. Navy* (Admiralty) (1886) 53 *Q.* What is a goring cloth? *A.* A side cloth of a topsail,..or lining of a topsail, called by sailmakers the leech lining.

Leeds (līdz). [Name of a city in West Yorkshire.] Used *attrib.* or *absol.* as the designation of a cream-ware type of pottery made at Leeds.

[**1783** *Hartley, Greens Trade Catal.* in *Art Jrnl.* (1911) Jan. 25/1 Designs of sundry Articles of Queen's or Cream colour'd Earthen-Ware, manufactured by Hartley Greens & Co., at Leeds Pottery: with A Great Variety of other Articles. The same Enamel'd, Printed or Ornamented with Gold to any Pattern; also with Coats of Arms, Cyphers, Landscapes, etc., etc. Leeds 1783.] **1863** W. CHAFFERS *Marks Pott. & Porc.* 133 *Leeds pottery*, earthenware, manufactured by Hartley, Greens, and Co. Leeds, 1786. This ware has much perforated or basket work. **1872** C. SCHREIBER *Jrnl.* (1911) I. 139 A very pretty Leeds sucrier and cover. **1876** *Ibid.* 485 We..arranged to come and look at his Leeds ware next week. **1903** MRS. H. WARD *Lady Rose's Daughter* xi. 169 The Leeds and Wedgwood dessert dishes that Cousin Mary Leicester had used for half a century. **1968** *Canad. Antiques Collector* June 17/2 What is Mocha Ware? Sometimes referred to as 'Leeds Ware' or 'banded creamware' it is a creamware decorated with seaweed or tree silhouettes. This was made from 1787 up to 1903.

Lee-Enfield (lī,e·nfīld). The names of J. P. *Lee* (1831–1904), Amer. designer of the bolt action, and *Enfield*, a town in Greater London, site of the British Royal Small Arms Factory, designers of the rifling form, used to designate a type of rifle used by the British Army in the S. African War and, modified, in the wars of 1914–18 and 1939–45. Also *Lee-Enfield bullet.*

1902 *Encycl. Brit.* XXXII. 241/1 The Lee-Metford Mark II. rifle has been further improved in its rifling to resist the wear of smokeless powder,..and is now known as the Lee-Enfield rifle. **1910** *Ibid.* I. 874/1 A cone-shaped sharp-pointed bullet, named the Spitzer bullet, has been

tried in the United States..in a Springfield rifle, which is practically identical with the British..Lee-Enfield. This bullet is lighter than the Lee-Enfield bullet. **1917** A. G. Empey *Over Top* 297 *Lee Enfield*, name of the rifle used by the British Army. Its caliber is ·303 and the magazine holds ten rounds. When dirty it has a nasty habit of getting Tommy's name on the crime sheet. **1959** [see *En-field]. **1966** *Guardian* 8 July 1/2 The Royal Navy laid the No. 4 short magazine Lee-Enfield ·303 service rifle to rest... The Army and the Royal Marines said goodbye to the rifle a few years ago. **1970** F. Wilkinson *Guns* 135 In 1895 the Lee-Enfield rifle was introduced and was to remain the standard arm until 1902 when a shorter version was approved. This, the Short Magazine Lee-Enfield, was to continue in service..through two world wars.

leegte, var. *laagte.

lee-lone, var. Lee-lane.

1893 R. L. Stevenson *Catriona* II. xxii. 265 What would become of you here, and you your lee-lone in a strange place? **1920** N. Munro in *Northern Numbers* 35, I heard a maiden sing, All in the lee-lone Sabbath morn. **1928** D. Byrne *Destiny Bay* i. § 19. 128 Will you.. leave your cousin Jenico and Miss Ann-Dolly by their lee lone? **1966** T. H. Raddall *Hangman's Beach* iv. xxvi. 399, I thought 'twas only love letters a gel went off tae read by her lee-lone.

Lee-Metford (lī,me·tfǒɹd). The names of J. P. *Lee* (see *Lee-Enfield) and W. E. *Metford*, used *attrib.* to designate a type of rifle in use before the Lee-Enfield rifle. Also *Lee-Metford bullet*.

1897 G. B. Shaw *Our Theatres in Nineties* (1932) III. 257 If he does not actually regard it [*sc.* the Bible] as an amulet, and believe that if a soldier carries it into battle it will magically attract and stop the Lee-Metford bullet. **1898** [see *dum-dum]. **1902** [see *Lee-Enfield]. **1967** *Everyman's Encycl.* VI. 202/2 The British War Office adopted..the Lee-Metford Mark I in 1888. In 1891 the Lee-Metford Mark II was adopted... This rifle was subsequently..improved, and became known as the Lee-Enfield rifle.

leep (līp), *v. Anglo-Indian.* [ad. Urdu (Hindi) *līpna.*] *trans.* To wash with cow-dung and water.

1895 Kipling *Second Jungle Bk.* 80 The big wicker-chest, leeped with cow-dung. **1920** *Blackw. Mag.* Oct. 464/1 As you smell the fresh leeped earth of the picquet floor.

leer, *sb.*³ Add: Also **lehr** (lɪ̄əɹ, lēəɹ). (Further examples.)

1908 W. Rosenhain *Glass Manuf.* x. 165 The split cylinders are taken to a special kiln, generally known as a 'lear', or 'lehr', where they are..raised to a dull red-heat. **1918** P. Marson *Glass* x. 72 These tunnels, or lehrs, are about 40 ft. long. **1937** *Nature* 18 Dec. 1072/1 There has been a corresponding improvement..in lehrs for annealing the finished product. **1943** *Amer. Speech* XVIII. 309/1 Among the latter were boys who carried hot glassware from the molds to the leer and toward the end of a shift they began a chant, 'Ten more trips to the layer O,' 'Nine more trips to the layer O,' and so on... They said 'layer' distinctly in two syllables. **1949** *Jrnl. Soc. Glass Technol.* XXXIII. 287 The term 'lehr' to denote an apparatus or plant for the continuous annealing of glass first appeared in factory usage in the U.S.A. between 1890 and 1900. The word arose most probably by corruption of the original form 'leer', but whether by accident or design is obscure. **1958** *Times* 22 Dec. 1/4 (Advt.), Practical experience of design and construction of glass furnace lehrs also essential. **1965** E. Tunis *Colonial Craftsmen* vi. 139/1 A boy carried the new bottle to the leer where he snapped the punty off its bottom. **1971** *Atom* May 118/1 A ribbon of glass up to 11 feet wide leaves the float tank and enters the annealing lehr at temperatures in the region of 600°C.

b. leer man, lehr man, one who works at a leer.

1849 A. Pellatt *Curiosities of Glass Making* 67 The instruction to the lear-man, or fireman, rather to run the risk of melting goods by excess of heat than subject them to fly by insufficient. **1912** G. Sowerby *Rutherford & Son* 27 The new lear man's shaping all right then. **1965** E. Tunis *Colonial Craftsmen* vi. 139/1 A leer man stood the bottle on a hot iron tray in the leer.

leerfish (lē·rfiʃ). *S. Afr.* [Partial tr. of Afrikaans *leervis.] A large game fish, *Hypacanthus amia*, of the family Carangidæ, found off the Atlantic coast of southern Africa.

1843 J. C. Chase *Cape Good Hope* II. 169 Leer Fish—A species of Pike, affording considerable sport to the angler. **1902** *Trans. S. Afr. Philos. Soc.* XI. 217 Probably the Cape Leer-fish was so named by the early Dutch sailors, who brought the name from the East Indies. **1930** C. L. Biden *Sea-Angling Fishes of Cape* ii. 54 For the past two or three generations the word has been commonly written and accepted by the English-speaking people as leerfish. **1957** S. Schoeman *Strike!* iii. 106 The average weight of leerfish is 20–35 lbs. **1973** *Eastern Province Herald* 28 Nov. 37 Out in the darkness came the unmistakeable sound of a leerfish hurling itself in frenzy after its prey.

‖ **leervis** (lē·rfəs). *S. Afr.* Also **leervisch.** [Afrikaans, f. *leer* leather + *vis* fish.] = prec.

1853 L. Pappe *Synopsis Edible Fishes Cape Good Hope* 24 *Lichia Amia*, Cuv. & Val. (Leervisch.).. Taken occasionally in Table Bay, but not in great repute, its flesh being deemed dry and rather insipid. **1913** W. W. Thompson *Sea Fisheries Cape Colony* 156 *Lichia amia* L... Leer-visch; Leather-fish; Garrick (Natal). **1945** *Cape Argus* 27 Jan., Many leervis, kob and yellowtail have fallen for spoons, spinners and wobblers of many kinds. **1951** *Cape Times* 13 Nov. 2/3 Anglers know Swartvlei as a place where the sporting *leervis* abounds. **1953** J. L. B. Smith *Sea Fishes S. Afr.* (rev. ed.) 222 The Leervis always seizes a fish across the middle and then works it about in the jaws until head-on for easy swallowing. **1956** *Cape Times* 2 Mar. 2/5 He caught a 32-lb. *leervis* near the lighthouse at Cape Agulhas. **1974** *Eastern Province Herald* 1 Aug. 21 In mid-December..leervis were caught in large numbers off the breakwater.

leery, *a.*² Add: (Earlier and later examples.) Also (esp. *U.S. slang*), doubtful, suspicious. Cf. *lairy *a.*²

1718 C. Hitching *Regulator* 20 The Cull is leery, *alias* the Man is shy. **1846** *Swell's Night Guide* 46 The president ..who is generally the most cheeky, *leary*, downy cove they can tumble to. **1896** Ade *Artie* iii. 29 The old lady's a little leary of me, but I can win her all right. *Ibid.* xii. 105 I'm leary of it. **1905** *Dialect Notes* III. 63 He is *leery* of book agents. **1909** R. A. Wason *Happy Hawkins* 122, I was rather leery about Jabez. **1923** L. J. Vance *Baroque* vi. 56 If you hadn't..made me leary that maybe you'd tip your friends off. **1942** E. Paul *Narrow St.* xx. 165 The Surrealists discovered that they were not, in fact, Communists and that Moscow was leery of their antics. **1956** B. Holiday *Lady sings Blues* (1973) xii. 108, I was leery of any man who could throw those things back at me in a quarrel. **1960** B. Crump *Good Keen Man* 113 Harry didn't entirely agree with my suggestion that [my dog] Flynn was probably a bit leery of boars since the one that 'killed' him at Maran. **1965** *Listener* 9 Sept. 391/3, I am..leary of theatrical revivalism. **1966** *Economist* 5 Feb. 489/1 At first, centre voters may be fed up with the government in power, but they are leery of voting for the other side, so they stop halfway and vote Liberal. **1969** *Southerly* XXIX. 9 Leery though I am of Greeks, Sophocles sums up my preoccupations effectively. **1970** *New Yorker* 10 Oct. 174/2 Many tennis authorities have been a little leery about placing her on a level with Lenglen. **1971** [see *Geheimrat]. **1973** *Tucson* (Arizona) *Daily Citizen* 22 Aug. 28/1 The Braunlichs will also tell you that, sad as it is, middle America is leery of things it gets for free.

2. *U.S. slang.* Careful.

1911 H. Quick *Yellowstone Nights* xii. 300 But be leery that we don't get stuck for non-performance.

lee side. Add: **b.** *Geol.* The 'down-stream' side of a mound of rock which has undergone erosion by a glacier.

1886 [see *drag-line* s.v. *drag *sb.* 9]. **1920** A. W. Grabau *Textbk. Geol.* I. xiv. 374 The eroded bottom of such a valley often shows hummocky surfaces, sloping and smooth on the side from which the glacier moved (stoss-side) and with striated surfaces, but rough and cliffed on the side away from the movement (lee side). **1969** J. L. Davies *Landforms Cold Climates* ix. 171 The characteristic roche moutonnée presents a streamlined appearance with smoothed, more gently sloping, upstream end and sides and a steeper lee side sometimes smooth but characteristically plucked.

left, *a., adv.*, and *sb.* Add: **A.** *adj.* **1.** Phr. *two left feet*: signifying a clumsy person.

1915 Wodehouse *Psmith Journalist* xviii. 132 Mr. Dawson..gave it as his opinion that one of the lady dancers had two left feet. **1959** E. L. Mascall *Pi in the High* 7 Or dance with two left feet the *valse triste.* **1975** D. Ramsay *Descent into Dark* iii. 92 Clumsy..you've got two left feet.

c. *left jabber*, a boxer whose characteristic punch is the left jab.

1950 [see *cross *sb.* 22 d].

3. *left bank*: applied *spec.* to a part of Paris lying south of the Seine noted for its 'advanced' intellectual views; = *Latin Quarter* (*Latin *sb.* 5); also *attrib.*; hence *left-bankish* adj.

1893 H. S. Edwards *Old & New Paris* I. iii. 10/1 On the 'left bank', ..stand the Institute, the Pantheon, [etc.]. **1911** W. J. Locke *Glory of Clementina Wing* ix. 129 Paris of the Left Bank, of the studios, of struggle and toil. **1929** E. Wilson *I thought of Daisy* iv. 243 She was staying ..in a little Left Bank hotel. **1932** 'F. Iles' *Before the Fact* ii. 42 Some unpretentious little restaurant on the left bank. **1943** D. Gascoyne *Poems 1937–42* 45 In a Left-bank café. **1949** *Oxf. Jun. Encycl.* III. 335/1 The streets.. on the left bank are noted for the numerous book-stalls. **1952** A. Wilson *Hemlock & After* II. iii. 168 She had carefully preserved her Left Bank student get-up for this bourgeois gathering. **1958** *Times Lit. Suppl.* 14 Feb. 85/1 The intense form of *Angst* that one associates..with French intellectualism is not confined to the Left Bank. **1958** *Manch. Guardian* 27 Feb. 7/6 The highly complicated 'left-bankish' and somehow heartless fairy story which it tells in its three acts grows no more likeable with renewed acquaintance. **1964** *Economist* 2 May 478/1 Mr Gomulka strongly criticised their 'left-bank' attitudes. **1974** 'S. Harvester' *Forgotten Road* vi. 72 Their meal took on a sort of Chelsea or Greenwich Village or Left Bank atmosphere.

b. (Further examples of *left* in political contexts.) Also **left-leaning** *a.*, sympathetic towards the left in politics.

1919 T. E. Lawrence *Let.* 27 Sept. (1938) 293 So long as we are the more liberal ('left' in the Parliamentary sense) we call the tune... Our remedy and safeguard will be to trend continually 'left'. **1953** M. Lowry *Sel. Lett.* (1967) 330, I am even 'left' of de Voto on the subject. **1957** J. Osborne *Entertainer* VIII. 62 A chap at my school ..managed to get himself in to the Labour Government, and they always said he was left of centre. **1961** *Times* 23 Jan. 13/6 The left-leaning Captain Kong Lae was, moreover, partly educated in Siam. **1962** J. Braine *Life at Top* x. 135, I asked the Warden who Graffham was. 'He's very Left,' the Warden said. **1962** *Listener* 19 July 87/1 A left-of-centre party not unlike the British Labour Party. **1964** Gould & Kolb *Dict. Social Sci.* 383/2 The word *left* was used in England from the 1920s onwards,..sometimes covering Communists and Socialists and sometimes Liberals as well. **1966** T. Pynchon *Crying of Lot 49* iii. 50 Peter Pinguid was really our first casualty. Not the fanatic our more left-leaning friends..chose to martyrize. **1972** *Times* 4 Aug. 13/4 The constitution of..the Donovan Commission, was on any showing a fair way left of centre.

c. Further special collocations: (in sport) *left arm, -armer, back, half (-back)*. Also *left field* (Baseball): the part of the outfield to the left of the batter as he faces the pitcher; also, a fielder in this position; also *fig.*, a position away from the centre of activity or interest; *left fielder*: a fielder in the left field; also *fig.*

1955 *Times* 9 May 15/1 Goddard opened the bowling with him, left arm over the wicket at a gentle medium pace. *Ibid.* 10 June 4/2 Splendid bowling by Hampshire's young, left-arm bowler Sainsbury, whose seven wickets for 25 runs was the best performance of his career. **1974** *Times* 11 Nov. 8/2 Titmus chopped Bright's orthodox left-arm spin into his stumps. **1960** E. W. Swanton *W. Indies Revisited* 277 New bowling talent will have to be unearthed, for instance..a slow left-armer. **1897** *Encycl. Sport* I. 419/2 [Assoc. Football] The left back and half-back deal with the opposing right wing. **1955** *Times* 9 May 14/3 Eckersley, the Blackburn Rovers left-back, who has not played for England since November, 1953, has been selected to accompany the Football Association party. **1960** B. Liddell *My Soccer Story* xvi. 98 The tragedy of Munich robbed England of one of her finest post-war left-backs in Roger Byrne. **1974** *Guardian* 18 May 19/2 Willie Ormond, the Scotland manager, has.. kept Danny McGrain..at left-back. **1857** *Spirit of Times* 29 Aug. 404/3 Enterprise Club. Maxfield, catcher;.. Webber, left field. **1867** H. Chadwick *Base Ball Player's Bk. Reference* 51 A ball similarly hit to the right or left fields. **1896** Knowles & Morton *Baseball* 77 Harry Athol..played left field for the Thespians in all their games. **1949** *Minot* (N. Dakota) *Daily News* 22 July 8/8 Marinari spoiled Lettau's chance for a no-hitter, lining a solid single to left field in the fifth frame. **1961** *Amer. Speech* XXXVI. 147 *Out in left field*, disoriented, out of contact with reality. **1970** *Time* 9 Mar. 19 An increasing number of candidates are emerging from leftfield to give voters surprising options. **1974** *Publishers Weekly* 11 Mar. 48/3 Novak's use of religious metaphor may put him in left field (Reinhold Niebuhr was there before him). **1867** H. Chadwick *Base Ball Player's Bk. Reference* 70 Suppose the left-fielder should be the third striker on the list. **1957** *Encycl. Brit.* III. 160/2 The outfielders are called right fielder, centre fielder and left fielder with relation to a man standing on home plate and facing out across the diamond. **1973** *Publishers Weekly* 29 Jan. 259/1 Sober, necktie-wearing citizens will get a bang out of the book, left-fielders not at all. **1897** *Encycl. Sport* I. 418/2 [Assoc. Football] Three half-backs are played nowadays... They are called..the right, centre and left half-back. **1914** *London Opinion* 19 Sept. 445/1 A 'rising young left-half' for Sludberry Rangers. **1960** B. Liddell *My Soccer Story* vi. 40 Bobby Paisley was at left-half.

4. *left-eyedness*; **left-brained**, having the left-hand side of the brain as the dominant half; **left-footer** *slang*, a Roman Catholic.

1890 W. James *Princ. Psychol.* I. ii. 39 Most people.. are left-brained, that is, all their delicate and specialized movements are handed over to the charge of the left hemisphere. **1902** *Daily Chron.* 22 May 3/4 Each half [of the cerebrum] governs the opposite side of the body, and ..as we are right-handed, so we may be called left-brained. **1937** S. T. Orton *Reading, Writing & Speech Probl. in Children* i. 52 A boy found..difficulty in using the rifle because of his right-handedness and left-eyedness. **1964** M. Critchley *Developmental Dyslexia* viii. 51 Others attached less importance to the role of left-handedness than to left-eyedness. **1944** J. H. Fullarton *Troop Target* 26 'What about the R.C.s?' 'Oh, yes. Leave the left-footers behind as gun-picquets.' **1959** I. & P. Opie *Lore & Lang. Schoolch.* xvi. 344 In Lancashire Roman Catholics are known as 'Micks', and in Dundee as 'Left-footers'.

B. *adv.* (Later example.)

1918 *Daily Chron.* 2 Dec., In Kiel, where the revolution started, matters appear to be going 'left' with a vengeance.

C. *sb.* **2. a.** (Further examples in *Boxing.*) Also, a blow dealt with the left hand.

1897 *Encycl. Sport* I. 136 (*heading*) Stop for lead-off at body with the left. **1912** *Chambers's Jrnl.* 394/2 Out went Reid's murderous 'left' to our unutterable surprise, and down went the man on the platform. **1914** J. H. & A. Lambert *Boxing* (ed. 2) 41 If possible send in a straight left to the head. **1930** *Daily Express* 8 Sept. 1/6 Siki fell to a left on the body and was counted out. **1948** 'P. Woodruff' *Whatever Dies* 126 An odious person who could be neatly floored by one skilful left to the chin. **1967** G. F. Fiennes *I tried to run a Railway* i. 5 Out shot a telescopic left, and I had the shiner of all time for weeks.

c. (Further examples.) Now usu. applied to a political group holding radical or socialist views.

1939 *John o' London's Weekly* 2 June 321/1 A defiant glare at the Left..with an equally defiant glare at the Right. **1940** W. Temple *Thoughts in War-Time* iii. 24 The Right tends to have a fuller sense of historical continuity than the Left. **1950** Theimer & Campbell *Encycl. World Politics* 260/2 The communists are referred to as the 'extreme' or 'far' left. **1971** W. Laqueur *Dict. Politics* 310 Popularly the Left has favoured rapid social change... During the thirties, Left was associated with opposition to fascism. **1974** 'W. Haggard' *Kinsmen* ix. 93 The tiresomely modern bishop..was..very far to the Left.

4. A shot fired at game with the left barrel

of a double-barrelled shotgun; a bird or beast hit by such a shot.

1893 H. A. MACPHERSON et al. *Partridge* II. iii. 131 Now thoroughly awake, you kill three neatly, quickly followed by a smart right and left—one in front and one behind—at a brace that come straight at you. **1908** R. H. BENSON *Conventionalists* I. iii. 82 On Saturday he had killed three rights and lefts, and had not missed more than one single bird flying alone. **1910** *Blackw. Mag.* Jan. 140/1, I got a right and left with the big gun. **1958** M. BRANDER *Rough-shooter's Sport* xx. 217 When..a covey of grouse was flushed.., I only managed to drop one bird. The others, however, performed more than adequately, each bringing down a right and left. **1974** *Field* 5 Dec. 1311/1 Congratulate anyone on a good piece of dog work..as one would if he achieved a right and left.

5. *Surfing.* The (use of the) left foot. Cf. *GOOFY *a.* 2.

1968 W. WARWICK *Surfriding in N.Z.* 17/3 Calculate where the waves are shaping up the best for your style of riding. Obviously..goofy footers will favour lefts. **1970** *Surf '70* (N.Z.) 17/2 Wayne Charlton was one of the best goofy footers to ever surf the left at Fitzroy.

left, *ppl. a.* Add: **1.** *left luggage* (earlier and later examples).

1861 H. RHYS *Theatr. Trip Canada & U.S.* xi. 96 Arrived at the depôt, I discovered in the doubtful light the 'left luggage' room. **1945** G. B. GRUNDY *55 Yrs. at Oxf.* 167 He left it in the left-luggage office. **1963** [see *baggage-room]. **1971** E. CANDY *Words for Murder Perhaps* xiii. 158 He..came straight back, leaving his case and holdall in the left luggage.

2. a, b. (Further examples.)

1873 'S. COOLIDGE' *What Katy Did* i. 7 In almost every large family, there is one of those..left-out children. **1908** *Westm. Gaz.* 18 Apr. 3/1 (*title*) The little brothers. Or, the land of the left-behind. **1909** *Daily Chron.* 14 Jan. 1/5, I believe the left-out millions are more miserable. **1941** E. BOWEN *Look at Roses* 242 Emma's left-behind silver things. **1965** *Economist* 21 Aug. 674/2 They [*sc.* Negroes who rioted, esp. in Los Angeles] believe—some of them rightly—that they could have risen out of the ghetto of the left-behind but for their colour. **1965** B. SWEET-ESCOTT *Baker St. Irreg.* i. 38 The section was for a few weeks engaged in organising 'left behind' parties all over the British Isles. **1974** W. FOLEY *Child in Forest* II. 220 Getting my swollen inflamed feet back into Leah's left-offs.

left-branching, *a. Linguistics.* [LEFT *adv.*] (Of grammatical constructions) having the majority of its constituents on the left of its tree diagram. Also **left-branching** *vbl. sb.*

1961 N. CHOMSKY in *Proc. Symposia Appl. Math.* XII. 14 Left-branching should offer no problem... A hearer will tend to group left-branching units of a complex sentence (as, e.g., in 'many more than half of the rather obviously much too easily solved problems') as units quite readily. **1965** —— *Aspects of Theory of Syntax* i. 13 A left-branching structure is of the form [[[···]···]···]—for example, in English, such indefinitely iterable structures as [[[[*John*]'s *brother*]'s *father*]'s *uncle*]... There are no clear examples of unacceptability involving only left-branching or only right-branching.

left hand. Add: **3. left-hand drive,** a (motor vehicle) steering system with the steering wheel and other controls fitted on the left side; also, such a vehicle. Hence **left-hand driving.**

1913 A. L. CLOUGH *Dict. Automobile Terms* 187 Left-hand Drive. **1931** *N.Y. Times* 19 July IX. 8/8 It was not..until 1909 that left-hand drive and centre control were introduced, reputedly by Henry Ford. **1933** P. MACDONALD *Mystery of Dead Police* vii. 51 It's a left-hand drive. **1956** *Collier's Year-Bk.* 670/1 Sweden is the only Scandinavian country with left-hand driving, and the desirability of changing to right-hand driving has been discussed off and on for many years. **1966** J. WEATHERHEAD *Force of Innocence* iv. 28, I was finding my left-hand drive difficult in London. **1975** *Guardian* 20 Jan. 7/3 All this year's production will be left-hand drive.

left-handed, *a.* Add: **3.** (Later examples.)

1914 'HIGH JINKS, JR.' *Choice Slang* 14 *Left handed compliment*, one that may be taken either as a compliment or in the opposite way. **1953** *Time* 3 Aug. 36/1 An enthusiastic patter of applause came from the British press, including a left-handed compliment from the *Manchester Guardian* that he was not at all like the movie-type American. **1972** *Ulster Folklife* XVIII. 94 In the dialect of Donegal..*left-handed* betokens 'malicious, underhand'; *a left-handed blessing* is a euphemism for a malediction or curse, and *a left-handed friend* is 'an enemy'. **1974** A. DOUGLAS *Noah's Ark Murders* vi. 54 'I'm not trying to date you.' 'Well, that's a left-handed compliment,' she complained.

5. (Later examples.)

1925 T. DREISER *Amer. Trag.* (1926) II. xxii. 308 The pleasures of this left-handed honeymoon were at full tide. **1935** A. J. POLLOCK *Underworld Speaks* 70/2 *Left handed wife*, a kept woman.

left-handed, *adv.* [f. LEFT HAND.] Towards the left; with the left hand.

1848 *Sporting Life* 1 Jan. 241/2 He also bats left-handed. **1851** *Illustr. London News* XVIII. 133/2 This nut is cut..left-handed. **1909** *Chambers's Jrnl.* Oct. 651/2 The great stag..swinging left-handed..passed Culworth. **1909** E. H. MILES *Lessons Lawn Tennis* (ed. 3) xv. 79, I do not know why ladies should not beat right-handed men players if the latter were compelled to play left-handed. **1928** *Observer* 19 Feb. 24/4 You leave the Oundle road and turn left-handed for Uppingham. **1929** *Morning Post* 30 Dec. 13/1 Hounds..swinging left-handed past Edgecote House. **1974** *Country Life* 7 Mar. 477/1 We rode left-handed beyond the Letham woods as our fox set his mask for Canty hall.

left-hander. Add: **a.** (Further examples.) Also in other games.

1937 [see *CHINAMAN 4]. **1937** S. T. ORTON *Reading, Writing & Speech Probl. in Children* i. 49 Prejudice..is so strong as to amount to the belief that the left-hander is abnormal. *Ibid.* 52 Parson..went so far as to hold that all left-eyed and right-handed individuals were native left-handers who had been shifted by training. **1940** G. MARX *Let.* 5 Sept. (1967) 25 A tennis player with the weirdest assortment of strokes... He's a left-hander. **1961** RUSSELL & ESPIR *Traumatic Aphasia* iv. 29 The left hemisphere is usually dominant..for left-handers. **1970** *Daily Tel.* 29 Dec. 10 Not all the evidence..supports his inference that left-handers have exceptional ability, even if they do range from Leonardo da Vinci to Sir Compton Mackenzie. *Ibid.*, A nice assortment of..40 offensive slang words for left-handers, from kack to cuddy-wifter. **1974** *Times* 6 Nov. 13 He continues to make runs for Western Australia..and has the advantage of being a left-hander.

d. A left-handed compliment.

1959 *Times* 28 Apr. 11/4 'Not bad' might appear a good enough specimen of the simplest type of left-hander.

leftie, var. *LEFTY.

leftish (le·ftiʃ), *a.* [LEFT *sb.* 2 c + -ISH[1].] Inclined to the political views of 'the left'. Hence **le·ftishness.**

1934 H. G. WELLS *Exper. Autobiogr.* II. ix. 809 The violent persecution of Jewish and leftish writers in Germany. **1934** WYNDHAM LEWIS *Let.* 29 Nov. (1963) 226 The strong *Leftish* political colouration of so much of the newest poetry. **1959** *Listener* 6 Aug. 195/1 There were leftish magazines on the tables. **1966** *Economist* 15 Oct. 254/2 This probably has little to do with the [Syrian] regime's 'leftishness'. **1972** *Observer* 6 Aug. 19/3 The leftish Left, the revolutionary Left.

Leftism (le·ftiz'm). Also **leftism.** [f. LEFT *sb.* 2 c + -ISM.] The political views or principles of 'the left'.

1920 *Oxf. Mag.* 19 Nov. 94/1 Mr. Clutton-Brock has consented to read a paper on 'Left-ism'. **1921** N. ANGELL *Fruits of Victory* v. 165 No sooner does the Left of some party break off and found a new party than it is immediately confronted by its own Leftism. **1945** 'G. ORWELL' in *Contemp. Jewish Record* VIII. 169 During the past few years there has been what amounts to a counter-attack against the rather shallow Leftism which was fashionable in the previous decade. **1960** *Guardian* 13 June 9/3 The 40th anniversary of the publication of Lenin's book on Leftism. **1967** C. SETON-WATSON *Italy from Liberalism to Fascism* iv. 160 Labriola was the first Italian to present socialism not as the natural offspring of the leftism of the Risorgimento but as a philosophical system. **1971** *Guardian* 4 Aug. 10/4 There is still a lot of old fashioned and sentimental Leftism (hanging over from much bad verse written in the late 1930s). **1973** *Listener* 19 July 91/2 The infantile Leftism of the fellow-traveller.

Le·ftist. Also **leftist.** [f. as prec.] An adherent of 'the left' in politics. Also *attrib.* or as *adj.*

1924 *Contemp. Rev.* July 20, I would support either a violent reactionary, or extreme Leftist. **1937** E. SNOW *Red Star over China* II. iii. 67 The Leftist Kuoming tang general. **1951** E. PAUL *Springtime in Paris* xi. 206 The anti-Communist Leftists, Existentialists, Trotskyists, Titoists and Anarchists published plans for a rival meeting. **1960** *Guardian* 12 Apr. 8/3 Most of the leaders of the Labour party were probably Leftist rebels at the age of twenty. **1960** *Economist* 8 Oct. 134/2 Many of the speeches were vaguely leftist. **1962** *Listener* 4 Jan. 36/2 It refutes the leftist legend that Dollfuss was simply a Fascist. **1964** L. NKOSI *Rhythm of Violence* 29 She's a bit of a Leftist, but I thought you wouldn't mind. **1967** H. V. DICKS *Marital Tensions* 61 This vivacious, carefree girl with her disdain for tradition was matched by this progressive, leftist scholar. **1974** *Times* 12 Oct. 5/4 It is difficult to find Spanish politicians who do not say they are leftists.

leftness (in Dict. s.v. LEFT *a.*, *adv.*, and *sb.*). (Further examples.)

1884 [see *BILATERALITY]. **1890** [see *DOWNNESS].

left-over, *a.* and *sb.* [LEFT *ppl. a.* 2. Cf. *LEAVE *v.*[1] 14 e.] **A.** *adj.* Remaining over; not used up or disposed of.

1897 R. M. STUART *In Simpkinsville* 65 A bundle of left-over flowers. **1905** *Westm. Gaz.* 28 Dec. 2/1 If..they find themselves with a left-over stock of life-force. **1907** *Smart Set* Feb. 13/1 She tacitly avoided him, and his left-over moments had..been spent philandering. **1967** N. FREELING *Strike Out* 103 The rice had left-over ham and chicken in it. **1968** *Listener* 4 Apr. 438 (*caption*) Is that leftover macaroni cheese..still in the fridge? **1972** *Guardian* 30 Dec. 13/3 Many senior EEC officials..make regular bookings out of Brussels, and the casual visitor has to battle for the left-over seats.

B. *sb.* Something remaining over; *esp.* a portion of some article of food left over from a meal. Freq. *pl.* Also *transf.*

1891 *Cassell's Family Mag.* May 374/1 They all like change of diet, so I provide all sorts of things, with the result that the 'left-overs', as I call them, are appalling. **1897** R. M. STUART *In Simpkinsville* 64, I try to keep the Potter's field a-bloomin' with my left-overs. **1906** *Daily Chron.* 19 Sept. 4/4 We are almost yawning at the 'left-overs' of the scandal banquet. **1950** H. J. MASSINGHAM *Curious Traveller* iv. 71 Now only the shoddy left-overs from the export trade can be bought at inflated prices. **1964** *Punch* 8 Jan. 73/2 Adlibbing madly on Mrs. Hannah Glasse's 'Domestic Cookery Made Easy' (1747) he will combine assorted garden leftovers, crab-apples, damsons, blackberries, radish-pods. **1974** *Sunday Express* 21 Apr. 23/1 (Advt.), As for the babies' left-overs—well, I really scoffed those.

b. A survival.

1902 KIPLING *Traffics & Discov.* (1904) 169 'E's a left-over from Majuba—one of the worst kind. **1911** L. ABBOTT *Amer. in Making* 94 The dread of this Executive power is a curious left-over from Colonial days. **1927** H. E. FOSDICK *Pilgrimage to Palestine* 252 In this ancient monastery these left-overs of a bygone age guard their relics. **1971** I. G. GASS et al. *Understanding Earth* vii. 102/1 Meteoritic debris (probably representing left-overs from the time of formation of the solar system).

leftward, *adv.* and *a.* Add: Freq. in political contexts: (tending) towards 'the left'.

adv. **1957** *Economist* 28 Dec. 1119/1 The Singapore city council elections last Saturday may be taken as an accurate indication of the political trend in the island colony. That trend is clearly leftward. **1973** *Listener* 15 Nov. 668/1, I was rather Conservative as a young man. I've moved gently leftward.

adj. **1936** M. SCHACHTMAN in J. G. Wright tr. *Trotsky's Third International after Lenin* p. xxii, In the message to the Sixth Congress entitled 'What Now?' Trotsky touches upon this Leftward evolution in the European working class. **1939** H. G. WELLS *Holy Terror* III. i. 220 The Group turned its attention to the existing leftward papers. **1949** I. DEUTSCHER *Stalin* 403 Stalin's leftward switch in Russia was not only an earnest affair; it had the grandeur of national drama. **1957** *Times* 11 May 7/2 It is no surprise that in the borough elections the leftward movement seen in national by-elections has been repeated—though not, it seems, carried any further. **1973** *Guardian* 10 Mar. 1/5 Mr Roy Jenkins..is calling on those who share his views..to dig in their feet against what is seen as a dangerous Leftward drift.

le·ftwardly, *adv.* = LEFTWARDS *adv.*

1908 HARDY *Dynasts* III. I. iii. 335 With that in eye he has bundled leftwardly Thomière's division.

le·ftwardness. *rare.* [f. LEFTWARD *a.* + -NESS.] The quality of being leftward in politics.

1944 *Politics* Sept. 247/2 What does *Politics* offer them? A center for leftwardness? **1966** *New Statesman* 5 Aug. 203/2 His leftwardness is smilingly excused, but we are not reminded that Eluard was a communist.

le·ftwards, *adv.* (Later example.)

1971 *Guardian* 3 July 11/8 When the Chinese civil war began in 1946 Liu wobbled to the Right... Then he lurched Leftwards.

left wing. [f. LEFT *a.* + WING *sb.*] **1.** In football and similar games: the position of a player on the left side of the centre(s); a player occupying this position; the part of the field in which a left wing normally plays. Cf. WING *sb.* 7 b.

1882 in Charles-Edwards & Richardson *They saw it Happen* (1958) 300 He was instantly robbed by Strachan, who passed it [*sc.* the football] to the left wing. **1889** [see WING *sb.* 7 b]. **1921** in B. James *England v Scotland* (1969) vi. 125 Remember he was against probably the finest left wing in the three countries; certainly the cleverest outside-left, Alan Morton. **1974** *Liverpool Echo* (Football ed.) 4 May 1/3 He raced down the left wing..to cross the ball into the goalmouth.

2. In Politics. (See LEFT *a.* 3 b.) Freq. *attrib.* Also *transf.*

1884 W. JAMES *Will to Believe* (1897) 171 In theology, subjectivism develops as its 'left wing' antinomianism. *Ibid.*, If the Hegelian gnosticism, which has begun to show itself here and in Great Britain, were to become popular philosophy, as it once was in Germany, it would certainly develop its left wing here as there, and produce a reaction of disgust. **1898** [see LEFT *a.* 3 b]. **1905** W. JAMES *Meaning of Truth* (1909) v. 124 If the formula ever became canonical, it would certainly develop both right-wing and left-wing interpreters. **1921** H. CRANE *Let.* 25 Dec. (1965) 74 You have met about all the personalities in the younger left-wing at all worth while. **1923** G. D. H. COLE *Trade Unionism & Munitions* p. i, One of the principal contentions of the 'left-wing' elements in the Trade Union and Socialist movements. **1940** W. TEMPLE *Thoughts in War-Time* iii. 23 The Left Wing tends to identify the Government and the community. **1957** *Times Lit. Suppl.* 1 Nov. 653/1 Mr Humphreys has been very ambitious here, in an attempt to analyse the relationships between a rich magazine publisher with Left-wing political ambitions and his family. **1972** *Times* 5 Sept. 2/3 The left-wing challenge over Europe is expected to unseat at least one member of the Labour Party National Executive Committee.

Also **left-wi·nger, -wi·ngery, -wi·ngism; left-wi·ngish** *a.*

Quots. 1891, 1896, 1967 are sense 1, the remainder sense 2.

1891 *Peel City Guardian* IX. 7/3 A beautiful bit of passing by the Peel left wingers. **1896** Left winger [see WINGER 2]. **1923** G. D. H. COLE *Workshop Organiz.* 17 The rise of 'left-wingism' inside the Trade Union movement. **1924** *Glasgow Herald* 5 Apr. 9 The unscrupulous, untiring representative of the leftest of left-wingers. **1951** R. CAMPBELL *Light on Dark Horse* 249, I have never been Left-Wingish. **1955** *Times* 2 May 8/5 Mr. Zilliacus is a left winger who has often been a thorn in the side of the party leadership. **1963** *Guardian* 10 May 22/7 Vague Left-Wingism. **1967** J. POTTER *Foul Play* (1968) viii. 90 Good left wingers are in short supply. **1968** *Economist* 7 Sept. 25

Voted on to the general council were Mr Cousins's new ally from the engineers, Mr Hugh Scanlon, and the draughtsmen's militant leader, Mr George Doughty. This gives the sensation of more imminent left-wingery. **1972** *Listener* 2 Nov. 615/3 A period atmosphere of Thirties left-wingery. **1975** *Daily Tel.* 22 Feb. 10/4 Perry Worsthorne was allowed about 30 seconds to question how far Jenkins' left-wingery was an opportunist gimmick, to 'shock and provoke' his opponents.

lefty (le·fti). Also **leftie.** [-Y[6].] **1.** A left-handed person. Also *attrib.* or as *adj.*

1886 *Sporting Life* 7 Apr. 2/4 In last Wednesday's [baseball] game Nashville presented her left-handed battery,..to offset our 'lefty' battery. **1927** *Glasgow Herald* 7 Apr. 12 He was a patriotic Roman youth who allowed his right hand to be burned off..and was henceforward designated by a term which..would be rendered by his comrades of to-day as 'Leftie'. **1969** *New Scientist* 6 Nov. 277/2 Such illustrious lefties as Leonardo da Vinci, Michelangelo..and Paul McCartney.

2. A left-winger in politics. Also *attrib.* or as *adj.*

1935 C. ODETS (*title*) Waiting for Lefty. **1937** in Partridge *Dict. Slang* (1951) 1097/2 (*caption*) Counterblast to lefties. **1939** R. CAMPBELL *Flowering Rifle* II. 40 As I who've lived beneath the two regimes And have not dreamed the Leftie Teacher's dreams. **1967** *Listener* 10 Aug. 164/1 The lefties are almost completely in control of the nation's communication. **1970** K. AMIS *What became of Jane Austen?* 204, I mean the kind of person who.. buys unexamined the abortion-divorce-homosexuality-censorship-racialism-marijuana package; in a word, the Lefty. **1972** *Times* 6 Oct. 14/7 A leader of the left who is no fair-weather Lefty but the genuine article. **1972** *Observer* 22 Oct. 29/1 These groups pump out quantities of magazines and news-sheets, frequently repetitive, full of Lefty names and too-ready inferences. **1974** *Oxford Times* 8 Mar. 11/3 This word, victimisation, has become a substitute, in leftie jargon, for just punishment.

leg, *sb.* Add: **2. a.** *on the leg,* also of a horse (example); *to give a person a leg up* (further examples); hence *leg-up* sb., a help, support, boost; *to hang a leg* (see HANG *v.* 4 c); *to have a leg*: to be physically attractive, to have a fine appearance (*Obs.*); *to show a leg*: to get out of bed; to make one's appearance; *to be tied by the leg*: to be prevented from doing something by some circumstance.

a **1817** JANE AUSTEN *Persuasion* (1818) II. vi. 116 She, poor soul, is tied by the leg. She has a blister on one of her heels. **1831** B. HALL *Fragments Voy. & Trav.* I. 247, I say, Master Doughy, do you mean to relieve the deck to-night? Here it's almost two bells, and you have hardly shewn a leg yet. **1832** F. TROLLOPE *Dom. Manners Amer.* I. xviii. 281 We should be obliged to pass the whole of Monday there, as the coach..would not arrive..till Tuesday morning. Thus..we were to be tied by the leg for four-and-twenty hours. **1854** 'C. BEDE' *Further Adventures Verdant Green* vii. 61 He used to sing out, 'You must show a leg, sir!' and..kept on hammering at the door till I *did.* **1865** MILTON & CHEADLE *N.W. Passage by Land* i. 13 The dogs kept tumbling off..until hauled back again with the help of a 'leg up' from the people inside [a stage coach]. **1879** G. MEREDITH *Egoist* I. ii. 16 And, says Mrs Mountstuart, while grand phrases were mouthing round about him '*You see he had a leg*'. **1901** *Chambers's Jrnl.* 27 July 554/2 He had..strong introductions to a great financier in Park Lane, who seemed to have good reasons for obliging him in such matters as club nominations and social 'legs-up' generally. **1901** J. N. MCILWRAITH *Curious Career R. Campbell* iv. 45 He might not have managed to mount had not Gib been at hand to give him 'a leg up'. **1908** *Westm. Gaz.* 28 Mar. 2/2 He first wore breeches at the Coronation of Queen Victoria, and there was a curious anticipation of a phrase immortal in literature in his statement that his first Court suit revealed to him 'that he had a leg'. **1916** 'TAFFRAIL' *Pincher Martin* ii. 19 All hands! turn out, turn out, turn out! show a leg, show a leg, show a leg! **1936** C. S. LEWIS *Allegory of Love* ii. 72 We can all but hear the voices shouting 'Show a leg—show a leg'. **1937** B. DE HOLTHOIR tr. *Duhamel's Pasquier Chron.* I. 73 Never mind, if you think it will give him a leg up. **1946** J. IRVING *Royal Navalese* 156 *Show a leg!*.. The boatswain's mates' early morning shout..is a direct link with pre-Nelsonic days when certain women were permitted to live on warships in harbour. **1950** A. L. ROWSE *England of Elizabeth* vi. 233 The family owed its leg-up in the world to Robert's grandfather. **1957** *New Yorker* 12 Jan. 25/1 For Nora, who came from a poor and an ugly lower-middle-class home, political action was a leg up. **1965** *Observer* (Colour Suppl.) 30 May 34 *On the leg.* A horse whose legs look too long for his body—he has a lot of daylight underneath him. **1969** 'P. ALDING' *Murder among Thieves* xii. 12 Kerr awoke to find someone was rocking his shoulders... 'Come on, me sleeping beauty, rise and shine, show a leg,' said P.C. Mottram, with indecent cheerfulness. **1969** *Listener* 9 Jan. 43/2 The boys are here..because local parents think it will give them a social leg-up. **1973** *Weekly News* (Glasgow) 11 Aug. 26/2 Then he got the leg-up on a horse called Native Copper. **1974** *Times* 5 Feb. 24/5 (Advt.), Want a leg up? There's more than one way with N.O.P. Secretary.

c. *on one's hind legs,* in a standing attitude (further examples); *not a leg to stand on* (earlier and later examples).

1594 NASHE *Unfort. Trav.* sig. B4 Faine he would have patcht out a polt-foot tale, but (God knowes) it had not one true leg to stand on. **1825** J. NEAL *Bro. Jonathan* I. 8 As if the Yankee man were determined to leave the.. brigadier without a leg to stand upon, as a lawyer would say. **1856** DICKENS *Dorrit* (1857) II. viii. 393 He had better confess, for he had not a leg to stand on. **1910** H. BELLOC *Pongo* xix. 29 The Pongo was to get on to his very short hind legs and talk of the gravity of the situation and all his party was to listen in awed silence. **1925** V. WOOLF *Mrs. Dalloway* 114 Solemnly Richard Dalloway got on his hind legs and said that no decent man ought to read Shakespeare's sonnets. **1944** E. S. GARDNER *Case of Black-Eyed Blond* (1948) xvi. 158 Mildred had gone to a lawyer, and the lawyer had advised her that she didn't have a legal leg to stand on. **1960** M. SPARK *Bachelors* ii. 21 She hasn't a leg to stand on in the case. He's divorcing her, she's not divorcing him. **1964** J. MASTERS *Trial at Monomoy* i. 26 That's why I'm on my hind legs now, asking you folks to keep calm. **1973** J. WAINWRIGHT *Pride of Pigs* 179 You haven't a leg to stand on... You don't even out-rank me.

14. d. *Lace-making.* A strand of the network which connects the patterns in lace. Usu. *pl.*

1865 F. B. PALLISER *Hist. Lace* xxii. 263 Early guipure of Venice or darned network, in which the raised flowers were strung together by legs or brides. **1900** E. JACKSON *Hist. Handmade Lace* 214 *Legs,*..the connecting threads thrown across spaces in needlepoint and bobbin laces. **1922** MRS. R. E. HEAD *Lace & Embroidery Collector* 232 *Brides.* Fr. Syns.: bars, legs (Eng.).

e. *U.S. Broadcasting.* A branch or supplementary network attached to the main network and providing coverage for a particular region (see also quot. 1937).

1937 *Printers' Ink Monthly* May 39/1 *Leg,* a regional chain, i.e., one link of stations in a network. **1951** E. E. WILLIS *Foundations in Broadcasting* iii. 47 Supplementary stations are added to the basic network in order to expand the coverage of a particular program. Often these supplementary stations are organised into groups or legs, which provide coverage of an entire section. The networks all have West Coast legs, for example. **1966** *McGraw-Hill Encycl. Sci. & Technol.* XI. 252/2 An appended supplementary network circuit, feeding more than one station from an intermediate point along a reversible or a round-robin system, is called the leg of a network. Network legs are usually..one-way circuits from the AT&T office to the leg office and the stations they feed.

15. c. A part of, or stage in, a journey, race, competition, etc.

1920 *Blackw. Mag.* Feb. 166/1 On each new 'leg' of our zigzags, our eyes were straining over ever-new horizons. **1927** *Nat. Geogr. Mag.* Aug. 185/2 (*heading*) First non-stop leg of the journey was 1,400 miles. **1938** W. L. HUGHES *Bk. Major Sports* xxx. 345 Each man on a relay team is said to run one leg of the race. **1953** R. CHISHOLM *Cover of Darkness* xiv. 151 We began a square search, flying five-minute legs. **1955** *N.Y. Times* 23 Jan. 3/6 Wiggins swam his leg of the relay in 56 seconds flat. **1958** *Times* 8 Sept. 6/3 Where an alien's visit to Britain was split into two parts by a trip to another country, each 'leg' of the United Kingdom visit had, by law, to be dealt with separately by the immigration authorities. **1972** *Nature* 31 Mar. 196/2 The first leg of this route traverses Arctic tundra regions of Alaska and Canada's Northwest Territories. **1973** C. BONINGTON *Next Horizon* xiii. 196 We squeezed out of the snow cave for the last leg down to Scheidegg.

17. leg art *slang* (orig. *U.S.*) = *CHEESE-CAKE 2; **leg drive,** in rowing, drive imparted by movement of the rower's legs; **leg-guard** (further examples); **leg man, woman** orig. *U.S.*, an assistant who does leg work, *spec.* a journalist who goes from place to place gathering information; **leg piece,** (*b*) (examples); **leg-pull** [f. the phr. *to pull one's leg*: see LEG *sb.* 2 a], the act of deceiving a person in a playful way, a humorous deception (so *leg-puller, -pulling* sbs.); **leg-rest** (earlier and later examples); **leg-ring,** an aluminium strip wrapped round a bird's leg to mark it; hence **leg-ringing** *vbl. sb.*; **leg-room,** space for the legs, *spec.* in a car; **leg-rope** *v.*, also *N.Z.*; **leg-rope** *sb.* (*Austral.* and *N.Z.*), a noosed rope for securing an animal by one hind leg; also **leg-roping** *vbl. sb.*; **legs eleven,** a jocular catch-phrase in the game of bingo (or housey-housey), etc., for 'eleven'; also *ellipt.* as *legs*; **leg shop** *colloq.*, a theatre in which 'leg-shows' are produced (*Obs.*); **leg-show** *colloq.* (orig. *U.S.*), a theatrical production in which dancing girls display their legs; **leg-stretcher,** (*a*) a walker; (*b*) a walk (see *to stretch one's legs* s.v. STRETCH *v.* 3 c); **leg woman** (see *leg man* above); **leg work,** work which involves running errands, going from place to place in search of information, etc.

1940 *Amer. Speech* XV. 359/1 *Leg art,* exploitation of sex appeal in pictures. **1958** *Spectator* 10 Oct. 481/1 The Cameo Royal, the leg-art cinema by London's Leicester Square. **1928** *Observer* 1 July 30/3 They are lacking in leg-drive, and their boat does not run evenly between the strokes. **1968** *Encycl. Brit.* XIX. 668/2 Fairbairn..emphasized leg drive and arm pull and considered smooth bladework more important than what he called the 'showy style' of body work. **1844** *Bell's Life* 12 May 1/3 (Advt.), Robert Dark, the Inventor and sole Manufacturer of..the improved leg guards, begs respectfully to inform the lovers of the Game of Cricket that they can be supplied at the shortest notice. **1890** [see *face-screen* (*FACE *sb.* 26)]. **1952** C. DAY LEWIS tr. *Virgil's Aeneid* VII. 160 Working polished leg-guards from malleable silver. **1923** *Nation* (N.Y.) 24 Oct. 454/2 Newsboys and 'legmen' and a foreign news service keep the streets of Mecca aware of all that goes on. **1951** E. PAUL *Springtime in Paris* xi. 195 The Paris police, leg men and cameramen from the Paris newspapers began tailing Nordmann and Tixier-Vignancour day and night. **1960** *Woman's Own* 5 Mar. 9/1 Jeannie supposed he'd have to get another secretary. He had two already, one more or less a leg-man, another who came in by the day. **1967** *Economist* 1 July 26/1 He was Mr Macmillan's leg man during the break-up of the Central African Federation. **1918** G. B. SHAW *Let.* Sept. in W. Loraine *Robert Loraine* (1938) xiii. 247 So long as you have a mouth left and one lung to keep it going, you will still be better than the next best: my pieces are not leg pieces. **1923** J. MANCHON *Le Slang* 179 *Leg-piece,*..ballet. **1915** *Truth* Nov. 848/1 What you describe as a swindle was only a brain-wave of mine ending in a leg-pull. **1938** *Times Lit. Suppl.* 12 Feb. 112/3 In point of fact they appear to have been no more than a not very subtle leg-pull. **1950** T. S. ELIOT *Cocktail Party* III. 148 You always did enjoy a leg-pull, Julia. **1965** M. SPARK *Mandelbaum Gate* iv. 106 Sometimes, Abdul, I wonder if you're just treating me to a big leg-pull. **1970** J. ARDAGH *New France* xi. 549 His whole operation might be partly a leg-pull at the expense of serious literature. **1923** *Motor Cycling* 7 Nov. 2/1 You are a confirmed leg-puller. Just fancy kidding me about the speed of the bus I bought from you. **1969** *Mind* LXXVIII. 31 Most samples are fair samples (God is not a leg-puller). **1908** *Westm. Gaz.* 30 June 2/1, I, too, have lived in Australia, where leg-pulling is one of the chief joys of life. **1926** T. E. LAWRENCE *Seven Pillars* IX. civ. 553, I could hardly tell my own self where the leg-pulling began or ended. **1946** *R.A.F. Jrnl.* May 178 'Liz' and 'Sally'..will take any amount of leg pulling—and give it. **1963** *Times* 30 May 17/2 Mr. Rovere is patently civilized, thoughtful and well-informed in his leg-pulling. **1833** J. C. LOUDON *Encycl. Archit.* III. vi. 1050 A Leg Rest..is sometimes used in dining-rooms by old gentlemen after the ladies are gone. **1854** MRS. GASKELL *North & South* (1855) II. v. 68 He was busy.. contriving a leg-rest for Dixon, who was beginning to feel the fatigues of watching. **1970** *Stoke Mandeville Dict. Managem. Paraplegic Patients* 23 *Leg-Rest,* attachment to wheelchairs used to keep a paralysed leg elevated. **1973** *Green Shield Stamps Catal.* No. 12. 133 (*caption*) Garden Chair with Leg Rest. Adjustable to 8 positions. [**1909** A. L. THOMSON in *Brit. Birds* II. 362 Various investigators..are endeavouring to obtain fuller and more accurate data with regard to migration, by liberating birds marked with metal foot-rings.] **1938** *Brit. Birds* XXXI. 242 Each bird was marked with a light, numbered, metal leg-ring of the British Birds Marking Scheme. **1959** *New Biol.* XXIX. 111 Leg-rings in different colours have been distributed to a large number of I.G.Y. bases in the hope that some of the mysteries associated with this bird's [*sc.* the Antarctic skua's] activities can be solved. **1963** *Times* 5 June 14/4 During the time he has been in Cyprus, Mr. Nicholson has helped in many major ornithological achievements, notably in the hazardous but successful leg-ringing of young Eleanora's falcons. **1928** *Punch* 18 Apr. p. xxii (Advt.), Carries four full-sized people. Ample leg-room... A wonderful performer for such a small horse-powered car. **1958** *Times* 19 Aug. 11/6 They [*sc.* Ford designers] succeeded in giving the passengers sufficient legroom. **1972** *Drive* Spring 147/3 The height, legroom and squab level of the driver's seat can be adjusted. **1878** E. S. ELWELL *Boy Colonists* 235 She kicked out at Ernest, who was trying to get the leg-rope on. **1911** H. FOSTON *In Bell Bird's Lair* 36 Each cow was to be carefully 'leg-roped'. *Ibid.*, Ted was shown how to 'leg-rope' a cow and bail up. **1950** *N.Z. Jrnl. Agric.* Feb. 169/2 Milk stools, door handles, leg ropes, posts and walls must be kept clean. *Ibid.* Nov. 465/3 The tail of the cow should be prevented from waving about and, if necessary, the animal comfortably leg-roped. **1963** *Landfall* Mar. 13, I..let the cow out into the race where, taking the leg-rope with her, she squittered off wild in the eyes. **1912** B. E. BAUGHAN in D. M. Davin *N.Z. Short Stories* (1953) 189 Much to my surprise, there was no leg-roping, and hardly any bailing-up [of the cows being milked]. **1919** W. H. DOWNING *Digger Dial.* 32 *Legs eleven,*..the number eleven in the game of 'house'. **1933** L. A. G. STRONG *Sea Wall* 256 A game of 'house' was in progress and a voice monotonously droned the numbers: '..legs... Kelly's eye.' **1945** E. WAUGH *Brideshead Revisited* II. i. 230 Kelly's eye—number one; legs, eleven; and we'll Shake the Bag. **1965** BROPHY & PARTRIDGE *Long Trail* 144 *Legs eleven,*..in the game of House, eleven. **1871** 'MARK TWAIN' *Screamers* xxviii. 144 They're playing 'Undine' at the Opery House, and some folks call it the leg shop. **1882** J. J. JENNINGS *Theatr. & Circus Life* 238 Burlesque with its blonde attributes kept the country in a rage..and the minor musical attractions of the *quasi* legitimate stage have usurped its principal feature—the leg show. **1900** *Amer. Jrnl. Sociol.* VI. 447 Next follows a cinematograph reproduction of a prize-fight, and then, in striking contrast with the first, a 'leg show' of the most shameless character. **1930** BROPHY & PARTRIDGE *Songs & Slang 1914–18* 137 At a leg-show of these days you saw far less of the female form than is now exhibited in the streets. **1930** J. DOS PASSOS *42nd Parallel* v. 420 Doc wanted to go to see a legshow. **1952** 'J. GUTHRIE' *Paradise Bay* vi. 57 He took me to exciting spectacles which I now know were leg shows. **1969** *Listener* 20 Mar. 399/1 We often use the cliché of the tired business-man to define the low response..that sustains leg-shows. **1616** T. CORYAT *Traveller for English Wits* 42 Your..most obliged Countreyman..the..Legge-stretcher of Odcomb in Somerset, Thomas Coryate. **1942** 'M. HOME' *House of Shade* iii. 57 Marigny was suggesting a leg-stretcher... The two made their way out to the glare of the sun. **1970** *Daily Tel.* 23 May 9 Now lonely, neglected, and often overgrown, they provide delightful leg-stretchers, on the springy turf, for the motorist with an hour or so to spare. **1960** M. G. EBERHART *Jury of One* (1961) i. 9 An old school friend, a fashion writer, had needed an assistant, a leg woman. **1891** *Dialect Notes* I. 207 Reporters characterize a task in which there is more running than writing by the expression *leg-work.* **1942** E. PAUL *Narrow St.* xxxi. 285 The Greek madonna did the leg work faithfully while La Absalom cackled orders through a rift in the portières. **1959** G. COBDEN *Murder for his Money* iv. 51 He wouldn't come himself for Patey was no man of action, but he might send..a man we used a great deal for leg work. **1972** *Daily Tel.* 21 June 13/8, 1,700 men..do the surveying leg-work needed for keeping local maps up to date. **1973**

L. HEREN *Growing up Poor in London* vii. 179, I would earn a few bob working on the edge of big stories... The reporters who came down from Fleet Street were nearly always willing to pay for leg work.

b. leg break (examples); hence *leg-breaker*, a leg-break bowler; **leg-cutter** (see quot. 1966); **leg glance, glide,** a shot in which the ball is glanced fine on the leg side; **leg play** (see quot. 1934); **leg side** = LEG *sb.* 6 b; **leg slip,** (a fielder in) a position corresponding to that of the slips (see SLIP *sb.*³ 14 a), but on the leg side; **leg spin,** a type of spin which causes the ball to turn from leg side to off (so *leg-spinner*); **leg-stroke** (examples); **leg stump** (later examples); **leg sweep,** a sweeping stroke which sends the ball to leg; **leg theory,** the technique of bowling to leg with a concentration of fielders on the leg side; **leg trap,** fielders stationed for catches close to the wicket on the leg side.

1888 A. G. STEEL in Steel & Lyttelton *Cricket* iii. 114 The 'leg break' ball is usually bowled from round the wicket. **1927** W. E. COLLINSON *Contemp. English* 19 Only gradually did the mysteries of yorkers, full tosses and leg-breaks penetrate to us. **1955** *Times* 9 May 15/1 Mansell.. bowled 17 steady overs of leg-breaks. **1969** M. PARKINSON *Cricket Mad* x. 57 We had our suspicions confirmed in the Indian's first over which contained five leg breaks. **1905** *Strand Mag.* June 703/2 Armstrong is a leg-breaker. **1956** R. ALSTON *Test Commentary* i. 13 Benaud, potentially a most dangerous leg-breaker. **1956** N. CARDUS *Close of Play* 37 What is action break? In what way is it a term with a meaning more demonstrable..than 'seamer' and 'leg-cutter'? **1963** *Times* 25 Apr. 4/5 He went to Lord's last year to play his first match for Warwickshire and within a couple of overs had bowled everything from a leg-cutter to an inswinger. **1966** B. JOHNSTON *Armchair Cricket* 102 *Leg-cutter,* is really a fast leg-break which is bowled by 'cutting' across the seam of the ball. **1883** *Cricket* 19 Apr. 39/1 Horan came in after lunch, and soon commenced to score in his own peculiar style, leg glances being his favourite stroke. **1966** B. CLOSE *Close on Cricket* iii. 35 *Leg glance,* this is a refined stroke played against a ball pitched on or outside the leg stump but not far enough up to drive efficiently. **1920** D. J. KNIGHT in P. F. Warner *Cricket* 33 The first of the leg strokes, the leg glide, is a glorious one to watch, and is exceedingly paying. **1955** *Times* 12 July 12/4 Just before luncheon he had lost Brookes, who, after a beautiful leg glide, missed one from Smith to be out leg before. **1888** R. H. LYTTELTON in Steel & Lyttelton *Cricket* xvi. 411 It is the bowlers who have most cause to grumble at the modern leg play. **1898** K. S. RANJITSINHJI *With Stoddart's Team* (ed. 4) v. 96 His [*sc.* S. P. Jones's] cutting and his leg play being particularly well-timed. **1928** *Daily Express* 28 June 3/4 If leg-play were more severely penalised and wickets less like polished concrete, the balance between bat and ball would be more redressed and the game restored to its former attractiveness. **1934** W. J. LEWIS *Lang. Cricket* 147 *Leg play,* 1. Stopping a breaking or curling ball with the leg instead of with the bat... 2. The playing of balls on the leg side. **1816** W. LAMBERT *Cricketer's Guide* (ed. 6) ii. 32 If the Ball should come 4 or 5 inches on the leg side, the Striker should move his right foot back at the moment of hitting, playing the Ball between his left leg and the wicket. **1956** N. CARDUS *Close of Play* 26 No opposing captain dreamed of setting a close leg-side field for him. **1969** P. POCOCK *Bowling* i. 19 The majority of seam bowlers swung the ball away from the batsman, using six fielders on the offside and three on the leg side. **1956** R. ALSTON *Test Commentary* xvi. 143 Miller swept him through the hastily retreating leg-slips. **1963** A. ROSS *Australia 63* vii. 134 Benaud gave Davidson his most aggressive field for some time; neither long leg nor third man, three slips, gully, leg slip and backward short leg. **1888** A. G. STEEL in Steel & Lyttelton *Cricket* iii. 116 The ball, coming from a great distance round the wicket and with a considerable amount of leg spin, would be gradually working away to the batsman's off side. **1966** B. CLOSE *Close on Cricket* v. 55 We have a quantity of good finger-spin bowlers but few leg-spin bowlers in first-class cricket. **1927** *Observer* 29 May 28/4 It was a clear case for old Brown's leg-spinners. **1965** P. WALKER *Winning Cricket* iv. 57 Nowadays you have to bowl leg spinners with the accuracy of an orthodox right hander to achieve even moderate success. **1906** *Westm. Gaz.* 12 July 4/1 This leg-stroke off a straight ball has two great merits—it scores runs and it puts the bowler off. **1955** *Cricket—How to Play* (M.C.C.) 47 (*heading*) Practising leg-strokes. **1937, 1956** Leg stump [see **Chinese cut*]. **1846** W. DENISON *Cricket Sk. Players* 17 His [*sc.* G. Brockwell's] 'leg sweeps' are very powerful, and generally speaking they are along the ground—not lifted. **1955** A. ROSS *Australia 55* xii. 168 His leg-sweep was comfortably finished before the ball had got anywhere near him. **1898** G. GIFFEN *With Bat & Ball* x. 153 Cooper bowled the leg-theory almost as remarkably as the off-theory is practised nowadays. **1923** *Daily Mail* 11 Aug. 7/4 Newman, following the fashion of the match, bowled the leg theory with a crescent of fieldsmen close in on the leg side. **1956** N. CARDUS *Close of Play* 26 He would have discovered a way of retaliation against leg-traps and leg-theories. **1923** *Wisden's Cricketers' Almanack* 329 His stock ball is the in-swinger and here again he often hits the wicket and has not got to rely on his leg-traps. **1924** N. CARDUS *Days in Sun* 50 The good balls were pushed for singles through the leg-trap—when they did not get wickets. **1953** R. WARNER *Escapade* II. iii. 93 It's a leg-trap... You see, my dear, the batsman is absolutely forced to play every ball to the leg. **1963** *Times* 5 June 4/2 He took a pace to Titmus only to turn him gently into the leg trap.

leg, *v.* Add: **5. b.** To seize or hold by the leg.

1876 *Coursing Calendar* 149 Birkdale..came round on the outside and legged the hare, which Stolen Moments killed. **1951** L. G. D. ACLAND *Early Canterbury Runs* 385 To *leg* a sheep is to haul him from the pen to the board by his hind leg, a practice much objected to, especially by owners of heavy sheep.

7. *Cricket.* To send to leg.

1902 *Westm. Gaz.* 11 July 5/2 The newcomer at once started scoring... Nicholl followed him by legging Hopley to the covered stands. **1903** *Star* 8 July 3/4 His first ball was legged by Ranji for what would really have been 3 with a couple of smart sprinters.

legal, *a.* Add: **1. e.** *legal cap*: ruled writing paper used chiefly for legal documents. *U.S.*

a **1877** KNIGHT *Dict. Mech.* I. 455/2 Foolscap and legal cap are of various sizes, from $7\frac{1}{2} \times 12$ to the size of a flat cap-sheet folded $8\frac{1}{2} \times 14$. **1902** W. N. HARBEN *Abner Daniel* i. 3 Old man Bishop..was carefully reading a long document written on legal-cap paper. **1937** E. J. LABARRE *Dict. Paper* 142 *Legal cap,* a size of paper 14″ × 8½″.

f. *legal beagle, eagle,* rhyming collocations designating a lawyer, *spec.* one who is keen and astute.

1949 *Law Library Jrnl.* XLII. 187/1 Legal Eagles and Stuffed Owls in Detroit. **1953** B. GLEMSER *Dove on his Shoulder* xii. 230 Since these letters are evidence they ought to be handed over to our legal beagles. **1961** I. T. ROSS *Requiem for Schoolgirl* vii. 118 He's got some sort of legal beagle who protects him. **1963** N. FREELING *Because of Cats* vii. 116 According to the legal eagles you'll never get away with prosecuting them. **1967** WODEHOUSE *Company for Henry* vii. 117 You allowed your mind to wander when the legal eagle was doing his stuff. **1968** M. ALLINGHAM *Cargo of Eagles* iv. 57 That's the only good thing I've ever heard about your infernal legal eagle. **1974** *Economist* 30 Nov. 75 Legal eagles agree... The meeting, only the second of the justice council in EEC history.., was civilised.

g. *legal positivism*: see *POSITIVISM.

2. a. *legal aid*: official assistance allowed under certain conditions towards the expense of litigation (cf. AID *sb.* 2 and *2 b); *legal capacity*: the authority under law of a person to engage in a particular undertaking, or maintain a particular status; *legal fiction*: see FICTION 5 a; *legal memory* (see quots.).

1890 (*title*) Constitution and bye-laws of the Deutsche Rechts-Schutz Verein (German Legal Aid Society). **1903** *Act 3 Edw. VII* c. xxxviii. § 1 Where it appears.. desirable in the interests of justice that [any poor prisoner] should have legal aid in the preparation and conduct of his defence, and that his means are insufficient to enable him to obtain such aid..the committing justices..may certify that the prisoner ought to have such legal aid. **1928** [see *INTERSTATE *a.*]. **1959** *Daily Tel.* 18 Mar. 19/6 In eight years legal aid has been given to more than 238,000 litigants. **1967** E. RUDINGER *Wills & Probate* 91 The other [leaflet] explained how to get legal advice under the legal aid scheme. **1971** 'M. UNDERWOOD' *Trout in Milk* ii. 27 Thanks to 'legal aid' it was much easier to get started at the criminal than the civil Bar. **1972** *Times* 28 Jan. 16/4 All concerned—the parties' advisers, the legal aid committees,..—should put children's cases at the top of the list.

1890 LELY & GEARY *Chitty's Pract. Treat. Law of Contracts* (ed. 12) vii. 194 The age of twenty-one years..has been fixed, as the period when an absolute and unlimited legal capacity to contract shall commence. **1968** *Lebende Sprachen* XIII. 82/2 The customer will bear any loss incurred by the bank resulting from the fact that the bank.. does not obtain knowledge of any restrictions of the customer's..legal capacity.

1861, 1876 [see FICTION 5 a]. **1937** R. H. LOWIE *Hist. Ethnol. Theory* v. 51 The same holds for the principle of legal fiction, which Maine also treated at length. **1966** BLACK & BROWN *Outl. Eng. Law* v. 43 Sometimes such a presumption takes the form of a *Legal Fiction.* For instance if two persons die in such a way that it is uncertain which of them died first the law presumes..that the younger outlived the older.

1766 BLACKSTONE *Comm.* II. II. iii. 31 It seems unaccountable, that the date of legal prescription or memory should still continue to be reckoned from an aera so very antiquated. **1882** *Encycl. Brit.* XIV. 650/1 By the Statute of Westminster the First,..the beginning of the reign of Richard I. was fixed as the date of limitation for such actions. This is the well known 'period of legal memory'. **1882** C. SWEET *Dict. Eng. Law* 525 When a person alleges in legal proceedings, that a custom or prescription has existed from time whereof the memory of man runneth not to the contrary..this is..called time of living memory, as opposed to time of legal memory, which runs from the commencement of the reign of Richard I. **1969** J. B. SAUNDERS *Words & Phrases legally Defined* (ed. 2) IV. 171/1 By the ancient rule of the common law, enjoyment of an easement has to be proved from time 'whereof the memory of man runneth not to the contrary', that is to say, during legal memory or since the commencement of the reign of Richard I.

5. b. The exact fare without any tip; a passenger who pays such a fare. Chiefly *taxi-drivers' slang.*

1923 J. MANCHON *Le Slang* 179 The legal = the legal fare. **1939** H. HODGE *Cab, Sir?* vii. 84 The last, and probably most common, cause of the inadvertent 'legal' is the super-sensitive meter. *Ibid.* 85 Some 'legals' are simply mean, and give excuses instead of a tip. **1963** M. LEVINSON *Taxi!* vii. 88 If his next passenger gives him another 'legal' (the exact fare) he will naturally take a very dim view.

legalese (līgǟlī·z). *colloq.* [f. LEGAL *a.* + -ESE.] The complicated technical language of legal documents.

1914 C. J. C. HYNE *Firemen Hot* 189 He signed his name at the foot of a bald formal agreement, written in the most incomprehensible legalese. **1966** A. SACHS *Jail Diary* xvii. 155 After all these weeks I am not used to reading legalese any more. **1967** 'J. H. ROBERTS' *February Plan* I. iii. 81, I won't go into the legalese, Mr. Corman, but he claims he had a contract with you. **1973** *Black Panther* 5 May 13/3 Is it any measure of excellence to assemble glossy paragraphs of smart untried legalese? **1973** *N.Y. Times* 11 Aug., Gordon Strachan spoke openly of his resort to legalese.

legation. 3. b. (Earlier examples.)

1832–3 *Reg. Deb. Congress U.S.* 22nd Congress 2 Sess. App. 90/2 The proceedings..are not recorded in the legation. *Ibid.,* The instructions are not in the legation [in London].

legend, *sb.* Add: **7. c.** The written explanatory matter accompanying an illustration, map, etc. Also *attrib.,* as *legend-line.*

1903 *Westm. Gaz.* 8 Jan. 2/1 The sort [of satire] I should employ if—if I were writing legend-lines for a halfpenny comic paper. **1951** D. BLAND *Illustration of Bks.* ix. 142 After the blocks have been made and the proofs approved, a paste-up should be prepared for the printer, to include legends or captions. **1963** *Which?* July 200/1 The symbols used on a map should be..explained clearly in the legend (or key). **1970** *Watsonia* VIII. 31 Figure 4. For legend see above. **1974** *Times Lit. Suppl.* 23 Aug. 910/5 The information provided in caption and legend is clear and exactly what is needed.

8. *legend-king, -lust; legend-haunted* adj.

1905 *Westm. Gaz.* 25 Mar. 5/3 Its famous, legend-haunted Jews' quarter. **1908** *Daily Chron.* 5 Oct. 7/1 As a poor and lonely boy he wove his day-dreams by the legend-haunted cliffs of Tintagel. **1930** BLUNDEN *Poems* 319 And thence, before to-morrow's dawn, it springs That they are one with elves and legend-kings. **1911** E. POUND *Canzoni* 42 Nay, on my breast thou must Forget and rest and dream there For thine old legend-lust.

b. Applied to the estimated or planned displacement, speed, etc., of a ship before construction or testing. Also *absol.*

1908 *Westm. Gaz.* 31 July 1/3 A ship.. in the Bay would exceed her legend speed by a knot or two. **1921** *Glasgow Herald* 17 Dec. 12 The British Government may construct two new ships, not to exceed 35,000 legend tons each. **1936** W. S. CHURCHILL in *Second World War* (1949) I. I. ix. 144 If you ask your people [the Admiralty] to give you a legend for a 16-inch-gun ship, I am persuaded they would show you decidedly better proportions than could be exhibited at 14-inch.

Legendre (ləʒā·ndr'). *Math.* The name of A. M. *Legendre* (see LEGENDRIAN *a.*), used *attrib.* and in the possessive to designate certain expressions investigated by him, esp. (*a*) the differential equation $(1-x^2)d^2y/dx^2 - 2xdy/dx + n(n+1)y = 0$, (*b*) its solutions $y = P_n(x)$, where $P_n(x)$ is a polynomial that is the coefficient of h^n in the expansion of $(1-2xh+h^2)^{-1/2}$, and (*c*) the associated functions $P_n{}^m(x)$, equal to $(1-x^2)^{m/2}\frac{d^m}{dx^m}P_n(x)$.

1875 I. TODHUNTER *Elem. Treat. Laplace's Functions* i. 1 The coefficient of α^n will be a function of x which we shall denote by $P_n(x)$, and shall call Legendre's Coefficient of the nth order. **1880** *Encycl. Brit.* XIII. 21/2 Legendre's function. **1885** A. R. FORSYTH *Treat. Differential Equations* v. 152 We have now obtained the complete integral of Legendre's equation in all cases when n is a real constant, by deducing two integrals which are linearly independent..of one another. **1902** *Encycl. Brit.* XXXII. 798/1 (*heading*) Legendre associated functions. **1930** *Engineering* 26 Dec. 812/3 There are also tables of Legendre functions. **1938** S. DUSHMAN *Elem. Quantum Mech.* vi. 153 The Legendre polynomials form an orthogonal system, since $\int_{-1}^{1} P_k(x)P_n(x)dx = 0$ (for $k \neq n$) [or] $= 2/(2k+1)$ (for $k = n$). *Ibid.* 158 Since the value of any function $P_k(\cos\theta)$ exhibits $k-1$ loops, there are $2(k-1)$ circles parallel to the nodal circles at which the function has the same absolute value. It is for this reason that the Legendre coefficients of zero order are known as zonal harmonics. **1953** A. D. & K. H. V. BOOTH *Automatic Digital Calculators* xvi. 189 The Legendre polynomials.. are such that, if any function is expanded in a series of the polynomials, the first n terms of this series will give the best nth degree polynomial approximation to the given function, in the least squares sense. **1962** CORSON & LORRAIN *Introd. Electromagn. Fields* iv. 172 The solutions of Legendre's equation are called Legendre polynomials, which we denote by $P_n(\cos\theta)$, there being a different polynomial for each value of the index n. **1970** G. K. WOODGATE *Elem. Atomic Struct.* ii. 17 The solutions are proportional to the associated Legendre functions.

Leger (le·dʒəɪ), *sb.*² Shortened f. *St. Leger* (see SAINT *a.* 4 c).

1871 [see EGG *sb.* 4 b]. **1880** TROLLOPE *Duke's Children* I. xvii. 206 Who would like to bet me fifteen to one in hundreds against the two events,—the Derby and the Leger? **1924** GALSWORTHY *Forest* II. i. 41 I'd give all mine [*sc.* my ancestors] to know what's won the Leger. **1961** F. C. AVIS *Sportsman's Gloss.* 230/2 *Leger Day,* the day upon which the St. Leger is actually run.

legger² (le·gəɪ). [f. LEG *sb.* + -ER¹.] **1.** In a slaughter-house, a butcher or packer who works on the legs of the carcasses.

1905 F. W. WILDER *Mod. Packing House* v. 116 The number of men necessary in [different sized] beef killing groups..are given in the following table... 2 front leggers ..3 hind leggers. **1923** R. A. CLEMEN *Amer. Livestock & Meat Industry* xv. 332 A string of butchers now follow each other in rapid succession. The 'leggers' remove the hind legs at the hoof and the forelegs at the knee. **1949** K. STRONACH in A. E. Woodhouse *N.Z. Farm & Station Verse* (1950) 188 The legger slits as a surgeon does And the puncher strips the pelt. **1966** *Mate* (Auckland) Aug. 42

Legger, the man who cuts out the legs from the newly killed lamb in the freezing works.

2. (See quot.)

1927 T. WOODHOUSE *Artificial Silk* 95 In the manufacture of stockings on such frames two machines are used... One of these machines, termed the 'legger', knits the upper and longer part of the stocking, whereas the other machine, termed the 'footer', knits the remainder of the stocking.

legger[3] (le·gəɹ). *U.S. colloq.* Shortened f. *BOOT-LEGGER. Also (with preceding hyphen) as the second element of *Combs.*, an illegal seller (of something indicated in the first element).

1926 [see *HIP *a.*]. **1929** *Variety* 5 June 58/2 Leggers claim the tonic is as potent as a fifth of gin selling for three times the price. **1934** *Time* 29 Jan. 49/1 Hundreds of U.S. citizens have smuggled copies through the customs or bought them from book-leggers. **1937** *Time* 4 Jan. 11/2 Unlike Prohibition's liquor 'leggers', they are not growing rich. **1945** *Chicago Daily News* 12 July 12/2 Most of the counterfeits have been used by steakleggers down East. **1945** MENCKEN *Amer. Lang.* Suppl. I. 366 But of more interest..are the words showing recent vogue affixes, *e.g.*..*-legger*, as in *bootlegger* and *meatlegger*. **1973** *Times Lit. Suppl.* 20 Apr. 451/5 A sinister group of organ-leggers who go beyond the resurrectionists and try to keep the hospitals supplied with adequate numbers of fresh organs for transplants.

legget (le·gət). Also leg(g)at(t), leg(g)et(t). [Etym. unknown.] In Thatching, a tool made from a flat board attached to a handle and studded with nails, used for dressing and driving the reeds into place. Cf. *LEDGER *sb.* 2 b.

c **1555** in *Norfolk Antiquarian Misc.* (1883) II. 9 A Cardynall legat & a trowell wᵗ suche other tooles. **1787** W. MARSHALL *Rural Econ. Norfolk* II. xxxii. 61 The eaves being thus completely set, they are adjusted and formed; .. nor are they formed by cutting; but by 'driving' them with a 'legget'. **1927** *Observer* 24 July 5/3 The tools and appliances used in Devon are more or less similar to those used in Norfolk. The 'leggett', however, is called a 'driff'. **1941** [see *BIDDLE]. **1949** K. S. WOODS *Rural Crafts Eng.* IV. xiii. 204 The beating tool is called a 'legatt'; it is a square of thick wood studded with horseshoe nails set alternately, nail and space, in the rows. **1961** *Guardian* 21 Sept. 5/2 Ramming home one corner with a Chaucerian tool known as a leggett. **1969** E. H. PINTO *Treen* XXV. 406 The leggat, legget or reed bat..is used for patting or beating reeds into position. **1971** *Country Life* 18 Nov. 1403/3 The Norfolk thatching reed is then beaten up tight under the hazel rods using an instrument called a leggett. **1972** *Daily Tel.* 28 Oct. 15/2 Each 'yelm' is pegged into place and beaten with a flat piece of wood or 'spud' (reed thatchers use a corrugated surface, called a 'leggat').

‖ **leggiero** (ledʒēə·ro), *a. Mus.* [It.] Of musical movement: light and nimble. Also used as *adv.*

1880 GROVE *Dict. Mus.* II. 113/2 Leggiero passages are usually, though not invariably, *piano*, and they may be either legato or staccato. **1939** *Internat. Cycl. Mus.* 988/2 *Leggiero* (Italian), lightly, usually applied to a rapid passage for the pianoforte. **1960** *Times* 4 June 9/5 Katchen's *leggiero* playing is predictably delightful.

legging, *sb.* Add: **b.** *Cricket* = PAD *sb.*[3] 3 c. Now *rare* or *Obs.*

1858 in *Cricket Q.* (1963) I. 21. **1875** *Baily's Monthly Mag.* May 11 Beldham also, without either leggings or gloves, scored 72 against Brown..when fifty-two years old. **1934** W. J. LEWIS *Lang. Cricket* 146 *Leggings*, leg-guards of a primitive type.

legging, *vbl. sb.* Add: **2.** Propelling a boat through a canal-tunnel by human labour (see quot. 1949). Cf. LEG *v.* 3. Also *attrib.*

1861 S. SMILES *Lives Engineers* II. VIII. x. 421 It [*sc.* the tunnel] was little larger than a sewer, and admitted the passage of only one narrow boat, seven feet wide, at a time, involving very heavy labour on the part of the men who worked it through. This was performed by what was called *legging*. **1949** *Archit. Rev.* CVI. 13/2 In the early tunnels towpaths were never constructed and boats were propelled through them either by shafting or legging... Legging was carried out by two men, one on each side of the boat lying on their backs and pushing against the tunnel sides with their feet. **1963** *Times* 4 May 6/4 They will stare in amazement at the legging boards used in the navigation of tunnels in the days when horse power meant what it said. **1975** *Times* 13 Mar. 4/7 The police have concentrated on the eighteenth-century 'legging' tunnel, built by Grindley, so called because boatmen had to propel their craft through by thrusting their legs against the roof.

3. *Austral.* and *N.Z.* Of dogs, the biting of an animal on the leg. Cf. *LEG *v.* 5 b.

1933 L. G. D. ACLAND in *Press* (Christchurch, N.Z.) 4 Nov. 15/7 Some dogs get a bad habit of biting sheep on the leg in yards; others of laming other dogs while fighting. Both these vices are called *legging*. **1960** [see *FORCE *sb.*[1] 7 e].

leggism (le·giz'm). *colloq.* [f. LEG *sb.* 5 + -ISM.] The practice, or an act, of 'black-legging' (Cf. BLACK-LEG, -LEGS 2).

1847 *Sporting Life* 28 Aug. 16/2 The system of adopting leggism as a legitimate part and parcel of horse-racing is one that must soon explode. **1896** FARMER & HENLEY *Slang* IV. 178/2 *Leggism*,.. the character, practices, or manners of a leg. **1937** PARTRIDGE *Dict. Slang* 477/1 *Leggism*, the art or the character of a 'leg'.

leggo (legōᵘ·), a representation of a colloq. or vulgar pronunciation of *let go!*

1884 'MARK TWAIN' *Huck. Finn* xxx. 310 Leggo the boy, you old idiot! **1889** J. K. JEROME *Three Men in Boat* ii. 24 What are *you* up to?.. leggo, can't you? **1906** KIPLING *Actions & Reactions* (1909) 207 Leggo my collar! **1932** L. GOLDING *Magnolia St.* II. xiii. 450 Leggo of my 'ead! **1961** 'F. RICHARDS' *Bunter the Ventriloquist* xxv. 145 'Ow! Leggo!' Bunter, wriggling, blinked round in alarm at the captain of the Remove. **1973** 'D. SHANNON' *Spring of Violence* (1974) x. 168 You're crazy, man. Leggo of me.

leggy, *a.* Add: Also *transf.*, long-stemmed.

1860 O. W. HOLMES *Prof. at Breakfast-Table* x. 310 The white meeting-house, and the row of youthful and leggy trees before it. **1932** *Times Educ. Suppl.* 9 July 267/4 If plants are crowded under glass they will grow 'leggy'. **1965** H. G. W. FOGG *Small Greenhouse* v. 39 Put the boxes, etc., on a shelf close up under the glass of the greenhouse, to prevent the seedlings from becoming drawn and 'leggy'.

legh (lī). Also **leigh.** [Etym. unknown.] = *Irish deer, elk* (*IRISH *a.* 2 b).

1774 T. WEST *Antiquities Furness* p. xlvi, That the legh was a native of Furness, is evident from the heads of those animals frequently found in Furness. **1795** A. RADCLIFFE *Journey* 483 A remarkably large breed of deer, called Leghs, the heads of which have frequently been found buried at a considerable depth in the soil. **1835** WORDSWORTH *Guide through District of Lakes* (ed. 5) ii. 38 The leigh, a gigantic species of deer which has long been extinct. **1974** J. W. SMYSER in Wordsworth *Prose Works* III. 403 Wordsworth drew on West for his information about the 'leigh'.

Leghorn. 1. (Earlier and later examples.)

1740 *Pennsylvania Gaz.* 22 May 7/2 Leghorn hats. **1742** *Boston News-Let.* 24 June 2/2 Just imported..from London..Leghorn Hats for women. **1969** GISH & PINCHOT *L. Gish* iii. 33 Dorothy and I were cool in our full-skirted summer frocks and wide-brimmed leghorn hats. **1975** R. PLAYER *Let's talk of Graves* ii. 46 Her big grey saucer eyes, shaded by the big Leghorn hat.

legion. Add: **1. b.** (Examples of *foreign legion*).

1897 E. A. BARTLETT *Battlefields Thessaly* vii. 144 There was a small foreign legion of about five hundred men, made up chiefly of Italians and English. **1924** M. MAGNUS (*title*) Memoirs of the foreign legion. **1957** P. KEMP *Mine were of Trouble* ii. 19 The Foreign Legion, or Tercio, was founded in the early 1920s by General Millán Astray. **1968** *Encycl. Brit.* XIII. 905/2 The term 'foreign legion' is often used for irregular volunteer corps of foreign sympathizers raised by states at war.

4. b. *Legion of the lost* (*ones*): people who are destitute or abandoned; *spec.* (see quot. 1961).

1870 D. J. KIRWAN *Palace & Hovel* xlii. 587 Those fair and frail members of the Legion of the Lost. **1892** KIPLING *Barrack-Room Ballads* 63 To the legion of the lost ones, to the cohort of the damned. **1899** —— *From Sea to Sea* I. ix. 299 Raising a Legion of the Lost for colonial service—of men who would do their work in one place for ever and look for nothing beyond it. **1961** PARTRIDGE *Dict. Slang* Suppl. 1167/1 *Legion of the lost, the*, those elderly or mentally infirm persons in homes or institutions who have been abandoned by relations and friends and who receive neither visits nor letters.

c. *American Legion*, a national association of ex-servicemen instituted in 1919 in the U.S.A.; *British Legion*, a similar association founded in 1921 and incorporated by Royal Charter in 1925 (since 1971 called the Royal British Legion); also *ellipt.*, as *Legion.*

1919 G. S. WHEAT *Story Amer. Legion* 8 At that dinner [in Paris, 16 Feb. 1919] the American Legion was born. *Ibid.* 32 That was the crux of the initial success of the Legion. **1921** *Times* 16 May 6/4 The arrangements for uniting various ex-Service men's societies into one big organization were completed..yesterday. The new organization will be known as the British Legion. **1953** *New Statesman* 13 June 696/2 A thousand business dinners, Legion reunions and family gatherings. **1968** *Encycl. Brit.* I. 764/1 Nonpolitical and nonsectarian, the American Legion's membership requirement is honourable service and an honourable discharge. **1970** *British Legion Jrnl.* Jan. 11/3 'Don' as he was affectionately known by all was a true member of the Legion, always to the fore in all branch and club activities. *Ibid.* 21 Are you going to Jersey for your holiday this year? The Appeals Department of the British Legion will send you..an interesting brochure. **1974** A. PRICE *Other Paths to Glory* vi. 72 Secretary of the Elthingham branch of the British Legion. *Ibid.* 73 He invariably sought information first from the local Legion secretary. **1974** T. KENRICK *Two for Price of One* xii. 101, I love my country... Been in the [American] Legion twenty years.

legionnaire (līdʒənēə·ɹ). Also **legionaire.** [ad. F. *légionnaire*, f. *légion* LEGION 1 b.] A member of the American, British, Foreign, or other Legion.

1818 SHELLEY *Let.* 20 Nov. (1964) II. 55 The marks of the chisels of the legionaires of the Roman Consul are yet evident. **1927** *Daily Express* 26 Apr. 1/5 Each legionnaire automatically becomes a member of the branch of the Canadian Legion nearest to the settlement on which he lives. **1927** *Daily Tel.* 14 June 7/2 The American Legion ..assembles in Paris in September... The legionnaires will be over two weeks on the Atlantic. **1932** KIPLING *Limits & Renewals* 322 His speech..ran From pure Parisian to gross peasant, With interludes North African If any Legionnaire were present. **1965** C. D. EBY *Siege of Alcázar* (1966) xi. 222 Captain Tiede and his Legionnaires filed into the Alcázar through the swimming pool door. **1974** *Northern Times* (Golspie, Sutherland) 23 Aug. 3/2 The Legion piper, Mr. Donnie McKenzie, played Mr. Bain's favourite pipe tune, while Legionaires paid their last respects.

legist. Add: *spec.* One of a group of legal philosophers in the early Han dynasty in China. Also *attrib.* or as *adj.*

1956 A. TOYNBEE *Historian's Approach to Relig.* ii. 22 In China the uncompromisingly rationalistic Legist school of philosophy was eventually driven off the field by a Confucian school which tempered its Rationalism with a conservative respect for a pre-rationalist tradition. **1957** *Chinese Culture* (Taipei) I. I. 77 As we know, School of the Legists prevailed during the earlier Han dynasty. **1965** *New Statesman* 24 Dec. 1004/1 Eventually the Romans did adopt that model but not, unfortunately, 'deliberately planned and executed in advance by an act of far-sighted and well-calculated statesmanship' (as Princes Hien and Hiao had done in China with the help of a 'sophist of the Legist school, Shang Yang').

legit., legit (līdʒi·t), colloq. abbrev. of LEGITIMATE *a.*, *sb.*, esp. of sense 2 b of the adj. Also in phr. *on the legit*, within the law.

1897 *National Police Gaz.* (U.S.) 26 May 6/1 Bob is envious of Corbett's success as a 'legit'. It pained him to see Jim strutting through four acts of a real play. *Ibid.*, Bob now wants to go into the 'legit'. **1904** *Daily Chron.* 22 Oct. 7/4 At the Hippodrome, four more 'legits' make their first appearance in 'variety'. **1908** 'ONE OF THE OLD BRIGADE' *London in Sixties* xiv. 177 Scene shifters, stage carpenters, actors, everything and everybody strictly 'legit' should have the preference of guzzling and swilling to the memory of the immortal poet. **1923** H. RUBY *Let.* 16 Aug. in G. Marx *Groucho Lett.* (1967) 184 He clicked as a legit actor on Broadway. **1931** G. IRWIN *Amer. Tramp & Underworld Slang* 138 *On the legit*, honest. **1936** N. COWARD *Tonight at 8.30* I. 93 When she stabs herself—she takes such a time about it—that's legits all over. **1946** MEZZROW & WOLFE *Really Blues* ii. 21 Once Sid got..a hundred cases of booze on the legit..but..would sooner have his throat cut than push them at legit prices at the drugstores. **1952** W. R. BURNETT *Vanity Row* (1953) v. 41 In the early 'twenties he'd served time..for bootlegging. .. Since then.., he'd been..on the legit. **1955** E. BOWEN *World of Love* xi. 206 Left no children—anyway, no legits. **1957** J. OSBORNE *Entertainer* v. 38 I'd gone legit. for a while..and I'd been in 'The Tale of Two Cities'. **1961** *Times* 29 Nov. 11/5 It provided funds for penetration into 'legit' business for the gang lords. **1965** J. B. PRIESTLEY *Lost Empires* I. ii. 16 She used to be legit and pretends to be very haigh-clarss,.. though she's only playing feed to a comedian. **1967** J. HORTON in T. Kochman *Rappin' & Stylin' Out* (1972) 22 Identified as white, a lame, and square, I had to build up an image of being at least 'legit' (not working for the police). **1969** B. MALCOLM in A. Chapman *New Black Voices* (1972) 384 First time I was sweet sixteen Marriage license, zircon ring—all legit. **1970** C. WOOD *Terrible Hard* viii. 112 I've never been 'legit' as you might say.., just an old-fashioned song and dance girl. **1972** R. HILL *Fairly Dangerous Thing* II. vii. 185 A business acquaintance. Runs an escort service. Legit. High class. **1972** *New Society* 7 Dec. 559/1 The age of legit drinking will come down from 18 to 17. **1973** 'H. HOWARD' *Highway to Murder* x. 127 This dough isn't strictly legit.

legitimacy. 2. (Earlier example.)

1812 *Niles' Reg.* I. 404/1, I never hear an American citizen speak of the '*legitimacy*' of princes without indignation or pity.

legitimate, *a.* Add: **2. b.** *legitimate drama* and absol. (Earlier and later examples.) Also in other collocations. So as *sb.*, an actor of legitimate drama.

1799 *Sporting Mag.* XV. 135/2 A lady to whom the public are so much indebted for the support which the legitimate drama has received from her exertions, and who..has disdained the pantomime and spectacle to which the German muse so often stoops. **1812** *Theatrical Inquisitor* Oct. I. 72 Mr. E treads closely upon the heels of the legitimate stage. **1838** DICKENS *Let.* 16 Jan. (1965) I. 355 Let the Legitimate Drama put this, and Joan of Arc..into her pipe. **1909** P. G. WILLIAMS in *Sat. Even. Post* 5 June 17/2 The vaudeville actor is much more thrifty than his colleague in the legitimate. **1933** P. GODFREY *Back-Stage* xvi. 207 The principal comedian of *Have a Nibble*..scandalizes the 'legitimates' by discarding the jacket of his sprightly plus-four suit. **1947** N. MARSH *Final Curtain* v. 84, I haven't got the wind for dancing.. and the 'legitimate' gives me a pain in the neck. **1952** *N.Y. Herald Tribune* 28 Aug. 16/7 A revision of New York City's building code to spur the construction of new legitimate theaters. **1968** *Globe & Mail* (Toronto) 17 Feb. 24 Nor is it [*sc.* the city] avoiding the inevitable responsibility of building a smaller legitimate house. **1972** *N.Y. Times* 3 Nov. 1/1 The new hotel would include..a legitimate theater. **1975** *Scottish Field* Jan. 9/1 With his feet now firmly planted in both acting spheres—the so-called legitimate theatre and the pantomime lark—this young-looking veteran [*sc.* Rikki Fulton]..feels fit to accept any professional challenge.

c. (Earlier example.)

1812 *Niles' Reg.* I. 404/2 The 'legitimate' sovereigns of Russia, Austria and Prussia.

e. In *Jazz colloq.*, designating 'serious' music as distinct from jazz or popular music.

1927 *Melody Maker* Apr. 359/2 The number lends itself exceptionally well to the symphonic treatment it has been given, the orchestration is very fine and the modulated passages and general arrangement make it, although a little too 'legitimate' for dancing, perfect from a concert point of view. **1933** *Fortune* Aug. 94 Other jazz heroes such as the Dorseys..have become more or less legitimate musicians for radio purposes. **1946** MEZZROW & WOLFE

Really Blues (1957) xvii. 341 The New Orleans drum patterns..were closest to 'legitimate' music. **1969** *New Yorker* 20 Dec. 52/3 It would have been interesting if he had made similar measurements during a performance by a 'commercial'—that is, a jazz or dance-band—player..to compare with those of a 'legitimate', or symphonic, player.

le·glessness. [f. LEGLESS *a.* + -NESS.] The condition of being legless.

1902 *19th Cent.* Feb. 254 Sir Richard Calmady's leglessness is never for an instant forgotten. **1911** G. B. SHAW *Doctor's Dilemma* Pref. p. xiv, The leg may mortify—it is always safer to operate—..evolution is towards motors and leglessness.

‖ **legong** (legǫ·ŋ). [Indonesian.] A stylized Balinese dance performed by young girls. Also *attrib.* Also, one of the performers of such a dance.

1926 E. MORDAUNT *Further Venture Bk.* xxiii. 291 For three days preparations have been going on for a..Legong ..given by a man who has won a law-suit. **1930** H. POWELL *Last Paradise* xii. 109 Runis and Madé Réi were nine years old... They danced the sacred traditional measures of the *legong*. **1937** M. COVARRUBIAS *Island of Bali* (1972) viii. 224 As the archetype of the delicate and feminine, the *legong* is the finest of Balinese dances... The *legong* is performed at feasts, generally in the late afternoon when the heat of the day has subsided. *Ibid.* 228 A very popular dance that seems related to the *legong* is the *djogèd*, performed by a girl in a variation of the *legong* costume and in the traditional *legong* steps. **1971** *Walkabout* (Austral.) Nov. 73/1, I was sitting at this beautiful bar, listening to the distant flurry of the Legong dance.

legouane, var. IGUANA. See also LEGUAN.

1790 E. HELME tr. *Le Vaillant's Trav. Afr.* I. 391 The Hottentot who fired at the Hippopotamus came home late..and was obliged to meet the sarcasms of my Hottentot wits, who tried to persuade him he had fired at a *Legouane* (a kind of large lizard, common in the rivers of Africa).

legrandite (ləgrǫ·ndəit). *Min.* [f. *Legrand*, the name of a 20th-c. Belgian mine manager who collected the first specimen + -ITE[1].] A basic hydrated zinc arsenate, $Zn_2AsO_4OH.H_2O$ occurring as colourless to yellow transparent monoclinic crystals at Lampazos, Mexico.

1932 DRUGMAN & HEY in *Mineral. Mag.* XXIII. 175 A chemical analysis..showed it to be indeed a new mineral, a basic zinc arsenate, and the name 'legrandite' is proposed for it in recognition of the collector. **1971** *Soviet Physics: Doklady* XVI. 421/2 Analyses of legrandite from various deposits reveal up to 2% Mn isomorphously replacing Zn.

legume. **2.** Delete *Obs.* and add later examples.

1870 J. YEATS *Nat. Hist. Commerce* II. 137 The legumes of temperate climates are familiar plants. **1969** *Oxf. Bk. Food Plants* 34/2 There are a number of other tropical legumes which are only of very minor or local importance as sources of food. *Ibid.* 44/1 Cowpea..is an annual legume, originating in Africa. **1974** A. HUXLEY *Plant & Planet* xxx. 365 Various legume seeds have proved the best sources [of vegetable protein] so far.

lehiite (lī·həi,əit). *Min.* [f. *Lehi*, the name of the city in Utah near which it occurs + -ITE[1].] A basic hydrated phosphate of calcium, potassium, sodium, and aluminium, of a white to grey colour.

1930 LARSEN & SHANNON in *Amer. Mineralogist* XV. 329 (*heading*) Lehiite, a new mineral. **1942** *Ibid.* XXVII. 294 Material identified by this writer as lehiite differs somewhat from that described by Larsen and Shannon. It forms dense, light gray layers on the outer shells of the nodules, and is made up of fine to moderately coarse fibers generally in subparallel bands. **1955** M. H. HEY *Index Min. Species* (ed. 2) 236 *Lehiite*, $(K,Na)_2Ca_5Al_8(PO_4)_8(OH)_{12}.6H_2O$ (?).

lehr, var. LEER *sb.*[3] (in Dict. and Suppl.).

‖ **Lehrjahre** (lē·ryārə), *sb. pl.* [G. *lehr(en* to teach + *jahre* years; cf. G. *lehrling* apprentice.] Apprenticeship, usu. *fig.*

1865 J. A. SYMONDS *Let.* 15 May (1967) I. 539 The retrospective view you take there of your last two years is the just one. They have been Lehrjahre in a high sense. **1891** E. B. BAX tr. *Schopenhauer's Sel. Ess.* p. x, They settled at Hamburg... It was here that Arthur Schopenhauer spent his *lehrjahre*. *a* **1892** G. C. ROBERTSON *Elem. Philos.* (1896) xx. 201 The Socratic stage (407–399)—his *Lehrjahre* as they have been called—when he was the pupil of Socrates. **1973** *Times* 14 June 16/2 Julian Fane has written an updated, nineteenth-century *Lehrjahre* book.

lehua (lehū·ă). [Hawaiian.] An evergreen tree, *Metrosideros collina*, of the family Myrtaceæ, native to the Polynesian and Melanesian islands of the Pacific Ocean and bearing panicles of scarlet flowers; also called *ohia* or *ohia lehua*.

1888 W. HILLEBRAND *Flora Hawaiian Islands* 125 *M[etrosideros] polymorpha*... The most generally prevailing tree on all Islands between 1500 and 6000 ft., usually gregarious. Nat[ive] name: 'Ohia lehua', or simply 'lehua'. .. The wood is very hard, furnishes the best fuel, and is also used for building houses. **1917** *Nature* 20 Sept. 57/2 Lehua, resembles, in the appearance of the trunk, our white oak, but bears beautiful clusters of scarlet flowers with long, protruding stamens. **1937** D. & H. TEILHET *Feather Cloak Murders* ix. 152 From the lehua trees the fragrance hung. **1965** M. C. NEAL *In Gardens of Hawaii* 637 The lehua, a favorite native Hawaiian tree, is the commonest kind..in some forests.

lei (lē[i]). [Hawaiian.] A Polynesian garland made of flowers, feathers, shells, etc., often given as a symbol of affection.

1843 J. JARVES *Hist. Hawaiian or Sandwich Islands* iii. 65 Garlands of flowers, necklaces of shells, and *leis*, beautiful wreaths fabricated from red or yellow feathers, encircled the limbs of the females. **1883** W. H. D. ADAMS *Mountains & Mountain-Climbing* 300 These crimson tassels, deftly strung on thread or fibres, are much used by the natives for their *leis*, or garlands. **1905** A. R. H. MONCRIEFF *World of To-Day* IV. 208 Bedecked by *leis*, garlands of bright flowers or feathers. **1956** J. MASTERS *Bugles & Tiger* xxii. 292 The garlands round my neck [at Honolulu] were called leis but they smelled much the same as the ones in India. **1966** MRS. L. B. JOHNSON *White House Diary* 25 Oct. (1970) 434 There were more 'Blue Ladies'—Mrs. Marcos' hostess committee—with fragrant leis of sampaguita for each of the First Ladies. **1970** N. ARMSTRONG et al. *First on Moon* xiv. 364 Jan Armstrong was wearing a carnation lei sent by friends in Hawaii. **1975** *Times* 2 May 7 (*caption*) Governor George Ariyoshi welcoming the Queen to Hawaii with a lei of orchids.

lei: see *LEU.

Leibnitz (ləi·bnits). *Philos.* Also **Leibniz.** [Name of the German philosopher and mathematician: see LEIBNITZIAN *a.* and *sb.*] *Leibnitz'(s) law*: the principle of the identity of indiscernibles (see INDISCERNIBLE *sb.* 2).

Leibniz is now the more usual spelling.

1941 O. HELMER tr. *Tarski's Introd. Logic* § 17. 55, *x=y* if, and only if, *x* has every property which *y* has, and *y* has every property which *x* has... [This] was first stated by Leibniz..and hence may be called Leibniz's law. **1965** *Philos. Rev.* LXXIV. 341 Physicalism violates Leibniz' law, which requires that if two things are identical they have all their non-intensional and nonmodal properties in common. **1968** *Aristotelian Soc. Suppl. Vol.* XLII. 99 Let us consider Leibniz's law firstly as a principle about the identity of individuals.

Leica (ləi·kă). [f. *Leitz* (see below) + CA(MERA.] The proprietary name of cameras made by the German firm of Ernst & Leitz Gesellschaft.

1925 *Brit. Jrnl. Photogr.* 26 June 387/2 New apparatus. .. Leica cine film camera... Quite an innovation in pocket cameras is one just issued by the well-known firm of Leitz, designed to take about 5 feet of ordinary standard perforated cinematograph film. **1930** *Trade Marks Jrnl.* 23 July 1135/1 Leica... Photographic cameras. Ernst & Leitz Gesellschaft mit beschränkter Haftung, (a Company organised under the laws of Germany),.. London,.. and Wetzlar, Germany; Manufacturers. **1933** W. ALEXANDER *Mod. Photogr. with Mod. Miniature Cameras* ii. 29 Leica and Contax have now become words.. familiar in the mouths of men throughout..the earth. **1934** H. NICOLSON *Let.* 9 Oct. (1966) 184 Lindbergh.. helped me to unload my Leica camera. **1936** P. FLEMING *News from Tartary* v. 36 The Leicas turned out very satisfactorily. **1948** 'N. SHUTE' *No Highway* v. 136 The print was an enlargement from a Leica frame. **1953** C. DAY LEWIS *Italian Visit* v. 53 Armed with good taste, a Leica and a guide. **1958** G. GREENE *Our Man in Havana* I. iii. 25 The victim's Leica had been smashed as well. **1959** P. H. JOHNSON *Unspeakable Skipton* vii. 57 An American..was photographing the swans with his Leica. **1973** R. THOMAS *If you can't be Good* (1974) iii. 28 Using.. an old Leica with some fast film, Sarah turned out striking, informal portraits.

Leicester. Add: Also **Leicestershire.** (Earlier and later examples of variety of sheep.) In *Austral.* and *N.Z.* freq. as *English Leicester*. Cf. **Border Leicester*.

1798 J. MIDDLETON *View Agric. Middlesex* xiii. 348 The Lincoln and Leicester sheep come to Smithfield in perfection. **1798** JANE AUSTEN *Let.* 17 Nov. (1952) 29 One of his Leicestershire sheep, sold to the butcher last week, weighed 27 lb. and ¼ per quarter. **1804** A. YOUNG *Gen. View Agric. Hertfordshire* 189 The cross is with the new Leicester: he sells no lambs. **1809** [see *KENT *sb.*[3]]. **1874** A. BATHGATE *Colonial Experiences* xv. 210 In cultivated lands the Leicester is the favorite. **1923** W. PERRY et al. *Sheep Farming in N.Z.* iv. 32 Thus Romney Marsh, English Leicesters, and Lincolns, have been improved or adapted to suit New Zealand conditions. **1950** H. G. BELSCHNER *Sheep Managem. & Dis.* ii. 21 The Leicester crosses well with the big-framed Merino, but it is not so much in favour for this purpose in Australia... The following description of the English Leicester is taken from the flock book of the Australian Society of Breeders of British Sheep. **1956** G. BOWEN *Wool Away!* (ed. 2) xii. 142 The English Leicester is another of the British breeds which has played a notable part in developing New Zealand's sheep farming, but is now more or less on the way out.

b. Leicester (occas. **Leicestershire**) **cheese,** a firm-textured full milk cheese originally made in Leicestershire.

1880 J. P. SHELDON *Dairy Farming* 241/1 The finest qualities of..Leicester cheese are generally admitted to be, with the single exception of genuine Stilton, the best cheese produced in these islands. **1902** *Encycl. Brit.* XXVII. 355/2 Derby cheese in its best forms is much like Leicester, being 'clean' in flavour and mellow. **1950** J. G. DAVIS *Dict. Dairying* 124 Leicester cheese is made from evening's and morning's milk. **1965** T. FITZGIBBON *Art Brit. Cooking* 133 Leicestershire cheese is a hard-pressed, flaky textured cheese..usually coloured a pale orange with annatto. **1970** *Guardian* 6 June 13/2 Leicester, an excellent dessert cheese with a mild flavour.

Leichhardt (ləi·kāɹt). The name of the German explorer of Australia, Friedrich Wilhelm Ludwig *Leichhardt* (1813–48), used *attrib.* in **Leichhardt-tree, -pine** to designate a tree native to Australia and India, *Nauclea orientalis*, of the family Rubiaceæ, which bears heads of yellow flowers; also *absol.*; **Leichhardt's bean** (see *BEAN *sb.* 4).

1860 F. VON MUELLER *Essay on Plants collected by Mr. Eugene Fitzalan* 12 The opportunity is an apt one for offering here some remarks on the 'Leichhardt-tree' of the settlers of Rockhampton. **1874** M. K. BEVERIDGE *Lost Life* 40 Groaning beneath the friendly shade That by a Leichhardt-tree was made. **1885** H. FINCH-HATTON *Advance Australia!* 258 The Leichhardt is a very symmetrical tree that grows to a height of about sixty feet, and has leaves rather like a big laurel. **1888** F. M. BAILEY *Queensland Woods* 76 *S[arcocephalus] cordatus*... Leichhardt-tree or Canary-wood... A large tree with a thick, soft, corky bark of a more or less yellowish colour. **1907** MRS. A. GUNN *We of Never-Never* 64 The camp had been fixed up in the silent depths of a dark Leichhardt-pine forest. **1908** E. J. BANFIELD *Confessions of Beachcomber* II. i. 252 'Koo-badg-aroo' (Leichhardt-tree, *Sarcocephalus cordatus*), resembling a strawberry in shape, but brown, spicy and hot. **1944** W. E. HARNEY *Taboo* (ed. 3) 27 Those huge Leichhardt trees..would then be fashioned into canoes.

leifite (lī·-, lēi·fəit). *Min.* [ad. Da. *leifit* (O. B. Bøggild 1915, in *Meddelelser om Grønland* LI. 427), f. the name of *Leif* Ericson (fl. 1000), Norse voyager: see -ITE[1].] An acidic aluminosilicate and fluoride of sodium occurring as colourless hexagonal prisms.

1917 *Jrnl. Chem. Soc.* CXII. II. 147 (*heading*) Leifite, a new mineral from Narsarsuk, Greenland. **1968** I. KOSTOV *Mineral.* II. v. 406 Leifite, $Na_2AlSi_4O_{10}F.H_2O_{<1}$, found as acicular hexagonal crystals in pegmatites is similar to cancrinite.

leigh, var. *LEGH.

leightonite (lēi·tǫ̆nəit). *Min.* [f. the name of Tomas *Leighton* (b. 1894), Chilean mineralogist + -ITE[1].] A hydrated sulphate of potassium, calcium, and copper found as transparent, pale blue to greenish blue, triclinic crystals at Chuquicamata, Chile.

1938 C. PALACHE in *Amer. Mineralogist* XXIII. 34 Leightonite, as the new species will be named, is triclinic, as shown by optical examination. **1962** *Canad. Mineralogist* VII. 276 It is interesting to note that leightonite has a chemical homologue—polyhalite, $K_2Ca_2Mg(SO_4)_4.2H_2O$. **1963** *Acta Crystallogr.* XVI. A10/1 Leightonite, $K_2Ca_2Cu(SO_4)_4.2H_2O$, is triclinic, but it is pseudo-orthorhombic (face-centred) to the extent that no departure from 90° has been found in the angles of the unit cell as determined by the usual X-ray diffraction techniques.

leio-. Add: leiotrichous *a.* (examples); hence **leio·trichy,** the condition of having straight lank hair.

1855 R. G. MAYNE *Expos. Lex. Med. Sci.* (1860) 581/2 *Leiotrichus*, having smooth hair: leiotrichous. **1909** Leiotrichous [see *CYMOTRICHOUS *a.*]. **1924** A. C. HADDON *Races of Man* (ed. 2) 5 For practical purposes these varieties of hair-form may be grouped as follows: (1) Leiotrichy.., or straight hair, [etc.]. **1935** HUXLEY & HADDON *We Europeans* iv. 114 Leiotrichy: the condition of straight lank hair, hanging straight down, as among the Chinese and certain other yellow-skinned peoples of Asia, and among the Eskimo. **1936** Leiotrichy [see *CYMOTRICHOUS *a.*].

Leishman (lī·ʃmăn, ləi·ʃ-). *Med.* The name of W. B. *Leishman* (1865–1926), British pathologist, used *attrib.* and in the possessive with reference to his work in pathology, as **Leishman('s) body** = *LEISHMAN–DONOVAN BODY; **Leishman('s) stain,** a mixture of eosin and methylene blue used to stain blood smears.

1903 *Brit. Med. Jrnl.* 28 Nov. 1401/1 (*heading*) Further notes on Leishman's bodies. *Ibid.*, There is never any contour line suggestive of a cell-wall, as with the Leishman bodies themselves. **1904** *Ibid.* 28 May 1250/1 A film prepared from the peripheral blood was examined.., Romanowsky and Leishman's stains being used. *Ibid.* 1252/1 These bodies stain purple or violet with the Leishman stain. **1961** *Lancet* 5 Aug. 315/2 In staining blood-films we obtained just as good results as with Leishman's stain prepared by the standard method. **1972** W. C. JOHNSON in J. H. Graham et al. *Dermal Path.* xix. 455/2 A definite diagnosis [of leishmaniasis] depends upon the demonstration of the Leishman bodies.

Leishman–Donovan body (-dǫ·nǒvăn-). *Med.* [f. prec. + the name of C. *Donovan* (1863–1951), Irish physician.] One of the numerous ovoid structures consisting of a single non-flagellated leishmania found in the macrophages of sufferers from leishmaniasis.

1904 *Brit. Med. Jrnl.* 28 May 1249/2 (*heading*) Note on the occurrence of Leishman–Donovan bodies in 'cachexial

fevers' including kala-azar. **1966** WRIGHT & SYMMERS *Systemic Path.* II. xxxix. 1601/2 (*caption*) Large numbers of Leishman–Donovan bodies are seen in the cytoplasm of many of the macrophages in this field.

leishmania (lī·ʃmæ·niă, ləiʃ-). *Zool.* and *Med.* Pl. **-ia, -iæ, -ias.** [mod.L., f. *LEISHMAN + -IA[1].] **a.** Any protozoon of the genus *Leishmania* (family Trypanosomidæ), comprising three species which are parasitic in man (and occas. other mammals), occurring as non-flagellated Leishman–Donovan bodies, and which are transmitted by sandflies of the genus *Phlebotomus*, wherein they occur as flagellated individuals in the alimentary canal. **b.** Any flagellate of the family Trypanosomidæ when existing in a leishmanial form.

[**1903** R. Ross in *Brit. Med. Jrnl.* 28 Nov. 1401/2 Laveran has given the name *Piroplasma donovani* to these organisms; and the specific name must therefore be permanently adopted. But if, as I suppose, they are found to belong to a new genus, it would be only fair to give the name *Leishmania* to that genus. In that event the full name would be *Leishmania donovani*, Laveran.] **1914** *Trop. Dis. Bull.* III. 141 Large numbers of leishmania were found in the lesions. **1926**, etc. [see *LEPTOMONAS]. **1952** M. E. FLOREY *Clin. Applic. Antibiotics* I. viii. 247 The lesion had again broken down and leishmania were found in smears. **1961** [see *LEPTOMONAD]. **1962** J. D. SMYTH *Introd. Animal Parasitol.* v. 63 Leishmanias are unusual in living entirely within the cells of the reticulo-endothelial system. **1968** E. J. L. SOULSBY *Helminths, Arthropods & Protozoa Domesticated Animals* 567 Endothelial and macrophage cells contain masses of leishmaniae.

Hence **leishma·nial, leishma·nian** *adjs.*, caused by leishmaniæ; typical of a leishmania as it occurs in man and other mammals (i.e. as a non-flagellated Leishman–Donovan body). Also **leishmani·asis** (pl. **-ases**) [-ASIS], **-manio·sis** (pl. **-oses**) [-OSIS], any of several diseases, principally kala-azar (visceral leishmaniasis), oriental sore (cutaneous leishmaniasis) and espundia (muco-cutaneous or American cutaneous leishmaniasis), which are caused by species of *Leishmania*; (**dermal**) **lei·shmanoid** [-OID, after VARIOLOID *a.* and *sb.*], a condition occurring as a sequel to kala-azar and characterized by an eruption of whitish patches on the skin.

1911 STEDMAN *Med. Dict.* 470/1 *Leishmaniosis*, infection with a species of *Leishmania*. **1912** *Trop. Dis. Bull.* I. 363 (*heading*) Fourth series of haematological researches on leishmanial anaemia. **1912** *Brit. Med. Jrnl.* 2 Nov. 1194/2 (*heading*) Papers dealing with leishmaniasis. **1914** *Chem. Abstr.* VIII. 1466 (*heading*) Possibility of the excitation of leucopoiesis in Leishmanian infection in childhood. **1916** *Jrnl. Amer. Med. Assoc.* 22 Nov. 1635/2 (*heading*) Tartrate of antimony and potassium in treatment of superficial leishmaniosis. **1920** W. E. MASTERS *Essent. Trop. Med.* i. 55 (*heading*) The leishmaniases. **1922** U. N. BRAHMACHARI in *Indian Med. Gaz.* LVII. 127/1 In view of the fact that the eruptions are due to leishmania infection whose virus has been modified by antimonial treatment, I propose to call this form of cutaneous leishmaniasis *dermal leishmanoid* just as small-pox modified by vaccination is called varioloid. **1942** [see *LEPTOMONAD]. **1966** WRIGHT & SYMMERS *Systemic Path.* II. xxxix. 1596/2 Cutaneous leishmaniosis (oriental or tropical sore) is caused by the protozoon, *Leishmania tropica*. **1967** A. C. ALLEN *Skin* (ed. 2) xiv. 541/1 The so-called post-kala-azar dermal leishmanoid is a familiar sequel of visceral leishmaniasis... The leishmanoid begins as patches of erythematous macules on the face and body. **1967** *New Scientist* 17 Aug. 349/2 Small rodents which are carriers of the disease leishmaniasis which causes suppurating sores in humans. **1968** E. J. L. SOULSBY *Helminths, Arthropods & Protozoa Domesticated Animals* 565 Developmental stages of the genus [sc. *Leishmania*] occur in the leishmanial form in vertebrates and in the leptomonad form in the insect vector and in culture. **1968** WEINMAN & RISTIC *Infectious Blood Dis. Man & Animals* I. viii. 160 These lack the physiological character possessed by the leishmanial parasites of mammals of being able to grow at temperatures of 34°–38°C.

Leisler (ləi·zləɹ). The name of the early 19th-c. German zoologist, T. P. *Leisler*, used in the possessive to designate **Leisler's bat**, a small black bat, *Nyctalus leisleri*, named after him in 1817 by H. Kuhl (*Deutsch. Fledermäuse* 38), and formerly called the hairy-armed bat.

1904 J. G. MILLAIS *Mammals Great Brit. & Ireland* I. 76 Leisler's Bat is considerably smaller than the noctule. **1910** G. E. H. BARRETT-HAMILTON *Hist. Brit. Mammals* I. 83 Leisler's Bat, or species closely resembling it, is found in the wooded districts of boreal and transitional Europe and Asia. **1941** H. CORY *Mammals Brit. Isles* 255 Leisler's Bat..is rare in England, but occurs in greater numbers in eastern Ireland. **1960** *Times* 14 June 14/7 Of the Leisler's bat..I recall no obvious distinguishing character.

leisure, *sb.* Add: **5. e.** *lady* (or *woman*) *of leisure*, a woman who has no regular employment or whose time is free from obligations to others.

1948 R. M. AYRES *Missing the Tide* v. 164 She was no longer a lady of leisure in her own house but a paid companion with irksome duties to perform. **1951** M. MCLUHAN *Mech. Bride* (1967) 40/1 The woman of leisure might wear long skirts, but the working woman was put into adolescent short skirts. **1955** L. P. HARTLEY *Perfect Woman* xxi. 190 Or as the lady of leisure, reading a book? **1975** D. RAMSAY *Descent into Dark* i. 26 She had a whole afternoon to play lady of leisure.

6. a. and **c.** (Further examples).

1816 JANE AUSTEN *Emma* I. ii. 25 He had still a small house in Highbury, where most of his leisure days were spent. **1899** T. VEBLEN (*title*) The theory of the leisure class. **1907** F. H. BURNETT *Shuttle* xxxiv. 347 In another generation there will be a male leisure class [in America]. **1907** BELLOC *Cautionary Tales* 31 Learn To pass your Leisure Time In Cleanly Merriment. **1912** J. H. MOORE *Ethics & Educ.* vi. 22 The school in its origin was a leisure-class institution. **1941** E. WILSON *Wound & Bow* i. 61 They [*sc.* Estella and Pip] are left with their leisure-class habits and no incomes to keep them up. **1947** O. BARFIELD in *Essays presented to Charles Williams* 121 It has no particular significance if poetry is to be regarded *only* as..a pleasurable way of diverting our leisure hours. **1951** M. MCLUHAN *Mech. Bride* (1967) 40/1 Competitive drives and ambitious impulses will be transferred increasingly to leisure and home occupations. **1954** *Encounter* Mar. 78/2 A master-race recruited solely from the leisure-class and endemic to English shores: 'Of such was The Breed.' **1961** D. JENKINS *Equality & Excellence* vii. 143 Problems of adjustment..connected with housing and leisure-time activities. **1963** *Punch* 15 May 710/3 Fashion shows of men's outerwear, underwear, leisure-wear, rainwear. **1964** A. WYKES *Gambling* iv. 80 Watching other people play games has been one of man's favorite leisure-time occupations for a long while. **1965** *New Society* 26 Aug. 5/3 Buxton is trying to..latch on to the leisure revolution, without becoming a coach tours nightmare. **1966** *Guardian* 16 Feb. 6/3 A case for subregional leisure centres—which would help people in small towns to feel less dependent on cities—was made out yesterday by Professor Arthur Ling. **1968** *Economist* 4 May 38/2 One should not conclude that Frenchmen have reached the stage of the fabled leisure civilisation. **1968** *Daily Tel.* 28 Dec. 21/1 The ever-increasing attraction of boating as a leisure-activity and a sport. **1969** *Times* 7 Nov. 14/2 With the increasing demand for leisure wear, formal wear people have softened their lines. **1972** *Accountant* 17 Aug. (Suppl.) 11/3 Expanding construction company specialising in growth market of the leisure industry. **1974** *Times* 12 Feb. 11/7 Silhouette's swimwear and leisurewear sales manager.

leisure (le·ʒĭŭɹ, U.S. lī·ʒ[1]ŭɹ), *v. rare.* [f. the sb.] **a.** *intr.* To have or enjoy leisure. **b.** *trans.* To make leisurely.

1928 BLUNDEN *Undertones of War* 304 There to tarry in careless ways,.. Leisuring after fiery days. **1929** BRIDGES *Testament of Beauty* i. 32 Science comforting man's animal poverty and leisuring his toil. **1970** G. F. NEWMAN *Sir, You Bastard* vi. 173 Sneed rose late..and leisured with the papers in the coffee-house opposite his flat.

leisured, *a.* Add: **2.** (*the*) *leisured class(es* (later examples).

1923 W. S. MAUGHAM *Our Betters* II. 85 American wealth has reached a pitch where it was bound to give rise to a leisured class. **1926** B. WEBB *My Apprenticeship* i. 9 The rulers of the country..ought in the main to be drawn from a leisured class. **1929** D. H. LAWRENCE *Pansies* 43 Obviously he's not one of the leisured classes. **1949** A. WILSON *Wrong Set* 111 The many leisured-class hypotheses by which Mr Cockshott obviously lived. **1960** M. BRADBURY *Phogey!* III. 105 The leisured classes demonstrated their leisure by indulgence in useless pursuits (personal relationships, scholarship, etc.).

leitmotiv. Add: (Later examples.) Also in extended use.

1896 H. ELLIS in *Savoy* I. 70 Zola..introduced this sort of *leit-motiv* into literature. **1898** G. MEREDITH *Let.* 6 July (1970) III. 1303, I long to hear from him of [the] Leitmotif—though indeed he has taken the world more or less into his confidence. **1899** KIPLING *Stalky & Co.* 84 A tune whose *leit-motif* was the word 'stinker'. **1912** WODEHOUSE *Prince & Betty* iv. 61 The name Scobell had been recurring like a *leit motif* in Mr Crump's conversation. **1937** KOESTLER *Spanish Testament* iv. 94 It provides the *leitmotif* of German foreign policy in Spain. **1955** *Times* 28 May 8/4 But the method remains, the orchestral tapestry of leitmotifs is more resplendent than ever, the drama is even more closely knit into the texture of sound. **1970** G. GREER *Female Eunuch* 151 Self-sacrifice is the leit-motif of most of the marital games played by women. **1972** *Composer & Conductor* Aug. 1/1 Ninety-nine music graduates out of a hundred..will say that the Leitmotiv (or Leitmotif, or leading motive)..was invented by Wagner. Wrong... The correct answer is: Friedrich Wilhelm Jähns, and even he applied it not to Wagner but to Weber. **1974** *Times Lit. Suppl.* 15 Feb. 162/4 There are plenty of *leitmotivs* which recur time and time again.

lek, *sb.*[1] Substitute for def.: A patch of ground used by groups of birds of certain species, esp. blackcock, during the breeding season, as a setting for the males' display and their meeting with the females; the display itself or the season during which it takes place. Also **lek** *v. intr.*, to take part in a pattern of behaviour centred upon a lek; **le·kking** *vbl. sb.*

1942 E. A. ARMSTRONG *Bird Display* xv. 215 The lek [of blackcock] is larger than the ruffs' assembly ground and the individual territories are not so clearly defined. **1964** A. L. THOMSON *New Dict. Birds* 432/1 The lek is usually maintained at the arena for considerable periods of time and many species revive the performance at the same display-ground year after year. *Ibid.* 432/2 During lek displays the birds tend to stimulate one another. **1970** *Country Life* 26 Feb. 490 (*caption*) A pair of blackcocks lekking. **1971** *Ibid.* 16 Sept. 693/2 Then came January, when instinct bade her [*sc.* a partridge] to that lekking field that had served as a partridge lekking area since time immemorial. **1972** C. WILLOCK *Death in Covert* (new ed.) i. 6 A randy old blackcock displaying triumphantly on a Highland lek. **1974** *Country Life* 26 Sept. 865/3 The strongest birds are nearest the centre of the [black grouse] lek because it is there that the females first land.

‖ **lek** (lek), *sb.*[2] Pl. **lekë, leks.** [Albanian.] A unit of currency in Albania.

1927 *Times* 18 Nov. 24/4 The monetary unit chosen is the gold franc (5 lek).., with a parity of approximately 25 to the £. **1937** M. COMENCINI *Coins Mod. World* 2 Albania Currency unit: the Franka Ari or Gold Franc of 5 Lek or 200 Qindar. One Lek corresponds to 8 5-Qindar Leku.. bronze coins. **1962** R. A. G. CARSON *Coins* 408 The republic of Albania, established in 1925, issued a coinage with the franka as the unit, divided into 5 lek, divided in turn into 40 qindar. **1966** *New Statesman* 8 Apr. 500/3 The plans are already drawn, 120 million lekë (nearly £500,000) promised by the state. **1967** *Spectator* 22 Dec. 775/3 Whitaker's [Almanack]..is no sure guide to the rate at which the British traveller can hope to exchange his pittance for Albanian *leks*. **1974** *Albania Today* (Tirana) Jan.–Feb. 16/3 The rate was fixed at 83.72 leks per ruble, as against 100 leks per ruble previously.

‖ **lekach** (le·kaχ). [Yiddish.] A traditional Jewish cake made with honey.

1932 L. GOLDING *Magnolia St.* III. viii. 573, I will fill large bags for them with *ingber* and *strudel* and *lekkach*. **1955** L. W. LEONARD *Jewish Holiday Cook Bk.* 20 A good standby for holiday entertaining is the traditional Lekach, or Honey Cake. **1960** S. BECKER tr. *Schwarz-Bart's Last of Just* (1961) v. 239 That's a *lekach*! A honey cake. **1973** CARR & OBERMAN *Gourmet's Guide to Jewish Cooking* 124 Foods associated with Rosh Hashanah are honey and honey cake (Lekach).

‖ **lekane** (leka·ni). *Gr. Antiq.* [ad. Gr. λεκάνη a bowl or dish.] A small shallow bowl, usually with handles and a cover. Also dim. **lekanis** (pl. **-ides**).

[**1905** H. B. WALTERS *Hist. Anc. Pott.* I. iv. 164 The word λεκάνη, however, seems to indicate a large bowl rather than a covered jar, and no satisfactory name has yet been found.] *Ibid.* 177 A method of divination sometimes practised..consisted in placing waxen images in a lekane full of water. *Ibid.* xi. 469 A new form is that known as the *lekane*, a jar for holding sweetmeats; it has vertical handles and a cover of elaborate form, often surmounted by a small vase. **1918** J. D. BEAZLEY *Attic Red-Figured Vases* xix. 188 Milchhöfer mentions four lekanides in the style of the Meidias painter. *Ibid.*, The toilet-vase called lekanis is rarely decorated with pictures before the free period. **1935** RICHTER & MILNE *Shapes & Names Athenian Vases* 23 The word λεκάνη..was widely used to signify flattish bowls employed for different purposes... The word lekanis, on the other hand, apparently signifies a bowl used for a special purpose. **1946** G. M. A. RICHTER *Attic Red-Figured Vases* 13 The lekanis [was] a covered dish often used as a wedding present. **1950** H. L. LORIMER *Homer & Monuments* vii. 448 The well-known Boeotian lekane in the British Museum. **1967** R. S. FOLSOM *Handbk. Gk. Pottery* 132 Shapes of pots: Kantharos, tripod pyxis, lekane, skyphos, and cup.

Lekhite, Lekhitic: see *LECHITIC *sb.* and *a.*

‖ **lekker** (le·kəɹ), *a.* *S. Afr. colloq.* [Afrikaans, f. Du. *lekker* (cf. G. *lecker*), rel. to Du. *likken* LICK *v.*] Pleasant, sweet, nice.

1900 A. CARTER *Let.* 8 Feb. (MS.), On Monday these left and in moving round the mountain was 'verneuked' as Hannes said 'lekker'. **1926** E. LEWIS *Mantis* II. viii. 123 To Mr Dan Hugo nothing tasted so *lekker* as a good cup of coffee at that hour. **1953** F. ROBB *Sea Hunters* viii. 137 'Fish soup and baked fish to follow. Lekker!' Olley drooled. **1961** *Personality* 16 May 27 It's a lekker language. **1963** A. SMITH *Throw out Two Hands* vii. 82 Charl Pauw..had the thickest of South African accents... 'But the place is lekker, I tell you, its lekker.' **1970** *Rand Daily Mail* 28 Feb. 7/4 Some South African English colloquialisms, again mainly of Afrikaans origin, he regards as downright 'barbarisms', such as..lekker.

lekker, var. *LECCER.

‖ **lekythos** (lī·kiþǫs, le·-). *Gr. Antiq.* Pl. **lekythoi** (-oi). Var. LECYTHUS.

1851 *Catal. Greek & Etruscan Vases Brit. Mus.* I. 27 Lêkythos... Clay ash-coloured; round the body brown and crimson bands. **1899** R. GLAZIER *Man. Hist. Ornament* 77 A vase produced specially for funeral purposes was the Athenian Lekythos, the body of which was covered with white slip, then painted in polychrome with subjects of singular appropriateness. **1931** *Times Lit. Suppl.* 31 Dec. 1054/1 Athenian white lekythoi. **1948** A. LANE *Greek Pott.* iv. 54 The white slip was easily chipped or abraded, and the technique was mainly reserved for..lekythoi that were buried with the dead. **1960** R. G. HAGGAR *Conc. Encycl. Cont. Pott. & Porc.* 246/2 *Lekythos*,..a narrow-necked flask or vase well adapted (from its long narrow neck) for the slow pouring of oil, chiefly used in funeral rites. **1972** *Oxf. Univ. Gaz.* CII. Suppl. No. 3. 20 White ground lekythos by the Inscription Painter, Attic, mid-5th century B.C.

Lem (lem). [f. the initials.] A lunar excursion module (*LUNAR *a.* 1 c). See also *L.E.M.* s.v. *L 7.

1962 *Listener* 26 July 150/2 We had a discussion of Project Apollo, the American scheme for getting a man

on the Moon. The secondary space-craft for this formidable task has been dubbed a 'lunar excursion module', or Lem for short. **1967** *Economist* 11 Nov. 627/1 The lunar excursion module—the Lem or bug—.. will make the actual touch-down on the moon when the great day comes.

‖ **lembing** (lĕmbi·ŋ). Also 9 **limbing, lambing.** [Mal. *lembing*.] A Malay spear characterized by a ridged blade.

1839 T. J. Newbold *Pol. & Statistical Acct. Straits of Malacca* II. xii. 211 The arms of the Orang Laut..are the limbing, or lance; the tampuling, a large hook, [etc.]. **1894** N. B. Dennys *Descr. Dict. Brit. Malaya* 370 For the javelin, or half-pike, the Malays have the name *lambing*. **1936** G. B. Gardner *Keris & Other Malay Weapons* iv. 85 Plate 80 shows an iron *lĕmbing*. **1947** R. O. Winstedt *Malays* ix. 165 The origin of the lance (*tombak*) and spear (*lembing*)..await study.

lemma². Add: **2.** *Bot.* In grasses, the lower bract of a floret.

1906 C. V. Piper in *Contrib. U.S. Nat. Herbarium* X. 8 We have taken the liberty to introduce the word lemma to apply to the ..'flowering glume' of authors. **1934** A. Arber *Gramineae* vii. 110 The idea that the grass flower is unique, and requires a special vocabulary..has led to..a series of names [for bracts], such as *gluma florifera, palea inferior, flowering glume* and *lemma*, of which the two latter are the more generally familiar in England and America. *Ibid.* viii. 141 In Ichnanthus the lemma may show remarkable winglike appendages at the base. **1968** F. W. Gould *Grass Systematics* ii. 51 Glumes, lemmas, and paleas are floral bracts. *Ibid.* 53 Lemma characters of taxonomic importance are shape, texture, size in respect to the glumes, nervation, awn development, and surface features.

lemmatization (le:mătəizēi·ʃən). [f. next + -ation.] The action or process of lemmatizing; an instance of this.

1967 *Computers & Humanities* II. 75 Method:... 3. Alphabetic sorting into word forms with context. 4. Lemmatisation. **1971** A. J. Aitken in R. A. Wisbey *Computer in Lit. & Ling. Res.* 14 The methods of lemmatization..so far mentioned necessitate informing the computer explicitly of the destination in terms of headword of every single instance of each word which it has to treat. **1972** *Computers & Humanities* VI. 212 Not all lemmas could, of course, be made to come out correctly from the computer... In fact, the accomplished wrong lemmatizations are more notable than the missing correct ones.

lemmatize (le·mătəiz), *v.* [f. Gr. λημματ-, λῆμμα Lemma¹ + -ize.] *trans.* To sort (words as they occur in a text) so as to group together those that are inflected or variant forms of the same word.

1967 *Computers & Humanities* II. 78 We have..tested programs for concordances, for lemmatizing with computer dictionary, and for transcribing from historical to phonologic alphabet. **1971** J. B. Carroll et al. *Word Frequency Bk.* p. xiii, The AHI Corpus is coded for capitalization. It is not parsed or lemmatized. **1971** A. J. Aitken in R. A. Wisbey *Computer in Lit. & Ling. Res.* 13 From a text prepared in this way the computer could deliver an output resembling a fully sorted collection for a traditional dictionary (already ordered and lemmatized) without further human attention. **1973** *Computers & Humanities* VII. 132 The vocabulary lists were next lemmatized by hand. *Ibid.*, The computer program made no attempt to lemmatize words or to distinguish homographs, but simply counted the number of occurrences of each distinct word-type.

Hence **le·mmatized** *ppl. a.*

1969 *Computers & Humanities* IV. 134 Method: Punching frequency lists and lemmatized texts; transferring to tapes; [etc.].

lemme (le·mi). Colloq. contraction of *let me* (see Let *v.* 12, 14). Cf. *gimme.

1876 'Mark Twain' *Tom Sawyer* ii. 19 Come now; lemme just try... Now lemme try. **1894** Kipling *Day's Work* (1898) 64 Lemme hide back o' you peoples, so's they won't see what I'm at. **1905** H. G. Wells *Kipps* I. i. 27 Ann—lemme kiss you. **1910** C. E. Montague *Hind let Loose* iv. 58 Lemme alone. I'm an old man. Gimme a drink. Lemme alone. **1923** 'R. Crompton' *William Again* iv. 64 'Lemme help!' he pleaded. **1930** E. Pound *XXX Cantos* xix. 86 And in came the street 'Lemme-at-'em' Like a bull-dog in a mackintosh. **1946** K. Tennant *Lost Haven* (1947) ii. 34 Lemme go... Oo-h, you're breaking my arm! Auntie, make 'im lemme go. **1972** C. Weston *Poor, Poor Ophelia* (1973) xxii. 138 Okay, man, lemme think.

lemming. Add: **1. b.** Used *fig.* to denote a person bent on a headlong rush, often towards disaster. Also *attrib.* or quasi-*adj.*; *lemming-like* adj.

[**1959** M. Gilbert *Blood & Judgement* iii. 35 Home-going office workers..potent in mass as a lemming migration.] **1968** M. Bragg *Without City Wall* I. x. 116 To opt out..in a way, you could say that was just as lemming-like as what *you're* doing. **1969** D. F. Horrobin *Sci. is God* i. 9 This lemming unconcern may have dangerous consequences. **1969** *New Yorker* 12 Apr. 61/2 In Dr. Langseth's view, going to the moon is an impulse ingrained in the national character, as though Americans were astronautical lemmings. **1970** *Islander* (Victoria, B.C.) 15 Feb. 12/1 No one had the slightest idea of what was happening, yet all had joined in the mad lemming-like scramble for the waterfront. **1970** P. Moyes *Who saw her Die?* xx. 256 It was Saturday, the lemming rush was in full spate, the suburbs pouring their millions in bus, tube. train and car into the central sea. **1972** 'J. Bell' *Death of Poison-Tongue* viii. 80 Lemmings..was only the present vogue word..to describe a collection of mindless people moved by a common purpose. **1972** *Guardian* 11 Dec. 12/6 The only way to stop multiple motorway crashes is by educating us all in roadcraft so that our individual intelligence becomes more powerful than our lemming instincts. **1975** *Sunday Times* 16 Feb. 51/1 Last week there were ample signs that the lemming-like rush to pile in at any price was wearing itself out.

lemna. Add to etym.: (Linnæus *Genera Plantarum* (1737) 417). (Earlier and later examples.)

1789 G. White *Selborne* II. liv. 269 Gold and silver fishes..will also feed on the water-plant called *lemna* (ducks' meat). **1801** M. Edgeworth *Belinda* II. xxi. 298 'This,' replied Belinda, 'is what "Th'unlearned, duck-weed; learned, lemma [*sic*], call," and it is to be found in any ditch or standing pool.' **1967** C. D. Sculthorpe *Biol. Aquatic Vasc. Plants* vii. 204 As a result of its small size and the ease with which it may be cultured..*Lemna* is eminently suitable for laboratory experiments.

lemon, *sb.*¹ Add: **1. b.** A person with a tart or snappy disposition (quot. 1863). More usually (*slang*), a simpleton, a loser; a person easily deluded or taken advantage of (see also quot. 1950).

1863 P. S. Davis *Young Parson* xxvii. 222 Mrs. Trimble ..had a great deal to say, and no little acrimony in her way of saying it. Indeed, she was what the knowing ones denominated 'a lemon'. **1908** J. M. Sullivan *Criminal Slang* 21 *Sucker* or *lemon*, a victim of criminals and tramps. **1916** J. B. Cooper *Coo-oo-ee* xiv. 208 There was always a danger of offending a man who has been runner-up in a boxing championship if you make him appear 'like a lemon'. **1931** Wodehouse *Big Money* i. 27, I don't know why it is, rich men's sons are always the worst lemons in creation. **1950** Partridge *Slang To-day & Yesterday* (ed. 3) iii. 313 If she is unpopular, she is *a pill, a pickle, a lemon.* **1966** J. Porter *Sour Cream* x. 137 Criminal carelessness, that's what it was! Leaving me standing here like a lemon. **1973** 'A. Hall' *Tango Briefing* i. 17 They'd sent me down to show me something and they knew I couldn't see it and I felt a bit of a lemon.

c. *slang* (orig. *U.S.*). Something which is bad or undesirable or which fails to meet one's expectations.

Phr. *the answer is a lemon*: used to denote that a reply is unsatisfactory or non-existent.

1909 *Sat. Even. Post* 20 Feb. 38/2 The wheel goes around; wherever the little indicator at the point of the pin stops, there is your prize—or your lemon. **1912** C. Mathewson *Pitching in a Pinch* x. 220 The papers were mentioning him as the '$11,000 lemon'. **1914** 'High Jinks, Jr.' *Choice Slang* 14 *Lemon*, a disappointment. **1922** M. Arlen *Piracy* I. v. 59 'What would happen if *we* went on strike?'.. No one among them..dreamed of answering. The answer was a lemon. **1927** *Daily Express* 13 Dec. 17/1 Middlesbrough seem to have 'picked a lemon', for the draw gives them South Shields as opponents. **1930** P. MacDonald *Link* iv. 75 The answer at first seems to be a lemon, but they're at least the sort of questions that make one think. **1931** *Morning Post* 19 June 6 'I sold five lemons for £210,' said a witness... 'Lemon' was a term used in the trade for second-hand cars of little value. **1959** M. T. Williams *Art of Jazz* (1960) ix. 85 This great record would have been a lemon commercially in 1925. **1961** C. Mabee *Seaway Story* vii. 70 He first politely wished success to New York's lemon, the new twelve-foot Erie Barge Canal. **1963** *Guardian* 21 Jan. 16/6 The French nuclear deterrent..is a military lemon of the first order. **1969** N. Freeling *Tsing-Boum* x. 68 One makes requests through official channels and the answer is a lemon. **1972** *Sat. Rev.* (U.S.) 17 June 7/3 Mechanics are less than delighted to see lines of lemons converging on their service department. **1972** *Sydney Morning Herald* 26 Aug. 1/2 The effect of this on consumers is too many lemons or part lemons coupled with near impossibility of obtaining redress from the manufacturer.

d. Phr. *to hand* (someone) *a lemon*: to pass off a sub-standard article as good; to swindle (a person), to do (someone) down.

1906 H. Green *At Actors' Boarding House* 36 Him gettin' handed a lemon in that English act, puts us up. [**1922** Wodehouse *Clicking of Cuthbert* x. 233 'It did indeed begin to appear as though our beloved monarch.. had been handed the bitter fruit of the citron.' The quaint old idiom is almost untranslateable, but one sees what he means.] **1939** E. S. Gardner *D.A. draws Circle* (1940) vi. 87 The way things are now, I co-operate with them. If they hand me a lemon, I can walk up and down the streets cussing them out for letting politics interfere with the administration of justice. **1970** *New Yorker* 12 Dec. 131/1 These senators felt that the President had handed them two lemons, had gone to the mat for his choices when he didn't have to.

e. *slang.* The head.

1923 Wodehouse *Inimitable Jeeves* i. 13 'What might you have missed?' I asked, the old lemon being slightly clouded. **1952** *Coast to Coast* 195 If you had any brains in that big lemon you'd wipe me. You'd get away.

f. *U.S. slang.* An informer, one who turns State's evidence (see also quot. 1931).

1931 *Amer. Speech* VI. 439 *Lemon*, one who testifies for the prosecution. **1935** G. Ingram *'Stir' Train* ii. 30 'You think you got the low-down on me: well, see me put it on you!' 'You talk like a "lemon"!' **1935** A. J. Pollock *Underworld Speaks* 70/2 *Lemon*, one who turns state's evidence.

5. a. *lemon cheesecake* (earlier example), *cordial, pie, sauce, tea* (later examples).

1728 E. Smith *Compleat Housewife* (ed. 2) 120 To make Lemon Cheese-cakes. **1836** *Mag. Domestic Econ.* I. 182 Lemon cordial. **1909** A. Arnold *Century Cook Bk.* Suppl. 584 Lemon pie. 2 lemons..sugar..butter..4 eggs..cornstarch. **1911** C. Harris *Eve's Second Husband* 154 Then you ate lemon pie, pound-cake and boiled custard. **1972** J. Potts *Trouble-Maker* (1973) ii. 10 Their first square meal in three days. Corn and chicken. Homemade relishes. Lemon pie. **1747** H. Glasse *Art of Cookery* ii. 36 To make Lemon-Sauce for boiled Fowls. **1861** Mrs. Beeton *Bk. Househ. Managem.* 220 (*heading*) Lemon sauce for boiled fowls. **1948** *Good Housek. Cookery Bk.* i. 15 Something piquant should be served with a dish that is very bland, as..lemon sauce with steamed sponge pudding. **1932** L. Golding *Magnolia St.* II. xi. 425 Reb Feivel sat sucking lemon-tea through a cube of sugar. *a* **1963** S. Plath *Crossing Water* (1971) 62 It'll be *lemon*-tea for me. **1975** *Times* 8 Feb. 7/4 There is no licence, but the lemon tea is fresh and good.

7. lemon cheese (curd), lemon curd, a confection made with lemons, butter, eggs, and sugar, and used as a spread or filling; **lemon cling** *U.S.*, a variety of clingstone peach; **lemon-drop** (examples); **lemon-game** *U.S. slang*, a type of confidence trick (see quots.); also *ellipt.* **lemon; lemon-house,** a building where lemons are stored; **lemon meringue (pie),** an open pie consisting of a pastry case with a lemon filling and a topping of meringue; **lemon oil,** an essential oil obtained from lemons; **lemon platt,** a flat sugar-stick, flavoured with lemon; **lemon-squeezer** (earlier and later examples); also *fig.*; also, *Austral.* and *N.Z. colloq.*, a hat with a peaked crown and broad flat brim worn by New Zealand troops; **lemon-thyme** (earlier and later examples); **lemon-verbena** (examples); also **lemon-scented verbena; lemon-wood** (later example); (*b*) a name for several tropical American trees or their light-coloured wood, esp. the Cuban *Calycophyllum candidissimum.*

1853 G. W. Francis *Dict. Pract. Receipts* (ed. 3) 211/2 Lemon cheese curd. **1891** R. Wells *Mod. Flour Confectioner* 101 Lemon cheese. **1909** *Daily Chron.* 17 Aug. 6/4 Boiling lemon cheese over a gas cooking apparatus. **1848** *Rep. Comm. Patents 1847* (U.S.) 196 Fifteen specimens.. of the lemon clinq..measured over a foot in circumference. **1895** *Army & Navy Co-op. Soc. Price List* 17/2 Lemon curd, for making Cheesecakes. **1948** J. Betjeman *Sel. Poems* 35 Lemon curd and Christmas cake. **1968** V. S. Pritchett *Cab at Door* iii. 36 On Thursday, she made her second baking, concentrating..on..her Eccles cakes, her puffs, her lemon-curd. **1807** M. E. Rundell *New Syst. Domestic Cookery* 203 (*caption*) Lemon drop. **1854** C. M. Yonge *Heartsease* II. xiv. 316 Here were some lemon-drops for papa. **1938** D. Runyon *Furthermore* x. 187 A young guy by the name of The Lemon Drop Kid, who is called The Lemon Drop Kid because he always has a little sack of lemon drops in the side pocket of his coat, and is always munching at same. **1908** J. M. Sullivan *Criminal Slang* 15 *Lemon game*, defrauding a sucker at a pool game. **1914** Jackson & Hellyer *Vocab. Criminal Slang* 55 *Lemon*,.. a confidence game in which skill at pool is the bait, though its successful negotiation is based upon the dishonesty or avarice of the victim. **1937** E. H. Sutherland *Professional Thief* iii. 68 The lemon is an agreement between the inside man, an expert pool player, and a prospect, by which the prospect will win bets on the pool games played by the expert. Through a supposed fluke the expert wins the game which the prospect had bet he would lose, and the prospect thereby loses his money. **1901** *Chambers's Jrnl.* Nov. 719/2 On the very day of the picking they must be carried to the lemon-house, and great care must be taken that the fruit is not exposed to the sun or bruised in any way. **1916** D. H. Lawrence *Twilight in Italy* 85 We passed through, and stood at the foot of the lemon-house. **1914** S. Lewis *Our Mr. Wrenn* i. 13 Hey, Drübel, got any lemon merang? Bring me a hunk, will yuh? **1922** *Hotel World* 15 Apr. 15/1 Lemon meringue pie. **1959** N. Mailer *Advts. for Myself* (1961) II. 126 There was roast chicken with stuffing, lemon meringue pie and chocolate cake. **1973** J. Wilson *Truth or Dare* vi. 75 It was lemon meringue pie for dinner. **1896** J. T. Law *Grocer's Manual* 408/2 The essence of lemon coming into commerce..is greatly made up of..the ethereal oil which is present in lemon oil. **1957** *Encycl. Brit.* XIII. 908/1 Among the important by-products resulting from the processing of lemons, after removal of the juice, are citric acid..lemon oil and pectin. **1916** Joyce *Portrait of Artist* (1969) i. 7 The moocow came down the road where Betty Byrne lived: she sold lemon platt. **1965** *Amer. N. & Q.* III. 117/2 'Lemon Platt', commonly sold as 'Yellow Man' at fairs in the North of Ireland,..derives its name..from its flavor. **1900** M. Thorn in W. D. Drury *Bk. Gardening* xi. 469 Lemon-scented Verbena should be represented in gardens where shrubs with fragrant leaves are cherished. **1969** D. Goold-Adams *Cool Greenhouse Today* xvii. 198 Lippia (Lemon-scented Verbena). Half-hardy deciduous shrub from Chile with insignificant flowers but grown in the greenhouse for the glorious scent of its crushed leaves. **1781** *Salem Gaz.* 3 July, Isaac Greenwood..makes Flutes.. Back-Gammon Boxes Men and Dies, Chess-Men, Billiard-Balls, Maces, Lemon Squeezers. **1856** 'Ockside' & 'Doesticks' *Hist. & Rec. Elephant Club* 118 One..had been hit over the head with the lemon-squeezer. **1887** *Century Mag.* Aug. 489/1 The 'Chunkers' were frequently of the 'lemon-squeezer' pattern. **1949** *Nat. Geogr. Mag.* Aug. 235 Knapsack's a Nuisance in the 'Lemon Squeezer' [*sc.* a narrow defile]. **1953** Baker *Australia Speaks* vii. 177 A few other words of wartime vintage..*lemon squeezer*, the peaked hat worn by New Zealand troops (apparently originated by the troops themselves). **1957** T. S. Eliot *On Poetry & Poets* 113 It might be called the lemon-squeezer school of criticism. **1959** B. Kops *Hamlet of Stepney Green* I. 10 Julius Caesar, such a silly geezer, caught his head in a lemon squeezer. **1964** *N.Z. News* 24 Nov. 2/1 The 'lemon squeezer' was no longer suitable headgear for ceremonial

rifle exercises and would never be worn by the New Zealand Army again, said the Chief of General Staff. **1629** J. PARKINSON *Parad.* cxxxi. 454 Lemon Tyme. The wilde Tyme that smelleth like unto a Pomecitron or lemon, hath many weake branches trayling on the ground. **1657** R. VERNEY in M. M. Verney *Mem.* (1894) III. xi. 409 Sweet Marjoram & Lemon Time. **1861** MRS. BEETON *Bk. Househ. Managem.* 220 *Lemon thyme.* Two or three tufts of this species of thyme, *Thymus citriodorus*, usually find a place in the herb compartment of the kitchen garden. **1971** *Country Life* 20 May 1252/2 Lemon-thyme has a lovely little golden cultivar which should be in all gardens. **1974** PAGE & STEARN *Culinary Herbs* 44 Those who find the flavour of garden thyme too dominating may prefer the milder and fruity flavour of lemon thyme. **1869** C. L. BRACE *New West* iii. 37 Lemonverbenas..are small trees. **1952** J. & L. BUSH-BROWN *America's Garden Bk.* (ed. 2) xxi. 723 Plants suitable for pot culture... Lemon Verbena. **1971** *Country Life* 20 May 1207/1 A huge lemon verbena (*Lippia citriodora*) is said to be pre-1903. **1924** RECORD & MELL *Timbers Trop. Amer.* 513 *Aspidosperma tomentosum* Mart... Lemon wood... Color mostly bright, clear canary-yellow. **1934** A. L. HOWARD *Man. Timbers of World* (rev. ed.) 148 Degame wood. *Calycophyllum candidissimum...* Lemon-wood. **1947** J. C. RICH *Materials & Methods Sculpture* x. 290 Lemonwood, also referred to as Degame, is a yellowish or creamy-white hardwood that is sometimes used for carving. Cuba is the major source of this wood. **1969** T. H. EVERETT *Living Trees of World* 162/2 The lemonwood of New Zealand..has masses of honey-scented yellowish green flowers and leaves that emit a lemon-like odor when bruised. **1972** *Handbk. Hardwoods* (Building Res. Establishment) (ed. 2) 66 Degame. *Calycophyllum candidissimum.* Other name: lemonwood (United States).

b. Abbrev. of LEMONADE, *lemon-juice*; also *bitter lemon*, a mineral drink.

1885 *List of Subscribers* (United Telephone Co.) p. xv. Kindly send us..one gross of seltzer, one gross of soda, one gross of lemon, and half that quantity of splits. **1898** J. D. BRAYSHAW *Slum Silhouettes* 228 'Oh! a lemon an' dash'll do me,' she says... So I calls fer two lemons, wiv a dash o' bitter. **1956** R. POSTGATE in C. Ray *Complete Imbiber* I. 182 'Port 'n lemon', which was an evidence of feminine folly some years ago, was I suppose a sort of proletarian equivalent of pink champagne. **1962** *Guardian* 27 Aug. 3/1 His sister..drinks nothing but orange juice or bitter lemon. **1965** I. FLEMING *Man with Golden Gun* viii. 110 Mr Hendriks..nursed a Schweppes Bitter Lemon.

lemonade. Add: **b.** *attrib.* and *Comb.*, as *lemonade bottle, crystal, powder, syrup.*

1972 *Country Life* 30 Nov. 1481/3 The screw-topped or marble-stoppered lemonade bottles of long ago. **1902** J. T. LAW *Grocer's Manual* (ed. 2) 528/2 *Lemonade powders* or *crystals*, these usually consist of a compound of.. bicarbonate of soda,..tartaric acid,..icing sugar,.. essence of lemon with..essence of pineapple. *c* **1938** *Fortnum & Mason Price List* 43/1 Lemonade crystals.. per bot. 9½d. **1896** J. T. LAW *Grocer's Manual* 413/1 *Lemonade powders*,..usually consist of a compound of.. bicarbonate of soda,..tartaric acid,..icing sugar. **1938** L. MACNEICE *I Crossed Minch* II. x. 140 A plump schoolgirl..had a tin..containing lemonade powder. **1822** M. EDGEWORTH *Let.* 20 Feb. (1971) 355 You are welcome to the lemonade-Syrop. I have sent my aunt another bottle.

lemony, *a.* Add: **b.** *Austral.* and *N.Z. slang.* Irritated, angry, esp. in phr. *to go lemony at*: to become angry with (someone).

1941 in BAKER *Dict. Austral. Slang* 31. **1946** D. STIVENS *Courtship of Uncle Henry* 75 He's as lemony as hell when he opens the door and doesn't say a word to me. **1945** BAKER *Austral. Lang.* vi. 121 A man in a temper is said.. *to go lemony*..at a person. **1952** *Coast to Coast* 97 Ironbark got lemony. He bellowed like a thousand bulls.

Lemuria (lĭmiūə·riă). [f. LEMUR + -IA[1].] A hypothetical continent stretching from Africa to south-east Asia, formerly supposed to have existed in the Jurassic period.

1864 P. L. SCLATER in *Q. Jrnl. Sci.* I. 219 In Madagascar and the Mascarene Islands we have existing relics of this great continent, for which as the original focus of the '*Stirps Lemurum*', I should propose the name Lemuria! **1876** A. R. WALLACE *Geogr. Distribution Animals* I. iv. 76 Lemuria..is undoubtedly a legitimate and highly probable supposition, and it is an example of the way in which a study of the geographical distribution of animals may enable us to reconstruct the geography of a bygone age. **1880** —— *Island Life* II. xix. 398 Atlantis is now rarely introduced seriously... But 'Lemuria' still keeps its place —a good example of the survival of a provisional hypothesis which offers what seems an easy solution of a difficult problem..long after it has been proved to be untenable. **1944** 'PALINURUS' *Unquiet Grave* iii. 85 To have set foot in Lemuria is to have been close to the mysterious sources of existence... Wild ghost faces from a lost continent who will soon be extinct. **1957** P. J. DARLINGTON *Zoogeogr.* x. 590 Some persons have claimed a broad connection or union of Africa, Madagascar, and India even in the Tertiary and have named it Lemuria, but there is decisive evidence against it.

lemurian (lĭmiūə·riăn), *a.* [f. LEMUR + -IAN; but sense 1 is derived from *LEMURIA.] **1.** (With capital initial.) Of or pertaining to *LEMURIA.

1871 *Nature* 30 Mar. 429/1 The Máldive and the Láccadive coral-islands belong strictly to the Lemurian region.. and I am not sure that the latter does not reach the mainland of India. **1893** A. NEWTON *Dict. Birds* 354 The hypothesis of a Lemurian continent was..unnecessary.

2. Of or pertaining to lemurs; characteristic of lemurs.

1891 *Ann. Rep. Board of Regents Smithsonian Inst. 1889–90* 621 An unsymmetrical face, the nasal overture of a pheleiform type, and lemurian attachment of the under jaw. **1893** A. NEWTON *Dict. Birds* 355 Lemurian remains have been found fossil in France.

lemurid (lĭ·miūrid, le·m-). [f. mod.L. family name *Lemuridæ*, f. *Lemur* (Linnæus *Systema Naturæ* (ed. 10, 1758) I. 29), ad. L. *lemures* ghosts.] A member of the family Lemuridæ.

1884 *American* VIII. 218 True monkeys are scarce, but galagos and certain other lemurids are common. **1972** T. A. VAUGHAN *Mammalogy* vii. 115/2 The fossil record of lemurids is from Pleistocene and sub-Recent deposits in Madagascar.

lemu·riform, *a.* [f. LEMUR + *i* + -FORM.] Resembling the lemurs. Also as *sb.*

1887 A. HEILPRIN *Geogr. & Geol. Distribution Animals* 174 Lemurs or lemuriform insectivores (Adapis, Necrolemur). **1972** *Nature* 24 Mar. 180/1 *Archaeolemur* and *Hadropithecus* are cited as the few lemuriforms with symphysal fusion. **1973** *Ibid.* 30 Mar. 353/1 The author has his first sub-order Prosimii embrace Tupaiidae and Tarsiidae as families of equal rank to five lorisiform and lemuriform families.

Lenape (lĕnā·pe). Also **Lenne-** or **Lenni-Lenape.** [See quot. 1819.] **a.** An Algonquian Indian people, also called Delaware Indians, formerly inhabiting the north-eastern United States; a member of this people. **b.** The language of this people.

1728 P. GORDON *Let.* 2 Sept. in S. Hazard *Pennsylvania Arch.* (1852) I. 230 Our Lenappys or Delaware Indians know nothing of it. **1785** T. JEFFERSON *Notes State Virginia* (1801) 198 Delawares, or Linnelinopies. **1819** J. HECKEWELDER *Hist. Indian Nations* (1876) p. xl, *Lenni Lenape* being the national and proper name of the people we call 'Delawares', I have retained this name, or for brevity's sake, called them simply *Lenape*, as they do themselves in most instances. Their name signifies 'original people', a race of human beings who are the same that they were in the beginning, unchanged and unmixed. *Ibid.* iii. 76 'It was we,' say the Lenape, Mohicans, and their kindred tribes, 'who so kindly received them on their first arrival into our country.' **1826** J. F. COOPER *Last of Mohicans* II. vii. 191 The Delaware, or Lenape, claimed to be the progenitors of that numerous people, who once were masters of most of the eastern and northern states of America. **1849** E. G. SQUIER in W. W. Beach *Indian Misc.* (1877) 9 (*heading*) A translation of the Walum-Olum, or bark record of the Lenni Lenape. **1885** D. G. BRINTON *Lenâpé & their Legends* iii. 35 *Lenape*, therefore, does not mean 'a common adult male', but rather 'a male of our kind', or 'our men'. **1888** BRINTON & ANTHONY (*title*) A Lenâpé-English dictionary. **1913** *Handbk. Indians of Canada* (Geogr. Board of Canada) 125/1 The early history of the Lenâpe is contained in their national legend, the Walum Olum. **1934** F. W. HODGE *McKenny & Hall's Indian Tribes of N. Amer.* III. 32 The Delawares were situated principally upon tide-water in New Jersey, Pennsylvania, and Delaware. Their own appellation of *Lenne Lenape*, or original people, has been almost forgotten by themselves, and is never used by the other tribes. **1959** E. TUNIS *Indians* 21/1 It was taken from the Lenape, an Algonquian language.

lenate (lĭnēi·t), *v. Phonology.* [f. L. *lēn*(*is* soft + -ATE[3].] = *LENITE *v.* Hence **lena·ted** *ppl. a.* Also **lena·tion** *sb.* = *LENITION.

1909 J. STRACHAN *Introd. Early Welsh* 12 When an adjective in the positive degree precedes, the noun is lenated. *Ibid.*, After proper nouns there is lenation of a following noun or adjective. *Ibid.* 13 In poetry, when the genitive precedes the noun, it may lenate. **1928** E. EKWALL *Eng. River-Names* p. lxxii, Quite different is the state of things in regard to lenated *t* (*d*). *Ibid.* p. lxxiii, British **b, d, g** were lenated to *v, ð, ʒ*, which latter often disappears.

lend, *sb.*[2] Add: (Further examples.) Also *Austral.* and *N.Z. colloq.*

1749 J. STEUART *Let.* 29 Dec. in *Publ. Scottish Hist. Soc.* (1915) 2nd Ser. IX. 464, I..sent him inclosed a letter..in which I desire the lend of 20£ sterlin for 18 months. **1946** F. SARGESON *That Summer* 77 Could you give me the lend of a bob? **1965** *Listener* 2 Sept. 339/1 Thanks for the lend of your earhole, mate.

lend, *v.*[2] Add: **2. e.** (Later examples.)

1940 *Times* 11 Dec. 5/4 In war-time a good many people take to what is vaguely called 'lending a hand' in the domestic circle. **1951** E. PAUL *Springtime in Paris* iv. 69 The local heroes all were known, except two passing strangers who had lent a hand at the barricade and died anonymously. **1961** NEW ENG. BIBLE *Luke* x. 40 Tell her to come and lend a hand.

h. *to lend colour* (*to*): see *COLOUR *sb.*[1] 12 e.

lend-lease. (Level stress.) = *LEASE-LEND. Also *attrib.* and in extended uses. Also as *vb.* So **lend-leased** *ppl. a.*

1941 *Economist* 15 Feb. 214/1 Future disposition of the armaments now being produced is before Congress in the 'Lend-Lease' Bill. **1942** *Times* (Weekly ed.) 9 Sept. 9/2 Thousands of barrage balloons were lend-leased to the United States soon after Pearl Harbour. *Ibid.*, Lend-leased British anti-aircraft guns help to defend American cities. **1942** *R.A.F. Jrnl.* 3 Oct. (recto rear cover), The combination of experienced pilots and planes in the fight to clear our side of the Atlantic is an element of the Lend-Lease programme in reverse. **1945** W. S. CHURCHILL *Victory* (1946) 178 Your friendship and great help as Lend-Lease Administrator and Secretary of State will always be remembered with gratitude. **1949** I. DEUTSCHER *Stalin* 512 More than 400,000 lorries were supplied to Russia under Lend-Lease. **1951** KOESTLER *Age of Longing* i. 18 Your hand, my child, is on lend-lease to a vicious old man. **1957** *Times Lit. Suppl.* 18 Oct. 625/1 Great Britain has undertaken to lend-lease to the United States nothing less than the Victorian Age in its entirety. **1962** *Listener* 15 Feb. 307/3 The abrupt ending of Lend-Lease. **1972** *National Observer* (U.S.) 27 May 3/1 Talks in the State Department are aimed at ending a U.S.-Soviet dispute over lend-lease that goes back to World War II. From 1942 to 1945, the United States supplied Russia with some $10.8 billion in military and civilian equipment under the lend-lease program.

lengenbachite (leŋĕnba·χəit). *Min.* [f. *Lengenbach*, the name of the quarry in Valais, Switzerland, where it was found + -ITE[1].] A sulphide of silver, copper, lead, and arsenic, $(Ag,Cu)_2Pb_6As_4S_{13}$, occurring as steel-grey blade-shaped crystals.

1904 *Nature* 1 Dec. 118/2 Mr. R. H. Solly exhibited and described various minerals from the Lengenbach quarry, Binnenthal. Three of these were new, viz. marrite and bowmanite..and lengenbachite. **1944** *Trans. R. Soc. Canada* XXXVIII. IV. 59 An *x*-ray study of lengenbachite shows that this mineral is monoclinic. **1969** *Mineral. Abstr.* XX. 227/2 Lengenbachite gave space group $P1$ or $P\bar{1}$, lattice constants of a subcell a' 35·10 ± 0·03, b' 5·75 ± 0·01, c' 36·92 ± 0·03Å, $\alpha' \sim 90°$, β' 92°35′, $\gamma' \sim 90°$.

length, *sb.* Add: **2. c.** *Bridge.* Four or more cards of the same suit held in a Bridge hand.

1927 M. C. WORK *Contract Bridge* iii. 43 The game-goer may be bid with a blank suit or a worthless singleton if the trump length be satisfactory. **1930** E. CULBERTSON *Contract Bridge Blue Bk.* xxii. 285 To build up, if possible, a great minor suit length in the strong hand. **1948** —— *Contract Bridge for Everyone* (1949) 77 When your principal length or strength is in the suit your opponent has bid, do not overcall. **1958** *Listener* 2 Oct. 541/1 West, from the bidding, is probably aware of his [*sc.* North's] great Club length. **1973** *Sunday Times* (Colour Suppl.) 20 May 90/2 It is easy to enter for East holding length in diamonds by playing the Ace and the Queen.

4. d. *Swimming.* The length of the swimming-bath taken as a measure of distance swum. Also *attrib.*

1912 F. SACHS *Compl. Swimmer* 237 They..arrange their races to suit the baths, and their handicaps..are measured by its length, *i.e.* '3 lengths (90 yards) handicap'. **1931** G. H. CORSAN *Diving & Swimming Bk.* viii. 74 Have the fastest swimmers swim a three lengths race. *Ibid.*, Finish with relay races of two lengths. **1972** B. TURNER *Solden's Women* xvii. 154 I'm not such a good swimmer as Patricia was. Three lengths at the baths is about my limit.

8. b. length-mark, a phonetic symbol used to indicate the relative length of a vowel sound.

1926 ARMSTRONG & WARD *Handbk. Eng. Intonation* p. vii, Length marks (: long and half-long) are used to indicate length only and not difference in vowel quality. **1932** D. JONES *Outl. Eng. Phonetics* (ed. 3) 65 The letter *i* without the length-mark stands for the members of the English *i*-phoneme used when the sound is relatively short. **1965** *English Studies* XLVI. 359 No allophonic length-marks are used.

10. (Later examples.) Hence *length bowler.*

1910 *Blackw. Mag.* Jan. 91/1 Only at the last gasp was any serious effort made to knock him off his length. **1937** *Daily Herald* 5 Jan. 14/1 [Verity] The best length bowler in England. **1956** N. CARDUS *Close of Play* 176 The old-fashioned 'length' bowlers, ball after ball on the same spot. **1958** D. BRADMAN *Art of Cricket* 97/1, I prefer to think in terms of a 'good length ball' and to define it thus—'The type of delivery which has the striker in two minds as to whether he should play forward or back.' **1969** *Listener* 1 May 622/3 At first Powell hit the ball all around the field and, just as it looked as if Miller might be finding his length, the item ended.

b. In racket games: the quality of making shots which pitch well back in the court and deny the opponent an easy return; the placing of a shot in this way; the 'form' required to make such shots consistently.

1924 G. W. HILLYARD *40 Yrs. Lawn Tennis* viii. 136 He..went on hitting..until he did get his 'length', and then it was..a case of woe betide the other man. **1930** *Morning Post* 19 July 14/6 The Italian's fine mixture of pace and length was pitted against Lott's youth, power, and cunning. **1948** S. NOEL *More about Squash Rackets* i. 24 Angles, drop-shots..and reverse angles are all the stock-in-trade of the professional, in addition to a sound length game. **1961** J. H. GILES *Squash Rackets* viii. 41 It [*sc.* the lob shot] can also be used as an attacking shot, providing as it does a complete change of pace and flight from the orthodox drive and length shots. **1964** R. LAVER *How to play Winning Tennis* vii. 57 You can get good length with the topspin I use. **1966** *Observer* 8 May 19/5 She was quick to switch from her steady baseline game into a counter attack whenever Miss Niessen lost her length.

11. c. *slang.* A penis; sexual intercourse; so *to slip* (someone) *a length*: (of a man) to have sexual intercourse with.

1949 PARTRIDGE *Dict. Slang* Add. 1173/2 *Slip* (her) *a length*, to coït with (a woman). **1952** C. MACINNES *June in Spring* vi. 156 'Is it hard to get a job on board a ship without experience?' 'Not if you work for nix and don't mind the stokers slipping you a length.' **1968** H. C. RAE *Few Small Bones* III. viii. 216 Beefy, randy-arsed wives crying out for a length. **1970** C. WOOD *Terrible Hard* v. 58 Come

on, Suggy, you're 'is batman, 'e's never slipped you a crafty length 'as 'e?

18. lengthman, a man appointed to maintain a certain stretch of road or railway.

The form *lengthsman* in quot. 1902 is an isolated use.

1902 *Times* 22 Sept. 2/5 Every lengthsman or fettler on the Government railway gets 8s. a day for eight hours' work. **1921** *Dict. Occup. Terms* (1927) § 577 *Lengthman*,.. an underman in a gang engaged on maintenance of a specific section..of permanent way. **1959** *New Scientist* 16 Apr. 852/1 The mixed plant community was largely maintained by..the regular cutting with scythe and sickle by ..the County Council 'lengthmen'. **1968** *Telegraph* (Brisbane) 3 June 18/1 Our legislators should modernise transport for railway lengthmen. **1970** *E. Anglian Daily Times* 31 Aug. 4/5 In days of cheaper labour many county council roadmen known as 'lengthmen' were each responsible for the maintenance of a limited number of miles of road in which they took great pride and knew all the peculiarities. **1971** *Times* 8 Apr. 15/3 An old man who lived at Spelbrook... His home was..the lengthman's cottage. **1972** L. Lamb *Picture Frame* xviii. 157 A road (or 'length') man, with broom and shovel strapped to his bicycle cross-bar.

Lengua (le·ŋgwa). [f. Sp. *lengua* tongue (see quot. 1904[1]).] **a.** A member of a tribe of South American Indians inhabiting the Paraguayan Gran Chaco area; also *attrib.* or as *adj.* **b.** The language of this tribe.

1822 S. Coleridge tr. *Dobrizhoffer's Acct. Abipones* I. 125 The equestrian nations remaining in Chaco, and still formidable to the Spaniards, are the Abipones,..and Oekakalots, Guaycurus, or Lenguas. **1904** W. B. Grubb *Among Indians Paraguayan Chaco* vii. 57 The *labret* is an extension of the lower lip, which has the appearance of a protruding tongue. Hence the Spanish term *Lengua* was applied indiscriminately by the early colonists to any tribe who adopted this custom. *Ibid.* x. 94 Unless the circumstances are known, some expressions in Lengua are quite meaningless. **1908** *Westm. Gaz.* 11 Sept. 8/2 During the past year sections [of the Bible] have been printed in Lengua, a language spoken by the Indians of the Paraguayan Chaco. **1911** J. G. Frazer *Golden Bough: Taboo* (ed. 3) ii. 38 The Lengua Indians of the Gran Chaco hold that the vagrant spirits of the dead may come to life again. **1950** J. G. Kerr *Naturalist in Gran Chaco* ix. 175 The main work of the Mission was..among a set of Lengua (i.e. Mushcui) Indians known as the Paisiapto or black-food people. **1973** B. J. Susnik in J. R. Gorham *Paraguay: Ecological Ess.* 121 (*table*) Lengua... Since 1850, contacts (bartering) with Spanish Americans.

Leninism (le·niniz'm). [f. *Lenin*, the assumed name of Vladímir Il'ích Ulyánov (1870–1924), the founder and leader of the Bolsheviks and of the Soviet State + -ism.] The political and economic doctrines of Marx as interpreted and applied by Lenin to the governing of the Soviet Union, to the theory of the international proletarian revolution, and to the dictatorship of the working class. So **Leninism–Stalinism,** Lenin's doctrines as interpreted and applied by Stalin.

1918 *Times* 19 Jan. 5/1 (*caption*) From Tsardom to Leninism. **1928** E. & C. Paul tr. *Stalin's Leninism* I. vi. 53 This second formulation was directed against some critics of Leninism, against the Trotskyists. *Ibid.* II. iii. 94 The endeavour of 'practical' persons to have no truck with 'theories' runs counter to the whole spirit of Leninism and is a great danger to our cause. **1935** *Economist* 12 Jan. 73/2 'Leninism' is a series of brilliant footnotes to the Marxist philosophy made by an experimenter. **1948** J. Towster *Political Power in U.S.S.R.* 3 The teachings of this theory are called Marxism, Leninism,..Marxism–Leninism, or Leninism–Stalinism. **1959** *Times Lit. Suppl.* 21 Aug. 479/3 The remainder of the book follows more familiar lines, Leninism being opposed to Stalinism. **1964** E. H. Carr *Socialism in One Country* III. I. xxxv. 500 In Bolshevik doctrine Leninism meant the adaptation of Marxism to the conditions not of a particular country, but of a particular historical period. **1966** P. Heath tr. *Wetter's Soviet Ideology Today* 328 If history has declined to develop in the manner prescribed by Marx, the endeavour must be made to adapt her to this plan. Hence the explicitly voluntaristic element in Leninism. **1966** L. Lempert tr. *Vinogradov's Socialist Nationalisation of Industry* 19 Leninism maintains, and historical experience confirms, that the ruling classes do not yield power of their own free will. **1971** *Times Lit. Suppl.* 21 May 589/1 Scholastic disputes about orthodoxy are no longer a feature of studies of Marxism and Leninism.

Leninist (le·ninist), *a.* and *sb.* [f. *Lenin* (see prec.) + -ist.] **A.** *adj.* Of, pertaining to, or characteristic of Lenin, his followers or his doctrine. Hence *Leninist–Marxist* (cf. *Marxist–Leninist* adj. s.v. *Marxist *sb.*[1] and *a.*[1]), *Leninist–Stalinist.* **B.** *sb.* A follower or supporter of Lenin or his doctrine.

1917 *Times* 10 Nov. 6/4 General Korniloff has been placed under the same ban as M. Kerensky, and renewed instructions for the arrest of both have been issued by the Leninist committee. *Ibid.* 23 Nov. 7/2 Trotsky, one of the Leninist chiefs, has just declared that violence done by his supporters is a right, but violence in resisting them is immoral. **1920** *Q. Rev.* Apr. 474 The Socialists and the Leninists. **1928** E. W. Dickes tr. *Marcu's Lenin* 187 The Leninists, as the closer adherents of Ulianov now called themselves. **1934** H. G. Wells *Exper. Autobiogr.* II. ix. 806 His [*sc.* Stalin's] was not a free impulsive brain nor a scientifically organized brain; it was a trained Leninist-Marxist brain. **1949** H. Read *Existentialism, Marxism & Anarchism* 16 Humanism is a term which..even an intransigent Marxist like Lukacs does not disdain—he calls the Leninist theory of knowledge a militant humanism. **1950** tr. *M. Djilas's On New Roads of Socialism* 29 The Soviet Government and the subordinate governments have..organized against her [*sc.* Yugoslavia] an economic blockade and violent pressure..by which all Leninist principles on relations amongst Socialist countries have been trampled underfoot. **1953** *Mind* LXII. 68 The Leninist..is able to demonstrate the inexorable nature of the 'withering away of the state'..because his definition of the state requires that it disappears when classes have been abolished. **1964** D. Caute *Communism & French Intellectuals* I. iii. 54 A demand that henceforth the intellectuals cultivate the spirit of the Party in the Leninist-Stalinist sense of the term. **1966** P. Heath tr. *Wetter's Soviet Ideology Today* ii. 32 If the Leninist concept of matter seeks to constitute a definition, it ought to explain what the nature of matter is. **1971** *Times Lit. Suppl.* 21 May 589/1 A critique of specific points of Leninist doctrine. **1973** E. Hyams *Final Agenda* ii. 20 He was a literal, not a nominal Leninist, and he believed..that wisdom.. lay in Lenin's profound distrust of the bureaucracy.

Leninite (le·ninəit), *a.* and *sb.* [f. *Lenin* (see above) + -ite[1].] = *Leninist *a.* and *sb.*

1917 *Times* 7 Dec. 7/3 Trotsky, on behalf of the Leninite 'Government', has telegraphed to all the representatives of Russia abroad. **1918** *Times* 1 Jan. 5/1 The Leninites.. earmarked for their own disposal both the food and the credits that had been set aside for the soldiers' sustenance. **1920** E. E. Cummings *Let.* 22 June (1969) 72, I do *not* need money..being a good (if innocuous) Leninnite [*sic*] or Trotskyite. **1920** *Glasgow Herald* 3 July 6 The Constitution of 1919 which recognised the existence of soviets, though not in the Leninite sense.

lenis (lī·nis), *a.* and *sb.* *Phonology.* [a. L. *lēnis* soft.] **A.** *adj.* Of one of two or more homorganic consonants: articulated with less energy. Opp. *fortis B. *adj.*

1929 G. K. Zipf in *Harvard Stud. Classical Philol.* XL. 63 Then, if our theory be true, the German *p* must be *fortis*, the German *b lenis*. *Ibid.* 64, I hazard the guess.. that the same condition of *lenis–fortis* obtains there also. **1962, 1964** [see *fortis B. *adj.*]. **1969** *Word* XXV. 20, l is sometimes realized as a very lenis unreleased t and ŋ as a nasalized vowel. **1971** F. W. Householder *Ling. Speculations* xi. 206 In Iranian Azerbaijani..the back velar stop is normally lenis only, unopposed by any fortis aspirated [*k*].

B. *sb.* (pl. -es). A lenis consonant.

1932 W. L. Graff *Lang.* vii. 274 In Alsace people..of French tongue often pronounce voiceless sounds or lenes as in Southern German. **1933** L. Bloomfield *Lang.* 99 Pressure and action are gentle in lenes, vigorous in fortes. .. In English the unvoiced stops are aspirated fortes, but other types occur as non-distinctive variants, notably the unaspirated lenis type after [s]. **1935** G. K. Zipf *Psycho-Biol. of Lang.* iii. 63 In the *voiceless fortes* and the *voiceless lenes* we have stops which differ appreciably in magnitude. **1965** *Amer. Speech* XL. 7 Four groupings within the lenes.

lenite (lī·nəit), *v.* *Phonology.* [Back-formation from *lenition.] **a.** *trans.* To make lenis in articulation. **b.** *intr.* (Of consonants), to become lenis. Hence **le·nitable** *a.*; **le·nited** *ppl. a.*

1912 F. W. O'Connell *Gram. Old Irish* 5 A true lenited *f* occurs in Modern Irish and is pronounced *h*. *Ibid.* 61 The absolute forms of the copula lenite the following anlaut. **1953** K. Jackson *Lang. & Hist. Early Brit.* 550 The Bretons lenited the consonants. *Ibid.* 556 British *c*, lenited to *g*. *Ibid.* 474 The consonants ordinarily regarded in Breton as lenitable. **1967** —— *Hist. Phonol. Breton* 309 The geminates, which were not lenitable, constitute a special case. **1971** *Canad. Jrnl. Ling.* Fall 20 Affrication of the yod element would create a consonant cluster which would not lenite. **1972** H. Kurath *Stud. Area Ling.* ix. 153 It should be further noted that 'lenited' /t, k/ appear as the voiced plosives /d, g/ only in the British branch of Insular Celtic.

lenitic (leni·tik), *a.* *Ecol.* [f. L. *lenitas* mildness + -ic.] Of fresh-water organisms or habitats: situated in still water. Cf. *lotic *a.*

1916 Needham & Lloyd *Life Inland Waters* vi. 315 Organisms..may be roughly divided into two primary groups for which are suggested the following names: I. *Lenitic* or still-water societies. II. *Lotic* or rapid-water societies. **1931** R. N. Chapman *Animal Ecol.* xiv. 285 Quantitative methods for the study of benthonic organisms have made important contributions to our knowledge of the quantity of life in lenitic environments.

lenition (lĭni·ʃən). *Phonology.* [f. L. *lēnis* soft + -ition, after G. *lenierung.*] In Celtic languages, the process or result of making or becoming lenis; softening of articulation; (see quots.). Also *attrib.*

1912 F. W. O'Connell *Gram. Old Irish* 5 In Old Irish a single consonant between two vowels was more loosely articulated than in absolute anlaut, and this phonetic change has been termed both *aspiration* and *lenition*. **1913** J. Morris-Jones *Welsh Gram.* § 103. 162 Continental scholars use 'Lenition' as a term embracing the Welsh 'soft mutation' and the corresponding Irish 'aspiration'. **1935** *Mod. Lang. Notes* L. 518 The term *lenition* might to advantage have been recorded; in recent Celtic grammars this term has taken the place of the older *aspiration*. **1953** K. Jackson *Lang. & Hist. Early Brit.* 424 IE. and Latin *d*..in lenition position initially and internally they became Late Brit. *d*. **1954** Pei & Gaynor *Dict. Ling.* 121 *Lenition*, in Celtic languages, the phonetic change which consonants undergo when occurring between vowels, as well as the change of the initial consonant of a word under the influence of the final sound of the immediately preceding word. **1963** J. P. Hughes *Sci. of Lang.* xiv. 251 A tendency arises..to shift the single medial consonant to a spirant... This process is prominent in the Celtic languages, and is known as *lenition*. **1971** *Canad. Jrnl. Ling.* Fall 17 There is some advantage to (1a), which treats lenition in terms of point of articulation classes.

leno. Add: (Earlier and later examples.) Hence, the type of weave used for this fabric. Also *attrib.* and *Comb.*, as *leno brocade, weave;* **leno loom,** a loom which produces leno weave.

1821 M. Browne *Diary* 11 Aug. (1905) 173 We at last got a leno cap and an under cap to wear with it. *c* **1828** J. R. Planché *Green-Eyed Monster* 8 Leno slip, over white satin, ornamented with leno puffs of white and pink. **1940** *Chambers's Techn. Dict.* 494/2 *Leno*, a fabric with an openwork or an embroidered effect, produced by cross-weaving; fabrics of this character that are of regular texture are usually termed *gauze*. *Ibid.*, *Leno brocade*, a brocade cotton, or cotton and rayon cloth, produced by a combination of ordinary and cross-weaving. **1964** H. Hodges *Artifacts* x. 141 Gauze or leno..is produced by crossing adjacent warps before passing the weft, and recrossing the warps again before passing the next weft. **1964** *McCall's Sewing* iv. 52/2 (*caption*) Leno weave; gauze weave. *Ibid.*, Some major fabrics woven on leno looms are marquisette, netting, mesh shirting. **1968** J. Ironside *Fashion Alphabet* 239 *Leno*,..a type of weave—an open-work fabric with warp yarns twisted before weaving.

lens, *sb.* Add: **1.** (Examples of wider applications of the word.)

1931 [see *electron lens* s.v. *electron[2] 2 b]. **1945** *Jrnl. Sci. Instrum.* XXII. 239/1 Another material useful for ultrasonic lenses, especially when the liquid is incompatible with plastics, is lithium. **1951** V. E. Cosslett *Pract. Electron Microsc.* ii. 35 Use is made of a surrounding shield of iron to concentrate the field into a small region near the middle of the lens. **1972** *Science* 16 June 1236/1 The spherical concave lens focused the sound at a nominal 3 cm from the transducer and provided a field 1 mm wide, extending from 2 to 4 cm in range.

2*. *Geol.* A body of ore or rock similar in shape to a biconvex lens.

1903 *Bull. U.S. Geol. Survey* No. 213. 113 The principal mines..have revealed valuable ore bodies of two great types, those which occur as lenses, roughly parallel to the bedding, and those which occur in fracture or fissure zones. **1935** *Economist* 21 Dec. 1283/3 Further lenses of valuable ore would be discovered in that section. **1939** *Proc. Prehist. Soc.* V. 40 Towards the top of the ferruginous gravels appears a lens of non-ferruginous, grey, clayey sand. **1969** Bennison & Wright *Geol. Hist. Brit. Isles* vi. 128 These Lower Palaeozoic rocks occur as discontinuous outcrops or lenses in what has been termed the Meneage Crush Zone... Included lenses may be up to 1 mile in length.

3. (sense 1, 1 b) *lens aperture, barrel, -board, -holder, mount, -work; lens-tube* (earlier and later examples); **lens cap,** a cap that fits over the end of a lens tube, used to protect the lens and, in early cameras without shutters, for regulating exposures; **lens coating,** a thin transparent coating applied to a lens to reduce reflection of light at its surface; **lens hood,** a tube, usually circular in cross-section and with outwardly sloping sides, fitted in front of a lens to shield it from light coming from outside the field of view; **lens louse** *slang* (see quots.); **lensman** = *camera-man* (*camera 3 d); **lens paper,** a kind of soft, thin, absorbent paper suitable for wiping lenses; **lens tissue** = **lens paper*; **lens turret,** a mounting fitted to the front of a camera and carrying several lenses, any of which can be brought into use by rotating the mounting.

1916 *Brit. Jrnl. Photogr.* LXIII. 166/2 (*heading*) Some matters concerning lens apertures. **1958** *Oxford Mail* 19 May 7/4 The length of exposure and the size of the lens aperture are linked to ensure that the right amount of light reaches the film at every shutter speed. **1971** L. B. Happé *Basic Motion Pict. Technol.* ii. 62 The brightness of the image formed by the lens is determined not only by the diameter of the lens aperture but also the size of the image. **1940** *Chambers's Techn. Dict.* 495/1 *Lens barrel*, the metal tube in which one or more lenses are mounted. **1958** *Newnes Compl. Amat. Photogr.* iv. 60 Camera body—the choice is between folding bellows or extending lens-barrel. **1967** Karch & Buber *Offset Processes* v. 143 The lens barrel contains a slot..used to insert filters for color work. **1892** *Photogr. Ann.* II. 289 The most important feature is the novel and convenient mode of attaching the front lens board to the baseboard. **1941** R. M. Allen *Photomicrogr.* ii. 67 Most manufacturers provide some type of fixture, preferably with focusing means incorporated in it, for carrying the lenses on the lens board. **1967** Karch & Buber *Offset Processes* v. 143 The lensboard, located directly in front of the copyboard, houses the lens. **1882** *Photogr. at Home: its Appliances & Apparatus for Amateurs* 11 A little shield covered with black velvet.. occupies the place of the ordinary lens cap. **1897** *Sears, Roebuck Catal.* 474/2 The front of the camera can be removed if desired and exposure made with a lens cap. **1965** Mrs. L. B. Johnson *White House Diary* 17 June (1970) 290, I wanted to be darned sure I didn't lose the lens cap on the camera. **1966** LaCour & Lathrop *Photo Technol.* iv. 48/2 It should seldom be necessary to clean a lens which has been protected from dust and fingerprints with a lens cap. **1952** C. B. Neblette *Photogr.* (ed. 5) ii. 48/1 Lens coatings are a remedial measure and do not entirely

remove reflections. **1966** LaCour & Lathrop *Photo Technol.* iv. 48/2 Finger prints on the lens..are detrimental to the lens coating. **1876** tr. *G. Tissandier's Hist. & Handbk. Photogr.* 223 The ordinary lens-holder being removed from the front of the camera. **1894** S. H. Gage *Microscope* (ed. 5) i. 4 (*heading*) Adjustable lens holder with universal joint. **1891** W. E. Woodbury *Encycl. Photogr.* 405 (*heading*) Lens screen or hood. **1908** *Brit. Jrnl. Photogr.* LV. 245/1 The lens-hood..has recently revived, owing to the necessity of shading the lens from direct light in the case of anastigmats which possess large aperture. **1955** E. Hillary *High Adventure* xii. 210, I clipped on [to my camera] the lenshood and ultra-violet filter. **1968** L. A. Mannheim tr. *Brandt's Photogr. Lens* xv. 166 Lens hoods not only have to shield the lens against stray light, but also protect it against accidental finger marks and rain or snow. **1928** *Amer. Speech* III. 368 Actors who strive for the most advantageous positions are also called 'lens lice'. **1950** J. Hall in *Daily Mail* 24 May, Bane of the news-reel cameraman is what he calls a 'lens louse'. They..never miss a chance of getting in front of a news-reel camera. **1951** *N.Y. Herald Tribune* 26 Aug. iv. 4/4 It was common to see a Leatherneck lensman wield a 45-automatic pistol in one hand and a 16-mm. camera in the other, firing both simultaneously at the enemy only a few hundred yards away. **1964** *Punch* 5 Aug. 183/1 He's one of the best lensmen in the business. **1972** I. Hamilton *Thrill Machine* vi. 27, I held back with the pen and ink men while the lensmen pushed forward to the press barricades. **1892** *Photogr. Ann.* II. 43 Unscrew the back combination and use the front alone *in situ*, thus gaining the length of the lens mount. **1938** H. Windisch *New Photo-School* vi. 166 A focusing screen is applied to the lens mount. **1972** Horne & Markham in A. M. Glauert *Pract. Methods Electron Microsc.* I. ii. iii. 354 Optical bench manufacturers make a large number of lens mounts and carriers. **1925** A. F. Collins *Amat. Photographer's Handbk.* iv. 61 Dirt that forms on the surfaces [of a lens] in an almost imperceptible film can usually be wiped off with a dry lens paper, which is a very soft Japanese tissue paper especially made for this purpose. **1973** *Nature* 27 July 233/1 Each portion [of ovary] was placed on defatted lens paper on a stainless steel mesh grid in a vitreosil dish. **1941** A. Sussman *Collins's Amat. Photographer's Handbk.* (rev. ed.) iii. 75 Use some dry lens tissue, or an old linen handkerchief that has been freshly laundered. **1955** S. C. Gilmour *Paper* 305 *Lens tissue*, British-made paper of very thin substance and transparent texture, resembling Japanese tissue. Long fibres, great strength for the substance, and extreme absorbency are characteristics. Used for cleaning optical and microscope lenses. **1858** Sutton & Worden *Dict. Photogr.* 260 The diaphragms within the lens-tube entirely prevent the reflection of light from the inside of the tube. **1918** Lens-tube [see *hood *sb.* 5 m]. **1971** L. B. Happé *Basic Motion Pict. Technol.* iv. 142 On 8 mm amateur cameras..the lens hood is usually limited to a deep flange extension to the lens tube itself. **1951** R. Spottiswoode *Film & its Techniques* iii. 64 Camera noise readily seeps through a lens turret and tends to interfere with dialogue recording. **1963** *Movie* July/Aug. 26/3 Brault's insistence on leaving in blank frames as he shifts the lens turret in mid-reel occasionally gets in the way. **1971** L. B. Happé *Basic Motion Pict. Technol.* x. 311 A lens turret mounting is often preferred for unit lenses and is more convenient for automated operations. **1888** G. M. Hopkins *Let.* 1 May (1938) 144 Photography proper now is mere scaffolding..a poor bastard art succeeds the lens-work and disguises what that gives.

lens (lenz), *v. Geol.* [f. the sb.] *to lens out* (intr.): of a body of rock: to become gradually thinner (along a particular direction) to the point of extinction.

1921 G. H. Cox et al. *Field Methods Petroleum Geol.* 11 The effects of irregularities in sands may be considered to be of three types; those in which the sand lenses out entirely, those in which it loses its porosity, and those in which the porous sand continues but is of changing thickness. **1965** G. J. Williams *Econ. Geol. N.Z.* viii. 108/2 Mining went down to the 500-ft level below which the calcite bodies themselves lens out—as proved by angled diamond drill-holes.

lensoid (le·nzoid), *a.* [f. Lens + -oid.] = Lentoid *a.*

1965 G. J. Williams *Econ. Geol. N.Z.* iv. 35/2 The quartz bodies are lensoid, seldom more than 5 ft in thickness, discontinuous longitudinally and overlapping in places. **1973** *Nature* 27 July 215/1 The cherts occur chiefly as intercalations, sometimes of wide lateral extent and sometimes lensoid, between the extrusives.

Lent, *sb.*¹ Add: **Lent-term** (examples).

1861 T. Hughes *Tom Brown at Oxf.* I. iv. 68 We're only half through Lent term. **1950** *Cambridge 1950* (Varsity) 8 The Cardinal's Ball..seems to have taken over the position of chief social event of the Lent term from the now banned Granta Ball. **1974** *Univ. Exeter Calendar 1974–5* 4 Wed. 8 [January] Lent term begins.

Lenten. Add: **B. 3. Lenten rose,** a variety of *Helleborus orientalis*, blooming in late winter and early spring.

1884 J. Wood *Hardy Perennials* 137 (*heading*) Helleborus Orientalis... Sometimes also called the Lenten Rose, as it may often be seen in flower during Lent. [**1897** S. Hibberd *Familiar Garden Flowers* I. 35 As the trumpet daffodils are called 'Lent lilies', so the spring flowering hellebores are called 'Lent roses'.] **1900** W. D. Drury *Bk. Gardening* x. 330 Equally deserving of praise are the Lenten Roses (*H. orientalis*), whose flowers embrace all the shades of rose and purple, as well as white and cream. **1948** P. M. Synge *Flowers in Winter* 57 Lenten Roses.. always look well in a mixed winter bowl of flowers. **1970** C. Lloyd *Well-Tempered Garden* v. 378 The main flush of blossom from Lenten roses is borne from February till April.

lentic (le·ntik), *a. Ecol.* [f. L. *lentus* slow, calm + -ic.] = *lenitic *a.*

1935 P. S. Welch *Limnology* ii. 13 The lentic environments, sometimes known as the standing-water series, include all forms of inland water (lakes, ponds, swamps, and their various intergrades) in which the water motion is not that of a continuous flow in a definite direction. **1940** L. H. Hyman *Invertebrates* I. iii. 80 Fresh-water habitats classify as lentic or standing-water bodies: lake-pond-swamp series, and lotic, or running-water formations. .. Among the smaller lentic environments, such as pools, ditches, ponds, and swamps, the animals are practically all littoral and benthonic. **1960** N. Polunin *Introd. Plant Geogr.* xv. 498 The stalks of inhabitants of swift currents tend to be much shorter than those of their lentic relatives.

lenticle (le·ntik'l). *Geol.* [ad. L. *lenticula* (see Lenticular *a.* and *sb.*).] A lentil (sense 4*) or a lenticular piece of rock.

1898 J. E. Marr *Princ. Stratigr. Geol.* iv. 35 The lenticles will be wider in a direction at right angles to that of the strike. **1902** *Encycl. Brit.* XXVIII. 654/2 Lenticles or eyes of uncrushed diorite may be traced. **1930** [see *hornblendite]. **1931** Cissarz & Jones *German-Eng. Geol. Terminol.* 179 Gash veins..are usually of small lateral and vertical extent, in the form of small lenticles.

lenticular, *a.* and *sb.* Add: **A.** *adj.* **1. b. lenticular stereoscope** (earlier example).

1852 *Phil. Mag.* III. 17 (*heading*) The lenticular stereoscope.

2. a. Delete *rare* and add further examples. Also, employing a lens or lenses.

1903 *Sci. Amer.* 7 Feb. 98/2 The lenses revolve at a given speed..proportioned to the diameter of the illuminant and the lenticular apparatus. **1961** *Listener* 26 Oct. 670/1 The first lenticular light-house.

2*. *Photogr.* **a.** Embossed with minute lenses, as *lenticular film*, a film having the non-emulsion surface formed into minute lenses (usually cylindrical lenses, giving a corrugated pattern), so that two or more images (as of different primary colours to make up a colour photograph) can be interspersed on the same area of film.

1934 *Photogr. Jrnl.* LXXIV. 206/1 The list of patents relating to the duplicating of lenticular films grows. **1950** A. W. Judge *Stereoscopic Photogr.* (ed. 3) xvii. 297 A more recent method of making Lenticular stereograms.. employs a lenticular screen, made up of contiguous cylindrical-type lenses, of very small width, placed in front of the sensitive emulsion. **1962** W. G. Hyzer *Engin. & Scientific High-Speed Photogr.* i. 42 A lenticular plate, comprised of an array of spherical lenslets, is employed to produce a corresponding array of spots on the photo-sensitive film. A primary lens having an aperture of *f*/6·3 is used to project the image of the event onto the front surface of the lenticular plate, whereupon each individual lenslet converges the image rays intercepted by its surface onto a tiny spot at the focal plane. Sequential images may be obtained by producing relative motion between the lenticular plate and the photographic emulsion. **1966** R. J. Ross *Television Film Engin.* xi. 445 A method of recording on 35 mm lenticular film was at one time employed by the National Broadcasting Company. **1967** *Electronics* 6 Mar. 79/1 (Advt.), The tube's light output is 30,000 foot lamberts, which results in a light level of 15-foot lamberts on a 3′ × 4′ lenticular screen.

b. Applied to a method of colour photography using a film with cylindrical lenticulations and filters with bands of the primary colours parallel to the lenticulations during exposure and projection.

1936 R. M. Fanstone *Colour Photogr.* xvii. 157 (*heading*) Lenticular colour photography. **1942** C. B. Neblette *Photogr.* (ed. 4) xxxii. 797 The Lenticular process is essentially a screen method in which the screen is formed optically on the emulsion during exposure. **1964** E. S. Bomback *Man. Colour Photogr.* iii. 56 The first commercial film based on the lenticular process was marketed by Kodak in 1928 as 16 mm. cine film..called Kodacolor.

lenticularity (lentikiŭlæ·riti). [f. Lenticular *a.* + -ity.] Lenticular form or quality.

1912 E. H. C. Craig *Oil-Finding* viii. 141 Many of the discrepancies between prediction and results nowadays are attributed to lenticularity of the oil-bearing strata. **1925** A. Beeby-Thompson *Oil-Field Explor. & Devel.* I. iv. 111 No cautious operators fail to appreciate the importance of lenticularity and lateral variation of sands. **1928** *Bull. Amer. Assoc. Petroleum Geologists* XII. 248 Lenticularity is a characteristic feature of the Lower Pico beds. **1965** G. J. Williams *Econ. Geol. N.Z.* xix. 345/1 Lenticularity of the sands may have prevented up-dip migration of the oil, although a slight arching of a 4° south-westerly dip may have assisted.

lenticulated (lenti·kiŭlēitėd), *a. Photogr.* [f. Lenticul(e + -at(e³ + -ed¹.] = *lenticular *a.* 2* a.

1925 *Brit. Jrnl. Photogr.* LXXII. 65/2 (*heading*) Lenticulated films for colour cinematography. **1950** A. W. Judge *Stereoscopic Photogr.* (ed. 3) xvii. 296 The positive (print or transparency) is viewed through a similar lenticulated screen to that used for the negative. **1970** R. J. Ross *Color Film for Color Television* xv. 147 (*heading*) Lenticulated film systems using black-and-white emulsions on a specially processed base material.

lenticulation (lentikiŭlēi·ʃən). *Photogr.* [f. Lenticul(e + -ation.] **a.** The condition of being lenticulated. **b.** Each of the minute lenses of a lenticular film.

1916 *Brit. Jrnl. Photogr.* LXIII. 117/2 It is known to obtain the lenticulation of such films by rolling them at a suitable temperature between a smooth cylinder and a cylinder carrying in intaglio the engraving of the embossing to be formed on the film. **1932** *Discovery* Dec. 383/1 If the embossed lenticular film is copied on another embossed film, the lenticulations, being so minute, give rise to interference or 'watering', which causes grave defects in the quality of the copy. **1975** *Movie Maker* Feb. 87/2 Many of these materials have a very bright surface with a whiter-than-white look.., and have some type of surface texture in the form of diamond shaped lenticulations or similar. *Ibid.* 90 (Advt.), 'Hi-Flect' Blankana-White with the unique hexagonal lenticulation

lenticule. Add: **b.** *Photogr.* A minute lens of a lenticular film; = *lenticulation b.

1942 H. C. Colton in C. B. Neblette *Photogr.* (ed. 4) xxxii. 799 Kodacolor film contained about 600 lenticules per inch. **1966** R. J. Ross *Television Film Engin.* xi. 445 A banded color filter acted on the light passing through the camera lens, with the bands parallel to the lenticules, producing three color separation records on a single frame of film.

lentigerous, *a.* (Example.)

1883 E. R. Lankester in *Encycl. Brit.* XVI. 680/2 The two lines of development of the Molluscan eye..the punctigerous and the lentigerous.

lentil. Add: **4*.** *Geol.* A mass of rock distinct in character and having the shape of a biconvex lens; *spec.* one regarded as a subdivision of a formation.

1895 J. W. Powell in A. Keith *Descr. Knoxville Sheet* (U.S. Geol. Survey Atlas), The kinds of rocks are indicated..by appropriate symbols... The following are generally used..Limestones..Lentils in strata. **1910** *Ann. N.Y. Acad. Sci.* XIX. 177 The gray sandstone of the Grès Noirs more than 20 feet thick, containing a thin irregular lentil of coal. **1953** *Bull. Amer. Assoc. Petroleum Geologists* XXXVII. 2410 Formations may be subdivided into members, lentils, 'tongues', beds, *et cetera.* **1970** *Earth-Sci. Rev.* VI. 275 Examples of informal rock units are:..(*b*) beds (e.g., quarry layer, coal beds, oil sands, tongues, lentils, etc.).

lento. Add: **b.** *Philol.* Applied to a word or phrase pronounced more slowly than in normal speech. Cf. *allegro B. 2.

1939 [see *allegro B. 2]. **1964** J. Vachek in D. Abercrombie et al. *Daniel Jones* 205 Yet the pronunciation with [əl], characteristic of a *lento* style of speech,.. can hardly be credited with exercising a decisive influence on the much more frequent *allegro* form with the syllabic [l̩]. **1968** *Language* XLIV. 87 Another main type of downdrift is in steps, with deliberate lento articulation. **1973** *Word 1970* XXVI. 39 The last two words in lento speech.

Lentz (lents). The name of Hugo *Lentz*, 20th-c. German engineer, used *attrib.* to denote a type of poppet valve invented by him for use in steam engines, and a locomotive valve gear employing such valves operated by a camshaft.

1925 *Marine Engineer* XLVIII. 19/2 In developing the Lentz poppet valve for marine engines, those first fitted were applied to engines of the triple and..quadruple-expansion types. **1930** *Engineer* 31 Jan. 132/1 L.N.E.R. locomotive with Lentz valve gear. **1949** C. J. Allen *Locomotive Pract. & Performance 20th Cent.* iv. 40 The most extensive application of poppet-valves to locomotives in Great Britain has been that of Lentz valves to the 'Hunt' class 4-4-0s of the late L.N.E.R. **1966** O. S. Nock *Brit. Steam Railway Locomotive 1925–65* viii. 99 (*caption*) L.M.S.R. Horwich 2-6-0 with Lentz R.C. poppet valve gear.

Lenz's law (le·ntsiz, le·nziz). *Electr.* [Named after H. F. E. *Lenz* (1804–65), German physicist, who first enunciated it (in *Ann. d. Physik u. Chem.* (1834) XXXI. 483).] The law that the direction of an induced current is always such as to oppose the change in the circuit or the magnetic field that produces it.

1866 E. Atkinson tr. *Ganot's Elem. Treat. Physics* (ed. 2) x. vi. 696 On the induction produced between a closed circuit and a current in activity when their relative distance varies, Lenz has based the following law, which is known as Lenz's law. **1931** L. B. Loeb *Fund. Electr. & Magn.* i. 35 Unless Lenz's law holds we could by induction effects get energy out of nothing. **1962** Corson & Lorrain *Introd. Electromagn. Fields* vi. 222 Lenz's law is a particular case of Le Chatelier's principle. **1973** *Physics Bull.* Dec. 715/2 Any change in the external field induces an appropriate supercurrent which (by Lenz's law) is just sufficient to counter the effect of the field variation.

Leonardesque (lī:ŏnāɹde·sk), *a.* [f. the name of *Leonardo* da Vinci (1452–1519) + -esque.] Resembling in subject or style, or in the manner of, the works of Leonardo da Vinci.

1864 Crowe & Cavalcaselle *New Hist. Painting Italy* II. xxii. 547 Nothing can exceed the Leonardesque precision of the drawing or the softness and fusion of the impasto. **1904** E. McCurdy *Leonardo da Vinci* 100 How eminently Leonardesque it was to make the angel point at S. John. **1939** *English* II. 276, I had early waited for a Leonardesque sweetness and subtlety which visited his

features. **1960** *Times* 24 Feb. 15/1 Sir Kenneth [Clark].. had for some time discerned a Leonardesque presence in the painting. **1971** A. Smart *Renaissance & Mannerism in Italy* xvi. 135 There is nothing here of Leonardo's mystery, but rather a calm objectivity and a cold grace that are the reverse of Leonardesque 'romanticism'.

Leonberg (lī·ǒnbɔ̄ɪg). The name of a town in south-western Germany used *attrib.* or *absol.* to designate a large dog, a cross between a St. Bernard and a Newfoundland, often golden in colour, of a breed first developed there about 1855. Also **Le·onberger.**

1907 K. Leighton *New Bk. Dog* xvii. 518/1 The Leonberg dog..is supposed also to be a worker among flocks and herds. **1945** C. L. B. Hubbard *Observer's Bk. Dogs* 179 The Leonberg is now regarded on the Continent as a distinct race. **1954** M. K. Wilson tr. *Lorenz's Man meets Dog* vii. 75 A great, strong Leonberger,.. a member of one of the largest breeds of dog, adopted as mistress the youngest sister. **1962** J. M. Bernstein tr. *Levi's Two-Fold Night* x. 86 Two enormous dogs..of the rare Leonberg breed. **1971** F. Hamilton *World Encycl. Dogs* 158 The popularity of the Leonberger increased and by 1872 other breeders were competing with similar crosses to obtain large, handsome, utility dogs.

leone (lī,ōu·n). [f. the name of Sierra *Leone.*] The principal unit of currency in Sierra Leone; a banknote of the value of one leone.

1964 *Times* 4 Aug. 6/5 The new basic unit is the leone with a value equal to 10s. **1972** *Whitaker's Almanack 1973* 987 Sierra Leone..Leone of 100 Cents.

Leonese (līǒnī·z), *a.* and *sb.* [f. Sp. *León*, the name of a town and region in Spain + -ese.] **A.** *adj.* Of or belonging to León, an ancient kingdom of Spain and now a province, or to the town of León in this region. **B.** *sb.* **a.** A native or inhabitant of León; also *collect.* **b.** The language of León, a dialect of Spanish with Portuguese affinities.

1845 R. Ford *Hand-bk. for Travellers Spain* II. viii. 558 The minor traits of Leonese character are influenced by local differences. *Ibid.* 559 The houses of the humble Leonese, like their hearts, are always open to an Englishman. **1865** H. O'Shea *Guide to Spain* 236/2 The present Jesuits..with their usual refinement, tact, and educational talents, will soon..ungothicise the good Leonese. *Ibid.* 245/2 The Leoneses differ considerably in character, according to the nature of the different regions which they inhabit. **1887** *Encycl. Brit.* XXII. 351/2 *Leonese.* Proceedings on inadequate indications, the existence of a Leonese dialect has been imprudently admitted in some quarters. **1893** H. E. Watts *Spain* ii. 52 Almanzor marched into the Christian kingdom,.. scattering Castilians and Leonese as the Goths had been scattered three hundreds years before. **1932** W. L. Graff *Lang.* x. 377 Spanish group, with the Castilian, Andalusian, Aragonese, and Leonese dialects. **1936** W. J. Entwistle *Spanish Lang.* v. 39 Mozarabic cooperation in many important settlements brought the use of Arabic terminology to a maximum in Leonese. **1964** *Archivum Linguisticum* 2 At that stage he [*sc.* Diez] did not yet identify the dialect at issue as Leonese.

leonine, *a.*[1] Add: **1. c.** Designating that form of leprosy called leontiasis, and the lion-like facies characteristic of it.

The allusion to the resemblance to the lion's face can be traced back to the ancient Arab physicians.

[**1749** J. Barrow *Dictionarium Medicum Universale, Leontiasis, Leontion,* or *Leonina lepra,* a name for Elephantiasis, or leprosy.] **1813** T. Bateman *Pract. Synopsis Cutaneous Dis.* 295 Haly Abbas says the countenance was called leonine, because the white of the eyes becomes livid, and the eyes of a round figure; and Avicenna observes that the epithet was applied to the disease, because it renders the countenance terrible to look at, and somewhat of the form of the lion's visage. **1867** *Rep. Leprosy* (R. Coll. Physicians) 242 The prominent blotches on the forehead gave a sombre character to his countenance; not as yet approaching the leonine expression of tubercular elephantiasis. **1899** T. L. Stedman *20th Cent. Pract.* XVIII. 623 The lower part of the frontal skin is drawn downwards and conceals the eyes, as in mad persons and lions. This is why the affection is also called leonine. **1959** R. G. Cochrane *Leprosy in Theory & Pract.* 367 The 'leonine' appearance in Hansen's disease is..attributable to the nodular leprosy. **1970** G. J. Hill *Leprosy in Five Young Men* 65 Patient 5 was a large dark-skinned man with moderately severe leonine facies.

leonite (lēi·-, lī·ǒnəit). *Min.* [ad. G. *leonit* (C. A. Tenne 1896, in *Zeitschr. d. deut. geol. Ges.* XLVIII. 637), f. the name of *Leo* Strippelmann, 19th-c. German salt-works director: see -ite[1].] A hydrated sulphate of potassium and magnesium, $K_2Mg(SO_4)_2.4H_2O$, found as transparent, colourless, or yellowish prismatic crystals.

1897 *Jrnl. Chem. Soc.* LXXII. ii. 269 There is no crystallographic relation between this mineral and blödite.., so that the older but unpublished name, leonite, is used in preference to kaliblödite. **1932** *Bull. U.S. Geol. Survey* No. 833. 44 In the Joe Mitchell well at a depth of 1,368 feet pale-yellow leonite with a waxy luster is intimately mixed with kainite... In places leonite occurs in larger blebs. **1970** *Mineral. & Petrogr. Acta* XVI. 14/2 This appears to be the first occurrence of leonite for Vesuvian fumaroles. Leonite is known to be associated in salt deposits of oceanic origin, at Stassfurt with halite, at Leopoldshall with kainite, and at Ascherleben.

leopard. Add: **2.** (Later examples.)

1920 *New Statesman* Apr. 20/1 For the moment the public is not likely to get a thorough grounding in economics, nor does the Press leopard show any signs of changing his spots. **1930** D. Jerrold *Lie about War* 35 As for the leopard who failed to change his spots, why blame the war? **1955** W. Gaddis *Recognitions* ii. v. 487 You wanted to marry a Christian, you wanted to marry a good Catholic. Well leopards can't change their spots. **1972** G. Oakley *Church Mouse* 20/2 The schoolmouse..said that..Sampson was a leopard in sheep's clothing and that a wolf couldn't change its spots. **1973** *Times* 21 Nov. 19/8 There is no evidence to show that the Communist Party leopard has changed its spots.

4. Delete †*Obs.* and add later examples. Also, the skin of the leopard; a coat made from this.

1924 *Vogue* early Sept. 42 (*caption*) Even smarter..is a suède coat lined and trimmed with leopard. **1930** M. Bachrach *Fur* xv. 197 All Leopards are open-handled and..there is very little natural grease on the skin. **1938** —— *Selling Furs Successfully* ix. 91 It is preferable when manufacturing Leopards into garments that as few seams as possible show after the garments are finished. **1951** R. T. Wilcox *Mode in Furs* vii. 157 Such peltries as bear, lynx, fox, wolf and goat were popular though lamb, civet cat and leopard are noted too [in the early 20th century]. *Ibid.* 208 (*caption*) Hooded circular cape of Somali leopard. **1973** E. McBain *Let's hear It* iii. 44 'My good jewelry.. [has] gone.' 'Anything else?' 'Two furs. A leopard and an otter.'

b. Delete † and substitute for def.: *attrib.* or quasi-*adj.* Made of leopard skin or material resembling leopard skin.

1938 M. Bachrach *Selling Furs Successfully* ix. 100 'This Leopard coat is rather heavy' is sometimes remarked by customers. **1951** R. T. Wilcox *Mode in Furs* vii. 199 (*caption*) Leopard jacket belted with dark blue antelope—leopard gloves with antelope palms. **1958** *Listener* 28 Aug. 316/3 Scowling Continental 'helps' in leopard slacks. **1974** *Times* 11 Nov. 28/7, 1 sable, skins worked down; 1 absolutely beautiful dark leopard coat. Both made by top furriers.

6. a. *leopard spot*; *leopard-coloured* (examples), *-spotted* adj.; **leopard-man,** a member of a leopard society (see below); **leopard-skin** *attrib.*, made of leopard skin; resembling a leopard skin in appearance; mottled; **leopard-skin chief, priest,** among the Nuer people of East Africa, a mediator or arbitrator who settles disputes (so called from the leopard skin which by custom he wears); **leopard society,** in West Africa, a native secret society whose members dress as leopards and attack their victims in the manner of leopards.

1847 Emerson *Poems* 73 Gayest pictures rose to win me, Leopard-coloured rills. **1889** W. B. Yeats *Wanderings of Oisin* 78 Or in autumnal solitudes Arise the leopard-coloured trees. **1929** F. W. Butt-Thompson *W. Afr. Secret Soc.* xiv. 283 *Tongo-players*, the Sierra Leonean society..said to have been started about the Eighties..as an organisation of leopard-men hunters. **1936** G. Griffin tr. *Schebesta's My Pygmy & Negro Hosts* iv. 67, I think that I have been the first to obtain any detailed information about these 'Anyoto'—the dreadful 'leopard-men'. **1973** G. Gale in Johnson & Gale *Highland Jaunt* ii. iv. 143 He now was happy..telling the bar about the Leopard Men in West Africa. **1895** F. B. & W. H. Workman *Algerian Memories* x. 93 Besides the oasis of Biskra..a number of others were visible, the dark colour of which, contrasting with the lighter hues of the plain, gave the leopard-skin appearance. **1929** E. Sitwell *Gold Coast Customs* 8 Courie shells..outline The leopardskin musty Leaves. **1975** *Times* 25 Feb. 6/7 Bagpipers of the Royal [Nepalese] Army in leopard-skin gaiters. **1940** E. E. Evans-Pritchard *Nuer* iv. 190 There is no central administration, the leopard-skin Chief being a ritual agent whose functions are to be interpreted in terms of the structural mechanism of the feud. **1956** —— *Nuer Relig.* iv. 110 In this particular ceremony several groups were opposed to each other, and the leopard-skin priest was acting in his priestly capacity as mediator between them. **1959** G. D. Mitchell *Sociol.* v. 89 If one man kills another he will go immediately to a person known as a leopard-skin chief... He is in no sense a chief but rather a person who performs certain ritual acts. **1915** K. J. Beatty *Human Leopards* i. 6 To deal with this extraordinary class of crime the Government of the Colony of Sierra Leone decided that drastic and exceptional legislation was necessary, and a Bill entitled the Human Leopard Society Ordinance, 1895, was introduced and passed. **1929** F. W. Butt-Thompson *W. Afr. Secret Soc.* i. 20 Most of the criminal associations are 'animal' societies... They include Alligator, Baboon, Boa, Leopard, Panther societies. **1968** *Encycl. Brit.* XIII. 975/2 There were many leopard societies, of which the most renowned was the *anyota* society of the Bali tribe, eastern Congo. **1939** T. S. Eliot *Old Possum's Pract. Cats* 13 Her coat is of the tabby kind, with tiger stripes and leopard spots. **1972** *Times* 23 Nov. 8/2 The presence of communist cadres within Government-held areas could produce more 'leopard spots', to use the accepted phrase, than the map [of S. Vietnam] suggests. **1931** V. Woolf *Waves* 239 Different lights fall, making the ordinary leopard-spotted and strange.

b. leopard frog *U.S.*, a green frog with black markings, *Rana pipiens*; **leopard lily** orig. *U.S.*, a name used for several spotted lilies, esp. *Lilium pardalinum* (cf. *panther-lily* (Panther 5)); **leopard-spotted goby,** a small brown goby with orange spots, *Gobius forsteri*, found close to the shore in parts of the western coast of Britain and France; **leopard-tree** *Austral.*, a name for either of two species of *Flindersia*, *F. maculosa* or *F. collina*; also used for the South American tree *Cæsalpinia ferrea*; **leopard-wood,** (*b*) *Austral.* = **leopard-tree.*

1839 D. H. Storer in Storer & Peabody *Rep. Fishes, Reptiles & Birds Mass.* 237 *Rana halecina*..[is] better known in this state as the leopard frog from its ocellated appearance. **1840** Thoreau *Jrnl.* 16 June in *Writings* (1906) VII. 141 Twelve hours of genial and familiar converse with the leopard frog. **1948** *Sierra Club Bull.* (San Francisco) Mar. 140 Migration is a part of the story of the American merganser, hibernation of the leopard frog. **1973** *Sci. Amer.* Oct. 26/3 The leopard frog (*Rana pipiens*) is particularly susceptible to a kidney carcinoma. **1902** *Out West* Sept. 349 The leopard-lily lights the heather dun. **1938** J. H. McFarland et al. *Garden Bulbs* 136 Lilium pardalinum. Sometimes called the Western Tiger Lily, this highly esteemed California native also has the common names of Leopard Lily and Panther Lily. **1949** H. Moldenke *Amer. Wild Flowers* 323 A great favorite of the Southeast is the leopard lily or pine lily, *L. catesbaei*, found in pinelands and acid swamps on the coastal plain from North Carolina to Florida and Louisiana. **1969** Hay & Synge *Dict. Garden Plants* 318/2 [*Lilium*] *pardalinum* Leopard Lily. Summer. Fl[ower] turkscap, orange flushed and spotted with red or maroon, pendulous. **1959** A. Hardy *Fish & Fisheries* x. 212 Mr. P. G. Corbin..is naming it after its discoverer, *Gobius forsteri*; it will also be known by the English name of leopard-spotted goby. **1971** *Nature* 30 Apr. 581/1 Closer examination should reveal the presence of the leopard-spotted goby along the Scottish west coast. **1927** *Austral. Encycl.* I. 474/2 *F*[*lindersia*] *maculosa* (Leopard Tree, so called from its spotted trunk) is a small tree (20–30 feet), found in the dry interior. **1933** *Bulletin* (Sydney) 20 Sept. 20/2 The leopard tree starts as a straggly, spiny bush, from the centre of which the stem shoots up. **1965** *Austral. Encycl.* V. 288/2 Leopard-tree, a name used for two species of *Flindersia*—the graceful inland *F. maculosa*, which has spotted bark, and the tall rain-forest species *F. collina* (broad-leaved leopard tree or leopard ash). The South American tree *Caesalpinia ferrea*, much grown as an ornamental flowering and shade tree in coastal Queensland, is also called leopard-tree and leopard-wood. **1888** F. M. Bailey *Queensland Woods* 76 *F*[*lindersia*] *maculosa*... Spotted tree or leopard-wood... Wood bright yellow, nicely marked. **1911** C. E. W. Bean '*Dreadnought*' *of Darling* xv. 140 It seems a wonder that Australians on the coast do not make a much bigger use of these delicate Western trees for their gardens, especially the leopard-wood. **1936** F. Clune *Roaming round Darling* xviii. 177 Spotted a splendid leopard-wood, reputed to attract lightning more than any other tree.

Leopardian (lī,ǒpā·ɪdiăn), *a.* [f. the name of Count Giacomo *Leopardi* (1798–1837) + -ian.] Of, pertaining to, or characteristic of the Italian poet and scholar Leopardi, or his works.

1881 *Fraser's Mag.* XXIV. 571 In England we have had as yet no notice of the flood of Leopardian recollections, memoirs, and posthumous correspondence that has recently appeared in Italy. **1934** *Times Lit. Suppl.* 21 June p. xi/1 This return to the Leopardian tradition in the more recent poets has been one of the most striking developments. **1947** *Horizon* Apr. 195 Articles and books have been written on 'Leopardian optimism'. **1970** I. Origo *Images & Shadows* viii. 181, I remember telling the distinguished Leopardian scholar and critic, Giuseppe de Robertis..that..I was just beginning a second life of the poet. He began to laugh. 'I see that you have caught it, too,' he said, '*il vizio leopardiano.*'

leotard (lī·ǒtāɪd). [The name of Jules *Léotard* (1830–70), French trapeze artist.] A close-fitting one-piece garment worn by acrobats and dancers; a similar fashion garment. So **le·otarded** *a.*

1920 J. W. Mansfield *Let.* Jan. (MS. in G. & C. Merriam Co. files), Leotards..are used by acrobats and aerial performers. **1930** *Theatre Arts Monthly* Jan. p. viii/3 (Advt.), The improved Nat Lewis leotards. Lovely, yet sturdily constructed for hard usage. **1939** Adeler & West *Remember Fred Karno* ii. 39 The gymnasts' costume worn by Westcott consisted of the classic leotard, a sort of vest specially designed to leave the arms free, spangled neckpiece and trunks. **1953** *Ballet Ann.* VII. 66/1 The simplest of costumes—white *tutus* for the girls, black *leotards* for boys. **1957** *N. Y. Times Mag.* 3 Mar. 42/1 (Advt.), Low and behold, the *leotard*..the shape they said could never be built into a corselette. **1957** *Life* 12 Aug. 91/2 (*caption*) Short skirt worn over striped leotards. **1957** *Vogue* 15 Aug. 42/1 (Advt.), Worsted knit leotard pants. **1958** *Daily Express* 8 Aug. 2/7 Leotards will be the rage with teenage girls this autumn—ballet tights made of stretch nylon. **1966** T. Pynchon *Crying of Lot 49* iii. 63 One of the girls, a long-waisted, brown-haired lovely in a black knit leotard. **1969** *Sears Catal.* Spring/Summer 21 Swimsuit. Knit of stretch nylon. Popular one-piece styling takes added fashion interest with its smart leotard look. Suit can also be worn as a leotard. **1972** *Listener* 20 Jan. 93/3 Leotarded, limbs akimbo. **1972** *Village Voice* (N.Y.) 1 June 40/4 Her dance, more leotarded than veiled, was attitude rather than movement.

Léoville (leovil). [Fr.] A red wine from any of three vineyards in the commune of Saint-Julien, district of Haut-Médoc, department of Gironde, France.

[**1833** C. Redding *Hist. Mod. Wines* v. 149 St. Julien de Reignac..is the eighteenth commune of the Medoc vine

country... The inferior growths of La Rose and Léoville are the produce of this commune.] **1875** TROLLOPE *Prime Minister* (1876) I. x. 155 'Oh yes, I remember the wine. You call it '57, don't you?' 'And it is '57;—'57, Léoville.' **1903** H. JAMES *Ambassadors* III. 73 Another degustation of the Léoville, another wipe of his mustache. **1966** H. YOXALL *Fashion of Life* xxv. 238 The Léovilles, it seems to me, are the characteristic wines of St Julien.

Lepcha (le·ptʃă), *sb.* and *a.* Also **Lapcha.** [Native name.] **A.** *sb.* A member of a Mongoloid people, native to Sikkim; the Tibeto-Burman language of this people. **B.** *adj.* Of or pertaining to this people or its language.

1819 F. HAMILTON *Acct. Kingdom Nepal* II. i. 118 The most eastern principality, in the present dominions of Gorkha, is that of the Lapchas, called Sikim. *Ibid.* 125 At this custom-house or mart is a Lapcha collector. **1839** *Jrnl. Asiatic Soc. of Bengal* VIII. 624 These neighbours of the hills are the Limboos, Kerantis, Lepchas, Murmis, and Bhotias. **1840** *Ibid.* IX. I. 393 Hill tribes,.. whose language, exhibiting a mere dialectic difference from the Lepcha, may be expressed in symbols not dissimilar. **1848** J. D. HOOKER in L. Huxley *Life J. D. Hooker* (1918) I. xiii. 256 The Lepchas or mountaineers of Sikkim I like extremely. **1862** H. DE SCHLAGINTWEIT et al. *Results Sci. Mission India & High Asia* II. 268, I had with me natives from a great variety of tribes, Górkhas, Kerántis, and Neváris from Nepál, and Límbus, Lépchas, and Bhútias from Síkkim. **1877** E. L. BRANDRETH in *Jrnl. R. Asiatic Soc.* X. I. 10 These determinatives are generally affixed in the languages of Nepál and in the Dhimal language; prefixed in the Lepcha language, [etc.]. *Ibid.* 15 In Lepcha, also, not only the adjective, but the demonstrative pronoun, as in Tibetan, follows the substantive. **1912** A. GORDON *Life A. H. Charteris* xiv. 339 The aboriginal Lepchas, a gentle race, are devil worshippers. **1940** F. S. CHAPMAN *Helvellyn to Himalaya* iv. 70 We wandered downhill to Dikchu...Most of the people here were sallow-faced Lepchas. **1948** D. DIRINGER *Alphabet* vi. 356 The Lepcha character seems to have been invented or revised by the Sikkim raja. **1965** *Evening Standard* 17 Sept. 6/2 The Sikkimese are Buddhists, and ethnically consist of Bhutias from neighbouring Bhutan; of Tibetans and of the neighbouring Lepchas. **1973** *Times* 12 Apr. 8/6 The Bhutias asserted themselves over the Lepchas, the aboriginal inhabitants, with whom they are now more or less integrated.

leper, *sb.*[2] and *a.* Add: Now often avoided in medical use because of its connotations. (Further examples of the *sb.*)

1948 R. G. COCHRANE in *Leprosy Rev.* XIX. 39, I feel that it is necessary for me to launch a protest at the constant use of the word 'leper' in medical literature. *Ibid.*, The Conference of the Leonard Wood Memorial held in Manila in 1931 recommended that the word 'leper' should not be used, but I fear this recommendation is completely ignored even by those leprologists who attended the conference. **1964** *Observer* 8 Nov. 33/5 To use the word 'leper' as a synonym for 'untouchable' is to perpetuate the ignorance and prejudice of former days. **1970** *Daily Tel.* 11 May 12/7, I regret to see that your columns have again been defaced twice by the word 'leper'... Its use has been banned by such..bodies as the World Health Organisation and the International Leprosy Association. **1970** *Ibid.* 21 May 18 Those most entitled to say whether they suffer more from the disease or from the stigma attached to the word 'leper' are the patients themselves. The campaign against the word was started by patients in the famous American leprosarium in Carville. **1974** *Ibid.* 30 Jan. 16 Like some friendly leper, Mr Mick McGahey, the Communist vice-president of the National Union of Mineworkers, moves among Labour politicians spreading terrified unease with every jovial slap on the back. **1974** *Times Lit. Suppl.* 15 Mar. 263/4 In 1941 the reappearance of leprosy led to the prohibition of the movement of Aborigines below the 20th parallel—the 'leper line'. **1975** *Daily Tel.* 11 Apr. 3/1 He decided to dedicate his life to the Indian people, and for many years was in charge of 13 hospitals, two for lepers.

lepido-. lepidocrocite, substitute for def.: a red to reddish-brown hydroxide of iron, FeO(OH), which is found as scaly or fibrous orthorhombic dipyramidal crystals, often in association with goethite, $HFeO_2$ (with which it was formerly identified); (add further examples); **lepidotri·chium** [Gk. θρίξ, τριχ- hair], (usu. in pl. **lepidotri·chia**) in most teleost fishes, the bony rays supporting the outer part of the fins.

1919 *Amer. Jrnl. Sci.* XLVII. 322 Optical studies of the reddish, scaly crystals called rubinglimmer and lepidocrocite, led Lacroix to propose that they be classed together as lepidocrocite and separated from goethite, with which they had formerly been identified. **1944** C. PALACHE et al. *Dana's Syst. Min.* (ed. 7) I. 644 The name goethite properly belongs to the species here described, since the name was originally given by Lenz to the material from Eiserfeld now known to be lepidocrocite. Goethite, however, is in general use to designate the compound $HFeO_2$. **1951** *Amer. Mineralogist* XXXVI. 31 Lepidocrocite has the hydrogen atom in a discrete OH group... Hence the decomposition of lepidocrocite occurs at a lower temperature than goethite. **1967** *New Scientist* 13 July 92/3 Professor Lowenstam has discovered that some chitons have a second iron mineral in their teeth—lepidocrocite. **1971** R. J. GETTENS *Two Early Chinese Bronze Weapons* iv. 23 The iron blade which served as the cutting edge has been drastically altered by corrosion... X-ray powder diffraction analysis of samples of rust showed that it consists of two hydrated iron oxides, goethite..and lepidocrocite. **1904** E. S. GOODRICH in *Q. Jrnl. Microsc. Sci.* XLVII. 472 In the majority of Teleostean fish the median and paired fins are covered with a smooth scaleless skin, below which lie the dermal fin-rays. For reasons which will appear later, I propose to call these rays the lepidotrichia. **1963** P. H. GREENWOOD *Norman's Hist. Fishes* (ed. 2) iii. 29 The outer part of the fin [of sturgeons] is supported not by horny rays but by bony fin rays, actually modified scales, called lepidotrichia.

lepidopteran, *a.* Add: (Later examples.) Also as *sb.*

1923 J. S. HUXLEY *Ess. Biologist* ii. 96 It is not only the burnt child who dreads the fire (although a study of moths and candles will convince us that 'Lepidopteran' cannot be substituted as subject of the proverb). **1971** *Nature* 13 Aug. 484/1 Similar responses of hymenopteran parasites to the mandibular gland secretions of their lepidopteran hosts may occur in other species. **1973** *Ibid.* 3 Aug. 253/1 One abundant lepidopteran is the southern armyworm, *Prodenia eridania*, a polyphagous species. **1973** PROCTOR & YEO *Pollination of Flowers* iv. 96 The lepidopteran proboscis is very differently constructed from that of the Diptera.

lepidopterist. (Later examples.)

1971 *Daily Tel.* (Colour Suppl.) 8 Jan. 21/2 If she is an amateur lepidopterist..the candids should obviously show her chasing butterflies. **1975** *Sci. Amer.* Jan. 92/3 The first person in the area who is known to have captured a dark-colored peppered moth was an active lepidopterist, R. S. Edleston, who obtained a specimen in 1849.

lepidopterology (le:pidǫptĕrǫ·lǒdʒi). [f. LEPIDOPTERA *sb. pl.* + -OLOGY.] The branch of entomology which deals with the study of Lepidoptera. Hence **le:pidoptero·logist; le:pidopterolo·gical** *a.*

1899 *Proc. 4th Internat. Congress Zool. 1898* 232 An important phenomenon that my studies in Lepidopterology have revealed. *Ibid.*, England and English-speaking America possess the greatest number of Lepidopterologists. *Ibid.* 337 Matters other than Lepidopterological must be settled by a general committee of Zoologists. **1921** (*title*) Bulletin of the Hill Museum: a magazine of lepidopterology. **1967** V. NABOKOV *Speak, Memory* (ed. 2) vi. 123 Since the middle of the century, Continental lepidopterology had been..a simple and stable affair. *Ibid.* 129 Among the very few lepidopterological images in English poetry, my favorite is Browning's.

leporicide. Add: **2.** [-CIDE 2.] The killing of hares. *nonce-wd.*

1914 W. DE MORGAN *When Ghost meets Ghost* I. xviii. 200, I..went..dreading that I should find Achilles [a dog] awaiting applause for an achievement in—in leporicide, I suppose.

lepospondyl (lepǫspǫ·ndil), *sb.* and *a.* [f. mod.L. name of suborder *Lepospondyli* (K. A. Zittel *Handbuch der Palæontologie* (1887–90) I Abth. III. 348), f. Gr. λέπος husk + σπονδύλος vertebra.] An extinct amphibian belonging to the suborder Lepospondyli, distinguished by vertebrae shaped like hourglasses; of or pertaining to an amphibian of this type. Also **lepospo·ndylous** *a.*

1901 H. GADOW in *Cambr. Nat. Hist.* VIII. iv. 79 The vertebræ [of Stegocephali] exhibit three types... 1. Lepospondylous and pseudocentrous.—The vertebra consists of a thin shell of bone surrounding the chorda dorsalis. **1902** C. R. EASTMAN tr. *Zittel's Text-bk. Palaeontol.* II. 118 (*caption*) Lepospondylous vertebrae of *Hylonomus.* **1933** A. S. ROMER *Vertebr. Paleontol.* v. 112 In the lepospondyls the vertebral centrum was a single hollow spool-shaped ossification. *Ibid.*, The divergence of the various lepospondyl groups must have taken place at an extremely early date. **1958** C. K. WEICHERT *Anat. Chordates* (ed. 2) xix. 850 Stegocephalia... Fossil forms: labyrinthodonts, lepospondyls, and phyllospondyls, varying primarily in structure of vertebral column. **1971** E. C. OLSON *Vertebr. Paleozool.* vii. 296 (*caption*) A lepospondyl (microsaur) skull. *Ibid.* 297 Like the other lepospondyls they [*sc.* *Lysorophus* and its relatives] are highly specialized.

lepper (le·pəɹ). A local variant of LEAPER, freq. of horses in hunting parlance.

1907 J. M. SYNGE *Playboy of Western World* III. 66 There you are! Good jumper! Grand lepper. **1920** *Baily's Mag.* Jan. 37/2 There are plenty of 'leppers' at Newmarket this season. **1931** A. J. CRONIN *Hatter's Castle* I. ii. 41 We'll kick off on the leppers. All aboard for the Donegal Hunt. **1937** R. WESTERBY *Wide Boys Never Work* 173 'I put a couple of nicker on Tenderloin. He's a good lepper at that.'.. 'Got all the jargon, haven't you? "Good lepper"!—strewth!' **1948** MENCKEN *Amer. Lang.* Suppl. II. 362 Among American horse fanciers a jumping horse is called a *lepper.*

leprolin (le·prolin). *Med.* [f. LEPRO(SY + -*lin*, after TUBERCULIN.] = *LEPROMIN.

1904 E. R. ROST in *Indian Med. Gaz.* XXXIX. 168/2 The next thing that was attempted was the manufacture of a leprolin on the lines of the manufacture of tuberculin. **1934** *Brit. Med. Jrnl.* 21 Apr. 703/2 The typical reaction to leprolin..when applied to healthy persons in an area free from endemic leprosy, differs from the intracutaneous tuberculin reaction in remaining for some days negative or doubtful. **1947** R. G. COCHRANE *Pract. Textbk. Leprosy* vii. 64 Neural (N) Type [of Leprosy]... These cases..are of relatively good prognosis as regards life.. and usually react positively to leprolin. [*Note*] Now termed lepromin. **1971** *Internat. Jrnl. Leprosy* XXXIX. 719/2 We deemed it worthwhile to determine the capacity of lymphocytes from leprosy patients to produce lymphotoxin in the presence of PHA and leprolin.

leprologist. Delete *rare* and add later examples.

1948 [see *LEPER *sb.*[2]]. **1950** G. W. MCCOY in R. L. Pullen *Communicable Dis.* xlii. 631 Promin..has been used in recent years by a group of leprologists working..at Carville, Louisiana. **1961** G. GREENE *Burnt-Out Case* v. i. 156 There is an old Danish doctor..who became a leprologist. **1970** *Daily Tel.* 21 May 18 Dr Browne is one of the leading leprologists in the world.

leproma. Add: Pl. **lepromas, lepromata.** (Earlier and later examples.)

1895 N. WALKER tr. *Hansen & Looft's Leprosy* ii. 5 The leprous nodes [of nodular Leprosy] or nodular Lepromata are of different size and colour; their consistence is at first firm and hard... Their form is usually semi-spherical, but they are often oblong. **1947** R. G. COCHRANE *Pract. Textbk. Leprosy* viii. 81 We are convinced..that the majority of lepromas commence from pre-lepromatous macules..; some, however, develop from the simple macular lesions. **1970** G. J. HILL *Leprosy in Five Young Men* iv. 103 The mixture [*sc.* lepromin] is essentially a sterile emulsion of lepromas—that is, nodules excised from patients with lepromatous leprosy.

lepromatous *a.* (further examples); also, characterized by or exhibiting lepromas: used *spec.* to designate one of the two principal forms of leprosy (see quot. 1938).

1938 *Internat. Jrnl. Leprosy* VI. 390 [Report of the Subcommittee on Classification of the First International Congress on Leprosy.] Objections have repeatedly been raised to both of the current names of the two types [of leprosy] (i.e., 'neural' and 'cutaneous')... It is the opinion of the committee... (*b*) That because 'cutaneous' has proved particularly confusing its use should be discontinued, and replaced by the term 'lepromatous'. *Ibid.*, Lepromatous (L) type.—All cases of the 'malignant' form of leprosy, relatively nonresistant and of poor prognosis, usually negative to lepromin, exhibiting lepromatous lesions of the skin and of other organs, especially the nerve trunks. **1962** *Lancet* 26 May 1116/2 If the altered tissue response could be maintained by repeated B.C.G. vaccination, this might prove a beneficial adjunct to chemotherapy in lepromatous leprosy. **1971** *Nature* 7 May 48/1 Leprosy, caused by *Mycobacterium leprae*, has two clinicopathological forms: lepromatous, associated with impaired delayed hypersensitivity, and tuberculoid, with intact cutaneous reactivity.

lepromin (le·promin). *Med.* Also **-ine.** [a. G. *lepromin* (P. Bargehr 1927, in *Zeitschr. f. Immunitätsf. und exper. Ther.* XLIX. 347): see LEPROMA and -IN[1].] A boiled saline extract of lepromatous tissue. So **lepromin test,** a test involving intradermal injection of lepromin and examination for a nodule at the site (see quot. 1951).

1932 *Monthly Bull. Philippine Health Service* XII. 300 The leprolin (lepromin) used by Mitsuda, Bargehr, de Langen, de Vogel, Mariani, Muir and Hayashi were prepared in different ways. **1940** ROGERS & MUIR *Leprosy* (ed. 2) 248 The lepromin test is thus of use in measuring the natural resistance of the patient to leprous infection. **1951** WHITBY & HYNES *Med. Bacteriol.* (ed. 5) xiv. 267 The lepromin test consists of the intradermal injection of a small quantity of the extract. The test is positive in milder types of leprosy and in many healthy contacts; it is negative in the more severe types of the disease which have a bad outlook. **1959** G. GREENE *Congo Jrnl.* in *In Search of a Character* (1961) 89 Lepromine used to determine the resistance of an undetermined patient. **1973** BRYCESON & PFALTZGRAFF *Leprosy for Students Med.* vi. 62 Infection with *M[ycobacterium] tuberculosis*, immunization with BCG or previous skin testing with lepromin may, but does not necessarily, induce lepromin positivity in a normal person.

lepropil (le·profil). [f. LEPRO(SY + -PHIL.] One who is attracted to sufferers from leprosy. So **lepropi·lia** [Gr. φιλία affection], such an attraction.

1959 G. GREENE *Congo Jrnl.* in *In Search of a Character* (1961) 24 Should one class Father Damien among the leprophils? **1961** —— *Burnt-Out Case* I. ii. 19 You know very well that leprophils exist... Schweitzer seems to attract them. They would rather wash the feet with their hair like the woman in the gospel than clean them with something more antiseptic. **1963** P. WEST *Mod. Novel* II. i. 97 Leprophilia is the extremist answer. **1964** P. FEENY *Fight against Leprosy* ix. 90 The most serious charge..is that he was a 'leprophil', that is, that he fell in love with leprosy... This disease does hold an inverted glamour for a handful of people. *Ibid.* 91 He [*sc.* Damien] rushed into his work on Molokai like a back-row forward rushing into a scrum. He saw suffering and ran to alleviate it... Leprophilia does not enter into it.

leprophobia (leprofōu·biă). Also **lepraphobia** (leprăfōu·biă). [f. LEPRO(SY + -PHOBIA; cf. LEPRA (*b*).] A morbid or insane fear of leprosy; *spec.* such a fear showing itself in the conviction of a person actually healthy that he is suffering from leprosy.

1894 GOULD *Dict. Med.* 670/1 *Leprophobia*, morbid or insane dread of leprosy. **1911** STEDMAN *Med. Dict.*, Lepraphobia. **1948** *Leprosy Rev.* XIX. 40 Euphemisms will not eradicate leprophobia. **1948** E. MUIR *Man. Leprosy* xiv. 98 Leprophobia may centre round any well-known symptom of leprosy. **1973** BRYCESON & PFALTZGRAFF *Leprosy for Students Med.* iv. 40 Do not treat for leprosy unless the diagnosis is established. Nothing is harder to cure than leprophobia.

leprosarium (leprosē°·riŏm). Pl. **leprosaria.** [f. L. *lepros(us* leprous + ARIUM.] A hospital for sufferers from leprosy.

1846 DUNGLISON *Dict. Med. Sci.* (ed. 6) 430/1 An hospital for the reception of the leprous, *Leprosarium.* **1927** *Lancet* 23 July 212/2 (*heading*) The leprosarium at Makogai. **1935** *Nature* 4 May 757/2 A leprosarium being provided at Darwin. **1938** *Internat. Jrnl. Leprosy* VI. 399 The services of an ophthalmologist, a rhino-laryngologist and a dentist should..be made available in all leprosaria. **1966** *New Statesman* 15 Apr. 525/3 (Advt.), We will channel your gifts... *Against disease.* To hospitals, clinics, leprosaria. **1970** [see *LEPER *sb.*² and *a.*].

leprosery, leproserie (leprǫ·səri). [ad. F. *léproserie* (also used) or Sp. *leprosería.*] A leper-house or -colony.

1884 *N.Y. Med. Jrnl.* 6 Sept. 275/2 In many parts of the country [*sc.* Brazil] *léproseries* have been established outside the city walls, to which are consigned all lepers excepting those of the very wealthiest families. **1891** J. L. ALLEN in *Century Mag.* Feb. 592 Mother Marianne would herself have written, but she was called away to the leprosery. **1897** *Dict. Nat. Biogr.* XLIX. 218/1 He founded the leprosery of St. Thomas the Martyr. **1961** G. GREENE *Burnt-Out Case* I. ii. 13 There was a rule that the leproserie should take contagious cases only.

leptazol (le·ptăzǫl). *Pharm.* [f. ANA)LEPT(IC *a.* and *sb.* + AZ(O- + -OL.] A white, crystalline, bicyclic compound, $C_6H_{10}N_4$, which stimulates the respiratory and motor centres, is used as an analeptic, especially after poisoning by narcotics, and was formerly employed in convulsive psychotherapy.

1946 *Analyst* LXXI. 308 Leptazol (pentamethylenetetrazole) is commonly encountered in the form of a 10% w/v solution containing 0·25% of sodium phosphate. **1953** *Brit. Jrnl. Psychol.* XLIV. 58 After an intravenous injection of Leptazol, given during the course of electroencephalographic studies, he had a generalized convulsion. **1968** W. C. BOWMAN et al. *Textbk. Pharmacol.* xxii. 603 In animals it [*sc.* meprobamate] protects against convulsions which occur after strychnine, leptazol and electric-shock.

leptocaul (le·ptokǫl), *sb.* and *a.* *Bot.* [f. LEPTO- + Gr. καυλός stem, stalk.] A tree having a relatively thin primary stem and branches; also *attrib.* or as *adj.* Hence **leptocau·lous** *a.*; **le·ptocauly** *sb.*, development of this type. Cf. *PACHYCAUL.

1949 E. J. H. CORNER in *Ann. Bot.* XIII. 392 Leptocauly. I use this name to indicate the modern tree with relative[ly] slender primary axis and branches in contrast with the pachycaulous cycad. *Ibid.* 393 The leptocaul, or modern tree, thus comes to dominate in height and spread and distribution.., forming the modern forests. **1964** E. J. H. CORNER *Life of Plants* ix. 154 'Leptocaul' (with thin primary stem) denotes the slender willow construction. *Ibid.* 155 Leptocaul plants predominate in temperate and subtropical climates. *Ibid.* (*caption*) Difference between pachycauly and leptocauly as shown by sections of the young twigs of figs. *Ibid.* xv. 275 Some of the herbaceous forms relate, like the banana, directly to the pachycaulous, others to the leptocaulous. **1973** F. EHRENDORFER in V. H. Heywood *Taxonomy & Ecology* xvi. 319 There is evidence for repeated changes from little-branched monopodial and pachycaulous types..to strongly branched, sympodial, leptocaulous, growth-forms. **1974** *New Phytologist* LXXIII. 977 Leptocauls do not become pachycaul on islands.

leptocentric *a.*: see *LEPTOME.

leptocephalus (leptose·fălŏs). [mod.L. (L. T. Gronovius *Zoophylacium Gronovianum* (1763) I. 135), f. LEPTO- + Gr. κεφαλή head.] The transparent leaf-shaped larva of a fish of the order Anguilliformes, or eels, or one belonging to the genus *Elops* or *Albula.* The larva was first described as a distinct genus; see *leptocephalan, leptocephalid* (LEPTO-), MORRIS *sb.*³

1769 T. PENNANT *Brit. Zool.* III. 125 We communicated it [*sc.* the fish] to that accurate Ichthyologist Doctor Laurence Theodore Gronovius, of Leyden, who has described it in his *Zoophylacium,* under the title of *Leptocephalus,* or small head. **1880** A. C. L. G. GÜNTHER *Introd. Study Fishes* xiii. 179 No instance is more remarkable than that of the so-called *Leptocephali,* which for a long time have been regarded either as a distinct group of Fishes, or as the larval stages of various genera of fishes. **1931** J. R. NORMAN *Hist. Fishes* xvi. 336 The first British *Leptocephalus* was discovered in 1763 by one William Morris near Holyhead. **1971** *Nature* 2 Apr. 278/3 In January 1930, the Danish Dana Expedition captured a leptocephalus on the Agulhas Bank, south of Africa, which was 184 cm long.

leptokurtic (leptokɒ̄·ɹtik), *a.* *Statistics.* [f. LEPTO- + Gr. κυρτ-ός bulging + -IC.] Of a frequency distribution or its graphical representation: having greater kurtosis than the normal distribution.

1905 K. PEARSON in *Biometrika* IV. 173 Given two frequency distributions which have the same variability as measured by the standard deviation, they may be relatively more or less flat-topped than the normal curve. If more flat-topped I term them platykurtic, if less flat-topped leptokurtic, and if equally flat-topped mesokurtic. **1954** *Brit. Jrnl. Psychol.* XLV. 96 These curves were clearly leptokurtic as well as skewed. **1966** *New Scientist* 28 July 213/1 The leptokurtic or 'peaked' distributions that geodesists often meet with.

Hence **le:ptokurto·sis** [*KURTOSIS], the property of being leptokurtic.

1907 *Phil. Mag.* XIII. 372 There is..sensible skewness and sensible leptokurtosis. **1937** YULE & KENDALL *Introd. Theory Statistics* (ed. 11) ix. 165 By a slip leptokurtosis is there [*sc.* in *Biometrika* (1905) IV. 169 ff.] inadvertently applied to distributions for which $\beta_2 < 3$ [instead of $\beta_2 > 3$]. **1949** DARLINGTON & MATHER *Elem. Genetics* 401 *Kurtosis,* the departure of a symmetrical frequency distribution from the normal by excess (platykurtosis) or deficiency (leptokurtosis) in its shoulders as opposed to tails and centre.

leptology. Add: †**2.** Used for *LEPTONOLOGY. *Obs. rare*⁻¹.

1928 *Amer. Naturalist* LXII. 208 The underlying basis of crystal form is now known... In fact, a complete science of the fine structure of matter—leptology—is being built up as a result of modern physical research.

leptome (le·ptōᵘm). *Bot.* Also **leptom.** [ad. G. *leptom* (G. Haberlandt *Physiologische Pflanzenanatomie* (1884) vii. 229), f. Gr. λεπτ-ός thin + *-OME.] (See quot. 1965.) So **leptoce·ntric** *a.*, having the leptome surrounded by hadrome.

1898 H. C. PORTER tr. *Strasburger's Text-bk. Bot.* 102 The vascular portion is also termed the xylem or hadrome, and the sieve-tube portion the phloem or leptome. **1902** *Encycl. Brit.* XXV. 409/1 The tissue developed to meet the demands for conduction..is known as leptom. **1914** M. DRUMMOND tr. *Haberlandt's Physiol. Plant Anat.* vii. 347 The protein-conducting elements..form..the delicate leptome portion..of the strand... If the leptome has no fibrous sheath, it of course becomes synonymous with phloem. *Ibid.* 349 If the hadrome is céntral and the leptome peripheral, the bundle may be termed hadrocentric. .. The opposite or leptocentric..condition is exemplified by the leaf-trace bundles in many monocotyledonous rhizomes. **1940** *Chambers's Techn. Dict.* 495/2 *Leptocentric vascular bundle,* a concentric vascular bundle, in which a central strand of phloem is surrounded by xylem. **1965** K. ESAU *Plant Anat.* (ed. 2) xii. 272 The term *leptom* deserves special mention. It refers..to the soft-walled conducting part of the phloem.

leptomonad (leptǫ·mŏnæ̆d). *Zool.* [f. LEPTO- + MONAD.] **a.** = *LEPTOMONAS a. **b.** Any flagellate of the family Trypanosomidæ when existing in an elongated form with a flagellum emerging from the anterior end and arising near a kinetoplast at this end, which form is assumed only in the invertebrate host (and in culture); freq. *attrib.* or as *adj.*

1909 *Jrnl. R. Microsc. Soc.* 362 (*heading*) New leptomonad in muscids. **1931** R. R. KUDO *Handbk. Protozool.* xi. 145 Genus *Leishmania* Ross... In culture the organism develops into leptomonad forms. **1942** D. L. BELDING *Textbk. Clin. Parasitol.* xi. 143 The species of the genus *Crithidia* occur in the leishmanian, leptomonad and crithidial forms. *Ibid.,* The species of the *Phytomonas* pass through both leishmanian and leptomonad stages. **1961** M. HYNES *Med. Bacteriol.* (ed. 7) xxviii. 433 In man leishmaniæ appear as ovoid organisms with no flagella, but in insects and in culture they turn into flagellated leptomonads. **1962** J. D. SMYTH *Introd. Animal Parasitol.* v. 52 Genus *Leptomonas.* The leptomonads are exclusively parasites of invertebrates. *Ibid.* 64 The morphological changes [of leishmanias] within the sandfly gut are simple. In the mid gut they become leptomonad flagellates which multiply rapidly, spreading forwards to enter the oesophagus and pharynx by the fourth or fifth day. When introduced into the mammalian skin by a bite, the flagellates become rounded and assume the leishmanial form.

leptomonas (leptǫ·mŏnæ̆s). *Zool.* Pl. **leptomonas.** [mod.L., f. LEPTO- + *-MONAS.] **a.** Any flagellate of the genus *Leptomonas* (family Trypanosomidæ), which comprises species parasitic in invertebrates (esp. in the alimentary tract of insects) and existing in both leptomonad and leishmanial forms. **b.** = *LEPTOMONAD b; freq. *attrib.* or as *adj.*

[**1880–1** W. SAVILLE-KENT *Man. Infusoria* I. 243 Genus IV. *Leptomonas,* S.K... Animalcules free-swimming, persistent in shape. elongate fusiform or aciculate, bearing a single long undulating flagellum at the anterior extremity, no distinct oral aperture yet detected. The above generic title combined with the following specific one is here introduced for the reception of the monoflagellate animalcule figured and briefly described..by O. Bütschli.] **1926** C. M. WENYON *Protozool.* I. 312 They are the true trypanosomes typically seen in the blood of vertebrates or their invertebrate hosts: the leptomonas, crithidia, and herpetomonas, which have only an invertebrate host..; the leishmania, which..have both a vertebrate and an invertebrate host..; and the phytomonas, which have both an invertebrate and plant host. *Ibid.* 319 Flagellates of the genus *Leishmania* resemble those of the genus *Leptomonas* in having only the leishmania and leptomonas forms. **1931** BLACKLOCK & SOUTHWELL *Guide Human Parasitol.* ix. 71 In *Phlebotomus argentipes* which has been fed experimentally on infected persons, the leishmania develop in the gut into leptomonas. **1942** J. T. CULBERTSON *Med. Parasitol.* ix. 86 The organisms of the genus *Leishmania*..have in their development only two stages: a leishmania and a leptomonas. **1971** BECK & BARRETT-CONNOR *Med. Parasitol.* iv. 38/2 *Phlebotomus* flies, while feeding, regurgitate leptomonas forms..into the wound.

lepton² (le·ptǫn). *Nuclear Physics.* [f. Gr. λεπτ-ός small, slight, slender + *-ON¹.] Any of the sub-atomic particles that do not participate in the strong interaction and have a mass less than that of a nucleon and a half-integral spin (viz. the electron, the muon, and the neutrinos, and their anti-particles); in recent use extended to include any other (hypothetical) particle, of whatever mass, which does not participate in the strong interaction. (Orig. introduced in a wider sense: see quot. 1948.)

1948 L. ROSENFELD *Nucl. Forces* p. xvii, This can be achieved..by postulating a special kind of interaction between a nucleon and a pair of light particles, or leptons, consisting of an electron and a neutrino. [*Note*] Following a suggestion of Prof. C. Møller, I adopt—as a pendant to 'nucleon'—the denomination 'lepton' (from λεπτός, small, thin, delicate) to denote a particle of small mass, irrespective of its charge. **1959** *Sci. News.* LII. 101 A similar conservation law holds for leptons, a group of particles including neutrinos, electrons, and muons. **1964** *Cambr. Rev.* 24 Oct. 53/1 The..equality of the Fermi coupling constant for many different particles, baryons, mesons and leptons. **1967** *New Scientist* 8 June 578/1 These, the leptons, consist of the electron, the muon, two types of the massless, chargeless neutrino..and the anti-particles of these four. **1969** R. E. MARSHAK et al. *Theory Weak Interactions Particle Physics* i. 2 The fact that the weak interaction takes place at approximately the same level of strength between leptons.., between leptons and hadrons.., and between hadrons is a major distinguishing feature of the weak interaction. *Ibid.* 7 The names lepton, meson, and baryon were originally invented to denote light, intermediate mass, and heavy particles respectively, but we now know that the particles in each of the three classes share certain important properties in common; both the leptons and baryons are fermions..whereas the mesons are bosons. However, of greatest importance is the presence of the strong interaction for the meson and baryon classes but not for the lepton class. **1971** *New Scientist* 17 June 669/3 If heavy leptons..exist, Pontecorvo argues that they must have neutrinos also. **1973** *Sci. Amer.* Oct. 111/2 There may well exist a spectrum of leptons of increasing mass. The heavy leptons, if they exist, could be produced, like muons, in pairs in electron-positron annihilation reactions. *Ibid.* Nov. 36/2 The few particles that feel only weak or electromagnetic forces are classed as leptons. Electrons, muons and neutrinos are the only known leptons.

b. lepton number, a quantum number assigned to sub-atomic particles that is ± 1 for leptons and 0 for other particles and is conserved in all known interactions.

1958 *Physical Rev.* CX. 1483/2 Such selection rules.. consist of giving opposite lepton numbers to μ^- and e^-. **1967** L. M. LEDERMAN in E. H. S. Burhop *High Energy Physics* II. 342 Conservation of lepton number now is a matter of N_μ and N_e being separately conserved. **1973** *Sci. Amer.* Aug. 33/2 The preference of the neutrino for the electron and of the antineutrino for the positron has been included in the theory of weak interactions by assigning a..lepton number to the various weakly interacting particles. The convention is that the electron and the neutrino have a lepton number of + 1, whereas their antiparticles, the positron and the antineutrino, have a lepton number of − 1.

Hence **lepto·nic** *a.*, of, pertaining to, or involving leptons; *leptonic number* = **lepton number.*

1957 *Ann. Physics* II. 422 Particles labelled by leptonic charge and electrical charge permit a complete identification with the known leptons. **1958** *Proc. 2nd Internat. Conf. Peaceful Uses Atomic Energy* (United Nations) 53 The law of conservation of leptons..states that if a leptonic number is assigned to each particle then the sum of leptonic numbers must be conserved in all reactions. **1969** *Nature* 23 Aug. 780/2 The Λ hyperon has leptonic decays of a very similar kind to those of the Σ.

† **leptono·logy.** *Obs. rare.* [ad. G. *leptonologie* (F. Rinne 1916, in *Neues Jahrb. f. Min., Geol. u. Paläont.* II. 48), f. Gr. λεπτός (neut. λεπτόν) small, slight, slender: see -OLOGY.] (See quot.)

1917 *Jrnl. Chem. Soc.* CXII. II. 166 Alongside the science of stereochemistry is developing a stereophysics, and these, together with the study of crystal structure, form a new branch of science, which the author terms 'Feinbaulehre der Materie' (the study of the ultimate structure of matter), or Leptonology.

leptosomic (leptosōᵘ·mik), *a.* [f. Gr. λεπτό-ς fine, small, thin + σῶμ-α body: see -IC.] In Kretschmer's system, designating a type of physique characterized by leanness and tallness. Also **leptosoma·tic** *a.*, in same sense.

Orig. used by Kretschmer as a synonym of asthenic (*ASTHENIC *a.* b) in his tripartite classification of human physique into pyknic, athletic (*ATHLETIC *a.* 3), and asthenic types. Later he employed a bipartite classification in which only pyknic and leptosomic types were recognized.

1936 E. MILLER in W. J. H. Sprott tr. *Kretschmer's Physique & Character* (ed. 2) 272 Kolle..[discovered] the existence of many cases with leptosomic physique who suffered from cyclothymia in one form or another. **1937** Leptosomatic [see *ATHLETIC *a.* 3]. **1959** *Chambers's Encycl.* XI. 335/1 The two characteristic types of physique

were termed the asthenic, or leptosomatic, and the pyknic respectively. **1960** J. Comas *Man. Physical Anthropol.* vi. 341 E. Schreider believes that Kretschmer's classification can be reduced to two bipolar types, pyknic and leptosomic, with the inclusion in the latter group of the following varieties: the asthenic, the true leptosomic and the athletic. It should be mentioned that in later editions of his book, Kretschmer abandoned the third (athletic) type, and fell back upon a dichotomy consisting of the pyknic and asthenic (leptosomic).

Hence **le·ptosome** *sb.*, (a person with) a leptosomic physique; also as *adj.*, = *leptosomic *a.*

1931 *Times Lit. Suppl.* 10 Dec. 1004/2 The two main classes of white man, which he calls 'linear' and 'lateral' (corresponding to the 'pyknic' and 'leptosome'..of other anthropologists). **1935** *Nature* 9 Feb. 236/1 Of Kretschmer's three types, the leptosome corresponds to the Nordic, the athletic to the Dinaric and the pycnic to the Mediterranean and the Alpine. **1960** J. Comas *Man. Physical Anthropol.* vi. 341 According to the Italian biotypologists, the average or normal type is located between the leptosomes (slender type) and the pyknics (broad type). **1971** J. Z. Young *Introd. Study Man* xxxix. 573 Kretschmer tried to force everyone into one of three classes, pyknic (round and fat), leptosome (long and thin), and athletic (broad and strong). *Ibid.* 576 Leptosomes were introverted.

leptospira (leptospəiᵊ·ră). *Bacteriology.* Pl. **-spiræ.** [mod.L., f. Gr. λεπτό-ς fine, small + σπεῖρα coil.] Any bacterium of the genus *Leptospira* (family Treponemataceæ), structurally similar to the genus *Spirochæta* and consisting of a few species either free-living or parasitic, of which *L. icterohæmorrhagiæ* is parasitic in rats and the cause of Weil's disease in man.

[**1917** H. Noguchi in *Jrnl. Exper. Med.* XXV. 759 It calls for a new genus, and on account of its fine and minute windings, the name *Leptospira* is suggested.] **1918** *Ibid.* XXVII. 588 Figs. 1 to 4 are intended to show the appearance of the leptospiræ in an air-dried specimen. **1922** *Lancet* 18 Nov. 1058/1 Uhlenhuth and Zuelzer record a leptospira (*L. pseudoicterogenes*) in salt springs. **1966** Wright & Symmers *Systemic Path.* I. xxi. 629 Leptospirae are demonstrable in the blood or urine in only half the fatal cases [of Weil's disease].

Hence **leptospi·ral** *a.*, of, characteristic of, or caused by leptospiræ; *leptospiral jaundice*, infectious or spirochætal jaundice, Weil's disease.

1924 *Brit. Med. Jrnl.* 23 Feb. 314/1 In sections of the liver..leptospiral forms were abundant. **1935** *Ibid.* 24 Aug. 339/1 Men who have been exposed to risk of leptospiral infection. **1937** *Proc. R. Soc. Med.* XXX. 746 Dr. J. Smith has informed us in a letter that he investigated an outbreak of leptospiral jaundice in a fox farm near Aberdeen, and that three foxes died of the disease. **1960** *Guardian* 10 Nov. 9/4 Leptospiral jaundice (Weil's Disease)..is contracted from the urine of rats. **1973** *Times* 31 Oct. 14/2 Some leptospiral serotypes cause serious disease in Man.

leptospire (le·ptospəiᵊɹ). *Bacteriology.* [Anglicized form of *leptospira.] = *leptospira.

1957 R. S. Breed et al. *Bergey's Man. Determinative Bacteriol.* (ed. 7) 907 Pathogenic leptospires were first isolated from human cases of Weil's disease... Since that time [*sc.* 1915] other leptospires..have been recognized as causing disease in man and other animals. **1969** *New Scientist* 20 Feb. 414/2 The leptospiral structures, too, bud out from the surface of the leptospire itself.

leptospirosis (le:ptospəiᵊrōu·sis). *Med.* and *Vet. Sci.* [f. *leptospir(a + -osis.] Infection with, or a disease caused by, leptospiræ.

1926 Stedman *Med. Dict.* (ed. 9) 558/2 *Leptospirosis*, infection with some species of *Leptospira*. **1934** *Brit. Med. Jrnl.* 7 July 10/1 Weil's disease (spirochaetal jaundice, infective jaundice, leptospirosis) has been recognized in many different countries. **1961** *Times* 6 Dec. 14/6 The bulls..have been tested for tuberculosis, brucellosis, and leptospirosis. **1970** *Daily Tel.* 11 May 12/7 In one area the Medical Officer of Health has made notifiable seven tropical diseases—plague, cholera, malaria, yellow fever, leprosy, typhus, and also leptospirosis. **1973** *Massey Ferguson Rev.* (N.Z.) Mar.–Apr. 8/1 Leptospirosis in man and cattle is recognised as a serious rural problem in parts of New Zealand.

leptotene (le·ptotīn). *Cytology.* [ad. F. *leptotène* (H. von Winiwarter 1900, in *Arch. de Biol.* XVII. 55): see Lepto- and *-tene.] The first stage of the prophase of the first meiotic division, in which the chromosomes are apparent as fine slender threads. Also *attrib.* or as *adj.*

[**1900** *Jrnl. R. Microsc. Soc.* 654 The reticulum gives rise to a chromatic thread.., which at first fills the nuclear cavity (leptotænic stage).] **1912** *Jrnl. Exper. Zool.* XIII. 360 The pre-synaptic leptotene. *Ibid.* 362 Are the leptotene-threads of this period chromosomes? *Ibid.* 368 Figs. 73 *a* and 73 *b* show two early leptotene-nuclei of this species. **1925** E. B. Wilson *Cell* (ed. 3) vi. 541 In the case of animals.. the leptotene-spireme is not continuous but consists of separate segments. **1964** G. H. Haggis et al. *Introd. Molecular Biol.* vii. 197 The chromosomes at leptotene must each consist of two chromatids so closely apposed as to give the appearance of a single structure. **1970** Ambrose & Easty *Cell Biol.* x. 325 The cell nuclei at this stage contain chromosomes in the form of very fine single threads, hence the name leptotene, meaning 'slender ribbon'.

lerky (lə̄·ɹki). [dial., of unknown origin.] In the Nottinghamshire area, the local name of a children's game (see quot. 1902).

1902 *Eng. Dial. Dict.* III. 576/1 *Lerky*, a noisy game, played with any old tin; this being placed in a ring, while all except one hide themselves, then rush out if unobserved and kick the tin out of the ring. Somewhat similar to hide-and-seek. **1913** D. H. Lawrence *Sons & Lovers* I. iv. 75 Paul was towed round at the heels of Annie, sharing her game. She raced wildly at lerky with the other young wild-cats of the Bottoms. **1969** I. & P. Opie *Children's Games* iv. 167 The game seems to have been well known in city streets before the First World War... Other names: 'Ecky'..'Kick the Bucket'..'Lerky' (Nottinghamshire).

lerp. *Austral.* Substitute for def.: A sweet secretion, or the scales formed from it, produced by larvæ of jumping plant-lice of the family Psyllidæ on the leaves of eucalypts and other plants. Also *attrib.* (Add later examples.)

1907 W. W. Froggatt *Austral. Insects* 363 Their popular name of 'Lerp Insects' [comes] from the habit of the larvae of many species of forming 'lerp scales', shell-like protective coverings formed from exudations from the insects. **1945** K. C. McKeown *Austral. Insects* 104 The Psyllidae, or Lerp-insects, form an important group in Australia. *Ibid.* 106 In its immature stages the insect lives as a squat little larva or nymph beneath the lerp-scale. **1962** *Proc. Linn. Soc. New South Wales* LXXXVII. 283 The encyrtid parasites described in this paper form one of the lesser groups of parasites of lerp-forming psyllids on eucalypts. **1965** *Austral. Encycl.* V. 290/2 Lerp-insects, a large and common group of jumping plant-lice..which suggest miniature cicadas... Some of them give themselves, through sugary exudations, protective and often picturesque coverings known as lerp scales. *Ibid.* IV. 479/2 The lerp scales secreted by the larvae are often of beautiful design and characteristic of the species. **1970** T. E. Woodward et al. in *Insects of Australia* (Commonwealth Sci. & Industr. Res. Organization) xxvi. 418/2 Lerp formation has probably evolved because of the need to protect the nymphs from desiccation. *Ibid.* 419/1 Most species of *Glycaspis* and *Lasiopsylla* are lerp-builders, but some form large bubble-shaped galls with an orifice at the base plugged with the same waxy or sugary material as is used by other species to build lerps.

Les (lez), **Les.,** colloq. abbrev. of *Lesbian *a.* 2 and *sb.* Also **Lesie, Lessie, Lessy.** Cf. *lez, lezz.

1929 M. Lief *Hangover* 235 'Certainly,' responded the Les, 'where is she?' **1959** C. MacInnes *Absolute Beginners* 52 Jill is a Les. and, what is more, you may not believe this, but a Les. ponce. **1965** L. Meynell *Double Fault* i. viii. 71 These Lessies are touchy; they just can't stand it when the girl friend leaves them. **1968** L. Berg *Risinghill* 122 What is a 'Lesie'..? **1972** L. P. Davies *What did I do Tomorrow?* vi. 74 There's so much homo and lessie stuff knocking about these days. **1972** *New Society* 11 May 301/1, I reckon she's a les you know. **1973** J. Jones *Touch of Danger* xxxii. 188 They're all leses, those extra-girl types.

Lesbian, *a.* Add: **b.** Short for *Lesbian wine.*

1775 E. Barry *Observations Wines of Ancients* vi. 99 The best Greek Wines, the Chian, Lesbian, Coan, &c. were equally prepared in the same manner. **1824** A. Henderson *Hist. Anc. & Mod. Wines* i. viii. 123 The dessert-wines most commonly mentioned as in use among the Greeks are the Thasian and Lesbian. **1846** R. Ford *Gatherings from Spain* xiv. 163 Manzanilla..may be compared to the ancient Lesbian, which Horace quaffed so plentifully in the cool shade, and then described as never doing harm.

2. (Freq. with small initial.) [After the alleged practice of Sappho, the poetess of Lesbos; cf. Sapphic *a.* and *sb.*, Sapphism.] Of a woman: homosexual, characterized by a sexual interest in other women. Also, of or pertaining to homosexual relations between women. Also as *sb.*, a female homosexual.

1890 Billings *Med. Dict.* II. 47/1 *Lesbian love*, tribadism. **1892** C. G. Chaddock tr. *Krafft-Ebing's Psychopathia Sexualis* v. 429 We are indebted to Parent-Duchalet ..for interesting communications concerning Lesbian love. **1925** A. Huxley *Let.* 21 Apr. (1969) 246 After a third-rate provincial town, colonized by English sodomites and middle-aged Lesbians, which is, after all, what Florence is, a genuine metropolis will be lively. **1931** R. Campbell *Georgiad* i. 13 No Lesbian governess had got the start of him. **1933** H. S. Walpole *Vanessa* iv. 781 She disliked people to take it for granted that unless she was Lesbian she was uninteresting. **1936** C. Day Lewis *Friendly Tree* i. 23, I shall never write real poetry. Women never do, unless they're invalids or Lesbians or something. **1940** 'G. Orwell' *Inside Whale* 132 Gruff-voiced Lesbians in corduroy breeches..could walk along the streets without attracting a glance. **1947** E. Taylor *View of Harbour* x. 170 '*I* think I look like a Lesbian,' Beth said doubtfully. **1972** *Jrnl. Social Psychol.* LXXXVII. 52, 50 adult female respondents who would define themselves ..as being Lesbian or homosexual or both. **1973** [see *homosexual *a.*]. **1974** *Ms* July 118/1 Testimony from a group of bright articulate lesbians covering: lesbian sexuality, problems of lesbian mothers..and the lesbian lifestyle.

Hence **Le·sbianism**, female homosexuality.

1870 A. J. Munby *Diary* 2 May in D. Hudson *Munby* (1972) 283 Swinburne..expressed a horror of sodomy.. and an actual admiration of Lesbianism, being unable..to see that that is equally loathsome. **1895** A. Douglas *Let.* in H. M. Hyde *Trials Oscar Wilde* (1948) 360 Thus in England there are no laws against 'Lesbianism' or intercourse of an erotic character between women, and yet there are several women in London whose friendship with other women does carry a taint and a suspicion, simply because these women are obviously 'sapphic' in their loves. **1897** H. Ellis *Stud. Psychol. Sex* I. iv. 82 Casanova remarked that the women of Provence are especially inclined to Lesbianism. **1965** [see *homosexual *a.*]. **1971** C. Wolff *Love between Women* iii. 40 No theory has so far been evolved which deals exclusively with lesbianism.

lesbic (le·zbik), *a.* = *Lesbian *a.* 2.

1892 D. H. Tuke *Dict. Psychol. Med.* II. 865/2 For many years a whole literature of romance and plays has been occupied in the description of Lesbic love, to the great damage of girls and neuropathic women. **1922** Joyce *Ulysses* 205 Sons with mothers,.. lesbic sisters, loves that dare not speak their name.

lesbo, colloq. abbrev. of *Lesbian *sb.* Also **lesbie.**

1940 J. O'Hara *Pal Joey* 175, I am all set to be m.c. in a crib where the Lesbos even come and watch the dress rehearsals. **1969** C. Himes *Blind Man with Pistol* xiii. 145 'One was a man; a good-looking man at that.' 'Man my ass, they were lesbos.' **1970** S. Ellin *Man from Nowhere* liv. 271, I don't dig Lesbies.

leschenaultia (leʃĕnǭu·tiă). Also **lechenaultia.** [mod.L. (R. Brown *Floræ Novæ Hollandiæ* (1810) 581), f. the name of L. T. *Leschenault* de la Tour (1773–1826), French botanist and traveller + -ia[1].] A herb or evergreen shrub of the Australian genus so called, belonging to the family Goodeniaceæ and bearing red, blue, white, or yellow flowers.

1825 *Curtis's Bot. Mag.* LII. 2600 (*heading*) Handsome Lechenaultia. **1916** L. H. Bailey *Stand. Cycl. Hort.* IV. 1844/2 The leschenaultias require special care in watering. **1955** A. Ross *Australia 55* 44 Thick clusters of blue and red leschenaultia. **1966** *Times* 11 Nov. (W. Austral. Suppl.) p. iv/2 The exquisite sky-blue leschenaultia, fragile as gossamer, shows its versatility by appearing, in different regions, in scarlet, crimson, blood-red, yellow, orange and green-blue. **1967** A. M. Blombery *Guide Native Austral. Plants* 279 It [*sc.* the genus] is probably best known by the Blue Lechenaultia of W[estern] A[ustralia]. **1972** *Southerly* XXXII. 18 The coffin draped in scarlet with a single bunch of blue leschenaultia, gathered by her friends in the hills.

Lesch-Nyhan (leʃ,nəi·hăn). *Med.* The names of Michael *Lesch* and William L. *Nyhan* (b. 1926), U.S. physicians, used with reference to a rare hereditary syndrome they described in 1964 which affects young boys (usu. causing early death) and is marked by compulsive self-mutilation of the head and hands, esp. the lips, together with mental retardation and muscular movements of choreiform and athetoid character.

1966 Reed & Fish in *Arch. Dermatol.* XCIV. 195/2 Indications are that this syndrome is probably sex-linked. .. Since Lesch and Nyhan first described the signs and symptoms as an entity, the condition should be called the Lesch-Nyhan syndrome. **1969** *Sci. News Let.* 11 Oct. 327 Skin cells from patients with a genetic defect known as the Lesch–Nyhan syndrome lack an enzyme essential for incorporation of purine bases into new nucleic acids. **1975** *Amer. Jrnl. Human Genetics* XXVII. 219 The mothers of Lesch–Nyhan cases will be either heterozygous (+/−) or homozygous normal (+/+). In the latter case the Lesch–Nyhan patient would have received a complete mutation from his mother.

Lesghian (le·zgiăn), *sb.* and *a.* Also **Lesghi(e), Lesghien, Lesgian, Lezg(h)ian, Lezgin.** [ad. Russ. *Lezgin.*] **A.** *sb.* A member of a tribe of the north-eastern Caucasus; also (in earlier quots.), one of a mountain people of Daghestan. Also, the language of these people. **B.** *adj.* Of or pertaining to these people. Also **Le·sg(h)ic** *a.*

1854 Max Müller *Suggestions in Learning Lang. Seat of War in East* 116 *Lesghic Branch.* Lesghistan, or the country of the Lesghi, also called Daghestan..lies between the rivers Koisu, Alazani, and the Caspian Sea. The Lesghi or Leski..may..be the same as the 'Legae' mentioned by Strabo. *Ibid.* 117 The Lesghians are Mahometans. **1875** C. Heneage tr. *M. von Thielmann's Journey Caucasus* I. iv. 280 The name Lesghie, used by the Russians in a general sense, and especially applicable to the inhabitants of Southern Daghestan, does not convey to the latter either the idea of a population or even of a single tribe. **1878** [see Finnic *a.*]. **1879** *Trans. Philol. Soc.* 1877–79 602 Here..*Lesghian* must be struck out, since it denotes no particular tribe or people. **1921** *19th Cent.* May 871 The bon-bons of the new faith were cast indiscriminately among Circassians,..Lesghiens..and Negroes. **1939** L. H. Gray *Foundations of Lang.* xii. 376 This alleged family has four sub-groups, characterised respectively by a sibilant.., a spirant plus a sibilant.., a spirant (e.g. in..Chechen, Avar, Lesghian..) and a spirant plus a sonant. **1959** B. Geiger et al. *Peoples & Lang. Caucasus* 38 Lezgian..has the status of a literary language in the Dagestan ASSR. **1968** *Encycl. Brit.* XIII. 1012/2 The Lezgian group of languages includes..the Agul, Tabasaran, Rutul, Tsakhur, Budukh and Dzhek languages.

Lesie, var. *Les.

lespedeza (lespedī·ză). [mod.L. (A. Michaux *Flora Boreali-Americana* (1803) II. 70), blunderingly (by a misreading of the surname) f. the name of V. M. de *Céspedez* (fl. 1785), Spanish governor of East Florida.] A herb or shrub of the genus so called, belonging to the family Leguminosæ, native to North America, Asia, or Australia, and bearing clusters of white, pink, or purple flowers; esp. a plant of this kind used in the southern United States as a hay or fodder crop; also called *bush clover*.

1891 *Garden & Forest* 25 Feb. 88/2 A tall, bushy Lespedeza (*L. Prainii*) is a highly ornamental shrub some ten feet high, bearing large panicles of fine purple-blue flowers. **1900** L. H. Bailey *Cycl. Amer. Hort.* II. 903/1 There are a number of native Lespedezas. **1929** W. Faulkner *Sartoris* (1932) 5, I expect every spring to find corn or lespedeza coming up in the hyacinth beds. **1943** J. S. Huxley *TVA* vi. 45 Lespedeza and other legumes.. bind soil and provide nitrates. **1965** Ripper & George *Cotton Pests Sudan* i. 6 Lespedezas, which come from China and Korea, are now widely used in the South East of the U.S.A. to renew worn out soil. **1975** *Country Life* 13 Feb. 373/1 In the crops of shot birds we found..the seeds of beggar weed, wild peas and lespedeza.

less, *a.* (*sb.*), *adv.*, and *conj.* Add: **A.** *adj.* **1. c.** (Later examples.) Now more frequently found but still regarded as incorrect.

1862 M. D. Colt *Went to Kansas* 84, I may see them all doing with still less comforts. **1873** *Nature* 1 May 15/2 The determination of position in the given manifoldness is reduced to a determination of quantity and to a determination of position in a manifoldness of less dimensions. **1874** *Rep. Brit. Assoc. Adv. Sci. 1873* 53 To return to the history of logarithmic tables to a less number of figures. **1904** *Amer. Jrnl. Philol.* XXV. 234 There might have been less barbed wire, less flaring flowers. **1971** *Guardian* 16 Dec. 16/1 The 47-page prospectus..shows that there are less restrictions..than is generally supposed. **1972** 'E. Lathen' *Murder without Icing* (1973) ii. 21 You've seen less hockey games than my wife.

4. (Examples of 'minus' sense.)

1869 *Bradshaw's Railway Manual* XXI. 304 Dividends were declared at the rate of 5 per cent. per annum in the preference shares, amounting, less income tax, to 1,218 *l.* **1910** *Chambers's Jrnl.* Oct. 661/1 If I borrow £100..I pay my interest, less tax. **1911** *Rep. Labour & Social Conditions Germany* (Tariff Reform League) III. vi–vii. 20 All meat is sold less the bone. **1930** *Times* 25 Mar. 24/2 A full year's dividend on the Preference Shares, less tax, absorbing £16,800. **1972** *Times* 2 Sept. 18/8 Cost of paint ..Less VAT input tax..£500.

7. b. (Later examples.)

1652 T. Gataker *Antinomianism* 5 In those words of mine nothing les was intended, then this Autor would.. enforce them to speak. **1836** C. Fox *Jrnl.* 23 Sept. (1972) 32 'A gentleman' was announced, who proved to be nothing less than Professor Sedgwick! **1856** Dickens *Dorrit* (1857) II. i. xxiii. 79 You couldn't do it when your Uncle George was living; much less when he's dead. **1863** J. A. Froude *Hist. Eng.* (ed. 3) II. xi. 298 But Elizabeth meant nothing less than to recall Sidney. **1865** *Daily Tel.* 2 Dec. 7/1 We may rest satisfied that the dispute will end in nothing less than a battle royal. *c* **1874** D. Boucicault in M. R. Booth *Eng. Plays of 19th Cent.* (1969) II. 174 You are not mistress in your own house, much less lady of the manor. **1895** *Bookman* Oct. 22/2 His policy became nothing less than a series of gigantic blunders.

C. *conj.* Delete † *Obs.* and read *Obs.* exc. *U.S. dial.* and *colloq.*

When written *'less* it represents a contracted form of *unless.*

1892 Kipling *Many Inventions* (1893) 41 'Less you want your toes trod off, you'd better get back. **1900** 'Flynt' & Walton *Powers that Prey* 62 If any of 'em knows us they'll beef dead sure, 'less we square 'em. **1929** W. Faulkner *Sound & Fury* 22 They wont know you got wet... Less me and Jason tells. **1973** *Black World* Apr. 61 Don't no broad be puttin' me down, less I go upside her head. **1973** J. Drummond *Bang! Bang! you're Dead!* xxxvii. 129 You gonna be like Jinx Janeiro soon, less you listen to me.

lessen (le·s'n), *conj. U.S. dial.* Also less'n. Unless. Cf. Less *conj.* (in Dict. and Suppl.).

1881 J. C. Harris *Nights with Uncle Remus* (1884) xix. 94 But less'n we gits dat Moon out er de pon', dey aint no fish kin be ketch. **1912** Mulford & Clay *Buck Peters* (1921) xxiii. 207 'Ain't that yore pinto?' queried Slick. 'Less'n I'm blind,' agreed the cow-punch. **1929** W. Faulkner *Sound & Fury* 35 And they aint going to be no luck in saying that name, lessen you going to set up with him while he cries. **1938** M. K. Rawlings *Yearling* iii. 23 None o' the dogs bayed him, Pa. Lessen I didn't hear, for sleepin'. **1970** H. Waugh *Finish me Off* (1971) 133 He's not bothering with girls less'n they're going to do him some good.

lesser, *a.* and *adv.* Add: **3.** *attrib.*, as *lesser breed*, applied allusively after Kipling (*Recessional*: see quot. 1897) to persons of inferior status; *lesser light*, applied allusively (after Gen. i. 16 'the greater light to rule the day, and the lesser light to rule the night') to a person of less eminence or importance.

1897 Kipling *Recessional* in *Times* 17 July 13/6 Such boasting as the Gentiles use Or lesser breeds without the Law. **1955** C. Pearl *Girl with Swansdown Seat* iv. 135 Wilfrid Scawen Blunt..was an English gentleman who shamed his class by championing the lesser breeds in Egypt and India. **1963** Brown & Foote *Early Eng. & Norse Studies* 39 The next stanza, which begins with the hope that the text will not be miswritten nor mismetred by scribes and lesser breeds without the law of final *-e.* **1971** A. Price *Alamut Ambush* ix. 113 The authentic supercilious voice of England—the lesser breeds shall not show unfitting qualities of sportsmanship towards each other! **1973** 'H. Howard' *Highway to Murder* vii. 82 You and your kind think you can order the lesser breeds around. **1608** Shakes. *Pericles* ii. iii. 41 None that beheld him, but like lesser lights, Did vaile their Crownes to his supremacie. **1873** R. Browning *Red Cott. Nt.-Cap* i. 34 Pilgrimage, Concourse, procession with, to head the host, Cardinal Mirecourt, quenching lesser lights. **1893** G. Moore *Mod. Painting* 45 In the seventeenth century were Poussin and Claude; in the eighteenth Watteau, Boucher, Chardin, and many lesser lights. **1906** Galsworthy *Man of Property* iii. v. 328 His interest was soon diverted from these lesser lights of justice by the entrance of Waterbuck, Q.C. **1943** K. Tennant *Ride on Stranger* xiii. 152 One of the lesser lights of the announcers' staff had his face slapped by a young lady. **1964** *Ann. Reg. 1963* 22 At all events the most senior Ministers..turned up on Saturday 27 April, and the lesser lights on the Sunday morning. **1974** *Times* 21 Jan. 14/7 His deepest affection was reserved for the Romantics—Coleridge, Shelley, Keats, and the lesser lights.

Lessie, var. *Les.

lessive. (Earlier example.)

a **1790** B. Franklin *Works* (1836) II. 104 One [way] is, to soak it [*sc.* the grain] all night in a *lessive* or lye.

lessness. (Further examples.)

1868 A. Sandeman *Pelicotetics* 188 The Multiple Test of the greaterness and lessness of the ratio. **1961** R. B. Long *Sentence & its Parts* iv. 99 Sometimes negation is semantically specialized to convey meanings of 'lessness', as in *I don't have a dime.* **1970** S. Beckett (*title*) Lessness.

lesson, *sb.* Add: **4. b.** *to read* (one) *a lesson*: see Read *v.* 11 b.

Lessy, var. *Les.

leste (le·ste). [a. Pg. *leste* east wind.] (See quot. 1967.)

1864 *Chambers's Encycl.* VI. 248/2 Sometimes a waft of the *lesté*, or east wind, raises it [*sc.* the temperature in Madeira] to 90°. **1911** *Encycl. Brit.* XVI. 499/2 The Leste is commonly accompanied by clouds of fine red sand. **1967** R. W. Fairbridge *Encycl. Atmospheric Sci.* 1155 *Leste.* This is a hot, dry, easterly wind occasionally encountered in Madeira and the Canary Islands at any season except in summer. Essentially it is an extension of the harmattan that blows across the Sahara and is accordingly hot and dry... It is similar to the sirocco of the Mediterranean and the leveche of Spain.

let, *v.*[1] Add: **12. e.** *let 'em all come*: a catch-phr. denoting cheerful defiance.

1903 *To-Day* 19 Aug. 99/1 'Let 'em all come,' said Billy Frew, cheerfully. **1909** J. R. Ware *Passing Eng.* 167/2 *Let 'em all come..*, cheery defiance. Outcome of the plucky way in which the British, in the first days of the new year, accepted the message of congratulation by the Emperor of Germany to President Kruger on the repulse of the Jameson raid.

14. a. Also (*U.S. colloq.*) in irregular phr. *let's you and me* (or *you and I*, or *us*): let us (do something).

1929 W. Faulkner *Sartoris* iii. 186 Let's you and I take 'em on for a set. **1950** J. D. Macdonald *Brass Cupcake* vi. 55 Let's you and me duck out of here. **1953** M. Dickens *No More Meadows* ii. 123 Let's you and me have a drink together first. **1961** R. B. Long *Sentence & its Parts* i. 23 In informal *let's us go too* strongly stressed *us* is an appositive which actually repeats its principal, the *us* of *let's.* **1964** Mrs. L. B. Johnson *White House Diary* 24 Mar. (1970) i. 101 Lady Bird, after this is over, let's you and me go out and have a drink.

18. e. (Earlier and later examples.) Also with following *adj.*

1812 M. Edgeworth *Absentee* in *Tales Fashionable Life* VI. xiii. 269, I didn't hide, nor wouldn't from any man living, *let alone* any woman. **1961** R. B. Long *Sentence & its Parts* xi. 264 The use of adjectives as complements of transitive verbs is quite limited... She isn't even pretty, let alone beautiful. **1966** *Listener* 20 Oct. 569/3, I cannot say that I ever felt anything like twice as old (let alone twice as wise) as my Polish friends. **1974** L. Deighton *Spy Story* ix. 100 He'd never be considered for a high security clearance, let alone a job in the Service.

20*. let drive (see Drive *v.* 11).

22. let go. c. Phr. *let it go at that* (see *go *v.* B. 21 e).

e. (Further examples.) *to let oneself* (or *it*) *go*: (*b*) to neglect one's appearance, personal habits, etc.

1923 A. Bennett *Riceyman Steps* v. i. 239 Her sole concern..was the condition of the shop. Ought she to clean it, or ought she to 'let it go'? **1960** *Woman* 23 Apr. 17/3 The first step towards 'letting yourself go'. **1963** N. Streatfeild *Vicarage Family* ii. 20 There is a flower garden. It's been let go rather but I saw some nice rose trees. **1970** G. Greer *Female Eunuch* 186 She tries not 'to let herself go', keeps young-looking. **1971** R. Rendell *One Across* v. 48 She's made a nice job of my hair, hasn't she? I wouldn't want Ethel to think I'd let myself go.

24*. let slide (see Slide *v.* 5 b).

29. let down. b. Add to def.: to fail in supporting, aiding, or justifying (a person, etc.); freq. in phr. *to let the side down.* Also *intr.*, to diminish, deteriorate; to relax. Chiefly *U.S.*

1913 E. C. Bentley *Trent's Last Case* xv. 307 That's good. I judged you would not let me down. **1925** W. Deeping *Sorrell & Son* xii. 110, I leave it to you, Stephen. I know you'll not let me down. **1927** *Daily Express* 12 Dec. 2/4 A boy who lets his group down..is made to feel ashamed of himself. **1952** M. Steen *Phoenix Rising* i. 22 Why..should she present herself to him against this sordid background..letting down her own side? **1958** 'A. Gilbert' *Death against Clock* x. 137 He couldn't guess his Frau was going to let down the side like that. **1969** *Guardian* 8 Sept. 7/2 'House and Garden' let the side down..by advancing very confident pro-reproduction arguments. **1971** J. Tyndall *Death in Lebanon* xii. 223 George..let the side down by his boat running out of juice. **1973** D. Robinson *Rotten with Honour* 20 You have a way of looking at people as if they're about to let the side down. **1974** N. Freeling *Dressing of Diamond* 99 He's my partner... He doesn't let me down, I won't let him down.

1866 'Mark Twain' *Lett. from Hawaii* (1967) 250 This Injun don't seem to know anything but 'Owry ikky', and the interest of that begins to let down after it's been said sixteen or seventeen times. **1870** —— *Lett. to Publishers* (1967) 33, I shall watch this Galaxy business pretty closely, and whenever I seem to be 'letting down', I shall withdraw from literature and recuperate. **1926** *Publishers' Weekly* 20 Feb. 563 Sales are increasing instead of letting down. **1964** Mrs. L. B. Johnson *White House Diary* 14 Jan. (1970) 45 The meeting had broken up a little after midnight, and after a little letting down.. Lyndon had arrived at 2 a.m. for—shall we call it dinner.

d. (*c*) *intr.* Of an aircraft or its pilot: to descend prior to making a landing. Cf. *let-down *sb.* 2.

1946 *Shell Aviation News* No. 100. 8/3 Another frequently used system was 'Lorenz' blind approach, which assisted aircraft to let-down in adverse visibility. **1947** *Jrnl. R. Aeronaut. Soc.* LI. 391/2 There remain the periods when so many accidents occur, just after taking off, or when the aircraft is letting down to land. **1958** 'N. Shute' *Rainbow & Rose* ii. 42 Over Macquarie Harbour I started to let down. **1971** K. Wheeler *Epitaph for Mr. Wynn* (1972) xxxii. 399 I'll be letting down now... On the ground in ten minutes.

g. Also, *to let* (a person) *down eas(il)y.*

1754 Richardson *Grandison* VI. xxii. 120 It will give him consequence in the eye of the world, and be a gentle method of letting his pride down easy. **1863** *Country Gentleman* 2 Apr. 227/3 The object of these ambiguous expressions is to 'let the applicant down easy'. **1866** *Harper's Mag.* Sept. 537/1 How to have the Colonel transferred, or 'let down easy',..was the question. **1907** [see *cotton *v.*[1] 8]. **1928** G. B. Shaw *Intelligent Woman's Guide Socialism* lvii. 274 The State..must let the loser down easily; and there is no other way of doing this except the way of purchase and compensation.

k. To lengthen (a garment); to lower (a hem) in order to lengthen a garment.

1890 *Monthly Packet* Christmas 182 Mrs. Thorpe was thinking that Babie's pink frock wanted 'letting down' an inch. **1952** E. Coxhead *Play Toward* v. 125 They both wore cotton [dresses], Sophia's showing where it had been let down, and Madeleine's dating back to the war years. **1953** K. Tennant *Joyful Condemned* xxxiii. 316 Philippa was..letting down the hem of Margot's green organdie. **1974** N. Freeling *Dressing of Diamond* 121 She liked to sit and sew; a frock whose hem needed letting down.

l. *to let one's hair down*: see *hair *sb.* 8 l.

m. To deflate (a tyre).

1968 M. Woodhouse *Rock Baby* ix. 91, I..hoped she hadn't had any bright ideas like letting down my tyres or removing the distributor cap. **1973** 'M. Yorke' *Grave Matters* v. i. 81 There was no trace of a hole in it [*sc.* a tyre] when the wheel was brought in for repair. It must have been let down. Deliberately.

31. let in. a. Also *fig.*, to include; to allow (someone) to share (confidential information, privileges, etc.). Freq. const. *on.*

1904 G. S. Porter *Freckles* xiv. 307, I guess you'll have to let me in on that, too. You mustn't be selfish, you know. **1910** E. A. Walcott *Open Door* xiii. 162 Let me in on the game, Tommy. **1923** L. J. Vance *Baroque* vii. 39 I'll let you in on a secret. **1928** E. Wallace *Double* xv. 239 He had been 'let in' by acquaintances on the Stock Exchange to several good things. **1942** Berrey & Van den Bark *Amer. Thes. Slang* § 197/5 *Inform; give inside information,*..let *or* leave in on.

c. (Further examples.)

1932 D. C. Minter *Mod. Needlecraft* 214/1 Joins can be made decorative by letting in a piping cord down the centre. **1968** J. Arnold *Shell Bk. Country Crafts* 257 Handles are constructed by letting in a cane as a foundation.

e. (Further examples of *to let* (*oneself* or a person) *in for.*)

1913 Galsworthy *Fugitive* ii. 48 Mr Malise, I know what I ought to be to you, if I let you in for all this. **1925** D. H. Lawrence *Let.* 29 Dec. (1962) II. 873 We sort of let ourselves in for these things. **1938** E. Waugh *Scoop* i. v. 86 We've been having a row with you lately. Something about a libel action one of our boys let you in for. **1955** *Times* 29 June 12/6 But never once has she let-in her passengers for a major breakdown in foreign parts, or otherwise far from home. **1971** E. Lemarchand *Death on Doomsday* i. 16 You're..spelling out the horrors we've let ourselves in for with appalling clarity. **1973** *Listener* 15 Nov. 661/1 Princess Anne, did you explain to Captain Phillips..what he was letting himself in for?

g. *Motoring.* To engage (the clutch) by releasing one's pressure on the clutch pedal.

1933 D. L. Sayers *Hangman's Holiday* 173 Mr. Egg acknowledged the courtesy with a wave of his smart trilby, and let his clutch in with quiet determination. **1960** I. Jefferies *Dignity & Purity* iv. 61, I let in the clutch and zoomed off. **1968** *Listener* 19 Dec. 811/2 The Fiddler chuckled as he let in the clutch. **1973** C. Egleton *Seven*

Days to Killing xx. 213 He slipped the handbrake, raced the engine and then let the clutch in fast.

h. As *ppl. adj.* (See quots.)

1882 J. SOUTHWARD *Pract. Printing* xxvii. 257 Let-in notes are, as the name indicates, let into the text. **1894** *Amer. Dict. Printing & Bookmaking* 336/1 *Let-in notes*, another term for cut-in notes, or those let into the text, as distinct from side notes. **1973** *Collins's Authors & Printers Dict.* (ed. 11) 247/2 *Let-in notes*,.. those let into the text, as distinct from side-notes.

32. let off. b. *to let off steam*: see *STEAM *sb.*

c. (Earlier examples.)

1814 J. CONSTABLE *Let.* 25 Oct. in *Corr.* (1964) II. 135 Mr. Roberson our curate was so polite as to ask me to dine with him as he had a party the other day, but I begged to be 'let off'. **1816** JANE AUSTEN *Emma* II. xiii. 244 It will be a good thing over..and I shall have been let off easily.

f. As *sb.* (*d*) (Earlier examples.) (*f*) A release or exemption from punishment or obligation. (*g*) *Rifle-shooting.* The pulling of the trigger.

1836 D. CROCKETT *Exploits & Adventures Texas* 52, I was for backing out and fighting shy; but there was no let-off, for the cock of the village..determined not to stay whipped. **1854** *Punch* 23 Sept. 114/2 A light let-off that will be for the murderer of more than half-a-million! **1864** in *Cricket Q.* (1963) I. 21 He had a couple of let offs. **1876** *Baily's Monthly Mag.* July 45 After this let off, Lord Harris hit in his usual free and dashing style. **1894** P. H. HUNTER *James Inwick* i. 10 He was ahint wi' his rent, and no' like to get muckle o' a let-aff frae the laird. **1913** A. G. FULTON *Notes on Rifle Shooting* 7 Position, holding, aim and let-off can be learned to perfection, and these things are the basis of successful Service rifle shooting. **1932** J. A. BARLOW *Elem. Rifle Shooting* ii. 9 Of the three essentials, holding should be placed foremost in order of importance, aiming next, and trigger pressing, trigger pulling, let-off, or whatever you like to call it, last. As far as possible I have purposely refrained from referring to let-off as trigger pressing. **1960** *Pistol Shooting* (Nat. Small-Bore Rifle Assoc.) (ed. 2) 21 The most difficult thing in shooting is to acquire an invariably good trigger let-off.

33. let on. a. For '*dial.* and *U.S.*' read 'orig. *dial.* and *U.S.*' (Further examples.)

1914 C. MACKENZIE *Sinister St.* II. IV. ii. 862 You'd better not let on you know he used to have a shop of his own. **1923** T. E. LAWRENCE *Let.* 5 Feb. (1938) 399 My private opinion is that she's read it, and he hasn't: and can't: but is much afraid to shock her by letting on. **1946** K. TENNANT *Lost Haven* (1947) xi. 173 Maybe Orry didn't like to let on he'd made a mistake in the first place. **1974** M. INGATE *Sound of Weir* viii. 62 'Would you say that he is very feeble?' 'Stronger than he lets on if you ask me. He don't need t' walk like that.'

b. To pretend. orig. *dial.* and *U.S.*

1822 J. GALT *Provost* xlvii. 354 The Provost maun ken nothing about it, or let on that he does na ken. **1828** *Yankee* (Portland, Maine) 23 Apr. 132/3 [In the South] to let on signifies to make believe. **1846** W. CROSS *Disruption* v. 48 She..had the sense to..let on to be just as ill pleased as her mistress. **1876** 'MARK TWAIN' *Old Times Mississippi* 137 If I wanted to..'let on' to prove what had occurred in the remote past..what an opportunity is here! **1929** *Randolph Enterprise* (Elkins, W. Virginia) 28 Mar. 1/1 We..found out that Mr. Van let on to take the proposal seriously. **1961** *John o' London's* 12 Jan. 41/4 In the positive it [*sc.* let on] means 'pretend' or 'simulate' as in 'He let on to be angry'.

34. let out. a. Also *fig.*, to excuse, to release (from some obligation). Also, to release (the clutch of a motor vehicle).

1869 B. HARTE *Luck of Roaring Camp* 41, I ran the whole way, knowing nobody was home but Jim,—and—and—I'm out of breath—and—that lets me out. **1884** 'MARK TWAIN' *Huck. Finn* vi. 43 They said he [*sc.* the Negro] could *vote* when he was at home. Well, that lets me out! **1922** WODEHOUSE *Girl on Boat* v. 101 But this is splendid! This lets you out. **1945** E. WAUGH *Brideshead Revisited* II. i. 222 Oh, that's quite different. It lets you out completely. **1958** C. WATSON *Coffin scarcely Used* vi. 63 The driver..glanced swiftly behind him before letting out the clutch. **1973** J. LEASOR *Host of Extras* viii. 152, I..let out the clutch and we were of. **1974** 'E. LATHEN' *Sweet & Low* xiii. 129 'They've started casting around for motives.' 'That lets all of us out.'

e. Add to def.: to slacken, *spec.* to increase the width of (a garment) by allowing extra material at the seams; to alter (the seams) in order to increase the width of a garment.

1791 F. BURNEY *Jrnl.* Dec. (1972) I. 97 Miss Cambridge said she thought I was grown fat... I assured her I had been obliged to have a Gown let out, that had been made last year. **1863** QUEEN VICTORIA *Let.* 22 Sept. in R. Fulford *Dearest Mama* (1968) 271 She has increased very much in size—her waist being quite broad and her clothes having all to be let out. **1877** A. SEWELL *Black Beauty* (*c* 1878, ed. 5) xxxiii. 158 When the crupper was let out a hole or two, it all fitted well. **1888** KIPLING *Under Deodars* (1889) 69, I shall say that I am going to Phelps's to get it [*sc.* a frock] let out. **1926** S. T. WARNER *Lolly Willowes* I. 17 Nannie would let out another tuck in Laura's ginghams and merinos. **1953** K. TENNANT *Joyful Condemned* xxxvi. 358 You've grown quite plump... I looked out a dress of mine... I'll let out the seams. **1974** R. HARRIS *Double Snare* viii. 54 'The dress is too tight...' 'Perhaps it could be let out.'

i. (Earlier example.) Also, to drive (a motor vehicle) very fast.

1849 F. PARKMAN *Calif. & Oregon Trail* 427 Let out your horse, man; lay on your whip! **1938** H. G. WELLS *Apropos of Dolores* vi. 321, I don't like these minor tracks. I can't let her [*sc.* his car] *out*. **1968** A. MARIN *Clash of Distant Thunder* (1969) xii. 91 There is a nineteen-kilometer stretch of road..that is almost straight, and I let the Alfa out all the way. **1970** 'D. HALLIDAY' *Dolly & Cookie Bird* iv. 50, I..overtook..the lorry..and then let her right out. I did a ton up that road, and probably more.

35. let up. b. (Earlier and later examples.) Also, to relax.

1787 G. WASHINGTON *Diaries* (1925) III. 185 The Plows, after the rain let up, proceeded to finish this part of field No. 5. **1841** J. F. COOPER *Deerslayer* I. vi. 172 Let up, you painted riptyles—let up! **1933** D. L. SAYERS *Murder must Advertise* v. 94 Never let up! Never go to sleep! **1936** H. HAGEDORN *Brookings* xv. 254 He was resourceful, steady, determined, he never let up on a man; and just wore people out. **1943** J. B. PRIESTLEY *Daylight on Saturday* xxx. 243 Bob's a chap that needs to let up, and now he can't let up... So he's angry inside all the time. **1970** C. MAJOR *Dict. Afro-Amer. Slang* 76 *Let up*, command to restrain from verbally abusing someone. **1974** E. LEMARCHAND *Buried in Past* viii. 138 The girl was..on the brink of tears... 'Why not let up a bit?' he suggested.

c. As *sb.* For '*U.S.*' read 'orig. *U.S.*' Add further examples.

1837 *Congress. Globe* 25th Congress 2 Sess. App. 47/3 There was no let up in the matter: the people had so ordered it, and the gentleman ought to be satisfied. **1841** J. F. COOPER *Deerslayer* I. viii. 240 There's no let-up in an Indian's watchfulness when he's on a war-path. **1891** E. ROPER *By Track & Trail* ix. 125 The snow was falling fast, and there was no appearance of a 'let-up'. **1892** *Eng. Illustr. Mag.* Sept. 884 (E.D.D.), There is no let-up, no change of undergarments, no camp. **1912** BELLOC *Green Overcoat* vii. 141 There was a gap in their conversation... A let up. An interval of repose. **1956** D. D. C. P. MOULD *Celtic Saints* xii. 126 The basis of Celtic prayer..is very simple... The background is ascetic, penitential, and without let-up. **1968** *Globe & Mail* (Toronto) 17 Feb. 23/5 The only let-up in policy is that non-profit groups get it [*sc.* a theatre] cheaper than shows booked by impresarios. **1973** *Nature* 21 Sept. 117/2 There is little prospect of a letup in fuel shortages for the next few years.

letch, see *LECH *sb.*[4]

letch *v.*, see *LECH *v.*

letchwe, var. *LECHWE.

let-down (le·t,daun), *sb.* [f. vbl. phr. *to let down* (LET *v.*[1] 29).] **1.** (See LET *v.*[1] 29 j.) Add further examples.

1933 N. COWARD *Design for Living* II. iii. 68 The human race is a let-down, Ernest; a bad, bad let-down! **1934** J. T. FARRELL *Young Manhood* ii. 41 He was lassitudinous in a mood of let-down, already lonesome for yesterday. **1938** J. STEINBECK *Long Valley* 135 Mike knew it was all over. He could feel the let-down in himself. **1946** W. STEVENS *Let.* 19 Feb. (1967) 523 There is not the..let-down between the two that one finds so often. **1960** M. SPARK *Bachelors* x. 182 And now *she's* in for a let-down, though she won't admit it. **1971** *Daily Tel.* 4 Nov. 8/4 What intrigues Mr Barstow is the inevitable let-down which is the result of getting older, of getting bored, of finding that passion can flicker out.

2. The descent of an aircraft or spacecraft prior to landing. Cf. *LET *v.*[1] 29 d (*c*).

1945 *Jrnl. R. Aeronaut. Soc.* XLIX. 74/1 Extra fuel to allow for errors in navigation, errors in weather forecasts and technical inabilities to make let-downs and landings through conditions of ice, clouds, or bad ground visibility. **1949** *Flight* 30 June 754/2 From its pilot, Col. Gray, we learned that, on the let-down from 35,000 ft, while the B-29 was still in formation, its port inner engine had over-speeded to 4,500 r.p.m. **1960** 'N. SHUTE' *Trustee from Toolroom* v. 97 The note of the engines changed as the let-down began. **1969** *Guardian* 13 Oct. 18/2 The precision of landing depends predominantly on the accuracy with which the spacecraft's orbital position is known at the moment let-down begins.

3. The action of a cow yielding milk. Cf. LET *v.*[1] 29 h.

1960 *Farmer & Stockbreeder* 5 Jan. 69/3 A time-lag between the end of let-down and stripping is too prevalent. **1965** LEE & KNOWLES *Animal Hormones* ii. 32 Thus the ejection of milk at suckling, or the 'let-down' of milk as it is referred to by agricultural workers, is a neurohormonal reflex.

Also *attrib.* or as *adj.*, in the senses of the vbl. phr. *to let down* or of the *sb.* (see above).

1907 M. C. HARRIS *Tents of Wickedness* II. vii. 193 The next was one of these 'let-down' mornings which every-body must remember having awakened to. **1945** E. BOWEN *Demon Lover* 72 The car was a two-seater, with a let-down hood. **1948** [see *fan marker* (*FAN *sb.*[1] 11)]. **1956** *Nature* 24 Mar. 582/1 In studying the function of the milk gland, with the view of increasing milk production, particular attention has been devoted in recent years to the milk-ejection mechanism (the let-down reflex). **1957** R. H. SMYTHE *Conformation of Dog* vi. 88 The exhibition Greyhound has always been noted for length of tibia, low set-on hocks, well let-down stifles. **1964** *Yearbk. Astron. 1965* 135 At a fixed height the lunar let-down engine will fire to reduce the descent rate and, landing legs having been extended, the vehicle will complete a vertical descent on to the lunar surface, hovering for short periods before making the final touchdown. **1973** M. MACKINTOSH *King & Two Queens* ii. 24, I had talked myself out of the let-down feeling and was determined to make the most of the trip. **1974** P. FLOWER *Odd Job* i. 6 Somebody had called it an escritoire... It had a letdown flap you could write on.

lethal, *a.* Add: **A.** *adj.* **1. c.** *lethal chamber*: also for the destruction of human beings, and *fig.*

1928 'M. HOFFE' *Many Waters* III. ix. 106 It [*sc.* the Bankruptcy Court] lacks of all the glitter of splendid sin; it is simply the paltry lethal chamber of the vanquished. **1933** *Punch* 4 Oct. 366/2 To a modern it is clear that age must be abhorrent. The best modern thought advocates a lethal chamber for all over fifty years of age.

d. *Genetics.* Of an allele or chromosomal abnormality (such as a deletion): resulting in the death of an individual possessing it before the normal span or before sexual maturity, or (if recessive) capable of causing such premature death when homozygous.

1917 *Proc. Nat. Acad. Sci.* III. 620 The difficulty which was experienced in getting pure stock was due to the fact that the chief factor for beaded—B_d'—is lethal, killing all flies homozygous for it. *Ibid.* 620 This remarkable genetic situation, wherein both types of homozygotes are prevented from appearing by the action of lethal factors lying in opposite chromosomes, may be termed a condition of 'balanced lethal factors'. **1939** STURTEVANT & BEADLE *Introd. Genetics* (1940) x. 160 It may be noted at once that the lethal genes ordinarily studied are recessive; a gene with a dominant lethal effect is necessarily lost before it can be studied. **1962** I. H. HERSKOWITZ *Genetics* xxviii. 239 Autosomes II, III, and IV of wild-type flies were individually made homozygous to detect the presence of recessive mutants..that are lethal (causing death of all individuals before adulthood), or semilethal (causing more than 90 and less than 100 per cent mortality before adulthood), or subvital (causing significantly less than normal but greater than 10 per cent survival to adulthood)... About 25% of all autosomes tested this way carried a recessive lethal or semilethal mutant. **1973** K. MATHER *Genetical Struct. Populations* ii. 21 Not all genes that affect viability are, however, completely lethal. Of some 3000 chromosomes tested in *Drosophila willistoni*.. over 35% carried genes that were lethal or semi-lethal. About half of the remainder carried other genes affecting the viability of flies homozygous for them.

B. *sb. Genetics.* A lethal allele or chromosomal abnormality (see *A. 1 d).

1917 *Proc. Nat. Acad. Sci.* III. 621 We must therefore believe that lethals are very frequent among recessive factors also. **1926** J. S. HUXLEY *Ess. Pop. Sci.* 59 Sometimes the impairment of vitality is so great that the organism pure for these factors cannot exist at all: such factors are styled lethals. **1934** *Mycologia* XXVI. 360 (*heading*) A lethal for ascus abortion in Neurospora. **1956** [see *DEFICIENCY 1 e].

lethal (lī·þăl), *v. rare.* [f. LETHAL *a.*] *trans.* To kill (animals) painlessly; = LETHALIZE *v.* So **le·thalling** *vbl. sb.*

1922 *Daily Mail* 7 Dec. 6 (Advt.), Cat. Dying from internal injuries..: Lethalled. **1925** *Observer* 27 Sept. 13/6 Proper lethalling establishments where cats can be put to sleep free of charge.

lethality. Delete *rare* and add further examples. Also *fig.*

1912 *Phil. Trans. R. Soc.* B. CCII. 2 The lethality of the venom was determined for frogs, rabbits,..and pigeons. **1930** G. BLAKE *Press & Public* 20 Mr. Baldwin..has lately discovered for himself the dread lethality of the powers I have described. **1953** *Sci. News* XXVIII. 18 Myxomatosis in the European rabbits is unique in its very high lethality. **1957** *Times* 26 Apr., Our early missiles will carry high-explosive warheads. Their lethality will be high. **1958** 'P. BRYANT' *Two Hours to Doom* 81 The radio-active cloud..would retain its lethality for hundreds of years. **1973** D. JORDAN *Nile Green* xxviii. 125 Significant strides have been made in the past two decades on the lethality of conventional and nuclear warheads.

lethally, *adv.* (in Dict. s.v. LETHAL *a.*). Delete † and add later example.

1971 *Nature* 10 Dec. 328/3 Lethally irradiated F_1 hybrid mice.

lethargy, *v.* (Later example.)

1893 F. THOMPSON *Poems* 75 It grew lethargied with fierce bliss.

lethed, *a.* Delete † *Obs. rare*$^{-0}$, substitute *rare*, and add example.

1895 F. THOMPSON *Sister Songs* 2 On the dull earth's lethèd ear.

let-in, *ppl. a.*: see *LET *v.*[1] 31 h; **let-off,** *sb.*: see *LET *v.*[1] 32 f.

let-out (le·t,aut), *sb.* [f. vbl. phr. *to let out* (LET *v.*[1] 34).] **1.** (See LET *v.*[1] 34 k.)

2. An excuse, a justification, a method of avoiding (a difficulty), a release from (an embarrassing situation). Also *attrib.*

1935 M. HODGE *Grief goes Over* in *Famous Plays* 331 That's not the trouble. I am glad she is. It's a let-out. **1942** H. C. BAILEY *Dead Man's Shoes* xx. 81 The open verdict let him out, old boy... He may want a good let out over Clavell. **1955** J. L. AUSTIN *How to do Things with Words* (1962) I. 10 Yet he provides Hippolytus with a let-out, the bigamist with an excuse for his 'I do' and the welsher with a defence for his 'I bet'. **1957** *Economist* 5 Oct. 17/1 And there is no easy let-out for the complacent in the notion that landladies are by definition a narrow-minded lot. **1961** *John o' London's* 17 Aug. 195/2 When we have made all possible allowance for apotropaic amulets..and any other let-out you can think up, we are left with a solid residue of crude, unimaginative..obscene paintings. **1971** C. BONINGTON *Annapurna South Face* xi. 138 'It would be best if you could stay at camp tomorrow and dig a platform for the second box before we arrive.' I was so tired that this sounded an easy let-out, and I

agreed. **1971** 'D. Halliday' *Dolly & Doctor Bird* xi. 153 Thanks for the let-out. I was just too bloody nosy. **1973** *Fremdsprachen* XVII. 57/1 It is understood that the proposed agreement would provide for a let-out clause. **1973** *Listener* 13 Sept. 346/3 The really essential problem is the increase of population..of the poor world. This is a very nice let-out for the rich countries.

3. *attrib.* or as *adj.* (See quot. 1954.)

1949 *Amer. Speech* XXIV. 92 A peltry is said to be let in if it is cut and resewed in such a manner as to fashion it broader and shorter than the original. Similarly, it is said to be let out if it is rendered longer and narrower than its first shape. **1954** Webster Add., *Let-out*, of furs, subjected to a method of preparation involving cutting the pelt in strips and reassembling them to form a longer, narrower piece in which good features of color and texture are emphasized. **1967** *Boston Sunday Herald* 7 May III. 3/3 (Advt.), The recent weakness in prices in the fur market enabled us to hand pick choice lush let out natural Mink Jackets.

letovicite (letǫvi·tsəit, -vi·səit). *Min.* [ad. G. *letovicit* (J. Sekanina 1932, in *Zeitschr. f. Krist.* LXXXIII. 117), f. *Letovic-e*, the name of its original locality in Moravia, Czechoslovakia + *-it* -ite¹.] An acid ammonium sulphate, $(NH_4)_3H(SO_4)_2$, found as colourless prismatic crystals in coal-mine waste-heaps.

1932 *Mineral. Abstr.* V. 145 Associated with this are gypsum and a new mineral (letovicite) as minute colourless pseudo-hexagonal plates. **1968** I. Kostov *Mineral.* II. ix. 503 Letovicite, lecontite, and mirabilite..are optically negative.

Letraset (le·trăset). The proprietary name of a system of alphabet transfers used for lettering.

1957 *Trade Marks Jrnl.* 27 Feb. 200/1 Letraset... Transfers. Art & Technics Ltd.,..London,..publishers. **1962** Hansell & Ollerenshaw *Longmore's Med. Photogr.* (ed. 7) xliv. 519 For both prints and slides it is a simple matter to produce a positive transparency at the same scale as the intermediate, with the lettering correctly disposed... Instant Letraset is well suited to all these requirements. **1964** *Trade Marks Jrnl.* 11 Mar. 397/1 Letraset Instant Lettering... Transfers (decalcomanias) of letters, numerals and punctuation symbols, in sheet form. Letraset Limited,..London,..manufacturers and merchants. **1966** R. Roberts *Typogr. Design* iii. 51 The invention of such hand transfer lettering systems as Letraset. **1971** *Physics Bull.* Sept. 527/2 His diagrams are beautifully drawn..with lettering carried out with stencils or even Letraset.

letshewe, var. *lechwe.

let's pretend (le:ts prĭte·nd), *sb. phr.* [f. Let *v.*¹ 14 a + -'s 3 + Pretend *v.* 3 d.] A game of pretence or make-believe. Also *attrib.*, *transf.*, and *fig.*

1948 *United Nations World* Dec. 92/1 The New Look.. was a 'Let's Pretend' fashion. **1963** *Ingenue* Dec. 45 A Short..wrap of let's-pretend beaver (called Norba). **1964** W. Golding *Spire* iv. 85 But there comes a point when vision's no more than a child's playing let's pretend. **1967** *Listener* 21 Sept. 371/1 The dividing line between reality and 'let's pretend'. **1969** N. Freeling *Tsing-Boum* xii. 85 Then—everything was queer then. Double-think and let's-pretend. **1970** *Guardian* 23 Dec. 9/6, I told all the children..that Santa Claus wasn't real but a let's-pretend person.

letter, *sb.*¹ Add: **1. c.** *letter-by-letter* (further examples).

1951 [see *comparatist]. **1961** T. Landau *Encycl. Librarianship* (ed. 2) 194/2 *Letter by letter filing*, a method of filing..entries in a list,..the basic principle being that each heading, whether consisting of one word or more, is regarded as one unit. **1964** F. Bowers *Bibliogr. & Textual Crit.* III. vii. 92 Palaeographical 'explanations' have a marked tendency to take it for granted that every letter must be confused with another, as if the scribe were puzzling out the word in detail, letter by letter... In reprints,.. the letter-by-letter misreading posited by palaeographers is impossible. **1967** Cox & Grose *Organiz. Bibliogr. Rec. by Computer* II. 13 The ability to sort word-by-word or letter-by-letter.

e. *colloq.* (freq. in *pl.*). A university degree or other honour (denoted by its initial letters following the name of the holder). Also (esp. *U.S.*), some other mark of distinction, usu. for achievement in sport, e.g. an abbreviation or monogram representing the name of a college or other institution.

1888 Kipling *Plain Tales from Hills* 54 It was pleasant to be singled out by a Commissioner with letters after his name. **1915** *Chicago Daily Maroon* 10 June 1/4 The Board of Athletic Control will meet today to award letters to this year's members of the track, baseball, tennis and gymnastic teams. **1951** Partridge *Dict. Slang* (ed. 4) 1098/2 *Letters*, degree-letters after one's name: coll.: mid-C. 19–20. **1964** Mrs. L. B. Johnson *White House Diary* 10 June (1970) 163 An Illinois boy, totally deaf, who had won awards in science and in English, and a school letter in wrestling, was scheduled..to become a scientist. **1970** *New Yorker* 23 May 54/1 He had earned his high-school letter in four sports. **1974** L. Lamb *Man in Mist* x. 66 The heads of departments knew me... Letters arter their names as long as Dick's hatband.

2. a. (Later examples.)

1854, 1884, 1892 [see *lift *v.* 3 g].

4. c. letter of credit: see Credit *sb.* 2 c and 10 b; **letter of intent**, a letter or similar document containing a declaration of the intentions of the writer.

1961 Webster, *Letter of intent*, a written authorization enabling officers of the federal government in time of imperative need for war materials and supplies to order the making or furnishing of such materials and supplies before the issuance of a formal contract and providing reimbursement for the contractor's expenses if no contract is subsequently issued. **1970** R. Johnson *Black Camels* v. 75 The news of his oil strike reached New York with a copy of the letter of intent he had exchanged with Sheikh Rasul.

d. (See quot. 1825.) *dial.* and *U.S.*

1825 Jamieson *Suppl.* s.v. *Letter*, a spark on the side of the wick of a candle; so denominated by the superstitious, who believe that the person to whom the spark is opposite will soon receive some intelligence by letter. **1854** B. F. Taylor *Jan. & June* 220 Two 'letters' are snuffed from the candles. **1902** in *Eng. Dial. Dict.*

e. An article, report, or the like, setting out the social, political, or cultural, etc., tendencies in a specified place.

1782 M. G. J. de Crèvecoeur (*title*) Letters from an American Farmer; describing certain provincial situations, manners, and customs, not generally known; and conveying some idea of the late and present interior circumstances of the British colonies in North America. **1848** *Manch. Guardian* 22 Nov. 5/1 (*heading*) Letters from London. (From a Private Correspondent.) **1874** Geo. Eliot *Let.* 7 Jan. (1955) VI. 4 The Parisian letter is nicely done... The single paragraph on the pressure of radiation is worth more than the price of the paper. **1913** W. J. Locke *Stella Maris* v. 52 He was..the contributor.. of a weekly London Letter to an American syndicate. **1955** *Radio Times* 25 Apr. 16/3 Letter from America, by Alistair Cooke. **1966** K. Martin *Father Figures* ix. 173 Dore was an excellent lobby correspondent, who for many years had written paragraphs about Parliament, mainly for the London Letter. **1974** *Spectator* 21 Dec. 787/3 American letter—The President gets smart—[by] Al Capp.

6*. = *French letter* s.v. *French *a.* 3.

c **1888–94** *My Secret Life* II. 318 My cock and the letter would not agree. **1916** [see *cap *sb.*¹ 13 d].

7. a. *letter-boy*, *-file* (later examples), *-form*, *-name*, *-post* (later example), *-sequence*, *-shape*, *-string*, *-tray*.

1816 Jane Austen *Emma* II. ix. 176 A stray letter-boy on an obstinate mule. **1895** *Montgomery Ward Catal.* 40/1 The 'Boss' File is the very best letter file ever sold at the price. **1911** O. Onions *Widdershins* 294 The shelf on which I kept my letter-files... My files contained..my agent's letters. **1955** E. Pound *Section: Rock-Drill* lxxxvii. 33 Windeler's vision: his letter file the size of 2 lumps of sugar, But the sheet legible. **1908** *Westm. Gaz.* 22 Aug. 14/1 He looks forward to the invention of letter-forms that will be much simpler and much more legible than the traditional symbols. **1937** *Discovery* Dec. 362/2 The letter-form of the calligrapher. **1963** *Times Lit. Suppl.* 4 Jan. 16/3 The changing use of type and letterforms in English. **1889** *Cent. Dict.*, Letter-name. **1934** Priebsch & Collinson *German Lang.* v. iii. 261 Rhyme-forms and spelling out names by means of new letter-names applied to the alphabet. **1961** R. B. Long *Sentence & its Parts* xvii. 388 Examples are *IQ* and *TV*, in which the component letters are given their individual letter-name pronunciations. **1929** D. H. Lawrence *Let.* 9 July (1962) II. 1163 If I seal them letter-post they may hold them and make more fuss. **1953** *Language* XXIX. 72 The letter-sequences QL, TSR, SSS..never occur in English spelling. **1964** W. R. Lee in D. Abercrombie et al. *Daniel Jones* 288 There are various letter-shapes to grasp. **1964** *Language* XL. 168 The omission of a given letter-string from a dictionary is no assurance that the combination is not an English word. **1907** *Yesterday's Shopping* (1969) 356/2 Letter Trays. Fitted with spring clip, 4to..0/9.

8. letter-balance (examples); **letter-ballot**, a ballot in which the papers are sent by post; **letter-bomb**, an explosive device sent through the post as a weapon of terror; **letter-box**, (*c*) *Mountaineering* (see quot. 1968); (*d*) in espionage (see quot. 1961); **letter-carrier** (later U.S. examples); **letter-man**, (*b*) *U.S.*, a sportsman who has received a letter of distinction (see sense 1 e above); **letter-mark**, a letter used as a contraction or symbol; **letter-perfect** *a.* (earlier example); (*b*) literally correct, verbally exact; *fig.* flawless, unexceptionable; **letter plate**, a plate for fixing to the outside of a door or wall and having a rectangular aperture, covered by a flap, through which letters may be put; **letter-scale**, a scale for weighing letters; **letter-space** *Printing*, a space inserted between the letters of a word; so **letter-spaced** *a.*, **letter-spacing** *vbl. sb*; **letter-weigher**, a device for weighing letters; **letter-weight** (examples); **letter-word**, a runic symbol or ideogram signifying both the name for something and a specific single letter; a word wholly or partly consisting of a letter or letters which are abbreviations in themselves.

1880 G. N. Lamphere *U.S. Govt.* 240/1 Supplying the post-offices entitled thereto with blanks,..twine, letter-balances, and cancelling-stamps. **1901** *Chambers's Jrnl.* Sept. 577/1 A German firm brought out a folding letter-balance, on the pan of which were engraved the British postal rates and the legend, 'Made in Germany'. **1961** *Lebende Sprachen* VI. 70/1 Letter scale (or: balance), die Briefwaage. **1898** *Engineering Mag.* XVI. 126/1 This resolution..submitted to the Society at large in the form of a letter-ballot. **1948** *Times* 4 Aug. 4/5 Each of the letter bombs which he has examined contained sufficient explosive to cause fatal injuries if detonated at close quarters. **1949** Koestler *Promise & Fulfilment* xiii. 149 His brother was killed by a letter-bomb sent by the Stern Group. **1972** *Times* 20 Sept. 1/3 One of the unexploded letter bombs. **1973** *Guardian* 28 June 26/5 A letter bomb exploded yesterday in the hands of a Londonderry solicitor..the first casualty of the letter-bomb campaign in Northern Ireland. **1974** *Ibid.* 26 Jan. 26/5 A letter bomb exploded at the head office of Pilkington Brothers, the glass manufacturers. **1951** E. Coxhead *One Green Bottle* iii. 78 The rib bore them upward, perpetually varied,..now parallel cracks, now a groove, now a letter box... The climb above the crux was even more delightful. **1955** J. Thomas *No Banners* xvi. 144 A circuit had to be organized into leak-proof compartments with letter-boxes or couriers as the only links between them. **1961** R. Seth *Anat. Spying* iii. 44 The 'letter-box' is a long-standing method of channelling information to the chief. It may be an accommodation address..or it may be a loose brick in a wall. Sometimes one member of a group acts as a 'letter-box' under his own name and at his home address. **1968** P. Crew *Encycl. Dict. Mountaineering* 79/1 *Letter-box*, a rectangular hole in a narrow rock ridge; a hole formed by jammed blocks or flakes of rock anywhere on a rock face. **1969** Hurd & Osmond *Smile on Face of Tiger* vii. 241 The silly girl popped out of the Home Office and they [*sc.* minutes] were in her usual letter-box within the hour. **1971** R. Petrie *Thorne in Flesh* xv. 187 Aury, apparently, had been a live letterbox for a French security organisation. **1967** *Boston Sunday Globe* 23 Apr. 13/1 Letter carriers in the 25 cities and towns in the Boston Postal District are delivering notices to 565,000 families and business firms, advising them of their own Zip code for use in return addresses. **1973** Wodehouse *Bachelors Anonymous* ix. 123 'You're American, aren't you?' said Amelia Bingham. 'I thought so. It was your saying "letter-carrier" instead of postman.' **1973** *Black Panther* 15 Sept. 5/2 Attrition is also used to get rid of workers, especially letter carriers. **1926** *Chicago Tribune* 19 Sept. II. 5/4 The letter men in the line are Wolf and Neff, guards, and Rouse, center. **1974** *Spartanburg* (S. Carolina) *Herald-Jrnl.* 21 Apr. B1/1 Now he is well on the way to becoming Spartanburg High School's first four-sport letterman in at least seven years. **1907** *Congregational Year Bk.* p. xxix, The following letter-marks and signs are adopted:—B. (Baptist); C.H. (Countess of Huntingdon's Connexion). **1845** *Ainsworth's Mag.* VII. 83 'I am letter-perfect,' said another [actor]. **1867** *Harper's Mag.* Aug. 405/1 Where [legal] papers are to be served, and copies must be letter-perfect. **1894** 'Mark Twain' in *Century Mag.* Apr. 822 Tom's conduct had remained letter-perfect during two whole months. **1929** F. M. Ford *Let.* 10 July (1965) 186 If you will send me the better copy to look through I will certainly make it as letter-perfect as I can. **1969** *Time* 31 Jan. 1 The performances by such Bergman regulars as Max von Sydow and Gunnar Björnstrand are letter-perfect. **1898** F. W. Macey *Specifications in Detail* 247 Knockers and letter plates are..made in iron and gun-metal, and vary in price from 3s. to £1 10s. **1923** *Work* 17 Nov. 161/2 A section through the door, showing the relative positions of the letter-plate and the box, is given by Fig. 3. **1971** *Country Life* 1 Apr. 752/3 Letter plates are easily bought. **1895** *Montgomery Ward Catal.* Index, Letter scale. **1900** A. Upward *Wonderful Career E. Lobb* 307 Be it enough To move the index of a letter-scale But in the estimation of a hair. **1961** Letter scale [see **letter-balance*]. **1934** Webster, Letter-space. **1967** Karch & Buber *Offset Processes* iv. 125 Modification is possible to condense, expand,..letter-space and drop-out shadows in Benday screens. **1959** R. Hostettler et al. *Technical Terms Printing Industry* (ed. 3) 120/2 One point letter-spaced, espacé un point. **1954** *Southward's Mod. Printing* (ed. 8) I. xxix. 178 Letterspacing. Spaces are also used for rendering uniform the thick perpendicular lines of capitals and fancy letters. **1961** T. Landau *Encycl. Librarianship* (ed. 2) 195/1 *Letter-spacing*, extra spacing between the letters of a word, especially in a running title or title-page. **1973** *Collins's Authors & Printers Dict.* (ed. 11) 247/2 *Letterspacing*,..shown in MS. by a stroke between letters, and # above (one word). **1862** *Illustr. Catal. Internat. Exhib., Industr. Dept., Brit. Div.* II. No. 5825, Inkstand, pen-tray, blotting-book, book-slide, letter-weigher. **1907** *Yesterday's Shopping* (1969) 366/2 Folding Portable Letter Weigher..to weigh up to 16 oz...each 1/8. **1880** Geo. Eliot *Let.* 7 Feb. (1956) VII. 249 He left me the beautiful letter-weight. **1923** P. Selver tr. *Čapek's R.U.R.* I. 5 A large 'knee-hole' writing-table on which stand an electric lamp,..letter-weight, [etc.]. **1927** Joyce *Let.* 2 Mar. (1957) I. 250 A Chinese student sent me some letterwords I had asked for. The last one is 山. It means 'mountain' and is called 'Chin'. **1934** Priebsch & Collinson *Germ. Lang.* v. 253 The emergence of 'letter-words' like *D-zug*..*L-zug*.. *P.S.*..*G.m.b.H.* **1948** D. Diringer *Alphabet* 519 A manuscript containing the poem..of King Alfred's time..which describes in verse each runic letter-word.

letter-card. (Later examples.)

1898 G. B. Shaw *Philanderer* II. 107, I wish you'd ask her not to write on letter-cards. **1939** E. Ambler *Mask of Dimitrios* x. 194 He bought a *pneumatique* letter-card. **1954** I. Murdoch *Under Net* viii. 116 We..bought two letter cards. **1971** D. Potter *Brit. Eliz. Stamps* ix. 94 A popular item in the suite of stationery is the familiar letter-card. They combine the convenience of envelope and paper with the secrecy of an ordinary letter.

lettergram (le·təɪgræm). [f. Letter *sb.*¹ + Tele)gram.] A telegram delivered by the postman with the ordinary mail. (Disused.)

1911 *World's Work* XVII. 447/2 'Lettergrams' of fifty words..for an inclusive fee of about two shillings over any distance. **1915** J. Webster *Dear Enemy* 19 When you feel so bursting with talk that only a hundred word telegram will relieve an explosion, at least turn it into a

night lettergram. **1921** *Chambers's Jrnl.* Dec. 834/1 An attendant handed him a night lettergram. **1966** *Commonwealth of Australia Post Office Guide* 294 Lettergrams are reduced rate messages which may be lodged only at capital cities and certain other offices having extended hours of service. They are transmitted by telegraph and delivered to addressees by the earliest post on the following working day.

letter-press. **1.** Substitute for def.: **a.** The text of a piece of printing, distinguished from illustrations, etc. **b.** Material printed from a relief surface, distinguished from lithographic or intaglio printing. Add further examples.

1892 A. POWELL *Southward's Pract. Printing* (ed. 4) i. 2 *Letterpress printing.* In this the subject is printed from a relief *above* the surface. *Ibid.* 3 Letterpress printing is done with types, blocks of wood, casts in metal, india-rubber, celluloid; electrotypes, &c. **1925** *Southward's Mod. Printing* (ed. 5) II. xxxiii. 274 These methods [of illustration] may be tabulated thus:—For printing by the letterpress method—Wood engravings; Engravings on type metal; Process blocks in line; Process blocks in half-tones... All the above blocks are in relief. **1939** *Guide Exhib. in King's Library* (Brit. Mus.) 9 The Old Testament types are explained in two paragraphs of woodcut letterpress in the upper corners of the design. **1946** W. L. HAYES in H. Whetton *Pract. Printing & Binding* xxv. 287/1 Relief printing, as its name implies, is that in which the printing surface stands in relief, that is, above the surrounding non-printing area; identified in this category is letterpress from type, plate, half-tone and line blocks, wood and lino cuts. **1959** *Penrose Annual* LII. 113 It was ..decided to use a plate etched as shallow as was practicable and to print by 'letterpress-offset'. **1966** *Print* (Wynkyn de Worde Soc.) iv. 39 The basic characteristic of the lithographic process is that the printing image is flat: not raised as in letterpress or recessed as in gravure. **1970** K. LINDLEY *Woodblock Engravers* ii. 29 They [*sc.* Bewick's woodcuts]..enabled the letterpress printer once more to think in terms of books equal to those with copperplate illustrations. **1971** M. MOORMAN in D. Wordsworth *Jrnls.* 107 In 1809–10 W[ordsworth] wrote the letter-press for Wilkinson's drawings of the Lake District.

letterset (le·tǝɹset). [f. *LETTER(-PRESS + *OFF)SET *sb.*] (See quot. 1963.) Cf. *DRIOGRAPHY.

1963 *Publishers' Weekly* 5 Aug. 87/1 A new name, 'Letterset', for what was formerly called 'dry litho' has been coined. Letterset refers to printing through the use of relief wrap-around plates and an intermediate blanket cylinder to transfer the image to the surface being printed. **1967** V. STRAUSS *Printing Industry* vi. 288/1 In 1962 Miehle and du Pont coined the term 'letterset'..for indirect relief printing. Dry offset of the past and contemporary letterset are based on the same principle but differ widely in actual performance. **1973** S. JENNETT *Making of Bks.* (ed. 5) x. 166 Indirect letterpress or letterset are terms used for letterpress printing on to a blanket cylinder and then on to paper, after the manner of litho offset; the printing surface is a shallow etched metal or plastic plate curved round the plate cylinder.

letting, *vbl. sb.*[1] **1.** (Later examples of *letting down.*)

1917 J. AGATE *Buzz, Buzz!* 9, I hold such statement of the actual and practical scope of current criticism not to be a letting-down of the art we hold dear. **1940** *Chambers's Techn. Dict.* 496/1 *Letting-down,* the process of tempering hardened steel by heating it until the desired colour is reached and then quenching. **1958** *Ibid.* 990/1 *Letting down,* the reduction of altitude from cruising height to that required for the approach to landing. **1966** J. & R. GODDEN *Two under Indian Sun* iii. 68 The letting down of hems or takings in, as dresses were handed down.

Letto- (le·to), combining form repr. mod.L. *Lettōn-, Letto,* used with adjs. or sbs. denoting other languages or peoples, signifying 'Lettish and..', as *Letto-Lithuanian, -Slavonic,* etc.

1880 A. H. SAYCE *Introd. Sci. of Lang.* II. vii. 107 The old middle or intransitive voice..has been lost in Keltic and Letto-Slavonic. **1913** L. W. LYDE *Continent of Europe* 419 These are the Letto-Lithuanians and Finnic (Esht) peoples of the Baltic Provinces. **1920** *Glasgow Herald* 21 July 8 A Polono-Lithuanian, a Polono-Lettish, and a Letto-Lithuanian question still unsettled. **1935** HUXLEY & HADDON *We Europeans* vii. 221 The Letto-Lithuanians tend to be of medium height, but taller where remote from Slav influence.

‖ **lettre** (letr'). The French word for 'letter' in: **a. lettre de cachet** (letr' dǝ kaʃe), lit. 'letter of seal', a warrant issued in the France of the *ancien régime* for the imprisonment of a person without trial at the pleasure of the monarch. Also *transf.* Cf. CACHET 1.

1718 VANBRUGH *Let.* 30 Aug. in *Athenæum* (1890) 30 Aug. 290/2, I am far from having the least doubt of his intentions to me; I fear only those same letters [*sic*] de cachet, that surprise folks every now and then. **1745** H. WALPOLE *Let.* 1 Aug. in *Corr.* (1941) IX. 23 Before the play itself is suppressed by a *lettre de cachet* to the booksellers. **1799** MALTHUS *Diary* 16 July (1966) 159 [Norway] These men seemed to have been placed by lettres de cachet exactly similar to those in France. **1824** SCOTT *Redgauntlet* III. vi. 163 There are sharp laws in France against refractory pupils—*lettres de cachet* are easily come by. **1849** THACKERAY *Pendennis* I. vii. 70 Why are there no such things as *lettres-de-cachet*—and a Bastille for young fellows of family? **1895** S. WEYMAN *From Mem. Minister of France* 138 M. de Clan..is for shutting him up. Getting a *lettre de cachet,*..and away with him. **1916** A. HUXLEY *Let.* 31 Mar. (1969) 96 A lettre de cachet from a Lord Lieutenant..can put one snugly away in the Jai! or Jug without any prospect of a trial for periods quite indefinitely coextensive with the war or even eternity. **1957** C. BROOKFIELD tr. *Durkheim's Professional Ethics & Civic Morals* vii. 87 Louis XIV, clearly, was able to issue his *lettres de cachet* against anyone he wished.

b. Used as the first element in **lettre bâtarde, lettre de forme, lettre de somme,** to designate groups of early type-faces based on manuscript forms then current, now more often described as *BASTARDA, *TEXTURA, and *ROTUNDA or fere-humanistica types.

1887 T. B. REED *Hist. Old Eng. Letter Foundries* i. 53 The Gothic letter employed by the inventors of printing for the *Bible, Psalter,* and other sacred works, was an imitation of the formal hand of the German scribes... This letter, as a typographical character, took the name of Lettre de Forme. *Ibid.,* The term [sc. *lettre de forme*]..was used by both Tory and Ycair to denote a class of letter which the former denominated *Canon,* or cut according to rule, as opposed to the more fanciful *lettres bâtardes. Ibid.* 54 The Lettre de Somme of the Germans..became in the hands of the fifteenth century printers a rival to the Gothic. **1922** D. B. UPDIKE *Printing Types* I. iv. 60 Fifteenth century Gothic type-forms may be roughly subdivided into Pointed, sometimes called *lettre de forme,* Round, sometimes called *lettre de somme,* and a vernacular Cursive black-letter, like the French *lettre batarde...* These three type-forms were the black-letter equivalents of the formal, less formal, and cursive manuscript-hands of the Roman period. *Ibid.* 63 The *lettre de somme* is said (without much authority) to derive its name from the *Summa* of St. Thomas Aquinas, for which..it was early employed. **1927** R. B. MCKERROW *Introd. Bibliogr.* 289 The *lettre de forme,*..derived from the most formal script, ..is in general of a rather narrow and pointed character, tending everywhere to angularity. *Ibid.,* Certain of the smaller sizes used by Wynkyn de Worde and Grafton.. seem very definitely to have that feeling of breadth and openness which is characteristic of the *lettre de somme. Ibid.,* The *lettre bâtarde* represents the cursive hand of its time. **1962** N. E. BINNS *Introd. Historical Bibliogr.* (ed. 2) xiv. 182 The rigid and formal types of this group are known as *Textura* types, or..*Lettre de Forme. Ibid.,* A broader, rounder, and less formal kind of type known as *Fere-Humanistica,* or *Lettre de Somme. Ibid.* 185 The early German and French printers also used various cursive types..known as *Bastarda,* or *Lettre Bâtarde.*

‖ **lettrine** (letrī·n). [Fr.] An initial letter, often decorated, and larger than the size of the text it accompanies.

1932 JOYCE *Let.* 11 Nov. (1957) II. 326 He liked her alphabet and has written to the manager of Burns and Oates about using these *lettrines* for a reprint of Chaucer's A.B.C. poem. **1934** *Ibid.* 25 Apr. (1966) III. 302, I enclose ..two *lettrines* of hers. **1970** *Private Library* III. 174 Wood engravings such as the 'lettrine' (initial letter) that figures at the beginning of this article.

lettrism (le·triz'm). Also in Fr. form **lettrisme.** [ad. F. *lettrisme,* f. LETTER *sb.*[1] + -ISM.] Applied to a movement in French art and literature, characterized by a repudiation of meaning, and the use of letters (sometimes invented) as isolated units. So **le·ttrist, lettriste** *sb.* and *a.*

1946 *Time* 2 Dec. 31/2 Lettrism, founded by Isidore Isou..is a theory of poetry as 'rhythmic architecture'. The rapidly growing hordes of Lettrists..prefer meaningless combinations of letters to dictionary words. **1948** *Spectator* 9 Apr. 432/2, I have been reading this week some poems written in the new mode of *'lettrisme'.* **1949** *Commentary* VIII. 183/2 'The new art,' declared Isou (his real name is Isidore Goldstein), 'accepts as its subject matter the letters reduced to, and become simply, themselves, replacing completely all poetic and musical elements which go beyond the letters in order to shape them into coherent works.' Thus was born Lettrisme, which may be regarded as a resurrection of some old avant-garde theories, or as a postwar symptom comparable to the explosions of Surrealism and Dada after World War I. **1951** *Amer. Mercury* LXXII. 659 In no time at all he [*sc.* Isidore Isou] was writing 'lettrist' poetry and he and his followers were assaulting the ears of everybody in the cafés of the Latin Quarter. **1962** *Times Lit. Suppl.* 13 Apr. 246/4 Hausmann's lettrist interview with some hypothetical French *lettristes.* **1964** *Ibid.* 3 Sept. 796/3 Lettrism is a creative movement..which claims to be able first to revolutionize every aesthetic discipline..from poetry to the theatre, by way of painting, and then to renovate the other cultural domains, whether philosophical or scientific. **1971** J. WILLETT in A. Bullock *20th Cent.* 244/2 The Lettrists in Paris and the Brazilian concrete poets of the 1950s, who were alike in their concentration on the appearance and sound of words or individual letters.

lettuce. Add: **1. b.** *slang* (orig. *U.S.*). Money.

1929 *Amer. Speech* June 357 If you wish to boast of having a great deal of money, you may speak of having.. wads of it, or a wad of lettuce, meaning a big roll of bills. **1932** J. DOS PASSOS *1919* 57 He still had more'n fifty iron men, quite a roll of lettuce for a guy like him. **1967** WODEHOUSE *Company for Henry* v. 84 How are you fixed for lettuce, Hank?.. Dough. Cash. Glue... Money. **1974** J. WAINWRIGHT *Cause for Killing* 216 'They spend money, in Beirut...' 'Phoenicia Street,' murmured Gantley. 'Anything... Any out-of-this-world luxury. Any service. Anything! You have the lettuce... Phoenicia Street can oblige.'

c. = **lettuce green.*

1963 *New Yorker* 1 June 115 *These* shirts..in..cedar, lettuce, navy or red.

3. lettuce green, a medium shade of green; also *attrib.*

1897 *Sears, Roebuck Catal.* 222/2 Delicate tintings of.. lemon, lettuce green, scarlet. **1929** E. WILSON *I thought of Daisy* i. 3, I saw lettuce-green cocktail glasses. **1970** *Guardian* 2 June 7/8 Mimosa, Lettuce Green, Lavender Blue. **1971** D. BEATY *Temple Tree* 157 A lettuce-green shirt.

letty (le·ti). *slang.* [ad. It. *letto* bed.] A bed, a lodging.

1846 *Swell's Night Guide* 71 While the old rum cull.. cannot wag from his Letty,..the accumulation of dirt thrives monstrously. **1875** T. FROST *Circus Life* xvi. 279 'Letty' is used both as a noun and a verb, signifying 'lodging' and 'to lodge'. **1933** E. SEAGO *Circus Company* v. 80 All the people of the smaller show dwell in wagons of their own, and do not seek for 'letties' in the town. **1957** J. OSBORNE *Entertainer* III. 77 *Jean:* We can't all spend our time nailing our suitcases to the floor, and shin out of the window. *Archie:* Scarper the letty.

let-up, *sb.*: see *LET *v.*[1] 35 c.

Letzeburgesch (letsǝbu·rgeʃ). Also **Letzeburg, Letzeburgisch, Lezebuurjesh,** etc. [Local name.] The name of the West Moselle Franconian dialect of German spoken by the natives of Luxembourg. Cf. *LUXEMBURGISCH.

1921 R. J. CASEY *Land of Haunted Castles* 152, I asked a young woman of Gosseldange..who..the 'Letzeburgers' were. She replied, proud of her ability to tell me in English: 'They are people who live in the Stadt Luxemburg... They speak a language that is very *difficile* to understand. It is not French. It is not German. It is not Luxemburg. It is Letzeburg.' **1944** *Luxembourg* (Geogr. Handbk. Ser. B.R. 528, Admiralty, Naval Intelligence Div.) 43 The native dialect, *Letzeburgesch,* is a Moselle Franconian dialect belonging to the West Middle German group. **1956** B. MILES *Attic in Luxembourg* xxviii. 215 Letzeburgesch, the Luxembourg dialect..although based upon old Teutonic origins,..borrowed extensively from Celtic, Roman and French. **1961** R. E. KELLER *German Dial.* 10 *Letzeburgisch* might be considered with some hesitation as a *Halbsprache* but *Schwyzertütsch* is for Kloss beyond the pale and he merely concedes that certain circumstances make it difficult to decide whether it might not after all qualify for the status of a *Halbsprache.* **1964** S. H. MULLER *World's Living Lang.* i. 16 The speech of 300,000 citizens of Luxemburg has diverged from standard German so much that it must be considered a distinct language, Luxemburgian (self-designation *lezebuurjesh*). **1965** W. B. LOCKWOOD *Informal Hist. German Lang.* 146 Some 300,000 persons..speak as their native idiom a now fairly uniform German dialect *Luxemburgisch* or, as they call it themselves, *Letzebursch.* **1972** *Guardian* 19 Sept. 14/3 The vast majority of Luxembourgers speak Letzeburgesch at home. **1973** *Times* 26 May (Benelux Suppl.) p. v/4 Luxembourg..is a case apart. Its 320,000 inhabitants speak a regional language called *Letzeburgisch* on which the official language, French, is superimposed.

leu (le·ˌu). Pl. **lei** (le·ˌi). [Rumanian, = lion.] The basic monetary unit of Rumania.

1879 *Coin Chart Manual* (N.Y.) 2 Value of U.S. Dollar. ..Roumania... 5 Lei 18⅛ Ben Paras. **1896** *Hist. Banking* III. VII. 333 Up to 1877 Roumania had no paper money. In that year, however, the Government issued non-compulsory notes of 5, 10, 20, 50, 100, and 500 lei. **1902** *Encycl. Brit.* XXXI. 291/1 In Rumania the unit of account is the *leu* of 100 *bani.* **1921** S. GRAHAM *Europe* viii. 107 The twenty, the hundred, the thousand-crown notes are almost identical... Roumanian lei are also much the same in appearance. **1940** G. CROWTHER *Outl. Money* viii. 305 Germany pushes up the value of the Reichsmark relatively to, say, the Roumanian leu; that enables her to quote a very attractive price, in lei, for wheat, without it costing her too much in Reichsmarks. **1967** *Economist* 19 Aug. (Suppl.) p. xlii/3 All families with a joint income of 2,000 lei..are now obliged to buy their flat.

Leucadian (l[i]ukē[i]·diăn), *sb.* and *a.* [f. *Leucadia* (see below) + -IAN.] **A.** *sb.* A native or inhabitant of Leucadia or Leucas, an island in the Ionian Sea. **B.** *adj.* Of or pertaining to Leucadia.

1615 G. SANDYS *Rel. Journey* I. 4 It was a custome amongst the Leucadians in their yearely solemnities, as a propitiatory sacrifice to Apollo, to throw some one from the top, condemned before for his offences. **1890** J. G. FRAZER *Golden Bough* II. iii. 213 From the Lover's Leap, a white bluff at the southern end of their island, the Leucadians used annually to hurl a criminal into the sea as a scapegoat. **1952** R. CAMPBELL tr. *Baudelaire's Poems* 181 Since then I watch on the Leucadian height. **1968** *Encycl. Brit.* XIII. 998/2 It was from the extremity..of this cape that in ancient times the 'Leucadian leap' was made, an ordeal whereby at the feast of Apollo accused persons were tried, those who survived the leap being picked up by boat.

leuchæmia. Add: Also **-emia.** The form **leuchæmia** is obs., and **leukæmia, leukemia** are the usual forms. [First formed as G. *leukämie* (R. Virchow 1848, in *Arch. f. path. Anat.* I. III. 563).] Substitute for def.: A progressive disease of man and other warm-blooded animals characterized by the hyperplastic transformation and greatly increased activity of leucopoietic tissue, leading to abnormal accumulations of leucocytes (freq. of immature or abnormal form) first at the site of leucopoiesis and then (usually) in the blood and elsewhere. (Further examples.)

1938 M. N. Richter in H. Downey *Handbk. Hematol.* IV. xlii. 2889 The type of cell and tissue primarily involved, the extent and distribution of infiltrations, and the presence or absence of immature cells in the peripheral blood make the lesions observed in different cases and different types of leucemia quite diverse, the only feature common to all being the increase in number of white corpuscles and their relative immaturity. **1942** C. L. Heel tr. *Engelbreth-Holm's Spontaneous & Exper. Leukæmia in Animals* i. 3 While leukæmia has not been observed in the lower vertebrates, the condition is known in many kinds of birds. *Ibid.* ii. 29 Detailed information is available about leukæmia in dogs, pigs, cattle, and..rodents. **1951** *New Biol.* XI. 97 In the treatment of leukaemia, a cancer-like disease of the white blood cells, several different classes of chemicals show some value. **1955** *Sci. News Let.* 19 Mar. 182/3 Leukemia, always fatal cancer of the blood, is showing up in survivors of the world's first military atom bombing. **1960** F. G. J. Hayhoe *Leukaemia* ii. 10 Patients with chronic leukaemias nearly always survive more than a year from the time of first symptoms, commonly for 3 to 5 years, and occasionally for very much longer. *Ibid.* 11 Subleukaemic and aleukaemic forms are more often encountered in the acute than in the chronic leukaemias, and they usually become fully leukaemic at a later stage in the progress of the disease. **1964** *Daily Tel.* 3 Jan. 13/3 A second British child suffering from leukemia ..arrived with his mother in Ajaccio, Corsica, to-day for treatment with a new serum which is claimed to cure the disease. **1966** Wright & Symmers *Systemic Path.* I. iv. 181/2 Post-mortem findings in acute leukaemia... Gross enlargement of the liver and spleen, such as is common in the chronic forms of leukaemia, is unusual.

leuchæmic, *a.* (In Dict. s.v. Leuchæmia.) Add: Now usu. **leukæmic, -emic** (see prec.). Add to def.: also, characteristic of or resembling leukæmia; *spec.* marked by an increased number of leucocytes in the blood. (Further examples.)

1922, 1946 [see *leucosis]. **1942** M. M. Wintrobe *Clin. Hematol.* xvi. 616 In many cases peculiarities can be observed in leukemic cells which are like those of neoplastic cells. **1949** [see *aleukæmic *a.*].

B. *sb.* An individual with leukæmia.

1964 *New Scientist* 13 Feb. 402/3 Nineteen of the 24 leukaemics were positive, one was doubtful and four were negative. **1973** *Nature* 12 Jan. 99/1 We have found that the response of lymphocytes from normals or leukaemics to low..doses of PHA [*sc.* phytohaemagglutinin] is often greatly reduced in the presence of serum obtained from patients with untreated AML [*sc.* acute myeloid leukaemia] and ALL [*sc.* acute lymphoblastic leukaemia].

leucin. Now always spelt **leucine.** Add to def.: an amino-acid that is one of the principal constituents of proteins. [First formed as F. *leucine* (H. Braconnot 1820, in *Ann. de Chim. et de Physique* XIII. 119).]

leuco-. Add: Many medical words with first element *leuco-* are also spelt *leuko-*. (*b*) In *Med.* used to represent 'leucocyte' (as in *leucopenia, -poiesis*). (*c*) In *Chem.* [after its use in *Dyeing*: see *b], used to form the names of some colourless compounds that are chemically transformed to coloured ones (as in *leucoanthocyanin*).

leu:coanthocya·nidin *Chem.*, any colourless substance which yields an anthocyanidin on heating with mineral acid; **leu:coanthocy·anin** *Chem.*, a leucoanthocyanidin; *spec.* any that is a glycoside; **leuco-, leukoci·din** († **-ine**) *Bacteriology* [a. F. *leucocidine* (H. van de Velde 1894, in *La Cellule* X. 434): see -cide 1], any leucotoxin produced by a microorganism; **leucocra·tic** *a. Petrol.* [ad. G. *leukokrat* (W. C. Brögger *Eruptivgesteine des Kristianiagebietes* (1898) III. 264), f. Gr. κρατ-εῖν to rule, prevail], (of a rock) light-coloured; rich in light-coloured minerals; **leu·coderm** (also *Leuco-*) *sb.* and *a.* [Gr. δέρμ-α skin], (of, pertaining to, or being) a person of a white-skinned race; **leucode·rmia** *Path.* = *leucoderma*; **leucodermic** *a.*, (*b*) (naturally) white-skinned; **leucopenia** (examples of the form *leukopenia*); **leucophore** [a. G. *leukophore* (R. Keller 1895, in *Pflügers Archiv Ges. Physiol.* LXI. 147)] = *iridocyte; **leu:copho·sphite** *Min.*, a hydrated basic phosphate of potassium and ferric iron found as white or greenish fine-grained masses; **leucoplacia**, now spelt *leuco-, leukoplakia*; (further examples); hence **leuco-, leukopla·kial** (now *rare*), **-pla·kic** *adjs.*; **leucoplast** (examples); **leuco-, leukopoiesis** (-poi,ī·sis) *Physiol.* [*-poiesis], the production of leucocytes; so **leuco-, leukopoie·tic** *a.*; **leuco·pterin** *Chem.* [*pterin], a white pigment found esp. in certain butterflies; 2-amino-4,6,7-trihydroxypteridine, $H_2NC_6N_4(OH)_3$; **leuco-, leuko-ta·xin(e** *Physiol.* [Gr. τάξις arrangement, order], a nitrogenous material found in injured tissue and inflammatory exudates which on injection causes inflammation, increase in the permeability of capillaries, and the attraction of leucocytes to the site; **leuco-, leukoto·xin** *Med.*, any substance which destroys leucocytes.

1935 G. M. & R. Robinson in *Jrnl. Chem. Soc.* 745 Probably class (b) [of leuco-anthocyanins] consists of relatively simple glycosides or diglycosides, whereas members of class (c) are sugar-free and should be regarded as leuco-anthocyanidins. **1962** J. Clark-Lewis in T. A. Geissman *Chem. Flavonoid Compounds* viii. 218 Choice between the terms leucoanthocyanin and leucoanthocyanidin seems so far to have rested on the preference of individual authors, but there are sound reasons for using leucoanthocyanidin for the sugar-free molecules, and as the general term, and for reserving the term leucoanthocyanin for leucoanthocyanidin glycosides. The terminations thus have the same significance as in anthocyanin and anthocyanidin. All the compounds of this class and known constitution so far discovered in nature are leucoanthocyanidins, i.e. do not contain sugar residues. **1967** J. B. Harborne *Compar. Biochem. Flavonoids* ix. 302 Leucoanthocyanidins (or condensed tannins) can be classified into three groups: (1) low molecular weight substances, which are probably dimers formed by linkage of a flavan-3,4-diol with a catechin.., (2) soluble oligomers, containing 4 to 8 flavan units, and (3) insoluble polymers (flavolans) of 10 or more units. **1967** *New Scientist* 4 May 270/3 The culprits that cause colour change in African mahogany are katechin and leucoanthocyanidin. **1920** O. Rosenheim in *Biochem. Jrnl.* XIV. 185 In the young leaf, however, the pseudobase does not occur in the free state, but in combination with either a carbohydrate or possibly another complex. For this combination the general name leuco-anthocyanin is proposed. **1960** L. H. Meyer *Food Chem.* vii. 251 Catechins and leucoanthocyanins are present in the tissues of those woody plants studied such as apples, peaches, grapes, almonds, and some pears, while they are absent in herbaceous plants. **1962** T. Swain in T. A. Geissman *Chem. Flavonoid Compounds* xvi. 536 It has been presumed by many workers that the term leucoanthocyanin, like the term catechin, refers to the monomeric C_{15} molecule. **1971** *Ann. de Technol. Agricole* XX. 32 Different methods for the dosage of leucoanthocyanins of white wines have been compared. **1894** *Jrnl. R. Microsc. Soc.* 732 The virulent cocci [of *Staphylococcus*]..secrete a special substance. This, which causes the death of the leucocytes, is termed 'substance leucocide' or leucocidine. **1909** J. G. Adami *Princ. Path.* I. iii. viii. 489 These leukotoxins are also known as leukocidins. **1970** Ambrose & Easty *Cell Biol.* xiv. 470 Some bacteria not only resist phagocytosis but produce substances, known as leucocidins, which kill phagocytes. **1909** A. Harker *Nat. Hist. Igneous Rocks* v. 112 The former [*sc.* camptonite, is] a melanocratic type..and the latter [*sc.* mænaite] leucocratic. **1954** H. Williams et al. *Petrogr.* ii. 33 In Johannsen's classification four rock classes are distinguished according to the volume-content of dark minerals, the limits being placed at 5, 50, and 95 percent. Shand also distinguishes four classes, but with different limits, as follows: leucocratic rocks, with less than 30 percent mafic minerals; mesocratic rocks, with 30–60 percent; melanocratic rocks, with 60–90 percent; and hypermelanic rocks, with more than 90 percent mafic minerals. **1965** G. J. Williams *Econ. Geol. N.Z.* xiv. 216/1 The Separation Point granite..is a massive white leucocratic soda-granite. **1924** A. C. Haddon *Races of Man* (ed. 2) 13 Occasionally in leucoderms, sometimes in Negroes, and as a rule in Mongoloid peoples, a fold of skin..covers the inner angle of the eye. *Ibid.* 84 The western steppe lands seem to have been the original home of fair (leucoderm) dolichocephals. **1935** Huxley & Haddon *We Europeans* iv. 115 A broad and convenient classification of skin-colour is as follows: (1) Leucoderms, or white-skinned (Caucasian) peoples; (2) Xanthoderms, or yellow-skinned peoples; (3) Melanoderms, or black-skinned peoples. **1888** *Syd. Soc. Lex.*, *Leucodermia*, see Leukoderma. **1908** *Practitioner* Aug. 349 They [*sc.* freckles] are an example of excess of pigment in the skin, a condition known as hyperchromasia, in contradistinction to achromasia, or leucodermia, in which there is a deficiency of pigment in the skin. **1926** H. H. Wilder *Pedigree of Human Race* vi. 348 Members of the Leucodermic race in Europe or America. **1961** R. D. Baker *Essent. Path.* ii. 18 In some inflammations the total white blood cell count is decreased (leukopenia). **1964** W. G. Smith *Allergy & Tissue Metabolism* ii. 16 Marked reductions in the number of leucocytes (leukopenia) and platelets (thrombocytopenia) circulating in the blood were described. **1924** L. Hogben *Pigmentary Effector Syst.* ii. 24 In the skin of the Chameleon there are present, immediately below the epidermis, cells charged with yellow pigment variously described as guanophores (Schmidt), leukophores or ochrophores (Keller), iridocytes (Pouchet), or interference cells (Brucke). **1963** M. Fingerman *Control of Chromatophores* i. 4 When the guanine consists of fine granules that can migrate the term leucophore is usually employed. **1932** E. S. Simpson in *Jrnl. R. Soc. W. Austral.* XVIII. 71 No previously described mineral approaches this in composition except minervite, a potassium aluminium phosphate, from which it differs in possessing a much greater basicity... It appears therefore to be a new species for which the name Leucophosphite is suggested. **1963** *Prof. Papers U.S. Geol. Survey* No. 475–C. 103/2 Leucophosphite and gypsum represent in large part only a recombination of the elements already present in the phosphatized wood when uplift of the enclosing Moreno Formation exposed it to weathering. **1972** *Amer. Mineralogist* LVII. 397 Leucophosphite, $K_2[Fe^{3+}{}_4(OH)_2(H_2O)_2(PO_4)_4].2H_2O$, possesses an atomic arrangement based on a discrete octahedral tetramer. **1920** W. E. Masters *Essent. Trop. Med.* vi. 477 Leucoplakia may also affect the penis, vulva and vagina. **1962** *Lancet* 1 Dec. 1170/2 Leucoplakia (or lichen sclerosus) diagnosed by the clinician on naked-eye appearances shows variable and non-specific histological features. **1962** *Ibid.* 8 Dec. 1228/2 Here operating is undesirable, except in those few patients in whom leukoplakia develops as well. **1973** *Daily Colonist* (Victoria, B.C.) 7 Sept. 2/1 Leukoplakia is a thickening of the membrane of a mucous surface, commonly on the lip or in the mouth. **1908** *Practitioner* Sept. 354, I believe that if sufficient examinations were made in syphilitic patients..leucoplakial patches would be found in the mucous membrane from time to time. **1923** *Surg. Gynecol. & Obstetr.* XXXVI. 189/1 The leukoplakial conditions of the urinary tract have received relatively little attention. **1907** *Arch. Middlesex Hosp.* IX. (6th Rep. Cancer Res. Lab.) 65 Those leucoplakic conditions of vulva, tongue, and lips which..often precede the development of squamous cell carcinoma. **1917** J. Bland-Sutton *Tumours, Innocent & Malignant* (ed. 6) xxx. 331 In some patients an ulcer appears in a leucoplakic patch. **1962** *Lancet* 1 Dec. 1170/2 If all vulvas described as leucoplakic on clinical grounds are subjected to biopsy, approximately 5% are found to be cancerous at the outset. *Ibid.* 8 Dec. 1228/2 Changes in vulval skin..are very common... Among other features, they are often white, but this does not mean that they are precancerous or leukoplakic. **1886** *Jrnl. R. Microsc. Soc.* 640 In the lower plants..the formation of leucoplasts is a subsequent process, a transformation of the coloured into a colourless chromatophore. **1887, 1902** Leucoplast [see *chloroplast]. **1964** *Oceanogr. & Marine Biol.* II. 199 All species [of the genus *Caulerpa* of green algae] possess amyliferous leucoplasts as well as the ordinary green plastids. **1913** Dorland *Med. Dict.* (ed. 7) 512/2 *Leukopoiesis*, production of leukocytes. **1942** M. M. Wintrobe *Clin. Hematol.* i. 26 Erythropoiesis in the spleen is at first more pronounced than leukopoiesis but it is short-lived. **1973** Woodliff & Herrmann *Conc. Haematol.* viii. 113 Disorders of leucopoiesis are usually reflected by changes in the peripheral blood. **1913** Dorland *Med. Dict.* (ed. 7) 512/2 *Leukopoietic*, forming or producing leukocytes. **1927** A. Piney *Recent Adv. Hæmatol.* iii. 35 Hyperplasias of a character similar to those occurring in the leucopoietic tissue may affect the erythropoietic one. **1973** Woodliff & Herrmann *Conc. Haematol.* viii. 113 A progressive malignant proliferation of the leucopoietic tissues. **1927** *Chem. Abstr.* XXI. 224 (*heading*) Leucopterin, the white wing pigment of cabbage butterflies (*Pieris brassicae* and *P. napi*). **1954** *Sci. News* XXXIV. 91 The purines and pterines contribute a major source of colour to the wings of butterflies... These compounds are only present in small amounts representing in the case of the white leucopterin of Pierid butterflies about 0·18 milligramme per specimen. **1937** V. Menkin in *Proc. Soc. Exper. Biol. & Med.* XXXVI. 167 For the sake of convenience the name leukotaxine is tentatively proposed for this active crystalline nitrogenous substance which is evidently released by injured tissue and is readily recovered in inflammatory exudates. **1947** *New Biol.* II. 135 The most reasonable hypothesis is..that leucotaxine is released from the killed and damaged cells of the injured skin we are considering, and is mainly responsible for the escape of fluid from nearby undamaged capillaries. **1957** *Amer. Jrnl. Physiol.* CLXXXIX. 99 (*caption*) A preliminary intravenous injection of 25 mg of cortisone acetate was performed in the tested rabbit to inactivate the masking effect of any leukotaxine possibly present in the acid exudate to be injected. **1964** W. G. Smith *Allergy & Tissue Metabolism* iii. 39 This material, which Menkin called leucotaxin, can upon injection into the skin induce increased capillary permeability and chemotactic attraction of polymorphs to the injection site. **1908** *Practitioner* Mar. 392 Roentgen-rays appear to lead to the production of veritable 'leucotoxins'. Normal leucocytes, exposed in vitro and in vivo to the action of such leucotoxins present in the serum of animals, which have been exposed to Roentgen-rays, undergo a specific disintegration. **1931** *Biol. Abstr.* V. 488/2 The virulent streptococci do not possess in the same degree the power of leukotoxin production. **1956** *Proc. Soc. Exper. Biol. & Med.* XCIII. 493/2 A leucotoxin develops in the blood of the rabbit in hemorrhagic shock, and..this leucotoxin severely impairs the antibacterial potential of the animal.

b. In Combs. in which *leuco* may be used *attrib.* (without a hyphen) as quasi-*adj.*, or be joined by a hyphen to the second element: chiefly in *Dyeing*, where *leuco* is used to denote the reduced, water-soluble colourless form of a dye which is fixed on the fibre and subsequently oxidized to the dye proper by the air; as *leuco-base* (so *leuco-basic* adj.), *-compound, -cyanide, -dye, -form, -fuchsin.*

1886 E. Knecht tr. *Benedikt's Chem. Coal-Tar Colours* 79 These compounds, called 'leuco-bases', are colourless and yield colourless salts with acids. By oxidation they are transformed..into the colour-bases, which differ from the 'leuco-bases' by containing one atom of oxygen. **1947** L. S. Pratt *Chem. & Physics Org. Pigments* viii. 140 The dyestuff is prepared by condensing *o*-chlorobenzaldehyde with dimethylaniline and then oxidizing the leuco base to the color base. **1958** J. R. Baker *Princ. Biol. Microtechnique* xvii. 309 Schiff's reagent..is often regarded as a leucobase, but this is an error; for a leucobase becomes coloured on oxidation and could not possibly serve in Feulgen's reaction. **1971** E. Gurr *Synthetic Dyes* 108 The leuco bases of triphenylmethane dyes (e.g. crystal violet and malachite green) are extremely light sensitive. **1956** *Nature* 14 Jan. 92/2 Leuco-basic fuchsin is specific for deoxyribonucleic acid. **1970** *Watsonia* VIII. 23 Root tips ..were..stained in leucobasic fuchsin. **1888** *Jrnl. Chem. Soc.* LIV. 493 The anthraquinone-dyes yield leucocompounds on reduction. **1906** *Notices Proc. R. Inst. Gt. Brit.* XVII. 107 What we are pleased to call leucocompounds, are in the majority of cases by no means colourless. Indigo-white itself is not white but yellow in its alkaline solution which we call a vat. Other vat-dyes have leucocompounds which are even more strongly coloured. **1961** Cockett & Hilton *Dyeing Cellulosic Fibres* viii. 280 All methods used in practice to apply vat dyes to cellulosic fibres involve, at some stage, the conversion of the insoluble vat dye to the soluble sodium salt of the so-called leuco compound of the dye. **1931** *Trans. Faraday Soc.* XXVII. 571 The pure alcoholic leuco cyanide solution is very suitable for a laboratory method [of measuring ultra-violet light]. **1965** J. Kosar *Light-Sensitive Syst.*

viii. 370 Aside from the photographic applications, light-sensitive leucocyanides are useful for detecting, measuring, and recording short wave ultraviolet light. **1954** *Textile Terms & Definitions* (Textile Inst.) 24 *Leuco dye*, a reduced form of dye from which the original dye may be regenerated by an oxidation process. **1973** J. F. WILLEMS in R. J. Cox *Proc. Symposium Photogr. Processing Univ. Sussex* 95 These leuco dyes are strong reducing agents, which in the adsorbed state on the silver halide grain start the development. **1959** *Nature* 15 Aug. 545/1 The production of a coloured dye by transformation of the leuco form. **1945** *Chem. Abstr.* XXXIX. 6288/1 (Index), Leuco-fuchsin. **1965** E. GURR *Rational Use Dyes Biol.* 94 Solutions of reduced dyes, such as Schiff's reagent (leuco fuchsin), leuco acid fuchsin and leuco patent blue in distilled water, are oxidized on heating and consequently restored in colour. **1967** *Jrnl. Med. Lab. Technol.* XXIV. 48 (*heading*) Nitric acid leucofuchsin technique for myelinated nerves.

leucocyte. Add: Also **leukocyte** (similarly **leukocytic**, etc.). (Further examples.)
1911 *Jrnl. Amer. Med. Assoc.* 25 Feb. 581/1 Alexin increases in the serum under conditions which favor disintegrating of leukocytes. *Ibid.*, The 'alexin' is synonymous with Metchnikoff's leukocytic ferment. *Ibid.*, Leukocytic extract is essentially the same in its action as alexin. *Ibid.*, The alexin varies with the degree of leukocytosis. **1947** Leukocytosis [see *GRANULOCYTOSIS]. **1951** A. GROLLMAN *Pharmacol. & Therapeutics* xxxi. 732 Mercurial poisoning is sometimes accompanied by a leukocytosis. **1971** J. SONG *Path. Sickle Cell Dis.* xviii. 355 Fever, vomiting, nausea, and leukocytosis. **1973** *Nature* 1 June 290/1 We cultured peripheral blood leukocytes for 24 or 48 h with phytohaemagglutinin.

leucosis. Add: Pl. **leucoses. d.** Also **leukosis**. [a. G. *leukosis* (Ellermann & Bang 1908, in *Centralbl. f. Bakteriol. Parasitenkunde u. Infectionskrankh.* (*Erste Abteil., Originale*) XLVI. 609).] = *LEUKÆMIA; *esp.* any of various leukæmic diseases of animals. Also *bovine leucosis,* a leukæmic disease of cattle; (*avian* or *fowl*) *leucosis complex,* a group of poorly-differentiated leukæmic diseases of poultry which are typically transmissible.
1922 V. ELLERMANN *Leucosis of Fowls & Leucemia Probl.* i. 9 Finally, it must be mentioned that Ellermann & Bang have proposed the word 'leucosis' as a common designation for leucemic and aleucemic cases, myeloses as well as lymphadenoses. **1927** A. PINEY *Recent Adv. Hæmatol.* iii. 35 The name 'leucosis' is suitable for all forms, either lymphatic or myeloid, and is much to be preferred to leukæmia. **1935** WHITBY & BRITTON *Disorders of Blood* xviii. 357 (*heading*) The leukæmias (leucoses). **1936** *Jrnl. Amer. Vet. Med. Assoc.* LXXXIX. 681 (*heading*) A study of transmissible fowl leukosis. **1941** *Ibid.* XCIX. 214/1 (*heading*) Studies on production of specific antibodies against the agent of the fowl-leucosis complex. **1943** BARGER & CARD *Dis. & Parasites Poultry* (ed. 3) vii. 177 The cause of the avian leukosis complex or fowl paralysis is a filter-passing agent. **1946** *Physiol. Rev.* XXVI. 48 The term leukemia or leukosis implies neoplasia of a blood cell (hemoblastosis) including both the aleukemic and leukemic types of the disease. **1960** *Proc. 7th Congr. European Soc. Haematol.* II. 291 (*heading*) The haematology of bovine leucosis. **1961** *Brit. Vet. Jrnl.* CXVII. 326 The separation of fowl paralysis granuloma from the leucoses has been suggested by Campbell. **1970** *Times* 13 Apr. 11/4 Only non-vaccinated maiden heifers and young bulls will be allowed in, and the stock will have to be cleared..of foot-and-mouth disease, tuberculosis, brucellosis, leucosis, leptospirosis, and Johnes disease.

leucotic (l*i*ūkǫ·tik), *a.* Also **leukotic.** [f. LEUC(OSIS + -OTIC.] Of, pertaining to, or affected with leucosis (in any sense).
1888 *Syd. Soc. Lex., Leucotic*, of, or belonging to, Leucoma. **1935** BARGER & CARD *Dis. & Parasites Poultry* vii. 162 The leukotic type of the disease. **1960** *Proc. 7th Congr. European Soc. Haematol.* II. 291 In 'leucotic' herds ..17 animals died. **1961** *Brit. Vet. Jrnl.* CXVII. 316 It has been calculated by Blaxland (1956) that seven to eight million pounds sterling are lost annually in Britain because of the leucotic complex, which in this particular context is taken to include the various types of fowl paralysis.

leucotomy (l*i*ūkǫ·tǫmi). *Surg.* [ad. F. *leucotomie* (E. Moniz *Tentatives Opératoires dans le Traitement de certaines Psychoses* (1936) viii. 195): see LEUCO- (here signifying the white matter of the brain) and -TOMY.] = *LOBOTOMY (in *spec.* sense).
1937 E. MONIZ in *Amer. Jrnl. Psychiatry* XCIII. 1379 (*heading*) Prefrontal leucotomy in the treatment of mental disorders. **1947** *Times* 13 Feb. 6/4 At intervals in the past 10 years details of the brain operation of leucotomy performed on patients with certain types of mental illness have appeared in the Press. **1950** M. GREENBLATT et al. *Stud. in Lobotomy* ii. 10 The English, however, use rather uniformly the more correct term 'leucotomy', in their description of the psychosurgical technic, whereas, in this country [sc. the U.S.A.], many still prefer the term 'lobotomy'. **1951** *Lancet* 21 July 91/2 (*heading*) Rostral leucotomy. **1958** *Listener* 5 June 931/2 People make moral objections to pre-frontal leucotomy even as a remedial measure. **1964** M. ARGYLE *Psychol. & Social Probl.* vi. 87 Other kinds of physical treatment, like insulin treatment and leucotomy, have declined in importance since the new methods have been discovered. **1967** [see *GYRECTOMY]. **1969** *Times* 22 Mar. 3/2 The symptoms of prefrontal leucotomy..include lack of inhibitions and inability to concentrate.

So **leu·cotome** [a. F. *leucotome* (E. Moniz 1936, in *Bull. de l'Acad. de Méd.* CXV. 390): see *-TOME[1]], an instrument used to perform leucotomy; **leuco·tomize** *v. trans.,* to perform leucotomy on; **leuco·tomized** *ppl. a.*
1937 E. MONIZ in *Amer. Jrnl. Psychiatry* XCIII. 1380 Sections were made in the subcortical white matter by a leucotome with a steel loop, tending to crush the white matter... At the present time we are using a leucotome with a steel band that cuts rather than compresses. **1951** *Lancet* 21 July 92/1 From the number of patients so leucotomised who have come to me for more extensive operations, the results do not appear very satisfactory. **1959** *Times* 24 July 4/4 Where not so long ago some of these patients might have been leucotomized we now no longer do so. **1964** M. ARGYLE *Psychol. & Social Probl.* xii. 149 Authoritarians, psychotics and leucotomized patients are all poor at person perception. **1969** *New Scientist* 30 Jan. 229/2 The destruction of localized areas in the brain has also been achieved by..the excision of a segment of tissue with an instrument (a leucotome).

leucovirus, var. *LEUKOVIRUS.

leucovorin (l*i*ūkǫ·vǒrin). *Biochem.* [f. mod.L. *Leuco(nostoc* (f. Gr. λευκο- LEUCO- + NOSTOC), the generic name + *citro)vor(um* (f. CITR-, CITRO- + L. *vor-āre* to devour + *-um*) the specific epithet, of the bacterium whose growth it was originally found to promote: see -IN[1].] = *folinic acid.
1951 H. P. BROQUIST et al. in *Federation Proc.* X. 167/1 A crystalline substance with the properties of the 'citrovorum factor' (CF) was prepared from pteroylglutamic acid... The amounts of this crystalline substance, 'leucovorin', required for half-maximum growth per ml. of PGA-deficient medium were 0·00015 μg. for *Leuconostoc citrovorum* 8081. **1954** *Poultry Sci.* XXXIII. 111/1 Leucovorin (synthetic citrovorum factor) appeared to be inferior to folacin in the nutrition of the chick. **1966** [see *FOLINIC *a.*]. **1971** *Cancer* XXVIII. 899/1 The combination of methotrexate with Leucovorin rescue is a well-tolerated therapeutic maneuver.

leukæmia. Now the usual form (with **leukemia**) of LEUCHÆMIA (q.v. in Dict. and Suppl.).

leukæmogenic (l*i*ūkī:mǫdʒe·nik), *a. Med.* Also **leukemogenic.** [f. *LEUKÆM(IA + -O + *-GENIC.] Capable of producing leukæmia; pertaining to the production of leukæmia.
1942 *Jrnl. Nat. Cancer Inst.* (U.S.) III. 231/2 Previous experiments indicated that X-rays are leukemogenic. **1953** *Cancer Res.* XIII. 267/2 Exposure to leukemogenic doses of x-rays. **1971** *New Scientist* 8 July 64/2 If these tumours were then removed.., these could then be shown to have leukaemogenic activity characteristic of leukaemia viruses. **1971** H. J. WOODLIFF *Leukaemia Cytogenetics* v. 47 Chromosomal abnormalities may be produced by many of the agents discussed above and many of these are also thought to be leukaemogenic, such as viruses, ionising radiation, chemicals and drugs. **1973** *Nature* 9 Feb. 397/1 Thymus dependent lymphatic leukaemia was induced [in mice] by irradiation or by a leukaemogenic virus.
So **leukæ·mogen,** a substance or agent capable of producing leukæmia; **leukæmoge·nesis,** the production or development of leukæmia.
1942 *Jrnl. Nat. Cancer Inst.* (U.S.) III. 239/1 A systematic study of changes in the blood pictures during the early phases of leukemogenesis was beyond the scope of this work. **1944** DORLAND & MILLER *Med. Dict.* (ed. 20) 804/1 Leukemogen. **1946** *Physiol. Rev.* XXVI. 48 Organisms are subject to accidental exposure to chemical, physical and other agents which may be powerful leukemogens. **1953** *Cancer Res.* 268/1 Genetic factors determine susceptibility to specific leukemogens. **1961** *Lancet* 30 Sept. 748/1 We have been interested in the role of the thymus in leukaemogenesis. **1971** *Brit. Med. Bull.* XXVII. 67/1 The back-lash effects could in fact be mistaken for the advent of a new leukaemogen. **1973** *Nature* 12 Jan. 95/1 Viruses are associated with leukaemogenesis in both laboratory and outbred animals.

leukæmoid (l*i*ūkī·moid), *a. Med.* Also **leuc-, -emoid.** [f. *LEUKÆM(IA + -OID.] Resembling (that found in) leukæmia but due to some other cause.
1926 *Amer. Jrnl. Med. Sci.* CLXXII. 529 Was it leukemia, simulating Banti's in an aleukemic early stage, or was it Banti's with a terminal leukemoid picture? **1940** *Acta Med. Scand.* CIII. 568 In another case of sepsis with marked hyperglobulinemia there was a leucemoid reaction with crowds of plasma cells. **1946** *Physiol. Rev.* XXVI. 62 The aerobic glycolysis values of preleukemic, leukemic and leukemoid lymph nodes, spleens and livers were 50 per cent to 100 per cent above normal. **1960** F. G. J. HAYHOE *Leukaemia* xvi. 318 The haematological findings in the myeloproliferative and lymphoproliferative syndromes provide a wide borderline between leukaemic and leukaemoid pictures,.. but we shall now be concerned with the unquestionably leukaemoid reactions occasionally observed in association with certain infections, metastasizing tumours, and some non-leukaemic blood diseases.

leuko-, var. LEUCO-.

leukocyte, -cytic, etc.: see LEUCOCYTE in Dict. and Suppl.

leukovirus (l*i*ū·kovəirŏs). *Virology.* Also **leuco-.** [f. *LEUKO- (in *LEUKÆMIA and *leukosis, *LEUCOSIS) + VIRUS.] Any of a group of pleomorphic viruses consisting of enveloped single-stranded RNA, different members of which cause leucosis or tumours in mammals and birds.
1968 F. FENNER *Biol. Animal Viruses* I. i. 26 The viruses which are associated with leukosis of chickens and murine leukemia have as their genetic material a molecule of single-stranded RNA of about 12 million daltons atomic weight. The pathogenic potential of both groups of agents is similar, as are the virions. These viruses can therefore be grouped together into a new group, for which we propose the name 'leukovirus'. *Ibid.* 28 Most infections with leukoviruses are latent for prolonged periods, but they may eventually cause fatal disease, usually apparent as a disturbance of the lymphoid or hemopoietic systems. **1970** *Nature* 14 Nov. 622/1 The RNA tumour viruses (leucoviruses) seem to have a different mode of replication from other RNA-containing viruses. **1971** MARAMOROSCH & KURSTAK *Compar. Virol.* xvi. 514 The more euphonious term *leukovirus* suggested by Fenner (1968) has recently been approved by the International Commission for the Nomenclature of Viruses and will be used here. **1972** *Sci. Amer.* Jan. 25/3 A group of viruses, variously called the RNA tumor viruses, the leukoviruses or the rousviruses.., replicate by another mode of information transfer.

lev (lev). Also (erron.) **leva.** Pl. **leva, levas, levs.** [Bulg. *lev* (pl. *leva*), lion.] The basic monetary unit of Bulgaria.
1902 *Encycl. Brit.* XXVI. 451/2 Bulgaria..has adopted the metric system... The monetary unit is the *lev*,.. nominally equal to the franc. **1908** *Daily Chron.* 31 Oct. 1/6 The East Roumelian tribute amounts to 2,951,000 leva. **1921** S. GRAHAM *Europe* ii. 33 Bulgarian francs or levas are..worth a bare three-farthings each today. **1928** *Daily Tel.* 16 Oct. 18 The Budget 1927–28 showed a surplus of sixty-five million levs. **1928** *Morning Post* 20 Oct. 11/5 The booty is estimated at many hundreds of thousands of levas (the leva is valued at about 600 to the £). **1959** *Chambers's Encycl.* II. 674/2 In May 1952 a drastic monetary reform was carried out whereby the lev was linked to the Russian rouble at the rate of 1·70 leva = 1 rouble. **1972** D. DAKIN *Unification of Greece* xiii. 188 Bulgaria had borrowed from France 245 million leva in 1904 and 1907.

|| **levada** (levā·dă). [Pg.] In Madeira, a canal for irrigation.
1885 J. Y. JOHNSON *Madeira* vi. 68 Besides the great levadas there are minor ones in every parish. **1920** *National Rev.* Nov. 408 Levadas are narrow canals cut out of the solid rock of volcanic basalt of which the island consists: watercourses of masonry, which intersect Madeira like a network, for the purposes of irrigation. *Ibid.* 409 One of the more hazardous levada walks. **1963** *Times* 28 Mar. 14/6 We..set off from the rest-house on the *levada* at Queimadas. **1975** *Country Life* 13 Feb. 400/1 Every farm is irrigated by levadas—a network of channels which carry rainwater down from the mountains.

|| **levade** (ləvā·d). [Fr., f. *lever* to raise.] (See quot. 1954.)
1944 E. BYNG *World of Arabs* 246 The three widely celebrated specialties of Vienna's 'Spanish' Riding School ..are known as the levade, the piaffe, and the capriole. **1953** G. BROOKE *Introd. Riding* vii. 69 A system that he believed would enable him to demonstrate the 'levade' and 'croupade' and similar gymnastics. **1954** A. PODHAJSKY *Spanish Riding School* (ed. 2) 22/1 Training above the ground is usually started either with the Levade or Pesade. In both these exercises which are constructed from the Piaffe, the hind quarters, deeply bent in the haunch, support the entire weight of the body, whilst the fore quarters with the fore feet drawn up under the body, rise more or less high above the ground; the duration of this position depends upon the dexterity and strength of the stallion. If the horse raises the fore quarters so high that his body reaches an angle of 45° with the earth, this is called 'Pesade'; on the other hand, if it raises the fore quarters less high, one speaks of a Levade.

Levallois (ləva·lwa). *Archæol.* [f. the Fr. place-name *Levallois* in north central France, NW. of Paris.] Used *attrib.* as a term for one of the main palæolithic cultures, post-Acheulian and pre-Mousterian. Hence **Levalloisean** (-wa·ziän), **-ian** *adjs.* Also **Levalloisoid** (-wa·zoid) *a.,* related to or similar to, this culture. Also in *Comb.,* as **Levalloiso-Mouste·rian** *a.*
1921 R. A. S. MACALISTER *Text-bk. European Archæol.* I. 239 The transition from Lower to Middle Palaeolithic is marked by the introduction of two important types of implement; the miniature coup-de-poing..and the Levallois scraper. **1932** [see *CLACTONIAN *a.*]. **1934** *Jrnl. R. Anthrop. Inst.* LXIV. 342 Partly Chellean, partly local Acheulean with a hint of Levalloisean. **1937** *Ann. Reg. 1936* 52 Associated with Levalloisian culture. **1937** GARROD & BATE *Stone Age Mt. Carmel* I. 1. ii. 8 The majority of these [sc. flints] were of Levalloiso-Mousterian type, but a fair number could be referred to the Lower Aurignacian. **1938** *Encycl. Brit. Bk. of Year* 49/1 A Mousterian using the Levallois technique. **1938** *Proc. Prehist. Soc.* IV. 19 A Levalloisian flake industry forms part of the latest Acheulian. **1952** *Ibid.* XVIII. 10 They include Acheulean hand-axes and Levalloisoid flakes. **1959** J. D. CLARK *Prehist. S. Afr.* ii. 40 The Middle Stone Age is essentially the time of the specially prepared core and the flake tool derived from it. This is the technique known in Europe as 'Levallois' technique' and in Africa

as 'prepared platform technique'. **1961** L. D. STAMP *Gloss. Geogr. Terms* 532 In East Anglia Clactonian is contemporaneous with Acheulian; Levalloisian with Mousterian.

levan (lī·væn). *Chem.* [f. LÆVO-, LEV(O- + -an, after *dextran*.] A lævulosan (fructan); *esp.* any fructan of the kind produced by certain bacteria, in which the linking of adjacent fructose units is between the second carbon atom of one unit and the sixth of the next.
1902 R. G. SMITH in *Proc. Linn. Soc. New South Wales* XXVI. 603 From a review of the lævo-rotatory gummy substances that are hydrolysed to levulose, it appears that this bacterial gum has not hitherto been described. I therefore propose for it the name levan, which was suggested by the polariscopic nature of the gum and derived glucose, and also from the fact that another bacterial gum, which is derived from dextrose, and which yields dextrose on hydrolysis, is known as dextran. **1948** W. PIGMAN *Chem. Carbohydrates* xv. 604 Fructosans or levans are found widely distributed throughout the plant kingdom..and generally serve as reserve polysaccharides in place of, or in addition to, starch. **1953** WHISTLER & SMART *Polysaccharide Chem.* xi. 276 D-Fructose polymers occurring in plants..are designated as fructans while those elaborated by microorganisms are called levans... Actually the levans are structurally similar to some of the plant polyfructoses. **1965** T. AKAZAWA in Bonner & Varner *Plant Biochem.* xii. 287 Although the size of these substances is small, 3–30 hexose residues per molecule, their structure is basically the same as that of the high molecular bacterial levan produced by several microorganisms... The name grass levan has therefore been given to this group of plant compounds. A further interesting point is..that fructosans of inulin type, $\beta\text{-}(2{\rightarrow}1)$, and of levan type, $\beta\text{-}(2{\rightarrow}6)$, are the main constituents of stem and ear tissues, respectively, of cereal plants.

levantinism (lĭvæ·ntiniz'm). [f. LEVANTIN(E *a.* and *sb.* + -ISM.] The spirit or culture of the Levant.
1949 KOESTLER *Promise & Fulfilment* III. iv. 330 What kind of a civilization will Israel's be? Will it be..the superficial veneer of Levantinism? **1961** *Guardian* 6 Feb. 8/2 Mr Ben-Gurion warned his countrymen against letting 'Levantinism' creep into their national life. **1973** *Observer* 6 May 6/6 Israel's leaders worry about 'levantinism'.

leva·ntinize, v. [f. as prec. + -IZE.] *trans.* To make Levantine in form or character.
1929 *Times* 5 Nov. 17/4 The Government's policy of 'Europeanizing' a somewhat levantinized Administration. **1930** *Times Lit. Suppl.* 4 Sept. 691/1 The rest of the Turks remained farmers..and thereby escaped the contamination of the Levantinized Ottomanism. **1946** KOESTLER *Thieves in Night* 112 Our small community will..become levantinised, submerged in the Arab sea.

|| **levari facias** (livā·ri fēi·ʃiæs). *Law.* [L., = to cause to be levied, f. *levari*, to be levied, f. *levāre* to raise + *facias* cause, 2nd pers. sing. pres. subj. of *facĕre* to do, make.] (See quot. 1768.)
a **1625** H. FINCH *Law* (1627) IV. xlvi. 471 A *Leuari facias*.. *Leuari facias* to leuie execution of the profits of his land and Chattels. **1768** BLACKSTONE *Comm.* III. xxvi. 417 A third species of execution is by writ of *levari facias*; which affects a man's goods and the *profits* of his lands, commanding the sheriff to levy the plaintiff's debt on the lands and goods of the defendant;.. little use is now made of this writ. **1818** [see FIERI-FACIAS]. **1888** *Encycl. Brit.* XXIV. 696/2 *Levari facias* is the means of levying execution for forfeited recognizances. **1959** JOWITT *Dict. Eng. Law* II, *Levari facias*..had been practically superseded before 1883 by the writ of *elegit*; and the Bankruptcy Act, 1883, s. 146 (2), enacted that it should no longer be issued in any civil proceeding.

|| **leveche** (leve·tʃe). [Sp.] A hot, dry, more or less southerly wind of south-eastern Spain, the local counterpart of the sirocco.
1887 *Encycl. Brit.* XXII. 296/2 The eastern part of this [southern] zone is the part of Spain which is liable to be visited from time to time by the scorching and blasting *leveche*, the name given in Spain to the sirocco. **1927** [see *GIBLI]. **1962** J. E. VAN RIPER *Man's Physical World* vii. 222/2 The Mediterranean area also is the home of a hot, searing, dust-laden wind off the Sahara, known in various localities as sirocco, khamsin, leveche, and samiel.

levee, sb.1 Add: **1. b.** *Geol.* A low broad ridge of water-laid sediment running along the side of a stream channel; also, any of various similar natural embankments, as those formed by mud flows or lava flows, or along a submarine channel.
1870 in L. C. Cramton *Early Hist. Yellowstone Nat. Park* (1932) 129 Passing over a sand levee, grown up with sagebrush, we found ourselves on the open beach of the great Yellowstone Lake. *Ibid.* 137 The shoreline is bordered by a levee of obsidian, lava pebbles, and calcareous fragments, cutting off and inclosing ponds of water behind it. **1910** *Proc. Indiana Acad. Sci. 1909* 260 Deltas occasionally take the form of long, narrow ridges upon one or both sides of a stream, resembling the natural levees in the 'goosefoot' of the Mississippi. **1942** *Jrnl. Geomorphol.* V. 222 (heading) Mudflow levees. **1957** G. E. HUTCHINSON *Treat. Limnol.* I. i. 99 Levees may form along the water courses. **1962** E. A. VINCENT tr. Rittmann's *Volcanoes* i. 33 When the supply of lava diminishes and finally comes to an end, the still-fluid lava inside the stream continues to flow out and the mantle of scoriae collapses, leaving a more or less even flow of scoriaceous block lava (clinker lava), flanked on both sides by upstanding block walls, called lava moraines (scoria moraines, lava levées). **1964** *Bull. Amer. Assoc. Petroleum Geol.* XLVIII. 1141/2 Trawl No. 23 was taken from a natural levee [of the Congo Submarine Canyon] and although the water depth was more than 500 fathoms greater than that of trawl No. 22, there was no marked decrease in diversity and abundance of animal life. **1968** R. W. FAIRBRIDGE *Encycl. Geomorphol.* 651/2 Alluvial streams flowing on flood plains commonly develop natural levees. Each levee is a low, wide ridge located immediately adjacent to the channel. **1972** G. A. MACDONALD *Volcanoes* v. 84 Overflows spread lava a few feet on either side of the river... Repeated overflows gradually build up natural levees.

levee, v.1 (Earlier examples.) Also, to shut or keep *off* by means of a levee.
1832 R. BAIRD *View of Valley of Mississippi* xxii. 269 Much has been done to levee or embank the Mississippi River. **1837** J. L. WILLIAMS *Territory of Florida* 45 Where there is clay enough in the soil, to form good embankments, the waters might be leveed off. **1847** J. PALMER *Jrnl. Trav. Rocky Mts.* 121 Several islands in the river might be leveed and successfully cultivated.
So **levee·ing** vbl. sb.
1845 *Indiana Senate Jrnl.* 364 An act to authorize the leveeing of Blue river, in Shelby county.

|| **levée en masse** (ləve aṅ mas). [Fr.] Mass mobilization, orig. in Revolutionary France, in response to invasion; = LEVY sb.1 3. Also *fig.*
1813 F. BURNEY *Let.* 12 Oct. (1905) VI. 95 Were he not essentially necessary in some department of civil labour and use, he would surely be included in some *levée en masse*. **1832** *Edin. Rev.* Apr. 254 A *levèe* [sic] *en masse* was decreed. The zeal of the Polish patriots was unbounded. **1895** T. A. WALKER *Man. Public Internat. Law* 135 It is, in fact, clear law that a combatant to be lawful must be formally authorised by a recognised Government, or be a member of a *levée en masse* rising on the approach of an invader. **1940** *Economist* 22 June 1067/1 There has been an outcry..for an immediate *levée en masse*, for the calling up now of every able-bodied man not busy on war work. **1943** J. M. THOMPSON *French Revolution* xxii. 424 A decree of February 24th, '93, ordered the levying of three hundred thousand men—..less than half the necessary number was procured. It became clear that the Convention must fall back on..a *levée en masse*, or wholesale compulsory enlistment. This plan..finally took shape in Carnot's decree, as it is generally called, of August 23rd. **1949** I. DEUTSCHER *Stalin* v. 143 They were the 'activists'..behind which there moved into battle a genuine political *levée en masse*. **1972** *Times* 29 Dec. 11/7 A levée en masse is one thing, assassination is quite another.

level, sb. Add: **2. b.** *on the level,* (in a) fair, honest, or straightforward (way); reliable, true. Freq. as *adv. phr.* = honestly; truthfully. *colloq.* (orig. *U.S.*).
1872 G. P. BURNHAM *Mem. U.S. Secret Service* p. vii, On the level, meeting a man with honorable intentions. **1896** ADE *Artie* vi. 50, I see barrel-house boys goin' around for hand-outs that was more on the level than you are. **1901** 'J. FLYNT' *World of Graft* iii. 89 When a man who has been a thief makes up his mind to quit stealing and live 'on the level', they say in the Under World that he has 'squared it'. **1932** A. J. WORRALL *Eng. Idioms* 50 You may be quite sure that the business is quite on the level. **1936** N. MARSH *Death in Ecstasy* xvii. 209 I've had no more'n my fair share. Same goes for Raveenje. He's on the level all right. **1958** R. GRAVES in *Times Lit. Suppl.* 15 Aug. p. x/3 He also prefers pools to premium-bond gambling—in which a bloke can't choose his own combination of numbers, so how does one know that it's on the level? **1970** G. F. NEWMAN *Sir, You Bastard* ii. 47 If you're on the level, we won't object. **1896** ADE *Artie* v. 42 On the level, I'm surprised you ain't on to that. **1914** WODEHOUSE *Man Upstairs* 63 'You look good to muh,' he said gallantly. 'The idea!' said Maud, tossing her head. 'On the level,' Mr. Shute assured her. **1923** R. D. PAINE *Comrades of Rolling Ocean* iii. 44 This was no fault of mine, on the level. **1931** E. LINKLATER *Juan in Amer.* III. iii. 231 'You're kidding,' said Buddy. 'On the level!' replied Olympia. **1942** T. RATTIGAN *Flare Path* II. ii. 137 On the level. I couldn't really.

3. d. A position (on a real or imaginary scale) in respect of amount, intensity, extent, or the like; the relative amount or intensity of any property, attribute, or activity. Freq. preceded by a sb. denoting the property, etc., referred to, as *danger, energy, noise level*.
1897 *Lancet* 5 June 1541/1 The pulse had been rising, and by 8.30 P.M. had reached its normal level (72 in the sitting posture). **1926** *Encycl. Brit.* III. 281/1 Nothing is to be gained by amplifying a signal below the 'noise level' at the location of the receiver. **1931** A. W. NYE in L. Cowan *Recording Sound for Motion Pict.* ii. 31 The sensation level of any sound reaching the ear is the number of decibels it is above the threshold level of audition. *Ibid.*, A change of the level of a sound by 1 db is approximately the smallest that the ear can detect. **1934** G. B. SHAW *On Rocks* I. 208 By the last returns the export of Spanish onions has again reached the 1913 level. **1935** [see *danger level* s.v. *DANGER sb. C]. **1942** W. B. BOAST *Illumination Engin.* x. 166 Recommended levels of illumination must provide an adequate safety factor..to maintain visibility well above threshold values for critical tasks. **1948** W. E. STYLER in M. Beloff *Hist.* xv. 320/1 Unemployment reached previously unknown levels, and overseas markets collapsed. **1958** H. G. M. SPRATT *Magn. Tape Recording* vii. 207 When recording it is essential to provide some means of indicating the level of the signal applied to the tape to ensure that it is neither too high nor too low. *Ibid.* 208 Low signal levels. **1967** [see *danger level* s.v. *DANGER sb. C]. **1968** MILLER & SAWERS *Technical Devel. Mod. Aviation* vii. 223 The level of general passenger comfort aboard the four-engined jets. **1971** *Times* 17 Mar. 21 (Advt.), I am encouraged by the current general level of orders and I am sure that because of the action which has been taken since the merger, [etc.]. **1973** HARRISON & WATERS *Burne-Jones* iii. 25 Possessing a high level of natural skill Edward Jones made rapid progress. **1973** *Nature* 23 Nov. 183/1 That could result in dangerous levels of sulphuric acid and sulphates in city air. **1974** *Daily Tel.* 11 Mar. 16 New house starts over the last three months are down to 40 per cent. of their level at this time last year.

e. *Physics.* More fully, *energy level.* An amount of energy associated with an atom or other quantized system and capable of being possessed by one of its constituents, being usu. measured relative to the minimum possible energy of that constituent; also, a discrete state of a quantized system characterized by such energy; *spec.* a state or group of states of an atom characterized by the quantum numbers n, L, S, and J, as distinguished from a 'term' (a group of levels: see *TERM *sb.*) and a 'state' so called (a constituent of a level: see *STATE *sb.*).
1922 A. D. UDDEN tr. *Bohr's Theory of Spectra* III. iv. 116 The values of the atomic energy corresponding to these [stationary] states are frequently referred to as the 'energy levels' of the X-ray spectra. **1925** RUSSELL & SAUNDERS in *Astrophysical Jrnl.* LXI. 69 When the series limit—or ionization level—can only be found inaccurately..the common convention of measuring terms from this level becomes inconvenient... A desirable alternative might be to set the zero-level at the *lowest* term and measure the others upward from this... In such cases, the numerical values referred to the lowest level might be called 'levels' to distinguish them from 'terms', referred to ionization as zero-point. **1926** R. W. LAWSON tr. Hevesy & Paneth's *Man. Radioactivity* vii. 75 This suggests that even in the nucleus of an atom there are different energy levels. **1934** H. E. WHITE *Introd. Atomic Spectra* v. 78 [In sodium] just as in hydrogen these energy levels represent certain possible energy states of an electron, and transitions between them represent spectrum lines. **1935** CONDON & SHORTLEY *Theory Atomic Spectra* iv. 122 All except s configurations split into two levels, corresponding to $j = l + \tfrac{1}{2}$ and $j = l - \tfrac{1}{2}$... The (one or) two levels to which each configuration is split are together said to constitute a doublet term. **1955** R. D. EVANS *Atomic Nucleus* iv. 122 After the emission of the β ray, each residual nucleus of Si^{28} is left in an excited level at about 1·78 Mev above its ground level. **1962** D. F. SHAW *Introd. Electronics* ix. 170 There are important modifications to the arrangement of energy levels when, as in a crystalline solid, the atoms are separated by distances of the same order of magnitude (10^{-8} cm) as the atomic diameters themselves... The valence electrons may no longer be associated with a particular atom. They become a group of 'free electrons' in energy levels which belong to the lattice as a whole. **1962** R. E. DODD *Chem. Spectroscopy* ii. 78 Transitions between rotational levels [of a molecule] without change in vibrational or electronic energy, give lines in the far infra-red and microwave region. **1970** G. K. WOODGATE *Elem. Atomic Struct.* i. 5 The spin–orbit interaction is the largest relativistic effect and is responsible for fine structure. Each term splits into levels whose separations are of the order of 1–$1{,}000$ cm^{-1}. *Ibid.* 6 The levels are split further into states by the application of a laboratory magnetic field... This is called the Zeeman effect.

f. *Statistics.* In full, *level of confidence* or *significance.* A number chosen as the maximum (or minimum) value of the probability with which any statistical result must be false (or true) for that result to be accepted as having been demonstrated.
1925 R. A. FISHER *Statistical Methods for Research Workers* vi. 157 Taking the four definite levels of significance, represented by P = ·10, ·05, ·02, and ·01, the table shows for each value of n, from 1 to 20, and thence by larger intervals to 100, the corresponding values of r. **1931** L. H. C. TIPPETT *Methods of Statistics* iii. 48 Adopting the 0·05 level of significance, a deviation in the mean greater than twice its standard error is statistically significant. **1937** YULE & KENDALL *Introd. Theory Statistics* (ed. 11) xxii. 425 There are..two values of P [sc. a probability] which are widely used to provide a rough line of demarcation between acceptance and rejection of the significance of observed deviations. These values are $P = 0\cdot05$ and $P = 0\cdot01$, and are said to define 5 per cent. and 1 per cent. levels of significance. **1950** W. FELLER *Introd. Probability Theory* I. vii. 142 However, no sample size can give absolute assurance that $|p'-p| < 0\cdot005$... Since absolute certainty is unattainable, we settle for an arbitrary confidence level α, say $\alpha = 0\cdot95$, and require that $|p'-p| < 0\cdot005$ with probability 0·95 or better. **1972** *Jrnl. Social Psychol.* LXXXVII. 39 The situations variable was significant at the ·01 level for all four dependent variables. *Ibid.* 48 A t value of 2·33 or greater indicates that differences between the high and low criterion group means are significant at the ·01 level of confidence.

g. Contextually in *Broadcasting*, etc.: the sound level or signal level as it shows up in the different pieces of equipment. Also *attrib.* in *level test*, a test of signal levels to determine whether changes in control settings, microphone positions, etc., are required.
1940 E. McGILL *Radio Directing* ix. 184 If many sound effects are devised it will be found that a great amount of rehearsal time will be consumed in trying to bring to perfection the levels and balances of sounds against orchestra

..under unfavorable acoustic circumstances. **1941** *B.B.C. Broadcasting Terms* 17 Level test. **1962** A. Nisbett *Technique Sound Studio* iv. 79 The purpose of control of levels and lining-up of equipment..is to make the best use of the region between which noise and distortion overtake the recording. **1966** *Listener* 4 Aug. 181/3 Delius's *Requiem*..seemed harassed by eccentric studio management, with levels all over the place. **1966** B. Glemser *Dear Hungarian Friend* xiii. 223 We must do a level test... Just talk naturally..and we will see what we pick up. **1969** J. Elliot *Duel* III. iii. 251 He wants you to say a few words..just for the level.

4. b. A plane or status in respect of rank or authority; position in a hierarchy. Freq. with a qualifying adj.

1933 L. Bloomfield *Language* iii. 49 Provincial colorings of standard English are tied up with differences of social level. **1937** A. Huxley *Ends & Means* x. 148 Examples of non-violence on the governmental level are seldom of a very heroic kind. **1944** *Amer. Speech* XIX. 234/1, I have often been amused at the constant recurrence of certain catchwords and phrases in [Government] memoranda... *level* ('This matter will be handled at the regional *level*'). **1945** *N.Y. Times* 24 June IV. 6/4 One of the reporters asks if he knows of any obstacle to our perfect cooperation with the Russians. Quick as a flash General Eisenhower replied, 'On my level, none.' **1948** Masterson & Phillips *Federal Prose* vi. 30 Until a program for personnel induction at the infant level can be coordinated with the Federal Prose tutorship objectives, this situation will continue to create embarrassments at the administrative and higher levels. **1952** *Economist* 20 Sept., How long it takes to get even a simple low-level decision. **1955** *Times* 10 May 10/1 The western Foreign Ministers have agreed in Paris to invite Russia to a four-Power conference, though the level at which the meeting should be held is not yet decided. **1960** *B.S.I. News* Jan. 9/2 This sort of progress can only be achieved through full consultation from and with users at the national level. **1962** *Sci. Survey* III. 263 There exist equally interesting relationships between odours and animal behaviours on a different and more profound level. **1971** *Guardian* 24 Sept. 22/7 On instructions from director-level, the estimates..had been prepared. **1974** *Daily Tel.* 1 Apr. 6/7 At the next level of responsibility are the 14 regional health authorities. **1974** *Nature* 17 May 210/2 In talking about the recognition of [alien] life at the microscopic level the decision is largely an aesthetic one. **1974** Green & Hooper *C. S. Lewis* x. 253 The stories can be read and enjoyed on at least two levels: by the child who perhaps knows nothing..of any of the authors whose works Lewis knew; and by the reader who knows many.

c. *Linguistics.* (See quots.)

1935 *Trans. Philol. Soc.* 61 Now to illustrate this empirical analysis of meaning at the phonetic, morphological, syntactical, and semantic levels. **1942** C. F. Hockett in *Language* Jan.–Mar. 3 Linguistics is a classificatory science. The starting-point in such a science is to define (1) the universe of discourse and (2) the criteria which are used in making the classification. Selection and preliminary ordering of data determine the *range* of analysis; the choice of criteria fixes the *level* of analysis. In linguistics there are various ranges,... and two basic levels, *phonological* and *grammatical*. **1958** C. Rabin in *Aspects of Translation* 130 Items which are the same at all levels (e.g. numbers) do not function as level-markers. **1959** M. Halle *Sound Pattern Russ.* i. 25 The rules of translation which make up the grammar can all be subsumed under the formula 'replace x by y under condition z'... A set of rules yielding representations of a particular type is called a *linguistic level*. **1964** E. Bach *Introd. Transformational Gram.* vi. 59 The word 'level' is also used occasionally in another sense to refer to the ordering of rules within a single level and also to the ordering of the PS, transformational, and phonological rules with respect to each other. **1964** M. A. K. Halliday et al. *Ling. Sci.* i. 10 From these three types of patterning are derived the three principal levels: substance, form and context. **1964** R. H. Robins *Gen. Ling.* 12 By extension the term level of language is used to designate those aspects of a language on which at any time the linguist is focusing his attention. **1969** *Pocket Oxf. Dict.* (ed. 5) (Suppl. Austral. & N.Z. Words) 1017 There are 'levels of usage' in Australia and New Zealand as there are elsewhere and the cautionary labels colloq., sl. (= slang), etc., are therefore employed here in the customary manner as a guide to currency. **1973** *Archivum Linguisticum* IV. 17 In the field of English intonation studies, bones of contention ..spring readily to mind: levels versus configurations.

12. level test (see *3 g); **level tube** = *bubble-tube* s.v. *Bubble *sb.* 6.

1890 Level tube [see *bubble-tube* s.v. *bubble *sb.* 6]. **1950** J. Clendinning *Princ. & Use of Surveying Instruments* v. 121 The level tube consists of a glass tube, partially filled with liquid, the inner surface of which is carefully ground.

level, *a.* and *adv.* Add: **A.** *adj.* **7. b.** (Earlier example.) So *level head,* a well-balanced person.

1869 'Mark Twain' *Innoc. Abr.* xl. 426 The wanderers were right, and the heads of the same were level. **1906** 'O. Henry' *Four Million* 204 James Williams belonged among the level heads.

9. (Earlier U.S. and later U.K. examples.) Also *levelest* in the same sense, and similarly *level worst,* etc.

Of these only *level best* is standard in the U.K.

1851 *An Arkansaw Doctor* 87 (Th.), We put our horses out at their level best. **1884** 'Mark Twain' *Huck. Finn* xxviii. 270 The old man..was on hand and looking his level pisonest. **1891** *Harper's Mag.* July 208/2 The pony will not do his level worst again. **1898** H. S. Canfield *Maid of Frontier* 97 She told me..that she was goin' to do her levelest to make our little home comfortable. **1920** Galsworthy *In Chancery* II. vii. 186 Val walked out behind his mother, chin squared, eyelids drooped, doing his level best to despise everybody. **1933** M. Lowry *Ultramarine* 205 You've been doing your level best to make life a misery to me since we left home. **1937** V. Bartlett *This is my Life* xi. 179 Everyone was doing his level best to make me feel nervous. **1953** R. Lehmann *Echoing Grove* II. 89 When the pain nagged he thought about the relation between worry and his acid juices, and did his level best to stop worrying. **1969** *Listener* 24 Apr. 556/1 He did his level best to suppress the views of other members of the embassy.

10. *level-backed, -balanced, -bellied, -browed, -grown, -lidded, -mouthed, -ranked, -tempered* adjs.; **level-compounded** *a. Electr. Engin.,* applied to a compounded generator in which the windings are such as to produce the same voltage on full load as on no load (and usually on intermediate loads also); = *flat-compounded* adj. s.v. *Flat *a.* 15; **level luffing,** luffing in which the load is maintained at constant height; freq. *attrib.,* as *level luffing crane.*

1926 Kipling *Debits & Credits* 232 Level-backed and level-bellied watch 'em move. **1917** D. H. Lawrence *Look! we have come Through!* 66 She Put back her fine, level-balanced head. **1938** Belloc *Sonnets & Verse* 199 Level-browed divine Touraine. **1915** W. T. Maccall *Continuous Current Electr. Engin.* viii. 204 The point, B, at which the generator is level-compounded, *i.e.* has the same P.D. as at no load, can be made to occur at any one load. **1957** A. T. Starr *Appl. Electr.* vii. 182 An over-compounded generator really acts as a level-compounded generator plus a booster. **1971** L. T. Agger *Introd. Electr.* xvi. 298 In the level-compounded generator L the p.d. on full load is the same as on no load, and it varies only slightly in between. This is useful where the load changes rapidly, as in traction systems. **1866** G. M. Hopkins *Jrnl.* (1959) 136 Beech branches..with level-grown pieces of pale window-like green. **1926** E. Bowen *Ann Lee's* 146 Miss Phelps' blue, calm, level-lidded eyes. **1922** H. H. Broughton *Electr. Handling of Materials* III. 33 Few level-luffing arrangements have been devised by crane makers on the Continent. **1963** R. Hammond *Mobile & Movable Cranes* iv. 110 Level luffing is achieved by the Babcock 'swan neck' supported by a fixed guy rope. **1971** *Engineering* Apr. 65 (Advt.), Level luffing cranes. **1948** C. L. B. Hubbard *Dogs in Brit.* 301 The muzzle is long, powerful and level-mouthed. **1867** G. M. Hopkins *Jrnls. & Papers* (1959) 153 Very level-ranked sunset. **1939** D. Cecil *Young Melbourne* i. 23 Level-tempered and rational, she found scenes and caprices as tiresome as they did.

level, *v.*[1] Add: **1. e.** *Phonology.* To alter (a sound) so that it falls together with a similar sound. Usu. const. *under.*

1884 H. Sweet *First Middle Eng. Primer* 5 The old diphthongs *ea, ēa, eo, ēo* became monophthongic, *ea* being levelled under O.E. *æ*, written *e* in M.E., and *ēa* under O.E. *ǣ*, so that such a pair as the O.E. *heard* and *þæt* were both pronounced with the same vowel. **1888** —— *Hist. Eng. Sounds* 178 In North. *ā* has been preserved unrounded up to the present day in the Scotch dialects, where it has been levelled under new long *â*. **1972** *English Studies* LIII. 503 There is, however, another type of development by which ME *ǭr* and ME *ōr* were levelled under the same sound as early as the fifteenth century.

3. Also *refl.*

1907 *Daily Chron.* 25 May 1/7 Another halfpenny may possibly be put on the loaf before prices level themselves again.

4. c. Also with *out.* (Further examples.)

1938 *Times* 24 Jan. 21/4 Later he took up with the heads of the motor industry..the question of their co-operating with the Government to level out the production and sales of cars. **1971** *Fremdsprachen* XV. 227/1 Much can be done to level out these differences by proper use of incentive and social purpose funds derived from the profits of enterprises.

d. To get rid of, put *away,* by levelling. Also *intr.,* with *away*: to become level.

1910 Galsworthy *Sheaf* (1916) 132 All the natural weaknesses and limitations of the dwellers shall be.. levelled away and minimized. **1921** —— *To Let* II. ii. 140 Those two crumpled rose leaves, Fleur's caprice and Monsieur Profond's snout, would level away if he lay on them industriously.

5*. *to level off* (or *out*): to bring an aircraft into horizontal flight (*intr.* and *trans.*); (of an aircraft) to assume horizontal flight, to flatten out.

1928 *Lit. Digest* 12 May 74/2 A 'pancake landing' occurs when the ship is leveled off several feet above the ground. **1928** *New Republic* 15 Aug. 331/2 In a straight dive down, coming out of a 'stall'..which stopped only when I levelled off and began to fly straight. *Ibid.*, When it gets into the diving position, it responds to all the controls and can be gradually levelled out. **1937** D. & H. Teilhet *Feather Cloak Murders* viii. 135 Climbing in the still blue atmosphere to five thousand feet, the ten-passenger Sikorsky amphibian levelled off above Honolulu. **1952** A. Y. Bramble *Air-Plane Flight* xviii. 306 Some airplanes take a considerable time to reach cruising air speed, with cruising power setting, after levelling off. **1963** Level off [see *auto-[1] b].

b. *fig.* To cease increasing or decreasing.

1958 *Listener* 10 July 40/1 If the recent signs of improvement in American business are not followed up, if production levels off again and unemployment rises.. then [etc.]. **1968** *Guardian* 24 Apr. 11/5 The American war effort can begin to level off and eventually to be reduced. **1968** *Times* 16 Dec. 7/1 Yields have been tending to level off, or even to fall. **1972** *Guardian* 21 July 21/5 There are a few signs..that the property market is beginning to level off and prices are steadying somewhat.

8. To be honest or truthful; to tell the truth, speak frankly, behave honestly or deal straightforwardly (*with*). *slang* (orig. *U.S.*).

1920 H. C. Witwer *Leather Pushers* (1921) 174 'Are you levelin' with the Kid in this one?' 'We level in all of 'em!' **1931** *Amer. Mercury* Dec. 416/2 Hymie, the mug, falls in love with her right off, Don't laugh, I'm levellin', honest to God. **1936** R. Chandler in *Black Mask* Mar. 28/1 'I was on the cops, but they bounced me.' I liked his telling me that. 'You must have been levelling,' I said. **1951** I. Shaw *Troubled Air* vii. 107 You're not levelling with me. **1962** K. Orvis *Damned & Destroyed* ix. 64 But see that you level with me about the new pusher. **1966** E. McGirr *Funeral was in Spain* 100 'Think Songbird was levelling?' 'Oh yes... Mr. Songbird wouldn't mislead you.' **1972** 'R. Crawford' *Whip Hand* I. viii. 49 I'll level with you. I've been paid to find your brother. **1973** *Tucson* (Arizona) *Daily Citizen* 22 Aug. 55/8 Not often enough will a company truly level with its employes. It won't say, 'These are hard times and here's why.' **1974** L. Deighton *Spy Story* iv. 97 I'd better level with you, son... From now on, control is through me.

le:vel-hea·dedness. [f. *level-headed* adj. (Level *a.* 10) + -ness.] Calmness or balance of mind or judgement.

1876 *Rep. Vermont Board Agric.* III. 156 That same steadiness, or, in horse parlance, level-headedness,.. is quite as essential on the race track..as any where else. **1886** *New Englander* (New Haven, Connecticut) Feb. 179 This unexampled success is due..to the levelheadedness of its clerical guardians. **1896** *Alma Mater* 11 Nov. 43/2 A man whose great characteristic is level-headedness. **1916** *Daily Chron.* 13 Oct. 4/5 The British Air Service is now a great army,.. all endowed with two sterling qualities required by the pilot of the air, courage and levelheadedness. **1927** *Daily Express* 9 Aug. 8/2 A tribute to the level-headedness of the country which in his puny way he tries to wreck. **1937** Koestler *Spanish Testament* iv. 84 English journalists..with their traditional feeling for level-headedness and decency, have often had to complain of this difficulty.

levelling, *vbl. sb.* Add: **2. b.** (Further examples.) Also with *off, out.*

1871 H. Sweet *King Alfred's West-Saxon Version of Gregory's Pastoral Care* p. xxxvii, The change is not phonetic,.. but is due to inflectional levelling, the nom. terminations being made uniform, regardless of gender. **1888** J. Wright *Old High-German Primer* 16 The regular operation of this law was often disturbed by new formations made by levelling. **1903** G. B. Shaw *Revolutionist's Handbk.* vii, in *Man & Superman* 201 To them the limit of progress is, at worst, the completion of all the suggested reforms and the levelling up of all men to the point attained already by the most highly nourished and cultivated in mind and body. **1932** F. R. Leavis in *Scrutiny* I. 137 Mass-production, standardization, levelling-down—these three terms convey succinctly, what has happened. **1953** *Manch. Guardian Weekly* 13 Aug. 7/2 Housewives..cheered the heavy drop in the price of beef and thankfully attributed it to..the 'levelling-off' of inflation. **1955** *Times* 17 Aug. 5/5 Efforts by the employers to make them [*sc.* piece rates] realistic have foundered on the insistence of the men that they shall be changed only by levelling up. **1962** Simpson & Richards *Physical Princ. Junction Transistors* vi. 112 The beginning of this levelling-off process can be seen in the figure. **1964** F. Bowers *Bibliogr. & Textual Crit.* I. ii. 13 This evidence also suggests that authors' papers and not a levelling-out scribal transcript formed the printer's copy. **1971** *Cabinet Maker & Retail Furnisher* 24 Sept. 518/1 Important social changes and a levelling-off of income groups are playing a strong part in the expanding consumer market. **1972** *Guardian* 30 Mar. 14/3 Labour came to office with a strategy of levelling-up, of faster growth to finance greater equality.

level-pegging, *vbl. sb.* (passing into *adv.*). (Level stress.) [Cf. Pegging *vbl. sb.*] On equal terms (competitively), neck-and-neck, neither falling behind nor getting ahead (used of two individuals, groups, etc.). Also (as a back-formation) **level-peg** *v.*

1927 W. E. Collinson *Contemp. Eng.* 30 Cribbage is scored with pegs on a triangular board with two rows of holes on each side and supplied us with the technical expressions: level pegging or neck and neck (*from the racecourse*), [etc.]. **1959** *Motor* 16 Dec. 704/1 Two competitors..[one of which] lost one less mark than [the other] on the fourth section which was the first section on which they were not level pegging. **1962** *Listener* 13 Dec. 1027/2 The sociologist is level-pegging with the psychologist to replace the priest in the cure-of-souls business. **1965** *Observer* (Colour Suppl.) 28 Mar. 16 While air and sea were roughly level-pegging at a million passengers each in 1958, last year's split was 3·5 million to the airlines and 714,000 to the sea. **1973** J. Wainwright *Touch of Malice* 155 They were level-pegging—in rank, in age and in service. **1974** *Listener* 21 Feb. 244/2 ITV first made the running in the coverage of election news... Initiative reverting to the BBC? Let's call it level pegging.

lever, *sb.*[1] Add: **3. f.** (Examples.)

1865 *N. & Q.* 27 Jan. 27/2 (Advt.), The prettiest gift for a lady is one of Jones's gold levers at 11*l* 11*s*. **1895** in *N. & Q.* (1941) 20 Sept. 160/1 It couldn't have been a stop watch. It was a lever.

5. lever frame: delete '*U.S.*' and add examples.

1869 *Bradshaw's Railway Manual* XXI. App. 116 (Advt.), Patent locking lever frames. **1950** *Times Rev. Industry* 21/1 All points and signals are worked from a

mechanical or manual lever frame. **1955** *Railway Mag.* May 307/2 At Stockport No. 2 signalbox, the existing mechanical lever frame has been retained. **1963** Kichenside & Williams *Brit. Railway Signalling* vi. 74 (*caption*) The interior of London Bridge signal box..showing the miniature lever frame.

lever, *v.* Add: **1. b.** To make way by leverage.

1883 S. Baring-Gould *John Herring* I. i. 9 When he took his weight off,.. the plough levered out of the ground.

2. Also *refl.* with *into*.

1910 *Westm. Gaz.* 24 Mar. 2/3 The Moderates have levered themselves into a position they have no claim to occupy on the Council.

le·verage, *v.* *U.S.* [f. the sb.] *trans.* and *intr.* To lever; *spec.* to speculate or cause to speculate financially on borrowed capital expecting profits made to be greater than the interest payable. Hence **le·veraged** *ppl. a.*; **le·veraging** *vbl. sb.*

1937 *Harper's Mag.* June 63 Acey leveraged the arm upward. **1957** *Robert R. Young & Alleghany Corp.* 2 Founded in 1929.., Alleghany was a classic example of the highly leveraged holding companies of that period. **1968** *N.Y. Times* 20 Feb. 64 Short-term trading,.. selling short and leveraging through borrowing are all speculative techniques which carry with them greater risk of loss. **1971** *Atlantic Monthly* July 49 He gave her the benefit of his experience, leveraging her up to the ears in convertible bonds. **1972** 'A. Smith' *Supermoney* iv. i. 209 The corporation discovered that the more it borrowed, the higher the earnings and the higher the stock, so it began to leverage. **1973** *N.Y. Law Jrnl.* 26 July 3/3 Tight credit tends to put some of the marginal builders (that are very highly leveraged and have tiny working capital positions) under additional pressures.

‖ **lever de rideau** (lĕve də rido). [Fr.] = *curtain-raiser*. Also *fig.*

1860 *Players* I. 107 As a lever de rideau it was favourably received. **1891** G. B. Shaw *How to become Mus. Critic* (1960) 193 Signor Lago has produced a few miserably-mounted fragments of worn-out Italian operas by way of *levers de rideau* for Cavalleria. **1906** W. de Morgan *Joseph Vance* v. 38 The Man went up into 'the Nursery' to look at the bricks in the chimney... This was a mere *lever-de-rideau*—the principal stage business of the day being an examination of the Drains. **1970** *Brewer's Dict. Phr. & Fable* (ed. 12) 638/2 *Lever de rideau*, a short sketch, etc., performed on the stage before the main play begins.

Leveresque (lĭvĕre·sk), *a.* [f. the name of Charles *Lever* (1806–72), Irish novelist.] Characteristic of the novels of Charles Lever in matter or style. Also **Le·verish** *a.*

1903 *Westm. Gaz.* 18 Mar. 4/2 There are some good stories, old or new, told in a racy and Leverish style. **1905** *Daily Chron.* 15 June 3/1 Of Anglo-Irish lords, of Leveresque landowners, of eighteenth-century spendthrifts. **1922** *Glasgow Herald* 6 June 3 The Leveresque pictures of Irish life.

Levers (lĭ·vəɹz). Also *erron.* **Leavers.** The name of John *Levers* (1786–1848), who effected improvements in lace-making machines in the early 19th c., used *attrib.*, *absol.*, or in the possessive in the names of the lace-making machinery he developed, and of the lace thus produced.

1828 J. Levers *Brit. Pat.* 5741 18 Dec., My improvements in machinery for making lace consist in a certain combination and arrangement of mechanism to be adapted to lace machines constructed upon the principle commonly called or known by the name of Levers' principle. *Ibid.*, The movements of all the working parts of an ordinary Levers' machine are well understood by practical mechanics. **1865** F. B. Palliser *Hist. Lace* xxxvi. 425 The machines now in use are the Circular, Leaver, Transverse Warp and Pusher. **1867** W. Felkin *Hist. Machine-Wrought Hosiery* xviii. 281 In February, 1835, T. Allcock.. took out a patent..for a new kind of Levers'. *Ibid.* xix. 294 Goods made upon Levers' Jacquard machines. *Ibid.* xxii. 329 Velvet patterns on circular Levers' bobbin net. **1890** *Chambers's Encycl.* VI. 474/2 The lace-making machine now principally used is known as the Levers machine. **1911** *Encycl. Brit.* XVI. 44/2 The Leavers lace machine does not make either a buttonhole stitch or a plait. **1959** D. E. Varley *Hist. Midland Counties Lace Manufacturers' Assoc.* i. 4 John Brown, John Leavers, and Clark and Mart, inventors of the traverse warp, the leavers and the pusher bobbin-net machines respectively, were all Nottingham artisans. **1968** J. Ironside *Fashion Alphabet* 235 *Leavers lace*, any lace made on the machine invented by John Leavers, an Englishman, in 1813. This was the first really satisfactory lace-making machine.

levigator (le·vigēˡtəɹ). [f. Levigat(e *v.* + -or 2 c.] An iron or steel disc, several inches thick and about a foot in diameter, which is rubbed over the surface of a lithographic stone to smooth it.

1914 H. J. Rhodes *Art of Lithogr.* ii. 11 The operator.. guides the revolving levigator (disc) over the surface, applying sand and water as required. **1965** Zigrosser & Gaehde *Guide to Collecting Orig. Prints* iv. 39 The metal [for a carbograph] is scratched with carborundum crystals and a levigator, producing a fair approximation of a mezzotint ground with much less labor and time. **1967** E. Chambers *Photolitho-Offset* i. 7 The method of preparing the stone for printing is..a mechanical operation in which a smaller stone, or a flat metallic jigger or levigator..is rubbed..over the surface.

Levi's, Levis (lī·vəiz). orig. *U.S.* Also (in *attrib.* use) **Levi, Levies,** and with small initial. [f. name of the original Amer. manufacturer, *Levi* Strauss.] A type of (orig. blue) denim jeans or bibless overalls, with rivets to reinforce stress-points, patented and produced as working clothes in the 1860s, and adopted as a fashion garment in the 20th century.

The form *Levi's* is a proprietary term in the U.S.

1926 R. Santee *Men & Horses* 125 My Levis was brand-new. **1928** *Official Gaz.* (U.S. Patent Office) 18 Sept. 519/1 Levi's..for Overalls. **1934** *Street & Smith's Western Story Mag.* 10 Mar. 132/1 The cowboy's..overalls are called 'Levi's' from the name of Levi Straus, of San Francisco, the pioneer overalls manufacturer of the West. **1935** *N.Y. Herald-Tribune* 28 Apr. xi. 13/2 Old timers advise the prospective dude rancher to..buy in the West a pair of Levi overalls. *Ibid.* 13/3 Levi's, or copper riveted, blue denim riding pants, have been found to be excellent. **1941** *Yankee* Dec. 39/1 Red-flannel underwear, Peavey axes, copper-riveted Levi's, etc. **1944** *Life* 15 May 66/2 Blue jeans ('levis') or corduroys, rolled at the bottom, are worn by almost all boys. **1950** *Time* 27 Feb. 88 When dude ranches became popular in the '30s, Haas introduced 'Levis for Ladies'. **1957** M. B. Picken *Fashion Dict.* 212/2 Levies, work pants of extra heavy denim, having pockets attached with rivets. Originally worn by ranchers, lumbermen, and industrial workers... Also overalls, especially the bibless type. **1957** J. Kerouac *On Road* (1958) iii. vi. 217 Dean was wearing washed-out tight levis and a T-shirt. *Ibid.* iv. iii. 266 Stan was wearing a levi outfit, jacket and all. **1961** *Sunday Express* 2 Apr. 14/6 The big rush this summer will be:—*for* parchment-coloured American Levi jeans. **1970** *Guardian* 15 Oct. 11 Whatever social stigma might have been attached to wearing a pair of blue jeans could hardly have been held to apply to 'white Levi's'. **1973** C. Bonington *Next Horizon* vii. 100, I can always see her in my mind's eye—bare footed, clad in a pair of old Levis and a simple sweater worn outside her trousers. **1973** E. Bullins *Theme is Blackness* 59 Her sandy hair is tied by a bandanna and the blue Levis are faded dull.

levitate, *v.* Add: **1.** (Later example.)

1971 *Daily Tel.* 19 Nov. 14/4 The demonstrators linked arms in a great circle..and repeated the invocation in the hope that the entire building would levitate.

2. b. Add to def.: Also in scientific use: To cause (something heavier than the surrounding fluid) to rise or remain suspended without visible means (e.g. using magnetic forces).

1952 *Jrnl. Electrochem. Soc.* XCIX. 206/2 Slugs of any shape of various conductive metals could be levitated in the space between the coils. **1961** *Ann. Reg. 1960* 398 Sceptre 4..was to be rebuilt with an aluminium ring 'levitated' inside its ring-shaped chamber. **1971** *Daily Tel.* 5 Apr. 7/2 Superconducting magnets are now being investigated to levitate fast-moving trains into the air above the rails. **1973** *Nature* 9 Feb. 359/2 It is now feasible both to levitate and to propel a hovertrain using only a linear induction motor.

fig. **1954** C. P. Snow *New Men* xxxiv. 240 The touch of the metal..levitated me to the forgotten happiness of a joyous summer night.

levitation. Add: **1.** (Later examples: in mod. use chiefly *transf.* from 1 b.)

1902 *Q. Rev.* July 125 Many such victims of levitation [*sc.* deep-sea fishes] have been picked up at sea. **1909** H. G. Wells *Tono-Bungay* iii. iii. 364, I lay in my customary glider position, horizontal and face downward, and the invisibility of all the machinery gave an extraordinary effect of independent levitation. **1966** *New Statesman* 18 Feb. 242/3 (Advt.), Atmospheric levitation. Learn to glide.

b. (Earlier example.)

1874 Geo. Eliot *Legend of Jubal* 191 On all points he adopts the latest views; Takes for the key of universal Mind The 'levitation' of stout gentlemen.

c. The process of raising or supporting by invisible means something heavier than the surrounding fluid. Cf. *levitate *v.* 2 b.

1939 *Gen. Electric Rev.* XLII. 231 (*caption*) As if by magic the shallow metallic dish rises into the air and appears to obey the gestures of the demonstrator's hand. Actually, the levitation results from a special application of electromagnetic principles. **1952** *Jrnl. Electrochem. Soc.* XCIX. 205 Stable levitation..of various metals in the solid state was obtained between the coils..both in air and in vacuum. **1952** *Jrnl. Appl. Physics* XXIII. 552/1 If electromagnetic levitation can be expanded to a larger scale, the following advantages can be anticipated: 1. The specimen touches no crucible or container during the heating, melting and drainage stages. 2. The heated or molten specimen can be protected by a suitable atmosphere or a vacuum. [Etc.] **1956** *Philips Res. Rep.* XI. 45 The possibilities..of levitation by auxiliary gravitational forces, by reaction forces and by forces in electromagnetic fields are investigated. **1961** *Lancet* 25 Nov. 1181/1 Levitation. It occurred to me that supporting a patient on air might solve some of the problems of nursing patients whose illness necessitates the avoidance of contact with their beds. **1971** *Observer* 28 Nov. 9/4 'Magnetic levitation'..could turn out to be the most important advance in transport technology since the internal combustion engine.

3. *fig.*

1909 *Q. Rev.* Jan. 78 In other words, it [*sc.* Labour] obeys its own law of economic levitation, if we may be permitted to coin a phrase. **1962** W. Nowottny *Lang. Poets Use* vi. 123 The poet..has not yet figured as one who soars into a sphere where diction takes forms so conspicuously unprosaic..that [etc.]... It is my purpose now to begin to enquire at what point levitation into such a sphere may be said to have taken place. **1966** *New Statesman* 28 Jan. 138/3 In his third phase..Tippett concentrates on the spiritual 'levitation' effected by his winging lines and springing rhythms.

So **levita·tional** *a.*, of or pertaining to levitation.

1903 *Edin. Rev.* Apr. 329 These people sought..for a levitational quality akin to the dormitive quality of opium, but never found it. **1912** J. Stephens *Crock of Gold* v. xiv. 206 Birds have atmospheric and levitational information which millions of years will not render accessible to us. **1969** *New Scientist* 17 Apr. 117/1 If the curve is anti-spatial (particle extinction) the field is anti-gravitational or levitational.

levitron (le·vitrǫn). *Physics.* [f. Levi(tate *v.* + *-tron.] A type of fusion reactor in which stability of the plasma inside a toroidal container is achieved by the combination of a magnetic field parallel to the sides of the torus, produced by an external winding, with a second field everywhere at right angles to the first, produced by a toroidal current-carrying core magnetically levitated inside the tube.

1960 Colgate & Furth in *Physics of Fluids* III. 999/2 The toroidal analog of the linear hard-core tube is the 'levitron', a toroidal pinch tube with a central ring core, levitated by magnetic field or held in place transiently by inertia. **1966** *McGraw-Hill Encycl. Sci. & Technol.* X. 234/2 Several Levitrons are built or under construction.

levity¹. Add: **4.** A saying or expression marked by levity.

1930 Blunden in *Nation* 6 Dec. 327/1 *Coleridge*, wonderfully well edited by his grandson.., lacks his epigrams and levities.

levodopa (lī:vodō͡u·pă). *Chem.* and *Biochem.* Also **lævo-** (*rare*). [f. Lævo-, levo- + *dopa.] The lævorotatory L form of dopa (see *L 7 c and *dopa).

1970 *Brit. Med. Jrnl.* 7 Feb. 331 (*heading*) Treatment of Parkinsonism with laevo-dopa. **1970** *Jrnl. Amer. Med. Assoc.* 16 Mar. 1857/3 Levodopa increased the severity of depression. **1971** *Lancet* 19 June 1272/2 It seems unlikely that levodopa will have a favourable therapeutic effect on acne vulgaris. **1972** *Approved Names 1970* (Brit. Pharmacopœia Comm.) Suppl. 1, *Levodopa*, (−)-3-(3, 4-Dihydroxyphenyl)-L-alanine. **1974** *Times* 8 Jan. 14/6 The weakness and tremor of Parkinson's disease are thought to be caused by a lack of the chemical dopamine. Treatment with levodopa corrects that deficiency, as the drug is converted to dopamine within the body.

levy, *sb.*² Add: (Earlier examples.) Also *local U.K.*, a shilling (*Obs.*).

1829 C. Sealsfield *Tokeah* II. ii. 22 'But them fips and levies,' throwing a dirty leather bag with a dozen small silver coins upon the table, 'must first go.' **1832** F. Trollope *Dom. Manners Amer.* I. 171 He drew from thence [*sc.* from his pocket] rather more dollars, half-dollars, levies, and fips, than his dirty little hand could well hold. **1864** Hotten *Slang Dict.* 170 *Levy*, a shilling.—*Liverpool.*

levy, *v.* Add: **1. f.** To impose a levy on (a person). Also *refl.*

1902 *Westm. Gaz.* 17 June 9/1 The members will be levied 1s. yearly to support their candidate. **1921** *Ibid.* 24 May 2/4 When the stoppage ceases the miners will levy themselves in order to meet these promissory notes.

levyist (le·vi,ist). [f. Levy *sb.*¹ + -ist.] One who imposes, or advocates imposing, a levy.

1923 *Glasgow Herald* 5 Mar. 4 Without the investment of money in any form which the levyist could reach.

lew, *sb.*² **2.** (Examples.)

1825 J. Jennings *Observations Dial. W. Eng.* 52 *Lew*, shelter; defence from storms or wind. **1863** [see Lee *sb.*¹ 1]. **1887** [see Lee *sb.*¹ 1 b]. **1899** W. Raymond *Two Men o' Mendip* i. 7 The primroses an' cowslips too be out beautiful in the lew between Black-rocks. **1909** S. Reynolds *Poor Man's House* vii. vi. 209 We crouched, all humped up, in the lew of a drifter's bows, whilst the rain water washed around our boots and coat-tails.

Lewis³ (lū·is). [f. the name of the inventor, Col. Isaac Newton *Lewis* (1858–1931) of the U.S. Army.] In full, *Lewis (machine) gun*. A light, magazine-fed, gas-operated, and air-cooled machine gun. So **Lewis-gunner** and other *attrib.* and *Comb.* uses.

1913 *Aeroplane* 4 Dec. 606 The Lewis Machine-Gun. **1914** E. A. Powell *Fighting in Flanders* iii. 72 The Lewis gun..is air-cooled. **1916** *War Illustr.* V. 11/2 Lewis gun-team. **1917** *Ibid.* VI. 466 A 'Lewis' gunner. **1919** *King's Royal Rifle Corps Chron. 1916* 81 Stokes mortars and Lewis gun fire subdued the enemy's resistance. **1923** Kipling *Irish Guards in Gt. War* I. 134 Strong training at bombing and Lewis-gunnery. **1926** T. E. Lawrence *Seven Pillars* (1935) xv. 104 If we strengthened them by light automatic guns of the Lewis type..they might be capable of holding their hills. **1937** *Granta* 3 Feb. 219/1 Memories of John taking command of two Lewis gun

crews in a dispersal under barrage fire. **1946** [see *BREN]. **1964** H. L. PETERSON *Encycl. Firearms* 190/1 The Lewis machine gun..was the first machine gun ever fired from an airplane (1912), and it was adapted for ground and naval use as well. **1974** M. BUTTERWORTH *Man in Sopwith Camel* vi. 58 Flip the cocking handles of the twin Lewises.

Lewis[4] (lū·is). *Chem.* [The name of Gilbert Newton *Lewis* (1875–1946), U.S. chemist, who introduced the concepts.] *Lewis acid,* any compound or ionic species which can accept an electron pair from a donor compound; similarly *Lewis base,* one which can donate an electron pair to an acceptor compound.

1944 I. M. KOLTHOFF in *Jrnl. Physical Chem.* XLVIII. 54 The following terminology is suggested. Acids which satisfy the Lewis definition are called Lewis acids or proto-acids. **1961** G. R. CHOPPIN *Exper. Nuclear Chem.* ix. 148 Ketones, ethers and many other oxygen containing organic solvents may act as Lewis bases. **1962** COTTON & WILKINSON *Adv. Inorg. Chem.* x. 179 Various Lewis bases, such as amines, phosphines, ethers, and sulfides, form 1:1 complexes with BX_3 compounds. *Ibid.* 180 There is good evidence that the relative strengths of the boron halides as Lewis acids are in the order $BBr_3 \geq BCl_3 > BF_3$. **1969** LOWRIE & CAMPBELL-FERGUSON *Inorg. & Physical Chem.* xix. 219/2 All Brønsted acids and bases are also Lewis acids and bases respectively. However, the term Lewis acid can be applied to substances which do not contain protons and are not therefore Brønsted acids. **1973** J. J. LAGOWSKI *Mod. Inorg. Chem.* xiv. 522 Cationic halogen species can be stabilized by Lewis bases.

lewis (lū·is), *v.* [f. LEWIS[1]] *trans.* To fasten by means of, or after the manner of, a lewis.

1837 *Civil Engin. & Arch. Jrnl.* I. 72/1 When the stone is broken..it is separated on the bed by a very large iron crowbar or gavelock, and this is either lewised or chained, and raised by the large crane or 'gin'. **1883** *Proc. Assoc. Municipal Engin.* IX. 88 The only ties are wrought-iron 'lewis' bolts, 'lewised' into the old arch stones and turned down and cemented into the new ones.

lewisia (lū,i·ziă, -i·siă). [mod.L. (F. Pursh *Flora Americæ Septentrionalis* (1814) II. 368), f. the name of Meriwether *Lewis* (1774–1809), American explorer + -IA[1].] A small perennial herb of the genus so called, belonging to the family Portulacaceæ, native to western North America, and bearing solitary or clustered pink or white flowers and leaves arranged in a rosette at ground level.

1863 *Curtis's Bot. Mag.* LXXXIX. 5395 *(heading)* Spatlum, or Reviving Lewisia. **1917** C. F. SAUNDERS *Western Flower Guide* 52 The large root of *Lewisia* is a conspicuous feature. **1961** *Amat. Gardening* 23 Dec. 2 The alpine gardener could feast on the roots of his lewisias. **1963** *Times* 11 May 11/5 Lewisias have come through with flying colours. **1974** J. BERRISFORD *Window Box & Container Gardening* vii. 60 In peaty composts..one might try..beautiful lewisias.

Lewisian (lū,i·siăn), *a. Geol.* [f. *Lewis,* name of the northern section of the largest island of the Outer Hebrides + -IAN.] Of, pertaining to, or characteristic of Lewis: applied to the earlier of the two main groups of Pre-Cambrian rocks in NW. Scotland. Also *absol.,* the Lewisian rocks or strata.

1859 R. I. MURCHISON in *Q. Jrnl. Geol. Soc.* XVI. 240 If this most ancient gneiss required a British name, it might indeed with propriety be termed the 'Lewisian System', seeing that the large island of Lewis is essentially composed of it..; but the term 'Laurentian' having been already applied to rocks of this age in North America by our distinguished associate Sir W. Logan, I adhere to that name. **1887, 1911** [see *HEBRIDEAN *a.* and *sb.*]. **1938** A. K. WELLS *Outl. Hist. Geol.* vi. 49 The dykes can be followed right up to the junction of the Lewisian with the Torridonian. **1943** *Jrnl. R. Anthrop. Inst.* LXXIII. 75/1 The inconceivably old Lewisian rocks of the north-west Highlands. **1957** G. E. HUTCHINSON *Treat. Limnol.* I. i. 57 Peach and Horne (1910) record many irregular basins formed in this way on the Lewisian gneiss of the western seaboard of Sutherland and Ross, and also in the Outer Hebrides.

lewisite[1] (lū·isəit). *Min.* [f. the name of W. J. *Lewis* (1847–1926), British mineralogist + -ITE[1].] An antimonate and titanate of calcium, iron, and sodium, $(Ca,Fe,Na)_2(Sb,Ti)_2O_7$, which is found as small yellow to yellowish brown octahedral crystals and may be regarded as a titanian romeite.

1895 HUSSAK & PRIOR in *Mineral. Mag.* XI. 83 We have given the name of Lewisite to this new titano-antimonate from Brazil in honour of Prof. W. J. Lewis, during whose tenure of office the study of Mineralogy in the University of Cambridge has been so much encouraged. **1932** *Mineral. Abstr.* V. 185 Lewisite is a cubic mineral, whose composition is probably $(Ca,Fe,Na)_2(Sb,Ti)_2(O,OH)_7$. **1951** C. PALACHE et al. *Dana's Syst. Min.* (ed. 7) II. 1022 Romeite... In Minas Geraes, Brazil, with cinnabar in eluvial sands at Tripuhy near Ouro Preto (lewisite).

Lewisite[2] (lū·isəit). Also **lewisite.** [f. the name of Winford Lee *Lewis* (1878–1943), U.S. chemist + -ITE[1].] A dark oily liquid (colourless when pure) which is a powerful respiratory irritant and causes painful blisters on contact with the skin; 2-chlorovinyldichloroarsine, $ClCH{:}CHAsCl_2$.

1921 FRIES & WEST *Chem. Warfare* ii. 23 One of the most interesting and valuable of the compounds which would have found extensive use had the War continued, is an arsenic compound called Lewisite. **1923** R. F. HORTON *Mystical Quest of Christ* xxi. 223 A new poison gas, called by the barbarous name Lewisite, is of such potency that, released over London by twenty or thirty aeroplanes, it would asphyxiate the whole population in three or four hours. **1937** A. HUXLEY *Ends & Means* xii. 216 In 1937 the 'instrument of God for the protection of the people' was all the armaments existing in 1914..plus arsenic smokes, plus Lewisite. **1938** *Times* 12 Jan. 11/6 There are probably millions of people..who do not realize..that the much discussed lewisite can be dealt with by a scrubbing brush and soap, if treated quickly. **1943** [see *B.A.L. s.v.* *B III]. **1970** *Amer. Rev. Respiratory Dis.* CII. 173 Almost one half of the men who had been exposed repeatedly to mustard gas or lewisite before 1945 had a persistent productive cough.

Lewisman (lū·is,mæn). [f. *Lewis* + MAN *sb.*[1]] A native or inhabitant of Lewis, the northern section of the island of Lewis with Harris in the Outer Hebrides.

1927 [see *FIFER[2]]. **1938** L. MACNEICE *I crossed Minch* i. 4 Drinking beer with some Lewismen while one of them sang a love-song in Gaelic. **1971** *Stornoway Gaz.* 10 July 4/1 The initiative for advancing the prosperity of Lewis must come from the Lewisman himself.

lewistonite (lū·istǫnəit). *Min.* [f. *Lewiston,* the name of the city in Utah, U.S.A., near which it was found + -ITE[1].] A basic phosphate of calcium, potassium, and sodium, $(Ca,K,Na)_5(PO_4)_3(OH)$, found as colourless to pale green hexagonal crystals; potassian hydroxyapatite.

1930 LARSEN & SHANNON in *Amer. Mineralogist* XV. 326 Some of the hexagonal prisms which are very much like the dehrnite have less alkali and much more water. Chemically they are so different from dehrnite as to give them species rank and the name lewistonite is proposed after Lewiston, Utah. **1942** *Ibid.* XXVII. 297 Lewistonite ..shows wide variation in its properties. Stout hexagonal crystals associated with oolites of pseudowavellite are divided into six biaxial negative segments. **1968** I. KOSTOV *Mineral.* II. ix. 458 Dehrnite and lewistonite for alkali-bearing apatites.

‖ **lex domicilii** (leks dǫmi·si·li,əi). *Law.* [L.] The law of the country in which a person is domiciled; the determination of the rights of a person by establishing where, in law, he is domiciled.

1832 BARNEWALL & CRESSWELL *Rep. Cases King's Bench* X. 909 The lex domicilii is to be regarded, yet it is not adverted to where the domicile was when the contract was entered into. **1961** *Times* 26 Oct. 19/2 Capacity and consent were matters that fell to be decided by the *lex domicilii.* **1965** *Mod. Law Rev.* XXVIII. v. 540 Unilateral acts of divorce, for example, the *talak* under Moslem law or the Jewish *gett,* have raised important questions whether an English court would recognise these acts as divorces obtained according to the *lex domicilii* of the parties.

lexeme (le·ksīm). *Linguistics.* [f. LEX(ICON + *-EME. Cf. *MORPHEME.] A word-like grammatical form intermediate between morpheme and utterance, often identical with a word occurrence; a word in the most abstract sense, as a meaningful form without an assigned grammatical role; an item of vocabulary.

1940 B. L. WHORF *Lang., Thought, & Reality* (1956) 160 C. F. Voegelin has accomplished the difficult and signal work of analyzing an immense number of baffling stem compounds of Shawnee into their component lexemes (stems) and other morphemes (formatives). **1946** M. SWADESH in C. Osgood *Ling. Struct. Native Amer.* 319 Lexeme building is accomplished mainly by readaptation of lexemes, paradigmatic forms, or syntactic constructions to new uses without change of form. **1950** *Archivum Linguisticum* II. 10 Discriminating between 'word' and 'lexeme'. **1954** S. NEWMAN in H. Hoijer *Lang. in Culture* 87 It is taken for granted..that no English lexeme is a perfect semantic equivalent of a Zuni lexeme. **1958** C. F. HOCKETT *Course in Mod. Ling.* xix. 171 The lexemes in the two-word sequence *twenty-eighth* are *twenty, eight,* and *-th... Red-haired* is two words; but it is a single minimum free form, since the ICs are *red hair* (free) and *-ed* (bound); and it is three lexemes, *red, hair,* and *-ed. Ibid.* 174 The definition of lexeme follows unpublished work of Bernard Bloch. **1963** *Amer. Speech* XXXVIII. 50 The meaning of *actor,* a minimum free form, is predictable from its structure, as is the meaning of *wants,* a lexeme. **1963** J. LYONS *Structural Semantics* iii. 40 Certain lexemes and expressions are quickly learnt. **1964** E. PALMER tr. *Martinet's Elem. Gen. Ling.* i. 25 A lexeme like *travaill-* is normally listed in the lexicon in the form *travailler.* **1968** J. LYONS *Introd. Theoret. Ling.* 197 The orthographic word *cut* represents three different inflexional 'forms' (i.e. three different grammatical words) of the lexeme *cut.* **1971** G. ANSRE in J. Spencer *Eng. Lang. W. Afr.* 156 If the phoneme is the minimal phonological unit and the morpheme is the minimal grammatical unit, then [the] lexeme will be the minimal lexical unit. **1971** *Archivum Linguisticum* II. 48 The view has already been expressed that words are names (of lexical items) derived from the combination of roots (or lexemes) and affixes (or morphemes). *Ibid.* 50 The concept and term of 'collocation' has to be seen partly in relation to that of 'root' or 'lexeme'.

lexemic (leksī·mik), *a.* and *sb. Linguistics.* [f. *LEXEM(E + -IC.] **A.** *adj.* Of or relating to lexemes. **B.** *sb. pl.* The branch of linguistics concerned with the study of lexemes.

1954 S. NEWMAN in H. Hoijer *Lang. in Culture* 89 The most difficult problem in this lexemic study is that of establishing valid methods. **1957** *Language* XXXIII. 588, I believe that..*all borrowing is lexemic,* i.e. a transfer of lexemes by imitation from one language into another, using 'lexeme' here to mean a free construction of one or more morphemes. **1962** E. F. HADEN et al. *Resonance-Theory for Ling.* iii. 37 The zero-resonance formula expresses the fact that in morphology *easily* and *gladly* are equivalent. Of course they can be dealt with separately in lexemics. **1963** J. LYONS *Structural Semantics* vi. 122 A definite level of analysis—phonological,..lexemic. **1973** *Archivum Linguisticum* IV. 119 These sememic graphs..must then be converted into syntactic or 'lexemic' representations.

‖ **lex fori** (leks fōə·rəi). *Law.* [L.] The law of the country in which an action is brought, as determining the nature and modes of the proceedings.

1836 H. WHEATON *Elem. Internat. Law* I. II. ii. 188 The extrinsic evidence by which the existence and terms of the contract are to be proved in a foreign tribunal is regulated by the *lex fori.* **1841** CLARK & FINNELLY *Rep. Cases Lords Appeals & Writs of Error* V. 13 The law on this point is well settled in this country, where this distinction is properly taken, that whatever relates to the remedy to be enforced, must be determined by the *lex fori,* the law of the country to the tribunals of which the appeal is made. **1960** *Times* 5 Mar. 10/2 Further the *lex fori*—English law—did not provide a cause of action and relief appropriate to the enforcement of the foreign right. **1970** *Internat. & Compar. Law Q.* XIX. 173 The Soviet system contains an extremely large number of imperative rules which impose the application of the *lex fori.*

lexic (le·ksik), *a. rare.* [f. Gr. λεξικ-ός: see LEXICON.] = LEXICAL *a.*

1900 *19th Ann. Rep. U.S. Bureau Amer. Ethnol. 1897–8* 832 Primitive languages are essentially structural or morphologic, only incidentally lexic.

lexical, *a.* Add: **1.** *lexical meaning,* the meaning of a base in a paradigm, e.g. of *love* in *loves, loved, loving,* etc.; *lexical change, class, form, item, morpheme, rule, set, unit, word* (see quots.).

1933 L. BLOOMFIELD *Lang.* x. 166 To contrast the purely lexical character of a linguistic form with the habits of arrangement to which it is subject, we shall speak of it as a lexical form. *Ibid.* xvi. 271 Languages with an elaborate part-of-speech system..have parallel forms with the same lexical meaning for use in different syntactic positions. *Ibid.* 277 The relative frequency of the various lexical and grammatical units (morphemes and tagmemes) in a language can be studied. **1942** BLOCH & TRAGER *Outl. Ling. Analysis* iv. 68 The meaning of the base itself..is called lexical meaning. **1951** G. A. MILLER *Lang. & Communication* iv. 89 In the Oxford English Dictionary there are nearly half a million lexical units. **1958** C. F. HOCKETT *Course in Mod. Ling.* 429 Back-formation can..lead to lexical change, in the form of new morphemes. **1962** H. C. CONKLIN in Householder & Saporta *Probl. Lexicogr.* 124 Minimally, a *lexical set* consists of all semantically contrastive lexemes which in a given, culturally relevant context share exclusively at least one defining feature. **1963** BLOOMFIELD & NEWMARK *Ling. Introd. Hist. Eng.* iv. 145 Lexical morphemes are those whose grammatical characteristics can be accounted for by identifying them as members of morphological classes. *Ibid.* vi. 257 All lexical units generated from the same grammatical unit by the same lexical rule are said to belong to a single lexical class. *Ibid.* 282 The lexical word *debtors* has the root *debt* and the affixes *-or* and *-s.* **1964** R. A. HALL *Introd. Ling.* liii. 254 Archaic features may be preserved in different lexical items in different places. **1965** N. CHOMSKY *Aspects of Theory of Syntax* ii. 85 The lexical rule..now allows us to insert *sincerity* for the first complex symbol. **1966** G. N. LEECH *Eng. in Advertising* ii. 21 There are thousands of examples of lexical items composed of a sequence of words: *put out* (= 'extinguish'). **1967** R. A. WALDRON *Sense & Sense Devel.* v. 102 A system of this kind, a limited group of words forming some kind of range or scale of mutually excluding terms is often called a *lexical set.* **1967** *Lingua* XVII. 34 Lexical words imply absence of grammatical meaning and vice versa. *Ibid.* 113 All members of the same paradigm are labeled as the same 'word' (lexical unit, lexeme). **1971** J. B. CARROLL et al. *Word Frequency Bk.* p. l, The basic color terms have often been studied as a lexical set, or semantic field. **1972** P. H. MATTHEWS *Inflectional Morphol.* ii. 11, I shall use orthographic forms in small capitals..to refer to Latin verbs *qua* lexical items.

Hence **le·xicalist** and **le·xicalness** (see quots.).

1967 *Lingua* XVII. 35 There seem to be degrees of both 'lexicalness' and 'grammaticalness' in English. **1970** N. CHOMSKY in Jacobs & Rosenbaum *Readings Eng. Transformational Gram.* 188 We might extend the base rules to accommodate the derived nominal directly (I will refer to this as the 'lexicalist position').

lexicalize (le·ksikăləiz), *v. Linguistics.* [f. LEXICAL *a.* + -IZE.] Usu. in *pass.* **1.** To accept into the lexicon, or vocabulary, of a language.

1937 C. E. BAZELL in *Jrnl. Eng. & Germ. Philol.* Jan. 3 But in a form early lexicalized a shortening previous to

the considerable dialectal differentiation of the dialects would be in harmony with Indo-European tendencies. **1954** Pei & Gaynor *Dict. Ling.* 122 *Lexicalize*, to incorporate a word, etc., into the lexicon of a language. **1972** A. Makkai *Idiom Struct. Eng.* 81 Should the morpheme *flation* become widely accepted.., it would be lexicalized, and Webster's new edition would list it. **1972** *Times Lit. Suppl.* 13 Oct. 1229/3 The uncharted waters of contemporary slang, where what appears ephemeral today may become lexicalized tomorrow, and conversely.

2. To express (a difference that is already expressed in the grammatical structure, or could be) by means of a different lexical item.

1968 J. Lyons *Introd. Theoret. Ling.* viii. 352 Consider the..two sentences:..*Bill died*..*John killed Bill.* In such instances, we may say that the relationship of the transitive to the intransitive is 'lexicalized'.

Hence **le·xicalized** *ppl. a.*; also **le:xicaliza·tion**, the action or process of lexicalizing.

1949 *Archivum Linguisticum* I. 10 The adverb differs from a combination of noun and case by a strong tendency to lexicalisation. *Ibid.* 181 'Immotive'..or 'lexicalised' words. **1961** *Brno Studies in English* III. 28 All this richness was gradually done away with (except for a very small number of adverbial or lexicalized survivals). **1968** J. Lyons *Introd. Theoret. Ling.* viii. 369 The difference between obligatory and optional 'lexicalization' in three-place constructions. *Ibid.*, *Kill* is the 'lexicalized' two-place causative form of *die.* **1971** F. W. Householder *Ling. Speculations* vii. 103 Lexicalization is here assumed to follow at least some transformations.

lexico- (le·ksiko). [f. Gr. λεξικό-ς.] In some mod. linguistic terms denoting 'lexical and..', as in *lexico-dynamics* (see quot.); *lexico-behavioural, -grammatical* adjs. See also *lexicostatistic *a.*

1964 E. A. Nida *Toward Sci. Transl.* iii. 36 Bloomfield ..sought to define the semantic value of symbols in terms of lexico-behavioral distinctiveness. **1970** Lancaster & Gillespie in *Ann. Rev. Information Sci. & Technol.* V. 38 The structure and uses of a large, dynamic controlled vocabulary for one-line implementation have been discussed by Harley and Lancaster... The authors have coined the term 'lexicodynamics' to express the concept of construction, maintenance, use and change of controlled vocabularies for IR purposes. **1953** Y. R. Chao in *Language* XXIX. 379 (*title*) Popular Chinese plant words, a descriptive lexico-grammatical study. **1964** E. A. Nida *Toward Sci. Transl.* xi. 243 In treating such lexico-grammatical features, both form and content must be dealt with, since special forms, e.g. poetry, liturgy, parables, proverbs, epigrams and epistolary formulae, are all important factors in determining meaning. **1971** *Archivum Linguisticum* II. 42 Valéry and also Eliot spoke, I believe, of their experience of composing first the formal rhythmic frame of a poem and letting the lexical and grammatical structures follow, but there are also discernible abstract arrangements of a lexico-grammatical order.

lexicology, lexicological, *a.* Add: (Later examples.) So **lexicolo·gically** *adv.*

1937 J. Orr tr. *Iordan's Introd. Romance Ling.* iv. 287 In some, the arbitrary character of the linguistic signs is more apparent..and these Saussure calls lexicological languages. **1949** *Jrnl. Theol. Stud.* L. 104 The fifth is devoted to doctrine; the sixth and seventh to remarks on syntax and lexicology respectively. **1952** *Archivum Linguisticum* IV. 71 Units which the application of formal and semantic criteria enables the grammarian to detach from lexicologically analysable groupings.

lexicon. Add: **1. b.** Also, the vocabulary or word-stock of a region, a particular speaker, etc.

1954 [see *European *sb.* 2]. **1963** *Amer. Speech* XXXVIII. 143 French-speaking Canadians..are developing a 'standard' form of Canadian French..with the same categories of variation (phonetics and lexicon) from the speech of the mother country as are found in American and Canadian English. **1972** *Archivum Linguisticum* III. 1 They constitute a regular part of his stylistic lexicon. **1973** K. Johnson in T. Kochman *Rappin' & Stylin' Out* 142 These racial-identity labels are part of what can be called 'the black lexicon' (words that are used exclusively by black people) formulated to designate concepts derived from the unique experience of black people within their culture. **1973** *Times* 31 July 6/7 He [*sc.* Mr. Ehrlichman] said the term 'deep six'—meaning throw in the river—had not been 'part of my lexicon'.

2. *Linguistics.* The complete set of meaningful units in a language; the words, etc., as in a dictionary, but without the definitions. (Opp. Grammar *sb.*)

1933 L. Bloomfield *Lang.* x. 162 The total stock of morphemes in a language is its lexicon. **1964** R. H. Robins *Gen. Ling.* 63 The categories of phonetics, phonology, and grammar are general; the components of the lexicon of a language are particular. **1968** J. Lyons *Introd. Theoret. Ling.* iv. 159 He can afford to make a less exhaustive classification of the lexicon.

3. (With capital initial.) The proprietary name of a game played with cards marked with the letters of the alphabet.

1932 *Trade Marks Jrnl.* 22 June 798 Lexicon... Card games. John Waddington Limited,..Leeds; manufacturers. **1945** D. Whitelaw *Lexicon Murders* i. 15 This card..was one from a pack of Lexicon cards, one bearing the letter V. *Ibid.* iii. 59 A Wop, eh...ever play Lexicon? **1960** *Guardian* 9 Dec. 9/7 Didn't we all learn to spell by playing Lexicon? **1965** R. Petrie *Running Deep* ii. 28 One of them produced a packet of Lexicon from her bag and spread the letters over the table. **1974** 'J. Le Carré' *Tinker, Tailor* xxii. 187 Smiley appeared to examine the lexicon cards, reading off the words longways and sideways.

lexiconize (le·ksikǫnəiz), *v.* [f. Lexicon + -ize.] **a.** *intr.* To compile a lexicon. **b.** *trans.* To reduce or make into (the form of) a lexicon.

1892 G. Meredith *Let.* 3 Jan. (1970) II. 1056 Your Lexiconizing is clever and I cannot go beyond it. **1908** F. Galton *Mem. my Life* 254 They admit of being so classified or 'lexiconised', that it would be possible for him to tell..whether a similar set had been already registered. **1952** C. P. Blacker *Eugenics: Galton & After* 49 Galton spent about eight years on this work... It was only in the last of these, the *Finger-Print Directory*, published in 1895, that the process of 'lexiconizing' or indexing the material was completed.

lexicostatistic (le:ksiko,stăti·stik), *a. Linguistics.* [f. *lexico- + Statistic *a.*] Of or relating to the statistics of vocabulary. Also **le:xicostati·stics** *sb. pl.* const. as *sing.*, a branch of linguistics closely allied to *glottochronology.

1952 M. Swadesh in *Proc. Amer. Philos. Soc.* XCVI. iv. 452 (*title*) Lexico-statistic dating of prehistoric ethnic contacts. **1956** S. C. Gudschinsky in *Word* XII. 175 Lexicostatistics is a technique which attempts to provide dates for the earlier stages of languages much as carbon 14 dating provides dates for archaeological finds. **1961** [see *glottochronology]. **1964** R. H. Robins *Gen. Ling.* viii. 318 The attempt to quantify linguistic divergence from a common source [etc.]..is known as lexicostatistics or glottochronology. **1965** *Canad. Jrnl. Ling.* Spring 94 Certain special methods, such as lexicostatistic list comparison, rest on comparative method. **1969** R. A. Hall in *Neuphilol. Mitt.* LXX. 199 Despite the failure of glottochronology, due to basic theoretical faults, a certain amount of interest has been maintained in other, less aprioristic aspects of lexicostatistics.

Also **le:xicostati·stical** *a.*, **le:xicostati·stically** *adv.*

1955 *Internat. Jrnl. Amer. Ling.* XXI. 138 (*heading*) Lexico-statistical skewing from dialect borrowing. **1963** *Language* XXXIX. 60 (*heading*) Lexicostatistically determined borrowing and taboo.

lexis (le·ksis). [ad. Gr. λέξις diction, word, f. λεγ- to speak.] **1.** The diction or wording, in contrast to other elements, of a piece of writing (see also quot. 1950).

1950 *Mod. Philology* XLVII. iv. 243/1, I have already distinguished, in the first part of this essay, between speech as action (*praxis*) and speech as meaningful (*lexis*). **1957** N. Frye *Sound & Poetry* p. xxiii, Singing and chanting are, in modern times, radically different methods of associating melos and lexis.

2. *Linguistics.* **a.** = *lexicon 2; items of lexical, as opp. esp. to grammatical, meaning; the total word-stock of a language. **b.** The study of words as lexical items.

1960 E. Delavenay *Introd. Machine Transl.* v. 67 During the early days of research the priority of lexis over morphology in preparing the way for machine translation was taken for granted. *Ibid.* 131 *Lexis*, used here, and by M.T. linguists, to designate the words of a language, contained in its dictionary or lexicon, as opposed to the morphology and syntax of that language. **1961** *Language* XXXVII. 325 A distinction..between grammar and lexis seems to be necessary if the patternings are to be economically stated or defined. **1962** R. Quirk *Use of English* v. 72 The word-stock—also known as the *vocabulary* or *lexis*. **1963** R. M. W. Dixon *Ling. Sci. & Logic* ii. 45 Theories of grammar and lexis are both needed. **1964** *English Studies* XLV. 24 Patterns of vocabulary, or *lexis*, which describe the company words keep. **1966** *Listener* 14 Apr. 534/2 Dr. Steiner's problems with the gaucho's lexis and the Amerindian's grammar..are linguistic and not literary problems. **1971** *E. Afr. Jrnl.* Mar. 35/2 Presentation of lexis is balanced by the introduction of grammatical structures.

‖ **lex loci** (leks lōᵘ·səi). *Law.* [L.] The law of the country in which a legal transaction is performed, a tort is committed, or a property is situated; freq. followed by a defining word or phrase.

1832 Barnewall & Cresswell *Rep. Cases King's Bench* X. 905 The decisions of both English and Scotch courts shew that the construction of personal contracts depends on the lex loci contractus. **1836** H. Wheaton *Elem. Internat. Law* I. ii. ii. 173 A necessary consequence of the rule relating to the application of the *lex loci rei sitæ.* **1848** Wharton *Law Lexicon* 375/1 All the formalities, proofs, or authentications of them [*sc.* contracts], which are required by the *lex loci*, are indispensable to their validity everywhere else. **1858** J. Westlake *Treat. Private Internat. Law* iv. 64 The fact of status must be referred to the domicile, but the incapacities attendant on the given status to the *lex situs* for immovable property, and to the *lex loci actus aut contractus* for other matters. *Ibid.* xi. 318 Both the form and the legality, the extrinsic and intrinsic validity, depended on the *lex loci celebrationis. Ibid.* 335 The *lex loci*..by which the conduct of married persons is to be regulated,..must always be referred, not to the place where the contract was entered into, but where it subsists for the time. **1896** A. V. Dicey *Digest Law Eng.* i. 66 '*Lex loci solutionis*' means the law of the country where a contract is to be performed. *Ibid.* xxvii. 669 It is not necessary that the *lex fori* and the *lex loci delicti* should be identical; it is sufficient if they are similar. **1970** *Internat. & Compar. Law Q.* XIX. 26 This at once gives rise to the problem whether it is the *lex fori* or *lex loci* which gives the plaintiff this cause of action.

ley (lī, lēⁱ). [Var. Lea *sb.*¹] The supposed line of a prehistoric track in a straight line usually from hilltop to hilltop with identifying points such as ponds, mounds, etc., marking its route (see also quot. 1932).

1922 A. Watkins *Early Brit. Trackways* 12 The sighting line was called the ley or lay. *Ibid.* 13 Previous writers, treating, say, of Roman or of mediæval roads, not knowing of the existence of the ley, assume that they are speaking of original primary structures, when they are only describing a route evolved from a number of the leys I describe. **1925** —— *Old Straight Track* 220 When you get a good ley on the map, go over it in the field, and fragments and traces of the trackways may be found, always in straight lines. **1932** D. Maxwell *Detective in Surrey* v. 86 A ley..is an invisible and imaginary line, drawn from one point in the landscape to another, mathematically straight... The key positions..are points where two or more leys cross... The crossing places..would be places of meeting. **1971** *It* 2–16 June 24/4 The leys..interlaced over the whole country. **1974** *Bookseller* 26 Jan. 192 (Advt.), Alfred Watkins' theory about leys which connect ancient sites.

ley, var. Lea *sb.*² (Later (non-*dial.*) examples.)

The form *lea* is now rarely used.

1932 *Discovery* Feb. 61/1 Some progressive farmers are alternating four years of corn-growing with four years of temporary grass leys, on which bullocks and grass-land sheep are fed. **1948** L. D. Stamp *Land of Britain* iv. 65 The length of time the grass is left down is usually determined by the farmer's own judgment..a common average being seven years. This is the system of 'leys' or 'ley farming'—taking the plough round the farm. **1957** *New Biol.* XXIV. 42 In many areas it was not convenient to change arable land to leys of any considerable duration. **1962** *Listener* 1 Feb. 214/1 The old permanent pastures are being replaced by temporary leys, with the plough 'going all round the farm'. **1972** *Oxford Times* 28 July 8 Don't be in a hurry to plough up and re-seed leys and permanent pastures.

ley, var. Lye *v.*² (See quot. 1823.) Hence **leyed** *ppl. a.* (cf. Lyed *ppl. a.*).

1823 E. James *Acct. Expedition Rocky Mts.* I. 114 Another very acceptable dish was called leyed corn. *Ibid.* 195 They sometimes prepare this hard corn for eating by the process of leying it, or boiling it in a ley of wood ashes for ..an hour or two. **1825** W. Biggs *Narr. Captivity among Kickapoo Indians* (1922) 35 Sandy hill cranes boiled in leyed corn.

leycesteria (lestīᵊ·riă). [mod.L. (N. Wallich in W. Carey *Roxburgh's Flora Indica* (1824) II. 181), f. the name of William *Leycester* (fl. 1820), Chief Justice of Bengal + -ia¹.] A shrub of the genus so called, belonging to the family Caprifoliaceæ, native to India, and bearing yellow or purple flowers; also called Himalayan honeysuckle or pheasant-berry.

1838 J. C. Loudon *Arboretum et Fruticetum Britannicum* II. 1060 The beautiful Leycesteria..is a rambling shrub, with the general appearance of a honeysuckle. **1899** G. Jekyll *Wood & Garden* ix. 101 We come back to Leycesteria, put rather in a place of honour. **1961** *Amat. Gardening* 23 Dec. 9 Quick growing shrubs which make long wands of growth annually..are..buddleia, leycesteria.

Leydig (ləi·dig). *Anat.* The name of Franz von *Leydig* (1821–1908), German anatomist, used *attrib.*, in the possessive, and with *of-*adjunct to designate various anatomical structures described by or associated with him, *esp.* the interstitial cell of the testis, a large, polyhedral cell occurring in large numbers in the connective tissue around the seminiferous tubules and believed to be the site of androgen production in the testis.

1904 *Amer. Jrnl. Anat.* III. 167 (*heading*) The embryonic development of the interstitial cells of Leydig. *Ibid.*, Boll..believed that Leydig's cells composed the walls of capillaries. **1936** Neal & Rand *Compar. Anat.* xii. 448 The interstitial Leydig cells of the testis. **1956** *Nature* 21 Jan. 144/1 In all cases the Leydig cell cytoplasm of the interstitium had become sprinkled with lipid droplets. **1962** *Gray's Anat.* (ed. 33) 1522 The interstitial cells of the testis (cells of Leydig) are large polyhedral cells lying in the connective tissue between the seminiferous tubules.

Leyland (lēⁱ·lănd). The name of Christopher John *Leyland* (1849–1926), of Haggerston Castle, used *attrib.* or in the possessive in **Leyland('s) cypress** to designate a hybrid conifer, × *Cupressocyparis leylandii* (*Chamæcyparis nootkatensis* × *Cupressus macrocarpa*), first raised by him from seedlings collected at Leighton Hall, Welshpool, in 1888.

[**1926** A. B. Jackson in *Kew Bull.* 114 As this new cypress has already been named *Cupressus Leylandii* by Mr. Leyland, we propose to describe it under that name.] **1933** W. J. Bean *Trees & Shrubs Hardy in Brit. Is.* III. 124 Leyland's Cypress..is a tree of dense pyramidal habit. **1960** N. J. Prockter *Garden Hedges* vi. 107 Leyland's Cypress..is still looked upon as something new, and I regret to say is at present little known. **1970** C. Lloyd *Well-Tempered Garden* iii. 215 The great

favourite now (although it is by no means new) is Leyland's cypress. **1974** A. MITCHELL *Field Guide to Trees of Britain* 68 At least three [hybrid cypresses] exist, but only one, the Leyland Cypress, is commonly grown.

lez, lezz (lez), varr. *LES. Also **le·zzy.**

1956 B. HOLIDAY *Lady sings Blues* (1973) ix. 90 I've known black chicks in show business who were as feminine as me, but before long they got acting like lezzies because it's so easy. **1958** F. NORMAN *Bang to Rights* III. 146, I didn't see why there should be a law against queers and lezes. **1966** I. JEFFERIES *House-Surgeon* iii. 37 'Is she like that with all the house-men?' 'Not the girls; she's lezzy as hell.' **1966** 'L. LANE' *ABZ of Scouse* 62 *Lezzy*, a lesbian woman. **1970** E. BERCKMAN *She asked for It* xi. 135 So you're a couple of Lezzes, you and little Monica?

L-form: see *L 6* c.

Lhasa (lā·sa). Also **lhasa, Lhassa.** The name of the capital of Tibet, used *attrib.* in **Lhasa apso** to designate a small long-coated dog, often gold or grey and white, belonging to a breed originally developed there, and formerly called the **Lhasa terrier,** a name also once used for the *Tibetan terrier* (*TIBETAN). Also *ellipt.*

1904 *C. B. Fry's Mag.* June 364/1 The little toy dog of Tibet, which Kennel Club edicts have declared shall properly be known as the 'Lhassa Terrier', is no novelty in our midst, although his numbers in an unkind climate possibly do not reach a round dozen. **1905** P. LANDON *Lhasa* I. 403 The Lhasa terrier is an entirely distinct breed. **1935** W. HUTCHINSON *Dog Encycl.* II. 1142/2 [The] Lhasa Apso..has only become known in England in very recent years. **1948** C. L. B. HUBBARD *Dogs in Brit.* 303 The Lhasa Apso has had many names given it in the course of its comparatively short British history. **1955** W. GADDIS *Recognitions* I. vi. 206 The lhasa turned to stare at the Coca-Cola machine. **1974** *Radio Times* 14 Feb. 3/2 Polluche is a Lhasa apso—literally translated, it means a Lhasa terrier.

Lhooshai, var. *LUSHAI *a.* and *sb.*

‖ **li³** (lī). [Chinese.] (See quots.)

1912 J. J. M. DE GROOT *Relig. of Chinese* iv. 95 The original *li* and *teh*, the only classical rules and ethics which keep man..in perfect harmony with the order of the universe. **1937** D. BODDE tr. *Fung Yu-Lan's Hist. Chinese Philos.* iv. 46 The 'Rites' (*Li*) were used in diplomatic relations. **1942** D. D. RUNES *Dict. Philos.* 168/1 *Li*, reason; law; the rational principle. This is the basic concept of modern Chinese philosophy. To the Neo-Confucians.., Reason is the rational principle of existence whereas the vital force (ch'i) is the material principle. **1953** *Oxf. Jun. Encycl.* V. 101/1 The word *li* used by Confucius, which is often translated by the English word 'religion', really means something more like ceremonial or ritual, the correct observance of which is needed for maintaining friendly relations with the Power or Powers of the unseen world. **1955** A. FANG in E. Pound *Classic Anthol.* p. xvi, Read in that context, Confucius must be understood as trying to integrate music with rites (*li*), just as he tried to integrate poetry with music. **1962** A. F. WRIGHT in Wright & Twitchett *Confucian Personalities* 7 The *li*, spread by fathers, village elders, and government officials, and supplemented by the discipline of ordered family life, would in turn foster social virtues: filial submission, brotherliness, righteousness, good faith, and loyalty.

liable, *a.* Add: **3. c.** *dial.* and *U.S.* Likely.

1886 F. T. ELWORTHY *West Somerset Word-Bk.* 433 Speaking of a wounded hen pheasant a farmer said, 'Tis very liable he's a-croped into one o' these here hovers. **1890** R. D. BLACKMORE *Kit & Kitty* I. ix. 95 Ould dog be put out at zix o'clock riglar, and 'tis liable he'll hurn straight to 'e. **1901** MERWIN & WEBSTER *Calumet 'K'* xi. 198 He's liable to call our men out to-night, ain't he? **1903** *N.Y. Even. Post* 22 Aug., Norman Hunter's new record..is liable to stand unmolested for many years. **1935** H. W. HORWILL *Dict. Mod. Amer. Usage* 189/1 'Boston is liable to be the ultimate place for holding the convention.' 'If the lawmakers get back before the frosts kill the vegetation, many of them are liable to think it a reproach to the nation that grass should be growing in the streets of the national capital.' **1957** B. & C. EVANS *Dict. Contemp. Amer. Usage* 273/1 An American might say *we are liable to be in Chicago next week* without meaning that that would be a calamity.

liaise (li,ē¹·z), *v.* orig. *Services' slang.* Also (erron.) **liase.** [Back-formation from LIAISON.] *intr.* To make liaison *with* or *between.* Hence **liai·sing** *vbl. sb.* and *ppl. a.*

1928 C. F. S. GAMBLE *Story N. Sea Air Station* xiii. 221 [Lord Fisher said in 1916] 'I want a soldier..to keep in touch with the Navy and so "liaise" or exchange inventions which may be suitable.' **1941** *Amer. N. & Q.* Dec. 141/1 The kind of grammatical economy found in a recent (British) Home Guard instruction sheet—in the event of certain circumstances, it stated, two groups were ordered to 'liase' with two others. **1942** *New Statesman* 1 Aug. 75/1 'To liaise'..was at first frowned on by the pundits: its usefulness..soon came to outweigh its objectionableness. **1942** *Tee Emm* (Air Ministry) II. 128 He then hurriedly climbed into a Spit and shot off to 'liaise' with his old Squadron. **1946** A. LEE *German Air Force* 25 Göring never acquired the happy knack of liasing satisfactorily with Germany's senior army generals. **1948** L. MACNEICE *Holes in Sky* 71 The liaising aircraft mounts. **1952** *World Rev.* Sept. 20 The manufacturer, too, has advertizing people on his own staff who liaise with the advertizing agency. **1958** L. DURRELL *Mountolive* vi. 139 For convenience it can work to us and liaise with our Service Departments. **1959** *Guardian* 15 Oct. 10/7 He would expect absolute obedience from his subordinates... It remains to be seen whether he could also 'liaise' successfully. **1962** *Times* 28 Mar. 3/1 He will liaise between the dressing room and the press. **1965** *New Statesman* 10 Dec. 919/3 Paris..was..in a state of great confusion... There seemed little liaising to be done. **1970** *Country Life* 1 Oct. 846/3 It would seem advisable for the host to detach well briefed members of the shoot staff to liase with the field trial stewards. **1974** *Times* 18 Feb. 20/8 It would seem that the Government statisticians do not: (a) Liaise with other departments, [etc.].

liaison. 2. a. Delete † and add later examples.

1870 *Putnam's Mag.* May 545/2 The knowledge gained from these new sources..has..given new zest to the alleged *liaisons* of the Republic. **1974** *Country Life* 5 Dec. 1814/2 Florence..remained..a home from home for the British... It is a liaison that seems to have lasted happily down the years.

b. (Earlier example.)

1816 BYRON *Let.* 24 Dec. in *Works* (1900) IV. 29 She is by far the prettiest woman I have seen here... I believe I told you the rise and progress of our *liaison* in my former letter.

3. *Phonetics.* Also in English contexts, and in *Music,* in wider sense.

1905 *Daily Chron.* 7 Feb. 4/7 The nightly false 'liaison' made by a clever actress... 'Take Lady Agatha-r-out,' she says with terrible distinctness. **1917** G. B. SHAW *How to become Mus. Critic* (1960) 292, I will not blame the singer for putting in a little *liaison* of her own at the reprise. **1929** *Amer. Speech* V. 87, I noticed recently a curious instance of consonant *liaison* (if that is the term for a carrying-over that is commoner in French than in English). **1962** *Listener* 6 Sept. 369/3 To our singers the style, the flavour, the true placing of the sounds, the liaisons—every aspect is elusive and deceptive.

4. *Mil.* Close connection and co-operation between two units, branches, allies, etc., esp. during a battle or campaign. Also *transf.*

1816 H. CLARKE *Hist. War* I. xliii. 702/1 Other advantages of a great and important nature arise from the combinations of the various corps of their invading armies maintaining their *liaison* or correspondence, by means of the..staff-establishments attached to every division. **1915** *Oxf. Mag.* 29 Oct. 18/2 The 'overseer' of the Press.. an unrivalled artist in the liaison of departments. **1920** G. H. PERRIS *Battle of Marne* xi. 225 With the I Army pulling north-west, the II Army pulling south-east,..how could anything more than a pretence of liaison be kept up? **1920** *Q. Rev.* July 138 It acted rather as a liaison between the Admiralty and the Press Bureau than as a branch of the latter. **1922** *Encycl. Brit.* XXXII. 967/2 The welfare supervisor..is thus able to refer all matters calling for attention direct to the general manager and may be regarded by him as a *liaison* between him and the various departments dealing with the women employees. **1930** A. W. MYERS *Lawn Tennis* ix. 113 Mind and body must be working in liaison. **1964** B. B. SCHOFIELD *Russ. Convoys* ii. 27 The main trouble during the first years of the war was the shortage of aircraft—otherwise the liaison between the two services was as good as it could be.

5. *attrib.* and *Comb.,* esp. **liaison officer,** an officer in the Services who is concerned with the liaison of units, etc.; also *transf.*

1915 'I. HAY' *First Hundred Thousand* xix. 285 He is one of that most efficient body, the French *liaison* officers, who act as connecting-link between the Allied Forces. **1916** *War Illustr.* 9 Dec. 405 (*caption*) Army liaison dog leaving with a message attached to his collar. **1917** *Times* 5 June 7/1 Members of Parliament have tended less and less in recent times to fulfil their primary duty as *liaison* officers between Parliament and the constituencies. **1918** *Daily Chron.* 19 June 2/2 This position as 'liaison Minister' between the House and the War Cabinet. **1930** *N. & Q.* 5 Apr. 250/2 This [book] is a *liaison* treatise of which ethics is the warp, and economics the very much less important woof, while the whole is coloured with a tinge of metaphysics. **1942** *R.A.F. Jrnl.* 3 Oct. 23 'L' [stands] for 'Liaison pilot'. **1946** *Sun* (Baltimore) 18 Feb. 11/5 The Navy has tabbed entertainment with the high-sounding name liaison unit. **1954** A. HUXLEY *Let.* Apr. (1969) 704 You unquestionably *are* the man to act as liaison officer between pure science and the rest of the world in this matter of the nature of the Mind. **1964** *Amer. Speech* XXXIX. 233 Compares duration of liaison consonants, as in *des airs,* with that of medial consonants, as in *désert.* **1966** *B.B.C. Handbk.* 75 The main duty of the department is to act in a liaison capacity. **1973** *Times* 14 Nov. 8/1 The Israeli liaison officer said he had still not received permission for the journalists to go on to Suez.

liar. Add: **1. a.** *I'm a liar,* (in trivial use) I am mistaken.

1940 *Sunday Express* 31 Mar. 3/5 'That's not my brother Sid you met in here last Thursday. Or was it Friday?' We said we didn't remember... 'I'm a liar. It was Wednesday.' **1972** W. GARNER *Ditto, Brother Rat!* xv. 105 Last winter, was it? No, I'm a liar. The spring. That's right.

c. Delete † *Obs.* and add **liar dice,** a gambling game resembling poker dice, in which the thrower conceals the dice thrown and sometimes declares a false score; also *ellipt.* (in *pl.*).

1946 J. SCARNE *On Dice* (ed. 2) xvii. 386 Liar or Doubting Dice. A popular game on transpacific liners and in the Far East, it is now gaining rapidly in popularity in the United States. **1956** M. MCMINNIES *Flying Fox* I. iv. 55 Everybody was round the bar playing liar dice. **1959** R. KIRKBRIDE *Tamiko* v. 37 'Which do you play, Balin?' 'Which?' 'Liars, Horses, Cameroon—.' 'I don't play dice.' **1966** O. NORTON *School of Liars* i. 2, I spent two months in graduating from the empty lounge to the bar, two more in..reaching the inner group, the liar-dice school. *Ibid.* ii. 23 We sat there playing liars until twenty past two. **1971** C. BONINGTON *Annapurna South Face* ix. 107 After the meal we played liar dice or Scrabble, with our tape-recorder blasting out music in the background.

d. *the liar* (Logic): the name of the paradox involved in a speaker's statement that he is lying or is a (habitual) liar; so *liar paradox, paradox of the liar.*

1871 T. M. LINDSAY tr. *Ueberweg's Syst. Logic* v. § 77. 245 This case happens when, and only when, the *truth of the judgment* is itself *the object of the judgment*, or belongs to the object of the judgment. The ancients have empirically discovered this case, without..giving an account of its logical nature. What is called '*The Liar*' represents it. Epimenides, the Cretan, says, all the Cretans are liars. **1906** J. N. KEYNES *Stud. & Exerc. Formal Logic* (ed. 4) App. B. 457 The sophism known as Ψευδόμενος or *The Liar.* **1908** B. RUSSELL in *Amer. Jrnl. Math.* XXX. 240 Hence his statement is false, and yet its falsehood does not imply, as that of 'I am lying' appeared to do, that he is making a true statement. This solves the liar. **1940** —— *Inquiry into Meaning & Truth* iv. 62 The inference from the paradox of the liar is..as follows. **1959** E. W. BETH *Found. Math.* VI. xvii. 485 The natural first reaction to the liar paradox is to ascribe the contradiction to the fact that the statement involved refers to itself. **1967** *Encycl. Philos.* V. 46/1 But one, the Liar,.. is still of great interest to us. **1970** R. L. MARTIN (*title*) The paradox of the liar. **1971** *Philos.* XLVI. 133 (*heading*) Tarski, Frege, and the liar paradox.

liatris (ləi,æ·tris, ləi·ătris). [mod.L. (J. C. D. von Schreber in *Linnæus's Genera Plantarum* (ed. 8, 1791) II. 542), of unknown derivation.] A North American perennial herb of the genus so called, belonging to the family Compositæ and bearing spikes or clusters of purple or white flowers.

1811 *Curtis's Bot. Mag.* XXXIV. 1411 (*heading*) Spiked Liatris. **1870** W. ROBINSON *Wild Garden* xv. 139/2 Plants for very moist rich soils... Liatris, in var. **1931** M. GRIEVE *Mod. Herbal* II. 746/2 Several varieties of *Liatris* are largely used in Southern United States to flavour tobacco. **1961** *Amat. Gardening* 14 Oct. 3/4 Cimicifugas, golden rods, liatris and lobelias.

lib, colloq. abbrev. LIBERATION, freq. preceded by *adj.* (as *gay lib*) or a *sb.* in the possessive (as *men's lib, women's lib*). See the defining words.

1970 *Atlantic Monthly* Mar. 116 The Lib Movement was rich in documentation of the conditioning processes. **1971** *Daily Tel.* 2 Dec. 7/2 Children's lib. notwithstanding, it would be hard to write a children's book without setting up some sort of standard for the child reader to admire. **1973** *Guardian* 3 Feb. 13/1 Lillian Thomas is a member of the Suffrage Fellowship Movement..and is delighted with the Libs. **1973** *Black World* Dec. 12/1 The various 'lib' movements, therefore, are white derivatives of the Black movement. **1974** *Listener* 25 Apr. 520/3 With Scots Lib, as with Women's Lib, it's no good the oppressors expecting the past to be forgotten when convenient.

liba·tionary, *a.* [f. LIBATION + -ARY¹.] = LIBATORY *a.*

1896 W. J. LOCKE *Study in Shadows* vi. 93 Mme. Popea scattered scraps of stuff about her room, in a kind of libationary joy. **1909** *Westm. Gaz.* 16 Feb. 5/2 The new Empress-Dowager had finished performing the libationary sacrifices to the memory of the late Empress-Dowager.

liba·tioner. [f. LIBATION + -ER¹.] One who pours out libations (to a god).

1920 *Brit. Mus. Return* 47 in *Parl. Papers* XXXVI. 673 Black stone squatting figure of Ser, a divine father and libationer of Amen.

li·bber, colloq. abbrev. *LIBERATIONIST. Cf. *LIB, *WOMAN *sb.*

1971 *Tel.* (Brisbane) 19 May 17/1 Women's libbers are preparing to do battle with the police in Baltimore. **1972** *Village Voice* (N.Y.) 1 June 26/4 Now the star-maker has decided to calm the libbers with another token. **1973** *Times* 1 Nov. 12/6 *The Female Woman* sorts out.. the contemporary confusion of ideas about the sexes which the Libbers have..worse confounded. **1973** *Daily Tel.* 24 Nov. 11/8 The..debate set things off by producing a truly appalling female whose anti-male views were so extreme and so crudely expressed that orthodox Libbers in the audience showed dismay.

liberal, *a.* and *sb.* Add: **A.** *adj.* **1.** (Further examples.) Freq. in *liberal arts.*

1753 W. SHIPLEY in D. G. C. Allan *William Shipley* (1968) 229 (*title*) Proposals for raising by subscription a fund to be distributed in premiums for the promoting of improvements in the Liberal Arts and Sciences, Manufactures, etc. **1906** P. ABELSON (*title*) The seven liberal arts, a study in mediæval culture. **1950** E. H. GOMBRICH *Story of Art* xv. 215 The so-called Liberal Arts such as rhetorics, grammar, philosophy and dialectic. **1951** [see *CLINIC *sb.*² 3]. **1961** *New Scientist* 16 Mar. 662/1 The better public schools..should be converted to liberal-arts colleges on the American pattern. **1965** *Listener* 11 Mar. 387/2 (Advt.), The major part of the work will be teaching Sociology,..but appropriately qualified candidates will be expected to teach Liberal studies. **1973** *Jrnl. Genetic Psychol.* CXXII. 183 The educational problems of the troubled liberal arts college student.

4. b. (Earlier and further examples.) Also in application to *Judaism.*

1823 (*title*) The liberal Christian. **1828** (*title*) Which society shall you join, liberal or orthodox? **1862** *Dublin Rev.* Nov. 48 Our friends the 'liberal' Catholics may be

interested in a note to F. Faber's treatise. **1876** O. B. Frothingham *Transcendentalism New Eng.* vi. 128 It may be inferred that Transcendentalism in New England was a movement within the limits of 'liberal' Christianity or Unitarianism as it was called. **1900** *Jewish Q. Rev.* July 618 (*heading*) Liberal Judaism in England. *Ibid.*, These liberal Jews have no organization. **1920** R. Macaulay *Potterism* vi. v. 253 Modernist liberal-catholic vicars asked him to preach. **1957** *Oxf. Dict. Chr. Ch.* 807/1 The 'Liberal Catholics' who formed a distinguished group in the RC Church in the 19th cent. were for the most part theologically orthodox, but they favoured political democracy and ecclesiastical reform... 'Liberal Protestantism'.. developed into an anti-dogmatic and humanitarian reconstruction of the Christian faith. **1965** *Sunday Times* 5 Feb. 5/3 A plan for a national conference of non-orthodox synagogues, Reform (progressive) and Liberal. **1968** B. M. G. Reardon (*title*) Liberal Protestantism. **1974** *Times Lit. Suppl.* 19 Apr. 424/4 Judaism is divided into Orthodox, Conservative and Reform varieties following the American terminology, and not into the British Orthodox, Reform and Liberal camps.

5. *Liberal-Labour*, of or pertaining to (persons associated with or sympathetic to) both the Liberal and the Labour parties. So *Liberal Labourism*. Cf. *Lib-Lab *a.*

1909 *Daily Chron.* 14 July 1/7 Mr. Hancock, the Liberal-Labour candidate for Mid-Derbyshire. **1929** M. Beer *Hist. Brit. Socialism* (new ed.) II. iv. xvi. 315 In 1898 Gladstone died, and with him one of the main pillars of Liberal Labourism disappeared from British politics.

6. *liberal-anarchic, -bourgeois, -cultural, -democratic, -empiricist, -humanist, -minded* (later examples), *-scientific* adjs.; *liberal-anarchism, -mindedness* (earlier example).

1964 *New Society* 13 Feb. 17/2 The progressive schools have been liberal-anarchic, the product of free enterprise in unorthodox educational ideas. *Ibid.*, Liberal-anarchism will no longer do. **1951** Koestler *Age of Longing* vi. 103 Where did you pick up this idea out of the liberal-bourgeois philosophy of law? **1953** A. K. C. Ottaway *Educ. & Soc.* v. 88 The supporter of the pure liberal-cultural tradition. **1940** Liberal-democratic [see *culture *sb.* 5 a]. **1949** *Mind* LVIII. 254 More than anyone, except perhaps Bertrand Russell, he [*sc.* L. T. Hobhouse] may be regarded as the inheritor of the liberal-empiricist mantle of John Stuart Mill. **1957** N. Frye *Anat. Crit.* 6 It would be easy to compile a long list of such determinisms in criticism, all of them, whether Marxist..liberal-humanist..or existentialist, substituting a critical attitude for criticism. **1925** Beerbohm *Observations* 16 Too proud to fight?.. or too liberal-minded?—or what? **1961** New Eng. Bible *Acts* xvii. 11 The Jews here were more liberal-minded than those at Thessalonika. **1971** 'D. Halliday' *Dolly & Doctor Bird* v. 71 Mini Adult Show for the Liberal Minded. **1783** *Gentl. Mag.* LIII. ii. 938 What the liberal-mindedness of the present age amounts to [etc.]. **1958** *Times Lit. Suppl.* 17 Jan. 26/4 The obvious charge which can be brought against this picture of a suppressed liberal-scientific element is the undeniable fact that it never showed any signs of formulating a practical alternative to current political or ethical machinery.

B. *sb.* **1. c.** In extra-European politics, and in wider application.

1832 *Liberal* (St. Thomas, Ontario) 20 Sept. 3/4 We shall first notice the slanderous imputations cast upon the Liberals, that they are a discontented set of men, ever on the watch to find occasion for complaint and clamour. **1854** *N.Y. Tribune* 22 Apr. 5/5 The 'Liberals' of Maine have called a 'State Democratic Mass Convention' at Portland. **1918** H. V. Evatt *Liberalism Austral.* x. 66 The Sydney press claimed that its own free traders were the Liberals. **1940** *N.Y. Times* 23 Jan. 20/4 Since then [*sc.* the Russian Revolution] Liberal has been a word of confusion. Everybody who was not a Conservative became a Liberal or Radical or Red, whichever came first to the mind. **1955** D. Viklund tr. Tingsten's *Probl. S. Afr.* x. 116 A Communist in South Africa is often, according to the general usage of the word, a liberal. **1957** *New Yorker* 12 Jan. 25/1 Both she and Robbie were campus liberals; they had met at a gathering that had something to do with the Spanish war. *a* **1964** H. Hoover in W. Safire *New Lang. Politics* (1968) 232/2 Fuzzy minded totalitarian liberals who believe that their creeping collectivism can be adopted without destroying personal liberty and representative government. **1969** *New Yorker* 14 June 44/2, I don't think he is a liberal. He's tight with his money, and he wants to see the poor work for their money.

liberalist. (Later examples.)

1958 A. Paton *Hope for S. Afr.* ii. 7 Further, the word 'liberal' has for the white enemies of South African Liberalism another meaning; it shares this further meaning with the words 'liberalist' and 'liberalistic'. This meaning is derogatory and carries the stigma of 'loose', 'careless', 'promiscuous'. **1972** *Times Lit. Suppl.* 27 Oct. 1272/2 Liberal or (in the pejorative corruption of her Afrikaner opponents) liberalist.

liberalistic, *a.* (Later examples.)

1958 [see prec.]. **1958** G. M. Carter *Politics of Inequality* iii. 104 W. A. Maree..brought out well the Nationalist view of the difference between what he called 'the liberalistic approach and the approach of nationalism' to education.

liberalization. Add: *spec.*, the removal by a government of restrictions placed upon the import of goods, the movement of capital, etc.

1940 *Economist* 5 Oct. 431/2 The liberalisation of bank loans to farmers still left unresolved the problem of the bad..credit proposition. **1961** *Ann. Reg. 1960* 496 During the year the liberalization of imports, especially from the dollar area, continued.

liberalize, *v.* Add: **1. d.** To remove restrictions on (the import of goods, outflow of capital, etc.). Also **liberalized** *ppl. adj.* (later example in the above sense).

1940 *Economist* 5 Oct. 431/2 All the joint-stock banks decided..to liberalise their policy of agricultural loans. **1955** *Times* 6 Aug. 6/3 The French Government has agreed to the German request that the 'liberalized' sector of French trade with the O.E.E.C. countries shall be restored.

liberaloid (li·bĕrăloid), *a.* [f. Liberal *a.* + -oid.] Resembling liberal (attitudes, etc.); in a bad sense, exhibiting liberal characteristics, pseudo-liberal.

1951 R. Campbell *Light on Dark Horse* xxiii. 346 The imbeciles of the King's Party in the French Revolution.. tamely handed over the keys of all the forts to the Reds because of the liberaloid mentality that they had acquired from reading the masturbations of that *pisse-froid* Rousseau. **1963** *Spectator* 29 Mar. 400 The mixture of French puritan bourgeois and liberaloid ideologist that emerges.

liberate, *v.* Add: **b.** To free (an occupied territory) of the enemy; also *ironically*, to subject to a new tyranny.

1944 G. B. Shaw *Let.* 4 Dec. in *To a Young Actress* (1960) 181 All your Italian friends must be starving now that we have 'liberated' them. **1955** *Ann. Reg. 1954* 303 Chu Teh..expressed China's intention of 'liberating' Formosa. **1961** *Listener* 28 Dec. 1100/2 President Sukarno's warning to Indonesian troops to be ready to 'liberate' West New Guinea. **1964** A. McKee *Caen* xix. 314 'This place sure has been liberated,' said an American M.P. to an H.C.R. crew, when eventually they reached the waste of brick and stone which had been Vire. **1971** A. Bullock *20th Cent.* iii. 76/2 The West had the great advantage of being liberated by the Americans and British, neither of whom wanted to stay. **1975** *Times* 1 May 1/2 At 11.30 am local time (03.30 GMT), according to Hanoi Radio, Saigon was 'liberated'.

c. To loot (property), to misappropriate. *slang.*

1944 *Daily Express* 7 Oct. 4/3 (*caption*) Excuse me, Canon, but I rather think you've liberated my matches. **1946** E. Linklater *Private Angelo* viii. 86 Those soldiers, who said they had liberated the turkeys and the geese, had taken a most drastic way of giving them their freedom. **1957** [see *careen *v.* 5]. **1965** G. Melly *Owning-Up* vi. 59 He..wore a sombrero liberated, I suspect, from the wardrobe of some Latin American group he had worked with in the past. **1970** *Daily Tel.* (Colour Suppl.) 1 May 9 Shoplifting—'liberating' to hippies—costs the English retail trade the staggering sum of £75 million a year. **1974** S. E. Morison *European Discovery of America: Southern Voyages* viii. 164 Drake's flagship *Golden Hind* carried no bell, but his men 'liberated' one from the church of Guatulco, Mexico, in 1579.

d. To free from social or male-dominated, etc., conventions. Freq. as *ppl. a.* Cf. *emancipated *ppl. a.* 2.

1970 R. Lowell *Notebk.* 191 The liberated girl with a build. **1970** *Globe & Mail* (Toronto) 25 Sept. 12/7 Liberated school. The co-eds from women's colleges in Virginia are going to attend formerly all-male Davidson College. **1970** *New Yorker* 5 Dec. 49/1 It is not only men liberated. It is *women* liberated. **1971** *E. Afr. Jrnl.* Mar. 9/1 Aunt Bimp..goes into the construction business .. She knows nothing about cement and sand but the corruption of the system has served to liberate her. **1973** D. Jordan *Nile Green* ix. 41 He resents me because I'm a liberated woman who can support herself. **1975** D. Ramsay *Descent into Dark* i. 25 Put '*Ms* Joyce Chandler'. Let them get the idea you're liberating yourself from the Kitchen on principle.

liberation. Also in the senses of *liberate *v.* b, c, and d.

1945 *Sun* (Baltimore) 28 Sept. 11/2 Liberation is only four months old. **1952** *Ann. Reg. 1951* 'Liberation' of the island [*sc.* Formosa] remained one of the primary stated objectives of the régime. **1956** *Ann. Reg. 1955* 314 On 15 August, the tenth anniversary of the 'Liberation' of Korea by the Soviet Russian army. **1966** *Punch* 5 Jan. 14/2 Each member of the crew would apply for his equipment to be 'written off', and for replacements to be issued. And each member of the crew would become the proud owner of the liberation loot. **1966** G. Jackson *Let.* 23 Feb. in *Soledad Brother* (1971) 94 Some..commit unpardonable crimes.. that must in the end bar them from partaking in the benefits of the liberation that is planned for tomorrow. **1967** *Daily Tel.* 14 Mar. 21/1 Negro and Puerto Rican parents who are organising a boycott of a school in Harlem began establishing 'liberation schools' today... They are demanding a say in running the school and in choosing a headmaster. **1970** [see *game-playing* sb. and adj. s.v. *game *sb.* 16 b]. **1971** *Black Scholar* Jan. 58/1 Those in the struggle have to deal with black separatists because they stand today as a potent obstacle to full black liberation. **1973** *Black Panther* 3 Mar. 8/1 The Black Panther Party is..an organization dedicated to the liberation of oppressed peoples in different communities. **1973** *Black World* Oct. 5 Development for us is liberation. It's liberating this person who, until now, has been suffering under colonialism..and under all kinds of superstitious beliefs. **1973** *Listener* 20 Dec. 841/1 The Arabs..are to give financial and diplomatic support to the African liberation movements.

liberationist. Add: Also, an advocate of women's liberation.

1970 G. Greer *Female Eunuch* 13 The organized liberationists are a well-publicized minority. **1971** *Guardian* 18 Jan. 9/2 The whole point..of bra-burning seems to have vanished from some English liberationist minds.

Liberian (ləibīə·riăn), *a.*[1] [f. *Liber(ius* (see below) + -ian.] Of or pertaining to Liberius (Pope, 352–66). So *Liberian basilica*, one of the early churches of Rome, formerly believed to have stood on the site of S. Maria Maggiore; *Liberian calendar*, a calendar attributed to the pontificate of Liberius; *Liberian catalogue*, a list of the Popes until and including Liberius.

a **1773** A. Butler *Lives Saints* (1779) X. 316 The Liberian calendar places him [*sc.* St. Callistus] in the list of martyrs. **1840** E. Cox tr. *J. J. I. von Döllinger's Hist. Church* I. i. 36 The Liberian catalogue would make him to have been bishop during the lifetime of the apostle. **1858** N. Wiseman *Recoll. Last Four Popes* ii. iv. 295 The recollection..will come back..in images..of solemn entrance into..an open basilica... The Liberian speaks to you of Bethlehem..the Sessorian of Calvary. **1913** E. R. Barker *Rome of Pilgrims & Martyrs* i. iv. 50 Philocalian (Liberian) Calendar of 354.—This Calendar is named *Liberian*, since it was compiled in 354 under Pope Liberius. It is called *Philocalian*, after its author Philocalus. *Ibid.* vi. 85 Sixtus III. (432–440) embellished the Liberian basilica. **1957** *Encycl. Brit.* VII. 4/2 Damasus was nominated.., but the intransigents of the Liberian party ..set up against him another deacon, Ursinus.

Liberian (ləibīə·riăn), *a.*[2] and *sb.* [f. *Liber(ia* (see below) + -ian.] **A.** *adj.* Of or pertaining to Liberia, a West African state founded in 1822, or its people. **B.** *sb.* A native or inhabitant of Liberia; also, a Liberian ship.

1854 A. H. Foote *Afr. & Amer. Flag* xxxiv. 386 The Liberians are freemen. *Ibid.* 388 Captain Cooper will not take exception at the remark, that it is 'the day of small things' with the Liberian navy. **1855** *Wesleyan-Methodist Mag.* I. 307 The Liberians..have acquired lands which no European power could peaceably gain from the natives. **1868** J. A. Horton *W. Afr. Countries* xvii. 270 The entrance to Monrovia, the capital of the Liberian Republic, reminds one of the entrance to a purely native town. **1882** *Encycl. Brit.* XIV. 508/1 The Liberian variety of coffee held in such high esteem. **1906** H. H. Johnston *Liberia* I. i. 7 The governing class..consists of approximately twelve thousand Negroes and Mulattos of American origin, to whom may be added..about thirty thousand 'civilised' Liberians of local origin. **1914** W. H. Page *Let.* 5 July in B. J. Hendrick *Life & Lett. W. H. Page* (1925) III. ix. 120 About half the Liberian Cabinet..have asked for an audience with me this week. **1944** *Amer. Speech* XIX. 164 In Liberia the descendants of returned American slaves who constitute the ruling caste of the country used to call themselves Americo-Liberians... But I am informed by Mr. Ben Hamilton, Jr., formerly of the Liberian consulate in Los Angeles, that..'Liberians consider the term Americo-Liberian opprobrious... Hence they prefer to be called civilized or Monrovian Liberians to distinguish themselves from the natives of the hinterland.' **1952** A. G. L. Hellyer *Sanders' Encycl. Gardening* (ed. 22) 121 *Coffea..liberica*, 'Liberian Coffee', white, fragrant, 15 to 20 ft., Trop. Africa. **1971** B. Callison *Plague of Sailors* iii. 98 Now, when you get aboard the Liberian... **1973** R. Thomas *If you can't be Good* (1974) ii. 13 A Dutch freighter, flying a Liberian flag of convenience. **1973** *Times* 17 Apr. (Liberia Suppl.) p. ii/6 By 1970..this group employed 1,500 Liberians and was the largest of Liberian concerns.

libertarian, *sb.* (*a.*). Add: **2.** (Further examples.) Also as *adj.*

1906 *Westm. Gaz.* 2 Oct. 2/1 No wonder the libertarian woman rebels. **1966** *New Statesman* 22 Apr. 602/2 She is a libertarian and was not happy under the dictatorship of Hassan II. **1969** *Listener* 15 May 666/1 The political activists..belong to what is known as the libertarian Left. **1972** *Science* 12 May 615/3 It gives fair play to the objections of civil libertarians. **1973** *Observer* (Colour Suppl.) 11 Nov. 44/4 Now he's suddenly the darling of the civil libertarians.

libertinous, *a.* Delete † *Obs. rare*$^{-1}$ and add later examples.

1906 *Daily Chron.* 14 Aug. 3/2 The tale of a bold bad knight, who made libertinous love to a virtuous young woman. **1966** *Punch* 30 Nov. 800/1 We red-eyed supporters of riotous and libertinous Sundays have no other lord before Ted.

li·bertist. *rare.* [f. Libert(y *sb.* + -ist.] An advocate of liberty.

1887 *Voice* (N.Y.) Aug. 11 But not for a moment can the radical personal libertist accept such a heresy.

liberty, *sb.*[1] Add: **5. b.** *to take liberties* (or *a liberty*) (further examples).

1749 J. Cleland *Mem. Woman Pleasure* I. 219, I had seen him taking the last liberties with my servant-wench. **1862** Borrow *Wild Wales* I. xii. 124 The creature [*sc.* a cat] soon began to take liberties, and in less than a week after my arrival at the cottage, generally mounted on my back, when it saw me reading or writing. **1924** A. A. Milne *When we were very Young* 57 Excuse me, Your Majesty, For taking of The liberty, But marmalade is tasty, if It's very Thickly Spread. **1967** *Listener* 23 Feb. 271/1 A scene in which he is wrongfully accused of 'taking a liberty' with one of the female guests.

9. d. *at liberty* (later examples).

1931 *Amer. Mercury* Nov. 351/1 *At liberty*, out of work. **1933** P. Godfrey *Back-Stage* v. 70 It takes many years before the superseded actors and actresses will admit to themselves that the professional terms 'at liberty' and 'disengaged' are no longer applicable to them in a temporary sense.

10. liberty act, a circus act performed by liberty horses; **liberty boat** *Naut.*, a boat carrying liberty men; **liberty bodice,** a close-fitting under-bodice; **liberty bond,** one of the interest-bearing bonds of the 'Liberty' loans issued by the U.S. government in 1917–18; **liberty boy,** (*c*) *U.S.* a supporter of a freedom movement; (*d*), (*e*) (see quots. 1826, 1842); **liberty cabbage** *U.S.*, sauerkraut; **liberty cap** (examples); **liberty horse** (see quot. 1946); **Liberty-loan,** one of the four issues of liberty bonds; **liberty man** (later examples); **liberty** (or **Liberty**) **ship,** a type of merchant vessel built in the United States by rapid mass-production methods during the 1939–45 war; also *ellipt.* **Liberty.**

1933 P. GODFREY *Back-Stage* xvii. 214 The training of a teom of spirited thoroughbreds for the 'Liberty' or 'Haute École' acts. **1837** *United Service Jrnl.* Aug. 474 They knew ..that the liberty-boat would be on shore for them at that hour. **1901** *Daily Chron.* 16 Nov. 4/3 The destroyer..ran down a liberty boat..with the loss of three lives. **1956** A. THORNE *Baby & Battleship* I. 33 They..had no intention of coming back until it was nearly time to catch the Liberty Boat. **1916** *Child* May 433/1 The 'Liberty Bodice' Factory, of Market Harborough, have made a speciality of the 'Liberty Bodice'... The bodice is made of durable but soft and elastic material, and is porous and pliable and arranged with well-placed straps carried over the shoulders to take the weight of underclothes and stand the pull of suspenders. **1932** S. GIBBONS *Cold Comfort Farm* xiv. 193 Give me my liberty bodice. **1968** J. IRONSIDE *Fashion Alphabet* 70 *Liberty bodice*, bodice to the waist,.. worn by girls. The bodice has built-up shoulders and buttons at front or back. It..has gone out of fashion for all but very young children. **1973** *Radio Times* 18 Jan. 18/1 (Advt.), The wiser you are, the more you appreciate the comfort of a liberty bodice. **1918** in WEBSTER Add., Liberty bond. **1919** E. E. CUMMINGS *Let.* 25 Nov. (1969) 64 Very nice of you all to include me in the liberty bond donation. **1922** *Encycl. Brit.* XXXI. 760/2 The Liberty Bonds and Victory Notes were issued under authority of the Acts of Congress approved April 24 1917, Sept. 24 1917, [etc.]. **1928** Liberty bond [see *DRIVE *sb.* 1 g]. **1774** in C. F. Aspinall-Oglander *Admiral's Widow* (1942) 51 They are distinguished here by the name of Tories, as the Liberty Boys—the tarring feathery gentry—are by the title of Whigs. **1781** S. PETERS *Gen. Hist. Connecticut* 393 The liberty boys were..honoured with the presence of ministers, deacons [etc.]. **1826** *New Monthly Mag.* II. 79 While the paying spectator..applauded, when his feelings prompted, the *liberty boy* [sc. free-ticket holder].., if he clapped at all, would clap with gloved hands. **1842** *N.Z. Gaz.* II. 112 People from ships called 'liberty boys' are only allowed to come on shore on Sundays for recreation. **1858** *Texas Almanac 1859* 33 The Liberty boys..joined Austin's Company. **1927** *Haldeman-Julius Q.* July–Sept. 7/2 Here we were..calling sauerkraut 'Liberty Cabbage'. **1967** *Listener* 18 May 642/1 In America it was more than a restaurant owner's life was worth to keep sauerkraut on the menu: it was changed to liberty cabbage. **1803** *Lit. Mag.* (Philadelphia) Dec. 172 A liberty pole..decorated with party coloured flags and liberty caps. **1835** *Mechanics' Mag.* 10 Jan. 256/2 It is wholly at variance with classic authority to place the Pileus or Liberty Cap on the head of the figure representing Liberty. **1843** L. M. CHILD *Lett. from N.Y.* xl. 274 This age and country, in which liberty-caps abound. **1930** E. SMITH *Red Wagon* xxvii. 225 The time came to exhibit his beloved liberty horses, four dapple-grey cobs exactly resembling painted rocking-horses. **1946** M. C. SELF *Horseman's Encycl.* 264 Liberty horses are those which perform in the circus without a rider. **1952** N. STREATFEILD *Aunt Clara* 103 The comedy horse turn was coming to an end, the liberty horses would follow. **1972** *New Statesman* 7 Jan. 14/2 Yasmin Smart is the only lady ring-master in the world... Since the age of 10 she has been learning to train Liberty horses. **1917** ADE *Let.* 12 June (1973) 64 We find it hard work to induce the farmers and other small investors to take the Liberty Loan bonds. **1921** E. L. BOGART *War Costs* 208 The First Liberty Loan Act of April 24, 1917, authorized a bond issue of $2,000,000,000 and advances to allies of $3,000,000,000. **1922** B. J. HENDRICK *Life & Lett. W. H. Page* II. xxii. 273 The American Government finally paid this over-draft out of the proceeds of the first Liberty Loan. **1909** *Daily Chron.* 25 Feb. 1/6 The packet boats which convey the 'liberty' men to Chatham after the day's routine. **1964** R. BRADDON *Year Angry Rabbit* xii. 110 A few hundred liberty men on each side.., their flights delayed by bad weather, returned to the firing line too late. **1941** *Marine Digest* 28 June 8/2 The emergency cargo ships, known as the EC-2 type, Liberty ships, will have an overall length of about 425 feet, width 57 feet, approximately 10,000 deadweight tons, and will be oil-burning. **1942** W. S. CHURCHILL *End of Beginning* (1943) 183 The launching of the *Patrick Henry*, the first Liberty ship. **1945** *Seafarers Log* 3/2 The first of the Liberties to be scrapped, the Banvard was delivered into service on April 8, 1943. **1961** W. VAUGHAN-THOMAS *Anzio* iv. 47 DUKWs were already chugging in from the big Liberty ships lying out to sea. **1966** C. R. TOTTLE *Sci. Engin. Materials* vii. 170 Some of the wartime 'liberty' ships fractured when lying in port, without operational loads.

Liberty (li·bəɹti), *sb.*² [The name of a London drapery firm, Messrs. *Liberty* and Co.] Used *attrib.* to designate materials, styles, colours, etc., characteristic of textile fabrics or articles sold by Messrs. Liberty.

1888 MRS. H. WARD *R. Elsmere* I. II. vii. 173 Bits of Liberty stuffs with the edges still ragged, or cheap morsels of Syrian embroidery. **1888** *Daily News* 23 Apr. 6/4 Her dress was of two kindred shades of almost indescribable colour, belonging to the class now commonly known..as Liberty tints. **1891** *Ibid.* 19 Jan. 3/1 'Liberty styles' are to be had in every large drapery establishment. **1892** 'F. ANSTEY' *Voces Populi* 2nd Ser. 112 Putting on a turban and a Liberty sash. **1892** G. & W. GROSSMITH *Diary of Nobody* ix. 126 Carrie has arranged some Liberty silk bows on the four corners. **1894** W. J. LOCKE *At Gate of Samaria* (1895) ix. 103 It had long been dismantled of the Liberty curtains, Persian rugs, and cheap Japaneseries. **1900** *Munsey's Mag.* July 517/2 Tying a brown liberty silk veil over my hair. **1901** *Daily News* 7 Mar. 8/4 Dresses and costumes (familiarly known as 'Liberty' gowns and frocks). **1903** A. BENNETT *Leonora* viii. 238 She had changed her Liberty dress for the dark severe frock of her studious hours. **1913** R. BROOKE *Let.* 22 Nov. (1968) 535 Hindus..in Liberty-coloured garments. **1923** R. MACAULAY *Told by Idiot* I. vi. 31 She looked round the Liberty room. **1957** M. B. PICKEN *Fashion Dict.* 283/1 *Liberty s[atin]*, trade name for soft, closely woven, piece-dyed satin fabric with raw-silk warp and single spun-silk filling. **1972** *Daily Tel.* 6 May 21/3 In spite of its French name, the 'new art' [sc. *art nouveau*] started in England and was originally known as the 'Liberty Style' deriving its name from the famous store which was started by Arthur Lazenby Liberty in 1875. Libertys sold many articles in this new style. **1973** *Country Life* 8 Feb. 365/2 Coat and skirt in a natural-coloured Swiss cloth with a lining and blouse in Liberty lawn.

b. Used *absol.*

1898 *Daily News* 19 Nov. 6/2 Another instance of the vogue enjoyed by English materials on the Continent is the universality of the word 'Liberty'. **1903** *Daily Chron.* 19 Sept. 8/4 Soft satin, called in Paris Liberty, is again being employed as a blouse fabric. **1909** *Westm. Gaz.* 1 Oct. 8/4 With pannier draperies over an under-skirt of Liberty.

‖ **liberum arbitrium** (li·bərʊ̆m āɹbi·triʊ̆m), Lat. phr. (occurring in Livy 4. 43. 5): full power to decide, freedom of action.

1652 N. CULVERWEL *Act of Oblivion* in *Lt. Nature* [II.] 38 The great Creator of Heaven and Earth, must wait upon mans *liberum arbitrium.* **1880** W. JAMES *Coll. Ess. & Rev.* (1920) 194 Shall I move my index finger or my little finger to show my '*liberum arbitrium indifferentiae*'?

libidinal (libi·dinăl), *a. Psychoanalysis.* [f. L. *libīdin-*, *libīdo* lust + -AL.] Pertaining to or connected with libido.

1922 J. RIVIERE tr. *Freud's Introd. Lect. Psycho-Anal.* 283 For a son, the task consists in releasing his libidinal desires from his mother, in order to employ them in the quest of an external love-object in reality. **1949** M. MEAD *Male & Female* xiii. 278 The pleasure of irresponsibility, untidiness, undirected libidinal behaviour. **1957** *Essays in Crit.* VII. 333 There remains the charge of brutality and its libidinal content. **1970** E. FROMM *Crisis of Psychoanal.* (1971) p. ix, One can speak of a non-neurotic character trait when libidinal impulses are transformed into relatively stable and socially adapted traits.

libido (libī·do, -əi·do). *Psychoanalysis.* [f. L. *libīdo* desire, lust.] Psychic drive or energy, particularly that associated with the sexual instinct, but also that inherent in other instinctive mental desires and drives. Also *transf.* and *attrib.*, as *libido theory.*

1909 A. A. BRILL tr. *Freud's Sel. Papers on Hysteria* vi. 147 The anxiety neurosis goes along with the most distinct diminution of the sexual libido or the psychic desire. **1913** C. G. JUNG in *17th Internat. Congr. Med.* XII. I. 66 This infantile fixation, which is understood as an unconscious attachment of the sexual libido to certain infantile phantasies and habits. **1922** J. STRACHEY tr. *Freud's Group Psychol.* 37 Libido is an expression taken from the theory of the emotions. We call by that name the energy..of those instincts which have to do with all that may be comprised under the word 'love'. **1929** *Encycl. Brit.* VIII. 399/2 The tenets of leading psycho-analysts assume a libido, with either one or two fundamental departments, sex, or sex and ego... The physiological basis of the libido and its emotions is hazy, to say the least. **1932** *Brit. Jrnl. Psychol.* Jan. 249 The attempt to find the foundation of group behaviour in instinctive tendencies fails, as does the psycho-analytic 'libido' theory. **1944** J. S. HUXLEY *On Living in Revolution* xv. 192 *Libido* is the nearest to such a term [*sc.* energy], but its use implies complete acceptance of orthodox psychoanalytic theory and has certain unsatisfactory connotations. **1953** *Encounter* Nov. 25/2 We accept the fact that our sexual libido is thwarted. It is time for us to recognise that our political libido is just as complex-ridden, repressed, and twisted, if not even more. *Ibid.* 26/2 The political libido can be defined as the individual's need to feel himself as part of a community, his urge to belong. **1971** *Sci. Amer.* Sept. 529/3 He shares the libido for new military systems that his entire guild displays. **1972** *Ibid.* Aug. 46/2 It has also been observed that removal of the ovaries does not reduce the libido of human females.

Lib-Lab (li:b,læ·b), *a.* Abbrev. of *Liberal-Labour* (see *LIBERAL *a.* 5); also as *sb.* Hence **Li:b-La·bbery.**

1903 *Review of Reviews* Aug. 113/1 The Progress of the Lib-Labs. The Lib-Lab party is carrying all before it. **1944** G. B. SHAW *Everybody's Pol. What's What?* xxx. 263 Despotic dictators came into fashion as fast as Lib-Lab prime ministers lost face. **1952** H. NICOLSON *King George V* vii. 94 Of the 53 Labour members elected in 1906, twenty-nine belonged to the Independent Labour Party and twenty-four were affiliated to the Liberal Party and known as 'Lib-Labs'. **1960** T. I. J. JONES in A. J. Roderick *Wales through Ages* II. 203 There were a few working class members of parliament before that date [*sc.* 1900]..but they counted themselves Liberals or at the most 'Lib-Lab'. *Ibid.* 205 The early years of the twentieth century saw the appearance of a new more militant type of leader ..and his appearance was to bring about the decline of the 'Lib-Lab' ideal. **1960** *Guardian* 18 Feb. 3/6 A famous 'Lib-Lab.' family. **1963** *Ann. Reg. 1962* 14 Mr Gaitskell stiffly shot down the idea of a formal Lib-Lab alliance. **1965** *Economist* 26 June 1496/1 This is the hoary dilemma of Lib-Labbery. **1970** *Guardian* 6 Aug. 10/3 North Cornish Liberals are to urge the Liberal Assembly to fight every parliamentary seat and to have no truck with Lib-Labbery. **1972** *Times* 30 Sept. 15/3 A Lib-Lab party would be well placed in terms of the central argument which is concerned with inflation. **1973** *Daily Tel.* 19 Oct. 16 Mr Wilson shudders at the very thought of a return to the old 'Lib-Lab.' combination.

library¹. Add: **1. b.** *free library* (examples).

1847 *Howitt's Jrnl.* I. 119/1 A scheme of free libraries. By Dr. Smiles. *Ibid.* 119/2 Samuel Brown, the author of the system of Free Libraries, (or, as he styled them, 'Itinerating Libraries',) was a merchant of the small town of Haddington. **1850** *Manch. Guardian* 28 Dec., A Free Library and Museum for Manchester. **1855** *Act* 18 & 19 *Vict.* c. 70, An Act for further promoting the Establishment of Free Public Libraries and Museums in Municipal Towns. **1902** *Daily Chron.* 4 Mar. 3/2 These things are surely axioms to the free-library reader. **1960** M. SHARP *Something Light* vi. 49 The meeting-place for intellectuals was the Free Library.

d. A theatre-ticket agency.

1827 W. CLARKE *Every Night Bk.* 108 It is..necessary ..to procure tickets of admission prior to the opening of the doors: they may be had at the libraries of Ebers, or Andrews, in old Bond Street. **1902** W. H. CHANTREY *Theatre Accounts* i. 7 The next source of income is derived from Library Bookings. It is usual for the management of a Theatre to allow a discount of from 5 to 10 per cent. upon seats booked by Libraries. **1959** *Financial Times* 23 June, The word 'library' is used in the trade to designate a central source of tickets—a 'ticket wholesaler' might be a better term. **1973** *Sunday Times* (Colour Suppl.) 28 Oct. 101/1 Ticket agencies..are..organised in the Combined Libraries Association ('library' is theatrical term for ticket agency).

2. b. (Later examples.)

1844 A. W. KINGLAKE *Eothen* xviii. 282 The books were thorough-bred Scotch... He prided himself upon the 'Edinburgh Cabinet Library'. **1974** *British Bks. in Print* I. p. ccxxvi/1 Home University Library. Oxf. U.P.

c. (*c*) A collection of films, gramophone records, music, etc.

1926–7 *Army & Navy Stores Catal.* 1095 Circulating library for music rolls. Arrangements can be made..for Members to subscribe to a Player Roll Library. **1937** *Amer. Speech* XII. 47/1 *Library*, collection of sheet music. **1957** *B.B.C. Handbk.* 101 Some types of material are recorded specially for the library, as for example, folk-music, dialect, natural history, and sound effects. **1962** H. ORTON *Survey Eng. Dial. Introd.* 20 The British Broadcasting Corporation's Permanent Sound-Record Library. **1969** *Listener* 12 June 836/3 Proms are no longer ..regarded as the poor man's record library. **1974** *Guardian* 26 Mar. 32/3 The transcription service..provides a library of BBC programmes on slow-speed recordings. **1974** *Times* 7 Oct. 13/4 Borrowers frequently make tape-recordings..from the material borrowed and can thus acquire..an extensive library of recorded music without paying the composer a penny.

2*. *Computers.* An organized collection of routines, esp. of tested routines suitable for a particular model of computer.

1950 *Proc. R. Soc.* A. CCII. 576 It is convenient to have a 'library' containing sub-routines for performing such standard operations as the evaluation of a sine, or a scalar product. **1951** *Ibid.* CCVI. 539 There are..some eighty sub-routines in the EDSAC library. **1951** *Math. Tables & Other Aids to Computation* V. 46 Routines for solving standard problems will be established on tape and stored in a 'library'. **1958** *Oxf. Mag.* 29 May 469/1 Their 'library' consists of 'routines', 'sub-routines', and even 'quickies', programmes already existing and tested. *Ibid.*, As the library grows in extent, programming for new problems becomes easier. **1964** F. L. WESTWATER *Electronic Computers* ix. 143 Soon, 'libraries' of standard subroutines were available for each particular computer. **1966** A. BATTERSBY *Math. in Managem.* viii. 195 Standard computing routines are always available for widely-used techniques such as network analyses or linear programming, and the range over which they extend is constantly widening. They are often referred to as 'library programs' or under the general term 'software'. **1967** *Technology Week* 23 Jan. 11/2 (Advt.), Software for Sigma 5 includes..a library of mathematical, business and utility routines.

3. *library book, card, centre, chair, committee, company, desk, house, material, stamp, style, table, ticket*; **library binding,** a special strong binding of books for lending libraries; **library edition,** an edition of good size and print and strongly bound, *spec.* a uniform edition of a writer's works; also (quot. 1917) an edition of a newspaper for depositing in certain libraries; **library frame, glasses, spectacles,** spectacles with heavy frames suitable for use when reading; **library shot** (see quot.); **library steps,** a step-ladder for use in libraries.

1903 J. D. BROWN *Man. Libr. Econ.* xxvi. 333 The principal leathers for public library bindings are pig-skin, Persian and Levant moroccos, and roan. **1952** W. MCGILL in *Library World* Dec. LIV. 90 (*heading*) A note on how some publishers produced reinforced or special library bindings for public libraries nearly 50 years ago. **1863** 'G. HAMILTON' *Gala-Days* 146 There was the long service, Sunday school and library books. **1916** A. BENNETT *Lion's Share* xxiv. 180 The women play golf all day on that

appalling golf course, and then after tea they go into the town to change their library books. **1973** K. Giles *File on Death* iii. 66 My old girl retires to bed around eight, with her library book. **1966** A. Sachs *Jail Diary* xviii. 164 The station commander..has spoken to his wife and she doesn't mind if I use one of the family's library cards. **1960** *Library Assoc. Rec.* Aug. 261/2 A library centre is a static service-point, whether or not under the control of paid staff, which does not comply with the definitions for full-time or part-time branches. **1883** *Heal & Son Catal.* 181 Dining room and library chairs. **1970** *Country Life* 31 Dec. 16/2 (Advt.), William IV mahogany library chair upholstered in antiqued Havana brown leather. **1831** *Congress. Rec.* 7 Feb. 618 It was referred to the Library Committee. **1965** D. Davinson *Academic & Legal Deposit Libr.* ii. 24 All British universities have a library committee formed from the Senate or similar body. **1745** B. Franklin *Let.* 11 Dec. in *Writings* (1905) II. 296 Our Library Company sends for about twenty pounds sterling worth of books yearly. **1837** W. Jenkins *Ohio Gazetteer* 99 The public institutions are a bank, a library company and a mechanics society. **1895** M. A. Jackson *Mem. Stonewall Jackson* (ed. 2) xi. 197 Between them is a library desk. **1869** Geo. Eliot *Let.* 19 Feb. (1956) V. 16 Ticknor and Field have intimated some intention to bring out a library edition of all my books. **1917** *Times* 2 July 1 (*top right-hand corner*) Library Edition. **1939** A. Huxley *Let.* 19 Feb. (1969) 440 The idea of a library edition makes me feel most horribly posthumous. **1960** S. Unwin *Truth about a Publisher* x. 150 They were..available only in the huge 38-volume Library Edition. **1948** *Optical Practitioner* II. vi. p. vi (Advt.), Frames of unusual design specially made... The '*London*' *Library* frame. **1962** L. S. Sasieni *Princ. & Pract. Optical Dispensing* i. 10 The heavy frame..is often called a 'library' frame. **1971** W. Garner *Andra Fiasco* ix. 56 She stared at him, reaching for a pair of library-frame glasses. **1959** *A.O.P. News* 31 Dec. 9/1 Modern spectacles for men, such as library glasses..can give the wearer a distinguished appearance. **1837** W. Jenkins *Ohio Gazetteer* 281 The library house is a handsome brick edifice. **1962** *Listener* 16 Aug. 259/2 John Elliot's production adroitly wove the tropical library material among the studio scenes. **1953** K. Reisz *Technique Film Editing* 280 *Library shot*, shot used in a film but not recorded specially for it; shot taken from a library or store of shots kept for future use. **1962** *Listener* 22 Feb. 346/1 The other, the one with the library spectacles, also lowered his paper. **1962** *Gloss. Ophthalmic Lenses & Spectacle Frames* (*B.S.I.*) 58 *Library spectacles*, spectacles of heavy weight with broad sides and usually of tortoiseshell or plastics. **1861** *Catal. Cathedral Libr. Calcutta* App. 120 To stamp the title page and other parts of each volume with the Library-stamp. *c* **1762** Ince & Mayhew *Universal Syst. Houshold Furnit.* 3/1 (*heading*) Plate XXII. Two Designs of Library Steps; the First intended for a large Room. **1793** T. Sheraton *Cabinet-Maker & Upholsterer's Drawing-Bk.* App. 9 There are other kinds of library steps which I have seen, made by other persons, but..these must have the decided preference. **1848** Thackeray *Pendennis* (1849) I. iii. 24 He would sit..perched upon the topmost bar of Doctor Portman's library steps with a folio on his knees. **1970** B. Cartland *Secret Fear* i. 5 He would notice the rosewood library steps below the place in the cabinet from which the book had been extracted. **1952** *Vision* VI. iii. 15/2 (*caption*) Heavy semi-rimless library style in dark mottled material. **1741** in *Publ. Colonial Soc. Mass.* (1925) XVI. 712 [The cross table was] compos'd of three Library Tables. **1853** Geo. Eliot *Let.* 29 Oct. (1954) II. 121, I wish to exchange my present one [*sc.* bookcase] for a Library Table, of which I am sorely in need. **1969** *Canad. Antiques Collector* Dec. 9/1 One of the most remarkable series of library tables (bureaux plats) to be found anywhere. **1971** *Country Life* 10 June Suppl. 52 (Advt.), A rare small George III library table with pull-out steps, reading top and two slides, constructed with fine quality solid mahogany. Height 32". Circa 1790. **1877** M. W. Chapman in H. Martineau *Autobiogr.* III. 63 Heaps of concert tickets, museum tickets, library tickets. **1950** O. Blakeston *Pink Ribbon* vi. 72 Amelia lent me her library tickets. **1965** C. Fremlin *Jealous One* xiv. 110 The usual contents of a hand-bag—comb, purse, powder compact, cheque book, library ticket.

Librium (li·briŏm). *Pharm.* Also **librium**. The proprietary name of a white crystalline compound, $C_{16}H_{14}N_3OCl.HCl$, used as a tranquillizer.

1960 *Official Gaz.* (U.S. Patent Office) 15 Mar. TM 90/1 Hoffman–La Roche Inc... *Librium* for psychotherapeutic agent. **1968** *New Scientist* 21 Mar. 623/2 Hostile tendencies can often be remarkably controlled by drugs, like Librium and diazepam, which are *not* sedatives, and which do not depress the general level of cerebral activity. **1970** *Times* 22 Sept. 10 In the first cafe he went into someone sold him six librium pills. 'It was my sort of cafe, my sort of people—of course they had gear.' **1972** T. P. McMahon *Issue of Bishop's Blood* (1973) xvi. 228, I decided the pills Dolly had left with Julio were Librium. I use them when the shakes get bad. **1975** N. Mitchison *All change Here* ix. 92, I took a tablet of librium, but had the father and mother of a nightmare.

Libyan, *a.* and *sb.* Add: (Earlier and additional examples.) Also, of or pertaining to (or an inhabitant of) the modern state of Libya.

1592 Nashe *Pierce Penilesse* 34 And such a spirit it was that possest the Libian Sapho, and the Emperorer Dioclesian. **1607** Topsell *Four-footed Beasts* 41 Beares are tamed..for sports among the Roxolani and Libians. *Ibid.* 115 The Lybian Roes..are..inferiour to the Lybian horses. **1725** E. Combe tr. *Huet's Weakness of Hum. Und.* 117 He might be call'd a Libyan, because he stay'd a long while at Cyrene, a City in Libya. **1882** [see *Kabyle]. **1921** *Handbk. Libya* viii. 147 Head-quarters of the Libyan Battalion. **1937** H. Pope *St. Augustine of Hippo* i. 18 In the purple-producing island of Girba.. Libyan was spoken, as Berber indeed is to this day. **1939** L. H. Gray *Found. Lang.* xii. 366 *Graffiti*..of uncertain date and in a script which marks them off from ancient Libyan and from modern Tuareg alike. **1956** H. S. Villard *Libya* xii. 154 In the suppression of native rebellions most of the educated Libyan leaders were exterminated. *Ibid.* 155 The Libyans..continue to place restrictions on the entry of Italian citizens into Cyrenaica. **1971** *Encycl. Judaica* XI. 205 During the Six Day War (1967)..widespread strikes of Libyan oil workers.. brought the flow of oil to a temporary stop. **1975** *Times* 11 Jan. 12/6 The Libyans, still the most active of the governmental supporters of Arab extremists.

Libyo-. Add: *Archæol.* **Libyo-Phœnician, Libyphœnician.** A Phœnician living in Libya, a person of mixed Libyan and Phœnician ancestry, or a Libyan vassal or ally of the Phœnicians.

1876 *Encycl. Brit.* V. 160/2 In Africa her [*sc.* Carthage's] subjects consisted of three classes—(1) Libyo-Phœnicians, [etc.]. **1948** *Antiquity* XXII. 142 Hanno tells us that he set sail..under orders..to proceed outside the Pillars of Heracles and found cities of Libyphoenicians. *Ibid.*, Libyphoenicians can mean either Phoenicians from Africa or African allies or vassals of the Carthaginians. **1962** D. Harden *Phoenicians* 223 Some think that it is the Berber inhabitants of the *territorium* who are the Libyphoenicians so frequently mentioned in ancient texts.

licence, *sb.* Add: **5.** *licence number, plate.*

1937 D. & H. Teilhet *Feather Cloak Murder* ii. 48 'Did you get the licence number?'..the grey car had vanished. **1972** L. Lamb *Picture Frame* xx. 178 We found his van... It was Mallender's licence number. **1926** *Amer. Speech* I. 686/1 American: Number plates. English: License plates. **1962** 'E. McBain' *Like Love* (1964) xiv. 189 You didn't happen to notice the licence plate number, did you? **1974** R. C. Dennis *Conversations with Corpse* xiv. 140, I..landed..a 1968 license plate.

li·cenceless, *a.* [f. Licence *sb.* 2.] Not possessing a licence.

1906 *Daily Chron.* 22 May 7/7 Six licenseless motorists on the Oxford to Birmingham highway were..discovered. **1923** *Glasgow Herald* 10 Oct. 7/1 Licenceless owners will make themselves liable to prosecution if discovered by the Post Office inspectors.

lichee, lichi, varr. Litchi in Dict and Suppl.

lichen, *sb.* Add: **3. b.** With mod.L. adjs., as **lichen planus**, a skin disease characterized by an eruption of wide, flat-topped, shiny, purple-coloured papules; **lichen simplex**, (*a*) a type of eczema characterized by the presence of small red papules; (*b*) (*lichen simplex chronicus*) a disorder characterized by areas of lichenification.

1798 R. Willan *Descr. & Treatm. Cutaneous Dis.* i. ii. 41 The extent of the disease being thus limited, I shall proceed to describe the varieties of it, which have occurred to my observation, under the denominations of Lichen simplex, Lichen agrius, Lichen pilaris, Lichen lividus, and Lichen tropicus. **1842** T. H. Burgess tr. *Cazenave & Schedel's Man. Dis. Skin* 191 Acute lichen simplex requires no other treatment than diluents and tepid baths. **1866** E. Wilson in *Brit. Med. Jrnl.* 13 Oct. 399/1 (*heading*) On lichen planus: the lichen ruber of Hebra. **1910** C. F. Marshall tr. *Gaucher's Dis. Skin.* 101 Lichen simplex may occur on all parts of the body, but it chiefly affects the forearms and dorsal surface of the hands, the neck and shoulders, the external and posterior surfaces of the legs, and the internal surface of the thighs. **1934** Dore & Franklin *Dis. Skin* viii. 121 Lichen planus is generally a chronic complaint. **1966** W. D. Stewart et al. *Synopsis Dermatol.* xxvi. 485 Lichen simplex chronicus..is a common pruritic disorder resulting in a localized patch of dermatitis that has a characteristic lichenification. **1971** *Acta Dermato-Venereol.* LII. 216/1 In an epidemiologic house-to-house survey..in Kerala in South India, 7639 individuals were examined for oral lichen planus.

5. lichen-acid, any lichen substance which is an acid; **lichen substance**, any of about 65 compounds, most of which are acids, which are found uniquely in lichens.

1893 *Jrnl. R. Microsc. Soc.* 497 (*heading*) New lichen-acid. **1967** M. E. Hale *Biol. Lichens* viii. 119 Lichen acids and pigments increase the opacity of the upper cortex. **1900** *Jrnl. R. Microsc. Soc.* 235 (*heading*) Lichen-substances. **1954** Asahina & Shibata (*title*) Chemistry of lichen substances. **1967** Lichen substance [see *depside].

lichenification (ləike:ni-, ləi:kĕnifikēi·ʃən). *Med.* [ad. F. *lichénification* (L. Brocq 1892, in *II. Internat. Dermatol. Congr.* 522), f. F. *lichen* Lichen *sb.*: see -ification.] Hardening and thickening of the skin caused by scratching or other continued irritation; an area of skin so affected.

1892 L. Brocq in *Brit. Jrnl. Dermatol.* IV. 326 At a certain time the skin shows quite a peculiar aspect, with a great exaggeration of its natural lines, representing a sort of network with meshes more or less large and regular, and a decided infiltration of the integuments... Such is the morbid process which I call Lichenification. *Ibid.* 329 In the second group..we only meet with the cutaneous lesions we have described as primary lichenifications. **1934** Dore & Franklin *Dis. Skin* iii. 41 The lichenification itself may be painted with crude coal-tar. **1968** A. J. Rook et al. *Textbk. Dermatol.* I. xii. 222/2 In all forms of lichenification pruritus is the predominant symptom. **1971** *Jrnl. Investigative Dermatol.* LVII. 299/2 Lichenification involves a change in the epidermis, characterized by hyperkeratosis, acanthosis and scattered parakeratosis.

lichenified (ləike·nifəid, ləi·kĕnifəid), *ppl. a. Med.* [f. Lichen *sb.* + -if(y + -ed[1] (to parallel *lichenification).] Showing lichenification.

1892 *Brit. Jrnl. Dermatol.* IV. 327 The cases entering into the second group, which we have called Secondary Lichenifications, are not of the nature of real and true lichens, but are simply lichenified dermatoses. **1927** R. C. Low *Common Dis. Skin* xii. 161 The situation of these lichenified areas, usually on the back of the neck, is a rare one in lichen planus. **1967** H. Montgomery *Dermatopath.* I. ix. 190/2 In my experience, one cannot distinguish between chronic lichenified disseminate neurodermatitis and localized forms of neurodermatitis histologically.

lichenized, *ppl. a.* (in Dict. s.v. Lichenize *v.*). Add: **b.** Of a fungus or an alga: living in association with (respectively) an alga or a fungus so as to form a lichen; adapted or evolved to live as a component of a lichen.

1942 *Proc. Sect. Sci. Kon. Akad. Wetensch. Amsterdam* XLV. 276 We believe to have found in the lichenized algal covers of Pleurococcus, Apatococcus and allied species, a better object of study in this respect. **1952** *Symbolae Bot. Upsalienses* XII. 10 It is certainly difficult in many cases to establish whether or not an organism should be regarded as a lichen. One type of questionable or easily misinterpreted cases is provided by such lichen-fungi as are sometimes lichenized and sometimes live without algae. *Ibid.*, A lichenized fungus means in the present paper always a fungus which lives in symbiosis (s. str.) with an alga and which is not a parasymbiont. **1960** *Amer. Jrnl. Bot.* XLVII. 677 (*heading*) Some new and interesting species of Trebouxia, a genus of lichenized algae. **1973** *Nature* 4 May p. xv (Advt.), Taxonomic research in the ascomycetous fungi or their lichenised relatives.

lichenometry (ləikĕnǫ·mĕtri). *Geol.* [f. Lichen *sb.* + -o + -metry.] The dating of moraines or other surfaces recently exposed for lichen colonization by measurement of the size of lichens growing on them.

1957 R. E. Beschel in *Arctic* (Montreal) X. 60/1 This method that I call lichenometry works well for the last 1,000 years under alpine conditions. **1967** *Jrnl. Glaciol.* VI. 818 The basic premise of lichenometry is that the diameter of the largest lichen thallus growing on a moraine, rock glacier or other surface is proportional to the length of time that the surface has been exposed to colonization and growth. **1973** *Oxford Times* 27 July 6/5 There will also be a botanical study of the glaciers and a lichonometry survey to assist the dating of withdrawal of ice.

Hence **lichenome·tric, -me·trical** *adjs.*

1958 *Arctic* (Montreal) XI. 254/1 (*heading*) Lichenometrical studies in West Greenland. **1959** *Biol. Abstr.* XXXIV. 861/2 In several glaciers of the group, a lichenometric study was performed. **1964** *Geogr. Bull.* (Ottawa) Nov. 80 (*heading*) A lichenometrical study of the north-western margin of the Barnes Ice Cap: a geomorphological technique. **1967** *Jrnl. Glaciol.* VI. 819 The wide geographic distribution of the species, together with its long life span and consistent size–age relationship make *R*[*hizocarpon*] *geographicum* ideal for lichenometric dating.

lick, *sb.* Add: **1.** (Later examples.) Also (*U.S. colloq.*) *a lick*, somewhat, a bit (usu. in neg. contexts).

1902 W. N. Harben *Abner Daniel* 94 But all day yesterday an' to-day he hain't worked a lick. **1919** H. L. Wilson *Ma Pettengill* vii. 215, I was fool enough to argue with him a bit, trying to see if he didn't have a lick of sense. **1938** C. H. Matschat *Suwannee River* vii. 110, I knocked him loose an' hit him a lick. **1939** Joyce *Finnegans Wake* 415 Seven bolls of sapo, a lick of lime, two spurts of fussfor. **1957** W. C. Handy *Father of Blues* v. 66 We had been complaining violently against an Irishman who couldn't cook a lick. **1971** *Black Scholar* Sept. 37/2 His grandfather was a preacher and he couldn't read a lick. **1973** *Black World* Jan. 63/2 His wife Fanny can't cook a lick. **1973** M. & G. Gordon *Informant* xlix. 188 If you've got a lick of sense, you'll mosey back into the woodwork.

b. (Further examples.) Also, a hasty tidying up, a casual amount of work.

1860 W. White *All round the Wrekin* xx. 207 We only gives the cheap ones a lick and a promise. **1899** E. F. Heddle *Marget at Manse* 43 That lassie gi'es a lick and a promise when I tell her to sweep! **1922** A. Bennett *Lilian* i. vi. 57 The dirty kitchenmaid was giving the stone floor of the porch a lick and a promise. **1934** L. A. G. Strong *Corporal Tune* iii. ii. 230 The room, instead of its usual vigorous cleaning, got what Nelly would have called a lick and a promise. **1942** C. Morley *Thorofare* xl. 355 You ought to be writing the Adventures of a Crustacean. You've only done a lick and a promise. There's six more inches to fill. **1948** M. McCarthy in *Partisan Rev.* May–June 325 The Dublin Gate players..had a slapdash style of acting that suggested an Irish housemaid flailing about with a dust-cloth—they gave their roles a lick and a promise and trusted to the audience's good-nature to take the will for the deed. **1967** V. Lincoln *Private Disgrace* (1968) xi. 91 She had only a basin of water and a rag with which to give the insides of the windows a lick and a promise. **1969** D. Clark *Death after Evensong* vi. 142 A pale sun gave Rooksby a lick and a promise of better things to come. **1972** J. Burmeister *Running Scared* iii. 51 The isolation ward..was given a lick and a promise once a month by an unsupervised maid.

2. (Further examples.) Also *Canad.*

1747 *Virginia Land Patents & Grants* in *Amer. Speech* (1940) XV. 280/2 Crossing the said Run above a Lick.

1750 T. WALKER *Jrnl. Explor.* (1888) 51 At the mouth of a Creek..is a Lick, and I believe there was a hundred Buffaloes at it. 1784 J. F. D. SMYTH *Tour U.S.A.* I. xviii. 141 Licks are particular places..where the clay or earth is impregnated with saline particles. a1816 B. HAWKINS *Sk. Creek Country* (1848) 29 Parallel with this, are some licks in post and red oak saplin flats. 1825 J. PICKERING *Jrnl.* 21 Dec. in *Emigration* (1830) v. 49 Deer will go miles to the salt spring, or 'licks' as they are called. 1832 J. MCGREGOR *Brit. Amer.* II. 556 Both buffalo and deer resort to them for the purpose of licking the salt off the shrubs hence the name *lick.* 1957 *Beaver* Summer 37/2 The goat evidently was headed for the same lick from which the sheep were returning.

b. = *lick-log.*

1920 WEBSTER *Lick*, an artificial saline preparation given to sheep and cattle to lick. c 1920 W. D. POWDRELL *Dairy Farming N.Z.* v. 38 A lick of rock-salt should be provided. 1950 *N.Z. Jrnl. Agric.* July 67/3 By using cobalt either as a topdressing, as a drench, or in licks all classes of stock could be run without any trouble [on this cobalt-deficient country]. 1963 *Times* 4 Feb. 4/7 A large feed block or lick is made available to cattle.

6. (Further examples.) Also *colloq.* and *N.Z.*

The phr. *to go* (or *run*, etc.) *for the lick of one's life* appears to be restricted to Australia and N.Z.

1809 T. DONALDSON *Poems* 135 Ere I get a pick, In comes young *Nannie* wi' a lick. 1835 *Gent's. Vade Mecum* (Philadelphia) 14 Feb. 3/4 When you come to put in the scientific licks, I squat. 1847 J. S. ROBB *Streaks of Squatter Life* 106 He was puttin' in the biggest kind a licks in the way of courtin'. 1851 —— in T. A. Burke *Polly Peablossom's Wedding* 111, I saw comin' my gray mule, puttin' in her best licks, and a few yards behind her was a grizzly. 1868 *Putnam's Mag.* June 715/1 The father..did an occasional 'lick of work' for some well-to-do neighbor. 1892 *Dialect Notes* I. 230 *To mend one's licks*, to quicken one's steps. 'When the dog got after me, I mended my licks.' 1905 *Dialect Notes* III. 86 You'll have to hit a different lick, if you expect to accomplish anything. 1906 H. D. PITTMAN *Belle of Bluegrass Country* xv. 224 I'll have to take care of the whole gang, and never get a lick of work out of one of them. 1932 W. FAULKNER *Light in August* (1933) i. 7 She's hitting that lick like she's been at it for a right smart while. 1934 J. MASEFIELD *Taking of Gry* 43 'They're [ships] going a good lick, sir,' I said. 1938 *Amer. Speech* XIII. 6/1 *Lick* n., an easy job. 'None of these jobs is a lick.' 1944 J. H. FULLARTON *Troop Target* I. v. 46 'Go for the lick of your life down the lane,' commanded Rangi. 1946 F. SARGESON *That Summer* 84 With all of us going for lick of our lives, there'd only be time for a wisecrack now and then. 1948 D. BALLANTYNE *Cunninghams* (1963) xviii. 203 Clive ran..full lick into the sea. 1949 *Marshfield* (Wisconsin) *News-Herald* 19 July 4/1 The power lobby got in its licks through a subcommittee of the Senate Appropriations Committee passing on the bill for funds for the Department of Interior. 1951 L. MACNEICE tr. *Goethe's Faust* I. 33 Lord, these strapping wenches they go a lick! 1966 *Sunday Mail Mag.* (Brisbane) 3 Apr. 6/3 A section of the miners agreed that the happiest solution to the sorry affair would be to lynch Mr. Chapple. The little Cornishman got wind of this thinking and, treating it seriously..went for the lick of his life. 1974 P. RUELL *Death takes Low Road* x. 127 Caroline contrived to be first down the gangway and set off along the quay at a good lick.

7. In jazz, dance-music, etc.: a short solo or phrase, usu. improvised and often interpolated into a piece of written music; = *BREAK *sb.*[1] 9 c; freq. in phr. *hot lick* (cf. *HOT *a.* 8 g).

1932 *Melody Maker* June 509 They manage to steal a 'lick' from an American record. 1933 *Metronome* Apr. 29 Please do not..think I want 'hot licks' to memorize in all keys. 1933 *Fortune* Aug. 47/1 His licks (musical phrases) are original. 1935 [see *GO *v.* 22 b]. 1935 [see *AD LIB. B *adj.*]. 1935 *Vanity Fair* (N.Y.) Nov. 38/3 Hot artists..add their licks to the exciting music that flourishes there. 1952 B. ULANOV *Hist. Jazz in Amer.* (1958) xix. 237 The panic was on to push vibrato aside, pick up his licks, and produce his sound. 1970 *Globe & Mail* (Toronto) 26 Sept. 27/3 The blues riff is even better, full of Charlie Parker-like bebop licks.

b. Plan, idea. *U.S. colloq.*

1955 S. ALLEN *Bop Fables* 54 So here's the lick. Take this beat-up bovine to market. 1970 C. MAJOR *Dict. Afro-Amer. Slang* 76 *Lick*, plan, idea, outline of a situation.

lick, *v.* Add: **1. b.** *to lick* (another's) *boots* = *to lick* (another's) *shoe; to lick the* (or *one's*, etc.) *chops* (*Jazz slang*), to tune up or warm up before a 'session'.

1890 KIPLING *Barrack-Room Ballads* (1892) 23 An' you'll lick the bloomin' boots of 'im that's got it. 1909 G. B. SHAW *Press Cuttings* 9 And now comes this unmannerly young whelp Chubbs-Jenkinson, the only son of what they call a soda-king, and orders a curate to lick his boots. 1930 —— *Apple Cart* I. 34, I had rather be a dog than the Prime Minister of a country where the only things the inhabitants can be serious about are football and refreshments. Lick the king's boots: that is all you are fit for. 1937 [see *CAT *sb.*[1] 2 c]. 1937 *Étude* Dec. 835/1 *Licking their chops*, getting warmed up to swing. 1959 J. BRAINE *Vodi* x. 138 He had to use his..willingness to lick anyone's boots, no matter how dirty, to get the money. 1970 C. MAJOR *Dict. Afro-Amer. Slang* 77 *Licking the chops*, the tuning up musicians do before a jam session. 1974 *Guardian* 19 Dec. 10/2 If Lifestyle (BBC-2) keeps licking boots like this, Cherry Blossom will sprout out of its ears.

7. Read: To run, ride, or move at full speed. orig. *dial.* (widespread outside the U.K.). Also in the U.S., *to lick it.* (Further examples.)

1850 L. H. GARRARD *Wah-to-Yah* i. 16 The mad animal ..charged. How they did 'lick it' over the ground! 1856 J. COLLIE *Poems* 124 Sae aff gaed Death what he cou'd lick. 1886 *Outing* Dec. 198/1 He'd nothin' ter do but ter lick it like blazes, with the little dog a-follerin' along. 1903 J. LUMSDEN *Toorle* IV. i. 76 Jock! lick awa' in, an' blaw up. 1947 'A. P. GASKELL' *Big Game* 80 He sped her [*sc.* a car] along. Boy, she can lick. 1953 M. TRAYNOR *Eng. Dial. Donegal* 169/1 *As hard as one can lick*, as fast as one can go. *To lick along*, to go fast. 1966 W. S. RAMSON *Austral. Eng.* iv. 65 *To lick*, meaning 'to travel fast' and common in..*as hard as one can lick.*

8. **lick-hole** *Austral.*, a place where lick-logs are placed for stock to lick; **lick-log** (earlier and later examples); *to stand up to one's lick-logs*, to make a firm stand; **lick-up,** (*c*) used *attrib.* to designate a type of paper-making machine (see quots.).

1928 'BRENT OF BIN BIN' *Up Country* ix. 143 No horse ..was safe..in the lick-hole country of its myriad spring-heads. Pool found a way with rock-salt to make the lick-holes a trap. 1936 M. FRANKLIN *All that Swagger* xvi. 148 A hint without evidence is a snake in the grass, like that boomer you dispatched to-day at the lickhole. 1834 D. CROCKETT *Narr. Life* 170, I was determined to stand up to my lick-log, salt or no salt. 1852 G. W. L. BICKLEY *Hist. Tazewell County* 226 Capt. Moore..was at a lick log ..salting his horses of which he had many. 1948 E. N. DICK *Dixie Frontier* 105 Small troughs were cut in the trunk of a fallen tree and occasionally salt was placed there, making what was known as a 'lick log'. 1929 CLAPPERTON & HENDERSON *Mod. Paper-Making* xv. 212 The 'lick-up' machine may have either a vat or Fourdrinier wet end, but it does not possess a wet press... On this type of machine the underside of the web sticks to the cylinder and receives the polished surface. 1952 F. H. NORRIS *Paper & Paper Making* xv. 208 The 'lick up' type of machine..may have either a cylinder mould to pick up the stuff out of a vat and form the paper as on a board machine, or it may have the normal Fourdrinier wet end. On a 'lick up' machine, the wet felt also acts as an over-felt, and as there is no wet press, the web is transferred to the wet felt at the top couch roll.

licker. Add: **a.** Also in sense 6 of the verb.

1894 A. MORRISON *Martin Hewitt* ii. 66 'There's no footprint here nor outside.'.. 'That's a licker,' he said. 1895 J. T. CLEGG *Works* I. 375 Iv that's ony credit to Walsden it's a licker to me! 1902 *Eng. Dial. Dict.* III. 587/1 Fatther, this sum is a licker; will yo' du it for mha? 1907 *Daily Chron.* 31 July 4/7 The licking his Majesty once suffered..[and] the half-crown the late Queen gave the licker for his pluck. 1908 A. S. M. HUTCHINSON *Once aboard Lugger* VI. viii. 456 Into a chair Bill collapsed... He gasped 'George, this is a licker, a fair licker.'

b. *licker-in*, the cylinder in a carding-machine which receives the cotton, wool, etc., from the feed-rollers and passes it on to the main cylinder. Also *attrib.*

1850 *Rep. Comm. Patents 1849* (U.S.) 198, I do not claim a licker-in, nor the first main cylinder as such. 1884 [see *BURRING *vbl. sb.*[1]]. 1884 W. S. B. MCLAREN *Spinning* 84 To assist the process..the licker-in rollers are sometimes made hollow, and steam is allowed to fill them. 1888 [see *BREAST *sb.* 9 h]. 1892 [see *GARNETT *sb.*]. 1946 A. J. HALL *Stand. Handbk. Textiles* iii. 101 The cotton in lap form from the scutching machine is fed on to one of the small rollers (termed the licker-in).

lickety (li·kĕti), *adv. colloq.* (chiefly *U.S.*). Also 9 **lickitie; lickerty, licketty, -ity, -oty.** [Fanciful; cf. LICK *sb.* 6 (in Dict. and Suppl.), *LICK *v.* 7.] Usu. prefixed to another word, as **lickety-split,** at full speed; headlong. Also (nonce-wd.) as *vb.* Also *lickety-cut, -smash, -wallop*, etc.

1817 D. MCKILLOP *Poems* 33, I rattl'd owre the A, B, C, as fast as lickitie An' read like hickitie. 1831 *Boston Even. Transcript* 4 June 2/2 He ran down the street licketty cut, and is probably at home by this time. 1847 J. S. ROBB *Streaks of Squatter Life* 116 Away they started, 'lickety-click', and arrived at the winning-post within touching distance of each other. 1848 in *Amer. Speech* (1935) X. 40 *Lickoty liner*, going very fast. 1858 *Harper's Mag.* May 766/2 There they had it, lickety-switch, rough-and-tumble. 1859 BARTLETT *Dict. Amer.* (ed. 2) *Lickety Split*, very fast, headlong; synonymous with the equally elegant phrase 'full chisel'. 'He went lickety split down hill.' 1863 L. M. ALCOTT *Hospital Sk.* iii. 40 When my mate, Eph Sylvester, caved, with a bullet through his head, I got mad, and pitched in, licketty cut. 1869 MRS. STOWE *Oldtown Folks* xxviii. 358, I tell you if they didn't whip up an' go lickety-split down that 'ere hill. 1886 [see *BUMP *v.*[1] 2 e]. 1897 [see *BAND *sb.*[3] 4 b]. 1911 R. D. SAUNDERS *Col. Todhunter* ix. 122 You're worse'n a old huntin' dog that goes sky-hootin' off lickety-split after a rabbit. 1928 'BRENT OF BIN BIN' *Up Country* ix. 141 They rattled the vehicle lickety-smash at a hand-gallop across the flower-strewn plains. 1934 W. SAROYAN *Daring Young Man* (1935) 131 And then he was running lickety split across the school grounds. 1949 O. NASH *Versus* 111 Firemen, what is your destination?.. You have lickety-splitted by so often that my thoughts Are utterly split-licketed. 1949 POWYS & BOLTON tr. *Guitry's Don't Listen Ladies* in *Plays of Year* I. 566, I was coming along the street not thinking of anything, and suddenly you came out and shot past me, lickerty-split. 1949 WODEHOUSE *Uncle Dynamite* iii. 48 If I was you, I'd hop into that car of yours and drive lickerty-split to London and get another bust. 1955 E. POUND *Classic Anthol.* II. 87 We took out our cars lickety-clickety at the call. 1960 V. NABOKOV *Bend Sinister* ii. 17 The old men overtook him in their turn, clattering lickety-split through the mist. 1961 B. FERGUSSON *Watery Maze* x. 245 While going lickety-spit..they had come up against the formidable 15th Panzer Grenadier Division.., and they were lucky not to have been chased into the sea. 1972 A. FOWLES *Double Feature* xiii. 240 If one of his outriders radios in that Chau Chieu is there he'll come licketty split. 1972 *Last Whole Earth Catalog* (Portola Inst.) 305/3 Just like that. Stopped in here a few minutes, then took off up that creek lickety-split.

lick-spittle. Add: **b.** The practice of toadying. Hence (or as a back-formation from the *vbl. sb.*) as *v. trans.*, to toady to (a person).

1914 A. HARRISON *Kaiser's War* 112 A social system of formality, lick-spittle, bullying, and brutality. 1927 *Daily Express* 2 May 12/3 Christ criticised the sins of the Church His mother attended, and got His reward. He did not lickspittle the wealthy.

licuala (likyuwā·lă). [mod.L. (C. P. Thunberg 1782, in *Kungl. Svenska Vetenskapsakad. Handl.* III. 284), f. Makassar *lekowala.*] A small palm tree of the genus so called, belonging to the family Palmaceæ, native to Malaysia, New Guinea, and northern Australia, and having fan-shaped leaves and prickly stalks.

1872 *Gardeners' Chronicle* 14 Dec. 1657/2 The Licualas are Fan Palms of Asiatic origin, requiring hothouse cultivation. 1900 L. H. BAILEY *Cycl. Amer. Hort.* II. 911/1 The large fan-shaped leaves of the Licualas are somewhat tender and easily injured. 1930 *Discovery* Nov. 380/1 A few *Licuala* and *Pinanga* palms were seen. 1952 'W. MARCH' *October Island* x. 125 Zalacca, pinanga, licuala, corypha, And the sealing-wax palm. 1966 E. J. H. CORNER *Nat. Hist. Palms* xiii. 310 When the forest is cleared, the thickets of *Licuala* may be left, and they catch the eye with their striking foliage and long sprays of pink, orange, and red berries.

lid, *sb.* Add: **1. b.** (Later example.)

1942 'B. J. ELLAN' *Spitfire!* p. x, Shut the *lid*, i.e., close the hood [over the pilot's cockpit].

e. In various slang or colloq. phrases with *down, off, on*, esp. *to put the lid on*, to bring to a close or climax; to conceal or 'clamp down on'.

1915 *Lit. Digest* 4 Sept. 467/1 In fact, excepting the ordinary saloons,..the 'lid' is down, secure and tight. 1964 J. P. CLARK *Three Plays* 13, I hope he keeps The lid down on his wife for I fear She is fretting already.

1873 M. F. MAHONY *Chron. Fermors* I. xii. 225 What wonder if the lid was constantly getting off her temper. 1904 *Public Ledger* (Philadelphia) 12 Sept. 16 Commissioner of Police McAdoo..has taken frequent occasions to deny that the 'lid' was off, to use the slang definition of a lax police administration. 1910 W. M. RAINE *Bucky O'Connor* 96 'Playing with the lid off back there, ain't they?' The sheriff's nod indicated the distant faro-table. *Ibid.* 218 I'll back that opinion with the lid off. 1926 A. HUXLEY *Let.* 14 Nov. (1969) 276 Then a vast book by the Italian Sociologist Vilfredo Pareto, very good..he really does take the lid off and show you the works. 1927 R. A. FREEMAN *Certain Dr. Thorndyke* II. xviii. 272 'My eye,' exclaimed Miller... 'This puts the lid on it—or rather takes the lid off.' 1951 E. PAUL *Springtime in Paris* ii. 17 A few jubilant days when the lid was off following Liberation. 1962 *Which?* May 160 (*heading*), 14 cars with the lid off. 1968 *Listener* 19 Dec. 819/2 Are you the Editor of the *Sunday Blast*, the paper that 'rips the lid off'? 1973 *N.Y. Law Jrnl.* 4 Sept. 5/3 Inevitably when the lid blows off and riots and bloodshed and vandalism begin, the courts will be called on to do something effective about it. 1974 'M. INNES' *Appleby's Other Story* ii. 15 What will happen, I ask myself, when the police take the lid off? What..will be the resulting smell?

1909 *Punch* 30 June 452/2 Your astonishing letter puts the lid on it. 1914 'HIGH JINKS, JR.' *Choice Slang* 14 *Lid* (*to put on*), to put the lid on a town means to close the saloons, gambling houses and all other resorts except summer resorts. 1914 G. B. SHAW *Misalliance* 77 *Tarleton.* .. Young man: youre a fool; but youve just put the lid on this job in a masterly manner. 1914 H. A. VACHELL *Quinneys'* II. xx. 288 'Blackmail!' gasped Quinney. 'I prefer to call it a weapon, sir, which you are forcing me, sorely against my will, to use.' 'This puts the lid on.' 1922 C. SIDGWICK *Victorian* ix. 69 'That puts the lid on,' said Jane... 'You've done for yourself now.' 1928 T. GANN *Discoveries Cent. Amer.* xii. 168 Then came the earthquake, which must fairly have put the lid on, as far as Uk was concerned. a 1930 D. H. LAWRENCE *Phoenix II* (1968) 236 Inland, in the isolation, the lid is on, and the intense watchful malice of neighbours is infinitely worse than any police system. 1930 J. BUCHAN *Castle Gay* xiv. 216 You can see for yourself how that would put the lid on it. 1966 MRS. L. B. JOHNSON *White House Diary* 6 Aug. (1970) 410 Liz came in with a harried look, wanting to know what she could tell the press. She needed to 'put the lid on' if Luci had departed. 1974 *Times* 6 Feb. 19/4 (*heading*) Putting the lid on distributors' profits.

f. A hat, a cap. *slang.* (Cf. *FLIP *v.* 9.)

1896 [see *GLAD *a.* 4 e]. 1916 *Story-Teller* Feb. 828/2 'Dash my wig—where's my lid...' He snatched his cap up off the bunk. 1916 C. J. DENNIS *Songs Sentimental Bloke* 21, I dips me lid. *Ibid.* Gloss. 125 *Lid*, the hat. *To dip the lid*, to raise the hat. 1929 WODEHOUSE *Mr. Mulliner Speaking* ix. 304 You've no idea what a blister you look in that lid. 1946 B. MARSHALL *George Brown's Schooldays* xlvi. 178 Keep that lid of yours off your bloody ears if you don't want to look like a rotten sheeny. 1956 B. HOLIDAY *Lady sings Blues* (1973) i. 11 All the big-time whores wore big red velvet hats then with bird-of-paradise feathers on them. These lids were the thing. 1960 WODEHOUSE *Jeeves in Offing* xii. 132 It is almost as foul as Uncle Tom's Sherlock Holmes deerstalker, which has frightened more crows than any other lid in Worcestershire.

g. (See quot. 1971.) *slang.*

1967 *Time* 8 Sept. 18 The high price of 'commercial' marijuana ($10 to $15 for a 'lid' from which some 40 cigarettes can be rolled). 1968 J. D. MACDONALD *Pale Grey for Guilt* (1969) xii. 152 We had almost two lids of Acapulco Gold. 1969 *Rolling Stone* 17 May 6/3 We've got

this guy rom Sand City we just caught with a lid. **1970** K. PLATT *Pushbutton Butterfly* (1971) iv. 43 He would be selling grass, meth, acid, lids, match boxes,.. or mescaline. **1971** E. G. LANDY *Underground Dict.* 120 *Lid*, one ounce of marijuana, a quantity by which it is sold.

lid, *v.* Delete *rare* and add later examples.

1913 *Chambers's Jrnl.* Oct. 729/2 The cans..then move along to be lidded. **1950** *N.Z. Jrnl. Agric.* Nov. 429 (*caption*) A case packed to the correct height is shown in the illustration. Severe damage may occur to fruit on the lidding press unless the pack is crowned correctly. **1959** *Listener* 22 Jan. 191/2 Lid the flan with pastry. **1960** *Encounter* Mar. 21/1 They lidded that box again.

lidar (ləi·dāɹ). [f. LI(GHT *sb.* + *RA)DAR.] A system for detecting the presence of objects or ascertaining their position or motion which works on the principle of radar, but uses laser radiation instead of microwaves.

1963 *Bull. Amer. Meteorol. Soc.* XLIV. 568/1 Scattering at 180°, or back-scattering, is the basis for both the microwave radar and the lidar (laser radar). **1963** *New Scientist* 20 June 673/3 The difficulties already encountered in detecting lidar pulses from the Moon will make astronomers wary of attempting to use such methods on the planets. **1968** *McGraw-Hill Yearbk. Sci. & Technol.* 228/1 The purpose of the lidar was to determine where the spray cloud drifted after release by the aircraft, so that the area of forest 'treated' could be accurately determined. **1970** *Daily Tel.* (Colour Suppl.) 28 Aug. 19/1 At Duisberg in the Ruhr a £20,000 laser system—called 'Lidar'..—which was supplied by a British firm, Laser Associates, monitors the pollution coming from industrial chimneys.

liddle (li·d'l), *a.* Representing a foreign or dialectal pronunciation of, or used hypocoristically for, LITTLE *a.* So **li·ddly** *sb.*, a little child.

1906 KIPLING *Puck of Pook's Hill* 224 Come along o' me while I lock up my liddle hen-house. **1929** R. HUGHES *High Wind in Jamaica* i. 8 Rachel, Edward, and Laura, the little ones (or Liddlies, as they came to be known in the family). **1941** M. TREADGOLD *We couldn't leave Dinah* vi. 106 They are nice liddle horses, *nicht wahr*, Karl? **1945** [see *CHUTZPAH]. **1970** C. DRUMMOND *Stab in Back* vii. 165 She takes 'er delicate liddle tray and bird-like appetite to one of the upstairs rooms. **1973** K. GILES *File on Death* v. 144 P'raps we could 'ave a liddle natter.

‖ **lidia** (lī·ðiă). [Sp., lit. 'fight'.] A bull-fight, esp. the earlier stages in which the cuadrilla prepare the bull for the faena; the process whereby the torero obliges the bull to conform to his movements. So **lidiador** (lī·ðiaðōᵊr), a torero considered as controlling his art and the actions of his picadors, and the responses of the bull.

1893 CHAPMAN & BUCK *Wild Spain* v. 57 It was a gay and imposing scene..when the *lidia*, or tournament, took place. *Ibid.* 59 De Bedoya's 'Historia del Toréo'.. gives Francisco de Romera as the first professional *lidiador* of the modern epoch. **1932** E. HEMINGWAY *Death in Afternoon* 445 *Lidia*, the fight... *Lidiador*, one who fights bulls. **1952** J. MARKS *To Bullfight* iv. 50 This task consists in calling the toreros to order if they infringe any of the rules that govern the course of *la lidia*, which is the actual conduct of the fight. **1957** A. MACNAB *Bulls of Iberia* i. 11 After a while they start learning to distinguish the cloth from the body. Some breeds..learn quickly, and unless the man knows his stuff properly ('gives correct *lidia*' is the technical expression), he is apt to find himself hanging on a horn. *Ibid.* xv. 230 Antonio is far too good a *lidiador* to..request the President to change the Act. **1967** MCCORMICK & MASCARENAS *Compl. Aficionado* i. 25 As with tragedy, the lidia to the noble bull has about it an aura of inevitability. *Ibid.* viii. 240 He wants the bull to follow the muleta smoothly, as he educated the animal to do throughout his entire lidia.

Lido (lī·do). [Venetian It. *lido*:– L. *litus* shore.] The name of a spit of land, a famous beach resort near Venice, now used *gen.* for: such a spit enclosing a lagoon; a bathing-beach or resort; a public open-air swimming-pool.

[**1611** CORYATE *Crudities* 160 Venice..is distant from the maine Sea about the space of 3 miles. From the which it is deuided by a certaine great banke called *litto maggior*, which is at the least fifty miles in length.] **1673** J. RAY *Observations Journey Low-Countries* 149 These Lagune are..separated from the main Gulf or Adriatic Sea by a bank of earth (il Lito or Lido they call it). *a* **1680** EVELYN *Diary* an. 1645 (1955) II. 433 A loud acclamation is Echod by the greate Guns of the Arsenale, and at the *Liddo*. **1860** E. HALL *Diary* 17 Oct. in O. A. Sherrard *Two Victorian Girls* (1966) II. 273 We took the boat to the Lido..and caught our first view of the Adriatic. **1930** *Morning Post* 16 July 5/4 The question of the safety of bathers in the Serpentine 'Lido' was raised at an inquest..yesterday. **1931** *Daily Express* 16 Oct. 8/2 £60,000 lido for England. The bathing pool and sunbathing beach which the Hastings Corporation has just decided to construct [etc.]. **1934** *Discovery* Aug. 215/1 The broad sandspit or *lido* separating the lagoons from the sea. **1935** 'N. BLAKE' *Question of Proof* xiii. 259 What are you doing with all those deck-chairs..? Going to set up as a Lido proprietor? **1953** B. GOOLDEN *Truth is Fallen* xi. 175 'I haven't got any bathing things here.' 'Why on earth should we want them? It is not a Lido.' **1961** *Guardian* 24 Apr. 7/3 The Lido deck. **1969** V. CANNING *Queen's Pawn* xiii. 231 He went..out on to the One Deck Lido. **1971** *Country Life* 6 May 1106/3 Luino is a clean and pleasant place with several hotels, a lido and camping. **1975** M. KENYON *Mr Big* xxi. 204 All his free time was spent..semi-nude at the Serpentine lido.

lidocaine (li·dokēin). *Pharm.* [f. ACETANI)-LID(E (from which the compound is derived) + -O + *-caine*, after COCAINE.] = *LIGNOCAINE.

1949 *Q. Cumulative Index Medicus* XLV. 105/1 *Lidocaine*, caudal anesthesia in delivery. **1954** *Jrnl. Pharmacol. & Exper. Therap.* CXII. 432 In spite of the wide application of lidocaine in dentistry and medicine, the physiological disposition of this drug has received only limited attention. **1972** *Sci. Amer.* Aug. 45/3 For heart-attack patients with normal or higher-than-normal heart rates lidocaine (a drug without any influence on the heart rate) is given intravenously almost universally in coronary-care units to suppress ventricular ectopic activity. **1972** *Chest* LXI. 682/1 We discuss and emphasize the danger of administering lidocaine in the presence of atrial tachyarrhythmias with rapid ventricular response.

lie, *sb.*¹ Add: **3. lie-detector** orig. *U.S.*, an instrument intended to indicate when a person is lying by detecting changes in his physiological characteristics.

1909 C. E. WALK *Yellow Circle* iv. 69 It is a lie detector. .. You set some wheels going. **1922** *Rep. 45th Ann. Meeting Amer. Bar Assoc.* 619 (*heading*) The Berkeley Lie Detector and other deception tests. **1933** *PMLA* XLVIII. 609 These views lead to such revolting pseudo-scientific nonsense as the use..of a *lie detector* apparatus in order to convict defendants. **1962** [see *GALVANIC *a.* a]. **1971** *Daily Tel.* 28 July 4/8 About 30 employees..have been given lie-detector tests in the fight against pilfering. It is believed to be the first use of 'polygraph interviews', as the tests are called, in New York shops. **1974** 'A. GARVE' *File on Lester* ii. 9 When a politician talks of frankness most voters reach for their lie-detectors.

lie, *sb.*² Add: **1.** *the lie of the land* (later examples).

1950 E. H. GOMBRICH *Story of Art* 1 To show the newcomer the lie of the land without confusing him with details. **1956** M. LOWRY *Let.* 13 Nov. (1967) 392 If anyone is to blame it is I, for not giving you the lie of the land before. **1966** D. VARADAY *Gara-Yaka's Domain* xi. 123 The quick powers of grasping a situation with which all game are endowed, showed themselves in the speedy summing-up by the leading boar, as he got the lie of the land.

4. (See also *LYE *sb.*²)

5. A period of resting or lying (esp. in bed). See also *lie-down, -in, -up* below.

1930 L. COOPER *Ship of Truth* i. 30 Sunday was their one chance of a long lie. **1938** D. DU MAURIER *Rebecca* xvii. 271 Have a good long lie tomorrow morning. Don't attempt to get up.

6. lie-about, an idle person, one of no fixed occupation, a disreputable 'character'; = *LAYABOUT; **lie-down** *colloq.*, a rest (on a bed, etc.); a form of protest in which the participants lie on the ground and refuse to move; **lie-in** *colloq.* = sense *5; also, as a form of protest, = prec.; **lie-up,** the fact of lying inactive in a place.

1937 M. ALLINGHAM *Dancers in Mourning* ii. 27 He took out a wallet which would have disgraced a lie-about. **1956** *Daily Mail* 26 Apr. 1/1 They are called champions of the prize ring but on Tuesday they appeared as two fat and horizontal lie-abouts. **1961** *Guardian* 27 Jan. 9/4 This former lie-about has got himself married. **1840** H. MOZLEY *Let.* 13 Oct. in D. Mozley *Newman Family Lett.* (1962) 93, I should be very glad of a lie down but cannot. **1850** C. KINGSLEY *Alton Locke* I. v. 80 You must keep moving all night..or else you goes to a twopenny-rope shop and gets a lie down. **1919** W. S. MAUGHAM *Moon & Sixpence* xlvii. 202 When..we hadn't even got the price of a lie down at the Chink's, he'd be as lively as a cricket. **1928** ST. JOHN ERVINE *Four One-Act Plays* 65 Yes, Aggie, you go an' 'ave a lie-down, see, and you'll be all right. **1936** *Time* 7 Dec., Second Sit-Down, Lie-Down... Twelve women and forty-five men, picketing the Berkshire Knitting Mills in Reading, Pennsylvania, by lying flat on its ice-covered front walk..were arrested. **1970** D. BALSDON *Oxf. Then & Now* III. v. 114 It is..the small body of demonstrators with whom we are here concerned —in particular the sit-down or lie-down to impede the Vice-Chancellor and Proctors in the exercise of their proper duties on November 5th, 1968. **1974** M. BIRMINGHAM *You can help Me* ii. 43, I won't risk our clients to you in your concussed state... Why don't you go and have a little lie-down? **1867** T. WRIGHT *Some Habits Working Classes* III. 206 The luxury of 'a long lie in', is the earliest and most universal of the delights of a working man's Sunday. **1916** 'TAFFRAIL' *Pincher Martin* xvi. 300 Lucky dogs!.. You've got a lie in. I envy you. This is a night for poor old Peter to be at sea. **1932** C. L. MORGAN *Fountain* II. iv. 120 He left orders you was both to have a lie-in this morning. **1959** G. FREEMAN *Jack would be Gent.* ix. 192 I'm going to 'ave a bit of a lie in..seeing I'm on 'oliday. **1964** *Tuscaloosa* (Alabama) *News* 20 Apr. 1/8 The reported demonstration plans grew —from an auto stall-in on access roads to the fair to sit-ins, lie-ins and alike on other major highways, bridges and in tunnels throughout the city. **1971** *Time* 27 Dec. 40 Last week pollution protesters staged a lie-in at government offices in Tokyo. **1908** J. W. TYRRELL *Across Sub-Arctics of Canada* (ed. 3) 222 The two hundred mile tramp..had hardened our muscles so much that, with the ten days' 'lie-up' on the bank of the Nelson River,..we were now in first-class walking trim. **1926** *Blackw. Mag.* Dec. 850/2 We settled ourselves down for a happy four months of 'lie-up'.

lie, *v.*¹ Add: **10. d.** (Later examples.)

1876 'MARK TWAIN' *Tom Sawyer* i. 4 But in spite of her, Tom knew where the wind lay, now. **1886** F. T. ELWORTHY *West Somerset Word-Bk.* 434 Which way do the wind lie 'smornin?

e. Of horses, yachts, etc., in a race: to occupy a specified ordinal position. Also *transf.*

1951 E. RICKMAN *Come Racing with Me* iii. 24 What is that with the light blue sleeves lying fourth? **1955** J. CHRISTOPHER *Year of Comet* ii. 49 Who's lying fourth? **1972** D. FRANCIS *Smokescreen* iv. 55 He took the first half mile without apparent effort, lying about sixth. **1974** *Country Life* 24 Oct. 1189/3 Busted is lying third in this year's table of sire's winnings.

12. (Later examples in legal use.)

1958 *Times* 26 Apr. 6/7 If a chief constable is dismissed by a county council an appeal lies to the Home Secretary. **1964** *Mod. Law Rev.* XXVII. III. 322 Nowadays, after the revival of certiorari as a remedy lying for intra-jurisdictional defects, the scope of review on habeas corpus must be defined with more accuracy. **1970** *Internat. & Compar. Law Q.* 4th Ser. XIX. II. 306 The *Erbersatzanspruch* lies against the heirs, and consists of a sum equal to half the value of the portion, to which a legitimate intestate heir would be entitled. **1971** *Mod. Law Rev.* XXXIV. VI. 691 Where X and Y have a regular course of dealing and are likely to make contracts in the future, a *quia timet* injunction will lie to prevent Z, a third party, from inducing breaches of such contracts as may be made in the future.

16*. lie about, to lie here and there; to be left lying carelessly or in disorder.

1852 C. KINGSLEY *Hypatia* (1853) I. xiii. 274 Why, these poor blackguards lying about are very fair specimens of humanity. **1891** R. BUCHANAN *Come live with Me* II. xiii. 168 Ye might leave it [*sc.* poison] lying about, and mischief might happen. **1891** W. MORRIS *News from Nowhere* v. 31 Most children, seeing books lying about, manage to read by the time they are four years old. **1934** G. B. SHAW *Simpleton of Unexpected Isles* i. 4, I hate to see dust lying about. Look! You could write your name in it.

21. lie down. a. Also, to give up; to be remiss or lazy.

1904 W. H. SMITH *Promoters* i. 21 When they finally lie down, we'll just say, 'All right, we'll go ahead alone.' **1916** *Lit. Digest* 8 Jan. 87/1 It is natural enough that the accusation of 'lying down' and quitting has been cast up in turn at each of the participants in the conference. **1918** E. POUND *Let.* 3 Apr. (1971) 134 It is the best that can be done. Hope Kahn won't think I am lying down on the job. **1926** J. BLACK *You can't Win* xiv. 193 An ambitious fighting young lawyer who never 'laid down' on a client.

d. (Further examples.)

1914 G. B. SHAW *Androcles* (1916) I. 17 You know, I should feel ashamed if I let myself be struck like that, and took it lying down. **1931** E. F. BENSON *Mapp & Lucia* viii. 229 She had to swallow her medicine... I had no idea..that she would take it lying down like that. **1974** M. GILBERT *Flash Point* viii. 64, I heard what the beak said to you. I had an idea you weren't going to take it lying down.

23. lie in. d. To remain in bed (after one's usual hour of rising). Cf. *lie-in* (*LIE *sb.*² 6).

1893–4 R. O. HESLOP *Northumb. Words* II. 449 *Lie*, in the combination *lie-in*, to sleep longer than intended. **1911** E. M. CLOWES *On Wallaby* v. 144 On Sundays her husband and son 'lay in', as she called it, till midday, while she gave them their breakfast in bed.

27. lie over. d. *U.S.* To suspend travelling; to stop.

1849 *Ex. Doc. 31st U.S. Congress 1 Sess. Senate* No. 64. 186 But I shall make an early drive and 'lie over' to-morrow at the first water. **1903** A. ADAMS *Log of Cowboy* 181 We overtook a number of wagons loaded with wool, lying over, as it was Sunday.

Lie (lī). The name of Sophus *Lie* (1842–99), Norwegian mathematician, used *attrib.* to denote certain concepts investigated by him, as **Lie algebra,** a vector space extending over a field in which a product operation (×) is defined such that for all x, y, z in the space $x \times y$ is bilinear, $x \times x = 0$, and $(x \times y) \times z + (y \times z) \times x + (z \times x) \times y = 0$; **Lie group,** a topological group in which it is possible to label the group elements by a finite number of coordinates in such a way that the coordinates of the product of two elements are analytic functions of the coordinates of the two elements and the coordinates of the inverse of an element are analytic functions of the coordinates of that element.

1935 *Bull. Amer. Math. Soc.* XLI. 344 A Lie algebra L over a non-modular field F will be called normal simple over F if H is an algebraically closed extension of F and L_H is a simple algebra. **1939** H. WEYL *Classical Groups* vii. 188 The process of averaging over a compact Lie group presupposes our ability to compare volume elements at different points of the group manifold. **1965** H. J. LIPKIN *Lie Groups for Pedestrians* i. 14 The use of the Lie algebra therefore simplifies the solution of the eigenvalue problem for the Hamiltonian by defining a number of integrals of the motion. **1967** G. STEINER *Lang. & Silence* 33 One cannot 'translate' the conventions and notations governing the operations of Lie groups..into any words or grammar outside mathematics. **1969** *Sci. News* 31 May 538 The mathematical name of these patterns is Lie groups or unitary symmetry groups. They have been used to predict the existence of new [subatomic] particles.

‖ **lié** (lie), *a.* [Fr., pa. pple. of *lier* to bind.] Connected with, intimately acquainted with, attached to (a person or group of persons).

1855 E. TWISLETON *Let.* 1 May (1928) xiv. 264 Milnes ..has always been *lié* with Lord Palmerston. **1897**

E. Dowson *Let.* c 14 Nov. (1967) 397, I gather he is rather *lié* with Whibley whom I greatly dislike & do not want to meet. **1906** W. de Morgan *Joseph Vance* xi. 86 In case it should strike you that I have said..very little about Nolly, I hereby declare that this is not because I did not love him, for we soon became very *liés*. **1947** E. Jenkins *Young Enthusiasts* 50 Alex and I..each had a young man... Alex was *liée* with a naval officer. **1955** A. L. Rowse *Expansion Eliz. Eng.* i. 22 Esmé Stuart was a danger: he was a Catholic and *lié* with the Guises.

‖ **Liebchen, liebchen** (lī·pχyen, lī·bχyen). [G.] A person who is very dear to another; a sweetheart, a 'pet', darling. Commonly used as a term of endearing address.

1876 Geo. Eliot *Dan. Der.* IV. viii. lxii. 232 'Stay a minute, *Liebchen*,' said Lapidoth. **1941** M. Treadgold *We couldn't leave Dinah* xv. 226 How providential that there should be this trustworthy boy to keep the *liebchen* so contented. **1972** G. Baxt *Burning Sappho* iv. 71 You are no fool, *liebchen*. You are the most clever woman in the world. **1972** J. Rossiter *Rope for General Dietz* xiii. 185 'Thank you, *Liebchen*,' she said softly.

‖ **lieber Gott** (lī·bəɹ gǫt). [G.] Dear God, chiefly as *int.*

1898 M. A. von Arnim *Elizabeth & her German Garden* 50 The April baby came..to ask about the *lieber Gott*, it being Sunday. **1912** R. Brooke *Old Vicarage Grantchester* (1916) 7 And I know How the May fields all golden show..Gild gloriously the bare feet That run to bathe... *Du lieber Gott!* **1929** R. Hughes *High Wind in Jamaica* v. 120 Lieber Gott! What do you think I am, eh? **1954** M. Stewart *Madam, will you Talk?* xxi. 160 Kramer snarled: '*Lieber Gott*, will you listen to me?' **1969** A. Marin *Rise with Wind* vi. 75 Weber said grimly, '*Lieber Gott*, what a profession to be in.'

Lieberkühn. Add: Also **-kuehn. 2.** *Anat.* The name of *Lieberkühn* used with *of*-adjunct, or occas. in the possessive, to designate the Lieberkühnian follicles or glands, as *crypts, follicles*, or *glands of Lieberkühn.*

1844 Dunglison *Dict. Med. Sci.* (ed. 4) 420/2 Lieberkuehn's glands or follicles. **1859** R. B. Todd *Cycl. Anat. & Physiol.* V. 346/2 The intestinal tubes—or, as they are commonly called, the follicles of Lieberkuehn—are the first to demand our notice. **1866** G. Harley *Histol. Demonstr.* 114 The arrangements of the various coats, and also the villi and Lieberkühn's follicles, can be seen under a low power. **1949** Adams & Eddy *Compar. Anat.* xi. 278 The glands of Lieberkühn, which supply the succus entericus, have their openings at the bases of the villi. **1970** C. K. Weichert *Anat. Chordates* (ed. 4) v. 189/2 The intestinal wall contains myriads of intestinal glands which are of two main types. The first of these are the simple tubular glands, or crypts, of Lieberkühn, found throughout the entire length of the small and large intestines.

Liebermann–Burchard (lī:bĕɹmæ̆nˌbu·ɹkāɹt). *Biochem.* [The names of Carl *Liebermann* (1842–1914) and H. *Burchard*, German chemists.] *Liebermann–Burchard reaction*, the reaction of unsaturated sterols with acetic anhydride and sulphuric acid in chloroform, which produces various coloured solutions; used esp. as a test for cholesterol, when a blue-green colour is produced; so *Liebermann–Burchard test.*

1904 W. R. Orndorff tr. *Salkowski's Lab. Man. Physiol. & Path. Chem.* ix. 92 (*heading*) Liebermann–Burchard reaction. **1915** Stedman *Med. Dict.* (ed. 3) 509/2 Liebermann–Burchard test. **1934** *Jrnl. Biol. Chem.* CVI. 746 The very weak color produced by digitonin with the modified Liebermann–Burchard reaction. **1956** E. V. Truter *Wool Wax* vii. 185 At present, the only technique for quantitatively determining alcohols of the isocholesterol group is based upon the spectrophotometric measurement of the colour developed in the Liebermann–Burchardt test. **1968** *Indian Jrnl. Med. Res.* LVI. 1776 A method for the estimation of total cholesterol in whole blood, serum or plasma, based on the Liebermann–Burchard reaction is presented.

‖ **Liebestod, liebestod** (lī·bəstōt). [G., lit. 'love's death'.] An aria or a duet proclaiming the suicide of lovers (see also quot. 1964); hence, such a suicide; also *fig.*

1889 G. B. Shaw *London Music 1888–89* (1937) 249 Isolde's Liebestod was a failure. **1928** in D. McCarthy *Drama* (1940) 112 Each pair sinks into the euthanasia of a matter-of-fact liebes-tod. **1947** A. Einstein *Mus. Romantic Era* xvi. 283 Yet this festival opera [*sc.* Aïda] ends *pianissimo* and *con sordini* with a *Liebestod*, which is not Romantically philosophical, but purely human. **1959** *Listener* 20 Aug. 280/2 Would the imagination..not die a *Liebestod* at the very moment it attains its goal? **1964** *Conc. Oxf. Dict. Opera* 223/2 *Liebestod*, the title used today for Isolde's death scene in Wagner's *Tristan und Isolde*, but used by Wagner of the mystic love duet in Act 2. **1971** G. Steiner *In Bluebeard's Castle* i. 25 It is permissible to see..in the Wagnerian *Liebestod* surrogates for the lost dangers of revolutionary action.

Liebfraumilch (lī·pfraumilχ, lī·b-). Also **Liebfrauenmilch.** [G., lit. 'milk of Our Lady'.] A white wine orig. produced at Worms; also loosely applied to German white wines.

1833 C. Redding *Hist. Mod. Wines* vii. 204 The Liebfrauenmilch..is a well-bodied wine, grown at Worms. **1846** Tennyson *Let.* 12 Nov. in H. Tennyson *Alfred Lord Tennyson* (1897) II. i. 6 Dickens..was very hospitable, and gave us biscuits..and a flask of Liebfraumilch. **1930** W. S. Maugham *Cakes & Ale* ii. 21 We want some of the Liebfraumilch, the '21. **1951** *Good Housek. Home Encycl.* 508/2 The best Hock, which is sold under a number of well-known names, e.g. Johannisberger,.. Liebfraumilch. **1967** A. Lichine *Encycl. Wines* 323/1 Rheinhessen wines, distinctive in their own right, are so named; the remainder call themselves Liebfraumilch. **1973** *Guardian* 28 June 11/6 Liebfraumilch is an invented name for almost any ordinary German white wine not worthy of its own district label.

Liebig. Add: *Liebig('s) condenser*, a device for condensing vapour, consisting of two concentric tubes, the vapour and condensate passing through the inner one and a cooling liquid through the outer one.

1867 Bloxam *Chem.* 46, A is a stoppered retort, the neck of which fits into the tube of a Liebig's condenser. **1903** S. Young *Fractional Distillation* i. 6 When a Liebig's condenser is used there is no advantage in having either the inner or the outer tube very wide. **1963** J. W. Davis *Adv. Level Pract. Chem.* 158 For preparations in an advanced level course the most suitable water-condensers are short Liebig condensers.

‖ **Liebling, liebling** (lī·pliŋ, lī·bliŋ). [G.] = *Liebchen, liebchen.

1868 C. M. Yonge *Chaplet of Pearls* I. vii. 79 She is a good little *Liebling*. **1970** J. Cleary *Helga's Web* iv. 60 'And you're not servile?' 'No, *liebling*.' **1972** J. Aiken *Butterfly Picnic* vi. 105 Is that you, Liebling?

‖ **Lied, lied** (līt). Pl. Lieder (lī·dəɹ). [G.] A song, esp. one characteristic of the German Romantic period. So **lieder-singer; lieder-singing** *vbl. sb.*

1852 J. C. Patteson *Let.* in C. M. Yonge *Life J. C. Patteson* (1874) I. iv. 89 He sang some of Medelssohn's [*sic*] Lieder very pleasantly. *Ibid. Let.* 115 As soon as a Lied or Sonata began, away would go my books. **1854** [see Seguidilla]. **1876** Stainer & Barrett *Dict. Mus. Terms* 274/2 The German lied, the sacred lied or chorale.. was founded upon the ecclesiastical modes and remained unchanged until the days of the Minnesingers. **1924** M. Kennedy *Constant Nymph* xvi. 222 She listened sadly to German Lieder. **1936** H. Read *Meaning of Art* (ed. 2) 53 Thus we read in our newspaper that Miss X 'is too deficient in variety of *tone-colour* to make a good lieder singer'. **1937** *Sunday Times* 21 Feb. 7/1 In Lieder singing the words, or rather what is at the back of the words, play a large part in determining the appropriate musical style. **1947** A. Einstein *Mus. Romantic Era* xiv. 184 Berlioz, of course, also wrote lieder and various other kinds of songs. **1955** *Times* 16 May 11/5 Programme included operatic arias,..two groups of lieder and English and Italian songs. **1959** *Times* 27 Apr. 5/6 (*heading*) Miss Gerda Lammas: a great Lieder singer. **1960** *Guardian* 22 Apr. 9/2 An intimate tone and style are..essential, to lieder singing. **1963** Auden *Dyer's Hand* 505 If one takes, say, a sea-shanty out of its proper context and listens to it on the gramophone as one might to a *lied* by Schubert, one is very soon bored. **1970** *New Yorker* 3 Oct. 36/1 Mother had a nice repertory of the more assailable lieder.

liegeful (lī·dʒfŭl), *a. rare.* [f. Liege *sb.* + -ful.] Loyal, faithful.

1872 A. de Vere *Legends St. Patrick* 72 If ye be liegeful; sirs, decree the day. *Ibid.* 155 Pure of heart, and liegeful unto Christ. **1887** —— *Legends & Rec. Church & Empire* 264 Liegeful I know hath been your wedded life.

lien[1]. Add: **2.** *fig.* (Later examples.)

1922 A. Bennett *Lilian* ii. v. 107 She had no lien, no attachment. **1925** *New Statesman* 3 Oct. 687/1 They desire two sets of negotiations to proceed simultaneously, and if they admit they may be pursued separately, there will nevertheless be so many liens between them, that the success of one will be dependent on the success of the other.

lieno-. Add: **lieno-renal** *a.*, pertaining to the spleen and the kidneys: applied *spec.* to a short ligament connecting the spleen and the left kidney.

1887 G. D. Thane *Ellis's Demonstrations Anat.* (ed. 10) viii. 475 The peritoneum may be followed..to the outer part of the left kidney, where it is reflected along the back of the splenic vessels to the spleen, forming one layer of the lieno-renal ligament. **1932** W. Wright in E. P. Stibbe *Pract. Anat.* 301 To the left it [*sc.* the cavity] is closed by the gastro-splenic omentum, the spleen, and a fold passing from the spleen to the left kidney, the lieno-renal ligament. **1967** G. M. Wyburn et al. *Conc. Anat.* i. 32/2 The lieno-renal ligament, which contains the splenic vessels.

lier, obs. var. Leer *sb.*[3] (in Dict. and Suppl.).

Liesegang (lī·zəgaŋ). *Physical Chem.* The name of Raphael Eduard *Liesegang* (1869–1947), German chemist, used *attrib.* (esp. in *Liesegang ring*) and in the possessive to designate (the formation of) concentric rings or parallel bands of precipitate following the diffusion, one into the other, of two dissolved substances that react to form a slightly soluble precipitate.

1913 *Chem. Abstr.* VII. 3797 The Liesegang figures produced on gelatin plates. **1917** M. H. Fischer tr. *Ostwald's Introd. Theoret. & Appl. Colloid Chem.* v. 215 A colloid-chemical method for discovering the addition of agar to fruit jellies and marmalades makes use of the influence which such addition has upon the form and the structure of Liesegang rings when formed in such jellies. **1932** *Jrnl. Physical Chem.* XXXVI. 299 The concentric rings in the 'common gall stones' of inflammatory origin are..a manifestation of the Liesegang phenomenon. **1944** A. van Hook in J. Alexander *Colloid Chem., Theoret. & Appl.* V. 517 Bucher..has devised a new method of blood analysis depending on the sensitiveness of Liesegang Ring formation to very slight variations in blood composition and quality. **1946** *Thorpe's Dict. Appl. Chem.* (ed. 4) VII. 307/2 A large number of stratified deposits occur in nature, and a study of Liesegang's rings has suggested explanations for some of these structures. **1953** *New Biol.* XV. 123 Periodic precipitations of the Liesegang type may occur. **1959** *Science* 15 May 1366/2 The best way to avoid the formation of multiple macroscopical Liesegang bands is to operate with equivalent concentrations of reagents. **1971** *Jrnl. Colloid & Interface Sci.* XXV. 591/2 The membrane-like behavior of the $PbCrO_4$ Liesegang ring system in agar gel has been confirmed..with a wide variety of inorganic ions.

lieutenant. Add: **2. c.** An officer in the Salvation Army.

1884 [see *captain *sb.* 5 b]. c **1897** A. E. Housman *Lett.* (1971) 45 Lieutenant Isabella..comes Dealing blows with her umbrella. **1970** *Guardian* 2 May 10/4, I love the Salvation Army through which I found my Saviour... Yours faithfully, Lars Juhlin. Lieutenant.

lieves, var. of *lieve* Lief *adv.* Cf. *leaves.

1863 'G. Hamilton' *Gala-Days* 241 We'd just as lieves work out of doors..as not.

life, *sb.* Add: **1. a.** *while there is life there is hope* (and similar phrases) (earlier and later examples); *there is life in the old dog yet* (and variants): an assertion of continuing competence, strength, etc., notwithstanding evidence to the contrary.

1539 R. Taverner *Erasmus's Proverbes* f. 36v, The sycke person whyle he hath lyfe, hath hope. **1671** J. Crowne *Juliana* v. 56 Madam, he breathes, and whilst there's life, there's hope. **1727** J. Gay *Fables* xxvii. 93 While there is life, there's hope, he cry'd. **1808** *Monthly Pantheon* I. 356/1 Whilst there is *life* you know there *are hopes*! **1859** S. Allen *Let.* 1 Dec. in D. Ayerst *Guardian* (1971) x. 134 'Are not the advertisements grand?'.. 'There is life in the old dog yet.' **1908** E. J. Banfield *Confessions of Beachcomber* ii. ii. 301 While there is life there is hope is evidently Nelly's creed. **1940** *Time* 15 July 49/1 Tallulah Bankhead demonstrated that there's life in Pinero's old girl yet.

c. (*a matter*, etc.) *of life and death*: also,..*of life or death.*

1837 Dickens *Let.* c 20 Apr. (1965) I. 249 It is matter of life or death to us, to know whether you have got Ainsworth's MS yet. **1898** W. J. Locke *Idols* x. 134 The marriage could be concealed no longer. It was a matter of life or death. **1950** K. Winsor *Star Money* iii. xxix. 249, I never have made any man a matter of life or death to me.

3. c. *for dear life* (examples); *anything for a quiet life; for once in his life.*

1624 T. Heywood *Captives* (1885) iii. iii. 169 Anythinge For a quiett lyfe. **1800** M. Edgeworth *Parent's Assistant* (ed. 3) VI. 123 Any thing for a quiet life. **1837** Dickens *Pickw.* xlii. 463 Anythin' for a quiet life, as the man said ven he took the sitivation at the light-house. **1843** W. T. Thompson *Major Jones' Chron. Pineville* 93 He..was climbing for dear life. **1846** 'Mrs. Markham' *Hist. Eng.* (ed. 12) xxxvi. 402 *George*. I think, mamma, that the fire of London was a happy event for the king, as it made him exert himself, for once in his life, to do some good. **1872** B. Jerrold *London* ii. 23 Hard-visaged men, breathlessly competing for 'dear life'. **1921** H. Crane *Let.* 17 Oct. (1965) 68 The man who would preserve them [*sc.* feelings] must duck and camouflage for dear life. **1968** 'L. Marshall' *Blood on Blotter* v. 40 I'm a born appeaser... Anything for a quiet life.

d. (Further example.) Phr. *not on your life*, not on any account, by no means.

1896 W. C. Gore in *Inlander* Jan. 149 'Say, Jack, are you going to bolt?' 'Not on your life.' **1905** *N.Y. Even. Post* 19 Aug. 2 The congressman was asked if there had been any gambling during the trip. 'Not on your life,' he said. **1913** Kipling *Divers. Creatures* (1917) 294 'Not on your life!' says Lundie. **1944** *Living off Land* iv. 62 Say that you are lost, properly bushed. You come across a river. Well, that river is not bushed—not on your life it isn't. **1962** F. Norman *Guntz* i. 7 My life (I thought) what chance am I going to have if I produce this letter. **1972** H. Carmichael *Naked to Grave* v. 56 'Why not get in touch with your lawyer?' 'Not on your life!.. It would be a tacit admission of my guilt.'

4. *spec.* in *Cricket*, that quality in the pitch which causes the ball to rise abruptly or unevenly after pitching.

1888 A. G. Steel in Steel & Lyttelton *Cricket* iii. 148 On wet hard wickets..there is still life and pace in the ground; but in the sodden dead state, directly the ball touches the ground it..loses all life and pace. **1906** A. E. Knight *Compl. Cricketer* 348 'Life' from the pitch implies the pitch and sting at or with which the ball leaves the ground.

5. a. (Further examples.)

1720 Defoe *Capt. Singleton* 73 These indeed were the Life and Soul of all the rest, and it was to their Courage that all the rest ow'd the Resolution they shewd. **1797** R. M. Roche *Children of Abbey* I. xvii. 309 They had assembled a number of their neighbours, among whom were a little fat priest, called Father O'Gallaghan, considered the life of every party, and a blind piper. **1814** Jane Austen *Mansf. Park* II. i. 9 Sir Thomas was indeed the life of the party. **1897** M. Corelli *Ziska* xv. 324 Armand Gervase..was making himself the life and soul of everything at the Mena House Hotel. **1932** L. Golding *Mag-*

nolia St. III. ix. 595 He's very much the official life-and-soul-of-the-party. **1939** [see *BORSCH]. **1965** *Melody Maker* 17 July 9 Offstage..Dudley doesn't strike you as being the life and soul of the party. **1970** G. GREER *Female Eunuch* 33 When the life of the party wants to express the idea of a pretty woman in mime, he undulates his two hands.

7. a. *as large as life* (further examples). Hence *larger-than-life*; so *larger-than-lifeness* (nonce). Also *life itself*.

1802 C. WILMOT *Let.* 17 Dec. in *Irish Peer* (1920) 129 A beautiful piece of clockwork representing Apollo with his lyre... It was as large as life. **1822** M. EDGEWORTH *Let.* 9 Mar. (1971) 368 We 6 went together to see Belzonis tomb—the model first and afterwards the tomb as large as life. **1836** T. C. HALIBURTON *Clockmaker* (1837) 1st Ser. 143 As large as life and twice as nateral. *c* **1840** LADY WILTON *Art of Needlework* xxi. 334 Birds..being, in proportion to other figures, certainly *larger* than life, and 'twice as natural'. **1871** 'L. CARROLL' *Through Looking-Glass* vii. 150 It's as large as life, and twice as natural! **1891** G. MOORE *Impressions & Opinions* 89 The illusion is complete; it is just, as the phrase goes, like life itself. **1898** G. B. SHAW *Mrs. Warren's Profession* II. i. 176 This is George Crofts, as large as life and twice as natural. **1926** G. HUNTING *Vicarion* i. 21 What she had seen and heard had been life itself! **1930** J. DOS PASSOS *42nd Parallel* 46 Doc Bingham was sitting as large as life in a rocking chair. **1937** M. ALLINGHAM *Dancers in Mourning* i. 12 A larger-than-life edition of his stage self. **1947** L. MACNEICE *Dark Tower* 70 Larger-than-lifeness need not be part of the recipe. **1953** K. AMIS *Lucky Jim* i. 7 Anyway, there it was in the *Post* as large as life. **1959** *Viewpoint* July 12 Larger-than-life faces on television. **1966** R. A. DOWNIE tr. *O. del Buono's Bond Affair* 18 Allen Dulles insisted on regarding James Bond as a larger-than-life character.

8. a. *of one's life*, denoting the most important event of its kind in one's life. See also TIME *sb.* 6.

1887 A. M. SULLIVAN *Let.* 13 Nov. in H. Keller *Story my Life* (1903) III. iii. 340 We took Helen to the circus, and had 'the time of our lives'! **1936** *Discovery* Jan. 14/2 They got the shock of their lives. **1939** W. SAROYAN (*title*) The time of your life. **1961** L. VAN DER POST *Heart of Hunter* i. 25 The men sat with their heads bowed over arms clasped round their knees like long-distance runners recovering from the race of their lives.

c. (Further examples.) In *Physics* applied *spec.* to the average duration of existence of the members of a population of identical particles or states (equal to the period in which the population decreases by a factor *e*).

The half-life is equal to the (mean) life multiplied by $\log_e 2$ (about 0·693).

1903 RUTHERFORD & SODDY in *Phil. Mag.* V. 607 In one gram of these elements less than a milligram would change in a million years. In the case of radium, however, the same amount must be changing per gram *per year*. The 'life' of the radium cannot be in consequence more than a few thousand years. **1926** R. W. LAWSON tr. *Hevesy & Paneth's Man. Radioactivity* vii. 64 In this so-called 'normal state' the hydrogen atom can persist permanently, whereas the 'life' of all other stationary states is very short. *Ibid.* xii. 111 Each group [of radioactive substances] is arranged in the order of diminishing half-value period, and begins with the member of longest life. **1926** *Sci. Abstr.* A. XXIX. 170 Using the observation that so long as these lines are absorbed, atoms must be in the s_3 and s_5 states, a determination is made of the mean life of these states. **1942** J. D. STRANATHAN *'Particles' of Mod. Physics* xiii. 535 There is some indication that the mean free path may be longer, and the mean life correspondingly longer, for high energy mesotrons than it is for low energy mesotrons. **1947** *Forum* (Johannesburg) 12 Apr. 15/3 Even with the aid of boreholes, which have yet to be sunk, the 'life' of the dam can be extended only until the end of September. **1958** *Times* 23 July 5/2 Its..turbo-jet engines will be permitted an initial 'life' between overhauls of 1,000 hours. **1968** M. S. LIVINGSTON *Particle Physics* x. 178 The quantity $2\pi\Gamma/h$ is the probability of decay per unit time, or the reciprocal of the mean life τ of the state. Mean life is defined as the time for the population of the state to be reduced to $1/e$ of its initial value... This means that, because of the finite lifetime of an excited state, the energy of the state cannot be sharply defined but is intermediate within the energy spread Γ. **1971** *Gloss. Electrotechnical Power Terms (B.S.I.)* IV. i. 26 *Life*, of a lamp. Time during which a lamp has been operated before becoming useless.

d. Imprisonment for life; a life sentence. *slang.*

1903 [see *CELL *v.* b]. **1924** E. WALLACE *Room 13* i. 10 He shot a copper and got life. **1967** [see *BLOW *v.*[1] 27 b]. **1975** *Times* 29 Apr. 4/6 Although the sentence is life, they all want parole.

9. So *a bad life, a first-class life*.

1921 A. HUXLEY *Let.* 23 Mar. (1969) 194 This perpetual lack of perfect physical health is intolerable. This was brought home to me more acutely than usual today by the refusal of the London Life Association to insure me... It is..humiliating to be a Bad Life. **1938** *Times Lit. Suppl.* 24 Sept. 618/2 Elizabeth all her days was reckoned a 'bad life'. **1970** *Times* 5 Dec. 9/3 If one is not accepted as a first class life, the most common procedure is for an insurance company to increase the premium.

11. *Cricket.* (Earlier and later examples.) Similarly in *Baseball*.

1865 *Bell's Life* 24 June 7/1 Mr. Voules (who had 'a life' when he had made but a single) was first to leave. **1868** *Cincinnati Commercial* 24 May 8/2 Meagher had a life given him by Gould not accepting the grounder Meagher hit to him, and Brainard's wild throw to first gave him his second. **1955** *Times* 9 July 4/5 Immediately after luncheon Goddard was given a life when he slashed at Tyson and Evans dropped a fast head-high catch. **1974** *Times* 25 Nov. 10/2 Ali also had a life from Barrett at mid-off.

12. a. *such is life!*: see SUCH *dem. adj.* and *pron.* 2; similarly *that's life, life's like that*; *to live one's (own) life*: to conduct oneself without reference to the opinions of others; *this is the life*: an expression of satisfaction; *it's a great life (if you don't weaken)*: an ironic comment on the difficulties of one's situation; *what a life!*: an expression of discontent; *how's life?*: how are you faring?

1796 W. J. TEMPLE *Diary* 7 Apr. (1929) 167 This interruption is very teasing; but such is Life. **1843** DICKENS *Mart. Chuzz.* (1844) xxix. 347 'Sairey,' says Mrs. Harris, 'sech is life. Vich likeways is the hend of all things!' **1849** N. KINGSLEY *Diary* (1914) 52 For my part [I] could almost wish myself in the same Latitude..but such is life. **1853** C. BRONTË *Villette* I. xiii. 229 Thinking meantime my own thoughts, living my own life, in my own still shadow-world. **1865** [see SUCH *pron.* 2]. **1903** 'T. COLLINS' (*title*) Such is life. **1911** D. H. LAWRENCE *White Peacock* III. iii. 397 At home you cannot live your own life. **1917** *Ladies' Home Jrnl.* Mar. 46 (Advt.), *This is the life.* There are two ways to live nowadays. One way is the life that is daily chock full of healthy activity, wholesome fun and lots of fresh air. **1919** J. BUCHAN *Mr. Standfast* v. 105 'Back to Glasgow to do some work for the cause,' I said lightly. 'Just so,' he said, with a grin. 'It's a great life if you don't weaken.' **1919** WODEHOUSE *My Man Jeeves* 234 She's glued to a chair, with this-is-the-life written all over her, taking it in through the pores. **1924** J. BUCHAN *Three Hostages* xvi. 227 That's life, my dear. We've got to go on to the finish anyhow, trusting that luck will turn. **1926** S. JAMESON *Three Kingdoms* x. 301 After all, she had chosen to stand apart from him and to live her own life, as the moderns have it. **1926** R. MACAULAY *Crewe Train* xi. 213 This was the life. **1930** J. B. PRIESTLEY *Angel Pavement* i. 49 She groaned as she stuck another sheet of paper into the typewriter. 'What a life!' **1933** D. L. SAYERS *Murder must Advertise* i. 10 There goes my thousand quid! Oh, well, that's life. **1935** N. L. MCCLUNG *Clearing in West* xxv. 205 Still Will had his own life to live and must make his own choice. **1935** N. MITCHISON *We have been Warned* v. 511 I've been very busy... How's life? **1943** K. TENNANT *Ride on Stranger* xviii. 202 Oh, it was a great life, if you liked that sort of a life. **1959** M. GILBERT *Blood & Judgement* ix. 102 We weren't sharing rooms... She was living her life, I was living mine. **1968** P. DICKINSON *Skin Deep* vii. 140 No, it's..not the sort of thing that makes the newspapers... Ah well, life's like that. **1970** *New Statesman* 26 June 924/3 Whatever Ned Kelly was really like.. he can scarcely have been like Mr Jagger... The famous last words 'Such is life'—could as well have been 'Pass the salt'. **1972** G. BELL *Villains Galore* viii. 104 'Nothing ventured, nothing lost either,' muttered Boote miserably. 'Gawd! What a life!' **1973** J. MCCLURE *Four & Twenty Virgins* ii. 22 The sports car accelerated away before she reached the end of the path. 'That's life,' said Kegg.

d. (Further examples.)

1851 H. MAYHEW *Mayhew's Characters* (1951) 309, I liked to see 'life', as it was called, and was fond of the company of women. **1918** C. MACKENZIE *Early Life Sylvia Scarlett* II. iv. 332 I've got a fancy..to show you a bit of life. **1937** A. CHRISTIE *Death on Nile* II. i. 41 He's made a good deal of money and he's seeing life, I fancy. **1972** L. MEYNELL *Death by Arrangement* i. 9 The spires of Oxford could go on dreaming..for all he cared; he set about getting himself a degree in the university of life.

e. *the life of the mind*: intellectual or aesthetic pursuits, scholarship; meditation, the realm of the imagination.

1926 E. HEMINGWAY *Men without Women* (1927) 216 Live the full life of the mind, exhilarated by new ideas. **1950** P. BOTTOME *Under Skin* xxiii. 204 If we try to escape into the life of the mind we find you there before us. **1972** G. WIGG *George Wigg* i. 28 He was an inspired teacher.. arousing in us a feeling for literature and poetry and the life of the mind. **1972** *Guardian* 1 Nov. 14/5 Universities exist to promote the life of the mind... They should create and discover knowledge.

13. (Later examples.) So *Life and Times*, a biography combined with a study of the public events of the character's lifetime; *life-and-work(s*, a biography combined with a study of the writings of the subject.

c **1889** W. PATER *Let.* 30 Apr. (1970) 94, I wish I could undertake a life for your admirable Series. **1933** J. THURBER (*title*) My life and hard times. **1951** G. GREENE *End of Affair* v. v. 204 'You seem interested in General Gordon.' 'They want me to do a Life.' **1957** *Times Lit. Suppl.* 25 Oct. 640/2 Mr Wilson's life-and-work summaries are excellent. **1959** *Listener* 9 Apr. 643/2 This is to be a life-and-works, not pure biography. *Ibid.* 3 Dec. 1005/1 It is a 'Life', not a 'Life and Times', that he has written. **1962** *Ibid.* 15 Nov. 804/1 To use a man's letters and all related correspondence to produce a reasonably short life and times. **1975** *Listener* 16 Jan. 93/1 *Cavafy* is..more biographical than critical, but a 'life' was needed and this is the fullest so far.

16. (Further, esp. 20th-c., examples.) **a.** *life-activity, -anger, -body, -centre, -chance, -course, -current, -demand, -drama, -electron, -flame, -flow, -habit, -idea, -instinct, -mate, -meaning, -mystery, -orientation, -path, -pattern, -principle, -quick, -responsibility, -situation, -space, -story, -stream, -stuff, -urge, -wish.*

1914 R. M. JONES *Spiritual Reformers 16th & 17th Cent.* p. xvii, Undivided faith attitudes always liberate within the field of consciousness energy for life-activity. **1937** R. A. WILSON *Birth of Lang.* 83 The modern error..of characterizing life-activity as mechanism. **1924** LAWRENCE & SKINNER *Boy in Bush* 203 It was the anger, the deep, burning life-anger which was the kinship. **1920** S. ALEXANDER *Space, Time & Deity* II. 355 Hunger and thirst..are the affections of its life-body. **1923** D. H. LAWRENCE *Birds, Beasts & Flowers* 54 Fragile-tender, fragile-tender life-body, More fearless than iron all the time. **1902** *Westm. Gaz.* 2 Apr. 10/2 As a life-centre Lake Eyre has long lost its importance. **1942** R. A. KNOX *In Soft Garments* xi. 85 We have got to go back to the life of Jesus of Nazareth, isolating the life-centre from which this vast organism of Christianity has sprung. **1944** *Politics* I. 273/2 However strongly life chances may be differentiated, this fact in itself..by no means gives birth to 'class action'. **1958** W. J. H. SPROTT *Human Groups* 60 The life-chances of children..are almost entirely determined by their position in the kinship scheme. *a* **1930** D. H. LAWRENCE *Phoenix* (1936) v. i. 609 This reversal of the life-course. **1970** R. J. HOLLINGDALE tr. *Schopenhauer's Ess. & Aphorisms* 144 The entire life-course, i.e., the inner and outer history, of each one [*sc.* man] differs.. from that of all the others. **1899** W. JAMES *Talks to Teachers* 257 The occasion and the experience..are nothing. It all depends on the capacity of the soul to be grasped, to have its life-currents absorbed by what is given. **1929** D. H. LAWRENCE *Pansies* 21 A new demand on his intelligence, A new life-demand. **1872** *Porcupine* 12 Oct. 443/2 He wanted to be left to work out his own Life-Drama. **1915** D. H. LAWRENCE *Rainbow* x. 262 On Easter Sunday the life-drama was as good as finished. *a* **1930** —— *Etruscan Places* (1932) 58 So within each man is the quick of him..some spark, some unborn and undying vivid life-electron. **1906** *Macm. Mag.* Apr. 436 Two of these life-flames were burning brightly..in the adjacent theatre. **1960** *Spectator* 14 Oct. 556 English is the true education of the life-flame. **1903** *Ibid.* 11 Apr. 565 The life-flow of justice..ceased to course through her heart. *a* **1930** D. H. LAWRENCE *Last Poems* (1932) 107 People who complain of loneliness must have lost..their life-flow Like a plant whose roots are cut. **1891** C. L. MORGAN *Animal Sk.* 214 To watch his life-habits with sympathetic interest. **1923** D. H. LAWRENCE *Kangaroo* xvi. 338 As some great life-idea cools down and sets upon them. **1908** E. F. BENSON *Blotting Bk.* i. 22 His was the hot blood that could do any deed when the life-instinct commanded it. **1922** Life instinct [see *death-instinct* (*DEATH *sb.* 19)]. **1906** *Westm. Gaz.* 17 Feb. 6/3 Each with the life-mate who should guide his way. **1922** JOYCE *Ulysses* 413 Faithful lifemate. **1923** D. H. LAWRENCE *Kangaroo* xii. 283 It is gruesome, with no life-meaning. **1927** —— *Lovely Lady* (1932) 230 He deemed it [*sc.* sex], as the Chinese do, one of the great life-mysteries. **1936** WIRTH & SHILS tr. *Mannheim's Ideology & Utopia* I. i. 22 The point of view of life-orientation and conduct. **1966** G. E. EVANS *Pattern under Plough* xii. 124 Only tremendous transformations of life-orientation have succeeded in tearing them away from this universal form of religiosity. **1950** *Psychiatry* XIII. 2 He [*sc.* Freud] provides the texts..for contradictory life-paths and social policies. **1955** AUDEN *Shield of Achilles* iii. 76 A fortuitous intersection of life-paths. **1920** T. P. NUNN *Education* i. 6 There is no limit to the number of life-patterns into which good or blameless actions may be woven. **1972** *Sci. Amer.* Jan. 39/1 Although sex-role ideology may be developed in early childhood, it is usually not until adolescence that a girl begins to apply her system of beliefs to her life pattern. **1851** H. MELVILLE *Moby Dick* III. xxi. 146 This same..cunning life-principle in him. **1950** L. S. THORNTON *Revelation & Mod. World* iii. 90 *Totality* and *identity* are two aspects of one life-principle by which the creative Word calls into himself that response which he creates. **1923** D. H. LAWRENCE *Stud. Classic Amer. Lit.* vi. 119 Nowadays society is evil. It finds subtle ways of torture, to destroy the life-quick, to get at the life-quick in a man. **1928** —— *Lady Chatterley* x. 131 What man with a spark of honour would put this ghastly burden of life-responsibility upon a woman. **1936** WIRTH & SHILS tr. *Mannheim's Ideology & Utopia* I. 10 Constantly varying social strata and life-situations. **1969** *America* 5 July 17/2 The mass media have formed many of our responses to life situations. **1935** *Psychol. Abstr.* Jan. 3/2 The psychological life-space (*Lebensraum*) is a general hodological space, which shows certain relativities. **1957** R. K. MERTON *Social Theory* (rev. ed.) 384 The social life-space of an individual. **1853** Life-story [in Dict.]. **1930** C. BEATON *Diary* Dec. in *Wandering Yrs.* (1961) 200 Buy her *Life Story* for three dollars. **1960** 'R. SIMONS' *Frame for Murder* xiii. 165 Squere..produced a bundle of papers. 'This is him. His entire life story.' **1879** BROWNING *Dramatic Idyls* 128 'Look unto me and be ye saved!' saith God: 'I strike the rock, outstreats the life-stream at my rod!' **1941** WYNDHAM LEWIS *Let.* 10 Aug. (1963) 295 The character..is so deeply stained with the deposits on the obscure bed of the life-stream. **1880** *Wesleyan-Methodist Mag.* Aug. 621/1 To say that the life-stuff of the lowest fungus and that of the most powerful human brain are *identical*, is absurd. **1956** A. H. COMPTON *Atomic Quest* 160 The life-stuff of intense effort. **1922** D. H. LAWRENCE *Let.* 21 Sept. (1962) II. 717 But I won't mention the life-urge any more. **1926** W. DE LA MARE *Connoisseur* 18, I had become an automaton—little better than a beetle obeying the secret dictates of what I believe they call the Life-Urge. **1944** R. LEHMANN *Ballad & Source* 13 A life-wish so crackling with energy that it could overcome no matter what minatory fate.

b. *life-affirming, -denying, -enhancing, -sapping* adjs.; *life-brightener, -denier, -enhancer.*

1947 A. EINSTEIN *Mus. Romantic Era* xii. 165 He became a priest, the 'Abbé Liszt', who sought in Rome a sort of defense against his overflowing, life-affirming virtuosity. **1966** *Observer* 6 Nov. 27/4 This instinctual, familial, life-affirming note of Tolstoy's. **1906** W. DE MORGAN *Joseph Vance* xxviii. 268 'Come, Joe, some news this time I hope!' I should have liked to be able to say yes, for he looked..as if he sadly wanted a life-brightener. **1922** JOYCE *Ulysses* 497 It's a lifebrightener, sure. **1955** L. P. HARTLEY *Perfect Woman* xxiii. 202 Jeremy, with his insistence on rules and regulations, his instinct for decorum in all things, seemed to her a spoil-sport and a life-denier. **1962** J. B. PRIESTLEY *Margin Released* II. v. 137 He would be twisted..malevolent, life-denying. **1973** *Times Lit. Suppl.* 21 Dec. 1554/1 Dame Rebecca's Augustine is.. introspective and life-denying, disgusted by physical existence... He bequeathed to posterity a complex of life-denying and art-denying ideas. **1955** S. SPENDER *Making of Poem* II. vi. 102 The golden Romantic poet then is more than life-enhancer... He is the magician who.. turns all his experience..into molten imagination. **1964**

Economist 8 Aug. 530/2 That purely modern life-enhancer, the private car. **1896** B. BERENSON *Florentine Painters* xi. 67 The contemplation of his [*sc.* Leonardo da Vinci's] personality is life-enhancing as that of scarcely any other man. **1960** *Guardian* 18 Nov. 7/6 His passionately serious novel..is a life-enhancing work. **1971** *Ibid.* 4 Jan. 10/2 The search for safer life-enhancing drugs. **1909** *Daily Chron.* 3 Sept. 1/1 The weather improved, but there still remained a light life-sapping wind which drove despair to its lowest recess. **1928** A. HUXLEY in *Sunday Dispatch* 16 Dec. 12/6 No people, it seems to me, has suffered more than the English from that life-sapping malady of too much machinery.

c. *life-clouded, -oriented, -sentenced* adjs.

1921 D. H. LAWRENCE *Tortoises* 18 Life establishing the first eternal mathematical tablet, Not in stone..or bronze, but in life-clouded..tortoise-shell. **1968** *Sun* (Baltimore) 4 July A 16/3 Speakers were using such terms..as life-oriented curriculum..and multi-media and multi-mode curriculum. **1901** *Chambers's Jrnl.* Nov. 744/2 This hapless man had completed seventeen of the twenty years which all life-sentenced prisoners must serve before release on license.

d. *life-blissful, -divine, -empty, -stupid* adjs.

1923 D. H. LAWRENCE *Birds, Beasts & Flowers* 54 Flaked out and come unpromised, The tree being life-divine, Fearing nothing, life-blissful at the core Within iron and earth. **1921** —— *Let. c* 8 May (1962) II. 653 Everybody nice, but rather spent, rather life-empty. **1922** —— *Fantasia of Unconscious* vii. 115 We are really far, far more life-stupid than the dead Greeks.

f. *life-class* (earlier and later examples), *-drawing.*

1891 A. BEARDSLEY *Let.* 13 Oct. (1971) 30, I eventually selected the Impressionist Academy as my school of art... It will not be so very long before I get into the life class. **1967** 'L. EGAN' *Nameless Ones* iv. 43 He was built like Tarzan, and could have earned a living posing for life classes. **1915** W. OWEN *Let.* 4 Apr. (1967) 329 Great talent in Life-Drawings and Oil Portraits; studied in Paris. **1956** K. CLARK *Nude* iv. 117 A splendid drawing of a nude model, one of the first 'life drawings' of a woman.

17. life-company, a life-insurance company; **life-craft,** a small craft, carried on board a larger one, by which escape may be made in an emergency; **life expectancy,** expectation of life; also *transf.* and *attrib.*; **life-force,** vital energy; so **life-forcer,** a believer in a philosophy of the *élan vital*; **life-gun,** a gun used for sending life-saving apparatus to ships; **life-history** (further examples); also *transf.* with reference to inanimate things; (*b*) life-story, the narrative of the career of a person; **life-index** (see quot. 1915); **life-insurance:** so *life-insurance policy* [POLICY *sb.*²]; also *fig.*; **life-member,** one who has acquired lifelong membership of a library, society, etc.; so **life membership; life net** *U.S.* (see quot. 1969); **life-office** (examples); **life-peer, -peerage** (later examples); so **life-peeress; life-policy** = **life-insurance policy*; **life-raft** (later examples; also in wider use); **life-ring** *N. Amer.*, a life-buoy; **life science,** any of the sciences (such as zoology, bacteriology, or sociology) which deal with living organisms; such sciences collectively; **life-span** [SPAN *sb.*¹ 4], lifetime; period of duration (of an animate or inanimate thing); **life-support** *a.*, applied to equipment designed to make possible the continued normal functioning of the body in hostile or dangerous environments; **life-tenant** (examples); so **life-tenancy; life test,** a test made on a sample of components in specified operating conditions, either for a certain length of time or until failure occurs, to determine the reliability of the components; hence (with hyphen) as *vb. trans.*, to perform a life test on; **life-testing** *vbl. sb.*; **life-token** = **life-index*; **life vest** *U.S.* = *life-jacket*; **life-world** *Philos.* [tr. G. *lebenswelt*], all the immediate experiences, activities, and contacts that make up the world of an individual, or of a corporate, life.

1907 *Westm. Gaz.* 10 Apr. 10/1 That is sufficient justification for the life-company amalgamation. **1970** *Sci. Jrnl.* June 9/1 Plastic lifecrafts carried aboard spaceships much as lifeboats are carried by ocean liners, have been advocated. **1970** *New Scientist* 22 Oct. 178/1 A computer would calculate the position of the lifecraft with an accuracy of one to ten miles. **1935** *Jrnl. Amer. Med. Assoc.* 17 Aug. 514/2 Today, life expectancy at birth is 57 years. **1956** A. H. COMPTON *Atomic Quest* 330 Life expectancy in our country increased by 50 per cent, from 46 years to 69 years. **1962** *Daily Tel.* 30 Apr. 24/3 Details of the Board's plans for closures in Scotland..await completion of a 'life-expectancy' survey. **1972** *Guardian* 15 Aug. 4/5 One of the reasons for higher life expectancy in India today is a better public health system. **1896** W. CALDWELL *Schopenhauer's Syst.* ix. 500 The will is the life-force that pulsates through man's nature. **1903** G. B. SHAW *Man & Superman* III. 109 And these are the creatures in whom you discover what you call a Life Force! *Ibid.* 137 Wagner once drifted into Life Force worship, and invented a Superman called Siegfried. **1920** D. H. LAWRENCE *Lost Girl* xii. 309 Even the will of God is a life-force. **1952** C. DAY LEWIS tr. *Virgil's Aeneid* VI. 137 The life-force of those seeds is fire, their source celestial. **1975** A. FRASER *Whistler's Lane* x. 160 The relentless, uncheckable advent of spring..this all-powerful life force which flowed so strongly. **1931** T. S. ELIOT *Thoughts after Lambeth* 9 These two depressing life-forcers [*sc.* Bertrand Russell and Aldous Huxley]. **1935** AUDEN & ISHERWOOD *Dog beneath Skin* I. (chorus betw. sc. ii & iii) 43 The naughty life-forcer in the norfolk jacket Was the rebels' only uncle. **1910** *Chambers's Jrnl.* Mar. 159/2 The life-gun which is used by the rescuers for shooting lines to the vessel. **1870** D. J. KIRWAN *Palace & Hovel* xxvi. 393 Those street hawkers..will relate their checkered life-histories with great eagerness. **1873** *Monthly Microsc. Jrnl.* X. 53 (*title*) Researches on the life history of a cercomonad. **1909** 'MARK TWAIN' *Is Shakes. Dead?* 141 Philosophers, burglars..surgeons—you can get the life-histories of all of them but one [*sc.* Shakespeare]. **1920** *Discovery* Apr. 111/2 The average value of the uranium present during the life-history of the mineral. **1927** R. FRY *Let.* 31 Aug. (1972) II. 609 The old man..poured out his whole life-history. **1935** B. MALINOWSKI *Coral Gardens* II. VI. 232 The development of speech within the life history of the individual. **1950** K. A. BISSET (*title*) The cytology and life-history of bacteria. **1962** Life history [see *ASTROPHYSICS]. **1884** STEEL & TEMPLE *Wide-Awake Stories* 404 Outside a person's life is an object which faithfully reflects the conditions of his life: this life-index is always very difficult of access. **1915** *Encycl. Relig. & Ethics* VIII. 44/2 'Life-token' or 'life-index' is the technical name given to an object the condition of which is in popular belief bound up with that of some person, which indicates his state of health or safety. **1862** R. H. NEWELL *Orpheus C. Kerr Papers* 1st Ser. 360 He's not an economical man if he don't destroy his life-insurance policy. **1891** E. G. WHITE in *Seventh-Day Adventist Bible Commentary* (1955) VI. 1070/2, I reprieve him from the condemnation of death giving him My life insurance policy—eternal life—because I have taken his place and have suffered for his sins. **1955** *Granta* 26 Nov. 20/2 I'm gonna sell 'em a life insurance policy. **1970** T. HUGHES *Crow* 29 Words came with Life Insurance policies—Crow feigned dead. **1867** *Harper's Mag.* Aug. 349/2 These life-members of my charity. **1907** R. FRY *Let.* 5 Mar. (1972) I. 282 I'm so glad they've made you a life member of the museum. **1926** A. E. HOUSMAN *Let.* 15 Jan. (1971) 233 You may be perplexed by communications from the London Library. I am taking steps to have you made a life member. **1972** H. KEMELMAN *Monday the Rabbi took Off* ii. 22 The by-laws made all past presidents life members of the board. **1859** in H. R. Fletcher *Story R. Hort. Soc.* (1969) xii. 187 It is proposed to raise the money by Donation, by Life Memberships of 40 Guineas and 20 Guineas. **1867** *Harper's Mag.* Aug. 349/1 A most laudable charity—put me down for a life-membership by all means. **1909** *Daily Chron.* 11 Mar. 6/3 New York... Many leapt from the windows and were caught in the life nets. **1947** *Chicago Tribune* 20 July (Comics) 4 Let's see some action—grab that life net! **1969** *Publ. Amer. Dial. Soc.* LII. 33 *Life net*, a net used to catch people who must jump from a building. **1879** Life-office [see **experience table*]. **1972** *Accountant* 28 Sept. 388/2 Rates of interest quoted by life offices at the moment are not so attractive as they were when borrow-all policies were popular. **1948** H. NICOLSON *Diary* 28 May (1968) 141 If they reform the House of Lords, they are certain to make me a life-peer. **1961** *Spectator* 20 Jan. 63 Six new life peers were created. **1973** *Times* 16 May 18/5 The making of life peers rather than hereditary peers (the present Conservative Government has given no hereditary titles) will gradually leave the Crown in increasing isolation as an hereditary institution. **1958** *Times* 24 July 8/7 (*heading*) Life peerages for four women. **1967** *Listener* 20 Apr. 533/1 Her Labour Party allegiance..took her through local government..to a life peerage. **1958** *Times* 24 July 8/7 The wives..of life peers, and the sons and daughters of.. life peers and life peeresses shall be treated..in the same way as the wives..and children of hereditary barons. **1881** *Harper's Mag.* Jan. 274/2 Most of their bargains with the public are made in the shape of life policies. **1907** 'MARK TWAIN' in *North Amer. Rev.* Jan. 14 If I hadn't taken out a life policy on this one the premiums would have bankrupted me long ago. **1942** *Mind* LI. 288 His watchword, in thinking not only of the means but of the ends of a life-policy, is 'here, or nowhere, is my America'. **1972** *Accountant* 28 Sept. 388/1 There are various schemes by which funds can be borrowed to buy shares at the outset, with a life policy being used to repay the loan in due course. **1903, 1922** Life-raft [see *CARLEY]. **1958** [see *air-sea rescue* (*AIR *sb.*¹ III. 1)]. **1962** S. CARPENTER in *Into Orbit* 60, I had a smaller version of it in my liferaft as part of the emergency kit. **1973** *Times* 9 Mar. 26/8 In emergency situations, such as aircrashes, liferafts are automatically inflated. **1912** L. J. VANCE *Destroying Angel* xiv. 189 He managed..to jam the life-ring over her head and under one arm before the next wave bore down upon them. **1972** *Daily Colonist* (Victoria, B.C.) 11 Jan. 7/1 The aircraft sighted..a life-ring bearing the ship's name. **1958** M. A. GRAUBARD (*title*) The foundations of life science. **1959** *Vistas in Astronautics* II. 139 (*heading*) The utilization of a satellite laboratory for life science studies. **1970** C. J. & O. B. GOIN (*title*) Man and the natural world: an introduction to life science. **1973** *Freedom* 2 June 3/4, I regard my own specialism, psychology, as a continuing part of the Darwinian revolution in the Life Sciences. **1918** W. B. YEATS *Per Amica Silentia Lunae* 38 Some.. have foreknown the event and pricked upon the calendar the life-span of a Christ, a Buddha, a Napoleon. **1937** B. H. L. HART *Europe in Arms* xxii. 290 He [*sc.* Napoleon] took short views, since his horizon was his own life-span. **1953** J. S. HUXLEY *Evolution in Action* iv. 103 Their life-span..may extend over several decades. **1957** G. E. HUTCHINSON *Treat. Limnol.* I. ii. 177 The life span of the lake. **1966** C. R. TOTTLE *Sci. Engin. Materials* x. 235 The life-span of the neutron depends on its kinetic energy, and on the material through which it passes. **1974** A. HUXLEY *Plant & Planet* xviii. 189 Plants are too varied to have an average lifespan. *Ibid.*, As soon as we move to multi-cellular plants the lifespans increase. **1959** *Adv. Space Sci. & Technol.* I. 174 (*heading*) Life support system. **1962** F. I. ORDWAY et al. *Basic Astronautics* xiii. 509 A life support system for a manned base on the Moon.. will be exceedingly complex. **1962** D. SLAYTON in *Into Orbit* 20 NASA decided we would adopt the U.S. Navy pressure suit for our spacesuit, so Wally Schirra..started work on the life-support system which we would need to keep the pilot alive and comfortable. **1969** *Guardian* 21 July 1/6 Before take-off the spacecraft's pressurisation system is tested while the astronauts are still in their life-support suits. **1970** *McGraw-Hill Yearbk. Sci. & Technol.* 280/2 All submersibles require life-support systems. **1908** *Westm. Gaz.* 24 Nov. 4/1 The life-tenancy individualism which Mr. Carnegie recommends to us is sharply distinguished from the feudal individualism which obtains in old countries. **1962** H. R. LOYN *Anglo-Saxon Eng.* iv. 178 An abbey or church..could receive estates as a gift, and then yield them back to the donor on a life-tenancy. **1837** Life-tenant [in Dict., sense 16 e]. **1973** *N.Y. Law Jrnl.* 4 Sept. 17/1 Ordinarily a life tenant of real property is entitled to collect all the income but must pay real estate taxes, mortgage interest if any, insurance cost and routine maintenance expenses. **1911** *Chem. Abstr.* V. 1371 (*heading*) Life test of metallic filament lamps. **1929** *Jrnl. Sci. Instrum.* VI. 247 The life test load accommodated by this regulator consists of twenty 2-volt 1-ampere miners' lamps screwed into bus bars. **1958** *Biometrika* XLV. 521 A second difficulty encountered in using conventional experimental methods in industrial life tests is the expense and time involved in waiting for all of the test items to fail. **1959** *Engineering* 20 Feb. 256/2 First on the market, some months ago, was the Hamilton electric watch, which was life tested for several years before the first one was sold, and which has proven itself a most reliable and accurate timekeeper. **1961** *Times* 31 May 18/4 Yet another machine life-tests switches. **1972** R. C. WINANS in D. Baker et al. *Physical Design Electronic Syst.* IV. viii. 368 As a control on time-dependent characteristics, life tests are made on samples from each production lot. These life tests are usually for periods ranging from 100 to 1000 hours, under maximum rated power, temperature, and/or voltage conditions. **1926** J. W. T. WALSH *Photometry* xvi. 449 An important branch of the work of a photometric laboratory is, frequently, the life testing of lamps. **1957** *Ann. Math. Statistics* XXVIII. 432 Life-testing situations where population properties are of greater interest than sample properties usually involve inanimate objects such as automobile tires, light bulbs, etc. **1899** R. C. TEMPLE in *Folk-Lore* X. 403 It now seems to have found a definite place among the recognized technicalities of writers on folklore under the guise of the life-token. **1915** Life-token [see **life-index*]. **1962** S. CARPENTER in *Into Orbit* 155 A tiny life vest which weighed less than a pound and could be folded up into a package not much bigger than a man's hand. **1970** *Washington Post* 30 Sept. D6/1 (Advt.), Fiberglas hardtop,..2 wipers, 6 life vests, 2 fire ext. and bell. **1940** A. SCHUETZ in M. Farber *Philos. Ess. in Memory E. Husserl* 173 Human existence itself is referred to an existent life-world as a realm of practical activity. **1960** D. CAIRNS tr. *Husserl's Cartesian Meditations* § 8. 19 Not just corporeal Nature but the whole concrete surrounding life-world is for me..only a phenomenon of being, instead of something that is. **1964** *Philos. Rev.* LXXIII. 418 Merleau-Ponty analyzes what..Husserl had termed the 'life-world' ('Lebenswelt'). **1969** M. FARBER in R. Klibansky *Contemp. Philos.* III. 167 There are life-worlds for ordinary experience, varying from person to person, from group to group, and from time to time. There are also life-worlds as viewed on the basis of the sciences. **1972** D. FØLLESDAL in Olson & Raul *Contemp. Philos. Scandinavia* 426 We all live in a 'life-world' which is constituted by everyone in community. The term 'life-world' ('*Lebenswelt*') first appeared in an unpublished article on Kant which he [*sc.* Husserl] wrote in 1924, and the life-world became the main theme of his last major work, *The Crisis of the European Sciences* (1936).

life-and-death, *a.* [See LIFE *sb.* 1 c.] Involving life and death; vitally important.

1822 MILL *Let.* 14 Nov. in *Works* (1963) XII. 14 The life-and-death style in which I speak and write about it [*sc.* the Utilitarian Society]. **1824** [see LIFE *sb.* 1 c]. **1834** HOOD *Tylney Hall* I. iii. 24 Joe made shift to explain that he was charged with what he called a life and death letter to Sir Mark. **1857** *Edin. Rev.* CVI. 198 The third, the part he assigned to himself in the life-and-death struggle of his country. **1857** *Chambers's Jrnl.* Nov. 338/1 These are really a life and death matter to our neighbours. **1888** MRS. H. WARD *R. Elsmere* II. III. xxiii. 226, I go about haunted by the *seriousness*, the life-and-death interest people throw into music. **1939** DYLAN THOMAS *Let.* 11 Sept. (1966) 236 If you look at *Tropic of Cancer*..not as a universal life-&-death book,..you must enjoy..it. **1951** S. SPENDER *World within World* ii. 97 At once I was aware of nature as a life-and-death force. **1973** *Times* 21 Dec. 4/2 On Christmas Day and Boxing Day..all inland telegram deliveries..will be suspended. Special arrangements will be made to deliver 'life and death' messages.

life cycle. Also life-cycle. [f. LIFE *sb.* + CYCLE *sb.*] **1.** *Biol.* (In Dict. s.v. LIFE *sb.* 17.)

1873 *Monthly Microsc. Jrnl.* X. 57 Thus the entire life cycle of this form is seen. **1894** [in Dict. s.v. LIFE *sb.* 17]. **1967** M. E. HALE *Biol. Lichens* ii. 27 The life cycle of fungi is completed when the vegetative thallus produces fruiting bodies that contain spores.

b. The course of human, cultural, etc., existence from birth or beginning through development and productivity to decay and death or ending.

1938 H. READ *Coll. Ess. Lit. Crit.* I. i. 19 The classical and romantic periods are related to each other in a 'life-cycle' which is the recurring cycle of the growth, maturity, and decay of culture. **1949** M. MEAD *Male & Female* xvi. 339 Here he is, only in middle age, and his life is over—.. no new fields to conquer... So while he is not out of a job ..the very nature of the life-cycle in America is such that he feels like an old man. **1959** G. D. MITCHELL *Sociol.* vi. 103 Religion is mostly important to mankind at times of personal crisis or when new and socially significant stages of the life-cycle are approached: at birth, initiation, marriage, death. **1967** B. S. COHN in P. Bohannan *Law & Warfare* 145 The general rule is that, when a household is celebrating a life-cycle rite, all adult males from the *khandan* and at least one adult male..from every other household in the hamlet is invited. **1969** W. E. MOORE in Lindzey & Aronson *Handbk. Social Psychol.* (ed. 2) IV.

xxxii. 316 A rather different perspective on social organization and social process results from dealing with the entire human life cycle.

2. *transf.*, esp. in *Econ.* and *Comm.*

1965 H. I. Ansoff *Corporate Strategy* (1968) ii. 31 Objectives..will vary from one type of firm to another depending on the firm's past profitability, its prospects, and its stage in the life cycle. **1969** J. Argenti *Managem. Techniques* 70 Many product life-cycles are declining. **1971** *Nature* 12 Feb. 486/2 The photo-oxidation of sulphur dioxide to sulphuric acid in the atmosphere is relevant both to the formation of aerosols in polluted air and to the life cycle of sulphur compounds in the atmosphere. **1971** *Daily Tel.* 21 June 17/6 The four-stage life-cycle of every [manufactured] product—exploration, growth, maturity, decline. *Ibid.* 17/8 Companies usually have a range of products at various stages of the life-cycle.

life-day. (Later examples.)

1893 'Mark Twain' *Lett.* (1917) II. 592, I shall tackle Adam once more... I've been thinking out his first life-days today. **1940** Auden *Another Time* 61 And we The life-day long shall part no more.

li·fe-form. Also **life form.** [f. Life *sb.* + Form *sb.*] **1.** *Biol.* A habit or vegetative form exhibited by any particular plant or which characterizes a group of plants.

Various life-form classifications have been proposed. That of C. Raunkiær (or a modification of his system) based upon the position of the buds relative to the soil surface during the unfavourable season is the one generally employed.

1899 *Natural Sci.* XIV. 109 Hence groups of similar adaptational form, 'Lebensform' of German authors, need by no means coincide with natural families or groups of species. For example, *Empetrum* and *Erica*, or *Aloe* and *Agave*, possess similar 'life-forms',..yet their floral characters indicate widely separate genetic affinities. **1913** *Jrnl. Ecol.* I. 16 (*heading*) Raunkiær's 'life-forms' and statistical methods. **1926** Tansley & Chipp *Study of Vegetation* ii. 11 Life form is the characteristic vegetative form of a species; in the first place whether it is a tree, shrub, herb, or a member of one of the lower group of the plant kingdom. **1960** [see *growth-form* s.v. *growth[1] 5]. **1964** V. J. Chapman *Coastal Vegetation* i. 9 There is no generally recognized life-form system for the algae. **1971** D. W. Shimwell *Descr. & Classification of Vegetation* iii. 74 Raunkiær..recognized fifteen main types of life form.

2. A living creature; any kind of living thing.

1905 *Daily Chron.* 17 Aug. 5/7 In the beginning, before life forms appeared, the sun shone on the ocean. **1908** *Lit. Guide* 1 Aug. 115/2 Proof..of an unbroken chain of psychical continuity between the lowest and highest life-forms. **1971** *Daily Tel.* (Colour Suppl.) 30 Apr. 17/3 If only..it were possible to introduce some terrestrial life-form on to Venus. **1971** I. G. Gass et al. *Understanding Earth* ix. 139/2 Once life had become universally distributed over the face of the globe, it must have prevented the further generation of new life-forms.

life-guard. 4. For *U.S.* read orig. *U.S.*, and add later examples.

1921 *Daily Tel.* 29 Aug. 9/6 They were sustained by this means until the life guards arrived to take the women ashore. **1933** *Boys' Mag.* XLVII. 122/1 When a party bathe, one or two of the best swimmers should be posted as life-guards. **1974** Hawkey & Bingham *Wild Card* xiii. 119 A guy who's drowning..who, if he's not subdued, will take the lifeguard down with him.

life-in-death. A phantom state, a condition of being or seeming to be neither alive nor dead; something having the form or appearance of the supernatural, an apparition, a spectre. Also, = *death-in-life* s.v. *death *sb.* 2.

1817 Coleridge *Anc. Mar.* in *Sibylline Leaves* 14 Her skin was as white as leprosy, The Night-Mair Life-in-Death was she, Who thicks man's blood with cold. **1901** *Daily Chron.* 27 Dec. 3/1 They lie in a sort of life-in-death until the touch of a mighty hand grants them their full development. **1904** *Ibid.* 22 Sept. 3/4 In a life-in-death existence she still languishes as an almost forgotten link with the past of forty years ago. **1925** R. W. Ketton-Cremer in *Oxf. Poetry* 22 From something not of earth, nor quite of Death—Some phantom Life-in-Death. **1932** W. B. Yeats *Words for Music* I, I hail the Superhuman; I call it Death-in-Life and Life-in-Death.

li·fe-line. [f. Life *sb.* + Line *sb.*[2]] **1. a.** (See Life *sb.* 17; also used by firemen.) (Earlier and later examples.) **b.** A diver's signalling line.

1700 in *N. & Q.* (1941) 12 July 22/2 Lyfline. **1790** *Gentl. Mag.* LX. in *N. & Q.* (1962) Jan. 17/1 A line..which was called his *Life-line*, as it was found..to have been serviceable in preserving ships and men. **1877** *Encycl. Brit.* VII. 297/2, *e* is the 'life' or 'signal' line, which is attached to the diver's waist, and by which he makes signals and is hauled to the surface. **1896** *Strand Mag.* XII. 351/1 As the strain of the air-pipe was downward, and that of the life-line upward, I concluded that the pipe must be fast below. **1904** *Daily Chron.* 26 Oct. 6/7 Fireman Herbert White lashed a branch hose to his body with a life-line. **1968** *Globe & Mail* (Toronto) 3 Feb. 11/4 Firemen..used a life-line gun to reach the boat and Mr. MacAdam. **1975** *Times* 6 Jan. 4/4 Lifelines used on Mr Heath's ill-fated yacht.. were yesterday called sub-standard by the British Safety Council.

2. In *Palmistry*: a mark on the palm of the hand supposed to indicate one's length of life.

1890 L. Cotton *Palmistry* II. 36 If the head line is separated, at its departure, from the life line, it indicates great self-confidence **1894** [see *head-line 5]. **1919** Beerbohm *Seven Men* 154, I had seen in my own hand..a clean break in the life-line. **1971** M. McCarthy *Birds of America* 312 He felt a sharp pain in..his palm, the part bounded by his life line.

3. *fig.* The line of life: see Line *sb.*[2] 1 g. Also, an essential supply route, a line of communication, etc.

1860 Hawthorne *Transformation* II. xiii. 209 If there were one of those friends whose life-line was twisted with your own, I am enough of a fatalist to feel assured that [etc.]. **1891** E. S. Ufford in I. D. Sankey *Gospel Hymns No. 6* 30 Throw out the Life-Line a-cross the dark wave, There is a brother whom some one should save. **1905** *Daily Chron.* 13 Feb. 3/1 Every man who has lived so long..and kept the life-line so straight and true as Mr. Holyoake. **1936** *Lit. Digest* 17 Oct. 13c Cut what Britain calls her 'life line'. **1941** *Times* (Weekly ed.) 15 Oct. 8 The King spent Wednesday at Liverpool seeing what is being done to hold this end of the Atlantic lifeline. **1963** *Times Lit. Suppl.* 1 Mar. 149/1 Liberals who keep a life-line open between the actual world..and the one they would like to see exist. **1970** *Daily Tel.* 7 Oct. 1/1 A £54-million 'lifeline' was thrown by the Government yesterday to the farming industry, which has been faced with having to cut back production because of rising costs. **1975** D. Ramsay *Descent into Dark* ii. 60 Who the hell thinks about honour when her lifeline's being cut?

lifemanship (ləi·fmǽnʃip). [f. Life *sb.* + *-manship.] Skill in getting the edge over, or acquiring an advantage over, another person or persons. So (as a back-formation) **li·feman.**

1950 S. Potter (*title*) Some notes on lifemanship. *Ibid.* 14 Day by day our centres send out young men, yes and women too, to assess the lifemanship approach. *Ibid.*, The Lifeman is never caddish himself. **1952** *Granta* 29 Nov. 8/2 They are the men who thought Lifemanship was something to practise rather than detect. **1953** *Encounter* Oct. 62/2 'Phoney' and 'corney'..are concepts, categories for criticising a whole school of bad 'lifemanship'. **1958** *Spectator* 29 Aug. 285/1 His narrative abounds in bashful lifemanship. **1959** *Times* 9 Apr. 15/3 You mean, don't you, that he was nearly the greatest European lifeman? **1964** *Discovery* Oct. 35/1 Lifemanship consists largely of a surreptitious and diplomatic control of what is ordinarily non-verbal and unconscious communication.

life-or-death, *a.* [See *life *sb.* 1 c.] = *life-and-death *a.*

1897 G. B. Shaw *Our Theatres in Nineties* (1932) III. 146 We should have had the ablest manager of the day driven by life-or-death necessity to extract from contemporary literature the proper food for the modern side of his talent. **1932** —— *Platform & Pulpit* (1962) 241 They will finally get rid of Parliament because they have a life-or-death pressure of necessity behind them. **1973** J. Wainwright *Touch of Malice* 134 The impression of life-or-death efficiency.

life-preserver. Add: **4.** *transf.* and *fig.*

1851 *London at Table* 1. 8 The 'life preserver', as the half-pint bottle has been termed. **1852** Geo. Eliot *Let.* 27 Mar. (1954) II. 15 Your cordial assurance..is one of those pleasant things—those life-preservers—which relenting destiny sends me now and then to buoy me up. **1941** J. Smiley *Hash House Lingo* 35 *Life preservers*, doughnuts. **1953** *Manch. Guardian Weekly* 14 May 11 Chambers admits that..he was busy preparing a 'life preserver' in the form of stolen documents he could use later to silence any-one who might rat on him.

lifer. Add: **3.** One who leads a life of a specified character.

Properly the second element of a compound.

1906 *Daily Chron.* 11 May 6/4 The Gospel did not commend itself to the simple lifers of the country-side, but spread like wildfire among the complex lifers of the Greek cities.

4. A life-peer.

1959 *Economist* 31 Jan. 397/1 An infusion of 'lifers'' half blue blood. **1969** *Sunday Tel.* 30 Mar. 2/8, I will not.. turn out for Lifers.

life-rent, *v.* [f. the sb.] *trans.* To assign in liferent; to use and enjoy property during one's life.

1700 *Edin. Gaz.* 2–5 Sept., The Lands of Hiltoun..presently Life-rented by the Lady Rosyth, are to be Set in Tack by way of publick Roup. **1819** Scott *Let.* 25 Nov. (1934) VI. 28 My wife's brother has left my children a considerable fortune which is at present life-rented by his lady. **1890** J. Rankine *Erskine's Princ. Law Scotl.* (ed. 18) 218 And money may be liferented, the interest..being due to the liferenter. **1937** *St. Andrews Citizen* 6 Mar. 2 The residue of his estate be life-rented to his sister.

li·fe-saver. [See Life *sb.* 16 b.] **1.** Something that may save one's life.

1883 [see Life *sb.* 16 b]. **1944** *Living off Land* v. 112 Failure to take a life-saver [*sc.* quinine or atebrine] on account of the bitter taste sounds childish yet there are such childish persons.

2. A person assigned to watch against accidents to bathers (at a beach resort, etc.). orig. *U.S.* (The customary term in Australia and N.Z.).

1887 *Courier-Jrnl.* (Louisville, Kentucky) 10 Feb. 8/3 The Police and the Life-Savers still prying into the mystery of Smyser's Pond. **1903** *Boston Even. Transcript* 20 Aug., According to a decision of the Election Commissioners a City Point life saver cannot vote. **1931** V. Palmer *Separate Lives* 99 'It's the life-savers!' he shouted. 'They're practising! Come on.' **1934** T. Wood *Cobbers* 169 You bask in the sun and watch the life-savers, picked volunteers. **1958** *Observer* 16 Nov. 27/2 He is a handsome cove, in the Australian surf life-saver tradition. **1963** V. B. Cranley *27,000 Miles through Austral.* xi. 78 A new life-boat donated to the local surf life-savers. Their performance of swimming and rescue work was really outstanding. **1967** C. O. Skinner *Madame Sarah* ix. 176 Madame Sarah was presented with a Life Saver's certificate. **1968** W. Warwick *Surfriding in N.Z.* 1 Since life-saving was practised in and around the sea, it was only natural that lifesavers were the first to try surfriding.

3. *fig.* Some quality, characteristic, or circumstance that helps a person to endure adversity.

1909 *N.Y. Herald* in *Daily Chron.* 8 Mar. 5/2 Both have that great life-saver for men who have to endure periods of stress and storm—a sense of humour. **1934** F. Scott Fitzgerald *Let.* 18 Dec. (1964) 258 Again thanks for the money. It was a life-saver. **1973** C. Egleton *Seven Days to Killing* ix. 101 He spotted a Falk street plan of Paris. It cost him six francs but it proved to be a life-saver.

li·fe-saving, *a.* [See Life *sb.* 16 b.] Of or pertaining to the saving of life from drowning, shipwreck, etc. Hence *life-saving station*, a coastal or beach building with life-saving equipment and life-savers. Also as *vbl. sb.*, the saving of life (from drowning).

1858 *Statutes at Large U.S.A.* XI. 320 Twenty-eight life-saving stations on the coast of New Jersey. **1877** *Harper's Mag.* Dec. 50/2 The life-saving car is passing from the vessel to the shore with living freight. *Ibid.*, The life-saving station. **1903** *N.Y. Times* 25 Sept. 14 The plight of the sloop had been signalled at the life-saving station at Sandy Hook. **1906** *Daily Colonist* (Victoria, B.C.) 30 Jan. 4/1 There should be somewhere within reach adequate life-saving stations. **1915** W. E. Dommett *Submarine Vessels* vii. 80 (*caption*) Bluejacket wearing life-saving helmet. **1931** V. Palmer *Separate Lives* 101 Dot and Peter were playing life-saving in the sand: Dot, lying flat on her back with her frock rucked up over her knees, and Peter restoring circulation the way he had seen the men do. **1932** N. Palmer *Talking it Over* 139 The same short stretch of surf..usually marked off short to give the life-saving patrol a chance of handling the crowd. **1933** *Boys' Mag.* XLVII. 122/1 Learn methods of life-saving as soon as possible. **1967** C. O. Skinner *Madame Sarah* ix. 175 Then came a delegation from the Life-Saving Society of Havre. **1973** A. Mann *Tiara* ii. 14 McCarthy had won prizes for swimming and life-saving.

Hence (as a back-formation) **li·fe-save** *v.* *trans.*, to rescue from death by drowning; to act towards as a life-saver. Also *intr.*

1938 'J. Bell' *Port of London Murders* x. 180 You mind what you're about. I'm not going to life-save you a second time. **1968** P. Dickinson *Weathermonger* i. 11 Geoffrey thought he might possibly be able to swim round to the harbour... But he couldn't do it if he had to lifesave Sally all the way. **1973** 'M. Hebden' *Dark Side of Island* iii. 32 Can you life-save?.. Are you a good swimmer?

life-size, *a.* Add: **B.** as *sb.* The size of life; a life-size portrait or statue. Also *fig.*

1850 *Art Jrnl.* 1 Mar. 95/2 A figure of life-size. **1864** *Illustr. London News* 16 July 55/1 Certain technical shortcomings are revealed by this first attempt by Mr. Mount in the life-size. **1885** W. M. Rossetti in *Encycl. Brit.* XVIII. 681/2 Cato as the emblem of wisdom, and (in life-size) numerous figures of classic worthies, prophets, and sibyls. **1959** *Spectator* 14 Aug. 181/2 This reduces M. Debré from the more-than-lifesize proper to all prime ministers..to more normal dimensions.

life-sized, *a.* [Life *sb.* 16 c.] = Life-size *a.*

1847 *Art Union* 1 May 149/2 A life-sized half-length figure. *Ibid.* 1 June 203/2 A life-sized cartoon. **1879** Clement & Hutton *Artists 19th Cent.* I. 26 'The Birds of America'..was completed in 1839.., containing 448 plates, life-sized and colored. **1898** H. A. Guerber *Story of Greeks* xxix. 69 The temple and grove [at Olympia] were ..adorned, with a great many statues representing the other gods and all the prize-winners, for it was customary to place a life-sized statue of each of them in this beautiful place. **1969** *Harper's Mag.* Feb. 106 Stuffed life-sized dolls drop to the floor of the stage.

li·fe-style. [f. Life *sb.* + Style *sb.* 24.] **a.** A term originally used by Alfred Adler (1870–1937) to denote a person's basic character as established early in childhood which governs his reactions and behaviour. **b.** *gen.* A way or style of living.

1929 A. Adler *Probl. Neurosis* [i. 7 The style of life is founded in the first four or five years of childhood.] *Ibid.* 8 This fragment of memory records the two typical motives of the main life-style. **1939** H. Orgler *Alfred Adler* i. 35 We have only really understood an individual when we have revealed the unitary life-style behind this ostensible duplicity. **1946** 'G. Orwell' *Crit. Ess.* 137 True to his life style, Koestler was..promptly arrested and interned by the Daladier Government. **1947** M. McLuhan in *Sewanee Rev.* LV. 11. 80 While ostensibly setting about the freeing of the slaves, they became enslaved, and found in the wailing self-pity and crooning of the Negro the substitute for any life-style of their own. **1950** Cole & Bruce *Educational Psychol.* i. 2 The teacher is confronted with such unique individuals, already shaped into recognizable life styles. **1952** M. Mackenzie *Contrast Psychol.* p. iii, The Freudian believes that the unconscious conflict, underlying an Anxiety State, springs from frustrated 'sexuality'; the Adlerian from an obstructed 'life style'. **1961** *Guardian* 22 Mar. 10/5 The mass-media..continually tell their audience what life-styles are 'modern' and 'smart'. **1972** *Jrnl. Social Psychol.* LXXXVI. 121 When a man's life style is incongruent with the demands of a task he must perform he will experience stress. **1972** M. Mead *Blackberry Winter* vii. 82 But in other ways those years in

Bucks County gave me a view of a much earlier life-style, one that corresponded with my grandmother's girlhood. **1973** T. Tobin in Ade *Lett.* 7 His commercial successes in the theater enabled him to become financially independent, and Ade chose the lifestyle with which he was most comfortable. **1973** *Times* 11 Apr. 18/4 (*heading*) Council of churches want freedom for students to create their own life-styles.

lifetime. Add: Also *attrib.* or as *adj.*, for the duration of a life, during one's life, while one is alive. Phrases: *all in a* (or *one's*) *lifetime*, implying resignation to whatever happens; *of a lifetime*, implying that an event, situation, or thing will never be equalled or repeated.

1849 N. Kingsley *Diary* (1914) 44 My consolation is that it is all in my lifetime and thus make myself quite contented. *Ibid.* 52 This must count as 'all in my lifetime'. **1898** F. P. Dunne *Mr. Dooley in Peace & War* 187 Well, tubby sure, 'tis thryin' to be dhrivin' a coal wagon or a sthreet-car; but 'tis all in a lifetime. **1929** Wodehouse *Mr. Mulliner Speaking* vii. 222 But let me tell you, my lad, that you're throwing away the laugh of a lifetime. *Ibid.* ix. 314 It must be a cocktail. The cocktail of a lifetime. **1961** —— *Ice in Bedroom* xxiii. 188 You take one step in its direction and you're going to get the headache of a lifetime. **1962** *Amer. Speech* XXXVII. 16 New England did contribute the largest number of white lifetime migrants to the state of New York. **1974** *Country Life* 2 May 1065/2 The gifts tax..would be a tax on lifetime gifts.

2. = Life *sb.* 8 c (in Dict. and Suppl.).

1858 [in Dict.]. **1920** *Discovery* Apr. 111/1 The helium now found in a mineral can be only a fraction..of the total amount which has been generated within it, and which alone could give a true estimate of its life-time. **1939** *Physical Rev.* LV. 506/1 The lifetime for a mesotron at rest has been estimated..to be of the order 2–4 × 10^{-6} sec. **1950** *Ibid.* LXXVII. 153/1 (*heading*) Lifetimes of mercury and potassium atoms in excited states. **1965** H. I. Ansoff *Corporate Strategy* (1968) ii. 24 If it turns out that the lifetime of some projects exceeds the budget period, the period is extended for purpose of analysis. **1968** [see *life *sb.* 8 c]. **1968** *Times* 29 Nov. 13/3 The running-down rate of the pulsar implies that it has a lifetime of the same order as the Crab nebula. **1972** *Sci. Amer.* May 50/1 The Viking spacecraft will consist of an orbiter and a lander, each with a lifetime of many months. **1974** *Daily Tel.* 17 Apr. 17/4 There is no possibility of action on the lines of the group's proposals in the lifetime of the present Parliament.

life-timer. [f. Lifetime.] One serving a life-sentence. (In quot. *fig.*)

1926 J. Black *You can't Win* v. 48 Life-timers of society, they were slowly sinking without a straw to grasp at.

li·fe-way. orig. *N. Amer.* [f. Life *sb.* + Way *sb.*[1]] Way or manner of life.

1961 in Webster. **1969** *Beaver* (Winnipeg) Spring 62/2 Wouldn't it be expected to contribute notably to an interpretation of their [*sc.* Eskimos'] life-ways in art? **1973** J. M. Anderson *Structural Aspects of Language Change* 203 Especially in regard to human lifeways and institutions, [etc.]. **1975** *Nature* 22 May 280/2 He [*sc.* Professor John Bowker (University of Lancaster)] drew attention to the extent to which religions function as bounded systems of information process, in which resources are made available to human beings for the construction of a lifeway from birth to death.

lifey, *a.* Delete 'Now *Sc.*' and add later *fig.* example.

1910 *Chambers's Jrnl.* Nov. 706/2 Those [sapphires] found in Ceylon, which are lighter in colour and 'lifier' than any of the others.

lift, *sb.*[2] Add: **1. b.** (Later examples.) Cf. *lift *v.* 11 e.

1929 M. de la Roche *Whiteoaks* v. 70 'Don't they ever send a car for you?' 'Good Lord, no. Sometimes I get a lift.' **1944** J. S. Huxley *On Living in Revolution* ix. 106 We found that a bus recorded on the time-table was in reality non-existent; cadged a lift on a road foreman's car to Denness. **1955** *Times* 26 Aug. 7/4 After giving a 'lift' to a hitch-hiker one will have lost only a tablespoonful or two of petrol, perhaps a teaspoonful of oil, and a saltspoonful or two of rubber off the car's tires. **1974** 'J. Le Carré' *Tinker, Tailor* xxxiii. 293 Declining a lift, Smiley said the walk would do him good.

2. b. Delete ?*U.S.* Also, a cheering or encouraging influence or effect, a sense of elation.

1861 T. Hughes *Tom Brown at Oxf.* I. xiv. 281 He heard Drysdale's view halloa above all the din; it seemed to give him a lift. **1873** A. G. Murdoch *Lilts on Doric Lyre* 10 Sae jist to gie their hearts a lift..They cannilie put owre a dram. **1887** [see *aspirational *a.*]. **1936** J. Dos Passos *Big Money* 498 Dick put down three bourbons in rapid succession but he wasn't getting any lift from them. **1951** E. Paul *Springtime in Paris* i. 12 Raoul realized that Katya got an enormous lift from secrecy and mystery, and helped her enjoy it. **1957** *Sat. Even. Post* 30 Mar. 102/2 The girl had to rush back to the pusher and complain that it didn't give her a lift. **1975** T. Allbeury *Palomino Blonde* xxiii. 135 Hallet had been demented with worry..and the 'lift' that he had got from his talk with Farrow had melted away.

5. d. (Earlier example.)

1829 J. Macauley *Nat. & Civil Hist. N.Y.* I. 170 This ..lock has an extent within the gates of one hundred and fourteen feet, with a breadth of thirty—the lift is nine feet.

e. (i) The upward force acting on an aircraft or other body in the air; *spec.* that produced by its motion through the air; the force on an aerofoil that acts at right angles to its direction of motion through a fluid.

1902 *Encycl. Brit.* XXV. 104/1 The sustaining power, or 'lift',.. in horizontal flight must be equal to the weight. *Ibid.*, The present data indicate that, with concave surfaces, angles of 2° to 5° will produce adequate 'lift'. **1919** H. Shaw *Text-bk. Aeronaut.* iii. 43 The upper surface of an aerofoil is considerably more important than the lower surface from the point of view of lift, as the suction over the top surface is numerically much greater than the pressure beneath. **1937** Dodge & Thompson *Fluid Mech.* vii. 127 Usually the component opposing the motion is referred to as the drag, while the cross-stream component is called the lift, even though it may not always be acting vertically upward. **1948** *Sci. News* VII. 23 In aerodynamics it is customary to resolve the reaction of the air on a surface into two components, namely lift, which is that part of the force acting upwards..and is thus desirable, and drag, which is the component at right angles to the lift and..resists the forward motion of the surface through the air. **1959** *Chambers's Encycl.* I. 110/2 In straight level flight the lift equals the weight. **1973** *Nature* 28 Sept. 182/1 Most flying insects depend, for their lift and thrust, on conventional aerofoil action which sets up a bound vortex around the moving wing to create a steady-state flow of air. **1974** *Encycl. Brit. Macropædia* I. 371/1 An airship derives lift from two sources: (1) by displacement of air as a balloon (static lift) and (2) from the reaction of airflow over its envelope and control surfaces when it is under way (dynamic lift).

(ii) The (maximum) weight that an aircraft can raise (including or, more commonly, excluding its own weight).

1910 *Blackw. Mag.* July 4/1 The compartments [of the Zeppelin] contained 351,150 cubic feet of hydrogen, giving a lift of eleven tons. **1929** *Nature* 14 Dec. 916/2 Recourse to the Servo-motor gear was not found necessary (if this holds good at full speed the gear may be removed, and then about ½ ton will be added to the useful 'lift'). **1971** *Daily Tel.* 19 Aug. 2/6 It is much lighter and can be lifted by the Puma tactical transport helicopter, which has a total lift of up to 5,500 lb.

f. *Pros.* An element of high intensity in an alliterative measure, marked by stress or tone. (G. *hebung*.) Cf. *dip *sb.* 1 g.

1894 [see *dip *sb.* 1 g]. **1927** E. V. Gordon *Introd. Old Norse* 293 The rhythm consists of regular alternation of strong and weak metrical elements, known as lift and sinking respectively. **1953** C. L. Wrenn *Beowulf* p. xxxvii, [Alliteration] is never repeated on the last lift. **1961** [see *dip *sb.* 1 g].

g. *Dance.* A movement in which a dancer lifts his partner in the air.

1921 *Dancing Times* Aug. 867/2 Miss Jules Andre.. filled the roll [*sic*] of 'boy' in..many..numbers. Her lifts and adage work were delightful. **1943** K. Ambrose *Ballet-Lover's Pocket-Bk.* 40 With the invention of each new ballet, new lifts are devised. **1944** 'Brahms' & 'Simon' *Titania has Mother* ii. 11 'He's a frightfully bad dancer, mother. His lifts!' She shuddered. **1950** *Ballet Ann.* IV. 69 She is equally at home in the most intricate acrobatic lifts..as [her body] is swung upwards in the air by her attendant cavaliers.

h. Transport by air (cf. *air-lift 2); also, a number of persons or an amount of supplies so transported. Cf. *lift *v.* 11 i.

1942 F. D Roosevelt in W. S. Churchill *Second World War* (1951) IV. xxx. 481 The following shipping can be made available by the United States..: Transports, other than combat leaders, with a lift of 52,000 men. **1947** Visct. Montgomery *Normandy to Baltic* 137 Our resources..made it impossible to fly in the whole of the Airborne Corps in one lift. **1947** M. Newnham *Prelude to Glory* ixiv. 350 The entire force was carried in one lift. **1949** *Flight* 15 Dec. 756/1 We eventually had sixteen crews, consisting of three members each, engaged wholetime on the Lift.

i. The establishment by a sheepdog of control over a flock of sheep. Cf. *lift *v.* 11 g.

1942 R. B. Kelley *Animal Breeding* xi. 115 A little 'eye'..can be associated meritoriously with a steady 'lift' and..restricts the dog from over-running a cast. **1946** F. Davison *Dusty* ix. 117 The [sheepdog] trial had four phases; the cast,..the lift, when the dog, having found them [*sc.* his sheep], established control over them; the fetch,..and the carry. **1955** *Galloway Gaz.* 1 Oct. 6 His dog 'Garry' won the Rosebowl for the best outrun and lift. **1964** *Weekly News* (Auckland) 29 Apr. 37/3 Fleet is losing points hand over fist now. He has failed to obtain a good 'lift': in other words he hasn't been able to head them unobserved and then start them moving gently and firmly. **1973** *Country Life* 25 Oct. 1292/1 From its position at 12 o'clock, the dog begins the critical 'lift', with a quiet authority that brooks neither refusal nor panic in the sheep.

10. b. chair-lift, a device for transporting people up a mountain slope, usually consisting of seats suspended from a continuously moving overhead cable; **ski-lift**, a chair-lift, or any of various types of apparatus for hauling skiers uphill. Also absol. *lift*.

1940 F. Elkins *Compl. Ski Guide* ii. 161 New 3500-foot 'T-bar' lift to connect with top of chair lift. **1947** *Penguin New Writing* XXX. 27 Dory found himself going up on the ski-lift with a Frenchwoman. **1953** C. J. Allen *Switzerland's Amazing Railways* viii. 93 A simpler application of the *téléphérique* principle is found in the chair-lift, known in French as a *télésiège* and in German as a *Sesselbahn*. **1955** W. Plomer *Shot in Park* 50 The ski-lift smoothly moves. **1958** *Times* 18 July 11/7 Skiing is also popular.. in the Thredbo Valley, where Australia's first chair lift, a mile long, began to work this winter. **1970** *Country Life* 17–24 Dec. 1214/3 Recently, Norway has been developing 'Alpine' resorts where the ski-lifts, the equipment and the ski-schools closely resemble good centres in the Alps. **1972** M. Yorke *Silent Witness* ii. 12 The lifts, and even the cable-car..had stopped, for the snow..had been falling steadily. **1972** D. Haston *In High Places* vii. 82 Once above the ski-lift level it was still possible to have the whole of a range to one's self on a certain day.

14. *spec.* of paper.

1808 C. Stower *Printer's Gram.* xvi. 405 Having thus doubled the first lift on the peel, he [*sc.* the warehouseman] raises it, holding it aslant, that the shorter fold of the sheets may open from the peel, in order to convey it over the pole. **1841** W. Savage *Dict. Art of Printing* 444 In the warehouse, each separate portion of printed paper, whether it consists of five or six sheets or more, that is placed upon the poles to dry, is termed a lift. **1861** [in Dict.]. **1888** C. T. Jacobi *Printers' Vocab.* 75 *Lift*, applied to a handful of printed work in the warehouse. **1967** V. Strauss *Printing Industry* x. 632 (*caption*) You see the lift of stock to be cut on the bed or table of the cutter. On the left the lift is lined up with one edge, in the rear it is lined up with another edge. **1971** D. Potter *Brit. Eliz. Stamps* xv. 175 Batches of 1,000 sheets are broken down into 'lifts' of 25.

18. (sense 10) *lift-boy, -button, -cage*; **lift coefficient** *Aerodynamics*, a ratio representing the lift developed by unit area of an aerofoil in relation to the air speed, and defined as the lift divided by the product of the aerofoil area (in plan) and the square of the air speed (and, in mod. use, by half the air density also); **lift-drag** *a. Aerodynamics*, relating to both lift and drag; applied *spec.* to the ratio of the lift to the drag; **lift-fan**, a fan in a hovercraft which provides the air-cushion; **lift-gate**, (*b*) a gate opening on to a lift (sense 10); (*c*) *U.S.* in a motor vehicle, a hinged back panel that opens upwards; **lift-slab** *attrib.*, applied to a labour-saving system of building whereby pre-cast components are raised by jacks to the position desired; **lift truck** = **fork-lift truck*; **lift valve**, a valve which opens by the valve head moving (vertically) out of its (horizontal) seat; **lift-web**, a strip of webbing joining the harness and the rigging lines of a parachute; **lift wire** *Aeronaut.*, a wire on a biplane or light monoplane that extends from the wing to the fuselage and is designed to transmit part of the lift to the latter during flight.

1904 'Saki' *Reginald* 15 Lift-boys always have aged mothers. **1967** L. Meynell *Mauve Front Door* vi. 82 Chauffeurs, waiters, lift-boys..they are the operators. **1955** W. Tucker *Wild Talent* xiv. 186 The man punched the lift button. **1970** P. Geddes *November Wind* vi. 64 Havill watched him press the lift button. **1951** R. Senhouse tr. *Colette's Last of Chéri* 213 The lift-cage heavily splashed with as much lacquer and gold as a sedan-chair. **1971** R. Petrie *Thorne in Flesh* xi. 145 A boy lounged on a stool in the silent lift-cage. **1919** H. Shaw *Text-bk. Aeronaut.* iii. 39 As the angle of incidence increases the lift coefficient also increases rapidly, until an angle of about 13° is reached, beyond which the coefficient increases less rapidly, and reaches its maximum value in the neighbourhood of 15°. **1933** *Techn. Rep. U.S. Nat. Advisory Comm. Aeronaut.* No. 463. 18 As speeds above half the velocity of sound are exceeded..the flow breaks down as shown by a drop in the lift coefficient. **1966** *McGraw-Hill Encycl. Sci. & Technol.* I. 85/2 The maximum lift coefficient (the stall value) of the wing is 1·1–1·5. **1919** Lift-drag ratio [see *ceiling *vbl. sb.* 6 b]. **1935** P. W. F. Mills *Elem. Pract. Flying* i. 6 Variations in incidence.. affect lift and drag disproportionately, and thus produce variations in the quantitative relation between lift and drag—that is to say, in what is called the lift-drag ratio. **1960** *Times Rev. Industry* Oct. 58/3 [The] airstream direction detector system..enables an aircraft to be flown on the best lift-drag curve to maintain economic flight conditions. **1962** *Flight Handbk.* (ed. 6) v. 98 The Republic AP-100, in which six J85 engines feed three lift fans. **1967** *Jane's Surface Skimmer Systems 1967–68* 49/2 A drive-shaft runs vertically upward to the 12-blade lift-fan. **1948** G. V. Galwey *Lift & Drop* i. 14 The crowd gathered at the lift gates. **1951** J. Wyndham *Day of Triffids* i. 19, I found a large '5' painted on the wall opposite the lift gate. **1961** Webster *Lift gate*, an upper rear panel (as on a station wagon) that opens upward as a tail gate opens downward. **1963** *Aerospace-Automotive Drawing Standards* (Soc. Automotive Engin.) 1 *Liftgate*, a hinged backwindow. **1970** *Motor Trend World Automotive Yearbk. 1971 Buyer's Guide* 112/3 The rear seat for a Gremlin is an optional extra along with the counter-balanced 'lift-gate' that comes with it. **1974** E. McGirr *Murderous Journey* 33 The liftman..was fiddling with the lift gate. **1951** (*title*) Youtz-Slick lift-slab building method (Inst. Inventive Res., San Antonio, Texas). **1960** *Economist* 22 Oct. 378/3 The 'lift slab' principle..was developed in America, the columns are first cast and erected, then pre-cast floor slabs are lifted by synchronised hydraulic jacks. **1962** *Daily Tel.* 30 Nov. 25/4 A 400,000-gallon watertank resting at the base of a tower before being raised 110 ft by the Lift Slab method... The 95 ft-diameter watertank was raised..in about 40 hours. **1963** H. Garner in R. Weaver *Canad. Short Stories* (1968) 2nd Ser. 56 Even with a lift truck hurrying the parts to the forge we were falling behind. **1971** [see *dozer[2]]. **1887** *Encycl. Brit.* XXII. 505/1 In many stationary engines lift or disk valves are used, worked by tappets, cams, or eccentrics. **1898** *Engineering Mag.* XVI. 108/1 Compression has been on the increase ever since the adoption of the lift valve. **1971** B. Scharf *Engin. & its Lang.* xii. 178 Poppet valves. These are spring loaded lift valves which are commonly used, e.g. in internal combustion engines. **1942** *Tee Emm* (Air Ministry) II. 134 Pass the left hand *in between* the left harness lift web and the body and grasp

the right harness lift web. **1947** M. Newnham *Prelude to Glory* viii. 33 To reduce the risk of backward landings men were told..if necessary to turn their bodies by manipulation of the parachute lift-webs. **1958** P. Kemp *No Colours or Crest* iii. 41, I took a frantic pull on my liftwebs to ease the impact. **1915** W. E. Dommett *Aeroplanes & Airships* ii. 26 When the machine is in flight, the upward pressure on the wings is taken by 'lift' wires or stays passing to a framework under the fuselage. **1942** C. C. Redman in R. A. Beaumont *Aeronaut. Engin.* xvii. 482/1 Wires running..inwards from the tip portions of the upper surfaces to inboard points of the lower surfaces adjacent to the fuselage—are known as 'flying' or 'lift' wires.

lift, *v.* Add: **1.** Occas., to lower after raising from an elevated position. Cf. quot. 1841.

1920 E. O'Neill *Beyond Horizon* ii. i. 73 Lifting Mary to the floor.

b. Also with *down*.

1838 Dickens *O. Twist* II. xxi. 25 Sikes dismounted.. holding Oliver by the hand..and, lifting him down directly, bestowed a furious look on him. **1890** A. Conan Doyle *Sign of Four* viii. 138 'He acted according to his lights,' said Holmes, lifting him [*sc.* a dog] down from the barrel. **1898** G. B. Shaw *Candida* i. 106, I cant lift a heavy trunk down from the top of a cab. **1920** E. O'Neill *Beyond Horizon* ii. ii. 95 He lifts her down to the grass. **1940** W. Faulkner *Hamlet* iii. i. 212 He finds the basket by smell and lifts it down from the limb and sets it before her.

f. To help (sick or weak cattle) to stand up. Cf. *lifting *vbl. sb.* 1 b.

1899 H. G. Graham *Social Life Scotl. 18th Cent.* I. 155 Cattle..after the long confinement and starving of winter, were mere skeletons, and required to be lifted on their legs when put into the grass.

g. = *face-lift* vb. (*face *sb.* 27). So **lifted** *ppl. a.* Also *transf.*

1922 *Ladies' Home Jrnl.* Sept. 28/2 For a skillful surgeon to 'lift' a woman's face—that is, to remove crescent-shaped pieces of skin, near the ears, and at the hair line, thus lifting the cheeks that have begun to sag and so removing the lines of age about the mouth—is actually a simple operation and practically without danger. **1928** G. B. Shaw *Let.* 31 May in *To a Young Actress* (1960) 127 How will you face old age: With a 'lifted' face, with grease paints and an iceball and rouge, with peroxided hair, an old hag..pretending to be a young witch. **1931** *Daily Express* 2 Sept. 3/5 A woman can now have her face lifted one day and appear among her friends the next. **1934** R. Macaulay *Going Abroad* i. 12 Mrs. Aubrey, bored, felt that they wanted her to have her face lifted, de-wrinkled ..and given a lick of paint. **1951** G. Mikes *Down with Everybody* 71 Modern nationalism is an attempt to see ourselves without the warts; and many historians, writers and poets are the masseurs and cosmeticians of the national beauty parlours, trying to dye our greying hair golden-blonde and trying to lift our faces. **1959** *Camb. Rev.* 30 May 549/2 Whole courts have had their faces lifted, with stone-work freshly dressed or replaced, stucco renewed. **1974** M. Cecil *Heroines in Love* vi. 149 She..could cling on to her youth..by having her face lifted.

h. (*not*) *to lift a finger*: see *finger *sb.* 3 a.

2. d. To raise in price, value, or amount. Also *ellipt.*

1907 *Daily Chron.* 7 Nov. 1/7 Home Rails were lifted all round..several rises being substantial. **1928** *Chambers's Jrnl.* Feb. 99/2 He kept on lifting the betting, merely to increase his plunder. *Ibid.* 115/2 Jackson..opened the pot for a pound. The American..raised it five, and Captain Reginald lifted another five. **1962** A. Nisbett *Technique Sound Studio* 272 To lift programme level 'a stop' is to increase it by turning the fader (potentiometer) from one stud to the next.

3. (i) Of an aircraft: to rise *off* the ground.

1879 *English Mechanic* 4 July 410/3 The small flying model..only just lifted off the pavement. **1899** H. G. Wells *When Sleeper Wakes* xxiv. 327 The aëropile..was running down its guides to launch. It lifted clean and rose. **1907** *Daily Chron.* 9 Oct. 4/5 She will have to get rid of at least 250 lb. of ballast before she will lift. **1973** J. Drummond *Bang! Bang! You're Dead!* xliv. 151 By the time Sorensen and Pittaway were lifting off the Wapping tarmac, certain constables..were already deploying... They saw the helicopter about the same time as Mariner did.

(ii) Hence in recent use *off* has changed from being a preposition to being an adverb in Astronautical contexts.

1959 W. A. Heflin *Aerospace Gloss.* 57/2 *To lift off*, to take off in a vertical ascent. **1961** Burchett & Purdy *Cosmonaut Yuri Gagarin* ii. 27 The giant ship lifts off..in a hurricane of white-hot flames. **1971** *Sci. Amer.* Oct. 49/2 On July 21, 1969, *Eagle* lifted off from the moon with its 22-kilogram cargo of lunar rocks and soil.

f. To rise in tone or volume of sound.

1912 Galsworthy *Inn of Tranquility* 157 He seemed to enjoy the sounds of conversation lifting round him. **1918** —— *Five Tales* 340 The wayward music lifted up again.

g. *Printing. intr.* Of a forme of type, to stay in one piece when raised from the surface on which it has been assembled; = Rise *v.* 13 c. Also *trans.*, to raise (lines of type), esp. in moving them from a composing stick to a galley, or in preparation for the distribution of used type.

1854 T. Ford *Compositor's Handbk.* 247 *Lift*, this term applies to the raising of a form from the stone. It is said to Lift when no letters drop out. The same term is applied at press when the pressmen are required to Lift a form before it is worked off. **1884** J. Gould *Letter-Press Printer* (ed. 3) 34 Before lifting the forme off the stone, raise it a little and observe carefully if any letters, &c., are loose and likely to fall out. If the forme 'lifts', take it from the imposing-stone to the proof-press. **1892** A. Powell *Southward's Pract. Printing* (ed. 4) xxi. 184 Lock up finally, so that the forme will lift. *Ibid.* 185 The next thing to be done is to 'see if it [*sc.* the forme] will lift'; that is, if it can be raised up from the imposing surface without any letters falling out. **1932** Sayers & Smart in W. Atkins *Art & Pract. Printing* I. iv. 48 If the job contains lines interspersed of the same size and fount (as in display) 'lift these and place together. **1961** H. W. Larken *Compositor's Work in Printing* viii. 95 When type matter is being lifted, it should be handled firmly. *Ibid.* 96 When lifting single lines from a galley or forme, use the side of the galley or the furniture. *Ibid.* 97 Type that is to be distributed should..be lifted in the same manner as that employed for removing it from the stick... The lifted type is allowed to rest on the third finger of the left hand. **1967** Karch & Buber *Offset Processes* 544 When each piece of type in a form stays in place after being locked in a chase, it is said to 'lift'.

8. Delete 'In early use' and add later examples.

1905 E. Wallace *Four Just Men* ix. 165 They was waitin' to cross towards Charing Cross Road when I lifted the clock. **1968** J. Lock *Lady Policeman* xix. 159 Goods from three or four stores would be found in them. Others would 'lift' a shopping bag first in which to put all the other 'lifted' goods. **1973** J. Wainwright *Devil you Don't* 107 Lift a bleedin' gun from somewhere.

11. (Later examples of sense 'to drive (cattle) away or to market'.) Also, to remove, discontinue (restrictions, an embargo, etc.).

1840 *Edin. Even. Courant* 19 Sept., We anticipate rather dull sales now, for a week or two, until the St Faith's droves are lifted. **1890** 'R. Boldrewood' *Squatter's Dream* iv. 45, I haven't lifted a finer mob this season. **1890** *Argus* (Melbourne) 14 June 4/2 We lifted 7000 sheep. **1906** *Daily Chron.* 12 Sept. 5/7 It was freely said that if we only applied the suspensions would be lifted. **1936** A. Russell *Gone Nomad* i. ii. 11, I hope his droving mission, that of 'lifting' a thousand head of cattle for the markets of the south, was attended with the success it merited. **1941** I. L. Idriess *Great Boomerang* x. 75 Red Bill and his gang lifted their cattle. They headed south-west and got safely across to the Paroo. **1974** *Nature* 25 Jan. 171/3 Even if the embargo is suddenly lifted, it will take several weeks for the oil to reach United States ports. **1974** *Daily Tel.* 4 Apr. 17/1 The university authorities yesterday lifted the temporary suspension on deliveries of supplies to the campus.

d. *Hunting.* (See quot. 1968.) Also, to disperse (scent).

1781 P. Beckford *Thoughts on Hunting* x. 147 By lifting his hounds too much, he will teach them to shuffle. **1843** *Ainsworth's Mag.* IV. 125, I seldom allow hounds to be lifted, except to a beaten fox. *Ibid.*, To lift, in that case, is proper and justifiable. **1863** C. Mordaunt *Diary* 6 Mar. in Mordaunt & Verney *Ann. Warwickshire Hunt* (1896) I. 264 [The hounds] had to be lifted several times to holloas. **1919** J. Masefield *Reynard* ii. 85 He heard the sounds Of a cantering huntsman, lifting hounds; The ploughman had raised his hat for a sign, And the hounds were lifted and on his line. **1929** *St. Andrews Citizen* 16 Mar. 7 Fife Foxhounds had three poor days last week. Although the weather was good, the bright, warm sunshine 'lifted' scent. **1968** J. Gordon *Beagle Guide* 172 *Lift*, to remove hounds from a lost scent with the idea of trying to hit the line further on.

e. To give a lift to (in a carriage, motor vehicle, etc.). Cf. Lift *sb.*[2] 1 b.

1884 E. W. Hamilton *Diary* 17 Aug. (1972) II. 672 A very hot walk. We got 'lifted' back in a carriage; and afterwards played lawn tennis. **1954** M. Sharp *Gipsy in Parlour* xxii. 211 Up she drove, lifted by Mr Simnel the chemist, Taunton-bound. **1959** I. Jefferies *Thirteen Days* vii. 87 He'd like to lift me back to Richon fairly soon as the roads were likely to tighten up during the day. **1960** *Sunday Express* 13 Nov. 14/5 A young R.A.F. hitch-hiker I 'lifted' from Shepherd's Bush to High Wycombe. **1965** I. Fleming *Man with Golden Gun* vi. 90 Get in the back. Lift you down to your car. **1971** M. Russell *Deadline* ii. 22 Can you lift me in your wagon, Wally?

f. *Artillery. trans.* and *intr.* To increase the range of fire from that being used at a given point in an attack.

1916 in A. Farrar-Hockley *Somme* (1964) iii. 94 Avoid a pause at 0000, at minus three in each field battery, where one section will lift on to the support line. **1917** J. Masefield *Old Front Line* ii. 30 The flash of our shells, breaking a little further off as the gunners 'lifted'. **1922** *Encycl. Brit.* XXX. 255/2 The bombardment is 'lifted' from the first line to reinforce that on the second line. **1962** *Ordnance Technical Terminol.* (U.S. Army Ordnance School) (AD 660 112) 176/2 *Lift fire*, to advance the range of fire by elevating the muzzle of a weapon. **1964** A. Farrar-Hockley *Somme* iii. 96 The 18-pounders lifted on time as they passed the wire. *Ibid.* 98 Some aghast to see the supporting artillery fire already lifting ahead of them.

g. Of a sheepdog: to establish control over a flock of sheep. Cf. *lift *sb.*[2] 5 i.

1921 *Kelso Chron.* 12 Aug. 2 This bitch started well... Her haulding, lifting, and penning were good, her bringing and driving very fair. **1942** R. B. Kelley *Animal Breeding* xiii. 127 When he [*sc.* a pup] has reached this point sit him down and make him lift the flock quietly. **1946** F. D. Davison *Dusty* ix. 90 The paddock, what with hills, broken ground and patches of scrub, was not the easiest in the world to lift sheep from. **1949** C. W. G. Hartley *Shepherd's Dogs* v. 33 Much will depend upon the manner in which the sheep are 'lifted'.

h. To arrest, take into custody.

1923 G. Watson *Roxburghshire Word-Bk.* 200 Tam's gruppen an' liftit. **1934** D. Allan *Hunger March* iii. ii. 208 They've lifted Smith. **1968** 'J. Ross' *Diminished by Death* ii. 27 The youth stood. 'Am I being lifted?' 'Not at the moment. You are helping us with our inquiries.' **1972** *Times* 24 Jan. 2/1 If you have a father who is lifted, he has sons and cousins who will take his place. **1973** 'J. Patrick' *Glasgow Gang Observed* iii. 32 A fund..to raise ten pounds bail money for two of their number who had been 'lifted' the night before for fighting.

i. To evacuate (soldiers) from a beach; to air-lift. Also *transf.* Cf. *lift *sb.*[2] 5 h.

1941 J. Masefield *Nine Days Wonder* 19 The first men lifted were not always soldiers. **1963** *Times* 24 Jan. 10/3 An emergency rail freighter service ordered by Lord Robens, chairman of the National Coal Board, is lifting thousands of tons of coal into the worst snowbound areas of south-east and south-west England. **1972** *Daily Tel.* 11 Apr. 17 Medical supplies, tents and food were being lifted in by helicopter last night.

12. a. Further examples of *Hort.* sense referring to potatoes, bulbs, etc. Also occas. *intr.*, in phr. *to lift well*, of the crops or plants concerned: to produce a good yield or be in good condition when lifted.

1888 L. Castle *Flower Gardening* 232 November... Lift Gladioli corms, storing them in a dry place; also Dahlia tubers. **1888** Hardy *Wessex Tales* II. 67 The next day went about his swede-lifting and storing. **1891** 'H. Haliburton' *Ochil Idylls* 106 The dreels [of potatoes] are to lift, An' the neeps are to pu'. **1931** *Morning Post* 19 July 5/1 What to do with the bulbs at this season when, apparently, they are sleeping, has for long been a rather controversial point. Should they be left or lifted? **1959** *Times* 7 Sept. 19/2 Some crops [of potatoes] in Lincolnshire are lifting well, others are below average. **1971** 'L. Black' *Death has Green Fingers* vii. 83 Suppose whoever it was had lifted the roses already. **1973** *Times* 20 Oct. 14/6 Nurseries..cannot lift and pack all their orders in a month.

14. lift-on, lift-off, used esp. *attrib.*, a method of hoisting containers from one vessel or vehicle to another; also **lift-on** *attrib.*; **lift-out** *attrib.*, made to lift out; **lift-up** *attrib.*, made to lift up.

1956 *Sun* (Baltimore) 16 Oct. 18/3 The relative merits of 'roll-on, roll-off' shipping, where trailers would be rolled aboard, and of 'lift-on, lift-off' service involving only a truck van. **1967** *Freight Management* Jan. 15/1 (Advt.), Last year Southampton handled thousands of containers by lift-on/lift-off. *Ibid.* 46/3 Basically roll-on is more expensive than lift-on. *Ibid.* 47/3 (*caption*) The tanks..can be used on both roll-on or lift-on vessels. **1968** *Economist* 14 Sept. p. xxxiv/1 The North Sea is now the focal point of a fight between two new forms of transport, the roll-on, roll-off ferry services..and lift-on, lift-off container services. **1969** *Jane's Freight Containers 1968–69* 73 (*caption*) Simultaneous roll-on and lift-on of trailers make possible a trip a week to Puerto Rico. *Ibid.* 160/3 Lift-on Lift-off Unitised Loads. **1926–7** *Army & Navy Stores Catal.* 314/2 These boilers are..fitted with a shaking grating and lift-out ashes pan. **1968** *Harrods Christmas Catal.* 3/4 Beauty case with inside pockets and lift-out tray. **1974** *Country Life* 14 Mar. (Suppl.) 41/1 Arm Chair with lift out seat covered in green velvet. **1917** *Installation News* Jan. 5/1 The Cabinets comprise a substantially constructed stained box, fitted with lift-up lid, lock and key. **1950** *N.Z. Jrnl. Agric.* Aug. 132/1 The lift-up gate opens by sliding up between guides fixed to uprights. **1956** *Railway Mag.* Feb. 121/1 There is a separate sheet steel case with lift-up cover containing the engineman's telephone. **1970** *Guardian* 19 Nov. 11/6 Two swing-out drawers, one with a lift-up mirror.

lifter. Add: **2. c.** *Cricket.* A ball, usu. one from a fast bowler, that rises sharply after striking the pitch.

1959 *Times* 28 July 4/7 He was caught off almost the only lifter of the day in his second [over]. **1974** *Daily Tel.* 12 June 34/1 Gavaskar got an awkward lifter from Old and gave a soft catch to the gully.

lifting, *vbl. sb.* Add: **1. b.** The raising of sick or weak cattle to enable them to stand. Cf. *lift *v.* 1 f. So *at the lifting*, very weak.

1812 W. Singer *Agric. County of Dumfries* 220 They become quite lean, almost 'at the lifting', as the farmers say. **1899** H. G. Graham *Social Life Scotl. 18th Cent.* I. 155 This period and this annual operation when all neighbours were summoned to carry and support the poor beasts, were known as the 'Lifting'. **1901** M. Franklin *My Brilliant Career* (1966) v. 18 My mother and father and I spent the day in lifting our cows... This cow-lifting became quite a trade.

c. In competitive walking, the raising of the rear heel before the front foot touches the ground.

1867 *Athlete 1866* 119 Lifting, the usual method of walking unfairly, is done by getting a spring from the toe of one foot on to the heel of the other. **1898** F. A. Cohen in W. A. Morgan *'House' on Sport* 433 What is technically called 'lifting' is, except perhaps in a final burst, seldom of any real advantage.

2. b. lifting beam, a beam, fitted to a crane hook, to which a load may be attached in two or more places; **lifting plate** (see quot. 1888); **lifting screw,** a hook with a threaded shank which can be screwed into an object to facilitate its lifting (see also *lifting *ppl. a.*).

1963 R. Hammond *Mobile & Movable Cranes* vi. 167 Aluminium-alloy lifting beams are very useful for getting the most out of crane-lifting capacity. **1969** *Jane's Freight Containers 1968–69* 130/1 There are new lifting beams used with existing straddle cranes to handle 24 ft. and 20 ft, containers. **1888** *Lockwood's Dict. Mech. Engin.* 208 *Lifting plates*, plates of wrought or malleable cast iron furnished with holes both for rapping and screwing, and let into or screwed on the faces of patterns; and by which they are lifted from the sand, a lifting screw being inserted into the tapped hole in the plate. **1925** J. G. Horner *Pattern Making* (ed. 5) iii. 56 Screws..either twisted into

the wood of the pattern or..fitting into corresponding tapped holes in the lifting plates attached to the pattern face, are used. **1885** —— *Pattern Making* xxii. 158 Figs. 206, 207 show two different forms of these [*sc.* rapping] plates, *a* being the plain hole for rapping, *b* the tapped hole for the reception of a lifting-screw. **1925** —— *Pattern Making* (ed. 5) iii. 59 A central hole bored through the boss for the lifting screw. **1944** E. D. Howard *Mod. Foundry Practice* 383/1 (Index), Lifting screw.

lifting, *ppl. a.* Add: Also, in *Aeronaut.*, providing lift; **lifting body,** a (wingless) spacecraft with a shape designed to produce lift, so that some aerodynamic control of its flight is possible within the atmosphere; **lifting screw,** a rotor operating in a horizontal plane so as to provide lift for a flying machine (see also *LIFTING *vbl. sb.*).

1902 F. Walker *Aërial Navigation* v. 79 The lifting screws. **1908** *Jrnl. R. Soc. Arts* LVII. 53/1 The Helicoptère, or lifting-screw flying machine. **1919** H. Shaw *Text-bk. Aeronaut.* ix. 111 In some machines it is arranged that the tail carries a portion of the load, when it is known as a 'lifting' tail. **1923** *Daily Mail* 12 Feb. 7 While aloft the pilot can change the action of his planes so that they cease to act as vertical lifting-screws and function like the surfaces of an aeroplane. **1935** P. W. F. Mills *Elem. Pract. Flying* i. 1 Aeroplanes..cannot fly backwards owing to their fixed thrust direction and the arrangement of their lifting surfaces. **1964** *Britannica Bk. of Year* 868/1 *Lifting body*, a wingless, somewhat bathtub-shaped vehicle for aerospace travel that combines some of the heat-handling capacity of a capsule with some of the maneuverability of a wingless aircraft. **1966** *McGraw-Hill Encycl. Sci. & Technol.* VI. 388/2 The disk loading [of a helicopter]..expresses the design gross weight as a function of the swept areas of the lifting rotor. **1969** K. Munson *Pioneer Aircraft 1903–14* 104/2 The Blériot III was also a floatplane, with annular lifting surfaces fore and aft. **1972** A. C. Kermode *Mech. of Flight* (ed. 8) xii. 390 These lifting bodies are but a step towards a shuttle service operating to and from a space station orbiting the earth.

li·ftless, *a.* [f. Lift *sb.*² 10 + -less.] Not provided with a lift.

1916 W. J. Locke *Wonderful Year* xvii. 245 She was living..on the fifth floor of a liftless block of flats in Wandsworth. **1921** *Spectator* 16 Apr. 484/2 In a liftless household.

lift-off, *a.* and *sb.* Also **liftoff, lift off.** [f. vbl. phr. *to lift off* (Lift *v.* 1 b, *3).] **A.** *adj.* Removable by lifting.

1907 *Yesterday's Shopping* (1969) 385/3 Art cloth box, with lift off lid. **1960** *Farmer & Stockbreeder* 16 Feb. 140/1 (Advt.), Lift-off wide doors..give remarkably easy access. **1970** *Gloss. Industrial Furnace Terms* (*B.S.I.*) 9 *ft-Lioff cover furnace*, a base over which a cover is placed for heating the charge; separate bases are normally available so that the same cover can be used for several charges. **1974** *Country Life* 6 June 1500 George III Decanter Stand... The lift off tray is divided into nine crenellated compartments.

B. *sb.* **1.** *Parachuting.* A method of leaving an aircraft by opening the parachute while standing on a wing, so as to be carried away by the air current.

1930 P. White *How to fly Airplane* xxii. 303 Two men are about to execute what is known as a 'lift-off' from the wings of a bombing plane. **1946** W. F. Burbidge *From Balloon to Bomber* iii. 46 There are two main methods of leaving aircraft. One is known as the 'lift-off' and in using this method the airman climbs on to the wing..and, by releasing his parachute, is lifted off. But this method has been superseded by the 'fall free'. **1957** *Encycl. Brit.* XVII. 252/2 In general use, there are two ways of leaving an aeroplane by parachute: (1) the drag-off or lift-off method, and (2) the jump or free-fall method.

2. [after *blast-off, *take-off.] The vertical take-off of a rocket, helicopter, or the like; the moment at which an aircraft begins to leave the ground.

1956 in W. A. Heflin *U.S. Air Force Dict.* 299. **1958** *Time* 8 Dec. 15/2 With great restraint, Shotwell and his 40-man launch team quietly waited in their bunker a full seven minutes after the lift-off before they dared shout. **1961** *Aeroplane* CI. 92/1 Lift-off took place at Cape Canaveral at 07.20 hrs. local time. **1962** *New Scientist* 22 Feb. 426/3 A plate in 10-gauge aluminium weighed 6·1 lb complete with nine-inch peg and gave adequate protection for fully 50 lift-offs [of VTOL aircraft] on grass. **1962** *Engineering* 27 July 99/1 The flow characteristic..is designed to facilitate part power operation and easy 'lift off' [of hovercraft] from the surface. **1966** J. A. Morris *Bird Watcher* (1968) ii. 27 The launch vehicle exploded soon after lift-off. **1967** D. P. Davies *Handling Big Jets* vii. 177 Take care when operating in cross winds. On take-off set in a little into-wind aileron control..; this will stop the down wind roll which will otherwise occur just before lift off. **1967** *New Scientist* 16 Nov. 406/1 From lift-off at Cape Kennedy..to splash-down in the Pacific Ocean northwest of Hawaii..the entire operation appears to have been an almost flawless performance. **1970** N. Armstrong et al. *First on Moon* xi. 245 If a serious malfunction should be detected, either by the men in Eagle or by the men on the ground, an immediate liftoff could be ordered.

b. *fig.* Initiation or commencement of activity; 'getting off the ground' (of a project or scheme).

1967 *Oxford Computer Explained* 7 Prior to lift-off on 1 August it was necessary that the actual stock in the warehouse be counted and the stock figures loaded to the computer. **1970** *Daily Tel.* 25 Apr. 17 (*heading*) Shell has lift-off with its space promotion. *Ibid.*, After weeks of harrowing doubt, the..'biggest, most widespread promotion the world has yet seen' achieves lift-off next week.

lig, *v.* Delete 'obs.' and add: Now freq. *colloq.*, to idle, to lie about.

Early examples of this form are cited in several sections s.v. Lie *v.*¹ A.

1960 *20th Cent.* Feb. 154 The ponce's air of having a function, an occupation..which totally distinguishes him from the mere 'ligging' layabout. **1967** *Melody Maker* 21 Jan. 6 When I was demobbed in 1960 I had no intention of going back to my trade as a fitter. I ligged around and joined Mike Peters. **1967** *Sun* 22 Feb. 6/6 *Lig, loon*, to kick one's heels or lounge about. **1969** *It* 4–17 July 10/2 It's a time for ligging in the streets and doing your thing, man.

ligamentum (li:gămeˑntŭm). *Anat.* Pl. **-menta.** [L. *ligāmentum* band, tie, bandage.] Used in numerous mod.L. collocations to designate ligaments of the body.

1713 W. Cheselden *Anat. Humane Body* i. ix. 30 One large Gland..seated in a Sinus at the bottom of the Acetabulum of the Os Innominatum, which is compress'd by the Ligamentum *Teres*. **1840** G. V. Ellis *Demonstrations Anat.* 128 The ligamentum nuchæ is a narrow ligamentous structure situated in the cervical region between the trapezius muscle of each side. **1877** W. Turner *Introd. Human Anat.* II. vi. 335 By its circumference or ciliary border the iris is not only continuous with the ciliary processes, but is connected by fibres, termed *ligamentum pectinatum*, with the posterior elastic lamina of the cornea. **1913** *Cunningham's Text-bk. Anat.* (ed. 4) 308 The laminæ of adjoining vertebræ are bound together by the ligamenta flava (O.T. subflava).., which consist of yellow elastic fibres. **1956** *Nature* 10 Mar. 467/2 Elastic fibres from ox ligamentum nuchæ, when treated with.. acetic acid solution.., are apparently devoid of collagen.

ligan, var. Lagan. (Later examples.)

1906 *Westm. Gaz.* 13 June 4/2 These are, says Mr. Clifford, the 'ligan' of history. **1909** *Daily Chron.* 20 Mar. 5/5 The custody of flotsam, jetsam, and ligan. **1952** *Brewer's Dict. Phr. & Fable* 534/2 *Lagan*, or *Ligan*, goods thrown overboard, but marked by a buoy in order to be found again.

ligand (li·gănd). *Chem.* [f. L. *ligand-us*, gerundive of *ligāre* to bind.] **1.** Each of the atoms or groups attached to the central (usually the metal) atom of a co-ordination complex.

1952 *Jrnl. Chem. Soc.* 4757 Inferences from spectral absorption to thermochemical stability are therefore very speculative, particularly if different types of ligand, say ions and neutral dipoles, are being compared. **1964** J. W. Linnett *Electronic Struct. Molecules* viii. 138 This implies that..the tendency to form a multiple bond is about the same for the PF_3 ligand as for CO. **1964** *Oceanogr. & Marine Biol.* II. 250 The relative accumulation factors for metals in marine organisms are related, in general, to the stability of the metal ions with ligands. **1971** *Arch. Biochem. & Biophysics* CXLVII. 226/1 At each monomer active site the two iron atoms can be bridged by two small, inorganic ligands.

2. Special Comb.: **ligand exchange,** exchange of ligands between complexes; **ligand field,** the electrostatic field produced by the ligands in the vicinity of the central atom; so *ligand field theory*, the branch of chemical theory which deals with the effect of ligands on the energy levels of the central atom or ion; *spec.* a theory based on an electrostatic model modified by molecular orbital considerations.

1964 *Jrnl. Amer. Chem. Soc.* LXXXVI. 765 (*heading*) Rates of rapid ligand exchange reactions by nuclear magnetic resonance line broadening studies. **1973** *Jrnl. Chromatogr.* LXXXVII. 513 A rapid ligand-exchange chromatographic method for the separation of α-amino acids from peptides is presented. **1956** *Nature* 18 Feb. 305/2 A proper consideration of the effect of the ligand-field explains why the six-coordinate complexes of nickel are equally stable with the cupric complexes. **1960** L. Pauling *Nature Chem. Bond* (ed. 3) v. 174 In some respects the ligand field theory is closely related..to the valence bond theory. **1966** Cotton & Wilkinson *Adv. Inorg. Chem.* (ed. 2) xxvi. 661 This modified CFT [*sc.* crystal field theory] is often called ligand field theory, LFT. However, LFT is sometimes also used as a general name for the whole gradation of theories from the electrostatic CFT to the MO [*sc.* molecular orbital] formulation. **1970** W. L. Jolly *Synthesis & Characterization Inorg. Compounds* xxii. 324 If we were able gradually to decrease the ligand field strength to zero, we would find that each term would gradually approach an energy corresponding to one of the states of the free ion. **1971** Orchin & Jaffé *Symmetry, Orbitals & Spectra* vii. 170 Interpretation of the spectra of inorganic complexes is greatly simplified and successfully integrated by the use of ligand field theory.

So **li·gancy** = *co-ordination number* s.v. *co-ordination 5; **li·ganded** *a.*, bound to a ligand or ligands.

1960 L. Pauling *Nature Chem. Bond* (ed. 3) ii. 63 A sharp distinction is to be made between the number of atoms bonded to a central atom (the ligancy or coordination number of the central atom) and the number of covalent bonds formed by the central atom (its covalence). *Ibid.* xiii. 538 The changes from the standard sodium chloride and rutile arrangements, with ligancy 6, to cesium chloride and fluorite, respectively, with ligancy 8, are nearly the same. **1965** Phillips & Williams *Inorg. Chem.* I. v. 157 The presence of shared edges and especially of shared faces in a coordinated structure decreases its stability; this effect is large for cations with large valence and small ligancy. **1967** *Jrnl. Biol. Chem.* CCXLII. 3705/2 If the αβ dimer that reacts with ligand is free in solution, the now liganded dimer, α*β*, can associate with another liganded dimer to produce a liganded tetramer, $\alpha_2{}^*\beta_2{}^*$. **1968** *Inorg. Chem.* VII. 1945/2 There are certain bonding situations common in boron chemistry and uncommon elsewhere that lead to unusual nomenclature problems. These include..excess connectivity or ligancy. **1973** *Jrnl. Molecular Biol.* LXXVI. 238 Hybrids formed in a mixture of HbS and CN met-Hb A would, upon deoxygenation, contain one liganded α chain and one liganded β chain.

ligase (li·gēiz, -ēis). *Biochem.* [f. L. *lig-āre* to bind + *-ase.] (See quot. 1961.)

1961 *Rep. Comm. Enzymes Internat. Union Biochem.* vi. 39 Enzymes catalysing the linking together of two molecules, coupled with the breaking of a pyrophosphate link in ATP, etc., will be known as ligases (pronounced with a short 'i' in English). These enzymes have hitherto been known as synthetases... A new systematic name was necessary. **1965** *Canad. Jrnl. Biochem.* XLIII. 1605 Succinate: CoA ligase (ADP)..catalyzes the formation of succinyl CoA. **1972** *Sci. Amer.* Jan. 31/1 The most unusual of them is an enzyme that is named polynucleotide ligase, which repairs breaks in DNA molecules.

liger (ləi·gəɹ). [f. Li(on *sb.* + Ti)ger *sb.*] The offspring of a lion and a tigress. Cf. *tigon.

1938 *Times* 28 May 7/7 Two young Whipsnade-bred tigresses have been sent to London with the intention that they shall be paired with lions to produce the so-called ligers. **1948** *Time* 17 May 27 Daisy, a Salt Lake City zoo tigress, gave birth to the first known liger..ever born in the U.S. **1964** *Sunday Mail Mag.* (Brisbane) 8 Nov. 4/6 A 'Liger' is the term applied to the result of a cross between a lion and a tigress. **1975** *Times* 17 Sept. 7/3 The world's only living liger, the cross-breed of a male lion and a female tiger, has died at a Japanese zoo. It was the last of a litter of three born on September 8.

ligger, *sb.* Add: **2. b.** (See quots.) *dial.*

1828 W. Carr *Dial. Craven* (ed. 2) I. 289 *Ligger*.., a branch cut or laid down horizontally in a hedge. **1869** R. B. Peacock *Gloss. Lonsdale* 51 *Ligger*.., a branch of thorn or other tree cut half through and laid along the top of a plashed hedge. **1898** B. Kirkby *Lakeland Words* 92 *Liggers*, long branches which a diker cuts partly through and ligs down to form a dike.

c. = *ledger *sb.* 2 b.

1953 J. Arnold *Countryman's Workshop* 160 *Liggers*, hazel strips which hold down thatch. **1965** J. G. Jenkins *Trad. Country Craftsmen* ii. 36 The method of making liggers is somewhat similar to that of spar making but the ends are bevelled for neat joining rather than pointed. **1966** *Punch* 10 Aug. facing p. 216 (Advt.), The ridge..is thickly capped with sedge grass.. and isgaily embellished with diamond and herring-bone patterns of 'liggers'. **1971** *Country Life* 18 Nov. 1403/3 The finish [of a thatch] that is visible consists of cleft hazel rods called liggers about four feet long neatly secured by spars, which gives a tidy and attractive appearance.

light, *sb.* Add: **1. i.** (Later examples.)

1866 'Mark Twain' *Lett. from Hawaii* (1967) 152 The sick Portyghee watched his chance..harnessed the provisions and ate up nearly a quarter of a bar'l of bread before the old man caught him, and he had more than two notions to put his lights out. **1891** *Star* 10 Feb. 3/6 He had been heard to say, 'I should like to put her light out,' and had fired at her bed-room window. **1910** W. M. Raine *Bucky O'Connor* 25 Mebbe I'd a-put his lights out for good and all. **1935** A. J. Pollock *Underworld Speaks* 92/2 *Put his lights out*, to kill. **1955** 'A. Gilbert' *Is she Dead Too?* vii. 133 Say she put out the old girl's light, that ain't going to encourage the widower to pay his addresses to her.

2. c. Now also, to reach a full understanding or realization; to be converted (esp. to Christianity).

1812 *Niles' Reg.* III. 195/2 It is indispensably necessary that every man should 'see the light'. **1889** *Kansas City* (Missouri) *Times & Star* 14 Oct., Up to a few weeks ago, he was opposed to a revival of navigation on the Missouri, but now he has seen the light and says he's for it strong. **1903** *N.Y. Even. Post* 10 Sept., It is altogether likely that they, too, will see the light before another week has passed. **1933** H. G. Wells *Shape of Things to Come* iii. iv. 275 Men who saw the light and spoke were only one species of a larger genus of human beings whose minds worked differently from the common man's. **1944** H. James et al. (*song-title*) I'm beginning to see the light. **1966** 'L. Lane' *ABZ of Scouse* 94 *See ther light*, to plead guilty or to reform.

5. b. *bright lights*: see *bright *a.* 10 b; *lights out* (Mil.): the last bugle-call of the day, giving the signal for all lights to be extinguished. Hence in non-military use.

1868 *Queen's Regulations Army* § 845 Between tattoo and reveille no trumpet or bugle is to be sounded,.. with the exception of the call 'lights out'. **1905** *Captain* XIII. 42/2 It's off... We aren't allowed to talk after lights-out! **1914** R. Brooke *Let.* 3 Oct. (1968) 621 Faint lights burning through the ghostly tents, and a distant bugler blowing *Lights Out*. **1922** C. E. Montague *Disenchantment* iv. 56 They would argue after Lights Out. **1942** *R.A.F. Jrnl.* 13 June 14 There would be no lights-out time, no check-up to ensure every man was in. **1950** A. Baron *There's no Home* ii. 19 The wooden gates.. could be closed every evening at Lights Out. **1965** G. Jackson *Let.* June in *Soledad Brother* (1971) 78 One of those tall ultrabright electrical fixtures used to illuminate the walls and surrounding area at night casts a direct beam of light in my cell at night... Consequently I have enough light, even after the usual twelve o'clock lights-out, to read or study by. **1969** I. & P. Opie *Children's*

Games viii. 246 The statues have to come to life, and do the things they think monsters or fairies..would do... The puller then commands 'Lights out'..and they have to close their eyes.

f. *out like a light* (with preceding verb or auxiliary): having lost consciousness, having fainted, or gone to sleep, at once.

1934 [see *GO *v.* 85 u]. **1956** B. HOLIDAY *Lady sings Blues* (1973) xix. 155 When it came time to come out for the third curtain call I said, 'Bobby, I just can't make it no further,' and I passed out like a light. **1964** R. BRADDON *Year Angry Rabbit* ii. 17 The Prof's out like a light. **1970** *Women's Household* July 10/3 That first night he came dashing in the house, made a running leap at the couch, and was out like a light! **1973** J. PHILIPS *Larkspur Conspiracy* I. iv. 75 He..lay down on his bed. He went out like a light.

g. Usu. *pl.* Traffic lights. Also *fig.*

1938 E. BOWEN *Death of Heart* III. vi. 439 The driver twitched his head once or twice. Then the lights went against him; he pulled up. **1963** A. HUNTER *Gently Floating* ii. 29 They came to the bridge, were halted by lights... The lights changed. Gently drove over. **1970** M. KENYON *100,000 Welcomes* i. 8 I'll drop you at the next lights. **1971** *Daily Tel.* (Colour Suppl.) 22 Oct. 7/2 That's right, you bumbling old fool, slow down as we come to the next lights and we'll miss the green. **1972** *Accountant* 19 Oct. 495/1 Stock markets have been in neutral waiting for the lights to change.

6. a. *to throw light upon* (earlier example).

1841 CARLYLE *On Heroes* v. 309 When he did speak, it was to throw new light on the matter.

e. (Earlier and later examples.)

1854 MRS. GASKELL *Company Manners* in *Househ. Words* 20 May 330/1 Why have we not oftener recourse to games of some kind. Wit, Advice, Bout-rimés, Lights..—every one knows these..if they would only not think it beneath them to be called upon..to play at them. **1937** H. G. WELLS *Brynhild* vii. 108 Valliant Chevrell was generally the director of his scenes [in a charade], but the direction of the first light was taken out of his hands. **1945** H. PHILLIPS *Word Play* xiv. 84 It is permissible to play tricks of this kind with the Lights—beheading or curtailing the words.

f. The answer to a clue in a crossword puzzle.

1925 'TORQUEMADA' *Cross-Words in Rhyme* Introd. Those who wish a separate entertainment..from each Light in their cross-words. **1965** *Listener* 16 Sept. 435/1 Some of the clues are two lines of verse, each by a different author. The names of the two authors have three or more consecutive letters in common and these letters form the light. **1967** *Sci. Amer.* Sept. 268/2 The horizontal words.. are called the cross-lights or simply the lights.

8. a. (Further examples.)

1887 *Lantern* (New Orleans) 7 May 3/1 Some of the leading lights of the National League. **1915** T. DREISER *Genius* II. xl. 469 What Eugene thought and what White thought of this prospective situation was that the other would naturally be the minor figure, and that he under Colfax would be the shining light. **1942** BERREY & VAN DEN BARK *Amer. Thes. Slang* §388/4 *Principal or most important person,*..leading card or light. **1943** K. TENNANT *Ride on Stranger* xvi. 180 An eminent legal light. **1974** E. AMBLER *Dr. Frigo* III. 240 The procession could ..move off. I was among the least of the lesser lights and so was among the first out.

12. *fig.* (Later examples.) Usu. opp. to *shade.*

1812 *Dramatic Censor 1811* 182 This may be what our modern playmakers call *light* and *shade.* **1937** *Printers' Ink Monthly* May 39/1 *Light and shade,* variations from quietness to tenseness, softness to shouting and which has a tendency to keep a production from a dull sameness. **1952** GRANVILLE *Dict. Theatr. Terms* 110 *Light and shade,* the niceties of intonation, inflection, modulation, etc., in the reading of a part.

15. a. *light-effect, -output, -ray, -scatter, -signal, -socket, -song, -source, -switch;* **b.** (objective) *light-absorber, -absorbing, -absorptive, -avoiding, -emitting, -gathering, -loving, -passing, -producing, -reflecting, -reflective, -refracting, -throwing* adjs.; (instrumental, etc.) *light-actuated, -sensitive, -stilled* adjs.

1957 *Technology* Dec. 361/2 Light absorbers for use in products affected by ultra-violet radiations from the sun. **1967** E. CHAMBERS *Photolitho-Offset* vii. 85 The term *density* refers to the light-absorbing ability of the [silver] layer. **1963** R. R. A. HIGHAM *Handbk. Papermaking* viii. 210 Opacity is dependent on the number of light-absorptive or -reflective fibre surfaces in a sheet. **1936** *Discovery* Nov. 358/1 Light-actuated apparatus for home use is now on the market. **1924** J. A. THOMSON *Sci. Old & New* xxvi. 142 The Fierasfer..is a light-avoiding fish, related to the sand-eel. **1965** B. E. FREEMAN tr. *Vandel's Biospeleol.* iv. 39 The light-avoiding planarians are simple to keep in captivity. **1902** *Westm. Gaz.* 29 Sept. 3/1 The energy required for producing pendulous movements of atoms and molecules giving light-effects must be very small as compared with the total energy employed. **1962** R. G. HAGGAR *Dict. Art Terms* 192/1 J. M. W. Turner..carried research into light effects further than any previous artist. **1964** *Oceanogr. & Marine Biol.* II. 351 The decrease in light-emitting capacity of a methanol solution of.. luciferin. **1869** *Chambers's Jrnl.* 10 Apr. 231/1 Under the high power and vast light-gathering capacity of Sir W. Herschel's four-foot reflector. **1960** *Farmer & Stockbreeder* 8 Mar. 134 The Meopta 12 × 60 has the rare combination of high magnification and brilliant light-gathering power even at night and under bad climatic conditions. **1895** J. H. & A. COMSTOCK *Man. Study Insects* xxi. 562 The Light-loving Anomala, *Anomala lucicola*..also feeds on the leaves of grape. **1974** A. HUXLEY *Plant & Planet* viii. 99 During the twelve-hour period of the average night.. the plant is regarded as 'dark-loving', while in the other twelve-hour period it is 'light-loving'. **1950** *Sci. News* XV. 43 The brightnesses thus catalogued are, however, only apparent... So, in order to compare the light-outputs of the stars, we introduce the idea of Absolute Magnitude. **1958** *Newnes Compl. Amat. Photogr.* 120 Recent developments have been in the direction of maintaining high efficiency and light-output operating at lower voltages. **1961** G. MILLERSON *Technique Television Production* iii. 38 Construction differences [in lenses]..can vary their respective light-passing abilities, although their stop numbers may be measurably identical. **1845** *Harmony of Comprehensible World* Essay II. XIII. 221 Between some bodies there may be no light-producing sympathy, because the mutual relations of their constituent molecules may not be such as to develope light. **1964** V. B. WIGGLESWORTH *Life of Insects* viii. 126 It is among the insects that some of the most brilliant and certainly the most complex types of light-producing organs are to be found. **1880** 'MARK TWAIN' *Tramp Abroad* I. xvi. 129 Of Light-rays was the Figure wove. **1950** *Sci. News* XV. 17 Light rays cannot bring about a photo-chemical change unless they are absorbed. **1854** GEO. ELIOT tr. *Feuerbach's Essence Christianity* v. 61 Tears are the light-reflecting drops which mirror the nature of the Christian's God. **1951** S. SPENDER *World within World* iii. 180 Their minds like little caves of calculating darkness which the light-reflecting snow has never penetrated. **1963** Light-reflective [see *light-absorptive* above]. **1889** E. CARPENTER *Civilization* 88 It [*sc.* modern science] takes the emerald, and breaks it up; treats of its color and light-refracting qualities. **1957** PARTRIDGE *English gone Wrong* ii. 29 The light-refracting heads of the Communist philosophers and propagandists. **1958** *A.M.A. Arch. Industr. Health* XVIII. 29/1 A plot of the light-scatter decay was divided into exponential portions by a slope-analysis method. **1961** G. MILLERSON *Technique Television Production* iii. 43 Optically speaking, there are several obvious causes for lack of clarity: dirty lenses, light-scatter in the lens. **1936** *Discovery* May 151/1 It was not until the appearance of a new type of light-sensitive cell, known as the rectifier or semi-conducting cell, that photo-electric exposure meters became popular. **1946** *Nature* 28 Sept. 454/2 *N. texana* also contains strains which have light-sensitive seeds. **1962** *Science Survey* III. 240 The retina is light-sensitive because it contains one or more photosensitive pigments located in its visual receptors. **1920** A. S. EDDINGTON *Space, Time & Gravitation* iii. 50 It would, in fact, be possible for an observer travelling along *NP* to receive a light-signal..announcing the event *O*, just as he reached *N*. **1930** *Morning Post* 19 July 13/6 An extension of the system of light signals for road traffic. **1964** *Amer. Jrnl. Physics* XXXII. 262/2 At an arbitrary instant *t*..a light signal *S* is emitted at the origin *A* of the coordinate system. **1960** H. PINTER *Caretaker* II. 48 There used to be a wall plug..but it doesn't work. I had to fit it in the light socket. **1935** A. H. HAFFENDEN (*title*) Light-song. **1946** L. B. LYON *Rough Walk Home* 27 Our anguish has a hand, that gropes For melody, for the light-song of the sun. **1903** *Edin. Rev.* July 113 Because a spectrum line changes with change of ..velocity of light source and other disturbing causes, the value of its record is thereby increased. **1961** G. MILLERSON *Technique Television Production* iii. 49 Prolonged static captions, and visible light-sources in the scene, are the worst offenders. **1938** W. DE LA MARE *Memory* 81 Peace beyond telling share with the light-stilled eye. **1892** F. C. ALLSOP *Pract. Electr.-Light Fitting* iii. 39 Lamp or branch switches are designated either by the number of lamps they are intended to control, or..by their current-carrying capacity. They are thus called 1, 2, or 3 light, or 1, 2, or 3 ampère switches. **1926** G. HUNTING *Vicarion* iv. 63 He went back to his light-switch, closed the closet door which stood ajar, and brought his chair toward them again. **1972** 'H. CARMICHAEL' *Naked to Grave* i. 14 He heard the click of a light switch in the bedroom. **1894** 'MARK TWAIN' in *Century Mag.* Jan. 336 He asked questions that would have brought light-throwing answers. **1902** *Westm. Gaz.* 1 July 2/1 An excellent translation of a light-throwing and thought-provoking book.

16. light-adaptation, self-adjustment of the eye to increased intensity of light by means of a decrease in the sensitivity of the retina; also, in extended use, any reversible change in an organism that occurs in response to increased light; so **light-adapted** *pa. pple.* and *ppl. a.*, in the state that results from light-adaptation; **light barrier,** (*a*) a limit to the resolution possible with an optical microscope arising out of the finite length of light waves (*nonce-use*); (*b*) the speed of light as the limiting speed attainable by any object; **light-box,** (*a*) (earlier example); (*c*) a box-like piece of equipment containing a light and usu. having translucent glass on one side which provides an evenly lighted surface; **light bucket** *Astr.* (*colloq.*), a telescope, regarded as a device for collecting and focusing a large quantity of low-intensity radiation; **light bulb** = *BULB *sb.* 4; **light-buoy,** a buoy equipped with a warning light which flashes intermittently; **light button,** a knob or disc which, when pressed, turns a light on or off; **light-change** *Astr.*, a change in the amount of light received from a variable star; **light check** *Theatr.* (see quot. 1952); **light cone** *Physics,* a surface in space-time which appears conical when represented in three dimensions and comprises all the world-points from which a light signal would reach a given point (defining the apex) simultaneously (and which therefore appear simultaneous to an observer at the apex); **light cord,** a cord which hangs from a ceiling or lamp stand and operates an electric light when pulled; **light cue,** (*a*) *Broadcasting,* a cue indicated by a light being switched on; (*b*) *Theatr.* (see quot. 1961); **light-cure** *rare* or *Obs.*, a cure effected by sunlight or artificial light; also *attrib.*; **light curve** *Astr.*, a graph showing the variation in the light received over a period of time from a variable star or other heavenly body; **light-demander,** a tree that will not tolerate shade; so **light-demanding** *a.*, of trees or, occas., other plants, needing full light; **light-fastness,** resistance to discoloration by light; so **light-fast** *a.*; **light-filter** *Photogr.* = *colour-filter* (see *COLOUR *sb.*[1] 18); **light-fixture,** the flex, socket, and other equipment which is used with a light bulb; **light fog** *Photogr.* (see quot. 1940 and FOG *sb.*[2] 4); **light-grasp** *Astr.*, light-gathering power (of a telescope); **light guide,** a cylinder or strip of transparent material, or a bundle of them, along which light can travel with little loss, by means of total internal reflection; **light gun** = **light pen*; **light meter,** an instrument for measuring the intensity of light; *esp.* an exposure meter; **light microscope,** a conventional microscope, in which ordinary light is used; **light organ,** in luminescent animals, the structure emitting light; **light pen,** a hand-held, pen-like device that incorporates a lens, photoelectric cell, and amplifier and may be used to feed information by wire to a data-processing system by placing or moving the tip on the screen of a cathode-ray tube or other surface so that electrical impulses are transmitted to the system; **light pipe** = **light guide*; **light-pressure,** pressure exerted on a body by light incident on it; **light quantum** *Physics* = *PHOTON; **light-scattering,** scattering of light, *spec.* of monochromatic light by a solution as a method of determining the molecular weight of dissolved polymers and investigating their conformation; **light-sensation,** in the study of visual perception, the sensation produced by light; **light show,** a display of changing coloured lights or varied film strips, freq. accompanying popular music; also *attrib.*; **light-stand,** a stand to support a light; **light station,** a group of buildings which includes a lighthouse and associated buildings for housing personnel, supplies, and equipment; **light-tight** *a.* (further examples); **light-time** *Astr.*, the time taken by light to travel from a distant source to the observer; **light trap,** (*a*) *Photogr.*, a device for excluding light from a room or other space without preventing access into it; (*b*) a device for attracting, catching, and sometimes killing, night-flying insects; so **light-trapped** *a.*, provided with a light trap; **light value** *Photogr.*, a number representing on an arbitrary scale the intensity of light from a particular direction; *light-value shutter,* a shutter having the aperture and shutter speed settings linked so that they can be altered together in such a way as to keep the amount of light admitted during an exposure constant; **light valve,** a device which regulates the amount of light passing through it according to the magnitude of an applied electrical signal; **light-well,** a shaft designed to admit light from above into inner rooms or a staircase of a building; **light-year,** add: it is approximately equal to $9{\cdot}46 \times 10^{12}$ km. ($5{\cdot}87 \times 10^{12}$ miles); also *fig.*; (further examples).

1900 W. H. RIVERS in E. A. Schäfer *Textbk. Physiol.* II. 1080 If the eye remained in a condition of light-adaptation, red and blue..became gradually blacker. **1962** H. C. WESTON *Sight, Light & Work* (ed. 2) i. 8 Thus, after full light-adaptation, complete dark-adaptation may require about an hour. **1964** *Oceanogr. & Marine Biol.* II. 352 Prolonged laboratory culture, starvation, and light- or dark-adaptation had relatively little effect on luminescent ability [of the copepod *Metridia lucens*]. **1900** W. H. RIVERS in E. A. Schäfer *Textbk. Physiol.* II. 1073 He found that in complete dark-adaptation the recurrent image followed the original immediately and was brighter than to the light-adapted eye. **1935** *Discovery* May 138/1 A source of light which is almost or quite invisible to a light-adapted eye, that is to one coming in from daylight, is quite obvious to a dark-adapted eye. **1950** *Sci. News* XV. 25 A [spontaneous] change in fixation direction is quite possible, particularly when the eye is not fully light-adapted or where there is too large an object for precise fixation. **1959** *Listener* 31 Dec. 1161/1 When one gets down to sizes round about the wavelength of light.. one runs into a barrier, which might be called the light barrier, that no microscope working by means of light can break through. **1964** M. MCLUHAN *Understanding Media* (1967) I. vi. 68 No further acceleration is possible this side of the light barrier. **1968** A. DIMENT *Great Spy Race* x. 180 The faster than light spaceships will bring the stars down into our backyard, for once one has broken the so-called 'light-barrier' there is no limit to speed. **1849** THACKERAY

Pendennis I. xix. 173 Helen..went for a light-box and his cigar-case. **1940** J. O. Kraehenbuehl *Electr. Illumination* viii. 108/2 The light boxes commonly used may be divided into two classes: those which are covered with some form of transmitting medium which is translucent.., and those which have prismatic lens plates. **1943** J. S. Huxley *TVA* 98 Note the flush light boxes with patent lenses at the side of the stairway. **1957** *Screen Printer & Display Producer* July 16/3 Pin-holes were spotted out over a lightbox before printing. **1962** H. C. Weston *Sight, Light & Work* (ed. 2) vi. 195 These devices consist of a light-box of suitable size, the cover-glass or vizor of which allows the emission of light in a regular pattern. **1968** *New Scientist* 31 Oct. 260/2 One piece of equipment is a 34-ft 'light bucket' for seeking out point sources of gamma rays in the universe. **1970** *Nature* 7 Feb. 492/2 Infrared telescopes, more properly called flux collectors—light buckets in the language of astronomy—are cheap compared with similar equipment for the visible spectrum. **1884** Light bulb [see Bulb *sb.* 4]. **1946** E. Hodgins *Mr. Blandings builds his Dream House* (1947) I. v. 78 The cost of your house doesn't get you moved into it with light bulbs in all the sockets. **1975** M. Kenyon *Mr Big* xix. 185 His muscled black tangled limbs trailing flex and popping lightbulbs from the overhead fixtures. **1894** W. Le Queux *Gt. War in Eng. in 1897* xxix. 236 A cruiser..was lying near the Herwit light-buoy. **1930** W. de la Mare *Desert Islands* 19 Light-ship or beacon or winking light-buoy rocked in the cradle of the deep. **1951** *Oxf. Jun. Encycl.* IV. 71/2 The older light buoys exhibit their light day and night; but they are gradually being superseded by buoys which automatically light up at sunset and extinguish themselves at dawn. **1929** D. Hammett *Dain Curse* x. 95 [My] hand touched the light button. I had sense enough to push it. Light scorched my eyes. **1970** R. Busby *Frighteners* xvii. 172 The time-switch light-button on the wall. **1890** A. M. Clerke *Syst. Stars* ix. 139 The light-change of S. Cancri, the second of the Algol variables, was discovered by Mr. Hind in 1848. **1928** *Publ. Washburn Observatory Univ. Wisconsin* XV. I. iv. 29 Ellipsoidal figure of the bodies would account for most of the light-change. **1933** P. Godfrey *Back-Stage* i. 18 'Light checks' are any alterations to the opening lighting of the scene. **1952** Granville *Dict. Theatr. Terms* 110 *Light check*, a dimming of lights. **1922** E. P. Adams tr. *Einstein's Meaning of Relativity* ii. 42 *P'* lies outside the 'light-cone'. **1964** A. O. Barut *Electrodynamics* i. 8 All time-like vectors are inside the light cone and the space-like ones are outside. **1964** *Listener* 17 Dec. 976/2 Encouragement also comes from the usual diagrams in physics text books representing such relativistic ideas as the 'light cone'. **1968** M. Lockwood *Accessory* (1969) iii. 74 She reached accurately for the hanging light cord. **1972** E. Page *Family & Friends* viii. 124 He pulled at the light cord, glanced at the clock. **1929** *Radio Times* 8 Nov. 389/1 They will sit at the [control] panel, flashing 'light cues', fading and cross-fading studios. **1930** L. Hartmann *Theatre Lighting* iii. 37 Light cues are written down during the progress of a rehearsal. **1961** Bowman & Ball *Theatre Lang.* 201 *Light cue*.., the cue for the commencement of some planned change in illumination. **1901** *Chambers's Jrnl.* Dec. 844/2 Hospitals..have already obtained apparatus for the light-cure of lupus. **1904** *Daily Chron.* 11 Apr. 5/3 Yesterday morning King Edward.. paid a lengthy visit to Professor Finsen's light-cure institution. **1890** A. M. Clerke *Syst. Stars* viii. 116 The light-curve [of U Geminorum] takes more or less the form of a double peak with a saddle between. **1956** *Astrophysical Jrnl.* CXXIII. 12 The light-curve for the 1952 eclipse, as measured in the Sudan, is much flatter than the curves..from the 1947 observations. **1968** *Project Icarus* (Mass. Inst. Technol.) i. 7 The rate of rotation of an asteroid and the axis of its rotation can be found approximately by careful analysis of the shape and variation of its light curve. **1975** *Sci. Amer.* Mar. 26/3 The X-ray light curve of Centaurus X-3 is the curve of a typical eclipsing binary system. **1891** W. Schlich *Man. Forestry* II. iv. 306 As regards light-requirement it [*sc.* the Weymouth Pine] stands half-way between light-demanders and shade-bearers. **1928** R. S. Troup *Silvicultural Syst.* v. 67 If the group system is applied to strong light-demanders, larger gaps would be necessary. **1966** *Times* 21 Apr. 16/6 Some trees are such emphatic light-demanders..that they will not thrive if there is any overhead shade. **1889** W. Schlich *Man. Forestry* I. ii. 117 Certain species [which] cannot thrive unless they enjoy a large measure of light throughout life..are called 'light demanding'. **1952** H. L. Edlin *Forester's Handbk.* viii. 113 Trees described as light-demanding will only succeed if grown in the open. **1964** *Oceanogr. & Marine Biol.* II. 213 In his [*sc.* Ernst's] opinion *Udotea* is a light demanding species [of green alga]. **1957** M. B. Picken *Fashion Dict.* 213/1 Lightfast. **1971** *Jrnl. Oil & Colour Chemists' Assoc.* LIV. 847 Bright red paints based on cadmium sulpho-selenide pigments, which are highly light-fast. **1913** C. E. Pellew *Dyes & Dyeing* iii. 63 The test for light-fastness is usually made by partially covering a dyed skein with a piece of wood.. and exposing it to direct sunlight. **1959** *B.S.I. News* June 4/1 The colour, colour-strength, transparency and light-fastness of these inks in terms of comparison with master standard inks. **1962** J. T. Marsh *Self-Smoothing Fabrics* vi. 75 Dimethylol dihydroxy ethylene urea appears to be quite outstanding in its effect on the light-fastness of dyed goods in general and those containing reactive dyes in particular. **1971** *Jrnl. Oil & Colour Chemists' Assoc.* LIV. 857 Better light-fastness of pigments, non-yellowing media..are thus seen to be important requirements. **1901** *Chambers's Jrnl.* June 367/2 For use either in orthochromatic or colour photography, light-filters..are now commercially produced. **1958** *Newnes Compl. Amat. Photogr.* iv. 83 The smaller increases in exposure needed when light-filters are employed. **1923** *T. Eaton & Co. Catal.* Spring & Summer 357/5 Light fixture, for dining-room or living-room. **1939** D. Parker *Here Lies* 27 He bought..storm-windows, and light-fixtures. **1889** E. J. Wall *Dict. Photogr.* 77 *Light fog* makes its appearance generally all over the plate. **1915** *Photo-Era* XXXV. 170/1 Plate and films must be loaded..with the utmost care to avoid light-fog. **1940** *Chambers's Techn. Dict.* 449/1 *Light-fog* (Photog.), fog in an emulsion, caused by intrusion of extraneous light into a camera or other apparatus which is intended to be light-tight. **1946** *Nature* 6 July 18/1 Wood..used the instrument in his charge for those types of astronomical observation for which it was eminently suitable by virtue of its short focal-length, large field of good definition and powerful light-grasp. **1961** *Listener* 7 Sept. 353/3 For televising relatively faint objects, such as planets, it is necessary to use a powerful telescope with considerable light-grasp. **1951** *Jrnl. Sci. Instrum.* XXVIII 188/1 (*heading*) A divided light guide for coincidence counting of scintillations due to alpha particles. *Ibid.*, A forked light guide was constructed from..Perspex rod. **1972** *Science* 9 June 1128/1 Luminescence was detected through a fiber-optic light guide. **1970** O. Dopping *Computers & Data Processing* xi. 179 An extension of the CRT terminal is the light pen, or light gun, which can be used for identifying details in the picture displayed by the computer and even for making sketches which the computer can record. **1972** *Computers & Humanities* VII. 5 With the use of a light gun the linguist can select from alternative expansions in phrase structure trees. **1921** *Gas Jrnl.* CLVI. 563/2 Mr. Haydn T. Harrison next interested the members with a description of the 'Benjamin' Lightmeter, which is a simple portable apparatus to measure illumination, and enable one to give intelligent and expert advice on factory lighting. **1943** D. Baker *Trio* ii. 92 A light-meter on a cord, some photographic lenses, an envelope full of negatives. **1973** A. Broinowski *Take one Ambassador* xiii. 211 Peering at the light-meter reading on his Asahi Pentax. **1941** Light microscope [see *electron microscope* s.v. *electron[2] 2 b]. **1961** *Lancet* 5 Aug. 295/1 There are great difficulties in interpreting the shapes of these small chromosomes because they are almost at the limit of light-microscope resolution. **1899** D. Sharp in *Cambr. Nat. Hist.* VI. v. 259 The structure of the light organs [of *Pyrophorus*] is essentially similar to that of the Lampyridæ. **1928** Russell & Yonge *Seas* 192 Some of these cuttlefish from the deep sea have over twenty light organs in various parts of the body. **1954** N. B. Marshall *Aspects Deep Sea Biol.* xi. 273 May not some of the light organs which stud the body [of certain fishes] also attract prey? **1969** R. F. Chapman *Insects* vi. 86 In most beetles the light organs are relatively compact. **1958** *Proc. IRE* XLVI. 1123/1 Narrow-based germanium photodiodes have been fabricated with intrinsic response times of less than 75 mμsec... They have been used with success in many applications among which are:.. detector in a transistorized 'light pen' for high-speed oscilloscope readout. **1964** *Discovery* Oct. 53/2 (*caption*) Display console of a computer which illustrates actual graphs, characters and drawings stored within the machine in digital form. The operator can make corrections to the display with a 'light pen' which automatically corrects the stored information. **1966** *Sci. Amer.* Sept. 95/2 The stylus-photocell arrangement called the light pen can be used to make the cathode-ray-tube display serve for the manual input of sketches and diagrams. **1973** *Courier & Advertiser* (Dundee) 21 Feb. 7/1 The 280's light pen will 'read' information from colour bar coded tags and data from 48 terminals can be fed into a central data unit and recorded on magnetic tape ready for computer processing. **1961** *Physical Rev.* CXXIII. 1150/2 A dielectric rod constitutes a waveguide (light pipe) and thus additional modes of propagation..are introduced. **1970** *New Scientist* 13 Aug. 340/1 Light can travel along a bundle of certain glass fibres—a light pipe. **1972** *Sci. Amer.* Sept. 112/2 Although light can be conducted through carefully fabricated pipes a centimeter or so in diameter with an attenuation of only a few decibels per kilometer..light pipes have the drawback that they must either be perfectly straight or be provided with optical means for bending the rays wherever the pipe bends. **1903** *Encycl. Brit.* Index, Light-pressure. **1908** *Westm. Gaz.* 23 Oct. 5/3 There is also a small and sharply curved envelope on the side of the nucleus [of the comet] towards the sun, the presumption being that the matter ejected from the head in this direction is quickly turned back by the 'light-pressure' exerted by the sun. **1968** R. A. Lyttleton *Mysteries Solar Syst.* v. 178 With comminution of cometary particles occurring mainly on the perihelion side of the orbit, light-pressure will automatically select all those of appropriate size and expel them from the comet. **1925** D. L. Thomson in J. A. Thomson *Sci. & Relig.* 211 It follows from the modern 'Quantum Theory' ..that there are 'smallest-possible' amounts of light, which we might call..light-quanta. **1938** R. W. Lawson tr. *Hevesy & Paneth's Man. Radioactivity* (ed. 2) ix. 105 According to this hypothesis, the emission of β-radiation is not a unitary elementary process like the emission of a light quantum, but a dual process consisting of the simultaneous emission of an electron and a neutrino. **1948** *Sci. News* VI. 75 In the quantum theory a light signal cannot be sub-divided indefinitely, but consists of finite units, so-called light quanta, or 'photons'. **1974** *Sci. Amer.* Oct. 68/1 Carbohydrates are the direct result of the photosynthetic activity of green plants... The energy needed to promote this reaction is provided by light quanta from the sun. **1926** H. C. Macpherson *Mod. Astron.* iv. 64 Dr. Wright, photographing Mars,..concluded that the Martian atmosphere was at least 120 miles in depth and possessed appreciable absorbing and light-scattering power. **1935** *Trans. Faraday Soc.* XXXI. 1324 We may therefore conclude that the main factor in the light-scattering of an isotropic protein is the molecular weight of the protein and that its scattering power is a true measure of its molecular dimensions. **1965** Peacocke & Drysdale *Molecular Basis Heredity* iv. 34 The hydrodynamic and light-scattering measurements both indicate that in solution its configuration is that of a stiffened coil, rather than that of a rigid rod or of a completely random coil. **1972** Billingham & Jenkins in A. D. Jenkins *Polymer Sci.* I. ii. 147 Despite the complexity and expense of the technique, light scattering remains one of the most useful techniques for the determination of weight average molecular weights of polymers. **1895** E. B. Titchener in *Amer. Jrnl. Psychol.* VII. 82 *Lichtempfindung*, light sensation. **1914** Williams & Waterlow tr. *Mach's Analysis of Sensations* x. 211 The habit of..giving attention to a large and spatially cohering mass of light-sensations. **1924** R. M. Ogden tr. *Koffka's Growth of Mind* iii. § 13. 134 The most varied light-, dark-, and colour-sensations. **1937** *Discovery* July 216/1 The nature of light-sensation, colour-tone, colour-blindness. **1966** E. Denson in *Berkeley Barb* 1 Apr. 4/1 Led by Tony Martin's light show, which fills the huge wall behind the bands and their 30 foot row of amplifiers and electronics with red shapes shifting in time to the music, the hall is filled with swaying, writhing people. **1967** *Ramparts* 9 Mar. 12/1 The light show atmospheric technique of projecting slides and wild colors on the walls during rock dances. **1969** *It* 11–24 Apr. 13/1 If it is regarded that lightshows began when the 'underground' or 'psychedelic' revolutions began, then it is doubtful that lightshows will ever recover from the damage inflicted during the capitalists' rape of those movements. **1971** E. E. Landy *Underground Dict.* 120 Light shows are given in auditoriums, coffeehouses, etc. They are put on for the purpose of simulating a hallucinogenic experience. **1836** N. P. Willis *Inklings of Adventure* I. 206 In another moment the light stand was swept from between us, and he struck me down with a blow that would have felled a giant. **1867** A. D. Whitney *Summer in L. Goldthwaite's Life* vi. 119 On this little green stood..a round white-pine light-stand with her work-basket and a few books. **1966** A. Feininger *Compl. Photographer* iv. 154 A boom extension arm that fits on a light stand is invaluable. **1953** *Aids to Navigation Manual* (U.S. Coast Guard) xxix. 3/1 The mission of a light station is to service, tend, and maintain a light on a fixed structure. **1956** *Navigation Dict.* (U.S. Naval Oceanogr. Office) 124/1 *Light station*, a group of buildings including a lighthouse and additional buildings housing personnel, fog signal, radiobeacon, and any other equipment associated with the lighthouse. **1969** *Islander* (Victoria, B.C.) 21 Dec. 16/1 It was December 1934 at Pachena Point, a lonely lightstation on Vancouver Island's stormy west coast. **1971** *Bahamian Rev.* Nov. 5/3 Mrs. Pierre grew up on light stations, as her father was a light-keeper. **1911** T. E. Lawrence *Let.* 31 Mar. (1938) 101 How to render light-tight a dark slide. **1942** *R.A.F. Jrnl.* 2 May 13 One of the..operators had just completed a spool, and my guide took it from her when she had fitted it into its light-tight case. **1970** *Jrnl. General Psychol.* LXXXII. 208 Behind the opening were a slide holder and a 12 volt d.c. light, both enclosed in a light-tight housing. **1920** A. S. Eddington *Space, Time & Gravitation* 12 But then you must know the speed of the earth through the aether. It may have shortened the light-time by going some way to meet the light coming from Arcturus. **1952** *Astrophysical Jrnl.* CXVI. 211 The problem of the determination of the light-time orbit will occur with increasing frequency as the observational data become more accurate and extend over greater stretches of time. **1968** P. R. Escobal *Methods Astrodynamics* vi. 185 (*heading*) Light time correction. **1906** R. C. Bayley *Compl. Photographer* ix. 99 Many otherwise efficient ventilating systems are rendered almost useless by the light trap. **1931** A. D. Imms *Recent Adv. Entomol.* vi. 141 In many countries practical entomologists have made use of light traps as a means for the quantitative attraction and destruction of noxious species of Lepidoptera. **1935** H. W. & M. Miles *Insect Pests Glasshouse Crops* iii. 54 Light-traps also attract the moths and might be used with advantage in cases of persistent infestation. **1965** M. J. Langford *Basic Photogr.* xv. 266 If..the darkroom is designed for entry or exit of staff without introducing light, some form of 'light trap' is essential. **1973** *Entomologist's Rec.* LXXXV. 95 On the night of May 19th I had an unusual, yet unfortunate, bonus of moths in my light trap. **1956** *Focal Encycl. Photogr.* 677/1 Many darkrooms..have light-trapped entrances so that the staff can pass freely in and out while sensitized materials are being handled. **1958** *Newnes Compl. Amat. Photogr.* iv. 75 The leading end of the film projects through a light-trapped slit, ready for loading into the camera. **1956** *Focal Encycl. Photogr.* 680/1 Exposure values, as used on shutters, are also frequently referred to as light values. **1957** T. L. J. Bentley *Man. Miniature Camera* (ed. 5) iv. 46 As the latest development in the between-lens type of shutter has come the so-called light-value shutter. **1958** *Newnes Compl. Amat. Photogr.* ii. 38 The light-value shutter is a modern device..designed to make speed and aperture setting more easy, and making use of the light value system. **1970** *Which?* June 186/2 You then point the meter at the subject and the needle will move along the light value scale... On some meters, instead of transferring the light value from one scale to another, you move a pointer until it overlaps the needle. **1928** *Trans. Soc. Motion Pict. Engin.* XII. 730 (*heading*) Sound recording with the light valve. **1932** *Discovery* July 234/2 Three light valves (each a specially developed form of Kerr cell) modulated the beams from the arcs. **1971** L. B. Happé *Basic Motion Pict. Technol.* v. 165 In variable density recording the intensity of illumination passing into this lens system from a lamp and condenser lens is modulated by a light valve consisting of a pair of narrow metal ribbons mounted under tension in a magnetic field at right angles to the direction of the film movement. **1925** V. G. Childe *Dawn European Civilization* v. 82 The palace was probably provided with a light-well and decorated with frescoes. **1958** *Listener* 23 Oct. 644/1 The nineteenth-century office block, with the quiet internal lawn shrunk to the scale of the light-well. **1949** A. Huxley *Let.* 26 Feb. (1969) 593 Hubble..showed us the first pictures taken by the 200 inch telescope... On the random sample selected, the nebulae went on with uniform density to a billion lightyears. **1957** I. Asimov *Naked Sun* (1958) i. 22 That..momentary transition through hyperspace that transferred a ship and all it contained from one point in space to another, light-years away. **1962** F. I. Ordway et al. *Basic Astronautics* vi. 289 (*caption*) Known stars within five parsecs (16½ light years) of the Sun. **1971** *Guardian* 22 July 11/4 Professor Peter Hungerford..said ..abortions should be the decision of the mother alone. This is light years from FPA policy. **1973** A. Holden *Girl on Beach* 143 He really is..a spare-time amateur art critic, light-years removed from a creative artist.

b. *Astr.* Combs. modelled on *light-year*, denoting the distance travelled by light in the time specified; so *light-day*, *-minute*, etc.

1923 G. D. Birkhoff *Relativity & Mod. Physics* ii. 20 Since it required $(t_2 - t_1)/2$ seconds for the light to travel from the one particle to the other, *B* must have been at a distance of $x = (t_2 - t_1)/2$ 'light-seconds' from *A* at the time *t*. **1925** D. L. Thomson in J. A. Thomson *Sci. & Relig.* 215 A light year is over five million million miles, and the sun is only eight-and-a-half light minutes from the earth. **1963**

Nature 18 May 651/2 If the flashes are real, either the optical source itself is of the order of light-days in size, or ..it must contain substructures of this scale. **1964** *Astrophysical Jrnl.* CXL. 15 Consider a region one light-month. i.e., 7×10^{16} cm, in radius. *Ibid.*, A maximum flash duration of only a few hours is possible for a region a light-month in radius. **1970** *Sci. Amer.* Dec. 25/3 The rapid changes in flux imply that if quasi-stellar objects are as remote as their red shifts indicate, they must have diameters reckoned in light-months, or even less. This means that such objects are on a scale only slightly larger than that of our solar system, which is about one light-day in diameter.

light, *a.*[1] Add: **2. b.** Applied to elements whose specific gravity (or atomic number) is relatively low; *light metal*, a metal of low specific gravity, esp. aluminium or magnesium; so *light alloy*, an alloy based on such a metal.

1912 Rosenhain & Archbutt in *Proc. Inst. Mech. Engin.* Apr. 323 It was decided in the first place to confine the investigations to alloys consisting principally of aluminium, which may be conveniently grouped under the term 'light alloys'. **1924** *Proc. Physical Soc.* XXXVI. 418 The other light elements, hydrogen, helium, lithium, carbon and oxygen gave no detectable effect beyond 7 cm. **1926** *Industr. & Engin. Chem.* Oct. 1016/1 The production of the light metals has only been rendered possible by the comparatively recent work of chemists and chemical engineers. **1936** R. P. Bell tr. *Bjerrum's Inorg. Chem.* 213 The metals fall naturally into two groups: the light metals with densities below four, and the heavy metals with densities above seven. The light metals are the most electropositive, i.e., they have a specially great tendency to form positive ions. *Ibid.*, The light metals react readily with many substances. **1948** 'N. Shute' *No Highway* i. 12, I couldn't find anything about light alloy structures in fatigue prior to the year 1927. **1949** A. J. Field tr. *A. von Zeerleder's Technol. Light Metals* i. 1 There is at the present time no standard value of this property [*sc.* specific gravity] recognized as a qualification for the title 'light metal'. **1959** *Times Rev. Industry* Apr. 55/1 Re-organization within the light-metal industries. **1962** *Appl. Spectrosc.* XVI. 162/1 The data..show the great advantage of using a chromium target tube for light element analysis. *Ibid.* 159/1 Light elements are defined as those elements having an atomic number less than 25. **1969** *Jane's Freight Containers 1968–69* 533/1 Containers: non-standard collapsible light-alloy.

4. *light line* = *light water-line* (see Light *a.*[1] 4).

1894 W. H. White *Man. Naval Archit.* (ed. 3) 47 The displacement of a ship between her light and load lines could be estimated, and would give the true 'dead-weight capability'. **1923** *Man. Seamanship* (Admiralty) II. 270 The portion of the ship's bottom, between the light and loadline, termed the *tapboot*, is difficult to protect from corrosion. **1948** R. de Kerchove *Internat. Maritime Dict.* 416/2 *Light line*, the line of immersion at which a vessel floats when in ballast draft or light trim.

c. *light industry*: an industry making use of relatively light and therefore easily handled materials. (Cf. Heavy *a.*[1] 5 b in Dict. and Suppl.)

1921 *San Francisco Chron.* 20 Sept. 22/1 There may be maintained in a Commercial District..Light Industries, clearly incidental to the operation of an Amusement Park. **1930** *Economist* 1 Nov. (Russ. Suppl.) 8/2 Only 22 per cent. is allotted to the building and equipment of factories devoted to 'light' industries. **1944** J. S. Huxley *On Living in Revolution* 128 Encouragement must be given to light and secondary industries, for only so can a reasonably balanced economy grow up in colonial areas. **1957** [see *heavy *a.*[1] 5 b]. **1961** E. A. Powdrill *Vocab. Land Planning* iv. 66 'Light industry' is any industry which does not commit a nuisance by noise, smell, fumes, soot or grit. **1974** E. Ambler *Dr. Frigo* iii. 156 The transformation he envisaged—roads, housing,..hydro-electric schemes, light industry, fertiliser plants.

6. Also *light car*, a small economical car made from light materials.

1908 *Westm. Gaz.* 16 Mar. 5/2 This being essentially a light-car year, more than ordinary interest is manifested in the 8-h.p. two-cylindered polished chassis. **1914** *Light Car Manual* 1 Manufacturers have..solved the difficulty of how to produce a car which shall give all the comfort anyone could desire, and yet..compare favourably with the cost..of a motorcycle and side-car. The whole secret of this solution is summed up in the words 'light car'. **1963** [see *fore-car* (*fore- 5)]. **1970** C. F. Caunter *Light Car* (ed. 2) p. xv, The popularity of the light car, particularly in its minicar form, had the effect in the 1960's of reducing the average size of motor cars in general.

b. Applied to small, relatively light-weight aeroplanes, such as most private (non-commercial) passenger aeroplanes.

1923 *Flight* XV. 168/1 For want of a better term we have referred to the machine as a 'light plane', much as in the automobile world cars below a certain size and weight are termed light cars. **1933** *Meccano Mag.* Mar. 192/1 Light aeroplanes will fly to and from these places from the main routes. **1965** Nayler & Ower *Aviation* v. 56/1 The Piper Aircraft Corporation led the world in the sales of light aircraft in 1959. **1971** P. J. McMahon *Aircraft Propulsion* xi. 331 Occasionally designers of light aircraft look to the possibilities of using automobile type engines as power units. **1971** *Flying* (N.Y.) Apr. 39/2 In fact, it may well be the best all-around lightplane in the world.

18. Also in phr. *light duty*: military service which does not entail full-time work.

1916 A. Huxley *Let.* 13 Feb. (1969) 91 He is still on light duty—so gets plenty of leave from Salisbury Plain. **1953** A. Baron *Human Kind* xiii. 100, I shouldn't be here by rights. I'm a light-duty man.

19. (Further examples.)

1827 L. T. Rede *Road to Stage* 16 In small theatres, the light comedian must play the seconds in tragedy. *Ibid.* 60 In light comedy it is continually requisite to execute music. **1841** Macaulay in *Edin. Rev.* Jan. 524 A great and rapid reform in..our lighter literature was the effect of his [*sc.* Collier's] labours. **1844** J. Cowell *30 Yrs. among Players* 43 The light and low comedy. **1872** D. G. Rossetti *Let.* 20 Sept. (1967) III. 1064 Your idea of George's possibly finding an outlet in light literature does not seem promising to me. **1874** W. Lennox *My Recoll.* I. 186 The highest walks of light tragedy. **1888** G. O. Seilhamer *Hist. Amer. Theatre* I. 23 Comedy parts or light tragedy roles. **1897** *National Police Gaz.* (U.S.) 26 May 6/4 Miss Blanche is, perhaps, the cleverest little lady on the burlesque and light comedy stage. **1929** *Radio Times* 8 Nov. 406/3 *Journey's End*..is not a memorial service; nor, at the other extreme, is it light entertainment. **1958** *Times Lit. Suppl.* 5 Dec. 701/3 The climax, both exciting and comic, just succeeds in lifting this novel out of the light-entertainment class. **1961** *John o' London's* 18 May 567/4 A more profitable career as a light-comedy lead. **1974** P. De Vries *Glory of Hummingbird* iii. 27 Some more pretty good nature lyrics and then a batch of light verse. **1975** *Times* 10 Feb. 3/7 Any programme of cuts..would have to be closely vetted by the IBA to ensure that they maintain a balance between light entertainment programmes and more serious productions.

b. *Light Programme*, one of the regular programme services of the B.B.C., chiefly featuring popular music and light entertainment. Also *ellipt.* as *the Light*. (On 30 Sept. 1967 its name was changed to 'Radio 2'.)

1945 *Radio Times* 27 July 1/1 Alongside these six regionalised Home Services there is to be available a new alternative, the BBC Light Programme... It will be built for the civilian listener. **1956** 'M. Innes' *Old Hall, New Hall* iii. iii. 205 No *real* American professor could be *quite* like that—not outside the Light Programme. **1959** S. Gibbons *Pink Front Door* iii. 37 He had missed a particularly good boxing match on the Light. **1962** L. Deighton *Ipcress File* xxviii. 180, I kept the radio tuned to the Light for the 6.30 bulletin. **1966** *B.B.C. Handbk.* 45 The Light Programme seeks to provide a friendly and companionable service for those who are in the mood for entertainment and relaxation. **1968** S. E. Ellacott *Everyday Things in Eng. 1914–68* xi. 162 At the end of the war the Home Service and the Light Programme were established (1945).

23. a. *light-density*, *-land* (later examples); **b.** *light-boned*, *-built* adjs.; **c.** Special Comb.: **light bread** *U.S.* (see quot. 1966); **light fantastic** (see Fantastic *a.* and *sb.* A. 6 b), as noun phr., the movements of dancing; **light-heavyweight** (see quot. 1954); also *attrib.*; also *ellipt.* as *light-heavy*; **light oil**, any of various fractions of relatively low specific gravity obtained by the distillation of coal-tar, wood-tar, petroleum, etc.; **light water**, (*a*) water containing the normal (about 0·02%) or less than the normal proportion of deuterium oxide (so *light water reactor*, a nuclear reactor in which the moderator is light water); (*b*) a foam formed by water and a fluorocarbon surfactant which floats on flammable liquids lighter than water and is used in fire-fighting.

1951 Auden *Nones* (1952) 14 Of light-boned children under great green oaks. **1974** J. Stubbs *Painted Face* ii. 48 She was light-boned and well-fleshed. **1821** *Western Carolinian* (Salisbury, N. Carolina) 27 Mar., Crackers and light Bread will always be found in his shop. **1880** 'Mark Twain' *Tramp Abroad* II. xlix. 225 Hot light-bread, Southern style. **1966** *Publ. Amer. Dial. Soc.* 1964 xlii. 20 *Lightbread*, any yeast-raised bread, to distinguish it from biscuit. **1970** C. Major *Dict. Afro-Amer. Slang* 77 *Light bread*, white bread. **1974** *Amer. Speech* 1971 XLVI. 62 The notion that *light bread* is a recessive term is especially plausible because baking is rarely done at home and because supermarkets sell *white bread* or simply *bread*. **1953** J. Cary *Except the Lord* v. 15 He was a light-built man, very dark in complexion, with a somewhat hollow face, and a long sharp chin. **1956** E. Muir *One Foot in Eden* 18 The crescent shadow Of the light-built bridge. **1967** *Times* 28 Feb. (Canada Suppl.) 35/3 This method of operation has implications..for light-density branch lines. **1967** *Jane's Surface Skimmer Systems 1967–68* 30/1 The H.M.2 is designed for ferry services on light density routes of short stage lengths. *c* **1843** J. S. Coyne *Binks the Bagman* (1852) i. 10 Then you're fond of sporting on the light fantastic? **1892** A. C. Gunter *Miss Dividends* ix. 128 'You dance very nicely,' she murmurs. 'Yes, for a man who has not tripped the light fantastic for years.' **1913** Galsworthy *Dark Flower* i. vii. 34 When I was your age I twirled the light fantastic with the best. **1953** K. Amis *Lucky Jim* x. 114, I thought you'd all be on the floor by now... I'm not going to permit any more of this skulking about in here. It's the light fantastic for you. **1974** L. Deighton *Spy Story* vi. 57 The inlaid sprung floor would still have supported a light fantastic or two. **1973** R. L. Simon *Big Fix* (1974) xv. 104 It was the guy..who looked like a promising light-heavy. **1975** M. Kenyon *Mr Big* vii. 63 'These the heavyweights?' 'Light-heavy. Watch Hudson, in the blue trunks.' **1903** *National Police Gaz.* (U.S.) 18 July 3/1 And now there is a new champion in a new class—George Gardiner, of Lowell, Mass., the holder of the light-heavyweight title. **1913** J. G. B. Lynch *Compl. Amat. Boxer* (App.) 234 Standard weights. .. Light-heavy weight, 12 stone 7 pounds and under. **1954** F. C. Avis *Boxing Reference Dict.* 77 *Light-Heavy-weight*, a standard weight division for professional boxers weighing more than 11 st. 6 lb. but not more than 12 st. 7 lb.; for amateurs 11 st. 11 lb. and 12 st. 10 lb. respectively. **1960** M. Golesworthy *Encycl. Boxing* 210/2 Light-heavyweight—Started in America in 1903 by Lou Houseman, manager of Jack Root, who had outgrown the middleweight division. The limit was set at 12 st. 7 lbs. (175 lbs.) and it remains at that figure today. The division was first recognised in Britain in 1913. **1968** *Encycl. Brit.* IV. 43/1 In 1920 light heavyweight competition was added. **1960** *Farmer & Stockbreeder* 29 Mar. 73/1 The only complaint—a little rain needed on some of the light-land farms. **1974** *Times* 15 Apr. 8/3 Dry weather over the past three weeks, rather too long a period for some light-land farmers, has made possible some catching up on the delays of March. **1867** Bloxam *Chem.* 452 The light oil which first passed over is rectified by a second distillation, and is then sent into commerce under the name of coal naphtha. **1898** F. H. Thorp *Outl. Industr. Chem.* 264 The distillate collected [from wood-tar] below 150°C. is called 'light oil', and is chiefly used as a substitute for oil of turpentine in varnish and paints. **1936** *Economist* 22 Feb. 399/2 Increasing demand for the heavier oils has enabled a higher proportion of refinery production to be marketed in that form, and has reduced the proportion subjected to 'cracking' to obtain light oils, such as motor spirit. **1964** N. G. Clark *Mod. Org. Chem.* xviii. 372 When light oil and crude benzole are distilled to give 'Benzole' for internal-combustion engines—over 70 per cent are treated in this way—a fraction embracing benzene, toluene, and the xylenes is collected. **1933** Light water [see *heavy *a.*[1] 2 d]. **1947** Crowther & Whiddington *Science at War* iii. 142 Vast quantities of water have been electrolysed, and separated into 'light water' and 'heavy water', the former containing hydrogen atoms of mass 1 only. **1956** *Nature* 4 Feb. 204/1 Studies have been made of the pressurized light-water reactor and of the sodium-graphite reactor. **1968** *Guardian* 21 Aug. 1/4 The air show's special fire brigade—using helicopters carrying 'light water'. **1971** *Sunday Times* 12 Dec. 45/6 American light water reactors are simple and in some ways cruder. **1972** *Aircraft Engineering* Jan. 28/1 Using Light Water aqueous film forming foam, the team cut a knock-down path to the cockpit within five seconds of reaching the fire. **1973** *Daily Colonist* (Victoria, B.C.) 7 June 42/2 The cost of a solar steam generating plant would now be about double the cost of light-water nuclear plants.

light, *a.*[2] Add: **2. b.** *light red*, (*a*) pale red; (*b*) a pale red or reddish orange pigment produced from iron oxides.

1803 J. C. Ibbetson *Accidence of Painting in Oil* 17 *Light red*, so called, is either calcined green vitriol mixed with a quantity of other substance, and called Venetian red; or calcined yellow oker. **1934** H. Hiler *Notes Technique Painting* ii. 125 *Light red, burnt ochre*... It is quite opaque, and may be defined as a scarlet modified by the addition of a little yellow and grey. **1958** M. L. Wolf *Dict. Painting* 142 The red iron oxides found as natural deposits include Indian red, light red,..and others of lesser importance. **1970** R. D. Harley *Artists' Pigments* ix. 109 Light red came into current use as a colour name during the eighteenth century, when it was generally used to indicate a brownish red prepared by burning yellow ochre.

3. *light-haired* (earlier example); **Light Sussex**, a white variety of hen.

1843 Mill *Logic* II. iii. xxiii. 149 The probability..that any given inhabitant of Stockholm is light-haired. **1909** T. W. Sturges *Poultry Manual* xiii. 359 The Light Sussex and the Buff Orpington are both blended in the White Orpington. **1938** L. Pearce-Gervis *Compl. Poultry Keeper & Farmer* vi. 153 The top prices..are still made by the Surrey Chicken... For this market either Pure Light Sussex or a cross in which there is a Sussex strain is necessary, for the white flesh must be maintained. **1965** P. Wayre *Wind in Reeds* xv. 224 A flock of four hundred Silky crossed with Light Sussex bantams.

light, *v.*[1] Add: **5. b.** (Earlier and later examples.) Also *to light in* (or *into*): to attack; to go at. *U.S. colloq.*

1866 'Mark Twain' *Lett. from Hawaii* (1967) 32 And you want to know what made me light out of bed so sudden last night? Only a 'santipede'. **1878** J. H. Beadle *Western Wilds* xii. 187 They double-quicked into town and lit in generally. **1889** K. Munroe *Golden Days* xiv. 156 You've got the levellest head of any man that ever lit into the diggings. **1917** Freeman & Kingsley *Alabaster Box* i. 3 He'll light into those hot doughnuts. **1948** 'J. Tey' *Franchise Affair* xxii. 262 The girl had lit out... She had dressed in a hurry and gone. **1967** *Boston Sunday Herald* 7 May iv. 5/5 Chris did demonstrate he is prepared for a scrap in the coming campaign when he lit into Mrs. Hicks' proposals. **1969** *Listener* 27 Mar. 433/2 Like a latter-day Huck Finn, he lights out for the territory. **1969** *New Yorker* 19 Apr. 81/1 If the astronaut missed mentioning a rock I knew was there, I'd light into him afterward, just like a football coach critiquing a fumble on a film of a game. **1973** *Observer* 15 Apr. 13/2 Inveighing against that new parliamentary building.. lighting into..the proposed gymnasium.

light, *v.*[2] **2. c.** (Further examples.)

1943 J. B. Priestley *Daylight on Saturday* ix. 55 Blandford opened..a very fine silver cigarette-box, and both men lit up and were then silent. **1959** C. Williams *Man in Motion* i. 6, I ripped open a packet of the cigarettes, found some matches..and lighted up. **1970** H. E. Roberts *Third Ear* 9/2 *Light up*, to light a marijuana cigarette.

lighter, *sb.*[2] Add: **1.** Also *lighter-up* (see quot. 1921).

1909 *Westm. Gaz.* 21 Apr. 8/1 Robert Brown, lighter-up [at locomotive shed] slight cut on left eyebrow. **1921** *Dict. Occup. Terms* (1927) § 709 Lighter-up, carries live coals from fire hearth in shed to engine fire box.

2. b. = *cigarette lighter* (see *cigarette 2); also any similar mechanical contrivance for

lighting a gas-fire, etc. So *lighter-fluid, -fuel,* the fuel used to work a lighter.

1895 *Montgomery Ward Catal.* Spring & Summer 554/2 There are two lighters, to be used with alcohol. **1907** *Yesterday's Shopping* (1969) 243/3 *The 'Telescopic' Gas Lighter.* The best substitute for matches. **1913** KIPLING *Divers. Creatures* (1917) 274 He smelt of rare soaps and cigarettes—such cigarettes as he handed me from a golden box with an automatic lighter. **1930** SAYERS & 'EUSTACE' *Documents in Case* xxxvii. 105, I came in to retrieve a garment or lighter that he had borrowed. **1947** 'N. BLAKE' *Minute for Murder* ii. 47 A thin cylindrical object..rather like a lighter-fuel container. **1955** W. GADDIS *Recognitions* II. i. 317 Setting fire to his hand dipped in lighter fluid. **1956** E. AMBLER *Night-Comers* iv. 85 She had a box of Kleenex and a can of lighter fluid... She began to wipe off the grease. **1959** *New Statesman* 19 Sept. 354/2 The pipe had an aircooled aluminium stem, the lighter was butane-fuelled and had a Cadillac 'V' on the side. **1960** 'H. CARMICHAEL' *Seeds of Hate* xix. 157 There had been a stain on the sleeve..and he had removed it with lighter fuel. **1961** *Esquire* Aug. 59/2 He kept the bottles on a shelf in a clump of lighter fluid and Never-Leak cans. **1974** M. GILBERT *Flash Point* xii. 102 'You haven't got a cigarette by any chance?'..Patrick got out his case. The girl..took one, and got out her own lighter.

li:ghter-than-ai·r, *attrib. phr. Aeronautics.* Designating a flying machine whose weight is less than the weight of the air which it displaces and which rises as a result of its own buoyancy; also applied to the use of such a machine or machines in flight.

[**1869** J. B. PETTIGREW in *Notices Proc. R. Inst Gt. Brit.* V. 103 A machine lighter than the air must necessarily rise through it. **1887** tr. *J. Verne's Clipper of Clouds* vii. 60 The first inventors did not think of apparatus lighter than air. *Ibid.* viii. 78, I solved the problem of aviation. That is what a balloon will never do, nor will any machine that is lighter than air.] **1903** *Work* 11 Apr. 155/1 The Barton Air Ship.. is a combination of the 'lighter than air' and 'heavier than air' system—that is to say, it is a machine in which a system of movable aeroplanes is interposed between the car and the balloon. **1907** *Daily Mail* 19 Mar. 5/6 The Berlin 'Zentralblatt für Bauverwaltung'..protests against the subsidising with State funds of airships, dirigible balloons, and other 'lighter-than-air' vehicles. **1912** S. F. WALKER *Aviation* i. 7 'Lighter than Air' apparatus which we call balloons. **1923** HART & LAIDLER *Elem. Aeronaut. Sci.* i. 8 The problem of 'lighter-than-air' flight. **1953** S. SPENDER *Creative Element* i. 28 Tennyson was thinking of a battle of lighter-than-air dirigibles. **1963** *Ann. Reg. 1962* 539 [Auguste Piccard.] He and his twin, Jean Félix, were intensely interested in lighter-than-air flight. **1974** *Times* 13 Feb. 14/3 The role of lighter-than-air craft as cargo carriers.

ellipt. **1887** tr. *J. Verne's Clipper of Clouds* v. 39 To these enthusiasts for 'lighter than air' a no less enthusiast for 'heavier than air' had said things absolutely abhorrent. *Ibid.* x. 94 In spite of all the jealousy of the two enemies of 'lighter than air', they could not help being surprised at the perfection of this engine of aerial locomotion. **1910** *Blackw. Mag.* Feb. 206/1 Neglecting the lighter than air as a military auxiliary.

light face. *Typogr.* [f. LIGHT *a.*¹ + FACE *sb.* 22.] A kind of type in which the letters are made up of thin strokes. Also *attrib.* Hence **light-faced** *a.* Cf. *heavy face* (FACE *sb.* 22, *HEAVY *a.*¹ 15).

1871 *Amer. Encycl. Printing* 275 *Light-Faces,* numerous varieties of job type, in which the lines of the letters are unusually light or thin. **1898** J. SOUTHWARD *Mod. Printing* I. xxii. 140 The first would be called a *light face,* and the second a *heavy face. Ibid.* xxiv. 155 In the case of light-faced letters, they are spoiled for good work after the first time of using. **1917** F. S. HENRY *Printing for School & Shop* vii. 90 Dainty, light-faced type. **1962** CORSON & LORRAIN *Introd. Electromagn. Fields* i. 1 Lightface type will indicate either a scalar quantity or the magnitude of a vector quantity. **1963** KENNEISON & SPILMAN *Dict. Printing* 115 *Light face,* descriptive of a type-face of fine appearance as opposed to medium and bold lines. **1970** W. P. JASPERT et al. *Encycl. Type Faces* (ed. 4) p. ix, We speak also of bold-faced and light-faced types, referring to the thickness or thinness of the strokes of the letter.

lighthouse. Add: **b.** *lighthouse keeper* (earlier example), *-man, -tender.*

1738 *Mass. Bay Acts & Resolves* (1904) XII. 513 That the sum of Fifty one Pounds..be paid..for his services as Light House Keeper. **1889** *Athenæum* 23 Feb. 257 (Advt.), The manners and ways of coastguardsmen, lighthousemen, and other amphibious creatures. **1901** *Daily Colonist* (Victoria, B.C.) 1 Nov. 3/2 The lighthouse-tender Manzanita called in yesterday morning for a short stay. **1921** *Ibid.* 16 Oct. 16/1 The lighthouse tender Berens then took up the search and..discovered the small boat sheltering behind Mouatt Reef. **1958** W. ARMSTRONG *True Bk. Lighthouses & Lightships* xiv. 142, I remembered, too, stories of how two lighthouse tenders and a pilot-cutter were sunk by mines in World War I. **1969** *Times* 19 Dec. 2/5 (*heading*) Lighthouse man missing.

lighting, *vbl. sb.*² Add: **1.** *attrib.* and *Comb.*: *lighting man, power, rate, socket, wire;* **lighting bridge** *Theatr.*, a narrow platform, suspended over a stage, on which lights are operated; **lighting cameraman** *Cinemat.* and *Television* (see quot. 1960); **lighting plot** *Theatr.* (see quot. 1961); **lighting tower** *Theatr.*, a tall structure on which lights are fixed.

1928 C. H. RIDGE *Stage Lighting* vii. 111 The roof and lighting bridge are all built in reinforced concrete. **1933** P. GODFREY *Back-Stage* iv. 43 Above the proscenium arch is the lighting bridge, which will accommodate as many as ten electricians with 'spotting lanterns'. **1967** *Punch* 16 Aug. 242/3 For *Figaro* and Verdi's *Macbeth* at the first [Edinburgh] festival twenty-one years ago, John Christie had to bring in a lighting bridge and sixty floods and perches from Glyndebourne. **1960** O. SKILBECK *ABC of Film & TV 78 Lighting Cameraman,* chief cameraman of a unit, who is responsible for ordering the illumination which gives pictorial quality to a shot. **1966** *Listener* 15 Dec. 889/3 The lighting cameraman can earn £1,000 a week on a major picture. **1972** A. FOWLES *Double Feature* iv. 67 I'd been Richard Powell, lighting cameraman. **1972** I. HAMILTON *Thrill Machine* vii. 30 For difficult interiors he should have had a lighting man, for interviews he should have had an audio man as well. **1931** C. S. PARSONS *Amat. Stage Managem. & Production* ii. 18 Lighting plots should always be well rehearsed. **1933** P. GODFREY *Back-Stage* iv. 44 The lighting-plot shows the position of every lamp, the colour of the medium, and the varying intensity of the light required. **1961** BOWMAN & BALL *Theatre Lang.* 201 *Lighting plot,*..a list, with diagrams, showing the lighting to be used in each scene of a production. **1884** F. KROHN tr. *Glaser de Cew's Magneto- & Dynamo-Electr. Machines* 183 A greater part of its lighting-power is due to the incandescence of the electrodes. **1928** *Chambers's Jrnl.* Jan. 21/1 An automatic regulator wherewith to make..and supply lighting power to the lamps. **1858** Lighting-rate [in Dict.]. **1928** *Chambers's Jrnl.* Jan. 79/1 All that has to be done to start charging is to insert the charger-plug in the nearest lighting socket. **1935** *Discovery* Nov. 326/2 A new power-driven spray-painting outfit which..can be run from an ordinary lighting socket. **1933** P. GODFREY *Back-Stage* iv. 43 In the wings stand a number of lighting towers twelve feet high, each capable of carrying a dozen 1000-watt flood lamps. **1967** R. COURTNEY *Drama Studio* ix. 76 At least one Lighting Tower is needed on the floor area. **1889** Lighting wire [in Dict.].

3. (Earlier example with *up*.)

1807 SOUTHEY *Lett. from Eng.* I. viii. 89 Between eight and nine the lighting-up began.., every window being filled with candles.

b. lighting-up time, the time when lights are switched on, esp. the time when lights on vehicles are required by law to be switched on.

1900 J. K. JEROME *Three Men on Bummel* iii. 55 On sunny afternoons you used to ride about with that lamp shining for all it was worth. When lighting-up time came it was naturally tired, and wanted a rest. **1935** H. G. WELLS *Things to Come* iii. 23 It [*sc.* a newspaper] should show the customary insets beside the title of the weather forecast and the lighting-up time. **1947** *Whitaker's Almanack* 150/2 The legal importance of *Sunrise* and *Sunset* is that the Road Transport Lighting Act, 1927 defines Lighting-up Time for vehicles as being from one hour after sunset to one hour before sunrise. **1957** *Times* 11 May 7/1 Lighting-up time, 9.8 p.m. **1963** *Times* 20 May 3/3 M.C.C., going in with three-quarters of an hour left, lost Atkinson before the umpires decided it was lighting-up time.

lightning. Add: **2.** Also, any strong, freq. low-quality, alcoholic spirit. Chiefly *U.S.* Cf. *chain-lightning* (s.v. CHAIN *sb.* 19 in Dict. and Suppl.).

1858 *Calif. Spirit of Times* (San Francisco) 7 Aug. 1/4 Having in his possession a few kegs of liquid lightning upon which he was avariciously desirous of reaping a speedy profit. **1873** J. MILLER *Life amongst Modocs* viii. 94 In one of the saloons where men were wont to..drink lightning. **1945** L. SHELLY *Jive Talk Dict.* 28/2 *Lightning and thunder,* whisky and soda. **1958** L. VAN DER POST *Lost World of Kalahari* ii. 53 The fiery Cape brandy known to us children as 'Blitz' or Lightning.

b. *pl.* One of the top grades of white jute.

1929 WOODHOUSE & KILGOUR *Spinning Flax & Jute* i. 2 (*caption*) Jute bale marks... Lightnings. **1929** *Observer* 17 Nov. 4/3 Jute... Lightnings November–December quoted £25. **1964** R. R. ATKINSON *Jute* i. 23 White jute is assorted into three main classes... The top class is sub-divided into Firsts, Lightnings, and Hearts.

3. c. *lightning-quick, -rapid* adjs.

1925 V. WOOLF *Common Reader* 41 That is the quality that first strikes us in Greek literature, the lightning-quick, sneering, out-of-doors manner. **1947** C. S. LEWIS *Miracles* xii. 118 What they painfully reconstruct from a million dots..he really produced with a single lightning-quick turn of the wrist. **1961** *Times* 25 Mar. 4/7 That strangely reluctant take-away of the club and the lightning-quick swing caused plenty of trouble yesterday. **1922** D. H. LAWRENCE *England, my England* 45 The officer was giving the last lightning-rapid orders to fire.

d. (Further examples.) Also, done, produced, or acting with the speed of lightning; spec. *lightning artist,* an artist who paints or draws pictures very quickly as an entertainment; *lightning-change,* a rapid change of costume made by an actor or performer; also *attrib.*; *lightning strike,* a sudden strike (STRIKE *sb.* 9) which takes place without any warning; *lightning tournament,* a Chess tournament in which each player must make his move within a prescribed few seconds; also *lightning chess, player,* etc.

1873 W. MATHEWS *Getting on in World* 242 Now.. people travel by 'lightning lines', going from New York to Chicago in twenty-nine hours. **1875** 'MARK TWAIN' in *Atlantic Monthly* Aug. XXXVI. 192/1 If one of the boats has a 'lightning' pilot, whose 'partner' is a trifle inferior, you can tell which one is on watch by noting whether that boat has gained ground or lost. **1889** G. O. SEILHAMER *Hist. Amer. Theatre* II. xxiii. 299 He may..be accorded the distinction of being the first 'lightning change artist' on the American stage. **1908** *Sears, Roebuck Catal.* 342/5 Silver Dip. The new lightning cleaner. **1910** *Year-Bk. Chess* 143 (*heading*) Two special lightning tournaments were held. **1920** *Radiograph* July p. ix/1 The first step was an endeavour to try to stigmatise the..action as 'A Lightning Strike'. **1927** W. E. COLLINSON *Contemp. Eng.* 70 A few technical expressions of the Halls which are commonly known to English townsfolk, but not likely to find their way into all the dictionaries, e.g...lightning artists (*caricaturists working at great speed*). **1927** E. GLYN *'It'* 240 She had promised to sit for him just for a lightning sketch. **1928** G. B. SHAW *Intelligent Woman's Guide Socialism* lxxxiii. 448 A lightning strike of waitresses in a restaurant. **1940** E. C. SHEPHERD *Britain's Air Power* 5 In the German 'Lightning War' on Poland the aeroplane was used to the full as an offensive weapon. **1945** *Tee Emm* (Air Ministry) V. 33 Fields, hedges and houses flash past at lightning speed under your wings. **1946** *Happy Landings* (Air Ministry) July 7/2 In addition to making a lightning survey of local air safety measures..a..lecture was given. **1948** C. DAY LEWIS *Otterbury Incident* iv. 39 Lightning sketches by Miss E. Toppingham. *Ibid.* 48 Toppy's sister, the lightning artist, had done particularly well. **1949** H. GOLOMBEK *World Chess Championship 1948* 24 He is..one of the world's best lightning players. **1951** 'ASSIAC' *Adventure in Chess* III. iii. 99 Most proficient at 'lightning Chess'. **1952** GRANVILLE *Dict. Theatr. Terms* 111 *Lightning-change artiste,* the (more usual) quick-change artiste, one who imitates..a number of well-known personalities. **1955** *Times* 3 Aug. 8/7 A shortage of labour caused a lightning strike of about 200 men at the Albert and William Wright docks at Hull to-day. **1971** E. PRITCHARD *Chess for Pleasure* xii. 148 In the evenings there may be *lightning* tournaments, when games are played at 10 seconds a move.

e. lightning beetle = *lightning-bug;* **lightning box,** a box used in producing stage-lightning; **lightning-bug** (earlier and later examples); **lightning conductor** (earlier and later examples).

1854 B. JAEGER *Life of N. Amer. Insects* 75 Some months since a lady..presented me two of these living Lightning beetles. **1825** P. EGAN *Life of Actor* ii. 67 Lightning boxes, sheep hooks, and three harlequin's bats. **1855** 'Q. K. P. DOESTICKS' *Doesticks, what he Says* xxvi. 237 The prompter was stretched on the top of a canvas volcano, with the bell-rope in his hand, and his hair full of resin, from the 'lightnin-box'. **1928** A. ROSE *Stage Effects* 26 Fig. 20 is a simple but useful and convenient form of lightning box... One or more electric lights are to be in the centre of the box. **1778** J. CARVER *Trav. N. Amer.* xviii. 491 The Lightning Bug or Fire Fly is about the size of a bee. **1842** *Southern Lit. Messenger* VIII. 199/2 It will never do to tell *us* that there is any humbug in this business, or even that it is a mere *lightning-bug.* **1936** T. S. ELIOT *Coll. Poems 1909–1935* 138 The small flare of the firefly or lightning bug. **1947** *Chicago Tribune* 21 June 2/4 He asserted that to 'talk about Henry Wallace intimidating Harry Truman on the veto is like describing a lightning bug as blotting out the rays of the sun'. **1971** *Lebende Sprachen* XVI. 10/1 US lightning bug—BE/US firefly. [**1791** E. DARWIN *Bot. Garden* I. Additional Notes 25 The design of these conductors is to permit the electric matter accumulated in the clouds to pass through them into the earth..and it would seem that the finer the point..the better, as it would take off the lightning while it was still at a greater distance.] **1814** W. BENTLEY *Diary* (1914) IV. 262 The post remained, retained on the side of the steeple by the Lightning conductors. **1967** *Everyman's Encycl.* V. 429/1 He [*sc.* B. Franklin] estab. the identity of lightning with electricity..and suggested the use of lightning conductors on large buildings.

lightning (ləi·tniŋ), *v.* [f. the sb.] = LIGHTEN *v.*² 6. Also *fig.*

1903 *Westm. Gaz.* 16 Nov. 8/2 The two metal balls.. thundered and lightninged as they delivered the message. **1926** H. CAINE in *Strand Mag.* Jan. 20/1 Mr. Gladstone leapt to his feet, whereupon the air of the House thundered and lightninged for a short ten minutes. **1935** in Z. N. Hurston *Mules & Men* (1970) I. i. 27 You know, when it lightnings, de angels is peepin' in de lookin' glass.

lightningy (ləi·tniŋi), *a.* [f. LIGHTNING + -Y¹.] Suggestive of lightning. (In comb. with *thunder.*)

1906 GALSWORTHY *Man of Property* II. ii. 141 They had never seen anyone look so thunder and lightningy as that little June!

lights, *pl.* Add: **b.** Colloq. phr. *to scare the (liver and) lights out of* (someone): to scare (someone) greatly.

1884 'MARK TWAIN' *Huck. Finn* xxix. 307 It most scared the liver and lights out of me. **1956** E. POUND tr. *Sophocles' Women of Trachis* 18 You might start by questioning Likhas, scare the lights out of him, and he might tell you.

lightship. Also *attrib.* and *Comb.*

1887 *Chambers's Jrnl.* 1 Jan. 1 (*title*) The lightshipman. **1904** *Westm. Gaz.* 8 Oct. 9/2 The light-ship men were unable to come on shore. **1905** *Daily Chron.* 10 Oct. 4/5 Such strictures upon the lightship keepers' employment would hold equally with reference to the crews of say the light vessels off the Scilly Islands. **1958** W. ARMSTRONG *True Bk. Lighthouses & Lightships* xiii. 131 'Better be safe than sorry' was always the unspoken motto of lighthouse and lightship men.

light-weight, *sb.* and *a.* Add: Also (without hyphen) **lightweight. A.** *sb.* In *Boxing,* now usu. a competitor weighing between 126 and 135 pounds. Also anything (e.g. a motorcycle) that is relatively light in weight.

1898 *Pearson's Mag.* Feb. 165/1 The torpedo-boat and the destroyer may fairly be called the light-weights of naval warfare. **1908** *Daily Report* 20 July 9/1 Light-weights of 2 h.p. are quite capable of averaging well over 20 m.p.h. **1960** M. Golesworthy *Encycl. Boxing* 211/1 *Weight Divisions...* Lightweight—1868 at 9 st. 7 lbs. (133 lbs.). 1912 raised to present limit of 9 st. 9 lbs. (135 lbs.) by Willie Ritchie.

b. *fig.* A person or thing of little importance, profundity, or intelligence.

1885 A. Edwardes *Girton Girl* III. xi. 205, I am not good at these high passions!..In everything I am a light weight... In life I walk gently. **1902** G. H. Lorimer *Lett. Self-Made Merchant* (1903) ii. 19 That is the spot where a young man has the chance to show that he is not a light-weight. **1951** A. L. Rowse *Eng. Past* 24 Harington was the Queen's godson—clever,.. naughty, a light-weight, perpetrator of puns and practical jokes. **1962** *Listener* 25 Jan. 185/2 Of the other stories in this book, those by the long-established writers..are light-weights. **1965** *English Studies* XLVI. 209 After Holiness or Justice, Courtesy may seem as something of a light-weight.

c. A garment, usu. a suit, made from light-weight material.

1972 J. Quartermain *Rock of Diamond* v. 26 He stood five ten clad in a dark-blue lightweight. **1973** R. Busby *Pattern of Violence* v. 80 He..picked up a man's suit jacket from the floor. It was a grey lightweight.

B. *adj.* (Further examples.) Also of clothes, fabrics, etc.

1892–3 *T. Eaton & Co. Catal.* Fall & Winter 31/2 Light weight overcoats in grey, brown, fawn. **1902** *Daily Chron.* 8 Nov. 8/3 Every woman who walks much clings to a light-weight Russian blouse. **1930** J. T. Hatfield et al. *Curme Vol. Ling. Stud.* 52 The intervening verbs are chiefly light-weight grammatical words. **1940** *Chambers's Techn. Dict.* 499/2 *Light-weight concrete* (Build.), concrete of low unit weight.., made by using aggregates such as pumice, sawdust, and cork, with cellular concrete. **1953** *News Chron.* 2 June 2/2 Squatting to drink it [*sc.* tea] in the light-weight (six pound) proofed cotton nylon tents. **1957** *Times Lit. Suppl.* 13 Dec. 751/2 One cannot reproach him with having produced a rather lightweight book. **1958** *Times* 10 Nov. 14/5 An entertaining, light-weight lecture recital by Mr. Antony Hopkins. **1963** A. J. Hall *Textile Sci.* iii. 158 In these days when light-weight apparel is much favoured the density of a textile fibre is important. **1968** M. Woodhouse *Rock Baby* xi. 109 He'd been.. wearing a lightweight raincoat. **1973** *Nation Rev.* (Melbourne) 31 Aug. 1443/3 A recent column attacking Whitlam for appearing on TV with 'a lightweight variety performer'.

Hence **light-weighted** *a.*, of light weight; carrying a light weight.

1867 J. R. Lowell in *Atlantic Monthly* Nov. 625/2 We ..see the rather light-weighted great man wheeled round the room..to converse with his guests. **1905** *Westm. Gaz.* 21 Mar. 8/2 The London and Brighton Handicap Steeplechase on Friday may be won by the light-weighted Dam.

ligno-. Add: **li:gnosu·lphonate,** any of the salts or esters of the lignosulphonic acids, some of which are used as adhesive binders, as pigment dispersants, in the tanning industry, and in the manufacture of vanillin; **li:gnosulpho·nic acid,** any of various compounds in which sulphonic acid groups are attached to lignin molecules, formed in the sulphite process for producing wood pulp.

1908 *Jrnl. Chem. Soc.* XCIV. i. 717 From the liquid obtained by boiling pine-wood with calcium hydrogen sulphite, the author has prepared barium lignosulphonate, $C_{40}H_{44}O_{17}S_2Ba$. **1952** F. E. Brauns *Chem. Lignin* v. 113 The isolation of a basic calcium lignosulfonate from a commercial spent liquor on a technical scale is carried out in the 'Howard process'. **1963** J. F. Harris et al. in B. L. Browning *Chem. Wood* xi. 578 Lignosulfonates, in particular the carbohydrate-free products, have found a variety of profitable applications. The most notable of these are their uses in oil well-drilling muds and in the production of synthetic rubber. **1908** *Jrnl. Chem. Soc.* XCIV. i. 717 In lignosulphonic acid, part of the sulphurous acid is tightly and part loosely bound. **1931** *Canad. Jrnl. Res.* V. 42 The first lignosulphonic acids studied were obtained by heating benzene-alcohol extracted spruce meal with sulphurous acid. **1967** Kirk & Othmer *Encycl. Chem. Technol.* (ed. 2) XII. 369 The sulfite process for producing pulp can lead to products which consist of lignosulfonic acids, or various lignosulfonates. These are commonly referred to in the trade as lignin sulfonic acids and lignin sulfonates.

lignocaine (li·gnokēin). *Pharm.* [f. Ligno- (as the L. equivalent of Xylo-, the compound having been orig. named *xylocaine* because of its chemical relationship to xylene) + *-caine*, after Cocaine.] A white crystalline aromatic amide, $(CH_3)_2C_6H_3NH{\cdot}CO{\cdot}CH_2{\cdot}N(C_2H_5)_2$, used as a local anæsthetic for the gums and mucous membranes, usually in the form of its hydrochloride and by injection, but also as tablets, sprays, or creams.

1954 *Anaesthesia* IX. 96 The development of a technique utilising the short acting relaxant suxamethonium chloride..and the analgesic lignocaine hydrochloride (Xylocaine). **1959** *Brit. Dental Jrnl.* CVI. 48/2 Extensive clinical experience has shown that procaine and, probably more so, lignocaine are really very satisfactory as local anæsthetic agents in dental practice. **1970** Passmore & Robson *Compan. Med. Stud.* II. viii. 6/1 Lignocaine..is therefore the safest drug in the treatment of acute ventricular arrhythmias even though it is toxic in high dosage.

lignum². (Later examples.)

1903 'T. Collins' *Such is Life* 79 When a certain class of bushman says 'mallee', he means any sort of scrub except lignum. **1933** *Bulletin* (Sydney) 13 Dec. 29/4 Beneath the surface is a mass of lignum roots. **1941** I. L. Idriess *Great Boomerang* xiii. 92 Carpeted with yellowish-green lignum —huge bunches of cane-like shrubs like man-high beehives.

ligroin (li·gro,in). *Chem.* Also **ligroïn.** [Etym. unknown: in quot. 1881 a. G. *ligroin.*] Any of various naphtha fractions with ranges of boiling points between 90 and 150°C, used as solvents.

1881 *Jrnl. Chem. Soc.* XL. 1181 The author has investigated the causes of explosions resulting from the products of the distillation of mineral naphtha when used for burning purposes. These products are known as 'gasoline', 'benzoline', 'ligroin', and 'lubricating oil'. **1942** H. Barron *Mod. Synthetic Rubbers* vii. 82 Straightforward rectification of petroleum yields: Petrol... Benzine... Ligroïn... Kerosene [etc.]. **1965** *Biol. Abstr.* XLVI. 680/2 Experimental solvent extractions of wood rosin from pine stump chips were carried out in ligroin at 0, 20, 50, and 80°C. **1968** B. J. Hazzard tr. *Asinger's Paraffins* iv. 402 Ligroin with a boiling range of 95–150°C (density= 0·745) containing 3·2 per cent of aromatics, 24·2 per cent of naphthenes, and 72·6 per cent of paraffins..can be 60–65 per cent nitrated in a single pass through the reactor.

ligularia (ligiŭlēᵊ·riă). [mod.L. (H. Cassini 1816, in *Bull. Sci. Soc. Philomatique* 198), f. L. *ligula* strap, referring to the shape of the ray-florets.] A herbaceous perennial plant of the genus so called, belonging to the family Compositæ, often native to China or Japan, and bearing yellow flowers.

1839 G. Don *Sweet's Hortus Britannicus* (ed. 3) 382 (*heading*) *Ligularia DC.* Ligularia (*ligula*, a little tongue; ray-flowers ligulate). **1862** *Curtis's Bot. Mag.* LXXXVIII. 5302 (*heading*) Kæmpfer's Ligularia. **1886** G. Nicholson *Illustr. Dict. Gardening* II. 263/1 Ligularias require generally a free, moist soil, and prefer a rather peaty one. **1966** J. Berrisford *Wild Garden* ii. 149 The ligularias are handsome plants for rich moist soil. **1971** *Country Life* 2 Sept. 567/2 My biggest colour splodges are..various yellow composites: heleniums..ligularias, [etc.].

Ligurian, *a.* and *sb.* Add: **b.** *sb.* Also, the Indo-European language of the ancient Ligurians; the Gallo-Italian dialect of this region.

1835 G. C. Lewis *Ess. Romance Lang.* i. 50 The diffusion of the Latin over Italy, in the place of the Etruscan, the Oscan, the Ligurian, and other native dialects, has been already noted. **1888** [see *Iapygian *a.* and *sb.*]. **1909** *Trans. Amer. Philol. Assoc.* XL. 81 The net result of the study is that by far the greater part of what is called Ligurian is strictly Gallic. **1927** C. H. Grandgent *From Latin to Italian* 6 In the northwest of Italy we find the Piedmontese dialect, and, to the south, along the Gulf of Genoa from Monaco to Carrara, the Ligurian. **1933** R. S. Conway et al. *Prae-Italic Dial. Italy* II. ii. 70 Of Ligurian properly so called very little can be said to be known. **1939** L. H. Gray *Foundations of Lang.* xi. 335 In the general area of Lago Maggiore, some seventy-two inscriptions..have been discovered... Their language may well represent the sole known remnants of Ligurian, which would seem to have stood midway between Italic and Celtic. **1968** *Encycl. Brit.* XII. 711/2 The dialects may be divided into six major classes: 1. Gallo-Italian: (*a*) Piedmontese; (*b*) Ligurian; (*c*) Lombard; (*d*) Emilian [etc.]. **1974** R. A. Hall *External Hist. Romance Lang.* iii. 51 Ligurian, used along what is now the Italian and French Riveria [*sic*], and perhaps to the north of this area in present-day Piedmont and Savoy.

ligustrum (ligʊ·strǒm). [L. *ligustrum* privet, adopted by Linnæus (*Hortus Cliffortianus* (1737) 6) and earlier botanists as the name of a genus.] = Privet¹.

1664 Evelyn *Kalendarium Hortense* in *Sylva* 71 July... Flowers in Prime, or yet lasting... Oleanders red and white, Agnus Castus, Arbutus, Yucca, Olive, Ligustrum, Tilia, &c. **1900** M. Thorn in W. D. Drury *Bk. Gardening* xi. 441 Ligustrums (Privets) are represented in many gardens only by *L. ovalifolium* (oval-leaved) and its golden-leaved form. **1957** *New Yorker* 23 Nov. 46/3 I've put four pyramid ligustrums on the sculpture balconies. We always use plants to bring out an exhibition. **1973** W. J. Bean *Trees & Shrubs Hardy in Brit. Is.* (ed. 8) II. 570 L[*igustrum*] *confusum* is..represented at Kew by a plant 10 ft high in the Ligustrum collection.

Lihyanic (liyā·nik), *sb.* Also **Lihyanite, Lihyanian; Lihyani** (liyā·ni). [f. Arab. *liḥyān* + -ic.] The name of an ancient Semitic language known only from north Arabian inscriptions of the 2nd and 1st centuries B.C. Also (all forms), as *adj.*

1911 *Encycl. Brit.* XXIV. 626/1 A more commendable proposal is to call the inscriptions Liḥyānī, since the tribe of Liḥyān is sometimes mentioned in them... Other brief inscriptions..have been discovered... Their writing is a somewhat later form of the Liḥyānī, and the dialect.. seems to be very similar to Liḥyānī. **1932** W. L. Graff *Lang.* xi. 402 From North Arabia we have a certain number of inscriptions dating from the 2d or 1st century B.C. and revealing a language, called Lihyanite, closely related to Arabic proper. **1936** *Encycl. Islam* III. 27/1 The Thamūdaean graffiti..are a development (later or parallel) of the Liḥyānī script. **1937** F. V. Winnett *Study of Lihyanite & Thamudic Inscriptions* 51 The earlier supplanting of Dedanite by Lihyanite points to a Lihyanite conquest of Dedan (al-'Ula) in the early 5th century B.C. **1939** L. H. Gray *Foundations of Lang.* 363 North Arabic is first recorded in Liḥyānian and Thamūdian inscriptions (the former between the second or first century B.C. and the fourth or sixth A.D...) and in Ṣafāitic graffiti. **1948** D. Diringer *Alphabet* ii. ii. 227 The Lihyanite inscriptions can be divided into two groups. **1968** *Encycl. Brit.* I. 663/2 The four South Semitic alphabets.. are known as Sabaean, Lihyanic, Thamudenic and Safahitic.

like, *a.*, *adv.* (*conj.*), and *sb.*² Add: **A.** *adj.* **1. b.** ¶ *like that*: spec. (usu. accompanying the crossing of the speaker's fingers) as an indication that two people described are very friendly or intimate; *like another* [cf. Fr. *comme un autre*]: that is ordinary or unexceptional; that is only one of a number of similar things, possibilities, etc.

1904 H. James *Golden Bowl* I. xiii. 236 Isn't the whole thing..perhaps but a way like another for their gaining time? **1926** F. Scott Fitzgerald *Great Gatsby* ix. 206 'We were so thick like that in everything'—he held up two bulbous fingers—'always together.' **1929** D. Hammett *Red Harvest* xxii. 219 'You're a friend of Whisper's?' 'You bet.' He held up two thin fingers pressed tightly together. 'Just like that, me and him.' **1936** D. Powell *Turn, Magic Wheel* i. 37 Theatrical people..just got here from London—they're like that with Cochrane—they know Dame Sybil Thorndike personally. **1966** I. Murdoch *Time of Angels* xviii. 193, I suppose it's a skill like another. **1971** M. Russell *Deadline* xv. 182 'Of course you had to get on terms with Gregory.' 'Now we're like *that*.'

2. e. Colloq. phr. (*a bit*) *more like* (*it*): nearer what it (etc.) should be or what is desired; better; also, closer to the truth. Cf. More *adv.* 1 h.

1888 Kipling *Phantom 'Rickshaw* (1889) 81 'That's more like,' said Carnehan. 'If you could think us a little more mad we would be more pleased.' **1891** S. Weyman *New Rector* II. xv. 12 'This is better than No. 383, Mrs. Baxter?' 'Well, sir,..it is a bit more like.' **1907** D. H. Lawrence *Phoenix II* (1968) 8 'Ah,' said Beelzebub, 'this is a bit more like it, a bit hotter. The Devils feel at home here.' **1962** D. Mayo *Island of Sin* viii. 63 Paid companion, hell. Whipping-boy was more like it. **1964** A. Wilson *Late Call* iv. 141 Shopping in the Town Centre provided something more like, and she ambled around, taking her time. **1968** P. Durst *Badge of Infamy* vii. 61 'Would you like some coffee?' 'Now that's more like it. Sure why not?'

9. b. (*be*) *like to do, have like to do*, be on the point of doing, almost do, look like doing. Cf. *like *v.*² 2. *U.S. colloq.*

1808 L. Summer in *Southern Hist. Mag.* (1892) I. 52 Strother was 150 votes behind Roberts & like to have lost his election in consequence of his opposing Madison. **1830** in *Jrnl. Illinois State Hist. Soc.* (1930–1) XXIII. 214 The boat went under a tree top and like to took me off. **1836** F. A. Chardon *Jrnl. Fort Clark* (1932) 70 Michael Belhumeres horse fell with him, had like to have broken his neck. **1854** in *Southwestern Hist. Q.* (1931–2) XXXV. 217 The supper—I had like to have said table-spread, for I can call it by no other name—it is a dirty old wagon cover sp[r]ead on the ground. **1855** in *Calif. Hist. Soc. Q.* (1929) VIII. 340 Like to never got back myself. **1884** 'Mark Twain' *Huck. Finn* xxxix. 396 We like to got a hornet's nest, but we didn't. **1889** 'C. E. Craddock' *Despot of Broomsedge Cove* xviii. 327 That's what like to have happened to me. **1916** 'B. M. Bower' *Phantom Herd* vi. 100, I like to died a-laughing. **1930** G. B. Johnson in B. A. Botkin *Treas. S. Folklore* (1949) iv. iii. 608 'I like to have got killed' means 'I almost got killed'. It is surprising how many phrases used by Negroes are exactly the phrases used by English folk. **1973** *Black World* Apr. 63 Damn brim like to covered broad street.

B. *adv.* **1. c.** *to know* or *read* (someone or something) *like a book*: to know very well, understand perfectly; *to speak* or *talk like a book*: (*a*) to talk elegantly; to use literary or pedantic language in conversation; (*b*) to speak knowledgeably and accurately. *colloq.*

1825 J. Neal *Bro. Jonathan* II. xxvi. 444 I can..read you off, like a book. **1829** *Mass. Spy* 28 Jan. (Th.), You talk like a book, Mr. Bond. **1833** J. Neal *Down-Easters* 26 An educated and travelled Yankee..talking like a book, even to his washerwoman. **1839** 'H. Franco' *Adventures H. Franco* I. xi. 73 'Know him like a book,' replied Mr. Lummucks. **1843** W. T. Thompson *Major Jones' Chron. Pineville* 74, I knows the Curloos like a book. **1844** T. C. Haliburton *Attaché* 2nd Ser. II. 176 Let a man or woman come and talk to me..and I'll tell you all about 'em right off as easy as big print. I can read 'em like a book. **1853** Lytton *My Novel* II. vii. xxi. 281 'If you can contrive to affect to be angry with him for his extravagance, it will do good.' 'You speak like a book, and I'll try my best.' **1875** [see Speak *v.* 1 d]. **1933** Wodehouse *Mulliner Nights* 101 That terrible old woman saw through my subterfuge last night. She read me like a book. **1940** H. G. Wells *Babes in Darkling Wood* i. i. 25 Don't you talk like a book, Mr Jimmy... Don't you go using long words. **1960** *Sunday Times* 27 Nov. 11 'Speaks Welsh like a book, the professor'—and, what's more, he also writes it like a book though he learnt it late in life.

d. *N. Amer. colloq.* Followed by an adj.: in the manner of one who is —— . Cf. *like crazy* (*crazy *a.* 4 c), *like mad* (Mad *a.* 1 c). Also in less analysable constructions.

1959 *She* May 21/2 Like wow...wonderful. **1961** G. Smith *Business of Loving* xi. 231 Sometimes we get rather soppy about each other..and laugh like young. **1962** [see *blow *v.*¹ 14 e]. **1970** *Time* 31 Aug. 19 Afterward, a girl

came up to me and said, 'You kinda look interested in this; did you know there are civil rights for women?' And I thought like wow, this is for me.

6. a. (Later examples.)

1941 *Coast to Coast* 192 She made a challenge of it, like she always does. **1961** *Word Study* Apr. 7/1 Like I said... The Beatnik School of Language Degradation must be responsible for the sudden mushrooming of the above expression. **1966** *New Yorker* 10 Dec. 149 Murray the K tells it like it really is. **1968** *Globe & Mail* (Toronto) 17 Feb. 34 (Advt.), Send for your copy now. Like we said, it's free. **1973** *New Society* 6 Dec. 608/1 His successors can build their modest, unpretentious monuments, like the British have been doing for years. **1974** 'E. LATHEN' *Sweet & Low* xviii. 174 Like I said, it was one o'clock... Everybody claims they were asleep.

e. Delete † (*obs.*) and add later examples.

1860 in Bartlett *Dict. Amer.* (ed. 3) 244 The old fellow drank of the brandy like he was used to it. **1886** *Harper's Mag.* June 109/2 None of them act like they belonged to the hotel. **1895** J. PRIOR *Renie* xvii. 191 'E made a noise like 'e were sorry or summat. **1898** H. S. CANFIELD *Maid of Frontier* 100, I sprung from the chair like a man had shot me through the head. **1932** T. S. ELIOT *Sweeney Agonistes* 30 When you're alone in the middle of the bed and you wake like someone hit you on the head. **1940** W. FAULKNER *Hamlet* I. i. 7 For a while it looked like I was going to get shut of it. *Ibid.* ii. 52 It seemed like we begun to hear it right away. **1969** *Observer* (Colour Suppl.) 23 Mar. 23/2 They look at me like I'm dirt. **1973** 'H. HOWARD' *Highway to Murder* vii. 76 That sounded like I was being left to hold the baby.

7. (Earlier and later examples.) Also, *colloq.* (orig. *U.S.*), as a meaningless interjection or expletive.

1778 F. BURNEY *Evelina* II. xxiii. 222 Father grew quite uneasy, like, for fear of his Lordship's taking offence. **1911** A. BENNETT *Hilda Lessways* I. vi. 49 He hasn't passed his examinations like... He has that Mr. Karkeek to cover him like. **1929** 'H. GREEN' *Living* vi. 57 'E went to the side like and looked. **1950** *Neurotica* Autumn 45 Like how much can you lay on [*i.e.* give] me? **1961** *New Statesman* 22 Sept. 382/2 'You're a chauvinist,' Danny said. 'Oh, yeah. Is that bad like?' **1966** *Lancet* 17 Sept. 635/2 As we say pragmatically in Huddersfield, 'C'est la vie, like!' **1971** [see *fighting chance* s.v. *FIGHTING *vbl. sb.* 3 b]. **1971** *Black Scholar* Apr.–May 26/1 Man like the dude really flashed his hole card. **1973** *Black Panther* 17 Nov. 9/4 What will be the contradictions that produce further change? Like, it seems to me that it would be virtually impossible to avoid some contradictions.

like, *v.*[1] Add: **6. a.** Colloq. phrases: *I like that!*, an ironical expression of surprise or disgust at someone's impudence, conceit, untruthfulness, etc.; (*to do*, etc., something) *and like it*, (to endure or perform something unpleasant) with a good grace, without complaint; *to like it or lump it*, see LUMP *v.*[2] 2. For *to know what one likes* see *KNOW *v.* 11 f.

c **1869** TAYLOR & DUBOURG in M. R. Booth *Eng. Plays of 19th Cent.* (1973) III. 255 *Lilian.* Bertie, you are a duffer. In these [arithmetic] questions the strength is always presumed to be equal. *Fitz-Urse.* I like that. As if one fellow was ever just as strong as another fellow. **1902** J. BRYNILDSEN *Dict. Eng. & Dano-Norwegian Lang.* s.v. *like*, *I ~ that..!* det var jo rart! **1927** A. B. COX *Mr. Priestley's Problem* ix. 146 'George, go and send them away.' 'Oh come,' protested George. 'I like that.' *a* **1930** D. H. LAWRENCE *Phoenix II* (1968) 182 'I feel so bare and brazen without a whiff of powder on my nose.' He gave a shout of laughter. 'I like that!' he said. **1941** H. G. WELLS *You can't be too Careful* III. vii. 138 'You *made* me.' 'I like that.' **1943** HUNT & PRINGLE *Service Slang* 11 *And like it!* A Naval expression anticipating a grouse and added to any instruction for an awkward or unwanted job. **1955** J. BINGHAM *Paton Street Case* vi. 97 'I'll have a pint.'.. 'You won't,' said Stan. 'It's May's birthday. You'll have a double Scotch, Len, and like it.' **1971** 'D. HALLIDAY' *Dolly & Doctor Bird* ii. 21 I'll do it again, and you'll stand by and like it. **1974** I. MURDOCH *Sacred & Profane Love Machine* 73 'If we didn't stupefy ourselves with drink we wouldn't get so comatose.' 'I like that. You taught me to drink.'

b. *if you like*: if you wish to phrase or consider something in a particular manner; often used as a vaguely intensive expression, = 'indeed', 'perhaps'. *colloq.*

1875 T. E. BRIDGETT *Our Lady's Dowry* II. xi. 336 They were placed in churches by simple faith, or credulity if you like, but not by wilful fraud. **1909** W. H. HUDSON *Afoot in Eng.* ii. 20 'What!' I exclaimed. 'Lady Y—: that funny old woman!' 'No—middle-aged,' he corrected... 'Very well, middle-aged if you like.' **1955** L. P. HARTLEY *Perfect Woman* xxxvi. 325 Eighteen years faithful to an unfaithful man: there was proof of staunchness, if you like! **1968** 'A. GILBERT' *Night Encounter* iii. 37 That was a surprise, if you like, you wouldn't have thought Mr. Nicholas had enough humanity in him to give her a child. **1970** *Sunday Times* (Colour Suppl.) 15 Mar. 25/1, I could tell you some stories about Max [Miller], but I won't. Used to make me laugh, though. He was real blue if you like. **1973** *Listener* 15 Nov. 664/1 *Princess Anne*: We're shown the best, if you like. But nonetheless it's life.

like, *v.*[2] **2.** (U.S. examples.)

1800 A. M. THORNTON in *Rec. Columbia Hist. Soc.* (1907) X. 117 Joe..said they liked to have been lost in Pohick run. **1854** J. E. COOKE *Virginia Comedians* I. xlix. 282 She liked to fainted just now.

-like, *suffix.* Add: **2. a.** (Further examples.)

1910 A. H. ADAMS *Galahad Jones* 208 I'd be useful-like to keep a look out. **1937** M. SCOTT *Barbara Prospers* 214 Her bein' shaky-like. **1953** 'N. BLAKE' *Dreadful Hollow* 38 We have a stronger parson now—more active-like.

b. (Further examples.)

1895 A. A. GRACE *Maoriland Stories* 105, I suppose you won't care to stop the night with a chap, friendly-like. **1907** W. H. KOEBEL *Return of Joe* 50 Things seemed panning out so strange-like. **1967** *Observer* 10 Sept. 17/3, I went out with her, but all the coloured girls began to look at me weird-like: I had to pack it up quick.

likelihood. 2. c. For '*Obs.* exc. *Sc.*' read 'Now *rare* exc. *Sc.*' and add further example.

1894 G. MEREDITH *Ld. Ormont* III. xii. 241 The likelihood is, she'll feel bound in honour to serve him faithfully for the rest of their wedded days.

likely, *a.* and *adv.* **A.** *adj.* **2. b.** Colloq. phr. *not likely*: certainly not; I refuse.

1893 G. B. SHAW *Widowers' Houses* II. iv. 47 Catch him going down to collect his own rents! Not likely! **1914** —— *Pygmalion* (1916) III. 153 Walk! Not bloody likely. .. I am going in a taxi. **1922** C. E. MONTAGUE *Disenchantment* x. 139 The German sentries said, 'Go back, or we shall have to shoot.' The Englishmen said 'Not likely!' advanced to the German wire, and asked again for an officer. **1934** G. B. SHAW *On Rocks* II. 240. Take the land with one hand and give back its cash value to the landlords with the other! Not likely. I ask you again, do you take us for fools?

B. *adv.* **2.** Now freq. in N. Amer.

1919 E. O'NEILL *Ile* in *Moon of Caribbees, etc.* (1923) 10 I'm afeard there'll be trouble with the hands by the look o' things. They'll likely turn ugly...if you don't put back. **1931** —— *Mourning becomes Electra* I. i. 37 You've likely heard gossip. **1963** *Monsanto Mag.* Mar. 10/2 Beams of different frequencies likely could be obtained by varying the lasing material slightly. **1964** *Amer. N. & Q.* Jan. 76/2 The American public never has understood, and likely never will, the chaotic and complex character of the Indian problem during the 19th century. **1970** *Toronto Daily Star* 24 Sept. 12/8 The heroin addict likely will retrace or repeat many strokes of the pen, showing he is not in full control of his neuromuscular functions. **1971** *Publishers' Weekly* 22 Nov. 14/1 It is possible to predict that within a few years the microfiche likely will move from the library into the study and home.

liker. (Further examples.)

1871 M. ARNOLD *Let.* 18 Aug. (1895) II. 62, I am one of the true likers of the Continent. **1890** W. C. GANNETT *Blessed be Drudgery* 41 Each of us is ringed about by two circles... The outer circle is the circle of our Likers, the inner is the circle of our Lovers.

likkewaan (li·kəvān). Also **lagavaan, likawaan.** [Afrikaans.] = LEGUAN. Cf. *IGUANA 2.

1907 P. FITZPATRICK *Jock of Bushveld* 315 There was not even a lagavaan slide, a game path, or a drinking place. **1914** *Farmer's Annual* (S. Afr.) 334 Likavaan Skin. How to cure it. Take a quantity of alum and place it along with a small quantity of water in an old iron pot. **1936** WILLIAMS & MAY *I am Black* xviii. 187 That boy was Shabala. It was he who had captured the likkewan [*in 1949 edition corrected to* likkewaan]. **1949** *Cape Argus Mag.* 14 May 10 The dour old likkewaan with his whiplash of a tail, can still be seen creeping through the shadows in search of birds' eggs to suck. **1971** H. C. BOSMAN *Bekkersdal Marathon* 123 'What I mean is all right, for instance,' Chris Welman continued, 'is to push a small likkewaan down the back of a visitor's neck, and to pretend to him that it's a mamba.'

likuta (likū·ta). Pl. **makuta.** [Native word; etym. uncertain; perh. f. Nupe *kuta* stone.] A coin and monetary unit introduced in the Democratic Republic of the Congo (now Zaïre) in June 1967, whose value is one hundredth of a zaïre.

1967 in WEBSTER Add. **1971** *N.Y. Times* 27 June 5 The monetary unit [of the Democratic Republic of the Congo] is the Zaire (Z.) divided into 100 makuta (K.) each worth two American cents. 'Makuta' is the plural form of the word 'likuta'. One Z. equals two U.S. dollars. **1972** *Times* 6 Dec. (Europe & Third World Suppl.) p. iii/2 (Advt.), The Zaire is divided into 100 Makuta and the Likuta (the singular of Makuta) in turn consists of 100 Sengi.

lil (lil), *a.* Also **li'l.** Colloq. contraction of LITTLE *a.*

1881 J. C. HARRIS *Nights with Uncle Remus* (1884) lx. 258 One ole Bear..hab one, two lilly Bear... Lil boy Bear, 'e des lahff'.. Lil gal Bear, 'e look skeer. **1912** C. E. MULFORD in *Pearson's Mag.* May 627/1 Purty, all right. Brown hair an' I reckon brown eyes. Nice li'l girl. **1912** C. MACKENZIE *Carnival* v. 54 Would you like him to give you a lil girl like me? **1932** L. GOLDING *Magnolia St.* III. iii. 516 Good ole Mick!.. Plucky lil bastard! **1953** K. TENNANT *Joyful Condemned* xxxix. 391 We'll go out and see your Mom. Take her a lil present, maybe. **1967** K. ALLSOP *Hard Travellin'* xxiii. 274, I can fiddle a li'l bit. **1967** PERRY & ALDRIDGE *Penguin Bk. Comics* iii. 99 Much of Li'l Abner has been absorbed into American folk-lore. **1969** 'I. DRUMMOND' *Man with Tiny Head* 7 Where's girl? Where's lil girl? **1975** M. KENYON *Mr Big* xviii. 165 Phoebe said, 'That's a helluva greeting for a li'l ladykin.'

lila (lī·la). *India.* [ad. Skr. *līlā* play, sport, amusement.] In Hindu mythology, the cosmic dance or playful activity of the Supreme Spirit manifested in the Universe (see quots.); also, the name of an Indian dance representing this.

1828 H. H. WILSON in *Asiatick Researches* XVI. 115 His [*sc.* Krishna's] feats, in which his juvenile characters are regarded, are his *Lilá*, or sport. **1861** —— *Ess. & Lect. Relig. Hindus* I. 124 In this description of creation.. the deity [*sc.* Krishna] is still spoken of as a young man... The acts of divinity are his *Lilá*, or sport. **1917** L. L. P. NOBLE in A. Coomaraswamy *Dance of Śiva* (1924) 63 The Spirit..is all rapture, all bliss, in this play (*lilā*) Free, divine, in this love struggle. **1924** A. COOMARASWAMY *Dance of Śiva* 62 The conception of the world process as the Lord's pastime or amusement (*lilā*) is also prominent in the Saiva scriptures. **1926** *Indian Art & Lett.* II. 78 The *Svabhāva*, or nature of Being-Power, is *Lilā*, or Play, a term which means free spontaneous activity. **1962** A. HUXLEY *Island* x. 167 Shiva-Nataraja dances the dance of endless becoming and passing away. It's his *lila*, his cosmic play. **1967** SINGHA & MASSEY *Indian Dances* xi. 109 Their dance is the *lila* or play of cosmic forces and serves as a preface to the drama which is to follow. **1972** N. HEIN *Miracle Plays of Mathurā* iv. 70 Not only Vishnu's creation of the cosmos is viewed as līlā, but also his actions within the cosmos when he enters his creation in the form of his various incarnations.

lilac. Add: **2. c.** The scent of lilac, esp. as used in cosmetics, etc.

1895 *Montgomery Ward Catal.* 259/3 Perfumes... White Lilac. **1898** *Illustr. London News* 1 Jan. 34 (Advt.), Lance Perfumes..acacia, violet, lilac..price one shilling. *c* **1938** *Fortnum & Mason Price List* 54/1 Soaps..Lilac. **1951** A. LANGENBACH *Wines Germany* xxviii. 126 The finest Rheingau growths..have a delicious lilac-like bouquet. **1972** *Guardian* 22 Aug. 9/4 Jackson's have revived the floral perfumes... The current range comprises sweetpea ..purple lilac, and jonquil.

3. *lilac-blossom*, *-time*; **lilac-breasted roller,** *Coracias caudata*, a bird found in the southern half of Africa.

1890 O. WILDE *Dorian Gray* ii. 15 Lord Henry..found Dorian Gray burying his face in the great cool lilac-blossoms. **1974** A. GOODARD *Vienna Pursuit* III. 115 Some lilac blossom had been blown..across the pavement. **1908** HAAGNER & IVY *Sk. S. Afr. Bird-Life* 29 The beautiful Lilac-breasted Roller (*C*[*oracias*] *caudatus*) is green, blue and brown, with the breast of a purplish-lilac tinge with white shaft-streaks, and the abdomen blue... This bird is not uncommon in the Transvaal bushveld. **1947** J. STEVENSON-HAMILTON *Wild Life S. Afr.* xxxiv. 293 The bright plumage..of the lilac-breasted roller. **1971** *Country Life* 28 Oct. 1126/2 [In Ethiopia] I first saw those gorgeously-coloured birds, the lilac-breasted rollers. **1906** W. ROBINSON *Eng. Flower Garden* (ed. 10) 881/1 To have a good Lilac-time it is essential to have the newer varieties raised in France. **1910** A. NOYES *Barrel Organ* in *Coll. Poems* I. 129 Go down to Kew in lilac-time (it isn't far from London!).

lilacky (ləi·lăki), *a.* Also **lilacy.** [f. LILAC 2.] Of a lilac colour.

1863 QUEEN VICTORIA *Let.* 23 Dec. in R. Fulford *Dearest Mama* (1968) 281 The sky is a leaden, lilacy blue—with no white clouds. **1910** *Westm. Gaz.* 19 Feb. 2/2 Walls on walls of lilacky limestone.

lilipi (li·lipi). Chiefly *N.Z. Hist.* Also **lilipu, lillipe, lillip(p)ee.** [Origin unknown.] (See quot. 1861.)

In quot. 1830, from a W. African context, *lilipee* may be some other word.

1830 H. CROW *Mem.* ix. 146 For the sick we provided strong soups and middle messes, prepared from mutton, goats'-flesh, fowls, &c. to which were added sago and lilipees. **1860** *Taranaki Punch* I. iv. 8 Something..that, although it is not lilipi yet, when pronounced by our old friend.., sounds very like it, namely 'lilly pay'. **1861** J. VON HAAST *Rep. Topogr. & Geol. Explor. Nelson Province* i. 22 [We confined] ourselves to a small pot of lillipe (or boiled flour) twice a day. **1874** L. J. KENNAWAY *Crusts* 147 The poor children..lived principally on heavy bread and '*lillippee*', (a mixture nothing more nor less than paper-hanging paste). **1880** J. C. CRAWFORD *Recoll. Trav. N.Z. & Austral.* 99 One old lady..presented us with a dish of *lillipee*, which is simply flour and water. **1915** J. HAY *Reminisc. Earliest Canterbury* i. 34 They [*sc.* the Maoris] were very fond..of wheat and sugar boiled together, to which they gave the name of 'Lilipu'.

lilium (li·liŏm). [L. *līlium*: see LILY. Adopted by Linnæus in his *Species Plantarum* (1753) I. 302 as the name of a genus.] = LILY 1.

1902 *Westm. Gaz.* 10 Dec. 10/1 Of all flowers none are affected by frost so much as roses,..violets, and liliums. **1903** *Ibid.* 26 Nov. 12/1 White liliums are fetching 4s. a bunch. **1923** *Chambers's Jrnl.* Dec. 786/2 The finest liliums and choice gladioli grow superbly. **1958** M. WEST *Second Victory* vi. 91 Hot-house blooms that must have come from a dozen private homes—cyclamen, orchids, liliums and azaleas. **1970** *Lily Year Bk.* XXXIII. 88 [In Australia] at least four leading lilium nurserymen of a decade ago no longer distribute lilium bulbs in appreciable numbers.

Lille (līl). The name of a city in the Nord department of France, used *attrib.* to designate a kind of pillow or bobbin lace.

1865 F. B. PALLISER *Hist. Lace* xvi. 211 The semé of little square dots on the ground—one of the characteristics of Lille lace—is still retained. **1900** E. JACKSON *Hist. Hand-Made Lace* 176 Lille laces have always been favourites in England, the black especially. **1953** M. POWYS *Lace & Lace-Making* iv. 31 The Lille lace edgings generally have a straight edge. **1960** *Connoisseur's Handbk. Antique Collecting* 164/1 *Lille lace*, pillow lace very popular in later 18th cent. England, made sometimes in black, but never as a dress lace.

Lillet (lī·le). Also **Kina Lillet.** the proprietary name of a French aperitif; also, a glass of this wine.

1930 H. Craddock *Savoy Cocktail Bk.* 41 *Campden Cocktail*, ½ Dry Gin. ¼ Cointreau. ¼ Kina Lillet. **1951** R. Postgate *Plain Man's Guide to Wine* iii. 59 St. Raphael is slightly sweeter, Byrrh and Lillet slightly sharper. **1960** *New Yorker* 29 Oct. 51/2 Sipping a Lillet-and-gin. **1972** N. Freeling *Long Silence* I. 59 Now—Campari, Lillet, Chambéry? **1973** *Vogue* Jan. 85/2 A twist of orange with Lillet.

lillipe, lillip(p)ee, varr. *lilipi.

lilly-pilly. Also lilli-pilli. Substitute for def.: An Australian evergreen tree, *Eugenia* (or *Acmena*) *smithii*, of the family Myrtaceæ, or the timber obtained from it. Also *attrib.* (Later examples.)

1881 *Off. Rec. Sydney Internat. Exhib. 1879* 723 Lilly Pilly. *Eugenia Smithii*... Forms a beautiful shrub when cut back... The wood makes good axe handles. **1936** F. Clune *Roaming round Darling* iii. 26 In 1881 King George V planted a lillipilli-tree. **1944** *Living off Land* ii. 45 Lilly-pilly or Brush Cherry. **1946** *Coast to Coast 1945* 56 A tree-fern, maidenhair in the mossy banks, and a clump of lilli-pillis marked the dell. **1965** *Austral. Encycl.* III. 412/1 *Acmena* is a small genus containing the common lilly-pilly (*A. smithii*), which is widely spread in eastern Australia along rivers and streams and in the rain-forests... It has small terminal sprays of insignificant greenish flowers followed by purplish to white fruits, and is much cultivated as a hedge plant. **1965** *Courier-Mail* (Brisbane) 16 Nov. 20 The feathered folk in the lilipillies of the great gully below began to welcome Piccaninny Daylight.

Li-Lo (ləi·lōu). Also **Lilo, lilo.** [f. *to lie low.*] The proprietary name of a type of air-bed or inflatable rubber mattress. Also *fig.*

1936 *Trade Marks Jrnl.* 16 Sept. 1150 Li-Lo... Air-beds, air-pillows and air-pillow-bags, all made principally of india-rubber. P. B. Cow & Company Limited,.. London,..manufacturers. **1939** 'N. Shute' *What happened to Corbetts* i. 1 Sophie their nurse was lying on a Li-Lo on the oil-stained floor, covered with an eiderdown. **1949** O. Lancaster *Drayneflete Revealed* 63 And Dido on her lilo à sa proie attachée. **1954** W. Noyce *South Col* iv. 58 The really experienced expeditioners, Ed and George Lowe, had their Li-Los inflated. **1960** V. Gielgud *To Bed at Noon* I. iv. 27 If the chairs were no more than adequate there were lilos and cushions in abundance. **1969** *Listener* 24 July 114/3 We've been looking at grand pianos... This is one likely spot where a nudist with an eye to the main chance might well secrete himself. A lilo across the wires. **1972** N. Bentley *Events of that Week* 39, I left Theresa on a Li-lo and put my sandals on. **1973** *Guardian* 13 Oct. 10/1 The social service Lilo has become too easy to loll on.

lilt, *v.* Add: **1. b.** Also with *out.*

1916 A. Bennett *Lion's Share* xxv. 191 Musa lilted out the delicate, gay phrases of Debussy.

3. (Later examples.)

1901 Kipling *Traffics & Discov.* (1904) 79 He lilted a little on his feet when he was pleased. *Ibid.* 80 He went to England, and he became a young man, and back he came, lilting a little in his walk.

lilting, *ppl. a.* Add: Also of one's gait: (sense 3 of vb.).

1903 *Longman's Mag.* Jan. 271 Swinging down the street with an easy lilting stride..marched two Englishmen, soldiers both. **1965** E. Bhavnani *Dance in India* xvi. 208 In a lilting change of movements, boys and girls hold hands or link arms and dance round and round in a circle.

lily. Add: **2. c.** The scent of lily of the valley, esp. as used in cosmetics, etc.

1890–91 *T. Eaton & Co. Catal.* Fall & Winter 42/2 Morse's perfumes..new-mown hay, lily of the valley, 25c. per bottle. **1970** *Guardian* 12 May 9/3 This..sprightly fragrance with..notes of carnation,..lily-of-the-valley and roses.

3. b. Used as a term of abuse, esp. of a man to imply lack of masculinity.

1923 G. Saintsbury *Second Scrap Bk.* v. 39 But in order once more to consider and console that lily, the Educational Expert, let us turn to 'grind'. **1929** Hostetter & Beesley *It's a Racket!* 231 *Lily*, an easy victim, exceptionally gullible person. **1930** D. H. Lawrence *Nettles* 19 And Mr. Mead, that old old lily Said: 'Gross! coarse! hideous!' **1933** S. Spender *Poems* 28 Here the pale lily boys flaunt their bright lips. **1958** J. Raymond *England's on Anvil!* 142 In this he differed from men like William ('Cory') Johnson, Oscar Browning, A. C. Benson and the rest of the Eton-and-King's lilies who were such a lush feature of the period.

4. d. *pl.* The bound feet of Chinese women, in allusion to their Chinese designation *kin-leen* 'golden water-lilies'. Also (in sing.) *attrib.* So **lily-footed** *a.*

1841 W. B. Langdon *Descr. Catal. Chinese Collection in Philadelphia* 15 The footstools upon which their 'golden lilies' rest, are covered with embroidered silk. **1886** C. M. Yonge *Chantry House* II. xx. 188 Is he going to wed a fair Chinese with lily feet? **1922** W. S. Maugham *On Chinese Screen* xviii. 72 They rest there for a while on their small feet, their golden lilies, gossiping elegantly. **1933** N. Waln *House of Exile* I. i. 26 We could not walk, as..Mai-da's mother..had 'lily' feet. **1937** E. Snow *Red Star over China* I. ii. 26 Yang Hu-Cheng..was a two-wife man. The first was the lily-footed wife of his youth.

4*. Phr. to *paint* (or *to gild*) *the lily*: to embellish excessively, to add ornament where none is needed.

1595 Shakes. *John* iv. ii. 11 To gilde refined Gold, to paint the Lilly; To throw a perfume on the Violet,.. Is wastefull, and ridiculous excesse. **1919** H. Jenkins *John Dene of Toronto* vii. 113 'Where's Finlay?' asked Colonel Walton. 'He's painting the lily... Seeing how near he can get to this Bergen fellow.' **1928** *Manch. Guardian Weekly* 28 Sept. 243/3 Nature and history have already been so kind to that ancient and charming townlet on the Dart that improvement would be a gilding of the lily. **1935** J. Buchan *House of Four Winds* 22 It's rather like painting the lily, you know. **1953** *Manch. Guardian Weekly* 19 Feb. 13/2 While it may seem to be painting the lily, I should like to add somewhat to Mr Alistair Cooke's excellent article. **1958** J. Raymond *England's on Anvil!* 15 In Englishing the passage, Peter Motteux..contrives at once splendidly to gild the lily and tone down the anti-Protestantism. **1968** *Encycl. Brit.* XII. 842/1 The favourite technique of decoration of Mogul jades is insetting with gold and precious stones..an example of painting the lily that would hardly have commended itself to the Chinese jade carver.

5. *lily-coloured, -green, -scented, -sweet, -yellow* adjs.; **lily-pad** (earlier and later examples); **lily-pond,** a pond in which water-lilies are grown; **lily-trotter,** a water-bird of the family Jacanidæ, esp. *Actophilornis africana*, found in tropical Africa, or *Microparra capensis*, the lesser lily-trotter, found in east Africa; also = Jacana.

c **1866** G. M. Hopkins *Poems* (1918) 9 Lily-coloured clothes provide Your spouse not laboured-at nor spun. **1875** Browning *Inn Album* ii. 72 My big and bony, here, against the bunch Of lily-coloured five with signet-ring. **1739** tr. *Art of Painting in Miniature* (ed. 4) 13 Lilly-Green, Sap-Green, and Gamboge..must be temper'd with fair Water only. **1965** S. Gibbons in J. Gibb *Light on C. S. Lewis* v. 87 Here she was, the right descendant of Grendel, with her lily-green complexion. **1843** *Knickerbocker* XXII. 1 Huge moccasin darting away beneath the dense reeds and lily-pads of the swamp. **1875** J. G. Holland *Sevenoaks* v. 65 A deer, feeding among the lily-pads. **1888** *Nation* (N.Y.) 19 July 57/2 The trout breaking at the edge of the lily-pads. **1946** K. Tennant *Lost Haven* (1947) 2 Shallow blue water from which the great white paper-barks tower shadowing the lily-pads. **1958** G. Durrell *Encounters with Animals* I. 38, I had watched her standing on the lily-pads. **1901** G. Jekyll *Wall & Water Gardens* xx. 161 Such a scene as Mr. Robinson's Lily pond in North Sussex..could scarcely be bettered. **1974** R. Harris *Double Snare* iv. 27 From the direction of the lily pond comes the croak of little frogs. **1796** Coleridge *Poems* 18 Summer's lily-scented plume. **1869** Browning *Ring & Bk.* III. vii. 50 The sword I wear shall pink His lily-scented cassock through and through. **1936** R. Campbell *Mithraic Emblems* 31 Out of a wound that never heals Rills forth the lily-scented blood. **1931** V. Woolf *Waves* 290 Let us commit any blasphemy of laughter and criticism rather than exude this lily-sweet glue. **1920** *Blackw. Mag.* May 649/2 The busy lily trotter, hurrying across the broad flat water-lily leaves. **1951** R. Campbell *Light on Dark Horse* 82 Those strange little birds, the lily-trotters. **1958** G. Durrell *Encounters with Animals* I. 35 It is with the aid of these long toes and the even distribution of weight that they give that the jacana manages to walk across water, using the water-lily leaves and other water-plants as its pathways. It has thus earned its name of lily-trotter. **1971** *Country Life* 30 Sept. 830/1 The lakes [in Tanzania] give you close views of ibises, egrets,..lily trotters. *c* **1865** G. M. Hopkins *Poems* (1948) 123 Lily-yellow is the west.

B. *adj.* **b.** *lily-faced* (later example); **lily-liveredly** *adv.*

1929 D. H. Lawrence *Pansies* 48 It's either you fight or you die, Die, die, lily-liveredly die. **1934** Dylan Thomas *Let.* 14 Jan. (1966) 92 As the black man must have first regarded the features of his lily-faced brother.

li·lying, *vbl. sb. rare*$^{-1}$. = *lily-work* (Lily A. 5).

1874 G. M. Hopkins *Jrnls. & Papers* (1959) 248 The touching and passionate curves of the lilyings in the iron-work.

lily-white, *a.* Add: **2.** In favour of, committed to, or pertaining to a policy of racial segregation. orig. *U.S.*

1903 *N.Y. Times* 23 Sept., The report that the President was seeking reconciliation with the 'Lilywhite' faction, which eliminated the negro from the last State Convention. **1909** *Westm. Gaz.* 13 Feb. 2/2 That..is what they call the lily-white policy!.. It is the unprincipled white politician who finds anti-negro agitation a popular plank in his platform. **1953** *Manch. Guardian Weekly* 8 Oct. 5/1 Before 1948 groups of landlords had managed to maintain 'lily-white' communities by signing 'restrictive covenants'. **1968** *Morning Star* 10 Aug. 1/1 While the lilywhite Republican convention was nominating Richard Nixon in an atmosphere of ballyhoo and frenzied hysteria, the same city of Miami saw Negroes demonstrating for their rights.

b. Irreproachable, lacking faults or imperfections.

1961 in Webster. **1970** *New Yorker* 9 May 33/3, I think the city should be lily-white on this, so the first thing I'm going to try to do is convert all our city vehicles to low-pollution engines. **1973** *Times* 18 Jan. 2/7 Robert Mark [the commissioner] is determined to have a lily-white police force. He will have a lily-white police force looking pretty in the street.

Lima. Add: **Lima bean** (earlier and later examples).

1819 [see *butter-bean]. **1831** M. Holley *Texas* (1833) xi. 123 He had known winters here so mild, as not to kill the Lima bean. **1969** *Northwest* (*Sunday Oregonian Mag.*) 14 Dec. 19/1 The pulp [of pawpaw] is yellow or orange and contains several brown seeds about the size and shape of a Lima Bean.

b. *ellipt.* = Lima bean. *U.S.*

1856 F. S. Cozzens *Sparrowgrass Papers* vii. 85 Put the Limas to the right..and as for the rest of the seeds sweep them into the refuse basket. **1865** *Trans. Illinois Agric. Soc.* V. 758 Pole Beans—Amongst these the Limas deservedly rank the highest. **1942** E. Paul *Narrow St.* vi. 51 The Épicerie Danton had limas, normal-sized and 'baby', Canterbury, scarlet runners, pintos, [etc.].

limb, *sb.*[1] Add: **2. b.** (Later examples.)

1885 in Farmer *Slang* (1891) II. 18/2 Between you'n me, red stockings ain't becomin' to all—ahem—limbs. **1898** M. Deland *Old Chester Tales* 237 But it was she who informed him that he might stay until his 'limb' permitted him to walk. **1902** H. L. Wilson *Spenders* xxxi. 369 One of my maids who slipped on the avenue yesterday and fractured one of her—er—limbs. **1904** *Courier-Jrnl.* (Louisville, Kentucky) 5 Sept. 1 Her limbs were void of shoes or stockings. **1924** W. M. Raine *Troubled Waters* i. 12 She dexterously arranged the skirt without being able to conceal some inches of slender limb rising from a well-turned ankle.

4. b. Also, the part of a compound core of a transformer, electromagnet, etc., on which a coil is wound.

1902 *Encycl. Brit.* XXVII. 584/1 These [portions] are: (1) the magnet 'cores' or 'limbs', carrying the exciting coils whereby the inert iron is converted into an electromagnet; (2) the yoke, which joins the limbs together and conducts the flux between them; and (3) the pole-pieces. **1934** H. Cotton *Design Electr. Machinery* viii. 162 With core-type transformers the cross-section of the limbs may be rectangular in the case of small transformers, but it is more usual to adopt for all sizes a cross-section which fits as closely as possible into a circumscribing circle. **1943** *Gloss. Terms Electr. Engin.* (*B.S.I.*) 40 Those parts of the [transformer] core surrounded by windings are termed legs or limbs and those not so surrounded are termed yokes.

d. *out on a limb*, in an isolated or stranded position; at a disadvantage. orig. *U.S.*

1897 A. H. Lewis *Wolfville* 59 Seven of us..seein' whatever can we tie down an' brand, when some Mexicans gets us out on a limb. **1934** *Amer. Speech* IX. 11/2 A player is *out on a limb* when he is allowed to play a hand at an overambitious contract. **1939** F. Scott Fitzgerald *Let.* Winter (1964) 50 She might not consider the rearrangement of someone else's words a literary composition, which would leave you out on a limb. **1943** J. B. Priestley *Daylight on Saturday* xxvii. 210 Somebody does something dam' silly, which probably means that some poor devils somewhere are left out on a limb. **1948** J. Steinbeck *Russ. Jrnl.* (1949) iii. 41 No one is willing to go out on any limb. No one is willing to say yes or no to a proposition. He must always go to someone higher. **1959** *Economist* 18 Apr. 214/2 President Nasser is out on a bit of a limb, but in this uncomfortable situation he can take comfort from the thought that there is still no other pan-Arab leader in sight. **1972** *Guardian* 7 Feb. 10/6 Once in the Commission, the British Civil Servant will feel out on a limb, away from the main-stream of his department. **1973** *Times* 23 May 16/5 At the international law of the sea conference Britain could find herself isolated and out on a limb.

5. *limb-dance, -fitter, -fitting*; **limb-bud** *Embryol.*, in an embryo, a small protuberance from which a limb develops; **limb-kinetic** *a. Path.*, denoting a form of apraxia (see quot. 1966); **limb-wood** (see quot.).

1906 G. R. Satterlee *Outl. Human Embryol.* v. 55 Outgrowths of mesenchyme occur from the lateral portion of the trunk. These projections are called the limb-buds, and are the *anlages* for the arms and legs. **1926** [see *cultivate *v.* 2 b]. **1965** L. B. Arey *Developmental Anat.* (ed. 7) xii. 210 The limb buds appear late in the fourth week as lateral swellings. *a* **1885** G. M. Hopkins *Poems* (1918) 79 While cripples are, while lepers, dancers in dismal limb-dance. **1967** *Economist* 8 Apr. 121/3 Hangers granted a rise..to its limb-fitters from the start of this year. **1920** *Glasgow Herald* 3 Dec. 8 The limb-fitting centres in the United Kingdom have been increased from 6 to 20. **1959** *Chambers's Encycl.* I. 652/1 Roehampton, the chief limb-fitting centre in England. **1914, 1933** Limb-kinetic [see *ideokinetic* adj. s.v. *ideo-]. **1966** *McGraw-Hill Encycl. Sci. & Technol.* I. 494/1 Several forms of apraxia are usually distinguished. The lowest order apraxia is called limb-kinetic or motor... Limb-kinetic apraxia refers to a loss of coordination usually affecting one upper limb only. Gross movements may be performed fairly well, whereas fine individual movements of the fingers are lost. **1901** J. Black *Illustr. Carpenter & Builder Ser.: Home Handicrafts* 62 [For mosaic work] black is obtained by using ebony or bog oak.. green, by.. a species of native green oak, known as 'limb wood'.

limb, *sb.*[2] Add: **4.** Special Comb.: **limb-darkening** *Astr.*, the apparent darkening of the face of the sun towards its edges.

1931 *Monthly Notices R. Astr. Soc.* XCI. 893, I (x) is of the form a–mx (limb darkening linearly proportional to distance from the centre). **1938** *Astrophysical Jrnl.* LXXXVII. 45 (*heading*) The effect of an adiabatic layer upon solar limb darkening. **1962** *Science Survey* III. 103 Visual observations..show that the sun's disc is brightest at the centre, becoming gradually dimmer towards the outer edge, or limb. This phenomenon is known as limb darkening, and is due to the fact that we look less and less deeply into the hotter layers of the sun as we view its surface more obliquely.

limb, *v.* Add: **1. b.** To remove branches from (a tree).

1835 H. Evans *Jrnl.* 2 July in *Mississippi Valley Hist.*

Rev. (1927) XIV. 202 Weather beaten cotton wood trees limbed and shattered by the storms of the prairies. **1839** E. HOLMES *Rep. Explor. Aroostook River* 53 The best mode undoubtedly is to fall the trees and '*limb*' them (that is, cut off the limbs,) in June. **1889** *Harper's Mag.* Jan. 231/1 It seemed to be built principally of alder poles well limbed off and placed, roughly speaking, side by side. **1971** *Timber Trades Jrnl.* 3 Apr. 58/2 The chainsaw has long been used for limbing hardwoods.

Limba[1] (li·mbă), *sb.* and *a.* Also **Limbah.** [Native name.] **A.** *sb.* **a.** A member of a West African people inhabiting Sierra Leone. **b.** The language of the Limbas. **B.** *adj.* Of or pertaining to this people or their language.

1902 *Encycl. Brit.* XX. 624/1 Sierra Leone is inhabited by about a dozen distinct African peoples, the most important being the Mende, Temne, Limba [etc.]. **1925** T. N. GODDARD *Handbk. Sierra Leone* III. 55 The *Limbas* may be found in the north of the Temne country. **1925** H. C. LUKE *Bibliogr. Sierra Leone* (ed. 2) 149 The Wesleyan Methodist Catechism in Limbah. **1951** K. L. LITTLE *Mende of Sierra Leone* 71 The Limba wear gowns of native cloth and tight shorts of the same material. **1954** R. LEWIS *Sierra Leone* xii. 118 When a Limba chief dies, weird moans issue from it [*sc.* a cave]. Limbas can hear the dead man being brought to Kumba the Krifi. **1964** C. FYFE *Sierra Leone Inheritance* 20 He killed the Limbas and sold them.

limba[2] (li·mbă). [f. Gabon name *limbo.*] The West African tree *Terminalia superba* or the hardwood obtained from it; = *AFARA.

[**1937** J. M. DALZIEL *Useful Plants W. Trop. Afr.* 83 The timber [of *Terminalia superba*] from the Belgian Congo is known as 'limbo (or limba) clair' when at least two-thirds of the diameter is light-coloured.] **1955** *Times* 6 May 12/6 Limba, a light honey-coloured hardwood from Africa. **1960** *House & Garden* Nov. 34/1 The new limba furniture has all the charm and grace one expects. *Ibid.*, An abundance of good designs in limba, tola, lacquer or oak.

limbal (li·mbăl), *a. Ophthalm.* [f. LIMB(US + -AL.] Of or pertaining to the limbus of the cornea.

1947 F. H. ADLER *Gifford's Textbk. Ophthalm.* (ed. 4) xi. 221 Fine capillary loops from the anterior ciliary vessels pass into the cornea, forming the limbal arcades. **1958** H. B. STALLARD *Eye Surg.* (ed. 3) viii. 570 The limbal incision covered by a conjunctival flap is preferable, for adjacent blood-supply is better and the firm closure of the wound is quicker than in the corneal section. **1972** *Virchows Archiv* A. CCCLV. 277 The limbal region of the bulbar conjunctiva was covered by a stratified squamous epithelium.

limbed, *a.* (Later examples.)

1899 *Echo* 9 Mar. 1/4 Every reader of Dickens remembers the frail ex-prisoner of the Bastille, white-haired and feeble-limbed. **1954** T. GUNN *Fighting Terms* 44 My hate throbs yet but I am feeble-limbed.

limber, *sb.*[1] Add: **3. limber-neck,** a kind of botulism affecting poultry, caused by the toxin produced by a type of the bacterium *Clostridium botulinum.*

1910 C. S. VALENTINE *How to keep Hens for Profit* 271 The disease called 'limberneck', in which the affected bird is unable to control the head, which droops to the ground, is said by many who have had large experience with it to be the result of stomach irritation brought on by eating maggots. **1927** E. T. BROWN *'How to do it' Poultry Bk.* xxiii. 242 Limberneck or false cholera..is due entirely to a form of poisoning. **1931** DICKINSON & LEWIS *Poultry Enterprises* ix. 216 When flies and maggots infest putrid meat and other spoiled feeds, fowls eating them are likely to show symptoms of limber neck disease. **1964** M. HYNES *Med. Bacteriol.* (ed. 8) xx. 296 These types [of botulism toxin] are also most often responsible for 'limber-neck' of chickens and ducks.

limber, *a.* Add: **4.** *limber-footed* (later example).

1904 *Westm. Gaz.* 8 May 14/2 Here leaps the limber-footed, listening hare.

limber, *v.*[1] Add: Also with *up*, and *intr.* Hence **li·mbering** *vbl. sb.*, **limbering-up** *vbl. sb.*

1901 *Daily Colonist* (Victoria, B.C.) 8 Oct. 3/2 When her machinery is limbered up after it has been used a while she will do much better. **1921** *Ibid.* 5 Apr. 10/2 During the recent fine weather several of the [tennis club] members have been out limbering up after the inactivities of the Winter months. **1921** *Blackw. Mag.* Aug. 262/1 Dempsey had passed the afternoon in a 'limbering-up hike'. **1927** *Dancing Times* Dec. 301/1 Most dance students know that limbering is the basis for every kind of dance work. **1929** WODEHOUSE *Mr. Mulliner Speaking* ii. 64 He waggled his right leg for a moment to limber it up, backed a pace or two and crept forward. **1957** *Oxf. Pocket Bk. Athletic Training* (ed. 2) 27 An athlete who fails to limber-up properly deliberately handicaps himself. **1962** *Listener* 29 March 566/1 As images and figures in compositions..they limber or stretch or occasionally pose. **1963** H. GARNER in R. Weaver *Canad. Short Stories* (1968) 2nd Ser. 23 The limbering up we were getting from our work. **1971** R. DENTRY *Encounter at Kharmel* i. 1 He did twenty four half knee-bends to limber up.

limbered (li·mbəɹd), *a.* [f. LIMBER *sb.*[1]] Having a limber.

1920 *Blackw. Mag.* Feb. 279/2, I lent him some men and a limbered waggon. **1942** *R.A.F. Jrnl.* 3 Oct. 18 The officers saw a German gun-team galloping their limbered gun away.

limberly (li·mbəɹli), *adv.* [f. LIMBER *a.*] In a limber or supple manner.

1891 *Harper's Mag.* Nov. 891/2 His long spare arms swing limberly before a long spare body. **1909** 'O. HENRY' *Roads of Destiny* xii. 186 They..slouched limberly over to the railroad eating-house. **1964** *N. Y. Times Mag.* 23 Aug. 30 It was sculpted to Chanel's small, athletic figure and moves with it as limberly as a leopard's own leopard skin.

limbic, *a.* Add: Also, of or pertaining to the limbic lobe or limbic system; *limbic system*, a region of the brain comprising the limbic lobe and certain neighbouring areas (see quot. 1967[1]).

1952 *Electroencephalogr. & Clin. Neurophysiol.* IV. 407 The limbic system is comprised of the cortex contained in the great limbic lobe of Broca..together with subcortical cell stations. **1957** H. H. JASPER et al. *Reticular Formation Brain* 665 There is no doubt that all the varied elementary somatomotor and vegetative mechanisms so clearly influenced by limbic stimulation remain essentially undisturbed after bilateral limbic lesions. **1967** C. R. NOBACK *Human Nervous Syst.* viii. 224/1 The difficult-to-define limbic system consists of the limbic lobe..some subcortical nuclei (septal nuclei and amygdala), and neural pathways to other nuclear stations of the brain... Some investigators include the 'other' nuclei (habenular nucleus, hypothalamus, midbrain tegmentum, thalamus, and interpeduncular nucleus) in the limbic system. *Ibid.* 226/2 The midbrain and thalamic reticular nuclei receive inputs from several limbic pathways. **1970** *Nature* 28 Feb. 797/1 Other behaviour patterns..have been elicited by stimulating hypothalamic and limbic regions in many species. **1971** J. Z. YOUNG *Introd. Study Man* x. 136 Sohilder's interpretation of the limbic system is as 'a mechanism for emotion'.

limbo[1]. Add: **2. c.** A type of anti-submarine mortar. Also *attrib.* or as *adj.*

1955 *Times* 20 June 4/6 The frigate Grenville fired live projectiles from her Limbo anti-submarine weapon. *Ibid.*, The Limbo.. is a multi-barrelled mortar of large calibre, linked automatically with a submarine detector of advanced design. **1956** *Jane's Fighting Ships 1956–57* 240/2 Have some side armour as well as deck protection; limbo type anti-submarine rocket throwers. **1957** *Jane's Fighting Ships 1957–58* 42/1 The two Limbos can each fire a pattern of large depth bombs with great accuracy. **1961** T. D. MANNING *Brit. Destroyer* 24 The Squid has been improved on by Limbo which..is not fitted in destroyers but only in frigates.

limbo[3] (li·mbo). [Native name.] A dance in which the dancer bends backwards and passes under a horizontal bar raised only a few inches off the ground. Also *attrib.*

1956 *Caribbean Q.* IV. III. & IV. 204 The firemen also had a characteristic dance similar to the 'limbo', with the body bent sharply backward, knees projecting, and lower legs almost on the pavement. **1958** *Daily Express* 22 Apr. 7/3 The Princess should take home with her memories of gay calypsos and limbos. **1963** *Pix* 2 Mar. 38 Peters said that he first encountered the Limbo on his Pacific cruise.. when it was merely known as 'going under the pole'. **1966** *Observer* 13 Feb. 40/4 Trinidad's champion limbo dancer.. can ease himself blindfold under a bar which is only 8 in. from the floor and is sometimes soaked in spirit and set alight. **1971** *Country Life* 18 Feb. 372 And watching limbo ladies slither and men blow fire. **1972** E. HARGREAVES *Fair Green Weed* i. 12 He..found the pair of them sitting on the patio, watching some limbo dancers on the beach. **1973** *Sunday Advocate-News* (Barbados) 21 Jan. 11/3 More variety should be introduced into these shows, including more steelband music, limbo dancing and folk dancing.

limbric (li·mbrik). (See quot. 1960.)

1930 *Economist* 18 Oct. 713/1 There is still some business to be done in other lines, such as mercerised cotton brocades and limbrics. **1940** *Chambers's Techn. Dict.* 500/2 *Limbric*, a plain grey cotton cloth of medium quality; used for curtains, etc. after being piece-dyed or printed. **1940** *Manch. Guardian Weekly* 25 Oct. 307 It seems unlikely..that the restrictions of silk piece-goods and made-up goods will cause a larger trade to be done in cotton poplins, cambrics, limbrics, etc. **1960** *Textile Terms & Definitions* (Textile Inst.) (ed. 4) 91 *Limbric*, a light-to-medium weight, closely woven, plain-weave cotton cloth made from good quality yarns.

Limbu (li·mbū), *sb.* and *a.* Also **Limboo.** [Native name.] **A.** *sb.* **a.** A member of a Mongoloid people of eastern Nepal; this people collectively. **b.** The Tibeto-Burman language of the Limbu people. **B.** *adj.* Of or pertaining to the Limbu people or their language.

1819 F. HAMILTON *Acct. Kingdom Nepal* i. 54 Among the Kirats was settled a tribe called Limbu... Their languages are said to be different. **1840** *Jrnl. R. Asiatic Soc. Bengal* IX. 495 The Limboos form a large portion of the inhabitants in the mountainous country lying between the Dood-Koosi and the Kanki rivers, in Nipal. **1854** J. D. HOOKER *Himalayan Journals* I. v. 138 The Limboo language is totally different from the Lepcha, with less of the *z* in it, and more labials and palatals, hence more pleasing. **1880** H. A. OLDFIELD *Sk. from Nipal* I. iii. 53 The country of the Kirantis and Limbus at the present time is divided into fifty-two small subahships. **1909** G. A. GRIERSON *Ling. Surv. India* III. I. 283 The Limbus are one of the principal tribes of Eastern Nepal... We have no information about the number of speakers of Limbu in Nepal. **1928** NORTHEY & MORRIS *Gurkhas* xv. 217 The Limbu race is now divided into a large number of tribes. These tribes were formerly centred, in groups, in ten different districts of the Limbu country. **1939** R. GODDEN *Black Narcissus* v. 54 She was learning to distinguish between the State natives and the hill clans, the Lepchas and Bhotiyas and Limbus. **1970** ROSE & FISHER *Politics Nepal* i. 12 The Limbus,.. are making a serious effort to revive their local language as a literary medium after long years of its suppression under Gorkha rule. **1971** K. KENT in C. Bonington *Annapurna South Face* App. H. 310 Later, the Eastern tribes (Rais and Limbus) were also recruited, and, together with some lesser-known but other martial tribes, also became known under the general title of Gurkhas.

Limburger (li·mbɒ̆ɹgəɹ). [a. Du. and G. *Limburger.*] **1.** *attrib.* with *cheese*, or *ellipt.* A soft strong-smelling cheese made in the province of Limburg in Belgium. Also *Limburg cheese.*

1817 C. CAMPBELL *Traveller's Compl. Guide through Belgium & Holland* (ed. 2) iv. 92 The disagreeable smell of the Limburg cheese, called *Herve*, though unpleasant to many, is justly ranked among the delicacies of the rich. **1859** W. H. J. WEALE *Belgium* p. xxvii, *Limburg* and *Herve cheese* are also very good, but their odour is intolerable. *c* **1870** *More Yankee Drolleries* II. 15 Limburger cheese, an abomination guilty of the most powerful odour. **1883** *Authors & Publishers* (G. P. Putnam's Sons) 45 The cheese-monger may not like either Stilton or Roquefort, he may even have his doubts as to the absolute wholesomeness of the more athletic brands of Limburger. **1887** *Harper's Mag.* Mar. 644/1 The obese Teuton delights in 'loud' Limburger and Gruyere. **1905** W. H. SIMMONDS *Pract. Grocer* III. 88 Limburger is a Belgian cheese of the soft class, which is allowed to ripen before use. **1908** [see *HAMBURGER 2]. **1966** MARQUIS & HASKELL *Cheese Bk.* III. 197 Strong cheeses like Limburger and Liederkranz are not for cocktail parties because after an hour or so at warm temperatures they will all but clear the room.

2. a. A native or inhabitant of Limburg. **b.** (Also **Limbu·rgerish.**) The dialect of the Limburgers. Also as *adj.*

1932 *Times Lit. Suppl.* 16 June 446/4 But this Limburgerish would not be a living language if it could be reduced to simple rules. *Ibid.*, Something for which Limburger grammarians have no doubt an appropriate name. **1963** N. FREELING *Gun before Butter* 51 He was no fool. A Limburger... The people from 'below the rivers' are quicker..than the Dutch of Holland.

limbus. 2. (Examples in *Anat.*)

1699 M. LISTER *Journey to Paris* 71 The Membrane or Valve on the Left side of the *Foramen Ovale*..extended almost over the hole, without any *Limbus* round its edges. **1877** W. TURNER *Introd. Human Anat.* vi. 368 Another membrane..arises from a denticulated spiral crest, the limbus or crista spiralis. **1954** S. DUKE-ELDER *Parsons' Dis. Eye* (ed. 12) i. 3 The cornea is set into the sclera like a watch glass so that the latter overlaps the cornea all round the periphery; the junction of the two tissues is known as the limbus. **1961** *Lancet* 22 July 166/2 The blade of the knife emerges 0·5–1·0 mm. on the corneal side of the limbus when the section is complete.

lime, *sb.*[1] Add: **3. e.** A vat containing a solution of lime for removing the hair from skins; the solution itself.

1885 C. T. DAVIS *Manuf. Leather* xxxii. 525 When sufficiently softened the skins are next placed in the 'limes'... The goat-skins remain in the 'limes' about 14 days. **1903** L. A. FLEMMING *Pract. Tanning* 6 When vat room is scarce, it is good practice to haul the skins out after they have been in the lime a few days. **1946** J. W. WATERER *Leather* II. ii. 137 The practice of passing the 'packs' of hides..through a series of liquors, commencing with an old or 'mellow' lime. **1969** T. C. THORSTENSEN *Pract. Leather Technol.* vi. 87 When the hide is introduced into the lime.

5. *lime-burning, -cask, -grout, -hater* (so *-hating* adj.), *-lover* (so *-loving* adj.), *-ooze*; *lime-free* adj.; **lime-rock** (earlier and later examples); **lime-silicate** *a. Petrol.*, applied to a rock which was originally an impure limestone or dolomite and has been thermally metamorphosed, with the result that the lime has combined with silica present as impurities to form calcium silicates; **lime-sink** (earlier example); **lime soap,** a mixture of insoluble calcium salts of fatty acids formed as a precipitate when soap is used in hard water and manufactured for various industrial purposes; **lime-soda** *attrib.*, applied to a process for softening water by treatment with lime and sodium carbonate; **lime-sulphur,** an insecticide and fungicide containing calcium polysulphides which is made by boiling lime and sulphur in water; **lime-work,** (*b*) (later example).

1860 J. S. C. ABBOTT *South & North* 196 [Slaves] employed..in lime-burning or fishing. **1865** MRS. STOWE *House & Home Papers* 94 Seating himself on a lime-cask which the plasterers had left. **1935** A. G. L. HELLYER *Pract. Gardening* iii. 34 It is wise to make enquiry when ordering rock plants and shrubs as to whether any of those supplied are likely to require lime-free soil. **1974** *Country Life* 28 Nov. 1639/1 *V[iburnum] furcatum*..needs a lime-free soil. **1875** R. R. BRASH *Eccl. Archit. Ireland* 8 The interior of the walls is filled with small stones and lime-grout. **1907** R. FARRER *My Rock-Garden* x. 148 The

plant [*sc. Cenisia excisa*]..is a real lime-hater. **1935** A. G. L. HELLYER *Pract. Gardening* xv. 112 The best plan is to set aside a portion of the rock-garden for lime-haters. *Ibid.* 284/1 (*index*) Lime hating plants. **1971** *Country Life* 18 Feb. 368/1 For some reason, many of the lime-hating shrubs have only white flowers. **1907** R. FARRER *My Rock-Garden* i. 12 At this point I will not embark on the awful question of lime-lovers and peat-lovers. **1971** MRS. D. UNDERWOOD *Grey & Silver Plants* iv. 35 The root fibres of the lime-lovers will wrap themselves round individual [limestone] chippings. **1916** *Nature* 2 Nov. 172/2 It seems probable from the evidence now before us that some of Forrest's newly discovered Chinese rhododendrons..must be reckoned as lime-loving species. **1956** MCCLINTOCK & FITTER *Collins' Pocket Guide Wild Flowers* 306 Limestone Polypody..is the lime-loving counterpart of the Oak Fern. **1974** *Country Life* 28 Nov. 1660/1 Used mushroom compost..is greatly appreciated by lime-loving cherries. **1867** J. N. EDWARDS *Shelby* xxix. 498 He..disappeared for a moment beneath lime ooze, half tanned hides and the smell of a charnel house. **1665** in *Early Rec. Providence* (Rhode Island) (1893) III. 66 Those Lime Rocks about Hackletons lime Killne shal be perpetually Common. **1969** *Islander* (Victoria, B.C.) 22 June 7/1 He had to tow empty scows from the cement works to Tod Inlet and back with full scows of limerock for making cement. **1888** J. J. H. TEALL *Brit. Petrogr.* 464/2 Lime-silicate hornfels. **1902** A. HARKER *Petrol.* (ed. 3) xx. 306 The carbonic acid is completely eliminated, and the whole converted into a lime-silicate-rock (the German 'Kalksilikathornfels' or 'Kalkhornfels'). **1965** G. J. WILLIAMS *Econ. Geol. N.Z.* x. 153/1 Lime-silicate dyke rocks in the ultramafic rocks of southern Westland. **1837** J. L. WILLIAMS *Territory of Florida* 9 Ponds and lime sinks are numerous between the..rivers. **1857** W. A. MILLER *Elem. Chem.* III. vi. 373 The tallow is melted by injecting hot steam into the vat which contains it, and milk of lime is added... An insoluble lime soap is thus formed. **1884** [in Dict. s.v. SOAP *sb.* 2]. **1918** C. M. WHITTAKER *Applic. Coal Tar Dyestuffs* iii. 36 Lime soaps may be removed by treatment with spirits of salts. **1952** KIRK & OTHMER *Encycl. Chem. Technol.* VIII. 524 The use of lime-soap thickened lubricants for the wheels of chariots dates back as far as 1400 B.C... In modern times, however, the manufacture of lubricating greases—also by means of lime soaps—started about 1854. **1961** COHEN & LINTON *Chem. & Textiles for Laundry Industry* iii. 46 Pure lime soap is more or less white when it is formed... If we accept a laundryman's concept of lime soap, on the other hand, we are talking about a dingy, gray, boardy impregnation that builds up in fabrics and defies all efforts to attain good whiteness. **1930** *Engineering* 15 Aug. 219/1 It [*sc.* the base exchange method] gives rise to no precipitate whatever, and this avoids what in the lime-soda process is often a cause of difficulty. **1950** B. E. HARTSUCH *Introd. Textile Chem.* iv. 92 The lime-soda method for softening water is the oldest and is still most used for very large softening plants. **1970** KIRK & OTHMER *Encycl. Chem. Technol.* (ed. 2) XXII. 98 The lime or lime-soda process is based upon precipitation of calcium as calcium carbonate and magnesium as magnesium hydroxide. **1907** *Bull. Bureau Chem., U.S. Dept. Agric.* No. 101. 12 The next set of experiments was to determine the composition of lime-sulphur mixtures boiled the same length of time.., but containing varying quantities of lime and sulphur. **1913** *Jrnl. R. Hort. Soc.* XXXIX. 378 It appears unsafe to spray many varieties of gooseberries with either lime-sulphur or liver of sulphur. **1937** A. M. MASSEE *Pests of Fruits & Hops* xiv. 266 In the post-blossom sprays..lime-sulphur is used as an acaricide as well as a fungicide, and it is then used at a strength of 1 per cent..for the control of the Fruit Tree Red Spider and Apple Scab. **1968** R. HAY *Gardening Year* 472/3 Lime sulphur can also be used against big bud mites on black currants, American gooseberry mildew and peach leaf curl. **1971** *Country Life* 1 Apr. 743/3 We struck east across the A515..to re-cross the road farther north by a limeworks.

lime, *sb.*[2] Add: **1. c.** *ellipt.* for *lime-green sb.* and *adj.* (LIME *sb.*[2] 2); also for LIME-JUICE, as in phr. *gin and lime*.

1923 *Daily Mail* 19 Feb. 1 (Advt.), Smart skirt... Colours: navy,.. gold, lime, cardinal and black. **1937** *Discovery* July 217/2 Dresses are burgundy, pine-blue, lime. **1938** L. MACNEICE *Earth Compels* 23 A gin and lime or a double Scotch. **1972** *Vogue* Jan. 12/2 The colours.. are remarkable—lime and raspberry, lemon, orange, rose.

2. lime-marmalade, marmalade made from limes; **lime-punch** (earlier example); **lime-squash,** a drink made with the juice of the lime (cf. *lemon-squash*).

c **1938** *Fortnum & Mason Price List* 44/1 Marmalade.. Lime—per glass 1/3. **1968** 'J. FRASER' *Evergreen Death* x. 80 He did like that lime marmalade they used to get. **1972** *New Statesman* 26 May 709/1 Coffee, bread and lime-marmalade. **1774** P. V. FITHIAN *Jrnl.* (1900) 206 We had after Dinner, Lime Punch and Madaira. **1909** *Daily Chron.* 15 June 4/4 For drinking, lime-squash is superior to lemon squash. **1939–40** *Army & Navy Stores Catal.* 28/2 Lime squash.

lime, *sb.*[3] Add: *lime-walk* (earlier examples), *-wood* (later examples).

c **1662** T. BROWNE *Let.* in *Works* (1931) VI. 307 Uncertain it is whether in any *Tilicetum*, or Lime-walk, abroad it be considerably exceeded. **1816** JANE AUSTEN *Emma* III. vi. 103 Some are gone to the ponds, and some to the lime walk. **1885** F. MILLER *Wood-Carving* iv. 27 Lime-wood was almost exclusively used by Gibbons in his drops and festoons of fruit. **1932** O. EVAN-THOMAS *Domestic Utensils of Wood* 118 Chrism spoon, limewood, entirely carved with sacred objects. **1965** J. ARONSON *Encycl. Furnit.* (1966) 285/1 *Limewood*, light-colored, close-grained wood that cuts as well across as with the grain, rendering it excellent for carving.

lime (ləim), *sb.*[5] Colloq. abbrev. of LIME-LIGHT. Freq. in *pl.* Also (in sing.) *attrib.* Phr. *in the lime* (Austral.), in the limelight.

1892 J. NIE *Robinson Crusoe* 6 Here! Where's the lime-light man? Of course, used up all his limes for Crusoe. **1895** B. DALY in Chevalier & Daly *A. Chevalier* II. 248 The footlights are turned low, and the hissing noise behind explains that Sam Pennett, the carpenter, is getting his limes ready for use. **1931** *Daily Express* 22 Sept. 17/1 She ..used to keep in her shop a working model of a theatre, complete to the last 'lime' and 'float'. **1935** RIDGE & ALDRED *Stage Lighting* iii. 18/2 Producers will frequently ask for the 'limes' when they mean front-of-house arc lanterns. **1941** BAKER *Dict. Austral. Slang* 43, *Lime, in the*, in the limelight. **1958** B. NICHOLS *Sweet & Twenties* xiii. 177 There was one figure which the limes should have picked out. **1961** PARTRIDGE *Dict. Slang* Suppl. 1169/2 *Lime, in the*, popular; much publicised: Australian... I.e. 'in the limelight'. **1966** *Guardian* 18 Feb. 10/5 At 16 he was a lime boy, looking after the lights.

lime, *v.*[1] **5. b.** Add to def.: To give (wood) a bleached effect by treating it with lime. Cf. *LIMED *ppl. a.* 2 b.

1966 M. M. PEGLER *Dict. Interior Design* (1967) 266 Woods other than oak can be limed.

d. (Later examples.)

1903 L. A. FLEMMING *Pract. Tanning* 6 The length of time to thoroughly lime the skins depends on the thickness of the skins. *Ibid.* 7 The best results accrue when only skins of like nature and size are limed..together. **1925** J. R. ARNOLD *Hides & Skins* 553 Hides and skins which are prepared for dehairing by sweating or painting..are also limed.

lime, *v.*[4]: see *LIMER[3].

limeade (ləimēɪ·d). [f. LIME *sb.*[2] 1 + -ADE 1 c.] A drink made from lime-juice sweetened with sugar.

1892 F. DAVIES *Temperance Drinks* 81 *Limeade*, plain syrup one gallon, lime-juice a quart, essence of lemon two ounces, essence of lime one ounce. **1936** J. DOS PASSOS *Big Money* 313 Give me a limeade and no sweetnin' in it. **1953** R. CHANDLER *Long Good-Bye* xiii. 79 She had finished her limeade. **1966** *Guardian* 28 Dec. 4/6 The abbot and I..shared a bottle of fizzy limeade.

Limean: see *LIMENIAN.

limed, *ppl. a.* Add: **2. b.** Of wood, esp. oak, that is treated with lime to give it a bleached effect.

1930 *Heal & Son Catal.* 17 Twin Bedsteads in Limed Oak. **1933** *Archit. Rev.* LXXIII. June 230 The Holy Table is in waxed and limed oak. **1952** J. GLOAG *Short Dict. Furnit.* 311 *Limed oak*, oak that has been pickled with a coating of lime... Limed oak surfaces are generally left unpolished. **1957** *N.Z. Timber Jrnl.* Oct. 73/1 *Limed oak*, chloride of lime and water applied to oak furniture to produce a bleached effect. **1973** A. ROOS *Dunfermline Affair* 162 The limed-oak furniture was all built in. Wardrobe, vanity units, dressing-tables.

Limehouse (ləi·mhaus), *v.* [*Limehouse*, a district in the east of London.] *intr.* To make fiery (political) speeches such as Mr. Lloyd George made at Limehouse in 1909. Also as *sb.* and **Li·mehousing** *vbl. sb.*

1913 *Daily Mail* 1 Aug. 5 (*heading*) Mr. Lloyd George himself again... Limehousing at Carnarvon. **1914** *National Rev.* June 543 Mr. Lloyd George went to Ipswich and Limehoused on the eve of the poll. **1920** *Glasgow Herald* 20 Mar. 7 It is exactly what he used to say in the old Limehouse days, though his Limehousing now is of a different kind. **1920** *Punch* 31 Mar. 259/1 Guerrilla tactics in the House, suspension, recognition, pacifism, office, original budgeting, limehousing.., social reform. **1932** *Times Lit. Suppl.* 9 June 426/2 He [*sc.* Bonar Law] introduced..a 'new acerbity' into Front Bench debating, or what his opponents might have called the Conservative counterpart of 'Limehouse'. **1937** PARTRIDGE *Dict. Slang* 484/1 *Limehouse*, 'to use coarse, abusive language in a speech'. **1963** *Punch* 16 Jan. 96/1 Enough of the actor to wallow in invective—'Limehousing' they called it.

limelight. Add to def.: Formerly much used in theatres to light up important actors and scenes, and so direct attention to them. Hence freq. *fig.*

1877 G. B. SMITH *Shelley* I. 45 Transcendent as were his virtues when compared with his faults, the lime-light of a malevolent scrutiny has been turned on the latter. **1881** P. FITZGERALD *World behind Scenes* I. 48 The use of so intense a light as the limelight has favoured the introduction of a new effect in the shape of transparent scenery. **1882** [in Dict.]. **1908** *Daily Chron.* 25 Jan. 3/2 The beauty of his person..helped to throw the limelight upon him. **1922** *Blackw. Mag.* Aug. 150/1 He did not..pose in the limelight to the same extent as his respected chief. **1934** A. HUXLEY *Let.* 1 Oct. (1969) 384 The town hardly gets its full share of the limelight because of the hero. **1952** GRANVILLE *Dict. Theatr. Terms* 111 *Fond of limelight*, greedy for notice. One who claims the centre of the stage. **1955** *Times* 5 May 16/2 German bonds took the limelight in the foreign bond market. *Ibid.* 17 June 9/3 The publicity given to the submission of identical tenders for public authorities' contracts has brought the question into the limelight. **1967** *Guardian* 3 Feb. 7/3 [He] did more than his bit of backing in to the limelight, and his declarations of his own genius aren't to everyone's taste. **1975** R. LEWIS *Double Take* iv. 127 In our business exposure to the limelight of the courts is like the kiss of death.

2. *attrib.*

1874 *Porcupine* 11 Apr. 26/3 And [he], with the willing aid of the stage-carpenter, scenic artist, and limelight man, has made our blood curdle. **1874** *Cassell's Mag.* May 432/1 The lime-light splendour of the tropics. **1876** *Porcupine* 22 Apr. 59/1 There is plenty of bustle and 'business', and lots of pistol-shots and obliging limelight rays. **1892** J. NIE *Robinson Crusoe* 6 Here! Where's the lime-light man? **1897** G. B. SHAW *Let.* 11 June (1965) 774 A ten inch moon, a limelight sky. **1938** W. LORAINE *Robert Loraine* 31 And recount the events of the evening—the mistakes of the limelight man, the hacking cough from the third row.

limelight, *v.* [f. the sb.] *trans.* To illuminate by limelight. Usu. *fig.* Also **li·melighted, -lit** *ppl. a.*; **li·melighting** *vbl. sb.*

1909 *Daily Chron.* 10 Apr. 4/6 The most limelighted person in Europe this morning is Queen Wilhelmina of Holland. **1909** *Westm. Gaz.* 10 Apr. 2/3 We had sympathised with the beautiful lime-lit heroine. **1927** *Daily Express* 21 Feb. 2/4 Unfeminine modern women go limelighting their way through the world. **1927** *Observer* 10 Apr. 29 This is not an occasion when the interests of motorists can be served by limelighting. **1940** *Nation* (N.Y.) 28 Sept. 263/1 What are the facts that justify these limelighted conferences in Berlin and Rome? **1964** *Punch* 12 Aug. 213/1 This keenness to pin something on the limelit.

Limenian (limī·niăn). Also **Limean** (limī·ăn). [f. *Lima*, capital of Peru: see below.] A native or inhabitant of Lima. Also *attrib.* Also the Spanish forms **limeño** (lime·nyo) a male, and **limeña** a female, native or inhabitant of Lima.

1824 B. HALL *Extracts Jrnl. Coasts Chili, Peru & Mexico* (ed. 2) I. iii. 90 San Martin's expedition took the Limenians quite by surprise; for they had always held Chili in contempt. **1856** C. R. MARKHAM *Cuzco & Lima* ix. 302 The Limenians, with all their indolence,.. bore themselves towards the Creoles with insolent pride. **1891** E. B. CLARK *Twelve Months Peru* iii. 55 It is considered highly improper for a Limeña, either married or single, to walk the streets alone. **1927** T. WILDER *Bridge San Luis Rey* I. 4 It was rather strange that this event should have so impressed the Limeans. *Ibid.* III. 49 Limean gossips.. declared them to be Castilian. **1962** N. MAXWELL *Witch-Doctor's Apprentice* ii. 13 Any place with no roads..and only one good hotel is not apt to be frequented by Limenos. **1971** *Guardian* 18 Aug. 3/2 [A] cynical Limeño lawyer. **1974** 'A. HAIG' *Peruvian Printout* 122 The car was a hired Cadillac... Few Limeños ever hired those vehicles; they were strictly for tourists.

limer[3] (ləi·məɹ). *West Indies.* [Etym. unknown.] A person who hangs about the streets. Hence (as a back-formation) **lime** *v.*[4] *intr.*, to hang about the streets; also **li·ming** *vbl. sb.*

Said to have been used in the 1940s but printed evidence is lacking.

1970 *Express* (Trinidad & Tobago) 6 Jan. 4 'Limers' are a menace on High Street at night. **1972** *Ibid.* 4 Feb. 21 One ride in a route taxi and a little liming in Frederick Street..would uncover whatever the wooding group may have forgotten. **1973** *Sunday Express* (Trinidad & Tobago) 1 Apr. (Suppl.) 13/1 Staying a minute more to lime. *Ibid.* 8 Apr. 13/3 Now I confess that in the past I have often had cause to voice a complaint about his penchant for ole talking and liming. **1974** *Sunday Advocate-News* (Barbados) 3 Mar. 16/6 The limers' attire ranges from the sophisticated to the ridiculous.

Limerick. Add: [The chief town of the county of Limerick in Ireland.] (Earlier examples.)

1896 A. BEARDSLEY *Let.* *c* 1 May (1971) 128 I have tried to amuse myself by writing limericks on my troubles. *Ibid.* 2 May 129 Your continuation of the limerick is superb.

2. Used *attrib.* to designate: **a.** Gloves of fine leather made originally at Limerick (see quot. 1960).

1804 M. EDGEWORTH *Pop. Tales* I. 245 Are you blind Mr. Hill? Don't you see that they are Limerick gloves? **1842** J. P. LAWSON *Gazetteer Ireland* 607/2 The glove trade ..has now declined, and those articles sold as Limerick gloves are actually manufactured at Cork. **1853** MRS. GASKELL *Ruth* II. vii. 173 She..brought down a pair of Limerick ones, which had been long treasured up in a walnut-shell. 'They say them gloves is made of chicken's-skins,' said Sally. **1960** CUNNINGTON & BEARD *Dict. Eng. Costume, Limerick gloves*, 2nd half 18th and 1st half 19th c...made of very fine leather, said to be made from the skins of unborn lambs.

b. A particular bend or pattern of fish-hook or a fish-hook with such a bend (said to have been orig. made in the town of Limerick) in which the wire of the hook is bent abruptly through a large angle behind the barb but thereafter is bent more shallowly to the point at which it continues as the straight shank. Also *ellipt.* as *sb.*, a Limerick hook.

1828 H. DAVY *Salmonia* 141, I have even made a hook, which..I think, I could boast as equal to the Limerick hooks. **1835** T. T. STODDART *Art of Angling in Scotl.* iii. 16 O'Shaughnessy's Limericks..are not always exactly the thing, excepting those used for salmon..which are really excellent. **1856** 'STONEHENGE' *Man. Brit. Rural Sports* 235/1 The round-bend hook is that which is most used in England, the Limerick pattern being chiefly in vogue in Ireland. **1928** *Chambers's Jrnl.* Jan. 2/2 He..picked out his lure without hesitation—a Number 5, Limerick-bend, double-hooked 'Blue Charm'. **1956** L. V. BATES *Artificial Flies* iii. 55 The Limerick is probably stronger but the fine elegant proportions of the Dee hook make for better hooking.

c. A type of embroidered lace made originally at Limerick. Also *ellipt.* as *sb.*

1842 J. P. LAWSON *Gazetteer Ireland* 607/2 Limerick lace has now obtained a high celebrity. This beautiful manufacture was introduced into the city in 1829 by Mr Walker, an English gentleman. **1886** B. LINDSEY *Irish Lace* ii. 9 A spirit of enterprise and commercial adventure..originated the Limerick manufacture. **1905** N. H. MOORE *Lace Bk.* 196 Limerick lace is a combination..of cut-work and embroidery, and hardly comes under our definition of lace. **1953** M. POWYS *Lace & Lace-Making* iv. 35 *Limerick lace*, embroidered net, Irish, 19th century... This type of lace is made in all the countries, including America and India. It is light, pretty and easy to produce. Limerick remains the finest of the kind. **1959** *Times* 21 Sept. 12/4 Her old family Limerick lace veil was held in place by a mother-of-pearl coronet. **1967** C. GASKIN *Edge of Glass* iv. 86 [Her] long ancient gown collared in yellowed Limerick lace.

limestone. Add: **c.** *limestone-cliff* (earlier example), *-land* (later example), *-water*; **limestone polypody**: substitute for def.: a fern, *Gymnocarpium robertianum*, restricted to areas of limestone rock; (later examples).

1699 M. LISTER *Journey to Paris* 88 The high Ragstone Mountains and Lime Stone Cliffs. **1811** *Niles' Reg.* 12 Oct. 101/1 Our steepest lime stone lands are very favorable to sheep. **1888** C. T. DRUERY *Choice Brit. Ferns* 118 The young fronds [of the Oak Fern] also, when unfolding, exactly resemble the pawnbroker's sign of three balls, which those of the Limestone Polypody do not. **1908** E. STEP *Wayside & Woodland Ferns* 87 The Limestone Polypody..will be found nowhere except on limestone rocks. **1960** P. TAYLOR *Brit. Ferns & Mosses* 164 The Limestone Polypody occurs in the mountains of Europe, temperate Asia and North America. **1831** J. M. PECK *Guide for Emigrants* 233 Those persons who have been unaccustomed to lime stone water..frequently have eruptions of the skin. **1872** E. EGGLESTON *End of World* ix. 65 Having..quaffed the hard limestone water.

Limey (ləi·mi). *colloq.* and *derogatory.* Also **limey.** [abbrev. LIME-JUICER.] **a.** In the former British colonies (esp. Austral., N.Z., and S. Afr.), an English immigrant. Also *attrib.*

The later examples prob. reflect the U.S. use in b.

1888 D. SLADEN *Austral. Ballads & Rhymes* 31 They'd seen old stagers and limey new chums. **1947** J. BERTRAM *Shadow of War* 251, I can remember scores of fights among the 'Limeys'. **1954** T. S. ELIOT *Elder Statesman* III. 93 Everyone would sneer at the fellow from London, The limey remittance man for whom a job was made. **1962** *Times* 6 Jan. 7/1 The [English] boys [at Sasolburg, Orange Free State] were constantly taunted by schoolmates as 'Pommie', 'Limey', and 'Rooinek'. **1964** O. E. MIDDLETON in C. K. Stead *N.Z. Short Stories* (1966) 198 We'd all be drawing the dole like every other mother-loving beachcomber in this..Limey hole!

b. *U.S.* An English ship; an English (or British) sailor; hence *gen.*, an Englishman, a Briton. Also *attrib.*

1918 A. N. DEPEW *Gunner Depew* 18 So, all over the world, British ships are called 'Lime-juicers' and their sailors 'Limeys'. *Ibid.* 48 Ask any Limey soldier and he will tell you the same. **1918** R. D. PAINE *Fighting Fleets* v. 87 Squads of the American navy patrol began to stroll about..displaying no sympathy..for the shipmate who..loudly announced that he could whip any three 'Limies' that ever trod a British deck. **1919** *Texas Rev.* IV. 86 In our fleet a British ship is regularly called a 'limey', from the old lime-juicers. The British seaman is likewise a 'limey'. **1924** *Chicago Tribune* 18 Oct. 1/5 (*heading*) Midway Signs Limey Prof. to Dope Yank Talk. **1930** J. DOS PASSOS *42nd Parallel* II. 169, I..shipped out East on a limey, on an English boat. **1921** E. LINKLATER *Juan in Amer.* II. vii. 115 'An Englishman,' he marvelled, 'the first limey I ever saw shot in Chicago.' **1933** 'J. SPENSER' *Limey* i. 4 'English, eh?' said the manager. 'I ain't too keen on you Limey's.' **1952** J. STEINBECK *East of Eden* lii. 498 Fights in the bar-rooms with the goddam Limeys. **1954** M. BRUCE *Tramp Royal* II. ix. 121 This ship differed from a Limey vessel in the way the watch bells are struck. **1955** G. GREENE *Quiet American* IV. ii. 241, I don't like Limies. **1968** M. PYKE *Food & Society* iii. 32 The pejorative identification of foreigners with unfamiliar foods. This makes..the English limies. **1969** *Listener* 26 June 881/3 Was it my limey accent that called it forth or did they say it to every customer? **1973** 'D. JORDAN' *Nile Green* xi. 49 Guy always plays up the limey accent when he's in the States.

limicole (ləi·mikōul). [f. mod.L. group-name *Limicolæ* (see quot. 1930), f. L. *līmus* mud + *colere* to inhabit.] An oligochæte worm living in mud or water.

[**1930** J. STEPHENSON *Oligochaeta* xvi. 607 Oligochaeta may be divided roughly into Terricolae and Limicolae—the earth-dwellers and the mud- and water-dwellers respectively.] **1963** R. P. DALES *Annelids* ix. 180 The common division of the Oligochaeta into the Microdrili or Limicoles (the aquatic families) and the Megadrili or Terricoles (the earthworms) is mainly one of convenience. **1965** B. E. FREEMAN tr. *Vandel's Biospeleol.* vii. 73 The limicoles are more interesting to the biospeleologist.

liminess (ləi·minės). [f. LIMY *a.*] The quality of being limy.

1902 E. A. WOODRUFFE-PEACOCK *Thoroughbreds & their Grass-Land* II. 7 Among plants..a score of species that could be named, suddenly appearing in a turf at once demonstrate a growing liminess in a clay soil.

liming: see *LIMER[3].

limit, *sb.* Add: **2. g.** In various card games, as (*a*) *Poker*, an agreed maximum stake or bet; so *attrib.*, as *limit game*; (*b*) *Bridge*, a call which shows that the strength of the caller's hand does not exceed a certain value; usu. *attrib.*, as *limit bid*, *raise*.

(*a*) **1892** W. J. FLORENCE *Handbk. Poker* 90 Before a game is commenced it is agreed that so many chips shall be the limit... No game ever should be played without a limit. **1928** *Chambers's Jrnl.* Jan. 116/1 Once again the betting came to Poker Jack, and this was his chance. He coolly raised Rymington the limit, and left his two opponents half-stupefied. **1963** *Esquire's Bk. Gambling* II. iv. 109 It is virtually impossible to bluff in a limit game. With a limit, poker is more like Screeno... Big Poker..as any unlimited-stakes player will be happy to tell you..requires the most brutality.

(*b*) **1959** REESE & DORMER *Bridge Player's Dict.* 138 A limit-bid is one that describes the strength of a player's hand within fairly narrow limits. *Ibid.*, A raise of partner's suit is generally a limit-raise, expressing the full value of the hand. **1959** *Listener* 24 Dec. 1118/2 Three Spades was a limit bid, which East might have passed. **1964** *Official Encycl. Bridge* 331/1 *Limit*, (1) the highest stake permitted in a bridge club... (2) A bid which shows a maximum as well as a minimum range of values in the bidder's hand. **1974** *Times* 23 Feb. 11/1 A player must take the decision whether..to go straight for a limit bid.

h. *colloq.* The very extreme; the last point or stage; the worst (etc.) imaginable or endurable; the maximum penalty. Phr.: *go the limit*, to behave in an extreme way; to last the stated number of rounds or the full time, as in a boxing match; to allow sexual intercourse; *over the limit*, having exceeded a stated bound or point. orig. *U.S.* (Apparently a fig. use of *2 g.) Cf. *the frozen limit* (*FROZEN *ppl. a.* 1 b).

1904 *Montgomery* (Alabama) *Weekly Advertiser* 26 Aug. 4 We can always depend on Kansas to go the limit in the freak line. **1906** *N.Y. Even. Post* 7 May 1 Desertion is bad enough..but to fire at one's comrades while in the act of turning against them is—well, the limit. **1907** *Westm. Gaz.* 16 Aug. 2/1 They [*sc.* wages] are low everywhere..but Belfast is what Americans would call 'the limit'. **1908** A. J. DAWSON *Finn* xxiii. 353 I'll be teetotally damned if that ain't the limit! *a* **1911** D. G. PHILLIPS *Susan Lenox* (1917) I. 389 We've made the plunge. We'll go—the limit. **1914** W. G. LAWRENCE in T. E. Lawrence *Home Lett.* (1954) 502 Bankers and business people of all sorts are the real limit. **1916** 'TAFFRAIL' *Pincher Martin* v. 79 Oh, to hell with you and your rotten excuses!.. You're about the frozen limit! **1919** G. B. SHAW *Heartbreak House* I. 18 Really! your father does seem to be about the limit. **1925** E. F. NORTON *Fight for Everest, 1924* 110 If vitality is low in the early hours at Camp III at 21,000 feet, it can be guessed how near the limit 6 a.m. found us at 27,000. **1925** G. MALLORY in *Ibid.* 237 That cutting against time at the end after such a day just about brought me to my limit. **1925** L. J. SMITS *Spring Flight* viii. 89 I'd marry a girl who had gone the limit just as willingly as I would a strict one, perhaps a little sooner. **1927** *Amer. Speech* III. 29 The boxer 'goes the limit' if he succeeds in lasting the specified number of rounds. **1947** 'N. SHUTE' *Chequer Board* iii. 68 If you get anything to go before court martial, for example, I'll see they get the limit. **1949** A. CHRISTIE *Crooked House* xvi. 126 This house is the absolute limit!.. I don't see why I should have to be burdened with such peculiar parents. **1966** *Daily Tel.* 11 Aug. 26/6 Attempting to drive while over the 80 mg/100 ml. limit can be punished... Being in charge of a vehicle while 'over the limit' can lead..to up to four months' imprisonment. **1968** N. BENCHLEY *Welcome to Xanadu* iii. 52 She'd heard girls in school talk about going the limit, or all the way.

5. limit dog, one shown in a class limited to dogs having certain required qualifications; **limit gauge** *Engin.*, a gauge used for determining whether a dimension of a manufactured item falls within the specified tolerance; so **limit gauging**, the use of limit gauges to ensure the interchangeability of parts; **limit load** *Aeronaut.*, the maximum load that an aircraft or part of one is expected to bear in particular conditions of operation; so *limit load factor*, the load factor corresponding to this load; **limit point** *Math.*, a point every neighbourhood of which contains a point (usu., a point other than the limit point) belonging to a given set; **limit switch** *Engin.*, a switch that prevents the travel of an object past some predetermined point and is mechanically operated by the motion of the object itself.

1903 *Forest & Stream* 21 Feb. 151/2 Limit dogs was won by St. Elvan. **1909** *Daily Chron.* 11 Feb. 5/6 The first prize for limit dogs over 45 lb. **1905** A. PARR *Machine Tools & Workshop Pract.* i. 10 (*caption*) Limit gauge. **1909** *Westm. Gaz.* 7 Dec. 5/1 When it comes to be measured in a special limit-gauge, the slightest discrepancy is discovered. **1970** W. J. PATTON *Mod. Manuf.* xvii. 454 Instead of measuring actual dimensions, we usually check conformity to tolerance specifications in a production run by fixed limit gauges, often termed 'GO' and 'NOT GO' gauges. **1920** *Proc. Inst. Mech. Engin.* Nov. 1076 Limit gauging may be applied to many kinds of fit. **1964** S. CRAWFORD *Basic Engin. Processes* xiv. 296 Limit-gauging systems have played an essential part in the development of the technique of quantity production. **1950** D. J. PEERY *Aircraft Struct.* iii. 69 The maximum loads which an airplane may be expected to encounter at any time in service are designated as limit loads or applied loads. The load factors associated with these loads are known as limit load factors... For loads which are under the control of the pilot, flight restrictions are used so that the limit load factor is never exceeded. **1967** *Technology Week* 23 Jan. 66/2 As an industry, we have done remarkably well, from a safety point of view, operating large aircraft with limit load factors of only 2·5 in rough air. **1972** T. H. G. MEGSON *Aircraft Struct.* xii. 413 Having decided on an ultimate load then the limit load may be fixed. **1905** *Trans. Amer. Math. Soc.* VI. 90 A geometrically closed set of points is a set that includes all its geometrical limit points. **1926** C. WALMSLEY *Introd. Course Math. Analysis* i. 44 For general sequences we define a limit (or limit point, limiting point, limiting value, limiting number) of any sequence s_1, s_2, s_3, . . as any number *L*, within an arbitrarily small neighbourhood of which..there lie numbers of the sequence; a number of the sequence itself not being a limit of the sequence unless it is repeated indefinitely often as a term of the sequence or there are other terms of the sequence within the arbitrarily small neighbourhood. **1959** E. M. PATTERSON *Topology* (ed. 2) ii. 29 The points $x = 0$ and $x = 1$ are limit points of the set $0 < x < 1$ on the Euclidean line; and in this case every point of *X* itself is also a limit point. **1930** *Engineering* 9 May 595/2 Automatic control at the end of travel is provided by geared limit switches, and intermediate positions are signalled by a travelling nut on the limit switch. **1956** *Railway Mag.* May 338/1 Limit switches are provided in the hoisting motion, and in the derricking motion, to limit the amount of travel in both directions. **1974** *BP Shield Internat.* Oct. 2 (*caption*) The computerised electronic requirement that operates all valves, limit switches, pressure transducers.

limited, *ppl. a.* Add: **2.** *limited edition*, an edition of a book, or reproduction of an object, limited to some specific number of copies; *limited express* or *train* (U.S.): cf. *limited mail* (in Dict.); *limited mail* (earlier example); *limited monarchy* (earlier examples); *limited war*, one in which the weapons used, the nations or territory involved, or the objectives pursued, are limited or restricted.

1648 R. FILMER (*title*) The anarchy of a limited or mixed monarchy. **1710** in T. B. Howell *State Trials* (1812) XV. 62 The nature of our constitution is that of a limited monarchy. *a* **1792** BURKE *Address Brit. Colonists N. Amer.* in *Works* (1812) V. 148 England has been great and happy under the present limited Monarchy. **1866** DICKENS *Mugby Junction* in *All Year Round* Extra Christmas No. 10 Dec. 17 Driving..at limited-mail speed. **1879** F. R. STOCKTON *Rudder Grange* ix. 93 Time flew like a limited express train. **1890** *Harper's Mag.* Aug. 409/1 Coming up by the limited train, Miss Lee was not favorably impressed. **1903** *Connoisseur* VI. 252/2 This library has the trail of the 'Limited Edition' serpent over it all. **1904** *Dial* (Chicago) 16 Oct. 238 It is not a book for the limited express. **1920** H. CRANE *Let.* 28 Jan. (1965) 32 A limited edition hastily gathered up would be the only possible method of presentation. **1930** Limited edition [see *HOG-WASH]. **1944** H. TREECE *Herbert Read* 41 The Quixote in him that writes prefaces to Limited editions. **1948** H. J. MORGENTHAU *Politics among Nations* xx. 291 Another variety of a limited war..has been well described. **1955** *Times* 4 July 9/7 Britain, then, has to be prepared for both nuclear and limited war. *Ibid.* 8 July 9/5 The recent war in Korea is an example of a major limited war, and the present operations in Kenya of a minor limited war. **1966** MRS. L. B. JOHNSON *White House Diary* 20 Aug. (1970) 413 It was a good speech [by Lyndon].. 'Perhaps it reflects poorly on our world that men must fight limited wars in order to keep from fighting larger wars.' **1971** *Ideal Home* Apr. 143 This Piccadilly mug is produced by Wedgwood in a limited edition of 4,000. **1972** *Country Life* 16 Nov. (Suppl.) 57/1 Pure silk 36 inch hand-rolled head-scarves, in four designs..and in limited editions for £12.50. **1973** *Daily Tel.* 27 Apr. 18 The National Maritime Museum..is adding two new clocks to its collection of historic timepieces next month. The two, however, are replicas of 18th-century clocks which..Thwaites and Reed are producing in limited editions.

b. *limited partnership*, inactive partnership, where liability is limited to the value of the capital contribution; so *limited partner*.

1907 *Act 7 Edw. VII* c. 24 § 1 This Act may be cited for all purposes as the Limited Partnerships Act, 1907. *Ibid.* § 4 Limited partners, who shall at the time of entering into such partnership contribute thereto a sum..valued at a stated amount and who shall not be liable for the debts or obligations of the firm beyond the amount contributed. **1931** *Pitman's Business Man's Guide* (ed. 9) 372/1 There is a further division into 'general' and 'limited' partners. The former correspond to the 'active' partners, and the latter to the 'sleeping' or 'nominal' partners. **1951** R. W. JONES *Thomson's Dict. Banking* (ed. 10) 381/1 The idea of the limited partnership has not appealed to the business world and..only some 1,300 such partnerships have been registered. **1970** *New Yorker* 10 Oct. 37/2 Richard Roth, Jr., a limited partner, joined the firm. **1973** *N.Y. Law Jrnl.* 31 Aug. 1/4 It omitted compensation agreements between Empire and its counsel..with whom Mr. Goldberg was then associated as a limited partner.

3. For 'quasi-*sb.*' read 'In *absol.* use'. Add later examples.

1910 KIPLING *Rewards & Fairies* 145 If you're off to Philadelphia..the Limited will take you there. **1913** E. WHARTON *Custom of Country* v. xliii. 556 A bigger and brighter blur ahead, into which they were plunging as the 'Limited' plunged into the sunset. **1938** S. V. BENÉT *Thirteen o' Clock* IV. 295 'Jerry Pye!' she said, 'I don't know what's come over you. You never take me on any limiteds!'

b. = *limited company.*

1905 *Westm. Gaz.* 20 Nov. 8/1 Company floaters have

gone very fast indeed, some limiteds, it is said, not having sufficient capital. **1907** *Daily Chron.* 26 July 3/4 This is my experience in a West-end house..classed with the Limiteds.

limiter. Add: **2. b.** *Electronics.* A device whose output is restricted to a certain range of values irrespective of the size of the input.

1919 R. STANLEY *Text-bk. Wireless Telegr.* (new ed.) II. xiv. 274 To a certain extent the H.F. amplifying valves of the Marconi Co., known as the V.24 type, are limiters, since their characteristic curves are of short range. **1930** H. M. DOWSETT *Handbk. Technical Instruction for Wireless Telegraphists* (ed. 4) xx. 297 Short wave signals vary greatly in intensity due to various causes, and the use of the limiter makes the signal currents more suitable for operating relays or recording apparatus. **1962** A. NISBETT *Technique Sound Studio* 258 Limiters are necessary in AM transmitters, and in the input to disc recorders in situations where overmodulation may occur by accident. **1972** *Sci. Amer.* Sept. 101/3 Since the amplitude of the FM carrier is constant, limiters can be used to reduce impulse noise.

limitrophe, *a.* and *sb.* Add: **A.** *adj.* (Earlier example.)

1763 EARL OF BUCKINGHAMSHIRE *Let.* 6 Dec. in *Despatches & Corr.* (1902) II. 113 The inconveniences which might arise if a country limitroph to Russia was governed by a sovereign allied and connected with the great European Powers.

B. *sb.* (Later example.)

1963 V. NABOKOV *Gift* iii. 155 Thus 'France' corresponded to his warningly raised eyebrows; some kind of 'limitrophes' to the hairs in his nostrils.

‖ **limmu, limu** (li·m*u*). *Assyriology.* [Assyrian *limmu* period, circuit, administrative year.] The year of office to which the holder gave his name; hence, the office itself. Cf. EPONYM 2.

1862 H. C. RAWLINSON in *Athenæum* 19 July 83/1, I am quite ready to abandon this notion if any more suitable explanation can be found of the office of *Limu*, from which the Assyrians commonly dated; but in the mean time I cannot accept of the unmeaning title of Eponymy, nor can I admit of the etymology which would make the *Limu* merely the 'seer' of the new moon. **1888** Z. A. RAGOZIN *Assyria* (ed. 2) v. 146 The year was then designated as the 'Limmu' of So-and-So. It is thought..that the magistrates themselves, in their capacity of time-keepers, had the special title of Limmu... Every king was *limmu* at least once, generally the second full year of his reign. **1901** R. W. ROGERS *Hist. Babylonia & Assyria* I. xii. 323 Historical inscriptions..often mention the *limmu* or eponym of a certain year, just as they give the name of the king who was reigning. **1956** A. TOYNBEE *Historian's Approach to Relig.* I. v. 57 The Assyrian list of holders of the office of *limmu*. **1963** F. S. LEIGH-BROWNE tr. *Læssøe's People Anc. Assyria* iii. 40 The Assyrians named the year after the official who (for that one year) occupied the office of *limmu*.

limnetic (limne·tik), *a.* [f. Gr. λιμνήτ-ης living in marshes + -IC.] Of, pertaining to, or living in the open part of a freshwater lake or pond, away from the margin or bottom.

1899 G. C. WHIPPLE *Microsc. Drinking-Water* viii. 105 The limnetic or pelagic organisms are those that make their home in the open water. They float or swim freely and are drifted about by every current... Then there are organisms that may be said to be facultative limnetic forms, that is, they are sedentary or free-swimming at will. **1903** *Amer. Naturalist* XXXVII. 503 This work is in the main an extension of Häcker's earlier papers..on the autonomy of the male and female pronuclei and of their derivatives in the development of limnetic Copepods. **1923** *Ecology* IV. 372 (*heading*) Limnetic A[ssociation]. **1955** C. C. DAVIS *Marine & Fresh-Water Plankton* i. 11 Horizontally, the relatively shallow area close to shore, characterized by rooted emergent or floating vegetation, is called the littoral region, while the region of open water is known as the limnetic (or pelagic) region... The limnetic region is much more extensive than the littoral in most lakes. **1957** G. E. HUTCHINSON *Treat. Limnol.* I. i. 19 The region has had a long limnetic history and has contained large tectonic lakes since the middle Tertiary.

limnic (li·mnik), *a. Geol.* [ad. G. *limnisch* (C. F. Naumann *Lehrb. d. Geognosie* (1850) I. II. iii. 814), f. Gr. λίμνη pool of standing water, marshy lake: see -IC.] Formed or laid down in an inland body of standing fresh water such as a lake or a swamp.

[**1911** *Proc. Amer. Philos. Soc.* L. 28 Naumann recognized the distinction between deposits formed on the sea border and those in fresh-water lakes... These types he terms paralisch and limnisch. *Ibid.* 29 The causes in paralisch areas are different from those in limnisch basins.] **1940** A. C. NOÉ tr. *Stutzer's Geol. Coal* vi. 159 Coal basins which have originated near the sea are called 'paralic basins'; and coal deposits which were formed inland..'limnic deposits'. This classification goes back to Naumann. Recent peat bogs can also be similarly classified. In the interior of a country—for instance, on the northern edge of the Alps—are found limnic moors, while the paralic moors are situated on the coast, as in Friesland. **1968** M.-TH. MACKOWSKY in Murchison & Westoll *Coal* xiv. 327 In the Upper Carboniferous large paralic coal deposits formed along the northern border of the Variscan mountains. Somewhat later the limnic coals of the Saar, Lorraine and central and south-eastern France developed in troughs between the mountains. **1971** *Nature* 30 Apr. 561/1 Tobien *et al.* have excavated a primitive, forest-adapted *Hipparion* fauna..from tuffaceous and limnic beds on the flank of the Höwenegg volcanic centre in southern Germany.

limno- (li·mno), comb. form of Gr. λίμνη lake, marsh, as in **li:mnobio·logy** *rare*, the biology of lakes and ponds; so **li:mnobiolo·gic, -biolo·gical** *adjs.*

1899 *Ann. Rep. Board of Regents Smithsonian Inst. 1897–98* 505 Switzerland has furnished perhaps the greatest number of investigators and stations for limnobiology. *Ibid.* 510 The Mount Prospect Laboratory,..placed under the direction of Mr. G. C. Whipple, whose contributions to limnobiologic questions are well known. **1909** *Cent. Dict.* Suppl., Limnobiological. **1957** G. E. HUTCHINSON *Treat. Limnol.* I. p. x, The first volume is intended to cover geographical and physico-chemical limnology, the second will deal with limnobiology and the ecological, typological, and stratigraphic problems of lake development.

limnology. Substitute for defs. of both senses a and b: (The study of) the physical, chemical, geological, and biological aspects of lakes and other bodies of fresh stagnant (sometimes also of fresh flowing) water. (Add earlier and later examples.)

1893 *Geogr. Jrnl.* I. 353 He [*sc.* Friedrich Simony]..became the founder of the special branch of science termed by Forel, Limnology, or the scientific study of lakes. **1929** *Jrnl. Ecol.* XVII. 106 A generation or so ago the general conception of the word limnology was that it covered the subject of the physiography of lakes, and that freshwater biology..was more or less a separate science... As the biology of fresh waters developed this branch of science was fairly often included within the range of the word limnology, but still the term continued to be frequently used for the physiographical aspect of lake investigations only, and the notion of limnology as a mere branch of physical geography separated from the biological side of the question persisted. That definition must now be entirely abandoned... The subject of limnology, then, is the study of everything connected with fresh waters—both stagnant and running—their geography, physical features, chemistry, biology, geology of the substrata and basins, in short the Natural History of fresh waters in the broadest sense of the word. **1938** *Jrnl. Wildlife Managem.* II. 94 (*heading*) Fish biology and limnology of Crater Lake, Oregon. **1946** *Nature* 21 Sept. 421/1 Up-to-date knowledge and theory of limnology—the freshwater equivalent of oceanography—has been combined with practical experience of waterworks. **1971** *New Scientist* 4 Feb. 236/1 The professor of limnology at the University of Lund.

So **limnolo·gical** *a.*, of or pertaining to limnology; **limnolo·gically** *adv.*; **limno·logist**, one who studies lakes.

1896 *Rep. 6th Internat. Geogr. Congr. 1895* 601 Such study [of British lakes] has been for the most part occasional and unsystematic, being only in rare cases worthy of being termed limnological. **1909** WEBSTER, Limnologically. **1910** MURRAY & PULLAR *Bathymetrical Survey Scottish Fresh-Water Lochs* I. 9 Several foreign limnologists have visited the Scottish lochs. **1933** *Geogr. Jrnl.* LXXXI. 380 A German limnological expedition was at work in the Dutch East Indies. **1957** G. E. HUTCHINSON *Treat. Limnol.* I. i. 22 Limnologically, this difference is not of any particular significance. *Ibid.* 27 The Lago di Nemi, famous in antiquity.., is also a lake of considerable limnological interest. **1967** *Economist* 29 July 414/3 The Lake Tahoe Area Council..has spent thousands of dollars on engineering and limnological studies. **1970** *Nature* 25 July 420/2 The English Lake District has been and is still a mecca for limnologists.

limnoplankton (li:mnoplæ·ŋktǫn). [a. G. *limnoplankton* (E. Hæckel 1891, in *Jenaische Zeitschr. Naturwiss.* XXV. 253), f. *LIMNO- + PLANKTON.] Plankton found in fresh water.

1893 G. W. FIELD tr. *Hæckel's Planktonic Stud.* in *Rep. U.S. Comm. Fisheries 1889–91* 580 The totality of the swimming and floating population of the fresh water may be called limnoplankton. **1909** GROOM & BALFOUR tr. *Warming's Oecol. Plants* xxxviii. 161 Limnoplankton appears to be one of the most cosmopolitan of formations. **1955** C. C. DAVIS *Marine & Fresh-Water Plankton* i. 28 The limnoplankton is the plankton of lakes.

limnoria (limnǭᵊ·riă). [mod.L. (W. E. Leach 1815, in *Trans. Linn. Soc. Lond.* XI. 370), ad. Gr. Λιμνορεια a water-nymph.] A marine isopod crustacean of the genus so called, which includes *L. lignorum*, a borer that attacks timber (= GRIBBLE[2]).

1868 BATE & WESTWOOD *Hist. Brit. Sessile-Eyed Crustacea* II. 353 Many kinds of wood, including old oak, are devoured by the *Limnoria*. **1936** *Times Lit. Suppl.* 18 Apr. 325/3 Against teredo's rival limnoria, luckily less wide-spread, no poison is effective. **1967** J. A. C. NICOL *Biol. Marine Animals* (ed. 2) v. 231 The gribble *Limnoria* is an isopod which tunnels into wood and feeds on wood particles.

limo (li·mo), colloq. abbrev. of *LIMOUSINE. *U.S.*

1968 *New Yorker* 23 Nov. 96 'You ride in the limo, dear,' he said,..helping her out of the Daimler. **1972** R. K. SMITH *Ransom* I. 18 If there's traffic too close to the limo, we forget it. **1972** *New Yorker* 23 Dec. 36/2 Just at the moment when the heavy groups freaking out in rented limos seemed to have wiped everybody out, this sing-song music..began to flower. **1973** R. MOORE *Fifth Estate* i. 16 The company should be sending a limo for me. I'd be happy to drop you off. **1975** *New Yorker* 24 Mar. 32/3 This place has got a laser beam on the perimeter to keep out marauders, as well as free Rolls-Royce and Mercedes limo service.

Limoges (limǭᵘ·ʒ). The name of a city in central France used (freq. *attrib.*) to designate painted enamels, porcelain, etc., made there.

1844 DISRAELI *Coningsby* II. v. viii. 310 He has..a collection of Limoges ware that is the despair of the dilettanti. **1856, 1861** [see *CHAMPLEVÉ *sb.* and *a.*]. **1870** C. SCHREIBER *Jrnl.* (1911) I. 77 Some beautiful Limoges enamels. **1938** [see *CHAMPLEVÉ *sb.* and *a.*]. **1963** L. DEIGHTON *Horse under Water* xvii. 71 Coffee came..in a silver pot attended by Limoges cups and saucers. **1966** MRS. L. B. JOHNSON *White House Diary* 23 Jan. (1970) 356 Exquisite Limoges—white with a chaste gold border—for her formal china. **1966** J. LAVER *Victoriana* 157 Royal Worcester patera of 1867 decorated in the 'Limoges enamel' style..suggested by the painted enamel work on copper which was carried out at Limoges during the Renaissance. **1973** *Country Life* 11 Oct. 1063 French lamp in white Limoges porcelain with sumptuous gold decorations..£14.95.

‖ **limon** (limoṅ). *Geol.* [Fr., = (*a*) silt, alluvium, (*b*) *limon*, loess:– L. *līmus* mud.] A fine sandy soil, probably of similar origin to loess, which is widespread in northern France and Belgium.

1890 *Rep. Brit. Assoc. Adv. Sci. 1889* 560 At the foot of the Alps,..the löss is dark grey; but west of the secondary chain the same deposit is yellowish, and composed almost entirely of silicious materials, with only a very little carbonate of lime. This *limon* or löss..is very generally modified towards the top by the chemical action of rain. **1931** H. ORMSBY *France* v. 168 Where the covering of *limon* was thick, on the lower slopes the farmer has been able to cover the scars of war with fields of grain. **1972** MANSFIELD & POWRIE *France & Benelux* viii. 137 The most typical of these chalklands is Picardy,..remarkably fertile, owing to the thick covering of *limon*.

Limousin (limuzæṅ). Also 8 **Lemosine, Limosine.** [Name of an old province in central France.] **1.** A native or inhabitant of the former province of Limousin or of the region round Limoges; also, the dialect of this region. Also *attrib.* or as *adj.*, of or pertaining to this region, its inhabitants, or their dialect.

1653 T. URQUHART tr. *Rabelais's Works* (1664) II. vi. 33 When all comes to all, thou art a Limousin, and thou wilt here by the affected speech counterfeit the Parisiens. **1706** J. STEVENS *New Spanish & Eng. Dict.* Pref., In Catalonia ..they have besides a peculiar language of their own... This is a sort of Limosine, or that of the Country of Limoges, being an old barbarous French, formerly brought into this Country out of France. **1716** C. CAMPBELL tr. *Dameto's Hist. Balearick Islands* I. v. 64 That which is in use at this time commonly called the Lemosine Language being originally from Limosin a Province of France, whose Capital is Limoge. **1787** A. YOUNG *Jrnl.* 10 June in *Trav. France* (1792) I. 18 Chestnuts on a calcareous soil, contrary to the Limosin maxim. **1911** S. M. HOGAN *St. Vincent Ferrer* iv. 29 St. Vincent himself tells us that he preached in his mother-tongue—Limousin. **1932** W. L. GRAFF *Lang.* 377 Provençal group, with different varieties: Provençal..Limousin, Gascon. **1964** *Archivum Linguisticum* XVI. 34 In quoting this dialect [*sc.* North Occitan] I give Limousin forms. **1968** F. WHITE *Ways of Aquitaine* IV. 55 The churches of the Limousin abbeys form a school of their own, deeply impressive because of their darkness and their strength. **1973** J. WAINWRIGHT *Devil you Don't* 62 The V.V.S.O.P. Cognac—pale, liquid ecstasy with a bouquet of Limousin oak.

2. An animal belonging to the French breed of beef cattle so called. Also *attrib.*

1970 *Times* 6 Apr. 10/7 The Limousin, a hardy, deep fawn coloured animal, is a beef breed which has impressed many visitors to Paris shows. **1971** *Country Life* 30 Dec. 1857/3 Limousins from the Limoges area..are the most recent invaders of the northern English counties. **1973** *Ibid.* 1 Mar. 548/1 A German Zimmenthal bull, and..a Limousin bull in France.

limousine (li·muzīn). [Fr., f. prec.] A (luxury) motor car with a compartment for the passengers and a separate compartment for the driver. Also *attrib.*

Orig. the driver's seat was outside though covered with a roof. Since the 1930s the word has been more usual in North America than in the U.K.; recently it has been used, esp. in the U.S., for vehicles conveying passengers to and from large airports.

1902 A. C. HARMSWORTH et al. *Motors* 55 With certain kinds of engines, too, it is difficult to adopt any other form of car than the Tonneau, or for the wet weather the Limousine. **1905** *Westm. Gaz.* 22 Nov. 9/2 A touring car.. fitted with a brougham or limousine body. **1916** A. BENNETT *Lion's Share* xxx. 217 A few days later an automobile—not Audrey's but a large limousine—bumped, with slow and soft dignity, across the railway lines. **1920** *Chambers's Jrnl.* May 279/2 He heard the purring of limousines gliding into Pall Mall. **1922** W. J. LOCKE *Tale of Triona* v. 47 Whom she saw drive away in luxurious limousines. **1960** I. WALLACH *Absence of Cello* (1961) 27 Marian..struggled to the bus [at N.Y. airport] that was known for some reason as a 'limousine'. **1968** *Globe & Mail* (Toronto) 3 Feb. 13/4 Limousine service..to take them to the nearest city bus stop. **1970** *Toronto Daily Star* 24 Sept. 38/1 Jones and most of the borough education directors—who are paid the same salary—are given chauffeur driven limousines. **1972** *Daily Tel.* 16 May 9/3 The open limousine was followed by one in which Prince Philip travelled with Mme Pompidou. **1972** *Times* 27 June (Tokyo Suppl.) p. vi/2 There are regular limousine services

from the airport. **1973** V. CANNING *Finger of Saturn* i. 10 The people from the limousine got out... The limousine driver watched them go. **1973** *Country Life* 13 Sept. 686 If the terms 'limousine' and '1½ litre' appear incompatible, see, sit in, and drive the Triumph 1500... In the generous luxury you get in a well-padded limousine..long-distance travelling is limousine-smooth. All the other limousine touches are there too.

b. limousine liberal: a wealthy liberal. *U.S.*

1969 *Times* 4 Nov. 10/5 The little man truly representing the ordinary people, hitting out strongly at Mr. Lindsay's 'limousine liberal' appeal. **1970** *N.Y. Times* 26 Oct. 36 Canada is most fortunate to have a Premier who is willing to tell the bleeding hearts and limousine liberals what he thinks of them.

limp, *a.* Add: **1. c.** *limp wrist* (see quot. 1960); also *transf.* and (usu. with hyphen) as *attrib. phr.*

1960 WENTWORTH & FLEXNER *Dict. Amer. Slang* 319/2 *Limp wrist* adj., homosexual; said of male homosexuals; effeminate... A homosexual or effeminate man. **1963** *Amer. Speech* XXXVIII. 171 An effeminate young man, a sissy.. *limp wrist.* **1969** *Guardian* 18 Mar. 1/3 Washington ..has concluded that if Britain continues to follow a 'limp wrist' policy after the open affront of the shooting affair, the gambling interests would draw obvious conclusions. **1970** C. MAJOR *Dict. Afro-Amer. Slang* 77 *Limp wrist*, having latent homosexual tendencies.

limp, *v.*[2] Add: **1. c.** *spec.* Of a damaged ship, aircraft, etc.: to proceed slowly or with difficulty.

1920 *Conquest* Apr. 291/3 The 'standard patch' has rendered invaluable assistance in helping stricken ships to limp into port. **1935** C. DAY LEWIS *Time to Dance* 37 But he tinkered and coaxed, and they limped Over the Adriatic on into warmer regions. **1971** *E. Afr. Standard* (Nairobi) 10 Apr. 1/1 Mr. Sprinzel, driving car No. 16, a Range Rover, with his co-driver David Benson, limped back to Nairobi yesterday afternoon. **1973** *Daily Tel.* 1 Jan. 1/4 The Fleetwood trawler Wyre Captain, 490 tons, limped into port at Thorshavn, Faroe Islands, yesterday, with a damaged bridge and no navigation instruments.

limpet. Add: **b.** Of officials alleged to be superfluous but clinging to their offices. Also *attrib.*

1905 *Westm. Gaz.* 9 Mar. 2/2 Lord Spencer..had some pertinent criticisms to make of the Limpet Government. **1922** *Daily Mail* 22 Nov. 8 He is rationing the departments and ejecting the 'limpets'. *Ibid.* 23 Nov. 10 Ministries are multiplying their accumulation of limpets and paying them too well. **1927** CARR-SAUNDERS & JONES *Survey Social Struct. Eng. & Wales* 54 After the war, attempts were made to rouse our animosity against 'limpets'.

c. limpet-hammer, a stone tool believed to have been used by prehistoric peoples to knock limpets off rocks.

1885 S. GRIEVE *Great Auk* 57 We were puzzling ourselves as to what could be the use of the numerous oblong stones we met with among the [limpet] shells, and..he.. informed us they were limpet-hammers. *Ibid.*, Subsequent enquiries have only helped to confirm us in the opinion that the large oblong stones found at Caisteal-nan-Gillean are really limpet-hammers.

2. A type of explosive device that is attached magnetically to a ship's hull; so *limpet bomb, charge, mine.*

1942 W. S. CHURCHILL *Secret Session Speeches* (1946) 50 Explosions occurred in the bottoms of the *Valiant* and *Queen Elizabeth*, produced by limpet bombs fixed with extraordinary courage and ingenuity. **1949** F. MACLEAN *Eastern Approaches* II. iii. 202 We fixed a couple of 'limpets' to her stern. These were half-spheres of metal, made to contain a pound or so of high explosive and fitted with a magnetic device to hold them to the side of the ship. **1955** J. THOMAS *No Banners* xix. 175 He wanted permission to use six limpet charges. **1959** *Chambers's Encycl.* IX. 428 Midget submarines placed these limpet mines which, being magnetized, clung to the hull and were fired by a time fuze. **1962** G. WELLER *All about Submarines* (1963) viii. 115 The German officers were sure that limpet mines had been attached to the keel of their battleship. **1971** D. BAGLEY *Freedom Trap* ix. 198 What do we use instead of a limpet?.. I can't invade her in the middle of the Grand Harbour.

limping, *ppl. a.* Add: **c.** *transf.* Of certain relationships that are held to be legal in one country but not in another.

1963 *Listener* 17 Jan. 122/1 There is probably no more embarrassing experience for a couple than to find that they are regarded as validly married in one country, but living in sin in another. Even worse, perhaps, is the position of a man regarded by one country's laws as divorced and therefore single, but by another country as married and liable to be convicted for bigamy if he remarries. This situation, vividly called 'the limping marriage', is deplored by most systems of law including our own. *Ibid.* 123/2 It goes some way towards mitigating the evil of the 'limping marriage'. **1970** *Internat. & Compar. Law Q.* XIX. I. 12 It was scarcely in the child's interests to make her a 'limping infant' by pronouncing an order which would be refused recognition in a country with which she had significant links. *Ibid.* 17 There was the particular danger..that the adoption order would not be recognised in some countries, producing a 'limping' adoption.

limu, var. *LIMMU.

linac (li·næk). *Physics.* [f. *lin*ear *ac*celerator.] A linear (i.e. straight) particle accelerator.

1950 *Amer. Jrnl. Physics* XVIII. 126/1 At Berkeley, L. W. Alvarez was the chief supporter of the 'linac', and he supervised the construction of the present 40-ft. machine. **1966** *New Scientist* 17 Nov. 359/2 Above the underground linac are two Van der Graaff accelerators. **1969** *Sci. Jrnl.* Jan. 55/1 Although many linear radio-frequency accelerators (called linacs) have been built, the more usual construction is circular so that the same field element can be used many times in the complete acceleration cycle.

linage. Add: **c.** Also, the charge made (by a newspaper, etc.) according to the number of lines occupied by an advertisement, etc.

1961 in WEBSTER. **1968** *Listener* 20 June 818/2 (Advt.), Linage 6s. 6d. a line. **1971** *Timber Trades Jrnl.* 14 Aug. 61 Linage. Minimum 20 words. 10p per word.

linalool (linæ·lo,ǫl). *Chem.* [a. G. *linalool* (F. W. Semmler 1891, in *Ber. d. Deut. Chem. Ges.* XXIV. 207), f. G. *linalo(ëol* linaloe oil + *-ol* -OL.] An optically active tertiary alcohol, $(CH_3)_2C{:}CH{\cdot}CH_2{\cdot}CH_2{\cdot}C(CH_3)OH{\cdot}CH{:}CH_2$, found in linaloe oil and used in perfumery: the *d*-isomer is *CORIANDROL and the *l*-isomer also occurs in the oils of rose, bergamot, lavender, and thyme.

1891 *Jrnl. Chem. Soc.* LX. I. 540 Linaloe oil appears to be a mixture of several compounds...The principal constituent which is termed linaloöl, boils at about 195–190° [*sic*]. **1922** *Jrnl. Amer. Chem. Soc.* XLIV. 2966 The odorous constituents of the peach consist chiefly of esters of the aliphatic terpene alcohol linalool. **1951** P. Z. BEDOUKIAN *Perfumery Synthetics & Isolates* 292 Commercial linalool is obtained from several sources, principally from oil of bois de rose, linaloe, shiu and coriander... Linalool occurs to the extent of about 80 per cent in the first two oils. **1968** *Times* 5 Nov. 17/2 Linalool and linalyl isobutyrate.. are both fragrant oils found in coriander and lavender.

Hence **li·nalyl**, the radical $C_{10}H_{17}$— present in ethers and esters of linalool.

1900 *Jrnl. Chem. Soc.* LXXVIII. II. 101 Analyses of two samples of essence of bergamot..show that during the process of ripening..the linalyl acetate increases from 33·8 to 37·3 per cent. **1964** *Economist* 26 Dec. 1448/1 Linalyl acetate goes into colognes to provide the lavender notes.

linamarin (linămæ·rin). *Chem.* [a. G. *linamarin* (Jorissen & Hairs 1891, in *Pharmaceut. Post* XXIV. 659), f. L. *līn-um* flax + *amār-us* bitter + -IN[1].] A bitter crystalline compound, $C_{10}H_{17}NO_6$, which occurs in flax; the glucoside of acetone cyanohydrin.

1892 *Jrnl. Chem. Soc.* LXII. I. 502 Linamarin forms groups of colourless needles having a cool and bitter taste. **1934** *Onderstepoort Jrnl. Vet. Sci. & Animal Industry* III. 116 The toxic substance present in the plant *Dimorphotheca cuneata* has been isolated and identified as the cyanogenetic glucoside 'linamarin'. **1964** D. D. DAVIES et al. *Plant Biochem.* x. 385 Feeding experiments have shown that the synthesis of the cyanogenetic glucosides, lotaustralin and linamarin, in *Trifolium repens* is related to the metabolism of isoleucine and valine. **1973** *Daily Colonist* (Victoria, B.C.) 18 July 18/4 Cassava's toxicity takes on a new importance. This toxicity is caused by a substance called linamarin..together with small amounts of a closely related substance, lotaustralin.

linchet: see *LYNCHET.

Lincoln[1]. Add: **1. Lincoln imp**, a grotesque carving in Lincoln cathedral; a door-knocker, ornament, or trinket modelled on this; also *attrib.*; **Lincoln Longwool**, a sheep of the breed so called, characterized by its large size and long fleece; **Lincoln Red**, an animal belonging to a breed of red shorthorn cattle so called, used as producers of both milk and beef; **Lincoln wool**, wool from a Lincoln Longwool.

1926–7 *Army & Navy Stores Catal.* 156/3 Bedroom door knockers..Lincoln Imp, 3¼ in., 1/6. **1941** E. BOWEN *Look at Roses* 245 They were mementoes—photos..a Lincoln Imp, a merry-thought pen-wiper. **1967** *Listener* 13 July 48/3 Lincoln Cathedral has its world famous devil—the Lincoln imp. **1894** *CGA Catal.* 46/1 Sheep. Lincoln Long Wool Shearling Rams, bred by owner; 1st and 2nd, £10. **1919** W. C. COFFEY *Productive Sheep Husbandry* xix. 163 Breeders in England organized the Lincoln Long-wool Sheep Breeders' Association in 1892. **1972** *Country Life* 16 Mar. 606/2 Lincoln Longwool and some of the white-faced breeds are used for crossing. **1903** *Farmer & Stockbreeder* 20 July 1195/3 The Lincoln Red is a profitable farmer's beast, growing to great weight. **1966** *Guardian* 13 July 18/1 Cockerington Earl..won the supreme championship of the Lincoln Red cattle. Lincoln Reds are the heftiest of the beef cattle. **1974** *Country Life* 17 Jan. 65/3 The stocky, sturdy, thick-coated Lincoln reds... Lincoln red cattle are..most attractive animals. **1930** L. G. D. ACLAND *Early Canterbury Runs* vii. 177 They cut over twelve hundred bales of Lincoln wool.

Lincoln[2] (li·ŋkǒn). Name of Abraham *Lincoln* (1809–65), sixteenth President of the U.S., in **Lincoln rocker**, a type of rocking-chair with straight upholstered back and seat and open arms, popular in the mid-19th c.

1952 J. GLOAG *Short Dict. Furnit.* 311 *Lincoln rocker*, a name occasionally used in the United States for a mid-19th century type of rocking chair. **1967** *Boston Sunday Herald* 26 Mar. I. 51/3 (Advt.), Grape carved Lincoln rocker.

Lincolnesque (liŋkǒne·sk), *a.* [f. the name of Abraham *Lincoln* (1809–65), 16th president of the U.S. + -ESQUE.] Resembling or having the qualities of Abraham Lincoln. So **Lincolnian** (liŋkōᵘ·niăn), *a.*

1910 H. P. WILLIS *Stephen A. Douglas* xiii. 283 A characteristic Lincolnian anecdote which the speaker applied to the repetition of the 'state fraud' of the Springfield resolutions. **1923** *Public Opinion* 15 June 565/3 That is Lincolnesque in its homeliness. **1962** E. AMES *Daughter of House* (1963) I. i. 30 The two long Lincolnesque furrows of the cheeks. **1963** *Economist* 20 July 257/2 The [Republican] party's Lincolnian heritage. **1968** MRS. L. B. JOHNSON *White House Diary* 9 Apr. (1970) 659 The star of that day was Hector Legge, of Dublin, Ireland, 'Dean' of the traveling journalists, a towering figure.. with a Lincolnesque face.

Lincolniana (li:ŋkǒniā·nă). [f. the name of Abraham *Lincoln* (see prec.) + *-IANA.] Matter such as books, objects, and writings, relating to or characteristic of Abraham Lincoln.

1921 *Double-Dealer* Feb. 67/1 Another notable essay in Lincolniana appears with the imprint of Walter M. Hill of Chicago—'The Assassination of Lincoln' by E. W. Coggeshall. **1932** *N. & Q.* 19 Nov. 366/2 A considerable amount of hitherto unprinted Lincolniana. **1949** *Jrnl. Illinois State Hist. Soc.* June 137 The volume is one of the few in the vast area of Lincolniana that influenced later research and publications. **1959** *Listener* 19 Feb. 326/1 That vast body of ephemeral Lincolniana.

Lincolnshire (li·ŋkǒnʃəɪ). The name of a county on the east coast of England, used *attrib.* in **Lincolnshire Curly-coat(ed)**, a pig of the extinct breed so called; **Lincolnshire limestone**, a bed of oolitic limestone of Upper Jurassic (Bajocian) age, extensively developed in Lincolnshire and adjoining counties; **Lincolnshire Longwool** = *Lincoln Longwool*; **Lincolnshire Red** = *Lincoln Red.*

[**1847** H. D. RICHARDSON *Pigs* iii. 36 The old Lincolnshire breed was light coloured, or even white, with, in most specimens, a curly and woolly coat.] **1917** W. POWELL-OWEN *Pig-Keeping* xi. 130 Lincoln Curly Coated. This Eastern counties breed is..most useful for crossing purposes. **1921** H. A. DAY *Pig-Keeping* 13 The Lincolnshire Curly-Coated. I see no reason why this breed should not be given a trial in districts where it is seldom met. **1972** *Country Life* 16 Mar. 606/2 Oxford Sandy and Black..are only one of five breeds of pigs that have become extinct, the others being the Cumberland, the Dorset Gold Tip, the Lincolnshire Curly Coat and the Yorkshire Blue and White. **1873** *Q. Jrnl. Geol. Soc.* XXIX. 226 The main feature of my Second Part will be the description and consideration of a series of beds grouped by Mr. Judd under the name of the 'Lincolnshire Limestone'. *Ibid.* 284 A few words as to the extent of the area occupied by the Lincolnshire Limestone. It ranges through the whole of the county of Lincoln, stretching into South Yorkshire on the north, and through Rutland into Northamptonshire on the south. **1969** BENNISON & WRIGHT *Geol. Hist. Brit. Isles* xiii. 301 The latter [*sc.* Collyweston Slate] forms a transition to the Lincolnshire Limestone which, appearing in Northamptonshire, thickens northwards to form the conspicuous west-facing escarpment on which Lincoln Cathedral stands. **1874** R. O. PRINGLE *Live-Stock of Farm* vii. 251 The old Lincolnshire long-wools were ungainly animals. **1897** W. HOUSMAN *Cattle* iii. 96 The excellence and purity of the Lincolnshire Red Shorthorn breed.

lincomycin (liŋkomǝi·sin). *Pharm.* [f. mod.L. *linco(lnensis*, specific epithet (see def.) + *-MYCIN.] An antibiotic, $C_{18}H_{34}N_2O_6S$, produced by cultures of the bacterium *Streptomyces lincolnensis* var. *lincolnensis* and given orally or by injection (usu. as the hydrate of the hydrochloride) to combat various Gram-positive bacteria, esp. staphylococci and streptococci.

1963 *Bacteriol. Proc. 1963* 94/1 Lincomycin, developed by The Upjohn Co., is a new antibiotic, chemically distinct from others now in use. **1966** *Practitioner* July 90 Lincomycin hydrochloride should prove useful in general practice against the common gram-positive infections. **1969** *New Scientist* 8 May 277/1 The group A haemolytic streptococci..are becoming increasingly resistant to tetracycline, erythromycin, and lincomycin. **1973** *Brit. Pharmacopœia 1973* 266/2 Lincomycin Hydrochloride is the monohydrate of the hydrochloride of methyl 6,8-dideoxy-6-(1-methyl-4-propyl-2-pyrrolidinecarboxamido)-1-thio-D-*erythro*-D-*galacto*-octapyranoside. **1975** *Daily Colonist* (Victoria, B.C.) 31 Jan. 3/6 Lee Smith said..that United States reports on the drugs clindamycin and lincomycin..were 'wildly exaggerated' in the news media.

lincrusta (linkrʊ·stă). Also **Lincrusta.** [f. L. *līn-um* flax + *crusta* rind, bark: after LINOLEUM.] A special type of thick embossed wall-paper.

1882 *Encycl. Brit.* XIV. 676/2 Mr. Walton, the original patentee of linoleum, has adapted a preparation of oxidized oil and cork or other thickening material embossed with patterns for wall decorations under the name of 'Lincrusta Walton'. **1891** *Jrnl. Soc. Chem. Industry* X. 150/2 Improvements in the Manufacture of Linoleum, Lincrusta, Cere-Cloth, and the like. **1921** *Spectator* 9 Apr. 464/1 'Lincrusta' wears so well that it seemed a sin to take it off. **1923** U. L. SILBERRAD *Lett. J. Armiter* i. 29 Semi-detached house, lincrusta dadoes, basement kitchen—it would suit him. **1939** *Archit. Rev.* LXXXVI. 258 *Lincrusta.* This is a plastic material from which a relief ornament is pressed. **1963** *Punch* 25 Sept. 457/1 He rolled

his eyes..towards the lincrusta ceiling. 1973 M. BENCE-JONES *Palaces of Raj* viii. 142 Lord Curzon replaced some of the Lincrusta with damask.

lindane (li·ndēin). [f. the name of Teunis van der *Linden* (b. 1884), Dutch chemist, who investigated the isomers of benzene hexachloride + *-ane* (perh. after *CHLORDANE).] The gamma isomer of benzene hexachloride, $C_6H_6Cl_6$, used as an insecticide; it is a colourless crystalline compound that is toxic to mammals but relatively harmless to plant life, and is used in the form of dusts, sprays, and aerosols.

1949 *Lindane* (Interdepartmental Comm. Pest Control, Bureau Entomol. & Plant Quarantine, U.S. Dept. Agric.) 3 The coined name, 'Lindane', is established for the gamma isomer of the chemical 1, 2, 3, 4, 5, 6-hexachlorocyclohexane of a purity not less than 99 percent. 1956 *Nature* 25 Feb. 367/1 In solid form 'Dieldrin' and 'Lindane' were the most effective toxicants against the larvæ of *Aedes aegypti* and *Culex fatigans*. 1961 *New Scientist* 6 July 26/3 A new liquid seed dressing..is based on lindane (a very pure form of gamma-BHC), which is considered to be the insecticide least hazardous to wild life. 1970 *Nature* 31 Oct. 403/2 Fresh and rain water in Britain contains small but not insignificant amounts of the chief persistent organochlorine pesticides, DDT, lindane and dieldrin.

Linde (li·ndə). The name of Carl P. G. R. von *Linde* (1842–1934), German physicist, used *attrib.* to designate a process for liquefying gases by means of repeated cycles of compression, cooling, and expansion, used in the extraction of nitrogen and oxygen from air by exploiting the difference in their boiling points.

1902 *Encycl. Brit.* XXX. 283/2 The efficiency of the Linde process is small, but it is easily conducted and only requires plenty of cheap power. 1928 J. K. ROBERTS *Heat & Thermodynamics* v. 111 Much less preliminary cooling is necessary to liquefy a gas by the Linde method than by the Cascade process. 1937 M. W. ZEMANSKY *Heat & Thermodynamics* xiv. 251 In the Linde process for the production of liquid air, the initial temperature, initial pressure and final pressure are chosen so that, after passing through a throttling valve, a drop in temperature is produced. 1968 B. J. HAZZARD tr. *Asinger's Paraffins* ii. 105 After the removal of carbon dioxide and benzene by washing, coke-oven gas is liquefied by the Linde process, all the constituents except the hydrogen and some nitrogen condensing.

lindgrenite (li·ndgrĕnəit). *Min.* [f. the name of Waldemar *Lindgren* (1860–1939), U.S. geologist + -ITE[1].] A basic copper molybdate, $Cu_3(MoO_4)_2(OH)_2$, found as transparent, green, monoclinic, platy or tabular crystals.

1935 C. PALACHE in *Amer. Mineralogist* XX. 491/2 The author takes great pleasure in designating this well-defined mineral lindgrenite in honor of Professor Waldemar Lindgren. His great contributions to the knowledge of the ore deposits and their paragenesis makes it peculiarly fitting that his name should appear in the special literature of mineralogy. 1953 *Amer. Mineralogist* XXXVIII. 905 The physical and optical properties of the Idaho lindgrenite are virtually identical with those of the Chilean material. 1955 *Mineral. Mag.* XXX. 726 This occurrence of lindgrenite at Brandy Gill is perhaps one of the most interesting additions to the remarkable number of rare and unusual minerals..in the Caldbeck district.

lindworm (li·ndwɒ̄ɹm). Also **lindorm.** [ad. Da. and Sw. *lindorm.* Cf. *LINGWORM.] A monstrous and evil serpent, common in Scandinavian legend.

1814 H. WEBER *Illustrations of Northern Antiquities* 60 The terms worm, drake, dragon, and serpent, are indiscriminately applied to these monsters, as well as lind-drake and lind-worm; probably from their haunt being generally under a linden or lime tree. 1896 W. A. CRAIGIE *Scandinavian Folk-Lore* 439 The lindorm is a favourite monster in Swedish as well as Danish tradition. 1910 F. BOND *Wood Carvings Eng. Churches* I. 63 When a wyvern has no wings as at Limerick, he is, in heraldry, a lindworm. *Ibid.*, No rigid distinction can be made between the dragon, wyvern, and lindworm. 1971 BARBER & RICHES *Dict. Fabulous Beasts* 97 *Lindorm*, a snake-like creature, which devoured cattle and ate bodies... The lindworm is a heraldic dragon or wyvern without wings, presumably the same as the lindorm.

Lindy Hop (li·ndi hǫp). Also **lindy-hop.** [f. *Lindy*, nickname of C. A. Lindbergh (1902–74), the American pilot who in 1927 was the first to make a solo non-stop transatlantic flight + HOP *sb.*[2] 2.] A Negro dance originating in Harlem (New York); also *attrib.* Also *ellipt.* **Lindy.** Hence **Lindy** *v. intr.*, to dance the Lindy Hop; **li·ndyhopper,** one who dances the Lindy Hop.

1931 *Zit's Theatrical Newspaper* 2 May 11 The winners of the all-Harlem Lindy Hop contest..drew rounds of applause nightly. 1936 *Life* 14 Dec. 64 The Lindy Hop originated at the Savoy. 1946 MEZZROW & WOLFE *Really Blues* (1957) xvi. 286 We'd get five teams of lindyhoppers from the Savoy Ballroom. 1948 K. DAVIS *Human Soc.* 79 The late and unlamented dance step called the 'Lindy Hop' was a fad. 1951 [see *JITTERBUG *sb.* 2]. 1959 *Sears, Roebuck Catal.* Spring & Summer 831/2 Betty White's Teen-Age Dance Book... Clear instructions for fox trot, lindy, mambo, cha cha, etc. 1969 *New Yorker* 15 Feb. 31/3 Their feet began to tap, and they tore into the Lindy. 1969 DISCH & SLADEK *Black Alice* ii. 19 No one could challenge his tango, but when he heard fast music his impulse was to lindy rather than to twist. 1970 G. GREER *Female Eunuch* 108 Here I am, a negro who cannot do the lindy-hop or sing the Blues! 1970 A. MILLER in A. Chapman *New Black Voices* (1972) 538 Few can ignore the effects of the cake walk, fox trot, lindy hop, the twist on the movement habits of people in the States. 1973 *Guardian* 7 Aug. 8/4 When I was a kid I would go and dance for the white folks. Do the splits and the Lindy Hop, and they would throw me pennies.

line, *sb.*[2] Add: **I. 1.** *spec.* as used by climbers (usu. opp. *rope*).

1907 *Yesterday's Shopping* (1969) 700/2 Fine alpine line. 1923 G. D. ABRAHAM *First Steps to Climbing* ii. 35 A light Alpine line is also supplied but that is mostly used by experts on exceptionally difficult courses... For the beginner the ordinary rope is advisable. 1935 D. PILLEY *Climbing Days* xi. 224 We set aside the ordinary Alpine rope, and used 120 feet of Alpine line. 1950 *Mountaineering Handbk.* (Assoc. Brit. Members Swiss Alpine Club) ii. 27 Line can be used on ice or rock..or for rappel slings... Doubled, it can be used as a light rope. 1957 CLARK & PYATT *Mountaineering in Brit.* ix. 160 One development in technique was..the increasing use of line in preference to full size rope.

e. (Earlier and additional examples.) Add to def.: A telephonic connection; an individual 'number' or extension. Cf. *hold the line* (*HOLD *v.* 6 h), *hot line* (*HOT *a.* 12 c). Also *fig.*, esp. in phr. *to get the lines crossed*, to become confused.

1847 *Handbk. to Electric Telegraph* 11 So rapid is the transmission of the electric current along the lines of wire, that..to carry the wires eight times round the earth.. would occupy but one second of time. 1900 C. H. CHAMBERS *Tyranny of Tears* I. 2 Miss Woodward. (*Speaking into telephone—very sweetly.*) ..Mr. Parbury's just coming in now—he'll speak to you—keep the line. 1921 *Conquest* Jan. 127/2 The 'busy tone' is sent back to the calling subscriber if the line he wants is busy. 1934 *Punch* 21 Mar. 332/1 The notepaper should carry—(1) The name of the firm. (2) Its address. (3) Fictitious address for creditors. (4) Telephone number (at least ten lines). 1944 H. MCCLOY *Panic* (1972) 15 Ronnie showed the doctor how to get an outside line and he dialled a number. 1951 *Oxf. Jun. Encycl.* IV. 448/1 The Post Office took over all 'trunk' long-distance lines in 1896, and 6 years later opened the first of several large London exchanges, the 'Central', with 14,000 lines. 1970 B. KNOX *Children of Mist* iv. 77 Thane lifted the telephone. When the desk constable answered he asked for a line... Then he began dialling. 1972 J. WILSON *Hide & Seek* iii. 61 What? I can't hear you. It's a terrible line. 1973 *Times* 16 Apr. 14/6 It clearly has the advantage of keeping all the lines from getting crossed and establishing the priorities of policy. 1973 K. ROYCE *Spider Underground* iii. 50 He told me he couldn't see me then and to get off the line. 1974 *Times* 15 Mar. 8/2 Mr Nixon has admitted that he ordered a cover-up of the plumbers' activities, but suggested that his staff got their lines crossed and took this to be an order to cover up the Watergate affair as well.

(ii) Hence, any wire or cable that serves as a conductor of electric current, for whatever purpose.

1886 G. KAPP *Electr. Transmission of Energy* viii. 205 Overhead lines, whether used for electric lighting or transmission of energy, are exposed to the effects of lightning. 1902 *Encycl. Brit.* XXV. 35/2 Alternate current is used for lighting and continuous current for the tramway line. 1920 *Whittaker's Electr. Engineer's Pocket-Bk.* (ed. 4) 407 Since the induced voltages due to lightning are the same whatever the working voltage of the line, the heavier insulation on extra high voltage lines renders them less subject to lightning trouble. 1930 *Engineering* 25 Apr. 548/2 Minimum expenditure on the transmission and distribution systems from those points, connoting the use of overhead lines. 1957 *Encycl. Brit.* XXI. 887/1 On the teleprinter at the other end of the line, the responses of the armature of a single electromagnet..cause the corresponding character to be printed. 1962 A. NISBETT *Technique Sound Studio* iv. 79 In a building the size of a broadcasting studio centre there is a danger not only of high frequency losses due to capacitance, but also induction of programme signals, hum, etc., from other lines.

II. 7. f. (Further examples.) Also in phr. (taken from American football, but influenced by sense *20 b) *to hold the line*, to maintain, support, a position, viewpoint, etc. In *Cricket*, the line of flight of the ball from the bowler's hand.

1887 [see DRIBBLE *v.* 4 a]. 1956 B. HOLIDAY *Lady sings Blues* (1973) xi. 102 But 52nd Street couldn't hold the line against Negroes forever. 1960 I. WALLACH *Absence of Cello* (1961) 48 Her voice had a factious quaver as she dug in and prepared to hold the line on Perry's team. 1961 *Times* 18 Aug. 3/3 At 18 Pullar was bowled by Davidson, playing across the line. 1962 *Listener* 19 Apr. 672/2 'Holding the line'..of costs, prices, and wages is vital to what he believes to be the continuance of American prosperity. 1963 A. ROSS *Australia 63* iii. 87 He moved solidly behind the line, early in position for anything that kept low. 1968 W. SAFIRE *New Lang. Politics* 190/2 'Holding the line against inflation' remains a cliché, taken from a football metaphor ('Hold-that-line!') which in turn comes from a military expression. 1969 *Times* 25 Aug. 9/2 Harris, eventually, was leg-before, hitting enthusiastically across the line.

g. *Ballet.* The total effect of the disposition of the dancer's limbs, body, and head in movement or repose. (Cf. sense 7 d.)

1912 J. E. C. FLITCH *Mod. Dancing & Dancers* xi. 170 Her purity of line is never broken by..inartistic feats of athletic dexterity. 1922 BEAUMONT & IDZIKOWSKI *Man. Classical Theatr. Dancing* 26 Beauty of line is one of the dancer's greatest assets. 1936 A. HASKELL *Prelude to Ballet* xvii. 85 Fluidity and large movements whose line can be extended indefinitely are the essential characteristics of the Russian School. 1948 *Ballet Ann.* II. 91 He has a fine classical technique and excellent line. 1960 *Times* 7 Mar. 3/7 She is already a dancer of great charm..with a particularly striking sense of line that showed to advantage in lifts.

h. *Mus.* Instrumental or vocal melody; a structured sequence of notes or tones.

1923 R. H. MYERS *Mod. Mus.* vi. 80 His music has line ..and the enormous merit of condensation. 1955 *Times* 26 Aug. 3/5 In spite of the cello's natural inclination to ruminative melancholy..it has plenty of cantilena... But it is line, always line, not harmony, that is the essence of the matter. 1961 *Listener* 14 Dec. 1046/3 What do singers mean when they talk about 'maintaining the line'? .. It means striking a level in the voice from which all expression is controlled. *Ibid.*, This 'line' of the singer is a physical conception. *Ibid.* 21 Dec. 1089/3 The music takes shape by means of a simple recitative-like vocal line, modal, flexible, limpid, with an orchestral part of matching directness and simplicity. 1962 *Radio Times* 22 Feb. 43/1, I was concerned at the time with the idea of inventing melodic line and harmonic texture directly from the fund of the twelve notes available within the octave. 1967 *Melody Maker* 28 Jan. 7/5, I consider jazz to be a lot of horns and one of those top speed bass lines.

i. Each of the narrow strips into which an image is divided for transmission and reproduction by television, corresponding to a single (usually side-to-side) passage of the scanning spot across the camera tube or picture tube: often with prefixed number, as *625-line(s)*, indicating the number of lines making up a complete picture.

1929 *Proc. IRE* XVII. 1586 He first arrived at a correlation between the number of 'halftone lines per inch' and the corresponding television 'scanning lines'. *Ibid.*, Halftones of letters and photographs were made up, and their appearance compared with the television image on a 48-line system of the same original. 1938 *Encycl. Brit. Bk. of Year* 633/2 The service was continued, using exclusively a standard of 405 lines 50 frames interlaced scanning. 1961 G. MILLERSON *Technique Television Production* ii. 20 To reduce flicker problems, the beam is made to read the odd lines (odd field) of the image first (i.e. lines 1, 3, 5,..) and then return to scan the even lines between them (i.e. lines 2, 4, 6,..). 1963 *Ann. Reg. 1962* 27 They duly authorized the B.B.C. to start a second television channel by 1964 on U.H.F. and with an improved picture of 625 lines. 1974 *Sci. Amer.* Jan. 115/2 Each 1·25-second signal comprises a 'line' of picture data that is analogous to the line of a television picture. About 850 lines..complete a weather-signal picture.

8. c. Delete the reference to Fraunhofer's lines (cf. *FRAUNHOFER) and add to def.: Hence in extended use, a component of emitted radiation at what is nominally a single discrete wavelength (in practice, over a narrow range of wavelengths containing one at which the intensity is a maximum). (Further examples.)

1932 *Sci. Abstr.* A. XXXV. 1561 (*heading*) Line emission in infra-red. 1962 *Science Survey* III. 67 For a normal lamp, emitting a line in the visible spectrum, the width..of the line would be of the order of 10,000 Mc/s. 1971 D. W. SCIAMA *Mod. Cosmol.* ii. 21 He calculated that a sensitive radio receiver should be able to detect the 21 cm line as emitted by clouds of hydrogen gas in the Galaxy. 1971 *Nature* 31 Dec. 505/2 The atoms made up of the smaller mass particles would then radiate their characteristic lines at longer wavelengths.

13. c. In *Politics* (orig. *U.S.*), a particular policy or set of policies which a politician may maintain or expect others to follow; = **party-line*. Also *transf.*

1892 *San Francisco Examiner* 9 Nov. 1/7 (*heading*) In the line! California joins the Democratic procession by a decisive majority. 1934 H. M. CHEVALIER tr. *Malraux's Man's Fate* 149 He knew, too, that Moscow would maintain its line. *Ibid.* 169 'There's a general line that directs us—must follow it.' 'And give up our arms! A line that leads us to fire on the proletariat is necessarily bad.' 1938 *Ken* (Chicago) 7 Apr. 46/2 The Intelligence Service of the Foreign Office is a state within a state, virtually Britain's second, secret Government as far as foreign policy is concerned. It often pursues a line different from the Government's policy. 1943 *San Francisco Chron.* 25 May 14/2 The Nazis have done Senator Happy Chandler of Kentucky the honor of picking up his line... Chandler's line may not get far in this country, but the Nazis are not slow to appreciate it. 1944 M. LASKI *Love on Supertax* v. 60, I think the line was made perfectly clear. 1955 *Times* 2 June 6/6 The issue before the court is not so much whether Mr. Lattimore is guilty under the indictment as whether such a nebulous charge as following the Communist 'line' is sufficiently defined to enable him to offer an adequate defence. 1958 *Economist* 29 Nov. 767/2 They think that the liberal line—uncontrolled immigration—can be held for a few more years, but not indefinitely. 1960 *News Chron.* 25 Feb. 2/5 Mr. Barber denied that a 'line' had been agreed on as to the shape of the reports to be sent by..British reporters. 1974 HAWKEY & BINGHAM *Wild Card* xxiii. 188 The official line on what had happened was, at best, grossly understated.

d. *transf.* A marked tendency, a policy or trend (in any activity). In weakened use (*slang*): a glib or superficially attractive mode

of address or behaviour, plausible talk. So *to do a line with* (Austral. and N.Z.), to (try to) enter into an amorous relationship with.

Not clearly separable from senses 28 a, b. Cf. also *to shoot a line* (sense 13 g below).

1903 'H. McHugh' *Out for Coin* vi. 83 Are you handing me a line of bogus conversation? 1920 F. Scott Fitzgerald *This Side of Paradise* I. ii. 76 Lordy, Isabelle—this *sounds* like a line, but it isn't. 1923 *Cosmopolitan* Apr. 82/1 'Where have I been all your life, good lookin'?' 'If you think that line will get you anything here, you're crazy!' 1933 J. G. Cozzens *Cure of Flesh* I. 61 He falls in love with Coral and says that some day, when he makes good, he will come back and marry her. Coral thinks it's just a line with him. 1941 *Illustr. London News* CXCVIII. 488/2 The jacket mentions Huckleberry Finn. Mr. Baum is not, of course, on that level; but that's his line. 1941 [see *knock *sb.*¹ 5]. 1942 T. Rattigan *Flare Path* I. 102 They'll think it's a line, sir. 1944 J. H. Fullarton *Troop Target* viii. 63 He was doing a heavy line with the saddler's daughter. 1946 F. Sargeson *That Summer* 91, I could do a line with Maggie. 1946 K. Tennant *Lost Haven* (1947) x. 156 Do you know young Len's doing a line with Gran'pa's little angel? 1953 *Encounter* Oct. 1/2 Appearing at this time, and amidst these problems, *Encounter* seeks to promote no 'line', though its editors have opinions they will not hesitate to express. 1956 A. L. Rowse *Early Churchills* ii. 33 He has a fine line in Churchillian invective. 1958 D. Reeman *Prayer for Ship* viii. 202 He gave me a terrific line about the hold-up. Said it was his partner's fault. But he promises definitely it'll be here tomorrow evening. 1967 *Observer* 6 Aug. 4/6 The sect's most telling line—plugged in all its broadcasts and pamphlets—is that the end of the world is due shortly, probably about 1975. The Arab-Israeli war in June was seen as the first step to Armageddon.

e. *to get a line on*, to acquire information about (a thing), to come to know. So *to give* (someone) *a line on. colloq.* (orig. *U.S.*).

1903 *Sun* (N.Y.) 18 Nov. 4 'These dressmakers'..cannot get a line on the styles except at the Horse Show. 1920 B. Cronin *Timber Wolves* 138 It ain't over wise to give anyone a line on to what's doing. 1923 R. D. Paine *Comrades of Rolling Ocean* iii. 41 How about these other birds. Give me a line on them. 1928 D. L. Sayers *Unpleasantness at Bellona Club* xiv. 165, I did tumble to it that you'd got a line on me when you sent me down with that detective fellow to Charing Cross. 1935 Wodehouse *Luck of Bodkins* v. 50 If you want to get a line on how she feels, she gave me a letter to give you... Here it is. 1942 *Penguin New Writing* XII. 85 'They got a line on him,' said the R.P. 1947 *Chicago Tribune* 22 July 1/5 If we can find any one who saw her at a dance after 10:30 p.m. we may be able to get a line on whom she was dancing with and whose company she was in when she left.

f. *to lay* (or *put*) *it on the line*: (*a*) to hand over money; (*b*) to state (something) clearly, plainly, or categorically; (*c*) (with direct object) to put (one's career, etc.) at risk. Also with *place*, and the verb *to be*. Chiefly *U.S.*

1929 D. Runyon in *Hearst's International* Aug. 73/1 My rent is away overdue for the shovel and broom..and I have a hard-hearted landlady... She says she will give me the wind if I do not lay something on the line at once. 1940 J. O'Hara *Pal Joey* 100 You fellows always put it on the line for me every pay day. 1950 J. D. Macdonald *Brass Cupcake* i. 13 Lay it on the line. You can't take it with you... Put it on the entertainment account. 1954 J. Symons *Narrowing Circle* xxxvii. 188 'I'll see you're not the loser. You put it on the line with Jake Beverley and he'll put it on the line with you...' 'Let me lay it on the line then, Jake.' 1956 E. Pound tr. *Sophocles' Women of Trachis* 17 Put it on the line, what do you know? Get it out clearly. 1967 'E. E. Sumner' *Chance Encounter* v. 94 I'll lay it on the line for you, if you like. Are you thinking of asking my girl to marry you? 1968 M. Luther King *Trumpet of Conscience* ii. 40 Our lives must be placed on the line if our nation is to survive its own folly. 1968 *Listener* 22 Feb. 244/3 America must fight in Vietnam..because it has laid its prestige on the line. 1968 *Guardian* 26 July 9/7 Mayor Stokes is putting his career on the line. And the people know it—they won't let him down. 1970 *Ibid.* 9 May 2/4 It was clear to the [American] President that his credibility was on the line with the leaders in Hanoi. 1972 *New Yorker* 26 Aug. 17/2 He had decided to put his artistic reputation as a talented and original director of opera on the line at the outset of his American career with an unorthodox..production of Bizet's 'Carmen'. 1972 J. Quartermain *Rock of Diamond* xxiv. 153 I'll lay it on the line, Raven. You can say yes or no. 1973 *Black Panther* 7 July 8/3 The situation is as bad as before the takeover and it only serves to give the Indian people more reason to put their life on the line. *Ibid.* 6 Oct. 3/2 Egil Krogh..put it squarely on the line: 'Anyone who opposed us we'll destroy.'

g. *to shoot a line* (cf. Shoot *v.* 23 g), to 'put on an act', to talk pretentiously, to boast. So *line-shoot* vb. (*-shooting* ppl. a. and vbl. sb.) and sb., *-shooter*; also *shooter of lines. colloq.*

Cf. sense 13 d above.

1941 N. Coward *Blithe Spirit* I. ii. 50 The whole thing's a put up job—I must say, though, she shoots a more original line than they generally do. 1942 *Penguin New Writing* XIII. 24 Occasionally..it publishes a serious article... But this is regarded as a 'bind',..while its author is invariably dismissed as a 'line shooter', i.e. a conceited person. *Ibid.*, The other day..our C.O. introduced a discussion on tactical evasion by saying: 'I do not want this to develop into a "line-shooting" competition.' 1942 *R.A.F. Jrnl.* 30 May 17 For keeping up the spirits, line-shooting is at least as good as beer-drinking. *Ibid.*, The man who shoots a heavy line about the work he is doing is probably very keen on his job. 1943 Hunt & Pringle *Service Slang* 44 *Lineshoot*, a tall story. 1944 G. Netherwood *Desert Squadron* i. 2 Some of the chaps also came from other well known fighter units. From the 'line-shooting' that ensued, one would think that the squadron which was then in the process of formation could never hope to be as well known as the one they had left—and so on and so forth. 1944 T. H. Wisdom *Triumph over Tunisia* 121 One of the most thorough and decisive of the air operations in the whole campaign was carried out by the Hurri-bombers. And this is no squadron line-shoot. 1946 G. Gibson *Enemy Coast Ahead* 144 These things were happening every night, so there was nothing to shoot a line about. 1951 M. Kennedy *Lucy Carmichael* VII. iv. 377 When Melissa shoots a line..don't protest or argue. Take it up and embroider it. 1952 T. Rattigan *Deep Blue Sea* I. 38 Funny thing about gongs. .. They don't mean a damn thing in war—except as a line-shoot, but in peace time they're quite useful. 1958 *Times Lit. Suppl.* 3 Oct. 564/2 A champion shooter of lines. In a party of outstanding climbers and travellers he could be relied on to cap any story. 1960 *Times* 19 July 18/4 One must bear in mind that what his Lordship had called..'shooting a line' was not necessarily inconsistent with a genuine belief. 1960 V. Gielgud *To Bed at Noon* I. xi. 73 He believed Tom to have been line-shooting as far as his swimming prowess was concerned. 1973 *Listener* 15 Mar. 342/1 [He] was an awful line-shooter. He claimed to have been at Oxford, but..he hadn't been at Oxford. 1973 *Times* 20 Sept. 20/8 He was awarded (his friends thought inadequately) the MBE by the British and by the French the Croix de Guerre. He never shot a line about his escapades but made them into entertaining stories.

14. b. *Fashion.* The outline or dominant features of composition of a dress or suit. Freq. with qualifying term or preceded by a letter of the alphabet (to indicate the outline shape of the garment). Cf. sense 23 a below.

1918 in C. W. Cunnington *Eng. Women's Clothes* (1952) iv. 141 What was called the '*barrel line*' brought out by Callot two seasons ago..certainly is a lovely line. 1930 *Times* 13 Mar. 11/6 The curved line was seen in all the long coats. *Ibid.* 27 Mar. 11/6 There is a distinguished coat in black matasol, which has a slimming line. 1932 *Punch's Almanack* 7 Nov. 8 (*caption*) The line of to day. 1955 *Britannica Bk. of Year* 489/2 Fashion produced a new 'line' in women's clothes, the *H-line*. 1958 *Woman's Own* 24 Dec. 14/3 Which year brought out the following trends: (*a*) the New Look; (*b*) the Trapeze Line; (*c*) the A-line. 1968 J. Ironside *Fashion Alphabet* 92 *Line*, the silhouette of a garment that makes it look fashionable or unfashionable. 1968, 1970 [see *empire *sb.* 8 b]. 1975 *Vogue* 1 Mar. 84/1 Overall, a clear narrowing of the silhouette, most marked at Saint Laurent, presaging an even sparer line for autumn.

17. b. (Earlier example.) Also ellipt. *the line.*

1779 in W. B. Reed *Life & Corr. J. Reed* (1847) II. 134 Perhaps we would be as well off with Mason and Dixon's line continued. 1845 F. Douglass *Narr. Life F. Douglass* xi. 101 We owe something to the slaves south of the line as well as to those north of it. 1909 'O. Henry' *Roads of Destiny* xxi. 358 If you had come from below the line, I reckon I would have liked you right smart. 1949 *Sat. Even. Post* 26 Mar. 38/2 The critic thunders, and below 'the line' the shades of Marse Robert and Jeff Davis inevitably are summoned forth to meet the charge.

c. *Bridge.* A line across a score-card. So *above the line*, denoting points scored for game, honours, overtricks, or rubber, or for the failure of opponents to fulfil their contract; *below the line*, denoting points scored for tricks bid and won, and counting towards game.

1905 H. A. Vachell *Hill* vii. 144 My partner..made the Little Slam, and scored nearly six hundred below the line. 1908, 1927 [see *contract *sb.*¹ 1 g]. 1933 A. G. Macdonell *England, their England* vi. 78 Gone down 650 points above the line whereas he ought to have made two no-trumps. 1967 P. Anderton *Play Bridge* i. 15 They win ten tricks so they score three times the value of Spades below the line, i.e. 90 points plus another 30 points above the line as a bonus for making one more than their contract. 1970 S. Hughes *Art of Coarse Bridge* i. 12 This kind of spectacular finale happens far more often than one might expect, but it takes an awful lot of scoring above the line before anyone actually has..the right cards to do it with.

d. In phrases indicating the boundary between a debit and a credit in one's account, or between ordinary and extraordinary expenditure. (See also quot. 1973.) Also *to pay on the line*, to pay promptly.

1934 J. O'Hara *Appointment in Samarra* i. 20 There were only a few of the Lantenengo crowd who could get a favour out of Ed without paying cash on the line for it. 1938 S. V. Benét *Thirteen o' Clock* 249, I kept on schedule with the work, but I couldn't with the money. Each week, I'd be just a little over the line. 1940 *Economist* 13 Apr. 683/1 The figures 'below the line' in the Exchequer Return show the result of the issue of the 4 per cent. 1948 *Ibid.* 31 Jan. 195/1 Aggregate Government expenditure, including..the 'below line' expenditure. 1959 N. Mailer *Advts. for Myself* (1961) 66, I paid on the line every time. 1966 A. Gilpin *Dict. Econ. Terms* 1 Since 1947 it has been customary for the British Budget to contain a full statement of the estimated expenditure and revenue for the following year, some items being shown as 'above-the-line'..and others as 'below-the-line'. Most current items appear above the line and most capital items below. 1973 *New Society* 28 June 736/2 The growth of petrol promotions has coincided with a growth of giveaways, gimmicks and competitions in the marketing of a wide range of products... Termed 'below-the-line' marketing, it is encroaching on the 'above-the-line' (advertising) share of manufacturers' marketing budgets.

III. 19. *spec.* = Queue *sb.* 3. *U.S.*

1930 M. Sullivan *Our Times* III. xii. 502 People..were herded by policemen into lines stretching away from the marble entrance. 1969 D. C. Hague *Managerial Econ.* xi. 222 The second kind of stock problem is the queueing problem... A queue (what Americans call a 'line')..will form. 1974 *State* (Columbia, S. Carolina) 15 Feb. 1-B/2 At least one employe went as far away as Forest Drive for gasoline and nearby stations, selling gasoline, quickly acquired lines. 1975 *N.Y. Times* 1 Apr. 35/5 It's to stand silently on unemployment lines with other surplus members of America's work force, waiting to sign for your unemployment check.

c. A row of machines or work stations where a product is progressively assembled, or a succession of operations performed on it, as it passes from one end to the other during manufacture or processing. Cf. **assembly line*, **production line.*

1926 *Encycl. Brit.* II. 822/1 All of these lines, with their various machines and operations, are converging on the point where the leaves are assembled into springs. 1937 *Times* 13 Apr. p. xii/2 The raw material is delivered at one end of the machining line with the component passing from machine to machine until it reaches the view table. 1940 *War Illustr.* 16 Feb. 113 In one of Britain's 'shadow' factories bombers on the line will soon be ready to take the air. 1971 *Cabinet Maker & Retail Furnisher* 24 Sept. 531/1 Features of the production facilities at the new factory.. include a fully automated machining line and the longest finishing line in the U.K.

d. In business or management organization, the chain of command or responsibility; the persons responsible for the administration and organization of a business (as opposed to the staff). Hence *line manager, management.*

1960 Nanassy & Selden *Business Dict.* 27 Following are the basic types of internal organization of a business: (1) *line*: The owner gives orders directly to the workers. As the business grows, the owner appoints a few executives, who are responsible to him... (3) *line-and-staff*: Authority flows from top to bottom, with responsibility falling on staff supervisors and special experts. 1964 M. Argyle *Psychol. & Social Probl.* viii. 111 In several British factories it was found that the division between 'line' supervisors and 'staff' technicians tended to disappear—technologists must have supervisory responsibility. 1967 C. Margerison in Wills & Yearsley *Handbk. Managem. Technol.* 25 The accountants considered that they had responsibility for the end-product and sought to control certain actions of line managers. Line managers resented this interference with their authority and started to obstruct the accountants in their ordinary accounting function. 1967 Coulthard & Smith in *Ibid.* 206 A good deal of the failure of these techniques stems from the inability of personnel men to convince line management of their own vital role combined with the assumption by line management that the creation of a specialist department covering personnel policies, training, management development, etc., automatically relieves them of responsibility. 1972 *Accountant* 28 Sept. 391/1 If the internal auditor sees himself as a someone who can review and report upon the functions of line management on matters other than security, then there is one fundamental issue that has to be faced. 1974 *Times* 25 Mar. 17/4 It was a pity that so few line managers were present as it was their present and future competence that was being discussed.

20. b. In the war of 1914–18, the trenches collectively; the front line. So *up the line* (see quots.).

1916 H. W. Fowler *Let.* 5 Mar. in *S.P.E. Tract* XLIII. (1935) 136 What may be going on up the line who knows? 1917 W. Owen *Let.* 4 Feb. (1967) 430, I am now indeed and in truth very far behind the Line; sent down to this old Town [*sc.* Abbeville] for a Course in Transport Duties. 1917 A. G. Empey *Over Top* 313 '*Up the line.*' Term generally used in rest billets when Tommy talks about the fire trench or fighting line. 1919 W. H. Downing *Digger Dial.* 52 *Up the line*, in action. 'Up the line, with the best of luck'—a satirical phrase applied to men who, after being for some time in a safe occupation, were returned to fighting units. 1964 B. Gardner (*title*) Up the line to death.

21. c. *all along the line* (further examples); also, *all* (*the way*) *down the line*. Also, *somewhere along the line*, at some point (in time).

1924 R. Fry *Let.* 27 June (1972) II. 553 Both he and Courbet did elaborate portraits of the same patron... Courbet wins all along the line. 1936 A. Huxley *Eyeless in Gaza* xxi. 297 A refugee from Germany... Aryan, but communist—ardently and all along the line. 1962 J. Wain *Sprightly Running* v. 189 There is always the wistful hope ..that these young will not merely benefit from meeting each other, but will, somewhere along the line, actually be *taught* something. 1965 *Listener* 16 Sept. 402/2 It is difficult to estimate its direct effect, because all along the line there are people working hard to try to make sure that those defects do not come back on the patient. 1965 *New Yorker* 20 Nov. 162/3 Somewhere along the line, the surf and wind went out of his playing. 1969 B. Turner *Circle of Squares* xviii. 143 I've helped him all along the line, not always knowing why. 1972 *Guardian* 6 July 2/2 It has been clear that they had had to refer to Moscow for instructions all along the line. 1975 N. Luard *Robespierre Serial* xi. 87 You've lied to me, all the way down the line. *Ibid.* xvi. 146 I'm not going to let that little bastard get away with it. He's screwed us all down the line from Riyadh to Geneva.

22. (Earlier U.S. examples.)

1786 *Mass. Centinel* (Boston) 11 Jan. 3/1 The new arrangement ordered by Congress, for the more safe and regular conveyance of the Mails, by the line of stages. 1818 *Niles' Reg.* XIV. 14/2 A regular line of waggons and packets are established between the city of New-York and Detroit. 1837 W. Jenkins *Ohio Gazetteer* 56 The post office is supplied by daily lines of Coaches from Cincinnati to Dayton.

23. a. *line by line*: delete † and add later examples (freq. used, with hyphens, *attrib.*).

Similarly *line for line* (also, with hyphens, *attrib.*). (For *line-for-line* in Fashion cf. sense *14 b.)

1876 J. Weiss *Wit, Humor, & Shakespeare* iii. 78 There was a worthy old deacon, who, repeating Watts's hymn line for line after his clergyman, said, 'Return, ye rancid sinners!' **1934** T. S. Eliot *Eliz. Ess.* 17 A line-by-line examination of almost any Elizabethan play..would be a fruitful exercise. **1951** L. MacNeice tr. *Goethe's Faust* 9, I aimed at a line-for-line translation. **1958** [see *fashion *sb.* 9 c]. **1964** E. A. Nida *Toward Sci. Transl.* ii. 17 Dryden felt that there were three basic types of translation: (1) metaphrase, a word-for-word and line-for-line type of rendering; (2) paraphrase..; and (3) imitation. **1969** *Guardian* 29 July 7/3 Line-for-line copies of his [couture] collection. **1971** *Computers & Humanities* VI. 7 Comparisons are made on a line-for-line basis. **1971** *Gloss. Electrotechnical, Power Terms (B.S.I.)* iii. iv. 13 *Line by line scanning*, scanning in which the sweep is effected in straight, substantially horizontal strips extending over the entire width of the picture. **1973** *Country Life* 6 Dec. 1970/1 A perfect line-for-line copy of a couture Dior trouser suit.

e. *pl.*, as an imposition (further examples).

1907 *Massacre of Innocents* ii. 13 Vardon, do me five hundred lines. **1914** 'I. Hay' *Lighter Side School Life* vii. 182 Mr. Duckworth..had occasion to set Master Smith fifty lines for inattention. **1959** I. & P. Opie *Lore & Lang. Schoolch.* xv. 325 At my junior school the boys had different doors from the girls and if a boy went through the girls' door he had a 100 lines to write out. **1961** D. Woodward tr. *Simenon's Premier* ii. 36 He took lessons without appearing to see his pupils..and his only reaction was, if one of them grew restless, to give him two hundred lines. **1974** *Age* (Melbourne) 12 Oct. 12/2 *Doing lines*, being kept in to write out good resolutions, such as 'I must not put squashed frogs in girls' sandwiches'.

IV. 24. c. Phr. *line of command.*

1930 *Nautical Mag.* Jan. 41 (*title*) The line of command. *Ibid.* 43 When the machinery fails, then the old line of command is called upon to take its full responsibility. **1962** *Rep. Comm. Broadcasting 1960* 161 in *Parl. Papers 1961–2* (Cmnd. 1753) IX. 259 The planning and operation of a national programme of television can never be simple, even when there is a single objective to be pursued, when effective control resides in a single authority, and when there is a direct line of command.

26. a. *line of communication*: see *communication 6 c.

b. *line clear*, a signal indicating that a line is unoccupied and that a train may therefore proceed; *line of rail* (see quot. 1965; cf. *end of steel*, s.v. *end *sb.* 6 e).

1869 *Cornh. Mag.* Mar. 282 Signalman at 3 tells signalman at 2, 'line clear, send train.' **1907** *Daily Chron.* 16 Oct. 7/4 Martin should have pulled up until he got the line-clear signal. **1936** *Gloss. Terms Railway Signalling (B.S.I.)* 9 The block indicator shows 'Line Blocked' or 'Normal', 'Line Clear' and 'Train on Line'. **1963** Kichenside & Williams *Brit. Railway Signalling* v. 46 The signal controlling entry to the block section can only be cleared ..when the block indicator for the section ahead is at 'line clear'. **1965** *Economist* 8 May 655/2 The figure [of unemployed] exceeds 75,000 and..they are concentrated in the few towns along the so-called line-of-rail, the thin strip of urbanisation in which is concentrated..the country's [*sc.* Zambia's] economic activity. **1971** *E. Afr. Jrnl.* Mar. 17/2 A few co-operatives, along the line-of-rail especially, produce poultry products for sale.

e. Chiefly *Canada* and *N.Z.* A settlement road, a bush road.

Such roads often later developed into roads of standard size and quality, and the word *line* appears in many road-names in both countries. The term may be of English dialectal origin.

1828 *Brockville* (Ontario) *Gaz.* 26 Dec. 3/4 A teamster by the name of M'Pherson from the Scotch Line. **1830** W. S. Moorsom *Lett. from Nova Scotia* ix. 344 The greater part of this line is either a rough horse-path, or in the same state as that described under the name of a 'new cut'. **1841** *N.Z. Jrnl.* No. 43. 224/2 Colonel Wakefield is also about to direct a line or bridle road (the basis of the future road) to be cut. **1853** J. M. Richmond in *Richmond–Atkinson Papers* (1960) I. iii. 133 There is what we call a *good* bush road to Rata Nui but beyond it there are two miles of bush walking along what is called a 'line'; a line is made by cutting the supple jacks and small shrubs with a bill-hook. **1863** E. H. Walshe *Cedar Creek* 103 They wished even for the corduroy expedient a little farther on, when the line became encumbered with stumps left from the under-brushing. **1880** W. H. Patterson *Gloss. Words Antrim & Down* 63 *Line*,..(2) a road. The new roads are so called. **1890** E. H. Searle *Angela* i. 2 This track was known to the neighbourhood as 'Mount's Line'. **1933** 'P. Slater' *Yellow Briar* 172 This grain was hauled down the 6th line and stored till the spring in Isaac Chafee's warehouse. **1943** *Amer. Speech* XVIII. 87 In some country districts [in New Zealand] (the Manawatu, for example) the roads are named *lines*—McDonell's Line, Richardson's Line, Union Line—presumably from early boundary or surveyors' lines. **1961** Price & Kennedy *Notes Hist. Renfrew County* [*Ontario*] 110 McNaughton's Plan of 1836 shows Queen's Line as an opened road. **1971** M. Tak *Truck Talk* 99 *Line*, a road, route or highway.

f. A row of traps or of poison bait.

Widely used in English-speaking areas outside the U.K.

1854 Mayne Reid *Young Voyageurs* 190 Moreover, he [*sc.* the wolverine] will follow the tracks of the trapper from one to another, until he has destroyed the whole line. **1871** R. L. Dashwood *Chiploquorgan* viii. 109 We followed an old 'sable line',..a line of traps set for that animal. **1949** *Sat. Even. Post* 22 Jan. 98/2 It is usually a glum day for the trapper when he pays his periodic visit to his line and sees in the snow the tracks of a wolverine joining the tracks that he made himself on his previous swing around. **1960** B. Crump *Good Keen Man* 31 Working from the same hut at first, we laid cyanide lines up every ridge within reach of the camp. The dodge was to work in pairs, one laying blobs of flour flavoured with oil-of-aniseed for bait, the other adding crushed cyanide to each heap of flour. We'd do this for three days, then go back over the lines cutting the ears off the dead possums for tokens. **1968** K. Weatherley *Roo Shooter* 39 Whenever a fox got on the line they lost about a quarter of their morning's catch. It would go round all the traps killing and tearing the rabbits until it was disturbed or caught in an unsprung trap.

g. A pipe or tube (of great or indefinite length in relation to its thickness).

1862 W. J. M. Rankine *Man. Civil Engin.* iii. ii. 739 From..reservoir to..town the main pipes may form a double line, so that in the event of a failure of one line, a supply..may be conveyed through the other line. **1895** W. T. Brannt *Petroleum* vii. 237 Beside the lines leading from the oil region to Baku..there are a number of branches which lead from the 21 principal lines to the refineries. **1921** W. F. Durand *Hydraulics of Pipe Lines* v. 231 The buried line cannot be inspected or repaired or repainted on the outside, and these conditions will.. reduce the serviceable life of the line. **1962** F. I. Ordway et al. *Basic Astronautics* x. 411 As the propellants flow through the feed lines to the pump a certain amount of pressure will be lost due to friction. **1966** A. E. C. Vizard in P. Hepple *Natural Gas* 55 By using large diameter lines at relatively high pressures the potential carrying capacity of a single line can be greater. **1974** *Sunday Express* 14 Apr. 1/3 Detectives investigating the death of a diver.. have found that his support line was cut. The line carried oxygen and communication cables to two divers 350 feet down.

h. *Golf.* (See quot. 1910.)

1887 W. G. Simpson *Art of Golf* ii. ix. 166 If their advice as to the line and strength be followed, and the putt comes off, it is supposed..that there was no other way of doing it. **1910** *Encycl. Brit.* XII. 223/2 *Line*, the direction in which the hole towards which the player is progressing lies with reference to the present position of his ball. **1971** Trevino & Fraley *I can help your Game* (1972) v. 72 (*caption*) The putt has been stroked but I maintain my immovable body position, concentrating on keeping the blade square to the line.

i. *up the line*: on leave. *Naut. slang.*

1942 *Gen* 1 Sept. 13/2 When a sailor goes on leave he goes 'up the line'.

j. Phr. *the end of the line* (*transf.* and *fig.*). Cf. *the end of the road* (*end *sb.* 3 h).

1948 *Amer. Speech* XXIII. 29 Calcutta commandos.. reached the End of the Line [*sc.* China] by flying..over the Hump. **1955** J. Potts *Death of Stray Cat* (1956) vii. 75 Lillian..turned to face Floyd, as a signal that this was the end of the line for him. **1959** E. Burgess *Divided we Fall* xx. 228 It looks like the end of the line for Roylake. Unless he can think up something—fast! **1967** Wodehouse *Company for Henry* v. 79 'Don't tell me we're there already.'.. 'Yes, this is the end of the line.' **1974** 'J. Graham' *Bloody Passage* x. 133 They have nowhere to go. This is—how do the Americans say it?—the end of the line.

28. b. (Further examples.) Also, *not one's line*, not one's vocation or calling, not among one's pursuits or interests; *to step* (or *get*, etc.) *out of line*, to behave in an unconventional or unexpected manner.

1791 J. Lackington *Mem.* xxv. 191, I cannot help noticing that in one of his [*sc.* Wesley's] publications (stepping out of his line) he betray'd extreme weakness and credulity. **1857** C. Kingsley *Two Yrs. Ago* I. p. xviii, 'He..wanted to call me out.' 'Did you go?'.. 'I told him that wasn't my line.' **1932** D. Runyon *Guys & Dolls* ii. 37 Reasonably safe for anyone who does not get too far out of line. **1937** M. Sharp *Nutmeg Tree* xix. 249 'Wouldn't you like to be Lady Waring?'.. 'No, I wouldn't..it's not my line.' **1938** D. Runyon *Furthermore* iii. 45 He is out of line in giving Frankie the hot foot. **1943** J. B. Priestley *Daylight on Saturday* xiii. 87 The welfare worker act.. wasn't her line at all. **1962** P. Gregory *Like Tigress at Bay* iii. 28 As long as he doesn't get out of line too often, I'll keep him on. **1962** J. Ludwig in R. Weaver *Canad. Short Stories* (1968) 2nd Ser. 244 Women weren't Sidney's line. **1973** N. Graham *Murder in Dark Room* viii. 58 You do it his way or else. I stepped out of line when I checked on Redman.

c. *line of business*: in the 18th- and 19th-century theatre, the kind of parts for which an actor or actress was specifically engaged. Cf. *business 20.

1775 F. Abington *Let.* in D. Garrick *Private Corr.* (1832) II. 106 Knowing the impossibility of my attempting that line of business while I am necessarily engaged in so many plays. **1807** A. Holbrook *Mem. Actress* 33 Another shocking custom is, that of giving no distinct line of business; for people, let them possess what talent they may, excel more in certain parts than in others. **1831** P. Egan *Show Folks* 27 Waiting in turn to engage young men for different '*lines of business*' to complete their companies. **1845** *Ainsworth's Mag.* VIII. 150, I have alluded to country actors..acting characters not in their 'line of business'. **1849** *Theatrical Mirror* 17 Sept. 20 We were surprised to see Mrs. W. Daly playing the part of Lady Macbeth, being quite out of her lines of business. **1901** C. Morris *Life on Stage* vii. 40 These were the principal 'lines of business', and in an artistic sense they bound actors both hand and foot.

d. Phr. *one's line of country*, one's pursuit, field of interest, area of study, etc. (Freq. in neg. contexts.) Also, *line of work.*

1861 T. Hughes *Tom Brown at Oxf.* III. viii. 138 This sort of thing isn't my line of country at all. **1926** R. Macaulay *Crewe Train* ii. v. 115, I don't advise you to join it [*sc.* the R.C. church]. I don't think it's your line of country, exactly. **1943** N. Balchin *Small Back Room* viii. 94 What? Pinching strange females?.. That's more his line of country than yours. **1951** W. Empson *Struct. Complex Words* 15 A mistake made by Richards..is a great deal more illuminating than the successes of other writers in this line of country. **1957** G. Faber *Jowett* v. 94 Josephine's absorption in her new 'line of work'. **1966** M. Brewer *Man against Fear* i. 15 I'd like to help... But it's not my line of country. Only the police can catch them. **1972** *News & Observer* (Raleigh, N. Carolina) 30 Dec. 4/3 No one lives in the sticks or is asked his line of work very often.

30. (Earlier and later examples.) Also, goods of a particular design.

1834 *Chambers's Edin. Jrnl.* III. 9/3 Even those [travelling salesmen] whose *line* seems the most hopeless and frivolous. **1930** H. Cousins in V. A. Demant *Just Price* v. 102 No business can expect that all its 'lines' will be successful. **1959** *Punch* 16 Sept. 177/1, I can do a nice line in powder compacts. **1971** *Cabinet Maker & Retail Furnisher* 1 Oct. 15/3 Rather than let a slow selling line stand on the shop floor it is reduced immediately.

b. The amount which one underwriter (or one company) accepts as his share of the total value of the subject matter covered by insurance.

1899 Hooper & Graham *Mod. Business Methods* 144 The names and the amounts on the back of a policy.. would appear thus... Each of the above persons is said to 'take a line' in the policy. **1905** [see **front-ranker*]. **1931** *Times* 14 Mar. 12/6 Many of those [*sc.* insurance companies] who have written large lines..are known to have been influenced by a desire [etc.]. **1974** W. L. Catchpole *Business Guide to Insurance* xxiv. 202 If the chosen underwriter..agrees to accept a substantial line at an equitable risk, he becomes the leading underwriter on the slip.

c. *line of credit*: a loan by one country to another, to be utilized by the second for buying goods from the first; credit extended by a bank to a commercial concern to a certain amount; the amount so extended.

1958 *Listener* 18 Sept. 407/1 A line of credit for £8,000,000 from Australia will have helped matters. **1971** *Daily Tel.* 1 Jan. 1/1 A total of 41 million Canadian dollars..was repaid on the Canadian line of credit.

31. *line-end* (later examples), *-length, -numbering*; *line-numbered* adj.

1908 *Daily Chron.* 23 Oct. 9/4 Now he types instead of stamping the last words so as to obtain an even line end. **1930** T. Sasaki *On Lang. R. Bridges' Poetry* i. v. 21 The strongest stress..is the one at the line-end. **1961** T. Landau *Encycl. Librarianship* (ed. 2) 226/1 *Line division mark*, a vertical line or double vertical lines used in bibliographical transcription to indicate the place of the ends of lines... Also called line end stroke, dividing stroke. **1905** *PMLA* XX. 814 The uniform background of the recurrent line-lengths. **1929** H. Crane *Let.* 30 Aug. (1965) 344 The line-lengths are longer than in any other section. **1905** *Academy* 14 Oct. 1072/2 We can see him turning over the page, line-numbered. **1959** *N. & Q.* Sept. 313/2 The recent line-numbered edition by W. J. B. Owen. **1953** Amos & Birkinshaw *Television Engin.* I. ii. 33 The system of line numbering must be explained... The lines are numbered according to the positions they occupy in the raster, number 1 being the top line and, in the British system, 405 the bottom line. **1966** *English Studies* XLVII. 296 His marginal references to Folio lines and passages (using the line-numbering of the Globe edition).

32. line angle *Dentistry*, the angle at the junction of two surfaces of a tooth or cavity; **line-at-a-time printer** = **line printer*; **line-backer**, in Amer. and Canad. football (see quot. 1961); **line-ball**: also in *Lawn Tennis*; **line blanking** *Television*, the suppression of signals that would contribute to the picture during fly-back of the scanning spot between the transmission of successive lines; freq. *attrib.*; **line block**, a block bearing a design in relief from which an illustration made up of lines without variations in tone may be printed; an illustration printed in this way; also *attrib.*; **line-book**, (*a*) *Printing* (*Obs.* exc. *Hist.*), a book in which compositors working in companionships (chiefly 19th c.) kept account of the lines of set type credited and debited to them; (*b*) (also **lines-book**) *R.A.F. slang*, a record of boasts (see 13 g, above); **line-bred** *a.*, produced by line-breeding; **line-camp** *N.Amer.*, a camp, esp. a cabin, for ranch hands in an outlying part of a large ranch; **line-casting** *a.*, of a composing machine, casting type a line at a time; so **line-cast** *a.*, **line-caster**; **line density**, also *gen.*, density or concentration of lines; **line drawing** (earlier and later examples); also *fig.*; **line-drawn** *a.*, made by line-drawing; **line-drive** *Baseball*, a ball driven straight and low above the ground; **line drop** *Electr. Engin.*, the voltage drop between two points on a transmission line (as a result of resistance, leakage, or other causes); **line-ending**, (*a*) = *line-filling*; (*b*) the end of a line of poetry; **line-engraved** *ppl. a.*, inscribed with a line engraving; **line-engraver**, one who does line engraving; **line engraving** (earlier example); **line-fence** *N. Amer.*, a boundary

fence between two farms or ranches; **line finder** *Telephony*, a selector which searches for the calling subscriber's line when he lifts his receiver so that the line can be connected to a group of selectors available to any caller; **line-finishing** = *line-filling*; **line frequency** *Television*, the number of scanning lines produced per second; **line gale** *U.S.* = *line-storm*; **line gauge** *Printing*, a ruler showing the size of a type or types; **line graph** = GRAPH *sb.*[1] 2 (in Dict. and Suppl.) (as distinguished from a *bar graph*, in which vertical rectangles represent the values of the dependent variable); **line haul** *U.S. slang* (see quots.); **line loss** *Electr. Engin.*, loss of electrical energy along a transmission line (as a result of resistance, leakage, or other causes); **line management, manager**: see sense 19 d above; **line officer,** a military or naval officer of the line; **line pipe,** pipe specially manufactured for use in pipelines; **line printer,** a printer that is capable of printing a whole line of characters in each cycle of operation and is usu. operated under the control of a computer; **line-ride** *v. intr. U.S.*, to perform the action of line-riding; **line-rider** *N.Amer.*, one engaged in line-riding; **line-riding** (earlier example); **line scan,** (*a*) the motion of a scanning beam or spot along a line; (*b*) the electrical signal which causes this; (*c*) an apparatus or technique which scans an object or scene line by line; so **line scanning** *vbl. sb.*; **line-sequential** *a. Television*, applied to a system of colour television in which each line of the picture is in one of the three primary colours, the colour changing for each successive line; **line shaft, shafting,** a shaft, or shafting, of relatively great length from which a number of separate machines are driven by countershafts or endless belts; **line-side** *attrib.*, adjacent to a railway line; **line space,** the space provided for a line of typescript; so *line-space lever, mechanism*, etc., the device that turns the platen of a typewriter to a new line of writing; **line-spacing,** the space between successive lines of typescript; *attrib.*, of the device that moves the platen to a new line; **line spectrum,** a spectrum containing lines distributed apparently at random (rather than in groups as in a band spectrum); hence, an emission (of light, sound, or other radiation) composed of a number of discrete frequencies or energies; **line-storm** (earlier and later examples); **line-synchronizing** *a. Television*, applied to a pulse transmitted in a television signal at the end of each line which initiates fly-back of the scanning spot in the receiver, so keeping the scanning process in synchronism with that in the transmitter; also abbreviated to **line-sync**; **line-tub,** a tub in which a whaling line is kept; **line-width** *Physics*, the width of a spectral line as measured by the difference in wavelength, wave number, or frequency between its two sides; **line-work** (later example); (*b*) (see quot. 1968); (*c*) work as a lineman. Also *LINE STANDARD.

1908 G. V. BLACK *Work on Operative Dentistry* I. 295 Line angles. **1930** W. H. O. MCGEHEE *Text-bk. Operative Dentistry* xi. 338 Flatten the gingival and axial walls, making a definite line angle at their junction. **1963** C. R. COWELL et al. *Inlays, Crowns, & Bridges* iii. 15 Complete the proximal box, using a chisel to plane its vertical walls and to sharpen the line angles. **1955** *Jrnl. Assoc. Computing Machinery* II. 294 Line-at-a-time printer (92 characters per line), operating at a speed of 150 lines per minute. **1963** GOULD & ELLIS *Digital Computer Technol.* xi. 141 The line-at-a-time printers have, in the main, been adapted from the tabulating machines of punched card practice. **1961** WEBSTER, *Linebacker*, a football player stationed within one to four yards of the line of scrimmage and expected to make quick tackles close to the line of scrimmage on running plays and to protect against short passes. **1968** *Globe & Mail* (Toronto) 13 Feb. 29/1 Darryl Burgess, a 225-pound linebacker from St. Mary's. **1969** *Eugene* (Oregon) *Register-Guard* 3 Dec. 10/2 Oregon linebacker Tom Graham..played well enough to make both UPI and AP All-Coast teams as a rookie. **1970** *Toronto Daily Star* 24 Sept. 18/5 We can always move Corrigall to linebacker. **1973** *Washington Post* 13 Jan. C5/4 The most misguided portion of the show comes during Jones' interviews of Jim Brown, the former football player-turned-actor, and Ray May, a linebacker for the Baltimore Colts. **1891** F. C. BURNAND *Miss Decima* 22 Chorus (outside—watching a game of Lawn Tennis).. Ah! 'Line' ball. **1952** HOWE & DUCLOUX tr. *Kerkhof & Werner's Television* iv. 76 The total line blanking of the picture signal is 0·15 L. **1957** AMOS & BIRKINSHAW *Television Engin.* (rev. ed.) I. ii. 31 The synchronising signals are not the only form of intelligence which must be transmitted between lines; an additional signal, known as the line-blanking signal, must also be inserted. **1966** G. H. HUTSON *Television Receiver Theory* I. iii. 31 The line blanking period is divided into..the front porch, the line sync. pulse and the back porch. **1896** A. BEARDSLEY *Let.* 29 Sept. (1971) 173 The rest of the drawing has come out so hardly and coldly in the line block. **1924** E. POUND *Let.* 3 Dec. (1971) 191, I think the idea of ten or twelve Blacks of size that cd. go by post, and that cd. be done in line block, might be useful. **1936** *Burlington Mag.* Mar. p. xiv/1 Line-block illustrations from the author's own drawings. **1956** *Nature* 18 Feb. 301/1 The illustrations are well chosen, both the line-blocks and the half-tones. **1972** P. GASKELL *New Introd. Bibliogr.* 272 The detail of all but the very best photographic line blocks tends to be slightly rougher at the edges than that of wood engravings. **1876** J. GOULD *Letter-Press Printer* 33 The system adopted in some of the smaller houses is for each compositor to make up and impose his own pages, the making-up being passed from one compositor to the companion who follows him, accompanied by the line book. **1942** *Observer* 4 Oct. 7/2 'There I was, upside down, in cloud, ten-tenths, at 1,500 ft...' But you never get to the end of your story if you were so foolish as to begin like that. 'Lineshoot!' they would cry. 'Line!' And most squadrons have a Line Book in which such statements are written down, to their authors' perpetual shame. **1943** C. H. WARD-JACKSON *Piece of Cake* 40 *Lines book*, in which are recorded exaggerated statements made at one time or another by Mess members. **1945** E. TAYLOR *At Mrs. Lippincote's* xxiii. 194 Quick, the line-book! **1972** P. GASKELL *New Introd. Bibliogr.* 193 He [*sc.* the clicker] kept an account of the number of lines that each man set, both in a line-book and by marking the copy. **1891** R. WALLACE *Rural Econ. Austral. & N.Z.* xxxi. 400 The impression that tuberculosis is more prevalent among high line-bred shorthorns than among the ordinary country-bred cattle. **1960** *Times* 19 Sept. 3/4, 20 dams were chosen..these being line-bred. **1971** *Amer. N. & Q.* Apr. 126/2 The quarter horse, developed from cross-breeding Spanish stock imported to America via Florida (Chickasaw horses) and what Nelson Nye calls 'line-bred orientals' from England, was originally a sport animal. **1888** *Century Mag.* Mar. 667/2 But some of the men are out in the line camps, and the ranchman has occasionally to make the round of these. **1949** *10 Story Western* May 12/2 He had been telling them all how he was going to winter here at the Buffalo Crossing line camp. **1963** R. D. SYMONS *Many Trails* v. 52 Most outfits had what they call 'line camps' strung along the limits of their range, from which 'line riders' operated. **1973** S. JENNETT *Making of Bks.* (ed. 5) xv. 286 The italic [of Linotype Baskerville] is a little loose fitting, its width, as in other line-cast type-faces, being governed by the roman. **1972** *Phys. Bull.* Sept. 533/1 These 'second generation' photosetters..are reasonably cheap and are considerably faster than the latest line-casters which are also tape driven. **1913** *Inland Printer* July 486 (Advt.), There are thousands of publishers all over the United States who have been waiting for a line-casting and composing machine so simple and easy to operate that it would prove practical in the small shop. **1916** LEGROS & GRANT *Typogr. Printing-Surfaces* iv. 15 Line-casting machine type-metal undergoes a wastage or depreciation. **1973** S. JENNETT *Making of Bks.* (ed. 5) v. 83 The Intertype Fotosetter was also an adaptation, of the Intertype line-casting machine. **1963** *Reshaping of Brit. Railways* (Brit. Railways Board) 65 Line densities are not the only measure of the use made of the railway. **1971** *Fremdsprachen* XV. 276 It can be used to restore old drawings and to improve line density for microfilming. **1891** A. BEARDSLEY *Let.* 25 Dec. (1971) 32, I am anxious to say something somewhere, on the subject of *lines* and line drawing. **1959** *Listener* 9 July 76/3 It [*sc.* an overture] is finer line-drawing than the Gordon Jacob work. **1966** *Ibid.* 6 Jan. 36/3 Over 300 [flowers] are illustrated in close-up colour photographs and 100-odd more in line drawings. **1967** E. SHORT *Embroidery & Fabric Collage* ii. 51 There is a tendency to produce line drawings which might just as well have been done with a pencil. **1903** *Westm. Gaz.* 17 Oct. 4/2 An order of the King in Council was published with two line-drawn illustrations. **1931** *Randolph Enterprise* (Elkins, W. Virginia) 9 July 5/3 Boyles turned in the star catch of the day by racing..to pull down a line drive with one hand. **1968** *Washington Post* 4 July C1/3 Mantle was safe as Ron Hansen's throw, after snagging a line drive by Andy Kosco, was a trifle tardy. **1894** Line drop [see *line loss* below]. **1962** *Newnes Conc. Encycl. Electr. Engin.* 86/1 D.C. boosters are normally low-voltage d.c. generators employed for adjusting a supply voltage, in line-drop compensation and as an aid in controlling the charging of large accumulator batteries. **1928** E. G. MILLAR *Eng. Illuminated Manuscripts XIVth & XVth Cent.* i. 9 Many of the line-endings..were added in the fifteenth century. **1962** W. NOWOTTNY *Lang. Poets Use* v. 120 The method he adopts is the eccentric placing of line-endings. **1802** *Monthly Mag.* XIV. 253/1 The best line-engraved prints preserved their superiority. **1881** *Stamp-Collector's Ann.* 5 The fall of the penny stamp and all its line-engraved family. **1936** *Discovery* Dec. 386/1 Practically all [18th-century tradesman's cards] are line- or stipple-engraved. **1965** *Stamp Collecting* ('Know the Game' Series) 44/1 Stamps printed from recess-plates are said to be line-engraved. **1873** *Illustr. London News* 15 Mar. 247/3 This eminent line-engraver. **1965** DOUGHTY & WAHL in D. G. Rossetti *Lett.* I. 9 Charles Warren (1767–1823), line-engraver and a noted illustrator. **1802** *Monthly Mag.* XIV. 253/1 The line engraving is now attaining its deserved preeminence. **1845** J. COMLY *Reader & Bk. Knowl.* 96 Always keep good line-fences. **1854** S. H. HAMMOND *Hills, Lakes & Forest Streams* xxv. 250 Later still, the old line fence was pulled away. **1893** E. R. YOUNG *Stories from Indian Wigwams* 34 One morning I.. went off to help a couple of Indians about their line fences. **1946** *Chicago Daily News* 23 Mar. 1/8 He got into an argument with the boy's parents over the building of a line fence between their properties. **1954** C. BRUCE *Channel Shore* 12 From there a person could look east and west along..the northern fields..separated by line fences. **1922** GLAZEBROOK *Dict. Appl. Physics* II. 834/2 The line finder corresponds to the answering plug in a manual exchange. **1950** J. ATKINSON *Herbert & Procter's Telephony* (new ed.) II. i. 19/2 If..the volume of traffic and the number of 1st selectors are considerable, then line-finders may become more expensive than subscribers' uniselectors. **1968** E. H. JOLLEY *Introd. Telephony & Telegr.* viii. 232/2 The subscribers' lines are multiplied over the bank of contacts of the line-finders so that each subscriber's line appears on each line-finder. **1906** E. JOHNSTON *Writing & Illuminating* xii. 205 Line-finishings are used to preserve the evenness of the text when lines of writing fall short. **1936** O. S. PUCKLE tr. *M. von Ardenne's Television Reception* i. 11 The total number of lines in the complete picture is 240, scanned sequentially and horizontally at 25 picture traversals per second... The line frequency is thus 6,000 impulses per second. **1973** *Newnes Colour Television Servicing Manual* I. i. 26/1 Sawtooth voltage at line frequency is developed across the inductive network. **1836** *Knickerbocker* VII. 17, I must take the oars myself, for that blamed line gale has kept me in bilboes.. a dog's age. **1948** *Words into Type* 544 *Line gauge*, a printer's measuring rule, marked off in nonpareils and picas, sometimes showing other type measurements also. **1967** KARCH & BUBER *Offset Processes* 544 *Line gauge*, a printer's ruler usually having 6 and 12 point graduations. Sometimes with other point scales, as: agate, 9-point, 10-point, etc. **1956** Line graph [see *DECODE *v.*]. **1972** *Scholarly Publishing* III. 274 Bar graphs, line graphs, pie charts, and other illustrative devices. **1942** BERREY & VAN DEN BARK *Amer. Thes. Slang* § 770 *Line haul*, a scheduled truck route. **1971** M. TAK *Truck Talk* 99 *Line haul*, a scheduled truck run or movement of freight between cities. **1894** A. T. SNELL *Electr. Motive Power* iv. 126 The line loss remains constant when the percentage of the line drop is kept the same for variations of supply pressure. **1953** C. F. HOCKETT in Saporta & Bastian *Psycholinguistics* (1961) 64/1 To supply one hundred-watt light bulb, a generator must transmit one hundred watts of power, plus a bit more to make up for line-loss. **1970** D. WATERFIELD *Continental Waterboy* iii. 29 And you have line loss, particularly with very long transmission lines. **1850** R. GLISAN *Jrnl. Army Life* (1874) i. 2 This rank.. avails its possessor..in everything except commanding troops when a line officer is present. **1909** *Westm. Gaz.* 1 Feb. 2/1 Wives of line-officers, engineers, servants. **1925** R. GRAVES *Welchman's Hose* 29 They hadn't one Line-officer left, after Arras. **1923** *Amer. Petroleum Inst. Bull.* 31 Dec. 117/2 The work of this committee has been..to the end that a specification might be had that would: (1) Minimize losses arising out of the use of casing line pipe, tubing and drill pipe, in oil field operations. **1930** L. D. BURRITT in Walker & Crocker *Piping Handbk.* xiv. 719 Line-pipe threads are of the same form and taper as American Standard threads, but the pipe is threaded with a longer length of thread than is standard pipe. **1967** *Times Rev. Industry* Feb. 45/3 The rising demand for line pipe made sense of a connexion between South Durham and Stewarts and Lloyds, which has been marketing X60 seamless line pipe up to 18 inches in diameter for many years. **1955** *Jrnl. Assoc. Computing Machinery* II. 294 Output: Line printer of a BULL tabulating machine. **1962** *Mod. Lang. Rev.* LVII. 171 The Cambridge Mathematical Laboratory possesses a line-printer which is directly operated by EDSAC 2. **1970** O. DOPPING *Computers & Data Processing* iv. 73 A normal speed for a computer line printer is 1,000 lines per minute. *Ibid.* xi. 164 A mechanical line printer has one printing device for each printing position in the line (for each 'column'). The number of printing positions is often between 100 and 160. **1883** *Rep. Productions Agric. 10th Census 1880* (U.S. Census Office) 971 The cattle-raisers were obliged to fence or to 'line-ride' to keep their cattle from trespassing. *Ibid.* 973 The cowboys engaged in this work are called 'line-riders'. *Ibid.*, The cattle of northwest Texas are in a large measure controlled or held on their ranges by a system of 'line-riding'. **1920** Line-rider [see *fence-rider* (*FENCE *sb.* 11)]. **1942** E. E. DALE *Cow Country* 119 This by no means did away with the work of the line rider, though it was made somewhat easier. **1963** Line rider [see *line-camp* above]. **1938** J. H. REYNER *Testing Television Sets* iv. 46 If the time base is operating the appropriate noise will be heard—a rapid ticking on the frame scan and a high squeal on the line scan. **1957** D. G. FINK *Television Engin. Handbk.* x. 12 The harmonic components of the line-scan spectrum may thus be thought of as carrier waves, each with a 60-cps modulation envelope. **1962** *Daily Tel.* 28 Aug. 13/5 Line scan is a system for reconnaissance and mapping at low levels. **1966** D. G. BRANDON *Mod. Techniques Metallogr.* 257 The line scans being automatically repeated 50 μm apart. **1971** *Daily Tel.* (Colour Suppl.) 22 Jan. 22/1 False colour photography.. does not record gradations of temperatures exactly, and these can be very important. The instrument which does this is the infra-red linescan, which scans the scene line by line like a television scanner, building up a composite picture from the heat records. **1935** *Television Today* I. 300/2 The line scanning is usually spoken of as the scanning motion. **1971** H. E. ENNES *Television Broadcasting* iii. 125 Picture information is contained in the fundamental and harmonics of the 60-Hz field frequency and the 15,750-Hz line-scanning frequency. **1949** *Electronics* Dec. 68/3 The change of color is introduced between successive lines in the scanning field, that is, the system is in the line-sequential class. **1965** G. DU CLOUX tr. *Holm's Colour Television Explained* (ed. 2) iii. 55 The R.C.A. appeared to have arrived at the ultimate solution with a line-sequential, or possibly even a dot-sequential system. **1881** *Spon's Dict. Engin.* Suppl. III. 1093 For the bearings of line shafts cast iron is..the best. **1936** Line shaft [see *jack shaft* s.v. *JACK *sb.*[1] 33 a]. **1974** *Encycl. Brit. Macropædia* XI. 253/2 In the days when all machines in a shop were driven by one large..prime mover, it was necessary to have long lineshafts running the length of the shop and supplying power..to shorter countershafts, jackshafts, or headshafts. **1872** J. RICHARDS *Treat. Wood-Working Machines* 95 Pulleys for line-shafting running at high speed should be light and true. **1966** *McGraw-Hill Encycl. Sci. & Technol.* XII. 240/2 The delivery of power to the machines in a shop has generally been converted from line shafting to individual electric motors for each machine. **1961** WEBSTER, *Lineside*, adjacent to a railway line. **1967** *Listener* 26 Jan. 123/1 This can be prodigiously expensive if it involves disturbance of lineside property. **1975** *Daily Tel.* 18 July

2/8 By next year it is expected that there will be fewer faults in the 547 lineside signals and 465 points controlled by the new box. **1951** *Oxf. Jun. Encycl.* IV 472/2 When it reaches the end, a line space lever is pushed to move the paper up to a new line and return the carriage to the right. **1962** *Which?* Dec. 357/1 Some of the models..had only two positions for their line space selector, the others all had three. **1957** *Encycl. Brit.* XXII. 645/1 The machine was soon renamed the Remington. Among its original features which were still standard..in the 1950s are the paper cylinder with its line-spacing and carriage-return mechanism. *c* **1961** *Imperial Type Faces* (Imperial Typewriter Co.), The number of words which can be typed on a quarto page..var[ies] according to the pitch of the letter and line-spacings. **1873** *Phil. Mag.* XLVI. 406 When the gas is near atmospheric pressure, the line-spectrum of nitrogen is brilliant. **1885** [see *BAND *sb.*² 13]. **1923** GLAZEBROOK *Dict. Appl. Physics* IV. 780/1 Luminous spectra can be divided into two classes, namely continuous spectra..and discontinuous spectra... Discontinuous spectra may be subdivided into line and band spectra. **1955** MILLER & NICELY in Saporta & Bastian *Psycholinguistics* (1961) 165/2 Acoustically, this means that the voiceless consonants are aperiodic or noisy in character, whereas a periodic or line-spectrum component is superimposed on the noise for voiced consonants. **1957** [see *BAND *sb.*² 13]. **1962** H. D. BUSH *Atomic & Nucl. Physics* iv. 96 There are two main features of a β-particle spectrum, a continuous spectrum with energies ranging from zero to a maximum value..and a line spectrum consisting of a number of discrete energies superimposed on the continuous spectrum. **1962** A. NISBETT *Technique Sound Studio* 254 A sound which is composed of individual frequencies (fundamental and harmonics or partials, or a combination of pure tones) has a line spectrum. Bands of noise have a band spectrum. **1850** N. KINGSLEY *Diary* (1914) 115 A fine day with a strong West wind; rather think the line storm is over. **1939** R. FROST *Coll. Poems* 38 The line-storm clouds fly tattered and swift. **1940** W. T. COCKING *Television Receiving Equipment* xix. 281 When a very large amplitude of line sync pulse is applied to the line generator it is tripped at half-line intervals during the frame sync pulses. **1969** C. R. G. REED *Princ. Colour Television Syst.* vi. 71 The line sync pulse duration is 4·7 μs. **1935** *Television Today* I. 300 The time duration of the line synchronising pulse is usually about 10 per cent. of that of each line. **1953** AMOS & BIRKINSHAW *Television Engin.* I. i. 16 A synchronizing signal is sent out every time the scanning beam at the transmitter reaches the end of a line; this signal is termed the line-synchronizing signal (abbreviated to line-sync signal) and has the function of initiating line flyback at the receiver. **1839** *Knickerbocker* XIII. 382 Line-tubs, water-kegs, and wafe-poles, were thrown hurriedly into the boats. **1851** H. MELVILLE *Moby Dick* III. xlviii. 287 Reaching out after the revolving line-tubs, oars and other floating furniture. **1946** *Nature* 28 Sept. 450/1 Measures of effective line-width, made..upon the brilliant reversal of the *Hα* (λ 6563) contour. **1962** *Science Survey* III. 67 The current reports of the line-width of the radiation produced by the helium-neon optical maser show the line-width is approximately one cycle per second. **1971** *New Scientist* 3 June 565/2 Molecular linewidths are of the order of 10^{-3} cm^{-1} at room temperature. **1972** *Physics Bull.* Feb. 83/2 A dye laser tuned to give a sodium linewidth of a hundredth of an ångstrom. **1904** *Brit. Printer* Apr. 86/2 Line work negatives are printed on to zinc. **1911** H. QUICK *Yellowstone Nights* ii. 32 I'm just through with a summer's line-work in the West. **1962** *Times* 10 Jan. 13/4 The pen drawing..is admirable..projecting in its free and open linework all the completeness of an oil composition. **1968** *Gloss. Terms Offset Lithogr. Printing* (*B.S.I.*) 10 *Line work*, copy or reproduction consisting of solid elements only, as distinct from half-tone.

line, *v.*² Add: **3. b.** *trans.* and *intr.* To guide or control a boat or canoe from the bank or shore of a stretch of inland water by means of a rope or ropes. *N. Amer.*

1907 J. G. MILLAIS *Newfoundland* 305 Several times they packed everything for a mile or two, but negotiated most of the worst rapids by 'lining' down them. **1912** H. FOOTNER *New Rivers of North* 125 No one has ever descended it alive, but there is a tradition that a party of Iroquois Indians in the 'company's' employ once lined a boat up. **1923** L. R. FREEMAN *Colorado River* 356 The low stage..gave them room to work below instead of lining from a ledge, eighty feet above the water. **1944** T. ONRAET *Down North* ii. 29 The skiff was too heavy for carrying, and to line it down as we had done in the rapids above was impossible. **1969** E. W. MORSE *Fur Trade Canoe Routes* I. i. 5 Provided that the shoreline was reasonably free of snags, the canoe was lined (tracked).

5. *to line out*: also, to delete, obliterate.

1963 S. WEINTRAUB *Private Shaw & Public Shaw* iii. 94 G.B.S...both edited and altered the language of the.. contract,..boldly lining out large passages and inserting new ones.

8. a. With *up*: more widely, to align, arrange, deploy, produce, or make ready (someone or something). orig. *U.S.* Also in various slang uses (see quots.). Also, to aim in a direct line *upon* an object.

a **1884** KNIGHT *Dict. Mech.* Suppl. 665/1 *Peep sight*, a form of hind sight for rifles. It has an opening through which the muzzle sight is lined upon the object. **1902** *Westm. Gaz.* 20 Aug. 8/2 (citing a New York newspaper), I..shall not really feel like myself till I get my coat off and line-up a few trust presidents in front of me for general inspection and drill. **1904** 'G. B. LANCASTER' *Sons o' Men* 41 They were fence-making down at the homestead, and there was no man in the district could line up standards in the same day with Muggins. **1906** *Forum* (N.Y.) Oct. 253 The university president must refuse to be lined up by any clique or party. **1910** *Chambers's Jrnl.* May 282/2 After the conflagration, the smaller débris is collected into heaps and reburned, until the ground is sufficiently cleared to admit of being lined up for planting. **1913** G. J. KNEELAND *Commercialized Prostitution N.Y.* 65 She was 'lined up' about a year ago by a gang that 'hangs out' in a cigar store on East 14th Street. Since then she has been a regular prostitute. **1926** J. BLACK *You can't Win* xiii. 181 We located a big poker game in a soft spot and decided to line up the players. **1931** W. G. MCADOO *Crowded Yrs.* x. 142, I did not see how Clark could possibly line up two thirds of the..votes. **1932** E. WALLACE *When Gangs came to London* viii. 58 You can tell the police all about this... But don't tell more'n the truth, or ever try to line me up by my voice. **1934** WODEHOUSE *Right ho, Jeeves* ix. 94, I tell you I have everything nicely lined up. **1939** COFFEE & COWEN *Family Portrait* II. i. 74 But I'd lined up a big job here—(*adds importantly*) with the Romans. **1941** BAKER *Dict. Austral. Slang* 43 *Line up to*, to approach, accost a person. **1953** E. TAYLOR *Sleeping Beauty* x. 175 Don't line up another one [*sc.* drink] for me. **1958** *New Statesman* 6 Sept. 263/1 Mr. Lim soon called for 'a united Socialist front', which would line up his Labour Front party with the right wing against the extreme left. **1962** A. NISBETT *Technique Sound Studio* 270 Sine tones are useful for studying frequency response and for lining up equipment. **1970** *Language* XLVI. 318 All of the sentences have been 'lined up' with respect to the end of phonation. **1973** G. GREENE *Honorary Consul* I. i. 26 It pays to be a consul. .. Permission to import a new car... I suppose he's got a general lined up in the capital to buy it.

c. *Baseball.* To hit a line-drive; to hit (a ball) hard and low. Freq. const. *out.*

1887 *Courier-Jrnl.* (Louisville, Kentucky) 26 May 2/6 He smashed the first ball that came over the plate, and lined out a beautiful hit past second base. **1948** *Daily Ardmoreite* (Ardmore, Okla.) 28 Apr., He..lined out to centerfield and walked twice in five trips to the plate. **1970** *Globe & Mail* (Toronto) 25 Sept. 31/3 Bob Robertson lined a double down the rightfield Line. **1972** *N.Y. Times* 4 June v. 2/5 Willie struck out, lined to Carty in left field, popped to second base and walked.

9. c. *line out* (*intr.* and *trans.*), to transplant (seedling trees) from beds into nursery lines, where they are grown on before being moved to their permanent situation.

1931 *Forestry* V. 17 Care in handling between lifting from seed-beds and lining out is of the utmost importance. **1938** C. P. ACKERS *Pract. Brit. Forestry* v. 180 Seedlings may be left for 1, 2, or 3 years in the seed-beds: they are then lined out and become transplants. **1957** *N.Z. Timber Jrnl.* Oct. 73/1 *Line out*, to transplant seedlings from seedbeds to rows in a nursery. This normally takes place after the first or second year in the seedbed; further lining out may take place again in the same or another nursery. **1970** H. L. EDLIN *Collins Guide Tree Planting & Cultivation* vi. 90 Trees are always transplanted in the nursery along straight lines, and the work is therefore often called lining-out.

‖ **linea** (li·niă). *Anat.* Pl. **lineæ**. [L. *līnea*: see LINE *sb.*²] Used in numerous L. or mod.L. collocations to designate lines apparent in or on the body, or structures which form a line.

1611 Linea alba [see LINE *sb.*² 1 c]. **1713** W. CHESELDEN *Anat. Humane Body* I. vi. 20 From the lesser Trochanter down the back-part of this Bone 'till within Four Inches of the End, is a Ridge call'd Linea Aspera. **1861** *Guy's Hosp. Rep.* VII. 297 Linear atrophy of the skin..refers to a condition resembling the *lineæ gravidarum*, but affecting both sexes, and probably all parts of the body. **1967** G. M. WYBURN et al. *Conc. Anat.* i. 7/2 A slight furrow formed by an underlying fibrous raphe, the linea alba, extends from the xiphoid process to the symphysis pubis. *Ibid.* vi. 159/1 Pectineus..is inserted into the femur above the linea aspera.

lineage. 2. c. Delete † *Obs.* and add: *Anthrop.* Patri- or matrilineal descent within a social group traced from a single ancestor; also occas. the traditional line of descent for the handing down of skills and knowledge pertaining to a particular craft or profession.

1871 L. H. MORGAN in *Smithsonian Contrib. Knowl.* No. 218. 151 There were but five other nations of the same immediate lineage of whom we have any knowledge. **1877** —— *Anc. Society* ii. 69 The gens came into being upon three principal conceptions, namely; the bond of kin, a pure lineage through descent in the female line, and non-intermarriage in the gens. **1934** R. H. LOWIE *Introd. Cultural Anthropol.* xiv. 254 A clan including only descendants of a single ancestor is a 'lineage'. Commonly it includes members of two or more lineages, but the concept remains the same. **1949** M. FORTES *Social Struct.* 62 Genealogies are cited to show that the founding ancestors of the lineages occupying the townships..came there some ten to twelve generations ago. **1951** R. FIRTH *Elem. Social Organiz.* ii. 53 The Tikopia lineages are patrilineal, membership being traced through the father along the male line to an original male ancestor. **1952** GERTH & MARTINDALE tr. *Weber's Anc. Judaism* I. ii. 28 Cain is the tribal father of the smith and the musician... It may, thus, be assumed that at the time of the establishment of this lineage such artisans, in Palestine as in India, were guest people. **1957** M. BANTON *W. Afr. City* vii. 123 Marriage is an arrangement between two lineages. **1963** *Listener* 7 Feb. 231/1 Arabic documents held by the mosques and the clerical lineages in Northern Nigeria and in Northern Ghana. **1971** *World Archaeol.* III. 217 Each village has a number of smiths of varying degrees of training and competence each assisted by novices who together form a lineage.

attrib.

1949 M. FORTES *Social Struct.* 65 Continuity in the social structure..is maintained by the lineage system. **1951** R. FIRTH *Elem. Social Organiz.* ii. 54 They and their immediate lineage members form a recognized class of 'chiefly houses'. **1957** V. W. TURNER *Schism & Continuity in Afr. Soc.* v. 152 They consolidate the rest of the.. lineage membership against them. **1964** GOULD & KOLB *Dict. Social Sci.* 391/2 Relations between the local groups, which may vary in size and locality over time, can none the less be seen as persistent and relatively stable. In this case lineages may compose a total structure or system, the lineage structure or the lineage system.

lineage, var. LINAGE.

lineal, *a.* and *sb.* Add: **A.** *adj.* **2. a.** (Further examples.)

1871 L. H. MORGAN in *Smithsonian Contrib. Knowl.* No. 218. 11 Every system of consanguinity must be able to ascend and descend in the lineal line through several degrees from any given person. *Ibid.* 46 If *Ego* is placed between the father and son the lineal and first collateral lines would become intelligible. **1929** *Encycl. Brit.* XIX. 84/1 The collateral kin of a generation were merged with the lineal.

B. *sb.* **2.** (Later examples.)

1881 E. W. HAMILTON *Diary* 3 Apr. (1972) I. 124 The Probate Duty is to be raised ½% all round, and the 1% (lineals) in the Legacy Duty scale is to be abolished; accordingly lineals will all benefit to the extent of ½%. **1909** *Hansard Commons* 29 Apr. 515/1 In the cases of spouses and lineals..I propose to exempt from the new.. duties all legacies.

linear, *a.* and *sb.* Add: **A.** *adj.* **2. b. Linear A**, the earlier of two related forms of writing discovered at Knossos in Crete by Sir A. J. Evans between 1894 and 1901; **Linear B**, the later form, found also on the mainland of Greece, and now shown to be a syllabary imperfectly adapted to the writing of Mycenæan Greek.

[**1902–3** A. J. EVANS in *Ann. Brit. School at Athens* IX. 52 This early system of linear script—which may be conveniently termed Class A as opposed to Class B of the latest Palace Period at Knossos—had a wide extension in the island.] **1907** R. M. BURROWS *Discoveries Crete* vi. 84 The linear writing of class A is now in regular use. *Ibid.* 92 The hoard of clay tablets..shows that its linear writing, called by Mr. Evans Class B, is more advanced. **1909** A. J. EVANS *Scripta Minoa* I. i. v. 31 Documents belonging to the Linear Class A only occur in this particular stratum... In deposits clearly belonging to the remodelled building the inscribed documents all belonged to Class B. *Ibid.* 35 Common to both the linear scripts A and B. *Ibid.* 36 The system of numerals..of the Linear Class B. **1948** A. E. KOBER in *Amer. Jrnl. Archaeol.* LII. 89 Inscriptions of Linear A have been found at several sites. **1950** E. L. BENNETT in *Ibid.* LIV. 81/1 Translations of and commentary upon additional Linear-B tablets from Knossos. *Ibid.* 204/1 The Linear A flourished in the rest of Crete.., and the Linear B at Knossos only. *Ibid.* 218/2 The Linear A ideogram L85 appears to have..the same form. *Ibid.* 219/1 The shapes of four other signs of Linear A..are reflected in the Linear B signs. **1952** J. L. MYRES *Evans' Scripta Minoa* II. 1 In this new 'Linear A' script about one-third of the signs are derived from linearized hieroglyphs. *Ibid.* 2 It was doubtless..local unconformity that provoked the drastic reform of the 'Linear B' script at Knossos. **1953** VENTRIS & CHADWICK in *Jrnl. Hellenic Stud.* LXXIII. 84 Evans believed that Linear *B*..was an administrative revision of Linear *A*, designed to express the same 'Aegean' language. **1966** C. H. GORDON *Evidence for Minoan Lang.* ix. 32 The Linear A and B texts overlap in time. **1972** *Sci. Amer.* Oct. 37/1 The Cretan system of writing, which we call Linear A, was crude but it was adequate for keeping rough accounts.

c. *Mus.* = *HORIZONTAL *a.* 4.

1944 W. APEL *Harvard Dict. Mus.* 409/1 *Linear counterpoint*, a term introduced by E. Kurth..in order to emphasize the 'linear', i.e., horizontal aspect of counterpoint. .. The term is also used..for what the Germans call *rücksichtsloser* (reckless) *Kontrapunkt*, i.e., the modern type of counterpoint which pays little attention to harmonic combination and euphony. **1955** [see *HORIZONTAL *a.* 4]. **1958** A. JACOBS *New Dict. Mus.* 211 *Linear counterpoint*, term—senseless, because all counterpoint is a matter of lines—sometimes used for a type of 20th-century counterpoint (e.g. Stravinsky's) held to be musically valid through the value of the separate lines themselves. **1959** *Listener* 8 Jan. 80/2 In the slow movement the orchestral texture begins in linear style, spare and canonic. **1962** *Ibid.* 18 Jan. 147/1 Linear and rhythmic techniques suggested by medieval music. *Ibid.* 147/2 A conscious employment of linear and metrical 'series' derived from Indian ragas and talas.

3. (Further examples.) Add to def.: capable of being represented by a straight line on a graph (in Cartesian co-ordinates); involving or possessing the property that a change in one quantity is accompanied by or corresponds to a directly proportional change in a related one.

1910 *Encycl. Brit.* IX. 146/2 The limiting tension beyond which the above law of proportionality [between tension and extension] fails to hold is often called the 'limit of linear elasticity'. **1940** *Chambers's Techn. Dict.* 503/1 *Linear amplification*, amplification in which the output current or voltage is strictly proportional to the input voltage. **1941** *Proc. R. Soc.* A. CLXXVII. 382 The disintegration of boron by slow neutrons has been investigated using an ionization chamber filled with boron trichloride in conjunction with a linear amplifier. **1942** *Electronic Engin.* XIV. 711/1 The conversion must be accomplished in a linear manner, i.e., the amplitude change is directly proportional to the frequency change. **1962** D. F. SHAW *Introd. Electronics* vii. 126 The preservation of the shape is a unique property of the sine wave and ..is a feature which it possesses for all linear circuits. *Ibid.* viii. 147 A circuit is linear if the individual components behave in such a manner that the amplitude of the current through each component is directly propor-

tional to the amplitude of the applied voltage and the relationship between the phases of the voltage and current is independent of the current and voltage magnitude. **1973** *Physics Bull.* Oct. 606/1 A linearizer circuit is used to ensure a true linear relationship between conveyor load and indicated reading.

c. *Educ.* Designating or pertaining to programmed learning aimed at step-by-step progress in which the material is broken down into small steps each of which must elicit a correct response before the next one is presented; freq. contrasted with branching methods.

For *linear programming* in a different sense see *7.

1958 B. F. SKINNER in *Science* 24 Oct. 974/2 A first step is to define the field. A second is to collect technical terms, facts, laws, principles, and cases. These must then be arranged in a plausible developmental order—linear if possible, branching if necessary. **1961** *Barron's Nat. Business & Financial Weekly* 30 Oct. 14/2 We are disciples of neither Crowder nor Skinner. Our programs will make use of either branching or linear techniques, depending on which seems best suited to the subject matter. **1962** A. A. LUMSDAINE in J. E. Coulson *Programmed Learning* 135, I believe that linear programs should almost invariably be constructed first, even if branching is later to be introduced. **1964** *Times Rev. Industry* Feb. 100/2 A novel feature is the method it uses—the linear (non-branching) technique of programmed learning. **1969** G. KENT *Blackboard to Computer* viii. 109 The basis of linear programming is that the subject matter to be understood is always presented to the student in small quantities. **1970** W. K. RICHMOND *Concept Educ. Technol.* iii. 103 That the majority of linear programmes are inordinately dull is, of course, a charge which will be strenuously denied by anyone who has laboured to produce one. *Ibid.*, This aseptic dullness is explained by the linear programmer's dependence upon a bird-brained psychology.

4. (Later examples.)

1923 C. R. STOCKARD in *Amer. Jrnl. Anat.* XXXI. III. 278 The two groups into which almost all ordinary persons fall more or less exactly may..be termed the Linear Type and the Lateral Type. The linear type is the faster growing high metabolizing thin but not necessarily tall group, while the lateral type is slower in maturing and is stocky and rounder in form. **1932** *Field Archæol.* (Ordnance Survey) 30 This term 'Linear Earthwork' is used to describe earthworks like Wansdyke..and the numerous Grim's Dykes... They consist of a bank and ditch and may be of any length from a few yards..to 10 miles. **1959** *Jrnl. Soc. Archit. Historians* XVIII. 40/1 Soria..customarily described his Linear City as a vertebrate animal. **1964** M. ARGYLE *Psychol. & Social Probl.* v. 62 Fewer of the delinquents are of linear (thin and bony) physique. **1966** *Guardian* 5 Apr. 2/6 A new linear city of half a million people..near Inverness..is the ambition of Professor Robert Grieve.

7. Special collocations: *linear accelerator* (see *ACCELERATOR e); *linear motor*, a motor (esp. an induction motor) which produces motion directly in a straight line (as opposed to rotary motion); *linear programming*, a mathematical technique for maximizing or minimizing a linear function (such as output or cost) of several variables (such as resources) when these are required to satisfy a set of linear equations and inequalities; (see also 3 c above).

1957 E. R. LAITHWAITE in *Proc. Inst. Electr. Engin.* CIV. A. 461/1 [The word 'linear' has already been used in connection with particle accelerators, but as there is little likelihood of confusion between these devices and electric motors, there appears to be no objection to the use of the word for the latter.] *Ibid.*, The use of linear motors as liquid-metal pumps is examined. **1966** *Listener* 13 Oct. 535/3 British Rail were the first to support Laithwaite's work on the linear motor, and suggested to him in 1960 its possible application to rail traction. **1973** *Sci. Amer.* Oct. 21/1 The evolution of electromagnetic flight is inextricably linked to the problem of propulsion. Two types of 'linear motor' are being studied for this application. One is called the linear induction motor, the other the linear synchronous motor. **1949** G. B. DANTZIG in *Econometrica* XVII. 203 It is our purpose now to discuss the kinds of restrictions that fit naturally into linear programming. **1953** COOPER & HENDERSON in W. W. Cooper et al. *Introd. Linear Programming* I. 1 Linear programming is concerned with the problem of planning a complex of interdependent activities in the best possible (optimal) fashion. **1966** A. BATTERSBY *Math. in Managem.* iv. 85 Transporting coal to power stations or gasworks, allocating cash to local branches, formulating foods and drawing up a maintenance schedule: these are all areas in which linear programming is at work today. **1967** E. DUCKWORTH in Wills & Yearsley *Handbk. Managem. Technol.* vi. 110 When the optimum order quantities have been decided, problems may occur in scheduling these through factories in the optimum manner... Quite complex methods of the linear programming or queueing theory type may be needed. **1971** *Sci. Amer.* Feb. 84/2 Among the intended tasks for ILLIAC IV is linear programming, a mathematical technique for allocating the use of limited resources to maximize or minimize a specified objective. *Ibid.* 85/2 In order to apply linear programming to an entire economic sector one must incur considerable expense in gathering the data to be used in the model.

linearism (li·nĭăriz'm). [f. LINEAR *a.* + -ISM.] Linearity; emphasis upon line or contour as opposed to colour or mass.

1935 *Archit. Rev.* LXXVII. 61 Far less of a constructor than a decorator, his famous 'linearism' was an echo of the same salient characteristic in Aubrey Beardsley's graphic designs. **1941** *Burlington Mag.* July 17/1 His bold method of brush drawing..is rendered possible by this two-dimensional linearism.

linearistic (linĭări·stik), *a.* [f. LINEAR *a.* + -ISTIC.] Pertaining to or characterized by a linear quality; of a linearized character.

1908 A. J. EVANS in R. R. Marett *Anthropol. & Classics* 41 Many of these signs are linearistic degenerations of animal figures.

linearity. Add: (Later examples.)

1947 A. EINSTEIN *Mus. Romantic Era* xvi. 245 Wagner wrote a Prelude..in the 'linearity' of which he seemed to overstep the stylistic limits of his own time. **1955** HOMANS & SCHNEIDER *Marriage, Authority & Final Causes* 20 Almost all the eastern Asian societies in which he finds mother's brother's daughter marriage preferred are organised in patrilineages. He concerns himself with linearity, [etc.]. **1958** *Times* 5 Dec. 8/6 Ectomorphy describes the linearity of the build. **1964** M. MCLUHAN *Understanding Media* xviii. 172 The linearity precision and uniformity of the arrangement of movable types.

b. *spec.* in *Math.* and *Physics*, the property of being linear in sense 3 of the adj. (in Dict. and Suppl.); proportionality of two related quantities (such as input and output).

1904 [see *EXTRAPOLATE *v.* 2 a]. **1943** *Electronic Engin.* XVI. 55/1 The insertion of a valve amplifier between the time base and the cathode-ray tube often involves some sacrifice in linearity. **1946** *Nature* 7 Sept. 330/2 Linearity is also important in the optical pick-up from the record, in the sense that the illumination of the photo-electric cell must be strictly proportional to the width of the white part of the illuminated area of the record. **1962** SIMPSON & RICHARDS *Physical Princ. Junction Transistors* xii. 269 Because the gain is high and the linearity fair, negative feedback may be used to exchange gain for linearity.

linearize, *v.* Add to def.: To make linear. Hence **li·nearized** *ppl. a.* (Further examples.)

1938 *Proc. Physico-Math. Soc. Japan* XX. 319 A method of linearization of wave equations for the electron. **1956** E. H. HUTTEN *Lang. Mod. Physics* iii. 94 Linearisation is a familiar trick in physics. **1957** L. FOX *Numerical Solution Two-Point Boundary Probl.* iii. 48 The only practical method of general application seems to be to 'linearize' the equations and solve them by an iterative process. **1962** W. B. THOMPSON *Introd. Plasma Physics* ii. 10 Then we obtain the linearized, approximate equations. **1968** CHOMSKY & HALLE *Sound Pattern Eng.* 391 What we have so far defined is simply a linearized version of rules of the form we have been discussing all along. **1969** *Physics Bull.* Nov. 463/1 Analysis is made difficult by the nonlinearity of the governing equations; any attempt to introduce approximations which linearize them seems to result in a loss of the basic features of the flow. **1969** *Canad. Jrnl. Ling.* XV. 25 It was speculated..that the reason that languages had embedding transformations..was to 'linearize' or spread out in linear form the deeply embedded concoctions which the human mind can produce. **1970** J. EARL *Tuners & Amplifiers* iv. 93 This can..reduce the distortion and linearise the power response. **1973** *Newnes Colour Television Servicing Manual* I. ii. 57/1 One half of the double triode is concerned essentially with linearising the field scan by means of negative feedback. **1973** *Physics Bull.* Oct. 606/1 Since the output from the digital ratemeter is nonlinear with load, it is necessary to use a short integrating time (about 0·1 s) in the ratemeter to obtain a true load signal after linearization.

Hence **li·nearizer,** that which linearizes, *esp.* a device which linearizes the response of a measuring instrument or other mechanism.

1973 [see *LINEAR *a.* 3]. **1973** *Physics Bull.* Dec. 745/1 The system is precalibrated for particular applications and has a built-in linearizer.

linearly, *adv.* Add: **d.** In a way that involves only terms of one dimension; in a linear or proportional manner.

1851 *Phil. Mag.* I. 295 If a quadratic function (U) be linearly converted into another (V), any minor determinant of any order of V must be a syzygetic function of all the minor determinants of U of the same order. **1859** G. SALMON *Lessons Introd. Mod. Higher Algebra* vi. 34 From the four equations thus formed we can eliminate linearly the four quantities, x^3, x^2y, xy^2, y^3. **1885** [see *LEGENDRE]. **1955** *Bull. Atomic Sci.* June 208/1 The extent of fall-out varies linearly with the fission yield of the bomb. **1963** *Amer. Jrnl. Physics* XXXI. 336/2 A necessary and sufficient condition..is that θ and T be related linearly. **1969** *Listener* 12 June 831/1 Criminals in human society..increase more rapidly than linearly with the total number of victims available. That is to say, if we double the population we more than double the number of criminals.

lineman. Add: **4.** *Amer.* and *Canad. Football.* A forward.

1907 *St. Nicholas* Sept. 1013/2 There was some discussion last year as to whether a line man could run from his position in the line and take the ball from the quarter. **1913** *Collier's* 13 Dec. 27/1 He was an aggressive, hard-fighting, and alert lineman, who did his best work under fire. **1959** *Times* 30 Nov. (Canada Suppl.) p. xx/2 There are five back-fielders and seven linemen. **1970** *Globe & Mail* (Toronto) 26 Sept. 35/5 The linemen and linebackers are all experienced. **1971** *New Yorker* 15 May 54/3 He was a forward, or lineman, in Rugby. **1972** *Nature* 2 June 297/3 Our manuscript read 'linemen', a designation for American football players who crouch in a line with hands on the ground prior to the attack.

linen, *a.* and *sb.* Add: **B.** *sb.* **3. a.** *to wash one's dirty linen in public*, to discuss an essentially private matter, esp. a dispute or scandal, in public.

1867 TROLLOPE *Last Chron. Barset* II. xliv. 2 There is nothing..so bad as washing one's dirty linen in public. **1931** *Times* 3 Aug. 9/1 If the Government had made tactful..representations..to the Holy See,..the whole matter could have been quietly settled without any washing of dirty linen in public. **1935** D. L. SAYERS *Gaudy Night* iv. 80 Even if the poison campaign led to no open disaster..a washing of dirty linen in public was not calculated to do Shrewsbury [College] any good. **1972** *Daily Tel.* 3 May 16, I know it is not done to wash dirty medical linen in public.

c. Abbrev. *LINEN-DRAPER b.

1955 J. PHELAN *Tramping the Toby* 223 *Linen*, a newspaper. **1962** R. COOK *Crust on its Uppers* i. 21 Everything they've ever read in a linen or a clever-clever book.

4. a. *linen-closet, -room, -tape, -thread.*

1885 'M. RUTHERFORD' *M. Rutherford's Deliverance* iii. 41 She cared nothing for the linen-closet, the spotless bed-hangings,..the true household gods of the respectable women of those days. **1955** W. TUCKER *Wild Talent* xiv. 181 The butler..saw Paul's questioning glance at the other two doors. 'The nearest one is a linen closet, sir,' he said. **1900** E. GLYN *Visits of Elizabeth* 33 Aunt Maria..said it was her day for seeing the linen-room. **1873** *Young Englishwoman* Mar. 150/2 A piece of linen tape..keeps the buttons securely in place. **1880** E. GLAISTER *Needlework* v. 49 The letters are made in linen tape, unbleached, the yellower the better. **1897** *Sears, Roebuck Catal.* 321/1 Marshall's Linen Thread (100 yd. spools, black only). **1908** *Westm. Gaz.* 28 Dec. 5/2 The whole front is a mass of hand embroidery done in heavy linen-thread. **1975** *Times* 6 Mar. 7/6 The greatest problem with owning old lace is getting it repaired... An added problem is the difficulty of obtaining the hair-fine linen thread.

5. linen basket, a receptacle for dirty clothing; **linen crash** = CRASH *sb.*[2]; **linen cupboard**, a cupboard designed to hold bed-linen and table-linen; also, the contents of such a cupboard; **linen duster**, a duster (see DUSTER 4) made of linen; **linen-horse** = HORSE *sb.* 7 c; **linen-press**, a frame or receptacle for pressing or holding linen; **linen shower** [*SHOWER *sb.*[1]] *N. Amer.*, a party at which a bride-to-be is given presents of household linen, etc.; **linen tea**, a tea arranged in order to provide house-linen for a crèche, day nursery, etc.

1907 *Yesterday's Shopping* (1969) 125/3 Linen baskets. Barrel shape, buff wicker. **1970** G. F. NEWMAN *Sir, You Bastard* viii. 239 He used his shirt to wipe his damp armpits, then threw it out on to the linen basket. **1895** *Montgomery Ward Catal.* 24/2 Linen crash or toweling. **1904** *Sci. Amer.* 21 May 409/3 The complainant, a manufacturer of linen crash, had adopted as a trade-mark the words 'Stevens Crash'. **1873** *Young Englishwoman* Mar. 155/1 The plain, economical housewife would do well to follow 'Myra's' plan of her linen-cupboard. **1939** A. THIRKELL *Brandons* ix. 234 She let Miss Morris help Nurse..to go through the linen cupboard and mark some new sheets. **1972** P. RUELL *Red Christmas* v. 48 The linen cupboard was, forecastably, full of linen. It was more of a room than a cupboard. **1867** *Galaxy* III. 635 His cloak..or linen duster..serves as a cover to hide the manipulations of his agile fingers. **1949** *Chicago Daily News* 11 Feb. 21/3 Grandma was a fashion plate in her smart linen duster for Sunday motoring. **1845** R. COBBOLD *Hist. M. Catchpole* II. xxv. 139 The large linen-horses belonging to the gaol stood in the passage. **1906** *Mrs. Beeton's Bk. Househ. Managem.* lxix. 1810 Silks..should always be dried in the shade, on a linen-horse. **1851** MRS. STOWE *Uncle Tom's Cabin* (1852) I. xviii. 296 The store-room, the linen-presses, the china-closet,..all went under an awful review. **1970** *Canad. Antiques Collector* June 4 (Advt.), Exceptional Pennsylvania walnut linen-press..Circa 1790. **1904** *N.Y. Tribune* 27 Oct. 7 The managers of the Home for the Friendless invite the public to a linen shower and reception. **1921** *Daily Colonist* (Victoria, B.C.) 3 Apr. 8/3 A delightful linen shower was given in honor of Miss Dorothy Woods, Thursday evening at the home of Mrs. B. E. Lefevre. **1974** *Evening Herald* (Rock Hill, S. Carolina) 18 Apr. 9/4 Hostesses for a linen shower were Mrs. H. D. Long and Mrs. Arthur Snyder. **1916** *Yorks. Post* 19 Apr. 4/7 The first crèche which held such a 'linen tea'... Yesterday's meeting was for the purpose of collecting house linen to furnish the place. **1948** Linen tea [see *kitchen tea* (*KITCHEN *sb.* 7)].

linen-draper. Add: **b.** A newspaper. *Rhyming slang.*

1857 'DUCANGE ANGLICUS' *Vulgar Tongue* 12 *Linen-draper*, paper. **1936** J. CURTIS *Gilt Kid* xxiv. 234 It might be just as well to keep under cover for a little until perhaps the linen-drapers gave him the office that the chase had not been taken up. **1972** *Lebende Sprachen* XVII. 8/3 *Linen draper*, paper.

li·ne-out. Pl. **line-outs, lines-out.** [f. the vbl. phr. *to line out* (LINE *v.*[2] 8 b).] In Rugby football: (see quot. 1900).

1889 [see TOUCH *sb.* 12]. **1900** A. E. T. WATSON *Young Sportsman* 284 *Line out*,.. the arrangement of forwards opposite to one another when the ball is about to be thrown in from touch. **1906** GALLAHER & STEAD *Compl. Rugby Footballer* v. 80 The line-out work. **1931** *Times* 16 Feb. 5/2 Barrington made a clever mark from a knock-on in a line-out, but failed with the kick at goal. **1955** *Times* 18 July 12/6 The Province won four scrummages and lines-out out of five. **1965** *New Statesman* 19 Mar. 465/1 Just before half-time Wales scored, and thereafter dominated the game, winning the line-outs by intelligent forward play. **1973** *Scotsman* 21 Feb. 18/6 He used to prefer being stationed at No. 7 but agrees that, with the

new laws tending so to compress the line-out, it is difficult to win much really usable ball from an opponent of markedly superior height.

liner[1]. Add: **3.** The lining of a garment, esp. one made of an artificial fibre. So *liner suit* (see quot. 1969).

1947 *Horizon* Sept. 203 They took off their helmet liners. **1962** F. I. ORDWAY et al. *Basic Astronautics* xiii. 517 The inner liner of the suit is of neoprene-coated fabric... The outer liner is an aluminized coverall. **1969** *Guardian* 7 Jan. 7/2 There is an undergarment called a liner suit which makes PVCs more comfortable to wear. It is a two-piece affair made from knitted nylon with the inside of cosy brushed cotton. **1970** *Washington Post* 30 Sept. B5/3 (Advt.), Zip-in-or-out orlon liner. **1971** C. BONINGTON *Annapurna South Face* 241, 4-oz. Dunloprufe nylon with open-cell foam liner. *Ibid.* 242, 1 pair overmitts [made of] proofed nylon with Borg fur liner.

4. In full, *liner note.* (See quot. 1953.) orig. *U.S.*

1953 *Britannica Bk. of Year* 638/1 *Liner*, the text accompanying an album of gramophone records. **1955** *Sat. Rev.* (U.S.) Jan. 41 The covers of these new jazz albums..are being covered..with thousands and thousands of words known as 'liner notes'. **1960** D. CERULLI et al. *Jazz Word* (1962) 106 They couldn't come up with any less information than on some liners today. **1968** *Jazz Monthly* Feb. 21/2 The enthusiastic sleeve note by Brian Rust suggests that he may be on the downward path towards acceptance of those degenerate swing bands whom he has damned in nearly all his liner writing! **1969** *Rolling Stone* 17 May 17/3 As Coleman observes in the liner notes, 'Ornette Denardo is hard to keep up with if you don't tell him what to do.'

liner[2]. Add: **7. b.** A cosmetic used for tinting a part of the face; a brush or pencil for applying this; *spec.* = **eye-liner, eyeliner.*

1926 M. SMITH *Bk. Play Production* xi. 182 Liners are smaller sticks of grease paints..used to make lines on the face, such as wrinkles, 'eyebrows', etc. **1958** OSBORNE & CREIGHTON *Epitaph G. Dillon* II. 44, I always touch mine up with a brown liner... The rings under my eyes. **1966** *Harper's Bazaar* Sept. 70/1 Wrapping up lid, indeed eye, in a cocoon of pale grey shadow and liner. **1972** *Daily Tel.* 24 Jan. 11/1 A narrower streak of colour on the lid by the lashes, in place of liner.

8. b. (Earlier examples.)

1829 W. N. GLASCOCK *Sailors & Saints* I. ii. 25 We *liners*, you know, are not in the habit of leading small craft to their anchorage. **1855** *Chambers's Jrnl.* II. 270/2 Not an hour was lost in expediting the fitting out of our liner, for war was raging.

c. One of the aircraft of a regular line, esp. one for passenger transport; an air-liner; a space-ship.

1905 KIPLING *Actions & Reactions* (1909) 125 A Planet liner, east bound, heaves up in a superb spiral and takes the air of us humming. **1919** H. GOLDING *Wonder Bk. Aircraft* 69 (*caption*) *Off!* The pilot of the 'liner' is just giving orders to remove the blocks from the wheels of the under-carriage. **1933** *Boys' Mag.* XLVII. 24/1 Mile after mile of seemingly endless country unfurled itself beneath the flying wings of the giant liner. **1951** A. C. CLARKE *Sands of Mars* iii. 24 The observation gallery..completely circled the liner. **1959** *Times Lit. Suppl.* 17 Apr. 230/3 These well-known liners were conceived with the future needs of the air lines in view. **1969** *New Scientist* 2 Oct. 20/2 The Boeing liner will have rather more than twice the capacity of the Concorde.

d. One of a fleet of lorries.

1955 *Times* 29 June 13/3 The commission have offered the trunk service vehicles, which provide regular daily services between certain towns..'liner' services, compared with 'tramps',..in relatively large lots together with their respective terminal depôts.

13. *attrib.*, as **liner train**, a fast through-running freight train made up of detachable containers on permanently coupled wagons.

1962 *Guardian* 30 Oct. 3/2 'Custom built' services..so that customers can..'buy space' on fixed formation trains —'liner trains'—whose wagons can..bear their name and line of business. **1963** *Reshaping of Brit. Railways* (Brit. Railways Board) 142 The description 'Liner Train' is applied to a conception of transport based upon joint use of road and rail for door-to-door transport of containerised merchandise, with special purpose, through-running, scheduled trains providing the trunk haul... The Liner Train..is a train of chassis which will remain continuously coupled... The speed will be a maximum of 75 and an average of 50 miles an hour. **1964** *Observer* 28 June 8/5 If Dr. Beeching's figures are accepted at their face value, the cost of carrying goods by liner trains will be so much less than by heavy lorries..that he should be able to undercut the roads by a comfortable margin. **1970** *Daily Mail* 16 Feb. 1/6 The plant sends rear axles and brake drums by liner trains to other Ford factories.

li·nerboard. [f. LINER[1] + BOARD *sb.*] A paper-board used as a facing on fibre-board.

1961 *Paper Technol.* II. II. 145 We have produced virtually every type of paper and board known today, for example, ranging from glassine to kraft liner board. **1969** *Jane's Freight Containers 1968–69* 439/2 Rectangular container, two layers corrugated fibreboard covered by linerboard. **1972** *Evening Telegram* (St. John's, Newfoundland) 28 June 4/3 What venture capital went into the Stephenville Linerboard Mill?

linesman. Add: **3. c.** In *N. Amer. Football*, (*a*) an official on the sideline with certain duties governed by the rules of the game (see quot. 1969[2]); (*b*) = *LINEMAN 4. In *Ice Hockey*, an official whose chief duty is to give offside decisions.

1897 *Encycl. Sport* I. 425/2 Two linesmen..mark the distance gained and lost, and are aids to the umpire. **1935** *Encycl. Sports* 528/1 The officials in this game are referee, umpire, linesman and two assistants, and a field judge. **1947** E. A. MCCOURT *Music at Close* 119 The crash of opposing linesmen, the spirited end runs, the long spiralling kicks awoke in him a strong desire to be a participant. **1955** *Globe & Mail* (Toronto) 31 Jan. 19/1 Flaman tried desperately to break from linesman Bill Roberts, who had put the clutch on the rampaging Bruin defenseman. **1969** *Official Rule Bk. Nat. Hockey League 1969–70* 44 The duty of the linesman is to determine any infractions of the rules concerning off-side play at the blue line, or center line, or any violation of the 'Icing the Puck' rule. **1969** *Official Playing Rules Nat. & Amer. Football Leagues* 93 Linesman is to mark with his foot..the yardline touched by forward point of ball at end of each scrimmage down. *Ibid.*, He and the Umpire are to determine whether ineligible linesmen illegally cross line prior to a pass.

4. One who attends to the upkeep of roadside verges.

1888 *Geysers & Gazers* 7 The road was impeded by a land-slip... As soon as we cleared one slip away, another came into view. I asked the driver why the linesman had not attended to the matter. **1971** *Country Life* 18 Nov. 1372/4, I was privileged to spend many hours in the company of a linesman... He was responsible for the upkeep of the roadside verges of some four to five square miles.

line standard. [LINE *sb.*[2]] **a.** *Metrology.* A standard of length in the form of a metal bar on which are engraved two lines, the distance between which (under specified conditions) is the standard length.

1888 *Encycl. Brit.* XXIV. 478/1 Standards of length are of two types, the defining points being either at a certain part of two parallel lines engraven in one plane (a line-standard), or else points on two parallel surfaces, which can only be observed by contact (an end-standard). **1906** HALLOCK & WADE *Outl. Evolution of Weights & Measures* x. 223 The line standard, of course, can be used with a microscope with cross-hairs, or a micrometer microscope, much more readily than an end standard. **1966** KAYE & LABY *Tables Physical & Chem. Constants* (ed. 13) 7 The yard equal to 0·9144 metre supersedes the definition in terms of the former imperial standard yard, a bronze line-standard constructed in 1845. **1967** A. J. T. SCARR *Metrology & Precision Engin.* v. 67 The calibration of a line standard is determined by comparison with a master scale.

b. *Television.* The number of lines constituting a complete picture.

1959 C. DANIEL in *Rep. Comm. Broadcasting 1960* (1962) 340 in *Parl. Papers 1961–2* (Cmnd. 1753) IX. 259 We understand that most of the rest of Europe are likely to adopt..a line standard of 625 lines. **1973** *Newnes Colour Television Servicing Manual* I. i. 2/2 The degaussing action takes place automatically when there is a change in the line standard during push-button selection.

li·ne-up. orig. *U.S.* [f. LINE *v.*[2] 8 a.] The assembling of a number of persons in a line, e.g. for inspection or identification; an instance of bringing into a line; a list of players in a game, orchestra, etc.; the players on such a list. Also of things. Also *fig.*

1889 *Kansas City* (Missouri) *Times & Star* 11 Mar., The line-up of the Kansas City ball club this season. **1904** *Springfield* (Mass.) *Weekly Republ.* 3 June 1 Thus we have a line-up of corporations against the people. **1907** J. LONDON *Road* 89 Then came the line-up, forty or fifty of us, naked as Kipling's heroes. **1911** H. S. HARRISON *Queed* xviii. 224 He studied his trustee list now more purposefully than he had ever pored over his faculty line up. **1913** G. J. KNEELAND *Commercialized Prostitution N.Y.* 62 Here they come to make deals for their women..or in vice resorts, to plan line ups when a 'young chicken' is about to be broken into the business. *Ibid.*, A 'line up' is the ruin of a girl who flirts with men and accepts their advances and immoral suggestions. Finally she yields to an invitation to visit a furnished room and the word quickly passes among the 'gang'. One by one the boys and men, perhaps only two or three, perhaps more, visit the room. **1914** J. B. BICKERSTETH *Land of Open Doors* 172 Guess I'm in the line up for hell all right—with no return ticket either. **1915** *Policeman's Monthly* Sept. 5 (*caption*) The famous 'line-up' at New York Police Headquarters. **1926** *Clues* Nov. 161/2 *Lineup*, suspects arrested the night before lined up for police inspection. **1928** A. G. HAYS *Let Freedom Ring* 289 The prisoners were brought before witnesses—not in a line-up with others of the same general type but separately. **1931** E. LINKLATER *Juan in America* II. xviii. 197 But she didn't know the line-up... It's Bauer that knows that, because Bauer's going to do the job. **1934** —— *Magnus Merriman* xxvi. 292 He knew the whole line-up from old man Plato to Bergson. **1938** *Amer. Speech* XIII. 71/1 *Line-up*, a record of all expected train movements for the day in the section where the gang is working. **1952** *Manch. Guardian Weekly* 10 Jan. 3 A police line-up. **1955** A. J. MCCARTHY *Jazzbook 1955* 39 The traditional line-up of trumpet, clarinet, trombone, piano, banjo, string bass and drums. **1965** J. POLLARD *Surfrider* ii. 18 The 'lineup' is where the waves line up to break. **1967** *Word Study* Mar. 1/2 To the general public, the English teacher is the witness qualified to identify the felon in a linguistic lineup. **1968** *Radio Times* 28 Nov. 55/4, 11.10. Late Night Line-Up. A last look around the daily scene. **1970** *Language* XLVI. 317 The negative and positive values of time refer to the computer 'line up' point. **1972** *Jazz & Blues* Sept. 11/3 This was the basic line-up which became the Domino band after the success of 'The Fat Man'. **1973** 'J. PATRICK' *Glasgow Gang Observed* v. 52 The phrase 'line-up'..was normally used to describe the queue of boys waiting to have sexual intercourse in one of the 'gang bangs'.

ling, *sb.*[1] Add: **3. ling-cod** *N. Amer.*, a North Pacific species of cod, *Ophiodon elongatus*, also called cultus cod. (Cf. sense 2.)

1955 W. DAWSON *Ahoy There!* 205 Besides salmon, we catch cod..ling-cod of up to (in our case) twelve pounds. **1964** *Canad. Geogr. Jrnl.* Mar. 91/3 This is particularly true in the case of the ling cod, the spear-fisherman's favourite quarry. **1971** *Islander* (Victoria, B.C.) 21 Mar. 2/3, I have taken in recent years, six species of rockfish..also lingcod.

Lingala (liŋgā·lă). Also **Ngala.** [Native name.] A Bantu language spoken by the Bangala people in the Mangala area of Zaïre, widely used in trade and public affairs. Also *attrib.* or as *adj.*

1903 W. H. STAPLETON *Compar. Handbk. Congo Lang.* p. 1, Bangala is a name originally given..to a people.. from the settlement of Mangala... The dialect chosen and called Ngala is spoken by the Boloki..and Bokomoi on the South bank. **1922** H. H. JOHNSTON *Compar. Study Bantu & Semi-Bantu Lang.* II. vi. 130 At present we can only surmise that Group KK contains the following sub-groups:..KK_4, the Lingala. **1945** C. M. DOKE *Bantu* 27 Ngala..is today called 'Lingala', though it is based on the speech of the Mangala people. **1965** *B.B.C. Handbk.* 103 Moscow radio started transmissions in..Lingala, Nepalese. **1973** *Black World* May 95/1 The Bolinga, the name for the Black Cultural Resources Center at Wright State University in Dayton, Ohio, is a Lingala word meaning 'love'.

lingberry: see *LINGONBERRY.

Lingby, var. *LYNGBY.

lingenberry: see *LINGONBERRY.

linger, *sb.* Add: **2.** *U.S.* (See quot.)

1895 *Nation* (N.Y.) 9 May 358/3 The enervating influence of the climate, giving rise to that which in the south-western United States is called the 'Texas lingers'.

linger, *v.* Add: **7. c.** *Hort.* To delay the blooming of (flowers) by artificial means.

1906 *Daily Chron.* 12 Sept. 4/4 If you force, you exhaust the [rose-]tree; it languishes. I prefer to 'linger' it.

lingerie. Add: **b.** *attrib.*

1866 MRS. GASKELL *Wives & Daughters* II. xxiv. 248 There was a 'lingerie' shop, kept by a Frenchwoman. **1905** *Daily Chron.* 13 Mar. 8/1 The lingerie blouse made a most emphatic appearance in Paris..this winter. *Ibid.*, It is the lingerie shirt that wins. **1909** *Westm. Gaz.* 22 Feb. 5/2 As to the lingerie gown, its importance in the wardrobe cannot be questioned. **1909** *Public Ledger* (Philadelphia) 24 June 7/7 (Advt.), Fine lingerie waists, trimmed with dainty laces & embroideries. **1909** *Daily Chron.* 10 Sept. 7/2 Embroider..if the sacque is of piqué or lingerie materials. **1964** *McCall's Sewing* ii. 30/1 *Lingerie hem*, a rolled hem that is caught with two overcast stitches at intervals of ⅛ to ⅜ inch gathering it in puffs. *Ibid.* 30/2 *Lingerie seam*, supposedly 'rip-proof'; made by pressing both edges of a seam to one side and top-stitching with a zigzag stitch along the edge. **1974** *Country Life* 3–10 Jan. 55/1 Harvey Nichols have.. palazzo suits by Mr Dino. In the lingerie department there are things by Iful, Yves Stillman, Leonara. **1974** *Evening Herald* (Rock Hill, S. Carolina) 18 Apr. 9/4 A lingerie shower was given by Mrs. Preston Ramsey and Mrs. Harold Wolfe.

lingering, *vbl. sb.* Add: **c.** *Hort.* Retarding the time of blooming by artificial means.

1907 *Daily Chron.* 13 Feb. 6/4 Lingering is retardation without frost; it keeps September roses blooming until January.

‖ **lingoa geral** (liŋgōu·ā dʒərā·l). Also **lingua geral.** [Pg., ad. *lingua geral*, lit. 'general language'.] A trade language based on Tupi and used as a lingua franca in Brazil.

1856 [see *JUPATI]. **1860** MAYNE REID *Odd People* 46 We shall use that [name] by which it is known in the 'Lingoa geral', and call it a *malocca*. **1876** *Encycl. Brit.* IV. 235/1 Most of the semi-civilized Indians of Brazil.. speak the Lingoa-Geral, a language adapted by the Jesuit missionaries from the original idiom of the Tupinambaras. **1932** W. L. GRAFF *Lang.* 431 The whole of Brazil that came into contact with the whites eventually became bilingual, knowing their own dialect and the Guarani *lingoa geral.* **1948** C. NIMUENDAJÚ in J. H. Steward *Handbk. S. Amer. Indians* III. 257 After their pacification, the *Mura* began to adopt the Lingua Geral... Later they substituted Portuguese for the Lingua Geral. *Ibid.* 311 *Tapanyuna* is not an *Apiacá* word, but a Lingua Geral term which means 'negro'. **1973** E. BROOKS et al. *Tribes of Amazon Basin in Brazil 1972* ii. 58 Tukano is still spoken widely among Indians of Santa Isabel..and many still speak *lingua geral*, the Jesuit's blend of Tupi and Guarani.

lingonberry (li·ŋǫ̆nberi). *Canad.* Also **lingberry, lingenberry.** [f. Sw. *lingon* mountain cranberry + BERRY *sb.*[1]] A dwarf variety of mountain cranberry, *Vaccinium vitis-idæa* var. *minus*, native to far northern temperate regions; also, another northern species of cranberry, *V. oxycoccus.*

1955 *Arctic Terms* 50/1 Lingberry, a name for the fruit

of the mountain cranberry. **1960** J. J. ROWLANDS *Spindrift* 156 In Sweden the cranberry is known as the lingonberry. *Ibid.* 161 This berry [*sc.* mountain cranberry] is probably close to the lingonberry of Scandinavian countries. **1961** *Harper's Bazaar* May 106/2 Sweden prides itself on..pancakes..dressed with lingonberries. **1970** *Beaver* Winter 23 Wild cranberries..are also known as lingenberries. **1971** D. NABOKOV tr. *Nabokov's Glory* (1972) vi. 24 Supper at the station (hazel hen with lingonberry sauce).

lingua. Add: **2. b.** (Examples of pl. form.)
1971 J. SPENCER *Eng. Lang. W. Afr.* 31 A very complex infrastructure of scores of vernacular languages as well as a number of regional lingue franche. **1974** R. A. HALL *External Hist. Romance Lang.* 21 The distribution of the Romance languages is best treated under four heads:.. (3) use as *lingue franche*.
fig. (Later examples.)
1955 *Times* 2 July 5/2 Cold war recrimination became the east–west *lingua franca*. **1958** *Times* 16 Sept. 3/2 Mr. Morrice handles them [*sc.* motifs] by cunningly intermingling realism with the *lingua franca* of ballet.

linguacious, *a.* Add: **1.** Also **linguaceous.** (Later examples.)
1827 J. F. COOPER *Prairie* I. xi. 329 On the summit, Obed fully expected to encounter Esther, of whose linguacious powers, he had too often been furnished with the most sinister proofs. **1950** J. Y. T. GREIG *Thackeray* xiii. 142 She needed it [*sc.* the gift of listening] with a witty and linguacious fellow for a husband. *a* **1953** DYLAN THOMAS *Quite Early One Morning* (1954) 64 And see, too, in that linguaceous stream, the tall monocled men..who lecture to women's clubs.

lingua geral: see *LINGOA GERAL.

lingually, *adv.* Add: **b.** On the lingual side; towards the tongue.
1902 *Dental Digest* VIII. 925, I have seen some cases of compound cavities which started at a point of structural defect perhaps two millimeters distant lingually from the contact. **1910** *Practitioner* Jan. 115 Internally (lingually), the neck of the tooth..is embraced by a thin shallow flap of gum. **1963** J. OSBORNE *Dental Mech.* (ed. 5) viii. 112 During eruption..the facial muscles push the teeth lingually. **1970** *Nature* 25 July 356/2 A crest extends lingually to delineate the extent of the talonid basin. **1971** *Ibid.*, 30 July 311/1 At the incisor sockets the alveolar margin seems to be preserved lingually but is broken labially.

Linguaphone (li·ŋgwăfōun). Also **linguaphone.** [f. LINGUA 2 + *-phone* after GRAMOPHONE.] The proprietary name of a language-teaching system based on the use of gramophone records in conjunction with textbooks (see quots.). Also *attrib.*
1908 *Westm. Gaz.* 29 Feb. 7/1 (Advt.), The Linguaphone. This machine..teaches languages by a marvellous system of phonographic records. **1913** *Chambers's Jrnl.* Nov. 830/2 In the linguaphone system..the records are prepared by distinguished speakers of the various languages. **1925** *Trade Marks Jrnl.* 4 Nov. 2397 Linguaphone..instruments and apparatus for teaching. Jacques Roston,..London,..teacher of languages and translator. **1926** *Glasgow Herald* 28 Feb. 9 The Linguaphone Institute has produced a system by means of which one can, in his own home, from book and gramophone record obtain a working knowledge of languages. **1936** P. FLEMING *News from Tartary* 162, I had left Peking with a minute.. Chinese vocabulary, based on the first half-dozen records of a linguaphone course. **1962** L. DEIGHTON *Ipcress File* xxv. 161 Suppose I buy you a Linguaphone course. **1966** A. E. LINDOP *I start Counting* xv. 174 They had bought some Linguaphone records—so everything was 'quel' this and 'quel' that. **1974** *Country Life* 14 Feb. 304/2 Brito e Cunha breaks off the native-tongue chat..for a caution of 'Hold hard!' or 'I say, sta-idy there!' in linguaphone Leicestershire.

linguate (li·ŋgwĕt), *a.* [f. L. *linguātus* (not recorded in this sense) or f. LINGU(A 1 + -ATE².] Tongue-shaped. As *sb.*, a tongue-shaped flint instrument.
1940 *Proc. Prehist. Soc.* VI. 8 Pointed linguates with untrimmed butts. **1963** S. PIGGOTT in Foster & Alcock *Culture & Environment* iv. 84 In Ireland, a fourth distinctive group of linguate daggers can be recognized.

linguatulid (liŋgwæ·tiŭlid), *sb.* and *a.* [f. mod.L. name of former class *Linguatulida*, f. the generic name *Linguatula* (G. F. von Froelich 1789, in *Naturforscher* XXIV. 148), f. L. *linguātus* 'having a tongue', eloquent.] A parasitic worm-like arthropod of the genus *Linguatula*, the adult form of which attacks the nasal passages of certain carnivorous mammals, esp. canids; also, a member of the group Pentastomida, including parasitic arthropods, most of which attack snakes; = *tongue-worm* (*b*) (TONGUE *sb.* 16). Also as *adj.*
1923 *Nature* 17 Mar. 381/2 (*title*) On the linguatulid arachnid, *Raillietiella furcocerca*. **1929** PATTON & EVANS *Insects, Ticks, Mites* I. 666 *Porocephalus* is the name of a Linguatulid genus. *Ibid.*, It [*sc.* a parasite] can hardly be acquired by eating the flesh of snakes, the commonest final host of these Linguatulids. **1942** *Ann. Trop. Med. & Parasitol.* XXXVI. 60 (*title*) Linguatulid infestations of man. **1961** C. H. POPE *Giant Snakes* (1962) 193 Linguatulids, some fifty species of which have been described, are degenerate arachnids closely related to ticks and mites.

linguine (liŋgwī·ne). Also **linguini.** [It., pl. of *linguina*, dim. of *lingua* tongue.] An Italian pasta made of tongue-shaped ribbons.
1948 LO PINTO & MILARADOVICH *Art of Italian Cooking* (1955) i. 24 *Linguini*, narrow, plain noodles cut about ⅛ inch wide. **1954** G. M. LAPOLLA *Good Food from Italy* 85 When peas are used, rarely is the sauce poured over the linguine or fettuccelle. **1965** M. ECHARD *I met Murder* (1967) vii. 59 Dining on fettuccine or linguini or ravioli. **1968** *N.Y. Times* 26 Jan. 22 The kitchen produces first-rate linguine with clam sauce. **1969** R. LOWELL *Notebk. 1967–68* (1970) 255 The ebb tide flings up wonders: rivers, linguini, Beercans, bloodstreams, eddies. **1972** R. K. SMITH *Ransom* I. 4 Just a little linguine, and a little veal parmigiana.

linguism. Restrict *nonce-wd.* to sense in Dict. and add: **2.** Advocacy of languages on a regional basis.
1967 *Economist* 18 Feb. 596/1 A good deal of the criticism heard..of Indian politics—for instance of 'linguism', 'casteism', and so on—is a roundabout way of wishing that human beings were different from what they are.

linguist. 2. Delete †*Obs.* and add later examples.
1922 O. JESPERSEN *Lang.* 64, I think I am in accordance with a growing number of scholars in England and America if I..apply the word 'linguist' by itself to the scientific student of language (or of languages). **1940** *Amer. Speech* XV. 187 The *Handbook* [of the Linguistic Geography of New England]..seems to suggest that American linguists are naïve. **1964** R. H. ROBINS *Gen. Ling.* 2 The general linguist, in the sense of the specialist or the student concerned with general linguistics. **1966** M. R. D. FOOT *SOE in France* viii. 212 He was a young linguist, a research student at Manchester University. **1966** *New Statesman* 11 Nov. 701/1 One or two of my friends even abandoned literature altogether and became fully fledged philologists—'linguists', as my companion at dinner would have said. **1973** A. P. SORENSEN in D. R. Gross *Peoples & Cultures of Native S. Amer.* 331 Some linguists wondered..whether the comparative method could or even should be applied to American Indian languages at all.
5. *attrib.* or appositive, as *linguist-anthropologist, -philologist, -reader.*
1951 S. F. NADEL *Found. Social Anthropol.* 46 The 'virtuosity' of the linguist-anthropologist..is only the fullest preparation for his task. **1960** *Amer. Speech* XXXV. 217 In a treatment of specific historical changes of morphemes and phonemes the linguist-philologist should attempt to recapture what actually happened. **1964** *Language* XL. 203 A sample passage from a 1956 article by Starkweather is enough to boggle the unprepared linguist-reader.

linguistic, *a.* and *sb.* Add: **A.** *adj.* (Later examples.)
1911 V. WELBY *Significs & Lang.* v. 17 The implicitly false mental image, source of the false linguistic image. **1921** E. SAPIR *Lang.* vi. 156 In a book of this sort it is naturally impossible to give an adequate idea of linguistic structure. **1935** B. MALINOWSKI *Coral Gardens* II. vi. v. 232 Within the linguistic theory of the present book, in which the distinction between 'form' and meaning is in the last instance illusory. **1936** J. R. KANTOR *Objective Psychol. Gram.* xiii. 195 It is undoubtedly necessary to include many other speech parts if we are to cover linguistic phenomena adequately. **1953** J. B. CARROLL *Study of Lang.* i. 5 It was only natural..that the engineer should have perceived the possibilities of developing various sorts of 'linguistic machines', such as a machine for instantly converting human speech into..printed alphabetic symbols. **1957** W. HAAS in *Studies in Ling. Analysis* (Philol. Soc.) 33 'Zero' in Linguistic Description stands for what is acoustically nothing. **1957** G. RYLE in C. A. Mace *Brit. Philos. in Mid-Cent.* 263 Philosophical problems are linguistic problems—only linguistic problems quite unlike any of the problems of philology, grammar, phonetics..etc., since they are..about the logic of the functionings of expressions. **1964** M. A. K. HALLIDAY et al. *Ling. Sci.* i. 18 If language is described according to the version of linguistic theory outlined, the task of the language learner..will be made easier. **1966** *English Studies* XLVII. 270 Instead of adverb transforms we find occasional instances of 'linguistic shortening', which in itself is a means of expressing emotiveness. **1967** R. TEXTOR *Cross-Cultural Summary* 67 The rationale for including linguistic affiliation is..that 'genetic relationships in culture and past historical connections among societies are commonly revealed..among the languages spoken by the peoples in question'. **1968** D. HYMES in *Internat. Encycl. Social Sci.* 366/2 Linguistic description has focused on the form of languages, neglecting the structuring of their use. **1968** CHOMSKY & HALLE *Sound Pattern Eng.* i. 4 The essential properties of natural language are often referred to as 'linguistic universals'. **1972** L. R. PALMER *Descr. & Compar. Ling.* ix. 227 Sound laws do not enable us to *predict* linguistic events as a law of chemistry predicts material change.
b. Special collocations: *linguistic analysis*, (*a*) the analysis of language structures in terms of some theory of language; (*b*) *Philos.*, analysis of language as the medium of thought; so *linguistic analyst*; *linguistic anthropology*, anthropological research based on the study of the language of a selected group; so *linguistic-anthropological* adj.; *linguistic atlas*, a set of tables or maps recording regional or dialectal variations of pronunciation, vocabulary, or inflexional forms; *linguistic form*, any unit or pattern of speech that has meaning; *linguistic geography*, the study of the geographical distribution of languages, dialects, etc.; so *linguistic geographer*, *linguistic-geographical* adj.; *linguistic map*, a map in a linguistic atlas; a map showing the distribution of linguistic features; *linguistic philosophy* = *linguistic analysis* (*b*); so *linguistic philosopher*; *linguistic psychology*, the study of human psychology through the data provided by language; cf. *PSYCHOLINGUISTICS; *linguistic science*, the science of language; the systematic study of linguistic phenomena; so *linguistic scientist*; *linguistic stock*, the group to which a set of related languages belongs.
1932 A. F. BENTLEY *Let.* 15 Nov. in Ratner & Altman *J. Dewey & A. F. Bentley* (1964) 51, I have at length found a region of investigation in which some tentative results can be secured, and I am permitting myself to send you a copy of the resulting book, *Linguistic Analysis of Mathematics*. **1943** *Amer. Speech* XXVII. 60/1 Outline of linguistic analysis. **1945** *Mind* LIV. 195 Positivists, as is well known, do not search for answers to the philosophical questions; what they try to bring about, in *all* cases, is the disappearance of the questions by means of what they call linguistic analysis. **1949** *Amer. Speech* XXIV. 55 His charts make it possible to suggest the potentialities of 'slur' as a factor in linguistic analysis. **1957** J. R. FIRTH in *Studies in Ling. Analysis* (Philol. Soc.) p. vi, Palatograms, kymograms..specifically keyed to the linguistic analysis. **1966** J. J. KATZ *Philos. of Lang.* iii. 16 The leading philosophical movements..have concerned themselves with what they call 'linguistic analysis'. **1945** *Aristotelian Soc. Suppl. Vol.* XIX. 7 If anyone was ever a 'linguistic analyst', surely Socrates was. **1957** G. RYLE in C. A. Mace *Brit. Philos. in Mid-Cent.* 263, I gather that at this very moment British philosophy is dominated by some people called 'linguistic analysts'. **1962** *Listener* 17 May 851/1 You might well meet a philosopher described as a linguistic analyst. **1964** E. A. NIDA *Toward Sci. Transl.* iii. 36 The linguistic-anthropological approach to meaning has in many respects paralleled developments in symbolic logic, though the immediate area of study in the two fields is different and the approach seemingly quite divergent. **1968** D. HYMES in *Internat. Encycl. Social Sci.* 354/2 Through Boas the interest became an intrinsic part of American linguistic anthropology. **1923** H. R. LANG in *Romanic Rev.* XIV. 264 It will be clear from this that the study of the charts of this linguistic atlas affords a deep insight into the various phases of the decline of the dialects of Italy. **1930** *Dialect Notes* VI. ii. 67 The Linguistic Atlas of New England will provide an organized collection of the present forms of the spoken language. **1939** *Amer. Speech* XIV. 64/2 Ten sets of 300 phonograph records representing all the present dialects of Germany. Recorded by Telefunken under the auspices of the Linguistic Atlas. **1952** DIETH & ORTON (*title*) A questionnaire for a linguistic atlas of England. **1954** G. BOTTIGLIONI in Martinet & Weinreich *Ling. Today* 261 The way in which the plan of a linguistic atlas is organized and carried out. **1975** *Times* 6 Jan. 4/7 The next project will be the publication of a complete linguistic atlas which will trace on maps not only the use of specific words but of dialect sounds as well. **1921** E. SAPIR *Lang.* iv. 62 Linguistic form may and should be studied as types of patterning, apart from the associated functions. *Ibid.* vi. 127 In dealing with linguistic form, we have been concerned only with single words and with the relations of words in sentences. **1943** *Amer. Speech* XVIII. 228 The flier forced down in Libya.., would have little interest in the linguistic form of the utterance, 'I am an American', in Arabic but he might forfeit his life by not knowing how to say it. **1964** M. A. K. HALLIDAY et al. *Ling. Sci.* i. 20 The least obvious distinction perhaps is that between grammar and lexis, since these are two aspects of linguistic form. *Ibid.* ii. 21 When we describe linguistic *form*..we are describing the meaningful internal patterns of language. **1952** *Word* VIII. iii. 275 Who but Rohlfs combines a background of solid 19th century German scholarship with a thorough training as a linguistic geographer? **1948** *Neophilologus* XXXII. 175 In the absence of English linguistic-geographical data, no more than tentative suggestions regarding the relation between English and its Continental cognates are as yet possible. **1926** *Germanic Rev.* I. iv. 281 Linguistic geography, as geography, is an aspect of human geography. **1930** *Dialect Notes* VI. ii. 74 A course in the methods and the interpretation of the results of linguistic geography. **1933** Linguistic geography [see *HISTORICAL *a.* 2 d]. **1934** H. KURATH in *Proc. Amer. Philos. Soc.* LXXIV. 228 Linguistic geography undertakes to ascertain the distribution of linguistic features (dialectal features). **1939** —— (*title*) Handbook of the linguistic geography of New England. **1954** G. BOTTIGLIONI in Martinet & Weinreich *Ling. Today* 255 Linguistic geography owes its origin to the comparative method. **1968** D. HYMES in *Internat. Encycl. Social Sci.* 359/2 Linguistic geography, or dialectology, and typological comparison, together with general linguistics, often are distinguished as well. **1944** *Amer. Speech* XIX. 135 The book includes sixteen linguistic maps and nineteen illustrations. **1951** *Mind* LX. 104 These words should rejoice the heart of any present-day Linguistic Philosopher. **1963** W. H. WALSH *Metaphysics* i. 16 The brief ascendancy of the Logical Positivists came to an end and their place was taken by the so-called Linguistic Philosophers. **1957** J. L. AUSTIN in *Proc. Aristotelian Soc.* LVII. 9 There are, I know, or are supposed to be, snags in 'linguistic' philosophy, which those not very familiar with it find, sometimes not without glee or relief, daunting. **1962** *Listener* 22 Feb. 353/1 He was reputed to be the high priest of linguistic philosophy. **1966** J. J. KATZ *Philos. of Lang.* iii. 15 The leading philosophical movements in twentieth-century philosophy have been referred

to..as 'linguistic philosophy'. **1953** J. B. CARROLL *Study of Lang.* iii. 70 The study of verbal behavior..has variously been called the *psychology of language, linguistic psychology*, or *psycholinguistics*. **1966** M. PEI *Story of Lang.* (rev. ed.) xii. 286 The number of unsolved problems in the field of linguistic psychology is tremendous. **1922** O. JESPERSEN *Lang.* 21 Nor did linguistic science advance in the Middle Ages. **1933** L. BLOOMFIELD *Lang.* ii. 21 Linguistic science arose from relatively practical preoccupations, such as the use of writing, the study of literature and especially of older records, and the prescription of elegant speech. **1938** *Year's Work Eng. Stud. 1936* 27 Philology (which scholars tend more and more to call 'linguistic science' or 'linguistics'). **1971** D. CRYSTAL *Ling.* 36 It is also sometimes called linguistic science. **1934** *Amer. Speech* IX. 88/1 Linguistic scientists will find a rich ground for study if they will stop thinking of the written or printed Standard Language as solely a secondary, or derivative, form of speech. **1921** E. SAPIR *Lang.* x. 221 What are the most inclusive linguistic groupings, the 'linguistic stocks', and what is the distribution of each. **1953** BEALS & HOIJER *Introd. Anthropol.* xvii. 524 As more and more languages are studied and compared intensively with each other, we may expect that the number of linguistic stocks will decrease.

B. *sb.* **b.** (Further examples.)

1847 in WEBSTER. **1902** *PMLA* XVII. 104 Both linguistics and literature are proper university studies. **1908** H. G. WELLS *War in Air* iii. § 4 He thought of himself performing feats with the sign language and chance linguistics. **1938** [see *linguistic science* above]. **1953** J. B. CARROLL *Study of Lang.* iv. 113 Linguistics thus appears to have a bearing on all the social sciences. **1964** M. A. K. HALLIDAY et al. *Ling. Sci.* i. 9 The term 'linguistic sciences' covers two closely related but distinct subjects: linguistics and phonetics. **1964** R. H. ROBINS *Gen. Ling.* ii. 66 The linguist..may have to rely on sciences other than linguistics and on unsystematized 'common sense'. **1972** L. R. PALMER *Descr. & Compar. Ling.* xiii. 300 There are few discussions of this subject [*sc.* etymology]..in modern handbooks of linguistics.

c. appositive and *Comb.*

1958 *College English* XX. 12/2 Linguistics-based metrical analysis. *Ibid.* 17/2 A few linguistics-manufactured accessories. **1965** *Canad. Jrnl. Ling.* Fall 40 The long history of the linguistics–literary study opposition.

linguistically, *adv.* (Later examples.)

1921 B. RUSSELL *Analysis of Mind* viii. 141 The subject ..is introduced, not because observation reveals it, but because it is linguistically convenient and apparently demanded by grammar. **1935** B. MALINOWSKI *Coral Gardens* II. VI. iv. 229 The magical word..has got some affinity with the name which linguistically defines the relation of man as speaker to the object addressed. **1942** *Language* XVIII. 7 Non-distinctive elements..are no more significant linguistically than is any other concurrent action of a speaker. **1956** E. H. HUTTEN *Lang. Mod. Physics* ii. 26 Truth is said to be linguistically neutral: whatever is true is true in any language. **1971** W. P. ROBINSON in W. H. Whiteley *Lang. Use & Social Change* 78 Linguistically, the code has the possibility of exploiting the full grammatical and lexical potential of the language.

linguistician. Delete *rare*$^{-1}$ and add earlier and later examples.

1895 E. W. FAY in *Amer. Jrnl. Philol.* XVI. 10 This identification of the earlier 'linguisticians' has been latterly abandoned. **1949** *Studies in Ling.* VII. 59, I intend to use *linguistician* regularly henceforth instead of *linguist* 'worker in linguistics'. **1950** *Ibid.* VIII. 1 To one of these, *linguistician*, I not only cannot subscribe [etc.]... This meaning, exemplified by such words as *mortician* and *beautician*, implies pretentiousness rather than precision. **1954** *English Studies* XXXV. 91 In the absence of any..description by native linguisticians, these observations by an experienced teacher of foreign students ..deserve the attention. **1967** C. L. WRENN *Word & Symbol* 7 If..texts may be properly explained by allegory and symbolism without any exact knowledge of their language, then the English language..may as well be left to the linguisticians.

li·ngworm. Also **lyngorm.** [ad. ON. *lyngormr* 'heatherworm'. Cf. *LINDWORM.] A fabulous serpent.

1870 MAGNÚSSON & MORRIS tr. *Völsunga Saga* xiii. 45 The fashion and the growth of him is even as of other lingworms. **1883** J. S. STALLYBRASS tr. *J. Grimm's Teutonic Mythol.* II. xxi. 690 The beautiful Thora Borgarhiörtr had a small lÿngorm given her, whom she placed in a casket, with gold under him. **1972** J. SIMPSON *Icelandic Folktales & Legends* iii. 103 The 'Heath Snake' mentioned here, the *lýngorm*, was a mythical creature which, like the dragon, had a particular affinity for gold.

linin. Add: **2.** *Cytology* (now chiefly *Hist.*). [a. G. *linin* (F. Schwarz 1887, in *Beitr. z. Biol. d. Pflanzen* V. 9), f. Gr. λίνον (= L. *līnum*) thread.] A substance which composes the fine threads seen in interphase nuclei; a thread or network composed of this substance (see quot. 1932).

1887 *Jrnl. R. Microsc. Soc.* 979 As components of the nucleus, Schwartz [*sic*] distinguishes the following substances:—..(3) linin and paralinin, the substance respectively of the nuclear threads, the 'nucleo-hyaloplasm' of Strasburger, and of the intermediate matrix or 'nuclear sap'. **1905** *Rep. Brit. Assoc. Adv. Sci.* 567 The nucleus contains an achromatic network—the linin—in which the chromatin granules are embedded. **1925** E. B. WILSON *Cell* (ed. 3) i. 88 The [nuclear] framework itself appears to consist of two constituents, namely, a continuous 'achromatic' basis, and of more or less discontinuous granules or clumps of 'chromatin' suspended in it... The first of these was found to be oxyphilic and was accordingly designated by Strasburger as nucleohyaloplasm, by Carnoy as the plasmatic network (composed of 'plastin') and later by Schwarz ('87) as linin, a term still in common use. **1932** C. D. DARLINGTON *Recent Adv. Cytol.* 498 *Linin*, a structural component of the nucleus. The term has been applied to the descriptions of various artefacts and has no definite meaning. **1948** W. ANDREW tr. *E. D. P. de Robertis's Gen. Cytol.* vii. 137 A fine lightly staining reticulum, the linin. **1969** BROWN & BERTKE *Textbk. Cytol.* 574/1 *Linin*, achromatic material connecting chromioles in the interphase nucleus, in contrast to only one substance, karyotin, composing the reticulum.

lining, *vbl. sb.*^{1} **5.** *lining paper* (later examples).

1938 *Burlington Mag.* July 34/2 Pasted inside [a hanging food cupboard] are the remains of a seventeenth-century lining-paper. **1962** F. T. DAY *Introd. to Paper* viii. 87 Rolls of lining papers of all kinds consume a large volume of paper in many grades.

lining, *vbl. sb.*^{2} Add: **1.** Also *lining-up*.

1940 *Chambers's Techn. Dict.* 503/2 *Lining-up*, the operation of arranging the bearings of an engine crankshaft, etc. in perfect alignment. **1959** W. S. SHARPS *Dict. Cinematogr.* 107/1 *Lining up*, the setting of camera or other controls, in order to obtain a correctly framed picture. **1967** E. CHAMBERS *Photolitho-Offset* v. 51 Modern layout and lining-up tables are in many respects similar to stripping benches or shiners, with straight edges often in the form of steel rules, and micrometer-adjustable.

4. (Later examples.)

1917 *Encycl. Relig. & Ethics* IX. 27/2 In the ordinary parish churches metrical Psalms only were sung. 'Lining out' by the 'clerk', or precentor, was the order, singing in unison without organ accompaniment the rule. **1968** P. OLIVER *Screening Blues* ii. 82 'Lining out' in which a lead singer paces a line and the congregation follows with the same line or a refrain response with a linear reply.

link, *sb.*^{1} **c.** Add to def.: In mod. usage sometimes treated as a singular.

1861 H. B. FARNIE *Fife Coast* 115 The links lying at the house door, is a very famous one in the annals of golf. **1890** H. G. HUTCHINSON *Golf* xiii. 311 The links of St. Andrews..holds premier place. *Ibid.* 317 It is a good links. **1904** *Daily Chron.* 20 Aug. 9/5 On a suburban links. **1919** WODEHOUSE *Damsel in Distress* x. 122 His first act.. had been to ascertain whether there was a links in the neighbourhood. **1933** H. S. COLT in M. A. F. Sutton *Golf Courses* 124 When..the links is stretched..an excellent test of golf is provided. **1972** R. QUIRK et al. *Gram. Contemp. Eng.* iv. 181 The following nouns invariably end in *-s*: alms..innings..links (..a golf-links).

link, *sb.*^{2} Add: **1. e.** *to let out the links,* to act with more power, to put more into something.

1839 *Spirit of Times* 6 Apr. 54/2 The horses came to the post... At this time Oscar began to let out a few additional links, and with a desperate rush parted company with Dandy, and won the heat handily. **1868** H. WOODRUFF *Trotting Horse* xxxiv. 282 Lancet..in the third heat, let out the links in such a manner that he trotted it in 2 m. 25½ s. **1880** P. H. BURNETT *Recoll. Old Pioneer* 110 [The buffaloes] let out a few more links, and ran much faster. **1942** *Dict. Amer. Eng.* III. 1429/1 *To let out links*, to make increased exertion or effort.

2. c. (Later examples.) Also *links of love*; (dial.) *link-hide, -meat.*

a **1825** R. FORBY *Vocab. E. Anglia* (1830) II. 197 *Link*, ..a sausage... We call two together a *latch of links*. In some other counties, a far more correct expression is used, 'a *link* of sausages'. **1869** R. B. PEACOCK *Gloss. Lonsdale* 51/2 *Links*, black puddings. **1891** 'H. HALIBURTON' *Ochil Idylls* 133 An' links o' puddin's, black to see, An' yowe-milk kebbuck. **1895** W. RYE *Gloss. E. Anglia* 129 *Link hides*, sausage skins, the intestines of a pig prepared and stuffed... *Link-meat*, mince-meat. **1922** JOYCE *Ulysses* 58 Shiny links packed with forcemeat fed his gaze. **1942** *Weekly Telegraph* (Sheffield) 28 Nov. 10/1 A war-time member of the naval service sends the following glossary, ..*links of love*, sausages. **1962** GRANVILLE *Dict. Sailors' Slang* 71 *Links of love*, sausages. Cf. *Bags of Mystery* and *Mystery Torpedoes*.

3. a. (Later examples.)

1905 H. W. NEVINSON *Bks. & Personalities* 172 Link by link from its small beginning we see the fateful chain of character wrought out. **1928** *New Ventures in Broadcasting* (B.B.C.) iv. 36 A link might be established with local groups. *Ibid.* App. B. 104 There is a very close link between the broadcasting company 'Ravag' and the Vienna Society for Popular Education. **1948** *Internat. Road Federation London Bull.* July–Dec. 9/1 When that is done the first link in the United States of Europe will have been forged. **1968** *Times* 19 Feb. 6/6 The contrast between most backbench speakers and the highly professional commentators who did the links was sharp. **1975** *Sunday Times* 23 Feb. 15/3 The major Press conference announcing the link between the kidnapping and the Dudley shooting produced..more than 700 lines of inquiry.

e. A means of travel or transport established between two particular places.

1869 *Bradshaw's Railway Manual* XXI. 115 The use of the intervening link from Askerne to Knottingley..is also permanently secured. **1928** *Econ. Geogr.* IV. 221 A river link..occurs between Tura and Tavda... These links are characteristic of undeveloped regions. **1934** *Highways & Bridges* 10 July 4/1 The opening of this important section..will prove..a road link of the greatest value. **1950** *Internat. Road Federation London Bull.* Jan. 10/2 A ferry link will cross Cabot Strait. **1961** *Assessment Highway Requirements S. Wales & Monmouthshire* (British Road Federation) 19 It is advised that the link between Haverfordwest..and Milford Haven..should be widened to provide a single 3-lane carriageway. **1975** *Vogue* 1 Mar. 139/2 (Advt.), Air-link services via Barcelona, Genoa, Marseilles.

f. A means of telecommunication established between two particular points.

1911 *World's Work* XVIII. 578/2 Signals had been flashed through the air from Canada to Great Britain and ..the Atlantic was spanned by a new and invisible link. **1926** *Encycl. Brit.* III. 1047/2 The superheterodyne method..is sometimes used for the 'wireless link' between studio and transmitting station in place of the land-line. **1928** *Daily Tel.* 23 Oct. 8/3 President Coolidge, speaking over the radio-link between White House and the workshop of the great inventor, lauded Mr. Edison as the embodiment of the finest traditions of American citizenship. **1957** *B.B.C. Handbk.* 59 The vision signals from remote outside broadcast points are carried back to the main television network by BBC microwave or VHF radio links. **1962** A. NISBETT *Technique Sound Studio* i. 18 The links between the various centres may be landlines or radio links. **1964** J. K. S. JOWETT in F. J. D. Taylor *Goonhilly Project* 2 A broadband link to the inland network..is used for demonstration purposes—in particular, transatlantic interchange of television programmes. **1972** *Sci. Amer.* Feb. 15/1 Microwaves do not bend with the curvature of the earth, so that for long links it is necessary to use repeaters that receive, amplify and retransmit the signal.

g. [tr. Russ. *zvenó*.] The name of a small labour unit on a collective farm in the U.S.S.R. Hence *link leader*; **link system,** a system of organizing collective farming into links.

1939 L. E. HUBBARD *Econ. Soviet Agric.* xvii. 165 Each brigade was further subdivided into a number of detachments known as *svena* or links, often consisting of relations or members of families living in close proximity. **1950** *Times* 22 Feb. 3/5 Mr. A. A. Andreev..was said to have encouraged during the past 10 years the 'link' system of labour, which..is less effective..than the..'brigade' system. The article blamed the 'link' system for a shortfall in grain and sugar beet deliveries. **1950** *Soviet Studies* I. 261 Piece-work for individuals and small groups was introduced and the work of the link came to be planned... 'Link', the smaller regular working group of collective farm members (averaging about ten people). Several 'links' make a 'brigade'. *Ibid.* 290 Much benefit was derived from..consultations of link leaders. **1958** R. D. LAIRD *Collective Farming Russ.* IV. ix. 125 As a result of the link system, labor discipline amounted to a major problem. *Ibid.* xi. 154 The brigade leader has a much greater opportunity to effect 'labor-discipline' than did the link leader. **1965** *Economist* 18 Dec. 1283/1 The 'links' are a veiled compromise between the American type of large-scale farming and the Soviet collective method.

h. In Hockey and in Association and Rugby Football = *LINKMAN^{2} b (*c*). Also *attrib.*

In some examples not a clearly distinguishable technical term.

1958 PELMEAR & MORPURGO *Rugby Football* VIII. 319 Next came the innovation of the stand-off half, thereby making two links. **1962** G. GREEN in B. Glanville *Footballer's Compan.* II. 209 Didi, floating about mysteriously in midfield, was always the master link. **1963** *Rugby World* June 24/3 Which is preferable—the fly-half as a link or as a tactical general and spearhead in attack? *Ibid.* 25/2 Neither..is primarily in the 'link' category. **1966** *Hockey Coaching* (Hockey Assoc.) II. 111 The half-back line is the link between the forwards and backs. **1969** B. JAMES *England v. Scotland* x. 233 The superiority of Baxter and Law, the Scottish midfield link players, over their English counterparts. **1970** *Cape Times* 28 Oct. 26/3 Finch has improved considerably since he was moved to right-back after filling the left-back and link positions. **1971** *Times* 15 Feb. 9/1 Rest were handicapped by Purdy, playing at link, with a hand which became increasingly painful.

7. link buttons, a pair of buttons linked by a thread, etc.; **link road,** a road serving to link two or more major roads or centres; **link rod,** (*a*) a rod which joins the levers on the steered stub axles of a motor vehicle; (*b*) each of the rods which connect pistons to wrist pins on the master rod in a radial internal-combustion engine; **link-verb** = COPULA 1; **link-word,** any part of speech performing a linking function.

[**1834** E. W. BRAYLEY *Graphic & Hist. Illustrator* 125 Linked Cloak Buttons.., of silver, and exactly alike.] **1895** *Montgomery Ward Catal.* 170 All our cuff buttons, except link buttons, have patent lever backs. *Ibid.*, (*caption*) Gold filled, engraved link buttons... $1.10. **1964** *McCall's Sewing* ii. 30/2 *Link buttons*, two flat buttons held together with several threads covered with blanket stitches. Used as cuff links. **1934** *Highways & Bridges* 24 July 5/2 New link road from the Bedford–Hitchin road..to the Bedford–Luton road;..a 60 ft. link road from the Bedford–Ampthill road..to the Luton road. **1948** T. SHARP *Oxf. Replanned* 9 The construction of the new Southern By-pass and the important link-road approximately along the line to Roman Way will make it even better for industrial purposes. **1961** *Assessment Highway Requirements S. Wales & Monmouthshire* (British Road Federation) 18 A similar problem exists on the link road between Treharris and Cardiff. **1970** *Milestones* Spring 35/1 A..link road from the M23 to the A23 near Gatwick airport will start from a roundabout over the motorway at Burstow. **1972** *Times* 26 Oct. 3/1 It was the eighth of 32 spans that make up the M4 link road bridge. **1925** W. DEEPING *Sorrell & Son* xv. 137 The driver of the lorry..was..repeating the same words over and over again... 'The bloomin' link-rod dropped. I can't think 'ow it came to 'appen. Just when they was passin' me—too. The bloomin' link-rod.' **1928** A. L. DYKE *Aircraft Engine Instructor* ii. 14 The master rod connects to the top or No. 1 piston. The other eight pistons are connected to the eight link rods, the other ends of which bear against bronze bushings on the knuckle pins. **1929** H. T. RUTTER *Mod. Motors* II. ix. 333 (*caption*) Front axle of Daimler, showing link rod. **1946** J. W. VALE *Aviation Mechanic's Engine Manual* i. 16 The master rod forms a bearing on the main crankpin and the remaining

link rods form a bearing on the knuckle pin arrangement of the master rod assembly. **1970** K. Ball *Fiat 600, 600D Autobook* ix. 108/1 Remove the cotter pins from the nuts securing the head pins of both link rod and nearside track rod. **1892** H. Sweet *New Eng. Gram.* I. 94 We call such verbs *link-verbs*, because they serve to connect the predicate with its subject. *To be* is a pure link-verb, that is, a pure form-word, devoid of independent meaning. **1933** O. Jespersen *Essent. Eng. Gram.* (1939) xiii. 126 It..serves to connect this with the subject as what is technically termed a *copula* or *link-verb*. **1963** F. T. Visser *Hist. Syntax* I. iii. 191 Link-verbs like *to abide*..differ from the link-verb *to be* in that their original meaning is not entirely lost. **1871** Link-word [in Dict.]. **1892** H. Sweet *New Eng. Gram.* I. 95 Other link-words, while having the same grammatical function of connecting subject and predicate, have also definite meanings of their own. **1947** W. S. Allen *Living Eng. Struct.* 235 'Who', 'what', 'which',..etc., are very important as link-words. **1968** *Brit. Med. Bull.* XXIV. 200/2 The computer compiles lists of the words used, and nouns, qualifying words and 'link' words can be sorted out by human intervention before retrieval programs are written.

link, *v.*[1] Add: **1. a.** (Later examples.)

1928 *New Ventures in Broadcasting* (B.B.C.) iv. 31 The aim of the B.B.C. is to link together the various national systems for the benefit of the Empire. **1935** R. C. Woodthorpe *Shadow on Downs* ix. 237 Men began to put up pillars of concrete and link them easily by girders of steel. **1959** *Science* 16 Oct. 954/3 Design effort must be directed toward ensuring that records can be linked in spite of such discrepancies. **1962** K. W. Gatland *Astronautics in Sixties* xi. 344 One proposed method of linking two vehicles in orbit has been outlined.

b. (Later examples.)

1962 *B.B.C. Handbk.* 47 All these studios outside London..can be linked into the network at short notice. **1968** *Globe & Mail* (Toronto) 17 Feb. B4 One of Mercantile's selling points, particularly to the Canadian export–import community, is that we can link into the Citibank international system. **1969** L. Jensen in J. N. Rosenau *Linkage Politics* v. x. 311 How a state links itself with the external environment depends upon what it believes will maximize its power.

2. Also followed by *together*.

1922 Joyce *Ulysses* 77 Those two sluts..linked together in the rain. **1962** K. W. Gatland *Astronautics in Sixties* xi. 341 The ability of two vehicles to match speed and link together in orbit.

3. a. *to link up*, to connect, combine, join *up*. *trans.* **1897** *Geogr. Jrnl.* IX. 364 The mouth of the valley ..which I visited for the purpose of linking up the rough survey Garwood and I made. **1927** E. O'Neill *Marco Millions* II. ii. 45 Their necks, waists, and right ankles linked up by chains. **1942** *R.A.F. Jrnl.* 2 May 11 Efforts are being made to link up other countries. **1942** *Tee Emm* (Air Ministry) II. 68 The fundamental method which links up all the information obtained.

intr. **1915** H. G. Wells *Boon* 211 Every one with ideas ..had to refer to that doctrinal core, had to link up to it. **1925** A. S. M. Hutchinson *One Increasing Purpose* I. xxiv. 147 Did I tell you that or has its connection with what you said only linked up in me since we parted? **1929** *Radio Times* 8 Nov. 393/3 Music lines through Belgium to the whole of Germany..are envisaged for..1930, while it may also be possible to link up to Scandinavia through Hamburg. **1974** 'E. Lathen' *Sweet & Low* xxiii. 217 The Russians and the Americans linked up in space... Every radio in New York was tuned to that docking.

b. *to link up with* (used as in sense 3 a): (*a*) in general contexts.

1899 E. G. White *Testimonies for Church* (1904) VIII. 188 You were willing to link up with them if they would second your propositions. **1903** *Studio* XXVIII. 159/1 To discuss the efforts of the lesser known men who link up the painters of 1830 with those of 1870. **1912** *Q. Rev.* July 231 The limit is entirely a question of alighting—a problem linked up with 'variable speed' aeroplanes. **1915** H. G. Wells *Boon* 174 Here is the sort of thing that I invite the intelligent reader to link up if he can with the very natural phenomenon of [etc.]. **1922** Joyce *Ulysses* 385 Our grandam, which we are linked up with by successive anastomosis of navelcords. **1928** *Sweet Shop* Nov. 6/3 The display man..should link up his shop with the advertisement. **1930** *Times* 15 Mar. 19/4 Our company has always been linked up with the trade to..South America. **1957** E. Bott *Family & Social Network* viii. 217 Many of the individuals and groups to which an urban family is related are not linked up with one another. **1967** E. Short *Embroidery & Fabric Collage* iii. 78 Napkins, teacosies, etc., can be designed to link up with the tablecloth or mats.

(*b*) By some means of transport or system of communication.

1907 *Jrnl. Soc. Arts* LV. 374/1 The linking up of railway stations with outlying country districts by means of mechanically propelled road vehicles. **1909** *Chambers's Jrnl.* XII. 658/1 It is freely mooted that Berlin and Munich will also be linked-up with this system [of airships]. **1910** *Ibid.* XIII. 329/1 Switches linked it [*sc.* a monorail system] up with other lengths of line. **1934** *Highways & Bridges* 24 July 4/4 A new road..would be needed..to link up with the main road. **1937** *Discovery* May 163/2 The network of air lines which now links up the United States with Central and South America. **1961** *Assessment Highway Requirements S. Wales & Monmouthshire* (British Road Federation) 3 Wasting money on local improvements which will not in the end link up with an overall system. *Ibid.* 16 It should link up with the bypass there.

‖ **link** (liŋk), *a.* [Yiddish, f. G. *link* left, left-handed, clumsy.] Not pious, not orthodox (in religion).

1889 *Referee* 3 Feb. 2/3 'Dolly', who was a Jewess, but one who was link rather than froom, was about forty years old. **1892** I. Zangwill *Childr. Ghetto* II. 90 'Suppose,' she said slowly, 'I wanted to marry a Christian?..if I was to marry a very *link* Jew, you'd think it almost as bad.' **1907** —— *Ghetto Comedies* ii. 380 But I am so *link* (irreligious).

linkage. Add: (Further examples.) Also, a link; an association or correlation; the process of linking or connecting (see also quots.). Also *attrib.*

1904 *Brit. & Colonial Printer* 10 Mar. 14/2 A linkage system transmits the movement to the slide bars. **1928** A. S. Eddington *Nature Physical World* xiv. 306 If the two structures were identifiable then the atom would involve a complete causal connection of the two types of phenomena. But apparently no such causal linkage exists. **1940** *Chambers's Techn. Dict.* 503/2 *Linkage* (Elec. Eng.), a measure of the product of the magnetic flux passing through a closed electric circuit and the number of turns in the circuit, the unit being one line passing through a circuit having one turn. **1957** *Educational & Psychol. Measurement* XVII. 207 (*title*) Elementary linkage analysis for isolating orthogonal and oblique types and typal relevancies. **1959** B. Higgins *Econ. Devel.* iv. xvi. 405 Any particular investment project may have both 'forward linkage' (may encourage investment in subsequent stages of production) and 'backward linkage' (may encourage investment in earlier stages of production). The task is to find the projects with the greatest *total* linkage. *Ibid.* xvii. 413 Favoring deliberate unbalancing of the economy to maximize the 'linkage' effects of investment. **1959** *Science* CXXX. 954/1 The term *record linkage* has been used to indicate the bringing together of two or more separately recorded pieces of information. **1962** K. W. Gatland *Astronautics in Sixties* xi. 344 Radar.. may be relied upon to achieve linkage of the spacecraft. **1962** *Which? Car Suppl.* Oct. 143/1 Modified carburettor and linkage to give smoother operation. **1963** F. W. Frey in L. W. Pye *Communications & Political Devel.* xvii. 301 The ratio of the number of existing power linkages..to the number of theoretically possible linkages. **1969** J. N. Rosenau (*title*) Linkage politics. **1970** *Nature* 24 Oct. 387/2 There follows a discussion of the linkages between population growth and food supplies.

b. *Genetics.* (An) association between characters in inheritance, such that if one parent has a pair of characters, there is a probability greater than 50% that any offspring inheriting one of the characters will also inherit the other, which effect is due to the two characters being controlled by alleles located on the same chromosome; formerly called (*gametic*) *coupling* (*coupling *vbl. sb.* 6 e); also, the amount or degree of this association (varying between 50% and 100%). Also *attrib.*

1912 *Biol. Bull.* XXIII. 175 There are no wingless black flies in the F_2 generation, which the Mendelian expectation calls for. Their absence can only be explained by strong linkage of the yellow factor and the factor for wings. *Ibid.* 178 There are actually 1,858 long grey flies to 916 long black, or a ratio of 2 to 1. This is the linkage ratio when two strongly or completely linked factors are concerned. **1915** T. H. Morgan et al. *Mechanism Mendelian Heredity* iii. 58 In the case of yellow and white just given the linkage between the two factors is very strong. **1928** *Hereditas* X. 126 The linkages P_1–V and B–V have been reported by Wellensiek. **1940** *Chambers's Techn. Dict.* 503/2 *Linkage group*, a group of hereditary characteristics which remain associated with one another through a number of generations. *Ibid.* 504/1 *Linkage map*, a diagram showing the position of the genes in a chromosome or group of chromosomes. **1958** *Oxf. Univ. Gaz.* 23 Apr. 892 Genetic investigations on mice with special reference to evolutionary processes and linkage. **1959** *Listener* 3 Dec. 967/1 We shall need to know how many chromosomes there are, and what may be the importance of the phenomenon called 'linkage' in keeping the genes on one chromosome together. **1970** Ambrose & Easty *Cell Biol.* x. 339 The genes [of *Drosophila*] fell into four linkage groups, which corresponded with the haploid number of four chromosomes. *Ibid.* 340 However far apart two genes are,..they will never show less than 50 per cent linkage due to multiple cross-overs.

linked, *ppl. a.* Add: **a.** (Later examples.)

1966 *Punch* 5 Oct. 506/2 Tiny terrace houses are now considered acceptable, at £12,000 to £20,000 a time, because they are called 'Town' or 'Linked' housing. **1970** P. Laurie *Scotland Yard* v. 123 Some traffic-light systems, like the linked set in Oxford Street, are extremely complicated.

c. Of industries: allied to and dependent on one another.

1942 S. Florence in H. B. Newbold *Industry & Rural Life* ii. 43 Certain industries may be linked to other industries..and all the linked industries would have to be dispersed together... An instance of such a complex of linked industries is found in Birmingham. **1961** Estall & Buchanan *Industr. Activity & Econ. Geogr.* v. 108 'Linked' or related industries often require similar types of labour skills... A further advantage is the easy interchange of materials and products between the linked establishments. **1961** E. A. Powdrill *Vocab. Land Planning* iv. 77 They [*sc.* factories] must be..near some other industry providing supplies or markets (i.e., 'linked').

linkedness (li·ŋktnės). [f. Linked *ppl. a.*] Interconnection.

1908 E. V. Lucas *Over Bemerton's* xiv. 137 (*heading*) The linkedness of life is illustrated.

linking, *vbl. sb.* Add: (Later examples.)

1929 C. J. Friedrich *Alfred Weber's Theory of Location of Industries* vi. 206 The connection is based..upon the linking of the market of the one with the other. **1957** E. Bott *Family & Social Network* iv. 99 Marriage becomes a linking of kin groups rather than..a union between individuals. **1960** J. H. Jones in E. Davies *Roads* ii. 26 Linking is the interconnection of two or more traffic signals in such a manner that the beginning of the green period at one signal is related to that of the previous signal.

Also **linking-up.**

1908 *Westm. Gaz.* 19 Nov. 10/4 The 'linking-up' Bill.. The process provided for by the [Electricity Supply] bill is known as 'linking-up'. **1909** *Daily Chron.* 19 Feb. 6/5 The increase in the traffic was..the natural result of the linking-up policy adopted. **1923** J. S. Huxley *Ess. Biologist* iv. 160 This first linking-up of sex with mind produced, eventually, a large proportion of the beauty of the organic world. **1934** *Highways & Bridges* 26 June 11/3 A 'Seven-Province Program' for the linking up of 13,670 miles of road. **1958** *Britannica Bk. of Year* 213/1 This linking-up was welcomed by delegates. **1972** *Radio Times* 7 Dec. 6/1 That's the date which has been set for the linking up in space of a Russian Soyuz with an American Apollo.

linking, *ppl. a.* Add: *spec.* **b.** *Gram.* = Copulative *a.* 1. Also *linking verb*.

1935 G. O. Curme *Parts of Speech* iv. 66 *Linking verbs*...The copula..performs..the function of announcing the predicate... Its use spread because there was an absolute need of such a linking word. **1952** A. H. Marckwardt *Introd. Eng. Lang.* ii. 115 Adjectives may also be..separated from the nouns they modify by a linking or copulative verb. **1967** W. N. Francis *Eng. Lang.* ii. 58 The construction is called *linking* or *copulative*... The following are typical linking constructions. **1972** R. Quirk et al. *Gram. Contemp. Eng.* xii. 820 The verb in sentences with subject complement is a 'copula' (or linking verb), which of itself has little meaning but functions as a link between the complement and subject.

c. *spec.* in *Broadcasting* and *Cinemat.*: providing continuity between programmes, scenes, etc., as music, camera shots, commentary.

1941 *B.B.C. Gloss. Broadcasting Terms* 17 *Linking Material*, words or music forming part of a continuity structure. **1960** N. Kneale *Quatermass & Pit* ii. 63 Fade in linking music. **1962** A. Nisbett *Technique Sound Studio* vii. 129 Trimming linking music to length. *Ibid.* viii. 136 Linking narration will..be necessary. **1967** *Listener* 6 Apr. 466/3 All the undeniably pretty pictures in the outdoor location and linking shots cannot breathe life into them.

d. *linking r*: a letter r in word-final position that is normally pronounced before a following vowel but is silent before a following consonant (as in *far, far away*).

1950 J. S. Kenyon *Amer. Pronunc.* (ed. 10) 164 Observe that linking *r* is the use between words of an *r* that is spelt and was formerly pronounced. *Ibid.* 165 Linking *r* is sometimes omitted in Southern British. **1956** D. Jones *Outl. Eng. Phonetics* (ed. 8) xxi. 196 When a word ending with the letter *r* is immediately followed by a word beginning with a vowel, then a *r*-sound..is usually inserted in the pronunciation... *r* inserted in this way is called 'linking *r*'.

li·nkman[2]. Also **link man.** [f. Link *sb.*[2] + Man *sb.*[1]] A person serving as a link between groups of people, etc.

Quot. 1909 prob. represents an extended use of Linkman (in Dict.).

1909 J. R. Ware *Passing Eng.* 168 *Linkman* (*W. London*), general servant about kitchen or yard. **1918** *Linkman* Apr. 1 (*title*) The Linkman—a literary and artistic quarterly review of congenial interests. **1969** *Guardian* 29 July 5/5 He is to..run an advice centre for residents, acting as a day-to-day 'link man' between the people and the available social and welfare services. **1972** *Where* May/June 150/3 We need a scheme which..makes Governors better linkmen between the school and their community. **1972** *Oxford Times* 20 Oct. 24/4 (*heading*) Social services Linkman. *Ibid.*, He will act as linkman between the department and volunteers. **1973** *Times* 20 Oct. 2/3 Mr Heaton, in his closing speech, claimed the prosecution had changed their allegations concerning his role in the burglary from perpetrator of the crime to link man and alibi for Miss Dugdale.

b. *spec.* (*a*) a commissionaire; (*b*) in Broadcasting, a person providing continuity in a radio or television programme consisting of several items; (*c*) in Hockey and Association Football, a player in any of the mid-field positions.

Sense (*a*) is probably an extended use of Linkman (in Dict.).

1939 H. Hodge *Cab, Sir?* xv. 222 A commissionaire is still a linkman to us. **1947** *Gloss. Technical Theatr. Terms* (Strand Electr. & Engin. Co.) 20 *Link men*, staff engaged at the Entrances and Exits of the theatre to pass the public to and from the street. **1960** *Listener* 23 June 1114/1, I must enter a protest against commentators, interviewers, announcers, link-men..and all the glorious company of contemporary communications. **1963** *Times* 25 May 3/6 McLintock is a foil and Gibson the link man. **1965** *Daily Express* 13 Aug. 15/5 Linkmen. 'They have to sort out the initial problems in defence,' said Wade, 'and then offer themselves as the focus for a pass from defence before going forward in supporting roles to the attack.' **1966** *Observer* 16 Oct. 23/5 There will be little change of format in the 26-week run. No chat, no singing, no dancing. No 'linkman' saying 'good evening' and 'goodnight'. **1968** K. Bird *Smash Glass Image* v. 59 One of my qualities as newsreader and linkman was that I remained cool in a crisis. **1968** *Listener* 10 Oct. 469/3 They seemed much more like linkmen waiting for tips outside an expensive hotel than dangerous and purposeful revolutionaries. **1970** *F.A. News* Apr. 340/1 In the days before 'sweepers' and 'link men', Clayton was the ideal old-type 'dual-purpose' wing half. **1974** *Listener* 10 Jan. 58/3 'Well.. can you answer very briefly..is Britain really on the edge

of disaster?'.. Timings, for linkmen, are of course inexorable.

Link Trainer (li·ŋk trē̆i·nəɪ). [f. Edward *Link*, its American inventor.] A flight simulator on which pilots are trained. Also *ellipt.* as **Link.**

1937 *Flight* 28 Oct. 416/2 Practice with a Link Trainer invariably results in a light touch upon the controls of a real aircraft whether flying blind or not. **1939** *War Illustr.* 4 Nov. 243 An ingenious apparatus used in the training of R.A.F. pilots is the Link Trainer. **1940** *Flight* 26 Dec. 548/2 After Link Trainer work, dual instruction in the air in turns, landings and spins, and ground instruction in parachutes, the pupil goes on his first solo. **1942** *R.A.F. Jrnl.* 18 Apr. 3 The lessons you learned on the Link Won't help you evade a Gremlin. **1943** *Ibid.* Aug. 36 Link Trainer Instructor....*Group* I. **1945** *Tee Emm* (Air *Ministry*) V. 41 Here's a nice little Link Trainer exercise. **1952** *New Biol.* XIII. 51 In some respects this apparatus resembled the Link Trainer, but for a number of reasons it was constructed so that, unlike the Link, it remained stationary. **1960** C. H. GIBBS-SMITH *Aeroplane* 299 *Link Trainer*, a synthetic training device, comprising a hooded cockpit, for training in instrument flying, radio aids, etc.

link-up (li·ŋk,ʌp). Also **linkup, link up.** [f. LINK *v.*[1]] The act or result of linking up; *spec.* (*a*) of troops, or in a military context; (*b*) of spacecraft.

1945 H. NICOLSON *Let.* 29 Apr. (1967) 452 You can imagine what an exhilarating week this has been. The surrounding of Berlin; the link-up with the Russian armies. **1945** W. S. CHURCHILL *Victory* (1946) 121 Russian and American troops made a link-up at Torgau. **1952** C. S. LEWIS *Let.* 2 Oct. (1966) 244 Much later..came the link-up between his.. interest in *Arthuriana* and a new interest in Byzantium. **1958** *Time* (Atlantic ed.) 26 May 20/3 Gaillard had moved to prevent any link-up between the insurgents in Algeria and their sympathizers in France. **1965** *New Scientist* 23 Dec. 852/2 In the technique used in the *Gemini* link-up, *Gemini VI* was first placed in an orbit which was.. elliptical. **1968** K. BIRD *Smash Glass Image* v. 64 What.. was the link-up between all these events and what had happened before I came away. **1969** *Daily Tel.* 17 Jan. 22 (*caption*) The link-up between the two Russian manned space-craft took place 150 miles above the earth yesterday. **1970** *Globe & Mail* (Toronto) 26 Sept. 10/3 In the Cambodian fighting, less than a mile had to be spanned for a linkup of Government forces. **1972** *Radio Times* 7 Dec. 6/3 It would be nice to believe that the space link-up is co-operation for co-operation's sake. **1973** D. FRANCIS *Slay-Ride* vii. 78 A world-wide racing investigatory link-up, something along the lines of Interpol.

lin-lan-lone. (Later example.)

1954 J. BETJEMAN *Few Late Chrysanthemums* 73 The dear old village! *Lin-lan-lone* the bells (Which should be six) ring over hills and dells.

linn[2]**.** (Later U.S. examples. Cf. *LYNN.)

1860 M. CURTIS *Woody Plants N. Carolina* 79 Southern Linn. (*T[ilia] pubescens*, Ait.)—This is confined to the Lower Districts of the Southern States. **1884** C. S. SARGENT *Rep. Forests N. Amer.* 514 A good deal of black cherry, lin, and locust.

lino[2] (ləɪ·no), colloq. abbrev. of LINOLEUM. Also **linoed, lino'd** *adj.*, covered with linoleum.

1907 C. E. DAWSON in *Process Engravers' Monthly* Jan. 15, I at last happened upon some samples of cork lino. **1920** *Glasgow Herald* 10 Apr. 4 The Earl caught the gloves, but the hat fell on the lino. **1933** R. C. HUTCHINSON *Unforgotten Prisoner* III. xiv. 420 He went up the lino'd stairs. **1966** M. PATTEN *Home Making in Colour* 36/2 Lino is easy to lay..and is a good background for rugs and carpets. **1966** J. CHAMIER *Cannonball* iv. 29 The edges of his coat swept papers skidding onto the linoed floor. **1973** P. DICKINSON *Green Gene* ix. 173 The lino-covered staircase. **1973** J. WAINWRIGHT *Pride of Pigs* 120 The usual collection of household goods..rugs, carpets and lino.

lino[3] (ləɪ·no), abbrev. of LINOTYPE.

1907 *Daily Chron.* 3 Dec. 4/4 He gave me a sketch of his paper. It was set up by 'linos'.

linocut (ləɪ·nŏkʌt). [f. LINO(LEUM + CUT *sb.*[2]] A design cut in relief on a block of linoleum; a print obtained from this. Hence **lino-cutting** *vbl. sb.*; **lino-cutter**, a person who makes linocuts; also, a tool used in lino-cutting.

1907 C. E. DAWSON in *Process Engravers' Monthly* Jan. 14 (*title*) Lino-cuts. A new method in blockmaking for posters and other bold work. *Ibid.* 16 This work, which I call *lino-cutting*, is..so easy that almost any simple design can be cut double crown size in an evening. *Ibid.* Feb. 28 Old chapbooks..are most usefully suggestive to the lino-cutter. **1919** R. FRY *Let.* 19 Nov. (1972) II. 471 Get Pamela to show you the lino-cut she did of a swan. **1927** C. FLIGHT *Lino-Cuts* iii. 19 The chief difficulties in lino-cut colour printing lie..in the arrangement of the design in form and colour. **1948** H. MISSINGHAM *Student's Guide Commercial Art* 71 *No. 5 lino cutter*, a sharp steel blade on a pen-nib shank, which can either be used in the normal lino tool handle or in a penholder. **1956** J. SYMONS *Paper Chase* xvii. 137 Round the walls were a variety of paintings ranging from *collages* to linocuts. **1972** J. MANN *Mrs Knox's Profession* xv. 116 One of those triangular blades screwed into a thick handle—a lino cutter. **1973** *Times* 6 Oct. 14/7 Miss Enid Lawrence..was a versatile artist, painter, lino-cutter... Her name is particularly associated with that of Claude Flight and the development of the lino-cut.

Linofilm (ləɪ·nŏfilm). *Printing.* [= *line o' film*, after LINOTYPE.] The proprietary name of an electronic photo-composing system. (See quots.) Also *attrib.*

1956 *Trade Marks Jrnl.* 5 Dec. 1212/2 Linofilm... Phototypographic machines and tape perforating machines for use in setting and composing type photographically. Mergenthaler Linotype Company.., Brooklyn, City and State of New York, United States of America; manufacturers. **1961** *Spectator* 14 Apr. 509/3 He referred to..lino-film, and the demarcation problems which must be solved if photo-composing is to continue. **1965** J. MORAN *Composition of Reading Matter* vii. 75 The Linofilm Magnetic-to-Punched Tape Converter accepts magnetic tape from standard computer and data processing equipment, and produced 15-hole Linofilm tape. **1973** S. JENNETT *Making of Bks.* (ed. 5) v. 86 Most electronic photo-composing machines, however, operate from punched tape only about an inch wide, with six to nine levels or rows of perforations..—the Linofilm, taking tape of fifteen levels, is a notable exception.

Linograph[1] (ləɪ·nŏgrɑf). *Printing.* [= *line o'* + -GRAPH, after LINOTYPE.] The proprietary name of an American composing machine which casts type a line at a time.

1913 *Inland Printer* May 240 (Advt.), The Linograph is now ready. **1931** *Brit. Printer* XLIII. 229/1 The author passes in review all the different types such as the Linotype, the Typograph, the Monotype,.. the American Linograph [etc.]. **1965** J. MORAN *Composition of Reading Matter* vi. 59 The Linograph closely resembled the Linotype, but differed in the arrangement of the magazine, which was vertical... The Linograph works were bought by Intertype in 1940.

linography (ləinǫ·grăfi). [f. L. *līn-um* flax (see LINE *sb.*[1]) + -GRAPHY.] (See quots.) Also **linograph**[2], a picture produced by linography.

1888 *Jrnl. Soc. Chem. Industry* VII. 588/1 Linography. This is a name given to photographing on linen or calico, to serve as a basis for painting in oil. **1945** E. EPSTEAN tr. *Eder's Hist. Photogr.* xxxvii. 325 Linography. Photographic reproductions (mostly enlargements) were produced on linen, to be afterwards colored, by a variation of Talbotypy... J. Lüttgens, in Hamburg, states that he used this process in 1856. **1970** *Canad. Antiques Collector* Dec. 26/1 Included in the collection were signed linographs, etchings and posters.

linolenic acid (linŏle·nik, -lī·nik). *Chem.* [tr. G. *linolensäure* (K. Hazura 1887, in *Sitzungsber. d. K. Akad. d. Wissensch.* (*Mat.-Nat. Kl.*) XCV. II. 1055), f. *linolsäure* LINOLEIC *acid* with insertion of *-en* -ENE.] A liquid unsaturated carboxylic acid, $C_{18}H_{30}O_2$, which is found as a glyceride in linseed and most other drying oils: 9,12,15-octadecatrienoic acid.

1887 *Jrnl. Chem. Soc.* LII. 913 The acids from drying oils contain both linolic acid, $C_{18}H_{32}O_2$, and linolenic acid, $C_{18}H_{30}O_2$. **1921** *Ibid.* CXIX. 1307 The product of the action of zinc on linolenic acid hexabromide was a mixture of α- and β-linolenic acids, although only the α-modification occurs naturally. **1951** R. MAYER *Artist's Handbk.* iii. 111 Poppy oil..owes its property of yellowing less than linseed oil to the smaller percentage of linolenic acid it contains. **1969** J. I. ROUTH et al. *Essent. Gen., Org. & Biochem.* xxxiii. 643 Unsaturated fatty acids such as linoleic and linolenic are essential components of cellular lipids that must be obtained in the diet, since they cannot be synthesized by the body.

Hence **linole·nate**, a salt or ester of linolenic acid.

1909 *Jrnl. Chem. Soc.* XCVI. I. 357 In the mixture of esters used about 22% was ethyl α-linolenate. **1950** *Jrnl. Nutrition* XLI. 485 When fed with suboptimum doses of linoleic acid, the resultant activity of the additional linolenate equalled that of linoleate.

Linotype. Substitute for def.: The proprietary name of a composing machine invented by Ottmar Mergenthaler (1854–99) that sets type line by line (see quot. 1892). (Further examples.) Also *attrib.* Hence **li·notyped** *ppl. a.*, of type set in this way; **li·notyper** = LINOTYPIST; **li·notyping** *vbl. sb.*, the process of setting type by the use of this machine.

1892 A. POWELL *Southward's Pract. Printing* (ed. 4) xxxii. 318 The Linotype..sets up not types, but type-matrices, and then, when a line is complete, passes the matrices on to a foundry which forms part of the apparatus, and a full line is cast... Distribution is avoided. The matter once used..is returned to the metal pot and melted ready for fresh work... The advantages of the machine are its great speed and the economy effected by melting instead of distributing. A disadvantage is the fact that.. there is no mode of correction other than to reset the whole line... Still,..the machine has decided merits. It is in use in many newspaper offices. *Ibid.* (Advt.), The result of a contest between four American Composing Machines..showed that on the Linotype the operator averaged 12,250 Ens an Hour, corrected matter. **1896** *Peterson Mag.* VI. 305/1 Stenographers, typewriters, compositors, and linotypers. **1902** A. W. BICKERTON (*title*) The perils of a pioneer: a protest in linotype proof. **1902** *U.S. Census Bull.* No. 242. 73 A new departure in the art of linotyping. **1903** *Stationer, Printer & Fancy Trades' Reg.* 1 Aug. 364/2 At present linotype operators work on piece, that is to say, they are paid according to the work they do. **1908** *Westm. Gaz.* 21 Apr. 7/2 The linotyped calumny of millionaire journalism. **1911** H. S. HARRISON *Queed* vii. 83 The little knot of linotypers and helpers..now listened. **1926** *Brit. Gaz.* 12 May 2/2 The *Thanet Advertiser*, Ramsgate, reports that its linotype operators have returned to work. **1946** A. MONKMAN in H. Whetton *Pract. Printing & Binding* iii. 33/1 As the name implies, the Linotype..is a slug-casting machine. Introduced about 1886 it is now used in practically every newspaper office and also in many general printing offices. **1951** E. PAUL *Springtime in Paris* xi. 211 Comrade Rappaport, a linotype operator from *L'Humanité*. **1963** W. CLOWES *Guide to Printing* iii. 22 The 'Linotype' machine incorporates both keyboard and caster. **1973** S. JENNETT *Making of Bks.* (ed. 5) iv. 68 The product of the Linotype is not a line of separate letters, but a solid metal strip, or 'slug', bearing on one of the long edges the characters that go to make up the whole line. **1974** *Northern Times* (Golspie, Sutherland) 21 June 5/2 His son..was a Linotype Operator on the 'N.T.' [*sc.* Northern Times].

linoxin. Substitute for entry:

linoxyn (linǫ·ksin). *Chem.* [a. Du. *linoxyne* (G. J. Mulder *Scheikundige Verhand. en Onderzoekingen* (1865) IV. I. 120), f. L. *līn-um* flax (see LINE *sb.*[1]): see OXY- and -IN[1].] Any of various gelatinous or resinous substances obtained by oxidation of linseed oil by air.

1876 J. HARLEY *Royle's Man. Materia Med.* (ed. 6) 714 By saponification linseed oil is resolved into glycerin and linoleic acid... This, when exposed in thin layers to the air, gradually increases in weight, and is converted into.. oxylinoleic acid, $C_{16}H_{26}O_5,H_2O$. At 212° it loses water, becomes of a blood-red colour, and forms linoxyn, $C_{32}H_{54}O_{11}$. **1925** *Jrnl. Soc. Chem. Industry* 7 Aug. 407T/2 When linseed oil is exposed for five or six days of warm weather in films so thin as to contain less than 0·05 g. of oil per 100 sq. cm. area, a linoxyn can be obtained from the dried (autoxidised) product having the formula $C_{57}H_{98}O_{20}$. **1969** R. F. LANG tr. *Henglein's Chem. Technol.* 774 Linoleum serves as floor covering and contains as basic materials linoxyn (oxidized linseed oil), cork flour, and resins. **1972** *Materials & Technol.* V. xiii. 439 The insoluble linoxyn is highly cross-linked and polymerised.

linsang. Substitute for first part of def.: A civet-like mammal of the genus *Prionodon*, which includes *P. pardicolor* of south-east Asia and *P. linsang*, found in this region and Sumatra, Java, and Borneo. (Add earlier and later examples.)

1821 T. HARDWICKE in *Trans. Linn. Soc.* XIII. 236 Viverra? Linsang... The general colour of the animal is a yellowish white. **1969** LD. MEDWAY *Wild Mammals Malaya* 91/1 Banded linsang... *Prionodon linsang*... In Malaya widespread on the mainland at all elevations but nowhere common.

Linson (li·nsǫn). The proprietary name of a tough fibrous paper fabric used esp. in bookbinding.

1948 *Trade Marks Jrnl.* 18 Feb. 127/2 Linson... Bookbinding materials. R. & W. Watson Limited,..Renfrewshire; manufacturers. **1952** A. W. LEWIS *Basic Bookbinding* ii. 11 Linson is available in numerous colours and surface finishes. **1957** *B.B.C. Handbook* 248 *Mrs. Dale's Diary*..ordinary edition, 6s. 3d., Linson bound, 3s. 7d. **1963** *Times Lit. Suppl.* 26 Apr. 316/1 Bound in Linson or one of its..equivalents. **1967** J. S. HEWITT-BATES *Bookbinding* (ed. 8) iii. 18 Non-woven materials such as Linson are ideal for school work.

lint[1]**.** Add: **4*.** The material which forms the bulk of the fibres in the cotton boll (cf. *LINTER[1] b), which is separated from the cotton seeds by ginning and which after processing is the ordinary cotton of commerce.

1877 *Encycl. Brit.* VI. 483/1 When this [*sc.* ginning] is done there remains of the bulk, as gathered from the tree, about one-third of clean cotton fit for manufacturing purposes, and two-thirds of seed. The separation of the seed from the lint is accomplished by different methods. **1883** 'MARK TWAIN' *Life on Mississippi* xxxiii. 325 In sixteen hundred pounds crude cotton four hundred are lint, worth, say, ten cents a pound. **1967** SHAW & ECKERSLEY *Cotton* iii. 10 The seed cotton..may be ginned three times but only the 'lint' from the first ginning is used in normal cotton spinning.

5. lint-head *U.S. dial.*, a worker in a cotton mill; (in contemptuous use) a person of whom one disapproves.

1933 E. CALDWELL *God's Little Acre* vii. 108 I'd rather be a God-forsaken lint-head and live in a yellow company house. **1940** C. MCCULLERS *Heart is Lonely Hunter* (1943) II. iv. 128, I would have just been a preacher or a linthead or a salesman. **1969** 'J. MORRIS' *Fever Grass* xvi. 138, I didn't kill that big linthead. *You* did!

linter[1]**.** Add: **b.** *pl.* A product composed of the short downy hairs or 'fuzz' adhering to the cotton seeds (from which it is removed by the linter), which is unsuitable for spinning into yarn and is used as a source of cellulose, etc.

1903 E. A. POSSELT *Cotton Manuf.* I. 49 The fibres, short or long, thus obtained, are technically known as 'Linters' and are delivered by the condenser of the linting machine as a sheet or film. **1904** L. L. LAMBORN *Cottonseed Products* iv. 50 The purpose of delinting is to remove more completely the short fibres which form the 'linters'... The products of delinting are the linters. **1927** T. WOODHOUSE *Artificial Silk* iii. 13 The short fibres from cotton seeds—to which the name of cotton linters has been given —are utilized for the cellulose solutions. **1967** SHAW & ECKERSLEY *Cotton* iii. 11 The 'linters' from the second and third ginning are used in the waste trade. **1972** *Sci. Amer.* Dec. 48/2 The early man-made fibers were essentially recast molecules of cellulose originating in wood fibers or cotton linters (very short fibers). **1974** *Ibid.* Apr. 52/1

Paper..has been and is made from rags, straw, cotton linters, bagasse..and flax.

lintling, var. LINTELLING *vbl. sb.*
1833 J. C. LOUDON *Encycl. Cottage, Farm, & Villa Archit.* 526 The cart-sheds to have a joist..built into the wall at each pillar, and chacked to the lintling beams.

‖ **Linzertorte** (li·ntsəɹtǭɹtə). [G., f. *Linzer* adj., f. *Linz* the name of an Austrian city + *torte* tart.] A kind of tart with a jam filling, decorated on top with strips of pastry in a lattice pattern.
1906 *Mrs. Beeton's Bk. Househ. Managem.* lii. 1542 Linzertorte. (German Gâteau.) **1936** LUCAS & HUME *Au Petit Cordon Bleu* 153 Linzertorte... Place a flan ring on to a baking sheet. Line carefully with the paste, fill with raspberry jam... Cover the top criss-cross with thin strips of paste. **1961** J. HELLER *Catch-22* (1962) xxiv. 249 *Linzer* and *Dobos Torten* from Vienna, *Strudel* from Hungary [etc.]. **1969** H. MACINNES *Salzburg Connection* iv. 47 What chance had she ever had of being taught how to run a house or bake Linzertorte?

lion, *sb.* Add: **10. a.** *lion-king, -limb, -mask, -paw*; **b.** *lion-taming* (examples); **c.** *lion-coloured* adj.; **d.** *lion-faced, -throated* adjs.
1920 E. POUND *Hugh Selwyn Mauberley* 25 The coral isle, the lion-coloured sand. **1964** *Listener* 30 July 163/3 Sun-swept, lion-coloured plains. **1856** C. M. YONGE *Daisy Chain* II. xix. 551 He leant on his lion-faced boy's arm, and walked down to the Minster. **1919** W. S. MAUGHAM *Moon & Sixpence* lv. 242 A look—how shall I describe it?—the books call it lion-faced. **1946** R. GRAVES *Poems 1938–45* 35 The Lion-faced Boy at the Fair. **1971** D. BEATY *Temple Tree* 232 Reincarnation. The new Lion King of Ceylon. **1972** *Times* 29 June 16/4 Their epics extol the 'Lion-king' Sundiata who founded the Manding Empire. **1885** G. M. HOPKINS *Poems* (1918) 62 Why wouldst thou..lay a lionlimb against me? **1906** *Westm. Gaz.* 9 May 8/2 A large vase decorated with lion-masks. **1933** *Burlington Mag.* July 36/1 The cabriole legs with their goats' heads and lion masks. **1934** *Ibid.* Oct. p. xv/2 The tripod terminates in lion-paw feet. **1972** *Country Life* 15 June (Suppl.) 43/2 Regency Rosewood Bookcase with..brass lion paw feet. **1870** O. LOGAN *Before Footlights* 354 After stating that lion-taming was a gift of nature with him. **1944** *Mind* LIII. 162 Others found it [*sc.* welfare] wholly comprehended in trout-fishing and lion-taming. **1927** E. SITWELL *Rustic Elegies* 91 Where two lion-throated fountains fell. **1957** R. CAMPBELL *Coll. Poems* II. 56 From lion-throated blooms ablaze.

11. lion comique *Obs.*, a leading comic singer in a music-hall or the like; **lion dance,** a traditional Chinese dance in which the dancers are masked and costumed to resemble lions; so **lion dancer; lion dog,** also, a dog belonging to one of several breeds resembling miniature lions in colour or type of fur, or once used for hunting in country inhabited by lions; **lion-head,** a variety of goldfish, *Carassius auratus*, having an enlarged head; **lion house,** a building in which lions are kept at a zoo; **lion-hunter** (earlier example); **lion-huntress,** a female 'lion-hunter'; **lion marmoset,** a small Brazilian monkey, *Leontideus rosalia*; = *lion-monkey*, MARIKINA.
1899 BEERBOHM *More* 120 The Lion Comique bawled out..some such crude, conventional ditty. **1927** *Observer* 11 Dec. 8 When did the music-hall die?.. Where is the 'lion comique'..? **1937** *N.Y. Times* 10 Feb. 2 The parades, according to a spokesman from the Chinese Benevolent Association, will take the form of lion dances. **1952** W. EBERHARD *Chinese Festivals* i. 57 The 'lion dance'..we still see in the streets of old Peking—and sometimes even in San Francisco's Chinatown. **1964** *Catal. National Museum Kuala Lumpur* 5/2 (*caption*) Lion dance tableau, authentically North China, is one of several in one main gallery. **1966** D. FORBES *Heart of Malaya* vi. 77 The Boat People of Hong Kong feast..with roast pig, lion dances and boat races on the twenty-third day of the third moon in our month of April. **1968** *Encycl. Brit.* VII. 33/1 In China itself there may be lotus dances, stilt dances, butterfly dances, lion dances (inspired by Buddhist stories from the parts of India where lions are known). **1927** BREDON & MITROPHANOW *Moon Year* xii. 394 Akin to the strolling players are the 'Lion Dancers' who wander from village to village. Each troupe is composed of two or three mountebanks with rude but picturesque properties. **1975** *Times* 17 Feb. 3/3 London's Chinatown in Soho celebrated the Chinese new year yesterday... Lion Dancers..wound and jigged all day around Gerrard Street. **1921** V. W. F. COLLIER *Dogs China & Japan* xii. 183 Tibetan lion-dogs are bred to resemble lions, and they, like the Chinese, appear to be willing to call any shaggy coated dog a lion-dog. **1938** E. C. ASH *New Bk. Dog* x. 430 Tibetan Lhasa Apso... This being the true Tibetan Lion-dog, golden or lion-like colours are preferred. *Ibid.* xi. 466 (*caption*) A Rhodesian Ridgeback (Lion Dog). **1958** *Bk. Dogs* (Nat. Geographic Soc.) 354/2 Ancient ancestors of the Peke were honored dogs of the imperial palace in Peking... At ceremonies two of these Lion Dogs preceded the emperor, two followed. **1971** DANGERFIELD & HOWELL *Internat. Encycl. Dogs* 284/1 Many breeds have been called lion dogs. With the exception of the Rhodesian Ridgeback, these have all been small dogs with a real, or imagined, lion-like aspect. **1928** *Daily Express* 5 July 8 Fancy goldfish can be very expensive... I paid £30 each for a lionhead and an oranda recently. **1972** Y. MATSUI *Goldfish Guide* xi. 176 The premier goldfish is the Ronchū or Lionhead. **1895** C. J. CORNISH *Life at Zoo* 64 The present Lion House, with its fine outdoor summer palaces, and itsi ndoor winter cages..seems to leave nothing to be desired. **1909** *Westm. Gaz.* 30 Jan. 7/1 We had better get them to the lion-house. **1974** *Times* 29 Apr. 10/8 Work to replace the outdated Lion House could not be started. **1829** R. C. SANDS *Writings* (1834) II. 199 During the interval..two lion-hunters..came into the box and introduced themselves. **1828** SCOTT *Jrnl.* 1 July (1941) 271 A professed lion-huntress, who travels the country to rouse the peaceful beasts out of their lair. **1850** THACKERAY in *Punch* 24 Aug. 89 The Lion-Huntress of Belgravia. Being Lady Nimrod's Journal of the Past Season. **1926** A. HUXLEY *Two or Three Graces* 229 The old familiar stories about that famous lion-huntress were being repeated. **1906** *Westm. Gaz.* 19 Feb. 12/2 Here may be seen the beautiful lion marmoset from Brazil. **1936** E. G. BOULENGER *Apes & Monkeys* vii. 195 Of the long-tusked marmosets, two of the most ornate are the 'emperor' and the 'lion'... The lion is one of the most vividly coloured of all mammals, the long silky fur being of a flaming orange hue. **1965** *Amer. Jrnl. Physical Anthropol.* XXIII. 261 (*title*) The skull of the lion marmoset, *Leontideus rosalia* Linnaeus.

lip, *sb.* Add: **1. d.** = EMBOUCHURE 3; the condition or strength of a wind instrumentalist's lips.
1889 in *Cent. Dict.* **1933** *Metronome* July 26 He's got the ideas, but his lip's weak yet. **1960** *Jazz Rev.* Nov. 10 My lip went bad after a year in the Earl Hines band. **1972** *Rolling Stone* 9 Nov. 10/2 Having not played for several months, Miles had lost the eternally fragile trumpeters' lip.

2. *a stiff upper lip* (later examples).
1969 C. BOOKER *Neophiliacs* vi. 134 The tradition of 'stiff upper lip' epics looking back to wartime greatness. **1973** G. GREENE *Honorary Consul* I. i. 11 *Machismo*..the Spanish equivalent of *virtus*..had little to do with English courage or a stiff upper lip. **1973** *Guardian* 10 Feb. 3/3 Stiff upper lip all round on Mrs Gandhi's taunt. **1973** *Times* 24 Dec. 14/4 (*heading*) How the Italians are facing up to austerity with a stiff upper lip.

3. d. A lawyer, esp. a criminal lawyer. *U.S. slang.*
1929 *Sat. Even. Post* 13 Apr. 54/3 A lawyer is a mouthpiece or a shyster or a lip. **1930** *Amer. Mercury* Dec. 456/2 Get a lip for a writ an' I'll lam. **1950** H. E. GOLDIN et al. *Dict. Amer. Underworld Lingo* 127/1 The lip took a hundred skins (dollars) and never showed (appeared) in court.

6. a. (*b*) Freq. in terms of Phonetics, as *lip-action, -closure, -consonant, -position, -protrusion, -rounded* adj., *-rounding, -spreading.*
1933 L. BLOOMFIELD *Lang.* vi. 107 It is relative tenseness, too, which in addition to lip-action, makes the Italian vowels very different from those of English. **1922** O. JESPERSEN *Lang.* 278 That lip-closure which is an essential part of the ordinary [m]. **1867** Lip consonant [see *BACK *a.* 1 c]. **1877** H. SWEET *Handbk. Phonetics* 32 Lip. S.G. *w* in '*wie*', '*wo*' is an example of a pure lip consonant. **1929** *Amer. Speech* IV. 414 The lip position of the Gascon sound was identical with that of the Parisian *b*. **1932** D. JONES *Outl. Eng. Phonetics* (ed. 3) xxi. 177 A correct English ʃ may be acquired by..retracting the tip of the tongue and exaggerating the lip-protrusion. **1921** E. SAPIR *Lang.* viii. 186 In *foti* 'feet' the long *o* was colored by the following *i* to long *ö*, that is, *o* kept its lip-rounded quality. **1910** *Mod. Lang. Rev.* V. 93 The lip-rounding is less energetic. **1950** D. JONES *Phoneme* xxxi. 224 A.. case..for representing the Japanese u by w on the ground that it has less lip-rounding than the European u-sounds. **1964** R. H. ROBINS *Gen. Ling.* 97 The English front vowels are mostly accompanied by lip-spreading. **1964** P. STREVENS in D. Abercrombie et al. *Daniel Jones* 121 Pupils may be exhorted to..'smile a little as you say that', in order to achieve voicing or lip-spreading.

7. lip-brush, a small brush used to apply lipstick; **lip-click,** a clicking noise made with the lips; **lip gloss,** a glossy cosmetic applied to the lips; **lip-line,** the outline of a person's lips; **lip microphone** (see quot. 1941); **lip pencil** (see PENCIL *sb.* 2 c); **lip-print,** the imprint made by a person's lips; **lip-read** *v. trans.* and *intr.*, to apprehend (someone, or what someone says) by observing the movement of the lips; so **lip-reader; lip-rouge,** red cosmetic for the lips; **lip-smacking,** the act of smacking one's lips (see SMACK *v.*² 1); also as *ppl. adj.*; **lip-sync(h), -synchronization** (see quots.); so **lip-sync** *v. intr.*, **lip-synchronized** *ppl. a.*, **lip-syncing** *vbl. sb.*
1947 *Glamour* Aug. 96 If you're aiming for makeup perfection..you'll naturally want the finest in lipbrushes. **1958** Lipbrush [see *AEROSOL 2]. **1960** *News Chron.* 21 June 6/2 Make the most of the mouth one has... This can only be done skilfully with a lip-brush. **1933** E. SITWELL *Eng. Eccentrics* 18 The lip-clicks of the earthworms which are, it may be, amongst the earliest origins of our language. **1939–40** *Army & Navy Stores Catal.* 437/1 Max Factor...Lip gloss—2/6. **1972** *Country Life* 4 May 1127/3, I have now come to..like lip gloss... These shiny lip colours have several good uses. You can use them alone for a pale, glossy look or you can put them over a lipstick to add gloss. **1972** *Vogue* June Special 90 Blueberry Wine Lipstick matching Lip Gloss. **1951** W. SANSOM *Face of Innocence* ii. 21 A smell of coffee and cigars blended with the black perfume and the red lipline of Eve's presence. **1960** *Farmer & Stockbreeder* 16 Feb. Suppl. 5/3 It is seldom the young who apply their lipstick badly. Their natural lip-line is still clear. **1941** *B.B.C. Gloss. Broadcasting Terms* 17 *Lip microphone*, type of ribbon microphone designed to be held close to the mouth and to eliminate extraneous sounds reaching it from either side. **1949** *Electronic Engin.* XXI. 354 There will be a commentator's box equipped with a lip microphone. **1904** Lip pencil [see s.v. PENCIL *sb.* 2 c]. **1948** *Woman & Beauty* Dec. 57 (*caption*) One of the new Gala lip pencils. **1934** 'J. RHODE' *Poison for One* II. ii. 92 Has it [*sc.* a drinking-glass] been examined for what I may term lip-prints? **1970** *New Scientist* 3 Sept. 455/2 They have collected lip prints from 280 people, using a technique akin to finger printing. **1892** *Strand Mag.* Mar. 250/2 He..lip read the advocates who examined him. *Ibid.* 251/1 He would like to test the lad's ability to speak, and to lip read. **1906** *Chambers's Jrnl.* 29 Dec. 80/1 An arithmetic class where questions..were not only heard (or, rather, lip-read) but answered. **1946** *Sat. Even. Post* 9 Mar. 10/2 Tele addicts contend they see football better than from any seat in the stadium, and can lip-read the signals. **1962** A. NISBETT *Technique Sound Studio* x. 170 My deaf friend preferred to switch it off and lip-read. **1973** C. CARFAX *Sleeping Salamander* vii. 66 Watching, I lipread rather than heard his words. **1912** *Strand Mag.* Jan. 15/1 In those days this youthful lip-reader had no name for her gift of seeing speech. **1941** V. WOOLF *Between Acts* 242 There was Dodge, the lip reader,..a seeker like her after hidden faces. **1974** R. C. DENNIS *Conversations with Corpse* ii. 10 A pity you aren't a lip reader. **1926** MAINES & GRANT *Wise-Crack Dict.* 11/1 *Leave a good impression*, use lots of lip rouge. **1930** J. DOS PASSOS *42nd Parallel* I. 76 She smeared liprouge on his nose. **1947** N. LINDSAY *Halfway to Anywhere* vii. 124 With lip smacking over swigs of cooking sherry, it was felt that luxury could go no farther. **1958** [see *CAPSULIZE *v.*]. **1966** AUDEN *About House* 21 Lip-smacking Imps of mawk and hooey. **1961** A. BERKMAN *Singers' Gloss. Show Business* 55 *Lip sync*, to move the lips in synchronization with a recorded sound; to pantomime with a recording. **1970** M. TORMÉ *Other Side of Rainbow* (1971) iii. 50 A decision was made to prerecord one of Judy's songs, which she would lip-sync on the show. While lip-syncing is anathema to most singers, it was Judy's particular teacup. **1972** *Cinema Rising* Aug. 2/2 A feature-length Western, and a lip-synch musical. **1959** W. S. SHARPS *Dict. Cinematogr.* 107/1 *Lip synchronization.* Abbreviated to Lip sync. The recording of sound, usually at the same time as its associated picture, so that on projection of the completed film, the words uttered synchronize exactly with the performer's lip movements as shown in the picture. **1957** MANVELL & HUNTLEY *Technique Film Music* ii. 27 *The Jazz Singer*..introduced in certain sequences lip-synchronized singing by Al Jolson.

lip, *v.*¹ Add: **2. c.** To insult, abuse, be impudent to (someone). *dial.* or *colloq.*
1898 B. KIRKBY *Lakeland Words* 93 He lipt mi rarely. **1902** *Eng. Dial. Dict.* III. 618/1 He's lipt mi as Ah was never lipt afoor. **1941** *Penguin New Writing* III. 65 Young Ernie was lippin' me just before you come in. **1972** A. DRAPER *Death Penalty* ii. 18 If anyone lips you, just swallow it.

lipase (li·pēⁱz, -s). *Biochem.* [a. F. *lipase* (A. A. M. Hanriot 1896, in *Compt. Rend.* CXXIII. 753), f. Gr. λίπ-ος fat: see *-ASE.] Any enzyme which catalyses the hydrolysis of fats and oils to fatty acids and alcohols; *esp.* one present in the pancreatic juice.
1897 *Jrnl. Chem. Soc.* LXXII. II. 150 The active enzyme, for which the name *lipase* is suggested, is also capable of acting..on the natural oils and fats. **1946** *Nature* 14 Sept. 375/1 It thus appears that there are at least two distinctly different enzymes (or enzyme systems) present in these glycerol extracts: (1) a lipase, hydrolysing esters of glycerol..; and (2) an esterase, hydrolysing esters of lower alcohols than glycerol. **1955** *Sci. Amer.* Oct. 70/2 Some enzymes (e.g., amylase and lipase) work in the digestive system, breaking up the crude food material into simpler parts which can be transported by the bloodstream. **1970** R. W. MCGILVERY *Biochem.* xvi. 342 The globule of stored triglyceride within an adipose tissue cell is not attacked by lipoprotein lipase... Breakdown of the stored material depends on the action of other lipases within the cell.

lipe, var. *LYPE.

lipid (li·pid). *Biochem.* Also **-ide** (-əid). [a. F. *lipide* (G. Bertrand 1923, in *Bull. de la Soc. de Chim. biol.* V. 102), f. Gr. λίπ-ος fat: see -IDE.

For the origin of the now more common form *lipid* see *Chem. & Engin. News* (1952) 5 May 1910.]

1. Any of the large group of fats and fat-like compounds which occur in living organisms and are characteristically soluble in certain organic solvents but only sparingly soluble in water; it is generally taken to include esters of higher aliphatic acids, together with various groups of related and derived compounds, and freq. also steroids and carotenoids.
1925 W. R. BLOOR in *Chem. Rev.* II. 244 Three terms have been suggested for the group, namely, 'Lipins' by Gies and Rosenbloom, 'Lipides' by the International Congress of Applied Chemistry, and the old term 'Lipoids' by the author. The term lipins has been used in a different sense by Leathes, and was later adopted by McLean in his monograph as a name for a subgroup containing the cerebrosides and the phosphatides. The term lipoids is understood by many to exclude the fats, although used in the wider sense by many workers on the Continent. For these reasons, and for the sake of uniformity, the author recommends the use of the term Lipides as the general group name. **1927** M. BODANSKY *Introd. Physiol. Chem.* iii. 49 The term 'lipides' or 'lipids'..referring to the fats and fat-like substances. **1937** *Nature* 6 Nov. 787 'Lipides' may be confused with 'lipins', and both these words together with 'lipoids' generally signify substances of a fat-like nature yeilding on hydrolysis fatty acids or derivatives

of fatty acids, and containing in their molecule either nitrogen or nitrogen and phosphorus... Some confusion may therefore arise since 'lipids' as used by the author signifies not only the above substances but also the simple fats and waxes and even the sterols. **1946** W. R. Fearon *Introd. Biochem.* (ed. 3) x. 172 The third great family of bio-organic compounds, namely, the lipides. **1954** A. White et al. *Princ. Biochem.* xviii. 453 Lipids are the most concentrated source of energy to the organism, yielding per gram over twice as many calories as do carbohydrates and proteins. **1955** J. A. Lovern *Chem. Lipids* ii. 37 Lipids by definition are soluble in the 'fat' solvents, such as ether, alcohol and chloroform. **1958** G. A. Maw *Aids to Org. Chem. for Med. Students* (ed. 5) p. xxxiv, Substances such as paraffin wax, petroleum jelly and mineral oils, although of a fatty or oily nature, are not classified as lipids since they do not occur in living material. **1961** *Chem. Abstr.* LV. 27470 Chemistry of lipides. **1968** Passmore & Robson *Compan. Med. Stud.* I. x. 5/2 The steroids form a large class of lipids, which includes the hormones of the adrenal and sex glands, vitamin D and the bile acids. **1973** *Sci. Amer.* Aug. 89/1 Today there are 10 well-characterized human diseases that are known to be caused by the excessive accumulation of lipids in tissue cells.

2. *attrib.* and *Comb.*, as *lipid storage* (freq. used *attrib.*, designating a disorder otherwise known as a *lipidosis); *lipid-soluble* adj.

1964 G. H. Haggis et al. *Introd. Molecular Biol.* vi. 151 Lipid-soluble substances are substances with a relatively high solubility in oils. **1955** H. J. Deuel *Lipids* II. vi. 623 (*heading*) Lipid storage under abnormal conditions. **1960** *Jrnl. Neurol., Neurosurg. & Psychiatry* XXIII. 211/2 The group of so-called lipid storage disorders..includes.. Hand-Schuller–Christian disease, gargoylism, Niemann-Pick's disease, Gaucher's disease, and amaurotic family idiocy. **1973** *Sci. Amer.* Aug. 88/1 When the enzyme that catalyzes a particular lipid reaction is inactive or absent, excessive amounts of that lipid begin to accumulate in certain tissues. In human beings lipid-storage disorders often result in mental retardation and enlargement of the spleen and the liver. Most of the known lipid-storage disorders are fatal.

lipidosis (lipidǭu·sis). *Med.* Pl. **lipidoses.** [f. *lipid + -osis.] Any disorder characterized by an excessive accumulation of a lipid in certain tissues.

1941 S. J. Thannhauser *Lipidoses* i. 2 A summary of the present knowledge..of lipid substances is.. an appropriate introduction to the group of diseases, which are called 'lipoidoses' or 'lipidoses'. **1961** R. D. Baker *Essent. Path.* iv. 47 The lipidoses are conditions in which fatty substances collect in macrophages, sometimes as part of the macrophage (reticulo-endothelial) system, sometimes in ectopic clusters of these cells and rarely in other types of cells. These diseases are also termed lipid-storage diseases. *Ibid.* 49 Niemann-Pick's Disease. This is a truly systemic lipidosis of the macrophage system, occurring typically in infants, with splenomegaly and hepatomegaly. **1966** Wright & Symmers *Systemic Path.* I. v. 245/1 Different lipids are concerned in each of the primary lipidoses, a different enzyme failure presumably being characteristic of each disease.

lipin (li·pin). *Biochem.* Also **-ine.** [f. Gr. λίπ-os fat + -in[1], -ine[5].] † **a.** Any lipid containing nitrogen. (Originally used more specifically: see quot. 1910.) *Obs.* **b.** = *lipid.

1910 J. B. Leathes *Fats* 3 Lipines [will be used] to denote compounds of fatty acids containing nitrogen but no phosphorus or carbohydrate group. **1911** Rosenbloom & Gies in *Biochem. Bull.* I. 51 We venture to propose the accompanying chemical classification of fats and the many substances related to or resembling them, which collectively can be very appropriately and conveniently called lipins. **1937** [see *lipid 1]. **1946** *Q. Jrnl. Microsc. Sci.* LXXXVII. 444 The lipines used in this investigation were lecithin, cephalin, sphingomyelin, and galactolipine, all obtained from the brains of sheep. **1952** *Chem. & Engin. News* 5 May 1910/1 'Lipide', however, has proved popular, replacing the older 'lipoid' and 'lipin', with a better defined meaning.

Lipiodol (lipəi·ǒdǫl). *Med.* Also **lipiodol.** [f. Gr. λίπ-os fat + Iod(ine *sb.* + -ol.] A proprietary name of a liquid containing about 40% iodine which is obtained by treating poppy-seed oil with iodine and is used as a contrast medium in radiography.

1923 *Brit. Med. Jrnl.* 4 Aug. 174/1 Between 1 and 2 c.cm. of lipiodol is injected into the spinal theca through a suboccipital puncture. **1925** *Trade Marks Jrnl.* 20 May 1096 Lipiodol... A pharmaceutical preparation for human use. Laurent Lafay,..Paris, France; chemist. **1928** Chandler & Wood *Lipiodol in Diagn. Thoracic Dis.* i. 1 The properties of lipiodol are opacity to the X-rays, a high specific gravity, an absence of any irritating action on mucous membranes, a reputed antiseptic and analgesic action, lubrication, and so firm a combination of the iodine with the oil that none of the ordinary effects of iodine are experienced. **1972** *Acta Chirurg. Scand.* CXXXVIII. 481/1 Oily contrast medium (lipiodol) injections from 10 to 30 ml were given in an attempt to demonstrate tumours..in the liver.

Lipizzan, Lippizan (li·pitsăn), *a.* [See -an.] Of or pertaining to Lipizza or Lippiza, the home of the former Austrian Imperial Stud, esp. designating a strain of horse originally bred there. So **Lipizza·na, Lippiza·na, -a·ner,** a horse of this breed; also *attrib.*

[**1911** M. C. Grimsgaard *Orig. Handbk. Riders* Suppl. 320 (*caption*) 'Muestoso-Moschina', a Lipizza stallion, one of the eight famous stallions at the..Spanish Court Riding-School in Vienna.] **1928** *Observer* 17 June 27/3 Twelve of the famous Lippizaner horses. *Ibid.*, The Lippizana is a perfectly separate and peculiar breed of horse, in appearance much like an Arab, but..more massive. **1946** P. Bottome *Lifeline* x. 100 Each horse was..a *Lippizaner.* **1954** A. Podhajsky *Spanish Riding School* (ed. 2) 4/1 General Patton..fulfilled the request made to him that the Lipizzan stud..be brought back to Austria. **1967** A. Arent *Gravedigger's Funeral* (1968) xii. 189 A Lippizaner, a white stallion from the Spanish Riding Academy in Vienna. **1971** *Islander* (Victoria, B.C.) 30 May 2/4 Those beautiful leaps and dancing steps made by the white Lipizzan stallions of the Spanish Riding School. **1972** *Guardian* 4 Oct. 4/6 The 58 photogenic white Lippizaner stallions of the Spanish Riding School which has just celebrated its four hundredth anniversary.

† **lip-lap** (li·plæp). *Obs.* Also **liplap.** [Native name.] In the Dutch East Indies, a half-caste or Eurasian; a child born in the East Indies.

1798 S. H. Wilcocke tr. *Stavorinus's Voy. E. Indies* I. ii. v. 315 Children born in the Indies, are nicknamed *liplaps* by the Europeans, although both parents may have come from Europe. **1893** *Academy* 11 Feb. 122 The acclimatisation..of liplaps, signos, and mannas, as the Dutch half-castes are variously called.

lipo-. Add: Also used in forming terms in *Biochem.* and other fields.

lipæ·mia (in Dict. as var. *lipohæmia*) (later examples); hence **lipæ·mic** *a.*; **lipoamide** (lipo͵ē̆i·məid) *Biochem.*, the amide of lipoic acid; **li·poate** *Biochem.*, the anion, or a salt or ester, of lipoic acid; **lipocaic** (-kē̆i·ik) *Biochem.* [see quot. 1936], a substance extracted from the pancreas which is found to prevent the accumulation of fat in the livers of animals from which the pancreas has been removed; **lipocho·ndrion** (pl. **-cho·ndria**) *Cytology* [ad. G. *lipochondrie* (E. Ries 1935, in *Zeitschr. f. Zellforschung u. mikrosk. Anat.* XXII. 528), f. Gr. χονδρίον, dim. of χόνδρος granule, prob. after G. *mitochondrie* *mitochondrion], a lipoid granule in the cytoplasm, esp. one seen in live preparations and possibly related to the Golgi apparatus; so **lipocho·ndrial** *a.*; **li·pochrome** *Biol.* [ad. G. *lipochrom* (C. F. W. Krukenberg *Vergleichend-physiologische Studien* II. iii. 93), f. Gr. χρῶμ-α colour], any of various mainly yellow or red pigments which are found naturally in both plants and animals and which are soluble in fats or fat solvents (see quot. 1951); **lipofu·scin** [Fuscin], any of various brownish pigments of animals, esp. those characteristically deposited in the cells during old age; (α-)**lipo·ic acid** *Biochem.*, a carboxylic acid, $S\text{–}S\text{–}CH_2CH_2CH(CH_2)_4COOH$, found in yeast and liver extracts which is a co-factor in the decarboxylation of pyruvate *in vivo*; **lipolytic,** substitute for def.: having the property of decomposing or hydrolysing fats (later examples); hence **lipo·lysis,** the hydrolytic breaking down of fat; **lipoly·tically** *adv.*; **li·pophile, lipophi·lic** *adjs.* [-phil, -phile], having an affinity for lipids; readily dissolving, or soluble in, lipids; **lipopho·bic** *a.* [-phobic], tending to repel lipids; not readily soluble in lipids; **li:popolysa·ccharide** *Biochem.*, any complex containing lipid and polysaccharide moieties; **lipopro·tein** *Biochem.*, any complex containing lipid and protein moieties, *spec.* one which is soluble in water or salt solution (as distinct from a proteolipid); **li:posarco·ma** (pl. **-o·mata**) *Path.* [Sarcoma], a sarcoma of fatty tissue; **lipo·sitol** *Biochem.* [*in)ositol], any phospholipid containing inositol in its molecule, *spec.* the one found in soy-beans; **li·poyl** *Biochem.* [-yl], the radical $C_7H_{13}S_2{\cdot}CO$— which is derived from lipoic acid.

1915 *Jrnl. Biol. Chem.* XXIII. 317 Alimentary lipemia is due to nothing more than the addition of these glycerides. **1961** *Lancet* 26 Aug. 492/2 After fat ingestion, visible lipæmia normally reaches a maximum in about four hours. **1906** *Bio-Chem. Jrnl.* II. 22 Case XV, also not lipaemic, was allowed a fat-rich diet, but five days later the lipaemic condition was absent, and has remained so. **1961** *Lancet* 26 Aug. 492/2 Sera from 10 patients..were visibly lipæmic before sodium *d*-thyroxine was given. **1960** *Biochim. & Biophys. Acta* XXXVII. 314 The turnover numbers at 25° vary from 1000 with dl-lipoic acid to about 80,000 with dl-lipoamide. **1972** *Zeitschr. für physiol. Chem.* CCCLIII. 875/2 We measured the overall reaction of the multi-enzyme complex.., the decarboxylase and the lipoamide oxidoreductase. **1954** V. H. Cheldelin in Sebrell & Harris *Vitamins* III. xviii. 580 The cyclic disulfide may react to produce an acyl lipoate. **1970** R. W. McGilvery *Biochem.* xi. 215 The oxidizing agent is a coënzyme containing a disulfide bond, lipoate, which is attached to a lysyl residue in the peptide chain of transsuccinylase. **1936** L. R. Dragstedt et al. in *Amer. Jrnl. Physiol.* CXVII. 180 We have chosen the name 'lipocaic' for this substance. It is derived from the Greek words 'λιπος', 'fat' and 'καιω', 'I burn'. A more general term suggesting that the hormone plays a rôle in the utilization of fat was sought but without success. **1955** H. J. Deuel *Lipids* II. vi. 672 A number of facts lead one to question whether or not lipocaic can be classified as a hormone in the usual sense of the word. **1936** *Biol. Abstr.* X. 219 During differentiation the cells..are relatively small..; ergastoplasm is absent and the reserve material consists of yolk globules and lipochondria. **1946** *Jrnl. Exper. Zool.* CI. 361 Apart from finding yolk, pigment granules, and mitochondria, these workers [*sc.* Ries and Fischer] observed large osmiophilic fat granules... These elements were called lipochondria. **1946** [see *liposome 1]. **1950** J. R. Baker in *Proc. Linn. Soc.* CLXII. 71 Since the particular artifact studied by Golgi represents so badly what is actually present in the living cytoplasm, it no longer seems desirable to connect the great neurologist's name with this cellular constituent. A descriptive name is surely preferable. Ries's name 'Lipochondrien' (Ries, 1935) is convenient, but a Greek ending is more suitable for a word that must be used internationally, I therefore suggest *lipochondrion* (plural *lipochondria*). **1968** [see *liposome 1]. **1971** *Acta Embryol. Exper.* 43 (*heading*) The cytoplasmic inclusions of the salamander oocyte. III. Lipochondria. **1946** *Jrnl. Exper. Zool.* CI. 390 Only lipochondrial substances were involved. **1887** *Encycl. Brit.* XXII. 420/2 A red pigment of the lipochrome series. **1928** [see *lipofuscin* below]. **1951** H. J. Deuel *Lipids* I. vi. 511 The term lipochrome was proposed by Krukenberg to cover a number of animal and plant pigments which had been known by such diverse names as luteins, carotin, zoonerythrin, tetronerythrin, chlorophane, xanthophane, and rhodophane. Although this designation was originally limited to pigments with yellow or reddish tints, by implication it obviously should include any fat-soluble pigment such as chlorophyll. **1968** Lipochrome [see *lipofuscin* below]. **1923** *Chem. Abstr.* XVII. 1667 Lipofuscin is not limited to ectodermal cells, although it is found there chiefly. **1928** *Amer. Jrnl. Path.* IV. 293 The pigment present in these last organs..is a yellow to brown granular substance which is frequently tinged with fat stains, and therefore has been called lipochrome in this country, and lipofuscin in Germany. These two names are used to designate the substance in most English and American literature, but they actually represent different pigments. **1964** *Oceanogr. & Marine Biol.* II. 408 Another brown pigment [in the echinoderm *Diadema*] appears to be a lipofuscin. **1968** Passmore & Robson *Compan. Med. Stud.* I. xiii. 16/1 Lipofuscin, one of the commonest cellular pigments, is known by a variety of names (wear and tear pigment, haemofuscin, lipochrome, brown atrophy and age pigment), a selection which demonstrates its complexity as well as ignorance of its function, and indicates that it contains some lipid and some iron. **1951** L. J. Reed et al. in *Science* 27 July 93/2 This work has led to the obtaining of a crystalline compound from processed insoluble liver residues, which is highly active for the growth of *Streptococcus lactis* in the absence of acetate... This compound is being called α-lipoic acid. *Ibid.*, The crystalline compound reported in this paper is designated as α-lipoic acid to indicate that it is the first member to be obtained of a series of chemically related substances which possess acetate-replacing and pyruvate oxidase factor activity. **1962** H. A. Krebs in A. Pirie *Lens Metabolism Rel. Cataract* 351 Cofactors such as..pyridoxal phosphate, or lipoic acid may play a role in controlling reaction rates by virtue of being shared cofactors. **1968** R. F. Steiner *Life Chem.* vi. 100 The reduced form of lipoic acid contains two sulfhydryl groups..and can accept an acetyl group from active acetaldehyde. **1903** Dorland *Med. Dict.* (ed. 3) 380/1 Lipolysis. **1907** *Science* 27 Sept. 413/1 Since the bile salts are known to increase lipolysis, the effects of the sodium salts of cholic, glycocholic and taurocholic acids in *n*/500 solutions were tested on lipolytic hemolysis. **1972** *Jrnl. Lipid Res.* XIII. 651 (*heading*) Effect of cell size on lipolysis and antilipolytic action of insulin in human fat cells. **1912** *Jrnl. Amer. Chem. Soc.* XXXIV. 845 Preparations possessing lipolytic activity. **1955** H. J. Deuel *Lipids* II. ii. 15 No correlation between sex, age, or food intake and lipolytic activity of adipose tissue was observed in rats. **1972** *Jrnl. Lipid Res.* XIII. 325 (*heading*) Hydrolysis of fully esterified alcohols..by the lipolytic enzymes of rat pancreatic juice. **1912** *Jrnl. Amer. Chem. Soc.* XXXIV. 829 Lipolytically inactive substances. **1917** *Jrnl. Biol. Chem.* XXIX. p. xxvi, Experiments..resulted in the production of lipolytically active substances by the action of alkali on castor bean globulin, caesin, and gelatin. **1938** A. D. Whitehead tr. *Jordan's Technol. Solvents* i. 12 The aliphatic..and aromatic..hydrocarbons..are electrically neutral or non-polar since they contain no hydrophile groups. They are therefore hydrophobic or lipophile. **1950** *Chem. & Engin. News* 26 June 2181 (Advt.), The Atlas HLB System..is based on the hydrophile–lipophile balance of each emulsifier. **1965** *Acta Endocrinol.* XLIX. 538 Whether these findings can be attributed to the lipophile properties of the sulphatide facilitating its entrance into the cell cannot be decided. **1946** *Arkiv för Kemi, Mineral. och Geol.* XXIIa. xviii. 29 The lipophilic end should contain an aromatic structure. **1954** Jirgensons & Straumanis *Short Textbk. Colloid Chem.* ii. 16 Substances which, like rubber, polystyrene or polyvinylchloride do not contain hydrophilic groups are insoluble in water. They are composed of lipophilic..groups such as CH_3, $—CH_2—$, and others, which have some affinity for the molecules of fats, fat solvents and other oils. **1971** *Nature* 21 May 186/2 Morphine has a highly lipophilic molecule. **1946** G. M. Sutheim *Introd. Emulsions* i. 4 Hydrophilic substances..are named oleophobic or lipophobic. **1961** E. O'F. Walsh *Introd. Biochem.* ii. 33 The polar end of the lecithin molecule, here represented as a Zwitterion, is hydrophilic and lipophobic. **1954** *Chem. Abstr.* XLVIII. 9453 Injection of a lipopolysaccharide from *Salmonella abortivoequina* increases the phagocytic activity of the granulocytes. **1958** *Immunology* I. 181 The stimulation of non-specific immunity by lipopolysaccharides could not be correlated with the serum properdin level at the time of challenge. **1970** W. J. Lennarz in S. J. Wakil *Lipid Metabolism* v. 164 Lipo-

polysaccharides, the complex heteropolysaccharides typical of Gram-negative enteric bacteria, are currently under extensive investigation. **1909** *Chem. Abstr.* III. 82 It is probable that in fatty degeneration there is a splitting off of fat from lipoproteins of this character. **1929** *Jrnl. Immunol.* XVI. 448 The constituents in fowl sera responsible for these non-specific precipitations are indicated to be lipo-proteins and neutral fats. **1955** H. J. DEUEL *Lipids* II. v. 371 The lipoproteins are widely distributed in living matter, where they occur in cell nuclei, mitochondria, cell membranes, chloroplasts, in egg yolk, in milk, and in blood. **1971** L. W. BURLEY in Johnson & Davenport *Biochem. Lipids* iv. 86 'Proteolipids'.. differ from lipoproteins in being soluble in certain organic solvents but insoluble in aqueous solutions. **1893** DUNGLISON *Dict. Med. Sci.* (ed. 21) 637/2 Liposarcoma. **1916** E. H. KETTLE *Path. Tumours* II. 94 Liposarcomata.. are undoubtedly rare. **1970** PASSMORE & ROBSON *Compan. Med. Studies* II. xxx. 16/2 Liposarcomata are most common in old men. **1943** D. W. WOOLLEY in *Jrnl. Biol. Chem.* CXLVII. 581 It is proposed to call the new substance soybean lipositol, since it is a lipid which contains inositol. **1949** H. W. FLOREY et al. *Antibiotics* II. xliv. 1386 The antibacterial activity of 50 units of streptomycin in 1 ml. was completely antagonized by as little as 0·2 μg. of lipositol. **1969** S. R. WILLIAMS *Nutrition & Diet Therapy* iii. 29/1 Other important phospholipids are cephalins and lipositols, which are like the lecithins except that they contain other factors in place of choline. **1960** *Biochem. Jrnl.* LXXVII. 347/1 There is a close correlation between the rates of the enzyme-catalysed oxidation of DPNH by the lipoyl derivatives used and the rates of reoxidation of the red intermediate..by the same lipoyl derivatives. **1970** R. W. McGILVERY *Biochem.* xi. 215 The reaction is now complete except for the regeneration of the original disulfide bond in the lipoyl group.

lipodystrophy (li:podi·strŏfi). *Path.* Also as mod.L. **li:podystro·phia.** [f. LIPO- + DYSTROPHY.] Any of various disorders of fat metabolism; *intestinal lipodystrophy*, a rare disease (usu. called Whipple's disease) of uncertain ætiology; chiefly of middle-aged men, presenting with joint pains, steatorrhœa, wasting, and lymph node enlargement; *progressive lipodystrophy* [tr. mod.L. *lipodystrophia progressiva* (A. Simons 1911, in *Zeitschr. f. d. ges. Neurol. u. Psychiatrie (Orig.)* V. 36)], a condition in which there is a progressive loss of subcutaneous fat, usu. from the upper half of the body while the lower half retains its fat. So **li:podystro·phic** *a.*

1907 G. H. WHIPPLE in *Bull. Johns Hopkins Hosp.* XVIII. 391/1 In searching for a name to designate this condition great difficulties were encountered. It would seem that no suitable name can be applied to it until the etiological factor is determined. The term *Intestinal Lipodystrophy* is suggested. **1925** *Q. Jrnl. Med.* XVIII. 224 Progressive lipodystrophy is a rare disease characterized by symmetrical and progressive loss of subcutaneous fat over the face, neck, arms, thorax, and abdomen, with a relative or absolute abundance of subcutaneous fat over the lower limbs. *Ibid.* 231 The active stage having ended, the lipodystrophic process becomes stationary. **1933** *Lancet* 23 Dec. 1417/1 The blood chemistry in lipodystrophia progressiva is normal. **1946** *Ibid.* 18 May 730/2 There is no satisfactory classification of the lipodystrophies. *Ibid.* 731/1, I venture to argue how Ziegler's lipodystrophic case might have a similar disturbance of fat-metabolism without an obvious lipæmia. **1964** *Pediatrics* XXXIII. 609/1 The syndromes of partial and total lipodystrophy have been reviewed... For inclusion in the syndrome of partial lipodystrophy symmetrical loss of fat from the face with or without truncal loss, but with retention of distal adipose depots was required. In total lipodystrophy fat loss was generalized. **1971** *Daily Colonist* (Victoria, B.C.) 28 Dec. 2/1 Lipodystrophy means a disturbance in the metabolism of fatty tissue.

lipoid, *a.* Add: (Further examples.)

1907 *Biochem. Jrnl.* II. 22 The lipöid material being mainly composed of an ester of cholesterin. **1946** *Nature* 13 July 41/1 Solution of the odorous substance in the lipoid or aqueous phase of these flagellæ is, therefore, the point from which all theories of osmic perception must proceed. **1974** *Ibid.* 1 Feb. 301/1 The uterine or milk glands in tsetse flies..release a nutritive liquid of proteinaceous and lipoid nature for the maturing intrauterine larva.

B. *sb.* [a. G. *lipoïd* (E. Overton *Studien über die Narkose* (1901) 54).] **a.** Any fat-like substance other than a true fat. **b.** = *LIPID.

1906 *Jrnl. Chem. Soc.* XC. II. 780 (*heading*) The influence of diffusibility and the solubility of lipoids on the rate of intestinal absorption. **1912** *Biochem. Bull.* I. 51 Fats and the substances resembling them ('lipoids'). **1925** [see *LIPID 1]. **1932** I. SMEDLEY-MACLEAN in *Ann. Rev. Biochem.* I. 135 The term lipoid is retained..to denote the ether-soluble constituents of a tissue, without regard to their nature. **1946** W. R. FEARON *Introd. Biochem.* (ed. 3) x. 173 Lipoids.—These are biological compounds resembling the lipides in certain physical properties, notably solubility in fats. **1952** [see *LIPIN]. **1955** GAIGER & DAVIES *Vet. Path. & Bacteriol.* (ed. 4) i. 6 All the normal body tissues contain fat in one form or another, the chief forms being neutral fat, fatty acids, soaps and lipoids (lecithin, cholesterol and myelin). **1958** *Times Lit. Suppl.* 17 Jan. 34/1 Living matter consists essentially of carbohydrates (or 'sugars'), lipoids (or 'fats') and proteins. **1971** *Nature* 9 July 138/3 'Lipoid' is used instead of the more usual 'lipid' throughout [the book].

lipoidal (lipoi·dăl), *a.* [f. prec. + -AL.] Resembling or containing fat.

1919 *Amer. Jrnl. Anat.* XXV. 251 Lipoidal vacuoles are becoming more abundant in the outer and especially the middle cortical zone. **1920** *Proc. R. Soc. Med.* XIII. (Path. Section) 8 The antitrypsin is lipoidal in nature. **1928** P. BAILEY in E. V. Cowdry *Special Cytol.* I. xv. 493 Small globules of lipoidal substances are seen in all the cells. **1954** A. J. MARSHALL *Bower-Birds* ii. 10 Considerable aggregations of heavily lipoidal Leydig cells can now be seen.

lipoidosis (lipoidōu·sis). *Med.* Pl. **lipoidoses.** [f. as prec. + -OSIS.] = *LIPIDOSIS.

1932 *Amer. Jrnl. Dis. Children* XLIV. 1117 Niemann-Pick's disease..is called phosphatide cell lipoidosis. *Ibid.*, Christian's disease..is called cholesterol cell lipoidosis. **1936** *Proc. R. Soc. Med.* XXIX. 585 The three principal types of these lipoidoses are Schüller-Christian's disease, the spleno-hepatomegaly of Gaucher and the splenohepatomegaly of Niemann-Pick. **1962** *Lancet* 13 Jan. 64/1 When infections, blood dyscrasias, lipoidoses, reticuloses, ..and congenital fibrosis..are excluded there remain some instances in which no obvious disorder can be demonstrated.

liposome (li·pŏsōum). *Biol.* [ad. G. *liposom* (E. Albrecht 1904, in *Verhandl. deutsch. path. Ges.* VI. 64): see LIPO- and *-SOME[4].] **1.** A natural globule of fat or lipid suspended in the cytoplasm of a cell.

1910 *Anat. Rec.* IV. 211 The protoplasm of renal cells, muscle fibers, etc., shows usually a large number of small more or less refractive droplets (liposomes) when examined in aqueous humor, or dilute potassium hydroxide. **1946** *Jrnl. Exper. Zool.* CI. 374 In the following discussion, while being aware of the arbitrariness of the choice, the term 'lipochondria' will be used as an alternative for 'lipoprotein bodies'. Their conversion product, the fat droplets, may be termed 'liposomes'. **1968** McGEE-RUSSELL & ROSS *Cell Struct.* xxvi. 351 The lipid inclusions of amphibian embryo cells have been studied by Holtfreter and Karasaki. Holtfreter called the larger bodies liposomes, and the small ones lipochondria.

2. A minute artificial globule consisting of one or more layers of phospholipid enclosing an aqueous core, used experimentally as a model for biological membranes.

1968 SESSA & WEISSMANN in *Jrnl. Lipid Res.* IX. 310 (*heading*) Phospholipid spherules (liposomes) as a model for biological membranes. *Ibid.*, Throughout this review, the artificial structures will..be referred to as 'spherules'. A. D. Bangham has used the term 'smectic mesophases', and colloquially we have called them 'liposomes' or 'Bangasomes'. As the literature dealing with these structures accumulates, the term 'liposome' is gaining favor, and should win general acceptance. **1970** *New Scientist* 11 June 511/1 In 1965 Alec Bangham..devised the 'liposome'. **1972** M. K. JAIN *Bimolecular Lipid Membrane* iii. 69 A large number of vesicles with cell-like geometry can be produced under suitable conditions by dispersing phospholipids in aqueous salt solutions above the phase-transition temperature of the lipid. These vesicles are generally termed liposomes, spherules, smectic mesophase, and sometimes Bangosomes (after Dr. Bangham).

lipotropic (lipotrōu·pik, -trǫ·pik), *a. Physiol.* [f. LIPO- + *-TROPIC.] Tending to prevent or remove an accumulation of excess fat in the liver. So **lipotro·pism**, lipotropic property or phenomena.

1935 C. H. BEST et al. in *Nature* 18 May 821/2 The term 'lipotropic' is used to describe substances which decrease the rate of deposition and accelerate the rate of removal of liver fat. **1945** *Jrnl. Biol. Chem.* CLX. 601 (*heading*) Growth and lipotropism. I. The dietary requirements of methionine, cystine, and choline. **1951** A. GROLLMAN *Pharmacol. & Therapeutics* xxvii. 607 Because of their lipotropic action, choline and, to a lesser extent, methionine and inositol have been used therapeutically in cirrhosis of the liver, hepatitis, [etc.]. **1953** *Canad. Jrnl. Med. Sci.* XXXI. 474 (*heading*) Further studies on lipotropism in the domestic duck. **1968** A. WHITE et al. *Princ. Biochem.* (ed. 4) xxi. 503 Any material capable of contributing methyl groups for choline synthesis has the property of being lipotropic.

Lippes loop (li·pēz lūp). [f. the name of its inventor, the American physician, Jack *Lippes*.] An intrauterine contraceptive device in the shape of a double s.

[**1962** J. LIPPES in C. Tietze *Intra-Uterine Contraceptive Devices* 71, I wanted a device such that the muscular contractions of the uterus would not press on the entire piece of plastic but on one section at a time only... With this in mind, I designed a device which I call a 'loop'.] **1964** *Lancet* 31 Oct. 958/1 The five types available are: the Margulies spiral, the Lippes loop, the Birnberg bow, the Hall-Stone stainless steel ring, and the Zipper nylon ring. **1966** E. MEARS in M. Pollock *Family Planning* iv. 50 With..the Lippes loop the inserter is loaded, introduced..beyond the internal os, rotated..and the device expelled by pushing the plunger. **1967** *Time* 7 Apr. 73 From Dr. Jack Lippes' labs in Buffalo came a series of double-S designs, now known as the Lippes loop, which has probably the widest acceptance both in the U.S. (150,000 users) and overseas (up to 4,000,000). **1971** H. J. DAVIS *Intrauterine Devices for Contraception* vi. 95 The shield..conforms most closely to the average uterine cavity size. The Lippes loop is the next most anatomically correct, commercially available device.

lipping, *vbl. sb.*[1] Add: **2.** A strip of wood or the like fixed to the edge of a board, door, table-top, etc.; the act of fixing such a strip.

1963 *Gloss. Terms Timber (B.S.I.)* 62 *Lipping*, a strip of wood or other material applied to the edge of a flush door, table top, etc. **1966** A. W. LEWIS *Gloss. Woodworking Terms* 53 *Lipping*, fixing a strip of solid wood to the edge of a board, usually by means of a tongue and groove. **1971** *Timber Trades Jrnl.* 14 Aug. 58/2 The pre-glued edging can be either conventional plastics or wood lippings.

Lippizan(a, Lippizaner: see *LIPIZZAN *a.*

Lippmann (li·pmæ̆n). *Photogr.* The name of Gabriel *Lippmann* (1845–1921), French physicist, used *attrib.* with reference to a method of colour photography invented by him in which colours are produced by interference effects in an emulsion containing very fine silver halide particles.

1902 *Westm. Gaz.* 26 Sept. 4/2 Among all experts in this branch of photography it is agreed that the Lippmann interference process is the only one which gives all the colours of Nature in a direct manner, but these experts are unfortunately also agreed that it is an exceedingly difficult process to work. **1908** *Astrophysical Jrnl.* XXVII. 346 This flexible silver mirror is immediately laid, silver surface down, on a wet Lippmann plate. **1936** R. M. FANSTONE *Colour Photogr.* ii. 7 The Lippmann Process presented difficulties, and was somewhat costly to work. **1942** C. E. K. MEES *Theory Photogr. Process* xxi. 872 A Lippmann emulsion..is practically grainless when properly prepared. **1963** F. W. H. MUELLER in *Photographic Theory: Liège Summer School 1962* I. i. 31 Lippmann emulsions, sometimes called grainless emulsions, contain very small silver halide crystals, 10 to 50 mμ in diameter, and are used for scientific purposes... They are chloride or bromide emulsions made by inversed or double jet addition. **1973** F. H. PERRIN in W. Thomas *SPSE Handbk. Photogr. Sci. & Engin.* xvii. 930 The finest grain is produced by procedures devised to make Lippmann color photographs.

lippy, *a.* Add: **2.** *colloq.* or *dial.* Impertinent, insolent; talkative, verbose.

1875 W. D. PARISH *Dict. Sussex Dial.* 70 *Lippy*, impertinent; apt to answer saucily. **1893** W. K. POST *Harvard Stories* 195 Ain't he getting pretty flip? The lippy dude! **1906** *Punch* 4 Apr. 250/3 'Aughty as teetotallers an' as lippy as Passive Resisters. **1968** V. CANNING *Melting Man* v. 128 You're a lippy bastard. **1971** R. ROBERTS *Classic Slum* 203 Any child who requested a book by title he at once designated as 'forward' or 'lippy'. **1971** R. THOMAS *Backup Men* iv. 32 It might learn them not to be so goddamned lippy.

lipstick (li·pstik), *sb.* Also **lip stick, lip-stick.** [f. LIP *sb.* + STICK *sb.*[1] 8.] A stick of cosmetic for colouring the lips, usu. a shade of pink or red; hence, cosmetic for the lips. Also *attrib.*

1880 E. JAMES *Amat. Negro Minstrel's Guide* 4 Prepared burnt cork, ready for use, 25 and 50 cents per box; lip sticks, 25 cts. *Ibid.* 8 An application of lipstick..around the natural part of the lips will extend that feature to a size quite remarkable. **1919** H. L. WILSON *Ma Pettengill* iii. 93 Metta was even using a lip stick! **1922** A. BENNETT *Lilian* II. vii. 116 She also knew what was the best lipstick. **1926** *Spectator* 18 Sept. 435/2 What is the matter with powder, paint and lipstick? **1942** D. POWELL *Time to be Born* x. 222 She applied a lipstick brush tenderly. **1962** F. I. ORDWAY et al. *Basic Astronautics* xiii. 521 Many are packaged in..devices resembling lipstick cases. **1966** AUDEN *About House* 46 Spotless rooms..Chill me, so do cups used for ashtrays or smeared With lipstick. **1973** *Country Life* 20 Sept. 831/2, I liked..the clear colours and good texture of the lipsticks. **1974** 'J. ROSS' *Burning of Billy Toober* xii. 113 There were two gilt lipstick cases.

Hence **li·pstick** *v. trans.* and *intr.*, to apply lipstick to (one's lips); **li·psticked** *ppl. a.*; **li·psticking** *vbl. sb.*; **li·psticky** *a.*, covered or sticky with lipstick; also *fig.*

1926 *Ladies' Home Jrnl.* Apr. 24 She..had recently lipsticked a red mouth into startling contrast to her natural pallor. **1928** *Sunday Express* 15 Apr. 15/4 She may be made of wax, with large, liquid eyes, a lipsticked mouth, and real hair. **1931** *Daily Tel.* 21 May 13/3 They chatted, smoked, 'lipsticked', read, sewed, [etc.]. **1931** *Punch* 28 Oct. 476/3 Her chronicle of minor adventures, if occasionally a shade too lip-sticky for all tastes, is thoroughly vivacious and entertaining. **1933** J. B. PRIESTLEY *Wonder Hero* vi. 249 The first thing she did was to give Charlie a large smacking lip-sticky kiss. **1940** A. G. MACDONELL *Crew of Anaconda* xxi. 260 Florinda did a little powdering and lipsticking. **1949** *Landfall* June 183 The lipsticky essays of her daughter into informed adolescence. **1960** *20th Cent.* Oct. 313 She would open her handbag, lipstick her mouth, and go home. **1966** J. B. PRIESTLEY *Salt is Leaving* i. 5 Sheila stopped lipsticking. **1969** *Daily Tel.* (Colour Suppl.) 5 Sept. 46/3 My eyes are still wandering over that lip-sticked mouth. **1974** *Listener* 17 June 69/1 Jonathan Miller used to imagine the BBC as an actual aunt, powdered and lipsticked and getting on in years.

Liptauer, liptauer (li·ptau,ər). Also **Liptai, Liptau, Liptoi.** [G., f. *Liptó* place-name in Czechoslovakia.] A soft cheese originally made in Hungary, usu. coloured and flavoured with paprika and other seasonings. Also *attrib.*

1902 J. T. LAW *Grocer's Manual* (ed. 2) 143/2 *Bringen* or *Liptau Cheese*, a Continental kind made in Hungary. Constituents:—Water, 34 per cent.; fatty matter, 28; Caseine, 23; salts, 5. **1935** M. MORPHY *Recipes of All Nations* 348 Liptauer cheese..which is extensively made in Germany and Austria, is of Hungarian origin. It is made from sour milk. **1955** G. FREEMAN *Liberty Man* I. ii. 32 The fillings came from a delicatessen. Liverwurst and liptauer cheese. **1964** *Punch* 19 Feb. 262/3 Mortadella,

lachscinken, kabanosi or Liptauer cheese. **1964** E. HUXLEY *Back Street New Worlds* vii. 75 In one [supermarket]..you can buy..Czech braun, gacciatori, or Liptauer cheese. **1967** T. A. LAYTON *Cheese & Cheese Cookery* 228 Liptoi is a goats' milk cream cheese; Liptoi is sold in Hungary packed in small bladders and owes its name to the county of Lipto (now in Czechoslovakia)... The German name of this cheese, *Liptauer*, is often used in shops and restaurants both in Hungary and abroad.

liquesce, *v.* Add: Also *fig.*, to merge *into.*

1920 *19th Cent.* Dec. 977 The perpetual tendency of privilege, royal as well as any other, to liquesce into the common stream of humanity.

liquescent, *a. transf.* (Later examples.)

1967 *Listener* 31 Aug. 287/3 Huge eyes fluctuating between fear and wonder and roguish amusement—liquescent, all light suddenly sinking out of them. **1969** *Daily Tel.* 10 Dec. 12/4 Debussy's 'Prélude à l'après-midi d'un faune' could scarcely have been bettered for delicate dynamic nuances and shapely liquescent phrasing.

liqueur, *sb.* Add: **2.** (Examples.) Also = **liqueur chocolate.*

1907 *Yesterday's Shopping* (1969) 937 Table glass services... 12 Clarets... 12 Champagnes... 6 Liqueurs... 12 Tumblers. **1925** *Heal & Son Catal.: Glass*, Table glass. ..Champagne..Claret..Sherry..Port..Liqueur..Tumbler. **1965** E. BROWN *Big Man* xi. 96 Andy took from his shoulder bag the box of liqueurs. **1967** K. GILES *Death in Diamonds* iii. 59 Elizabeth was..eating chocolates. 'My present to myself,' she said, 'Austrian Liqueurs and none for pigs.' **1968** G. BEARD *Mod. Glass* ii. 101 (*caption*) Automatic production six sizes of 'Five Star' 1 oz. liqueur to 12½ oz. goblet.

3. liqueur chocolate, a chocolate with a liqueur filling; **liqueur-glass** (earlier and later examples).

1904 'SAKI' *Reginald* 84 Some liqueur chocolates had been turned loose by mistake among the refreshments—really liqueur chocolates, with very little chocolate. **1950** O. BLAKESTON *Pink Ribbon* vii. 76 Some flying beetle, rather like a small liqueur chocolate, zoomed past my ear. **1969** J. ELLIOT *Duel* I. iii. 74 A small box of liqueur chocolates..shaped like miniature bottles. **1850** E. RUSKIN *Let.* 9 Mar. in M. Lutyens *Effie in Venice* (1965) I. 155 The little Liqueur glasses of Rossolio. **1904** 'SAKI' *Reginald* 16 There are liqueur glasses, and crystallized fruits. **1962** E. O'BRIEN *Lonely Girl* iv. 48 Joanna opened the wine and served it in liqueur glasses to make it go far. **1975** *Sunday Times* (Colour Suppl.) 23 Feb. 11/4, 6 sherry glasses which when half filled double superbly as liqueur glasses.

liquid, *a.* and *sb.* Add: **A.** *adj.* **6.** (Later examples.)

1930 J. M. KEYNES *Treat. Money* II. xxv. 67 On the other hand, bills and call loans are more 'liquid' than investments. **1962** C. H. KREPS *Money* I. i. 12 The assets categorized as near money are those that are highly liquid; that is, they are convertible into money quickly, easily, and without loss. **1974** *Times* 12 Nov. 14/4 These small engineering businesses..are now..low on liquid assets.

7. liquid air, air in a liquid state; **liquid compass,** a form of magnetic compass used in ships in which the card and needle are mainly supported by floating in a bowl filled with liquid; **liquid controller** *Electr.* = **liquid rheostat*; **liquid crystal** *Physical Chem.* [tr. G. *flüssiger krystall* (O. Lehmann 1890, in *Ann. d. Physik und Chem.* XL. 404)], a turbid liquid that exhibits double refraction (indicative of internal anisotropy and hence some degree of ordering in its structure, as in an ordinary crystal) and exists as a distinct state of certain pure substances between the melting point and some higher temperature, at which it becomes an ordinary liquid; **liquid extract** (occas. as one word) *Pharm.* = *fluid extract* s.v. *FLUID *a.* 1 a; **liquid fire,** any very 'fiery' (in taste) or highly combustible liquid, now *esp.* one that can be sent as a burning jet in warfare; **liquid fuel,** fuel that is a liquid, now esp. as used in rocketry; so **liquid-fuelled** *a.*; **liquid glue,** glue that keeps a liquid form till applied; **liquid lunch** *colloq.*, a midday meal at which drink rather than food is consumed; **liquid manure** *Hort.*, a water extract of manure used as a fertilizer; **liquid oxygen,** oxygen in a liquid state; **liquid paraffin** *Pharm.*, an almost tasteless and odourless oily liquid that consists of hydrocarbons obtained from petroleum and is used as a laxative and in dressings; **liquid petrolatum** *N.Amer.* = **liquid paraffin*; **liquid rheostat** *Electr.*, a rheostat which uses an electrolyte solution as the resistive element; **liquid soap,** soap in liquid form; **liquid starter,** a liquid rheostat used as a starter of an electric motor.

1899 *McClure's Mag.* XII. 397 (*heading*) Liquid air. A new substance that promises to do the work of coal and ice and gunpowder, at next to no cost. *Ibid.* 399/1 A liquid-air engine, if powerful enough, will compress the air and produce the cold in my liquefying machine exactly as well as a steam engine. **1901** *Daily Colonist* (Victoria, B.C.) 6 Oct. 3/4 The most sensational thing in the scientific world today is liquid air. **1925** E. F. NORTON *Fight for Everest, 1924* 91 Waiting for us with hot soup in a liquid-air flask. **1946** *Nature* 20 July 105/1 A laboratory liquid-air plant utilizing Freon-12 as a pre-cooling fluid has been designed and is now being constructed. **1865** *Rep. Brit. Assoc. Adv. Sci. 1864* 14 The distinctive peculiarities of the liquid compass are an air-tight metallic case, within which is placed the magnetic needle, and of such size and weight as to be of very nearly the same specific gravity as the liquid in which it is intended to float. **1959** E. C. GOLDSWORTHY *Seamanship & Navigation* iii. 41 This liquid compass is preferred to the dry-card compass where there is much vibration, as the liquid damps the oscillations of the card caused by the movements of the vessel. **1916** C. C. GARRARD *Electr. Switch & Controlling Gear* v. 357 The rating of the liquid controller is, therefore, based upon the maximum horse-power dissipated. **1957** W. J. JOHN *Mod. Electr. Engin.* II. iii. 58 (*caption*) A liquid controller of the type shown here provides smooth control from normal down to crawling speed. **1891** *Jrnl. Chem. Soc.* LX. I. 250 Liquid crystals, when heated between cover glasses slightly above the point where they pass into ordinary liquids, retain on cooling the original direction of their optical axes. **1938** *Ann. Reg. 1937* 352 Tobacco mosaic virus is a nucleoprotein of special character, existing as mesomorphic fibres in the cell sap and spontaneously forming liquid crystals of gigantic cell-size when isolated. **1962** *Times* 30 Apr. 7/1 When detergents are mixed with a limited amount of water, several distinct 'mesomorphic' phases may be formed. These phases are also known as 'liquid crystals' because some of their properties are akin to those of a solid while others are characteristic of a liquid. **1972** *Physics Bull.* May 279/1 These fascinating compounds can no longer be regarded as freaks of nature, for out of every two hundred organic compounds at least one may be a liquid crystal. **1864** *Brit. Pharmacopœia* 219 (*heading*) Liquid extract of Bael. **1930** J. W. COOPER *Pharmacy* xiii. 115, 1,000 grm. of couch grass is used to produce 1,000 mil. of liquid extract. **1935** Liquidextract [see *FLUID *a.* and *sb.* A. 1 a]. **1968** *Biol. Abstr.* XLIX. 1161/1 This liquid extract [from the bark of *Oroxylon indicum*] lowered the vascular permeability of rats sensitized with egg protein. **1604, 1667** Liquid fire [in Dict., sense A. 1]. **1815** J. SMITH *Panorama Sci. & Art* II. 579 It is in this way that the various kinds of cordial waters are prepared... The term liquid-fire has not unaptly been given them. **1838** E. EDEN *Let.* 28 Nov. in *Up Country* (1866) I. xxvi. 282 Runjeet produced some of his wine, a sort of liquid fire. **1862** *Temple Bar* July 512 Ordinary phosphorus is readily soluble in bisulphide of carbon: when thus in solution constituting the liquid denominated by Captains Disney and Norton 'liquid fire'. **1915** *Illustr. London News* 13 Mar. 321 The enemy attacking a trench into which they had sent liquid fire. **1889** GROVES & THORP *Chem. Technol.* I. 293 (*caption*) Liquid fuel. **1912** W. S. CHURCHILL *Let.* 11 June in *World Crisis 1911–14* vi. 32 This liquid fuel problem has got to be solved. **1913** *Chem. Abstr.* VII. 3827 One of the principal differences between solid and liquid fuels is in the proportion of C combined with H. **1920** *Conquest* Nov. 47/2 In the near future liquid fuel will have to be 'rationed' again. **1935** *Jrnl. R. Aeronaut. Soc.* XXXIX. 507 Germany consumes two million tons of liquid fuel per year. **1946** *Jrnl. Brit. Interplanetary Soc.* VI. I. 2 At first the research was conducted with powder rockets, but after a few years a change was made to liquid fuel. This was at first tried out on a test bench, and then, in July, 1929, what is claimed to be the first liquid-fuel rocket to take-off was launched near Worcester—but it exploded at 900 feet. **1963** BIRD & HUTTON-STOTT *Veteran Motor Car* 75 Daimler's 'high speed' liquid-fuel engine. **1966** *Electronics* 17 Oct. 35 For the next decade, at least, liquid fuel will propel United States astronauts into space. **1969** *Times* 3 June (Suppl.) p. ii/4 Goddard launched on March 16, 1926, the world's first liquid fuel rocket. **1960** *Times* 18 Oct. 13/6 The Minuteman cannot carry as large a warhead as the liquid-fuelled i.c.b.m.s. **1967** *Technology Week* 20 Feb. 3/2 The hardened, storable liquid-fueled *Titan* carries the largest U.S. missile warhead and can also reach targets beyond the range of the current *Minuteman I*. **1875** E. SPON *Workshop Receipts* 41/1 Liquid glue... Soft water, 1 quart; best pale glue, 2 lbs.; [etc.]. **1927** KNIGHT & WULPI *Veneers & Plywood* xxv. 276 Probably the general public..thinks of liquid glues, whenever glue is mentioned, but such preparations are in no way typical of manufacturing materials or procedures. **1966** *McGraw-Hill Encycl. Sci. & Technol.* VI. 219/2 Liquid glue is commonly made from fish collagen because this has little tendency to gel, but it can also be made from animal glue by treatment with acid or certain salts to inhibit gelation. **1970** G. F. NEWMAN *Sir, You Bastard* ii. 65 The caretaker, aroused from his post-liquid-lunch slumber, confirmed that the couple had parted. **1972** B. EVERITT *Cold Front* vii. 55 He..refused all offers of liquid lunches and bore me off..for a great deal of solid pasta. **1837** C. W. JOHNSON (*title*) On liquid manures. **1842** J. C. LOUDON *Suburban Horticulturist* iii. 59 Arrangements should be made for collecting all the liquid manure into two adjoining tanks. **1869** S. R. HOLE *Bk. about Roses* vi. 83 The rich extract, full of carbonate of ammonia..may be used..as liquid manure in the Rosary. **1911** O. ONIONS *Widdershins* 247 The hares and foxes were down four days ago, and the liquid-manure pumps like a snow man. **1914** J. LONDON *Let.* 21 Sept. (1966) 429, I have a fairly decent brood-barn, with liquid-manure tank attached. **1973** R. GENDERS *Epicure's Garden* II. 167 An occasional application of liquid manure will also prove beneficial. **1878** *Jrnl. Chem. Soc.* XXXIV. 10 A jet of liquid oxygen escaping from the tube when the pressure was taken off. **1885** [see REFRIGERANT *sb.* 3]. **1919** *Chem. Abstr.* 791 Spontaneous explosion of the charcoal in liquid-oxygen containers. **1954** *Economist* 11 Sept. 12/1 Rocket motors do not need atmospheric oxygen, although they frequently carry liquid oxygen, and rocket power is, unlike jet power, effective in outer space. **1956** *Spaceflight* Oct. 5/1 Propellants which are in common use to-day (e.g. liquid oxygen and petrol) yield exhaust velocities of the order of 2½ km./sec. **1884** *Jrnl. Chem. Soc.* XLVI. 1073 The 'liquid paraffin' of the German Pharmacopœia, is an oily liquid consisting of a mixture of hydrocarbons of the methane series. **1943** J. B. PRIESTLEY *Daylight on Saturday* ii. 6 She was a dark girl with a long sad nose, and dosed herself with liquid paraffin. **1962** *Which?* Jan. 26/2 Liquid paraffin is the only common lubricant laxative. **1905** *Pharmacopœia U.S.* 336 Liquid Petrolatum, a mixture of hydrocarbons, chiefly of the methane series, obtained by distilling off most of the lighter and more volatile portions from petroleum, and purifying the liquid residue. **1926** *Daily Colonist* (Victoria, B.C.) 20 Jan. 7/3 (Advt.), Liquid petrolatum, heavy, special at 53¢. **1951** A. GROLLMAN *Pharmacol. & Therapeutics* xix. 386 Liquid petrolatum is also available in the form of a flavored emulsion. **1905** P. DAWSON in M. Maclean *Mod. Electr. Pract.* VI. v. iv. 214 Amongst the advantages claimed for liquid rheostats may be mentioned the gradual variation of the resistance, their compactness and cheap first cost, and the absence of damage from sparking when the current is interrupted. **1957** W. J. JOHN *Mod. Electr. Engin.* II. iii. 59/1 A common method of providing resistance is by means of a liquid rheostat, consisting of a tank of electrolyte containing two electrodes, one fixed and one movable. **1600** Liquid sope [in Dict. s.v. SOAP *sb.* 2]. **1907** *Yesterday's Shopping* (1969) 536/3 Moline, a liquid soap, delicately perfumed for the toilet. **1920** A. KEANE tr. *Deite's Man. Toilet Soap-Making* (ed. 2) 236 The liquid soaps are mostly solutions of potash soaps in glycerine, sugar, or alkali and strong alcohol solutions. **1966** J. S. COX *Illustr. Dict. Hairdressing* 90/2 *Liquid soap shampoo.* The base is usually green soft soap and sometimes in addition either cocoanut oil, olive oil or eucalyptus oil. **1907** G. W. O. HOWE tr. *Thomälen's Text-bk. Electr. Engin.* 453/1 (Index), Liquid starter. **1916** C. C. GARRARD *Electr. Switch & Controlling Gear* v. 353 The liquid starter, in which a solution of caustic soda or washing soda replaces the resistance wire or grids as used in the ordinary form of starter, is the most rugged of all forms of starting gear. **1932** E. MOLLOY *Pract. Electr. Engin.* IV. 1319/2 Liquid starters are best suited for medium and large-size motors which require to be started infrequently.

B. *sb.* **3.** *liquid-cooled, -filled* adjs.; *liquid-cooling*; **liquid-drop,** used *attrib.* in *Physics* to denote a theoretical model in which an explanation of the properties and behaviour of the atomic nucleus is sought by likening it to a droplet of liquid, as regards the forces between its constituents; **liquid–liquid** *a.*, pertaining to or involving two different liquids, or liquids in two different ways.

1931 *Jrnl. R. Aeronaut. Soc.* XXXV. 180 The developments to be described are..applicable to all water or liquid-cooled engines. **1967** *Jane's Surface Skimmer Systems 1967–68* 25/1 The power plant..comprises a 240 hp Rolls-Royce LV-8 liquid-cooled eight-cylinder engine. **1933** J. D. FRIER *Aero Engines* I. vii. 94 A great advantage of liquid cooling is that..the engine temperature is limited to the boiling-point of the liquid employed. **1960** *McGraw-Hill Encycl. Sci. & Technol.* IV. 604/2 In liquid cooling, the engine and radiator may be separated and each placed in the optimum location. [**1939** MEITNER & FRISCH in *Nature* 11 Feb. 239/1 On account of their close packing and strong energy exchange, the particles in a heavy nucleus would be expected to move in a collective way which has some resemblance to the movement of a liquid drop.] **1939** BOHR & WHEELER in *Physical Rev.* LVI. 426 On the basis of the liquid drop model of atomic nuclei, an account is given of the mechanism of nuclear fission. **1955** R. D. EVANS *Atomic Nucleus* xi. 365 The liquid-drop model is the antithesis of the independent-particle models. The interactions between nucleons are assumed to be strong instead of weak. **1970** D. F. JACKSON *Nucl. Reactions* ii. 17 The static liquid drop model of the nucleus.. was the first successful nuclear model and was used to describe the bulk properties of nuclei such as nuclear masses and binding energies. **1960** E. L. DELMAR-MORGAN *Cruising Yacht Equipment & Navigation* ii. 33 The liquid-filled 'dead-beat' instrument [*sc.* compass] has now taken its place. **1967** KARCH & BUBER *Offset Processes* iv. 128 Modification of copy is effected simply by liquid-filled cylindrical lenses or prisms in front of the copy or film. **1940** GLASSTONE *Text-bk. Physical Chem.* x. 725 (*heading*) Distribution in liquid–liquid systems. **1951, 1952** [see *gas-liquid* adj. (*GAS *sb.*[1] 7)]. **1958** *Chambers's Techn. Dict.* 991/1 *Liquid–liquid extraction*, process whereby two non-mixing liquids are brought together for an exchange of substances dissolved in them. **1968** COULSON & RICHARDSON *Chem. Engin.* (ed. 2) II. xii. 486 The separation of the components of a liquid mixture with a solvent in which one or more of the desired components is preferentially soluble is known as liquid–liquid extraction. This process has been..very extensively applied to the separation of hydrocarbons in the petroleum industry.

liquidate, *v.* Add: **7.** [after Russ. *likvidírovat'* to liquidate, wind up.] To put an end to, abolish; to stamp out, wipe out; to kill.

1924 *Yale Rev.* XIII. 477 In this way the 'Labor Opposition', the 'Workers *Pravda*', and a few other recalcitrant groups were all 'liquidated'. **1926** C. SHERIDAN *Turkish Kaleidoscope* xvi. 125 The evening paper, *L'Akcham*, came out with large headlines: 'How to Liquidate a Strike'. **1930** *Economist* 1 Nov. (Russ. Suppl.) 2/2 Only in 1929, when the growth of the Socialist section of agriculture was enabling the State to become independent of the supplies of the Kulaks, could the Government begin to 'liquidate' them. **1939** V. A. DEMANT *Relig. Prospect* iv. 90 The Trotskyists..are 'liquidated' as being insufficiently dialectical to see that the policy of the Russian State at any moment has absolute finality. **1943** C. S. LEWIS *Abolition of Man* iii. 37 Once we killed bad men: now we liquidate unsocial elements. **1957** PARTRIDGE *English gone Wrong* ii. 31 *Liquidate*, therefore, is an erudite synonym of 'to wind up', hence, in its euphemistic transferred sense, it means 'to eradicate in a thoroughly ruthless manner', 'to destroy, especially by mass murder'. **1970** *Nature* 26 Dec. 1248/2 All existing sources of industrial pollution are to be 'liquidated'. **1971** *Sunday Times* 13 June 12/6 When the army units fanned out in Dacca on the evening of March 25..many of them carried lists of people to be liquidated.

liquidating *vbl. sb.* and *ppl. a.* (Later examples.)

1931 *Economist* 20 June 1331/1 The market capitalisation of the common shares of these concerns was equal to only 74 per cent. of the 'liquidating value' of the assets behind them. **1964** *Ann. Reg. 1963* 103 It provided that.. the permanent heads of the three territorial Treasuries would constitute a liquidating agency to wind up the affairs of the Federation. **1975** [see *LIQUIDATOR c].

liquidation. Add: **2. b.** *Chess.* The partial clearing of the board, by an exchange of pieces, to obtain an obviously winning position; simplification.

1965 LOVE & HODGKINS *Further Chess Ideas* xv. 124 Sometimes, too, under pressure of an enemy attack and with good end game prospects if ever one should be reached, wholesale exchanges are most welcome. This is called liquidation. **1965** W. H. COZENS tr. *Euwe & Kramer's Middle Game* II. x. 185 The problem of liquidation is to select the precise moment when pieces, or some particular piece, should be exchanged... Judicious liquidation involves steering a middle course between the one extreme of premature simplification and the other extreme of interminable 'wood shifting'. **1966** *New Statesman* 2 Dec. 854/3 True enough, White is a P up, but the Black heavy artillery is well placed. Yet, hey presto: a miraculous 'liquidation', and a won ending in a few moves.

3. Also, the selling of certain assets in order to achieve greater liquidity. (See quot. 1965.)

1909 *Westm. Gaz.* 2 Mar. 4/2 As many people..think that the word 'liquidation' must necessarily be associated with bankruptcy.., I am asked to state officially that the liquidation of the old company is only one step in the course of reconstruction for the purpose of obtaining fresh capital. **1929** *Observer* 17 Nov. 4/2 The Rhodesian share market was in a depressed condition, owing to the liquidation taking place on American account. **1939** J. A. SCHUMPETER *Business Cycles* I. iv. 149 Abnormal liquidation destroys many things which could and would have survived without it. **1965** *McGraw-Hill Dict. Mod. Econ.* 299 *Liquidation*, the process of selling assets, such as inventories or securities in order to achieve a better cash position.

b. [f. *LIQUIDATE *v.* 7.] The action or process of abolishing or eliminating; the doing away with or killing of unwanted persons.

1925 tr. *L. Trotzky's Whither England?* vi. 145 History is liquidating liberalism and preparing for the liquidation of pseudo-labor pacifism. **1932** *Week-end Rev.* 2 Jan. 24/1 The Russians..took starvation almost as a matter of course, just as they..take as a matter of course the liquidation of unfortunate individuals with contra-revolutionary idealogies. **1949** F. MACLEAN *Eastern Approaches* I. ii. 24 There was nothing new in the 'liquidation', as it was called, of public figures. For some years past numerous politicians and others had met with this fate, variously branded as 'Trotskists' [*sic*], 'wreckers',..and so on. **1952** *Sat. Rev.* (U.S.) 20 Sept. 37/1 Liquidation..was extended ..to persons in..the Party... The liquidation occurred during the purges (a revolting combination).

4. The action or fact of partaking of an alcoholic drink. *rare.*

1889 F. E. GRETTON *Memory's Harkback* 311 As regards *liquidation*, champagne..is now almost as *vin ordinaire*. **1909** 'O. HENRY' *Roads of Destiny* vii. 106 His desire for liquidation was expressed so heartily that I went with him to a café..where we had some vile vermouth and bitters.

liquidator. Add: (Later examples.)

1965 SELDON & PENNANCE *Everyman's Dict. Econ.* 260 The Official Receiver is appointed provisional liquidator, and his appointment may be confirmed or he may be replaced at the first meeting of the creditors. **1971** *Daily Tel.* 9 Feb. 15/5 The creditors' call for a provisional liquidator for Mineral Securities..followed on intense activity ..with leading Australian international financiers. **1971** *Times* 10 Dec. 8/6 The appointment of a provisional liquidator and special manager was essential in order to collect those balances and get the other assets in.

c. A person who implements a policy of liquidation. Cf. *LIQUIDATE *v.* 7.

1949 [see *GRAVE-DIGGER 3]. **1963** *Listener* 24 Jan. 171/1 The psychotic actions of totalitarian liquidators. **1975** J. GARDNER *Killer for Song* ii. 16 Special Security had employed him as an agent—a liquidating agent, designed, quite literally, to cut down security risks. They had even called him the Liquidator.

liquidity. Add: **1. d.** *Econ.* The interchangeability of assets and money; hence **liquidity preference**, the holding of assets in money or near-money in preference to securities or interest-bearing investments; **liquidity ratio**, that proportion of total assets which is held in liquid or cash form, esp. by a bank.

1923 R. G. HAWTREY *Currency & Credit* (ed. 2) v. 83 The liquidity of the Bank of England is secured by its power of printing notes, and the interchangeability of its deposits with cash is absolute. **1925** G. G. MUNN *Bank Credit* i. 9 Gold is the ultimate in liquidity, the ultimate intermediate of exchange, and is *ipso facto* irredeemable. **1936** J. M. KEYNES *Gen. Theory Employment* xiii. 168 Liquidity-preference is a potentiality or functional tendency, which fixes the quantity of money which the public will hold when the rate of interest is given. *Ibid.* xvii. 241 Money itself rapidly loses the attribute of 'liquidity' if its future supply is expected to undergo sharp changes. **1940** *Economist* 27 Jan. 152/1 The attainment of a more than adequate liquidity ratio is perhaps the main feature..over the past year. **1940** G. CROWTHER *Outl. Money* ii. 76 The more highly developed banking systems are more prone to suffer from such a 'liquidity preference' than the less developed countries. **1958** *Economist* 26 July 281/2 The real spark-plug of expansion—improved international liquidity—cannot be discussed in the Commonwealth context alone. **1961** *Ann. Reg. 1960* 488 The 'liquidity ratio' is the proportion of 'liquid assets', i.e. cash, short money and bills, to gross deposits. **1962** C. H. KREPS *Money* I. i. 12 One view of the fundamental nature of interest regards interest as compensation for loss of liquidity. *Ibid.*, Using this liquidity-preference approach, we may say that wealth held in absolutely liquid form—in the form of money, that is—yields its owner no income. **1969** *Times* 5 May (Suppl.) p. iv/3 The market would lose its liquidity... As liquidity declined.., public confidence would lessen considerably. **1972** *Accountant* 23 Mar. 385/1 It was necessary to increase liquidity during the year to finance the continuing substantial capital programme.

liquidize, *v.* Add: Also *intr.*, to become liquid.

1969 *Sunday Times* (Colour Suppl.) 9 Feb. 13/2 The lettuce liquidising in the vegetable compartment.

b. [f. *LIQUIDIZER.] To purée, emulsify, or blend in a liquidizer. Hence **li·quidizing** *ppl. a.* and *vbl. sb.*

1959 *Which?* June 49/1 It was satisfactory in its mixing and liquidizing. **1966** *Punch* 2 Nov. 676/3 A very nice Melde dish is made by heating the vivid green..liquidised leaves with cheese to serve on toast as 'Anglo-Saxon Rarebit'. **1972** S. ATTERBURY *Waste Not—Want Not* II. 53 After liquidising, pour the soup into a saucepan. *Ibid.* 54 Do not add too much liquid before the pods are liquidised or the subtle flavour might be swamped. **1972** BEALE & JOHNSTON *Mixer & Blender Cookery* xxi. 132 Liquidize ½ or 1 banana and add to thick custard. **1972** *Garde ta Foie!: Cambridge Cookery Bk. for Shelter* (Cambridge Shelter Group) 7 Stew gently with lid on until soft. Sieve or liquidise. **1973** *Daily Tel.* 27 Jan. 1/2 After his thirst and hunger strike ended, MacStiofain was given soups, tea and liquidised vegetables.

liquidizer (li·kwidəizəɹ). [f. LIQUIDIZ(E *v.* + -ER[1].] A machine used in the preparation of food, to make purées, emulsify, etc. Also *attrib.*, as *liquidizer attachment*.

1950 *Consumers' Res. Bull.* (U.S.) Feb. 9 (*heading*) 'Liquefiers', 'liquidizers', or 'blenders'. **1958** *Observer* 24 Aug. 7/5 The most usual 'extras' are mincers, juice squeezers, and liquidisers—the last consisting of whirling blades inside a glass goblet, to make purées, soups, drinks, etc. **1962** *Which?* May 144/2 All the mixers had liquidiser attachments, and we tested them to see how well they pulped tomatoes, made breadcrumbs, chopped nuts, ground coffee beans, chopped parsley and crushed ice. **1969** H.-P. PELLAPRAT *Everyday French Cooking* 48 Put through a fine sieve or the liquidiser. **1972** BEALE & JOHNSTON *Mixer & Blender Cookery* iv. 20 The liquidizer reduces dried peas beans, lentils, rice, etc., into powder speedily.

liquidus (li·kwidŭs). [L. *liquidus* LIQUID *a.*, adopted in this sense (in G.) by H. W. B. Roozeboom 1899, in *Zeitschr. f. phys. Chem.* XXX. 387.] A line in a phase diagram, or a temperature (corresponding to a point on the line), above which a mixture is entirely liquid and below which it consists of liquid and solid in equilibrium; freq. *attrib.* as *liquidus curve, temperature.* Also (more fully *liquidus surface*), an analogous surface in a three-dimensional phase diagram.

1901 *Proc. R. Soc.* LXVIII. 174 Cooling curves will.. give the approximate moment of complete solidification of an alloy, and enable us to plot in a rough way the 'solidus' curve, as Roozeboom calls it; but the solidus curve thus obtained is not nearly so accurate as the 'liquidus' or freezing-point curve. **1923** GLAZEBROOK *Dict. Appl. Physics* V. 245/2 The liquidus and the solidus meet, in the case under consideration, at the points A and C, which are the melting points of the pure metals, and B, which is known as the eutectic point. **1948** GLASSTONE *Textbk. Physical Chem.* (ed. 2) x. 762 Separation of solid.. commences at *y* and is complete at *z'*; for this reason the liquidus curve is sometimes called the freezing-point curve, and the solidus curve is called the melting-point curve. **1960** C. J. PHILLIPS *Glass: Industr. Applic.* v. 54 The viscosity at the liquidus temperature is high enough to prevent nucleation. **1967** A. H. COTTRELL *Introd. Metall.* xvi. 252 (*caption*) Liquidus surface of a eutectic system. **1972** *Physics Bull.* Nov. 352/3 Glass is a metastable state; it can be brought to the stable state by holding at temperatures near the liquidus.

liquor, *sb.* Add: **7.** *liquor-bar, house, law, licence, question, -saloon* (earlier example), *-seller* (examples), *-selling, -shop* (later examples), *-store* (later examples), *trade, traffic* (earlier and later examples); **liquor prescription** *Canad. Hist.*, a doctor's prescription of alcohol for 'medicinal' purposes, to evade the prohibition regulations.

1813 W. DUNLAP *Mem. G. F. Cooke* II. xxx. 278 The fountain of mischief, the liquor-bar, was shut. **1924** W. M. RAINE *Troubled Waters* ii. 21 The postmistress handed him a letter and two circulars from liquor houses. **1852** *Boston Bee* 29 July, The Life Boat..takes the Bee to do, for its course in relation to the Liquor law. **1858** A. LINCOLN *Coll. Works* (1953) II. 493, I do not believe in the right of Illinois to interfere with..the Liquor Laws of Maine. **1866** G. MEREDITH *Let. c* 27 Nov. (1970) I. 345 You will become a fanatical Retired Admiral advocating Maine Liquor laws for every natural appetite on earth. **1908** *Daily Chron.* 27 Feb. 4/4 Certain liquor-law restrictions which had existed under the second Empire. **1975** *Listener* 16 Jan. 76/1 The counties would have.. their own educational system, their liquor laws. **1850** *Hunt's Merchant's Mag.* XXII. 87 (*caption*) Statistics of Liquor Licenses in New York City. **1956** B. HOLIDAY *Lady sings Blues* (1973) xix. 157 According to the law.. nobody who has a police record can hold a liquor licence. **1971** *Sunday Express* (Johannesburg) 28 Mar. (Homefinder) 7/2 (Advt.), 1. Dance hall. 2. Restaurant—Liquor licence. **1921** *Daily Colonist* (Victoria, B.C.) 18 Mar. 1/3 The suspension of 19 physicians in Manitoba for unlawfully issuing liquor prescriptions has resulted from an inquiry. **1855** Liquor question [see *liquor-shop* below]. *c* **1918** C. STELZLE *Why Prohibition!* 291 Michigan was about to vote on the liquor question. **1863** *Daily Even. Bulletin* (San Francisco) 29 Sept. 3/2 At 1 o'clock they went into a liquor saloon kept by a woman on Kearny Street. **1855** P. T. BARNUM *Life* 359 The liquor seller, the moderate drinker, and the indifferent man. **1877** *Harper's Mag.* Dec. 146/2 A method which practically makes the government the liquor-seller. *Ibid.*, All liquor-selling is not equally dangerous to the community. **1855** 'Q. K. P. DOESTICKS' *Doesticks, what he Says* xxxi. 276 The great excitement was on the liquor question; it was Noggs and no liquor shops, or Boggs and a few liquor shops. **1877** J. HABBERTON *Jericho Road* xix. 167 There was not even a streak of light visible under the door of any liquor-shop in the town. **1911** *Encycl. Brit.* XVI. 769/2 The effect has been a very large reduction in the number of liquor shops. **1855** 'Q. K. P. DOESTICKS' *Doesticks, what he Says* xii. 98 Fire in a liquor-store—hose burst; brandy 'lying round loose'. **1887** *Nation* (N.Y.) 15 Dec. 468/3 To keep a liquor-store in Philadelphia. **1939** F. P. GROVE *Two Generations* 39 Take the proceeds to the liquor store. **1964** *Calgary Herald* 24 July 23/2 A liquor store on the site would devalue residential property to the immediate west. **1972** R. BLOCH *Night-World* (1974) xi. 72 He passed the lights of the liquor store. **1908** *Daily Chron.* 12 May 4/4 Unfortunately for the Labour party they have got entangled with the liquor trade vote. **1848** J. MARSH (*title*) A discourse on the extent and evils of the Sunday liquor traffic in cities. **1877** *Harper's Mag.* Dec. 146/2 This work is a compilation of evidence on 'the problem of law as applied to the liquor traffic'. **1915** W. J. BRYAN *Mem.* 2 Oct. (1925) 434 The brewers and distillers were connecting them with the liquor traffic to their detriment.

liquordom. (Later example.)

1918 T. H. WALKER *Principal J. Denney* 119 His hatred of liquordom..sprang from devotion to his Master.

liquorice, licorice. Add: **4.** *liquorice all-sorts* (see *all-sorts* s.v. *ALL E. 13), *drop, jujube, lozenge, lump, toffee, treasure, -water* (earlier and later examples); **liquorice bootlace** = *BOOT-LACE c; **liquorice-stick,** (*a*) in Dict. (later examples); (*b*) *Jazz slang*, a clarinet.

1928 *Sweet Shop* Nov. p. ii (Advt.), Original Liquorice All Sorts. **1931** [see *all-sorts* s.v. *ALL E. 13]. **1946** *R.A.F. Jrnl.* May 162 His C.O...with the broad ring and a row of gongs that reminded Joe of liquorice all-sorts. **1952** *Blackw. Mag.* July 30/2 Lollipops, pincushions, liquorice boot-laces, bottles of home-made wine. **1956** 'R. CROMPTON' *William & Space Animal* v. 135 Doughnuts an' trifle an' liqu'rice boot laces. **1906** 'O. HENRY' *Four Million* (1916) 173 Liquorice drops—the kind that make your cheek look like the toothache. **1967** R. MACKAY *House & Day* 74 Have you licorice drops? **1891** *Confectioners' Union* IV. 530 (Advt.), Goods packed in 4 lb. boxes.. Bright liquorice jujubes. **1857** J. A. SYMONDS *Let.* 25 Jan. (1967) I. 86 Will you send me also another box of Liquorice Lozenges. **1893** *Official Catal. Internat. Manufacturing Confectioners Exhib.* 60 (Advt.), Linseed Liquorice and Chlorodyne Lozenges. **1926** 'R. CROMPTON' *William—the Conqueror* iii. 54 Large paper bags of bullseyes, liquorice lumps, barley sugar and chocolate cigars. **1879** Liquorice-stick [see **goose-yoke*]. **1935** *Vanity Fair* (N.Y.) Nov. 71/3 *Agony pipe, wop stick,* and *licorice stick* for clarinet. **1958** N. D. HINTON in *Publ. Amer. Dial. Soc.* XXX. 39, I have found a common belief that jazzmen refer to a clarinet as a 'licorice stick'... Jazz musicians do in fact use these terms ..in a very peculiar way. **1967** C. DRUMMOND *Death at Furlong Post* iv. 39 Bee dispensed liquorice sticks..and fizzy drinks. **1930** *Confectioners' Union Directory Trade Marks & Trade Names* 18/2 (Advt.), Buttered Liquorice Toffee in Dainty Pieces. **1924** 'R. CROMPTON' *William—the Fourth* viii. 125 'Have a liquorice treasure?' she said. **1860** DICKENS *Gt. Expect.* (1861) I. ii. 29 That intoxicating fluid, Spanish-liquorice-water. **1913** C. MACKENZIE *Sinister St.* I. iv. 59 They used to go calling up and down, 'Fine liquorice-water!.. Bring out your pins and have a bottle of liquorice-water.' **1960** *Guardian* 6 Dec. 7/2 The bottles of liquorice-water which provided grog for his young games of pirates.

lira. Add: **2.** A monetary unit in Turkey.

1871 *Murray's Handbk. Turkey in Asia* (new ed.) 27 The coinage consists of copper, silver, and gold, at the rate of 100 piastres to the Turkish pound or *lira.* **1884** F. BOYLE *On Borderland betwixt Fact & Fancy* 237 The high wall on our left was that of the pasha's grounds. The one-eyed calender informed me that he could get permission to visit them next day, for a baksheesh of two liras. Thirty-six shillings seemed too much to pay for a stroll through a burnt-up garden. **1904** *Daily Chron.* 17 Feb. 3/6 A thousand Turkish liras weigh about 14 lb. **1912** T. E. LAWRENCE *Let.* 10 Feb. (1938) 136 The foot seal must be worth a lira at the least. **1975** J. RATHBONE *Kill Cure* III. vii. 128 'How much?'..'Forty dollars or twenty-five sterling. Turkish lira, much more.'

lirate (ləiə·rĕt), *a.* [f. L. *līra* ridge, furrow: see -ATE[2].] Of a shell: having ridges. Hence **lira·tion**, marking of this kind.

1894 J. W. TAYLOR *Monogr. Land & Freshwater Mollusca Brit. Isles* I. I. 28 Cingulate, or Lirate, when the whorls are furnished with spiral ribs or ridgings. **1901** *Proc. Zool. Soc.* II. 357 *Actis calotropis*... A very delicate species, vitreous,..delicately spirally lirate. **1904** *Ann. &*

Mag. Nat. Hist. 7th Ser. XIII. 459 This liration bears small tubercles connected by short cross-ridges with the dentations of the keel.

‖ **lirio** (li·ryo). [Sp. *lirio* iris.] The American Spanish name for the water hyacinth, *Eichhornia crassipes.*

Quot. 1844 refers to a different plant, perhaps the frangipani, *Plumeria rubra.*

[**1844** J. G. F. Wurdemann *Notes on Cuba* v. 140 The quaint lirio's trumpet-shaped flowers painted yellow and red, and bursting in bunches from the blunt extremities of each leafless branch.] **1926** D. H. Lawrence *Plumed Serpent* v. 94 A long canal paved with bright green leaves from which poked the mauve heads of the lirio, the water hyacinth.

Lissajous (li·saʒu). The name of Jules Antoine *Lissajous* (1822–80), French physicist, used *attrib.* and in the possessive to designate the plane figures (mostly crossed loops and simple curves) traced by a point executing two independent simple harmonic motions at right angles to one another and with frequencies in a simple numerical ratio (described by Lissajous in *Compt. Rend.* (1855) XLI. 814).

1877 Rayleigh *Theory of Sound* I. p. vii, Lissajous' Figures. **1902** *Encycl. Brit.* XXV. 50/1 If both forks vibrate, an observer looking through the microscope sees the bright point describing Lissajous figures. **1939** *Brit. Jrnl. Psychol.* Oct. 129 The frequency of the tones employed.. is checked by obtaining a Lissajous's figure against a constant frequency source applied to the other deflectors of the cathode-ray tube. **1943** *Electronic Engin.* XVI. 170 Two measuring techniques for the Lissajous' figures produced on the oscilloscope screen are described. **1973** *Sci. Amer.* Aug. 76/2 The two tones were next matched precisely on a cathode ray oscilloscope by tuning the generated tone until a clear Lissajous figure with a ratio of 1:1 appeared repeatedly on the screen.

lissoir (liswā·r). *Archæol.* [Fr.] A smoothing, polishing tool.

1911 W. J. Sollas *Ancient Hunters* viii. 214 A small object, about the size and shape of the human tongue, possibly the end of a 'lissoir' (smoothing implement). *Ibid.* xii. 368 The ivory 'lissoir' or smoother of the Eskimo..is represented in the Magdalenian industry. **1932** *Jrnl. R. Anthrop. Inst.* LXII. 265 Skin-rubbers were made from antler of *Dama Mesopotamica*, cut obliquely and smoothed, in the manner of the Magdalenian *lissoir.* **1937** Garrod & Bate *Stone Age Mt. Carmel* I. I. ii. 15 Bone points and pierced animal teeth and a *lissoir* of *Dama Mesopotamica* antler. **1964** *New Scientist* 9 Apr. 88/1 A single, well-used bone-tool came to light; it appears to be a sort of 'lissoir' for working leather thongs.

lissom, *a.* Hence li·ssomely *adv.*

1902 W. de la Mare *Songs of Childhood* 54 Though danced she lissomely. **1927** M. Sadleir *Trollope: a Comm.* 322 Trollope worried to find it limping on its way, when usually his stories moved so lissomely.

list, *sb.*³ Add: **2. d.** (Further examples.)

1809 Jane Austen *Let.* 24 Jan. (1952) 257 We..could have staid longer but for the arrival of my List shoes to convey me home. **1856** Dickens *Dorrit* (1857) I. xiii. 106 Mr. Casby rose up in his list shoes. **1908** A. Bennett *Old Wives' Tale* IV. iii. 480 Sophia wore list slippers in the morning. It was a habit which she had formed in the Rue Lord Byron—by accident rather than with an intention to utilize list slippers for the effective supervision of servants.

3. (Later examples.)

1855 P. T. Barnum *Life* 109 Mallet had agreed..to deliver twelve yards of broadcloth 'lists' to Shepard. **1886** F. T. Elworthy *West Somerset Word-Bk.* 442 In flannels and in wool-dyed cloths it is usual to have a list or narrow border on each side of the cloth.

list, *sb.*⁶ Add: **a.** In specific senses. (*a*) The titles of the books (to be) published by a particular publisher. So *autumn list,* *backlist, *spring list.*

1860 G. H. Lewes *Let.* 4 Jan. in Geo. Eliot *Lett.* (1954) III. 243 It will be well now to begin announcing it in lists —if not the title at any rate the fact of a new novel being in the press. **1919** *Publisher's Let.* Aug. in T. S. Eliot *Waste Land Drafts* (1971) p. xvi, Mr. Eliot's work is no doubt brilliant, but it is not exactly the kind of material we care to add to our list. **1922** T. S. Eliot *Let.* 25 June in *Waste Land Drafts* (1971) p. xxii, Knopf said that it was too late for his autumn list this year. **1930** E. Waugh *Vile Bodies* ii. 28, I suppose you could get the book rewritten in time for the Spring List? **1938** H. R. Dent in J. M. & H. R. Dent *House of Dent* xxiii. 300 It used to be said..that a publisher kept poetry on his lists more for the look of the thing than anything else. **1951** M. Sharp *Lise Lilywhite* xix. 161 Mr Villiers..published chiefly poetry... He had no list, in the trade sense, nor had he travellers. **1964** R. Church *Voyage Home* viii. 166, I should send the book to the house of Dent, whose list it would suit admirably. **1967** E. Grierson *Crime of One's Own* viii. 60 Christmas operated like a guillotine on the Autumn lists, leaving only a bare four weeks of selling time.

(*b*) An official register of buildings of architectural or historical importance that are statutorily protected from demolition or major alteration. Cf. *list *v.*⁴ 1 e.

1947 *Act* 10 & 11 *Geo. VI* c. 51 §30 With a view to the guidance of local planning authorities..in relation to buildings of special architectural or historic interest, the Minister shall compile lists of such buildings, or approve.. such lists compiled by other persons or bodies of persons. *Ibid.*, So long as any building..is included in any list compiled or approved under this section, no person shall execute..any works for the demolition of the building or for its alteration or extension in any manner which would seriously affect its character. **1968** P. Ward *Conservation & Devel. Historic Towns & Cities* III. 98 Lansdown Parade..is also a Grade II listed building on the Ministry of Housing and Local Government's list of architecturally or historically important buildings.

(*c*) In the National Health Service, a general practitioner's register of patients.

1949 *Britannica Bk. of Year* 412/2 Doctors starting their careers..had few patients on their lists. *Ibid.* 413/1 The doctor was free to accept or reject anyone applying to go on his list. **1971** *Reader's Digest Family Guide to Law* 242 A doctor..does not have to give reasons for his refusal to accept a patient on his list. **1974** M. Birmingham *You can help Me* iii. 56, I asked him if he did not sometimes hanker after..a few wealthy private patients so that he could afford to keep his list shorter.

d. list-betting, betting on the list of horses displayed in a list shop; **list broker,** a trader in mailing lists; so **list-broking** *vbl. sb.*; **list house** = **list shop*; **listman,** one who works in a list shop; a bookmaker; **list price** (examples); **list shop,** an illegal betting shop where prices on future important races were displayed; **list system** (also *party list system*), a system of voting, common in continental W. Europe, in which voters cast their vote for a list of candidates rather than for an individual candidate; so **list vote, voting.**

1874 *Porcupine* 18 July 248/2 Mr. Chaplin, M.P., with other horse-owners, have..chuckled greatly at the prospect of list-betting no longer interfering with their speculations. **1928** *Daily Express* 24 Mar. 1/1 The..gaming laws..were primarily intended only to abolish notorious gaming houses and list-betting in shops and houses. **1959** *Economist* 7 Feb. 498/1 Publishers now send out circulars to people on mailing lists, bought from a growing class of 'list brokers'. **1967** *Guardian* 27 Dec. 4/2 She is a list broker, which means that she trades in names and addresses. *Ibid.* 4/4 The magnitude of list-broking in the United States. **1970** *Daily Tel.* 12 Oct. 17/3 'List broking' in this country could well develop into the sophisticated service industry it is in America. **1902** 'N. Gubbins' *Dead Certainties* 71 Most of the 'list-houses' (in Long Acre and elsewhere), whose name was legion, had their shutters up on the morning after Lord Zetland's horse had defeated Pitsford. **1922** *Daily Mail* 6 Nov. 11 Most of the listmen got scared to death over particular animals in these final handicaps. **1937** Partridge *Dict. Slang* 486/1 *Listman*, a ready-money bookmaker. **1871** *English Mechanic* 10 Nov. 206/2 The list price for a ½ horse-power engine is £60. *c* **1883** J. Montagu *Let.* in Troubridge & Marshall *John Lord Montagu of Beaulieu* (1930) 30 Now my old machine [*sc.* tandem bicycle] cost £26 list price, and we finally got it for £23:10s. owing to discount for ready money. **1928** *Publishers' Weekly* 30 June 2603 The reprint is usually about one-third of the list price of the earlier edition. **1955** *Radio Times* 22 Apr. 51/1 Hand in an old electric shaver.. and claim £2 allowance off the list price of a Remington 60. **1967** *Autocar* 28 Dec. 38/3 All 'list' prices are taken from *Autocar*'s 'Recommended New Car prices'. **1875** *Encycl. Brit.* III. 619/1 'List shops', where the proprietors kept a bank against all comers, and backers could stake their money in advance on a horse..sprung up..leading to..flagrant dishonesty. [**1901** T. R. & H. P. C. Ashworth *Proportional Representation* vii. 162 The *Liste Libre*, or Free List system,..applies the proportional principle not to individual candidates but to parties.] **1908** J. King *Electoral Reform* vii. 87 In the Party List System the elector gives his vote for the party list, on which the candidate is enrolled, when he gives a vote to any candidate. **1911** *Encycl. Brit.* XXXIII. 115/2 In the 'list systems'..candidates are grouped in lists. **1926** Hoag & Hallett *Proportional Representation* v. 60 Most of the countries which use list systems..have been successful in securing reasonable accuracy in the assignment of seats to parties. **1971** G. K. Roberts *Dict. Political Analysis* 115 *List system*, a system of election, based on proportional representation of parties or similar groups, each of which presents a list of candidates. The voter then casts his vote for one of these lists. **1911** J. H. Humphreys *Proportional Representation* viii. 180 List votes form a pool from which the candidates of the list draw in succession as many votes as are necessary. **1954** B. & R. North tr. *M. Duverger's Pol. Parties* I. i. 44 The list vote (*scrutin de liste*), operating within the framework of a large constituency, obliges the..local branches of the party to establish amongst themselves a strong system of articulation within the constituency, so that they can agree upon the composition of the lists. *Ibid.* 45 Belgium, where at the end of the nineteenth century party structure was amongst the strongest in Europe: it coincided with list-voting. **1958** W. J. M. Mackenzie *Free Elections* ix. 75 List voting is almost always associated with formulae for distributing seats.

list, *v.*⁴ Add: **1. c.** *U.S.* To place (a property) in the hands of a real-estate agent for sale or rent; to add to the list of properties advertised by a real-estate agent. Cf. *listing *vbl. sb.*² 3.

1906 W. A. Carney *Real Estate Business* v. 20 A real estate broker..should have listed considerable property. *Ibid.* 21 He can sometimes list a real bargain. **1908** *Amer. Real Estate Seller* July 2 Every real estate dealer should have a form contract and use it. He should not list a property that he has not a contract on. **1909** *Ibid.* Aug. 6 The real estate dealers should combine and pass a resolution to list property exclusively. **1911** *National Realty Jrnl.* Mar. 14/2 The land owner, the investor, will also find it to his interest to recognize an active agent and list property with him. **1921** J. B. Spilker *Real Estate Business* v. 25 Only those properties which in the mind of the sales manager are saleable, and only those properties which are secured at a fair price and reasonable to both the buyer and seller, should be listed for sale. **1945** G. H. Beurhaus *Who handles your Real Estate?* (rev. ed.) vi. 19 The broker..proceeds to list property. **1972** J. L. Gale *Listing Real Estate* p. xix, Once we learn the ground rules for listing residences, we can then go on and successfully list property of any kind.

d. To enter (a name and address) in a telephone directory.

1959 R. Stout *Crime & Again* 91 'I'll see if she's listed.' I went to my desk for the Manhattan phone book. **1971** *Post Office Telephone Directory Section 101: London Postal Area* 12/1 A special Greater London Business directory has been introduced, listing certain businesses within about thirty miles of Charing Cross.

e. To protect (a building, etc.) by placing it on a statutory preservation register. Cf. *list *sb.*⁶ a (*b*).

1968 *Act Eliz. II* c. 72 § 52 A building which, immediately before the date of the compulsory purchase order, was listed. *Ibid.* § 54 Matters which may be taken into account by the Minister in listing buildings. **1972** E. Lemarchand *Cyanide with Compliments* vi. 74 The lovely little seventeenth-century timber-framed house... It's recently been listed. *Ibid.* xiii. 170 Some local preservation enthusiasts succeeded in getting the house listed as of architectural and historic interest. **1973** *Daily Tel.* 24 Mar. 14/6 Church House..was listed on Feb. 27 because of its architectural or historic merit. But workmen knocked a hole through the front wall on Tuesday.

listed, *ppl. a.*¹ Add: **2.** Included in a list, directory, or catalogue; *listed building,* one protected from demolition or major alteration by being included in an official list of buildings of architectural or historical importance.

1907 *Installation News* Jan. 11/1 Conduits have now to be manufactured to exact listed diameters. **1965** H. I. Ansoff *Corporate Strategy* vi. 117 Investment funds which trade in listed securities have the additional advantage of knowing the full field of choice. **1968** R. H. McCall in P. Ward *Conservation & Devel. Historic Towns & Cities* III. 110 Of 439 Listed buildings in the City [*sc.* Winchester], 9 on the Statutory List have been wholly or partly demolished. **1971** P. Gresswell *Environment* 150 There are now about 120,000 'listed' buildings in England. *Ibid.*, An owner can also be threatened with compulsory purchase if he fails to keep a listed building in reasonable repair. **1973** *Country Life* 29 Mar. 866/2 The highest price, about £54,000, was paid for the Wealden farmhouse, a listed building that probably dates from the 17th century.

listed, *ppl. a.*² Add: **b.** *Basket-making.* Having an extra (decorative) skein on a handle.

1912 T. Okey *Introd. Basket-Making* xii. 145, I have carried out a listed handle with skeins of ordinary chair cane. **1953** [see *listing *vbl. sb.*⁴].

listen, *sb.* Add: **2.** (Earlier and later examples.)

1788 'Aspasia' in *Amer. Museum* IV. 565 Every time the door opens, or a foot is on the stairs, you are on the listen. **1935** *World-Radio* 5 July 9/1 People like me, who..are constantly on the listen with half an ear for something. **1968** J. Philips *Hot Summer Killing* (1969) III. ii. 138 Take a listen while I try to find Jerry. **1968** C. Watson *Charity ends at Home* x. 122 So what I did was to pull off to the side and have a proper listen under the lid. **1970** P. Bair *Tribunal* II. i. 60 'Did you have a nice talk?' 'I had a long listen.' **1971** *It* 2–16 June 19/3 Give it a listen.

b. listen-in, a period of listening to a broadcast, telephone conversation, etc. Cf. *listen *v.* 2 e.

1922 *Daily Mail* 30 Nov. 7 A listen-in. The Queen.. listened to a recitation sent out from Marconi House. **1946** *Philadelphia Bulletin* 1 Aug. 3 An occasional listen-in on the..[telephone] line later convinced company men.

listen, *v.* Add: **2. c.** Also, *to listen out,* to listen for a sound, e.g. on a radio receiver.

1910 A. Bennett *Clayhanger* III. v. 362 Don't latch the door. Pull it to. I'll listen out. **1945** *Tee Emm* (Air Ministry) V. 35 Owing to the fact that they were listening out on channel 'A' instead of channel 'B', he failed to make contact. **1946** L. E. O. Charlton *R. Air Force July 1943 to Sept. 1944* 21 (*caption*) This photograph..depicts a scene in the flying control room—'listening out' to bring the Lancasters back to base. **1959** *Listener* 16 July 111/3 Initially I was afraid that the work would founder in an over-poetic fog but Mr. Bradnum was wisely listening out for. **1971** J. Wainwright *Last Buccaneer* I. 49 We need receiving equipment to listen-out—to pinpoint every wavelength. **1974** D. Kyle *Raft of Swords* xiii. 140 He searched the air waves... For several days he had 'listened out' to a Russian ship with three operators aboard.

e. *to listen in,* to listen to a broadcast programme, etc.; to listen secretly to a telephone conversation. Also const. *to, on,* and *transf.*

1905 *Electrician* 20 Jan. 532/1 At the end of the first section the operator on the ship listened in for a reply. At last he took off the telephone. **1915** A. F. Collins *Bk. Wireless* p. vii, A boy sitting..at home with..a telephone receiver to his ear *listening-in* to the news of the world. **1920** *Wireless World* Jan. 594/2 While 'listening-in', the switch..is placed over to the right. **1926** *Daily Chron.* 13 May 3/1 By the primitive process of passing it from lip to lip the news sped 'like wildfire' amongst the London millions who were not listening in, but were just sitting in their offices or lunching in the restaurants, or walking about the streets. **1928** *Chambers's Jrnl.* Jan. 27/2 None

of us could help 'listening in' to the fun that was going on in the kitchen. **1931** *Boys' Mag.* XLV. 99/2 Patients..are able to listen-in to the Radio programmes by means of headphones. **1939** MRS. BELLOC LOWNDES *Diary* 5 Oct. (1971) 180, I asked him if he ever listened in, whereupon he said in an explosive tone: 'never'. I observed that one learnt a great deal from listening in. **1973** 'H. CARMICHAEL' *Too Late for Tears* xv. 175 His wife wasn't involved... If she had been she wouldn't have wanted us to listen-in on that phone conversation. **1973** 'M. INNES' *Appleby's Answer* v. 49 They have forgotten about you and resumed their tittle-tattle. Whereupon you listen in. **1973** *Radio Times* 15 Nov. 73/3 For thousands of children..who 'listened in' each Friday afternoon, Romany *was* the countryside.

f. *spec.* To listen to a broadcast programme.
1929 *Radio Times* 8 Nov. 395/3 We sat listening..with a portable set. **1935** *World-Radio* 5 July 19/3 (Advt.), Below 100 Metres, Listen to the World. **1936** *B.B.C. Empire Broadcasting* 2 Dec. 2/3 Your greeting, Big Ben, and then the National Anthem, moved us profoundly—it took quite a time to listen without real emotion. *Ibid.* 9 Dec. 2/1 Whenever there was a sporting commentary a host of people used to come to my bungalow to listen. **1946** *B.B.C. Year Bk.* 11 With the restoration of peace there was a natural tendency for the citizens of other countries to listen, at first, only to their own newly freed broadcasting services. **1970** *B.B.C. Handbk.* 98 There is magic in ensuring that most people in the world can listen in a language they can really understand.

4. *intr.* To sound (in a certain way). Freq. with *to* = to strike (one) as. *U.S.*
1908 K. MCGAFFEY *Sorrows of Show Girl* 78 That listened very well indeed, and we all climbed into a cabbage and vamped over. **1912** C. MATHEWSON *Pitching in a Pinch* vii. 143 All is fair in love, war, and baseball except stealing signals dishonestly, which listens like another paradox. **1923** R. D. PAINE *Comrades of Rolling Ocean* xiv. 250 Here's where I slip it out..to help square the repair bill for my joy-ride. How does it listen to you? **1923** L. J. VANCE *Baroque* xxvii. 174 [It] don't listen reasonable to me. **1945** MENCKEN *Amer. Lang.* Suppl. I. 317 It has been suggested..that *it listens well* may be from *es hört sich gut an.*

listenable (li·s'năb'l), *a.* [f. LISTEN *v.* + -ABLE.] Easy or pleasant to listen to; willing to listen. Hence **listenabi·lity,** the quality of being listenable.
1920 C. MORLEY *Haunted Bookshop* vi. 95 He felt very talkative, as most older men do when a young girl looks as delightfully listenable as Titania. **1946** *Newsweek* 18 Feb. 90 In listenability, it is more like the Concerto for Orchestra. **1958** *Oxford Mail* 12 Aug. 6/6 Viewers are invited to..listen to..works carefully selected from the classics for their 'listenable' qualities. **1964** *Listener* 31 Dec. 1066/2 Talks producers might take a little more trouble in making them [*sc.* scripted talks] listenable, if they were given credits in *Radio Times*. **1966** G. N. LEECH *Eng. in Advertising* iii. 27 Characteristics of advertising language..readability (or 'listenability'). **1970** *Guardian* 9 June 8/2 Berta was full of listenable opinions on her father. **1971** *Hi-Fi Sound* Feb. 78/2 It can be seen how singularly useless the THD results are, when attempting to assess the 'listenability' of an amplifier.

listener. Add: **3.** One who listens to a broadcast. Also *attrib.* Also *listener-in*. Cf. *LISTEN *v.* 2 e, f.
1922 *Daily Mail* 21 Nov. 7 The limited service has already established itself in high favour with 'listeners-in'. **1923** *Radio Times* 28 Sept. 12/1 It seems to me that the B.B.C. are mainly catering for the 'listeners' who own expensive sets. **1926** *Daily Chron.* 13 May 3/1 By the magic of wireless it was, perhaps, the listeners-in who heard it first. **1929** *Radio Times* 8 Nov. 388/1 The recent broadcasting of *Aida* has prompted a Forest Hill listener to send in..a very delightful story. **1936** *B.B.C. Ann.* 87/2 The BBC has recently established, at its Head Office, a special unit, with the object of co-ordinating information ..and studying new methods of 'listener research'. **1950, 1951** [see *AUDIENCE 7 d]. **1970** *B.B.C. Year Bk.* 23 For the great majority of listeners..there will be little evidence of sudden upheaval.

Hence **li·stenership,** the estimated number of listeners to a broadcast programme or to radio (*spec.* as opp. to television).
1943 *Business Week* 30 Jan. 44 Increased emphasis on news broadcasts and commentators boosted listenership particularly between 5 and 7 p.m. **1958** *New Statesman* 2 Aug. 142/2 In America, reports *Time*, sound-radio is enjoying a 'spectacular comeback'; latest figure of 'listenership' show it 'up 8 per cent over last year, 25 per cent over its pre-TV peak in 1947'. **1971** *Daily Tel.* 17 Apr. 19/2 Listenership levels are still an imponderable. It is unlikely that the British public will listen to local radio as much as, say, the Americans.

listening, *vbl. sb.* Add: **b. listening key** *Teleph.* (see quot. 1940); **listening post** *Mil.*, an advanced position used to discover movements or the disposition of the enemy; also *transf.*
1906 J. POOLE *Pract. Telephone Handbk.* (ed. 3) x. 159 (*heading*) Kellogg combined listening and ringing key. **1940** *Chambers's Techn. Dict.* 505/1 *Listening key*, the lever key which the operator throws, to put her head-set on to a cord circuit and speak to a subscriber. **1916** *War Illustr.* V. 69/1 At a listening-post. **1928** BLUNDEN *Undertones of War* xv. 167 The men lying at each listening-post were freezing stiff. **1945** *Life* 19 Nov. 119/2 The barbed wire was up everywhere, and the few listening posts that we did have at Vichy, at General Weygand's North African Headquarters—were in perpetual danger of sabotage by the well-meaning but essentially stupid remonstrances of the more emotional Left press. **1961** *Guardian* 29 May 9/5 Vienna is Europe's busiest listening post. **1965** MRS L. B. JOHNSON *White House Diary* 3 Nov. (1970) 335 John Gronouski was seated on my left and I enjoyed hearing him talk about Poland and how it serves as a sort of listening post for what is going on in Red China. **1971** J. TUNSTALL *Journalists at Work* iii. 86 Fairly standard features are centres like Hong Kong and Beirut which are used as 'listening posts' and jumping-off points for covering China and South East Asia, and the Middle East respectively. **1972** *Guardian* 25 Jan. 15/8 Paris uses the Commission mainly as a listening post to find out what the others are up to.

2. (Also *listening-in*.) The action of listening to a radio broadcast, a record-player, etc.; also, the action of listening (esp. secretly) to a telephone conversation. (Cf. *LISTEN *v.* 2 e, f.) Also *attrib.* and *transf.*
1904 *Electr. World & Engin.* 7 May 875/2 The removal of the operator's plug, or her 'listening-in', restores the circuits to their proper condition for subsequent use. **1921** *Wireless World* 10 Dec. 581/1 'Listening in' was indulged in. **1925** A. HUXLEY *Those Barren Leaves* II. v. 149 But of what use is leisure, when leisure is occupied with listening-in and going to football matches? **1927** *Sat. Even. Post* 24 Dec. 80/2 These telephones were connected with a listening-in device concealed behind a picture on the wall. **1929** *Radio Times* 8 Nov. 389/3 The sounds heard had emerged from the loud-speaker of the caretaker... The caretaker was extremely annoyed at this interruption to his listening. **1939** *War Illustr.* 21 Oct. p. ii/1 Its [*sc.* the B.B.C.'s] dud programmes have led to a great falling-off in listening. **1940** *Manch. Guardian Weekly* 2 Feb. 83 From South West Germany it is stated that controllers have been appointed in blocks of flats to supervise the listening-in. **1941** *B.B.C. Gloss. Broadcasting Terms* 17 *Listening log*, list, in prescribed form, of the broadcast programmes heard by one person over a period of time. **1951** J. B. PRIESTLEY *Festival at Farbridge* II. ii. 217 Dan Cobbley was another radio personality, although he was on a lower listening figure level. **1957** *Encycl. Brit.* X. 619/2 The new possibilities for continuous listening helped enormously. On the debit side was the tendency especially of solo artists to record whole programs on LP disks, repeating endlessly the same established repertoire. **1966** *Listener* 10 Feb. 221/3 The portrayal of..the jostling and jockeying of the foreign ambassadors, made really good listening. **1969** *John Edwards Mem. Foundation Q.* V. IV. 126 The transcriptions of the songs..are as nearly accurate as I can make them. After countless listenings I still can't make out some of the words. **1971** *Gloss. Electrotechnical, Power Terms* (*B.S.I.*) III. ii. 31 *Listening-in*, listening to a call in progress.

listening, *ppl. a.* Add: **b.** (Also *listening-in*.) That listens to a broadcast, recording, etc.
1926 *Punch* 14 July 39 (*caption*) *Husband* (to listening-in Wife). 'What's the matter, dear? Is it bad news or Stravinsky?' **1935** *Discovery* Sept. 277/2 They are providing ever better products and service to enable the listening public to get more enjoyment from the 'audio' programmes. **1941** *B.B.C. Gloss. Broadcasting Terms* 17 *Listening group*, group of listeners meeting regularly with the twofold object of hearing a particular series of broadcast talks..and engaging in discussion. **1957** *B.B.C. Handbk.* 104 Audience Research set up permanent Listening Panels to report their reactions to the programmes they heard. **1970** *Ibid.* 112 A special listening section keeps track of the activities of foreign radio stations. **1974** *Times* 30 Nov. 10/4 The practitioners [of religious broadcasting]..are impeded by some notion of what the listening public expects their output to be.

lister[3]**.** Add: (Examples.) Also *attrib.*
1887 *Sci. Amer.* LVI. 6/3 When grain is planted by the so-called 'combined lister and drill', the listing forms a ditch or furrow several inches deep, in which the seed is deposited. **1897** *Sears, Roebuck Catal.* 157/2 (*heading*) Subsoil lister with wood beam complete with runners. **1946** *Harper's Mag.* Oct. 307/2 In my day a lister cost $20 —a great deal of money, indeed. **1949** *Lubbock* (Texas) *Morn. Avalanche* 23 Feb. II. 6/4 Lister shares for any make tractor $3·50 each.

listerella (listəre·lă). *Bacteriology.* Pl. **-ella, -ellæ.** [mod.L., f. the name of Joseph (later Lord) *Lister* (1827–1912), English surgeon + L. *-ella* (see -EL²).] = *LISTERIA.
[**1927** J. H. PIRIE in *Publ. S. Afr. Inst. Med. Res.* III. xx. 164 The 'Tiger River Disease' is present among gerbilles... The causative organism of this disease is a small Gram-positive bacillus, for which, from its most striking pathogenic effect, I propose the specific name *hepatolytica*, and the generic name, *Listerella*, dedicating it in honour of Lord Lister, one of the most distinguished of those connected with bacteriology whose name has not been commemorated in bacteriological nomenclature.] **1940** *Vet. Jrnl.* XCVI. 330 *Listerella* were recovered from the uteri of the sheep slaughtered immediately after aborting. [**1940**: see *LISTERIA.] **1948** *Jrnl. Bacteriol.* LV. 471 (*heading*) A new technique for isolating listerellae from the bovine brain.

Hence **li:sterello·sis** [-OSIS] = *LISTERIOSIS.
1939 *Science* 6 Oct. 337/1 More recently Biester and Schwarte reported spontaneous bovine listerellosis in Iowa. **1940** [see *LISTERIA]. **1948** *Jrnl. Bacteriol.* LV. 473 Listerellosis as manifested in the ovine is extremely acute. **1961** R. D. BAKER *Essent. Path.* ix. 190 Infection with the small gram-positive rod, *Listeria monocytogenes* (listerellosis) is limited largely to meningitis, although it apparently causes abortions and stillbirths.

listeria (liste·riă). *Bacteriology.* Pl. **listeria, -ias.** [mod.L., f. *LISTER(ELLA + -IA¹ (see quot. 1940).] Any bacterium of the genus *Listeria*, formerly called *Listerella*, esp. *L. monocytogenes* which is a widespread pathogen of man and animals.
[**1940** J. H. PIRIE in *Science* 19 Apr. 383, I have been informed..that the new name *Listerella* which I proposed for a genus of bacteria in 1927 had already been given to a Mycetozoan by Jahn in 1906 and to one of the Foraminifera by Cushman in 1939. My proposed name, therefore, becomes a homonym, but as the genus has acquired some importance in both human and veterinary pathology and references to 'Listerellosis' are becoming fairly common in literature, I think that a name as near to my original proposal as possible is desirable. I therefore propose *Listeria*, as the name for the genus of bacteria as defined by me in Publication No. XX of the South African Institute for Medical Research.] **1961** *Lancet* 2 Sept. 514/1 The amniotic fluid was examined again..and listeria grew copiously from it.

Hence **liste·rial, liste·ric** *adjs.*, caused by or derived from listerias; **listerio·sis,** infection with or disease caused by listerias.
1941 *North Amer. Vet.* XXII. 545 (*heading*) An outbreak of listeriosis in sheep. **1961** *Jrnl. Clin. Path.* XIV. 193 (*heading*) Human listerial meningitis. **1961** tr. *H. P. R. Seeliger's Listeriosis* 144 A generalized listeric septicaemia. *Ibid.* 145 [Seeliger] established that 'Granulomatosis infantiseptica' was a listeric infection. **1961** *Lancet* 2 Sept. 515/1 Listeriosis should no longer be considered a rare disease in man. **1972** *Amer. Jrnl. Vet. Res.* XXXIII. 591 (*heading*) Effects of listerial hemolysin on rabbit heart. **1972** *Obstetr. & Gynecol.* XL. 91 (*heading*) Listeriosis as a cause of fetal wastage. *Ibid.* 96/1 Penicillin or tetracycline..should be started immediately when the possibility of Listeric infection is entertained.

Listerize, *v.* (Earlier example.)
1888 *19th Cent.* June 846 In this way the patients are 'Listerized', to use a hospital term.

listing, *vbl. sb.*² Add: **3.** *N.Amer.* The placing of a property on the list of a real-estate agent; an estate agent's register of properties that he has for sale; a property so listed. Cf. *LIST *v.*⁴ 1 c.
1906 W. A. CARNEY *Real Estate Business* v. 21 Where values are changing it is necessary to confirm and correct the listings every month or two. **1909** *Amer. Real Estate Seller* Aug. 6 It may be well to explain exclusive listing here... When you have a piece of property to sell and you empower one and only one agent to dispose of it for you—your property is being listed exclusively. **1925** P. L. MELBERG *Realty Salesman* 138 Well bought is half sold can be applied to listings also; a good exclusive listing is half sold. **1926** HINMAN & DORAU *Real Estate Merchandising* vii. 95 Every administrator of the policies of a real estate firm will have to make a decision for or against multiple listing. **1950** C. URBAN *Successful Real Estate Practice* 78 Many brokers will take a listing at any price, hoping to get some offer the owner will accept. **1968** *Globe & Mail* (Toronto) 17 Feb. 45 (Advt.), To inspect this new listing please call Viola Roper. **1972** J. L. GALE *Listing Real Estate* p. xix, Listings are the inventory, the stock on the shelves, the merchandise of the real estate broker.

4. An entry in a catalogue, telephone directory, or other list.
1962 K. ORVIS *Damned & Destroyed* v. 443, I..reached out for the telephone directory. Helen Ashton had no listing. **1965** J. CLAPP (*title*) College textbooks, Supplement I: a classified listing of 9,500 textbooks used in 36 colleges. **1969** *John Edwards Mem. Foundation Q.* V. IV. 125 This complete listing of Cash's recordings was compiled by John Smith. **1971** *Amer. N. & Q.* Sept. 10/1 Every Lowe listing [in a bibliography] is found either in the main body or in an appendix. **1971** *Post Office Telephone Directory Section 101: London Postal Area* 6 The alphabetical listings under 'Telephone Service'.

listing, *vbl. sb.*³ Add: The action of LIST *v.*³ 4.
1805 R. PARKINSON *Tour Amer.* 165, I was near two months getting a plough made, therefore I hired for the listing (as they call it). **1887** *Sci. Amer.* LVI. 6/3 The drawback to this listing is due to the fact that close to the edges of the furrow on each side, a row of weeds springs up. **1935** *Nature* 17 Aug. 253/1 One of the processes whereby the drift of loose soil has been to some extent countered. This process, known to farmers as 'listing', consists of specially deep ploughing with the aid of motor-driven tractors... The furrows may be as many as fifteen feet apart.

li·sting, *vbl. sb.*⁴ *Basket-making.* [f. LIST *v.*³ + -ING¹.] (See quots. 1912, 1953.) Hence **listing-skein.** Cf. *LISTED *ppl. a.*² b.
1912 T. OKEY *Introd. Basket-Making* 153 *Listing*, an additional skein or skeins worked in with the lapping of skein handles. **1953** A. G. KNOCK *Willow Basket-Work* (ed. 5) 36 *Listing*, a method of adding a raised form of ornamentation to a lapped handle by the use of one or more additional skeins, called listing-skeins... The listing on any handle can be added after the handle has been lapped. *Ibid.*, Diagram 26 shows a simple listed handle employing three listing-skeins. **1961** L. G. ALLBON *Basic Basketry* vii. 53 Another method of decorating a wrapped handle would be with listing. **1972** D. WRIGHT *Baskets & Basketry* ii. 61 Listing is worked over the interwoven No. 3 or 4 cane.

listing, *ppl. a.*² [f. LIST *v.*⁵ + -ING².] Of a ship: heeling, inclining to one side.
1923 *Public Opinion* 30 Mar. 312/3 Six projectiles struck the listing Iowa.

Lisztian (li·stiăn), *a.* (*sb.*) [f. the name of *Liszt* (see below) + -IAN.] Of, pertaining to, or characteristic of the Hungarian pianist and composer Ferencz (Franz) Liszt (1811–86) or his music. Also as *sb.*, an adherent or imitator of Liszt.

1890 G. B. Shaw *London Music 1888–89* (1937) 308 Such Lisztian hero-worshippers as Herr Stavenhagen and the late Walter Bache. **1921** A. Huxley *Crome Yellow* xxi. 227 A brilliant Lisztian tremolo. **1934** C. Lambert *Music Ho!* iii. 163 The Lisztian symphonic poem. **1947** A. Einstein *Mus. Romantic Era* vii. 70 Genuine Lisztians or innovators like Smetana..wrote no more symphonies. **1947** N. Cardus *Autobiogr.* 208 In the 'Sanctus' we have the original prototype of how many Lisztian and other symphonic-poems. **1963** *Times* 24 Jan. 14/5 The late Lisztian keyboard style. **1971** *Daily Tel.* 26 Apr. 9/1 [He] produced moments of Lisztian abandon in which the whole orchestral palate crowded in on the keyboard.

lit, *ppl. a.* Add: (Further *fig.* examples.)
1922 M. A. von Arnim *Enchanted April* i. 17 She listened to her impetuous, odd talk and watched her lit-up face. **1936** R. Campbell *Mithraic Emblems* 18 My own lit heart, its rays of fire.
b. *slang.* Drunk (see also quots. 1933 and 1971). Freq. const. *up.*
1914 'High Jinks, Jr.' *Choice Slang* 14 Lit up, intoxicated. **1918** J. M. Grider *War Birds* (1927) 82 We walked into the vamp's house. We all got lit and had a hell of a time. **1922** *Daily Mail* 16 Dec. 10, I am afraid I was rather tight—certainly lit up. **1933** *Amer. Speech* VIII. ii. 27/1 When one has contracted the habit or is under the immediate influence of the drug, he is *all lit up.* **1938** G. Greene *Brighton Rock* iii. i. 109 If I hadn't been a bit lit this wouldn't have happened. **1939** M. Allingham *Mr. Campion & Others* i. ii. 37 Driving round the country with a topper over your eyes and a blanket round your neck at three o'clock in the morning... You *must* have been lit. **1948** Wodehouse *Spring Fever* xviii. 189 A lit-up Augustus Robb should, he considered, provide a spectacle which nobody ought to miss. **1949** E. Hyams *Not in our Stars* xvii. 220 Some of the lads a bit lit, eh? Who's this in the hedge? **1971** E. E. Landy *Underground Dict.* 121 Lit up,.. under the influence of a narcotic.

lit., Lit., colloq. abbrev. of (*a*) Literature. Cf. *Eng. Lit. (*b*) Literary *a.* Also used *absol.* = literary student, literary magazine. Also *lit. crit.,* literary criticism; *lit. ed.,* literary editor; *lit. sup.,* literary supplement.
(*a*) **1850** [see *Eng. Lit.]. **1870** Geo. Eliot *Let.* 11 Feb. (1956) V. 77 The lentisc or mastich tree..figures both in Greek and Roman lit. **1946** L. Durrell *Let.* 20 Oct. in *Spirit of Place* (1969) 87 In Athens I am going to see Seferis and Katsimbalis and give modern lit a bashing with them. **1959** *Observer* 8 Mar. 22/2 Chadwick's opposition to tacking on 'Lit' to 'Lang', followed by his decision to leave the English Tripos. **1964** W. Markfield *To Early Grave* (1965) xii. 252 Perhaps if I should ever give a regional lit course. **1973** P. Geddes *Ottawa Allegation* xiii. 173 She..worked in publishing... She was into Canadian Lit. before he could draw breath. **1975** *New Yorker* 21 Apr. 103/3 You don't get much of that in Russian lit.
(*b*) **1895** W. B. Yeats *Let.* 20 Jan. (1954) II. 245 Not one word was said about the Irish Lit Society and Prof Dowden expressed scorn for the Irish Lit movement. **1895** W. C. Gore in *Inlander* Nov. 64 Lit, literary student. **1900** *Dialect Notes* II. 45 Lit, n., the Literary Monthly, Quarterly, etc., a student publication. **1930** *English Jrnl.* XIX. 632 Whatever wit or lightness of heart characterizes the magazines appears in the East; the Western 'lits' are in dead earnest. **1932** H. Nicolson *Diary* 19 Oct. (1966) 122 Kingsley Martin..wants me to become the literary editor... But I..could not expect to make more than £1,000 a year as Lit. Ed. **1932** V. Woolf *Let.* in K. Martin *Editor* (1968) i. 30, I used to try to write regularly for *The Times Lit. Sup.* **1935** N. Mitchison *We have been Warned* iv. 437 He showed her his reviews... The *Lit. Sup.* had been dull, the *New Statesman* annoying. **1936** L. C. Douglas *White Banners* viii. 171 Naturally the 'Lits' began to view Professor Ward with a new respect. **1962** M. Drabble *Summer Bird-Cage* xi. 206 'I could have guessed that from his books. They lack compassion.' 'How beautifully, how lit. critically you put it.' **1963** 'N. Blake' *Deadly Joker* ii. 33 The Americans had..begun to make an industry of lit. crit. **1968** *Lebende Sprachen* XIII. 110/2 Jet-age litcrit. **1968** E. McGirr *Lead-Lined Coffin* ii. 44 Rostron sat making derisive noises over the Sunday lit. sups. **1973** *Times Lit. Suppl.* 6 Apr. 401/5 The refingered worry-beads of lit-crit jargon.

litchi. Add to etym.: [First used as a generic name in P. Sonnerat *Voyage aux Indes Orientales* (1782) III. 255.] Substitute for def.: The fruit of an evergreen tree, *Litchi chinensis,* of the family Sapindaceæ, native to southern China but widely cultivated in tropical countries elsewhere; the fruit is a large berry with a rough, brown skin and sweet, white flesh, which is eaten fresh or preserved. (Later examples.)
1908 *Daily Chron.* 12 Nov. 3/4 Lychees, pine-apples, pears, cranberries, dates, figs, medlars and mangos swell the number of fruits. **1933** *Punch* 9 Aug. 142/2 We never dreamed that it [*sc.* tinned fruit] would appear..in such dazzling variety..from loquats to li-chees. **1938** *Nature* 14 May 866/2 The litchi has arrived in much larger quantities lately and been much appreciated. **1953** R. Campbell *Mamba's Precipice* 137 Monkeys lived on the beautiful lychees and loquats. **1965** *Listener* 1 July 23/2 You'd never know, looking at me, I had..eaten lychees in a town called Reading. **1969** *Oxf. Bk. Food Plants* 104/1 Litchis are most usually eaten fresh, but are also sometimes canned for export or preserved in syrup. **1972** A. F. Simmons *Growing Unusual Fruit* 175 The litchee can..be grown in Britain in a large green-house.

-lite. Add: Also used in forming the names of some rocks, as *IJOLITE, Phonolite.

literacy. Add: Also *transf.*
1943 *Amer. Mag.* Mar. 103/1 To help many of the poverty-stricken peoples to set their feet on the path of education, manual dexterity, and economic literacy. **1962** *B.B.C. Handbk.* 33 Our skills in the understanding of the medium [*sc.* television] and our own literacy in it are growing all the time. **1969** *Times* 4 Nov. 25/2 A project aimed at raising the level of economic literacy.

literæ humaniores, var. *Litteræ humaniores.

literal, *a.* and *sb.* Add: **A.** *adj.* **3. e.** literal-minded *a.,* having a literal mind; characteristic of one who takes a matter-of-fact or unimaginative view of things. Hence *literal-mindedness.*
1869 *Wesleyan-Methodist Mag.* Jan. 28 An old friend, whom we used to call 'Bacon', because he..was a literal-minded man. **1905** J. L. Lowes in *PMLA* XX. 816 A strangely literal-minded, not to say naïve, interpretation of the charming fiction of the Prologue. **1927** *Glasgow Herald* 31 Oct. 10 The gentleman married the lady on the strength of her literal-mindedness. **1941** [see *Analyst 6]. **1944** *Mind* LIII. 238 One of my aims is..to formulate, in a manner which is freed from all merely technical literal-mindedness, the epistemological idea and significance of pure semantics. **1957** *Essays & Stud.* X. 18 It delivers us from too much matter-of-fact and from the dreary flats of literal-mindedness. **1974** M. Fido *R. Kipling* 80/2 'If you won't retract the lies..I'll blow out your goddam brains!' 'If I don't do certain things, you'll kill me?' Rudyard asked, with infuriating English primness and literal-mindedness.
B. *sb.* **3.** *Computers.* An operand in a program which directly specifies the value of a constant, or defines itself rather than serving as an address or label.
1960 *Nebula: a Programming Lang.* (Ferranti, Ltd.) iii. 5 A literal need not always be a numerical quantity. For example, the item address may have a value which is '216 London Road' and this whole phrase (viz., 216 London Road) is then a literal. **1962** D. N. Chorafas *Programming Syst. for Electronic Computers* ix. 107 Commercial Translator distinguishes among three different types of constant: defined constants, literals and basic constants. *Ibid.,* A literal is a purely numerical constant which is introduced in a procedure statement as the need arises. **1968** S. M. Bernard *System/360 COBOL* I. 52 A literal is a self-defining value; that is, it does not have to be separately defined by the programmer. 1. Non-numeric literals... 2. Numeric literals. **1968** N. Chapin *360 Programing* ii. 19 The symbolic addresses used by the programer take four main forms: self-defining values, literals, symbolic names, and relative addresses. **1970** O. Dopping *Computers & Data Processing* xix. 311 In certain languages..a literal must be surrounded by quotation marks. In those systems, the literal may even begin with a letter. In that case, we could..write the instruction print 'sum' for ordering the computer to print the word sum. **1971** L. Coddington *Quick COBOL* ii. 16 Literals are: 777, which is a numeric literal..and alphanumeric literals (YES, NO, SMITH, ZZZZ) which consist of letters... They are not true data-names: 'SMITH' is not only the name of a location in store, but the contents of that location. The numeric literals need no explanation.

literally, *adv.* **3. b.** (Further examples of the improper use.)
1902 *Daily Chron.* 10 Dec. 7/2 A contemporary states that Kubelik has been 'literally coining money' in England. **1906** *Westm. Gaz.* 15 Nov. 2/1 Mr. Chamberlain literally bubbled over with gratitude. **1922** R. Macaulay *Mystery at Geneva* xiv. 72 The things 'they' say! They even say..that 'literally' bears the same meaning as 'metaphorically' ('she was literally a mother to him,' they will say). **1960** V. Nabokov *Invitation to Beheading* iii. 31 And with his eyes he literally scoured the corners of the cell. **1973** *Good Food Guide* 176 'Crabs and lobsters are literally to be found crawling round the floor waiting for an order,' reports an early nominator.

literarism (li·tĕrăriz'm). [f. Literar(y *a.* + -ism.] = Literaryism.
1942 Partridge *Usage & Abusage* 173/1 Literarisms are either the journalese of the literary (these literarisms might also be stigmatized as high-brow) or such unusual words as are used only by the literary or learned. **1963** A. Huxley *Lit. & Sci.* i. 5 Snow or Leavis? The bland scientism of *The Two Cultures* or, violent and ill-mannered, the one-track, moralistic literarism of the Richmond Lecture? **1970** F. R. Leavis in *Times Lit. Suppl.* 23 Apr. 441/4 The term 'literarism' was in fact coined by the late Aldous Huxley for use against me.

literary, *a.* Add: **3. b.** *literary dinner, luncheon, party, prize.* Also *literary adviser:* one who gives advice or information on literary matters; *literary agent* (see quot. 1960); also *literary agency; literary circle* (see Circle *sb.* 21); *literary criticism* = Criticism 2 (of works of literature); so *literary critic, literary-critical* adj.; *literary editor:* (*a*) the editor of the literary section of a newspaper; (*b*) the editor of a book of collected writings; so *literary-edit* vb., *-editorship; literary executor* (see Executor 3); *literary world* (see World *sb.* 16 b).
1831 M. Edgeworth *Let.* 6 Jan. (1971) 469 He..criticises so well—not as a mere literary critic appealing to authorities. **1840** Macaulay in *Edin. Rev.* Jan. 520 In 1698, Collier published his 'Short View..', a book which threw the whole literary world into commotion. **1845** H. C. Robinson *Diary* 27 Jan. (1967) 234 Mrs. Jameson.. is now received in the highest literary circles. **1851** *N. & Q.* 28 June 527 (Advt.), Literary Agency—Mr. F. G. Tomlins..is desirous to make it known that a Twenty years' experience with the Press and Literature,..enables him to give advice and information to Authors, Publishers and Persons wishing to communicate with the Public. **1853** C. M. Yonge *Heir of Redclyffe* I. xv. 251 She was..the leading lady of the place.., giving literary parties, with a degree of exclusiveness that made admission to them a privilege. **1857** G. H. Lewes *Let.* 11 Feb. in Geo. Eliot *Lett.* (1954) II. 295 When I am no longer here to act as go-between he [*sc.* Geo. Eliot] must, I think, become his own literary Agent. **1862** —— *Let.* 10 May in *Ibid.* (1956) IV. 31 Smith again offered me the editorship of the C[ornhill] M[agazine] which I again declined; but accepted the post of Literary Advisor. **1868** Literary executor [see Executor 3]. **1876** Geo. Eliot *Let.* 2 May (1956) VI. 244 One cannot escape seeing and hearing something of political and literary criticism. **1883** Trollope *Autobiogr.* II. xiv. 88 Literary criticism.. has become a profession,—but it has ceased to be an art. **1885** Literary circle [see Circle *sb.* 21]. **1904** A. Bennett *Great Man* x. 98 Henry had learnt for the first time what a literary agent was. **1912** R. Brooke *Let.* 25 Nov. (1968) 408 German literary circles are..entirely cut off from English. **1919** 'C. Dane' *Legend* 84 You know I'm literary executor? **1919** Mrs. Belloc Lowndes *Diary* 10 July (1971) 91 The great literary prizes awarded in the last fifty years by the French Academy. **1923** Literary-edit [see *art-edit* v. (*Art sb.* V)]. **1931** R. Campbell *Georgiad* iii. 51 O Dinners! take my curse upon you all, But literary dinners most of all. **1932** H. Nicolson *Diary* 23 Feb. (1966) 110 Leonard Woolf has an idea that I should take on the literary editorship of the *New Statesman.* *Ibid.* 19 Oct. 122 Round to the *New Statesman.* Kingsley Martin indicates that he wants me to become the literary editor when Ellis Roberts goes. **1936** *Discovery* Jan. 28/2 The literary executors of the late Professor Hicks are to be congratulated. **1936** 'E. M. Delafield' *Provincial Lady in Amer.* 116 Literary luncheon really important function will receive wide press publicity letter follows Stop Very sincerely Katherine Ellen Blatt. **1937** F. M. Ford *Let.* 17 Feb. (1965) 271 The eccentric Principal, Brewer, who once humorously subedited—or rather literary-edited the *Spectator* for three weeks. **1940** 'M. Innes' *There came both Mist & Snow* x. 114 The young man..had just that deference which I am accustomed to meet with from young critics at literary parties. **1941** 'G. Orwell' in *Listener* 29 May 768/1, I am speaking on literary criticism. **1941** V. Nabokov *Real Life S. Knight* (1945) i. 6 Last winter at a literary lunch, in South Kensington, a celebrated old critic..was heard to remark..'A dull man.' **1950** 'E. Crispin' *Frequent Hearses* i. 12 I'm acting as literary advisor in connexion with a film they're making. **1960** G. A. Glaister *Gloss. Bk.* 238/1 *Literary agent,* an agent, paid on a commission basis, who acts for an author by submitting his work to, and dealing with a publisher; and who may arrange the sale of translation or other rights. **1962** J. B. Priestley *Margin Released* iii. ii. 158 Most of my meetings with authors took place..at literary parties. **1965** *Philos. Rev.* LXXIV. 208 Literary-critical description..is what is needed. **1965** L. Sands *Something to Hide* i. 14 She had attended a dull literary luncheon. **1967** *Guardian* 14 Sept. 2/5 A highlight of the literary world..a Foyles Luncheon. **1968** *Writers' & Artists' Year Bk.* 242 Literary agents exist to sell saleable material. *Ibid.,* Adamastor Press and Literary Agency Ltd. **1968** K. Martin *Editor* i. 7 Raymond Mortimer..was the sort of literary editor with whom I scarcely ever wanted to interfere. **1969** A. G. Thomas in L. Durrell *Spirit of Place* 11, I have had one advantage not generally available to literary editors. When work on this book was well advanced Durrell came to stay with me..and I was able to consult him. **1971** D. Crystal *Ling.* 107 An 'objective correlative' (to apply T. S. Eliot's literary critical term in a context where it was never intended). **1972** A. Christie *Elephants can Remember* i. 11 I'm always being asked to literary lunches. **1972** *Guardian* 1 Dec. 13/2 The Marxist writer, John Berger, had arrived at the National Liberal Club to receive the Guardian literary prize for his novel 'G'. **1973** *Listener* 15 Feb. 211/2 I've never been a great one for going out in literary circles, but I did know Wells very well, and I knew Galsworthy slightly. **1973** J. Goodfield *Courier to Peking* ii. 23 There's lots of people I must talk to... I'm his literary executor. **1975** A. Clarke *My Search for Ruth* xii. 111 A terrifying woman at a literary party.
4. (Earlier example.) Also, *literary gent* (colloq.): one who prides himself on his literary accomplishments.
1785 *Daily Universal Reg.* 1 Jan. 1/1 This Day is published..by the Literary Society, *Modern Times..*a Novel. **1850** Thackeray *Pendennis* II. xxxiv. 336 Doctor Johnson has been down the street many a time with ragged shoes... You literary gents are better off now. **1937** 'G. Orwell' *Road to Wigan Pier* xii. 243 Ten years ago.. the typical literary gent wrote books on baroque architecture. **1967** L. Woolf *Downhill all Way* i. 106 Being also what I call a literary gent, he [*sc.* James Stephens] used to fill me alternately with depression and irritation.
5. Of painting, sculpture, etc.: that depicts or represents a story.
1928 *Morning Post* 20 Oct. 10/6 The music is too 'literary', but its craftsmanship and imagination are undeniable. **1931** C. Holmes *Gram. Arts* vii. 118 The intrusion of 'literary' elements into the arts has long been suspect. **1962** R. G. Haggar *Dict. Art Terms* 196 *Literary art...* The term is frequently used in a pejorative sense, but most romantic painting is dependent upon a text. **1970** *Daily Tel.* 8 June 12/8 It is accepted by many as a compliment rather than as an insult to describe a painting as literary.
Also as *sb.,* a literary club or society; a literary person. *U.S.*
1904 *Dialect Notes* II. 419 We organized a literary at the school-house. **1923** U. L. Silberrad *Lett. J. Armiter* vi.

145 Obstacles..may be a blessing in disguise to half-baked literaries. **1928** *Amer. Speech* IV. 130 In many districts a 'literary' is held every Friday night, when the 'Sandhillers' of this district recite and sing and debate. **1936** E. G. BARNARD *Rider Cherokee Strip* 157 We spent a happy winter at this work and visiting our neighbors and going to the 'literaries' and dances.

‖ **litera scripta** (li·tĕră skri·ptă). [L.] The written word.

1864 J. S. LE FANU *Uncle Silas* I. xxi. 256 Henceforward all is circumstantial evidence..except the *litera scripta*, and to this evidence every note-book, and every scrap of paper..must contribute..what it can. **1910** R. BRIDGES in *Essays & Stud.* I. 48 The *litera scripta* has an enormous power.

literate. Add: **B.** *sb.* **4.** (*Lady*) *Literate in Arts*, the title conferred on the holder of a higher certificate for women issued at St. Andrews University. Abbrev. *L.L.A.*

This diploma was discontinued in 1931.

1881 *St. Andrews Univ. Cal.* 203 Any Candidate who passes in four subjects, [etc.]..will receive the title of Literate in Arts (L.L.A.). **1891** R. F. MURRAY *Scarlet Gown* 122 An L.L.A. is a Lady Literate in Arts. **1901** *Daily Record* 30 July 3 Lady Literates in Arts. **1931** *L.L.A. Examination, Diploma, & Title for Women* (Univ. St. Andrews) 8 There is no limit as to age in the L.L.A. Examination.

‖ **littérateur.** An occas. spelling (in English works) of LITTÉRATEUR.

1806 [see LITTÉRATEUR]. **1895** E. DOWSON *Let.* 22 Dec. (1967) 335, I suppose you have heard of the abortive petition which he started among French litérateurs for the grace of Oscar? **1925** W. STEVENS *Let.* 14 Oct. (1967) 245, I have seen very few litérateurs during the last year or two.

literation. Add: (Examples.)

1918 HARDY in T. H. Ward *Eng. Poets* V. 174 His aim in the exact literation of Dorset words is not necessarily to exhibit humour and grotesqueness. **1928** J. SYKES *Mary Anne Disraeli* ix. 85 'D'Israeli and Mrs. D'Izzy'—an unusual form of literation of the familiar diminutive.

b. The method or style of making letters.

1926 *Times Lit. Suppl.* 10 June 390/2 To sacrifice..the exquisite literation that in the old hands delights us like a poem.

literature. Add: **3. b.** (Later examples.)

1939 [see *NORMALIZABLE *a.*]. **1969** [see *DÉCOLLEMENT 2]. **1971** *Nature* 25 June 499/1 We have searched the literature for reliable radiometric ages for Late Pre-Cambrian glaciogenic rocks, but they seem to be rare. **1973** *Sci. Amer.* June 55/3 A voluminous scientific literature accumulates each year on the normal vibrational modes of molecules in liquids and on optical phonons in crystals.

c. (Later examples.)

1938 WODEHOUSE *Code of Woosters* i. 8 It is some literature from the Travel Bureau. **1962** *Observer* 4 Mar. 37/1 (Advt.), Full details and literature from: Yugoslav National Tourist Office. **1973** D. FRANCIS *Slay-Ride* vii. 78, I talked my throat dry, gave away sheaves of persuasive literature.

literatus. (Later examples.)

1972 *Times Lit. Suppl.* 19 May 563/3 He had already made himself the universal literatus. *Ibid.* 28 July 880/2, I join with a literatus in conversation about the trash we read in childhood.

lites. Delete 'obs.' and add later example.

1963 B. VESEY-FITZGERALD *Cat Owner's Encycl.* 69 Lungs (commonly known as 'lites'), whether of cow, sheep or horses, are strongly to be recommended.

‖ **litham** (liþā·m). Also **lisam.** [ad. Arab. *liṯām* veil.] A veil of cloth wound round the head leaving only the eyes uncovered and worn by the men of the Tuareg people of the central Sahara desert.

1839 E. W. LANE tr. *Thousand & One Nights* I. vi. 467 The Khaleefeh then put on himself the fisherman's jubbeh and turban, and, having drawn a lithám over his face, said to the fisherman, Go about thy business. **1855** R. F. BURTON *Pilgrimage* I. xii. 346 This veiling the features is technically called *Lisam*: the chiefs generally fight so, and it is the usual disguise when a man fears the avenger of blood, or a woman starts to take the *Sar*. **1879** *Encycl. Brit.* IX. 129/1 The *litham* or shawl-muffler of the Tuareg, wound round the mouth to keep out the blown sand of the desert. **1903** W. J. H. KING *Search for Masked Tawareks* xv. 220 He stood..slightly raising with his long slender fingers the upper fold of his *litham* or mask. **1966** M. WOODHOUSE *Tree Frog* xxi. 157 Mohammed Jalil al Murzuq sat still..the veil, the *litham* drawn across his face.

lithian (li·þiăn), *a.* *Min.* [f. LITH(IUM + *-IAN 2.] Of a mineral: having a (small) proportion of a constituent element replaced by lithium.

1930 W. T. SCHALLER in *Amer. Mineralogist* XV. 571 Lithium—lithian. **1953** *Ibid.* XXXVIII. 91 The following characteristics of lithian muscovite illustrate its close structural similarity to normal muscovite. **1964** *Ibid.* XLIX. 398 (*heading*) Lithian hureaulite from the Black Hills.

lithic, *a.*[1] **2.** (Further examples in *Archæol.*)

1946 F. E. ZEUNER *Dating Past* vii. 208 The lithic industries of the Grotte de l'Observatoire were described by Boule. **1971** *Nature* 6 Aug. 383/2 Although other human remains that may be attributed provisionally to *Homo erectus* have been found at Olduvai,..the discoveries at [site] WK are the first occasion on which a well represented lithic industry has been directly associated. **1971** *World Archaeol.* III. 144 There is a need for studies of lithic technology.

lithifaction (liþifæ·kʃən). [f. LITHI(FY *v.* + -FACTION (cf. *petrifaction*).] = LITHIFICATION.

1893 *Compte Rendu 5me Sess. Congrès Géol. Internat.* 160 The formations of the Coastal plain range in age from Pleistocene to early Cretaceous or late Jurassic..; all, indeed, are commonly unconsolidated and lithifaction is local and exceptional. **1971** I. G. GASS et al. *Understanding Earth* xix. 264/1 Sediments in various degrees of lithifaction. **1972** *Islander* (Victoria, B.C.) 1 Oct. 13/3 According to James T. Fyles, geologist with the department of mines, these concretions are formed during the process of lithifaction of sand.

lithification. (Earlier and later examples.)

1872 *Amer. Jrnl. Sci.* Dec. 468 Even the former moderate temperature..would be sufficient to produce incipient change—at least lithification, if not metamorphism. In fact, lithification of sediments will probably take place under heavy pressure even at ordinary temperature. **1971** I. G. GASS et al. *Understanding Earth* xiii. 165/1 The lithification of the soft sediments after deposition.

lithify, *v.* Add: Chiefly as **li·thified** *pa. pple.* and *ppl. a.* (Further examples.)

1937 *Geogr. Jrnl.* LXXXIX. 9 This is the normal beach-rock—lithified sands containing a few boulders of coral here and there. **1963** D. W. & E. E. HUMPHRIES tr. *Termier's Erosion & Sedimentation* x. 215 When clays are lithified by compaction and cementation, they become mudstones or limestones with fossil mud cracks on their surfaces. **1971** *Nature* 2 Apr. 287/1 The rock was thus almost certainly lithified during the lower relative sea level of the Pleistocene.

lithiophorite (li:þi,ǫ·fŏrəit). *Min.* [ad. G. *lithiophorit* (O. Breithaupt 1870, in *Jrnl. f. prakt. Chem.* CX. 205): see LITHIUM, -O, and -ITE[1].] A basic oxide of aluminium, lithium, and manganese $(Al,Li)MnO_2(OH)_2$, found as bluish-black monoclinic crystals.

1871 *Jrnl. Chem. Soc.* XXIV. 205 Lithiophorite is amorphous, occurs in compact botryoïdal and reniform masses, in flat shell-like forms, and in pseudomorphs after calcspar. **1932** *Amer. Mineralogist* XVII. 149 Material which in the past has been classified as psilomelane may actually be..lithiophorite, previously considered as a variety of psilomelane containing lithium and aluminium, but which the *x*-ray pattern shows to be a distinct mineral. **1952** *Acta Crystallogr.* V. 676/2 Lithiophorite has a layer structure with alternate sheets of MnO_6 and $(Al,Li)(OH)_6$ octahedra placed one on top of the other. **1970** *Mineral. Mag.* XXXVII. 618 Lithiophorite..is one of the major mineral forms of nodular manganese in Australian soils.

lithistid, *a.* and *sb.* Add to etym.: [(O. Schmidt *Grundzüge einer Spongien-fauna des Atlantischen Gebietes* (1870) ii. 21).] (Example of sb. and later example of adj.)

1885 J. E. TAYLOR *Our Common Brit. Fossils* i. 26 Sections of it show it to belong to the *lithistids*. **1972** P. MEGLITSCH *Invertebr. Zool.* (ed. 2) v. 98/2 Desmas are often cemented together to form a solid meshwork, or lithistid skeleton.

litho (li·þo, now more usually ləi·þo). Add: Also, abbrev. of LITHOGRAPHIC, LITHOGRAPHY (in Dict. and Suppl.). (Further examples.)

1903 *Brit. Printer* Jan. 40/1 The *Gazette* is the organ of the litho trade. **1915** *Southward's Mod. Printing* (ed. 3) II. xxxiii. 284 A number of transfers may be laid down on the stone, and from such litho prints there is, of course, no impression on the back. **1946** A. KIRK in H. Whetton *Pract. Printing & Binding* xvi. 190/1 Part of the very extensive mail-order catalogue business of America..is printed from the web by litho-offset at very high speeds. **1948** *Sci. News* VII. 100 A simple processing technique resulted in litho printing plates ready for use. *Ibid.*, Litho printers. **1965** S. C. GILMOUR *Paper* (ed. 2) xix. 236 Litho offset ink is normally stiffer than that used for letterpress. **1972** *Nature* 17 Mar. 101/2 This printing is done quite quickly by the Ordnance Survey by litho directly from the typescripts. **1973** *Times Lit. Suppl.* 7 Dec. 1492/2 One other contributory factor has been the growth of film-setting, which composes letters directly on to film, whence they can be directly transferred to a litho printing plate. *Ibid.* 1518/1 Letterpress, although progressively eroded by litho, still prints about 50 per cent of bookwork.

Also (abbrev. of LITHOGRAPH *v.* 1) as *vb.*

1934 J. A. LEE *Children of Poor* (1949) vi. 205, I would print or litho intricate design in varied colour.

litho-. Add: **li·thofacies** *Geol.*, a facies (*FACIES 2 b) distinguished by its lithological character (see quot. 1949[2]); **lithogenesis** (examples); also, the formation of rock; **lithogeny,** (*b*) *Geol.* (*rare*) = *lithogenesis* (in Dict. and Suppl.); **lithophane** (examples); also **lithophanie; li·thophil(e, lithophi·lic** *adjs. Geol.* and *Chem.* [ad. G. *lithophil* (V. M. Goldschmidt 1923, in *Skrifter utgit av Videnskapsselsk. I. Mat.-nat. Kl.* III. 5); see -PHIL, -PHILE], applied to elements which are commonly found as silicates and are supposed to have concentrated in the outermost zone when the earth was molten; **li·thopone** [Gr. πόνος work, anything produced by work], a mixture of zinc sulphide and barium sulphate used as a white pigment in paint, linoleum, and printing ink, and as a filler in paper; **li·thosere** *Ecol.* [*SERE], a plant succession having its origin on bare rock; **li·thosol** *Soil Sci.* [*-SOL], any azonal soil consisting largely of imperfectly weathered rock fragments; **lithosphere,** add: in mod. use, usu. applied to the crust and the upper part of the mantle; formerly also used for the crust together with the whole interior portion of the earth, or the crust together with the entire mantle; (further examples); hence **lithosphe·ric** *a.*; **li:thostrati·graphy** *Geol.*, stratigraphy based on the physical and petrographic characters of rocks, rather than on fossils; so **li:thostratigra·phic, -gra·phical** *adjs.*; **lithotint** (later examples); so **li·thotinted** *ppl.a.*

1946 M. KAY in *Progr. Rep. Res. Comm. Amer. Assoc. Petroleum Geologists* 15 Jan. 4 The forms present in any population are influenced by age, but also by habitat reflected in lithology (lithofacies). **1949** R. C. MOORE in *Mem. Geol. Soc. Amer.* XXXIX. 16 It seems clear that 'facies' should not be used in double manner to refer also to this type of differentiation, and I suggest the term 'lithofacies'..as appropriate for such meaning. *Ibid.* 32 The rock record of any sedimentary environment, including both physical and organic characters, is designated by the term 'lithofacies'. **1958** *Bull. Amer. Assoc. Petroleum Geologists* XLII. 2729 The term lithofacies seems to have been introduced by the Russian geologist Eberzin (1940: *fide* Markevich, 1957). When and by whom it was launched in America is not clear from available references. Soon after 1945 it appeared in publications and was used in the sense given above. **1968** R. W. FAIRBRIDGE *Encycl. Geomorphol.* 92/1 (*heading*) Braided stream lithofacies. **1909** *Cent. Dict.* Suppl., *Lithogenesis*, the production or origin of minerals or rocks; lithogenesy. **1937** WOOLDRIDGE & MORGAN *Physical Basis Geogr.* vi. 82 The period of lithogenesis, during which the rocks later to form the range are accumulated. **1956** 'H. MACDIARMID' *Stony Limits & Scots Unbound* 42 All is lithogenesis—or lochia, .. Stones blacker than any in the Caaba. **1963** D. W. & E. E. HUMPHRIES tr. *Termier's Erosion & Sedimentation* 405 The cycle of geological phenomena comprises lithogenesis or petrogenesis, orogenesis, then glyptogenesis. **1888** J. J. H. TEALL *Brit. Petrogr.* 437 *Lithogeny*, that department of petrology which treats of the formation of rocks. **1958** *Contrib. Cushman Found. Foraminiferal Res.* IX. 106/2 The Illinois cyclothem comprises a widely consistent, repetitious succession of rock types whose lithogeny records the environmental changes of the place and time in considerable detail. Various aspects of the lithogenesis, biology, and ecology of the sedimentary units in the Illinois and related kinds of cyclothems have been described. **1947** M. PENKALA *Europ. Porc.* 32 The lithophane process..involved the use of white biscuit plaques of varying thickness. **1960** R. G. HAGGAR *Conc. Encycl. Cont. Pott. & Porc.* 269/1 Some of the German porcelain factories made effective use of the lithophane for lamp shades and sconces. **1970** G. SAVAGE *Dict. Antiques* 244/2 Lithophanes were first modelled in translucent wax, the object of the craftsman being to remove sufficient wax to give the desired amount of light transmission, building up his picture from dark and light passages. **1866** W. CHAFFERS *Marks Pott. & Porc.* (ed. 2) 431 At the Berlin manufactory *Lithophanie* was invented. **1904** E. DILLON *Porcelain* xvi. 264 Another application of porcelain was to the 'transparencies' or *lithophanie*, in which the design, as seen by transmitted light, was given by variations in the thickness of the paste. **1923** *Mineral. Abstr.* II. 159 Corresponding with the zones of the earth postulated in the preceding papers, the chemical elements are divided into four main groups: (1) Siderophil elements..; (2) Chalcophil elements ..; (3) Lithophil elements of silicate fusions (O, Si, Ti, F, Cl, Al, Ce, Na, K, Be, Mg, Ca, V, &c.); (4) Atmophil elements. **1950** RANKAMA & SAHAMA *Geochem.* iv. 91 The lithophile metals form ions of the noble-gas type having 8 electrons in the outermost shell. **1965** PHILLIPS & WILLIAMS *Inorg. Chem.* I. xvi. 598 Goldschmidt quoted the following elements: Fe Co Ni [etc.]..as concentrating in terrestrial sulphides (chalcophil) rather than in silicates (lithophil). **1973** *Nature* 28 Sept. 204/1 The entry into or rejection of lithophile ions from silicate lattices is dependent on size and valency *inter alia*. **1971** *Ibid.* 27 Aug. 606/1 Elements like Be and Th..are strongly lithophilic under both crustal and mantle conditions. *a* **1884** KNIGHT *Dict. Mech.* Suppl. 551/2 Lithopone. **1902** *Jrnl. Soc. Chem. Industry* 31 Mar. 427/1 'Lithopone' is prepared by mixing together solutions of barium sulphide and zinc sulphate, the precipitate of $ZnS,BaSO_4$ being then washed, dried, and ignited. **1923** U. R. EVANS *Metals & Metallic Compounds* II. 156 Lithopone is a comparatively cheap pigment, and is much used for flat wall paints and the cheaper grade of enamel paints. **1961** J. P. CASEY *Pulp & Paper* (ed. 2) III. xx. 1830 Lithopone has been known to cause trouble in coated offset papers by reacting with the acid in the fountain water. **1916** F. E. CLEMENTS *Plant Succession* ix. 182 While the surfaces of rock and of dune-sand may be almost equally dry, the differences of hardness and stability result in very dissimilar adseres. These may be distinguished as lithoseres..and psammoseres. **1960** N. POLUNIN *Introd. Plant Geogr.* xi. 325 As a characteristic xerosere we will take a lithosere initiated on bare rock. **1939** *U.S. Dept. Agric. Yearbk. 1938* 1171 *Lithosols* (skeletal soils), an azonal group of soils having no clearly expressed soil morphology and consisting of a freshly and imperfectly weathered mass of rock fragments. **1968**

H. C. T. STACE et al. *Handbk. Austral. Soils* iii. 35 Lithosols are found throughout Australia wherever natural erosion has been active enough to maintain a thin soil cover. **1893** A. GEIKIE *Text-bk. Geol.* (ed. 3) 38 (*heading*) The solid globe or lithosphere. **1910** LAKE & RASTALL *Text-bk. Geol.* i. 8 The Lithosphere or solid part of the earth, so far as it is open to our inspection, consists of rocks. **1950** RANKAMA & SAHAMA *Geochem.* ii. 32 The Sial crust, which is the surface layer of the silicate shell of the Earth (the lithosphere), is composed of three groups of rocks of different origin. **1957** G. E. HUTCHINSON *Treat. Limnol.* I. iv. 222 The water content of the major part of the lithosphere, the great mantle of ultrabasic rock which composes most of the earth, is unknown. **1971** I. G. GASS et al. *Understanding Earth* xvi. 248/1 As a result of seismological studies, it has been realised that the Earth's outermost skin, or lithosphere, which exhibits appreciable strength and rigidity, extends well beneath both continental and oceanic crusts to depths of 50 or even 100 km. **1973** M. W. MCELHINNY *Palaeomagnetism & Plate Tectonics* v. 156 In this 'new global tectonics'.., now generally referred to as Plate Tectonics, it is supposed that a mobile, near-surface layer of strength (the lithosphere) plays a key role... The lithosphere, which generally includes the crust and uppermost mantle, has significant strength, and is of the order of 100 km thickness. The asthenosphere, which is a layer of effectively no strength on the appropriate time scale, extends from the base of the lithosphere to a depth of several hundred kilometres. **1970** *Nature* 5 Sept. 1016/1 At ridge crests the lithospheric plates are thinned by the elevation of the geotherms as a result of mantle upwelling and emplacement. **1971** I. G. GASS et al. *Understanding Earth* xi. 153 (*caption*) Biospheric, lithospheric and atmospheric evolution on the primitive Earth. **1950** *Bull. Amer. Petroleum Geologists* XXXIV. 2365 Our repeated efforts to treat stage and zone as true time-stratigraphic units have met with failure. Since these are biostratigraphic or lithostratigraphic in character..we have no logical choice but to place them also in a category by themselves. **1970** *Earth-Sci. Rev.* VI. 270 The formation is the fundamental unit in lithostratigraphic classification. **1964** J. CHALLINOR *Dict. Geol.* (ed. 2) 144/2 Lithostratigraphical unit. **1969** *Proc. Geol. Soc.* Aug. 141 For the description of stratified rocks lithostratigraphical procedure is already generally agreed. **1956** *Bull. Amer. Assoc. Petroleum Geologists* XL. 2711 (*heading*) Factors in lithostratigraphy. **1969** *Proc. Geol. Soc.* Aug. 155 The boundaries between stages are based on biostratigraphy where possible, and on lithostratigraphy otherwise. **1938** *Archit. Rev.* LXXXIV. 177/3 Hullmandel's lithotint process, patented in 1840,..used a resin solution..which could be painted on to the polished tint stone so that it printed a modulated, instead of a flat tint. **1969** D. BLAND *Hist. Bk. Illustration* (ed. 2) vii. 250 The forerunner of the chromo-lithograph was the lithotint. *Ibid.* 251 One of the best litho-tinted books is *Original Views of London as it is* (1842).

lithodipyra (li:þodipəiə·rə̆). [mod.L., f. LITHO- + DI-² + Gr. πῦρ fire, as repr. 'stone twice fired'.] The name given to a kind of artificial stone by members of the Coade family when in 1769 they took over the factory in Lambeth where it was made (until *c* 1837), which stone (also called *Coade stone*) was claimed to have greater frost and heat resistance than natural stone and was much used for statues, monuments, and decorative work.

c **1778** (*title*) Coade's lithodipyra or artificial stone manufactory. For all kinds of statues, capitals, vases, tombs, coats of arms, & architectural ornaments &c. &c. **1910** *N. & Q.* 2 July 15/1 A monument to Edward Wortley Montagu, made of Coade's Lithodipyra, is in the west walk of the Cloisters of Westminster Abbey. **1928** *Connoisseur* Oct. 81 (*caption*) Plaque in Lithodipyra, from a design by J. Bacon, R.A. installed on the east front of Hooton Hall, Cheshire 1788. **1954** *Archit. Rev.* CXVI. 296/1 George Coade died in 1770 and can, therefore, have had little to do with the development of 'Coade's Lithodipyra Terra-Cotta or Artificial Stone Manufactory'.

lithograph, *sb.* **1.** (Earlier and later examples.)

1828 DISRAELI *Voy. Capt. Popanilla* ix. 96 It was a sublime lithograph. **1970** *Oxf. Compan. Art* 666/1 Lithographs have..taken on a number of appearances, ranging from simple linear designs made with pen or crayon to colour prints with the most varied effects of transparency and texture.

lithographed, *ppl. a.* (Earlier examples.)

1826 DISRAELI *Viv. Grey* I. II. x. 151 A bundle of Stewart Newton's beauties, languishing, and lithographed. **1829** H. C. ROBINSON *Diary* 13 Aug. (1967) 102 Knebel had shown me a lithographed manuscript.

lithographic, *a.* Add: **1.** (Further examples: cf. *LITHOGRAPHY 3.)

1885 *List of Subscribers, Classified* (United Telephone Co.) (ed. 6) 123 Lithographers and Lithographic Printers. **1892** A. POWELL *Southward's Pract. Printing* (ed. 4) i. 3 Lithographic printing is done with stones, zinc plates, &c. **1915** *Southward's Mod. Printing* (ed. 3) II. xxxiii. 281 Rotary lithographic machines work from zinc or aluminium plates carried on a plate cylinder. **1970** E. A. D. HUTCHINGS *Survey of Printing Processes* v. 75 Lithographic plates are made from both zinc and aluminium. **1972** P. GASKELL *New Introd. Bibliogr.* 269 Nineteenth-century lithography was a separate trade... Towards the end of the century, however, powered lithographic cylinder machines were developed which had a productivity comparable with that of the letterpress machinery of the period, and they were followed around 1900 by lithographic rotaries which ran at yet higher speeds. These new machines, used in conjunction with photographic transfer methods of plate preparation, pointed the way to the integration of lithographic with general letterpress printing which took place during the first half of the twentieth century. **1973** *Brit. Printer* July 68/3 It was only with the increase in lithographic printing that photosetting began to 'find its feet'.

4. lithographic offset = *OFFSET *sb.* 10 b; **lithographic paper,** paper suitable for lithographic printing; **lithographic varnish,** a preparation of linseed oil used in inks for lithographic printing.

1915 *Southward's Mod. Printing* (ed. 3) II. xxxiii. 282 Lithographic Offset Printing. Offset printing is popularly supposed to have owed its introduction to a 'miss' made in printing on a lithographic cylinder machine. **1946** H. WHETTON *Pract. Printing & Binding* 446/1 Lithographic offset printing. **1960** G. A. GLAISTER *Gloss. Bk.* 239/2 Modern lithographic offset printing is mostly done in rotary presses. **1937** E. J. LABARRE *Dict. Paper* 167/1 Since the introduction of the offset printing process, however, all papers have become possible as 'lithographic' papers. **1963** R. R. A. HIGHAM *Handbk. Papermaking* vii. 202 Lithographic papers..are similar to offset cartridge, but generally cheaper and in a lighter substance. **1903** A. SEYMOUR *Pract. Lithogr.* x. 52 The most useful and the commonest form of reducing medium is a linseed oil product, known in its prepared state as a lithographic varnish. **1951** R. MAYER *Artist's Handbk.* x. 312 Lithographic varnishes, from which many types of inks for other printing purposes are also made, are heat-bodied linseed oils.

lithographically, *adv.* (Further examples.)

1952 in G. H. Bourne *Cytol. & Cell Physiol.* p. iv, (*Imprint*) First edition 1942. Reprinted (with corrections) 1945. Second edition 1951. Reprinted lithographically.. at the University Press, Oxford, 1952 from corrected sheets of the second edition. **1965** *Economist* 6 Mar. 1026/2 No model of Picasso can hide in obscurity and the olive-shaped outline of the head of Françoise Gilot is known, lithographically, to millions. **1967** E. CHAMBERS *Photolitho-Offset* xvii. 264 The artist has complete freedom of expression and application to produce an image from which impressions can be obtained lithographically.

lithography. Add: **3.** Also, a planographic printing process using metal or plastic plates with a sensitized coating on which the matter to be printed is fixed chemically, before the non-printing areas of the plates are damped and the remainder printed with greasy inks on flat-bed or cylinder presses. Cf. *DRIOGRAPHY, *OFFSET *sb.* 10 b, *PHOTOLITHOGRAPHY.

1906 *Brit. Printer* Dec. 296/2 The tendency of the day is undoubtedly towards..the utilization of lithography by typographers doing certain classes of work. **1932** *Jrnl. Soc. Chem. Industry* 9 Sept. T313/1 Lithography is based essentially on the adsorption of fatty acids by the metal. **1946** A. KIRK in H. Whetton *Pract. Printing & Binding* xvi. 190/1 Although the printing of daily newspapers is outside the present scope of lithography, the uninterrupted weekly production of *The Australian*, Melbourne, since 1929 may be instanced as but one outstanding achievement..in this direction. **1973** *Brit. Printer* July 68/3 The radically reduced cost of photosetting machines in recent years, their improved capability, and the continuing growth in the use of lithography have all been instrumental in increasing the demand for photosetting and allied equipment.

Lithol (li·þǫl). *Dye Chem.* Also **lithol.** Any of various azo pigment dyestuffs, many of which are the salts of diazo coupling compounds of β-naphthol and aromatic amino-sulphonic acids. *Lithol red*, any of various salts of the diazo coupling compound of 2-naphthyl-amine-1-sulphonic acid with β-naphthol, used as red pigments of moderate colour fastness.

Formerly a proprietary name in the U.S.

1903 *Official Gaz.* (U.S. Patent Office) 16 June 1891/1 Dyestuff. Badische Anilin & Soda Fabrik, Ludwigshafen, Germany. Filed April 24, 1903... The word 'Lithol'. Used since June 6, 1901. **1930** A. W. C. HARRISON *Manuf. Lakes & Precipitated Pigments* xii. 146 Lithol red being the most profitable of all the bright pigment reds, as regards such desirable qualities as strength, price and reasonable fastness to light in full shades, it is made in larger quantities than any other pigment red. *Ibid.* xiii. 176 Two cheaper bright yellows which may be used are Pigment Chlorine G.G. and Lithol Fast Yellow G.G., which are formaldehyde condensation products. **1947** L. S. PRATT *Chem. & Physics Org. Pigments* viii. 116 Lithols, as a class, are prepared by coupling the diazonium salts of Tobias acid..with β-naphthol, and then converting the resulting practically insoluble sodium lithols into the corresponding barium, calcium, or strontium products. *Ibid.*, The lithols are the most important single group of organic pigment colors. **1967** KARCH & BUBER *Offset Processes* vii. 269 Lithol reds range in shades from an orange to deep maroon. In between these extremes are some very brilliant and deep shades which are used where extreme permanency to light is not important.

l·ithoprint, *v.* [f. LITHO(GRAPHY + PRINT *v.*] *trans.* To print by photolithography, usu. in reference to the production of copies of a typescript by this means. Also as *sb.* = LITHOGRAPH *sb.* Hence **li·thoprinting** *vbl. sb.*

1935 *Amer. Botanist* Jan. 39 The book is lithoprinted from type-written copy. **1947** *Amer. Speech* XXII. 136 It is too bad that this most important of volumes on its subject could not have been put in more solid form than lithoprinting. **1957** TRAGER & SMITH *Outl. Eng. Struct.* 7 The preliminary drafts were reproduced in lithoprinted form. **1969** *Sunday Times* 6 Apr. 30 His enchanting drawings (transformed into big, clear-coloured lithoprints in limited editions of 100 each) are in a gallery run by his mother. **1971** *New Scientist* 28 Jan. 206/2 The several hundred local natural history publications, often duplicated or lithoprinted, offer an easy first outlet for young artists.

lithops (li·þǫps). [mod.L. (N. E. Brown 1922, in *Gardeners' Chron.* 28 Jan. 44/2), f. Gr. λίθος stone + ὤψ face.] A small succulent plant of the genus so called, belonging to the family Aizoaceæ, native to Namaqualand, South Africa, and resembling small stones.

[**1922** *Gardeners' Chron.* 28 Jan. 44/2 Lithops, N. E. Brown. Very dwarf succulent plants, in nature growing buried in the ground with their tops scarcely, or not at all, rising above the level of the surface. *Ibid.*, Dr. Marloth is quite wrong in his identification of the plant, which I have no doubt whatever is a species of Lithops.] **1938** H. A. DAY *Flowers of Desert* iv. 148 It is most difficult to tell which are plants and which are pebbles when the two are mixed, as they are in the habitat of the *Lithops*, for the plants grow in the stony deserts of South Africa. **1966** E. PALMER *Plains of Camdeboo* xvi. 269 We have never found a Lithops on Cranemere, the nearest species that we know of being Burchell's Lithops to the north and another species, *Lithops terricolor*, to the west.

lithospermum. Add to etym.: [Adopted by Linnæus in his *Systema Naturæ* (1735) as the name of a genus.] Substitute for def.: A herb or sub-shrub of the genus so called, belonging to the family Boraginaceæ, native to Europe, northern Asia, or North America, and bearing white, yellow, or blue flowers. (Later examples.)

1900 J. M. ABBOTT in W. D. Drury *Bk. Gardening* ix. 295 Lithospermums are showy rockwork plants. **1937** *Daily Express* 10 May 12/4 The lithospermum's name [*sc.* 'Heavenly Blue'] is no exaggeration of its colour. **1966** J. BERRISFORD *Wild Garden* 11. 166 With their brilliant blue flowers and evergreen leaves the lithospermums are most desirable garden plants.

lithothamnion (li:þoþæ·mniǫn). [mod.L. (R. A. Philippi 1837, in *Arch. Naturgesch.* III. 387), f. LITHO- + Gr. θάμνος shrub.] A calcareous, marine, red alga of the genus so called. Also *attrib.* Hence **lithotha·mnic** *a.*

1895 G. MURRAY *Introd. Study Seaweeds* 241 *Lithophyllum* forms thin stony plates of erect habit, while *Lithothamnion* gives rise to massive stony branches. **1935** J. E. TILDEN *Algae* viii. 362 Portions of the *Lithothamnion* crust were kept for many months. **1967** *Oceanogr. & Marine Biol.* V. 551 Both fauna and flora of this lithothamnic bottom are very abundant. **1972** *Sci. Amer.* June 62/1 A hitherto minor group of coralline red algae, the lithothamnions, now began to play an increasingly important role.

Lit. Hum. Abbrev. of *LITTERÆ HUMANIORES.

1939 L. MACNEICE *Autumn Jrnl.* xii. 49 If it were not for Lit. Hum. I might be climbing A ladder with a hod.

litmus. Add: *fig.*, as in *litmus test.*

1957 *Essays in Crit.* VII. 80 Their possession is as good a cultural litmus test as any I can think of. **1971** *Daily Tel.* Nov. 13/2 The litmus test comes with the old issue of whether the NUS should re-join the IUS. **1972** *Times* 21 Nov. 21/7 The litmus test will be the effect of the rise from 4p to 10p in the basic charge for an inpayment.

litoptern (litǫ·ptɜːn). *Palæont.* Also **litopternan.** [f. mod.L. name of order *Litopterna* (F. Ameghino 1889, in *Actas Acad. Nac. Córdoba* VI. 492), f. Gk. λῑτός smooth + πτέρνη heel-bone.] An extinct South American ungulate mammal of the order so called. Hence **litopternine** (litǫ·ptɜːnəin) *a.*

[**1891** E. D. COPE in *Amer. Naturalist* XXV. 688 The articulation in the Litopterna is of ungulate character.] **1925** C. R. EASTMAN tr. *Zittel's Text-bk. Palaeontol.* III. 123 The Litopternine suborder of ungulates is restricted to South America. **1927** HALDANE & HUXLEY *Animal Biol.* xi. 243 (*caption*) Extinct South American Litopternan. **1933** A. S. ROMER *Vertebr. Paleontol.* xvi. 316 Small litopterns..present in the oldest known Tertiary beds of South America, had primitive bunodont cheek teeth. **1971** *Nature* 15 Jan. 172/1 In some mammals, tapirs, elephants, the extinct astropotheres, pyrotheres, and litopterns, the external nares are posterior and large.

‖ **lit-par-lit** (l*i*parl*i*), *a. Geol.* [Fr., = 'bed by bed'.] Designating the intrusion of innumerable narrow, more or less parallel, sheets or tongues of magma into the bedding of rocks. Also as *adv.*

1896 *Q. Jrnl. Geol. Soc.* LII. 635 In..1890..Mr. Horne obtained confirmatory evidence of the 'lit par lit' introduction of granitic materials into the crystalline schists south-west of Strath Halladale. **1902** *Ibid.* LVIII. p. lxxv, M. Michel Lévy recognizes two types of intermixture: the one taking place by superposition, the other by injection lit par lit... In the latter type the compound rock consists of alternating folia of granite and sedimentary material. **1909** F. H. HATCH *Text-bk. Petrol.* (ed. 5) I. 18 When the intrusion is repeated between many planes of stratification, it is known as *lit-par-lit* intrusion. **1925** B. N. ODELL in E. F. Norton *Fight for Everest 1924* 291 It is composed of dark horizontally banded biotite gneiss alternating with bands of light granite, though in the upper part of the cliff the latter is represented by pegmatite, and the whole appears to represent a large-scale

example of *lit-par-lit* injection. **1962** A. E. J. & C. G. ENGEL in A. E. J. Engel et al. *Petrologic Stud.* 42 The amphibolites are only locally shredded, injected *lit-par-lit*, or replaced by granite. **1968** K. R. MEHNERT *Migmatites* ix. 278 Banded gneisses and migmatites of the 'lit-par-lit'-type follow.

litre². Add: (Earlier and later examples.)

In 1901 the litre was redefined as the volume of a kilogramme of water under specified conditions (see quot. 1957), which made it equal to approximately 1·000,028 cubic decimetres; this definition was abandoned in 1964 in favour of the original one (see quot 1965).

1797 *Jrnl. Nat. Philos.* Aug. 197 A vessel of a cubical form, having for its side one decimetre, or a cylindrical vessel of the same solid contents, has received the name of litre. It contains about two pounds of water, or twenty-five ounces of wheat. **1902** *Nature* 10 Apr. 538/1 Annexe iv..recapitulates the decisions of the Troisième Conférence Générale held at Paris last October, as to the definitions of the metric units, metre, kilogramme and litre. **1923** GLAZEBROOK *Dict. Appl. Physics* III. 777/2 The definition of the litre has no reference to the units of length, and the original intention that it should be equal to 1 cubic decimetre has been quite abandoned. *Ibid.* 778/2 In his final résumé of the whole observations M. Benoit gives 1 litre = 1000·027 c.c. as the most probable value. **1957** E. R. COHEN et al. *Fund. Constants Physics* ii. 5 The liter is defined as the volume of a kilogram of water, at standard atmospheric pressure and at the temperature of its maximum density, approximately 4°C. On a level of sufficient precision this is an ambiguous definition, since it does not specify the isotopic constitution of the water... We adopt..1 liter = 1000·028 ± 0·004 cm³. **1965** *Nature* 6 Feb. 553/1 The twelfth General Conference of Weights and Measures was held..during October 6–13, 1964... Resolution 6 (the litre) abolished the definition of the litre established in 1901 by the third General Conference, declared that the word 'litre' can be used as a special name given to the cubic decimetre and recommended that the name 'litre' shall not be used to express the results of volume measurements of high precision... It now reverts to its original meaning. The intention is that this litre shall only be used for ordinary transactions in trade and not for scientific purposes. **1969** *Physics Bull.* Feb. 58/2 It was a regrettable international decision in 1964 which reinstated the name litre for a cubic decimetre.

b. Preceded by a number or a word denoting a number so as to form adjs. denoting the capacity (i.e. the inside volume of the cylinders) of a motor vehicle or its engine, and used *ellipt.* for a vehicle having the specified engine capacity.

1927 A. HUXLEY *Let.* 25 Feb. (1969) 284 We have gone and bought a really rather tremendous car—an Itala six cylinder two-litres. **1951** *Engineering* 26 Oct. 533/2 It is a full six-seater, powered by a new 3-litre six cylinder engine developing 90 brake horse-power at 4,100 r.p.m. **1955** *Times* 3 May 10/5 Bruigi, driving a three-litre Ferrari, crashed into a cement road sign near Teramo. **1974** *Country Life* 17 Jan. (Suppl.) 34/1 Put the Triumph 2000 beside any other 2-litre in its class and there's very little in it for mpg.

litter, *sb.* Add: **6.** (sense 4) *litter-bag, -basket, -bin, -box, -bug* (*BUG *sb.*² 4 a), *-carrier, -cart, -lout*; (sense 5) *litter-mate, -sister.*

1968 *Punch* 19 June 892/2 Drop it sadly in your heavy white kraft paper car litterbag. **1958** J. CANNAN *And be a Villain* vii. 160 Oh, the mess they leave on our little common..in spite of the litter baskets. **1972** J. BROWN *Chancer* xiv. 191 There's a row of litter baskets each side of the gates. **1947** *Archit. Rev.* CII. 198 (*caption*) On the right a typical litter-bin. **1972** *Guardian* 28 Jan. 5/6 Clerical staff..have been..sweeping up, and emptying litter bins. **1953** *News Chron.* 2 June 4/4 What a mess there will be on Coronation Day unless people use the litter-boxes. **1947** *N.Y. Herald-Tribune* 16 Feb. 2/7 (*heading*) 47,000 subway 'litterbugs' pay $107,000 in fines in 1946 drive. **1959** *Times* 23 July 7/7, I rate such persons in the same category as litter bugs. **1971** *Guardian* 8 Dec. 24/8 He picks up any litter he can find..and he is apt to give litter-bugs a severe dressing-down. **1915** J. LONDON *Let.* 26 Jan. (1966) 445 He has no litter-carriers to carry manure. **1967** Litter-cart [see **cloth-capped* adj.]. **1927** *Children's Newspaper* 25 June 8/2 It is time the Litter Lout was taken seriously in hand. **1972** *Guardian* 29 Mar. 24/1 The packaging industry had been made a scapegoat for the actions of the litter lout. **1921** *Genetics* VI. 122 These are assumed to be litter-mates for whom all or nearly all tangible environmental factors may be assumed to be in common. **1946** *Nature* 24 Aug. 258/2 A biological test of a solution in arachis oil of the vitamin A thus obtained showed growth-promoting activity in rats (ten litter-mate growth comparisons) of the order indicated by spectroscopic assay. **1972** *Sci. Amer.* Feb. 22/3 Rodents are small, inexpensive and bear large litters, so that littermates with the same genetic background can be assigned to different conditions. **1960** *Farmer & Stockbreeder* 1 Mar. 79/2 Mr. G. H. Lewis was not to be denied in the junior class, litter-sisters from him..taking first and second places. **1973** *Country Life* 15 Feb. 385/1 Miss S. G. Weall's fawn dog..collected two firsts and his litter sister..two seconds.

litter, *v.* Add: **6. a.** Also with *over.*

1888 MRS. H. WARD *R. Elsmere* I. i. iv. 90 The house was littered over with stanzas from the opening canto of a great poem on Columbus. **1890** A. CONAN DOYLE *Sign of Four* v. 84 The table was littered over with Bunsen burners, test-tubes, and retorts.

‖ **litteræ humaniores** (li·tərəi hiumæni,ōə·riz). Also **literæ humaniores.** [L., lit. 'more humane letters'.] The humanities, secular learning as opposed to divinity; esp., at the University of Oxford, the study of Greek and Roman classical literature, philosophy, and ancient history; also, = *Greats* (GREAT C. 10).

1747 CHESTERFIELD *Let.* 24 Nov. (1932) III. 1057 Studies of the *Literæ Humaniores*, especially Greek. **1760** STERNE *Tr. Shandy* (ed. 3) II. xii. 61, I would not depreciate what the study of the *Literæ humaniores*, at the university, have done for me. **1883** *Sat. Rev.* 3 Nov. 581/2 We cannot conceive a better accompaniment to the study of *literæ humaniores*. **1907** 'B. BURKE' *Barbara goes to Oxf.* 43 'Greats', you must know, is a nickname for the school of 'Literae Humaniores'. **1911** BEERBOHM *Zuleika D.* iii. 30 He..was reading, a little, for Literae Humaniores. **1926** FOWLER *Mod. Eng. Usage* 240/2 *The Humanities*, or *Litteræ humaniores*, as an old-fashioned name for the study of classical literature. **1962** K. CHORLEY *Arthur Hugh Clough* iv. 72 In Clough's day there were but two schools open to men reading for honours—namely, Mathematics and *Literae Humaniores*. **1965** J. A. W. BENNETT in J. Gibb *Light on C. S. Lewis* 48 But *litterae humaniores* were his foundation, and they did in every sense make him more humane, enlarging his responses not restricting them. **1972** *Univ. Oxf. Examination Decrees* 1. 120 The Subjects of the Honour School of Literæ Humaniores shall be (I) Greek and Roman History, (II) Philosophy, (III) Greek and Latin Literature.

li·tterer. [f. LITTER *sb.* 4 + -ER¹.] One who throws or drops litter.

1928 *Sunday Dispatch* 29 July 12/2 Every corner of the finest streets in London is disfigured with the..manifold refuse of the litterer. **1958** *Observer* 10 Aug. 8/7 The Act.. includes parish councils among the authorities empowered to proceed against litterers.

littering, *vbl. sb.* Add: **1. d.** The action of throwing or dropping litter.

1960 *Times* 14 Sept. 12/7 There is something of the threat of doom in the perfunctory notice of New York pavements 'Littering 25 dollars'. **1970** D. E. WESTLAKE *Hot Rock* (1971) I. i. 13 He threw the Kleenex on the sidewalk. Littering. **1972** *Jrnl. Soc. Psychol.* LXXXVII. 324 The interview dealt with littering...'should it be everyone's responsibility to pick up litter?'

little, *a., adv.*, and *sb.* Add: **A.** *adj.* **1. b.** (Further examples.)

1785 J. LATHAM *Gen. Synopsis Birds* III. I. 90 Little Egret... Size of a Fowl: length near a foot: weight one pound. **1802** G. MONTAGU *Ornith. Dict.* I. s.v. *Egret*, Little Egret. **1908** R. LYDEKKER *Sportsman's Brit. Bird Bk.* 248 Of the little egret..sixteen individuals appear to have been recorded from the British Islands during the last century. **1919** Little-smelt [see *GRUNION]. **1953** *Calif. Almanac* 36/2 On certain moonlit nights in the spring great numbers of small fish, termed 'grunion' or 'little smelt' appear along the beaches. **1971** *Country Life* 18 Feb. 356/3 Neither the little egret nor the common heron have been proved to breed in the [Ebro] delta, though both are present.

c. *Little Witham*: in phrases.

1560 J. HEYWOOD *Fourth Hundred Epygrams* sig. A7 Whens come great breeches? from little wittam. **1595** R. WILSON *Pedlers Prophecie* sig. B4ᵛ At litle Wytham seuen yeares I went to schoole. *a* **1661** FULLER *Worthies* (1662) Lincs. 153 *He was born at Little Witham*... It is applyed to such people as are not overstock'd with acutenesse. **1787** GROSE *Provincial Gloss.* s.v. *Essex*, He was born at Little Wittham. A punning insinuation that the person spoken of wants understanding. Ray places this proverb in Lincolnshire. **1932** E. WEEKLEY *Words & Names* x. 151 The stupid are said to be 'born at Little Witham'.

2. ¶ b. *little language*: also *transf.*

1863 *Fraser's Mag.* Feb. 152/1 She carried on hip a prize baby, a most 'doody' thing, to quote the 'little language'. **1866** MRS. GASKELL *Wives & Daughters* II. xxiv. 244 Some innocent sentences of love,..little sentences in 'little language' that went home to the squire's heart. **1922** O. JESPERSEN *Lang.* viii. 144 It would not do, however, for the child's 'little language' and its dreadful mistakes to become fixed. **1944** H. G. WELLS *'42 to '44* 142 The first thing two lovers set about doing is..to devise a little language of their own.

c. In collocations *little brother, sister*: younger (cf. 2 a). Also *fig.*

1611 BIBLE *Song of Solomon* viii. 8 We haue a little sister, and shee hath no breasts. **1799** JANE AUSTEN *Let.* 21 Jan. (1952) 57 Our own particular little brother got a place in the coach last night. **1859** THACKERAY *Virginians* II. xii. 93 Your brother and mine are gone to see our little brother at his school at the Chartreux. **1876** C. M. YONGE *Womankind* xvi. 126 In no case should they go without a more real chaperon than a maid or a little sister's governess. **1940** G. B. SHAW *Geneva* (1946) IV. 123 Ruritania is, so to speak, our little sister, and..if you laid a finger on her..we should be obliged to knock the stuffing out of you. **1949** R. CHANDLER (*title*) The little sister. **1974** *Country Life* 21 Nov. 1573/3 At present this dehydrated food is only available to caterers and food manufacturers, although its little sister Vegex (dehydrated vegetarian version) is on sale in some health-food shops.

d. *little brother* (see quot. 1928 and cf. *BIG *a.* 3 g); also *attrib.* and in extended use.

1928 *Daily Tel.* 10 July 16/2 Ninety-six youths will leave Tilbury to-day to take up farm work in Australia... Captain R. T. Thornton..will visit many of the 1,400 'Little Brothers' who have gone to the Commonwealth. **1962** *Times* 25 Apr. 11/6 'Little brother' organizations formed mostly of young people.

e. Phr. *to laugh like little Audrey*: to laugh heartily (esp. at a serious situation). Also *attrib.*, of a type of joke, a *CRUELLIE.

1939 C. MORLEY *Kitty Foyle* xiv. 153 She laughs like Little Audrey. **1959** I. & P. OPIE *Lore & Lang. Schoolch.* v. 82 Crazes for limericks, Little Audrey jokes, Knock-knocks, and Shaggy Dog stories. **1972** J. AIKEN *Butterfly Picnic* ix. 165 If I choose to..laugh like little Audrey when I'm all knotted up..who the hell's got the right to forbid me?

13. Little American (cf. *Little Englander*), **Americanism; little black dress** (or *frock*, etc.), a simple black garment suitable for a woman to wear at most kinds of relatively formal social engagements; **little chief hare** *N. Amer.* [tr. Chipewyan *bucka-thrae-ggayaze*], a North American pika, *Ochotona princeps*; **little death** [cf. F. *petite mort*], a weakening or loss of consciousness, spec. in sleep, during an orgasm, etc.; **Little Entente**: see *ENTENTE (quot. 1923); **little green man,** an imaginary inhabitant of outer space; an imaginary person of peculiar appearance (in quot. 1906 an actual person tattooed green); **little house**: delete (now *dial.*) and substitute (now *Austral., N.Z.*, and *dial.*); (further examples); **Little Irelander** (cf. *Little Englander*); **little Joe,** in the game of Craps (see quots.); **little magazine,** a name designating any of various periodicals devoted to serious literary or artistic interests (see also quots.); also *attrib.*; so (as colloq. abbrev.) **little mag; Little Mary** *colloq.*, the stomach; **(poor) little me** († I), used to convey the speaker's mock-depreciation of (and the supposed vulnerability of) himself; **little mother,** a young girl who behaves maternally towards her younger brothers or sisters, or her dolls; **little Neddy** (also **little Ned**) [*NEDDY 3], one of a number of committees under the National Economic Development Council; **little old** (followed by a pronoun or a name): used as an endearing or mock-depreciatory mode of reference; **little Orphan(t) Annie,** the name of an orphan child in a poem by J. W. Riley and a strip-cartoon by Harold Gray, used allusively in various senses (see quots.); **little review** = **little magazine*; **little science,** term used of scientific and technological investigation that does not require large resources; **little season,** a fashionable season in London in the winter; **little theatre,** a small playhouse, esp. one used for dramatic experiment (in quot. 1771 the name of an actual theatre); also *attrib.*; **little Venice,** a name given to various local areas felt to resemble Venice in canal scenery; also *attrib.*; **little Willie,** a term first used of Crown Prince Friedrich Wilhelm Viktor August Ernst of Germany (1882–1951) and applied to persons as a term of disparagement and to weapons (see quots.); (quot. 1907 is prob. an unconnected casual use); **little woman,** (*a*) one's wife, freq. with *the*; (*b*) a private dressmaker or odd-job woman.

1904 *Press* (Philadelphia) 11 Aug. 6 Judge Parker's whole contention is that of the little American. *Ibid.*, His little Americanism invites fuller discussion. **1902** H. JAMES *Wings of Dove* xviii. 427 She might fairly have been dressed tonight in the little black frock..that Milly had laid aside. **1949** D. SMITH *I capture Castle* xi. 192 Perhaps it gives you a glorious, valuable feeling to wear little black suits of fabulous price. **1951** *Woman & Beauty* May 1/2 Invest your all in one good little black dress. **1968** J. IRONSIDE *Fashion Alphabet* 19 *Little black dress.* This highly useful garment was at first almost the trademark of the British designer, Molyneux, who perfected it as an 'after 6' look in the cocktail party era between 1920 and 1939. The ultimate in sophistication then, it is still much in demand. **1973** *Country Life* 13 Dec. 2067/1, I have included a little black dress in my photographs this week, because I think it is the right alternative to glitter for winter '73. **1868** *Proc. Calif. Acad. Sci.* IV. 6 *Lagomys princeps* Richardson—'Little Chief Hare'; Rat-rabbit. **1898** F. RUSSELL *Explor. Far North* p. vi, The timid squeak of the little chief hare was often heard. **1947** V. H. CAHALANE *Mammals N. Amer.* 581 Some imaginative naturalist has given the animal the title of 'little chief hare'. **1960** *Canad. Audubon* Jan.–Feb. 28/3 The industrious little pika has yet another name, the Indian name, 'Little Chief Hare'. **1932** A. HUXLEY *Brave New World* v. 89 The sexophones wailed like melodious cats under the moon, moaned in the alto and tenor registers as though the little death were upon them. **1939** —— *After Many a Summer* II. ii. 198 Like all the other addictions, whether to drugs or books, to power or applause, the addiction to pleasure tends to aggravate the condition it temporarily alleviates. The addict goes down into the valley of the shadow of his own particular little death. **1959** W. GOLDING *Free Fall* v. 108 The little death shared or self-inflicted was neither irrelevant nor sinful. **1959** D. KROOK *Three Traditions Moral Thought* x. 275 That other aspect of the sexual act that Augustine finds so disturbing, that oblivion which the poets called the 'little death', the overwhelming of the will and the reason, need have no terror in it. **1969** G. SIMS *Sand Dollar* x. 126 She attained her climax with a deep shudder... Her features took on a delicate nature in the 'little death'. **1971** R. RENDELL *One Across* III. xxi. 166 A little death would make the unbearable present pass... The pubs wouldn't be open yet. **1973** D. BAGLEY *Tightrope Men* i. 9 That everyday miracle of the reintegration of the psyche after the little death of

sleep. [**1906** KIPLING *Puck of Pook's Hill* 185 The little green man orated like a—like Cicero.] **1961** PARTRIDGE *Dict. Slang* Suppl. 1170/2 *Little green men*, mysterious beings alleged to have been seen emerging from flying saucers. **1966** K. GILES *Provenance of Death* iv. 121 Are you saying you are being watched perhaps by little green men? **1967** M. KENYON *Whole Hog* iv. 42 There was a desert-island cartoon..and a little-green-men-from-Mars cartoon. **1969** C. HODDER-WILLIAMS *98·4* iv. 46, I wasn't at the Cape, nor Atlantis, nor a lunatic asylum for little green men with antennae. **1971** 'H. CALVIN' *Poison Chasers* iii. 36 We been reading too many books about little green men from Mars. **1972** *Daily Tel.* 25 Sept. 7/7 Neither he, nor I, believes that 'little green men' from Mars..are watching us and closely inspecting our planet. **1789** J. PARKER in *New England Hist. & Geneal. Reg.* (1915) LXIX. 305 Charles worked on my Little house. **1939** L. MANN *Mountain Flat* ii. 23 A gate led from the first yard into another in which were the pig sty, the hen-house, the tool-shed and what they called jocosely 'the little house'. **1939** F. THOMPSON *Lark Rise* i. 10 Later, the place of honour in the 'little house' was occupied by 'Our Political Leaders', two rows of portraits on one print. **1941** BAKER *N.Z. Slang* vi. 53 Other expressions..to make a sale, to vomit; little house, a privy;..poled for stolen. **1927** *Sunday Times* 13 Feb. 5/1 This may not be pleasing to certain little Irelanders who wish us to live in complete isolation. **1890** *Dialect Notes* I. 61 *Big Dick*: 10; *little Joe*: 4. **1926** T. S. STRIBLING *Teeftallow* viii. 67 The shooter..was half drunk,..chanting at each shot, 'Come up, Little Joe! Don't deceive yo' pappy!' **1968** *Scottish Daily Mail* 16 July 2/1 If you throw crap dice and a combination of seven is showing on top, what is facing down? .. Little Joes? **1962** *Listener* 24 May 920/2 Shaw had no use for the 'little mag' mentality. **1900** *Book-Lover* (San Francisco) Autumn (recto rear cover), To quote its publishers we may tell our friends *Impressions* is a little magazine, simply done to tell the truth about books and other matters. **1913** *Writer's Mag.* Oct. 140/1 *The Black Cat* externally is the same little magazine that it has been for years. **1926** *Atlantic Monthly* Mar. 391/2 As these little magazines often contain only thirty-two pages, cost..two or three cents a copy to produce, and sell for fifteen..you can afford to dispense with advertisements. **1947** *Partisan Rev.* XIV. 473 This group formally includes members of the faculties of the universities and the few writers in the larger cities who do independent critical work pitched beyond the level of commercialism. These find their outlet in the little magazines. **1952** *Times Lit. Suppl.* 29 Aug. Suppl. p. xlvii, The birth of the Little Magazine may also now be seen in retrospect as heralding the decline of the greater. **1958** *Spectator* 18 July 116/3 Little-magazine society. **1971** *Ann. Rep. Curators Bodl. Libr. 1969–70* 39 Acquisitions in contemporary literature of the United States and the Commonwealth, including 'little magazines'..continued. **1972** *Guardian* 30 Aug. 8/2 Little magazines have been the pioneers of twentieth-century literature from Wyndham Lewis's Blast in the First World War to F. R. Leavis's Scrutiny in the thirties and forties and on to the present day. **1903** *Punch* 14 Oct. 258/1 And what is the subject of the piece [Barrie's *Little Mary*]? Who is Little Mary? It is nobody: it is simply a nursery name that the child-doctor invents as a kind of polite equivalent to what children ordinarily allude to as their 'tum-tum'. *Ibid.*, Good-natured British audiences have strong Little Maries. **1905** *Daily Chron.* 8 Nov. 6/5 To wear it over their chest, not to speak of Little Mary, as people all now call their other danger spot. **1923** U. L. SILBERRAD *Lett. J. Armiter* iv. 82 Then I get a cold in Little Mary, my vulnerable spot. **1933** W. H. HARRISON *Humour in East End* 18 'I've got a little Mary too!' Swift as lightning came the reply, with a shrewd glance at a corpulent waistcoat: 'Not arf yer ain't, guv-nor.' **1781** N. MUNDY *Let.* 21 Oct. in A. E. Newdigate-Newdegate *Cheverels* (1898) iii. 48 How very Ill poor little I am used kick'd quite out & not allowed room. **1818** M. EDGEWORTH *Let.* 15 Oct. (1971) 126 Could I four years ago have believed if it had been prophecied to me that I poor little i should this day have been driving about London with Honora *alone*? **1895** A. W. PINERO *Second Mrs. Tanqueray* III. 111, I really thought you'd forgotten poor little me. **1899** R. WHITEING *No. 5 John St.* xxx. 267 The wonder why the irresponsible..powers could not let 'poor little me' alone. **1913** A. BENNETT *Regent* I. iii. 68 'What about poor little me?' cried the driver, who was evidently a ribald socialist. **1923** E. BOWEN *Encounters* 9 *Nobody* takes *any* notice of little me. **1961** M. BEADLE *These Ruins are Inhabited* (1963) ix. 124 A cold snap prompted the writing of some poor-little-me letters home. **1968** A. DIMENT *Bang Bang Birds* viii. 149 He had had instructions from his bosses to liquidate little me. **1828** M. WILMOT *Let.* 23 Apr. (1935) 316 Blanche..is the little *Mother* of the house upon the occasion. **1897** *Sears, Roebuck Catal.* 333/1 Little Mother's Outfit... Contains..a 'Little Mother's Fashion Book', showing designs and directions for making dolls' dresses. **1967** A. WILSON *No Laughing Matter* II. 70 Sukey had better deal with them. She likes being the little mother. **1963** *Daily Tel.* 18 Oct. 31/3 The committee will be among the first 'little Neddies' set up under the auspices of the National Economic Development Council. **1964** *Economist* 5 Dec. 1112/1 The 'little Neds' (the separate councils..for different industries). **1967** *Punch* 24 May 766 The Little Neddy for the hotel and catering industry has just published the result of a survey it commissioned among foreign travel agents. **1969** *Times* 13 Jan. 11/3 Even a small shift in the distribution of domestic resources could meet the needs of the expansion postulated by Little Neddy, provided the profits were already there. **1905** Little old [see *MONEY *sb.* 6 a]. **1961** C. COCKBURN *View from West* vii. 71 Iceland.. was menacing poor little old England in a truly devilish manner. **1966** J. POTTS *Footsteps on Stairs* (1967) xiv. 177 Why couldn't I have been looking out for little old me? **1968** J. SANGSTER *Touchfeather* vi. 54 He wasn't carrying a gun, probably considering that with just little old me to look after he didn't need to. **1973** A. ROSS *Dunfermline Affair* 80 Askwith and Gibson made polite noises, but little old Abbie refused to dissemble. **1973** *Guardian* 12 Mar. 9/1, I started at 15..and it was three or four years before I got a little old machine of my own. [**1913** J. W. RILEY *Poems* 9 Little Orphant Annie's come to our house to stay. **1924** H. GRAY in *Daily News* (N.Y.) (Pink ed.) 5 Aug. 26 (*title of cartoon strip*) Little Orphan Annie.] **1938** D. SMITH *Dear Octopus* I. 39 You stood there in the doorway..looking exactly like little Orphan Annie. **1952** M. STEEN *Phoenix Rising* vi. 142, I won't have my friends..made uneasy by your bogey tales. You're worse than Little Orphant Annie! **1960** *Woman* 20 Feb. 6/3 She cast herself in the rôle of Little Orphan Annie. **1965** *Newsweek* 19 July 58/1 A Little Orphan Annie dress by Mary Quant or Caroline Charles will do, or for the male, a set of Mod threads. **1966** M. G. EBERHART *Witness at Large* (1967) i. 13 You'll soon be out of a job, Little Orphan Annie. *Ibid.*, It was true that I was in a position of Little Orphan Annie in my relationship to the Esseven family. **1914** (*title*) The little review. **1958** *Times Lit. Suppl.* 24 Jan. 37/3 As Mr. Granville Hicks has pointed out, the 'little reviews' themselves have become erudite, careful, critical not creative, moved more by the spirit of Sainte-Beuve than by that of Baudelaire. **1961** A. M. WEINBERG in *Science* 21 July 162/1 We must make Big Science flourish without..allowing it to trample Little Science—that is, we must nurture small-scale excellence as carefully as we lavish gifts on large-scale spectaculars. **1963** D. J. PRICE (*title*) Little science, big science. **1970** *Sunday Times* (Colour Suppl.) 16 Aug. 22/2 Little Science changed into recognisable Big Science during the Second World War. **1972** *Science* 9 June 1084/1 There is no question that for nearly every scientist the personal joys of little science are greater than those of big science. **1928** *Daily Tel.* 3 Jan. 1/5 Lady Chamberlain's Tuesday afternoon At Homes at the Foreign Office..were one of the features of the 'little season'. **1938** *Burlington Mag.* Feb. p. xvii/1 Highly successful sales..in the so-called 'little season' which ended just before Christmas. **1959** J. FLEMING *Miss Bones* xiv. 150 This..is the Little Season, as it's known. There are numerous Embassy parties..first nights at the theatres..and what have you. **1771** SMOLLETT *Humph. Cl.* I. 246 His detestation of the mob..has prevented him from going to the Little Theatre in the Hay-market. **1813** JANE AUSTEN *Pride & Prej.* III. ix. 166 London was rather thin, but however the little Theatre was open. **1912** M. B. LEAVITT *50 Yrs. Theatr. Managem.* xxxvii. 574 'Little Theatres' have for some time been playing important rôles in the dramatic life of Paris, Berlin and London. **1914** *Writer's Mag.* Jan. 327/2 (*caption*) The 'little' theater movement expanding. **1916** *Stage Year Bk.* 45 Another little theatre, the Portmanteau.. opened its doors with a programme of one-act plays. **1929** [see **community theatre*]. **1958** *Listener* 21 Aug. 283/2 The shabby treatment accorded here to our little theatres. **1965** E. O'BRIEN *Aug. is Wicked Month* ii. 22 She worked for a little theatre magazine. **1971** *Author* LXXXII. 118 A trusting author, Mr. X, wrote a 'philosophical' conversation-piece which was staged at a London little theatre. **1973** *Philadelphia Inquirer* (Today Suppl.) 7 Oct. 49/1 There is only one fully funded..little theatre in the Philadelphia area. **1934** M. ALLINGHAM *Death of Ghost* i. 2 Little Venice [on the Regent's Canal] in 1930... The room..took up the entire first floor of the old house on the canal. **1951** D. NEWTON *London West of Bars* xxii. 323 Robert Browning, back from Italy, settled for a time in a tall house overlooking 'Little Venice'. **1960** C. MACINNES *Mr. Love & Justice* 21 Edward was sitting with his girl in the park at Little Venice, up by the Harrow road. **1968** *Guardian* 12 July 20/6 The justices granted a provisional restaurant licence for two barges to be moored..near the lock of the Rochdale Canal... It was hoped this section of the canal..would become a Little Venice patronised by yachtsmen. **1970** *Ibid.* 8 Aug. 7/3 It has taken a solid anniversary to bring the Little Venice Boat Show back to London... The anniversary signals the completion in 1820 of the Regent's Canal. **1907** F. H. BURNETT *Shuttle* xxiii. 229 Little Willie's not quite as easy as he looks. **1915** D. O. BARNETT *Let.* 27 May (1915) 154 At intervals of about twenty minutes last night they fired a *Little Willie* on to our trench. *Ibid.* 8 June 166 Our fieldgun H.E. shell is a very fine thing, more powerful than the German one (otherwise known as *Little Willie*). **1925** A. CHRISTIE *Secret of Chimneys* xii. 121 That some one unlatched the window..to make it look like an outside job—incidentally with me as Little Willie. **1925** FRASER & GIBBONS *Soldier & Sailor Words* 304 *Big and Little Willie*, names given the Kaiser and German Crown Prince in a series of cartoons... The names soon..were applied to a variety of objects. For instance, two experimental tanks, which were begun on about August, 1915... 'Little Willie' first 'moved' on September 8th. **1927** 'D. YATES' *Blind Corner* iv. 125 'God give it's Little Willie,' said Ellis, and sucked in his breath. 'I'd like to meet him like this.' **1965** BROPHY & PARTRIDGE *Long Trail* 145 *Little Willie, Big Willie*, the Crown Prince and the Kaiser. Journalese. So used occasionally by the troops, who applied the terms to all manner of things: e.g. a long-range naval gun operating on the Western Front. **1624** J. CHAMBERLAIN *Let.* 20 Mar. (1939) II. 551, I send Dr. Bargraves sermon and the little womans worke for my Lady. **1795** W. B. STEVENS *Jrnl.* 18 Aug. (1965) III. 280 The Little Woman's passions swell... She is expecting her Husband to be her Slave. **1801** M. O'CONNELL *Let.* 6 Nov. in D. O'Connell *Corr.* (1972) I. 63 Complying with the earnest request of your *little woman* whose entire happiness is wrapped up in you. **1852** DICKENS *Bleak Ho.* (1853) xxxii. 314 My little woman will be looking for me, else. **1936** 'R. WEST' *Thinking Reed* viii. 262 We went off to a little woman who does manicures. **1959** *Sunday Express* 26 July 10/5 I've..found a 'little woman' —one of those treasures who will dressmake at home. **1970** G. GREER *Female Eunuch* 286 Loving mockery of the little woman. **1973** G. GREENE *Honorary Consul* IV. i. 175 The material was quite inexpensive, and I had it run up by a little woman.

14. little-bitty: see *BITTY *a.* 3; **little-boy** *attrib.*, pertaining to, suited to, or resembling a small boy; infantile; so **little-boyish** *a.*; **little-boy-lost**: used (without hyphens) as a title of literary works by William Blake and other writers after him; *attrib.* or as *adj. phr.*, resembling a small boy who has lost his way; also *absol.*; **little boys' room** (cf. **little girls' room*), a genteelism for a gentlemen's lavatory; **little-girl** *attrib.*, resembling or characteristic of a little girl, e.g. a type of collar, a voice; so **little-girlish** *a.*; **little-girlhood, -girlishness**; **little-girl-lost** (cf. **little-boy-lost*); **little girls' room**, a genteelism for a ladies' lavatory.

1847 THACKERAY *Van. Fair* (1848) v. 39 Out of the little-boy class into the middle-sized form. **1923** D. H. LAWRENCE *Stud. Classic Amer. Lit.* (1924) vii. 143 Old-fashioned Nathaniel, with his little-boy charm. **1929** —— *Phoenix II* (1968) 537 Men..spend years training up the little-boy-baby-face type, till they've got her perfect. Then the moment they marry her, they want something else. **1951** M. MCLUHAN *Mech. Bride* (1967) 68/2 The male tends to assume the little-boy role. **1955** E. BLISHEN *Roaring Boys* iv. 182 Two faces, well-washed and little-boyish. **1968** H. WAUGH *30 Manhattan East* (1969) 149 That little-boy quality that wasn't little-boyish at all. **1789** W. BLAKE *Songs of Innocence* in *Compl. Writings* (1972) 120 (*title*) The little boy lost. **1905** W. H. HUDSON (*title*) A little boy lost. **1949** M. LASKI (*title*) Little boy lost. **1957** R. HOGGART *Uses of Literacy* ix. 235 An appearance compounded of the metallically-cynical and the little-boy-lost. **1957** *Numbers* VII. 4 The strand of dark hair..made him appear slightly dishevelled and rather little-boy-lost. **1961** J. PUDNEY *Thin Air* viii. 95 The-little-boy-lost look ..which..brought out the mother in most women. **1967** V. CANNING *Python Project* ix. 186 Having that little-boy-lost feeling and knowing that all the world is against you. **1973** 'B. MATHER' *Snowline* iv. 51 He was beginning to realize his aloneness. Little boy lost in a big strange country. **1957** A. WILSON *Bit off Map* 145 'Hullo,' said Sylvia, 'I expected Victor.' 'He's gone to the little boy's room,' said the girl. 'He'll be back in a jiffy.' **1973** W. FAIRCHILD *Swiss Arrangement* vi. 74 He bought me this jumbo cornet... I took it into the little boys' room with me... In case it started to melt while I was having a pee. **1973** M. WOODHOUSE *Blue Bone* ii. 15 Rodway pulled up in a lay-by. 'All out for the little boys' room,' he said. **1864** C. M. YONGE *Trial* I. xiii. 263 Gertrude did not like people in the 'little girl' stage. **1896** E. TURNER *Little Larrikin* xiii. 149 Isn't he a bit like your little-girl ideal man? When you were seventeen..and had ideals? **1938** *Chatelaine* July 27/1 Last year it was the Little Girl Look. **1939** M. B. PICKEN *Lang. Fashion* 95/3 *Little girl collar*, narrow, round collar, smaller than Peter Pan or Buster Brown. **1949** M. MILLER *Sure Thing* (1950) 69 Her voice was a little-girl voice. **1967** MRS. L. B. JOHNSON *White House Diary* 5 Jan. (1970) 470 In came Lynda..wearing mesh hose and little-girl flat shoes. **1925** 'R. CROMPTON' *Still—William* viii. 134 His ideal of little-girlhood was Joan, dark haired and dark-eyed and shy. **1945** 'O. MALET' *My Bird Sings* I. iv. 30 Camille, glad of her still unquestioned little-girlhood, kept out of the way. **1901** A. F. BROWN *Lonesomest Doll* 35 Clotilde soon became little-girlish again. **1936** C. DAY LEWIS *Friendly Tree* iv. 58 Anna felt absurdly obedient and little-girlish. **1962** I. MURDOCH *Unofficial Rose* xiii. 122 She spoke with a little-girlish satisfaction. **1974** M. HIGGINS *Changeling* xiv. 75 You've done something to your hair..it's too little-girlish. **1936** J. CURTIS *Gilt Kid* v. 58 It was obvious that she was playing little girlishness for all that she was worth. **1936** C. DAY LEWIS *Friendly Tree* xiii. 190 You can be the little girl lost, and I'll be the policeman who finds you. **1963** *Guardian* 18 Jan. 4/6 Her little-girl-lost brand of charm. **1963** 'G. BLACK' *Dragon for Christmas* xi. 173 If ever there was a little girl lost it was Mei Lan. She had known love and the Kiangsi opera and been cut off from both. **1974** M. HIGGINS *Changeling* ix. 46 That little-girl-lost look you have. **1949** M. MILLER *Sure Thing* (1950) 267 'Look, where are you going?' 'To the little girls' room.' **1959** P. H. JOHNSON *Humbler Creation* vi. 43 'I wonder where on earth she's gone?'..'Probably to the little girls' room.' **1975** A. THACKERAY *One Way Ticket* I. 10, I just saw Maggie disappear into the little girls' room.

B. *absol.* and *sb.* **4.** (Further *Proverbs.*)

1791 J. O'KEEFFE *Wild Oats* v. iii. 64 It isn't much, but every little helps. **1840** MARRYAT *Poor Jack* xiii. 90 It's a very old saying, that every little helps. **1872** S. HALE *Lett.* (1918) 84, I get fearfully tired, and a very little Abbey goes a long way with me. **1873** 'MARK TWAIN' in 'Mark Twain' & Warner *Gilded Age* xxiv. 226 Every little helps, you know. **1910** E. M. FORSTER *Howard's End* xxiv. 201 Dolly's a good little woman..but a little of her goes a long way. **1936** 'G. ORWELL' *Let.* 14 Feb. in *Coll. Ess.* (1968) I. 163, I expect I can either review it or get it reviewed... Not that that gives one much of a boost, but every little helps. **1951** J. MASTERS *Nightrunners Bengal* I. i. 3 A little of Caroline Langford went a long way. **1967** V. CANNING *Python Project* iv. 63 Carry on. Every little helps. You might turn up something.

little, *v.* (Later *poet.* examples.)

1928 HARDY *Winter Words* 194 Can littlest life beneath the sun More littled be? **1957** A. CLARKE *Later Poems* (1961) 61 Yet, littling by itself, I found one That had never run to town.

little-go. Add: **3.** *transf.* (various senses).

1852 MRS. GASKELL *Let.* 19 May (1966) 191, I (boldly) asked them all to come here..so we had an impromptu *little-go* last night. **1858** *Leisure Hour* 15 July 448/1 This preliminary spread, or 'little go'. **1909** J. R. WARE *Passing Eng.* 169/1 *Little go*, first imprisonment, first invented by a fallen university man. **1960** WENTWORTH & FLEXNER *Dict. Amer. Slang* 321/1 *Little go*, an unimportant, unexciting, or incomplete attempt, effort, task, or performance.

little man. Add: **2.** Also, a person working or producing on a small scale; a small craftsman or tradesman; a local man available to do light work.

1825 H. WILSON *Mem.* IV. 103 That little man in St. James's Street, who sells box-combs. **1890** W. BOOTH *In Darkest Eng.* vi. 214 Would it not be possible..to establish..a Poor Man's Bank..doing for the 'little man' what all the banks should do for the 'big man'? **1937** *Ann. Reg. 1936* II. 63 The potential customers being most numerous among the 'little men', *i.e.*, small shopkeepers and owners

of one-man businesses. **1952** *Economist* 30 Aug. 514/1 Diversified investment buying by the general public, especially by the 'little man'. **1959** *Motor Manual* (ed. 36) xiii. 269 For cars so built it is seldom possible to have an adequate towing bracket made up by the 'little man round the corner' who happens to have a welding plant and some iron. **1962** *Guardian* 12 Dec. 4/4 What most of us have to do is to find a 'little man' who will oblige with a bit of painting in his spare time. **1966** *Listener* 15 Sept. 382/2 The Bideford 'little man' who fears competition.

b. The undistinguished and ordinary 'man in the street'.

1933 E. SUTTON tr. H. Fallada *(title)* Little man, what now? **1935** *New Statesman* 8 June 857/1 The old *noli-me-tangere* John Bull has disappeared, and his place has been taken by the all-enduring Little Man. **1936** 'G. ORWELL' *Keep Aspidistra Flying* iii. 64 To turn into the typical little bowler-hatted sneak—Strube's 'little man'. **1941** AUDEN *New Year Let.* III. 52 The hitherto-unconscious creed Of little men who half succeed. **1946** *R.A.F. Jrnl.* May 162 Joe represents the typical 'little man' in blue, doomed to a lowly rank. **1952** M. LASKI *Village* xiii. 187 The element of the ordinary man, the little man, taking matters into his own hands. **1960** *Times* 28 Sept. 15/4 Its central episode is the rebellion of a 'little man' against the anonymity and dreariness of his life. **1975** *Times* 2 Jan. 13/3 Mr [Charlie] Chaplin's indomitable little man beset by adversity.

5. A young male child: see MAN *sb.*^{1} 4 f.

Little Neck. *U.S.* The name of a locality in Long Island, used *attrib.* in **little neck clam** to designate small specimens of the quahog, *Mercenaria mercenaria*, or other similar clams. Also *absol.*

1884 *Bull. U.S. Nat. Mus.* No. 27. 234 Another name [for the small round clam] is 'Little Neck', derived originally from a neck of land on the north shore of Long Island, known as Little Neck, whose clams had a superior flavour. **1899** J. HATTON in *People* 17 Dec. 2 Regret was expressed that New York did not possess the English sole ..but there was good compensation in the little-neck clam and the bass. **1910** *Chambers's Jrnl.* July 430/2 In the restaurants the British visitor will invariably be confronted with the possibilities contained in 'little neck clams',..and so on. **1935** J. C. LINCOLN *Cape Cod Yesterdays* 49 Everyone eats oysters and Little Necks *au naturel.* **1972** *Guardian* 1 Sept. 9/1 Clams from the Maine coast, Quahogs, 'steamers', Littlenecks.

little people. 1. Fairies, gremlins.

1726–31 [in Dict. s.v. LITTLE *a.* 13]. **1897** E. PHILLPOTTS *Lying Prophets* x. 101 The li'l people takes all manner o' shaapes. **1941** [see *GREMLIN 1]. **1973** *Times* 17 Mar. 14/8 The two larger clovers..were said to afford protection against 'unkind Little People'. **1973** *Stornoway Gazette* 19 May 6/2 As a writer, and collector of unusual information, I would be interested to hear from people who have seen the 'little people' or any strange, apparently non-human beings, under any circumstances whatever.

2. Children.

1752 M. W. MONTAGU *Let.* 22 July (1967) III. 15 How often do I fancy to my selfe the pleasure I should take in seeing you in the midst of your little people! **1876** C. M. YONGE *Three Brides* I. xvii. 282 My little people are so anxious to have me with them. **1934** H. G. WELLS *Exper. Autobiogr.* II. viii. 602 The Bastable family she created is still a joy to little people between ten and seventeen. **1972** A. ROUDYBUSH *Sybaritic Death* (1974) ii. 7 Tiled Beatrix Potter bunnies still scampered around the frieze..and windows, barred to prevent accidents to little people. **1975** *Sunday Times* 30 Mar. 8/1 (Advt.), Big savings for little people from Boots.

3. The poor; ordinary or undistinguished people.

1827 [see LITTLE *a.* 8 b]. **1901** C. MORRIS *Life on Stage* xxiv. 195, I hear many tales of the insolence of stars—of their..injustice to 'little people' as the term goes. **1951** M. McLUHAN *Mech. Bride* (1967) 66/1 Her allies are the little people, who..have to contend with the frustrations brought about by bureaucratic bungling.

Littler (li·tləɹ). The name of William *Littler* (1724–84), English potter, used in the possessive to denote a rich blue colour applied to porcelain or stoneware.

1957 MANKOWITZ & HAGGAR *Conc. Encycl. Eng. Pott. & Porc.* 130/2 *Littler's blue*, a brilliant 'royal' blue or lapis-lazuli found on porcelain attributed to Longton Hall, and on salt-glazed stoneware believed to have been made by William Littler & Aaron Wedgwood, c. 1750. **1971** *Country Life* 28 Oct. 1124/1 William Littler..was the originator of a rich blue enamel which has come down in collectors' jargon as 'Littler's blue'.

Little's disease. *Med.* [Named after William John *Little* (1810–94), English physician, who described it.] Cerebral spastic paralysis of infants.

1885 *Boston Med. & Surg. Jrnl.* CXII. 217/1 *(heading)* Cases of congenital muscular rigidity, or Little's disease. *Ibid.*, This 'congenital muscular rigidity' was first described as an affection by Little, of London, in 1853, and Rupprecht ..suggested that the name of Little's disease be applied to it. **1887** *Buck's Handbk. Med. Sci.* V. 200/2 Little's disease. Spasmodic tabes of children. **1938** *Times Lit. Suppl.* 22 Jan. 50/2 Recent researches would appear to have established that the trouble from which Byron suffered was not an ordinary club-foot: that he was the victim of some obscure nervous malady—Little's disease, otherwise spastic paraplegia, has been suggested. **1964** S. DUKE-ELDER *Parsons' Dis. Eye* (ed. 14) xxxiv. 549 Congenital spastic diplegia (*Little's disease*), a bilateral spastic paralysis present from birth, considered at one time to be due to meningeal hæmorrhage as a result of birth injury, is probably a degenerative cerebral process of obscure ætiology.

littly, littlie (li·tli), *sb.* [f. LITTLE *a.* + -Y^{6}, -IE]. A small child or person; *pl.*, small children, the younger children of a family, etc.

1893–4 R. O. HESLOP *Northumb. Words* II. 453 *Littlie*, a smaller person than others. **1961** A. UPFIELD *Bony & White Savage* v. 41 How's she? How's the littlies? **1967** B. JEFFERIS *One Black Summer* vi. 122 Can you see Hilary instructing the littlies at Sunday school?

littly (li·tli), *adv.* [f. LITT(LE *a.* + -LY^{2}.] In a small, modest, undistinguished way.

1897 F. THOMPSON *New Poems* 137 Littly he sets him to the daily way. **1905** BEERBOHM *Around Theatres* (1924) II. 177 To strut agreeably, littly, as in the average production.

littorina (litŏrəi·nă, -ī·nă). [mod.L. (A. d'A. de Férussac *Tableaux Systématiques des Animaux Mollusques* (1822) p. xxxiv), f. L. *lītus* shore.] **1.** A gastropod mollusc of the genus so called; = PERIWINKLE^{2} 1.

[**1820–5** J. & G. B. SOWERBY *Genera Recent & Fossil Shells* plate 211 As the name implies, the Littorinæ are found on and near the shore.] **1857** L. REEVE *Conchologia Iconica* X. s.v. *Littorina*, plate 1, species 1 *(heading)* The bubbled Littorina. **1963** D. W. & E. E. HUMPHRIES tr. *Termier's Erosion & Sedimentation* iii. 64 The Littorinas of California..have each been able to dislodge 0·3 gm of grains in twenty-four hours.

2. Littorina (or **Litorina**) **sea**, the Baltic sea at the end of the Boreal period. Also *Littorina beach, minimum, period, stage, transgression* (see quots.).

1921 R. A. S. MACALISTER *Text-bk. European Archæol.* I. ii. 43 The Baltic Sea became of much the same configuration as at present, but rather larger in extent and more salt; the name given to this stage of its history, once more derived from the name of its mollusc, is *Littorina Sea*. The greatest depression of this phase of land-movement may be called the *Littorina Minimum*. The Littorina period is also known as the *Tapes* period. **1928** C. DAWSON *Age of Gods* iii. 48 The climate of Scandinavia became much warmer, owing perhaps to a change in the ocean currents... This is the Litorina stage, named after the periwinkle which now inhabited the warmer waters of the Baltic. **1949** W. F. ALBRIGHT *Archaeol. of Palestine* iii. 62 Pottery came into use in an early phase, scarcely later than about 4500 B.C., at the height of the Litorina period. **1954** S. PIGGOTT *Neolithic Cultures* i. 2 The Litorina Transgression of the Baltic. **1963** D. W. & E. E. HUMPHRIES tr. *Termier's Erosion & Sedimentation* i. 26 Corresponding to the Calaisian are the *Littorina* beaches.

littorinid (litǫ·rinid). [f. mod.L. family name *Littorinidæ*, f. generic name *Littorina* (see prec.).] A marine snail of the family Littorinidæ.

1948 *Austral. Jrnl. Sci. Res.* B. I. 191 The Supralittoral is the region above high-water spring tide levels which has been invaded by only a few typically marine animals, chiefly gastropods. The species are Littorinids, and one might call this the Littorinid zone. **1952** *Jrnl. Ecol.* XL. 87 We agree..in defining the upper limit of the littoral.. as the region where littorinids become dominant. **1964** V. J. CHAPMAN *Coastal Vegetation* ii. 37 The littorinids do not penetrate them [*sc.* lichen zones] under normal conditions. **1974** *Nature* 3 May 11/3 Littorinids are present on the rock shores of all continents.

liturgical, *a.* Add: *Liturgical Movement* (see quot. 1957).

1929 *Tablet* 17 Aug. 197/2 The proficiency of these youngsters has been acquired in our Catholic schools, the grand hope of the Liturgical Movement, and Catholic girls are not lagging behind Catholic boys. **1935** A. G. HEBERT *Liturgy & Society* v. 126 The so-called Liturgical Movement is concerned with things vastly more important than mere ritualism. **1957** *Oxf. Dict. Chr. Ch.* 815/1 *Liturgical Movement*, a Movement of which the object is the restoration of the active participation by the people in the official worship of the Church. **1959** *Times Lit. Suppl.* 29 May 325/3 Since the war the landscape of Christianity has been unmistakably changing..under the gradual pressures of that climate of opinion generally called the Liturgical Movement.

liturgism (li·tɒɹdʒiz'm). [f. LITURGY + -ISM.] Excessive concentration on liturgy; a disproportionate concern with liturgical detail.

1926 *Q. Register* Feb. 117 With this prevailing liturgism, religion ceased to be an important force in common life. **1953** E. L. MASCALL *Corpus Christi* iii. 79 It is possible to point to parishes whose priest is an enthusiastic amateur liturgiologist, where the layfolk have to adapt themselves at regular intervals to fresh modifications in the rite and ceremonies of the Mass in agreement with the stage now reached by their pastor in his researches. Liturgism of this kind is simply individualism run riot.

Litvak (li·tvǫk). Also **Litvok.** [Yiddish, f. Pol. *Litwak* Lithuanian.] A Jew from Lithuania or its neighbouring regions.

1892 I. ZANGWILL *Childr. Ghetto* I. 38 To a Dutch or Russian Jew, the 'Pullack', or Polish Jew, is a poor creature; and..the 'Pullack' looks down upon the 'Litvok', or Lithuanian. **1970** L. M. FEINSILVER *Taste of Yiddish* 10 Four major dialects developed. Of these, the one spoken by so-called Litvaks, the Jews of Lithuania, White Russia and Northeastern Poland, is essentially 'standard' or literary Yiddish. **1970** I. SIEFF *Mem.* i. 5 'What can you expect? He's a Litvak.' A kind of Scot in Jewry? Whatever the reason, many Litvaks led the way in emigration when the circumstances were most daunting. **1971** B. MALAMUD *Tenants* 209 A middle-aged Litvak, a stocky man in mud-spotted trousers.

Litz (lits). *Electr.* Also **litz.** [f. *LITZ(ENDRAHT.] Used *attrib.* to designate wire composed of many fine strands twisted together and individually insulated, so as to reduce the skin effect and the associated increase in resistance at high frequencies.

1927 *Wireless World* 13 Apr. 447/1 *(heading)* Preparing Litz wire. **1928** *Observer* 17 June 26/3 The most efficient inductance to use in a 'tuned anode', radio-frequency amplifying circuit is one wound with 'Litz' wire. **1959** K. HENNEY *Radio Engin. Handbk.* (ed. 5) iii. 2 Since the smaller the conductor, the less the skin effect, if the conductor is broken down into many small strands, twisted..and each strand insulated from the others, the skin effect is lessened. Such wire is known as 'litz' wire. **1968** *Radio Communication Handbk.* (ed. 4) iv. 14/2 Tuned circuits of higher *Q* than can readily be obtained in the conventional type of i.f. transformer (even when wound with Litz multi-stranded wire).

litzendraht (li·tsĕndrāt). *Electr.* [a. G. *litzendraht* Litz wire, f. *litze* braid, cord, lace, strand + *draht* wire.] Litz wire.

1921 J. H. MORECROFT *Princ. Radio Communication* ii. 124 It is..important in getting the stranded wire (sometimes called litzendraht) to see that..it is made up of a great number of well-insulated strands..properly interwoven. **1933** K. HENNEY *Radio Engin. Handbk.* vii. 151 The former [*sc.* skin] effect is minimized by the use of conductors with insulated strands—so-called *litzendraht.* **1962** *Newnes Conc. Encycl. Electr. Engin.* 445/2 *Litzendraht*, stranded cable for high-frequency currents.

livability: see *LIVEABILITY.

livant, var. LEVANT *v.*^{1}

1912 D. H. LAWRENCE *Let.* c 5 Nov. (1962) I. 154 F. had carefully studied *Anna Karenina*, in a sort of 'How to be happy though livanted' spirit. *Ibid.*, I am the fellow she livanted with.

live, *a.* Add: **2. b.** (Earlier and later examples.)

1857 *Knickerbocker* L. 456 A neighbouring bath-house, kept by a live Yankee of the name of Martin. **1870** *Scribner's Monthly* I. 71 Quite as likely..the 'advanced' preacher selects a 'live' subject, a theme for the times. **1932** E. V. LUCAS *Reading, Writing & Remembering* 45 A varied, learned and very live and amusing book would be the result. **1973** *Times* 26 Apr. 9/8 Bungebah..could be a 'live' Imperial Cup prospect one day.

c. Corresponding to actual facts.

1927 CARR-SAUNDERS & JONES *Survey Social Struct. Eng. & Wales* 152 The Unemployment figures were obtained by taking an average of the 'live registers' of the employment exchanges in Great Britain. **1931** *Times Educ. Suppl.* 9 May 166/3 The 'live' register has, it is true, dropped from 923 to 757, but these figures are now swollen..by the children who left school at the Easter recess.

d. Of a performance, heard or watched at the time of its occurrence, as distinguished from one recorded on film, tape, etc. Also quasi-*adv.*

1934 *B.B.C. Year-Bk.* 248 Listeners have..complained of the fact that recorded material was too liberally used.. but..transmitting hours to the Canadian and Australasian zones are inconvenient for broadcasting 'live' material. **1937** M. LOWELL *Listen In* 109 People do not like 'canned' entertainment when they can obtain 'live' entertainment just as easily. **1944** *Ann. Reg. 1943* 348 It was still felt..that attendance at concerts and listening to 'live' performances belonged to a better order of things. **1947** *Penguin Music Mag.* II. 21 The standard of playing ..has suffered..because..there was an unprecedented demand for live performances. **1953** [see *3-D, 3 D* (*D III. 3)]. **1953** E. SMITH *Guide Eng. Traditions* 11 The development of the gramophone and wireless broadcasting.. has made many thousands familiar with the great musical composers and anxious to hear 'live' performances of their works. **1955** *Radio Times* 22 Apr. 15/2 At the moment, Northern Ireland has no means of originating 'live' television programmes. **1958** *Listener* 25 Sept. 463/2 Long experience of the effect of gramophone record sales and broadcasts provides pretty convincing evidence that they have strengthened rather than sapped the general interest of the public in attending live performances. **1970** *New Scientist* 2 July 13/1 We now accept full live coverage of soccer games in Mexico as a matter of course. **1974** *Daily Tel.* 2 May 13/5 Live entertainment is to return to the London Casino,..since 1953 the home of Cinerama. **1974** *Times* 14 Nov. 8/8 The hearing was televised live. **1975** *Daily Tel.* 18 Apr. 13/2 When people spoke 'live' or on tape it was often difficult to hear what they were saying.

4. For 'Charged with electricity' read: Connected to a source of electrical potential. In a single-phase supply: being the conductor on which the supply voltage is developed (with respect to the neutral). Also *ellipt.*, a live conductor or terminal. (Further examples.)

1913 D. S. MUNRO *Pract. of Electr. Wiring* xx. 181 When the neutral wire is itself practically at earth potential there are, of course, increased risks, if the live wire be in contact with its metal cover. **1938** J. W. SIMS *Electr. Installations* 148 When the fuse unit is enclosed in an iron case there should be an inch clearance all round any live part. **1966** J. F. WHITFIELD *Electr. Install. & Regulations* vi. 123 Two-pin sockets and plugs. Live and neutral only are catered for in these

units. **1970** *Which?* Aug. 256/2 Britain objected to black for the live, since in Britain it was being used for the neutral. **1973** G. BURDETT *Householder's Electr. Guide* vi. 34 Two-core sheathed flex is now made with the new core colours of brown for the 'live' core and blue for the neutral.

6. Applied *spec.* to an axle.

1875 [in Dict.]. **1903** *Work* XXV. 199/3 The two systems of driving are the live axle and the double sprocket chain. **1904** A. B. F. YOUNG *Compl. Motorist* (ed. 2) iv. 116 The driving of the rear wheels being direct through a powerful chain and live axle. **1929** NEWTON & STEEDS *Motor Vehicle* xxi. 259 A live axle is one that rotates or houses shafts that rotate, while a dead axle is one that does not rotate or house rotating shafts. **1963** BIRD & HUTTON-STOTT *Veteran Motor Car* 8 In modern usage 'live axle transmission' means the combination of propellor shaft and bevel- or worm-geared live axle—but many chain-driven cars also had live axles of a different sort. **1971** *Daily Tel.* 24 Mar. 11/3 It has a water cooled engine driving the rear wheels and a live rear axle.

7*. *Acoustics.* Of a room or enclosure: having a relatively long reverberation time (opp. *DEAD *a.* A. 14 b).

1931 L. COWAN *Recording Sound for Motion Pict.* xviii. 266 The music is reproduced in the live end, which would correspond to the stage of an auditorium, and the microscope is placed in the comparatively deader end, which would correspond with the audience position. **1962** A. NISBETT *Technique Sound Studio* ii. 33 The answer might at first sight appear to be to do away with reverberation entirely and try to create entirely 'dead' studios... But listening tests indicate that most people prefer a moderately 'live' acoustic. **1974** *Which?* Aug. 243/3 In a very live room—one with a lot of hard surfaces that can reflect sound—upper and middle frequencies will stand out more.

8. live action (see quot. 1960); also *attrib.*; live fence orig. *U.S.*, a hedge; also *live-fencing*; live load *Engin.*, a temporary or varying load imposed on a structure by its being put to use (cf. *dead load* s.v. *DEAD *a.* A. 29); live weight, the weight of an animal before it is slaughtered and prepared as a carcase; also *attrib.* and as quasi-*adv.*; live wire (see sense 4) orig. *U.S., fig.* esp. a person full of energy; also (with hyphen) *attrib.*

1957 MANVELL & HUNTLEY *Technique Film Music* iii. 136 A great deal of Hollywood's comedy music is linked with the cartoon world and..a number of techniques associated with the animation studios are increasingly employed during the making of live-action scenes. **1960** O. SKILBECK *ABC of Film & T.V.* 79 *Live action*, normal cinematography as opposed to Animation, Titles, etc. **1964** *Listener* 5 Nov. 735/3 There was a very long-drawn-out rescue scene in which live-action and graphics were mingled in a fashionable but not here very convincing way. **1804** J. ROBERTS *Pennsylvania Farmer* 84 When the hedge is full grown, then there is a perfect live fence. **1858** J. A. WARDER *Hedges & Evergreens* i. i. 13 Live-fences, or —as they are commonly called—Hedges, are a means of enclosure that belongs to an advanced state of civilization. **1866** *Bull's Wellington* (N.Z.) *Almanack* 28 Sow..furze for live fences. **1882** W. D. HAY *Brighter Britain!* 192 We have done something towards making live-fences. **1958** *Chambers's Techn. Dict.* 991/1 *Live fence* (Highways), a hedge. **1829** *Mass. Spy* 25 Mar. (Th.), Messrs. G. Th. and Son have imported 75,000 hawthorns, for 'live fencing'. **1866** Live load [see *FACTOR *sb.* 8]. **1908** M. S. KETCHUM *Design of Highway Bridges* ii. 41 The live loads on railway bridges are properly a series of moving concentrated loads. **1918** COWLEY & LEVY *Aeronautics* viii. 163 When the aeroplane is just smoothing out from a steep dive the angle of attack is suddenly increased and the loading rapidly attains a value which in practice is several times its normal. This [*sic*] in all essentials a live load is allowed for in the safety factor. **1974** *Sci. Amer.* Feb. 93/1 A building must ordinarily sustain three kinds of force. The first is the 'dead load' of the structure itself and its fixed contents; the second is the 'live load' of the building's occupants and of such movable components as elevators. ..The third force is produced by the movement of air. **1852** *Trans. Mich. Agric. Soc.* III. 151 Two hundred lambs..weighing some one hundred pounds..live weight. **1960** *Farmer & Stockbreeder* 12 Jan. 50 More than 3½ lb. of food to make 1 lb. of liveweight gain. **1971** *Farmers Weekly* 19 Mar. 85/1 The cost per pound of gain would exceed the price per pound liveweight received at slaughter. **1972** *Country Life* 30 Nov. 1504/2 These small birds [*sc.* turkeys]..are killed out..when they achieve liveweights of about 8½ lb. **1903** 'H. MCHUGH' *Back to Woods* 12 Bunch went down to the skating pond one day with $18 and picked four live wires at an average of 8 to 1. **1903** *Everybody's Mag.* IX. 30/1 If you cut 'Browny' you cut a live wire and were socially paralyzed. **1909** *Sat. Even. Post* 13 Mar. 24/1 As a legislator..he was probably known to many people as an aggressive 'comer' of the live-wire kind. *a* **1911** D. G. PHILLIPS *Susan Lenox* (1917) II. v. 110, I sized you up as a live wire the minute I saw you. **1931** A. CHRISTIE *Sittaford Mystery* xxiv. 197 He appears to be one of the live wires of this investigation. **1935** AUDEN & ISHERWOOD *Dog beneath Skin* I. ii. 39 And I'm the live wire of the *Evening Moon*. **1952** J. C. MASTERMAN *To teach Senators Wisdom* i. 17 He was, if anyone was, the live wire of the Senior Common Room. **1971** *Daily Tel.* 21 Aug. 14/4 The live-wire management here will miss few opportunities given the right political and economic background in which to operate. **1973** D. FRANCIS *Slay-Ride* x. 121 Our Lars was a live wire once himself. Did a lot of motor racing.

live, v.¹ 2. Also in phr. *to live off the country* (or *the land*): to obtain sustenance from the produce of the countryside without payment.

1884 *Century Mag.* Feb. 503/1 In his marches he had been obliged to live, to a great extent, off the country.

1913 H. FOOTNER *Jack Chanty* 68 The Indians..live off the land during the summer. **1934** *Discovery* Mar. 63/1 It is possible to 'live off the land' to an extent never dreamed of by earlier explorers. **1949** *Milwaukie* (Oregon) *Rev.* 4 Aug. 1/4 The main cause for the Communist army success was the fact that it was well fed, living off the country as it marched through China. **1966** *Globe & Mail* (Toronto) 5 Jan. 25/3 Eskimos in the area [Boothia Peninsula] live off the land.

3. b. *live and let live* (later examples); also *attrib.*

1928 BLUNDEN *Undertones of War* xv. 161 Our future.. depended on the observance of the 'Live and Let Live' principle. **1936** 'R. WEST' *Thinking Reed* xii. 418 Servants ..haven't the live-and-let-live of equals. **1957** L. F. R. WILLIAMS *State of Israel* 217 The belief that he was on the point of reaching some kind of live-and-let-live understanding with Israel. **1959** *Films & Filming* May 22/3 Father, in spite of the live-and-let-live attitude of his brother, persecutes the elderly Dr. Boris Winkler. **1972** J. BROWN *Chancer* iii. 46 What's got into you, love?.. I thought you were always one for live and let live. **1975** J. AIKEN *Voices in Empty House* vi. 161 It takes all sorts, as I always say. Live and let live.

4. b. Also, *to live dangerously*: to take risks habitually; to live with little regard for one's safety.

[**1910** T. COMMON tr. *Nietzsche's Joyful Wisdom* 219 The greatest enjoyment of existence is to *live in danger*!] **1930** A. HENDERSON *Contemporary Immortals* 78 The numerous attempts at assassination give point to Mussolini's avowed motto, after Nietzsche: 'To live dangerously!' **1938** L. MACNEICE *I crossed Minch* vii. 93 The young people lack spirit... If only they would appreciate 'living dangerously'! **1939** F. SCOTT FITZGERALD *Let.* 7 Oct. (1964) 407, I have 'lived dangerously' and I may quite possibly have to pay for it. **1962** *Listener* 9 Aug. 226/1 The spectators in the Bridgearama theatre saw the British pair..living dangerously. **1969** *Outdoor Life* Mar. 88/2 To fish the stream when the water is running full pipe is to live dangerously.

f. (*c*) *to live it up*: to live gaily and extravagantly.

1951 *San Francisco Examiner* 14 Feb. 12 Lieutenant Thumhill is really livin' it up! **1957** P. FRANK *Seven Days to Never* vii. 200 They come to Havanna to live it up. They live about two years in two days. **1959** H. HOBSON *Mission House Murder* iii. 24 Off-key characters who live it up like crazy. **1961** C. MCCULLERS *Clock without Hands* xiii. 249 Nobody lives for always, but when I live to live it up. **1970** N. ARMSTRONG et al. *First on Moon* ii. 39 Those who lived it up in the cocktail lounges that night were also emotionally moved. **1973** C. BONINGTON *Next Horizon* xiv. 203 We certainly had little chance of living it up on our *Daily Telegraph* expense accounts.

5. *spec. to live one's own life*: to follow one's own plans or principles; to live independently.

1853 C. BRONTË *Villette* I. xiii. 229 Thinking meantime my own thoughts, living my own life in my own still, shadow-world. **1893** O. WILDE *Lady Windermere's Fan* II. 56 There are moments when one has to choose between living one's own life..or dragging out some false..existence that the world in its hypocrisy demands. **1921** R. MACAULAY *Dangerous Ages* iii. 52 Now I must Live my own Life, as the Victorians used to put it. **1933** 'E. CAMBRIDGE' *Hostages to Fortune* IV. ii. 221 All Jane's set, with their ceaseless chatter about..living their own lives, .. had that macabre, sullen look.

8. b. *where one lives*: at or to the right or vital point. *U.S. slang.*

1860 J. G. HOLLAND *Miss Gilbert's Career* xxii. 386 When that little wife of mine says, 'Tom you're a good fellow, God bless you,' it goes right in where I live. **1878** J. H. BEADLE *Western Wilds* xxxvi. 597 The Mormons never got a cent of it. This hurt Brigham—right where he lived. **1886** *Century Mag.* Feb. 511/1 If I could only have reached him where he lives, as our slang says. **1900** 'FLYNT' & WALTON *Powers that Prey* 122 'Sock it to him!' 'Hit him where he lives!'

9. Also, *to live and learn*: a catch-phr. used, freq. on the acquisition of some new knowledge, to indicate that one learns through experience; *I'll* (or *he'll*, etc.) *live*: there is no need for serious worry or concern (freq. used in a trivial way).

c **1620** in *Roxburghe Ballads* (Ballad Soc.) (1871) I. 60 A man may liue and learne. **1803** Mrs. WILMOT *Let.* 6 Aug. in *Russ. Jrnls.* (1934) I. 32 Humph! thinks I. One must live and learn. **1844** [in Dict.]. **1849** DICKENS *Dav. Copp.* (1850) xx. 208 Live and learn. I had my doubts, I confess, but now they're cleared up. **1956** J. SYMONS *Paper Chase* xi. 88 'Are you hurt?' 'I shall live.' **1957** A. HUXLEY *Let.* 12 Dec. (1969) 836 Problems which I have been trying to solve for the last four months, without any success; for they are, so far as I can see, insoluble. So there we are. One lives and learns. **1963** N. FREELING *Gun before Butter* iii. 145 'Potato salad.. doesn't sound much fun.' 'I'll live.' **1967** O. HESKY *Time for Treason* xviii. 146 'Better, darling?' Miller asked Miriam anxiously... 'Yes, she'll live,' Tami said sourly. **1971** M. MCCARTHY *Birds of America* III Well, live and learn! **1972** 'R. CRAWFORD' *Whip Hand* I. vi. 34 The doctor asked him how he felt. 'I'll live.'

12. Delete 'Of shop-assistants' (since *to live in* is now used more generally). Add further examples. Also, *spec. to live together*, to cohabit. Also *transf.*, to have its place.

1813 JANE AUSTEN *Pride & Prej.* III. xv. 266, I..am only concerned that their living together before the marriage took place, should be so generally known. **1875** [in Dict.]. **1879** TROLLOPE *John Caldigate* III. viii. 106 They had not become man and wife... They had lived together. **1890** J. WATSON *Nature & Woodcraft* vi. 71 The farm servants of Cumbria 'live in'. **1891** [in Dict.]. *a* **1916** H. JAMES *Sense of Past* (1917) IV. iii. 242 A pot of

about the size..of that one..with something or other on the cabinet or wherever, the place where it 'lives', as we say, rather branching out on either side of it. **1919** N. FRY *Let.* 6 Oct. (1972) II. 457, I don't think they're married; they've lived together for twelve years. **1938** E. BOWEN *Death of Heart* III. vi. 426, I should like to know how she knew I'd been at her diary. I put it back where it lives. **1953** A. UPFIELD *Murder must Wait* v. 45 The nurse girl..didn't live in... She came every day. **1958** J. CANNAN *And be a Villain* i. 37, I couldn't find any brandy. Do you know where it lives? **1961** N. STREATFEILD *Silent Speaker* iv. 61 Mrs. Simpson had led Olivia into the little room where the vases lived. **1963** M. MCCARTHY *Group* ii. 42 She and Dick had 'lived together' on quite a different basis. **1971** *Woman's Own* 27 Mar. 21/3 One advantage of the permissive society is that it's all right to live together before marriage. **1971** *Daily Tel.* 16 Oct. 2/8 The development is designed..to provide extra accommodation for undergraduates to enable all 400 to 'live in'.

12*. *to live with*: **a.** To live with as if husband and wife; to cohabit with (COHABIT *v.* 2).

1749 J. CLELAND *Mem. Woman Pleasure* III 36. I had now liv'd with Mr. Norbet near a quarter of a year. **1813** JANE AUSTEN *Pride & Prej.* III. viii. 147 She was more alive to the disgrace, which the want of new clothes must reflect on her daughter's nuptials, than to any sense of shame at her eloping and living with Wickham, a fortnight before they took place. **1854** GEO. ELIOT *Let.* 23 Oct. (1954) II. 179 If you hear of anything that I have said..in relation to Mr. Lewes beyond the simple fact that I am attached to him and that I am living with him,.. believe that it is false. **1871** [see *ALLOW *v.* 7]. **1879** TROLLOPE *John Caldigate* II. iii. 33 Did she ever live with you?.. As your wife? **1923** D. H. LAWRENCE *Stud. Classic Amer. Lit.* vii. 123 Do you imagine Adam had never lived with Eve before that apple episode? **1928** E. WALLACE *Flying Squad* xvi. 159 People are under the impression that you're living with me. **1963** M. MCCARTHY *Group* i. 11 The knowledge..of Kay's having 'lived with' Harald filled them with a sudden sense of the unsanctioned. **1972** M. J. BOSSE *Incident at Naha* 31 'Virgil asked me to live with him two months ago,' I stated.

b. *fig.* To put up with; to come to terms with. *colloq.*

1937 T. S. ELIOT in B. Dobrée *From Anne to Victoria* xliii. 603 Were one a person who liked to have busts about, a bust of Scott would be something one could live with. **1941** F. D. ROOSEVELT *Let.* 1 July in H. L. Ickes *Secret Diary* (1955) III. 567 Both of these are elements that we have to live with whether we like it or not. **1961** *Listener* 2 Nov. 694/2 We know that, on account of the balance of military power, we have got to live with it [*sc.* Communism]. **1964** 'W. HAGGARD' *Antagonists* ii. 16 That was awkward, but the experienced Mr Palliser could live with it. **1965** *Ottawa Jrnl.* 29 Apr. 25/3 Canada is so bound by the General Agreement on Tariffs and Trade that in effect it would have to live with its big auto deficit with the U.S. if there were no U.S.–Canada agreement. **1973** J. PORTER *It's Murder with Dover* vi. 56 Gary was illegitimate... Not that I ever made any secret about it. It was something Gary had to learn to live with.

c. *to live with oneself*: to retain one's self-respect.

1962 P. GREGORY *Like Tigress at Bay* xiv 143 Would he be able to live with himself, later? **1971** 'J. J. MARRIC' *Gideon's Art* xi. 98, I think he'll find it difficult to live with himself if he's taken off the job]. **1973** R. PERRY *Ticket to Ride* ii. 32 The note of hysteria in her voice stopped me dead. The sensible thing to do would have been to continue on my way but if I did I knew I'd find it awfully difficult to live with myself.

liveability, livability (livăbi·liti). [f. LIV(E)-AB(LE *a.* + -ILITY.] **a.** Survival expectancy, *spec.* that of poultry. **b.** Suitability for habitation.

1914 *Springfield* (Mass.) *Republican* 28 June II. 9/2 You increase the egg yield, the fertility of eggs for hatching and the 'livability' of every chick hatched. **1922** E. W. NELSON in V. Stefansson *Northward Course of Empire* p. xviii, He [*sc.* Stefansson] has developed here and elsewhere the story of the 'livability' of the Far North, and shown that this hitherto dreaded region offers a welcome. **1934** W. A. LIPPINCOTT *Poultry Production* (ed. 5) iv. 133 The livability or vigor of a given chick might be looked upon as a part of its individuality. **1945** NELSON & WRIGHT *Tomorrow's House* vi. 75/2 Soft, general illumination which can give this room the same air of livability as the living-room itself. **1950** *N.Z. Jrnl. Agric.* Apr. 331/1 This trial..is..a means of measuring the productive powers, the livability, and the quality of pullets intended as breeding stock. **1960** *Farmer & Stockbreeder* 8 Mar. 158/1 Spinks pullets are uniform, batch after batch, giving high egg production, good size and liveability. **1971** *Farmers Weekly* 19 Mar. 90/2 What about liveability, egg numbers, egg size and feed conversion?

li·ved-in, *a.* [Cf. LIVE *v.*¹ 12 b.] Occupied, inhabited.

1873 'S. COOLIDGE' *What Katy did at School* i. 3 The lived-in-look of the best parlor. **1950** C. EDWARDS in M. Cecil *Heroines in Love* (1974) viii. 203 Your home has that wonderful lived-in feeling. **1960** *House & Garden* July 50/1 Halls..can insulate the more lived-in parts of the house. **1970** *Daily Tel.* 19 May 16/4 It [*sc.* a play] has a lived-in look and all the acting is robustly expressive. **1975** *New Yorker* 21 Apr. 103/1 Mr. Ritman has a knack for making his sets look lived in.

live-in (li·vin), *a.* [f. vbl. phr. *to live in* (LIVE *v.*¹ 12).] Resident, residing in the establishment (as opp. to living out or at home). So **li·ve-out** *a.*, that lives out.

In quot. 1966 used in the sense 'deliberately living in as a form of protest'. Cf. *-IN *suffix*³.

1955 'C. H. ROLPH' *Women of Streets* 148 Worked for four months as live-in domestic. **1966** *Maclean's Mag.* 18 June 1 The 'live-in' principles used by civil rights workers in the southern United States. **1969** *New Yorker* 18 Jan. 41 He has a live-out cook, but he likes to bend over the stove himself. **1970** *Daily Tel.* (Colour Suppl.) 9 Jan. 19/1 In 1920..the House at Maiden Bradley was run with the help of 26 live-in staff. **1971** H. WAUGH *Shadow Guest* ii. 10 We had a live-in couple to cook and caretake and a live-out woman to clean.

liveness. Add: (Further examples.) Also *attrib.*

1926 N. M. GUNN *Grey Coast* ii. 21 That liveness of the body with its whirl and suppressed gaiety. **1931** L. COWAN *Recording Sound for Motion Pict.* xviii. 261 (*heading*) Liveness of sets. **1940** *Scrutiny* IX. 94 A translator of Mr. Archer's liveness of interest and taste. **1961** *Jrnl. Acoustical Soc. America* May 604 Liveness effects on the intelligibility of noise-masked speech.

liver, *sb.*¹ Add: **7.** *liver extract, paste, pâté, pudding* (earlier examples); *liver-shaped* adj.; **liver money** (see quots.); **liver pad** (earlier example); **liver rot** (later examples); also, a type of anæmia in sheep, cattle, and, occasionally, other animals, caused by the liver fluke, *Fasciola hepatica*; **liver salt,** a powder with purgative properties which is intended to be taken, in solution, for the relief of dyspepsia or a bad 'liver'; usu. short for the proprietary name *Andrews Liver Salt* and used in *pl.*; **liver sausage** [tr. G. *leberwurst*], a soft sausage filled with cooked liver, or a mixture of liver and pork, with various seasonings; cf. *LIVERWURST; **liver-spots,** read **-spot** and add: also, one of the small brown spots characteristic of this condition; (further examples); **liver-spotted** *a.*, having liver-coloured spots or liver-spots.

1910 MARTINDALE & WESTCOTT *Extra Pharmacopœia* (ed. 14) 820 Early cases of cirrhosis have been well treated with glycerinated liver extract. **1959** *Brit. Med. Jrnl.* 28 Mar. 833/2 Parenteral liver extracts still enjoy some popularity. **1935** R. M. *Trawler* 132 Firstly, there is the 'liver-money'. The livers of all fish caught..are taken aft and tried down for the oil they produce... The proceeds of sale are divided among the crew. **1962** J. TUNSTALL *Fishermen* ii. 55 *Liver money*, received for the amount of cod and haddock livers landed. **1879** G. W. PECK *Peck's Fun* 38 A boarder at a Leadville hotel investigated his beef-steak and found that it was a fried liver pad. *c* **1938** *Fortnum & Mason Price List* 51/1 *Potted meats*..Liver Paste—per tin 1/-. **1961** M. SPARK *Prime of Miss Jean Brodie* iv. 121 Some sandwiches of liver paste. **1964** S. BELLOW *Herzog* (1965) 70 Cheese, liver paste, crackers. **1935** E. CRAIG *Family Cookery* 50 *Calf's liver pâté*... Put the liver, uncooked bacon and ham twice or three times through a mincer. **1951** E. DAVID *French Country Cooking* 222 *Liver pâté*. The French Amieux brands are always reliable. **1964** 'J. MELVILLE' *Murderers' Houses* iv. 75 Velia was making a liver pâté for Sunday supper. **1716** C. LUDWIG *Teutsch-Englisches Lexicon*, *Leberwurst*, a haggass or haggess, a liver-pudding, a pudding made of liver and lights or lungs. **1723** J. NOTT *Cook's & Confectioner's Dict.* sig. S2ᵛ To make Liver Puddings. Boil a Hog's Liver..; take an equal Quantity of grated Bread, two Pound of Beef-suet. **1937** A. FRASER *Sheep Farming* xvi. 144 Liver-rot has at one time or another caused tremendous losses among sheep. **1972** *Country Life* 2 Mar. 524/2 In the early 19th century men were still prepared to argue that liver-rot was due to poisonous dew. **1896** *Trade Marks Jrnl.* 10 June 517 Andrews Liver Salt.. purifies & strengthens the whole system... A medicinal preparation for human use. The firm trading as Andrews & Co.,..Newcastle-on-Tyne; manufacturers. **1938** L. MACNEICE *I crossed Minch* x. 140 De Valera's sham industries—putting liver salts into tins. **1951** J. B. PRIESTLEY *Festival at Farbridge* III. iii. 584 The High Street chemist who had sold him shaving soap and liver salts. **1969** M RUSSELL *Hunt to Kill* II. 116 'I'm fine. Bit of a gut-ache. Too much booze.' 'Get home, take liver-salts.' **1855** GEO. ELIOT in *Fraser's Mag.* June 706/1 He is enthusiastic about the delights of dining on *blaukraut* and *leberwurst* (blue cabbage and liver sausage). **1868** [see *blood-sausage* (*BLOOD *sb.* 19)]. **1965** *House & Garden* Jan. 60 Liver sausage ranges in seasoning from extremely bland to highly spiced and pungent. **1971** *Sunday Times* (Colour Suppl.) 27 June 50/3 Liver sausages are found in every European country. **1942** S. SPENDER *Ruins & Visions* III. 51 A tree..rotted By a liver-shaped fungus on the bank. **1954** M. RICKERT *Painting in Brit.: Middle Ages* viii. 197 The border..contains some motifs found earlier in East Anglian manuscripts, as the little round liver- and heart-shaped leaves. **1964** 'E. MCBAIN' *Axe* vi. 101 He wore a dark black suit and he kept his hands, brown with liver spots, tented in front of his face. **1971** *Physics Bull.* July 410/3 Seborrheic keratosis, commonly called liver spot—a blemish occurring frequently in the middle aged and aged. **1973** N. GRAHAM *Murder in Dark Room* iv. 24 He had a thin, yellow face dotted with liver spots. **1922** R. LEIGHTON *Compl. Bk. Dog* vi. 86 Prince IV..a liver-spotted specimen. **1971** V. CANNING *Firecrest* i. 7 Everything about him was contained, precise and impeccable..the fingernails of his liver-spotted hands immaculate. **1975** D. BAGLEY *Snow Tiger* xxiv. 205 Critchell placidly continued to fill his pipe with liver-spotted hands.

liverishness. [f. LIVERISH *a.*] Symptoms attributed to disordered condition of the liver.

1904 *Westm. Gaz.* 5 Oct. 10/1 Ordinary attacks of liverishness or biliousness are swiftly dispersed. **1928** *Daily Express* 14 July 15/7 Yellow, perhaps, suggests liverishness. **1930** R. LEHMANN *Note in Music* v. 199 Never, he thought, would he forget..his liverishness.

Liverpool (li·vəɹpūl). [The name of an English city on the River Mersey.] **1.** Applied *attrib.* to the delftware and porcelain manufactured in Liverpool in the eighteenth century. Also *ellipt.*

1863 W. CHAFFERS *Marks Pott. & Porc.* 130 *Liverpool*. A pottery, called Herculaneum, was established on the Mersey by Richard Abbey, in 1794. **1869** C. SCHREIBER *Jrnl.* 5 Nov. (1911) I. 60 A Liverpool printed mug of Gen. Wolfe. **1957** MANKOWITZ & HAGGAR *Conc. Encycl. Eng. Pott. & Porc.* 131/2 Liverpool is at times difficult to distinguish from Bristol. **1964** M. DRABBLE *Garrick Year* iv. 56 One of my Liverpool ware teapots was broken. **1972** *Country Life* 6 Jan. 21/3 Liverpool or Delft tiles decorate the fireplace surround. **1972** *Collector's Guide* Aug. 9/1 (Advt.), An extremely rare Liverpool Vase, c. 1760 (William Ball's factory).

2. Special combs.: **Liverpool button** (see quot. 1896); **Liverpool house** *Naut.*, a deck-house; **Liverpool pantile,** a hard ship's biscuit; **Liverpool pennant** (see quot. 1933); **Liverpool sound,** the music, popular in the early 1960s, played by pop singers and groups in Liverpool, chiefly the Beatles; **Liverpool weather** *Naut. colloq.*, windy and 'dirty' weather.

1896 FARMER & HENLEY *Slang* IV. 212/1 *Liverpool-button*, a kind of toggle used by sailors when they lose a button. **1908** E. NOBLE *Grain Carriers* III. i. 146 Shanghaied crews are usually persons dressed in a rag and a Liverpool button. **1869** in C. N. Longridge *Cutty Sark* (1933) II. 205 Liverpool house fitted on centre 30 feet long. **1948** R. DE KERCHOVE *Internat. Maritime Dict.* 422 *Liverpool house*, a superstructure extending from side to side and situated amidships in large (steel built) sailing vessels. **1902** in B. Lubbock *Round the Horn* viii. 311 He handed me a regular bad-looking Liverpool pantile from the bread-barge. **1925** B. HAYES *Hull Down* iii. 28 The biscuits, commonly called 'Liverpool pantiles', were so hard you could break them only with a hammer. **1933** J. MASEFIELD *Bird of Dawning* 287 *Liverpool pennants*, rope yarns used instead of buttons. **1963** *Daily Mail* 20 Sept. 10/4 It's been boys, boys, boys from Merseyside who have dominated pop music since the 'Liverpool sound' started to carry all before it towards the end of last year. **1963** *Daily Tel.* 10 Dec. 13 A show by the Beatles, the 'Liverpool sound' group, was not typical of 'pop' concerts. **1929** F. C. BOWEN *Sea Slang*, Liverpool weather. **1934** G. H. GRANT *Consigned to Davy Jones* (1935) xviii. 260 If we was on a windbag..it would be what we calls Liverpool weather.

liverwurst (li·vəɹvūᵊrst, -wɒ̄ɹst). [Partial tr. of G. *leberwurst*.] = **liver sausage*.

1869 *Atlantic Monthly* Oct. 483/1 Our Dutch neighbors make *liver-wurst* ('woorsht') or meat pudding, omitting the meal, and this compound stuffed into the large intestines, is very popular in Lancaster market. **1929** E. WILSON *I thought of Daisy* iii. 150 The boy-friend's passed out! Too many of those rich liverwurst sandwiches! **1934** H. MILLER *Tropic of Cancer* 41 Throw in some sweetbreads,..Throw in some fried liverwurst. **1945** S. LEWIS *Cass Timberlane* (1946) vi. 39 Coca-Cola, liverwurst, stuffed olives, and chocolate layer cake. **1954** P. HIGHSMITH *Blunderer* (1956) xxii. 139 Kimmel ordered a liverwurst sandwich. **1965** A. ROUDYBUSH *Season for Death* (1966) xix. 111 Spreading two slices of rye bread thickly with liverwurst.

livery, *sb.* Add: **2. c.** An emblem, device, or distinctive colour on a vehicle, product, etc., indicating its owner or manufacturer.

1938 H. A. VALLANCE *Highland Railway* xiv. 155 He introduced on the Highland Railway the style of painting which was afterwards so well-known on the south coast. Passenger engines were painted yellow... For goods engines a dark green livery was adopted. **1966** J. THOMAS *Callander & Oban Railway* x. 169 The Caledonian 2–4–2 tanks..had the plain conical chimney..and the Prussian-blue passenger livery then standard on the line. **1970** *Guardian* 27 July 16/2 The Antonovs [*sc.* planes] are painted battleship grey, with red hammer and sickle emblems, not the normal livery of Aeroflot passenger aircraft. **1972** *Times* 13 Oct. 17/7 London Transport's intention can be simply stated. It is that the livery of the bus fleet will remain red, with a very strictly limited number offered to advertisers for all-over painted designs. **1973** *Times* 1 Dec. 17/7 As the designers responsible for the BEA livery we were invited, along with two other design groups, to make proposals for 'British Airways'. **1974** P. LOVESEY *Invitation to Dynamite Party* ii. 22 An enormous express locomotive painted in the brilliant golden ochre and dark olive green livery of the London, Brighton and South Coast Railway Company.

9. (Examples.) Also *attrib.*

1845 F. DOUGLASS *Narr. Life F. Douglass* 16 His stable and carriage-house presented the appearance of some of our large city livery establishments. **1888** C. D. FERGUSON *Experiences Forty-Niner* i. 15 We placed our horses in a livery on Third street. **1902** W. N. HARBEN *Abner Daniel* 29, I could 'a' gone to a livery an' ordered out a team. **1903** A. ADAMS *Log of Cowboy* xiii. 81 Long before we reached the Mulberry, a livery rig came down the trail to meet us. **1936** E. G. BARNARD *Rider Cherokee Strip* 210 They met a traveling man who was driving a good livery team to a buckboard. **1940** W. FAULKNER *Hamlet* ii. 32 The village consisted of a livery barn and lot and a contiguous shady through grassless yard.

10. *livery horse* (earlier example).

1838 H. COLMAN *1st Rep. Agric. Mass.* (Mass. Agric. Survey) 17 The number of stage and livery horses kept in the county cannot fall short of one thousand,..who depend on the purchase of hay.

livery, *a.* **2.** (Examples.)

1937 in PARTRIDGE *Dict. Slang* 487/2. **1968** R. JEFFRIES *Traitor's Crime* ii. 34 You had too much port: port always makes you livery.

lives, *U.S.* var. of *lieve(s)*, LIEF *adv.*

1772 M. MASCARENE *Let.* 14 Sept. in *Mass. Hist. Soc. Coll.* (1914) LXXI. 189, I had full as lives have it [*sc.* the portrait] on a larger [plate]. **1856** A. CARY *Married* 22, I would just as lives stand here as not. **1858** J. R. LOWELL *Two Gunners* in *Poetical Wks.* II. 126 I'd jest ez lives eat tripe. **1891** *Harper's Mag.* Oct. 820/1, I will get Provided Usher to watch with me. He'd just as lives.

livett, var. LIBBET¹.

1908 G. SANGER *70 Yrs. a Showman* xiv. 48 We could see the big sticks—'livetts' they were termed—hurtling towards..the prizes.

liveyere (li·vyəɹ). *Canad.* Also **liveyer, livier, livyer(e.** [Prob. f. the phr. *live here* (see below).] (See quot. 1909.) Also a permanent resident (as opp. to visiting fishermen, etc.).

Dict. Canadianisms suggests that the term 'may be < *livier* < OF *livree* (cp. *livery*), formerly in English villages a manorial worker having certain hereditary rights to a cottage and a small piece of land, thus being regarded as a permanent resident'. But cf. LIVIER in Dict.

1863 J. MORETON *Life & Work in Newfoundland* iii. 35 It is said of any uninhabited place that there are no *liviers* in it. **1881** EARL OF DUNRAVEN in *19th Cent.* IX. 93 A 'livier' signifies a person who lives all the year around in a locality, in contradistinction to one who visits it during the fishing season. **1895** W. GRENFELL *Vikings of To-day* 57 The summer Labrador settlements are on islands or outside headlands, and here both Newfoundlanders and 'Livyeres' dwell, the latter retiring up the bays and inlets, to be nearer wood and game, when the former return to Newfoundland. **1901** *Chambers's Jrnl.* Jan. 68/2 The residents along this coast are termed 'livyres' (live heres), to distinguish them from the nomadic fisherfolk. **1905** N. DUNCAN *Dr. Grenfell's Parish* i. 12 The shore fishermen of the remoter Newfoundland coasts, the Labrador 'liveyeres', the Indians of the forbidding interior. **1907** D. WALLACE *Long Labrador Trail* xxiii. 273 Even tea and molasses, usually found amongst the 'livyeres' (liveheres) of the coast, were lacking. **1909** *Toilers of Deep* July 176/1 The permanent inhabitants of the Labrador coast, the 'liveyers' are about three thousand in number. **1925** *Dialect Notes* V. 335 *Livyere*, one who lives here (in Newfoundland), usually an outport man. **1955** *Arctic Terms* 50/1 *Liveyere*, a corruption of 'live here', used in south-eastern Labrador to designate a semisettled inhabitant who customarily has a summer dwelling near coastal fishing grounds and a winter dwelling in an inland valley or in a mission settlement. **1966** A. R. SCAMMELL *My Newfoundland* 47 The steamer had just turned the point, whistled hoarsely a couple of times to alert the livyers. **1969** H. HORWOOD *Newfoundland* xxv. 204 Most of the Livyers today are black-haired and a little darker than most Europeans... But many Livyers with blond hair, blue eyes, and fair skin keep cropping up too.

livid, *a.* Add: **c.** Furiously angry, as if pale with rage. *colloq.*

1912 *Collier's* 9 Mar. 21/1 He sprang to his feet, livid. 'That's a lie,' and he stopped suddenly, startled by his own violence. **1918** C. MACKENZIE *Early Life Sylvia Scarlett* II. ii. 292 He was livid with fury. He asked if I thought he was made of money. **1936** M. KENNEDY *Together & Apart* II. 151 Betsy is *livid*. She says now she will fight to the last ditch to get complete custody of the children. **1949** R. CHANDLER *Little Sister* ii. 10 Orrin would be absolutely livid. Mother would be furious too. **1959** J. VERNEY *Friday's Tunnel* xxiv. 214 Friday's livid because he thinks you've punctured his bike. **1973** 'D. SHANNON' *No Holiday for Crime* (1974) x. 162 Mr. MacFarlane would be livid to have it [*sc.* whisky] impounded as evidence.

living, *vbl. sb.* Add: **1. d.** *living-in, -out* (further examples).

1942 *R.A.F. Jrnl.* 13 June 14 The misunderstanding has arisen..over the living-out system on which the Commandos work. The men are neither billeted nor fed by the Army. **1955** M. LASKI *Apologies* 59 I'd never have living-in servants again. **1962** L. DEIGHTON *Ipcress File* xi. 71 Murray decided that this was a good time to ask about his living out allowance. **1970** 'J. BELL' *Hydra with Six Heads* vii. 76 There was a living-in cook. **1974** 'P. B. YUILL' *Bornless Keeper* viii. 71 Check with Exeter [Gaol] he isn't on their wonderful living-out rehabilitation scheme.

7. a. *living-dining room*; **b.** *living price* (earlier example); **living area** = **living space* (*c*); **living floor** *Archæol.*, the site of a prehistoric camp indicated by bones, tools, etc., found there; **living space,** (*a*) tr. *LEBENSRAUM; (*b*) space for accommodation; (*c*) a habitable area in a room or house; **living standard** [cf. STANDARD *sb.* 12 a], the level of consumption in terms of food, accommodation, clothing, services, etc., estimated for a person, group, or nation; **living wage** (earlier and later examples).

1962 *Listener* 18 Jan. 135/1 A new house..which I recently visited is centred on a large living area. **1965** in P. Jennings *Living Village* (1968) 103 The garages are built at road level, and the living areas of the houses are built over the garages. **1969** K. GILES *Death cracks Bottle* vii. 74 The inglenook which the architect had fashioned in the living area. **1933** *Archit. Rev.* LXXIV. 20 The exhibit is part of a projected structural unit which includes

an entrance hall and kitchen in addition to the living-dining room. **1945** Nelson & Wright *Tomorrow's House* iv. 41/1 The living-dining-room was a makeshift..but nevertheless an expedient to save space and money. **1968** *Globe & Mail* (Toronto) 17 Feb. 45 (Advt.), Living-dining room with open fireplace. **1946** *Nature* 2 Nov. 637/2 In 1943, further evidence was obtained pointing to the conclusion that on the site, now known as Glorgesailie site 10, there was a series of actual living floors or camp sites of Acheulean men. **1947** L. S. B. Leakey in *E. Afr. Ann. 1946–7* 69/1 On the ancient land surfaces were uncovered the actual 'living floors' or camp sites of ancient Acheulean hunters. **1965** Hole & Heizer *Introd. Prehist. Archeol.* iii. 35 The amount of bone and stone tools suggests seasonal, or perhaps permanent year-round camps. In Africa these are called 'living floors'. **1834** *Congress. Globe* 3 May 362/2 Mr. Forsyth said that..70 to 76 cents was a very living price for fish oil. **1939** W. S. Churchill *Into Battle* (1941) 127 The Swiss..may rob them of their living-space. **1944** F. Clune *Red Heart* 20 The Australian native..can make a 'living-space' in a country where white people can't. **1959** *Listener* 10 Dec. 1032/1 The 5,000 or so species of pest insects are man's most dangerous competitors for food and living space on this planet. *Ibid.* 17 Dec. 1071/1 The bed-sitting-room was divided by curtains into three living-spaces. **1959** *Chambers's Encycl.* IV. 338/2 Hitler's next objective was to sweep Czechoslovakia out of the road to 'living space' in the east. **1961** L. D. Stamp *Gloss. Geogr. Terms* 296/2 *Living space*, an English translation of the German *Lebensraum* but most authors prefer to use the German word when discussing its geopolitical implications. **1961** *Listener* 28 Dec. 1110/1 Architects will be able to plan, on the ground floor, one, two, or three living spaces—for example, a kitchen partially opening into a dining-room, with a separate living-room. **1966** *Ibid.* 19 May 729/3 The average living space per person in Moscow is officially admitted to be eight square metres. **1972** M. Jones *Life on Dole* i. 15 There might have been a couple of lodgers, unmarried men..whose living space was a cot in the corner. **1957** P. Worsley *Trumpet shall Sound* vi. 121 The aim of the Government was to raise living-standards to those of the Europeans. **1964** Gould & Kolb *Dict. Social Sci.* 690/1 The concept of *living* standards, or levels, would include and perhaps emphasize, 'material' quantitative elements such as the consumption of goods and services. **1968** *Listener* 10 Oct. 469/3 This was the chief reason..why..Western achievements and Western living standards were so consistently lied about. **1974** *Times* 16 Jan. 13/2 Improving personal living standards. **1888** E. Bellamy *Looking Backward* xxviii. 450 The wonder to me is, not that industries conducted as these are do not pay you living wages, but that they are able to pay you any wages at all. **1967** *Listener* 23 Feb. 248/1 Some of them already have to work up to fifty-six hours a week to make up their weekly pay to a living wage of £20. **1974** *Guardian* 31 Jan. 13/8 Another miner..sounds bitter... 'We are broken down old men; we're limping and we are injured. And all we want is a living wage.'

living, *ppl. a.* Add: **2. b.** *living fossil*: a plant or animal that has survived the extinction of others of its group.

1935 C. J. Chamberlain *Gymnosperms* iv. 61 The cycads of today may well be called 'living fossils'. **1953** J. S. Huxley *Evolution in Action* v. 127 There is the persistence of a few survivors from a once-abundant group—so-called 'living fossils', like the duckbill platypus; and that of a whole successful group. **1955** *Sci. Amer.* Apr. 108/2 A living fossil is defined as an organism that has survived beyond its era. A standard example is the tuatara of New Zealand, which looks like a lizard but is in fact the 'sole survivor of an order of reptiles which flourished in the great Age of Reptiles and is now extinct except for this one species'. **1966** C. A. W. Guggisberg *S.O.S. Rhino* ii. 31 The two-horned Sumatran rhinoceros..has come to us practically unchanged from the Tertiary Age, another 'living fossil'. **1974** *Encycl. Brit. Micropædia* VI. 276/3 Living fossil, an organism long believed extinct that is discovered to be still in existence.

c. *the land of the living* (further examples). See also Land *sb.* 3 c.

1708 Lady Cave *Let.* in M. M. Verney *Verney Lett.* (1930) I. xiv. 266 Sir Thomas is glad to hear Col. Oughton is in the land of the living..having not heard a word from him. **1925** E. Phillpotts *Voice from Dark* ii. 22 And is Mr. Bitton still in the land of the living? **1964** *Roman Breviary* 346 P, You are my refuge, my portion in the land of the living.

f. *living corpse*; *living dead*: as *adj. phr.*, having lost hold of life, not using one's life abundantly; as *sb. phr.*, such people.

1860 J. W. Palmer tr. *Michelet's Love* iv. viii. 243 It may be said that she came out of the asylum a living corpse, and it was not long before she died in reality. **1917** R. Graves *Fairies & Fusiliers* 28 You'll find me buried, living-dead In these verses that you've read. *a* **1930** D. H. Lawrence *Last Poems* (1932) 168, I know the unliving factory-hand, living-dead millions Is unliving me, living-dead me, I, with them, am living dead. **1958** *Listener* 14 Aug. 225/2 What they thought of 'squares', and the living dead in general.

3. *living chess*: a game of chess in which living persons act as the chessmen; *living newspaper* (see quot. 1966); *living theatre*: the theatre, as opposed to the cinema.

1905 *Lasker's Chess Mag.* II. iii. 131 So that the reader may visualize the phases through which the game has passed we will show two historical cameos of living chess. **1929** *Brit. Chess Mag.* LXIX. 126 A picturesque display of living chess was given by the schoolboys. **1935** *N.Y. Times* 31 Dec. 10/1 Elmer Rice, regional director, announced that..the Biltmore will open before the end of January with the first topical production of the unit known as the 'Living Newspaper'. The initial show..will offer in graphic terms the background of the Italo-Ethiopian war. **1938** *Times* 28 Dec. 11/3 The 'living' theatre, as it has come to be called in distinction from the cinema, must be in a very healthy condition. **1940** *Ann. Reg. 1939* 40 The Chancellor made the entertainment tax lighter for the 'living theatre'. **1941** J. S. Huxley in *Fortnightly* July 11 The theatre project indeed began to create new types of popular drama like the Living Newspaper, which undoubtedly stimulated social self-consciousness. **1963** *Guardian* 12 Mar. 2/6 It was deplorable that Plymouth had no living theatre. **1966** J. R. Taylor *Penguin Dict. Theatre* 159 *Living newspaper*, a sort of topical documentary revue in a series of short scenes based on current social and political problems, devised in the 1930s in the U.S.A. by the Federal Theatre, and used elsewhere for propaganda during the war. **1970** A. Sunnucks *Encycl. Chess* 291 *Living chess.* During the past 600 years the game played with living pieces has from time to time been presented in different countries. **1971** J. Willett in A. Bullock *20th Cent.* 243/1 The Theater Project..evolved a new form of lecture-cum-sketch in the Living Newspaper.

6. *living picture*, (*a*) = *tableau vivant* (Tableau *sb.* 4); (*b*) a motion-picture.

1875 *N.Y. Herald* 24 Nov. 2/4 Mr. Matt Morgan's Classical Tableaux of Living Pictures, illustrated by a Corps of Beautiful Ladies. **1895** G. B. Shaw in *Sat. Rev.* 6 Apr. 443/2, I sat out the entire list of sixteen 'Living Pictures'. Half a dozen represented naiads, mountain sprites, peris, and Lady Godiva, all practically undraped. **1897** *Knowledge* 1 Sept. 216/2 Last winter saw the 'living pictures' adopted as the craze of the season for music-halls, bazaars, and variety entertainments generally. **1897** *Sears, Roebuck Catal.* 342/2 [The book] includes also elaborate directions for exhibiting Living Pictures and Tableaux. **1899** H. V. Hopwood *Living Pictures* vi. 207 The first requirement in the projection, as in the taking, of Living Pictures is absolute rigidity of the apparatus. **1906** J. A. Manson *Indoor Games* 30 Living Pictures, or Tableaux Vivants, if considered as an indoor game, must be placed on the highest level... It need hardly be said that neither acting nor speech is required in a living picture. **1962** E. Larsen *Film Making* i. 18 Soon nearly every variety show contained 'living pictures' as a programme item.

living-room. Also living room. [Living *vbl. sb.* 7.] **1.** A room that is set aside for ordinary social use (as opp. to a bedroom, etc.).

1825 [in Dict. s.v. Living *vbl. sb.* 7]. **1857** C. Vaux *Villas & Cottages* 119 Under the..living-room is a basement-kitchen. **1867** 'T. Lackland' *Homespun* i. 139 The joy with which grand parents welcome us in the great living-room. **1879** F. R. Stockton *Rudder Grange* i. 7 There was a kitchen, a living room, a parlor and bedrooms. **1911** C. Harris *Eve's Second Husband* 310 She occupied one chair in the living room all day. **1911** H. S. Harrison *Queed* xix. 239 Queed..went upstairs to the comfortable living-room. **1917–18** *T. Eaton & Co. Catal.* Fall & Winter 416/4 Massive living-room arm chair. **1931** A. J. Cronin *Hatter's Castle* i. i. 12 The common room, the living room of the house where its inhabitants partook of meals, spent their leisure and congregated in their family life. **1933** *Discovery* July 218/2 The growing popularity of the living-room as the central dominant feature of the modern dwelling..has completely altered the design of the house. **1933** H. Walpole *Vanessa* ii. 287 The room at the top of the first stairflight that had once been the drawing-room with the fine gilt chairs,..the rosy cupids on the ceiling, was now the general living-room. **1953** G. Greene (*title*) The living room. **1967** E. Short *Embroidery & Fabric Collage* iii. 78 [The cushion] can transform a divan from a bed into an acceptable piece of living-room furniture. **1971** *Daily Tel.* (Colour Suppl.) 12 Nov. 30/1 In the living-room is the Steinway upright.

2. tr. *Lebensraum.

1938 *Times* 18 Nov. 17/6 The Danube valley and the Balkans are..the natural 'living-room' of industrial Germany. **1940** 'G. Orwell' in *New English Weekly* 21 Mar. 321/1 Hitler envisages, a hundred years hence,..a continuous state of 250 million Germans with plenty of 'living room'. **1942** E. Paul *Narrow St.* xxxiv. 305 The leaders had told them Hitler would behave, if appeased, that he did not want their lands and goods but only 'living room'.

Livingstone (li·viŋstǒn). [Origin unknown.] A name used *attrib.* to designate the **Livingstone daisy**, a small, annual, succulent plant, *Dorotheanthus bellidiformis* (*Mesembryanthemum criniflorum*), native to the Cape Province of South Africa, and bearing daisy-like flowers.

1934 B. P. Mansfield in *Gardeners' Chronicle* 19 May 330/1 The Livingstone Daisy. From..seed catalogues.., I gather that *Mesembryanthemum criniflorum* is introduced as a 1934 novelty. **1950** W. E. Shewell-Cooper *Compl. Gardener* iii. 243 The 'Livingstone Daisy' is a delightful annual with fairy-tale flowers in many lovely shades of pink, crimson, pale or golden-yellow or apricot. **1960** *House & Garden* Aug. 53/2 South Africans like..the Livingstone Daisy. **1971** *Daily Colonist* (Victoria, B.C.) 16 May 36/5 There is another Mesembryanthemum, *M. criniflorum*, known as the Livingstone Daisy, which is a delightful little spreading carpeter.

Livonian (livōu·niăn), *sb.* and *a.* [f. med.L. *Livonia*, Livland, a former Baltic province of Russia.] **A.** *sb.* **a.** A native or inhabitant of Livonia. **b.** The language of the Livonian people. **B.** *adj.* Of or pertaining to Livonia, or to the Livonian people or their language.

1652 Heylyn *Cosmographie* ii. 167 Derpt or Derbren..situate on the Beck..in the midst of the Province; and taken at the same time by the Moscovite; who transporting the Livonians into other places, planted these parts with Colonies of his own people. **1677** [see Prussian *sb.*]. **1757** J. Dyer *Fleece* iv. 139 The Livonian gulph Receives her sails. **1824** J. D. Cochrane *Narr. Journey Russia & Siberian Tartary* I. 23 A young Livonian Baron..gave me letters of recommendation to the frontiers of Siberia. **1841** [see Lettish *a.* (*sb.*)]. **1872** [see Lettic *a.* (*sb.*)]. **1882** *Encycl. Brit.* XIV. 723/2 [The] plateaus..of Haanhoff and of the Livonian Aa. *Ibid.* 724/1 The Livonians..have nearly all passed away. **1926** *Spectator* 31 July 176/1 If one of their German servants or retainers wanted to marry a Livonian girl the Lutheran priest would seek to stop him. **1933** L. Bloomfield *Lang.* 68 The other languages of the Baltic branch, Carelian,..Ludian, Vepsian, Livonian, [etc.]. **1936** *Times Lit. Suppl.* 27 June 532/2 Descended, to quote his own words, from 'a middle-class East Prussian, a Westphalian peasant's son, a Livonian *bourgeoise* and a Livonian noblewoman'. **1954** *Trans. Philol. Soc.* 86 In the Livonian dialect of Lettish all gender has vanished, a state of affairs clearly due to the influence of Livonian, a Finno-Ugrian, genderless language. **1972** W. B. Lockwood *Panorama Indo-European Lang.* 140 Languages belonging to the Baltic division of Finnic... The best known of the languages concerned is Livonian which in the thirteenth century still predominated in the area of the Gulf of Riga, i.e., in the historic province of Livonia. It is not yet entirely extinct.

Livornese (livoɹnī·z), *sb.* and *a.* [f. name of the Italian city of *Livorno* (Leghorn) + -ese.] **A.** *sb.* The people of Leghorn. **B.** *adj.* Of or pertaining to Leghorn.

1819 Shelley *Let.* 17 Nov. (1964) II. 157 The astonishment of the Livornese when she returns from her cruise. **1821** *Ibid.* 8 June 296 The Livornese merchants, who sell board & lodging. **1912** N. Douglas *Fountains in Sand* vii. 78 The old distinction between Livornese and Tunisian Jews is slowly becoming effaced.

‖ **livre de chevet** (livr də ʃəvɛ). [Fr., lit. pillow-book.] A bedside book; a favourite book.

1923 A. Huxley *On Margin* 122 For some days I made Dr. Legat's book my *livre de chevet*. **1939** *Times Lit. Suppl.* 13 May 284/1 It may also be recommended as a *livre de chevet*. **1958** L. Durrell *Mountolive* v. 111 It was Darley..who introduced me to the current Alexandrian *livre de chevet* which is a French novel called *Moeurs*. **1972** *Times Lit. Suppl.* 5 May 529/2 To restore the *Heroides* to its rightful place as a *livre de chevet* for the literary connoisseur.

‖ **livre de circonstance** (livr də sirkoństańs). [Fr.] A book composed or adapted for the occasion.

1945 *Yale Rev.* Winter 356 It is one of those rare *livres de circonstance* with a relevance that may extend far beyond the moment to an entire generation. **1957** C. Vereker *Devel. Political Theory* iii. 93 Begun as a *livre de circonstance*, Hooker's great work raised most of the abiding problems of political authority. **1973** *Times Lit. Suppl.* 1 June 606/5 Mr Neelkant's *livre de circonstance* provides a good deal of ammunition for defenders of the Indo-Soviet Treaty by setting out in detail the many ways in which Russian aid has contributed to India's industrial development.

livyer(e, varr. *Liveyere.

‖ **liwa** (lī·wa). [Arab. *liwā'*.] A province or large administrative district in any of several Arabic-speaking countries.

1925 S. H. Longrigg *Four Centuries Mod. Iraq* 308 In 1872 he was Mutasarrif of his own Liwa. **1931** *Special Rep. Progress of 'Iraq, 1920–1931* (Colonial Office) vi. 49 It has been pointed out above that in 1921 the country was divided into 10 liwas. **1957** *Encycl. Brit.* XII. 590C/2 Tobacco is grown in the Sulaimaniya and Ariba *liwas* [of Iraq]. **1959** *Chambers's Encycl.* VII. 705/2 The administration [of Iraq] is centralized, the *mutasarrifs* of the *liwas*..being all appointed from Baghdad. **1962** *Times* 14 Aug. 9/7 The main centre of activity has now shifted northwards to the *liwa* of Mosul. **1974** *Internat. Jrnl. Middle East Stud.* V. 165 Stafford at the time was the Administrative Inspector of the *liwas* of Mosul and Arbil.

lizard. Add: **1. d.** Lizard skin. Also *attrib.*

1895 *Montgomery Ward Catal.* 100/1 Ladies' pocket books... Light American lizard grained leather. **1926–7** *Army & Navy Stores Catal.* 495/3 Manicure cases... Polished lizard with silver gilt fittings. **1957** M. B. Picken *Fashion Dict.* 215/1 *Lizard*, leather made from lizard skins. **1968** J. Ironside *Fashion Alphabet* 238 *Lizard*, scaly skin of the lizard from Java and India. Used mainly for shoes and handbags, it is harsh and not pliable. **1974** A. Laski *Night Music* 134 Her good navy lizard shoes and bag.

2. b. *Austral.* and *N.Z. slang.* A musterer of sheep; a man employed to maintain boundary fences.

1931 'W. Hatfield' *Sheepmates* xv. 121 You'd be better out in the camp with me than crawlin' around a fence like a fly-catcher lizard. **1933** L. G. D. Acland in *Press* (Christchurch, N.Z.) 4 Nov. 15/7 *Lizard*, slang for musterer, I suppose, because they both crawl over the hills. **1937** A. W. Upfield *Winds of Evil* xviii. 175 What bloke wouldn't be depressed at coming down to a fence lizard?.. Come down to fencin' and you want to know why a bloke's depressed. **1945** Baker *Austral. Lang.* ii. iii. 63 Shepherds have been known variously as *lizards*, *crawlers*.

c. = **lounge lizard*.

1935 E. Pound *Let.* Feb. (1971) 269 Alas, as you are writing English, you can't call *them there bloody* gallants, 'cake-eaters' or 'lizards', 'dudes', 'gigolos', 'young scum' [etc.].

8. lizard-bird (later example).

1911 Kipling in Fletcher & Kipling *School Hist. Eng.* i. 9, I remember the bat-winged lizard-birds.

lizardite (li·zăɹdəit). *Min.* [f. *Lizard*, the name of a peninsula in Cornwall + -ITE[1].] A basic silicate of magnesium, $Mg_3Si_2O_5(OH)_4$, which is a variety of serpentine.

1956 WHITTAKER & ZUSSMAN in *Mineral. Mag.* XXXI. 122 A new name is desirable by means of which specimens [of serpentine] possessing the single-layer ortho-cell can be distinguished from chrysotile and from antigorite. Since a well-known locality for serpentine minerals is the Lizard area of Cornwall, England, and since specimens of the subgroup in question are known to occur there.., the name lizardite would seem appropriate. **1967** *Prof. Papers U.S. Geol. Survey* No. 384B. 101/1 We have further investigated this stability using lizardite from the type locality at The Lizard, Cornwall, England..and natural admixtures of lizardite and clinochrysotile from Snarum, Parish of Buskerud, Norway, from New Almaden mine, Santa Clara County, Calif., and from Forest Hills, Hartford County, Md. **1968** *Zeitschr. für Kristallogr.* CXXVI. 163 The measured *x* and *z* parameters of single-layer lizardite from Raduša chromite Mine, Yugoslavia, indicate a distortion of the basic serpentine layer similar to that found in chrysotiles.

Lizzie (li·zi). *slang.* Also **lizzie.** [Abbrev. of the female Christian name *Elizabeth.*] **1.** A lesbian. Also, an effeminate young man; also *lizzie boy.*

1905 *Dialect Notes* III. 87 *Lizzie* (*boy*), an effeminate young man. **1912** N. L. MCCLUNG *Black Creek Stopping-House* xi. 98 She's married to a no-good Englishman, a real lizzie-boy. **1949** A. WILSON *Wrong Set* 98, I wish you wouldn't talk to those Lizzies. **1966** J. B. PRIESTLEY *Salt is Leaving* vi. 75 She has a Lizzie crush on me. **1970** J. SYMONS *Man who lost his Wife* I. x. 70 You'd never have thought I was a lizzie, would you? And butch at that.

2. A motor car, esp. an early model of a 'Ford'. Also *Tin Lizzie.*

1913 'B. L. STANDISH' *The Desert* (Advt. on rear cover), So, when you get tired of rolling around in your Lady Lizzie..hie yourself to the nearest news dealer. **1915** *Chicago Herald* 2 Nov. 4/2 You're right about the guy who is able to make a tin lizzie out of the cans they tie to him. **1922** *Blackw. Mag.* Jan. 37/2 We then prepared to start for home; but 'Lizzie'..refused..to think of starting. *Ibid.* Feb. 253/1 An extra bad pothole put Lizzie's back axle out of action. **1949** D. M. DAVIN *Roads from Home* 233 The pace they drove their old tin lizzies. **1956** J. TICKELL *Moon Squadron* 39 These special duty 'Lizzies' had to be stripped of all guns, armour and wireless equipment—except radio telephones—in order to allow room for the passengers.

3. (See quot.)

1925 FRASER & GIBBONS *Soldier & Sailor Words* 145 *Lizzie*, a big gun: also its shell. A term originating at the Dardanelles and suggested by the firing of the big fifteen-inch guns of H.M.S. *Queen Elizabeth.*

4. Lisbon wine.

1934 M. ELLISON *Sparks beneath Ashes* 182 She drinks 'Lizzie' and methylated spirit. **1936** J. CURTIS *Gilt Kid* v. 48 A glass of cheap Lisbon red wine, lizzie they called it.

llama. b. (Earlier example.)

1864 'P. PATERSON' *Glimpses Real Life* xxv. 244 The hosier's bill is £70—all kinds of stockings, silk,..embroidered, striped, llama,..and otherwise.

llano. Add: Hence **Llane·ro, llane·ro**, an inhabitant of a *llano* (see also quot. 1878).

1878 A. H. KEANE in H. W. Bates *Cent. Amer.* 519 (*heading*) American tribes and languages... Llaneros... An Apache tribe. **1908** *Daily Chron.* 27 Oct. 4/6 The llanos,.. on which the llaneros live a precarious life. **1910** *Encycl. Brit.* II. 158/2 The chief divisions of the Apaches were the Arivaipa,..Llanero, [etc.]. **1960** H. S. FERNS *Brit. & Argentine* iii. 96 Now José Paez, the *llanero*, began to rally the cowboys to the side of the revolution. **1973** *Country Life* 20 Dec. 2114 Simon Bolivar..was..one of the greatest horsemen who ever lived... His outstanding skill..enabled him to control the wild Llaneros of the coastal plains who..were the backbone of his army.

Lloyd-Georgian (loid,dʒǭ·ɹdʒiăn), *a.* and *sb.* [f. the name of David *Lloyd George* (1863–1945), British politician.] **A.** *adj.* Of, pertaining to, or associated with Lloyd George. **B.** *sb.* A follower or supporter of Lloyd George or his policy.

1909 *Daily Graphic* 12 Oct. 6/2 The self-sacrificing Ministerial millionaires..with the Lloyd-Georgian iron entering into their souls. **1928** [see *ASQUITHIAN *a.* and *sb.*]. **1928** *Daily Tel.* 25 Sept. 12/2 The kaleidoscopic contortions of Lloyd-Georgian politics. **1963** [see *DRESSAGE].

So **Lloyd-Georgeite** = **Lloyd-Georgian* sb.; **Lloyd-Georgery** [-ERY 2], **Lloyd-Georgism**, the political policy of Lloyd George.

1910 *Blackw. Mag.* Dec. 772/2 Lloyd Georgism (not Liberalism) was defeated in the Division last January. **1921** *Spectator* 19 Mar. 352/1 They must now be counted as Lloyd Georgeites rather than as Unionists. **1958** *Ibid.* 11 July 48/1 Most of his time was spent talking..second-rate Lloyd-georgeries about the opinions of posterity.

lloydia (loi·diă). [mod.L. (R. A. Salisbury 1812, in *Trans. Hort. Soc. Lond.* I. 328), f. the name of Edward Lhwyd or *Lloyd* (1660–1709), Welsh antiquary and Keeper of the Ashmolean Museum, who discovered the British species on Snowdon.] A small alpine bulbous plant of the genus so called, belonging to the family Liliaceæ, native to the northern hemisphere, and bearing white or yellow flowers; also called the Snowdon lily or mountain spiderwort.

1850 HOOKER & ARNOTT *Brit. Flora* (ed. 6) 442 Lloydia... *L. serotina* Reich. (Mountain L[loydia])... On the Welsh mountains, rare. **1866** LINDLEY & MOORE *Treas. Bot.* II. 690/2 Lloydia. A liliaceous plant, from five to six inches high. **1956** WALTERS & RAVEN *Mountain Flowers* v. 104 The Devil's Kitchen is well named, and I wish anybody luck who tries to find *Lloydia* in flower there. **1966** W. CONDRY *Snowdonia National Park* vi. 112 Lhuyd found quantities of the tiny lily later called Lloydia in his honour.

Lloyd Morgan's canon (loid mǭ·ɹgănz kæ·nən). *Psychol.* [f. the name of Conwy *Lloyd Morgan* (1852–1936), British psychologist.] (See quot. 1937.)

[**1894** C. LLOYD MORGAN *Introd. Compar. Psychol.* iii. 53 In no case may we interpret an action as the outcome of the exercise of a higher psychical faculty, if it can be interpreted as the outcome of the exercise of one which stands lower in the psychological scale.] **1937** *Discovery* May 162/1 No action must be interpreted as a higher psychological process if it can be interpreted as one lower in the scale. This is known as 'the Lloyd Morgan canon'. **1964** A. KOESTLER in *Listener* 14 May 786/2 A principle which became a kind of eleventh commandment for psychologists, known as 'Lloyd Morgan's canon'. **1968** E. BORING in *Internat. Encycl. Social Sciences* X. 495/2 He [*sc.* Lloyd Morgan] is best known for what has come to be called Lloyd Morgan's canon, which demands parsimony in the inference of an animal's place on the scale of mind from its behavior.

Lloyd's (loidz). [f. the name of Edward *Lloyd* who opened a coffee-house in London in 1688, and supplied shipping information to his clients.] Name of a London association of underwriters and agency for arranging insurance (formerly marine insurance only, but now nearly all kinds); it also issues daily shipping intelligence, as *Lloyd's List* (of which the occasional newspaper *Lloyd's News* was a precursor). *Lloyd's Register* (*of Shipping*), an independent society which surveys ships to ensure compliance with standards of strength and maintenance; its annual classified list of such ships. Also *Lloyd's policy*, an insurance policy underwritten by Lloyd's; so *Lloyd's underwriter.*

1819 M. EDGEWORTH *Let.* 4 Mar. (1971) 174 He won £30,000 by a bit of gambling insurance on 2 missing.. ships. The ships re-appeared... He never could shew his face at Lloyds afterwards. **1829** G. GRIFFIN *Collegians* (ed. 2) II. xxvi. 248 A more crazy and precarious mode of conveyance could not be found, even among the ships marked with the very last letter in Lloyd's list. **1833** [see UNDERWRITER 2]. **1846** [see REGISTER *sb.*[1] 4 c]. **1876** F. MARTIN (*title*) History of Lloyd's and of marine insurance in Great Britain. **1882** J. ASHTON *Social Life in Reign of Anne* I. xviii. 224 Lloyd's was then in Lombard Street, and indeed to this day, on Lloyd's policies, is stated that this policy should have the same effect as if issued in Lombard Street. **1911** *Encycl. Brit.* XV. 833/2 Lloyd's... Originally a mere gathering of merchants..in a coffee-house kept by..Edward Lloyd in Tower Street, London, the earliest notice of which occurs in the *London Gazette* of the 18th of February 1688. *Ibid.* XIX. 554/2 In 1696 Edward Lloyd..started a thrice-a-week paper, *Lloyd's News*, which..was the precursor of the *Lloyd's List* of the present day. *Ibid.* XXIV. 957/2 *Lloyd's Register*, as at present constituted, has existed since 1834. **1922** *Ibid.* XXXI. 492/1 Lloyd's underwriters have shown a great deal of enterprise in accepting risks of a novel kind. **1959** *Chambers's Encycl.* VIII. 623/2 The incorporation of Lloyd's as a chartered body on 25 May 1871.

Lo, *sb. U.S.* [Humorously from Pope's line '*Lo*, the poor Indian', etc., *Essay on Man* I. 99.] An American Indian. Also *Mr.* (or *Mrs.*) *Lo.*

1871 *Republican Rev.* (Albuquerque, New Mexico) 2 Sept. 1/4 Cowardly Lo prefers to attack none but very small parties of teamsters, farmers, or lone mail riders. **1873** G. W. PERRIE *Buckskin Mose* vi. 88 This document set forth that the bearer was a good Lo. *Ibid.*, He appeared again at the head of our train, in the company of thirty or forty other Los. **1874** J. G. MCCOY *Hist. Sk. Cattle Trade* 260 Crossing the plains was an undertaking fraught with great danger; especially as Mr. Lo was decidedly fond of horses. **1880** A. A. HAYES *New Colorado* (1881) iii. 40 Colonel Craig..and his men began, not unsuccessfully, the repression and suppression of Mr. Lo. **1885** [see *EVOLUTE *v.* 2]. **1904** *Minneapolis Daily Times* 12 June 6 The march of civilization has convinced Lo that fighting is not as profitable as it used to be. **1904** *N.Y. Even. Post* 6 Aug., On Florida's shield stands a placid and buxom Mrs. Lo, with fringed skirt falling to the knee. **1947** R. P. T. COFFIN *Yankee Coast* 220 He..went to join Lo, the Poor Indian on the Happy Hunting Grounds.

lo, *int.*[1] Add: **b.** Freq. in phr. *lo and behold* (usu. jocular).

1808 LADY LYTTELTON *Let.* June in *Corr.* (1912) i. 20 Hartington..had just told us how hard he had worked all the morning..when, lo and behold! M. Deshayes himself appeared. **1841** LYTTON *Night & Morning* II. iii. v. 144 The fair bride was skipping down the middle..when, lo and behold! the whiskered gentleman..advanced..and cried—'*La voilà!*' **1849** DICKENS *Dav. Copp.* (1850) xxii. 234 What does he do, but, lo, and behold you, he goes into a perfumer's shop. **1930** J. B. PRIESTLEY *Angel Pavement* ii. 60 And then—lo and behold—it was there all the time. **1947** T. WILLIAMS *Streetcar Named Desire* x. 151 You come in here and sprinkle the place with powder and spray perfume and cover the light-bulb with a paper lantern, and lo and behold the place has turned into Egypt and you are the Queen of the Nile!

lo, 'lo, *int.*[2] Colloq. abbrev. of HALLO, HALLOA, HELLO, HULLO, HULLOA *ints.*

1921 J. DOS PASSOS *Three Soldiers* I. i. 13 ''Lo, buddy,' came a voice beside him... 'Goin' to the movies?' **1922** JOYCE *Ulysses* 287 Lo, Joe, says I. How are you blowing? **1938** F. D. SHARPE *Sharpe of Flying Squad* ii. 16 ''Lo,' said Moisher. ''Lo,' said Harry. **1968** R. CLAPPERTON *No News on Monday* viii. 99 ''Lo, son. You the detective?' he murmured.

loa[1]. Substitute for etym. and def.: [Native name in Angola, used as a specific name in *Filaria loa* (T. S. Cobbold *Entozoa* (1864) xiv. 389) and as a generic name in *Loa loa* (C. W. Stiles 1905, in *Bull. U.S. Dept. Agric. Bur. Anim. Ind.* no. 79. 50).] A filarial worm of the monotypic genus so called, found in tropical Africa and infecting the eyes and subcutaneous tissues in man. Also *attrib.* (Add earlier and later examples.)

1864 T. S. COBBOLD *Entozoa* xiv. 389, I had independently arrived at the conviction that the *Loa* was a totally distinct worm from the *Filaria oculi*. *Ibid.*, The parasite in question is rather more than an inch in length, it is.. termed *Loa.* **1958** *Ann. Trop. Med. & Parasitol.* LII. 158 (*title*) The relationship between human and simian Loa in the rain-forest zone of the British Cameroons. **1971** PRICE & HOPPS in R. A. Marcial-Rojas *Path. Protozoal & Helminthic Dis.* lii. 917/1 (*heading*) The eye worm, loa worm. *Ibid.*, He [*sc.* Guyot] described the worm under the native name 'loa'.

loa[2] (lōᵘ·ă). Pl. **loa** or **loas.** [ad. Haitian Creole *lwa.*] A deity in the voodoo cult of Haiti.

1933 J. H. CRAIGE *Black Bagdad* xv. 267 Thanks to the spells I have made in your behalf, the *loas* have held their hands over you, and you are free. **1937** M. J. HERSKOVITS *Life in Haitian Valley* II. iv. 81 The ordinary plates or calabashes on which food is offered the *loa*, or African deities. **1959** H. CHARTERIS tr. *Métraux's Voodoo in Haiti* iii. 120 A *loa* moves into the head of an individual having first driven out..one of the two souls that everyone carries in himself. **1960** *Spectator* 5 Aug. 218/3 The peculiar congregation, led by the Voodoo Priestess, start summoning up their favourite spirits or 'loas', who—dead on cue—take possession of the celebrants one after another. **1966** *Punch* 10 Aug. 235/3 The 'loa', the demon-gods who take possession of the initiates at Voodoo ceremonies and impose on them their own voice, features, and character.

load, *sb.* Add: **2. c.** The material carried along by a stream in suspension, by saltation, or by traction (by some writers material carried in solution is included); the amount of material so carried; hence, by extension, the material carried by various other natural agents of transportation, as glaciers, winds, and ocean currents.

1888 J. W. POWELL in *Science* 16 Nov. 229/2 In erosion and corrasion the material which is transported may be called the 'load'. The load is transported by two methods, a portion floats with the water, and another portion is driven along the bottom. **1907** R. D. SALISBURY *Physiogr.* iv. 122 The sediment moved by a stream, whether in suspension or at the bottom, is its load. **1950** W. H. TWENHOFEL *Princ. Sedimentation* (ed. 2) vi. 226 These figures show that the suspended loads of rivers draining dry areas are larger than the dissolved loads. *Ibid.* 227 The loads of standing bodies of water are small in terms of any unit of volume... There is not a great deal of information respecting loads in the open ocean away from shallow water. **1968** R. W. FAIRBRIDGE *Encycl. Geomorphol.* 627/2 Load is an additional variable which changes together with flow along a stream wherever it is joined by a tributary. **1970** *Jrnl. Glaciol.* IX. 227 (*heading*) Contrast between the debris loads of polar and temperate glaciers.

3. f. *Electr. Engin.* The electric power that a generating system is delivering or required to deliver at any given moment; **base load**, the minimum value of the load during any period, generally met (in a grid system) by the continuous operation of the most efficient stations, without the intermittent and varying contribution of the less efficient ones.

In the earliest quots. identical with 3 c (quot. 1900 for which belongs here).

1888 *Proc. Inst. Mech. Engin.* Oct. 508 The efficiency of its working was limited to a constant load and a uniform speed, as when the dynamo was supplying a constant current with constant pressure. *Ibid.*, In many electric lighting installations..motors were required that would work economically between wide variations of load. **1891** *Min. Proc. Inst. Civil Engin.* CVI. 15 The cost of labour per unit..would continue to decrease as long as the duration of maximum load increased, up to a certain limit. **1894** [see *BOOSTER 2]. **1903** *Electr. World & Engin.* 23 May 866/2 It is necessary at times of fall and winter peak loads to operate the steam plants in the three combination sub-station and subsidiary steam plants which the company was operating three years ago. **1928** *Daily Express* 4 June 15/3 We have, in twenty-six years, built up a huge base-load..with an annual output of over 25,000,000 units. **1956** *Nature* 4 Feb. 204/2 The prospect of competitive

nuclear power with low operating costs means that this plant will carry the base load. **1966** *Economist* 14 May 734/1 Running charges have, since 1961, differed by day and by night, since costs for the best, base-load stations at night are so much lower than the average running costs in the mixed bag of stations, from good to awful, used by day. **1974** *Times* 15 Jan. 14/3 A mass switch-off..which would record several million watts being wiped off the national energy load.

g. *Electronics.* An impedance or circuit that receives the output of a transistor or other device, or in which the output is developed.

1918 *Physical Rev.* XII. 180 Variations in potential difference are set up between cathode and grid, and these cause variations in the current in the circuit *FPR*, the power developed in the load *R* being greater than that fed into the input circuit. **1931** *Proc. IRE* XIX. 49 With the pentode..the maximum output was obtained at approximately a 10,000-ohm load. **1943** C. L. Boltz *Basic Radio* xv. 243 In a receiver the load on the output is a loud-speaker or telephone. **1957** B. I. & B. Bleaney *Electr. & Magn.* xiv. 362 In many applications the size of the load is fixed; if, for example, the load is a loud-speaker, its impedance..is generally in the range 5 to 15 ohms. **1962** Simpson & Richards *Physical Princ. Junction Transistors* xi. 251 We require a current in the load of 2 mA. *Ibid.*, Since R_{e1} is assumed to be by-passed by a capacitor, the a.c. load consists of $R_{c1}+R_{e1}$.

h. Colloq. phr. *to take a load off* (*one's feet*): to sit or lie down; to relax.

1945 A. Kober *Parm Me* 35 How's about taking a load off your feet? **1968** J. Hudson *Case of Need* III. i. 175 'Sit down,' she said. 'Take a load off.'

4. Esp. in phr. (*to take*) *a load off one's mind*: (to bring someone) relief from anxiety.

1852 Lytton *My Novel* (1853) III. x. vi. 132 It is a load off one's mind. **1857** Dickens *Perils Eng. Prisoners* iii, in *Househ. Words* Extra Christmas No., 7 Dec. 31/2 It takes a load off my mind to leave her in your charge. **1951** E. Caldwell *Episode in Palmetto* vii. 136 It's a big load off my mind to hear you say that.

b. *slang.* An occurrence of venereal disease; = *dose *sb.* 2 d. Cf. Load *v.* 4 (quots. 1799, 1818).

[**1878** *N. & Q.* 10 Aug. 105/1 *Load*, an eruption, measles, smallpox.] **1937** Partridge *Dict. Slang* 488/1 *Load*, a venereal infection. **1965** F. Sargeson *Mem. Peon* ii. 28 They displayed their rubber goods, and..were doubly protected against finding themselves landed with either biological consequences or a load.

c. An amount of work, teaching, etc., to be done by one person; freq. with defining word prefixed, as *case-load, teaching-load, work-load.*

1946 *Nature* 17 Aug. 216/2 The scientific study of conditions affecting the work-load involved in various processes. **1950,** etc. [see *case-load* s.v. *case *sb.*[1] 14]. **1958** J. C. Herold *Mistress to an Age* (1959) III. xiv. 294 His teaching load amounted to three and a half hours daily for five days a week. **1961** *Lancet* 5 Aug. 303/1 He cemented the relationships by careful inquiry into examinations and study load. **1964** in *Rep. Comm. Inquiry Univ. Oxf.* (1966) II. 450 Please give as accurate estimates as you can for your average weekly load this term. **1966** *Ibid.* 465 A quarter were critical of the heavy teaching load with its consequent adverse effects on research. **1971** *Black Scholar* Jan. 64/2 (Advt.), Normal load is 6 courses per year. **1971** *Sat. Rev.* (U.S.) 18 Dec. 56/2 Teaching loads at white schools often are only a fraction the size of those at black schools.

5. a. Delete 'Now only *dial.* and *U.S.*' and add later examples; now esp. with *on.* Also, a satisfying amount to eat; (*U.S. slang*) a dose of narcotics.

1897 Barrère & Leland *Dict. Slang* II. 22/1 A man who walks unsteadily, owing to intoxication, is said to have a load on. **1922** Joyce *Ulysses* 160 After their feed with a good load of fat soup under their belts. **1929** J. B. Priestley *Good Companions* I. i. 26 You've got a load on and no mistake. **1929** [see *bang *sb.*[3]]. **1934** J. O'Hara *Appointment in Samarra* (1935) vii. 202 What a load you had. Did you get home all right? **1942** Wodehouse *Money in Bank* (1946) xxvi. 229 Drunk!..He's got a load on that would sink an ocean liner. **1948** V. Palmer *Golconda* ix. 65 We're not to blame if men get a load on and begin to fight. **1968** C. Nicole *Self Lovers* ii. 38 I'm sorry about last night. I was carrying a load. Else I'd have recognised you.

6. *a load*: delete † and add later examples; esp. a great quantity of something undesirable or nonsensical.

1943 C. H. Ward-Jackson *Piece of Cake* 41 *Load of guff*, a lot of humbug or nonsense. **1964** [see *crap *sb.*[1] 7 b]. **1965,** etc. [see *cod, abbrev. of *codswallop]. **1967** *Jazz Monthly* Dec. 12 Playing a load of rubbish, while sounding quite competent to the casual listener. **1968** [see *cobbler 1 c]. **1974** A. Morice *Killing with Kindness* iv. 38 No man is an island... That's what Mike used to say. Mind you, I always thought it was a load of rubbish.

7. e. Phr. *to get a load of* (freq. *imp.*): to look at, perceive, make oneself aware of, scrutinize; to listen carefully to. *slang* (orig. *U.S.*).

[**1929** D. Hammett *Dain Curse* (1930) xix. 217 The red-head nurse was getting a load at the keyhole.] **1929** D. Runyon in *Hearst's International* Oct. 64/1, I am not so sure..Blake will care to be anybody's husband, and especially Madame La Gimp's after he gets a load of her. **1941** I. Baird *He rides Sky* 143 What do you think would have happened if Queen Bess had got a load of the Air Force? **1958** E. Dundy *Dud Avocado* I. ix. 157 Come over here... Get a load of this script. **1966** [see *casting-couch* s.v. *casting *vbl. sb.* 4]. **1972** D. Bloodworth *Any Number can Play* xxii. 221 Get a load of that chick over there.

8. *load-bearing, -carrying* adjs.; **load-carrier,** a vehicle with the capacity to accommodate a load; **load cast** *Geol.*, a rounded protrusion on the underside of a stratum (usu. one of sandstone), owing to its having sunk before consolidation into the underlying bed (which is usu. shale); so **load-casted** *a.*, modified or covered by a load cast; **load-casting,** the formation of load casts; **load-cell,** an electronic device for weighing large quantities of material; **load factor,** for 'production' read 'productive capacity' and add: also, in *Aeronaut.*, (*a*) the ratio (or its reciprocal) of the weight of an aircraft to the maximum the wings can support, or that of the force exerted on a part of the structure in ordinary horizontal flight to that exerted in some other condition; (*b*) the ratio of the number of passenger seats occupied to the number available; (earlier and additional examples); **load line,** (*b*) *Electronics*, a straight line that crosses the characteristic curves (of output voltage against output current) of a valve or transistor and has a gradient and position determined by the load, so that it represents the possible operating conditions of the device; **load-shedding,** reduction of the supply of electric current over a specific area, esp. with a view to reducing consumption; also *transf.* and *fig.*; also *load-spreading.*

1925 Hull & Ingberg *Fire Resistance of Concrete Columns* 658 Pittsburgh gravel concrete was used in the load-bearing portion and cinder concrete from bituminous cinders in the outer portion. **1947** *Horizon* Oct. 63 No columns or load-bearing walls intervene. **1961** *Architect & Building News* 21 June 822/1 The building has massive load-bearing walls facing on to the Fellows' Garden and the College Park. **1974** *Times* 18 Feb. 12 Facilities include such items as load-bearing ceiling girders. **1962** *Times* 3 May 19/4 The rear seat can be folded flat to convert the car into an exceptionally roomy load-carrier. **1974** *Country Life* 21 Nov. 1579/3 A very comfortable car and a handy load carrier. **1960** R. W. Marks *Dymaxion World of B. Fuller* 55/1 For this reason the truss has an enormous load-carrying ability. **1953** P. H. Kuenen in *Bull. Amer. Assoc. Petroleum Geologists* XXXVII. 1048 The base is sharply cut and flat or forms pockets in its substratum, 'flow casts' in Shrock's terminology (1948). As this term tends to cause confusion it is here suggested to call them 'load casts'. **1969** Bennison & Wright *Geol. Hist. Brit. Isles* v. 101 Sedimentary structures, including flute casts, load casts, graded bedding, etc., have been described from the arenites. **1957** *Jrnl. Geol.* LXV. 248/1 (*heading*) Load-casted current markings. **1972** F. J. Pettijohn et al. *Sand & Sandstone* iv. 123 Load-casted ripples. **1953** *Bull. Amer. Assoc. Petroleum Geologists* XXXVII. 1051 They were not formed after deposition by load casting. **1972** F. J. Pettijohn et al. *Sand & Sandstone* iv. 124 If one turbidite flow follows on the heels of another, conditions are more favorable for load-casting. **1958** *Engineering* 28 Feb. 39 (Advt.), A standard range of loadcells designed for industrial weighing. **1891** R. E. B. Crompton in *Min. Proc. Inst. Civil Engin.* CVI. 3 What, for want of a better term, is hereafter called the 'load-factor', that is, the relation which the actual output of a plant..bears to what would be its output if worked continuously day and night, at the full load. **1922** *Encycl. Brit.* XXX. 21/2 The 'load factor' is the number of times the weight of the craft which the wings will support; a measure of the strength. **1943** *Jrnl. R. Aeronaut. Soc.* XLVII. 195 Allowing for the 65 per cent. load factor which seems to be about the maximum that can be expected on any commercial service under normal peacetime conditions, that would call for an aircraft providing accommodations for 57 passengers. **1950** Load factor [see *limit load* s.v. *limit *sb.* 5]. **1962** *Times* 16 May 15/3 The passenger load factor (the proportion of passenger capacity used) dropped by 1·7 per cent. to 48·1 per cent. **1970** D. Waterfield *Continental Waterboy* iii. 29 The B.C. Power Commission has a load factor of around 52%. **1931** *Proc. IRE* XIX. 49 The maximum output will be obtained when the slope of the load line equals minus the slope of the plate current curve. **1962** Simpson & Richards *Physical Princ. Junction Transistors* vii. 140 The straight line passing through the battery-voltage point..has a slope $(-1/R_l)$ corresponding to the resistance R_l of the load and is called the load line. **1947** *Times* 10 Feb. 2/2 If the saving that was essential was not forthcoming the company would have to resort to load shedding or temporary cuts in supply. **1948** *Ann. Reg. 1947* 8 The cuts in coal and the 'load-shedding'—a term now incorporated into the vocabulary of the citizen—were due to 'the wretched private coal-owners'. **1963** *Guardian* 29 Apr. 8/6 Lord Longford has announced his resignation as chairman... This is part of the load-shedding of some of his extensive social work. **1951** *Engineering* 6 Apr. 402/2 Electricity load spreading..necessary..owing to heavy demand for electricity.

load, *v.* Add: **3. c.** *Electr.* To provide with additional inductance (e.g. by means of a loading coil) in order either to counteract the effect of capacitance and so reduce the distortion and attenuation of signals (in the case of a telephone line or other transmission line), or to reduce the resonant frequency (in the case of an aerial); more widely, to provide with a load (*load *sb.* 3 g) consisting of any kind of impedance.

1901 M. I. Pupin in *Trans. Amer. Inst. Electr. Engin.* XVII. 452 Though a given cord may be properly loaded for some wave-length it will not be properly loaded for shorter wave-lengths. **1922** Glazebrook *Dict. Appl. Physics* II. 852/2 The effect of loading a line in such a way is approximately the same as though inductance were uniformly distributed along the circuit. **1923** E. W. Marchant *Radio Telegr.* iii. 26 The frequency of the oscillation in the aerial can be varied by varying its inductance; that is, coils of copper tube may be inserted which will have the effect of 'loading' it, and so bringing down the frequency of the oscillations. **1962** *Newnes Conc. Encycl. Electr. Engin.* 846/1 Some low-frequency lines are 'loaded' with added inductance to give some approximation to the distortionless condition. **1970** J. Earl *Tuners & Amplifiers* iv. 82 Each source, whether it be radio tuner..or ceramic pickup or tape head, requires to be loaded by a specific value of impedance or within a range of impedance.

4. Also *to load up with* (something).

1880 'Mark Twain' *Tramp Abroad* xxxviii. 435, I loaded them up with paragoric and put them to bed. **1892** —— *Amer. Claimant* iii. 21 He loads up the house with cripples and idiots and stray cats. **1943** K. Tennant *Ride on Stranger* (1968) i. 3 Other men get married without being loaded up with kids, kids, and then more kids.

5. b. To insert a photographic film or plate in (a camera); also with the film as object.

1902 *Year Bk. Photogr.* 13 (Advt.), The 'Roll Film' Automan will be preferred by many on account of the ease with which it may be loaded and unloaded in daylight. **1936** *Discovery* Aug. 237/1 This unique camera..weighs 305 pounds when loaded. **1956** A. L. M. Sowerby *Dict. Photogr.* (ed. 18) 88 A long roll of film..was loaded into the camera at the factory.

c. To fill (a tobacco-pipe).

1927 'F. Lonsdale' *On Approval* II. 66 He crosses to stool down R, and loads his pipe.

9. a. (Earlier example.)

1870 J. K. Medbery *Men & Mysteries Wall St.* 136 To 'load' one's self with stocks is to buy heavily.

11. *Psychol.* To weight (a result or outcome), to contribute to or be correlated with; also *intr.* (const. *on*), to be correlated (with something else).

1931 *Psychol. Rev.* XXXVIII. 408 The ministry is loaded high for interest in people and in language but low for science. **1952** R. B. Cattell *Factor Analysis* xviii. 340 The factor loading (situational index) is not a measure of the mean amount of the contribution of the factor to the situation. For example, the discovery that in a certain collection of books, the factor of weight is loaded 0·6 in thickness and only 0·2 in height simply indicates that for a given weight (overall size) these books vary more in thickness than they do in height—as books on a tidy shelf should. **1970** Liebert & Spiegler *Personality* vi. 132 As part of the factor analysis, the ratings on each of the 50 trait elements, on which the subjects were rated, were correlated with each of the factors which had been found... The elements which loaded (correlated) most highly both in a positive and in a negative direction (recall that the magnitude of a correlation is independent of its sign) are listed in Table 6–3. **1971** *Jrnl. Gen. Psychol.* LXXXIV. 242 Both of these [test variables] were originally predicted to load the insight factor. **1972** *Jrnl. Social Psychol.* LXXXVIII. 190 The items loading on Factor I seem to reflect the parent's interests.

loadability (lōᵘdăbi·lĭti). [f. Load *v.* + Ability.] The degree of ease with which goods may be loaded or transported.

1945 F. Hamann *Air Words* 35/1 *Loadability.* (1) Cargo volume of commercial aircraft. (2) Ease of access in aircraft. **1955** *Times* 10 June 3/1 The definition of loadability..should include other traffic characteristics such as bulk in comparison to weight, stowage potential, [etc.]. **1960** *Economist* 22 Oct. 392/3 Generally, road hauliers would like to charge more for the smaller loads ('loadability' is as important by road as by rail). **1967** *Freight Management* Jan. 46/2 As far as loadability is concerned, roll-on offers many advantages. **1974** *Country Life* 26 Dec. 2019/3 The Citroen Safari for sheer loadability with comfort.

loadberry (lōᵘ·dbĕri). *Shetland dial.* Also **lodberry.** [Cogn. w. Norw. dial. *ladberg*, ON. *hlaðberg* a lading-rock, a natural quay or pier.] A flat rock forming a natural landing-place; *spec.* a small enclosed landing-place for the unloading of boats.

1764 in W. R. Mackintosh *Glimpses Kirkwall* (1887) 173 The said loadberry or north east part of the Ness of Quanterness. **1871** *Black's Picturesque Tourist of Scotl.* (ed. 19) 596 Lerwick is now before us, a great portion of the houses lining the shore, and standing in the sea, with loadberrys and piers attached. **1950** *Menzies' Guide to Shetland* 10 The most interesting feature of this part of the town [*sc.* Lerwick] is the series of lodberries, or enclosed courtyards with wooden doors surmounting steps down to the water. **1975** *Country Life* 13 Feb. 367/1 Many of these houses had their own slipways with stores or lodberrys.

loaded, *ppl. a.* Add: **1. d.** *fig.* Charged with some hidden implication or underlying suggestion; biased, prejudiced.

1942 *College English* Oct. 16 General Semantics..being metaphysical in a particularly partial and dogmatic sense ..can yield us only a vocabulary of 'loaded' general words, calculated to distort rather than to illuminate the writings of any other school. **1957** *Observer* 29 Dec. 9/2 Is our popular preference for plays of less blatant sexuality a mark of higher civilisation or merely of greater hypocrisy? Is the Dionysiac cult..more childish or simply more honest than the religious practices that have succeeded it in the West?..

These are loaded questions, I admit. **1958** *Times* 7 July 13/2 You cannot solve the riddle of he universe by giving the answer 'Yes' or 'No' to a loaded question. **1961** *Listener* 7 Dec. 991/3 He chose to use emotionally loaded words like 'scare' and 'infection'. **1975** D. Bagley *Snow Tiger* xi. 96 It is improper of Mr Smithers to ask such a loaded question... He is usurping the function of this commission.

2. Of a camera: with a film inserted. Of a film: inserted (in a camera) (cf. *load *v.* 5 b). In *Electr.*, of a telephone line, etc. (cf. *load *v.* 3 c). In insurance: of a life (cf. Load *v.* 10).

1888 *Judge* (U.S.) 20 Oct. 27/1 (Advt.), The Kodak Camera..Loaded for 100 instantaneous views. **1901** *Trans. Amer. Inst. Electr. Engin.* XVII. 475 Propagation of electrical waves over a periodically loaded loop..is compared to that over a uniform loop. **1903** *Phil. Mag.* V. 313 The loaded line discussed in this paper is an electrical circuit of two long parallel conducting wires having self-induction coils inserted at regular intervals. **1922** *Encycl. Brit.* XXXII. 709/2 In 1911 Messrs. Siemens introduced a form of balata dielectric as a substitute for gutta-percha in loaded submarine cables... The effect was to reduce materially the attenuation constant and increase the range of speech in loaded cables. **1928** *Daily Express* 10 May 11/6 The application was refused in the first instance, and only afterwards accepted as a 'loaded' life. **1937** *Discovery* Apr. 112/2 Little..envelopes, in which glass plates and flat films are sold ready loaded. **1968** *Radio Communication Handbk.* (ed. 4) xvi. 33/1 While the centre loaded aerial may be the best radiator, on the lower frequency bands, particularly 1·8 Mc/s and 3·5 Mc/s, mechanical considerations may have to influence the loading coil position.

3. b. Drugged; under the influence of drugs; containing a drug. *U.S. slang.* (Cf. *load *sb.* 5 a.)

1923 J. F. Fishman *Crucibles of Crime* vi. 126 It was discovered that each of them [*sc.* handkerchiefs] has a small ink mark in one of the corners..these handkerchiefs had been dipped in cocaine... The mark in the corner notified the 'snowbird' that it was 'loaded'. **1928** J. Tully *Circus Parade* xviii. 237 When guys are loaded up on heroin it'll give 'em more nerve. **1953** W. Burroughs *Junkie* xii. 120 To get really loaded, you would need four papers. *Ibid.* xv. 147 He was loaded on H and goof-balls. **1962** K. Orvis *Damned & Destroyed* xi. 74 'I'm gorgeous,' she said. 'Loaded and gorgeous.'

4. Rich; extremely wealthy. *slang* (orig. *U.S.*).

[**1910** O. Johnson *Varmint* iv. 60 He's just loaded with the spondulix.] **1948** *Call-Bulletin* (San Francisco) 16 July 10/4 Lonely but loaded, a carpenter newly returned from Guam was taken for a ride by six young women. **1949** A. Hynd *We are Public Enemies* i. 20 The boys were loaded after the safety deposit opening and the money was burning their pockets. **1952** 'J. Tey' *Singing Sands* xi. 172 He slapped his pocket, 'I'm loaded.' **1957** C. MacInnes *City of Spades* i. iv. 23 'Is your Dad rich?'.. 'He's reasonably loaded.' **1971** D. O'Connor *Eye of Eagle* v. 32 Adriana's a very popular girl and there are guys here who are absolutely loaded.

loader[1]. **3.** Add to def.: Applied similarly to other things, such as agricultural machinery (e.g. *front-end loader* s.v. *front *sb.* (and *a.*) 14), washing machines (e.g. **front-loader*); see also *side-loader* s.v. *side *sb.*[1] 27. (Further examples.)

1968 *Which?* May 149/1 This [washing] machine is a top loader, but has a horizontal stainless steel drum. **1975** *Radio Times* 22–28 Feb. 56/1 Fully automatic top-loader. Takes loads of 4 lbs., 7 lbs., or 10 lbs... 7 programme automatic front loader. Takes load of 9 lbs.

4. Special comb.: **loader gate** *Coal-mining*, a passage along which coal is conveyed away from a long-wall face.

1964 A. Nelson *Dict. Mining* 258 *Loadergate*, a gate road equipped with a gate conveyor or a gate-end loader; the gate to which the face conveyors deliver their coal. **1973** *Times* 3 May 4/1 Then I saw all the loader gate workmen running towards me. Someone shouted 'run, water has broken in.'

loading, *vbl. sb.* Add: **1. f.** *Electr.* Addition of inductance, or the inductance added (see *load *v.* 3 c); any impedance that acts as a load (*load *sb.* 3 g).

1903 *Phil. Mag.* V. 325 Loading..presents the greatest possibilities upon long cable circuits. **1922** Glazebrook *Dict. Appl. Physics* II. 850/2 The increase in voltage resulting from the increased impedance..increases the leakage losses, and these set a limit to the possible improvement in transmission efficiency by loading. **1959** K. Henney *Radio Engin. Handbk.* (ed. 5) xxviii. 29 Uniformly surrounding the conductor with a thin layer of magnetic material of high permeability..is known as continuous loading. This has been used, to some extent, in the construction of some long submarine-cable circuits for telegraphy as well as telephony. However, loading is usually introduced in telephone circuits by connecting loading coils in series with the conductors at intervals. **1968** *Radio Communication Handbk.* (ed. 4) xvi. 34/1 With a centre loaded coil on 3·5 Mc/s it may be possible to vary the transmitter frequency over about 25 kc/s before it becomes essential to re-adjust the loading. **1973** *Physics Bull.* Dec. 716/1 This changes the impedance of the loop and hence it alters the loading of the RF circuit and this can be detected in the RF drive output.

g. The (maximum) current or power that an electrical appliance is designed to take.

1938 E. M. Ackery *Electr. Heating for Public & Commercial Libraries* iv. 42 The coke-boiler was replaced by a 400 gallon thermal storage tank, fitted with immersion heaters with a total loading of 100 kw. **1951** *Good Housek. Home Encycl.* 310/1, 2 or 3 kilowatts is a sufficient loading for the average-sized tank. **1973** *Daily Tel.* 4 Dec. 11/4 Fan heater with loading of 2 kw: 1·8p an hour (2 units).

4*. The weight supported by a wing divided by its area. More fully **wing loading* (cf. **power loading*).

1918 [see *live load* s.v. *live *a.* 8]. **1919** H. Shaw *Text-bk. Aeronaut.* xv. 181 The loading of a machine, which is the weight carried per unit area of surface, varies in different types. **1936** *Discovery* Mar. 73/2 Most birds fly at a loading of $1\frac{1}{2}$ to $2\frac{1}{2}$ lb. per sq. ft. **1973** *Sci. Amer.* Dec. 103/2 The glider can travel much faster than the vulture at a given gliding angle. This is owing partly to..its higher wing loading (the ratio of weight to wing area).

4.** *Psychol.* The extent to which any given factor or variable contributes to or is correlated with some resultant quality or overall situation, usu. represented by a number arrived at by statistical analysis of the results of a series of tests.

1931 *Psychol. Rev.* XXXVIII. 407 Our next problem is to assign a weight or loading of each of the general factors to each of the variables... Engineering, for example, has a high loading of interest in science, a rather low loading of interest in language. **1935** L. L. Thurstone *Vectors of Mind* viii. 201 (*heading*) The elimination of negative factor loadings. **1947** L. E. Tyler *Psychol. Human Differences* xv. 364 The task of the factor analyst then becomes one of determining these weights or loadings. The raw material for the mathematical work in each case is the original table of intercorrelations. **1952** [see *load *v.* 11]. **1971** *Jrnl. Gen. Psychol.* LXXXV. 72 The loadings have been rounded to two figures and the order of both factors and variables rearranged to facilitate inspection. *Ibid.* 212 Because many of the memory tests require recall of the items memorized, and because the operations of divergent and convergent production are so much dependent upon retrieval of information from the memory store, it might be expected that..either production tests would have some memory loadings, or memory tests would have some loadings on production factors.

5. *loading-board, -tool, -tower, -yard*; **loading bay**, a bay (Bay *sb.*[3]) or recess in a building where vehicles, etc., are loaded and unloaded; **loading coil** *Electr.*, an inductance coil used in the loading of telephone lines or aerials (see sense *1 f and *load *v.* 3 c); **loading gauge** *Railways*, (*a*) the maximum height and width allowed for rolling stock to ensure adequate clearance under bridges and in tunnels; (*b*) a device suspended over railway lines for checking the dimensions of rolling stock.

1963 *Listener* 31 Jan. 202/2 The whole street is sometimes used as an open-air loading bay and temporary warehouse. **1971** R. Busby *Deadlock* x. 152 The roller doors of the loading bay were shut. **1910** W. M. Raine *Bucky O'Connor* 36 The loading board was lowered and the horses led from the car. **1901** *Ann. Rep. Amer. Telephone & Telegr. Co.* 4 The efficiency of these lines will be largely increased by the use of 'loading coils'. **1922** Glazebrook *Dict. Appl. Physics* II. 853/1 Loading coils are encased in iron cases and are mounted in manholes—if the circuit..is a cable circuit—or are mounted at the cross-arms of poles if the circuit..is an open-wire line. **1974** *Encycl. Brit. Micropædia* VI. 286/1 Auto radios generally use loading coils because whip antennas are much too short to resonate at broadcast frequencies. **1883** F. S. Williams *Our Iron Roads* (ed. 4) 266 Among the minor appurtenances of a railway station is the wagon loading gauge. **1901** *Young Engineer* I. 53 The fire-box may be extended to the full width of the loading gauge. **1930** *Engineering* 22 Aug. 230/2 The upper part [of a coke wagon] slopes inward to suit the loading gauge. **1874** J. W. Long *Amer. Wild-Fowl Shooting* 20, I usually made a practice of reloading as fast as possible between shots, carrying an ammunition-box and loading-tools with me. **1901** *Chambers's Jrnl.* May 12/1 Steam-cranes and movable loading-towers..lower the coal into the hold of the vessel. **1909** *Westm. Gaz.* 9 June 11/1 Between them is a loading yard 200 ft. by 60 ft.

loadmaster (lōu·d,mɑːstəɹ). *Aeronaut.* [f. Load *sb.* + Master *sb.*[1]] The crew member of an aircraft who is responsible for the load or cargo.

1961 *Newsweek* 6 Mar. 9 The United Nations and C-130 loadmasters did most of the work. **1967** *New Scientist* 17 Aug. 328 The aircraft [*sc.* Douglas C-47s] carry a crew of eight—pilot, co-pilot, navigator, flight mechanic, load master (who also drops the flares), two gun loaders, and a Vietnamese Air Force liaison officer. **1973** *Daily Tel.* 2 Oct. 2 If she passes her 14-week officer training course she will join an aircrew as a loadmaster. **1974** *Ibid.* 22 Feb. 14/4 Flying Officer Howard has logged 3,500 flying hours all over the world as an air loadmaster in VC-10s of No. 10 Squadron based at Brize Norton. The job, formerly known as air quartermaster, was given air crew status in 1962.

loaf, *sb.*[1] Add: **2. e.** Minced or chopped meat moulded into the shape of a loaf and cooked; generally eaten cold, in slices. Usu. with qualifying word, as *beef, ham, meat, veal loaf.*

[**1787** Lady Newdigate *Let.* 21 Oct. in A. E. Newdigate-Newdegate *Cheverels* (1898) v. 71 We made an excellent Dinner upon our Cold Loaf.] **1895** 'M. Ronald' *Century Cook Bk.* 308 Liver loaf, or false pâté de foie gras..is better cold with salad, or used like pâté de foie gras. A loaf of any game may be made in the same way. **1902, 1907** [see *ham loaf* s.v. *ham *sb.*[1] 3]. **1939** Auden & Isherwood *Journey to War* 90 We had fruit-juice, meat-loaf, salad and cake. **1964** J. Masters *Trial at Monomoy* iv. 140 She stared at rows of Spam, corned beef, meat loaf, ham loaf. **1975** *Times* 7 Mar. 5/2 She recommended home-made vegetable soup and meat loaf, followed by apple or rhubarb crumble.

f. *slang.* [Prob. from *loaf of bread*, rhyming slang for 'head'.] The (human) head; hence, the mind, common sense; *esp.* in phr. to *use one's loaf.*

1925 Fraser & Gibbons *Soldier & Sailor Words* 145 *Loaf*, head, *e.g.*, 'Duck your loaf—*i.e.*, keep your head below the parapet'. **1938** J. Curtis *They Drive by Night* xiv. 155 Bloody seconds counted in a job like this. You certainly had to use your loaf. **1943** Hunt & Pringle *Service Slang* 44 *Use your loaf* is the injunction often heard when someone is particularly slow in following orders. But this phrase, in its finer meanings, says: 'Use your common sense. Interpret orders according to the situation as you find it, and don't follow the book of words too literally.' **1949** 'N. Blake' *Head of Traveller* ii. 36 Do try to use your loaf. **1957** P. Frankau *Bridge* 73 He uses his loaf where you and I just muddle along. **1971** B. W. Aldiss *Soldier Erect* 79 You want to use your bloody loaf, Stubbs, or we'll never win this war the way you're carrying on. **1973** *Jewish Chron.* 2 Feb. 12/1 Use your loaf. Didn't Sir Jack Cohen of Tesco..start the same way?

g. *loaf o(f) bread*: rhyming slang for 'dead'.

1930 Brophy & Partridge *Songs & Slang 1914–18* 137 Loaf o' Bread, dead. **1935** Auden & Isherwood *Dog Beneath Skin* III. i. 123 O how I cried when Alice died The day we were to have wed! We never had our Roasted Duck And now she's a Loaf of Bread.

6. *loaf-tin*; **loaf-cake**, a plain cake made in the form of a loaf.

1828 E. Leslie *75 Receipts* 62 Loaf Cake. **1844** *Knickerbocker* XXIV. 423 The biscuit would not rise, her loaf-cake was heavy. **1906** Kipling *Puck of Pook's Hill* 195 Hobden said that the loaf-cake..was almost as good as what his wife used to make. **1941** F. M. Farmer *Boston Cooking-School Cook Bk.* (ed. 7) 624 Loaf and layer cakes. **1883** *Facts, or Experiences Recent Colonist N.Z.* iii. 30 The materials required are:—..one deep tin-pan, six loaf tins, one wooden spoon. **1932** E. Craig *Cooking with E. Craig* 305 Place..in a greased loaf tin. **1972** K. Stewart *Times Cookery Bk.* xviii. 235 Divide the dough... Place carefully in..two small, greased, 1 lb loaf tins.

loafer. Add: (Earlier U.S. examples.)

1830 *Mechanic's Press* (Utica, N.Y.) 10 July 274/1 Nor are they topers at taverns, or *benchers* at groceries, or loafers who 'chase misfortune o'er the towpath'. **1835** *Knickerbocker* VI. 63 The late Ben Smith, Loafer. I present an outline sketch of one of that species of the *genus homo*..which Custom has christened with the expressive appellation of Loafer!

2. [cf. Sp. *lobo* wolf.] A timber wolf, *Canis lupus nubilus*, found in the south-western part of North America; = Lobo. Also *attrib.*

1878 McDanield & Taylor *Coming Empire* v. v. 314 The Mexicans call these big wolves 'lobos' and the Texans call them 'loafers' which is a corruption of the Mexican word. **1908** *Sat. Even. Post* 4 July 16/3 One of the loafers had run in, leaping out of the black like a streak of gray light. **1948** *Ibid.* 10 July 80/3 With loafers,..mountain lions or bears, he was absolutely ruthless. **1974** *Islander* (Victoria, B.C.) 16 June 13/2 The lobo wolf derived its name from a word in the Blackfoot Indian language meaning 'buffalo wolf' and sounding like 'lobo', the Spanish word for wolf. They were also known as the buffalo grey or loafer wolf as they followed migrations of bison.

3. Usu. *pl.* The proprietary name of a shoe for wearing on informal occasions.

1939 *Trade Marks Jrnl.* 19 Apr. 520/2 *Loafer.* Boots, shoes, slippers, sandals, leggings and gaiters. Fortnum and Mason Ltd.—London. **1948** M. Sturges-Jones *In Wedlock Wake* 11 Pullover sweaters, bobby socks, and leather loafers. **1963** T. Pynchon *V* vi. 136 Profane kicked off his shoes—old black loafers of Geronimo's—and concentrated on dancing in his socks. **1971** 'V. X. Scott' *Surrogate Wife* 161, I saw him standing there in lean slacks..and suède loafers. **1972** *Last Whole Earth Catalog* (Portola Inst.) 406/2 The big thing for guys is jeans or slacks, button-down shirts or T-shirts and brown loafers without socks.

b. A type of jacket for informal wear.

1959 *Trade Marks Jrnl.* 19 Aug. 688/2 *Loafers...* Jackets. Chas. MacIntosh & Company Limited,..London. **1969** P. Roth *Portnoy's Complaint* 125 My clip-on tie and my two-tone 'loafer' jacket.

loafery. Add: **b.** A place where people loaf.

1898 *Daily Tel.* 10 Feb. 7/3 The Whitechapel Guardians have been considering a proposal to call their workhouse by another name... Perhaps 'House of Repose' or 'The Loaferies' would be appropriate. **1903** *Liberty Rev.* July 7 A new trap is set for it—the free loafery at the corner.

loaiasis (lōuᵃ,əi·ăsis). *Path.* Also **loasis** (lōu,ēi·sis), **loiasis** (lōu,əi·ăsis). [mod.L., f. Loa + *-iasis.] Infection with, or disease caused by, loas.

1913 Castellani & Chalmers *Man. Trop. Med.* (ed. 2) lx. 1442 (*heading*) Loasis. **1919** *Ibid.* (ed. 3) lxxxviii. 1972 Löiasis is a subcutaneous and subconjunctival filariasis caused by *Loa loa*. **1923** E. A. & T. M. Neatby *Man. Trop. Dis. & Hygiene* 382 The species responsible for the filariases and loasis. **1956** *Nature* 25 Feb. 367/1 Studies on loiasis in the Cameroons and Nigeria. **1961** *Lancet* 5 Aug. 323/2 In 1948 Gordon started an investigation of the African filarial infection, loaiasis. **1963** T. J. Brooks *Essent. Med. Parasitol.* III. 259 Loaiasis, or eye worm infection.

loa loa (lōu·ă lōu·ă). [Taxonomic name of the causative organism: see *LOA[1].] = *LOAIASIS.

1923 E. A. & T. M. NEATBY *Man. Trop. Dis. & Hygiene* 396 Loa loa is a filarial infection, confined to West Africa, the worm (*Filaria loa*) resembling *F. bancrofti.* **1963** *Times* 8 Feb. 15/7 It was found that exactly the reverse held true for the form of filarial disease in West Africa, known as loa loa. Here the number of microfilariæ in the bloodstream is maximal at noon and minimal at midnight.

loam, *sb.* Add: **5.** *loam-foot.*

1940 T. S. ELIOT *East Coker* i. 8 Lifting heavy feet in clumsy shoes Earth feet, loam feet, lifted in country mirth. **1955** D. DAVIE *Brides of Reason* 28 Come with me by the self-consuming north (The North is spirit), to the loam-foot west And opulent departures of the south.

loam, *v.* Add: **3.** *Austral. intr.* and *trans.* To search (a region) for gold by washing the loam from a hill's base until the increasing number of gold grains leads to the lode. So **loa·ming** *vbl. sb.*

1916 R. MACKAY *Recoll. Early Gippsland Goldfields* vi. 29/2 The science of loaming was either then unknown, or known to very few. *Ibid.* 30/1 The loaming system will tire the strongest and most wiry man that ever swung a pick. **1935** *Bulletin* (Sydney) 13 Feb. 21/1 He'll be loaming up a hill and following a trace, Until he gets above the gold. **1953** *People* (Austral.) 23 Sept. 39/1 Loaming for gold he explains, entails, roughly, taking samples of loam from the topsoil, washing it in a dish, counting the colors and following them in intensity until a likely spot to sink a shaft is found. **1966** 'J. HACKSTON' *Father clears Out* 50 Old Tom was to make himself useful about the plant, and loam the surrounding country for the reef.

Loamshire (lōu·mʃər). Name given to an imaginary rural county, much used in novels and plays; also (*pl.*) a regiment from this county. Also *attrib.*

1859 GEO. ELIOT *Adam Bede* I. v. 108 He was only a captain in the Loamshire Militia. *Ibid.* xii. 230 Jolly housekeeping—finest stud in Loamshire. **1866** —— *Felix Holt* I. i. 18 Transome Court was a large mansion..with a park and grounds as fine as any to be seen in Loamshire. **1912** G. W. E. RUSSELL *Afterthoughts* xvii. 158 In Loamshire 'my foot is on my native heath', and I have been renewing my youth by contact with my early friends. **1920** 'SAPPER' *Bull-Dog Drummond* i. 24 Captain Hugh Drummond, D.S.O., M.C., late of His Majesty's Royal Loamshires. **1954** K. TYNAN in *Observer* 31 Oct. 6/1 Look about you; survey the peculiar nullity of our drama's prevalent *genre*, the Loamshire play. **1962** *Listener* 6 Dec. 959/1 They [*sc.* English novelists] also have to avoid the pitfall of regionalism and dialect. They have to avoid Loamshire. **1974** GREEN & HOOPER *C. S. Lewis* x. 247 In the version which Green read..Digory..stayed in a farm cottage with an old countryman called Piers and his wife, who spoke with a rather laboured 'Loamshire' accent.

loan, *sb.*[1] **5.** *loan-market*; **loan-blend,** a compound word consisting of both native and foreign elements; a hybrid (see HYBRID *sb.* 2); **loan capital,** the part of the capital of a company or the like that is borrowed for a specified period; **loan-farm** *S. Afr.*, land loaned to a farmer by the government; **loan-form,** a form adopted by one language from another; **loan-place** *S. Afr.* = **loan-farm*; **loan-shark** orig. *U.S.* (see quot. 1928 and SHARK *sb.*[1] 2); so **loan-sharking** *sb.*, lending money at exorbitant rates of interest; **loan-shift,** a change in the meaning of a word resulting from the influence of a foreign language; a word so affected; **loan-translation** [= G. *lehnübersetzung*], an expression adopted by one language from another in more or less literally translated form; a *CALQUE.

1950 *Language* XXVI. 215 Loanblends show morphemic substitution as well as importation. **1974** R. A. HALL *External Hist. Romance Lang.* 9 On occasion, a newly formed word may consist, in part, of a native term ..and, in part, of a borrowing. The result is a *loan-blend*, as in Fr[ench] *bar-serveuse* 'bar-maid', with the first part of the loan-compound kept and with the second part replaced by Fr. *serveuse* 'maid, waitress'. **1848** *Bradshaw's Railway Almanack* (ed. 2) 57 The guarantee is extended to the payment of interest on £1,000,000 (the authorized Loan Capital) at whatever rate it may be borrowed. **1964** *Financial Times* 31 Jan. 19/5 No share or loan capital of the Company or any of its subsidiaries has within two years preceding the date hereof been issued or is proposed to be issued for cash or otherwise. **1804** J. BARROW *Acct. Trav. S. Afr.* II. 380 The number of these loan farms registered in the office of the receiver of the land revenue, on closing the books in 1798, were..1832. **1955** J. H. WELLINGTON *S. Afr.* II. III. xiv. 208 To create a stable border farming population in the place of the cattle farmers trekking from loan farm to loan farm, land was offered to settlers on a quit-rent basis. **1966** E. PALMER *Plains of Camdeboo* ii. 21 Probably in the 1770's the land was issued as a loan place and became the temporary property of one farmer. Loan farms were apportioned in the simplest possible way and were held at a nominal rent. **1902** *Amer. Anthropologist* IV. 31 Penobscot *nachigadonkak* is a Passamaquoddy loan-form. **1844** MILL in *Westm. Rev.* XLI. 593 The already existing pressure upon the loan market. **1870** J. K. MEDBERY *Men & Mysteries Wall St.* 11 Its loan market holds the keys of trade. **1844** J. BACKHOUSE *Narr. Visit Mauritius & S. Afr.* 585 A *loan place* which is a place obtained from the Government, that has not yet been surveyed, is half-an-hour's walk in every direction from the house or centre. **1939** J. S. MARAIS *Cape Coloured People* iv. 140 During the previous twenty years land had been granted to farmers as 'loan places'. **1905** TAYLOR & GIBSON *Log of Water Wagon* 41 Loan sharks have been following the Lithia all day. **1911** *Collier's* 4 Feb. 8/1 Mr. Ham became interested in the 'World's' lucrative and lengthy list of loan-shark advertisements. **1913** *Munsey's Mag.* Nov. 218/1 In New York the loan-sharks were doing a business of twenty million dollars per annum. *Ibid.* 221/1 At the convention of the Legal Aid Society in Pittsburgh..the loan-shark evil was discussed. **1928** *Daily Tel.* 5 May 9/5 It is hoped by this plan virtually to put out of business the 'loan shark', who exacts usurious rates of interest from the person of small means. **1972** *Sunday Sun* (Brisbane) 27 Aug. 22/1 He was a loan-shark extortionist, and he had a very cute way of making sure customers paid up. **1970** *New Yorker* 15 Aug. 24/1 Other illicit activities engaged in by Cosa Nostra ..included..hijacking, loan-sharking. **1971** *Daily Colonist* (Victoria, B.C.) 10 Sept. 25/5 We are all aware that narcotics, prostitution, gambling and loansharking make up the bankroll of organized and syndicated crime. **1950** *Language* XXVI. 220 Loanshifts in general occur most readily when there is both phonetic and semantic resemblance between foreign and native terms. **1964** *Ibid.* XL. 95 The problems of translators and their role in introducing neologisms and loanshifts. **1974** R. A. HALL *External Hist. Romance Lang.* 9 French *réaliser* 'to bring into existence' has..undergone a shift of meaning to 'become aware', under the influence of Eng[lish] *realise.* Such a process of reinterpretation is known as a *loan-shift*, and its result as a *calque.* **1933** L. BLOOMFIELD *Lang.* xxv. 456 The Slavic languages translate the term [sc. *conscientia*] by 'with' and 'knowledge', as in Russian ['so-vest] 'conscience'. This process, called loan-translation, involves a semantic change: the native terms or the components which are united to create native terms, evidently undergo an extension of meaning. **1958** C. RABIN in *Aspects of Translation* 140 Loan-translation (calque)..is very common [in modern Hebrew]. We find, for example, *gan yeladim* 'garden of children', which (except for the difference in the..order of elements) reproduces G. *Kindergarten* even to the pl. of *Kinder.* **1964** C. BARBER *Ling. Change Present-Day Eng.* IV. 101 Another type of loan from a foreign language is the *calque* or *loan-translation.* **1965** *Ulster Dialect Archive Bull.* (Ulster Folk Museum) IV. 11 Fairy lore appears in *fergorta*..occurring also as a loan-translation *hungry-grass.* **1974** *Verbatim* Dec. 2/1 Hebrew..has a little series, mostly loan translations,..on a semantically similar pattern.

loasis, var. *LOAIASIS.

lob, *sb.*[2] **6. lob-tailing** *vbl. sb.* and *ppl. a.* (earlier and later examples); so **lob-tail** *v. intr.*

1933 B. WILLOUGHBY *Alaskans All* 134 Nearby, a third [whale] would pop up and 'lob-tail'—that is stand on its head with its tail out flaying the sea with thundering blows that sent clouds of spray in every direction. **1851** H. MELVILLE *Moby Dick* II. xliv. 298 Five great motions are peculiar to it [*sc.* the tail of a whale]... Fourth, in lob-tailing. **1937** *Discovery* Oct. 310/1 In 'lobtailing', it [*sc.* the cachalot] stands on its head with its tail some thirty feet out of the sea.

lob, *sb.*[5] **1.** (Earlier examples.)

1851 J. PYCROFT *Cricket Field* ix. 178 Practise high lobs —a most useful variety of ball. **1865** F. LILLYWHITE *Guide to Cricketers* 59 A good lob-bowler and excellent long-stop. **1871** 'THOMSONBY' *Cricketers in Council* 40 The best lob bowlers by a mere turn of the wrist impart an enormous amount of twist to the ball. *Ibid.*, 'Lob' bowling is, we believe, rather undervalued at the present day.

lob, *v.* Add: **3. b.** *to lob* (*in*), to arrive. *Austral. slang.*

1916 C. J. DENNIS *Songs Sentimental Bloke* 56 'Twas at a beano where I lobs along To drown them memories o' fancied wrong. *Ibid.* 125 *To lob*, to arrive. **1934** *Bulletin* (Sydney) 12 Dec. 25/2 Scrubby lobs in one sundown while Old Dave is over with the storekeeper. **1950** K. S. PRICHARD *Winged Seeds* ii. 24 You never knew who'd lob into the camp. **1970** *Sunday Truth* (Brisbane) 5 July 30/5 When they had 15 pines on board, the farmer lobbed on the scene.

4. b. To send (a player) a lobbed ball.

1921 A. W. MYERS *20 Yrs. Lawn Tennis* 135 Having discovered the wisdom of lobbing Barrett, Hackett.. allowed McLoughlin to kill anything smashable. **1928** *Daily Tel.* 5 June 17/1 As soon as one is certain of not being lobbed. **1972** D. DELMAN *Sudden Death* (1973) vi. 170 He lunges for the backhand volley... He is off balance, out of position, and I lob him wickedly.

lobar, *a.* Add: **b.** *spec.* in *Path.* Applied to an acute form of pneumonia lasting about nine days, most commonly caused by pneumococcal infection, and marked by fever, pains in the chest, coughing, and blood-stained sputum, and by inflammation concentrated in one lobe of the lung.

1858 J. COPLAND *Dict. Pract. Med.* II. 761/2 The French pathologists, and after them some recent English writers, have distinguished the disease [*sc.* pneumonia] into lobar, lobular, and vesicular... Of these the lobar is the most common. **1873** [in Dict.]. **1876** J. S. BRISTOWE *Treat. Theory & Pract. Med.* iii. 406 Lobar pneumonia commences with hyperæmia of the small vessels which are distributed in the walls of the air-cells and bronchial passages. **1961** R. D. BAKER *Essent. Path.* ix. 151 There may be lobar pneumonia in one lung and lobular in another. Lobar pneumonia has this difference, that almost all cases are caused by the pneumococcus, whereas many cases of lobular pneumonia are caused by other bacteria, such as streptococci or staphylococci. **1966** WRIGHT & SYMMERS *Systemic Path.* I. x. 368/2 In most cases the onset of lobar pneumonia is abrupt.

lobate, *a.* Delete *Nat. Hist.* and add further examples.

1919 D. W. JOHNSON *Shore Processes* iv. 188 Where the current of a river's distributaries strongly predominate[s] over shore currents and wave attack, the delta shoreline will be of the 'lobate' type, as in the case of the Mississippi delta. **1933** SCHUCHERT & DUNBAR *Textbk. Geol.* (ed. 3) xix. 430 When the ice later retreated northward over the Great Lakes region, its front became deeply lobate. **1957** G. E. HUTCHINSON *Treat. Limnol.* I. i. 85 Genuine morainic dams are probably commoner in regions of moderate preglacial relief that has been covered by continental ice sheets or by large lobate glaciers. **1967** *New Scientist* 2 Feb. 263/2 The hills in the north of the ring define lobate shapes in a manner highly reminiscent of viscous lava flows on Earth.

lobby, *sb.* Add: **3. b.** (Earlier example.)

1808 *Deb. Congress U.S.* 2 Feb. (1852) II. 1536 If we move to Philadelphia we shall have a commanding lobby.

c. In extended use: a sectional interest (see INTEREST *sb.* 4), a business, cause, or principle supported by a group of people; the group of persons supporting such an interest.

1952 *Economist* 26 July 254/2 American..interests have maintained their effective lobby against the project [*sc.* the St. Lawrence Seaway]. **1954** *Ibid.* 7 Aug. 425/1 M. Mendès-France..has to face powerful colonial lobbies in parliament. **1958** *Listener* 21 Aug. 273/1 The United States Government, sensitive to the Jewish lobby.. backed the Jews. **1959** *Ibid.* 4 June 968/2 They even tackled the vested privileges and subsidies of the powerful alcohol lobby. **1971** *Daily Tel.* 9 Mar. 10/6 The anti-pollution lobby might claim that a spot of exaggeration is justified in such a cause.

4. lobby chest (see quot. 1803); **lobby man,** (*a*) *U.S.* (see quot. 1934); (*b*) a lobbyist.

1803 T. SHERATON *Cabinet Dict.* 261 Lobby chest, is a kind of half chest of drawers, adapted for the use of a small study, lobby, or small lodging room. **1970** *Canadian Antiques Collector* Nov. 15/2 All sorts of compact, changeling furniture..lobby chests and Rudd's tables, [etc.]. **1934** WEBSTER *Lobbyman*, one who works as attendant or porter, or does chores, in a lobby. **1958** *Times Lit. Suppl.* 21 Feb. 93/4 The high-pressure methods of the United States lobby-men, whose contacts and antecedents are open to inspection.

lobby, *v.* For *U.S.* read orig. *U.S.* Add: **1.** (Further examples.) Also *transf.*

1955 *Times* 17 June 4/6 M.P.s were lobbied yesterday by delegates of the Uganda National Congress. **1971** P. GRESSWELL *Environment* 154 We can always lobby our councillors. **1974** *Times* 18 May 8 [Wilberforce] was lobbying heads of state.

2. (Earlier and later examples.)

1837 *Cleveland* (Ohio) *Herald* (Weekly ed.) 6 Oct. 2/6 Gen. Bronson..spent a considerable portion of the last winter in Columbus, lobbying to procure the establishment of a Bank at Ohio City. **1916** GALSWORTHY *Sheaf* iii. 55 Animals..cannot lobby in the House of Commons, withdraw votes or commit outrages. **1962** *Listener* 20 Dec. 1041/1 In France the planners, being part of the civil service machine, have always been able to lobby from inside.

lobby-gow (lǫ·bi,gau·). *U.S. slang.* [Etym. unknown.] An errand-boy, messenger; a hanger-on, underling, esp. in a opium den or in the Chinese quarter of a town.

1906 I. SWIFT *Sketches of Gotham* 41 The lobbygows—the errand men of the Chinese—the whites, who execute commissions for them,..saw and noted this Queen also. *a* **1911** D. G. PHILLIPS *Susan Lenox* (1917) II. x. 248 The lobbygows—men who live by lying in wait in the darkness to seize and rob the lonely, friendless fast woman. **1911** C. B. CHRYSLER *White Slavery* xi. 80 A 'lobbygow'—a Chinaman who acts as stool pigeon and informer for the police. **1911** G. BRONSON-HOWARD *Enemy to Society* ix. 295, I 'ain't gunna have her think Stevey's tied up with a bunch of lobby-gows. **1930** D. H. CLARKE *Louis Beretti* ii. 22 He ran errands for the girls, which made him a lobby-gow in the original meaning of the word. **1956** 'T. BETTS' *Across Board* xii. 177 He flung away fortunes in grubstakes to bums, heels, and lobby-gows.

lobbyist. Add to def.: Also, one who promotes a 'lobby' (see *LOBBY *sb.* 3 c).

1945 *Sun* (Baltimore) 23 Oct. 1/4 Hoffman identified Arundel in a House speech as a Washington 'lobbyist' who, he was informed, picked up the $75,000 check which paid for the festivities. **1961** *Encounter* Jan. 6/2 Skilful lobbyists with large funds and a powerful influence on the Algiers administration. **1971** *Nature* 4 June 278/2 The food industry lobbyists convincingly argue that the FDA is not responsibly handling the authority it already has. **1971** *Daily Tel.* 9 Nov. 15/6 Legislative provisions, which are promoted by a group of hysterical lobbyists who are spreading the fear of a world catastrophe because of chemical poisoning. **1974** 'R. B. DOMINIC' *Epitaph for Lobbyist* i. 6, I don't like high-powered lobbyists and their greasy favors.

lobe. Add: **1. i.** *Electr.* A portion of the radiation pattern of an aerial which represents a group of directions of stronger radiation and is bounded on each side by directions in which there is minimum radiation.

1926 *Bell Syst. Techn. Jrnl.* V. 297 It is interesting to observe the variation in the diagrams... A lobe starts as a small bud, it grows in size until it reaches the unit circle,

it then becomes dented. **1947** J. S. Hall *Radar Aids to Navigation* i. 13 All antennas radiate small amounts of power in directions other than the main lobe. **1959** Davies & Palmer *Radio Stud. Universe* iii. 39 In the simplest form of interferometer each narrow lobe of the aerial polar diagram produces its own small drift curve. **1968** *Radio Communication Handbk.* (ed. 4) xiii. 40/2 With increased spacing between the two aerials, more lobes appear... This type of pattern is not very useful, but if the intervening space is filled with aerials spaced λ/2, one pair of lobes grows at the expense of all the others, giving a sharp main beam with a number of relatively small minor lobes.

j. *Calligraphy.* A curved projecting part of a letter.

1957 N. R. Ker *Catal. Manuscripts Containing Anglo-Saxon* p. xxvii, In minuscule of the eighth and ninth centuries **a** is a pointed letter, the back of which projects above the place at which it is joined by the lobe. **1969** M. B. Parkes *Eng. Cursive Bk. Hands 1250–1500* p. xxvi, The letter b comprises a stem or mainstroke which rises above the general level of the other letters and a lobe made with a curved stroke to the right of the stem.

lobectomy (lǝbe·ktǒmi). *Surg.* [f. Lob(e + *-ectomy.] Excision of a lobe of some organ, esp. of a lung or the brain.

1911 Dorland *Med. Dict.* (ed. 6) 464/1 *Lobectomy*, excision of a lobe of a gland, as the thyroid. **1932** *Arch. Surg.* XXV. 898 (*heading*) Lobectomy and pneumectomy in dogs. **1940** *Brit. Jrnl. Psychol.* XXX. 371 Thirty-two cases, each representing a partial lobectomy. **1949** *Amer. Jrnl. Physiol.* CLVII. 135 Liver lobectomy. **1965** [see *computer 2 b]. **1967** S. Taylor et al. *Short Textbk. Surg.* xvi. 208 Treatment is wide removal of the tumour with surrounding healthy lung... Lobectomy may suffice, but pneumonectomy may be required.

lobelia. b. (Earlier example.)

1849 N. Kingsley *Diary* (1914) 94 Lobelia is the great cure, but some are against it.

loblolly. Add: **1. b.** *U.S. colloq.* A mud-hole.

1865 *Memphis* (Tennessee) *Daily Argus* 19 Nov. 3/1 We noticed a party of two or three men attempting to clean off one of them..but as fast as they cleaned away the loblolly, the lob-lolly rolled back again. **1899** Ade *Doc Horne* i. 6 In those days a mud-hole with this deceptive dry crust on top was called a 'loblolly'. **1903** A. Adams *Log Cowboy* xi. 164 His ineffectual struggles caused him to sink farther to the flanks in the loblolly which the tramping of the cattle had caused. **1944** in *Publ. Amer. Dial. Soc.* ii. 58.

3. (Read) = *loblolly pine.*

1819 E. Dana *Geogr. Sk. Western Country* 195 Contiguous to the Florida line, a space, occupying in width from 50 to 60 miles, is timbered with cypress, loblolly, and long and short leafed pine.

lobo. Add: (Further examples.)

1918 C. E. Mulford *Man from Bar-20* ix. 88 What you saw was a bear or a lobo or a cougar come up to see th' fire. *Ibid.* 93 The lobo wolf in the canyon. **1973** R. D. Symons *Where Wagon Led* i. v. 79 But there were still a few buffalo wolves about. We called them lobos.

b. *transf.*

1907 'O. Henry' *Heart of West* 220 I'm not one of them lobo wolves..who are always blaming on women the calamities of life.

lobola. Add: Also **loboler, lobolo.** (Earlier and later examples.) Also, the price or present given for a bride according to this custom. Also *attrib.*

1825 N. Isaacs *Jrnl.* 25 Oct. in *Trav. E. Afr.* (1836) I. iii. 49 Jacob had become enamoured of Enslopee's sister, and had sent three head of cattle to 'Lololer'. **1905** *Westm. Gaz.* 19 Apr. 9/2 The native custom of passing cattle, known variously as 'lobolo', 'ikazi', and 'bohadi', in connexion with marriage. *Ibid.* 8 Sept. 5/1 Many of the natives are able to find the lobola for the luxury of additional wives. **1953** D. Lessing *Five* v. 248 And when our sister marries, he will have her cattle and her lobola money. **1957** G. Muldoon *Trumpeting Herd* ix. 95 According to the Angoni custom, the aunts and not the parents are responsible for fixing the Lobola, or payment for the bride. **1971** *Weekend World* (Johannesburg) 9 May 9/6, I have since paid part of the lobola to her parents. **1972** *Police Rev.* 24 Nov. 1520/3 [Rhodesia] A man may take, under tribal rites, as many wives as he can afford and he pays a bride price (called lobolo) for each.

lobotomy (lǫbǫ·tǒmi). *Surg.* [f. Lob(e + -o + -tomy.] Incision into a lobe; *spec.* incision into the frontal lobe of the brain, esp. in the treatment of mental illness.

1936 Freeman & Watts in *Med. Ann. District of Columbia* V. 326 (*heading*) Prefrontal lobotomy in agitated depression. **1946** *Lancet* 29 June 953/2 Pain of organic disease relieved by prefrontal lobotomy. **1950** [see *leucotomy]. **1972** *Lancet* 8 July 69/2 Schizophrenia is no longer a standard reason for performing any kind of lobotomy. **1973** *Nature* 23 Mar. 222/3 Unlike the classical lobotomy operation, which reached its height of popularity in the 1950s and was used on up to 50,000 people in the US, psychosurgery now rarely involves actually cutting into the brain.

fig. **1959** N. Mailer *Advts. for Myself* (1961) 91 Success had been a lobotomy to my past, there seemed no power from the past which could help me in the present. **1972** *Village Voice* (N.Y.) 1 June 80/2 Even private screenings are not immune to artistic lobotomy, out-of-focus, and other chronic hazards.

Hence **lobo·tomize** *v. trans.*, to perform lobotomy on; **lobo·tomized** *ppl. a.* (also *fig.*, sluggish, stupefied).

1943 *Jrnl. Amer. Med. Assoc.* 27 Nov. 810/1 The lobotomized individual is friendly, good natured and indifferent to others' opinions. **1952** B. Wolfe *Limbo* (1953) xxii. 368, I can tell you a thing or two about lobotomizing little rapists down to good little pacifists. **1955** *Sci. Amer.* June 34/3 One interesting case was that of a lobotomized patient. When she was given LSD, she reverted to her pre-lobotomy depression. **1963** H. C. Shands in H. I. Schneer *Asthmatic Child* vi. 78 Her brother had developed an intractible schizophrenic illness and had been lobotomized. **1971** 'T. Coe' *Jade in Aries* (1973) iv. 38 Manzoni can have our unfortunate friend committed, castrated, lobotomized and deported.

fig. **1953** W. Burroughs *Junkie* (1972) ix. 84 One night, I got lobotomized drunk in Frank's and went to a queer bar. **1968** *N.Y. Times* 5 Feb. 29 It was the life and times of a tightly clustered and rather faceless group, which ended with a robotlike square dance. Mr. Sheppard's lobotomized shuffle was a joy to watch. **1971** *Atlantic Monthly* Apr. 50 [He] was explaining his reasons for calling the police onto the campus, a speech greeted for the most part with a lobotomized silence.

lobster¹. Add: **2. b.** A slow-witted, awkward, or gullible person; a fool, dupe; a bore. *U.S. slang.*

1896 Ade *Artie* x. 91 Every time I ever see him he was a lobster. **1900** —— *Fables in Slang* 54 He went to College, where he proved to be a Lobster. **1947** T. H. White *Elephant & Kangaroo* (1948) xix. 157 When she was giving breakfast to Father Byrne, after a Station, she used to lean forward whenever the old lobster spoke. **1965** *English Studies* XLVI. 468 The noun 'lob' 'dupe' became the root of *lobster* 'dupe; victim'.

5. *lobster mayonnaise, patty, soup*; **lobster bisque,** a thick cream soup made of lobster; hence, the colour of this soup; **lobster cocktail:** see *cocktail 4; **lobster Newburg,** lobster cooked in a thick cream sauce containing sherry or brandy; **lobster thermidor,** cooked lobster mixed with a cream sauce, returned to its shell, sprinkled with cheese, and browned in the oven.

1895 'M. Ronald' *Century Cook Bk.* 569 Lobster bisque. **1929** E. Wilson *I thought of Daisy* i. 8 She seemed appetizing in her lobster-bisque dress. **1967** L. Deighton *London Dossier* 49 Bentley's'..sells lobster bisque freshly tinned. **1974** *Times* 15 Jan. 14/8 Their amazing lobster bisque did much to console me. **1889** A. B. Marshall *Cookery Bk.* vi. 100 Lobster Mayonnaise à l'Osborne. *Ibid.* 101 Lobster Mayonnaise with Aspic. **1913** J. Vaizey *College Girl* xxvii. 368 Iced soup, lobster mayonnaise, salmon and green peas. **1969** *Queen* 17–30 Sept. 50/3, I would not dispute the quality of the lobster mayonnaise at the Marbella Club. [**1895** 'M. Ronald' *Century Cook Bk.* ii. iii. 139 Lobster à la Newburg.] **1914** 'Saki' *Beasts & Super-Beasts* 172 The lobster Newburg and the egg mayonnaise. **1968** H. Franklin *Crash* vii. 82 We..had a dozen oysters, Lobster Newburg and Chablis from the barrel. **1817** I. D'Israeli *Curiosities of Lit.* III. 240 Keep up the fire, and lively play the flame Beneath those lobster-patties. **1845** E. Acton *Mod. Cookery* (ed. 2) xvi. 349 For lobster patties, prepare the fish as for a *vol-au-vent*, but cut it smaller. **1942** Mrs. Belloc Lowndes *Let.* 19 Nov. (1971) 235 There were lobster patties, and queer looking Maid of Honour cakes. **1972** C. Drummond *Death at Bar* i. 36 A large tray of lobster patties. **1723** J. Nott *Cook's & Confectioner's Dict.* sig. S3ᵛ (*heading*) To make Lobster Soop. **1865** R. Riddell *Indian Domestic Econ.* (ed. 6) 37 Lobster soup. [Recipe.] **1960** *Good Housek. Cookery Bk.* (rev. ed.) 78/1 Simple lobster soup. **1973** J. Cleary *Ransom* iii. 74 Lobster soup—why the hell did I buy that? **1933** E. A. Robertson *Ordinary Families* xiii. 291 Lobster thermidor always brings on a sort of gastric aphasia. **1969** R. Airth *Snatch!* ix. 90 She'd made this lobster thermidor.

lobstering, *vbl. sb.* (Later examples.)

1957 *Times Lit. Suppl.* 8 Nov. 676/2 The story opens with lobstering in the Orkneys. **1971** *Country Life* 9 Dec. 1643/1 There is good lobstering and mackerel fishing for the retired.

lobsterish (lǫ·bstǝriʃ), *a.* [f. Lobster¹ + -ish¹.] Resembling a lobster; red-faced.

1914 Chesterton *Wisdom of Father Brown* x. 259 [He] thrust his laughing, lobsterish face into the room. **1946** G. Millar *Horned Pigeon* x. 140 Clifton, a bald, lobsterish little man with freckles all over his muscle-rounded back.

lobstick, var. *lop-stick* (*lop *sb.*³ 4).

local, *sb.*¹ The generally accepted form is now **locale** (see quot. 1926). (Further examples.)

1926 Fowler *Mod. Eng. Usage* 331/1 The 'erroneous form' (OED) *locale* is recommended... If something happens in a locality, the locality becomes that something's locale, or place of happening. **1957** *New Statesman* 2 Nov. 551/3 Madison Avenue is already associated in the public mind (more than subliminally) with tricky manœuvring, having all but replaced Wall Street as a suspect locale. **1970** S. J. Perelman *Baby, it's Cold Inside* 226 My existence would acquire new purpose..if I could visit the actual locale of the movie. **1973** *Nature* 6 July 61/1 These locales were chosen with considerable attention to site safety.

local, *a.* and *sb.*² Add: **A.** *adj.* **2. a.** *local time* (later examples).

1968 H. Franklin *Crash* i. 9 Our estimated time of arrival at Cairo is 17.45 local time, 15.45 G.M.T. **1973** 'E. Ferrars' *Small World of Murder* ii. 20 She had not adjusted her watch to local time. **1974** 'A. Haig' *Peruvian Printout* 99 Arrive Lima 0730hrs local time.

c. *local authority*, an administrative body in local government (cf. Authority 3). Also *attrib.*

1861 Mill *Repr. Govt.* xv. 273 Things..which would be best left to local authorities if there were any whose authority extended to the entire metropolis. **1897** *Lancet* 20 Feb. 537/1 [A Bill] which has for its object the superannuation of the officers and servants of local authorities. This latter term has a wide significance, as it includes practically all local bodies having sanitary and parochial functions, outside boards of guardians and other authorities, to which the Poor Law Officers Superannuation Act of last session relates. **1909** *Daily Chron.* 22 July 5/3 There would soon be a growth in the number of local authority training colleges. **1937** *Discovery* Jan. p. viii, The difficulty of persuading local authorities to provide funds. **1956** J. M. Richards in A. Pryce-Jones *New Outl. Mod. Knowl.* 380 The best British local-authority housing. **1972** M. Gilbert *Body of Girl* iv. 40 We put her into a local authority home..and she stayed there until she was fourteen. **1973** *Inverness Courier* 31 July 4/4 It was noted with regret that a teacher from Kingussie High had been offered, but turned down, a local authority house, and it was left with the Clerk to tell the county housing factor.

d. *local call*, a telephone call within a prescribed area around a telephone exchange (opp. a long-distance call); *local cluster* Astr., a cluster of stars (within the Galaxy) to which the sun belongs; also = **local group*; *local exchange* (see quot. 1940); *local group* (also with capital initials) Astr., the cluster of about twenty galaxies to which our own galaxy belongs; † also = **local cluster*; *local line*, a railway line used by local or stopping trains (opp. *main line*); *local paper*, a newspaper distributed only in a certain area and usu. featuring local, as distinct from national, news; *local radio*, radio that serves a local area only; *local room* U.S., the reporters' room in a newspaper office; *local supercluster* or *supergalaxy* Astr., a supercluster to which it is thought the 'local group' belongs; *local talent*, talented people, *spec.* (*colloq.*) the attractive women, in a particular locality.

1927 E. Murray *Post Office* viii. 138 A fixed annual charge for the installation together with a uniform fee for each effective local call. **1975** D. Bagley *Snow Tiger* xv. 124 The exchange has a bank of batteries... We're all right for local calls. **1922** H. S. Jones *Gen. Astron.* xiv. 359 We must therefore conclude that our stellar universe has a longest diameter of at least 300,000 light-years... It seems probable that the Sun is near the centre of a large local cluster situated eccentrically in this larger system. **1938** W. M. Smart *Stellar Dynamics* i. 2 There is some evidence that the stars in the neighbourhood of the sun form a loose cluster—known as the local cluster—with characteristics of distribution somewhat different from those of the galactic system as a whole. **1971** *New Scientist* 29 July 245/1 The Supergalaxy is, in turn, composed of smaller clusters of galaxies, including the local cluster of about a dozen members, our Galaxy being one of them. **1940** *Chambers's Techn. Dict.* 507/2 *Local exchange*, the exchange to which a given subscriber has a direct line. **1918** J. C. Kapteyn in *Astrophysical Jrnl.* XLVII. 106 Within this boundary the Bo–B5 stars are about 12 times and the B8–B9 stars about 5·7 times more numerous than in the surrounding regions. This alone proves..that we have to do with a local group which probably does not extend in depth much farther than it does laterally. **1922** H. S. Jones *Gen. Astron.* xiv. 359 On the above hypothesis it must be assumed that the B-type stars belong mainly to the local group, for stars of this type do not increase in number with decreasing apparent magnitude as rapidly as do other types. **1936** E. Hubble *Realm of Nebulæ* vi. 125 The known members of the 'local group' are the galactic system with the Magellanic Clouds as its two companions; M31 with M32 and NGC 205 as its companions; M33, NGC 6822 and IC 1613. **1939** Skilling & Richardson *Astron.* xvii. 543 The two large spirals.., M31 and M33, belong to what Hubble calls the Local Group of nebulae. **1965** *Listener* 2 Dec. 891/2 The Andromeda Spiral and the [Magellanic] Clouds belong to what is termed the 'local group'. **1971** D. W. Sciama *Mod. Cosmol.* iii. 40 They [*sc.* galaxies] show considerable clustering, ranging from pairs of galaxies through clusters with fifteen or twenty members like the local group, up to clusters such as the one in Virgo containing several thousand galaxies. **1869** *Bradshaw's Railway Manual* XXI. 86 The question was accordingly referred to the arbitration of Captain Galton, who decided that the Midland might work the local line with Cheltenham..but that it ought not to work the main line. **1967** G. F. Fiennes *I tried to run a Railway* iv. 43 At Seven Kings we went down the local line. **1837** Dickens *Pickw.* xlix. 532 If it gets into one of the local papers, it will be the making of me. **1883** Local paper [see Paper *sb.* 8]. **1947** G. Greene *19 Stories* 78 No book-shops, just *Film Fun* and the local paper. **1967** R. Rendell *New Lease of Death* ix. 88 Elizabeth Crilling sat..reading the Situations Vacant in last week's local paper. **1966** *Economist* 1 Oct. 22/2 That aim should be the creation of a legal framework within which it would be possible to establish, without subsidy, a large number of low-powered local radio transmitting stations. **1971** *Guardian* 17 Nov. 10/6 The real question..is whether local radio can make a good profit and still be local radio. **1974** *Ibid.* 23 Mar. 10/1 Capital Radio, the general commercial radio in London..[is] in competition with four BBC networks and BBC Local Radio. **1890** *Scribner's Monthly* Aug. 157/2 We were all talking about it one night ..in the local room. **1903** E. L. Shuman *Pract. Journalism* 90 Almost the only open door to the editorial room is through the local room. **1948** *Chicago Tribune* iv. 18 Jan. 2/3 The usual banter that goes on in a local room after presstime. **1958** *Nature* 29 Nov. 1479/2 We assume that the local supercluster is in a state of differential rotation

and differential expansion about its centre in the Virgo cluster. **1971** *New Scientist* 29 July 245/1 They analyse the distribution, first of normal bright galaxies known to belong to a local supercluster of galaxies, and then of quasars and some peculiar galaxies. **1953** *Astron. Jrnl.* LVIII. 30 (*heading*) Evidence for a local supergalaxy. **1974** *Encycl. Brit. Macropædia* VII. 830/1 Evidence found in the early 1950s gave strong support to the concept of a 'local supergalaxy'. **1947** M. GILBERT *Close Quarters* xii. 175 You can play darts and engage the local talent in gossip. **1972** R. QUILTY *Tenth Session* 138 He's not the sort who would import local talent just for the hell of it. **1975** *Times* 18 Feb. 13/3 So much 'local' talent, so much unearthed by chance... Is the crafts revival the illustration of the desire for independence and self-sufficiency?

4. b. Radio and Television. *local oscillator*, an oscillator in a receiver that generates oscillations (*local oscillations*) with which an incoming signal is heterodyned.

[**1908** R. A. FESSENDEN in *Electrician* 4 Sept. 787/2 The heterodyne receiver, in which a local field of force actuated by a continuous source of high-frequency oscillations interacts with a field produced by the received oscillations and creates beats of an audible frequency.] **1913** *Proc. IRE* July 102 In the apparatus using a local oscillation generator in combination with a standard rectifier receiver electrical beats are produced and utilized. **1919** R. STANLEY *Text-bk. Wireless Telegr.* (new ed.) II. viii. 143 With an independent local oscillator C.W. reception can take place with very loosely coupled circuits. **1931** [see *HETERODYNE *a.*]. **1967** WHARTON & HOWORTH *Princ. Telev. Reception* v. 74 The function of the mixer is to multiply together the received and local oscillator signals so as to produce an output at the intermediate frequency. **1972** *Sci. Amer.* Feb. 76/1 Radio telescopes receive signals that are at too high a frequency to be recorded directly on magnetic tape. Independent local oscillators must therefore be used to 'heterodyne' the radio-frequency signal.. to a much lower intermediate frequency.

e. local colour, (*c*) something picturesque in itself. Also *local colouring, colourist.*

1854 *Chambers's Jrnl.* 7 Jan. 8/2 Local colouring—*couleur locale*—is a modern expression signifying the accordance..of the adjuncts in a work of art..with the.. subject. **1904** F. M. COLBY *Imaginary Obligations* 7 Stupendous 'local color' work going on at every railway junction, and you heed it not. **1912** A. T. SLOSSON (*title*) A local colorist. **1934** *Amer. Speech* IX. 111/2 Villages with 'local color'. **1949** A. HUXLEY *Let.* 6 Mar. (1969) 593 About the country in which they lived you might consult, for local colour, a travel book by..Freya Stark. **1959** *Listener* 15 Oct. 616/1 [Henry] James never needed such ironic advice, since he was not a local colourist.

B. *sb.* **2. e.** (Earlier and later examples.) Also, a train which stops at all or most of the stations on a line (opp. an *express train*).

1879 WEBSTER Suppl., *Local*..an accommodation railway train, which receives and deposits passengers and freight along the line of the road. **1955** AUDEN *Shield of Achilles* i. 21 Any junction at which you leave the express For a local that swerves off soon into a cutting. **1975** S. JOHNSON *Urbane Guerilla* I. 21 The downtown local was already at the platform.

g. A local branch of a trade union. *N. Amer.*

1888 *Nation* (N.Y.) 3 May 356/3 The Knights of Labor have locals of engineers and firemen. **1911** M. W. OVINGTON *Half a Man* 98 Strong organizations in the South, as the bricklayers, send men North with union membership, who easily transfer to New York locals. **1949** *Newsweek* 18 Apr. 29/1 The local announced..miners would refuse to work in the pits with him. **1967** *Boston Herald* 1 Apr. 1/7 Nicholas P. Morrissey, New England regional director of the Teamsters Union, said Boston Local 25 will vote Sunday at 10 a.m. in the Charlestown armory. **1971** D. RAMSAY *Little Murder Music* 121 Statement of Detective Anthony Crawley, deputed to question members of Local 6, American Federation of Musicians. **1972** *Evening Telegram* (St. John's, Newfoundland) 24 June 3/2 A trawler.. had taken aboard approximately 100,000 pounds of fish, according to Jack Dodd, president of the fishermen's local.

h. (Usu. *the local.*) The public house in the immediate neighbourhood. *colloq.*

1934 *Evening News* 11 Sept. 10/1 After a modest beer or two at the 'local', bedtime calls about nine o'clock. **1937** 'T. SHY' in L. Russell *Press Gang!* 178 What about a snort at the local? **1943** *R.A.F. Jrnl.* Aug. 4 Someone..has done him a good turn by..standing him a drink in the 'local'. **1954** L. M. BOSTON *Children of Green Knowe* 120 The story about it is widespread. It has been told me in much the same form in different 'locals' all over the country. **1957** J. BRAINE *Room at Top* x. 92 The Siege Gun was our local. **1970** G. GREER *Female Eunuch* 142 Women don't nip down to the local.

localitis (lōᵘkăli·tis). *colloq.* [f. LOCAL *a.* + -ITIS.] (See quots.)

1943 *Newsweek* 12 Apr. 18 The 'Pacific first' strategists are now reduced to those afflicted with *localitis*, a military disease..common to those, usually in remote spots, who see their local areas as the axial hub of all strategic movements. **1961** WEBSTER *Localitis*, undue concern (as on the part of a military commander) with a particular area or the problems of a particular situation resulting in failure to visualize adequately the whole of which it is a part. **1962** *Listener* 8 Nov. 747/1 He was suffering from the complaint known in the Foreign Service as 'localitis'—such an intense obsession with his own particular field that he could not see beyond it. **1964** *Economist* 25 July 396/1 Among the world's occupational diseases, there is one that afflicts ambassadors. Americans call it 'localitis'..when an envoy is so captivated by the country..to whom he is accredited that he keeps urging his home government to follow a policy which that country would favour.

localizability (lōᵘ:kăləizăbi·lĭti). [f. LOCALIZABLE *a.* + ABILITY.] The quality of being localizable.

1957 *Think* May 10 Whitehead's reference to the fallacy of simple location, the reminder that existence need not be tied to localizability, was useful in its day. **1966** *Amer. Philos. Q.* III. 233/2 Spatial localizability..is not so shared. **1969** *Nature* 21 June 1207/1 Since the early days of quantum theory there has been much discussion concerning the concept of the localizability of a particle. **1972** *Science* 12 May 592/3 The ultimate localizability of space-time measurements.

localizer (lōᵘ·kăləizəɹ). [f. LOCALIZ(E *v.* + -ER¹.] One who or that which localizes; *spec.* in *Aeronaut.*, a device for transmitting a narrow vertical radio beam along a runway by means of which an incoming aircraft can be brought into line with it and any lateral deviation automatically corrected. (In quot. 1872, 'a reporter of local items'.)

1872 *Newton Kansan* 22 Aug. 3/1 This quiet season.. furnishes poor food for localizers. **1889** *Cent. Dict.*, *Localizer*, a small coil of definite resistance placed at each station of an electric fire-alarm system, which is brought into the circuit when the alarm is given, thus enabling the observer at the receiving-station to know the locality from which the alarm is sent. **1892** MRS. M. BUTLER *Jrnl.* 26 Jan. in H. Tennyson *Tennyson & his Friends* (1911) 216 He [*sc.* Tennyson]..preferred to believe that Homer's descriptions were entirely imaginary. When I said that I thought that a disappointing view, he called me 'a wretched localizer'. **1942** H. L. SMITH *Airways* 364 On the landing field engineers placed a 'localizer', which was a radio device emitting a peculiar beam. **1945** *Aeronautics* Feb. 29/3 The equipment linked up as a whole is then designed to guide the aircraft steadily along a localiser beam to keep it in dead line with the centre of the runway. **1946** *Jrnl. R. Aeronaut. Soc.* Oct. 750/1 The first radio aid to approach and landing, consisting of a Marconi very high frequency track beacon or 'localiser' with associated marker beacons, was installed at Heston aerodrome in 1935. **1965** *Sun* 28 Oct. 8/5 As the plane approaches London Airport it fixes on a 'localiser' beam which brings it into line with the runway.

locally, *adv.* Add: **4.** Also *Comb.*

1896 R. S. S. BADEN-POWELL *Jrnl.* 5 Dec. in *Matabele Campaign* (1897) xix. 480 The locally-born children are as healthy..as you could wish. **1955** J. BETJEMAN in R. S. Thomas *Song at Year's Turning* 11 Locally-printed volumes. **1968** *National Fisherman* Aug. 26-A/3 U.S. firms are willing and ready to buy locally caught tuna. **1975** *Country Life* 16 Jan. 143/1 Perhaps Jay was asked ..to revise a locally-made design.

locant (lǫ·kănt). *Chem.* [f. L. *locant-*, *locans*, pres. pple. of *locāre* (see LOCATE *v.*).] A number or letter in the name or cipher of a compound that indicates the position in its molecular structure of a constituent atom or group.

1946 G. M. DYSON in *R. Inst. Chem. Lect. New Notation Org. Chem.* 10 A number immediately preceding a symbol is referred to as a locant, as, for example, in '2ZN' or '6, 7QC'; in the second example both 6 and 7 are locants. **1952** *Chem. & Engin. News* 2 June 2337/1 He [*sc.* G. M. Dyson] also thinks that a subscript might be used to indicate a number of identical locants; for example 1,1,1,2,2,3,3,4-octachloro- might be written $1_3,2_2,3_2,4$-octachloro-. **1965** *Nomencl. Org. Chem.* (I.U.P.A.C.) C. 29 The starting point and direction of numbering of a compound are chosen so as to give lowest locants to the following structural factors (if present). **1968** R. S. CAHN *Introd. Chem. Nomencl.* (ed. 3) viii. 79 Locants used for the ring system are the usual numerals—the '2' in the examples above refer to the 2-position of the naphthalene nucleus.

Locarno (lǒkā·ɹno). The name of a town in Switzerland used to designate the conference held there and the treaties signed as a result in 1925 between Germany and several other European countries for the preservation of peace and the continuation of existing territorial boundaries. So *transf.*, a similar conference, treaty, or agreement. Hence **Loca·rnist** *sb.*, a supporter or advocate of the policy adopted at the Locarno Conference; also as *adj.*; **Loca·rnize** *v. intr.*, to settle disputes by pacific means.

1926 *Glasgow Herald* 19 Feb. 8 Sir Austen had called Locarno only a beginning... Some business men, having settled a quarrel among themselves, said that they had 'Locarnized'. *Ibid.* 5 Mar. 9 We shall go to Geneva to work there as 'Locarnists' in the Locarno spirit. **1927** *Daily Tel.* 21 June 13/3 After Locarno there was..a genuine desire to get on better terms with the Reich. *Ibid.*, The demand for the evacuation of the Rhineland..has met with opposition, even in strongly Locarnist quarters. *Ibid.* 6 Sept. 9/5 All the talk about Eastern or Danubian Locarnos is very much in the air, when even the Western Locarno is seen to be in difficulties already. **1937** *Ann. Reg. 1936* [74] The answers of Germany and Italy to the invitation sent on July 24 to a new 'Locarno' Conference were still being awaited. *Ibid.* [189] The Hitler Government could count on the help of Italy in its negotiations for a new Locarno Pact. **1937** KOESTLER *Spanish Testament* ii. 60 The Europe of the Locarno period..would have reacted..with a storm of indignation. **1971** A. BULLOCK *20th Century* 72/1 Stresemann had refused to conclude an Eastern Locarno which would mean accepting Germany's postwar frontiers with Poland and Czechoslovakia, and in April 1926 he balanced his acceptance of Locarno by a new treaty of friendship with Soviet Russia.

locatable (lǒkēⁱ·tăb'l), *a.* Also **locateable.** [f. LOCAT(E *v.* + -ABLE.] Capable of being located.

1936 *Discovery* Apr. 122/1 Thus we find..four parallel alleys, or 'zones', locatable at the 'wavelength' for the stream. **1964** *English Studies* XLV. 250 Any locatable regional dialect. **1968** E. RUSSENHOLT *Heart of Continent* III. vii. 101 Officials of 'the Company' and some free traders are locateable.

locater, var. LOCATOR (in Dict. and Suppl.).

location. Add: **5.** (Earlier and later S. Afr. examples.) For 'Also..natives.' read 'Also, in South Africa, the quarters or area set apart for black South Africans; occas. also used of an area in which Coloureds live.'

1833 G. GREIG *S. Afr. Almanac & Directory* 191 The population consists of a mixture of Bastards and Hottentots, who are divided into about 60 parties, each of which has a district location allotted to it. **1835** D'URBAN in W. M. Macmillan *Bantu, Boer, & Briton* (1929) 128 He may be placed in a location in His Majesty's Colony [*sc.* the Cape]. **1851** J. J. FREEMAN *Tour S. Afr.* xv. 361 They are located by the Government, and on these locations they cultivate lands and build their native huts. **1926** O. SCHREINER *From Man to Man* II. ix. 316 You..stood looking down at the..little brown huts of the Kaffir Location sleeping at your feet. *Ibid.*, A Kaffir servant might be seen hurrying from the Location to the town. **1945** R. HARGREAVES *Enemy at Gate* 241 The 'location' occupied by the half-breed fraternity. **1961** T. MATSHIKIZA *Chocolates for my Wife* v. 45 Several beasts were sacrificed and thousands of location residents partook of the traditional royal roast. **1971** *Rand Daily Mail* 4 Sept. 5/1 Transkeians were against the establishment of locations in their territory.

c. In the production of motion pictures, an exterior place, away from a film-studio, where a scene is filmed; freq. in phr. *on location.* Also *attrib.* orig. *U.S.*

1914 *Scribner's Mag.* Mar. 276/1 It was his duty..to pick out 'locations', as are called the scenes and backgrounds of a moving-picture play. **1918** H. CROY *How Motion Pictures are Made* v. 120 If an exterior is chosen for the first scenes it has been selected in advance by the 'location man' and the director. *Ibid.* iv. 148 Now many actors are..in the studio or on location. **1928** 'I. HAY' *Poor Gentleman* iii. 42 They're converting the whole place into what is called a Location, where they can stage dramas of English country life. **1935** *Time* 8 July 32/3 The fault most likely to creep into pictures made on location comes from their producers' natural reluctance to throw away bits of local color even when these impede their story. **1957** M. SUMMERTON *Sunset Hour* iv. 62, I have been working hard... Working out location shots. **1971** *Daily Tel.* (Colour Suppl.) 12 Nov. 51/1 On location in Yugoslavia and at Pinewood Studios I talked to four people deeply involved in the filming of *Fiddler on the Roof.* **1973** J. LEASOR *Host of Extras* iii. 41 I'm hiring them out to a film company. Two weeks guaranteed, on location. Corsica.

7. The action of discovering, or the ability to discover or determine, the position of a person or thing.

1900 *Geogr. Jrnl.* Oct. 382 These birds [*sc.* penguins] must have a wonderful power of location. **1962** A. NISBETT *Technique Sound Studio* 259 The script is also marked ..with notes for quick groove location. *Ibid.* 276 These help in the exact location of editing points on tape.

locational (lǒkēⁱ·ʃənăl), *a.* [f. LOCATION + -AL.] Of or pertaining to location.

1909 in *Cent. Dict.* Suppl. **1926** *Cleaning & Dyeing World* Oct. 19 He has one advantage, however, which the extensive advertiser does not have, and that is locational identification. **1957** *Economist* 5 Oct. 15/1 These two locational accidents could have served as the theme of the conference. **1960** ROBBINS & TERLECKYJ (*title*) Money metropolis: a locational study of financial activities in the New York region. **1971** *Nature* 18 June 426/2 In the population sector, locational attraction is a function of existing floorspace and available land in a zone.

locator. Add: Also **locater.**

4. Something which locates; *spec.* a device for indicating the position or direction of something. Also *attrib.*

1902 *Cyclists' Touring Club Gaz.* Aug. 359/1 A spicule of flint..pierced my tube, but kindly remained in evidence as a locater. **1919** *Nature* 30 Oct. 182/1 Sound-locators were also used to board anti-submarine craft. **1951** *Gloss. Aeronaut. Terms* (*B.S.I.*) III. 29 *Locator beacon*, a non-directional radio-beacon of low power, associated with a recognized instrument landing system. **1971** J. B. CARROLL et al. *Word Frequency Bk.* p. xix, The editorial outputs prepared from the tape files included..a locator list that can be used to determine the source of every token in the Corpus. **1973** *Black Panther* 21 July p. B, The automatic car locator system.

loc. cit. (lǫk sit), abbrev. of L. *loco citato* or *locus citatus*, '(in) the place cited', i.e. in the book, etc., that has previously been quoted.

1854 H. H. MILMAN *Hist. Latin Christianity* I. II. iii. 149 In the words of the ecclesiastical historian,.. by such a deed a deep stain was fixed on Cyril and the Church of Alexandria. [fn.] Socrat. loc. cit. **1937** M. LEACH *Amis & Amiloun* p. xc, Kölbing, *loc. cit.*, and also in his edition of *Amis and Amiloun.* **1969** Y. KAMISAR in A. B. Downing *Euthanasia* 132 Chesterton, 'Euthanasia and Murder', loc. cit.

Loch Fyne (lǫχ fəin). The name of a sea loch in West Scotland, used *attrib.* to designate a

type of fishing-boat having a standing lug mainsail.

1906 *Yachting Monthly* II. 15/1 The first boat built on Loch Fyne lines, and approximating in size to the ordinary fishing boat, was the May. *Ibid.* 19 Col. Dunlop's Loch Fyne ketch Marsailidh. **1930** *Ibid.* XLIX. 209/2 More odd rigs have been tried out here than in any other class in existence, including split lugs, Loch Fyne skiff rigs, and sprit sails. **1974** R. SIMPER *Scottish Sail* 31 The Loch Fyne skiffs were rather lightly constructed and seem not to have lasted very long.

Lochinvar (lǫkinvā·ɹ). The name of the hero of a ballad in Sir Walter Scott's *Marmion*, used allusively for a young male eloper; also *transf.* (see also quot. 1951).

1879 C. M. YONGE *Magnum Bonum* I. xii. 233 His bride..had had a young Lochinvar, and even in her wedding dress, favoured by sympathising servants, had escaped down the back stairs of a London hotel, and been married at the nearest Church. **1890** 'R. BOLDREWOOD' *Colonial Reformer* III. xxviii. 129 Much he marvelled at this Australian edition of 'Young Lochinvar'. **1906** 'O. HENRY' *Four Million* (1916) 125 He..received the hearty thanks of the backyard Lochinvar. **1936** J. BUCHAN *Island of Sheep* ix. 170 The young Lochinvar business was rather out of my usual line. **1951** E. HILL *Territory* 311 Lochinvars sold the women to the drovers and the stations at £10 a head. *Ibid.* 444 *Lochinvar, the*, old time term for catching lubras to work cattle, etc. **1966** [see *EXTRAMURAL *a.* b]. **1970** *New Yorker* 3 Oct. 83/1 The majority of young artistic Lochinvars..have turned..to the tools and processes of modern industrial technology. **1972** 'J. & E. BONETT' *No Time to Kill* iv. 45 She looked.. expectant, waiting..for the return of her young Lochinvar. But young Lochinvar..had found another bride, and she had married Eldred.

Lochlann (lǫ·χlan). *Hist.* [a. Irish *Lochlann* Scandinavia, *Lochlannach a.* and *sb.* Scandinavian.] A viking, (ancient) Scandinavian, Norseman.

1857 W. REEVES *Adamnan's Life St. Columba* 332/2 About the same time the Fortrenns and Lochlanns fought a battle. **1861** F. O'CURRY *Lect. Manuscript Materials Anc. Irish Hist.* x. 225 A book for the saints, and a book for the Fomorians, Lochlanns or Danes. **1880** W. F. SKENE *Celtic Scotl.* I. I. vi. 304 Forty-eight of the number of Icolumkill slain by the Lochlanns. **1905** *Westm. Gaz.* 15 Aug. 2/1 The ships of the Lochlanns lie in the river, and never send a man against her. **1922** JOYCE *Ulysses* 46 Galleys of the Lochlanns ran here to beach, in quest of prey.

lochlet (lǫ·χ,lėt). *rare.* [f. LOCH[1] + -LET.] A little loch.

1925 A. S. ALEXANDER *Tramps across Watersheds* 40 These lochlets with their ancient relics are mostly meadows now.

Loch Ness. [LOCH[1].] The name of a loch in Scotland used *attrib.* of a water-monster alleged to exist in its waters. Also *fig.*

1933 *Inverness Courier* 9 June 5/5 The Loch Ness 'monster' was seen near the west end of the Loch. **1934** *Discovery* Jan. 14/1 That elusive creature the sea-serpent is again in the news, this time in the shape of the Loch Ness 'monster'. **1937** *Ibid.* Nov. 334/2 Though the Loch Ness monster itself were laid before him in all its magnitude, he would still surely find an outlet..for his nervous, driving, shrewish disposition. **1959** A. HARDY *Fish & Fisheries* xiv. 364, I am deliberately not discussing the so-called Loch Ness monster. If there is some strange creature there it is clearly not a sea-beast bigger than a seal which might make its way up the shallow River Ness. **1965** *New Society* 9 Sept. 7/3 Britain's brain drain appears, then, to be something of a Loch Ness monster. It surfaces sporadically, then vanishes from view. **1971** *Stornoway Gaz.* 10 July 1/6 Preparations are now complete and they set off in a few days' time to try and capture that elusive denizen of the deep—the Loch Ness Monster.

lock, *sb.*[2] Add: **1. b.** *lock and key*, delete 'rarely *attrib.*' and add: also *fig.* (freq. *attrib.*) with allusion to the structural complementarity or mutual specificity of a lock and its key.

[**1894** E. FISCHER in *Ber. d. Deut. Chem. Ges.* XXVII. 2992 Um ein Bild zu gebrauchen, will ich sagen, dass Enzym und Glucosid wie Schloss und Schlüssel zu einander passen müssen, um eine chemische Wirkung auf einander ausüben zu können.] **1901** C. A. MITCHELL tr. *Oppenheimer's Ferments* v. 65 Two haptophore groups coinciding with one another ('lock and key') and a subsequently active zymophore group. **1924** K. G. FALK *Chem. Enzyme Actions* (ed. 2) v. 116 E. Fischer's lock-and-key simile for the mutual getting together of substrate and enzyme, each fitting in with the other, gives a mechanical picture of the action. **1950** *Sci. News* XV. 120 So far, blood group antibodies have been described as having the property of reacting by agglutination with red cells which contain the specific antigen, and with no others, on the lock-and-key principle. **1969** *Times* 25 Apr. 13/6 It seems that some of the proteins in the mixture are able to recognize and bind to certain sites on the RNA molecule by a lock-and-key mechanism. **1974** *Physics Bull.* Dec. 581/1 The lock and key interaction between enzyme and substrate does not usually involve strong covalent bonds.

5. *lock, stock, and barrel* (earlier and later examples). Also as *advb. phr.* (See also STOCK *sb.*[1] 28 b.)

1842 W. T. THOMPSON *Major Jones' Courtship* (1844) 66 All moved, lock, stock, and barrel. **1855** S. A. HAMMETT *Wonderful Adventures Captain Priest* xii. 76 He sold off his feathered stock, 'lock, stock, and barrel'. **1909** [see *CAGEY *a.*]. **1961** B. FERGUSSON *Watery Maze* xii. 292 One of the ministries would take over lock, stock and barrel the administration. **1974** P. ERDMAN *Silver Bears* i. 12, I bought us a Swiss bank: lock, stock and barrel.

10. Add. to def.: also, a similar chamber used between air at atmospheric pressure and either water (e.g. outside a submarine) or a vacuum (e.g. outside a spacecraft).

1914 S. F. WALKER *Submarine Engin.* iii. 35 The air lock ..is a chamber with doors at each end, arranged so that only a small quantity of air or water can enter each time the lock is opened. **1959** 'WYNDHAM' & PARKER *Outward Urge* ii. 66 The duty-man operated the lock, and presently Troon was outside. **1961** E. LEYLAND *Crash Dive* viii. 91 Taking the place of the Twill Trunk..came the Escape Chamber method, a permanent chamber or lock entered by way of a watertight door.

11. b. *lock and block* (*system*): a system of railway signalling by which a train does not enter a section of line until the preceding train has left it, the signal being locked at 'danger' and only released when the preceding train leaves the section.

1902 *Encycl. Brit.* XXXIII. 146/2 'Lock-and-block' has been used to a limited extent on a good many lines in England and a half-dozen in America. **1905** *Westm. Gaz.* 12 Jan. 7/2 The failure was partly due to faulty line circuits of the lock and block instruments. **1950** *Engineering* 1 Dec. 436/1 Signals..operated mechanically..with the Sykes lock-and-block system. **1956** *Railway Mag.* Nov. 748/1 The Sykes lock-and-block, although old fashioned, ..has a long record of reliable service in the operation of dense traffic.

c. *Rugby Football.* A player in the second row of the scrummage (see quots.); this position. Also *attrib.*, as *lock-forward, -man.*

1906 GALLAHER & STEAD *Compl. Rugby Footballer* vii. 100 Working the [New Zealand] Scrum... The lock [etc.]. *Ibid.* 104 Immediately behind these hookers..is he whom we call the lock man... His duty is to hold or lock the two hookers. *a* **1914** J. E. RAPHAEL *Mod. Rugby Football* (1918) xvii. 225 The middle man in the second row, the 'lock', bound the 'hookers' together, not his own row. **1956** V. JENKINS *Lions Rampant* ii. 23 Mr Siggins..was one of the finest lock-forwards of his day. **1959** *Times* 10 Sept. 4/3 It was strange to see the former hefty England wing, Woodward, at lock in the blues' scrummage. **1971** *Sunday Express* (Johannesburg) 28 Mar. 20/6 Springboks fullback Ian McCallum, prop Hannes Marais and lock Frik du Preez are in the opening fixture.

12. a. Delete † *Obs.* and add later examples.

1954 E. DOMINY *Teach Yourself Judo* iii. 41 There are only a few basic types of lock and these can be developed by anyone sufficiently interested. **1974** 'J. LE CARRÉ' *Tinker, Tailor* xxii. 189 Guillam selected Tarr's right arm and flung it into a lock against his back, bringing it very near to breaking. **1974** P. ERDMAN *Silver Bears* xiii. 143 He would sooner see the whole bank go down the drain.. than get beaten by us. Unless we develop an even better lock on him—and that won't be easy.

15. b. The turning of the front wheels of a motor vehicle to change its direction of motion; the full extent of such turning.

1908 *Autocar Handbk.* (ed. 2) xvi. 123 There should be plenty of 'lock' for the wheels, which, with an inconsequence not unusual in our language, means that the wheels shall be quite free to be deflected through a large angle. **1939** L. MACNEICE *Autumn Jrnl.* xxiv. 79 The quick lock of a taxi. **1959** *Observer* 1 Mar. 21/5 From lock to lock it takes 3⅝ turns, allowing prompt correction if a heavy throttle foot should provoke tail wag on a slippery surface. Turning circle is 37 ft. **1967** *Autocar* 28 Dec. 10/2 The 35 ft 3 in. mean turning circle with 4·25 turns lock-to-lock is not excessive. **1974** L. MEYNELL *Fairly Innocent* xi. 148, I must have got on to the wrong lock... I don't really understand about going backwards.

18. (Later example.)

1922 JOYCE *Ulysses* 509 Mary Shortall that was in the lock with the pox.

19. a. (sense 9) *lock-bar, -bridge, -canal, -charge, -cut, -house* (example), *-pen, -station, -thief, -wall.*

1923 F. L. PACKARD *Four Stragglers* 312 The lock-bar worked through the side of the pier wall. **1865** DICKENS *Mut. Fr.* II. iv. i. 162 He crossed back by his plank lock-bridge to the towing-path side. **1903** *Westm. Gaz.* 2 Jan. 3/1, I imagine that the Panama waterway is to be a lock canal. **1877** J. HABBERTON *Jericho Road* ii. 20 Dont you b'leeve she could run the dam at Mount Zion, and dodge paying lock-charges? **1905** *Westm. Gaz.* 16 Aug. 5/3 Motor boats..probably find their way down lock-cuts made more difficult and tedious than before. **1908** *Daily Chron.* 30 Apr. 1/2 An assistant lockkeeper..found the body of a child floating in the lock-cut. **1865** Lock-house [in Dict., sense 9 d]. **1907** *Westm. Gaz.* 20 Aug. 12/1 The lock-pen..opens and shuts now to let through the *Queen Elizabeth* in solitary state. **1863** E. E. HALE *If, Yes & Perhaps* (1868) 16, I would start in the morning to walk to the lock-station at Brockport on the canal. *Ibid.* 22 At night I walked the deck till one o'clock..to keep guard against the lock-thieves. **1885** WARREN & CLEVERLY *Wand. 'Beetle'* 61 He ran along the lock-wall to open his gates when he saw us coming.

20. lock-box *U.S.*, a delivery letter-box provided with a lock; **lock-in,** the action or fact of locking in a person or thing (see LOCK *v.*[1] 2 and *3 e); also *attrib.*; **Locknit,** the proprietary name (but see quot. 1935) of a fabric knitted with an interlocking stitch; also **lock-knit**; freq. *attrib.*; **lock-nut,** add: also, a nut specially designed to prevent accidental loosening once it has been tightened; (further examples); **lock-step** (further example); also *fig.*, a rigid or unchanging pattern; also *attrib.*, rigid, unchanging.

1872 E. CRAPSEY *Nether Side N.Y.* 150 C. H. Chester, M.D., Lock Box 4, Reading, Pa. **1906** M. E. FREEMAN *By Light of Soul* 384 She saw one letter slanted across the dusty glass of the box. It was not a lock box, and she had to ask the postmaster for the letter. **1955** E. POUND *Section: Rock Drill* lxxxviii. 42 A First Folio (Shx) in his lock-box. **1920** *Contemp. Rev.* Dec. 823 To the lock-out of the masters, the workers replied with the 'lock-in' movement—the temporary capture of the factories and workshops. **1970** *Globe & Mail* (Toronto) 25 Sept. B7/6 There may be some giving in on peripheral items such as reducing the length of lock-in clauses. **1973** *Times* 25 Jan. 23/5 First, there is the 'lock-in' factor. Given additional tax burdens, the first reaction of any jobber is to feel less inclined to sell. **1935** *Trade Marks Jrnl.* 8 May 588/2 *Lansil Locknit.* Registration of this Trade Mark shall give no right to the exclusive use of the word 'Locknit'. Knitted piece goods composed wholly or mainly of artificial silk. Cellulose Acetate Silk Company, Ltd...Lancaster. **1936** *Times* 14 Feb. 9/5 A three-piece in pale blue chalk stripe locknit and plain jersey. **1951** *Good Housek. Home Encycl.* 231/1 Lock-knit or open weave articles should be dried flat. **1952** 'J. TEY' *Singing Sands* vi. 93 Hams hung from the roof among strings of locknit undergarments. **1973** R. RENDELL *Some lie & Some Die* ix. 84 Passing her iron across a pair of pink locknit knickers. **1907** *Westm. Gaz.* 21 Nov. 4/2 The steering is..of the worm and segment type, the adjustment of which is easily effected by releasing a lock-nut and slightly turning the steering column. **1964** S. CRAWFORD *Basic Engin. Processes* xiv. 304 The rollers are secured by tightening the locknut with the special adjusting key. **1972** *Practical Motorist* Oct. 162/3 If this resistance is felt *before* the vertical position of the lever is reached, or if no resistance is felt at all, adjustment can be made by loosening the lock-nut 'C'. **1836** T. POWER *Impressions Amer.* I. 379 They [*sc.* convicts] were marched from the building in squads, using what is called the 'lock-step', and were jammed together as closely as they could possibly travel. **1955** *Sci. News Let.* 16 Apr. 255 A 'what will people think' disease is driving us all, cab driver as well as scientist, toward straitjacketed thinking and lock-step living. **1963** *New Society* 7 Nov. 19/1 The prescribed lock-step of school life. **1971** *New Yorker* 30 Oct. 155 Mrs. Handy's lockstep methods (copy the great novelists, read the 'Masters of the Far East', stay away from girls) produced a handful of published novels. **1972** *Business Week* 18 Mar. 32/1 The break could occur if Ireland did not follow Britain into the EEC. For the republic marches in an economic lookstep with Britain. **1973** *Where* Apr. 109/3 Students working.. in their own way, and at their own pace, freed from the 'lock-step' of the classroom. **1973** *Time* 25 June 74/1 The 'whole thing' was an attempt..to break what he calls 'the lockstep'—the educational process that leads in a straight line from kindergarten through graduate school, and often onward into the walled-in offices of academia.

lock, *v.*[1] Add: **3. e.** Const. *in.* To trap or fix firmly or irrevocably; to fix in position.

1953 BERREY & VAN DEN BARK *Amer. Thes. Slang* (1954) § 623a/7 *Locking in*, adjusting the televised image for a clear picture. *Ibid.* § 623a/10 *Locked in*, televised image properly synchronized. **1959** *Economist* 16 May 634/2 This may tend to 'lock in' many traders with their present holdings. **1968** *Sunday Times* 3 Mar. 51 The Extra campaign had to be aggressive because people are so locked in to coupons. **1968** *Telegraph* (Brisbane) 8 Nov. 14/7 Anything I knew..was too late to help Ford. They already were locked in on their program. **1972** *Sci. Amer.* Nov. 96/3 Lowering its temperature back to normal locks in any deformations due to loadings.

5. lock out. c. *Electronics* and *Computers.* Temporarily to prevent the operation or use of. Cf. *LOCK-OUT 2.

1953 R. C. WALKER *Relays* viii. 222 Voltage selective systems have been devised in which the value of the applied voltage actuates one of a group of thermistors and locks out all the others. **1962** *Gloss. Terms Automatic Data Processing* (*B.S.I.*) 47 During an autonomous peripheral transfer, the storage blocks concerned may be locked out to prevent reference to those blocks until completion of the transfer. **1972** *Computer Jrnl.* XV. 194/2 Another circumstance in which an investigation..is called for is when a record that has been locked out preparatory to being updated remains locked out for an unreasonable time.

6. *to lock up* (Printing): (later examples).

1927 R. B. MCKERROW *Introd. Bibliogr.* I. ii. 16 The furniture employed to fill up the chase is 'locked up' by the insertion and driving home of wedges or 'quoins'. **1972** P. GASKELL *New Introd. Bibliogr.* 80 The quoins were driven home with a mallet and 'shooting stick' to lock the forme up tightly.

7. d. (Earlier U.S. examples.)

1839 *Hist. Virgil A. Stewart* 23 (Th.), They are enemies, and let them lock horns. **1855** *Knickerbocker* XLVI. 95 As neither of the trains stop at way-stations, I expect nothing more than to see the two lock horns at the corner of my kitchen.

12. *to lock on to*: **a.** *intr.* Of radar or other equipment: to locate and then to track automatically; to accept as a target or reference object that is thereafter maintained as such (usu. automatically).

1949 *Jrnl. R. Aeronaut. Soc.* May 439/2 The aerial system has been designed to 'lock on' to the responder signal and to 'follow it' during its motion through the atmosphere quite automatically and with great accuracy. **1964** *Discovery* Oct. 7/3 The stabilized instrument platform has been developed..to lock on to the sun (or moon) within two minutes of lift-off. **1966** *New Scientist* 25 Aug. 405

Stars were often mistaken for aircraft lights. In 27 cases pilots chasing a target aircraft had 'locked on' to a star for periods between one and ten minutes and actually tried to fly up to it. **1968** *Times* 10 Dec. 6/7 The satellite was to have used six star trackers which would lock on to reference stars.

b. *trans.* To cause (a piece of equipment) to lock on to some object.

1954 K. W. Gatland *Devel. Guided Missile* (ed. 2) iv. 118 After a short period, radar tracking and aiming devices are 'locked on' to target, and from then on the whole attack is automatic. **1964** *Guardian* 1 Dec. 1/4 Their fourth attempt to 'lock' Mariner-4 on to the star Canopus. **1971** *Nature* 8 Oct. 367/3 The flight took place aboard a Skylark sounding rocket, which was stabilized and 'locked on' to the strong X-ray source Sco X-1 during the four minutes of observing time.

lockage. Add: **2. e.** The passage (of a vessel) through a lock.

1913 J. B. Bishop *Panama Gateway* v. iv. 375 The average number of lockages through the..Canal..was 39 per day.

locked, *a.*² **2.** (Earlier example.)

1819 D. Thomas *Trav. Western Country* 30 The milldams on this stream are locked.

locked, *ppl. a.* Add: **d.** *locked-coil*: used *attrib.* to denote a rope or cable which has the outer strands of such a shape as to lock together and form a smooth cylindrical surface.

1885 *Cassell's Family Mag.* Dec. 59/1 A new kind of rope, called the locked-coil rope, has recently been brought out. **1952** T. Bryson *Mining Machinery* (ed. 3) x. 246 The desire to increase further the wearing surface of ropes led to construction of locked-coil ropes.

e. *locked-room*: used *attrib.* to denote a mystery, or a mystery story, involving a locked room.

1942 H. Haycraft *Murder for Pleasure* vi. 104 *The Mystery of the Yellow Room*..remains..the most brilliant of all 'locked room' novels. **1954** J. Symons *Narrowing Circle* iii. 14, I listened to the dictabook on my desk, which was a deliberately old-fashioned locked-room style detective story. **1965** 'D. Shannon' *Death-Bringers* (1966) vii. 83 He'd never believed there were such things as Locked Room mysteries in real life. **1970** —— *Unexpected Death* (1971) xiii. 194 Lock the door on the outside and shove the key under the door. No locked-room puzzle.

f. *locked groove*: on a gramophone record, a circular groove into which the normal spiral groove runs.

1958 in *Chambers's Techn. Dict.* Add. **1962** A. Nisbett *Technique Sound Studio* xii. 207 On disc, using locked grooves to provide rhythmic repetitions.

g. With *in*: of a surfer, enveloped in and being carried along on a wave.

1965 *S. Afr. Surfer* I. iii. 7 Its breathlessly fast hollow waves afford the lucky surfer an easy 300 yard locked-in ride. *Ibid.* 33 Each situation, from being locked-in to wiped-out, is entirely dependent on how the surfer uses the wave. **1971** *Studies in English* (Univ. of Cape Town) Feb. 27 If the wave is very hollow, as at Gansbaai, then the wave may arch over the surfer and he will get covered up and enjoy a tube ride. This is called being locked in.

locker, *sb.*¹ **7.** *locker-room* (later examples).

1906 *Westm. Gaz.* 11 July 8/1 Two extra payments are a penny for a bath, including towel and soap, and 6d. deposit for the use of a large locker in the locker room. **1931** *Maclean's Mag.* 1 Aug. 28/4 Mere males are lucky to find sanctuary in locker room, grill and bar. **1934** [see *bathroom]. **1972** *Newsweek* 10 Jan. 30/2 On one side of the crowded Kansas City locker room, veteran quarterback Lenny Dawson dressed hurriedly and disappeared.

lock-on (lǫ·kǫn). [f. vbl. phr. *to lock on* (*to*): see *lock *v.*¹ 12.] **1.** (The commencement of) automatic tracking.

1960 *Aeroplane* 4 Mar. 278/1 The Bloodhound target radar lock-on technique will be demonstrated and a model of the missile is to be 'fired'. **1967** *Sci. Amer.* May 83 (Advt.), When an air-to-air training missile 'sees' its target, a new microminiaturized signal amplifier..tells the pilot that lock-on has been achieved. **1971** *Time* 15 Feb. 8 As *Antares* swooped below that altitude, its radar remained inactive. 'C'mon, radar,' Mitchell implored. 'Get the lock-on.'

2. The establishment of a rigid physical connection.

1967 *Sunday Times* 23 Apr. 8 Back at the surface, a lock-on device enables divers to transfer to a larger chamber on board, releasing the sub to return to work with a fresh diving team. **1968** *New Scientist* 6 June 509/1 As it will need to contend with the underwater currents playing around the submarine, it will need extremely sensitive means of controlling its position just before lock-on. **1969** *Jane's Freight Containers 1968–69* 574/2 The top lift cradle has..power-guided lock-on at each of the four corners. Safe lock-on indicators are monitored by the operator in the cab.

lock-out. Add: Also **lockout.** (Earlier and later examples.)

1854 *Westm. Rev.* V. 120 How far the 'lock-out' has been forced upon the masters by partial 'strikes' of the men,.. what proportion of the workpeople have been victims rather than combatants 'locked-out',..these are some among many much disputed points. **1889** [see *close-down]. **1926** *Times* 5 May 2/1 Lord Gainford, speaking for the mine owners, said the notices which were put up were not lockout notices. **1955** *Times* 17 Aug. 7/2 The employers announced that the strike would be met by a lockout, and there seems to be no prospect that they will change their attitude. **1970** T. Lupton *Managem. & Social Sci.* (ed. 2) iii. 62 The hidden sanction of strike or lockout always underlies bargaining. **1971** *Daily Tel.* 20 Oct. 16 It is somewhat exceptional in industrial relations for employers to resort to a lock-out in reprisal against strikes and overtime bans. **1974** *Socialist Worker* 9 Nov. 16/1 Truck workers at British Leyland's AEC plant marched through Southall last Thursday chanting and determined after the month-long lock-out.

2. *Electronics* and *Computers.* The automatic temporary prevention of the operation or use of a relay or other device. Usu. *attrib.*

1924 T. Croft *Electr. Machinery & Control Diagrams* vii. 213 When current passes through the contactor, both the closing and the lockout portions of the switch are magnetized. **1945** '*Electr. Engineer' Ref. Bk.* vii. 105 When the directional relay closes contacts for fault current fed out of the feeder, the secondary coil operates the associated attracted armature relay which initiates a lockout operation. The overcurrent relay cannot operate because the secondary coil is not connected to the series coil. **1952** I. Frazee et al. *Automotive Electr. Syst.* vii. 369 Vibrating and lockout circuit breakers consist of a coil winding and a set of contact points... When current in excess of the rated value flows..a plunger..opens the contact points. **1960** *McGraw-Hill Encycl. Sci. & Technol.* XIII. 348/2 The problem in all applications of lockout circuits is that of concurrently competing circuits, among which one has to be picked for some action. **1961** N. Chapin *Programming Computers for Business Applic.* viii. 198 The high-speed transfer-of-data phase during which the buffer empties into or fills from high-speed storage..is sometimes called the lockout phase. **1972** *Computer Jrnl.* XV. 194/2 The information in the record is then read, any necessary checking done, and the update performed. The updated version of the record is then inserted in the file and finally the lockout is cancelled.

lockschen, lockshan, lockshen, varr. *lokshen.

locksman² (lǫ·ksmæn). [f. pl. of Lock *sb.*¹ + Man *sb.*¹] In Kingston, Jamaica, a member of the Ras Tafari cult who wears his hair long and plaited as a mark of his membership.

1960 M. G. Smith et al. *Ras Tafari Movement in Kingston, Jamaica* iv. 23 The Locksmen, whose hair is matted and plaited and never cut, neither their beards. **1966** *Guardian* 3 Feb. 8/1 The long-haired Rastas, the Locksmen, are the ones Jamaicans laugh at in the streets.

lock-up, *sb.* (*a.*). Add: **1. a.** (Earlier and later examples.) Also *attrib.*

1845 T. J. Green *Jrnl. Texian Expedition* xvii. 300 To elude the vigilance of the officer at lock-up time. **1910** A. Huxley *Let.* 5 June (1969) 37 To crown all we were 5 minutes late for lock-up! **1914** 'I. Hay' *Lighter Side School Life* iv. 104 Rules, roll-calls, bounds, lock-ups. **1968** *Eton College Chron.* 22 Mar. 6221, Sat. Mar 23 Lock-up, 7.15 p.m.

b. Also *attrib.*

1908 *Daily Report* 26 Aug. 5/4 As a promising speculative lock-up holding, the shares are worth buying at the present prices. **1929** *Observer* 17 Nov. 4/3 The shares may be regarded as a good lock-up investment.

c. *Printing.* The action of preparing plates or formes for printing or placing them in the press; also, a contrivance for holding the plates or formes in a press. Also *attrib.* Cf. Lock *v.*¹ 6 (in Dict. and Suppl.).

1888 C. T. Jacobi *Printers' Vocab.* 76 *Lock-up chases*, special chases made in order to dispense with large quantities of furniture in filling up spare room in formes or on the press. *Lock-up iron*, the iron stick used for tightening up formes as they stand instead of laying them up. **1925** H. Crane *Let.* 4 May (1965) 203 Lockup & Presswork.. $40.00. **1960** G. A. Glaister *Gloss. Bk.* 240/2 *Lock-up table*, any of several varieties of imposing surface specially equipped for the accurate imposition of formes for colour registration. **1964** *Gloss. Letterpress Rotary Printing Terms* (*B.S.I.*) 15 Lock-up. 1. A mechanical arrangement for holding the printing plates or formes on the press. 2. The action of locking the printing plates or formes on the press. **1967** Karch & Buber *Offset Processes* ii. 23 The form of hot type is locked up in a chase with 'furniture' (blocks of wood or metal) and quoins by the lock-up man. *Ibid.* 24 This [*sc.* preparation of printing surfaces] includes lock-up and imposition.

2. b. (Earlier and later examples.)

1839 *Knickerbocker* XIV. 110 He was seized, and carried to the 'lock-up'. **1972** *Police Rev.* 8 Dec. 1599/1 There would be a chance to run these establishments as if they were something more constructive than mere lock-ups. **1973** R. Busby *Pattern of Violence* i. 14 Sam..was at present residing within the central lock-up in..police headquarters, ready to appear before the court.

c. Short for **lock-up garage.*

1910 *Bradshaw's Railway Guide* Apr. 1036 Southgate Private Hotel..Lock-up for Bicycles. *Ibid.* 1070 Motor garage, with 12 lock ups. **1973** E. Lemarchand *Let or Hindrance* ix. 103 'Was the car standing out while you were in Cornwall?' 'No. They gave me a lock-up.' **1974** G. Mitchell *Javelin for Jonah* v. 68 We followed Jonah.. to the garages..frisked him and pinched the key to his lock-up.

4. *lock-up book, cubicle, garage, prisoner*; lock-up shop (further examples).

1870 G. H. Lewes *Diary* 22 Nov. in Geo. Eliot *Lett.* (1956) V. 123 Bought Polly a Lock-up book for her Autobiog[raphy]. **1910** *Bradshaw's Railway Guide* Apr. 1019 Most up-to-date Motor Garage, with lock-up Cubicles. **1935** *Archit. Rev.* LXXVIII. 168/1 A general garage and a number of private lock-up garages. **1963** *Times* 21 Feb. 8/7 The rent of all council houses and lock-up garages provided by Maidstone Town Council is to be increased by 12½ per cent. **1846** D. Corcoran *Pickings* 33 To the right of the column we perceived a prisoner whom we at once knew was above and beyond the ordinary class of lock-up prisoners. **1906** *Daily Chron.* 10 Dec. 5/7 Many people patrolled the district in which Fell's warehouse and Beardwood's lock-up shop are situated. **1947** Lock-up shop [see *amusement 7].

loco, *sb.*¹ Add: **a.** *loco-plant, loco-weed*: (earlier and later examples).

1879 *Special Rep. U.S. Dept. Agric.* No. 12. 211 The losses among cattle, caused by eating the poisonous loco weed, will perhaps not exceed 1 per cent. **1884** *Amer. Naturalist* XVIII. 1148 Experiments..prove that *Crotalaria sagittalis*, the Rattle-box, is a 'loco-plant'. **1904** 'O. Henry' in *McClure's Mag.* Apr. 617/1 If you have ever seen a horse that has eaten loco-weed you will understand what I mean when I say that the passengers get locoed. **1948** *Miami* (Okla.) *Daily News-Rec.* 30 June 8/2 Little is heard today of the once troublesome loco weed. **1955** W. Foster-Harris *Look of Old West* ix. 260 The most famous of the lethal stuff is undoubtedly loco, or crazy, weed... Loco grows all over the West, and a locoed horse is easy to spot.

c. loco weed = *marijuana, marihuana.

1935 A. J. Pollock *Underworld Speaks* 72/2 *Loco weed*, mariahuana; hemp; hashish. **1960** *Time* 25 Jan. 87/2 In U.S. slang marijuana is called..loco weed. **1972** *Sunday Sun* (Brisbane) 2 July 14/3 Detectives from the CIB Drug Squad in Brisbane are becoming quite familiar now with words like..rope and locoweed.

loco, *sb.*³ Add: (Earlier and later examples.)

1833 S. Breck *Recoll.* (1877) App. 274 With the *loco*.. he may start from one city in the morning and return again in the evening. **1869** *Bradshaw's Railway Manual* XXI. 14 Supt. of Loco. Dept., C. K. Domville, Belfast. **1955** *Times* 28 May 10/2 The last named company received important contracts including one for 94 diesel electric locos for the Irish State Transport. **1974** A. MacLean *Breakheart Pass* iv. 63 To haul this heavy load with a single loco?.. Thirty hours, I'd say.

b. lo·co-spotting, train-spotting; the action of noting the numbers (and sometimes other details) of locomotives seen; so **loco-spotter,** (as back-formation) **loco-spot** *v.*

1959 *Junior Radio Times* 25 Sept. 1/1 What is the loco-spotter looking for? Chiefly the engine number, which normally is painted on the cab side and also on the smoke-box door; secondly, the name if the engine has one; and thirdly, the code of the shed to which the engine is allocated. *Ibid.*, One of the objects of locospotting is to see—or 'cop'—all the engines in a particular class, marking off the number of each engine as it is observed. **1960** W. E. Hildick *Boy at Window* xvii. 131 It was a train the boy remembered well from his loco-spotting days. **1968** *Listener* 21 Mar. 368/2, I loco-spotted 45076..and 45254. **1971** *Where* Dec. 365/3 They..for many years ran the Loco Spotting Club.

loco (lōᵘ·ko), *a.* orig. *U.S.* [a. Sp. *loco* (see Loco¹). Cf. Locoed *ppl. a.*] Mad, insane, off one's head.

1887 *Outing* X. 7/1 You won't be able to do nuthin' with 'em, sir; they'll go plumb loco. **1904** Conrad *Nostromo* i. vi. 37 He was old, ugly, learned—and a little 'loco'—mad, if not a bit of a sorcerer. **1910** C. E. Mulford *Hopalong Cassidy* iv. 38 Are you loco? Do you mean to let th' rest of th' outfit see that? **1922** *Chambers's Jrnl.* Mar. 167/2 Some of them would be loco over it. **1929** Ade *Let.* 8 Feb. (1973) 139 We have gone a little loco on shopping, because..prices seem low. **1934** R. Macaulay *Going Abroad* i. 13 The young people were, so far as anyone could judge, completely loco. **1965** D. Francis *Odds Against* 124 He'd been quietly going loco and making hopeless decisions. **1973** 'A. Hall' *Tango Briefing* iv. 46 You heard of ergot?.. There was a case in France, remember? Half a village went loco.

loco (lōᵘ·ko), *adv. Mus.* [It. *al loco*, at the place.] (See quots.)

1801 Busby *Dict. Mus.*, *Loco*,..a word in opposition to *8va Alta*, and signifying that the notes over which it is placed are not to be played an octave higher, but just as they are written. **1970** *Oxf. Compan. Mus.* (ed. 10) 578/2 *Loco*.., 'place', used after some sign indicating performance an octave higher or lower than written and reminding the performer that the effect of that sign now terminates. Often the expression used is *Al loco*, 'at the place'.

loco-descriptive, *a.* (Later example.)

1966 *English Studies* XLVII. 68 Loco-descriptive poems of and guides to the Lakes.

locoman². [Loco³.] A driver of a locomotive; an engine-driver.

1941 *Penguin New Writing* XII. 9 We loco-men carry on whatever the conditions overhead. **1970** *Daily Mail* 3 Mar. 1/2 Locomen at King's Cross plan a one-day stoppage today which will hit services to the North and some commuter trains. **1972** *Guardian* 14 Aug. 1/1 The locomen's union insists that drivers should be paid more money.

locomobile. Add: **b.** *sb.* (Examples.) Also *attrib.*

1895 W. R. Fisher *Schlich's Man. Forestry* V. 748 The elevator and macerating cylinder are driven by a locomobile. **1900** *Sci. Amer.* 27 Jan. 54/1 The steam carriage which is popularly and commercially known as the 'Locomobile'. **1900** *Sun* (N.Y.) 23 May 7/6 A locomobile operator was arraigned for driving a locomobile, which is a steam automobile. **1915** *Lit. Digest* 21 Aug. 387/2 Goodyear Cord Tires... Adopted for the new Locomobile as

standard equipment. *a* 1936 KIPLING *Something of Myself* (1937) vii. 177, I bought me a steam-car called a 'Locomobile', whose nature and attributes I faithfully drew in a tale called 'Steam Tactics'. **1962** R. B. FULLER *Epic Poem on Industrialization* 169 No, the ephemeralization Of doing more with less, Took gold along with tonnage And three-ton Locomobiles.

locomote, *v.* (Earlier and later examples.)
1834 *Knickerbocker* IV. 20 Who but our author would represent him [*sc.* a bard], 'locomoting' on a long, dog-trot over the bogs of his neighborhood. **1894** *Proc. R. Soc.* LV. 163 They [*sc.* the leucocytes]..do not locomote over the floor of the counter. **1970** *Amat. Photographer* 22 Apr. 9/3 That foot..pointing daintily downward; except for a prima ballerina I've never yet seen a dame who could locomote like that. **1974** *Nature* 15 Mar. 240/1 Colchicine and vinblastine caused the ruffling activity of fibroblasts locomoting in culture to spread from a restricted area to all parts of the edge of the cells.

locomotive. Add: **B.** *sb.* **1.** (Later examples.)
1959 E. K. WENLOCK *Kitchin's Road Transport Law* (ed. 12) 26/1 No one under 21 is allowed to drive a locomotive, motor tractor or heavy motor car on a road. **1971** *Morning Star* 3 July 3/3 More classes of vehicles will be able to use motorways... They include 'locomotives', which are load-carrying vehicles weighing more than 7¼ tons.
c. *U.S. slang.* A cheer. Also *attrib.*
1901 *Princeton Alumni Weekly* 131/2 But he saw you trying to join in a locomotive cheer last Saturday. **1907** *Ibid.* 321/2 The boys gave a rousing locomotive and then stood in silence. **1961** WEBSTER, *Locomotive*, a cheer characterized by a slow beginning and a progressive increase in speed and used esp. at school and college sports events.
4. *locomotive works.*
1848 *Mass. Private & Special Statutes* 13 Mar., A corporation, by the name of the Boston Locomotive Works, for the purpose of manufacturing locomotive engines. **1889** G. FINDLAY *Working & Managem. Eng. Railway* vii. 118 Crewe, which previous to the establishment of the locomotive works was inhabited only by a few farmers and cottagers, has now developed into a flourishing town. **1966** G. F. ALLEN *Brit. Rail after Beeching* xii. 357 Of the Southern Region's locomotive works, Brighton had already been shut down and Ashford (Kent) had been slated for closure.

loco-move, *v.* (Later example.)
1873 LELAND *Egyptian Sk.-Bk.* 88, I only remember one instance when a man who made locomotion his business was unwilling to locomove.

locoum (lōᵘ·kŭm). Also **locum, lokoum, loukoum**(i. [Turk. *lokum.*] Turkish delight.
1887 F. M. CRAWFORD *Paul Patoff* III. xxiii. 239 Two little white saucers filled with pieces of loukoum-rahat, the Turkish national sweetmeat, commonly called by schoolboys fig-paste. **1894** [see *DELIGHT *sb.* 4]. **1913** *Chambers's Jrnl.* Apr. 313/2 The elemes and locoums, packed respectively in layers and in cubes. **1921** S. GRAHAM *Europe* ii. 38 Pride intervenes only to stop them begging... But you see the nicest of girls with pinched white faces trying to sell *loukoum*. **1960** *Spectator* 8 Jan. 51/1 In Istanbul,..go for Turkish delight,..a quite different confection from what passes as Turkish delight in Britain. You ask for *lokoum*. **1962** J. FLEMING *When I grow Rich* iv. 53 A little *locum* for a friend..a present of a little Turkish delight. **1967** *Vogue* Jan. 4/2 A coral crusted dish of loukoumi. **1970** SIMON & HOWE *Dict. Gastron.*, Turkish delight, the popular English name of Turkey's sweetmeat *rahat lokum.* **1972** J. RATHBONE *Trip Trap* vi. 65 A servant poured Turkish coffee; *lokoum* was offered in tiny silver dishes.

locule. = LOCULUS 2. (Later examples.)
1953 *New Biol.* XIV. 44 The cotton fruit, called a boll, is divided into three or four locules, each with several seeds. **1967** M. E. HALE *Biol. Lichens* ii. 28 The locules in the stroma are separated by branched pseudoparaphyses.

locum. Add: **b.** Short for LOCUM-TENENCY.
1903 *Lancet* 9 May 101/2 (Advt.), Hospital Locum wanted..for three weeks or less. **1946** *Ibid.* 2 Mar. 322/2 When doing a locum I attended a family of actors.

locum tenens. Add: **b.** The post of a locum tenens; a locum-tenency.
1899 *Lancet* 5 Aug. 86/2 (Advt.), Locum Tenens or good Assistantship by doubly-qualified man. **1908** A. S. M. HUTCHINSON *Once aboard Lugger* vi. vi. § 2. 437 There's this locum tenens I was going to take up in the North.

locum-tenent. Add: **b.** = LOCUM TENENS.
1899 *Lancet* 19 Aug. 547/1, I met with a serious accident ..in consequence of which I had to engage a locum-tenent. *Ibid.*, This sort of thing should make men very careful as to locum-tenents before engaging them.

locus, *sb.*¹ Add: **1. b.** *Genetics.* A site or position on a chromosome at which a particular gene is located; *loosely*, a gene.
1913 *Jrnl. Exper. Zoöl.* XV. 591 White and eosin are allelomorphic to each other, that is, they occupy the same locus in the sex chromosome. **1915** T. H. MORGAN et al. *Mechanism Mendelian Heredity* ii. 37 There are three pink eye colors in Drosophila, one whose locus is in the third chromosome (pink). *Ibid.* vii. 155 A mutant factor is located at a definite point in a particular chromosome; its normal allelomorph is supposed to occupy a corresponding position (locus) in the homologous chromosome. **1919** *Anatomical Rec.* XV. 358 In another case of duplication the duplication piece contains only the locus for sable as far as known. **1949** [see *ALLELOMORPH]. **1962** *Lancet* 6 Jan. 10/1 The colour-blind locus is thought to be about 10 units of crossing-over from the locus for hæmophilia and about 25 units from the locus for Duchenne's type of muscular dystrophy. **1970** *Nature* 25 July 342/1 Considerable numbers of gene loci are required to code for the primary structures of the immunoglobulin molecules made in any one organism. **1971** *Ibid.* 13 Aug. 498/1 Haemoglobin type in sheep is controlled by a pair of alleles at a single locus.
c. *locus of control* (Psychol.) (see quot. 1972¹).
1966 MANDLER & WATSON in C. D. Spielberger *Anxiety & Behavior* 286 A locus of control scale has been developed which differentiates individuals according to the degree to which they appraise themselves or the environment to control the occurrence of reinforcement. **1971** *Jrnl. Gen. Psychol.* LXXXV. 98 There is movement from external to internal locus of control from trial to trial. **1972** I. G. SARASON *Personality* (rev. ed.) i. 9 Locus of control refers to the degree to which an individual sees himself in control of his life and the events that influence it. **1972** *Jrnl. Social Psychol.* LXXXVI. 233 The work of Rotter and his associates on perceived locus of control has resulted in a considerable body of evidence.
4. locus classicus (earlier example); **locus communis** (later example); **locus desperatus** (see quot. 1966); **locus standi** (later examples).
1853 BAGEHOT *Coll. Works* (1965) I. 202 These lines are, as it were, the *locus classicus* of fairy literature. **1843** MILL *Logic* II. v. ii. 339 *Loci communes* of bad arguments on some particular subject. **1922** F. KLAEBER *Beowulf* 214 This passage remains..a 'locus desperatus'. **1966** A. J. BLISS *Dict. Foreign Words & Phrases Current Eng.* 231 *Locus desperatus*, a passage in a text transmitted by manuscript whose meaning is so corrupt as to be almost beyond conjecture. **1969** *English Studies* p. lxxv, The result is an editorial 'locus desperatus' which still to some extent defies repeated scrutiny and modern photographic aids. **1969** R. RENEHAN *Greek Textual Crit.* 2 The textual critic..must decide in each case whether the original reading..has been or can be recovered by modern conjecture or whether the passage is a *locus desperatus.* **1970** *Anglia* LXXXVIII. 367 Faced with such a *locus desperatus*, even a conscientious editor might decline to grapple afresh with the battered folio. **1911** J. WARD *Realm of Ends* x. 212 Death..means that the soul in consequence, so far as it is thus deprived of its *locus standi*, is..in the position of a deserter from the general order. **1974** *Times* 9 Feb. 20 The power of the Department [of Trade and Industry] should, of course, be discretionary but the Panel should be given a *locus standi* with the Department.

locust, *sb.* Add: **5. b.** (Earlier and later examples.)
1863 D. M. BARNES *Draft Riots N.Y.* 82 Go in they did forthwith, and, where moral suasion had failed, the locusts succeeded. **1865** G. A. SALA *My Diary in Amer.* II. 211 The New York policeman wears a handsome uniform. At his side hangs a club or bludgeon... This club is made of 'locust wood'..and by rowdies the policeman is often generically called..a 'locust'. **1904** *N.Y. Tribune* 19 June 4 The policemen did not carry their 'locusts'. **1930** E. H. LAVINE *Third Degree* 78 A detective picked out the largest and heaviest locust in the group.
6. locust-bean (later examples); **locust-borer** (examples); **locust stick** = *locust club*; **locust wood,** the wood of a locust-tree; **locust years,** years of poverty and hardship (see also quot. 1962¹).
1958 L. DURRELL *Balthazar* ii. 32 He would pick a stick of sugar-cane off a stall as he passed..or a sweet locust-bean. **1972** *Country Life* 30 Nov. 1481/1 Locust beans don't attack the teeth as jube-jubes did. **1839** H. COLMAN *2nd Rep. Agric. Mass.* (Mass. Agric. Survey) 100 Locust-Borer... [He] washed his locust trees with spirits of turpentine, and in that way compelled the borer to leave them. **1972** SWAN & PAPP *Common Insects N. Amer.* 448 Locust borer: *Megacyllene robiniae*... The larvae bore in the sapwood of black locust. **1919** WODEHOUSE *Coming of Bill* (1920) I. i. 15 The policeman..relieved his feelings by dispersing the crowd with well-directed prods of his locust stick. **1742** W. ELLIS *Timber-Tree Improved* II. xxxii. 166 Where the Natives can't get Locust-wood, they use this to make their Bows. **1874** *Rep. Vermont Board Agric.* II. 777 *Clytus robiniae.* The larvae feed upon locust wood. [**1611** BIBLE Joel ii. 25 And I will restore to you the yeeres that the locust hath eaten.] **1948** W. S. CHURCHILL *Second World War* I. I. v. 52 (*heading*) The Locust Years, 1931–1935. **1962** *Listener* 19 July 107/3 Sir Winston Churchill applied the phrase, the locust years, to the middle thirties, when vigorous rearmament should have begun. **1962** W. MCELWEE (*title*) Britain's locust years, 1918–1940. **1964** P. MAGNUS *King Edward VII* xiii. 244 (*heading*) Locust years. **1970** *Times* 27 May 8 Yet before these locust years of Labour, we had the Conservative years of rising prosperity.

locustal (lǫkʊ·stăl), *a.* [f. LOCUST *sb.* + -AL.] Of, pertaining to, or connected with locusts.
1891 *Chambers's Encycl.* VII. 187/1 Temperature may also have something to do with locustal migrations.

locustarian. (Example.)
1895 *Nature* 5 Dec. 108/1 Mr. Scudder..has given much attention to the sounds made by locustarians.

locutionary (lǫkiū·ʃənări), *a. Philos.* [f. LOCUTION + -ARY¹.] Of or pertaining to an utterance by a speaker. Cf. *ILLOCUTIONARY *a.*
1955 J. L. AUSTIN *How to do Things with Words* (1962) viii. 94 The act of 'saying something'..I call, i.e. dub, the performance of a locutionary act. **1962** *Times Lit. Suppl.* 21 Sept. 743/2 A locutionary act is the speaker's act of saying whatever it is he says. **1973** *Ibid.* 5 Oct. 1161/5 The locutionary act was the act of saying something—i e, the act of uttering sounds as constituting a sentence.

lodberry, var. *LOADBERRY.

Loddon (lǫ·dən). The name of a tributary of the River Thames, used *attrib.*, esp. in **Loddon lily,** to designate the summer snowflake, *Leucojum æstivum*, a small, white-flowered, bulbous plant once common on the banks of this river.
1882 *Dickens's Dict. Thames* 28/3 It [*sc.* the summer snowflake] is very abundant in the meadows by the Loddon, and hence called 'Loddon lilies'. **1938** R. GATHORNE-HARDY *Wild Flowers Brit.* viii. 53 The Loddon Lily is to be found principally on the tributaries and main river of the Thames Valley. **1971** *Country Life* 2 Sept. 575/1 On the banks of the River Loddon linger a few 2 ft.-high clumps of the snowy-white Loddon lily, or summer snowflake, *Leucojum aestivum.* **1973** *Times* 15 Dec. 10/7 The Loddon or Summer Snowflake Leucojum aestivum used to grow in great numbers on the banks of the Loddon near Reading. It has now become quite scarce.

lode. Add: **6. lode-light,** a light said to be seen sometimes above a vein of ore.
1883 *Encycl. Brit.* XVI. 443/1 The appearance of the so-called lode-lights may be explained by the production of phosphoretted hydrogen. **1894** C. LE N. FOSTER *Ore & Stone Mining* 107 Appearances of flame above mineral veins..are sufficiently well established to have received a special name 'lode lights' in Cornwall.

loden (lōᵘ·dən). [a. G. *loden* thick woollen cloth.] A heavy waterproof woollen cloth. Used *attrib.* to designate garments made of this material, as *loden cloak, cloth, coat, jacket, mantle, skirt*; also *absol.* Also, a dark green.
1911 GALSWORTHY *Little Dream* in *Plays* (1929) 204 There enters a lean, well-built, taciturn young man dressed in Loden. **1914** G. ATHERTON *Perch of Devil* II. 354 She..wrapped herself in a dark lodenmantle, a long cape with a hood that she had worn..in Bavaria. **1916** J. BUCHAN *Greenmantle* vii. 98 Long shooting capes made of a green stuff they call *loden. Ibid.* xv. 196 Blue jeans, *loden* cloak. **1920** D. H. LAWRENCE *Women in Love* xxix. 450 The two..daughters of the professor, with their plain-cut, dark blue blouses and loden skirts. **1951** V. NABOKOV *Speak, Memory* iv. 61 He wore an ulster unless the weather was very mild, when he would switch to a kind of greenish-brown woollen cloak called a *loden.* **1952** *New Yorker* 13 Dec. 128/2 A rugged coat for the country, made in Austria of greenish or brownish loden cloth and cut something like a hunting coat. **1956** *San Francisco Examiner* 9 Sept. I. 21 (Advt.), The original Alpine Lodencoat. **1957** *Times* 25 Nov. 11/1 This coat is reversible, in loden cloth and water-proofed poplin. **1964** *N.Y. Post* 4 Nov. 11 Russ Togs in black, brown, loden, navy, and menswear grey. **1966** *Listener* 3 Nov. 641/1 People dressed in green Loden jackets. **1969** R. T. WILCOX *Dict. Costume* (1970) 198/1 *Loden*, a waterproof cloth resembling Irish frieze, made by the Tyrolean peasants from the wool of their mountain sheep. It is woven and dyed in several colors but especially a bluish green known as loden green. **1973** *Guardian* 10 Apr. 13/1 The greatest source of inspiration is the traditional Loden coat.

lodge, *sb.* Add: **4. b.** A residence or hotel. (Freq. as the second element of house- or hotel-names.)
1818 JANE AUSTEN *Persuasion* III. ii. 31 As to her young friend's health, by passing all the warm months with her at Kellynch-lodge, every danger would be avoided. *Ibid.* v. 80 Anne walked up..to the Lodge, where she was to spend the first week. **1854** DICKENS *Hard Times* I. iii. 12 To his matter of fact home, which was called Stone Lodge, Mr. Gradgrind directed his steps. He had..built Stone Lodge. **1869** *Bradshaw's Railway Manual* XXI. 307 Directors... W. C. Stobart Esq., Etherley Lodge, near Bishop Auckland. **1953** A. CHRISTIE *Pocket Full of Rye* iv. 24 *Call* it a lodge, indeed! Yew Tree Lodge!.. The house was what he..would call a mansion. **1971** *Author* LXXXII. 173 In hotels and auto lodges he listens to many a late-night argument. **1972** *Automobile Assoc. Members' Handbk.* 1972–73 154/1 Linton Lodge, Linton Road [Oxford].
7. (Later examples.)
1969 in Halpert & Story *Christmas Mumming in Newfoundland* 181 The (Protestant) Society of United Fishermen..soon had no fewer than forty-two lodges. **1970** *Britain: Official Handbk.* (H.M.S.O.) xvi. 428 The basic unit of organisation in most British trade unions is the local branch (sometimes called a lodge). **1974** *Socialist Worker* 7 Dec. 8/3 And there were more than 30 other workplace units—such as chapels and lodges—represented.
15. (sense 7) *lodge-meeting, official, room*; (sense 10) *lodge-cover, -covering, -fire, -skin, -trail.*
1878 J. H. BEADLE *Western Wilds* ix. 137 The former [*sc.* buffaloes] furnished them with food, clothing, lodge-covers,..and a dozen other conveniences. **1847** F. PARKMAN in *Knickerbocker* XXX. 234 The squaws of each lazy warrior had made him a shelter..by stretching..the corner of a lodge-covering upon poles. **1837** W. IRVING *Capt. Bonneville* I. 111 Knots of gamblers will assemble before one of their lodge fires, early in the evening. **1903** C. T. BRADY *Bishop* iii. 47 Most of the Churches have a week-night prayer-meeting, and the other nights are taken up with lodge meetings. **1926** *Scribner's Mag.* Sept. 327/2 A lodge meeting to the average negro is one of the big events of the week. **1933** J. BUCHAN *Prince of Captivity* II. i. 147 The weekly lodge meetings. **1909** *Daily Chron.* 30 Dec. 1/4 The fifteen lodge officials and delegates prosecuted for offences against the Industrial Disputes Act. **1974** *Times* 6 Dec. 3/1 All lodge officials are completely vindicated. **1911** J. C. LINCOLN *Cap'n Warren's Wards* vi. 88 I'm more used to lodge rooms than I am to clubs. *a* **1831** J. SMITH *Jrnl.* in M. S. Sullivan *Trav. J. Smith* (1934) 4 They [*sc.* Indian lodges] do not smoke except from a sudden

change of wind and then no longer than it takes a squaw to spread a smoke wing of the Lodge skin. **1891** *Century Mag.* Mar. 776 We had already devoured..a small sack made of smoked lodge skin. **1845** J. C. FRÉMONT *Rep. Exploring Expedition* 114 We resumed our journey.. following an extremely good lodge-trail.

lodgement. Add: **1. d.** *Mining* = LODGE *sb.* 13 a.

1883 W. S. GRESLEY *Gloss. Terms Coal Mining* 159 *Lodgment* (S[cotland]), see *sump* and *lodge.* **1886** J. BARROWMAN *Gloss. Scottish Mining Terms* 43 *Lodgment*, a reservoir or storage place underground for water for convenience of pumping.

5. lodgement-level (see quot. 1877).

1877 *Encycl. Brit.* VI. 63/2 Driving a gallery..along the course of the coal seam, which is known as a 'dip head level', and a lower parallel one, in which the water collects, known as a 'lodgment level'. **1886** J. BARROWMAN *Gloss. Scottish Mining Terms* 43 *Lodgment-level*, a room driven level course at a short distance to the dip of a pit and used for storage of water.

lodge-pole, *sb. N. Amer.* **1.** (See LODGE *sb.* 15.)

1805 M. LEWIS in Lewis & Clark *Orig. Jrnls. Lewis & Clark Expedition* (1904) II. 88 Found a new indian lodge pole today. **1855, 1865** [in Dict. s.v. LODGE *sb.* 15]. **1903** A. ADAMS *Log of Cowboy* xxi. 330 He..with The Rebel went back about a mile to a thicket of lodge poles. **1946** G. FOREMAN *Last Trek of Indians* 242 They pulled down the lodges of three of their villages and sold the lodgepoles and lumber.

2. lodge-pole pine, a pine native to mountainous regions of north-west America, *Pinus contorta* var. *latifolia.*

1859 G. A. JACKSON *Diary* 9 Jan. in *Colorado Mag.* (1935) XII. 205 Cut the top off a small lodge pole pine. **1884** C. S. SARGENT *Rep. Forests N. Amer.* 564 The forests largely composed of the lodge-pole pine..cover the outlying eastern ranges of the Rocky Mountains. **1905** *N.Y. Even. Post* 29 Apr., The lodgepole pine..bears the common name of 'lodgepole' from the fact that the Indians used its long slender trunks as supports for their wigwams, or lodges. **1949** *Sierra Club Bull.* (San Francisco) June 6 Lodgepole pines, singing birds and scampering chipmunks, ..all familiar elements of the mountain scenes. **1964** *N.Z. News* 24 Nov. 3/1 The lodgepole pine, becoming common on the Waiouru Plains and a cause of concern because of its possible spread in the South Island, is in fact a favoured species for pulping in U.S. **1972** *Islander* (Victoria, B.C.) 23 Jan. 6/1 Amongst the lodge-pole pines and blue spruce. **1972** *Country Life* 7 Dec. 1559/1 Foresters in Scotland can be criticized for planting an excess of sitka and Canadian lodgepole pine.

lo·dge-pole, *v. U.S.* [f. prec.] *trans.* To beat with a lodge-pole. Hence **lodge-poling** *vbl. sb.*

1848 G. F. A. RUXTON in *Blackw. Mag.* LXIV. 139 Nor are they [*sc.* squaws] so schooled to perfect obedience to their lords and masters as to stand a 'lodge poling'. **1850** L. H. GARRARD *Wah-to-Yah* (1927) ix. 116 Often..their negligent spouses are lodge-poled (beaten) for such accidents. **1968** *Amer. Speech* XLIII. 218 It was customary to discipline a squaw by *lodge-poling* her, and the term became figurative for any beating.

lodgerdom (lǫ·dʒəɹdəm). [f. LODGER + -DOM.] Lodgers collectively; the world of lodgers; a district in which lodgers are common.

1905 *Daily Chron.* 6 Mar. 4/6 Even dingy Lodgerdom would disclaim the place. **1907** *Ibid.* 23 May 3/3 A very pleasant, humorous-pathetic story of lodgerdom. **1927** *Observer* 14 Aug. 6 Discomfort..that goes with the bondage of..lodgerdom.

lodging, *vbl. sb.* Add: **6. lodging-hall** *U.S.*, a lodging-house; **lodging paper,** a handbill advertising lodgings; **lodging turn,** an occasion or period for which a railway employee has to lodge at his place of destination before returning to his place of departure.

1860 J. G. HOLLAND *Miss Gilbert's Career* xii. 208 We left Arthur Blague..sitting on his bed in the lodging-hall. **1817** JANE AUSTEN *Sanditon* vii, in *Minor Works* (1954) 402 No fewer than three Lodging Papers staring me in the face at this very moment. **1952** *Ann. Reg. 1951* 15 Economy measures, some of which (such as more lodging turns) had caused serious strikes. **1955** *Ann. Reg. 1954* 30 About two-thirds of the..footplate men..came out on strike against the introduction of new 'lodging turns', i.e. nights spent, usually in railway hostels, away from home.

lodging-room. (Later U.S. examples.)

1849 *Ex. Doc. 31st U.S. Congress 1 Sess. House* No. 5. II. 1089 One hewed-log lodging-room for hired men. **1906** *Springfield* (Mass.) *Republ.* 7 Feb. 2 Lodging Rooms to Let.

lodicle, var. LODICULE (in Dict. and Suppl.).

1888 *Encycl. Brit.* XXIV. 531/2 Within the pale[a] are two minute, ovate, pointed, white membranous scales called 'lodicles'.

lodicule. Substitute for def.: A green or white scale, the lowest part of a grass flower. (Later example.)

1968 F. W. GOULD *Grass Systematics* ii. 55 Lodicules play a role in the opening of the flower at anthesis.

loerie (lu·ri). *S. Afr.* Also **loorie, lourie.** [Afrikaans, f. Du. *lori* LORY.] = TOURACO.

1798 A. BARNARD *Jrnl.* in A. W. C. Lindsay *Lives of Lindsays* (1849) III. 408, I began to collect my Cape trifles for my friends at home,—some beautiful loories alive—some still more beautiful swallows dead. **1810** W. J. BURCHELL *Jrnl.* 7 Dec. in *Trav. S. Afr.* (1822) I. ii. 20 In the aviary, I saw the *Touracoo*, called *Loeri* by the colonists. **1812** [see LORY]. **1850** J. S. CHRISTOPHER *Natal* 33 The beautiful and soft-voiced loerie, the golden cuckoo, the green pigeon..and many others too numerous to particularise. [**1908** *East London* (Cape Province) *Dispatch* 4 Dec. 4 The *vlei-lourie*, perhaps better known hereabouts as the 'rain-bird', the natives regarding it as a weather prophet.] **1932** *Discovery* July 230/2 The Louries, magnificent in green, blue and carmine..nest outside the door of the mission [at Kilimanjaro]. **1950** *Cape Argus Mag.* 18 Mar. 7/7 Loeries with their beautiful crimson-and-green plumage fill the air with their liquid call. **1957** V. W. TURNER *Schism & Continuity in Afr. Soc.* x. 293 The woman may dream that her dead relative has appeared to her equipped like a hunter, wearing the red wing-feather of a lourie in her hair. **1971** *Evening Post* (Port Elizabeth, S.A.) *Suppl.* 12 June 5 When we think of birds in general, it is the pleasanter members of that enormous family that come to mind—the brilliantly-plumaged sunbird, the dove, the loerie.

loess. Delete 'found in the valley of the Rhine and of other large rivers' and substitute: which occurs extensively from north-central Europe to eastern China, in the American mid-west, and elsewhere, esp. in the basins of large rivers, and which is usually considered to be composed of material transported by the wind during and after the Glacial Period. (Add further examples.)

1882 F. RICHTOFEN in *Geol. Mag.* IX. 302, I believe I am correct in stating that, among those who have had extensive experience in Loess regions, all who have pronounced an opinion of late years are agreed that subaërial deposition is the only mode of origin by which all its peculiar features can be easily explained. **1906** *Westm. Gaz.* 4 Dec. 2/1 North of the river [*sc.* the Hwang Ho] we come into the land of the loess, a loose light soil of prodigious fertility and the joy of the agriculturist. **1938** C. L. WHITTLES tr. *Reifenberg's Soils Palestine* ii. 25 Microscopic examination shows that loess consists mainly of extremely small particles of quartz together with calcareous particles which frequently, from their markings, etc., have been derived from fossils. **1972** J. G. CRUICKSHANK *Soil Geogr.* ii. 59 During the deglaciation phases of the Pleistocene glaciations, wind-blown silt was deposited on a spectacular scale in extensive, stoneless loess.

loessial (lö·siăl), *a.* [f. LOESS + -IAL.] Composed of loess.

1928 *Bull. Amer. Soil Survey Assoc.* IX. 34 These [*sc.* glacial soils] include the till, moraine, drumlin..and other typical forms and a portion of the loessial deposits. **1974** *Nature* 22 Mar. 320/2 Silt, in excess of that which could be derived from weathering of the substrata and generally considered loessial, is found in many British soils.

loessic (lö·sik), *a.* [f. LOESS + -IC.] = *LOESSIAL *a.*

1909 in *Cent. Dict.* Suppl. **1940** *Nature* 6 July 14/1 In periglacial regions such arid episodes are represented by loessic deposits. **1952** F. E. ZEUNER *Dating Past* (ed. 3) vi. 158 The Middle Older Loess of the section is a complex of loessic hillwash material derived from higher up the slope, and of brecciated loess with large molluscan shells, interrupted by a brown soil.

lo-fi (lōu·fəi·). *colloq.* [Repr. *low fidelity*, after *HI-FI.] Sound reproduction less good in quality than 'hi-fi'. Also *attrib.* or as *adj.*

1958 *Observer* 15 June 14/6 For heaven's sake let us have the real Bob Cats, even in lo-fi, and let the record companies make their issues under that kind of policy. **1967** *Sat. Rev.* (U.S.) 29 July 53 Despite Mr. Kolodin's warning of the 'lo-fi', we would urge the purchase of this set as a significant item in Toscanini's recorded legacy. **1968** *Which?* Oct. 312/1 You can buy your hi-fi equipment one piece at a time, and play it through the 'lo-fi' parts of, say, your old radio. **1970** *Daily Tel.* 16 Mar. 24/3 It was because of the cassette's 'lo-fi' that Philips first attacked the bottom end of the market. **1970** J. EARL *Tuners & Amplifiers* v. 100 The medium-frequency a.m. system is.. possibly adequate for 'lo-fi' reception on small transistor sets.

loft, *sb.* Add: **5. d.** A place where sails are manufactured; = *sail-loft.*

1938 T. NORTH *Yacht Sails* xii. 113 When a new sail leaves the loft it should be perfect. **1959** W. R. BIRD *These are Maritimes* iii. 92 He learned his trade in his father's loft in West Pubnico... There are only two other 'lofts' in the Maritimes. **1973** *Observer* (Colour Suppl.) 3 June 18/3 His personal sails are no better than his customers'. 'They go through the loft as part of the system.'

7. c. *fig.* Elevation, uplift.

1925 *Brit. Weekly* 12 Nov. 159/2 We need more loft in our thinking than our fathers had.

8. loft-bombing (see quot. 1956).

1956 *Time* 24 Sept. 36 Its [*sc.* a low-flying fighter-bomber's] bombing can be made extremely accurate, but if it uses any ordinary bombing system, such as dive-bombing, it is apt to be vaporized by the fireball springing up under its tail. The best way to avoid this misadventure is 'loft-bombing', which uses the speed of the airplane to make the bomb behave like an artillery shell. *Ibid.*, The main advantage of loft-bombing..is not the range of the bomb, but the time that it spends in the air while the airplane is making its get-away. **1960** *Aeroplane* XCIX. 352/2 The first L.A.B.S. manœuvre was completed by an A3D, in which loft bombing had been pioneered by Cmdr. H. F. Lang.

loft, *v.* Add: **2.** (Later example.)

1951 E. SEWELL in *Durkett's Reg.* July 105 Blenheims will keep till Christmas, if lofted cool and dry.

3. Also in other games.

1927 [see *INFIELDER 2]. **1950** W. HAMMOND *Cricketers' School* facing p. 96 W. Hammond hits a 6; position correct for lofting the ball over mid-on. **1963** *Times* 8 June 4/2 Soon afterwards Hunte lofted Allen over mid-off for four, before Allen for the second time in the day, had the last word with a batsman trying to attack him. **1970** *Globe & Mail* (Toronto) 28 Sept. 18/6 Rookie Paul McKay lofted the final Hamilton punt, a high 47-yard spiral. **1972** J. MOSEDALE *Football* vi. 91 Tittle lofted the ball..over the heads of the other players. **1974** *News & Reporter* (Chester, S. Carolina) 22 Apr. 10-A/6 Guy Meadow lofted a sacrifice fly and Clayton, up for the second time in the inning, singled again.

b. *transf.* and *fig.*

1883 J. MARTINE *Reminisc. Haddington* 120 He [*sc.* a goat]..thought nothing of pouting and 'lafting' folk. **1902** BARRIE *Little White Bird* xxiv. 282 We had lofted him out of the story, and did very well without him. **1948** G. H. JOHNSTON *Death takes Small Bites* v. 110 Her eyes, bright with strain, lofted above the murals to the great range behind the town. **1952** [see *day-beam* s.v. *DAY *sb.* 23 a, b]. **1960** L. P. GARTNER *Jewish Immigrant* ix. 251 The banner of the Hebrew national..renaissance was lofted. **1971** D. MEIRING *Wall of Glass* vii. 57 He would..loft his bag up the hotel stairs himself..instead of handing it to the orderly.

lofted, *ppl. a.* Add: **2. c.** Of a ball: hit into the air. Also in other games.

1904 *Daily Chron.* 20 Aug. 9/5, I saw a lofted ball..miss the head of a player in front by not more than six inches. **1955** *Times* 29 June 4/3 He made the winning hit, a lofted straight four, on the stroke of time. **1963** *Times* 27 May 5/3 The same player scored from a 30-yard penalty, while Ramsden replied with a well lofted hit from 40 yards.

lofting, *vbl. sb.* Add: **2*.** *Aeronaut.* The action of a loftsman.

1939 *Jrnl. R. Aeronaut. Soc.* XLIII. 140, I should like to mention two or three operations coming under the control of the engineering department... One of these is the mould loft. The art of lofting as it is now generally followed in American aircraft production was, of course, borrowed from the ship-building industry. **1956** W. A. HEFLIN *U.S. Air Force Dict.* 304/1 *Lofting*, as applied to airplanes, the act or process of laying out full-size drawings of an airplane that is to be built, of designing and making templates, etc. **1972** *Lebende Sprachen* XVII. 73/2 The production of aircraft part drawings, preparation of magnetic tape for machine-tool control, and many lofting, drawing and checking jobs are to be automated.

lofting (lǫ·ftiŋ), *ppl. a.* [f. LOFT *v.* + -ING².] Of a stroke in golf: that lofts.

1905 *Westm. Gaz.* 25 Aug. 3/1 Why to go for a low-running shot or for a high lofting shot, respectively.

loftsman (lǫ·ftsmæn). *Shipbuilding* and *Aeronaut.* [Cf. *mould-loft* s.v. MOULD *sb.*³ 17.] One who reproduces a draughtsman's specifications for a ship or aircraft in full size on the floor of a mould-loft.

1901 T. WALTON *Steel Ships* vii. 178 After the plans of a vessel have been prepared in the drawing office, the first man who takes her in hand is the loftsman. His domain is the mould loft, where..he proceeds to reproduce the 'lines' plan upon the loft floor to actual size. *Ibid.* 180 The loftsman's work is to rectify any..irregularities, and to produce perfect harmony and fairness in all lines which make up the form of the hull. **1909** WEBSTER, *Loftsman*, one who lays down the lines of a ship in a shipbuilding loft. **1921** *Dict. Occup. Terms* (1927) § 668 s.v. *Scriever*, *Loftsman*, lays off from plans, on wooden floor,..outlines of ship frames and plates, [etc.]. **1947** *Aircraft Engin.* July 222/1 The loftsman would simply pass a curve pleasing to the eye through a few points determined by the designer. **1955** *Times* 13 July 2/5 Aircraft Loftsmen for the Aircraft Full-scale Layout Section. **1957** *Technology* Apr. 53/2 At a single step the loftsman will become a white collar worker, no longer grubbing about on hands and knees on a dirty floor marking off a life-size scrieve board. **1974** *Sci. Amer.* May 16/3, I worked for eight years..as lumberman, machinist, machine designer and loftsman before retiring to college.

log, *sb.*¹ Add: **1. b.** *as easy* (or *simple*) *as falling* (or *rolling*) *off a log.*

1839 *Picayune* (New Orleans) 29 Mar. 2/2 He gradually went away from the Lubber, and won the heat, 'just as easy as falling off a log'. *c* **1880** 'MARK TWAIN' *Speeches* (1923) 97 A man who could have elected himself Major-General Adam or anything else as easy as rolling off a log. **1904** 'A. DALE' *Wanted: a Cook* 207 It was so easy that the inelegant simile of 'rolling off a log' impressed me as being absolutely justifiable. **1913** F. H. BURNETT *T. Tembarom* xvii. 223, I dropped into it by accident,..and that made it as easy as falling off a log. **1949** N. MARSH *Swing, Brother, Swing* iv. 67 Don't keep asking if I can understand things that are as simple as falling off a log. **1973** *Times* 10 Feb. 11/3 Acting? said Ernest Borgnine. Why, there was nothing to it, really. 'For me,' he said, 'it's as easy as falling off a log.'

g. *Surfing.* (See quots.)

1967 J. SEVERSON *Great Surfing* Gloss., *Log*, a very heavy surfboard. **1970** *Studies in English* (Univ. of Cape Town) I. 28 His board may be described as a barge or a log, both of which describe a big cumbersome surfboard, one that is difficult to manoeuvre.

4*. A piece of quarried slate before it is split into layers.

1725 D. EATON *Let.* 13 Feb. (1971) 9 The reason why the slaters could not go on was bycause they could not run their slate out of the log for want of frost. **1939** *Evening News* 2 Feb. 8/6 When the slate is taken to the surface it is called 'log', and is then left in the 'slate-patch' to wait for the frost to break it into layers. **1946** N. WYMER *Eng. Country Crafts* x. 108 Then the props are systematically removed, and the slate is allowed to crash down, breaking up into large slabs which can be levered up and roughly broken by hammer into 'logs'. **1975** *Times* 9 Aug. 12/7 Collyweston slate is unusual in that it is produced by the action of frost on the stone logs.

6. d. Any record in which facts about the progress or performance of something are entered in the order in which they become known; e.g. (*a*) a record of what is found, or how some property varies, at successive depths in drilling a well; a graph or chart displaying this information; (*b*) a record kept by a lorry driver in which details of journeys are noted; (*c*) a record kept of what is broadcast by a radio or television station from moment to moment.

1913 *Jrnl. Geol.* XXI. 671 This company has prepared logs of various..salt wells. **1920** L. S. PANYITY *Prospecting for Oil & Gas* xiii. 162 It is the duty of the driller..to keep a record or log of the well. This consists in noting the various formations drilled through, the casing points, and the showings of water, oil or gas. **1924** G. W. GRUPP *Econ. Motor Transportation* ix. 187 Nothing is more interesting than..making..a motor-truck performance log. **1925** K. G. FENELON *Econ. Road Transport* 241 A daily log prepared by the driver of each vehicle, showing the nature of the work performed, the tonnage carried, the time taken, etc. **1937** *Printers' Ink Monthly* May 39/2 *Log*, an account of every minute of broadcasting, all errors being considered. An accurate journal required by law. **1956** *Nature* 21 Jan. 120/2 The study of these continuous velocity logs in conjunction with seismic reflexion records shot from the surface is leading to a better understanding of the origin of reflexions. **1957** M. R. J. WYLLIE *Fund. Electr. Log Interpretation* (ed. 2) II. 105 Even in dirty formations the neutron log can sometimes give a fairly good estimate of porosity. *Ibid.* 110 Logs which make use of the scattering of gamma-rays to determine the density of formations penetrated by boreholes..are rapidly being improved in efficiency. **1960** J. M. WELLER *Stratigr. Princ. & Pract.* xvii. 614 Electric logs consist of curves that are continuous records of self-potential and resistivity measured in wells and plotted against depth... In a general way..they indicate differences in lithologic characters of strata and many lithologic changes are shown with great precision. **1963** *Amer. Speech* XXXVIII. 44 *Log, log book*, the driver's daily report required by the I.C.C. **1965** W. S. BARRY *Airline Managem.* x. 149 Station logs report troubles that have occurred during embarkation or disembarkation. **1968** *Radio Communication Handbk.* (ed. 4) xx. 4/2 Log Keeping. The Post Office requires all amateurs to keep a log book containing full details of all transmissions... Entries must be made at the time of operation, and no gaps should be left in the log. **1974** *Sci. Amer.* May 133/3 These men filled out sleep logs (for pay) and answered many questions.

8. (in sense 'made of logs'): *log barn, barrack, building, causeway, chapel, church, city, college, heap, kitchen, meeting-house, pen, pound, prison, room, shanty* (earlier example), *stable, tavern, tenement, wall, way* (later examples); (in sense 'for use in dealing with logs') *log skid*.

1795 *Pittsburgh Gaz.* 6 June 1/2 To be Sold..two cabins, a log barn. **1845** S. JUDD *Margaret* I. iii. 12 On the east side of the road was a log barn. **1948** *Time* 11 Oct. 21/1 A country which still remembered Indians, wild turkeys, log barns, [etc.]. *a* **1861** T. WINTHROP *Life in Open Air* (1863) 32 All residents of Damville dwelt in a great log-barrack. **1806** Z. M. PIKE *Acct. Expeditions Sources Mississippi* I. App. 36 [The fur-trading establishment] at Lower Red Cedar Lake..consists of log buildings. **1828** *Gore Gaz.* (Ancaster, Ontario) 18 Oct. 134/2 The stumps are all taken out—and the log causeways, where these are necessary—are covered with a thick coat of earth. **1831** T. BUTTRICK in R. G. Thwaites *Early Western Trav.* (1904) VIII. 54 In some places, in low grounds, there would be log-causeways for a considerable distance. **1810** F. ASBURY *Jrnl.* (1821) III. 298 Saturday, at William Adams's log-chapel I preached to a small assembly. **1847** F. PARKMAN in *Knickerbocker* XXIX. 313 We found the log-church ..belonging to the Methodist Shawanoe Mission. **1895** M. A. JACKSON *Mem. Stonewall Jackson* (ed. 2) 382 The little log church is..full. **1817** S. R. BROWN *Western Gaz.* 106 Vangeville,—A log city..has fifteen or twenty old log houses. **1795** P. FRENEAU *Poems* 374 On the Demolition of a Log-College. **1850** W. H. FOOTE *Sk. Virginia* 349 Could we..look into the school of the worthy pastor, then gaining its eminence as 'a log college'. **1818** L. D. CLARKE in *Firelands Pioneer* (1920) XXI. 2324, I spread ashes where log-heaps had been burned. **1819** E. DANA *Geogr. Sk. Western Country* 36 The Creoles never having before smelted, except by throwing the ore into log heaps. **1856** A. CARY *Married* 295 Having made a log-heap fire, Martin put the table-cloth about his shoulders. **1933** E. C. GUILLET *Early Life Upper Canada* 277 In new settlements during July the whole countryside was illuminated by the burning of log heaps. **1874** E. EGGLESTON *Circuit Rider* v. 56 The wide old log-kitchen, with its loom in one corner. **1948** *Florida Hist. Q.* July 40 Close to many of the larger houses were log kitchens where cooking and eating took place. **1823** *Baptist Mag.* IV. 74 We have a good log meeting-house on Salt Creek. **1789** M. L. WEEMS *Let.* in *M. L. Weems: Works & Ways* (1929) III. 148, I lodged in a log-pen. **1832** *Louisville Directory* 102 The ditch was surmounted by a breast work of log pens filled with the earth obtained from the ditch. **1853** 'P. PAXTON' *Stray Yankee in Texas* 118 A fish spear is to him [*sc.* the old Texan] a groin,..a house no house, but a log-pen. **1737** in *Coll. New Hampsh. Hist. Soc.* (1863) VII. 358 A log pound 30 ft. square, six feet high, with a good gate, and a lock and key. **1802** G. BARRINGTON *Hist. N.S. Wales* 184 (Morris), The governor resolved on building a large log prison. **1845** C. M. KIRKLAND *Western Clearings* 212, I went to prison; nothing but a log prison. **1743** D. BRAINERD *Let.* 30 Apr. in J. Edwards *Acct. Life D. Brainerd* (1749) 201 It is a Log-Room, without any Floor, that I lodge in. **1903** S. E. WHITE *Conjuror's House.* x. 119 Virginia entered a small log room..and sat down in a musty red armchair. **1847** H. HOWE *Hist. Coll. Ohio* 492 They fell to work..erecting bark huts and log shanties. **1923** Log-skid [see *BREAK-DOWN 3]. **1957** *N.Z. Timber Jrnl.* Oct. 73/2 *Log skids*, a platform on which logs are stacked in the forest to assist loading on to trucks. **1834** *Southern Lit. Messenger* I. 120 In the log stable..I saw a number of them. **1810** F. CUMING *Sk. Tour Western Country* 44 We stopped to feed our horses at a small log tavern. **1874** E. EGGLESTON *Circuit Rider* xvi. 147 Marton was conducted three miles down the river to a log tavern. **1829** J. F. COOPER *Borderers* III. i. 27 The log tenement, the stacks, ..were sending forth clouds of murky smoke. **1841** —— *Deerslayer* (ed. 2) I. ii. 47 The furniture was of the strange mixture that it is not uncommon to find in the remotely situated log-tenements of the interior. **1840** *Knickerbocker* XVI. 247, I looked around on the bare log-walls and ceiling. **1822** Logway [see *ground-hornet* (*GROUND *sb.* 18 b)]. **1874** B. F. TAYLOR *World on Wheels* II. vii. 245 Days when, over the old road, ran the yellow mud-stained coach,..pitching along its log-ways. **1973** A. PRICE in *Winter's Crimes* 5 202 The driver..had driven the cart off the logway.

b. *log-heaving, -raising; log-hauler, -lumberer.* **c.** *log-built* ppl. a.

1835 C. F. HOFFMAN *Winter in West* I. 79 We stopped to breakfast at a low log built shantee. **1937** *Discovery* Nov. 344/2 This sole surviving example of the log-built churches, once common in the forest region of Essex. **1919** W. T. GRENFELL *Labrador Doctor* (1920) xiii. 233 The log-hauler would not deliver the goods to the rotary saw. **1962** *Amer. Speech* XXXVII. 134 *Log hauler*, an engineer on a logging train. **1823** W. FAUX *Memorable Days Amer.* 180 Log-heaving, that is, rolling trees together for burning, is done by the neighbours in a body, invited for the purpose. **1909** *Westm. Gaz.* 11 Aug. 5/1 The pulp-maker..is not content, like the log-lumberer, to remove the grown trees, but takes the young plants as well. **1864** 'E. KIRKE' *Down in Tennessee* iii. 43 In April, 1862, he and his band came upon a party of neighbors collected at a log raising in Fentress County. **1897** E. W. BRODHEAD *Bound in Shallows* 169 Law, the log-raisin's and corn-huskin's they used to have!

9. **log-basket**, a basket, or similar receptacle, for holding logs by a fire; **log-canoe, -cock** (earlier examples); **log-deck** (see quot.); **log-drive** (see DRIVE *sb.* 3); **log-headed** (later example); **log-man,** (*a*) (later example); **log-paddock**, a small field fenced in with logs; **log-rule** (see quot. 1905); **log-runner**, read: *Austral.*, a ground-dwelling bird of the genus *Orthonyx* found in northern New South Wales, Queensland, and New Guinea; add examples; **log-running**, the operation of sending logs down a river; **log-scale** (see quot. 1905); **log sheet**, a log-book in which the driver of a commercial motor vehicle enters particulars of his working and rest hours; **log-slate** (earlier example).

1902 *Westm. Gaz.* 17 Dec. 8/2 A really nice log-basket in wrought iron. **1972** *Country Life* 14 Dec. 1697/2 A split-willow log basket—22 in. long, 18 in. wide and 12 in. high, it costs £4.00. **1752** P. STEVENS in N. D. Mereness *Trav. Amer. Colonies* (1916) 315, I..set out..in the morning accompanied by an officer and ten soldiers, who brought us in two log canoes. **1806** M. LEWIS in Lewis & Clark *Orig. Jrnls. Lewis & Clark Exped.* (1905) IV. 132 The large woodpecker or log cock. **1853** 'P. PAXTON' *Stray Yankee in Texas* 58 (Th.), The log-cock, with his gaudy head-dress. **1905** *Terms Forestry & Logging* (U.S. Dept. Agric. Bureau Forestry) 42 *Log deck*, the platform upon a loading jack. **1904** *N.Y. Even. Post* 3 May 2 The annual log-drives have begun in the upper Hudson watershed. **1926** *Spectator* 24 July 149/1 Anyone..would have been thought log-headed or obstinate. **1845** C. M. KIRKLAND *Western Clearings* 175 He turned his hand to the plough, and was the 'patient log-man' of a poverty-stricken household. **1900** H. LAWSON *On Track* 29 He was putting up a two-rail fence along the old log-paddock. **1895** *Montgomery Ward Catal.* 369/1 Log rules, either Scribner or Doyle scale. **1905** *Terms Forestry & Logging* (U.S. Dept. Agric. Bureau Forestry) 15 *Log rule*, 1. A tabular statement of the amount of lumber which can be sawed from logs of given lengths and diameters. 2. A graduated stick for measuring the densities of logs. The number of board feet in logs of given diameters and lengths is shown upon the stick. **1898** E. E. MORRIS *Austral Eng.* 272/1 *Log-runner*, an Australian bird, called also a Spine-tail. **1901** A. J. CAMPBELL *Nests & Eggs Austral. Birds* I. 252 A nest I found in the Big Scrub, Richmond River, which I believe belonged to the Orthonyx, or Log Runner, was in a damp situation. **1931, 1934** [see *CHOWCHILLA]. **1965** *Austral. Encycl.* V. 359/1 Log-runners construct large domed nests of leaves and moss, with a side-entrance placed usually on the ground or on the top of a low stump. **1878** *Lumberman's Gaz.* 6 Apr., The Green Bay *Advocate* of March 28 says that log-running is commencing all around. **1901** S. E. WHITE *Westerners* xxi. 199 In the log running Michail Lafond was the man always called upon to skim over the bobbing logs. **1877** *Mich. Supreme Court Rep.* XXXVI. 168 The scale of the manufactured lumber exceeded the log scale. **1905** *Terms Forestry & Logging* (U.S. Dept. Agric. Bureau Forestry) 42 *Log scale*, the contents of a log, or of a number of logs considered collectively. **1958** *Listener* 14 Aug. 226/2 The lights come on in the cabs [of the lorries], while the drivers make out their log sheets. **1959** E. K. WENLOCK *Kitchin's Road Transport Law* (ed. 12) 78/2 A current record (popularly known as a log sheet) containing the prescribed particulars must be compiled by the driver of every vehicle, [etc.]. **1964** *Times* 11 Feb. 11/6 The practice of keeping duplicate sets of log sheets,..is so common that it is hardly remarked upon. **1834** *Knickerbocker* III. 83 Adding on the log-slate another 'ditto' to the long column of them.

log (lǫg), *sb.*[3] and *a.* Also † **log.** (with point). Abbrev. of LOGARITHM, LOGARITHMIC *a.*

See the last paragraph of the note to LOGARITHM; (*log* is no longer confined to a position before a number).

1631 [see LOGARITHM]. **1805** J. W. NORIE *Epitome Pract. Navigation* Expl. Tables p. xv, Thus the log. of 295 is 2·469822. **1858** I. TODHUNTER *Algebra for Schools* 308 Given log 2 find log ·0025. **1890** G. F. MATTHEWS *Man. Logarithms* 18 How many positive integers are there whose logs. to the base 3 have 6 for a characteristic? **1960** F. LAND *Lang. Math.* ix. 119 Either of the forms $1296 = 6^4$ or $4 = \log_6 1296$ describes the relationship between the number 1296, the base 6 and the index 4. **1971** *Nature* 17 Dec. 419/2 At every stage in dark adaptation, the log threshold for test flash detection..is raised in proportion to the log brightness of the after image.

1785 C. HUTTON *Math. Tables* 150 To find the log. sine of 1° [etc.]. *Ibid.*, To find the log. tang. of 2° [etc.]. **1805** J. W. NORIE *Epitome Pract. Navigation* Expl. Tables p. xv, The log. sine of 3 points is 9·744739. **1890** G. F. MATTHEWS *Man. Logarithms* 49 The Logarithm of the sine of A is called the logarithmic sine of A and written log sin A. **1967** *Oceanogr. & Marine Biol.* V. 134 In a recent account of headland-bay beaches Yasso (1965) found that their plan geometry, which results from wave movements, closely fits a log-spiral. **1974** *Daily Tel.* 14 May 3 (Advt.), At last there's a pocket calculator which gives you log and trig functions instantly..at a price that makes sense.

2. Special Comb.: **log log,** (*a*) *sb.*, the logarithm of the logarithm (of a number); also *attrib.*, indicating or involving such quantities; (*b*) *adj.* (usu. hyphenated), applied to a graph or to graph paper having a logarithmic scale along both axes; **log-normal** *a.* (*Statistics*), such that the logarithm of the variate is distributed according to a normal distribution; hence **log-normally** *adv.*; **log phase** *Biol.* = *logarithmic phase* s.v. *LOGARITHMIC *a.*; **log table,** a table of logarithms; usu. *pl.*

1910 *Encycl. Brit.* IV. 975/1 Dr John Perry added log log scales to the ordinary slide rule in order to facilitate the calculation of a^x..according to the formula $\log \log a^x = \log \log a + \log x$. **1933** S. DAWSON *Introd. Computation of Statistics* i. 28 Log.-log. paper, in which both sets of values are represented by lines proportional to their logarithms. **1957** KENDALL & BUCKLAND *Dict. Statistical Terms* 169 *Loglog transformation*, the transformation of a probability *P*..according to the formula $Y = \log_e(-\log_e P)$. **1962** *Lancet* 5 May 949/2 An exponential function yields a straight line when plotted on log-linear graph paper, while a power law function gives a straight line when plotted on log-log paper. **1966** D. G. BRANDON *Mod. Techniques Metallogr.* 209 The slope of the log–log plot of the current–voltage characteristic near the threshold field ..is of the order of 30. **1945** J. H. GADDUM in *Nature* 20 Oct. 465/1 It is proposed to call the distribution of *x* 'lognormal' when the distribution of log *x* is normal. *Ibid.*, Examples of lognormal distributions have been found in estimates of the numbers of plankton caught in different hauls of the net, and in the amounts of electricity used in medium-class homes in the United States. **1951** *Biometrika* XXXVIII. 434 It is assumed that the population distribution of abundance is log-normal. **1971** J. B. CARROLL et al. *Word Frequency Bk.* p. xxi, This model.. is called the lognormal model, because it postulates that the total vocabulary underlying a corpus is distributed according to the familiar 'normal distribution' when the logarithms of the frequencies are used. **1945** J. H. GADDUM in *Nature* 20 Oct. 465/1 The size of the particles of silver in a photographic emulsion were lognormally distributed. **1951** *Biometrika* XXXVIII. 427 (*heading*) The expected frequencies in a sample of an animal population in which the abundances of species are log-normally distributed. **1967** *Proc. Ussher Soc.* I. 277 Testing on a logarithmic scale, however, reveals the existence of two lognormally distributed populations with a discontinuity at about 0·15% Mg. **1938** H. L. HIND *Brewing* I. xv. 367 This method..was termed the Log phase method because it is used to measure acidity during the logarithmic phase of the growth of the bacterium in wort. **1959** F. S. STEWART *Bigger's Handbk. Bacteriol.* (ed. 7) i. 10 The log phase is of relatively short duration, lasting at most for some hours. **1974** *Nature* 4 Jan. 67/1 Stationary and log-phase cultures of *E. coli* B, *E. coli* K 12 Sr..and *B. subtilis* were exposed to 160° C. *c* **1935** J. A. HAMMERTON *New Popular Educator* 467/1 For practical purposes the indices of 10 have been tabulated in what are called Tables of Logarithms... The student now needs this tool, 'log tables'. **1962** R. B. FULLER *Epic Poem on Industrialization* xx. 143 Napier developed between 1614–1620 His logarithms, his complete log tables. **1969** D. C. HAGUE *Managerial Economics* vi. 132 Given time, patience and log tables, we could draw up a table like Table 7 for ourselves.

log, *v.*[1] Add: **1. b.** (Earlier and later examples.) **c.** To remove the logs or trees from (an area). Also const. *off, over, up.* Chiefly *N. Amer.*

1717 in *Mass. House of Representatives Jrnl.* (1919) I. 272 Bridger [is trying]..to compel the Inhabitants..to Pay Him Forty Shillings..for each Team they send to Log and get Timber. **1818** L. D. CLARK in *Firelands Pioneer* (1920) XXI. 2322 He and Lines went logging of the land to sow with wheat. **1829** J. MACTAGGART *Three Yrs.*

Canada II. 206 When the large wood is hewn down and *logged*, that is, cut into lengths and laid round these stacks in a rude pile, the fire can more readily be applied to them. **1829** in E. C. Guillet *Valley of Trent* (1957) 355 After this we logged up and cleared three acres. **1833** *Chambers's Edin. Jrnl.* II. 167/2 He..acquaints his neighbours around him, according to the extent of the land he has to log. **1839** A. Langton *Jrnl.* in *Gentlewoman Upper Canada* (1950) 114 Six or seven acres were logged up during the day. **1902** S. E. White *Blazed Trail* ii. 5 We own, however, five million on the Cass Branch which we would like to log on contract. **1904** —— *Blazed Trail Stories* iii. 46 Suppose you log a knoll which..must grow at least a half million. **1919** B. W. Sinclair *Burned Bridges* 302 As soon as the land is logged off it is open for soldier entry. **1921** H. Kephart *Camping & Woodcraft* (new ed.) I. 113 With this one tool a good axeman can..quickly fell and log-up a tree large enough to keep a hot fire before his lean-to throughout the night. **1948** *Milwaukee* (Wisconsin) *Jrnl.* 18 July 6/5 By 1889 he had built a farm home and 'tourist home' from timber he had cut and logged himself. **1959** A. McLintock *Descr. Atlas N.Z.* 45 Once provisional State forest was logged over for timber it was then released for agricultural development. **1963** E. C. Guillet *Pioneer Farmer* I. 318 Some men were known to log several acres a year entirely alone—without even oxen.

d. *to log up* (see quots. 1889 and 1905). So logging-up. *N.Z. colloq.*

1889 *Colonia* I. 1. 26 'Logging-up' is generally done in the autumn, when there are strong gales of wind blowing. The bush which has been felled in the winter, is set fire to, and after a day or two when the ground is sufficiently cool for walking on, the still-burning logs are rolled together and piled up with rubbish, so that they may be burnt clean away. **1891** R. Wallace *Rural Econ. Austral. & N.Z.* xv. 232 When the burning is badly done the seed cannot be properly sown; the rubbish lies thick over the ground and the whole has to be gone over again and 'logged-up', else the land is thrown temporarily out of use.. while the owner waits for the remaining rubbish to decay. **1905** J. M. Thomson *Bush Boys N.Z.* ii. 32 These [big unburned trees] are 'logged-up' afterwards, that is rolled together and piled round the stumps, so as to dry thoroughly preparatory to 'firing' them again. **1908** B. E. Baughan *Shingle-Short* 84 [Trees] logged up for burning.

4. (Later example.)

1839 C. F. Briggs *Adventures Harry Franco* I. xix. 194 The captain ordered Mr. Ruffin to log me, and swore he would send me back to the States in irons.

5. (Further examples, other than *Naut.*)

1924 J. Bruce *Power Station Efficiency Control* v. 105 If an analysis is to be made of the boiler-room operating results, the indications from the various instruments must be carefully logged at least every half-hour. **1966** Rubin & Haller *Communication Switching Syst.* viii. 294 Every message which is accepted into the system is logged on a storage device. **1969** Bennison & Wright *Geol. Hist. Brit. Isles* i. 18 One further parameter of particular importance in logging bore-hole strata is the measurement of thermal conductivity. **1974** *Physics Bull.* Jan. 30/2 Up to now data from brake tests have been logged using ultraviolet recorders or human observers.

b. Also, to travel at (a certain speed) as measured by a log; to 'do'. Also of an aircraft or pilot: to attain a cumulative total of (so many hours, miles, etc.) in the air. Also *transf.*, of a machine and the time spent in operation.

1928 *Chambers's Jrnl.* Feb. 116/2 The liner was logging a steady seventeen knots. **1955** *Times* 22 Aug. 8/5 During the past five days..Secretary of State for Air, who has been learning to fly, has logged 13 hours' solo flying, it was stated yesterday by an Air Ministry spokesman. **1956** *IRE Trans. Electronic Computers* V. 138/2 To date 670 hours of operation have been logged on this unit since debugging. **1966** *Listener* 4 Aug. 179/2 The *Graf Zeppelin*.. was the first aircraft to log over a million miles. **1972** *Lebende Sprachen* XVII. 73/2 Over the past two years, our HS 125s..have proved themselves to be increasingly valuable as management tools while logging more than 1,200 trouble-free hours.

loganberry. Substitute for def.: [f. the name of J. H. *Logan* (1841–1928), American lawyer and horticulturist, who first cultivated it.] A fruit produced by crossing a raspberry with a blackberry, or the plant producing it. (Add earlier and later examples.) Also *attrib.*

1893 *Bull. Calif. Agric. Exper. Station* No. 103. 3 The Logan Berry..[has] the shape of a blackberry, the color of a raspberry, and a combination of the flavors of both. **1897** *Gardeners' Chronicle* 24 July 47/1 One of the most interesting of recent contributions from American experiment-stations is Professor L. F. Kinney's bulletin on the Logan-berry. This fruit has been..much talked of in recent years. **1926** *Daily Colonist* (Victoria, B.C.) 11 July 3/2 The Growers' Wine Company, with headquarters in this city, starting out this season with the objective of putting up 100,000 gallons of loganberry wine, has already more than 50 per cent. of that production. **1929** D. H. Lawrence *Phoenix II* (1968) 539 Women..aren't something new on the face of the earth, like the loganberry or artificial silk. **1929** J. Masefield *Hawbucks* 154 Would you care to have some loganberry plants? **1944** E. Carr *House of All Sorts* 151 The seasoned widow brought loganberry wine of her own brew. **1973** R. Genders *Epicure's Garden* i. 67 The loganberry..has been widely grown for bottling and canning.

logarithmic, *a.* Add: *logarithmic amplifier* Electr., an amplifier which produces an output in logarithmic proportion to the input; *logarithmic decrement*: see *decrement 2 b; *logarithmic phase* Biol., the period during which the population of a culture of bacteria increases exponentially with time.

1914 *Jrnl. Hygiene* XIV. 260 This selected strain holds the field during the second or logarithmic phase. **1938** Logarithmic phase [see *log phase* s.v. *log *sb.*[3] and *a.* 2]. **1954** C. P. Snow *New Men* vi. 101 There was one of those counters whose ticking I had come to expect in any Barford laboratory; there was a logarithmic amplifier, a D.C. amplifier..which would give a measure..of the 'neutron flux'. **1957** C. Wu in C. F. Bonilla *Nucl. Engin.* iv. 128 When a wide range of the neutron flux, as much as six to eight decades, is to be measured, a logarithmic amplifier must be used. **1971** J. S. Hough et al. *Malting & Brewing Sci.* xviii. 480 The next stage is the dividing of the cells at a constant rate, referred to as the 'exponential phase' or 'logarithmic phase'.

logatom (lǫ·gætǫm). *Telephony.* [f. Gr. λόγ-ος word + Atom.] A meaningless syllable formed arbitrarily, usually from initial and final consonants and a vowel, for use in testing telephone systems.

1937 W. H. Grinsted in *Siemens Mag.* (Engin. Suppl.) Jan. 4/2 Measurements are easier and more definite if one goes to the limit of intelligibility or uses nonsense syllables (logatoms). *Ibid.* 8/2 A few approximate contour curves, ..for logatom articulation, have been plotted. **1942** Knight & Prickett *Poole's Telephone Handbk.* (ed. 8) xx. 491 These syllables are composed of consonant, vowel and consonant, based on the esperanto alphabet, which are termed logatoms. **1973** D. L. Richards *Telecommunication by Speech* iii. 165 Table 3.13 shows also a list of English single syllable words, which have been constructed by selecting from the English logatoms just described those that were actual English words.

Logbara, var. *Lugbara *sb.* and *a.*

log-book. Add: **1.** (Further example.)

1813 *Theatrical Inquisitor* II. 362 It [*sc.* the voyage] was divested of all log-book lumber.

b. *Aeronaut.* A book in which particulars of aircraft flights, flying hours, etc., are recorded.

1911 R. M. Pierce *Dict. Aviation* 150 *Log-book*, a book in which the particulars of a balloon-trip or airship-flight are entered or kept. **1917** Grahame-White & Harper *Air Power* iv. viii. 154 Turning to his log-book, he will look up this sign, and identify the place on the coast he is approaching. **1951** O. Berthoud tr. *Clostermann's Big Show* 19 Flying hours..quickly mounted up in my pilot's log-book.

c. (*a*) The registration book of a motor vehicle. (*b*) (See quot. 1971.)

1958 *Listener* 20 Nov. 835/2 The internal combustion engine, or 'I.C.E.' as my log-book calls it. **1963** *Amer. Speech* XXXVIII. 44 *Log book*, the driver's daily report required by the I.C.C. **1965** *Mod. Law Rev.* XXVIII. v. 571 English lawyers will still have to admit that a car's logbook is not admissible evidence of the engine number. **1971** M. Tak *Truck Talk* 100 *Log book*, the daily log in which truckers list their activities. **1973** *Times* 28 Nov. 9 Vehicle Registration Documents (Logbooks) will be stamped by the post office to record each issue of [petrol] coupons.

log cabin. orig. *U.S.* [See Log *sb.*[1] 9.] A cabin, or small house, built of logs.

1770 in H. R. Shurtleff *Log Cabin Myth* (1939) 25 The court doth appoint..to agree with a workman to build a log cabbin..for a Court House. **1803** F. Asbury *Jrnl.* (1821) III. 119 Kindness will not make a crowded log cabin, twelve feet by ten, agreeable. **1817** S. R. Brown *Western Gaz.* 48 There are six families living in log cabins. **1835** *Southern Lit. Messenger* I. 546 Most of the log cabins have been exchanged for neat white cottages. *Ibid.* II. 53 We behold the low log-cabin of a school-house. **1881** W. M. Thayer (*title*) From log-cabin to White House: the story of President Garfield's life. **1937** A. Huxley *Let.* 3 June (1969) 421 We have a log cabin..on Frieda Lawrence's ranch. **1970** *Globe & Mail* (Toronto) 28 Sept. 26/6 (Advt.), Advertiser..has original log cabin for disposal. **1974** *Guardian* 23 Jan. 11/1 America has always frenetically nurtured its pioneer myths... Log cabins, and old Abe Lincoln.

attrib. **1819** R. L. Mason *Narr. in Pioneer West* (1915) 54 It is very common for a log cabin tavern without a door or window (perhaps a log out to answer both purposes) to sup and lodge twenty persons. **1840** *Nashville* (Tennessee) *Whig* 17 Aug., They are the representatives of a hardy race of honest log cabin pioneers. **1840** *Boston Atlas* 11 Sept., Crow,.. For the Party laid low By the log-cabin boys Of old Tippecanoe. **1841** *Congress. Globe* 22 June 92 Mr. Clark of New York said all this log-cabin slang was quite out of date. **1887** [in Dict. s.v. Log *sb.*[1] 9]. **1965** A. Colby *Patchwork Quilts* 78 Log cabin quilts were popular in England and America from about the middle of the nineteenth century, and were so called because the square blocks were composed of a square centre patch surrounded by strips of material or 'logs'..overlapped..in much the same fashion as the log cabins were built. **1973** *Sat. Rev. World* (U.S.) 4 Dec. 46/3 Boulder Flat, a log-cabin settlement at 11,000 feet, from which the last inhabitant departed more than one hundred years ago.

loge[2]. Add: **1. b.** A concierge's lodge.

1969 *Guardian* 2 Aug. 3/7 The tiny loges, ill-lit and ill-ventilated, in which too many concierges are condemned to live. **1972** R. Mayne *Europeans* v. 72 The views of the man in the street, or the woman in the concierge's *loge*.

2. (Later examples.)

1900 Ade *More Fables* (1902) 188 When he was in a Loge at the Play-House with Exclusive Ethel and her Friends. **1904** A. Bennett *Great Man* xxiv. 260 They occupied a 'loge' in the..Folies-Bergère. **1968** *Globe & Mail* (Toronto) 17 Feb. 24 (Advt.), Loges $5.00. **1974** *Plain Dealer* (Cleveland) 13 Oct. C2/2 The goal..is to keep the building occupied at least 300 nights a year. Naturally, it won't be completely finished for the Sinatra opener. The loges won't be ready.

logged, *ppl. a.* Add: **b.** Also *logged-off.*

1908 *Chambers's Jrnl.* 2 May 352/1 The people who are taking up the 'logged-off' lands are usually accustomed to getting along in a small way. **1911** *U.S. Dept. Agric. Farmer's Bull.* No. 462. 5 The merchantable timber has been stripped from large areas, leaving what is known as 'logged-off' or 'cut-over' land. **1921** *Daily Colonist* (Victoria, B.C.) 25 Mar. 4/3 The report contains a great array of information referring to the sub-division of logged-off lands and expired timber licences for settlement on the coast.

logged, *a. U.S.* [f. Log *sb.*[1] + -ed[2].] Built of logs.

1784 Washington *Diaries* (1925) II. 294 A Logged dwelling house with a punchion Roof. **1834** *Knickerbocker* III. 32 Immediately on the road, appeared a large rude double logged cabin. **1972** J. Bunting *Lionheads* 155 The bunker, a mud carapace with logged sides, is ten meters inland.

logger, *sb.*[1] Add: **2.** = *data logger* (*datum 3).

1958 L. E. C. Hughes *Electronic Engineer's Ref. Bk.* 832 Another service..by an automatic logger..is to provide the equivalent of the manuscript log of, say, temperatures in a much more useful form. **1967** *Times Rev. Industry* Apr. 63/3 The basic logger..can be connected to up to 20 data channels to monitor, for instance, the operation of a small process plant.

loggerhead. Add: **2. b.** (See quot.)

Known to be older than 1885.

1909 A. C. Fox-Davies *Compl. Guide Heraldry* 193 The leopard's face... For some unfathomable reason these charges when they occur in the arms of Shrewsbury are usually referred to locally as 'loggerheads'.

3. b. (See quot.)

1904 *Athenæum* 27 Feb. 280/1 The inkstands..include many of the top of the prototypes of the circular heavy inkstand, still used, and known to many under the old name of 'loggerheads'.

6. b. (*b*) (Later examples.)

1870 *Amer. Naturalist* III. 159, I saw a Loggerhead attack a snake. **1906** *N.Y. Even. Post* 8 Aug. 2 Charleston S.C. pet canaries are being killed by a bird that is known as the 'loggerhead'. A loggerhead strikes at the canaries through the bars of the cage. **1939** Forbush & May *Nat. Hist. Birds Amer.* 398 The Loggerhead is an indefatigable destroyer of grasshoppers, for which it seems ever on the watch.

8. *to be at loggerheads* (later examples).

1955 *Bull. Atomic Sci.* Mar. 90/3 Uranium men and oil and gas producers had long been at loggerheads due to the fact these natural substances frequently occur on the same site, though at different horizons. **1955** *Times* 19 May 4/2 The jury would not have much difficulty in getting rid of that suggestion, because those two were obviously at loggerheads. **1975** J. Gardner *Killer for Song* i. 13 'James, it's good to see you.' His expression was at loggerheads with the words.

loggia'd, *a.* Provided with loggias.

1903 *Westm. Gaz.* 9 Dec. 3/1 A great loggia'd palace, gaunt, time-stained, damp-eaten.

logginess. [f. Loggy *a.* 2.] A state of heaviness or sluggishness.

1924 *Scribner's Mag.* July 88/2 He ate sparingly.. rather as insurance against any sensation of logginess. **1969** P. Highsmith *Tremor of Forgery* xxv. 237 He awakened with the now familiar logginess of brain that always took fifteen seconds to clear.

logging, *vbl. sb.* Add: **2*.** The process of taking and recording information about something. (Cf. Log *v.*[1] 5 in Dict and Suppl., *log *sb.*[1] 6 d.)

1941 F. H. Lahee *Field Geol.* (ed. 4) xviii. 574 For.. learning more about the lithology and fluid content of rocks in the walls of a bore-hole, and..for more accurately fixing the top and bottom contacts of rocks of varying character..electrical surveying, or electrical logging..has become common practice. **1958** L. E. C. Hughes *Electronic Engineer's Ref. Bk.* 832 With the aid of the automatic logging control..the alarm circuits on each unit controller trigger off printed messages. **1965** G. J. Williams *Econ. Geol. N.Z.* xvi. 255/1 Down-hole resistivity logging.. showed that the kerogen content of the shale is thin-bedded, and that it can be measured rapidly by this means. **1967** *Electronics* 6 Mar. 269/1 Suggested applications include scanning, multiplexing..data logging..and telemetering.

3. *logging-chain, company, establishment, railway, swamp, wheel.*

1825 A. Anderson *Diary* 10 Sept. in G. Sellar *Narr.* (1916) vii. 103 Walked to Toronto... Am no judge of oxen... Besides them had to pay for logging-chain and an ox-sled. **1905** *Terms Forestry & Logging* (U.S. Dept. Agric. Bureau Forestry) 36 *Dump hook*, a levered chain, grab hook attached to the evener to which a team is hitched in loading logs. A movement of the lever releases the hook from the logging chain without stopping the team. **1910** J. Hart *Vigilante Girl* xxvi. 356 He was carrying in his hand a light logging-chain which was attached to his ankles. **1949** *Sat. Even. Post* 15 Jan. 71/2, I rushed around to the toolbox, dragged out one of the heavy logging chains. **1903** A. B. Hart *Actual Govt. Amer. Colonies* 326 Logging companies buy up immense areas of land for timber. **1948** *Time* 9 Feb. 36/3 Logging companies protested it was a poor policy to rob them of 800 loyal, trained workers when there was a shortage of labor. **1851** J. S. Springer *Forest Life & Forest Trees* 67, I have seldom taxed my judgement as severely on any subject as in judiciously locating a logging establishment. **1888** J. Muir *Picturesque Calif.* 460 It is moved from camp to

camp by the 'logging' railway. **1926** *Daily Colonist* (Victoria, B.C.) 7 July 1/7 Construction of logging railways and similar facilities will be proceeded with..for the reopening of the logging camps in September. **1969** *Islander* (Victoria, B.C.) 9 Mar. 12/1, I used shank's mare along the logging railway to what was referred to as Headquarters Camp. **1848** BARTLETT *Dict. Amer.*, *Logging swamp*, in Maine, the place where pine timber is cut. **1851** J. S. SPRINGER *Forest Life & Forest Trees* 46 We have sometimes heard the voice of prayer even in the logging swamp. **1905** *Terms Forestry & Logging* (U.S. Dept. Agric. Bureau Forestry) 42 *Logging wheels*, a pair of wheels, usually about 10 feet in diameter, for transporting logs.

loggy, *a.* Add: **2.** (Later examples.)
1886 *Outing* VIII. 58/1 They do very well sailing free but on the wind are loggy. **1902** *Westm. Gaz.* 18 Oct. 2/2 They seemed..'loggy' and slow to get going. **1966** H. MARRIOTT *Cariboo Cowboy* vii. 66 A fellow doing quite a bit of riding needs two or three horses at least, because riding one horse day after day makes the horse loggy and leg-weary.

3. Abounding in logs.
1851 A. O. HALL *Manhattaner* 2 The sandy, boggy, loggy, grassy, and snaggy strips of land.

log-house. (See LOG *sb.*[1] 9.) (Earlier and later examples.)
1662 in H. R. Shurtleff *Log Cabin Myth* (1939) 80 As fare Westwardly as the logg house. **1784** J. F. D. SMYTH *Tour U.S.A.* II. 9 Constructing temporary habitations (log houses) to reside in. **1879** A. W. TOURGÉE *Fool's Errand* vii. 34 This log house had..given way to a more pretentious structure of brick. **1965** MRS L. B. JOHNSON *White House Diary* 7 Sept. (1970) 318, I arrived at Honeymoon Cabin, a real log house. **1974** 'S. HARVESTER' *Forgotten Road* v. 54 Clusters of log houses..formed the village.

Logian (lǫ·dʒiăn), *a.* [f. *logi-a* LOGION + -AN.] Containing the Logia of Jesus.
1909 V. H. STANTON *Gospels as Hist. Documents* II. 48 To call the source we are considering simply 'the Logian document' cannot, I think, be open to the same objection. **1911** J. C. HAWKINS in *Stud. Synoptic Probl.* 107 The convenient practice which has grown up of calling it the 'Logian source'. **1921** *Contemp. Rev.* Mar. 263 An expanded form of the original Greek Logian document.

logic, *sb.* Add: **1. a.** Also, since the work of Gottlob Frege (1848–1925), a formal system using symbolic techniques and mathematical methods to establish truth-values in the physical sciences, in language, and in philosophical argument. (Later examples.)
1903 B. RUSSELL *Princ. Math.* I. i. 4 But now Mathematics is able to answer, so far at least as to reduce the whole of its propositions to certain fundamental notions of logic. **1932** LEWIS & LANGFORD *Symbolic Logic* v. 118 This logistic method requires that the first branch of logic to be developed should be the calculus of propositions. **1967** A. E. BLUMBERG in *Encycl. Philos.* V. 13/1 What distinguishes modern from ancient and traditional logic is not only its reliance on symbolic techniques and mathematical methods but also its vastly greater formal power and range of application. **1969** F. MONDADORI in R. Klibansky *Contemp. Philos.* III. 352 The phenomenological foundation of logic will make a basic use of Gödel's theorem.

2. b. In phr. *the logic of* ——, indicating the application of logical methods to other subjects of investigation or study; the inferential procedures or structure of some field of inquiry.
1845 MILL in *Westm. Rev.* XLIII. 319 By the logic of a science we understand its method; its particular modes of investigation, and the nature of its evidence. **1882** A. BAIN *John Stuart Mill* iii. 87, I was at the meeting, and listened to Herschel's address. One notable feature in it was the allusion to the recent works on the Logic of Science, by Whewell and Mill especially. **1934** *Mind* XLIII. 101 Little puzzles about the logic of classes. **1937** A. SMEATON tr. *Carnap's Logical Syntax of Lang.* IV. § 70. 256 All the foregoing systems of the logic of modalities.. have, it seems, applied the quasi-syntactical method. **1942** R. G. COLLINGWOOD *New Leviathan* xxxi. 252 As mathematics is the logic of physics, so law is the logic of politics. **1945** *Mind* LIV. 175, I now regard semantics as the fulfilment of the old search for a logic of meaning, which had not been fulfilled before in any precise and satisfactory way. **1971** KOPNIN & NARSKY in R. Klibansky *Contemp. Philos.* IV. 321 The elaboration of these problems has led to the necessity of investigating the logic of contemporary scientific knowledge.

3. b. Phr. *the logic of the situation*, the facts which dictate what action is rationally to be taken.
1876 W. JAMES *Coll. Ess. & Rev.* (1920) 34 The very essential logic of the situation demands that we wait not for any outward sign. **1945** K. R. POPPER *Open Soc.* II. xiv. 90 The detailed determination of his action by what we may call the logic of the situation. **1946** E. WILSON *Mem. Hecate County* (1951) iv. 117 The logic of the situation impelled me to force her backwards, dropping one hand to her waist. **1960** *Rep. Proc. Conf. Univ. U.K.* 58 For the ambitious young man, the logic of the situation (which fortunately doesn't wholly govern his conduct) is this: time given to teaching is time taken from research; and his future depends not on teaching, but on research. **1961** *Observer* 19 Nov. 11/8 He said that Mr. Gaitskell had taken up the position of outside-right, and that the logic of the situation was for him to reorganise his team so that it would at least be facing in the same direction. **1969** H. PERKIN *Key Profession* v. 214 The logic of the situation was that the C.A.T.s should seek to complete their upgrading by seeking recognition as universities.

3*. *Computers* and *Electronics.* The system or principles underlying the representation of logical operations and two-valued variables by electrical or other physical signals and their interactions; the forms and interconnections of logic elements in any particular piece of equipment, in so far as they relate to the interaction of signals and not to the physical nature of the components used; also, the actual components and circuitry; logical operations collectively, as performed by electronic or other devices.
1950 W. W. STIFLER *High-Speed Computing Devices* v. 62 For the convenient operation of a general-purpose machine, they [*sc.* Burks, Goldstine, and von Neumann] point out, it is essential that some steps be taken to translate the nonconforming command quoted above to the same stereotype form. This translation of description of all possible operations to prescribed forms has been called the logic of the machine by these authors, and the term is now in general use. **1952** *Math. Tables & Other Aids to Computation* VI. 42 It is possible, with this new approach, to obtain many of the advantages of a digital computer and also the essential advantages of an analog differential analyzer. The result is a different type of digital 'logic' from that used in the general purpose digital computer. **1954** *IRE Trans. Electronic Computers* Mar. 33/2 The authors have presented the more general aspects of the machine in block diagram form and in addition have given pertinent illustrations of the instrumentation of the logic. **1956** *Ibid.* IV. 134 (*caption*) Logic for self-timing full length carry. **1962** SIMPSON & RICHARDS *Physical Princ. Junction Transistors* xvi. 401 If we now define the most positive value of the output to represent a 'one' and the most negative value a 'zero' in a binary system of arithmetic (the positive logic system) the emitter followers form an 'AND' gate, i.e. all *n* inputs must be 'one' if the output is to be 'one'. **1967** *Electronics* 6 Mar. 26 Santa Clara was making milliwatt resistor–transistor logic for the project. **1968** *Proc. Inst. Electr. Engin.* CXV. 1385/2 He separated the ternary circuits into two sets of binary circuits, one based on a positive logic and the other on a negative one. Then he used translating circuits between the two logics and achieved a true ternary output with the aid of a combining circuit. **1970** *New Yorker* 11 Apr. 34 The computer logic is so fast that it has to loaf at several intervals while the input and output devices..are printing information. **1971** *New Scientist* 25 Mar. 692 The technology [of fluidics] was developed basically to provide a system of control logic and power amplification in the adverse environment of space. **1973** *Nature* 20 Apr. 494/2 The transistor has endowed tremendous scope for performing electronic functions (for example switching, which permits binary logic, and amplifying, which makes possible many other forms of signal processing).

b. *attrib.*, as *logic design, designer, diagram, function, module, network, operation, state*; **logic circuit**, a circuit for performing logical operations and consisting of one or more logic elements; **logic element**, a device (usu. electronic) for performing a logical operation, in which the past or present values of one or more inputs determine the values of one or more outputs in accordance with a simple scheme which most commonly involves, in effect, only two possible values for the signals; **logic gate**, a logic circuit that is a gate (*GATE *sb.*[1] 8 g).
1953 *Communications & Electronics* (N.Y.) Nov. 593/1 The search for simple abstract techniques to be applied to the design of switching systems is still..in its early stages. The problem in this area which has been attacked most energetically is that of the synthesis of efficient combinational that is, nonsequential, logic circuits. **1959** K. HENNEY *Radio Engin. Handbk.* (ed. 5) ix. 7 Very complicated logic circuits involving many thousands of diodes have been assembled for use in electronic computers. **1968** *Times* 18 Oct. 16/5 Computer logic circuits based on the ternary system of arithmetic have been devised by two engineers... They have devised logic circuits that perform the basic arithmetical operations in ternary numbers. **1956** *IRE Trans. Electronic Computers* V. 132/2 The evolution of a set of standard logical circuit blocks allows this design without direct reference to the circuits, thus reducing logic design to the application of a set of rules expressing the input and output capabilities of each of the logical circuit blocks. **1972** D. ZISSOS *Logic Design Algorithms* p. v, Complex switching circuits are used extensively, not only in the logic design of systems such as digital computers and message-switching networks, where they are the subject of study by specialist logic designers, but also for purposes of industrial control and automation. **1956** Logic designer [see *LOGICAL *a.* 1 b]. **1962** *Gloss. Terms Automatic Data Processing* (*B.S.I.*) 59 *Logic diagram*, a graphical representation of the logic design. **1971** J. H. SMITH *Digital Logic* iv. 54 There are a number of different circuits which will carry out this function and it is normal to use the symbol of the circuit employed when drawing logic diagrams. **1959** C. V. L. SMITH *Electronic Digital Computers* iv. 106 This technique makes it possible to make large arrays of logic elements in very compact form. *Ibid.* (*heading*) Symbols for logic elements. **1969** P. B. JORDAIN *Condensed Computer Encycl.* 291 A sequential logic element has an output determined by present and past input signals: it has some degree of retention, or memory. **1971** *New Scientist* 25 Mar. 692 The technology of fluidics is divided into..pure fluidic techniques which use a logic element with no moving parts, and the method using moving part logic. **1959** K. HENNEY *Radio Engin. Handbk.* (ed. 5) ix. 7 Since diodes have two distinctly differing impedance levels, they lend themselves to use in performing predetermined decision or logic functions just as switches or relays may. **1961** *Times* 3 Oct. (Computer Suppl.) p. v, What the technical terms (binary, logic gates, programme and many others) mean. **1967** *Electronics* 6 Mar. 45/3 Each cell will have a working structure, or 'base', of 13 logic gates, plus 13 flip-flops. **1971** J. H. SMITH *Digital Logic* iv. 40 It is usually unnecessary to design logical circuitry today, as many manufacturers supply logic modules to carry out the more common forms of logic. **1974** *Physics Bull.* Mar. 113/1 Ortec will be displaying the new fast logic modules in the M300 series. **1961** *Engineering* 17 Feb. 269/1 The first step in designing the computer was the synthesis of the logic network to perform the necessary functions. **1970** *Nature* 12 Sept. 1092/2 The most exciting possibility for these devices lies naturally in their use as shift registers and for logic operations in computers. **1973** *Sci. Amer.* Nov. 14/1 (Advt.), In a digital circuit, the important thing is to know the logic state of a node, whether it's above the threshold voltage and therefore a logic high, or below the threshold voltage and therefore a logic low.

5. *logic-book*; (sense 3) *logic-chopper, -chopping*; **logic-tight** *a.* [after WATERTIGHT *a.* 1], impervious to logic or reason.
1685 tr. *Arnauld & Nicole's Logic* 17 We should give a reason for omitting so many questions as are found in the common Logic-Books. **1895** W. JAMES *Coll. Ess. & Rev.* (1920) 394 An hypothesis, we are told in the logic-books, ought to propose a being that has some other constitution and definition than that of barely performing the phenomenon it is evoked to explain. **1906** *Daily Chron.* 13 Mar. 6/2 Mr. Balfour..made his reappearance in his old part of the Logic-chopper. **1924** R. GRAVES *Mock Beggar Hall* 32 Put it another way, thou logic-chopper. **1956** J. BLISH *Earthman, Come Home* i. 33 You have no ties, no faith. You will have to excuse ours. We cannot afford to be logic-choppers. **1904** W. JAMES in *Mind* XIII. 458 This is a kind of intellectual product that never attains a classic form of expression when first promulgated. The critic ought therefore not to be too sharp and logic-chopping in his dealings with it. **1960** KOESTLER *Lotus & Robot* I. iii. 132 The Schoolmen confined themselves to verbal logic-chopping. **1912** B. HART *Psychol. Insanity* vi. 82 The delusion is preserved in a logic-tight compartment. **1968** P. MCKELLAR *Experience & Behaviour* x. 269 The widespread tendency..to surround their favourite beliefs with logic-tight compartments.

logical, *a.* (and *sb.*). Add: **1.** (Further examples.)
1847 J. D. MORELL *Hist. View Philos.* (ed. 2) I. i. 95 To Logic, Hobbes devoted a considerable share of attention. The peculiarity of his logical system lies in the theory, that reasoning is merely a numerical calculation. **1905** B. RUSSELL in *Mind* XIV. 490 The distinction of primary and secondary occurrences also enables us to deal with..the logical status of denoting phrases that denote nothing. **1922** E. P. ADAMS tr. *Einstein's Meaning of Relativity* i. 1 The object of all science, whether natural science or psychology, is to co-ordinate our experiences and to bring them into a logical system. **1939** *Mind* XLVIII. 304 To say that a term is of such and such a type or category is to say something about its 'logical behaviour', namely, about the entailments and compatibilities of the propositions into which it enters. **1966** W. V. QUINE *Ways of Paradox* viii. 67 This condition is met by the usual logical languages, and presumably it can be met likewise by languages adequate to science in general.

b. *Computers* and *Electronics.* Of or pertaining to the logic (*LOGIC *sb.* 3*) of computers and similar equipment; designed to carry out processes on electrical or other signals analogous to the processes of reasoning, deduction, etc., employed in (formal) logic; *logical element* = *logic element* (*LOGIC *sb.* 3* b); *logical operation*: see *7; *logical shift*, a displacement of the digits of a sequence by a specified number of positions in a way that is not equivalent to multiplication by an integral power of the base; *esp.* a cyclic shift, in which digits taken from one end reappear, in the same order, at the other end.
In some of the uses below *logical* can equally well be regarded as having the sense of LOGICAL *a.* 1.
1946 BURKS, GOLDSTINE, & VON NEUMANN (*title*) Preliminary discussion of the logical design of an electronic computing instrument. (Rep. submitted to U.S. Army Ordnance Dept., PB 96703.) **1946** GOLDSTINE & VON NEUMANN *Princ. Large Scale Computing Machines* in J. von Neumann *Coll. Works* (1963) V. 23 The Memory Organ... In performing an operation (arithmetical or logical) it is usually necessary to store the quantities entering into it. **1950** [see *COINCIDENCE 7 b]. **1956** *IRE Trans. Electronic Computers* V. 132/2 One of the important properties of a digital computer is that it may be assembled simply and easily from a few well-chosen functional circuits. Each of these circuits represents a logical element that is useful to the system or logic designer in planning a computer. **1958** GOTLIEB & HUME *High-Speed Data Processing* iii. 34 A concise and informative way of describing a computer is to draw its logical diagram which shows the paths and effects of the various signals through it. Logical diagrams are built up largely of gates. *Ibid.* v. 89 In a logical or cyclic shift the digits lost off one end of the number appear at the other end. **1962** *Newnes Conc. Encycl. Nucl. Energy* 671/2 Such a system is sometimes referred to as a logical switching system because the output responses are related by fixed rules to the inputs from the measurement channels. **1964** F. L. WESTWATER *Electronic Computers* iii. 49 The practical engineer must have the last word. Not infrequently, a design engineer will ask the logical designer to make alterations for various reasons. **1970** O. DOPPING *Computers & Data Processing* vii. 117 In the logical shift, all bits take part and zeroes are shifted in at one end. This kind of shift is suitable for handling non-arithmetic information. **1971** J. H. SMITH *Digital Logic* vii. 133 The reader using logical gating

should analyse his specifications to eliminate the trivial and reduce the circuit as far as possible.

2. (Earlier and additional examples.)

1588 A. Fraunce *Lawiers Logike* f.120, I haue, for examples sake, put downe a Logicall Analysis of the second *Aegloge* in Virgill. **1828** Mill in *Westm. Rev.* IX. 144 Those who maintain, that to perform the logical analysis of an argument, in the manner pointed out by the syllogism, is not the best means of discovering whether it contain a flaw. **1958** G. J. Warnock *Eng. Philos. since 1900* ix. 120 The narrowly logical, context-neglecting manner adopted by the practitioners of 'logical analysis'.

7. Special collocations (see also sense *1 b): *logical addition*, the formation of a logical sum; *logical atomism* (see *atomism 1 b); *logical constant* (see quots. 1903, 1914); *logical construction*, an entity theoretically superfluous in that any statement referring to it can be replaced by an equivalent statement making no reference to it; *logical empiricism*, the name given to philosophical theories which replaced those of logical positivism (see quots. 1936, 1937); so *logical empiricist*; *logical fiction* = **logical construction*; *logical form*, the form, as distinct from the content, of a proposition, argument, etc., which can be expressed in logical terms; *logical grammar*, the rules of word-use in a proposition upon which its logical, as opposed to its purely grammatical, sense or meaning is held to depend; so *logical-grammatical* adj.; *logical implication*, implication which is based on the formal and not the material relationship between propositions; *logical machine*, an apparatus designed to facilitate logical calculations; also *transf.*; *logical multiplication*, the formation of a logical product; *logical operation*, an operation of the kind dealt with in logic (such as conjunction or negation); any analogous (non-arithmetical) operation on numbers, esp. binary numbers, in which each digit of the result depends on only one digit in each operand; *logical paradox* (see quot. 1967); *logical positivism*, the name given to the theories and doctrines of philosophers active in Vienna in the early 1930s (the Vienna Circle), which were aimed at evolving in the language of philosophy formal methods for the verification of empirical questions similar to those of the mathematical sciences, and which therefore eliminated metaphysical and other more speculative questions as being logically ill-founded; hence *logical positivist*; *logical product*, the conjunction of two or more propositions, or the intersection or two or more sets (written $p \wedge q$, $p \cap q$, $p.q$, pq, p and q); *logical structure*, the formal framework of logical rules to which a theory, language, proposition, etc., must conform in order to have truth-value; *logical subject*, the subject which is implied in a sentence or proposition, or which exists in the deep structure of a sentence; *logical sum*, the disjunction of two or more propositions, or the union of two or more sets (written $p \vee q$, $p \cup q$, p or q, $p+q$); *logical syntax* (see quot. 1934); *logical truth*, that which is true in logical or formal terms regardless of material meaning; *logical word*, a word of the type which gives logical context or form to a proposition but which, by itself, is non-representational and without meaning (see quot. 1940).

1868 C. S. Peirce in *Proc. Amer. Acad. Arts & Sci.* VII. 250 Let $a + b$ denote all the individuals contained under *a* and *b* together. The operation here performed will differ from arithmetical addition in two respects: 1st, that it has reference to identity, not to equality; and 2d, that what is common to *a* and *b* is not taken into account twice over... The process denoted by + ..I shall call the process of logical addition. **1903** B. Russell *Princ. Math.* ii. 18 From this point we can prove the laws of contradiction and excluded middle and double negation, and establish all the formal properties of logical multiplication and addition—the associative, commutative and distributive laws. **1970** O. Dopping *Computers & Data Processing* i. 23 In Boolean algebra..instead of the usual mathematical operations, there are certain logical operations; the most common ones of these are logical addition, logical multiplication, and negation. **1914,** etc. Logical atomism [see *atomism 1 b]. **1973** E. Gellner in Horton & Finnegan *Modes of Thought* 179 The..formal fact of the existence and nature of the mosaic's framework itself. This vision is shared by classical empiricism and by doctrines such as 'logical atomism'. **1903** B. Russell *Princ. Math.* i. 3 Pure Mathematics is the class of all propositions of the form '*p* implies *q*', where *p* and *q* are propositions containing one or more variables, the same in the two propositions, and neither *p* nor *q* contains any constants except logical constants. And logical constants are all notions definable in terms of the following: Implication, the relation of a term to a class of which it is a member, the notion of *such that*, the notion of relation, and such further notions as may be involved in the general notion of propositions of the above form. **1914** —— *Our Knowl. External World* vii. 208 Such words as *or, not, if, there is, identity, greater, plus, nothing, everything, function*, and so on, are not names of definite objects, like 'John'..but are words which require a context in order to have meaning... 'Logical constants', in short, are not entities. **1922** tr. *Wittgenstein's Tractatus* 69 My fundamental thought is that the 'logical constants' do not represent. That the *logic* of the facts cannot be represented. **1958** G. J. Warnock *Eng. Philos. since 1900* x. 125 We thus get a distinction between so-called 'logical constants', the irreplaceable words on which the validity of general patterns of inference depends, and items of non-logical vocabulary. **1965** B. Mates *Elem. Logic* iv. 49 The logical constants occurring in ϕ are understood in the way usual among logicians (i.e., '$\vee$' as standing for 'or', '—' for 'not', the universal quantifier for 'all', etc.). **1883** F. H. Bradley *Princ. Logic* 236 To show a new relation of elements in a logical construction is demonstration in the sense of reasoning. **1914** B. Russell *Our Knowl. External World* iv. 101 The only justification possible must be one which exhibits matter as a logical construction from sense-data. **1936** A. J. Ayer *Lang., Truth & Logic* iii. 73 The English State..is a logical construction out of individual people. **1956** J. O. Urmson *Philos. Analysis* iii. 36 If '*X*' is an incomplete symbol then *X*s are logical constructions. Thus if the expression 'the average man' is an incomplete symbol we may say that the average man is a logical construction. **1936** A. J. Ayer *Lang., Truth & Logic* 10 Our own logical empiricism to be distinguished from positivism. **1937** *Mind* XLVI. 345 Logical Empiricists are not attempting to be metaphysical, when they distinguish between language and reality. On the contrary, the distinction refers only to certain rules of usage for statements and modes of speech. Since we have investigated the rules of speech in empirical sciences, we are justified in calling our viewpoint 'Logical Empiricism'. **1966** J. J. Katz *Philos. of Lang.* iii. 16 The chief reason for this failure on the part of *logical empiricism*..and *ordinary language philosophy*..was that both were governed in their inferences..by an assumption about the nature of language. **1936** *Mind* XLV. 545 J. Somerville [in] 'The Social Ideas of the Wiener Kreis's International Congress' reflects on the Paris Congress 1935, [and] announces that the 'logical positivists' desire to repudiate Comte and to be henceforth known as 'scientific' or 'logical' empiricists. **1967** *Philos.* XLII. 293 A failure to work out in detail the consequences of logical empiricist principles for ethics. **1843** Mill *Logic* I. iii. v. 404 This tendency shows itself very visibly in the different logical fictions which are resorted to even by philosophers... Thus, rather than say that the earth causes the fall of bodies, they ascribe it to a *force* exerted by the earth, or an *attraction* by the earth. **1918** B. Russell in *Monist* XXVIII. 512, I believe that series and classes are of the nature of logical fictions. **1933** L. S. Stebbing *Mod. Introd. Logic* (ed. 2) 502 To say that the table is a logical fiction (or construction) is not to say that the table is fictitious..it is rather to deny that, in any ordinary sense, it is an object at all. *Ibid.*, 'Logical fiction' may be taken to be an unfortunate synonym for 'logical construction'. **1840** Mill in *Westm. Rev.* XXXIII. 266 A truth..to be believed in opposition to all that appears proof to the mere understanding; nay, the more to be believed, because it cannot be put into words and into the logical form of a proposition without a contradiction in terms. **1967** A. E. Blumberg in *Encycl. Philos.* V. 13/2 Logic confines itself to those arguments whose validity rests exclusively on the logical form of the statements composing them... There is still no fully satisfactory account of logical form. **1922** tr. *Wittgenstein's Tractatus* 55 A symbolism..which obeys the rules of logical grammar—of logical syntax. **1962** L. J. Cohen *Diversity of Meaning* iii. 81 The most obvious fault in the doctrine of logical grammar is that it suggests the conceptual study of meanings to be concerned with something that is timeless and unchanging. **1937** *Atlantic Monthly* CLIX. 49/2 The logical-grammatical construction involved is so commonly mishandled in current American speech and print. **1887** A. Seth *Hegelianism* v. 172 In the first sense..development means simply logical implication. **1904** B. Russell in *Mind* XIII. 209 It would seem that..logical implication is a simple notion, into whose composition the notion of terms does not enter. **1934** Cohen & Nagel *Introd. Logic* i. 9 (*heading*) Logical implication does not depend on the truth of our premises. **1870** W. S. Jevons in *Proc. R. Soc.* XVIII. 167 To explain the nature of the logical machine alluded to, it may be pointed out that the third of the fundamental Laws of Thought allows us to affirm of any object one or the other of two contradictory attributes. **1883** F. H. Bradley *Princ. Logic* 344 We shall discuss the Indirect Method, and with it the claims of the Logical Machine. **1943** *Mind* LII. 319 He is thus stymied at the outset, and being neither a logical machine nor an esthetic idiot he is likely to feel uncomfortable about it. **1868** C. S. Peirce in *Proc. Amer. Acad. Arts & Sci.* VII. 251 Let *a, b* denote the individuals contained at once under the classes *a* and *b*... If *a* and *b* were independent events, *a, b* would denote the event whose probability is the product of the probabilities of each. On the strength of this analogy..the operation indicated by the comma may be called logical multiplication. **1903, 1970** Logical multiplication [see *logical addition* above]. **1885** C. S. Peirce in *Amer. Jrnl. Math.* VII. 186, I prefer not to assign determinate values to **f** and **v**, nor to identify the logical operations with any special arithmetical ones. **1932** Lewis & Langford *Symbolic Logic* i. 7 It would have coincided with what we now know as symbolic logic. That is, it would have been an organon of reasoning in general, developed in ideographic symbols and enabling the logical operations to be performed according to precise rules. **1960** M. G. Say et al. *Analogue & Digital Computers* vii. 165 A zero input digit to this unit gives a one-digit output and a one-digit input gives a zero output. This is the logical operation 'not'. **1970** Logical operation [see *logical addition* above]. **1904** W. James *Ess. Radical Empiricism* (1912) i. 11 'Representative' theories of perception avoid the logical paradox, but on the other hand they violate the reader's sense of life, which knows no intervening mental image. **1954** I. M. Copi *Symbolic Logic* 332 These two kinds of paradoxes were first explicitly distinguished by F. P. Ramsey in 1926. Since then those of the first kind have been known as 'logical paradoxes'. **1967** J. van Heijenoort in *Encycl. Philos.* V. 45/2 In logic the word [*sc.* paradox] has taken on a more precise meaning. A logical paradox consists of two contrary, or even contradictory, propositions to which we are led by apparently sound arguments. **1931** Blumberg & Feigl in *Jrnl. Philos.* XXVIII. 281 To facilitate criticism and forestall even more unfortunate attempts at labelling this aspect of contemporary European philosophy, we shall employ the term 'logical positivism'. **1934** *Philos. Rev.* XLIII. 125 The logical positivism of the Vienna Circle..is based..upon this consideration of empirical meaning. **1968** M. Black *Labyrinth of Lang.* vi. 147 Logical Positivism has seen its best days. **1931** *Jrnl. Philos.* XXVIII. 291 The principle of causality is for the logical positivist not a categorical necessity of thought. **1967** J. Passmore in *Encycl. Philos.* V. 55/1 The logical positivists ordinarily took for granted the substantial truth of contemporary Science. Thus, it was a matter of vital concern to them when it became apparent that the verifiability principle would rule out as meaningless all scientific laws. **1868** C. S. Peirce in *Proc. Amer. Acad. Arts & Sci.* VII. 411 The numerical rank of a logical product depends on the identity or diversity..of parts of the factors. **1903** B. Russell *Princ. Math.* ii. 21 Most of the propositions of the class-calculus are easily deduced from those of the propositional calculus. The logical product or common part of two classes *a* and *b* is the class of *x*'s such that the logical product of '*x* is an *a*' and '*x* is a *b*' is true. Similarly we can define the logical sum of two classes (*a* or *b*). **1955** A. N. Prior *Formal Logic* I. i. 7 We may also have a conjunction or logical product of more than two propositions, the analogy with arithmetical multiplication still holding. **1959** Logical product [see *logical sum* below]. **1871** A. C. Fraser *Life Berkeley* ii. 39, I have tried elsewhere..to explain the logical structure of the *Essay on Vision*. **1918** B. Russell in *Monist* XXVIII. 510 The first thing to do would be to discover the kinds of atoms out of which logical structures are composed. **1943** *Mind* LII. 26 Linguistic structure, though at times it conceals or distorts, has to be taken as capable of revealing logical structure, otherwise the study of logic would be impossible. **1970** L. J. Cohen *Implications Induction* i. 6 Many propositions are never hypothesised at all, even if alike in logical structure to those that are. **1898** *Mind* VII. 34 (*heading*) On the logical subject of the proposition. **1903** B. Russell *Princ. Math.* iv. 44 Every term..is a logical subject. **1933** [see *grammatical *a.* 1 b]. **1965** N. Chomsky *Aspects of Theory of Syntax* i. 23 In (8i) [*sc.* 'I persuaded a specialist to examine John'] the phrase 'a specialist' is the Direct-Object of the Verb Phrase and the logical Subject of the embedded sentence. *Ibid.* iv. 163 It seems that beyond the notions of surface structure..and deep structure (such as 'logical subject'), there is some still more abstract notion of 'semantic function' still unexplained. **1868** C. S. Peirce in *Proc. Amer. Acad. Arts & Sci.* VII. 411 The numerical rank of a logical sum depends on the identity or diversity..of the integrant parts. **1903** [see *logical product* above]. **1959** C. V. L. Smith *Electronic Digital Computers* ii. 32 Given two binary words..it is possible to generate a third word each bit of which is the logical sum or the logical product or, indeed, any Boolean function of the bits in the corresponding position of the given words. Operations of this sort may be called 'logical operations'. **1963** G. T. Kneebone *Math. Logic* ii. 53 In older accounts of symbolic logic, the terms 'logical sum' and 'logical product' are often used where 'disjunction' and 'conjunction' would now be preferred. There is indeed an analogy between the arithmetical operations of addition and multiplication. **1922** Logical syntax [see *logical grammar* above]. **1934** R. Carnap in *Philos. Sci.* I. 9 By the 'logical syntax' (or also briefly 'syntax') of a language we shall understand the system of the formal (i.e. not referring to meaning) rules of that language, as well as..the consequences of these rules. **1945** *Mind* LIV. 172 The weaknesses of the argument might be due in part at least to a certain poverty in the technical equipment of 'logical syntax'. **1970** L. J. Cohen *Implications Induction* i. 6 Some elementary principles in the logical syntax of experimental support. **1818–19** Coleridge *Philos. Lect.* (1949) ix. 276 This necessarily led men..to doubt whether a logical truth was necessarily an existential one, i.e. whether because a truth was logically consistent it must be necessarily existent. **1877** W. S. Jevons *Princ. Sci.* (ed. 2) viii. 153 Nothing is more certain than logical truth. **1943** *Mind* LII. 272 An exhaustive formulation of logical truth remains a worthy undertaking. **1940** B. Russell *Inquiry into Meaning & Truth* 20 We pass from the primary to the secondary language by adding what I shall call 'logical words', such as 'or', 'not', 'some', and 'all', together with the words 'true' and 'false' as applied to sentences in the object-language. **1958** S. E. Toulmin *Uses Argument* iv. 149 The validity of syllogisms being closely bound up with the proper distribution of logical words within the statements composing them. **1972** *Sci. Amer.* Sept. 82/3 Language performs this miraculous function largely through such little particles as 'if', 'when', 'not', 'therefore', 'all' and 'some', which have been called logical words because they account for the ability of language to formulate logical inferences (also known as syllogisms).

logically, *adv.* Add: Phr. *a logically perfect language*: a language in which the grammatical structure of sentences would be identical with their logical structure.

1918 B. Russell in *Monist* XXVIII. 520 In a logically perfect language the words in a proposition would correspond one by one with the components of the corresponding fact, with the exception of such words as 'or', 'not', 'if'. .. The language which is set forth in *Principia Mathematica*..aims at being that sort of a language that, if you add a vocabulary, would be a logically perfect language. **1922** —— in Wittgenstein *Tractatus* Introd. 7 He is concerned with the conditions which would have to be fulfilled by a logically perfect language. **1939** M. Black in Copi & Beard *Ess. Wittgenstein's Tractatus* (1966) 97 This view of the character of Wittgenstein's investigation..may have

been suggested by Russell's own attempts to construct a logically perfect language. **1953** *Mind* LXII. 13 They have even gone so far as to suggest that philosophers should invent a logically perfect language as a substitute for ordinary speech. **1971** A. Flew *Introd. Western Philos.* xi. 388 One..of the many projects of Leibniz..was to develop a logically perfect language in which the truth or falsity of any proposition would be obvious from the symbols alone.

logicism (lǫ·dʒisiz'm). [f. Logic *sb.* + -ism.] The theory of Frege that a set of axioms for mathematics could be deduced from a primitive set of purely logical axioms, so that mathematics was essentially a part of logic.

1937 A. Smeaton tr. *Carnap's Logical Syntax of Lang.* v. § 84. 325 What should a logical foundation of mathematics achieve? On this question there are various views; the fundamental antithesis between them is particularly clearly brought out in two doctrines, *logicism*, which was founded by Frege (1884), and *formalism*, represented by Frege's opponents. (The designations 'logicism' and 'formalism' only appeared later.) **1970** A. E. Blumberg tr. *Stegmüller's Main Currents Contemp. German, Brit. & Amer. Philos.* viii. 327 The modern philosophy of mathematics is characterized by the fact that various schools have been formed to overcome the difficulties occasioned by the antinomies. The oldest of these schools is logicism and goes back to Frege. **1973** *Sci. Amer.* Apr. 103/2 Typically the choice is determined by one's degree of sympathy with one or another of three modern schools of mathematical thought: logicism, formalism and intuitionism.

logicist (lǫ·dʒisist), *sb.* and *a.* [f. Logic *sb.* + -ist.] **a.** *sb.* A (formal) logician; a mathematician who uses the methods or accepts the theory of logicism. **b.** *adj.* Of or pertaining to logicism. Also occas. **logici·stic** *a.*

a **1910** W. James *Some Probl. Philos.* (1911) v. 82 Hibben and the logicists seem to believe that conception, if only adequately attained to, might be all-sufficient. **1916** J. Dewey *Ess. Exper. Logic* 65, I am not questioning the right of the physicist, the mathematician, or the symbolic logicist to go ahead with accepted objects and do what he can with them. **1937** A. Smeaton tr. *Carnap's Logical Syntax of Lang.* v. § 84. 326 The sentence..can be derived with the help of the logicist system. **1952** S. C. Kleene *Introd. Metamath.* I. iii. 44 The logicistic definition of natural number now becomes predicative. **1956** E. M. Hutten *Lang. Mod. Physics* vi. 231 Our understanding of what statistical inference can do is obscured..by the logicist scheme of taking all hypotheses as universal implications, e.g. (x)(fx ⊃ gx). **1973** *Sci. Amer.* Apr. 109/3 In the 'new math' the logicist theory that natural numbers are derived from the quantification of classes was at last put into educational practice.

logicize, *v.* Delete *rare* and (in sense 2) *nonce-use* and add further examples. (See also quot. 1919.) Hence **lo·gicized** *ppl. a.*, **lo·gicizing** *vbl. sb.*

a **1910** W. James *Mem. & Stud.* (1911) xv. 393 All these tricks for logicizing originality, self-relation, absolute process, subjective contradiction, will wither in the breath of the mystical fact. **1919** B. Russell *Introd. Math. Philos.* i. 7 Frege, who first succeeded in 'logicising' mathematics, *i.e.* in reducing to logic the arithmetical notions which his predecessors had shown to be sufficient for mathematics. **1924** C. K. Ogden tr. *Vaihinger's Philos. of 'As If'* III. iv. 360 This creating, logicizing, arranging, falsifying, is the best guaranteed reality. **1937** [see *arithmetize *v.* 2 a]. **1957** J. Passmore *100 Yrs. Philos.* vi. 149 It is in the writings of G. Frege that the fundamental problems of a logicised mathematics first clearly emerged.

logico-. (Later examples.)
Used with adjs., sbs., and occas. with advbs. as second elements.

1858 A. De Morgan *On Syllogism* (1966) 89, I distinguish the two sides of logic as the *logico-mathematical* and the *logico-metaphysical*, frequently dropping the prefix *logico*. **1898** J. A. Hobson *John Ruskin* xiii. 319 No one..more subtly practised the vital as distinguished from the logico-mechanical method of teaching. *c* **1905** C. S. Peirce *Coll. Papers* (1933) IV. I. ix. 274 Dr. Georg Cantor, the great founder and *Hauptförderer* of the logico-mathematical doctrine of numbers. **1918** C. I. Lewis *Survey Symbolic Logic* p. v, Treatises..bristling with logico-metaphysical difficulties. **1922** D. Ainslie tr. *Croce's Aesthetic* (ed. 2) II. v. 229 The same criticism.. must have extended to the logico-grammarians of Port-Royal. **1930** T. Sasaki *On Lang. R. Bridges' Poetry* 3 The following different lines of approach are possible: (1) Logico-psychological [etc.]. **1931** J. Wisdom *Interpretation & Analysis* 13 The logico-analytic philosophers are constantly asking questions such as 'What does "This is a chair" mean?' **1935** *Mind* XLV. 263 It is only from a footnote that we learn that Pareto had realized the importance (and difficulty) of the 'theorem' that 'the logico-experimental truth of a theory and its social utility are independent'. **1937** *Mind* XLVI. 253 This book should prove stimulating to scientists, methodologists, and philosophers of all kinds, speculative, critical, or logico-positivist. **1938** C. Morris *Found. Theory of Signs* § 5. 92 The logico-grammatical structure of language. **1940** W. V. Quine *Math. Logic* 127 The atomic formulae formed by flanking 'ε' with variables happen merely to be the ones appropriate to logico-mathematical matters. **1943** H. Read *Educ. through Art* iii. 70 What is now suggested, in opposition to the whole of the logico-rationalistic tradition, is that there exists a concrete visual mode of 'thinking'. **1946** *Mind* LV. 44 It refers only to a very small group of Logico-Analytic philosophers. **1949** *Mind* LVIII. 397 The latest logico-analysts avowedly make use of utterances that are as NonSensical as those of the metaphysician. **1951** *Mind* LX. 24 The Logico-positivist proposes not to *speak* of 'inference'. **1952** *Mind* LXI. 574 The great logico-philosophical revolution of the last half century, initiated by Frege and Russell. **1958** W. Stark *Sociol. of Knowl.* II. viii. 320 If we study social reality as all reality should be studied, namely 'logico-experimentally', i.e. truly scientifically, we find..that human action is controlled by a set of drives. **1958** *Listener* 27 Nov. 879/1 The kind of thinking which I have called metaphysical thinking can lead to positive achievements, where both the system-philosophies and logico-linguistic investigations fail. **1970** J. N. Findlay tr. *Husserl's Logical Investigations* II. vi. viii. 826 The purely logico-grammatical laws which, as laws of complication and modification, distinguish the spheres of sense and nonsense. **1971** P. F. Strawson (*title*) Logico-linguistic papers.

lo·gily, *adv.* [f. Logy *a.*] In a dull or heavy manner.

1912 J. London *Son of Sun* viii. 326 The schooner,.. from the weight of water on her decks, behaved logily.

logistic, *a.* and *sb.* Add: **A.** *adj.* **3. a.** *logistic curve*: also [after F. *logistique* (P.-F. Verhulst 1845, in *Nouv. Mém. de l'Acad. R. des Sci. et Belles-Lettres de Bruxelles* XVIII. 8)], a curve described by the equation $y = K/(1 + Ae^{a-bt})$, where K, A, a, and b are constants, which approximates an exponential curve for small values of t, has a point of inflexion at $t = a/b$, and as t increases approaches $y = K$ asymptotically. Hence *logistic growth, law*, etc.

1925 G. U. Yule in *Jrnl. R. Statistical Soc.* LXXXVIII. 11 The logistic curve implies that, if we could plot the instantaneous percentage rate of increase of the population at any moment of time against the magnitude of the population, the resulting points should lie on a straight line, a line sloping downwards from left to right, since the rate of increase falls as the population increases. **1928** R. Pearl *Rate of Living* vii. 132 The growth of the stem follows a logistic curve. **1930** W. R. Inge *Christian Ethics & Mod. Probl.* v. 252 Professor Raymond Pearl, of Baltimore,..has evolved a theory that the growth of population follows what he calls a logistic curve, apparently independent of human volition. **1947** *Jrnl. R. Statistical Soc.* CX. 134 A most important..paper of Feller..on the application of Markoff processes to a series of population problems normally treated in a deterministic manner leading to exponential or logistic laws of growth. **1969** Sladen & Bang *Biol. of Populations* vi. 72 Pearl used the logistic equation of Verhulst, which is $dN/dt = rN(K-N)/K$. The first part, $dN/dt = rN$, is the exponential equation for growth. K is a constant concerned with realization of the potential, and N is the number of individuals in the population. **1974** *Encycl. Brit. Macropædia* XIV. 831/1 (*caption*) Logistic growth of a laboratory population of the small fruit fly.

d. Of or pertaining to mathematical or symbolic logic.

1918 C. I. Lewis *Survey Symbolic Logic* vi. 343 The logistic method is..applicable to any sufficiently coördinated body of exact knowledge. **1934** *Mind* XLIII. 101 First, he presents 'the basic calculus of exact logic by the logistic method'. **1963** H. B. Curry *Found. Math. Logic* i. 21, I shall discuss briefly the three principal varieties of higher-order logistic calculus.

4. Connected with or pertaining to logistics (cf. *logistics *sb. pl.*[2]).

1934 in Webster. **1957** *Listener* 14 Nov. 774/2 [Of local elections in Ethiopia] Everything had to be improvised; the logistic problems of this complicated terrain had to be solved as much as the psychological. **1958** *Times* 3 Nov. 11/7 When Montgomery, promised extra logistic support, fixed the date for Arnhem, Patton decided to get his forces so involved beyond the Moselle that Supreme Headquarters would find it impossible to find that extra support at his expense. **1971** *Sci. Amer.* Dec. 106/2 The Gombe Stream Centre, which arose from her work, is now a thriving institution with a dozen students and an entire little village of logistic and touristic support.

B. *sb.* **2.** (Later examples: cf. sense *A. 3 a.)

1925 G. U. Yule in *Jrnl. R. Statistical Soc.* LXXXVIII. 5, I have relegated to Appendix II some discussion of the mathematics of the curve, which, following Verhulst, we may term a 'logistic'. **1928** R. Pearl *Rate of Living* vii. 132 The seedling growth curves are slightly asymmetrical, but to a first approximation are sufficiently well graduated by the simple logistic $y = K/(1 + e^{a+bx})$. **1974** *Nature* 3 May 12/3 In the absence of competition..the growth rate conforms to the logistic.

3. c. (usu. *sing.*) Mathematical or symbolic logic (see quot. 1918).

[**1905** *Philos. Rev.* XIV. 445 A logical renaissance must be noted... I give it the name of 'logistique' from an old word which appears to be revived. *Ibid.* 453 In the 'Logistique' (the revival of the word was recognized by the congress) the presence alone of MM. Peano, Couturat, [etc.].. was sufficient to guarantee the interest and importance of the questions treated.] **1918** C. I. Lewis *Survey Symbolic Logic* i. 3 Logistic would not have served our purpose because 'logistic' is commonly used to denote symbolic logic together with the application of its methods to other symbolic procedures. Logistic may be defined as *the science which deals with types of order as such.* It is not so much a subject as a method. **1933** *Mind* XLII. 117 Prof. Scholz writes throughout as an enthusiastic student of symbolic logic, or—to use the name more commonly employed on the Continent—Logistic. **1936** A. J. Ayer *Lang., Truth & Logic* iii. 88 The best-known example of such a symbolism [*sc.* artificial language symbolism] is the so-called system of logistic which was employed by Russell and Whitehead in their *Principia Mathematica.* **1956** A. Church *Introd. Math. Logic* (rev. ed.) I. 57 The word 'logistic'..originally meant the art of calculation or common arithmetic. Its modern use for mathematical logic dates from the International Congress of Philosophy of 1904. **1956** E. H. Hutten *Lang. Mod. Physics* ii. 34 There are still people who believe that Gödel's theorem represents the ultimate failure of logic and mathematics. But, to paraphrase Mark Twain, the reports of the early demise of logistic are greatly exaggerated.

logistical, *a.* Delete ? *Obs.* and add: **3. b.** = *logistic *a.* 3 d; of or pertaining to logicism.

1932 H. W. B. Joseph in *Mind* XLI. 439 And it would be consonant so far with the logistical doctrine that pure mathematics is just logic, or an outgrowth of logic. **1943** *Mind* LII. 264 The 'logistical thesis' that mathematics is reducible to logic. **1966** W. V. Quine *Ways of Paradox* viii. 64 (*heading*) A logistical approach to the ontological problem.

4. Pertaining to *logistics *sb. pl.*[2]; = *logistic *a.* 4.

1934 in Webster. **1957** *Economist* 7 Sept. 838/3 Soldiers who can, without any lessening of their primal martial qualities, handle their logistical and procurement problems. **1966** *Listener* 13 Jan. 65/2 You would..allow more time than six months for the 190,000 American troops to effectively dismember the 165,000 Viet Cong troops, an enemy which possesses all the strategical and logistical advantages. **1972** *Sci. Amer.* Feb. 77/3 Logistical problems such as transporting magnetic tapes and fragile equipment..proved to be as much of a challenge as technical considerations. **1975** *Listener* 9 Jan. 41/1 Sven Hedin in 1927..could show his journeys through East Asia, China and Mongolia with all the emphasis on the logistical dramas.

logistically (lŏdʒi·stikăli), *adv.* **1.** [f. Logistical *a.* + -ly[2].] In a logistic manner.

1932 Lewis & Langford *Symbolic Logic* v. 118 The logistically derived calculus of classes. **1933** *Mind* XLII. 32 We must hold constantly in mind that this logic is to be developed logistically.

2. [Cf. *logistics *sb. pl.*[2]] Connected with or from the point of view of logistics.

1956 R. Braddon *Nancy Wake* xviii. 212 A situation both logistically valuable and humanly comic. **1960** *Daily Tel.* 10 Oct. 24/6 The American official position has always been that it would be impractical, even logistically, to withdraw American troops from Germany and concentrate them, say, in Alsace Lorraine. **1966** M. R. D. Foot *SOE in France* x. 308 It turned out logistically impracticable. **1971** J. B. Carroll et al. *Word Frequency Bk.* p. xviii, Choosing *k* based on the length of individual texts was rejected as being unacceptably laborious and logistically impossible. **1971** *Physics Bull.* Dec. 726/1 If industrial work is to be done by universities, it must be set up and supported in such a way as to be logistically viable.

logistician (lǫdʒisti·ʃən). [f. Logistic *a.* + -ian.] One skilled in logic or logistics.

1932 *Mind* XLI. 433 Logisticians are the last persons who should quarrel with a notational convention whereby a syllogistic 'calculus' can be simplified. **1936** Ogden & Richards *Meaning of Meaning* (ed. 4) v. 95 Logisticians will only be logical when they admit that universals are an analogous convenience. **1937** *Mind* XLVI. 244 Prof. Scholz, who is editing the series of logistical studies to which this work belongs, has the rare distinction of being both an accomplished logistician and an erudite philosophical scholar. **1966** W. V. Quine *Ways of Paradox* viii. 65 Such conformity was the logistician's objective when he codified quantification.

logistics, *sb. pl.*[2] Add to def.: The organization of supplies, stores, quarters, etc., necessary for the support of troop movements, expeditions, etc.

1944 A. H. Burne *Art of War on Land* i. 10 All this must be superimposed on his knowledge of the material conditions—'the logistics' of the situation, as pointed out by Lord Wavell. *Ibid.*, Logistics, the science of moving and supplying troops. The term was invented by Baron de Jomini, but is seldom used in this country. **1947** D. S. Ballantine (*title*) U.S. naval logistics in the Second World War. **1947** Crowther & Whiddington *Science at War* 117 The Americans use the word 'logistics' to describe the technique of packing stores... It is derived from the French '*maître du logie*'. **1963** Mrs. L. B. Johnson *White House Diary* 27 Dec. (1970) 21 Bess Abell..and some Filipino stewards arrived at the Ranch yesterday and got preparations under way for Chancellor Ludwig Erhard's visit—the vast logistics of deciding who was going to stay where. **1966** *Aviation Week & Space Technol.* 5 Dec. 22/1 The new plan is to provide, essentially, separate modules for each of at least three major experimentation areas—astronomy and biology, earth resources, including meteorology, and orbital operations and logistics. **1971** *Daily Tel.* 8 May 8/6 He was responsible for the administration and logistics of the mine-sweeping forces in the operation Neptune (the invasion of North-West Europe in 1944).

log-jam. [f. Log *sb.*[1] + Jam *sb.*[1]] **1.** An accumulation of logs in a river; a place where logs become jammed. Cf. *jam *sb.*[1] 1.

1885 E. L. Dorsey *Midshipman Bob* (1886) i. 73 His father got killed in a log-jam. **1897** Kipling *Five Nations* (1903) 39 Do you know that racing stream With the raw, right-angled log-jam at the end? **1900** *Jrnl. School Geogr.* (U.S.) Apr. 153 The breaking of a log jam or an ice dam on one of our rivers. **1940** J. Buchan *Memory Hold-the-Door* v. 101 He could do what the lumberman does in a log-jam, and pick out the key log which, once moved, sets the rest going. **1957** G. E. Hutchinson *Treat. Limnol.* I. i. 115 The successive formation of log jams.

2. *fig.* An obstruction or blockage; a delay; a deadlock. Cf. *jam *sb.*[1] 1 b.

1890 W. James *Princ. Psychol.* I. xi. 451 But at intervals an obstruction, a set-back, a log-jam occurs. **1907** *Springfield* (Mass.) *Weekly Republ.* 14 Feb. 8 The congressional log-jam which held back all legislature for

nearly a week was finally broken Thursday afternoon. **1935** *Economist* 4 May 1009/1 A number of corporate refunding issues have been successfully offered.., leading the Secretary of the Treasury to affirm that the 'log-jam in the capital market' has at last been broken. **1951** M. Lowry *Let.* 5 June (1967) 245 There is a kind of log jam in my work. **1962** *Listener* 5 Apr. 597/2 Nothing is likely to break the Arab-Israeli log-jam until the Arabs achieve a greater measure of unity. **1965** *Ibid.* 20 May 737/2 Something may have happened to show us what Mr Ian Smith's electoral victory really means and how the political log-jam has begun to move. **1973** I. M. Sinclair *Vienna Convention on Law of Treaties* v. 139 Informal meetings among leading delegations failed to move the log-jam.

loglet (lǫ·glėt). [f. Log *sb.*¹ + -let.] A little log.

1914 W. De Morgan *When Ghost meets Ghost* II. vi. 504 She brought a couple of young loglets to keep a little life in the fire.

logo (lǫ·go). Abbrev. of *logogram 2 c or *logotype 2. Also *attrib.*

1937 *Advertising & Selling* 1 Jan. 29 He wrote the first ad ever written for that new-fangled mechanical pencil called 'Eversharp'. Designed a logo for it, too. **1960** O. Skilbeck *ABC of Film and T.V.* 79 *Logo*, the layout of a sponsor's name, brand or slogan. **1967** T. Harknett *Two-Way Frame* xii. 92 An eight-wheeled trailer lorry and a five-ton van, both with the company logo on the side. **1969** *Guardian* 27 May 5/8 Almost every page carries that arch public relations device, an image-making logo. **1970** *Cabinet Maker & Retail Furnisher* 25 Sept. 628 (*caption*) A stylised version of the letter A is the logo used as a feature on Arkana's fleet of vans. The van body is in silver, with the cab and the logo in blue. **1971** *B.S.I. News* Dec. 4/2 With a single gold motif drawn from the Institution's crest and logo, these ties are now available. **1975** *Times* 13 Jan. 13/4 A national airline decided.. to have their logo printed on the cover of book matches.

logocentric (lǫgose·ntrik), *a.* [f. Gr. λόγο-ς reason + *-centric.] Centred on reason.

1939 V. A. Demant *Relig. Prospect* v. 124 The connection of this biocentric dogma with a dogma of becoming is obvious. In what respects is the rational, logocentric tradition against which it revolts related to a true dogma of being? **1951** *Mind* LX. 575 Terminating in a logocentric predicament. **1952** [see *biocentric *a.*].

logogram. Add: **2. b.** *Philol.* A symbol or character used, alone or in combination, as the graphic representation of a whole word as a single letter.

1933 L. Bloomfield *Lang.* 287 The Egyptians.. represented words not always by one symbol, but also by various arrangements of logograms. **1939** L. H. Gray *Foundations of Lang.* 360 Akkadian as written contains many Sumerian logograms. **1963** Bloomfield & Newmark *Ling. Introd. Hist. Eng.* ii. 35 Mesopotamian and Egyptian peoples developed a rebus technique by which signs for whole words (logograms) could be put together to form longer words.

c. *gen.* A symbol, as found in road-signs, advertising, &c., designed to represent in simple graphic form an object, concept, or attitude.

1966 *Sunday Times* 27 Feb. 11/2 Labour's original badge..has progressively turned into what the trade calls a logogram.

logographic, *a.* **2.** (Later example.)

1970 *Language* XLVI. 959 It now appears that the Proto-Indian script is a purely logographic script based on the so-called rebus principle.

logology. 2. (Later examples.)

1943 *Jrnl. R. Anthrop. Inst.* 5 Logology = the general study of linguistic elements of culture. **1961** K. Burke (*title*) The rhetoric of religion: studies in logology.

logopedics (lǫgopī·diks), *sb. pl.* [f. Gr. λόγο-ς word, speech, after Orthopædics, -ped-.] (See quot. 1951.) Also **logope·dia** [-ia¹], in the same sense.

1923 Dorland *Med. Dict.* (ed. 12) 622/1 Logopedia, logopedics. **1951** S. D. Robbins *Dict. Speech Path. & Therapy* (1961) 67 *Logopedia, logopedics*, the study and correction of speech and voice defects and disorders as a general field of knowledge. **1960** F. T. Wien (*title*) Current problems in phoniatrics and logopedics. **1969** J. H. van Thal *Elem. Logopedics* i. 10 Logopedics, which is widely used in many countries..is more comprehensive ..than any other term in current use.

logophobia (lǫgǒfōᵘ·biă). [mod.L., f. Gr. λόγο-ς word + -phobia.] Fear or distrust of words.

1923 [see *God-box* (*God *sb.* 16 a)]. **1933** H. R. Huse *Illiteracy of Literate* 48 The fear behind this logophobia is that secret names can be used in incantations. **1959** W. H. Mittins in Quirk & Smith *Teaching of English* iv. 126 The interest generated by such an approach might even help to overcome that language-resistance—the Americans call it 'logophobia'—which some teachers claim to be meeting more and more.

logopœia (lǫgǒpī·yă). [a. Latinized form of Gr. λογοποιία f. λόγος word + ποιεῖν to make + -ια abstract fem. ending.] (See quot. 1929.)

1929 E. Pound in *N.Y. Herald-Tribune* 20 Jan. xi. 5/4 Logopoeia, 'the dance of the intellect among 'words, that is to say, it employs words not only for their direct meaning, but it takes count in a special way of habits of usage, of the context we *expect* to find with the word... It holds the æsthetic content which is peculiarly the domain of verbal manifestation and can not possibly be contained in plastic or in music. **1934** —— *ABC of Reading* iv. 21 You still charge words with meaning mainly in three ways, called phanopoeia, melopoeia, logopoeia. **1957** N. Frye *Anat. Crit.* 244 The context that Ezra Pound has in mind when he speaks of the three qualities of poetic creation as *melopoeia, logopoeia,* and *phanopoeia.*

logorrhœa, logorrhea (lǫgǒrī·ă). [f. Gr. λόγο-ς word + ῥοία flow, stream (prob. after Diarrhœa).] Excessive volubility accompanying some forms of mental illness; also *gen.*, an excessive flow of words, prolixity. So **logorrhœ·ic, logorrhœ·tic** *adjs.*

1902 Baldwin *Dict. Philos. & Psychol.* II. 30/1 Logorrhea refers to the excessive flow of words, a common symptom in cases of mania. **1907** *Daily Chron.* 13 Feb. 7/4 In the case of a man suffering from the insanity known as logorrhea the ideas come rapidly tumbling over each other. **1935** *Punch* 5 June 662/2, I have invented logorrhœa—or, if you prefer it, logorrhage. Like pyorrhœa.., it afflicts three out of four. **1960** *Spectator* 21 Oct. 591 Protective shields against the prevailing logorrhoeic fall-out. **1965** *Listener* 14 Jan. 62/3 No one could, or would want to, surpass that logorrhoetic master, except himself. **1965** W. R. Brain *Speech Disorders* (ed. 2) v. 56 Patients with sensory or Wernicke's aphasia or jargon aphasia include logorrhoeic patients with abundant paraphasias and serious defects of comprehension. **1970** *Daily Tel.* 5 Feb. 6/4 We are left with a tedious tale of complicated intrigues written by an author suffering from acute logorrhoea. **1970** Hinsie & Campbell *Psychiatric Dict.* (ed. 4) 751/2 Also known as *logorrhea*..[tachylogia] is characteristic of the manic phase of manic-depressive disorder.

logotherapy (lǫgǒþe·răpi). *Psychol.* [ad. G. *logotherapie* (V. E. Frankl *Ärztliche Seelsorge* (1947)), f. Gr. λογό-ς reason + Therapy.] An existential type of psychotherapy which maintains that man's mental health depends on awareness of meaning in his life.

1948 *Amer. Jrnl. Psychotherapy* 685 To help his patients in their spiritual distress the author [*sc.* Frankl] uses the art of reasoning, i.e., 'logotherapy', and as his method is principally based on an explanation of the meaning of existence, he calls it 'Existential Analysis'. **1953** *Ibid.* VII. 10 To overcome psychologism we have introduced a psychotherapeutic method which we have called *Logotherapy*, an heuristic opposite to psychotherapy in its hitherto accepted narrow psychological sense. Logotherapy is to be understood as a therapy which derives from spiritual sources, and aims toward a spiritual goal. **1964** I. Lasch tr. *Frankl's Man's Search for Meaning* II. 98 In logotherapy the patient is actually confronted with and reoriented toward the meaning of his life. *Ibid.* 99 According to logotherapy, this striving to find a meaning in one's life is the primary motivational force in man. **1968** Reinecke & Bailey tr. *Rudin's Psychotherapy & Relig.* ix. 188 We should not bypass Viktor Frankl's logotherapy, since this is the approach which most encompasses the spiritual dimensions of man. **1972** W. C. Coe *Challenges Personal Adjustment* vi. 141 V. E. Frankl.. has developed what he calls 'logotherapy'. Its aim is to provide meaning..to man's existential being, uniqueness, and responsibility for self-actualization.

logotype. Add: **2.** = *logogram 2 c.

1957 *Archit. Rev.* CXXII. 421 These air outlet grills carry the company's loggotype [*sic*] (the three letters IBM which are the company's 'signature') in the form of magnetic plate, the position of which can be adjusted. **1968** *Heidelberg News* (Heidelberg Printing Machinery Co.) Sept. 2/2 It could concentrate its resources, as some printers have already done, on creating house styles, designing company logotypes, [etc.]. **1970** *Railway World* Apr. 166 A tatty sign affixed to the inside of the station windows (latterly in magnificent British Rail character-less logotype). **1970** *Sat. Rev.* (U.S.) 12 Sept. 94/1 The familiar *Life* logotype appears in the upper left corner. **1974** *Globe & Mail* (Toronto) 8 Feb. 12/5 The symbol was designed by Burton Kramer and Allan Fleming, authors of a number of other visual identikits including Canadian National Railways' CN logotype.

log-roller. 1. (Further examples.)

1897 [see *back-scratching *vbl. sb.*]. **1966** *Listener* 3 Mar. 324/1 Whether as editor,..impresario, log-roller, or friend, Ford seems to have been mixed up with almost every major writer of his time. **1968** *New Scientist* 5 Sept. 474/2 The same old professional log-rollers are going to say lightly-disguised variations of the thing they said to the same applauding audiences they met somewhere else last year. **1974** *Listener* 10 Jan. 54/3 D. G. Rossetti.. would set Swinburne and the rest of his..practised log-rollers to promote his discovery.

log-rolling. 2. For *U.S. slang* read *colloq.* (orig. *U.S.*). Add further examples. Also *attrib.* or as *adj.*

1838 J. A. Quitman *Let.* 13 Dec. in J. F. H. Claiborne *Life & Corr. J. A. Quitman* (1860) I. 165 Tending to promote combinations and log-rolling schemes. **1860** S. Mordecai *Virginia* xxx. 303 But the log-rolling system of Virginia has diverted her energies from the completion of any one useful work. **1869** *Atlantic Monthly* Sept. 365/2 The log-rolling lobby generally exerted their powers upon objects which possessed a public character. **1889** G. B. Shaw *London Music 1888–89* (1937) 245, I received them with imprecations, having exhausted every form of words that logrolling amenity could take. **1914** W. B. Yeats *Responsibilities* 78 Log-rolling cranks and faddists. **1919** *New Statesman* 2 Aug. 437/2 There is no such thing as gratitude in politics—a fact which is perhaps the chief security we have against a universal orgie of log-rolling. **1929** A. Douglas *Autobiogr.* xxxiii. 222, I was involved in half-a-dozen controversies which covered matters of principle and the welfare of letters, as opposed to log-rolling and corrupt cliques. **1932** N. M. Butler *Looking Forward* vi. 87 This is no time..to permit log-rolling combinations of special interests to use public authority for their own benefit. **1957** J. S. Huxley *Relig. without Revelation* vi. 136 Politics would degenerate into a game of log-rolling. **1967** V. Nabokov *Speak, Memory* (ed. 2) xiv. 284 In their attitude toward literature they were curiously conservative; with them soul-saving came first, logrolling next, and art last. **1975** *N.Y. Times* 4 Mar. 33/3 In fact, a logrolling system, from which women rarely benefit, is the norm for faculty hiring.

Logudoro (lǫgudōᵊ·ro). The name of a town or area of Sardinia, used *attrib.* to designate the dialect or language used there. Hence **Lo:gudore·se, Lo:gudore·sian** *adjs.*

1849 J. W. Tyndale *Island of Sardinia* II. vi. 264 (*heading*) The Logudoro dialect. **1885** R. Tennant *Sardinia* v. 63 The rendering of the Lord's prayer in Sarde or Logudoro language, (so called to distinguish the Sarde proper from its northern and southern dialects) will give the best idea of the composite character of the language. **1946** Priebsch & Collinson *German Lang.* (ed. 2) i. 14 The Logudoresian dialect retains certain relict-words with affinities in Basque. **1952** *Archivum Linguisticum* IV. i. 92 Alghero, in Logudorese territory,..was an important centre of Catalan influence. **1954** Pei & Gaynor *Dict. Ling.* 190 The most important [Sardinian dialects]..are: Campidanese..and Logudorese (Logudoresian), spoken in the southern and central parts of the island. **1965** W. S. Allen *Vox Latina* i. 14 The Logudoro dialect of Sardinia.

logwood. Add: **3.** The extract of logwood used for colouring or dyeing. Also *attrib.*

1876 [see **chrome-black*]. **1880** *Encycl. Brit.* XIII. 80/1 Such an ink is costly..on account of the concentrated condition in which the logwood must be used. **1935** C. A. Mitchell *Documents & their Sci. Exam.* 56 Iron logwood inks have a greenish shade which gradually becomes black as the writing dries. **1966** J. S. Cox *Illustr. Dict. Hairdressing & Wigmaking* 91/1 Logwood... Used in the 19th cent. for dyeing hair. **1969** T. C. Thorstensen *Pract. Leather Technol.* xi. 173 Logwood has been extensively applied in the development of base colors in upper leathers, particularly calf.

logy, *a.* For *U.S.* read *N. Amer.* and add further examples.

1907 J. G. Millais *Newfoundland* 339 Logy, heavy, dull. Thus, a *logy* day. **1935** H. Davis *Honey in Horn* iv. 37 Ordinarily he could have out-wrestled her..but he was fagged and logy. **1955** *U.S. Bureau Amer. Ethnol. Bull.* No. 159. 277 Mrs. Murphy informed me that Ute medicine men placed a root (unidentified) in the mouth of an opponent's race horse to make it logy. **1955** W. Gaddis *Recognitions* II. i. 291 And do you feel run down at the end of the day? that dull logy tired feeling that just seems to creep through you? **1973** E. Pace *Any War will Do* (1974) II. 97 The heat, the flies, the logy ground swell.

Lohan (lō·hān). [Chin.] = *Arhat, Arahat.

1878 H. A. Giles *Gloss. Far East* 81 'Lohan cash' were cast in the reign of the Emperor K'ang Hsi, and were thus honourably named because believed to contain gold. **1880** J. Edkins *Chinese Buddhism* 5 Among [those]..who have gone deeper than the others into the profundities of Buddhist doctrine, are included those called..by the Chinese, P'usa and Lohan. **1905** *Daily Chron.* 26 Oct. 3/3 To call the Lohans or disciples of Buddha, 'Genii awaiting transformation into Buddhas' sounds as strange as if the twelve Apostles were described as awaiting transformation into Christs. **1936** *Discovery* Jan. 23/1 These T'ang figures and the great pottery Lohan, the Buddhist priest in contemplation, all live. **1964** M. Medley *Handbk. Chinese Art* 47 They [*sc.* Arhats] are called Lohan by the Chinese. **1971** L. A. Boger *Dict. World Pott. & Porc.* 201/2 The images of the Lohan are derived chiefly from the art work of one or two painters of the T'ang dynasty.

loiasis, var. *loaiasis.

‖ **loi-cadre** (lwa kadr'). *Fr. Pol.* [Fr.] A general outline law, the principles of which can be applied by the government in succeeding parallel situations.

1953 *Ann. Reg. 1952* 202 Eight votes of confidence. On the first—to empower the Government to draw up skeleton laws (*lois cadres*) reorganizing the nationalized industries. **1957** *Observer* 27 Oct. 15/6 It was a 'Loi-Cadre' for Algeria which provoked the collapse of the French government. **1967** *Economist* 29 Apr. 435/2 The French have long used and abused the technique of decree-laws and *loi-cadres* to overcome the difficulties of inefficient rule by the assembly. **1968** *Encycl. Brit.* I 624A/1 De Gaulle ignored a *loi-cadre*, laboriously passed by the French National Assembly, which provided for the setting up of regional assemblies in Algeria.

loid (loid). *Criminals' slang.* Also **'loid.** [Shortened f. Cellu)loid *sb.*] A celluloid strip used by thieves to force open a spring lock. Also *attrib.* Also as *v. trans.*, to break open (a lock) by this method; to let (oneself) in by this method. Hence **loi·ding** *vbl. sb.*

1958 M. Procter *Man in Ambush* xvi. 202 You said you could use a loid. Let's see you open that door. **1960** *Observer* 24 Jan. 5/5 Got yer stick (jemmy)? Got yer 'loid (celluloid strip for spring locks)? **1968** 'G. Bagby' *Another Day* vi. 107 What point..could there be in changing the cylinder..when..my visitor had managed

entry by..'a loid job?'. He had worked a strip of heavy celluloid in over the lock tongue and pushed it back. *Ibid.* ix. 174, I loided myself into my apartment. **1968** *Observer* 10 Mar. 25/4 Mortice deadlocks with five or more levers, difficult to pick and impossible to loid. *Ibid.* 25/5 Doors are opened by picking, loiding, or using a false key. **1968** B. TURNER *Sex-Trap* xiv. 134 'Have you got keys to all Creedy's places?' 'Beatty has. I use a loid myself.' He showed a tapered wedge of blank celluloid.

loin, *sb.* Add: **3.** *loin-rag* (= *loin-cloth*), *-steak*.

1929 D. H. LAWRENCE *Escaped Cock* II. 49 He peeped round..adjusting his loin-rag. **1938** R. GRAVES *Coll. Poems* 184 Nor yet that brooding Hindu heat For which a loin-rag and a dish of rice Suffice until the pestilent monsoon. **1868** *Rep. Iowa Agric. Soc. 1867* 127 The reason.. is the same that persons have for preferring loin-steaks to those cut from just aft of the horns.

loiner (loi·nəɹ). *slang.* [Origin uncertain.] An inhabitant of Leeds, West Yorkshire.

1950 M. MARPLES *University Slang* 180 *Loiner*,..possibly a corruption or mispronunciation of *oiner*. **1967** P. RYAN *How I became Yorkshireman* iii. 16 The lunchtime audience of Leeds loiners applauded vociferously. *Ibid.* ix. 59, I ran through the ranks of rumbling loiners and out into the eternal, grey twilight of Leeds.

loiter, *v.* Add: **1. a.** Freq. in legal phr. *to loiter with intent* (to commit a felony).

1891 *Act* 54 & 55 *Vict.* c. 69 § 7 The provisions [shall be] applied also to every suspected person or reputed thief loitering about or in any of the said places and with the said intent. **1899** C. ROOK *Hooligan Nights* i. 16 You get lagged for loiterin' wiv intent to commit a felony or some dam nonsense like that. **1952** *Economist* 26 Jan. 207/3 Montgomery is always suspected of loitering with intent. **1957** [see *CASE *v.*[2] 5].

2. b. (Later example with *out*.)

1863 LYTTON *Caxtoniana* I. 50 The little lake..on the banks of which I loitered out my schoolboy holidays.

‖ **lokal** (lokā·l). [Ger.] A local bar, a night-club.

1903 *Pop. Sci. Monthly* Dec. 126 The entire body, like a German scientific gathering, gravitated after adjournment to a summer garden or winter 'Lokal'. **1931** WYNDHAM LEWIS *Let.* 7 Feb. (1963) 200 If Miss Hamilton insists upon..robbing the night *lokals* of Berlin of foreign custom, I at least will have nothing to do with it. **1947** L. HASTINGS *Dragons are Extra* vii. 157 Tourists were filling the *lokals* in the evenings. **1949** A. WILSON *Wrong Set* 170 Her later life of boites and lokals. **1969** A. GLYN *Dragon Variation* viii. 229 Drinking beer in a keller, singing German songs, drinking wine or apfelsaft in a Schwabing *lokal*, and singing quite different songs.

‖ **lokanta** (lokæ·ntă). [Turk.] In Turkey: a restaurant.

1954 M. GOUGH *Plain & Rough Places* ix. 142 The courtyard..is occupied, in summer-time, by the *lokanta*—the restaurant. **1964** D. C. HILLS *My Trav. Turkey* xi. 120 We had hardly sat down in the *lokanta* when a gendarme captain swooped on me. **1969** 'A. GARVE' *Ascent of D. 13* ii. 23 He descended the rock in time to lunch at a small *lokanta*, on watermelon, *shish kebab* and yoghurt. **1969** *Daily Tel.* 4 Jan. 15/3 There are many nearby *lokantas* where you can try Turkish food and wines.

lokoum, var. *LOCOUM.

‖ **Lok Sabha** (lǫk sā·bă). [Skr. *lok* people + *sabhā* assembly, council.] The lower house of the Indian parliament.

1954 BINANI & RAMA RAO *India at Glance* (rev. ed.) 178 House of the People... Called Lok Sabha with effect from May 14, 1954. **1960** *Guardian* 24 Nov. 11/5 The Loksabha ..endorsed the Indian Government's..policies pursued during the current session of the UN. **1969** *Times* 13 Oct. (Indian Suppl.) 6/4 The fact that no Harijan or tribal member was elected to the Lok Sabha in the 1967 general election from a general seat is significant. **1971** *Femina* (Bombay) 2 Apr. 15/1 Mrs. Indira Gandhi announced the dissolution of the Lok Sabha. **1972** *Times of India* 28 Nov. 8/2 As soon as Mrs. Gandhi finished her statement in the Lok Sabha, the former minister for parliamentary affairs, Mr. Raghuramaiah, rose to seek some clarifications to assuage feelings in Andhra.

‖ **lokshen** (lǫ·kʃən), *sb. pl.* Also **lockschen, lockshan, lockshen.** [Yiddish, pl. of *loksh* noodle.] Noodles. Also *attrib.*, esp. *lokshen soup*.

1892 [see *FARFEL]. **1934** L. J. GREENBERG *Jewish Chron. Cookery Bk.* 167 Thickly grease a pudding basin and sprinkle thickly with brown sugar; then put in a layer of lockshen. **1964** G. SIMS *Terrible Door* xii. 67 Come on: the lockshan soup, the potato lutkas, are calling! **1969** *Coast to Coast 1967–68* 179 After the prayers Mrs Katzen served traditional fare; tonight it was lokshen soup, chopped herring, [etc.]. **1973** *Jewish Chron.* 20 July 23/3 He is not a man to decry lokshen soup.

Lolita (lǒlī·tă). The name of a novel (1958) and its main character by Vladimir Nabokov (1899–) about a precocious schoolgirl seduced by a middle-aged man, used to designate people and situations resembling those in the book. Also *attrib.* and *Comb.*

1959 *Encounter* Feb. 31/2 The melodrama turns this country of common routines into Lolitaland. **1960** B. FRETCHMAN tr. S. de Beauvoir (*title*) Brigitte Bardot and the Lolita syndrome. **1960** *Spectator* 25 Nov. 843 A nymphomaniac launched into her life's work by a Lolita-ish experience with the man who wanted to marry her mother. **1964** C. DALE *Other People* v. 113 He drew back. .. This was June from next door, a sweet kid but a schoolgirl... Christ, he wasn't a Lolita type! **1967** H. HUNTER *Case for Punishment* viii. 134 Jack Carter's our first assistant and he's absolutely head over heels in love with Jinnie Turner of the sixth form. A real Lolita affair. **1972** *Guardian* 25 Jan. 9/2 Louis Feraud..includes a group of dresses called schoolgirl frocks... Lolita lives again and one longs for the innocence of St Trinian's. **1975** *Listener* 6 Mar. 305/1 Chaplin had an uncontrollable infatuation with young girls... But his Lolita-like relationships in real life rarely matched the spiritual purity of love-on-the-screen.

lollapaloosa, etc.: see *LALLAPALOOSA.

lollie, var. *LOLLY[1].

lollipop, *sb.* Add: **a.** (Earlier and later, incl. *attrib.*, examples.) Restrict *dial.* to sense in Dict. and add: now a sweet or water-ice on a stick.

1784 *London Chron.* 17–20 Jan. 72/3 She confessed.. that a certain person..had enticed her to commit it [*sc.* the robbery], and given her sweetmeats, called lolly-pops. **1845** THACKERAY *Legend of Rhine* ix, in *George Cruikshank's Table-Bk.* Sept. 193 Ask the youth whether the lollypop-shop does not attract him? **1944** W. DE LA MARE *Coll. Rhymes & Verses* 41 A bottle of lollipops loved by Bess Stood apart on a window shelf. **1953** C. T. WILLIAMS *Chocolate & Confectionery* vi. 104 The B.C.H. Hollow Sleeve Drop Roller Machine may be augmented by a special attachment for the production of lollipops. **1959** [see *BRICK *sb.*[1] 4]. **1959** N. MAILER *Advts. for Myself* (1961) 401 He is as pretentious as a rich whore, as sentimental as a lollypop. **1962** *Spectator* 13 Apr. 463/2 What will inevitably be known as the 'lollipop' tax. **1965** HUTTON & BODE *Simple Sweetmaking* iv. 39 The lollipops have wax or cellophane paper twisted or tied round them. **1970** P. VILLIARD *Pract. Candymaking Cookbk.* v. 62, I am going to start your candymaking career off with some recipes for lollipops... You will need a supply of lollipop sticks.

b. Also, a showy or non-serious performance. Also *attrib.*

1952 J. MASEFIELD *So Long to Learn* 203 Many of the speakers were of a kind that I called 'lollipop-speakers': they spoke every kind of verse as if it were a caramel to be sucked, without any glimmering of a notion that the words had any meaning. **1958** *Times* 16 Oct. 4/6 His [Beecham's] reluctance to offer 'lollipop' encores. **1959** *Punch* 16 Sept. 172/2 That will be no more than the 'lollipop' innings of a Compton, the once-in-a-while reappearance of a Cotton or a Kyle. **1972** *Times* 3 July 12/2 Colin Carr chose, mistakenly for a student, a lollipop, a Popper Polonaise, rather than good red meat, but it served to show off an enviable fluency on the instrument.

c. *attrib.*, spec. of or pertaining to a person using a circular sign on a stick to stop traffic so that children may cross the road. Less commonly (occas. in non-attrib. use), the pole bearing a disc used by such a person.

1959 *Courier & Advertiser* (Dundee) 28 Mar. 5/6 These old people, commonly called 'lollipop men', ..do a good job. **1960** S. POTTER *Lang. in Mod. World* iv. 49 The traffic warden (or lollipop-man as the children affectionately call him) in his white overall makes himself prominent by raising his red disk on high: 'Stop, children crossing.' **1969** *Sunday Times* 9 Mar. 5 Top-hatted they stream from the school, one boy picks up the lollipop sign—which is hidden in a bush—and traffic is brought to a halt. **1969** *Courier-Mail* (Brisbane) 23 June 7/7 Civilian wardens to supervise school crossings..were used extensively overseas, and were known as 'lollipops' from the big discs on long poles they used to control vehicular traffic through school crossings. **1970** *Sunday Times* 25 Jan. 13 Mr. Blackmore, holding the lollipop that stops most traffic, said, 'That offside brake seems to be pulling.' **1971** *Daily Tel.* 27 July 13/1 (*heading*) Drivers must stop for lollipop men. *Ibid.*, Drivers stopped at school crossings by lollipop patrols must not proceed until the 'Stop, children crossing' sign has been taken away. **1972** *Sat. Titbits* 21 Oct. 20/1 Outside the school a 'lollipop lady' was holding up the traffic. **1972** *Times* 16 Dec. 12/2 We were on the lollipop patrol escorting the kids when they all scattered. **1973** *Daily Tel.* (Colour Suppl.) 16 Mar. 9/4 They watch the children in and out of school, something which on the mainland is done by a single elderly man with a 'lollipop stick'.

lollop, *sb.* Add: **2.** A trifling lazy person.

1896 in FARMER & HENLEY *Slang* IV. 223/2. **1919** H. L. WILSON *Ma Pettengill* iv. 125 Of course the poor lollop had never been able to think under any circumstances.

lolly[1]. Add: Also **lollie. a.** (Further, incl. Austral. and N.Z., examples.) Now usu. = *LOLLIPOP *sb.* a.

In Australia and N.Z. the usual sense is 'sweetmeat'.

1854 C. SPENCE *Clara Morison* II. ix. 102 Fanny ran away to the nearest lolly shop, and all her brothers and sisters followed her. **1860** C. M. YONGE *Friarswood Post Office* vii. 112 You may take your choice—gingerbread-nuts, or bits of cocoa-nut; or, what's jolliest, lollies with gin inside 'em! *Ibid.* x. 189 The children..bought all the 'lollies'. **1864** H. WEATHERLEY *Treat. Art Boiling Sugar* 5 Whether they consist of the 'Loggets' or 'Cushies' of the Eastern part..the 'Humbugs' or 'Lollys' of the South.. they each have their votaries. **1874** V. PYKE *Adventures G. W. Pratt* III. iv. 78 One of them filled her lap with cakes and 'lollies' for the 'bairnie'. **1886** A. R. BUTLER *Glimpses Maori Land* iii. 42 A friend of mine goes to the stores..and says, 'I want some lollies.' **1898** 'H.' *Grain of Gold* ii. 4 The first part of every child's education.. was to catch the old man by the coat tails and get a pat on the head and a 'lollie'. **1899** *Bulletin* (Sydney) 28 Jan. 11/3 A crowd of well-dressed women amused themselves by throwing lollies, bits of ginger, and small fruits into the mouths of a straw-hat push on the other side. **1911** E. M. CLOWES *On Wallaby* v. 136 Men, when they wanted to show their appreciation of her services, sent her a box of sweets—or lollies, as they are called out here. **1915** [see *CHUCK *v.*[2] 2 e]. **1935** 'G. ORWELL' *Clergyman's Daughter* ii. 131 London hawkers would come with baskets of doughnuts or water ices or 'halfpenny lollies'. **1936** C. R. ALLEN *Poor Scholar* i. 17 Even Herby fought down a longing for liquorice as they went by his favourite 'lolly' shop. **1955** *Times* 13 June 4/4 The 'real menace of sweets' to dental health was the constant sucking of lollies or other sweets, particularly at night. *Ibid.* 6 Aug. 8/4 A merry little cottage is painted in clear white and lolly pink. **1959** B. COMYNS *Vet's Daughter* xii. 100 A scraggy woman with a fringe, dressed in lolly pink. **1961** *Coast to Coast 1959–60* 161 Anyway, Vivi, you look nice in those new shoes. Here's threepence for lollies. **1964** *Weekly News* (Auckland) 10 June 3/3 The most popular event was a giant lolly scramble. Hundreds of children spent a few minutes of furious activity seizing their share of about 7000 sweets tossed among them. **1969** M. DRABBLE *Waterfall* 87 He had acquired eleven wooden lollie sticks. **1969** *Landfall* XXIII. 99 What was an award for merit promises now to become a lolly-scramble. **1972** J. WILSON *Hide & Seek* i. 8 She looked longingly at the ice-cream van... 'Can I have a lolly?'

b. In Cricket, an easy catch. Also as *adj.* Cf. *DOLLY *a.* b.

1924 H. DE SÉLINCOURT *Cricket Match* v. 160 He..hit it—a 'lolly' into the hands of point. **1960** J. FINGLETON *Four Chukkas to Austral.* xv. 128 May did not last long.. giving Benaud a lolly-catch at gully-slip.

c. *slang.* Money. Also *attrib.*

1943 M. HARRISON *Reported Safe Arrival* 61 This 'ere bloke touches the Guv'ment fer a nice drop er lolly. **1958** *Spectator* 14 Feb. 194/2 Next year's Budget gives fistfuls of lolly away to everybody. **1965** *Listener* 28 Oct. 677/2 A young English con-man..stands to gain lots of lovely lolly. **1971** *Ink* 12 June 14/1 Bernie's salesmen kept bringing in the lolly during the..boom. **1973** *Scotsman* 13 Feb. 8/3 The rank and file Bishops would be better off, financially, if they accepted jobs as Principals in the Egg, Poultry and Potato Division of the Ministry of Agriculture... In terms of lolly they would be better off as Senior Officers in the Land, Drainage and Water Supply Division of the Ministry. **1973** G. MOFFAT *Deviant Death* i. 14 There's only one person bringing in the lolly in that house.

lolly[2] (lǫ·li). *Canad.* [Shortened f. LOBLOLLY. Cf. *E.D.D.*] (See quots.)

1792 G. CARTWRIGHT *Jrnl.* I. p. xii, *Lolly*, soft ice, or congealed snow floating in the water when it first begins to freeze. **1889** W. H. WITHROW *Our own Country: Canada* 68 The distance to Cape Traverse is about nine miles, part solid ice, part drifting ice, part water, and sometimes a great deal of broken ice or 'lolly'. **1895** *Dialect Notes* I. 379 *Lolly*, ice and snow in the water along the shore... It is the hardest kind of thing to get the boat through. **1963** *Amer. Speech* XXXVIII. 299 *Lolly*, soft ice beginning to form in a harbor.

lollygag, var. *LALLYGAG *v.* and *sb.*

Lolo (lōᵘ·lōᵘ). [Native name.] The name of an aboriginal people of south-western China, of a member of this people, and of their Tibeto-Burmese language. Also *attrib.* or as *adj.*

1736 R. BROOKES tr. *Du Halde's Gen. Hist. China* I. 59 The Nation of the Lolos rul'd in Yun nan, and was govern'd by different Sovereigns. **1878** H. A. GILES *Gloss. Far East* 81 *Lolos*, wild hill tribes of Szechuan and Yünnan. **1898** A. R. COLQUHOUN *China in Transformation* i. 24 It is clear there are but three great non-Chinese races in Southern China—the Lolo, the Shan and the Miao-tzu. **1901** E. H. PARKER *China* i. 8 Among the mountains of north-east Yün Nan and south Sz Ch'wan, the powerful confederation of so-called Lolo tribes still maintains its independence. **1933** L. BLOOMFIELD *Lang.* iv. 70 The other two groups [of *Tibeto-Burman*], *Bodo-Naga-Kachin* and *Lo-lo*, consist of lesser dialects. **1937** E. SNOW *Red Star over China* v. 194 Moving..into Szechuan..[the Reds] soon entered the tribal country of warlike aborigines, the White and Black Lolos of Independent Lololand. **1948** D. DIRINGER *Alphabet* I. ix. 141 The languages of the Lolo-Mo-so group belong to the Tibeto-Burmese sub-family of the Tibeto-Chinese family of languages... Lolo is itself a sub-group of various languages, spoken by about 1,800,000 people in the south-western provinces of China. **1966** R. & D. MORRIS *Men & Pandas* iii. 47 Lieutenant J. W. Brooke was murdered in 1910 by the Lolos. **1968** *Encycl. Brit.* V. 567/2 The Tibeto-Burman branch of the Tibeto-Chinese language family falls into three groups: the Tibetan, the Yi (formerly called Lolo) and the Kachin.

loma (lōᵘ·mă), *sb.*[2] *U.S.* (chiefly S.-Western). [Sp., f. *lomo* back, loin, ridge.] A broad-topped hill or ridge.

1849 *Picayune* (New Orleans) 4 May 2/3 [They] were riding quietly along the Loma Blanca, (white hill,) when they came suddenly upon a party of eight or ten Indians. **1863** *Ex. Doc. 37th U.S. Congress Sp. Sess. Senate* No. 1. 20 The new road is to follow the bottom at the edge of the *lomas*. **1923** C. F. SAUNDERS *Southern Sierras Calif.* 75 All about are rounded hills, or lomas, rising in baldness. **1941** *Harper's Mag.* Oct. 498/1 Stand on the 'knoll' at Yucca Loma, drink in the desert, and then look down at your feet.

Loma (lōᵘ·mă), *sb.*[3] and *a.* Pl. **Loma, Lomas.** [Native name.] **A.** *sb.* The name of a people inhabiting the border regions of Liberia, Sierra Leone, and the Republic of Guinea, and of their language. **B.** *adj.* Of or pertaining to the Loma or their language.

1957 *Encycl. Brit.* XX. 624/1 Above the plateau surface rise many mountain ranges, the highest of which are the Loma mountains. **1964** E. A. NIDA *Toward Sci. Transl.* ix. 198 In a language such as Loma, spoken in Liberia, it is impossible to duplicate these sequences. **1969** *Liberian Studies Jrnl.* I. 25 The Kpelle, Loma, Bandi and Mende are included in the Southwestern Mande group. *Ibid.* 37 The people of eastern Lukasu and Yawiyasu have several linguistic similarities to the Loma people. **1970** D. DALBY *Lang. & Hist. Afr.* 112 The Loma syllabary (with a total of at least 185 characters) was devised in the 1930's.. reputedly inspired by a dream.

Lombard, *sb.*¹ and *a.* Add: **1. c.** The language of this people. Also *attrib.* or as *adj.*

1598 FLORIO *Worlde of Wordes* 3 How may we ayme at the Venetian, at the Romane, at the Lombard..at so manie, and so much differing Dialects..as be used and spoken in Italie? *Ibid.* 132/2 *Fio*.. In Lombard Italian for *Figlio*, a sonne, a childe. **1878, 1880** [see *EMILIAN *a.* and *sb.*]. **1936** G. F.-H. & J. BERKELEY *Italy in Making* II. 353 All this he told me in Lombard dialect of which every word had to be translated into Italian by his son.

B. 1. b. *Lombard band* (see quots. 1959).

1936 A. W. CLAPHAM *Romanesque Archit.* ii. 28 The so-called Lombard bands and wall-arcading..are distinctive of the first Romanesque style. **1959** *Chambers's Encycl.* I. 558/2 Shallow external pilasters cutting the wall-surface into bays and commonly called 'Lombard bands'. **1959** E. A. FISHER *Introd. Anglo-Saxon Archit. & Sculpture* 26 Lombard band ornamentation consisted of vertical pilaster strips of slight projection which divided a wall into bays.

Lombard-street. (Further examples.)

1815 *Pancratia* (ed.2) 367, 9th [round]—Lombard-street to a China orange; Molineux was dead beat. **1821** P. EGAN *Real Life London* I. vi. 83 Beat him hollow, it was all Lombard-street to a china orange. **1892** *Evening Standard* 9 Nov. 1/1 We describe the betting upon a moral certainty as being All Lombard-street to a China orange. **1974** *Times* 30 Nov. 10/5 If you didn't already know..then it's most of Lombard Street to a China Orange you'd never find out.

Lombardy. The name of a region of northern Italy, used *attrib.* in **Lombardy poplar,** to designate a columnar variety of poplar, *Populus nigra* var. *italica* (or *P. italica*), which was introduced from Italy to other countries. Also *absol.*

1766 [see POPLAR 1 b]. **1797** S. DEANE *Newengland Farmer* (ed. 2) 267 The Lombardy Poplar begins to be propagated in this country. **1799** JANE AUSTEN *Let.* 17 May (1952) 62 The drawing-room window..commands a perspective view of the left-side of Brock Street, broken by three Lombardy poplars in the garden of the last house in Queen's Parade. **1882** [see POPLAR 1 b]. **1917** L. M. MONTGOMERY *Anne's House of Dreams* vii. 58 The Lombardies down the lane, tall and sombre. **1957** M. HADFIELD *Brit. Trees* 151 The Lombardy poplar was once generally held to be a sport from the southern European black poplar. It is now said to be a true species. **1969** T. H. EVERETT *Living Trees of World* 94/1 The Berlin poplar, a tree of columnar growth and bright green foliage [is] believed to have the Lombardy poplar and *P. laurifolia* as its parents. **1974** A. MITCHELL *Field Guide to Trees of Britain* 27 A narrow, columnar or spire-like tree, like a Lombardy poplar, looks much taller than it really is.

Lombrosian (lǫmbrǭ·ziǎn), *a.* [f. the name of Cesare *Lombroso* (1836–1909), Italian physician and criminologist + -IAN.] Of or pertaining to Cesare Lombroso and to his theories of the physiology, psychology, and treatment of the criminal; also as *sb.*, an adherent or follower of Lombroso or his theories. Hence **Lombro·sianism; Lombro·sic** *a.*, of or pertaining to Lombrosianism.

1906 JOYCE *Let.* 19 Aug. (1966) II. 151 He was ridiculing lombrosianism and antimilitarism. **1914** *Everyman* 16 Jan. 451/2 The 'conclusions' have been so recently published that Lombrosians and anti-Lombrosians must be..excused if they ask for time. **1922** G. B. SHAW in S. & B. Webb *Eng. Prisons under Local Govt.* p. lxii, The stigmata of the Lombrosic criminal. **1973** *Listener* 8 Nov. 624/1 'We don't go in for the Lombrosian type of nonsense of measuring skulls any more,' protest our present-day criminologists.

lomi-lomi. (Earlier and later examples.)

1850 W. COLTON *Deck & Port* xi. 347, I was..determined to try..the bath and the 'lomi-lomi'. **1951** *Amer. Speech* XXVI. 23 Other common Hawaiian words are.. *lomilomi* (massage).

Lomongo: see *MONGO¹.

lomonosovite (lomǫ·nosǫvəit). *Min.* [ad. Russ. *lomonosovit* (V. I. Gerasimovsky 1941, in *Dokl. Akad. nauk SSSR* XXXII. 498), f. the name of Michael *Lomonosov* (1711–65), Russian mineralogist: see -ITE¹.] A phosphate, silicate, and oxide of sodium and titanium, $Na_5Ti_2(Si_2O_7)(PO_4)O_2$, found as dark brown triclinic crystals in the Kola peninsula, U.S.S.R.

1941 V. I. GERASIMOVSKY in *Compt. Rend. (Doklady) de l'Acad. des Sci. de l'URSS* XXXII. 498 The pegmatite patches..are composed of hackmanite..with a very considerable content of chinglusuite and lomonosovite (a sodium phosphate-titanium silicate). **1966** *Geochem. Internat.* III. 197 It is better to interpret lomonosovite as an inorganic clathrate of murmanite structure and sodium phosphate, with the possible formation of intermediate compounds between lomonosovite and sodium-poor lomonosovite.

London. Add: **London-bottled** *a.*, (of a wine) bottled in London; **London bridge,** a children's singing game; **London broil** *U.S.* (see quot. 1969); **London fog,** a dense fog once peculiar to London and large industrial towns; **London gin,** a dry gin; **London plane,** *Platanus* × *hispanica* (*P.* × *acerifolia*), a hybrid of *P. occidentalis* and *P. orientalis*, often planted as a street tree; **London shrinking,** a finishing process applied to fabric to prevent shrinkage; also **London-shrunk** *a.*

1959 *Times* 21 Sept. 13/2 London-bottled, it costs about 10s. **1972** *Guardian* 24 Feb. 11/2 The difference between London-bottled and château or domaine-bottled wine of the same vineyard..cannot be stated in hard terms. **1972** *House & Garden* Feb. 111/1 With London-bottled clarets starting at £1.50 and château-bottled at £2.50, the prices were not excessive. [**1827** R. THOMSON *Chronicles of London Bridge* 152 'Here follows the ancient Music to the Song and Dance of London Bridge is broken down.'.. 'A choice piece of simple melody, indeed,' said Mr. Postern,.. 'but you called it also a dance, Mr. Barbican; pray was it ever adapted to the feet, as well as to the tongue?'] **1894** A. B. GOMME *Traditional Games* I. 199 It is singular that the verses of this game [*sc.* 'Hark the robbers'], also enter into the composition of 'London Bridge is broken down'. It is probable, therefore, that it may be an altered form of the game of 'London Bridge'. **1909** *Encycl. Relig. & Ethics* II. 852/1 The singing game known as 'London Bridge' has many variants in the different localities where it is played, but fundamentally the theme is the same. **1939** F. THOMPSON *Lark Rise* ix. 159 Well-known games still met with at children's parties, such as 'Oranges and Lemons', 'London Bridge'. **1969** I. & P. OPIE *Children's Games* viii. 235 A singing game such as 'London Bridge is Falling Down'. **1969** R. & D. DE SOLA *Dict. Cooking* 143/1 *London broil*, large flank steak broiled, then cut in thin slices diagonally across the grain for serving. **1973** E.-J. BAHR *Nice Neighbourhood* ii. 24 We cooked a London broil out on the grill and ate on the patio. **1974** *Columbia* (S. Carolina) *Record* 24 Apr. 14-B/1 Most steak buffs have their favorite cut, and this brings up something I haven't been able to figure out: the names they give steaks. I'm told that Britons had never heard of London broil until some Yank informed them what it was. **1830** M. EDGEWORTH *Let.* 8 Dec. (1971) 445 It is so very dark in a thick London fog that I can scarcely see what I write. **1887** [see FOG *sb.*² 2]. **1906** W. MARRIOTT *Hints to Meteorol. Observers* (ed. 6) 67/1 *London fog*, the dry, gloomy, irritating fog peculiar to London and other large towns, aggravated by smoke. **1931** E. E. CUMMINGS *Let.* 7 Jan. (1969) 120 A London fog struck the ville at the very moment of departure. **1972** E. ROUTLEY *Puritan Pleasures of Detective Story* iii. 36 Holmes..has moral status, and that makes one feel safer when one sets out with him into another London fog. **1920** G. SAINTSBURY *Notes on Cellar-Bk.* vii. 104 Gin, whether 'squareface' or London or Plymouth, [costs] not much more than half a crown. **1954** M. SHARP *Gipsy in Parlour* xxiv. 230 'Devon cider be a powerful brew,' said my Aunt Charlotte... 'London gin's a sight worse,' retorted Clara. **1963** A. L. SIMON *Guide Good Food & Wines* 721/1 *London Gins*, which differ according to the Distilleries responsible for them. **1970** *House & Garden* Nov. 126/2 The type of gin in most general use is London Dry... Though a few countries ..deem 'London' to indicate a geographical origin,..the term London Dry Gin is mainly accepted as indicating a type of gin. **1860** T. RIVERS in *Gardeners' Chronicle* 21 Jan. 47/1 (*heading*) The London Plane trees. **1885** G. S. BOULGER *Familiar Trees* 1st Ser. 23 Most of our London Plane-trees belong to an intermediate form. **1930** A. D. WEBSTER *London Trees* 92 The Maple-leaved or London Plane stands first in the list of select trees for planting in towns. **1970** *Nature* 21 Mar. 1159/2 The London plane has proved extremely valuable as a tree that will endure the difficult environments of modern cities. **1957** *Textile Terms & Definitions* (Textile Inst.) (ed. 3) 61 *London shrinking*, a finishing process. **1940** *Chambers's Techn. Dict.* 509/2 London-shrunk (*Textiles*), a term used in the woollen and worsted trades to indicate that a fabric has been specially treated in order to prevent shrinkage during make-up and when worn. **1950** '*Mercury*' *Dict. Textile Terms* 323/2 *London shrunk.* The dry cloth to be shrunk is folded between an upper and lower layer of wet cloth. The cloth is then dried naturally, and afterwards pressed. **1968** J. IRONSIDE *Fashion Alphabet* 239 *London-shrunk*, a process for shrinking wool fabric before tailoring.

Londonish (lɒ·ndəniʃ), *a.* [-ISH¹.] Pertaining to or characteristic of London; exhibiting features or aspects of London.

1838 *Civil Engin. & Arch. Jrnl.* 154/2 A modest porch below, and a *neat* viranda—something of that sort, spruce and Londonish. **1852** GEO. ELIOT *Let.* 23 June (1954) II. 37 Not that I don't like him..but I want nothing so Londonish when I go to enjoy the fields. **1922** *Sketch* 1 Nov. 194/3 A few mellow Cockney vowels to make us feel cosy —Londonish. **1925** W. DEEPING *Sorrell & Son* vi. 56, I had been getting a little—Londonish—shall we call it. **1927** *Observer* 6 Nov. 9/4 The Cromwell-road is at once the most English and the most Londonish of our thoroughfares. **1956** M. STEWART *Wildfire at Midnight* iii. 32 You look a bit Londonish, if I may say so.

Londonization. (Further examples.)

1959 *Daily Tel.* 21 Nov. 15/2 Mr. Grimond..said Londonisation of the whole of the country must be prevented. **1962** *Rep. Comm. Broadc. 1960* (Cmnd. 1753) xiii. 139 The dangers of Londonisation are less than those of isolation.

Londony (lɒ·ndəni), *a.* [-Y¹.] Suggestive of London or its characteristics.

1884 L. TROUBRIDGE *Life amongst Troubridges* (1966) 169, I thought him so very smart and Londony. **1907** D. O'CONNOR *Peter Pan Picture Bk.* 27 They made a chimney out of John's tall hat, which he had been Londony enough to bring with him. **1920** J. GALSWORTHY *In Chancery* I. x. 88 Rather pale she looked and Londony. **1949** D. SMITH *I capture Castle* xiv. 263 A cool breeze was blowing in from the Park, smelling of dry grass and petrol—a most exciting, Londony smell. **1974** C. MILNE *Enchanted Places* x. 69, I hated wearing overcoats in the country... Overcoats were Londony things.

lone, *a.* Add: **1. b.** *fig.* (Earlier example.) Also *attrib.*

1879 B. F. TAYLOR *Summer-Savory* xv. 122 In fact, in pretty nearly all his plays he had a 'lone hand'. **1888** KIPLING *Barrack-Room Ballads* (1892) 118 A lone-hand raid of the rearmost cart. **1916** *Brit. Dominions Year Bk. 1917* 243 Lone-hand raids on Constantinople. **1922** JOYCE *Ulysses* 455 This is a lonehand fight.

3. b. *lone star*, the single star on the state flag of Texas, hence called the *Lone Star State*. Also *Lone Star Stater*, a Texan.

1843 W. B. DEWEES *Lett. from Early Settler Texas* (1852) 246 The lone star of Texas shall continue to wave proudly in the air as long as one brave Texan remains to defend it. **1845** *Congress. Globe* 28th Congress 2 Sess. App. 78/3 The 'lone star' has found a place upon the democratic banners. **1848** *Ibid.* 30th Congress 1 Sess. App. 973/1 Texas was then a 'lone star'. She is now one of thirty. **1860** *Ibid.* 5 Dec. 11/3 There is a clog in the way of the lone-star State of Texas in the person of her Governor. **1873** J. H. BEADLE *Undevel. West* 805, I am proud to find him in honor and position among the 'Lone Star Staters'. **1873** Z. N. MORRELL *Flowers & Fruits* (ed. 2) 20 Sam. Houston was then in Texas..intending..to set in motion 'a little two-horse republic under the Lone Star'. **1886** B. P. POORE *Perley's Reminisc.* I. 315 It took him only from February 28th to April 12th to conclude the negotiation which placed the 'Lone Star' in the azure field of the ensign of the Republic. **1909** 'O. HENRY' *Roads of Destiny* xvi. 267 The Lone Star State never yet failed to grant relief, [etc.]. **1943** B. HOUSE (*title*) I give you Texas: 500 jokes of the Lone Star State. **1971** *Times* 21 Sept. (Ireland Suppl.) 1/4 Two experts from Texas are using Cork as a base..appropriate, since co Cork has always had some of the aggressive independence of the lone star state.

c. *lone wolf*, (orig. *U.S.*) *fig.* (*a*) one who mixes little with others, keeps himself to himself; (*b*) a criminal who operates alone; also *attrib.* Hence (with hyphen) as *v. intr.*, to live, work, operate, etc., alone.

1909 F. H. TILLOTSON *How to be a Detective* 130 Occasionally the police run across Panhandlers known as 'lone wolves'—that is they do not mix with others of their class. **1927** *Dialect Notes* V. 454 *Lone wolf*, a bandit or house breaker who works without confederates. **1931** *Times Lit. Suppl.* 28 May 415/3 He was the 'lone wolf' of the campaign for federation. **1938** *Amer. Speech* XIII. 195 Lone-wolf v. **1938** E. BOWEN *Death of Heart* II. iv. 249, I am quite enough of a lone wolf as it is. **1944** R. F. ADAMS *Western Words* 93/1 *Lone-wolfing*, living alone, avoiding companionship of others. **1950** 'S. RANSOME' *Deadly Miss Ashley* iii. 35 He had been given hardly a dime's worth of information by the lone-wolf doctor. **1953** A. BARON *Human Kind* xvii. 121 They despised his ignorance, his vices and his pitiless lone-wolf philosophy. **1955** *Publ. Amer. Dial. Soc.* xxiv. x. 166 She is..a kind of *lone wolf* thief. **1955** *Times* 11 July 10/1 A 'lone wolf' terrorist. **1959** ANON. *Streetwalker* viii. 154 He's no lone wolf from Leeds or anywhere else. **1959** N. MAILER *Advts. for Myself* (1961) 408 The lone-wolf hope that we can begin to explore a little more. **1966** J. PHILIPS *Wings of Madness* II. iv. 131 You are in very serious danger if you try to lone-wolf it. **1966** G. BURNETT *Dead Account* vii. 51 Remember what I said..no lone-wolfing, no withholding information. **1970** G. F. NEWMAN *Sir, You Bastard* i. 19 An individualist to be watched unless he should develop into too much of a lone wolf. **1973** J. ROSSITER *Manipulators* ii. 21 Detective Inspector De Moro..had given him a preliminary reprimand about lone-wolfing operations.

e. *lone pair* (Physical Chem.): a pair of electrons in the outer shell of an atom which are not involved in bonding.

1923 *Chem. & Industry Rev.* 2 Nov. 1051/1 A basic substance is one which has a lone pair of electrons which may be used to complete the stable group of another atom. **1964** J. W. LINNETT *Electronic Struct. Molecules* ii. 31 In ammonia there are, therefore, three shared-pairs and one lone-pair.

6. b. More recently also in form *lone* (and *lones*).

1902 KIPLING *Just So Stories* 197 They walked in the Wet Wild Woods by their wild lones. *Ibid.* 206 This is the picture of the Cat that Walked by Himself, walking by his wild lone through the Wet Wild Woods. **1908** *Westm. Gaz.* 28 May 2/4 The roads are dusty and dry When you walk 'em all by your lone. **1910** W. M. RAINE *Bucky O'Connor* 21 But why for do they let a sick man like you travel all by his lone? **1917** W. J. LOCKE *Red Planet* vi. 75 After five minutes on my lones, I felt as if I should go off my head. **1941** W. DE LA MARE *Coll. Poems* 7 As she asks in her lone, This old, desolate crone.

lonely, *a.* Add: **1. b.** Colloq. or dial. phr. *on one's lonely(-o)*: on one's own; alone. Cf. LONE *a.* 6 b in Dict. and Suppl. (prob. infl. by *only*).

1919 D. H. LAWRENCE *England my England* (1922) 61 Oh, I'm going home by myself to-night—all on my lonely-O. **1924** 'K. MANSFIELD' *Something Childish* 61 So you're on your lonely, missus? *a* **1930** D. H. LAWRENCE *Phoenix*

(1936) v. 594 A child was to be given a lump of soft clay and told to express himself, presumably in the pious hope that he might model a Tanagra figure or a Donatello plaque, all on his little lonely-o.

6. lonely-heart, a sentimental name for a friendless person; so (**Miss**) **Lonelyhearts**, a journalist who gives advice in a newspaper or magazine to people who are lonely or in difficulties; also *transf.* and *attrib.*; also **lonely-hearted** *a.* (and *absol.*).

1863 Lonely-hearted [in Dict.]. **1904** W. DE LA MARE *Henry Brocken* 200 Criseyde..the lonely-hearted. **1931** R. CAMPBELL *Georgiad* i. 15 More lonely hearts are linked by the Reviews Than by the 'Link' or 'Matrimonial News'. **1933** 'N. WEST' (*title*) Miss Lonelyhearts. *Ibid.* 14 *Miss Lonelyhearts* tells the story of a reporter,..detailed to write an agony column and answer daily the letters desperate with human misery addressed to his paper. **1938** G. GREENE *Brighton Rock* I. i. 9 Come on over here, lonely heart. **1955** W. GADDIS *Recognitions* III. ii. 749 Down the bar, the Big Unshaven Man was offered a job writing the lonely-hearts column for a newspaper in Buffalo. **1956** A. WILSON *Anglo-Saxon Att.* I. iii. 59 You're so busy being Miss Lonelyhearts to your public. **1958** M. DICKENS *Man Overboard* ii. 31 Rose's weekly show was a toothsome mixture of soap opera and a Lonely-hearts column. **1959** 'N. BLAKE' *Widow's Cruise* 29 He might just be the fulsome, pathetic lonely-heart he appeared to be. **1959** T. GRIFFITH *Waist-High Culture* (1960) ii. 25 With a fellow lonely-heart,..he would drive out to remote lakes. **1959** *Listener* 28 May 924/2 The office of Connie, the girl who writes the 'Lonely Hearts' column. **1975** *Times* 1 Mar. 8/4 *Music Through Midnight*..the BBC's Miss Lonelyhearts spot. The other two nights there is *Contact*, a radio advice and counselling column.

loner (lōᵘ·nəɹ). [f. LONE *a.* + -ER¹.] A person who avoids company and prefers to be alone.

1947 *New Republic* 22 Dec. 7 Big John has decided to become a 'loner' for keeps. **1961** *Guardian* 26 Oct. 7/1 The American ex-patriates along the Seine..are what James Jones calls 'loners'. **1964** L. LINTON *Of Days & Driftwood* xviii. 88 There are many 'loners' dotted around the coastal area, only accessible by boat. **1970** *Daily Tel.* (Colour Suppl.) 3 July 7 On course, as in private life, he is a loner, a man of few words who finds it impossible to chat and joke with the crowds. **1971** *Universe* 25 June 13/5 Mr Paisley is a bit of a maverick, a loner who won't be tied by party trappings. **1971** *Country Life* 29 July 278/1 A loner done to death by his fellows for stepping out of line. **1972** *Daily Mail* 30 Oct. 7/2 By nature I'm a loner.

lonesome, *a.* Add: **1. b.** *by* (or *on*) *one's lonesome*, all alone, without company or assistance. (Cf. *LONE *a.* 6 b). *colloq.*

1899 C. J. C. HYNE *Further Adventures Capt. Kettle* ii. 31 No, Kettle, if I'm to get well, some white man will have to go up by his lonesome for me, and square that witch doctor by some trick of the tongue. **1908** *Daily Chron.* 13 Aug. 5/7 Then, parting from him,..I went, all by my lonesome, along the Madeira Walk. **1920** B. CRONIN *Timber Wolves* 125 'When I marry Amelia Peters,' says George, 'you can hit the trail on your lonesome.' **1953** H. MILLER *Plexus* (1963) xii. 442 That evening I wandered off by my lonesome. **1973** G. BEARE *Snake on Grave* ii. 10 One of Rommel's 88's had taken care of his old man somewhere in the Western Desert, and that had left Latch on his lonesome.

c. *lonesome for.*

1905 *Smart Set* Sept. 74 [He]..had become exceedingly lonesome for the nice young man. **1935** M. DE LA ROCHE *Young Renny* xi. 98 Bob has gone in to see Lizzie. She's feeling a bit lonesome for a sight of him.

long, *a.*¹ Add: **A. 1. c.** *to make a long arm* (examples); *the long arm of coincidence* (earlier and later examples); *to make a long nose* (later examples); *long in the tooth*: (orig. of horses) displaying the roots of the teeth owing to the recession of the gums with increasing age; hence *gen.*, old.

1852 THACKERAY *Esmond* I. ii. 50 She was lean, and yellow, and long in the tooth; all the red and white in all the toyshops of London could not make a beauty of her. **1854** C. M. YONGE *Heartsease* I. ii. 11. 146 Rising, and making a long arm, he deposited them on the top of a high wardrobe. **1860** [see *ARM *sb.*¹ 2 b]. **1884** [see ARM *sb.*¹ 2 b]. *c* **1888** C. H. CHAMBERS *Capt. Swift* (1902) II. 29 I'm not safe here. This place is a hornet's nest. The long arm of coincidence has reached after me. **1895** G. B. SHAW *Our Theatres in Nineties* (1932) I. 229 Mr. Jerome..has discovered that in working the familiar but safe stage trick of *dénouement* by coincidence, the long arm cannot be too long. **1919** J. C. SNAITH *Love Lane* xxi. 106 One of the youngest R.A.s on record, but a bit long in the tooth for the army. **1932** J. CONQUEST *Village Pompadour* xxv. 183 Long in the tooth, he escaped the traps laid by widow, débutante and free-lance. **1933** 'R. CROMPTON' *William—the Rebel* x. 187 They merely made long noses at the Outlaws. **1936** W. S. MAUGHAM *Cosmopolitans* 213 Go on... The long arm of coincidence was about to make a gesture. **1942** *R.A.F. Jrnl.* 27 June 20 Izzy Grant saw one [*sc.* a Gremlin]..making a long nose at him as he went into the ditch. **1951** 'E. CRISPIN' *Long Divorce* xii. 141 'That's stretching the long arm of coincidence rather far.' 'It's pulling the damned thing right out of its socket.' **1957** J. BRAINE *Room at Top* xii. 124 A trifle long in the tooth, mark you, but she has style, real style. **1963** A. HUXLEY *Let.* 17 Nov. (1969) 964 Talk about the long arm of coincidence! The mail which brought your note..brought..at the same time a letter from Betty Wendel. **1972** *Sunday Express* 24 Dec. 2/5 To be honest I am getting quite long in the tooth and this is a method of bringing children into my Christmas. **1973** 'B. MATHER' *Snowline* vii. 83, I made a long arm for the telephone.

f. Also *long manure.*

1839 J. BUEL *Farmer's Compan.* xx. 198 Great economy in dung may be effected by feeding these crops with the long manure of the yards and stables, instead of summer-yarding it.

5. b. *long purse*, one in which there is plenty of money; *long shillings*, good wages.

1809 M. L. WEEMS *Life F. Marion* iii. 26 Great Britain the nation of the longest purse in Europe. **1871** *Scribner's Monthly* II. 551 For longer purses there are hard woods in all combinations. **1910** 'SAKI' *Reginald in Russia* 105 The long arm, or perhaps one might better say the long purse, of diplomacy at last effected the release of the prisoners. **1910** *Chambers's Jrnl.* Sept. 603/2 There are 'long shillings' to be earned at the docks, but no easy ones; and the work is not only hard but dangerous. **1955** J. I. M. STEWART *Guardians* I. ix. 97 Lady Elizabeth's generalisation that here—in point of the long purse—was a particular in which Quail himself must lead any field.

c. *long suit, fig.* one's strong point.

1895 W. C. GORE in *Inlander* Dec. 114 *Long suit*, something one is familiar with or expert in. **1903** A. ADAMS *Log of Cowboy* xiv. 218 Young Pete..assured our foreman that the building of bridges was his long suit. **1916** E. V. LUCAS *Vermilion Box* 26 Organizing has always been your long suit. **1923** U. L. SILBERRAD *Lett. J. Armiter* iv. 82 Charity's evidently your long suit. **1934** M. V. HUGHES *London Child of Seventies* vi. 72 'Can you do simple long division?' 'Oh, yes, Dym,' said I hopefully, for that was my long suit. **1959** N. COWARD *Look after Lulu!* II. 68 Oh Lord! That's a teaser—arithmetic's never been my long suit.

d. *long chance*, one involving considerable uncertainty or risk.

1907 S. E. WHITE *Arizona Nights* I. xiii. 191 He's plumb scared at the prospect of suffering anything, and would rather die right off than take long chances. *Ibid.* II. iv. 262 He's one of those long-chance fellows. **1938** H. NICOLSON *Let.* 17 Feb. (1966) 322, I do not think there is going to be a war yet. Not by a long chance. **1971** D. EDEN *Afternoon Walk* ix. 125 It would be a long chance that the one I just saw was the same one.

7. a. Also used advb. without preceding *a* in Jamaican English (see also quot. 1961).

1942 L. BENNETT *Jamaica Dial. Verses* 21 Me did tink me always hear sey Missis Queen bannish slavery lang time. **1961** F. G. CASSIDY *Jamaica Talk* vi. 107 *Long time* means long ago ('Him gone long time'). **1971** *Jamaican Weekly Gleaner* 3 Nov. 5/1 Tams are also in (well, we did have that long time).

c. Colloq. phr. (orig. *U.S.*) *long time no see*, a joc. imitation of broken English, used as a greeting after prolonged separation.

1900 W. F. DRANNAN *31 Yrs. on Plains* (1901) xxxvii. 515 When we rode up to him [*sc.* an American Indian] he said: 'Good mornin. Long time no see you.' **1939** R. CHANDLER in *Sat. Even. Post* 14 Oct. 72/4 Hi, Tony. Long time no see. **1940** [see *HIYA *int.*]. **1959** D. BEATY *Cone of Silence* viii. 105 'Hello, Clive.' 'Long time no see.' **1959** C. MACINNES *Absolute Beginners* 68 Hail, squire... Long time no see. **1971** D. E. WESTLAKE *I gave at the Office* (1972) 164 'Hello, Arnold,' I said... 'Long time no see.'

8. (Earlier and later examples of *longest day.*)

1774 J. ANDREWS *Let.* 11 Aug. (1866) 340, I shall never get the idea out of my mind the longest day I have to live. **1836** A. H. CLOUGH (*title*) The longest day. A poem written at Rugby School. **1911** H. S. HARRISON *Queed* xxv. 321 You'd be a marked man to the longest day you lived. **1962** *Times* 27 Sept. 16/4 Mr. Darryl Zanuck's three-hour film, *The Longest Day*,..attempts to recapture some of the immensity of the D-Day operations.

9. c. *long on*: possessing a copious quantity of, having plenty of. Cf. *short on*, also *short of* (SHORT *a.* 18 e). orig. *U.S. slang.*

1913 KIPLING *Divers. Creatures* (1917) 286 He was long on Kings. And Continental crises. **1929** W. R. BURNETT *Little Caesar* IV. vi. 147 You're long on regard yourself, ain't you Rico? **1938** S. CHASE *Tyranny of Words* vii. 78 Governor Lehmann, deficient in logic but long on human understanding, commuted the sentence. **1967** 'H. HOWARD' *Routine Investigation* ix. 97 The battered Dodge may not have been long on looks, but it started first time. **1969** *Guardian* 22 Jan. 1/7 The new team is admittedly long on business management and short on statesmanship. **1973** *Good Food Guide* 429 Two inspectors describe it [*sc.* a restaurant] as long on gemütlichkeit and short on good cooking.

15. *long-exposure, -period, -range* (further examples), *-stay*; also **long-day**, (*a*) having a long working-day; (*b*) of plants, needing a long period of light each day before flowering.

1892 Long-day [in Dict.]. **1920** GARNER & ALLARD in *Jrnl. Agric. Res.* XVIII. 559 It will be convenient to use the expressions 'long day' as meaning exposure to light for more than 12 hours and 'short day' as referring to an exposure of 12 hours or less. *Ibid.* 578 Hibiscus is a striking example of a long-day plant. **1947** *Sci. News* IV. 129 By and large, short day plants flower if they receive 8–9 hours of light a day, and long day plants flower if they receive 14–16 hours of light a day. **1966** G. E. EVANS *Pattern under Plough* xiv. 146 Practical observations on a long-day plant, the lettuce. **1972** *Nature* 21 Apr. 407/1 It would be interesting to know whether other long day and short day plants exhibiting a photoperiodic response..behave in the same way as *Sinapis*. **1975** *Listener* 6 Mar. 319/1 The BBC requires Fitters (Shift-working)... The rate of pay is £62.42 p.w. for long-day shift working. **1902** *Chambers's Jrnl.* Nov. 706/2 A long-exposure survey of the whole heavens with one of the most modern photographic telescopes would indicate, I am convinced, no fewer than five hundred million stars. **1903** A. M. CLERKE *Probl. Astrophysics* 348 The typical long-period variable is Mira Ceti. **1923** P. B. BALLARD *New Examiner* 107 Long-period testing. **1968** R. A. LYTTLETON *Mysteries Solar Syst.* iv. 109 The advent of the vast majority of comets, the so-called long-period comets, cannot be predicted. **1854** Long-range [see *ASPHYXIANT *a.* and *sb.*]. **1932** J. BUCHAN *Gap in Curtain* i. 64, I..set myself..to a long-range forecast—what would be likely to happen on June 10th a year ahead. **1958** *New Statesman* 18 Jan. 59/1 Never mind your long-range missiles, Johnson said in effect. **1966** T. PYNCHON *Crying of Lot 49* iii. 67 Incest or no, the marriage must be; it is vital to his long-range political plans. **1966** *Punch* 3 Aug. 186/1 According to the long-range forecast, there's a wettish month ahead. **1971** C. BONINGTON *Annapurna South Face* iii. 33 The Nepalese authorities..did not normally allow expeditions to use long-range radios in Nepal. **1952** C. P. BLACKER *Eugenics* xi. 316 Long- and short-stay residential nurseries. **1970** *Guardian* 9 July 3/2 In France today..two thirds of the beds in mental hospitals are occupied permanently by long-stay patients. **1972** *Ibid.* 16 Feb. 7/3 Allegations of ill-treatment are confined to four of the long-stay wards. **1974** *Advocate-News* (Barbados) 19 Feb. 1/2 Meanwhile, during the year under review, a total of 189,000 'long-stay' visitors came to Barbados.

16. *long-barrelled, -billed* (earlier and later examples), *-descended, -grained* (also *-grain*), *-lashed, -leafed, -leaved* (further examples), *-rooted, -skirted, -sleeved* (later examples), *-spooned, -trousered.*

1902 *Daily Chron.* 20 Mar. 3/1 The rests for the long-barrelled muskets disappeared just at the beginning of the war. **1969** F. WILKINSON *Flintlock Pistols* 26 Pair of long-barrelled 17th century pistols of very fine quality. **1594** BARNFIELD *Affect. Sheph.* II. ix. 13 (Arber), Wilt thou set springes..To catch the long-billd Woodcocke? **1822** J. FOWLER *Jrnl.* (1898) 148 We thear for the first time seen the long Billed Bird;..the bill about one foot in length. **1970** S. TRUEMAN *Intimate Hist. New Brunswick* xi. 144 Some seafowl, like the..long-billed curlew, had become either extremely scarce, or extinct over the years. **1847** EMERSON *Poems* 53 He would come in the very hour.. And tell its long-descended race. **1866** MRS. GASKELL *Wives & Daughters* I. xxiii. 260 Osborne was to do great things..marry a long-descended heiress. **1892** 'MARK TWAIN' *Amer. Claimant* xix. 180 Every man is made up of hereditaries, long descended atoms and particles of his ancestors. **1831** J. M. PECK *Guide for Emigrants* II. 156 The long grained Virginia corn is chiefly produced. **1970** 'D. HALLIDAY' *Dolly & Cookie Bird* iii. 33 You all meet over the trolleys with your long-grain rice sacks at the mainline Cash & Carry. **1974** *Times* 10 Jan. 10/1 With long grain rice, when correctly cooked, the grains remain separate. **1856** J. G. WHITTIER *Panorama* 128 A pleased surprise Looked from her long-lashed hazel eyes. **1913** C. MACKENZIE *Sinister St.* I. II. ii. 167 The long-lashed blue eyes and rose-leaf complexion. **1963** J. FOUNTAIN in B. James *Austral. Short Stories* 277 Her long-lashed eyes modestly lowered. **1819** E. DANA *Geogr. Sk. Western Country* 173 The long leafed pine is a stately tree, from 60 to 80 feet, clear of limbs. **1778** G. WHITE *Let.* 3 July in *Selborne* (1789) II. xli. 235 *Drosera rotundifolia*, round-leaved sundew. [*Drosera*] *longifolia*, long-leaved ditto. **1785** H. MARSHALL *Arbustrum Americanum* 83 Long-leaved Mountain Magnolia or Cucumber Tree. **1832** D. J. BROWNE *Sylva Amer.* 228 This invaluable tree is..called Long-leaved Pine, Yellow Pine, Pitch Pine and Broom Pine. **1942** W. DE LA MARE *Songs of Childhood* 86 The twilight rain shone at its gates, Where long-leaved grass in shadow grew. **1953** E. SITWELL *Gardeners & Astronomers* 3 The long-leaved planets in our garden-shed. **1964** W. L. GOODMAN *Hist. Woodworking Tools* 21 Inside the court there was a long-leaved olive tree. **1579** T. LUPTON *Thousand Notable Things* II. 28 If the disease be so long rooted. **1902** W. JAMES *Varieties Relig. Experience* xi. 264 It costs, then, nothing..to renounce long-rooted privileges and possessions. **1960** *Farmer & Stockbreeder* 26 Jan. Suppl. 4/1 Long-rooted carrots only grow well in deep, sandy soil. **1821** M. EDGEWORTH *Let.* 19 Dec. (1971) 296 Very long skirted coat which he holds up often by tucking one hand under inside the bottom of the waist behind. **1921** D. H. LAWRENCE *Tortoises* 13 A gentleman in a long-skirted coat. **1974** R. HARRIS *Double Snare* xv. 105 Students..accompanied by their sandalled, long-haired, long-skirted birds. **1897** R. M. GILCHRIST *Peakland Faggot* 95 Vignettes akin to those one sees on the porcelain faces of old Derbyshire 'long-sleeved clocks'. **1903** G. F. ABBOTT *Tale Tour Macedonia* 221 A long-sleeved black jacket. **1964** O. COBURN tr. *Braun-Ronsdorf's Wheel of Fashion* 263/1 The basque bodice, high-necked, long-sleeved and ever more tight-fitting. **1876** J. MACGREGOR *Rob Roy on Baltic* 286 A long, narrow, light racing-canoe, with a long-spooned paddle. **1964** *Seventeen* Jan. 46 Something very big in beach fashions—Petti's new long-trousered Surfer! **1967** A. WILSON *No Laughing Matter* III. 362 The long-trousered suit that he had worn this holidays. **1974** I. MURDOCH *Sacred & Profane Love Machine* 104 A thin long-trousered boy.

18. long-acting *a. Pharm.*, having effects that last a long time; **long and short stitch**, in embroidery, a flat stitch used for shading; **long-arm**, (*a*) a long-barrelled gun, as a musket, rifle, etc.; (*b*) a device used as an extension of the arm, e.g. a pole fitted with a hook, shears, etc., for lifting objects to, cutting branches, etc., at a height beyond the ordinary reach of the arm; freq. *attrib.*; **long Bertha** = *Big Bertha* (s.v. *BERTHA²); **long blow** *Austral.* and *N.Z.* [*BLOW *sb.*¹ 1 c], a stroke of the shears in sheep-shearing which cuts away the fleece from rump to neck; **long bond** *Comm.* (see quot. 1948); **long card** *Contract Bridge* (see quots.); **long-case clock** = *grandfather's clock* [GRANDFATHER 5], also

ellipt. *long-case*; **long chain** *Chem.* [*CHAIN *sb.* 5 g], a relatively large number of atoms (usu. of carbon) linked together in a line; freq. *attrib.* (usu. hyphenated); **long chair** = CHAISE-LONGUE; **long chalk** (see CHALK *sb.* 6 b); **long cist** *Archæol.*, a type of megalithic tomb having a long and narrow chamber to which there is direct entry; **long clothes** (earlier and later examples); also *fig.*; **long cross,** (*a*) *Printing* (see quot. 1884); (*b*) *Numism.*, a cross of which the arms extend to the outer circle on a coin; **long deal,** in card-playing (see quot.); **long drawer,** a drawer which extends the full width of a chest, wardrobe, etc.; **long dress,** a floor- or ankle-length dress, usu. worn as evening dress; **long ear,** a translation of the native name for a member of an extinct people which inhabited Easter Island and was distinguished by artificially lengthened ears; **long fallow** (see quots.); **long-fed** *a.* (see quot. 1969); **long Forties** *Naut.* (cf. FORTY *sb.* 4); **long glass,** (*a*) a full-length looking-glass; (*b*) a drinking-glass approximately three feet long for holding a yard of ale (cf. YARD *sb.*[2] 9 c); **long grass,** used *gen.* of grass or grass-like growth, typical of certain areas in Africa, tall enough, for example, to conceal animals; **long green** *U.S. slang*, dollar-notes, money (cf. *GREEN *sb.* 7 d); **long-haul** *attrib.* (see *HAUL *sb.* 1 c); **long-house,** (*b*) (earlier examples); also, a long dwelling-house in other areas, esp. a large communal village house in certain parts of Malaysia and Indonesia; **long ink** *Printing* (see quots.); **long john,** usu. in *pl.*, (*a*) a type of long, warm underwear; (*b*) a children's game; (*c*) (in *sing.*) a long coffee table; also *long John table*; (see also sense *18 c); **long jump,** also (with hyphen) as *vb.*; **long-keeping** *a.*, able to be kept for a long time; **long lady** = *farthing-candle* (FARTHING *sb.* 5); **long legs** *W. Afr. colloq.* (see quot. 1971); **long-life** *a.*, remaining serviceable (quot. 1946 = remaining radioactive) for an unusually long time; **Long March,** *spec.* the year-long retreat of the Chinese Communists across south-western China during the period of Nationalist government; also (not always with capital initials) in other contexts; **long mirror** = **long glass* (*a*); **long paddock** *Austral.* and *N.Z. slang* (see quot.); **long-persistence** *a.*, applied to a screen of a cathode-ray tube on which a spot remains luminous for a relatively long period after the electron beam has moved elsewhere; **long pull,** (*a*) *Printing*, in the operation of the hand-press, a pull on the bar almost to its fullest extent; (*b*) the practice in public houses of giving over-measure to attract custom; **long rains** [cf. RAIN *sb.*[1] 2 b], in tropical countries, the rainy season; **long-room** (later examples); **long s,** a lower-case form of the letter s, printed ſ, no longer in general use; **long sauce** (see SAUCE *sb.* 4 a); **long service,** (*b*) also used to denote a less specific period of service; **long ship,** (*b*) *Naval slang* (see quots.); **long-short,** (*a*) (earlier example); **long short story,** a short story (see *SHORT *a.* 26) of more than average length, a novella; also **long-short** *ellipt.*; **long sight** (see also *SIGHT *sb.*[1]); **long silk** *attrib.* of cotton, long-stapled; **long sleeve,** a sleeve which extends to the wrist; also (with hyphen) *attrib.*; **long slide** *Curling* (see quots.); **long-small,** a length of rod used in basket-making; **long song** (see quot.); **long-splice** *Naut.* (see quot. 1968); also as *vb.*; **long-staple** *a.* (earlier examples); also *ellipt.*; **long-stop** (see sense *18 d); **long-straw** *Thatching* (see quot. 1968); **long-straws,** the drawing of straws as a game; **long-sweetening,** (*a*) (earlier and later examples); **long-termer,** a person who is serving a long prison-sentence; **long-time** *a.*, also, extending for a long time into the future; requiring a long time; **long-timer** = **long-termer*; **long twelves** *Printing*, a duodecimo (12mo) imposition scheme with the forme arranged in two rows of six long narrow type pages as opposed to three rows of four shorter and broader pages in standard 12mo schemes; **long verse** = *LONG-LINE 3; **long wave,** a wave of relatively long wavelength; *spec.* in *Broadcasting*, a radio wave with a wavelength longer than about one kilometre (but less than ten kilometres, in mod. use); freq. *attrib.* (usu. hyphenated); **long week-end,** a week-end holiday of more than the usual length; *fig.* the period between the wars of 1914–18 and 1939–45; **long-wool** (earlier examples of sense *b*).

1951 A. GROLLMAN *Pharmacol. & Therapeutics* vi. 143 For prolonged mild sedation..small doses of a long-acting barbiturate are useful. **1971** D. CLARK *Sick to Death* ii. 35 Sally was on long-acting insulin. That means she only had to inject twice a day. **1848** E. C. P. in C. H. Hartshorne *Eng. Medieval Embroidery* 121 'Long and short' stitch is employed for shading. **1960** [see *brick-stitch* (*BRICK *sb.*[1] 10)]. **1967** E. SHORT *Embroidery & Fabric Collage* iv. 91 The ones in existence depict the Buddha life size, the large areas of colour being filled in solidly in chain, satin, and long-and-short stitch. **1675** in *Public Rec. Colony of Connecticut* (1852) II. 270 Such Troopers as shall neglect to prouide themselues with long armes, viz. a carbin or muskett..shall be disbanded. **1952** GRANVILLE *Dict. Theatr. Terms* 113 *Long-arm*, a long wooden pole used for clearing borders and ceilings, that foul the lines in the flies. **1969** E. H. PINTO *Treen* 406 *Long-arms*, the trigger action, long-arm hook,..for removing objects from crowded windows, was a useful and necessary device in Victorian times... It is still made in modified form, to assist invalids in picking up objects which are otherwise out of reach. **1972** D. W. BAILEY *Brit. Mil. Longarms 1815–65* 9 The barrels of military longarms were officially 'browned' from 1815. **1973** *Times* 14 July 12/1 Gang mowers and long-arm rotary cutters for roadside banks and verges. **1919** G. B. SHAW *Peace Conf. Hints* vi. 75 Within range of Long Bertha. **1929** H. B. SMITH *Sheep & Wool Industry Austral. & N.Z.* (ed. 3) x. 77 The shearer now gets in a long blow with the machine, running from the britch end to the top of the neck. **1949** P. NEWTON *High Country Days* v. 49 Laying his sheep full length he swung into the 'long blow'—from rump to neck. **1952** J. CLEARY *Sundowners* iii. 138 Paddy was beginning the longest cut, the 'long blow', from the flank to the top of the head. **1956** G. BOWEN *Wool Away!* (ed. 2) iii. 36 If you see a shearer with a good long blow he is usually a good shearer. **1948** G. CROWTHER *Outl. Money* (ed. 2) ii. 73 Those that mature within five years are known as Short Bonds. Medium Bonds run from five to about twenty years, and all above that are Long Bonds. **1936** E. CULBERTSON *Contract Bridge Complete* i. 39 Low cards established from four-card or longer suits. They are called *long* cards. **1959** C. H. GOREN *New Contract Bridge in Nutshell* (1960) 13 What is a long card? In the trump suit, long cards start at the fifth card. In a side suit, the fourth card is considered a long card. **1892** Long-case clock [see *GRANDFATHER 5]. **1899** F. J. BRITTEN *Old Clocks & Watches* 320 Some of the earliest long-case clocks were liberally embellished with marqueterie. **1972** *Country Life* 9 Mar. 546/3 Strictly speaking, all clocks of this type should be called longcases, although since Victorian times they have been known to the general public as 'grandfathers'. **1972** B. LOOMES *Yorks. Clockmakers* 10 Very few longcase clocks were made after 1860. **1930** *Biochem. Jrnl.* XXIV. 113 A peculiar long-chain fatty acid. *Ibid.* 114 The two long chains are connected to polar groups. **1951** *Sci. News* XXII. 98 The configuration in space of the long chains, formed by the linking together of successive amino-acids, which seem to be a common feature of all proteins. **1964** G. H. HAGGIS et al. *Introd. Molecular Biol.* ix. 216 Nucleic acids are long-chain molecules, and the individual units linked together to form these chains are called nucleotides. **1974** *Sci. Amer.* Mar. 72/3 The useful properties of a polymer depend almost entirely on the presence of long chains. **1891** KIPLING & BALESTIER *Naulahka* (1892) vi. 54 It was full of white men..lying in the verandah in long chairs. **1929** E. BOWEN *Last September* iv. 41 Help Uncle Richard in with the long chair. **1956** E. AMBLER *Night-Comers* viii. 195 One of the long chairs was lying across the balustrade. **1925** V. G. CHILDE *Dawn European Civilization* xiii. 213 The long cists in North France, Belgium, Hessen, and Sweden have a holed-stone for the doorway **1963** *Field Archaeol.* (Ordnance Survey) (ed. 4) 113 In Scotland, Wales, the Isle of Man, and the South-west of England burials in long cists which are coffin-like arrangements of stone slabs are frequently met with. **1819** KEATS *Let.* 24 Sept. (1958) II. 215 A child in a[r]ms was passing by his chair..in the nurses a[r]ms—Lamb took hold of the long clothes saying 'Where, god bless me, Where does it leave off?' **1861** DICKENS *Gt. Expect.* II. xvi. 254 He had just finished putting somebody's hat into black long-clothes, like an African baby. **1932** *Times Lit. Suppl.* 29 Sept. 676/3 Fibonacci, the first Christian writer to give a systematic exposition of the Hindu numerals, without which analysis might still have been in its long-clothes. **1683–4** J. MOXON *Mech. Exerc. Printing* (1962) 267 Then he [*sc.* the Press-man] Folds a sheet of the Paper he is to Work long-ways, and broad-ways, and lays the long Crease of it upon the middle of the Long-Cross. **1755** J. SMITH *Printer's Gram.* 261 They [*sc.* compositors] lessen the Furniture on both sides the Long Cross, to enlarge the Bottom Margin. **1884** J. GOULD *Letter-Press Printer* (ed. 3) 166/1 *Longcross*, the bar that divides a chase the longest way. **1924** *Southward's Mod. Printing* (ed. 5) I. xl. 246 (*caption*) Long cross. **1904** C. L. STAINER *Oxf. Silver Pennies* 50 Long cross voided, each limb terminating in crescent. **1972** *Oxf. Univ. Gaz.* CII. Suppl. No. 3. 50 A selection of 23 silver 'long-cross' pennies (1247–78) from a hoard found at Colchester. **1898** H. S. CANFIELD *Maid of Frontier* 86 It was what is termed a 'long deal', that is, no winning or losing card had slipped from the dealer's carelessly careful hands. **1810** E. WEETON *Let.* 11 May (1969) I. 261 You will find the necessary keys for the three long drawers. **1928** A. M. M. DOUTON *Bk. with Seven Seals* 19 They are in the top long drawer. **1975** *Country Life* 20 Feb. 426/2 The chest..has one long drawer..and below that are two deeper drawers. **1949** N. MARSH *Swing, Brother, Swing* iii. 40 She climbed into a long dress, six years old. **1954** J. MASTERS *Bhowani Junction* xxxii. 275 There's a dance to-night... Please come. Long dress. **1973** H. MCCLOY *Change of Heart* ix. 102 Long dress? Surely not in these days for a family dinner at home? **1891** W. J. THOMSON in *Rep. U.S. Nat. Museum (1889)* 529 This unsatisfactory state of affairs was brought to an end..by a desperate battle, in which the 'long ears' had planned the utter annihilation of their enemies. **1919** K. ROUTLEDGE *Mystery of Easter Island* xviii. 282 The Long Ears suddenly appear on the island at a much later time. **1958** T. HEYERDAHL *Aku-Aku* xi. 353 The mayor..and his ancestors who had made the great statues on Easter Island called themselves long-ears. Is it not strange that they should bother to lengthen their ears so that they hung down to their shoulders? **1960** G. E. EVANS *Horse in Furrow* x. 131 A bastard summer-land is so called to distinguish [it] from a true summer-land or long fallow. **1971** *World Archaeol.* III. 135 They [*sc.* the Tifalmin] practise long-fallow cultivation, clearing a patch of forest and abandoning it after two or three years, probably for fifteen years or more. **1909** *Daily Chron.* 12 Oct. 4/4 Long-fed beef, as fed by English farmers, cost 21s. 3d. **1969** NEUMANN & SNAPP *Beef Cattle* (ed. 6) xi. 303 If cattle are fed finishing rations for 8 to 10 months, they are spoken of as 'long-fed' cattle. **1776** T. PENNANT *Tour in Scotl. & Voy. Hebrides 1772* II. 145 Quantities of white-fish..might be taken on the great sand banks off this coast. The long Fortys extend parallel to it. **1928** C. F. S. GAMBLE *Story N. Sea Air Station* xii. 183 The Grand Fleet was ordered to rendezvous in the 'Long Forties'; the Battle Cruiser Fleet to join farther south. **1843** C. RIDLEY *Let.* Nov. in *Cecilia* (1958) xii. 141 Little Matt..always gives himself a kiss in the long glass. **1883** J. BRINSLEY-RICHARDS *Seven Yrs. at Eton* xxix. 322 There was a way of holding the long glass at a certain angle by which catastrophes were avoided. **1942** G. MITCHELL *Laurels are Poison* xvii. 186 Have a look at yourself in the long glass. **1953** *Word for Word: Encycl. Beer* (Whitbread & Co.) 37/1 *Yard of ale*, known also as a long glass..held between 2$\frac{3}{4}$ and 3$\frac{1}{2}$ pints. **1858** E. H. D. DOMENECH *Missionary Adventures Texas & Mexico* iv. 276 The way of the long grass is not easy. **1863** *Macm. Mag.* Nov. 27/2 The long grass swarmed with hog-deer. **1912** D. CRAWFORD (*title*) Thinking Black: 22 years without a break in the long grass of Central Africa. **1961** *Listener* 7 Sept. 346/1 This is the Africa of the 'long grass' such as *Hyparrhenia* and *Echinochloa* into which, half a century ago, one would have romantically disappeared. The areas of long-grass plains in the Sudan have to be experienced to be believed. **1964** C. WILLOCK *Enormous Zoo* i. 14 Much of it is long-grass country. **1896** ADE *Artie* ix. 79, I never see him do a stroke of work, but he can always make a flash o' the long green. **1903** A. H. LEWIS *Boss* xiv. 174 I'd naturally s'ppose that when you went ehy on th' long green, you'd touch th' old gentleman. **1946** S. NEWTON *Paul Bunyan* x. 63 We'll be there tomorrow afternoon with Napoleon and the long green. **1928** *Electrical Communication* VII. 1. 62 Long Haul Single Channel Carrier Telephone Systems Connect Melbourne with..Victoria and South Australia. **1957** [see *HAUL *sb.* 1 c]. **1961** *Economist* 11 Nov. 575/2 The [airport] buildings themselves are expected to be adequate to meet all long-haul traffic until 1970. **1974** *Times* 5 Jan. 9/2 Other long-haul operators to be recommended..*Kenton Travel International*..offer a round-the-world trip starting at £795. **1975** *Islander* (Victoria, B.C.) 17 Aug. 3/3 Expenses of the long-haul teamsters who rested and stabled their horses there. **1751** C. GIST *Jrnls.* (1893) 51 They marched in under French Colours and were conducted into the Long House. **1753** G. WASHINGTON *Diaries* (1925) I. 50 We met in Council at the *Long House*. **1894** *Sarawak Gaz.* 1 May 67/1 The practice of herding together in 'long houses' prevents mental and moral improvement and hinders advance in gardening and planting and agricultural developement generally. **1905** *Chambers's Jrnl.* Oct. 714/1 The grim line of trophies hanging in the village long-house. **1912** HOSE & MCDOUGALL *Pagan Tribes Borneo* I. iv, The Kenyah village frequently consists of a single long house. **1937** *Discovery* Sept. 257/1 Anga, our guide, who was head of the community on the opposite hill, invited us to visit his Longhouse... This dwelling place was cleverly constructed of bamboo and palm leaves (*atap*). **1949** B. A. ST. J. HEPBURN *Handbk. Sarawak* xix. 180 The 'long-house' system ensures that the individual incapacitated by illness or accident cannot be ignored or abandoned. **1961** *Listener* 9 Nov. 757/1, I came to my first long house after a journey of hours down the famous Rejan River, in the British territory of Sarawak in Borneo. **1965** C. SHUTTLEWORTH *Malayan Safari* ii. 32 The walls and roofs of the long-houses were built of palm leaves. **1966** G. E. EVANS *Pattern under Plough* v. 72 The Welsh long-houses..with long sides and opposite doors providing a passage from side to side, and dividing the building roughly in two. **1971** *Lady* 15 July 88/3 The longhouse is an object lesson in community living. **1967** KARCH & BUBER *Offset Processes* 545 *Long ink*, ink that can be drawn out into a long thin string—such ink has considerable tack which will pull a plate clean and sharp. **1970** E. A. D. HUTCHINGS *Survey of Printing Processes* 200 *Long ink*, an ink which will flow freely from a knife... Such an ink will, when dabbed on a finger and thumb, stretch out without breaking as these digits are drawn apart. **1943** T. R. ST. GEORGE *C/o Postmaster* 12 Some odd garments affectionately known as 'longjohns'. **1961** A. SMITH *East-Enders* ix. 156 In the living room there would be..a long John table, a small cocktail bar. **1961** *Sunday Express* 24 Sept. 20 'Longjohn' coffee table. **1962** W. SCHIRRA in *Into Orbit* 47 We..stripped down to our long johns so that the technicians could plaster us all over with strips of wet paper. *Ibid.* 49 A series of waffle-weave patches on our long john underwear helps to keep the oxygen moving. **1964** *Spectator* 14 Feb. 217 The long john is a homely woollen undergarment of rustic provenience. **1969** J. GARDNER *Founder Member* vii. 115 Boysie picked up the clothes... A suit of woollen long johns, a pair of heavy calf-length stockings. **1970** G. E. EVANS *Where Beards wag All* xix. 219 The boys played *Long Johns* which they did as they walked along the road throwing the marbles ahead of them. **1971** *New Yorker* 4 Dec. 102/1 (Advt.), One-piece waist-to-toe Lightweight Long Johns with ribbed dress socks. **1972** *Guardian* 30 Nov. 15/6 (Advt.), Big Long John in opulent teak finish... This elegantly styled occasional table..47″ × 17″ overall width by $14\frac{3}{4}''$ high. **1934** R. CAMPBELL *Broken Record* v.

116 An Impala..can long-jump thirty-seven feet without a run. **1963** *Times* 4 Feb. 3/4 He long jumped 26 ft. 10 in. for a world's best indoor performance. **1860** *Trans. Mich. Agric. Soc.* X. 229 That it is impossible to raise winter apples in the South, and that it is necessary to look to the North for a supply of long-keeping varieties. **1861** Mrs. Beeton *Bk. Househ. Managem.* 589 As late or long-keeping potatoes, the Tartan or Red-apple stands very high in favour. **1970** *Guardian* 6 June 12/4 Long-keeping cream..keeps longer than fresh cream but a shorter time than sterilised cream. **1896** Farmer & Henley *Slang* IV. 228/2 *Long-lady*, a farthing candle. **1953** A. Jobson *Househ. & Country Crafts* vii. 81 A farthing candle was known as a Long Lady. **1971** A. Kirk-Greene in J. Spencer *Eng. Lang. W. Afr.* 144 'Long legs' is a commonplace [in West Africa] for using influence in high places to secure a service. **1973** *Listener* 14 June 782/3 'Long leg' is a Nigerian colloquialism denoting corruption. **1928–9** *T. Eaton & Co. Catal.* Fall & Winter 245/2 The famous long-life Minerva Batteries. **1946** *Physical Rev.* LXX. 987/1 (*heading*) Long-life radio-iodine. **1966** *Daily Tel.* 7 Nov. 17/1 The association has already announced plans to buy a half-share in a Liverpool creamery and manufacture 'long life' milk for export to the Middle East and other tropical areas. **1969** *Guardian* 1 Aug. 7/6 Some bread is certainly tasteless but it's the prepacked sliced long-life cotton wool wadding that most people prefer. **1971** *Ibid.* 9 Aug. 7/5 Children may increasingly find themselves drinking longlife or dried milk next term. **1906** Kipling *Puck of Pook's Hill* 168 'Few people nowadays walk from end to end of this country.'.. 'The greater their loss. I know nothing better than the Long March when your feet have hardened.' **1937** E. Snow *Red Star over China* I. i. 19 The historic Long March of 6,000 miles, in which they crossed twelve provinces of China..and triumphantly emerged at last into a powerful new base in the North-west. *Ibid.* IV. vi. 180 The Long March..was begun in October 1934..the Red Army at last reached northern Shensi in October 1935. **1967** L. Deighton *Expensive Place* xxxvi. 217 The Long March meant the Nationalists killed two and a half million. **1970** *Guardian* 14 May 9/3 [Regis] Debray..overestimates the capacity of Latin Americans to envisage a 'long march'. Most Latin American revolutionaries..think mostly about the short, sharp blow that will lead to quick success. **1972** *Times* 23 Oct. 12/1 Mr Chou held a number of important posts and travelled widely before the Long March. *Ibid.* 27 Dec. 6/3 The MPLA had originally been based on the Congo (Zaire) but, after differences, had carried out the traditional 'Long March' (so beloved by revolutionaries when attempting to found a new state) to new bases in Zambia. **1973** *Times* 1 Oct. 6/5 The 'long march' on Besançon yesterday, organized by the leading French trade union organizations, proved a striking demonstration of the impact the six-month-old struggle of the Lip watch plant workers has had throughout France. **1869** L. M. Alcott *Little Women* (1871) II. i. 6 There were no..long mirrors, or lace curtains in the little parlour. **1960** D. Lessing *In Pursuit of English* iv. 138 All her games were centred around the long mirror. **1933** L. G. D. Acland in *Press* (Christchurch, N.Z.) 4 Nov. 15/7 *Long paddock, the.* Slang for the road. People turn stock out on it, or travel them on it, to get cheap grazing. **1960** *Jrnl. Acoustical Soc. Amer.* XXXII. 1065 An instrument is described which extracts from the complex speech wave..information related to the subjective pitch of a sound. It then displays this information on the long-persistence screen of a revolving cathode-ray tube in such a manner that a continuous graph of pitch vs. time is obtained. **1966** D. G. Brandon *Mod. Techniques Metallogr.* v. 236 Visual observation of the image, even on a long-persistence screen, is very difficult at small probe diameters. **1683–4** J. Moxon *Mech. Exerc. Printing* (1962) 261 A long or a Soaking or Easie Pull, is when the Form feels the force of the Spindle by degrees, till the Bar comes almost to the hither Cheek of the Press, and this is also call'd a Soft Pull. **1770** P. Luckombe *Conc. Hist. Printing* 500 *Long pull* is when the bar of the Press requires to be brought close to the cheek to make a good impression. **1888** C. T. Jacobi *Printers' Vocab.* 77 *Long pull*, when the bar-handle of a press is pulled right over. **1901** *Contemp. Rev.* Mar. 355 The unlettered barmaid..tiring of handling the taps and the long-pull. **1909** *Daily Chron.* 30 Aug. 5/3 As the law stands magistrates have no power to stop the 'long pull'. **1964** *New Statesman* 21 Feb. 283/3 In 1921 a Licensing Act made this permanent—under the homely caption 'Long Pull Prohibited'. **1963** A. Smith *Throw out Two Hands* vi. 70 The plan was to take off from Zanzibar on January 1st... There was so much to be done before the long rains began. **1970** *Kenya Farmer* Feb. 3/2 If the long rains fail altogether—a most unlikely event—then a shortage would follow at the end of this year. **1841** *Knickerbocker* XVII. 458 In the long room of the Village Inn. **1870** J. K. Medbery *Men & Mysteries Wall St.* 22 A chamber is provided at the Exchange, where members may bargain with members at any hour throughout the day. This is known as the Long Room. **1962** S. Potter in L. Frewin *Boundary Bk.* 21 It is not the slightest use simply making vague references to the Long Room. **1808** C. Stower *Printer's Gram.* vi. 143 Since the very general introduction of round, in the room of long s's, many [type] cases have been made upon a plan different from the original ones. **1894** [see Serif]. **1914** A. E. Housman *Let.* 8 Mar. (1971) 410 His date..cannot be much earlier than 1800, as he seems not to use the long *s* except when *t* follows. **1960** G. A. Glaister *Gloss. Bk.* 241/1 It was not until John Bell's edition of Shakespeare in 1775 that the long s was generally discarded. **1830** William IV in W. A. Steward *War Medals* (1915) 348 Discharged soldiers receiving a gratuity for meritorious conduct shall be entitled to wear a medal having on one side the words For Long Service and Good Conduct, and on the other in relief the King's Arms. **1925** A. J. Toynbee *Survey Internat. Affairs 1920–23* II. 109 Immediate legislation for the abolition of conscription and for setting up a long service army as provided in the Treaty. **1937** B. H. L. Hart *Europe in Arms* xii. 158 From that time onward the army became professional and long-service. **1916** M. T. Hainsselin *In Northern Mists* xvi. 63, I say, Padre, this is a pretty long ship, isn't it?.. Don't you know that 'a long ship' means one where it is a long time between drinks? **1946** J. Irving *Royal Navalese* 110 *Long ship*, a ship, or party, in which there is a long interval between..drinks. **1840** *Knickerbocker* XVI. 22 A buxom, rosy-cheeked girl, with a blue-striped long-short..was busied around the fire-place. **1906** J. London *Let.* 15 Dec. (1966) 235 *The Times Magazine*..bought..one of my best long-short-stories. **1924** F. M. Ford *Let.* 18 Sept. (1965) 162 As for the novel: Hemingway..gave me the impression that it was a long-short story. **1942** 'G. Orwell' in *Partisan Rev.* IX. 159 The paper shortage..may possibly bring back the 'long-short story', a form which has never had a fair deal in England. **1959** *News Chron.* 7 Oct. 8/5 Long shorts by Arthur Miller and Saul Bellow. **1870** J. Yeats *Nat. Hist. Commerce* II. ii. 200 The long silk cotton of Algeria partakes at the same time of the character of the long silk staple of Georgia. **1814** Jane Austen *Let.* 9 Mar. (1932) II. 93 Mrs. Tilson had long sleeves too, & she assured me that they are worn in the evening by many. **1897** *Sears, Roebuck Catal.* 241/2 Ladies' Long Sleeve Vests...high neck and long sleeves with elastic ribbed cuffs. **1957** M. B. Picken *Fashion Dict.* 215/2 *Long sleeve*, sleeve which ends ½ inch below wrist joint. **1962** *Canada Month* Apr. 26/3 The west..introduced the long slide now about twice the distance the old-style curler slides before launching his stone. **1969** R. Welsh *Beginner's Guide Curling* xii. 85 The delivery called the 'Slide' or the 'Long Slide' was introduced by Canadian curlers. **1912** T. Okey *Introd. Basket-Making* vii. 76 Some Luke, Long Small and Threepenny will be needed, and a few small two yearling sticks. **1953** A. G. Knock *Willow Basket-Work* (ed. 5) 9 The old trade names ..three feet, Tacks; four feet, Short-Small; five feet, Long-Small. **1856** *Chambers's Jrnl.* 28 June 402/1 An item in those streaming fathoms of verse technically known as 'long songs', in which as many as a hundred favourite ditties are sold for a penny. **1883** *Man. Seamanship for Boys' Training Ships R. Navy* (1886) 106 To form a long-splice with a piece of three and four-strand rope... Unlay the ends of the two ropes to the required distance [etc.]. *Ibid.* (*heading*) How do you long-splice a three or four-strand rope together? **1968** E. Franklin *Dict. Knots* 19 *Long splice*, a splice which has no apparent thickening of the rope at the points of joining. **1802** J. Simons *Let.* 15 Dec. in J. Steele *Papers* (1924) I. 341 Long Staple Cotton is in demand. **1843** *Knickerbocker* XXI. 39 It is here that the most valuable product of our country, the long staple cotton, is raised. **1867** *Harper's Mag.* Aug. 349/1 A bale of uplands cotton..demanding to be bought at the price of long-staple. **1947** *Agriculture* LIII. 448 (*heading*) Estimate no. 1. Long straw method (unclipped surface). **1963** *Times* 22 Apr. 9/2 For the customer it means a neater job and a roof that will last anything from 35 to 60 years instead of the 10 to 20 years of the traditional long-straw thatch. **1968** J. Arnold *Shell Bk. Country Crafts* xiii. 185 One notices that long-straw has a looser, more plastic appearance, compared with the stiff, 'close cropped', brush-like texture of reed. **1835** R. M. Bird *Hawks of Hawk-Hollow* I. ii. 33 Shall we sit down here, and play long-straws for sweethearts? **1714** in *N. Carolina Colonial Rec.* (1886) II. 132 Let who will go unpaid, Rum, long Sweet'n alias Molasses..must be had. **1936** M. Mitchell *Gone with Wind* xxi. 352 The sorghum used for 'long sweetening' did little to improve the taste. **1956** B. Holiday *Lady sings Blues* (1973) xviii. 142 Quite a few girls, especially long-termers in the joint, were lovers. **1970** Long-termer [see *Fantasy *v.* 1 a]. **1927** Carr-Saunders & Jones *Survey Social Struct. Eng. & Wales* xx. 228 This is no indictment of the usefulness of long-time forecasts, because it is in any case impracticable to plan so far ahead. **1944** C. Sandburg in B. A. Botkin *Treas. Amer. Folklore* p. vi, A longtime book is this. One reading won't do for it. **1971** B. Malamud *Tenants* 13 Long voyage in a small room. There's a long-time book to finish. **1907** J. London *Road* (1914) v. 139, I know that the long-timers got more substantial grub, because there was a whole row of them on the ground floor in our hall. **1952** 'J. Henry' *Who lie in Gaol* viii. 133 The long-timers are allowed to plant a few things in a plot there if they want to. **1770** P. Luckombe *Conc. Hist. Printing* 414 (*caption*) A sheet of long twelves. **1888** C. T. Jacobi *Printers' Vocab.* 77 *Long twelves*, a plan of imposition whereby the pages are laid down in two long rows of six pages. **1972** P. Gaskell *New Introd. Bibliogr.* 81 Long twelves (long 12°), when the sheet is folded once across the shorter side and five times across the longer, again making twelve leaves, twenty-four pages. **1871** H. Sweet in W. C. Hazlitt *Warton's Hist. Eng. Poetry* II. 3 Each long verse has four accented syllables. **1889** C. W. Kent *Elene* 8 The so-called 'long-verse' consists of two hemistichs. **1839** *Trans. Cambr. Philos. Soc.* VII. 95 Any particle *P* revolves continually in a circular orbit... The radius of this circle, and consequently the agitation of the fluid particles, decreases very rapidly as the depth *c* increases, and much more rapidly for short than long waves, agreeably to observation. **1895** H. Lamb *Hydrodynamics* viii. 276 Waves whose slope is gradual and whose length λ is large compared with the depth *h* of the fluid, are called 'long waves'. **1909** E. B. Titchener *Text-bk. Psychol.* I. 60 Let us take..a chart or projection of the solar spectrum, and let us work right through it, from the left or long-wave to the right or short-wave end. **1928** D. Brunt *Meteorol.* v. 38 The term 'low temperature radiation' [is frequently used] to denote the long-wave radiation of bodies at relatively low temperature. **1928** *Chambers's Jrnl.* Jan. 79/1 Many foreign long-wave stations have also been clearly heard with this set. **1963** *Meteorol. Gloss.* (Meteorol. Office) (ed. 4) 155 *Long wave*, in synoptic meteorology, a smooth, wave-shaped contour pattern on an isobaric chart with a wavelength of the order of 2000 km. .. Some four or five such waves..typically extend across a hemispherical chart. **1974** *Encycl. Brit. Macropædia* III. 311/1 [Broadcasting.] Long waves range from 30 to 300 kilohertz; medium waves from 300 kilohertz to three megahertz; and short waves from three to 30 megahertz. **1927** M. Kennedy (*title*) A long week-end. **1933** H. G. Wells *Shape of Things to Come* III. § 8. 317 The old British institution of the *long week-end* flourishes. **1940** Graves & Hodge (*title*) The long week-end: a social history of Great Britain 1918–1939. **1944** Blunden *Cricket Country* xiv. 149 The name, 'The Long Week-End', has been devised to characterise the period between the two great wars. **1968** 'E. Peters' *Grass Widow's Tale* ii. 24, I'm heading north..for a long week-end. **1859** *Trans. Illinois Agric. Soc.* III. 458 The Longwools attain to greater size and shear a larger fleece. **1877** J. Darby in J. Coleman *Sheep & Pigs Gt. Brit.* II. v. 50 The best flocks of Devon Longwools are..derived solely from Leicester and Bampton—a most valuable cross in every respect... During the past fifteen years these sheep have been designated 'Devon Longwools'.

b. longspur, read: a bunting of the genus *Calcarius*, esp. *C. lapponicus*, the Lapland bunting; (later examples).

1917 T. G. Pearson *Birds Amer.* III. 22 Shore Larks that feed up and down the wintry seashore of New England and the middle states have also many Longspurs among them. **1953** D. A. Bannerman *Birds Brit. Is.* I. 314 While *Calcarius lapponicus* is the sole Palæarctic representative of the genus, the Nearctic fauna includes two other 'Longspurs'—as they are called in America. **1973** R. D. Symons *Where Wagon Led* I. iv. 45 The sun hit the top of the gray-green sage and the longspurs fluttered overhead.

c. longjohn, a tropical South American tree, *Triplaris surinamensis*, of the family Polygonaceæ; **long-leaf pine** *U.S.*, *Pinus palustris* (also *long-leafed*, *-leaved pine*: see sense *16); **long-pod** (later example).

1910 *Chambers's Jrnl.* Feb. 88/2 Impenetrable jungle, consisting mostly of chinchilla or sand box-trees, with now and then a sand-cocoa or a longjohn. **1969** S. M. Sadeek *Windswept & Other Stories* 30 We will build a nice house..with bamboo and longjohn. *a* **1816** B. Hawkins *Sk. Creek Country* (1848) 60 [On] the uplands to the south are the long-leaf pine. **1901** [see *laurel oak* (*Laurel *sb.*[1] 6)]. **1904** T. E. Watson *Bethany* I. i. 8 Ours was just a plain house..of timbers torn from the heart of the long-leaf Georgia pine. **1969** T. H. Everett *Living Trees of World* 50/2 The longleaf pine, an open-headed kind that reaches 120 feet in height and has a natural range from Virginia to Florida and Mississippi is the most important timber tree of the south-eastern United States. **1972** *Country Life* 13 Jan. 104/4 A dependable way to ensure early pickings of broad beans..is to sow the seeds now..for which purpose I prefer longpod varieties.

d. long field (earlier example); also **long-fielder**, **-fieldsman**; **long-hop** (also in *Fives*), a ball which a player has ample time to hit after it bounces; **long-stop** (earlier example); also *fig.* a last resort, e.g. in an emergency; also (in literal sense) **long-stopper**; *long-stopping* vbl. sb. (earlier example).

1816 W Lambert *Cricketer's Guide* (ed. 6) iii. 44 *Long field off side* this man should stand on the off side, between the middle wicket man and bowler at a considerable distance in the Field, so as to cover them. **1897** K. S. Ranjitsinhji *Jubilee Bk. Cricket* ii. 55 Nearly all good long-fielders take the ball, in catching, with their hands close to their bodies about chest-high. **1920** P. F. Warner *Cricket Reminisc.* xiv. 91 Never had he been a long-fielder. **1790** *Reading Mercury* 8 Mar. 3/3 He was the swiftest bowler and best long fieldsman at that time in the kingdom. **1900** A. E. T. Watson *Young Sportsman* 237 s.v. *Fives*, C..must above all avoid so returning it [*sc.* the ball] that it comes into the middle of the outer court as a long-hop. **1767** R. Cotton *Cricket Song* ix, in F. S. Ashley-Cooper *Hambledon Cricket Chron.* (1924) 184, I had almost forgot—they deserve a large bumper—Little George, the long Stop, and Tom Sueter, the Stumper. **1957** *Listener* 5 Sept. 349/1 Like all sorts of longstop laws we keep on the statute-book, but hardly ever use. **1962** *Punch* 11 Apr. 558/1 The National Assistance Board..is the long-stop of the Welfare State. **1973** *Times* 9 Nov. 1/5 The two uninvolved unions may..provide a long-stop cover. **1891** W. G. Grace *Cricket* x. 258 The most expert long-stoppers at the time when long-stop was even of more importance than the wicket-keeper. **1832** P. Egan *Bk. Sports* 348/2 Dick's shin-breakers stop'd them short In 'midst of their long-stopping!

B. 4. b. In the Morse code, a dash (opp. 'short'); a long buzz, etc., sounded as a signal.

1875 W. Thomson *Pop. Lect. & Addresses* (1891) III. 128 [It] renders quick and sure Morse signalling by longs and shorts impracticable. **1902** Kipling *Traffics & Discov.* (1904) 192 In longs and shorts, as laid down by..Mr. Morse. **1916** [see *Buzz *v.*[1] 9]. **1926** R. W. Hutchinson *First Course Wireless* 112 The key in the primary circuit enables the train of sparks to be continued for a long or a short period of time, thus producing the 'longs' and 'shorts', *i.e.* the 'dashes' and 'dots' of the Morse Code. **1943** F. J. Salfeld in *Penguin New Writing* XVII. 41 The alarm sounded: a series of urgent longs on the buzzer. **1948** 'J. Tey' *Franchise Affair* x. 112 Do you know morse?.. I shall hoot the initials of your beautiful name on the horn... Two longs and three shorts. **1973** J. Drummond *Bang! Bang! You're Dead!* xxxviii. 134 A buzzer sounded..two longs, two shorts, another long.

7. (Earlier and later examples.)

1848 J. H. Newman *Loss & Gain* I. x. 71 'Reding ought to live here all through the Long,' said Tenby: 'does any one live through the Vacation, sir, in Oxford?' **1852** C. A. Bristed *Five Yrs. in Eng. Univ.* (ed. 2) 37 For a month or six weeks in the 'Long' they rambled off to see the sights of Paris. **1857** Mrs. Gaskell *Let.* 7 Dec. (1966) 490 Arthur Stanley..has just been spending the 'Long' at Moscow. **1861** D. G. Rossetti *Let.* June (1965) II. 406 Amateur workmen..offered on all hands, chiefly university men who stayed in Oxford that 'Long' for the purpose. **1863** G. M. Hopkins *Let.* 22 Mar. (1956) 15 The probability is I shall not see you for an age, unless we manage to meet in the Long. **1920** G. Saintsbury *Notes on Cellar-Bk.* x. 158 A mixture..first imparted to me..by a very amiable Dorsetshire farmer whom I met while walking from Sherborne to Blandford in my first Oxford 'long'.

8. b. *pl.* Long trousers. *colloq.*

1928 *T. Eaton & Co. Catal.* Spring & Summer 219/3 Flannel longs..boy's long trousers made from grey union flannel. **1947** D. M. Davin *Gorse blooms Pale* 57 His first

suit of longs, all neatly pressed. **1954** 'A. GARVE' *Riddle of Samson* i. 15 A pair of grey flannel shorts that looked as though they'd been cut down from 'longs'. **1962** B. HARRISSON *Orang-Utan* i. 37 They wanted to buy smart shorts (or, better still, longs), shirts and tie, a radio.

10. b. *pl.* Long-term stocks.

1964 *Financial Times* 12 Mar. 21/1 Partly reflecting technical influences, gilt-edged continued to gain ground, with the 'longs' closing up to $\frac{7}{16}$ better. **1969** *Daily Tel.* 16 Sept. 2 The 'longs' and undated stocks were particularly prominent and Treasury 6¾ p.c. 1995–98 rose a full point. **1972** *Times* 17 June 23/3 The 'longs'..closed 'uneasily steady', dealers said.

long, *adv.* Add: **1. b.** Also, *long as*, ellipt. for *so* (or *as*) *long as*.

1807 WORDSWORTH *To Small Celandine* in *Poems* I. 22 Long as there's a sun that sets Primroses will have their glory. **1938** G. GREENE *Brighton Rock* I. i. 22 'It's all right,' he said, 'long as you are here.'

2. b. (Later examples.)

1849 THACKERAY *Pendennis* I. xxv. 239 She fairly told Pen one day..that she felt herself breaking, and not long for this world. **1933** J. MASEFIELD *Bird of Dawning* 43 He was shocked by the roaring wash of the water coming into the after hold. 'She's not long for this world,' he muttered. **1968** L. GOODMAN *Sun Signs* (1970) 193 These people either radiate incredible vitality or else complain that they're not long for this world.

7. (Later example.)

1887 W. MORRIS tr. *Homer's Odyssey* XII. 251 As the fisher sits on the headland with a rod that reaches long.

9. a. *long-awaited, -dead, -departed, -felt, -gone, -held, -lost* (as *sb.*), *-waited, -wearing.*

1914 *Times* 25 Aug. 6/4 The long-awaited battle is begun. **1974** *Melody Maker* 23 Mar. 19/3 The release of Jackson Browne's long awaited album 'For Everyman'. **1905** *Daily Chron.* 14 Nov. 3/4 The old Franciscan.. mourned frantically for his long-dead brother. **1937** AUDEN in Auden & MacNeice *Lett. from Iceland* i. 21 Scribbling to a long-dead poet. **1974** A. PRICE *Other Paths to Glory* I. vii. 79 The two long-dead riflemen. *c* **1838** E. BRONTË *Compl. Poems* (1941) 77 Old Hall of Elbë, ruined, lonely now;..Home of the departed, the long-departed dead. **1869** 'MARK TWAIN' *Innoc. Abr.* xi. 102 Their long-departed owners seemed to throng the gloomy cells. **1952** R. CAMPBELL tr. *Baudelaire's Poems* 19 Sweeping the far-off skylines with a gaze Regretful of Chimeras long-departed. **1862** A. LINCOLN *Ann. Message to Congress* in *Evening Star* (Washington, D.C.) 1 Dec. 1/2 The judicious legislation of Congress..has satisfied..the long felt want of an uniform circulating medium. **1936** *Discovery* Mar. 83/2 To satisfy a long-felt want on the part of the serious student. **1950** W. DE LA MARE *Inward Compan.* 25 A happy house in that long-gone sunshine. **1943** D. GASCOYNE *Poems 1937–42* 33 With long-held burning breath. **1960** R. W. MARKS *Dymaxion World of B. Fuller* 117/2 Fuller's long-held theory that energy in gases evolves unique local patternings. **1853** MRS. GASKELL *Cranford* xv. 308, I could no longer confirm her belief that the long-lost was really here. **1920** M. BEERBOHM *And Even Now* 80, I was always in hope that when next the long-lost turned up..I should *see* him. **1928** *Publishers' Weekly* 16 June 2425 The long-waited reminiscences of the British Prime Minister. **1972** *Buenos Aires Herald* 4 Feb. 6/4 The long-waited inauguration in July of the Peligre Hydroelectric Dam. **1908** *Westm. Gaz.* 16 Apr. 4/2 Greasers are fitted everywhere to..add to the long-wearing life of the parts. **1963** *New Yorker* 23 Nov. 15 (Advt.), Our famous shirts..are made ..of exclusively woven, long-wearing materials. **1975** *Country Life* 2 Jan. 32/1 The engine is..low-revving and long-wearing.

long distance. A. 1. (See LONG *a.*[1] 15.) (With hyphen.) Forming combinations used attrib. or as quasi-adj., esp. (*a*) of a telephone call; (*b*) of a race; (*c*) of a journey.

1884 *Whitaker's Almanack* 385/1 In America some remarkable trials of long distance telephoning have taken place. **1886** *Sci. Amer.* 2 Oct. 208/2 There is a popular belief that the long distance telephone is crowding the telegraph to the wall. **1887** [in Dict. s.v. LONG *a.*[1] 15]. **1897** [see *CENTURION 3]. **1908** *Sat. Even. Post* 26 Sept. 15/3 A long distance line can only be used by one person at a time. **1919** [see *CEILING *vbl. sb.* 6 b]. **1923** [see *all-red* adj. (*ALL E. III. 13)]. **1925** W. J. BRYAN *Mem.* 487 After the meal he made several long distance telephone calls. **1926** *Times* 6 May 3/4 The following other long-distance trains will also run, calling at the principal stations. **1929** *Daily Express* 7 Nov. 2/5 A Socialist member's resolution urging the nationalisation of railways and long-distance road transport was debated. *Ibid.* 11/3 The airship has now to compete with the flying boat as a long-distance craft. **1933** *Discovery* Apr. 131/2 The 'bypath' system gives faster service on local and long-distance calls. **1934** *Ibid.* Nov. 316/2 This railcar recently set up a world's record for long-distance running. **1934** [see *door-to-door* attrib. (*DOOR 8)]. **1935** *Discovery* Dec. 352/1 Long-distance flight. **1935** G. GREENE *England made Me* ii. 47 Put through any long-distance calls. **1959** A. SILLITOE (*title*) The loneliness of the long-distance runner. **1960** *Guardian* 13 June 3/3 Walking down a long-distance Russian train is apt to be..dull. **1961** *Times* 3 Oct. (Computer Suppl.) p. vi/4 Long-distance telephone calls. **1961** L. VAN DER POST *Heart of Hunter* I. i. 25 The men sat with their heads bowed over arms clasped round their knees like long-distance runners from the race of their lives. **1968** *National Fisherman* Aug. 15-A/3 Formosa and South Korea started long-distance tuna fishing later than Japan. **1975** J. RATHBONE *Kill Cure* II. i. 53 A long distance call from Ankara to Istanbul involved time and trouble.

2. A long-distance telephone (call). Also as *adv.*, by long-distance telephone.

1904 'MARK TWAIN' *$30,000 Bequest* (1906) viii. 44 Aleck's imaginary brokers were shouting frantically by imaginary long-distance, 'Sell! sell!' **1920** WODEHOUSE *Jill the Reckless* (1921) xx. 295 Calling Izzy on the long distance. **1923** —— *Inimitable Jeeves* xv. 196 He became a sort of Voice Heard Off, developing a habit of ringing me up on long-distance. **1961** WEBSTER, Called her up long-distance. **1969** A. GLYN *Dragon Variation* v. 147 He went straight to the telephone and called New York long-distance.

B. As *v. trans.* To make a long-distance telephone call to (a person); to report by means of such a call.

1945 *Time* 6 Aug. 79/1 Henry J. Kaiser last week long-distanced an old friend. **1950** *Newsweek* 30 Oct. 61 A UP staffer simply copied the story as it came in, went to an open phone, and long-distanced it to UP in San Francisco in a few seconds. **1965** E. LACY *Double Trouble* viii. 79 My own family is down in the Bahamas, and I long-distanced them.

longer (lǫ·ŋgəɹ), *sb.*[3] *Canad.* (Atlantic Provinces). [f. LONG *a.*[1] + -ER[1].] A long pole or piece of timber used for fencing, a fishing stage, etc.

1772 G. CARTWRIGHT *Jrnl.* 17 Apr. (1792) I. 216 At noon I..searched the woods..where I found some good longers, and boat-hook staffs. **1837** *Times* (Halifax, Nova Scotia) 25 July 235/1 The skeleton of a man was found in the woods..by a man and boy who were cutting longers. **1878** *North Star* (St. John's, Newfoundland) 30 Mar. 3/2 On the afternoon of their death, the deceased.. left home for the woods to draw 'longers' across the pond. **1973** *Canad. Antiques Collector* Jan.–Feb. 13/2 Fences of longers made from spruce or marsh juniper meet and sometimes mingle with the hedgerows.

longeron (lǫ·ndʒĕrǫn). [a. F. *longeron* stringer, beam, (longitudinal) member.] A frame member running lengthways along a fuselage.

1912 *Flight* 13 July 626/1 In front, the four longerons are assembled into a specially designed pressed-steel housing. **1915** W. E. DOMMETT *Aeroplanes & Airships* ii. 26 The framework has as its ground-work four members running fore and aft known as 'longerons'. **1931** J. E. YOUNGER *Airplane Construction & Repair* viii. 130 Longerons are usually made of ash. **1962** F. I. ORDWAY et al. *Basic Astronautics* xi. 444 (*caption*) Space frame and longerons. **1966** E. V. RICKENBACKER *Rickenbacker* (1968) vi. 107 The explosive bullet had hit the longeron just behind me.

longeur: see *LONGUEUR.

lo·ng-hair, *sb.* Also **longhair.** [f. LONG *a.*[1] + HAIR *sb.*] **1.** A cat with long fur. Also *attrib.*

1893 J. JENNINGS *Domestic or Fancy Cats* ii. 6 The several varieties which range under Long-hair embrace Persian, Angora, Chinese, Indian, French, and Russian. **1935** E. B. SIMMONS *Cats* xxviii. 143 The long-hair standard demands a body that is low on the legs. **1948** P. M. SODERBERG *Cat Breeding* 78 Long-hairs need constant attention from the brush. **1958** *Listener* 28 Aug. 298/2 Pedigree cats are divided into two categories: long-hairs and short-hairs. **1972** M. BABSON *Murder on Show* viii. 94, I was in the Cream and Blue-Cream Longhair aisle, cheering the lot of a lonely little Cream Longhair.

2. a. A 'brainy' person, an æsthete, an intellectual; also, a devotee of classical (as opp. to popular) music. (Freq. used contemptuously.) Also *attrib.*

1920 S. LEWIS *Main St.* xxiii. 281 I'm surprised to find you talking like a New York Russian Jew, or one of these long-hairs! **1930** E. FERBER *Cimarron* xxiv. 378 These were the reformers—the long-hairs—fanatics. **1936** *Amer. Mercury* XXXVIII. x/2 *Long hair*, a symphony man. **1938** *Manch. Guardian Weekly* 2 Sept. 188/4 Very few [swing players] are 'long hairs' (people who like classical music). **1950** BLESH & JANIS *They all played Ragtime* (1958) x. 208 Victor has withheld the records..because of fear of insulting the long-hairs. **1955** R. BLESH *Shining Trumpets* (ed. 3) xiii. 314 One can understand why Scott Joplin..could praise ragtime..and could heap fiery denunciation on its 'long-hair' detractors. **1957** O. NASH *You can't get there from Here* 84 So what do you want on yours—a lot of pinko longhairs, or red-blooded athletes and drum majorettes? **1958** OSBORNE & CREIGHTON *Epitaph G. Dillon* II. 57 Intense students, incompetent longhairs, and rather flashy deadbeats. **1960** 'W. HAGGARD' *Closed Circuit* xvi. 192 All those longhairs advising us. **1967** *Listener* 16 Feb. 236/3 He planned to become a 'long hair' musician... He wanted to be a composer of symphonies.

b. A hippie, a beatnik.

1969 *Rolling Stone* 17 May 6/1 Would hippies and long-hairs sit on the youth commission? **1972** *Last Whole Earth Catalog* (Portola Inst.) 215/1 Long-hairs are doing new stuff with their bodies and nervous systems that occasionally needs medical attention or perspective. **1972** 'R. LLEWELLYN' *Night is Child* (1974) i. 13 The noise of the band, a group of longhairs in..girlish duds, velvets, silks and falderals.

long-haired, *a.* (Stress variable.) Also **long haired, longhaired.** [f. LONG *a.*[1] + HAIRED *a.*] Having long hair; *spec.* applied, at various times, (*a*) to Merovingians; (*b*) (freq. derog.) to æsthetes and intellectuals; (*c*) to cats with long fur; (*d*) to classical (as opposed to popular) music and musicians; (*e*) to beatniks and hippies. Sometimes without reference to the actual length of the hair: with or of intellectual or æsthetic pretensions. Spec. *long-haired chum* (see quot. 1890).

1552, etc. [in Dict. s.v. LONG *a.*[1] 16]. **1872** GEO. ELIOT *Middlem.* I. II. xix. 340 Romanticism..was fermenting still..in certain long-haired German artists at Rome. **1881** W. S. GILBERT *Patience* I. 11 The peripatetics Of long haired aesthetics Are very much more to their taste. **1889** H. WEIR *Our Cats* 16 Long-haired cats..are very diversified, both in form, colour, and the quality of the hair. **1890** BARRÈRE & LELAND *Dict. Slang* II. 27/2 *Long-haired chum* (tailors), a young woman, a young lady friend. **1914** C. MACKENZIE *Sinister St.* II. xiii. 769 After a year with long-haired students I want a change. **1915** J. E. PATTERSON *Epistles from Deep Seas* 262 Goin' to have a 'long-haired chum', are we. **1917** 'TAFFRAIL' *Off Shore* 92 Some sort of a friendship, platonic or otherwise, with a 'long-haired' pal. **1922** S. LEWIS *Babbitt* xiv. 184 The long-haired gentry who call themselves 'liberals'..and 'intelligentsia'... Irresponsible teachers and professors constitute the worst of this whole gang. **1935** *Vanity Fair* (N.Y.) Nov. 71/3 Straight or commercial musicians are often derisively called *salon-men* or *long-haired boys*. **1943** G. W. WILLIS *Tangleweed* xii. 174 It ain't a song. It's a composition. Long-haired. **1955** J. CANNAN *Long Shadows* iii. 33 The long-haired fraternity hold the art of the camera in contempt—it rivals their daubs. **1959** C. MACINNES *Absolute Beginners* 157 Archeology, and long-haired music, and all those sorts of thing. **1959** *Times* 22 Nov. 5/6 Since the result of the general election..some of the long-haired boys in our movement have been holding inquiries and assessing blame for our defeat on everyone but themselves. **1962** J. M. WALLACE-HADRILL (*title*) The long-haired kings. **1963** *Listener* 7 Feb. 264/2 It [*sc.* jazz] has begun an unwise flirtation with 'long-haired music'. **1965** M. MORSE *Unattached* i. 59 Howard..found the atmosphere so sombre, long-haired and tedious that he quickly left. **1972** ING & POND *Champion Cats of World* 73 A definite breeding programme has begun in an endeavour to popularize once more the original long-haired cats. **1975** J. SYMONS *Three Pipe Problem* ii. 15 Sir Pountney was..opposed..to long-haired students, and to spineless intellectuals.

long-horn. [LONG *a.*[1] + HORN *sb.*] **1.** A breed of beef cattle, orig. English, now common in the U.S., raised especially in the south-western states. Also *attrib.* and *transf.*

1834, etc. [in Dict. s.v. LONG *a.*[1] 18 b]. **1901** W. A. WHITE in *McClure's Mag.* Dec. 145/2 The picture of Tom Platt..standing at the head of a drove of wild-eyed human long-horns, as if to keep them from a stampede. **1903** A. ADAMS *Log of Cowboy* xxii. 353 There were lots of old long-horn cowmen living in the town. *Ibid.* 356 Some of those old long-horns didn't think any more of a twenty-dollar gold piece than I do of a white chip. **1949** O. NASH *Versus* 24 The big dog is to her Like a scarlet rag to a Longhorn. **1955** *Sci. News Let.* 22 Jan. 61/1 The longhorn first landed in this country when the animals were brought to America in 1521 by Gregorio Vallalobos, a governor-general sent to 'New Spain'. **1972** *Sat. Rev.* (U.S.) 6 May 20/3 Those are white-faced Herefords and black Angus... Don't see many longhorns anymore. **1974** *Sunday Times* (Colour Suppl.) 28 July 18 (*caption*) Longhorn Bull Hillpatrick at Cotswold Farm Park, near Cheltenham: a survivor from the Stone Age?

2. long-horn(ed) beetle = LONGICORN *sb.*

1840 J. & M. LOUDON tr. *Köllar's Treat. Insects* 15 The family of the long-horned beetles, (*Cerambycidæ*). **1894** *Insect Life* VI. 219 A Cerambycid or long-horned beetle; in pods of Enterolobium from Paraguay. **1936** *Forestry* X. 49 Longhorn beetles—Cerambycidae..are large, conspicuous, and easily recognized by their long horns or antennae. **1966** A. W. LEWIS *Gloss. Woodworking Terms* 5 Longhorn beetle. Black and grey beetle about 1 in. long which sometimes attacks the softwoods used in buildings. **1968** R. D. MARTIN tr. *Wickler's Mimicry in Plants & Animals* viii. 86 The long-horned beetle *Erythrus rotundicollis* also resembles the same bug.

3. The long-eared owl, *Asio otus*.

1856 [in Dict. s.v. LONG *a.*[1] 18 b].

4. long-horn(ed) grasshopper, a grasshopper of the family Tettigoniidæ (formerly called Locustidæ), having very long antennæ.

1893 *Insect Life* V. 271 The large Locustidæ, or long-horn grasshoppers, are very appropriately called 'cradlers' from the resemblance of the ovipositor of the female to a grain cradle. **1920** W. J. LUCAS *Monogr. Brit. Orthoptera* 5 Locustodea (Long-horned Grasshoppers). **1972** L. E. CHADWICK tr. *Linsenmaier's Insects of World* 80/2 In contrast with ordinary grasshoppers, most of which live on the ground, the long-horned grasshoppers do more climbing. **1972** SWAN & PAPP *Common Insects N. Amer.* 74 The tettigoniids, or longhorn grasshoppers, may be distinguished from the acridids, or grasshoppers, by their long filamentous antennae.

longifolene (lǫndʒifōᵘ·līn). *Chem.* [f. mod.L. *longifol-ia*, specific epithet of the pine *Pinus longifolia* from which the oil was first isolated (f. LONGI- + *-folia*, f. L. *folium* leaf) + -ENE.] A colourless, somewhat viscous oil that is present in the turpentine oil from some species of pine and is a tricyclic sesquiterpene, $C_{15}H_{24}$.

1920 J. L. SIMONSEN in *Jrnl. Chem. Soc.* CXVII. 573 The sesquiterpene for which the name longifolene is proposed has..only been cursorily examined. **1962** E. L. ELIEL *Stereochem. Carbon Compounds* x. 298 Among natural products, polycyclic bridged systems are exemplified by..the sesquiterpenoids longifolene and cedrene.

longitude. Add: Also with pronunc. (lǫ·ŋgitiūd).

longitudinal, *a.* and *sb.* Add: **A.** *adj.* **2.** (Further examples in *Geomorphol.*)

1822 Conybeare & Phillips *Outl. Geol. Eng. & Wales* p. xxiv, The longitudinal valleys are those which pursue a course parallel to the direction of the chains [of hills] which bound them. **1924** *Bull. Seismol. Soc. Amer.* XIV. 28 Tectonic earthquakes have also been divided into longitudinal and transverse earthquakes according as they are associated with the strike or transverse faults of a district. **1937** [see *concordant *a.* 4]. **1937** Wooldridge & Morgan *Physical Basis Geogr.* xxi. 354 The conception of truly longitudinal coasts as characteristic of the Pacific Basin breaks down on the coasts of Eastern Asia. **1971** C. R. Twidale *Structural Landforms* i. 11 Cross joints which cut vertically across the lineation or foliation of the rock; and longitudinal joints, which run parallel to such textural features in a vertical plane.

4. Involving information about an individual or group at different times throughout a long period (obtained by repeated examination or by eliciting recall on one occasion).

1949 B. J. Underwood *Exper. Psychol.* v. 117 Most researches in the past have been concerned with cross-sectional analyses of the organism, i.e., the capacity of the organism at the moment. When we study the influence of learning on these processes we are interested in the longitudinal aspects, i.e., how they developed. **1958** M. Argyle *Relig. Behaviour* vi. 59 These longitudinal studies can supply important supplementary information. **1962** *Arch. Gen. Psychiatry* VI. 328/1 Longitudinal studies of the urinary excretions of tryptamine and total indole-3-acetic acid..were made on 20 male schizophrenic patients. **1973** *Sci. Amer.* Sept. 35/3 Mathematical curves have been fitted with great success to measurements of individuals followed during the adolescent spurt... Such serial studies of individuals are called longitudinal, as opposed to the studies of populations called cross-sectional, in which each child is measured only once.

B. *sb.* **2. b.** *Aeronaut.* A longeron, esp. one in an airship.

1911 *Aero* May 38/1 There are three main longitudinals, which are of ash rebated for the reception of the diagonal cross-pieces. **1914** H. M. Buist *Aircraft in German War* i. 21 (*in figure*) Longitudinal. **1919** *Jane's All the World's Aircraft* 37a/1 Fuselage longitudinals and struts have sections of I-shape. **1950** *Gloss. Aeronaut. Terms (B.S.I.)* 1. 50 *Longitudinal*, a girder on the outside of the hull structure running fore and aft. **1973** D. H. Robinson *Giants in Sky* ii. 31 The hull was identical with that of the LZ 2, the dimensions, the number of longitudinals and ring frames being identical with those of the ships lost at Kisslegg.

long knife. [f. Long *a.*^{1} + Knife *sb.*] **1.** *N. Amer. Hist.* (Freq. *pl.*, and with capital initials.) A name given by North American Indians to white settlers, esp. of Virginia, or white soldiers. In Canada, *spec.* a citizen of the United States.

1774 J. R. Peyton *Let.* 10 Oct. in J. L. Peyton *Adventures my Grandfather* (1867) 143 The white troops, or 'Long Knives',..imagined no enemy was near. **1784** D. Boon in J. Filson *Discovery Kentucke* 62 The savages now learned the superiority of the long knife, as they call the Virginians, by experience. **1827** J. F. Cooper *Prairie* I. v. 135 If the Tetons lose their great chief by the hands of the Long-knives, old shall die as well as young! **1838** A. Jameson *Winter Stud. & Summer Rambles Canada* III. 55 A distinguished Pottowottomie warrior..was..a good friend to the Long-knives, (The Americans). *Ibid.* 142 The Indians gave the name of Cheemokomaun (Long Knives, or *Big Knives*) to the Americans at the time they were defeated by General Wayne..in 1795, and suffered so severely from the *sabres* of the cavalry. **1908** W. R. Nursey *Story Isaac Brock* xviii. 100 'My object,' said Brock, addressing the Indians, 'is to assist you to drive the "Long-knives" from the frontier.' **1959** R. Gant *World in Jug* 38 Paleface, hear me. Do not send pony soldiers and long knives against my nation. **1959** N. Sluman *Blackfoot Crossing* 33 Crowfoot says that the border—the medicine line—protects his people from the Long Knives. **1972** J. Mosher *Some would call it Adultery* iii. xvi. 147 Brought General Terry and his 'Long Knives', as the Indians called U.S. Cavalry, 'up across the border, Mounted Police or no'.

2. Phr. (*night of*) *the long knives*: a treacherous massacre (as, according to legend, of the Britons by Hengist in 472, or of Ernst Roehm and his associates by Hitler on 29–30 June 1934); hence used allusively of any similarly decisive or ruthless action.

The massacre of the Britons is described by Geoffrey of Monmouth in *Historia Regum Britanniæ* Bk. vi. xv.

1862 Borrow *Wild Wales* II. xx. 226 Hengist had commanded..that..each Saxon should draw his long sax, or knife,..and should plunge it into the throat of his neighbour... This infernal carnage the Welsh have appropriately denominated the treachery of the long knives. **1891** E. C. Brewer *Historic Note-Bk.* 531/2 *Long Knives* (*The Plot or Treachery of the*). This was a treacherous conference to which Geoffrey of Monmouth tells us the chief Britons were invited by Hengist at Ambresbury; others say by Vortigern. Beside each Briton a Saxon was seated, armed with a long knife; and, at a given signal, each Saxon slew the Briton seated by his side. Geoffrey tells us the signal was the utterance of these words: *Nemet oure Saxas*, and that the number massacred was 460. **1936** R. Olden *Hitler the Pawn* xvi. 378 The consequence is massacre, 'the night of the long knives', a St. Bartholomew's night. **1937** S. H. Roberts *House Hitler Built* ii. iii. 114 Such seem to have been the facts of this 'Night of the Long Knives' (the name given to it by Hitler and taken from one of the earliest marching songs of the Nazis). **1960** 'W. Haggard' *Closed Circuit* iii. 29 Many would die in any night of the long knives. **1961** G. Thomas *Keep in Plays of Year* XXIV. 217 This is the night of the long knives and they all landed on Con. **1967** W. R. Manchester *Death of President* i. i. 93 His popularity margin with state voters was..wider than those of Connally or Kennedy-Johnson... He could be fairly confident of surviving the long knives of Austin. **1967** *Economist* 22 July 313/2 A government that can provide some degree of stability may be forgiven its day of the long knives—if the exercise is not repeated. **1968** J. Bingham *I love, I Kill* iv. 44 There was not the 'night of the long knives' feeling you get when a commercial management has ten thousand smackers at stake. **1968** *Sunday Times* 1 Dec. 11/5 The Long Knives flashed last week at Bush House. **1973** *Times* 18 June 1/7 They both lost their jobs last April 30, the night of the long knives when a whole series of officials suddenly resigned. **1973** R. Payne *Life & Death of Hitler* 274 The historical event known as the Night of the Long Knives took place in broad daylight.

long-legged, *a.* Add: **b.** Hence *long leg* (see quots.). *slang.*

1929 F. C. Bowen *Sea Slang* 85 *Long leg*, a big difference in the draught forward and aft in a sailing ship. **1961** F. H. Burgess *Dict. Sailing* 137 Any sailing vessel that draws a lot of water is said to have a long leg.

long-line, long line. 2. a. For def. read: A line of manuscript or type that runs across the page without columnar division. Also (with hyphen) *attrib.* Add further examples.

1914 E. A. Loew *Beneventan Script* xi. 289 The oldest extant Beneventan MSS. are written in long lines and not in two or more columns. **1939** W. H. P. Hatch *Princ. Uncial Manuscripts New Testament* 17 It was soon found that a wide column and a long line are more convenient for the reader. **1964** Dean & Legge *Rule of St. Benedict* p. xviii, The Douce Rule has thirty long lines to the page.

3. In Old English verse, two half-lines considered as a unit. Cf. G. *langzeile.*

1868 W. W. Skeat in Hales & Furnivall *Bp. Percy's Folio MS.* III. p. xxiv, There has been much discussion as to whether alliterative poems should be printed in couplets of short lines, or in long lines comprising two sections. **1877** H. Rehrmann *Essay concerning Anglo-Saxon Poetry* 9 All words of a long line are fit for alliteration that distinguish themselves in the verse by natural gravity or grammatical accent. **1929** W. E. Leonard in Malone & Ruud *Studies Eng. Philol. in Honor of F. Klaeber* 7 The law of the meter remains, an eight-beat long-line. **1970** *Rev. Eng. Studies* XXI. 133 The metrical division between two verses (hemistichs) of an alliterative long line.

lo·ngliner. Chiefly *N. Amer.* Also **long-liner.** [f. Long-line 1 + -er^1.] One who fishes with a long-line; a fishing vessel which uses long-lines.

1909 *Westm. Gaz.* 3 June 14/3 Dog-fish, these terrors to netsmen and long-liners. **1919** W. T. Grenfell *Labrador Doctor* (1920) x. 183 The Hearn long-liners and trawlers, who were just beginning their vast fishery in those waters. **1955** *Fishermen's Advocate* (Port Union, Newfoundland) 14 Jan. 10/5 Three new longliners are now under construction. **1959** *Globe Mag.* (Toronto) 12 Sept. 21/2 Groundfishing operations—draggers with their great, bottom-scraping nets, and longliners with multiple lines armed with hundreds of baited hooks—were the principal targets. **1969** *Guardian* 8 Mar. 7/5 Off this place the professional Japanese long-liners have taken swordfish in excess of a thousand pounds. **1974** *Nat. Geographic* Jan. 114/2 The boat is of the type still called a long-liner, from a time when the crews of such boats fished with lines and hooks. **1974** *Sci. Amer.* Mar. 119/1 The yellowfin-tuna fishery on the Pacific Equator, worked only recently by American and Japanese long-liners, is plainly disclosed in the Nantucketers' logbooks.

Hence **longlinerman**, a member of the crew of a longliner.

1955 *Fishermen's Advocate* (Port Union, Newfoundland) 14 Jan. 7/3 The courses, while aimed at longlinermen, were made available to all who wished to attend.

Longmyndian (lǫŋmi·ndiăn), *a. Geol.* [f. *Long Mynd* (see def.) + -ian.] Applied to a thick series of non-fossiliferous sedimentary rocks in the west Midlands, now believed to be of Pre-Cambrian age, whose main outcrop forms the hills of the Long Mynd in southern Shropshire (Salop). Also *absol.*

1888 C. Callaway in *Trans. Shrops. Archæol. & Nat. Hist. Soc.* XI. 239 We are able to determine the relative ages of the three most ancient rock-systems in the region, viz., the Malvernian, the Uriconian, and the Longmyndian... The great series which forms the Longmynd Hills was referred..to the Lower Cambrian; but until good evidence of its age is obtained, I have thought it better to use a local designation. *Ibid.* 240 The Longmyndian conglomerates are largely derived from the Uriconian. **1929** Evans & Stubblefield *Handbk. Geol. Gt. Brit.* iii. 20 The outcrop of the Longmyndian Rocks at Church Stretton forms the wild, moorland tract called the Longmynd. **1967** D. H. Rayner *Stratigr. Brit. Isles* ii. 45 The structures in the Longmyndian pediments..suggest strongly that the western part of the Wentnor outcrops are inverted. **1969** Bennison & Wright *Geol. Hist. Brit. Isles* iii. 67 The Longmyndian is in the form of a very large syncline.

long-neck. Add: **2. b.** In full, *long-neck clam.* An elongated, thin-shelled clam, *Mya arenaria*, found on the eastern coast of North America; = *long clam* (Long *a.*^{1} A. 18 b).

1905 *Bull. N.Y. State Mus.* No. 71. 22 The soft or long-neck clam, Mya, is capable of locomotion only when very small. **1910** J. L. Kellogg *Shell-Fish Industries* 281 Mya, in different localities, is known as the clam, the soft clam, the long neck, long clam, squirt clam. **1923** D. K. Tressler *Marine Products of Commerce* 533 *Mya arenaria* commonly called soft clam, long clam, long neck..is found from South Carolina to the Arctic Ocean. **1970** R. Lowell *Notebk.* 200 File upon file, the beds of long-neck clams.

† **long nine.** *Obs. U.S.* [f. Long *a.*^{1} 1 + Nine *sb.* 4 b.] A kind of cheap cigar.

1830 N. Dana *Mariner's Sk.* 213 (Th.), The fourfold row of long-nine-smoking beaux, that are regularly drawn up on Sunday forenoon in Market Square. **1835** *Harvardiana* I. 157 (Th.), He unfolded the wrapper; it contained two long-nine segars. **1851** *Yale Lit. Mag.* June 315 Pete had, as he always had after breakfast, a cigar in his mouth, a long nine. **1879** *Bradstreet's* 31 Dec. 3/3 Boys smoke 'long nines' while they still wear jackets.

‖ **longo intervallo** (lǫ·ŋgo intəɹvæ·lo). [Lat., lit. 'at a great distance'.] At some remove, though there is a gulf between them (of two persons, places, etc., being compared).

1693 Dryden tr. *Juvenal's Satires* (Dedication) p. iii, The most Vain, and the most Ambitious..have yielded the first place without dispute; and have been arrogantly content, to be esteem'd as second to your Lordship, and even that also, with a *Longo, sed proximi Intervallo.* **1890** W. James *Princ. Psychol.* II. xx. 227 Almost all subsequent progress has been made in Germany, Holland, and, *longo intervallo*, America. **1923** *Spectator* 17 Feb. 294/1 In casual passages *The Orissers* may seem dull, pompous and even ridiculous; but as a whole it has a strange power, a conviction and an intensity of imagination that mark it off from other novels and link it, *longo intervallo*, with *Moby Dick* and *Wuthering Heights.* **1935** J. C. Masterman *Fate cannot harm Me* ii. 44, I remember asking him once..who were his literary idols among the moderns. 'Well,' he said, 'Max Beerbohm of course..and then, but *longo intervallo*, P. G. Wodehouse.'

long-playing, *a.* [Long *adv.* 9 a.] That plays for a long time; *spec.* designating or pertaining to a microgroove gramophone record designed to be played at $33\frac{1}{3}$ revolutions per minute. Cf. *L.P.* (*L 7).

1912 *Talking Machine News & Jrnl. Amusements* Nov. 529/1 The Petmecky Needle, which plays ten times, is the subject of an interesting little leaflet... Users interested in this long-playing needle should ask their dealers for full particulars. **1929** *Wireless Mag.* Oct. 252 (*heading*) Long-playing dance records. **1931** *Electronics* Dec. 236/1 Long-playing records... Already announced is a phonograph record that will play for 15 minutes. **1948** *Electronic Engin.* XX. 333 A new library of recorded music has been announced..which consists of a series of long-playing 10 and 12 in. records run at $33\frac{1}{3}$ r.p.m. **1951** *Ann. Reg. 1950* 386 An important advance was made by the introduction of 'long-playing' records containing about 20 minutes of music in place of the $4\frac{1}{2}$ minutes hitherto available. **1958** V. Bellerby in P. Gammond *Duke Ellington* ii. 151 With the advent of the Long Playing record he has shown himself ready to compose well outside his former 'three-minute' form. **1968** P. Oliver *Screening Blues* ii. 81 Singers who have been recently recorded under the more liberal circumstances of the long-playing era. **1972** *Gramophone* Oct. 834/2 (Advt.), Trade in your unwanted classical long-playing records..for guaranteed unplayed new records.

So **long-play** *a.* = *long-playing *a.*; also *ellipt.* as *sb.*, long-playing records collectively; **long-player**, a long-playing record.

1954 F. Ramsey (*title*) A guide to longplay jazz records. **1957** M. Goff (*title*) Short guide to Long Play. **1958** *Times* 19 Apr. 7/3 Already tape recording is hard on the heels of the long-play record and stereophonic reproduction promises to invade both. **1958** *New Statesman* 3 May 580/2 The Rank Organisation..has decided to start a record club..which will issue long-players. **1958** I. Murdoch *Bell* xiv. 187 I'll..put on my new long-player. **1962** A. Nisbett *Technique Sound Studio* 273 Long Play tape gives 50% more recording time on a spool than standard play. **1962** R. Douglas-Home *Sinatra* i. 8 The buying of long-players was (and still is) an expensive pursuit. **1968** *Blues Unlimited* Sept. 26 Phillips was introduced to long-play by Origin with two of his less impressive pieces. **1975** M. Kenyon *Mr Big* ii. 18 He chose a long-player of Carroll Gibbons and his Savoy Orpheans.

long run, long-run. Add: **2.** *Theatr.* A long period of being presented on the stage; a play or entertainment presented for a long period. Also *attrib.*

1714 [see Run *sb.*^{1} 18]. **1883** D. Cook *On Stage* I. ix. 203 These are the days of 'long runs', when but one or two plays can be produced in a season. **1896** [see Run *sb.*^{1} 18]. **1901** Beerbohm *Around Theatres* (1924) I. 320 The long-run system is often deplored on the ground that the mimes 'walk through' their parts. **1909** *Westm. Gaz.* 22 Apr. 2/3 Half the week is to be given to 'long-run' plays; the other half to new plays, revivals, and the classical drama. **1967** *Oxf. Compan. Theatre* (ed. 3) 195/2 Alfred Butt presented Laurette Taylor in *Peg o' My Heart.* This had a long run and was then transferred to the Globe.

B. *adj.* Taken or considered in the long run; = *long-term *a.*

1904 W. James *Meaning of Truth* (1909) iii. 89 Abstract truth, truth verified by the long run, and abstract satisfactoriness, long-run satisfactoriness, coincide. **1931** A. L. Rowse *Politics & Younger Generation* 7, I have had in mind the necessity of a long-run view of politics. **1946** J. S. Huxley *Unesco* i. 19 Long-run human progress. **1957** K. R. Popper *Poverty of Historicism* i. i. 6 There is no long-run uniformity in society on which long-term

generalizations could be based. **1969** D. C. HAGUE *Managerial Econ.* II. iii. 61 With many industrial goods, long-run costs will be constant or falling. **1975** *Times* 6 Jan. 12/6 We need..restraint from business and labour in which their longrun interests are elevated over..short-run interests.

long-running, *a.* [LONG *adv.* 9 a.] Continuing for a relatively long period of time; *spec.* of a play: having a large number of consecutive performances.

1956 *Nature* 21 Jan. 142/1 This is precisely the case in a long-running crossing experiment with strains *H*..and *O*. **1968** G. C. RAMSEY *Agatha Christie* iv. 50 It is..poetic justice that the most famous play in the English language should have supplied the title for the longest-running play in England. **1972** *Guinness Bk. Records* (ed. 19) 98/2 The longest-running musical show ever performed in Britain was *The Black and White Minstrel Show*. **1975** *Listener* 6 Feb. 166/2 A long-running and repetitive weekly discussion.

longshanks. Add: **1. b.** Hence applied generally to a tall or long-legged person, often as a term of derision.

1699 B.E. *New Dict. Canting Crew, Long-shanks,* long-legged. **1915** *Dialect Notes* IV. 206 There comes long-shanks across the fields. **1939** F. THOMPSON *Lark Rise* ii. 32 The two tamer children..would make a dash on their long stalky legs for their own garden gate followed by.. cries of 'Long-shanks! Cowardy, cowardy custards.' **1954** J. R. R. TOLKIEN *Fellowship of Ring* xi. 193 He was smoking a short black pipe. As they approached he took it out of his mouth and spat. 'Morning, Longshanks!' he said. **1959** I. & P. OPIE *Lore & Lang. Schoolch.* ix. 169 In the following [terms] the chief emphasis is on height, 'Lofty' being the most popular nickname, followed by 'Long-shanks'.

long-shore, *attrib. phr.* Add: Also **longshore, 'longshore. 1. b.** *Physical Geogr.* Moving, taking place, or laid down more or less parallel to a shore.

1837 [in Dict., sense 1]. **1910** V. CORNISH *Waves of Sea* vi. 179 When, at sea, the wind is obliquely on-shore there is not only a 'longshore current.., but waves also break obliquely. Their effect to drive shingle along the shore is then obvious to the eye. **1952** R. F. PEEL *Physical Geogr.* xv. 253 Longshore drift..is often the main factor controlling the supply of shingle to beaches. **1964** V. J. CHAPMAN *Coastal Vegetation* viii. 193 Long-shore movement of beach material takes place..at the upper limit of the waves. **1968** R. W. FAIRBRIDGE *Encycl. Geomorphol.* 58/1 Currents from both flanks later build up the long-shore bar, both trough and bars being affected by long-shore currents, and the troughs are scoured by water escaping laterally behind the bars from the beach zone and longshore drift-currents bringing sand.

lo·ngshoring. [f. LONG-SHORE *attrib. phr.* (*sb.*) + -ING¹.] The type of work done at a port; the occupation of a longshoreman.

1926 *Daily Colonist* (Victoria, B.C.) 1 July 7/1 Two men were injured while doing longshoring work on Monday. **1930** C. S. JOHNSON *Negro in Amer. Civilization* (1931) iv. 53 In a study of the conditions of the longshoring industry of the Chicago port in 1915 by Charles B. Barnes, 100 workmen were interviewed.

long shot. Also **long-shot, longshot.** [f. LONG *a.*¹ + SHOT *sb.*¹] **1.** (In Dict. s.v. LONG *a.*¹ 18.)

2. Something incredible or very unlikely; a far-fetched explanation; a wild guess; *spec.* a bet laid against considerable odds; = OUTSIDER 1 b. See also SHOT *sb.*¹ 9 d in Dict. and Suppl. Also *attrib.*

1867 [in Dict. s.v. LONG *a.*¹ 18]. **1869** *Leisure Hour* May 326/1 He may also..learn to systematise his turf speculations, may know when it is prudent to 'back a jockey' or a long shot. **1906** 'O. HENRY' *Four Million* (1916) 33 A few long-shot winners at the New Orleans race-track. **1939** *Sun* (Baltimore) 30 Nov. 24/7 The long shots won the first and second races. **1955** *Sci. Amer.* Feb. 47/2, I made the first test very simple, because the whole idea seemed a long shot. **1970** *Globe & Mail* (Toronto) 26 Sept. 38/1 The other sign that fall has arrived is a sudden surge of long-shots from Western Canada speeding across the finish line in first place. **1971** *Publishers' Weekly* 23 Aug. 45/2 Since establishing his company nine years ago, Grossman has played hunches and longshots. **1975** *New Yorker* 20 Jan. 81/1 It was a day for long-shot players.

3. A cinema or television shot which includes figures or scenery at a distance; opp. *CLOSE-UP. orig. *U.S.*

1922 *Sci. Amer.* Sept. 177/1 A quarter of a mile away, from which distance some of the so-called 'long shots' were filmed by the cameraman. **1930** *Sunday Times* 12 Oct. 4/3 Some of the close-ups are brilliantly clear and fascinating in detail, some of the long shots blurred and vague. **1934** *B.B.C. Year-Bk.* 58 The first television programme was transmitted... New ways of using photo cells enabled artists to be followed from 'long shot' to 'close up' and vice versa. **1962** *Movie* Sept. 7/3 The last shot of the film is a longshot of a general advance. **1974** *Times* 19 Jan. 9/7 We got Griffith in long shot winding up like a clock gone haywire.

long-standing. 2. (Earlier and later examples.)

1814 JANE AUSTEN *Mansf. Park* II. ix. 196 In spite of every long-standing expectation. **1848** MILL *Pol. Econ.* I. xi. 208 A long-standing and hereditary confidence in the safety of funds when trusted out of the owner's hands. **1975** *Times* 15 Jan. 14/1 The holing of the Japanese supertanker, Showa Maru, on a rock off Singapore last week is bound to reactivate sharply a long-standing conflict of views over control of the nearby Malacca Straits.

long-tail. Add: **1.** *spec.* a greyhound. Also *attrib.*

1876 *Coursing Calendar* 12 The former Duke of Hamilton..and others of their day, were followers of the 'long tails' on the very same ground. **1927** *Daily Express* 25 May 12 A little more foresight..might have made 'rag running' a very popular entertainment, commanding as much notice as the sport of long-tail racing. **1930** BILLIS & KENYON *Pastures New* vi. 102 Some high-priced coursing dogs,—longtails as they were called—were brought into the colony.

b. Read: The long-tailed duck, *Clangula hyemalis*. (Later examples.)

1919 J. MASEFIELD *Reynard* 93 Some longtails prinking. **1958** D. A. BANNERMAN *Birds Brit. Isles* VII. 141 A number of immature long-tails may be seen in the Channel from November onwards.

c. The white-tailed tropic bird, *Phaëthon lepturus*.

1905 *Chambers's Jrnl.* May 367/1 The tropic bird commonly called 'longtail'. **1960** J. BOND *Birds W. Indies* 22 White-tailed Tropicbird... Local names:.. Boatswain Bird; Long-tail.

4. long-tail pair *Electronics* = *long-tailed pair* (*LONG-TAILED *a.* 3).

1946 *Electronic Engin.* XVIII. 298/2 Each of the amplifiers..embodies a 3-stage network, employing valves (EF. 50) in a long-tail pair connexion... The circuiting is such that the amplifiers respond to difference of signal potential between the input terminals, being several hundred times less sensitive to variations of the potential of the two terminals together with respect to ground. **1971** J. H. SMITH *Digital Logic* iv. 70 Transistors T_2 and T_3 form a long tail pair where a fixed current is passed through R_3 into either T_2 or T_3, so that either one or the other transistor will conduct, but not both.

long-tailed, *a.* Add: **3. long-tailed pair** *Electronics*, a pair of identical valves (or transistors) with their cathodes (or emitters) connected together to a large resistor and usu. with their anodes (or collectors) connected to equal loads. Cf. **long-tail pair*.

1947 *Electronic Engin.* XIX. 272/1 The type of circuit used is based on what is generally referred to as the 'long-tailed pair' and owes its inception to the late A. D. Blumlein. **1970** J. SHEPHERD et al. *Higher Electr. Engin.* (ed. 2) xxii. 713 Drift [in a d.c. amplifier] cannot be reduced by straightforward feedback since this reduces the gain in proportion; the technique of compensation may however be employed. In this method drift in one part of a circuit is balanced against drift in another part. The long-tailed or emitter-coupled pair circuit..is an example.

long-term, *a.* [f. LONG *a.*¹ + TERM *sb.*] Lasting for, pertaining to, or involving a relatively long period of time; maturing or becoming effective only after a long period. Also quasi-*advb.*

1908 *Daily Chron.* 24 July 1/6 The long-term men, who wore blue cotton overalls marked with the broad arrows, were in the rear. **1909** *Westm. Gaz.* 2 June 5/2 Mr. Fielding was able to place a 2½ per cent., long-term loan in London. **1937** *Discovery* June 178/1 A long-term programme of development. **1942** C. S. LEWIS *Screwtape Lett.* xiv. 73 It is His long-term policy..to restore to them a new kind of self-love. **1956** C. AUERBACH *Genetics in Atomic Age* 65 Thus each species has to strike a balance between the short-term requirement for a low frequency of mutation and the long-term requirement for an ample store of mutant genes. **1956** *Planning* XXII. 38 The more specific the investment the greater the need for forecasting, especially long-term. **1959** A. LEJEUNE *Crowded & Dangerous* xii. 134 The long-term future could look after itself. **1969** *Listener* 5 June 786/3 The difficulty in getting both politicians and the bureaucracy to think long-term, particularly on financial affairs. **1971** *Jrnl. Gen. Psychol.* LXXXV. 51 Short-term memory is required to act as..a cue to recall data from long-term storage. *Ibid.*, The effectiveness of extracting information from long-term memory may depend on short-term load. **1972** *Accountant* 23 Mar. 383/2 Valuation of long-term contracts. **1972** *Listener* 21 Dec. 854/2 Courses of action are followed without regard for their long-term consequences. **1974** *Times* 28 Dec. 9/6 Ordinary table wines..must not be kept long-term in the refrigerator.

Long Tom. Add: **1.** (Earlier example.)

1832 M. SCOTT *Tom Cringle's Log* xi, in *Blackw. Mag.* July 27/2 The long Tom must be a tearer to pitch its mouthful of iron this length.

2. (Earlier examples.)

1839 *Amer. Railroad Jrnl.* VIII. 98 The Long Tom.. consists merely of a trough. **1852** *Elora* (Ontario) *Backwoodsman* 17 June 2/4 The plough is a far more profitable instrument than 'the long Tom' or 'the rocker'.

4. *Austral.* A marine fish of the family Belonidæ.

1883 [in Dict., sense 3]. **1908** E. J. BANFIELD *Confessions of Beachcomber* I. iv. 154 The 'long tom' (*Zylosurus*, sp.) or alligator-pike, which shoots from the water. **1934** *Bulletin* (Sydney) 24 Jan. 20/2 The slender Long Tom must in future be known as *Lewinichthys ferox*... On the other hand the stout Long Tom is to be styled *Lhotskia macleayana*. **1965** *Austral. Encycl.* V. 362/2 Long toms or Needle-fish, members of the family Belonidae, in England and America called garfish... Long toms have the habit of leaping from the water, when either pursuing or being pursued.

5. *slang.* A particularly high-powered telephoto camera lens.

1968 'J. WELCOME' *Hell is where you find It* iv. 58 There were Rollieflexes, a Leica, a Long Tom for peeping, a couple of polaroids. **1968** 'O. MILLS' *Sundry Fell Designs* xiii. 142 Russ, grinning, remembered a Long Tom lens he had seen in the hands of one of the photographers. **1973** R. BUSBY *Pattern of Violence* x. 165 The long tom lenses and the barrels of the TV cameras peering down into the cleared arena.

Longton Hall (lǫ·ŋtŏn hǭl). The name of a house in Staffordshire where the first Staffordshire porcelain was manufactured; hence *attrib.* of the porcelain manufactured there. Also *ellipt.* Longton.

1757 *Public Advertiser* 4 Apr. 3/3 A Quantity of new and curious Porcelain or China, both useful and ornamental, of the Longton-Hall Manufactory, which has never been exposed to public View. **1885** C. SCHREIBER *Jrnl.* 27 Feb. (1911) II. 469 A certain Longton Teapot, which we had discovered among her china. **1925** W. W. WORSTER tr. *Hannover's Pott. & Porc.* III. xx. 533 A mode of decoration probably peculiar to Longton Hall is the application of designs like those on Battersea or Staffordshire enamels, in white enamel pigment on a strong blue ground. **1961** *Connoisseur* Dec. p. xiv (Advt.), A rare Longton Hall Vase finely painted with flowers. **1973** *Times* 14 Nov. 21/5 For Longton Hall a small melon tureen..made a record price at £4,000.

longuette (lǫŋge·t). [f. F. *longuette* somewhat long, longish.] A midi dress, a midi skirt.

1970 *New Yorker* 10 Oct. 167/1 A photographer hopped among them adding to the bulging dossier of *Women's Wear Daily* evidence of the arrival of its 'longuette'. **1971** *Time* 29 Mar. 29 Along Belgrade's Terazije, maxicoats and Longuettes, velvet knickers and leather gaucho pants abound.

longueur. Add: (Earlier and later examples.) Also in extended use, of music, etc.

The form *longeur* in quots. 1959 and 1970 is *erron.*

1791 H. WALPOLE *Let.* 26 May (1905) XIV. 437 Boswell's book is gossiping;.. but there are woful longueurs, both about his hero and himself. **1866** *Nation* (N.Y.) 16 Aug. 127/2 In what other writer than George Eliot could we forgive so rusty a plot, and such *langueurs* [sic] of exposition? **1892** I. ZANGWILL *Childr. Ghetto* I. 5 The terrible *longueurs* induced by the meaningless ministerial repetition of prayers already said by the congregation. **1950** 'G. ORWELL' *Shooting Elephant* 41 A kind of pattern ..survives the complications and the *longueurs* [in *King Lear*]. **1952** 'M. COST' *Hour Awaits* 251 This sense of impending pause in herself—this *longueur* of spirit. **1958** *Times* 22 Dec. 5/5 Should the recitalist be an imperfect executant, the audience must listen for much too long a period, with only one interval to alleviate the *longueurs*. **1959** *Guardian* 2 Nov. 7/1 One was aware of extensive stretches in which nothing historically worth while seemed to be going on—longeurs which the Director of History..would not have tolerated in his scenario. **1963** *Times Lit. Suppl.* 18 Jan. 40/3 Some of his own early experiences were clearly embedded: the longueurs of the middle-class Sunday, the deadly frustrations of office routine. **1970** *Times* 29 May 7/2 Despite the show's contradictions and longeurs, it does at least attempt something audacious and original. **1971** *Guardian* 18 Feb. 9/8 There are so many longueurs in most of the originals that one can hardly jib at Miss Wilson's frequent condensations. **1974** *Times* 6 Mar. 14/8 A perfect committee man, he would remain wholly silent—and even asleep—during the *longueurs* not unknown in university meetings.

longward(s (lǫ·ŋwǭɹd(z)), *adv.* [f. LONG *a.*¹ + -WARD, or -WARDS.] Towards longer wavelengths; on the long-wavelength side *of*.

1971 D. W. SCIAMA *Mod. Cosmol.* ix. 132 Because of the red shift the emission is spread out longwards of 21 cm. **1974** *Nature* 22 Feb. 513/1 Since the first report of a diffuse ultraviolet background, there have been several measurements attempted, both longward and shortward of Lyman α.

longyi (lǫ·ŋyī), var. LUNGI. Cf. *LUNGYI.

1908 H. JONES *Let.* 2 May in H. J. W. Hetherington *Life & Lett. Sir H. Jones* (1924) II. 203 The boxers, all naked except for their ornamental silk *longyis* tied up hard between their legs and around their middle. **1934** [see *ARAKANESE *a.* and *sb.*]. **1947** 'N. SHUTE' *Chequer Board* 105 A green *longyi* wrapped around her waist and falling to her feet. **1957** R. MASON *World of Suzie Wong* II. ii. 17 A Burmese woman..with her bright red *longyi* taut over her thighs. **1959** *Times* 10 Dec. 11/2 Burma, where men wear the *longyi*. **1971** *Nat. Geographic* Mar. 304/2 He wears the Burmese national costume, a wrap-around skirt called a *longyi*, derived from India, and a short formal jacket with three pockets and cloth buttons, derived from China.

Lonk (lǫŋk). [dial. var. of *Lank*, the first syllable of *Lancashire*: see *E.D.D.*] A large-sized variety of mountain sheep which originated in Lancashire or Yorkshire; the wool of this variety of sheep.

1863 in W. Fream *Youatt's Compl. Grazier* (1893) 473 If the Lonks be as hardy as they are good, they must be the most valuable sheep for the hills that we have at present. **1866** *Jrnl. R. Agric. Soc.* II. 367 The hill ranges of Yorkshire and Lancashire are believed to be the earliest home of the Lonks. **1911** *Chambers's Jrnl.* Dec. 778/2 The lonk is believed to have come originally from the Yorkshire hills. **1940** *Chambers's Techn. Dict.* 510/2 *Lonk*, wool that comes from the large type of mountain sheep of the same name, reared on the Lancashire and Yorkshire

moorlands. **1968** FRASER & STAMP *Sheep Husbandry* (ed. 5) ii. 110 The Lonk. Another horned and black-faced breed is native to a rather confined hill district of Lancashire and Yorkshire. It is a big sheep, handsome, with very clearly differentiated black-and-white markings on face and legs, strong-boned and active. **1972** J. WAINWRIGHT *Night is Time to Die* 7 The dark patch could be a sheep... Ye-es—it *could* be some stupid, wandering Lonk. **1974** *Times* 23 Feb. 14 Several farmers may turn out their Swaledale or Scottish Blackface, Herdwick or Lonk sheep onto one moor.

lonnin(g, var. LOANING *sb.*

Cf. the 14th–17th cent. examples with similar spellings in Dict. s.v. LOANING *sb.* and in *Dict. Older Sc. Tongue.*

1808 R. ANDERSON et al. *Ballads in Cumberland Dial.* 23 In dark winter neeghts i' the lonnins. **1849** F. T. DINSDALE *Gloss. Teesdale* 81 It's a lang lonnin that has nivver a turn. **1896** F. M. T. PALGRAVE *List Words Hetton-le-Hole* 29 *Lonning*, 'laning', i.e. lane... 'We find swiney up Mousely (Moorsley) lonen.'—Extract from boy's essay on Wild Flowers. **1933** *Times Lit. Suppl.* 6 Apr. 243/2 This is for those whose feet leave the road at the first chance and strike up through lonnins and intakes to untrodden ground. **1971** *Country Life* 9 Sept. 630/1 We came to the lonnin that turns away from the river and leads beside the church towards the dale road.

Lonsdale (lǫ·nzdēil). The title of Hugh Cecil Lowther (1857–1944), fifth earl of *Lonsdale*, used *attrib.* to denote any of various belts conferred upon professional boxing champions of the United Kingdom. Also *transf.* So *to give* (someone) *the Lonsdale* (slang), to dismiss, repudiate, 'throw out' (cf. *BELT *sb.*[4]).

1910 *Daily Graphic* 18 Oct. 10/4 At the National Sporting Club..last evening, the contest was decided for the Bantam-weight Championship of Great Britain, the winner of which also holds the Lonsdale belt for that weight. **1914** *Boxing's Bk. Records* 9 (*caption*) Lonsdale Belt Holders. **1958** F. NORMAN *Bang to Rights* III. 167, I can always give her the Lonsdale after a week or two. **1959** C. MACINNES *Absolute Beginners* 77 The Wiz was wearing a gladiator Lonsdale belt with studs on it. **1973** *Country Life* 26 July 249/1 The traditional Lonsdale Belt..with its enamel portrait of the 5th Earl.

lontar (lǫ·ntaɹ). [Malay.] = PALMYRA; also, a manuscript written on leaves of this palm.

1820 J. CRAWFURD *Hist. Indian Archip.* I. IV. 443 The *Lontar*, (*Borassus flabellifer*), the *Tar*, or Tal of Western India, grows abundantly in the Indian islands. **1935** I. H. BURKILL *Dict. Econ. Products Malay Peninsula* I. 348 Lontar is also the best-known Malayan name. **1937** M. COVARRUBIAS *Island of Bali* (1972) vii. 193 In Singaradja there is a library of these manuscripts,..where are preserved some splendid old *lontars* with illustrations... These are masterpieces of the art of illustration, with miniature pictures incised with an iron style on the blades of the *lontar* palm. **1952** 'W. MARCH' *October Island* i. 11 He moved majestically towards the four tall lontar palms. **1953** C. A. GIBSON-HILL *Malay Arts & Crafts* § Hats & Dish-covers. Other fibres are employed, including strips from the Lontar Palm. **1961** P. KEMP *Alms for Oblivion* ix. 152 You know about *lontars*? Good. Well, in one important *lontar* is written, 'It is fair to lie to wifes [*sic*] and enemies.'

loo (lū), *sb.*[3] [Hind., f. Skr. *ulkā* flame.] The name given in Bihar and the Punjab to a hot dust-laden wind.

1888 KIPLING *Phantom 'Rickshaw* 78 The *loo*, the red-hot wind from the westward, was booming among the tinder-dry trees. *a* **1936** —— *Something of Myself* (1937) iv. 98 A hot wind, like the *loo* of the Punjab. **1954** O. H. K. SPATE *India & Pakistan* ii. 55 In the NW hot weather depressions generally take the form of violent dust-storms... Such dust-storms are distinct from the *loo*, a very hot dust-laden wind which may blow for days on end. **1965** E. AHMAD *Bihar* iv. 45 The hot scorching 'loo' winds of the Bihar plains during late April and May have an average velocity of 5–10 miles per hour. **1974** M. PEISSEL *Great Himalayan Passage* xi. 175 The Loo is caused by the hot expanding air of the Indian plains rushing into the cool hills.

loo (lū), *sb.*[4] [Etym. obscure.] A privy, a lavatory. Also *attrib.* and *Comb.*

A. S. C. Ross's examination of possible sources in *Blackw. Mag.* (1974) Oct. 309–16 is inconclusive: he favours derivation, in some manner that cannot be demonstrated, from *Waterloo*.

[**1922** JOYCE *Ulysses* 556 O yes, *mon loup*. How much cost? Waterloo. Watercloset. **1932** N. MITFORD *Christmas Pudding* ix. 137 The absence in his speech of such expressions as 'O.K. loo'..'we'll call it a day'.] **1940** —— *Pigeon Pie* ii. 27 In the night when you want to go to the loo. **1943** C. BEATON in *Horizon* Jan. 37 They had dressed, teeth brushed, breakfasted, had visited the loo, and were on their precarious journey all in a question of fifteen minutes. **1944** AUDEN *For Time Being* (1945) 20 Between the bottle and the 'loo' A lost thing looks for a lost name. **1954** KOESTLER *Invis. Writing* xxxix. 419 The story of 'the loo-tank papers'..is another instance of the cloak-and-dagger atmosphere. **1955** G. FREEMAN *Liberty Man* II. vi. 113 Johnnie, do take him to the loo, there's a good boy. **1957** P. WILDEBLOOD *Main Chance* 57 The loo's on the landing, if you want to spend a penny. **1960** C. MACKENZIE *Greece in my Life* 23, I think I should sigh for the old Grande Bretagne Hotel in spite of the squalor of the loo which was no paradise for dysentery. **1971** *Petticoat* 17 July 31/2 You can wait until he goes to the loo or, if he appears to have a bladder like an ox, send him to the kitchen for more coffee. **1972** *Guardian* 23 Feb. 18/5 Matching bathmats (£2.20)..and loo seat covers (£1.80 and £1.12). **1973** E. MCGIRR *Bardel's Murder* iv. 85 A neighbouring cat had come through the window and made away with the loo brush. **1974** *Observer* 28 Apr. 28/6 The loo rolls unfurling across the pitch.

loo, var. LEW *a.*[1] (Further examples.)

Several examples (-1881) in Dict. s.v. LEW *a.*[1]

1889 'M. GRAY' *Reproach of Annesley* (ed. 5) VI. iii. 276 'Tis fine and loo here,.. and you med set down and hrest. **1892** H. C. O'NEILL *Devonshire Idyls* 7 His house..was 'loo' from the cold north winds. **1906** *Daily Chron.* 16 Aug. 3/6 It is cool and pleasant to find a 'loo' corner on the Esplanade [in Penzance]. **1963** NANCE & POOL *Gloss. Cornish Sea-Words* 109 *Loo*,.. (2) lee, sheltered out of a wind.

looard, var. LEEWARD *a.* (*sb.*) and *adv.*

1886 in H. BAUMANN *Londinismen* 100/1. **1910** 'O. HENRY' *Whirligigs* ii. 33 Morgan lived in a bamboo shack to 'loo'ard'. **1963** NANCE & POOL *Gloss. Cornish Sea-Words* 109 *Looard*, leeward, is common sea-language.

looder, var. LOWDER (in Dict. and Suppl.).

looey (lū·i). *N. Amer. slang.* Also **looie, louie.** [f. LIEU(TENANT with pronunc. (lū-) + -Y[6], -IE.] A lieutenant.

1916 *Rio Grande Rattler* 11 Oct. 5 The 'Looey' gaily saunters from his tent. **1920** J. DOS PASSOS *One Man's Initiation: 1917* vii. 86 Our louie's name's Duval. **1928** W. H. UPSON *Me & Henry & Artillery* 120 Then the looeys started hollering to the sergeants. **1935** A. J. POLLOCK *Underworld Speaks* 73/1 *Looie*, a police lieutenant. **1942** M. HARGROVE *See Here, Private Hargrove* lxiii. 182 How would you like a second looey's commission? **1967** I. A. BARAKA in W. King *Black Short Story Anthol.* (1972) 119 Jimmy Lassiter, first looie. **1974** *Weekend Mag.* (Montreal) 27 Apr. 10/1 One scrap of the rarely-talked-about reality: after being a private 14 months, Angus was commissioned in the field as second looey.

loogan (lū·gǎn). *U.S. slang.* [Etym. unknown.] In derogatory use: a fellow, a 'fool'.

1929 D. RUNYON in *Hearst's International* July 126/3 The poor loogan she is marrying will never have enough dough to buy her such a rock. **1932** J. T. FARRELL *Young Lonigan* ii. 86 Bill's a loogin who always tries to wise-crack. **1933** 'P. CAIN' *Fast One* 200 There's Rose, with his syndicate behind him, and all the loogans he's imported from back East.

looie, var. *LOOEY.

look, *sb.* Add: **1.** Phr. *if looks could kill* (or *slay*): used to denote an expression of hostility in a look.

1913 F. L. BARCLAY *Broken Halo* xxxvii. 372 If looks could slay, Margaret would not have left that room alive. **1922** F. HARRIS *My Life & Loves* I. ii. 37 When they let me up, I looked at Jones and if looks could kill, he'd have had short shrift. **1943** K. TENNANT *Ride on Stranger* iv. 31 Just then she saw me..and if looks could have killed!

2. c. Also in pl., esp. in *from* or *by the looks* (*of*).

1883 R. CLELAND *Inchbracken* iv. 28 It micht be e'en a bairn by the looks o' the bun'le. **1923** 'B. M. BOWER' *Parowan Bonanza* v. 54 You're just ahead of a big storm, by the looks, Mr. Rayfield. **1975** J. SYMONS *Three Pipe Problem* ix. 65 Acting doesn't pay too well from the looks of it.

e. Colloq. phr. *for the look of the thing*: for the sake of appearances.

1876 TROLLOPE *Prime Minister* IV. xiii. 217 'I shall go down and vote for them of course,' said Mr. O'Mahony, 'just for the look of the thing.' **1910** 'SAKI' *Reginald in Russia* 63 He often wished, for the look of the thing, that people would sometimes burn candles at his shrine. **1924** M. KENNEDY *Constant Nymph* xv. 212 Save for the look of the thing she had no particular wish for a reconciliation. **1940** L. H. MYERS *Pool of Vishnu* IV. v. 191 Why are they willing to die, and to send those whom they love to their death, for the sake of—what shall I call it?—the look of the thing?

f. *Fashion.* With defining word(s): an appearance or effect indicated by the preceding word(s). Occas. without defining word (quot. 1973).

1938 [see *little-girl* attrib. (*LITTLE *a.* 14)]. **1939** *Vogue* 15 Apr. 2 (Advt.), Accent on That Fresh Young Look. **1940** *Mademoiselle* Mar. 56 Formold created for you that Tall Look of 1940. **1948** *Vogue* Mar. 41 The New Look has fined down... Length has crystallized into eleven inches from the ground for formal wear. **1966** *Listener* 3 Feb. 171/1 This year..the geometrical look is in. **1971** *Daily Mail* 3 Feb. 3 A specially-created hair-style to complete the hot-pants look. **1973** *Sunday Times* 28 Jan. 43/2 The clothes are created on them, and a whole look is painstakingly put together. **1974** *Country Life* 17 Jan. 107/1 The peasant look in knitwear.

look, *v.* Add: **1. a.** ¶ Colloq. phrases: *as quick* (or *soon*) *as look at you* (or *him*, etc.): very rapidly and readily; 'at the drop of a hat'; *not to know which way to look*: to be embarrassed; *not to look at* (someone): to find unattractive, to show no sexual interest in (someone); occas. in positive contexts.

1814 JANE AUSTEN *Mansf. Park* I. v. 101 She came up to me..and talked and laughed till I did not know which way to look. I felt that I must be the jest of the room. **1817** M EDGEWORTH *Harrington* xi. 247 Nor did I know well which way to look, when his lordship..asked Miss Montenero if she could possibly imagine that any such vulgar prejudices existed. **1861** C. M. YONGE *Young Step-Mother* xxviii. 420 Albinia did not know which way to look when all was ascribed to Mr. Kendal's great kindness to him. **1888** 'R. BOLDREWOOD' *Robbery under Arms* II. iii. 46 He was awful shook on Mad; but she wouldn't look at him. **1894** SOMERVILLE & 'ROSS' *Real Charlotte* II. xx. 78 There was no other woman here that signified except Miss Dysart, and it didn't seem likely she'd look at him. **1922** JOYCE *Ulysses* 347 Give it to him too on the same place as quick as I'd look at him. **1926** I. MACKAY *Blencarrow* xi. 105 Supposing Kathrine wouldn't look at him in any case? **1937** M. SHARP *Nutmeg Tree* xx. 266 If I married you I'd never look at another man so long as I lived. **1941** H. NICOLSON *Diary* 8 July (1967) 177 He then stalks out of the room. We are left ashamed and wretched and do not know which way to look. **1946** E. O'NEILL *Iceman Cometh* (1947) III. 167 From what I've seen of 'em..they'd run over you as soon as look at you. **1955** J. I. M. STEWART *Guardians* III. ii. 214 The novelists ..constantly endow sensitive women with husbands whom, in fact, they would never *look at.* **1971** M. TORRIE *Bismarck Herrings* xi. 156 Threatened to report you to the council as soon as look at you, she did. **1973** W. M. DUNCAN *Big Timer* iv. 29 You have to watch it nowadays. Jump you as soon as look at you. **1974** P. DICKINSON *Poison Oracle* ii. 37 Will she even look at a male chimp? Doesn't she think she's human?

h. (Later examples.)

1947 A. MENEN *Prevalence of Witches* ii. 36 Suddenly his eyes looked mischief again. **1956** H. GOLD *Man who was not with It* (1965) vi. 53, I looked a question at her.

4. a. (Further examples.) *looky here* U.S. regional variant of 'look here'; also *look-a-here.* Also, *look who's* (or *what's*) *here*: see who (or what) is here.

1872 [see *gum-game* (*GUM *sb.*[2] 9)]. **1876** 'MARK TWAIN' *Tom Sawyer* x 94 And besides, look-a-here—maybe that whack done for *him*! **1925** E. O'NEILL *Desire under Elms* I. ii. 20 Looky here! Ye'd oughtn't t' said that, Eben. **1935** Z. N. HURSTON *Mules & Men* I. iv. 95 'Looka here, folkses,' Jim Presley exclaimed. 'Wese a half hour behind schedule.' **1943** 'C. DICKSON' *She died a Lady* v. 38 Looky here... Burn it all, all I was tryin' to do was see what she'd do flat out on an open road. **1945** A. KOBER *Parm Me* 75 'Well, look who's here!' exclaimed the host. **1949** N. MARSH *Swing, Brother, Swing* iii. 48 'Well, well, well,' he said. 'Look who's here.' **1969** *Listener* 1 May 614/1 Look, my Bill doesn't include any blanket condemnation of unofficial strikes. **1971** *Black Scholar* June 54/2 Lookahere, Dr. Hare, I don't have a picture at this time. **1973** *Black World* Apr. 62 Lookahere Sammy... I'm glad to see ya. **1973** G. SIMS *Hunters Point* xiii. 115 Look, we don't have to sit here. We could go down to the beach. **1974** *Daily Mail* 1 Oct. 8/5 *Look you!* Plaid Cymru protested to the BBC yesterday over the timing of its only party political broadcast.

6. a. *to look babies*: delete † and add later example.

1957 J. BRAINE *Room at Top* xi. 107, I could see my face in her pupils... 'You're looking babies,' she said.

d. For † *Obs.* read *rare*, now *dial.*

1879 *Boy's Own Paper* 18 Jan. 14/3 [The monkeys] both set to work and 'look fleas' in the hare's fur. **1961** F. G. CASSIDY *Jamaica Talk* vii. 148 A very common usage makes *look* into a transitive verb meaning look for, gather: 'Arthur and I joined a group of boys to *look wood*.'

10. a. (Further examples.) Also, (*it*) *looks like*: it seems likely. *colloq.* (chiefly *U.S.*).

1910 W. M. RAINE *Bucky O'Connor* 55 Your cook, Anderson, kid-napped the child, looks like to me. **1929** J. BUCHAN *Courts of Morning* 13, I admitted that it looked like it, and said that if Blenkiron had been captured by bandits..his captors had done the worst day's work of their lives. **1936** M. MITCHELL *Gone with Wind* I. i. 11 Don't it look to you like she would of asked us to stay for supper? **1970** N. MARSH *When in Rome* v. 127 'Wouldn't it be a yell if..you were The Man?' 'Do I look like it?' **1972** G. BROMLEY *In Absence of Body* viii. 101 'And now I suppose you've got to find a replacement?' 'Looks like it.' **1973** *Guardian* 31 Jan. 4/7 Looks like your child's birthday is news again this year.

b. (Later example.)

1973 A. BROINOWSKI *Take One Ambassador* ii. 21, I look like being in and out of the office a lot in the next few days.

18. d. *to look on* (or *to*) *the bright* (or *worst*, etc.) *side*: to regard or consider something with optimism (or dismay, etc.). Cf. SIDE *sb.*[1] 10.

a **1784** JOHNSON in E. Fuller *Thesaurus Quots.* (1941) 667/1 The habit of looking on the best side of every event is worth more than a thousand pounds a year. **1833** W. F. HOOK *Let.* 9 Dec. in W. R. W. Stephens *Life & Lett. W. F. Hook* (1878) I. iv. 258, I am a bit of an optimist, I always look to the bright side of things. **1839** [see *BRIGHT *a.* 1 e]. **1848** J. RUSKIN *Let.* 17 Mar. in M. Lutyens *Ruskins & Grays* (1972) xi. 98 My disposition is to look to the worst side of things and..I feared you were entirely ruined. **1852** MRS. STOWE *Uncle Tom's Cabin* II. xxiv. 82 Well, of course, if you can look on the bright side, pray do. **1914** R. FROST *North of Boston* 69 But I don't count on it as much as Len. He looks on the bright side of everything. **1942** 'P. WENTWORTH' *Pursuit of Parcel* xi. 51 Well, ducks, I shouldn't take on. Look on the bright side.

22. b. *to look towards a person* (later examples). Also, *to look at* (a person).

1880 STEVENSON & HENLEY *Deacon Brodie* I. 24 Deacon, I looks towards you. **1890** B. L. FARJEON *Mystery of M. Felix* I. iii. 26 Mrs. Middlemore,..you're a lady after my own heart... Here's looking towards you. **1910** A. NOYES *Coll. Poems* I. 241, I looks to-wards you, Prester John, you've done us very proud! **1930** J. DOS PASSOS *42nd Parallel* I. 119 'Pard, have that on me.'.. 'Thanks, here's lookin at you.'

c. (Examples.)

1879 A. W. TOURGEE *Fool's Errand* xliv. 330 There could be nothing looking towards marriage between us.

1903 A. T. HADLEY *Relations between Freedom & Responsibility* 15 A series of negotiations rather than discussions, looking toward compromise rather than toward mutual enlightenment. **1904** T. N. PAGE in *McClure's Mag.* 621 The South regarded jealously any teaching of the Negroes which looked toward equality. **1932** T. J. GRAYSON *Leaders & Periods Amer. Finance* xiii. 278 The thing to do was to take no precipitate action looking toward resumption.

30. look around. b. = *look round* (sense *42 c). Also, to search about *for*.

1883 'MARK TWAIN' *Life on Mississippi* xliii. 437 I'll look around a little, and if I can't do better I'll come back and take it. **1927** H. CRANE *Let.* 14 Mar. (1965) 290 I'm looking around for some sort of 'avocation'. **1974** 'M. INNES' *Appleby's Other Story* x. 81 Upper servants are frequently left in residence as caretakers... If it happens at Elvedon, it will give you time to look around.

32. look back. e. (Later examples.)

1928 *Observer* 17 June 27/4 Since they adopted the bold experiment..of changing the date of their regatta.. Marlow Amateur Regatta has never looked back. **1936** 'N. BLAKE' *Thou Shell of Death* i. 17 His origin is shrouded in mystery... Turned up suddenly in the R.F.C. early in the war, and never looked back. **1949** *Radio Times* 15 July 17/1 Jules Verne..wrote *Five Weeks in a Balloon*, scored an immediate success, and never looked back. **1973** *Times* 23 Apr. 4/7 The play ran into the war, and she has never looked back.

33. look down. e. (Earlier examples.)

1812 *Niles' Reg.* III. 45/2 Volunteer companies..are rolling to the frontiers, in force sufficient to look down opposition. **1837** *Knickerbocker* IX. 361 We're a free trader..and are forced to go well armed, to look down all resistance. **1838** J. F. COOPER *Homeward Bound* I. viii. 194 If the people cannot control and look down peculiarity ..one might as well live in a despotism at once.

37. look in. c. [After *listen in*, *LISTEN *v.* 2 e.] *intr.* To watch a television programme. *colloq.*

1927 *Pictorial Weekly* 5 Mar. 100/1 We shall then 'look-in' by wireless and see events and scenes at a distance. **1928** *Daily Sketch* 7 Aug. 11/1 The public..can 'listen-in' or 'look-in' to the transmissions. **1950** *Ann. Reg. 1949* 418 At the end of October there were..206,000 [television] sets licensed and..as many as a million people regularly looking-in. **1959** J. BOLAND *Operation Red Carpet* v. 67, I often look-in when he's on.

42. look round. c. (See quot. 1914.)

c **1869** TAYLOR & DUBOURG in M. R. Booth *Eng. Plays of 19th Cent.* (1973) III. 250 I've begged and prayed to him for time—only to look round. **1914** *Conc. Oxf. Dict.* Add., *Look round*, (esp.) examine the possibilities &c. with a view to deciding on a course. **1950** J. CANNAN *Murder Included* i. 8 Hugo..is out of the army and looking round; there was some talk of him starting a dairy herd. **1974** 'R. TATE' *Birds of Bloodied Feather* iii. 74, I looked round for a job and found a modest occupation.

43. look through. d. *to look right* (or *straight*) *through* (a person): to pretend not to see (someone), to ignore (someone) deliberately.

1959 B. KOPS *Hamlet of Stepney Green* I. 9 Like me? He never even sees me. He looks straight through me. **1963** P. WILLMOTT *Evolution of Community* ix. 98 It's awful when they look right through you, because they think you're not as good as them. **1973** G. MITCHELL *Murder of Busy Lizzie* ii. 26 Clothilde's straight-laced mamma boycotted Eliza..and Clothilde..looked straight through the poor woman.

45. look up. e. (Earlier example.)

1806 R. COCHRANE *Let.* 6 Jan. in J. Steele *Papers* (1924) I. 461 One cause why it has been so low at this market was the scarsity of salt; our river is now full enough for Boats to run, I think the Article will look up.

47. Further collocations used attributively or as sbs.: **look-ahead**, an action of judging what can happen or is likely to happen in the (immediate) future; **look-and-say**, a method of teaching reading by identifying each word as a whole (as opposed to treating a word as a series of separate letters needing to be spelt); **look-around, -round** [cf. *to look (a)round*, senses 30, 42 (in Dict. and Suppl.)], an inspection, scrutiny, search; **look-through** *Papermaking* (see quots.).

1963 I. FLORES *Logic Computer Arithmetic* iv. 78 Another solution is to examine the inputs to a number of stages and, somehow, simultaneously predict the carry outputs for this group of stages. This is called the carry lookahead. *Ibid.* v. 83 Let us examine an adder which performs the carry function with a lookahead on several levels. **1967** A. BATTERSBY *Network Analysis* (ed. 2) xii. 210 The effect of a 'look ahead' decision rule is shown. **1973** *Sci. Amer.* June 93/3 Since the number of legal moves available to a player at each turn averages about 30, a full look-ahead to a depth of four would require examination of about 30^4, or 810,000 moves. **1909** B. DUMVILLE *Sci. of Speech* xii. 167 The books on school method usually mention three methods of teaching to read—the Alphabetic, the Look-and-Say, and the Phonic. **1964** M. CRITCHLEY *Developmental Dyslexia* iv. 16 Many have blamed the analytic, look-and-say, 'flash' or global systems of teaching—whereby the child learns to identify each word as a whole. **1973** *Guardian* 7 Mar. 5/2 The use of highly speculative Gestalt psychology as the theoretical basis for 'look and say' methods. **1947** *Ann. Reg. 1946* 157 Field-Marshal Smuts found time to fly to Berlin for what he described as a 'private look around' with no special..objectives. **1967** M. MCLUHAN *Medium is Massage* 10 'The Medium is The Massage' is a look-around to see what's happening. **1914** R. FROST *North of Boston* 65 We took one look round. **1932** J. BUCHAN *Gap in Curtain* ii. 97 He hoped, while in the country, to have a look round. **1937** E. J. LABARRE *Dict. Paper* 149/1 *Look-through*, a term applied to the appearance of paper when held to the light, thus disclosing the texture or formation. **1973** C. COHEN *Watermarks* (William Sommerville & Son Ltd.) 8/1 *Look-through*, the appearance of a sheet of paper when held up to the light: may be clear or mottled.

look-a-here: see *LOOK *v.* 4 a.

look-alike. *N. Amer.* [LOOK *v.* 9 + ALIKE *a.*] Something or someone that closely resembles another in appearance. Also *attrib.* or as *adj.*

1947 *Time* 1 Dec. 78 Lisle Maxwell Sanders..is often called 'Mr. Kieran' for his famed look-alike. **1949** J. ROEBURT *Tough Cop* xvi. 180 There were enough look-alikes in the flat photography of the period to puzzle me. **1961** M. BEADLE *These Ruins are Inhabited* (1963) ii. 31 Those look-a-likes, the two-shilling piece and the half-crown. **1969** L. GREENBAUM *Out of Shape* (1970) xxv. 175 Asher was flanked by his pregnant wife and a long-haired student. Except for the wife's stomach, the two women were look-alikes. **1972** *Islander* (Victoria, B.C.) 27 Feb. 10/3 This is the critical test, such misleading lookalikes as serpentine and its brother, bowenite, permitting no passage of light even through the finest sliver. **1974** *Publishers Weekly* 11 Feb. 62/3 He meets Gabrielle, Simone's look-alike sister, and falls in love all over again.

looker, *sb.* Add: **1. b.** (Further examples.) Also **looker-out,** in the book-trade, one who looks out wanted volumes from stock; **looker-upper** *colloq.*, one who looks something up.

1826 *New Monthly Mag.* XVII. 241, I have always casual lookers-in, and it is my cue..to keep..an open house. **1836** *Scottish Christian Herald* I. 286/2 Like the keepers of a puppet-show, to extort money from every looker-in. **1901** *Daily Chron.* 4 Dec. 9/2 (Advt.), Lookers-up (2 experienced); also several boys in beer factory. **1926** W. J. LOCKE *Old Bridge* II. viii. 134 The result..if sought, is there for the looker-round to behold. **1939** H. HODGE *Cab, Sir?* ii. 20 At the blind corners, where the separate sections are too far apart to keep in touch, there's a 'looker-out'. He waves up the cabs from one section to another. **1951** 'J. TEY' *Daughter of Time* vii. 91 'Marta.. said you wanted something looked up.' 'And are you a looker-upper?' **1961** *Evening Standard* 14 July 19/4 Publisher has vacancy for warehouse-man to train as looker-out.

d. looker-in: a viewer of television. Also (now *rare*) *looker.*

The more usual word is *viewer.*

1927 *Pictorial Weekly* 5 Mar. 101 A speech which the 'looker-in' can actually see being delivered. **1928** *Daily Tel.* 30 Oct. 12/5 This afternoon 'lookers-in' will be given a chance of seeing the first still pictures to be publicly broadcast in this country. **1933** *Radio Times* 14 Apr. 72/2 *The First Television Revue*..should draw the majority of Britain's 'lookers' to their receivers. **1953** *Sunday Times* 25 Jan. 9/4 Producers should never allow themselves to be influenced by the knowledge that their audience contains many doggedly *literal* lookers. **1959** *Listener* 16 July 100/3 If the looker-in [of a televised church service] can only be a looker-on it would be better if he did not watch.

3. A person, usu. a woman, of particularly pleasing appearance. *colloq.* (orig. *U.S.*).

1893 S. CRANE *Maggie* v. 41 The young men of the vicinity said, 'Dat Johnson goil is a puty good looker.' **1898** E. N. WESTCOTT *David Harum* 322, I was alwus a better goer than I was a looker. **1909** E. RICKERT *Beggar in Heart* 207 She isn't much of a looker—my missus has other points than looks. **1923** L. J. VANCE *Baroque* vii. 65 Just because daughter's a swell looker don't make father out an innocent. **1933** AUDEN *Witnesses* in *Listener* (Poetry Suppl.) 12 July p. ii, The days went by, he grew mature; He was a looker you may be sure. **1947** J. STEINBECK *Wayward Bus* vii. 80 She was a looker too—fine well-filled legs with rounded thighs. **1971** R. PARKES *Line of Fire* iv. 42 Bit of a looker... Otherwise..a ranking detective on a priority case, would hardly have bothered driving her home. **1973** *Washington Post* 5 Jan. 8/2 Sandra Archer, who plays the heroine from the Peace Corps..is such a looker that she can't help but make the Quest for Revolutionary Consciousness appear hopelessly glamorized.

looker (lu·kəɪ), *v. dial.* [f. the sb.] *trans.* and *intr.* To tend and guard (farm animals).

1887 PARISH & SHAW *Dict. Kentish Dial.* 95 *Looker*, to perform the work of a looker. 'John? Oh! he's *lookering*.' **1961** *John o' London's* 5 Oct. 400/3 In East Sussex a shepherd is still called a 'looker' and his occupation 'lookering'. **1962** R. JEFFRIES *Exhibit No. 13* x. 97 Jones was 'lookering' his bullocks. The ministry man was due.. and..the bullocks had to be treated with all possible care and attention.

look-in, *sb.* **2.** For def. read: *colloq.* An opportunity to take part in something, usually with a chance of success; a share of attention. Add later examples.

Quot. 1870 replaces that in Dict.

1870 *Bell's Life* 12 Feb. 3/6 If Fawcett imagines he has got a look in, Mullins will fight him for all the money he can get together. **1902** KIPLING *Traffics & Discov.* (1904) 27 We might even be able to give our Native Army a look in. **1905** *Official Guide Nat. Assoc. Professional Baseball Leagues* 58 With a team which never had a look-in for anything better than cellar championship..the club made money. **1911** G. B. SHAW *Getting Married* 244 We shall none of us have much of a look-in when Mrs. George comes. **1916** *Lit. Digest* 1 Jan. 7/2 Between Colonel Roosevelt and the diplomatic correspondence of this epoch the dictionary business is getting a look-in all right. **1916** 'TAFFRAIL' *Pincher Martin* xvii. 330 It's time we had a look in at something. **1936** *Times Lit. Suppl.* 17 Oct. 837/1 The faithful, unmarried lover who never gets a look-in. **1964** *Word Study* Apr. 1/1 Nor would a quack bonesetter get a look-in at a position in a modern clinic. **1968** *Listener* 26 Sept. 390/1 An acknowledged modern artist gets a look-in at illustration 52.

looking, *vbl. sb.* Add: **1. d. looking-in** *Television* = *VIEWING *vbl. sb.* Also *attrib.*

1926 *Daily Herald* 31 Dec. 1/2 It is predicted that before many years have passed the family looking-in set will be as common in the home as is now the listening-in set. **1927** *Pictorial Weekly* 5 Mar. 101/2 'Looking-in' on Mr. Baird's apparatus is an interesting experience. **1951** *Ann. Reg. 1950* 414 From America came alarming reports of the craze for looking-in. **1957** R. HOGGART *Uses of Literacy* vi. 156 An undiscriminating looking-in, night after night, at T.V.

looking-forward. [f. LOOKING *vbl. sb.* + FORWARD *adv.*] The action of looking forward; an anticipation of future events.

1837 DICKENS *Let.* 3 Nov. (1965) I. 328 Anxious lookings-forward to the pleasure of your society. **1867** *People's Hymnal* 205/2 One the earnest looking forward, One the hope our God inspires. **1871** [see LOOKING *vbl. sb.* 1 b]. **1915** BEERBOHM *Lett. to R. Turner* (1964) 242 Well, dearest Reg, again all apologies..and all lookings-forward to later on. **1955** E. BOWEN *World of Love* xi. 221 Were there not those who said that everything *has* already happened, and that one's lookings-forward are really memories?

looking-glass. Add: **5. looking-glass image** *rare* = *mirror image*; **looking-glass world** (or **land**), a vision of the world as it would be if seen, reversed, through a looking-glass.

1929 A. HUXLEY *Do what you Will* 44 The professional Don Juan destroys his spirit as fatally as does the professional ascetic, whose looking-glass image he is. **1896** B. BERENSON *Italian Painters of Renaissance* (1930) II. ii. 63 He cannot persuade himself of the unreality of Looking-Glass Land until he has touched the back of the mirror. **1909** CHESTERTON *Tremendous Trifles* 234 Always the Kingdom of Heaven is 'at hand', and Looking-glass Land is only through the looking-glass. **1911** —— *Innocence of Father Brown* viii. 225 An unspeakable certainty that there was something still unexplained... Could not be fully explained by his fancy about 'looking-glass land'. **1871** 'L. CARROLL' *Through Looking-Glass* xii. 218 You've been along with me, Kitty—all through the Looking-Glass world. **1963** *Daily Tel.* 15 Aug. 18/1 It is quite conceivable that there might exist a kind of looking-glass world, in which all matter is made up from anti-matter. **1967** 'A. GILBERT' *Visitor* xii. 203, I felt as if I were in a Looking-Glass world where everything goes the wrong way.

lookit (lu·kit). *U.S. colloq.* [f. LOOK *v.* with arbitrary final element.] **a.** *int.* Listen! **b.** *v. trans.* Only in imp.: look at (something or someone).

1917 *Dialect Notes* IV. 396 *Look-at*, used among school children for *look!*.. Cf. *look-it* in Mass., Mich. **1925** T. DREISER *Amer. Trag.* (1926) I. xiv. 103 Oh, isn't that just the classiest, darlingest little coat you ever saw! Oh, do look at those sleeves... Lookit the collar. And the lining! And those pockets! **1926** *S.P.E. Tract* XXIV. 124 *Lookit*, listen to me. **1927** M. OSTENSO *Mad Carews* (1929) iv. 49 But lookit! Lookit the nice stockin's Mrs. Bowers made for ye. **1938** D. BAKER *Young Man with Horn* IV. iv. 242 'Lookit the jig-men,' Olga said. 'I thought you'd give us the go-by.' **1966** M. BREWER *Man against Fear* i. 8 Lookit my hair—whiter it gets every day. **1968** [see *JEEZ(E *int.*]. **1972** D. BLOODWORTH *Any Number can Play* xxiii. 231 Just get a load of that stuff, will you? It's not even killing the lousy jungle, lookit. It's bringing it alive!

look-out. Add: (Now usually stressed *loo·k-out.*) **2. a., b.** (Further N. Amer. examples.)

1888 *Century Mag.* Feb. 498/2 These lookouts or forerunners having returned, the herds are set in motion as early in the spring as may be. **1893** *Harper's Mag.* May 939/2 By each dealer's side sits the 'lookout'..lazily looking on in the interests of such fair play as is consistent with professional gambling. **1935** A. J. POLLOCK *Underworld Speaks* 73/1 *Look-out*, gambling house employee who observes the bets of players and the pay-off of dealers for regulatory purposes. **1955** J. S. GOWLAND *Smoke over Sikanaska* 16 The look-out had to be an expert woodsman, be able to read meteorological instruments, have an excellent degree of physical fitness and good eyesight. **1961** *Canada Month* 6 Oct. 42/3 However, the forestry people want money to buy greater preparedness through more lookouts, men, planes and equipment.

look-over. [f. LOOK *v.* 19.] An examination, a survey.

1909 R. A. WASON *Happy Hawkins* 183 Then I..took a stroll around to see that no one had been givin' us the look-over. **1916** 'B. CABLE' *Action Front* 216, I want you to go down quickly and have a look over at the new ground. **1952** *Irish Digest* Feb. 8/2, I have myself treated one farmer..who was sent to me for a general 'look over'. This disclosed a malunited fracture of the ulna.

loo·k-see. *slang.* Also **looksee.** [Pidgin-like formation from LOOK *sb.* or *v.* + SEE *v.*] **1.** A survey; a tour of inspection, a reconnaissance; an investigation. Also *rare* (quot. 1926), appearance, looks.

1883 *Boy's Own Paper* 22 Dec. 185/1, I 'spec she just come here to makee look see how de people get on. **1906** J. LONDON *Let.* 25 Apr. (1966) 204 Would you care to have a look-see at it for publication in the magazine? **1908** *St.*

George's Rev. I. 156 China..opium problem... It was my business to go out there and have what my John would call a 'look-see'. **1924** *Blackw. Mag.* Sept. 356/2, I sat up, and had a look-see. The ground sheet was crawling with scorpions. **1926** M. LEINSTER *Dew on Leaf* 82, I distrust the look-see of things. **1927** *Observer* 9 Oct. 22 We must be grateful to the B.B.C. for letting us have a 'looksee', as the Chinese say. **1928** *Sat. Even. Post* 4 Feb. 105/3 And I can take a look-see at what they're doing in aviation over there. **1939** J. PASCOE *Unclimbed N.Z.* v. 67 A hurried reconnaissance, or in Colonial argot, a 'look-see', disclosed that. **1942** C. BARRETT *On Wallaby* iii. 52 We had a looksee at Merre Gudda, which, the blacks say, is a haunted cave. **1943** C. H. WARD-JACKSON *Piece of Cake* 41 *A look-see*, a reconnaissance. Thus, 'Let's get some facts first; go down to the flights and take a look-see.' **1957** I. CROSS *God Boy* (1958) xv. 123 I'll wander up and have a look-see. **1967** B. COPPER *No Flowers for General* xi. 142 I'll have a looksee at the front. **1968** A. DIMENT *Bang Bang Birds* ii. 13, I took a long looksee through my ..binoculars.

2. (See quot.) *rare.*

1925 FRASER & GIBBONS *Soldier & Sailor Words* 147 *A look see*, a telescope, a periscope.

3. *attrib.*

1929 *Amer. Speech* V. 149 Several pidgin English terms are now accepted American slang:..'chow-chow' for food, and 'look-see man' for tourist or sightseer. **1971** M. TAK *Truck Talk* 101 *Look-see window*, a window in the rear of the sleeper that assists the driver in backing up by increasing his visibility. **1973** *Times* 17 May 27/2 As a result of his 'look-see' trip Lewis..came back home with around £100,000 worth of export orders. **1973** *Sci. Amer.* Oct. 114/1 'Look-see' diagrams that offer visual proof of complex algebraic formulas.

look-up (lu·kʌp). [f. vbl. phr. *to look up* (see LOOK *v.* 45).] **1.** A call, a visit. *rare.*

1855 D. G. ROSSETTI *Let.* 25 Nov. (1965) I. 278 Hughes ..gave them a look up about it. **1888** 'R. BOLDREWOOD' *Robbery under Arms* I. xiv. 191 We foraged up Aileen's mare, and made it up to ride over to George Storefield's, and gave him a look-up.

2. The action of (or a facility for) looking something up in a dictionary, file, etc.; retrieval of information about items in an ordered collection. Freq. *attrib.*

1948 *Math. Tables & Other Aids to Computation* III. 157 Operations such as division, square root, table look-up, etc., where the required time cannot be predicted. **1958** A. D. BOOTH in *Aspects of Translation* 88 All that had been produced was a programme which would enable a computing machine to perform look-up operations which a human translator would perform with a dictionary. **1960** E. DELAVENAY *Introd. Machine Transl.* vi. 93 An appreciable amount of time will thus be saved in dictionary look-up. **1964** *Discovery* Oct. 55/1 The programme does this in several stages: (1) a dictionary look-up which provides information about parts of speech, [etc.]. **1967** COX & GROSE *Organiz. Bibliogr. Rec. by Computer* iv. 79 These citations are then found in the main file by a 'look-up' procedure. **1971** A. J. AITKEN in R. A. Wisbey *Computer in Lit. & Ling. Res.* 14 In addition, TLF also has a computer 'look-up' which in effect lists certain predictable collocations of certain common function words so that the computer can subdivide its examples according to these collocations.

looky here: see *LOOK *v.* 4 a.

loom, *sb.*[1] Add: **5*.** *Electr.* **a.** Flexible tubing which is fitted over the ordinary insulation of an electric wire to provide additional protection.

1917 A. L. COOK *Interior Wiring* xiii. 235 For wires carrying more than 300 volts or for damp places, flexible conduit or armored cable must be used. The flexible tubing used is sometimes called 'circular loom'. **1939** H. P. RICHTER *Pract. Electr. Wiring* xi. 158 Where wires cross each other, slip loom over both wires.

b. A group of parallel insulated wires bound together into a bundle; (see also quot. 1949).

1949 *Gloss. Aeronaut. Terms* (*B.S.I.*) II. 23 *Loom*, one or more cables pre-assembled for installation in an aircraft. **1962** *Which? Car Suppl.* Oct. 139/1 A wiring loom prevented the dipstick being removed or replaced easily. **1972** C. E. JOWETT *Electronic Engin. Processes* iv. vi. 141 The forming of looms should preferably be by means of plastic ties, at an approximate pitch of 25 to 38 mm.

6. *loom-room*; **loom-house** (earlier U.S. example); **loom-state** *a.*, of woollen fabrics, in the state in which they came from the loom, untreated.

1819 *Western Rev.* I. 303 The other two young women slept in a loom house adjoining. **1845** *Knickerbocker* XXV. 448, I went out to look at the loom-room. **1961** BLACKSHAW & BRIGHTMAN *Dict. Dyeing* 101 *Loomstate*, woven fabrics in the condition in which they come from the loom. For practical purposes the term is synonymous with *Grey* (adjective). **1972** *Times* 9 May 20/6 Lists of cotton 'grey' (loomstate) goods.

loon, *sb.*[2] Add: **1. b.** In phrases with *loon's* (see quots.). Also freq. *as crazy as a loon* (in reference to its actions in escaping from danger and its wild cry) and varr.; so, *as drunk as a loon*; *to hunt the loon* (see quot. 1880).

1830 *Kentucky Intelligencer* (Flemingsburg) 29 May 4 Patton informed me that McLaughlin had just gone from Elizabethville, and was 'drunk as a loon'. **1834** C. A. DAVIS *Lett. J. Downing* 42, I saw thru' it in a minute, and made it all as strait as a loon's leg. **1834** S. SMITH *Sel. Lett. J. Downing* 110 He begun to sing out like a loon for us to come and take him. **1840** C. F. HOFFMAN *Greyslaer* I. I. xi. 129 After tramposing for twenty-four hours on a stretch, with not even a loon's nap at the end of it. **1845** C. M. KIRKLAND *Western Clearings* 83 Why, you're both as crazy as loons! **1865** 'MARK TWAIN' in Harte & 'Twain' *Sk. Sixties* (1926) 163 Our reserve..came filing down the street as drunk as loons. **1880** *Harper's Mag.* Dec. 31 Miss Lois had been hunting the loon with a hand-net—a Northern way of phrasing the wearing of the willow. **1931** W. FAULKNER *Sanctuary* vi. 57 You're as crazy as a loon. **1934** J. T. FARRELL *Young Manhood* xxiv. 398 Jesus, I'm drunk as a loon. I'm drunk, Kelly. Drunk. **1951** *Publ. Amer. Dial. Soc.* xv. 66 Crazy as a loon.

c. *transf.* A crazy person; a simpleton.

Perhaps influenced by LOONY, LUNY *a.* and *sb.*

1885 'C. E. CRADDOCK' *Prophet Gt. Smoky Mts.* xii. 230 But ye air a smart man ter that loon, fur..he dunno he air a loon. **1918** C. SANDBURG *Cornhuskers* 99, I am a loon about the sea. **1945** *Coast to Coast 1944* 72 There we were, bottled up in camp because the loon in charge couldn't get the order signed for the trucks to leave.

2*. An early type of guided missile developed by the U.S. Navy.

1947 *Newsweek* 17 Mar. 64/2 The Navy also displayed a 'bat bomb' and a 'loon', two hitherto secret radio-controlled missiles. **1951** COGGINS & PRATT *Rockets, Jets, Guided Missiles & Space Ships* iii. [28/1] Later the [U.S.] Navy built its own improved version of the V-1, called the 'Loon'. It can be launched from a submarine far at sea in a surprise attack against a harbor or convoy. **1952** *Jane's Fighting Ships 1952–53* 410/1 'Loon' missile is contained in a watertight steel hangar and takes off from a ramp fixed to the submarine's deck.

loon (lūn), *sb.*[4] *colloq.* [f. the vb.] *pl.* A style of close-fitting casual trousers widely flared from the knees to the ankles. Also (in *sing.*) *attrib.*, as *loon pants, trousers.*

1971 *Melody Maker* 13 Nov. 50 (Advt.), New velvet and cord loon pants with 28″ flare... New cotton drill loons and military trousers. **1972** *Guardian* 15 Aug. 17/3 As dead as tucked up loon pants. **1974** 'D. CRAIG' *Whose Little Girl are You?* v. 94 They had bloody long-hairs in the police now and kids in loon trousers. **1974** D. WINSOR *Death Convention* xii. 98, I wriggled into a pair of brown velvet loons, dropped a cream lace tunic over them.

loon (lūn), *v.* [Etym. unknown.] *intr.* Esp. of young people: to spend one's leisure time in a pleasurable way, e.g. by dancing to popular music; to lie *about* or wander *about*. So **loo·ner**, one who loons; **loo·ning** *vbl. sb.* Cf. *LOON *sb.*[4]

1966 *Melody Maker* 30 July 8/6 The younger members of the MM staff spend a lot of time doing something called 'looning'. To judge by their general condition the next morning I gather this is what used to be known as 'raving'. **1969** *It* 4–17 July 12/2 It's sort of music essentially to loon about to. **1969** *Daily Tel.* 14 July 11 (*heading*) Long enough to loon in. *Ibid.*, A fashion designer..has just completed his first collection of clothes aimed purely for after work. He calls them 'looning' clothes. **1969** *Melody Maker* 13 Sept. 12/4 In the company of looners like Eric Burdon and Brian Auger, Zoot was the king looner. Zoot became a much beloved symbol of good fun and good time music. **1971** *It* 2–16 June 21/3 Children and the younger adults alike looning about in wonderful costumes.

loony, luny, *a.* and *sb.* Add: **c. loony bin** [*BIN *sb.* 7], a facetious term for a mental hospital; also *fig.* and *ellipt.*; **loony-doctor** *slang*, a doctor who treats mental illnesses, a psychiatrist.

1919 WODEHOUSE *My Man Jeeves* 195 If you're absolutely off your rocker, but don't find it convenient to be scooped into a luny-bin, you simply explain..it was just your Artistic Temperament. **1921** —— *Indiscretions of Archie* xxv. 303 Nine out of ten of them had views on Art which would have admitted them to any looney-bin, and no questions asked. **1938** J. PHELAN *Lifer* xix. 201 Left him behind us there, we did, stone balmy. Finished in a loony. **1942** N. STREATFEILD *I ordered Table for Six* 216 Mrs. Framley must have thought him fit for a looney bin. **1959** *New Statesman* 28 Mar. 434/3 In short, I do not want men to live for ever in a sort of global loony-bin. **1962** J. SYMONDS *Bezill* 68 Yes, Aunt Marion. She's locked up, you know, in the looney bin. **1974** *Times* 9 Feb. 10/4 (*heading*) In the looney bin. **1925** WODEHOUSE *Carry on, Jeeves!* vi. 139 Old Sir Roderick, who's a loony-doctor and nothing but a loony-doctor, however much you may call him a nerve-specialist. **1936** BENTLEY & ALLEN *Trent's Own Case* iv. 39 'Once, I remember, he said that the worst of these loony-doctors——.' 'Did he say "loony-doctors"?' **1960** WODEHOUSE *Jeeves in Offing* ii. 18 She's browsing with Sir Roderick Glossop, the loony-doctor.

loop, *sb.*[1] Add: **1. e.** *U.S.* The looped portion of a lasso. **f.** = NOOSE *sb.* 1.

1907 S. E. WHITE *Arizona Nights* I. v. 93 Some few whirled the loop, but most cast it with a quick flip. **1933**, etc. [see *HONDA]. **1944** *Living off Land* vii. 138 Knots.. nooses (or loops). **1970** G. R. STEWART *Amer. Place-Names* 264/1 *Loop* Texas: so called because the post-master-to-be, at the time of suggesting a name, was playing with the loop of his lasso.

4. d. (ii) *Electr.* A point on an aerial at which the current or the voltage is a maximum.

1922 GLAZEBROOK *Dict. Appl. Physics* II. 1034/1 A standing wave forms on the simple antenna just as in an organ-pipe with stopped end, there being a node of current at the upper end and a loop at the earthed connection. **1928** [see *FEEDER 10 b]. **1968** *Radio Communication Handbk.* (ed. 4) xiii. 3/1 At positions of current loops, the current-to-voltage ratio is high and the wire will behave as a low impedance circuit.

e. Add to def.: Hence in *Electr.*, any complete circuit or path for a current.

1909 WEBSTER, *Loop*, a complete electric circuit. **1922** GLAZEBROOK *Dict. Appl. Physics* II. 659/1 If a stout wire be temporarily used to connect the two banks of plates inside, the condenser may be measured as a loop at telephonic frequencies. **1967** *Electronics* 6 Mar. 132/1 The feedback loop is formed by connecting the amplifier's inverting input (pin 2) to potentiometer. **1970** J. EARL *Tuners & Amplifiers* iv. 95 Small mains currents can flow in the loops formed by the several earths, and these can induce hum into the system.

f. Also, a similar path described by an aeroplane. (Cf. *LOOP *v.*[1] 6.) Phr. *to knock* [KNOCK *v.* 6 e] *for a loop* and varr.

1913 *Aeroplane* 25 Sept. 350/2 M. Pégoud succeeded in looping the loop completely. **1923** *Cosmopolitan* Apr. 84/1 It took Hurricane Sherlock just two boisterous rounds to smite 12-Punch O'Bernstein 'for a loop', as Hurricane put it. **1936** J. G. BRANDON *Pawnshop Murder* v. 46 Something had happened which had knocked even the imperturbable Wibley for the loop. **1968** J. WAINWRIGHT *Web of Silence* 126 Have you lost your marbles, Pewter?.. Have you gone for a complete loop? **1969** E. AMBLER *Intercom Conspiracy* (1970) vi. 110, I was really confused. That memorandum threw me for a loop. **1971** *Country Life* 18 Feb. 374/2 It was over Tewkesbury that I pointed my nose at the Mill and did my first loop. **1973** D. RAMSAY *Deadly Discretion* 153 That little charade of hers had knocked him for a loop.

g. *Skating.* A curve crossing itself, or any of several elaborations upon this.

1869 VANDERVELL & WITHAM *Syst. Figure-Skating* x. 187 The Large Loop. This being done entirely on one edge throughout, requires some medium degree of speed. **1901** *Encycl. Sport* IV. 370/1 Loops are of three kinds—the ordinary variety, the turn loop, and the bracket loop. **1935** *Encycl. Sports* 560/1 'Loop' is effected by over-balancing the body and recovering equilibrium by a quick turn of the foot. **1962** T. D. RICHARDSON *Art of Figure Skating* vii. 60 Loops are not skated in the normal positions..and what is more, they require an entirely different timing. **1973** *Times* 7 Feb. 15/8 Hoffmann was fourth in the rocker but skated the best loops.

h. A configuration in finger-prints.

1880 H. FAULDS in *Nature* 28 Oct. 605/1 The right ring-finger..has an oval whorl, but the corresponding left finger shows an open loop. **1894** 'MARK TWAIN' in *Century Mag.* June 235 The bewildering maze of whorls or curves or loops which constituted the 'pattern' of a 'record' stand out bold and black. **1938** G. W. WILTON *Fingerprints* xvi. 78 Galton had experimented only with thumbprints, grouping his lineations into three classes of arches, loops and whorls. **1970** P. LAURIE *Scotland Yard* ix. 193 There are two basic finger-print patterns: loops, where the lines turn through two right angles, and triradii.

i. A slack length of film, flexible strip, or the like left between two mechanisms to allow for a difference between the supply and take-up motions, esp. (in cinematographic equipment) one between a sprocket that turns continuously and one that turns intermittently.

1912 F. A. TALBOT *Moving Pict.* vii. 70 A slight loop is made at either end of the gate. **1939** SPENCER & WALEY *Cinema To-Day* ii. 25 A flickering motion of these loops absorbs the difference between the steady feed of the sprocket wheels and the intermittent feed of the claw. **1962** G. A. T. BURDETT *Automatic Control Handbk.* ix. 54 When metal strip is being wound or reeled it is usual to form loops in the feed line to allow for flexibility and avoid undue tension.

j. = *loop aerial* (see *6).

1922 GLAZEBROOK *Dict. Appl. Physics* II. 1058/1 Before the advent of high amplification, it was impracticable to use single loops of manageable dimensions. **1936** *Jrnl. R. Aeronaut. Soc.* XL. 175 To obtain a full direction finding service, it is usual to instal an external circular loop which can be rotated and orientated by the operator when taking a bearing. **1966** *McGraw-Hill Encycl. Sci. & Technol.* I. 445/2 Use of small loops concealed within the set is a standard practice for broadcast receivers in areas where signal strength is high.

k. A length of film or magnetic tape whose ends have been joined to form an endless strip, so that continuous repetition of the recording is made possible (e.g. in rehearsing the synchronization required for dubbing a foreign-language sound track).

1931 K. F. MORGAN in L. Cowan *Recording Sound for Motion Pict.* x. 151 The machine is provided with a film elevator attachment for running a continuous loop of sound track. This attachment is particularly useful for the dubbing of continuous background sounds. **1951** R. SPOTTISWOODE *Film & its Techniques* xii. 355 It is most important [in dubbing]..not to upset the recording order of an emotional scene which has had to be broken down into several loops. **1959** HALAS & MANVELL *Technique Film Animation* xix. 216 Each pencil-test is shot on negative and projected in loops so that it can be viewed over and over again. **1962** A. NISBETT *Technique Sound Studio* 258 A tape loop may be used (*a*) to provide a repeated sound structure or rhythm (in radiophonics), (*b*) for an 'atmosphere' track where this is regular in quality, (*c*) in tape delay techniques. **1968** *Punch* 31 Jan. 153 At the Rank Organisation's Pinewood Studios they tell how Sophia Loren dubbed sixty-four loops in an hour and a half, against an average of ten or twelve loops an hour.

l. A sequence of control operations or activities in which each depends on the result of the previous one; *esp.* (more fully *closed loop*), one in which there is feedback, the result of a later operation being made to affect

one earlier in the sequence, usu. so as to maintain the output at a desired level.

1945 L. A. MacColl *Fund. Theory Servomechanisms* viii. 70 This procedure of adding feedback loops to internal parts of a servomechanism is employed frequently when it is necessary to take special steps to insure that the performances of those parts shall be accurate and reliable. **1948** Brown & Campbell *Princ. Servomechanisms* vii. 227 Figure..shows internal loop within a main closed loop. **1954** M. H. Lajoy *Industr. Automatic Controls* i. 9 The automatic washing machine which operates on a time basis and is not dependent upon whether or not the clothes are clean is an open loop system. **1962** F. I. Ordway et al. *Basic Astronautics* ix. 366 There are two basic control systems: the open-loop system and the closed-loop system. The open-loop system is familiar to us all. Examples of this are..a light switch, or the horn button on an automobile... In the closed-loop system a portion of the output is sensed and fed back to the input. The input is then altered to achieve a co-ordinated response at the output... A good example is the modern air conditioning system in which room air is fed back to the thermostat control. **1971** J. Z. Young *Introd. Study Man* vii. 107 Certain cells in the hypothalamus..are very sensitive to slight rises in temperature above the normal (37°C). They then discharge nerve impulses that set in action the mechanisms that cool the body, such as sweating. This cools the blood and switches off the hypothalamus. In order to study such closed-loop feedback systems engineers use the device of 'opening' the loop. This has been done..by putting heating electrodes in the hypothalamus and arranging that they keep it at a constant temperature a few tenths of a degree above normal in spite of the cooling blood.

m. *Computers.* A sequence of instructions which is executed repeatedly (usu. with an operand that changes in each cycle) until some previously specified criterion is satisfied.

1947 Goldstine & von Neumann in J. von Neumann *Coll. Works* (1963) V. 86 When a simple induction takes place, C travels during each step of the induction over a certain path, at the end of which it returns to its beginning. Hence this path may be visualized as a loop. We will call it an induction loop or a simple induction loop. **1954** *First Gloss. Programming Terminol.* (Assoc. Computing Machinery) 12 *Loop*, the repetition of a group of instructions in a routine. **1955** R. K. Richards *Arithmetic Operations in Digital Computers* xii. 359 Any one program may contain many loops which may interlock one another in a complex manner. **1964** C. Dent *Quantity Surveying by Computer* iii. 28 It will be seen that *s* in instruction 4 is reduced by unity at every cycle of the loop, by reason of instruction 7, and that eventually..the conditional jump instruction will decide that the number stored by instruction 5 is negative. Control then proceeds with the next sequence according to instruction 9. **1969** P. B. Jordain *Condensed Computer Encycl.* 294 The terminating condition test is usually the last instruction of the loop, but it may be anywhere. **1970** O. Dopping *Computers & Data Processing* xiv. 215 Loops..are basic to the economy of automatic data processing. It costs a few dollars to have an instruction written, but the computer executes it at a price which may be only a fraction of a cent below what the same operation would cost if it were executed by a human being. The only way of amortizing programming is to arrange for most instructions to be repeated a great number of times.

n. *Nuclear Engin.* A system of pipes passing through or associated with a reactor that forms a closed circuit (under operating conditions).

1957 *New Scientist* 23 May 33/1 The chemical behaviour of such systems has to be investigated in a reactor by passing a pipe containing a portion of the system under investigation through or close to the reactor core. Such a pipe, with the necessary measuring equipment, is called a test loop. **1958** H. Etherington *Nucl. Engin. Handbk.* v. 142 To satisfy the demand for testing operation under conditions of high temperature and pressure in those reactors using a primary water loop, high-pressure loops have been developed. Questions of fuel stability, heat transfer, water chemistry, radiation-accelerated corrosion, fission-product leakage, and fuel stability under desired operating conditions may be answered in high-pressure water loops. **1974** *Times* 21 Jan. 15/2 The CEGB's first two plants..would be the 52nd and 53rd of their type—the Westinghouse four-loop design, in which a single reactor is linked to four steam-generating boilers. **1974** *Encycl. Brit. Macropædia* XII. 897/1 Pressurized water both cools the reactor and carries away the fission-produced heat through the primary system (or loop) to a heat exchanger. .. The pressurized water then circulates back through the reactor in a constant cycle. In the secondary loop (which is sealed off from the radioactive primary coolant water) the water boils and expands into steam.

o. A type of intra-uterine contraceptive device. Cf. *Lippes loop.

1962 [see *Lippes loop]. **1965** *Guardian* 28 May 6/3 The medical council has authorized the intra-uterine contraceptive device... The IUCD would nearly always prevent pregnancy... The 'loops'..cost only a few pence. **1967** *Times* 9 Oct. 4/4 [Pakistan] Although the 1970 target of 500,000 vasectomies and five million loop insertions might seem low,..the main object was to retard or halt the growing birth rate. **1971** *Petticoat* 17 July 6/4 There's one excellent method (the coil or loop) only suitable for someone who's already had a baby. **1974** *Guardian* 25 Mar. 10 Will the loop make your periods more painful? If you have comfortable periods before you have a loop fitted, you are unlikely to develop painful periods afterwards.

6. *loop-handle, -head, -lock, method, -net, road, system, way*; **loop aerial, antenna** *Radio*, an aerial consisting of one or more loops of wire; **loop film,** a loop (sense *4 k) of cinematographic film; **loop-line,** (*a*): for 3 c read 4 e; (examples); **loop pile** (see quot. 1963); **loop-stitch**: also as *v. trans.*, to connect or attach by means of loop-stitches; so **loop-stitching,** such work; **loop system,** a method of connecting electrical supply points (as lamp roses) by taking the wires to each point from terminals at its switch and at the previous supply point, instead of making a separate joint elsewhere in the circuit; **loop yarn** (see quot. 1940).

1913 *Year-Bk. Wireless Telegr.* 314 For the directive aerial, the writer had been employing a closed circuit or loop aerial, tuned with a condenser. **1966** J. P. Hawker *Outl. Radio & Television* xxii. 367 The main advantage of the loop aerial is the two sharp null positions as the loop is rotated, occurring when the plane of the loop is parallel to the wave front. **1968** M. Woodhouse *Rock Baby* xiii. 131, I packed the D.F. set, the loop aerial, and the little transceiver into my rucksack. **1906** J. A. Fleming *Princ. Electr. Wave Telegr.* iv. 280 (*caption*) Stationary potential oscillations set up on loop antennæ. **1932** F. E. Terman *Radio Engin.* xvi. 588 All practical direction-finding systems make use of a loop antenna. **1968** A. L. Weeks *Antenna Engin.* ii. 56 Small loop antennas are frequently employed for low-frequency receiving applications. **1940** *Chambers's Techn. Dict.* 510/2 *Loop film*, the same as band film or cycle film. **1957** *Oxf. Pocket Bk. Athletic Training* (ed. 2) 9 Get a loop film taken of your technique at normal and slow motion speeds. **1949** W. F. Albright *Archaeol. of Palestine* vi. 115 These craters were supplied with two tilted horizontal loop-handles. **1969** E. H. Pinto *Treen* 387 Some 19th-century planes have 17th-century type 'loop' handles. **1876** J. S. Ingram *Centenn. Exposition* ix. 318 These were the larger and most important part of the exhibit, while the rest was made up of..prop nuts, loop heads, offsets and stay ends. **1859** G. A. Sala *Twice round Clock* 261 Then from the beginning of Italian opera in England, a grand trunk line extending to our days, I shunt off on to innumerable little branches and loop-lines. **1869** *Bradshaw's Railway Manual* XXI. 115 A loop line from Peterborough, through Boston and Lincoln, rejoining the main line at Retford. **1908** *Daily Chron.* 16 May 1/5 The loop-line railway linking up all the railway termini. **1956** *Railway Mag.* Nov. 745/1 The up main and goods loop lines were destroyed or heavily damaged for about 70 yd. **1970** *Ibid.* Oct. 585/2 Passenger trains were diverted over the loop line via Lochwinnoch which is rarely used by other than freight services. **1888** G. M. Hopkins *Poems* (1918) 90 Then with loop-locks Forward falling..his twiny boots Fast he opens. **1901** L. W. Waterhouse *Conduit Wiring* 51 The wiring in this building has been carried out entirely on the 'loop' method, there being no joints in any of the wires or cables. **1869** *Game Laws Illinois* in *Fur, Fin & Feather* (1872) 175 That it shall be unlawful..to take or catch fish..by means of any seine, gill-net, tramel net, pike-net, or loop-net. **1924** R. Beaumont *Carpets & Rugs* vii. 262 The loop pile may wear flat or bare, but it remains part of the carpet structure. **1963** *Which?* Mar. 69/1 A loop pile carpet has closed loops while a cut pile has the top of the loop cut open. **1909** *Daily Mail* 5 Aug. 5/2 To construct loop-roads for fast motor traffic round villages. **1960** *New Left Rev.* July–Aug. 23/1 Loop roads for buses would penetrate some distance into the pedestrian precinct. **1963** *Times* 7 Mar. 7/4 Whether the town is to have a loop road or.. the High Street is to be widened. **1973** M. Yorke *Grave Matters* iv. ii. 76 He took the loop road that led away from the village. **1932** D. C. Minter *Mod. Needlecraft* 189/1 In fig. 30 the patch edge..is loop-stitched to the paper. **1951** *Good Housek. Home Encycl.* 213/2 The wrong side of the garment is neatened by loopstitching the two raw edges together. **1969** *Jane's Freight Containers 1968–69* 544/1 One such hook and, at the other end, loop-stitching for permanent fixing to container sides. **1896** R. Robb *Electr. Wiring* v. 119 The object of confining this construction to the loop system is to prevent joints being made in concealed places. **1925** G. A. Willoughby *House Wiring* ii. 73 The loop system of wiring does away with this possibility of fire, because the wires are looped from outlet to outlet and all joints are made within outlet boxes. **1929** *Times* 1 Nov. 18/3 Traffic proceeding towards London is being diverted at Hatton cross roads, *via* Cranford-lane to the Bath road and London (A.A. loop-way). *Ibid.*, A.A. loop-way signs. **1940** *Chambers's Techn. Dict.* 511/1 *Loop yarn*, a fancy yarn, with small loops; composed of three threads folded together, one of which is an effect thread and forms the loops, which are bound by another thread. **1957** Simpson & Weir *Weaver's Craft* (ed. 8) xvi. 214 *Curl or Loop Yarn* is made by turning a comparatively thick thread around a much finer ground thread so as to form a succession of curls or loops along the surface of the yarn. **1964** [see *bouclé *a.*].

loop, *v.*[1] Add: **5.** (Earlier example.)

1837 J. Kirkbride *Northern Angler* 3 Loop on the dropper-flies; the tail-fly should also be looped.

b. **loop in.** *trans.* (i) To connect into an electric circuit by the loop system.

1893 W. J. Hopkins *Telephone Lines & their Properties* xiii. 203 It was the custom..to 'loop in' the several telephones, that is, to place them in series. **1899** W. P. Maycock *Electr. Wiring* iii. 242 At A, three lamps *L* and switches *S* are 'looped in' to one fuse *F*. **1965** J. H. M. Sykes *Beginner's Guide Electr. Wiring* v. 113 Lighting circuits may be looped in, using three-plate ceiling roses, to avoid the necessity for joints.

(ii) To form (a wire) into a loop and insert it into a terminal.

1911 A. Bursill *Princ. & Pract. Electr. Wiring* vi. 37 The wires must never be cut where they are looped-in. **1952** W. E. Steward *Mod. Wiring Pract.* 140 Frequently, the description of this [*sc.* looping-in] system given in books on wiring methods tends to create a false impression in the mind of the reader. From these descriptions it would appear that one length of cable is bared at intervals and looped in at switch and lighting terminals. In practice, when wiring in conduit, the two lengths of wire forming the loop are threaded in separately and the junction is made at the switch, light, or other terminal. **1967** G. A. T. Burdett *Electr. Installations* 226 (*heading*) Looping-in the cable.

6. *to loop the loop*, to perform the feat of circling in a vertical loop, orig. on a specially prepared track (see Loop *sb.*[1] 4 f), later in an aeroplane. Also *transf.*, *fig.*, and as *sb.*

Orig. a fairground phrase.

1902 *Strand Mag.* June 708 (*heading*) Looping the loop on a bicycle. *Ibid.* 708/1 'Looping the loop' in America has become even more popular than shooting the chutes. *Ibid.* 708/2 At first he could not induce the ball to loop the loop. **1903** G. Bell *Let.* 8 July (1927) I. 166 We went on a switchback that looped the loop... Hugo..was distinctly conscious of being upside down..for the fraction of a second. **1903** *Outing* XLII. 552/1 He knows how to win the steeplechase..and has been 'thrown out' for standing up in the loop-the-loops. [**1908** A. Bazin in *L'Aérophile* 15 May, Pourquoi pas 'looping the loop' tout de suite?] **1911** A. P. Thurston *Elem. Aeronaut.* iii. 33 A glider..can be made to 'loop the loop', or follow any curve of a number of curved paths. **1913** [see *loop *sb.*[1] 4 f]. **1922** A. S. Eddington *Theory of Relativity* 3 The planets literally looped the loop in fantastic curves called epicycles. **1922** Wodehouse *Clicking of Cuthbert* ix. 209 A girl of such pronounced beauty that Ramsden Waters' heart looped the loop twice in rapid succession. **1935** [see *falling *ppl. a.* 5 b]. **1940** O. Nash *Face is Familiar* (1954) 10 It's pleasant to loop the loop, To daringly seize The flying trapeze With a cry of Allez-oop! **1960** B. Keaton *Wonderful World of Slapstick* (1967) 73 The climax of the act came when he started doing loop the loops, riding upside down. **1961** [see *aerobatics *sb. pl.*]. **1968** *Michelin Guide N.Y. City* 124 Coney Island..scenic railways, loop-the-loops and Ferris wheels compete with phantom trains, tunnels of love, sputniks.

7. *intr. Computers.* To execute a loop (*loop *sb.*[1] 4 m).

1958 Gotlieb & Hume *High-Speed Data Processing* vi. 98 A common procedure is to use one sequence of instructions, cycling or looping through this sequence as often as required. **1969** P. B. Jordain *Condensed Computer Encycl.* 293 The ability to loop, and thus reuse instructions without duplicating them and wasting memory, is probably the single most important advantage gained by stored-program computers.

loop, *v.*[3] [f. Loop *sb.*[2] Cf. Looped *ppl. a.*[2]] *trans.* To furnish with loop-holes.

1846 Z. Taylor *Let.* 9 Nov. in *N.Y. Morn. Express* (1847) 22 Jan. 2/3 The houses are of stone..all looped up for musketry.

‖ **loop** (lōᵘp), *int. S. Afr.* [Afrikaans, f. Du. imp. of *lopen* to walk.] A word of command to an animal to move forward.

1811 W. J. Burchell *Jrnl.* 18 June in *Trav. S. Africa* (1822) I. viii. 169 Philip mounted his seat,..with an animated voice calling out to the oxen, *Loop!* **1927** W. Plomer *I Speak of Afr.* i. 40 'Loop!' he ordered in a loud voice. Shilling cracked his whip and shouted to the oxen. The voorlooper's head could just be seen through a forest of horns. **1937** F. B. Young *They seek a Country* ii. i. 162 'Ay, Blauwberg, would you?' (The long lash curled in the air like a salmon cast and stung the off-leader's muzzle.) '*Loop*, you devils, *loop*!'

looped, *ppl. a.*[1] Add: **5.** Intoxicated, drunk. *slang* (chiefly *U.S.*).

1934 in M. H. Weseen *Dict. Amer. Slang* xviii. 279. **1951** 'M. Spillane' *Big Kill* ii. 46 The sap sounded half-looped. **1959** A. Bailey *Making Progress* vi. 63 Slater..was almost looped on the Veuve Clicquot. **1962** J. Potts *Evil Wish* ii. 28 Joe had gotten looped and called here. **1973** 'R. Macdonald' *Sleeping Beauty* xxxviii. 221 The message ..didn't come through too clear. She talked as if she was slightly looped.

looper[1]. Add: **1.** Also *attrib.*

1840 J. & M. Loudon tr. *Köllar's Treat. Insects* iii. 212 The most ruinous insect for fruit-trees is assuredly the green looper-caterpillar. **1932** E. Step *Bees, Wasps, Ants* 184 A more striking..case is that of some 'looper' caterpillar,..from which a hundred *Microgaster* larvæ have broken out. **1964** V. B. Wigglesworth *Life of Insects* x. 149 We have a whole series of insect larvae, of Noctuid moths, of 'looper' or Geometrid caterpillars, saw-fly larvae and others, all of which resemble pine needles.

3. *Aeronaut.* One who loops the loop, or who has done so; a machine specially adapted for looping the loop.

1914 *Aeroplane* 15 Jan. 63/1 Two more names have been added to the roll of loopers. *Ibid.* 12 Mar. 284/2 Mr. Hucks..first flew his two-seater, and later on the 'looper' at 700 feet, made one loop.

loop-in. [f. vbl. phr. *to loop in* (see *loop *v.*[1] 5 b).] A connection between two lengths of wire made at a terminal in the loop system. Usu. *attrib.*, as *loop-in system* = *loop system* (s.v. *loop *sb.*[1] 6).

1908 *Installation News* II. 86/2 In comparing the third method with the second, which is the usual method of loop-in wiring adopted, it will be found that there is a saving of wire in the new method. **1911** A. Bursill *Princ. & Pract. Electr. Wiring* vi. 35 Fig. 18 shows four lamps connected in parallel on the loop-in system. **1960** E. L. Delmar-Morgan *Cruising Yacht Equipment & Navigation* xvii. 187 Even with the 'loop in' system one or at most two pairs of fuses will be sufficient. **1967** G. A. T. Burdett *Electr. Installations* 224 To overcome the inherent dangers of using an ordinary three-plate ceiling rose as a looping-in point for the live feed an entirely new purpose-made loop-in ceiling rose has been introduced.

Ibid. 226 More recent patterns..have a fourth terminal which is intended for the earth continuity conductor loop-in.

looping, *vbl. sb.*[1] Add: (Later examples.)

1914 *Isis* (Oxf.) 28 Feb. 5/1 The 'looping' looked simplicity itself. A sudden plunge straight towards the earth ..a sudden reversal and a perpendicular climb, which gradually brought the airman upside down and..a second downward plunge. 1929 E. Wilson *I thought of Daisy* III. 123 'I'm not out for any looping,' said Daisy... 'I think I'll go home and go to bed.' 1964 E. Bach *Introd. Transformational Gram.* iii. 46 Care must be taken to ensure that unwanted recursion (looping) does not occur.

c. looping in (cf. *loop *v.*[1] 5 b), connection by the loop system.

1899 W. P. Maycock *Electr. Wiring* iii. 243 The advantages of looping-in, as applied to the interconnection of switches and ceiling roses. 1902 F. C. Raphael *'Electrician' Wireman's Pocket Bk.* 33 (*caption*) Simplex looping-in ceiling rose. 1930 —— *Electr. Wiring of Buildings* ii. 23 Looping in has become absolutely general, for not only does it save the danger of bad joints, but it is actually less expensive than to make joints. 1967 [see *loop-in].

looping, *ppl. a.* Add: Also *looping caterpillar* = Looper[1] 1.

1875 Huxley & Martin *Course Elem. Biol.* x. 95 The polypes..are capable of crawling about by a motion similar to that of the looping caterpillar.

loopist (lū·pist). *rare.* [f. *loop *v.*[1] 6 + -ist.] = *looper[1] 3.

1914 *Aeroplane* 15 Jan. 63/1 One of the latest loopists is M. Galtier, who on January 7th looped the loop at Chateaufort.

loopy, *a.* Add: **3.** *slang.* Crazy, 'cracked'.

1925 Fraser & Gibbons *Soldier & Sailor Words* 147 *Loopy*, silly, daft. 1928 E. Waugh *Decline & Fall* I. xiii. 145 He'll get off on a plea of insanity. Loopy, you know. 1942 'M. Innes' *Daffodil Affair* II. 40 One does not want a loopy colleague when embarked upon so distinctly rummy an investigation as the present. 1957 I. Cross *God Boy* (1958) vi. 44 Honestly, the pair of them were looking at me as though I was loopy. 1961 P. White *Riders in Chariot* iv. 88 'I will not waste my breath arguing with loopy Louie,' replied Mrs Jolley. 1970 *New Yorker* 15 Aug. 68/2 The wife..is mad neither in the sense of loopy nor in the sense of furious. 1973 A. Hunter *Gently French* xiv. 125 He was loopy over her. If she said jump, he'd fall off a cliff.

loorie, var. *loerie.

loose, *a.* Add: **1. a.** *spec.* of horses etc.: allowed to run free in travelling or marching.

1845 J. C. Frémont *Rep. Exploring Expedition* 10 A few loose horses, and four oxen..completed the train. 1843 *Oregon Hist. Soc. Q.* (1901) II. 191 About fifty wagons, with those who had large droves of loose cattle, now left. 1846 W. G. D. Stewart *Altowan* II. i. 41 The neighing of the loose troops, that ever and anon, broke forward to snatch the opportunity of browsing ere the crowd advanced. 1885 *Outing* VII. 21/2 All drove pack and loose animals before them.

l. Of money, cash, etc.: in relatively small denominations; in coins (as opp. to notes). So *loose change* (orig. *U.S.*), a quantity of coins kept or left in one's pocket, etc., for casual use.

1811 Jane Austen *Sense & Sens.* I. xvii. 217 My loose cash would..be employed in improving my collection of music and books. 1827 A. Sherwood *Gazetteer Georgia* 112 It would be a kind of generous charity, to leave with the tavern-keepers..some of the loose change. 1872 E. Eggleston *End of World* 173 Unless he means to part with all his loose change. 1895 A. Machen *Three Imposters* 81 He never returned, but his watch and chain, a purse containing three sovereigns in gold, and some loose silver, with a ring..were found three days later. 1927 C. A. Siringo *Riata & Spurs* v. 54 That little burg saw the need of saloons and dance-halls to relieve the cowboy of his loose change. 1950 Wilkinson & Frisby *They're Open* ii. 19 *Capacious left-hand pocket*,..in order that a large bulk of loose change may be carried. 1970 G. F. Newman *Sir, You Bastard* viii. 245 He got rid of the loose change in his pocket. 1973 *Woman's Own* 4 Aug. 36 (Advt.), The clip-to coin section is just the right size for all your loose change.

m. *Gram.* Of certain syntactical elements: not essential to the meaning or construction, etc.

1932 E. Kruisinga *Handbk. Present Day Eng.* (ed. 5) II. III. 235 The members of a loose group may be connected by other words or not... We distinguish *linked* groups and *unlinked* groups. 1933 O. Jespersen *Essent. Eng. Gram.* xxxiv. 357 A non-restrictive (or loose) clause, ..may be left out without injury to the precise meaning of the word it is joined to, as in 'The Prince of Wales, who happened to be there, felt sorry for the prisoners.' 1961 R. B. Long *Sentence & its Parts* iii. 68 They [*sc.* subordinate interrogatives] function also as loose adjuncts... We went with Larry, *who knew everyone.* 1972 Hartmann & Stork *Dict. Lang. & Ling.* 135 *Loose apposition*, a word or phrase used in apposition and often separated by sustained juncture in speech or by commas in writing.

3. a. (Later example.)

1908 *Animal Managem.* 17 The skin..when handled, should feel 'loose' and freely movable over the structures beneath.

9. loose back, a method of binding the spine of a book to make it open more easily; **loose body** *Med.* = *joint mouse* (*joint *sb.* 15); usu. *pl.*; **loose coupling** *Electr.* (see *coupling *vbl. sb.* 6 f (i)); **loose cover,** a detachable cover for a chair, couch, or car seat; also *attrib.*; **loose-fill, loose fill,** a type of house insulation (see quot. 1964); also *attrib.*; **loose head,** see *head *sb.* 26 c; **loose-housing,** a method of housing cattle in winter in partly covered barns with access to a feeding area, in which the cows are not confined to a single stall; also *attrib.*; hence **loose-housed** *a.*; **loose scrummage, loose scrum,** in *Rugby Football*, a scrum formed by the players round the ball during play, and not ordered by the referee: opp. *set scrum*(*mage*); hence, **loose scrummaging; loose smut,** a disease of cereals, esp. barley and wheat, caused by the fungus *Ustilago nuda*; **loose whale,** a whale which remains beside its harpooned mate.

1923 H. A. Maddox *Dict. Stationery* 46 *Loose back*, also termed open or spring back. *Ibid.* 47 A loose back may be created by simply casing the book... The spring or loose back is actually bound into the book. 1956 *Bookman's Conc. Dict.* 277 *Spring Back*, an inner joint in a bookbinding which allows the book to open flat; known as Hollow or Loose Back. 1961 T. Landau *Encycl. Librarianship* (ed. 2) 268/2 *Open back*, a style of construction in which the cover is separated from the spine of the book by a special lining... Also called Hollow and Loose Back. 1886 H. Marsh *Dis. Joints* xv. 185 On examining his joint when the acute attack has gone off, the patient detects the loose body, and learns that it shifts its position. *Ibid.* 183 (*caption*) Specimens of the loose bodies found in the knee joint in Mr. Smith's case. 1952 [see *joint mouse* s.v. *joint *sb.* 15]. 1961 R. D. Baker *Essent. Path.* xxi. 578 Portions of the damaged articular cartilage, or fragments of the thickened peripheral bone, break off and become loose bodies in the joint cavities. 1876 M. W. Cook *Tables & Chairs* i. 52 You may prefer to have your curtains, as well as the loose covers, of chintz. *Ibid.* 56 Nothing now-a-days looks so nice and ladylike, or is so economical as well-fitting loose covers. 1911 F. B. Jack *Woman's Bk.* 613/2 Loose covers are not much used nowadays, and, at the best, they soon get out of order and become shabby looking. 1929 *Radio Times* 8 Nov. 438/1 Odd Jobs about the House—II, A Few Hints on Loose Cover Cutting. 1936 R. Lehmann *Weather in Streets* I. v. 104, I might keep her on for the sewing. She's very clever at loose covers. 1953 M. Sheridan *Furnisher's Encycl.* IX. iii. 414 A loose cover service may substantially increase the furnisher's business. 1959 *B.S.I. News* Nov. 20 Specifies..maximum foreign matter content for..loose cover cloths made from cotton. 1973 A. Broinowski *Take One Ambassador* xii. 206 Comfortable upholstery, not bottomlessly soft, with well-cut linen loose covers. [1949 *Building Digest* IX. 305 The flat roof has..a loose vermiculite filling.] 1950 *Archit. Rev.* CVIII. 332/2 A 4 in. thickness of vermiculite loosefill for instance has the same thermal insulation as 24 times that thickness of concrete. 1956 *Good Housek. Home Encycl.* (ed. 4) 170/2 'Loose fill' which is poured or packed.. between the joists. 1964 J. S. Scott *Dict. Building* 198 *Loose-fill insulation*, insulating materials such as granulated cork, loose asbestos..vermiculite. Loose fill is placed between rafters or studs to increase the insulating value of a dry air space. 1969 *Daily Tel.* 16 Sept. 15 Most householders can climb into their lofts and lay mineral wool or glass fibre over the joists, or loose-fill between them. 1907 'Old International' *Rugby Guide* 62 It was discovered that on the flank of the row where the ball came into the scrum there was a head overhanging the side of the scrum. This head was given the appellation of 'loose head'. 1917 [see *head *sb.* 26 c]. 1927 [see *hooker[1] 6]. 1960 C. Venables *Instructions to Young Rugger Players* iii. 37 When the two scrummages are formed they pack down and, of course, the heads of the two front rows are interlocked. But, with three men in each row, this clearly means that one man in each row will have his head free. This is known as the 'loose head' and it is on that side that the scrum half will put the ball in, for the good reason that his own hooker will be nearer to the ball than the hooker on the other side. 1960 E. S. & W. J. Higham *High Speed Rugby* xiv. 191 The *loose-head prop* puts the *inside* foot forward. *Ibid.* 195 We will refer to the hooker who has the loose head..as the 'loose-head hooker'. 1960 *Farmer & Stockbreeder* 5 Jan. 53/1 Half [the herd] is loose-housed and zero-grazed. *Ibid.* 12 Jan. 78/1 Three sides of the yard accommodating the 55 pedigree..Friesians loose-housed are filled by the covered lying shed. 1963 C. T. M. Herriott tr. *Craplet's Dairy Cow* v. xvii. 374 Loose-housed animals are less nervous than those kept in byres. 1946 *Agric. Engineering* XXVII. 499/2 The loose-housing barn and milking parlor seemed to offer a possible improvement. 1948 *Pop. Bull. Washington Agric. Exper. Station* No. 190 (*title*) The loose housing and feeding of dairy herds. *Ibid.* 2 Loose housing is becoming popular. 1963 C. T. M. Herriott tr. *Craplet's Dairy Cow* v. xvii. 369 Loose housing provides a well-compacted, thoroughly decomposed manure. *Ibid.*, Cows to be kept under a loose housing system can become accustomed to communal living. 1874 G. H. West *Rugby Union Football Ann.* 66 A light and very useful forward, especially in a loose scrummage. 1936 Loose scrummage [see *heel-back* (*heel *sb.*[1] 25)]. 1952 *Rugby Union Football* ('Know the Game' Series) (ed. 2) 26 A 'loose' scrum..is formed by..players closing round the ball when it is on the ground. 1958 Pelmear & Morpurgo *Rugby Football* VIII. 339 Loose scrummaging (now sometimes known as 'rucking') was becoming the half-back's delight. 1960 E. S. & W. J. Higham *High Speed Rugby* xiv. 201 It is possible to build up a loose scrum in two ways. 1890 *2nd Ann. Rep. Kansas State Exper. Station 1889* 213 The loose smuts are four closely allied species found on oats, wheat, and barley. 1909 *Bull. Bureau Plant Industry, U.S. Dept. Agric.* No. 152. 7 The loose smut..is easily distinguished from the covered smut by its earlier appearance, by its olive-green spore-mass.., and by the early shedding of the spores. 1924 *Jrnl. Agric. Res.* XXIX. 263/1 Formaldehyde and some of the organic mercury compounds have been found to control the loose-smut of barley in certain varieties. 1968 *Times* 16 Dec. 7/1 Loose smut in barley..has become a serious problem again because of the preponderance of susceptible varieties. 1903 F. T. Bullen in *Strand Mag.* Nov. 539/1 All through the combat..the whale-fishers will be closely beset by the 'loose' whale.

10. d. loose-ended *a.*, ended or finished off in a slack, untidy, or inconclusive way; also *fig.*; hence **loose-endedness; loose-footed** *a.* (later examples); **loose-knit** *a.*, connected in a tenuous or ill-defined way; not closely linked; **loose-lipped** *a.*, (*a*) loose-tongued; uninhibited in speech; (*b*) having full lips; **loose-mouthed** *a.* = **loose-lipped* adj.; **loose-skinned** *a.*, having skin wrinkled or hanging in folds.

1867 J. R. Lowell in *Atlantic Monthly* Jan. 24 Loose-ended souls, whose skills bring scanty gold. 1937 *Times Lit. Suppl.* 15 May 379/1 The weaving of three themes through the tenuous and loose-ended plot. 1944 *Horizon* IX. 286 My purpose is to indicate..how we loose-ended mortals are dealt with. 1905 *Proc. Roy. Soc.* LXXV. 378 There was no slackness or loose-endedness about him either physically or intellectually. 1968 *Punch* 3 Jan. 4/2 The problem, which mightn't worry some people but had teased me for a fortnight by its sheer loose-endedness. 1878 J. H. Beadle *Western Wilds* ii. 38 Every loose-footed man wanted to go. *Ibid.* xxviii. 442 Loose-footed young men erect a cabin, barely habitable in good weather. 1927 G. Bradford *Gloss. Sea Terms* 104/2 *Loose-footed*, a fore and aft sail not laced to (or without) a boom. 1948 R. de Kerchove *Internat. Maritime Dict.* 433/2 *Loose-footed*, an expression used for denoting a fore-and-aft sail in which the foot is not laced to the boom. 1906 T. Hardy *Dynasts* II. I. vii. 42 As he shatters the moves of the loose-knit nations to curb his exploitful soul's ambitions. 1957 E. Bott *Family & Social Network* iii. 94 Networks become loose-knit when people move from one place to another... If both husband and wife have moved considerably before marriage, each will bring an already loose-knit network to the marriage. 1963 *Times* 11 Mar. 3/5 The Welsh forwards performed doughty deeds individually, but were too loose-knit to hold their opponents, which was bad luck on D. C. T. Rowlands, whose most effective game thrives on a dominant pack. 1968 *Daily Tel. Mag.* 8 Nov. 27/4 The ARB team is loose-knit and embraces a cross-section of specialists. 1919 J. Masefield *Reynard* 33 Loose-lipped with song and wine and revel. 1924 W. de la Mare *Ding Dong Bell* 70 Hook-nosed was I; loose-lipped. 1924 Compton Mackenzie *Heavenly Ladder* xiii. 186 It was sad to see a young woman of thirty so loose-lipped and blowsy. 1928 *Daily Mail* 13 Aug. 5/1 Her mastery of what Sir William Watson has called the loose-lipped lingo of the streets. 1934 H. G. Wells *Exper. Autobiogr.* II. ix. 679 If I were to put my reputation before my autobiographical rectitude, I think I should just let this little volume decay and char and disappear... Most of it is very loose-lipped indeed. 1934 W. B. Yeats *King of Great Clock Tower* 29 Had de Valera eaten Parnell's heart No loose-lipped demagogue had won the day. 1872 J. G. Whittier *Pennsylvania Pilgrim* in *Poet. Wks.* (1874) 447 We may trace How loose-mouthed boor and fine ancestral grace Sat in close contrast. 1931 W. Faulkner *Sanctuary* xxii. 203 You'll know I ain't loose-mouthed. 1938 *Times Lit. Suppl.* 18 June 415/4 Were all Roman aristocrats loose-mouthed and pot-bellied? 1950 D. Gascoyne *Vagrant* 53 He is apt to get oddly pedantic about the proprieties while even more loose-mouthed than ever. 1906 *Westm. Gaz.* 14 June 4/2 This old man had a full, loose-skinned face, with a comic mouth and forlorn eyes. 1909 *Ibid.* 5 Jun. 2/2 The sail heaved like a gigantic loose-skinned animal awakening. 1937 V. Woolf *Years* 397 His swarthy wrinkled face.. always made her think of some loose-skinned, furry animal. 1941 Blunden *Thomas Hardy* v. 110 Hands very white and soft and loose-skinned.

B. quasi-*sb.* and *sb.* **1. a.** *on* (or † *upon*) *the loose*: (*b*) of women: living by prostitution; (*c*) *gen.*, not tied down; not answerable to anyone.

1749 J. Cleland *Mem. Woman Pleasure* II. 9 The giddy, wildness of young girls once got upon the loose. 1859 Hotten *Dict. Slang* 70 *On the loose*, obtaining a living by prostitution, in reality, on the streets. The term is applied to females only. 1879 *Roget's Thesaurus* 330 Impure; unclean &c...; on the streets, on the *pavé*, on the loose. 1890 Barrère & Leland *Dict. Slang* II. *Loose, on the*,..getting a living by prostitution. 1914 G. B. Shaw *Fanny's First Play* III. 201 Do you mean to say that you went on the loose out of pure devilment? 1935 N. Ersine *Underworld & Prison Slang* 51 Ted is *on the loose.* 1949 Partridge *Dict. Underworld* 483/2 *On the loose*, obtaining a living by prostitution. 1951 E. Paul *Springtime in Paris* i. 12 Just then Raoul was spending all his free time with the peace posters and Katya stayed at home. When the roles were reversed, and Katya was on the loose, no one knew precisely what she was about. 1958 *Times Lit. Suppl.* 30 May 293/2 A group of young Americans.., some being genuinely on the loose or moving from job to job. 1970 V. Canning *Great Affair* xvii. 319 There was a little mistiming at Sokota so your friend King Alfy is on the loose.

2. (Further examples.)

1894–5 *Rugby Union Football Handbk.* 11 'Offside' is still penalised in the loose, but not Solon himself..could define where a scrummage ends and the loose begins. 1922 'Touch Flag' *Mod. Rugby Tactics* 49 Dangerous attacks frequently originate from chance openings in the loose. 1963 *Rugby World* Aug. 8/3 Wightman and Rogers impressed in the loose for England. 1974 *Country Life* 5 Dec. 1717/1 The All Blacks..were..gaining their expected supremacy at the line-out and in the loose.

loose, *v.* **4.** Delete ? *Obs.* and add later examples.

1916 'Boyd Cable' *Action Front* 48 The artillery made a regular practice of loosing off a stated number of rounds

per night. 1944 *R.A.F. Jrnl.* Aug. 286 Dropped our bomb-load..an' loosed off all our ammo.

b. (Examples with *off*.) Also *loosing off*.

1906 *Westm. Gaz.* 9 Mar. 4/1 The man for whom the whole of shooting is comprised in the gunning—in the 'loosing off', as he will call it. 1926 *Punch* 28 July 86/2 The bowler would acquire the trick of looking at one [wicket] while really he was loosing off at the other. 1928 BLUNDEN *Undertones of War* ii. 8 The howitzer loosing off occasionally outside punctuated these amenities. 1946 J. IRVING *Royal Navalese* 110 *To loose off*, to open fire.

12. Also in phr. *loose-all*, the signal to stop work given in the pits.

1911 D. H. LAWRENCE *White Peacock* vii. 485, I heard the far-off hooting of the 'loose-all' at the pits, telling me it was half-past eleven. 1913 —— *Sons & Lovers* ii. 30 Some men were there before four o'clock, when the whistle blew loose-all.

loose-leaf, *a.* Of a note-book, file, or the like: made to facilitate the insertion or removal of each leaf separately. Also as *sb.*

1902 *Accountant* 29 Nov. 1240/1 The difficulty he mentions is partly met by using a 'loose leaf' Ledger. 1907 *Daily Chron.* 6 Dec. 11/4 'Loose-Leaf' notebooks and diaries,..in which pages can be taken out or added at will, have already won a well-deserved popularity. 1917 H. B. TWYFORD *Purchasing & Storing* 409 A copy of every printed form used should be posted on a loose-leaf sheet. 1930 'J. J. CONNINGTON' *Two Tickets Puzzle* xv. 232 Dr. Selby-Onslow nodded again: crossed the room to his desk; and pulled from a drawer a large loose-leaf volume. 1937 I. O. EVANS *Cigarette Cards* 122 Sheets made up in this fashion could also be filed after the manner of the loose-leaves. 1955 W. GADDIS *Recognitions* II. vi. 559 In the window was a large loose-leaf book, whose lined pages were filled in a cramped round hand. 1967 *Listener* 21 Sept. 370/2 The large loose-leaf notebook in which he wrote rehearsal notes. 1971 *Ann. Rep. Curators Bodl. Libr. 1969–70* 49 Transferring of the old handlists to typescript sheets in looseleaf binders continued. 1975 *BSI News* May 6/3 The third revision of BS 2782 *Methods of test for plastics* is being issued in a loose-leaf form.

loosely, *adv.* Add: **6.** *loosely-knit* adj. Cf. *loose-knit* adj. s.v. *LOOSE *a.* 10 d.

1935 HUXLEY & HADDON *We Europeans* i. 13 It [*sc.* group-sentiment] has spread beyond the family, the tribe, the loosely-knit federation of tribes to the yet more extensive aggregate, the nation. 1957 C. HUNT *Guide to Communist Jargon* xlvi. 153 It [*sc.* the Decree of the Central Committee] replaced the loosely-knit Union of Proletarian Writers by a single Union of Soviet Writers.

loosen, *v.* Add: **7.** *absol.* with *up.* **a.** To give money willingly, to talk freely, etc. *U.S. colloq.*

1908 K. McGAFFEY *Sorrows of Show-Girl* xi. 125 Loosen-up... You've got to donate for a couple of tickets to the annual benefit. 1911 G. S. PORTER *Harvester* xx. 516 You're tight-mouthed... Loosen up! 1923 R. D. PAINE *Comrades of Rolling Ocean* xi. 187 Somebody will have to loosen up to pay for the damage to my nervous system. 1922 C. SANDBURG *Slabs of Sunburnt West* 6 Come across, kick in, loosen up. Where do you get that chatter? 1927 *Ladies' Home Jrnl.* 114 That is the first time he has ever loosened up. 1949 WODEHOUSE *Uncle Dynamite* i. 8 You will generally find women loosen up less lavishly than men.

b. In *Sport* or *Dancing*, to exercise the muscles before concentrated physical effort, to limber up. Also *loosening-up* vbl. sb. and ppl. adj.

1955 M. GILBERT *Sky High* xii. 165 The General came to a stop in the middle of his loosening-up exercises. 1956 R. ALSTON *Test Commentary* xvi. 139 Lindwall was given a couple of loosening-up overs. 1973 M. RUSSELL *Double Hit* viii. 55 Make it an hour. I'll be twenty minutes loosening up... I'm after the exercise.

Looshai, var. *LUSHAI *a.* and *sb.*

loot, *sb.*² Add: **2.** *slang.* Money.

1943 HUNT & PRINGLE *Service Slang* 44 *Loot*, Scottish slang for money received on pay day. 1956 B. HOLIDAY *Lady sings Blues* (1973) ii. 16 There was nothing to do except for Mom to go back slaving away as somebody's maid. In Baltimore she couldn't make half the loot she could up North. 1959 *Encounter* Oct. 73/1 MacInnes's teen-agers..are all economically self-supporting, in their own phrase, they've got the loot. 1968 J. SANGSTER *Touchfeather* xiii. 141 When you've got his sort of loot I don't suppose it matters. 1973 *Center City Office Weekly* (Philadelphia) 9 Oct. 3 Jefferson Medical College picks up $362,949 in loot for..continuing research in hemophilia.

loot (lūt), *sb.*³ *U.S. Mil. slang.* Shortened from Amer. pronunciation of LIEUTENANT 2.

1898 F. P. DUNNE *Mr. Dooley in Peace & War* 11 R-run over an' wake up th' loot at th' station. 1918 *Stars & Stripes* 27 Dec. 7 He's a loot-colonel now and a D.S.C. 1921 B. MATTHEWS in *S.P.E. Tract* v. 6 In the United States this officer is called the *lootenant*, which the privates of the American Expeditionary Force in France habitually shortened to '*loot*'. 1944 K. LEVIS in Murdoch & Drake-Brockman *Austral. Short Stories* (1951) 423 Some nitwit of a loot's in charge that don't know a bush track from Pitt Street. 1948 J. G. COZZENS *Guard of Honor* 331 Don't thank the loot!

lop, *sb.*³ Add: **4. lop and top,** waste branches cut from timber trees, usually after the trees have been felled; **lop-stick** (earlier and later examples); also **lobstick.**

1892 Lop and top [in Dict., sense 1]. 1938 C. P. ACKERS *Pract. Brit. Forestry* vi. 194 Lop and top may be overcome either by burning or by stacking it in 'trenches'. 1972 *Country Life* 30 Mar. 789/3 'Lopp and Topp'—the side and top branches—were the college property and if from ash or oak fetched 8s. to 9s. 6d. a load. 1821 N. GARRY *Diary* 19 Aug. (1900) 149 After Dinner we observed that two of our Men had lopped away the Boughs and all the Lower Branches of two Trees leaving a Top. This is called a Lop-Stick. 1847 J. B. NEVINS *Two Voy. Hudson's Bay* iv. 90 Two gentlemen were travelling a short time since, and lobsticks were cut for them. 1873 G. M. GRANT *Ocean to Ocean* vii. 196 There is an old superstition that your health and length of days will correspond to your lobstick's. 1923 *Beaver* Aug. 421 To commemorate this great battle, three lobsticks were cut on each side of the river. 1949 *Argosy* Apr. 13 On the far side of the lake, if you must portage, use the 'lop-stick' mark. This is made by cutting all branches from one side of a tall tree which may be seen either from water or land. Its unnatural appearance attracts the eye; the side from which branches are cut indicates the direction of portage. 1964 *Islander* (Victoria, B.C.) 18 Oct. 1/12 There was a tradition among the Northern Indians that a lobstick honouring an individual would fall when its sponsor died.

lop, *v.*² Add: **2. b.** *to lop down*, to sit down, to lie down. *U.S. colloq.*

1839 C. M. KIRKLAND *New Home* ii. 17 Jist come in, and take off your things, and lop down, if you're a mind to. 1861 MRS. STOWE *Pearl of Orr's Island* I. viii. 67 Ruby said she thought she'd just lop down a few minutes on the old sofa. 1892 F. P. HUMPHREY *New Eng. Cactus* 34 You'd best lop down on the lounge and get a nap.

4. *lop-brimmed* adj.

1901 S. E. WHITE *Westerners* xvi. 131 His broad hat—straight-brimmed in a lop-brimmed camp—was pushed to one side.

lope, *sb.* Add: **2.** (Further examples.) Now used chiefly of people.

1809 M. L. WEEMS *Life F. Marion* xii. 108 He dashed off at a charging lope. 1910 C. E. MULFORD *Hopalong Cassidy* xxi. 135 As he rode at an easy lope he kept a constant lookout for signs of rustling. 1953 R. CHANDLER *Let.* 15 Mar. in *R. Chandler Speaking* (1966) 28 Walks with a forward-leaning lope, huh? 1961 L. VAN DER POST *Heart of Hunter* I. ii. 25 The others followed close on her heels with a strange stumbling lope. 1973 *Houston* (Texas) *Post* 14 Oct. (Spotlight Suppl.) 15/4 Somehow..Hero Hazard reaches the Sphinx..and evades the grisly Arab agents after a lope up and down the Great Pyramid.

loper¹. 3. (Later examples.)

1952 J. GLOAG *Short Dict. Furnit.* 323 Sliding rails which pull out from the carcase of a bureau to support the fall are called lopers. 1963 *Times* 20 Apr. 11/7 The bureau bookcase has continuously changed its outline, wood and fashionable finish according to the dictates of fashion, but apart from the invention, in this century, of the automatic opening loper, no basic improvement in it has been found possible between the reigns of Queen Anne and Queen Elizabeth II. 1971 *Canad. Antiques Collector* Mar. 10/1 The name 'pembroke' should be saved for a particular sort of small 4-legged dropleaf tables, usually with a drawer, the leaves supported on lopers (pull-out bars).

loper² (lǭu·pəɹ), var. LOOPER². *S. Afr.*

1886 P. GILLMORE *Hunter's Arcadia* iii. 18, I quickly substituted cartridges of lopers (buckshot) for the No. 3 that my chambers had previously contained. 1932 C. FULLER *Louis Trigardt's Trek* x. 120 They espied a fully armed Native and scared him away with a charge of *lopers*.

lopolith (lǫ·polįþ). *Geol.* [See quot. 1918 and -LITH.] A large intrusive mass similar to a laccolith but having the base centrally sunken.

1918 F. F. GROUT in *Amer. Jrnl. Sci.* CXCVI. 518 Professor John Barrell has suggested that as igneous forms they deserve a distinct name... The name proposed by the writer is 'lopolith' (from [Greek] λοπάς, a basin, a flat earthen dish, and λίθος, a stone). *Ibid.*, Pronunciation, lŏ'polith. 1962 [see *INTRUSIVE *sb.*]. 1972 M. P. BILLINGS *Struct. Geol.* (ed. 3) xvi. 343 In plan, lopoliths are arcuate or circular.

Hence **lopoli·thic** *a.*

1959 *Econ. Geol.* LIV. 1208 Cooling of a lopolithic mass would proceed under the influence of two cooling gradients. 1968 R. W. FAIRBRIDGE *Encycl. Geomorphol.* 281/2 The second type [of intrusive dome mountain] is the complex laccolith (or lopolithic) intrusion with broad sill-type interfingering tongues of igneous material penetrating the surrounding sediments.

loppage. (Later example.)

1911 FLETCHER & KIPLING *School Hist. Eng.* ii. 32 Laws they made in the Witan, the laws of flaying and fine—Common, loppage and pannage, the theft and the track of kine.

loppiness. *rare.* [f. LOPPY *a.*³] The quality of being loppy or choppy.

1908 *Daily Chron.* 10 Aug. 1/4 He complained that the loppiness of the water had taken the strength out of him.

loppy (lǫ·pi), *sb. Austral. slang.* [Prob. from LOPPY *a.*¹] A handyman on rural stations.

1898 *Bulletin* (Sydney) 1 Oct. 14/3 A few more Western Queensland slang words... In a shearing shed: The boss is the 'finger', the shearers the 'brutes', the rouseabouts 'leathernecks', 'spoonbills', 'loppies' or 'Jacks'. 1933 *Ibid.* 8 Feb. 21 The loppies, who are meek and spry To shearers and the rest, Are perky chaps when I am by.

lop-sidedness. (Earlier and later examples.)

1843 H. JAMES *Let.* 11 May in R. B. Perry *Tht. & Char. W. James* (1935) I. 46 Thought heaped up to topheaviness and inevitable lopsidedness. 1946 *Nature* 21 Dec. 890/2 He makes, incidentally, a powerful case for some attempt to redress the lopsidedness of scientific advance.

lop-stick: see LOP *sb.*³ 4 (in Dict. and Suppl.).

loquat. (Earlier and later examples.)

1820 *Trans. Hort. Soc. London* III. 229 You desire me [*sc.* Lord Bagot] to give you some information as to my mode of treating the Lo-quat. *Ibid.* 301 In 1813 ripe fruits of the Lo-quat were presented to the Horticultural Society by Lord Bagot. 1884 tr. *J. J. Rein's Japan* I. vii. 139 A Japanese fruit-tree, the Loquat (Eriobothrya japonica Lindl.), which the English have transplanted to their tropical and subtropical colonies. 1969 *Oxf. Bk. Food Plants* 104/2 Loquat..is also sometimes known as Japanese medlar... The yellow pear-shaped fruits are the size of crab apples and have a sweetish acid flavour.

loquence (lǭu·kwĕns). *rare.* [ad. late L. *loquentia*: cf. LOQUENCY.] Speaking; talk.

1677 T. HARVEY tr. *Owen's Epigrams* 199 Thy Tongue is loose, thy Body close; Both ill: With Silence this, with Loquence that doth kill. 1886 R. F. BURTON tr. *Arabian Nights* VIII. 346 When the Princess Miriam beheld Nur al-Din and heard his loquence and verse and speech, she made certain that it was indeed her lord Nur al-Din.

Loran (lǭə·-, lǫ·ræn). orig. *U.S.* Also **loran.** [f. the initial letters of *lo*ng-*ra*nge *n*avigation.] A hyperbolic navigation system employing the difference in the times of arrival of pulsed radio signals from different stations. Freq. *attrib.*; also *ellipt.* for a Loran receiver.

[1942 (*title*) Development of airborne receiver model LRN-1: report on project 191. (Radio Corporation of Amer. License Div. Lab. Rep. No. 207 (PB 32732), 9 Sept.).] 1943 (*title*) Development of Loran receiver trainer: report on project 191 (extension). (Radio Corporation of Amer. License Div. Lab. Rep. (PB 23321), 17 Mar.) 1945 *Tuscaloosa* (Alabama) *News* 18 Oct. 5 In the airplane, a loran receiver measures the difference in radio wave travel time in millionths of a second. 1945 [see *HYPERBOLIC *a.* 2 b]. 1946 J. P. BAXTER *Scientists against Time* ix. 151 The beauty of Loran for wartime use was that the ship or plane which used it emitted no signal that might give away its position. 1960 M. SHARCOTT *Place of Many Winds* i. 6 We passed Spring Island, where there is a Department of Transport Loran station. 1966 *McGraw-Hill Encycl. Sci. & Technol.* VII. 585 The distance at which reliable loran fixes are generally obtained is about 800 nautical miles over water from the pair of transmitting stations during daytime and about 1500 miles at night. 1972 K. CAMPBELL *Thunder on Sunday* 11 'Get a Loran fix.'.. Peter Spence had his face glued into the rubber eye-piece of the Loran... He counted the jumping electric lines and the long number blips... He then transferred his eyes to the Loran map.

lorandite (lǭə·răndəit). *Min.* [ad. Hung. *lorandit* (J. Krenner 1894, in *Matemat. és Természett. Értesitö* XII. 473), f. the name of *Loránd* Eötvös, 19th-century Hungarian physicist: see -ITE¹.] A sulphide of thallium and arsenic, $TlAsS_2$, found as scarlet monoclinic crystals.

1895 *Mineral. Mag.* XI. 32 Professor Krenner, of Budapest,..describes a mineral containing no less than 59·5 per cent. of thallium, to which he has given the name Lorandite. 1946 [see *CROOKESITE]. 1957 *Contrib. Mineral. & Petrol.* XVI. 45 A new find of the thallium-arsenic-sulphosalt mineral lorandite in the Triassic dolomite of the famous Lengenbach quarry in Binnatal, Ct. Wallis (Switzerland) is described.

lord, *sb.* Add. **2.** *lord and master* (later examples). Also, a husband (now usu. *joc.*).

1665 R. VERNEY *Let.* 5 June in M. M. Verney *Mem.* (1899) IV. iv. 122 Peg Gardner saw your Lord and Master with some gentlemen in Parke. 1739–40 RICHARDSON *Pamela* (1740) II. 251 Your lord and master came in very moody. 1816 JANE AUSTEN *Emma* III. xvi. 300, I am waiting for my lord and master. 1864 C. M. YONGE *Trial* I. vii. 126 She was not going to be one of the womankind sitting up in a row till their lords and masters should be pleased to want them! 1922 JOYCE *Ulysses* 639 The erring fair one begging forgiveness of her lord and master. 1961 [see *DROIT¹ 1 b]. 1975 P. HARCOURT *Fair Exchange* II. 121 'You're a Counsellor, a senior official..what advice would you give?'..'I can't see our lords and masters asking me.'

3. *Lord of the Manor*: rhyming slang for 'tanner' (sixpence, now equal to 2½ pence); also (*ellipt.*) *Lord.*

1839 H. BRANDON *Poverty, Mendicity & Crime* 163/2 *Lord of the manor*, sixpence. 1882 *Sydney Slang Dict.* 5/2 *Lord of the Manor*, sixpence. 1933 *Times Lit. Suppl.* 16 Nov. 782/1 Twenty years ago you might hear a sixpence described as a 'Lord' meaning 'Lord of the Manor'; that is, a tanner. 1972 *Lebende Sprachen* XVII. 8/3 *Lord of the Manor*, tanner (*old sixpence*).

6. b. Also *lord* (or *lor'*) *lumme* (= lord love me).

1902 E. NESBIT *Five Children & It* ii. 61 'Lor' lumme,' said Billy Peasemarsh, 'if there ain't another on 'em!' 1903 J. LONDON *People of Abyss* i. 8 Lord lumme, but it'll be the last I see af you if yer don't py me. *Ibid.* iv. 31 'Lor' lumme,' she laughed.

9. b. *House of Lords.* Also, a lavatory. *slang.*

1961 in PARTRIDGE *Dict. Slang* Suppl. 1139/1. 1967

Listener 21 Dec. 802/2 In between you have the Business Man Jocular: 'I say, where's the geography, old son?' or 'When you need the House of Lords, it's through there.' **1969** J. ALEXANDER *Where have All Flowers Gone?* I. 46 Half way up the stairs there was a lavatory... 'The House of Lords,' said Jake.

12. d. *Lord of the Flies*, a name for Beelzebub [tr. Heb. *ba'al-zĕbhūbh*: see BEELZEBUB]; also, used allusively of the book (1954) by William Golding (1911–) of the same name, in which a group of schoolboys marooned on an uninhabited tropical island revert to savagery and primitive ritual. (Use in quot. 1971 is *joc.*)

1931 A. HUXLEY *Cicadas* 37 But 'tis the shitten Lord of Flies Who with his loathsome bounties now fulfils On us their prayers. **1948** —— *Ape & Essence* (1949) 69 Such.. is the inscrutable justice of the Lord of Flies. *Ibid.* 90 The Lord of Flies, who is also the Blowfly in every individual heart. **1965** *Listener* 24 June 933/1 The ship's figurehead.., removed from its place by the children, becomes a kind of Lord of the Flies. **1967** J. BLACKBURN *Flame & Wind* II. 72 Beelzebub—the Lord of the Flies—the Prince of the Hebrew devils. **1969** I. & P. OPIE *Children's Games* 13 Such accounts..have..influenced educational practice..leading us to believe that a *Lord of the Flies* mentality is inherent in the young. **1971** *Guardian* 9 Feb. 8/4 Instead of the orgasmic moment, we arrive at Mr Neville's playtime: the lord of the flies.

13. c. Lord Derby, a large green and yellow-skinned variety of cooking apple, or the tree that produces it.

1876–85 HOGG & BULL *Herefordshire Pomona* II. plate 73 Lord Derby. The origin of this apple is unknown. It has probably been cultivated in the orchards for some years, without special notice. **1933** HALL & CRANE *Apple* ii. 27 Some varieties, like Lord Derby, have a markedly upright habit. **1962** *Listener* 27 Sept. 495/1, I am thinking of cooking apples like..that good old-fashioned one, Lord Derby. **1966** C. R. THOMPSON *Pruning Apple Trees* II. 194 There are a few varieties from which large apples are wanted early in the season, such as early Victoria and Lord Derby.

14. c. *Lord Muck*, a pompous self-opinionated man (see quot. 1966). *slang.*

1937 in PARTRIDGE *Dict. Slang* 539/1. **1955** J. THOMAS *No Banners* xxix. 287 Hey, Lord Muck! May we have the honour of introducing ourselves? **1966** 'L. LANE' *ABZ of Scouse* 63 *Lord Muck of Muck Hall*, a bombastic person; a swollen-headed man who likes to assert his authority.

16. lord and lady (duck) *N. Amer.*, a pair of harlequin duck, *Histrionicus histrionicus.*

1770 G. CARTWRIGHT *Jrnl.* 29 July (1792) I. 20, I shot four eider ducks, and seven lords and ladies. **1835** E. WIX *Six Months Newfoundland Missionary's Jrnl.* (1836) 162, I had a fine view of a patch fox in my walk, saw several seals, and some of those very beautiful birds, called by the people of Newfoundland 'lords and ladies'. **1930** *Canad. Geogr. Jrnl.* I. 32/2 The Harlequin Duck..is known to trappers and prospectors in the far west as 'Lord and Lady Duck'. **1959** W. L. MCATEE *Folk-Names Canad. Birds* (ed. 2) 16 Harlequin Duck [is also called] lord and lady (Usually in the plural, 'lords and ladies'. In allusion to the handsome plumage.)

Lord Lieutenant. Add: **1. c.** (Later examples.) The position is now mainly ceremonial, though he retains some of his former powers (see quots.), including the recommendation of persons for appointment as justices of the peace.

1962 W. O. HART *Hart's Introd. Law Local Govt. & Admin.* ii. 64 With the disappearance of the militia the lord lieutenant has ceased to have a county force to command. His position has come to be largely one of great honour with no active duties to perform. **1963** *Times* 10 May 19/2 At the moment it was contemplated that there would be one lord lieutenant for the Greater London area, with a number of deputy lieutenants to assist him. **1963** K. B. SMELLIE *Hist. Local Govt.* iii. 42 The Lord Lieutenant and the Sheriff have mainly ceremonial duties. **1972** *Whitaker's Almanack 1973* 631 The duties of the Lord Lieutenant are to advise the Lord Chancellor as to the appointment of magistrates to the county bench... The Lord Lieutenant is usually a peer or baronet..and is often appointed *custos rotulorum* (keeper of the records).

lordosis. Add to def.: (occurring as a physical deformity).

b. A temporarily assumed posture, characteristic of some female mammals during mating, in which the back is arched downwards; the assumption of such a posture.

1941 *Endocrinology* XXIX. 411 Two males exhibited lordosis and hopping behavior typical of the sexually-receptive female [rat]. **1947** *Physiol. Rev.* XXVII. 243 Some female rats in heat display lordosis each time they are mounted by the male. **1965** *Science* 15 Jan. 306/3 Frequency of lordosis, ear-wiggling, and crouching (all indications of receptivity) were recorded. **1968** M. DIAMOND *Perspectives in Reproduction & Sexual Behavior* xx. 321 Normal males [*sc.* rats] rarely exhibit lordosis. **1971** *New Scientist* 13 May 370/3 The rats with no sense of smell were much more likely to show the typical lordosis (a posture where the belly is lowered and the rump stuck up in the air) that is normal in sexually receptive animals.

lordotic *a.* (examples, corresponding to sense *b of the sb.).

1971 *New Scientist* 13 May 370/3 With these animals removal of both olfactory lobes increased the likelihood of going into a lordotic posture. **1972** *Science* 5 May 519/1 After a 9-hour delay, the typical lordotic reactions and sticky estrous discharge had generally disappeared.

Lord's (lǭɹdz). Also **Lords.** The cricket ground at St. John's Wood, London, named after its founder Thomas *Lord* (1757–1832); now the headquarters of the Marylebone Cricket Club.

1799 *Times* 1 June 3/4 The colours..were presented.. to the corps in Lord's cricket-ground. **1823** H. BENTLEY *Cricket Matches played by Mary-le-bone Club*, Lord's.—26th August, 1793. Eleven of England against Twenty-two of the County of Middlesex. **1863** A. J. MUNBY *Diary* 10 July in D. Hudson *Munby* (1972) 167 Miss Williams had asked me to go with her party to the Eton and Harrow cricket match at Lord's. **1910** *Blackw. Mag.* 90/1 The Australians had won the toss at Lords... Our visitors had already on a Lords wicket pretty thoroughly extended a M.C.C. eleven. **1930** E. WAUGH *Labels* 88 There was an interval, during which everyone..strolled about..as people do at Lord's between the innings. **1959** *Listener* 19 Feb. 344/1 He loyally goes through the motions, military and social (Bank Picquet, Tower Guard, débutantes' balls, Ascot, Lord's), that are required of him. **1972** K. WARD *Put Lock On!* ix. 99 When there's a Test on at Lords..radio stations cater to the thousands who sit up until dawn.

lordship, *sb.* **6.** Add after 'royalty': (on a mine or a book). (Earlier examples.)

1859 J. BLACKWOOD *Let.* 18 Sept. in Geo. Eliot *Lett.* (1954) III. 160 Your warning voice about G.E.'s new novel keeps me uncertain. I incline to offer £3000, or £2000 with a lordship not to begin until so many are sold. **1861** STEPHENS & BURN *Bk. Farm-Buildings* 171 The contractor will have Kinpurney quarry, free of lordships, for all the stones necessary. **1886** J. BARROWMAN *Gloss. Scottish Mining Terms* 43 *Lordship*, rate per ton or other measure paid to the proprietor of minerals, royalty.

lordy, *int.* orig. *U.S.* = LORD *sb.* 6 c. Also *lordy me* (= lord help me).

1853 *Southern Lit. Messenger* Oct. 602/2 On the sofa.. you sank down and bounded up and said Lordy! **1857** *Knickerbocker* L. 236 O Lordy me Sir! I'm so dreadful afeard you're both on you Dorrites! **1897** R. M. STUART *In Simpkinsville* 155 Lordy, but it all takes my breath away. **1926** S. ANDERSON *Let.* 25 Apr. in R. L. White *S. Anderson/G. Stein* (1972) 52 It was a beautiful story, beautifully done. Lordy but that man can write. **1928** *Sat. Even. Post* 12 May 20/3 But seven hundred dollars and his pocket piece back again! Phew! Lordy! **1959** N. MAILER *Advts. for Myself* (1961) 198 Well, Lordy-me.. I could introduce you to a good many of us. **1968** *Melody Maker* 30 Nov. 25/7, I have..seen many blues groups and have yet to hear one shouting 'Lordy, Lordy, yes'. **1973** *Bulletin* (Sydney) 25 Aug. 44/2 Oh lordy, that buffet car. **1973** E. TAYLOR *Serpent under It* (1974) xiv. 209 Lordy, ma —if you pamper me like this you'll unfit me for ordinary existence. **1974** N. FREELING *Dressing of Diamond* 88 A kidnapping... And lordy, it's the child of a magistrate.

Lorelei (lōᵊ·rĕləi). *German Mythol.* Also 9 **Loreley.** [Name of a rock on the Rhine near Coblenz.] A legendary woman with long blonde hair who sat on the Lorelei rock and with her fine singing distracted boatmen, so that they drowned when their ships foundered on the rock. Also *transf.* Cf. SIREN *sb.* 2.

1878 *Chambers's Encycl.* VIII. 745/1 The Loreley of the Rhine is only a river-siren, though a more exquisite enchantress than ever Greek fancy conceived. **1910** 'O. HENRY' *Strictly Business* (1917) i. 10 Instead of being motoring bacchanalians and diamond-hungry *loreleis* they are businesslike folk. **1927** N. WAINWRIGHT tr. *Dekobra's Madonna of Sleeping Cars* ix. 125 My little Lorelei had unfastened her hair, which fell in a blonde cascade. **1965** 'A. GILBERT' *Passenger to Nowhere* iii. 42 Probably thought you were the original Lorelei. **1971** R. SALE *Man who raised Hell* III. vii. 249 She..evolved into the most devastating Lorelei of Mayfair, with an utterly intriguing contempt for the men she could so easily fetter.

Lorentz (lǫ̈re·nts). *Physics.* The name of H. A. *Lorentz* (1853–1928), Dutch physicist, used *attrib.* to designate various concepts and phenomena described by him, as **Lorentz (–FitzGerald) contraction** = **FitzGerald contraction*; so *Lorentz-contract* vb. trans.; **Lorentz-covariant, -invariant** adjs., covariant, or invariant, under a Lorentz transformation; so *Lorentz-covariance*; **Lorentz transformation** [named in Fr. by H. Poincaré 1905, in *Compt. Rend.* CXL. 1505], the set of equations which in the special theory of relativity relate the space and time co-ordinates of one frame of reference to those of another moving rectilinearly with respect to the first; **Lorentz triplet,** a group of three spectral lines produced by the splitting of a single line with the frequency of the middle one by a magnetic field (the Zeeman effect, first interpreted by Lorentz).

¶ See also *LORENZ.

1908 *Sci. Abstr.* A. XI. 687 The equations for moving bodies, when subjected to a Lorentz transformation, are converted into the corresponding equations for the transformed quantities. **1916** *Monthly Notices R. Astron. Soc.* LXXVII. 155 The well-known Lorentz-contraction. **1920** [see *COVARIANT B]. **1922** A. D. UDDEN tr. *Bohr's Theory of Spectra* II. iii. 47 it follows immediately from this result according to the principle of correspondence that each fine structure component must be expected to split up into a normal Zeeman effect (Lorentz triplet). **1923** C. D. BROAD *Sci. Thought* iv. 135 The Lorentz–Fitzgerald Contraction, if taken as a physical fact, affects all kinds of matter equally. **1955** R. PEIERLS *Laws of Nature* vi. 126 When one first hears of this 'Lorentz contraction' it sounds most artificial and unreasonable. **1955** W. HEISENBERG in W. Pauli *Niels Bohr* 21 Such an interpretation..would destroy..just the decisive symmetry property of the theory of relativity, namely the Lorentz invariance, and it must therefore be considered inappropriate. **1955** W. PAULI *Ibid.* 35 Lorentz-invariant quantized field theories. **1955** J. LINDHARD *Ibid.* 189 The reason for this is that the field acting on an electron is Lorentz contracted. **1964** E. A. POWER *Introd. Quantum Electrodynamics* iii. 23 The former is the more deep and can be made explicitly Lorentz covariant. **1965** P. CAWS *Philos. of Sci.* xxii. 167 Einstein found the Lorentz transformations at hand when he needed them. **1970** G. K. WOODGATE *Elem. Atomic Struct.* viii. 147 This so-called Lorentz triplet of one π and two σ lines is characteristic of the 'normal' Zeeman effect in electric dipole radiation. **1970** *Nature* 17 Oct. 272/3 Measuring scales..are assumed to be Lorentz-contracted by a factor $(1-\omega^2r^2/c^2)^{1/2}$.

Lorenz (lǫ̈re·nts). *Physics.* Also (erron.) **Lorentz.** The name of L. V. *Lorenz* (1829–91), Danish physicist, used *attrib.* and in the possessive to designate the ratio $k/\sigma T$ (k = thermal conductivity, σ = electrical conductivity, T = temperature), which has approximately the same value for many metallic elements over a wide range of temperatures.

1922 GLAZEBROOK *Dict. Appl. Physics* I. 459/2 They found that for seven pure metals..the value of Lorenz's constant $K/\lambda T$ was nearly the same over the range 18° to 100°C. **1966** C. R. TOTTLE *Sci. Engin. Materials* v. 122 The electron influence on the thermal conductivity of metals is normally far greater than the lattice contribution. When this is the case, the Lorentz constant holds reasonably well. **1966** PHILLIPS & WILLIAMS *Inorg. Chem.* II. xix. 23 On the free-electron theory [of metals] it is predicted that there should be a direct relation between the thermal, k, and electrical, σ, conductivities... The Lorenz number, $k/\sigma T$, has the theoretical value of $2{\cdot}45\times10^{-8}$ watt ohm deg^{-2}.

lorgnette. (Further examples.)

[**1776** *Monthly Rev.* LIII. 536 Concerning Achromatic spying Glasses... We have thus translated the word *Lorgnettes.*] **1803** *Lett. Miss Riversdale* III. 320 Mr. Drummore moved on..with his lorgnette to his eye, scrutinising every dish. **1859** G. A. SALA *Twice round Clock* 253 Surveyed, through powerful-lensed lorgnettes. **1952** H. INNES *Campbell's Kingdom* 75 To my astonishment she quizzed me through a gold lorgnette as I entered the room. **1970** V. CANNING *Great Affair* vi. 104 My aunt.. favoured Edwardian dress.., feathered hats, lorgnettes, [etc.].

lorie, var. LORY.

1848 H. W. HAYGARTH *Recoll. Bush Life Austral.* xii. 139 The lorie, with his splendid livery of blue and green.

loris. Add to etym.: [Used as a mod.L. generic name (E. Geoffroy Saint-Hilaire 1796, in *Mag. Encycl.* I. 48).] Substitute for def.: **a.** A small arboreal primate of the genus so called, distinguished by grey or black fur, large eyes, and thin limbs, and found in Sri Lanka (Ceylon) and southern India; also called *slender loris* **b.** A larger primate of similar form but heavier build, belonging to the genus *Nycticebus* and found in south-east Asia; also called *slow loris.* (Further examples.)

1827 E. GRIFFITH tr. *Cuvier's Animal Kingdom* I. 229 The Loris, commonly, Lazy Monkeys. **1909** E. PROTHEROE *Handy Nat. Hist. Mammals* iii. 73 The Slender Loris is a small animal only eight or nine inches long. **1967** J. R. & P. H. NAPIER *Handbk. Living Primates* II. 206 The Slender Loris is not a particularly successful animal in captivity owing to delicacy and irascible temper. **1972** T. A. VAUGHAN *Mammalogy* vii. 119 Lorises occur in Africa south of the Sahara, in India, Ceylon, and South-east Asia.

lorisid (lōᵊ·risid), *sb.* and *a.* [f. mod.L. family name *Lorisidæ*, f. generic name *Loris* (see above).] **A.** *sb.* A member of the family Lorisidæ, which includes lorises, pottos, and, in certain classifications, galagos. **B.** *adj.* Of or pertaining to this family.

1969 *Nature* 22 Nov. 821/1 Lorisid primates. *Ibid.*, The only lorisids which live in open country today are some of the galagines of Africa. **1970** *Ibid.* 25 July 356/1 The talonids of tarsiids, plesiadapids and lorisids. **1972** *Ibid.* 24 Mar. 180/2 Unlike the condition of the symphysis in living tarsiers, lorisids or lemur..show distinct separation of the superior and inferior transverse tori.

lorisoid (lōᵊ·risoid), *sb.* and *a.* [f. mod.L. name of suborder *Lorisoidea*, f. generic name *Loris* (see above).] **A.** *sb.* A member of the suborder Lorisoidea, introduced by C. Tate Regan in 1930 and used in some recent classifications of primates. **B.** *adj.* Of or pertaining to this suborder.

1930 C. T. REGAN in *Ann. & Mag. Nat. Hist.* VI. 385 The continent formed by the union of Africa and South America..was the original home of the Lemuroids and Lorisoids. *Ibid.* 387 In the Eocene there were in existence animals with many Lorisoid characters. **1953** W. C. O.

HILL *Primates* I. 101 Their [*sc.* dwarf-lemurs'] general affinities are certainly more lemuroid than lorisoid. *Ibid.* 105 Lorisoids tend to possess more rounded heads, with shorter faces, than the average lemuroid. **1965** *Punch* 21 Apr. 580/1 Dr. Manley's studies on social behaviour and reproductive patterns in lorisoid primates have been extended to include the Angwantibo. **1970** *Nature* 25 July 355/2 Such diverse groups of primates as the omomyids, most lemuroids, lorisoids or the platyrrhines.

Lorraine (lǫrē^{i}·n). The name of a province in NE. France used *attrib.* in *Lorraine cross* = *cross of Lorraine* (CROSS *sb.* 18). Also *cross Lorrain(e)*.

1830 T. ROBSON *Brit. Herald* III. Gloss., *Cross patriarchal* or *double cross*, (French, *croix double*) composed of one piece in pale, and two transverse horizontal pieces... But French heralds form their cross patriarchal somewhat different, and often call it a *cross Lorrain.* **1894** GOUGH & PARKER *Gloss. Terms Heraldry* 173 It is often blazoned as a *cross Lorraine.* **1920** WEBSTER, Lorraine cross. **1970** *Guardian* 13 Nov. 1/1 Lorraine crosses, the symbol of the Gaullist Resistance.

Lorrainer (lǫrē^{i}·nəɹ). [f. *LORRAINE + -ER^{1}.] A native or inhabitant of Lorraine. Also *attrib.* Cf. *LOTHARINGIAN *sb.* and *a.*

1743 *Gentl. Mag.* Aug. 447/1 Of the Lorrainers..it is affirmed, that they are with Difficulty restrained from declaring in favour of their Sovereign. **1903** F. W. MAITLAND in *Cambr. Mod. Hist.* II. xvi. 574 The Lorrainers were not France. **1933** KIPLING *Souvenirs of France* ii. 58, I love that imperturbable Lorrainer [*sc.* Poincaré]. **1966** M. R. D. FOOT *SOE in France* vii. 163 He was one of three brothers, barons of Lorrainer origin, landed gentry of the Limousin.

lorry, *sb.* (The form *lorry* is now usual.) Delete '*local*' and add: **1. b.** A large motor vehicle for carrying goods, etc., by road. Also *attrib.*

1911 *Encycl. Brit.* XVIII. 927/2 (*caption*) Halley's van or lorry chassis. **1915** *Autocar Handbk.* (ed. 6) i. 11 Commercial motor vehicles, such as heavy motor lorries..are not *specifically* dealt with. **1925** *Morris Owner's Manual* p. xiv (Advt.), Morris cars vans & lorries. **1930** *Amer. Speech* V. 274 American English has universally chosen *motor truck* and *truck* rather than *auto-truck* or the British *lorry.* **1955** *Times* 23 May 4/4 He spoke from a lorry on Waun Y Pound, a mountain top between Tredegar and Ebbw Vale. **1972** *Guinness Bk. Records* (ed. 19) 130/2 The world's largest lorry is the M-200 Lectra Haul built by Unit Rig and Equipment Co. of Fort Worth, Texas with a capacity of 200 tons.

3. *lorry driver, driving, load; lorry-borne* adj.; **lorry-bus,** a lorry used as a vehicle for public transport; also **lorribus; lorry-hop** *v.*, to hitch-hike by lorry; so **lorry-hopping** *vbl. sb.*; **lorry-jump** *v.* = **lorry-hop* vb.; so **lorry-jumping** *vbl. sb.*; **lorry park,** an open space or lot reserved for the parking of lorries.

1937 B. H. L. HART *Europe in Arms* xxiv. 323 The inability of these temporarily lorry-borne infantry to attack effectively after they had dismounted. **1943** *R.A.F. Jrnl.* Aug. 7 Our aircraft..have operated against..armoured formations and lorry-borne infantry. **1919** *Daily Mail* 12 June 4/4 In the welter of London's crowded streets we grasped at the relieving 'lorribus' (the converted Army lorry doing the duty as an emergency omnibus). **1963** *Economist* 23 Nov. 758/2 Ghana's ubiquitous lorry-buses, or mammywagons. **1926** *C.M.U.A. Jrnl.* Apr.–May 29 It sometimes happened that a lorry driver, arriving at noon, was told to go away and return next morning, as railway trucks were being loaded. **1972** *Times* 30 Nov. 5/6 Lorry drivers will meet dockers' representatives to-morrow. **1937** D. L. SAYERS *Busman's Honeymoon* viii. 166 Odd jobs of lorry-driving and taxi-work. **1975** J. WAINWRIGHT *Square Dance* 246 Shurrup, lad... Stick to lorry-driving, and learn. **1933** A. G. MACDONELL *England, their England* xvii. 286 He walked a bit from Alton, and then lorry-hopped, in army fashion, as far as..Alresford. **1947** *Penguin New Writing* XXI. 98 An ex-convict..who lorry-hops across England in order to escape the police. **1925** FRASER & GIBBONS *Soldier & Sailor Words* 147 *Lorry hopping* (or *jumping*), a familiar term at the Front for travelling by begging 'lifts' from passing transport vehicles. **1928** BLUNDEN *Undertones of War* 201 By luck or judgment in lorry-hopping..one reached Boulogne. **1931** *Times Lit. Suppl.* 12 Nov. 899/3 She 'hitch-hiked', the American equivalent for 'lorry-hopping'. **1947** L. HASTINGS *Dragons are Extra* v. 101 He..lorry-jumped his way back to his own battery. **1963** *Guardian* 6 Apr. 4/5 The moral dangers of young girls 'lorry jumping' or frequenting roadside cafés. **1928** C. T. BRUNNER *Probl. Motor Transport* vi. 101 The expense of railway transport,..could be reduced by packing the goods in containers..of a weight which would constitute a lorry load. **1972** *Times* 30 Nov. 23/4 Mr John Peyton..has actively stimulated opposition to the present EEC proposals for standardizing lorry loads. **1968** *Listener* 14 Mar. 335/1 Eight caravans..had been parked as a final gesture of despair in the middle of a Walsall Corporation lorry park. **1971** *Daily Tel.* 13 Sept. 3/6 Recommendations..to replace traditional transport cafés with a network of guarded lorry parks. **1974** *Ibid.* 9 Mar. 2/5 The removal of guard dogs, closed circuit television and the £1 parking fee at a high security lorry park has led to a record number of lorries using it.

lorry (lǫ·ri), *v.* [f. the sb.] *trans.* To transport or convey by means of a lorry or lorries. Hence **lo·rried** *ppl. a.*

1920 *Blackw. Mag.* Jan. 125/1 They were 'lorried' to the Lys front. **1949** W. S. CHURCHILL *Second World War* II. II. xxiii. 416 Tanks..and artillery in front, and with lorried infantry in the centre. **1958** G. DONALDSON *Shetland Life under Earl Patrick* 61 Only since such calls [at individual ports] ceased have all goods for places on the Mainland been landed at Lerwick and then lorried to their destinations. **1975** *Daily Tel.* 9 Sept. 12/6 There will be in 1 British Corps, three lorried infantry battalions.

lose, *sb.*^{2} Add: *lose bet, game,* one in which the loser of the game wins the stakes.

1964 A. WYKES *Gambling* vi. 143 (*caption*) A 'lose' bet is that the shooter will throw a crap. **1971** *Jrnl. Gen. Psychol.* LXXXV. 268 High-risk bets are again more typical of the lose game.

lose, *v.*^{1} Add: **3. b.** Phr. *to lose one's nerve* (NERVE *sb.* 10): to become scared, uneasy; *to lose sleep over* (or *about, for,* etc., something): to worry about (something) (usu. in negative contexts).

1912 *Chambers's Jrnl.* Nov. 739/1 There's nothing here to lose one's nerve about. **1934** G. B. SHAW *Too True to be Good* III. 86 When I was wounded and lost my nerve for flying, I became an army chaplain. **1942** H. C. BAILEY *Dead Man's Shoes* iv. 19 'I'd like to know why you didn't tell me.' 'You told me not to lose any sleep over it.' **1944** 'N. SHUTE' *Pastoral* ii. 41 'I wasn't losing any sleep for them.'..'Those two have been at this for years.' **1959** [see *CHANCER *sb.*]. **1959** N. MAILER *Advts. for Myself* (1961) 241 It's not the sort of thing I lose sleep over. **1967** J. PORTER *Dover & Unkindest Cut of All* x. 109 Dover hadn't lost any sleep over them... 'You can't win 'em all,' he used to say. **1971** *Guardian* 10 July 9/1 Stolid and conservative Midwesterners..never lost much sleep over the Negroes' troubles. **1974** *Ibid.* 18 Mar. 6/5 Although increasing restrictions on immigration..had been criticised ..it is doubtful whether the immigrants themselves have lost much sleep over them. **1975** *Times* 24 Feb. 14/7 You just have to get straight back on, or else you lose your nerve. The others are far more concerned with the loose horse than the girl lying face down in the dirt.

f. Also with *off.*

1874 *Rep. Vermont Board Agric.* II. 717, I think that tin buckets are preferable for catching sap to wooden ones, as they..have no hoops to lose off. **1906** *Dialect Notes* III. 145 A wheel lost off as they were driving to town.

j. *to lose a dinner* (or *a meal*): to vomit (what one has recently eaten).

Examples are *Austral.* and *U.S.*

1941 BAKER *Dict. Austral. Slang* 44 *Lose a meal,* to vomit up food. **1952** M. R. RINEHART *Swimming Pool* xxv. 227 I'm going to lose my dinner.

4. c. (20th-cent. examples with *in.*)

1902 *Chambers's Jrnl.* July 441/2 A bird does not gather speed when sailing in the air, as a falling stone would, neither does it lose in pace. **1913** *Q. Rev.* Oct. 413 As a consequence the work loses in freshness and even in clearness. **1947** *Harrap's Stand. French & Eng. Dict.* II. 728/2 The incident did not lose in the telling... To lose in value, in interest.

d. orig. *U.S. to lose out*: to be unsuccessful, to fail.

1858 H. BUSHNELL *Sermons for New Life* ix. 176 The child brought up a thief gets an infinite power of cunning..and loses out just as much in the power of true perception. **1909** 'O. HENRY' *Roads of Destiny* iv. 66, I know you've lost out some by not having me to typewrite 'em. **1913** E. D. BIGGERS *Seven Keys to Baldpate* xiii. 165 But it's over, and you've lost out. **1930** C. JOHNSON *Negro in Amer. Civilisation* (1931) xxvi. 396 Is it not true that the Negro female is losing out in personal service? So often newspapers are specifying white in their want ads. **1942** E. PAUL *Narrow St.* xvii. 133 Daladier made a bid for the premiership and lost out because Briand would not play ball with him. **1947** 'G. ORWELL' *Eng. People* 38 The American tendency is to burden every verb with a preposition that adds nothing to its meaning (*win out, lose out, face up to,* etc.). **1959** *Encounter* Sept. 16/1 It will probably lose out in the competition. **1963** S. DOUGLAS *Years of Combat* x. 251 Tracers might come whistling past one's ears, indicating all too clearly that the enemy..was on the attack. If that happened it meant that we had lost out in the preliminary tactical manoeuvrings. **1966** *Listener* 10 Mar. 337/2 It could be that both China and America are losing out to the Russians. **1971** *Guardian* 23 July 5/2 We are going to lose out unless the Government are prepared to do a tremendous public relations job for the tourist industry here. **1972** *Newsweek* 10 July 15/2 Rep. Bella Abzug..lost out in her bid for a second term in Congress. **1973** *Times* 30 June 13/6 The monstrous proliferation of redundant prepositions in the ever more popular usages 'check up on', 'lose out to', 'meet up with'.

e. Of a clock, watch, etc.: to become slow (SLOW *a.* 12); to indicate a time earlier than the correct time. Also *trans.*, to run slow by the amount of (a specified period).

1861, 1870, 1917 [see *GAIN *v.*^{2} 3 d]. **1955** *Oxf. Jun. Encycl.* VIII. 81/2 A pendulum clock with a steel rod loses 2½ seconds per day for a rise of temperature of 10°F. **1972** *Which?* Aug. 244 At the same time each day the amount they had gained or lost was noted, and they were wound.

9. b. Delete † *Obs.* and add later examples. Esp. in phr. *you('ve) lost me* = 'I failed to follow what you were saying'.

1962 L. DEIGHTON *Ipcress File* vii. 42 'They have money..to investigate what they call "synthesised environment".' I said, 'You've lost me now—without trying.' **1967** H. VAN SILLER *Biltmore Call* 103 Frazer.. looked up, frowning. 'You've lost me. What do you mean, exactly?' **1970** R. LEWIS *Wolf by Ears* i. 11 You will have to be a little more explicit in your statements. I'm a bit lost. *Ibid.* 17 'You've lost me.' 'Put simply, it's this way.' **1973** *Observatory* Oct. 162 You lost me at one stage.

loser. Add: **2. d.** *a bad, poor* (or *good*) *loser*: a person who loses with bad (or good) grace.

1892 A. W. PINERO *Magistrate* I. 28 I hate a bad loser, don't you, Guv? **1917** *Dialect Notes* IV. 326 *Loser* n., differentiated as good loser and bad loser. Not local. 'Those college boys are good losers and do not complain at defeat, but the academy boys..are sure bad losers.' **1931** D. L. SAYERS *Five Red Herrings* xiii. 146 He was a bad loser. A slice off the tee..would put him off his game for the afternoon. **1947** 'G. ORWELL' *Eng. People* 14 The admiration for a 'good loser'. **1951** [see *CLOBBER *v.*^{2}]. **1973** A. MANN *Tiara* xvii. 164 The British were always talking about 'being a good loser'. **1973** *Radio Times* 20–27 Dec. 10/1, I like to win at things. But..I'm a good loser.

e. An unsuccessful or incompetent person, a failure.

1955 *Amer. Speech* XXX. 304 *Loser,*..someone..hopeless. **1959** *Ibid.* XXXIV. 154 Those limited in ability or old-fashioned in dress or manners, [are] losers. *Ibid.*, The opposite of a B[ig] M[an] O[n] C[ampus] is a loser. **1972** *Melody Maker* 25 Nov. 53 (*heading*) Jiving K. Boots. The adventures of a loser musician. **1974** J. STUBBS *Painted Face* xiii. 180 Poor fellow... A born loser, every time.

4. *U.S. slang.* A convicted criminal, a person who has served a sentence in prison. So *two-time* (or *three-time,* etc.) *loser,* a person who has been in prison twice (or three, etc., times).

1912 D. LOWRIE *My Life in Prison* xi. 127 T'day some four 'r five time loser'll drive up with a year. *Ibid.* xxvii. 337 He was a 'ten-time loser' the last time I saw him; *i.e.*, he had served nine previous terms at either San Quentin or Folsom. **1914** JACKSON & HELLYER *Vocab. Criminal Slang* 56 *Loser* noun, current amongst prison habitues. An ex-convict... Examples: 'Three-time losers cop life in some states.' **1926** *Clues* Nov. 161/2 *Loser,* one who has served a prison sentence. **1931** *Amer. Speech* VII. 117 *Two-time loser,* a prisoner who has been convicted twice. 'He's a two-time loser; got the book the second time.' **1939** E. S. GARDNER *D.A. draws Circle* (1940) xii. 213 He's a two-time loser. **1950** H. E. GOLDIN *Dict. Amer. Underworld Lingo* 129/1 *Loser,* anyone convicted of a felony. (A second felony conviction makes one a 'two-time loser'; a third conviction, a 'three-time loser', etc.) 'I'm a four-time loser on the next pinch (arrest).' **1973** *Houston* (Texas) *Chron. Texas Mag.* 14 Oct. 4/1 Bob, a three-time loser with a long line of busts and drug abuse..was sick of his life.

5. *Bridge.* **a.** A losing card.

1917 E. BERGHOLT *Royal Auction Bridge* (ed. 2) 56 The opponent will be able to make two tricks in that suit before Y has had a chance of discarding his two losers. **1921** F. IRWIN *Compl. Auction Player* ii. 48 You hold five losers. That is a two-bid, no more. **1964** *Contract Bridge* ('Know the Game' Series) (ed. 2) 29/1 You should not play any trumps but utilize them to ruff losers. **1964** *Official Encycl. Bridge* 334/1 At no trump, all cards below the ace and not in sequence with it are possible losers.

b. loser-on-loser (see quot. 1964).

[**1929** *Auction Bridge Mag.* Jan. 328/1 (*title*) Discarding a loser on a loser...discarding a losing card on a loser.. may be the only play to secure the contract or game.] **1947** T. REESE *Reese on Play* xi. 162 Loser-on-loser play makes the hand against any defence... Some very complicated positions can arise after a loser-on-loser elimination. **1964** *Official Encycl. Bridge* 334/1 *Loser on loser,* the act of playing a card that must be lost on a losing trick in some other suit.

loseyite (lō^{u}·zi,əit). *Min.* [f. the name of Samuel *Losey* (*c* 1833–1906), U.S. mineral collector + -ITE^{1}.] A basic carbonate of zinc and manganese, $(Zn,Mn)_7(CO_3)_2(OH)_{10}$, found as bluish-white monoclinic crystals at Franklin, New Jersey, U.S.A.

1929 BAUER & BERMAN in *Amer. Mineralogist* XIV. 150 This mineral is named loseyite in honor of Mr. Samuel R. Losey, a native of Franklin and for many years, until his death, an ardent collector of the minerals occurring there. **1968** I. KOSTOV *Mineral.* II. xi. 542 Loseyite is also monoclinic (*A2/a*), found as bluish white radiating bundles of lath-like crystals.

loss, *sb.*^{1} Add: **4. c.** *to cut one's loss(es)*: to cease carrying on a losing transaction.

1912 *Q. Rev.* Jan. 287 It is now made the basis of the argument that England should 'cut her loss', and Ireland be sent adrift. **1926** T. E. LAWRENCE *Seven Pillars* (1935) VIII. xciv. 519 Feisal had..made one of his lightning decisions to cut the loss; a wise decision, though it hurt us sorely. **1927** *Daily Express* 13 July 8/2 The only reasonable thing is for Great Britain to..cut her losses, and bring the whole matter to an end. **1939** 'G. ORWELL' *Coming up for Air* II. vii. 123 The trouble over Joe aged Father a great deal. To lose Joe was merely to cut a loss, but it hurt him. **1944** A. BRYANT *Yrs. of Victory* ii. 39 Bonaparte..saw that he was beaten and, like the great man he was, cut his losses. **1969** *Listener* 28 Aug. 269/1 For this reason the CIA is cutting its losses, reducing its labyrinthine commitments.

5. c. (Examples.) *dead loss*: see *DEAD *a.* 30.

1940 W. FAULKNER *Hamlet* I. i. 16 Major De Spain's barn taken fire and was a total loss. **1943** *Scrutiny* XI. 288 If you apply serious standards, then P. G. [Wodehouse] is a total loss.

d. *one person's loss is another's gain*: a semi-proverbial expression. Also with non-personal subject and complement.

1914 G. B. SHAW *Misalliance* 41 It civilizes them. And it uncivilizes us. Their gain. Our loss. **1925** *New Yorker* 22 Aug. 9/1 When the fighting was over she remained... Our loss was their gain. **1949** B. A. BOTKIN *Treas. S. Folklore* II. i. 147 What is history's loss is folklore's gain. **1973** *Times* 22 Jan. 9/5 (*heading*) Newcastle's loss is Doncaster's gain.

10. *attrib.* and *Comb.* **loss leader** *Comm.*, an article put on sale at a non-profit-making

price in order to attract potential buyers of other articles; also *transf.*; hence **loss-leading** *vbl. sb.*; **loss-maker,** a business, etc., consistently working at a loss; **loss-making** *vbl. sb.*, the making of a loss (in business, etc.); also as *ppl. a.*, that makes a loss.

1922 HAYWARD & WHITE *Chain Stores* vii. 109 Many chains have a fixed policy of featuring each week a so-called 'loss leader'. That is, some well known article, the price of which is usually standard and known to the majority of purchasers, is put on sale at actual cost to the chain or even at a slight loss..on the theory..that people will be attracted to this bargain and buy other goods as well. Loss leaders are often termed 'weekly specials'. **1942** H. LEVY *Retail Trade Assoc.* xviii. 211 Prohibitions on 'loss leaders'. **1958** *Times* 15 Dec. 9/3 No doubt price cutting in individual lines often goes beyond the point where it is justified by reduction in direct cost: it is in part the loss-leader technique. People are attracted into a shop by some very low prices, and buy many other articles which give a handsome margin. **1969** *Daily Tel.* 7 Mar. 19 Sir Stanley Raymond, chairman of the Gaming Board, said yesterday he was convinced that Bingo was often used as a 'loss leader' to induce housewives into 'hard' gambling. In many cases Bingo provided only half of the takings in clubs. **1970** *Ibid.* 15 May 21/5 Some would like to see bank charges on personal accounts reduced or abolished, as a 'loss leader' to the existing personal customers. **1971** *New Scientist* 21 Jan. 102/1 The ranks of loss leaders and unrepeatable offers. **1964** *New Statesman* 28 Feb. 343/1 This concession was necessary to get any bill past his own back-benchers; and there are a few more..concessions..in particular a ban on loss-leading. **1968** *Daily Tel.* 12 Nov. 17/8 Only a madman or a company making a genuine attempt at loss leading would reduce rates. **1971** *Guardian Weekly* 23 Jan. 22 What happens when two companies, both lossmakers, merge into one? The answer, as often as not, is one big loss-maker. **1973** *Times* 24 Aug. 17/2 The company declined to give reasons for its withdrawals except to say that the bookstalls did not fit into its 'economic pattern' or plans for the future. It said the stalls were not lossmakers. **1971** *Sunday Times* 15 Aug. 41 He started by picking up a 40% stake in the lossmaking Carson's chocolate business in March 1964. **1974** *Times* 7 Mar. 19/6 The company has been loss-making since 1971.

lossless, *a.* Restrict † *Obs.* to sense in Dict. and add: **b.** *Electr.* Characterized by or causing no dissipation of electrical or electromagnetic energy.

1952 *Proc. IRE* XL. 1651/1 If..the system is lossless, then the transverse electromagnetic (TEM) mode can be propagated. **1962** CORSON & LORRAIN *Introd. Electromagn. Fields* xi. 357 Lossless dielectrics, good conductors, and low-pressure ionized gases. **1969** P. M. CHIRLIAN *Basic Network Theory* i. 46 Inductors and capacitors are called lossless elements.

loss-proof (lǫ·sprūf), *a.* [f. LOSS *sb.*[1] + PROOF *a.* 1 b.] Guaranteed against loss, inflation, fluctuation in market value, etc.

1963 *New Yorker* 8 June 107 (Advt.), Travelers cheques ..Loss-proof and theft-proof. **1969** *Daily Tel.* 22 Nov. 14 (Advt.), The guaranteed loss-proof investment that *grows* despite Stock Market ups and downs.

lossy (lǫ·si), *a. Electr.* [f. LOSS *sb.*[1] + -Y[1].] Characterized by or causing dissipation of electrical or electromagnetic energy.

1948 H. A. LEITER in Smullin & Montgomery *Microwave Duplexers* ix. 378 Lossy cables are used..in order to isolate the oscillator from effects of mismatch in the unit under test. **1949** L. L. LANGTON *Radio-Frequency Heating Equipment* v. 76 A lossy capacitor. **1969** *Sci. Jrnl.* Dec. 44/3 At optical frequencies a metal transmission line structure would be very 'lossy' and only transparent dielectric materials such as glass can be considered. **1970** J. EARL *Tuners & Amplifiers* iv. 94 Most transformers are 'lossy' at the sub-bass end of the spectrum.

lost, *ppl. a.* Add: **1.** (Later examples of *lost soul.*)

1895 [see *BOOZE *sb.* 1 c]. **1923** D. H. LAWRENCE *Ladybird* 224 The lost-soul look of the men. **1937** *Discovery* May 150/2 It emits a weird screaming wail like a lost soul.

2. (Earlier and later examples of *lost ball.*) *to get lost*: see *GET *v.* 33.

1809 *Laws of Cricket* (rev. ed.), If lost Ball is call'd, the Striker shall be allowed four, but if more than four are run before lost Ball is call'd, then the Striker to have all they have run. **1967** *Laws of Cricket* ('Know the Game' Series) 15 If a ball in play cannot be found or recovered, any fieldsman may call 'Lost Ball', when 6 runs shall be added to the score.

6. lost cause, a cause (CAUSE *sb.* 11) that has failed or that is unlikely to succeed; *spec.* the cause of the South in the American Civil War (1861–65); **lost generation,** *spec.* that of the period of the 1914–18 war, a high proportion of whose men were killed in the trench warfare; also used more generally of any generation judged to have 'lost' its values, etc.; **lost property,** lost articles found but not claimed; so *lost property department, office,* an office dealing with (the disposal of) lost property; **lost river** *U.S.*, a river which disappears into the ground and re-emerges elsewhere; **lost rock** *U.S.*, a travelled boulder; **lost stone** *U.S.* = **lost rock*; **lost wax** = *CIRE PERDUE; **lost weekend,** one spent in dissolute living; also *transf.*

1865 M. ARNOLD *Ess. Criticism* p. xix., Oxford...home of lost causes, and forsaken beliefs, and unpopular names, and impossible loyalties! **1866** E. A. POLLARD (*title*) The lost cause. **1901** 'MARK TWAIN' *Speeches* (1923) 231 You testify by honoring two of us, once soldiers of the Lost Cause. **1914** *Times Lit. Suppl.* 7 Aug. 378 Oxford has often been called 'the home of lost causes', or, as Mr. Cram puts it, 'of causes not lost but gone before'. **1933** C. MACKENZIE (*title*) The lost cause. A Jacobite play. **1938** J. BETJEMAN *Oxf. Univ. Chest* v. 112 Wytham and Binsey are the less hackneyed of Oxford's lost causes on the edge of Oxford. **1940** C. F. ADAMS *And Sudden Death* xvii. 155 Why should I go round championing a lost cause? **1948** D. WECTER in J. G. Kerwin *Civil–Military Relationships in Amer. Life* 31 Their late adversaries, the United Confederate Veterans, licked their wounds and dwelt lovingly upon the Lost Cause. **1949** D. S. FREEMAN in B. A. Botkin *Treas. S. Folklore* p. viii, Perhaps every land that has the tradition of a Lost Cause builds its monuments in a certain sentimental determination and seeks through its memorials both to exemplify and to perpetuate its ideal. **1926** E. HEMINGWAY *Sun also Rises* (*title-page*), 'You are all a lost generation.'—Gertrude Stein in conversation. **1930** R. MACAULAY *Staying with Relations* iv. 57, I was nineteen when the affair [*sc.* the war] ended... I belong practically to the Lost Generation. **1939** C. DAY LEWIS *Child of Misfortune* II. i. 146 'Ha,' Alec yelled. 'We're the Lost Generation.' **1951** E. PAUL *Springtime in Paris* xi. 197 The era of the Lost Generation and the notorious expatriates. **1959** *Listener* 15 Oct. 616/2 Thomas Wolfe, F. Scott Fitzgerald, Sinclair Lewis, Ernest Hemingway, and Katherine Anne Porter—members of the so-called 'lost generation', strove and strayed on the left banks between the wars. **1969** [see *HIPPIE, HIPPY *sb.* and *a.*]. **1970** D. T. TURNER in Z. N. Hurston *Mules & Men* 11 New York was an exciting place for young black intellectuals and artists during the mid-Twenties. Afro-American culture had been rediscovered... The 'Lost Generation' danced wildly to jazz rhythms. **1844** A. W. KINGLAKE *Eothen* xxii. 340 The Governor..saw the value which I set upon the lost property. **1922** JOYCE *Ulysses* 56 His lost property office secondhand waterproof. **1923** H. C. BAILEY *Mr. Fortune's Practice* vi. 156 He was only calling on the lost property department to leave a lady's bag. **1941** V. NABOKOV *Real Life S. Knight* (1945) x. 86 She fails to get the..job in the lost property office. **1959** *Manch. Guardian* 7 Aug. 12/2 A home-made double bass..will be included in a lost property sale. **1971** 'A. GARVE' *Late Bill Smith* ii. 49 Everyone with any kind of problem was bringing it to Sue. She was harbour-master, postmaster, nurse, lost property office. **1843** 'R. CARLTON' *New Purchase* I. ix. 58 Out come the mole rivers that have burrowed all this time under the earth, and which, when so unexpectedly found are styled out there,—'lost rivers'! And every district of a dozen miles square has a lost river. **1872** R. W. RAYMOND *Statistics of Mines* 197 The great 'lost river' which bursts out of the vertical side of the cañon of the Snake. **1831** J. M. PECK *Guide for Emigrants* II. 136 Scattered over the surface of our prairies are large masses of rock, of granitic formation, roundish in form, usually called by the people *lost rocks*... These stones are denominated *boulders* in mineralogy. **1857** *Trans. Illinois Agric. Soc.* II. 347 Another curiosity is the boulders, or 'lost rocks', as they are frequently called, which are found on the surface of the earth in the middle and northern sections of Illinois. **1819** H. C. MCMURTRIE *Sk. Louisville* 29 (Th.), [Certain stones] in the Illinois and Missouri territories are denominated lost-stones, from their being strangers to the soil where they are found. **1933** H. F. LENZ *Alfred David Lenz Syst. Lost Wax Casting* 9 The modeling wax for casting in the 'cire perdue' or 'lost wax' method has several requirements. **1947** J. C. RICH *Materials & Methods of Sculpture* vi. 146 The 'lost-wax' or *cire-perdue* process is the traditional method of casting in bronze... The ancient Egyptians employed the lost-wax method, casting over ash cores. **1972** *Times* 28 Sept. 18/6 The bronzes were made by the lost-wax process in which the mould is destroyed. **1944** C. JACKSON (*title*) Lost weekend. **1947** M. MCCARTHY in *Partisan Rev.* May–June 303 It was..comic that a man should have one name..for his wife..and another..for trips and 'lost' week ends. **1955** KOESTLER *Trail of Dinosaur* 56 He is the classic type who becomes addicted to the Communist drug, and never finds his way back from the lost weekend in Utopia. **1960** K. AMIS *Take Girl like You* xix. 229, I quite expected to find you on the couch this morning, especially after your lost-weekend act. **1968** A. MACLEOD *Dam* iii. 32 I'll have to go down to the pub and replenish the stock... And that will mean another bloody lost weekend. **1969** 'E. LATHEN' *Come to Dust* iii. 34 He seems to feel that if Patterson emerges from some lost weekend, the press will seize on his connection with Neil Marsden. **1975** M. KENYON *Mr Big* vii. 65 The *Express* used one paragraph headed Lost Weekend.

‖ **los von Rom** (lōs fǫn rōm). [Ger., = 'free from Rome'.] A slogan used by and applied to a movement which arose in Austria and Germany at the end of the 19th c., seeking to reduce the political influence of the Roman Catholic Church. Also used allusively of other policies of this kind.

1899 *Times* 8 Apr. 8/2 The really significant feature of the conversion of Herr Wolf, the Pan-Germanic member of the Reichsrath, and perhaps the most active promoter of the 'Los von Rom' agitation, is..his acceptance by the Evangelical community. **1920** W. T. WHITLEY in *Encycl. Relig. & Ethics* XI. 326/2 This Los von Rom movement seems..to have been anti-Slav, and reinforced Protestants quite as much, the tendency being to pave the way for these provinces to join the German Empire. **1923** G. M. TREVELYAN *Manin & Venetian Revolution of 1848* ix. 165 Irritated by the Pope's Italian nationalism, the German Catholics might drift toward the position of *los von Rom.* **1957** *Oxf. Dict. Chr. Ch.* 822 *Los von Rom*... The Movement, which owed its name to the shout of a student at the Deutscher Volkstag at Vienna (1897), came to have its centre at Innsbruck. **1963** *Listener* 28 Feb. 360/1 None of the Five, not Dr Adenauer nor any other German, is likely to cry '*los von Rom*'.

lot, *sb.* **1. e.** Delete *rarely*, and add later examples.

1870 [see THROW *v.*[1] 41 e]. **1927** *Daily Express* 15 June 11/7 Mr. Patrick O'Maille..threw in his lot recently with Professor Magennis' party, Clainn Eireann.

2. d. Also in colloq. phr. *to be* or *to have had* (one's) *lot.*

1960 *Observer* 24 Jan. 5/2 When the bogies sus you and take your trousers to the forensic lab you've had your lot. **1961** J. MACLAREN-ROSS *Doomsday Book* I. vii. 77 Any trouble, mush, and it's your lot. *Ibid.* II. v. 156 That's your lot, Marsh! This isn't one of your crime-plays, d'you hear. **1968** *Listener* 18 July 77/2 'Mummy, Tristram has just dropped your handbag into something rustic.' 'Right, that's your lot. Into the car, and we'll get back to civilisation.' **1973** *Times* 12 Dec. 2/7 Hate slogans scrawled on a blackboard. One read, 'Tina Wilson is going to be done over,' and another, 'Tina Wilson has had her lot tonight.'

6. a. (Earlier and later examples of *across* or *cross lots.*) Also *attrib.*, as *lot gate.* **b.** Also, land round a film studio where outside filming may be done.

a **1852** F. M. WHITCHER *Widow Bedott Papers* (1883) xxii. 87 You see yer uncle and me went hum by the turnpike instid o' gwine cross lots. **1854** *Jrnl. Discourses* I. 83 [I dreamed that] I cut one of their throats from ear to ear, saying, 'Go to hell across lots.' **1858** J. R. LOWELL *Two Gunners* in *Poetical Works* II. 125 Joe looked roun' And see (acrost lots in a pond..) A goose. **1887** *Scribner's Mag.* Dec. 735/1 He'd have had to foot it by the path 'cross lots... He's sold his hoss. **1928** 'R. WEST' *Strange Necessity* 205 The worst of making war, as of acting for the 'movies', is the amount of waiting around on the lot. **1929** W. FAULKNER *Sartoris* IV. 281 Restless hounds waited for them at the lot gate. **1937** PARTRIDGE *Dict. Slang* 538/1 The most picturesque phrase of all is 'the lot', which is always used to describe the company's land surrounding the studio. It has been in use since the days when..hard-pressed pioneers rented vacant building lots. **1938** M. K. RAWLINGS *Yearling* xv. 153 As he clicked the lotgate, doves flew from the pines with a whistling of wings. **1948** 'N. SHUTE' *No Highway* vi. 151 Don't you ask me why, I'll tell you when I see you on the lot. **1966** *Listener* 15 Dec. 880/1 Many lots are devoted to the less arduous and expensive work of turning out films for television networks. **1969** in Halpert & Story *Christmas Mumming in Newfoundland* 174 Then commenced the chase, up lanes, 'across lots', down lanes.

8. b. (Later examples.)

1936 W. R. TITTERTON *Chesterton* I. ii. 30 If I quoted much of that marvellous essay I should have to quote the lot. **1956** H. & M. WILLIAMS *Plays of Year* XV. 178 It was to be a big wedding—the full treatment—Royalty—the lot. **1958** *Listener* 3 July 10/2 They are said to cure everything from rheumatism to ringworm, colic to snake-bite.. —the lot. **1961** [see *CROAK *v.* 5]. **1970** *Times* 7 Jan. 7/5 The death of his father..triggers off a crisis for him too, producing a temporary breakdown, dismissal from his job, separation from his wife, the lot. **1974** 'P. B. YUILL' *Bornless Keeper* vii. 65 They've searched the island twice —helicopters, dogs, the lot.

9. (Later examples.) Also with *adj.* as (*this, that*) *little lot.*

1898 J. D. BRAYSHAW *Slum Silhouettes* 141 Yus, it's a nobby little turn-out, ain't it?.. Mine? Lor' luv a duck! No, that's Sal Hogan's little lot. **1920** J. MANDER *Story N.Z. River* v. 76, I just love you, lots. **1957** 'J. WYNDHAM' *Midwich Cuckoos* iii. 24 That there Miss Ogle ain't 'alf goin' to cop 'erself a basinful of 'Er Majesty's displeasure over this little lot. **1961** B. CRUMP *Hang on a Minute* 91 Have a bo-peep at this little lot, Jack, called Sam from the back of the truck. **1965** [see *BUSTER 2 b]. **1968** *Listener* 1 Aug. 148/1 Mr Donoghue, like any good critic, doesn't mean us, he means you lot. **1975** P. G. WINSLOW *Death of Angel* 125 A group of lads she doesn't care about... Next stop Wormwood Scrubs, that little lot.

10. lot-jumper *U.S.*, one who appropriates another's lot.

1869 *Overland Monthly* III. 63 Then there had been a lot jumper's fight down at the end of the street. **1889** in J. B. Thoburn *Stand. Hist. Oklahoma* (1916) I. xx. 223 Gamblers, liquor dealers,.. lot-jumpers. **1931** G. F. WILLISON *Here they dug Gold* 241 Counterfeiters, lot-jumpers, mine-jumpers,.. and ruffians in general.

lotaustralin (lōᵘtau·strălin). *Chem.* [f. mod.L. *Lot-us*, the generic name, + *austral-is*, the specific epithet (see AUSTRALIAN *sb.* and *a.*), of the lotus (LOTUS 5) from which it was first isolated: see -IN[1].] A toxic crystalline compound, $C_{11}H_{19}NO_6$, which occurs in *Lotus australis* and in white clover (*Trifolium repens*).

1938 FINNEMORE & COOPER in *Jrnl. Soc. Chem. Industry* May 165/1 The cyanogenetic constituent is in the main composed of the glucoside of the cyanohydrin of methyl ethyl ketone. This is new and it is proposed to call it lotaustralin. **1964**, **1973** [see *LINAMARIN].

Lotharingian (lōᵘþări·ndʒiăn), *sb.* and *a.* [f. *Lotharingia* (see below) + -AN.] **A.** *sb.* A native or inhabitant of the ancient duchy of Lotharingia in northern Europe, situated between the Rhine and the Scheldt from Frisia to the Alps. **B.** *adj.* Of or pertaining to Lotharingia or its inhabitants, or to modern Lorraine (see quot. 1969). Cf. *LORRAINER.

1607 TOPSELL *Four-f. Beasts* 46 They [*sc.* beavers] are vsed by the Lotharingians and Sauoyens for meat allowed to be eaten on fish-daies. **1883** *Encycl. Brit.* XV. 5/1 By the treaty of Bonn (921) the Lotharingian duchy was ceded formally to France. *Ibid.*, The ever-restless spirit of the Lotharingians broke out into new commotions. **1909** J. H. B. MASTERMAN *Dawn Mediæval Europe* xxiii. 216 Louis the German and Charles both fell upon his [*sc.* Lothair's] Lotharingian lands like birds of prey. **1959** *Chambers's Encycl.* VIII. 694/1 In a struggle with the turbulent Lotharingian magnates, the young king was killed. **1964** *Times Rev. Industry* Jan. 73/3 The river Our ..is situated within 100 miles of the Belgian coalfields, the Ruhr, the Lotharingian steel industry,.. and the Luxembourg iron industry. **1969** *Listener* 6 Feb. 165/2 In this new economic Europe, which hinges on the Rhine and the Rhône—the Lotharingian axis, as it's sometimes called—Brittany tends to feel even more isolated.

lotic (lōᵘ·tik), *a. Ecol.* [f. L. *lōtus* washing (Needham & Lloyd *Life of Inland Waters* (1916) vi. 315).] Of fresh-water organisms or habitats, situated in rapidly moving water. Cf. *LENITIC *a.*

1916 NEEDHAM & LLOYD *Life Inland Waters* vi. 363 The animals of lotic societies are mainly small invertebrates. **1931** R. N. CHAPMAN *Animal Ecol.* xvii. 347 Along the shores of the Great Lakes there are lotic communities where the wave action is incessant, thus producing the fundamental conditions of a lotic environment and presenting an exception to the general statement that all lotic environments are streams. **1970** F. J. & W. B. VERNBERG *Animal & Environment* ii. 44 Fresh-water systems are generally divided into two groups based on the activity or rate of movement of the water: (1) standing quiet (lentic) waters..; and (2) flowing (lotic) waters.

lotong (lotǫ·ŋ). Also **lutung.** [Malay.] A leaf monkey of the genus *Presbytis*, esp. *P. obscurus.*

1821 T. S. RAFFLES in *Trans. Linn. Soc.* XIII. 247 *Simia maura?* Linn. Lotong of the Malays. **1824** T. HORSFIELD *Zool. Res. Java* s.v. *Semnopithecus Maurus.* The name of the latter [monkey] is Lutung; but the Malays and Europeans apply this name to both species... In Sumatra the name of the 'Maure' is Lotong. **1839** T. J. NEWBOLD *Pol. & Statistical Acct. Straits of Malacca* I. vii. 432 Of the genus Semnopithecus are..the Lotong, or Semnopithecus Maurus, of F. Cuvier; the kra, etc. **1903** J. L. BONHOTE in *Fasciculi Malayenses: Zoology* I. 6 The lôtong is very generally distributed over those parts of the Peninsula that we visited. **1936** G. B. GARDNER *Keris & Other Malay Weapons* v. 95 They have a curved iron handle forged on, resembling the tail of a *lotong* monkey. **1965** C. SHUTTLEWORTH *Malayan Safari* 10 A *lotong* (leaf monkey) chattered its alarm call near by.

lotsa (lǫ·tsă). Colloq. contraction of *lots of.*

1927 [see *HOT *a.* 1 e]. **1945** A. KOBER *Parm Me* 18 Mmm, is good the cake... You must use lotsa ecks [*sc.* eggs] fa such a cake. **1967** 'P. CHAMBERS' *Bad die Young* x. 146 We got lotsa time. **1969** in Halpert & Story *Christmas Mumming in Newfoundland* 88 The social drinkers soon left, even though the host was protesting that there was 'lotsa time to stay'. **1971** *It* 9–23 Sept. 4/2 The Notting Hill Carnival was lotsa fun for seven days and nights.

lotta (lǫ·tă). Also **lotter.** Colloq. contraction of *lot of.*

1906 E. NESBIT *Railway Children* viii. 175, I gets a lotter green paint and I paints her stem to stern. **1928** [see *BULLSHIT 1]. **1944** C. HIMES *Black on Black* (1973) 198 Lotta hustlers up there. **1945** A. KOBER *Parm Me* 34, I hadda do a lotta talking to get her to come. **1965** 'D. SHANNON' *Death-Bringers* (1966) xiii. 164 A lotta people know my name who I don't know. **1969** *Coast to Coast 1967–68* 9 No, I'm a lotta things, but I ain't crazy. **1971** *Black World* Apr. 56 Lotta big talk, but when you get there nothin is happenin.

lotus. Add: **3. c.** The plant treated symbolically in Hindu and Buddhist thought; also, in Yogic exercises, a bodily position said to resemble the lotus blossom. Cf. *lotus gospel, pose*, etc. in *6.

1848 J. D. HOOKER *Himalayan Jrnls.* Nov. (1854) I. x. 229 Low stone dykes, into which were let rows of stone slabs, inscribed with the sacred 'Om Mani Padmi om'.—'Hail to him of the lotus and jewel.' **1887** E. ARNOLD (*title*) Lotus and jewel, containing 'In an Indian temple', 'A casket of gems'..with other poems. **1949** S. MUZUMDAR *Yogic Exercises* 103 There are insuperable impediments because of which many will fail to master the Lotus. **1973** R. RENDELL *Some lie & some Die* xviii. 183 Vedast..had taken up a Yoga position, a half-Lotus, on the floor.

6. (*Buddhism* and *Yoga*) *lotus gospel, pose, position, posture, seat, throne.*

1911 E. A. GORDON (*title*) The Lotus Gospel or Mahayana Buddhism and its symbolic teachings. **1966** 'A. HALL' *9th Directive* ii. 17 He sat with his legs crossed under him in the Lotus pose. **1962** T. C. LETHBRIDGE *Witches* v. 57 There are so many ways in which the Indian gods agree with those of Western Europe, even to their sitting in the 'lotus' position. **1964** I. FLEMING *You only live Twice* i. 21 Since Bond had arrived in Japan he had assiduously practised sitting in the lotus position. **1968** *Guardian* 29 Feb. 8/4 Sitting in the lotus position..concentrating upon one's navel and repeating the mystic syllable, 'Om, Om'. **1884** RAM CHANDRA BOSE *Hindu Philos.* vi. 177 It is called Padmásana (lotus-posture), and is highly beneficial in overcoming all diseases. **1965** W. SWAAN *Jap. Lantern* xii. 136 Ideally, one should assume the cross-legged 'Lotus Posture' familiar from Buddha images. **1937** F. YEATS-BROWN *Yoga Explained* ii. 71 (*caption*) The pupil is shown in the Lotus Seat, padmasana, but any comfortable position can be adopted. **1911** E. B. HAVELL *Ideals Indian Art* iii. 32 The whole spirit of Indian thought is symbolised in the conception of the Buddha sitting on his lotus-throne.

lotus-eating, *vbl. sb.* Add: Hence (as a back-formation) **lotus-eat** *v. intr.*

1898 W. J. LOCKE *Idols* v. 64 'What have you been doing with yourself all this time?' she said... 'Oh, Lotus-eating, generally,' he replied. **1911**——*Glory of Clementina Wing* xv. 211 The week had evidently passed pleasantly for Quixtus... He was lotus eating. **1972** J. POTTER *Going West* 60 Every dream fades. If he drank and lotus-ate, he would think. **1973** 'B. MATHER' *Snowline* xix. 231 Hippies..come here..from Bombay—lotus-eat for a month..and off they go.

louche. Delete *rare* and add to def.: Also, dubious, shifty, disreputable.

1873 G. H. LEWES *Diary* 16 Jan. in Geo. Eliot *Lett.* (1956) V. 368 The whole thing appeared *louche* and unpromising. **1905** G. B. SHAW *Lett. to G. Barker* (1956) 53 You could play Snobby. I want a slim, *louche*, servant-girl-bigamist, half-handsome sort of rascal. **1921** A. HUXLEY *Crome Yellow* xvii. 182 There had seemed to be something a little *louche* in the way she had suddenly found herself alone with Ivor. **1945** AUDEN *Sea & Mirror* ii. 46 A quick cold clasp now and then in some *louche* hovel. **1945** E. WAUGH *Brideshead Revisited* 236, I knew of a louche little bar quite near here. **1959** P. H. JOHNSON *Humbler Creation* xlviii. 328 As if he were an unfrocked priest due for reception into the world of the *louche* and the lost. **1970** *Times* 7 Mar. (Saturday Suppl.) p. iv/6 There is plenty of marvellous delicate comedy and superbly *louche* menace. **1974** *Daily Tel.* (Colour Suppl.) 14 June 30/4 His louche greeting, 'Ladeez and Gentle*men*' was a byword among..BBC Light Programme listeners.

‖ **loucherbem** (lūʃebęm). Also **loucherbème.** [f. Fr. *boucher* butcher.] The name given to a type of French slang formed by the transposing of certain letters and addition of others.

1937 J. ORR tr. *Iordan's Introd. Romance Lang.* iv. 360 The butchers of La Villette speak, or spoke, a slang called *loucherbem*, or *largongi*... The process..is a deliberate modification of an existing word. **1938** I. GOLDBERG *Wonder of Words* viii. 155 In French there is the *loucherbème* language, so called because its model of transformed words is *boucher*. **1939** L. H. GRAY *Foundations of Lang.* 31 Only in a few instances do they actually change the form of words, as in the relatively recent French *loucherbème*. **1942** PARTRIDGE *Usage & Abusage* (1947) 160/2 *Gibberish* is applied..to the Loucherbem of the Paris butchers (*loucherbem* for *boucher* is itself Loucherbem).

Loucheux (lū·ʃö), *sb.* and *a.* [Canad. Fr., f. F. *louche* squint-eyed (see quot. 1828).] **A.** *sb.* **a.** A North American Indian people inhabiting the Yukon and Mackenzie River areas. **b.** The language of this people. **B.** *adj.* Of, pertaining to, or designating this people or their language.

1828 J. FRANKLIN *Narr. Second Expedition Polar Sea* i. 23 The fact is, that Loucheux, or Squinter, was intended to convey the sense of the Indian name..Deguthée Dennee, which means, 'the people who avoid the arrows of their enemies, by keeping a look out on both sides'. *Ibid.*, The tribe of Indians whom Mackenzie calls the Quarrellers, but whom the traders throughout the fur country name the Loucheux. *Ibid.* 29 The Red River contributes its waters to the Mackenzie..and..is remarkable as being the boundary between the lands claimed by the Loucheux Indians and those of the Esquimaux. **1867** *Ann. Rep. Board of Regents Smithsonian Inst. 1866* 311 The physical characteristics of the Loucheux nation are..the same as those of the other aborigines of North America. *Ibid.*, The Loucheux language is a dialect of the Chepewyan. *Ibid.*, The Loucheux, though sunk in barbarism, are rather more intelligent than the other tribes. *Ibid.*, The Loucheux proper is spoken by the Indians of Peel's river. **1890** J. G. FRAZER *Golden Bough* II. iii. 127 The Loucheux and Hare-skin Indians..are forbidden by custom to eat the sinew of the legs of animals. **1921** E. SAPIR *Lang.* iv. 71 Such languages as Navaho,..Chipewyan, Loucheux. **1971** *Times* 22 Feb. (Canada Suppl.) p. v/1 In the north of the Yukon close by the Alaska border, a small band of Loucheux Indians have stood up to be counted: they do not want oil and gas exploration in their territory. *Ibid.*, The caribou move..through these flats, and the Loucheux take about 1,000 of them a year for food.

loud, *a.* Add: **6.** *loud-mouthed* adj. (further examples); *loud-talking* adj.; **loud-mouth** [f. the adj.], a person given to loud and self-assertive talk; hence as *vb.*, to talk in this manner, to bluster; **loud-mouthing** *vbl. sb.*

1934 J. O'HARA *Appointment in Samarra* iv. 111 He was a loud-mouth and a good one-punch fighter. **1940** J. B. PRIESTLEY *Postscripts* 17 You will find that the laziest loud-mouth in the workshop has suddenly been given power. **1950** A. LOMAX *Mister Jelly Roll* (1952) v. 235 Morton, the old whorehouse pianist who seemed to be trying to loud-mouth his way back to big time. **1959** *Daily Mail* 31 Jan. 4/2 These 625 vain, devious loud-mouths..are our elected representatives. **1968** M. RICHLER *Cocksure* ix. 52 We are most decidedly not done for. My goodness, the last loudmouth to make that mistake was Hitler. **1867** TROLLOPE *Last Chron. Barset* I. xli. 353 How, from the abjectness of his own humility..he would rebuke the loud-mouthed triumph of the bishop's wife. **1924** G. B. SHAW *St. Joan* I. i. 7 The self-assertive, loud-mouthed, superficially energetic, fundamentally will-less Robert. **1966** *Listener* 27 Oct. 609/1 The Surrey amateur with an Oxford background and the loud-mouthed crowd from the foundries suddenly coalesced. **1971** C. BONINGTON *Annapurna South Face* vii. 85 He was well built, very self-confident yet not loudmouthed. **1950** W. L. JAMES in A. Dundes *Mother Wit* (1973) 431 Famous among those yet surviving names are 'corn field holler'..and 'loud mouthing'. **1973** *Daily Tel.* (Colour Suppl.) 26 Jan. 7/3 Money talks and there will be a lot of loud-mouthing before the future of the fourth channel is settled. **1848** MRS. GASKELL *Mary Barton* I. i. 3 Merry and somewhat loud-talking girls. **1925** T. DREISER *Amer. Trag.* (1926) I. I. ix. 56 He was too smooth and loud-talking.

loud, *adv.* Add: **1. d.** *out loud*, aloud, without restraint. Cf. OUT-LOUD.

1821 M. EDGEWORTH *Let.* 22 Nov. (1971) 277 Lord Andover in the presence of Lord and Lady Suffolk and speaking *out loud* said 'Miss Dutton..be so good to walk with me into the library.' **1844** [see OUT-LOUD]. **1881** TROLLOPE *Ayala's Angel* III. xlix. 67 He knew it would make me laugh out loud. **1924, 1933** [see *CRY *v.* 21 e]. **1939** G. B. SHAW *In Good King Charles's Golden Days* II. 104 Even a dissolute court, as they say mine is—I suppose they mean a court where bawdy stories are told out loud instead of whispered. **1941** [see *CRY *v.* 21 e].

e. Phr. *loud and clear*: (said, etc.) in a way that reduces or avoids confusion or misunderstanding; (esp. in radio or telecommunication) (heard or received) loudly and clearly; also *transf.*

1871 'L. CARROLL' *Through Looking-Glass* vi. 133, I said it very loud and clear; I went and shouted in his ear. **1940** H. G. WELLS *Babes in Darkling Wood* II. ii. 256 I'd have to play the Star Spangled Banner, loud and clear, one hundred per cent. **1958** 'CASTLE' & 'HAILEY' *Flight into Danger* ix. 123 Hullo, Vancouver. 714 answering. Receiving you loud and clear. Over. **1959** *Listener* 19 Feb. 319/1 It seems desirable to say so loud and clear. **1962** L. DEIGHTON *Ipcress File* vii. 43 Dalby looked up. 'You are receiving me?' 'Loud and clear,' I said. **1962** A. SHEPARD in *Into Orbit* 104, I also contacted..the chase planes—and heard them loud and clear. **1963** J. N. HARRIS *Weird World Wes Beattie* (1964) iii. 25 The fact is I remember that black Dodge loud and clear. **1970** C. COLLINGWOOD *Defector* iv. 33, I read you loud and clear. Now, suppose something does go wrong, what do I do? **1972** D. LEES *Zodiac* 90 They don't seem able to make up their minds whether to warn me off or knock me off but I do get the message loud and clear and..I'm going.

louderback (lau·dəɹbæk). *Geol.* [Named after G. D. *Louderback* (1874–1957), American geologist.] A cap of old lava on a tilted fault-block.

1930 W. M. DAVIS in *Bull. Geol. Soc. Amer.* XLI. 299 It seems to me highly appropriate that the lava sheets, which were thus spread unconformably on the Powell surface of the worn-down King mountains, and which now cover the back slopes of the tilted Gilbert blocks, should be called Louderbacks, after their discoverer. **1965** W. D. THORNBURY *Regional Geomorphol. U.S.* xxiv. 473/2 Some of the range have lava caps, called by Davis (1930) louderbacks. **1968** R. W. FAIRBRIDGE *Encycl. Geomorphol.* 679/1 Since the original [lava] flow would normally have filled a valley, the louderback is usually also a form of inverted topography.

loud-hail, *v.* [Back-formation from next.] *trans.* and *intr.* To speak or call through a loud-hailer; to address (someone) through a loud-hailer; also *fig.* Also **loud-hailing** *ppl. a.* and *vbl. sb.*

1943 *Combined Operations, 1940–42* (Ministry of Information) xvii. 130 We 'closed' the 'Calpe', struggling with our loud-hailing equipment which remained resolutely silent. **1964** R. PETRIE *Murder by Precedent* i. 19 I'd just left again and gone to Despatch when they loud-hailed me. **1965** *Listener* 3 June 837/1 Ku Klux Klan men, assorted torchbearers,.. and a loud-hailing director. **1969** C. CARFAX *Silence with Voices* xviii. 129 She went back into the cabin after Dr Ford loud-hailed her. **1969** J. ELLIOT *Duel* I. ii. 43 'The extraordinary thing is ——' Harry loud-hailed so that people at the next table were forced to listen.

loud-hai·ler. [f. LOUD *a.* 1 + HAILER.] A megaphone or other device for amplifying the voice, especially as used at sea. Also *transf.* and *attrib.*

1941 *Illustr. London News* 20 Sept. 366/3 Orders, signals and instructions..given over about one-eighth of a mile of water, orally, by the 'Loud Hailer' from Captain to Captain. **1943** *Combined Operations, 1940–42* (Ministry of Information) xvii. 131 'Maintain a smoke screen half a mile inshore and to the westward,' came over the loud hailer from the 'Calpe'. **1955** G. FREEMAN *Liberty Man* i. 2 Two metallic pipe-notes sounded through the loud-hailer system. **1956** J. MASTERS *Bugles & Tiger* xxii. 283, I heard a loud hailer calling my name. **1959** C. MACINNES *Absolute Beginners* 13 There was a loud-hailer echo up and down the flights. **1971** B. W. ALDISS *Soldier Erect* 241 They were allowed to use loud-hailers, even if the Japs would not trust them with rifles. **1971** *Daily Tel.* 16 Apr. 17/3 [He] alerted the Thames Coastguard..and then used a loudhailer to direct them to the highest point on the sandbank. **1973** C. BONINGTON *Next Horizon* xix. 264 John..ran out with the loud-hailer, shouting..the conventional form of greeting.

loudness. Add: Also, the (great or small) extent to which a sound is heard as loud. (Further examples.)

1937 *Ann. Reg. 1936* 65 It was suggested that an overall loudness of 90 phons at a lateral distance of 18 ft. should be the maximum permitted for a private car running on full throttle at 30 m.p.h. **1948** P. M. MORSE *Vibration & Sound* (ed. 2) vi. 226 Corresponding to the physical quantities intensity and frequency are the physiological (or, rather, psychophysiological) quantities loudness and pitch. *Ibid.* 227 The bottom curve, for zero loudness, is the threshold of hearing, below which a sound ..is inaudible to the average person. **1959** *Chambers's Encycl.* XII. 728/1 It is important to distinguish between sound intensity—a physical quantity measurable in definite physical units; and loudness—the magnitude of the auditory sensation produced by that sound and therefore a subjective quantity depending upon personal judgements. **1961** G. A. BRIGGS *A to Z in Audio* 117 Although loudness depends primarily on actual intensity, it is also strongly affected by frequency. **1962** A. NISBETT *Technique Sound Studio* xi. 196 Equal loudness from the two voices will not generally be required.

2. attrib., as *loudness level, scale*; **loudness control**, a device on an audio amplifier which corrects for the change in quality of reproduced sound at low volumes by boosting the bass (and often also the treble) relative to the middle frequencies, either combined with a volume control or as a separate on–off switch.

1961 G. A. BRIGGS *A to Z in Audio* 117 When the volume is turned down, music tends to sound thin and emaciated. The effect may be counteracted to some extent by bass and treble boost in the amplifier. A loudness control is a device which automatically applies bass and treble boost as volume is reduced. **1970** J. EARL *Tuners & Amplifiers* i. 18 An idea which is popular in Europe and America (though not often liked in Great Britain) is the so-called loudness control. *Ibid.*, Some amplifiers are equipped only with a loudness control, while others feature the ordinary (non-compensated) volume control which can be changed to loudness control action by means of a switch. **1975** *Gramophone* May 2026 (Advt.), Separate loudness control. **1938** *Bell Lab. Rec.* XVI. 213/1 The intensity level of the 1000-cycle reference tone was defined as the loudness level of this tone, and any other sound which is judged by listeners to be equally loud is said to have an equal value of loudness level. *Ibid.* 214/2 The unit to be used for intensity level measurements is the decibel, but the unit to be used for the equivalent loudness level measurements is the phon. **1934** *Discovery* Dec. 346/2 The number of phons and decibels coincides for the loudness scale applying to the frequency 1,000 cycles per second, but for no other frequency.

loud-speaker (laudspī·kəɹ). Also **loud speaker, loudspeaker**. [f. LOUD *a.* + SPEAKER.] **1.** Any instrument for converting variations in an applied electric current or voltage (of appropriate magnitude and frequency) into corresponding sound waves that are able to be heard at a distance from the instrument.

Loud-speaking (see next) was formerly the usual term employed to refer to such instruments. Quot. 1884 is an isolated early example of *loud-speaker*.

1884 *English Mechanic* 26 Sept. 95/3 Before troubling to make or buy a 'loud speaker', 'Pathologist' might try the following dodge... Fix an ordinary 'toy' telephone over one ear... Fasten the end of the string from the 'toy' to the centre of the diaphragm of the Bell..and, at the middle of the string, hang a small weight..to keep it taut... The voice is almost..as clear as when using the Bell direct. **1920** *Telegraph & Telephone Jrnl.* VI. 111/2 It was quite remarkable how far and how distinctly it was possible to hear the talk from the loud-speakers. **1923** *Daily Mail* 1 Mar. 9 For each concert there will be seating accommodation..for 1,000 people, and to these the concert will be delivered by powerful loud speakers. **1924** *Wireless Weekly* 8 Oct. 745/1 Loud speakers of all kinds are an outstanding feature of the show. **1930** J. BUCHAN *Castle Gay* xiii. 208 Their ears were greeted by the bray of a loud-speaker to which the wives by their house-doors were listening. **1931** B. BROWN *Talking Pict.* v. 117 In some form or other the dynamic or moving coil loud speaker, well known in radio, is..always used for sound picture work. **1943** J. B. PRIESTLEY *Daylight on Saturday* v. 27 They were now putting canned music over the loud speakers. **1957** L. F. R. WILLIAMS *State of Israel* ix. 158 Regulations strictly forbid..loudspeakers in their [*sc.* the polling stations'] immediate vicinity. **1970** J. EARL *Tuners & Amplifiers* iii. 76 Headphones..can nowadays give a subjective impression of quality, spaciousness and stereo effect equally as good as the best loudspeakers.

2. attrib., as *loud-speaker enclosure, system, unit, van*.

1962 A. NISBETT *Technique Sound Studio* iv. 76 A manufacturer of loudspeaker enclosures invited members of the public to judge and compare the quality of three different stereo speaker systems. **1971** *Daily Tel.* (Colour Suppl.) 22 Oct. 57 (Advt.), Twin sealed loudspeaker enclosures, each containing 2 speakers (bass and treble). **1958** *Times Lit. Suppl.* 10 Oct. 583/2 The installation of loudspeaker systems in churches has rendered..manner even less important than matter in sermons than ever before. **1970** J. EARL *Tuners & Amplifiers* i. 25 A loudspeaker *system* is a box, usually called enclosure or cabinet, carrying a socket or couple of terminals at the rear with a grille at the front through which the sound comes. Such a loudspeaker system is scientifically designed in conjunction with the loudspeaker units inside. **1925-6** T. *Eaton & Co. Catal.* Fall & Winter 391 This Loud Speaker Unit when attached to your gramophone tone arm, makes the horn act as a loud speaker. **1970** Loudspeaker unit [see *loud-speaker system* above]. **1945** H. NICOLSON *Let.* 3 July (1967) 474 One of my workers said something mean on the loud-speaker van. **1973** J. DRUMMOND *Bang! Bang! You're Dead!* xlii. 144 A police loudspeaker van..pointed out that nothing could be gained by further resistance.

loud-speaking (lau·dspī·kiŋ), *a.* Also without hyphen (as one word). [f. LOUD *adv.* + SPEAKING *ppl. a.*] Speaking loudly (in quot. 1855, *fig.*); *spec.* (the usual sense), capable of producing sound that can be heard at a distance; fitted with or employing a loud-speaker.

1855 [see LOUD *adv.* 3]. **1879** *Telegraphic Jrnl.* VII. 112/2 The new telephone receiver of Mr. Edison is, undoubtedly, the greatest step..towards rendering the telephone a loud-speaking instrument. **1897** *Pearson's Mag.* July 51/1 This head-gear would hardly be necessary if a loud-speaking telephone were employed. **1921** *Sci. Amer.* Dec. 100/3 With a loud-speaking telephone on the living-room table and with a simple receiving set the members of the family can receive all the news..followed by a musical program. **1923** *Radio Times* 28 Sept. 14 A loud-speaking equipment that will enable all..to hear perfectly without headphones. **1951** *Catal. of Exhibits, South Bank Exhib., Festival of Britain* 82/2 Combined two-way loudspeaking intercommunication from bridge to selected points. **1960** *20th Cent.* Apr. 308 Loud-speaking cars toured hour by hour, giving names of known survivors.

louie, var. *LOOEY.

Louis heel. Also **Louis Quinze heel.** [f. the name of Louis XV (1715–74), King of France, in whose reign it became fashionable.] A type of heel used on a woman's shoe (see quot. 1968).

1872 *Young Englishwoman* Dec. 651/1 She knows that it is impossible to walk gracefully with the high-pointed heel, and never wears any but the demi-talon Louis Quinze. **1901** F. H. BURNETT *Making of Marchioness* I. ii. 30 'She's got Louis Quinze heels,' returned his Lordship. **1906** *Daily Chron.* 23 Feb. 6/5 From the pretty shopgirl..to the daughter of the upper classes the Louis heel is regarded amongst women as a pedestal of superiority to be appropriated for personal adornment. **1968** J. IRONSIDE *Fashion Alphabet* 136 It is of any height or shape... Its character is defined by the sole material which..is attached to the breast (front) of the heel by adhesive... But the term 'Louis' is generally applied to a high heel with curved waist, flared at the base.

Louisianian (luˌīz-, luˌiziæ·niăn, luˌiziā·niăn), *a.* and *sb.* [f. *Louisiana* (see below), named after Louis XIV of France.] **A. adj.** Of or pertaining to the State of Louisiana at the mouth of the Mississippi. **B. sb.** A native or inhabitant of Louisiana.

1775 J. ADAIR *Hist. Amer. Indians* 240 The illustration of this may..shew our southern colonies what they may still expect from the masterly abilities of the French Louisianians. **1835** J. H. INGRAHAM *South-West* I. ix. 101 Americans; that is to say, Anglo-Americans as distinguished from the Louisianian French. **1854** C. E. A. GAYARRÉ *Hist. Louisiana (French Domination)* I. 13 Is not this the very poetry of landscape, of Louisianian landscape? **1945** *Chicago Daily News* 26 July 2/3 The slow but straight-talking Louisianian is extremely popular with his junior officers. **1949** B. A. BOTKIN *Treas. S. Folklore* iv. i. 552 Marylanders grow lyrical over Brunswick stew..and Louisianians, over the superiorities of the Cajun and Creole cuisine. **1967** Mrs. L. B. JOHNSON *White House Diary* 5 Dec. (1970) 597 This is a warm, loving, family-type house..crowded to the limit with..Louisianians.

Louis-Philippe (luiˌfilī·p). The name of Louis-Philippe, King of France from 1830 to 1848; used *attrib.* or *ellipt.* to designate the style of architecture, furniture, and interior decoration characteristic of his reign.

1908 A. BENNETT *Old Wives' Tale* iii. 307 He minutely examined his mouth in the glass of the Louis Philippe wardrobe. **1919** W. S. MAUGHAM *Moon & Sixpence* xi. 46 It was a very small room, overcrowded with furniture of the style which the French know as Louis Philippe. **1951** N. MITFORD *Blessing* II. iv. 183 To be able to tell at a glance whether an object was Louis XV or Louis Philippe, First or Third Empire. **1970** *Oxf. Compan. Art* 441/1 The slightly monotonous interiors..foreshadow the bourgeois interiors of Louis-Philippe. **1975** *Country Life* 6 Feb. (Suppl.) 31/2 Five piece gilt suite of the Louis Philippe period.

loukoum(i, varr. *LOCOUM.

loulou (lū·lū). [Fr., f. *loup* wolf.] A nickname for a Pomeranian dog.

1894 G. DU MAURIER *Trilby* II. vi. 208 The same old couples petting the same toutous and loulous! *Ibid.* (*footnote*), Loulou—a Pomeranian dog. **1916** E. V. LUCAS *Vermilion Box* ccv. 237 One of our sights for visitors here is a dog. A real dog, not a toutou or a loulou, but a great collie kind of thing.

lounge, *sb.* Add: **2. b.** The drawing-room of a private house; the public sitting-room in a hotel or institution. Also *transf.*

1881 [in Dict., sense 2]. **1908** *Daily Chron.* 13 Nov. 4/6 London hotels are extending their lounges. **1938** E. BOWEN *Death of Heart* II. i. 186 The sea..seemed an annexe of the livingroom... She learned later that Daphne called this the lounge. **1954** J. BETJEMAN *A Few Late Chrysanthemums* 94 It's ever so close in the lounge dear, But the vestibule's comfy for tea. **1965** M. BRADBURY *Stepping Westward* iv. 181 Expressly for the purpose of hunting down Walker and bringing him to the English

department faculty lounge, wherein the faculty were even now assembled. **1973** *Houston* (Texas) *Chron. Mag. People, Places, Pleasures* 14 Oct. 21/1, I am in a mobile lounge which is about to roll out from Dulles Airport to the supersonic Concorde. **1973** *Times* 8 Dec. 26/4 Burns Hotel.. Licensed restaurant, bar lounge.

c. Ellipt. for *lounge-coat, *-jacket, -suit*.

1893 J. TOMLIN *Bond St. Syst. Cutting* 44 There are many different styles in which the Lounge is produced. **1905** *Daily Chron.* 16 Mar. 8/7 (Advt.), Good coat presser and baister for lounges and morning coats. **1928** *Tailor & Cutter* 29 Nov. 899/3 I'll take the lad; and..in six calendar months he will be able to make a lounge. **1968** A. A. WHIFE *First Course Gentlemen's Garment Cutting* (ed. 4) 69 The Reefer, Sports Jacket, Hacking Jacket..are designed on lines which originate in the basic structure of the Lounge.

3. (Earlier and later N. Amer. examples.)

1830 J. F. WATSON *Ann. Philadelphia* 183 Formerly they had couches of worsted damask..in lieu of what we now call sophas or lounges. **1845** *Knickerbocker* XXV. 446 The hard-bottomed chairs were the same, and the lounge, and the tall mahogany clock. **1915** in B. A. Botkin *Treas. S. Folklore* (1949) III. ii. 538 He stayed in the barn nights ..and slept on an ol' lounge he carried out from the house. **1972** E. STAEBLER *Cape Breton Harbour* xvi. 142 There is always some one sitting on the rocker or on the wooden lounge built into the corner.

4. *lounge-jacket, -wear*; also (sense *2 b) *lounge-diner* (also *lounge/diner*), *-hall*; **lounge bar**, a bar in a public-house which is furnished with the amenities of a lounge; **lounge lizard** *slang* (orig. *U.S.*), a man who spends his time idling in fashionable society, esp. in search of a wealthy patroness.

1937 *Hotel & Catering Management* Sept. 23/1 Smokeroom or lounge bars are obviously larger than cocktail bars, and provision has to be made for the serving of draught beers. **1971** 'H. CALVIN' *Poison Chasers* vii. 83 Two of the security men..came into the public bar, and the rest of the customers..went into the lounge bar. **1961** *Evening Standard* 3 July 23/4 (Advt.), Modern s/d house... Hall, lounge/diner, kitchenette. **1966** Loungediner [see *garden gnome* s.v. *GARDEN sb.* 6]. **1974** *Country Life* 7 Mar. (Suppl.) 21/1 Excellent Family House.. study/TV room, 31 ft. lounge/diner, breakfasting kitchen. **1910** *Bradshaw's Railway Guide* Apr. 1046 Lord Warden Hotel... Orchestra plays..in the beautiful lounge hall every evening. **1933** D. C. PEEL *Life's Enchanted Cup* xi. 126 This house..contained..what house agents now call a lounge-hall. **1939** O. LANCASTER *Homes Sweet Homes* 66 The luxury flat..is divided up..into a dining-room, drawing-room, lounge-hall, three bed, two bath, a kitchen and all the usual offices. **1887** E. B. GILES *Hist. Cutting in Eng.* I. 70 When repose is required [we use] the lounge jacket or dressing gown. **1899** R. WHITEING *No. 5 John St.* xxviii. 284 The billycock and the lounge jacket are, I think, my strong point. **1918** *Hatchet* 4 Apr. 39/1 (*caption*) Nautical lounge lizards. **1921** *Daily Colonist* (Victoria, B.C.) 10 Apr. 4/4 The delicate, poetic cast of features, and the misplaced eyebrow adorning the nether lip of these lounge lizards, denizens of dansants and cabarets. **1926** *Punch* 17 Nov. 534/1 Formal recognition of those firmly attached appendages of Society, the lounge-lizards. **1973** *Times* 29 Dec. 7/7 The £50 a week contract which.. lets her keep her lounge lizard husband, Queckett, in the manner to which he is accustomed, lacks conviction. **1969** *Sears Catal.* Spring/Summer 3 Now—and all through the summer—Sears has the answer to just what you're looking for in loungewear. **1974** *News-Palladium & Herald-Press* (Benton Harbor, Mich.) 8 May (Advt. Suppl.), See this utterly feminine loungewear in enchanting prints.

lounger. Add: **b.** An article of furniture or of dress designed to be used for relaxation.

1964 G. SIMS *Terrible Door* xviii. 98 She wore..blue woollen stockings and highly polished, brown moccasin loungers. **1969** *Sears Catal.* Spring/Summer 3 Ankle length loungers with their own carefully constructed Bra sewn right in. **1969** A. LASKI *Dominant Fifth* v. 182, I am sitting in a lounger under an umbrella. **1971** *Daily Tel.* 11 May 13/5 The best 'loungers' are those which allow the legs to be raised slightly above the body.

lounging, *vbl. sb.* Add: **b.** *lounging-chair* (later example), *-coat, robe, -room*.

1971 *Daily Tel.* 11 May 13/5 Now, this year, Vogue have a lounging chair which lets you get your head down. **1920** B. E. STEVENSON *Gloved Hand* 11, I paused only to open my bag, change into a lounging-coat, and brush off the dust of the journey. **1960** *Harper's Bazaar* Oct. 87 A chiffon lounging coat printed with cinnamon flowers. **1908** *Sears Roebuck Catal.* 1117 (*heading*) Long kimonos or negligees and bath or lounging robes. **1945** R. CHANDLER *Let.* 13 Oct. in *R. Chandler Speaking* (1966) 44 The great man appeared.., clad in an expensive lounging robe. **1863** Mrs. GASKELL *Dark Night's Work* iv. 42 He used the study for a smoking and lounging-room principally. **1887** C. D. WARNER *Their Pilgrimage* (1888) i. 2 In the spacious office and general lounging-room, sea-coal fires glowed in the wide grates.

loungy (lau·ndʒi), *a.* [f. LOUNGE *sb.* + -Y[1].] Suggestive of lounges or lounging.

1911 CHESTERTON *Innocence of Father Brown* v. 124, I mean little, loungy men, who had just enough to live on and had nothing to do but lean about in bar-rooms and bet on horses.

‖ **loup** (lū), *sb.*[4] [Fr., lit. 'wolf'.] In full, *loup de mer*. The sea-bass, *Dicentrarchus labrax*, found off the coasts of western Europe and in the Mediterranean.

1766 SMOLLETT *Trav.* I. xviii. 291 One of the best fish of this country, is called *Le Loup*, about two or three pounds

in weight; white, firm, and well-flavoured. **1938** E. Bowen *Death of Heart* I. iv. 76 Filing off wet third-class decks of lake steamers, choking over the bones of *loups de mer*. **1966** P. V. Price *France: Food & Wine Guide* 44 The *loup de mer*, so often found grilled over fennel sticks all over the south, is a sort of sea-perch or sea-bass. **1969** J. Elliot *Duel* I. v. 117 Keith..had lines out trolling for *rouget* and *loup de mer*. **1969** *New Yorker* 27 Sept. 120/2, I have seen more herbs thrown on the coals beneath, somewhat as fennel is blazed under a *loup*, the wolfish sea bass, at its last minutes on the grill.

loupe (lūp). [Fr.: cf. Loop *sb.*[4]] A small magnifier used by a watchmaker or jeweller.

1909 in *Cent. Dict.* Suppl. **1940** C. McCullers *Heart is Lonely Hunter* (1943) II. ii. 105 He noticed the distorted look of Kelly's right eye as it appeared through his watchmaker's loupe. **1949** H. C. Weston *Sight, Light & Efficiency* iv. 122 Simple spectacle loupes are generally made to give a magnification of 2¼ or 2½. **1962** R. Webster *Gems* II. xxxiii. 598 It is now possible to discuss the various types of simple microscopes, such as the ordinary magnifiers with which jewellers are so familiar. These magnifiers, or loupes as they are sometimes called, must be considered with two points of view in mind. **1964** E. Bruton *Finsbury Mob* viii. 111 On an old kitchen table were a pair of jeweller's scales, a loupe,..various other bits of jewellers' paraphernalia, and a packet of detergent.

loup-garou. (Later examples.)

1939 H. M. Miner *St. Denis* vii. 136 The devil, in various forms, and *loup-garous* were abroad in the land and were a considerable problem. **1961** R. M. Patterson *Buffalo Head* ii. 69 Jerome, certain that the loup garou had come for him at last, backed closer to the fire.

lourie: see *Loerie.

louse, *sb.* Add: **3. louse-borne** *a.*, of diseases: transmitted by lice.

1919 W. Byam et al. (*title*) Trench fever: a louse-borne disease. **1942** *Times* 21 Sept. 5/3 Typhus, which is louse-borne,..was overcome by active measures of disinfestation. **1964** M. Hynes *Med. Bacteriol.* (ed. 8) xxi. 322 *Trep. recurrentis obermeieri* is typical of the louse-borne disease. **1970** *Control of Communicable Dis. in Man* (Amer. Public Health Assoc.) (ed. 11) 275 (*heading*) Typhus-fever, epidemic louse-borne. **1974** Passmore & Robson *Compan. Med. Stud.* III. xii. 75/1 Louse-borne relapsing fever is a disease of cold weather.

louse, *v.* Add: **3.** With *up*. To infest with lice. orig. *U.S.*

1931 *San Francisco Examiner* 29 Jan. 34/4 Lousey, now fixed in Broadway actor jargon, is from small time troupers... The Maine tavern keeper who refused lodging to a repertoire company..explained: 'The last troupe loused up the beddin'.' **1931** *Gang World* Jan. 14 The precinct was fumigated yesterday, an' you ain't gonna louse it up again. **1955** R. P. Hobson *Nothing too Good for Cowboy* i. 15, I got loused up in that cabin once. **1968** *Listener* 9 May 601/2, I was occasionally loused-up myself, and people, rather than pass me, used to go on the other side of the road.

b. *slang.* To spoil, to mess up. Const *up*. Also **loused-up** *a.* orig. *U.S.*

1934 J. O'Hara *Appointment in Samarra* ii. 61 There's fifty bucks in it for you on account of lousing up your date. **1938** *Amer. Speech* XIII. 195 Louse up the show. **1948** *Sat. Even. Post* 25 Sept. 41 The hospital field is loused up enough. **1957** F. & R. Lockridge *Practise to Deceive* (1959) ii. 29 Of all the loused-up operations. **1958** E. Dundy *Dud Avocado* II. i. 185 He said if I'm really serious about getting a part..the easiest way to louse it up would be to turn up with a hundred other people. **1959** *Tamarack Rev.* XII. 24 What a way to louse up this new magenta outfit... You'd think she'd spent her afternoon at a Yiddish tear-jerker. **1959** 'S. Ransome' *I'll die for You* x. 119 Had a rough time getting her to come back... Damned if I'll let you louse me up now. **1967** [see next]. **1969** *N.Y. Rev. Bks.* 10 Jan. 38/2 It is safe to predict that President-elect Nixon will look for some outstanding public figure for this job, even though it may louse up the table of organization. **1972** *Human World* Nov. 48 If..he tries to sabotage his actions —he louses up a machine he is purporting to work, for example [etc.]. **1973** R. Ludlum *Matlock Paper* i. 7 A loused-up army record. **1975** *New Yorker* 5 May 115/1 The picture is a cheerfully loused-up reworking of the legend of King Arthur's Grail hunt.

louser. (See under Louse *v.*) Also, one who spoils things: used as a general term of abuse. Also **louser-up**.

1960 B. Moore *Luck of Ginger Coffey* iv. 86 You louser. ..What the hell do you know about love? All you want is to get up some woman's skirts. **1966** A. Prior *Operators* viii. 110 He entered her, cursing all women... The sluts, bags, lousers, slags. **1967** C. Cockburn *I, Claud* xxxv. 438 Hardly anyone can be packed off to some social equivalent of the Russian 'virgin lands' for lousing things up, because almost every louser-up can convincingly claim that he was not really responsible for the thing that happened. **1968** 'N. Blake' *Private Wound* vii. 108 If any of you lousers interfere I'll plug him in the belly.

lousy, *a.* Add: **1. d.** 'Swarming' with; abundantly supplied with (money, people, etc.); full of. Const. *with*. *slang* (orig. *U.S.*).

1843 *Spirit of Times* 4 Mar. 7/3 He was lousy with money, and dared any man to face him. **1856** *Democratic State Jrnl.* (Sacramento, Calif.) 6 Oct. 2/3 The bed of the river is perfectly 'lousy' with gold. **1864** A. J. Munby *Diary* 15 July in D. Hudson *Munby* (1972) 199 Why Sir, these unfortunates are all over the place: the ground (he added with a gesture of disgust) is *lousy* with them. **1928** S. Vines *Humours Unreconciled* i. 13 The Totsuka Club was..in the words of Mr. Podler, 'just lousy with liars'. **1934** V. M. Yeates *Winged Victory* xix. 150 And if the Dover Patrol was costly in life, were not shipping magnates lousy with shekels? **1936** W. Holtby *South Riding* II. i. 89 Leckton told me last month they threw in sixteen and a half couple of hounds and couldn't see a dog. Lost in thistles and willow herb—but lousy with foxes. **1956** R. Braddon *Nancy Wake* xiii. 153 The town was lousy with Germans, she noted.

2. Delete 'Now *rare*' and add further examples. Also, inferior, poor, bad; ill; in low health or spirits.

1822 D. O'Connell *Let.* 22 May in *Corr.* (1972) II. 391 Perhaps to save some lousy postage you wrote across the letter. They stop all such letters in France. **1849** A. Gordon *Diary* 12 July in W. E. Woodward *Way Our People Lived* (1944) viii. 268, I wish I could never hear the word *lousy* again. I am willing to bet that Tommy Plunkett uses it fifty times a day, but he is no worse than the others. It is 'lousy' this and 'lousy' that. The rain is lousy, the trail is lousy, the bacon is lousy, and Gus Thorpe, losing in the card game, has just said that he has had a lousy deal. **1922** Joyce *Ulysses* 18 You come along with your lousy leer and your gloomy jesuit jibes. *a* **1930** D. H. Lawrence *Last Poems* (1932) 197 Oh great god of the machine What lousy archangels and angels you have to surround yourself with! **1932** N. Mitford *Christmas Pudding* xiv. 220, I still think it's lousy of you not to have taken me last night. **1933** 'N. West' *Miss Lonelyhearts* (1949) 46, I felt swell before you came, and now I feel lousy. **1937** L. Bromfield *Rains Came* I. xxxix. 170 Life is so short and so lousy. **1950** 'S. Ransome' *Deadly Miss Ashley* xv. 171 She felt too lousy to come to work. A foul cold, she said. **1959** J. Braine *Vodi* xi. 153 A dirty rotten little whore, who couldn't wait six months for her husband, not six lousy months before she went off with another man. **1959** R. Gant *World in Jug* 136 That sudden, nervous sweep which made him to my mind one of the lousiest drivers in Paris, city of lousy drivers. **1968** K. Weatherly *Roo Shooter* 23 You're not a bad bastard, Hunter,..in spite of your lousy cooking. *Ibid.* 74 'I got fifty-two last night,' he said... 'I only got a lousy twelve,' replied Hunter. **1973** P. Moyes *Curious Affair of Third Dog* xi. 148 A brisk, pretty, coloured nurse came in... 'Ah, you're awake... How do you feel?' 'Lousy,' said Henry.

B. As *adv.* 'Lousily', extremely. Chiefly *N. Amer.*

In quot. 1971 a mere intensive.

1932 *Amer. Speech* VII. 436 A man drunk is..'lousy drunk'. **1936** C. Day Lewis *Friendly Tree* xiv. 210 Well, not lousy-drunk. Just comfortable. **1971** D. Heffron *Nice Fire & Some Moonpennies* iv. 33 But she didn't lousy come to school that day! What a blow.

‖ **loutrophoros** (lūtrǫfōə·rǫs). *Cl. Antiq.* [Gr. λουτρο-φόρος, f. λουτρόν water for a bath + -φορός bearing.] A tall two-handled vessel used for carrying water to the nuptial bath.

1896 C. H. Smith in *Catal. Greek & Etruscan Vases Brit. Mus.* III. 366 Beside her is a box or table on three legs terminating in lions' paws, on which stand a pyxis and an oinochoè with tall handle and neck (loutrophoros?). **1931** *Times Lit. Suppl.* 16 July 563/2 A splendid loutrophoros by Polygnotus. **1935** Richter & Milne *Shapes & Names Athenian Vases* 5 *Loutrophoros*,..tall vase with high, funnel-shaped neck, slender body, and flaring mouth. Water was brought in it from the fountain Kallirrhoe for the nuptial bath, and it was placed on tombs of unmarried persons. **1967** R. S. Folsom *Handbk. Greek Pott.* 157 The loutrophoros usually was an amphora, but sometimes the form appears as a hydria with three handles.

louver. Add: The form *louvre* is now usual in the U.K. and *louver* in the U.S.

4. Add to def.: Also used for other purposes, e.g. to deflect air issuing from an opening or to prevent the direct passage of light through it. Used in *sing.* in same sense; also, an individual slat or strip of such an arrangement. (Further examples.)

1833 J. C. Loudon *Encycl. Cottage, Farm & Villa Archit.* 1128/2 *Louvre*, see *Luffer-boards*. **1920** W. Neubecker *Pract. Sheet Metal Duct Construction* xiv. 155 (*caption*) Formation of movable louvre. *Ibid.*, When movable louvres are used they are pivoted on rods. **1923** *Man. Seamanship* (Admiralty) II. 282 An ideal system of ventilation for a small compartment. A small adjustable flap and louvre..is fitted in the supply trunk. **1933** Moyer & Fittz *Air Conditioning* ix. 236 The two-point thermostat *A* is located near the fresh-air intake louver. **1957** *Economist* 23 Nov. 710/1 Heat is distributed not only in conventional radiators but through louvres in the skirting board. **1966** D. F. Galouye *Lost Perception* xvi. 169 He had managed to..check on the intake louvre... The simple removal of four screws would unfasten the grating and provide access to the ventilation duct. **1968** *Autocar* 25 Jan. 30/2 The wheels splashed through puddles..and steam blew back from the bonnet louvres. **1972** *Sci. Amer.* June 127/3 The temperature probes can be housed in a box that has louvers large enough to ensure the free circulation of air.

5. *louvre door, screen, slat;* **louvre damper,** a louvre the inclination of whose slats may be varied to regulate the flow of air through them.

1920 W. Neubecker *Pract. Sheet Metal Duct Construction* xv. 160 (*caption*) Louvre dampers for large size ducts. **1953** N. W. Kay *Mod. Building Encycl.* 410/1 Louvre door. **1967** *Boston Sunday Herald* 26 Mar. III. 5/7 (Advt.), Set up louver door. **1948** C. Isherwood in *Penguin New Writing* XXXIV. 127 Movable louvre-screens take the place of port-holes. **1969** *Sears Catal.* Spring/Summer 910 Louver slats fitted into 1⅛-in. thick frame.

louvered *ppl. a.* (also, esp. in the U.K., **louvred**) (further examples of sense b).

1898 F. W. Macey *Specifications in Detail* 264 Louvred doors are generally required for ventilation in various places. **1934** H. M. Vernon *Princ. Heating & Ventilation* ix. 170 A fresh-air shaft may be necessary, with a louvered opening above the level of the building. **1950** *Engineering* 7 Apr. 376/2 The long-distance transport of fruit and vegetables is being investigated..with special reference to the performance of a new type of louvred van. **1969** *Daily Tel.* 14 Jan. 15/4 Wardrobes..are better with louvred doors. **1972** *Gloss. Electrotechnical, Power Terms (B.S.I.)* IV. iii. 21 *Louvered ceiling*, luminaire system comprising a large installation of louvres above which are mounted the lamps.

lovally: see *Loverly *a.*[2]

Lovat (lɒ·văt). The name of a place in Inverness-shire, used *attrib.* and *ellipt.* to denote a muted green colour, a tweed (suit), or another garment or material of this colour.

1907 *Daily Chron.* 21 Nov. 7/4 The famous 'Lovat' shades of tweed are very popular among lady motorists. **1911** *Daily Colonist* (Victoria, B.C.) 5 Apr. 2/5 (Advt.), Sweater Coats—New consignment, white, navy, lovat and camel hair, for ladies and gentlemen. **1914** C. Mackenzie *Sinister St.* II. III. xi. 719 This world of light-green Lovat tweeds, of fashionable rusticity. **1922** J. Buchan *Huntingtower* i. 16 A most disreputable tweed suit..had once been what..is called a Lovat mixture, but was now a nondescript sub-fusc. **1930** H. Nicolson *Diary* 22 Feb. (1966) 42 The Prime Minister appears in Lovat plus-fours. **1937** D. L. Sayers *Busman's Honeymoon* iv. 87 Will you wear the Lovats or the grey suit? **1940** *Illustr. London News* CXCVII. 640 (Advt.), Overcoats... A wide choice of brown, fawns, greys or lovat. **1953** J. Trench *Docken Dead* vi. 81 He wore a shapeless suit of Lovat tweed. **1969** J. Wood *Three Blind Mice* i. 9 He wore..lovat-green socks.

love, *sb.*[1] Add: **1. e.** Also *love from...*

1785 Lady Newdigate *Let.* May in A. E. Newdigate-Newdegate *Cheverels* (1898) iv. 67 Love from all here Adieu. **1913** W. Owen *Let.* 19 Oct. (1967) 202 Love, Hopes, and Kisses from your own Wilfred. **1921** A. Huxley *Let.* 21 Nov. (1969) 205, I will telephone or write about both these dates. Love from Aldous. **1949** D. Smith *I capture Castle* xi. 188 Dear Cassandra, it was nice of you to write... Love from Neil.

4. *for love* (later example in weakened sense); *love at first sight*: the action or state of falling in love with someone whom one has never previously seen; *love's young dream*: the relationship of young lovers; the object of someone's love, a man regarded as the perfect lover.

c **1374** Chaucer *Troilus & Criseyde* II. 667 This was a sodeyn love, how mighte it be That she so lightly lovede Troilus Right for the firste sighte; ye, pardee? *a* **1593** Marlowe *Hero & Leander* (1598) I. 175 Where both deliberat, the loue is slight, Who euer lov'd, that lov'd not at first sight? **1822** Hazlitt *Table-Talk* II. xvi. 354, I do not think that what is called *Love at first sight* is so great an absurdity as it is sometimes imagined to be. *a* **1834** Love's young dream [in Dict.]. **1839** [see *Beat *v.*[1] 10]. **1868** W. Collins *Moonstone* I. vii. 91 You have heard of beautiful young ladies falling in love at first sight, and have thought it natural enough. **1898** J. K. Jerome *Second Thoughts* 155 The stout lady, now regarded as a would-be blighter of love's young dream, was hustled into the back seat. **1903** Kipling *Traffics & Discov.* (1904) 132 'Do you want a tow to Brixham?'.. 'What for?'.. 'For love; for nothing.' **1920** Galsworthy *Skin Game* I. 33, I don't mean any tosh about love's young dream; but I do like being friends. **1937** D. L. Sayers *Busman's Honeymoon* xv. 307 There now!.. If there ain't love's young dream a-comin' up the path. **1952** *Scrutiny* XVIII. 273 We know that what we have here is no drama of romantic love-at-first-sight. **1961** C. McCullers *Clock without Hands* iv. 89 In early youth, love at first sight, that epitome of passion, turns you into a zombie. **1966** L. Southworth *Felon in Disguise* viii. 121 It calls for a sweetheart act, a proper 'Love's Young Dream' routine. **1975** D. Bagley *Snow Tiger* xvi. 138 Don't you believe in love at first sight?

7. a. *for the love of Mike*: for goodness' sake! (A colloq. exclamation of exasperation or surprise, with no notion of the literal sense; prob. f. Mike *sb.*[4])

1922 Joyce *Ulysses* 763 O move over your big carcass out of that for the love of Mike listen to him. **1925** T. Dreiser *Amer. Trag.* (1926) I. I. ix. 57 For de love o' Mike, will you listen to dat, now. **1934** J. Brophy *Waterfront* i. 14 For the love of mike..shut those blasted windows. **1935** W. D. Hubbard *Thousandth Frog* i. 7 Dick could not repress an exclamation of astonishment. 'For the love of Mike. Look at them.' **1941** *Penguin New Writing* VIII. 91 Well, for the luvva Mike! **1942** *R.A.F. Jrnl.* 3 Oct. 11 Tired? Well for the love of mike! What about me? **1957** A. MacNab *Bulls of Iberia* xv. 181 For the love of Mike, let's hope he's brave.

g. *to make love*: now more usually, to copulate.

1950 M. Peake *Gormenghast* xxix. 173 One of the Carvers made love to her and she had a baby. **1966** Auden *About House* 15 Stocktaking, horseplay, worship, making love. **1967** B. Wright tr. *Queneau's Between Blue & Blue* xiv. 151 When you make love on a bunk,..the man has to bump his head. **1971** *Daily Tel.* 15 Jan. 17/1 Couples who make love frequently are more likely to have sons than those who do so less often.

9. a. (Later examples as a term of endearing address.)

1895 A. W. PINERO *Second Mrs. Tanqueray* III. 104 Paula love, I fancied you and Aubrey were a little more friendly. 1966 *New Yorker* 29 Jan. 22/3 'Sit over here, love,' he said as another actress entered. 1967 *Listener* 5 Oct. 429/3 Lovely, loves, I loved it. And Alison here was hysterical, weren't you, Alison? 1975 J. SYMONS *Three Pipe Problem* iii. 25 But Sher. love, it was only a read-through. You don't expect me to *act*.

f. *love in disguise*: (see quots.).

1877 E. S. DALLAS *Kettner's Bk. of Table* 282 *Love in disguise* is a calf's heart stuffed, then surrounded with forcemeat, next rolled in vermicelli, lastly deposited in a baking dish..and sent to the oven. 1958 W. BICKEL tr. *Hering's Dict. Cookery* 451 *Love in disguise*, calf's heart, soaked in water, larded, boiled until tender, dried, coated with veal forcemeat, rolled in crushed raw noodles, roasted in butter in oven and basted frequently.

15. a. *love-allegory, -bed* (later examples), *-bite, -bond, -charm, -dance, -drug, -duel, -duet, -flight, -game, -look, -lyric, -magic, -marriage, -poet, -poetry, -secret, -sonnet, -talk, -theme.*

1933 R. TUVE *Seasons & Months* iv. 189 All this is to be found in the love-allegory of the *Golden Targe*. 1934 DYLAN THOMAS *18 Poems* 19 Invisible, your clocking tides Break on the lovebeds of the weeds. *a* 1963 S. PLATH *Crossing Water* (1971) 33 Musky as a lovebed the morning after. 1749 J. CLELAND *Mem. Woman Pleasure* II. 63 Then the turtle-billing kisses, and the poignant painless love-bites. 1903 H. ELLIS *Stud. Psychol. Sex* III. 71 We may find references to love-bites in the literature of ancient as well as of modern times... In the Indian *Kama Sutra* of Vatsyayana a chapter is devoted to this subject. 1972 *Daily Tel.* 29 Jan. 3/1 Once I saw her sitting in class with a love bite on her neck. 1951 L. MACNEICE tr. *Goethe's Faust* II. v. 295 Rapture which yearns ever, Love-bond which burns ever. 1889 *Cent. Dict.*, Love-charm. 1935 *Amer. Speech* X. 119/2 Certain generic epithets.. have become so conventionalized that they too tell their tales... Love thief, love nest, love lure, love charm, love potion. 1948 B. G. M. SUNDKLER *Bantu Prophets S. Afr.* vi. 222 Various Native 'Chemist' shops sell..love-charms. 1911 J. A. THOMSON *Biol. Seasons* II. 233 The long larval period of two or three years in the water, and the short aerial love-dance lasting for an evening or two. 1934 *Discovery* Nov. 309/1 For a few weeks they [*sc.* the termites] revive their ancestral free-living life in a mad love-dance. 1959 *Chambers's Dict.* Suppl., *Love-drug*, dagga. 1969 *Rolling Stone* 17 May 3/4 The new 'love drug', MDA (3,4-methylenedioxy-phenyl-iso-propylamine). 1880 'MARK TWAIN' *Tramp Abroad* 58 This was not a love duel, but a 'satisfaction' affair. 1932 R. CAMPBELL *Taurine Provence* ii. 44 The great 'Lou Pouvenco'..bore a small fortune between his horns, until he was killed in a love-duel by a younger rival. 1946 *Essays & Stud.* XXXI. 105 Anyone who takes the trouble to get the score of Verdi's *Otello*, and compare the love-duet at the end of the first act, in particular Otello's solo passages, with the last but two and last but one paragraphs of the *Anna Livia* episode, will discover some very interesting similarities in phrasing. 1975 *Times* 12 Feb. 23/6 The dance of Discord and War..has to be reconciled by the love duet. 1908 E. J. BANFIELD *Confessions of Beachcomber* I. vii. 232 The love flight of the green and gold butterfly. 1936 *Brit. Birds* XXIX. 307 The love-flights of many species depend on a subtle change in the character of the wing-beat, most marked perhaps in the waders. 1925 F. HARRIS *My Life & Loves* I. 182, I waited a little while and then began the love game. 1973 B. FREEMANTLE *Goodbye to Old Friend* iv. 54 He wondered if Anne were playing some odd kind of love game. 1637 S. RUTHERFORD *Let.* 10 June (1891) clxxv. 331 Any little communion with Him [*sc.* Christ], one of His love-looks, should be my begun heaven. 1904 *Windsor Mag.* June 305/2 Do you think I don't know a love-look when I see it? 1856 *National Rev.* III. 372 The love-lyric..is probably the most intense expression of primitive passion. 1962 L. DURRELL *Spirit of Place* (1969) 19 He had just published a sequence of love-lyrics called *Kingcup*. 1974 P. DICKINSON *Poison Oracle* ii. 44 You get a basic story, but inside it you get dramatic sections and love lyrics. 1949 M. MEAD *Male & Female* iii. 56 How the ..human sacrifice or love-magic fitted into the whole. 1850 THACKERAY *Pendennis* II. xxi. 209 Look at your love-marriages... The love-match people are the most notorious of all for quarrelling afterwards. 1973 *Archivum Linguisticum* IV. 93 A love-marriage (as opposed to an arranged marriage). 1923 J. M. MURRY *Pencillings* 224 Love poets are seldom the singers of happiness in love. 1965 *New Statesman* 16 July 87/2 Donne..has a title to be our greatest love poet. 1865 *Reader* 20 May 561/2 Claim passionate tenderness as especially feminine, and the inquiry is made whether all the best love-poetry in existence..has not been written by men. 1872 GEO. ELIOT *Middlem.* III. v. xlvii. 75 Verifying in his own experience that higher love-poetry which had charmed his fancy. 1971 *Guardian* 14 July 11/2 The best of his [*sc.* Attlee's] poems are political ballads... The others (not so good) run even to love poetry. 1754 RICHARDSON *Grandison* I. xxxvii. 265 And has he, can he have, *so many* Love-secrets, and yet..not let them transpire to such a sister? 1923 R. GRAVES *Feather Bed* 25 This meek exnovice rifled Of her love-secrets? 1870 D. G. ROSSETTI *Let.* 26 Feb. (1965) II. 804 The love-sonnets are the preponderant portion. 1958 BLUNDEN *War Poets* ii. 15 In the pre-war poems of Brooke something like a premonition can be seen recurring. A love-sonnet dated 1909 powerfully includes it. 1862 G. MEREDITH *Mod. Love* xxxiii. 65 My wife, read this! Strange love talk, is it not? 1968 'N. BLAKE' *Private Wound* v. 69 She used none of the experienced woman's verbal tricks to arouse me, none of the shameless, titillating, love-talk. 1938 R. GRAVES *Coll. Poems* p. xxi, With the love-theme went the old fear-theme, sharpened rather than blunted by the experiences of peace. 1957 MANVELL & HUNTLEY *Techniques Film Music* i. 21 Examples of original music by Griffith and Briel included a prominent love-theme (for the Little Colonel and Elsie Stoneman).

c. *love-lighted, -lit, -starved* adjs.

1785 T. DWIGHT *Conquest of Canäan* (1788) III. 78 For earth too bright were these love-lighted fires! 1904 *Daily Chron.* 9 Feb. 5/2 Peering through the pale miracle of spring at his violets,..his blear eyes love-lighted. 1855 J. R. LOWELL *In-doors Out* in *Uncoll. Poems* (1950) 107 No glimmering beacon's love-lit rays Will homeward guide the wand'rer's feet. 1948 BLUNDEN *Shakespeare to Hardy* (1964) 208 Here she is in her father's garden, flowering, love-lit, awaiting the slow old Nurse. 1909 *Westm. Gaz.* 24 July 2/1 Love-starved young Keats hath cast his gift of clay. 1955 *New Yorker* 25 June 59/1 The heroine is a love-starved American secretary.

16. love-affair (earlier *sing.* and later *fig.* examples); **love beads**, a necklace of coloured beads worn as a symbol of universal love; **love-book**, (*b*): delete *nonce-use* and add earlier and later examples; **love comic**, a comic (sense *B. 2) in which the principal ingredient of the stories is love; **love-curl**, a lovelock, esp. on the forehead; **love draught**: delete † and add later examples; **love-hate**, (orig. a psychoanalytic) term used to describe ambivalent feelings of love and hate existing towards the same object; freq. *attrib.*; so as *vb.*; also *love-hatred*; **love-interest**, a theme or episode in a story, film, etc., of which the main element is the affection of lovers; **love-juice** restrict † to sense in Dict. and add: (*b*) an aphrodisiac; (*c*) a sexual secretion; **love-life**, relations between the sexes as they affect a particular person; **love-nest**, a secluded retreat for (esp. illicit) lovers; **love-object**, the object on which love is centred; **love-pass** = *love-passage*; **love-passage** (earlier example); **love-play**, wooing, caressing, spec. **foreplay*; also *fig.*; **love-scene** (earlier and later examples); **love-seat**, a special form of arm-chair (also, of sofa) designed for two occupants; **love-spoon**, a wooden spoon, sometimes with a double bowl, carved for presentation to one's intended wife; **love-up** [cf. *LOVE *v.*¹ 1 d] *slang*, an act of caressing, hugging, etc.

1862 *National Rev.* XIV. 220 They have suggested that some irregular love-affair was unprosperous. 1969 *Times* 25 Mar. 9/4 The crazy world of Erogenous Zones [*sc.* a play] is the result of 25-year-old Mike Stott's love affair with American strip cartoons. 1974 *Times* 4 Dec. 17 This century's love-affair with the motor-car. 1968 *Daily Colonist* (Victoria, B.C.) 20 June 1/5 Love beads, draped on him by Pierre Trudeau, adorn former Prime Minister Pearson at Toronto political rally. 1969 R. LOWELL *Notebk. 1967–68* (1970) 217 Our love-beads Rattling together to show that we were young. 1973 'B. MATHER' *Snowline* xiii. 155 Weirdo fringed shirts, headbands, love beads..as unsavoury a bunch of love children as I have ever seen. 1587 F. CLEMENT *Petie Schole* 36 Bookeloue I say, but I meane not louebookes, which..be the enemies of vertue. 1936 C. S. LEWIS *Allegory of Love* iv. 172 Hence those strange comings and goings in every medieval love-book. 1951 M. MCLUHAN *Mech. Bride* (1967) 151/2 It recently shifted a large section of its enterprises from murder to love comics. 1970 G. GREER *Female Eunuch* 214 The market is contested by ..love comics and fotoromance. 1850 H. MELVILLE *White Jacket* II. xxxvii. 240 Many sailors, with naturally tendril locks, prided themselves upon what they call love curls. 1926 T. E. LAWRENCE *Seven Pillars* (1935) lxxxvi. 479 In command was young Metaab, stripped to his skimp riding-drawers for hard work, with his black love-curls awry. 1841 BORROW *Zincali* I. II. i. 228 The women.. dealing in love draughts and diablerie. 1906 *Westm. Gaz.* 27 Aug. 3/1 The love-draught which Tristram and Iseult drink together. 1925 J. RIVIERE et al. tr. *Freud's Coll. Papers* IV. 79 So the second antithesis, love–hate, reproduces the polarity pleasure–pain, which is bound up with the former. 1937 H. NICOLSON *Diary* 16 June (1966) 302 Goering..has the love-hate complex of the average German bourgeois for England. 1950 E. J. SIMMONS *Dostoevsky* xix. 315 Versilov's..love-hate relations with Katerina which conclude with his mad attempt to murder her. 1967 A. WILSON *No Laughing Matter* II. 216 *She* love-hates him enough to be unable to leave him. 1972 LD. ROBENS *Ten Year Stint* ii. 15 My personal relationship with the men and their leaders was schizophrenic—a sort of love-hate relationship. 1951 H. HATFIELD *Thomas Mann* iii. 36 The protagonists in *Two Friends*, a novella of the love-hatred between a responsible burgher and a ne'er-do-well, afford a certain parallel to Thomas and Christian Buddenbrook. 1961 *Times* 18 Mar. 11/4 The love-hatred of Isolde for Tristan. 1892 H. JAMES *Notebks.* (1947) 129 There must be a 'love-interest'—which is one and the same with the other parts of the situation. 1938 R. G. COLLINGWOOD *Princ. Art* v. 84 The cinema, where it is said to be a principle accepted by almost every manager that no film can succeed without a love-interest. 1961 C. S. LEWIS *Exper. in Crit.* iv. 38 The story of excitement or mystery usually has a 'love interest' tacked on to it. 1973 *Time Out* 2–8 Mar. 59/3 'Love-interest' rears its inept head just as the medical satire should show its teeth. 1896 FARMER & HENLEY *Slang* IV. 241/1 Love-juice. 1965 J. GASKELL *Fabulous Heroine* 59 The sheets smelt of linen instead of love-juice. 1968 L. BERG *Risinghill* 122 'What is "love-juice"?' 'The liquid produced in the vagina of a woman when she is sexually excited.' 1972 'R. CRAWFORD' *Whip Hand* I. ix. 54 She was drugged by love-juices and on the brink of sleep. 1972 *Pussycat* XXXIII. LIX. 7/2, I could feel his lovejuice so hot, trickling down into the start of my stomach. 1919 M. K. BRADBY *Psycho-Anal.* v. 59 The character and development of the infantile love for father and mother will have an influence on the whole love-life of later years. 1934 'R. WEST' *Mod. Rake's Progress* 74 Ecclesiastics..called out to sanctify the love-life of our puny little George. 1959 A. CHRISTIE *Cat among Pigeons* viii. 89 Even Games Mistresses may have their love lives. 1972 T. ARDIES *This Suitcase* xiii. 140 He's the guy who's trying to break up my love life. 1919 U. SINCLAIR *Brass Check* xi. 65 So before long we began to notice dark hints in the newspapers; such esoteric phrases as 'Sinclair's love-nest'. 1970 G. GREER *Female Eunuch* 154 Nobody knew of his love-nest. 1972 'H. HOWARD' *Nice Day for Funeral* ix. 124 Pamela and Frankie were sharing a love-nest at Lakeland Towers. 1923 J. T. MACCURDY *Probl. Dynamic Psychol.* xvi. 191 The 'sentiment of love'.. consists in identification with the love object. 1925 J. RIVIERE et al. tr. *Freud's Coll. Papers* IV. 45 In the choice of their love-object they have taken as their model not the mother but their own selves. 1960 C. DAY LEWIS *Buried Day* vii. 137 When it became apparent that..as a love-object, I myself was unsatisfactory, she started on dogs. 1967 M. E. ROMM in C. W. Wahl *Sexual Probl.* 221 Fetishism is..the utilization in sex of a substitute for the love object. 1973 S. FISHER *Female Orgasm* xv. 437 Orgasm difficulties were observed to be linked to concern about the instability or potential loss of love objects. 1872 HARDY *Under Greenwood Tree* I. I. viii. 113 Good luck attended Dick's love-passes during the meal. He sat next Fancy. 1845 C. M. KIRKLAND *Western Clearings* 106 No one..had ever been able to ascertain whether there had actually been any 'love-passages' between them or not. 1911 Love-play [see *COURTING *vbl. sb.* 3]. 1944 T. RATTIGAN *While Sun Shines* II. 226 You're both very much mistaken if either of you imagines that you're going to have twopence-worth of verbal loveplay with my fiancée on my telephone. 1963 A. HERON *Towards Quaker View of Sex* 55 Adult heterosexuality presents fewer problems where early love play is tolerated than where it is suppressed. 1964 L. NKOSI *Rhythm of Violence* 46 Lili: Jo, I don't want to play. Jojozi: [tries to kiss her.] Not even love-play? 1639 MASSINGER *Unnat. Combat* III. iii. 181, I will bring you Where you..may see The love-scene acted. 1818 *Theatrical Inquisitor* XIII. 183 Love-scenes..which both French and English writers..regard as absolutely essential to their drama. 1932 R. CAMPBELL *Taurine Provence* 37 Read his [*sc.* Shaw's] miserable love-letters (published) and his 'love-scene' between Caesar and Cleopatra. 1975 *Country Life* 6 Feb. 326/2 Intimate, tender love-scenes. 1904 Love-seat [see *double chair* (*DOUBLE *a.* A. 6)]. 1915 F. W. BURGESS *Antique Furnit.* 205 Such settees which closely resemble an adaptation of two single chairs, are commonly called 'love-seats'. 1970 *Canad. Antiques Collector* Dec. 21/1 A Victorian love seat Mr. Daniel saw being hauled away in a garbage truck. 1973 'D. HALLIDAY' *Dolly & Starry Bird* x. 151 Johnson.. kissed her, and then..found a love seat and dropped there beside her. 1918 W. R. BUTTERFIELD in *Connoisseur* Aug. 191/1 At first,..love-spoons did not differ greatly from the wooden spoons in ordinary use in the household. 1968 J. ARNOLD *Shell Bk. Country Crafts* 193 The Welsh carvers ..produced a great deal of fine work, amongst which were the celebrated love-spoons. 1972 *Country Life* 20 Jan. 160/2 These [*sc.* stay busks] were rather in the manner of Welsh love-spoons and were made by young men for their intended marriage partners. 1953 'CADDIE' *Sydney Barmaid* xxv. 136 Come on, wot about a little bit of a luv-up? 1968 M. ALLWRIGHT *Roundabout* ix. 65 He looked so beaten by the world that I wanted to gather him in my arms on the spot and give him a good love-up.

b. love-bush, the Jamaican name for DODDER *sb.* 1.

1814 J. LUNAN *Hortus Jamaicensis* I. 266 Cuscuta Americana... The negroes of Liguanea mountains call it love-bush. 1954 *Farmer's Guide* (Jamaica Agric. Soc.) 582 The common Love-bushes of Jamaica comprise about four species of *Cuscuta*. 1962 S. WYNTER *Hills of Hebron* ii. 35 Pale yellow tendrils of the 'lovebush' wrapping themselves around the prickly arms of the cactus.

love, *sb.*² [Of obscure origin.] One of a set of transverse beams supporting the spits in a smoke-house for the curing of herring.

1865 [see SPIT *sb.*¹ 4 d]. 1895 A. PATTERSON *Man & Nature on Broads* 44 A savoury bloater, fresh down from the 'loves', is engrossing our own attentions. 1962 GRANVILLE *Dict. Sailors' Slang* 73/2 *Loves*, wooden splines in a herring curing loft on which the fish are suspended to dry.

love, *v.*¹ Add: **1. d.** With *up*. To caress, fondle; to engage in love-play with. *colloq.* (orig. *U.S.*).

1921 J. DOS PASSOS *Three Soldiers* II. iii. 83 You said you were goin' back and love up that goddam girl. 1928 *Dialect Notes* VI. 62 If a hillman [in the Ozarks] does admit that he loved a woman he means only that he caressed and embraced her—and he usually says that he *loved her up*. 1932 K. S. PRICHARD *Kiss on Lips* 167 Why don't you give her a hug..love her up a bit? 1957 J. BRAINE *Room at Top* xix. 166 If you love me up, I'll be as warm as toast. 1968 M. ALLWRIGHT *Roundabout* ix. 59, I never meant any harm; it was just as if he was a puppy I was loving up.

2. b. (Earlier and later examples.)

c 1810 W. HICKEY *Mem.* (1913) II. i. 10 Lord love your honour, to be sure I will. 1821 SCOTT *Pirate* I. i. 15 But, Heaven love you, Mr Mertoun, think what you are purposing. 1898 J. D. BRAYSHAW *Slum Silhouettes* 1 Mister Bloomfiel'? Lor' lummy! there ain't no misters 'ere. *Ibid.* 141 Mine? Lor' luv a duck! No, that's Sal Hogan's little lot. 1916 'TAFFRAIL' *Pincher Martin* xii. 218 'Lord love us!..d'you mean to say'—Words failed him. 1922 JOYCE *Ulysses* 176 Lord love a duck, he said, look at what I'm standing drinks to! 1934 T. S. ELIOT *Rock* ii. 65 What's that? Lor-love-a-duck, it's the missus! 1938 'J. BELL' *Port of London Murders* xv. 247 ''Lor love us!' I says to meself. 'Something's up.' 1954 W. SANSOM (*title*) Lord love us. 1955 M. ALLINGHAM *Beckoning Lady* iv. 55 Orf come 'is 'at, and lord luva duck!

d. *he loves me, he loves me not*, etc.: a formula used in divining-games. Also *transf.*

[1909 A. E. GILLINGTON *Old Hampshire Singing Games* facing p. 1 Then they say 'David Bailey' (Boy's name), Do you love me? Yes, No, etc. till the skipping girl stops.

The two trilling the rope say—'Alma Bailey' (Girl's name), Do you love him? Yes, No, etc.] **1946** A. Uttley *Country Things* v. 64 He loves me. He don't. He'll have me. He won't. He would if he could, But he can't. **1959** I. & P. Opie *Lore & Lang. Schoolch.* xv. 339 Much energy and calculation is devoted to skipping through the alphabet... the following sequence being that used by an 11-year-old Portsmouth girl: Does he love me? Yes, no, yes, no... Will he marry me? Yes, no, yes, no. **1971** *Guardian* 10 July 11/2 Eric Lubbock's private game of 'he loves me, he loves me not' with press and politicians is coming to a blessed end.

e. Phrases. *an* (or *as*) *you* (or *thou*, etc.) *love me*, if (or since) you love me: used as an imprecation; *to love and leave you*: a formula of departure; *love them and leave them*, etc.: seduce and abandon women.

1818 Carlyle *Early Lett.* (1886) 148 Send a letter quickly, an thou love me. **1823** J. F. Cooper *Pioneers* I. i. 28 Natty—you need say nothing of the shot, nor of where I am going—remember, Natty, as you love me. **1885** R. Holland *Gloss. County of Chester* 212 *Love you and leave you*, a common saying when any visitor is going to take his departure. 'Well a' mun *love ye, and leave ye*.' **1917** 'S. Rohmer' *Si-Fan Mysteries* xxxv. 264 But in waiting for one who is stealthily entering a room, don't, as you love me, take it for granted that he will enter *upright*. **1930** *Amer. Speech* Dec. 92 Love 'em and leave 'em. **1938** W. G. Hardy *Turn back River* 33 Love 'em and leave 'em; that was the idea. **1946** K. Tennant *Lost Haven* (1947) xvi. 259, I wouldn't try to keep me if I was you... Love me and let me leave. **1960** K. Amis *Take Girl like You* ii. 36 I'm afraid I shall have to love you and leave you. **1967** J. Morgan *Involved* 11 'Dewi, I have to love you and leave you,' Frankie said. 'I'm supposed to be on duty.' **1975** H. McCutcheon *Instrument of Vengeance* vii. 123 'I have many interests.' 'But no girls? ..You just love them and leave them, no?'

loveable, etc.: see Lovable, etc.

love-bird. Add: **2.** A lover.

1911 *Maclean's Mag.* Nov. 39/2 Seems as if I'd lighted on a pretty nest of love-birds. **1949** A. Hynd *We are Public Enemies* iv. 121 Ma barged in on the love birds. **1974** J. Mitchell *Death & Bright Water* xx. 242 'Lovebirds, lovebirds,' Randy Blythe said. Callan sat up, one arm still round Helena.

loved, *a.* Add: **1. c.** *loved one.* (i) A beloved, a lover; *pl.*, one's family or relations. (ii) A dead relation (spouse, etc.). Freq. with capital initials.

1862 M. B. Chesnut *Diary* 9 June (1949) xiv. 240 How many, many of your friends and loved ones this scrap of paper may tell you have gone to their death. **1879** Geo. Eliot *Let.* 20 Feb. (1956) VII. 104, I want, if I can, to write a '*characteristik*' of my loved one—no memoir, but a brief sketch. **1906** Chesterton *Charles Dickens* viii. 187 To ask for the loved one, and then not to dare to cross the threshold. **1926** A. Huxley *Jesting Pilate* iv. 272 Lay the Loved Ones to rest in — Graveyard, the Cemetery Unusual. **1938** D. Castle *Do Your Own Time* iii. 35, I sat idly drawing designs on my writing-paper while nineteen heartsick men began writing to their loved ones. **1948** E. Waugh (*title*) The loved one. **1968** *Guardian* 17 Aug. 8/1 Montpellier has just acquired..Europe's first funeral parlour on the American model..the Loved Ones make their final appearances in rooms done up in sky blue, water green, pink, or beige. **1971** *Progress* (Cape Town) May 8/3 In many cases these people would have to travel more than two or three hundred miles to be with their loved ones. **1973** *Advocate-News* (Barbados) 22 Jan. 12/1 (Advt.), For a smaller charge, we do not only intimate about the Birth, Baptism, Confirmation, Marriage and Death of your loved ones in our Classified Columns we also give a lasting record of the event for posterity.

love-feast. 2. and **3.** (Later examples.)

1870 [see *Ebenezer 1]. **1876** *Solano Republican* (Suisun, Calif.) 24 Aug. 2/1 A regular old-fashioned Democratic love-feast was engaged in by the many-scarred war-horses of the party. **1882** *19th Cent.* Nov. 740 They who turn aside to attend a Ranters' Love-feast..must be wrong in the head. **1909** F. Calhoun *Miss Minerva* 96 She was always on hand at the Love Feast and the Missionary Rally. **1922** G. Edwards *From Crow-scaring to Westminster* iii. 35 One form of [Primitive Methodist] service was called a 'love-feast' at which small pieces of bread were taken round with water. **1943** K. Tennant *Ride on Stranger* iii. 28 Aunt Edith beamed over the love-feast. **1948** *Minneapolis Star* 17 Sept. 1/3 Senator Joseph H. Ball and Gov. Luther Youngdahl had a sort of love feast at the capitol Thursday. **1973** 'S. Harvester' *Corner of Playground* I. v. 47 Several of their customs had Egyptian overtones, including a 'love-feast'..close to the Pharaonic *agapes*.

love-in (lɒ·vˌin). [*-in[3].] A gathering for the purpose of establishing and enjoying love relationships.

1967 *Times* 28 Mar. 4/7 The 'love-in' in Elysian Park, Los Angeles, was equally odd but caused no more than a traffic jam. **1967** *Observer* (Colour Suppl.) 3 Dec. 12/1 The imitation 'Love-in' at the Alexandra Palace..attracted 'horrible yobs'. **1971** M. Butterworth *Flowers for Dead Witch* ix. 127 We had a few love-ins up on the cliffs... We'd go for moonlight swims, and then dry off with a little horseplay.

lovekin (lɒ·vkin). Also **lovekins.** [f. Love *sb.* + -kin.] A lover.

1922 Joyce *Ulysses* 418 Reels off a credit. Lovey lovekin. **1925** T. Dreiser *Amer. Trag.* II. ii. xliii. 36 He'll be with me most of the time—the lovekins will.

Lovelace (lɒ·vlēɪs). The name of Robert *Lovelace*, a character in Richardson's *Clarissa Harlowe* (1747–8), used allusively for 'a seducer'.

[**1751** Richardson *Clarissa* (ed. 3) VIII. 294 Ladies.. should rather prefer the honest heart of a Hickman..than the volatile mischievous one of a Lovelace. **1812** Shelley *Let.* 11 June (1964) I. 305, I regard charges of resembling Lovelace with contemptuous indifference.] **1850** Thackeray *Pendennis* II. ix. 92 If Arthur had been the most determined *roué* and artful Lovelace who ever set about deceiving a young girl, he could hardly have adopted better means. **1944** S. Putnam tr. *E. da Cunha's Rebellion in Backlands* II, iv. 127 A scandal in which a certain local bigwig, a police sergeant, was *magna pars*, the Lovelace of the episode.

lovelify (lɒ·vlifəi), *v. rare.* [f. Lovel(y *a.* + -ify.] *trans.* To render lovely. So **lo·velified** *ppl. a.*, **lo·velifying** *vbl. sb.*

1897 G. B. Shaw *Our Theatres in Nineties* (1932) III. 73 Life, death, love and mankind are no longer themselves: they are glorified, sublimified, lovelified. **1935** *Punch* 17 July 65/1, I have heard of a 'Hairdresser and Beautician' who offers to 'lovelyfy' the ladies of Manchester; and, from New York of a Youthifying Beauty Cream. And here is a pretty piece from *The Windsor Magazine*:— 'A hand-cream..has a lovelifying effect on hands roughened from gardening.'

lovely, *a.* Add: **3. a.** *absol.* or *sb.* A woman or girl of glamorous loveliness, esp. one who takes part in an entertainment or 'show'. Also *transf.*

1933 [see *frippet]. **1938** Auden & Isherwood *On Frontier* III. ii. 108 It [*sc.* the working class] prefers our larger and livelier organs of enlightenment, which can afford snappier sports news,..and bigger photographs of bathing lovelies. **1940** H. G. Wells *Babes in Darkling Wood* II. i. 143 Not for many years have I had that hungry craving for everything, give and receive, from another human being. I can't imagine the man. What a marvel, what a lovely he'd have to be! **1957** J. Braine *Room at Top* xvi. 150, I was taking Susan not as Susan, but as a Grade A. lovely, as the daughter of a factory-owner. **1966** T. Pynchon *Crying of Lot 49* iii. 63 One of the girls, long-waisted, brown-haired lovely in a black knit leotard. **1967** *Stage* 2 Mar. 7/1 The six lovelies comprising Marie de Vere's Ballet Montparnasse. **1974** *Times* 22 Jan. 11 Gone are the remorseless parade of whey-faced classic lovelies, each indistinguishable from the other.

lover[1]. Add: **2. c.** A pimp. *U.S. slang.*

1904 'No. 1500' *Life in Sing Sing* 250/1 *Lover*, a man who receives support from a prostitute. **1963** R. I. McDavid *Mencken's Amer. Lang.* 727 A pimp is a.. McGimp, fish and shrimp, lover, Latin lover and many others.

d. As a form of address (to a lover, or casually). *colloq.* (orig. and chiefly *U.S.*).

1911 G. S. Porter *Harvester* x. 194 'Hello, lover!' cried Doctor Carey... 'Are you married yet?' **1920** F. Scott Fitzgerald *This Side of Paradise* II. i. 209 *Rosalind*: Lover! Lover! I can't do with you, and I can't imagine life without you. **1959** N. Mailer *Advts. for Myself* (1961) 389 Maybe I wouldn't hear all the jazz you hear, lover, but I could develop her talent. **1963** D. Heyes *12th of Never* (1964) v. 31 'You got it, lover,' the waitress said. **1966** L. Deighton *Billion-Dollar Brain* iv. 41 It's nothing like that, lover. I'm not going to get myself hurt. **1972** J. Burmeister *Running Scared* iv. 72 She swung her legs off the bed. 'How about some coffee, lover?'

4. lover boy, man *slang* (orig. *U.S.*), a lover, an attractive man, a woman-chaser; also used as a form of address; **lovers' lane**, a road or any other secluded place to which lovers resort; **lover's (lovers') quarrel**, a dispute between lovers; also *transf.*

1677 (*title*) The lovers quarrel: or, Cupids triumph. **1823** C. Lamb *Let.* 9 Jan. (1935) II. 364 Henceforth I retract all my fond complaints of mercantile employment; look upon them as lovers' quarrels. **1842** Lytton *Zanoni* I. ii. ii. 137 The mysterious warning of Zanoni then suddenly occurred to him; he had forgotten it in the interest of his lover's quarrel with Viola. **1881** *Golden Gate Gaz.* (San Francisco) 26 Oct. 2/2 Sunday afternoon as a young lady and gentleman were promenading through 'Lovers' Lane' they were attacked by a ferocious dog. **1918** Barrie *What Every Woman Knows* iv. 134 There is a romantically damp little arbour at the end of what the villagers call the Lovers' Lane. **1941** *Time* 25 Aug. 41/1 In England, a young pair who had had a lovers' quarrel took 50 years to cool off, finally got the knot tied. **1942** R. Frost *Witness Tree* 52, I had a lover's quarrel with the world. **1947** *News of World* 26 Jan. 3/6 Her..body..was found in a 'lovers' lane' on an empty building site. **1952** S. Ellin *Key to Nicholas Street* I. i. 14 Here was lover boy walking around with milady's key. **1958** M. Procter *Man in Ambush* xvi. 196 Lover boy's been talking to you. Take no notice. **1959** C. Williams *Man in Motion* iii. 26 He's a Lover Boy, one of those big, flashy, conceited types that has to..give all the girls a break. **1961** H. S. Turner *Something Extraordinary* ii. 28 Clive..has never been able to stop her calling him 'loverboy' in tones of scorn. **1966** J. Pearl *Crucifixion P. McCabe* (1967) ix. 136 How would I know that I'd find Donna Lord parked in a lovers' lane at Briarwood Lake? **1968** L. Deighton *Only when I Larf* xvii. 226 'There's no hurry, loverman,' she said. **1972** F. Warner *Lying Figures* II. 9 Out on the prowl tonight, lover-boy? **1972** J. Brown *Chancer* xv. 208 Our arty friend, lover man, he was running a photography business. **1974** *Daily Tel.* (Colour Suppl.) 18 Jan. 34/4 Elisabeth Foster's body was found on January 3, 1972, under a hedge by a 'lovers' lane' near the picturesque village of Wrea Green.

lovering (lɒ·vəriŋ), *vbl. sb.* [f. Lover[1] + -ing[1].] Courting, fondling. Also *attrib.*

1884 in R. Lawson *Upton-on-Severn Words* 22. **1907** *Daily Chron.* 27 Nov. 3/3 Where the schoolboy demands gore in his books, she asks for 'lovering', as she calls it. *Ibid.*, Let him only think of the possibilities of that new 'mixed' school, where the headmaster kept a 'lovering table', at which dined the spoony couples. **1919** Galsworthy *Saint's Progress* I. ii. 20 Between these two young people no actual word of love had yet been spoken. Their lovering had advanced by glance and touch alone. **1922** C. Orr *Kate Curlew* xi. 178 She's nae objections to a bit of lovering behind her sister's coats. **1926** R. Macaulay *Crewe Train* II. ix. 169 People like the lovering couple usually stayed out..for long hours on end.

loverly, *a.*[2] Also **lovally.** Repr. a Cockney pronunc. of Lovely *a.*

1907 [see *jellied *a.* 3]. **1937** in Partridge *Dict. Slang* 497/2. **1956** Lerner & Loewe *My Fair Lady* (1958) I. i. 13 All I want is a room somewhere, Far away from the cold night air;.. Oh, wouldn't it be loverly? **1968** J. Wainwright *Web of Silence* 28 He 'ad the ackers—believe me—wiv a car like that... A loverly job, it was.

lovership. (Earlier example, used as a form of address to a lover.)

1837 F. Trollope *Vicar of Wrexhill* III. xiv. 325 Your lovership must excuse me if I declare that it is my intention to accompany the young lady myself.

lovescape (lɒ·vskēɪp). *rare.* [f. Love *sb.* after Landscape.] A view or prospect of love.

1876 G. M. Hopkins *Wreck of Deutschland* xxiii, in *Poems* (1967) 59 With the gnarls of the nail in thee, niche of the lance, his Lovescape crucified. **1969** *Punch* 19 Feb. 286/1 It is finely elegiac and the townscapes and lovescapes are vivid.

loveward(s (lɒ·vˌwəɹd(z)), *adv. rare.* [f. Love *sb.* + -ward or -wards.] Towards love.

1927 Joyce *Watching Needleboats at San Sabba* in *Pomes Penyeach*, I heard their young hearts crying Loveward above the glancing oar. **1971** G. M. Brown *Fishermen with Ploughs* 76 The children of the valley Drifted lovewards.

lovey-dovey (lɒ·viˌdɒ·vi), *sb.* and *a.* [f. Lovey + Dovie, dovey.] **A.** *sb.* = Lovey; also, brotherly love.

1819 [see Dovie, dovey]. **1904** *Daily Chron.* 26 Mar. 6/5 We will..love one another as much as we can, lovey dovey. **1946** H. L. Mencken in *Life* 5 Aug. 46/2 And bring in a reign of peace, prosperity and lovey-dovey.

B. *adj.* Fondly affectionate; namby-pamby.

1886 *Harper's Mag.* Dec. 134/1, I would wear gray, which mamma prefers, but which I think looks lovey-dovey. **1900** H. Lawson *On Track* 65 Just as lovey-dovey talk is important to her and nonsense to you. **1967** 'D. Shannon' *Chance to Kill* (1968) vii. 91 You want to act all broad-minded and lovey-dovey with the dinges, O.K., but I got a right to feel how I like too. **1969** *Sunday Times* (Colour Suppl.) 19/3 There had been a fight. 'There was none of the usual lovey-dovey stuff between them.' **1973** 'H. Carmichael' *Too Late for Tears* viii. 99 This woman hadn't been all lovey-dovey with her husband... They'd been squabbling for months.

So **lo·vey-do·veyness** [-ness], a state of maudlin sentimentality.

1923 D. H. Lawrence *Stud. Classic Amer. Lit.* x. 210 He [*sc.* Melville] wanted the lovey-doveyness of perfect mutual understanding. **1968** *Punch* 29 May 788/3 The fond pleasures, dear upsets and general lovey-doveyness of family life.

loving, *ppl. a.* Add: **4.** *Comb.*, as *loving-heartedness*; *loving-hearted*, *-kind*, *-kindly* adjs.

1903 Hardy *Dynasts* I. I. vi. 33 In its early, loving-kindly days Of gracious purpose. **1909** *Westm. Gaz.* 27 Feb. 4/3 The loving-hearted but hot-tempered musician who was head of the Conservatoire at Naples. **1909** R. Brooke *Coll. Poems* (1918) 99 Quiet and strange, and loving-kind, you sleep. **1926** *Contemp. Rev.* Feb. 226 It may have been the *sirocco*, which never makes for loving-heartedness. **1960** *Clergy Rev.* Jan. 14 More's way, detached, peaceful and loving-kind, must have set him dreaming.

low, *a.* and *sb.* Add: **A.** *adj.* **2. f.** Also *Comb.*, as *low-back*, *-central*, *-front*, *-mid*, *-rising*, used chiefly attributively or quasi-adj.

1924 H. E. Palmer *Gram. Spoken Eng.* I. 13 Low-Rising. Nucleus-tone. **1934** J. J. Hogan *Outl. Eng. Philol.* 14, æ: low-front. **1934** Webster, Low-back, low-central. **1944** T. H. Wetmore in *Studies in Speech & Drama in Honor of A. M. Drummond* 244 (*title*) The dialectal significance of the non-phonemic low-back vowel variants before R. **1951** Z. S. Harris *Methods Struct. Ling.* vi. 57 Low-rising intonation. **1962** *Amer. Speech* XXXVII. 165 The low-central free vowel /ɑ/. **1962** Low-front [see *high *a.* 4 b]. **1965** *Language* XLI. 346 A low-back /ə/. *Ibid.*, In disyllabic words, Ngbaka shows only four sequences: high–mid, mid–high, mid–low, and low-mid. **1970** *Publ. Amer. Dial. Soc. 1968* L. 13 Sometimes.. it occurs as a retracted low-front or as a low-central monophthong.

h. Phr. *low to paper*: of type, of less than normal height.

[**1683–4** J. Moxon *Mech. Exerc. Printing* (1962) 346 Low against Paper.] **1888** *Encycl. Brit.* XXIII. 698/2 Types lower than the ordinary dimension are said to be *low to paper*, and if surrounded by higher types will not give a perfect impression. **1922** D. B. Updike *Printing Types* I. ii. 34 The standard height-to-paper is 0·918 inch.

Types exceeding or falling short of this measurement are termed respectively 'high-to-paper' and 'low-to-paper'.

7. c. (Later example.)

1912 *Chambers's Jrnl.* Aug. 533/1 He may feel that he is the superior in every way of some of the 'low whites' with whom he comes into daily contact.

12. b. *low on*: deficient in, short of. *colloq.*

1966 *Listener* 23 June 926/2 Low on credibility however was *They Were So Few.* **1969** *Ibid.* 22 May 732/2 Her difficulty is that she is incapable of fulfilling herself, partly because she seems to be low on energy. **1974** J. Wainwright *Evidence I shall Give* xxxv. 200 He brewed instant coffee. He was low on sugar.

20. *low-altitude, -angle, -budget, -calorie, -consumption, -contrast, -cost, -density, -drag, -energy, -fat, -field, -flux, -impedance, -income, -intensity, -noise, -price, -rank, -rental, -risk, -status, -sulphur, -temperature, -tension* (later examples), *-value, -velocity, -voltage, -wage, -wattage, -wing.*

1925 R. W. G. Kingston in E. F. Norton *Fight for Everest 1924* 286 Low-altitude deserts. **1966** *Electronics* 3 Oct. 181 Dornier System GmbH last year made a successful low-altitude recovery with a paraglider that unfolds its wings for descent. **1971** C. Bonington *Annapurna South Face* iii. 34 He [*sc.* Kelvin Kent] had also organized our low-altitude porters, whose job it was to carry all the gear up to Base Camp. **1907** *Yesterday's Shopping* (1969) p. xliii/4 Low angle planes. **1956** *Nature* 17 Mar. 500/1 Low-angle X-ray patterns from two durains of different rank. **1966** *Electronics* 14 Nov. 48 An antenna lacking the low-angle coverage..would not be able to communicate with the satellite unless the plane flew farther south. **1958** R. Sill in *Film Daily Yearbk. Motion Pict.* 985/1, 20th Century Fox..proclaimed that it has budgeted $65,000,000 for the production of 65 features this year, including 25 from..Regal Films, which specialize in low-budget films. **1961** B. Paulu *Brit. Broadcasting in Transition* vii. 129 Audiences seem to show no more enthusiasm for high-cost television than low-budget radio music. **1973** E. Bullins *Theme is Blackness* 129 Short, low-budget films that could be distributed nationally. **1969** *Lancet* 8 Dec. 1190/2 On low-calorie high-fat diets, fat and thin subjects developed the same levels of ketones in the blood. **1970** *Sunday Times* 26 Apr. 28/2 Jars of low-calorie instant soup. **1960** *Farmer & Stockbreeder* 8 Mar. 61/1 The north-east, a low-consumption area. **1975** *Times* 11 Mar. (Italian Industry Suppl.) p. v/1 Petrol has never been cheap in Italy, so low consumption motors were developed there. **1966** D. G. Brandon *Mod. Techniques Metallogr.* i. 14 The curves for a 'soft', low-contrast, fast emulsion and a 'hard', high-contrast, slow emulsion are shown. **1934** H. L. Ickes *Diary* 10 Mar. (1953) I. 152 Obviously it wasn't a model of low-cost housing for people on the very lowest rung of the economic order. **1960** *Times* 21 Nov. (Canada Suppl.) p. xiii/7 Efficient and low-cost producers. **1969** *New Statesman* 11 Apr. 506/1 There is no cheaper way of running a radio station than sitting a low-cost young man in a studio to talk about his breakfast and his fan mail. **1960** *New Left Rev.* May–June 70/2 Low density, two-storey three-bedroom housing. **1962** F. I. Ordway et al. *Basic Astronautics* iii. 58 Since it [*sc.* the Moon] is a low-density world, there is little likelihood of extensive concentrations of metallic iron and nickel. **1964** *Ann. N.Y. Acad. Sci.* CXV. 569 The resulting digital data, when stored on low-density (200 characters per inch) digital tape, would fill 84 digital tapes. **1962** F. I. Ordway et al. *Basic Astronautics* xi. 428 An aerodynamic shroud..provides a low-drag housing for the entire vehicle. **1971** *Flying* Apr. 2/1 A low-drag high-speed wing. **1942** J. D. Stranathan *'Particles' of Mod. Physics* xiii. 535 The mean free path may be longer, and the mean life correspondingly longer, for high energy mesotrons than it is for low energy mesotrons. **1960** *Farmer & Stockbreeder* 8 Mar. 149/2 A low-energy ration contained 750 cal per lb. **1960** *Times* 20 Sept. (Pure Food Suppl.) p. iii, None of the low-fat girls had better skins than at the start of the experiment. **1972** J. Ball *Five Pieces Jade* xii. 150 He poured some cornflakes into a bowl, covered them with..low-fat milk. **1962** Corson & Lorrain *Introd. Electromagn. Fields* iii. 91 All that varies from one *O'* to another is the fact that sometimes the point lies in a high-field region, within a molecule, for example, and other times it lies in a low-field region. **1956** *Nature* 4 Feb. 205/2 The rent of experimental facilities in [the nuclear reactor] DIDO may vary from £100 a day down to £10 a day for those in less-attractive low-flux positions. **1962** Simpson & Richards *Physical Princ. Junction Transistors* ii. 26 The device thus passes most of the emitter current from a low-impedance generator to a high-impedance load. **1952** M. Laski *Village* xvi. 219 Roy Wilson may start in a low-income group, but if he can make a success, well, he's worth more than people who can't. **1971** *Guardian* 7 July 24/4 Up to 60,000 children in low income families have lost their right to free school meals. **1953** N. Tinbergen *Herring Gull's World* xiii. 109 Low-intensity copulations can be seen early in the season. **1964** P. Delattre in D. Abercrombie et al. *Daniel Jones* 51 Very low-intensity vowel. **1971** D. E. Westlake *I gave at the Office* (1972) 14 Marijuana was legal in the United States until 1935, and it was just a sort of low-intensity fact in American culture. **1961** *Times* 5 Apr. 6/4 Special 'maser' low-noise amplifiers will be used in the reception of the very weak signals from the satellites. **1851** in O. Hudson *Martin Tupper* (1949) x. 121 Shepherd's mammoth low price clothing emporium, Chesnut street above Third. **1944** A. G. Hatcher in *Mod. Lang. Notes* LIX. 516, I have seen..*low-price shoes.* **1968** D. E. Allen *Brit. Tastes* viii. 204 Low-price catering. **1956** *Nature* 17 Mar. 501/1 The decreased intensity of the diffuse scattering [of X-rays] at very low angles for the low-rank coals. **1965** *Times Lit. Suppl.* 25 Nov. 1057/3 Artistic low-rental areas. **1951** S. A. Stouffer in Parsons & Shils *Toward Gen. Theory Action* iv. v. 492 Low-risk and high-risk situations. **1956** J. Klein *Study of Groups* vii. 102 One thus obtains four types of sub-groups: high-status mobile, and non-mobile; low-status mobile, and non-mobile. **1974** J. Burnett *Useful Toil* i. 31 Farm labouring gradually sank during the course of the [nineteenth] century into a low-status occupation. **1965** G. J. Williams *Econ. Geol. N.Z.* xviii. 322/1 The coal is a low-sulphur lignite of lower grade than the lignites of Benhar and Mataura. **1909** *Installation News* III. 133/2 The low-temperature system of healing by means of convectors. **1957** R. Hoggart *Auden* iii. 32 He seems to be aiming not at a widely-acceptable demotic speech but at a low-temperature verse of intelligent observation and comment. **1948** *Penguin New Writing* XXXV. 93 Poetry of a kind which is at present particularly in need of rescue from oblivion: what may be called low-tension poetry. **1957** *Railway Mag.* Mar. 159/2 A cubicle containing the majority of the low-tension control equipment is housed in a van compartment in the motor coach. **1962** A. Battersby *Guide to Stock Control* viii. 76 At the other end of the scale, spare parts should be in the low-value, long-residence class. **1956** *Nature* 21 Jan. 120/2 In areas where deep weathering or drift presents difficult low-velocity-layer correction problems, the reflexion times down to a known shallow marker-bed will give the necessary corrections for the deeper horizons. **1975** N. Luard *Robespierre Serial* vi. 45 A low-velocity handgun. **1922** Glazebrook *Dict. Appl. Physics* II. 748/1 On low-voltage alternating-current systems these [switches] consist of movable blades bridging two contacts. **1971** L. Payne *Even my Foot's Asleep* i. 7 The soft glow of a low-voltage lamp. **1920** *Act* 10 *Geo. V* c. 10 § 1, Part of the contributions payable in respect of low-wage earners. **1971** *Times* 19 Mar. 6 There had been a suggestion that steel might be imported from low-wage producers like Japan. **1962** A. Wise *Death's Head* xi. 131 A few low-wattage wall lights. **1971** W. Hanley *Blue Dreams* xix. 314 Erotic light..suffused the rooms, cast by the low-wattage red light bulbs. [**1923** *Flight* XV. 122/2 The choice of low wing position has doubtless been made mainly on account of a desire to keep the wing in one piece.] **1942** *R.A.F. Jrnl.* 16 May 15 This is a conventional two-seater low-wing monoplane. **1950** *Gloss. Aeronaut. Terms* (*B.S.I.*) I. 30 *Low-wing monoplane*, a monoplane in which the main planes are located at or near the bottom of the fuselage.

21. *low-ceiled, -eaved, -powered, -priced* (later examples), *-sided, -sized, -studded, -toned* (later examples), *-vaulted, -voiced* (later examples), *-waisted.*

1904 W. de la Mare *Henry Brocken* 106 The room in which we sat was low-ceiled and cheerful. **1905** *Westm. Gaz.* 20 May 5/3 Low-eaved houses, cobbled streets, and quiet squares. **1903** *Daily Chron.* 3 Aug. 3/7 A motor-car, however low-powered or slow it may be. **1953** R. Lehmann *Echoing Grove* 211 Put a frame round the amorphous semi-transparent mass of low-powered energy that seemed himself. **1972** 'G. North' *Sgt. Cluff rings True* xv. 114 The glow from a low-powered bulb in a standard lamp. **1895** *Montgomery Ward Catal.* 5/1 This is one of the best made low priced suitings that we ever received. **1923** *Radio Times* 28 Sept. 22/2 Headphones specially low priced at 24/– per pair. **1874** J. W. Long *Amer. Wild-Fowl Shooting* 78 A small, low-sided boat..might be.. dangerous on large waters. **1882** Nodal & Milner *Gloss. Lancs. Dial.* 186 *Low-sized*, little, short of stature. **1907** Joyce *Let.* 1 Mar. (1966) II. 218 They were low-sized and quince-coloured. **1938** S. Beckett *Murphy* 97 A low-sized corpulent middle-aged woman. **1854** B. P. Shillaber *Life & Sayings Mrs. Partington* 16 A tall man could not stand erect in the low-studded room. **1884** Low-studded [see Studded *ppl. a.* 6]. **1934** E. Wharton *Backward Glance* x. 251 It was a tiny garden patch, and a few steps brought us to the door of a low-studded cottage in a gap of the hanging woods. **1909** R. Fry *Let.* 15 Jan. (1972) I. 310 The *Fur Jacket* ..is..exceedingly low-toned. **1941** *B.B.C. Gloss. Broadcasting Terms* 18 *Low-toned*, manifesting a form of frequency distortion in which the lower audio-frequencies are accentuated. **1969** *Word* XXV. 155 Possessive prefixes are usually low-toned. **1869** J. R. Lowell *Foot-Path* in *Under Willows* 225 Those angel stairways in my brain, That climb from these low-vaulted days To spacious sunshines far from pain. **1895** A. W. Pinero *Second Mrs. Tanqueray* ii. 63 She is a low-voiced, grave girl. **1953** 'N. Blake' *Dreadful Hollow* 148 He stared up at her, and caught Charles's low-voiced words. **1923** A. Huxley *Antic Hay* ix. 124 Low-waisted summer frocks. **1966** *Guardian* 27 July 6/4 A long, lean, low-waisted jumper top. **1974** *Country Life* 24 Oct. 1242/3 The long, low-waisted black jersey evening dress.

22. *low-burning.*

1904 E. Rickert *Reaper* 8 His mother sat by the low-burning peat. **1974** E. Hardwick *Seduction & Betrayal* 131 Miss Kilman..is hanging on..to a low-burning encounter with religion.

23. low-alloy *a. Metallurgy*, containing a small proportion of alloying elements; **low-bush** *N. Amer.*, used *attrib.* to designate low-growing plants or their fruit, esp. **low-bush blackberry**, one of several species of *Rubus*; **low-bush blueberry**, a variety of *Vaccinium angustifolium*; **low-bush cranberry**, in Canada, *Viburnum edule*; **low comedy**, also *attrib.*; **low definition**: see *Definition 5 c; **low-fidelity** *a.*, characterized by an absence of 'high fidelity' (see *high fidelity); **low gear**: see *Gear *sb.* 7 b; **low grade** *Philol.* [Grade *sb.* 9 a], a reduced form, generally represented by [ə], in an ablaut series; **low-key** *Photogr.* (see quot. 1959); also *attrib.* and *fig.*, esp. muted, restrained, of modest ambition; so **low-keyed** *a.* (in *fig.* senses); **low-loader**, a lorry with a low deck (usu. without sides) to facilitate loading of heavy loads, esp. other vehicles; **low-loss** *a. Electr.*, characterized by or causing little dissipation of electric or electromagnetic energy; **low maple** *U.S.*, the mountain maple, *Acer spicatum*; **low-molecular** *a. Chem.*, having a low molecular weight; **low-neck**, a low-necked dress; **low-pass** *a.*, denoting a filter that attenuates components with a frequency greater than some cut-off frequency and passes components of lower frequency; **low profile**, (*a*) *attrib.* of a motor-vehicle tyre, having a relatively great width in proportion to its height; (*b*) (of or pertaining to) a low-keyed and unobtrusive policy, restrained or inconspicuous behaviour, etc.; **low quarters** (Quarter *sb.* 20 c] *pl. U.S.* (see quots. 1916, 1971); also **low-quarter** *attrib.*; **low-residue** *a.*, (of a meal or diet) designed to give rise to relatively little fæces and urine; **low-rise** *a.*, of a building: low, of one storey or few storeys; also *transf.*; as *sb.*, a low building; **low-yield** *a.*, producing little, giving a low return; *spec.* applied to a nuclear weapon having a relatively low explosive force.

1931 *Iron Age* CXXVIII. 1142/1 The low alloy steels were described [by H. J. French] as those containing usually no more than 6 or 7 per cent of the alloying metal. **1956** W. D. Hargreaves in D. L. Linton *Sheffield* 287 Rotherham produces about a million tons per year of carbon and low alloy steel. **1972** *Jrnl. Austral. Inst. Metals* XVII. 175/1 Where additional durability is required, a widely employed technique is to use a low-alloy 'marine grade' of steel. **1833** C. P. Traill *Let.* 18 Apr. in *Backwoods of Canada* (1836) 144 The low-bush cranberries are brought in great quantities by the Indians to the towns and villages. **1857** A. Gray *First Less. Bot. & Vegetable Physiol.* 122 *R*[*ubus*] *trivialis*, Michx. (Low Bush-Blackberry). **1891** J. M. Coulter *Bot. W. Texas* I. 104 Low bush blackberry. A southern blackberry, apparently common in eastern, southern, and western Texas. **1958** *Edmonton* (Alberta) *Jrnl.* 26 July 39/6 For the most part, housewives pick high and low bush blueberries..and in the fall, low bush cranberries. **1962** M. E. Murie *Two in Far North* i. i. 15 And sometimes had time to pick a handful of bright red low-bush cranberries. **1969** E. H. Pinto *Treen* 91 The harvesting of lowbush blueberries..begins in Maine in late July and August. **1849** *Theatrical Mirror* 17 Sept. 19 Whether in consequence of the non-arrival of the second low-comedy man, I would undertake his part in the last piece. **1886** in J. R. Ware *Passing Eng.* (1909) 171/2 The success of *Indiana* mainly depends upon the extravagant humours of the chief low-comedy merchant. **1906** E. Dyson *Fact'ry 'Ands* xviii. 239 Feathers had some reputation as a yarn spinner. His low-comedy style was popular. **1961** *John o' London's* 6 July 8/2 She lacks the low-comedy sense which Kingsley Amis shows in his poetry. **1947** *Amer. Speech* XXII. 132 The relatively low-fidelity aluminum disks might not always record it clearly enough to interfere with established habits of transcription. **1962** Simpson & Richards *Physical Princ. Junction Transistors* xviii. 451 For low-fidelity communication links using portable equipment a narrow-band FM system..may be used. **1963** T. Pynchon *V* v. 113 Each anchor man had a walkie-talkie, tied in on a common network to Zeitsuss's office and a low-fidelity 15-inch speaker mounted on the ceiling. **1901** *Jrnl. Gmc. Philol.* III. 265 Skr. *i*: Gr. *α*<*ə*, as low grade of a long vowel. **1907** *Mod. Philol.* V. 269 OE. *þwinan*, pre-Germ. *tu̯ino-* may represent the low grade of a base *tā-u̯o-* from *tā-u̯o-* from *tā-*. **1895** *Leeds Mercury* Suppl. 5 Jan. (E.D.D.), Sarah wor in a varry low key. **1907** *Westm. Gaz.* 19 Jan. 14/2 There is not the slightest reason why we should not exploit this low-key type of picture. **1953** K. Reisz *Technique Film Editing* i. 65 The elegant low-key lighting (which is utterly unrealistic). **1959** W. S. Sharps *Dict. Cinematogr.* 108/1 *Low-key*, the term applied when a majority of the tones in the subject or image lie at the dark end of the grey scale. **1965** *Listener* 2 Dec. 934/3 Pleasant, low-key entertainment. **1972** *Guardian* 11 July 12/2 With the UDA building its barricades, how long can the 'low key' phase last. **1960** R. Davies *Voice from Attic* 19 Nothing could be farther from my intention, and I know that many readers are happiest with a low-keyed and antitheatrical approach to their pleasure. **1969** *Daily Tel.* 11 Feb. 16/1 A fairly low-keyed inquiry. **1973** *Publishers Weekly* 30 May 40/3 A girl spending the winter recovering from a long illness, and her pet hamster are the elements in this low-keyed fantasy. **1927** *Times* (Weekly ed.) 3 Nov. 495/4 Two open coaches mounted on six-cylindered low-loader commercial chassis. **1960** *Guardian* 23 Nov. 11/4 Efforts were still being made to tow the low loader out of the hedge. **1973** J. Leasor *Host of Extras* i. 23, I may have to carry them [*sc.* old cars] round the country on a low loader to show them to someone who can't come to London. **1928** *Times* 23 Mar. 20/1 The effect of connecting up a valve amplifier with a highly efficient tuned circuit employing a coil of the low-loss type. **1946** *Nature* 9 Nov. 671/1 The oxides in powder form were mixed in various proportions with a low-loss, non-magnetic binder, paraffin wax. **1962** Corson & Lorrain *Introd. Electromagn. Fields* xii. 418 This type of wave guide is found in almost all types of electronic equipment for use both at low and at high frequencies. The medium of propagation is a low-loss dielectric. **1813** H. Muhlenberg *Catal. Plant.* 95 Mountain maple or low maple. **1832** D. J. Browne *Sylva Amer.* 102 It is sometimes called Low Maple, from the dwarfish stature of the tree. **1897** G. B. Sudworth *Nomencl. Arborescent Flora U.S.* 282 *Acer spicatum*. Mountain Maple... Low Maple (Tenn.). **1946** *Nature* 28 Dec. 925/1 Crystallization phenomena in rubbers show certain similarities to, but also striking differences from, crystallization in ordinary low-molecular systems. **1866** Low-neck [in Dict., sense A. 1 c]. **1909** *Englishwoman* Apr. 319 Magazines with 'types of beauty'—in tights, ballet dancers' skirts or low-necks. **1922** Low-neck [see *bathing-suit* (*Bathing *vbl. sb.* 2)]. **1929** J. H. Morecroft *Elem. Radio Communication* vii. 250 A simple calculation, say, of the low-pass type, will show the reason for the particular performance of filters. **1950** *Engineering* 17 Feb. 186/3

The model..consists essentially of a headpiece made up of successive layers of flexible material, felt and iron arranged so as to constitute a low-pass acoustic filter. Such a filter does not cause appreciable attenuation of the low and voice frequencies, but cuts out those frequencies which give rise to harmful shrillness. **1964** *Language* XL. 203 'Content-free speech' has also come to refer to doctored recorded corpora of speech which have been run through low-pass filters, so that features conveying affective qualities are retained while linguistic intelligibility is suppressed. **1967** *Guardian* 25 Sept. 3/8 A production Aston Martin..with..low profile tyres. **1970** *Ibid.* 24 Aug. 3/2 The Nixon doctrine of 'low profile' involvement, in other words a maximum of aid and a minimum of US troops. **1971** *Publishers' Weekly* 6 Dec. 19/2 Los Angeles..more than lives up to its reputation as a low-profile, seemingly endless sprawl with no center. **1972** *Times* 2 Aug. 14/5 Whittaker Hunt has been adopting an altogether lower profile. **1973** *Listener* 4 Jan. 7/3, I admire the brisk creativeness of American English. 'Low profile' is a perfectly vivid phrase for 'conciliatory demeanour'. **1880** 'MARK TWAIN' *Tramp Abroad* 275 He wore very low-quarter patent-leather shoes. **1916** *Dialect Notes* IV. 269 *Low-quarters*, Oxford shoes. 'He wears *low quarters* all the year round.' [New Orleans; Also N. Car.] **1971** *Current Slang* (Univ. S. Dakota) VI. 7 *Low quarters*, army dress shoes. **1962** A. SHEPARD in *Into Orbit* 98, I had a low residue breakfast of orange juice, a filet mignon wrapped in bacon, and some scrambled eggs. **1971** *New Scientist* 11 Mar. 551/2 Waste can be minimised by the careful planning of low-residue diets..but it will always present a problem [in space flight]. **1957** *Fortune* Sept. 213/2 What kind of people..prefer 'high-rise' apartment buildings, what kind of people prefer two-to-five-storey 'low-rise' houses? **1967** *London* (Ontario) *Free Press* 23 June 38/4 Hip Briefs for today's low-rise trousers. **1971** *Rand Daily Mail* (Home Owner) 27 Mar. 7/4 High rise for young couples or old folk, low-rise for couples with older children. **1972** *Sat. Rev.* (U.S.) 17 June 47/2 The finished units..were stacked 3-high..to form low-rise garden units. **1957** *Wall St. Jrnl.* 25 Jan. 1/3 Only low-yield nuclear tests will be conducted at the Frenchman's Flat Proving Ground... The announcement added high-yield devices (hydrogen bombs) are never tested in Nevada. **1959** *Times* 20 Oct. 19/3 Substantial two-way business in industrial shares partly reflected switching out of low-yield shares into higher yielding second rankers. **1972** *Sat. Rev.* (U.S.) 6 May 31/2 Localized Soviet attacks would be countered..by the Pentomic army equipped with a variety of sophisticated, low-yield nuclear weapons.

B. *sb.* **3. a.** *spec.* in E. Anglia, a hollow or valley between dunes; a pool left by the tide in such a hollow. (Further examples.)

1855 *Trans. Philol. Soc.* 33 [Norfolk words.] *Low*, a loch left by the tide on the shore. **1878** MILLER & SKERTCHLY *Fenland* ix. 291 The Tides..having a larger and deeper channel run with greater velocity into Lynn Deeps, and set westward through the lows in the sands into Boston Deeps, the Tide being about 20 minutes later there than in Lynn Deeps. **1929** *Jrnl. Ecol.* XVII. 138 Very characteristic of the Blakeney dunes are the 'lows'—narrow valleys between the dune-ridges, corresponding to the 'slacks' of the west-coast dunes. The lows differ from slacks in not being permanently moist..and in being liable to flooding by unusually high tides. **1964** V. J. CHAPMAN *Coastal Vegetation* vi. 156 After flooding by the tide, water may remain in the low for some time. **1970** G. E. EVANS *Where Beards wag All* xxi. 240 These men lived in these huts which they'd placed down there in the Low.

b. Also, an area of low gravitational field strength.

1966 *McGraw-Hill Encycl. Sci. & Technol.* 166/2 Gravity maps display highs and lows. **1972** *Nature* 3 Mar. 24/1 The main feature of the present map..is the large gravity 'low' in the Moray Firth.

c. A low point or minimum in price, temperature, numbers, or the like. Cf. *all-time* adj. (*ALL E. 13).

1911 *N.Y. Times* 20 Sept., Calumet and Hecla opened 17 points off at 373, which is 47 points above the established low of 1897. **1929** *Observer* 17 Nov. 3/4 The sharp rally..called the weighted average of eight leading industrial stocks up to 149·0 from the new low of 133·0. **1933** A. R. LONGWORTH *Crowded Hours* viii. 133 In 1906 the finances of the Longworths, though they were on the way, had not reached their present 'low'. **1934** WODEHOUSE *Thank You, Jeeves* xiv. 203 But the heart was still sinking. And when I heard him snort emotionally in the darkness it touched a new low. **1953** —— *Performing Flea* 193 The population of Dormitory 309 fluctuated between a high of 68 and a low of 57. **1955** *Ann. Reg. 1954* 82 The death rate fell to a new low of 8·7 per thousand. **1964** *Financial Times* 3 Mar. 2/6 A new low for many years was reached in stocks of refined tin in London Metal Exchange official warehouses last week. **1968** *Globe & Mail* (Toronto) 17 Feb. 1/6 The predicted high for Elliot Lake today is 5 below; the low tonight 20 below. **1971** *Sci. Amer.* Sept. 107/2 The interior temperature of the house sometimes reached 80 degrees, and the nightly lows were seldom below 70. **1973** *Jrnl. Genetic Psychol.* CXXII. 186 Scores could range from a high of 64..to a low of 1.

5. = *low gear* (see *GEAR *sb.* 7 b).

1934 in WEBSTER. **1968** C. NICOLE *Self Lovers* ii. 30 He descended the hill from his house in low, partly to minimise the potholes..and partly to enjoy the view. **1970** T. HILLERMAN *Blessing Way* xiii. 119 Put it in low and angle to the left. **1973** 'A. HALL' *Tango Briefing* viii. 96, I dragged the manual into low to kill the rest of the speed.

low, *adv.* Add: **5.** *low-cut, -flying, -growing* (later examples), *-hung* (later examples), *-paid* (also *absol.*), *-ranking, -slung, -trained* (also as pa. pple.), *-yielding*; **low-flung** *a. U.S. colloq.*, of low character or standing.

1897 *Sears, Roebuck Catal.* 203/3 Men's low cut canvas pumps. **1932** 'E. M. DELAFIELD' *Thank Heaven Fasting* II. iii. 44 Lady Marlowe, superb..in her low-cut green satin, with an emerald tiara. **1962** P. GREGORY *Like Tigress at Bay* iv. 40 Steve was forced to admit to himself that she presented a beautiful picture, sitting there in the spotlight in her low-cut, strapless gown. **1843** *Missouri Reporter* (St. Louis) 11 Apr. (Th.), Here we have a beautiful specimen of the dishonesty and low-flung slang of the clique. **1844** *Knickerbocker* XXIII. 506 Who wants a parcel of low-flung 'outside barbarians' to go in cahoot with us? **1853** J. G. BALDWIN *Flush Times Alabama* 24 He..denounced Jefferson as a low-flung demagogue. **1861** *Oregon Argus* 28 Dec. (Th.), It would be impossible to attempt a controversy with such low-flung dogs. **1963** *Times Lit. Suppl.* 8 Feb. 95/2 The low-flying beginning of this book is much better than its high-flying philosophic end. **1906** *Westm. Gaz.* 26 May 11/3 The topmost bough of some low-growing tree or shrub. **1958** W. J. STOKOE *Caterpillars Brit. Moths* (new ed.) I. 299 Greater plantain (*Plantago major*) and other low-growing plants. **1916** D. H. LAWRENCE *Amores* 104 The low-hung lamps stretched down the road..as I hastened to meet The low-hung light of her eyes. **1924** E. SITWELL *Sleeping Beauty* xvi. 54 It seemed a low-hung country of the blind. **1964** W. L. GOODMAN *Hist. Woodworking Tools* 138 Comparatively low-paid labourers. **1974** *Times* 5 Dec. 4/4 The TUC had..recognized the low-paid as a special case. **1958** W. J. H. SPROTT *Human Groups* ix. 152 The less popular members of the consistently low-ranking teams did not change their allegiance. **1931** *Morning Post* 21 Aug. 11/7 His low-slung car simply hurtled down the straight and was lost to view. **1965** G. MCINNES *Road to Gundagai* ii. 31 A very full, low-slung muskmelon moon. **1973** 'R. MACLEOD' *Nest of Vultures* ii. 30 Sleek Ferraris, opulent Rolls-Royces and an occasional low-slung Lamborghini. **1869** *Rep. Comm. Agric. 1868* (U.S. Dept. Agric.) 249 Low-trained hedges may be necessary where land is limited in area, and high in price. *Ibid.*, Evergreens or shrubs may be formed, trimmed, and low-trained a long time without pleaching. **1946** *Nature* 23 Nov. 762/2 The replacement of existing virus-infected, low-yielding clonal stocks of raspberries is a pressing necessity. **1968** *Economist* 2 Mar. 61/2 Town and City has always been a favourite low-yielding property share.

b. Also *low-flying* (so *low-fly* vb.), *-loading*.

1881 O. WILDE *Poems* 69 Young Mercury Low-flying to the dusky ford of Dis. **1949** *Happy Landings* July 8/1 One pilot, low flying over the Continent, had his aircraft blown-up. **1958** G. DUTTON in B. James *Austral. Short Stories* (1963) 288 He low-flies through the unforeseeable complications of tree and rock. **1942** *Tee Emm* (Air Ministry) II. 78 The pilot who is recklessly daring..in properly authorised low-flying practices. **1945** *Ibid.* V. 33 There is..a fascination about low-flying. **1940** *Chambers's Techn. Dict.* 512/2 *Low-loading amplifier*, a more recent name for a loaded push-pull amplifier. **1962** *Times* 8 May 16/5 The luggage boot, with its flat, low-loading floor.

low, *v.*³ (Further examples of *'low*.)

1881 J. C. HARRIS *Nights with Uncle Remus* (1884) xvi. 81 Brer Fox 'low dat he know dat ar place same ez he do he own tater-patch. **1911** G. S. PORTER *Harvester* xvi. 367 She 'lowed to make him a big man. **1938** [see *JES, JES']. **1948** G. V. GALWEY *Lift & Drop* iv. 65 Wind's backed four points... We've got to 'low for it.

lowan (lōu·ǎn). *Austral.* [Aboriginal name.] = *mallee bird, fowl, hen* (MALLEE²).

1861 H. W. WHEELWRIGHT *Bush Wanderings* iv. 63 The lowan is a plain dull-coloured bird, brownish black, a little larger than the common fowl. **1888** 'R. BOLDREWOOD' *Robbery under Arms* II. ii. 23 The lowan (Mallee hen, they're mostly called) and tallagatta (brush turkey) were thick enough in some of the scrubby corners. **1939** *Nature* 12 Aug. 272/2 It [*sc.* Wyperfeld (Mallee) National Park, Victoria] is probably..the last home of that wonderful bird—the mound builder called the lowan, which incubates its eggs in the vegetative centre of mounds which it builds. **1963** [see *incubator-bird* (*INCUBATOR 5)].

low-boy. **2.** For *U.S.* read orig. *U.S.*, and add later examples.

1929 *Burlington Mag.* LIV. 313 The 'Lowboy'..is the pendant piece to the 'Highboy' and also has no counterpart in England. **1970** *Canad. Antiques Collector* May 11/2 Rare William and Mary lowboy of excellent proportions in burr-walnut and inlays of herringbone. **1973** *Country Life* 29 Mar. (Suppl.) 31/2 Queen Anne walnut two drawer lowboy..Height 2 ft. 3 ins. **1975** *Times* 6 Feb. 9/1 Hand made, hand finished traditional lowboy, in walnut.

lowbrow, low-brow (lōu·brau), *sb.* and *a. colloq.* (orig. *U.S.*). [f. LOW *a.* 1, in contrast with *HIGHBROW, HIGH-BROW *sb.* and *a.*] **A.** *sb.* One who is not, or does not claim to be, highly intellectual or æsthetically refined.

1906 S. FORD *Shorty McCabe* iii. 64 The spaghetti works was in full blast, with a lot of husky low-brows goin' in and out. **1907** *Collier's* 30 Mar. 23/2 The overwhelming majority of Low Brows, who never read 'Peer Gynt'. **1914** 'HIGH JINKS, JR.' *Choice Slang* 15 *Low brow*, an uneducated person usually prone to exhibit his deficiencies. **1915** E. WALLACE *Melody of Death* ii. 20 If you only knew how the low-brows are pitying you..you would not be posing for a picture of 'The Ruined Gambler'. **1926** *Glasgow Herald* 13 Mar. 4 The highbrows will be overwhelmed..: the lowbrows will be unmoved. **1927, 1929** [see *broadbrow, broadbrow* (*BROAD *a.* D. 2)]. **1935** *Discovery* Sept. 281/1 If we can persuade the lowbrows and free-livers of the present day that there is something heroic, even sporting, in the cultivation of the higher regions of the mind, we shall have won more than half the battle. **1947** [see *CLASSICAL *a.* 6 c]. **1953** [see *Aunt Edna* (*AUNT 6)]. **1974** *Times* 30 Nov. 8/2 They considered themselves lowbrows and..preferred a rattling good yarn to all that highbrow twaddle.

B. *adj.* Of, pertaining to, or characteristic of a lowbrow; not highly, or not pretentiously, intellectual; unrefined, unæsthetic. Also quasi-*advb.*

1913 H. A. FRANCK *Zone Policeman 88* i. 28 With all its excellences it would be unjust to complain that the Zone 'Y.M.' is a trifle 'low-brow' in its taste. **1914** S. LEWIS *Our Mr. Wrenn* v. 61 You ain't neither too highbrow or too lowbrow. **1923** *Spectator* 22 Sept. 391/2 Often the sole reason why he [*sc.* the man of genius] does not write 'low-brow' is because he cannot. **1928** *Collier's* 10 Nov. 30/1 The doctor who is sufficiently adventurous, or lowbrow, to visit a soda-fountain occasionally. **1934** S. R. NELSON *All about Jazz* i. 24 From the many attempts of our leaders to substitute..'symphonic syncopation', 'modern rhythm', and the like, it is obvious that the much-maligned and obvious 'low-brow' caste of the word has rendered it necessary for us to designate our music with something that is emphatically not—jazz! **1963** [see *HIGHBROW, HIGH-BROW B. *adj.*]. **1974** *Country Life* 9 May 1126/2 Another enormous price was the £22,000 paid..for a mid-18th-century print of an actor by Toyonobu;..but, as all the subjects of such prints..seem to me to represent deplorably ham actors, I remain wholly unimpressed. Now I come to think of it, what a low-brow criticism.

absol. **1927** *Daily Express* 7 May 9/6 Our aim will be..to steer a course between the 'highbrow' and the 'low-brow' in music.

So **low·browism**, the condition of being low-brow; lack of interest in intellectual or æsthetic matters.

1931 A. HUXLEY *Music at Night* 222 The snobbery of culture..has now to wrestle with an organized and active low-browism. **1946** *Amer. Speech* XXI. 121 The Australian dislike of elegance and affectation leads to a general 'low-browism' of expression and a careless enunciation. **1957** R. HOGGART *Uses of Literacy* x. 255 At a time when it is so easy to be led into arrogant low-browism, some retain an idealistic love for 'things of the mind'. **1971** *Listener* 2 Dec. 763/3, I am not at all arguing for a populist lowbrowism.

low-browed, *a.* **1.** (Earlier, later, and *absol.* examples.)

1855 J. E. COOKE *Ellie* 71 The man, who was a coarse, low-browed fellow. **1905** *McClure's Mag.* May 20/1 Exactly the type of low-browed ruffian and professional thug that they were hiring over there. **1936** G. B. SHAW *Shaw on Theatre*(1958)251 The simplicity of the lowbrowed.

low-country. Add: **1.** (Later examples.)

1797 *Last Advice of C. Pettigrew to Sons* (MS.) (D.A.E.), You may think it best to sell your possessions in this low country, and to move westwardly. **1823** E. JAMES *Acct. Expedition Rocky Mts.* I. 38 Here commences the low country, which extends west to the Mississippi. **1828** W. CARR *Dial. Craven* (ed. 2) I. 302 *Low-country*, East Riding of Yorkshire, being, in general flat, particularly when contrasted with this mountainous district. **1874** 'H. CHURTON' *Toinette* x. 114 He came from somewhere down in the low country. **1963** R. I. MCDAVID *Mencken's Amer. Lang.* vi. 299 Low Country, especially in the South, denotes the Coastal Plain of South Carolina and Georgia, as distinguished from the Piedmont or Up Country. **1974** *State* (Columbia, S. Carolina) 15 Feb. 17-A/8 Sen. Strom Thurmond, R-S.C., said Thursday arrangements have been made for an additional 1.4 million gallons of gasoline for the South Carolina Low-country.

3. *S. Afr.* = *LOWVELD. Cf. *BUSHVELD b.

1879 [see *BUSHVELD]. **1929** D. REITZ *Commando* xiv. 126 Our road ran through the Sabi low country teeming with big game of all descriptions. **1930** *Official Year Bk. S. Afr.* No. 11. 18 The Low Country stretches from the Limpopo valley behind the escarpment past the eastern end of Zoutpansberg southwards to meet the South-Eastern region below the escarpment east of Carolina. **1947** J. STEVENSON-HAMILTON *Wild Life S. Afr.* xxiii. 189, I have weighed a good number of low-country leopards immediately after death.

lowder. Add: Also **looder**.

1881 *Contemp. Rev.* Aug. 190 The cure for this was to throw a fire-brand down the 'lighting-hole' in the 'looder'. **1899** J. SPENCE *Shetland Folk-Lore* 172 In a corner of the looder stood a toyeg..containing as much corn as would be a hurd o' burstin. **1910** *Old-Lore Misc.* III. i. 9 The table or bin on which the quern stands is called lūðr in Edda and looder in Orkney.

low down, *a.* and *adv.* Add: **a.** (Later examples.) **b.** (Earlier U.S. and later examples.)

In quot. 1850 in *b used in the geographical sense, and in quot. 1908 in a physical sense.

a. 1935 [see *GROWL *v.*³ 3]. **1959** 'F. NEWTON' *Jazz Scene* 291 The widespread practice of equating joy with height..and grief with depth... Thus the quality most desired in the old blues is that it should be *low-down* or *dragging*.

b. 1850 *Congress. Globe* 25 Apr. 821/1 The 'low down' Virginia Democracy had to yield to the western mountain Democracy. **1865** *Nation* (N.Y.) I. 586 His manners and conversation, showed him to be a good-deal above that class commonly called 'low-down, triflin' people', or poor white trash. **1869** *Overland Monthly* III. 130 There are the delusive 'kettlings', among the 'low-down' people. **1908** *Sears, Roebuck Catal.* 604/2 The closet..is a syphon jet bowl with a low down tank and seat. **1915** F. M. HUEFFER *Good Soldier* III. i. 140 Low-down Bowery tough. **1916** 'TAFFRAIL' *Pincher Martin* xii. 214 They considered that Pincher had played them a low-down trick in ignoring their charms and in going elsewhere for an object for his affections. **1928** *Variety* 15 Aug. 49/4 There were as many as 35 or 40 dark-skinned musicians on the stand, kidding around and giving their conception of low-down tunes. **1968** *Blues Unlimited* Sept. 10 John Lee Hooker comes here a lot, an' he plays some really lowdown things.

low·-down, *sb. slang* (orig. *U.S.*). [f. the adj. or adv.] The fundamental, though not gene-

rally known, facts *on* (about) a person, situation, etc.; the 'inside story'.

1915 *San Francisco Call & Post* 2 Dec. 12 (*caption*) Aw, give us the low down on them, Bill. **1920** *Collier's* 15 May 57/2 He calls me back, and in about twenty minutes I have got the low down on Monsieur Kane Halliday. **1924** WODEHOUSE *Leave it to Psmith* ix. 184 Listen, Ed, while I slip you the low-down. **1930** *Punch* 5 Feb. 144/1 Our own book, Percival and I have decided, is to be called the Low-down on Taxi-drivers. **1930** ADE *Let.* 19 Dec. (1973) 149 You certainly shattered some of my early idols, although I think I had figured out the low-down on most of them before I read your book. **1935** AUDEN & ISHERWOOD *Dog beneath Skin* I. ii. 34 The Old Man sent for me before I left. Wants me to get the low-down on the Dripping merger. **1939** *War Illustr.* 18 Nov. p. ii/3, I have often smiled in recollecting this bit of 'low down' on the exile of Doorn—possibly for the first time here divulged. **1946** R. CAMPBELL *Talking Bronco* 13 To have the low-down from their cross-Fates, Predicting tons of human phosphates Imported here in flesh and bone. **1957** N. MICKLEM *Box & Puppets* v. 102, I was occasionally able to do him some slight service in return by giving him 'the low-down' on theologians about whom he was required to compose orations. **1959** G. JENKINS *Twist of Sand* iv. 73 I'll give the low-down, charts, position, damage and all the rest of it. **1973** M. MACKINTOSH *King & Two Queens* x. 147 One of his minions will..give me the official low-down on Fisher. Possible police record, etc.

lower, *a.* (*sb.*) and *adv.* Add: **A.** *adj.* **2.** (Examples of *lower income, middlebrow, middle-class, working-class.*)

1852 H. MARTINEAU *Let.* 7 Apr. in R. K. Webb *H. Martineau* (1960) x. 301 Thinking men & women of the *lower middle*, & working classes. **1861** MILL *Repr. Govt.* iii. 67 A benefit of the same kind..is produced on Englishmen of the lower middle class by their liability to be placed on juries and to serve parish offices. **1881** LADY MONKSWELL *Diary* 26 Apr. in E. C. F. Collier *Victorian Diarist* (1944) 52 Presently an old lady, rather 'lower middle class', with grey hair & no cap, appeared and welcomed us. **1930** *Archit. Rec.* Feb. 113/1 The wages of the lower income groups will indeed have to be raised. **1937** *Daily Tel.* 15 Oct. 22/5 'American Dream' has many of the hall-marks of a lower-middlebrow best-seller. **1951** M. McLUHAN *Mech. Bride* (1967) 35/2 Kindly human thoughts such as keep ordinary men in the lower-income brackets. **1968** D. LAWTON *Social Class, Lang. & Educ.* ii. 7 The lower working class consists of groups traditionally outside the educational system. *Ibid.* v. 78 The typical lower working-class environment. **1971** R. ROBERTS *Classic Slum* vii. 105 Before 1914..lower-working-class men did not generally shave themselves, but patronised a barber twice a week. **1972** A. DAVIDSON tr. *Moravia's Two of Us* i. 10, I was struck by his language, half courtly, half bureaucratic and, in any case, lower middle-class. **1973** *Guardian* 19 Apr. 4/4 Mario Biaggi, probably the most popular candidate for Mayor of New York among the city's lower income white population.

3. a. Delete † *Obs.* and add later examples.

1921 *Chambers's Jrnl.* 30 July 545/1 Appreciation of beauty..is that which most distinguishes the humans from their lowers. **1967** *Listener* 21 Dec. 802/1 If a man spoke rather loudly..keeping his vowels open, then he was an Upper. If he attempted this and just failed, then he was a Middle. If..his voice carried the flavour of the area in which he was born, then he was a Lower.

c. A lower plate of artificial teeth.

1878 C. HUNTER *Mech. Dentistry* i. 7 For edentulous uppers or lowers plaster is employed. **1939** A. THIRKELL *Before Lunch* vi. 162 'And how are the new lowers?'..Mrs. Pucken smiled broadly with a slightly seasick motion of her lower teeth. **1963** J. OSBORNE *Dental Mech.* (ed. 5) ix. 170 In function there is a tendency for upper dentures to be moved forwards and lowers backwards.

5. b. With duplication of *lower*: belonging in the lower reaches of a 'lower' class or grade.

1955 T. H. PEAR *Eng. Social Differences* iii. 89 There are few serious impersonations of the lower-lower class. **1970** 'D. CRAIG' *Young Men may Die* ix. 68 We languish at an almost unbelievable and entirely unspeakable lower-lower-middle Costa Blanca resort.

B. *adv.* **b.** *Comb.*

1960 F. C. STERN *Chalk Garden* vii. 74 *P[aeonia] obovata alba*..is a lower-growing plant with rather smaller flowers. **1972** *Guardian* 24 Nov. 10/1 Lower-paid hospital workers are resorting to a series of unofficial strikes. **1972** *Times* 24 Nov. 2/7 Incomes standstill blow to lower-paid clergymen. **1975** *Times* 3 Jan. 2/3 Teachers should be looking after their lower-paid colleagues. **1975** *Times* 11 Jan. 7/6 Show a minimum by bidding Two Hearts or a near minimum by bidding Two Diamonds (a lower ranking suit).

lower, *v.* Add: **1. e.** To drink (beer or other liquor); to empty (a bottle or glass of liquor) by drinking. *colloq.*

1895 *Punch* 27 July 39/1 If you'd just seen me lower the beer. **1899** C. ROOK *Hooligan Nights* iv. 63 Out comes a bloke wiv a razzo like 'arf a boiled beetroot.... Looked as if you wouldn't like to pay for the 'arf of what 'e could lower. **1920** 'SAPPER' *Bull-Dog Drummond* ii. 64 During the time that he took to drink a mild nightcap, Mr. Benton succeeded in lowering three extremely strong glasses of spirit. **1933** A. G. MACDONELL *England, their England* vii. 113 The gallant Major..had already lowered a quart and a half of mild-and-bitter. **1962** 'L. GREX' *Terror wears Smile* ix. 143 He could lower a whole bottle of three-star brandy without batting an eye. **1974** P. LOVESEY *Invitation to Dynamite Party* v. 56 He's more accustomed to lowering pints than lifting weights.

f. *to lower the boom*: to inflict a physical defeat *on* (someone), to treat someone severely, to put a stop to an activity. *N. Amer. slang.*

1950 *Western Folklore* Apr. 118 *Lower the boom.* In a fight, to knock out your adversary with one punch. 'I sure lowered the boom on him. He had to take down his pants to blow his nose.' **1951** *New Yorker* 30 June 21/1 Just as they were about to pawn my studs.., my patience evaporated and I lowered the boom on them. **1963** J. N. HARRIS *Weird World Wes Beattie* (1964) xv. 186 Wes had been borrowing from everybody and his brother, and the boys had lowered the boom on him. **1973** *Times* 14 July 5 Senator Inouye asked if President Nixon's actions, after being told all by Mr Dean, could be considered as 'lowering the boom'—the phrase used by the former Attorney General, Mr John Mitchell, in his testimony this week.

4. e. *Phonetics.* To replace (a sound) with an allophone or phoneme of lower tongue position (Webster).

1888 H. SWEET *Hist. Eng. Sounds* 21 In diphthongs of the (ij)-type there is a tendency to make the cleaving more distinct to the ear by divergence, the first element being lowered and retracted. **1927** E. V. GORDON *Introd. Old Norse* iv. ii. 255 Neither *i* nor *u* was lowered if *i* or *j* stood in the next syllable. **1959** A. CAMPBELL *Old Eng. Gram.* 122, *ǣ* had been unrounded to *ĕ*, and *ȳ* unrounded and lowered to *ĕ*.

lowest, *adv.* (Later examples.)

1926 *Daily Chron.* 13 May 1/7 Any such agreement should..not adversely affect in any way the wages of the lowest-paid men. **1974** *Guardian* 24 Jan. 4/3 His scheme would help the lowest paid. **1975** *Times* 8 Mar. 7/7 East.. invited a switch to the lowest-ranking suit.

Lowestoft (lōu·stǫft). The name of a town in Suffolk, used *attrib.* or *ellipt.* to denote a soft-paste porcelain made from 1757.

1790 E. GILLINGWATER *Hist. Acct. Lowestoft* ix. 423 It was agreed upon to open a subscription..in order to raise a sum sufficient for building a man of war..on which occasion the town of Lowestoft subscribed as follows:—Mr Walker, for the proprietors of the Lowestoft porcelain manufactory £10 10s. 0d. **1875** L. TROUBRIDGE *Life amongst Troubridges* (1966) 106 Two pretty old Lowestoft bowls. *Ibid.* 9 June 120 In the window was a most beautiful tea-set of old blue Lowestoft. **1912** C. MACKENZIE *Carnival* xviii. 181 'But what a terrible teapot.'.. 'It's old Lowestoft.' **1968** R. H. R. SMITHIES *Shoplifter* (1969) 8 A small irregular pair of Georgian silver candlesticks flanked a bowl of armorial Lowestoft..the gold tracery glittering against the ultramarine glaze and the creamy porcelain. **1974** *Country Life* 6 June 1517/2 Rare Lowestoft coffee pot..circa 1776.

low fre·quency. [f. LOW *a.* + FREQUENCY 4.] **1. a.** A frequency (see FREQUENCY 4 b in Dict. and Suppl.) having a relatively small number of cycles in a second; applied esp. to an electric current or voltage, an electromagnetic wave, or a sound wave. Abbrev. **L.F.*, esp. in radio and telecommunications, where it also refers specifically to electromagnetic waves of 30–300 kilohertz.

1900 M. A. OUDIN *Stand. Polyphase Apparatus* xiv. 242 Transmissions of power are accomplished at a comparatively low frequency. **1928** *Daily Mail* 25 July 18/1 The best Gramophone and Wireless Sets at present in use fail to reproduce the low-frequency of bass notes in anything like proper proportion. **1933** *B.B.C. Year-Bk.* 384 Actually the microphone responds from very low frequencies up to about 8000 cycles per second. **1934** [see *HIGH FREQUENCY 1 a]. **1943** C. L. BOLTZ *Basic Radio* vii. 121 In considering an imaginary capacitance, that of a tumbler switch,..we judged its capacitance in thousandths of a μμF. At low frequencies the reactance of such a switch is in perhaps millions of megohms. **1960** H. CARTER *Dict. Electronics* 169 *Low frequency.* (1) A relative term used to distinguish waves or oscillations of a particular frequency or band of frequencies from those of higher frequencies. (2) More specifically applied to radio waves of frequencies between 30 and 300 kc/s, corresponding to the long wave range. (3) The term is also loosely applied to the audio-frequency signals in a radio receiver to distinguish them from the 'high frequency', i.e. the radio- and intermediate-frequency signals. **1962** A. NISBETT *Technique Sound Studio* iv. 78 The second harmonic [of the mains frequency] is generally the most serious component [of hum] except in certain types of hi-fi loudspeaker cabinet which provide a high output at low frequencies.

b. A low rate of occurrence, in space or time.

1935 [see *HIGH FREQUENCY 1 b].

2. *attrib.* (usu. with hyphen). **a.** In sense *1 a.

1900 *Engineering* 28 Sept. 412/3 Low frequency induction telegraphy experiments..were not considered in this report. **1920** H. M. DOWSETT *Wireless Telegr.* v. 118 Low-frequency amplification is the process applied to the signal current after its form has been altered by rectification so that it can affect a telephone. **1923** *Radio Times* 28 Sept. 36 Its volume is limited only by the amount of low frequency amplification employed in the receiving set. **1926** J. S. HUXLEY *Ess. Pop. Sci.* xvii. 191 The special sense-organs for perceiving low-frequency vibrations in water which, like a herring or any other fish, it [*sc.* the tadpole] carries on a 'lateral line' along its flank. **1934** *B.B.C. Year-Bk.* 385 The output from the microphone is taken to a two-stage low-frequency amplifier. **1941** *Electronic Engin.* XIV. 404 Low frequency response is expressed in the form of a curve showing variation in power output at different frequencies. **1964** W. JASSEM in D. Abercrombie et al. *Daniel Jones* 344 The level of this low-frequency noise in the spectrum is 20–25 db below the peak at the higher frequencies. **1973** BOYD & PARKES *Dark Number* viii. 83 Some stimuli are so reverberant they just hum on as a low-frequency signal programmed into your unconscious.

b. In sense *1 b: occurring rarely, involving relatively few instances.

1957 *Publ. Amer. Dial. Soc.* XXVIII. 78 Low-frequency verbs like *asseverate, reiterate, aver,* etc.,..would rarely be initials without *that*, or parentheticals. **1963** ERVIN & MILLER in J. A. Fishman *Readings Sociol. of Lang.* (1968) 79 The evidence..reveals a high degree of similarity in the existence of such sequences of high-frequency and low-frequency items. **1971** *Brit. Med. Bull.* XXVII. 19/1 Much of the risk to people from tribes where the frequency [of cancer of the penis] is high is lost when they move to low-frequency areas.

low-grade, *a.* [LOW *a.* 20.] **a.** Of low or inferior quality.

1878 [see *HIGH-GRADE *a.*]. **1879, 1899** [see LOW *a.* 20]. **1926** J. S. HUXLEY *Ess. Pop. Sci.* iv. 39 If the good types are now crossed together, a stock will be produced..not containing harmful recessive factors and therefore not continually producing a certain proportion of low-grade individuals. **1940** J. H. JAGGER *English in Future* i. 12 Low-grade mental vocabularies consist of the auxiliary words common to all of us. *a* **1963** L. MACNEICE *Astrol.* (1964) ii. 46 The Moon is especially responsible for rather low-grade persons. **1964** *Ann. Reg. 1963* 389 Going on from this, scientists found strains of bacteria which throve on the normally poisonous metal copper, and began research into the possibility of pumping solutions of such bacteria into cracks in rocks above low-grade copper ore. **1974** E. MCGIRR *Murderous Journey* 93 A cheap low-grade snooper.

b. Not high in amount or degree of intensity. Cf. LOW *a.* 9.

1940 A. HUXLEY *Let.* 24 Apr. (1969) 452 There seems to be some kind of long-standing low-grade infection at work. **1950** A. L. ROWSE *England of Elizabeth* p. viii, The accumulation of capital then—as against its erosion in a low-grade consumption now. **1961** *Lancet* 19 Aug. 402/2 Because of continuing low-grade colonic obstruction,..the left colon was excised.

low-headed, *a.* [LOW *a.* 21.] **a.** Of trees: havinga low crown of foliage.

1861 *Trans. Illinois Agric. Soc.* IV. 328 Plant dwarf, or dwarfed, low-headed cherries, only. **1869** *Rep. Comm. Agric. 1868* (U.S. Dept. Agric.) 201 The silk tree (*Albizzia julibrissin*) is a low-headed, spreading tree, possessed of the most graceful foliage.

b. *transf.* Favouring low-headed trees.

1865 *Trans. Illinois Agric. Soc.* V. 205 We have never.. been identified with the ultra low headed orchardists.

c. Of animals: carrying their heads low.

1932 W. FAULKNER *Light in August* xiv. 311 The low-headed and eager dogs..began to bay.

lowland, *sb.* and *a.* Add: **A.** *sb.* **1.** *sing.* (Earlier U.S. examples.)

1841 THOREAU *Jrnl.* 8 Feb. in *Writings* (1906) VII. 207 Upland and lowland, forest and field have been ransacked. **1843** *Knickerbocker* XXII. 5 Everywhere, in lowland and highland,.. nothing is more evident than the ..degradation of the negro.

2. (Later examples.)

1938 DUKE OF MONTROSE in R. Bain *Clans & Tartans* 11 The Tartan as a dress properly belongs to the Highlands, and not to the Lowlands. **1961** C. R. MACKINNON *Highlands in Hist.* 95 Montrose had mustered his army at Blair Atholl, and decided to open his campaign in the Lowlands in order to encourage the king's supporters in the south.

b. *pl.* The Low Countries.

c **1685** in *Roxburghe Ballads* (Ballad Soc.) (1887) VI. II. 421 And it is called the Sweet Trinity, And was taken by the false Gallaly, sailing in the Low-lands. **1923** G. B. HARRISON *Shakespeare's Fellows* iii. 100 Between his service in the Lowlands and the success of *Every Man in his Humour*, 1598, he had tried acting. **1961** T. HENROT *Belgium* 28 Some fifteen Spanish grandees were named successively governors of the Spanish Low Lands.

low-level, *a.* [LOW *a.* I and II.] Situated near or below ground level; *fig.* not advanced in skill, culture, etc.; low-ranking, unobtrusive, restrained.

1881 W. D. HAY *300 Years Hence* vii. 149 The Sahara Desert, or rather the low-level parts of it. **1908** *Chambers's Jrnl.* Sept. 647/1 The conformation of the barrier which it pierces compelled an abnormally long low-level tunnel. **1910** *Jrnl. R. Inst. Brit. Archit.* Apr. 472 The scheme [of Leonardo da Vinci] comprises a system of low-level streets for commercial purposes, and an upper residential stratum. **1914** W. OWEN *Let.* 2 Feb. (1967) 232 Once fixed in a low-level Rut one is ever-after straightened there;—straightened intellectually and socially as surely as financially. **1923** OGDEN & RICHARDS *Meaning of Meaning* vii. 255 A useful low-level shorthand. **1930** *Times Educ. Suppl.* 11 Jan. p. i/2 We saw low-level sea ice. **1941** *Flight* 9 Jan. 23/1 During such low-level attacks it was easy to see what damage had been done, and there is a vivid report from an aircraft which roared over a main railway station at just below 100 feet. **1955** *Bull. Atomic Sci.* Jan. 5/1 Finally, the long-range genetic danger of exposure of mankind as a whole to low-level, but widespread and persistent radioactivity—the most ominous but least well understood of all dangers of the new age—is only beginning to be dimly perceived. **1955** T. H. PEAR *Eng. Social Differences* xi. 264 An atmosphere of low-level excitement. **1964** E. BACH *Introd. Transformational Gram.* iv. 59 Thus a 'high-level' rule is a rule that is placed earlier in an ordered list than a 'low-level' rule. **1972** *Village Voice* (N.Y.) 1 June 53/2 Lee is obsessed with a woman who has let him down; Harry, who would rather sleep than hear the horny details, tells him, 'Obsession is low-level awareness.'

low·-life, *a.* and *sb.* [LOW *a.* 20.] **A.** *adj.* Coarse, disreputable, vulgar.

1794 [see LOW *a.* 20]. **1861** M. B. CHESNUT *Diary* 8 Dec. (1949) 171 Mr. Shuford he goes for low life things, hurting

people's feelings. **1885** [see Low *a.* 20]. **1910** G. B. SHAW *Brieux: a Preface* 16 Servants, solicitors, and other low life personages. **1931** W. FAULKNER *Sanctuary* xxvi. 265 A durn low-life Jew. **1939** *Time* 18 Dec. 21/1 There can be nothing very awful about even such ostentatiously 'low-life' dives as the Nut Club in Greek Street. **1959** P. BULL *I know Face* xi. 198 Soho low-life stories. **1964** *English Studies* XLV. 368 Could minor low-life characters speak at once so feelingly and with our own voice, to their mistress, at a tragic climax? **1972** *Listener* 10 Aug. 184/3 Low-life action and local vernacular.

B. *sb.* Pl. usu. *low-lifes.* A coarse, vulgar, or no-good person. (Esp. in Jewish use.)

1911 M. GLASS *Potash & Perlmutter* i. 8 'If you think Pincus Vesell done me up good, Noblestone,' Potash said, 'you are mistaken. I got better judgment as to let a low-life like him get into me.' **1932** L. GOLDING *Magnolia St.* II. xiv. 467 *Nu*, and what do you expect from such a low life? **1933** *Omaha* (Nebraska) *World-Herald* 25 Oct., Police Commissioner Bolan in opening a school of correct English for policemen yesterday, remarked that such study would 'refine the tastes' of the men, but his noble prospect left most of the city's lowlifes cold. **1955** J. POTTS *Death of Stray Cat* (1966) xxii. 209 Why, that low-life! Stealing my stuff. **1959** H. PINTER *Birthday Party* (1960) III. 50 Keep an eye open for low-lives, for schnorrers and for layabouts. **1964** *Amer. Folk Music Occasional* I. 7 It would be an error to conclude that such songs are found only among the low-life. **1971** *Black World* Apr. 38/2 Our responsible leaders sniffed their disdain of the low-lifes and begged aristocrats for white-collar jobs.

lowly, *a.* Add: **2. b.** Of plants or animals, comparatively undeveloped.

1876 *City-Road Mag.* Jan. 44/2 There can be very little doubt that lowly forms can exist..at temperatures not much below 150° Fahr. **1886** A. GEIKIE *Class-Bk. Geol.* xv. 293 The progress of life from its earliest appearance in lowly forms of plant or animal has been continuous. **1912** *Q. Rev.* Apr. 528 The most conspicuous physical features in Europe..had no existence when these lowly organisms lived and died. **1927** PEAKE & FLEURE *Apes & Men* 13 Birds first appear in the Jurassic system, while traces of lowly mammals have been found from the Trias onwards.

lowveld (lōᵘ·felt, -velt). *S. Afr.* Also hyphenated and with capital initial(s). [ad. Afrikaans *Laeveld* low country.] The low-lying region of the eastern Transvaal and of Swaziland; also applied to corresponding regions of adjoining territories. Freq. *attrib.*

1878 A. AYLWARD *Transvaal of Today* iii. 44 Bushveld and Lowveld are convertible terms. **1905** *Transvaal Agric. Jrnl.* Oct. 141 (*title*) Notes on the native flora and crops of the Lowveld of the Eastern Transvaal. **1929** J. STEVENSON-HAMILTON *Low-Veld* 1 The Transvaal Province of the Union of South Africa is divided into three zones of altitude known respectively as High, Middle, and Low Veld... It is not unusual to hear an altitude of three thousand feet referred to as 'Low-Veld'... The Low-Veld of the Transvaal lies approximately between the twenty-second and the twenty-sixth parallels of south latitude. **1931** *Discovery* Aug. 259/2 At Barberton [Transvaal], where problems connected with the improvement of cottons for low-veld areas are dealt with. **1949** *Cape Argus Mag.* 5 Nov. 9/5 The lowveld hills around Umgungundhlovu. **1959** *Cape Times* 4 Feb. 1/1 Mr. Ray Stockil yesterday announced his intention to retire as Leader of the Opposition in the Southern Rhodesia Parliament and to devote his attention to the economic development of the lowveld of the country. **1968** C. BURKE *Elephant across Border* v. 189 A shallow ravine, covered in those lowveld succulents which are able to grow out of small patches of moss and cracks in the rock.

lox (lǫks, el ōᵘ eks), *sb.*¹ Also **LOX.** [orig. f. *l*iquid *o*xygen e*x*plosive; later interpreted as repr. *l*iquid *ox*ygen.] **a.** An explosive device which uses liquid oxygen as an oxidant (see quot. 1946).

1923 *Chem. Abstr.* XVII. 2646 Wood pulp as an ingredient renders LOXs less sensitive to detonation. **1933** *Mining & Metall.* XIV. 368/1 This research was to be centered upon the absorbent material used in the manufacture of LOX cartridges. **1946** G. J. YOUNG *Elem. Mining* (ed. 4) v. 127 Lox consists of a canvas cartridge filled with granular carbonaceous material, moistened, which when soaked in liquid oxygen, removed from the soaking box, and placed in the drill hole can be detonated and is an effective blasting agent. **1966** S. FORDHAM *High Explosives & Propellants* v. 63 A type of explosive..which achieved popularity for a time and is still used in some countries, is the liquid oxygen explosive or LOX.

b. Liquid oxygen, esp. when used as a rocket propellant.

The 1923 example may have been intended in sense a.
1923 *Chem. Abstr.* XVII. 2646 The ballistic pendulum was found suitable for tests of LOX explosives. **1940** *News* (San Francisco) 3 Oct. 19/4 That liquid is called liquid oxygen, or 'L-O-X', as the mining men say. **1949** *Time* 6 June, The Viking burns alcohol and 'lox' in a single combustion chamber. **1959** *Adv. Space Sci. & Technol.* I. 193 Existing LOX systems probably will not function properly under weightlessness. **1962** *Flight Internat.* LXXXI. 168/2 The Buccaneer is the first Naval aircraft to use lox.

Hence as *v. trans.*, to fuel with liquid oxygen; **lo·xing** *vbl. sb.*

1961 A. B. SHEPARD in *Astronauts* Suppl. 4 The Redstone was loxed. **1962** J. GLENN in *Into Orbit* 187 One of the loxing valves stuck and the technicians had to shift a smaller valve to complete the loading process. **1970** R. TURNILL *Lang. of Space* 72 Loading the lox into the launch vehicle's fuel tanks from a ground supply is referred to as loxing.

lox (lǫks), *sb.*² Pl. **lox, loxes.** [f. Yiddish *laks*, f. G. *lachs* salmon.] A kind of smoked salmon.

1941 S. LONGSTREET *Last Man around World* xii. 135 Listen, you lox-eater—until last year you thought herring was the only thing they took from the sea. **1950** F. ALLEN *Let.* Oct. in G. Marx *Groucho Lett.* (1967) 73 At the stage delicatessen..the lox is running good and the cream cheese is spreading easily. **1961** B. MALAMUD *New Life* (1962) 121 I'll bet lox to bagels that Gerald will get more for the department. **1969** A. GLYN *Dragon Variation* ix. 293 He..folded himself on to a stool at the counter, and ordered coffee and a bagel with lox. **1972** *Times* 21 July 12/8 Where in Paris,..can one enjoy a breakfast of beigles, lox (Yiddish for salmon) and cream cheese? **1973** *Daily Colonist* (Victoria, B.C.) 16 Sept. 35/5 The bagel.. often is eaten with smoked salmon or lox from Nova Scotia.

loyal, *a.* Add: **3.** spec. *loyal toast*, a toast proposed and drunk (in the U.K. and British Commonwealth) to the monarch or (elsewhere) to some other important personage.

1799 *Times* 1 June 3/4 Many Loyal Toasts were given, and the day spent with great conviviality. **1835** [in Dict.]. **1858** [see *HIGHLAND *a.* 2 a]. **1970** M. KELLY *Spinifex* xi. 166 'Gentlemen—' Matsuda barked.. 'The Loyal Toast!' **1972** *Guardian* 9 May 15/4 It was the most miserable meal I have ever presided over, and I had not the heart to propose the Loyal Toast at the end. **1974** *Ibid.* 25 Jan. 10/4 The time was come for toasts and speeches. After the Loyal Toast, Blackadder clipped his cigar.

loyalty. Add: **2. a.** *spec.* Of government employees.

1955 *Bull. Atomic Sci.* Apr. 132 Commissioner Murray, concurring in the result, found Dr. Oppenheimer a risk on grounds of loyalty which he newly defined as obedience to security regulations. **1956** M. GRODZINS *Loyal & Disloyal* v. 230 Loyalty-security programs threaten to cripple the entire foreign service. *Ibid.* 231 Governments must guard themselves against harm and destruction, and there can therefore be no criticism of the objectives of loyalty investigations for government employees and scientists who work on government projects. **1964** GOULD & KOLB *Dict. Social Sci.* 397 In the United States since the end of World War II, loyalty has been an important issue in politics... Under President Truman..there was an elaborate procedure for determining the 'loyalty' of servants of the U.S. government.

b. loyalty oath *U.S.*, an oath, usually mandatory, required of a prospective public employee or other person in which he swears to abstain from subversive activities.

1952 M. MCCARTHY in *Reporter* (N.Y.) 8 July 32/2 In order to..work for the Columbia Broadcasting System you have to sign a loyalty oath which is presented with your contract. **1969** L. GREENBAUM *Out of Shape* xxii. 162 The older man had his contract terminated under a clause dealing with loyalty oaths. Apparently he was a card-carrier and hadn't said so. **1971** M. MCCARTHY *Birds of America* 250 Berkeley is horrible... You have to swear a loyalty oath... It's natural that the students would finally rebel. **1973** *Black Panther* 12 May 6/1 After signing a loyalty oath to the school, students are required to present two identification cards, one issued since November 16th, before gaining entrance to the campus.

Lozi (lōᵘ·zi). [Native name.] **A.** *sb.* **a.** A Bantu people inhabiting Zambia. **b.** Their language. **B.** *adj.* Of or pertaining to the Lozi.

1948 M. GUTHRIE *Classification Bantu Lang.* 53 Nominals are used as sentences. For example,..in Lozi..*ze kilitipa* 'these are the knives'. **1949** M. GLUCKMAN in M. Fortes *Social Struct.* 146 The Lozi..call them *Mawiko*, 'the people of the West'. *Ibid.*, I worked through Lozi, a lingua franca which most Wiko men..speak and understand. *Ibid.* 151 The hostility of the Wiko..to their Lozi and Kwongwa neighbours. **1953** D. T. COLE in D. Hymes *Lang. in Culture & Society* (1964) VIII. 549/1 These [languages] include..Lozi of Barotseland in Northern Rhodesia. **1959** G. D. MITCHELL *Sociol.* 82 We shall be concerned with the Lozi system, which since British influence has undergone some modifications. **1967** *Economist* 11 Nov. 617/1 The..conference..saw Barotseland's Lozi leaders lose much of their status in the party... Barotseland's development is lagging behind..because of ..Lozi cultural indifference... Mr Kaunda could galvanise the Lozis into political co-operation. **1972** *Times* 18 Sept. 12/4 President Kaunda of Zambia has had to face..a Lozi challenge.

LSD² (e:lesdī·). Also (*rare*) L.S.D. [f. G. *l*yserg*s*äure-*d*iäthylamid, lysergic acid diethylamide.] Lysergic acid diethylamide (see *LYSERGIC *a.*). Freq. with the number 25 appended.

[**1947** W. A. STOLL in *Schweizer Arch. für Neurol. und Psychiatrie* LX. 279 Dieser Stoff ist das Lysergsäure-diäthylamid (LSD).] **1950** *Diseases Nervous Syst.* XI. 243/1 We believe that L.S.D. 25 is a drug which induces a controllable toxic state within the nervous system, that re-activates anxiety and fear with apparently just enough euphoria to permit recall of the provoking experiences. *Ibid.* 243 Supplies of L.S.D. 25 for this study were made available by the manufacturer, Sandoz Pharmaceuticals, New York City. **1955** *Sci. News Let.* 26 Feb. 135/1 LSD has been used by psychiatrists recently to bring on a mental disease state in healthy persons in the hope of learning more about how to treat or prevent real mental sickness. **1958** A. HUXLEY *Let.* 11 Jan. (1969) 843 A session with an RC psychiatrist, who had reluctantly submitted to taking LSD25. **1962** *Observer* 15 July 1/5 The American Medical Association has given a warning that use of the drug known as LSD-25, or lysergic acid, can lead to suicide, and that LSD-25 has joined the ranks of black-market drugs like marijuana and heroin. **1964** *Daily Tel.* 28 Mar. 9/3 The tablets are believed to be a solid form of LSD, lysergic acid diethylamide. They can be obtained in certain clubs and public houses in London and other big cities. **1964** D. F. DOWNING in M. Gordon *Psychopharmacol. Agents* I. xiii. 569 The effective oral dose in man amounts to 0·02–0·05 mg and (+)-LSD-25 is therefore 10^4 times as active as mescaline in causing a psychotomimetic effect and the most powerful psychotomimetic substance known. **1965** *New Scientist* 22 Apr. 225/1 Bizarre though the symptomatology may seem, the intensive research which has taken place in the 23 years since LSD 25 was discovered has failed to reveal any seriously deleterious effect which the drug may have on brain chemistry or biophysics. **1966** *Daily Tel.* 31 Mar. 25 New York County Medical Society has called for severe penalties against the illicit manufacture, distribution and sale of the hallucination-producing drug known as LSD. It has described the drug as 'far more dangerous than heroin'. **1968** A. HOFMANN in A. Burger *Drugs affecting Cent. Nervous Syst.* II. v. 205 In the case of a very intensive reaction to LSD, the normal feeling of the identity with the own self is weakened (depersonalization). The test person at the same time appears to himself as a stranger watching him and judging his actions coolly and critically. *Ibid.*, LSD produces a state of hypersuggestibility, which is characterized by an enormous sensitiveness to the influence of sensory and cognitive stimuli and which is of decisive importance for the use of LSD as an adjuvant in psychotherapy. **1973** E. BULLINS *Theme is Blackness* 162 Not many of us smoked as much pot as before. And L.S.D. almost disappeared from our circle.

Ltd., abbrev. of LIMITED *ppl. a.* (sense 2 b).

1900 *Times* 19 Oct. 12/1 (Advt.), Employees of Bovril Ltd...are not eligible to compete. **1922** JOYCE *Ulysses* 152, I am hastening to purchase the only reliable ink-eraser *Kansell*, sold by Hely's Ltd, 85 Dame Street. **1967** *Times Rev. Industry* Feb. 37 (Advt.), Dictation systems Dictaphone Company Ltd. **1974** *Spectator* 22 June 774/3 Chater & Scott Ltd... Specialists in motoring books.

luau (lū·au). [ad. Hawaiian *lu'au.*] **a.** A party or feast with Hawaiian food and usually accompanied by Hawaiian entertainment; also *attrib.* **b.** A cooked dish of young taro leaves served with coconut cream and octopus or chicken.

1843 L. SMITH *Diary* 3 Aug. in M. D. Frear *Lowell & Abigail* (1934) 168 The table..was..loaded with an immense quantity of food—pigs, turkies,..taro, luau, etc., etc. **1853** *Putnam's Mag.* II. 19/1 It was on a Saturday afternoon in the year 1852, that a merry party of us started forth to attend a *luau* or native feast, given by a chief who lived some miles from Honolulu. **1905** *Hartford* (Connecticut) *Courant* 24 Apr. 8/5 A *luau* is a square meal with roast pig and poi in it. **1951** H. WOUK *'Caine' Mutiny* 62 Willie and Keefer..full of hog meat and whisky which they had consumed at a hilarious luau. **1957** *New Yorker* 19 Jan. 14 Choose from a range of restaurants..from quaint Japanese tea house to lively Hawaiian luau. **1960** *Ibid.* 26 Mar. 152 (Advt.), Luau dinners and after theater suppers. **1964** *Asia Mag.* 16 Aug. 20/1 In the old days, the luau was an expression of thanksgiving to the gods. Today, it is a feast for sight and palate. *Ibid.*, Guests sit cross-legged around the low luau table and eat with their fingers. **1966** *New Yorker* 22 Oct. 20 (Advt.), Charge everything from a surfboard to a luau on your American Express Credit Card.

lubber, *sb.* Add: **2. b.** **lubber-grasshopper** (earlier and later examples); **lubber-lift** *v.* (see quot. 1905).

1877 *Field & Forest* II. 160 The 'Lubber' grasshopper [is the] large grasshopper *Romalia microptera.* **1962** METCALF & FLINT *Destructive & Useful Insects* (ed. 4) xii. 577 Large and small, lubberly grasshoppers often invade cotton from near-by waste lands and defoliate the plants... Lubber grasshoppers, differential grasshoppers. **1797** *Spirit of Farmer's Museum* (1801) 85 Our Democrats begin to muster, Rolling around an anxious eye, Some 'lubber lifting' power to spy. **1905** *Terms Forestry & Logging* (U.S. Dept. Agric. Bureau Forestry) 42 *Lubber lift*, to raise the end of a log by means of a pry, and through the use of weight instead of strength.

lube (liūb, lūb), *sb.* and *v.* Chiefly *N. Amer.* and *Austral.* Colloquial shortening of LUBRICANT *sb.*, LUBRICATION, LUBRICATE *v.* (cf. *HYDRO-LUBE). Freq. *attrib.*, as *lube bay, job, oil.*

1947 *Lubrication Engin.* Sept. 26 (*heading*) Lube spots. **1951** *Chem. & Engin. News* 24 Dec. 5456/1 (*heading*) Synthetic lube oil announced by Defense Department. **1956** *Ibid.* 3 Sept. 4247/2 (*heading*) Better lubes needed. **1957** CASAMASSA & BENT *Jet Aircraft Power Syst.* (ed. 2) xiv. 195/1 On the rear face are mounted the main lube and scavenge pump [etc.]. **1961** B. MALAMUD *New Life* (1962) 259 He had once lubed Levin's car. **1962** *Engineering* 31 Aug. 285/2 A reinforced plastic coating can be laid on without putting the tank out of commission if the products are crude or lube oils. **1964** *N.Z. Listener* 11 Dec. 5/1 A new office girl passed the lube-bay... Windy was so upset he got grease all over everything. **1965** J. M. CAIN *Magician's Wife* (1966) xv. 115 I'm just about due, I think, for the works—wash, lube job, tyre checks, gas—the usual. **1973** R. HAYES *Hungarian Game* liii. 323 The grease nipples were dry; the car needed a lube. **1973** *Tucson* (Arizona) *Daily Citizen* 22 Aug. 60/1 (Advt.), Clean and lube backing plates.

lubfish, var. LOBFISH.

1817 SCOTT *Rob Roy* I. ii. 32 Stockfish—Titling—Cropling—Lub-fish.

lubra. Add: **b.** More generally: a woman. *Austral. slang.*

1966 W. S. RAMSON *Austral. Eng.* 129 *Gin* and *lubra* are used of Aboriginal women and occasionally, though only in slang and never as a compliment, of women in general.

lubric, *a.* **3.** Delete †*Obs.* and add later example.

1909 J. JUSSERAND *Lit. Hist. Eng. People* III. 436 Here we have a Bellario, all virtue and sweetness..opposed to a series of lubric and ferocious monsters.

lubricate, *v.* Add: **2. c.** To grease the palm of; to bribe.

1928 *Daily Express* 12 July 1/1 He made specific charges. One was that taxicab proprietors have to 'lubricate' Scotland-yard before their taxicabs are passed for licensing.

lubricating, *ppl. a.* (Further examples.)

1867 *Amer. Jrnl. Sci.* XCIII. 348 The lubricating oils are of very low specific gravity. **1974** *Sci. Amer.* May 97/1 As lubricating oil circulates through a machine it picks up myriads of wear particles.

lubrication. Add: Also *attrib.*

1906 *Westm. Gaz.* 23 July 8/2 Motor-'buses, fitted with the new automatic lubrication appliance. **1907** *Ibid.* 13 Nov. 9/1 The lubrication system..can be regulated to suit all engine speeds. **1951** M. MCLUHAN *Mech. Bride* (1967) 124 He brings you our 78 years of lubrication experience. **1975** *D. Bristow's Catal. Miscellany* 1/75 14 (*Operation manual*). The Singer Car..with lubrication chart loosely inserted.

lubricational (liūbrikēi·ʃənăl), *a.* [f. LUBRICATION + -AL.] Of, pertaining to, or for lubrication.

1909 *Westm. Gaz.* 18 Nov. 4/2 An automatic lubricational oil pump is fitted at the end of the cam-shaft.

lubritorium (liūbritōᵊ·riŏm). Chiefly *U.S.* Also **lu·britory.** [f. LUBRI(CATE *v.* + *-torium* as in *auditorium, sanatorium.*] A greasing bay in a service station; a service station.

1930 *Amer. Speech* V. 329 In New Philadelphia, Ohio, there is a 'lubritorium' which I presume is intended to assist automobiles to a proper degree of lubricity. In Ann Arbor, Michigan, there is a 'Lubritory' which serves the same purpose. **1942** BERREY & VAN DEN BARK *Amer. Thes. Slang* §544 *Lubritory*, a gas station. **1954** *Encounter* June 13/1 The effort to 'professionalise' work has become the major means of giving one's job a badge of honorific quality... So the garage becomes the 'lubritorium'. **1963** *Punch* 24 Apr. 579/3 The sign outside a Glasgow service station: Lubritorium. **1969** M. PEI *Words in Sheep's Clothing* (1970) xxi. 209 'Lubritorium' is so much more learned a word than 'service station'. **1969** *West Australian* 5 July 71/5 (Advt.), Lubritorium and driveway attendant..required.

Lucanian (lukēi·niăn), *sb.* and *a.* [f. *Lucania*, name of a district of southern Italy, also called Basilicata.] **A.** *sb.* A member of the Lucani, a branch of the Sabelline race, inhabiting Lucania. **B.** *adj.* Of, pertaining to, or belonging to Lucania; *spec.* **Lucanian ox, cow** (see quots.).

1709 [see *APULIAN *a.* and *sb.*]. [**1797** *Encycl. Brit.* X. 314 *Lucæ boves* denoted elephants; first seen in Pyrrhus's wars in Lucania, whence the appellation (Pliny).] **1863** W. K. KELLY *Curiosities Indo-European Trad. & Folk-Lore* i. 5 The Romans gave the name of Lucanian *ox* to the elephant. **1878** J. R. KING tr. *Cicero's Philippic Orations* XIII. v. 230 He..took possession of his estates in the Lucanian territory. **1879** LEWIS & SHORT *Latin Dict.* 1079/1 *Luca bos*, Lucanian cow, for elephant (because the Romans first saw this animal in Lucania, in the army of Pyrrhus). **1907** A. E. ZIMMERN tr. *Ferrero's Greatness & Decline Rome* I. iv. 85 The Samnites and Lucanians, who were still under arms, sent ambassadors. *Ibid.* v. 89 Only the Samnites and the Lucanians, as being still in revolt, were to be excepted. **1949** *Oxf. Classical Dict.* 313/1 The Romans first encountered elephants ('Lucanian oxen') in Pyrrhus' army, but seldom used them in battle. *Ibid.* 514/2 Lucanian communities had an official known as *meddix*. **1957** *Encycl. Brit.* XIV. 456 The Social War, in which the Lucanians took part with the Samnites. **1960** *Times* 29 June 15/7 Slogans on the walls of a Lucanian town: 'We are Italians too.'

lucanid (lukēi·nid), *a.* and *sb.* [f. mod.L. family name *Lucanidæ*, f. generic name *Lucanus* (J. A. Scopoli *Entomologia Carniolica* (1763) 1), f. L. *Lūcānus* Lucanian, f. *Lucania* (see prec.).] **A.** *adj.* Of or pertaining to a stag-beetle of the family Lucanidæ. **B.** *sb.* A member of this family.

1925 A. D. IMMS *Gen. Textbk. Entomol.* 512 Lucanid larvae inhabit the rotting wood of trees or their roots. **1932** J. S. HUXLEY *Probl. Relative Growth* vii. 208 A peculiarly interesting example..is provided by the Lucanid beetle *Cyclommatus tarandus*, with markedly heterogonic male mandibles. **1959** E. F. LINSSEN *Beetles Brit. Is.* II. 115 While not having the extraordinarily developed mandibles of male Lucanids, there is in the present family [*sc.* Scarabæidæ] a great complexity of 'outgrowth-horns'.

Lucas (liū·kăs, ‖lūka). *Math.* The name of F. Édouard A. *Lucas* (1842–91), French mathematician, used *attrib.* to designate (*a*) the sequence of integers 1, 3, 4, 7,..., formed in the same way as the Fibonacci numbers; (*b*) the sequences generated by the recurrence relation $u_{n+2} = Pu_{n+1} - Qu_n$ when $u_0 = 0$, $u_1 = 1$ (the Fibonacci numbers being a particular case corresponding to $P = 1$, $Q = -1$) and when $u_0 = 2$, $u_1 = P$, which are respectively defined by $u_n = (a^n - b^n)/(a - b)$ and $u_n = a^n + b^n$ ($n = 0, 1, 2,..$), where *a* and *b* are the roots of $x^2 - Px + Q = 0$.

[**1919** L. E. DICKSON *Hist. Theory Numbers* I. xvii. 393 (*heading*) Recurring series; Lucas' u_n, v_n.] **1953** *Scripta Math.* XIX. 278 (*heading*) Linear expressions for the powers of Fibonacci and Lucas numbers. *Ibid.*, The *i*th term of the Lucas sequence 1, 3, 4, 7... **1954** *Duke Math. Jrnl.* XXI. 608 If any term of (W) vanishes, (W) is essentially the well-known Lucas sequence $L_n = (\alpha^n - \beta^n)/(\alpha - \beta)$. **1961** *Pacific Jrnl. Math.* XI. 385 It would be interesting to make a numerical study of several recurrences..to endeavor to find out whether the two Lucas sequences 0, 1, P,... and 2, P, $P^2 - 2Q$,... and their translates are essentially the only ones for which a global characterization of the divisors is possible. **1966** OGILVY & ANDERSON *Excursions in Number Theory* 164 The Lucas numbers satisfy the same recursion relation as the Fibonacci numbers, but have starting values $L_1 = 1$, $L_2 = 3$. **1972** P. RIBENBOIM *Algebraic Numbers* i. 8 Prove: (a) Two consecutive Lucas numbers are relatively prime. (b) $b_n{}^2 - b_{n-1}b_{n+1} = (-1)^n.5$ for every $n \geqslant 1$.

Lucca (lu·ka). [The name of a city and province in northern Italy.] *Lucca lamb*, a variety of processed lambskin, used mainly to make headwear; *Lucca oil*, a superior quality of olive oil.

1725 J. STEUART *Letter-Bk.* (1915) 238 A Chist of finest Cucca [*sic*] oil. **1734** C. MORTIMER in W. Ellis *Mod. Husbandman* (1750) VII. II. 84 His Wife rubbed in..the Sallad-oil (which I had bought by the Name of Lucca-oil). [**1861** S. SMITH in Mrs. Beeton *Bk. Househ. Managem.* 244 Four times the spoon with oil of Lucca crown, And twice with vinegar.] *c* **1938** *Fortnum & Mason Price List* 52 (*caption*) Superfine Lucca oil. **1956** J. G. LINKS *Bk. Fur* ii. 52 Persian lamb..and all the odd varieties of processed lamb (beaver, Tuscan,..Lucca and..others). **1962** —— *How to look at Furs* (rev. ed.) 108 The merino can be sheared less or more than it is in the case of beaver lamb. If it is sheared less, the result is often called by such names as Lucca lamb or Tuscan lamb (Italian lambs are often treated in this way). **1966** J. S. COX *Illustr. Dict. Hairdressing* 92 *Lucca oil*, olive oil. **1970** *Kay & Co. (Worcester) Catal.* 1970–71 Autumn/Winter 287/1 Lucca Lamb Fur Hat. Get the feel of luxury with this fashionable..hat made in real Lucca lamb.

Hence **Lu·ccan** *a.* and *sb.*

1911 H. GERARD tr. *Maurel's Little Cities of Italy* I. I. vi. 63 Mirrors planted by the Luccan army on the towers of Asciano. *Ibid.*, The Luccans added a charming porch of elegant proportions. *Ibid.* 69 Matteo must have wandered often about the Luccan country. **1936** *Times Lit. Suppl.* 29 Aug. 690/2 He..finds the Pisan school Byzantine and the Luccan Roman. **1961** C. C. BAYLEY *War & Society in Renaissance Florence* i. 7 Florence emerged..with only a secondary prize, the former Luccan dependency of Pistoia. **1968** E. HYAMS *Mischief Makers* iv. 51 Olives yielding an oil of almost Luccan quality.

Lucian. Add: **Lucianesque**, in a Lucianic style; **Lucianic** *a.* (later examples); **Lucianism**, admiration and emulation of Lucian.

1922 P. S. ALLEN *Erasmus* 6 The outcome of his thoughts ..was a Lucianic composition, *Moriae Encomium*. **1925** A. M. HARMON tr. *Lucian* IV. 111 The source and character of the reply contribute a truly Lucianic fillip of surprise. **1937** C. R. THOMPSON (*title*) Lucian and Lucianism in the English Renaissance: an introductory study. **1962** R. P. ADAMS *Better Part of Valor* IV. 48 Erasmus couples Lucianic irony and his own special form of wit. **1969** G. HOLMES *Florentine Enlightenment 1400–50* iv. 112 *Momus* is the most substantial of his Lucianesque creations.

Lucianist[1]. Add: **b.** A student, admirer, or emulator of Lucian.

1940 C. R. THOMPSON *Translations of Lucian* i. 1 Erasmus..was the paramount Lucianist of the Renaissance. **1941** H. H. HUDSON tr. *Erasmus's Praise of Folly* p. xix, Enough has been said, though more is available, to prove him a Lucianist. *Ibid.* p. xx, Rabelais..was both a Lucianist and an Erasmian. **1946** L. F. DEAN tr. *Erasmus's Praise of Folly* 17 By 1506 he had become a thorough Lucianist.

Lucianist[2]. Add: (Later examples.)

1805 H. ADAMS *View Relig.* I. 187/2 *Lucianists*, so called from Lucianus, a disciple of Marcion. **1824** C. BUCK *Theol. Dict.* (ed. 2) 313/2 *Lucianists*,..a sect so called from Lucianus,..a heretic of the second century, being a disciple of Marcion, whose errors he followed. *Ibid.*, There was another sect of Lucianists, who appeared some time after the Arians. They taught, that the Father had been a Father always,..even before he begot the Son, as having in him the power and faculty of generation. **1874** J. H. BLUNT *Dict. Sects* 262 *Lucianists*, a section of the Marcionites, followers of Lucian... The particular tenet by which the Lucianists were distinguished from the Marcionites..was that, in the resurrection from the dead, neither the actual body nor the actual soul..would arise. **1882** H. M. GWATKIN *Stud. Arianism* ii. 31 Disciples of Lucian—Eusebius.., Menophantus.., and Leontius... These are all the Lucianists whom we can trace. *Ibid.* iii. 73 Eusebius himself was the ablest of all the Lucianists. **1903** J. F. BETHUNE-BAKER *Introd. Early Hist. Christian Doctrine* xii. 163 The Lucianists thought that logic could settle everything. **1958** J. N. D. KELLY *Early Christian Doctrines* III. ix. 230 He and Eusebius.., he implied, were 'fellow-Lucianists', and Eusebius is elsewhere described as a disciple of Lucian. **1960** A. BULL tr. *Ricciotti's Age of Martyrs* v. ii. 265 The Origenists and the Lucianists were interested to see whether or not the unity of God..could be reconciled with their particular school.

Hence **Lucia·nic** *a.*[2]

1882 H. M. GWATKIN *Stud. Arianism* iii. 72 We find him using the Lucianic creed. **1903** J. F. BETHUNE-BAKER *Introd. Early Hist. Christian Doctrine* xii. 174 The Lucianic origin of the Creed has, however, been called in question in recent times. *Ibid.* 175 The Fourth Creed assigned to this Council, which might be Lucianic. **1962** *Catholic Dict. Theol.* I. 139 They could never hope to pass off the rambling and old-fashioned Lucianic creed as one that would now rally all theologians of the West.

luciferase (liusi·fĕrēiz, -s). *Biol.* [ad. F. *luciférase* (R. Dubois 1887, in *Compt. Rend.* CV. 691): see next and *-ASE.] Any enzyme which catalyses a reaction by which a specific luciferin produces light.

It was formerly believed that a single enzyme, luciferase, was common to all organisms which produce light.

1888 *Jrnl. R. Microsc. Soc.* 26 From the luminous parts of the animal the author [*sc.* R. Dubois] has succeeded in extracting two substances, the contact of which in the water, determines the appearance of the light. One of them was obtained in the crystalline state... It is soluble in water, and hardly soluble in alcohol; it may be called luciferine. The other body is an active albuminoid of the class of soluble ferments, and may be called luciferase. **1920** *Nature* 26 Aug. 843/1 The production of light by animals is due to the burning or oxidation of a substance called luciferin in the presence of an enzyme or catalyst called luciferase. **1952** [see *LUCIFERIN]. **1971** *Country Life* 9 Sept. 605/1 The luciferin, or light-producing material, in a glow-worm's body is oxidised and broken down, with the aid of an enzyme called luciferase, to release light energy with practically no wastage.

luciferin (liusi·fĕrin). *Biol.* Formerly also **-ine.** [ad. F. *luciférine* (R. Dubois 1887, in *Compt. Rend.* CV. 691), f. L. *lūcifer* light-bearing: see -IN[1].] Any substance which is present naturally in an organism (such as the glow-worm) and which when oxidized in the presence of a specific enzyme (a luciferase) is capable of producing light.

It was formerly believed that one single substance, luciferin, was common to all organisms which produce light.

1888, 1920 [see *LUCIFERASE]. **1952** E. N. HARVEY *Bioluminescence* p. xi, Luciferin and luciferase are general names used for these compounds manufactured by luminous animals, but it is probable that the luciferin or luciferase from a species in one group may be quite different chemically from that in another. **1954** HARVEY & TSUJI in *Jrnl. Cell. & Compar. Physiol.* XLIV. 71 Luciferin may properly be defined as the oxidizable substance supplying molecules capable of absorbing enough excess energy to emit in the visible region. **1966** JOHNSON & HANEDA *Bioluminescence in Progress* 10 Bacterial luciferin has become a matter of definition... $FMNH_2$ may be considered the 'luciferin' of this system. **1971** [see *LUCIFERASE].

Lucite (liū·səit). Also **lucite.** [f. L. *luc(i)-*, *lux* light + -ITE[1].] A proprietary name for a solid, transparent plastic that is a methyl methacrylate resin; perspex.

1937 *Official Gaz.* (U.S. Patent Office) 6 July 9/1 E. I DuPont de Nemours and Company. Lucite. For thermoplastic synthetic resin material, known as methyl methacrylate, in the form of sheets, rods, and tubes, and in powdered or granular form. **1939** *Reader's Digest* Feb. 81/1 Light flows through rods made of Lucite, a du Pont plastic, as water flows through a pipe. **1953** J. Y. COUSTEAU *Silent World* 89 Through the lucite windows [of the *Bathyscaphe*] the pilots could look into a landscape lighted by exterior floodlamps. **1973** R. HAYES *Hungarian Game* xv. 98 The system had two Lucite indicators, one red the other green.

luck, *sb.* Add: **3.** *as (good, ill) luck would have it*: by (good, ill) fortune; *best of Arab* (or *Welsh*) *luck*: cf. *BRITISH *a.* 6; *better luck another* (or *next*) *time*: an expression of encouragement to endure a disappointment; *devil's own luck*: uncannily good luck; *good luck to* (a person or thing): see *GOOD LUCK; *just my* (or *his, our,* etc.) *luck*: typical of my (his, our) bad luck, or occas., of my good luck; *(one's) luck is in*, or *is/runs out*: luck is on one's side, or, one has come to the end of one's run of luck; *luck of the draw*: an expression of resignation to chance; *no such (good) luck*: the thing is beyond the power even of good fortune, unfortunately not; *push* (or *crowd, ride*) *one's luck*: to expect or count on an even better run of good fortune than one has had already; cf. *to push one's fortune* (PUSH *v.* 11 b); *you never know your luck*: you cannot be sure that luck won't change for the better, you may be lucky.

1598 SHAKES. *Merry W.* III. v. 83 As good lucke would haue it..they conuey'd me into a bucke basket. **1680** A. RADCLIFFE in Rochester *Poems* 147 As luck wou'd have it in came Will. **1687** J. PHILIPS tr. *M. de Cervantes's Don*

Quixote I. I. ii. 9 As ill luck would have it, it happen'd to be upon a Friday Night. **1854** E. TWISLETON *Let.* 29 June (1928) 213 They..asked us to a dinner a fortnight off, when as ill-luck would have it, we were engaged. **1855** F. W. FABER *Growth in Holiness* xvi. 297 When we fall we must rise again, and go on our way, wishing ourselves, after a Christian fashion, better luck another time. **1857** C. M. YONGE *Dynevor Terr.* II. xii. 176 'When you break down anywhere, send me a telegraph.' 'No such good luck,' sighed Clara. **1858** TROLLOPE *Doctor Thorne* II. iv. 74 No harm had been done, and he might have better luck next time. **1862** W. COLLINS *No Name* I. I. xi. 150 All *he* ever said was, better luck next time. *c* **1874** D. BOUCICAULT in M. R. Booth *Eng. Plays of 19th Cent.* (1969) II. 190 Well, as the divil's luck would have it, there was only ..a tailor's thimble, an' they couldn't get it full. **1891** E. DOWSON *Let.* 30 June (1967) 205, I came here..& found as luck would have it a Rosière going on. **1892** R. L. STEVENSON *Let.* 29 May (1911) IV. 54 No such luck; the ship delayed, and at last, about three, I had to send them home again. **1898** J. D. BRAYSHAW *Slum Silhouettes* 29 Well, yer never know yer luck; an' his was 'ard enuff, Gawd knows. **1901** ADE *Forty Mod. Fables* 156 Adams had a Run of Luck and he crowded it. **1903** G. B. SHAW *Man & Superman* I. 21 'She'll marry you.'.. 'No such luck, Jack!' **1907** —— *John Bull's Other Island* IV. 82 He has the divil's own luck, that Englishman, annyway. **1909** GALSWORTHY *Strife* I. 195 Just our luck, the men finding a fanatical firebrand like Roberts for leader. *a* **1911** D. G. PHILLIPS *Susan Lenox* (1917) II. xxi. 494 Don't be a fool. Let's push our luck, now that things are coming our way. **1916** A. BENNETT *These Twain* III. xx. 488 You never know your luck. If she'd been free I might have been fool enough to get married. **1923** *Brewer's Dict. Phr. & Fable* (new ed.) 689/1 *He has..the devil's own luck*, he is extraordinarily lucky; everything he touches turns to gold. **1926** J. BUCHAN *Dancing Floor* I. ii. 53 Something about the features..struck me as familiar. As luck would have it, it turned out to be Vernon. **1927** E. O'NEILL *Marco Millions* I. iii. 45 Better luck next time. He'll learn! **1928** —— *Strange Interlude* VIII. 274 The damned radio has to pick out this time to go dead!.. Just my luck! *a* **1930** D. H. LAWRENCE *Phoenix II* (1968) 146 Gilbert at her side took step after step, and thought to himself his luck was out as regards women. **1938** R. D. FINLAYSON *Brown Man's Burden* 60 Just my luck to be caught in a thunderstorm. **1938** G. GREENE *Brighton Rock* III. i. 99 'You ever come across this Kolley Kibber?' she asked. 'No such luck,' the barman said. **1956** J. POTTS *Diehard* vii. 116 He paused. Was he pushing his luck too far? **1959** 'J. WELCOME' *Stop at Nothing* i. 11 He had never won the Derby and..had..announced that he would not die until he did. As he must by now be touching eighty.., this was pushing his luck pretty hard. **1963** A. SMITH *Throw out Two Hands* vii. 79 If our luck was in we might hit Madagascar, but there is quite enough luck needed in ballooning without attempting to stretch it, and to hope for a landfall on a solitary island. **1966** 'S. HARVESTER' *Treacherous Road* xix. 183 And the best of Arab luck to you, mate. **1966** M. R. D. FOOT *SOE in France* x. 341 *Cinema-phono* had never been a lucky circuit, and its luck now ran out altogether. **1967** *Listener* 23 Nov. 667/2 As luck, or history, if you like, would have it, the Russian Revolution coincided with the spread..of wireless telegraphy. **1967** 'J. ASHFORD' *Forget what you Saw* iii. 14 You never know your luck—one of these days we might actually set sail. **1967** M. CHILDS *Taint of Innocence* (1968) iii. 177 'It's so unfair.' 'Well, the luck of the draw.' **1969** 'A. GARVE' *Boomerang* iii. 132 'Anything else?' 'I don't think so—Except to wish you the best of Welsh luck!' **1970** N. MARSH *When in Rome* v. 127 Don't tell me you *are* the Lord Chamberlain... It would have been just my luck. **1972** M. BABSON *Murder on Show* v. 58 My luck was in and I caught a taxi. **1973** 'H. HOWARD' *Highway to Murder* iii. 37 Some say first impressions are best. Mine have been wrong as often as they've been right, so I guess it's the luck of the draw. **1974** I. MURDOCH *Sacred & Profane Love Machine* 75 If I..was never heard of again. Thank you very much! No such luck! **1975** J. SYMONS *Three Pipe Problem* xv. 131 You ain't going to find no killer... I reckon this is some amateur riding his luck.

luck, *v.* Restrict *Obs.* exc. *dial.* to senses in Dict. and add: **1. c.** (Later examples.)

1946 MEZZROW & WOLFE *Really Blues* 376 Luck up on: get by luck, come into possession of unexpectedly. **1962** E. LACY *Freeloaders* i. 9 This is the best writing pad I've ever lucked up on. **1971** *Black World* Apr. 56 All of em hopin to luck up on a few grand by hittin on me. **1973** *Black Panther* 29 Sept. 2/3 Riggs happened to luck up on a good hustle by attacking women's rights in tennis.

e. *to luck out* (U.S.), to achieve success or advantage by good luck in a difficult, testing, or dangerous situation.

1954 *Amer. Speech* XXIX. 303 He lucked out on the final examination... I just 'lucked out' on that shot... He really 'lucked out'. He didn't get any Saturday classes. **1967** *Boston Sunday Herald* 7 May VI. 8/4 If you luck out, good. If not, you've still got your original bookings. **1971** J. BALL *First Team* (1972) xxi. 317 Since we pretty much had to choose one from one..it looks as if we lucked out. **1972** J. WAMBAUGH *Blue Knight* (1973) ii. 22, I started making inquiries..and damned if I didn't luck out and get steered into a good job.

f. *to luck into*, to acquire by good fortune.

1959 *Time* (Atlantic ed.) 6 July 15/1 Loveless..lucked into booming revenues from old taxes as..Iowa expanded. **1966** S. MORROW *Moonlighters* (1967) ix. 98 He lucked into a prime location there. **1970** J. POTTS *Affair of Heart* viii. 63 The rent was fantastically low; she had lucked into it a couple of years ago through an artist friend.

Lucky (lʌ·ki), *sb.*³ [ellipt. f. *Lucky Strike*, a U.S. brand of cigarettes.] A Lucky Strike cigarette.

1934 A. HUXLEY *Beyond Mexique Bay* 153 If Luckies are to sell here, they will have to be put under the patronage of Saint Joseph. **1949** O. NASH *Versus* 139 As a Lucky Striker, Whenever I offer smart folk a Lucky [etc.]. **1953** A. BARON *Human Kind* 184 He fumbled for a packet of Luckies and offered Casey a fresh cigarette. **1963** 'D. RUTHERFORD' *Creeping Flesh* i. 63 I smoked six Luckies. *Ibid.* 80 A packet of Luckies, please. **1969** N. FREELING *Tsing-Boum* xxii. 160 Those French ones—no thanks. I only smoke Luckies, really.

lucky, *a.* Add: **1. e.** *lucky him* (or *you*, etc.): phrases expressing envy at another's good fortune.

1857 C. M. YONGE *Dynevor Terr.* II. xi. 171 She's..the finest figure in the whole county; lucky him who gets her. *Ibid.* xii. 176 Lucky you to have work at home, and to stay with it. **1893** W. ELWIN *Let.* 4 May in E. Lutyens *Blessed Girl* (1953) x. 190 Lucky you to be mothered by Betty. **1965** A. ROUDYBUSH *Season for Death* (1966) xxviii. 165 'I'm going to the flicks.' 'Lucky you. God bless!' **1972** R. HILL *Fairly Dangerous Thing* I. iv. 36 'I'm busy every night but tonight.' 'Lucky you,' said Joe.

3. (Further examples.)

1905 A. BURVENICH *Eng. Idioms* 219 To be born under a lucky star. **1911** C. E. W. BEAN *'Dreadnought' of Darling* xxxv. 317 The Australian should probably thank Providence and his lucky star. **1920** W. J. LOCKE *House of Baltazar* xv. 187 It doesn't seem to be one of the House of Baltazar's lucky days. **1959** J. BRAINE *Vodi* xxv. 261 Thank your lucky stars to be well out of it. **1973** A. BEHREND *Samarai Affair* xii. 115 Richardson wondered if this was going to be his lucky day.

7. lucky dip: see *DIP *sb.* 1 h; **lucky dog,** someone considered by others to be lucky.

1841 S. BAMFORD *Passages in Life of Radical* (ed. 2) I. xxix. 175 They were a set of 'lucky dogs'... They escaped. **1844** [in Dict., sense 1]. **1922** JOYCE *Ulysses* 634 You were a lucky dog if they didn't set the terrier at you directly you got back.

lucky-bag. Add: **1.** (Further examples.)

1891 *Confectioners' Union* IV. 530/1 (Advt.), Farthing Goods... Pick-me-up Lucky Bags. **1927** W. E. COLLINSON *Contemp. Eng.* 20 The term lucky bag is still used to denote a bag stuffed full of miscellaneous objects. **1931** A. UTTLEY *Country Child* iii. 37 There the paper bag lay, 'Monster Lucky Bag', with some others..on the counter, asking her to open it. **1968** 'E. PETERS' *Grass Widow's Tale* vii. 90 This trifle, hardly too big to have fallen out of a child's lucky-bag. **1973** *Dalesman* May 144/1, I well remember..the lucky bags which cost a ha'penny. These bags were pink, yellow or green and contained some sweets and a little novelty or toy.

2. (Earlier U.S. examples.)

1832 E. C. WINES *Two Yrs. in Navy* (1833) I. 55 All property that falls in his [*sc.* the master-at-arms'] way for which he cannot find an owner, is thrown into the 'lucky bag'. **1840** *Southern Lit. Messenger* VI. 233/2 Every man-of-war, you know, has her lucky bag, containing a little of every thing, and something belonging to everybody.

luculia (lukū·liă). [mod.L. (R. Sweet *Brit. Flower Garden* (1826) II. 145), f. *luculi swa* native name of *L. gratissima* in India.] A large deciduous shrub of the genus so called, belonging to the family Rubiaceæ, native to northern India and China, and bearing corymbs of fragrant pink flowers.

1826 R. SWEET *Brit. Flower Garden* II. 145 (*heading*) Delightfully fragrant Luculia. **1885** W. J. MAY *Greenhouse Managem.* (ed. 2) vi. 236 The best place for Luculias is in the beds or borders of a conservatory where they have plenty of room to grow. **1962** *Amat. Gardening* 21 Oct. (Suppl.) 32/3 The luculias need plenty of room and are best planted out in a well drained, peaty soil in the greenhouse.

Lucullan (liukʌ·lăn), *a.* [L. *Lucullanus*, *Lucullianus*.] = LUCULLIAN, -EAN *a.*

1857 BOSTOCK & RILEY tr. *Pliny's Nat. Hist.* VI. XXXVI. ii. 307 The largest of these columns, pillars of Lucullan marble..were erected in the atrium of Scaurus. *Ibid.* viii. 325 L. Lucullus was consul; the same person who gave its name, it is very evident, to the Lucullan marble. **1909** G. G. RAMSAY tr. *Tacitus' Annals* II. XI. xxxii. 41 Messalina took herself off to the Lucullan Gardens. **1913** *Chambers's Jrnl.* 11 Jan. 87/1 Two thousand pounds for a really Lucullan feast as planned..by one who plans them constantly. **1935** *Times Lit. Suppl.* 11 Apr. 245/2 This is definitely a Lucullan book, of use only to the hostess with a chef and a large staff. **1935** J. M. COBBAN *Senate & Provinces* iv. 116 Clodius and his fellows were acting at the direct instigation of the 'anti-Lucullan' party at Rome. *Ibid.* 123 Pompey..whom we have seen to be the prime force behind the anti-Lucullan movement. **1966** *Punch* 4 May 669/3 He gives us a Lucullan feast of stories, but my favourite is the tale of Mrs. Keppel.

Lucu·llic, *a.* = prec.

1904 J. MCCABE tr. *Haeckel's Wonders of Life* xi. 98 The careful choice and preparation of savoury food..was just as important..as it is to-day in royal banquets or the Lucullic dinners of millionaires.

‖**lucus a non lucendo** (lū·kɒs a nǫn lūke·ndo, liū·kɒs ēi nǫn liūse·ndo). [L. phr., 'a grove, (so-called) from the absence of *lux* (light)', discussed by Quintilian in *De inst. oratoria* i. 6. 34.] A paradoxical or otherwise absurd derivation; something of which the essence or qualities are the opposite of what its name suggests. Also **lucus a non.**

1711 ADDISON *Spectator* 8 May, He composed an..Epic Poem..consisting of four and twenty Books, having entirely banished the Letter *A* from his first Book, which was called *Alpha* (as *Lucus a non lucendo*) because there was not an *Alpha* in it. *c* **1728** SWIFT in W. King *Dreamer* 88 And make his ignorance discerned, To get the name of council learned; (As *lucus* comes *à non lucendo*). **1749** FIELDING *Tom Jones* III. VIII. iv. 172 This Sun, into which Jones was now conducted, was truly named as *Lucus a non lucendo*; for it was an Apartment into which the Sun had scarce ever looked. **1823** BYRON *Don Juan* VI. lv. 240 Thus..has been shown 'Lucus a *non* Lucendo', *not* what *was*, But what *was not*; a sort of style that's grown Extremely common in this age. *Ibid.* XI. xxi. 54 Through Groves, so called as being void of trees, (Like *lucus* from *no* light;). **1845** R. FORD *Hand-bk. Trav. Spain* II. 941 *St. Jean de Luz*..is not a 'city of light', but of 'mud', and a Lutetia or lucus a non lucendo. **1848** J. R. LOWELL *Fable for Critics* 69 'Illustrations'..are said to illustrate, because, as I view it, Like *lucus a non*, they precisely don't do it. **1904** W. F. H. KING *Classical & Foreign Quotations* 186 To the *Lucus a non lucendo* principle, as it is called, are referred all such paradoxical derivations and descriptions which involve a contradiction in the mere stating of them. **1924** A. HUXLEY *Little Mexican* 13 Their philology was the picturesque *lucus a non lucendo*, bloody from by-our-Lady type. **1958** R. LIDDELL *Morea* III. 219 Was its name Hydraea (watery), a *lucus a non lucendo*—it is singularly waterless today.

luderick (lū·dərik, lʌ·drik). *Austral.* Also **ludrick.** [Aboriginal name.] A perciform herbivorous food fish, *Girella tricuspidata*, which has a dark-coloured back and silvery belly; also called blackfish, black bream or perch.

1898 E. E. MORRIS *Austral Eng.* 275/2 Luderick, or Ludrick, an aboriginal Gippsland name for a local variety of the fish *Girella simplex*. **1951** T. C. ROUGHLEY *Fish & Fisheries Austral.* 92 In 1947, when a conference of fisheries officials from all Australian States was held to discuss the question of the diversity of the names of fish in the various States, it was decided to adopt the Victorian name of 'luderick' for this fish throughout Australia... The luderick is an estuarine fish found in all Australian States, but it occurs in its greatest numbers in New South Wales, southern Queensland, and Victoria. **1969** *Man* (Austral.) Mar. 12/2 Over the seasons you get a variety of fish you'd be scratching to find anywhere else—drummer, luderick, [etc.].

Ludian (liū·diăn). Also **Lüd, Lude, Ludic, L'üdikš, Lüdish.** [f. Olonetsian *liüdi* (? ad. Russ. *ljudi*, people) + -AN, -IAN.] A language of the Finnish group of the Finno-Ugrian family of languages, used by a small number of speakers in the region of Olonets, now in the north-west part of the Russian Socialist Federation of Soviet Republics.

1921 M. STENBÄCK in T. Homén *East Carelia & Kola Lapmark* II. ii. 122 Among the Onega Wepsians... Those who speak Wepsian are said to speak *l'üdikš*. **1933** L. BLOOMFIELD *Lang.* 68 The other languages of the Baltic branch [of the Finnish-Lapponic languages], *Carelian, Olonetsian, Ludian, Vepsian, Livonian, Ingrian*, and *Votian*, are far smaller, and some of them are near extinction. **1939** L. H. GRAY *Foundations of Lang.* 369 The languages of the Uralic family are as follows: (1) *Finnish* group: Finnish proper.., Karelian.., Olonetzian, Ingrian, Lüdish, Vepsian, [etc.]. **1954** PEI & GAYNOR *Dict. Ling.* 127 *Ludian*, a dialect (also called *Lüdish*) of the Finnish group of the Finno-Ugric (or Uralic) sub-family of the Ural-Altaic family of languages. **1955** B. COLLINDER *Fenno-Ugric Vocab.* p. ix, Lude.., spoken in the region west of lake Onega, is a kind of intermediary between Olonets and Veps. **1959** *Chambers's Encycl.* XIV. 200/2 Lüd, spoken to the north and west of Petrozavodsk. **1967** D. S. PARLETT *Short Dict. Lang.* 81 *Ludian* 10 th[ousand] speakers in region of Olonets (north east of Leningrad on shore of Lake Ladoga) of a series of patois, basically northern Vepsian but with influences of Carelian, and forming a transition between the two. Impregnated with Finnish and Russian. **1974** *Encycl. Brit. Micropædia* V. 709/3 Ludic, a minor group of dialects spoken to the south of Karelian, is considered to be a blend of Karelian and Veps.

ludic (liū·dik), *a.* [ad. F. *ludique*, f. L. *lūdĕre* to play.] Of or pertaining to undirected and spontaneously playful behaviour.

1940 HINSIE & SHATZKY *Psychiatric Dict.* 323/2 This excess-energy must be expended (without purpose) in some way, most usually in play-activity, called *ludic activity*. **1969** P. L. BERGER *Rumor of Angels* iii. 76 Ludic, or playful, elements can be found in just about any sector of human culture. **1971** D. G. BOYLE *Lang. & Thinking in Human Devel.* vi. 65 Ludic play and symbolism are among the defining characteristics of humanity. **1972** *Times Lit. Suppl.* 3 Mar. 234/5 Poetry is sacred..for the same reasons that eroticism is sacred: it is ludic, that is to say useless. **1973** M. AMIS *Rachel Papers* 207 My existence, too, was a prismatic web of mendacity—but for me it was..far more ludic, literary, answering an intellectual rather than an emotional need.

Ludlovian (lʌdlōᵘ·viăn), *a. Geol.* [f. *Ludlovia*, med.L. name of Ludlow, town in Salop (Shropshire) in the vicinity of which are exposures of this series: see -IAN.] Of, pertaining to, or designating the latest of the three divisions of the Silurian, preceding the Downtonian (or the second latest, if the Silurian is taken to include the Downtonian). Also *absol.*

1855 J. PHILLIPS *Man. Geol.* vi. 104 This stage contains no less than seventy-eight species—the genera being mostly Wenlockian and Ludlovian. **1946** L. D. STAMP

Britain's Struct. xii. 109 Though various divisions of the Silurian have been proposed the old three-fold one into: (3) Ludlow Series or Ludlovian; (2) Wenlock Series or Wenlockian; (1) Llandovery Series or Valentian; has stood the test of time and is most convenient. **1969** Bennison & Wright *Geol. Hist. Brit. Isles* vi. 121 There is..an almost perfect transition in the Welsh Borders from the Ludlovian into the Dittonian reflecting a gradually changing environment from marine to non-marine. *Ibid.* 120 *Monograptus scanicus* suggests a low Ludlovian age for these deltaic deposits.

ludo. (Later examples.)

1955 L. P. Hartley *Perfect Woman* xxxvi. 324 The four ludo-players identified her. **1973** *Times* 4 Oct. 2/5 Pedestrians feel like pawns on a vast spongy chess and ludo board. **1975** R. Player *Let's talk of Graves* iv. 108 Our dear Miss Grigg produced a new Ludo set and..a few crackers.

Ludolph (lū·dǫlf). [The name of *Ludolph* van Ceulen (1540–1610), who was born at Hildesheim (Germany), taught mathematics in the Netherlands, and calculated π to 35 decimal places.] *Ludolph's number*; the number π (see Pi *sb.*).

[**1887** *Encycl. Brit.* XXII. 434/2 In Germany the 'Ludolphische Zahl' is still a common name for the ratio.] **1894** F. Cajori *Hist. Math.* 154 The value of π is therefore often named 'Ludolph's number'. **1959** *Webster's Biogr. Dict.* s.v. *Ceulen, Ludolph van*... Known for computations of the value of π (Ludolphian, or Ludolph's number).

Hence **Ludo·lphian** *a.*

1886 G. S. Carr *Synopsis Pure & Appl. Math.* I. ii. 901/1 (Index), Ludolphian number. **1905** *Westm. Gaz.* 14 Oct. 3/1 The history of the search for this ratio, the Ludolphian number..is practically the early history of mathematics itself. **1953** H. Eves *Introd. Hist. Math.* iv. 92 Ludolph van Ceulen of Germany computed π to 35 decimal places by the classical method, using polygons having 2^{62} sides. He spent a large part of his life on this task and his achievement was considered so extraordinary that the number was engraved on his tombstone, and to this day is frequently referred to in Germany as 'the Ludolphian number'.

Ludwig's angina (lu·dvigz ændʒəi·nă). *Path.* [tr. mod.L. *angina Ludovici*, f. the name of W. F. von *Ludwig* (1790–1865), German surgeon, who described it in 1836.] Severe inflammation of the tissues of the floor of the mouth (usu. caused by streptococci).

[**1875** *Brit. Med. Jrnl.* 25 Dec. 778/2 (*heading*) A note on Angina Ludovici. **1885** *Lancet* 26 Sept. 571/2 (*heading*) Two cases of angina Ludovici.] *Ibid.*, Ludwig's angina is a name applied to the condition known as submaxillary cellulitis. **1939** *Bull. Hist. Med.* VII. 1124 Ludwig's Angina is a comparatively rare disease despite the fact that the disease picture is fairly well known to all students of medicine. **1971** D. F. Mitchell et al. *Oral Diagn.* (ed. 2) xiv. 344 In this case, all of the spaces of the floor of the mouth (submandibular, sublingual, submental) are involved and the condition is called Ludwig's angina.

Ludwigsburg (lu·dvigzbʊ̈ɹg). The name of a town in Württemberg used *attrib.* or *absol.* to designate a variety of hard-paste porcelain made there from 1758 to 1824, characterized by its suitability for figure-modelling.

1863 W. Chaffers *Marks Pott. & Porc.* 185 Ludwigsburg, or Louisburg, called also Kronenburg porcelain. **1960** R. G. Haggar *Conc. Encycl. Cont. Pott. & Porc.* 188/1 (*caption*) Ludwigsburg porcelain miniature group. *Ibid.* 189/1 Ludwigsburg porcelain Chinese groups. *Ibid.* 273/1 Ludwigsburg models were reproduced at Amberg.. during the nineteenth century.

‖**lues Boswelliana** (liū·īz bǫzweliē̆i·nă, -ā·nă). [f. Lues: cf. Boswellian *a.*, *-iana.] A disease of admiration; a biographer's tendency to magnify his subject.

1834 Macaulay in *Edin. Rev.* Jan. 508 Biographers, translators, editors,—all, in short, who employ themselves in illustrating the lives or the writings of others, are peculiarly exposed to the *Lues Boswellianæ*, or disease of admiration. **1928** [see *furor 4]. **1931** *Times Lit. Suppl.* 8 Oct. 765/3 Though he decidedly comes to praise Caesar, not to bury him, he avoids any excessive *lues Boswelliana*.

lueshite (liū·əʃəit). *Min.* [a. F. *lueshite* (A. Safiannikoff 1959, in *Bull. d. Séances, Acad. r. d. Sci. d'Outre-Mer* V. 1255), f. *Lueshe*, name of a locality north of Goma in eastern Zaïre where it was discovered: see -ite[1].] A black orthorhombic niobate of sodium, $NaNbO_3$.

1961 *Mineral. Mag.* XXXII. 966 Lueshite. **1968** I. Kostov *Mineral.* I. 250 The chief minerals [of the perovskite group] are perovskite ($CaTiO_3$), lueshite ($NaNbO_3$), and loparite ($NaCeTi_2O_6$).

luff, *v.* Restrict *Naut.* to senses 1 to 4 and add: **3. b.** To obstruct (an opponent's yacht which is attempting to pass to windward on the same course) by sailing one's own yacht closer to the wind.

1912 Heckstall-Smith & Du Boulay *Compl. Yachtsman* xiii. 299, I make it a fixed rule to luff every vessel that attempts to pass me to windward. **1960** E. Schiøttz *Pract. Yacht Racing* ix. 89 If a yacht clear astern sails between two yachts ahead she has no right to luff the windward one. **1965** *Sailing* ('Know the Game' Series) (ed. 2) 34/1 A yacht may luff a yacht clear astern or a windward yacht, until helmsman of windward yacht comes abreast of the mainmast of the leeward yacht.

5. *trans.* To alter the inclination of (the jib of a crane or derrick); to raise or lower in a vertical plane. Also with adverbs, as *luff in*, to raise (the jib), so moving the hook nearer to the operator; similarly *luff out*.

1913 H. Wilda *Cranes & Hoists* ii. 128 The lifting and lowering of the load is effected by means of multiple pulley blocks, the horizontal movement of the load by luffing the jib. **1922** H. H. Broughton *Electr. Handling of Materials* III. ii. 32 The load follows a horizontal path when luffing-in the jib. **1932** S. J. Koshkin *Mod. Materials Handling* v. 78 A derrick boom can be changed in inclination, or luffed, to give one of the components of motion to the load. *Ibid.* 80 The boom is luffed-in or out as little as possible. **1963** R. Hammond *Mobile & Movable Cranes* vi. 180 This arrangement reduces the power required to luff in the jib.

luffing *vbl. sb.* (further examples: cf. sense *5); so *luffing-in, -out*; **luffing crane**, a crane whose jib can be luffed in operation.

1913 *Engineering* 9 May 632/1 Most of these luffing-cranes are now fitted with some sort of compensating gear to keep the load approximately level while the luffing operation is being carried out. *Ibid.*, Greater acceleration in luffing is also obtained. **1922** H. H. Broughton *Electr. Handling of Materials* III. ii. 41 The design is exceedingly simple, the level path being obtained by the automatic paying-out or taking-in of the load rope during the operations of luffing in and luffing out respectively. **1963** R. Hammond *Mobile & Movable Cranes* vi. 181 The luffing motion control equipment consists of a negative-phase sequence panel, with contactors to give plain rotor-controlled 'luffing in' and 'luffing out' by the unbalancing of the stator voltages of the motor through an inbuilt transformer. **1967** *Courier-Mail* (Brisbane) 8 July 1/9 The cries of wharf laborer Derek Beuttel, 54, were not heard by fellow workmen because of the noise of three large luffing cranes.

‖ **luftmensch, luftmensh** (lu·ftmenʃ). Pl. **luftmenschen.** [Yiddish, f. G. *luft* air + *mensch* person.] An impractical visionary.

1907 I. Zangwill *Ghetto Comedies* 240 The word 'Luftmensch' flew into Barstein's mind. Nehemiah was not an earth-man... He was an air-man, floating on facile wings. **1960** *Commentary* June 530/1 The revolutionary student, the nihilist-anarchists, the *Luftmenschen.* **1966** *New Society* 12 May 11/2 Americans, children of the soil, have become traders in air, advertising men, *luftmenschen.* **1968** L. Rosten *Joys of Yiddish* 212 The prototype of the luftmensh was one Leone da Modena,.. who listed his skills and cited no fewer than twenty-six professions... Why would so accomplished a man be classified as a *luftmensh*? Because out of all twenty-six professions.., he barely made a living. **1969** *Sat. Rev.* (U.S.) 26 Apr. 44/2 Menachem-Mendl, *luftmensch* extraordinary, a veritable Don Quixote of Eastern European commerce.

‖ **Luftwaffe** (lu·ftvafə). [G., 'air-weapon'; cf. Lift *sb.*[1]] The German air force before, and until the end of, the 1939–45 war. Also *attrib.*

1935 *Times* 23 May 15/1 The armed forces are henceforth known collectively as the Wehrmacht (Defence Force) and consist of the Army (*Heer*), Navy (*Kriegsmarine*), and the Air Arm (*Luftwaffe*). **1939** *War Illustr.* 21 Oct. 169 The German Luftwaffe—literally 'air weapon' —has been built up by Field-Marshal Goering and General Milch into a formidable force both in size and quality. **1941** *Ann. Reg. 1940* 66 The repulse..broke down the legend of the invincibility of the German *Luftwaffe.* **1941** H. G. Wells *You can't be too Careful* vi. 244 The Luftwaffe he [*sc.* Goering] had launched. **1942** *Electronic Engin.* XV. 240 Generally the receiving valves are..similar to those used in German Luftwaffe sets. **1946** *R.A.F. Jrnl.* May 174 One Group alone has disposed of thousands of tons of Luftwaffe equipment. **1957** *Encycl. Brit.* I. 453/1 As soon as the arms limitation of the Versailles treaty had been repudiated, Germany embarked upon the creation of a great Luftwaffe.

lug, *sb.*[1] Add: **3. lug-pole** *U.S.* (= sense 1).

1773 *Mass. Gaz.* 4 Feb. (Suppl.) 1/2 A Defect in the Chimney, by Reason of the Wooden Lug-pole burning out. **1848** D. Drake *Pioneer Life Kentucky* (1870) v. 107 The tea kettle swung from a wooden 'lug pole'.

lug, *sb.*[2] Add: **2.** (Later examples.)

The statement in Dict. 'In Sc. the only word in use, *ear* being *obs.* exc. in combination' is no longer true. In Scotland as in England *lug* in this sense is *colloq.* or *joc.*

1908 *Old-Lore Misc.* I. vii. 270 Lang an last, da laird grippit him be da lug. **1916** 'Taffrail' *Pincher Martin* ii. 28 Give 'im a clip under the lug! **1922** *Banffshire Jrnl.* 26 Sept. 6 An' hame-brewn sets th' lugs a crackin'. **1922** Joyce *Ulysses* 192 Has the wrong sow by the lug. *Ibid.* 261 Cowley's red lugs and Adam's apple in the door of the sheriff's office. **1939** —— *Finnegans Wake* 500 The snare drum! Lay yer lug till the groun.

3. d. *to put* (or *pile*) *on lugs*, to put on airs. *U.S. slang.*

1889 K. Munroe *Golden Days* xvii. 188 If you notice me..piling on any lugs..you just bump me down hard. **1896** Ade *Artie* vi. 54 The family did n't put on no such lugs in them days. **1903** A. Bennett *Leonora* iv. 106 American women..put on too much lugs, at any rate for an Englishman. **1905** *Springfield* (Mass.) *Weekly Republ.* 15 Sept. 12 Dr. Hall puts on no 'lugs', and is not above sitting on a cracker barrel in a country grocery for a chat with old acquaintances. **1920** S. Lewis *Main St.* 326 Oh, the lugs he puts on—belted coat, and piqué collar.

e. A demand for borrowed or exacted money. Esp. in phr. *to put the lug on*, to extort, to put pressure on. *U.S. slang.*

1929 D. Runyon in *Hearst's Internat.* Aug. 73/2 Why do you not put the lug on him? **1935** A. J. Pollock *Underworld Speaks* 84/2 *Out on the lug*, engaged in begging racket. *Ibid.* 93/1 *Put the lug on*, to borrow; to beat up a racketeer with blackjack or brass knuckles for muscling in on forbidden territory. **1936** *Kansas City* (Missouri) *Star* 15 Oct. 6/1 Indiana uses the 'Lug'. **1938** *Kansas City* (Missouri) *Times* 14 Feb. 1/6 The Democratic organization's lug on all city and county employees..for its campaign fund..has been started. **1940** *Topeka* (Kansas) *State Jrnl.* 26 Mar. 1/8 Shakedowns in Topeka are known to have ranged from $20 to $50 monthly, depending on the amount of illegal business done by the individuals on whom the lug was put. **1973** M. Truman *Harry S. Truman* vii. 129 My father also knew, from his inside contacts with Missouri Democrats, that the governor..was 'putting the lug' (to use Missouri terminology) on state employees to contribute to his campaign fund.

4. (Earlier U.S. examples.)

1835 J. Martin *New Gazetteer Virginia* 175 An eminent tobacco manufacturer of Richmond has offered the inhabitants of this district to take all of their tobacco, (lugs included) at $10 a hundred. **1851** *Southern Planter* (Richmond, Virginia) June 192/1 We quote lugs $5 25 to $7.

4*. Chiefly *N. Amer. slang.* Used contemptuously of a person: a lout, a sponger.

1931 *Broadway Brevities* 19 Oct. 2/1 Is his only sin the fact that he was born a lug? **1935** A. J. Pollock *Underworld Speaks* 73/2 *Lug*, an incapable person who frequently borrows small sums of money. **1936** R. Chandler *Black Mask* June 24/1 The girl snapped at me: 'Is this lug your partner?' **1952** *Landfall* VI. 265 Now there's your sermon!.. No, no, no. These lugs would never understand. **1953** K. Tennant *Joyful Condemned* xxix. 284 The big fellows slip through my fingers, leaving some tough lug to take the rap. **1968** B. Turner *Sex Trap* xi. 98 'The other lug's at June's,' Louis said. **1973** *Hansard* (Canada) 20 Mar. 2388/1, I will stand down when Mr. Speaker tells me to, not when you lugs tell me to. **1973** 'B. Mather' *Snowline* x. 116 Any other names you can come up with?.. You don't owe these lugs anything.

5. lughole *dial.* and *colloq.*, ear-hole; **lug sole** *N. Amer.* (see quot. 1961).

1895 J. S. Fletcher *Wonderful Wapentake* 72 I'll come ..and pelt thi lughoil for tha. **1898** B. Kirkby *Lakeland Words* 96 Stuff thi lug-whols wi' woo. **1966** F. Shaw et al. *Lern Yerself Scouse* 20 *Is lugole*, his ear. **1973** *Times* 25 Aug. 10/8 A session with *Hello, Cheeky* is like being exposed to some noisy, rude and unstoppable urchin who wins you round or at least averts a skull-shattering clout about the lughole simply because he will go on regardless. **1961** Webster, *Lug sole*, a thick rubber sole that has deep indentations in a pattern designed to provide good footing and is used on sport and work shoes. **1970** *Toronto Daily Star* 24 Sept. 16/2 (Advt.), Heavy duty lug sole.

Luganda (l[i]ugæ·ndă). A language of the Bantu group, spoken in Uganda.

1889 R. P. Ashe *Two Kings of Uganda* p. ix, *Buganda* is the country itself, '*Muganda*' a native of the country, '*Baganda*' the plural of '*Muganda*', and '*Luganda*' is the language. **1902** *Encycl. Brit.* XXXIII. 541/2 The languages spoken in the Uganda Protectorate belong to the following stocks:—... *Bantu* (Lu-Ganda, [etc.]). **1933** L. Bloomfield *Lang.* iv. 67 The languages of the Bantu family,.. are very numerous,..; among the better known are *Luganda*, [etc.]. **1955** *Times* 6 July 8/3 Similar statements have been prevalent in Luganda newspapers and in the resolutions of some district councils outside Buganda. **1966** B. Kimenye *Kalasanda Revisited* 15 His Luganda was spoken with a sharp accent. **1971** *Guardian* 22 Apr. 10/3 He was brought up at Bombo in Buganda and speaks excellent Luganda.

Lugbara (lugbā·ră), *sb.* and *a.* Also **Logbara, Lugbware, Lugwari. A.** *sb.* **a.** A people inhabiting the border area of Uganda and Zaïre; a member of this people. **b.** The Sudanic language of this people. **B.** *adj.* Of or pertaining to this people.

1925 R. E. McConnell in *Jrnl. R. Anthrop. Inst.* LV. 439 The Lugwari Tribe of the West Nile District of Uganda does not seem to have been described, so I venture to record some notes. *Ibid.* 442 Though not aggressive, the Lugwari are a fearless and warlike people in defence. *Ibid.* 448 The Lugwari women very usually wear large clumsy iron rings around their ankles. **1932** C. G. & B. Z. Seligman *Pagan Tribes Nilotic Sudan* viii. 282 Rain-stones..said to be of Bari origin..taken from the Lugbware some years previously. **1933–5** A. N. Tucker in *Bull. Sch. Oriental Stud.* VII. 868 The Lugbara (also called 'Lugwari') live in the North-East Congo..and extend into the West Nile District of Uganda. **1935** Thomas & Scott *Uganda* v. 86 Languages of the Moru-Madi group [are spoken] by the Lugbara..and Lendu..of the West Nile. **1953** Trowell & Wachsmann *Tribal Crafts Uganda* i. 57 The Madi and Lugbara smoke their tobacco in a water-cooled pipe with a small clay bowl. **1959** *Chambers's Encycl.* XIII. 257/1 Sudanic languages... Sudan-Nile (Lugbara, Logo, Lendu, Baka in Belgian Congo and the Sudan). **1960** J. P. Crazzolara (*title*) A study of the Logbara, Ma'di, language, grammar and vocabulary. **1971** *Sunday Nation* (Nairobi) 11 Apr. 14/2 On January 25, 1971, a modestly educated Lugbara voice haltingly read out to the nation eighteen reasons why the army had taken over power. **1974** *Guardian* 26 Mar. 1 Amin's recent policy of cracking down on Lugbara officers. *Ibid.*, Ondoga was a Lugbara from the western Nile.

luge (lūʒ), *sb.* [Swiss dialect.] A sledge, of Swiss origin, of the bob-sleigh type. Also *attrib.*

1905 *Sci. Amer.* Suppl. 15 Apr. 24488/1 The 'luge' is a small sled peculiar to the Grisons. **1907** *Ladies' Field* 19 Jan. 278 On the ascent the luge flies straight up into the

air. **1919** *Daily Mail* 10 Dec., (*caption*) A pair of winter holiday-makers in Switzerland enjoying a run on a Canadian luge. **1968** *Globe & Mail* (Toronto) 13 Jan. 41/4 Canada's luge team..will be announced Monday. The Canadian luge championships are scheduled Sunday.

Hence **luge** *v. intr.*, to toboggan on a luge. Also **lu·geing, lu·ging** *vbl. sb.*, **lu·ger.**

1907 *Ladies' Field* 19 Jan. 278 The gentle art of Luging... Les Avants is the most obvious place from which to luge... Caux is the only other [place] where lugers assemble in force. **1909** *Westm. Gaz.* 26 Jan. 5/2 Les Avants.. has one of the finest natural luging courses in Europe. **1924** *Yorksh. Post* 28 Jan. 10/7 There is good curling, bob sleighing, and lugeing. **1927** *Daily Express* 28 Dec. 3/1 Youths..'luged' in a reckless, haphazard style.

Luger (lū·gəɹ). Also (erron.) **Lueger, Lüger.** The name of G. *Luger*, German firearms expert, used *attrib.* or *absol.* to designate a German type of automatic pistol. Cf. *PARABELLUM.

1904 W. B. WALLACE *Text Bk. Small Arms* 178 The Borchardt Leuger or 'Parabellum' automatic pistol belongs to Class I. **1912** H. M. RIDEOUT *William Jones* 139 For arms he carried only a Luger pistol. **1933** 'P. CAIN' *Fast One* 229 Faber lifted the flap of the right side pocket, slipped a black Luger out onto the seat beside him. **1934** D. TEILHET *Talking Sparrow Murders* ii. 34 A short Lüger thudded to the floor. **1947** *Landfall* I. 264 He held a Lueger pistol. **1957** 'D. RUTHERFORD' *Long Echo* viii. 159 He picked up the Luger and began to extract the magazine. **1961** *Sunday Express* 12 Mar. 17/8 Two middle-aged men..shoot at one another, one with a Luger and the other with a ·38. **1970** R. A. STEINDLER *Firearms Dict.* 171/2 s.v. *Pistole Parabellum.* The name of Georg Luger has been linked to the gun to such an extent that the gun is often simply called the 'Luger'. **1975** P. SOMERVILLE-LARGE *Couch of Earth* iii. 39, I would have expected..a Luger or a Walther.

luggage. Add: **4.** *luggage boot, -grid, -rack, -rest, -train* (earlier and later examples); **luggage locker**, a locker (sense 5) at a railway station, air terminal, etc., for use by passengers.

1972 *Country Life* 7 Dec. 1592/3 The luggage boot is.. fairly well filled by the spare wheel. **1907** *Westm. Gaz.* 12 Feb. 4/2 A telescopic luggage-grid capable of taking heavy trunks. **1928** Luggage grid [see *GRID 9]. **1969** *Guardian* 21 Aug. 9/6 The dreary rows of luggage lockers. **1971** M. KELLY *25th Hour* i. 9, I drove to the main station..and..I put my case in a luggage locker. **1905** *Daily Chron.* 18 May 4/5 Holding on..to the luggage-rack in the narrow..boxes which serve for [train] compartments. **1928** *Chambers's Jrnl.* Jan. 21/2 Just below the luggage-rack is an indicator by which the passenger may control the amount of steam entering the radiator. **1973** C. WILLIAMS *Man on Leash* (1974) i. 5 The room was cool... He dropped the bag on a luggage rack. **1941** 'N. BLAKE' *Case of Abominable Snowman* viii. 83 That luggage-rest..at the end of the bed. **1846** R. FORD *Gatherings from Spain* v. 49 A handful of opponents..may..burn the engines.., particularly smashing the luggage train. **1899** O. WILDE *Importance of being Earnest* III. 127 Apprised, sir, of my daughter's sudden flight.., I followed her at once by a luggage train.

lugger, *sb.*[1] Add: Also in *beef, ship lugger.*

1904 *Sun* (N.Y.) 5 Aug. 1 It was reported that beef luggers in all the cold storage plants were to be called out. *Ibid.* 11 Aug. 3 The men who are called ship luggers, and who load meat aboard the steamships.

lugger, *sb.*[2] (Earlier example.)

1757 *Gentl. Mag.* Jan. 45/2 On the 25th inst. a French lugger drove a vessel ashore at Hastings.

Lugol (lu·gǫl). [The name of Jean *Lugol* (1786–1851), French physician.] *Lugol's iodine, solution*, a solution of 5% iodine and 10% potassium iodide in water, which is used for the internal administration of iodine and as a biological stain.

1880 P. SQUIRE *Compan. Brit. Pharmacopœia* (ed. 12) 177 (*heading*) Lugol's solution. **1917** *Jrnl. Pharmacol.* IX. 363 The increase in resistance to Lugol's solution did not go beyond three times. **1948** L. MARTIN *Clin. Endocrinol.* iv. 83 If thyroidectomy be chosen for a case of thyrotoxic heart failure, it is best to secure the maximum improvement possible with strict rest in bed, digitalis, and the mercurial diuretics before giving Lugol's iodine. **1961** *Lancet* 23 Sept. 688/1, 30 minims Lugol's iodine were administered intravenously during the night. **1972** *Acta Path. & Microbiol. Scand.* A. LXXX. 185 The substance displays some properties similar to those of classic amyloid, such as..responsiveness to methyl-violet, iodine green and Lugol's solution.

lugubre. (Later example.)

1835 J. ROMILLY *Diary* 26 Feb. (1967) 69 In a fly..to drink tea with Mrs Clarkson..the affair most lugubre.

Lugwari, var. *LUGBARA *sb.* and *a.*

Luian, var. *LUVIAN *sb.* and *a.*

Luing (liŋ). [Name of an island in the Hebrides.] The name given to cattle evolved from a crossing of the beef shorthorn and Highland breeds. (See quots. 1970.)

1970 *Times* 8 July 2/4 The Luing (pronounced Ling) bred from the Highland and the Beef Shorthorn, confined itself to the new commercial cattle section... Some purists have queried whether it is..a breed within the strict meaning of the term. **1970** *Radio Times* 24–30 Oct. 51/1 The three Cadzow brothers..had to create the first new beef cattle breed for nearly two centuries—Luing cattle. To accomplish their task they turned the Hebridean island of Luing into a huge experimental ranch. **1971** *Country Life* 6 May (Suppl.) 32b, 87 arable acres support the hill flock and herd of pedigree Luing. **1972** *Field* 7 Dec. 1352 (*caption*) A new breed of beef cattle, the Luing. The breed was evolved by the Cadzow brothers..on the island of that name in the Inner Hebrides... The Luing is based on beef Shorthorn *x* Highland.

Luiseño (luisenʸo). Also **San Luiseño.** [Sp., f. *San Luis Rey*, a mission established in S. California in 1798.] The name, orig. San Luiseño, given to a tribe of the Shoshone Indians; a member of this tribe or the language spoken by them. Also *attrib.* or as *adj.*

1858 *Daily Even. Bulletin* (San Francisco) 5 Nov., The true native Americans of the wild forests—such as the Yumas,..San Luiseños,..predominate. **1875** H. H. BANCROFT *Native Races Pacific States* I. iv. 460 The villages of the San Luiseños are in a section of country adjacent to the Cahuillas. **1884** H. H. JACKSON *Ramona* 244 In the Luiseno tongue that is Majel. **1965** R. F. SPENCER et al. *Native Americans* vi. 263/1 The Luiseño myth of their origins revealed a surprising loftiness of concept. *Ibid.* 264/2 These events have combined to substantially eliminate the Luiseño as an ethnic and cultural group. **1965** *Canad. Jrnl. Ling.* Spring 139 The Luiseno sub-branch of languages in South-western California.

Lukan, var. LUCAN *a.*

Lukanism (liū·kăniz'm). [f. *Lukan* LUCAN *a.* + -ISM.] A form of expression characteristic of St. Luke.

1919 S. C. CARPENTER *Christianity acc. Luke* 69 There are in the passage certain Lukanisms of style.

Lukanize (liū·kănəiz), *v.* [f. as prec. + -IZE.] *trans.* To invest with a Lucan character.

1919 S. C. CARPENTER *Christianity acc. Luke* 81 It would no doubt be possible to assert that he determined at all costs..to Paulinize and Lukanize the Master.

‖ **lukiko** (luki·ko). Also **lukiiko.** [Luganda, = audience-hall, council, levee.] A levee; the council or parliament of the Buganda people of Uganda.

1889 R. P. ASHE *Two Kings of Uganda* vi. 53 He, like us, has come to 'kika', that is to present himself at Mutesa's grand 'lukiko', or levee. **1902** *Encycl. Brit.* XXXII. 539/1 The native parliament or 'Lukiko' was reorganized and its powers were defined. [**1904** G. R. BLACKLEDGE *Luganda-Eng. Vocab.* 51/1 *Lukiko*, audience room, council, levee.] **1955** *Ann. Reg. 1954* 122 It was suggested..that..the Lukiko should be given the opportunity to decide whether to recall the exiled Kabaka or to elect a new Kabaka, as a constitutional monarch. **1955** *Times* 3 Jan. 7/3 The compromise was not made public until after the Great Lukiko had debated the Namirembe reforms. **1969** *Times* 15 Sept. (Uganda Suppl.) p. ii/3 The Buganda Lukiko (Parliament) is not the only regional body to have suffered an eclipse. **1971** *Sunday Nation* (Nairobi) 11 Apr. 11/4 The Lukiiko..demanded that Obote's government should quit the soil of Buganda.

lulav (liū·lāv). Also **lulab, lulov.** [Heb. *lūlābh* branch.] (See quot. 1959.)

1892 I. ZANGWILL *Childr. Ghetto* I. 265 He bore to synagogue the tallest *Lulav* of palm-branches. **1893** *Ibid.* (ed. 3) 409 *Lulov*, palm-branch dressed with myrtle and willow, and used at the Feast of Tabernacles. **1959** D. D. RUNES *Conc. Dict. Judaism* 157/1 *Lulav*, palm frond, one of four species waved at Sukkoth services (others are citron, myrtle, willow). These plants are interpreted as representing various types of man. **1972** C. RAPHAEL *Feast of Hist.* iii. 72/1 An oil lamp..bearing symbols familiar in Jewish art, including..a *lulav* for Sukkot. **1973** *Jewish Chron.* 10 Aug. 18/5 Succot is a festival of thanksgiving for the harvest... What is the lulav for? *Ibid.*, The lulav represents the palm-tree and its dates are delicious. **1973** *Synagogue Light* Sept. 50/1 The required length of the stock of a Lulab, besides its upper leaves, should measure four hand-breadths.

Lullian, *a.* Add: (Later examples.)

1933 *Times Lit. Suppl.* 29 June 433/2 No records remain to us of the early Centenaries, but their nature can be safely deduced from that of the Lullian cult, which was practised for hundreds of years both in Majorca and on the mainland. **1946** E. A. PEERS *Fool of Love* vii. 108 He rifled the Lullian library of the College of Sapiencia. *Ibid.* 109 With Pasqual began a new orientation of Lullian studies.

Hence **Lu·llism**, the philosophy or beliefs of Raymund Lull or his followers.

1929 E. A. PEERS *Ramon Lull* xviii. 377 Ample evidence exists, supplied alike by the friends of Lullism and its enemies, as to the veneration with which its author was regarded. **1933** *Times Lit. Suppl.* 29 June 433/3 That Lullism could survive so long,..is an astonishing testimony to the hold which the Doctor Illuminate had upon his fellow-countrymen. **1946** E. A. PEERS *Fool of Love* vii. 109 At this very time Lullism was taking a fresh impetus both in Spain and abroad. **1954** T. MAYNARD *Long Road of Father Serra* (1956) ii. 27 Students from all over Spain were attracted to this main center of Lullism.

lulu (lū·lu). orig. *U.S. slang.* [Of obscure origin.] A remarkable or wonderful person or thing; freq. used ironically; also *attrib.*

1886 *Lantern* (New Orleans) 10 Nov. 6/3 Farrell's two baser was a lu-lu. **1896** ADE *Artie* ix. 76 Mebbe you think I ain't got a lulu of a head on me this morning. **1904** 'O. HENRY' *Cabbages & Kings* xvii. 301, I smelt a million violets. She was a lulu. I told her I came in a private yacht. **1922** H. TITUS *Timber* iii. 38 *She's* a lulu though! **1940** R. STOUT *Over my Dead Body* xiii. 176 You certainly picked a lulu for an adopted daddy. **1946** J. IRVING *Royal Navalese* 111 *Lulu*, a lady of infinite allure but questionable character. **1963** *Economist* 9 Nov. 578/1 Its own rationale..of why it suddenly became obligatory for [oil] companies to consult governments before changing prices ..might be described as a lulu performance. **1968** *Jazz Monthly* Oct. 19/2 A muddle unparalleled in the history of jazz record issues—and there have been some Lulus—seems to have taken place. **1969** *Islander* (Victoria, B.C.) 13 July 6/1 His first job was, to use modern parlance, a lulu—census taker for the Island's west coast. **1971** *Black Scholar* Sept. 43/2 Joyce, honey, when you goof, its a lulu. **1972** D. SALE *Love Bite* iv. 50, I do hope you're not scared of earth tremors... This one was a real lulu. **1974** *Evening News* (Edinburgh) 23 Nov. 8/4 There are some parts of a new book on spying that aren't fit to be printed. .. This one is a lulu. As long as two years ago, legal proceedings were initiated.

‖ **luluai** (lu·luai). *New Guinea.* [Native name.] A man appointed by the administration to be responsible for the maintenance of order in a village; a village headman.

1924 J. AINSWORTH *Rep. Administrative Arrangements Natives New Guinea* 17/1 in *Austral. Parl. Papers 1923–4* IV. 1819 A luluai or kukurai is the political head of the particular section of which he is either the hereditary or appointed headman. **1930** M. MEAD *Growing up in New Guinea* 372 *Luluai*, headman of village. **1937** *Official Handbk. New Guinea* IV. 302 For the purpose of local government, the Administration has appointed two native representatives in each village. The senior of these is called a '*luluai*' and the junior, his assistant, a '*tul-tul*'. The work of the *luluai* is that of a village headman. **1957** M. WEST *Kundu* v. 63 There is a luluai in every village appointed by the Kiap in Goroka. **1965** *Sunday Mail* (Brisbane) 10 Oct. 2 In the next village the headman, the 'luluai', had a wife who was dying of kuru. **1970** L. P. MAIR *Austral. in New Guinea* (ed. 2) v. 72 The native authorities were known..as luluais..and tultuls... The luluais are responsible for good order and control in the villages.

Lulworth (lɒ·lwəɹþ). The name of Lulworth Cove, Dorset, used *attrib.* in **Lulworth skipper** to designate a butterfly, *Thymelicus acteon*, of the family Hesperiidæ (cf. SKIPPER *sb.*[1] 2 c), first found there in 1833 by J. C. Dale.

1833 J. CURTIS *Brit. Entomol.* X. 442 (*heading*) The Lulworth Skipper. **1894** W. FURNEAUX *Butterflies & Moths* 199 The Lulworth Skipper..is a very local species. **1945** E. B. FORD *Butterflies* vii. 149 In England the Lulworth Skipper only flies within a mile or two of the sea. **1973** T. G. HOWARTH *South's Brit. Butterflies* 27 The Lulworth Skipper... The coloration of this butterfly is somewhat dingy.

lumbar, *a.* and *sb.*[1] Add: **A.** *adj.* **b.** Of, pertaining to, or performed on or within the spinal cord in the lumbar region.

1895 *Brit. Med. Jrnl.* Suppl. 27 Apr. 65/2 Fürbringer.. recalls how Quincke, in 1891, at Wiesbaden, made known his method of lumbar puncture in cases of meningitis of various kinds. **1947** *Physiol. Rev.* XXVII. 253 The bitch exhibits normal estrous and mating despite complete lumbar section. **1963** *Lancet* 12 Jan. 116/1 In three infants the fundus oculi was examined, and in two a lumbar puncture was done.

lumber, *sb.*[1] Add: **3.** (Later examples.)

1928 *Chambers's Jrnl.* Feb. 119/1 Behind the lumber grand-stand, which..resembled every natural wooden grand-stand in the world, stretched a grass meadow. *Ibid.* 120/1 We found Miss J. and Miss N. in a home where the lumber had mellowed—featuring an entrancing tint. **1941** *Sun* (Baltimore) 15 Oct. 5/5 They take nuts and bolts out of packing cases, pick up broken and abandoned field telephone wire along the roadsides, whittle scrap lumber with penknives and produce workable Morse sending keys. **1945** J. J. MATHEWS *Talking to Moon* 66, I had lumber left over from the building of the chicken and pheasant houses. **1965** *Globe & Mail* (Toronto) 5 Jan. B5 A company that will manufacture prefabricated homes in the United Kingdom with Canadian lumber.

4. (sense 1) *lumber-cellar, -house* (earlier and later examples) (cf. LUMBER-HOUSE); *lumber-headed* (earlier example); (sense 3) *lumber-business, -king* (examples), *-merchant* (earlier example); **lumber baron** *U.S.*, a leading or wealthy timber merchant; **lumber-carrier,** (*b*) a vehicle for carrying lumber; **lumber-jack** (earlier and later examples); freq. *lumberjack* (unhyphenated); **lumber jacket** orig. *N. Amer.*, a warm jacket of the type worn by lumbermen; **lumber-mill** (earlier example); **lumber-port,** (*a*) a port-hole in the bow or stern of a ship for loading or unloading timber; (*b*) a seaport from which lumber is shipped; **lumber-raft,** a raft made of logs, boards, or the like; **lumber town** *U.S.*, a town chiefly engaged in the timber trade; **lumber-trade** (earlier and later examples); **lumber-wagon** *N. Amer.*, a springless wagon of a type used for hauling lumber or for general transport (see also quot. 1962); **lumber-yard** *N. Amer.*, a timber-yard.

1888 *N.Y. Life* 18 Feb. 27/2 One of the..lumber 'Barons' of Michigan. **1948** *Time* 29 Nov. 24/1 In many ways he seemed a throwback to the lumber barons, the cattle kings and the mining magnates who had ruled the West before him. **1792** J. BELKNAP *Hist. New-Hampshire* III. 211 Husbandry..is much preferable to the lumber business. **1896** *Vermont Agric. Rep.* XV. 79 Gov. Woodbury has spent years as superintendent of the Burlington branch of J. R. Booth's gigantic lumber business. **1928** *Collier's* 29 Dec. 5/4 On the left were rows of twenty-foot lumber piles, trams laid between them, and electric lumber carriers rolling on the trams. **1832** *Chambers's Edin. Jrnl.* 24 Mar. 59/2 Stone bottles..collected from all the lumber-cellars in the country. **1910** *Daily Chron.* 18 Jan. 3/4 A cramped and pokey lumber-cellar. **1818** T. G. FESSENDEN *Ladies' Monitor* 38, I would not wish your pedant lumber-headed. **1720** in A. McF. Davis *Tracts Currency Mass. Bay* (1902) 385 Hemp, Flax, Turpentine.. to be stored up in the Lumber-house. **1899** H. B. CUSHMAN *Hist. Indians* 162 A lumberhouse and granary, each 18 × 20 ft. **1831** in E. C. Guillet *Valley of Trent* (1957) VI. 236 My misfortunes have been brought upon me chiefly by an incorrigible..race of mortals called *lumberjacks*, whom, however, I would name the Cossacks of Upper Canada. **1902** S. E. WHITE *Blazed Trail* 41 Typical native-born American lumber-jacks powerful in frame. **1972** *Daily Colonist* (Victoria, B.C.) 2 Feb. 16/5 She later became a lumberjack and spent three months in the woods. **1939** *These are our Lives* (Federal Writers Project, N. Carolina) 107 He was dressed in riding breeches and leather lumber-jacket. **1943** *R.A.F. Jrnl.* Aug. 16 They wore lumber jackets. **1952** S. KAUFFMANN *Philanderer* (1953) vii. 107 He went into the middle of the group and squatted next to Jake (he still remembered the smell of the woollen lumber-jacket). **1956** T. H. RADDALL *Wings of Night* 70, I pulled on my old lumber jacket and went out to do the firewood chore. **1968** J. IRONSIDE *Fashion Alphabet* 37 In its modern meaning, the lumber-jacket is very similar to an anorak. It is a short, straight jacket, reaching to the hips, with a centre-front fastening (usually zipped) and buckled at the sides to make it fit snugly. **1975** P. SOMERVILLE-LARGE *Couch of Earth* ix. 148 A black and red lumber-jacket, the sort American hunters wear. **1889** W. H. WITHROW *Our Own Country: Canada* 372 One of the great lumber-kings of the country. **1941** *Yankee* Dec. 19/3 They were..Anderton's lumber kings; so nobody minded their smelling strongly of horses, even in the Methodist basement. **1789** *Boston Directory* 181 Dillaway, Samuel, lumber-merchant. **1830** *Deb. Congress U.S.* 11 Mar. 606/2 You will not find..such constant, unceasing labor as in our lumber mills. **1838** *Yale Lit. Mag.* III. 76 The pirates had knocked out the lumber port, with the intention of sinking her [*sc.* a ship]. **1883** *Wheelman* I. 333 Calais [in Maine], the great lumber port of this part of the country. **1837** W. JENKINS *Ohio Gazetteer* 62 The Hockhocking river..furnishes..a downward navigation for flat boats and lumber rafts. **1898** Lumber-raft [in Dict.]. **1961** B. FERGUSSON *Watery Maze* v. 111 Irrawaddy lumber-rafts. **1880** *Harper's Mag.* Aug. 354/1 A cheerful little lumber town lying high among the hills. **1904** S. E. WHITE *Blazed Trail Stories* I. 3 The sawdust streets..of the lumber town were filled with people. **1972** R. NEELY *Sexton Women* (1974) ii. 12 She had been..brought up in a lumber town..near the Oregon border. **1689** in *Mass. Hist. Soc. Coll.* (1834) 3rd Ser. I. 98 They are supplied.. with the lumber trade. **1732** COL. DUNBAR *Let.* 25 Aug. in *Calendar State Papers* (*Colonial Ser.*) (1939) 201 The undertaker for the masting has and does carry on a greater lumber trade than any man in N. Engld. **1963** *Canada Month* Nov. 22/1 The lumber trade furnished employment for thousands of lumber jacks, river drivers, and sailors. **1831** S. STODDARD *Diary* 30 Nov. in *Mich. Hist. Mag.* (1927) XI. 472 Breakfast swallowed we stepped into our next rig, which was a lumber wagon drawn by two very good horses. **1887** C. D. WARNER *Their Pilgrimage* (1888) xiii. 288 At this season one meets them [*sc.* the hop-pickers] on all the roads driving from farm to farm in lumber wagons. **1902** E. BANKS *Autobiogr. Newspaper Girl* 1 Gathered about the little village station in hard-seated lumber-wagons. **1961** *Edmonton* (Alberta) *Jrnl.* 24 July 11/7 They forded the North Saskatchewan River in a lumber wagon. **1962** *Amer. Speech* XXXVII. 270 *Lumber wagon*, an old, broken-down automobile, particularly one that rides rough. **1786** *Maryland Jrnl.* 4 Apr. (Th.), Lumber-yard, at the head of Baltimore Bason. **1851** C. CIST *Sk. Cincinnati in 1851* 207 Connected with the machinery is a lumber yard. **1961** W. E. GREENING *Ottawa* 108 The district close to the lumberyards was full of waterfront dives. **1973** C. WILLIAMS *Man on Leash* (1974) iv. 52 Lew was..running a lumberyard and building supply here.

lumber, *sb.*[2] Restrict † *Obs.* to senses 1 a and 2, and add: **1. b.** *to be in lumber* (further examples); also, to be in trouble.

1963 J. PRESCOT *Case for Hearing* viii. 125 My poor old dad was in and out of lumber all his life. **1965** A. PRIOR *Interrogators* xi. 202 We're out on a limb hoping for a confession, and if we don't get it we're in dead lumber. **1967** 'M. CARROLL' *Begotten Murder* iv. 104 It rather looks to me as if someone is trying to get Susan in lumber. **1972** L. HENDERSON *Cage until Tame* vi. 43 I've got to keep at it. Break my bloody leg or something stupid like that and I'm in lumber.

3. *slang.* A house or room; *spec.* one where stolen property is hidden; a house used by criminals.

1753 J. POULTER *Discoveries* (ed. 2) 33 They pike up the Prancers, that is, go up Stairs, and fisk the Lumbers, that is, search the Rooms. *a* **1790** H. T. POTTER *New Dict. Cant & Flash* (1795) 40 *Lumber*, a house convenient for the reception of swindlers, sharpers, and cheats. **1800** G. PARKER *Life's Painter* xiv. 117 Have you any body in the lumber behind the bar? *Ibid.* xv. 140 *Lumber*, a room. **1846** *Swell's Night Guide* 34 The polka is greatly in favour with the femmes of this lumber. *Ibid.* 74 His long room, or 'slanging lumber', is the scene of many a choice spree and downey movement. **1923** S. T. FELSTEAD *Underworld of London* iii. 108 The proprietor of the 'lumber', where stolen property is stored pending a suitable buyer, also wants his whack. **1938** F. D. SHARPE *Sharpe of Flying Squad* xiv. 151 Her husband was taken into custody at a 'lumber' (hide-out for stolen property) in Walthamstow. **1950** R. FABIAN *Fabian of Yard* xxxiv. 206 *Lumber*, address used by a prostitute for her profession only.

lumber, *v.*[1] Add: **2.** (Later U.S. examples in special senses.)

1855 J. E. COOKE *Ellie* 207 Keeping the footman lumberin at the knockers on both sides o' the street. **1890** *Dialect Notes* I. 65 'Listen how he lumbers', said of a deep-mouthed dog's barking when he has treed a 'coon or 'possum. **1904** T. WATSON *Bethany* (1920) 165 And he himself did not always know what he had on his mind until he pushed back his specs, and began to 'lumber' [= hold forth].

lumber, *v.*[2] Add: **1. a.** (Further examples.) Now usu., to leave (someone) *with* something unwanted or unpleasant; to get (someone) into trouble or difficulties; freq. *pass.*

1924 E. WALLACE *Room 13* i. 9 'If they lumbered you with the crime, it was because you was a mug,' said Lal complacently. 'That's what mugs are for—to be lumbered.' **1951** A. BARON *Rosie Hogarth* III. iv. 180, I suppose you're afraid... Of getting lumbered, eh? **1958** T. HALL in P. Gammond *Decca Bk. Jazz* xix. 233 Poor old Don Rendell..got really lumbered. He left his clarinet with Gee's with the proviso that it would be forfeited if the trousers and windcheaters weren't returned by the following Monday. Needless to say, they weren't. **1961** SIMPSON & GALTON *Four Hancock Scripts* 35/2 Every time I travel on a train I get lumbered with a carriageful of the most miserable-looking bunch of face-aches you've ever seen in your life. **1964** G. DAVIS *Friday before Bank Holiday* i. 11, I want to realise on the cottage..but I'm lumbered unless I can find another home for Fiddler. **1968** J. LOCK *Lady Policeman* xii. 113, I tell him I'm lumbered for court in the morning.

3. b. *trans.* To go over (ground) cutting the timber on it.

[**1831** *Trans. Lit. & Hist. Soc. Quebec* II. 269 His intention..was to clear land and lumber some.] **1851** J. F. W. JOHNSTON *Notes N. Amer.* I. 52 We clean up two or three acres every year of the lumbered land (land from which the timber has been cut). **1871** R. L. DASHWOOD *Chiploquorgan* v. 60 This part of the country has bever been 'lumbered', being too difficult of access. **1900** *U.S. Dept. Agric. Yearbk.* 365 The cut-over lands..which..have been lumbered heavily, not only for timber but also for fuel. **1971** *Lebende Sprachen* XVI. 9/2 This valley was lumbered in 1955. We lumbered more than a million acres last year.

lumber, *v.*[3] Add: Also, to arrest, imprison.

1882 *Sydney Slang Dict.* 6/1 *Lumber*, to take or carry away to the lock-up. **1931** *Police Jrnl.* Oct. 501 Did the detective (busy) arrest (lumber) Jack? **1953** K. TENNANT *Joyful Condemned* ii. 17 Don't you worry about the police. If there's a warrant out for you..they'll lumber you sooner or later. **1961** B. CRUMP *Hang on a Minute* 136 We were sneaking into the church to bunk down last night when the johns lumbered us. **1970** M. KENYON *100,000 Welcomes* iv. 30 We're pros—twice in twelve years I've been lumbered... Only twice in twelve years screwing.

lumbriculus (lʌmbri·kiŭlʌs). [mod.L. (A. E. Grube 1844, in *Archiv für Naturgeschichte* X. 207), f. mod.L. *Lumbricus* (cf. LUMBRICUS) the name of a genus of earthworms + *-ulus*.] An aquatic, oligochæte worm of the genus so called, resembling an earthworm.

1901 [see *DIVISION 1 f]. **1927** HALDANE & HUXLEY *Animal Biol.* ix. 172 The same (multiplication) would have been true if instead of a Planarian you had cut up the little polyp Hydra, and almost the same with the smaller Annelid worms such as Lumbriculus. **1963** R. P. DALES *Annelids* viii. 154 *Lumbriculus* has been found capable of regenerating the head twenty-one times in succession.

lumbrous, *a.* (Earlier example.)

1836 J. HILDRETH *Dragoon Campaigns Rocky Mts.* I. iii. 26 Our lumbrous vessel heavily groped her way through the waters.

lumen. Add: **2.** [First adopted, in Fr., by A. Blondel 1894, in *La Lumière électrique* 7 July 10.] A unit of luminous flux (now incorporated into the International System of Units), equal to the flux emitted by a point source of intensity one candela (formerly, one candle) into a solid angle of one steradian.

The total flux emitted by a source of one candela is 4π (= about 12·57) lumens.

1898 *Astrophysical Jrnl.* VII. 300 Luminous current is defined as the rate at which luminous energy is emitted by a point-source through a solid angle of one steradian. Unit: The luminous current of one candle, i.e., of one Hefner lamp. Name: 'Lumen'. Proposed by L. Weber. **1937** *Times* 13 Apr. p. iv/2 Electric discharge lighting.. has been recently installed to give an even and intense illumination of 1,120,000 lumens so that any flaw or defect in the panels being produced may be detected at once. **1953** AMOS & BIRKINSHAW *Television Engin.* I. vii. 125 The efficiency of electric lamps is usually expressed in lumens per watt... For gas-filled lamps the efficiency increases steadily with the rating and is approximately 10 lumens per watt for 25 W lamps, 13 lumens per watt for 100 W lamps and 17·5 lumens per watt for 1 kW lamps. Thus a 100 W lamp radiates a total of 1,300 lumens and is equivalent to a source of $1{,}300/4\pi$, i.e., approximately 100 candle-power. **1974** *Which?* Mar. 88/3 The long-life bulbs gave a light output of about 600 lumens after one hour of life.

3. Special Comb.: **lumen-hour,** the quantity of light corresponding to a flux of one lumen radiated for one hour; similarly **lumen-second.**

1925 *Trans. Illuminating Engin. Soc.* (U.S.) XX. 630 The Lumen-hour is the unit of quantity of light. It is equal to a flux of one lumen continued for one hour. **1975** *Times* 21 Mar. 20/3 The public wanted a certain package of candlepower (expressed in lumens); the industry assured certain fixed wattages, and then aimed at the minimum cost per lumen-hour for those wattages. **1930** tr. *L. P. Clerc's Photogr.* ii. 7/2 The unit of exposure is the lumen-second or candle-metre-second. **1958** *Newnes Compl. Amat. Photogr.* x. 110 The light output of a flash-bulb is measured in lumen seconds.

‖ **lumen siccum** (liū·men si·kʌm). [L., = dry light.] The dry light of rational knowledge or thought.

1605 BACON *Adv. Learn.* II. f.48 But this same *Lumen siccum*, doth parch and offend most mens watry and soft natures. **1819** COLERIDGE *Philos. Lect.* (1949) xiii. 374 Must there not be some power, call it with Lord Bacon the '*lumen siccum*'; or 'the pure light', with Lord Herbert;.. that stands in human nature but in some participation of the eternal and the universal by which man is enabled to question, nay to contradict, the irresistible impressions of his own senses, nay, the necessary deductions of his own understanding? **1946** *Mind* LV. 285 Taylor's intellect was no *lumen siccum*, but was always strongly personal in its approach and attitude.

lumeter (liū·mītəɹ). [f. L. *lūm-en* light + -METER.] = *LUXMETER.

1911 *Trans. Optical Soc.* XII. 104 Messrs. R. & J. Beck, Ltd., the makers of the 'Lumeter' instrument. **1923** L. C. MARTIN *Colour* 178 The lumeter reads in foot-candles, that is to say the brightness which a perfectly reflecting and diffusing surface would have if illuminated by so many foot-candles. **1947** *Brit. Jrnl. Psychol.* XXXVIII. 89 The apparatus was calibrated for intensity of illumination (as this would appear to the subject's eye) by placing a lumeter in the position of the tube T.

lumichrome (liū·mikrōum). *Chem.* [ad. G. *lumichrom* (P. Karrer et al. 1934, in *Helv. Chim. Acta* XVII. 1010), f. L. *lūmi(n-, lūmen* light + Gr. *χρῶμ-α* colour.] 6,7-Dimethylalloxazine, $C_{12}H_{10}N_4O_2$, a crystalline compound that is formed by ultra-violet irradiation of riboflavin in acidic solution and shows a sky-blue fluorescence.

1935 *Chem. Abstr.* XXIX. 798 Straw-yellow crystals of lumichrome..are obtained by irradiating solns. of lactoflavin with sunlight. **1949** *Proc. Soc. Exper. Biol. & Med.* LXX. 585/2 The presence of lumichrome crystals in the media containing riboflavin after growth of the tubercule bacillus indicated that the loss of the vitamin was due to conversion to lumichrome. **1962** S. UDENFRIEND *Fluorescence Assay in Biol. & Med.* xiv. 460 Fresh milk and cream emit greenish-yellow fluorescence which is due mainly to riboflavin. When exposed to daylight for appreciable periods of time or irradiated in any other way, the fluorescence turns from yellow to blue. The latter is characteristic of lumichrome. **1972** *Plant Physiol.* XLIX. 991/2 The present report establishes the formation of lumichrome, presumably from either free or bound riboflavin, by the action of light on etiolated shoots of corn and oats and on yeast cells.

Lumière (liūmiēəɹ). *Photogr.* The name of the brothers Auguste (1862–1954) and Louis (1864–1948) *Lumière*, French photographers, used *attrib.* to denote a process of colour photography invented by them involving a colour screen consisting of a glass plate coated with a mixture of starch grains dyed in the primary colours which was placed in front of the panchromatic emulsion on exposure and for viewing; also applied to plates used in this process. Cf. *AUTOCHROME *a.* and *sb.*

1907 *Westm. Gaz.* 24 Aug. 14/2 In some respects the new Lumière process is old. *Ibid.* 20 Sept. 4/3 Even in the case of the Lumière plate a keen eye can detect the red and blue grains upon the lighter portions. **1920** *Chambers's Jrnl.* Apr. 238/2 Twelve volumes, illustrated by 1260 plates of his [*sc.* Burbank's] most beautiful creations, reproduced in colour from original *lumière* plates. **1955** G. R. SHARP tr. *Lorelle's Colour Bk. Photogr.* 199 In the Lumière process a transparent film base carries a mosaic pattern of microscopic coloured filters which is coated with a fine grain panchromatic emulsion. **1966** LACOUR & LATHROP *Photo Technol.* xv. 194/2 To produce the Lumiere Autochrome plate, starch grains were pulverized and one third dyed blue, one third dyed green and the remaining grains dyed red. The colored grains were remixed and spread in a very thin layer on a glass plate.

lumiflavin (liūmiflē·i·vin). *Chem.* [f. L. *lūmi(n-, lūmen* light + *FLAVIN 2.] 6,7,9-Trimethylisoalloxazine, $C_{13}H_{12}N_4O_2$, a crystalline compound that is formed by ultra-violet irradiation of riboflavin in alkaline solution and shows a yellow-green fluorescence.

1934 *Chem. Abstr.* XXVIII. 2036, 1000 l. whey yields 170 mg. pure lumiflavin. **1946** *Jrnl. Biol. Chem.* CLXII. 96 Lumiflavin can either inhibit or stimulate the use of riboflavin or FAD by *Lactobacillus casei*, depending upon the relative amounts of lumiflavin present. **1956** *Jrnl. Biochem.* (Tokyo) XLIII. 643 To estimate the fluorescence

of flavin separately from similar fluorescent substances in living body, the procedure of converting flavins to lumiflavin is of excellent one [*sic*]. **1962** S. Udenfriend *Fluorescence Assay in Biol. & Med.* vii. 243 Riboflavin can also be converted to the more highly fluorescent derivative, lumiflavin, by photodecomposition in alkaline solution, the formation of lumiflavin involving cleavage between the ribitol and flavin ring.

luminaire (liū·minē°ɹ). orig. *U.S.* [Fr.; see Luminary *sb.*] An electric light and its fittings; such a lighting unit. Cf. Luminair.

1921 *Trans. Illuminating Engin. Soc.* (U.S.) XVII. 249 The matter of a generic term for 'lighting unit' was considered by the Committee... The suggested term 'luminaire' was deemed to be the most acceptable... It is not a coined word but is a term already in use in the French language. **1925** M. Luckiesh in Cady & Dates *Illuminating Engin.* ix. 363 In school lighting..luminaires should not be spaced farther apart than a distance of 1·5 times their elevation above the desk-tops. **1933** *Trans. Illuminating Engin. Soc.* (U.S.) XXVIII. 274 A luminaire is a complete lighting unit consisting of a light source, together with its direct appurtenances, such as globe, reflector, refractor, housing and such support as is integral with the housing. **1940** *Chambers's Techn. Dict.* 513/2 *Luminaire*,.. a term sometimes used in America to denote an electric-light fitting. **1960** *How TV Works* iv. 24 The ceiling of a large studio such as Studio 6 in Manchester..may be fitted out with up to a hundred different lights, or 'luminaires' as they are more often called. **1971** *Daily Tel.* 21 Aug. 10 The British Standards Institution's committee responsible for electric light fittings has announced that in the interests of international standardisation it recommends the use of the word 'luminaire' instead of 'lighting fittings' in future. **1971** *Bahamian Rev.* Nov. 32/2 The 'Night Guard' luminaire is turned on automatically at dusk and switched off automatically at dawn, providing night-long security and safety. **1972** Henderson & Marsden *Lamps & Lighting* xix. 341 Luminaires can be divided into two categories: those which are essentially decorative and those which are essentially functional. Decorative luminaires are usually in the form of an assembly of decorative components around a light source, ranging from a simple pendant to the large..prestige chandelier. **1973** *Times* 1 Feb. 22/8 It is preposterous for BSI to force *luminaires* upon us.

Luminal (liū·minæl), *sb. Pharm.* Also **luminal.** [prob. f. L. *lūmin-, lūmen* light (as a rendering of Phen-) + *-al².] A proprietary name of phenobarbitone.

1912 *Trade Marks Jrnl.* 20 Mar. 402 Luminal... A medicine for human use as a sedative and hypnotic. The Bayer Company, Limited,..Manchester; manufacturers. **1928** *Daily Express* 7 Dec. 12 Gave him five grains of luminal. He'll sleep for a few hours and wake up penitent. **1937** *Times* 6 Sept. 7/5 For the defence, it was suggested that the shock of the collision, together with the use of luminal (a narcotic), would account for the symptoms. **1951** 'E. Crispin' *Long Divorce* iv. 37 As a doctor, she had remedies to hand—barbitone, nembutal, luminal. **1960** W. G. Lennox *Epilepsy* II. xxvi. 860 Luminal (Winthrop-Stearns) is phenobarbital that costs more.

luminance. Add: **2.** *Physics.* The amount of luminous flux emitted by unit area of a source into unit solid angle (the objective analogue of subjective brightness).

1950 Jenkins & White *Fund. Optics* (ed. 2) vii. 104 To distinguish it from the visual sensation of brightness, it is usually termed the luminance in the technical literature, but..we shall use the commoner name brightness, with the understanding that..the photometric quantity..is meant. **1952** *Electronics* Nov. 208/2 Luminance is a purely photometric quantity. Use of this name permits brightness to be used entirely with reference to the sensory response. **1957** V. J. Kehoe *Technique Film & Television Make-Up* viii. 95 As to..the reception of a color telecast on a monochromatic receiver, only the luminance portion will be supplied to the single electron gun in the monochrome tube to produce a black-and-white version of the signal. **1968** *Sci. Amer.* Nov. 8/2 Consider two areas that have the same luminance but one of which is seen against a dark background while the other is seen against a light background. The former will appear to be brighter. **1970** *Jrnl. Gen. Psychol.* LXXXII. 111 Midway between these red apertures a yellow spot, three minutes of arc in diameter and 3·1 ftL in luminance, provided the fixation. **1972** *Sci. Amer.* June 101/1 Measurements of a photograph of the vase..showed that the luminance of the moon was 15 foot-lamberts and the space one moon diameter below was 20 foot-lamberts. The contour effect is so strong that the apparent brightness of the two areas is just the reverse of the objective luminance.

luminarism (liū·minăriz'm). [-ism, after Luminarist.] The art or doctrine of the luminarists.

1903 *Edin. Rev.* Oct. 373 We shall probably hear less of Turner as the pioneer of impressionism, luminarism, and pre-Raphaelitism. **1953** *New Republic* 6 July 18 In our own art the progression from linear to formal, formal to coloristic, and finally to the complete luminarism of the 1870s has been a slow process.

luminism (liū·miniz'm). [f. L. *lūmin-, lūmen* light + -ism.] = *luminarism.

1905 *Sat. Rev.* 11 Feb. 174 And now, stated in general terms, what is the principle of Monet's luminism? **1920** *Glasgow Herald* 27 Aug. 4 The world of art has given us Futurist, Cubist, Vorticist, luminism and others. **1927** F. J. Mather *Hist. Mod. Painting* 365 The theoretical Cubists merely turned upon the prevailing Expressionism the criticism which Cézanne had applied to Luminism. **1970** R. Lowell *Notebk.* 245 One misses Emerson drowned in luminism.

luminize (liū·minəiz), *v.* [f. L. *lūmin-, lūmen* light + -ize.] *trans.* To make luminous; to apply a luminous substance to.

1958 *Oxford Mail* 9 July 1 Home radiation hazard in luminizing clocks. **1959** *Times* 30 Apr. 6/5 A Swiss firm was using strontium to luminize their watches. **1967** *Health Physics* XIII. 613/2 Where large numbers of the same type of dial are to be luminised, the paint is often applied by machine.

Hence **lu·minized** *ppl. a.*, **lu·minizing** *vbl. sb.*; **lu·minizer**, one who luminizes objects.

1958 *Times* 20 June 11/7 Luminizing belongs to the daunting group of hazards associated with radiation. **1958** *Ann. Rep. Chief Inspector of Factories on Industr. Health 1957* 36 in *Parl. Papers 1958–9* (Cmnd. 558) XIII. 183 The case of a female luminiser, aged 42, is of special interest. **1959** *New Scientist* 19 Nov. 980/2 The clock industry has its own luminizing regulations. **1967** *Health Physics* XIII. 613/1 It was possible to make body radioactivity measurements on almost all the personnel employed on luminising in these workshops. *Ibid.* 613/2 Radium luminous compound is usually obtained by the luminiser in the form of a powder. *Ibid.* 614/1 In some cases the rest periods are spent on work with luminised articles.

luminol (liū·minǫl). *Chem.* [f. L. *lūmin-, lūmen* light + -ol.] A pale yellow crystalline bicyclic hydrazide, $C_8H_7N_3O_2$, which gives a blue luminescence when oxidized in alkaline solution and is used in the determination of oxidizing agents and metal ions.

1934 E. H. Huntress et al. in *Jrnl. Amer. Chem. Soc.* LVI. 241/1 It is the purpose of the present note to offer an improved method for the synthesis of this material [*sc.* 3-aminophthalhydrazide], which in the interest of simplicity we have long referred to as 'Luminol'. **1965** *Analytical Biochem.* XII. 309 This assay [for hematin iron] is based on the luminescence of alkaline luminol in the presence of hematin iron and hydrogen peroxide. **1970** R. P. Wayne *Photochem.* iv. 120 The oxidation of luminol ..in alkaline solution by ferricyanide..is one of the best-known chemiluminescent reactions. **1974** *Nature* 25 Jan. 193/2 Using a ^{60}Co-γ-source, irradiated saccharides give a bright blue light (≈4,460 Å) when they are dissolved in luminol solution.

luminophore (liū·minǒfō°r). Also **-phor.** [f. L. *lūmin-, lūmen* light + -o + -phore.] **a.** A luminescent substance.

1907 *Jrnl. Chem. Soc.* XCII. ii. 419 The addition of sodium or potassium sulphate to the mixture intensified both this green phosphorescence and that due to the luminophore added. **1930** *Chem. Abstr.* XXIV. 785 (*heading*) Contribution to the preparation of luminophores. **1950** H. W. Leverenz *Introd. Luminescence of Solids* v. 147 Luminescent materials in general (luminophors).. have the additional property of being able to convert part of the absorbed primary energy into emitted luminescence radiations whose spectral characteristics are determined almost entirely by the luminophor. *Ibid.*, The generic term *luminophor* is subclassified into fluorophors..and phosphors. **1968** *Proc. Internat. Conf. Luminescence, Budapest 1966* I. 1290 Precipitates of uniform size..are demanded especially by the luminophore industry.

b. A group of atoms in a molecule which is considered to be responsible for its luminescence.

1910 *Encycl. Brit.* X. 72/1 H. Kauffmann..suggested that the property [of fluorescence] is due to the presence of at least two groups. The first group, named the 'luminophore', is such that when excited by suitable aetherial vibrations [it] emits radiant energy; the other.. acts with the luminophore in some way or other to cause the fluorescence. **1949** P. Pringsheim *Fluorescence & Phosphorescence* v. 392 The strong absorption of visible light which is characteristic of dyes was ascribed to the presence of certain unsaturated groups, such as the azo group —N=N—, the ethylene group —HC=CH—, and the carbonyl group >C=O, which were called chromophors. These chromophors were at first supposed also to be the carriers of fluorescence as 'luminophors'.

luminosity. Add: **1. b.** The effectiveness of light of any particular wavelength in producing the sensation of brightness when perceived.

[**1888** *Amer. Jrnl. Sci.* CXXXVI. 359 While..the luminosity of any spectral ray increases proportionately to the heat in this ray, and indeed is but another manifestation of the same energy..there is..a failure to recognize how totally different optical effects may be produced..according to the wave-length.] **1898** *Astrophysical Jrnl.* VII. 303 That particular property of any color which determines its value as an illuminant is called its 'luminosity'. **1936** *Proc. R. Soc.* A. CLV. 664 The relative luminosity (visibility) in the red region has been measured..as far as 770 *mμ*. In this paper an account is given of measurements up to 900 *mμ*. At this wavelength the relative luminosity is one-sixty millionth of that at 556 *mμ*. **1950** F. H. Adler *Physiol. Eye* xx. 645 The luminosity of any one wave length is usually compared to that of 550 *mμ*. **1966** C. W. Wilman *Seeing & Perceiving* xiv. 116 Curve *Ph* in Fig. 78 represents the relative luminosity (brightness) of various parts of the spectrum.

c. *Astr.* The intrinsic brightness of a heavenly body (as distinct from its apparent brightness, diminished by distance); the rate of emission of electromagnetic radiation (visible or invisible) within any part of the spectrum.

1906 *Astrophysical Jrnl.* XXIII. 248 Prevailing opinion ..admits the presence in the heavens of at least a few stars of extraordinary intrinsic brilliancy... stars having a luminosity exceeding that of the Sun by ten-thousand fold or more. **1924** H. Dingle *Mod. Astrophysics* vi. 74 By brightness we mean—at present, at any rate—the apparent brightness of a star, which will be determined by the star's distance from us as well as by its intrinsic luminosity. **1930** R. H. Baker *Astron.* ix. 369 The apparent magnitude of a star relates to its brightness as we observe it, depending on its real brightness, or luminosity, and on its distance. **1974** *Nature* 1 Mar. 34/2 We have..assumed a thermal spectrum, with an electron temperature of 2×10^6 K, in deriving an upper limit to the X-ray luminosity of the source. *Ibid.*, A 3σ upper limit was obtained to the source luminosity of $4{\cdot}0\ (\pm 1{\cdot}0) \times 10^{32}$ erg s^{-1} for the energy range 0·5 to 1·5 keV.

3. Special Comb.: **luminosity curve**, a graph showing how emitted energy, or perceived brightness, varies with wavelength; **luminosity function** *Astr.*, a function giving the number or proportion of heavenly bodies with an absolute magnitude equal to, or greater than, any chosen value.

1886 Abney & Festing in *Phil. Trans. R. Soc.* CLXXVII. 425 By successive alterations in the distance of the comparison-light other pairs of points in the spectrum are determined until the limits of the visible spectrum are reached. The curves of intensities of different parts of the spectrum plotted from these observations will be found to be fairly smooth. This curve we call the 'luminosity curve'. *Ibid.* 452 We..determined the luminosity-curve of a candle. **1900** *Astrophysical Jrnl.* XI. 220 (*heading*) Determining the luminosity curve of the solar spectrum. **1937** *Nature* 6 Mar. 409/2 The maximum of this luminosity curve was at 510 *mμ*. This was a mean value for forty-eight young observers. **1941** J. D. Cobine *Gaseous Conductors* xiii. 514 The luminosity curve for an incandescent lamp is shifted slightly toward the long wave lengths compared with sunlight. **1951** *Proc. IRE* XXXIX. 1143/2 The luminosity curve expresses the relation..between the luminance and the radiance of spectrum colors. *Ibid.* 1144/1 Based on the new definition of the lumen, and on the new International Temperature Scale, the peak value of the luminosity curve corresponds to 680 lumens per watt. **1924** *Astrophysical Jrnl.* LIX. 13 The comparison.. is easily made with the aid of what may be called the apparent luminosity function..which expresses the frequencies of absolute magnitudes among the stars brighter than m_0. **1958** *Ibid.* Suppl. III. 211 Distances of galaxies are correlated with their apparent magnitude; however the uncertainty of the luminosity function of galaxies complicates and weakens the statistical treatment.

luminous, *a.* Add: **1.** (Further examples.)

1877 W. H. Balmain *Brit. Pat. 4152* 7 Nov., My invention relates to a method of rendering paints, varnishes, whitewashings, and temperings luminous, and consists in the introduction into ordinary paints, varnishes, or washes of a phosphorescent substance, by which means the object to which the paint, or varnish, or wash is applied is made visible in the dark and more or less capable of imparting light to other objects. **1926** R. W. Lawson tr. *Hevesey & Paneth's Man. Radioactivity* xxv. 194 These radioactive 'luminous substances' differ from the phosphorescent substances formerly used, in that they do not require previous illumination. **1929** *Jrnl. Amer. Med. Assoc.* 9 Feb. 466/1 (*heading*) Occupational poisoning in manufacture of luminous watch dials. **1953** Kirk & Othmer *Encycl. Chem. Technol.* X. 658 Of increasing commercial importance are the luminous pigments which produce fluorescent and phosphorescent effects of value in interior decoration, for direction signs and safety devices, television picture tubes, special military applications, and the like. **1958** *New Statesman* 28 June 846/3 The sins of the hitch-hiking undergraduates were drainpipes, luminous socks, and frying sausages in their bedrooms. **1969** R. F. Lang tr. *Henglein's Chem. Technol.* 546 Radium salts are used..for manufacturing luminous paint mixed with ZnS and CaS. **1975** K. Barclay tr. *Orum's Whipping-Boy* xi. 82 My alarm clock has a luminous dial.

d. *luminous efficiency*, (of radiant energy) the ratio of the luminous flux to the total flux; (of a light source) the ratio of the luminous flux to the total flux emitted by, or power supplied to, the source.

1902 *Encycl. Brit.* XXVIII. 89/1 The luminous efficiency of any source of light, that is to say, the percentage of rays emitted which affect the eye as light compared with the total radiation, is dependent upon its temperature. In an ordinary oil lamp the luminous rays do not form much more than 3 per cent of the total radiation. **1927** H. N. Russell et al. *Astron.* II. xvi. 529 The luminous efficiency of sunlight is obtained by dividing the total luminous flux by the total radiant flux..and comes out 100 lumens, or about 8 candles per watt. **1961** Carnt & Townsend *Colour Television* iii. 55 Objects moving across the screen may..leave a yellow trail..as the red and green phosphors continue to glow after the blue phosphor has ceased... The luminous efficiency of these phosphors is low, only a few per cent of the electrical energy being converted into radiant energy... Ten or so lumens per watt can be obtained at 20 kV.

lumirhodopsin (liū:mirodǫ·psin). *Biochem.* Also **lumi-rhodopsin.** [f. L. *lūmi(n-, lūmen* light + *rhodopsin.] An orange intermediate that is formed when rhodopsin is bleached by light and changes spontaneously to metarhodopsin.

1950 G. Wald et al. in *Science* 17 Feb. 180/1 On exposing the solution to light at these low temperatures, the maximum shifts about 5 *mμ* toward the blue, rising about 5% in height in cattle rhodopsin, falling about this amount in frog rhodopsin, still with little change in shape. This is the light reaction. We shall call its product lumirhodopsin. **1975** *Nature* 3 Jan. 56/2 Lozier and Stoeckenius have observed [in *Halobacterium halobium*] four

spectrally distinct intermediates analogous to the rhodopsin, prelumirhodopsin, lumirhodopsin and metarhodopsin of invertebrates.

lumisterol (liū·mi·stĕrǫl). *Biochem.* [ad. G. *lumisterin* (A. Luttringhaus 1931, in *Chemiker-zeitung* 12 Dec. 956/2), f. L. *lūmi(n-, lūmen* light + *-sterin* after CHOLESTERIN, *ERGOSTERIN, with altered ending (see *-STEROL).] A steroid alcohol, $C_{28}H_{44}O$, which is a stereoisomer of ergosterol and occurs as an intermediate when this is converted to vitamin D_2 by ultra-violet irradiation and warming.

1932 *Nature* 20 Feb. 277/1 In lumisterol the crystals are fine needles with *b* as needle axis. **1949** W. H. EDDY *Vitaminology* iii. 46 Lumisterol can be converted into calciferol and may form with it an addition compound consisting of one part lumisterol and one part calciferol... This addition compound..was called vitamin D_1. **1967** W. R. BUTT *Hormone Chem.* xi. 235 It has been established that acetate is the primary carbon source of cholesterol, there being probably about thirty separate reactions involved in the pathway through squalene and lumisterol to cholesterol. **1970** R. A. MORTON *Fat-Soluble Vitamins* 187 The compound originally called vitamin D_1 was later found to be a mixture of ergocalciferol (D_2) and lumisterol, a photodecomposition product of D_2.

lumme (lʊ·mi), *int.* Also **lummy.** A corruption of (*Lord*) *love me.*

1898 J. D. BRAYSHAW *Slum Silhouettes* 146 Wot! Pay for me death? Oh, lummy! not me. **1921** H. WILLIAMSON *Beautiful Yrs.* xviii. 205 He's an awful liar, you know, but can't he half climb a tree! Lumme, much better'n I can! **1934** P. ALLINGHAM *Cheapjack* xxii. 297 You've forgotten all about sister Alice! Lumme, you must get 'er something. **1935** D. L. SAYERS *Gaudy Night* xvii. 370 'Lor' lumme!' I says, 'there's old Winderpane gawn.' **1942** *R.A.F. Jrnl.* 3 Oct. 33 Two years ago..they set London on fire... Lumme, that was a night. **1963** *Times* 4 Mar. 5/2 A pitch which has evoked from Trueman the classic comment: 'Lumme! A green dusty.'

lummox (lʊ·məks). *dial.* and *U.S.* Also **lommocks, lommox, lummicks, lummux,** etc. [Of obscure formation. Goes with the dial. verb *lummock* to move heavily or clumsily.] A large, heavy, or clumsy person; an ungainly or stupid lout.

a **1825** R. FORBY *Vocab. E. Anglia* (1830) II. 201 Look o' yin great lummox, lazing and lolloping about. **1854** A. E. BAKER *Gloss. Northamptonshire Words* I. 402 A great fat lommocks. **1854** 'Dow Jr.' *Patent Sermons* IV. 149 (Th.), Man in his original state is little more than a big lummux of a baby. **1857** J. G. HOLLAND *Bay Path* 381 (Th.), I hope you'll leave somebody else to home besides this lazy lummox. **1893** W. K. POST *Harvard Stories* 186 Well, don't you be such a lazy lummox. **1919** H. L. WILSON *Ma Pettengill* iii. 92 Oswald is a big fair-haired lummox that sings tenor in the Presbyterian choir. **1924** F. HURST (*title*) Lummox. **1934** [see *GORMLESS *a.*]. **1952** J. STEINBECK *East of Eden* xvii. 172 Those great lummoxes would chew a little thing like you to the bone. **1953** K. TENNANT *Joyful Condemned* vi. 54 There's that settee. .. This big lummox..can sleep on that. **1957** J. BRAINE *Room at Top* iv. 45 The big lummox standing possessively beside her. **1971** T. KILROY *Big Chapel* vi. 123 And that other lummox backing him up good-oh!.. A fine pair of cross-fire merchants the two of them! **1973** A. GARNER *Red Shift* 55 You big lummox,.. He's talking about the Irish.

lump, *sb.*[1] Add: **1. a.** (Earlier example of *lump of sugar.*) Also *ellipt.*, = *lump of sugar.*

1728 E. SMITH *Compleat Housewife* (ed. 2) 213 When 'tis fine draw it into dry Bottles, and put a Lump of Sugar into every Bottle. **1899** H. JAMES *Awkward Age* III. xi. 101 Sugar?—isn't that the way to say it? Three lumps? *a* **1916** 'SAKI' *Toys of Peace* (1919) 24 Little friendly questions about weak or strong tea, how much, if any, sugar, milk, cream, and so forth. 'Is it one lump? I forgot.' **1922** H. S. WALPOLE *Cathedral* I. v. 85 No, I'm afraid I don't—thank you, Mrs. Sampson. One lump, please.

f. = *lump work* (LUMP *sb.*[1] 8). Of persons: those who contract to do work 'in the lump', i.e. for a lump sum.

[*a* **1852** H. MAYHEW *London Labour* (1861) II. 330/1 The first man who agrees to the job takes it in the lump, and he again lets it to others in the piece.] **1902** *Eng. Dial. Dict.* III. 691/1 You can do it either by the day or lump. **1969** *Daily Mail* 3 Sept. 2/1 He then spelt out exactly how the thousands of 'labour only' sub-contractors—'The Lump' in building trade slang—deprive the Treasury of more than £3 million a year. **1970** *Daily Tel.* 27 May 11/1 In the building industry, the outgoing government argues, this employment of a quarter of a million men—known as 'the Lump' because it accepts a lump sum for its work and attends to its own tax and social insurance problems—has resulted in widespread tax and National Insurance evasion. **1972** *Times* 21 Nov. 21/2 They attribute much of the confusion in the building 'jungle', as they often call it, to the operations of the 'lump', the growing number of labour-only sub-contractors and 'self-employed'. **1973** *Guardian* 22 Feb. 9/5 A Bill which would prohibit 'lump' labour in the building and construction industry was given a formal first reading in the Commons... There had been a definite increase in the lump in the past 10 years. **1974** *Shelter News* Easter 3/2 Some companies already party to the agreement admit a limited use of lump labour and argue very convincingly that they have little choice if they are to meet completion dates.

g. *U.S. slang.* A parcel of food given to a tramp or vagrant. Cf. Eng. dial. *lump,* a luncheon (see *E.D.D.*).

1912 D. LOWRIE *My Life in Prison* ix. 105, I noticed he had a lump (lunch) with him. **1914** JACKSON & HELLYER *Vocab. Criminal Slang* 56 *Lump,* current chiefly amongst yeggs, hobos, and the indigent. A donation of victuals intended for consumption outside the house. **1926** J. BLACK *You can't Win* vi. 67 She'll give you a sit-down for yourself, chances are, but bring back a 'lump' for us. **1931** 'D. STIFF' *Milk & Honey Route* xiv. 161 It may be that he has the boy along only to wash his clothes or to bum his lumps. **1967** K. ALLSOP *Hard Travellin'* xviii. 214, I met a husky burly taking of his rest And he flagged me with a big lump and a can.

h. *pl.* Hard knocks, scolding.

1935 *Jrnl. Abnormal Psychol.* XXX. 363 *Lumps, get the,* to [be] beaten up. **1949** [see *FOOT *sb.* 29]. **1970** J. H. GRAY *Boy from Winnipeg* 32 My father would sit and take his verbal lumps, saying nothing. **1971** B. MALAMUD *Tenants* 130 Now I take my lumps, he thought. Maybe for not satisfying Mary.

4. b. (Earlier example.)

1849 N. KINGSLEY *Diary* (1914) 53 The farther north we get the more our anxiety is increased, as those big lumps are not quite eradicated from our minds yet.

5. d. (Later examples.)

1923 H. G. WELLS *Men like Gods* I. viii. 143 We shall all be..judged in a lump. **1934** G. B. SHAW *Too True to be Good* Pref. 9 The unqualified assertion that the rich, in a lump, are miserable.

7*. *slang.* The workhouse (see also quot. 1933).

1874 HOTTEN *Slang Dict.* 219 *Lump,* the workhouse; also called the Pan. **1898** J. D. BRAYSHAW *Slum Silhouettes* 146 If Sal can't bury me, the 'Lump''ll have to. **1933** 'G. ORWELL' *Down & Out* xxxii. 236 These..are some of the cant words now used in London... The lump —the casual ward. **1972** G. F. NEWMAN *You Nice Bastard* 347 *In the lump,* in the workhouse.

8. *lump-lac, -tobacco;* **lump-sugary** *a.*, suggestive of lump-sugar.

1815 KIRBY & SPENCE *Introd. Entomol.* I. x. 317 In this country..it is distinguished by the names..Lump-lac when melted and made into cakes. **1873** *Beeton's Dict. Commerce* s.v. *Lac,* Lump lac is the deposit [of lac] formed into cakes. **1909** *Chambers's Jrnl.* Sept. 585/2 The body has a dry, lump-sugary appearance. **1851** C. CIST *Sk. Cincinnati in 1851* 244 Charles Bodmann..manufactures lump tobacco.

lump, *sb.*[2] Add: **1.** (Later examples.)

1844 *Knickerbocker* XXIV. 471 We discussed the merits of dun-fish,..lump, halibut,..and trout. **1867** [see *BAGATY, BAGGETY]. **1969** A. WHEELER *Fishes Brit. Isles & N.-W. Europe* 345 (*heading*) Lumpsucker (Sea Hen, Hen-fish, Lump).

2. lump-fish, lump sucker: later examples.

1969 H. HORWOOD *Newfoundland* 223 A lumpfish that I weighed on a pier-head in Conception Bay a few years ago went over thirty pounds. **1972** *Country Life* 30 Nov. 1541/3 You can afford to entertain with the real thing [*sc.* Sevruga caviar] and not pass off Danish Lumpfish roe (dyed black) as a substitute. **1974** *Observer* (Colour Suppl.) 15 Dec. 76/2 The lumpfish, known also as the cock- or hen-paddle on account of the thick crest shaping its back, is a creature of character. *Ibid.*, There is lumpfish caviare, which comes dyed black, and pearly, in small glass pots from Iceland and Denmark. **1959** A. HARDY *Fish & Fisheries* x. 193 Another surprise in this first haul was a lumpsucker *Cyclopterus lumpus* which I had previously decided to leave out of the book, thinking it to be an entirely coastal species... Its body is covered with little protuberances giving it a somewhat toad-like appearance; but it is bright with a pink hue on its lower parts. **1974** *Observer* (Colour Suppl.) 15 Dec. 76/2 They [*sc.* the female lumpfish] swim off leaving the males in charge, who cling to the rock by means of a suction disc between the pelvic fins—hence yet another name, lumpsucker.

lump, *v.*[3] Add: **2. a.** *spec.* in *Taxonomy*: To classify (plants and animals) without using minute variations as a basis for the establishment of a large number of different species or genera. Cf. LUMPER *sb.* 3 (in Dict. and Suppl.).

1893 [in Dict.]. **1945** A. YOUNG *Prospect of Flowers* xx. 151 Our Village Schoolmistress carries lumping to an extreme degree. **1962** MACKWORTH-PRAED & GRANT *Birds S. Third Afr.* I. p. xi, It will be noted that we have not followed the modern trend of 'lumping' species and that we keep specific rank in this work for more birds than is usual nowadays. **1973** *Nature* 30 Mar. 353/1 The general absence of subgenera and species groups [in Chiarelli's classification of primates], combined with some tendency to 'lump' has meant the virtual disappearance of certain significant distinctions.

6. (Influenced by LUMPER *sb.* 1.) To act as a lumper, to load or unload cargoes. Hence, (*colloq.*) to carry or shift (something heavy) *about.* Also **lu·mping** *vbl. sb.*

1890 BARRÈRE & LELAND *Dict. Slang* II. 33/2 (Thieves), to *lump* the lighter, to be transported. In this case to *lump* signifies to load. **1905** *Westm. Gaz.* 10 Oct. 10/1 He..soon had the squad of irregulars at hard work 'lumping' as heartily as any gang of dock labourers. **1911** 'KIWI' *On Swag* 14 For a month or so [I] was lumping on the wharf at the Spit. **1925** A. B. ARMITAGE *Cadet to Commodore* vi. 43, I earned sixteen shillings a week by 'lumping' in the docks. **1946** K. TENNANT *Lost Haven* (1947) xiii. 201 'I promised her a salmon.' He felt a fool lumping the great thing about.

lumped, *ppl. a.* Add: **2.** *Electr.* (Containing impedances or circuit elements) localized at a particular point or points, rather than distributed uniformly throughout part of a circuit.

1912 A. E. KENNELLY *Applic. Hyperbolic Functions to Electr. Engin. Probl.* iii. 35 This semi-angle cannot be correct, because it is based on a lumped leakance instead of a distributed leakance as assumed. **1948** E. G. BOWEN *Text-bk. Radar* xiii. 439 The units are connected by a low impedance coaxial cable which..is equivalent to a lumped capacity at video frequencies. **1967** *Electronics* 6 Mar. 163/1 Factors that combine to make analysis of crosstalk difficult are:.. The distributed, rather than lumped, nature of the inductances and capacitances of the circuits involved. **1973** B. KINARIWALA et al. *Linear Circuits & Computation* i. 4 We will confine ourselves to the discussion of lumped circuits—that is, circuits composed entirely of lumped elements.

lumpenproletariat (lʊ·mpənprōulĭtēə·riăt). [a. G. *lumpenproletariat* (K. Marx 1850, in *Die Klassenkämpfe in Frankreich* and 1852, in *Der achtzehnte Brumaire des Louis Bonaparte*), f. *lumpen,* rag (*lump* ragamuffin: see LUMP *sb.*[1]) + *proletariat* (see PROLETARIATE, -AT).] A term applied, orig. by Karl Marx, to the lowest and most degraded section of the proletariat; the 'down and outs' who make no contribution to the workers' cause. So **lu·mpenproleta·rian** *a.* and *sb.* Also **lu·mpen** *a.*, boorish, stupid, unenlightened, used derisively to describe persons, attitudes, etc., supposed to be characteristic of the lumpenproletariat; also *ellipt.* or as *sb.*

1924 H. KUHN tr. *Marx's Class Struggles France* I. 38 The financial aristocracy, in its methods of acquisition as well as in its enjoyments, is nothing but the reborn *Lumpenproletariat,* the rabble on the heights of bourgeois society. **1936** R. GESSNER *Some of my Best Friends are Jews* xxii. 306 No bandits dared attack her desperate inhabitants, the rough and dangerous Jews who had become lumpen-proletarians under the Czar. **1937** F. BORKENAU *Spanish Cockpit* i. 15 A not unimportant number of these 'lumpenproletarian' elements have joined the anarchist movement. **1940** 'G. ORWELL' *Inside Whale* 132 The lumpen-proletarian fringe..composed partly of genuine artists and partly of genuine scoundrels. **1942** *New Statesman* 17 Oct. 255/1 He [*sc.* Hitler] mixed with the *Lumpen-proletariat,* the nomadic outcasts in the no-man's-land of society. **1944** KOESTLER in *Horizon* Mar. 167 Thus the intelligentsia..becomes the Lumpen-Bourgeoisie in the age of its decay. **1948** J. STEINBECK *Russ. Jrnl.* (1949) ix. 220 This journal will not be satisfactory either to the ecclesiastical Left, nor the lumpen Right. **1949** A. WILSON *Wrong Set* 57 Like called to like. The Colonel's lady and Lily O'Grady were both 'lumpen' under the skin. **1958** *Time* 28 June 35/3 At his cinematic best a shaggy lumpen-proletarian helplessly meshed in the woof of modern life..Charlie Chaplin. **1963** D. MACDONALD *Against Amer. Grain* i. 58 The spoofs of Dada have now become the serious offerings of what one might call the lumpen-avant-garde. **1969** R. BLACKBURN in Cockburn & Blackburn *Student Power* 186 Regis Debray has suggested that the lumpen-bourgeoisie of Latin America substitute police vigilance for an authentic class consciousness. **1970** *New Yorker* 18 July 22/2 Cope, a well-known proponent of lumpen aesthetics, had met the challenge with cool authority. **1971** P. KAVANAGH *Triumph of Evil* (1972) ii. 19 The rightist reaction of the white *lumpenproletariat* is easily imagined. Their instinctive response is racist and anti-intellectual. **1972** *Times Lit. Suppl.* 6 Oct. 1202/4 The *lumpenbourgeoisie,* behind a variety of leaders, is sick of dissent—student demonstrations, anti-apartheid, pornography, drug-taking, immigration, strikes, and crime. **1972** *Times* 14 Nov. 14/8 The underlying antipathy..towards the *lumpen* masses. **1973** *Ann. N.Y. Acad. Sci.* CCXI. 128 Fortunately for a lumpen linguist like me, my job doesn't require exercise of the vernier virtuosity that one sees in Linguistic Atlas maps and synopses. **1974** *Black Panther* 27 Apr. 13/2 The outlaw and the lumpen will make the revolution. The people, the workers, will adopt it. **1974** *Listener* 2 May 598/2 These institutions are likely to be manipulated only by a comparatively favoured group in society..leaving a real *lumpen* element at the bottom.

lumper. Add: **3.** *Taxonomy.* Substitute for def.: A taxonomist who is unwilling to use minute variations as a basis for the establishment of a large number of different species or genera. (Later examples.)

1945 A. YOUNG *Prospect of Flowers* xx. 151 Botanists are divided into two classes, 'splitters' and 'lumpers', 'splitters' being those who split plants into a large number of species and sub-species, while 'lumpers', impatient of minute distinctions, are inclined to lump them together. **1967** A. W. JONES *Introd. Parasitol.* xxix. 419 The more conservative taxonomists, called irreverently 'lumpers', defended established categories from attack by the radical 'splitters'. **1972** *Sci. Amer.* Nov. 60/2 One can use the work of many different taxonomists, without regard to whether they are 'lumpers' or 'splitters' in their method of classification, as long as the work is self-consistent.

lumpers (lʊ·mpəɪz), *sb. pl. slang.* [f. *lump sum*: cf. *-ER[6].] A lump sum paid as compensation for loss of employment.

1960 *Economist* 23 July 352/2 They all give the impression that they remain happiest when a colonial official takes his 'lumpers' (lump sum compensation) and retires for good. **1963** *Punch* 17 July 77/2 The civil servants.. deprived..of their career, have the consolation of their 'lumpers'—..up to £10,000. **1965** *New Society* 11 Nov. 11/2 The settler saw the official receive the 'golden handshake' or 'lumpers'.

lumpless (lʊ·mplės), *a.* [f. LUMP *sb.*[1] + -LESS.] Having no lumps.

1908 *Daily Chron.* 3 Mar. 8/1 As soon as the ingredients are fairly worked into a lumpless, creamy whole, stop beating.

lumpy, *a.* Add: **1. b.** Also of broken weather.

1928 *Sat. Even. Post* 10 Mar. 8/1 'Had good weather?' 'Lumpy weather all the way.'

2. Applied to a person.

1926 A. BENNETT *Lord Raingo* I. xxxviii. 216 The fair but lumpy young woman silently left the room. **1928** E. O'NEILL *Strange Interlude* I. 14 Pretty vicious face under caked powder and rouge..lumpy body. **1934** *Times Lit. Suppl.* 8 Mar. 162/2 In the early nineties I was looking at Rubens's 'Rape of the Sabines' in the National Gallery, when a British workman beside me remarked, 'Lumpy lot to lift, eh?' **1959** I. & P. OPIE *Lore & Lang. of Schoolch.* ix. 168 The unfortunate fat boy..is known as..lumpy. **1973** *Observer* 5 Aug. 18/7 Lumpier and mousier, the girl grooms socialised affectionately with their ponies.

luna. 3. (Earlier and later examples.)

1869 *Amer. Naturalist* II. 679/2 Luna moth. **1876** *Field & Forest* II. 72 Mr. Rodgers..gives the history of the Luna moth. **1948** *Natural Hist.* Dec. 451/1 The Hercules moth is a close relative of the well-known Luna moth. **1972** SWAN & PAPP *Common Insects N. Amer.* 267 Luna Moth: *Actias luna*... Wings are delicate green, shading to pale gray, with transparent eyespots... Larva..resembles the Polyphemus larva except that Luna has yellow lateral stripe and no oblique stripes on the side. **1974** A. DILLARD *Pilgrim at Tinker Creek* x. 159 Luna moths are those fragile ghost moths, fairy moths, whose five-inch wings are swallow-tailed, a pastel green bordered in silken lavender.

lunabase (liū·năbēis). *Astr.* [f. L. *lūna* moon + BASE *sb.*[1] (as the sb. corresponding to the adj. *basic*, in the petrographic sense).] The lunar maria or lowlands (the dark-coloured regions as seen from the earth).

Orig. proposed for the rock composing them (see quot. 1944).

1944 J. E. SPURR *Geol. applied to Selenology* II. iv. 20 The differently colored formations which largely make up the marking of the lunar 'map' have, in the Imbrian study (volume I), been interpreted as probably corresponding to two main types of terrestrial rock: the light-gray 'uplands' as siliceous, the dark mare as basic or basaltic... In future descriptions the light-colored rocks may be called lunarite. The dark-gray mare..may be called imbase... In the mare formations south of the Mare Imbrium, a later, darker phase of presumably basic rock..may safely, and briefly, be called novabase (later lunar basaltic rock). And the inclusive term for both would be lunabase (lunar basaltic rock). **1966** *Earth Sci. Rev.* I. 231 Spurr (1944) gave the name 'lunarite' to the more highly reflective parts [of the moon's surface], and the name 'lunabase' to the darker parts. Large areas of lunarite are referred to as 'continents', and specific areas of lunabase are called 'maria'. **1967** *New Scientist* 2 Feb. 263/2 The mountains [on the moon] end with steep terminal slopes of 20° or so, which cannot be due to erosion as a result of melting by subsequent lavas from the mare region (the dark lunabase).

lunanaut: see *LUNARNAUT.

Luna Park. The name of an amusement centre on Coney Island, Brooklyn, New York; also *transf.*, any such entertainment park. Also as *v. intr.*

1911 H. HAWTHORNE *New York* viii. 53 Luna Park and Dreamland are large sections of Coney..within whose gates are real fairylands of plaster palaces. **1921** A. HUXLEY *Crome Yellow* ii. 8 The lights of Luna Park. **1930** J. COLLIER *His Monkey Wife* iii. 33 The Fun Fairs and Luna Parks of the carnal capitals of Europe. **1936** F. CLUNE *Roaming round Darling* xxiv. 244 Over a by-wash, then, Luna-parking down a big dipper, belly half-way up the other side. **1956** M. DUGGAN *Immanuel's Land* 90 Up at Tibidabo in the empty luna-park an aluminium aeroplane turns slowly at the end of a long pole. **1957** A. HEPBURN *Compl. Guide N.Y. City* (new ed.) 109 Biggest and best of the amusement centers are Steeplechase, Luna Park, Dreamland. **1967** G. GREENE *May we borrow your Husband?* 10 As squalid as a closed fun-fair with Lunar [*sic*] Park boarded up.

lunar, *a.* and *sb.* Add: **A.** *adj.* **1.** (Further examples.)

1958 *Observer* 17 Aug. 1/6 It was new moon on Friday, and the 'lunar probe' must be launched in the next two or three days or postponed for a month. **1971** *Sci. Amer.* Oct. 49/3 Type *D* material consisted of miscellaneous fines smaller than a centimeter in diameter, material sometimes called lunar soil. **1972** *Science* 2 June 1014/3 It is appropriate to define the base of the 'lunar crust' at the discontinuity at 65 km.

b. lunar orbit, (*a*) the orbit of the moon around the earth; (*b*) an orbit around the moon; **lunar window,** a launch window for a mission to the moon.

1728 *Chambers's Cycl.* II. 578/1 The transverse Diameter of the Lunar Orbit. **1834** [in Dict., sense 1]. **1968** *Guardian* 28 Dec. 9/1 The Lunar Landing Module..will shuttle two astronauts from lunar orbit, down to the moon's surface. **1969** *Daily Mail* 14 Jan. 1/2 For us, lunar orbit was the busiest time of the flight. **1969** *New Scientist* 17 July 114/2 They are inserted into an elliptical lunar orbit varying between 60 and 170 nautical miles above the Moon's surface. **1969** *Guardian* 15 Jan. 18/2 A lunar window exists for Russia at the moment. **1970** N. ARMSTRONG et al. *First on Moon* ii. 33 The time of launch..had been chosen with great care. The date and the hour had been fixed to take full advantage of the so-called 'lunar window'.

c. Employed in or relating to travel to or from the moon or on its surface; *lunar* (*excursion*) *module*, a module designed to take an astronaut from an orbiting spacecraft to the moon's surface and back (abbrev. *LM*, *LEM* (*L 7)).

1962 *Daily Tel.* 17 July 17/6 If anything should go wrong with the lunar space-craft and the astronauts found themselves unable to take off, from the moon, unmanned supply vehicles would be sent. **1962** *New Scientist* 19 July 123 At a hundred miles or so from the lunar surface retro-rockets will slow the craft into a lunar orbit. It will then be split in two, to form a mother craft and a lunar excursion module. **1965** *Punch* 20 Jan. 84/1 The great Apollo 'lunar project' by which the Americans, bless them, still hope to land a man, alive, on the Moon in 1970. **1966** *Electronics* 3 Oct. 134 The Lunar Excursion Module of the Apollo program has to descend safely as well as take off and rendezvous with the command module for the long trip home. **1967** *Technology Week* 20 Feb. 16 (*caption*) Full-size mockup of Apollo Telescope Mount..is based on Apollo Lunar Module and is being used for placement of instruments. **1969** *Daily Mail* 14 Jan. 5/2 We were to test the lunar module, the vehicle which will land on the Moon, in a high Earth orbit. **1970** N. ARMSTRONG et al. *First on Moon* i. 20 By 1962..the future programs were well designed and the lunar mission was going to become a reality. **1971** *New Scientist* 3 June 574/1 Special wire mesh wheels have been built for America's Lunar Roving Vehicle which..is to drive around the lunar surface during the Apollo 15 mission in July. **1972** *Daily Tel.* 24 Apr. 1/4 They climbed into the lunar rover to drive 3·3 miles to North Ray Crater. **1975** S. JOHNSON *Urbane Guerilla* v. 181 Neil Armstrong at last stepped down from the lunar module *Eagle* on to lunar soil.

B. *sb.* **2. b.** *colloq.* A look.

1906 GALSWORTHY *Man of Property* i. 21 Now and then he would level his umbrella and take a 'lunar', as he expressed it, of the varying heights. **1938** N. MARSH *Artists in Crime* v. 65 Let us take what used to be called a 'lunar' at the case. **1950** 'J. GUTHRIE' *Is this what I Wanted?* iii. 71 Charles took a lunar.

lunarite (liū·nărəit). *Astr.* [f. L. *lūna* moon + -ITE[1].] The lunar uplands (the light-coloured regions as seen from the earth).

Orig. proposed for the rock composing them (see quot. 1944).

1944, 1966 [see *LUNABASE]. **1967** *New Scientist* 2 Feb. 263/3 In a few places the lunarite [lava] flows seem to dip under the lunabase of the surrounding plain, indicating that the lunarite and lunabase flows may at an early time have been contemporaneous.

lunarnaut (liū·năɹnǭt). Also **lunanaut.** [f. LUNAR *a.* + *-naut*, after *aeronaut, astronaut*.] One who travels or has travelled to the moon.

1965 *Guardian* 30 Aug. 12/1 The moon men (or lunarnauts, as they will doubtless come to be called) must be able to park their spacecraft. **1966** *Electronics Weekly* 27 July 29/2 (*heading*) Lunanauts will land with a reassuring 'bump'. **1969** *Scottish Daily Mail* 13 Jan. 2/6 Lunarnaut Frank Borman warned today that space flights are 'chancy'. **1971** *Daily Tel.* 30 Jan. 3/3 The Command and Service Module orbit the Moon while the lunarnauts carry out experiments and walk on its surface.

lunarscape (liū·năɹskēip). [f. LUNAR *a.* + SCAPE *sb.*[3]] A picture or view of the moon's surface; the lunar landscape.

1965 *Newsweek* 25 Jan. 89 No one knows in detail what the lunarscape is like. **1966** *Punch* 27 Apr. 636/1 Superb blending of the Op and the Pop, comprising pointillist lunarscape in Coke bottle-tops. **1967** *Time* 25 Aug. 38 Lights flashed everywhere, bounding off the Day-Glo lunarscapes along the wall. **1970** *Guardian Weekly* 15 Aug. 12 The moon began to show out over the North Sea... Through my powerful binoculars I was able to study its face. The lunarscape looked like some great contoured globe. **1971** *New Scientist* 22 Apr. 224/1 These [paintings] include some dramatic lunarscapes.

lunate (liū·nēit), *sb. Archæol.* [f. the adj.] A small prehistoric stone (usu. flint) artifact which was probably used as an arrow-head and has an elongated half-moon shape with the straight edge unworked and the curved edge sharpened by chipping.

1932 *Jrnl. R. Anthrop. Inst.* LXII. 261 A fair proportion of lunates and other microliths showed a peculiar retouch... The back of the implement is not blunted in the ordinary way, but is trimmed obliquely from both surfaces, the result being to make it sharp instead of blunt. **1949** W. F. ALBRIGHT *Archaeol. of Palestine* iii. 59 The Natufian was a thorough-going microlithic culture, consisting largely of flint blades and points, most typical of which is the so-called lunate, a crescent or arc-shaped blade, probably used to tip reed arrows. **1960** K. M. KENYON *Archaeol. in Holy Land* ii. 36 Most characteristic of all are the lunates, very fine little flakes with a straight edge and a crescent-shaped back.

lu·nately, *adv. rare.* [f. LUNATE *a.*] In a crescent form.

1872 H. C. WOOD *Contrib. Hist. Fresh-Water Algæ N. Amer.* 109 Cells..more or less lunately curved.

lunatic, *sb.* Add: **1. c. lunatic fringe,** a minority group of fanatical adherents to a political or other movement or set of beliefs; also *attrib.*; **lunatic soup** *Austral.* and *N.Z. slang*, alcoholic drink.

1913 T. ROOSEVELT *Hist. as Lit.* 305 There is apt to be a lunatic fringe among the votaries of any forward movement. **1936** *Economist* 4 Jan. 3/1 Dr. Townsend has now left all his rivals behind in competition for the votes of the lunatic fringe. **1945** 'G. ORWELL' *England your England* (1953) 56 The lunatic fringe even contrived to be simultaneously pro-Russian and pro-Nazi. **1951** E. PAUL *Springtime in Paris* iii. 59 Most of the paintings are imitations of other paintings, either conscious or unconscious, ranging from primitives and false primitives to the latest lunatic fringe. **1953** *Manch. Guardian Weekly* 21 May 15/4 Five [letters]..refer to his 'plug-ugly tactics', the 'lunatic fringe' brand of anti-communism. **1958** *Times* 9 Sept. 9/3 The lunatic fringe of society, to which only too many irresponsible hoaxers here and in America belong, finds the telephone its best friend. **1968** *Guardian* 12 Dec. 9/1 Lunatic-fringe Utopians call for something entirely new. **1969** *Observer* 23 Nov. 25/3 Views like these, as anyone who has listened to a few conversations on the verandahs of suburban Kingston will recognise, aren't lunatic fringe. **1970** *Ibid.* 11 Oct. 32/3 Both sides..have what you might call lunatic fringes; on the middle-aged right there are those who would lynch anyone with long hair, on the young left..there are those who refuse to state their case rationally. **1973** D. RAMSAY *Deadly Discretion* 175 Antique shops were magnets for the lunatic fringe. **1933** *Bulletin* (Sydney) 6 Sept. 42/1 Lunatic soup, as the few fellows about who knew him as Darkie called the brandy he drank. **1941** BAKER *Dict. Austral. Slang* 45 *Lunatic soup*, cheap red wine.

lunation. 2. Delete † *Obs.* and add later example.

1953 A. C. CLARKE *Prelude to Space* xxii. 115 If..there's a last-minute hold-up, launching will be delayed.., at the most, thirty-six hours. After that we'll have to wait for the next lunation—that is, for four weeks... We're anxious to land in daylight.

lunch, *sb.*[2] Add: **2.** (Later examples.) Now in common use for LUNCHEON 2. Also, a light meal at any time of the day.

1936 *S.P.E. Tract* XLV. 183 In several..instances a word has been liberated in America from the restrictions that limit its application in England; for example..*lunch*. **1950** E. A. MCCOURT *Home is Stranger* (1951) viii. 124 At midnight the womenfolk hurried out to the hall to prepare lunch. **1951** *Good Housek. Home Encycl.* 540 *Lunch*, the midday meal..may cover anything from the sandwich lunch taken by some office and factory workers to the fairly elaborate formal meal given when guests are entertained at a public function or private party. **1960** S. PLATH *Colossus* (1967) 20, I open my lunch on a hill of black cypress. **1964** L. DIACK *Labrador Nurse* I. vii. 37 After a 'lunch' (i.e. a snack), all hands..would set to work. **1965** J. S. GUNN *Terminol. Shearing Industry* I. 36 *Lunch*, a light snack which was taken at the mid-morning or mid-afternoon break... Lunch was food taken at any time away from main meals, even in the evening. **1968** *New Society* 22 Aug. 265/2 Though the U still have lunch (not dinner) in the middle of the day and U-dogs still have their dinner then, U-children have changed; they no longer have mid-day dinner, in the nursery, but have lunch with their mothers.

b. *out to lunch*: insane; stupid, unaware; socially unacceptable. *N. Amer. slang.*

1955 *Sci. Digest* Aug. 33/1 'Out to lunch' refers to someone who, in other years, just wasn't 'there'—and he is told immediately to 'Get with it!' **1959** *She* May 21/2 *Out to lunch* has nothing to do with social life but implies one is not in the groove. **1966** *Toronto Daily Star* 16 June 74/2 A girl who would be attracted to Bud's mean streak and bad temper must be a little out to lunch. **1974** *Melody Maker* 13 July 13/5, I think he's out to lunch. He's blown out—completely.

3. *lunch-bell, -box, -break, -cake, -can, -counter, -date, -hour, -house, -money, -pail, -party, -room, -stand, -tin, -wagon.*

1875 MRS. STOWE *We & Neighbors* v. 67 The ringing of the lunch bell interrupted the conversation. **1864** *Rep. Comm. Patents 1862* (U.S.) I. 158 *Improved Lunch Box*... This invention consists of an arrangement of dishes, cups, etc., arranged within a case for the use of travellers. **1921** *Daily Colonist* (Victoria, B.C.) 23 Oct. 6/1 (Advt.), Folding lunch boxes. **1970** G. GREER *Female Eunuch* 233 Her house is ideally a base which her tired-warrior hunter can withdraw to..while he..is prepared by laundry and toilet and lunch-box for another sortie. **1960** *News Chron.* 14 June 6/6 Half of today's secretaries are married women and rely on the lunch break to do..their shopping. **1971** C. STORR *Thursday* xii. 133 She timed herself to reach the [building] site just before the lunch break. **1886** M. L. DODS *Handbk. Pract. Cookery* (new ed.) 219 Lunch Cake,.. Bake in a moderate oven for one hour and a quarter. **1901** *Daily Colonist* (Victoria, B.C.) 27 Oct. 7/2 Our buns, scones and lunch cakes are the acme of perfection. **1951** *Good Housek. Home Encycl.* 540/2 *Lunch cake*, a fairly plain, substantial fruit cake. **1897** R. M. STUART *In Simpkinsville* 14 They'd give him biscuits out o' their lunch-cans. **1869** *Demorest's Young Amer.* Oct. 460 (*caption*) Eating at a small lunch counter or eating-saloon. **1904** G. S. FULLERTON *Syst. Metaphysics* xv. 242 To obtain a sandwich from the woman at the lunch-counter. **1934** *Archit. Rev.* LXXVI. 159/1 (*caption*) Lunch counter with recessed stainless steel front. **1960** *New Statesman* 26 Mar. 435/2 Possibly President Eisenhower will be a shade or two happier when a coloured Georgian and a white Georgian, seated on adjacent stools, have pie and coffee at a Woolworth lunch-counter in Atlanta—and possibly he may not. **1970** *Times* 23 Mar. 13/3 A nostalgic echo of those days when it seemed that all

we had to do to achieve integration was to sit down at enough lunch counters together. **1933** *Radio Times* 14 Apr. 95 A tragic lunch date. **1968** *Listener* 25 July 103/3 A message came regretting he could not keep our lunch date, because he must be sure to cast his vote. **1908** Kipling *Lett. of Travel* (1920) 129 Canadian Clubs.. assemble their members during the mid-day lunch-hour. **1909** H. G. Wells *Ann Veronica* xiv. 302 She waited in the laboratory at the lunch-hour. **1929** *Radio Times* 8 Nov. 426/1, 1.15–2.0. A lunch hour concert. **1959** J. O'Donovan *Visited* xviii. 116 Edith sat by the phone all the lunch-hour. **1846** *Knickerbocker* XXVIII. 558 The following parody was found inscribed on the newspaper-board of a 'lunch-house' in Saint Louis, Missouri. **1902** G. H. Lorimer *Lett. Merchant* viii. 108 One of those fellows..goes around and makes the boys give up their lunch money to buy flowers. **1955** M. Gilbert *Sky High* x. 144 Sixpence a week and their lunch money. That's all they get. **1891** M. E. Wilkins *New Eng. Nun* 44 Matilda came in her voluminous alpaca, with her tin lunch-pail on her arm. **1926** E. Hemingway *Torrents of Spring* x. 71 He set down his lunch-pail. **1964** M. Gallant in R. Weaver *Canad. Short Stories* 2nd Ser. (1968) 77 There was an unbridgeable gap..between the girl whose father went off to work with a lunch pail and the daughter of a man who ate..in the company cafeteria. **1884** F. M. Crawford *Amer. Politician* I. iii. 43 At a lunch party..they sat and talked about pictures. **1936** H. Nicolson *Let.* 19 Feb. (1966) 244, I gave a lunch-party. **1961** New Eng. Bible *Luke* xiv. 12 When you give a lunch or dinner party. **1830** *N.Y. Mercantile Advertiser* 16 Aug. 4/6 His Breakfast, Lunch and Dining rooms are capacious and comfortable. **1919** Lunch room [see *hole *sb.* 7 b]. **1958** *New Statesman* 1 Feb. 143/1 By the end of the novel, Flem..having by trickery acquired a half-interest in a Jefferson lunch-room has taken himself off to the county seat. **1887** C. B. George *40 Yrs. on Rail* v. 79 Superintendent Johnson..noticed this lunch-stand, with its modest, yet appetizing display. **1950** *N.Z. Jrnl. Agric.* Aug. 191/1 Lunch tins which can be painted attractive colours are easily washed, inexpensive, and light and convenient to carry. **1894** *Life* 4 Oct. 215/1 'That, my dear,' responded Adalbert, 'is a lunch wagon.' **1959** N. Mailer *Advts. for Myself* (1961) 69 Inside, out of the rain, the lunch wagon was hot and sticky.

luncheon. Add: **2. b.** *U.S.* Applied to a late supper.

1903 *Boston Even. Transcript* 3 Oct. 5 At this table, from 9 o'clock until midnight, a bountiful standing luncheon was served continuously.

3. *luncheon-basket* (earlier and later examples); **luncheon-car,** on a railway train, a restaurant-car where luncheons are provided; also *attrib.*; † **luncheon-dinner** = *lunch-dinner* (Lunch *sb.*² 3); **luncheon meat,** a type of pre-cooked meat containing preservatives; **luncheon voucher,** a money voucher given to employees which is exchangeable for meals at certain restaurants.

1859 Queen Victoria *Jrnl.* 7 Oct. in D. Duff *Victoria in Highlands* (1968) 159 Our pony carried the luncheon baskets. **1958** J. Cannan *And be a Villain* i. 15 Ah, the Victorian railways!..the luncheon baskets you wired ahead for. **1903** A. Bennett *Leonora* vii. 203 The express, with its two engines, its gilded luncheon-cars, and its post-office van. *Ibid.* 204 Catching the luncheon-car attendant by the sleeve. **1909** *Westm. Gaz.* 8 Sept. 2/1 A new luncheon-car express, starting from King's Cross at 1.5 p.m. **1970** *Country Life* 31 Dec. 1293/1 On the next stage north there was a luncheon car, and at The Mound he ate his lunch. **1819** M. Edgeworth *Let.* 4 Mar. (1971) 178 After luncheon-dinner I finished at Oxford. **1882** W. D. Hay *Brighter Britain!* I. ii. 25 There are three common meals—breakfast, luncheon-dinner, and dinner-supper. **1945** 'R. Crompton' *William & Brains Trust* ix. 166 Although it meant opening her last remaining tin of Luncheon Meat. **1953** J. Hunt *Ascent Everest* iv. xii. 155 Over our bacon and, possibly, eggs or fried luncheon meat. **1957** E. Craig *Collins Family Cookery* 814 Dice luncheon meat and use as a filling for bread. **1960** A. E. Bender *Dict. Nutrition* 76/2 *Luncheon Meat*..must have a meat content not less than 80%. **1955** *Evening Standard* 28 Oct. 15/3 (*heading*) Doorman/timekeeper for staff and goods entrance... Pension scheme, welfare fund, luncheon vouchers, etc. **1966** A. La Bern *Goodbye Piccadilly* v. 48 Their wallets contained more luncheon vouchers than treasury notes. **1973** *Times* 24 Jan. (Security Conf. Printing Suppl.) p. i/3 The notes in our wallets, stamps for letters..luncheon vouchers..are a few of the little pieces of paper so essential to modern life.

luncheonette. orig. *U.S.* [Luncheon 2 + -ette.] A small restaurant or snack bar serving light lunches.

1924 *Public Opinion* 11 July 31/2 Luncheonettes supply icecream soda and a ham sandwich. **1930** J. O. Dahl (*title*) Soda fountain and luncheonette management. **1939** C. Morley *Kitty Foyle* viii. 74 Sparta's, a Greek candy and luncheonette a block farther up Main. **1959** *New Statesman* 24 Oct. 534/3 They sleep late, meet on the corners, drift in and out of the poolrooms and the luncheonettes. **1969** *New Yorker* 20 Sept. 38/2 A luncheonette, where a couple of young men in shirt sleeves sat hunched over the counter eating..noodle soup. **1972** *Daily Tel.* 10 Apr. 9/8 France is to have 100 quick-lunch restaurants *à l'Anglaise*. .. These luncheonettes will all be along France's main highways. **1974** D. Ramsay *No Cause to Kill* i. 44 She didn't care for luncheonette food.

lunching, *vbl. sb.* [f. Lunch *v.*] The action of taking lunch. Also *attrib.*

1920 R. L. Alsaker *Maintaining Health* 271 Lunching before going to bed is a bad habit. **1968** *Economist* 18 May 74/2 One can see bloated central staffs, outside directors who are appositely called 'lunching directors' and cannot control their management colleagues in any way.

lu·nchless, *a.* [f. Lunch *sb.*² + -less.] Having had no lunch; without lunch.

1904 Kipling *Traffics & Discov.* 339, I found myself stranded, lunchless, on the sea-front. **1920** Galsworthy *In Chancery* iii. i. 244 Sitting lunchless in the hall of his hotel. **1958** E. Newby *Short Walk in Hindu Kush* ii. 17 In my lunchless state I envied them.

lu·nch-time. [f. Lunch *sb.*² + Time *sb.*] The time at which lunch is eaten. Also *attrib.*

1859 Geo. Eliot *Let.* 10 Oct. (1954) III. 180 He can't take us wrongly any day either at 1 o'clock, (lunch-time) or at half past 5 (dinner). **1866** G. M. Hopkins *Lett. to R. Bridges* (1955) 5 He..left me at lunch-time. **1890** [see Lunch *sb.*² 3]. **1909** H. G. Wells *Ann Veronica* xiv. 290 Capes came into the laboratory at lunch-time. **1929** *Radio Times* 8 Nov. 389/2 The lunch-time programme arranged by Mr. Christopher Stone. **1957** Manvell & Huntley *Technique Film Music* 235 Kisenga, an African musician..is seen playing this work in a reconstruction of the war-time National Gallery lunch-time concerts. **1963** *Times* 22 May 9/5 We'll be at the coast by lunchtime and the children can't wait for a swim and neither can I. **1968** J. Bingham *I love, I Kill* xv. 222 Have me thrown out, boyo. If you hurry up, it'll make the lunchtime editions. **1971** D. Crystal *Ling.* i. 11 There is at least one teachers' common-room..where problems of etymology..provide the normal, lunch-time gossip.

‖ **lundum** (lu·ndəm). [Pg.] A primitive Portuguese song and dance, from which the *fado* probably developed.

1936 R. Gallop *Portugal* xi. 252 The *lundum*..shared the affections of the Lisbon populace from the last quarter of the eighteenth to the middle of the nineteenth century. The *lundum* came to Portugal from Brazil... It reached Brazil from the west coast of Africa. **1957** R. Campbell *Portugal* ix. 191 It was this crossing of the primitive sensual ferocity and black, wailing misery of the negro *lundum*..that gave us the *fado*. **1957** [see *belly-dancing s.v. *belly *sb.* 17]. **1969** S. Bradford *Portugal & Madeira* 27 With them [*sc.* Angolan slaves] went memories of their native dances, one of them being the lundum, a dance of Congolese origin.

lunette. Add: **15.** *Physical Geogr.* A broad shallow mound of wind-blown material built up along the leeward side of a lake basin, esp. in arid parts of Australia, and typically having a crescent shape with the concave edge of the crescent along the lake shore.

1940 E. S. Hills in *Austral. Geographer* III. vii. 15 (*title*) The lunette, a new land form of aeolian origin. *Ibid.* 15/1 Along the eastern shores of almost every lake and swamp in the plains of northern Victoria there occurs a crescentic ridge of silty clay or clay 'loam'... It is..proposed to designate them by a new term—*lunette*. **1942** C. A. Cotton *Geomorphology* (ed. 3) xx. 275 Dust captured from the air during gales that produce dust storms is brought down by spray whipped up from lakes, so that crescentic mounds of loamy material of this origin grow up immediately to leeward of the lakes. Being rarely more than 20 or 30 feet high these broad mounds are not conspicuous unless they rise from very level plains, as is the case in south-eastern Australia, where there are many examples of such landscape forms, there termed lunettes. **1957** G. E. Hutchinson *Treat. Limnol.* I. i. 127 The most important type of wind action in forming lake basins..is deflation or wind erosion. The clearest evidence of this process is provided by those cases in which the deflated material is piled up as a curved mound of sand or *lunette*..along the lee shore of the depression.

lung. Add: **6. a.** *lung cancer, function.* **b.** *lung-breathing, -bursting* adjs.

1907 *Westm. Gaz.* 1 June 16/3 The complete proof of this evolution of the lung-breathing four-footed creatures of the earth from purely aquatic forms has been lost. **1949** *Oxf. Jun. Encycl.* II. 359/2 If the larval form [of the Axolotl] is kept..it will gradually turn into the mature, lung-breathing salamander. **1971** S. Cavell *World Viewed* vii. 41 Baudelaire's..lung-bursting inflation of Delacroix. **1973** C. Bonington *Next Horizon* xxi. 286 The last length of rope..was the most strenuous of all, taking two hours of lung-bursting effort to reach the top. **1926** *Jrnl. Amer. Med. Assoc.* 17 July 147/1 A diagnosis of endothelioma has been made frequently in primary lung cancers. **1953** *Newsweek* 25 May 60 Dr. Alton Ochsner..believes that lung cancer..'is unquestionably due to the carcinogenic effect of cigarette smoking'. **1975** 'G. Black' *Big Wind* ii. 39 When she was still a deb..lung cancer was still diagnosed as galloping consumption. **1966** *Lancet* 24 Dec. 1386/1 Systematic lung-function studies were not carried out in these patients.

7. lung book, a lamellate respiratory organ found in spiders, scorpions, and certain other arachnids; cf. *book-lung* (*book *sb.* 18); **lung-fish** (later example); **lung fluke,** a parasitic trematode flatworm of the genus *Paragonimus*; also *attrib.*; **lung snail,** a snail of the order Pulmonata (see Pulmonate *sb.*).

[**1861** J. Blackwall *Hist. Spiders Great Brit.* i. 4 The internal organs of respiration in connection with the anterior pair of stigmata present the appearance of membraneous sacs formed by lamellæ applied to one another like the leaves of a book.] **1881** E. R. Lankester in *Q. Jrnl. Microsc. Sci.* XXI. 541 The lamellæ of the Scorpion's lung-book. **1932** Borradaile & Potts *Invertebrata* xv. 447 The spiders, at least, have passed through a primitive lung-book stage from which they have not all emerged. In fact they show all the stages of replacement of lung books by tracheae. **1971** *Nature* 12 Feb. 455/1 The species [*sc. Micrathena gracilis*, a spider] possesses a well-developed stridulatory organ with a file on the cover of the lung book (the respiratory organ). **1968** A. S. Romer *Procession of Life* viii. 165 The dipnoans owe their popular name of lungfishes to the fact that, except for two ray-finned fishes..they are the only living fishes to possess these air-breathing structures. **1900** Stiles & Hassal in *16th Ann. Rep. Bureau Animal Industry, U.S. Dept. Agric.* 560 (*title*) The lung fluke (*Paragonimus westermanni*) in swine and its relation to parasitic hemoptysis in man. **1931** *Jrnl. Amer. Vet. Med. Assoc.* LXXVIII. 229 (*title*) Lung flukes of the genus Paragonimus in American mink. **1937** *Discovery* Feb. 34/2 The lung-fluke disease, or paragonim[i]asis, of which they [*sc.* mitten crabs] are a carrier in China, does not really threaten Europe as yet. **1970** *Black's Vet. Dict.* (ed. 9) 516/1 Lung flukes attack cats, dogs, pigs, and man in the Far East and the United States. **1909** *Westm. Gaz.* 26 June 15/2 The land and most of the freshwater snails belong to the lung snails, the gills being reduced to a mere vestige.

Lung-ch'üan (luŋtʃuā·n). The name of a district in the province of Chekiang, China, used to designate a type of Chinese celadon ware produced mainly during the Sung dynasty (A.D. 960–1279).

1904 E. Dillon *Porcelain* v. 63 Lung-chuan ware was made during Sung times. **1936** *Burlington Mag.* Jan. 9/1 The lovely green celadons of Lung-ch'üan... Soon it may be possible to identify the celadons made at the different factories of the Lung-ch'üan district. **1960** H. Hayward *Antique Coll.* 62/1 Typical [of Celadon wares] are..the much-exported Lung-chüan celadons of the Sung and Ming dynasties. **1971** L. A. Boger *Dict. World Pott. & Porc.* 56/1 The characteristic Sung Lung-ch'üan celadon has a body that approaches a white porcelain in character, but its main glory rests in the radiant, light bluish-green glaze.

lunge, *sb.*² **2.** (Earlier example.)

1845 J. J. Hooper *Taking Census* in *Some Adventures Simon Suggs* 155 That was a most unfortunate lunge I made into that hole in the river.

lunge, *sb.*³ Substitute for def.: Either of two large North American freshwater fishes, *Salvelinus namaycush*, a char or lake trout found in northern lakes, or *Esox masquinongy*, a pike found in the Great Lakes. (Earlier and later examples.)

1851 *Vermont Laws* 49 Such person or persons shall forfeit and pay..the sum of one dollar for each trout or lunge so taken. **1857** *Porter's Spirit of Times* 11 Apr. 86/3 The lower end of the lake..is supplied with the large cat-fish,..Oswego, black, longe, great-bass, pike-perch, perch, &c. **1902** *Jrnl. Amer. Folk-lore* Oct. 246 *Longe* or *lunge*, a common abbreviation of *muskelunge* (*maskalonge*) among English-speaking people in the region about the Great Lakes. **1953** *Canad. Geogr. Jrnl.* XLVII. 17/1 Recently, thanks to government hatcheries, 'lunge has been added to the menu.

lungful. Add: (Later examples.) *spec.* a quantity of inhaled cigarette-smoke.

1942 *R.A.F. Jrnl.* 3 Oct. 33 The little man accepted a cigarette.., drawing down a lungfull of smoke. **1964** 'E. Lathen' *Accounting for Murder* (1965) xiv. 128 He sucked a healing lungful of smoke. **1973** A. Hunter *Gently French* ii. 20 He pulled in a contemptuous lungful. **1973** P. Malloch *Kickback* xxix. 154 Hold your breath all the time. You don't want to get a lungful.

‖ **lung-gom-pa** (lu·ŋgɒmpa). Also **lung-pa.** [Tibetan.] A Tibetan monk who has the mystical power of walking many miles at great speed without stopping.

1931 A. David-Neel *With Mystics & Magicians in Tibet* vi. 200, I met the first *lung-gom-pa* in the Chang thang of Northern Tibet. *Ibid.*, The feat expected from the *lung-gom-pa* is one of wonderful endurance rather than of momentary extreme fleetness... True *lung-gom-pas* must be very rare. **1937** *Times Lit. Suppl.* 7 Aug. 579/1 He claims to have seen *lung-gom-pas* on two occasions. These are hermits who are said to have gained the power of travelling a hundred miles a day on their own feet. **1952** E. Mossbacher tr. *Maraini's Secret Tibet* iii. 51 *Lung-pa*, ..the 'wind-men'—monks who, after years of extreme asceticism and strenuous preparation, succeed in freeing themselves almost completely from the weight of the human frame and are therefore able to travel hundreds of miles in a single day. **1954** W. Noyce *South Col* iii. 39 On the boat we read two books about Buddhism. I read of 'tumo'..and 'lung-gompa', the art of going into a trance and travelling many miles at incredible speeds.

lungy, *a.* Add: **b.** Coming from the lungs.

1909 *Westm. Gaz.* 21 Apr. 2/1 As the armed companies turned this corner of the narrow road a lungey Oriental cheer..saluted each. **1935** 'R. Crompton' *William—the Detective* ix. 211 Sounds lungy to me.

lungyi (lʊ·ŋyī), var. Lungi. Cf. *longyi.

1906 W. del Mar *Romantic East* i. 8 The lungyi.. whenever the wearer can afford it, is of thin silk and is simply a square of about five feet..put on like a petticoat and folded in over the right hip. **1948** *Amer. Speech* XXIII. 228/2 *Longyi, lungyi*, Burmese skirtlike attire which falls to the ankles. The national dress, worn by both sexes. **1959** *Times* 19 Mar. 14/6 The Burmese in their gaily coloured *lungyis*.

lunik (liū·nik). *Astronautics.* Also **Lunik.** [f. L. *lūn-a* moon + *-nik, after *sputnik*, or ad.

Russ. *lúnnik* (similarly f. Russ. *luná* moon).] Any of a series of Russian spacecraft sent to or close by the moon.

1959 *Daily Tel.* 5 Jan. 16/6 The Russians had a word for the moon rocket soon enough: Lunik. Unlike Sputnik the word was not official. *Ibid.*, The only vocal demonstrations..were from the generation still young enough to qualify for..trips..aboard Luniks. **1959** H. NICOLSON *Let.* 14 Sept. (1968) 370, I hate the lunik for having bumped into the radiant moon. **1961** *Ann. Reg. 1960* 388 The Russians attempted no further 'lunik' shots. **1964** *Yearbk. Astron. 1965* 70 The Russians se[n]t up their Moon probe Lunik III, which represented the greatest triumph in space research up to that moment. [**1966** *Ann. dell'Istituto Univ. Orient., Sezione Slava* IX. 213 From the evidence presented above the fact seems to emerge that, even if *lunnik* was coined in Moscow on the morning of 3 January 1959, it was simultaneously fabricated in the West.] **1967** *Punch* 28 June 937/1 The Luniks were soon joined by American Surveyors and Lunar Orbiters and by the end of 1966, by no stretch of poetic imagination could the moon be described as companionless.

lunk (lɒŋk). *colloq.* (orig. *U.S.*) [Abbrev. of LUNKHEAD.] A slow-witted, unintelligent person.

1867 *Harper's Weekly* 25 May 330/2 They're tigers, you thick-headed lunk. **1907** J. MASEFIELD *Tarpaulin Muster* iv. 70 He's dead all right... He might ha' known..going alone among them Indians... None but a red-headed runt'd have been such a lunk as to try it. **1931** F. HURST *Back St.* II. xxvi. 231 What a lunk he continued to be! **1955** W. GADDIS *Recognitions* I. vii. 229 Most artists have a great lunk of a man they trail around with them, they never know what to do with him, he gets drunk, he gets into trouble. **1975** *New Yorker* 24 Mar. 93/3 He looks incredulous, as if he couldn't figure out how he got turned into such a lunk.

lunker (lʌ·ŋkəɹ). *N. Amer. colloq.* [Origin unknown.] An animal, esp. a fish, which is an exceptionally large example of its species; a 'whopper'. Also *attrib.*

1912 *Dialect Notes* III. 582 Isn't that calf a lunker. **1920** *Outing* July–Aug. 197, I said that I caught trout in a tin pan, and here's the proof. This old lunker of a rainbow gave me a bath. **1947** *Sports Afield* Dec. 21/1 A bronzed lunker came out of the shadowy depths and smashed the pigskin. **1968** *Globe & Mail* (Toronto) 3 Feb. 33/5 The area has been dubbed lunker country and anglers find it's more than just a slogan. **1972** *Angling Times* 6 Apr. 14/3, I shall be going out..in search of these lunker bass.

lunkhead. Delete '*colloq. U.S.*' and substitute '*colloq.* (orig. *U.S.*)'. Add earlier and later examples.

1884 'MARK TWAIN' *Huck. Finn* xxii. 225 So the duke said these Arkansaw lunkheads couldn't come up to Shakespeare. **1908** *Daily Chron.* 23 July 3/2 Now do you see, you lunkhead? **1934** WODEHOUSE *Right Ho, Jeeves* v. 52 A lunkhead capable of mucking things up as Gussie had done. **1951** E. PAUL *Springtime in Paris* ix. 165 They are not all lunkheads or mountebanks. **1966** *Punch* 7 Dec. 868/1 The poor lunkhead's concerns soon get lost under all the modelling and backlighting.

lunokhod (liū·nǒkǫd, -χǫd). *Astronautics.* Also (as the proper name of individual vehicles) with capital initial. [a. Russ. *lunokhód*, f. *luná* moon + *-khod*, suffix denoting something that travels (f. *khodít'* to go).] A type of Russian self-propelled, radio-controlled vehicle for transmitting information about the moon as it travels over its surface.

1970 *Guardian* 18 Nov. 1/2 Russia is likely to try to bring its moon crawler Lunokod-1 back to earth. **1973** *Nature* 30 Nov. 241/2 The thickness of the regolith decreased as the lunokhod approached the rille and the lip consisted of a rock 'border' with boulders of at least 1 to 2 m. *Ibid.*, Magnetometer experiments, a new feature of Lunokhod-2.

lunula. Add: **5.** *Archæol.* A gold, crescent-shaped, neck ornament found in archaeological sites of the Early Bronze Age.

1719 J. HARRIS *Hist. Kent* I. II. 249/1 Many also of the *Lunulae* were found here. **1773** *Archæologia* II. 37 The small circular plates at the extremities of the Lunula. **1867** *Archæol. Jrnl.* XXIV. 197 In another remarkable discovery of golden relics.., namely the two *lunulæ* found at Padstow.., the precious deposit was likewise accompanied by an object of bronze. **1911** *Encycl. Brit.* II. 353/1 The flat, crescent-shaped, diadem-like objects called 'lunulae', which are..characteristic of Ireland. **1939** G. CLARK *Archaeol. & Society* v. 133 If the distribution of crescentic jet necklaces and the gold 'lunula' ornaments are together plotted on the map they will be found to coincide closely with the distribution of food vessels.

Luo (lū·o), *sb.* and *a.* Also **Luoh, Lwo.** **A.** *sb.* **a.** The name of an East African people in Kenya and the upper Nile valley; a member of this people. **b.** The Nilotic language of this people. **B.** *adj.* Of or pertaining to the Luo or their language.

[**1905** C. ELIOT *E. Afr. Protectorate* viii. 148 Whereas the villages in the north are surrounded with mud walls, those of the Ja-luo are protected by a thick-set hedge of euphorbias and aloes.] **1911** *Encycl. Brit.* XV. 565/1 *Jur*, the Dinka name for a tribe of negroes of the upper Nile valley, whose real name is Luoh, or Lwo. **1942** *E. African Ann. 1941–2* **17**/1 The Luo are a Nilotic negro tribe of agriculturalists living in the hot fertile country east of Lake Victoria. **1957** W. M. HAILEY *Afr. Survey* (rev. ed.) iii. 98 There are language committees concerned with the Kikuyu and Luo languages and an increasing volume of vernacular literature is being produced. **1964** C. WILLOCK *Enormous Zoo* v. 85 A mixed horde of Kikuyu, Luo and one Turkana appeared armed with pangas. **1968** *New Scientist* 12 Dec. 599/3 The Luo, the second largest tribe in Kenya after the Kikuyu. **1968** Y. R. CHAO *Lang. & Symbolic Syst.* 99 Dinka and Luo..have almost 1 million speakers each. **1969** *Listener* 24 July 100/1 Mboya was the only Luo leader of stature still in the party hierarchy. **1970** *Guardian* 6 June 9/6 Josphat shouted something in Luo which I did not hear. **1970** *Language* XLVI. 402 Some of the so-called prefixing forms of Luo are almost isomorphic semantically with their suffixal counterparts in Tarascan.

lupinosis (liūpinōu·sis). [f. LUPINE, LUPIN *sb.* + -OSIS.] Poisoning of animals, esp. sheep, after ingestion of lupines, either that caused by the presence of lupine alkaloids in the lupines, or (and now usu. spec.) that caused by toxins produced by a fungus of the genus *Phomopsis* growing on lupines.

1899 E. V. WILCOX in *Bull. Montana Agric. Exper. Stat.* No. 22. 39 The symptoms have become so well known and are so constant and uniform that the disease caused by the lupine poisoning has been called lupinosis. **1905** MOUSSU & DOLLAR *Dis. Cattle, Sheep, Goats & Swine* II. vii. 242 The symptoms of lupine poisoning are so well known in Europe that chronic lupine poisoning has been given the name lupinosis. **1928** W. C. MILLER *Black's Vet. Dict.* 571/2 In Europe, by far the greater number of cases [of poisoning by lupines] are of a chronic type, which results in the production of a train of symptoms to which the name 'lupinosis' has been given. **1943** *N.Z. Jrnl. Agric.* LXVII. 83/3 There was considerable swelling about the head, and the skin came off the ears and the nose and also along the top of the head. These symptoms are identical with those described as occasionally occurring in cases of lupinosis. **1961** *Jrnl. Austral. Inst. Agric. Sci.* XXVII. 62/1 In 1880, 14,138 of a total number of 240,000 sheep in one district in Pomerania died of lupinosis. **1966** *Brit. Vet. Jrnl.* CXXII. 508 Lupinosis of sheep was shown to be due to the grazing of dead standing lupin roughage which had been exposed to rain after drying off in the spring. **1967** *Adv. Veterinary Sci.* XI. 86 Two distinct forms of injury are recognized in animals ingesting one or more of the several parts of lupines. The first of these is due to the pharmacologic activity of the bitter principle (a variable mixture of alkaloids) and has become variably known as lupine poisoning, alkaloidal poisoning, American lupinosis, or lupine madness. The second is an icteric disease caused by a hepatotoxin which was designated..as 'ictrogen'... The disease was called 'lupinosis', or sometimes more specifically, 'European lupinosis'. **1972** *Mycologia* LXIV. 316 Typical signs of lupinosis were produced experimentally in Merino ewes fed either naturally infected lupines or pure cultures of the fungus [sc. *Phomopsis leptostromiformis*] on autoclaved white lupine seeds.

lupulone (liū·piŭlōun). *Chem.* Also **-on** (-ǫn). [ad. G. *lupulon* (W. Wöllmer 1916, in *Ber. d. Deut. Chem. Ges.* XLIX. 781), f. mod.L. *lupulus*, used either as the specific epithet of the hop, *Humulus lupulus*, or † as a name for the genus *Humulus* (cf. L. *lupus* hop): see -ONE.] A bitter, crystalline, cyclic ketone, $C_{26}H_{38}O_4$, that is an important constituent of hops and has strong antibiotic activity.

1919 *Chem. Abstr.* XIII. 495 The so-called α- and β-bitter acids..are more appropriately termed 'humulone' and 'lupulone'. **1937**, etc. [see *HUMULONE]. **1967** *Chem. Rev.* LXVII. 26/1 While lupulone crystallizes from the soft resin of continental European hops, British and American hops yield cohumulone.

lupus. Add: **4. b.** Used in various mod.L. (or sometimes Englished) collocations to designate various forms and manifestations of *lupus vulgaris* or to designate various other skin diseases: **lupus erythematosus** [tr. F. *lupus érythémateux* (Casenave 1850, in *Gaz. des Hôpitaux* 27 July 354/3): see ERYTHEMATOUS *a.*], a disease which is now considered to be manifested in two related forms, that of chronic discoid *lupus erythematosus*, which usu. involves only the skin and causes scaly red patches to form esp. on the face, and that of systemic *lupus erythematosus*, which produces a similar skin condition but involves the connective tissues generally and is attended by widespread symptoms of illness, esp. fever, malaise, and arthralgia; **lupus vulgaris**, a tuberculous disease of the skin, characterized by the formation of brownish nodules; = LUPUS 4.

1852 *Med. Times & Gaz.* XXVI. 141 (*heading*) Treatment of lupus exedens. **1857** *Lancet* 1 Aug. 116/2 (*heading*) Horrible deformity from lupus vorax. **1860** *Boston Med. & Surg. Jrnl.* LXII. 462 In lupus vulgaris it [*sc.* a liquid remedy] is seldom used, but in lupus erythematosus it may be considered a true specific. **1878** *Lancet* 13 July 35/1 (*heading*) Clinical lecture on disseminated follicular lupus. **1883** *Med. Chron.* (Baltimore) I. 271 (*heading*) Notes of a case of erythematous lupus complicated by the tubercular syphiloderm. **1947** *Sci. News* IV. 106 Tuberculosis can attack not only the lungs but also most other parts of the body—bones and joints, kidneys, glands, brain, and skin. In the last mentioned the disease is known under the Latin name of Lupus vulgaris. **1966** WRIGHT & SYMMERS *Systemic Path.* II. xxxix. 1547 In systemic lupus erythematosus the skin manifestations are merely part of a much more widespread disorder. **1974** PASSMORE & ROBSON *Compan. Med. Stud.* III. xxxi. 47/2 Lupus vulgaris most commonly begins in childhood.

‖ **lur**[1] (lūᵊɹ). Also **lure** (liūᵊɹ). Pl. **lurer, lures, lurs.** [Da., Norw., and Sw.] A Bronze Age musical instrument of the horn family found in Scandinavia.

1876 STAINER & BARRETT *Dict. Mus. Terms* 275/2 *Lures*, ancient Scandinavian trumpets. **1879** GROVE *Dict. Mus.* I. 56/2 There is a Swedish instrument of this kind called *Lure*. **1955** *Times* 24 May 5/5 The *lur* is still occasionally used in Denmark. **1961** C. W. MONK in A. Baines *Mus. Instruments* xi. 277 Some examples of the Danish Bronze Age *lurs*, cast in the shape of a mammoth tusk, have mouthpieces astonishingly like modern melodic brass instruments. **1968** G. JONES *Hist. Vikings* I. i. 18 The long, slender, gracefully curved lurs or trumpets. **1970** BRAY & TRUMP *Dict. Archaeol.* 136/1 Lurer come from the peatbogs of Denmark and are almost invariably found in pairs.

Lur[2] (lūᵊɹ). A member of an aboriginal people inhabiting Luristan in western Iran. Chiefly in *pl.*

1845 *Encycl. Metrop.* XXIII. 272/2 The Lurs are divided into the Písh-kúh..and Pusht kúh. **1909** *Daily Chron.* 18 Feb. 5/1 Colonel Bell formed a favourable opinion of the Lurs as a whole. **1965** B. SWEET-ESCOTT *Baker St. Irreg.* iii. 89 Most of the Persian troops had not been paid for several weeks, and..when the surrender had taken place.., they had promptly sold their rifles to the neighbouring Lurs and Kurds.

Lurex (liū·reks). Also **lurex.** The proprietary name of a type of yarn which incorporates a metallic thread; also, fabric made from this yarn.

1945 *Official Gaz.* (U.S. Patent Office) 16 Oct. 360/1 The Dobeckmun Company, Cleveland, Ohio... Lurex. For yarn and thread comprised either in whole or in part of laminated film having a metallic appearance, including gimp comprised of a filament of yarn spirally overwrapped with coated or laminated foil which has been slit to a narrow width, said overwrapping imparting a metallic appearance. **1958** *Spectator* 12 Dec. 853/1 The party from the Camberwell Jazz Club, dressed in Italian-cut jackets shot with lurex, were not enthusiastic. **1965** *Guardian* 31 Mar. 15/2 Far away in the Outer Hebrides, the crofter weavers have found pleasure as well as profit in weaving 'Lurex' threads into tweeds of an altogether new lightness and beauty. **1967** *Spectator* 4 Aug. 139/3 The curtain rises on Donald Pleasance, in lurex dressing-gown,.. kneeling before a marble urn and listening to Verdi. **1973** *Guardian* 18 June 15/2 Plain snakeskin Lurex blousons.

Lurgi (lūᵊ·ɹgi, lʌ·ɹgi). The name of the *Lurgi* Gesellschaft für Wärmetechnik m.b.H., of Frankfurt, W. Germany, used *attrib.* to denote a method of gasification suitable for low-grade coal such as lignite by reaction with steam and oxygen at high pressure; so *Lurgi gas, plant.*

1934 ROBERTS & JENKNER *Internat. Coal Carbonization* xi. 249 In the Lurgi process the heat transference occurs directly by means of hot gaseous products of combustion, which pass through the coal. **1950** D. A. TOWNEND in D. H. Bangham *Progress Coal Sci.* xxvi. 436 Lurgi gas from brown coal has the following composition. **1950** WARING & FOSTER in Foster & Lund *Econ. of Fuel Gas from Coal* v. 81 Table 17 gives..the average analyses of the gas from the Lurgi plant at Bohlen. *Ibid.* 83 The economic advantage of the Lurgi process is that gasification of a cheaper, low-rank fuel is possible and that a comparatively high-Btu gas is delivered under pressure without the expense of carburetion with oil. **1973** *Nature* 7 Dec. 326/2 The well established Lurgi process is used to gasify the coal almost completely and a gas of low calorific value..is produced. *Ibid.*, The Lurgi process converts almost all the coal into gas, unlike the system used to manufacture town gas which produces coke and tar as well. **1974** *Sci. Amer.* Mar. 20/2 In some places Lurgi plants made a gas that was distributed as city gas.

lurgy (lʌ·ɹgi). Also **lurgi.** Usu. in phr. *the dreaded lurgy.* A fictitious, highly infectious disease invented and made a byword by the Radio Goons (*GOON 4).

1954 *Radio Times* 9 Nov. 20/3 The Goon Show... Poor Arnold Fringe is suddenly stricken with the Dreaded Lurgi. .. Within a few days Lurgi has claimed nine thousand victims. **1969** I. & P. OPIE *Children's Games* ii. 75 (*heading*) The dreaded lurgy. **1971** *It* 15–29 July 5/3 The youth of Australia have been saved once more from the dreaded lurgy, marijuana. **1974** H. MACINNES *Climb to Lost World* ix. 149, I was beginning to feel weak and knew that I had caught the dreaded swamp lurgy.

luringly (liūᵊ·riŋli), *adv.* [f. LURING *ppl. a.* + -LY[2].] In a luring or enticing manner.

1897 J. L. ALLEN *Choir Invisible* xvi, This second image ..drawing always nearer, summoning him more luringly. **1961** R. CRAFT *Diary* 31 Oct. in Stravinsky & Craft *Themes & Episodes* (1966) II. 203 He talks luringly of the Favors of a houri.

Luristan (lūəristā·n). The name of a district in western Iran used *attrib.* to designate the engraved bronze articles and castings, of the twelfth century B.C., found in the region.

[**1935** L. BINYON *Spirit of Man in Asian Art* iv. 105 Persian art, as we see it in the bronzes of animals recently discovered in Luristan, propagated its motives of design among the outlying, unsettled, still nomad tribes.] **1961** *Times* 6 June 22/7 (Advt.), A pair of unique Luristan bronze cheekpieces from a bit. **1970** *Oxf. Compan. Art* 830/1 Scientific excavations..have been held to show (though it is still unproven) that the Luristan bronzes are the handwork of the Medes, an Indo-European people who ..began to infiltrate into Persia at about this period. **1971** *Ashmolean Mus. Rep. of Visitors* 1970 16 *Purchased*: seventeen 'Luristan' and 'Amlash' bronzes, Iran, late 2nd to early 1st millennium B.C.

lurk, *sb.*[1] Add: **2.** (Earlier example.)

c **1842** *Exposure of Impositions practised by Vagrants* 5 Persons who go on this lurk, generally represent themselves as Captains or Masters of merchant ships which have been wrecked, and they have, of course, lost all their property.

b. Chiefly *Austral.* and *N.Z. slang*. A scheme, 'dodge', plan of action, ruse (not necessarily implying fraud). (See also quot. 1941.)

1916 C. J. DENNIS *Songs Sentimental Bloke* 125 *Lurk*, a plan of action. **1918** [see *JERRY *v.*]. *c* **1926** [see *FREEZE *sb.*[1] 1 (i)]. **1938** *Observer* 13 Nov. 11/3 *Dart*, a scheme or racket; *lurk*, ditto. **1941** BAKER *Dict. Austral. Slang* 45 *Lurk*, a 'dodge', scheme, racket. 2. A hanger-on, an eavesdropper or sneak. **1953** A. UPFIELD *Murder must Wait* xvii. 149 Thanks a lot for the antidote... It is one hell of a good lurk. **1961** *N.Z. Listener* 17 Mar. 3/1 The Navy..is just a good lurk for those who want to delve deep into the public purse. *Ibid.* 15 Sept. 29/2, I suspect Barry Crump found he was on a good advertising lurk when he was interviewed for *Book Shop*. **1966** B. COOPER *Drown him Deep* xx. 165 She was a very rich girl indeed, and Hilary, with considerable influence over her, might well be on to a very good 'lurk'. **1967** C. DRUMMOND *Death at Furlong Post* xv. 182 If the hounds were out, the lurk was to get ahead of them and go to earth.

c. *Austral. and N.Z. slang.* A job.

1916 C. J. DENNIS *Songs Sentimental Bloke* 20, I found 'er lurk Wus pastin' labels in a pickle joint. *Ibid.* 125 *Lurk*, a regular occupation. **1958** R. STOW *To Islands* 126 'What's your lurk, mate?' 'Me? Stockman on a mission.' **1965** *Telegraph* (Brisbane) 2 June, O'Grady's current lurk is holidaying as an unpaid deck hand on the South Molle cruise ship Crest while he absorbs sunlight and material for a new book.

4. *slang.* A hiding-place; a 'hang-out'.

1906 E. DYSON *Fact'ry 'Ands* viii. 97, I come out frim me lurk, 'n' went over ther ground. **1924** *Chambers's Jrnl.* 20 Sept. 683/2 Why did the old beggar come to this secret lurk in the East End and disguise himself? **1972** *N.Z. News* 26 Jan. 4/1 The first bar I saw was the Cockney's Pride—a completely new lurk for me. **1974** J. GARDNER *Return of Moriarty* 32, I met her in a servant's lurk.

lurk, *v.* Add: **5.** [Perh. connected with LURCH *v.*[2]] In pa. pple.: beaten, lost (in a game of chance) (see also quot. 1929). *slang.*

1917 M. T. HAINSSELIN *Grand Fleet Days* xx. 172 'What-Ho!'..said the Admiral, 'not a bad idea at all! Let's have a garden..' '——' said the Watch-keepers, in the sheltered seclusion of the wardroom, knowing full well that they would be lurked for the digging. **1929** F. C. BOWEN *Sea Slang* 87 *Lurked, to be*, to be ordered to do some unpleasant job without a chance of avoiding it. **1938** C. MORGAN *Flashing Stream* III. 222 Four straight aces. Good enough? You're lurked, Sandford. **1946** J. IRVING *Royal Navalese* 111 The man who 'cuts' for drinks and loses is 'lurked for the round'.

lurker[1]. **2.** (Earlier and later examples.)

c **1842** *Exposure of Impositions practised by Vagrants* 4 Lurkers are persons who go about with briefs, containing false statements of losses by fire, shipwrecks, accidents, &c. **1925** H. LEVERAGE in *Flynn's* IV. 869/2 *Lurker*, a swindler. **1973** G. BUTLER *Coffin for Pandora* i. 27, I knew the lingo. A macer was a cheat or a sharper and a lurker was a man with a story of hard luck to tell.

lurkingly, *adv.* (Later example.)

1929 R. B. C. GRAHAM *Thirty Tales & Sk.* 178 They eyed the women just as a starving dog looks at a butcher's shop, sideways and lurkingly.

lu·rkingness. [f. LURKING *ppl. a.* + -NESS.] The quality of lurking.

1912 GALSWORTHY *Inn of Tranquility* 51 The mist.. seemed to have in its sheer silence a sort of muttered menace, a shuddery lurkingness.

lu·rkman. *Austral. slang.* [f. LURK *sb.*[1] + MAN *sb.*[1]] (See quot.)

1945 BAKER *Austral. Lang.* vii. 138 We are..originators of the following terms for various sharpers, tricksters and others who live by their wits: *spieler*..*lurk man*..and *amsterdam*.

lurrier (lʋ·riəɹ). [f. LURRY *v.* + -ER[1].] An operative in textile-printing (see quot. 1897).

1897 C. F. S. ROTHWELL *Printing Textile Fabrics* 34 The lurrier brings the colour required from the colour shop, the pieces and back-greys from the stock room, and also does any odd jobs required by the printer. **1921** *Dict. Occup. Terms* (1927) § 399 *Lurrier, lurryman*, colour carrier.

Lusatian (liusēi·ʃiăn), *sb.* and *a.* [f. med.L. *Lusatia* + -AN.] **A.** *sb.* A native or inhabitant of Lusatia, name of a former region of eastern Germany between the Elbe and the Oder; = WEND *sb.* 1. **b.** The West Slavic language spoken in Lusatia. **B.** *adj.* Of or pertaining to Lusatia or its inhabitants.

1555 R. EDEN tr. *Martyr's Decades of Newe Worlde* 290 The Slauon tounge..vsed of..the Bohemians, Lusacians, Silesians, Morauians, [etc.]. **1862** R. G. LATHAM *Elem. Compar. Philol.* 766 Lusatian language. **1877** A. H. KEANE tr. *Hovelacque's Sci. of Lang.* 275 The Sorbian, or Sorabian, called also Wendic, or Lusatian comprises two distinct varieties, High and Low Sorbian. *Ibid.* 276 About the middle of the sixteenth century the Lusatian territory was twice as extensive as at present. **1921** *19th Cent.* May 894 We need only except Lessing, who was a Lusatian. **1933** L. BLOOMFIELD *Lang.* iv. 60 One of these, *Lusatian* (*Wendish, Sorbian*), survives as a speech-island of some 30,000 persons in Upper Saxony. **1949** *Archivum Linguisticum* I. i. 89 In view of the scarcity of Lusatian literature it is to be regretted that no selections have been supplied. **1972** W. B. LOCKWOOD *Panorama Indo-European Lang.* 158 Slavonic in Lusatia—it may be termed Sorbian or Lusatian as well as (Lusatian) Wendish—falls into two divergent dialect groups.

lush, *sb.*[2] Add: **1. c.** A habitual drunkard, one addicted to drink.

1890 J. A. RIIS *How Other Half Lives* (1891) xix. 221 The first long step in crime taken by the half-grown boy.. is usually to rob a 'lush', i.e., a drunken man who has strayed his way. **1899** ADE *Doc Horne* i. 1 'My uncle didn't think so,' remarked the lush. *Ibid.* iv. 39 The drinking man, often mentioned as the lush. **1945** J. STEINBECK *Cannery Row* xxix. 124, I don't like to leave the place without a man. Some lush might get smart and the kids couldn't handle him. **1958** J. & W. HAWKINS *Death Watch* (1959) 135 She took a drink now and then, but she wasn't a lush. **1958** *Spectator* 14 Feb. 210/1 Some high-class Hollywood bitches and lushes. **1972** D. DELMAN *Sudden Death* (1973) iii. 94 He's a drunk, ain't he?.. He's a lush. And a lush is a lousy security risk.

2. lush-head, -hound, a drunkard; **lush-roller, -worker,** one who steals from drunks.

1925 H. LEVERAGE in *Flynn's* IV. 869/2 *Lush-roller*, one who robs drunken men. **1930** Lush-worker [see *GLOM *v.*]. **1935** G. INGRAM *'Stir' Train* ii. 31 He's a 'lush-hound' and I knew he must be a coward. **1945** L. SHELLY *Jive Talk Dict.* 29/1 *Lush head*, chronic drinker. **1946** MEZZROW & WOLFE *Really Blues* (1957) Dedication, To all the junkies and lushheads in two-bit scratchpads. **1948** MENCKEN *Amer. Lang.* Suppl. II. 682 A *creep-joint* or *panel-house* is one in which patrons are robbed, a *roller* or *mush-worker* is a girl who robs them, and a *lush-worker* is one who specializes in drunks. **1957** *Amer. Speech* XXXII. 278 *Zoot suit* meaning flashy clothes, and *lushhead* or *lush* for drunkard are no longer considered good jazz lingo, though they are or were in common nonjazz usage.

lush, *a.*[1] Add: **2. d.** Also, luxurious; of a woman: sexually attractive.

1939 *Punch* 8 Nov. 517/1 Business-men from neutral countries should be met with red-carpeted gangways and military bands, and passed in lush motor-cars from one feast to the next. **1942** [see *BINT *sb.*[2]]. **1958** *Economist* 8 Nov. 497/2 The egg board's lush new London headquarters.

lush, *v.*[2] Add: **3.** With *up*. **a.** *intr.* To get drunk. **b.** *trans.* To ply with drink, to make (a person) drunk. **c.** *trans.* To provide with a luxurious standard of living.

1926 MAINES & GRANT *Wise-Crack Dict.* 10/2 *Lush up*, to get drunk. **1927** K. NICHOLSON *Barker* 150 *Get lushed up*, become intoxicated. **1927** *Punch* 25 May 573/1 He at once enclosed a bit of tennis-lawn for them [*sc.* rabbits] as a *manège*..and altogether lushed them up to the good things of this world. **1933** WODEHOUSE *Mulliner Nights* ii. 48 If I lush this cat up satisfactorily, shall I not be in a position later on to make a swift touch? **1952** W. R. BURNETT *Vanity Row* (1953) xv. 107 Mr. Hobart got so lushed up... He was spilling drinks down the front of his shirt. **1959** R. GANT *World in Jug* 39 By that time Andy Mendoza had got himself lushed up and started careening around the set playing a slow drag. **1960** *News Chron.* 9 Apr. 3 (*caption*) You are lushed up on the good life and are convinced that we never had it so mechanised and marvellous. **1961** WODEHOUSE *Ice in Bedroom* i. 8, I see you're lushing up the dumb chums.

Lushai (lu·ʃai), *a.* and *sb.* Also **Lhooshai,** etc. [Native name.] **A.** *adj.* Of or pertaining to a mountainous region in India between Burma and Bangladesh, its inhabitants, or the language spoken by them. **B.** *sb.* **a.** A native or inhabitant of this region. **b.** The Tibeto-Burman language spoken there.

1862 C. U. AITCHISON *Coll. Treaties India* I. 77 On the southern frontier of Cachar lies the territory of the Lhooshai Kookees... Timber merchants are..in the habit of employing Lhooshais in felling the trees in their forests. **1868** *Ann. Indian Administration* XII. 86 Mr. N. T. Davey remarks on the difficulties..likely to result in an attempt to explore..the hilly tract lying between Cachar and Chittagong. These hills are inhabited by the Looshais. **1873** E. BALFOUR *Cycl. India* III. 499/1 In the beginning of 1871, the Looshai made a prolonged raid on the North-East Provinces of British India, but were driven back. **1874** T. H. LEWIN *Progressive Colloq. Exercises in Lushai Dial.* 3 The Lushai dialect is in fact the *lingua frânca* of the country. The clan-name Lushai probably means 'the decapitators', being derived from 'lú' a head and 'shá' or 'shát' to cut. **1876** W. W. HUNTER *Statistical Acct. Bengal* VI. 59 The Lusháis or Kukís are a powerful and independent people, split up into different clans. **1887** C. A. SOPPITT *Short Acct. Kuki-Lushai Tribes* i. 2 The Lushai people have only been known to us within comparatively recent years. *Ibid.* 4 In Hill Tipperah there are three tribes, named Paitu, Omroi, Korêng, all nearly connected with the Lushais. *Ibid.* 79 (*heading*) Comparison of the dialects of the Kuki Lushai tribes and of the language known as Lushai. **1890** KIPLING *Barrack-Room Ballads* (1892) 17 We've chivied the Naga an' Looshai, we've give the Afreedeeman fits. **1910** *Encycl. Brit.* I. 773/1 The inner line formerly maintained along the Lushai border has since 1895 been allowed to fall into desuetude, but Lushais visiting Cachar are required to take out passes from the superintendent of the Lushai hills. **1915** *Encycl. Relig. & Ethics* VIII. 198/1 The Lushais are a superstitious people, and believe firmly in witchcraft. **1959** P. C. CHOUDHURY *Hist. People of Assam* iv. 95 The Central Chin group..includes the Lushāis and other allied peoples. **1972** *Language* XLVIII. 476 The most useful Kukish language for comparative purposes has hitherto been Lushai. **1972** W. B. LOCKWOOD *Panorama Indo-European Lang.* 227 To the south of these places [*sc.* Manipur and Tripura], in the southern tip of Assam, the local language is Lushai with 250,000 speakers. **1974** *Encycl. Brit. Micropædia* VI. 396/3 Lushai villages traditionally were situated on the crests of hills or spurs and..were fortified by stockades. *Ibid.*, The Kuki clans have been largely absorbed by the Lushai, adopting the Lushai customs and language.

lu·sher. [f. LUSH *v.*[2] 2.] One who is excessively self-indulgent, especially one who drinks excessively.

1895 G. MEREDITH *Amazing Marriage* II. xxxi. 80 The suspicion cast on the dreary lusher was the wife's wild shot at her husband. **1914** *Dialect Notes* IV. 110 Once all the politicians, nearly, were lushers. **1928** M. C. SHARPE *Chicago May* 288/1 *Lusher*, lone drinker.

lushy, *a.*[1] Add: Also as *sb.*, a drunkard. *U.S.*

1944 *New Yorker* 8 July 28/2 All our horn blowers were lushies. **1945** L. SHELLY *Jive Talk Dict.* 13/2 *Lushie*, a drunkard. **1946** MEZZROW & WOLFE *Really Blues* (1957) 94 The lushies didn't even play good music.

Lusitanian, *a.* Add: **2.** *Biol.* Of plants or animals, having their origin in south-western Europe, esp. Portugal.

1907 R. F. SCHARFF *European Animals* v. 88 Almost all the members of that South-western, or Lusitanian, element in our fauna have a discontinuous range, which is a sure indication of great antiquity. **1927** PEAKE & FLEURE *Hunters & Artists* 38 It is a remarkable fact that the west of the Spanish peninsula and the south-west corner of Ireland share several peculiar plants and animals, such as the winter strawberry, the London pride, the great spotted slug, and a peculiar lacustrine shellfish. This so-called 'Lusitanian' association may be supposed to have lived on the Atlantic coast-lands of the Ice Age. **1935** *Discovery* Nov. 318/1, I look upon it [*sc.* the field cricket] as clearly a member of that group which Scharff has called Lusitanian. **1970** *Watsonia* VIII. 93 Several of the main phytogeographical elements in the British flora, including the Lusitanian, are represented in this section.

Luso- (lū·so). [f. *Lusitania* = Portugal.] In *Comb.*: of Portugal, Portuguese.

1951 SMITH & MARCHANT *Brazil* v. 146 The Brazilian Negroes are blending physically and culturally with the national types, mostly Luso-Brazilian ethnically. **1957** R. CAMPBELL *Portugal* 20 The Luso-Spanish sieges of Numantia. **1958** *Archivum Linguisticum* X. i. 30 The Luso-Hispanic frontier. **1964** *New Statesman* 3 Apr. 514/1 Portugal's assertion of complete Luso-African unity. **1969** J. MANDER *Static Society* ii. 79, I have stressed the unity that Latin America possesses in virtue of its Luso-Hispanic inheritance. **1973** *Black World* Sept. 19/1 [Jorge de Lima] taught Luso-Brazilian literature at the Federal and National Universities.

lusting, *vbl. sb.* (Later examples.)

1895 KIPLING *Seven Seas* (1896) 82 The lying, and the lusting, and the drink. **1909** *Westm. Gaz.* 18 Aug. 2/3 Thou art grim with the lusting of gain.

lustre, *sb.*[1] Add: **1. e.** In ceramics, the surface sheen produced by glazing; the material used for glazing. Also *ellipt.*, = *lustre ware* below. Hence *lustre-glazed, -painted* adjs.

1829 S. SHAW *Hist. Staffordshire Pott.* x. 227 The Lustre of our day is a good red clay body, with a fine brown glaze; upon which is laid, for Gold Lustre, a very thin coating of a chemical mixture containing a small quantity of Gold in solution. **1892** J. R. & F. KIDSON *Hist. Notices Leeds Old Pott.* 87 The Agate ware made at the Leeds Pottery was contemporary with the earliest makes of their Silver Lustre. **1897** *Sears, Roebuck Catal.* 681/2 Luster band, open Meakin's English-ware... The decorations are of a heavy luster band and a flower sprig in luster which resembles gold very closely. **1939** *Burlington Mag.* May 227/2 A lustre-glazed tile made at Valencia in the late fifteenth century. **1961** *Antiquaries Jrnl.* XLI. 9 A lustre-painted bowl of Malaga ware in the Staatliche Museen, East Berlin. **1969** G. LEWIS *Collector's Hist. Eng. Pott.* xvi. 157 The newly introduced technique of electro-plating made the silver lustre less popular and production ceased. **1973** *Country Life* 11 Nov. 1049/1 Morris's philosophy extended as much to..rush-bottomed chairs as to gold lustre.

7. *lustre bowl, china, jug, mug, tea-pot, tile*; **lustre ware** (further examples); *spec.* pottery which is given a metallic lustre by the application of a metal oxide to its surface; also *transf.*

1908 *Sears, Roebuck Catal.* 359/4 Iridescent luster bowl

made of the most select Bavarian china. **1952** M. Laski *Village* viii. 136 The furniture..consisted of..a painted pine corner cupboard with..some genuine old lustre china inside. **1908** J. M. Synge *Lett. to Molly* (1971) 276 Look round in Galway for lustre jugs or Irish curios. **1971** 'E. Ferrars' *Stranger & Afraid* i. 16 A good deal of clutter, in the way of Staffordshire teapots, lustre mugs, Bohemian glass and photographs. **1935** N. Mitchison *We have been Warned* i. 107 Miss Waterhouse would now be giving.. strong tea to her weaving class, pouring steadily from a beautiful lustre tea-pot. **1943** D. Welch *Maiden Voy.* vi. 46, I was only talking about the lustre teapot... It's shiny stuff—like metal, only china. **1933** *Burlington Mag.* Nov. 224/1 These spiral scrolls and leaves are familiar..in the thirteenth century lustre tiles. **1875** E. Meteyard *Wedgwood Handbk.* 312 After the commencement of the present century lustre-wares were generally made throughout the Potteries. **1938** *Times Lit. Suppl.* 17 Sept. 595/4 The household of the meek Jewish tailor and the home of the jolly publican are shining pieces of cockney lustre-ware. **1961** *Antiquaries Jrnl.* XLI. 1 A large cover of Hispano-Moresque lustreware, imported from Malaga. **1971** *Canad. Antiques Collector* Jan. 17/1 English lustre ware affords a fascinating variety of colour, charm and decoration for the collector.

luteal (liū·tiăl), *a.* [f. L. *lūte-us* yellow (in mod.L. *corpus luteum*: see *corpus 2) + -al.] Of or pertaining to the *corpus luteum*.

1927 *Amer. Jrnl. Anat.* XL. 211 The inhibitory effect of luteal tissue upon follicular development does not explain why certain animals have an anoestrum. **1932** E. Allen *Sex & Internal Secretions* xvi. 794 The lutenizing [*sic*] factor will not cause the luteal change in the ovary of an immature animal. *Ibid.* 795 During the luteal phase the so-called 'B' factor is utilized. **1939** S. R. M. Reynolds *Physiol. Uterus* iii. 69 The action of the luteal hormone. **1966** *Ann. Rev. Physiol.* XXVIII. 60 Prolactin may stimulate luteal function in the ferret. **1969** K. W. McKerns *Gonads* iii. 72 (*heading*) Factors affecting luteal activity in intact rabbits.

lutecium, var. *lutetium.

luteinization (liū:tīnəizēi·ʃən). *Physiol.* [f. Lutein + -ization.] The formation of lutein in the cells that remain of the Graafian follicle after expulsion of the ovum, during which process the follicle is converted into the *corpus luteum*; the formation of a *corpus luteum.*

1929 *Anatomical Rec.* XLIII. 239 (*heading*) The origin of the corpus luteum in the rat as indicated by studies upon the luteinization of the cystic follicles. **1931** *Amer. Jrnl. Physiol.* XCVII. 292 It [*sc.* the luteinizing hormone] does, however, cause luteinization of the follicles which are produced by the gonad stimulator. **1967** G. S. Richardson *Ovarian Physiol.* ii. 22 Increased follicular growth without luteinization or corpus-luteum formation. **1968** Passmore & Robson *Compan. Med. Stud.* I. xxxvii. 18/2 Following ovulation and subsequent luteinization of the follicle, oestrogen synthesis is supplemented by the production of progestagens.

Hence **lu·teinize** *v. trans.*, to cause (a tissue associated with the *corpus luteum*) to form lutein; **lu·teinized** *ppl. a.*; **lu·teinizing** *ppl. a.* and *vbl. sb.*; *luteinizing hormone,* a glycoprotein hormone secreted by the adenohypophysis which in the female helps to induce ovulation and brings about the formation of the *corpus luteum,* and in the male promotes the secretion of androgen by acting on the Leydig cells of the testis (abbrev. LH (*L 7)).

1929 *Anatomical Rec.* XLIII. 242 The cells of either the granulosa or the theca have become luteinized. **1931** *Amer. Jrnl. Physiol.* XCVII. 291 (*heading*) The gonad stimulating and the luteinizing hormones of the anterior lobe of the hypophesis [*sic*]. *Ibid.* 294 This preparation.. does luteinize the follicles produced by the gonad stimulating fraction. *Ibid.*, The water soluble preparation contains primarily the gonad stimulating hormone with little or none of the luteinizing substance. *Ibid.* 295 Stimulation to luteinizing activity. **1935** *Endocrinology* XIX. 45 The ovary of the infantile rat can be luteinized to a much higher degree than was found in the above experiments with urine. **1966** *Ann. Rev. Physiol.* XXVIII. 61 Heavily luteinized ovaries. **1969** K. W. McKerns *Gonads* x. 279 Some 95 percent of the ovarian tissue consisted of luteinized cells. **1970** *Sci. Jrnl.* June 47/1 Three gonadotrophic hormones are produced by the anterior section of the pituitary gland: the mammotrophic hormone, prolactin, the follicle stimulating hormone (FSH) and the luteinizing hormone (LH). **1970** *Nature* 26 Sept. 1344/2 In the cyclic female albino rat, a release of pituitary luteinizing hormone (LH) occurs on the afternoon of proestrus.

luteo-. Add: **b.** Also before a vowel **lute-.** Used as the combining form of *corpus luteum* (*corpus 2), as in **luteo·lysis** *Physiol.* [*lysis 3], degeneration of the *corpus luteum,* such as occurs when the discharged ovum is not fertilized; so **luteoly·tic** *a.* [*-lytic], bringing about or sufficient to bring about luteolysis; **luteo·ma** *Path.* [*-oma], an ovarian tumour consisting of cells resembling those of the corpus luteum.

1961 J. W. Everett in W. C. Young *Sex & Internal Secretions* (ed. 3) I. viii. 537/1 By luteolysis we shall refer to corpus luteum regression in any of its manifestations. **1965** *Endocrinology* LXXVI. 1218/1 The luteolysis induced by estrogen. **1971** *Nature* 23 Apr. 526/1 We have measured the output of prostaglandin from the uterus in one condition which is associated with premature luteolysis, uterine distension. **1974** *Ibid.* 10 May 176/2 In many species luteolysis is dependent upon the presence of the uterus and an intact utero-ovarian vasculature. **1961** *Recent Progress Hormone Res.* XVII. 122 This experiment.. argues against the possibility that the luteolytic effect of progesterone is due to a direct action on the corpus luteum. **1965** *Endocrinology* LXXVI. 1214/1 Particular attention was focused on establishing the luteolytic dose of estradiol cyclopentylpropionate. **1971** *Nature* 23 Apr. 526/1 Prostaglandin $F_{2\alpha}$..has a luteolytic action in various species including the guinea-pig. **1931** R. J. E. Scott *Gould's Med. Dict.* (ed. 3) 749/1 *Luteoma,* a tumor developing from the corpus luteum. **1947** *Radiology* XLIX. 280/1 Figure 10 shows a mixed luteoma and tubular adenoma. **1966** R. W. Evans *Histol. Appearances Tumours* (ed. 2) xxviii. 666 There exists a rare though well-recognized ovarian tumour which, because of its debatable nature and genesis, has been variously and confusingly called: adrenocorticoid tumour or hypernephroma of ovary, virilizing lipoid-cell tumour, luteoma, androgenic hilus-cell tumour and masculinovoblastoma.

luteotrophic (liū:tĭotrōu·fik), **-tropic** (-trōu·-pik, -trǫ·pik), *a. Physiol.* [f. *luteo- b + *-trophic, *-tropic.] Maintaining or capable of maintaining the *corpus luteum* and thus counteracting luteolysis during pregnancy; *luteotrop(h)ic hormone,* such a hormone which in rats and mice is produced by the adenohypophysis and which is probably identical with the hormone prolactin of other animals, including man (though attempts to demonstrate that prolactin is luteotrophic in these other animals have failed) (abbrev. LTH (*L 7)).

1941 E. B. Astwood in *Endocrinology* XXVIII. 310 In speaking of a substance which will maintain the functioning of formed corpora lutea it has been found convenient to use the term 'luteotrophic' substance or 'luteotrophin'. **1955** *Jrnl. Endocrinol.* XIII. 19 Cutuly (1941) found that luteotrophic hormone stimulates corpora lutea of hypophysectomized rats sufficiently to allow implantation. **1961** *Recent Progress Hormone Res.* XVII. 120 The luteinizing hormone..may be luteotropic in animals other than rats and mice. **1964** H. H. Cole *Gonadotropins* i. 1 We know nothing of other possible pituitary luteotropic hormones. **1964** *Endocrinology* LXXV. 625/1 Such extracts have been shown to be luteotrophic in hypophysectomized rabbits. **1968** Passmore & Robson *Compan. Med. Stud.* I. xxxvii. 16/2 The factors which control the maintenance and regression of the corpus luteum are not understood, but during pregnancy a placental gonadotrophin exerts a powerful luteotrophic effect.

Hence **lu:teotro·phin, -tro·pin,** any substance exerting a luteotrophic effect; *spec.* = **luteotrop(h)ic hormone.*

1941 [see *luteotrophic *a.*]. **1945** *Index-Catal. Library Surg.-General's Office, U.S. Army* 4th Ser. IX. 1323/1 Luteotropin: see Pituitary hormone. **1961** *Recent Progress Hormone Res.* XVII. 120 LH may have the dual role of causing ovulation and of acting as a luteotropin. **1961** W. C. Young *Sex & Internal Secretions* (ed. 3) I. viii. 530/2 The term luteotrophin was proposed by Astwood (1941) to refer to a substance that maintains function of corpora lutea, in distinction to substances that cause them to form. It is now conceded that the substance described in that paper was probably the lactogenic hormone... Although lactogen seems to be the hypophyseal luteotrophin in rats, such is not necessarily true for all species... Nevertheless, the expression luteotrophin in the generic sense continues to be desirable. **1965** *Endocrinology* LXXVI. 1218/1 It therefore appears..that a hypophysial luteotropin is only necessary for a short period after ovulation.

lutetium (liutī·ʃiəm, -siəm). *Chem.* Also **lutecium.** [ad. F. *lutécium* (G. Urbain 1907, in *Compt. Rend.* CXLV. 761), f. F. *Lutèce,* L. *Lutēt-ia* (see Lutetian *a.*): see -ium.] A rare metallic element that is the heaviest member of the lanthanide series and forms colourless salts in which it is trivalent. Atomic number 71; symbol Lu.

1907 *Jrnl. Chem. Soc.* XCII. ii. 956 (*heading*) A new element: lutecium, resulting from the decomposition of Marignac's ytterbium. **1929** *Encycl. Brit.* XIV. 490/2 Lutecium occurs along with ytterbium, erbium, etc., in the minerals gadolinite, euxenite, xenotime, etc. It is separated from the other members of the group by the fractional crystallization of the bromates, lutecium bromate being the most soluble passes into the mother-liquor. **1939** *Physical Rev.* LVI. 21 The half-life of the natural radioactivity of lutecium..is..$7{\cdot}3 \pm 2 \times 10^{10}$ years for Lu^{176}, which probably is the active isotope. **1952** *Chem. & Engin. News* 7 July 2843/2 The table of international atomic weights, as published by the 'Comptes Rendus' of the New York meeting of the Union for 1951.. shows changes in the weights of seven elements... Lutetium replaces lutecium, to agree with the original Latin spelling Lutetia..instead of the French Lutèce. **1973** J. J. Lagowski *Mod. Inorg. Chem.* xvi. 604 Lutetium, the first element which follows the lanthanides, starts the last *d*-series, but it forms a M^{3+} cation with a filled 4*f* orbital. Thus, lutetium on the basis of its atomic and ionic radii also appears to be a member of the lanthanide series.

luthier. (Later examples.)

1932 *Times Lit. Suppl.* 4 Feb. 68/2 That [knowledge] which comes from the long practice of the craft of the *luthier.* **1951** H. M. Robinson *Cardinal* ii. 183 With two luthiers in the house, a violin ought to get finished once in a while. **1974** *Daily Colonist* (Victoria, B.C.) 1 Sept. 16/8 Dunn learned to make the 16th-century instruments while sharing a shop with Canadian luthier Ray Nurse and now makes about 20 a year.

lutite (lʋ·təit). *Geol.* Formerly also **-yte.** [f. L. *lut-um* mud + -ite[1] 2 b.] = Pelite. So **luta·ceous** *a.* [-aceous] = Pelitic *a.*

1904 A. W. Grabau in *Amer. Geologist* XXXIII. 242 The third texture [*sc.* that of 'rock flour or impalpable powder'], finally, may be designated by the term *lutaceous,* (from *lutum,* mud), and for consolidated rocks of this type the term *lutyte* may be used, irrespective of chemical composition. Pelyte has been used particularly for argillaceous rocks of the group. **1941** F. H. Lahee *Field Geol.* (ed. 4) 785 These terms [*sc.* psephite, psammite, pelite] are derived from the Greek. The equivalent terms, derived from the Latin and preferred by some geologists, are rudite.., arenite.., and lutite. **1959** W. W. Moorhouse *Study of Rocks in Thin Section* xviii. 334 The clastic sediments are classified according to size as rudytes (rudaceous), which are conglomerates, arenytes (arenaceous) which are sands, and lutytes (lutaceous), which are shales and muds. **1970** *Nature* 14 Mar. 1068/2 A sediment core..reveals the top 20 cm to be a greyish-brown fossiliferous lutite.

Lutomer (liū·toməɹ). Also **Ljutomer.** The Slovene name for the region of Slovenia in which wine is produced; used *attrib.* for the wine produced there.

Before the creation of Yugoslavia in 1918 both the region (then part of Austria) and the wine were known by their German name *Luttenberg.*

[**1851** C. Redding *Wines* (ed. 3) xi. 288 The Luttenberg wines of Lower Styria are among the first.] **1954** 'Bon Viveur' *A.B.C. of Wine Drinking* 74 *Lutomer Riesling,* sweetish—definitely—fairly sturdy and with a slight bouquet. **1965** *Sun* 23 Jan. 6/6 The favourite white, Lutomer Riesling, that great party standby. **1970** L. W. Marrison *Wines for Everyone* ix. 122 One has the feeling that in those restaurants where carafe wines are available, the white is more likely to be lutomer riesling than graves or mâcon. **1971** J. Jeffs *Wines of Europe* 499 In a tasting of 1958 wines in 1964, the best was undoubtedly a lutomer traminer which..was very well balanced.

lutulent, *a.* (Later *literary* example.)

1922 Joyce *Ulysses* 377 Exterior splendour may be the surface of a downwardtending lutulent reality.

lutz (luts). [prob. f. name of Gustave *Lussi* (1898–), Swiss figure skater, who invented it.] A jump in ice-skating in which the skater takes off from the outside back edge of one skate and lands, after a complete rotation in the air, on the outside back edge of the opposite skate.

1938 D. Cummings *Figure Skating* xv. 83 Similar to the flip jump is the *Lutz*; but it is more difficult. **1940** M. Y. Vinson *Advanced Figure Skating* vi. 175 A really fine lutz ..is the ambition of every jumper. **1959** *Times* 12 Mar. 4/4 The title therefore was not awarded, in spite of Jones's splendid free skating programme, which included a fine.. lutz. **1964** *Times* 3 Feb. 3/5 There was a momentary unsteadiness in landing the double lutz, but all her other jumps were splendidly executed. **1976** *Times* 19 Jan. 9/6 The rather perilous landing of a double lutz.

luv (lʋv, luv). Spelling used to represent an affectionate, dialectal, or colloquial, etc., occurrence of the word *love*: esp. freq. as a term of address.

1898 J. D. Brayshaw *Slum Silhouettes* 35 They say as luv is blind. **1909** R. Brooke *Let.* 21 Aug. (1968) 174 Boxer's in Luv. **1957** J. Braine *Room at Top* vi. 52 T'lad's cum to enjoy hisen, 'aven't you, luv? **1966** 'L. Lane' *ABZ of Scouse* 63 *Luv,* ironical term of affection applied to the opposite sex. Often used by waitresses as in *what'll yer 'ave luv?* **1968** A. Clarke *Darkened Room* x. 126 The nurses called me 'Luv' or 'Dear'. **1972** G. Bell *Villains Galore* xiii. 205 Watch that money, luv! It's not safe there.

Luvian (lū·viăn), *sb.* and *a.* Also **Luwian, Luian.** [f. G. *Luvisch, Luvier* from *Luvia,* name given to part of Asia Minor: see E. Forrer in *Mitteilungen Deut. Orient-Gesellschaft* (1921) LXI. 20–39: see -ian.] **A.** *sb.* **a.** A member of an Anatolian people contemporary with the Hittites, known from cuneiform inscriptions. **b.** The language of the Luvians. **B.** *adj.* Of or pertaining to the Luvians or their language.

[**1923** H. R. Hall in Buckler & Calder *Anatolian Studies* 168 Although until we have the cuneiform texts before us it is quite impossible to control the work of Forrer..yet, whatever we may think at present of his elaborate analysis of the eight languages which he thinks the Hittites or their subjects spoke,..'Ur-Luvisch', 'Luvisch',..and so on, yet the rough historical results.. can no doubt be accepted without demur.] **1924** *Cambr. Anc. Hist.* II. xi. 253 More [tablets], however, are couched in some six native allied dialects, according to the latest decipherers.., who agree in regarding the dialects as Indo-European... To the six dialects they give the names Kanesian, Luvian, [etc.]. **1933** C. D. Buck *Compar. Gram. Greek & Latin* 15 Closely related to the cuneiform Hittite are the hieroglyphic Hittite and Luwian. **1934** Webster, *Luian,*..an ancient language of the Hittite empire. **1939** L. H. Gray *Foundations of Lang.* xi. 324 There are also Hittite inscriptions in pictographic or hieroglyphic characters... Their language may be akin to that seen in the thus far scanty fragments of *Luian* or *Luvian,* closely related to Hittite. **1952** O. R. Gurney

Hittites i. 18 Other Indo-European dialects (Luwian, Palaic, Lycian, and 'Hieroglyphic Hittite') established themselves in other parts of Anatolia. **1961** L. R. PALMER *Mycenaeans & Minoans* 26 The possibility..that the predecessors of the Greeks were Luvians from western Asia Minor should please both philologists and archaeologists. **1963** —— *Interpretation Mycenaean Greek Texts* 339 The word [*sc. a-ja-me-na*] may be a Luvian loan-word (*a-ja* 'do, make') in the sense 'wrought'. This possibility is strengthened by the fact that *kuwana-* occurs in Luvian and is held to be the source of Greek *κύανος*. **1966** J. PUHVEL in Birnbaum & Puhvel *Anc. Indo-European Dial.* 238 This linguistic division of the substrata is indirectly discernible in the divergent Hattic, Kaneshite, and Luwian pantheons within the hospitality of the state cults of the Hittite empire... 'Hieroglyphic Hittite' is in reality a dialectal form of Luwian ('East' or 'Late' Luwian). **1973** K. A. KITCHEN in D. J. Wiseman *Peoples of Old Testament Times* 67 Goliath (*Golyat*) is claimed as a dissimilated form of a Walwatta.., from a Luvian base *walwi/a*.

Luwian, var. *LUVIAN *sb.* and *a.*

lux (lɒks), *sb. Physics.* Pl. **lux.** [L., = 'light'.] A unit of illumination (now incorporated into the International System of Units) equal to the illumination of a surface all of which is one metre from a uniform point source of light of unit intensity (now one candela), i.e. (as now defined) one lumen per square metre.

1889 *Engineering* 13 Sept. 313/1 Mr. Preece was not.. fortunate with his unit of surface illumination, the 'lux' being the illumination produced by a lamp of one Carcel power at a distance of one metre, which is practically the same illumination as that afforded by an English standard candle at a distance of 1 ft... It is probable, sooner or later, that such a unit will be adopted. **1897** *Jrnl. Inst. Electr. Engin.* XXVI. 638 It was proposed by the Committee of the International Congress of Geneva that M. A. Blondel should present a report, with..a complete system of defining the dimensions and units of photometry... This report was submitted for examination of a commission..and was accepted... Lux = Lumen/Square metre. **1911** A. P. TROTTER *Illumination* ii. 17 Sir William Preece ..adopted the Carcel-metre, and he showed that it was equal to a standard candle of 1·058 foot. At the Paris Electrical Congress of 1889 he adopted the name 'lux' for this... The unit of illumination produced by a bougie-décimale at a metre has been called a bougie-metre, and the name 'lux' was revived at the Geneva Congress of 1896 and was applied to this unit... This lux is, roughly, one-twelfth of a foot-candle, or about one-fourteenth of Preece's lux. The illumination produced by a Hefner at a metre has also been called a 'lux', and it seems probable that the International candle at a metre may be called an International lux. **1927** *Forestry* I. 87 Experiments carried out..in a light intensity of 48,000 lux. *Ibid.*, The lux is a light intensity produced by a light of one candle-power at a distance of one metre. Forty-eight thousand lux is roughly equivalent to full sunlight at noon in midsummer in Germany. **1953** AMOS & BIRKINSHAW *Television Engin.* I. 279, 1 lux = 1 lumen per square metre = 0·0929 foot-candle. **1970** *Nature* 26 Dec. 1349/2 On many days during the growth of these plants light intensities reached 80,000 lux.

luxe. 1. Delete † *Obs.* and add later examples. Also *attrib.* or quasi-*adj.*

1908 *Westm. Gaz.* 28 July 11/3 We possess..a special department for hiring out luxe carriages. *Ibid.*, One of our Charron luxe cars fills all the essentials of a gentleman's private car. **1932** R. FRY *Let.* 26 Apr. (1972) II. 667 Epidauros..was all on a grand scale and tremendous *luxe* in the architecture. **1959** *N.Y. Times* 8 Nov. 1. 98 (Advt.), The incomparable beauty and luxe of silk. **1961** *Ibid.* 26 Nov. 1. 91 (Advt.), The great revival of the luxe little mesh evening bag. **1967** L. DEIGHTON *London Dossier* 124 Jermyn Street..is a thoroughfare resonant with *luxe.* **1968** L. DURRELL *Tunc* iii. 94 For tonight the Pera hotel.. will enable you to rest. There is every luxe. **1974** *New Yorker* 3 June 98/2 He looks round his palace of a house with sniffly and quite unfair resentment, considering its comfort and luxe.

Luxembourgeois (lɒ·ksĕmbuɹʒwā), *a.* Of or pertaining to Luxemb(o)urg or to its inhabitants. Also as *sb. pl.*, the natives or inhabitants of Luxemb(o)urg.

1905 T. H. PASSMORE *In Further Ardenne* v. 121 If its effects upon conduct be any test of a religious system, Luxembourgeois Catholicism comes out brightly, for in the matter of honesty and chastity the people are resplendent. **1951** T. EDWARDS *Belgium & Luxembourg* vii. 80 A playground for both Luxembourgeois and Belgians. **1971** *Guardian* 8 June 11/4 Though the Luxembourgeois run the hotel, all have English as a working language. **1973** *Sunday Times* 21 Jan. 24/6 Many Luxembourgeois aristocrats have long ago departed.

Luxembourger (lɒ·ksĕmbɒ̄ɹgəɹ). A native or inhabitant of Luxemb(o)urg.

1913 G. RENWICK *Luxembourg* i. 38 During the two previous reigns German influence was supreme at Court. .. But..that is so no more, and to be a Luxembourger is not now a drawback. **1942** *R.A.F. Jrnl.* 16 May (recto rear cover), Luxembourgers paid tribute to fallen R.A.F. pilots and were punished for their gesture. **1951** W. J. TAYLOR-WHITEHEAD *Luxembourg* 1. ii. 24 The Luxembourgers work hard, and they work long (though sometimes irregular) hours. **1956** B. MILES *Attic in Luxembourg* i. 3 Redouté, the rose-painter, was a Luxembourger. **1972** R. MAYNE *Europeans* vi. 164 Some European officials.. smiled at Luxembourgers' accents in French or German. **1973** *Guardian* 23 Mar. 15/7 The Luxembourgers have been saying that they will sign, only if the bank has its headquarters in their capital.

Luxemburgisch (lɒksĕmbɒ̄·rgiʃ). Also **Luxembourgish.** [f. *Luxemb(o)urg* + -ISH¹.] = *LETZEBURGESCH.

1957 *B.B.C. Handbook* 251, 1940... 30 Nov. Luxembourgish broadcasts (as part of Belgian Service) began. **1961** R. E. KELLER *German Dial.* 10 These two dialects—or languages—are the daily medium of *all classes* of 300,000 people in the case of Luxemburgisch and of over three million people in the case of *Schwyzertütsch.* **1965** [see *LETZEBURGESCH].

luxmeter (lɒ·ksmītəɹ). Also **luxometer.** [f. *LUX *sb.* (+ -O) + METER *sb.*³] An instrument for measuring the luminance (brightness) or illuminance (illumination) of a surface.

1910 H. M. HOBART *Dict. Electr. Engin.* II. 319/2 *Luxmeter, photometric.* This is a photometer of the 'cat's-eye type'. **1912** W. C. CLINTON tr. *Bloch's Sci. of Illumination* v. 101 A further development..in the direction of greater portability and lightness has been made in the luxometer. **1915** GASTER & DOW *Mod. Illuminants* vii. 261 Another small instrument of the surface-brightness type, the 'Luxometer', has recently been introduced. **1932** *Proc. Internat. Illumination Congr., 1931* I. 215 Two types of luxmeter have been studied: the luxmeter with a scale of illuminations, and the luxmeter with a single comparison illumination, controllable either by the distance of the lamp or by the interposition of a photometric wedge. **1967** E. CHAMBERS *Photolitho-Offset* vii. 85 Meters can be purchased for measuring the number of Lux (luxmeters) or [*printed* of] foot-candela (foot-candela meters).

luxury. Add: **7.** *attrib.*, as *luxury coach, cruise, duty, edition, flat, liner, shop, tax, trade. Comb.*, as *luxury-loving* adj.

1936 O. LANCASTER *Progress at Pelvis Bay* 61 As many as fifty or sixty..luxury coaches leave daily from the square. **1941** N. COWARD *Australia Visited* 1. 5 Society ladies returning home exhausted after a lightning luxury cruise. **1971** E. CANDY *Words for Murder Perhaps* iv. 50 The drug pusher, the criminal classes. You don't get that sort of person in good hotels or on luxury cruises. **1904** *Hansard Commons* 19 Apr. 564 An article of luxury which might very fairly pay a luxury duty. **1930** T. E. LAWRENCE *Lett.* (1938) 709 We must do our best to get the whole of the luxury edition placed before the date of publication. **1937** *Night & Day* 9 Dec. 12 Luxury flat. A story by K. K. Busvine. **1939** O. LANCASTER *Homes Sweet Homes* 66 The luxury flat..is divided up with fiendish ingenuity into a dining-room, drawing-room, lounge-hall, three bed, two bath, a kitchen and all the usual offices. **1958** *New Statesman* 5 Apr. 439/2 A luxury-flat developer ..instructed his architects to do neo-Georgian. **1934** G. B. SHAW *Too True to be Good* Pref. 11 The rich tourists in the palace hotels and luxury liners. **1947** L. MACNEICE *Dark Tower* 50, I followed you—but not on a luxury liner. Mine was a cargo boat. **1959** N. MARSH *Singing in Shrouds* iii. 38 A luxury liner and organised fun would be more his cup-of-tea. **1899** 'MARK TWAIN' in *Forum* Mar. 32 We are..the most luxury-loving people on the earth. **1927** H. WADDELL *Wandering Scholars* i. 25 It was an apple-orchard in blossom to his luxury-loving, exquisite and peaceful soul. **1962** H. R. LOYN *Anglo-Saxon Eng.* ii. 69 The gold coinage, papyrus, fine stuffs and spices point to the existence of a luxury-loving aristocracy. **1935** N. MITCHISON *We have been Warned* IV. 349 Turning..to Mayfair, they began to pass the discreet and rather impressive luxury shops. **1973** S. JACKMAN *Guns covered with Flowers* vi. 74 The luxury shops and the department stores. **1904** *Hansard Commons* 19 Apr. 564 The luxury tax at that time was 6*d.* **1974** R. JEFFRIES *Mistakenly in Mallorca* xiii. 122 The large cars on national or tourist plates whose owners were not forced to pay the luxury taxes that all Spaniards had to. **1905** *Westm. Gaz.* 9 Jan. 3/1 Their action deprives of employment persons who were..employed in luxury trades. **1966** G. GREENE *Comedians* I. iii. 84, I can see great possibilities of improvement. My mother was not catering for the luxury-trade.

ly, abbrev. *LANGLEY.

1959 S. L. HESS *Introd. Theoret. Meteorol.* ix. 131 The rate of receipt of solar energy is nearly constant at the equator where it varies between 790 and 895 ly day⁻¹. **1963** G. L. PICKARD *Descriptive Physical Oceanogr.* v. 51 One langley (ly) is one gram calorie per square centimetre.

lycænid (ləisī·nid), *sb.* and *a.* [f. mod.L. family name *Lycænidæ*, f. the generic name *Lycæna* (J. C. Fabricius 1807, in *Mag. für Insektenkunde* VI. 85), f. Gr. *λύκαινα* she-wolf.] **A.** *sb.* A butterfly of the family Lycænidæ, which includes the blues and the hairstreaks. **B.** *adj.* Of or pertaining to this family.

1892 W. L. DISTANT *Naturalist in Transvaal* 68, I have often mistaken it for a large Lycænid. **1913** *Oxf. Univ. Gaz.* 4 June 950/1 A beautiful series of 84 Lycaenid butterflies from the Nicobar Islands. **1972** L. E. CHADWICK tr. *Linsenmaier's Insects of World* 197/1 (*caption*) The hairstreaks, a large group of the lycaenids, spend most of the time in bushes and trees. **1974** *Nature* 1 Mar. 16/3 Eliot's paper is designed to evoke thought and curiosity about his lycaenid butterflies.

lycaon (likēi·ǫn). [mod.L. (S. Brookes in E. Griffith et al. tr. *Cuvier's Animal Kingdom* (1827) V. 151), f. Gr. *λυκάων*, L. *lycāon* a wolf-like animal.] A wild dog of the monotypic genus so called, found in Africa south of the Sahara; the African hunting dog.

1827 E. GRIFFITH et al. tr. *Cuvier's Animal Kingdom* V. 151 (*heading*) Burchel's Lycaon. **1915** ROOSEVELT & HELLER *Life-Hist. Afr. Game Animals* I. viii. 265 The skull of *Lycaon* is easily recognizable from that of a wolf or a jackal. **1945** C. L. B. HUBBARD *Observer's Bk. Dogs* 187 *Lycaon* is the most peculiar and interesting of all dog-like carnivores native to Africa. **1958** *Listener* 16 Jan. 102/2 The four-legged animal which deals out more destruction than almost any other is the lycaon, or wild dog.

Lycaonian (likēiōu·niăn), *a.* and *sb.* Also **Lykaonian.** [f. L. *Lycaonia*, Gr. *Λυκαονία* Lycaonia + -AN.] **A.** *adj.* Of or pertaining to ancient Lycaonia in southern Asia Minor, its inhabitants, or the language spoken by them. **B.** *sb.* **a.** The language of Lycaonia. **b.** A native or inhabitant of Lycaonia.

1582 BIBLE (Reims) *Acts* xiv. 10 And the multitudes when they had seen what Paul had done, lifted vp their voice in the lycáonian tongue. **1890** W. M. RAMSAY *Hist. Geogr. Asia Minor* 392 When, in 361–2, it was found advisable to divide further the large province of Isauria, all the Lykaonian cities were taken from it and from Pisidia. **1893** —— *Church in Roman Empire* ii. 57 Greek then, and not Latin or Lykaonian, would be the common language of these two classes of the population. **1911** [see *ICONIAN *a.* and *sb.*]. **1926** *Public Opinion* 25 June 582/1 The two gods to whom the Lycaonians..were accustomed to pray. **1957** *Encycl. Brit.* XIV. 511/2 The Lycaonians were to a great extent independent of the Persian empire... The mention of the Lycaonian language in the Acts of the Apostles..shows that the native language was spoken by the common people at Lystra as late as A.D. 50.

lyceal (ləisī·ăl), *a.* [f. LYCÉE + -AL.] Of or pertaining to the French Lycées or similar establishments.

1904 G. S. HALL *Adolescence* I. 345 Marro tabulated the conduct of 3,012 boys in gymnasial and lyceal classes in Italy from eleven to eighteen years of age.

‖ **lycéen** (liseaṅ). [Fr.: see LYCÉE.] A pupil at a *lycée* in France.

1883 H. JAMES *Little Tour in France* (1885) xiii. 90 Little pale-faced *lycéens*..who are about to be restored to those big educative barracks. **1909** *Daily Chron.* 23 Sept. 4/4 One is naturally led to inquire what steps are taken to ensure the discipline of the Lycéens out of school. **1971** G. STEINER *In Bluebeard's Castle* iv. 85 The Victorian public-school boy, the *Gymnasiast* or *lycéen.* **1974** *Guardian* 26 Mar. 4/4 A background of marching lycéens and charging police, not to speak of protesting school masters.

lyceum. Add: **4. b.** *lyceum bureau, hall, lecture, lecturer, lecturing, system* (earlier example).

1924 I. S. COBB *Kansas* ii. 20 Fate, personated by the booking agency of a lyceum bureau, decreed that I should jump out of the Teutonic comforts of St. Louis. **1831** *Mass. Private & Special Statutes* 4 Mar., They are hereby made a corporation, by the name of Lyceum Hall,..for the purpose of affording means..for the prosecution of literary and scientific studies [etc.]. **1837** H. MARTINEAU *Society in America* I. 1. iii. 61, I attended another Lyceum lecture in Massachusetts. **1922** L. MUMFORD in H. E. Stearns *Civilization in U.S.* 6 The Lyceum lecture..was taken as a soporific rather than a stimulant. **1844** *Knickerbocker* XXIV. 294 The remark of a lyceum lecturer upon matrimony. **1881** *Harper's Mag.* Mar. 628/2 During the days of his lyceum lecturing, no man was more popular [than Dr. Chapin] upon the platform. **1843** 'R. CARLTON' *New Purchase* I. 174 The common school system, the lyceum system.

6. (With capital initial.) The name of a theatre near the Strand in London, used *attrib.* to denote a performance characteristic of those given at this theatre, esp. of the melodramatic type associated with Henry Irving; also *transf.*

1898 G. B. SHAW *Let.* 29 Jan. in C. St. John *Ellen Terry & Bernard Shaw* (1931) 294 Henry [Irving]..is as much behind the times now as Pinwell's and Fred Walker's and Mason's pictures are (I always call them the Lyceum school). **1898** —— *Plays Pleasant & Unpleasant* p. xix, Popular entertainments like Gounod's opera or the Lyceum version, in which poetry and philosophy are replaced by romance. **1901** —— *Three Plays for Puritans* p. xi, I found that the whole business of stage sensuousness, whether as Lyceum Shakespear, musical farce, or sham Ibsen, finally disgusted me. **1936** 'N. BLAKE' *Thou Shell of Death* xiii. 229 Tones that would have done credit to a Lyceum melodrama. **1964** 'A. GILBERT' *Knock knock, who's There?* i. 21 This wasn't a cosy pub..it was all set for a Lyceum melodrama.

Lycian (li·siăn), *sb.* and *a.* [f. L. *Lycia*, Gr. *Λυκία* Lycia + -AN.] **A.** *sb.* **a.** A native or inhabitant of ancient Lycia in south-west Asia Minor. **b.** The language and script used in Lycia. **B.** *adj.* Of or pertaining to ancient Lycia, its inhabitants, or the language and script used by them.

1598 CHAPMAN tr. *Homer's Seaven Bookes of Iliades* 45 Sarpedon had the Lycians charge. **1607** TOPSELL *Four-f. Beasts* 115 These beasts are..plentifull..in Lycia:..the Lycian Roes doe neuer goe ouer the Syrian Mountaines. **1718** POPE tr. *Homer's Iliad* XVI. 570 Two sounding Darts the Lycian Leader threw. **1839** C. FELLOWS *Jrnl. Excursion Asia Minor* viii. 229 On the side of the tomb..under two lines of the peculiar characters of this town, (perhaps Lycian,) is a group of figures. **1841** —— *Acct. Discoveries Lycia* vii. 168 The tedious, but..useful occupation, of copying the Lycian inscription. **1845** [see *BILINGUAL *a.* 2]. **1883** *Encycl. Brit.* XV. 92/2 It [*sc.* Lycia] was..inhabited from a very early period by a distinct people,

known to the Greeks as Lycians. *Ibid.* 94/1 A few of these inscriptions are fortunately bilingual, in Greek and Lycian. **1913** H. R. Hall *Anc. Hist. Near East* vi. 270 There is a reference to Lycian pirates in another letter. **1933** [see *Carian *sb.* and *a.*]. **1941** [see *Ilian *a.* (*sb.*)]. **1948** D. Diringer *Alphabet* 464 The Lycian alphabet..is certainly of Greek origin. **1951** J. B. Bury *Hist. Greece* (ed. 3) viii. 337 Cimon..constrained the Lycian communities to enrol themselves in the confederacy of Delos. **1972** R. Meiggs *Athenian Empire* xvii. 307 The Lycians also had ceased to bring their tribute. *Ibid.*, The Carian and Lycian coasts were being used by pirates. **1973** *Times* 1 Oct. 17/6 Lycian is an Indo-European language and belongs to the Luwian sub-group of Anatolian. *Ibid.*, It would be important to know in which of the two Lycian dialects the inscription is written.

lycid (li·sid), *a.* and *sb.* [f. mod.L. family name *Lycidæ*, f. generic name *Lycus* (J. C. Fabricius *Mantissa Insectorum* (1787) I. 163), f. Gr. proper name *Λύκος*, L. *Lycus*: see -id³.] **A.** *adj.* Of or pertaining to a beetle of the family Lycidæ. **B.** *sb.* A beetle of this family.

1932 J. S. Huxley *Probl. Relative Growth* vii. 237 See.. Mjöberg's discussion (1925) on the larviform females of certain Lycid beetles. **1934** Webster, *Lycid n.* and *adj.* **1962** *New Scientist* 6 Dec. 577/1 The cerambycid beetle *Elytroleptus ignitus* is a mimic of the lycid beetles *Lycus loripes* and *L. simulans*... They are typical cases of Batesian mimicry, the cerambycids being palatable to predators but gaining protection by looking like the distasteful lycids. **1972** L. E. Chadwick tr. *Linsenmaier's Insects of World* 165/1 There are a great many mimetic forms that resemble protected beetles (such as the already-mentioned lycids).

lycomarasmin (ləi:kɒmăræ·smin). *Chem.* Also † **lyco-marasmine.** [ad. G. *lyco-marasmin* (Plattner & Clauson-Kaas 1945, in *Experientia* I. 196), f. mod.L. *lyco-persici* varietal or specific epithet (taken as gen. of *lycopersicon*: see *lycopersicin) + Gr. *μαρασμ-ός* withering + -in¹.] A phytotoxic dipeptide, $C_9H_{15}N_3O_7$, which contains glycine and aspartic acid residues and was isolated from *Fusarium bulbigenum* var. *lycopersici*, the fungus which causes tomato wilt.

1945 *Experientia* I. 196 On hydrolysis lyco-marasmine yields glycine, aspartic and (probably) pyruvic acid and ammonia. **1956** *Ann. Rev. Microbiol.* X. 361 Lycomarasmin, therefore, causes iron deficiency in the stem and iron excess in the leaves. **1972** S. A. J. Tarr *Princ. Plant Path.* xiii. 236 Lycomarasmin is a dipeptide which brings about wilting and yellowing of tomato cuttings, and its phytotoxicity is increased in the presence of iron.

lycopene (ləi·kɒpīn). *Chem.* [f. *lycop(in + -ene.] A polyunsaturated hydrocarbon, $C_{40}H_{56}$, which is a red carotenoid pigment present in tomatoes and many berries and fruits.

1935 *Jrnl. Biol. Chem.* CXII. 424 In an investigation of the plastid pigments of marsh dodder,..α- and β-carotenes, γ-carotene, lycopene, and rubixanthin have been isolated. **1950** *Genetics* XXXV. 209 Tomatoes which contain principally *beta*-carotene differ from those which contain mostly lycopene by a single incompletely dominant gene. **1972** Goodwin & Mercer *Introd. Plant Biochem.* xi. 279 The conversion of phytoene into coloured carotenoids involves a stepwise desaturation to neurosporene and lycopene which are then converted into the cyclic carotenoids.

lycopersicin (ləi:kɒpɜ·ɪsikin). *Chem.* [f. mod.L. *lycopersic-on*, the name of the genus to which the tomato belongs, f. Gr. *λύκο-ς* wolf + *περσικ-ός* peach (f. *Περσίς*: see Persian *a.* and *sb.*): see -in¹.] **a.** = *lycopene.

1913 B. M. Duggar in *Washington Univ. Stud.* I. 23 Since the pigment derived from the tomato has now been demonstrated to be distinct from carotin.., and since it was first described in the tomato, it seems well to suggest that, in view of the inappropriateness of the earlier terms, lycopersicin should be adopted instead.

b. = *tomatin.

1945 G. W. Irving et al. in *Science* 6 July 9/1 We have obtained from the expressed juice of Pan American tomato plants..a preparation which..possesses marked fungistatic activity toward Fol. This antibiotic agent, which will be designated 'lycopersicin', occurs throughout the mature plant. **1946** *Jrnl. Bacteriol.* LII. 601 In a recent publication..this substance was referred to as 'lycopersicin'. Inasmuch as it has since been learned that the term 'lycopersicin' was once used..as a synonym for 'lycopene', the red pigment of the tomato, the designation of the antibiotic agent has been changed to 'tomatin' to avoid possible confusion.

lycopin (ləi·kɒpin). *Chem.* [f. mod.L. *lycopersicon* (see *lycopersicin) + -in¹.] = *lycopene.

1903 C. A. Schunck in *Proc. R. Soc.* LXXII. 174 Believing that this substance has not been isolated before, or if it has, has been mistaken for carotin, I venture to apply to it the name *Lycopin*. **1965** Bell & Coombe tr. *Strasburger's Textbk. Bot.* 43 Over seventy different carotinoids are known. Of these we need refer here only to the carotin of the carrot.., to the lycopin of the tomato and other red fruits, and to the yellow violaxanthin.

Lycra (ləi·kră). Also **lycra.** A proprietary name of an elastic polyurethane fibre and fabric used esp. for underwear and swimming costumes.

1958 *Official Gazette* (U.S. Patent Office) 18 Nov. TM 87/1 E.I. du Pont de Nemours and Company... Lycra. For synthetic fibers and filaments for generalized use in the industrial arts. First use Feb. 3, 1958. **1959** *Trade Marks Jrnl.* 8 Apr. 380/2 Lycra... Raw or partly prepared natural or synthetic fibres; and untwisted and unspun filaments;..E. I. Du Pont De Nemours and Company. **1961** *Harper's Bazaar* Sept. 103 Lycra, the ultimate in lightweight power. **1963** *Guardian* 8 Nov. 12/4 Proofed.. lycra jersey ski pants. **1968** *Vogue* 15 Apr. 23/2 This.. pantie-corselette..of softest lycra power net. **1972** *Country Life* 18 May 1275/3 Beachwear in newest Lycra material, light but giving corselette support.

lyctus (li·ktɒ̆s). [mod.L. (J. C. Fabricius *Entomologia Systematica* (1792) I. ii. 502), f. Gr. *Λύκτος*, L. *Lyctus* name of a city in Crete.] A wood-boring beetle of the genus so called; a powder-post beetle. Also *attrib.* Hence **ly·ctid** *sb.*, a beetle of the family Lyctidæ; as *adj.*, of or pertaining to this family.

1917 *U.S. Dept. Agric. Farmers' Bull.* No. 788 (*title*) Powder-post damage by *Lyctus* beetles to seasoned hardwood. **1926** E. O. Essig *Insects Western N. Amer.* 438 The European lyctus..can be separated by the single row of large round shallow punctures on the elytra. **1936** *Discovery* Feb. 42/1 The Powder-Post or Lyctus beetles are menacing timber-yard pests. **1958** *Times Rev. Industry* May 18/3 Death watch beetles and furniture beetles..are joined by..the lyctus beetle. **1959** E. F. Linssen *Beetles Brit. Is.* II. 63 The dust made by Anobiid larvae is granular, that of the Lyctid grubs is a fine powder. **1963** N. E. Hickin *Insect Factor in Wood Decay* v. 134 Lyctid beetles are small.

Lycurgan (ləikɜ̄·ɪgăn), *sb.* and *a.* Also **Lycurgean, Lycurgian.** [f. L. *Lycurgus*, Gr. *Λυκοῦργος* traditional lawgiver and founder of the Spartan constitution, dated in antiquity variously to the ninth and eighth centuries B.C.] **A.** *sb. rare.* An adherent of Lycurgus or his methods. **B.** *adj.* Of, pertaining to, or characteristic of Lycurgus, or the constitutional innovations attributed to him; harsh, severe.

1584 W. Allen *True Defence Eng. Catholiques* vii. 149 By the meanes of such Lycurgians as this, we haue in England new lawes against al claime of iurisdiction spiritual or temporal, that can be made by anie person whosoeuer, borne out of the Realme. **1846** G. Grote *Hist. Greece* II. ii. vi. 454, I incline to adopt the opinion of Thucydides as to the time at which the Lycurgean constitution was introduced at Sparta. **1934** [see *die-hardism]. **1956** A. Toynbee *Historian's Approach to Relig.* 242 The Lycurgean régime at Sparta was exceptional. **1962** *Listener* 30 Aug. 323/2 The Lycurgan training for public service enriched Greek 'paedeia'. **1970** *Oxf. Classical Dict.* (ed. 2) 1007/2 Proposals to revive the strictness of the Lycurgan training..were obstructed by the ephors.

lyddite, *v. rare.* [f. the sb.] *trans.* To destroy, wreck, etc., by the explosion of lyddite.

1906 F. Campbell *Dearlove* 78 She was pleased they had not dynamited or lyddited him.

lydite (li·dəit). *Min.* Also 9 **lydit.** [f. Lyd(ian *a.* and *sb.* + -ite¹.] = *Lydian stone* (s.v. Lydian *a.* 3).

1816 R. Jameson *Syst. Mineral.* (ed. 2) I. 192 Lydit. **1861** H. W. Bristow *Gloss. Mineral.* 223/2 Lydian Stone ..Lydite. **1907** *Q. Jrnl. Geol. Soc.* LXIII. 31 It is by no means a pure sand; there are no 'lydite' or other pebbles. **1948** *Proc. Prehist. Soc.* XIV. 129 Brown and purple quartzite cobbles, pieces of vein quartz and of lydite. **1968** *Mineral. Abstr.* XIX. 333/1 Six chemical analyses of phyllites and clay slates are listed; these are in zeolitic and greenschist facies and contain grapholite-bearing lydites.

lye, *sb.* Add: **4.** *lye-cask, hominy, -leach.*

1821 W. B. Dewees *Lett. from Early Settler Texas* (1852) 20 Our subsistence was principally upon..a kind of lye hominy seasoned with hickory nut kernels. **1843** 'R. Carlton' *New Purchase* I. ix. 63 A lie-cask, or rather, an inverted pyramidical box to contain ashes. **1847** J. O. Halliwell *Dict. Archaic & Provincial Words* Lie-leach. **1854** M. J. Holmes *Tempest & Sunshine* xv. 202 Now be keerful and not run afoul of the plaguey lye leech! **1919** J. P. Dunn *Indiana* II. 1170 A woman situated like Mrs. McCoy, in her Indian boarding school, with no food but lye hominy in the house..'degraded her soul' by cooking lye hominy. **1948** E. N. Dick *Dixie Frontier* 290 Lye hominy was made by soaking the whole grains of corn in lye water to remove the hulls.

lye, *sb.*², var. Lie *sb.*² 4.

1855 Ogilvie *Imp. Dict.* Suppl., *Lye*, a term employed, in *railway lang.*, to denote the sidings or short offsets from the main line, into which trucks may be run for the purpose of loading or unloading. **1901** *Daily Record* (Glasgow) 31 Aug. 3 A boy..was accidentally killed at the lye of South Renfrew Station on Thursday night.

lying, *vbl. sb.*¹ Add: **3. lying-in-state,** (of the corpse of a public figure) being on display for public tribute before burial.

1923 W. de la Mare *Riddle* 241 Positive constellations of candles as if for a Prince's..lying-in-state. **1947** M. Field *Boys' & Girls' Film Bk.* 67 When he died thousands of people went to his lying-in-state. **1972** *Whitaker's Almanack 1973* 565/2 The Duke of Windsor's lying-in-state took place in St. George's Chapel, Windsor.

lying-in. b. (Further examples.)

1823 J. Constable *Let.* 24 Aug. in *Corr.* (1964) II. 282 Miss Cookson is on a visit with another lying in sister. **1861** D. G. Rossetti *Let.* 20 Apr. (1965) II. 396 Dr. Babington, head of the Lying-in Hospital. **1912** *Q. Rev.* July 60 A slight increase in the ratio of lying-in claims to the number of members... A lying-in benefit of 30s. **1964** D. Owen *Eng. Philanthropy* I. ii. 50 The years 1749–65 saw the founding of..the British Lying-In (1749), the City of London Lying-In (1750),..these in addition to the Lying-In Charity,.. established in 1757. **1975** *Country Life* 2 Jan. 50/3 Villages which had a mutual aid or 'lying-in society'.

Lyle gun (ləil gʊn). [Named from its inventor D. A. *Lyle* (d. 1937) of the U.S. Ordnance Dept.] A cannon, invented in 1877, designed to project a rope from the shore to a stranded ship to facilitate salvaging and rescue operations.

1880 *Ann. Rep. U.S. Life-Saving Service* 109 The keeper ..then proceeded to charge the Lyle gun. **1899** *Ibid.* 471 The sample submitted is designed for use with the 2½-inch Lyle gun. **1911** *Encycl. Brit.* XV. 606/2 The keeper fires a line over the wreck with the Lyle gun, a small bronze cannon..having an extreme range of about 700 yards. **1927** G. Bradford *Gloss. Sea Terms* 106/2 *Lyle gun*, a life-saving gun designed to shoot a projectile with a line attached. This line..establishes a connection with a stranded ship by which an endless line and tail block is hauled off and afterwards a hawser. **1944** H. Norby *Questions & Answers* vi. 128 No part of Lyle gun equipment is to be used for any other purpose.

Lylian (li·liăn), *a.* Also **Lylyan.** [f. the name of John *Lyly* (*c* 1554–1606), English dramatist and novelist.] Of, pertaining to, or having the characteristics of John Lyly or his works.

1923 E. K. Chambers *Eliz. Stage* III. 36 The plays of the Lylyan school..illustrate very precisely, on the side of staging, that blend of the classical and the romantic tempers which is characteristic of the later Renaissance. **1928** E. A. Gerrard *Eliz. Drama* II. i. 145 The scene between Lucilla and the Enchanter is purely Lylian. **1959** *Times* 1 Sept. 11/2 It was Lyly who opened the door for Shakespeare, and when he was forced to abandon the Lylian view he abandoned comedy. **1962** G. K. Hunter *John Lyly* iv. 164 The approach to Alexander is underlined for us in a typically Lylian way. *Ibid.* iv. 218 With typical Lylian balance the action returns to the point from which it started.

Lyman (ləi·măn). *Physics.* The name of Theodore *Lyman* (1874–1954), U.S. physicist, used *attrib.* to designate a series of lines (individually designated alpha, beta, etc.) discovered by him in the ultraviolet part of the spectrum of atomic hydrogen, with wave numbers represented by the formula $R(1 - 1/m^2)$ (where R is the Rydberg constant and $m = 2, 3, \ldots$), the first line of which has a wavelength of 121·6 nanometres.

1922 *Encycl. Brit.* XXXII. 559/2 The formulæ for the hydrogen series are as follows:—Lyman series: $\nu = N/1^2 - N/m^2$ $(m = 2, 3, \ldots)$. Balmer series: $\nu = N/2^2 - N/m^2$ $(m = 3, 4, \ldots)$. Paschen series: $\nu = N/3^2 - N/m^2$ $(m = 4, 5, \ldots)$. **1929** J. K. Robertson *Introd. Physical Optics* xviii. 359 Lines of the Lyman series arise from electron drops from outer orbits to the innermost or normal orbit, for which $k = 1$. **1959** *Sunday Times* 5 Apr. 8/3 The sun itself has been photographed in the extreme ultra-violet (the Lyman-alpha) region of the spectrum. **1967** W. R. Hindmarsh *Atomic Spectra* ii. 13 Ritz..proposed his well-known combination principle in 1908; he recognized that the wave-numbers of the lines could always be represented as a difference between two terms... It was with the use of this principle that the Paschen, Lyman, Brackett and Pfund series in the spectrum of hydrogen were predicted ..before they were known experimentally. **1968** G. M. B. Dobson *Exploring Atmosphere* (ed. 2) viii. 158 Another possibility is that the very strong radiation which is given out by hydrogen in the sun, at a wavelength of 1216 Ångstrom units (known as the Lyman alpha line) produces the *D* region [of the ionosphere].

lymph. Add: **5. lymph node,** any of several small rounded gland-like structures of the lymphatic system, which are disposed along the course of the lymph vessels and which are responsible for removing foreign bodies from the lymph stream and for producing lymphocytes and antibodies; a lymph gland.

1892 *Proc. N.Y. Path. Soc. 1891* 65 (*heading*) Large-celled indurative hyperplasia of the lymph nodes. **1925** *Jrnl. Amer. Med. Assoc.* 28 Feb. 669/2 The cervical, axillary, epitrochlear and inguinal lymph nodes were moderately enlarged. **1955** *Sci. News Let.* 18 June 393/2 Antibodies, he found, are formed in lymph nodes, better known to the layman as glands. **1961** H. A. Skinner *Origin Med. Terms* (ed. 2) 259/2 All of the early writers seem to have adhered to the term [lymph] gland..and the term has been continued, although there is no indication of any gland function. This was a matter of vigorous debate at the anatomical congress at Basle [in 1895]..and Toldt especially advocated use of the term 'lymph node'. On the last ballot his suggestion was voted down by a large majority. In the Nomina Anatomica adopted at Paris in

1955 the term node was approved. **1972** J. W. SHIELDS *Trophic Function Lymphoid Elem.* xi. 71 The lymph nodes are characteristically oriented to receive substrate more or less directly from the peripheral tissues.

lymphadenopathy (li:mfædi̇̄nǫ·pāþi). *Med.* [f. LYMPH + ADENOPATHY.] Disease of the lymph nodes.

1920 *Bull. Johns Hopkins Hosp.* XXXI. 413/2 An acute infection associated with lymphadenopathy and lymphocytosis. **1973** *Nature* 27 July 206/2 The pertinent findings on physical examination were marked gingival hypertrophy, lymphadenopathy, petechiae of the lower extremities, and hepatomegaly.

lymphangiography (li:mfændʒi͵ǫ·grăfi). *Med.* [f. LYMPH + ANGIOGRAPHY.] A technique or procedure for demonstrating and examining the lymph vessels *in vivo* by injecting a contrast medium into them and examining them with X-rays; an examination by this technique.

1941 DORLAND & MILLER *Med. Dict.* (ed. 19) 830/1 *Lymphangiography*, the roentgenologic visualization of lymphatic vessels following the injection of contrast medium. **1952** *Clin. Sci.* XI. 13 (*heading*) Lymphangiography in man. **1961** *Radiology* LXXVI. 179/1 Lymphangiography, the radiographic demonstration of the lymphatic system by intralymphatic injection of contrast material, has opened a new field of investigation. **1973** J. F. MEANEY et al. *Complications & Legal Implications Radiologic Special Procedures* ix. 92 Lymphangiography is usually considered a relatively simple procedure. *Ibid.*, Many outpatients having lymphangiographies do not have their temperatures recorded.

Hence **lympha·ngiogram**, a radiograph taken by this technique; **ly:mphangio·grapher**, one who carries out or employs lymphangiography; **lympha:ngiogra·phic** *a.*; **lympha:ngiogra·phically** *adv.*

1955 *Brit. Med. Jrnl.* 16 Apr. 941/1 (*caption*) Normal lymphangiogram: 6 ml. of 70% diodone was injected and the films were exposed one minute later. **1964** *Clin. Radiol.* XV. 346/1 We have encountered only one serious reaction during our series of fifty-five lymphangiograms. **1967** A. RÜTTIMANN *Progress Lymphology* 127 (*heading*) Lymphangiographic evaluation of lymphoma. **1968** *Proc. Conf. Lymph & Lymphatic Syst.* vii. 154 Kinmonth and associates reported the largest series of patients studied lymphangiographically. **1973** J. F. MEANEY et al. *Complications & Legal Implications Radiologic Special Procedures* ix. 99 Every lymphangiographer should be aware of the potential danger.

lymphangitis. Add: Also **-angiitis.** (Earlier and later examples.)

1842 DUNGLISON *Dict. Med. Sci.* (ed. 3) 425/2 Lymphangeitis. **1889** *Syd. Soc. Lex.* Lymphangiitis. **1960** R. A. RUNNELLS et al. *Princ. Vet. Path.* xxii. 691/1 Epizootic lymphangitis is a chronic suppurative infection of horses, mules, and donkeys caused by the fungus *Zymonema farciminosum.* **1966** WRIGHT & SYMMERS *Systemic Path.* I. xxvi. 803/2 Elephantiasis of the penis and scrotum... Repeated attacks of lymphangiitis and the presence of a sufficient number of worms may, in the course of time, block so many lymph channels that chronic oedema develops.

lympho- (li·mfo), comb. form of LYMPH 3, used in numerous biological and medical terms, as **ly·mphoblast** *Biol.* [-BLAST], any cell which is a precursor of a small lymphocyte; so **lymphobla·stic** *a.*; **ly:mphoblasto·ma** *Path.* [*-OMA], malignant proliferation of lymphoblasts; **lymphoge·nic** [*-GENIC], **lympho·genous** [*-GENOUS], (*a*) producing lymph or lymphocytes; (*b*) arising in, produced by, or disseminated via the lymphatic system; **ly·mphokine** *Immunol.* [f. Gr. κινεῖν to move], any of various soluble substances released by lymphocytes following activation by contact with an antigen which are thought to be involved in cell-mediated immunity but to lack the antigen-specificity of antibodies; **lymphope·nia** [*-PENIA], reduction in the number of lymphocytes in the blood; **lymphopoiesis** (-poi͵ī·sis) [*-POIESIS], the formation of lymphocytes; so **lymphopoie·tic** *a.*

1909 *Cent. Dict.* Suppl., Lymphoblast. **1935** *Jrnl. Amer. Med. Assoc.* 7 Sept. 765/2 Lymphoblasts approach the structure of myeloblasts. **1962** *Lancet* 27 Jan. 206/2 In the early stages of the production pathway, the lymphocytes are large and possess an intensely basophilic cytoplasm; these are the cells which have often been called lymphoblasts. **1905** *Ibid.* 12 Aug. 465/2 Dr. Jones concluded,..secondly, that apparently a lymphoblastic marrow was usually accompanied by an increased production of erythroblasts, but that, on the other hand, a leucoblastic marrow was not associated with increased erythroblastic production. **1961** *Ibid.* 5 Aug. 291/2 In 2 cases biopsy of a lymph-gland was undertaken and reported as lymphoblastic lymphoma. **1920** *Jrnl. Urol.* IV. 137 (*title*) Lympho-blastoma (lympho-sarcoma) of the prostate. **1926** *Jrnl. Amer. Med. Assoc.* 17 Apr. 1185/1 Lymphoblastoma, a name considered by some as synonymous with malignant lymphoma..may include lymphatic leukemia (lymphocytic and lymphoblastic), aleukemic lymphatic leukemia (pseudoleukemia, aleukemic lymphadenosis), lymphocytoma, Hodgkin's disease (lymphogranuloma), lymphadenoma, lymphomatosis, lymphosarcoma, round cell sarcoma, leukosarcoma and lymphadenosarcoma. **1970** S. D. KOBERNICK tr. *Masson's Human Tumors* II. x. 353 The structure is very simple: a chaotic mixture of small cells with round nuclei, larger in lymphoblastomas than in lymphocytomas. **1901** Lymphogenic [see *LYMPHOMATOSIS]. **1968** *Proc. Conf. Lymph & Lymphatic Syst.* viii. 173 Experimental animals with lymphogenic encephalopathy have decreased response to pain. **1889** *Syd. Soc. Lex.*, *Lymphogenous*, producing lymph. **1909** *Practitioner* Nov. 656 The unilateral distribution of renal tuberculosis..is explained by lymphogenous infection. **1935** N. P. SHERWOOD *Immunol.* iii. 59. The four avenues [of spread of infectious agents] commonly mentioned are surface spread, dissemination by way of the lymphatics (lymphogenous), blood stream (hematogenous) and direct extension to adjacent tissues. **1968** *Proc. Conf. Lymph. & Lymphatic Syst.* viii. 169 (*heading*) Lymphogenous encephalopathy. **1969** D. C. DUMONDE et al. in *Nature* 4 38/1 In the guinea-pig these four phenomena are mediated by cell-free soluble factors, which are generated during interaction of sensitized lymphocytes with specific antigen, but which are expressed without reference to immunological specificity. The generic term 'lymphokine' is suggested to describe this group of biological activities. **1973** *Ibid.* 2 Mar. 22/2 When T cells are activated by antigen, they proliferate..but they..do not become antibody-secreting cells. They do, however, secrete a variety of non-antigen-specific factors ('lymphokines') such as migration inhibition factors (MIF), chemotactic factors, cytotoxic factors and mitogenic factors, at least some of which presumably play a role in cell-mediated immune responses, for which T cells are primarily responsible. **1974** *Sci. Amer.* Apr. 36/2 Transplantation antigens and other foreign material ..stimulate the production and release of 'sensitized' lymphocytes, or effector cells... In addition to killing graft cells directly the sensitized lymphocytes secrete a variety of chemical agents called lymphokines, some of which act directly on the foreign cells and some of which attract other leukocytes..which digest damaged cells and cell fragments. **1909** *Cent. Dict.* Suppl., Lymphopenia. **1921** *Lancet* 10 Dec. 1205/2 The blood content passes from exhibiting a lymphopænia to a lymphocytosis. **1964** L. MARTIN *Clin. Endocrinol.* (ed. 4) i. 35 A leucocytosis of 10–15,000 per c.mm. is usual with a polymorph excess, lymphopenia and eosinopenia. **1918** STEDMAN *Med. Dict.* (ed. 5) 569/1 *Lymphopoiesis*,..the formation of lymphocytes. **1968** PASSMORE & ROBSON *Compan. Med. Stud.* I. xxvii. 2/2 In the lymphoreticular organs the reticulum cells..also differentiate into stem cells which divide and mature to form lymphocytes in the process known as lymphopoiesis. **1915** J. E. R. MCDONAGH *Biol. & Treatm. Venereal Dis.* xv. 144 (*heading*) Syphilis of the lympho- and haemopoetic [*sic*] system. **1966** M. W. ELVES *Lymphocytes* iii. 71 The lymphopoietic role of the thymus.

lymphocyte. Substitute for def.: A kind of small leucocyte which has a single round nucleus and little or no granulation in the cytoplasm, constitutes about a quarter of the total leucocytes in the blood stream, is found in large numbers in the lymph nodes and other lymphoid tissue, and is a major agent in most immunological processes. *Large lymphocytes*, which constitute a small proportion of the total number of lymphocytes, are larger than and apparently the precursors of the *small lymphocytes*, which constitute the bulk of them. (Earlier and later examples.)

1890 *Jrnl. Morphol.* IV. 108 It is quite generally agreed that the origin of the white corpuscles of the blood is to be found in the lymph leucocytes, or lymphocytes, to borrow a convenient term... The lymphocytes are characterized by a vesicular nucleus, usually with a nucleolus and a scanty reticulum, and by a very small protoplasmic envelope. **1891** *Rep. Lab. R. Coll. Physicians Edin.* III. 118 If this view of the nature of leucocytes is accepted, we at once realise the futility of the attempts..to establish distinctions between the leucocytes found in different situations,—the white blood corpuscles, the wandering cells in the tissues, the lymphocytes of the lymph, lymph-glands and spleen, the thymus-cells, the marrow-cells, &c. **1905** A. STENGEL tr. *Ehrlich's Dis. Blood* 71 At the introduction to this chapter it was pointed out that a retrograde movement in hematology is in progress which attempts to establish the derivation of all the white blood-cells from the lymphocytes. **1913** GULLAND & GOODALL *Blood* II. vii. 58 Large lymphocytes have the same general characters as the small lymphocytes. **1962** *Lancet* 26 May 1098/2 The blood-picture was:..eosinophils 2%, lymphocytes 11%, monocytes 1%, [etc.]. **1968** PASSMORE & ROBSON *Compan. Med. Stud.* I. xxvii. 4/2 Lymphocytes, or more properly small lymphocytes, to distinguish them from their immediate precursors, the medium and large lymphocytes, are formed in the cortex of lymph nodes by the maturation and division of lymphoblasts and lymphoid stem cells. **1970** *Courier-Mail* (Brisbane) 28 Jan. 30 Unfortunately this desensitisation technique seems to affect only a proportion of the recipient's lymphocytes: the remainder attack the transplant.

So **ly:mphocyto·ma** (pl. **-o·mas, -o·mata**) *Path.* [*-OMA], malignant proliferation of lymphocytes; any condition characterized by this; a tumour composed of lymphocytes; **ly:mphocyto·matous** *a.*

1908 OSLER & MCCRAE *Syst. Med.* IV. 827 The hyperplastic and neoplasm-like conditions of the lymph nodes depending upon an overgrowth of cells of the type of lymphocytes..are here brought into one general class, the lymphocytomata. This includes all the lymphocytomatous tumors classed variously as lymphoma, lymphadenoma, lymphosarcoma, pseudoleukæmia, adenia, lymphadenomatosis, lymphomatosis, etc. **1920** J. E. R. MCDONAGH *Venereal Dis.* iv. 55 (*heading*) Syphilitic lymphocytomata. **1949** *Year Bk. Radiol.* 406 The medical profession has believed that no attempt at treatment of lymphoid tumors (lymphosarcoma, lymphocytoma, Hodgkin's disease and macrofollicular lymphoma) will be successful.

lymphœdema (limfi̇̄dī·mă). *Path.* Also **lymphedema.** [f. LYMPH + ŒDEMA.] Œdema resulting from obstruction of lymph vessels or lymph nodes.

1889 *Syd. Soc. Lex.*, Lymphœdema. **1961** *Lancet* 19 Aug. 408/1 The XO female was noted to have peripheral lymphœdema and neck-webbing at birth. **1968** *Proc. Conf. Lymph & Lymphatic Syst.* vii. 153 In 1892, Milroy reported congenital, bilateral lymphedema of the legs in twenty-five of ninety-two members of one family.

Hence **lymphœde·matous** *a.*

1934 *Arch. Internal Med.* LIV. 614 Lymphedematous swelling..is present at birth. **1962** D. I. ABRAMSON *Blood Vessels & Lymphatics* xxiv. 733 The protein content of tissue fluid from the lymphedematous area was similar to that of the serum.

lymphogranuloma (li:mfogræniŭlōᵘ·mă). *Path.* [f. *LYMPHO- + GRANULOMA.] Used, usu. with mod.L. or Eng. adjs., to designate any of three diseases (see quot. 1958), esp. *lymphogranuloma venereum* (or *lymphogranuloma inguinale*), a venereal disease, esp. of the tropics, caused by micro-organisms of the group Chlamydiæ, and manifested esp. as inflammation, followed by suppuration and breakdown, of the lymph nodes and lymph vessels, particularly in the inguinal region.

1924 J. SCHAUMANN in *Brit. Jrnl. Dermatol.* XXXVI. 515 When in November 1914, I described the disease I proposed designating by the anatomico-clinical name of benign lymphogranuloma, I had already detected the essential characteristics, which justified its classification amongst lymphadenic affections. **1932** DEWOLF & VAN CLEVE in *Jrnl. Amer. Med. Assoc.* 24 Sept. 1065/1 They [*sc.* Durand, Nicolas, and Favre] chose the name 'subacute inguinal lymphogranulomatosis' for the disease, a rather unfortunate designation because of the confusion to which it may lead. We have chosen the shorter designation, 'lymphogranuloma inguinale', as this name is becoming more widely used by European writers. **1958** R. W. RAVEN *Cancer* II. xxiv. 473 Few medical terms can have such different meanings in different countries as lymphogranuloma. When used without qualification, in English-speaking countries, 'lymphogranuloma' usually refers to 'lymphogranuloma inguinale' (Nicolas–Favré disease); in most European countries it implies Hodgkin's disease ('lymphogranuloma malignum') but in Scandinavia it refers to sarcoidosis ('lymphogranuloma benignum'). **1960** J. MARSHALL *Dis. Skin* xxv. 630 (*heading*) Hodgkin's disease (malignant lymphogranuloma of Paltauf–Sternberg). **1967** A. C. ALLEN *Skin* (ed. 2) xi. 423/1 At different stages in the evolution of the information on the disease, stress was placed on the involvement of one organ over others, as indicated by the application of the terms 'uveoparotid fever', 'osteitis tuberculosa multiplex cystica', 'lupus pernio', and 'benign lymphogranuloma'. **1974** PASSMORE & ROBSON *Compan. Med. Stud.* III. xiii. 13/2 Lymphogranuloma venereum. Alternative names for this disease are lymphogranuloma inguinale and tropical bubo. It is caused by *Chlamydia* or *Bedsonia.*

lymphogranulomatosis (li:mfogræniŭlomătōᵘ·sis). *Path.* [f. *lymphogranulomat-*, taken as stem of prec. + -OSIS.] Used, usu. with mod.L. or Eng. adjs., to designate any of three diseases, viz. *lymphogranulomatosis benigna*, sarcoidosis; *lymphogranulomatosis inguinalis* [tr. F. *lymphogranulomatose inguinale* (Durand et al. 1913, in *Bull. et Mém. Soc. méd. d. Hôp. de Paris* XXXV. 274)], lymphogranuloma venereum; *lymphogranulomatosis maligna*, Hodgkin's disease.

1911 DORLAND *Med. Dict.* (ed. 6) 470/1 *Lymphogranulomatosis*..Hodgkin's disease. **1915** J. E. R. MCDONAGH *Biol. & Treatm. Venereal Dis.* xlvi. 550 This case..would probably have been called lymphogranulomatosis on the Continent, and lymphadenoma or Hodgkin's disease affecting the skin in this country. **1926** *Arch. Dermatol. & Syphilol.* XIV. 36 In January, 1913, Nicolas, Durand and Favré published a report concerning a series of cases of lymphatic enlargement of the groins which they named 'lymphogranulomatosis inguinalis'. **1932** [see *LYMPHOGRANULOMA]. **1935** *Brit. Jrnl. Dermatol.* XLVII. 225 The symptomatic triad of benign lymphogranulomatosis. *Ibid.*, I attributed the diabetes to the presence of lymphogranulomatosis benigna in this organ. *Ibid.* 227 The polynuclear leucocytosis in malign lymphogranulomatosis (Hodgkin's disease). **1971** BRUNSON & GALL *Concepts of Dis.* xxv. 925/1 In the United States and Great Britain, Hodgkin's disease is regarded generally as a malignant neoplasm; in Germany it is considered to be a peculiar inflammatory process and is designated by the term *lymphogranulomatosis.* **1973** R. B. SCOTT *Price's Textbk. Pract. Med.* (ed. 11) ix. 874 Sarcoidosis. *Synonyms.* Lymphogranulomatosis benigna [etc.].

lymphography. Add: **2.** A technique similar to lymphangiography but including demonstration and examination of lymph nodes.

1935 DORLAND & MILLER *Med. Dict.* (ed. 17) 776/1 *Lymphography*, roentgen visualization of the lymph vessels and nodes after the injection of a contrast medium. **1969** *Brit. Med. Jrnl.* 6 Dec. 579/1 Lymphovenous shunts have been detected in patients by lymphography with Ultrafluid Lipiodol. **1973** J. F. MEANEY et al. *Complications & Legal Implications Radiologic Special Procedures*

ix. 96 Fraimow et al. demonstrated the physiologic effects of lymphography on the lungs.

lymphomatosis (limfomătōu·sis). *Path.* [f. *lymphomat-* (taken as stem of mod.L. LYMPHOMA) + -OSIS.] Any of various diffuse neoplastic or hyperplastic disorders originating in lymphoid tissue.

1900 DORLAND *Med. Dict.* 368/2 *Lymphomatosis*, general lymphatic engorgement. **1901** *Encycl. Medica* VII. 196 Among them [*sc.* synonyms of lymphadenoma] are adenia, lymphadenia, lymphogenic diathesis, lymphadenosis, lymphoma, lymphomatosis, pseudo-leukemia, lymphosarcoma, and the non-committal Hodgkin's disease. **1933** *Jrnl. Exper. Med.* LVIII. 254 Lymphomatosis (lymphoid leukosis) of chickens is identical with the similar disease of mammals. **1947** *Radiology* XLIX. 354/1 Terminal changes were mainly of two types: generalized atrophy (premature aging) and mediastinal lymphomatosis. **1961** *Brit. Vet. Jrnl.* CXVII. 323 Much confusion has resulted from the use of the term 'visceral lymphomatosis', which some workers understand to be a genuine lymphoid leucosis, whilst others use it to designate the visceral lesions associated with fowl paralysis. **1965** *New Scientist* 17 June 800/2 The three main leukaemias of poultry —lymphomatosis, erythroblastosis and myeloblastosis. **1970** JUBB & KENNEDY *Path. Domestic Animals* (ed. 2) I. iv. 386/1 All primary tumours of the lymphoreticular tissues are malignant... These tumours occur in all domestic animals... Very many names have been applied to them depending on the pattern of growth, the presence or absence of 'leucaemic' changes in the circulating blood, and the judgement of the observer on what was the chief cell involved. In the following discussion we shall include them all in the designation lymphomatosis.

lynchet. Now the usual form of LINCHET. Delete *'dial.'* and add: **2.** (Later *attrib.* example.)

1917 J. MASEFIELD *Old Front Line* 42 The line of the lynchet-top merges into the slope behind it.

b. *Archæol.* A cultivation terrace. Also *attrib.*

1796 *Gentl. Mag.* LXVI. 822/1 On the declivities of the elevated and chalky tracts of Wiltshire, Dorsetshire, and other counties, there very frequently occurs a beautiful assemblage of *terraces*, mostly horizontal, and rising in a continued series like the steps of Egyptian pyramids... These, which are commonly arable,..are popularly called *lynchets*... They are generally regarded in the neighbourhood as the offspring of human exertion in remote ages, to facilitate and extend the dominion of the plough. **1869** D. MACKINTOSH *Scenery Eng. & Wales* IV. ii. 89 Many terraces are still cultivated but..there is..a general desire to plough down the 'lynchets' (as they are locally called), and..formerly their number was much greater than at present. **1908** A. H. ALLCROFT *Earthwork of Eng.* ii. 40 All but the very summits of the highest Downs were early ploughed, and the lynchets must in many cases be of mediæval, if not of Saxon date. **1953** R. J. C. ATKINSON *Field Archaeol.* (ed. 2) 19 When lynchets (cultivation terraces) are photographed facing a setting sun, the sloping faces of the terraces..will reflect more light than the surrounding ground. **1954** M. BERESFORD *Lost Villages* ix. 297 On the valley sides are lynchet-like terraces which look as if they mark where the ploughs moved. **1968** J. ARNOLD *Shell Bk. Country Crafts* 13 Celtic farmers increased the areas of their arable land by excavating some of the hillsides and making terraces or lynchets.

Hence **ly·nchetted** *ppl. a.*, of land: cultivated in this way.

1928 *Antiquity* June 171 To the south and west of the lynchetted area lies what is known as 'The Druid's Circle'. **1933** *Ibid.* VII. 494 The..rarity in Cumbria of the lynchetted form of settlement. **1954** S. PIGGOTT *Neolithic Cultures* ii. 33 Certain types of settlement, characterized by huts within irregular lynchetted areas, may be Neolithic in date.

lynching, *vbl. sb.* (Earlier examples. Also *lynching-bee.*)

1836 D. CROCKETT *Exploits & Adventures Texas* vii. 103 This is what we call Lynching in Natchez. **1837** *Southern Lit. Messenger* III. 648 The outrages of the borderers, the frontier law of 'regulation' or 'lynching', which is common to new countries all over the world, are ascribed to slavery. **1900** *Congress. Rec.* 31 Jan. 1369/1 They have sometimes had 'lynching bees',..they have sometimes lynched men for murder, for arson, for rape. **1903** C. T. BRADY *Bishop* ix. 172, I don't join no more lynchin'-bees. **1943** *Christian Cent.* 1 Dec. 1/2 Evidently there is a widespread and growing fear lest the United Nations..let loose in Europe what might turn out to be little less than a gigantic lynching bee.

Lynch law. Add: Now usu. **lynch law.** (Earlier and later examples.)

The particulars supplied by Ellicott, together with other evidence, clearly establish the fact that the originator of Lynch law was Captain William Lynch (1742–1820) of Pittsylvania in Virginia. According to Ellicott, 'this self-created judicial tribunal was first organised in the state of Virginia about the year 1776'; an article in the *Southern Lit. Messenger* (1836) II. 389 gives the date definitely as 1780.

1811 A. ELLICOTT in C. V. Mathews *A. Ellicott* (1908) 220 Captain Lynch just mentioned was the author of the Lynch laws so well known and so frequently carried into effect some years ago in the southern States in violation of every principle of justice and jurisprudence. **1902** J. LONDON *Daughter of Snows* 284 It's lynch law, you know, and their minds are made up. They're bound to get me. **1963** *Times* 18 Apr. 9/1 It smacks more of lynch law than the reasoned kind of wisdom one hopes for in our elected officials. **1974** *Times* 28 Nov. 8/7 Mr Jeremy Thorpe.. urged..that the hijackers of the British Airways VC10 should not be handed over to the 'lynch law' of the Palestine Liberation Organization.

Judge Lynch (earlier example); **lynch mob,** a mob intent on lynching.

1838 H. MARTINEAU *Retrospect of Western Travel* II. 87 A distant Lynch mob was outraging..a free and innocent citizen. **1840** W. G. SIMMS *Border Beagles* 248 The murmurs began to close with the ominous inquiry after that venerable border magistrate, Judge Lynch. **1972** B. GARFIELD *Line of Succession* (1974) III. 255 If he pulls through alive you'll just have to hold off a lynch mob.

Lynch-like, *a.* [f. *Lynch*: see LYNCH LAW.] Characteristic or suggestive of Judge Lynch.

1837 R. M. BIRD *Nick of Woods* I. 221 Since Stackpole, having endured the penalty for stealing him, considered himself as having a legal, Lynch-like right to the animal, which no one could dispute.

lynch-man. [Cf. LYNCH LAW.] One of the early administrators of lynch law.

1811 A. ELLICOTT in C. V. Mathews *A. Ellicott* (1908) 221 The Lynch-men associated for the purpose of punishing crimes in a summary way without the tedious and technical forms of our courts of justice. *Ibid.* 222, I should not have asserted it as a fact had it not been related to me by Mr. Lynch..together with several other Lynch-men as they are called.

Lyngby (li·ŋbi). Also **Lingby.** [See quot. 1964.] Used *attrib.* or *ellipt.* to designate a mesolithic culture of the Baltic area or its artefacts (see quots.).

1925 V. G. CHILDE *Dawn European Civilization* i. 11 The..Lingby culture..belongs to the end of the ice-age or the very beginning of the Ancylus period. **1936** J. G. D. CLARK *Mesolithic Settlement of N. Europe* ii. 70 The tanged flake from Christiansund..is often spoken of as 'a Lyngby point'. *Ibid.* iii. 79 Our knowledge of the Lyngby culture apart from the reindeer antler objects is slight. **1951** A. COATES *Prelude to History* x. 253 To the east several cultures, the Ahrensburg..in north Germany, Lyngby in Jutland and Swiderian in north Poland, derive from the East Gravettian of the upper palaeolithic. **1964** W. L. GOODMAN *Hist. Woodworking Tools* 12 Their earliest tools, made of reindeer antler, with the stump of the brow tine sharpened to a cutting edge, are known as 'Lyngby axes', from the site at Norre-Lyngby, in Denmark, where they were first found.

lyngorm: see *LINGWORM.

lynn, U.S. var. of LINN² (in Dict. and Suppl.). Also *attrib.*

1787 W. SARGENT in *Mem. Amer. Acad. Arts & Sci.* IX. 158 Lynn,..a light white wood very proper for finishing the inside of dwelling houses. **1796**, etc. [see LINN²]. **1819** E. DANA *Geogr. Sk. Western Country* 84 Sugar maple, black and white walnut,..lynn, sycamore, cotton wood. **1819** E. EVANS *Pedestrious Tour* 299 Here are the lynn tree, gum tree, [etc.]. **1839** in *Trans. Mich. Agric. Soc.* (1855) VI. 263 The table lands are mostly timbered with the varieties of oak, beech, maple, lynn, hickory. **1849** E. CHAMBERLAIN *Indiana Gazetteer* (ed. 3) 170 The other forest trees..are ash, walnut,..lynn, [etc.]. **1886** *Harper's Mag.* June 58/2 Ropes are made of lynn bark.

lyochrome (ləi·ŏkrōum). *Biochem.* [ad. G. *lyochrom* (Ellinger & Koschara 1933, in *Ber. d. Deut. Chem. Ges.* LXVI. B. 317), f. Gr. λύ-ειν to loosen + -O + Gr. χρῶμ-α colour.] = *FLAVIN 2.

1933 *Chem. Abstr.* XXVII. 2167 The name lyochrome is proposed for pigments of this class. **1938** [see *INTRAVITAL *a.*]. **1964** WAGNER & FOLKERS *Vitamins & Coenzymes* iv. 48 The term 'lyochrome' was rejected, and the designation 'flavin' was adopted for these growth-promoting water-soluble pigments. **1974** *Encycl. Brit. Macropædia* IV. 922/2 (*heading*) Flavins (lyochromes).

Lyonnais (lī,ŏnē·, ‖ li,onę), *sb.* and *a.* Also **Lyon(n)ese** (lī,ŏnī·z); (fem.) **Lionnoise, Lyonnaise, Lyonoise.** [Fr.] **A.** *sb.* A native or inhabitant of the city of Lyons (Fr. *Lyon*), or the former province of Lyonnais, in eastern France; these people collectively; also, the French dialect of this area.

1653 [see *ANGEVIN *a.* and *sb.*]. **1768** STERNE *Sentimental Journey* II. 201 The maid was a Lyonoise of twenty, and as brisk and lively a French girl as ever moved. **1777** P. THICKNESSE *Year's Journey* II. xliii. 78 Two harangues made by the Emperor Claudius in the senate, in favour of the Lyonoise. **1867** C. M. YONGE *Pupils of St. John* xv. 249 To Irenæus and his Lyonnese such falsehood was the next thing to apostasy. **1868** J. S. NORTHCOTE *Celebrated Sanctuaries of Madonna* iv. 134 The devotion of the Lyonnese..clung rather to the crypt and the image of St. Pothinus. *Ibid.* 142 Suchet was a Lyonnese by birth. *Ibid.* 146 Nor must we..fail to notice the last ornament presented to the sanctuary by the piety of the Lyonnese. **1955** J. THOMAS *No Banners* xvii. 156 Fernande continued in her archaic *Lyonnais*: 'Joe's been arrested, too.' **1960** L. DURRELL *Spirit of Place* (1969) 327 No traveller will repeat these words to a Lyonnais without provoking the passionate cry: 'Unjust!' **1966** *Observer* 30 Oct. 5/2, I saw between 15,000 and 20,000 *Lyonnais* in the square. *Ibid.*, The *Lyonnaises* peered into an English bathroom in the Ideal Home Exhibition House. **1972** *Guardian* 11 Mar. 15/1 The nineteenth century writer, Edouard Aynard, described the Lyonnese as 'a northern race astray in the south'.

B. *adj.* Of, pertaining to, or characteristic of Lyons or its inhabitants; *spec.* designating either of two styles of book-binding associated with Lyons.

1801 C. WILMOT *Let.* 13 Dec. in *Irish Peer* (1920) 17, I have issued forth betimes, under the conduct of a Lyonese Laquais de Place. **1867** C. M. YONGE *Pupils of St. John* xiv. 224 The whole..day..was spent by this Lyonnese multitude in baiting these..men. **1893** S. T. PRIDEAUX *Hist. Sk. Bookbinding* i. 46 The Lyonnese binders..used very fine stamps. **1894** H. P. HORNE *Binding of Bks.* ii. 77 The use of azured tools..became a characteristic of Lyonese bindings. **1928** E. P. GOLDSCHMIDT *Gothic & Renaissance Bookbindings* I. 317 These bindings are generally referred to as being in the 'Lyonnese' style. It is quite possible that a good many may come from Lyons, but I have never found any proof for this. **1960** E. A. LOWE *Eng. Uncial* 3 The collection of Concilia in the sixth-century Paris MS. Lat. 12097 written mostly in half-uncial has many pages in almost contemporary uncial. Experts consider the collection Lyonese. **1960** L. DURRELL *Spirit of Place* (1969) 328 The first steam-powered boat was Lyonnais in conception and design. De Jouffroy of Lyons built it. **1966** M. R. D. FOOT *SOE in France* viii. 215 He made firm friends with two Lyonnais business men. **1972** R. COBB *Reactions to French Revolution* ii. 51 The 29 Mai..would *never* be forgotten,.. another example no doubt of Lyonnais particularism.

b. *Cookery.* Designating food, esp. sliced potatoes, cooked or served with onions, or with an onion sauce. Freq. placed after the sb., and as *à la Lyonnaise.*

1846 C. E. FRANCATELLI *Mod. Cook* 8 Lyonnaise Sauce. Peel..onions... Slice them... Fry them... put them into a small stewpan, with..brown sauce. [**1846** A. SOYER *Gastronomic Regenerator* 470 (*heading*) Pommes de Terre à la Lyonnaise.] **1866** H. ST. CLAIR *Dainty Dishes* 130 Potatoes à la Lyonnaise..are very good to eat with cutlets. **1877** E. S. DALLAS *Kettner's Bk. of Table* 359 *Lyonnese Potatoes* (Pommes-de-terre à la Lyonnaise).— These are cooked potatoes combined with cooked onions. **1939** A. SIMON *Conc. Encycl. Gastron.* I. 34 *Lyonnaise*, Sauce. A white wine and onion sauce. **1960** E. DAVID *French Provincial Cooking* 228 What is to be served after these sausage dishes?.. No dish requiring potatoes after the Lyonnais one. **1974** *Times* 2 May 8/1 Lyonnaise potatoes... Fried potatoes made with blanched raw potatoes... Sauté potatoes with onion.

Lyons (ləi·ənz, liòn). Also **Lyon.** [F. *Lyon* Lyons, a city in France.] Used *attrib.* to designate various products associated with the city (see quots.); also *absol.*

1765 STERNE *Tr. Shandy* VII. xxxi. 162, I could.. sometimes not so much as see even a Lyons-waistcoat, but this remembrance..would present itself. **1778** F. BURNEY *Evelina* I. xvi. 100 We found her..very busy in wiping her negligee..as she said it was a new Lyon's silk. *Ibid.* III. xxi. 234 'Twill be a most excellent opportunity of shewing off her best Lyons' silk. **1851** MAYHEW & BINNY *1851* xvi. 160 The jewels and the tapestry, and the Lyons silks, are not now the sole objects of attraction. **1855** DICKENS *Dorrit* (1857) I. i. 6, I can cut my bread..like Lyons sausage. **1869** 'MARK TWAIN' *Innoc. Abr.* (1870) xxx. 244 Lyons velvets rank higher in America than those of Genoa. **1872** *Young Englishwoman* Dec. 646/1 Lyons grosgrains and moire silks. **1874** W. CROOKES *Pract. Handbk. Dyeing & Calico-Printing* II. iii. 195 (*heading*) Aniline blues... *Lyons blue* (Girard and De Laire). **1895** *Brit. Warehouseman* Feb. 13/2 A triple-pleated blouse of purple Lyons velvet was worn. **1902** S. J. WEYMAN *In Kings' Byways* I. 161 The hiding-places..had been.. contrived to hold runlets of Nantz and bales of Lyons. **1908** A. BENNETT *Old Wives' Tale* III. vi. 385 She bought ..coffee, Lyons sausage, dried prunes. **1914** F. W. ATACK tr. *Wahl's Manuf. Org. Dyestuffs* III. xvi. 171 The monophenyl- and monotolyl-derivatives [of Pararosaniline] occur..in the dyestuffs known as Phenyl violet,..Lyons blue, etc. **1924** A. T. DE MOUILPIED *Quest for Colour* iv. 20 Summary of the more important discoveries in the history of synthetic organic dyestuffs... 1860 Bleu de Lyon—a spirit soluble blue derived from Magenta. [Discoverer] Girard and De Laire. **1952** 'P. WENTWORTH' *Brading Collection* xi. 66 Great ladies..had bought changeable silks there, and fine Lyons velvet. **1959** D. OGRIZEK *France Observed* 211 The contribution local artists have made towards enhancing the prestige of Lyons silk has always been recognised. **1960** E. DAVID *French Provincial Cooking* 225 Randall & Aubin..sell a coarsely-cut garlic-flavoured sausage which is not unlike the Lyon sausage. **1971** *Colour Index* (Soc. Dyers & Colourists) (ed. 3) V. 5573 Commercial name..Lyon Blue..C. I. Solvent Blue 3.

lyophile (ləi·ŏfəil), *a.* [ad. G. *lyophil* (Freundlich & Neumann 1908, in *Zeitschr. f. Chem. und Ind. d. Kolloide* III. 81/2), f. Gr. λύ-ειν to loosen; see -PHIL, -PHILE.] **1.** *Physical Chem.* = *LYOPHILIC *a.*

1915 W. W. TAYLOR *Chem. Colloids* i. 7 The term *lyophile* has been applied to those systems in which there is a marked affinity between the phases and *lyophobe* to the others. **1927** H. S. VAN KLOOSTER tr. *Kruyt's Colloids* i. 10 Emulsoids, or lyophile colloids,..form disperse systems in which the properties of the dispersing phase are considerably modified by the disperse colloid. **1941** R. J. HARTMAN *Colloid Chem.* xviii. 358 The terms lyophobe ('hatred' toward external phase) and lyophile ('love' toward external phase) were suggested by Freundlich.

2. *Biol.* and *Med.* Also **lyophil** (-fil). Of, pertaining to, or employing lyophilization; lyophilized.

1934 S. MUDD et al. in *Jrnl. Immunol.* XXVI. 341 (*heading*) The preparation, properties and applications of lyophile serum proteins and complement. **1949** *Jrnl. Bacteriol.* LVII. 575 The lyophil process has been shown to be a successful method for the preservation of yeast cultures in a viable state. **1958** *Angiology* IX. 189/2 The condenser

system of the lyophile apparatus should be cleaned and dried before re-use. **1961** *Phytopathology* LI. 259/1 (*heading*) Observations on lyophil preservation and storage of Pythium species.

lyophilic (ləiǒfi·lik), *a. Physical Chem.* [f. *LYOPHIL(E *a.* + -IC.] Of a dispersed colloidal phase: having an affinity for the dispersion medium; not readily precipitated out by small quantities of electrolyte. Also applied to sols containing such a phase, which generally have a lower surface tension and a higher viscosity than the dispersion medium and which give gels on evaporation or cooling.

1911 [see *LYOPHOBIC *a.*]. **1938** H. L. HIND *Brewing* I. vi. 111 The complex carbohydrates and proteins belong to the class of lyophilic colloids, which is much the more important class in brewing. **1940** GLASSTONE *Text-bk. Physical Chem.* xiv. 1210 Substances which most readily form lyophilic sols are those of high molecular weight; each particle, therefore, consists of a small number of molecules and in some instances possibly of only one large molecule. **1959** [see *LYOPHOBIC *a.*]. **1969** G. D. PARFITT *Dispersion of Powders in Liquids* iii. 81 Solutions of macromolecules and association colloids are of the lyophilic type and form spontaneously when the components are brought into contact.

lyophilization (ləiǫ:filəizēi·ʃən). *Biol.* and *Med.* [f. *LYOPHIL(E *a.* + -IZATION.] = *FREEZE-DRYING *vbl. sb.*

1938 *Jrnl. Allergy* X. 3 The chief advantage of lyophilization lies in the means it offers to preserve antibodies and other labile serum components..over extended periods of time. **1949** E. P. ABRAHAM et al. in H. W. Florey et al. *Antibiotics* II. xv. 638 Solvent transfer and lyophilization still form the basis of all commercial penicillin production, processes. **1958** W. C. FRAZIER *Food Microbiol.* xvi. 214 Milk and other liquid dairy products may be dried by lyophilization. **1967** *Oceanogr. & Marine Biol.* V. 164 Lyophilization is probably the gentlest way to dry a tissue and is essential if delicate materials are to be preserved.

lyophilize (ləiǫ·filəiz), *v.* [f. *LYOPHIL(E *a.* + -IZE.] *trans.* To subject to lyophilization; to freeze-dry.

1938 *Jrnl. Allergy* X. 3 In each instance a negative Kahn reaction was obtained on the 'immune' serum before it was lyophilized. **1949** A. G. SANDERS in H. W. Florey et al. *Antibiotics* II. xvi. 684 Spores from these fungi can be lyophilized, that is, dried from the frozen state, without impairing their vitality. **1973** LANDHUIS & IDE in J. A. Capella et al. *Corneal Preservation* xii. 141 Tissue lyophilized without pretreatment in glycerin became hard, took longer to rehydrate, and healed more slowly.

Hence **lyo·philized** *ppl. a.*; also **lyo·philizate** [after *filtrate*, *precipitate*, etc.], a substance or material which has been lyophilized; **lyo·philizer**, an apparatus for carrying out lyophilization.

1938 *Jrnl. Allergy* X. 9 Patients to be treated with lyophilized immune serum were selected. **1963** *Problemy Gematol. i Pereliv. Krovi* VIII. vi. 62 Both homogenates and lyophilizates may be used as a source of erythroplastin in experimental research and clinical laboratory tests for hemostasis. **1967** *Oceanogr. & Marine Biol.* V. 163 In a lyophilizer the water is sublimed away during a drying period lasting several hours but the tissue is at zero degrees as long as ice is present. **1971** *Times* (Suppl.) 27 July p. iii/6 Problems concerning skin replacement in burns have been tackled..where the preparation of lyophilized (freeze dried) and deep frozen skin has been successful. **1972** *Nature* 14 Apr. 347/1 The lyophilizate was then redissolved to give a final concentration of 5 × SSC. **1972** IZAK & LEWIS *Mod. Concepts in Hematol.* 76 Lyophilization was performed in a Virtis batch lyophilizer.

lyophobe (ləi·ǒfōᵘb), *a. Physical Chem.* [ad. G. *lyophob* (Freundlich & Neumann 1908, in *Zeitschr. f. Chem. und Ind. d. Kolloide* III. 81/2), f. Gr. λύ-ειν to loosen: see -PHOBE.] = *LYOPHOBIC *a.*

1915 [see *LYOPHILE *a.* 1]. **1927** H. S. VAN KLOOSTER tr. *Kruyt's Colloids* i. 10 The suspensoids, or lyophobe colloids ..are systems in which most of their physical properties differ only slightly from their dispersion media. **1941** [see *LYOPHILE *a.* 1].

lyophobic (ləiǒfōᵘ·bik), *a. Physical Chem.* [f. *LYOPHOB(E *a.* + -IC.] Of a dispersed colloidal phase: not having an affinity for the dispersion medium; readily precipitated out by small quantities of electrolyte. Also applied to sols containing such a phase, which generally have a similar surface tension and viscosity to those of the dispersion medium, and which on evaporation or cooling give solids which cannot readily be reconverted into sols.

1911 H. FREUNDLICH in *Chem. News* 22 Sept. 140/1 Colloidal solutions stand between these two extremes. One class, distinguished from coarse suspensions only by the ultramicroscopic dimensions of their particles, are termed 'Suspension-colloids' or 'Lyophobic Sols'. These include colloidal metals, sulphides, and many hydroxides. 'Emulsion-colloids', or 'Lyophilic sols', which include albumin, gelatin, starch, &c., approach more nearly to the true solutions. **1959** K. J. MUSELS *Introd. Colloid Chem.* viii. 181 If we consider a paraffinic solvent,..the alcohol group is now lyophobic and the hydrocarbons are lyophilic. **1968** *Physics Bull.* Nov. 377/1 The stability of lyophobic colloids, like a quartz suspension or gold sol, is due to the competition between electrostatic forces of repulsion.. and the van der Waals attraction.

lyotrope (ləi·ǒtrōᵘp), *a. Physical Chem.* [ad. G. *lyotrop* (H. Freundlich *Kapillarchemie* (1909) 54), f. Gr. λύ-ειν to loosen + τροπή turn, turning.] = *LYOTROPIC *a.* 1.

1915 W. W. TAYLOR *Chem. Colloids* i. 8 Among the reactions in which this lyotrope influence has been recognised are the following: the catalysis of esters, the inversion of cane sugar, the setting of gelatine, and the heat-coagulation of albumin. **1965** *Biol. Abstr.* XLVI. 480/2 Hofmeister's lyotrope salts modify the molecular structure of erythrocyte stroma protein.

lyotropic (ləiǒtrǫ·pik, -trōᵘ·pik), *a. Physical Chem.* [f. *LYOTROP(E *a.* + -IC: see *-TROPIC.] **1.** Associated with the change of internal pressure of a solution from that of the solvent which is caused by the solute. *Lyotropic series*, a series in which ions are arranged in order of their lyotropic effects, esp. their ability to cause precipitation of a lyophilic sol.

1924 W. A. PATRICK in H. S. Taylor *Treat. Physical Chem.* II. xx. 1285 Those properties of solutions or liquids that are in causal relation to the forces of molecular attraction are termed lyotropic. We thus have two great groups of properties of solutions, the colligative, and the lyotropic. **1925** G. BARGER tr. *Freundlich's Elem. Colloid Chem.* 27 The characteristic series of cations and anions so obtained..are called the lyotropic series. **1926** H. S. HATFIELD tr. *Freundlich's Colloid & Capillary Chem.* 49 We can therefore distinguish from the group of properties which are comprehended in the van't Hoff theory a second independent group, which are due to the change of the internal pressure by the solute. These properties will be described as lyotropic; the influence of the solute upon the surface tension, the compressibility, the solubility of difficultly soluble substances, and others will be called lyotropic influences. **1937** *Chem. Rev.* XX. 170 The numbers obtained in the case of salting-out experiments with lyophilic colloids play an important part in other lyotropic phenomena. *Ibid.* 179 Since the heat of hydration of ions depends on the electric field which surrounds them, the lyotropic effects are beyond doubt caused by the different electric field strengths of the ions. **1956** *Bacteriol. Rev.* XX. 51/2 Attempts have been made to correlate the toxicity of various salts to the lyotropic..series. **1970** *Biochemistry* IX. 2802/1 We have adopted an approach to the elucidation of lyotropic mechanism in which the effects of related perturbants on a standard collagen-buffer system have been compared.

2. Of a mesophase: having its phase transitions readily effected by a change of concentration. Also applied to the mesomorphism exhibited by such a mesophase.

1933 *Trans. Faraday Soc.* XXIX. 1008 (*heading*) Lyotropic mesomorphism. **1966** *Molecular Crystals* II. 55 Lyotropic systems are also thermotropic and it is the cooperative action of the temperature and of the solvent which enables them to pass successively from the solid crystalline state to the liquid crystalline state and to the isotropic liquid or dissolved state. **1969** *Analytical Chem.* Nov. 26A/3 Liquid crystals are divided into two major groups. One of these is identified as thermotropic, indicating that the class is prepared by heating... Lyotropic liquid crystals constitute the second major group and are prepared by mixing two or more components. In two-component systems involving water the second component is generally an amphiphile. Lyotropic systems can be large in number and varied in composition. **1974** P. G. DE GENNES *Physics Liquid Crystals* i. 5 For all the systems listed in this section, the transitions are induced most easily by changing the concentration of rods rather than the temperature; for this reason they are commonly called lyotropic. *Ibid.* 6 Depending on which..conditions hold, amphiphilic compounds may be lyotropic or thermotropic.

lyotropy (ləiǫ·trǒpi). *Physical Chem.* [f. *LYOTROP(E *a.* + -Y³.] The change of internal pressure brought about in a solution by the solvent or solvents; the mechanism by which this is brought about.

1927 H. S. VAN KLOOSTER tr. *Kruyt's Colloids* xvii. 237 Lyotropy, therefore, is probably not a hydration pure and simple, but one that orients the dipoles of water. **1937** *Chem. Rev.* XX. 169 (*heading*) Quantitative lyotropy.

lype (ləip). *Sc.* Also **lipe.** [See LIPE *sb.*¹] Part of the roof of a mine rendered dangerous by faults in the rock.

1835 *Trans. Highland Soc.* X. plate ix (*caption*) Lipes or 'glazed backs'. Dislocations or 'hitches'. **1883** W. S. GRESLEY *Gloss. Terms Coal Mining* 163 *Lypes*,..irregularities in the *roof* indicating danger from *falls*. **1912** G. CUNNINGHAM *Verse* 70 'Boot up steps and doon steps, and veezes and lypes. **1920** A. H. FAY *Gloss. Mining & Mineral Industry* 411/1 *Lype* (Scot.), an irregularity in the mine roof... A projecting rock in a mine roof that may fall at any time. Usually in the plural, and sometimes spelled Lipe. **1952** B. HOLMAN *Behind Diamond Panes* 82 All the care in roof support did not prevent a 'fall' because of a 'greasy lipe'.

lyric, *a.* and *sb.* Add: **A.** *adj.* **1.** *lyric drama, lyric stage*: examples.

1825 W. AYRTON *Let.* 5 Apr. in J. Ebers *Seven Yrs. King's Theatre* (1828) 255 Signor Tramezzani,..one of the finest singers and actors that ever graced the lyric stage, took the character of Guglielmo. **1842** *Ainsworth's Mag.* I. 183 Still we hail with undiminished delight the lyric drama. **1877** G. B. SHAW *How to become Mus. Critic* (1960) 22 The most exciting situation in lyric drama—the duet in the fourth act of Les Huguenots. *Ibid.* 28 It requires a faculty for light comedy, which is almost unknown on the lyric stage. **1938** *Oxf. Compan. Mus.* 526/2 *Lyric Drama*, another name for opera, covering all kinds. The term is applied not so much to any particular work as to the whole class—i.e. opera as distinct from the spoken play. **1957** *Oxf. Compan. Theatre* 589/1 Beethoven's..solitary contribution to the lyric stage, 'Fidelio' (1805). **1958** A. JACOBS *New Dict. Mus.* 218 *Lyric drama*, occasional synonym for opera (especially in French, as *drame lyrique*); hence also *the lyric stage*, i.e. the operatic stage.

B. *sb.* **4.** The words of a popular song; freq. *pl.* Also *attrib.*, as *lyric-writer*.

1876 STAINER & BARRETT *Dict. Mus. Terms* 276/2 *Lyric*, poetry or blank verse intended to be set to music and sung. **1927** *Melody Maker* Aug. 759/3 On July 8 Edgar Leslie, the prolific and most successful lyric writer in America, arrived in London. **1933** *Punch* 16 Aug. 180/3 The gramophone plunged fervently into that lyric called 'I've Got a Date with an Angel'. **1934** C. LAMBERT *Music Ho!* IV. 272 The lowbrow poet—the type of writer who in the nineteenth century produced 'Champagne Charlie' and now produces revue lyrics. **1938** *Oxf. Compan. Mus.* 526/2 Another well-known poet constantly advertises himself in the British musical press as 'Lyric Author...2,000 songs...not one failure to give great pleasure'. **1946** E. O'NEILL *Iceman Cometh* (1947) II. 132 They all join in a jeering chorus, rapping with knuckles or glasses on the table at the indicated spot in the lyric. **1958** *Times* 2 Aug. 7/4 Teenagers in Minneapolis, believing that the words of some 'pop' songs can encourage juvenile crime, have.. 'opened a nation-wide "better lyrics" contest'. **1967** *Listener* 3 Aug. 130/1 Having introduced a new sound in the music, they saw that they had next to change the type of lyric. **1968** *Ibid.* 7 Nov. 610/1 According to Mick Farren, lyric-writer of the Deviants: 'Pop music is..the last free medium.' **1972** *Jazz & Blues* Sept. 12/1 The banality of the lyrics. **1973** *Listener* 19 Apr. 522/1 The bo' weevil fugues..in blues lyrics.

lyricist. Add: **b.** A writer of lyrics (*LYRIC *sb.* 4).

1909 *Pall Mall Gaz.* 12 Apr. 4/3 No doubt it could be paralleled in the works of our own music-hall 'lyricists'. **1932** *Amer. Speech* VII. 243 Scores of ways of saying 'I Love You' have been invented by the lyricists of popular songs. **1963** *Movie* Apr. 11/3 Music by Joseph Kosma. Lyricist: Jacques Prevert. English lyrics by Johnny Mercer, sung by Nat King Cole. **1971** *Daily Tel.* 11 Oct. 15 'Jesus Christ, Superstar', a 'folk opera' depicting the last seven days of Christ,..is making a fortune for its composer and lyricist.

lysate (ləi·zēⁱt). *Biol.* [f. LYS(IS + *-ate*, after *filtrate, precipitate.*] A solution or preparation containing the products of lysis of cells, esp. bacterial cells.

1922 *Brit. Med. Jrnl.* 19 Aug. 298/2 The other point is the question of the effect of dispersion of the lysate—that is, the bacterial bodies in the emulsion used. **1954** *Sci. News* XXXIII. 91 This process of bacterial destruction is called 'lysis'; the resulting liquid is a 'lysate', and may contain over a hundred thousand million bacteriophage particles per cubic centimetre. **1973** *Nature* 12 Jan. 96/1 These antibodies gave strong reactions with ultrasonic lysates of both normal and CML leucocytes.

lyse (ləiz), *v. Biol.* [Back-formation from *LYSIS 3: cf. *analysis/analyse, catalysis/catalyse*, etc.] **1.** *trans.* To bring about lysis of (a cell, etc.).

1927 *Brit. Jrnl. Exper. Path.* VIII. 121 It [*sc.* an active phage] lysed certain laboratory strains of coliform bacilli. **1947** *New Biol.* II. 75 Fleming made the observation that the small bacterial colonies close to the mould colony were being 'lysed' (dissolved). **1967** *New Scientist* 13 July 97/1 It will burst open or lyse the offending bacteria. **1970** *Nature* 16 May 594/1 They lysed algal cells by treatment with penicillin.

2. *intr.* To undergo lysis (sense *3).

1933 *Jrnl. Infectious Dis.* LII. 272 The tendency of placental blood to lyse was found to be overcome by this use of hypertonic salt solution. **1971** *Nature* 22 Jan. 272/2 Many bacteria lyse when growth of the cultures ceases. *Ibid.* 26 Nov. 231/2 When leaves of these two species were slowly dried.., chloroplast lamellae and mitochondrial cristae often disintegrated or lysed while tonoplasts.. usually remained intact.

So **lysed, ly·sing** *ppl. adjs.*

1922 *Brit. Med. Jrnl.* 19 Aug. 290/1 The filtrate contains the bacteriophagic principle as active as the lysed non-filtered culture. **1924** *Jrnl. Bacteriol.* IX. 401 It is established that, though non-lysing, they carry *some* lytic agent. **1929** *Jrnl. Path. & Bacteriol.* XXXII. 41 The type of resistant colony is related to these characteristics of the lysing phage. **1934** *Biol. Rev.* IX. 338 Phage particles just liberated from a lysing bacterium are more active. **1949** H. W. FLOREY et al. *Antibiotics* I. i. 36 The lysates were known as Sentocym preparations, with a prefix to indicate the type of lysed organism which they contained.

Lysenkoism (ləise·ŋkoˌiz'm). [f. the name *Lysenko* (see below) + -ISM.] Belief in or advocacy of the views of the Russian agronomist T. D. Lysenko (b. 1898), who opposed modern genetics and advocated neo-Lamarckian views and who for a time achieved great influence in Soviet Russia. Cf. *MICHURINISM.

1948 *Discovery* Nov. 325/1 The opponents of Lysenkoism did not remain silent. **1962** *New Scientist* 11 Jan.

101/2 It would mean that if genes can be offset by a non-hereditary factor, that very factor could in effect become hereditary... This, surely, would be Lysenkoism, or an aspect of it. **1969** I. M. LERNER tr. *Medvedev's Rise & Fall T. D. Lysenko* vi. 136 The period of absolute domination of Lysenkoism in Soviet biology and agronomy was relatively short-lived. **1974** *Nature* 11 Oct. 558/1 A convinced anti-Lysenkoist, whose career suffered considerably during the years of Lysenkoism, Astaurov became a focus for the anti-Lysenkoist reaction.

Hence **Lyse·nkoist,** one who believes in or advocates the views of Lysenko; also as *adj.*

1949 *Jrnl. Heredity* XL. 197/1 The Lysenkoist offensive is a two-pronged attack. **1950** *New Biol.* VIII. 6 The argument between Lysenkoists and geneticists is in the tradition of those great controversies which periodically ruffle, sometimes convulse, the progress of a science. **1969** *Nature* 13 Sept. 1182/1 He describes the total failure of.. attempts to breed cows with high butter-fat by hybridization with Jerseys by Lysenkoist principles. **1973** *New Yorker* 24 Sept. 119/1 In 1971..Lysenkoists were still accusing classical geneticists of failure to achieve practical results.

lysergic (ləisə̄·ɹdʒik), *a. Chem.* [f. *lys* (in HYDROLYSIS) + ERG(OT *sb.* + -IC.] *lysergic acid*: **a.** A crystalline tetracyclic compound, $C_{16}H_{16}N_2O_2$, containing the indole nucleus and occurring in two enantiomorphic forms, the dextrorotatory one being produced by the hydrolysis of ergot alkaloids.

1934 JACOBS & CRAIG in *Jrnl. Biol. Chem.* CIV. 547 A new substance was obtained..which possessed both acid and basic properties and which we have named lysergic acid. **1961** *New Scientist* 2 Nov. 278 The alkaloids of ergot are all derivatives of lysergic acid, an indole compound. **1964** D. F. DOWNING in M. Gordon *Psychopharmacol. Agents* I. xiii. 572 Lysergic acid derivatives with biological activity are..known to occur both in fungi and higher plants. The most active hallucinogenic substance (LSD-25) has, however, been obtained only by synthesis from (+)-lysergic acid. **1969** T. A. BAN *Psychopharmacol.* xviii. 347/1 Lysergic acid diethylamide, or, as commonly referred to, LSD_{25}, is a synthetic product prepared from lysergic acid.

b. Used *ellipt.* for *lysergic acid diethylamide*, or (less commonly) any derivative of the acid.

1952 *Jrnl. Mental Sci.* XCVIII. 314 High doses of glucose raising the blood sugar above 200 mgm. inhibit the action of lysergic acid (LSD. 25). **1954** *Brit. Jrnl. Psychol.* XLV. 274 The visions produced by such drugs as mescaline and lysergic acid. **1955** *Sci. Amer.* June 39/1 The creation of experimental psychoses with lysergic acid thus opens the way to studying treatments and the nature of mental illness. **1957** J. S. HUXLEY *Relig. without Revelation* vii. 168 Mescalin and lysergic acid induce remarkable intensifications and modifications of consciousness, including often a sense of transcendence of self. **1958** *Sunday Times* 1 June 7/5 Lysergic acid should be tried for its extraordinary property of resurrecting childhood. **1962** [see *LSD[2]]. **1964** *New Statesman* 28 Feb. 347/3 (Advt.), Author seeks objective confirmation of subjective mystical experience under Lysergic Acid (LSD 25). **1969** T. A. BAN *Psychopharmacol.* xviii. 348/1 Other lysergic acids. Besides LSD_{25} there are at least eight other lysergic acid derivatives with psychotomimetic properties. **1972** *Daily Tel.* (Colour Suppl.) 11 Aug. 12/3 The acids, like the barbiturates and amphetamines, are synthetically produced, and the best known is lysergic acid, LSD.

Hence **lysergic acid diethylamide** (dəi,e·þil-, dəi,ĕþəi·lămaid), the diethylamide of lysergic acid (in which the group $—N(C_2H_5)_2$ replaces the hydroxyl group of the acid), an extremely powerful synthetic hallucinogen which can produce profound changes in perception (esp. vision) and mood, with psychotic symptoms resembling those of schizophrenia, and which has been given orally in psychotherapy, usu. as the water-soluble tartrate, a colourless odourless powder; also called *LSD[2], *LYSERGIDE.

1944 *Chem. Abstr.* XXXVIII. 1502 With $NHEt_2$ condensation gave *d*-lysergic acid diethylamide. **1950** *Diseases Nervous Syst.* XI. 241/1 Occasionally, it was observed that patients were able to verbalize the repressed components of their conflicts during a toxic delirium. This led us to consider various drugs that might induce a transitory delirious state. It was during this search that the Sandoz Company called to our attention and made available d-lysergic acid diethylamide (L.S.D. 25). **1955** *Sci. News Let.* 2 July 4/1 LSD, short for lysergic acid diethylamide, is a chemical that produces hallucinations and delusions in healthy persons like those in mental sickness. **1965** *New Scientist* 22 Apr. 224/3 Lysergic acid diethylamide (LSD 25) and mescaline are..often called 'psychotomimetic', because some of the symptoms which they produce create certain resemblances to schizophrenic illness. **1967** *Economist* 7 Oct. 20/1 The coming thing is lysergic acid diethylamide (LSD). **1969** [see sense a above]. **1971** *Nature* 29 Jan. 347/1 Small doses (~100 μg) of lysergic acid diethylamide (LSD) taken orally cause hallucinations and distortions of visual perception in man. *Ibid.* 16 July 191/1 Lysergic acid diethylamide (LSD-25) is believed to cause chromosome abnormalities.

lysergide (ləisə̄·ɹdʒəid). *Pharm.* [f. *LYSERG(IC *a.* + AM)IDE.] = **lysergic acid diethylamide.*

1965 *Jrnl. Amer. Med. Assoc.* 11 Jan. 93/1 Lysergic acid diethylamide..is the most potent of the hallucinogenic drugs. and is also referred to as LSD-25, lysergide, and delysid. **1968** M. SHEPHERD et al. *Clin. Psychopharmacol.* viii. 188 Lysergide has been administered to patients suffering from many types of mental illness. *Ibid.* 190 The dangers of lysergide therapy have been repeatedly stressed.

lysin. Delete entry in Dict. and see next and *LYSINE.

lysin (ləi·sin). *Biol.* Also †**-ine.** [ad. G. *lysine* (W. Kruse 1893, in *Beiträge zur path. Anat. und zur allgemeinen Path.* XII. 339), f. *lysis* LYSIS: see -IN[1].] Any substance (as a bacteriolysin or hæmolysin) which is able to lyse cells; *spec.* an antibody with this ability.

1900 A. C. JONES tr. *Fischer's Struct. & Functions Bacteria* xvii. 168 To formulate a theory of immunity that shall not be lost in clouds of hypothesis is at present impossible. The alexines, antitoxines, lysines, and anti-lysines, that the wordy research of the last few years has given us, are at present quite unknown. **1902** *Brit. Med. Jrnl.* 5 Apr. 845 Some immune serums appear to exercise an agglutination of the red cells immediately before the lysin action. *Ibid.* 12 Apr. 920 [The first-mentioned poisons] as well as..the lysin of cholera belong to the lysin group. **1922** *Brit. Jrnl. Exper. Path.* III. 259 Gengou ..has described a bacteriolytic substance which he has found in extracts of leucocytes. He found, however, that the lysin was absorbed by saturation with the microbe. **1954** A. WHITE et al. *Princ. Biochem.* xxiv. 658 If the cells are lysed, the antibodies are lysins. **1966** *McGraw-Hill Encycl. Sci. & Technol.* VII. 637/2 Lysins vary in the range of host species whose cells they will attack and in their requirements for accessory factors for lysis; the immune lysins are strictest in their requirements.

lysine (ləi·sīn). *Chem.* Also †**-in.** [ad. G. *lysin* (E. Fischer 1891, in *Arch. f. Anat. u. Physiol., physiol. Abtheil.* 269), prob. f. *lysatinin* LYSATININE: see -INE[5].] An amino-acid, $COOH·CH(NH_2)·(CH_2)_3·CH_2NH_2$, which is probably a constituent of all proteins.

1892 *Jrnl. Chem. Soc.* LXII. 1500 Not lysine, but lysine carbonate..was obtained. **1897** [see LYSATININE]. **1919** Lysin [see *HISTIDINE]. **1946** *Nature* 7 Sept. 349/2 Destruction of lysine by heat has been observed in milk, casein and oat protein. **1964** *Economist* 4 July 70/3 Lysine, a chemical that has great potentialities as a protein-forming additive for animal feedstuffs. **1965** LEE & KNOWLES *Animal Hormones* ii. 33 The structural formula of vasopressin is the same in all mammals except in the pig and the hippopotamus, where the amino acid arginine is replaced by lysine. **1973** *Daily Colonist* (Victoria, B.C.) 29 Sept. 28/1 Lysine is one of the amino acids that is an essential component of protein in human nutrition.

lysis. Add: **3.** *Biol.* [perh. derived from the suffix *-lysis* in *bacteriolysis, hæmolysis* (see *-LYSIS 2).] The disintegration or dissolution of cells or cell organelles; *esp.* the dissolution of bacterial cells brought about by bacteriophage.

1902 *Jrnl. Exper. Med.* 17 Mar. 4 That complete agglutination has no effect upon subsequent solution (lysis) of the corpuscles will be shown when treating of the latter phenomenon. **1922** *Brit. Med. Jrnl.* 19 Aug. 296/2 The Twort phenomenon and the d'Herelle phenomenon are identical. They are two different aspects of..the transmissible lysis of bacteria. **1922** *Brit. Jrnl. Exper. Path.* III. 258 The lysis takes place with dead as well as with living bacteria. **1937** *Jrnl. Immunol.* XXXII. 1 (*heading*) A natural hemolysin from the rat producing nuclear lysis of chicken erythrocytes. **1940** *Jrnl. Gen. Physiol.* XXIII. 643 (*title*) The growth of bacteriophage and lysis of the host. **1970** *Nature* 11 July 138/1 Certain antibiotics can cause physical disintegration or 'lysis' of cells when added to growing cultures of sensitive bacteria.

-lysis (lisis). A word-forming element [f. Gr. λύσις a loosening, parting] in many technical terms, primarily denoting decomposition, disintegration, dissolution.

1. In words in which the first element indicates the agent; e.g. (in *Chem.*) ELECTROLYSIS (*c* 1840), *HYDROGENOLYSIS; (in *Biol.*) *BACTERIOLYSIS (sense 1), *BIOLYSIS.

2. In words in which the first element indicates the substance or object affected; e.g. (in *Chem.* and *Biochem.*) *FRUCTOLYSIS, *GLYCOLYSIS (1892); (in *Biol.*) *BACTERIOLYSIS (sense 2), *HÆMOLYSIS (cf. *LYSIS 3). **b.** In a few terms in *Surg.* *-lysis* denotes surgical detachment of a part indicated by the first element, as **cardiolysis.*

3. In words in which the first element indicates some other characteristic; e.g. (in *Biol.*) *AUTOLYSIS, *HETEROLYSIS (sense 1); (in *Chem.*) *HETEROLYSIS (sense 2), *HOMOLYSIS. (CATALYSIS (1836) was adopted directly from Gr. κατάλυσις dissolution.)

lyso- (ləi·so), a comb. form of LYSIS (sense *3), used to form various biological and biochemical terms, as **lysole·cithin** *Biochem.*, any compound obtained from a lecithin by the hydrolytic removal of one of the two fatty acid groups.

1923 LEVENE & ROLF in *Jrnl. Biol. Chem.* LV. 743 Thus the product was a mixture of several substances, which we propose to name lysolecithin and lysocephalin. Inasmuch as lecithins differ in the nature of their saturated fatty acids, it is probable that there exist several lysolecithins. **1972** *Sci. Amer.* Jan. 88/3 Lecithin, like the bile salts, is synthesized by the liver, and after it is secreted into the small intestine an enzyme secreted by the pancreas converts lecithin to lysolecithin. This substance breaks up cells by removing the lipids from their membranes.

lysogenesis (ləisodʒe·nėsis). *Bacteriology.* [f. *LYSO- + -GENESIS.] Orig., the production of lysis or a lysin; in mod. use = *LYSOGENY.

1901 *Lancet* 19 Oct. 1031/1 Agglutination..is not concerned in lysogenesis, which is a function of the action of immune body to addiment alone. **1902** *Encycl. Brit.* XXVI. 68/1 It has been completely established that in this phenomenon of lysogenesis [*sc.* dissolution of bacterial cells] there are two substances concerned, one specially developed or developed in excess, and the other present in normal serum. **1932** *Jrnl. Path. & Bacteriol.* XXXV. 855 The use of *B. sanguinarium* as an indicator of lysogenesis arose out of previous work..on the characteristics of a lysogenic enteritidis strain. *Ibid.* 862 The phenomenon of lysogenesis. **1951** *Jrnl. Bacteriol.* LXII. 293 (*heading*) Studies on lysogenesis. I. The mode of phage liberation by lysogenic *Escherichia coli*. *Ibid.*, The stable association of a bacteriophage with a bacterial strain, known as lysogenesis, has received scarce attention. **1968** A. L. SMITH *Microbiol. & Path.* (ed. 9) xxvi. 278/1 This kind of phage is referred to as a prophage, and this condition of mutual tolerance is termed lysogeny or lysogenesis.

lysogenic (ləisodʒe·nik), *a. Biol.* [f. *LYSO- + *-GENIC.] Pertaining to, or capable of producing or undergoing, lysis (sense *3); *spec.* applied to a bacterium which, without being attacked by a phage, can lyse and liberate phage, an effect which is due to the ability of such a bacterium to carry, through an indefinite number of generations, a phage which is integrated with the bacterial genome and normally replicates synchronously with it but which may, under a suitable stimulus, become detached from the bacterial genome, replicate rapidly, and lyse the bacterial cell.

1899 [see *immune body* s.v. *IMMUNE *a.* (*sb.*) 3 b]. **1902** *Encycl. Brit.* XXVI. 68/1 The first of these is the lysogenic action, which consists in the production of a change in the corresponding bacterium whereby it becomes granular, swells up, and ultimately may undergo dissolution. *Ibid.*, Lysogenic action is not confined to the case of bacteria, but obtains also with other organised structures. **1911** STEDMAN *Med. Dict.* 499/1 *Lysogenic*, relating to the formation of lysins. **1929** *Austral. Jrnl. Exper. Biol. & Med. Sci.* VI. 277 (*heading*) Observations on a permanently lysogenic strain of *B. enteritidis gaertner*. **1929** J. H. DIBLE *Recent Adv. Bacteriol.* iv. 73 Of greater interest are certain strains which, whilst themselves resistant, have incorporated with them the lytic principle, which remains present through future subcultures. These are the 'lysogenic' strains of Bordet. **1930** F. M. BURNET in *Syst. Bacteriol.* (Med. Res. Council) VII. xxxix. 494 There are some bacterial strains that it is impossible to deprive of lysogenic power. **1934** *Biol. Rev.* IX. 346 The ability of certain bacterial strains, so-called lysogenic bacteria, to liberate phage during their growth. **1953** [see *INDUCTION 9 d]. **1953** *Cold Spring Harbor Symp. Quant. Biol.* XVIII. 71/1 It is possible that the phage population is heterogeneous, containing lytic, lysogenic, etc. phages. **1965** *New Scientist* 21 Oct. 167/2 Strains of bacteria carrying prophage DNA are described as 'lysogenic'. **1970** PASSMORE & ROBSON *Compan. Med. Stud.* II. xviii. 101/2 The prophage is normally inhibited from replication in the lysogenic state by the presence of virus-specified repressor substance that controls the operon for the structural gene. **1971** LECHEVALIER & PRAMER *Microbes* xli. 430/1 Such phages (e.g., coliphage λ) are called lysogenic viruses.

Hence **lysogeni·city, lyso·geny,** the state or property of a bacterium of being lysogenic; the phenomenon of lysis of a lysogenic bacterium with the subsequent release of phage.

1932 *Jrnl. Path. & Bacteriol.* XXXV. 857 Double lysogenicity, *i.e.* the production of two distinct phage types by a single strain, is relatively common. *Ibid.* 857 In certain important bacterial groups lysogenicity is a normal characteristic. **1934** *Biol. Rev.* IX. 347 It was found that another group of Salmonellas..did show the existence of a common type of lysogenicity. **1954** *Genetics* XXXIX. 429 (*heading*) Segregation of lambda lysogenicity during bacterial recombination in *Escherichia coli* K12. **1956** *Nature* 14 Jan. 92/1 The occurrence of lysogeny in *SU*298 was demonstrated. **1962** *Lancet* 19 May 1054/2 Little is known about the mechanism of induction of tumours by viruses, and..it seems clear that nothing directly akin to bacteriophage lysogeny occurs. **1970** PASSMORE & ROBSON *Compan. Med. Stud.* II. xviii. 101/2 When a bacteriophage infects a sensitive bacterium, it can either replicate and lyse the host cell..or it may be incorporated in the host genome in a state of lysogeny.

lysogenization (ləisǫ:dʒĕnəizē̆i·ʃən). *Bacteriology.* [f. *LYSOGEN(IC *a.* + -IZATION.] The process by which a bacterium acquires a phage which becomes stably integrated into its genome; the establishment of the lysogenic state.

1953 *Cold Spring Harbor Symp. Quant. Biol.* XVIII. 71 (*heading*) Studies on lysogenization in *Escherichia coli.*

1970 *Nature* 17 Jan. 226/1 The parallels between the lysogenization of bacteria by bacteriophage and the transformation of cells in tissue culture by DNA tumour viruses are too compelling to ignore.

Hence **lyso·genize** *v. trans.*, (of a bacteriophage) to become stably integrated into the genome of (a bacterium); also *absol.*; **lyso·genized** *ppl. a.*; **lyso·genizing** *vbl. sb.*

1953 *Cold Spring Harbor Symp. Quant. Biol.* XVIII. 71/1 There do occur, however, *lambda* mutants that lysogenize poorly or not at all. *Ibid.*, Different strains of artificially lysogenized bacteria. **1957** *Virology* III. 42 (*heading*) Mutations in a temperate bacteriophage affecting its ability to lysogenize *E. coli.* **1961** *Jrnl. Molecular Biol.* III. 399 (*heading*) A mutation affecting the DNA content of bacteriophage lambda and its lysogenizing abilities. **1971** *Nature* 5 Nov. 12/1 The Paris group..set about isolating mutants of this phage which by lysogenizing CRT46 cells can cause the cells to replicate at 42° C.

lysosome (lǝi·sǒsōum). *Biol.* [f. *LYSO- + *-SOME⁴.] A cytoplasmic cell organelle widely found in animal tissues which contains hydrolytic enzymes enclosed in a membrane.

1955 C. DE DUVE et al. in *Biochem. Jrnl.* LX. 615/2 For practical purposes, it is proposed to refer to these granules as lysosomes, thus calling attention to their richness in hydrolytic enzymes. **1970** *Sci. Jrnl.* Aug. 15/4 The invader is met by the lysosome, engulfed and destroyed by the enzymes.

Hence **lysoso·mal** *a.*

1957 *Symp. Soc. Exper. Biol.* X. 59 All the lysosomal enzymes..were recovered to a large extent in the parenchymal cells. **1965** *Listener* 18 Mar. 404/1 Amoebae or other protozoa take particles into food vacuoles, release lysosomal enzymes into the vacuoles and so digest the particles.

lysozyme (lǝi·sǒzǝim). *Biochem.* [f. *LYSO- + *-EN)ZYME.] Any of various similar enzymes of relatively low molecular weight which are widely found in animal and plant tissues and secretions and which are capable of hydrolysing a particular mucopolysaccharide found in the cell walls of certain Gram-positive bacteria and hence of lysing such bacteria.

1922 A. FLEMING in *Proc. R. Soc.* B. XCIII. 306 In this communication I wish to draw attention to a substance present in the tissues and secretions of the body, which is capable of rapidly dissolving certain bacteria. As this substance has properties akin to those of ferments I have called it a 'Lysozyme', and shall refer to it by this name throughout the communication. **1934** J. H. PARSONS *Dis. Eye* (ed. 7) x. 144 The tears are not a good culture medium, and though they contain traces of lysozyme, they cannot be regarded as actively bactericidal. **1949** H. W. FLOREY et al. *Antibiotics* I. p. v, No consideration has been given to antibacterial substances of animal origin, such as lysozyme. **1962** FLORKIN & MASON *Compar. Biochem.* III. viii. 413 *Ficus* lysozyme is different from the egg white enzyme. **1965** PEACOCKE & DRYSDALE *Molecular Basis Heredity* xii. 144 Similar studies have been initiated on the genetically controlled structure of the lysozyme produced in bacteria infected by normal and mutant T4 bacteriophage.

lytic (li·tik), *a.* [ad. Gr. λυτικ-ός able to loose.] **1.** *Med.* Of, pertaining to, or causing a lysis (sense 2).

1889 *Syd. Soc. Lex.*, *Lytic*, of, or belonging to, a loosing or dissolving. **1907** *Practitioner* Apr. 500 It boots little whether that increase in heat [during fever] is due to an excessive production, as the 'genetic' protagonists proclaim, or an inadequate dissipation, as their 'lytic' opponents contend. **1962** *Lancet* 26 May 1123/2 Ice placed inside the oxygen tent and cold sponging are remarkably efficient in lowering the temperature of these infants to 86–88°F (31°C)... In our experience 'lytic' agents are not required.

2. *Bacteriology.* Pertaining to or causing lysis (sense *3); **lytic cycle**, the sequence of events that takes place from the infection of a bacterium by a virulent phage to lysis of the bacterium and the release of progeny phage.

1902 *Jrnl. Exper. Med.* 17 Mar. 281 Only when the lytic serum is very fresh will solution be effected. **1922** *Brit. Jrnl. Exper. Path.* III. 259 The lytic substance, lysozyme, is very stable. **1925** C. H. BROWNING *Bacteriol.* ix. 214 He concluded that the agent causing this solution or lytic action was a living virus. **1946** *Nature* 23 Nov. 745/1 The lytic effect of certain myxobacteria upon the true bacteria (eubacteria) has been known for some years. **1963** *Biol. Abstr.* XLI. 1198/2 Studies on control of enzyme induction and initiation of lytic cycle in a lysogenic bacterium. **1968** R. RIEGER *Gloss. Genetics & Cytogenetics* 34 The introduction by infection of the genetic material of virulent phages into a susceptible host results invariably in the death and dissolution of the cell with the release of (100–10000) new phages ('lytic cycle'). **1972** *Nature* 24 Mar. 144/3 It is much more likely that the tails kill sensitive cells either by injecting lytic enzymes or by acting at the cell surface.

-lytic (li·tik), ending of adjs. corresponding to sbs. that end in *-LYSIS (some of the earliest examples of which, ANALYTIC, CATALYTIC, correspond to Gr. originals in -λυτικός: cf. *LYTIC *a.*).

lytically (li·tikăli), *adv. Bacteriology.* [f. *LYTIC *a.*: see -LY².] (By infection) with a lytic phage.

1967 *Jrnl. Virol.* I. 917/2 The enzyme..in lytically infected cells is dependent on virus genome for its development. **1969** A. M. CAMPBELL *Episomes* i. 5 Such specialized transduction is not observed with lytically grown phage. **1972** *Jrnl. Molecular Biol.* LXX. 68 The sequences of SV40 RNA which appear only late in lytically infected cells.

lyxoflavin (liksoflēi·vin). *Biochem.* Also **-flavine.** [f. *LYXO(SE + *FLAVIN 2.] A yellow crystalline flavin, $C_{17}H_{20}N_4O_6$, which is a lyxose derivative and occurs in heart tissue.

1949 *Arch. Biochem.* XXII. 64 We have succeeded in isolating L-lyxoflavine from the human heart muscle. This compound was obtained in the form of monoclinic crystals. **1953** *Proc. Soc. Exper. Biol. & Med.* LXXXII. 590/2 Relatively large amounts of lyxoflavin are required for such growth stimulation, and since available evidence indicates that the compound does not occur naturally, it cannot be considered a vitamin. **1963** J. P. LAMBOOY in Florkin & Stotz *Comprehensive Biochem.* XI. ii. 31 Lyxoflavin stimulates a small increase in the growth rate of rats, chicks, and pigs when adequate amounts of riboflavin are present in the diet.

lyxose (li·ksōuz,-s). *Chem.* [a. G. *lyxose* (Fischer & Bromberg 1896, in *Ber. d. Deut. Chem. Ges.* XXIX. 581), f. *xylose* XYLOSE by reversal of the first syllable.] A crystalline pentose sugar, $C_5H_{10}O_5$, which differs from xylose in the configuration of the carbon atom adjacent to the aldehyde group, is rare in nature, and is obtained synthetically by degradation of the calcium salt of galactonic acid.

1896 *Jrnl. Chem. Soc.* LXX. I. 348 The lactone can be reduced with 2½ per cent. sodium amalgam at 0° to the sugar, lyxose. **1961** *Tetrahedron* XV. 80 This is the first time that L-lyxose..has been found in a natural product [*sc.* curamycin].

M

M. Add: **II. 4*.** Further symbolic uses in science.

a. In *Physics M* is used to designate the series of X-ray emission lines of longer wavelength than the *L*-series obtained by exciting the atoms of any particular element (cf. *L 6* a); these arise from electron transitions to the atomic orbit of third-lowest energy, with principal quantum number 3, which is thus termed the *M-shell*, and electrons in this shell *M-electrons*. **M-capture,** the capture by an atomic nucleus of one of the *M*-electrons.

1911 C. G. BARKLA in *Phil. Mag.* XXII. 408 From the similarity of the behaviour of all the elements we must then admit..the possibility of further series M, N, &c. **1923** H. L. BROSE tr. *Sommerfeld's Atomic Struct. & Spectral Lines* iii. 145 Electronic transitions that end in the M-shell, furnish differences of energy that correspond to emissions of lines of the M-series. **1924** *Phil. Mag.* XLVIII. 722 Krypton..has 2 K, 8 L, 18 M, and 8 N electrons. **1924** R. W. G. WYCKOFF *Struct. Crystals* ii. 72 The M-lines have been observed from the elements from dysprosium..to uranium. **1934** H. E. WHITE *Introd. Atomic Spectra* xvi. 306 Like the *K* and *L* series lines, the *M* series lines follow nearly straight lines on a Moseley diagram. **1968** *Physical Rev.* CLXVI. 944/2 The predicted exchange–overlap correction..is even larger for M capture than for *L* capture. **1970** E. P. BERTIN *Princ. & Pract. X-Ray Spectrometric Analysis* i. 27 An electron that has enough energy to expel a *K* electron obviously can also expel any *L* or *M* electron.

b. In *Physics m* and *M* denote magnetic quantum numbers, corresponding to the component of an angular momentum (often indicated by a subscript) in some physically distinguished direction (usu. that of a magnetic field). [Introduced by A. Landé 1921, in *Zeitschr. f. Physik* V. 233.]

m is usually used for a single particle, and *M* for an assemblage of particles.

1923 *Jrnl. Optical Soc. Amer.* VII. 415 The numbers at the left show the magnetic quantum number *m* characterizing each level. **1926** *Proc. R. Soc.* A. CXII. 80 It is necessary also..to take into consideration the effect of the orientation of orbits with respect to an imaginary magnetic field, and such orientation involves a fourth quantum number *m*, which in turn is itself composite and is equal to the vector sum of two subsidiary quantum numbers m_a and m_s. **1962** H. D. BUSH *Atomic & Nucl. Physics* ii. 38 It is necessary to characterize electrons in atoms by four quantum numbers *n, l,* m_l, m_s. **1967** W. R. HINDMARSH *Atomic Spectra* I. vi. 72 We can also perform a simple calculation for the case where the Zeeman splitting is large compared with the hyperfine structure but still small compared with the fine structure. In this case the quantum numbers M_J and M_I (which defines the *z*-component of the nuclear spin) are well defined, but not *J* and *I*.

5. M. = member, as in M.B.E., Member(ship) of the Order of the British Empire, M.C., Members of Congress (examples), M.I.A.E., Member of the Institute of Automobile Engineers, M.I.C.E., Member of the Institution of Civil Engineers, M.I.E.E., Member of the Institution of Electrical Engineers, M.I.M.E., Member of the Institute of Mechanical Engineers, Member of the Institute of Mining Engineers, M.I.Mech. E., Member of the Institution of Mechanical Engineers, M.I.Struct.E., Member of the Institution of Structural Engineers, M.J.I., Member of the Institute of Journalists, M.L.A., Member of the Legislative Assembly, M.L.C., Member of the Legislative Council, M.P.P., (in Canada) Member of Provincial Parliament, M.R.C.S. (examples), M.V.O., Member of the Royal Victorian Order.

m- (Chem.) = META- 6 b; M = middling: of paper, showing slight imperfections; M. or m. = million (£300 m. = three hundred million pounds); M = morphine.

M.A., mental age; M.A.D., MAD, magnetic anomaly (or airborne) detector (or detection); M. and D., medicine and duty, marked on a serviceman's sick report when he is feigning illness; M. and V., meat and vegetable(s); M.A.P., Ministry of Aircraft Production; M.A.S.H. (*U.S.*), Mobile Army Surgical Hospital; M.A.T.S. (*U.S.*), Military Air Transport Service; M.C., Military Cross (established 1915); M.C.C., Marylebone Cricket Club, the governing body of English cricket; the official title of touring teams generally deemed to represent England; Mcf, mcf, etc., a thousand cubic feet; so MMcf(d), etc., a million cubic feet (per day); MCP, male chauvinist pig; M.C.P.A., 2-*m*ethyl-4-*c*hloro*p*henoxy*a*cetic-acid (salts and esters of which are used in sprays as herbicides); M.C.R., middle common room (in the University of Oxford); M.C.U. (*Photogr.*), medium close-up; M.D., Managing Director; m.d., mental, or mentally, deficient or defective; M.D., Musical Director; M-day, mobilization day; m.e. (*Bibliogr.*), marbled edges; M.E., medical examiner; M.E., Middle English (see ENGLISH *sb.* 1 b); mF (also mf, etc.), microfarad; M.F., m.f., motherfucker; M.F., M.G., machine-finish(ed), -glazed (*MACHINE 9 c, 10); M.F.N., most favoured nation; M.F.V., m.f.v., motor fleet vessel; motor fishing vessel; M.G., machine-gun; M.G. (*Building*), make good; M.G.B. [Russ. *Ministérstvo Gosudárstvennoĭ Bezopásnosti*], Ministry of State Security; M.G.C., machine-gun company; m.g.d., million gallons per day; M.G.M., Metro-Goldwyn-Mayer (a film company); freq. *attrib.*, esp. to denote a roaring lion used as a symbol by this company; MHD, magnetohydrodynamic(s); M.H.W., mean high water; M.I., Military Intelligence (followed by numerals which indicate departments); M.I.5, M.I.6, sections of Military Intelligence which (until 1964) dealt with matters of state security; cf. **D.I.*; M.I., Mounted Infantry; MIA, missing in action; MICR, magnetic ink character recognition; mip, mean indicated pressure; MIRV, multiple independently targeted reentry vehicle (a type of missile); hence as *vb. trans.*, to equip with multiple independently targetable warheads; so *MIRVed* ppl. adj., *MIRVing* vbl. sb.; M.I.T., Massachusetts Institute of Technology; M.K.S., m.k.s., metre-kilogramme-second; M.L., motor launch; M.L.D., MLD, minimum lethal dose; M.L.F., multilateral force; M.L.W., mean low water; M.M., Military Medal (established 1916); mm., millimetre (examples); m.m.f., M.M.F., magnetomotive force; M.M.P.I., Minnesota Multiphasic Personality Inventory; M.O., mass-observation; M.O., medical officer; m.o., modus operandi; M.O., m.o. (*Chem.*), molecular orbital; M.O., money order; M. of I., M.O.I., Ministry of Information; M.O.H., Medical Officer of Health; M.O.L., manned orbiting (or orbital) laboratory; M.O.S. (*U.S. Mil.*), Military Occupational Specialty; MOS(T), metal-oxide-semiconductor (transistor); M.O.T., MoT, Ministry of Transport; also *ellipt.*, a Ministry of Transport test to establish the roadworthiness of a motor vehicle; also *attrib.*; m.p., M.P., melting point; M.P., military police(man); m.p.g., miles per gallon; m.p.h., miles per hour; so as *v. intr.* (nonce), to travel; M.Q. (*Photogr.*), metol-hydroquinone; M.R.A., Moral Rearmament, *BUCHMANISM; M.R.B.M., medium range ballistic missile; mRNA († M-RNA), messenger RNA; M.R.P. [Fr. *Mouvement Républicain Populaire*], Popular Republican Movement, the Christian Democratic Party of France under the Fourth Republic; M.S. (*Photogr.*), medium shot; M.S., minesweeper; M.S., morphine (sulphate); MS, multiple sclerosis; MSG, monosodium glutamate; MSH, melanocyte-stimulating hormone; M.S.I. [It. *Movimento Sociale Italiano*], Italian Social Movement, the Fascist Party of Italy under the Republic; M.T., machine translation; M.T., motor transport; M.T.B., motor torpedo boat; M.T.C., Mechanized Transport Corps; M.T.I., m.t.i., moving-target indication (a radar system that gives prominence to moving objects); M.V.D. [Russ. *Ministérstvo Vnútrennikh Del*], Ministry of Internal Affairs, replacing the N.K.V.D.; M.Y.O.B., mind your own business. Also *M AND B, *MS², *MUSA².

1889 G. M'GOWAN tr. *Bernthsen's Text-bk. Org. Chem.* xvii. 329 The xylene of coal tar consists of a mixture of the three isomers, *m*-xylene being present to the extent of 70 to 85 p.c. **1929** L. A. COLES *Introd. Mod. Org. Chem.* xxvii. 327 *m*-Dinitrobenzene is always prepared by the nitration of benzene in two stages. **1968** R. O. C. NORMAN *Princ Org. Synthesis* xi. 368 The t-butyl group is removed by re action with more of the starting *m*-dialkylbenzene. **1971** *Nomencl. Org. Chem.*(I.U.P.A.C.) (ed. 3) A. 18 The position of substituents is indicated by numbers except that *o-* (*ortho*), *m-* (*meta*) and *p-* (*para*) may be used in place of 1,2-, 1,3-, and 1,4-, respectively, when only two substituents are present. **1894** *Amer. Dict. Printing & Bookmaking* 354/1 *M paper*, paper which is not up to the highest standard of the manufacturer. **1937** E. J. LABARRE *Dict. Paper* 170/1 M paper is that which is not up to the first sorting, but in which the imperfections are trivial. **1948** *Words into Type* 545 M's or M paper. Paper not up to the standard quality. **1934** WEBSTER, *M*,..mega- (million). **1955** *Times* 3 May 10/3 (*heading*) $1M. declined. *Ibid.* 9 May 8/2 $28m. for aid to Spain. *a* **1912** W. T. ROGERS *Dict. Abbrev.* (1913), *M.*, morphin. **1914** JACKSON & HELLYER *Vocab. Criminal Slang* 60 *M*, or *Morph*, used by morphine fiends. Sulphate of morphia. **1922** M (= morphine) [see C (*C III. 3)]. **1935** A. J. POLLOCK *Underworld Speaks* 74/1 *M.*, morphine (a white alkaloid derived from opium). **1953** W. BURROUGHS *Junkie* xii. 125 When I have an H or M shooting habit I am non-sociable. **1940** R. S. WOODWORTH *Psychol.* (ed. 12) iv. 111 Of the two measures, MA and IQ, which is the better index of intelligence? **1960** J. B. CARROLL in Saporta & Bastian *Psycholinguistics* (1961) 340/1 There has been much interest in the relation between language maturity and measures of intellectual functioning such as MA or IQ. **1952** *Coronet* May 78/1 Scientists..thought, a compasslike magnetic device could be made to respond to even as small a body of metal as a submarine.... U.S. Navy engineers tried dangling the tiny magnetic element on the end of a hundred-foot cable, through which electrical impulses traveled to a recording instrument in the plane. It worked, and MAD (magnetic air-borne detector) was soon helping our Navy send U-boats to the bottom. **1967** *Sunday Mail Mag.* (Brisbane) 22 Jan. 6/3 The long metal shape of a sub shows up distinctly as MAD passes over the hull. **1968** A. HINE *Magnetic Compasses & Magnetometers* xi. 308 The purpose of M.A.D. is to find small irregularities in the general pattern of the Earth's magnetic field, which are associated with ferro-magnetic deposits of rock and oil-bearing strata. **1917** A. G. EMPEY *Over Top* 299 *M. and D.*, what the doctor marks on the 'sicker' or sick report when he thinks Tommy is faking sickness. **1919** W. H. DOWNING *Digger Dial.* 33 *M. & D.*, medicine and duty. A familiar sick-parade slogan. **1935** G. BLAKE *Shipbuilders* 256 If that wound's not healed by to-morrow it's M. and D. for you. **1925** FRASER & GIBBONS *Soldier & Sailor Words* 148 *M and V*, a familiar expression for the tinned meat and vegetable ration. **1944** *R.A.F. Jrnl.* Aug. 260 We are given..a hot tin of M. & V. (Meat and Vegetable: you pour it into your mess tin and eat it with a spoon). **1944** A. JACOB *Traveller's War* 273 The spearhead of the Eighth Army will eat a Christmas dinner of tinned meat and vegetable stew (the famous 'M. and V.'), biscuits and tinned fruit and tea. **1972** A. NEAVE *Flames of Calais* iii. 34 By nightfall my troop was cooking M & V beneath the plane trees of the market place. **1942** PARTRIDGE *Dict. Abbrev.* 60/1 M.A.P. **1946** *Happy Landings* (Air Ministry) July 1/2 Returning to England as Controller of Research and Development at M.A.P. **1953** *Economist* 14 Nov. 505/2 The Ministry of Aircraft Production. The problems that will confront the Atomic Energy Corporation have a family likeness..to those of MAP. **1950** *Army Information Digest* Dec. 51 Critical cases are flown by..helicopter direct to Mobile Army Surgical Hospitals (MASH). **1970** *Monthly Film Bull.* (Brit. Film Inst.) July 140/2 *M-A-S-H*, U.S.A., 1969 Director: Robert Altman... Hawkeye Pierce, Duke Forrest and Trapper John McIntyre arrive to join the 4077th Mobile Army Surgical Hospital in Korea, and are kept busy operating on wounded men sent back from the front lines. **1955** R. J. SCHWARTZ *Compl. Dict. Abbrev.* 109/1 MATS. **1958** *Times* 24 July 9/7 M.A.T.S...has to have up-to-date aircraft capable of carrying freight as well as troops. **1917** *Illustr. London News* 30 June 759/1 The five classes of the Order [of the British Empire] are:..4. Officers (O.B.E.), 5. Members (M.B.E.). **1936** *Discovery* Sept. 292/1 Major A. B. Klein, M.B.E. **1955** *Times* 8 July 15/2 Mr. Stace has recently been honoured with the M.B.E. and we are all extremely gratified that such an honour should have been conferred on another stalwart of the industry. **1972** *Times* 6 Dec. 32/3 In proud and ever loving memory..of Capt. John Henry Brunt, V.C., M.C...and his beloved father, T. H. Brunt, M.B.E. **1832** *Boston Even. Transcript* 29 June 2/2 Two bundles were lately received at the Opeloasas post office, franked 'H. A. Bullard, M.C.' which contained two Marseilles vests for children in that parish. **1904** *N.Y. Even. Post* 23 Sept. 5 John Wesley Gaines, M.C., made a careful study some years ago of the evils of a President's eligibility to reëlection. *a* **1917** M.C. [see *D.S.O.* (*D III. 3)]. **1969** S. MAYS *Fall out Officers* viii. 51 He's only got one eye and a lump shot aff his knee; both shot aff when he got his M.C. **1862** *Lillywhite's Cricket Scores* I. 128 Neither the M.C.C. books or 'Bentley' gave the name of the ninth batsman on the M.C.C. side. **1972** *Times* 6 Dec. 11/1 MCC's outcricket tightened up after an alarming start. **1960** V. B. GUTHRIE *Petroleum Products Handbk.* III. 43 *Mcf*, 1,000 cu ft. *Ibid.* XVII. 18 *MCF*, abbreviation for thousand cubic feet. **1975** *Economist* 30 Aug. 8/3 Someone has interpreted mcf as million cubic feet whereas according to American practice this means 1,000 cubic feet. **1971** *Publishers' Weekly* 1 Nov. 22 MCPs, you should know by now, are Male Chauvinist Pigs, an epithet that has grown so common it is now abbreviated. **1946** G. BLACKMAN in *Jrnl. Ministry of Agric.* LIII. 17 These names..are unlikely to be remembered, so that the abbreviations MCPA and DCPA can perhaps serve better. *Ibid.*, White charlock, corn buttercup and shepherd's needle are best destroyed with MCPA. **1958** *New Biol.*

XXVI. 45 The selective growth regulating herbicides such as M.C.P.A...and 2,4-D..are the most commonly used herbicides on pastures and the buttercup species differ in their sensitivity to these. **1971** *Arable Farmer* Feb. 12/2 MCPA, discovered during the war and still widely used alone or in mixture for cereals. **1966** *Rep. Comm. Inquiry Univ. Oxf.* II. 483 For those who enjoy the college atmosphere and who belong to a college which has a MCR *and* which is usefully situated in relation to their living accommodation or place of work, this can largely supply their need. **1959** W. S. Sharps *Dict. Cinematogr.* 110/2 *M.C.U.*, abbreviation for Medium Close-up. **1955** R. J. Schwartz *Compl. Dict. Abbrev.* 110/2 *MD*..; Managing Director. **1963** *Times* 14 May p. i/4 (Advt.), Do give this a little thought and perhaps you might have a word with the Managing Directors of some of the subsidiary companies. .. Have you talked to the M.D.s about it? **1942** Partridge *Dict. Abbrev.* 61/1 *M.D.*,..mentally deficient. **1968** 'L. Black' *Outbreak* xiv. 137, I just don't see..how the m.d. ward got infected. **1971** *Oz* May 5/1 He is classified in Orange County..as MDSO (mentally defective sexual offender). **1927** *Melody Maker* Apr. 397/1 It would be useless for any M.D. to call a rehearsal and run through music *before* seeing the 'subject' he has to accompany. **1967** *Stage* 2 Mar. 3/2 Ernest Woodhouse the MD of Creswell Colliery Band. **1937** *Reader's Digest* Aug. 97 M-day in America. **1970** N. Armstrong et al. *First on Moon* i. 18 That was M day, and a good one to remember. *a* **1912** W. T. Rogers *Dict. Abbrev.* (1913) 123/1 *m.e.* (book), marbled edges. **1952** J. Carter *ABC for Bk.-Collectors* 12 *M.e.*, marbled edges. **1961** Webster, *ME*,..medical examiner. **1968** H. Waugh *30 Manhattan East* (1969) 120 I'll give your boss the M.E.'s verdict as soon as I get it. **1874** H. Sweet in *Trans. Philol. Soc. 1873–4* 526 The word *gréét* [in the eighteenth century] = M.E. *grèèt* (O.E. *grēat*) is an example of exceptional retention of the older *éé*. **1927** *Englische Studien* 10 Nov. 74 The investigations which have been published hitherto with a view of classifying the ME. dialects by the aid of place-name material. **1972** M. L. Samuels *Ling. Evol.* v. 85 The plural *-eþ* had been replaced by *-en* in the Midlands, and early ME texts from East Anglia show this feature as their only distinction of number. **1914** E. A. Dawe *Paper* 157/2 (*index*) Machine finish (M.F.). **1965** S. C. Gilmour *Paper* (ed. 2) xix. 218 M.F. papers are much used for printing formes of type with line blocks. **1892** C. T. & W. H. Jones *Telegr. Connections* 15/2 On one end of the condenser will usually be found a stamp like this: 2·5 M.F. The microfarad (for which M.F. stands) is the one-millionth part of a farad. **1911** L. W. Bishop *Wireless Operators' Pocket-Bk.* v. 62 The highest capacity of a variable condenser should not be over ·004 mf. **1940** *Chambers's Techn. Dict.* 544/2 *mF.*, *μF.*, abbrev. for micro-farad. **1958** *Times Rev. Industry* May 32/1 Single phase 26V current in conjunction with a 1·5 mf tuning capacitor. **1969** C. M. Rodgers *Songs of Blackbird* 38 None of us can relax until the last m.f.'s Been done in. **1971** B. Malamud *Tenants* 165 The blacks have to murder you white MF's for cripplin our lives. **1973** S. Henderson *Understanding New Black Poetry* 44, I am not speaking merely of words like 'nigger' and 'the big M.F.', as Ron Welburn calls it. **1942** Partridge *Dict. Abbrev.* 62/1 *M.F.N.*, most favoured nation. **1961** *Times* 16 May 15/7 Consequently, the M.F.N. concept is not helpful. **1948** *Hansard Commons* 8 Mar. 971/1, I hope I shall be able to satisfy the hon. Gentleman with the figures for..the number of fishery protection vessels. We have now.. eight ships plus two M.F.V.s. **1949** P. F. Anson *Scots Fisherfolk* 84 The fleet has also been increased by the addition of a large number of Admiralty-built, diesel-motor vessels (M.F.V.s), originally used by the Navy, but since allocated to fishermen. **1973** A. MacVicar *Painted Doll Affair* xiii. 148 They're at sea in that m.f.v. **1974** 'M. Hebden' *Pride of Dolphins* ii. ix. 188 They were moving up astern of a big grey-painted vessel..an ex-naval M.F.V. **1914** E. A. Dawe *Paper* iv. 25 The paper passing round this heated cylinder is dried, and glazed on one side, hence the term M.G., or machine-glazed paper. **1937** E. J. Labarre *Dict. Paper* 170/2 Characteristic of machine glazed papers (abbr. M.G.) is that they are only glazed on one (the under) side, the other being in the (rough) condition in which it comes from the wet end of the machine. **1965** S. C. Gilmour *Paper* (ed. 2) xix. 236 Litho posters are generally printed on M.G. paper. **1915** D. O. Barnett *Let.* 8 July 207 I'm going to be M.-G. officer. **1969** S. Mays *Fall out Officers* xx. 154 Sergeant Yardley of M.G. Squadron. **1940** *Chambers's Techn. Dict.* 544/2 *M.G.* (Build.), abbrev. for make good. **1950** Webster Add., M.G.B. **1974** T. P. Whitney tr. *Solzhenitsyn's Gulag Archipelago* I. i. iv. 145 The MGB wasn't interested in the truth and had no intention of letting anyone out of its grip once he was arrested. **1917** W. Owen *Let.* 12 Feb. (1967) 433 We have a Canadian,..various M.G.C.'s, a S.W.B. **1963** F. D. Fawcett *Cycl. Initials & Abbrev.* 97/2 *MGC*, Machine Gun Corps, disbanded 1922. **1955** *Times* 7 July 1/5 (Advt.), The extent of the supply works to be supervised and maintained include the following... Ultimate maximum output of finished water 21·5 m.g.d. **1935** Ade *Let.* 27 June (1973) 186 The sad facts in regard to *The County Chairman* are that M.G.M. bought the talking rights and recently sold them to Fox. **1952** S. Kauffmann *Philanderer* (1935) iv. 68 What we want is some kind of gimmick or slogan or handle for the public to tie on to with this thing... Like 'Ask the man who owns one'. Or the M.G.M. lion. A trade-mark. **1974** W. Garner *Big enough Wreath* xvi. 250 He'd allowed his *id* an MGM roar. **1974** P. M. Hubbard *Thirsty Evil* i. 14 Jimmy was my agent... We had not reached the point yet where he had to haggle with M.G.M. over the film-rights. **1960** *Aeroplane* XCIX. 837/2 The latter included ion-drive, solar propulsion, plasmajet propulsion, photon-drive, and MHD (Magneto-hydrodynamic) propulsion. **1965** *New Scientist* 3 June 652/2 By passing the exhaust gases from the MHD generator into a conventional steam-raising plant, an overall thermal efficiency of 55 per cent might be achieved. **1974** *Nature* 1 Mar. 89/3 In the post-war years Ferraro did much to encourage research in MHD. [**1920** *Tide Tables* (Admiralty, Hydrographic Dept.) I. p. xxi (*heading*) M.H.W.S...M.H.W.N.] **1923** N. Davey *Stud. Tidal Power* iv. 63 Taking the M.H.W. and M.L.W. areas of the estuary at Salcombe..the half-tide outflow system will utilise a mean average of 49% of the maximum valume of water above M.L.W.S. level. **1964** V. J. Chapman *Coastal Vegetation* ii. 19 It is possible to regard the littoral as extending from mean high water (M.H.W.) to mean low water (M.L.W.); alternatively, it can be defined as reaching from extreme high water mark (E.H.W.M.) to extreme low water mark (E.L.W.M.). Most of the early ecological work is based upon one of these two definitions. **1939** D. Wheatley *Sixty Days to Live* vi. 58 'It's a matter which may affect the welfare of the whole nation. I really mean that'. 'Well, if you put it that way. Is this M.I.5, or something?' **1940** H. Innes *Trojan Horse* ii. 32 The search of a representative of M.I.5. **1963** V. Gielgud *Goggle-Box Affair* xiii. 126 He ultimately opted for Polish nationality, promising apparently to do occasional jobs for M.I.6 on the side. **1964** M.I.5 [see D.I. (*D. III. 3)]. **1965** B. Sweet-Escott *Baker St. Irreg.* iii. 85 M.I.9..had the job of helping allied prisoners of war to escape. **1901** Kipling *Five Nations* (1903) 164 (*title*) M.I. **1929** J. Buchan *Courts of Morning* ii. i. 177 They've first-rate cavalry, but indifferent M.I. **1946** *Newsweek* 6 May 36/2 From D Day until May 6, 1945..more than 10 per cent of the total casualties were listed as MIA. **1970** *Sunday Mail* (Brisbane) 8 Feb. 5/1 Diana O'Grady has groped through 34 months as the wife of an MIA (missing in action). *a* **1912** W. T. Rogers *Dict. Abbrev.* (1913) 125/1 *M.I.A.E.*, Member of the Institute of Automobile Engineers. **1935** *Discovery* Sept. 276 H. Warren, M.I.E.E., M.I.A.E. **1885** *List of Subscribers, Classified* (United Telephone Co.) (ed. 6) 89 *Engineers* (Civil)... Lowe J. E., M.I.C.E., M.I.M.E. (of Bolling & Lowe). **1966** MICR [see *magnetic *a.* 1]. **1970** O. Dopping *Computers & Data Processing* iii. 62 MICR readers do not utilize the information contained in the vertical distribution of ink. They analyze only the horizontal distribution. *a* **1912** W. T. Rogers *Dict. Abbrev.* (1913) 125/2 *M.I.E.E.*, Member of the Institute of Electrical Engineers. **1937** *Discovery* Apr. p. xxviii/1 Professor John Hollingworth, M.A., D.Sc., F.C.G.I., M.I.E.E. *Ibid.*, Professor Dempster Smith, M.B.E., M.Sc.Tech., M.I.M.E. **1909** *Cent. Dict.* Suppl., M.I.Mech.E. **1961** Webster, mip. **1962** *Engineering* 23 Nov. 662/2 A series of marine engines of various sizes, all having the high mip pressure of 10·4 kg per sq. cm. **1967** *Technology Week* 20 Feb. 12/3 A program to demonstrate the feasibility of a solid propellant Post Boost Control System (PBCS) to deliver Multiple Independent Re-entry Vehicle (MIRV) payloads is expected to be funded shortly. **1968** *N.Y. Times* 3 Nov. iv. 7 MIRVing the Polaris system allows a dozen warheads to be fitted to a single Poseidon missile. **1970** *Time* 20 Apr. 22 Each MIRVed rocket is capable of carrying a number of warheads. **1974** L. Deighton *Spy Story* xii. 119 Can they retarget the MIRVs before launching? **1974** *Times* 5 Mar. 7/3 The multiple independently targeting technology for warheads (Mirvs) is the most striking Soviet advance adduced in the report. **1974** *Nature* 6 Dec. 431/1 Proposals for SALT–2 now include multiple warheads in the list of constraints,..presumably because it is considered economically desirable not to go the whole way on MIRVing. **1975** *Sci. Amer.* Jan. 48/1 The tentative agreement represents an incremental advance for arms control..in that for the first time it includes strategic bombers and limits at least the number of missiles that can be MIRVed. **1937** *Discovery* Mar. p. xx/1 W. B. McKay, M.Sc.Tech., M.I.Struct.E. **1950** J. D. MacDonald *Brass Cupcake* (1955) xii. 124 Very distinguished Boston type. Taught mathematics at M.I.T. **1954** D. Riesman *Individualism Reconsidered* v. 303 The M.I.T. students who brought us together dreamed up the whole idea, then found the means to implement it. **1968** Chomsky & Halle *Sound Pattern Eng.* p. x, The general point of view that underlies this descriptive study is one that several of us have been developing for more than fifteen years, at M.I.T. and elsewhere, at first independently, but increasingly as a joint effort. **1909** *Cent. Dict.* Suppl., MJI. **1935** *Engineering* 26 July 95/1 This new system has been designated the Giorgi-M.K.S. system, and in it the practical electrical units are essential constitutional elements in one-to-one relation, with the result that the numerical conversion factors need no longer be..memorised. **1963** Jerrard & McNeill *Dict. Sci. Units* 15 The Giorgi or M.K.S. system attracted little attention until about 1935 but after this interest in them [*sic*] increased and in 1948 the 9th International Conference on Weights and Measures adopted the M.K.S. definition as their definition of the ampere. **1968** M. S. Livingston *Particle Physics* xii. 208 In the rationalized mks system of electromagnetic units, charge becomes a fourth fundamental quantity. **1942** Partridge *Dict. Abbrev.* 63/1 *M.L.*,..motor launch. **1945** 'N. Shute' *Most Secret* i. 4 The *Raumboot* is rather like our own M.L., isn't it? **1897** *Medicine Hat* (Alberta) *News* 8 Apr. 4/2 Another of our M.L.A.'s is to join his confreres in the new Western Eldorado, the marvellously rich Kootenay. **1933** *Bulletin* (Sydney) 6 Sept. 12/3 The combination of the guillotine and the division system is being developed to a stage when the main duty of an M.L.A. will be to sit on a bench and be counted like a sheep. **1970** *Globe & Mail* (Toronto) 26 Sept. 8/2 Indeed the new talk about Fraser power has been met with instant avowals of undying opposition from some of the Government's own MLAs in the Fraser Valley. **1971** *Sunday Australian* 8 Aug. 7/2 He is an old family friend and 'retainer' of Norman Smith, Labor MLA for the Mt Isa area from 1940 to 1960. **1849** *Niagara* (Ontario) *Chron.* 25 Oct. 3/2 J. Leslie, M.L.C. **1930** L. G. D. Acland *Early Canterbury Runs* ii. 29 He..was a member of the old Provincial Council and an early M.L.C. **1971** *Hindustan Times Weekly* (New Delhi) 4 Apr. 3/4 Two MLAs and one MLC of Uttar Pradesh..joined the Congress (N) today. **1901** M.L.D. [see *addiment]. **1928** L. E. H. Whitby *Med. Bacteriol.* xx. 198 One M.L.D. is that amount of toxin which, on subcutaneous inoculation, will with certainty cause the death of a 250 gm. guinea-pig within four days. **1961** N. G. Pandalai *Textbk. Bacteriol.* (ed. 2) xii. 245 While the M.L.D. of atropine for an adult person is 130 mg., of strychnine 30–40 mg., and of cobra venom 4·4 mg., the M.L.D. of the crude tetanus toxin is only 0·2 mg. or even less. **1973** White & Tinbury *Essent. Immunol. & Microbiol.* ii. vii. 120 The ultimate measured effect of toxin is the MLD. **1963** *Times* 10 June 10/5 Thus the first and perhaps most important objection to the multilateral force (M.L.F.) has been largely removed. **1904** *Amer. Jrnl. Sci.* XVII. 335 The datum plane used..is mean low water—M.L.W.—at the Battery as used by the Department of Docks and Ferries. **1923, 1964** M.L.W. [see *M.H.W.* above]. **1933** M.M. [see *Minnie', minnie]. **1971** D. Niven *Moon's a Balloon* v. 63, I caught a glimpse of the medal ribbons of the D.C.M. and M.M. on his chest. **1878** *Jrnl. R. Microsc. Soc.* I. 355 A quarter of a century ago..Harting proposed..micro-millimetre... Thus we had *m.* for the metre, *mm.* for the millimetre, and *mmm.* for the micromillimetre. **1897** *Sears, Roebuck Catal.* 583/1 Pin Fire Pistol Cartridges... In sizes 7 M-M is 32 caliber, 9 M-M is 38 caliber, 12 M-M is 44 caliber. **1971** *Guardian* 16 Dec. 1/2 The police did not identify the weapon but said that the ammunition was 9 mm. **1973** G. G. Spalding in P. Hepple *Outlook for Natural Gas* iv. 55 (*heading*) Estimated well deliverability (MMCFD). **1974** *Petroleum Rev.* XXVIII. 792/2 The field came on production in September 1971 and is currently producing 560 MMcfd. **1975** *North Sea Background Notes* (Brit. Petroleum Co.) 19 Under this agreement, BP undertook to deliver at least 50 million cubic feet of gas a day for a period of 15 years. Later revisions to the contract have resulted in a present commitment of 168 mmcfd as the basic contract rate. **1893** R. M. Walmsley *Wormell's Electr. in Service of Man* ii. 392 The number of lines..which a magnetomotive force (M.M.F.) can set up depends not only on its own magnitude but on the reluctance..of the path provided. **1962** *Newnes Conc. Encycl. Electr. Engin.* 467/1 The m.m.f. per metre length of path is H.., the value of H determining the magnetic flux density $B = \mu H$ at the point, where μ..is the absolute permeability of the medium. **1946**, etc. MMPI [see *Minnesota]. **1948** *Psychol. Bull.* XLV. 402 This would seem to indicate that..the MMPI scales do not actually differ from each other as they are supposed to. **1970** *Jrnl. Gen. Psychol.* LXXXIII. 70 Noting the discrepancy between behavior and test data (in this instance, the MMPI), Peterson..also concluded that the manifestations of psychosis in the MMPI..were instances of inaccurate diagnosis. **1939** Madge & Harrisson *Britain, by Mass-Observation* i. 10 Through M-O you can already listen-in to the movements of popular habit and opinion. **1971** *Guardian Weekly* 10 Apr. 18/1 The MO reports now held by Sussex University have been cleverly worked over. **1916** F. M. Ford *Let.* 19 Dec. (1965) 80 The M.O. who has just sounded my poor old lungs again says I am to be sent to Nice. **1924** *Army Q.* Oct. 138 Stop a minute—give this chit to the M.O. **1944** *Living off Land* v. 97 Day's travel from the nearest M.O. **1974** S. Gulliver *Vulcan Bulletins* 23 You have to get your ideas sorted out not to spend your time in the MO's queue asking for tranquillisers. **1955** R. J. Schwartz *Compl. Dict. Abbrev.* 114/3 *MO*,..method of operation (*modus operandi*). **1956** 'E. McBain' *Cop Hater* (1958) vii. 66 It was possible that the two deaths were unrelated..but not very probable. The m.o. was remarkably similar. **1974** R. Edwards *Dixon of Dock Green* 108 His m.o. was to pull two or three jobs in a line and then fade from the scene. **1937** *Trans. Faraday Soc.* XXXIII. 1481 The *m.o.* solution depends essentially upon the solution of a one-electron problem. **1947** *Q. Rev.* I. 151 The energy of a M.O. is lowest..when the component atomic orbitals overlap one another as much as possible. **1968** R. O. C. Norman *Princ. Org. Synthesis* ii. 35 In the lower-energy MO, termed the $\sigma 1s$ bonding orbital.., there is an accumulation of charge in the region between the nuclei. **1909** J. Joyce *Let.* 4 Sept. (1966) II. 246, I received your M.O. for £3.5.0. **1940** H. Nicolson *Diary* 3 Aug. (1967) 104, I am feeling very depressed by the attacks upon the Ministry of Information... Since the M. of I. should be an offensive instrument, its value to our war-effort will be diminished by this constant sniping from the rear. **1942** E. Waugh *Put out more Flags* 169, I will say for the Ministry of Information they were uncommon civil. Not at all like they are here. At the M. of I. they were never too busy to see one. **1909** *Cent. Dict.* Suppl., MOH. **1911** G. B. Shaw *Doctor's Dilemma* Pref. p. lxxii, When one of the first-rate posts becomes vacant, all the leading M.O.H.s compete for it. **1961** *Lancet* 19 Aug. 440/1 She worked as assistant M.O.H. and inspector of midwives in Manchester. **1939** *War Illustr.* 18 Nov. p. iii/2 M.O.I., Ministry of Information. **1957** J. Braine *Room at Top* x. 100 A MOI poster. **1963** *Aviation Week & Space Technol.* 16 Dec. 30 As described by Defense Secretary McNamara, the system, called MOL for manned orbiting laboratory, will consist largely of hardware already under development. **1965** *Sci. News Let.* 2 Jan. 6/2 The most immediate USAF manned space project is the Manned Orbital Laboratory (MOL), scheduled for some time between 1967 and 1969. In the MOL two men will spend 30 days in orbit around the earth, studying both outer space and each other's reactions to it. **1969** *Times* 13 June 7/6 The cancelled Manned Orbiting Laboratory (M.O.L.) of the U.S. Air Force. **1955** R. J. Schwartz *Compl. Dict. Abbrev.* 115/2 *MOS*,..Military Occupational Specialty. **1969** I. Kemp *Brit. G.I. in Vietnam* iii. 43 'What's your M.O.S.?' he barked. 'Operations and Intelligence Assistant, First Sergeant.' **1964** R. D. Lohman in *Semiconductor Products* May 31 The metal-oxide-semiconductor (MOS) transistor is a new semiconductor device which combines many advantages of vacuum tubes and bipolar transistors. *Ibid.*, A typical n-channel MOS. **1967** Millman & Halkias *Electronic Devices & Circuits* xiv. 384 There are two types of field-effect transistors, the junction field-effect transistor (abbreviated JFET, or simply FET) and the insulated-gate field-effect transistor (IGFET), more commonly called the metal-oxide-semiconductor (MOS) transistor (MOST or MOSFET). **1971** *New Scientist* 8 July 77/2 With the very high-precision masking now used in MOS techniques the space between metallised paths can be 0·0003 in or less. **1973** *Sci. Amer.* Aug. 54/2 Today virtually all desk calculators and all pocket calculators are designed around MOS circuits. **1955** R. J. Schwartz *Compl. Dict. Abbrev.* 115/2 *MOT*,.. Ministry of Transport. **1968** *Listener* 13 June 787/3 The annual MoT test could incorporate a check on noise, and any vehicle which had become noisier..than its original design limits would fail the test. **1971** *Exchange & Mart* 15 July 67 (Advt.), Spot cash!! For any make of Car or Van in any condition e.g. Failed M.O.T. and Damaged Vehicles. **1972** A. Aird *Automotive Nightmare* ii. 41 The inclusion of other items, and in particular corrosion, in the MOT test would also significantly increase the repair demand. **1973** J. Morris *Age of Arthur* 178 The roads are shown as classified by the Ministry of Transport (MoT). **1885** *Phil. Mag.* XX. 513, 2 [exceptions] are due to the m.p. of carbon tetrabromide, CBr_4, being too high. **1947**

Sci. News IV. 153 A polisher using a powder of oxamide (M.P. 417° C.)..did not produce any effect on speculum metal (M.P. 745° C.) or copper (M.P. 1,083° C.). **1917** A. G. Empey *Over Top* 300 M.P., Military Police. Soldiers with whom it is unsafe to argue. **1967** *Coast to Coast 1965–66* 22 A bloody M.P. I suppose, that's what you were. **1972** D. E. Westlake *Cops & Robbers* (1973) vi. 91 What I really wanted was to drive a tank, but I wound up an (M.P. **1931** *Daily Express* 28 Apr. 2/1 Petrol consumption ..averages 20–26 m.p.g. **1955** *Times* 30 Aug. 11/5 The petrol consumption is claimed to be at the rate of 100 m.p.g. on long journeys and 90 m.p.g. in town. **1973** *Country Life* 20 Sept. 802/3 The engine..is very thirsty for its size, giving me 14 mpg overall and nearer 12 mpg in town driving. **1909** *Cent. Dict.* Suppl., m.p.h. **1935** *Discovery* Oct. 293/2 Speed was increased by only two m.p.h. **1942** *R.A.F. Jrnl.* 16 May 9 The qualities of this type of aircraft are judged..by its m.p.h., manoeuvrability and ascending speed. **1960** Wodehouse *Jeeves in Offing* xix. 185, I deposited Upjohn at the 'Bull and Bush' and started m-p-h-ing homeward. **1975** *Guardian* 20 Jan. 7/3 The car with..a top speed of 107 mph, is aimed initially at the American market. **1826** *Colonial Advocate* (Toronto) 9 Feb. 2/4 John J. Lafferty, Esq. M.P.P. was called to the chair. **1970** *Toronto Daily Star* 24 Sept. 35/1 Lewis, MPP for Scarborough West. *a* **1912** W. T. Rogers *Dict. Abbrev.* (1913) 129/1 *M.Q.*, Metol-Quinol (Developer). **1940** *Chambers's Techn. Dict.* 561/1 *M.Q.*, an abbrev. for metol-quinol or metol-hydroquinone developers. **1939** *Nation* (N.Y.) 5 Aug. 135/1 M.R.A. and Hollywood were made for each other. **1949** *New Statesman* 15 Oct. 422/1 The success of M.R.A...is so brilliant that one cannot understand why the world is still in such a mess. **1969** *Listener* 3 July 19/3 Less than 1 per cent of our members are associated with MRA. **1960** *Acronyms Dict.* (Gale Research Co.) 126 MRBM... Medium Range Ballistic Missile. **1961** *Ann. Reg. 1960* 167 Opposition to giving M.R.B.M.s to NATO was partly emotional. **1848** Thackeray *Pendennis* (1849) I. ii. 10 A professional friend, M.R.C.S. **1936** *Discovery* June 182 Winifred de Kok, M.R.C.S., L.R.C.P. **1961** M-RNA [see *messenger RNA* (*messenger 7)]. **1965** *Jrnl. Molecular Biol.* XI. 187 A very small proportion of rapidly labeled RNA can be identified as M-RNA in the cell cytoplasm. **1965** *Ibid.* XIV. 257 [They] have presented evidence for the attachment of ribosomal particles to mRNA while the RNA is still attached to its DNA template. **1970** Ambrose & Easty *Cell Biol.* iv. 129 When the code has been transcribed from DNA on to mRNA, the latter leaves the nucleus, passing through the nuclear membrane into the cytoplasm. **1946** *Ann. Reg. 1945* 172 The Socialist Party (S.F.I.O.) and Christian Democrats (M.R.P.) were in favour of *Yes.* **1958** *Spectator* 30 May 676/3 Feelings within the MRP were stiffening as in the Socialist Party. **1953** K. Reisz *Technique Film Editing* iv. 87 *M.S.* Father, daughter and doctor. **1923** *Man. Seamanship* (Admiralty) II. 177 The executive officer of a minesweeping vessel should first ascertain the allowed establishment of M/S stores. **1953** W. Burroughs *Junkie* (1972) v. 52, I was getting sick and wondered if I would get home to the M.S. I had stashed in my apartment. **1969** R. R. Lingeman *Drugs from A to Z* 176 When used by addicts, morphine is most commonly in the form of a salt, e.g., morphine sulfate (the origin of M.S., a slang term for morphine), which is soluble in water and hence injectable. **1955** *Sci. News Let.* 14 May 311/3 The search for twins with MS, or multiple sclerosis, has yielded 33 identical sets so far, but the National Multiple Sclerosis Society would like to locate about 350 more, fraternal as well as identical. **1959** *Observer* 29 Mar. 8/4 Best results are obtained by dissolving M.S.G. in the cooking liquor and adding towards the end of cooking. **1969** *New Scientist* 6 Mar. 505/2 Every packet soup, fish-finger and chicken croquette contains a dose of MSG to..'wake up all the flavour *nature* put in your food'. **1953** MSH [see **melanocyte-stimulating hormone*]. **1958** MSH [see *melatonin]. **1965** Lee & Knowles *Animal Hormones* x. 128 As in amphibians, the elasmobranch skin colour is controlled by the level of MSH. **1955** M. Grindrod *Rebuilding of Italy* viii. 79 The MSI had..by 1952..built up some sort of status for itself. **1959** *Engineering* 6 Feb. 184/2 MT is discussed in two general chapters, on dictionary searching, the 'stem-ending' method of analysis, identification of idioms and a possible method for resolving multi-meanings. **1966** Y. Bar-Hillel in *Automatic Transl. of Lang.* (NATO Summer School, Venice 1962) 20 On the other hand, the number of research groups which have taken up MT as their major field of activity is still on the increase. **1917** 'Contact' *Airman's Outings* 167 The Squadron Commander meets us... 'Seen anything?' he asks. 'Fourteen trains and some M.T.,' I reply. **1946** *R.A.F. Jrnl.* May 174 There are W.A.A.F. clubs,..W.A.A.F. on M.T. **1947** L. Hastings *Dragons are Extra* i. 25 He collected second-hand cars.... Tinkering them up, and practising the same sort of cannibalism that long after became an M.T. necessity in modern war. **1938** *Jane's Fighting Ships* 140 A number of the M.T.B's of the Thornycroft type are still in existence. **1944** *R.A.F. Jrnl.* Aug. 265 Cargo vessels, with M.T.B.'s weaving among them, leaving long white wakes. **1955** 'N. Shute' *Requiem for a Wren* 128 Left Gosport in an M.T.B. **1942** Partridge *Dict. Abbrev.* 65/2 MTC. **1944** M.T.C. [see *Croix de Guerre]. **1956** *Electronic Engin.* XXVIII. 15 A further important feature of this equipment is the m.t.i. (moving target indicator) system, which is more effective in removing unwanted clutter and permanent echoes, and more stable in operation than any other previous type. **1966** *McGraw-Hill Encycl. Sci. & Technol.* VIII. 620/1 MTI is almost a necessity when moving targets are being sought over a region from which the ground clutter echoes are very strong. **1949** Koestler *Promise & Fulfilment* 262 At the bottom of their hearts they know quite well what the M.V.D. has in store for them. **1959** *Listener* 4 June 996/3 One falls into the hands of the M.V.D. **1902** *Encycl. Brit.* XXXI. 339/2 The Royal Victorian Order..consists of.. knights commanders (K.C.V.O.), commanders (C.V.O.), and members of the fourth and fifth classes (M.V.O.), the distinction between these last divisions lying in the badge and in the precedence enjoyed by the members. **1915** *Dialect Notes* IV. 246 *N.o.y.b.*, none of your business. Also *m.y.o.b.*, mind your own business. **1951** P. Branch *Lion in Cellar* xvi. 184 'Who are you?'..'M.Y.O.B.' **1972** J. Wilson *Hide & Seek* i. 8 'I had to go and collect something,' Alice mumbled. 'What?' 'M.Y.O.B.' 'Don't be cheeky.' **1974** L. Meynell *Fairly Innocent Little Man* xi. 140 'M.Y.O.B.,' Hooky said, 'if you know what that means.' 'At school we say it means Mess Your Own Breeches.'

b. Abbrev. for Master: M.A.A., Master-at-Arms; M.B.A., Master of Business Administration; M.C. (earlier and later examples; also as *v. trans.* and *intr.*); M.Ed., Master of Education; M.Litt. (*magister litterarum*), Master of Letters; M.R., Master of the Rolls; M.S. (*U.S.*), M.Sc., Master of Science.

1916 'Taffrail' *Pincher Martin* vii. 117 'Petty Officer William Weatherley,' the M.A.A. went on, 'requests hextension o' leaf till two p.m. on Monday.' **1934** Webster *M.B.A.*, Master in, *or* of, Business Administration. **1965** *New Statesman* 26 Nov. 828/3 Even those few firms that give lip service to the idea of business schools are unwilling to regard a good MBA degree as representing more than one or two years of 'relevant experience'. **1790** E. Sheridan *Jrnl.* 5 Jan. (1960) 192 It was Tyson's Benefit, and as he is my acquaintance, independent of being M:C:, it was but decent that at least one of us should appear there. **1812** *Dramatic Censor 1811* 470 They are no more..co-equal with what they were, than the M.C. of a watering-place is on a par with the late Earl of Chesterfield in mind and manners. **1937** A. Upfield *Mr. Jelly's Business* viii. 74 Almost seventy people waiting for the M.C. to announce the first dance. **1938** *New Yorker* 22 Oct. 23/3, I m.c'd and they had a couple of kids from the local dancing school doing tap. **1950** Webster Add., *m.c.*, *MC*, or *M.C.*...v.i. & t. **1954** E. Warner *Trial by Sasswood* (1955) x. 185 He was to m.c. an assemblage in the market compound. **1968** *Listener* 5 Sept. 307/1 With his mutton-chop whiskers John Peel appropriately looks like an MC at an Edwardian music hall. **1934** Webster, *M.Ed.*, Master of Education. **1937** *Discovery* June p. xlviii/1 G. P. McHugh M.Sc., Ph.D. (Lond), M.Ed. (Dunelm). **1909** *Cent. Dict.* Suppl., M.Lit. **1955** R. J. Schwartz *Compl. Dict. Abbrev.* 113/3 *M Litt*, Master of Letters. **1895** *Funk's Stand. Dict.*, M.R. **1964** *Mod. Law Rev.* XXVIII. iii. 274 Lord Denning M.R. said that Silverthorne was liable. **1909** *Cent. Dict.* Suppl., M.S. **1955** *Sci. Amer.* Sept. 36/3 He was born in Miami, Fla., and has a B.S. and an M.S. in physics from the University of Florida. **1909** *Cent. Dict.* Suppl., M.Sc. **1936** *Discovery* May 156 Julius Grant, Ph.D., M.Sc., F.I.C.

d. m = Milli-, as in mA, milliampere(s); mg, mgm, milligram(s); ml, millilitre(s); mm (see sense 5 a in Dict.); mrad, millirad(s).

1896 T. E. Herbert *Electr. in Applic. to Telegr.* iii. 27 1/1000 ampere or 1 m.a. **1927** *Wireless World* 16 Nov. 670/1 The..three valves..draw a high-tension current totalling 2 or 3 mA. **1970** *Which?* June 183/2 Even at maximum volume most transistor radios will not use more than 100 mA. **1894** J. Walker tr. *Ostwald's Man. Physico-Chem. Measurements* iii. 39 The correction is 0·00014, i.e. 0·14 mg. per gram. **1951** *Good Housek. Home Encycl.* 339/2 Its vitamin C content is low—1 mg. per oz. **1968** *Listener* 28 Nov. 703/1 The good effects of last year's Road Safety Act, making it an offence to drive with a level of alcohol in the blood of more than 80 milligrammes per 100 millimetres [*sic*], may be wearing off. This may well be because 80mg/100ml is such a high level. **1909** *Cent. Dict.* Suppl., *mgm.*, an abbreviation of *milligram.* **1939** *Nature* 11 Mar. 442/1 It is..possible to carry out exact estimations of carbon..using 2–3 mgm. of material. **1892** G. Collar *Notes on Metric System* 7, 10 millilitres (ml.) make 1 centilitre (cl.). **1968** ml [see *mg* above]. **1961** *New Scientist* 11 May 297/1 The average exposure in the course of radiological procedures was only of the order of 20 mrad annually, which is far less than the 100 mrad from natural background sources to which we are subjected. **1970** mrad [see *dose *sb.* 1 b].

e. M = Mega- b, as in MeV (also Mev, etc.), million electron volt(s); MHz, megahertz; MW, megawatt(s).

1934 *Physical Rev.* XLVI. 1109/2 The spectrum.. indicates gamma-ray lines of roughly 2, 4, 5·5 and 7 m.e.v. *Ibid.*, (*heading*) Energy in MEV. **1955** *Bull. Atomic Sci.* May 171/3 U-238 does not undergo fission with neutrons below 1·1 Mev. **1964** Heisenberg in *Cambr. Rev.* 24 Oct. 48/1 A mass difference up to 400 MeV. **1951** *Physica* XVII. 213 Measurements have been carried out on paramagnetic resonance absorption in iron ammonium alum at a frequency of about 9200 MHz. **1970** *E. Afr. Standard* (Nairobi) 2 Jan. 11/7 (Advt.), B.B.C. listeners can also hear programmes in English for East Africa between 7.30 and 8.45 p.m. on 15·42 MHz. **1956** *Proc. CERN Symposium* I. 22/2 Production of the flutter fields by pole-face windings..would require ~ a few MW of power per pole face. **1962** *Newnes Conc. Encycl. Electr. Engin.* 324/1 Fuel-fired steam power stations..are now built for outputs up to 1,000 MW or more.

f. Designating a motorway. Also *fig.* and *Comb.*

1959 *Times* 10 Nov. 6/5 Two people were injured in an accident on the London–Birmingham motorway, the M.1, yesterday. **1963** *Listener* 10 Jan. 100/2 Some of the by-ways of sound radio—by-ways to me but no doubt a positive M1 to thousands of others—can be rewarding. **1964** *Daily Tel.* 3 Mar. 21/1 (*heading*) M-drivers 'can stop if drowsy'. **1966** 'A. York' *Eliminator* iv. 72, I would have thought you'd have wanted to try her on the M. **1973** *Guardian* 26 May 8/5 Bartholomew's new Motorway Atlas..is a useful tool for those who go up and down the Ms all the time.

'm. = Madam *sb.*

1864 J. S. Le Fanu *Uncle Silas* I. iv. 37 He bowed gravely, with a: 'Yes, 'm—shall, 'm.' **1933** E. A. Robertson *Ordinary Families* vii. 140 Her submissive 'Yes 'm' and 'No, miss'. **1945** in B. A. Botkin *Treas. S. Folklore* (1949) ii. iv. 352 Mr. Linktum come down. Yes'm, Mr. Abe Linktum and his partner, Horace Greeley, comed down.

m'. = My *poss. adj.*

1712 [see My *poss. adj.* 1 β]. **1837** J. F. Cooper *England* II. xii. 51, I take it, the polite way of pronouncing this word is by a sort of elision—as m'horse, m'dog, m'gun. *Ibid.*, I think more noble peers, however, said '*me* lurds', than 'm' lurds'. **1852** Dickens *Bleak Ho.* (1853) i. 4 'Mr. Tangle,' says the Lord High Chancellor... 'Mlud,' says Mr. Tangle. **1907** R. Brooke *Let.* 12 Aug. (1968) 99 M'uncle is changing his house or face or wife or something. **1908** [see *house *sb.*[1] 4 c]. **1914** [see *æsthete]. **1942** G. Greene *Brit. Dramatists* 33 Lady Teazle 'm'ludding' and flirting a fan. **1945** E. Waugh *Brideshead Revisited* i. ii. 47 A series of harrowing interviews with m'tutor. **1967** *Guardian* 31 July 5/1, I remember him playing the part of a prosecuting counsel..full of patronising 'M'luds'. **1968** A. Diment *Gt. Spy Race* vii. 103 Why, chappie in m'tutors, doing four years in the Scrubs. **1970** O. Norton *Dead on Prediction* v. 84 Not evidence, m'dear. Is it? **1972** J. Porter *Meddler & her Murder* iii. 39 Allow me to carry the tray for you, Eve, m'dear.

ma, *sb.* Add: **a.** Also a familiar shortening of (or substitute for) Mrs. Also applied *colloq.* to a middle-aged or elderly woman, esp. one in authority.

1932 J. Cary *Aissa Saved* xxxvii. 196 You come now, ma; she very sick. **1943** K. Tennant *Ride on Stranger* iii. 27 'What-ho, Ma,' came a howl from the kitchen. 'Coming.' Beryl appeared wiping her hands. **1951** J. Common *Kiddar's Luck* xi. 161 My father called them the Ma gang, because they had a habit of always alluding to each other as Ma This and Ma That. *Ibid.*, It was becoming fairly regular to see Ma McGrewin, or Ma Smailes, or Ma Forbes sitting boldly by the fireside. **1966** Wodehouse *Plum Pie* v. 124 'Did Ma Purkiss make a speech?' 'Yes, Mrs. Purkiss spoke.' **1974** M. Babson *Stalking Lamb* xvi. 120 'Here, Ma,' Aaron said, 'I've brought company.'

b. *Austral.* (With capital initial.) Popular name for New South Wales. So *Ma State.*

1934 *Bulletin* (Sydney) 24 Jan. 25/1 The Cabbage Gardeners will have to be licked outright if Ma is to have a hope. **1945** Baker *Austral. Lang.* 187 *New South Wales*, New South, the Ma State or Ma. **1949** *Geogr. Mag.* Feb. 373 *New South* and *The Ma State*, New South Wales (oldest state in the Commonwealth).

ma. (mēi), *a.* Colloq. abbrev., in some schools, of *major* = the elder of two namesakes.

1932 Wodehouse *Louder & Funnier* 12 Faber *ma* was so annoyed by his snorts and chuckles that he hit him over the head with a *croisson* or small French roll. **1963** *Times* 5 June 14/3 There was gentler satire from McGavin ma. with John Betjeman's 'Village Inn'.

maa (mā), *v.* [Echoic, in imitation of the sound made by a sheep or goat. Cf. Mae *v.*] *intr.* To bleat. Hence as *sb.* and **maa·ing** *vbl. sb.*

1827 Darley *Sylvia* ii. i. 34 It will make me *ma-a* like a he-goat on a rock-top when he misses the beard of his charmer. **1886** J. Stewart *Twa Elders* 147 The boys would maa and bleat. **1922** Joyce *Ulysses* 162 All are washed in the blood of the lamb, bawling maaaaaa. **1928** *Blackw. Mag.* Mar. 324/1 Poor old goat!..His caperings were fantastic, his *maaings* continuous. **1940** N. Marsh *Surfeit of Lampreys* (1941) xvii. 268 'M-a-a-ah,' said Rattisbon with a formidable and sheep-like cry.

maalesh, var. *maleesh *int.*

maar (māɹ). *Geol.* Pl. ‖ **maare, maars.** [G. dial., 'crater-lake'.] **a.** (Usu. with capital initial.) One of the craters or crater-lakes of the Eifel district in Germany. **b.** Any volcanic crater which does not lie in a cone and was formed by a single explosive event (and is usu. occupied by a lake).

1826 *Edin. Jrnl. Sci.* V. 152 The craters of this country [*sc.* Prussia] have nearly, without exception, become bodies of water, or *Maare*, as they are called by the natives. *Ibid.* 154 To the S.E. of Steffler, lies a small *maar*, or crater-lake. *Ibid.* 156 The water in the three lakes appears to stand at the same level... One only, the Schalkenonchrener maar, has any visible outlet. **1882** A. Geikie *Text-bk. Geol.* 560 Occasionally, as in some of the Maare of the Eifel, these non-volcanic fragments constitute most of the débris. **1895** *Bull. Philos. Soc. Washington* XII. 251 The maars are of still rarer occurrence, and represent the antithetic phase of volcanism. **1933** R. A. Daly *Igneous Rocks & Depths of Earth* viii. 161 Maars are relatively flat-floored craters of explosion at vents that are either coneless or else provided with inconspicuous cones. *Ibid.*, Reck has recently published..fine illustrations of maars in Abyssinia. **1968** R. W. Fairbridge *Encycl. Geomorphol.* 681/1 Maare sometimes resemble calderas. **1971** *Nature* 30 July 330/2 The lake occupies the crater of a maar—a volcanic eruption crater lying below the general level of the surrounding country and surrounded by a low tuff ring.

maas (mās). *S. Afr.* Also **amaaz, amas, amasi.** [f. Zulu (*pref.*) *ama-* + *si* milk.] Thickened sour milk.

1833 S. Kay *Trav. Caffraria* i. v. 121 Their general diet extremely simple. This ordinarily consists of milk, which ..they invariably use in a sour curdled state. It is called *amaaz*, and rendered thus thick and acidulous by being kept in leathern sacks or bottles. **1857** *Cape Monthly Mag.* I. 289 The men are not allowed to drink any amasi or thick sour milk from a kraal of which they may think of courting a girl. **1882** W. R. Ludlow *Zululand & Cetewayo* vii. 73 Maas, which is the chief food of the Zulus, where there are large herds of cattle, is most delicious and nourishing food. **1946** J. Hertslet *Bantu Folk Tales* v. 61

A wether had been killed and a large piece of its meat was put with the maas and beer. **1952** S. Cloete *Curve & Tusk* (1953) iii. 33 He ate..maas, the sour thickened milk of the indigenous people. **1953** R. Campbell *Mamba's Precipice* ii. 24 They solidified the milk in calabashes and called it *Maas.* **1967** O. Walker *Hippo Poacher* 18 He provided them with *amasi* or sour milk.

maasbanker (mā·sbaːŋkər, mǫsbǫ·ŋkəɹ). Also **maasbancker, maasbank, marsbanker, masbanker, massbanker.** [Afrikaans, f. Du. *marsbanker* Mossbunker.] The South African name for the scad or horse mackerel, *Trachurus trachurus.*

1727 J. G. Scheuchzer tr. *Kæmpfer's Hist. Japan* I. I. xi. 136 *Adsi* is the *Maasbancker* of the Dutch. **1843** J. C. Chase *Cape Good Hope* II. 169 Maasbank..June..Like Mackarel, but stronger, not always wholesome. **1853** L. Pappe *Synopsis Edible Fishes Cape Good Hope* 25 *Caranx Trachurus* Lacep. (Maasbanker; Bastard Mackerel.)..Caught in winter at both ends of the Colony. Its flesh is well flavoured and wholesome. **1902** *Trans. S. Afr. Philos. Soc.* XI. 215 The Maasbanker..is identical with the Maasbanker (*Caranx trachurus*) of Holland, and indeed is to be found almost everywhere within the temperate and tropical zones of both hemispheres. **1930** C. L. Biden *Sea-Angling Fishes of Cape* vii. 146 The English horse-mackerel is the masbanker of the Cape (*Trachurus trachurus*). **1947** *Cape Times* 2 May 9 Maasbankers continue to be plentiful. **1953** *Ibid.* 20 May 4/4 The Government has limited the number and capacity of plants which may be used for the manufacture of fish meal and fish oil from pilchards and massbankers. **1959** G. Jenkins *Twist of Sand* ii. 43 We'd had a fair haul of pilchard, stockfish and maasbanker. **1970** *Cape Times* (S.A. Fishing Rev.) 28 Oct. 2/2 The purse seine boats..hunt the shoals of pilchard, mackerel, maasbanker and anchovy along the West Coast. **1972** L. G. Green *When Journey's Over* (1973) xii. 148 Nelson saw snoek and *marsbankers* in boxes and barrels or hanging up to dry.

Maastrichtian, var. *Maestrichtian *a.*

‖ **maat** (māt). *S. Afr.* [Afrikaans = Mate *sb.*[2] 1.] A companion, partner, friend.

1812 W. Burchell *Trav. S. Afr.* 24 July (1822) II. 466 Another chieftain who was his *maat* (partner, or agent). *Ibid.* 555 Thus a Hottentot..when he visits Litakun..goes directly to the house of his correspondent, whom he calls his *maat* (a Dutch word identical with 'mate'). **1827** G. Thompson *Trav. S. Afr.* (ed. 2) I. xii. 238 Many of the Bechuanas selected *maats* or comrades..from among their allies. **1932** C. Fuller *Louis Trigardt's Trek* x. 124 We drank it as my *maats* had just come to my wagon.

mabela (mabī·la). *S. Afr.* Also **mabbele.** [ad. Zulu *i(li)bele*, pl. *amabele.*] Indian millet, *Sorghum vulgare*, or the meal or porridge made from it. Also *attrib.*

1824 W. J. Burchell *Trav. S. Afr.* II. xviii. 586 The plant resembles... Maize or Indian corn... The Bichuanas call it *mâbbêlě*..and are fond of chewing the stalk. **1939** A. W. Wells *S. Afr.: Planned Tour* xx. 228 (*caption*) Natives in a valley of mealies and mabela corn near the Caledon River. **1946** *Cape Argus Mag.* 14 Dec. 4/5 He..set before him on a stool a bowl of mabela, a flat scone toasted on the coals and a calabash bowl of milk.

mac[1]. Add to def.: Also a familiar form of address used to any stranger.

1937 Partridge *Dict. Slang* 503/1. **1962** L. Deighton *Ipcress File* xxv. 158 'Make on the feet, mack,' he said. **1963** *Landfall* XVII. 14 You'd only to hear my father..to know where he stood, solid for intolerance, mac, but solid. **1965** *Sc. Nat. Dict.* VI. 169/2 *Mac,*..in colloq. use applied in Eng. to anyone known or thought to be a Scotsman, in Scot. common as a fam. form of address to any stranger. **1968** *New Yorker* 16 Mar. 42 For the last time, Mac—we don't have any mead. **1973** J. Wainwright *Pride of Pigs* 128 The bouncer..tapped him on the shoulder and said: 'Hey, mac.'

mac, var. *mack *sb.*[5]

macabre, *a.* Add: **1.** (Later examples.)

1870 C. M. Yonge *Caged Lion* ix. 166 It is the Danse Macabre... It was invented as a warning to those of sinful life. **1938** *Oxf. Compan. Mus.* 251/1 *Danse macabre.* The idea of Death as a dancer, or as a fiddling inciter to the dance, is very ancient. **1955** *Times* 19 May 3/7 This *danse macabre* could only have been written by a poet. **1966** *Listener* 17 Nov. 746/3 An *Allegretto* in G minor—a waltz-like *danse macabre*—which quotes the opening of the first cello concerto. **1974** H. Waugh *Parrish for Defence* (1975) i. 5 The hours before dawn belonged to the souls of the dead... The restless whirling of their frenzies would be the *Danse Macabre.*

2. Hence as *sb.*; also **maca·brely** *adv.*

c **1920** T. E. Lawrence *Lett.* (1938) facing p. 233 It's just struck me that there's all the elements of a macabre in the passage which R. G. censored. **1948** F. R. Leavis *Great Tradition* i. 19 The unfortunate *macabre* of the cab-journey. **1961** A. Wilson *Old Men at Zoo* ii. 107 The black suit she wore, against which her white face..stared out so macabrely. **1964** *Economist* 24 Oct. 365/2 This is where [it]..might become most macabrely relevant. **1968** D. Francis *Forfeit* xiii. 163 What he said..was macabrely at variance with the way he said it.

macadamia (mækădēi·miă). [mod.L. (F. von Mueller 1858, in *Trans. Phil. Inst. Victoria* II. 72), f. the name of John *Macadam* (1827–65), Scottish-born chemist, who was secretary of the Philosophical Institute of Victoria at that time.] An evergreen tree of the Australian genus so called, of the family Proteaceæ, esp. *Macadamia ternifolia*, the Queensland nut, which bears white-fleshed nuts in hard shells. Also *attrib.*

1904 J. H. Maiden *Forest Flora New South Wales* I. 217 Mr. Betche and I described a *Macadamia*..from Camden Haven, N.S.W. **1929** M. D. Frear *Our Familiar Island Trees* 64 Perhaps the best of these [recent introductions to Hawaii] is the Macadamia Nut, sometimes called the Queensland Nut from its native habitat. **1949** S. A. Clark *All the Best in Hawaii* xx. 207 Macadamia nuts call for special pause and explanation, for mainlanders seem rarely to have heard of them... A man named E. W. Jordan brought some of these nuts from Tasmania to Honolulu about the year 1890. *Ibid.* 208 Some smooth-leaf varieties of macadamia produce smaller and less sweet nuts. As a delicacy..macadamia nuts, salted and bottled, have hardly three decades of history... Several Honolulu concerns ship bottled macadamias anywhere. **1955** W. Gaddis *Recognitions* II. i. 295 She returned to her desk..took a macadamia nut from the jar. **1963** *Economist* 14 Dec. 1198/3 Oils are available..from..macadamia nuts. **1969** *Coast to Coast 1967–68* 4 He could hear the familiar morning sounds through that hush,..the sow's demanding squeals, the butcher-birds and magpies in the macadamia-trees. **1970** *Daily Colonist* (Victoria, B.C.) 23 Dec. 4/1 Economies [made by United Air Lines] have ranged from cancelling routes..and ceasing to serve macadamia nuts—a Hawaiian delicacy—with drinks.

macaroni. Add: **8*.** An Italian. *slang.*

1845 [see *frog[1] 3 b]. **1901** 'L. Malet' *Hist. R. Calmady* v. x. 461 You don't suppose I mean to stand here till the second anniversary of the Day of Judgment, watching your blithering chicken-shanked macaronies suck rotten oranges, do you? **1942** E. Paul *Narrow St.* xxix. 266 'Cut the throats of the macaronis,' Madame Absalom said. She disliked Italians slightly more than the rest of the human race. **1946** D. Hamson *We fell among Greeks* viii. 91 They dropped us practically on to the Italian garrison at Karpenísi... Doug was playing hidey-ho with a couple of macaronis, taking potshots round bushes at each other.

8.** Nonsense, meaningless talk. *slang* (chiefly *Austral.*).

1924 Lawrence & Skinner *Boy in Bush* iii. 46 Yes. Jam, macaroni, cockadoodle. We're plain people out here-aways, not mantle ornaments. **1941** Baker *Dict. Austral. Slang* 45 *Macaroni*, nonsense, foolishness. **1945** —— *Austral. Lang.* vi. 128 *Macaroni*..and *borak* cover the same meaning of misleading chatter. **1965** J. von Sternberg *Fun in Chinese Laundry* (1966) iv. 67 What is flashed from the projector overhead will be the same old macaroni.

9. (sense 1) *macaroni pudding, soup*; **macaroni cheese**, a savoury of which the principal ingredients are macaroni and cheese.

[**1769** E. Raffald *Experienced Eng. Housekeeper* xii. 261 To dress Macaroni with Permasent Cheese... Boil it.., pour it on a Plate, lay all over it Permasent Cheese toasted.] **1877** Trollope *Is he Popenjoy?* (1878) I. i. 2 It is as though one were asked to eat boiled mutton after woodcocks, caviare, or maccaroni [macaroni, 1877 *serial publ.*] cheese. **1934** A. Ransome *Coot Club* iii. 40 Tell her we won't be late. Macaroni cheese to-night. **1972** B. Nilson *Pears Bk. Light Meals* xii. 184 Macaroni cheese with ham. **1861** Mrs. Beeton *Bk. Househ. Managem.* xxvii. 654 *Sweet macaroni pudding...* Put the macaroni, with a pint of the milk, into a saucepan with the lemon-peel. **1963** N. Heaton *Puddings* II. 56 *Macaroni Pudding.* .. When cool, add the beaten egg and the sugar. **1845** E. Acton *Mod. Cookery* (ed. 2) ii. 11 *Maccaroni soup.* Throw four ounces of fine fresh mellow maccaroni into a pan of fast-boiling water. **1949** H. Smith *Master Bk. Soups* xv. 198 *Thick Macaroni Soup.* Prepare 3 pints of good gravy. .. Garnish with 6 ozs. macaroni cooked in salted water.

Macartney. Add: **b. Macartney rose,** an evergreen white-flowered climbing rose, *Rosa bracteata*, introduced in 1795 by Lord Macartney.

1811 *Curtis's Bot. Mag.* XXXIV. 1377 Macartney's [*sic*] Rose... Native of China, whence it was introduced by Lord Macartny [*sic*], on his return from his embassy to that country. **1837** [in Dict. s.v. Rose *sb.* 3]. **1908** H. H. Robbins *Our First Ambassador to China* p. viii, The design on the cover of the book is one adapted from a sprig of the original Macartney rose, growing in the North of Ireland. **1955** C. C. Hurst in G. S. Thomas *Old Shrub Roses* ix. 93 So many different species have been concerned in the nineteenth and twentieth centuries... Macartney Roses from *R*[*osa*] *bracteata* [etc.]. **1974** *Country Life* 21 Mar. 631/1 The Macartney Rose, *Rosa bracteata*, belongs essentially to late summer..an exquisite creature with large white blooms and golden stamens.

Macassar. Add: **1. Macassar ebony,** the dark-coloured wood of *Diospyros celebica* and related species from Celebes and the Andaman Islands.

1889 G. S. Boulger *Uses of Plants* vii. 177 Those [sticks] most commonly cut out of the solid log are Oak..home-grown; Ceylon or Macassar Ebony..; and the Palmyra Palm. **1920** A. L. Howard *Man. Timbers of World* 76 (*heading*) Ebony, macassar... This wood is imported in large billets and round logs... The colour ranges from dark brown to black, and a large proportion of the logs are streaked with yellow or yellowish brown, some very handsomely figured pieces being occasionally found. **1936** *Nature* 9 May 790/2 Counter front..in finely figured macassar ebony. **1947** J. C. Rich *Materials & Methods of Sculpture* x. 288 Macassar ebony, or Coromandel,..is considered by many wood carvers to be inferior to African ebony. **1972** *Handbk. Hardwoods* (Building Res. Establishment) (ed. 2) 68 In Macassar ebony pale to medium brown zones contrast with black wood.

2. Also **Macasar, Makasar, Makassar, Mangkasar, Mungkasar.** A native or inhabitant of Macassar; the name of their language. Also *attrib.* or as *adj.*

1808 *Asiatick Researches* X. 194 The dialect of Mungkásar or Macassar, the bravest and most renowned of the Búgís tribes, differs..from the Búgís proper... I have formed a short radical vocabulary of both the Búgís and Mungkásar [languages]. **1816** T. S. Raffles *On Malayu Nation* 125 To the collection that has already been made of the various laws and usages of the Malays, Sumatrans, Javanese, Bugis, Macasars and Sulus, may be added the compendium of the Muhammedan law of inheritance. **1817** —— *Hist. Java* II. xi. 162 By the aid of the Dutch..the Makásar chief was driven from his post. **1840** J. Brooke *Jrnl.* 14 Feb. in R. Mundy *Narr. Events Borneo & Celebes* (1848) I. vii. 106 From his residence at Tetiagi..he transmits information to the Makassar government. **1886** *Misc. Papers relating to Indo-China* (Straits Branch R. Asiatic Soc.) I. xii. 108 The descriptive catalogues of the extensive Bugis and Makassar literature..may now be consulted. **1911** *Encycl. Brit.* V. 598/1 The Macassars are well-built and muscular, and have in general a dark-brown complexion. **1968** *Ibid.* V. 132/2 They [*sc.* the Toradja tribe] came under a Bugis and Makasarese civilizing influence... The Bugis and Makasars..came into touch with Hindu culture in southern Celebes..and later were converted to Islam. *Ibid.* XIV. 654/1 Gaily coloured, plaited basketry is an outstanding feature of Makasarese markets... The people, the Mangkasaras or Makasars, are a branch of the Malay people, similar to but not identical with the Bugis, who inhabit the same region.

Macassarese (măkæsărī·z). Also **Makas(s)arese. a.** The Macassar people. **b.** Their language. Also *attrib.* or as *adj.*

1880 [see *Dyak]. **1948** D. Diringer *Alphabet* vii. 430 The Macassarese and the Buginese..are the most important and the most advanced peoples of the island [*sc.* Celebes]... Macassarese is spoken nowadays in all the districts from Balu Kumba to Segere. **1959** *Chambers's Encycl.* III. 211/1 The peoples of the south (Buginese and Macassarese) are Moslems. **1968** [see *Macassar 2].

McBurney's point (măkbɒ̄·ɹnīz). *Surg.* and *Anat.* Also **McBurney point.** [f. the name of Charles *McBurney* (1845–1913), U.S. surgeon, who described it in 1889.] A point on the surface of the abdomen situated along a line from the umbilicus to where the anterior superior spine of the right ilium can be felt and at a distance of 1½ to 2 inches from this spine, which point normally lies directly above the appendix and is the point of maximum tenderness in appendicitis.

1890 L. A. Stimson in *N.Y. Med. Jrnl.* 25 Oct. 449/2, I found him..very weak, with marked tenderness and slight deep induration at a point midway between the umbilicus and the right anterior superior spine of the ilium... For the sake of brevity, and as a proper recognition of the value of this symptom, I shall speak of this point as 'McBurney's point'. *Ibid.* 450/1 The McBurney point was well marked. **1910** *Practitioner* Feb. 261 In peritonitis the pain is situated over the inflamed viscus, *e.g.* at McBurney's point in appendicitis. **1972** *Sci. Amer.* Aug. 122/2 Draw a line from the navel to the frontal protuberance of the right hipbone. Place your finger about one and a half inches from the bony end. That is McBurney's point.

macca (mæ·kă). [f. Macaw[2].] **1.** A Jamaican name for the palm *Acrocomia sclerocarpa*, distinguished by its prickles; hence, used for the prickles of other plants and animals. Also *attrib.*

1873 [implied in sense *2]. **1910** Anderson & Cundall *Jamaica Anancy Stories* 31 De man dat hab on boot must go befo' so' mash macca. **1946** E. N. Burke *Stories told by Uncle Newton* I. 17 There was soft grease—applied warm—for prickles ('macca' to us children) in the fingers or toes. **1956** J. Hearne *Stranger at Gate* xvii. 131 They went through the bush..the dry *macca* crunching beneath their shoes. *Ibid.* xxxi. 239 If I have to walk a hundred mile on macca thorn, I am going to be dere. **1961** F. G. Cassidy *Jamaica Talk* i. 7 A thoroughly Jamaican word ..is *macca*, which now means any kind of prickle, thorn, bur, or sharp spine on plants or animals... It is used in many combinations too, like *macca breadfruit, macca yam, macca fern.*

2. macca-fat, a Jamaican name for the fruits of certain oil-yielding palms, esp. those of the genus *Acrocomia* and the oil palm, *Elæis guineensis*; **macca-fat palm,** one of these trees. Cf. *macaw-fat* (Macaw[2]).

1873 C. J. G. Rampini *Lett. from Jamaica* 71 Clumps of wild ginger, Macca-fat palms,—surely the most graceful of all that graceful tribe. **1961** F. G. Cassidy *Jamaica Talk* i. 7 The *macaw tree* [is]..also called the *macca-fat palm* in Jamaica. *Ibid.*, The two most prominent features of these trees [are]—the fruits (not dates, but a similar nut-like berry with an edible rind, the *macca-fat* of today) and the thorns.

Maccabean, -æan (mækăbī·ăn), *a.* and *sb.* [f. *Maccabee + -an.] **A.** *adj.* Of or pertaining to Judas Maccabæus or the Maccabees. **B.** *sb.* = *Maccabee.

1821 R. Laurence *Bk. of Enoch* 207 Between the period of the captivity, and the rise of the Maccabæan dynasty. **1840** J. H. Howlett *Metrical Chronol.* (ed. 3) 16 Under the Maccabaean princes, what did the Jews become? **1845** [see *Maccabee]. **1890** Church & Seeley (*title*) The hammer, a story of Maccabean times. **1920** *Q. Rev.* July 4 His [*sc.* Disraeli's] party reaped the benefit of

his Maccabean courage. **1952** GERTH & MARTINDALE tr. *Weber's Anc. Judaism* IV. xiv. 360 The high priest Onias, who in the confusion of Maccabean party struggles had escaped to Egypt..had not scrupled to build a temple there. **1973** [see *HASMONEAN *sb.* and *a.*].

Maccabee (mæ·kăbī). *Jewish Hist.* [ad. L. *Maccabæ-us*, Gr. *Μακκαβαῖος*, the epithet of the Jewish patriot Judas.
'The source of the name is uncertain, but it is most natural to connect it with *maqāb*, "hammer".' 1883 *Encycl. Brit.* XV. 130/2.]
A supporter or successor of Judas Maccabæus, the leader of a religious revolt against Antiochus IV, 175–164 B.C., as recorded in the Books of the Maccabees.
1375 BARBOUR *Bruce* I. 465 Thai was lik to the Machabeys, That, as men in the bibill seys [etc.]. *a* **1420** WYCLIF *1 Macc.* (*heading*) Here biginnith the firste book of Machabeies. **1550** *Briefe & Compendiouse Table, Concordaunce Bible* Title-page, The thirde boke of the Machabees. **1614** RALEGH *Hist. World* I. II. x. 377 Then Modin the Natiue Citie of the Macchabees. **1702** R. L'ESTRANGE tr. *Josephus' Works* 1058 Flavius Josephus, his discourse of the Maccabees. **1845** *Encycl. Metrop.* IX. 643/2 Hence, all who fought under that standard were called Maccabees, or Maccabeans. **1920** H. F. HENDERSON *Relig. in Scotl.* i. 16 The patriotism of the Jew, especially in the age of the Maccabees, was an ardent passion that enabled him to overcome enemies four times his number. **1956** W. R. FARMER (*title*) Maccabees, Zealots, and Josephus. An inquiry into Jewish nationalism in the Greco-Roman period.
transf. and *attrib.* **1865** *Sunday at Home* 194/2 But at length one of the Maccabee princes..subdued them. **1883** *Encycl. Brit.* XV. 131/1 The Vatican [MS.] does not contain the Maccabee books. **1959** *Listener* 20 Aug. 292/2 The Maccabees of this small but resolute movement.. were the Aaronsohn family.

Maccabiah (mækăbī·ă). [f. *Maccabi*, the name of an Israeli sporting organization + *-ah* Heb. adj. ending.] In full, *Maccabiah Games.* A sporting contest, modelled on the Olympic Games, for Jewish athletes, and held at four-yearly intervals in Israel.
[**1962** *New Jewish Encycl.* 299/1 The major project of the Maccabi is the organization of Maccabiads, or 'Jewish Olympics'.] **1963** J. COMAY *Introducing Israel* viii. 129 The Maccabiah, an 'Olympic Games' for Jewish athletes.. takes place in the huge Ramat Gan Sports Stadium. **1969** *National Herald* (New Delhi) 29 July 10/3 The kindling of the Maccabiah flame was followed by the release of hundreds of doves. **1973** *Black Panther* 11 Aug. 12/3 Israel has declared that athletes from Rhodesia who took part in the so-called Maccabiah Games had no official status.

McCarthyism (măkā·ɹþi,iz'm). [f. the name of Joseph R. *McCarthy* (1908–57), U.S. senator + -ISM.] The policy of hunting out (suspected) Communists and removing them from Government departments or other positions. Hence **McCa·rthyist** *a.*, of or pertaining to McCarthyism; **McCa·rthyite**, one who gave support to such a policy; also *attrib.* and *transf.*
1950 *N.Y. Post* 5 Apr. 44/1 To call McCarthyism a fascist atmosphere would be descriptive enough. **1951** [see *big lie* (*BIG *a.* B. 2)]. **1952** *N.Y. Times* 26 Oct. I. 70/7 McCarthyism breeds fear, suspicion and unrest. It turns neighbor against neighbor and makes every American a suspected traitor until and unless he can prove his innocence by McCarthyite standards. **1952** *San Francisco Examiner* 18 Sept. 3/6 The McCarthyites unquestionably have an appeal, Senator Lehman conceded, since they come before the people as super-patriots. **1953** *Ibid.* 23 July 20/8 The editorial denounced a House committee investigation of Communistic clergymen... The 'Daily Worker' called it 'the new McCarthyite drive against the integrity and independence of the church'. **1954** *Encounter* Aug. 10/1 For the unlucky rest of us, McCarthy and McCarthyism—the proper noun and the common one—are familiar to excess. **1954** RORTY & DECTER *McCarthy & Communists* 118 They are not so much *pro*-McCarthyites as anti-anti-McCarthyites (opponents of all who oppose McCarthy). **1955** H. READ *Grass Roots of Art* (rev. ed.) iv. 85 We are at once struck by the fact that whatever the political ideology may be—socialist, fascist, communist, or MacCarthyist—..all express one opinion about art. **1957** *Times Lit. Suppl.* 27 Dec. 782/2 Has this book been written to add fuel to McCarthyist flames that have long been dying away in the United States? **1959** *Ibid.* 6 Nov. p. xix/3 The whole academic community is only now emerging from the shock of the assault on the academies that was one of the most sinister results of 'McCarthyism'. **1960** *20th Cent.* June 578 People who were not active McCarthyites..were none the less sources of strength for him. **1971** *Guardian* 19 Jan. 10/2 Once people start.. wondering about their neighbours, a McCarthyite infection could take hold. **1973** *Ibid.* 18 June 4/4 A tradition of paranoia out of which grew McCarthyism and many earlier witch-hunts. **1973** *Times Lit. Suppl.* 6 July 765/1 The tendency is timeless—and by no means sinister or subversive even in McCarthyite terms.

‖ **macchia** (ma·kiă). [Corsican It.] = *MAQUIS I.
[**1868** J. A. SYMONDS *Let.* 4 May (1967) I. 805 The sea shore [of Corsica]..is a tangle of sweet & splendid flowers. .. The whole air is fragrant with multitudinous scents wafted from these 'macchi', as the natives call them.] **1924** A. HUXLEY *Let.* 3 Dec. (1969) 238 The mountain is covered with woods of cork trees and a kind of macchia or bush of fragrant shrubs. **1936** *Nature* 2 May 735/2 Such characteristic native vegetation as the beautiful 'fijnbos' (the macchia or maquis of the south-west Cape) may be irretrievably damaged by fire. **1962** *Times* 24 Mar. 11/4 A cottage lost in the *macchia*. **1966** C. MACKENZIE *My Life & Times* V. 133 One looked down..into the *macchia* of Ventrosa.

McCoy (măkoi·). In the colloq. phr. *the real McCoy* (or *Mackay, McKie*): the 'genuine article', the real thing.
Its origin remains uncertain: see, for example, *Amer. Speech* (1958) XXXIII. 297 f.
1883 R. L. STEVENSON *Lett. to C. Baxter* (1956) 123 For society, there isnae sae muckle; but there's myself—the auld Johnstone, ye ken—he's the real Mackay, whatever. **1922** *Collier's* 7 Oct. 26/2 'At's the real McCoy you got there, brother!..Comes right down from Canada! **1930** *Amer. Mercury* Dec. 456/2 *McCoy*, genuine liquor. 'This is McCoy. You can't fake Quebec wrappers.' **1934** M. ALLINGHAM *Death of Ghost* v. 68 There's something very attractive about the real McKie when you meet it. **1935** R. C. WOODTHORPE *Shadow on Downs* xii. 298 It looks like the real Mackay. A lovely colour. **1940** *Penguin New Writing* I. 73 'You look the real McCoy, now,' he said. **1942** C. BARRETT *On Wallaby* v. 103 It's the real Mackay we've got, Chas.; didn't it spring out of the wall? **1949** N. MARSH *Swing, Brother, Swing* vi. 140 If I could pick my work I'd be in an outfit that went for the real mackay. **1952** W. R. BURNETT *Vanity Row* (1953) v. 43 A real gentleman... Not a phony... He was the real McCoy. **1959** L. BERNSTEIN *Joy of Mus.* (1960) 167 The operetta score..was musically elaborate, closer to opera, even containing finales, with everybody *singing* his way through the plot, vocalizing different sentiments at the same time —the real contrapuntal McCoy. **1972** *Guardian* 17 Feb. 10/3 Sadler's Wells is playing host to the regal offspring Royal Ballet, and not, please note, a second eleven but the real Macoy.

mace, *sb.*[1] Add: **5. mace-reed** = REED-MACE.
1901 G. MEREDITH *Reading of Life* 126 A hundred mares, all white! their manes Like mace-reed of the marshy plains Thick-tufted, wavy.

Mace (mēis), *sb.*[5] In full, *Chemical Mace.* The proprietary name of a chemical preparation used as a disabling weapon by being sprayed at a person's face; also *attrib.* Hence (usu. with small initial) as *v. trans.*, to attack with this liquid.
1966 *Official Gaz.* (U.S. Patent Office) 22 Nov. TM 174, SN 233,338. General Ordnance Equipment Corp., Pittsburgh. Pa. Filed Nov. 26, 1965. Chemical Mace. The word 'Chemical' is disclaimed apart from its use with the mark. For Non-Explosive Defensive Weapons in the Nature of Tear Gas Packaged in Aerosol Containers. **1966** *Law & Order* June 50/3 The development..of the Chemical Mace, a liquid, long range, selective, tear gas projector is an event of considerable importance to law enforcement. **1967** *N.Y. Times* 3 Aug. 17/2 The gas is called Mace and it comes in a small black aerosol container like a hair spray can. **1968** *Listener* 9 May 595/3 A new anti-riot chemical called Mace. Sprayed like tear gas it turns the victim temporarily blind. **1968** *Sun* (Baltimore) 18 Sept. A.14/6 Scores of innocent adult bystanders.. were clubbed, maced, arrested. **1969** E. AMBLER *Intercom Conspiracy* (1970) vii. 143 The stuff was..some kind of chemical Mace or nerve gas. **1970** W. WAGER *Sledgehammer* (1971) xvi. 103 Williston raised the can of Mace, aimed for his enemy's eyes and nose. **1971** *Harper's Mag.* Sept. 63 He responded to foul and abusive language by Macing an old woman's hot dog. **1972** J. ROSSITER *Rope for General Dietz* i. 16 The two pen-shaped aerosols of Mace chemical gas I invariably carried. **1973** *Black Panther* 25 Aug. 2/2 They feel that because they are in power they can call ten or 20 pigs for just one man, mace him, beat him up and call him profane names.

Macedo- (mæ·sĭdo), combining form of MACEDONIAN *a.*[1] in the names of dialects spoken in Macedonia, an area in the central Balkans (see *MACEDONIAN *a.*[1] and *sb.*[1]), as *Macedo-Bulgarian, -Illyrian, -Rumanian, -Rumanic.*
1861 MAX MÜLLER *Lect. Sci. of Lang.* v. 182 This Romance language is spoken in Wallachia and Moldavia, and in parts of Hungary, Transylvania, and Bessarabia... It is divided by the Danube into two branches: the Northern or Daco-romanic, and the Southern or Macedoromanic. **1880** A. H. SAYCE *Introd. Sci. of Lang.* II. vii. 120 The Danube divides it [*sc.* Rumanian] into two branches, the northern or Daco-Rumanic, and the southern or Macedo-Rumanic, the latter of which abounds with Albanian and Greek words. **1908** T. G. TUCKER *Introd. Nat. Hist. Lang.* 240 A southern division [of Rumanian]..is formed by the *Macedo-Roumanian* (or *Vlach*) of parts of Roumelia, Macedonia, and Thessaly. **1937** J. ORR tr. *Iordan's Introd. Romance Ling.* ii. 95 The current forms in Macedo-Rumanian. *Ibid.* iii. 267 The five Macedo-Rumanian, the two Megleno-Rumanian, and the two Istro-Rumanian localities. **1948** L. SPITZER *Linguistics & Lit. Hist.* 3 Meyer-Lübke would quote..Macedo-rumanian. **1949** ENTWISTLE & MORISON *Russ. & Slavonic Lang.* vii. 370 It is the pronunciation current in Macedo-Bulgarian dialects. *Ibid.* 374 The forms in *-m* are widely distributed in Bulgarian dialects, and are universal in Macedo-Bulgarian. **1959** G. NANDRIS *Handbk. Old Church Slavonic* I. 20 It [*sc.* epenthetic *l*] is dropped as a rule in Macedo-Bulgarian. **1960** R. AUTY *Ibid.* II. 10 The researches of Vatroslav Oblak showed the affinities of O[ld] C[hurch] S[lavonic] with present-day Macedo-Bulgarian dialects. **1965** G. Y. SHEVELOV *Prehist. Slavic* 611 There are also two small peripheral areas with a tendency to self-isolation from the other Slavs..: West Baltic and Macedo-B[ul]g[arian]. **1966** E. G. POLOMÉ in Birnbaum & Puhvel *Anc. Indo-European Dial.* 70 Pisani preferred to consider the former as Macedonian,..without, however, connecting *siiri-* with 'Macedo-Illyrian' *Σίρρας*. **1966** H. BIRNBAUM *Ibid.* 161 We can..assume here the existence of certain C[ommon] Sl[avic] dialect groups... These dialect groups will be shown to correspond to East Slavic.., Lekhitic.., Sorbian.., Czechoslovak.., Slovenо-Serbocroatian.., and Macedo-Bulgarian. **1967** D. S. PARLETT *Short Dict. Lang.* 103 Macedo-Rumanian (or Arumanian), in Albania, Thessaly, Macedonia. **1972** W. B. LOCKWOOD *Panorama Indo-European Lang.* 45 Macedo-Rumanian or Aromunian..is the language of the Aromuni, the Rumanians of the south.

macédoine (masedwan). [Fr., f. *Macédoine* Macedonia, with reference to the diversity of peoples in the Macedonian empire of Alexander the Great] **1.** Mixed fruit or vegetables cut up into small pieces. Also *attrib.*
1846 C. E. FRANCATELLI *Mod. Cook* 32 White macedoine of vegetables. *Ibid.*, Garnish of brown macedoine. Prepare the vegetables for the *Macedoine* according to the directions given in the preceding recipe. **1855** E. ACTON *Mod. Cookery* (rev. ed.) xxiii. 453 Jelly of two colours, with *macedoine* of fruit. **1894** L. HERITAGE *Cassell's New Universal Cookery Bk.* 67 Soup with Macédoines. *Ibid.* 1127 Macédoine of Fruits. **1895** 'M. RONALD' *Century Cook Bk.* 378 Macédoine salad. **1960** *Good Housek. Cookery Bk.* (rev. ed.) 313/2 Macédoine of fruit.
2. *fig.* A medley or mixture of unrelated things.
1820 H. LUTTRELL *Advice to Julia* 18 Such is the tattle of our beaus. These simple elements compose..The *Macedoine* of London-talk. **1857** G. C. MUNDY *Our Antipodes* (ed. 4) 10 Now for a *macédoine* of advertisements, word for word as entered. **1925** *Glasgow Herald* 3 Nov. 10 Europe contains as many different types of features,..as India. But there are few parts of Europe which present such a mosaic, or macédoine, of contrasts side by side. **1974** *Times* 30 Apr. 8/5 Ann Buck designs in what I call the *macedoine* style, with all sorts of bits and pieces of fabric welded into a garment.

Macedon. For 'Macedonia' read 'ancient Macedonia' and add later examples of sense 2.
1940 A. H. M. JONES *Greek City* i. 8 As king of Macedon he [*sc.* Alexander] could draw as he wished on the resources of Macedonia. **1969** A. TOYNBEE *Some Probl. Greek Hist.* IV. ii. 426 The invaders found the entire manpower of Macedon arrayed against them. **1969** 'M. RENAULT' *Fire from Heaven* (1970) vi. 275 In Athens, the marble tablet which witnessed the peace with Macedon had been torn down, in formal declaration of war. **1972** F. W. WALBANK *Polybius* i. 26 Polybius describes with amazement Demetrius of Phalerum's prophecy of the future downfall of Macedon.

Macedonian, *a.*[1] and *sb.*[1] **A.** *adj.* For 'a country north of Greece' read 'an ancient country north of Greece; now, a geographical area in the central Balkans lying astride the frontiers of southern Yugoslavia, northern Greece, and southwestern Bulgaria; also, the name of a province in Yugoslavia' and add further examples.
1946 [see B. c below]. **1958** *Listener* 4 Dec. 912/2 The first Macedonian dictionary is being prepared, there are newspapers in the Macedonian language, and Skopje has acquired a brand-new Macedonian university. **1974** *Encycl. Brit. Micropædia* VI. 442/1 Yugoslav Macedonia contains the great majority of the Macedonian people.
B. *sb.* **a.** (Later examples.)
1844 [see *EPIROT]. **1897** W. E. GLADSTONE *Let.* 19 Jan. in *Macedonian Question* (1902) 3 Why not Macedonia for the Macedonians as well as Bulgaria for the Bulgarians and Servia for the Servians? **1902** N. BUXTON *Ibid.* 44 There is, moreover, a certain enmity in Bulgaria towards the Macedonians. **1935** S. CHRISTOWE *Heroes & Assassins* vii. 116 The Macedonians took as their motto 'Liberty or Death'. **1950** E. BARKER *Macedonia* ii. 23 After King Alexander instituted his dictatorship in January 1929.. the Macedonians began to settle down and to accept Yugoslav rule passively. **1966** D. DAKIN *Greek Struggle in Macedonia* xii. 307 There seems also to have been some conflict between the National Greeks and the Greek Macedonians over the question of leadership. **1971** PALMER & KING *Yugoslav Communism & Macedonian Question* iv. 64 Evidently there was no attempt by the Macedonians to proclaim an independent or autonomous state, as the Croatians did. **1974** *Encycl. Brit. Micropædia* VI. 442/1 In the Greek province are Slavic speakers, Macedonians, and Pomaks, or Bulgarian-speaking Muslims.
b. The language of ancient Macedonia, recorded in fragmentary remains, and usually regarded as a variety of Greek within the Indo-European family.
1556 [in Dict., sense A]. **1933** C. D. BUCK *Compar. Gram. Greek & Latin* 14 Languages for which Illyrian origin is claimed or disputed are Venetic and Messapian in ancient Italy, Macedonian, and Albanian. Macedonian, that is, the native speech of the Macedonians as distinguished from the Attic *κοινή* which they came to adopt as their official language, is known from proper names and rather numerous glosses. **1939** L. H. GRAY *Foundations of Lang.* 330 The relation of Macedonian to Greek is uncertain. **1966** E. G. POLOMÉ in Birnbaum & Puhvel *Anc. Indo-European Dial.* 70, *σιβύνη* and *σιγύνη* are both occasionally ascribed to Macedonian by scholiasts and lexicographers. **1972** W. B. LOCKWOOD *Panorama Indo-European Lang.* 6 Since Macedonian was in contact with Illyrian and Thracian, borrowings from these languages could account for the exotic strain... It is to be assumed that the Macedonian dialect (or language) succumbed to Attic Greek.. during the Hellenistic Age.
c. The modern language of the province of Macedonia in Yugoslavia and adjacent areas of Bulgaria and Greece. Also *attrib.* So *Macedonian-speaking.*

1946 R. CAPELL *Simiomata* II. 85 A Macedonian nationalist, one Gotchi, has been leading a band of Macedonian-speaking Andartes. **1955** R. JAKOBSON *Slavic Lang.* (ed. 2) 15 Still preserved is the nasal component in ..some border dialects of Slovenian and Macedonian. **1964** M. PARTRIDGE *Serbo-Croatian* 13 Together with Bulgarian, Macedonian and Slovene, Serbo-Croatian belongs linguistically to the southern branch of the Slavonic group. **1972** W. B. LOCKWOOD *Panorama Indo-European Lang.* 162 The greatest concentration of Macedonian speakers was found in that part of the province which passed to Serbia. In 1945, this area became the Macedonian Constituent Republic of Yugoslavia with Macedonian as its official language. The number of speakers exceeds one million. **1974** *Encycl. Brit. Micropædia* VI. 442/2 Macedonian became the official language of the People's Republic of Macedonia, an autonomous area in Yugoslavia, when it was established in the 1940s.

Macedonian, *sb.*² (Earlier example.)
1559 [see *EUNOMIAN *sb.* (*a*.)].

Macedonic (mæsɪ̆dǫ·nik), *a.* [a. L. *Macedonic-us*, Gr. *Μακεδονικ-ός* Macedonian.] = MACEDONIAN *a.*¹
1859 E. MASSON tr. *Winer's Gram. New Testament Diction* I. 33 The previously distinct dialects..were blended into a popular spoken language, with a predominance of the Macedonic variety.

maceral (mæ·sĕrăl). *Geol.* [f. L. *mācer-āre* MACERATE *v.* + -AL, after MINERAL *sb.*] Any of the microscopic structural constituents of coal.
1935 M. C. STOPES in *Fuel in Sci. & Pract.* XIV. 11/1 To..construct an acceptable petrological classification, therefore, a prime need became obvious, viz., a word to cover all petrological units seen in microscopic sections of coals, as distinct from the visible units seen in hand specimens... I now propose the new word 'Maceral' (from the Latin, macerare, to macerate)... The word 'macerals' will, I hope, be accepted as a pleasantly sounding parallel to the word 'minerals', conveying the suggestions of the fundamental difference between them. *Ibid.*, The concept behind the word 'macerals' is that the complex of biological units represented by a forest tree which crashed into a watery swamp and there partly decomposed and was macerated in the process of coal formation, did not in that process become uniform throughout but still retains delimited regions optically differing under the microscope, which may or may not have different chemical formulae and properties. These *organic* units, composing the coal mass I propose to call *macerals*, and they are the descriptive equivalent of the *inorganic* units composing most rock masses and universally called *minerals*. **1970** *Nature* 11 July 194/2 The petrographic components (macerals) of coals possess different stability ranges.

macerate (mæ·sĕrĕ̄it), *sb.* [f. the vb., after *precipitate, filtrate*, etc.] A product obtained by maceration.
1961 in WEBSTER. **1974** *Nature* 27 Sept. 294/2 In scanning electron microscopical (SEM) investigations of Precambrian sedimentary rocks, the risk of contamination during the preparation of rock macerates is extremely high. **1975** *Ibid.* 20 Mar. 184/2 Nitrate production was depressed when *Hyparrhenia* root macerate was added to soils.

macerator. Add: **c.** A pulping machine. *U.S.*
1912 *Publishers' Circular* 12 Oct. 503 Then the macerator, the greatest consumer of contemporary literature, takes them [*sc.* books] to its bosom.

Mach (māk, mæk, ‖ māχ). The name of Ernst *Mach* (1838–1916), Austrian physicist and philosopher: **a.** Used, usu. *attrib.*, to designate certain concepts associated with his work on aerodynamics, as **Mach('s) angle**, the angle between a generator of the Mach cone and its axis; **Mach cone,** a cone that extends backwards from a body moving at supersonic speed and coincides with the shock wave it produces, separating a region affected by the motion (inside the cone) from a region unaffected by it (outside the cone); **Mach('s) number,** the ratio of the relative speed of a body and a fluid to the speed of sound at the same point; so *Mach one, two* (or *1, 2*), etc., a speed corresponding to a Mach number of one, two, etc.
1930 DOUGALL & DEANS tr. *Ewald's Physics Solids & Fluids* v. 261 During a small interval of time *r*, a point source of disturbance expands to a sphere of radius *cr*, the centre of which has moved through a distance *qr*. The cone touches this sphere, so that sin $a = cr/qr = c/q$.. *a* is called Mach's angle. **1933** *Proc. R. Soc.* A. CXXXIX. 307 The Mach cone $x = y$ and $z = 1$ would satisfy the required conditions. **1937** DODGE & THOMPSON *Fluid Mech.* xiii. 370 The ratio V/c will be found to appear in all flow problems where compressibility is an important factor. It is known as Mach's number..in honor of the Austrian scientist. **1938** *Jrnl. R. Aeronaut. Soc.* XLII. 194 The part of the wave at a distance from the shell moves normal to itself with the speed of sound and this fact determines the angle it makes with the direction of motion of the shell (the 'Mach angle'). **1947** *Time* 8 Sept. 76/2 During both flights it reached 'mach ·828'. **1948** 'N. SHUTE' *No Highway* 34 It was diving at round about Mach unity, and the wings came off. **1953** *Sci. News* XXIX. 93 The non-dimensional quantity $M = V/a$ is defined as the 'Mach Number' of the flow. **1957** *Spaceflight* I. 51/1 In a rocket exhaust where the gases are moving at 6,000 ft./sec.,..the velocity of sound is 2,000 ft./sec., so the Mach No. is 3. **1967** *Technology Week* 23 Jan. 29/2 (Advt.), McDonnell testing and development facilities range from man-rated space chambers to Mach 28 wind tunnels.

b. Used, usu. *attrib.*, to designate an optical illusion first investigated by Mach (in *Sitzungsber. der K. Akad. der Wissensch. (Math.-Natur. Cl.)* (1865)), in which a place where the spatial rate of variation of surface brightness abruptly increases or decreases (as at the inner and outer edges of an indistinct shadow) may appear extra dark or bright to an extent that cannot be accounted for simply in terms of the objective variation in brightness.
1932 W. M. DEANS tr. *Pohl's Physical Princ. Mech. & Acoustics* i. 4 Mach's bands have led to much trouble in the carrying out of physical observations. **1936** *Brit. Jrnl. Psychol.* XXVII. 103 The same generalizations can be made about the Mach effect on a rotating colour wheel. **1965** GRAHAM & BROWN in C. H. Graham et al. *Vision* xvi. 474/2 Mach rings with spatial variations in color. **1965** F. RATLIFF *Mach Bands* ii. 43 The Mach bands appear at once in the shadow cast on a piece of white paper by the edge of a card held under a fluorescent desk lamp, which provides an extended source of light. Covering the ends of the lamp, which usually are not uniformly bright, somewhat enhances the effect. **1970** —— in Cohen & Seeger *Ernst Mach* 32 The Mach bands are one of the most compelling of all the visual 'illusions', and have been mistaken for objective physical phenomena.

machærodont, *a.* Add: Also **machairodont.** Also as *sb.*
1889 NICHOLSON & LYDEKKER *Man. Palæont.* (ed. 3) II. 1448 The extinct Machærodonts or Sabre-toothed Tigers. **1925** C. R. EASTMAN tr. *Zittel's Text-bk. Palaeont.* III. 75 A possible derivation of both Felines and Machairodonts may be from Dinictis. **1973** *Nature* 3 Aug. 311/2 A minimum of twenty-three large mammal species were represented, including at least five extinct forms—a large baboon (?*Simopithecus*), a sabretooth cat (machairodont), [etc.].

machair (maχē̆ə·ɹ). *Sc.* Also **machaire, machar, machir, machirr.** [Gael. *machair*, Ir. *machaire*.] A flat or low-lying coastal strip of arable or grassland usually overlying shell sand. Also *attrib.*
1684 A. SYMSON in A. Mitchell *Geogr. Coll. relating to Scotl.* (1907) II. 86 These three parishes last described.. are commonly called the Machirrs or Machirrs of Whithern, which word Machirrs, as I am informed, imports white ground, and indeed those parishes, contain by far much more arable and white land, than up in the Moors, though the parishes there be much larger. **1878** *Q. Jrnl. Geol. Soc.* XXXIV. 848 Benbecula..has only one hill; and if we except the 'Machair', as the 'good land' along the west coast is called, all the rest of the island consists of low-lying moor, bog, and lake, with long shallow inlets of the sea straggling in. *Ibid.* 849 Adjoining the sandy shores are the delightful 'machairs', with their wealth of bright colour; while inland from the 'machairs' stretch the brown sombre peat and moorland. **1899** *Blackw. Mag.* Feb. 423/2 The burial-ground..occupied a little knoll in the middle of the 'machar', close to the sea (*machar* is the fine sweet pasture or links lying along the shore). **1924** *Glasgow Herald* 15 Mar. 4 In Highland glens or by the machirs of the Western Isles a crone..will still be consulted as if she were the Delphic sibyl. **1930** J. BUCHAN *Castle Gay* xvii. 271 The machars, yellowing with autumn, stretched for miles before him. **1955** F. F. DARLING *West Highland Survey* 21 There is a sufficiency of shell among the sand to encourage a fairly typical *machair* flora. *Ibid.* 51 The introduction of rabbits in the nineteenth century has gone a long way towards ruining the agricultural potential of the island, as these animals have created several small deserts on the *machair*. **1958** *Irish Times* 7 June, The term 'machaire' is used by English-speakers here to denote 'coastal strips of pasture land'. **1971** *Country Life* 24 June 1606/1 Her parents complained of attempts to put holiday caravans and a public lavatory on the machair. **1973** *Stornoway Gaz.* 3 Mar. 6/2 We are appealing to any reader (rugby enthusiast or not) who might be able to suggest (or lend) any reasonably flat area of ground—a stretch of machair or croftland—within, say, five miles of Stornoway.

mâche (maʃ). Also **mache.** [Fr.] = CORN-SALAD.
1830 [see *lamb's lettuce* s.v. LAMB *sb.* 7 b]. **1961** *Harper's Bazaar* June 84/2 Other salad greens..watercress, and French *mache*. **1962** S. COMBES *Dict. Cuisine French* 44/2 *Mâche*, lamb's lettuce, corn-salad. **1964** *Harper's Bazaar* Sept. 125/2, I like a green salad..lettuce or *mâche* or endive.

macheer (mătʃīə·ɹ). *Western U.S.* Also **machere.** [Corruptly ad. Sp. *mochila*.] A leather flap attached to a saddle. Also *attrib.*
1847 *Calif. Star* (San Francisco) 21 Aug. 2/3 [A] man declares his *macheres* (saddle cover) was stolen from under him, although seated upon his horse and his horse in motion. **1853** G. D. BREWERTON *Overland with Kit Carson* (1930) 49 Our saddles were of the true Mexican pattern, wooden trees covered with leathers called *macheers*. *a* **1861** T. WINTHROP *John Brent* (1883) v. 45 Showers shrank his buckskins and soaked the macheers of his saddle to mere pulp. **1873** J. MILLER *Life amongst Modocs* 50 The Prince unfastened his cloak from the macheers behind my saddle. **1927** C. M. RUSSELL *Trails plowed Under* 166 I've seen bronc riders use an old macheer saddle with a Texas tree.

‖ **macher** (ma·χəɹ). *U.S.* [Yiddish, f. G. *macher* maker, doer.] A man of importance, a bigwig; a braggart. Often *derogatory*.
1930 *Amer. Speech* VI. 126 A *Macher*..from the German word... Literally translated the word means 'maker' and idiomatically..is used derisively, referring to a braggart. **1964** S. BELLOW *Herzog* 87 He's a fine fellow... Not like that *macher*, Alexander. Always some scandal about him. **1964** W. MARKFIELD *To Early Grave* (1965) ii. 29 A man who sat on every board and committee, a powerful *macher* in Jewish communal affairs, who had passed around word that he needed a speech-writer. **1969** D. S. DAVIS *Where Dark Streets Go* (1970) i. 10 His father's a big *macher* in the union. **1973** *Jewish Chron.* 2 Feb. 19/3 It doesn't matter a tinker's cuss whether you amend the constitution to call the chairman president, macher or grand panjandrum.

machete (mătʃe·tĭ). Now the more usual form of MATCHET.
1832 M. R. MITFORD *Lights & Shadows Amer. Life* III. 215 The monteros drew their *machetes*, the sharp broadswords they usually carry about with them. **1854** [see MATCHET]. **1956** H. G. DE LISSER *Cup & Lip* v. 66 A dozen black men rushed forward, two with upraised machetes. **1958** J. COPE *Golden Oriole* xxiii. 131 On the far side of the wooden building an old man hired by Chipi was slowly chopping with a machete at the tropical growth. **1962** S. WYNTER *Hills of Hebron* ii. 29 The shadow of a man flung across the dirt track as he stalked along, one hand swinging free, the other with his machete held at the ready. **1973** *Black World* Sept. 12/2 The blade of the machete has a deeper significance in the song of the cane cutter.

Machian (mā·kiăn), *a.* and *sb.* [f. *MACH + -IAN.] **A.** *adj.* Of, pertaining to, or characteristic of Ernst Mach (see *MACH) or his theories or ideas. **B.** *sb.* A follower or adherent of Mach or his ideas.
1927 D. KVITKO tr. *Lenin's Materialism & Empirio-Criticism* i. 69 We shall confine ourselves to those opinions which reveal the 'subjective' ignorance of our Machians. *Ibid.* ii. 85 Your statement..is utterly fallacious, and follows only from your Machian position. **1938** A. FINEBERG tr. *Lenin's Materialism & Empirio-Criticism* i. 82 Karl Pearson, the English Machian, who avoids all philosophical artifices. *Ibid.* iii. 169 James Ward...does not controvert Mach, but..utilises the entire Machian trend in physics in his fight against materialism. **1941** *Mind* L. 82 The Machian positivists of Peirce's day denied that there are 'really' any natural laws. **1958** *Victorian Stud.* I. 253 Russell's own theory of knowledge underwent an increasingly Machian development from *Our Knowledge of the External World*..to the *Analysis of Mind*, in which a full-blooded neutral monism of Mach's variety is expounded. **1963** K. R. POPPER *Conjectures & Refutations* vi. 173 In our own day essentialism has been dethroned; a Berkeleian or Machian positivism or instrumentalism has..become fashionable. **1974** *Nature* 11 Jan. 99/2 Relation (8) may be looked upon either as an equipartition between the gravitational energy and the energy of expansion according to Einstein's equations or as a Machian relation determining the gravitational constant in terms of the matter content of the Universe.

‖ **machila** (măʃī·lă). Also **machilla.** [Pg., perh. f. Tamil *macil, mañcil* stage in a journey, f. Hindi *manzil*, f. Arabic.] A conveyance, usually for one person, used in Africa, consisting of a hammock slung between two poles, carried by two or more bearers.
1884 MRS. M. A. PRINGLE *Towards Mountains of Moon* vii. 89 The Portuguese [in Quilliman] go from house to house in a sort of palanquin, called here a *machilla* (pronounced *masheela*). **1897** H. H. JOHNSTON *Brit. Cent. Afr.* iv. 91 We then started for Kotakota, Jumbe's men insisting on carrying me in a machilla. **1900** GROGAN & SHARP *From Cape to Cairo* 168 [He] obtained..a team of boys to carry me in a machila to the highlands of Kivu. **1944** J. C. HEENAN *Cardinal Hinsley* 64, I have now travelled in Africa in every kind of conveyance—ox carts, glorified perambulators, machilla. **1952** S. CLOETE *Curve & Tusk* (1953) iv. 38 We will carry you, Lord, we will carry you in a machila, a hammock.
b. *attrib.*, as *machila-carrier*, etc.
1900 GROGAN & SHARP *From Cape to Cairo* vi. 57 [He] utilized the bandsmen when off duty as machila-carriers. **1906** R. C. F. MAUGHAM *Portuguese E. Afr.* 14 Machilla-travelling on the Frontier.

machinability (măʃī:năbi·lĭti). [f. MACHIN(E *v.* + ABILITY.] The ability to be cut by machine tools.
1921 *Glasgow Herald* 22 Sept. 5 The influence of lead on the greater possibility of liquation from gun metal castings, the easier machinability, expected minimised corrosion and improvement for bearings. **1940** [see *GRAPHITIZER]. **1941** F. T. SISCO *Mod. Metall. for Engin.* x. 159 It is impossible to evaluate the machinability of ferrous or non-ferrous materials by a single laboratory test. **1961** *Jrnl. Iron & Steel Inst.* CXCVII. 171/1 The machinability of nodular cast iron is compared with that of steels of similar microstructure and mechanical properties. **1968** A. KOBAYASHI in *Encycl. Polymer Sci. & Technol.* VIII. 349 The machinability of polyester cast resin is relatively poor.

machinable (măʃī·năb'l), *a.* [f. MACHIN(E *v.* + -ABLE.] Capable of being cut by machine tools.
1917 *Sci. Amer. Suppl.* 16 June 374/2 If well handled in the cupola the product will be strong and machinable. **1930** *Engineering* 23 May 676/2 The resistor of a new electric furnace..is a new machinable alloy of iron with

several other metals. **1951** Woldman & Gibbons *Machinability & Machining of Metals* i. 1 The most machinable metal is the one which will permit the fastest removal of the greatest amount of material per grind.

machine, *sb.* Add: **1. a.** *machine-for-living(-in)* [tr. F. *machine à habiter* ('Le Corbusier' *Vers une Architecture* (1923) p. ix)], a house. Also in imitative phrases.

1931 A. Huxley *Music at Night* 217 In Le Corbusier's phrase, a house is a 'machine for living in'. **1934** —— *Beyond Mexique Bay* 132 Le Corbusier himself could hardly have done the trick better: King's is the perfect machine-for-praying-in. **1960** R. W. Marks *Dymaxion World of B. Fuller* 22/1 The house was actually the world's first tangible embodiment of what one French architect hopefully designated as a 'Machine-for-Living'. **1966** 'J. Melville' *Nell Alone* vii. 75 The whole house was..a machine for Mrs Richier to live in.

b. Short for *bathing-machine* (earlier and later examples).

1788 E. Sheridan *Jrnl.* (1960) iv. 114, I went down to the bathing House where I found a great Number of Ladies and Gentlemen waiting to take their turn in the Machines. **1825** E. Weeton *Jrnl.* 14 June (1969) II. 384 Southport..is sadly exposing..and the modest complain much, gentlemen's and ladies' machines standing promiscuously in the water! **1870** G. Meredith *Lett.* (1970) I. 426 We have a flat sandy shore, and you see half a dozen fat men at a time scampering out of the machines.

c. A motor car. *U.S.*

1901 *McClure's Mag.* XVIII. i. 21/2 His assistant crouching at his feet out of range of the swift-flying currents of air produced by the mad flight of the machine. **1912** *Collier's* 21 Sept. 37/2 Leslie, Lanagan, and I hurried in the chief's machine to the Swanson home. **1915** *Sat. Even. Post* 3 Apr. 62/2 The reliability of the machine was so amazing that, in seven years of business, not a single breakdown had been reported. **1919** *Ibid.* 25 Jan. 45/3 As I neared my own house I slowed the machine.

3. Delete † *Obs.* and add later examples.

1941 G. Marx *Groucho Lett.* (1967) 48 They will wind up at Las Vegas playing the machines. **1962** *Gloss. Terms Automatic Data Processing* (*B.S.I.*) 92 *Tabulator* (*accounting machine*), a machine which reads data from a medium ..and produces lists, tables or totals. **1968** *Times* 11 Oct. 8/2 Thorpe has analysed the fish-calls of 40 sandwich terns by means of a sound spectrograph, a machine which analyses sounds, in terms of their pitch and loudness and produces a graphical representation of the sound. **1970** *Washington Post* 30 Sept. B.14/1 The stoves, the refrigerators and other machines. **1973** *Black Panther* 14 Apr. 6/1 The Visiting Room containing tables and chairs and machines for snacks and soft drinks.

4. b. A bicycle (earlier and later examples); a flying-machine, an aircraft; a mechanical printing press; a fire-engine (U.S.); a typewriter; a calculating machine or computer. Also short for *shearing-machine* (Austral. and N.Z.).

1659 T. St. Serf tr. *Cyrano de Bergerac's Govt. World in Moon* sig. D3v, I caused a Machine to be made of Iron.. and being well seated in the seat, I cast my Magnetique Bowl into the Air. **1679** R. Hooke in *Phil. Coll. R. Soc.* I. 15 A Machin newly Invented for Flying in the Air. **1751** R. Morris *Narr. Life J. Daniel* xii. 170 He had brought his machine to absolute perfection, and..had been making an experiment for flying in it. **1809** *Nicholson's Jrnl. Nat. Philos.* Nov. 172 It may be of some amusement to some of your readers to see a machine rise in the air by mechanical means. *Ibid.* 173 The little machine is completed. **1825** T. C. Hansard *Typographia* 699 The machine being put in motion, the paper which is to be printed is laid upon a board, passed through, and receives the impression on one side. *Ibid.* 700 One machine was to perform the work of eight presses. *Ibid.* 712 My machine has had a trial of six months: its ordinary speed is..at an average of two thousand impressions, or one thousand perfected sheets per hour. **1832,** etc. [see *calculating machines* s.v. *calculating *vbl. sb.*]. **1833** *Penny Mag.* Monthly Suppl. Nov.–Dec. 508/2 One thousand perfect copies..could only have been daily produced at one press by the labour of two men. The machine produces sixteen thousand copies. *c* **1848** B. A. Baker *Glance at N.Y.* (*c* 1857) 9 I've made up my mind not to run wid der machine any more. **1859** Bartlett *Dict. Amer.* (ed. 2) 259 *Machine*, the name for a fire-engine among the New York 'b'hoys'. **1871** *Porcupine* 29 July 276/1 Tantalising the toll-bar keepers on a 'machine'. **1891** W. D. Howells in 'Twain' & Howells *Mark Twain–Howell's Lett.* (1960) II. 639 The machine with which this letter is written is a Hammond. **1892** A. Powell *Southward's Pract. Printing* (ed. 4) ii. 11 Presses..are of two kinds, (a) hand presses and (b) mechanical presses. The latter are, in England, usually called 'machines' or 'printing machines'. *Ibid.* xlviii. 429 The one-side, single-cylinder machine, which is generally referred to when a cylinder machine, or, indeed, 'a machine', is mentioned among printers. **1899** *Northern Times* (Golspie, Sutherland) 22 June 1/1 (Advt.), Splendid cycles... Boys' machines at £5 10s. **1900** F. M. Ford *Let.* Oct. (1965) 10 My dear Galsworthy, Excuse my writing by machine; Christine at this moment monopolizes the only pen there is in the house. **1909** *Aeronautics* Dec. 151 Any machine—'plane or dirigible. **1915** *Southward's Mod. Printing* (ed. 3) II. i. 1 In the printing office the hand press is spoken of as the 'press' and the machine press as the 'machine'... The press can be worked by hand power only; the machine may be driven by steam, gas, or other motive power. **1919** 'Boyd Cable' *Old Contemptibles* viii. 124 He paid more attention now to watching for enemy machines, and never failed..to rush his pilot to a machine and into the air if a German was reported in sight. **1927** H. Crane *Let.* 30 Mar. (1965) 295 I'm *so* unhappy without a machine. Hope I get my new one soon. **1940** *Bulletin* (Sydney) 10 Jan. 16/1 'Anyone,' [Old Harry] declared, 'could put up tallies with machines. With the tongs now—'.. Harry produced half a dozen pairs of tongs and some sheep. **1944** 'N. Shute' *Pastoral* iv. 89 The machine before them opened out and trundled down the runway. **1946** V. S. Gandert0n in H. Whetton *Pract. Printing & Binding* x. 114/2 Work on the principle of matching the new sheet to the machine, not the machine to the sheet. **1946** *Ann. Computation Lab. Harvard Univ.* I. Foreword, Harvard University's need for a machine such as the IBM Automatic Sequence Controlled Calculator has long been a matter of discussion. **1954,** etc. [see *machine code, instruction*, etc., in sense *10]. **1956** G. Bowen *Wool Away!* (ed. 2) i. 9 Relative quality of workmanship between blades and machines is a debatable point. **1957** D. D. McCracken *Digital Computer Programming* ii. 14 The first two digits [of the instruction]..tell the machine what to do. **1960** N. R. Scott *Analog & Digital Computer Technol.* v. 170 Instructions to the machine consist of combinations of these addresses with code numbers designating the arithmetical operations to be performed. **1970** E. A. D. Hutchings *Survey of Printing Processes* iv. 58 The inking unit is situated at the top of the machine, above the type-bed. **1970** O. Dopping *Computers & Data Processing* xix. 306 A company which changes computers normally changes to a machine which is considerably faster than the old one. **1972** *Daily Tel.* 5 Aug. 9/3 For us, it was back to our bicycles. We stacked our machines in the back of the car and set off for gently contoured Norfolk.

e. *slang.* The penis; a condom (see also quot. 1896).

1749 J. Cleland *Mem. Woman Pleasure* I. 200 Coming out with that formidable machine of his, he lets the fury loose. **1785** Grose *Dict. Vulgar T.*, *Machines*,..See *Cundum*. *c* **1863** Philo cunnus *Festival of Passions* II. 12, I then seized his stiff machine in my grasp. **1896** Farmer & Henley *Slang* IV. 262/2 *Machine*,..1. The female *pudendum*... 2. The *penis*.

f. *N.Z. colloq.* A totalizator.

1889 G. P. Williams in A. E. Woodhouse *N.Z. Farm & Station Verse* (1950) 26 What a lot [of money] you left behind in the 'machine'. **1891** Williams & Reeves *In Double Harness* 8 When racing was developed by the aid of the 'machine'. **1900** J. Scott *Tales Colonial Turf* 218 The bookmakers would not pay 30–1 as the machine is doing.

6. b. [A Gallicism.] A painting of large size.

1932 R. Fry *Characteristics French Art* iii. 62 He was too poor in spirit ever to try, himself, to paint one of the big machines which made one an historical painter. **1965** *Listener* 28 Oct. 672/1 The small pictures and the *machines* appear to be the different sides of the same coin.

8. For *U.S.* read orig. *U.S.*, and add further examples. Also *transf.*

1884 *Tit-Bits* 28 June 164/3 The Business Machine was furious. He said that [etc.]. **1941** *Ann. Reg. 1940* 281 Britain unaided could not hold out against the spectacular German machine. **1942** *R.A.F. Jrnl.* 18 Apr. 13 It dared to oppose the Nazi war machine. **1948** P. D. Whitting in M. Beloff *Hist.* xvi. 338/1 Hitler, backed by a finely organized propaganda machine, could rouse the German nation to frenzied hatred of one country after another. **1965** *New Statesman* 7 May 706/1 To some people who have observed the scope and method of operations at Transport House, the question is not simply one of finding new custodians to mind the party machine. It is whether that machine ought not to be taken apart and entirely reconstructed. **1972** *Guardian* 28 Oct. 13/4 The Labour machine had failed to pick up..the magnitude of the swing towards Cyril Smith. **1973** *Black Panther* 20 Oct. 17/3 The 'Miracle Mets'..surprised everyone by..swamping the 'Big Red' Cincinnati machine in the National League playoffs.

9. a. (sense 3) *machine aesthetic, art, form, sculpture*; (sense 4) *machine house, part, -power, -process*; (sense 4 b) *machine embroidery, lace, stitch*; (sense 8) *machine candidate, party, power*; *machine-like* adj. (earlier and later examples).

1945 H. Read *Coat of Many Colours* lxvii. 320 (*heading*) Machine aesthetic. **1967** *Listener* 8 June 745/3 The Bauhaus is one thing, and the machine aesthetic..is another. **1973** *Times* 8 Aug. 10/4 In Léger's writings of the Twenties, it is not so much speed as the mass-produced object and the 'machine aesthetic' which occupies his attention. He saw the mass-produced object as the surfacing of an anonymous natural beauty of man-made forms independent of the self-conscious architect-designer. **1945** H. Read *Coat of Many Colours* lxvii. 323 What the critics of machine art object to..is not the fact of standardization, but rather the failure to reproduce certain qualities which they regard as essential to art. **1959** —— *Conc. Hist. Mod. Painting* vi. 213 [The Bauhaus] established for the first time a course in basic design that could serve as a training for the machine art of an industrial civilization. **1950** *Economist* 9 Dec. 1004/1 The two machine candidates in New York City. **1960** G. Lewis *Handbk. Crafts* 66 The word 'machine', perhaps, makes this sort of embroidery sound dull and mechanical, but in actual fact machine embroidery is decorative, exciting and creative, and has the added advantage that it is relatively quick to do. **1973** 'E. Ferrars' *Foot in Grave* vi. 104 I'll write and I'll paint, and I'll take up machine embroidery. **1909** W. R. Sorley *Interpretation of Evolution* 29 Instinct..impresses the machine-form upon portions of the external world, as in the bird's nest or beaver's dam. **1955** P. Heron *Changing Forms of Art* 70 They are the crystallized thoughts of an inventor, but one who is aware of the beauty of the machine-forms which come to him out of the blue. **1808** J. Steele *Let.* 31 Aug. in *Papers* (1924) II. 562, I bought them [*sc.* steelyards]..last winter for the use of my Machine house. **1913** J. Vaizey *College Girl* xxvi. 360 'A neck arrangement', composed of the cheapest of machine lace. **1698–1712** Shaftesbury *Philos. Regimen* (1900) 114 Machine-like to be moved and wrought upon, wound up and governed exteriorly, as if there were nothing that ruled within or had the least control. **1932** E. Bowen *To North* xv. 151 Machine-like efficiency is not, she had been given to understand, compatible with high intelligence. **1944** *Horizon* Feb. 97 What society wants is the machine-part which does the job. **1972** *Sci. Amer.* June 122/3 A distributor of bearings and similar machine parts. **1858** *N.Y. Daily Tribune* 1 Nov. 7/6 Both of these alleged swindlers are prominent members of the 'Masheen' party of the First Ward. **1924** *Army Q.* Oct. 38 The replacement of muscle-power by machine-power is the cardinal fact in every department of material life. **1937** B. H. L. Hart *Europe in Arms* xxiii. 312 As was inevitable, machine-power overcame an ill-equipped opponent. **1951** S. Spender *World within World* v. 284 The new phase of domination, and threat by machine-power politics. **1968** *Brit. Med. Bull.* XXIV. 189/1 The first industrial revolution is largely the history of enlisting machine power in the performance of many thousands of tasks. **1935** *Burlington Mag.* July 48/2 One familiar with machine-processes. **1970** *New Scientist* 12 Mar. 513 The ultimate comment on technology came from the American artist Tinguely who built machine-sculptures that could be exhibited only once—because they destroy themselves. **1934** Webster, Machine stitch. **1964** *McCall's Sewing* vii. 98/2 Use a fine machine-stitch..and a fine machine needle.

c. *machine-driller, -knitter, -printer*; *machine-darning, -knitting, -moulding, -printing* (earlier and later examples), *-production, -riveting, -switching*; *machine-coated, -finished, -generated, -glazed, -knitted, -printed, -processable, -readable, -set, -tooled* adjs.; *machine-darn, -knit, -mould* vbs.

1963 R. R. A. Higham *Handbk. Papermaking* ix. 228 To the papermaker, the term *machine-coated* signifies a paper which has been coated on the paper machine as an integral part of the papermaking process. To the printer, however, machine-coated means a class of paper. **1932** D. C. Minter *Mod. Needlecraft* 182/2 This type of tear may also be machine-darned. *Ibid.* 177/2 Machine-darning is suitable for table-linen. **1967** E. Short *Embroidery & Fabric Collage* i. 17 (*caption*) Motif on net with machine darning and cut work. **1906** *Westm. Gaz.* 11 Jan. 3/1 The wages of machine-drillers on the surface are 10s. a day. **1892** W. W. Greener *Breech-Loader* 52 The machine-made and machine-finished gun may be distinguished: First, by [etc.]. **1960** *Gloss. Paper, Stationery* (*B.S.I.*) 17 *Machine-finished* (*M.F.*) *paper*, paper treated mechanically on a paper-machine to obtain a smoother and more uniform appearance on both sides than on the unfinished paper. **1973** S. Jennett *Making of Bks.* (ed. 5) xi. 182 Machine-finished Papers (or M.F.) have the normal finish of the paper-making machine. The surface is moderately smooth and shiny, but not glossy. **1961** F. Kaufman *Electronic Data Processing & Auditing* vii. 117 The loss of a machine-generated decision is surely no worse than the failure of careless or overburdened people to make such decisions. **1914** Machine-glazed [see *M.G.* s.v. *M 5]. **1959** *Gloss. Packaging Terms* (*B.S.I.*) 66 *Machine glazed* (*M.G.*) *paper or board*, paper or board which has had one side made smooth and glossy by drying on a heated, polished metal cylinder, forming part of the drying section of the machine. The other side remains relatively rough. **1962** F. T. Day *Introd. to Paper* iv. 44 The M.G. high-speed single-cylinder paper making machine illustrated here is a standard type of equipment employed in the mill for making thin machine glazed papers. A popular name for the M.G. or cylinder machine is the 'Yankee'. **1927** T. Woodhouse *Artificial Silk* 83 Enormous lengths were machine-knitted into hose and half-hose. *Ibid.* 79 The utilization of artificial silk yarn for hand-knitted and machine-knitted articles. *Ibid.* 83 If a machine-knitter does not wind the yarns in his own mill, he can have them supplied in the form of bottle bobbins. **1886** *Family Friend* Jan. 87/1 Machine-knitting. **1927** T. Woodhouse *Artificial Silk* 86 In machine-knitting several courses are formed simultaneously. **1922** *Encycl. Brit.* XXX. 36/1 By 1915–6 cast-iron cylinders were cast from metal patterns and machine-moulded. **1888** *Lockwood's Dict. Mech. Engin.* 217 *Machine-moulding*, ..embraces the moulding of wheels and ordinary work by the aid of special machines. **1949** F. Bowers *Princ. Bibliogr. Descr.* x. 355 It seems necessary for the purposes of descriptive bibliography to draw a chronological line after which the methods of description for machine-printed books will in general hold. **1963** *Times Lit. Suppl.* 26 Apr. 312/1 Machine-set and machine-printed books. **1909** *Westm. Gaz.* 24 Sept. 8/1 An old man..described as a machine-printer. **1825** T. C. Hansard *Typographia* 714 Machine printing will..be only applicable to works of extensive sale. **1892** A. Powell *Southward's Pract. Printing* (ed. 4) liii. 467 (*heading*) Some difficulties in machine printing. **1972** P. Gaskell *New Introd. Bibliogr.* 260 Inks for machine printing differed little from those for the hand-press period. **1967** Cox & Grose *Organiz. Bibliogr. Rec. by Computer* vii. 185 The B.N.B. machine-processable records. **1971** J. B. Carroll et al. *Word Frequency Bk.* p. ix, Machine-processable data for lexicography. **1898** J. A. Hobson *John Ruskin* ix. 217 The 'driving' tendency of modern machine-production. **1931** L. Watt *Future of Capitalism* iv. 42 This 'dilemma' of technological unemployment (unemployment resulting from the development of machine-production) would..face any form of economic organisation. **1961** *Times* 30 Oct. (Computer Suppl.) p. ix/6 The three basic types of machine-readable document. **1971** *Computers & Humanities* V. 301 To collect in machine-readable form a million-character corpus of modern vernacular literature. **1888** *Lockwood's Dict. Mech. Engin.* 217 *Machine-riveting*, riveting performed by a single application of steady pressure at the same instant upon the tail and the head of a rivet. **1908** Kipling *Lett. of Travel* (1920) 154 The brittle pulp-paper, the machine-set type, are all as standardised as the railway cars of the Continent. **1967** Karch & Buber *Offset Processes* iii. 47 The layout man may choose to use proofs (also called proof-press prints). These proofs may be hand-set, machine-set or both. **1922** Glazebrook *Dict. Appl. Physics* II. 834/1 Several types of machine switching or automatic exchange systems have been devised, but in each of them the principle is to move the terminal of the calling line to that of the called line, which is fixed. **1950** J. Atkinson *Herbert & Procter's Telephony* II. i. 1/1 The idea of automatic or machine switching is by no means new. **1962** *Times* 3 Mar. 11/3 Hook-making..is a high-speed machine-tooled operation.

10. machine age, a name given to an era notable for its extensive use of mechanical devices; also *attrib.*; **machine code,** a code (CODE *sb.*[1] 3 b or *3 c) prepared by or for the use of a machine; *spec.* = **machine language*; so; *machine-coded* adj.; **machine finish,** a moderately smooth finish that paper has after leaving the machine on which it was made (see quots. 1937, 1960); **machine-hours,** hours during which a machine operates; **machine instruction** *Computers,* an instruction (*INSTRUCTION 4 c) in a machine language; **machine language** *Computers,* a language (*LANGUAGE *sb.* 1 d) that a particular computer can handle or act on directly, without further translation; **machine-oriented** *a. Computers,* (of a computer language) devised in the light of the requirements of a particular kind of computer; **machine-pistol,** a submachine-gun; **machine proof** = *press-proof* (PRESS *sb.*[1] 16 b); **machine-room** *Printing,* the room in which printing presses are operated; **machine-shop** (earlier U.S. example); **machine-time,** time during which a computer is in use; **machine translation,** translation by a computer; **machine word** see *WORD *sb.*; **machine-work,** (*b*) (examples).

1922 L. MUMFORD in H. E. Stearns *Civilization in U.S.* 11 These buildings..shall embody all that is good in the Machine Age. **1934** H. READ *Art & Industry* I. i. 6 Has he [*sc.* the artist] any function in a machine-age society? **1967** SINGHA & MASSEY *Indian Dances* i. 36 Shaivism itself, under the impact of the new materialistic machine age had lost its religious fervour. **1954** *First Gloss. Programming Terminol.* (Assoc. Computing Machinery) 4 *Computer code* (*Machine code*), the code representing the operations built into the hardware of the computer. **1958** G. GREENE *Our Man in Havana* I. iv. 45 Of course it's [a book-code] not so hard to break as a machine-code. **1971** LOWE & HIDDEN *Computer Control in Process Industries* v. 108 The machine language, or machine code,..is the repertoire of instructions for the basic operations that the central processor is designed to perform. **1964** F. L. WESTWATER *Electronic Computers* ix. 144 A special routine called a 'compiler'..produced an efficient machine-coded program from the pseudo-code. **1907** CROSS & BEVAN *Text-bk. Paper-Making* (ed. 3) x. 270 The mill or machine finish is one which can be varied within wide limits. **1937** E. J. LABARRE *Dict. Paper* 170/1 Machine finish is the surface of the paper (1) as it leaves the last drying cylinder of the paper machine; (2) as it leaves the calenders immediately following the paper-machine. **1960** G. A. GLAISTER *Gloss. Bk.* 245/1 *Machine-finish,* paper made smooth, but not glossy, by receiving the normal finish of a Fourdrinier paper-making machine which completes its process by passing the paper over heated drums and through steel calendering rolls. These smooth the surface to the required degree. **1921** EGGLESTON & ROBINSON *Business Costs* 377 Direct labor and overhead... Machine Hours 30. **1966** A. BATTERSBY *Math. in Managem.* vii. 173 For the sake of simplicity, we may choose to use a measure such as 'idle machine-hours', on the grounds that a reduction in idleness will automatically bring down operating costs. **1956** Machine instruction [see *LANGUAGE *sb.* 1 d]. **1970** Machine instruction [see *MICROPROGRAMMER]. **1949,** etc. Machine language [see *LANGUAGE *sb.* 1 d]. **1967** A. HASSITT *Computer Programming* ii. 41 There are a series of programs..which accept Fortran statements as data and produce machine language statements as output. *Ibid.,* Although there are many different machine languages, many concepts are common to all of these languages. Some of the common ideas are binary arithmetic, index registers, memory addresses, [etc.]. **1968** *Brit. Med. Bull.* XXIV. 192/1 The user prepared his program in a..computer language..which the computer itself translated into its own basic machine language. **1967** D. WILSON in Wills & Yearsley *Handbk. Managem. Technol.* iii. 47 These programs are often referred to as problem-oriented languages, as opposed to the lower-level assembly or autocoder languages which are more commonly used at present and are machine-oriented. **1970** O. DOPPING *Computers & Data Processing* xiv. 227 When problem-oriented programming languages..are used instead of simple machine-oriented languages, programming time is often reduced drastically. **1940** *Illustr. London News* CXCVI. 786 (*caption*) Much has been heard of the machine-pistols used by Nazi parachutists. **1962** *Spectator* 1 June 710/1 A Police State that tries to stop runaway schoolboys with machine-pistol fire. **1973** M. WOODHOUSE *Blue Bone* xiv. 153 A man with red hair and a machine pistol. **1951** S. JENNETT *Making of Bks.* vi. 88 The machine proof..is pulled immediately before the forme goes on the press, or while it is actually on the press. **1961** T. LANDAU *Encycl. Librarianship* (ed. 2) 233/1 *Machine revise,* a proof printed when the forme is on the printing machine... Also called machine proof. **1833** *Penny Mag.* Monthly Suppl. Nov.–Dec. 510/1 We will conduct our readers to Mr. Clowes's printing establishment, where there are more printing machines at work than at any other office in the world... Upon entering the machine-room the stranger will naturally feel distracted by the din of so many wheels and cylinders in action. **1904** *Brit. Printer* Feb. 6/2 One of the strong points of the establishment—its machine-room accommodation—is examined. **1946** V. S. GANDERTON in H. Whetton *Pract. Printing & Binding* x. 128 (*caption*) A fine example of a modern letterpress machine room. **1972** P. GASKELL *New Introd. Bibliogr.* 294 The machine-room overseer, an important man who ran the hand-press department as well as the machine-room. **1827** *Aurora* (Philadelphia) 25 July 1/3 A Machine Shop, from 60 to 70 feet long and 20 feet wide, two stories high. **1968** *New Scientist* 12 Sept. 548 In my environment the majority of user time, not machine time but user time, is spent in writing and running short programs. **1973** *Computers & Humanities* Mar. 198 The operation that consumes most machine time is the verification of Rule II, where we test that each sentence is contained in the union of at most three others. **1949** W. WEAVER in Locke & Booth *Machine Transl. of Lang.* (1955) 20 Mr. Max Zeldner, in a letter to the *Herald Tribune* on June 13, 1949 [*published* June 26], stating that the most you could expect of a machine translation of fifty-five Hebrew words which form the 23d Psalm would start out Lord my shepherd no I will lack [etc.]. **1956** *Nature* 7 Jan. 1/1 Dr. Booth is optimistic that even the problems of machine-translation of literary work may prove less complex than they at present appear. **1960** E. DELAVENAY *Introd. Machine Transl.* 123 Machine translations today are still very imperfect. **1968** J. LYONS *Introd. Theoret. Ling.* iv. 159 The automatic analysis of written texts for the purpose of machine-translation. **1861** B. HEMYNG in H. Mayhew *London Labour* (1862) Extra vol. 222/1 She then supported herself and her child by doing machine-work for a manufacturer. **1867** A. D. WHITNEY *Summer in L. Goldthwaite's Life* i. 10 No machine-work, but all real dainty finger-craft.

machine, *v.* Add: **2. a.** Also with *in.*

1894 J. E. DAVIS *Elem. Mod. Dressmaking* 47 Tacking is not strong enough to hold sleeves well to the arm-hole for machining-in.

b. *absol.* To manufacture things by machinery.

1916 H. G. WELLS *Mr. Britling* I. i. 16 They had standardised and machined wholesale, while the British were still making the things one by one.

4. a. Delete *nonce-use* and add later example. **c.** To render mechanical; to treat as if machinery.

1916 F. M. FORD *Let.* Sept. (1965) 72 The French Press ..continues to blaze and coruscate about my gifts... Of course these salvos are a little machined by the French Govt. **1916** H. G. WELLS *Mr. Britling* I. ii. 67 The reality of life is adventure, not performance. What can be ruled about can be machined. **1919** J. L. GARVIN *Econ. Found. Peace* 183 As they drilled under arms or machined their Socialism. **1959** *Listener* 19 Nov. 868/2 'The new poets,' Apollinaire wrote in 1917, 'will one day machine poetry (*machiner la poésie*) as the modern age has machined the world.'

machine-gun, *sb.* (see MACHINE *sb.* 10.) Add earlier and later examples. Also *fig., attrib.,* and *Comb.*

Some more recent types of machine-gun can be fired from the hip and are adaptable for firing single shots.

1870 *Jrnl. R. United Service Inst.* XIV. 504 Machine Guns: The 'Gatling Battery'—The Agar and Claxton Guns —The French and Montigny Mitrailleurs. **1882** *Army & Navy Mag.* Dec. 195 Machine-guns, which have an effective range not differing materially from that of small arms, would..have to advance with infantry. **1906** *Westm. Gaz.* 4 Oct. 2/3 Motor-bicycles, those machine-gun terrors of the road. **1909** *Ibid.* 9 Dec. 5/1 Experiments carried out with the machine-gun fitted aeroplane. **1915** R. W. CAMPBELL *Private Spud Tamson* xix. 288 Z-r-r-p—Z-r-r-p—Z-r-r-p spat the machine-gun batteries behind the little knolls. **1919** 'BOYD CABLE' *Old Contemptibles* ix. 146 The steady postman's-knock *rat-tat-tat* of machine-guns. *Ibid.* xvi. 255 The rifle and machine-gun fire rose again. **1928** H. LASKI in *Holmes–Laski Lett.* (1953) II. 1077 They cross-examined me with machine-gun rapidity. **1937** KOESTLER *Spanish Testament* v. 104 Militiamen were frequently obliged to smoke out the machine-gun nests set up in the monasteries. **1941** *Ann. Reg. 1940* 154 [France] sent..5,000 machine-gun rifles. **1955** S. SPENDER *Coll. Poems 1928–53* 99 Machine-gun anger quickly scythed the grasses. **1970** *Toronto Daily Star* 24 Sept. 3/3 They put their machine-gun nests on roofs and in the rooms and gardens of private houses. **1972** 'E. LATHEN' *Murder without Icing* (1973) iii. 30 Convulsions on one level or another could be expected with..machine-gun rapidity. **1973** *Times* 14 Nov. 8/1 The Israelis..have reinforced their machinegun posts beside the road.

So **machine-gun** *v. trans.,* to turn a machine-gun on, to fire at with a machine-gun; **machine-gunning** *vbl. sb.*; **machine-gunner,** one who operates a machine-gun. Also *fig.*

1915 R. BROOKE *Let.* 29 Jan. (1968) 658 There's a good chance of my going to Hythe for a fortnight to learn machine-gunning. **1915** 'I. HAY' *First Hundred Thousand* xix. 279 The machine-gunner is a more or less accepted nuisance by this time. **1917** 'CONTACT' *Airman's Outings* 185 Other guerilla work is done by craft which..machine-gun whatever worth-while objects they spot. **1918** E. M. ROBERTS *Flying Fighter* 38 Whatever they saw was sure to be machine-gunned. **1930** J. B. PRIESTLEY *Angel Pavement* ii. 76 They sweep, lash, and machine-gun the streets with rain. **1942** *R.A.F. Jrnl.* 2 May 5 Our work was mainly bombing and machine gunning, to weaken the will of the enemy. *Ibid.* 16 May 21, I ..maintained my course to machine-gun the decks. **1955** *Times* 25 June 6/3 He said that a conspiracy was hatched last November for a military revolt... The aim was to murder the President of the Republic through air bombardment or land action and to intimidate civilians by air bombing or machine-gunning the streets. **1967** B. PATTEN *Little Johnny's Confession* 17 The last young thigh..machineguns you down. **1970** T. HUGHES *Crow* 24 The face Of a machine-gunner a long burst not long enough. **1972** *Daily Tel.* 1 June 2/8 This was followed by a machine-gunning of the Spanish Embassy on December 3. **1973** D. LEES *Rape of Quiet Town* vi. 102, I aimed at one of the machine-gunners.

machi·neless, *a.* [f. MACHINE *sb.* + -LESS.] That does not use or does not require a machine or machines. Spec. *machineless waving* (see quot. 1966); also *ellipt* as *sb.*.

1909 in WEBSTER. **1926** *United Free Ch. Miss. Rec.* May 201/1 It was a machineless age, the world moved at a slow pace. **1933** *Catholic Med. Guardian* Apr. 90 Catholic Law Associations..advocate the return to machineless handicrafts. **1942** *Horizon* July 58 One of Thelma's ladies was settin' over yonder..gitting a machineless. **1966** J. S. COX *Illustr. Dict. Hairdressing* 93/1 *Machineless waving,* (1) Hot permanent waving in which the required heat is either generated chemically in a pad applied to the hair, or by means of a pre-heated metal clamp. (2) Cold Permanent Waving.

machi·ne-wash, *v.* [f. MACHINE *sb.* + WASH *v.*] *trans.* To wash in a washing-machine. So **machi·ne-wa·shable** *a.*

1960 *Farmer & Stockbreeder* 26 Jan. (Suppl.) 4/3 Some drip-drys can be successfully machine-washed. **1962** *N.Y. Post* 9 Oct. 54 Stretch-ever elastic made without rubber so you can machine-wash it. **1963** *New Yorker* 8 June 87 Guaranteed machine-washable. **1970** *Guardian* 28 May 11/5, I doubt if you would really machine-wash a child's walking shoe. *Ibid.* 16 June 13/2 In Welsh peasant cotton, machine washable. Jacket with inset waistband. **1975** *Country Life* 13 Mar. 673/3 Machine-washable continental quilts.

machinofacture (mǎʃī:nofæ·ktiŭɪ, -tʃiŭɪ). [f. MACHINE *sb.* + -O + FACTURE.] The making of articles by machine; mechanization.

1903 L. F. WARD *Pure Sociol.* 26 The invention of tools, instruments, utensils, missiles, traps, snares, and weapons comes under this head, crowned by the era of machinofacture, artificial locomotion, and electric intercommunication. **1928** E. & C. PAUL tr. *Marx's Capital* xiii. 403 An organised system of working machines which are one and all set in motion by the transmitting mechanism from a central automaton, constitutes the fully developed form of machinofacture.

machir(r), varr. *MACHAIR.

Machism (mā·kiz'm, -χ-). [f. name of Ernst *Mach* (see *MACH) + -ISM.] The theories of Ernst Mach, esp. his concept of empiriocriticism.

1927 D. KVITKO tr. *Lenin's M̶a̶t̶e̶r̶i̶a̶l̶i̶s̶m̶ & Empirio-Criticism* i. 69 In philosophical literature, writers of various tendencies have long since discovered the chief sin of Machism in spite of all its covering. **1949** P. FRANK *Mod. Sci. & its Philos.* x. 194 A logical contradiction exists only between a metaphysically conceived Machism, which is then subjective idealism, and a metaphysically conceived materialism, which accepts only matter as having existence. **1968** *Listener* 14 Nov. 648/3 Lenin was particularly incensed at Machism, and wrote his *Materialism and Empiriocriticism* against Mach and Avenarius. **1972** J. T. BLACKMORE *Ernst Mach* xiv. 214 If we may define 'pure Machism' as a phenomenalism hostile to atomism and theoretical physics, [etc.].

machismo (mǎtʃī·zmo). [Mexican-Sp., f. *mach(o* masculine + *-ismo* -ISM.] The quality of being *MACHO; male virility, masculine pride. Also *attrib.*

1948 B. GRIFFITH *Amer. Me* 50 Machismo makes a boy swear big round oaths as a youngster. **1962** *Listener* 12 Apr. 649/1 The Mexican obsession with the concept of *machismo,* of masculinity. **1967** MCCORMICK & MASCAREÑAS *Compl. Aficionado* iii. 74 To bite the cape like an animal while folding it is false machismo. **1969** J. MANDER *Static Society* i. 56 The exaggerated masculinity, the famous *machismo,* of the Mexican. **1969** A. MARIN *Rise with Wind* v. 63 The bus driver..drove with Latin *machismo* through a tangle of narrow streets. *Ibid.* x. 125 A eunuch was without *machismo,* that peculiar combination of pride and virility that was the essence of manliness. **1971** *Guardian* 20 July 11/8 The contradictions, hypocrisy, and 'machismo' ideal in Puerto Rican culture. **1973** GAGNON & SIMON *Sexual Conduct* (1974) viii. 251 In the prison, toughness may substitute for intercourse as a measure of *machismo.*

Machmeter (mā·k-, mæ·kmītəɪ mā·χ-). *Aeronaut.* Also **Mach meter.** [f. *MACH + METER *sb.*[3]] An air-speed indicator that reads directly in Mach numbers.

1947 *Jrnl. R. Aeronaut. Soc.* LI. 734/1 An instrument known as a Mach meter, which indicates the Mach number of flight at any height, has already been developed and is now being fitted in certain high-speed aircraft. **1948** 'N. SHUTE' *No Highway* xii. 305 What was the Machmeter showing? **1958** 'P. BRYANT' *Two Hours to Doom* 118 He watched the Machmeter carefully as it moved up from point nine. **1964** J. E. D. WILLIAMS *Operation of Airliners* xx. 320 The indication of the Mach meter is not..instantaneously responsive to changes of engine thrust. **1975** L. J. CLANCY *Aerodynamics* iii. 32 A Machmeter..depends on measurements of total and static pressure by the pitot-static tube.

macho (matʃo, mæ·tʃo), *sb.* and *a.* orig. *U.S.* [Mexican-Sp. *macho,* a male animal or plant; *adj.,* masculine, vigorous.] **A.** *sb.* A man; *spec.* a 'tough guy'; also, manliness, virility; an impression of this. **B.** *adj.* Ostentatiously or notably manly and virile.

1928 *Nation* 29 Feb. 233/2 The Machos (Americans) have taken El Chipote. *Ibid.* 11 Mar. 288/1 Here was I in their midst, a Macho Yankee Gringo, yet treated with consideration. **1951** *Sat. Rev. Lit.* 22 Sept. 15/2 In the Continente, men were supposed to be *machos*—males—and the women were supposed to bear their children, besides keeping their houses, and awaiting with patience their returns from the beds of their mixed-breed mistresses, or the battlefield. **1959** N. MAILER *Advts. for Myself* (1961) 19 Every American writer who takes himself to be both major and *macho* must sooner or later give a *faena*

which borrows from the self-love of a Hemingway style. *Ibid.* 418 'Man, you can take care of yourself,' he said with glee. 'I don't know about that,' I answered, obeying the formal minuet of the *macho*. **1964** *Punch* 25 Mar. 444/1 A quality much prized in Mexico called *macho*, namely 'masculinity, virility'. **1964** S. BELLOW *Herzog* 157 Provided that he remain *macho* she would listen with glistening eyes. *Ibid.* 186 A prince of the erotic Renaissance, in his *macho* garments. **1968** T. HOWARD *Black Light* xix. 163 The medical practitioner had to salvage a little of that all-important Latin-American *macho*—or manliness. **1972** *Publishers' Weekly* 23 Oct. 40/2 Reveals the *macho* of the sport for what it is: gridiron Darwinism, young athletes psyched out of their skulls. **1972** *New Yorker* 2 Dec. 159/3 And so we have separate cultures—black-*macho* movies and white-*macho* movies, equally impoverished, equally debased. **1975** *Ibid.* 14 July 65/1 She [*sc.* Greta Garbo] played opposite Clark Gable once, and the collision, though heated, didn't quite work; his macho directness—and opacity—reduced her from passionate goddess to passionate woman.

machree (măkrī·). *Ir.* Also **Machree, ma chree, mochree.** [Ir.-Gaelic *mo chroidhe* (of) my heart, my dear.] My dear! Often in phr. *Mother Machree.*

1829 G. GRIFFIN *Collegians* (ed. 2) II. xx. 92 Coax him, *ma chree, ma lanuv*, to gi' me the price o' the whiskey. *Ibid.* xxiv. 195 Oh, ma chree, m'asthora... What ails you? **1831** S. LOVER *Legends & Stories Ireland* p. xxiii, *Machree*, my dear. *Ibid.* 89 They wint to the wine-cellar, but, jew'l machree, they soon run back into his room. **1866** MRS. GASKELL *Wives & Daughters* II. xvi. 160 Thanks to you, little Molly—cuishla ma chree, pulse of my heart. **1918** N. MUNRO *Jaunty Jock* 159 'I could live on the berries.., I love them!' 'Doubtless, mochree,' would he answer her, laughing. **1918–19** *T. Eaton & Co. Catal.* Fall & Winter 389/2 Vocal Records... Mother Machree (Tenor). **1952** E. O'NEILL *Moon for Misbegotten* (1953) 132 In a minute you'll start singing 'Mother Machree'! **1970** M. KENYON *100,000 Welcomes* iv. 32 'You ever been to Ireland, Louie?'..'Every year... Ol' Mother Machree. And see the Micks get stoned.' **1973** *Listener* 1 Mar. 277/2 The Celtic Revival, born as it was of romantic nationalism—Mother Machree, Kathleen ni Houlihan and the whole pack of Gaelic Norns started calling to us.

‖ **macht-politik** (ma·χt,pǫlītīk). Also **macht politik, machtpolitik.** [G., f. *macht* power, strength + *politik* policy, politics.] Power politics; strength as a potential factor to use in gaining a desired result.

1916 J. W. HEADLAM in Prince von Bülow *Imperial Germany* (rev. ed.) p. xxiii, Let us consider these things purely as a balance-sheet of loss and gain according to the undiluted principles of 'Macht-Politik'. **1940** *Horizon* May 326 Our leaders display not the qualities of *Macht-politik*, but the caution of the peaceful negotiator. **1958** *Times Lit. Suppl.* 11 Apr. 190/4 Indeed, the uniformly cynical *Machtpolitik* practised by every leading actor in the drama is profoundly depressing. **1964** P. MEADOWS in I. L. Horowitz *New Sociol.* II. 456 A space age revolution.. in which the technological *Machtpolitik* of space conquest is also serving as a relatively moral equivalent for war. **1969** J. MANDER *Static Society* vi. 179 Naked *machtpolitik* ..calls countervailing forces into being. **1973** *Times* 26 Oct. 20/1 The Chinese, in a gesture of fastidious distaste, abstained from the Security Council resolution on the reasonable grounds that although it was in effect a blatant example of Soviet-American *macht politik* it would be perverse to vote against it simply on that account.

Machzor (mā·χzǭɹ). Also **Machsor, Maḥzor.** Pl. **-im.** [Heb. *maḥzor* a cycle.] In Jewish liturgy, the name for the books of prayers and readings used on various occasions in the liturgical year; usu. used *spec.* for the book of prayers for use at festivals.

1864 *Chambers's Encycl.* VI. 155 Later, the term [sc. *Siddurim*] was restricted to the weekday ritual, that for festivals being called *Machsor* (Cycle). **1883** *Encycl. Brit.* XV. 292/2 The *Maḥzor*, meaning prayer-book, is capable of division..into..the Smaller and the Larger. The Smaller Maḥzor contains ordinary prayers,..with the poetical insertions and lessons from the Pentateuch and the Prophets... The Larger Maḥzor..embodies the ordinary prayers..for the whole year, and the lessons..for all feasts and fasts and..other occasions. **1891** M. FRIEDLÄNDER *Jewish Relig.* 391 The *Machzor*..or Prayer-book for the Holy-days contains numerous additions to the ordinary prayers. **1892** I. ZANGWILL *Childr. Ghetto* I. 276 Three sets of Machzorim, or Festival Prayer-Books. **1893** —— *Ghetto Tragedies* 66 She bent her eyes downwards on her neighbour's *Machzor.* The woman immediately pushed the prayer-book more towards Rebecca. **1973** *Synagogue Light* Sept. 42/2 The festival prayer book, the Machzor, is used during the High Holidays because many additional prayers not recited throughout the year are read on these days. **1974** *Encycl. Brit. Micropædia* VI. 505/3 *Maḥzor*.., originally a Jewish prayer book arranged according to liturgical chronology and used throughout the whole year... *Maḥzor* has come to mean the festive prayer book, as distinguished from the Jewish prayer book (Siddur) used on ordinary sabbaths and on week-days.

McIntosh (mæ·kintǫʃ). Also **MacIntosh, Mackintosh.** The name of John *McIntosh* (b. 1777), Canadian farmer, used *attrib.* in **McIntosh Red** to designate a red-skinned variety of eating apple or the tree producing it, first developed on his farm. Also *absol.*

1878 *Canad. Horticulturalist* Mar. 42 Winter apples; here my list will be small, but I think reliable: Talman's Sweet, Pomme Grise, American Golden Russet, and McIntosh Red. **1908** *Busy Man's Mag.* Feb. 89 The First McIntosh Red Tree in Canada. **1910** L. WOOLVERTON *Canad. Apple Grower's Guide* 190 McIntosh [is] a very fine dessert apple for early winter use. **1932** [see *DELICIOUS *a.* 2 b]. **1933** M. DE LA ROCHE *Master of Jalna* xii. 136 He extracted a large, perfectly shaped MacIntosh Red from his pocket. **1965** MRS. L. B. JOHNSON *White House Diary* 15 Jan. (1970) 221 Our best brands are Northern Spies and MacIntosh Reds. **1969** *New Yorker* 20 Dec. 76/2 Already on our six acres..we have planted..a MacIntosh apple. **1970** *Globe & Mail* (Toronto) 28 Sept. 5/2 (*caption*) Alison Loates..found a bright-red McIntosh was her fancy.

mack, *sb.*[4] (Later examples.)

1926 MAINES & GRANT *Wise-Crack Dict.* 11/1 *Mac*, man who lives off the earnings of a woman. **1931** G. IRWIN *Amer. Tramp & Underworld Slang* 125 *Mac*, a pander; a lover or associate of lewd women. No doubt from the French word for this class, 'maqereau'.., although the shorter word has been in use in America for years. **1950** BLESH & JANIS *They all played Ragtime* (1958) ii. 39 The dapper, foppish 'macks'..in their Stetsons, box-back coats, and St. Louis 'flat' shoes got their gambling stakes from the girls. **1972** T. KOCHMAN *Rappin' & Stylin' Out* 243 'Pimp', or 'mack man'..a person of considerable status in the street hierarchy, who, by his lively and persuasive rapping ('macking' is also used in this context), has acquired a stable of girls to hustle for him and give him money. **1973** *Washington Post* 21 Apr. D 7/2 Now comes 'The Mack', a movie about the rise and fall of a sweet pimp named Goldie.

mack (mæk), *sb.*[5] Also **mac.** A common abbrev. of MACKINTOSH 2 and 3.

1901 'R. ANDOM' *Troddles & Us & Others* xxi. 245 It rained pretty steadily... Murray and Wilks, having left their 'macs.' behind, were constrained to spend one solid day loafing about the..inn premises. **1902** *Captain* VII. 468/1 Who said you might wear my mackintosh?.. Suppose you give it up... Buck up. It looks like rain... Mack up, please. I want it. **1917** A. G. EMPEY *From Fire Step* 170 In front of the door stood an officer in a mack (mackintosh). **1923** *Daily Mail* 12 Feb. 12 (Advt.), Girls' Mack Capes with Hoods... All guaranteed waterproof. **1929** GALSWORTHY *Roof* iii. 54 'Have we got to dress?'..'No; bung on your mack and shoes.' **1963** *Times* 15 May 14/6 Small knots of mac-clad farmers. **1973** A. BEHREND *Samarai Affair* viii. 85 Richardson slipped on his mack and went round to India buildings. **1974** D. WINSOR *Death Convention* ii. 10, I had dug my hands in my mac pockets.

Mack (mæk), *sb.*[6] [f. *Mack*, name of manufacturer.] The proprietary name of several types of heavy vehicle, as lorries, tractors, etc. Also *attrib.*

1913 *Hand Bk. Gasoline Automobiles* (U.S. Automobile Board of Trade) 165 (*caption*) Mack 2-ton truck. **1921** *Official Gaz.* (U.S. Patent Office) 4 Jan. 192/1 International Motor Company, New York, N.Y... Mack.. [for] Motor-Trucks. Claims use since about Oct. 13, 1911. **1930** J. DOS PASSOS *42nd Parallel* v. 401 Charley..started to help clean the parts of the carburetor of a Mack truck. **1948** PARTRIDGE *Dict. Forces' Slang* 114 *Mack*, a ten-ton lorry. (Army.) **1959** E. K. WENLOCK *Kitchin's Road Transport Law* (ed. 12) 85/1 Mack type N.M. heavy artillery tractors may be used for snow ploughing, or grit or salt distribution on frosty roads, notwithstanding their excess width. **1962** *Times* 27 Nov. 13/3 A fleet of 'Macks'—snow-shifters. **1971** M. TAK *Truck Talk* 103 *Mack*, a popular, economical and long-wearing make of tractor, the one best known to the public... The Mack engine has a characteristic sound. .. The Mack trademark is a bulldog. **1972** MARSHALL & BISHOP *Lorries, Trucks & Vans* 123 No other name can surely be more autonomous with the US truck industry than Mack. 'Built like a Mack' is still a phrase used by Americans to signify something solid or sturdy. **1973** *Trade Marks Jrnl.* 13 June 1141/2 Mack... Commercial motor road vehicles and parts and fittings therefor.. Mack Trucks, Inc..., Allentown, State of Pennsylvania, United States of America; manufacturers.

Mackay: see *MCCOY.

mackayite (măkəi·əit). *Min.* [f. the name of John W. *Mackay* (see quot. 1944[2]) + -ITE[1].] A green hydrated tellurite of ferric iron, perhaps $Fe_2(TeO_3)_3.xH_2O$.

1944 FRONDEL & POUGH in *Amer. Mineralogist* XXIX. 217 The new mineral described here under the name mackayite was found in specimens from two deposits in Goldfield, Nevada. *Ibid.* 218 At the instance of Mr. C. D. Woodhouse, the writers propose the name mackayite for the species after John W. Mackay (1831–1902), a mining operator who in a few years amassed a great fortune on the Comstock Lode, Nevada. The name is intended to recognize Mackay's financial endowment of the School of Mines of the University of Nebraska. **1968** I. KOSTOV *Mineral.* 518 Mackayite is tetragonal.., found as short prismatic green crystals.

McKenney (măke·ni). [f. the name of W. E. *McKenney* (1891–1950), who popularized it.] The name given to a suit preference signal in Bridge, devised by the American player Lavinthal in 1934. Freq. as *McKenney convention.*

1952 I. MACLEOD *Bridge is Easy Game* xiii. 158 You should study and play what is called the 'McKenney' suit preference signal. *Ibid.* 159 East must make a 'McKenney' by throwing the Jack of Diamonds calling for a Spade switch. There is a danger that a McKenney signal may be confused with the ordinary demand for the suit to be continued. **1959** *Listener* 20 Aug. 298/3 Many partnerships, therefore, have a rule, 'No McKenney at trick 1'—McKenney being an alternative name for a suit preference signal. **1964** *Official Encycl. Bridge* 341/2 *McKenney*, standard term in Great Britain for the suit preference signal... McKenney's support..caused the convention to be called in European countries the McKenney convention. **1965** *Listener* 3 June 842/1 The convention known as the McKenney convention is a form of suit-preference signalling, publicized by McKenney, but invented by another American player, Hy. Lavinthal. It differs from other suit-signalling conventions in as much as the signals relate to suits other than that played.

mackerel[1]. **1. a.** For '*Scomber scomber*' substitute '*Scomber scombrus*' and add: Also used for other fishes of similar appearance belonging to the family Scombridæ. (*Austral.* and *N.Z.* examples.)

1838 J. S. POLACK *New Zealand* I. ix. 322 The *pátiki*.. is equally excellent with the European fish [sole], as are also the *mackarel*, of which there are several varieties. **1843** E. DIEFFENBACH *Trav. N.Z.* II. 209 *Scomber loo*.. (*Scomber scombrus*, Solander, Pisc. Austr., p. 31.) Solander observed this mackerel in Queen Charlotte's Sound. **1886** R. A. SHERRIN *Handbk. Fishes N.Z.* 61 In season mackerel are often found between Cape Colville and the Great Barrier. **1951** T. C. ROUGHLEY *Fish Austral.* 96 Common mackerel (Slimy mackerel—*Pneumatophorus australasicus*). The common mackerel (of the family Scombridæ) is found in all Australian States and occurs in great numbers, particularly round the southern half of the continent where it inhabits ocean waters no great distance from the coast. **1960** DOOGUE & MORELAND *N.Z. Sea Anglers' Guide* 250 Common mackerel..is the mackerel of English-speaking countries... Other names: *Pneumatophorus japonicus*; southern mackerel, English mackerel, frigate mackerel; tawatawa (Maori).

c. Phr. *Holy Mackerel*, an exclam. expressing wonder or astonishment.

1899 ADE *In Babel* (1903) 111 Hot? Holy sufferin' mackerel! Me pushin' up the lid..to get a little fresh air. **1944** T. RATTIGAN *While Sun Shines* II. 218 Holy mackerel! A Duke! **1958** 'J. BROGAN' *Cummings Report* xviii. 189 Holy mackerel! What a way to run an army! **1961** *Amer. Speech* XXXVI. 40 *Holy Mary* is probably the idea underlying *holy Moses* and *holy mackerel.*

4. *mackerel fleck*; **mackerel shark,** substitute for def.: a shark of the family Lamnidæ, esp. a mako shark (*MAKO[1]) or the porbeagle, *Lamna nasus* (examples); **mackerel-skied** *a.*, having, or characterized by, a mackerel-sky.

1940 R. GIBBINGS *Sweet Thames run Softly* xx. 182 Tall nimbus clouds reared their heads towards the mackerel flecks in the upper air. **1819** *Plough Boy* I. 135 The revenue cutter brought in two very strange fish, found eating a dead horse, supposed to be mackerel sharks. **1959** A. HARDY *Fish & Fisheries* iv. 73 The inclusion here [*sc.* in the British list] of the mako or mackerel shark, *Isurus oxyrinchus*, is a surprise. **1971** *Islander* (Victoria, B.C.) 17 Oct. 6/1 A..fisherman..found a drift bottle inside a mackerel shark. **1921** W. DE LA MARE *Mem. Midget* xxxviii. 255 One mackerel-skied afternoon, Mrs. Monnerie and I and Susan were returning across the Park.

mackereling, *vbl. sb.* Add: Also **mackerelling.** (Earlier and later examples.)

1856 J. REYNOLDS *Peter Gott* xiv. 167 When fishermen can make as much in a few weeks at mackerelling, as in as many months at codfishing,..they prefer to run their chance in the former. *Ibid.*, Mackerelling is often called a lottery. **1880** *Harper's Mag.* Sept. 510/1 Among the rest are two of the singular 'porgy steamers' turned to mackereling. **1881** S. P. MCLEAN *Cape Cod Folks* iii. 62, I was going mackerellin' with ye myself that time. **1952** *Gloucester* (Mass.) *Daily Times* 20 Mar. 8/7 His present seiner is the Jean and Patricia which stays with mackereling only.

b. A mackerel-like effect.

1866 G. M. HOPKINS *Jrnls. & Papers* (1959) 139 Scud spots etc, and some very faintly made out mackerelling. .. Bright, with mackerelling now and then. **1883** —— *Let.* 21 Dec. in Hopkins & Dixon *Corr.* (1955) 165, I have further noticed streamers, fine ribbing or mackerelling, and other..textures.

McKie: see *MCCOY.

Mackinaw. Add: Also **Macinac, Macinaw, Mackina,** and with lower-case initial. Also, a heavy woollen cloth, now usu. with a plaid design; *pl.*, garments made of this cloth. **Mackinaw (boat),** (*b*) a schooner-rigged boat formerly used on the Great Lakes; **Mackinaw coat** (or **jacket**), a thick double-breasted jacket; also *ellipt.*; **Mackinaw shirt,** a plaid woollen shirt; **Mackinaw skiff** = *Mackinaw* (*boat*) (in Dict.); **Mackinaw trout** (further examples); also, a North American char, *Cristivomer namaycush.*

1812 J. G. LUTTIG *Jrnl. Expedition Upper Missouri* (1920) 54 The Mackina Boat took 5 hunters to the Island. **1822** L. CASS *Let.* 4 Oct. in *Wisconsin State Hist. Soc. Coll.* (1911) XX. 287 The heavy Mackinac blankets are almost impervious to the rain, and are universally worn by the Indians in this quarter. **1826** T. FLINT *Recoll.* 102, I have seen a Mackinaw skiff, carrying five tons, which came from the lakes into the Chicago of Michigan. **1836** in *Mass. Hist. Soc. Proc.* (1892) 2nd Ser. VII. 276 Covering, a cotton counterpane, a sheet.., besides my own great coats and green Mackinaw. **1840** *Southern Lit. Messenger* VI. 604/1 The celebrated Mackinaw trout, so called after the town, near which they are found, is generally caught by the hook. **1841** *Western Herald & Farmers' Mag.* (Sandwich, Ontario) 31 Mar. 3/2 They have also a large

assortment of blankets..of the real Mackinaw. **1842** *Southern Lit. Messenger* VIII. 586/2 A party of six..had occasion..to ascend the Missouri, in a Mackinaw [boat], with the purpose of trading. **1872** Mackinaw blanket [see *blanket coat* s.v. *BLANKET *sb.* 7]. **1887** *Rep. U.S. Comm. Fisheries* 24 At Duluth, Minnesota, the mackinaw boats average about 32 feet in length. **1900** *Atlantic Monthly* LXXXV. 102/1 It is then the woodsman dons his Mackinaw jacket. **1902** J. LONDON *Daughter of Snows* 316 He was interrupted by a warm-complexioned man clad in faded mackinaws. **1902** S. E. WHITE *Blazed Trail* 16 They all wore heavy blanket Mackinaw coats. *Ibid.* 375 A tall..individual dressed in a faded mackinaw and a limp slouch hat. **1912** J. SANDILANDS *Western Canad. Dict.* 28 *Mackinaw*, a heavy woolen cloth much in favour among lumberjacks. A lumberjack speaks of his thick winter jacket as his mackinaw. **1916** H. KEPHART *Camping & Woodcraft* I. 147, I usually discard the sweater in favor of a mackinaw shirt. **1920** S. LEWIS *Main St.* 230 He had given up..wearing red mackinaws in lumber-camps. **1930** J. DOS PASSOS *42nd Parallel* I. 101 A young man, his head and ears huddled into the collar of a mackinaw. **1938** E. HEMINGWAY *Fifth Column* (1939) 479 He wore..a mackinaw shirt. **1941** L. D. BALDWIN *Keelboat Age* 50 The Mackinaw boat in use on the Missouri was an adaptation of the flatboat and of the Mackinaw skiff. **1945** R. W. SERVICE *Ploughman of Moon* 157, I couched on the floor, lying on a buffalo-robe and wrapped in a mackinaw blanket. **1956** J. S. GOWLAND *Sikanaska Trail* 44 A guard in plain clothes brought along my mackinaw jacket. **1961** E. HUNTER *Mothers & Daughters* I. 9 She had hardly ever seen him without his hooded Mackinaw. **1961** *Vancouver Sun* 17 Aug. 23/1 The laker (mackinaw trout) is a record. Largest Canadian sport-caught lake char..is an 87 pounder. **1964** *Atlantic Advocate* July 77/1 William M...was operating the mill and producing a large red and black check design for Mackinaw or cruiser cloth. **1968** R. F. ADAMS *Western Words* (ed. 2) 187 The Mackinaw was a flat-bottomed boat with a pointed prow and a square stern... A large Mackinaw was as much as 50 or 60 feet long. **1971** J. MCDOUGALL *Parsons on Plains* i. 1 My first recollections are of stumps, log heaps,..bateaux, Mackinaw boats. **1973** D. MACKENZIE *Postscript to Dead Let.* 9 He was..wearing a red-and-grey mackinaw over a shirt without a tie. **1973** J. RYDER *Trevayne* (1974) xxxiv. 264 A man in a mackinaw coat and a fur cap.

mackinawite (mæ·kinǭəit). *Min.* [f. *Mackinaw*, the name of a mine in Snohomish County, Washington + -ITE¹.] A black tetragonal iron sulphide.

1962 H. T. EVANS et al. in *Program Ann. Meetings Geol. Soc. Amer.* 47A Recently, another iron sulfide mineral, mackinawite, very similar in physical properties to valleriite, but containing no copper.., has been identified from the Mackinaw Mine, Snohomish County, Washington. **1969** *Amer. Mineralogist* LIV. 1190 Information about the occurrence, optical properties, microhardness and cell-size is given for a nickelian mackinawite (Fe 38·1%, Co 3·3%, Ni 18·7%) from Vlakfontein in the Transvaal. *Ibid.*, This mackinawite was examined in reflected light in both air and oil. It shows the very strong pleochroism and anisotropy characteristic of this mineral. **1970** *Nature* 15 Aug. 700/1 Modern surface sediments containing H_2S are often coloured black by fine grained, iron monosulphide minerals such as mackinawite, $Fe_{1+x}S$, and greigite, Fe_3S_4.

mackintosh. Add: **2.** Now freq. used to designate any type of rain-proof coat.

1895 *Montgomery Ward Catal.* 296/3 Men's Double Texture Mackintosh Box Coats, double breasted, all wool black tricot.., fancy plaid lining, silk velvet collar. **1897** *Sears, Roebuck Catal.* 188/2 Ladies' Single Military Cape Mackintosh. Made from extra fine all wool Scotch mixed cheviot, with fine, soft dressy finish. **1956** A. S. C. ROSS in N. Mitford *Noblesse Oblige* 30 *Burberry* and *raincoat* are of the same genre, *macintosh* or *mac* being normal.

mackintoshed (mæ·kĭntǫʃt), *a.* Also **macintoshed.** [f. MACKINTOSH + -ED².] Wearing, or protected by, a mackintosh.

1904 J. VAIZEY *More about Pixie* xxiv. 257 The cloaked and mackintoshed figures..seemed all black, all the same. **1927** *Daily Mail* 30 June 9/4 Mackintoshed enthusiasts occupied them [*sc.* boats]. **1962** *Punch* 21 Nov. 751/1 Macintoshed ruthless plainclothesmen. **1963** *Times* 25 Apr. 6/1 They sauntered self-consciously off, mackintoshed and blackbooted, to mingle with the unsuspecting crowd.

Mackintosh Red: see *MCINTOSH.

mackintoshy (mæ·kintǫʃi), *a.* [f. MACKINTOSH + -Y¹.] Of, belonging to, or suggestive of mackintoshes; characterized by or given to wearing mackintoshes.

1939 'G. ORWELL' *Coming up for Air* IV. vii. 279 The gas-bill and the school-fees, and the mackintoshy smell. **1941** E. BOWEN *Look at Roses* 253 'They're mackintoshy sort of people,' she said.

McLeod (măklau·d). Also erron. **Macleod.** [Name of Herbert *McLeod* (1841–1923), English scientist, who invented the instrument in 1874 (*Phil. Mag.* XLVIII. 110).] *McLeod gauge*: a type of mercury-in-glass manometer for the absolute measurement of low pressures, in which a fixed large volume of the gas to be measured is compressed by the mercury into a small volume and the resulting pressure found from the height of the column of mercury it supports, the desired pressure then being obtained by multiplying this by the ratio of the smaller to the larger volume in accordance with Boyle's law.

1880 J. E. H. GORDON *Physical Treat. Electr. & Magn.* II. xxxv. 83 The apparatus is in connection with a McLeod gauge, by means of which pressures to 0·00005 millim. can be determined. **1923** *Proc. Cambr. Philos. Soc.* XXI. 505 The residual pressure of the gas in the box was measured by a Macleod gauge. **1971** *Sci. Amer.* Aug. 114/2 Although the McLeod gauge indicates absolute pressure and is universally used for calibrating other instruments, it is inconvenient to operate.

maclock, var. *MUCKLUCK.

McLuhanism (măklū·ăniz'm). The social ideas of the Canadian writer H. Marshall *McLuhan* (1911–), such as that the effect of the introduction of the mass media is to deaden the critical faculties of individuals. Hence **McLuhane·sque** *a.*; **McLu·hanite** *a.* and *sb.*, of or pertaining to, an adherent of, McLuhan; **McLu·hanize** *v. trans.*, to convert to McLuhanism; to render in a manner typical of McLuhan.

1967 *Punch* 4 Oct. 520/1 Most of us 20th-century electric circuitry villagers by now have got at least the drift of McLuhanism. **1967** *Spectator* 10 Nov. 571/2, I am leaving on one side all McLuhanite arguments that books are on the way out. **1967** *Observer* 10 Dec. 24/3 A suitably McLuhanesque fanfare. **1968** *Listener* 4 Jan. 8/1 Then there is Father Walter Ong, whom Martin Dodsworth once McLuhanised into 'the Ong with the numinous prose'. *Ibid.* 6 June 722/3 The demolition of fashionable McLuhanite myths about television has been another of the year's benefits. *Ibid.* 751/1 It was really a kind of McLuhanesque exercise in the depiction of the influence of media on people's lives. **1968** *Punch* 17 July 100/3 Mr. Turner and director Peter Hammond had bravely attempted to McLuhanise the intractably literary. **1970** *Times* 31 Mar. (Australian Suppl.) p. vi/8 The thesis of Australia in the seventies as a model McLuhanized society is fervently denied by publishers. **1971** *Guardian* 14 Jan. 7/1 McLuhanites and Orwellians are likely to block our view of their masters' arguments. *Ibid.* 1 Nov. 9/1 One occasionally wonders whether the image—as in some McLuhanesque lens—is not more important than its object. **1972** *Ibid.* 8 Feb. 4/6 It is on the basis of evolution ..and not instant McLuhanism that the Swiss delegation has opened negotiations at Brussels. **1973** *Ibid.* 19 Feb. 8/6 Designers on a newspaper—whatever McLuhanesque horror next?

maclura (măklⁱūᵊ·ră). [mod.L. (T. Nuttall, 1818), f. the name of William *Maclure* (1763–1840), American geologist.] A deciduous North American tree, *Maclura pomifera*, of the genus so called, belonging to the family Moraceæ and bearing an inedible fruit resembling an orange; the Osage orange or bow-wood. Also *attrib.*

1818 T. NUTTALL *Genera N. Amer. Plants* II. 233 Maclura. (Bow-wood, Yellow-wood.) **1857** *Trans. Illinois Agric. Soc.* II. 222 A few Maclura hedges are growing. *Ibid.* 302 Mr. Tisdell has two hedges of the maclura growing on his farm. **1858** J. A. WARDER *Hedges & Evergreens* 21 The division of the prairies into twenty-acre lots, by the dense hedges of maclura. *Ibid.* 52 The cost of the maclura hedge.

M'Naghten rules (măknǭ·t'n). Also **McNaghten, MacNaughten, Macnaughton,** etc., **rules** (or **case,** etc.). [Named after Daniel *M'Naghten* who was tried for murder in 1843 and acquitted on a plea of insanity.] Name applied to the answers given in the House of Lords in 1843 after the trial of Daniel M'Naghten for the murder of Sir Robert Peel's secretary, Edward Drummond, when five questions were put respecting crimes alleged to have been committed by persons suffering from insanity; subsequently used as criteria for judging an accused person's responsibility for his actions.

[**1843** *Times* 14 Mar. 4/3 Last night the Lord Chancellor ..brought forward the circumstances of M'Naughten's trial for the consideration of the Peers... He proceeded to caution their Lordships against supposing that, even if the verdict in M'Naughten's case should appear to have been given upon faulty or inconclusive evidence, it would be necessary to alter the law upon the subject.] **1892** D. H. TUKE *Dict. Psychol. Med.* I. 318/1 Juries are never, at the present day, charged strictly in conformity with the McNaghten rules. [**1902** *Encycl. Brit.* XXIX. 491/2 The answers [by Chief Justice Tindal] to these questions are commonly called 'The rules in Macnaughton's case' and they still nominally contain the law of England as to the criminal responsibility of the insane.] **1958** B. HAMILTON *Too Much of Water* xii. 271 So long as the McNaughton rules run, I don't think he's got a *chance* of Broadmoor. **1959** JOWITT *Dict. Eng. Law* II. 1122/2 In R. v. *McNaghten* or *M'Naghten* or *Macnaughten* (1843)..a discussion took place in the House of Lords upon the direction to the jury..and as a result a series of questions was put to the judges. The answers of the majority constitute the 'McNaghten Rules', and have been accepted as laying down the law as to insanity with reference to criminal responsibility. **1959** *Listener* 24 Sept. 481/1 Insanity in this context was until lately very narrowly defined by the McNaghten rules. **1962** *Lancet* 1 Dec. 1148/1 Giving the background to present-day legal views on diminished responsibility, the McNaughten rules, uncontrollable impulse, and psychopathy. **1968** N. WALKER *Crime & Insanity in Eng.* vi. 105 It is difficult to find a clear statement of the medical objections to the M'Naghten Rules at this date. *Ibid.* 107 Mr Justice Bray explained the M'Naghten Rules to the Gloucester jury. **1971** *Reader's Digest Family Guide to Law* 773/1 The McNaughten Rules can be applied to all offences, but they are rarely used in anything but murder cases. **1973** *Times* 24 May 12/7 What emerges clearly from the Canadian trial is the immense benefit to both doctors and lawyers in *this* country from the subsidence of the McNaghten rules and the introduction of the plea of diminished responsibility.

Mâcon (mā·koṅ). [Name of a city in the department of Saône-et-Loire, France.] A wine of Burgundy, produced in the district around Mâcon.

[**1699** M. LISTER *Journey to Paris* 161 The White Wines of value are those of *Mascon* in *Burgundy*.] **1863** T. G. SHAW *Wine* viii. 258 A bottle of the homely Mâcon, instead of the elegant Beaujolais, had to be called for. **1908** CHESTERTON *Man who was Thursday* viii. 155 Draining a glass of Mâcon. **1963** *Spectator* 1 Mar. 275, I chose a Macon from the wine-list and subsequently paid £1 for it. **1967** A. LICHINE *Encycl. Wines* 336/2 A slightly lesser amount [of wine] will be sold simply as Mâcon with no other indication of source. **1972** H. W. YOXALL *Enjoyment of Wine* xv. 117 A glass or two of cool, light, dry wine—a young moselle, a muscadet, a mâcon blanc..—is a first-rate aperitif.

macon (mē̆i·kən). [f. M(UTTON + B)ACON.] During the 1939–45 war: mutton salted and smoked like bacon.

1939 *Daily Express* 22 Nov., *Macon* has now been adapted by other newspapers as a name for mutton bacon. This is only the latest of many words and phrases originally coined in this office which have later been used generally. **1939** *News Rev.* 30 Nov. 15 Macon, the Scottish dish which may eke out any wartime shortage of bacon. Macon is mutton cured in the same way as bacon. **1939** *Times* 7 Dec. 10/4 Macon was introduced..at the Savoy Hotel yesterday... Mr. Cecil Rodd, introducing macon.. said he did not pretend to know how the word macon came into being; it just happened. **1968** *Punch* 7 Feb. 177/2 The Ministry of Food then stood in for Mrs. Beeton, instructing them how to..work wonders with such unlikely raw materials as macon (bacon made from mutton, children)..and..coelacanth.

Maconochie (măkǫ·nǒki). *colloq.* [The name of the makers, *Maconochie* Brothers, of London.] **1.** Meat stewed with vegetables and tinned, esp. as supplied to soldiers on active service; a tin of such meat. Also *Maconochie ration.*

1901 'LINESMAN' *Words by Eyewitness* i. 9 The hungry shelterers trooped back to their 'dixies', and wasted not a thought upon them [*sc.* shells], until the 'Maconochie' had vanished. **1915** F. H. LAWRENCE in T. E. Lawrence *Home Lett.* (1954) 689 We have found several tins of Maconochie Rations & also Jam in the house. **1917** 'I. HAY' *Carrying On* viii. 220 How would a Maconochie apiece suit your boys? **1940** 'GUN BUSTER' *Return via Dunkirk* II. xix. 225 He manages to scrape together two tins of Maconochie (stew), a tin of cold potatoes,..and some 'issue biscuits'. **1954** W. FAULKNER *Fable* 61 His company commander was shaving out of a Maconochie tin.

2. *joc. slang.* The stomach. Also *Maconochie Cross, Medal* (see quots.).

1919 W. H. DOWNING *Digger Dial.* 32 *Maconochie*,.. stomach. *Ibid.*, *Maconochie Cross*, Military Cross. *Maconochie Medal*, Military Medal. **1925** FRASER & GIBBONS *Soldier & Sailor Words* 149 *Maconochie*..was also sometimes used for stomach, *e.g.*, 'He got hit in the Maconochie'. **1965** BROPHY & PARTRIDGE *Long Trail* 147 *Maconochie Medal*, the Military Medal; *Maconochie Cross*, the Military Cross.

‖ **macoumère** (makumē̆r). *West Indies.* Also **macomère, macoumere.** [French Creole.] A god-mother, or the mother of one's god-child; more generally applied to any female friend of a family, or as a derogatory term for an old woman or gossip.

1942 H. C. GORDON *West Indian Scenes* xix. 217 *Macomère Crab*, who was a kind soul, complied with her request. **1952** S. SELVON *Brighter Sun* vi. 95 And is why you looking at me so, *macoumère*? **1960** *Tamarack Rev.* XIV. 22 This time so, they ain't bothering about the other people in the queue at all, they mauvalanging and bursting out in some loud kya-kya laugh like them macoumere in the market in..Trinidad.

macrergate (mækrə̄·ɪgē̆it). *Ent.* Also **macroërgate** [ad. G. *makroergate* (E. Wasmann 1895, in *Biol. Centralbl.* XV. 606), f. Gr. μακρ-ός large + ἐργάτης worker.] A large worker ant.

1901 W. M. WHEELER in *Amer. Naturalist* XXXV. 879 The larger macroërgates are nearly eight times as large as the normal workers. **1910** —— *Ants* vi. 97 The *macrergate* is an unusually large worker form which in some species is produced only in populous or affluent colonies. **1915** H. ST. J. K. DONISTHORPE *Brit. Ants* 40 The macrergate is larger in stature than the normal worker of the species in question.

macro (mæ·kro), *sb.* [f. the prefix MACRO-.] **1.** *Computers.* A macro-instruction. Freq. *attrib.*

1959 *Jrnl. Assoc. Computing Machinery* VI. 132 The built-in system macro instructions in SCAT presently consist of (1) two macros for generating the..standard entry and exit from subroutines, (2) a set of debugging macros [etc.]. 1961 LEEDS & WEINBERG *Computer Programming Fund.* iv. 103 The assembly program can be instructed to recognize this instruction sequence through the use of a single form called a macro-instruction... Recognition of the 'macro' form causes the assembly program to assemble the corresponding sequence of one or more machine instructions. 1963 L. SCHULTZ *Digital Processing* xi. 240 To avoid having to write the groups repeatedly, the programmer..instructs the machine to establish a table in which it stores the group of instructions. To identify the group, he assigns a code name, called a macro name. *Ibid.*, The programmer writes one instruction (a macro) and the machine 'generates' several. 1966 *New Scientist* 27 Oct. 162/3 In the ICT command language it is possible to define new commands in the language in terms of those already defined. An example of this 'macro' facility is given here... The effect is to allow the user to condense a long and complicated job description into a shorthand phrase of his own choice. The use of 'macros' in this way makes it extremely easy for the user to set up his own conventions. 1970 O. DOPPING *Computers & Data Processing* xix. 324 As an advantage of automatic coding, it is sometimes pointed out that the macros and subroutines are tested and error-free, in contrast to home-made subroutines. 1972 J. J. DONOVAN *Systems Programming* iv. 111 In employing a macro, the programmer essentially defines a single 'instruction' to represent a block of code. For every occurrence of this one-line macro instruction in his program, the macro processing assembler will substitute the entire block.

2. *Photogr.* (See *MACRO- 2 c.)

macro-. Add: **1. b.** *macrochromosome, macrovegetation*; **ma·croform** (see quot.); **ma·crofossil** *Palæont.*, a fossil discernible to the naked eye; **ma·cro-instruction** *Computers*, an instruction in a programming or source language which is equivalent to a specified set of ordinary instructions in an object language (which may be the source language or machine language); freq. as two words (cf. *MACRO *sb.* 1); **macro·phagous** *Zool.* [-PHAGOUS], feeding on relatively large pieces of food; **macrotri·chium** *Ent.* [Gr. θρίξ, τριχ- hair], usu. in pl. **macrotri·chia**, in certain insects, the larger hairs on the body, esp. those on the surface of the wings.

1905, 1969 Macrochromosome [see *microchromosome* s.v. *MICRO- 1]. 1967 *Anglo-Amer. Catal. Rules: Brit. Text* 267 *Macroform*, a reproduction large enough to be easily read by the unaided eye. Used in contradistinction to 'microform'. 1937 G. D. HANNA in Camp & Hanna *Methods in Paleont.* II. 79 Under the term macrofossils it will be desirable to treat together many of the larger groups of invertebrates such as the Mollusca, Brachiopoda, Echinodermata, Bryozoa, and Crustacea... All forms more than 10 mm. in diameter will be treated as macrofossils. 1969 BENNISON & WRIGHT *Geol. Hist. Brit. Isles* ii. 34 The larger fossils (macrofossils) of the Chalk are largely neritic. 1974 A. HUXLEY *Plant & Planet* ii. 9 Tertiary and Cretaceous sediments in Venezuela and Borneo..yielded a detailed pollen record but virtually no macro-fossils. 1959 Macroinstruction [see *MICRO-INSTRUCTION]. 1959, 1961 [see *MACRO *sb.* 1]. 1961 *Times* 3 Oct. (Computer Suppl.) p. x/5 Through the use of these macro-instructions the computer can be given the semblance of being a much more powerful machine than it really is. 1970 O. DOPPING *Computers & Data Processing* xix. 312 By introducing macro instructions in the source language, the designer can bring about the same ease of programming as could be achieved by giving the computer a more powerful operation list than it really has. But naturally, one does not get the same advantages in terms of economy of memory space and computer time as would be obtained if the more powerful instructions were really built into the machine. 1972 Macro instruction [see *MACRO *sb.* 1]. 1949 I. F. & W. D. HENDERSON *Dict. Sci. Terms* (ed. 4) 240/1 Macrophagous... Feeding on relatively large masses of food; *opp.* microphagous. 1951 M. ABERCROMBIE et al. *Dict. Biol.* 130 All land animals are macrophagous. 1964 *Oceanogr. & Marine Biol.* II. 396 He [*sc.* A. R. Fontaine] finds both microphagous and macrophagous mechanisms are used in this species [*sc. Ophiocomina nigra*]. 1934 C. H. CURRAN *Families & Genera N. Amer. Diptera* 487 Macrotrichia—The larger microscopic hairs on the surface of the wings. 1957 RICHARDS & DAVIES *Imms's Textbk. Ent.* (ed. 9) I. 12 Setae or Macrotrichia are commonly known as hairs and each arises from a cup-like pit or alveolus. *Ibid.* 38 Macrotrichia or true setae..are found on the main veins and their branches,..less frequently on the wing-membrane. 1970 E. F. RIEK in *Insects of Australia* (Commonwealth Sci. & Industr. Res. Organization) xxxvii. 875/2 Hooked macrotrichia may occur over most of the fore margin of the hind wing [in Hymenoptera]. 1958 *Jrnl. du Conseil Internat. Explor. de la Mer* XXIV. 32 Samples of macrovegetation were collected in the spring. 1960 *Oikos* XI. 183 (*heading*) Subaquatic macrovegetation in Ösbysjön, Djursholm.

d. macrocra·nial *a.*, having a long skull; macrocephalic; **macropha·llic** *a.*, having a large phallus.

1902 *Biometrika* Aug. 462 Dolichocephaly and chamaecephaly in both races are associated with macrocranial characters. 1907 *Practitioner* Aug. 318 The population of the south-west of Scotland, exclusive of Glasgow, is long-headed or macrocranial. 1970 F. SNOWDEN *Blacks in Antiquity* 23 The circumcised and macrophallic Ethiopians. 1972 *Sunday Times* 23 Apr. 43 Commercial porn.. with its inevitable distortions, brutalised women and macrophallic faceless men.

e. Terms in which *macro-* indicates subject-matter treated on a larger scale, or more comprehensive phenomena or levels of treatment, than is implied either by the word to which *macro-* is attached or by the corresponding term beginning *micro-*, as *macro-planning, -sociology* (hence *-sociological* adj.); *macro-historical* adj.; **ma·croclimate**, the general climate of a relatively large area; so **ma:croclima·tic** *a.*; **ma:cro-evolu·tion**, evolutionary change over a long period, leading to the appearance of new groups of plants or animals; **ma·crophysics**, the part of physics that is concerned with bodies and phenomena on a macroscopic scale; so **macrophy·sical** *a.*

1939 *Geogr. Jrnl.* XCIII. 463 As in all local climates strong departure from the macroclimate develops in the climates of cities in calm cloudless weather. 1967 M. J. COE *Ecol. Alpine Zone Mt. Kenya* 59 This remarkable contrast between the micro- and macroclimates of these areas is expressed even more clearly by Mani. 1971 J. Z. YOUNG *Introd. Study Man* xxxviii. 544 The British..move with less protection in their damp but equable macroclimate. 1939 *Ecology* XX. 30 Microclimate..makes it possible for smaller groups of preclimax vegetation to persist as relict colonies long after macroclimatic changes have shifted formations. 1946 S. A. WILDE *Forest Soils* iii. 21 Macroclimatic soil-forest zones. 1939 *Ann. Reg. 1938* 369 The gene theory was applied increasingly to problems of macro-evolution. 1940 R. GOLDSCHMIDT *Material Basis of Evolution* iii. 8 Microevolution..has been used..for evolutionary processes observable within the span of a human lifetime as opposed to macroevolution, on a geological scale. 1972 *Listener* 3 Aug. 138/2 There may be a different mechanism for grand heroic macro-evolution and for ordinary humdrum everyday evolution at species or sub-species level. 1955 *Bull. Atomic Sci.* Feb. 42/2 There are some who profess to see in matters of culture, in matters precisely of the arts and sciences, a certain macro-historical pattern, a grand system of laws which determines the course of civilization and gives a kind of inevitable quality to the unfolding of the future. 1902 MANN & MILLIKAN tr. *Drude's Theory of Optics* p. vii, Pure electromagnetic experiments lead to conclusions in what may be called the domain of macrophysical properties only. For the explanation of optical dispersion a hypothesis as to the microphysical properties of bodies must be made. 1956 E. H. HUTTEN *Lang. Mod. Physics* v. 179 Two micro-physical events are connected in a different way from two macro-physical events. 1960 *Times* 15 Mar. 2/2 A study of the relationships between the macro-physical properties of soils and the physical chemistry of their colloidal constituents. 1909 *Cent. Dict.* Suppl., Macrophysics. 1936 *Discovery* Mar. 96/2 Thirteen unsolved problems are listed, ranging from those concerning the creation of the universe..to the structure of the atom, from macrophysics and astronomy *via* biology..back to physical science again. 1956 *Nature* 18 Feb. 321/1 Mr. F. H. Ludlam..pointed out that the partitioning (into micro-, macro- and synoptic-physics) of cloud studies.. must not be made too rigid. 1966 *Economist* 11 June 1206/1 To mention only a few [contributions], largely concerned with macro-planning: welfare-theoretical problems and planner's and consumer's sovereignty are the theme of Joan Robinson. 1973 *Financial Times* 26 Mar. 16/4 The macro-planning functions of the metropolitan county (mainly transport and town and country planning, together with fire and police, consumer protection, [etc.]). 1951 R. FIRTH *Elem. Social Organiz.* i. 18 If the distinguishing feature of the anthropologist is micro-sociological technique, his theory is macro-sociological. 1970 *New Society* 5 Feb. 232/3 The approach, the initiated will recognise, is essentially macrosociological. 1941 G. GURVITCH in *Jrnl. Philos.* XXXVIII. 486 Macrosociology is the study of the world of groups and of global societies, each of which are microcosms of the forms of sociality. 1958 W. STARK *Sociol. of Knowl.* i. 20 It might be useful..to call the one the macrosociology of knowledge, because it fixes its attention on the inclusive society.

2. Combs. in which *macro* can be regarded as a separable element having adjectival force, with the meaning: macroscopic, large-scale; overall, comprehensive; large. Hence used as an independent word not preceding the sb. it qualifies.

1934 WEBSTER, *Macro* adj. = *macro-*. 1937 *Mind* XLVI. 327 Quantum mechanics, moreover, claims applicability not only to micro-processes; it also contains laws of mechanics which are applicable to macro-processes. 1954 *Gloss. Terms Iron & Steel* (*B.S.I.*) I. 19 *Macro etch test*, etching with acids or other reagents to reveal the macro structure, flow lines and/or defects. 1957 C. DAY LEWIS *Poet's Way of Knowl.* 14 Until recently the scientist has sought for general laws governing macro-events, and has drawn from them inferences about individual events. 1959 K. R. POPPER *Logic Sci. Discovery* II. viii. 196 Observable physical effects are interpreted as 'macro laws'. 1961 G. H. ORCUTT et al. *Microanalysis Socioecon. Syst.* p. xv, Given the possibility of experimentation at both micro- and macrolevels, it has been possible for the physical sciences to achieve great successes at both levels without the necessity of predicting aggregate behavior on the basis of knowledge about microbehavior. 1962 J. T. MARSH *Self-Smoothing Fabrics* xv. 263 This type of staining test..does, however, demonstrate irregularity of distribution on a macro-basis as distinct from a micro-basis, and provide useful evidence of uneven impregnation during padding, or of resin migration during drying. 1966 *McGraw-Hill Encycl. Sci. & Technol.* XI. 143/2 The instruments and apparatus used in microanalytical work are to some extent miniature replicas of macro instruments and apparatus. 1967 COX & GROSE *Organiz. Bibliogr. Rec. by Computer* v. 107 Before I move from the macro-level of the overall design of a MARC service to the minutiae of record data content and file organization. 1967 D. WILSON in Wills & Yearsley *Handbk. Managem. Technol.* iii. 47 The logic for the individual programs is expressed in terms of macro and micro block-diagrams. The macro block-diagrams show the main logic for a particular program and may be prepared by the systems analyst; the micro block-diagrams show the detailed logic for program coding and will be prepared by the programmer. 1970 *Guardian Weekly* 18 Apr. 15 Revolutions, including the Russian one, made the mistake of insisting that the macro-change, of the whole system, should come before micro-change, of the life style. 1971 *New Scientist* 21 Jan. 100/1 Undoubtedly a number of serious macro-problems face the Ulster community. *Ibid.* 100/2 In the absence of a knowledge of these macro-changes, systems will continue to evolve on the basis of year-to-year crisis decisions. 1971 *Good Motoring* Sept. 9/2 As vehicle speeds rise from 25–30 mph to 60–70 mph, however, tyre grip in wet weather diminishes unless there is also 'macro' or large-scale roughness of the surface. 1973 A. E. WILKERSON *Rights of Children* 307 These issues..reflect the necessity for a macro-approach to child welfare. 1974 *Times Lit. Suppl.* 8 Mar. 242/5 The forms and methods of economic management, both micro and macro.

b. *Chem.* Of or pertaining to macroanalysis. Cf. *MACRO-SCALE.

1933 *Biochem. Jrnl.* XXVII. 434 The present micro-method for urea in 0·2 cc of blood compares very favourably with the comparatively macro-method of Van Slyke and Cullen. 1938 ARTHUR & SMITH *Semi-Micro Qualitative Analysis* I. 3 Dealing with samples of only 3 to 5 mg. (compared with the usual 0·5 to 1·0 g. macro sample), the micro method consumes much less time for reactions.. and in many other ways proves superior to the macro methods. 1946 MELDRUM & DAGGETT *Textbk. Qualitative Analysis* i. 2 The two..generally applicable methods of qualitative analysis of inorganic materials are the macro and the semimicro methods. 1974 [see *MICRO- 8 b].

c. *Photogr.* Denoting apparatus or procedures used in macrophotography, as **macro lens** (also *ellipt.* as *macro*), a lens suitable for taking photographs unusually close to the subject.

1956 *Focal Encycl. Photogr.* 688/1 A camera with back focusing is a great advantage in macro work. 1961 L. A. MANNHEIM tr. *Croy's Camera Close Up* 85 The maximum aperture of a macro-lens depends..on its design. *Ibid.* 88 Macro-exposures. Exposures in close-up work have to allow for..the subject and its lighting..and the scale of reproduction. 1968 GAUNT & PETZOLD *Pict. Cycl. Photogr.* 425/2 The main requirement for a macro-camera is adequate lens extension. 1971 *Amat. Photographer* 13 Jan. 80/1 (Advt.), 50 mm f/3·5 Macro. 1974 *Ibid.* 29 May 8/1 The picture on the left could only have been taken with a macro lens. *Ibid.*, It's impossible to combine macro and telephoto in one lens.

macroanalysis (mækrоˌæ̆næ·lĭsis). *Chem.* [f. *MACRO- 1 e + ANALYSIS.] Quantitative analysis of samples of the size for which the older chemical techniques were usually developed, commonly 0·1–1 gramme.

1938 MELDRUM & FLOSDORF *Qualitative Analysis Inorg. Materials* I. 7 Microanalysis may be applied when the amount of material available..is very small... Many of the reactions are essentially the same as those used in the systematic macroanalysis. 1955 [see *MICRO- 8 b]. 1966 *McGraw-Hill Encycl. Sci. & Technol.* XI. 143/1 Methods of quantitative analysis vary with the amount of sample taken and of constituent being determined. A macro-analysis (decigram analysis) uses a sample of about 0·1–0·5 gram.

macrobiotic, *a.* and *sb.* Add: **a.** *adj.* **2.** Of or pertaining to a Zen Buddhist dietary system intended to prolong life, comprising pure vegetable foods, brown rice, etc. Also as *sb.*, a follower or adherent of this system; **macrobiotics** *sb. pl.* (const. as *sing.*), the use or theory of such a dietary system.

1936 L. P. WEAVER tr. *Székely's Cosmos, Man & Society* III. ii. 207 (*heading*) Macrobiotics, the optimal and omnilateral correlations of longevity. 1965 W. DUFTY *You are All Sanpaku* (Eng. version of *Y. Sakurazawa's Zen Macrobiotics*) 178 Macrobiotics is not the kind of vegetarianism which is merely sentimental. 1968 *New Yorker* 10 Feb. 22 Macrobiotic. That means she'll eat fish. 1969 *Listener* 17 July 79/3 Macrobiotics is a life science discovered in Japan by Georges Ohsawa and it's based on the two pillars of philosophy and diet—the staple food being brown rice. 1970 M. SPARK *Driver's Seat* 48 Rice, unpolished rice is the basis of macrobiotics... It is a cleansing diet. Physically, mentally and spiritually. 1970 *Time* 16 Nov. 59 Most macrobiotics, as Ohsawa's devotees call themselves, try to follow his other nine diets, which are graduated from six to minus three to include increasing amounts of fish and vegetables—organically grown—along with brown rice. 1971 *Courier-Mail* (Brisbane) 10 May 9/4 Macrobiotic nibblers of seeds, bean curd, kale, other seaweeds and brown rice, are spreading their message of love and peace by feeding. 1971 *Daily Tel.* 18 Oct. 4/6 The macrobiotic diet, a rigid system based on vegetables and cereals..is denounced..by the American Medical Association as bad for health and even potentially lethal. 1972 *Guardian* 1 Dec. 11/2 Right now she is into the Zen macrobiotic brown-rice bit. 1973 'P. REID' *Harris in Wonderland* vii. 55 Supper ..was macrobiotic, leeks and brown rice on a wooden plate. 1975 *Listener* 1 May 589/3 Macrobiotics crumbling to death in the name of good health.

macrocarpa (mækrŏkā·ɹpă). [mod.L., specific epithet of *Cupressus macrocarpa* (T. Hartweg 1847, in *Jrnl. Hort. Soc.* II. 187), f. Gr. μακρό-ς large + καρπός fruit.] An evergreen

tree, *Cupressus macrocarpa*, native to the Monterey peninsula of California and widely cultivated elsewhere, esp. as a fast-growing hedge or wind-break; = *Monterey cypress*. Also *attrib.*

[**1866** 'SENILIS' *Pinaceæ* 73 It [*sc.* large-coned cypress] is to be found in two forms. *Macrocarpa*, when raised from seed, has a distinct, continuous, and erect leader with the side branches regularly disposed and gracefully drooping.] **1905** *Daily News* 12 Feb. 4/6 The Bird only moved from a macrocarpa tree to the cypress and lime trees. **1922** *N.Z. Jrnl. Agric.* 20 Mar. 176 The macrocarpa is very rapid in its growth. **1935** *Discovery* Dec. 375/1, I have found macrocarpa hedges a very popular breeding place for various species. **1937** 'R. HYDE' *Persephone in Winter* 42 The faint wet tang of macrocarpa leaves. **1948** J. BETJEMAN *Sel. Poems* 78 Those macrocarpas still survive the gales They must have had last winter. **1950** *N.Z. Jrnl. Agric.* Feb. 163 Good, well-kept shelter belts of macrocarpa. **1959** A. MCLINTOCK *Descr. Atlas N.Z.* p. xiii, Plantations and shelter belts of introduced (exotic) trees, mainly radiata pine and macrocarpa, break up the farmlands. **1966** G. W. TURNER *Eng. Lang. Austral. & N.Z.* iv. 82 Children..grew up among the pine and macrocarpa hedges or bleak unsheltered paddocks which replaced the bush.

macrochoanite (mæːkrokōᵘ·ănəit). *Palæont.* [f. MACRO- + Gr. χοάν-η funnel + -ITE¹ 2 a.] A nautiloid cephalopod once included in a sub-order Macrochoanites, in which each septal neck reaches back into the preceding one. Hence **maːcrochoani·tic** *a.*, (having septal necks) characteristic of a macrochoanite.

1883 A. HYATT in *Proc. Boston Soc. Nat. Hist.* XXII. 260 We, therefore, divide the Ellipochoanoida into the true Microchoanites,..and the Macrochoanites. *Ibid.*, In the more complicated forms of Goniatitinæ, while the young are quite generally macrochoanitic, the later larval stages and the adults are universally short funnelled. **1964** C. TEICHERT in R. C. Moore *Treat. Invertebr. Paleont.* K 39/1 Macrochoanitic necks are found only in the Endocerida. *Ibid.* 95/1 Hyatt distinguished the Bactritidae as 'Macrochoanites'.

macroco·smically, *adv.* [f. MACROCOSMIC *a.*: see -LY².] In relation to the macrocosm.

1881 [see *MICROCOSMICALLY *adv.*]. **1939** C. WILLIAMS *Descent of Dove* 128 Considered macrocosmically or microcosmically.

macrocyclic (mækrosəi·klik), *a.* [f. MACRO- + CYCLIC *a.*] **1.** *Bot.* Of a rust fungus: having a long life cycle.

1926 ARTHUR & KERN in *Mycologia* XVIII. 90 The vegetative body is either long-cycle (macrocyclic), consisting of two unlike and discontinuous generations, or short-cycle (microcyclic), consisting of one continuous generation. *Ibid.* 91 We are indebted to Dr. G. Lagerheim, of Stockholm, for the suggestion of the terms macrocyclic and microcyclic which seem to us to be very appropriate and satisfactory. **1929** [see *ÆCIUM]. **1950** E. A. BESSEY *Morphol. & Taxon. Fungi* xii. 396 Rusts possessing such a cycle are called macrocyclic or long-cycle rusts. **1970** J. WEBSTER *Introd. Fungi* 376 It is also believed that forms with shorter life cycles arose..from macrocyclic ancestors.

2. *Chem.* Containing or being a ring composed of a relatively large number of atoms.

1947 R. L. WAKEMAN *Chem. Commercial Plastics* xi. 225 Macrocyclic esters can thus be formed, containing even as many as 16 or more members in the ring. **1960** [see *MACROLIDE]. **1964** M. HYNES *Med. Bacteriol.* (ed. 8) x. 137 These substances, as well as erythromycin, have a macrocyclic lactose ring, and are sometimes termed macrolides. **1972** BANTHORPE & CHARLWOOD in A. A. Newman *Chem. Terpenes* vii. 377 The macrocyclic compound cembrene.. is probably derived from GGPP.

Hence (as a back-formation) **ma·crocycle**, a macrocyclic compound or molecule.

1956 *Nature* 14 Jan. 70/1 Synthesis of azaporphins and related macrocycles. **1971** *Ibid.* 17 Sept. 183/1 Several [antibiotics] have structures made up of two types of chemical entity; for example..the macrolides (macrocycles attached to carbohydrate residues). **1974** *Chem. Rev.* LXXIV. 351/2 Christensen and coworkers have discussed for several classes of macrocycles their unique ion binding properties.

macrocyte. Add: Hence **macrocytic** (-si·tik) *a.*, typical or characteristic of a macrocyte; characterized by macrocytes; **macrocytosis** (-səitōᵘ·sis) = MACROCYTHÆMIA.

1893 DUNGLISON *Dict. Med. Sci.* (ed. 21) 656/2 *Macrocytosis*, condition in which the red corpuscles are increased in size, becoming macrocytes. **1930** DAVIDSON & GULLAND *Pernicious Anæmia* xi. 237 We would describe the condition as a macrocytic hæmolytic anæmia. **1930** M. M. WINTROBE in *Proc. Soc. Exper. Biol. & Med.* XXVII. 1072 The first and most obvious group [of anemias], which can be called macrocytic, includes the cases of pernicious anemia, sprue, and a case of pernicious anemia of pregnancy. **1932** *Jrnl. Exper. Med.* LVI. 551 Evidence that a normal red corpuscle could change into a macrocytic or a microcytic form. **1947** *Radiology* XLIX. 289/2 Macrocytic anemias appeared in certain animals on chronic exposure to doses in the range under discussion. **1962** *Lancet* 12 May 1004/2 Clinical and hæmatological examinations..showed anæmia with..macrocytosis, and reticulocytosis. *Ibid.* 1 Dec. 1142/2 The peripheral blood is not strikingly macrocytic. **1968** J. H. BURN *Lect. Notes Pharmacol.* (ed. 9) 79 In pernicious anaemia there is enough haemoglobin but too few red cells. The red cells are swollen (macrocytic) and hyperchromic.

maːcro-econo·mics, *sb. pl.* (usu. const. as *sing.*). Also **macroeconomics.** [f. MACRO- + ECONOMIC B. *sb.* 2 c.] The science or study of the economy as a whole. Opp. *MICRO-ECONOMICS *sb. pl.* So **maːcro-econo·mic** *a.*

1948 *Econometrica* XVI. 309 (*heading*) Some conditions of macroeconomic stability. **1948, 1949** [see *MICRO-ECONOMICS *sb. pl.*]. **1957** *Economist* 5 Oct. 36/3 The macroeconomic prophets, having seen their forecasts repeatedly falsified, have lost something of their confidence. **1961** G. ACKLEY *Macroecon. Theory* i. 4 Macroeconomics deals with economic affairs 'in the large'. It concerns the over-all dimensions of economic life. **1966** *Listener* 3 Mar. 312/2 Even within the field of what we call macro-economics—the study of what determines the over-all level of activity and other aspects of the economy as a whole—there have been considerable elements of continuity. **1969** *Daily Tel.* 1 Nov. 10 The Government may be difficult to challenge in matters of macro-economics or high finance. When it comes to the practical mechanics of daily life, however, in which a convenient coinage matters a great deal, the public is the best judge. **1971** *New Scientist* 15 Apr. 147/1 The pundits argue about the overall, macro-economic effects of the budget. **1975** *Times* 16 July 15/5 The wonderful world of established macro-economics—no serious unemployment, no intolerable inflation, no controls.

macroërgate, var. *MACRERGATE.

macrogametophyte (mækrogǽmī·tofəit). *Bot.* [f. MACRO- + *gametophyte* (s.v. GAMETE).] = *MEGAGAMETOPHYTE.

1931 *Bot. Gaz.* XCII. 23 (*heading*) Development of the macrogametophyte and embryo of *Daucus carota*. **1938** G. M. SMITH *Cryptogamic Bot.* II. vii. 193 The developing embryo of *Selaginella* always pushes deeply into the macrogametophyte by means of a suspensor.

macroglobulin (mækroglǫ·biŭlin). *Biochem.* [ad. G. *makroglobulin* (attributed to Pedersen and Waldenström by Waldenström 1948, in *Schweiz. Med. Wochenschr.* 25 Sept. 928/2): see MACRO- b and GLOBULIN.] Any of the immunoglobulins of very high molecular weight (about 1,000,000 or more).

1952 J. WALDENSTRÖM in *Adv. Internal Med.* V. 408 Pedersen compared this normally occurring macromolecule with the pathologic so-called 'macroglobulin' found in the disease described by us as macroglobulinemia. **1961** [see *macroglobulinæmia* below]. **1967** *Times* 21 Nov. 3/6 As well as these small antibody molecules, the body produces much larger antibodies, called macroglobulins.

So **maːcroglobulinæ·mia** [ad. G. *makroglobulinämie* (J. Waldenström 1948, in *Schweiz. Med. Wochenschr.* 25 Sept. 928/2)], an excess of macroglobulins in the blood; esp. (more fully *Waldenström's macroglobulinæmia* or *syndrome*) a disease similar to myelomatosis but less often fatal; **maːcroglobulinæ·mic** *a.*

1949 K. PEDERSEN in *Jrnl. Franklin Inst.* CCXLVIII. 570 In a few rare cases of essential macroglobulinemia.., a very high concentration of the 20 S component has been found. **1961** *Lancet* 5 Aug. 289/2 While there can be no doubt that Waldenström's syndrome exists, it seems that such increases in macroglobulins are not confined to a single disease entity. The term macroglobulinæmia will therefore be used in this paper to refer to the presence in the serum of increased amounts of macroglobulins, regardless of the clinical associations. *Ibid.* 290/1 On paper electrophoresis, macroglobulinæmic sera yield patterns which are indistinguishable from those found in multiple myeloma. **1971** D. HAWKINS in S. O. Freedman *Clin. Immunol.* vi. 179 Patients with Waldenstrom's [*sic*] macroglobulinemia may have proteinuria and even nephrotic syndrome.

Maːcrolepido·ptera, *sb. pl. Ent.* [f. MACRO- + LEPIDOPTERA *sb. pl.*] A collective term for the larger butterflies and moths.

1882 W. F. KIRBY *European Butterflies & Moths* p. iii, The present work is designed to provide entomologists.. with a comprehensive illustrated guide to the study of European Macro-Lepidoptera. **1907** R. SOUTH *Moths Brit. Isles* 1st Ser. 6 Quite a number of the species included in that division [*sc.* Micro-lepidoptera] are actually larger than the many kinds that were placed in the other contingent styled Macro-lepidoptera. **1946** *Nature* 12 Oct. 498/2 A well-worked group of insects such as the Macrolepidoptera affords admirable material for faunistic comparisons. **1955** E. B. FORD *Moths* p. xv, The Macro-Lepidoptera are an artificial assemblage, consisting of an arbitrary selection of certain families, and parts of families, without scientific validity. **1972** L. E. CHADWICK tr. *Linsenmaier's Insects of World* 226/2 These families [*sc.* Microlepidoptera] consist of very small species, yet they are in no way separated from the others (the 'Macrolepidoptera').

macrolide (mæ·krŏləid). *Pharm.* [ad. Polish *makrolid* (Z. Katula 1958, in *Postępy Hig. i Med. Dosiviadczalnej* XII. 491): see MACRO- and LACTIDE.] Any of a class of antibiotics containing macrocyclic lactone rings.

1960 *Biol. Abstr.* XXXV. 4202/2 From the fermentation products of various strains of *Streptomyces* there have been isolated several dozen antibiotics, whose common characteristic is a macrocyclic lactic ring. These antibiotics are called macrolides. **1967** [see *ERYTHROMYCIN]. **1968** *New Scientist* 28 Mar. 678/2 Tylosin is a macrolide antibiotic, and organisms resistant to it are often cross-resistant to other macrolides, such as erythromycin, oleandomycin, and spiromycin.

macromolecule (mæːkromǫ·lĭkiŭl, -mōᵘ·lĭkiŭl). *Chem.* [f. MACRO- + MOLECULE.] † **a.** A group of chemical molecules in a crystal bound together in a characteristic shape, which was once believed to account for the symmetry of the crystal. *Obs.*

1886 G. J. STONEY in *Rep. Brit. Assoc. Adv. Sci. 1885* 989 In iron pyrites, FeS_2, the hemihedral form which is characteristic of this mineral..can be traced on from the chemical molecule FeS_2 through a macromolecule which includes six of these as sub-molecules, and which is connected with the other similar macromolecules in a regular way.

b. [ad. G. *makromolekel* (Staudinger & Fritschi 1922, in *Helv. Chim. Acta* V. 788).] A molecule composed of a very large number of atoms and having a high molecular weight (e.g. a molecule of a polymer, a protein, or a nucleic acid).

1935 *Nature* 19 Oct. 626/1 The now generally accepted view that the polymers and condensates must be regarded as constituted of macromolecules formed by the polymerization or condensation of single units. **1957** *New Biol.* XXIII. 66 Proteins are macromolecules normally built up from hundreds or thousands of individual amino acid molecules, and possessing molecular weights in the range of 10,000 to several millions. **1959** *Sunday Times* 5 Apr. 8/6 The macromolecules that are thought to have been the progenitors of living matter. **1969** *Sci. Jrnl.* Nov. 15/3 The two key macromolecules of living things, proteins and nucleic acids, principally play the parts of catalyst and information carriers respectively.

So **maːcromole·cular** *a.*, of, pertaining to, or consisting of a macromolecule or macromolecules.

1931 *Chem. Rev.* VIII. 409 The physical properties of rubber..indicate..that it is macromolecular. **1958** *New Scientist* 26 June 256/2 We know how the macromolecular mechanism of the chromosomes reshuffles the genes when the sperm and the eggs are formed. **1964** G. H. HAGGIS et al. *Introd. Molecular Biol.* iv. 80 The helix is emerging today as a fundamental feature of macromolecular structure at several levels. **1970** *New Statesman* 20 Mar. 406/3 Otto Wichterle, director of Macromolecular Chemistry in Prague.

macronutrient (mæːkroniū·triĕnt). *Plant Physiol.* [f. MACRO- + NUTRIENT *sb.*] Any of the chemical elements (as potassium, nitrogen, calcium, sulphur, phosphorus, or magnesium) which are normally taken up by plants as inorganic salts and which are required for growth and development in relatively large amounts (rather than trace amounts).

1942 *Bot. Gaz.* CIII. 651 An extensive experiment in plant nutrition was designed in order to examine the effects of varying concentrations of macro-nutrient elements in the nutrient medium on the ascorbic-acid content of tomato fruits. **1970** *Nature* 25 July 376/1 The lack of macronutrients especially N, P and K, and sometimes micronutrients.

macropædia (mæːkropī·diă). [f. MACRO- + Gr. παιδεία learning.] The main section of the 15th edition of the *Encyclopædia Britannica* (published in 1974) in which information is presented in the form of extended articles. (Cf. *MICROPÆDIA, *PROPÆDIA.) Hence **macropæ·dic** *a.*

1974 *Times* 12 Jan. 12/1 Finally, there is macropaedia, 19 volumes of substantive essays ranging the world of learning, with articles from 750 to 250,000 words each. Twelve articles are book length. *Ibid.* 16 Jan. 14/4 The *Encyclopaedia Britannica*..proclaimed the imminent publication of a new edition..the macropaedia, supplying knowledge in depth, with 19 volumes. **1974** *Times Lit. Suppl.* 11 Oct. 1120/4 Some sorts of item, those needing more than 750 words but less than full-scale Macropaedic attention,..get Procrustean treatment.

macrophage. Add: Hence **macropha·gic** *a.*

1904 *Brit. Med. Jrnl.* 10 Sept. 562/1 The lymph glands and other macrophagic organs. **1971** *Nature* 5 Feb. 412/2 A sparse scattering of cells, presumably macrophagic or inflammatory.

maːcrophoto·graphy. [f. MACRO- + PHOTOGRAPHY.] Photography in which objects are reproduced larger than or at their actual size but without the degree of magnification that use of a microscope would give.

1889 E. J. WALL *Dict. Photogr.* 114 *Macro-photography*, a term used to denote the enlargement of the negative. **1940** A. L. M. SOWERBY *Wall's Dict. Photogr.* (ed. 15) 438 *Macro-photographs*, term applied to photographs of small objects reproduced at or about natural size. Macrophotography occupies a position intermediate between ordinary photography, in which objects are much reduced, and photo-micrography, in which objects are shown greatly enlarged. **1958** *Newnes Compl. Amat. Photogr.* xiv. 147 Macrophotography, showing all the colour variations of a natural subject in close-up, is a fruitful field. **1964** *Times Rev. Industry* Apr. 42/2 Representatives..demonstrating photomicrography, oscillography, macrophotography and general industrial photography to present or potential Polaroid users in industry. **1967** *Pix* 6 May 24 It might be said that photomacrography (or macro-photography) is that area of close-up photography which lies between what can be done by a simple dioptre lens (close-up attachment lens) and what requires the attachment of the camera to a microscope (i.e., photomicrography).

So **ma:cropho·tograph**, a photograph produced by macrophotography.

1900 DORLAND *Med. Dict.* 370/1 *Macrophotograph*, an enlarged photograph. **1933** *Burlington Mag.* Jan. 15/2 A wealth of information is recorded by the X-rays, macrophotographs, micro-photographs and details. **1940** [see above]. **1973** *Sci. Amer.* Feb. 63/2 (Advt.), Macrophotographs (formerly up to 10 times actual size) can now be made up to 14·8 times actual size.

macropsia (mæ̆krǫ·psiă). *Ophthalm.* [f. MACRO- + *-opsia*, as in MEGALOPSIA.] = MEGALOPSIA.

1890 BILLINGS *Med. Dict.* II. 96/1 *Macropsia*, a condition of vision in which objects appear abnormally increased in size. **1899** [see MICRO- 3]. **1961** A. HUBER *Eye Symptoms in Brain Tumors* i. 24 The usual hallucinations and the phenomena of micropsia and macropsia actually bring us to the symptomology of disturbances of the higher visual functions.

macro-scale (mæ·kroskē̆l). Also **macro scale, macroscale.** [f. MACRO- + SCALE *sb.*³] A large or macroscopic scale; *spec.* in *Chem.*, the scale of macroanalysis.

Macro is freq. apprehended as an adj. qualifying *scale* (cf. *MACRO- 2).

1931 J. W. BROWN in C. A. Mitchell *Recent Adv. Analytical Chem.* II. xv. 304 Developments in the application of general macro-scale chemical methods of qualitative and quantitative analysis to amounts of material 50, 100 or 1,000 times smaller. **1941** J. H. REEDY *Elem. Qualitative Analysis* (ed. 3) 2 Formerly chemical analysis was carried out on a 'macro' scale, using considerable amounts of material. **1964** N. G. CLARK *Mod. Org. Chem.* xxiv. 496 Quantitative analysis was originally designed to be performed on a sample of 0·4–1·0 g for each elemental determination (only carbon and hydrogen are estimated on the same sample); this is called the macro-scale. **1968** C. A. DOXIADIS *Between Dystopia & Utopia* 52 Also, we should not forget that projecting in the macro-scale..is easier than in the micro-scale. It is easier to predict where the future population will settle in one generation than what type of house, or dress, a certain lady is going to like next year. **1970** *Interior Design* Dec. 767/1 Nevertheless, changes will occur, of course, but on a micro- not macro-scale. **1972** *Physics Bull.* Nov. 668/1 A polymer crystallized from the melt will show, on a macroscale, random crystalline orientation.

macroscopic, *a.* Add: Also *fig.*, general, comprehensive, concerned with large units.

1931 M. DOBB in W. Rose *Outl. Mod. Knowl.* II. xiv. 623 Those macroscopic, as distinct from microscopic, issues of the economic order. **1960** E. DELAVENAY *Introd. Machine Transl.* 132 Macroscopic study concentrates on large-scale aspects of phenomena—for instance macroscopic linguistics bears on very general statistical rules of language. **1963** *Listener* 10 Oct. 536/2 The problem is to explain *macroscopic individuality* (in common usage) in terms of microscopic non-individuals, rather than the other way round. **1964** I. L. HOROWITZ *New Sociol.* 3 The rationalists, or 'macroscopic' tendency, concerned with developing 'general theories' of human behavior.

macrosegment (mæ·krosegmĕnt). *Linguistics.* [f. MACRO- + SEGMENT *sb.*] A continuous unit of speech between two pauses, with a single intonation.

1958 C. F. HOCKETT *Course in Mod. Ling.* iv. 38 The stretch of material spoken with a single intonation is called a *macrosegment*. *Ibid.* 41 Though the center of an intonation is by definition the most prominent syllable in the macrosegment, it need not carry the highest pitch. **1963** [see *MICROSEGMENT]. **1964** K. L. PIKE in D. Abercrombie et al. *Daniel Jones* 430 The total phonemic phrase (i.e., the macrosegment including the sum of units between primary juncture,..) in unemotional speech has an overall intonation contour. **1965** *Language* XLI. 244 A major segment (..Hockett's macrosegment) consists of a series of pitch levels terminated by a major juncture. **1971** *Ibid.* XLVII. 739 In the nucleus column for macrosegment and mega-segment, a O symbol occurs with no explanation given.

macroseism (mæ·krosəiz'm). *Geol.* [f. MACRO- + SEISM.] A major earthquake; in mod. use (*rare*), any earthquake, as opposed to an imperceptible earth tremor (cf. *MICROSEISM).

1903 *Sci. Amer.* Suppl. 2 May 22855 Prof. Milne pointed out the distinction which exists between macroseisms, or large earthquakes, and microseisms, or small earthquakes. The former he described as world-shaking disturbances. **1907** *Jrnl. Geol.* XV. 401 Great confusion exists because of the different uses of the terms 'macroseism' and 'microseism', as well as the adjectives derived from them. The usage here is that of both Milne and de Montessus, which makes 'macroseism' apply to the greater disturbance on the ground. **1924** *Bull. Seismol. Soc. Amer.* XIV. 29 Various useful compounds [of *seism*] have been suggested, such as..*macroseism*, de Montessus, 1907, for an ordinary sensible earthquake. **1972** *Gloss. Geol.* (Amer. Geol. Inst.) 424/1 *Macroseism*, a syn. of *earthquake*, as opposed to *microseism*.

Hence **macrosei·smic** *a.*, of or pertaining to a macroseism or (in mod. use) those effects of an earthquake that are perceptible without the aid of instruments; **macrosei·smically** *adv.*

1903 *Nature* 9 July 235/1 This is probably true for other phases of motion, and it has also been shown to exist for macro-seismic disturbances. **1907** *Jrnl. Geol.* XV. 408 Macroseismic origins. **1938** *Nature* 1 Oct. 624/1 The region over which the shock was felt macroseismically extended as far as the island. **1940** *Ibid.* 6 Jan. 14/1 On the basis of the macroseismic data, the accompanying sketch map showing the isoseismal lines has been constructed. **1947** K. E. BULLEN *Introd. Theory Seismol.* xv. 252 Macroseismic data..usefully supplement the data obtained from seismographs. **1973** *Nature* 17 Aug. 384/2 Fairly complete pictures of what are now termed the macroseismic aspects of Britain's larger earthquakes.

macrosmatic, *a.* Delete '*rare*' and substitute for def.: *Zool.* Having well-developed olfactory organs. Also *fig.* (Add earlier and later examples.)

1890 W. TURNER in *Jrnl. Anat. & Physiol.* XXV. 106, I propose..to arrange the Mammalia in relation to the development of the olfactory apparatus into three groups: —(a) Macrosmatic, where the organs of smell are largely developed, a condition which is found..in the majority of mammals. [Etc.] **1894** *Proc. Zool. Soc.* 9 *Echidna*..is, to use Turner's nomenclature, 'macrosmatic'. **1924** *Jrnl. Comparative Neurol.* XXXVII. 318 Even macrosmatic animals like dogs and fishes locate odorous substances by random seeking reactions, not by direct orientation. **1962** *Science Survey* III. 260 Cats and dogs, most of the predators, rodents and deer, and many others are called macrosmatic because a large part of their nasal labyrinths are covered with a special olfactory epithelium. **1968** *Times* 5 Oct. 20/7 [Orwell is] a macrosmatic writer tracking down the stench of hypocrisy or the gangrene of intellectual treachery. **1971** *Nature* 16 Apr. 432/1 Groddeck argued that man is as macrosmatic as the dog.

macrospore. a. Substitute for def.: = *megaspore* (s.v. *MEGA-). (Add further examples.)

1955 G. M. SMITH *Cryptogamic Bot.* (ed. 2) II. x. 281 The heterospory was pronounced [in the fossil fern *Archaeopteris*], the macrospores having a diameter about ten times that of microspores. **1965** [see *megaspore* s.v. *MEGA-]. **1974** *Mycopathologia et Mycologia Applicata* LIII. 56 Some fungi..produce two spore states which are similar in type but differ in size. The large septate spores are frequently referred to as macrospores and the smaller, nonseptate spores as microspores. The term macrospore is also used infrequently as synonymous with chlamydospore... This latter usage seems undesirable.

macrosporophyll (mæ:krospǫ·rŏfil). *Bot.* [f. MACRO- + *sporophyll* (s.v. SPORO-).] = *megasporophyll* (s.v. *MEGA-).

1888 *Encycl. Brit.* XXIV. 130/2 Carpel = leaf bearing macrosporangia (macrosporophyll). **1955** G. M. SMITH *Cryptogamic Bot.* (ed. 2) II. viii. 201 According to the nature of their sporangia, the sporophylls are called macrosporophylls and microsporophylls.

ma·crostructure. Also **macro-structure.** [f. MACRO- + STRUCTURE *sb.*] Large-scale or overall structure; *spec.* the structure of a metal that is visible (on polished and etched surfaces) to the naked eye or under low magnification.

1920 *Glasgow Herald* 18 Dec. 4 The lecturer spoke of microscopical methods, of macro-structure, and dealt with the variation of physical properties of steel. **1930** *Engineering* 14 Mar. 357/1 Macrostructure of cast alloys. **1960** E. H. GOMBRICH *Art & Illusion* xi. 365 Van Gogh's own [accent] can be forged with relative ease. But then his swirling lines still belong to the macrostructure of his style. **1964** *English Studies* XLV. (Suppl.) 180 Bogard also rejects the possibility of Shakespeare having influenced the macro-structure of Webster's tragedies.

b. *concr.*

1956 *Nature* 14 Jan. 81/1 The protein and its associated copper bonds..are stable or protected in highly organized macrostructures such as mammalian melanin granules.

So **ma:crostru·ctural** *a.*

1893 [see *MICROSTRUCTURAL *a.*]. **1963** J. WIESENFARTH *Henry James & Dramatic Analogy* i. 15 One of the principles of James's dramatized novel is that it should always represent. Such macrostructural devices as scenes and pictures..are integral elements by which this ideal is realized. **1964** *English Studies* XLV. (Suppl.) 188 It is strange that no one appears to have taken much interest in the macro-structural relations between his plays and those of other Elizabethan and Jacobean dramatists. **1974** B. JESSOP *Traditionalism, Conservatism & Brit. Political Culture* ii. 42 This requires macrostructural analysis as well as survey analysis.

macula. Add: **1.** *Anat.* Any of various structures which have the appearance of a spot; *spec.* the *macula lutea* (see below).

1901 *Phil. Trans. R. Soc.* B. CXCIV. 74 Fundus oculi (right eye) of the Lemurine Dourocouli. The macula is present, but the macula ring has disappeared. **1932** S. ZUCKERMAN *Social Life Monkeys* x. 153 Since the eyes of the lower mammal are usually set more to the sides than to the front of the head..a specially sensitive area or macula is not developed. **1952** *Sci. News* XXIII. 73 When an object is fixed, the eyes are directed towards it in such a way that it is focused on the central spot of the retina—the area for acute vision, known as the macula. **1964** [see *CRISTA].

2. *Anat.* and *Path.* Used in various mod.L. collocations, as **macula densa** [(K. W. Zimmermann 1929, in *Zeitschr. f. mikrosk.-anat. Forschung* XVIII. 529), f. L. *densus* thick, dense], a small mass of cells of uncertain function closely associated with the juxtaglomerular cells; **macula lutea** [L. *luteus* yellow], an oval, yellowish area near the centre of the retina, where visual acuteness is most pronounced; the yellow spot.

1836–9 R. B. TODD *Cycl. Anat. & Physiol.* II. 530/1 Its bottom..presents a sieve-like spot, *macula cribrosa*. **1848** DUNGLISON *Dict. Med. Sci.* (ed. 7) 370/1 *Foramen centrale et limbus luteus retinæ*; the central foramen and yellow spot of the retina; discovered by Sömmering. Macula lutea. **1857** *Ibid.* (rev. ed.) 560/2 *Maculæ albæ*, white spots, seen on serous membranes..and which appear to be the result of previous inflammatory action. **1942** *Lancet* 3 Oct. 394/2 Zimmerman [*sic*] first recognised the different appearance of the cells of the distal tubule most closely applied to the afferent arteriole in its juxtaglomerular portion. In this part, the ordinary tubular cells seem aggregated, and become in some species much higher and more columnar. Because of this grouping together of nuclei, and the impression of increased density of epithelial cells produced, Zimmerman called this the macula densa. **1952** Macula densa [see *JUXTAGLOMERULAR *a.*]. **1962** *Gray's Anat.* (ed. 33) 1302 The pyramid and adjoining part of the elliptical recess [of the internal ear] are perforated by a number of holes (macula cribrosa superior). **1967** G. M. WYBURN et al. *Conc. Anat.* viii. 206/2 In the centre of the retina is the yellow spot, the macula lutea. **1968** Macula densa [see *JUXTAGLOMERULAR *a.*].

macular, *a.* Add: *spec.* of or pertaining to the *macula lutea*.

1909 M. GREENWOOD in L. Hill *Further Adv. Physiol.* 397 If there is a good deal of macular pigmentation the mixed light undergoes selective absorption. **1932** S. ZUCKERMAN *Social Life Monkeys* x. 166 Monkeys have hands and, what the handed prosimiæ lack, macular vision to guide their manipulations. **1961** R. D. BAKER *Essent. Path.* iv. 49 In Tay–Sachs disease..lipids are collected in ganglion cells..and in the macula of the retina (macular star).

maculate, *ppl. a.* Add: Now chiefly *lit.* and *poet.* (Later examples.)

1919 T. S. ELIOT *Sweeney among Nightingales* in *Poems*, The zebra stripes along his jaw Swelling to maculate giraffe. **1932** W. FAULKNER *Light in August* (1933) xiii. 300 Leaning in the window, breathing the hot still rich maculate smell of the earth. **1964** C. S. LEWIS *Discarded Image* vii. 161 In Shakespeare's *Lucrece* we need to know fully who the 'spotted princess' (719–28) is: Tarquin's Reason, rightful sovereign of his soul, now maculate. **1965** E. BISHOP *Questions of Travel* 22 House, open house.. Darkened and tarnished By the warm touch Of the warm breath, Maculate, cherished, Rejoice!

maculate, *v.* Add: Now *rare.* (Later examples.)

1737 A. BAXTER *Inquiry Human Soul* (ed. 2) II. 202 *Lucretius* tells us maculating dreams accompany youth. *a* **1945** E. R. EDDISON *Mezentian Gate* (1972) ii. 21 That were to maculate the purity of your own proper nature.

maculature. Delete † *Obs.*⁻⁰ and add: **2.** *Engraving* (see quots.).

1904 *Burlington Mag.* V. 70 One of these [impressions of the Hundred Guilder Plate]..is a 'maculature', an impression on a sheet of ordinary paper passed over the plate to remove the ink. **1914** *Brit. Mus. Guide Processes of Engraving* 52 A maculature is another form of weak impression. A copper plate needs to be inked between each impression. Sometimes a second impression is taken from the plate before re-inking, as a means of extracting the remainder of the ink from the lines. This is called a maculature.

maculopapule (mæ:kiŭlopæ·piŭl). *Med.* [f. MACUL(A + -O + PAPULE.] A maculopapular lesion. So **ma:culopa·pular** *a.*, having characteristics of both a macule and a papule; characterized by such lesions.

1900 DORLAND *Med. Dict.* 370/2 Maculopapule. **1905** GOULD *Dict. New Med. Terms* 347/1 Maculopapular. **1912** H. FRENCH *Index Differential Diagn. Main Symptoms* 424 If a macule takes on a slight degree of elevation it is sometimes styled a maculo-papule. *Ibid.* 528 If the lesions, originating as erythematous macules, do not take on the full character of papules, they are said to be maculopapular. **1928** C. P. EMERSON *Physical Diagn.* iii. 82 There may be some maculopapules or true papules on the palms or soles. **1962** *Lancet* 12 May 998/2 He had a scattered maculopapular rash over the trunk. **1968** *Biol. Abstr.* XLIX. 4986/2 The scales are grayish in appearance in chronic squamous maculopapular dermatoses.

macumba (măku·mbă). Also **makumba.** [Pg.] A religious cult-practice of the Negro population of Brazil characterized by sorcery, ritual dancing, and the use of fetishes. Also *attrib.*

1939 *Peabody Bull.* Dec. 8 The frenzy of a *macumba* or the tropical sensuality of a son. **1941** *Survey Graphic* Mar. 181 The religious *macumba* or *candomblé* found in the morros (the hills) combines Catholicism with African and Indian magic rituals. **1948** H. MIELCHE *From Santos to Bahia* vii, Once a year..for four days the city surrenders to the spell of Makumba. **1951** SMITH & MARCHANT *Brazil* v. 145 Brazilian *macumbas* and *candomblés* are undergoing rapid changes. There is a curious fusion..with other religions and cults, especially with Catholicism and Spiritualism. **1963** *Guardian* 4 June 7/1 Some of the most striking scenes are depictions of the macumba rites. **1964** *Listener* 6 Aug. 211/1 They had penetrated a *macumba* temple in Rio de Janeiro. **1969** J. MANDER *Static Society* vii. 211 The Brazilian North-East, where Voodoo or *makumba* cults flourish. **1971** *Daily Colonist* (Victoria, B.C.) 23 May 33/3 The people of Bahia are..devotees of Macumba, that unique north east Brazilian blend of voodoo and Christianity.

Macushi (măkū·ʃi). Also **Macusi. a.** A Carib Indian people inhabiting Guyana (formerly

British Guiana) and Brazil; a member of this people. **b.** The language of this people. Also *attrib.* or as *adj.*

1881 *Encycl. Brit.* XII. 828/2 In British Guiana the Carib tribes are the Ackawais and Caribisi of the coast and forest regions, the Arecumas and Macusis of the savannah region. **1934** E. WAUGH *Handful of Dust* v. 273 She Macushi woman. All these people Macushi people. *Ibid.* 274, I wish I could speak Macushi. **1934** —— *Ninety-two Days* iii. 78 There was a large Indian village. These were sophisticated Macushis who were in constant contact with the ranches. *Ibid.* 89 He was at work on a translation of the scriptures into Macushi. **1974** H. MACINNES *Climb to Lost World* iv. 57 A Macusi Indian..had been taken to England by some missionaries.

macushla (mäku·ʃlä). *Anglo-Ir.* [f. Ir. *mo* my + *cuisle* vein, pulse (of the heart). Cf. *ACUSHLA.] (My) dear heart; darling. (Used as a term of address.)

1887 W. B. YEATS *Dawn-Song* in *Irish Fireside* 5 Feb. 83/3 Wake, *ma cushla*, sleepy-headed. **1918–19** *T. Eaton & Co. Catal.* Fall & Winter 369/2 Vocal Records... Macushla (Tenor). **1946** A. SETON *Turquoise* viii. 115 Sure, and ye're a foine figger of a woman yourself, macushla. **1950** O. NASH *Family Reunion* (1951) 89 In a word, Macushla, There's a scad o' things that to make a house a home it takes.

mad, *sb.*[2] (Earlier and later U.S. examples.)

1834 in J. S. Bassett *Southern Plantation Overseer* (1925) 65, I will be darnde if I can do anything with them and they all ways in the mads. **1867** W. L. GOSS *Soldier's Story* xiv. 258 The Colonel has got his mad up. **1878** E. B. TUTTLE *Border Tales* 50 A grizzly will stand in the middle of the road, growling and getting his mad up. **1916** H. L. WILSON *Somewhere in Red Gap* ii. 57 She kept her mad down better. She set there as nice and sweet as a pet scorpion. **1950** J. D. MACDONALD *Brass Cupcake* (1955) iii. 25 When I want a personality course, friend, I'll go to someone who hasn't a mad on at the world. **1973** M. & G. GORDON *Informant* xxxiii. 128 Well, thanks a lot! I go through hell for you and you take your mad out on me.

mad, *a.* Add: **1. b.** (Earlier examples.)

1605 SHAKES. *Lear* II. iv. 289 O Foole, I shall go mad. **1782** COWPER *Poems* I. 314 What! hang a man for going mad? Then farewell British freedom. **1795–1804** W. BLAKE *Vala* I. in *Compl. Writings* (1972) 265 Thou wilt go mad with horror if thou dost Examine thus Every moment of my Secret hours. **1839** in *Amer. Speech* (1965) XL. 130 O dear, I shall go mad, My husband is so crazy.

fig. **1901** G. B. SHAW *Three Plays for Puritans* Pref. p. xxix, Besides, I have a technical objection to making sexual infatuation a tragic theme. Experience proves that it is only effective in the comic spirit..but..to worship it, deify it, and imply that it alone makes our lives worth living, is nothing but folly gone mad erotically. **1914** —— *Parents & Children* in *Misalliance* p. cii, The sort of Rationalism which says to a child 'You must suspend your judgment until you are old enough to choose your religion' is Rationalism gone mad. **1923** L. W. REESE *Wild Cherry* 21 The weather has gone mad with white. **1949** T. RATTIGAN *Playbill* 56 The lighting for this scene has gone mad.

4. c. (Examples.)

1776 [see *music-mad* s.v. MUSIC *sb.* 12 b]. **1825** H. WILSON *Mem.* I. 41 One of her new admirers, who, being flute-mad, and a beautiful flute player, was always ready. **1848** [see *woman-mad* adj. s.v. WOMAN *sb.* 7]. **1904**, etc. [see *man-mad* adj. s.v. *MAN *sb.*[1] 20]. **1943** E. M. ALMEDINGEN *Frossia* ii. 58 Look at all this promiscuity... They have all gone sex-mad. **1946** K. TENNANT *Lost Haven* (1947) 8 All the family were horse-mad. **1974** 'P. B. YUILL' *Bornless Keeper* xiii. 129 Perhaps you can save her from a sex-mad rabbit and win her undying love.

5. (Further examples.)

1887 F. FRANCIS *Saddle & Mocassin* 111 The more he studied it [*sc.* the bill] the madder he got. **1902** W. JAMES *Varieties Relig. Experience* xi. 264 He can't 'get mad' at any of his alternatives; and the career of a man beset by such an all-round amiability is hopeless. **1925** E. WALLACE *King by Night* viii. 32 Don't get fresh with that girl of mine... You just get mad at her. **1939** [see *CHISEL *v.*[1] 4]. **1956** M. DUGGAN in C. K. Stead *N.Z. Short Stories* (1966) 90 Are you mad at me? Simpson asked. **1962** H. HOOD in R. Weaver *Canad. Short Stories* (1968) 2nd Ser. 210 'Why is Daddy mad?' said Deedee. '*I'm not mad*' **1973** *Black World* June 57/1 Gloria mad at me three days now.

8. Also (*as*) *mad as a cut snake* (Austral.), † *Ajax, a hornet* (U.S.), *a meat axe* (chiefly Austral. and N.Z.), *a wet hen.*

1588 SHAKES. *L.L.L.* IV. iii. 7 By the Lord this Loue is as mad as Aiax, it kils sheepe. **1607** CHAPMAN *Bussy d'Ambois* III. 468 Murther market folkes, quarrell with sheepe, And runne as mad as Aiax. **1732** T. FULLER *Gnomologia* 140 Love is as mad as Ajax; it kills Sheep, so it kills me. **1823** J. DODDRIDGE *Dialogue of Backwoodsman & Dandy* in *Logan* 42 Every body that was not ax'd was mad as a wet hen. **1855** T. C. HALIBURTON *Nat. & Hum. Nat.* I. 85, I feel as mad as a meat axe. **1902** W. N. HARBEN *Abner Daniel* 54 The Colonel is as mad as a wet hen about the whole thing. **1919** MENCKEN *Amer. Lang.* 80 In the familiar simile, *as mad as a hornet*, it [*sc.* the word *mad*] is used in the American sense. **1923** WODEHOUSE *Inimitable Jeeves* xviii. 249 My uncle will be as mad as a wet hen when he finds out that he has been fooled. **1927** *Amer. Speech* II. 360 He was as mad as a hornet when he heard how the election went. **1932** 'W. HATFIELD' *Ginger Murdoch* 30 'But you're mad!' said Mick, 'mad as a cut snake!' **1946** J. FOUNTAIN in *Coast to Coast 1945* 252 The cow's mad—mad as a meat-axe! **1951** S. MACKENZIE *Dead Men Rising* 203 'Mad as a cut snake,' Johnson said admiringly, 'and there's not a better feller in the whole camp.' **1963** *Moderna Språk* LVII. I. 10 *As mad as a cut snake*: 'mad' is used in the sense of 'angry', and the phrase means 'extremely angry'. **1970** D. M. DAVIN *Not Here, Not Now* v. iii. 263 She's mad as a meataxe anyway about the whole idea. **1971** *Wall St. Jrnl.* 22 July W. 1/4 The chicken farmers of Quebec..are as mad as, well, a wet hen.

9. *mad-afraid, -keen* adjs.; **mad minute** *Army slang*, a minute of rapid rifle-fire or frenzied bayonet-practice (see quots.); **mad money** *colloq.*, money for use in an emergency; *spec.* (see quot. 1922); **mad scientist**, a scientist who is mad or eccentric, esp. so as to be dangerous or evil: a stock figure of melodramatic horror-stories; freq. *attrib.*

1895 KIPLING *Seven Seas* (1896) 90 When the steers are mad-afraid. **1949** A. CHRISTIE *Crooked House* xvi. 126 She's mad keen on this detecting stuff. **1974** L. LAMB *Man in Mist* xiii. 88 Derek Boots was not exactly the type to join us here... I was not so mad keen on him. **1917** A. G. EMPEY *Over Top* 298 *Mad minute*, firing fifteen rounds from your rifle in sixty seconds. A man is mad to attempt it, especially with a stiff bolt. **1942** in Baker *Austral. Lang.* (1945) viii. 155 *The mad minute*, bayonet drill. **1945** C. H. B. PRIDHAM *Superiority of Fire* vi. 57 By 1914, many men in each regiment could exceed even twenty rounds in the 'mad minute'. **1964** C. FALLS in S. Nowell-Smith *Edwardian England* xiv. 537 Reservists and young soldiers alike could shoot steadily and accurately at a relatively slow rate for long periods, or in emergency fire what they called their 'mad minute'. **1965** BROPHY & PARTRIDGE *Long Trail* 147 *Mad minute*, a newspaper phrase for British rapid fire during the Retreat from Mons... The name was also applied to the frenzied minute spent charging down the assault course, bayoneting straw-filled dummies, representing enemy soldiers. **1922** *Dialect Notes* V. 148 *Mad money*, money a girl carries in case she has a row with her escort and wishes to go home alone. **1933** PARTRIDGE *Slang To-day & Yesterday* v. 285 *Mad money*, return fare, it being very generally believed by the New Zealand troops..that every English girl infallibly carried her return fare in case her soldier friend became *mad*, i.e., acted with an excessive freedom of manner. **1943** J. STEINBECK *Once there was War* (1959) 136 He has a nest egg or mad money. **1962** L. DEIGHTON *Ipcress File* x. 61, I think he grabs an S.I. now and again when he needs some mad money. **1970** 'D. SHANNON' *Unexpected Death* (1971) ix. 135, I haven't even a dime of mad money with me, hope I don't need it. **1972** O. SELA *Bearer Plot* i. 15, I reached for the wad of notes Keith kept as mad money. **1940** 'N. BLAKE' *Malice in Wonderland* III. xviii. 282 A sort of mad-scientist motive for the whole series of outrages. **1963** 'G. BAGBY' *Murder's Little Helper* (1964) iv. 36 The whole idea smacked too much of some mad-scientist fable out of a comic strip. **1972** B. TURNER *Solden's Women* ix. 82 He would have passed for the mad scientist in one of those films which star giant insects.

mad, *v.* **1.** (Later U.S. examples.)

1873 M. HOLLEY *My Opinions* 249 At the same time it madded some of the Republicans. **1893** 'O. THANET' *Stories Western Town* 31, I madded him first; I was a fool. **1916** H. L. WILSON *Somewhere in Red Gap* vi. 268, I think to find him all madded up and mortified; but he's strangely cheerful for one who has suffered. **1924** W. M. RAINE *Troubled Waters* vi. 59 O' course, it ain't that any of them's afraid to mad that crazy gunman, Tait.

Madagascan (mædăgæ·skăn), *a.* and *sb.* [irreg. f. *Madagascar* (see next) + -AN.] **A.** *adj.* Of or pertaining to Madagascar (now the Malagasy Republic). **B.** *sb.* A native or inhabitant of Madagascar.

1886 *Ibis* 135 The alternative hypothesis..that the Madagascan and Columbian species [of Snipes] have changed. **1890** *Cent. Dict.*, *Madagascan*,..a native or an inhabitant of Madagascar. **1953** L. D. STAMP *Africa* xx. 511 Every Madagascan farm has a few pigs. **1973** *Listener* 20 Sept. 369/1 The Madagascan revolt, in which eighty thousand were killed. **1973** *Country Life* 20 Dec. 2122/2 The Japanese..have developed a real yen for it [*sc.* Beaujolais]. So have the Madagascans, the Tahitians and the Nationalist Chinese.

Madagascar (mædăgæ·skăɹ). The former name of the Malagasy Republic, a large island off the east coast of Africa, used *attrib.* in special collocations, as **Madagascar cat**, the ring-tailed lemur, *Lemur catta*; **Madagascar (clove) nutmeg, manna** (see quots.); **Madagascar periwinkle**, a tropical plant (*Vinca rosea*) with white or rose-coloured flowers.

1900 H. A. BRYDEN *Animals Afr.* 12 Some of these curious lemurs, which are usually known as 'Madagascar Cats'. **1866** LINDLEY & MOORE *Treas. Bot.* I. 28/2 One species, *A[gathophyllum] aromaticum*, grows in Madagascar... The fruit..encloses a kernel of an acrid caustic taste, known as Madagascar clove nutmegs. **1889** *Cent. Dict.*, *Dulcitol*,.. is commercially obtained from an unknown plant in Madagascar, and in the crude state is called *Madagascar manna*. **1821** M. BROWNE *Diary* (1905) 104 There were..myrtles, beautiful campanulas, geraniums, Madagascar periwinkles, etc.

Madagascarian (mædăgæskēᵊ·riăn), *a.* [f. prec. + -IAN] = *MADAGASCAN *a.* Also **Madaga·scarene, Madaga·scrian** *sbs.* = *MADAGASCAN *sb.*

1824 M. A. HEDGE *Radama* iv. 78 The first order is usually composed of those termed the white Madagascrians. **1856** C. NORDHOFF *Merchant Vessel* xix. 246 The natives..are mostly black, the descendents of Madagascarenes. **1875** *Encycl. Brit.* III. 758/2 Madagascar, the Comoros, and the widely-scattered Mascarene Islands constitute a fifth Subregion,..and for this we may most reasonably use the name 'Madagascarian'. **1893** A. NEWTON *Dict. Birds* II. 347 Those [genera] belonging to the insular or Madagascarian Subregion.

‖ **madal** (madā·l). Also **madāla, maddale.** A double-headed drum used in Nepal and eastern India. Cf. *MRIDANGAM.

1914 A. H. F. STRANGWAYS *Mus. Hindostan* ix. 228 The *maddale* (*mṛdānga*-shape) hollowed out of a tree. **1954** J. MASTERS *Bhowani Junction* 329 My Birkhe beat cheerfully on a madal, which is a deep and narrow Gurkha drum. **1960** S. PRAJÑĀNANANDA *Hist. Devel. Indian Mus.* i. 7 The different musical instruments of folk-music like *ekatāra*,..*madāla*,..etc. bear testimony to..the cultural taste and outlook of the peoples of Bengal. **1969** *Illustr. Weekly India* 27 July 33/1 They assemble..and dance—both men and women—to the accompaniment of the *madal* (the Santali drum). **1971** K. KENT in C. Bonington *Annapurna South Face* App. H. 314 Most boys [in Nepal] learn to play the flute and *madal*—a double-ended drum, with one end slightly smaller than the other.

madam, *sb.* Add: **3. c.** (*d*) A brothel-keeper; cf. *MADAME 4. (*e*) Nonsense, humbug. *slang.*

(*d*) *a* **1911** D. G. PHILLIPS *Susan Lenox* (1917) I. xxi. 393 The madam fixes things so that every girl always owes her money. **1912** T. DREISER *Financier* xlvi. 510 In a few moments the 'madam', as the current word characterized this type of woman, appeared. **1918** C. GARNETT tr. *Dostoevsky's White Nights* 117 Before me was standing a person with a stupid smile, the 'madam' herself. **1926** J. BLACK *You can't Win* iv. 30 The following week I called at Madam Kate Singleton's... In a minute the madam came down. **1959** N. MAILER *Advts. for Myself* (1961) 279 A rather remarkable woman who had been the madam of a whorehouse. **1960** AUDEN *Homage to Clio* 85 Henry Adams Was mortally afraid of Madams: In a disorderly house He sat quiet as a mouse. **1962** *Punch* 30 May p. xiii/1 Barbara Stanwyck as Lesbian madam of New Orleans brothel. **1975** *Daily Tel.* (Colour Suppl.) 18 July 7/1 The oldest girl is a woman, maybe Czechoslovakian, maybe the madam.

(*e*) **1927** E. WALLACE *Feathered Serpent* xvii. 218 'I was getting a hundred quid for this job..and I couldn't turn him down.' 'The usual "madam"!' sneered the inspector. 'It's not "madam", Mr. Brown,' said Jerry earnestly, 'though I admit it sounds as likely as cream in skilly; but it's true.' **1932** A. GARDNER *Tinker's Kitchen* 284 Madam = made up story; flattery. **1936** J. CURTIS *Gilt Kid* ii. 18 'What did the old boy say?' 'Just the usual madam.' **1965** *Sunday Times Mag.* 11 July 21 Both sides are expert with the madam—a form of kidology which seems to come naturally to most Merseysiders. **1973** J. WAINWRIGHT *Touch of Malice* 130 It was not the sort of place conducive to putting over a spot of old madam. The normally glib flannel tended to stick in his throat and the guff and eyewash hadn't enough elbow-room to..sound..feasible.

4. (*b*) **madam-shop** [MADAM *sb.* 3], a small shop which sells ready-to-wear clothes for the fashionable woman of mature taste.

1952 *Times Lit. Suppl.* 28 Nov. 778 The juggling with couture dressmakers..and owners of 'madam shops' in order to keep them contented with their share of reporting. **1963** *Harper's Bazaar* Feb. 20/3 The sight of two assistants in one of those little madam shops fitting girdles on to plastic models. **1965** *Guardian* 16 July 8/5 Boutiques are nothing new in Manchester. There is a stalwart 'madam shop' tradition; little shops for women of substance. **1966** H. W. YOXALL *Fashion of Life* viii. 68 The contemporary Madam Shops, so aptly named,..are enjoying a new popularity. **1967** *Guardian* 30 Mar. 5/1 The madam shops... Shops catering for women over 25 who want to dress in fashion, and can afford to.

madame. Add: **4.** = *MADAM *sb.* 3 c (*d*).

1871 *N.Y. Herald* 29 July 6/2 The Madame..sent her to an infamous den in Forsyth Street kept by a Mrs. Hines. **1922** V. WOOLF *Jacob's Room* ix. 171 Only Madame herself..had about her that leer, that lewdness. **1934** A. WOOLLCOTT *While Rome Burns* 157 Visiting the local Maison Tellier..and taking the madame and all her girls out duck-shooting. **1961** M. JONES *Potbank* xxvi. 111 Her behaviour..made me think of a *madame* in the more discreet sort of brothel. **1969** G. GREENE *Trav. with my Aunt* I. viii. 83 There was a discipline in the old-time brothels. The madame..played a rôle similar to that of the headmistress of Roedean. **1975** *Sunday Times* 12 Jan. 37/2 She plays the part of the notorious Xaviera Hollander, New York call-girl and *madame*.

madarosis. (Further examples.)

1902 GOULD & WARREN *Internat. Text-bk. Surg.* (ed. 2) II. xxvii. 864 The affection may go on until nearly all the eye-lashes are lost and the lids left bald—madarosis. **1956** 'H. MACDIARMID' *Stony Limits & Scots Unbound* 39 Nor.. can we..Shut our eyes despite their madarosis of the sun. **1972** A. SORSBY *Mod. Ophthalm.* (ed. 2) II. xx. 557 (*caption*) Leprosy showing lagophthalmos and madarosis of brows and lashes.

madbrain. A. *sb.* Delete † *Obs.* and add later example.

1876 G. MEREDITH *Beauch. Career* II. xvi. 285 He began to think her lost beyond hope, embarked for good and all with the madbrain.

madcapery (mæ·dkæpĕri). Also **madcappery.** [f. MADCAP *sb.* + -ERY.] The behaviour of a madcap; mischievous or reckless conduct.

1905 D. SLADEN *Playing Game* xii. 139, I wondered what madcapery Rich had been up to. **1966** *Punch* 20 April 586/2 Seeing the two plays in such quick succession ..does provide an opportunity to follow in one long sweep the two stages of Prince Hal's progress from madcappery to maturity.

maddening, *ppl. a.* Add later examples of the sense 'irritating, annoying, vexatious'.

1896 A. Beardsley *Let.* c 25 Oct. (1971) 188 Dent must be simply maddening. **1925** N. Coward *Vortex* II. 55 'Have you only one set, Florence?'.. 'Yes, isn't it maddening? Clara promised to bring hers down but forgot.' **1944** —— *Middle East Diary* 36 So many of my Naval friends are here and it's maddening that I shall have no time to go and visit them. **1947** A. Huxley *Let.* 19 Jan. (1969) 565 There will still be revisions to do on the screen play..maddening work, resembling jig saw puzzles rather than literature.

madder, *sb.*[1] Add: **4. madder-bleach,** a special method of bleaching cotton; **madder-print,** madder-printed cloth or cotton (*Cent. Dict.* 1890).

1909 L. A. Olney *Textile Chem. & Dyeing* II. 58 The Madder Bleach... In calico printing..where a particularly clear and white ground is desired this form of bleach is used.

maddery (mæ·dəri), *a. Nonce-wd.* [f. Madder *sb.*[1] + -y[1] 2.] = Madderish *a.*

1873 G. M. Hopkins *Note-bks. & Papers* (1937) 186 Its dewlaps and bellyings painted with a maddery campion-colour.

madding. Add: **1.** Esp. in phrase *far from the madding crowd* (see quot. 1749 in Dict.), a conventional phrase denoting a secluded place removed from public notice.

1874 Hardy (*title*) Far from the madding crowd. **1889** J. K. Jerome *Three Men in Boat* i. 9, I..suggested that we should seek out some retired and old-world spot, far from the madding crowd, and dream away a sunny week among its drowsy lanes. **1944** F. Clune *Red Heart* 14 People..far from the madding crowds, west of the Darling River. **1952** G. Sarton *Hist. Sci.* I. xvi. 397 He [*sc.* Plato] did not want to teach in the streets and markets, but on the contrary in a place that was sufficiently distant from the madding crowd and secluded.

mad-doctor. For def. read: A physician who specializes in disorders of the mind; a psychiatrist. (Add further examples.)

1852 Dickens & Wills *Curious Dance round Curious Tree* in *Househ. Words* 17 Jan. 385/1 Nothing was too wildly extravagant, nothing too monstrously cruel, to be prescribed by mad-doctors. **1877** J. M. Granville *Care & Cure of Insane* I. 2 It must never be forgotten that the so-called 'mad doctors' have been the first to press this truth on the profession. **1890** (*title*) Mad doctors by one of them, being a defence of asylum physicians. **1972** C. Achebe *Girls at War* 9 That humble practitioner who did the miracle became overnight the most celebrated mad-doctor of his generation.

made, *ppl. a.* Add: **3. b.** Of bills of exchange: (see quots.).

1868 E. Seyd *Bullion & Foreign Exch.* 89 The foregoing Foreign Bills of Class 2 are called *drawn* Bills, being usually negotiated from the Drawer direct to a London Foreign Banker; but where such drafts are made in the Country, and sent up to a correspondent in London, who then negotiates the same with his own Indorsement on them, they are called *made* Bills. *Ibid.* 90 Bills drawn abroad and payable abroad, but negotiated in the United Kingdom, are also *made* Bills.

5. b. *made to measure*: see Measure *sb.* 2 a; also (usu. with hyphens) *attrib.*; *made to order*: see Order *sb.* 24 c; also (usu. with hyphens) *attrib.*; so *made-to-order-ness*, the state or condition of being made to order.

1960 *Sunday Express* 24 July 12/6 Made-to-measure tweed skirt. **1973** *Guardian* 26 Feb. 3/3 Good lighting is made-to-measure lighting..the result of applying a lighting engineer's expertise to your particular office problem. **1974** *Country Life* 3–10 Jan. 58/1 Made-to-measure..corsets, brassieres, maternity foundation. **1921** *Daily Colonist* (Victoria, B.C.) 3 Apr. 9/1 (Advt.), Ladies' and gents' smart made-to-order spring suits made with particular care to every detail. **1947** 'G. Orwell' *England your England* (1953) 8 There was the made-to-order stuff which I produced quickly. **1973** *Amer. Speech* 1969 XLIV. 277 Or the phrase used in a television advertisement for 'Sentry—the made-to-order insurance'. **1973** R. Stout *Please Pass the Guilt* (1974) ii. 11 He sat..in his made-to-order chair. **1923** *Glasgow Herald* 8 Nov. 4 There is an air of cynical made-to-order-ness about the second [poem].

7. c. *to have* (*got*) *it made*, to be sure of success; to have it easy, to have no more obstacles to overcome. *colloq.* (orig. *U.S.*).

1955 in *Amer. Speech* May 118. **1960** J. Updike *Rabbit, Run* (1961) 108 Say. You really think you have it made. **1961** J. Heller *Catch-22* (1962) vi. 51, I had it made, I tell you. Fifty grand a year I was knocking down, and almost all of it tax-free. **1967** A. Diment *Dolly Dolly Spy* vi. 85 The money you earn is fantastic... You've got it made, mate. **1968** —— *Gt. Spy Race* iii. 45 She had..big, well-proportioned hips. I tell you, if the derrière gets with-it again this bird had it made. **1972** 'H. Howard' *Nice Day for Funeral* iii. 49 This was the kind of set-up half the dames I know would've given their back teeth for. I had it made. **1974** *Times Lit. Suppl.* 8 Mar. 227/2 The abstentions of 1972 were due not to this disillusionment but to an overwhelming conviction that Mr Nixon had it made, so why take time..to go out and vote?

9. *made-over* (examples); **made-up,** (*e*) of articles of trade, ready-made, not made to measure; also **made-up tie,** a tie, esp. a bow-tie, with a fixed bow or knot; (*f*) of stakes, arranged after the original programme of races is drawn up; (*g*) of a book, with its deficiencies made good by the insertion of a leaf, etc., from another copy of the same edition.

1912 R. A. Wason *Friar Tuck* xxx. 208 When Jim came back he was a made-over man, and everyone asked him if he had religion. **1916** J. E. Wells *Man. Writings Middle Eng.* 294 A copy, and perhaps a somewhat made-over copy of an earlier text. **1929** W. K. Gregory *Our Face from Fish to Man* II. 153 Even the most imposing human faces are but made-over fish traps. **1967** A. Lewin *Unaltered Cat* I. ii. 24 A place very like her own, a made-over brownstone only two blocks away. **1725** M. W. Montagu *Let.* c 10 June (1966) II. 53, I wish you would lay out part of my Money in a made up Mantua and petticoat. **1849** *Theatrical Programme* 16 July 55 (Advt.), The immense patronage they have received this season in their made-up skirt-rooms. **1876** *Coursing Calendar* 110 In the made-up stakes for puppies Mr. Farmer's brace..made a good display. **1883** *Graphic* 14 Apr. 395/4 (Advt.), A full assortment of made-up articles of the best and most suitable description. **1895** *New Rev.* June 631 It is an odious fact that this country spends about a million and a half a year in the purchase of made-up clothes from Germany. **1913** C. Mackenzie *Sinister St.* I. II. ii. 171 The boys..bought made-up bow-ties of purple and pink that were twisted round the stud with elastic. **1913** R. B. McKerrow in *Trans. Bibliogr. Soc.* XII. 303 The cruder sort of made-up copies that one often finds in the second-hand market. **1929** J. Buchan *Courts of Morning* 25 Sandy in a greasy dress suit and a made-up black tie. **1952** J. Carter *Bks. & Bk.-Collectors* (1956) vi. ii. 195 The..language of book-collectors..is thickly encrusted with jargon... 'Made-up,' says one, with a sniff. 'Q6 is a cancel as usual,' says another. **1972** M. Gilbert *Body of Girl* v. 52 He was wearing a blue suit,..a flannel shirt and a made-up bow tie.

10. Colloq. phr. *made of money*, extremely rich, very wealthy.

1849 D. W. Jerrold (*title*) A man made of money. **1855** Mrs. Gaskell *North & South* I. xii. 143 'I shall order horses.' 'Nonsense, John. One would think you were made of money.' **1876** Trollope *Prime Minister* III. xv. 254 You're living here in a grand house, and your father's made of money. **1895** Mrs. H. Ward *Story B. Costrell* ii. 35 You don't care, not you!—one 'ud think yer were made o' money. **1918** C. Mackenzie *Early Life Sylvia Scarlett* II. ii. 292 He asked if I thought he was made of money and could buy top-hats like matches. **1967** E. Coxhead *Thankless Muse* iv. 103 'Then why don't we keep it?' 'You think Clare's made of money, I suppose?' **1975** C. Egleton *Skirmish* x. 104 Book him into a hotel..but nothing fancy, we're not made of money.

Madeira[1]**.** Add: **2. c.** Madeira sauce, a rich brown sauce made with Madeira and served with braised or roast meats.

1872 R. C. Smith *Madeira & its Associations*, The lively Frenchman..dwells upon the virtues of delicious Madeira. He offers at once to despatch his grandfather in Madeira sauce. *A la Sauce Madère on mangerait son grandpère.* **1877** *Cassell's Dict. Cookery* 57/1 *Beef, Lumber, in Madeira Sauce*..Prepare a sauce with brown stock or broth, some butter, flour, cayenne pepper, salt, pepper, and a glass of Madeira. **1946** G. Millar *Horned Pigeon* xix. 305 She followed this with kidneys and a Madeira sauce. **1956** L. Diat *French Cooking for Home* 43 Boiling spoils the flavour of Madeira Sauce.

madeleine (mæ·dlēⁱn). Also **madeline.** [F., prob. f. name of *Madeleine* Paulmier, 19th-c. French pastry-cook.] A (kind of) small rich cake baked in a shell-shaped tin. Sometimes (with allusion to Proust, quot. 1922) taken as typical of something that strongly evokes memories or nostalgia. Also, in English cooking, a kind of baked pudding or small fancy cake.

1845 E. Acton *Mod. Cookery* xviii. 473 (*heading*) Madeleine puddings. (To be served cold.) **1846** C. E. Francatelli *Mod. Cook* 404 Madeleines..are made with the same kind of batter as Genoese cakes, to which currants, dried cherries, candied peel or angelica, may be added. **1902** G. H. Ellwanger *Pleasures of Table* vi. 169 Dumas tells the story of the excellent cake called madeleine, an entremets which all who have been in France will remember. **1922** C. K. S. Moncrieff tr. *Proust's Swann's Way* I. 61 And suddenly the memory returns. The taste was that of the little crumb of madeleine..my aunt Léonie used to give me, dipping it first in her own cup of..tea. **1939** O. Lancaster *Homes Sweet Homes* 42 The flavour of Bordeaux pigeon summons with all the completeness of Proust's tea-soaked madeleine an unforgettable cloud of Mons. Doré's angels hovering over the Colosseum. **1948** *Good Housek. Cookery Bk.* 577 Dip a cherry in a little jam, place on top of each madeleine and put on 2 leaves of angelica. **1958** *Spectator* 1 Aug. 174/1 We all have our little fragment of *madeleine* that brings back a dearly remembered but half-forgotten past. **1960** E. David *French Provincial Cooking* 32 At the little town of Commercy originated the small, fragile, shell-shaped cakes called madeleines so beloved of French children... (How the English madeleine, a sort of castle pudding covered in jam and coconut, with a cherry on the top, came by the same name is something of a mystery.) **1962** *Punch* 21 Mar. 462/1 It may be said—if it may then Proust has certainly said it—that the intensity of nostalgic emotion has little to do with the quality of the material which evokes it. (I dare say that madeleine cakes are very nasty.) **1972** 'M. Innes' *Open House* I. ii. 12 He might have been Proust's Marcel, hard upon imbibing the displeasing little sopped *madeleine* which brought his childhood flooding back to memory.

‖**madérisé** (maderize), *a.* [Fr.] Of wine, affected with maderization (see below). So **ma·derize** [F. *madériser*] *v. intr.*, to become *madérisé.*

1941 Schoonmaker & Marvel *Amer. Wines* 219 The French also describe a white wine which has been too long in barrel..as *madérisé*, or 'madeiraed'. **1950** O. A. Mendelsohn *Earnest Drinker* xx. 189 When a white wine starts to go a brownish colour and gets a curious..musty smell about it, it is called *Madérisé* and means that the wine is on the road downhill. **1958** A. L. Simon *Dict. Wines* 105/2 *Madérisé*, the polite French word to use to describe the bottle stink of a wine which has been kept too long. **1961** W. E. Massee *Wines & Spirits* 10 A white table wine that has maderized is undrinkable. **1972** H. W. Yoxall *Enjoyment of Wine* v. 39–40 White wine deepens its tone with age and becomes what they call maderisé, though not all white wines that are so darkened acquire the musty taste of a truly maderized wine.

maderization (mădīərəizēⁱ·ʃən). [ad. F. *madérisation* (also used), f. Madeira[1] 2 + -ization.] A brown discoloration in white wines often appearing after overlong or unsuitable storage.

1951 R. Postgate *Plain Man's Guide to Wine* iv. 76 The only noticeable change is an occasional darkening of colour, called *madérisation.* **1952** H. W. Allen *White Wines & Cognac* ii. 53 Still without a hint of *madérisation* and golden as sunlight. **1952** A. Lichine *Wines of France* i. 7 A characteristic called maderization after Madeira wine, whose colour they take. **1959** W. James *Word-bk. Wine* 113 *Maderization*, a flaw in white wines caused by their absorption of too much oxygen during vinification or maturation; the wine turns rusty in the bottle, and takes on a brown colour and a musty, flat, taste; when much advanced there may be some resemblance to a very poor madeira. **1971** *Times Lit. Suppl.* 12 Mar. 297/2 Such a bouquet suggests maderization, and I cannot believe that a lover of German wines would enjoy this very much. **1973** *Vogue* 15 Apr. 153/3 Old champagne can be great. It goes brown with age, and turns sweeter and heavier—a condition known as 'maderization'.

madhead[2]**.** After '*Obs.*' add 'exc. *dial.*'

1959 *New Statesman* 26 Dec. 904/3 He'd quietened down now though, and butter wouldn't melt in his mouth, he said..after all his stories about him being a madhead. **1959** I. & P. Opie *Lore & Lang. Schoolch.* ix. 170 Red heads attract a barrage of nicknames..glow-worm, mad head [etc.].

madhouse. Add: **a.** (Later examples.)

1916 G. B. Shaw *Androcles & Lion* Pref. p. lxiii, One person in every five dies in a workhouse, a public hospital, or a madhouse. **1922** Joyce *Ulysses* 358 The nobleman with the foreign name..had to have her put into a madhouse, cruel only to be kind. **1929** F. N. Hart *Hide in Dark* v. 182 It seems fairly essential to get at what facts are available..if some of us aren't to wind up in a madhouse. **1955** G. Willans *Fasten your Lapstraps!* i. 23 There is a dull sound of barley sugar being crunched and gum chewed—the whole place..is like a Victorian madhouse. **1971** J. Namier *Lewis Namier* xiii. 234 To L insanity was man's ultimate degradation; a madhouse, however well appointed, was hell.

b. *fig.* A scene of uproar or confusion bewildering to the onlooker.

1919 G. B. Shaw *Heartbreak Ho.* III. 95 Is this England, or is it a madhouse? **1929** H. Crane *Let.* 7 Feb. (1965) 335 This City [*sc.* Paris], as you know, is the most interesting madhouse in the world. **1946** E. O'Neill *Iceman Cometh* (1947) III. 160 God, I'm glad I'm leaving this madhouse! **1956** R. Braddon *Nancy Wake* xiv. 155 The Moulins railway junction was a mad-house of torn and tangled lines and shattered rolling stock. **1973** *Radio Times* 26 Apr. 48/1 They [*sc.* chefs] roast and stew and bake in a kind of madhouse of shouted commands, cancelled orders and frayed tempers.

Ma·dison. orig. *U.S.* [Origin unknown.] A group dance, popular in the 1950s and 1960s.

1962 *Listener* 27 Dec. 1074/2 Girls in traditional Kimono dancing the twist or the Madison. **1966** *Punch* 25 May 768/2 We found the Bishop and Dolly Girl an hour later. She was teaching him the rudimentary technique of The Madison. **1968** M. & J. Stearns *Jazz Dance* 4 Before and during Presley's initial success, the first wave of dances became popular. Group dances such as the Madison and the Birdland arrived first. **1969** C. Booker *Neophiliacs* vii. 177 In the same month of October [1962]..the unknown Beatles first joined the fashionable beat of the Madison in the charts.

Madison Avenue (mæ·disən æ·vĭniu). The name of a street in New York City, which is the centre of the American advertising business; hence *allusively*, (American) advertising generally, the advertising business; *collect.*, American advertising agents. Also *attrib.*

1955 H. Kurnitz *Invasion of Privacy* (1956) v. 39 A tall, lean young man..dressed in the dark grey and neat stripes of a Madison Avenue advertising executive. **1957** J. Blish *Fallen Star* ii. 33 We had..Madison Avenue gossip..for lunch. **1958** J. K. Galbraith *Affluent Society* xviii. 200 The violent mores of Hollywood and Madison Avenue. **1959** N. Mailer *Advts. for Myself* (1961) 404, I kept expecting him to go Madison Avenue, I was certain he would sell out sooner or later. **1959** V. Packard *Status Seekers* (1960) i. 12 Madison Avenue has been busily trying to understand our tastes and buying behaviour. **1960** *Guardian* 15 Oct. 6/5 An Eisenhowerish vocabulary which..sometimes has more of a Madison Avenue ring. **1961** [see *Harley]. **1970** *Times* 24 Aug. 15/5 Britain's Madison Avenue widely predicted that after a decent interval, *Ad Weekly* would also attempt something spectacular. **1972** *Jazz & Blues* Sept. 9/2 We know what's wanted. I had something to offer Madison Avenue.

madly, *adv.* Add: **2.** Colloq. uses. **a.** Passionately, fervently (cf. quot. 1590 in Dict.).

1767 BOSWELL *Let.* 30 Mar. (1924) I. 108, I was so madly in love as to think of marrying her. 1880 O. C. STONE *Few Months New Guinea* iv. 55 The natives..seem madly fond of *kuku* [*sc.* tobacco], and would pawn their very clothes for it if they wore any. 1888 W. S. GILBERT *Trial by Jury* 12, I love him—I love him—with fervour increasing, I worship and madly adore. 1924 A. CHRISTIE *Man in Brown Suit* ii. 19, I could never marry a man unless I loved him madly. 1959 [see *BEETLE *sb.*[2] 2 b]. 1974 M. CECIL *Heroines in Love* v. 151 Upper-class heroines.. were never 'in love', always 'madly in love'.

b. Extremely, very, 'awfully'.

1888 H. JAMES *Reverberator* II. i. 16, I was not madly impatient to see you married. 1902 G. BELL *Lett.* (1927) I. vii. 130 It is a madly interesting place. 1935 N. MARSH *Enter Murderer* ii. 31 She's madly keen on criminology. 1937 C. CONNOLLY in L. Russell *Press Gang!* 79 Hubert said Balliol was perfect for case-histories like mine, but I realised I should find it madly ungay. 1945 N. MITFORD *Pursuit of Love* ix. 73 It's madly wearing to the optic nerve centres. 1954 J. B. PRIESTLEY *Magicians* i. 20 Mavis..brightened up like a touched-off firework and was at once, in her own phrase, 'madly gay'. 1967 [see *DRAGGY *a.* b]. 1974 *Radio Times* 3 Jan. 5/4 Mr Williams's facial mobility is *madly* impressive.

mado (mā·do). *Austral.* [Aboriginal name.] A small marine fish, *Atypichthys mado* (or *A. strigatus*), found in southern Australian and northern New Zealand waters.

1898 E. E. MORRIS *Austral Eng.* 277/2 *Mado*, a Sydney fish, *Therapon cuvieri*, Bleek; called also *Trumpeter-Perch*. 1906 D. G. STEAD *Fishes of Australia* 134 The mado is a handsome little fish, having alternate brown and yellow longitudinal stripes along the body. 1958 *Austral. Encycl.* V. 458/2 *Mado*, a small fish (*Atypichthys mado*) very common round wharf-piles and in inlets along the coasts of the southern half of Australia. 1960 DOOGUE & MORELAND *N.Z. Sea Anglers' Guide* 229 Mado..yellow with longitudinal brown streaks..Distribution: North Island south to about East Cape. Also occurs in Australian waters.

Madonna. Add: **4.** *Madonna-like* adj.; **Madonna blue**, a shade of deep blue; **Madonna lily** (earlier and later examples).

[1930 MAERZ & PAUL *Dict. Color* 198/2, 1917 Madonna.] 1932 A. CHRISTIE *Peril at End House* vii. 85 She was wearing a gown of Madonna blue. 1935 *Times* 2 Oct. 17/4 A Madonna-blue lining. 1971 N. FREELING *Over High Side* II. 110 Twilight had fallen, of a pure madonna blue. 1850 MRS. GASKELL *Let.* 24 Jan. (1966) 101 She was a madonna-like person with a face..full of thought and gentle love. 1895 G. B. SHAW *Let.* 20 Mar. (1965) 502 You must..be sweet..and Madonna like. 1909 M. DIVER *Candles in Wind* I. iv. 40 The soft brown hair..giving a Madonna-like air of purity to the oval face. 1966 'R. STANDISH' *Widow Hack* vi. 65 She has large, generous features which compose themselves in a Madonna-like serenity. 1877 E. S. PHELPS *Story of Avis* ix. 172 An exquisite motion which an artist..would not have wasted..on anything less than a Madonna lily. 1963 W. BLUNT *Of Flowers & Village* 173 My whole room is scented by a great pot of Madonna lilies. 1974 *Country Life* 21 Mar. 632/1 A child in a bonnet creeps shyly down the path, dwarfed by the Madonna lilies.

Madras. Add: **1.** Also, **Madras cotton**, cotton fabric produced in Madras, *esp.* the brightly checked or striped cottons the colours of which run together in laundering. Also **Madras** *ellipt.*

1890 L. HEARN *Two Years in French West Indies* 216 The making-up of the Madras into a turban is called 'tying a head'. 1897 *Sears, Roebuck Catal.* 216/3 French Madras is a fine soft finished fabric with the colors woven through. .. Light colors, plaids or stripes. 1921 *Daily Colonist* (Victoria, B.C.) 22 Oct. 7/2 (Advt.), 50-Inch Colored Madras at $1.50 a Yard..this Madras will make beautiful side curtains. 1942 J. HOYE *Staple Cotton Fabrics* vii. 148 When made in fancy weaves and of fine yarns, they are known as Madras ginghams. 1962 L. DEIGHTON *Ipcress File* xxviii. 177 A bright Madras jacket. 1964 HOLLEN & SADDLER *Textiles* (ed. 2) 153/2 The imported Indian madras, today, is handwoven with white warp and colored filling 'guaranteed to bleed'. 1968 H. WAUGH *Con Game* iii. 34 Three pairs of men's shoes and one wrinkled Madras jacket. 1972 *Vogue* Feb. 86 Madras checked safari jacket, unlined seersucker.

Madrasi (mădræ·si), *a.* and *sb.* Also **Madrassi, -assee.** [Urdu *Madrasī*, f. *Madras* the city in southern India.] **A.** *adj.* Of or pertaining to Madras. **B.** *sb.* A native or inhabitant of Madras.

1878 *Chambers's Jrnl.* Feb. 115/1 English, after the rickety fashion of a Madrassee, Sam spoke fairly enough. 1879 H. HARTIGAN *Stray Leaves* 2nd Ser. 129 While ruminating, a Madrasi servant came out. 1921 *Contemp. Rev.* Sept. 291 'Western civilisation,' said an eminent Madrasi the other day, 'has led to war.' 1924 *Blackw. Mag.* Aug. 227/2 The officer commanding..Madrasi Christians, will not admit this. 1971 R. RUSSELL tr. *Ahmad's Shore & Wave* v. 49 His partner, a solemn-looking, bald Madrasi, was suffering all this in silence.

madrigalesque (mædrigăle·sk), *a.* [f. MADRIGAL *sb.* + -ESQUE; cf. F. *madrigalesque* f. It. *madrigalesco*.] Having the features or characteristics of madrigals.

1911 *Encycl. Brit.* XVII. 295/2 Long afterwards we occasionally meet with the word again, when a 17th or 18th century composer sets to some kind of accompanied singing a poem of madrigalesque character. 1924 W. H. HADOW *Music* iv. 99 A pleasant light comedy set to madrigalesque music with a real sense of characterization.

madrilene (mædrilī·n, -lē·n), *sb.* Also **madrilène.** [ad. F. (*consommé à la*) *madrilène*, f. Sp. *Madrileño, -leña* of Madrid.] A clear soup which is usually served cold (see quot. 1907).

1907 G. A. ESCOFFIER *Guide Mod. Cookery* xiii. 224 *Consommé a la madrilène.* Add four oz. of raw tomato and one oz. of capsicum to the consommé per every quart of the latter. Mix these ingredients with the clarification, and serve as cold as possible. 1931 J. BERJANE *French Dishes for Eng. Tables* i. 13 Consommé Froid aux Tomates, or Madrilène. 1952 S. KAUFFMANN *Philanderer* (1953) xi. 183 He found a lot of food in the icebox and had fixed some madrilène and a big salad and some fruit cup by the time she arrived. 1955 E. BOWEN *World of Love* v. 96 Terence..began to spoon up liquidly-jellied madrilene. 1956 A. L. SIMON *Wine & Food Menu Bk.* 182 Consommé madrilène..should be rather highly seasoned and its colour should be not more than just a maiden's blushing pink. 1964 A. LAUNAY *Caviare & After* 135 *Madrilène* (*à la Madrilène*), dishes flavoured with tomato juice or clear soups flavoured with tomato juice and usually served chilled.

Madrilenian (mædrilī·niăn), *a.* and *sb.* Also **Madrileñan, Madrilene, Madrilenean.** [f. Sp. *Madrileño, -leña* of Madrid, the capital of Spain.] **A.** *adj.* Of or pertaining to Madrid. **B.** *sb.* A native or inhabitant of Madrid.

1841 BORROW *Zincali* I. II. ii. 241 The Madrilenian Gypsy women are indefatigable in the pursuit of prey. 1846 R. FORD *Gatherings from Spain* xviii. 254 This bit of land was taken possession of by a worthy Madrilenian. 1873 BROWNING *Red Cott. Nt.-Cap* I. 42 Father Miranda, goldsmith of renown: By birth, a Madrilene. 1882 F. R. MCCLINTOCK *Holidays in Spain* 20 The carriages and horses of the Madrilenian high-life are as good as anything to be seen in Hyde Park. 1889 M. S. VAN DE VELDE *Cosmopolitan Recoll.* II. iv. 135 One of the unsavoury apartments is occupied by Señor de Castellan—a gentleman, a scholar, and an officer in the navy—who was once the most conspicuous figure in the Madrilene world of fashion. 1909 *Daily Chron.* 2 July 3/1 A far better opportunity..of seeing the inner life of a Madrilenean family of distinction. 1921 J. B. TREND *Pict. Mod. Spain* 65 Some critics have accused Baroja of distorting the Madrileñan character. 1957 A. MACNAB *Bulls of Iberia* xii. 129 Vicente Pastor... A Madrilenian born and bred,..had the dry, dominating, Castilian style in the ring. 1972 *Times* 11 May (Spain Suppl.) p. vii/2 Madrilenians take their bullfighting seriously. 1974 *Times* 2 May 17/2 Madrid's residents are crowded... Few Madrilenians live in one-family homes.

Madrileño (mædrilē·nʸo). Fem. **Madrileña** (-lē·nʸă). [Sp.] = *MADRILENIAN *sb.*

1832 E. C. WINES *Two Yrs. in Navy* (1833) I. x. 307 The tragedian was a *Madrileno*, as nearly all the actors on the Spanish stage are. 1866 MRS. W. P. BYRNE *Cosas de España* I. viii. 180 The Madrileños and Madrileñas were already sunning themselves in the bright morning air. 1903 L. WILLIAMS *Toledo & Madrid* II. i. 117 Both were *Madrileños*, and taught the sciences at Toledo and Granada. 1932 E. HEMINGWAY *Death in Afternoon* v. 50 Madrileños love the climate. 1943 E. A. PEERS *Spain in Eclipse* I. iv. 85 'Han pasado, han pasado..' shouted crowds of Nationalist Madrileños. 1950 G. BRENAN *Face of Spain* v. 101 Mr. Washbrook is a New Englander..his wife is a handsome and vigorous Madrileña. 1965 C. D. EBY *Siege of Alcázar* (1966) i. 28 Swarms of Madrileños of the lower classes were arguing along the curbs. 1975 *Times* 19 Apr. 12/4 Do as the Madrileños do: punctuate your perambulations at the various bars.

Madurese (mædiŭrī·z), *a.* and *sb.* [f. *Madur(a* + -ESE.] **A.** *adj.* Of or belonging to Madura, an island lying off the north-east coast of Java. **B.** *sb.* **a.** A native or inhabitant of Madura. **b.** The Austronesian language of Madura. Also **Madu·ran.**

1817 T. S. RAFFLES *Hist. Java* I. ii. 59 The Madurese.. display a more martial and independent air..than the natives of Java. *Ibid.* viii. 359 In the provinces east of Surabáya, the language partakes much of the Madurese. 1853 J. R. LOGAN in *Jrnl. Indian Archipelago* VII. 33 Anam heads are common in eastern Java and especially amongst the..Madurans. 1878 R. N. CUST *Sk. Mod. Lang. E. Indies* ix. 137 The Javanese is the chief Language of the island of Java... Its Character..is used by the Sundanese, Balinese, Madurese, and the people of Lombok. *Ibid.* 138 The Madurese..has one Dialect, the Sumanap. 1880 *Encycl. Brit.* XIII. 607/1 The limits of the Madurese area are not so easily given. 1933 L. BLOOMFIELD *Lang.* iv. 71 The languages of the great islands of the East, such as..Maduran. 1969 *Language* XLV. 685 Although there is still much of Madurese morphology which requires further description, this study goes far beyond anything done for Madurese heretofore.

maduro (madū·ro). [Sp., = ripe, MATURE *a.*] A dark-coloured cigar.

1889 L. FRIEDLANDER *Tobacconist* (ed. 5) 28 M.. Maduro—very dark brown. 1908 S. FORD *Side-Stepping with Shorty* vii. 106 The spots of him that you could see.. was the colour of a twenty-cent maduro cigar. 1939 C. GRAVES *Cigars & Man* 16 The two remaining darker shades, Colorado-Maduro and Maduro are seldom met with in England. 1957 C. MACKENZIE *Sublime Tobacco* xiv. 240 '1 pound full Cabañas'... These may have been Maduro, the darkest of all, which are never seen to-day.

maduromycosis (ma·duroməikōu·sis). *Path.* [mod.L., f. MADUR(A + -O + MYCOSIS.] A chronic destructive infection of the foot (rarely of other parts) that is accompanied by many discharging sinuses and is caused by various actinomycetes and fungi; also called *Madura foot* when appropriate.

1916 CHALMERS & ARCHIBALD in *Ann. Trop. Med. & Parasitol.* X. 170 But confusion may arise between the terms 'Mycetoma' and 'True Mycetoma', and, therefore.. we suggest the word 'Maduromycosis' instead of True Mycetoma. 1937 *Nature* 27 Feb. 377/2 Maduromycosis, a fungus disease affecting the legs of human beings. 1961 R. D. BAKER *Essent. Path.* ix. 213 Maduromycosis or mycetoma is an infection of an extremity, usually the lower, as the result of a puncture wound.

maemae, var. *MAIMAI.

maestrale (məistrā·le). Also **maestral, maestro** (məi·stro). [It. *maestrale*, f. L. *magistrāl-is*, f. *magister* MASTER *sb.*[1]] The name of a wind experienced in the Mediterranean (see quot. 1944). Cf. MISTRAL.

1766, 1813 [see MISTRAL]. 1902 *Encycl. Brit.* XXX. 622/1 In summer a north-west 'trade' wind, the Maestro occurs in the Adriatic. 1920 *19th Cent.* Aug. 288 The waves ..on the beaches of Corfu..come in with a pleasant surge when the northerly *maestro* is blowing. 1944 *Italy* (Geogr. Handbk. Ser. B.R. 517, Admiralty, Naval Intelligence Div.) I. v. 415 The *maestro* (or *maestrale*), although bearing the same name as the mistral of the Rhône valley, is not to be confused with it. The name is given to NW. winds in the Adriatic, and NW., N., and NE. winds in Liguria and Tuscany. In the west the maestrale is a winter wind (Genoa), but is less cold and dry than the mistral proper. In the Adriatic it is a summer wind. 1967 D. S. WALKER *Geogr. Italy* (ed. 2) iii. 224 The influence of persistent winds (especially the *maestrale*) is apparent in the tortured shapes of the trees.

‖ **maestria** (maˌe·striă). [It.] Skill, mastery.

1876 STAINER & BARRETT *Dict. Mus. Terms* 279/1 *Maestria* (It.), skill, address, authority. 1921 R. FRY *Let.* 15 Mar. (1972) II. 505 He [*sc.* Derain] 's becoming more and more Baroque... It may be dangerous with his incredible *maestria*. 1928 *Daily Express* 16 Jan. 4 Sir Charles..can occasionally be persuaded to render the 'Volga Boatmen's Song', which he sings with incomparable maestria. 1938 *Daily Tel.* 25 July 9/1 While admiring the maestria of this piece of writing by Mr. Shaw I find in it..several inaccuracies. 1955 TAYLOR & KERR *Mus. Lovers' Encycl.* 633/1 Maëstria.

Maestrichtian (māstri·χʸtiăn), *a. Geol.* Also **Maastrichtian.** [ad. F. *maestrichtien* (A. Dumont 1849, in *Bull. de l'Acad. R. d. Sci.*, etc., *de Belgique* XVI. II. 360), f. *Maestricht* (now *Maastricht*), the name of a city in SE. Holland; see -IAN.] Of, pertaining to, or designating a division of the Upper Cretaceous in Europe that is now regarded as a stage lying next below the Danian. Also *absol.*

1885 A. GEIKIE *Text-bk. Geol.* (ed. 2) 834 In the Cotentin, a limestone with *Baculites anceps, Scaphites constrictus*, and other fossils has been paralleled with the Maestricht chalk (Maestrichtian sub-stage). 1931 GREGORY & BARRETT *Gen. Stratigr.* xi. 171 The Senonian deposits in the N.E. of France and Belgium were those of a shallow sea, such as the phosphatic chalks of the Campanian and the limestone 'tuffau' of the Maastrichtian. 1967 D. H. RAYNER *Stratigr. Brit. Isles* x. 337 Maastrichtian chalk is rare in Britain but small remnants of the lower zone (*Belemnitella lanceolata*) are known from the Norfolk coast and north-eastern Antrim. 1971 *Nature* 19 Feb. 553/2 Although disputed by some, the latest Cretaceous and earliest Tertiary (Maestrichtian and Danian stages) have generally been recognized as a brief interval during which many organisms underwent a severe attenuation in diversity or became extinct. 1975 *Ibid.* 6 Mar. 50/1 By about 70 Myr ago (late Cretaceous: Maastrichtian) there seems to have been a gap large enough to have prevented east–west migration of marine reef colonies.

maestro. Add: **a.** Also with pronunc. (məi·stro). Pl. **maestri, maestros.** (Further examples.)

1947 *Penguin Music Mag.* IV. 44 The maestros on the rostrum. 1952 J. K. SHERMAN (*title*) Music and maestros.

b. *transf.* A master or leader in any art, profession, etc.

1938 M. ALLINGHAM *Fashion in Shrouds* xv. 238 The old *maestro* allows beautiful suspect to slip through nicotine-stained fingers. 1942 BERREY & VAN DEN BARK *Amer. Thes. Slang* § 629 Coach; trainer; manager.. *maestro*. 1945 R. CHANDLER in *Atlantic Monthly* Nov. 51/3 There is no reason to expect from the anonymous toilers of the screen a quality which we are very obviously not getting from..the sulky maestri of the little magazines. 1945 S. LEWIS *Cass Timberlane* (1946) xix. 114 Reverence for jazz and familiarity with such contemporary maestri as Benny Goodman and Pee-wee Russell. 1952 PHILLIPS & REESE *Bridge with Mr. Playbetter* xxix. 123 'Perhaps, if you lead a low Diamond originally,' answered the maestro. 1953 *Proc. Geologists' Assoc.* LXIV. 139 That maestro of Highland tectonics, Sir Edward Bailey. 1958 *Listener* 2 Oct. 537/3 The 'Ted Ray Show' came back with the maestro in full hilarity. 1960 V. NABOKOV *Invitation to Beheading* xix. 193 We beseech you, be calm, maestro. If something was not just right, it was the fault of the director. 1964 L. NKOSI *Rhythm of Violence* 64, I deman' an explanation why my bottle is being impounded... Ah, the maestro needed a shot in the arm too! 1971 *Sunday Nation* (Nairobi) 11 Apr. 26/1 Anyone willing to part with a work of the maestro is asked to contact the Society.

maestro: see *MAESTRALE.

‖ **maestro di cappella** (maę·stro di kape·lă, məi·stro —). *Mus.* Also **maestro di capella.** [It., lit. 'master of the chapel'.] = *Kapellmeister* (see KAPELLE); choir-master; musical director, conductor.

1724 *Short Explication Foreign Words in Musick Bks.* 44 *Maestro,* is Master. Thus, *Maestro de capella,* is Master of the Chapel Musick or Master of Musick only, meaning thereby one of the first Rank. **1774** 'J. COLLIER' *Mus. Trav.* 16 All the musicians of Britain..together with every *Maestro di Capella* in Italy. **1880** J. H. SHORTHOUSE *John Inglesant* xxiii. 316 The elder, whose name was Giacomo Andria, was maestro di capella of one of the churches. **1947** C. GRAY *Contingencies* 98 In 1850, Raimondi became *maestro di cappella* at St. Peter's in Rome. **1964** *Conc. Oxf. Dict. Opera* 238/2 The *Maestro di cappella* was orig. the equivalent of the German Kapellmeister..but today the term is used only with reference to religious music.

Maeterlinckian (mēⁱtəɹli·ŋkiăn, mā·təɪ-), *a.* [f. *Maeterlinck* (see below) + -IAN.] Of, pertaining to, or having the characteristics of Maurice Maeterlinck, Belgian author (1862–1949), or his writings.

1895 G. B. SHAW *Our Theatres in Nineties* (1932) I. 189 The Maeterlinckian treatment of Pelléas et Mélisande. **1904** W. L. COURTNEY *Devel. M. Maeterlinck* 35 It is hardly a characteristic example of the Maeterlinckian drama. **1909** *Times Lit. Suppl.* 22 Apr. 150/2 Conflicting with the spirit of mystery and fascinating Maeterlinckian unreality. **1933** *Ibid.* 5 Oct. 657/2 The old haunted house of the Harveys on the Quay, with its Maeterlinckian terrors for a sensitively imaginative child. **1974** P. DE VRIES *Glory of Hummingbird* (1975) xiii. 173 On the one hand, flocks of Maeterlinckian bluebirds fresh descended from heaven; on the other, a passel of pubescent near-villains queuing up for release from hell.

Mae West (mēⁱ west). *slang* (orig. *R.A.F.*). [f. the professional name of an American film actress and entertainer (1892–), with reference to her curvaceous figure (see quot. 1941).] An inflatable life-jacket, orig. issued to R.A.F. men in the war of 1939–45, later in more general use where the risk of drowning is involved.

1940 *Reader's Digest* May 31/2 The aviators have adopted amusing novelties. For example..*Mae West* for a life jacket. **1941** *N.Y. Times Mag.* 27 July 21/2 One can understand..why an airman's life-belt should be a 'Mae-West'. It..gives the wearer a somewhat feminine figure. **1942** *R.A.F. Jrnl.* 16 May 33 A second more determined pull opened it [*sc.* the parachute] at about 400–500 feet. The pilot did not inflate his Mae West. **1945** *Daily Mirror* 15 Aug. 3/3 McGarvey discarded his Mae West and swam to the vessel. **1952** T. J. MULVEY *These are your Sons* v. 100 When you are flying over the hills of Korea, Mae Wests are a poor substitute for parachutes. **1958** M. DICKENS *Man Overboard* x. 152 I'm glad I wasn't in your submarine, Ben. I'd have worn a Mae West all the time. **1971** *Daily Tel.* 16 Jan. 21/8 He was burned about the face and floated in his 'Mae West' until rescued by the Air-Sea Rescue Service. **1974** *Times* 4 Sept. 1/8 One of them had a Mae West on with the words, 'Morning Cloud' written across it.

‖ **mafeesh** (măfī·ʃ), *a.* and *int.* Also **mafish, mefeesh.** [ad. colloq. Eastern Arab. *mā fī-š* there is nothing.] (See quot. 1925.)

1855 R. F. BURTON *Pilgrimage to El-Medinah & Meccah* I. i. 11 When a little boy, presuming that the occasion might possibly open the hand of generosity, looked in my face and exclaimed 'Bakhshish', he obtained in reply 'Mafish'; which convinced the bystanders that the sheep-skin contained a real sheep. **1897** A. CONAN DOYLE *Tragedy of Korosko* (1898) viii. 225 'But what..about the three ladies?' The black soldier shrugged his shoulders. 'Mefeesh!' ['Mafeesh!', 1897 serial publ.] said he. 'One of them is old, and..there are plenty more women if we get back to Egypt.' **1916** C. J. DENNIS *Moods of Ginger Mick* (1918) 135 *Mafeesh,* finish; I am finished. **1919** W. H. DOWNING *Digger Dial.* 32 Mafish.., finish, finished. **1924** KIPLING *Debits & Credits* (1926) 318 As soon as he reached the place it was *mafeesh* with him, as usual... You never noticed him. *Ibid.* 320 House, two ricks an' stable *mafeesh,* the big glasshouse with every pane smashed. **1925** FRASER & GIBBONS *Soldier & Sailor Words* 150 *Mafeesh,* (*Arabic*). Dead. Done with. Finished. Used colloquially everywhere on Eastern Fronts... It had other meanings: 'I can't', 'I know', 'Get out', 'Go to hell', [etc.]. **1931** T. R. G. LYELL *Slang* 497 *Mafeesh,* old lad—nothing doing! I gave away the last of them a week ago.

mafficker. (Example.)

1910 *Blackw. Mag.* July 9/2 The 'mafficker' may hereafter come within sight of the enemy.

mafia. Add: Now usu. with pronunc. (mæ·fiă, ma·fiă). Delete ‖ and (from def.) 'erroneously'. Also in the U.S. and elsewhere, and *transf.* (Further examples.) Hence also **mafio·sa** (fem.), **ma·fiaist,** a member or supporter of the mafia; **ma·fiaism,** the doctrines or practices of the mafia. Also *attrib.* and *transf.*

1924 A. CHRISTIE *Poirot Investigates* iii. 92 Suddenly they learn that one of these secret societies, the Mafia, or the Camorra..is on their track. **1927** *Daily Tel.* 22 Nov. 7 Thuggism meant an end to human life; Mafiaism poisoned every department of it. **1948** *Oxf. Jun. Encycl.* I. 135/2 Through a secret society called the Mafia, they [*sc.* the Czechs and Slovaks] gave help to the Allies against the Austrians and Germans. **1948** E. L. IREY *Tax Dodgers* (1949) vii. 145 His gunmen shot the Mafiaists out of the top rung of the underworld. **1959** *Times Lit. Suppl.* 9 Oct. 575/1 Mr. Maxwell also prints statements by members of the ruling classes and outsiders: a nun, a priest, a semi-*mafioso* doctor, a Tuscan *carabiniere.* **1965** J. WAINWRIGHT *Death in Sleeping City* I. 75 She was born into the Mafia. She was a Mafiosa... He was a lousy Mafioso—because he wasn't all rotten. **1967** *Times* 28 Feb. (Canada Suppl.) 29 Their Mafia-conscious compatriots south of the border. **1967** *Listener* 20 Apr. 529/2 He [*sc.* J. F. Kennedy] was constantly personalizing the office he held, filling the White House with his 'Irish mafia',..extending the influence of the Kennedy court to cover the whole range of American cultural and intellectual activity. **1969** C. DRUMMOND *Odds on Death* v. 118 No law enforcement agency had ever learned to cope with *mafiosi.* **1970** *New Yorker* 3 Jan. 44 The composers' Mafia, with its dedication to atonality and the production of new noises, holds no terrors for him. **1970** E. TIDYMAN *Shaft* (1971) vi. 92 If a Mafia don was breaking his kid into the business today, he would break him in through the Harvard Business School. **1971** M. MCCARTHY *Birds of America* 263 I'm prepared for attacks, naturally, from the academic Mafia. **1971** P. ZIEGLER *King William IV* xiii. 162 It was the turn of the Ultra Tories. This mafia of malcontents..pledged themselves to destroy the Duke [of Wellington]. **1972** 'J. RIPLEY' *My Word you should have seen Us* 88 The F.B.I. know Joseph Colombo as a Capo Mafioso. **1973** *Guardian* 16 Feb. 13/8 British Brussels is..split on the issue of the TUC's participation in Europe. The Labour Party mafia is oversensitive about the TUC. **1974** *Sumter* (S. Carolina) *Daily Item* 24 Apr. 12A/4 Another top Mafioso, Aniello Dellacroce, just finished an income-tax sentence in the Atlanta pen. A few days before his release, another Mafioso leader, Frank Valenti, was locked behind federal bars.

mafic (mæ·fik), *a. Min.* [f. MA(GNESIUM + L. *f-errum* iron + -IC.] Pertaining to, containing, or designating the dark-coloured minerals of igneous rocks, which are predominantly ferromagnesian in character. Opp. *FELSIC *a.*

1912 W. CROSS et al. in *Jrnl. Geol.* XX. 561 We suggest the term..*mafic* for the group of modal ferromagnesian minerals of all kinds. **1920** [see *FEMIC *a.*]. **1926** [see *ANKARAMITE]. **1969** *Nature* 20 Dec. 1153/1 The lavas are intruded by ultramafic and mafic bodies and dyke swarms. **1970** *Ibid.* 31 Oct. 413/1 The African rifts are sites of under-saturated, predominantly mafic volcanics erupted in comparatively small volume from single vents. **1971** I. G. GASS et al. *Understanding Earth* v. 83/1 The oceans, with their thin (about 5 km) mafic crust.

mafioso: see MAFIA in Dict. and Suppl.

mafish, var. *MAFEESH *a.* and *int.*

‖ **ma foi** (ma fwa), *int.* [Fr., lit. 'my faith'.] On, upon my word (see WORD *sb.* 15 a). Cf. † MAFEY *int.*

c **1400** *Brut* 17 'Ma foy,' quod þe fader, 'y may no more axen.' **1778** F. BURNEY *Evelina* I. xiv. 76 '*Ma foi,* Sir,' answered she, '..none of my acquaintance is in town.' **1791, 1842** [see MAFEY *int.*]. **1868** C. M. YONGE *Chaplet of Pearls* II. xxxvi. 159 [He] had the civility to give me a guide and an escort... *Ma foi!* I believe they were given to..take me by indirect roads. **1906** BARONESS ORCZY *I will Repay* xvii. 197 'A splendid combination, *ma foi!*' said Merlin. **1928** A. CHRISTIE *Mystery of Blue Train* xxvii. 221 This time, *ma foi,* I thought we had got him.

mafoo (mā·fū). Also **ma-fu.** [ad. Chinese *ma-fu,* f. *ma* horse + *fu* servant, labourer.] A Chinese groom, stable-boy, or coachman.

1863 G. FLEMING *Trav. Mantchu Tartary* ii. 16 Ma-foo, as he was soon christened, from his occupation as horse-keeper. **1880** W. GILL *River of Golden Sand* II. viii. 310, I at first rode a hired pony, and my new Ma-Fu walked on in front leading the grey. **1890** BARRÈRE & LELAND *Dict. Slang* II. 37/2 *Mafoo* (pidgin), horse-boy, groom. **1924** *Blackw. Mag.* Feb. 232/2 Let them send word to the mafoo to have the ponies saddled. *Ibid.* Aug. 265/2 He borrowed Cantegril's famous two-horse barouche, all complete, with its variegated *mafoos.* **1939** 'A. BRIDGE' *Four-Part Setting* xxiii. 313 They dismounted and left the mafoos and ponies in an open grassy space.

mag (mæg), *sb.*⁵ *Astr.* Also **mag.** (with point). Abbrev. of *magnitude(s)* (MAGNITUDE 3 a).

1840 *Mem. R. Astron. Soc.* XI. 283 (*heading*) Relative order of mag. as observed. **1851** *Monthly Notices R. Astron. Soc.* XI. 187 A double star..appearing to the naked eye as a bright 4 mag., and designated by A as 3·4. **1918** *Astrophysical Jrnl.* XLVII. 264 The absolute magnitudes of the bulk of the A stars lie within a range of 2·6 mags. **1972** *Nature* 22 Dec. 439/2 The distribution of galaxies brighter than 16 mag is..not especially isotropic.

mag (mæg), *sb.*⁶ Also **mag.** (with point). Colloq. abbrev. of MAGNETO.

1920 *Blackw. Mag.* Nov. 562/2 Having wrestled for an hour with the mags., they were eventually induced to give forth reluctant sparks. **1930** [see *DIFFERENTIAL *a.* and *sb.* B. 4]. **1943** *R.A.F. Jrnl.* Aug. 11, I could see her eyes intent on the rev counter as she cut out first one mag, then the other. **1958** 'CASTLE' & 'HAILEY' *Flight into Danger* i. 16 Each engine has two magnetos... In the run-up each engine in turn is opened to full throttle and each of the mags tested separately. **1973** E. ARNOLD *Proving Ground* (1974) iv. 61 Sayers pulled off the throttle and cut off the mag.

mag (mæg), *sb.*⁷ Also **mag.** (with point). Colloq. abbrev. of MAGNESIUM, often used for *magnesium alloy.*

1969 C. TRICKEY *Building & Racing 850 Mini* i. 10/2 While, naturally, mag. alloy wheels are highly desirable from other points of view, the steel ones are obviously the best choice for a formula which is trying to keep costs to a minimum. **1970** *Telegraph* (Brisbane) 8 Dec. 14 Many 'mag' wheels sold as extras for hotted-up cars are made of cast aluminium. They cost about $40 each. Genuine magnesium alloy wheels, as used on racing cars, cost about $120 each. **1973** D. J. ABODAHER (*title*) Mag wheels and racing stripes.

Magar² (mā·gāɹ). Also **Muggur. a.** A member of one of the tribes of western Nepal, of Mongol origin and noted for their prowess in fighting. **b.** The language spoken by this tribe. Also *attrib.* or as *adj.*

1811 W. KIRKPATRICK *Acct. Kingdom Nepal* vii. 220 Besides the Sanskrit,..the principal vernacular languages of this country are, the Purbutti, the Newar, the Dhenwar, the Muggur, [etc.]. **1833** B. H. HODGSON in *Jrnl. Bengal Asiatic Soc.* II. 219 Both Gúrúngs and Magars still maintain their own vernacular tongues, Tartar faces, and careless manners. *Ibid.* 221 The attachment of the Magars to the house of Gorkhá is but recent, and of no extraordinary or intimate nature. **1859** R. G. LATHAM *Descriptive Ethnol.* II. xlii. 403 Gorkha, so far as it was other than Hindu, seems to have been chiefly Magar. **1877** L. H. MORGAN *Anc. Society* III. vi. 513 If the organizations..of ..the Magars of Nepaul..were examined upon the original evidence, it is highly probable that they would be found exactly analogous to the Iroquois tribes. **1911** *Encycl. Brit.* XIX. 379/2 The Gurkhalis, Magars, and Gurungs are Hindus, but..the Magars will eat pork but not buffalo's flesh. **1950** T. LONGSTAFF *This My Voyage* v. 93 Besides speaking Khaskura..he was familiar with the peculiar dialects of the Magars and Gurungs, two of the most redoubtable of the fighting clans. **1971** C. BONINGTON *Annapurna South Face* iv. 47 Our porters were recruited in the main from two different tribes, the Magars and the Gurungs. **1971** J. PEMBLE *Invasion of Nepal* i. 9 Lévi thought that the Mongolian Magar tribesmen were the earliest inhabitants of the western hills.

magazine, *sb.* Add: **5. c.** = **magazine programme.*

1936 *Radio Times* 30 Oct. 88/2 'Picture Page'. A Magazine of Topical and General Interest. **1949** *Ibid.* 15 July 12/2 Music Magazine. A weekly review. **1953** *Ann. Reg. 1952* 360 The establishment of the radio magazine *New Soundings.* **1957** *B.B.C. Handbk.* 153 *Family affairs*: a weekly magazine for mothers with children. **1975** *ITV Evidence to Annan Committee* 46 A thirty-minute news magazine is taking shape for 6 pm transmission.

6. b. (Later examples.)

1915 'I. HAY' *First Hundred Thousand* vii. 77 Pumpherston graciously accepted the charger of cartridges.., rammed it into the magazine, adjusted the sights,..and fired his first shot. **1919** 'BOYD CABLE' *Old Contemptibles* xvii. 277 Carruthers..took a box of cartridges from a niche in the wall, and proceeded to recharge his magazine. **1964** H. L. PETERSON *Encycl. Firearms* 255/1 This turret system was revived many years later as a practical magazine for the Lewis machine gun.

d. Also, in a camera, projector, etc.

1889 *Judge* (U.S.) 22 June 180/2 Every operator can develop and print his own negatives and refill his magazine. **1958** *Amat. Photographer* 31 Dec. 3/2 (Advt.), The Hanomatic slide changer is complete with a plastic magazine holding 36 slides. **1964** C. WILLOCK *Enormous Zoo* v. 77 John Buxton used up one magazine of film and then reloaded with terrible precision. **1967** H. M. R. SOUTO *Technique Motion Pict. Camera* i. 13 The first mechanism has the task of drawing the unexposed film (or raw stock) from the storage chamber, called a *magazine,* and after exposure, driving it into a similar magazine.

7. (sense 5 b) *magazine rack, -reader, table*; (sense 6 b) *magazine slot*; **magazine cover,** the cover, freq. pictorial, of a magazine; **magazine programme,** a periodical broadcast programme comprised of varied items of entertainment linked together as a single series (see quot. 1941); **magazine rights,** the rights of publishing matter in a magazine; **magazine section,** a section included in some newspapers the contents of which resemble a magazine; **magazine story,** a story written for publication in a magazine.

1938 *Toronto Daily Star* 30 Dec. 12/6 Famous Hollywood Glamour Girls. Magazine cover models. **1942** E. PAUL *Narrow St.* xvi. 124 Mireille was not the most attractive, from the magazine-cover standpoint. **1951** M. MCLUHAN *Mech. Bride* (1967) 120/2 The feminine images of our ads and magazine covers. **1941** *B.B.C. Gloss. Broadcasting Terms* 18 *Magazine programme,* programme made up of miscellaneous items (e.g. talks, interviews, musical acts), loosely related one to the other by a compère or by other means of presentation. **1970** *Times* 23 Feb. 25/3 B.B.C. Newcastle..will have its own budget which will be sufficient to allow the production of another 30-minute weekly magazine programme. **1972** P. BLACK *Biggest Aspidistra* III. iv. 175 Godfrey Bazely, a Midland Region broadcaster..loved the world of farming... The BBC gave him a new magazine programme aimed at farmers and their families. **1917–18** *T. Eaton & Co. Catal.* Fall & Winter 416/1 Morris Chair... Paper and magazine rack under arm. **1955** E. BOWEN *World of Love* II. 42 One or two ruched taffeta cushions and a magazine-rack..survived from her few attempts to bring the room into line with her ideas. **1969** *House & Garden* Apr. 160/2 Magazine rack in Afrormosia. **1833** MILL *Let.* 24 Sept. in *Works* (1963) XII. 179 They would not be attractive to the bulk of Magazine-readers. **1882** W. JAMES *Will to Believe* (1897) 109 Thousands of innocent magazine readers lie paralyzed and terrified in the network of shallow negations which the leaders of opinion have thrown over their souls. **1909** *Westm. Gaz.* 14 July 11/2 In America 'magazine rights'

did not necessarily mean publication by instalments. The term was used to distinguish magazine rights from newspaper syndicate rights. **1959** N. Mailer *Advts. for Myself* (1961) 158 Sam throws the Magazine Section away... Sam is enraged at editorial dishonesty. **1969** *Listener* 30 Jan. 148/1 Leavis did not apologise that his terms of reference should be the Robbins Report and Harold Wilson and the magazine sections of the English Sundays. **1910** Kipling *Land & Sea Tales* (1923) 178 The tiny twenty-two cartridge had dropped into the magazine-slot. **1858** J. A. Froude *Let.* 17 Jan. in J. W. Cross *George Eliot's Life* (1885) II. viii. 4, I had made acquaintance with 'Janet's Repentance', and had found there something extremely different from general magazine stories. **1885** C. M. Yonge *Nuttie's Father* II. ii. 23 The hero of many a magazine story. **1932** Q. D. Leavis *Fiction & Reading Public* I. iii. 47 The magazine story is almost without exception a commercial article. **1942** Magazine story [see *exclusive A. *adj.* 9]. **1966** H. Roth *Button, Button* (1967) i. 15 A small, locked safe..unnoticeable..because the top was extended to make it look like a magazine table. **1967** A. Diment *Dolly Dolly Spy* xi. 145 The magazine table caught them neatly behind the naked knees and..they overbalanced.

magazinedom (mægăzī·ndəm). [f. Magazine *sb.* 5 b + -dom.] The world or sphere of magazines.

1890 *Review of Reviews* I. 9/1 Such a guide to magazinedom as you propose to establish would be extremely useful. **1902** *Tablet* 22 Sept. 448 It is the very romance of magazinedom. **1907** *Daily Chron.* 19 Feb. 3/2 It is true that magazinedom is very crowded, but there is always room at the top.

magaziny. Add: (Later examples.) Also **magaziney.**

1938 *New Statesman* 8 Jan. 56/2 Nor is *The Best Poems* negligible. It is magaziny, but contains respectable work by De la Mare [etc.]. **1941** *Scrutiny* IX. 379 He [*sc.* Mr. Plomer] attempts also pseudo-ballads made to the Auden formula, which are amusing in a magaziny way. **1961** *Times Lit. Suppl.* 23 Jun. 385/1 Of these fourteen pieces at least eight are almost defiantly magaziny. **1966** *Punch* 9 Mar. 362/3 The violence seems somehow bookish and the literary chat magaziney.

Magdalenian (mægdălī·niăn), *a.* and *sb.* *Archæol.* Also **Madelainean, Madelenian.** [ad. F. *magdalénien* (G. de Mortillet, *c* 1867), f. the place-name *La Madeleine* in the department of Dordogne, France: see -an.] **A.** *adj.* Of or belonging to the Lower Palæolithic culture represented by remains found at La Madeleine. **B.** *sb.* A man or woman of this culture.

1885 A. Geikie *Text-bk. Geol.* (ed. 2) vi. 914 Those [deposits] which contain well-finished implements associated with carved bone and ivory, as at the caves of La Madeleine (Périgord), have been called Magdalenian. **1896** A. H. Keane *Ethnol.* 87 Madelenian or Third Cave Age. **1904** [see Solutrian, Solutrean *a.*]. **1911** W. J. Sollas *Anc. Hunters* 323 The Magdalenians were quite capable of making respectable buckles or fibulæ. **1920** *Q. Rev.* Oct. 376 We are moved by a greater number of artistic qualities than were the Magdalenian reindeer men. **1956** H. Read *Art of Sculpture* ii. 28 This highly stylized figure anticipates the schematic character of the later Magdalenian figures. **1963** *Field Archaeol.* (Ordnance Survey) (ed. 4) 21 From the period of the Magdalenians who were hunting and making their wonderful cave paintings in France round about 20,000 B.C...there is very little in Britain... A few typical Magdalenian objects have been found in Mendip caves. **1973** *Listener* 10 May 606/2 The Magdalenian hunters of southern Europe fifteen thousand years ago invented the harpoon.

mage. **2.** Delete † *Obs.* and add later example.

1877 Smith & Wace *Dict. Christian Biogr.* I. 477/2 The author of that superstition was Masdec,..a mage, who gathered the credulous around him.

Magen David (māge·n dāvī·d). Also **Mogen David** (mǫ·gən dǫ·vid). [Heb. *māghēn Dāwīdh* shield of David, f. *Dāwīdh* David, king of Judah and Israel, d. circa 973 B.C.] A six-pointed star symbolizing Jewishness or Zionism.

1904 *Jewish Encycl.* VIII. 251/2 *Magen Dawid* ('David's Shield'), the hexagram formed by the combination of two equilateral triangles. **1934** *Encycl. Jewish Knowl.* 324/2 *Magen David*... During the World War it was used..as equivalent to the Red Cross, such organizations described themselves as the 'Red Magen David'. **1964** W. Markfield *To Early Grave* (1965) vi. 109 During the Sinai campaign she beat two Egyptians to death with a *Mogen David* she herself welded together from a pair of captured gasoline drums. **1972** C. Raphael *Feast of Hist.* (dust-jacket), The 'square' Magen David on the jacket appears in some Jewish manuscripts from late-fifteenth-century Portugal. **1975** *Jewish Chron.* 7 Feb. 21/5 Can anyone explain why Jewish greetings cards should be so expensive?.. Why should the addition of a..Magen David make them so much dearer than their non-denominational counterparts?

mageship (mēi·dʒ,ʃip). [See -ship.] The position or function of a mage.

1875 E. Dowden *Shakspere: his Mind & Art* i. 37 Prospero must forever have remained somewhat apart and distinguished from other Dukes..by virtue of the enchanted island and the marvellous years of mageship.

magged, *a.* Add: **b.** Irritated; exhausted, jaded.

1839 F. Trollope *Fragment* in *Dom. Manners Amer.* (ed. 5) 272 Mrs. Rapp... We shall be right down magged without her... Angelina... It won't convene for me to be mixing doe cakes..all day. **1903** *Eng. Dial. Dict.* IV. 7/2 I'm quite magged with my day's glanin'.

Maggid (mā·gid). Also **Magid, m-.** Pl. **Maggidim.** [Heb. *maggīdh* narrator.] An itinerant Jewish preacher.

1892 I. Zangwill *Childr. Ghetto* I. 35 The central place of honour which befits a Maggid. **1902** H. Hapgood *Spirit of Ghetto* x. 289 He was sitting opposite an old 'magid', or wandering preacher. **1941** G. G. Scholem *Major Trends Jewish Mysticism* ix. 329 Rabbi Baer the *Maggid*, or popular preacher. **1960** L. P. Gartner *Jewish Immigrant* iv. 105 Hirsch Dainow (1833–1877), a recently arrived Maggid of some note.

maggie. Add: **2. b.** *dial.* and *Austral.* A magpie.

1825 J. T. Brockett *Gloss. North Country Words* 131 *Maggy*, a magpie. **1878** *Zoologist* Sept. 332/1 Magpie. *Piet*; *Maggie.* **1934** *Bulletin* (Sydney) 19 Sept. 21/2 Out maggie went backwards through the door, arguing every inch of the ground. **1965** *Jrnl. Lancs. Dial. Soc.* Jan. 7 *Maggie*: Tunstall, Burton, Hornby, Bentham, [etc.].

4. In full, *Maggie Ann* (also *Maggy Anne*). Margarine. *colloq.*

1933 Partridge *Slang To-day & Yesterday* 385 *Maggie Ann.* Margarine: C20. **1959** I. & P. Opie *Lore & Lang. Schoolch.* ix. 163 Margarine or 'marg' is 'Maggy Anne'. **1971** D. Lees *Rainbow Conspiracy* vi. 91 Sam never paid him enough to put maggy on his bread.

maggoty, *a.* Add: **2*.** *Austral.* and *N.Z.* Also **maggotty.** Angry, bad-tempered, esp. in phr. *to go maggoty*, to lose one's temper.

Dialectal evidence of this use is presented in *Eng. Dial. Dict.*

1919 W. H. Downing *Digger Dial.* 33 *Maggotty*, angry. **1936** F. Sargeson *Conversations with Uncle* 24 There was a shearer who used to go maggoty if a lamb wouldn't sit still. **1951** D. Stivens *Jimmy Brockett* 31, I didn't need to, but I shaved every day and my old man made me maggotty by asking me one day, 'Do you shave up or down?' **1959** D. Forrest *Last Blue Sea* 74 He's down there..going maggotty about doctors and Japs and boongs.

maghemite (mæ·ghī·məit). *Min.* [f. Mag(netite + *hem-atite* (var. Hæmatite) + -ite[1].] A modification of ferric oxide, Fe_2O_3, belonging to the spinel family, which is found as brown isometric crystals, is highly ferromagnetic, and is principally an alteration product of magnetite.

1927 P. A. Wagner in *Econ. Geol.* XXII. 846 The interesting form of ferric oxide under discussion appears to be identical in atomic structure with magnetite, but has the chemical composition and the physical properties of hematite... It is desirable that it should have a distinctive designation... I would suggest *maghemite.* **1944** *Trans. Geol. Soc. S. Afr.* XLVI. 30 Maghemite is the commonest and most widely distributed mineral in the Bushveld magnetic iron ores. **1962** W. A. Deer et al. *Rock-Forming Min.* V. 73 Maghemite is metastable, and inverts to haematite (α-Fe_2O_3) on heating.

Maghribi (magri·bī), *sb.* and *a.* Also **Maghrabee, Maghrabi, Maghrebi.** [Arab. *maġribi*, lit. 'western'.] **A.** *sb.* **a.** A native or inhabitant of the Maghrib, a region of north-western Africa, including Morocco, Algeria, and Tunisia. **b.** The Arabic spoken in this region. **B.** *adj.* Of or pertaining to the Maghribi or their language.

1840 E. W. Lane tr. *Arabian Nights' Entertainments* II. xviii. 600 The people of Western Africa... Called by the Arabs 'El-Maghrib'. This name is generally given to the districts of Northern Africa west of Egypt. The inhabitants of those parts are called 'Maghrabees'. **1855** R. F. Burton *Pilgrimage to El-Medinah & Meccah* I. viii. 228 We lay down upon the sand, to rest among a party of Maghrabi pilgrims travelling to Suez. **1898** A. J. Butler tr. *Ratzel's Hist. Mankind* III. v. v. 196 The Islamite world witnessed a great struggle for supremacy between.. the Maghrebin in the west, the Mashrikin in the east. **1948** D. Diringer *Alphabet* II. iv. 272 Kufic gave rise to a number of varieties,..in northern (known as Maghribi, or western) and central Africa. **1969** *Word* XXV. 116 In many varieties of Maghribi Arabic when it co-occurs with a sibilant in the same word.

Maghzen (ma·χzən). Also **Maghasen, Makhzen, -an.** [Arab. *makzan.*] The Moroccan government; the dominant official class in Morocco; irregular Algerian horsemen in the service of France. Also *transf.*

1854 J. R. Morell *Algeria* xxi. 392 Immediately that the tribes were subdued, the victors required them to supply irregular horsemen, called *makhzen* or *goum*, to attack the refractory. **1874** tr. *G. Rohlfs's Adventures Morocco* ix. 193 Every day at midday on his return from the Maghasen (palace of the Sultan and seat of government) I was called. **1894** G. Montbard *Among Moors* 169 A knot of soldiers of the Maghzen are plunging their horses into the stream. **1901** *Chambers's Jrnl.* 6 July 504/1 Laraiche, once offered to the British Maghzen (Government) in return for help against the enemies of the Sultan. **1930** *Economist* 24 May 1179/1 This loan of 62,500,000 francs was originally contracted by the Maghzen of Morocco. **1973** R. E. Dunn in Gellner & Micaud *Arabs & Berbers* 92 At the 'national' level it influenced foundation of the *makhzan*'s policies towards the Saharan region, especially in relation to the southward expansion of French Algeria.

magic, *sb.* Add: **1. d.** *like magic*: without any apparent explanation; with incredible rapidity. (Cf. Like *a.*, etc. B. 1 b.)

1857 *Knickerbocker* Jan. 98 Broiled chicken and oysters ..disappeared from before us like magic. **1900** *Congress. Rec.* 9 Jan. 704/2 Germany's Chinese trade is increasing like magic.

4. **magic-man**, a magician, sorcerer; also *fig.*

1905 *Westm. Gaz.* 6 Apr. 3/2 Disease was thought to be a visitation of supernatural wrath, to be appeased by offerings to the priests and magic-men of the time. **1923** R. Graves *Whipperginny* 51 Time and Space, folly's wonder, Three-card shufflers, magic-men! **1959** Halas & Manvell *Technique Film Animation* v. 62 Magic-men, mummers and actors wore masks in earlier times to typify ..the farcical, the comic, the eccentric, the pathetic, the tragic and the insane in human portraiture.

magic, *a.* Add: **2.** *magic box*: applied *colloq.* to various, esp. electronic, devices; *magic carpet*: a legendary carpet on which a person could be transported wherever he wished; also *transf.* and *fig.*; *Magic Marker*: the proprietary name of an instrument, consisting of a tube of quick-drying ink and a felt-tipped pen, used for marking objects; also *magic marker*.

1897 Kipling *Capt. Cour.* ix.189 From San Diego to Sixteenth Street, Chicago, let the magic carpet be laid down. Hurry! oh, hurry! **1909** H. G. Wells *Tono-Bungay* iv. i. 434, I had to come off my magic carpet and walk once more in the world. **1931** *Times Lit. Suppl.* 20 Aug. 625/2 His Magic Carpet is a book of travels, by means of which he is transported into lands that he is fated never to see. **1935** A. J. Pollock *Underworld Speaks* 74/2 *Magic box*, crooked farobank box in which 53 instead of 52 cards are manipulated by dealer. **1935** J. Hargan *Gloss. Prison Lang.* 5 *Magic-box*, coil arrangement which starts any car—without the aid of key. **1936** *Daily Tel.* 15 Aug. 15/5 (*heading*) Nicknames of the freight expresses... The Magic Carpet is not from Arabia, but Kidderminster, bringing fine weaves to London's floors. **1945** *Daily Mirror* 15 Aug. 4/2 Most sensational development was the 'Magic Box', which gave our pilots a picture of the ground beneath them even though it was hidden by darkness and cloud. **1959** *20th Cent.* Nov. 325 Both radio receivers and television sets have been known and called for brief periods 'magic boxes'. **1960** *Guardian* 22 Mar. 10/4 The job of the 'magic boxes' in the wheelhouse is to take some of the chance out of trawling. **1960** D. Lessing *In Pursuit of English* vi. 204 The yapping..of the..puppies distracted Flo from her magic box. **1960** L. Meynell *Bandaberry* viii. 127, I had suddenly an immense desire to get on a magic carpet and float away..to some carefree place. **1956** *Official Gaz.* (U.S. Patent Office) 4 Dec. TM5/2 Speedry Products, Inc., Richmond Hill, N.Y... *Magic Marker.* Applicant disclaims the term 'Marker' apart from the mark as a whole. For Felt Nib Marking Pens Comprising Small Containers for Such Ink, Equipped with Caps and having Felt Nibs at their Ends for Marking. First use on or about Sept. 1, 1952. **1962** L. Deighton *Ipcress File* xxxii. 209 A slim green file; on the cover it said 'Henry' in magic-marker lettering. **1964** 'S. Forbes' *Long Hate* (1966) ii. 16 Block letters. Magic Marker, unquestionably. Children used Magic Markers in school these days. **1971** R. Russell tr. *Ahmad's Shore & Wave* vii. 59 Nur Jahan felt as though she were on a magic carpet soaring towards the sky. **1971** C. Bonington *Annapurna South Face* App. B 255 Magic markers 20. **1973** 'J. Patrick' *Glasgow Gang Observed* xiii. 120 With chalk, magic markers, but most often with..aerosol spray paint, the pitch was marked out with slogans. **1974** D. Mackenzie *Zaleski's Percentage* iv. 94 That restaurant's his magic carpet. If they take it away from him, he'll never stop falling.

3. *magic circle*: (*b*) the title of a society of conjurers; (*c*) a circle used in magic as a protection against evil; (*d*) a small group of people who are privileged to receive confidential information, make important decisions, etc.

1912 *Magic Wand* Aug. 377/2 (*heading*) 'The Magic Circular'.—A monthly review of the magic art, issued for private circulation only amongst members of the Magic Circle. **1934** Webster, *Magic circle*, 1. a. A circle drawn by a magician about any person or place, within which demons raised by incantations were believed to have no power. b. A clearly defined place, group, or the like, entrance into which is regarded as desirable, pleasing, etc. **1955** *Radio Times* 22 Apr. 32/3 All this week magicians from all over the world are gathering to celebrate the Golden Jubilee of the Magic Circle. **1965** *Listener* 10 June 859/1 Kaiser wrote a series of plays centred on the love of two people. The pattern is throughout the same: the lovers are enclosed in a kind of magic circle which isolates them from the rest of the world. **1971** G. Mitchell *Lament for Leto* ii. 51 He..was an amateur conjuror and.. was 'on the fringe of the Magic Circle'. **1973** *Jrnl. Genetic Psychology* CXXII. 168 The complete, circular form of the Ufos is reminiscent of the mandala or 'magic circle': i.e., totality. **1974** E. Ambler *Dr. Frigo* I. 65 Could he have concluded belatedly that letting me into the magic circle had been a mistake..? **1974** *Times* 13 Nov. 16/7 The Tories..would be making a profound mistake if they were to take the right to decide their leader out of the exclusive hands of the elected MPs and put it back into those of some kind of new-furbished Magic Circle.

4. *magic (chain-)stitch* (see quot. 1900).

1900 Day & Buckle *Art in Needlework* 41 A playful variation upon chain-stitch..is effected by the use of two

threads of different colour... The light thread disappears, and comes out again to the left of the dark one... This 'magic stitch'.. is to be found in Persian, Indian, and Italian Renaissance work. **1934** M. THOMAS *Dict. Embroidery Stitches* 34 *Chain stitch—chequered*, also known as *magic stitch* and *magic chain stitch*. **1957** M. B. PICKEN *Fashion Dict.* 329/2 *Magic Chain-stitch*... Chain-stitch worked with two threads of different colors in one needle.

5. *Nuclear Physics.* Applied to a set of numbers which correspond to nuclei of exceptional stability when either the number of protons or the number of neutrons in it is equal to one of the set (now taken to be 2, 8, 20, 28, 50, 82, 126, and perhaps 184); hence applied to nuclei containing such a number of protons or neutrons; *doubly magic*, containing a magic number of protons and also a magic number (not necessarily the same) of neutrons. Occas. extended to an analogous set of numbers (see quot. 1974) for electrons in atoms.

1949 O. HAXEL et al. in *Physical Rev.* LXXV. 1766/1 A simple explanation of the 'magic numbers' 14, 28, 50, 82, 126 follows at once from the oscillator model of the nucleus. **1956** *Nature* 28 Jan. 159/1 The current work on fast-neutron capture..refines the earlier studies by D. J. Hughes of the variation of cross-section with atomic weight which..throws more light on the magic-number nuclei. **1969** *Physics Lett.* XXVIIIB. 544/2 Since the nucleon shells at $Z=114$, $N=184$ are not as 'magic' as those at $Z=82$, $N=126$, we would not expect an unusually small capture cross section for $^{294}110$. **1969** *Nature* 27 Dec. 1253/2 In calcium-40 which, like lead-208, is doubly magic and so a suitable isotope for nuclear structure calculations, the protons have been found to bunch together towards the centre of the nucleus. **1971** *Ibid.* 12 Feb. 451/2 One complication is that for heavier nuclei, the magic numbers probably differ for neutrons and protons. **1971** *Physics Bull.* Dec. 711/2 Much interest has been aroused by the prediction that the nucleus ($A=298$, $Z=114$) may be a doubly magic nucleus.., which could involve an island of stability in the mass region around 300. **1974** *Encycl. Brit. Micropædia* VI. 484/1 The magic numbers for atoms are 2, 10, 18, 36, 54, and 86.

magic (mæ·dʒik), *v.* [f. the sb.] *trans.* To transform, make, etc., (as if) by magic; also *to magic* (something) *away*, to cause, as if magically, to disappear.

1906 KIPLING *Puck of Pook's Hill* 304 There was Oak and Ash and Thorn enough in that year-end shower to magic away a thousand memories. **1909** L. M. MONTGOMERY *Anne of Avonlea* xxiv. 282, I actually have a half-guilty feeling as if I had 'magicked' it [*sc.* a storm] up. **1925** W. DE LA MARE *Miss Jemima* 31, I discovered, as if the Fairy Creature herself had magicked it there..a large hay-wain. **1952** A. GRIMBLE *Pattern of Islands* v. 104 A steel hook bought from a trade-store could only be magicked once, as a finished article. **1957** J. FRAME *Owls do Cry* ix. 38 It was to have these things sitting in their head, like a charm, to magic away the drudgery. **1966** *New Statesman* 25 Nov. 792/2 Children, who are still capable of being magicked, will, I hope, get it for Christmas. Though it's not a children's book. **1972** *Times* 16 Feb. 13/3 We cannot magic them away. **1973** D. FRANCIS *Slay-Ride* iv. 56 He magicked some huge open sandwiches on about a foot of French loaf.

magical, *a.* **3.** *magical circle*: also = **magic circle* (sense *c*).

1915 *Encycl. Relig. & Ethics* VIII. 322/1 The famous constituent of the mediaeval magical circle.

Hence also **magica·lity,** magical power or quality.

1924 W. J. LOCKE *Coming of Amos* iv. 43 An untouched cheque-book of whose magicality he was innocently certain.

magic eye. [f. MAGIC *a.* + EYE *sb.*[1]] **a.** A miniature cathode-ray tube used as a tuning indicator on a radio receiver, or to indicate the correct adjustment of other electrical equipment.

Magic Eye is registered as a proprietary name in the U.S.

[**1936** *Official Gaz.* (U.S. Patent Office) 6 Oct. 21/1 RCA Manufacturing Company, Inc.,..*Magic eye* for radio receiving sets of the type equipped with cathode ray tubes for resonance indication and accessories and parts thereof.] **1937** *Night & Day* 26 Aug. 28/1 Should one..plump for the [wireless] set with a 'mystic eye', or are those which boast a 'magic eye' or an 'electric eye' to be preferred? **1939** *Proc. IRE* XXVII. 631/2 The ground wave alone was introduced into a receiver which had a 'magic eye'. With this wave, the 'eye' remained exactly fixed in deflection. **1962** A. NISBETT *Technique Sound Studio* v. 100 A 'magic eye' is a useful guide, but should not be relied on unless the recordist is quite sure of what its indications mean in terms of the particular programme material. **1968** *Radio Communication Handbk.* (ed. 4) ii. 20/2 Magic-eye tubes are often used as voltage indicators in a.f. and r.f. measuring equipment and also widely as indicators of signal level for tape recorders.

b. A photo-electric cell or similar electrical device used for identification, detection, or measurement.

1938 *Sun* (Baltimore) 22 Feb. 20/3 Eleven pairs of 'magic eyes'..have counted approximately 7,000,000 motor vehicles during the last year. **1945** *Nature* 15 Sept. 320/2 The aids to the bombing of invisible targets which were variously called 'H_2S', the 'gen-box', 'Mickey' and the 'Magic Eye'. **1958** *Times* 2 May 7/2 The large radio antenna carried on the superstructure of the Victorious.. was a form of 'magic eye'. **1962** *Daily Tel.* 26 Oct. 17/7 The 'magic eye' records the wagon numbers of freight vehicles moving at speeds up to 100 mph. **1974** *Country Life* 6 June 1449/1 An automatic 'magic eye' lets in exactly the right amount of light every time you want to take a picture.

magic lantern. Add: Also *fig.*

1775 *Morning Chron.* 29 May 1 (Advt.), At Marylebone Gardens, To-morrow..will be presented The Modern Magic Lantern..being an attempt at a Sketch of the Times in a variety of Caricaturas. **1840** C. FOX *Jrnl.* 21 July (1972) 100 We are all shadows in the magic lanthorn of Time. **1933** S. SPENDER *Poems* 28 Where magic-lantern faces skew for greeting.

magic-lantern *v.* Delete (*nonce-wd.*) and add further example.

1935 W. EMPSON *Poems* 29 All those large dreams by which men long live well Are magic-lanterned on the smoke of hell.

magico- (mæ·dʒiko). Combining form of MAGICAL *a.* with other adjs. as *magico-erotic, -oriental, -profane, -religious.*

1915 *Encycl. Relig. & Ethics* VIII. 258/2 These are of a magico-erotic nature, and, like similar rites among savages, are founded on the belief that the ghost can cause fruitfulness, or perhaps may incarnate himself in the barren woman who performs the rite. **1930** *Times Lit. Suppl.* 27 Nov. 1004/3 As against the 'magico-oriental' view of the image maintained by the Iconoclast stands the Platonism of the image-worshipper. **1941** *Jrnl. R. Anthrop. Inst.* LXXI. 85/2 Numerous acts and ceremonies..which the European..would place under the category of magico-profane, magico-religious ideas or superstition. **1908** *Man* VIII. 46 The magico-religious ideas and practices of savage and proto-historic man. **1922** *Nature* 29 Apr. 540/2 The complex and inexorable system of magico-religious *gennas*. **1967** C. L. WRENN *Word & Symbol* 17 Anglo-Saxon magico-religious arts.

Magid, var. *MAGGID.

Maginot (‖ maʒino, mæ·dʒinōᵘ). The name of a French minister of war, André *Maginot* (1877–1932), used to designate the line of fortifications (*Maginot Line*) built before the war of 1939–45 along the north-eastern borders of France, and in which the French placed excessive confidence. Also *transf.* (designating other similar lines of defence) and *fig.*

1936 *Times* 30 Oct. 15/4 The Maginot Line. M. Daladier ..inspected the recently completed frontier fortifications between Maubeuge and Valenciennes. **1937** A. VAGTS *Hist. Militarism* xii. 457 The American coast is the Maginot Line of the United States. **1938** *Nation* (N.Y.) 23 July 78 Little Steel's Maginot Line against unionism. *Ibid.* 83/2 Along the border the Czech Maginot Line is artfully concealed. **1940** *Economist* 27 July 118/1 Sea-power is no Maginot Line to lull us again into lethargy. **1940** L. B. NAMIER in *19th Cent.* Nov. 468 Her [*sc.* France's] system of alliances in East-Central Europe was as imperfect and as deceptive as her Maginot line later on. **1947** C. S. LEWIS *Miracles* xiv. 146 The belief that nothing but Nature exists and that if anything else did she is protected from it by a Maginot Line. **1972** *Times* 14 Nov. 17/2 The Dow has still to close above what is jestfully known on Wall Street as the 'Maginot Line' of 1,000. **1973** B. FREEMANTLE *Goodbye to Old Friend* i. 14 He..lifted out his tray containing pens..and set it..at the head of the blotter. My Maginot Line, he thought. Behind the tray, I'm safe. **1975** *Guardian* 27 Jan. 4/3 Casemate 35/3, a key heavy gun emplacement in the Maginot Line.

Hence *attrib.* and *Comb.*, as **Maginot-minded** *a.*, obsessed with the inviolability of the Maginot Line; *Maginot(-Line) complex, mentality*, etc.: indicating an obsession with defence (of the status quo, etc.) as an attitude of mind.

1940 *Economist* 13 July 37/1 The efficacy of blockade is a mirage, a delusion comparable to the Maginot-complex that bemused and enervated France. **1942** *Ann. Reg. 1941* 79 People began to wonder whether the Government had not become 'Maginot-minded'. **1955** *Bull. Atomic Sci.* Mar. 81/1 Maginot-line mentality..denotes..a one-sided preoccupation with putting all reliance on a single strategy. **1962** *Listener* 24 May 893/1 Defence is only relevant to my present argument as evidence of the Maginot attitude of the old and Great Powers. **1962** *Observer* 1 July 7/1 There is also the danger that a national shelter programme could lead to a Maginot Line psychology. **1973** *New Society* 13 Sept. 632/2 The NGA has been attacked by the non-craft unions for having a 'Maginot line mentality'.

magisterially, *adv.* Add: **1.** (Later examples.)

The dominant sense now is 'authoritatively'.

1963 *Times* 4 Mar. 14/2 M. Planchon, who wrote every word of the text and was responsible for every step of the choreography, rarely stumbles and magisterially weaves the disparate threads into one homogeneous pattern. **1972** *Times* 15 June 7/3 These dons, judges and headmasters.. who moved so magisterially within their cathedral closes, [etc.]. **1975** *Gramophone* Oct. 633/3 The new Karajan reading is certainly magnificent, magisterially played by the finest orchestra in the world.

magistery. Add: **5.** = MAGISTERIUM 2.

1899 C. B. PALLEN tr. *Sarda y Salvany's What is Liberalism?* xxxii. 105 The Church alone possesses supreme doctrinal magistery in fact and in right.

magistral, *a.* **1. a.** (Later example.)

1942 PARTRIDGE *Usage & Abusage* (1947) 5, I obtained permission from..eminent scholars..to quote at length from their magistral works.

magistrate, *sb.* Add: **3.** *magistrates' court*: a court for the trial of minor offences and small civil cases and for the preliminary hearing of more serious cases.

1867 T. W. SAUNDERS *Practice in Magistrates' Courts* (ed. 3) i. 1 The various kinds of magistrates' courts—petty and special sessions—quarter sessions—clerk to the justices. *Ibid.*, It is..the design of the following pages to treat of the *practice* of the magistrates' courts as we find these courts established. **1904** J. F. & B. E. CRUMP *Magistrate's Pocket Manual* xii. 47 There is perhaps even greater need to observe the spirit of these instructions in the Magistrates' Courts, because..rough and uncultivated manners..make so great a strain on the patience and self-control of the Bench. **1952** *Act 1 Eliz. II* c. 55 § 38 Where a person is taken into custody for an offence without a warrant and is retained in custody, he shall be brought before a magistrates' court as soon as practicable. **1959** JOWITT *Dict. Eng. Law* II. 1341/2 *Petty sessional court*, a court of summary jurisdiction consisting of two or more justices..now known as the magistrates' court. **1965** *New Statesman* 10 Dec. 920/2 The police courts, reborn as magistrates' courts in 1952, are still police courts not only to those who never frequent them but also to the old lags who frequent them most.

4. *Sc. slang.* In full, *Glasgow magistrate.* A herring.

1833 *Chambers's Edin. Jrnl.* 2 Nov. 314/2 My neighbour, thinking it absurd to mince such a matter as a *Glasgow Magistrate*, handed up a whole one to the chairman. **1874** HOTTEN *Slang Dict.* 177 *Glasgow Magistrate*, a salt herring. When George IV. visited Scotland, a wag placed some salt herrings on the iron guard of the carriage belonging to a well-known Glasgow magistrate, who made one of a deputation to receive his Majesty. **1890** BARRÈRE & LELAND *Dict. Slang* II. 38/1 *Magistrate* (Scotch slang), a herring. **1895** J. NICHOLSON *Kilwuddie* (ed. 4) 119 Ham's unco dear, sae, if ye like, we's hae a 'magistrate'. **1950** *Scots Mag.* Dec. 171 Herring were cured there by Walter Gibson, a merchant of Glasgow and Provost of that city in 1688, and it is perhaps because of Provost Gibson that salt herring acquired their nickname of 'Glasgow Magistrates'.

Maglemose (mæglәmōᵘ·sә). [The Danish place-name *Maglemose* (great moss) near Mullerup on the west coast of Sjælland.] Used *attrib.* to designate the Mesolithic culture of northern Europe represented by bone implements and microliths found at Maglemose.

1915 W. J. SOLLAS *Anc. Hunters* (ed. 2) 544 The Maglemose industry is widely distributed around the Baltic. **1921** M. C. BURKITT *Prehistory* xii. 155 These..formed the Maglemose culture along the shores of the Baltic. **1931** *Times Lit. Suppl.* 8 Jan. 23/1 Azilian and Maglemose man. **1932** *Antiquity* VI. 218 It proves..that during the Maglemose period, there was fresh water at a spot now many feet below the sea. **1948** A. L. KROEBER *Anthropol.* (rev. ed.) xvi. 668 For the first time we find European habitation sites along beaches (Ertebølle and Asturian phases of Mesolithic culture), river mouths (Azilian), on lake and bog shores (Maglemose).

Maglemosian (mæglәmōᵘ·siăn), *a.* and *sb.* Also -ean. [f. prec. + -IAN.] **A.** *adj.* = prec. **B.** *sb.* A person of the Maglemosian culture; the culture itself.

1918 in WEBSTER Add. **1921** M. C. BURKITT *Prehistory* xiii. 163 The first culture found is the so-called Maglemosean. **1925** V. G. CHILDE *Dawn European Civilization* i. 9 The Maglemosians had axes and adzes and their command over nature was thereby enormously extended. **1943** J. & C. HAWKES *Prehist. Brit.* i. 26 The Maglemosians probably crossed the area now covered by the North Sea as fishers and fowlers. **1949** W. F. ALBRIGHT *Archaeol. of Palestine* iii. 62 If we allow the Tahunian a time spread of between one and two thousand years (say about 6000–4500 B.C.) it would have been roughly contemporary with the late Maglemosean. **1954** S. PIGGOTT *Neolithic Cultures* i. 14 The Star Carr discoveries in Yorkshire have shown that cultures of Maglemosean affinities were established in what is now eastern England at least as early as the beginning of Boreal times. **1970** *Guardian* 5 Aug. 18/4 An almost complete skeleton of an elk..unearthed near Blackpool..belongs to the early mesolithic period which began around 8000 B.C... This new find is the first evidence that this maglemosian culture extended to what is now the North-west of England.

maglev (mæ·glev). Also **mag-lev.** Abbrev. of *magnetic levitation* (see *LEVITATION 1 c).

1973 *Financial Times* 7 Sept. 25/7 Krauss-Maffei expects to be running a 20-passenger 'maglev' vehicle capable of speeds up to 250 mph later this autumn. **1973** *Sci. Amer.* Oct. 18/3 Two entirely different approaches to magnetic levitation (which is often shortened to 'maglev') are being pursued. **1974** *Globe & Mail* (Toronto) 16 May 4/4 The Canadian program is aimed at the development of mag-lev vehicles which will travel at 300 miles an hour, carrying about 100 passengers each.

magma. Add: **3. a.** In mod. use: A hot, fluid or semi-fluid material beneath the earth's crust from which igneous rocks are believed to be formed by cooling and solidification and which erupts as lava. (Further examples.)

1944 A. HOLMES *Princ. Physical Geol.* iii. 28 A volcano

is essentially a rift or vent through which magma (molten rock material highly charged with gases) from the depths is erupted at the surface. **1955** *Sci. News Let.* 19 Mar. 187/3 The liquefied material forms a fluid mass, called magma, that is lighter than the overlying rocks and tends to rise at an opening. Magma is called lava when it reaches the earth's surface. **1971** I. G. Gass et al. *Understanding Earth* xxi. 310/2 At the close of volcanism, the magma in these chambers will also solidify to coarse-grained rocks having the same composition as the lavas which previously were being erupted.

5. *fig.*

1928 R. A. S. Macalister *Archæol. of Ireland* iv. 219 A conglomerate of lazy abbreviations..studded in a repulsive magma of exotic gibberish. **1933** H. G. Wells *Shape of Things to Come* III. §1. 261 The need for a planned 're-nucleation' in the social magma that arose out of this dissolution.

6. *attrib.*, as (sense 3) *magma reservoir*.

1909 A. Harker *Nat. Hist. Igneous Rocks* ii. 36 At the depth at which we suppose a large magma-reservoir to be situated the conditions would be quite different. **1971** I. G. Gass et al. *Understanding Earth* xxi. 303/1 Because these volcanoes are large and their volcanic history is long, the magma reservoirs beneath them..have fractionated, giving rise to diversified lava assemblages.

magmatic *a.* (examples).

1890 in *Cent. Dict.* **1903** Geikie *Text-bk. Geol.* (ed. 4) II. 808 (*heading*) Magmatic ores. **1910** *Encycl. Brit.* III. 513/2 The modifications of the granite are ascribed to magmatic segregation (chemical and physical processes which occasioned diffusion of certain components towards the cooling surfaces). **1933** *Geogr. Jrnl.* LXXXI. 332 Magmatic movement, however caused, has been a factor in the formation of the Rift Valleys. **1957** G. E. Hutchinson *Treat. Limnol.* I. i. 33 Intermittent volcanic activity.. repeatedly drew off material from the magmatic reservoir. **1971** I. G. Gass et al. *Understanding Earth* i. 24/1 Quartz and nepheline if brought into contact at magmatic temperatures react to give albite.

magmatism (mæ·gmătiz'm). *Geol.* [f. L. *magmat-*, *magma* (see Magma) + -ism.] **a.** The theory advocated by magmatists.

1948 *Q. Jrnl. Geol. Soc.* CIII. 140 Dr. Reynolds 'tolls the knell' of the passing theory of 'magmatism' as an all-embracing explanation of the origin of all plutonic rocks. *Ibid.* 141 A new era in petrogeny, an era in which 'magmatism' will become incorporated with 'transformism', plutonic processes will become closely linked with metamorphic processes, and petrogenesis..will become an integral part of a wider science of geochemistry.

b. Motion or solidification of magma; magmatic activity.

1952 H. Ramberg *Orig. Metamorphic & Metasomatic Rocks* 3 (*heading*) Natural boundary between metamorphism and magmatism. **1970** Clifford & Gass *Afr. Magmatism & Tectonics* p. vii, Studies..to illustrate the relationship between two important geological processes —magmatism and tectonics. **1974** *Nature* 19 Apr. 650/1 Seismicity, tectonism and magmatism are now concentrated near plate margins.

magmatist (mæ·gmătist). *Geol.* [f. as prec. + -ist.] One who believes that many granitic rocks, or plutonic rocks in general, were formed from magma.

1947 *Geol. Mag.* LXXXIV. 209 Much of the disagreement..arises from a belief on the part of the Magmatists that Hutton proved the magmatic origin of granite. **1947** *Q. Jrnl. Geol. Soc.* CII. 443 He agrees with the 'magmatists' that 'the now classical views of Sederholm, put forth in explanation of the pre-Cambrian granite phenomena of Finland, are reasonable and may be applied..to other Archaean formations, such as the Canadian Shield'. **1957** H. H. Read *Granite Controversy* iii. 154 The inability of the magmatists to interpret the plain field-facts arises.. from the inertia of a century of belief in the magmatic origin of all granitic rocks.

‖ **magna cum laude** (mæ·gnā kɒm lǭ·di, mæ·gnā kum laudi), *phr.* Chiefly *U.S.* [L., 'with great praise'.] With great distinction; with a high level of achievement: designating a degree, diploma, etc., of a higher standard than the average. Also *transf.* and *fig.*

1900 *Dialect Notes* II. 13 A few words or phrases of direct Latin importation used at some of the older institutions...more commonly *cum laude*, *magna* or *summa cum laude* for the degree of honor attained in studies. **1933** Balmer & Wylie *When Worlds Collide* i. 22 He was graduated from Harvard with a *magna cum laude*. **1963** M. McCarthy *Group* v. 102 He was angry because Helena had failed to get *magna cum laude*, when a lot of the Jewish girls had. **1973** *Physics Bull.* Feb. 116/3 From 1911 to 1914 he was an 1851 Exhibition research scholar in physics, and spent the period in Göttingen taking special advanced courses in a variety of subjects and carrying out research on *Die Struktur des Gels der Kieselsäure*, for which he was awarded the degree of PhD 'magna cum laude'. **1973** E. Pace *Any War will Do* (1974) i. 47 The minute I heard poor Ollie shout, I knew you had passed. And when the counter splintered, you got magna cum laude.

magnaflux (mæ·gnăflɒks). Also **Magnaflux.** [f. *magna-*, taken as comb. form of Magnetic *a.* + Flux *sb.*] A method of testing metal parts for internal or surface defects by magnetizing the metal and observing the pattern assumed by a magnetic powder that is applied to it (either directly, or in oil that is used as a bath or sprayed on the metal). Usu. *attrib.*

1938 *S.A.E. Jrnl.* May 36/1 Another method of magnetic testing..involves the use of Magnaflux in which the parts to be inspected are first longitudinally or circularly magnetized... When properly magnetized, defects result in local flux leakage. Magnaflux powder, being of high magnetic permeability..adheres along the lines of flux leakage. **1940** Crump & Maul *Our Airliners* vii. 139 Every piece is measured and checked for wear and many of the parts go to the magnaflux tank. **1946** *Jrnl. R. Aeronaut. Soc.* L. 535/2 Japanese designers considered that all important parts should be hardness-tested after heat treatment; that welded primary structures should be magnaflux tested; and casting radiologically examined. **1963** Jones & Schubert *Engin. Encycl.* (ed. 3) 783 Although the Magnaflux method of inspection has been universally adopted throughout the aircraft industry it is by no means confined to it.

magnalium (mægnēi·liɒm). [f. Magn(esium + Al(umin)ium.] A light aluminium-based alloy containing some magnesium.

1900 *Motor-Car World* I. 90/1 Magnalium is a new alloy of aluminium with from ten to thirty per cent. of its weight of magnesium. **1910** *Encycl. Brit.* I. 708/2 This alloy, under the name of magnalium, is coming into use for small articles in which lightness and rigidity have to be combined. **1948** J. J. Stevens tr. *A. von Zeerleder's Technol. Aluminium* ii. 20 The binary aluminium-magnesium alloys, which were developed in 1899 by Mach under the name 'Magnalium', exhibit rising mechanical properties with rising magnesium content... After 1910 these alloys fell out of favour owing to low corrosion resistance.

‖ **magna mater** (mæ·gnă mēi·təɹ, mæ·gnă mā·təɹ). [L., lit. great mother.] A mother-goddess, a fertility deity; also *transf.*

1728 [see Great A. *adj.* 12 b]. **1845** *Encycl. Metrop.* XVII. 481/2 *Cybele*, otherwise known as Ops, Rhea, Vesta,..Idæa Mater, Magna Mater, Mater Deorum, Bona Dea, and Tellus. **1896** [see *fieldstone]. **1919** J. Buchan *Mr. Standfast* xxi. 356 There was a strange cult in the ancient world, the worship of *Magna Mater*—the Great Mother. **1962** 'M. Innes' *Connoisseur's Case* viii. 92 She was a kind of *magna mater* whose true sphere was a teeming nursery. **1974** *Times Lit. Suppl.* 13 Sept. 977/3 In Frieda [von Richthofen]'s case this was a straightforward matter. Like other *magnae matres* of the time (Mr. Green discusses Alma Mahler, Isadora Duncan, Lou Andreas-Salome and Mabel Dodge Luhan), she sought to enhance life by erotic love.

magnateship (mæ·gnēitʃip). [See -ship.] The dignity or position of a magnate.

1916 W. J. Locke *Wonderful Year* i. 4 The vast, original Margett had retired..to county magnateship. **1937** *Sat. Rev. Lit.* 24 Apr. 14 The Ball Brothers glass jar magnateship.

magnesian, *a.* Add: **2.** *Min.* [See *-ian 2.] Of a mineral: having a (small) proportion of a constituent element replaced by magnesium.

1930 W. T. Schaller in *Amer. Mineralogist* XV. 571/2 Magnesium-magnesian. **1951** C. Palache et al. *Dana's Syst. Min.* (ed. 7) II. 503 Cuprian melanterite and pisanite are obtained from solutions containing added copper sulfate; and magnesian and other compositional variants may be similarly obtained by appropriate additions. **1968** I. Kostov *Mineral.* ii. ix. 498 Kirovite a magnesian variety [of melanterite].

magnet. Add: **4.** *magnet-drawn* adj.

1923 R. Graves *Whipperginny* 43 She was magnet-drawn by his least wish. **1952** R. Campbell tr. *Baudelaire's Poems* 67 When to a cherished cat my gaze Is magnet-drawn.

magnetic, *a.* and *sb.* Add: **A.** *adj.* **1.** (Selected further examples; see also the sbs., and sense *5).

1926 *Jrnl. Iron & Steel Inst.* CXIV. 112 The concentrate from the magnetic separation is always mixed with much water, and cannot on that account be directly used. **1964** F. L. Westwater *Electronic Computers* iv. 65 If we now suppose that we have another electro-magnet which we can call a 'reading' magnet or magnetic head as it is more usually termed, when the magnetised spot of wire passes under the reading head there will be a change of magnetic flux through the coils on the head. **1964** T. W. McRae *Impact of Computers on Accounting* i. 6 The current vogue is to use magnetic storage devices which employ the principle of magnetic hysteresis or retained magnetism. The more popular of these devices are: 1. Magnetic tape. 2. Magnetic drum. 3. Magnetic disks. 4. Magnetic cards. 5. Magnetic core (i.e. ferrite core). **1966** A. Battersby *Math. in Managem.* viii. 200 An alternative to optical scanning is to use characters printed in magnetic ink. The micr system (Magnetic Ink Character Recognition) is mainly used by banks, and the specially designed characters are now becoming a familiar feature of our cheque-books. **1967** D. Wilson in Wills & Yearsley *Handbk. Managem. Technol.* iii. 42 Many data processing installations are now planning to use magnetic disks or magnetic cards for the first time. **1970** *Sci. Amer.* Feb. 29/2 By 1972, if not sooner, it should be economic to replace the standard magnetic-core memory of the computer (the type of memory in which tiny magnetic rings of ceramic are threaded on a matrix of thin wires) with a series of LSI memory modules. **1971** J. H. Smith *Digital Logic* vi. 126 A variation of the drum is the magnetic disc, very much like a long playing record, but again coated with magnetic material. A whole stack of these discs are normally assembled to give a reasonably fast memory of very large capacity.

5. Special collocations (see also sense 1 in Dict. and Suppl.): **magnetic anomaly,** a local deviation from the general pattern of the earth's magnetic field; **magnetic bottle,** a magnetic field that confines a plasma inside it to a restricted region; **magnetic brake,** a friction brake that is actuated magnetically; **magnetic bubble,** a small, mobile region of reverse magnetization in a very thin sheet of magnetic material in which the magnetization is perpendicular to the sheet and predominantly in one direction; **magnetic drum** *Computers*, a cylinder that can be rotated and has a magnetizable outer surface on which data can be recorded on circular tracks by means of a set of fixed heads (one opposite each track); **magnetic induction** (see *induction 10 b); **magnetic lens,** (a device producing) a magnetic field capable of focusing a beam of charged particles; **magnetic memory,** (*a*) a dependence of the magnetic state of a body on its previous magnetic history; (*b*) *Computers*, a memory (sense *2 d) that employs the magnetic properties of bodies; **magnetic mine,** a submarine mine that is detonated by the approach of a magnetized body such as a ship; **magnetic mirror,** (*a*) a magnetized surface that reflects light; (*b*) a magnetic field that causes approaching charged particles to be reflected; **magnetic moment** (see *moment *sb.* 8 c); **magnetic quantum number,** the quantum number *m* (see *M 4* b); **magnetic resonance accelerator** = *cyclotron; **magnetic stripe** (see *stripe *sb.*³); **magnetic tape,** tape (now usu. of plastic) coated or impregnated with a magnetic material, or made of magnetic material, for use as a recording medium.

1899 *Jrnl. Brit. Astron. Assoc.* IX. 134 (*heading*) Magnetic anomalies in Russia. **1929** Eve & Keys *Appl. Geophysics* ii. 38 Three auxiliary magnets of different strengths are usually carried in order to provide for the measurement of large magnetic anomalies and thus extend the range of measurement. **1971** *Nature* 5 Feb. 374/2 The magnetic evidence for seafloor spreading is based on the pattern of the linear magnetic anomalies which lie over and to the sides of mid-oceanic ridges. **1957** *Sci. Amer.* Aug. 80/2 Since no conceivable material will withstand the temperature of these [thermonuclear] reactions, the hope is to contain them in a 'magnetic bottle' that will take advantage of the plasma's response to electromagnetic forces. **1967** *Science Year* 341 No one yet knows how to confine a hot plasma in a 'magnetic bottle' long enough for the energy liberated by relatively infrequent thermonuclear reactions to overcome the inevitable loss from electromagnetic radiation and from plasma escaping from the bottle. **1922** Glazebrook *Dict. Appl. Physics* II. 323/1 In magnetic brakes..an electromagnet..is held just above the rail to which it is attracted upon excitation. **1970** *Nature* 10 Oct. 114/1 Magnetic bubbles, small stable regions of reverse magnetization in a highly anisotropic ferrimagnetic sheet, were described by Dr F. C. Rossol. **1971** *Sci. Amer.* June 78/1 A promising alternative..exploits a new technology in which data bits are stored in the form of magnetic 'bubbles' moving in thin films of magnetic material... The bubbles are stable over a considerable range of conditions and can be moved from point to point at high velocity. **1950** W. W. Stifler *High-Speed Computing Devices* xiv. 304 A rotating magnetic drum..is a static storage system, according to this definition, because data recorded on the drum are static with respect to the surface of the drum. **1955** *Sci. Amer.* June 98/2 For the larger, intermediate-speed memory of a computer the favorite device at present is the magnetic drum. **1968** *Brit. Med. Bull.* XXIV. 192/1 Different users require.. different combinations of back-up storage (magnetic tape units,..magnetic drum units, and so on). **1919** *Phil. Mag.* XXXVIII. 709 Such a 'magnetic lens' is not of much immediate value as the magnetic spectrum of positive rays is very complex. **1966** *McGraw-Hill Encycl. Sci. & Technol.* VIII. 33/2 Magnetic lenses are employed as condensers, objectives, and projection lenses in magnetic electron microscopes, as final focusing lenses in the electron guns of cathode-ray tubes, and for the selection of groups of charged particles of specific velocity in velocity spectrographs. **1887** *Jrnl. Soc. Telegr. Engin.* XVI. 523 No matter how treated, a piece of soft iron has a 'magnetic memory'. **1947** L. B. Loeb *Fund. Electr. & Magn.* (ed. 3) xvii. 242 A continuous curve is retraced that never restores the magnetic material back to its zero value. This behavior can be ascribed to a sort of 'magnetic memory' of the substance. **1957** *Economist* 30 Nov. 797 The electronic valves, transistors and magnetic memories used in the modern computer have been developed from knowledge gained from other spheres of electronic applications. **1939** *News Rev.* 30 Nov. 13/1 We already know the secrets of the magnetic mine. **1939** *War Weekly* 1 Dec. 185/1 The new magnetic mine is said to be in use by the Germans at the present time. **1974** *Encycl. Brit. Micropædia* VI. 910/2 Three common types of naval mine are in use, classed by their method of detonation: magnetic mines, pressure mines, and acoustic mines. **1894** *Jrnl. Inst. Electr. Engin.* XXIII. 448 (*heading*) Researches on the reflection of polarised light from magnetic mirrors. **1952** R. F. Post in *Classified Conf. Thermonucl. Reactors held at Denver June 28, 1952* (AEC Rept. Wash.–115) 83 A second possible attack on the problem of containment of a linear discharge at its ends is through the use of what might be called an 'enhanced magnetic mirror'. The ordinary 'magnetic mirror' effect has been known for some time. **1956** L. Spitzer *Physics of fully Ionized Gases* i. 11 The constancy of the magnetic moment has the immediate result

that gyrating particles will tend to be reflected from regions of increasing magnetic field... Such a reflecting region may be called a 'magnetic mirror'. **1966** *McGraw-Hill Encycl. Sci. & Technol.* X. 388/1 The 'mirror machine' (invented by R. F. Post) allows confinement [of the plasma] in a tube with ends 'plugged' by magnetic mirrors... A magnetic mirror is merely a localized region where the magnetic field is made much stronger than average, so that charged particles tend to be reflected as they approach the mirror. **1923** Magnetic quantum number [see *M 4* b]. **1961** POWELL & CRASEMANN *Quantum Mech.* x. 355 Since the single electron in these atoms has zero angular momentum in the ground state, the magnetic quantum number must be $m=0$. **1935** Magnetic resonance accelerator [see *CYCLOTRON]. **1968** F. KERTESZ *Lang. Nucl. Sci.* (Oak Ridge Nat. Lab. TM 2367) 17 A number of the accelerators..have names ending in '...tron', recalling the generic term *cyclotron* or magnetic resonance accelerator. **1937** *Bell Syst. Techn. Jrnl.* XVI. 165 (*heading*) Sound recording on magnetic tape. **1942** *Jrnl. R. Aeronaut. Soc.* XLVI. 68 This paper described an electro-magnetic method of producing and controlling reverberation by the use of a magnetic tape recording system. It consists of recording a sound pattern magnetically on steel tape. **1957** *Economist* 30 Nov. 807/2 The computer, in turn, produces the instructions on magnetic tape which is read by the control apparatus of the cutting machine. **1958** *Listener* 16 Oct. 605/1 Stereophonic magnetic tape recordings have been available for some time. **1967** C. BERNERS-LEE in Wills & Yearsley *Handbk. Managem. Technol.* i. 6 It may well be that the data already exists on magnetic tape in a computer installation.

B. *sb.* **3.** (Further example.)

1971 *Nature* 26 Nov. 187/2 Gravity and magnetics have theorems which limit the amount of interpretation which can be applied to observations of potentials and in general geophysicists work within the confines of these restrictions.

4. *pl.* Magnetic devices or materials.

1965 *IEEE Trans. Magnetics* Mar. 3/1 The name became Magnetics Group, and its scope:..treatment of all matters in which the dominant factors are the fundamental developments, design, and certain applications of magnetic devices. **1971** *Physics Bull.* Nov. 646/1 The size of the magnetics market however does not hold any reassurances for research.

5. *pl.* Magnetic properties or phenomena collectively.

1972 *Nature* 22 Dec. 438/1 They have recorded bathymetry, magnetics and gravity along a profile over a ridge striking N 50° W. **1974** *Ibid.* 4 Jan. 9/1 A new geophysical model for the Red Sea is presented in Fig. 5... The synthetic magnetics is compared with the observed. The fit of the anomalies for the older crust is not quite so good as for the Gulf data.

magnetician. (Examples.)

1838 *Ann. Electr. Magn. & Chem.* II. 53 Had Mr. Clarke, the 'magnetician', known that fact, he might have saved himself the trouble. **1846** C. FOX *Jrnl.* 13 Oct. (1972) 168 Mineral veins, however, a quite different case; infinite scope therein for Papa and all Magneticians. **1897** *Proc. R. Soc.* LX. p. x, His first paper on that subject..was completely overlooked by magneticians. **1939** *Geogr. Jrnl.* XCIII. 157 Gilbert the magnetician. **1966** *McGraw-Hill Encycl. Sci. & Technol.* IV. 20/1 One of these [components], called variation by the navigator and magnetic declination by the magnetician, is the angle between magnetic and geographic meridians. **1970** *Nature* 29 Aug. 982/2 He found that magneticians were far readier to collect than to interpret data, and set himself to analyse geomagnetic variations.

magnetization. Add: **2.** Special Comb.: **magnetization curve,** a graph of magnetic induction against magnetic field strength in the same region.

1890 J. HOPKINSON in *Proc. R. Soc.* XLVIII. 2 A magnetisation curve is all that I have obtained free from doubt; the sample was heated and its magnetisation determined at various temperatures for a force of 0·50. **1968** C. G. KUPER *Introd. Theory Superconductivity* v. 86 Figure (5.5) shows a typical magnetization curve for a small cylinder in a transverse field.

magneto, *sb.* Add: *spec.* one in an internal-combustion engine employing spark ignition.

1902 J. E. HUTTON in A. C. Harmsworth et al. *Motors* viii. 154 The magneto is driven off the main shaft of the engine..by means of a chain. **1929** A. HUXLEY *Let.* 22 Feb. (1969) 307 At Albengo on the Italian riviera, our magneto suddenly gave out. Short circuit, something fused. **1959** *Motor Man.* (ed. 36) vi. 169 Special equipment is needed to develop the high tension required for ignition... There are two systems. One, commonly known as coil ignition, takes in low tension current from the battery and converts it to high tension. The other depends upon a magneto-electric machine—a magneto, for short—which is driven by the engine and generates high-tension current. **1971** *Arable Farmer* Feb. 49/1 On external types of magneto..the points are normally accessible by removing the end cover.

b. *attrib.*, as **magneto ignition,** in some internal-combustion engines, ignition by means of a voltage generated by a magneto that is driven by the engine.

1902 J. E. HUTTON in A. C. Harmsworth et al. *Motors* viii. 159 The magneto ignition system, which is applied to all the new model motor-engines of M. Mors, consists of a magneto-electric rotary machine, combined with a series of mechanical contact-breakers. **1905** *Westm. Gaz.* 12 Dec. 4/2 The all but universal use of magneto-ignition. *c* **1933** E. MOLLOY *Mod. Motor Repair* III. 877/1 The distance of the gaps..should be adjusted as accurately as possible to between ·015 to ·018 in.; if the engine is fitted with magneto ignition. **1966** *McGraw-Hill Encycl. Sci. & Technol.* VIII. 52/2 The higher cost of magneto ignition is not warranted in modern automobiles, where storage batteries are required for other electrically operated equipment.

magneto-. Add: *magneto-induced* adj.; **magne:toca·loric** *a.* [ad. F. *magnétocalorique* (Weiss & Piccard 1918, in *Compt. Rend.* CLXVI. 352)], applied to the reversible change of temperature that accompanies a change in the magnetization of a paramagnetic or ferromagnetic material; **magne:toca·rdiogram** *Med.*, a record of the variations in the magnetic field of a patient's body that occur as a result of the beating of the heart; so **magne:toca·rdiograph,** an instrument used to make such records; **magne:tocardiogra·phic** *a.*, **-cardio·graphy**; **magne:toche·mistry,** the branch of science concerned with the relation between magnetism and chemical phenomena, molecular and atomic structure, etc.; so **magne:toche·mical** *a.*; **magne:to-explo·der,** a magneto-electric apparatus for firing an explosive charge; **magne:to-io·nic** *a.*, of or pertaining to the joint effect of a magnetic field and ionized gas (e.g. in the ionosphere) on the propagation of radio waves; **magne:to-mecha·nical** *a.*, pertaining to the interrelation of magnetic and mechanical properties, esp. the magnetic moment and angular momentum of an atom or particle; *spec.* applied to the ratio of these quantities (or its reciprocal); **magneto-optics,** substitute for def.: the branch of physics which deals with the optical effects of magnetic fields; (further examples); **magne:toresi·stance,** dependence of the electrical resistance of a body on an external magnetic field; **magne:toso·nic** *a.*, pertaining to or designating a type of magnetohydrodynamic wave that has two speeds of propagation (both functions of the magnetic field strength and the speed of sound in the fluid), can travel in any direction relative to that of the field, and is characterized by a displacement of the fluid in any direction in the plane defined by the directions of propagation and of the field except the direction normal to the former; **magne:tosta·tics** [after ELECTROSTATICS], the branch of physics dealing with unchanging magnetic fields; so **magne:tosta·tic** *a.*, **-sta·tically** *adv.*; **magne·totail** [TAIL *sb.*[1]], the broad, elongated part of the magnetosphere that extends from the vicinity of the earth in a direction away from the sun; **magne:totellu·ric** *a.*, pertaining to or designating a technique for investigating the electrical conductivity of the earth by measuring simultaneously fluctuations in its magnetic and electric fields at the surface; hence **magne:totellu·rics** [-IC 2], the branch of geophysics concerned with this.

1921 *Sci. Abstr.* A. XXIV. 724 (*heading*) Magnetocaloric effect. **1937** J. W. T. SPINKS tr. *Herzberg's Atomic Spectra & Atomic Struct.* vi. 211 The magnetocaloric effect [in paramagnetic substances] is so small at room temperature that it cannot be observed. **1965** A. H. MORRISH *Physical Princ. Magn.* iii. 83 Since for a normal paramagnetic salt $(\partial M/\partial T)_H$ is negative, an increase in the field produces a heating and conversely decreasing H gives rise to a temperature drop. This is often called the magnetocaloric effect. The important application of this effect is in the production of temperatures below 1°K. **1963** BAULE & MCFEE in *Amer. Heart Jrnl.* LXVI. 95/1 The electromotive forces of the heart set up currents in the torso which in turn produce magnetic fields. These fields are exceedingly small... Nevertheless, they may be detected, as is shown by the magnetocardiogram. **1971** *New Scientist* 10 June 631/2 As well as being more convenient, a magnetocardiogram (MKG) is faster to take than an electrocardiogram. **1963** *Amer. Heart Jrnl.* LXVI. 96/2 The magnetocardiograph offers the potentiality of detecting otherwise 'silent' components of the electromotive forces of the heart. **1967** *N.Y. Times* 6 May 33 Dr. Cohen said..it is..too early to assess the long-range potential of the magnetocardiograph. **1970** *Amer. Heart Jrnl.* LXXIX. 231/2 Since the electromotive surface representing the activation boundaries lies in the heart, electrocardiographic or magnetocardiographic lead fields need only be known within this region. **1967** *Bull. Exper. Biol. & Med.* LXIV. 1024 Magnetocardiography is also valuable as an addition to electrocardiography. **1911** *Jrnl. Chem. Soc.* C. II. 367 (*heading*) Magneto-chemical researches on the atomic structure of the halogens. **1943** P. W. SELWOOD *Magnetochem.* iii. 58 The dimerization of free radicals and of other paramagnetic molecules is one of the most fruitful fields for magnetochemical research. **1972** *Indian Jrnl. Chem.* X. 726/2 A magnetochemical study of these derivatives has also been carried out to get some information about the nature of bonding of the metal ions with the polyphosphate chain. **1914** *Chem. Abstr.* VIII. 2648 (*heading*) Magneto-chemistry. **1937** *Nature* 20 Mar. 489/1 By magnetochemistry is meant the examination of the problems of chemical structure in the light of magnetic measurements and modern magnetic theory. **1969** *Jrnl. Leeds Univ. Union Chem. Soc.* XI. 42 The earliest significant work on magnetochemistry was probably by Faraday who devised a method for measuring susceptibility which is still used today. **1973** *Nature* 31 Aug. p. xi (Advt.), Magnetochemistry, especially the study of metal–metal interactions in paramagnetic clusters. **1869** *Chambers's Jrnl.* Apr. 271/2 A magneto-exploder.. was shewn, which will fire a fuse, and consequently a cannon. **1908** *Installation News* II. 149/2 Water-tight bells and magneto exploders for blasting purposes. **1871** *Eng. Mechanic* 3 Feb. 480/1 He is referring to a galvanic, and not a magneto-induced current. **1925** APPLETON & BARNETT in *Electrician* 3 Apr. 398/1 The same theory (for which we propose the name magneto-ionic theory) has also been independently put forward by Messrs. Nicholls and Schelling ('Nature', March 7th, 1925). **1932** E. V. APPLETON in *Jrnl. Inst. Electr. Engin.* LXXI. 645/2 It is highly probable that interference between the various magneto-ionic components of singly- and multiply-reflected downcoming waves is partly responsible for resultant intensity fading. **1973** *Physics Bull.* May 291/3 A first start is made to the problem of the transfer of radio emission in a pulsar magnetosphere by applying the method of magnetoionic theory. **1925** *Sci. Abstr.* A. XXVIII. 611 Magneto-mechanical anomaly of the atom. **1930** Magneto-mechanical [see *GYROMAGNETIC *a.* 1]. **1950** W. FINKELNBURG *Atomic Physics* iii. 153 The magnetic moment of paramagnetic atoms is due to the electron rotating in its orbit or to the spin of the electron. The so-called magnetomechanical parallelism enables us to distinguish between these two contributions to the atomic magnetism. **1953** [see *GYROMAGNETIC *a.* 1]. **1958** CONDON & ODISHAW *Handbk. Physics* IV. viii. 136/1 Because of the magnetomechanical interactions.., internal stresses due to cold-working, impurities, precipitates, etc., contribute a spatially varying component of the short-range energy. **1913** P. ZEEMAN *Res. Magneto-Optics* p. xi, To the memory of this sage [*sc.* Faraday]—..the pioneer in magneto-optics as in so many things, I have ventured to dedicate this volume. **1960** *Physical Rev. Lett.* IV. 357 (*heading*) Photon momentum effects in the magneto-optics of excitons. **1930** L. W. MCKEEHAN in *Physical Rev.* XXXVI. 949 The magneto-resistance effect in non-ferromagnetics is only measurable with accuracy in very intense magnetic fields. **1961** *Engineering* 22 Dec. 823 One of the first practical devices to use the phenomenon of magnetoresistance is a voltage regulator. **1966** *New Scientist* 3 Feb. 286/2 The magnetoresistance effect in semiconductors, which has recently been shown to exist at frequencies well up into the microwave region. **1962** W. B. THOMPSON *Introd. Plasma Physics* v. 84 There is remarkably little evidence for the propagation of magnetosonic waves through a plasma. *Ibid.* 91 In the magnetohydrodynamic case, there are three possible parametrizing velocities C_s, C_A and the magnetosonic speed $C_T = \sqrt{(C_A^2 + C_s^2)}$. **1971** *Nature* 13 Aug. 443/3 The Crab pulsar..seems to be associated with a series of wisps of gas... Wisps 2, 3 and 4 have been generated by the magnetosonic waves which this motion of Wisp 1 produces. **1893** *Notices Proc. R. Inst. Gt. Brit.* XIII. 348 Magnetostatic screening by soft iron would follow the same law as electrostatic screening, if the magnetic susceptibility of the iron were infinitely great. **1950** *Physical Rev.* LXXV. 156 The domain patterns..represent configurations of low magnetostatic energy. **1969** M. A. UMAN *Lightning* 101 The magnetostatic field present during a lightning discharge is directly proportional to the discharge current. **1960** *Physical Rev. Lett.* V. 47/1 The figure of 10^{-8} erg/cm^3 represents..a solar wind flux sufficient to compress the geomagnetic field magnetostatically to $\sim 9R_e$ if we utilize the usual model. **1897** A. G. WEBSTER *Theory Electr. & Magn.* ix. 353 (*heading*) Parallel treatment of electrostatics and magnetostatics. **1952** E. G. RAMBERG tr. *Sommerfeld's Electrodynamics* I. 40 In most treatments the analogy between electrostatics and magnetostatics is emphasized. **1968** J. C. ANDERSON *Magnetism* i. 10 In magnetostatics it is convenient to define a magnetic pole strength, q, analogous to electric charge. **1971** *Daily Tel.* 4 Aug. 4/3 This region's outlines become distorted by a varying stream of electrified atomic particles from the Sun called solar wind. It sweeps part of the magnetosphere..into a tear-drop shape which scientists would now refer to as the Earth's magnetotail. **1973** *Nature* 9 Mar. 79/2 The multiple satellite mission will help unravel the spatial and temporal variations of the radiation belt, the magnetopause, the bow shock and magnetotail. **1953** L. CAGNIARD in *Geophysics* XVIII. 605 (*heading*) Basic theory of the magneto-telluric method of geophysical prospecting. **1967** L. R. ALLDREDGE in Matsushita & Campbell *Physics of Geomagn. Phenomena* I. I. ii. 55 Smith et al...describe instrumentation for magnetotelluric experiments for which simultaneous measurements of geomagnetic micropulsations and telluric currents are made. **1971** *Nature* 3 Sept. 13/1 To learn something about the behaviour of the upper mantle..Tammemagi and Lilley..have made four magnetotelluric soundings at 150 km intervals roughly along the latitude of Canberra. **1960** *Jrnl. Geophysical Res.* LXV. 4202/1 Useful field results have not been numerous in the literature, and field magnetotellurics is still in the developmental stage. **1967** A. T. PRICE in Matsushita & Campbell *Physics of Geomagn. Phenomena* I. II. iii. 295 There is, at present, much activity in the theory and practice of magnetotellurics, which should greatly help the task of unravelling and interpreting many geomagnetic phenomena.

magnetogyric (mægnī:todʒəiə·rik), *a. Physics.* [f. MAGNETO- + Gr. γῦρ-ος ring, circle + -IC.] **1.** Pertaining to or exhibiting the Faraday effect (*FARADAY 1).

1904 A. SCHUSTER *Introd. Theory Optics* xii. 272 All substances turn the plane of polarization when they are traversed by light in the direction of a magnetic field. They become therefore 'magneto-gyric'. *Ibid.* 290 A simple and rational connexion between the Zeeman effect and magneto-gyric properties.

2. Applied to the ratio of the magnetic moment of an atom or particle to its angular momentum.

1965 M. G. SCROGGIE *Electron in Electronics* ix. 204, γ_s,

the magnetogyric ratio for spin, is different from the orbital γ, being practically twice as large. **1967** Condon & Odishaw *Handbk. Physics* (ed. 2) VIII. ix. 113/1 The term $g_N(e/2Mc)$ is often replaced by γ, the magnetogyric ratio; hence, $\mu = \gamma\hbar I$. **1972** *Science* 27 Oct. 364/1 As long as $\mathbf{H}_1$ is applied, **M** precesses.. at a frequency given by the Larmor relation $\omega_R = \gamma H_1$ (in radians per second) where γ is the magnetogyric ratio of the nucleus. **1974** *McGraw-Hill Yearbk. Sci. & Technol.* 314/2 Compared to H^1, the C^{13} nuclei are much weaker magnets. The magnet strength (magnetogyric ratio γ) is only about ¼ that of protons.

magnetohydrodynamic (mægnī:tohəidrodəinæ·mik), *a.* [f. Magneto- (repr. *electromagnetic*) + Hydrodynamic *a.*] = *hydromagnetic *a.* Abbrev. MHD (see *M 5).

1943 [see *hydromagnetic *a.*]. **1950** H. Alfvén *Cosmical Electrodynamics* iv. 76 This coupling between mechanical and electromagnetic forces produces a type of wave motion, called magneto-hydrodynamic waves. **1960** *Times* 14 Apr. 2/2 (Advt.), Central Electricity Generating Board. .. Teams are being formed to work on the following projects:—..Magnetohydrodynamic generation. Fundamental research on (relatively) low temperature plasmas and their interactions with magnetic fields [etc.]. **1961** *Engineering* 16 June 817/3 The magnetohydrodynamic prospect, direct generation by passing hot gas through a magnetic field. **1962** F. I. Ordway et al. *Basic Astronautics* vi. 287 In a binary system, the angular momentum of the main star seems to have been transferred to the orbital motion of the second star. The means by which the angular momentum was shuffled off is not entirely clear, but magnetohydrodynamic or viscous effects could have played the key role. **1971** I. G. Gass et al. *Understanding Earth* vi. 94/2 Runcorn has re-examined the possibility of exciting the wobble [of the rotating earth] by the effects of magnetohydrodynamic turbulence in the fluid outer core.

Hence **magne:tohydrodyna·mical** *a.*, **-dyna·mically** *adv.*

1953 L. H. Aller *Astrophysics* ix. 354 Alfvén suggested a theory of sunspots based on magneto-hydrodynamical waves. **1959** *Jrnl. Geophysical Res.* LXIV. 1220/1 The entire medium can..be stirred up without requiring any magnetohydrodynamical work. **1962** W. B. Thompson *Introd. Plasma Physics* iv. 58 The possibility of producing a magnetohydrodynamically confined plasma has stimulated an enormous research effort in plasma physics.

magnetohydrodynamics (mægnī:tohəidrodəinæ·miks), *sb. pl.* (const. as *sing.*). [f. prec.: see -ic 2.] The more usual name for *hydromagnetics *sb. pl.*

1950 *Sci. Amer.* Oct. 39/3 Among these [theories] one can mention the magneto-hydrodynamics of charged particles proposed by the Swedish cosmologist H. Alfven. **1958** *Observer* 7 Sept. 13/5 'Magnetohydrodynamics', a branch of theoretical physics which combines classical theory of the behaviour of water and of magnetic fields,.. is becoming one of the most elaborate and enthralling branches of science. **1973** M. Harwit *Astrophysical Concepts* vi. 194 Magnetohydrodynamics..tells us that the presence of a force, such as a gravitational or electrostatic force, acting normal to the magnetic field, can produce a drifting motion.

Hence **magne:tohydrodyna·micist**, one who studies magnetohydrodynamics.

1955 *Sci. Amer.* Feb. 41/1 How the corpuscles travel through space is still in dispute. The Alfvén school of 'magneto-hydrodynamicists', for instance, maintains that the Chapman–Ferraro theory is basically incorrect, and that the solar corpuscles, as well as cosmic rays, are accelerated by magnetic and electrical fields in space.

magneton (mæ·gnėtǫn). *Physics.* [ad. F. *magnéton* (P. Weiss 1911, in *Compt. Rend.* CLII. 189), f. *magnéti-que* Magnetic *a.*: see *-on¹.] Any of several units of magnetic moment used in atomic and nuclear physics: *Bohr magneton* [*Bohr], a unit that arises naturally in Bohr's theory of the atom, equal to $eh/4\pi m$ (where e and m are the charge and mass of the electron, and h is Planck's constant, in S.I. units), i.e. about $9{\cdot}27 \times 10^{-24}$ joule per tesla; *nuclear magneton*, a unit used for expressing nuclear magnetic moments, defined analogously to the Bohr magneton with the mass of the proton replacing that of the electron and equal to about $5{\cdot}05 \times 10^{-27}$ joule per tesla; *Weiss magneton* [named after P. Weiss (see above)], a disused unit (equal to approximately one-fifth of a Bohr magneton) arrived at as the highest common factor of the measured magnetic moments of the atoms of various elements.

At first often regarded as a 'particle' or 'atom' of magnetism.

1911 *Sci. Abstr.* A. XIV. 191 The author [*sc.* P. Weiss] is led to postulate the existence of a common constituent of magnetic materials—the elementary magnets of [*sic*] which he terms *magnétons*, and which are to be found in the atoms of all magnetic substances. *Ibid.* 243 (*heading*) Size of the magneton deduced from the coefficients of magnetisation of solutions of iron salts. **1915** *Proc. Physical Soc.* XXVII. 430 A further comparison with experimental determinations is rendered possible by assuming that the magnetic moment of an electron revolving with the unit of angular momentum is equivalent to 5 magnetons. **1917** R. W. Hutchinson *Adv. Textbk. Magn. & Electr.* II. 313 This fundamental magnet he calls the 'magneton'. Calculation shows that iron, nickel and magnetite contain 11, 3, and 7 of these magnetons per molecule respectively. **1919** *Nature* 6 Nov. 227/2 The suggestion, first proposed by Weiss, that there exists a natural unit of magnetism called the magneton, analogous in some respects to the atom of electricity, still lacks definite proof. **1923** Bohr magneton [see *Bohr]. **1927** N. V. Sidgwick *Electronic Theory of Valency* 208 The Bohr magneton..is almost exactly five (4·96) times the Weiss magneton. **1932** J. H. Van Vleck *Theory Electr. & Magn. Susceptibilities* ix. 228 Although many molecules are still found to have moments which are integral multiples of the Weiss magneton within the experimental error, this is probably fortuitous, for there are many reasons for believing the Weiss magneton phenomenon to be spurious. **1935** *Physical Rev.* XLVII. 745/2 Using the value 3/2 for the spin of K^{39} and 0·0152 for $\Delta\nu$ we get 0·39 nuclear Bohr magnetons for the magnetic moment of the K^{39} nucleus. *Ibid.* 801/1 We obtain a value of 3·14 nuclear magnetons for the magnetic moment of the Li^7 nucleus. **1962** H. D. Bush *Atomic & Nucl. Physics* iii. 60 For all nuclei, including the proton the magnitude of the moment is not an integral multiple of the nuclear magneton. **1973** *Nature* 26 Jan. 239/1 Quantum fluctuations of the electromagnetic field close to the particle [*sc.* a free electron] imply an apparent increase in its magnetic moment beyond the value of one Bohr magneton implied by the unmodified Dirac theory.

magnetopause (mægnī·topǭz). [f. Magneto- + Pause *sb.*] The outer limit of a magnetosphere.

1963 Sonett & Abrams in *Jrnl. Geophysical Res.* LXVIII. 1243/2 We call the region discussed in this paper the magnetopause (the transition region between the magnetosphere proper and the interplanetary medium). **1969** *Physics Bull.* Feb. 54/1 The third spacecraft..is intended to investigate the 'solar wind' of low energy protons and electrons together with the geomagnetic cavity or magnetopause, where these particles are just in balance with the earth's magnetic field. **1971** I. G. Gass et al. *Understanding Earth* xviii. 259/2 The solar wind protons are reflected at the magnetopause, and so never enter the magnetosphere.

magnetophone. Add: **2.** An early form of moving-coil microphone.

1922 *Encycl. Brit.* XXXII. 528/1 The behaviour of microphones in this respect was often unsatisfactory, and telephone earpieces, or magnetophones, were frequently substituted for them. This results in diminished sensitivity, but the binaural effects are much improved. **1929** J. A. Ratcliffe *Phys. Princ. Wireless* v. 73 A microphone of quite a different type is much used at the present day for broadcasting. It is known as the magnetophone, and consists of a small coil of very light aluminium wire attached to the back of a freely moving diaphragm. The coil is placed between the poles of an electro-magnet. **1931** *B.B.C. Year-Bk.* 445/2 The magnetophone is relatively insensitive, and its output requires considerable amplification. **1962** *Listener* 8 Nov. 765/3 Two of the earliest [*sc.* BBC microphones] are to be seen..: Round-Sykes 'magnetophone', [etc.].

3. Also **-phon.** [a. G. *magnetophon.*] A tape recorder. (Used chiefly as a rendering of the German or with reference to German machines.)

1946 *Wireless World* Feb. 53/1 The equipment, known as the magnetophone, uses a thin plastic tape, about 0·25 in. wide, coated with a metallic powder film. **1949** *Electronic Engin.* XXI. 124/3 Sound recorders of the magnetophone type make use of two oscillatory currents in the recording head. **1953** F. Spandöck in E. G. Richardson *Technical Aspects Sound* I. xv. 410 After the Second World War magnetophones were built in many countries in many different forms. **1954** *Sci. Abstr.* B. LVII. 245/1 The various tests carried out on magnetophones, microphones and amplifiers are enumerated. **1974** *Encycl. Brit. Macropædia* XVII. 55/2 The Magnetophon Company of Germany succeeded in producing a magnetic film-coated tape that constituted a low-cost recording medium. During World War II the magnetophon, using the coated tape, served the Nazi propaganda organizations well.

magnetoplumbite (mægnī:toplʋ·mbəit). *Min.* [ad. G. *magnetoplumbit* (G. Aminoff 1925, in *Geol. För. i Stockholm Förh.* XLVII. 289), f. Gr. μάγνητ-, μάγνης Magnet + L. *plumb-um* lead: see -ite¹.] A strongly magnetic greyish black oxide of manganese, lead, titanium, and ferric iron occurring as acute dipyramidal crystals.

1926 *Chem. Abstr.* XX. 1194 (*heading*) A new oxide mineral from Långban, magnetoplumbite. **1944** C. Palache et al. *Dana's Syst. Min.* (ed. 7) I. 728 Adelsköld,.. (1938), gives *C6/mmc* as the space group of an artificial material supposedly the same as magnetoplumbite... The supposed composition $PbFe_{12}O_{19}$, by analogy with so-called β-alumina, proposed by Adelsköld (1938) is not indicated by analysis. **1968** I. Kostov *Mineral.* II. iv. 259 Magnetoplumbite has a perfect {0001} cleavage.

magnetosphere (mægnī·tosfiəɹ). [f. Magneto- + Sphere *sb.*] The region surrounding the earth or a heavenly body in which its magnetic field is effective and prevails over magnetic fields due to other causes (in the case of the earth not spherical but much elongated on the side away from the sun).

1959 T. Gold in *Jrnl. Geophysical Res.* LXIV. 1219/1 The region above the ionosphere in which the magnetic field of the earth has a dominant control over the motions of gas and fast charged particles..is known to extend out to a distance of the order of 10 earth radii; it may appropriately be called the magnetosphere. **1962** *Flight Internat.* LXXXI. 222 Instead of distinct inner and outer [radiation] belts, the picture now appears to be of one large region in which particles of different characteristics are trapped. Different types of particles have been observed at 1½ Earth radii (from the centre of the Earth), three radii, four radii (the older concept of the outer belt) and between six radii and the outer edge of the magnetosphere, as the region is now known. The outer limit varies from day to day but is at approximately 8–12 Earth radii. **1967** *New Scientist* 26 Jan. 198/1 Like the Earth, Jupiter is expected to have a 'magnetosphere' with a 'tail' pushed away from it by the solar wind. **1971** I. G. Gass et al. *Understanding Earth* xviii. 260/1 The Van Allen belts are zones of stably trapped particles within the magnetosphere. **1971** *Nature* 13 Aug. 443/3 Much work needs to be done to investigate the kinds of plasma instabilities that can occur in the magnetospheres of neutron stars.

Hence **magnetosphe·ric** *a.*

1961 *New Scientist* 19 Jan. 167/2 What have been termed 'magnetospheric waveguides' may provide new methods of radio communication between the northern and southern hemispheres. **1969** *Physics Bull.* June 223/1 Instabilities..occur in both laboratory and magnetospheric and interplanetary plasmas. **1974** *McGraw-Hill Yearbk. Sci. & Technol.* 277/2 The so-called whistlers in the kilohertz frequency range, as well as the long-period waves,..have become important tools in magnetospheric exploration both from the ground and from satellites.

magnetostriction (mægnī:tostri·kʃən). [f. Magneto- + L. *strictiōn-em* drawing or pressing together (f. *stringere* to draw together, draw tight).] A dependence of the state of strain of a body (and hence its dimensions) on its state of magnetization. Freq. *attrib.*

1896 *Phil. Mag.* XLI. 454 (*heading*) On the effects of magnetic stress in magnetostriction. **1926** *Jrnl. Iron & Steel Inst.* CXIII. 657 A reciprocal relation between magneto-striction and the effect of stress on magnetisation was investigated experimentally. **1937** *Nature* 18 Dec. 1068/2 A magnetostriction oscillator has been developed which produces intense audible vibrations of frequencies of 8000 cycles per second, capable of fracturing glass. **1959** H. Barnes *Oceanogr. & Marine Biol.* 74 The magneto-striction effect depends upon the fact that when certain metals, notably nickel, are placed in a varying magnetic field they undergo mechanical changes; nickel itself contracts in an increasing and expands in a decreasing magnetic field. As with the mechanical changes brought about by the piezo-electric effect, these also may be transmitted to a medium and, if they are sufficiently rapid, ultrasonic waves are produced. **1966** C. R. Tottle *Sci. Engin. Materials* vi. 138 Iron crystals expand along the direction of magnetization and contract at right-angles to it, whereas nickel contracts along the magnetization direction and expands perpendicular to it. This phenomenon is known as magnetostriction.

Hence **magne:tostri·ctive** *a.*, of, exhibiting, or employing magnetostriction.

1911 *Chem. Abstr.* V. 1550 (*heading*) A study of the Joule and Wiedemann magnetostrictive effects in steel tubes. **1939** *Nature* 11 Mar. 416/1 Pierce and the late J. H. Vincent independently developed similar oscillators based upon the magnetostrictive properties of iron and nickel and their alloys. **1951** *Electronic Engin.* XXIII. 16 The maximum dimensional change is obtained when the magnetostrictive element is excited at its natural resonant frequency. **1964** T. W. McRae *Impact of Computers on Accounting* i. 6 The Ferranti 'Pegasus' introduced the so-called magnetostrictive delay line store, whereby a mechanical stress wave passing along a wire represents a bit.

magnetron (mæ·gnėtrǫn). *Electronics.* [f. Magnet(ic *a.* + *-tron.] A diode with a cylindrical anode surrounding a coaxial cathode in which the flow of electrons is controlled by a magnetic field applied parallel to the axis, and now usu. designed to produce microwave pulses of high power.

1924 *Sci. Monthly* XVIII. 650 As the negatively charged grid cuts off the current of the three-element tube, so an external magnetic field will also do it in the two-element tube... Such a device, called a magnetron, was shown. **1945** *Times* 15 Aug. 2/1 In July 1940, Professor J. T. Randall, of Birmingham, produced a magnetron which was the first high-power generator of centimetric waves in the world. The magnetron remains the heart of every modern Radar equipment. **1958** *Engineering* 7 Feb. 174/3 The machine [*sc.* a linear accelerator] is of the travelling-wave type, using radio-frequency power generated by a magnetron valve operating at a frequency of 3,000 Mc/s. **1971** *New Scientist* 1 Apr. 36/1 Outred is developing microwave cavity sources using very high-powered (kilowatts) magnetrons for the infrared spectroscopy programme.

magnitude. Add: **2. c.** The intrinsic size of an earthquake or underground explosion (as distinguished from the intensity of its effects at any particular place), usu. expressed by a number that is a logarithmic function of the maximum resulting seismometric deflection adjusted to allow for distance.

1935 C. F. Richter in *Bull. Seismol. Soc. Amer.* XXV. 1 In the course of historical or statistical study of earthquakes in any given region it is frequently desirable to have a scale for rating these shocks in terms of their original energy, independently of the effects which may be produced at any particular point of observation. On the suggestion of Mr. H. O. Wood, it is here proposed to refer to such a scale as a 'magnitude scale'. *Ibid.* 2 The requirements of research..call for some estimate of the magnitude, in the sense here used, of each important shock in the California region. **1947** K. E. Bullen *Introd. Theory Seismol.* xiv. 234 The smallest earthquakes

reported felt are of magnitude 1·5;..those of magnitude 4·5 are capable of causing slight damage near the epicentre. **1959** B. F. Howell *Introd. Geophysics* ix. 125 Values of magnitude calculated at different observatories, using different seismometers at one observatory, or even different phases (body or surface waves) on the same seismogram, may be different. **1971** *Daily Colonist* (Victoria, B.C.) 7 Feb. 1/1 The quake had a magnitude of 6·7 on the Richter scale. **1972** *Sci. Amer.* Jan. 14/3 Underground explosions in the megaton range can have a body-wave magnitude of 6·5 to 7.

3. a. (Further examples.) Now regarded as a number on a continuous scale representing the negative logarithm of the brightness, such that a decrease of five magnitudes represents a hundred-fold increase in brightness and a decrease of one magnitude an increase of 2·512 times.

Before decimal or fractional numbers were used there was an intermediate stage illustrated by quots. 1796, 1826 (and also 1851).

1796 W. Herschel in *Phil. Trans. R. Soc.* LXXXVI. 168, 1.2m for instance, denotes that a star so marked is between the first and second magnitude. 2.1m signifies the same thing, with an intimation that the star so marked is nearly of the second magnitude, but partakes still something of the lustre of a star of the first order. **1826** J. F. W. Herschel in *Mem. R. Astron. Soc.* II. 444, I shall extend the examination to all stars of the 8th and (8·9) magnitudes; those of the 9th however not included. **1851** *Monthly Notices R. Astron. Soc.* XI. 187 The differences.. clearly show that widely different *scales* of magnitude have been adopted. *Ibid.*, This triple star..is designated by Argelander..as of magnitude 5·4 (or about 4·7). **1897** D. P. Todd *New Astron.* xvi. 423 Even the surpassing brilliancy of the sun can be indicated on the same scale; the number −25·4 expresses his stellar magnitude. **1930** R. H. Baker *Astron.* i. 20 The magnitude of the brightest star, Sirius, is −1·6; Canopus is −0·9. **1967** C. M. Huffer et al. *Introd. Astron.* xvii. 248/2 The photoelectric photometer, under the best conditions and by averaging several observations, can make measures down to 0·001 magnitude in accuracy.

magnolia. Add: **b*.** The colour of magnolia blossom, usu. a shade of pale pink. Hence *attrib.* passing into *adj.*, of the colour of magnolia blossom.

1931 *Daily Chron.* 21 May 6/1 A gown of pale magnolia-pink satin. **1963** *Times* 25 Apr. 6/6 For her wedding yesterday Princess Alexandra chose..a traditional dress ..fine cotton lace..faintly tinted with magnolia. **1971** R. Fuller in *Listener* 28 Oct. 583/1 My study has been repainted 'Magnolia'... Magnolia shows bright enough, if really Only off-white. **1974** 'S. Harvester' *Forgotten Road* xii. 137 The pale blue cotton shirt had been replaced by one of a droopy magnolia tint.

magnolious (mægnōu·liəs), *a. slang.* [Humorously f. Magnolia + -ous.] Magnificent, splendid, large. Hence **magno·liousness** [see -ness], the fact or quality of being magnolious.

1865 G. A. Sala *My Diary in Amer.* 114 But..she might be the sheriff's daughter.., accustomed to go out on Sundays with a 'magnolious' parasol and a 'spanglorious' crinoline. **1913** *Dialect Notes* IV. 19 *Magnolious*, very fine, magnificent. Used in Wyoming. 'How do you like my suit?' 'It's *magnolious*.' **1921** Joyce *Lett.* (1957) I. 173 With many thanks again and wishes for your magnolious expansiveness. *Ibid.* 175 Best wishes for your continued magnoliousness. **1942** Berrey & Van den Bark *Amer. Thes. Slang* § 29/5 *Magnificent*,..magnolious, phenomenal, red-hot.

magnon (mæ·gnɒn). *Physics.* [f. Magn(etic *a.* or Magn(etism + *-on[1].] The quantum or quasiparticle associated with a spin wave in a magnetic material.

1941 *Jrnl. Physics* (Moscow) IV. 358/1 Such magnetic excitations will be called..'magnons' (this name was suggested by L. Landau). **1971** *Nature* 18 June 424/2 Light scattering research has been revolutionized by the introduction of the laser... Scattering from magnons or spin waves has furthered understanding of antiferromagnetic materials and their phase transitions. **1973** *Sci. Amer.* Jan. 91/1 Phonons and magnons are typical examples of quasiparticles that are bosons.

magnoperate, *v.* Add: **3.** *intr.* (*nonce-use.*) To act in a grand manner.

1926 J. Agate *Contemporary Theatre 1925* 18 Everything about Richard is magnificent... He may be said not to act, but to magnoperate.

Also (as *nonce-wds.*) **magnopera·tion**, a great 'operation', a *magnum opus*; **magno·perator**, a great 'operator'; **magno·perous** *a.*, ? operating in a grand manner.

1928 Beerbohm *Seven Men & Two Others* (1950) 230 Mr. Nat Heinz, the famous 'Firsts Agent', had recently come over from New York... I wrote at once a respectful note to this magnoperator. **1930** *Times* 28 Mar. 15/4 Not until the very last volume did Sir John Fortescue seek the help of a 'devil' in any part of his 'magnoperation'. **1939** Joyce *Finnegans Wake* I. 57 The shadow of the huge outlander,..magnoperous, had bulked at the bar of a rota of tribunals.

magnox (mæ·gnɒks). *Nuclear Engin.* Also **Magnox.** [f. *mag*nesium *no ox*idation.] Any of various magnesium-based alloys containing a small proportion of aluminium that were developed for the containers of the fuel in nuclear reactors. Freq. *attrib.*

1953 *Technical Memorandum Min. of Supply, Div. of Atomic Energy (Production), Res. & Devel. Branch, Metall. Lab.* 30 Dec. 1 A magnesium alloy 'Magnox E'. **1955** *U.K. Atomic Energy Authority Rep. SCS-M-301* (*title*) The spectrographic determination of aluminium and beryllium in magnox alloys. **1957** *Financial Times Ann. Rev. Brit. Industry* 15/3 Materials able to stand up to much higher temperatures than..the present metallic uranium fuel and Magnox cans. **1962** *Economist* 2 June 913/1 Assumptions about the cost of nuclear generation of electricity by the magnox systems are unduly conservative. **1971** *Nature* 28 May 233/1 The UK had then just announced plans for its first nuclear power programme based on magnox reactors.

magnum (mæ·gnɒm), *a.* [Cf. Magnum.] (Freq. with capital initial.) Of a cartridge: adapted so as to be more powerful than its calibre suggests. Of a gun: designed to fire such cartridges. Also *absol.*

Magnum is registered as a proprietary name in the U.S. **1935** *Official Gaz.* (U.S. Pat. Office) 26 Mar. 718/2 Smith & Wesson, Inc., Springfield, Mass. Filed Feb. 20, 1935. *Magnum* for Revolvers. Claims use since Dec. 28, 1934. **1937** P. B. Sharpe *Compl. Guide Handloading* xxx. 286/1 A Magnum load..is anything which is 'stepped up' in power and should be so treated by the handloader. **1962** *Amer. Speech* XXXVII. 267 A ·357 Magnum bullet. **1970** *New York* 16 Nov. 50/1 A picture of Huggins and his Magnum on the floor of UCLA. **1971** V. Canning *Firecrest* xiii. 188 Guards who carried twelve-bore shotguns and ·375 Magnum rifles. **1973** *Black Panther* 31 Mar. 6/3 It was a magnum type revolver bullet that killed Carr. **1973** G. C. Nonte *Firearms Encycl.* 157 While magnum cartridges are legion in the rifle field, there are currently only three used in handguns.

Magnus effect (mæ·gnɒs efekt). [Named after Heinrich G. *Magnus* (1802–70), German scientist, who first described it.] The effect of rapid spinning on a cylinder or sphere moving through a fluid in a direction at right angles to the axis of spin, which results in a sideways force at right angles to both the direction of motion and the axis of spin and towards the side where the peripheral motion of the body is in the opposite direction to its overall motion.

1921 tr. *Cranz & Becker's Handbk. Ballistics* I. 314 A quantitative theory of the deviation of a sphere under the influence of the adhering air (Magnus effect) was attempted ..by Tait. **1925** *Flight* 8 Jan. 14/1 It does not appear to be until quite recently that the idea of applying the Magnus effect has occurred to anyone. **1943** R. C. Binder *Fluid Mech.* xi. 143 The Flettner rotor, which employs the Magnus effect, has been applied to the propulsion of marine vessels. Vertical cylinders are extended some distance above the deck. Each cylinder is rotated about its axis by a small motor, and an air force is produced for moving the craft. **1973** *Sci. Amer.* Apr. 121/2 The drag of the turbulent wake and the sidewise forces of the Magnus effect (the name given the transverse forces produced by the flow pattern around a spinning ball) are carefully considered. They are at the heart of baseball, tennis, golf and high-quality soccer.

Magosian (magōu·siăn), *a. Archæol.* [f. the place-name *Magosi* in Uganda + -an.] Of, pertaining to, or designating a stone-age culture in Uganda.

1932 Wayland & Burkitt in *Jrnl. R. Anthrop. Inst.* LXII. 369 The Magosian Culture of Uganda... Magosi, an outpost of the King's African Rifles in Karamojo (North-East Uganda), is situated 160 miles due north of the centre of Mount Elgon and less than 5 miles to the west of the..escarpment that forms the boundary between Uganda and..Kenya Colony. **1946** *Ibid.* LXXVI. i. 60/1 The Magosian culture was first noticed at Sawmills..by Jones in 1924. At that time..it was not even given a name. **1959** J. D. Clark *Prehist. S. Afr.* ii. 40 We find a similar link between the Middle and the Later Stone Ages. These are the various forms of the Magosian Culture and they are now placed in the Second Intermediate stage. This culture is named from the small rock cistern in north-eastern Uganda, excavated by Wayland. **1968** *Encycl. Brit.* II. 232/2 In the final stages of the Middle Stone Age, known as the South African Magosian, microlithic elements appear, just as in the case of east Africa. **1970** Bray & Trump *Dict. Archaeol.* 120 The sequence continued with Sangoan, followed by Early Middle Stone Age (Lupemban) industries related to those of the Congo, then Magosian.

magpie. Add: **3. a.** and **b.** (Later examples.)

1917 G. W. E. Russell *Politics & Personalities* iv. ix. 357 The most hideous of all known costumes—the episcopal 'Magpie'—costs £100. *Ibid.* 360 Carrying with his own apostolic hands the sacred appliances of Mitre or Magpie. **1920** P. Dearmer *Ornaments of Ministers* (new ed.) plate 29 (*caption*) The..figures of the two bishops well illustrate the 'magpie' dress. **1923** *Brewer's Dict. Phr. & Fable* (new ed.) 700/2 Formerly bishops were humorously or derisively called magpies because of their black and white vestments.

8. Add: *magpie-minded* adj.

1955 G. A. N. Lowndes *Brit. Educ. Syst.* iii. 49 Satisfying his curiosity..with unrelated snippets of knowledge which may lead to his becoming magpie-minded.

b. *attrib.* and quasi-*adj.*: with allusion to the acquisitiveness, curiosity, etc., of the magpie.

1808 M. Wilmot *Russ. Jrnls.* (1934) iii. 371 He deplores ..the Magpye mingle of foreign expressions with the language of the Country. **1901** G. B. Shaw *Caesar & Cleopatra* ii. 114 He maintains an air of magpie keenness and profundity. **1936** P. Fleming *News from Tartary* iii. ii. 116 All our actions..were closely scrutinized..by the Chinese with ill-concealed amusement and a magpie curiosity. **1940** *Proc. Prehist. Soc.* VI. 120 Beaker people ..showed a magpie acquisitiveness for other people's chattels. **1953** R. Lehmann *Echoing Grove* ii. 32 Where does she get this magpie streak from?.. But Mother hoarded, didn't she? **1962** G. K. Hunter *John Lyly* iv. 162 A variety of elements which would appeal to the magpie taste for classical motifs. **1974** 'J. Le Carré' *Tinker, Tailor* xv. 125 That whole magpie collection of tattered hotel junk.

c. Used *attrib.* of something with black and white colouring.

1885 Kipling *Phantom 'Rickshaw* (1889) 9 My eye was arrested by the sight of four *jhampanies* in 'magpie' livery... Was it not enough that the woman was dead.., without her black and white servitors re-appearing? **1923** *Daily Mail* 28 Mar. 11 *Magpie Millinery.* Black and white millinery is popular at all seasons. **1932** *Daily Tel.* 25 Apr. 4/5 Black and white is to continue its long reign this summer. Charming examples of this smart, practical 'magpie' fashion will be found at most inexpensive prices. *Ibid.* (Advt.), Ermine that imparts the fashionable magpie effect. **1942** H. J. Massingham *Field Fellowship* ii. 58 Moreton Old Hall in Cheshire is the conventional example of the magpie style. *Ibid.*, We find the wood-workmanship of the Avon Valley carried to the utmost pitch of elaboration and complexity... This is the country of the 'magpie' timber-framing. **1971** J. S. Gunn *Opal Terminol.* 26 *Magpie*, black and white patch formed together.

magslip (mæ·gslip). [said to be f. Mag(netic *a.* + **slip(-ring.*] A kind of electric motor designed so that, when it is operating as a receiver, the angular position of its rotor is maintained the same as that of the rotor of a similar motor electrically connected to it and operating as a transmitter; *orig.* applied to a particular design of receiver in which the rotor is a simple magnetic member without windings polarized by a fixed coil and moved by a three-phase stator.

1947 *Electronic Engin.* XIX. 259/1 Small instruments of the magslip or selsyn type, in which shaft position corresponds to the angular datum of the input quantity. **1950** *Engineering* 29 Dec. 557/3 The forces developed by the gyroscopes are..small and therefore have to be amplified. This is achieved by means of a sensitive hydraulic-motor unit developed by the Admiralty, the signals being transmitted from the gyroscope to the hydraulic unit by a system of 'magslips'. The magslip is, of course, well known as a device for the electrical transmission of angular displacements. **1954** *Jrnl. Brit. Interplanetary Soc.* XIII. 281 Running up the axis of the life compartment and projecting through the nose is the coelostat tube topped by a semi-elliptical mirror which can be tilted and rotated by a servo magslip motor thus allowing viewing in all directions. **1962** J. Bell in G. A. T. Burdett *Automatic Control Handbk.* iv. 11 Magslips were developed for use in the Royal Navy for transmission of bearing, range and elevation data between observing instruments, calculating tables, searchlights and guns. **1967** M. Healey *Princ. Automatic Control* xiv. 261 Some confusion existed over terminology, but military specifications have led to standardisation of sizes, voltages, frequencies, etc., so that older units such as Selsyns and Magslips are similar in principle but different in size.

magsman. Add: **2.** *Austral.* A story-teller, raconteur.

1944 W. E. Harney *Taboo* (ed. 3) 56 We were discussing dreams... It was the Doc's subject and he was..'giving it hell'. I let him go—with his complexes and repressions, but I was itching to have my say, for I too am a good 'magsman'. **1963** —— *To Ayers Rock & Beyond* v. 45 We would sit around the camp-fire to sing songs or recite our favourite poems... I am pretty sure that this bush school of oral teaching was the starting point with many a bush-poet and magsman, such as I, who kept up the yarning into later days. **1967** *Telegraph* (Brisbane) 8 Apr. 4/1 Hardy..became the official yarn-spinning champion of Australia today. He won the magsman's championship in Darwin.

‖ **magtig** (ma·χtiχ), *int. S. Afr.* [Afrikaans, shortened form of *allamagtig* Almighty *a.*] An exclamation of astonishment, awe, etc.

1891 B. Mitford *Weird of Deadly Hollow* viii. 77 *Magtag!* It's all through the *vrouw-menschen*. Whoever heard of bringing *vrouw-menschen* out springbok-hunting! **1925** W. Plomer *Turbott Wolfe* iii. 141 '*Magtig!*' he said, 'supposing Jacop dies—.' **1927** —— *I Speak of Afr.* i. 53 Magtig! but he's a strong man! **1943** 'B. Knight' *Covenant* (1944) ii. iii. 64 A hundred and fifty! *Magtig*, that is a lot to lose. **1948** *Sunday Times* (Johannesburg) 17 Oct. 21 If only Oom Piet were a reasonable man. But, magtig, what's the good of wishing that? **1973** S. Cloete *Company with Heart of Gold* 126 *Magtig*, what is a farm if there is no one to leave it to?

Magyar, *sb.* and *a.* Add: **B.** *adj.* **2.** *Dressmaking.* Of or pertaining to a style of blouse, bodice, etc., in which the sleeves are cut in one piece with the main part of the garment. Also *ellipt.* as *sb.*

1911 *Daily Colonist* (Victoria, B.C.) 5 Apr. 24/1 (Advt.), Evening gown of grey chiffon..with low neck and magyar sleeves. **1912** *Home Chat* 13 Apr. 112/2 Take away the lace insertion, and you get a quite plain little Magyar of white muslin. **1912** A. J. Reeve *Elem. Dress Pattern-Making* 17 The Empire yoke may be cut Magyar style if preferred. *Ibid.* 19 Magyar Blouse. Cut from Blouse Pattern. **1923** *Daily Mail* 19 June 15 A tight-fitting bodice which buttons down the back, the bolero bodice,

and cross-over magyar. **1952** *Woman's Jrnl.* June 73/3 Asta's interpretation is in white fleecy wool, with..magyar sleeves and immensely wide cuffs. **1958** V. CLIFFE *Making your own Clothes* iii. 42 It is not at all difficult, especially if you begin with what is known as a Magyar blouse. **1964** N. BRAY *More Dress Pattern Designing* xiii. 150 (*heading*) The kimono or magyar block. **1968** W. CLARK *Dressmaking Techniques for Trade Students* 33 The magyar is not to be confused with a Dolman sleeve which, although cut in one with the bodice, is closer fitting. **1972** H. STANLEY *Modelling & Flat Cutting for Fashion* viii. 93 Variations of style in category (b) are limited to the Kimono (or Magyar) and to styles with gussets of differing shapes.

mah (mā, *unstressed* mă), var. MY *poss. adj.* Common in written Black English. Cf. *ma* s.v. MY *poss. adj.*

1933 J. M. BREWER in *Publ. Texas Folklore Soc.* XI. 101 Yuh kin sow in mah fiel' ef yuh wants to. **1935** Z. N. HURSTON *Mules & Men* I. i. 31 Nobody don't want to buy *mah* ole rusty toe. **1938** C. HIMES *Black on Black* (1973) 168 Mah belly feels lak mah throat wus cut. **1953** S. A. BROWN in A. Dundes *Mother Wit* (1973) 41/2 Ah wuz settin' in de do' wid mah pipe. **1966** E. BULLINS *Theme is Blackness* (1973) 25 Now, brothers and mah good sisters, now are we really honest? **1966** M. THELWELL in A. Chapman *New Black Voices* (1972) 141 Ah *kno-o-ows* in mah heart she would. **1968** *Esquire* Apr. 88/2 To those so blessed as to have had bestowed upon them at birth the lifetime gift of soul, these are the most communicative and meaningful sounds..: the familiar 'mah' instead of 'my'.

Mahabharata (mahabā·ratā). Also **Mahābhārata, Mahabharat.** [Skr., 'the great history of the Bharata dynasty'.] An ancient Hindu epic.

1784 W. HASTINGS *Let.* 4 Oct. in C. Wilkins tr. *Bhăgvăt-Gēētā* (1785) 6 The Măhābhārăt contains the genealogy and general history of the house of Bhaurut, so called from Bhurrut its founder. *Ibid.* 11 The Măhābhārăt..is said to consist of more than one hundred thousand metrical stanzas, of which he [*sc.* Wilkins] has at this time translated more than a third. **1788** *Asiatick Researches* I. 351 The next in celebrity [to the *Ramayana*], if it be not superior in reputation for holiness, was the Mahábhárata of Vyása. **1795** C. WILKINS (*title*) The story of Dooshwanta and Sakoontalā extracted from the Mahābhārata, a poem in the Sanskreet language. **1863** M. WILLIAMS *Indian Epic Poetry* 16, I come now to the Mahá-bhárata or Great Bharateid, that is, the great poem which describes the achievements, mutual rivalries, and contests of the descendants of Bharata. **1894** J. C. OMAN *Gt. Indian Epics* II. i. 91 Of the one hundred thousand verses of the *Mahabharata* not more than a fourth part is concerned with the main story of the epic. **1901** E. W. HOPKINS *Gt. Epic of India* ii. 63 The later Rāmāyana..unquestionably betrays acquaintance with the Mahābhārata. **1931** E. J. THOMAS *Song of Lord* 22 In Book VI of the *Mahābhārata* begins the account of the great battle, probably a real event of prehistoric times. **1948** S. RADHAKRISHNAN *Bhagavadgītā* 14 The authorship of the *Gītā* is attributed to Vyāsa, the legendary compiler of the *Mahābhārata*. **1967** SINGHA & MASSEY *Indian Dances* II. viii. 88 Plays were written with themes from other sacred works such as the *Mahabharata*, the *Shiva Purana* and the *Bhagavad Purana*. **1972** P. HOLROYDE *Indian Mus.* iii. 75 Musical instruments had already been mentioned in the *Upanishads* (*c.* 600 BC) and in the *Mahabharat* (*c.* 500 BC–AD 200). **1972** M. SHEPPARD *Taman Indera* 69 The patrons of the Javanese and Balinese shadow plays seem always to have preferred the Mahabharata, with its plethora of gods and heroes. **1973** J. A. B. VAN BUITENEN *Mahābhārata* I. p. xiii, The central story of *The Mahābhārata* takes its matter from the legitimacy of the succession to the kingdom of Kurukṣetra in northern India.

mahaila (mahəi·la). Also **mahailah, maheila, maheileh, mahela(h), mehala.** [App. f. Arab *safīna mahīla* ship treated with bitumen; cf. Arab. *muhl(a)* liquid pitch.] A large river sailing-boat used in Iraq.

1904 H. V. GEERE *By Nile & Euphrates* vi. 86 On the Shatt el-Arab many varieties of native craft are to be seen, *dhows, mehalas.* **1916** T. E. LAWRENCE *Home Lett.* (1954) 319 The bellam is the passenger boat..and the Mahaila the cargo boat. Mahailas sit on the water like the scooped third of a melon-rind. **1922** *Blackw. Mag.* Jan. 10/2 They were..waiting for a mahaila to pass on her way upstream. **1952** E. F. DAVIES *Illyrian Venture* iii. 44 The Nile showed up.., and mahelas with their lateen rig were sailing downstream. **1969** R. MILLAR *Kut* i. 9 Townshend ..improvised a mock fleet from the few available river steamers and disguised *mahailas* (small river dhows).

Mahal. Add: **4.** The name of a type of coarse-woven carpet made in villages near Arak, Iran. Also *attrib.*

1911 G. G. LEWIS *Pract. Bk. Oriental Rugs* xiii. 201 Mahal is but a trade name. **1913** W. A. HAWLEY *Oriental Rugs* 286 If the field has concentric medallions, the rug may be a..Mahal. **1931** A. U. DILLEY *Oriental Rugs & Carpets* iv. 121 With us Mahal means the lowest grade of Sultanabad weaving. **1967** K. LARSON *Rugs & Carpets of Orient* 104/1 *Mahal*, made in: the districts of Mahallat, Muskabad and Dulakhoo. **1972** P. L. PHILLIPS tr. *Formenton's Oriental Rugs & Carpets* 150 Mahal carpets are easily recognizable because of their large knots and their softness.

Mahamad (mā·hămād). Also **Ma'amad** and with small initial. [mod.Heb. *ma'amad.*] The body of trustees ruling a Sephardic synagogue; freq. in phr. *gentlemen of the Mahamad.* Also *attrib.*

1831 *Ascamot, or Laws & Regulations Jewish Congregation* v. 37 The institution of the *Mahamad* in this congregation is very ancient... The *Mahamad*..is composed of the four *Parnassim* and a *Gabay*, elected annually. **1893** I. ZANGWILL *Childr. Ghetto* (ed. 3) I. 8 The blue-blooded Dons, 'the gentlemen of the Mahamad', who ruffled it with swords and knee-breeches in the best Christian Society. **1904** *Jewish Encycl.* VIII. 259 The mahamad exercised over the members of the congregation a despotic control which degenerated into a sort of police supervision. **1923** *Public Opinion* 17 Aug. 161/1 The gentlemen of the Mahamad had sent a call to members of the Spanish and Portuguese Jews' Congregation of London to assemble at their ancient burial-ground in Mile-end Road. **1944** *New Judaea* May 125/2 The Sephardim were to learn that..the Haham..would brook no trespass by the *Mahamad.* **1971** *Encycl. Judaica* XI. 638/1 One of the characteristic features of *ma'amad* policy was that on completion of its term of office the *ma'amad* itself appointed its successors.

Maharana (maharā·na). [Hindi, f. *mahā* great + *rānā* (dial. var. of *rājā*) RAJA(H).] = MAHARAJA(H), *spec.* in the title of the Maharana of Udaipur.

1823 J. MALCOLM *Mem. Cent. India* I. viii. 342 The old chief immediately unbuckled his sword, which..he laid at the feet of the Maha Rana... Maha Rana means Great Prince, the title by which the rulers of Odeypoor are always distinguished. **1876** L. ROUSSELET *India & Native Princes* xiv. 168 In my conversations with the Maharana I learnt several curious particulars concerning the fauna of the country. **1899** KIPLING *From Sea to Sea* I. 65 To return..to modern Udaipur... The Maharana and the Prime Minister..divide the power of the State. **1906** W. CROOKE *Things Indian* 398 Udaypur, the greatest of all, who claims descent from the god Ráma, and has a pedigree dating back to 144 A.D., calls himself Mahárána. **1971** *Femina* (Bombay) 2 Apr. 65/2 A former palace of the Maharana of Udaipur, the Lake Palace Hotel is presently run by the Maharana himself.

Maharanee. Add: Also **maharani.** (Earlier and later examples.)

1855 H. H. WILSON *Gloss. Judicial & Revenue Terms* 318/1 *Mahárání*,.. the principal wife of a Rájá, or a queen in her own right: applied also in courtesy to Hindu ladies of rank, although not of princely dignity. **1924** J. BUCHAN *Ld. Minto* x. 280 The Maharani sang Scots songs to him from behind the *purdah.* **1938** W. V. GRIGSON *Maria Gonds of Bustar* i. 3 The late Chief, Maharani Prafulla Kumari Devi, at her accession in 1924 was the last legitimate survivor of one of the most ancient royal families of southern India. **1971** R. RUSSELL tr. *Ahmad's Shore & Wave* ix. 110 God knows how many maharanis' hearts he had conquered.

Maharashtri (maharā·ʃtrī). Also **Maharastri** (-st-). [Skr. *Mahārāshṭrī* f. *Mahārāshṭra* Great Kingdom.] The Prakrit language of the Maharashtra region of India, the modern descendant of which is Marathi (MAHRATTI).

[**1803** H. T. COLEBROOKE in *Asiatick Researches* VII. 227 The Mahárāshtra or Mahrátta is the language of a nation which has in the present century greatly enlarged its antient limits.] **1880** A. F. R. HOERNLE *Compar. Gram. Gaudian Lang.* p. xviii, There are in reality only two varieties of Prákrit. One includes the Şaurasenī and the (so-called) Mahárāshṭrī. **1900** R. B. JOSHI *Comprehensive Marathi Gram.* i. 35 Our present Marathi is derived from the Maharashtri through the Apabransha form of that Prakrit language. **1903** *Indian Antiquary* XXXII. 189 It will be seen that Marâthî occupies exactly the same position within the modern Indo-Aryan vernaculars as Mâhârâshṭrî among the Prâkrits. **1968** *Encycl. Brit.* XVIII. 429/1 Later, Māhārāṣṭrī was especially used in composing lyric poetry, possibly on the basis of a popular oral lyric in the dialect; it began to flourish in the 3rd–4th centuries A.D.

Maharashtrian (maharā·ʃtriăn), *a.* and *sb.* Also **Mahrashtrian.** [f. *Maharashtra* a region of India + -IAN.] **A.** *adj.* Of, pertaining to, or characteristic of Maharashtra. **B.** *sb.* A native or inhabitant of Maharashtra. Cf. *MAHARASHTRI.

1957 *Ann. Reg. 1956* 103 Maharashtrian demonstrations took place outside Parliament House in Delhi. **1958** A. TOYNBEE *East to West* xxxii. 99 But how is one to dispose of a great city in which labour is Maharashtrian while capital is Gujerati? **1965** P. ROBINSON *Pakistani Agent* i. 8 Parulekar was a slightly-built Mahrashtrian in his late twenties. *Ibid.* viii. 106 The brassière, worn high in the Mahrashtrian style. **1969** *Capital* (Calcutta) 27 Feb. 358/1 In Bombay, the Shiv Sena, in its attempt to drive out all the non-Maharashtrians from the city, committed atrocities on them. **1969** *Enactment* (Delhi) Nov. 12/1 He is an 'invader' in Bombay just as the Maharashtrian is an 'invader' in Ahmedabad. **1971** *Hindustan Times Weekly Rev.* (New Delhi) 4 Apr. p. iv/5 A Maharashtrian girl married to a Saraswat..felt that 'marriage is mostly give and take'. **1971** *Femina* (Bombay) 30 Apr. 7/1, I was sitting and chatting with a group of friends, all of whom were Maharashtrians.

maharee, mahari, varr. *MEHARI.

Maharishi (mahari·ʃi). Also 9 **Maharshi.** [Skr. *mahārshi*, f. *mahā* great + *ṛishi* inspired sage.] The title of a Hindu sage or holy man. Also in more general use: (the title of) a popular leader of spiritual thought or opinion. Cf. *GURU.

1785 C. WILKINS tr. *Bhăgvăt-Gēētā* 144 *Măhărshēēs*, great saints, of whom there are reckoned seven, who were at the creation produced from the mind of Brăhmā. **1810** E. MOOR *Hindu Pantheon* 94 The terms *Devarshi, Rajarshi, Maharshi*, are nearly synonimous with *Rishi*; meaning saint, deified saint, or great sage. **1855** H. H. WILSON *Gloss. Judicial & Revenue Terms* 318/1 Maharishi. **1966** C. F. LUTES in Mahesh Yogi *Sci. of Being* (rev. ed.) 13 It was in Madras, in 1958, that Maharishi founded the Spiritual Regeneration Movement. **1968** *Listener* 4 Jan. 8/1 The Dial Press..have published as 'A Brahmin Book' *McLuhan hot & cool*, the new 'critical symposium' on Maharishi McLuhan. **1970** K. PLATT *Pushbutton Butterfly* (1971) ix. 107 Testimonials of faith and gratitude to Guru Maharishi Viparina. **1972** *Guardian* 1 Nov. 10/6 The Beatles..turned to the Maharishi, but he let them down.

Mahatma. Add: **1.** (Further examples.)

1855 *Daily News* 14 Feb. 5/2 Teacups are found by Mahatmas where no teacups should have been, unless they were either miraculously created or surreptitiously introduced. **1909** [see *HIGHER *a.* 2]. **1961** A. H. NETHERCOT *First Five Lives of Annie Besant* v. 295 (*heading*) The Chela of the Mahatmas.

2. A title indicative of love and respect conferred on revered persons in India; applied freq. to Mohandas Karamchand Gandhi (1869–1948).

1931 *Manch. Guardian* 11 Aug. 8/2 The great soul in the insignificant-looking body is the distinguishing mark of the Mahatma. **1948** C. LESLIE *Goat to Kali* v. 203 His casual mention of great names convinced her that he was an intimate friend of them all: of the Mahatma, of Nehru, of Subhas Bose. **1949** H. N. BRAILSFORD in H. S. L. Polak et al. *Mahatma Gandhi* viii. 96 On 9 January, 1915, ..Gandhi landed in Bombay... Soon after..in a published letter, the poet Rabindranath Tagore conferred on him the title of 'Mahatma', of which the literal meaning is 'great soul'. It is the custom among Indians to bestow such distinctions on leaders whom they love and admire. *c* **1949** P. YOGANANDA *Autobiogr. Yogi* xliv. 352 Mr. Desai led us..to the writing-room where, cross-legged, sat Mahatma Gandhi... He never refers to himself as 'Mahatma'. He has made some humble, and witty, protests about the title. **1973** J. FERGUSON *Politics of Love* iv. 104 This is why Mahatma Gandhi said 'If you Christians rely on soldiers for your safety, you are denying your own doctrine of the Cross.'

Mahayana (mahayā·nă). [Skr. *mahāyāna*, f. *mahā* great + *yāna* vehicle.] The 'Great Vehicle', a name given to the more general form of Buddhism practised in northern Asia. Cf. *HINAYANA. Also *attrib.* So **Mahaya·nian** *a.*, **Mahaya·nism, Mahaya·nist** *a.* and *sb.*, **Mahayani·stic** *a.*

1868 [see *HINAYANA]. **1883** MAX MÜLLER *India* iii. 87 The Northern conquerors..seem to have made a kind of compromise with Buddhism, and it is probably due to that compromise, or to an amalgamation of Saka legends with Buddhist doctrines, that we owe the so-called Mahâyâna form of Buddhism. **1891** W. W. ROCKHILL *Land of Lamas* 105 A curious perversion of the Mahāyānist doctrine of the *Kāyatraya.* **1907** [see *HINAYANA]. **1907** D. T. SUZUKI *Outl. Mahayana Buddhism* 21 The idea is distinctly Mahayanistic. **1927** A. HUXLEY *Proper Stud.* v. 187 In the first century of our era..the Mahayana or Great Vehicle was created, and Buddhism became an entirely new religion. **1945, 1951** [see *HINAYANA]. **1956** A. TOYNBEE *Historian's Approach to Relig.* I. vii. 89 The Mahayanian Buddhists in China. **1961** J. MASTERS *Road past Mandalay* xiii. 162 They worshipped God according to the rites of the Mahayana and Hinayana. **1971** *Sun* (Ceylon) 17 Sept. 5/6 This impact of Japan and Mahayana Buddhism on him opened a further avenue for his missionary zeal. **1973** *Times* 14 Apr. (Nepal Suppl.) p. ii/3 Although several early statues of the historic Buddha Sākyamuni survive, the favourite motifs of Mahāyāna art were the five Celestial or Dhyāni Buddhas and the Bodhisattvas, whose images became the centres of devotional cults.

Mah Jong, mah-jong (mā dʒǫ·ŋ). Also **mah jongg, mah jongh,** etc., and as one word. [Chinese *ma-ch'iao* (Shanghai dial. *-tsiang*) sparrows (f. *ma* hemp + *tsiang* small birds), the name of the game.] An old Chinese game resembling certain card games, introduced into Europe and America in the early 1920s. The 136 or 144 pieces used in the game are known as tiles, and they are divided into five or six suits. The object of the players, usually four in number, is to build a hand containing four sets of three tiles and a pair. Also *attrib.*

1922 R. E. LINDSELL (*title*) Ma-Cheuk or Mah-Jongg. **1923** CHIANG LEE *Mah Jong* 7 Mah Jong, or Mah Tsiong (Sparrows), as it is pronounced in the city of Ning Po where it received its name and modern form, has been in vogue in China as a card game for about eight centuries. **1923** *Daily Mail* 23 June 6 There will be..demonstrations of Mah Jongg, the wonderful Chinese game which threatens to oust Bridge. **1923** JOYCE *Let.* 2 Nov. (1966) III. 82, I have prepared a nice intricate Mah Jongg puzzle for myself. **1931** *Times Lit. Suppl.* 7 May 365/2 Particularly interesting are his snapshots of modern China's methods of civil warfare (hireling warriors firing harmless fusillades in the intervals of their mah jongh). **1963** J. KIRKUP *Tropic Temper* 63 Two old men were playing mah-jong. **1967** *Guardian* 16 Aug. 6/6 Following the traditional 'Cleansing of the Tiles' the North Cotswold Mah-Jongg Canton started another session last Wednesday at their Stow-on-the-Wold tryst. **1967** D. & E. T. RIESMAN *Conversations in Japan* 116 The favourite pre-war game, mah-jongg, still popular with many. **1971** K. HOPKINS *Hong Kong* 246 The interests of these 'unions' centre on..

mahjong. **1972** *Straits Times* (Malaysian ed.) 22 Nov. 21/7 The $10,000 hold-up of mahjong players at the Keong Kee sawmill's recreation club.

Hence **Mah Jong** *v. intr.*, to complete one's hand at the game of Mah Jong.

1923 J. BRAY *How to play Mah Jong* 12 Each player in turn draws a tile and discards one in place of this until some player completes his hand; i.e. 'Mah Jongs'. *Ibid.* 21 None of the following tiles in the hand assist so far in Mah Jonging (completing the hand)..and may be discarded. **1924** M. C. WORK *Mah-Jongg Up-to-Date* I. 32 The Chinese word 'Woo' (meaning peace) has been extensively used by many American writers in the same sense as it is used by Chinese players; viz., to Mah-Jongg, to win the game, to go out. **1933** E. TALBOT *Mah-Jong made Easy* 31 Sometimes a player collects tiles that will give a small mah-jong to oneself and discards those of high value that give another player the opportunity of making a big hand, even if he does not mah-jong. **1966** 'HAN SUYIN' *Mortal Flower* I. 24 Everyone..shopping, tea-ing, mahjonging or donkey-riding.

Mahlerian (mālīə·riăn), *a.* and *sb.* [-IAN.] **A.** *adj.* Of, pertaining to, or characteristic of the Austrian composer Gustav Mahler (1860–1911) or his music. **B.** *sb.* An admirer or adherent of Mahler; an exponent of Mahler's music. Also **Ma·hlerish** *a.*, resembling the classical-romantic style of Mahler; **Ma·hlerite** *sb.* = *MAHLERIAN *sb.*

1947 D. NEWLIN *Bruckner, Mahler, Schoenberg* v. 130 The typically Mahlerian direction..sets the stage for a mysterious march-like beginning, likewise typically Mahlerian. **1948** *Penguin Music Mag.* VI. 132, I am no ardent Mahlerite. **1959** *Listener* 27 Aug. 333/2 He [*sc.* a conductor] was a great Mahlerian. *Ibid.* 10 Dec. 1052/3 Almost a Mahlerish work. **1962** *Times* 2 Feb. 13/2 Mahlerites are likely to owe their allegiance to the prewar gramophone records conducted by Dr. Bruno Walter. **1962** *Listener* 25 Oct. 695/1 We hear an eclectic, youthful style penetrated by what we recognize as the unmistakable and emerging Mahlerian voice. **1963** *Times* 7 Mar. 8/3 Emotionally the music lacks the concentrated intensity of anguish to win it Mahlerian popularity. **1971** *Guardian* 17 Apr. 8/1 Does he then consider that composer's [*sc.* Shostakovitch's] expiatory fifth symphony better music than his weird Mahlerian fourth? **1974** *Times* 18 Apr. 7/7 Blaukopf has heeded the lesson and his essay has a proper Mahlerian sharpness to it.

mahogany. Add: **3. b.** *colloq.* = BAR *sb.*[1] 28.

1936 N. COLLINS *Trinity Town* i. 18 From the moment Mr. Primrose appeared behind his own mahogany and superseded the barmaid, he dominated everything. **1955** *Punch* 4 May 557/1 Every interval sees twenty orchestral players with their elbows on the mahogany and off-duty singers in full fig on high stools being selectively sweet about their rivals.

7. mahogany birch *U.S.* (examples); **mahogany flat** *slang*, a bed-bug.

1813 H. MUHLENBERG *Catal. Plant.* 88 *Betula lenta*.. soft birch,..black birch,..sweet birch,..or mahogany birch. **1908** N. L. BRITTON *N. Amer. Trees* 256 The cherry birch, or Black birch,..is also called Sweet birch and Mahogany birch. **1864** HOTTEN *Slang Dict.* 176 *Mahogany flat*, a bug. **1942** BERREY & VAN DEN BARK *Amer. Thes. Slang* § 120/60 *Bedbugs*,..flats, mahogany flats. **1952** *New Biol.* XIII. 86 The abdomen [of the bed-bug] when empty is flat (hence the name 'mahogany flat'). **1959** SOUTHWOOD & LESTON *Land & Water Bugs* 188 Bedbug. Also known as 'wall lice', 'mahogany flats' and 'crimson ramblers' these insects have been carried all round the world. **1967** B. J. BANFILL *Pioneer Nurse* v. 61 Until two months ago we had only a log shanty. Somehow the Mahogany Flats took over and we had to burn it.

mahoohoo, var. *MOHOOHOO.

mahorka (măhǭ·ɹkă). Also **makharka, makhorka.** [Russ. *makhórka* shag.] A coarse tobacco smoked in Russia mostly by soldiers and peasants. Also *attrib.*

1902 R. N. BAIN tr. *Tales from Gorky* ix. 263 The chums were going along the high-road smoking *makharka* cigars of their own manufacture. **1949** I. DEUTSCHER *Stalin* i. 22 The circles met in the workers' own overcrowded slum-dwellings and filled the air with the biting smoke of *makhorka*. **1951** KOESTLER *Age of Longing* iv. 68 The tall old man with the dignified stoop, the mahorka smell and the sparkling, close-set eyes. *Ibid.* vi. 94 Old Arin sat down on the foot of the bed, smoking his mahorka cigarettes. **1962** *Listener* 2 Aug. 182/2 The sights and sounds of St Petersburg—..the smell of Mahorka tobacco and of the droshkies. **1964** *Sunday Mail Mag.* (Brisbane) 22 Nov., Villagers in the Caucasus have been smoking a mossy mixture known as mahorka.

Mahsud (mā·sūd). Also **Mahsood.** A member of one of the principal tribes of Waziristan in north-west Pakistan, noted for their bellicosity. Also as *adj.*

1873 E. BALFOUR *Cycl. India* (ed. 2) V. s.v. *Wazira*, The Wazeeri are divided into three great divisions, or Usman kheyl, Ahmedzye, and Mahsood. **1882** H. B. ROWNEY *Wild Tribes India* II. i. 120 The Wuzeerás... are a bold and ferocious people... The principal tribal divisions among them are: the Máhsuds, Áhmedzyes, Othmánzyes, and Bithunnees. **1895** *Blackw. Mag.* July 79 The Mahsud headmen solemnly bound themselves to renounce looting the Powindah caravans. **1898** H. W. MILLS *Pathan Revolt N.-W. India* (ed. 3) iv. 22 Even after the Mahsuds had attacked Wano, Waziristan was not permanently occupied. **1909** *Daily Chron.* 2 June 1/7 The Mahsuds, who have been causing trouble on the Indian frontier, are said to have secured 10,000 rifles. **1920** *Blackw. Mag.* Oct. 445/1 You take the road to Mahsudland. *Ibid.* 457/2 The half-veiled, unfriendly, grey Mahsud hills. **1924** [see *BRAHUI *sb.* and *a.*]. **1957** R. HILTON *N.-W. Frontier* x. 133 The 20th Punjabis..hustled the mob of Mahsuds out of the camp at the points of their bayonets. **1963** *Listener* 10 Jan. 96/2 A column was out against refractory Mahsuds.

mahwa. Add further variant spellings: **moa, mohua, mohur, mohwa, mowra, mowrah.**

1. Substitute for def.: A large tree, *Madhuca latifolia*, native to India and belonging to the family Sapotaceæ, which bears fleshy, edible flowers and is used as a timber-tree; also, a smaller, related tree, *Madhuca butyracea*, the Indian butter tree, native to Nepal, whose seeds yield an oily, butter-like substance. Also *attrib.* (Further examples.)

1889 G. S. BOULGER *Uses of Plants* III. 139 The Mahwa, besides its saccharine flowers, yields 33 per cent. of a butter from its seeds, used in India as food, and now imported for soap and candle making. **1907** B. M. CROKER *Company's Servant* xii. 108 A sickly tamarind and two frail gold mohur trees. **1920** *Nature* 1 Apr. 147/1 The possibility of utilising the mowra flowers of India for the purpose [of manufacturing alcohol] is discussed... They are used by the natives as a foodstuff, and especially for the preparation by fermentation of an alcoholic liquor called daru or mohwa spirit. **1922** W. SCHLICH *Man. Forestry* (ed. 4) I. II. 134 Mention should be made of the flowers of..the 'mohwa' tree, the corolla of which is eaten fresh or dried, or distilled into intoxicating liquor. **1934** 'G. ORWELL' *Burmese Days* ii. 20 Gold mohur trees like vast umbrellas of bloodred bloom. **1951** *Dict. Gardening* (R. Hort. Soc.) III. 1229/2 *M[adhuca] latifolia.* Mahwah or Moa... The fl[owers] are edible and the wood valuable. **1954** J. MASTERS *Bhowani Junction* xxvii. 234 There was a gold mohur tree in bloom, its branches leaning out. **1964** R. PERRY *World of Tiger* x. 142 The oak-like mohua tree..carries a tremendous weight of flowers—a hundredweight or more on a single tree. **1971** *Illustr. Weekly India* 18 Apr. 35/1 Toddy and mohua liquor are also sometimes drunk.

3. mowrah meal, the dried and powdered residue of the seeds of the mahwa tree, after the oil has been extracted, used as a pesticide to kill worms in turf.

1939 R. B. DAWSON *Pract. Lawn Craft* xxv. 180 Mowrah meal..does not maintain the turf in worm-free condition for longer than about two years. **1948** I. G. LEWIS *Turf* xii. 121 The residue of an Indian bean after the oil has been extracted for commercial purposes, Mowrah Meal is a material which is entirely safe to use. **1973** R. GROUNDS *Perfect Lawn* viii. 73 Mowrah meal applied in summer or autumn..will effectively reduce the worm population.

Mahzor, var. *MACHZOR.

mai (mai). Shortened form of MATAI.

1831 G. BENNETT in *London Med. Gaz.* 12 Nov. 184/2 *Podocarpus Species*... This tree, the Mai or Matai of the natives of New Zealand, is an unpublished species of Podocarpus. **1845** [see *HINAU]. **1855** R. TAYLOR *Te Ika a Mani* 440 Matai, mai.., a tree with a fine thick top, and leaf much resembling that of the yew. **1874** LINDLEY & MOORE *Treas. Bot.* II. Suppl. 1315/1 Mai (N. Zeal.), *Podocarpus spicata.* **1946** *Jrnl. Polynesian Soc.* LV. 145 Matai, a tree (*Podocarpus spicatus*), black-pine: often shortened to māi.

maid, *sb.*[1] Add: **8.** *maid service.*

1951 *N.Y. Times* 28 Oct. VIII. 19 (Advt.), Shamrock apartment hotel... Maid service. **1968** *Globe & Mail* (Toronto) 17 Feb. 49/1 (Advt.), Prince Carlton Hotel Ltd. Rooms. Maid service, telephones. **1969** 'O. BLEECK' *Brass Go-Between* (1970) vi. 69 In addition to daily maidservice, the Adelphi offered a restaurant and bar. **1971** *Country Life* 23 Dec. 1814/4 [Villa]..Sleep 10, c.h.w., refrigerator, maid service. **1973** H. NIELSEN *Severed Key* v. 60, I wonder if this place provides maid service.

maid, *v.* Add: **1.** (Later examples.)

1936 M. MITCHELL *Gone with Wind* iv. 63 My Prissy been maidin' fo' Miss India fo' a year now. **1958** V. P. JOHNS *Servant's Probl.* i. 11 During the two months I've been maiding for Mr. Atterbury, one or the other of them have been in every day.

3. *trans.* To wait on (a person) as a maid.

1909 R. HICHENS *Bella Donna* xxi. 228, I must learn to maid you. **1929** 'R. OKE' *Frolic Wind* v. 83 It was, of course, certainly untrue that she had a fourth to maid her. **1934** A. CHRISTIE *Murder on Orient Express* III. iv. 219 Susanne..used to look after my clothes and maid me. **1949** C. H. B. KITCHIN *Cornish Fox* xi. 164 What would happen to the Colonel after the wedding?.. Upton wouldn't be at all pleased if Delia continued to 'maid' her father from Southview.

Hence **mai·ding** *vbl. sb.*

1900 [see MAID *v.* 1]. **1921** *Chambers's Jrnl.* 1 Jan. 73/1 If you require 'maiding', you tell the lady of the bureau of your floor, and she supplies you with an attendant. **1955** 'C. H. ROLPH' *Women of Streets* vi. 78 Maiding to a prostitute is a definite job.

maiden. Add: **A.** *sb.* **1. c.** *the answer to a maiden's prayer*, an eligible bachelor. Also *transf.*

1935 *Mademoiselle* Aug. 15 Here, you Freshmen, Seniors, et al, is the answer to a maiden's prayer. **1957** J. FLEMING *Maiden's Prayer* II. 109 You're the answer to a maiden's prayer, dear heart. No need for you to do a stroke of work, you can marry money and live the life of a gentleman. **1971** J. BRUNNER *Honky in Woodpile* xi. 83, I was still in college. Thought he was the greatest.. answer to a maiden's prayer! **1974** A. PRICE *Other Paths* II i. 112 You're the answer to a maiden's prayer.

9. b. A strawberry plant bearing its first crop. Also *attrib.*

1928 *Daily Express* 28 May 5/3 The 'runners' are laid from the 'maidens' or last year's [strawberry-]beds. **1974** *Times* 13 July 11/3 Another advantage of growing only maiden strawberries is that it gives us one more crop to work into our programme of crop rotation... I have now decided..to grow only maidens—that is, to take one crop off a plant and then discard it.

c. Short for *maiden bell* (see sense *B. 4 f).

1909 *Daily Chron.* 1 Oct. 7/5 The High Wycombe 'tenor'..thus issues proudly from the Whitechapel Foundry a 'maiden'.

10. a. *maiden-catching, -eyed, -folded, -furled, -hued* adjs.; **maiden-thought** *poet.*, Keats's term for the stage of human development after 'the infant or thoughtless Chamber', one of innocent, untarnished hope.

1957 AUDEN & KALLMAN *Magic Flute* I. i. 28 Had I a maiden-catching net, Fair maids by dozens I should daily get. **1930** J. MASEFIELD *Wanderer of Liverpool* 24 The maiden-eyed morning. **1916** D. H. LAWRENCE *Amores* 100 Then lets her black hair loose, the darkness fall About her from her maiden-folded bands. **1876** G. M. HOPKINS *Wreck of Deutschland* xxxiv, in *Poems* (1967) 62 The heaven-flung, heart-fleshed, maiden-furled Miracle-in-Mary-of-flame. **1913** E. F. BENSON *Thorley Weir* i. 21 The dog-rose spread its maiden-hued face skywards. **1818** KEATS *Let.* 3 May (1958) I. 281 We no sooner get into the second Chamber, which I shall call the Chamber of Maiden-Thought, than we become intoxicated with the light and the atmosphere. **1954** L. MACNEICE *Autumn Sequel* 22 The Customs Office of Maiden-thought.

b. maiden's wreath, a perennial herb of the genus *Francoa*, bearing pink or white flowers in spikes or racemes; cf. *bridal wreath* (*BRIDAL *a.* 2 c).

1893 W. ROBINSON *Eng. Flower Garden* (ed. 3) 419/1 Francoa (Maiden's Wreath).—Chilian plants of the Saxifrage family... They are rather tender. **1908** G. JEKYLL in *Colour Flower Garden* xiii. 116 Maiden's Wreath (*Francoa ramosa*) is a plant for many uses. The foliage, though sparing in quantity, is distinct and handsome. The long flower-stems are flung out with a kind of determination of character. **1952** A. G. L. HELLYER *Sanders' Encycl. Gardening* (ed. 22) 198 Francoa (Maiden's Wreath; Bridal Wreath).

B. *adj.* **2.** *maiden name* (earlier and later examples).

1689 S. SEWALL *Diary* (1878) I. 305 Visited Cousin Powers, and Cous. Lapworth, whose maiden name was Ann Lee. **1862** BORROW *Wild Wales* III. v. 41, I asked her her maiden name. **1922** JOYCE *Ulysses* 366 Her maiden name was Jemima Brown And she lived with her mother in Irishtown.

4. b. (Earlier *Cricket* example.)

1851 J. PYCROFT *Cricket Field* iv. 58 In point of style the old players did not play the steady game with maiden overs as at present.

f. In Bell-founding: (see quots.).

1901 H. E. BULWER *Gloss. Technical Terms Bells* 2 *Maiden bell*, a bell that requires no tuning after it comes from the mould. **1910** *Encycl. Brit.* III. 688/1 The metal is then boiled and run molten into the mould... When extricated it ought to be scarcely touched and should hardly require tuning. This is called its maiden state. **1912** H. B. WALTERS *Church Bells Eng.* ii. 47 Sometimes a whole peal used to be turned out so nearly correct that no tuning was needed; such bells were known as a 'maiden peal'.

5. d. (Earlier example.)

1596 SHAKES. *I Hen. IV*, v. iv. 132 Full bravely hast thou flesht thy Maiden sword.

maiden aunt (mēⁱ·d'n ānt). [f. MAIDEN *a.* 1 + AUNT.] An unmarried aunt. Hence **mai:den-au·ntishly** *adv.*, in a manner characteristic of maiden aunts; primly.

1709 PRIOR *Henry & Emma* in *Poems on Several Occasions* 244 The ancient Maiden Aunt. **1711** [see AUNT 1 a]. **1758** [see MAIDEN *sb.* and *a.* B. 1]. **1847** C. M. YONGE *Scenes & Characters* xiii. 158 That worst of plagues, a prying maiden aunt. **1917** T. S. ELIOT *Prufrock* 33 Miss Helen Slingsby was my maiden aunt. **1928** *Observer* 22 July 7 Camberley..was rather like a shocked maiden aunt, who had been forced to look on at something not quite 'nice'. Maiden-auntishly she took up again the knitting of the Franco-German War. **1938** W. S. MAUGHAM *Summing Up* 176, I..ask myself whether in another forty years the bright young things of current letters will appear as jejune as do now their maiden aunts of The Yellow Book. **1975** *Harper's & Queen* May 137/3 As for aged relations, maiden aunts in whose name so much is suffered, Miss Charlton hasn't got any.

maidenhair. Add: **5. b.** A woman's pubic hair.

1928 D. H. LAWRENCE *Lady Chatterley* xv. 265 That's where to put forget-me-nots, in the man-hair, or the maiden-hair. *a* **1930** —— *Last Poems* (1932) 14 The dim blotch of black maidenhair like an indicator, Giving a message to the man.

maidenhead[1]. Add: **1.** Also = HYMEN[2] 1. (Further examples.)

1592 SHAKES. *Rom. & Jul.* I. i. 23, I will bee civill with the Maids, and cut off their heads..the heads of the Maids, or their Maiden-heads. **1867** R. G. LATHAM *Dict. Eng. Lang.*, *Maidenhead*,..Virginity..the hymen, or virginal membrane. **1928** F. W. S. BROWNE tr. *T. H. van de Velde's Ideal Marriage* II. iv. 57 Within this space is the sexual orifice... In maidens this is closed by the *hymen*.. or virginal membrane, popularly called 'maidenhead'.

maiden's blush. Add: **1.** Also *maiden-blush rose.*

1861 C. M. YONGE *Stokesley Secret* ii. 35 The standard maiden-blush rose. **1928** D. H. LAWRENCE *Let.* 14 Nov. (1962) II. 1100 Those maiden-blush roses.

3. Either of two Australian trees with pinkish wood, *Sloanea australis,* of the family Elæocarpaceæ, or *Euroschinus falcatus,* of the family Anacardiaceæ.

1884 A. NILSON *Timber Trees New South Wales* 54 *E[chinocarpus] Australis.*—Maiden's Blush.—A beautiful tree, sometimes attaining a height of 150 feet. **1965** *Austral. Encycl.* I. 174/2 It [sc. *Euroschinus falcatus*] is variously known as pink poplar, ribbonwood, Donnelly's cedar and most generally perhaps as maiden's blush, though this last vernacular is now retained for a very different tree, *Sloanea australis. Ibid.* III. 364/2 *S[loanea] australis* (maiden's blush or bush alder) is a small tree with showy flowers, found in the coastal brush forests from Illawarra in southern New South Wales to Queensland.

4. *Austral.* (See quots.)

1941 BAKER *Dict. Austral. Slang* 45 *Maiden's blush,* ginger beer and raspberry. **1961** PARTRIDGE *Dict. Slang Suppl.* 1177/1 *Maiden's blush,* ginger beer and raspberry cordial: Australian. **1966** G. W. TURNER *Eng. Lang. Austral. & N.Z.* vi. 116 *Maiden's blush* (a drink, either of port and lemonade or rum and raspberry).

maiding: see under *MAID *v.*

maidless (mēⁱ·dlės), *a.* [f. MAID *sb.*[1] + -LESS.] Not having or without a maid-servant.

1892 C. M. YONGE *That Stick* I. xi. 117 My Lady could not well be allowed to go maidless. **1909** *Daily Chron.* 19 Aug. 7/3 The clever housekeeper knows the value of saying to the cook—or family, if maidless—'It is going to be so hot that we'll have cold meals.' **1926** *Public Opinion* 23 Apr. 410/3 The maidless mother is the chief victim of the storm. **1973** *Sci. Amer.* June 10/1 My outside interests are those one acquires in raising four children (a geologist, an astronomer, a mathematician and a violinist) and running a busy, exciting, maidless household.

maid of honour. Add: **2.** (Further examples.) No longer restricted to Richmond, Surrey.

1942 MRS. BELLOC LOWNDES *Let.* 19 Nov. (1971) 235 There were lobster patties, and queer looking Maid of Honour cakes. **1960** *Good Housek. Cookery Bk.* (rev. ed.) 394/1 Maids of Honour..3 oz. butter, 2 eggs,..1 oz. blanched almonds..puff pastry, [etc.]. **1966** J. DOS PASSOS *Best Times* (1968) i. 11, I had so many little cheesecakes called Maids of Honor that I felt a bit sick.

3. The principal unmarried female attendant on the bride at a wedding; a bridesmaid. Also *fig.*

1895 in *Funk's Stand. Dict.* **1906** M. E. FREEMAN *Light of Soul* 348 Lily asked Maria to be her maid of honor. She planned to be married in church. **1911** H. S. HARRISON *Queed* xxi. 267 A victoria containing two lovely young girls sponsor and maid of honor for South Carolina. **1922** JOYCE *Ulysses* 321 The maids of honour..sisters of the bride, wore very becoming costumes. **1974** 'R. B. DOMINIC' *Epitaph for Lobbyist* x. 90 The maid of honour and the bridesmaids passed by... Betty Jo appeared on the arm of her father..floating in a cloud of white.

‖ **maiko** (mǝi·ko). [Jap.] A girl who is being trained to become a geisha.

1904 R. J. FARRER *Garden of Asia* xii. 111 They are but Maiko—geisha so young and untried as to be beneath Japanese consideration. *Ibid.* 113 She rises.., flanked by the two Maiko. **1938** BUSH & KAGAMI *Japanalia* 69/1 Young apprentice geisha are called *Maiko* in Kyōto and *Hangyoku* in Tōkyō. **1966** P. S. BUCK *People of Japan* (1968) vii. 93 Young geisha, or *maiko,* usually dance with some gaiety. **1971** *Vogue* Dec. 92/1 An apprentice Geisha is a Maiko—a girl usually between seventeen and twenty.

mail, *sb.*[3] Add: **2.** Also (orig. *U.S.*) without article.

1873 J. H. BEADLE *Undevel. West* xxii. 441, I think this office gives us three times as much mail as that at Salt Lake. **1913** *U.S. Official Postal Guide* July 12 The postage on fourth-class mail may be prepaid by..ordinary postage stamps. **1941** *Men Only* Sept. 12 Forwarding mail is another job that usually falls to the Mess Secretary.

b. For *U.S.* read orig. *U.S.* (Earlier and later examples.)

a **1844** M. C. FIELD in S. F. Smith *Theatr. Apprenticeship* (1846) 204 He walks as if he had the missing mail in his pocket and an extra to issue immediately. **1873** T. B. ALDRICH *Marj. Daw* 163, I go over to K— for my mail. **1941** *Men Only* Sept. 12 Although the addressee has made half a dozen moves since leaving the Mess, he expects his mail to reach him without delay. **1953** *Manch. Guardian Wkly.* 3 Sept. 7/4 Mr. Lattimore..had his personal mail forwarded to the White House.

c. Used as the name of a newspaper.

1789 (*title*) The Evening Mail. **1823** (*title*) Waterford Daily Mail. **1896** (*title*) The Daily Mail. **1896** LLOYD GEORGE *Family Lett.* (1973) 108 There are excellent reports in the Mail & S.W. Daily News of Saturday's meeting at Barry. **1922** JOYCE *Ulysses* 242 Look here Martin, John Wyse Nolan said, overtaking them at the *Mail* office. **1975** *Times* 10 Apr. 17/4 The tremendous financial support that the *Daily Mail* has received..from its readers for its Vietnam Orphans Fund.

4. b. *mail boat* (earlier and later examples), *-boy, carriage, -hack, matter* (later example), *-plane, room* (later examples), *-van, wagon* (earlier examples); *mail-carrying* adj.; **mail-bag** (earlier example); **mail-box** (examples of *b*); **mail-car,** (*c*) *Austral.* and *N.Z.*, a motor vehicle used for the conveyance of the mail (and also sometimes of passengers); **mail-catcher** (earlier example); **mail-contract,** a contract for the conveyance of postal matter; **mail cover** *U.S.*, the monitoring of all mail sent to a specified address; **mail-day,** the day on which mails are dispatched or received; **mail drop** [*DROP *sb.* 17 d], a place where mail may be left to be collected by another person; **mail order** orig. *U.S.*, an order for goods sent to a business house by post; hence as *v. trans.*; also **mail-order firm, house,** one transacting business mainly by post; so *mail-order business, catalogue*; **mail-rider** (earlier and later examples); **mail-road** (earlier example); **mail run** *Austral.* and *N.Z.*, = *mail-route*; **mail-slot** *U.S.*, = *letter-slit*; **mail stage** (later examples); **mail-time,** the time mails take to pass between two places; **mail truck,** a motor vehicle used for the conveyance of mail.

1812 *Theatrical Inquisitor* I. 273 The majority of readers..ramble through books as post-boys ride through towns..and..can tell you as little of the contents as those who carry the mail-bags can of the letters. **1795** in R. Putnam *Mem.* (1903) 397 It has been suggested to me that the mail boats are much too heavy for pushing with the requisite speed. **1933** L. A. G. STRONG *Sea Wall* 1 He did not even heed the mailboat, as she glided gracefully in..to the harbour. **1872** *Rep. Comm. Patents 1870* (U.S.) II. 751/1 In a mail-box, the arrangement herein shown and described..for the purpose of guiding and holding the mail matter. **1922** M. B. HOUSTON *Witch-Man* xix. 260 She stopped now at the foot of Little Glory to look in the mail-box. Always she brought him his mail now. **1973** 'H. HOWARD' *Highway to Murder* x. 128 One of the mail boxes said Miss Thorpe's flatlet was on the third floor. **1842** in J. S. Buckingham *E. & W. States Amer.* II. 118 [I] saw descending the hill..the mail-boy on his horse at full speed. *a* **1861** T. WINTHROP *John Brent* (1883) xvii. 159 Jake Shamberlain aint a hog, and his mail boys aint of the pork kind. **1874** *Congress. Rec.* 15 Apr. 3099/1 Hitherto seven [officers] were known as mail-boys and the others as mail-messengers. **1907** N. MUNRO *Daft Days* i. 3 The tune of the mail-boy's song. **1942** C. ASTON in *N.Z. New Writing* I. 55 Martin heard the mailcar go past. **1945** C. MANN in Murdoch & Drake-Brockman *Austral. Short Stories* (1951) 261 Sent by the mail-car up to Town. **1947** 'A. P. GASKELL' *Big Game* 48 She had returned from town.. in the mailcar. **1860** J. G. HOLLAND *Miss Gilbert's Career* x. 166 The Crampton line of public travel and mail carriage was only one of the many tributaries to the great trunk lines. **1909** *Westm. Gaz.* 1 June 8/3 The various lines of passenger and mail-carrying steamers. **1875** *Chicago Tribune* 18 Sept. 5/3 The Post-Office Department has introduced the use of a 'mail-catcher'. *a* **1861** T. WINTHROP *John Brent* (1883) vi. 50 His ranch is down the valley, towards Pravo. He owns half the United States mail contract. **1965** *N.Y. Times* 24 Feb. 26 When a person is subjected to a mail cover, the Post Office records the name and address of anyone sending mail to him, as well as the postmarking and the class of mail. **1974** *Daily Tel.* 29 Jan. 17/4 The FBI began its investigation of Miss Paton as a result of a 'mail cover' on the New York headquarters of the party. **1855** J. EVANS *Let.* 15 June in G. N. Jones *Florida Plantation Rec.* (1927) 131 People will be there [*sc.* at the post office] every Mail day. **1926** [see *BACK BLOCKS, BACKBLOCKS *sb. pl.*]. **1933** B. WILLOUGHBY *Alaskans All* 102 Everywhere in the land mail-day is the most longed-for, the most important day the Alaskans know. **1972** *Time* 17 Apr. 45/1 It is hiring a full-time employment counselor to help them find new jobs if they are fired, and even has a special mail drop to receive anonymous tips. **1973** *Sat. Rev. World* (U.S.) 4 Dec. 46/2 Today's students traveling abroad use American Express offices as a mail drop. **1909** 'O. HENRY' *Roads of Destiny* x. 165 One afternoon Jimmy Valentine..climbed out of the mail-hack. **1906** *Churchman* 10 Nov. 724 All mail matter for the secretary of the convention should be addressed to [etc.]. **1867** *Commercial & Financial Chron.* V. 26/2 Mail and telegraph orders will receive our personal attention. **1875** *Chicago Tribune* 8 July 6/3 Few buyers were present and the 'mail order' business also was light. **1897** *Sears, Roebuck Catal.* 579 There was a time when the consumer paid what was asked... [This] is radically changed,—changed by the Mail Order Business. **1906** S. E. SPARLING *Introd. Business Organiz.* 318 The mail order is based almost exclusively upon circular advertising, and while the mail-order firms employ general publicity, they rely almost exclusively upon circularization in developing and holding the trade. **1916** H. L. WILSON *Somewhere in Red Gap* v. 175 Hetty Daggett..orders this [skirt] by catalogue, ..from the mail-order house in Chicago. **1928** *Collier's* 29 Dec. 7/1 Wasn't it my suggestion that marriage be turned over to the mail-order houses? **1930** J. B. PRIESTLEY *Angel Pavement* iv. 167 He read all the advertisements in his newspaper, which specialised on Saturdays in the mail-order business. **1968** 'N. BLAKE' *Private Wound* iv. 64 A brand-new suite of furniture which looked as if it had been mail-ordered out of a catalogue. **1969** *Times* 7 Nov. 14/7 The sophisticated stores—even the better mail order catalogues—want to know what is happening. **1972** *Guardian* 23 Feb. 11/3 Allcraft..mail-order a candle-making kit. **1926** *Daily Colonist* (Victoria, B.C.) 2 July 1/5 Vessel expected to arrive here on July 12—Mr. Wells and Mr. Evans then to leave on mail plane. **1931** C. KELLY *U.S. Postal Policy* vii. 137 At the great airports may be seen the alert, efficient, young eagles who pilot the mail planes. **1940** *Jrnl. R. Aeronaut. Soc.* XLIV. 743 The design of a high-speed mailplane for overnight trans-Atlantic services. **1801** in C. Cist *Cincinnati in 1841* (1841) 177 The mail-rider..from the upper route. **1846** *Knickerbocker* XXVI. 52 The mail-rider sank down apparently through the solid ground with his horse and saddle-bags. **1944** F. CLUNE *Red Heart* 81 The far-western mail-rider who, once a fortnight, jogged over the red-soil plains. **1818** in H. B. Fearon *Sk. Amer.* 430 About three miles from the great mail road to Cincinnati. **1911** *Daily Colonist* (Victoria, B.C.) 7 Apr. 7/2 Came before the police magistrate yesterday to answer to the charge of wrecking the mail room of the steamer, throwing mail bags over board, and generally making things interesting. **1968** *Punch* 21 Feb. 270/3 The Mail Rooms (I believe you call them Dispatch Rooms).. were crowded. **1946** M. TRIST in Murdoch & Drake-Brockman *Austral. Short Stories* (1951) 418 A mail run used to be a mail run in those days. **1961** B. CRUMP *Hang on a Minute* 88 [He was] doing the Whenuaroa mail-run in a flash new truck. **1957** J. KEROUAC *On Road* (1958) 183 He peeked down through her mail-slot. **1821** T. NUTTALL *Jrnl. Trav. Arkansa* i. 35 On the morning of the second of October 1818, I took my departure from Philadelphia in the mail stage. **1834** *Southern Lit. Messenger* I. 181, I took my seat in the mail stage, and travelled three hundred miles without once going to bed. **1912** *Chambers's Jrnl.* Jan. 5/2 The mail-time between that town [*sc.* Villa Rica] and London will be reduced from thirty days to about eighteen. **1961** L. VAN DER POST *Heart of Hunter* I. vii. 112 Catch the fortnightly mail truck to Ghanzis. **1963** A. LUBBOCK *Austral. Roundabout* 44 Twice a week, the mail-truck from Bourke brought out their stores and fresh vegetables. **1909** *Chambers's Jrnl.* June 343/2 Mail-vans in large numbers..are now being driven by mechanical power. **1959** *Times* 2 Apr. 10/4 A Post Office spokesman said that the mailvan had previously collected three bags from a firm in Bell Street. **1831** *Boston Even. Transcript* 23 June 2/1 We..were carted thence in the mail waggon to Sandwich. **1871** E. EGGLESTON *Hoosier Schoolmaster* (1872) xvii. 135 You can git on the mail-wagon that passes there about five o'clock.

mail, *v.*[4] For *U.S.* read orig. *U.S.* Add later examples.

The usual word in the U.K. is still *post.*

1948 H. T. MOORE in D. H. Lawrence *Lett. to B. Russell* 8 Lawrence is telling Lady Ottoline that Russell, who has mailed him the synopsis of his lectures..still needs to break away. **1968** M. RICHLER in R. Weaver *Canad. Short Stories* 2nd Ser. 170 Once more Mervyn mailed off his novel.

mailabi·lity. *U.S.* [f. MAILABLE *a.*] The quality or fact of being mailable.

1883 *U.S. Official Postal Guide* Jan. 664 Mailability of Doubtful Matter. **1903** *Publishers' Circular* 3 Mar. 275/3 As the card does not bear on the address side the words 'United States of America', its mailability is not affected by my circular of the 16th ult. **1944** *Newsweek* 29 May 72 Manhattan's postmaster, Albert Goldman, doubtful as to the mailability of 'Strange Fruit'. **1968** *U.S. Postal Bull.* LXXXIX. No. 20226, 2/1 (*heading*) Mailability of concealable firearms.

mailed, *a.* **1.** Delete † *Obs.* and add later example.

1922 JOYCE *Ulysses* 305 With his mailed gauntlet he brushed away a furtive tear.

2. *mailed fist,* (a threat of) armed force or superior might.

1897 [in Dict.]. **1898** *19th Cent.* Jan. 164 Japan is a foe who will not be terrified by the mailed fist of Germany. **1898** *Review of Reviews* Mar. 214 Prince Henry of the mailed fist has by this time reached his destination. **1920** M. BEER *Hist. Brit. Socialism* II. III. i. 16 The first rude contact with the mailed fist brought him back to the sober realities of life.

mailer[2]**.** Add: **4.** *S. Afr.* A person who purchases liquor from a bottle-store and resells it to an illicit liquor dealer or shebeener.

1950 *Cape Times Week-end Mag.* 17 June 5 As soon as the bottlestore opens, the *mailer* is there. He gets his regulation two bottles and takes this to the shebeen. Then he goes to another bottlestore for a further two bottles. And so he goes on the whole day. **1950** [see *DOP *sb.*[3] 2]. **1959** *Cape Argus* 14 Nov. 2/9 When we stopped the delivery the shebeens arranged for mailers to get the liquor for them.

mailing, *vbl. sb.*[2] Add: **mailing list** orig. *U.S.*, a register of addresses to which goods and postal matter may be sent; **mailing shot** *Advertising,* material dispatched to potential customers as part of an advertising campaign.

1909 *Daily Chron.* 12 Oct. 4/5 In the States there are 600,000 farmers on the mailing list. **1928** *Publishers' Weekly* 26 May 2201 It is proposed that the booksellers of the country place in this Clearing House..duplicates of their mailing lists. **1961** *Lebende Sprachen* VI. 70/1 Office furniture, machines and supplies..mailing list. **1968** *Heidelberg News* (Heidelberg Printing Machinery Co.) Sept. 3/3 The primary aim of a mailing shot is to obtain sales leads. So include a reply paid card and only as much information as is needed to provoke interest. **1969** *Times* 5 Nov. 21/2 A gift offer of a beauty pack with a new bathroom cleaner, real shillings back in an off-pack offer for the bleach, mailing shots, and trade press advertising. **1972** *Times* 30 Nov. 23/5 They decided to go ahead with a 10,000 mailing shot, coupled with..advertisements. **1973** *Sat. Rev. Society* (U.S.) May 68/2 Ask to be put on the mailing list for Selected U.S. Government Publications.

‖ **maillot** (mayo). [Fr. (13th c. in Robert, but the undermentioned senses are not recorded in Fr. before the 19th c.), lit. 'swaddling clothes'; prob. alteration of *maillol, maille* mesh, mail (see MAIL *sb.*[1]).] **1.** Tights.

Romance etymologists mention, but have not verified the existence of, the Maillot referred to in quot. 1936.

1888 H. JAMES in *Cent. Mag.* Apr. 872 The hungry conjurer, the gymnast whose *maillot* is loose, have something of the glamour of the hero. [**1936** A. HASKELL

Prelude to Ballet 101, 1801..An important development of costume affecting the dance is the invention of tights by Maillot, costumier of the Paris Opera.] **1939** in WEBSTER Add.

2. A tight-fitting, usu. one-piece, swimming costume.

1928 *Daily Express* 30 June 5/3 Dressmakers have prepared for these holiday-makers most delightful bathing outfits, and mannequins walk in maillots, bathing caps and wraps. **1928** *Daily Mail* 9 Aug. 3/4, I have heard of a wonderful eelskin maillot. **1960** 'J. & E. BONETT' *No Grave for Lady* v. 79 Lumina, in a white maillot, was.. wincing as her bare feet met the sharp stones. **1974** F. SELWYN *Cracksman on Velvet* II. 80 She was dressed in the latest Parisian *maillot*... It was hardly to be imagined that so fragile a costume would survive a single immersion in sea-water.

3. A jersey, 'top'.

1948 A. WAUGH *Unclouded Summer* iv. 65 At a gala evening where the men would discard their *maillots* for starched linen. *Ibid.* 78 His heart was thudding against the cotton of his *maillot*. **1955** *Times* 29 July 9/4 This is the *maillot jaune*, the yellow jersey which the rider, who is so far ahead on aggregate, is privileged to wear as the emblem of leadership. **1955** D. BARTON *Glorious Life* vi. 74 In a not quite clean maillot and a seersucker skirt.

maimai (məi·məi·). *N.Z.* Also **maemae, mai mai, mimi.** [Alteration of Austral. Aboriginal *mia-mia* MIA-MIA.] A makeshift Maori shelter of sticks, grass, etc. (see quots. 1863, 1873). Hence, in more recent use, a duckshooter's hide or stand.

1863 S. BUTLER *First Year in Canterbury Settlement* v. 72 The few Maories that inhabit this settlement..always go on foot, and we saw several traces of their encampments—little *mimis*, as they are called—a few light sticks thrown together, and covered with grass, affording a sort of half-and-half shelter for a single individual. **1873** J. H. H. ST. JOHN *Pakeha Rambles through Maori Lands* ix. 153 In the days of bush fighting it used to be a common occurrence at the end of a day's march, when the maemae's had been knocked up by the side of a stream, to see three or four of the men gravely set to work with pannikin ..and 'wash' for a prospect. **1963** *Weekly News* (Auckland) 15 May 27 W. Porter operated successfully from a well-made maimai in the shallows of the Waikato River. **1966** J. K. BAXTER *Pig Island Lett.* 43 He needs the maimai's breast of shade.

main, *sb.*[1] **8.** Add to def.: The pl. *mains* is freq. used, esp. *attrib.* and in *Comb.*, in a collective sense: the public supply, esp. the electricity supply.

1929 *Radio Times* 8 Nov. 433/1 Faultless Radio, coupled to an all-mains system of current supply, operating..without mains hum. **1930** *Morning Post* 18 Aug., With any good receiver, costing from about £12 for a battery-operated model, to £30 for a mains-model, several foreign stations may be regularly well received. **1936** *Discovery* July 203/1 It is still safer to switch off the current at the mains. **1959** *Times* 26 Aug. 5/4 A transistor radio receiver will soon be a serious challenge to the mains-driven sound radio receiver. **1962** *Which?* Aug. 261/1 The voltage will probably be fixed—a mains voltage of 200 to 250 volts. **1968** *Listener* 22 Aug. 239/1 At the airport there were lights—not from the mains, but from a generator. **1969** *Soviet Weekly* 13 Sept. 12 You rent a cottage with mains water and a gas cooker for 32 to 38 roubles a month. **1971** 'H. CALVIN' *Poison Chasers* xii. 161 There was an old-fashioned mains radio on the sideboard, and I switched it on. **1975** *Daily Tel.* 13 June 13/4 Villages on high ground at the end of the mains system have been temporarily without supplies, the South West Water Authority announced.

main, *a.* Add: **1. e.** (Later example.)

In context *arch.*

1922 JOYCE *Ulysses* 339 And he answered with a main cry: *Abba! Adonai!*

11. main beam, (*a*) *Building* (see quot. 1940); (*b*) the undipped beam of the headlights of a motor vehicle; **main chancer** [*CHANCER *sb.*], an opportunist, one who has an eye to the main chance; **main course, dish,** one of a number of substantial dishes in a large menu; the principal dish of a meal; also *fig.*; **main crop,** the chief crop, excluding the early and late varieties or sections; also *attrib.* (usu. as one word); **main drag** (see *DRAG *sb.* 3 e); **main frame** *Computers* (see quots. 1964, 1970); **main man** *U.S. slang* (see quot. 1970); **main plane** *Aeronaut.*, a principal supporting surface of an aircraft (as distinguished from a tail plane); also *mainplane*; **main range** *Austral.* and *N.Z.*, the principal ridge of a chain of mountains; **main sequence** *Astr.*, in the Hertzsprung–Russell diagram of stellar magnitude against spectral type or decreasing surface temperature, a continuous band of star types extending from the upper left of the diagram (hot, bright stars) to the lower right (cool, dim stars) to which most of the stars in the neighbourhood of the sun belong; freq. *attrib.* (usu. hyphenated); **main squeeze** *U.S. slang*, an important person; also (with pun on SQUEEZE *sb.* 2 b) a man's principal woman friend (see also quot. 1941).

1940 *Chambers's Techn. Dict.* 522/1 *Main beam*, in floor construction, one of the principal beams transmitting loads direct to the columns. **1964** *Which?* Apr. 47/2 Our drivers particularly liked the headlamps of the *BMC Bluebird* and *Commer* on main beam and also found their dipped beam better than the other caravans. **1967** *Autocar* 28 Dec. 2/2 The little trio of warning lights—red for ignition, green for blinkers and blue for main-beam—are set..into the walnut of the facia. **1940** 'N. BLAKE' *Malice in Wonderland* I. vii. 95 There was a terrific row on the local council... Beauty-snobs versus main-chancers. **1974** *Publishers Weekly* 5 Aug. 57/1 Candid but never mean-spirited, O'Brien comes across as a deeply dedicated party man who is far more than a main-chancer. **1889** A. FILIPPINI *Table* 21 French dinners are generally served in three main courses, viz., *Relevés*, *Entrées*, and *Rotis*; all the rest are considered side courses. **1936** E. CRAIG *Woman, Wine & Saucepan* i. 17 If the courses are few, choose one wine, red or white, according to what you are serving as the main course. **1967** *Guardian* 22 July 4/5 As low as 5s for a main course (meat balls, potato salad). **1970** 'M. UNDERWOOD' *Silent Liars* II. xii. 134 How many more main courses to come? **1782** MAWE & ABERCROMBIE *Every Man his own Gardener* (ed. 9) 119 Onions or leeks for the main crop should be sown the beginning or middle of this month. **1859** R. THOMPSON *Gardener's Assistant* 249 The main crop of the Long Horn, Altrincham, and other large sorts [of carrots] for winter use, should be sown [etc.]. **1877** S. HIBBERD *Amateur's Kitchen Garden* 49 The second early and main crop sorts [of peas]. **1883** *Culture of Vegetables & Flowers* (Sutton & Sons) 147 Potatoes for main crops should now be got in. **1908** *Daily Chron.* 2 Oct. 3/5 The 'White City' potato..is confidently expected to surpass all the maincrop varieties hitherto produced. **1942** *R.A.F. Jrnl.* 18 Apr. 8 There should be full scale raking down of land and sowing of maincrop Carrots, Onions.. and Lettuce. **1962** *New Scientist* 12 Apr. 31/2 Arran Pilot, an early potato, which develops more rapidly than main-crop varieties. **1971** *Arable Farmer* Feb. 35/2 Maris Piper. Early maincrop. **1957** A. MACNAB *Bulls of Iberia* viii. 81 Three modes: the high spectacular curtain-raisers, the low dominating 'benders', and the main dish or *natural* passes with the breast pass as their natural complement. **1972** J. BALL *Five Pieces Jade* x. 118 A small, intimate meal was waiting in basic Japanese style... There was no evident main dish as in Western dining. **1964** *Gloss. Data Processing & Communication Terms* (Honeywell Inc.) 27/1 *Main frame*, (1) the central processor of the computer system. It contains the main storage, arithmetic unit and special register groups... (2) All that portion of a computer exclusive of the input, output, peripheral and in some instances, storage units. **1970** A. CHANDOR et al. *Dict. Computers* 245 *Main frame*. Originally implied the main framework of a central processing unit on which the arithmetic unit and associated logic circuits were mounted, but now used colloquially to refer to the central processor itself. **1973** *Ann. N.Y. Acad. Sci.* CCXI. 282 The development of small main-frame computers called 'minicomputers'. *Ibid.* 283 Their chief advantages are small size, low price—as low as $2500 for a main frame. **1974** *Sci. Amer.* Apr. 79/1 The laboratory station mainframe has the essentials built-in (power supply, logic state indicators and programmers, and pulse sources to provide active stimulus for the student's circuits). **1967** I. A. BARAKA in W. King *Black Short Story Anthol.* (1972) 126 'Hey, man, I saw that d' fagit Bobby Hutchens down in the lobby with a real D.C. queer.'.. 'Hey man you cats better cool it... You talkin' about Ray's main man. You dig?' **1970** C. MAJOR *Dict. Afro-Amer. Slang* 79 *Main man*, favorite male friend; one's hero. **1910** R. FERRIS *How it Flies* xx. 464 *Main plane*, the principal supporting surface of an aeroplane. In the biplane, or the multiplane type, it denotes the lowest surface, unless some other is decidedly larger. **1913** A. E. BERRIMAN *Aviation* iii. 21 The presence of the two main planes as the distinguishing feature of biplanes. **1946** *Happy Landings* (Air Ministry) July 5/1 The aircraft.. was seen..minus the port outer mainplane and engine. **1973** *Nature* 14 Sept. 95/1 A further important observation was of a 20 cm ball which appeared at a height of about 50 cm over the trailing edge of the mainplane of an aircraft in flight. **1888** 'R. BOLDREWOOD' *Robbery under Arms* II. iii. 52, I say,..we haven't made any mistake—crossed over the main range and got back to the coast, have we? **1950** *N.Z. Jrnl. Agric.* Jan. 19/1 The barren and unproductive land consists of bare mountain tops, and native bush areas on the slopes of the main ranges. **1971** *N.Z. Listener* 19 Apr. 56/4 A *main range* is the major backbone of any individual group of mountains. [**1926** A. S. EDDINGTON *Internal Constitution of Stars* vii. 151 The three stars belong to what is now called the 'main series' running from types *O* and *B* down the dwarf series to type *M*.] **1927** P. DOIG *Outl. Stellar Astron.* I. i. 10 The dwarf branch is now more frequently referred to as the 'main sequence', a name due to Eddington. **1962** F. I. ORDWAY et al. *Basic Astronautics* vi. 284 A new star not yet hot enough to initiate thermonuclear reactions obtains its luminosity from gravitational contraction. Later, as the star heats up, thermonuclear reactions commence; and it joins the main sequence. **1966** *McGraw-Hill Encycl. Sci. & Technol.* XIII. 106/2 Stars that do not belong to the main sequence fall into two main groups: red giants..and white dwarfs... Modern theoretical work indicates that red giants and white dwarfs began their stellar careers as normal main-sequence stars and owe their distinctive properties to evolutionary changes incident on the exhaustion of nuclear energy sources. **1896** ADE *Artie* vii. 63, I went in and asked the main squeeze o' the works how much the sacque meant to him. **1927** D. HAMMETT in *Black Mask* Feb. 12/2 Vance seems to be the main squeeze. **1941** J. SMILEY *Hash House Lingo* 36 *Main squeeze*, hostess. **1970** H. E. ROBERTS *Third Ear* 9/2 *Main squeeze*, a man's closest woman friend.

main (mē¹n), *v.* [f. *main road* (MAIN *a.* 8 b).] **1.** *trans.* To convert into a main road.

1927 *Daily Tel.* 7 June 11/3 The widening and 'maining' of the road leading to the Royal Hotel corner. **1930** *Jrnl. Town Planning Inst.* XVI. 102/1 It is reported that the process of 'maining' roads has been steady and continuous. **1969** A. BIRD *Roads & Vehicles* iii. 40 The new county councils were made responsible for maintaining all 'main' roads in their counties, though it was left to them to determine which should be 'mained'.

2. *slang.* To insert (heroin or a similar drug) into a vein; to mainline.

1970 *Time* 16 Mar. 17 All my friends were on heroin. I snorted a couple of times, skinned a lot, and after that I mained it. **1972** J. BROWN *Chancer* v. 69 The bastard, he mained me. I said to skin it, but he mained it. First time. **1973** *Daily Mail* 3 Apr. 19/4 *Maining*, injecting straight into the vein.

Maine (mē¹n), *sb.*[2] *U.S.* **a.** The name of the State of *Maine* used in *Maine* (*liquor*) *law*, a law forbidding the manufacture or sale of intoxicating liquors; hence applied to similar laws (see quot. 1897).

1852 *Lantern* (N.Y.) I. 119/2 Does the Maine Law, in abolishing the use of liquors, include the Cotton-Gin? **1853** *Illustr. London News* 26 Nov. 438/1 The Earl of Harrington approves of a Maine law for England. **1855** *Knickerbocker* XLV. 479 They have the Maine Law down below. **1860** W. L. SARGANT *Robert Owen & his Social Philos.* xix. 216 Nor had he had recourse to a Maine law. **1864** T. H. NICHOLS *40 Yrs. Amer. Life* I. 76 But drunkenness becoming common,..spirits were banished, the apple orchards cut down,.. 'Maine Laws' were finally passed. **1871** *Scribner's Monthly* I. 673 Its special suggestiveness resides in the fact that it originates with the friends of the Maine law. **1897** *Encycl. Social Reform* 1107/1 A prohibitory law was passed in Maine in 1846, and in 1851 a more stringent one, including the provision for the seizure and destruction of intoxicating liquors (known as the 'Maine Law'..) was enacted... Vermont in 1852, New Hampshire in 1855, and Connecticut in 1854, passed the Maine law. **1960** R. K. WEBB *H. Martineau* xi. 346 She saw the Maine Law..as the exercise of the will of a democratic people.

b. *Maine law man*: a prohibitionist.

1858 *Leisure Hour* 3 June 352/2 Upon the extensive mines..are large numbers of teetotallers and Maine Law men.

mainland. Add: **1. c.** *Canad.* That part of British Columbia on the mainland of Canada, as opposed to Vancouver Island.

1921 *Daily Colonist* (Victoria, B.C.) 26 Mar. 5/4 Vancouver Island has done a great deal to support the Mainland in the past, and is doing so at present. The Mainland is no good to us.

d. The continent of Australia, as opposed to Tasmania.

1934 T. WOOD *Cobbers* xiii. 164 They are tied to Australia—'the mainland', they call it... 'The mainland' is an object of suspicion, envy, and dislike. **1944** *Living off Land* v. 102 So far as malaria is concerned, there's not much of it on the mainland. **1958** C. KOCH *Boys in Island* 15 He lived in an island. At six years old he knew about that. He heard it at school, and knew about it from Uncle Charlie's talk about the Mainland, Australia. **1968** G. DUTTON *Andy* 200 Soon as I blew from the boob, I headed down for the Old Tassy... I'll get over on the Mainland soon, or up the islands.

e. *N.Z. colloq.* The South Island.

1949 *Journeys* XXXIV. 56 I'm sure South Islanders are right in claiming that they live on the 'mainland'. **1965** *Weekly News* (Auckland, N.Z.) 10 Feb. 3/1 Greater numbers of adventurous North Islanders than ever before have crossed the seas this summer to the 'mainland'.

2. b. Special combs., as **mainland China,** the People's Republic of China, as opposed to Taiwan; hence *mainland Chinese*.

1967 *Guardian* 14 July 5/3 She lived in Hongkong and.. visited Japan, Korea, and what is known as 'Mainland China'. **1972** *Korea Herald* 17 Nov. 2/2 (*caption*) Chiao Kuanhua, first vice foreign minister of mainland China is greeted Tuesday by David Scotfox on behalf of Alec Douglas-Home at London airport. **1973** J. GOODFIELD *Courier to Peking* iii. 42 Teh Chang..went to mainland China... He was from Hong Kong. **1975** *Times* 3 Mar. 14/5 Mainland China is about to fight back against..the degenerate Hong Kong cult of violence, *Kung fu*. **1966** C. ISRAEL *Hostages* 38 World War III won't begin..until everyone has a chance to see what happens when the Mainland Chinese take their seat in the General Assembly. **1972** W. GARNER *Ditto, Brother Rat!* xxi. 159 Chinese, right? Mainland Chinese, too, I'd say.

mainlander (further examples).

1941 BAKER *Dict. Austral. Slang* 45 *Mainlander*, a person living on the Aust. continent, in contrast to one living in Tasmania or an island dependency. **1966** *Tribune* (Palmerston North, N.Z.) 1 Apr. 8/7 It's great what a pause in the wrong place does to the meaning of a phrase. Judging by a news announcer on Tv. the other night we can now lay claim to being Mainlanders. The news item doesn't matter but in the script were the words 'Palmerston, North Otago'. **1969** *Times* (Taiwan Suppl.) 9 Dec. p. iii/2 Taiwan's population today is 13.6m.—10.1m. native-born Taiwanese and 3.5m. mainlanders. **1971** *Guardian* 5 Nov. 21/3 If the mainlanders do not deliver on the current promises, the Taiwanese will be further disillusioned.

ma-in-law, colloq. abbrev. of MOTHER-IN-LAW.

1961 in PARTRIDGE *Dict. Slang* Suppl. **1971** R. RENDELL *One Across* v. 45 We've got some old tab coming here. ..Pal of my ma-in-law's. **1971** J. TYNDALL *Death in Lebanon* x. 181 So Ma-in-law has been quick to take her revenge. **1974** *People's Jrnl.* (Inverness & Northern Counties ed.) 29 June 4/2 My ma-in-law used to say.. 'Fierce is the light which beats upon the throne.'

main line. [f. MAIN *a.* + LINE *sb.*[2] 26 b.] **1.** The principal line of a railway.

1841 [see Line sb.^{2} 26 b]. **1865** [see Main a. 8 b]. **1880** *Harper's Mag.* July 196/2 The main line will soon have reached the Rio Grande Valley. **1959** *Chambers's Encycl.* XI. 488/2 The first lengthy main line, the Grand Junction, was opened in 1837. **1970** O. S. Nock *Rail, Steam & Speed* i. 17 A 'Gladstone' gliding effortlessly down one of the 1 in 264 banks of the Brighton main line.

b. *transf.* A principal route, connection, conduit, family, etc. *U.S.*

1845 *Hunt's Merchant's Mag.* XIII. 127 The main line of state works of Pennsylvania extends from the city of Philadelphia..to the city of Pittsburg. **1925** *Amer. Speech* I. 136/1 The cable that hauled the logs was called 'the main line'. **1945** S. J. Perelman *Crazy like Fox* 124 Why not follow the example of glamorous Mrs Barney Kessler, socially prominent matron of the Main Line. **1952** *Sunday Times* 3 Feb. 5/4 'Main line'..in America..is widely applied to important roads or conduits or arteries of one kind or another.

c. A large or principal vein, into which drugs can readily be injected; hence, an intravenous injection of drugs; the act or habit of making such an injection. *slang* (orig. *U.S.*).

1933 *Amer. Speech* VIII. ii. 27/2 The *main line* is the blood vessel into which the injection is made. **1938** *Amer. Speech* XIII. 182/2 From my dropper I'll shake the dust, From my spike I'll scrape the rust, And my old main-line I'll bust. **1953** W. Burroughs *Junkie* (1972) iii. 33, I began shooting in the main line to save stuff and because the immediate kick was better. **1959** 'E. McBain' *Pusher* iv. 36, I gave him a snort... He got on mainline a couple of weeks later. **1968** 'J. Welcome' *Hell is where you find It* xiv. 165 What about the purple hearts? Gone on main line yet? **1970** *Sunday Times* 8 Mar. 1/2 She was taking big doses of heroin..by mainline-injection into a vein—every four hours.

2. *attrib.* or quasi-*adj.* (often with hyphen). **a.** Of or pertaining to the main line of a railway.

1879 E. J. Simmons *Mem. Station Master* (1974) viii. 124, I couldn't take charge of this main-line station if you gave me all the world. **1884** R. Pike *Railway Adventures & Anecdotes* 93 A gentleman..got into a first-class carriage ..with the intention of proceeding home by one of the main line down trains. **1926** *Daily Express* 11 May 1/1 Great improvements in the main line train services continue to be made throughout the country. **1958** *New Statesman* 11 Oct. 484/2 Wuhsi..apparently sees a foreigner rarely although it is a large main-line city. **1969** M. Gilbert *Etruscan Net* i. i. 13 At main line stations they have a nose for these things.

b. *transf.* and *fig.* Principal; occupying a principal or important position; also, 'middle-of-the-road', 'mainstream'.

1941 Blunden *Thomas Hardy* iii. 42 Here he wrote one of his main-line novels. **1941** *Time* 20 Jan. 77 High life in Philadelphia's Main Line society. **1958** *Listener* 13 Nov. 775/1 Asimov's two books..in addition to being main-line science fiction, are also 'whodunits' in the classic tradition. **1963** *Guardian* 29 Apr. 9/1 She is from a wealthy main-line Philadelphia family. **1965** P. Freund *Spymaster* 114 His family, though not Main Line, was acceptable. **1968** *Punch* 11 Sept. 378/3 The enthusiasm of American main-line politicians for TV is said to be waning. **1972** *Times* 15 Apr. 16/4 The 'mainline Christian churches', say these young folk, have sold out to the 'establishment'.

c. Of, pertaining to, or characterized by the intravenous injection of drugs. Also *fig.*

1938 *Amer. Speech* XIII. 187/2 *Main-line shooter*, a vein-shooter. **1944** R. A. Moore *Textbk. Path.* xlvii. 522 On occasion, as in 'main-line' drug addicts, the fungus may be introduced directly into the blood. **1957** J. Kerouac *On Road* (1958) 173 A big shot of heroin in the main-line vein. **1969** *Daily Tel.* 29 Jan. 21/7 He was allowed a daily prescription of three grains—18 pills—of heroin. These were dissolved and injected directly into the bloodstream, which was known as the 'mainline' method. **1969** *Punch* 26 Feb. 295/3 Flattery is the mainline drug of the theatre —there is no one connected with that ridiculous institution who does not need his fix. **1972** *Times* 10 Apr. 10/4 As a mainline addict of BBC news..it has taken a week of comparing news on the two channels..to push me into the ranks of the deserters. **1974** G. Jenkins *Bridge of Magpies* iii. 46 Then you'll be like that poor bugger coming off now in the boat. Started smoking grass. Grew the stuff..in a potty in his cottage... He's on to mainline stuff now.

main-line, *v. slang* (orig. *U.S.*). Also (without hyphen) **mainline**. [f. prec.] *trans.* and *intr.* To inject (a drug or drugs) intravenously. So **main-liner**; **main-lining** *vbl. sb.*

1934 *Detective Fiction Weekly* 21 Apr. 113/2 The addict who shoots stuff into the veins is said to be a gutter, or mainliner. **1938** *Amer. Speech* XIII. 187/2 If you can main-line a cube of that stuff, it is on the house. **1950** R. Chandler *Let.* 18 May in *R. Chandler Speaking* (1966) 79, I don't think any writer could think up an expression like 'mainliner' for a narcotic addict who shoots the stuff into a vein. **1951** *N.Y. Times* 27 June 19/1 An intravenous injection of the drug..is called 'mainlining'. **1959** A. Bestic *Girl Outside* xiii. 213 She took to the needle. She's what they call a mainliner. **1959** 'E. McBain' *Pusher* viii. 77 Snorting?.. Skin pops?.. Larry, Larry, are you mainlining? **1964** B. Ellis *I came back from Hell* iii. 24 She was only skin-popping in those days (injecting her arms), not mainlining (injecting her veins). **1967** M. M. Glatt et al. *Drug Scene* v. 58, I don't know how much longer I would have lasted before I would have tried to mainline. *Ibid.* 59 Peter was revolted by the sight of someone else 'mainlining hard drugs' yet, whilst under the influence of hashish, he thought that he might go on to try mainlining for a bigger kick. **1970** N. Marsh *When in Rome* v. 126 The big leap. Pothead to main-liner. **1971** *Nature* 5 Nov. 14/3 The serious possibilities were raised of teratogenicity, tachycardia (especially if main-lining ever started), brain damage, [etc.]. **1972** M. Pereira *Singing Millionaire* vii. 71 He made himself a fix..and he mainlined it. **1974** D. Gray *Dead Give Away* ii. 23 What about the ones that can't cope in the rat race?.. The meths drinkers, the mainliners?

mainpast (mē̆i·npɑst). *Law. Obs.* exc. *Hist.* [ad. AF. *meynpast*, f. med.L. *manupastus*, f. L. *manū* abl. of *manus* hand + *pāstus*, pa. pple. of *pāscere* to feed (cf. Pasture *sb.*).] A man's household; a domestic; a dependant.

Anglo-Norman examples are cited in *Mod. Lang. Notes* (1932) June 375–6.

1865 F. M. Nichols tr. *Britton* I. i. ii. 13 Let the coroner inquire of whose tithing or whose mainpast such fugitive was. **1891** Maitland & Baildon tr. *Court Baron* (Selden Soc.) 53 Thy son who is thy mainpast entered the lord's garden. **1895** Pollock & Maitland *Hist. Eng. Law* I. ii. iii. 555 The head of a household answers for the appearance in court of the members of his household, his servants, his retainers, those whom his hand feeds, his *manupastus* or *mainpast*. **1909** W. S. Holdsworth *Hist. Eng. Law* III. ii. 295 We can see traces of the older principles under which he was held to be liable in the rule which made him responsible for the doings of his household or 'mainpast'. **1961** R. F. Hunnisett *Medieval Coroner* iv. 64 They [*sc.* the coroners] had to inquire in whose tithing or mainpast the outlaw had been and enrol it, in order that it might be amerced at the eyre for his flight.

mainprize, *v.* For '*Obs.*' read '*Obs.* exc. *Hist.*' and add later examples.

1865 S. Dobell *Life & Lett.* (1878) II. iii. 272 Not Moses only or Elias, But Heaven mainprized, and every standing saint Astonied into marble. **1895** Pollock & Maitland *Hist. Eng. Law* II. ii. ix. 582 If a man was arrested he was usually replevied (*replegiatus*) or mainprised (*manucaptus*), that is to say, he was set free so soon as some sureties (*plegii*) undertook (*manuceperunt*)..his appearance in court. **1904** M. Bateson *Borough Customs* (Selden Soc.) I. 99 If distress be delivered by pledge or mainprise of any one, if he who is..mainprised does not come to justify himself..let his..mainpernours be distrained to produce him.

main stem. [Main *a.* 8 b.] The principal stem; also *transf.* and *fig.* in various (chiefly *U.S. slang*) senses, as a main street, main line of a railway, pre-eminent person, etc.

1832 *Amer. Railroad Jrnl.* I. 804/2 The western fork.. connects it with the main stem. **1900** Ade *Fables in Slang* iv. 24 To grow up and be the Main Stem, like Mr. Jeffries. **1900** 'Flynt' & Walton *Powers that Prey* x. 250 Investigations that have been begun in 'the main stem'. **1907** J. London *Road* (1914) vii. 218 The kids began 'battering' the 'main-stem'. **1923** D. H. Lawrence *Birds, Beasts & Flowers* 42 Each single twig, Each one setting off straight to the sky As if it were the leader, the main-stem, the forerunner. **1928** [see *fold *v.*^{1} 5]. **1931** [see *drag *sb.* 3 e]. **1941** J. Smiley *Hash House Lingo* 36 *Main stem*, principal street of a city. **1945** E. T. Wallace *Barington* 62 The hog bounced us around and finally got back on the main stem. **1959** *Times Lit. Suppl.* 6 Nov. p. xxii/1 London audiences were listening to a play called *Broadway*.. typical of drama at that time in and around the Main Stem.

main stream. Also mainstream, main-stream. [Main *a.* 8 b.] The principal stream or current (of a river, etc.). Also *transf.* and *fig.*, the prevailing direction of opinion, fashion, society, etc.; *spec.* of jazz: see quot. 1960^2. Also *attrib.* Hence **mai·nstreamer**, a musician, etc., who is in the 'main stream' of his profession.

1667 [see Main *a.* 8 b]. **1831** Carlyle in *Foreign Q. Rev.* viii. 355 But after Luther's day, the Didactic Tendency again sinks to a lower level; mingles with manifold other tendencies; among which, admitting that it still forms the main stream, it is no longer so pre-eminent, positive, and universal, as properly to characterize the whole. **1865** M. Arnold *Ess. in Crit.* 171 Byron and Shelley will be long remembered..for their..Titanic effort to flow in the main stream of modern literature. **1938** F. M. Ford *Let.* Oct. (1965) 302 The very considerable influence that Mr. Pound..exercised on literary mainstreams. **1952** *New World Writing* Apr. 33 Negro artists, in moving out into the mainstream of American culture, should gain a sense of solidarity with both the national and the general world of art. **1957** S. Dance in S. Traill *Concerning Jazz* 55 Mainstream jazz, typified by musicians like Basie, Ellington..Armstrong. **1957** *Jazz News* Apr. 2/3 Rising like a Pheonix [*sic*] from the dying embers of the British modern jazz world is a musical form that has been tagged 'Mainstream'. **1958** 'E. Crispin' *Best SF Three* 9 Main-stream fiction..has been almost uniformly catatonic in its withdrawal from environment. **1960** W. Naylor *Silver Birch Anthol.* 7 Ask him a question on a comparatively minor issue and time and time again he will use it as a tributary through which to return to the mainstream of his philosophy. **1960** *Sunday Times* 11 Sept. 37/1 Very broadly you can break up jazz asymmetrically into the big, simple, driving noise of the traditionalists and the smaller, sophisticated, elegiac sound of modern jazz. In between, there is a discernible third group of 'mainstream' enthusiasts. **1961** *New Left Rev.* July–Aug. 42/2 Humph is authentic mainstreamer: he's been influenced by everything in jazz up to the moment. **1966** R. Ellison in A. Chapman *New Black Voices* (1972) 407 The main stream of American literature is in me, even though I am a Negro, because I possess more of Mark Twain than many white writers do. **1969** *Listener* 26 June 904/3 Gesualdo.. belongs less to the mainstream of music than to one of its smaller and more wayward canals. **1973** C. Bonington *Next Horizon* xxii. 297 A climber who had always been on the outside of the mainstream British climbing scene. **1974** *Listener* 10 Jan. 54/2 Dick Taverne..possesses a rigid habit of mind, so far quite alien to mainstream British politics.

Main Street, main street. [Main *a.* 8 b.] **a.** The principal street of a town, esp. in the U.S.; freq. used as a proper name.

In quots. 1598–1743 preceded by an article and not a special collocation.

[**1598** Florio *Worlde of Wordes* 327/2 *Rióne*, a maine streete, a high way. **1687** S. Sewall *Diary* (1878) I. 183 At night a great Uproar and Lewd rout in the Main Street. **1698** *Rec. East Hampton, N.Y.* (1887) II. 434 Ten Acres of Land..[bound] on the west with the Maine Street of the said Town. **1717** in *Narragansett Hist. Reg.* (1884–5) III. 279 In or through the Main street, called Hope street, in this town [*sc.* Bristol, R.I.]. **1741–3** [see Main *a.* 8 b].] **1810** F. Cuming *Sk. Tour Western Country* 194 Main street, parallel to Water street, is one hundred feet wide. **1817** S. Brown *Western Gazetteer* 92 Main street presents to the traveller as much wealth, and more beauty than can be found in most of the Atlantic cities. **1855** *Knickerbocker* XLVI. 328 Louisville is an imposing, wealthy city. Main-street, in its entire extent would do honor to any metropolis in America. **1888** 'R. Boldrewood' *Robbery under Arms* II. iii. 54 Go on down Main Street (the first street in a diggings is always called Main Street). **1889** W. D. Howells *Hazard of New Fortunes* I. i. xi. 106 You know the kind of street Main Street always used to be in our section—half plank-road..and the rest mud-hole. **1892** Kipling *Lett. of Travel* (1920) 8 Every..thing, is reported, digested, discussed, and rediscussed up and down Main Street [in Vermont]. **1961** L. Mumford *City in Hist.* iii. 74 It was rather a Broad Ways..it served as the classic 'Main Street'. **1968** *Michelin Guide N.Y. City* 78 Before the Revolution..Greenwich Street, which then bordered the Hudson and its warehouses, was 'Main Street'. *Ibid.* 82 Mulberry Street is the Italian 'Main Street': colorful shops offer national specialities. **1973** A. Broinowski *Take One Ambassador* vii. 86 You should see this station in rush hour. It's like Main Street Christmas Eve.

b. Used allusively, esp. since the publication in 1920 of Sinclair Lewis's novel *Main Street*, as a symbol of mediocrity, parochialism, or materialism in small-town life. Also *attrib.*

[**1855** *N.Y. Tribune* 31 Dec. 4/4 It has risen to its present position of bloated arrogance and swaggering insolence by the liberal and unstinting patronage it has received from the full purses and free hands of Eastern men in Main street and elsewhere.] **1916** 'B. M. Bower' *Phantom Herd* i. 5 You'll have to let me weed out some of these Main Street cowboys. **1920** S. Lewis (*title*) Main Street. **1931** *Times Lit. Suppl.* 9 Apr. 282/3 He dislikes uniformity, mass-control, Main-street and Rotarian ideals. **1948** *Time* 6 Dec. 20/3 Harry Truman has never lost his great respect for Marshall, nor is he unmindful of the prestige and authority Marshall carries on Main Street as well as in Moscow. **1972** B. Garfield *Line of Succession* (1974) ii. 126 The President..was an amalgam of liberal traditions..and the values of Main Street. **1973** T. H. White *Making of President 1972* (1974) ix. 231 From faculty club to student union, from bar to parlor, from Wall Street to Main Street, all wanted out of Vietnam.

Hence **Main Streeter, Mai·nstreeter**, a typical inhabitant of a small American town; one who shares the values of Main Street (sense *b). Also **main-street** (*N. Amer.*) *v. intr.*, to campaign in main streets during an electoral campaign; hence **main-streeting** *vbl. sb.*

1934 Webster, Main Streeter. **1945** *Sat. Rev.* (U.S.) 6 Oct. 8/2 His books started some Americans laughing at others and made it possible for people to realize that somebody else was a Main Streeter. **1947** *Time* 27 Jan. 4/3 It has raised the hope of this Mainstreeter from Podunk to its highest ebb since the era of Wendell Willkie's 'One World'. **1966** *Maclean's Mag.* 1 Jan. 31 Though she [*sc.* Olive Diefenbaker] refuses to speak in public she mainstreets better than The Chief [*sc.* John Diefenbaker]. **1967** *Canad. Ann. Rev. 1966* 133 Duff Roblin, whose rural mainstreeting, recorded bagpipe accompaniment, and unflagging oratory had won him his fourth personal victory in a row. **1971** *Time* 14 June 20 Boston has witnessed a merry binge of mainstreeting, leafletting and parties with some of the excitement of a mayoral election. **1974** *Globe & Mail* (Toronto) 5 June 8/3 New Democratic Party Leader David Lewis traded polemics with Parti Quebecois supporters in Montreal's working-class St. Jacques district yesterday before doing some mainstreeting not far from the area where he lived as a young immigrant half a century ago.

maintain, *v.* Add: **9. c.** To give a drug to (an individual, esp. a drug addict) in maintenance doses so as to sustain a particular therapeutic effect. Cf. *maintenance 7 c.

1957 *Jrnl. Amer. Med. Assoc.* 14 Dec. 1970/1 The current discussion..can be reduced to the desirability and feasibility of treating the addict as a total person,..withdrawing drugs.., or of maintaining him on an appropriate amount of drugs if it is determined he cannot be successfully cured of his addiction. **1971** *Nature* 22 Oct. 558/2 The recipient dogs were anaesthetized with intravenous thiopentone and maintained with halothane, nitrous oxide and oxygen through an endotracheal tube. **1972** *Science* 26 May 881/1 In April 1971, a program was inaugurated to maintain at least 20,000 addicts on methadone in New York State alone.

maintained school (see quots.).

1944 in *Parl. Papers 1943–4* (Cmd. 6523) (*title*) Principles of government in maintained secondary schools. **1960** *Where?* iii. 15/1 *Maintained school*, a school maintained by a local education authority, including county, voluntary aided, and voluntary controlled schools. **1966** *Rep. Comm. Inquiry Univ. Oxf.* I. 74 It is also likely that the swing to science has played some part in raising the

rate of recruitment from maintained schools. **1973** *Guardian* 25 Apr. 15/4 The 12-man governing board of Sacred Heart (a Catholic maintained school).

maintainability (mēin-, mĕntēⁱ·năbi·lĭti). [f. MAINTAINABLE *a.*; see *-BILITY.] The quality of being easily maintained; capability of being maintained.

1943 *Sci. Amer.* June 250 Engineering..determines the serviceability and maintainability of new types of equipment. **1971** *New Scientist* 3 June 574/3 Every project should have goals for reliability..and 'maintainability'. **1974** *Daily Colonist* (Victoria, B.C.) 9 Oct. 3/2 It demonstrates the maintainability of the Candu reactor system.

maintenance. Add: **3.** Freq. *attrib.*

1884 *List of Subscribers* (London & Globe Telephone Co.), In case of unsatisfactory service..send complaint in writing..to London and Globe Telephone and Maintenance Company, Limited. **1942** *Aeronautics* May 40/1 The public does not hear very much about the Maintenance Command of the Royal Air Force. **1957** *Ann. Reg. 1956* 67 A prolonged ban on overtime working by the maintenance men. **1958** *Listener* 23 Oct. 650/1 Maintenance engineers at London Airport vote unanimously to continue their strike. **1970** *E. Afr. Standard* (Nairobi) 23 Jan. 18/2 (Advt.), Applicants..should have at least five years' experience, either in a supervisory capacity or as a maintenance engineer in sole charge of a plant. **1974** *Times* 7 Mar. 1/1 Maintenance workers will be allowed into the pits during the weekend.

7. b. (Further examples.) Also *maintenance order*: a court order, in the case of a broken marriage, compelling the husband to pay the wife a regular fixed sum for her maintenance.

1803 G. COLMAN *John Bull* IV. 42 I'll settle a separate maintenance upon ould mother Brulgruddery [*sc.* his wife]. **1866** *Act* 29 & 30 *Vict.* c. 32 § 1 It shall be lawful for the Court to make an order on the husband for payment to the wife during their joint lives of such monthly or weekly sums for her maintenance..as the Court may think reasonable. **1907** *Act 7 Edw. VII* c. 12 § 1 The court may ..make an order on the husband for payment to the wife ..for her maintenance. **1920** *Act* 10 & 11 *Geo. V* c. 33 § 10 The expression 'maintenance order' means an order other than an order of affiliation for the periodical payment of sums of money towards the maintenance of the wife or other dependants of the person against whom the order is made. **1960** M. SPARK *Bachelors* vi. 88 But there's usually a question of maintenance orders. I distinctly recall his being described as a bachelor. **1971** *Reader's Digest Family Guide to Law* 265/2 In many cases a wife will be left, after a separation, with insufficient money for her own day-to-day expenses. Her need for maintenance will be even more urgent if she is taking care of any children of the marriage... She can apply to the local magistrates' court or to a divorce court for a maintenance order. **1973** *Times* 14 Mar. 20/4 To qualify for maintenance a wife does not have to ask for a divorce.

c. The action of providing (a person) over a period of time with doses of a drug sufficient to maintain its effect on the body while usu. being less than the dose given initially; usu. *attrib.*, as *maintenance dose.*

1936 STEDMAN *Med. Dict.* (ed. 13) 319/2 *Maintenance dose*, the dose given in a protracted case of illness, to keep the patient under the influence of the drug after this has been attained by the initial dosage. **1963** *Brit. Pharmaceutical Codex* 683 Dose [of propylthiouracil]. Controlling dose, 200 to 600 milligrams daily; maintenance dose, 50 to 200 milligrams daily. **1965** *Jrnl. Amer. Med. Assoc.* 23 Aug. 648/1 Addicts coming to a maintenance program usually fear that physicians will not prescribe enough medication. **1971** *Nature* 29 Jan. 290/2 The committee believes that the British system of maintenance, in which an addict is supplied with daily doses of heroin, and the methadone maintenance treatment,..both have their advantages and drawbacks.

‖ **maintien** (mañtiañ). [Fr.] Bearing, deportment.

1849 GEO. ELIOT *Let.* 4 Oct. (1954) I. 313 Those happy souls..who do really effect much good, simply by their calm and even *maintien.* **1889** G. B. SHAW *London Music 1888–89* (1937) 73 Josabeth had the *maintien* of the French stage in a degree that would have enraptured A. B. Walkley.

Maioli (māyǭ·li). The name of Thomas Mahieu (fl. 1549–72), latinized as *Maiolus*, French book-collector and secretary to Catherine de Médicis, used *attrib.* to designate a French style of book-binding with elaborate gold tooling, used for some of the books in his library. Also *absol.*

[**1837** 'J. A. ARNETT' *Inquiry into Nature & Form of Bks. of Ancients* vi. 142 Another patron, of the name of Maioli, is well known, from his bindings, though of his personal history no traces are left.] **1890** *Catal. Exhib. Recent Bk.-Bindings 1860–9* (Grolier Club) 37 [Book] Brown morocco..Sides decorated with a Maioli design. **1894** W. S. BRASSINGTON *Hist. Art of Bookbinding* xiii. 178 (*caption*) Maioli binding, Italian, early sixteenth century. **1928** E. P. GOLDSCHMIDT *Gothic & Renaissance Bookbindings* I. 105 Both the Groliers and the Maiolis were made by the same binders and gilders at the same time. **1961** J. P. HARTHAN *Bookbindings* (ed. 2) 12 The 'atelier au trèfle' which supplied bindings to Grolier and Henri II is probably the source also of these fine Maioli bindings.

maiosis, maiotic, obs. varr. *MEIOSIS 3, *MEIOTIC *a.* 2.

‖ **maire**² (mḗr). [Fr.; see MAYOR.] A mayor; the chief municipal officer of a French town or of one of the arrondissements or districts of Paris.

1790 H. WALPOLE *Let.* 30 Aug. (1905) XIV. 289 At Marseilles..a Monsieur Cazalet..had been invited to dine with the *maire*! *a* **1861** A. H. CLOUGH *Poems* (1862) 239 Their *maire*, he said, could neither write nor read. **1900** C. M. YONGE *Modern Broods* xiii. 121 She gabbled away most eloquently to the Maire, almost as fluently as a born Frenchwoman. **1955** *Times* 22 Aug. 8/6 As a record of continuous office-holding it is overshadowed by that of Edmond Mathis, maire of Ehuns in the Haute-Savoie from 1878 to 1953. **1964** C. MACKENZIE *My Life & Times* III. i. 31 Monsieur Boeuf the *maire*, who looked exactly like his name. **1974** S. SHELDON *Other Side of Midnight* ii. 55 Let's get married by some *maire* in the country.

‖ **mairie** (mḗ·ri). [Fr., f. *maire* mayor (see prec.).] In France, a town hall; a public building housing the municipal offices of a town or arrondissement and often also serving as the official residence of the mayor.

1864 DICKENS *Mrs. Lirriper's Legacy* i, in *All Year Round* Extra Christmas No., 1 Dec. 8/2 The Major went down to the Mairie. **1896** E. DOWSON *Let. c* 25 Apr. (1967) 359 In his official capacity I cannot reach him, although I call daily at the mairie & at his house. **1925** E., O., & S. SITWELL *Poor Young People* 13 Outside the mairie of this country place. **1935** W. FORTESCUE *Perfume from Provence* 82 The mysteries in the Mairie having been performed, the procession..went into the church, where the Marriage Mass was celebrated. **1966** N. FREELING *King of Rainy Country* 96 A real French country mairie with grandiose pillars outside to support the dignity of the Republic. **1974** *Times* 16 Apr. 5/1, I found M. Jarrot at the *mairie* of Montceau-les-Mines.

maison. Delete *Sc. Obs.* and add later examples. Now usu. in the sense of a business (esp. a fashion) house or firm.

1922 JOYCE *Ulysses* 165 He went on by la Maison Claire. **1932** 'E. M. DELAFIELD' *Thank Heaven Fasting* I. ii. 32 The tall, yellow-headed assistant from the Maison Leroy in Sloane Street..twisted the hot irons in and out of her hair. **1935** A. CHRISTIE *Death in Clouds* xiii. 138 I'll easily get what I want from Henri's or the Maison Richet. **1966** J. S. COX *Illustr. Dict. Hairdressing* 94 *Maison...* A mode of address used by many fashionable hairdressers of the Victorian and Edwardian periods... The intention was to convey to the public that the firm had a knowledge of French hair styles... An example was *Maison Stephens et Cie.*, Queen's Road, Clifton. **1968** *Listener* 29 Aug. 280/2 The *spécialité* of this particular *maison* is the primal bourgeois myth, the Dick Whittington legend brought up to date. **1970** 'J. & E. BONETT' *Sound of Murder* ix. 112 In gold letters on a heart-shaped label were the words 'Maison Petronelle—Nail Lacquer'. **1971** D. AYERST *Guardian* xxiii. 330 Dresses by 'Maison N'Importe' and all the rest of it.

2. *Comb.* **maison close** [lit. 'closed house'], a brothel; **maison de couture,** a fashion house; **maison de passe** [lit. 'house of passage'], a brothel (see quot. 1967); **maison de santé** [lit. 'house of health'], a nursing home; also, *euphem.*, a home for the mentally sick; **maison tolérée** [lit. 'tolerated house'], a licensed brothel.

1939 E. AMBLER *Mask of Dimitrios* vii. 126 Your *maison close* must have proved disappointing. The inevitable Armenian girls, of course. **1950** *Landfall* IV. 124 The squalid harlot in the *maison close.* **1961** *Guardian* 10 Feb. 9/4 Toulouse-Lautrec..became..an inhabitant of the *Maisons Closes* where the girls regarded him as an amiable ..mascot. **1927** E. HEMINGWAY in *Scribner's Mag.* Apr. 359/2 The American lady had bought her own clothes for twenty years now from the same maison de couturier [*sic*] in the Rue Saint Honoré. **1933** A. CHRISTIE *Lord Edgware Dies* xii. 107 The name of Lao Tse would suggest to her a prize Pekingese dog, the name of Molière a *maison de couture.* **1964** A. ADBURGHAM *Shops & Shopping* xxi. 247 Paul Poiret..described..a visit paid to his *maison de couture* by Margot Asquith. **1970** S. J. PERELMAN *Baby, it's Cold Inside* 53 The rigors of squiring her through a score of *maisons de couture*, jewelers', and millinery shops were..unimaginable. **1960** B. MARSHALL *Divided Lady* xxix. 99 The hotel we drew up at eventually reminded me of a *maison-de-passe* I used to know in Barcelona. **1967** L. DEIGHTON *Expensive Place to Die* x. 71 It's not a brothel... It's a *maison de passe*. It's a house that people go to when they already have a girl with them. **1841** POE *Murders in Rue Morgue* in *Tales* (1845) 142 Some raving maniac escaped from a neighbouring *Maison de Santé.* **1859** *Times* 5 Feb. 5/6 (Advt.), Maison de Santé, or Residence for Invalids. **1910** W. J. LOCKE *Simon* xxiv. 337 He seemed to be happy enough at the *maison de santé.* **1940** JOYCE *Let.* 3 Nov. (1966) III. 496, I had arranged for the reception at a Swiss *maison de santé.* **1942** 'A. BRIDGE' *Frontier Passage* vii. 125 We don't want him shut up in a *maison de santé* for spy mania. **1893** G. B. SHAW *Let.* 12 Dec. (1965) 412 A woman of bad character, proprietress of two *maisons tolérées* in Brussels. **1927** *Observer* 11 Dec. 20/2 Agreement on that point [*sc.* that abolition of the licensed houses of prostitution decreases the white slave traffic] greatly strengthens the hands of the League in working for the abolition of the maison tolérée. **1970** K. CHESNEY *Victorian Underworld* x. 343 Conditioned by her existence in a *maison tolérée*,..she was very much in the hands of the bawd to whom she was consigned.

maisonnette. Add: **2.** (Usu. in the form *maisonette.*) A part of a residential building which is let separately, usu. distinguished from a flat by not being all on one floor.

1912 *Chambers's Jrnl.* Feb. 144/2 Flats or maisonettes, such as Queen Anne's Mansions, Westminster, London. **1919** T. S. ELIOT *Whispers of Immortality* in *Poems*, Grishkin has a maisonette. **1923** A. HUXLEY *Antic Hay* ix. 129 'It's a dr-dreadful little maisonnette,' she explained. 'Full of awful things. We had to take it furnished.' **1957** *New Yorker* 5 Oct. 171/1 Le Corbusier wisely utilized the type of apartment the English call the maisonette, with a narrow private stairs to connect upper and lower rooms. **1959** *Times* 28 May 13/5 To-day one sees maisonnettes advertised as such but also covering a range of separate living accommodation from the hotch potch of the converted house to the modern slab block of flats. **1961** L. MUMFORD *City in Hist.* Note to plate 51, The London County Council's Roehampton estate, with its mixture of tower apartments and lower houses and maisonettes. **1975** J. SYMONS *Three Pipe Problem* iii. 22 Why did wretched house agents insist upon using not the word rooms, nor apartment, nor even flat, but the atrocious *maisonette*?

Maithili (mai·tili). The name of a dialect of Bihari, one of the Indo-Aryan group of languages; also, the name of its script.

1881 G. A. GRIERSON *Introd. Maithili Lang. of N. Bihar* I. i. 5 The Maithilí character is nearly the same as Bangálí, differing only in one or two letters. *Ibid.* ii. 8 Words derived direct from the Saṃskṛit, which were originally neuter, become masculine in Maithilí. **1928** *Funk's Stand. Dict.* 1494/3 Many lyrics in Maithili script date from the 15th century. **1948** D. DIRINGER *Alphabet* II. vi. 365 The Oriya, Maithili and Early Manipuri characters seem...to be somewhat connected with the Bengali script. **1962** D. C. SWANSON in Householder & Saporta *Probl. Lexicogr.* I. 74, I have been unable to elicit any ['diminutive' suffixes] from speakers of..Maithili. **1968** *Encycl. Brit.* III. 606/1 Maithili is the dialect of the old country of Mithila or Tirhut, famous from ancient times for its learning... The only dialect which has any real literature is Maithili.

‖ **Maitrank** (mai·traŋk). [G., f. *Mai* May + *trank* drink, beverage.] = *May-drink* (MAY *sb.*³ 5 a).

1858 GEO. ELIOT *Jrnl.* in J. W. Cross *George Eliot's Life* (1885) II. viii. 41 Delicious *Mai-trank*, made by putting the fresh *Waldmeister*—a cruciferous plant with a small white flower..into mild wine, together with sugar. **1897** G. DU MAURIER *Martian* 273 You might sit for sixpence in a pretty garden and drink coffee, beer, or Maitrank. **1899** G. JEKYLL *Wood & Garden* vi. 60 The pretty little Woodruff..revives memories..of Maitrank, that best of the 'cup' tribe of pleasant drinks, whose flavour is borrowed from its flowering tips.

‖ **maître** (mḗtr'). [Fr., = master.] **1.** *slang.* Also **maître d', maitre de** (mḗtr' də or dī). Used *ellipt.* for *MAÎTRE D'HÔTEL 2.

1899 R. WHITEING *No. 5 John St.* xviii. 188 But the viands! Some of them, as the maître is so good as to tell me..come straight from Paris. **1953** P. ADLER *House is not Home* (1954) i. 16 Hat-check girls, waiters, the maître d', some nicely-dressed people..all spoke to Harry. **1959** *Guardian* 12 Dec. 3/1 The maître de (they do not bother about the 'hotel' bit) ushered..parties..to tables. **1967** C. DRUMMOND *Death at Furlong Post* iv. 56 A very large steak..made with great blobs of butter by a spivvy little *maître* with a spirit stove. **1969** A. GLYN *Dragon Variation* vii. 208 The *maître d'*, who knew her well, greeted her and led her to her usual table on the north side. **1973** M. CATTO *Sam Casanova* iv. 74 With the help of the *maître* who looked after the cellar they chose a fabulous Chateau d'Yquem. **1973** W. MCCARTHY *Detail* iii. 161 I've just brought over a new maître de, a young Italian fellow who will be running the place [*sc.* a restaurant]. **1974** *Publishers Weekly* 17 June 10/1 The sort of lady who is instinctively escorted to corner tables by *maîtres d'*.

2. The title and form of address of a French lawyer.

1883 C. M. YONGE *Stray Pearls* I. xvi. 211 Technically he [*sc.* a lawyer] was only Maître Darpent, and his mother only would have been called Mademoiselle. Monsieur and Madame were much more jealously limited to nobility than..now. **1910** BARONESS ORCZY *Lady Molly of Scotland Yard* vi. 148, I hear from Maître Vendôme that he has safely received my letter. *Ibid.* 165 He was met by his late aunt's lawyer, Maître Vendôme. **1957** D. DU MAURIER *Scapegoat* xxiii. 305 The lawyer bowed. 'You will have the kindness, Maître, to see that notification of the death goes to the newspapers.' **1971** *Guardian* 15 Sept. 2/6 Maître Nicolet then said in court that the centre of the European gang was a Frenchman.

3. a. maître d'armes (mḗtr' dārm) [lit. 'master of arms'], a fencing instructor.

1896 G. A. HENTY *Through Russian Snows* vii. 143 The veterans were always ready to give him lessons with the sabre or rapier in addition to those he received from the *maître d'armes* of the regiment. **1932** *Times Lit. Suppl.* 24 Mar. 220/2 He will by then be lost in a maze of technical terms..and will fly to a *maître d'armes* for instruction. **1956** J. D. AYLWARD *Eng. Master of Arms* ix. 110 He was ..abreast of the progress made during the seventeenth century by the great French *maîtres d'armes.* **1961** F. C. AVIS *Sportsman's Gloss.* 194 *Maître d'Armes*, a master of arms or fencing master.

b. maître de ballet (mḗtr' də bale) [lit. 'ballet-master'], originally one who composed and superintended the production and performance of a ballet; now, a trainer of ballet dancers; hence **maîtresse de ballet,** the female counterpart.

1823 T. CREEVEY *Let.* in *Creevey Papers* (1903) II. iii. 64 Yesterday I spent a very amusing hour with Sefton at the Opera House, seeing the *maitre de ballet* manœuvre about 50 *figurantes* for the approaching new ballet of *Alfred.* **1828** J. EBERS *Seven Yrs. King's Theatre* xii. 351 An amiable and able individual..has experienced the com-

mon fate of mortality; I mean M. Boisgerard, the second Maître de Ballet. **1845** *Morning Post* 9 Apr. 5/5 *Maîtres de ballet* have to begin a new course of study. **1913** A. E. Johnson *Russ. Ballet* 3 But though his [*sc.* Noverre's] ambition as a *maître de ballet* outran his perceptions as an artist,..he initiated and firmly established a new form of art. **1915** M. E. Perugini *Art of Ballet* xxxiii. 278 A wise choice was made in the selection of the late Madame Katti Lanner as *maîtresse de ballet.* **1959** *Times* 1 Sept. 11/3 Under its *maître de ballet*..it has reached international standards. **1975** *Times* 27 May 11/5 Hu's fight master is a former Peking *maître de ballet.*

maître d'hôtel. Add: **2.** A hotel manager; now usually the manager of a hotel dining-room, a head waiter.

1891 R. H. Savage *My Official Wife* iv. 43 The attentive *maître d'hôtel* flew past us and threw open the door of a splendid apartment. **1907** E. Glyn *Three Weeks* i. 17 Her red wine the *maître d'hôtel* poured into her glass himself. **1923** M. Arlen *These Charming People* 85 The agreeable and polished M. Risotto, prince of *maître d'hôtels*, chanced by our table. **1959** T. S. Eliot *Elder Statesman* I. 9 The *maître d'hôtel* And the waiters all seem to be your intimate friends. **1973** D. Miller *Chinese Jade Affair* xvii. 157 The 'canard aux navets' was brought to the table by the Maître d'Hotel himself.

3. *attrib.* (See quots.)

1845 E. Acton *Mod. Cookery* (ed. 2) iv. 107 *French Maître d'Hotel*, or *Steward's Sauce.* Add to half a pint of rich, pale veal gravy,..salt, minced parsley, and lemon-juice. **1861** Mrs. Beeton *Bk. Househ. Managem.* x. 223 *Maître d'Hôtel Butter*, for putting into Broiled Fish just before it is sent to Table. *Maître d'Hôtel Sauce (Hot)*, to serve with Calf's Head, Boiled Eels, and different Fish. **1951** *Good Housek. Home Encycl.* 543/2 Simply prepared dishes garnished with maître d'hôtel butter. **1965** *House & Garden* Dec. 84/2 *Maître d'hôtel.* If given this name, a dish will probably be fairly quickly and simply cooked—a grill or something like that—and it will include parsley in some form or other. When used to describe butter, it means that the butter has been seasoned, has chopped parsley and lemon juice worked into it and is then put to get cold so that it can be made into pats. **1974** *Times* 6 Nov. 14/8 My salmon steak with maître d'hotel butter was good.

‖ **maîtresse** (mɛ̄trɛs). [Fr., mistress.] Used in phrases, as **maîtresse en titre** [lit. 'mistress in name'], an official or acknowledged mistress; **maîtresse femme**, a strong-willed or domineering woman.

1839 Thackeray *Catherine* in *Fraser's Mag.* July 104/1 We had a great mind to make..Mrs. Catherine *maîtresse en titre* to Mr. Alexander Pope. **1853** C. Brontë *Villette* III. xxxii. 83 Ah! I know you well..cette maîtresse-femme, my cousin Beck herself. **1876** C. M. Yonge *Womankind* xxii. 179 There are four kinds of wives—the cowed woman, the dead-weight, the *maîtresse femme*, and the helpmeet. **1925** W. J. Locke *Great Pandolfo* xix. 240 She had been the *maîtresse en titre* of one of his friends. **1929** S. Runciman *Emperor Romanus Lecapenus* ii. 42 At first Leo did not dare to marry her: though he took her to the Palace as an acknowledged *maîtresse en titre.* **1929** C. L. Thomson *Jane Austen* i. 50 The wonderful heroine [of *Corinne*], a *maîtresse femme* like Mme de Staël herself. **1931** *Times Lit. Suppl.* 9 July 544/1 She tells of..dwarf, and cicisbeo, and maîtresse en titre. **1936** G. B. Shaw *Millionairess* Pref. 105 In the humblest cabin that contains a family you may find a *maîtresse femme* who rules in the household by a sort of divine right. *Ibid.* 107 Queen Elizabeth was a *maîtresse femme.* **1953** M. Steen *Anna Fitzalan* iii. 72 For two and a half years Anna fulfilled.. the functions of a nurse, as well as those of a *maîtresse en titre* of Evan's household. **1964** *Guardian* 26 Oct. 16/8 An accredited speech-writer is, like a 'maitresse en titre', an offence to public morals. **1973** D. Chandler *Marlborough* i. 5 Arabella [Churchill] was..combining the roles of maid-of-honour to the Duchess and *maîtresse-en-titre* to the Duke, to whom she bore several children. **1973** E. Hyams *Final Agenda* viii. 98 The widow was a *maîtresse femme* whose place in the hierarchy was three steps higher than that of her..husband.

Maitreya (məitrēi·yă). [Skr., f. *maitrī* friendship.] In Buddhist theology, the name of the Buddha who will appear in the future; also, an artistic representation of this future Buddha.

1889 M. Monier-Williams *Buddhism* iv. 135 Gautama is the fourth Buddha of the present age... He is to be followed by the fifth Buddha, Maitreya (a name meaning 'full of love towards all beings'). **1923** A. B. Keith *Buddhist Philos.* xvii. 289 We have the Buddha's own authority for the advent of Maitreya. **1933** E. J. Thomas *Hist. Buddhist Thought* xiii. 168 As a part of this doctrine of a succession of Buddhas arose the belief in a future Buddha, Metteyya, or Maitreya. **1961** *Guardian* 23 Mar. 11/3 A seated Maitreya in gilt bronze, Silla—early seventh century. **1972** P. M. Bartz *S. Korea* 142/1 The figures are *miroks*, images of Maitreya, the Buddha of the future. **1972** D. Bloodworth *Any Number can Play* iii. 17 The guru strikingly resembled the Maitreya who would one day come to herald an age of happiness.

maize. Add: **3.** (Further examples.) Freq. denoting a colour of cloth or dress-material.

1838 E. Grosvenor *Jrnl.* 9 June in G. Huxley *Lady Elizabeth & the Grosvenors* (1965) iii. 78 Succeeded in finding..a maize and silver gown. **1853** Mrs. Gaskell *Cranford* xiii. 244 If a happy sea-green could be met with, the gown was to be sea-green; if not she inclined to maize. **1858** Geo. Eliot *Scenes Clerical Life* I. ii. 32 Maize is a colour that decidedly did *not* suit his complexion. **1923** *Daily Mail* 15 June 6 (Advt.), Crepe de Chine..newest shades, including: Pale Pink,..Maize, Lemon. **1970** *Cape Times* 28 Oct. 19/3 (Advt.), Rambler Rogue, 1970, 5500 miles, maize with cognac trim. **1975** *New Yorker* 26 May 54/1 (Advt.), Our all silk honan tie... Navy, red, brown, maize, rust, bottle green.

4. *maize-yellow.*

1897 C. T. Davis *Manuf. Leather* (ed. 2) 607 Light ochre yellow, maize yellow to dark gold ochre yellow.

Maje·stic, *sb.* [f. the adj.] A variety of potato, producing light-skinned, kidney-shaped tubers.

1917 T. W. Sanders *Bk. Potato* (ed. 3) xviii. 99 *Majestic*, tubers, oval-shaped; hardy, strong grower; enormous cropper; fine quality and appearance. **1926** R. N. Salaman *Potato Varieties* xxvi. 285 Majestic has attained great popularity, and today is one of the most widely grown field crop potatoes in the country. **1956** S. M. Gault *Vegetables* x. 203 *Main Crop.* Majestic, a heavy cropping white kidney, with shallow-eyed large tubers. **1963** *Times* 22 Apr. 2/6 Majestic, which takes up over 50 per cent of the maincrop acreage, was introduced in 1912.

majesticalness. (Later example.)

1905 *Westm. Gaz.* 19 Apr. 1/3 The majesticalness of this master-work of human genius and human sorrows.

majesty. Add: **2.** *His Satanic Majesty* (examples). Also *his sable majesty* (see *sable *a.*).

1751 Richardson *Clarissa* (ed. 4) IV. 126 To be sure, Jack, she means to do great despight to his Satanic Majesty in her hopes of reforming me. **1922** Joyce *Ulysses* 325 The priests and bishops of Ireland doing up his room in Maynooth in his Satanic Majesty's racing colours.

majlis (ma·dʒˌlis). Also **madjlis, majlas, majliss, medjelis, medjliss, mejliss, mezlis.** [Arab. *majlis.*] An assembly or council; *spec.* the national assembly in Iran; also, a reception-room.

1821 G. F. Lyon *Narr. Trav. N. Afr.* vi. 261, I found Mukni sitting in the greatest agitation, pale, and alone in the Mezlis, or Court of his Castle, and scarcely able to welcome me. **1830** J. L. Burckhardt *Notes on Bedouins & Wahábys* 291 At his evening assemblies (*madjlis*), everybody sat down where he could find a convenient place. **1855** R. F. Burton *Pilgrimage* II. xv. 36 The Shaykh..led me up to the *majlis*, which was swept and garnished with all due apparatus for the forthcoming reception ceremony. **1870** *Once a Week* 7 May 303/2 'To-morrow,' we said, 'at the *Medjliss* hour, we will be punctual.' **1885** E. Balfour *Cycl. India* (ed. 3) II. 799/1 *Majlas*, Arab., is an assembly. **1911** *Encycl. Brit.* XXI. 198/2 By a rescript dated the 5th of August [1906] Muzzafar-ud-Dīn Shah gave his assent to the formation of a national council (*Majlis i shora i milli*). **1920** *Glasgow Herald* 29 Nov. 11/2 The British Government expects the Mejliss to meet within a month to decide whether it wishes to ratify the Anglo-Persian agreement. **1925** *Lit. Digest* 27 June 19/2 Premier Riza Khan replied in the Medjelis that..he would proclaim Persia a republic. **1940** F. Stark *Winter in Arabia* 160 There in the Mansabi majliss they sit. **1955** *Times* 22 June 11/3 The lead..has been taken up by the Majlis, where a strong group of Government supporters has been formed. **1964** *Ann. Reg. 1963* 296 The Majlis was opened on 6 October, thus bringing to an end a period of some two and a half years during which the Constitution had been suspended. **1972** *Daily Colonist* (Victoria, B.C.) 12 Mar. 28/1 [Bahrein] There is an air of desert democracy mixed with a certain noblesse oblige about the majlis, the formal Arab court session in which the ruler sits on his throne. **1973** *Nat. Geographic* Feb. 227/2, I found him presiding over the *majlis*, the open meeting attended by petitioners and friends each day [in Oman]. **1974** *Christian Science Monitor* 5 Dec. 3F/2 Colorful Arab dhows sail past concrete skyscrapers outside the windows of the Majlis.

major, *sb.*¹ Add: **1. c.** An officer in the Salvation Army.

1907 G. B. Shaw (*title*) Major Barbara. **1970** C. Bramwell-Booth *Catherine Booth* vi. 377 The Army Mother gave colours to..Major Rose Clapham and her assistants who were to establish the work in South Africa. **1975** *Times* 30 Apr. 9/3 Major Eva den Hartog, of the Dutch Salvation Army, has spent the last 17 years at the disaster centres of the world.

d. Major Mitchell *Austral.* = *Leadbeater's cockatoo* (*leadbeater¹).

1898 E. E. Morris *Austral Eng.* 280/1 *Major Mitchell*, vernacular name of a species of Cockatoo, *Cacatua leadbeateri*... It was called after the explorer, Major (afterwards Sir Thomas) Mitchell, who was Surveyor-General of New South Wales. The cry of the bird was fancifully supposed to resemble his name. **1911** C. E. W. Bean *'Dreadnought' of Darling* xvii. 169 We came across a flock of 'Major Mitchells',..white and pink, and exceedingly pretty when they fly and show the whole expanse of their pink feathers. **1953** A. Moorehead *Rum Jungle* iii. 40 Two of the Major Mitchells lighted on my shoulder. **1966** *Times* 28 Mar. (Austral. Suppl.) p. xvi/5 The Major Mitchell or pink cockatoo.

e. (See quot. 1919.)

1910 R. Blatchford *My Life in Army* xvii. 52 The 'major' meant well. **1919** *Athenæum* 25 July 664/1 *'Major'*, for Sergeant-major—a polite form of address by an N.C.O. **1925** Fraser & Gibbons *Soldier & Sailor Words* 150 *Major, the*, the usual name among N.C.O.'s colloquially for the Sergeant Major.

major, *a.* and *sb.*² Add: **A.** *adj.* **I. 1. a.** *major road*, esp. in phr. *major road ahead* used on traffic signs (until 1967).

1930 *Highway Code* 7 It is the duty of a driver on a minor road when approaching a major road *to go dead slow.* **1937** R. F. Broad *Motor Driving made Easy* (ed. 6) v. 61 The *Halt at Major Road Ahead* sign..enforces a definite standstill upon road users. **1950** *N.Y. Times* 20 Apr. 1/5 Railroad firemen and engineers called a strike against four major roads for Wednesday. **1967** L. Meynell *Mauve Front Door* xi. 137 Sidney Street runs into Falloden Street at right angles; there isn't any sort of traffic sign ('Halt' 'Major Road Ahead' or anything like that). **1968** *Highway Code* 14 You must..be ready to stop to let traffic on the major road go by first. **1972** A. Draper *Death Penalty* v. 37 Hudson drove the car at full speed, not even bothering to halt at the major road ahead.

c. Also *ellipt.* in other sports, for *major penalty, score*, etc.

1951 *Football Record* (Melbourne) 8 Sept. 18 They opened with four behinds, and then rattled on sixteen majors. **1962** *Kingston* (Ontario) *Whig-Standard* 28 Dec. 9/7 Kingston took 21 penalties and Gananoque sat out 14 sentences, including a misconduct to James McGlade for incurring his second major of the game. **1969** *Sun-Herald* (Sydney) 13 July 48/2 Goals by Brian Douge and Ray Wilson seemed to put the seal on the match for Hawthorn until a last-minute burst by the Dons took them to within a straight goal, with two majors by Blethyn. **1970** *Toronto Daily Star* 24 Sept. 17/5 Peter Murray of Jarvis raced 23 yards for a third-quarter major, then quarterback Mike Chrzan sneaked from three yards in the fourth, Lang converting. **1970** *Globe & Mail* (Toronto) 25 Sept. 33/3 Parkdale quarterback Rich Chudziak tossed a 38-yard pass to Wally Lytwynec, who ran 30 yards for the major.

d. In Bridge. *major suit*: spades or hearts (tricks taken by the declarer when these are trumps score more points than when clubs or diamonds are trumps). Also *ellipt.*

1916 R. F. Foster *Auction Bridge for All* vii. 27 High cards, two sure tricks, are just as necessary in the major suits as in the minor suits. **1927** M. C. Work *Contract Bridge* ii. 11 Many find it easier to remember 20 for Minors, 30 for Majors and 35 for No Trump. **1958** *Listener* 9 Oct. 572/3 It would give an exaggerated picture to reverse by following One Diamond with Two of a major. **1973** *Country Life* 13 Dec. 2048/1 Many pairs reached Six Diamonds, which is an inferior contract... It scores less than the major suit slam. **1974** *Times* 27 Apr. 10/3 After opening a strong No Trump without a four-card major, I rarely know how much strength to read into my partner's second response.

e. N. Amer. *major league*, the highest division of teams in baseball, etc. Also *attrib.*

1942 *Sun* (Baltimore) 3 Apr. 18/6 The pitching machine now used in several major league training camps. **1947** *Partisan Rev.* XIV. 258 He concealed his fear most of all from himself by means of his devotion to professional sports, major league baseball especially. **1963** C. Anderson *Young Sportsman's Guide Baseball* ii. 17 A vast number of the current major league players had participated in the American Legion sponsored Leagues. **1968** *Globe & Mail* (Toronto) 17 Feb. 35 (Advt.), Start with the finest beaches in Florida, add great fishing,..major league baseball, greyhound and horse racing. **1971** H. Seymour *Baseball* II. p. vi, I..scouted unofficially..for two major-league clubs.

B. *sb.*² **6.** orig. *U.S.* In some universities, a subject to which special attention is given during a certain period of study. Also, this subject seen as a qualification. Also, a student thus specializing.

1890 in T. W. Goodspeed *Hist. Univ. Chicago* (1916) 142 A subject taken as a major requires eight or ten hours classroom work or lecture work a week. **1907** *Columbia Univ. Catal.* Mar., Open only to students taking a major in the Department of English. **1926** [see *elective *sb.* 2]. **1948** *Democrat* 5 Aug. 1/7 Mr. Gray will receive the Bachelor of Science degree with a major in business administration. **1949** *Daily Ardmoreite* (Ardmore, Okla.) 25 Jan. 6/6 McLaurin is a Negro education major at the University of Oklahoma who is receiving instruction in a separate classroom. **1953** *Manch. Guardian Weekly* 24 Dec. 14/3 Courses for the 'English major'. These are courses in phases of English literature designed largely..for those who are 'majoring' in English. **1959** *Times* 8 Sept. 3/2 (Advt.), Royal Australian Air Force. Education Officers required with Majors in Maths or Physics. **1961** *New Statesman* 3 Mar. 338 In English Studies the 'major' could be English literature. **1964** L. Nkosi *Rhythm of Violence* II. ii. 38 She has been campaigning among Afrikaner students... Sarie is a Social Science major! **1972** *Jrnl. Social Psychol.* LXXXVII. 91 Three female upperclass psychology majors served as experimenters. **1972** *N.Y. Times* 3 Nov. 22/4 The regulars are unhappy..that the McGovern organization has selected as its two district coordinators a shaggy-headed political-science major at Brooklyn College who sometimes tours the neighborhood in dungarees, [etc.]. **1973** *Black World* Mar. 62 He is presently a theater-arts major at Los Angeles Community College.

7. A major company, organization, etc.

1968 *Wall St. Jrnl.* 24 Apr., Says a Columbia Pictures Corp. screen writer: 'You can be sure what Russ is doing today will be done by the majors tomorrow.' **1968** *Blues Unlimited* Sept. 29 Apart from Goldstar, the major outputs were from the majors in Hollywood. **1973** *Time* 25 June 85/2 In some cases, asserted his Connecticut counterpart, Robert Killian, 'the majors are taking over the choice locations, putting up giant 20-pump stations with 24-hr. service and are replacing the small dealers'. **1974** *ITV 1974* 10/2 The [Independent Television] Authority.. created a system made up of several large so-called 'network companies' (sometimes also called the 'majors') and a number of smaller 'regional companies' (sometimes called the 'minors')... The five major companies..are the main providers of network programmes to be used by the whole service. **1974** *Spartanburg* (S. Carolina) *Herald* 24 Apr. A2/2 Of the four majors reporting so far, only Exxon showed a decline from the fourth-quarter profits, while Amoco's net rose 81 per cent.

major, *v.* Add: **3.** *intr.* Of a university student: to take, or qualify *in*, a major course of study. Also *transf.* orig. *U.S.*

1924 P. Marks *Plastic Age* xvii. 185 Having decided to major in English, he found that he was required to take a composition course the second half of his sophomore year. **1927** *Brit. Weekly* 1 Sept. 470/2 It is a thesis for the Th.D. degree, for which he has already stood the examination, 'Majoring' in Greek New Testament at Louisville. **1929** *Publishers' Weekly* 20 July 252 Bulbous-headed adolescents who have majored in English descend in shoals. **1955** W. Gaddis *Recognitions* i. i. 7 As a youth in a New England college he had..majored in classical poetry. **1958** *Times Lit. Suppl.* 5 Sept. 502/2 He majored in forgery and illegal entry inside several specially recommended prisons. **1965** *Listener* 25 Feb. 290/2 A student who in the School of Social Studies 'majors'—Sussex seems to revel in this transatlantic noun-verb—in history also reads various 'contextual' subjects. **1971** *Progress* (Cape Town) May 1/2 He majored in Afrikaans at Witwatersrand University. **1972** *Daily Tel.* 12 June 21/2, I am studying A levels in geography, English and art, with a view to majoring in geography. **1973** *Amer. N. & Q.* 83/1 For both B.A. and M.A., Eliot majored in literature.

Majorcan (mădʒǭ·ɹkăn, măyǭ·ɹkăn), *sb.* and *a.* Also 7 **Majorkine.** [f. *Majorca* the name of one of the Balearic Islands + -an.] **a.** *sb.* A native or inhabitant of Majorca. **b.** *adj.* Of or pertaining to Majorca. Cf. *Mallorcan *sb.* and *a.*, *Mallorquin *sb.* and *a.*

1697 H. Maundrell *Jrnl.* 27 Apr. in *Journey from Aleppo* (1703) 123 We..were very courteously receiv'd by the Guardian, Father Raphael, a Majorkine by birth. **1848** E. J. Sabine tr. *A. von Humboldt's Cosmos* II. 147 One maritime people after another, Phoenicians,.. Majorcans,..and Spaniards, made successive efforts to penetrate onwards in the Atlantic Ocean. **1858** *Leisure Hour* 18 Feb. 103/2 This Majorcan driver said he had always thought a Protestant meant 'somebody who does not accept the Bible'. **1873** *Gentl. Mag.* Feb. 219 The family of Napoleon I. was originally native of that island *i.e.* Majorcan. **1876** C. T. Bidwell *Balearic Islands* 105 Myrtle-covered posts, in the use of which the Majorcans display natural skill. *Ibid.* 111 Majorcan carpets and matting cover the floors. **1935** J. A. Fraser *Spain & W. Country* ix. 106 The five following treatises of the great Majorcan [*sc.* Ramon Lull]. **1965** *New Statesman* 14 May 766/3 There is some farcical reporting of Majorcan dialogue. *Ibid.* 767/1 The Majorcans believe in being 'formal' as the Spaniards also do. **1973** *Times* 2 June 13/7 A Majorcan official remarked that the British went about as though they owned the country.

major-domo. Add: **c.** *U.S.* In south-western states, an overseer on a farm or ranch; also, the water-master or official in charge of irrigation in New Mexico.

1834 in *Calif. Hist. Soc. Q.* (1929) VIII. 228 Four ranchos, each one made up of an Indian village, a house for the *mayordomo* directing it, [etc.]. **1836** D. B. Edward *Hist. Texas* ix. 291 Having thus glanced at the Major domo, we shall take a peek at his Locum tenens. **1902** F. H. Newell *Irrigation in U.S.* 107 He is usually known as the 'water master' or 'ditch-rider'; or, in Spanish-speaking communities as majordomo. **1910** J. Hart *Vigilante Girl* xiv. 195 Arthur's chair was taken to the *portal*, where they found the major-domo and a group of *vaqueros* waiting. **1948** P. Johnston *Lost & Living Cities Calif. Gold Rush* p. ii, The precious metal was found..by Francisco López, majordomo of San Gabriel Mission, in Placerita Canyon.

majorette (mēⁱdʒəre·t). orig. *U.S.* [f. Major *sb.*[1] + -ette.] = *drum-majorette.

1941 *San Francisco Examiner* 20 Apr. (Amer. Weekly Section) 4/1 During the past few years the drum major.. has given way to the so-called majorette. **1951** M. McLuhan *Mech. Bride* (1967) 122/1 The majorette is no man beater. **1959** *Times* 30 Nov. (Canada Suppl.) p. xx/4 Each club has a band and a corps of bare-legged prancing girls called majorettes. **1960** *Wanganui* (N.Z.) *Photo News* 13 Feb. 30 (*caption*) Coach of the Wanganui Majorettes. **1973** *Sat. Rev. Society* (U.S.) May 64/1 A bubbly ex-majorette named Linda.

majoritarian (mădʒǫ:ritēᵊ·riăn), *a.* [f. Majorit(y + *-arian* as in *libertarian*, etc.] Governed by or believing in decision by a majority; supporting the majority party. Also as *sb.*

1918 J. Buchan *Nelson's Hist. War* XX. 118 Early in June came the delegation of the German Majority Socialists, which included—besides Scheidemann, the Majoritarian leader—that Hermann Müller who, on the eve of the declaration of war, had invited the French Socialists to vote against war credits. **1957** *Britannica Bk. of Year* 512/1 Some new words arose from politics and world affairs... Majoritarian was an adjective meaning ruled by the beliefs of the majority. **1964** Gould & Kolb *Dict. Social Sci.* 484/2 The idea of party responsibility..aims at facilitating the practice of majoritarian democracy. **1965** *Listener* 21 Jan. 113/3 The fateful divide in the pre-revolutionary Russian Social-Democratic movement between the Mensheviks (i.e., minoritarians) and the Bolsheviks (i.e., majoritarians)..went far deeper than a purely political argument. **1971** P. Worsthorne *Socialist Myth* viii. 196 The idealistic disillusion with majoritarian democracy. **1972** *Mod. Law Rev.* XXXV. i. 73 In exercising their discretion the courts have normally adopted a posture which is both 'legalistic' and 'majoritarian'.., majoritarian in the sense that the views of the majority have been treated as the most probative..factor.

Hence **majorita·rianism**, belief in, or the existence of, rule or decisions by a majority.

1961 in Webster. **1968** A. Lijphart *Politics of Accommodation* vii. 125 In short, the rule is majoritarianism tempered by the spirit of concurrent majority. **1968** *Internat. Encycl. Social Sci.* IX. 537/2 Opponents of strict majoritarianism advance numerous arguments. First, they point out that the majoritarian principle might be used to destroy the conditions of its own existence, such as freedom of association and expression. **1975** *N.Y. Times* 28 Mar. 27/3 The public interest defined as the greatest happiness for the greatest number..has hardened into an increasingly impervious 'majoritarianism'.

majority. Add: **2.** Also *transf.*

1909 *Westm. Gaz.* 28 Sept. 5/1 The majority celebration of the pneumatic tyre promises to be the biggest trade function on record. **1939** F. M. Ford *Let.* 25 May (1965) 324 If it [*sc.* the book] did not see the light until its majority it will become almost a historical novel. **1965** *Listener* 1 July 10/1 It is sad that, as it approaches its majority, this organisation should have run into deep waters.

3. *absolute majority* (examples).

1888 J. Bryce *Amer. Commonwealth* I. v. 55 Neither Polk in 1844, nor Taylor in 1848,..had an absolute majority of the popular vote. **1971** G. K. Roberts *Dict. Political Analysis* 120 In politics..the number of votes constituting a majority is equal to 50 per cent plus one of votes cast (sometimes referred to as an 'absolute majority').

7. *majority-rule, -vote*; **majority calling,** in Bridge (see quot. 1964); **majority carrier** *Electronics*, a charge carrier of the kind carrying the greater proportion of the electric current in a semiconducting material (i.e. an electron in *n*-type and a hole in *p*-type material); **Majority-Socialist,** one who, after the division of the German Socialists during the 1914–18 war, acted with the larger party; **majority verdict,** the verdict of the majority of a jury; also *transf.*

1927 *Daily Express* 28 June 1/7 The system of 'majority calling' at auction bridge, the adoption of which in this country was first advocated by the 'Evening Standard'. **1929** *Laws Contract Bridge Portland Club* 6 While, at the Portland Club, 'value calling' is invariably played at 'Auction', 'majority calling' is being used at 'Contract'. **1964** *Official Encycl. Bridge* 343/1 *Majority calling*, the principle by which any bid outranks any other bid at a lower level, regardless of scoring value. **1951** W. Shockley et al. in *Physical Rev.* LXXXIII. 151/2 The density of minority carriers is much smaller than the density of majority carriers in each region. **1962** Simpson & Richards *Physical Princ. Junction Transistors* vi. 100 Using equation (1.11) with the assumption that the conductivities in emitter and base are decided practically entirely by their majority-carrier densities, we obtain γ_0= [etc.]. **1893** B. R. Tucker *Instead of Bk.* 169 Rule is evil, and..it is none the better for being majority rule. **1959** *Chambers's Encycl.* XI. 701/1 When such deep and permanent cleavages are absent, majority rule seems more likely to secure more equal freedom than any other, at least if free discussion and airing of grievances are presupposed. **1968** J. R. Pennock in *Internat. Encycl. Social Sci.* IX. 536 The term 'majority rule' stands for a rule of decision making within a specified group. At its simplest, the rule requires that the votes of each member shall be counted as equal to that of every other and that no vote or decision by a minority may override that of a majority. By extension, majority rule is sometimes contrasted with any rule requiring that decisions be unanimous or by any number larger than a simple majority. **1972** *Guardian* 28 Jan. 10/1 The Smith regime..is proving..how slender is the hope of orderly progress towards majority rule. **1918** J. Buchan *Hist. War* XX. 125 The great governing parties, apart from the Conservatives on the extreme right and the Minority Socialists on the extreme left, were the Catholic Centre, the Radicals, the National Liberals, and the Majority Socialists. **1923** E. A. Ross *Russ. Soviet Republic* 20 At this time [*sc.* 1918] a Soviet was formed in Berlin, to which members of even the Majority Socialists adhered. **1972** S. Delmer *Weimar Germany* i. 6 Ebert and his 'Majority' Socialists called on him [*sc.* Prince Max] to hand over power to them. **1905** *Westm. Gaz.* 7 Apr. 5/2 The jury..sent in to court to inquire if the parties would accept a majority verdict. **1966** H. Kalven et al. *Amer. Jury* xxxvi. 461 Numerous states allow for a majority verdict in civil cases. **1973** 'D. Halliday' *Dolly & Starry Bird* vi. 82 We can all go home and finish our knitting if the majority verdict prefers it. **1927** *Chambers's Jrnl.* 602/2 Now he had the majority vote. **1953** B. M. Cross *Legislative Struggle* xviii. 380 In committee sessions, disputed questions are decided by a majority vote. **1965** *Wireless World* Sept. 419 This is a triplicated system with a majority vote scheme for ensuring correct operation. **1973** *Listener* 20 Dec. 841/2 [An] impeachment resolution.. requires a simple majority vote.

makak, var. *mocock.

‖ **makan** (ma·kan). *Malaysia.* [Cf. Malay *makan* to eat; *makanan* food.] Food.

1927 R. J. H. Sidney *In Brit. Malaya To-Day* 233 His stomach may become distended with some of the weird mixtures..from the School *makan* shop. **1963** J. Kirkup *Tropic Temper* 101, I wander back to the hotel for my makan. (Cold turkey.) **1971** *Carry Singapore in your Pocket* (Singapore Tourist Promotion Board) (ed. 3) 29 Watch a meal of noodles being fried in 5 minutes at the 'makan' (food) stall.

‖ **makara** (mʌ·kără). Also **Makara.** [Skr.] A mythical Hindu sea-animal, variously represented in Indian art; the equivalent of Capricorn in the signs of the zodiac.

1873 E. Balfour *Cycl. India* (ed. 2) III. M 58/2 Kama ..bears on his banner the fish Makara, an aquatic monster something like the sign of the zodiac Capricornus. **1901** A. C. Gibson tr. *Gruenwedel's Buddhist Art India* ii. 57 The sea-elephant, Makara, a creature formed of the forepart of an elephant with the body and tail of a fish..has been retained everywhere in Indian art. **1934** *Burlington Mag.* Oct. 164/1 But essentially Indian is the Makara, a phantastic animal which, since the days of King Asoka, has played a part in Indian art; it is seen on toranas of all times;..it followed the spread of Indian art to the islands, ..whilst it lives a prolific life on all sorts of minor objects in Ceylon. **1969** A. K. Coomaraswamy *Introd. Indian Art* (ed. 2) ix. 42 Decorative work with *makaras* and other marine monsters [is] represented. **1971** *Illustr. Weekly India* 11 Apr. 67/2 (*December 21 to Jan. 19*) *Capricorn* (*Makara*). Frankness with friends may make you happy till midweek. **1972** *Oxf. Univ. Gaz.* CII. Suppl. No. 3. 54 A fine terracotta relief in the form of a *makara*.., formerly part of an architectural frieze..was also acquired.

Makassar, Makas(s)arese: see *Macassar, *Macassarese.

make, *sb.*[2] Add: **2. a.** *spec.* with implied reference to the manufacturer or source of manufacture; = Brand *sb.* 6.

1909 Webster, *Make*,..often referring to quality or origin of a manufactured article; as, whose *make* is it? **1937** *Discovery* Feb. 61/2, I tested the records on four different makes of gramophone. **1937** J. Betjeman *Continual Dew* 5 Talk of sports and makes of cars In various bogus Tudor bars. **1975** 'D. Craig' *Dead Liberty* xix. 108 It would be better not to park the same..vehicle in that street again... He wished now he had not mentioned the make.

8. *on the make* (earlier and later examples); also, intent on winning someone's affections; seeking sexual pleasure; improving, advancing, getting better.

1869 J. R. Browne *Adventures Apache Country* 507 'Oh, you're on the make, are you?'..'Why, yes, to be candid, I'd like to make fifty thousand or so.' **1874** Hotten *Slang Dict.* 221 Any one is said to be 'on the make' who asks too high a price for his goods, or endeavours in any way to overreach. **1918** Barrie *What Every Woman Knows* ii. 55 There are few more impressive sights in the world than a Scotsman on the make. **1929** J. P. McEvoy *Hollywood Girl* (1930) 41 Jimmy..said Buelow was on the make for me or he wouldn't have wasted that much time on me. **1934** J. O'Hara *Appointment in Samarra* (1935) vii. 212 It's the first time I ever knew of you going on the make for some dame. **1955** *Times* 12 May 7/3, I think we are on the make and that, on balance, the tide is running in our favour. **1967** N. Freeling *Strike Out* 77 He struck me always as a sly nasty fellow, a bootlicker, always on the make. **1973** 'A. Blaisdell' *Crime by Chance* vii. 126 You mean he was still on the make? At his age? **1973** W. M. Duncan *Big Timer* xxii. 150 Riordan was on the make. He'd found out something he could use. **1974** R. Adams *Shardik* li. 426 Insinuating, dandified, with the manners, at once familiar and obsequious, of a presuming servant on the make.

10. = *declaration 8 b (see also quot. 1964).

1902 J. B. Elwell *Bridge* 13 In considering a heart make, the dealer should be influenced by the general strength of his hand and by the number of honours he holds in the trump suit. **1905** R. F. Foster *Compl. Bridge* 316 The declaration is often called the make. **1964** *Official Encycl. Bridge* 343/1 *Make...* As a noun, it means a successful contract, but usually a hypothetical one in the post-mortem: 'Five diamonds would have been a make.' **1974** *Country Life* 17 Jan. 98/3 Four Spades is a make, but Five Clubs is the safer sacrifice.

11. A (sexual) conquest; *spec.* a woman of easy virtue. Cf. *make *v.*[1] 65 *slang* (orig. *U.S.*).

1942 Berrey & Van den Bark *Amer. Thes. Slang* § 439/1 Woman of easy morals..*make.* **1951** *Landfall* V. 98 'A widow's an easy make,' He said, 'you pedal and let her steer.'

12. An identification of, or information about, a person or thing from police records, finger-prints, etc. *slang* (orig. *U.S.*).

1950 in Wentworth & Flexner *Dict. Amer. Slang* (1960) 332/1 We got a make on his prints. **1959** 'E. McBain' *Pusher* vii. 62 Couldn't get a make on those fingerprints. **1965** 'L. Egan' *Detective's Due* (1966) vii. 71, I think this is too good to be true, but we'll get a make on it just for fun. *Ibid.* 80 The D.M.V. just came through with a make on that plate number... It belongs to a fifty-five two-door Ford. **1967** W. Pine *Protectors* ix. 82 We've got a make on Beth Paget. She's on our files. **1972** R. K. Smith *Ransom* iv. 175 We got a make on the Chevvy... Stolen last week. **1973** *Daily Colonist* (Victoria, B.C.) 6 Sept. 4/5 For years authorities have been trying to get a better 'make' on motorists who sidestep the law by picking up a licence in a nearby state after theirs has been revoked.

13. *make and mend*: the action of making and repairing clothes; spec. *Naut.*, a period set apart for seamen to repair their clothes; hence, a period of leisure; a half-holiday; also *attrib.* and as vb.

1884 W. D. Howells *Rise S. Lapham* (1885) i. 5 She cooked, swept, washed, ironed, made and mended from daylight till dark. **1899** *Navy & Army Illustr.* 14 Oct. 107 (*caption*) Thursday has been in the Navy, ever since King William IV..first instituted the practice, regularly observed as 'make and mend' day. **1903** Kipling *Traffics & Discov.* (1904) 154 I'm going to ask this young gentleman to breakfast, and then we'll make and mend clothes till the umpires have decided. **1916** 'Taffrail' *Pincher Martin* xv. 273 Th' navy's 'avin' its make an' mend, an' carn't be disturbed. **1925** Fraser & Gibbons *Soldier & Sailor Words* 150 *A make and mend*, a naval holiday. In

old days..usually on a Thursday. Now-a-days..the weekly half holiday (often transferred to a Saturday) continues to be known as a 'Make and Mend'. **1935** *New Survey London Life* IX. iv. xiii. 423 On Tuesday afternoon I go to the make-and-mend class. **1942** F. G. Hackforth-Jones *One-One-One* xxi. 193 Saturday too, when all on board H.M.S. *Empire* were supposed to be enjoying a well-earned 'make and mend'. **1943** *Our Towns* (Women's Group on Public Welfare) ii. 60 Any 'Make and Mend' organisation evolved during the war should form the basis of a permanent service. **1955** *Times* 12 July 9/6 They.. move out to their 'sun-porch', usually a clearing in the forest where they spend their time in 'make-and-mend'.

make, *v.*[1] Add: **1. d.** (Later example.) For *slang* read *colloq.*

1934 T. S. Eliot *Rock* i. 13, 'e was a fine fellow on one side and as bad as they make 'em on the other.

3. b. *to be made for each other* (or *one another*): to be such as to harmonize perfectly or form an ideal combination; to be ideally suited: usu. of a specified man and woman.

1751 Richardson *Clarissa* (ed. 3) III. 328 Her features are all harmony, and made for one another. **1857** Dickens *Let.* Sept. (1938) II. 887 Poor Catherine and I are not made for each other, and there is no help for it. **1927** J. N. McIlwraith *Kinsmen at War* xvii. 172 She and Stephen were made for one another. **1971** D. Clark *Sick to Death* iv. 82 When two people—what's the popular phrase?—are made for each other, these things happen.

29. b. (Later examples.) Also, in milder sense, to 'acquire', manage to get. (See also quots. 1926, 1953.)

1914 D. O. Barnett *Lett.* (1915) 13 The company made a dog the other day, but it was claimed almost at once, so we haven't got a mascot. **1926** J. Black *You can't Win* i. 5, I was an expert house burglar..carefully choosing only the best homes... I 'made' them in the small hours of the night. *Ibid.* vi. 74 Better wait till night if you want to make a train. **1928** Kipling *Limits & Renewals* (1932) 53 I've made a temp'ry collar and lead off Probert. **1946** G. Millar *Horned Pigeon* ii. 16 Skinner and I were both good at what the Army calls 'making things', which is what the civilian would call 'finding' or even 'stealing' things. *Ibid.*, Potatoes and onions I had 'made' from the food-dumps round Alexandria. **1953** W. Burroughs *Junkie* (1972) iii. 34 Taking junk hidden by another junkie is known as 'making him for his stash'. *Ibid.* 158 *Making Cars*... Breaking into parked cars and stealing the contents.

39. Delete † *Obs.* and add N. Amer. examples. (See also *Dict. Canadianisms.*)

1856 J. Reynolds *Peter Gott* 43 Since the last war with England, the fishermen from the States have not been allowed to make their fish upon the shores of the British Provinces. **1909** E. C. Robinson *In Unknown Land* 30 A fisherman comes here to 'make' fish, not to catch them. **1923** *Canad. Fisherman* 243/1 It is a new departure for Newfoundland green fish to be taken to Europe to be 'made'. **1971** S. E. Morison *European Discovery Amer.: Northern Voy.* xiv. 491 In our times 'making fish', as the Maine people call curing cod, haddock, and pollock in the sun, is simple enough... You simply soak the gutted, split, and washed fish in brine for two or three days, slack-salt them, and spread them on home-made flakes to be cured in the sun. **1974** *Nat. Geographic* Jan. 122/1 Many south coast men [in Newfoundland] have to 'make' fish—that is, preserve their own.

46. a. (Further examples.) Phr. *to make one's day*: to render a day delightful or redeem it from routine, dullness, or banality. Similarly, *to make one's evening*, etc.

1903 A. Bennett *Leonora* vi. 168 The conductor..told her..that she had simply made the show. **1909** F. Barclay *Rosary* xxiv. 252, I knew her presence made my day and her absence meant chill night. **1935** Wodehouse *Luck of Bodkins* i. 15 That..will be great. That will just make my day. **1942** M. Dickens *One Pair of Feet* ix. 194 If she could put you in the wrong in front of Sister, her day was made. **1942** T. Rattigan *Flare Path* i. 113 We've got some nice cheerful news for you boys. It's going to make your evening. **1953** X. Fielding *Stronghold* 220 For Ioanna, the evening had been made. **1958** *Listener* 16 Oct. 623/2 What made the programme was the alternation of argument with recorded extracts from the conference itself. **1959** *Ibid.* 6 Aug. 223/3 It [*sc.* a play] didn't make my day. **1970** H. McLeave *Question of Negligence* (1973) xviii. 141 Get him to..show us his scar... Go on, dare him. It'll make the evening.

51. f. *U.S. Underworld slang.* To recognize or identify (a person, etc.). Cf. *make *sb.*[2] 12.

1906 A. H. Lewis *Confessions of Detective* 222 You wouldn't have come within a block of him. In the language of the guild, Sorg, he would have 'made you' and got away. **1908** J. M. Sullivan *Criminal Slang* 16 *Make one*, identify a person. **1914** Jackson & Hellyer *Vocab. Criminal Slang* 57 You had better ring up (disguise) so he won't make you. **1955** *Publ. Amer. Dial. Soc.* xxiv. 81 The victim then can possibly identify, or *make*, the tool if he is arrested. **1971** 'O. Bleeck' *Thief who painted Sunlight* (1972) xiv. 127 I'm a pretty good tail. You didn't make me. **1973** 'D. Shannon' *Spring of Violence* (1974) vi. 107 'Have you made the gun?' 'Right off. It's a Hi-Standard revolver.'

53. e. *to make believe* (further examples).

1902 G. B. Shaw *Mrs. Warren's Profession* Pref. p. xxiii, At such plays we do not believe: we make-believe. **1904** Kipling *Traffics & Discov.* 334, I did all that..just to make believe. **1925** S. Lewis *Martin Arrowsmith* xxxii. 386, I make believe read my French books. **1951** G. Greene *End of Affair* i. vi. 37 As long as I could make-believe that love lasted, I was happy. **1974** J. Wainwright *Hard Hit* 38, I make-believe I am giving it careful thought.

f. *to make do*: to manage *with* (what is available, esp. an inferior substitute). Also *absol.*, esp. in phr. *to make do and mend*: to repair for continued use (cf. *make *sb.*[2] 13); also as *sb. phr.* See also *make-do.

[**1899** E. Wharton *Greater Inclination* 87 She had.. accepted it [*sc.* marriage] as a provisional compensation,—she had made it 'do'.] **1927** *Observer* 28 Aug. 16/4 The listener who was content to receive only the programmes from his local station..could make do with a very simple and inefficient form of direct-coupled tuning arrangement. **1934** J. Marston *Andromeda* xii. 156 She had already had experience..in 'making do' on a small income. She 'made do' now, with a skill which impressed..Letty. **1941** *New Statesman* 26 Apr. 431/1 It should be no great hardship for the community to make do with the same housing accommodation that it enjoyed in 1938. **1947** I. Brown *Say Word* 105 This age of bits and pieces, queues, rationing, and make-do-and-mend. **1958** *Technology* Jan. 375/4 We may put all our energy into making real the ideal technical schools of 1944, or we may make do and mend by integrating technical studies in..grammar..schools. **1961** New Eng. Bible *Luke* iii. 14 No bullying; no blackmail; make do with your pay! **1967** A. Wilson *No Laughing Matter* iv. 414 You *are* lucky. Having a family to make do and mend for. **1968** M. Woodhouse *Rock Baby* vi. 51 Rasmussen had to make do with four eggs and only half a dozen rounds of toast because I was there.

65. b. (Further examples.) Also *fig.*, to achieve, accomplish, reach. Freq. *to make it*, to reach a certain place; to succeed in traversing a specified distance; to achieve a desired object; to be successful; *spec.* to achieve sexual intercourse.

1885 [see *bullocky *a.* 2]. **1905** R. Beach *Pardners* (1912) ii. 56 We can't make it over into Mexico without being caught up. **1912** R. A. Wason *Friar Tuck* xxvi. 187 Badger-face tried to raise himself on his elbow, but he couldn't quite make it. **1916** H. L. Wilson *Somewhere in Red Gap* i. 25, I hurried home to get a bite to eat and dress and make the party. **1925** E. Hemingway *In Our Time* (1926) ix. 121 It looked like him or the bull and then he finally made it. **1928** [see *best *adv.* 3 b]. **1935** L. A. G. Strong *Seven Arms* 46 No matter if they can't make it in the day, sleeping out won't hurt them. **1938** G. Greene *Brighton Rock* i. i. 20 'Will you be there?' 'No,' Hale said. 'I can't make it.' **1951** N. M. Gunn *Well at World's End* xviii. 148 He had..found out that we could make Pamplona that day and asked if we were game. **1955** W. Gaddis *Recognitions* i. vii. 266 But I have to make a train, he said. **1957** J. Kerouac *On Road* iii. viii. 225 They went to a parking lot in broad daylight..and there, he claims, he made it with her in nothing flat. **1959** N. Mailer *Advts. for Myself* (1961) 217, I knew *The Deer Park* had damn well better make it or I was close to some serious illness. *Ibid.* 295 The hipster's belief that when he really makes it, he will be able to turn his hand to anything. **1967** *Field & Stream* June 96/3, I hope he makes it through the winter. **1968** *Observer* 28 Jan. 12/3 A flood of letters has convinced us that we are providing a useful service and this view was confirmed a week ago when we 'made it' in the House of Commons. **1970** G. Greer *Female Eunuch* 159 His wife, who had been a trendy catch ten years before, was not making it so well. **1970** G. F. Newman *Sir, You Bastard* viii. 202 Billie would eventually get the sheet changed..or Mrs Basil, whoever made the scene first. **1970** *Observer* 20 Sept. 26/1 Bombers.. lurching along the runway like a swarm of crippled insects, until finally they make it into the air. **1973** *Weekly News* (Glasgow) 11 Aug. 3/1 She's been a member [of the Glasgow Police Judo Club] for the past three years and managed to make the team which gave a display at the last Police Tattoo. **1973** *Times* 12 Nov. 15/7 Only those undergraduates most likely to make the team are engaged. **1973** *Times Lit. Suppl.* 16 Nov. 1389/2 He finally makes it with long-desired Rachel.

c. To be successful in advances to (a member of the opposite sex); to win the affection of; *spec.* to persuade (a person) to consent to sexual intercourse; to seduce. *slang* (orig. *U.S.*).

1918 H. C. Witwer in *Amer. Mag.* June 110/3 Look at that big stiff tryin' to make the dame! **1921** *Sat. Even. Post* 1 Oct. 17/1 She give up trying to make me and got off at Albany. She was a good looker but I have no time for gals that tries to make strangers on a train. **1926** Anderson & Stallings *What Price Glory* i, in *Three Amer. Plays* (1926) 7 God! I guess even Lippy could make a kid if she slept on the other side of a paper wall. *Ibid.* 8 This broad I was trying to make insisted on riding on the merry-go-round. **1926** S. Lewis *Mantrap* xii. 155 The guys..think they can make you P.D.Q. [*sc.* pretty damn quick], even if they're old and fat. **1930** E. Rice *Voy. to Purilia* ii. 27 Never before had I seen a face so disfigured by unbridled lust! 'Looks as if he's trying to make her,' shouted Johnson. **1952** L. A. G. Strong *Darling Tom* xiv. 116, I don't say I'd always have been content with thoughts of you, or that, if you'd stayed lost, I mightn't have tried to make you. **1959** P. H. Johnson *Humbler Creation* xxvi. 187 Young Fraser tried to make her once. **1969** E. Goffman *Where Action Is* 200 James Bond makes the acquaintance of an unattainable girl and then rapidly makes the girl.

66. *to make time* (*with*) (a person): to make advances to (a member of the opposite sex); to court or flirt with; also = sense 65 c above. *N. Amer. slang.*

1934 G. & S. Lorimer *Stag Line* iv. 122 'You can't make any time with me,' I said giving him a lazy smile. 'I belong to another.' **1953** W. Burroughs *Junkie* (1972) xiv. 141 At another table two young men were trying to make time with some Mexican girls. **1962** E. Lucia *Klondike Kate* viii. 171 The ranchers and cowpokes came in for a peek, and to make time if they could. **1962** J. Potts *Evil Wish* xii. 159 She decided that Joe was lying... Probably making time with some kid half Marcia's age. **1971** E. Bullins in W. King *Black Short Story Anthol.* (1972) 82 Say, are ya makin' much time with mah little sister? There was a guarded flash in his eyes. **1971** 'D. Shannon' *Ringer* (1972) viii. 140 Frankly, he'd have liked to make time with that girl, but she'd turned up her nose at him. **1973** D. Hughes *Along Side Road* (1974) ii. 16 Which I'll bet he did if he wanted to make time with her, eh?

70. *to make as if* (later examples).

1919 V. Woolf *Night & Day* iv. 53 Denham..made as if he were tearing up handfuls of grass..from the carpet. **1957** 'M. Yourcenar' *Coup de Grace* 86 With her foolish bundle she looked like a discharged servant-girl; shifting it from one arm to the other she made as if to escape. **1971** *Leader* (Durban) 7 May 9/2 The girls want to look like boys and the boys make as if they are girls.

b. *to make like*: to pretend (to be), to behave like or as if; to imitate. *colloq.* (orig. *U.S.*). Cf. sense 73 a in Dict.

a **1881** S. Lanier *Poems* (1892) 179 Then he..made like he neither had seen nor heerd. **1928** J. Peterkin *Scarlet Sister Mary* x. 100 Mary made like she was nearly dead. **1939** J. Steinbeck *Grapes of Wrath* xxiii. 396 This rich fella..makes like he's poor. **1953** P. Frankau *Winged Horse* iii. i. 177 Couldn't make like nice when the old boy said he knew I'd be..ready for my native land again. **1956** B. Holiday *Lady sings Blues* (1973) iii. 34 The next time around she made like a big shot and started the ball rolling by handing me a big tip. **1968** W. Warwick *Surf-riding in N.Z.* 20/3 On a large wave it is also possible to spread your arms and legs out and make like a bird in flight. **1968** M. Woodhouse *Rock Baby* xxiii. 227 Well, you aren't making much noise... For a guy who was making like an avalanche an hour back.

72. (Later examples.)

1910 Belloc *Verses* 3 The tide is making over Arun Bar. **1956** C. Willock *Death at Flight* viii. 104 We shall build this into a platform..in order to give us a little extra height when the tide makes.

b. Of ice: to form. *N. Amer.*

1784 N. Webster in E. E. Ford *Notes Life N. Webster* (1912) I. 88 Cold; ice makes in the river. **1817** *Montreal Herald* 8 Feb. 2/5 The ice having made in the bay, has added greatly to the gaiety of the place. **1888** J. McDougall *George Millward McDougall* 114 As soon as the snow falls and ice makes, dogs will become the means of transport for the most part. **1890** *N.Y. Tribune* 12 Dec. 3/3 Several good guides..will assist him in an attempt to reach Kadiak Island by crossing Alaska Peninsula before the ice makes. **1933** E. Merrick *True North* ii. 86 A gray day, ice making everywhere. **1971** J. McDougall *Parsons on Plains* iv. 31 After ice makes, the fish freeze almost as soon as you take them out of the water.

82. make with —. d. [tr. Yiddish *mach mit.*] To bring into operation; to use, affect; to concern oneself with. *slang* (orig. *U.S.*).

1940 J. O'Hara *Pal Joey* 131 The poor man's Bing Crosby is still making with the throat here in Chi. **1943** *Amer. Speech* XVIII. 46 'To make with the mouth', meaning 'to give the bird, to give forth a Bronx cheer'. *Ibid.*, Come, Baby, make with your hands. **1959** W. Burroughs *Naked Lunch* 80 A. J., surrounded and fighting against overwhelming odds, throws back his head and makes with the hog-call. **1962** L. Deighton *Ipcress File* xviii. 114 Dalby had changed into a red Hawaiian shirt... 'You're making with the native costume?' **1964** 'C. E. Maine' *Never let Up* xv. 149 Don't be a Smart Alick. Make with the alcohol. I haven't got all night. **1972** 'H. Howard' *Nice Day for Funeral* xi. 148 Make with the feet into your bathroom. **1972** D. Lees *Zodiac* 118 When people like Zodiac make with the dreams you have to listen. **1974** 'A. Gilbert' *Nice Little Killing* i. 6 Make with the feet, sugar... You're embarrassing Jim. Time his place closed.

86. make down. b. (Example.)

1877 'S. Tytler' *Childhood 100 Yrs. Ago* i. 19 Old clothes of their seniors carefully kept and 'made down' for their descendants.

91. make out. c. (*b*) Delete 'Chiefly *U.S.*' and add further examples; *to make it out* (example).

1861 W. Collins *Tom Tiddler's Ground* iv, in *All Year Round* Extra Christmas No., 12 Dec. 22/1 They were artisans and farm-labourers who couldn't make it out in the old country. **1916** 'Boyd Cable' *Action Front* 7, I took a fancy to seein' how the engines made out under war conditions. **1931** W. G. McAdoo *Crowded Yrs.* v. 55 Without my wife's..help I could not have made out at all. **1932** Wodehouse *Hot Water* x. 170 'How did you make out?' 'Oke. I'm in the Château.' **1935** M. M. Atwater *Murder in Midsummer* vii. 64 Uncle Will can go to hell; we'll make out somehow. **1939** D. Parker *Here Lies* 116 With that big yard and all, I think we'll make out all right. **1942** J. Dill in W. S. Churchill *Second World War* (1951) IV. ii. xxv. 397 Leaving us with limited American assistance to make out as best we can against Germany. **1951** E. Paul *Springtime in Paris* ii. 37 We made out all right, with a hare paté, onion soup, a rare sirloin steak.., a slice of Port Salut, [etc.]. **1959** *Observer* 17 May 1/1 Whitsun seemed a good occasion to learn how Shakespeare and tourism were making out. **1965** *Listener* 16 Sept. 433/3 Sibelius might not have made out very well as an opera composer had he chosen to do so. **1966** Bereiter & Engelmann *Teaching Disadvantaged Children* i. 2 How do you think they'll make out there?

(*c*) *spec.* To gain sexual satisfaction; to have sexual intercourse (*with*). *slang* (orig. *U.S.*). Cf. *making *vbl. sb.*[1] 10 b.

1939 I. Baird *Waste Heritage* vii. 99 Oh, say, how'd you make out with Hazel? **1961** *Times* 27 Apr. 17/2 The detailed accounts of how he 'made out' sexually and emotionally with some sixteen different girls. **1962** *Amer. Speech* XXXVII. 39 When I was young, if one 'made out', his accomplishment was a good deal more total than was implied by either *to neck* or *to pet*, or both.

92. make over. d. Delete 'Now only *U.S.*' and add further examples.

1903 H. James *Ambassadors* viii. 111 The new quantity was represented by the fact that Chad had been made

over. **1928** R. MACAULAY *Keeping Up Appearances* ix. 94 Feeling..in need of restoration, she..had a small port. That's better, she agreed with herself..makes you feel quite made over. **1936** 'J. TEY' *Shilling for Candles* xvi. 180 She..never recognized Chris... She'd heard that they made you over in Hollywood. Perhaps that was it. **1958** *Technology* Jan. 375/4 Had we better do what we can to 'make over' the traditional grammar school for an age of scientific industry? **1972** *Daily Tel.* (Colour Suppl.) 8 Sept. 26/1 A sewing machine stands on a table with a limp-looking dress, in the process of being 'made over', hanging on a nearby chair.

96. make up. i. (*b*) (Earlier and later examples.) Also, of a woman: to apply cosmetics to (one's face). Hence **made-up** *a.*

1808 *Monthly Pantheon* I. 346/1 Yes, she produces a good effect!—she's well *made up*! *a* **1817** JANE AUSTEN *Persuasion* (1818) IV. x. 222 Morning visits are never fair by women at her time of life, who make themselves up so little. If she would only wear rouge. **1926** GALSWORTHY *Silver Spoon* III. vi. 258 Marjorie Ferrar stepped into the Box, not exactly nervous, and only just 'made-up'. **1930** V. SACKVILLE-WEST *Edwardians* i. 15 She was heavily but badly made-up, with a triangle of red on either cheek. **1945** S. LEWIS *Cass Timberlane* (1946) xlvii. 333 Small white wool socks..to be worn with bare legs that were made-up to look tanned. **1968** A. MUNRO in R. Weaver *Canad. Short Stories* 2nd Ser. 295 The women's faces in the room, made up some time before, have begun to show the effects of heat.

(*c*) (Further examples.)

1901 C. MORRIS *Life on Stage* v. 26 Of course when you are making up for a character part you go by a different rule. **1931** *Daily Tel.* 21 May 13/3 She came to a car in which one girl was smoking a cigarette and two others were busily 'making up'.

ma:ke-and-brea·k. Also without hyphens. [f. the vbs. as used in *to make contact* (MAKE *v.*¹ 8), *to break contact* (BREAK *v.* 29): see CONTACT I c.] **a.** The alternate making and breaking of electrical contact. Freq. *attrib.*

1857 *Chambers's Jrnl.* 22 Aug. 121/1 The transmission of the current having..to be made through a make and break key of metal. **1875, 1898** [see MAKE *sb.*² 9]. **1904** A. B. F. YOUNG *Compl. Motorist* (ed. 2) 197 The time of firing is controlled by a simple 'make-and-break' commutator placed on the half-time shaft. **1911** *Encycl. Brit.* XXVI. 520/2 In Squier and Crehore's 'Synchronograph' system 'sine waves' of current, instead of sharp 'makes and breaks',..are employed for transmitting signals. **1938** *Archit. Rev.* LXXXIII. p. lviii, A semi-rotary quick make-and-break switch. **1958** *Newnes Compl. Amat. Photogr.* 120 To charge a large capacitor from accumulators requires a more complex power pack which includes a make-and-break coil, transformer and rectifier.

b. An apparatus for automatically making and breaking electrical contact.

1908 *Daily Chron.* 7 Nov. 3/3 The 'make and break' or commutator..is..frequently placed in an inaccessible position. **1911** A. B. SMITH *Mod. Amer. Telephony* xxv. 689 The circuit consisted of an induction coil..and mechanical 'make and break' that gave 10,000 sparks per second. **1929** *Times* 5 Nov. 7/5 The distributor and make-and-break are easily seen. **1970** K. BALL *Fiat 600, 600D Autobook* xi. 138/2 Failure of the horn to operate may be due to..dirty contacts on the horn make-and-break.

make-belief. Delete '*rare*' and add further examples.

1909 *Westm. Gaz.* 20 Aug. 4/1 The contempt with which all things are remembered, to which cling suggestions of the theatrical and the make-belief. **1960** J. RAE *Custard Boys* II. xix. 212 He had been my guide through the days of make-belief and blinkered memory. **1971** *Daily Tel.* 11 Oct. 9/1 That great reservoir of make-belief which lies hidden in so many children.

make-believer, -believing. (Further examples.)

1907 G. B. SHAW *Major Barbara* Pref. 149 The romantic make-believer lay outside the pale of sympathy in literature. **1909** *Times Lit. Suppl.* 18 Mar. 105/2 A little make-believing girl, not unlike..the make-believing child of the 'Child's Garden of Verses'. **1954** T. S. ELIOT *Confid. Clerk* I. 40 It begins as a kind of make-believe And the make-believing makes it real. **1957** L. MACNEICE *Visitations* 17 Coral islands of first love Where makebelieving boy and girl Assume the music of the spheres.

make-do (mēⁱ·k,dū·). [f. *to make do*: see *MAKE *v.*¹ 53 f.] A makeshift; a temporary expedient. Also *attrib.* or quasi-*adj.*, characterized by makeshift methods. So *make-do-and-mend* (cf. *MAKE *v.*¹ 53 f).

1895 *Dialect Notes* I. 372 These 'ere make-dos are no 'count. **1916** KIPLING *Tales of 'Trade'* 13 The full tale of their improvisations and 'make-do's' will probably never come to light. **1923** *Daily Mail* 12 Feb. 4 When..prices steadily mounted to their peak, thousands of careful housewives adopted what was known as a 'make-do' policy. **1944** in R. W. Zandvoort et al. *Wartime English* (1957) 151 This garment is being made in the Make-do-and-Mend Department of the store from an old costume. **1948** *Times* 19 Aug. 5/2 Large schemes..must be ruled out; make do and mend must take their place. **1961** L. MUMFORD *City in Hist.* xiv. 420 The spirit of make-shift and make-do too often prevailed.

make-ready. 2. Delete *U.S.* and add further examples. Also *attrib.*

1915 *Southward's Mod. Printing* (ed. 3) II. iii. 39 As a preventive against slurring through baggy tympans as much of the make-ready as is practicable should be done at the back of the forme. **1946** *N. & Q.* 9 Mar. 93/1 Most early books are marked by bad paper, brownish ink, poor typography, lack of care in 'make-ready', and crude illustrations. **1959** *Times* 14 Jan. 12/4 A saving of 50 hours' make-ready time. **1967** KARCH & BUBER *Offset Processes* ii. 24 Makeready can be mechanical..with the 3 M makeready machine. **1970** E. A. D. HUTCHINGS *Survey of Printing Processes* 200 *Make-ready*, specifically, all operations carried out on the production machine from receipt of the job to the start of the production run.

makeshift. Add: **2.** Also *transf.*, of a person. Quot. 1848 may belong to sense 1.

1848 [see WIRE-PULLER]. **1912** [see *GAWD]. **1920** H. CRANE *Let.* 22 Dec. (1965) 50, I..hope that I have not been relinquished as one of Akron's temporary 'make-shifts' or 'reliefs'. **1951** E. PAUL *Springtime in Paris* ix. 162 Dr. Thiouville..completed his studies under the De Gaulle régime and the first few Middle-of-the-Road make-shifts.

make-up. Add: **1.** *spec.* The character or temperament of a person (cf. quot. 1821 in Dict.). Also *transf.*

1898 [see *GET *v.* 73 b]. **1908** W. MCDOUGALL *Introd. Social Psychol.* iv. 117 Constitutional conditions..that exert a constant influence..responsible for much in the mental make-up of the adult. **1928** *Morning Post* 23 Mar. 15 M. Poincaré..works alone, and has nothing of the people's tribune in his make-up. **1942** *R.A.F. Jrnl.* 13 June 5 The lack of conscience in the make-up of the Japanese. **1965** G. N. GARMONSWAY in Bessinger & Creed *Medieval & Ling. Stud.* 140 He becomes the prototype of the more ruthless type of Germanic hero, with a touch in his make-up of the berserk or ruffian. **1975** *Country Life* 6 Feb. 343/1 Dogs possessing faults in their make-up..are liable to pass them on to their offspring.

b. The balancing of accounts at the end of a certain period; cf. MAKE *v.*¹ 96 j. Also *attrib.*

1952 *Economist* 21 June 839 Electricity repayments by B.E.A. completed by the date of the May make-up. **1975** *Guardian* 20 Jan. 12/2 On the latest make-up date, the banks' acquisitions of interest-bearing liabilities were..higher.

2. b. Also used by women generally.

1932 'N. SHUTE' *Lonely Road* vii. 135 She had made herself look quieter than before. It may have been that she had less make-up on. **1959** J. BRAINE *Vodi* xxi. 229 Her mother would..put on a little makeup. The lipstick and rouge seemed to give the large face..not less but more dignity. **1974** *Listener* 7 Nov. 603/3 We've all got our 'titfers' on, four layers of make-up, every jewel we can find.

d. The action or process of 'making up' with cosmetics, etc.

1890 *Cent. Dict.*, *Make up*,..the preparation of an actor for impersonating the character assigned to him, including dress, painting and altering the appearance of the face, etc. **1922** J. ERSKINE *Coll. Poems* 120 If this world be a stage, what hours we give To tedious make-up in the tiring-room. **1930** *Punch* 8 Jan. 47/2 One 'make-up' each morning, says Popkin, is plenty. **1951** *Good Housek. Home Encycl.* 20/2 It is a good idea to have also a magnifying mirror for shaving or make-up. **1974** *Country Life* 28 Nov. 694/3 A cleanse and make-up from £2.50, a make-up lesson £5.

e. A make-up room; the place where an actor or the like is 'made up'; the work of such a place. *colloq.*

1960 *Guardian* 5 May 9/4, I..lost no time phoning Groucho, who was 'in make-up'. **1967** M. SHULMAN *Kill 3* III. viii. 146 'She's been to make up?' 'Only a bit of powder. We thought the wan look was best.' **1972** *New Statesman* 28 Apr. 554/3 There are still important women in BBC TV. They have four of the top 70 jobs, to do with planning, education and children's programmes. And Head of Make-up, of course. **1973** *Listener* 20 Dec. 838/3 They've got a new girl in make-up here and I'm not sure whether she has caught the Ronnie Corbett look.

4. b. *colloq.* or *dial.* Something (esp. food) made up from odds and ends. Also *attrib.*

1854 A. E. BAKER *Gloss. Northamptonshire Words* II. 6 *A make-up dinner*, a dinner composed of scraps and remnants. **1877** J. M. NEILSON *Poems* 48 The treacle mak'-up on the candyman's stand. **1924** 'L. MALET' *Dogs of Want* v. 129 The sort of refreshments caterers supply at a public entertainment like this—left-overs and make-ups, from the local restaurants.

5. b. Replacement of the water lost from a boiler or the like by evaporation, leakage, etc.; water added for this pupose.

1930 *Engineering* 10 Jan. 56/1 Others..treat the entire boiler feed water, including condensate and make-up, [etc.]. **1971** *Sci. Amer.* May 71/2 The amount of water required for 'makeup' in a large cooling tower is considerable. **1972** R. G. KAZMANN *Mod. Hydrol.* (ed. 2) iv. 133 A 500 megawatt plant will use 500,000 gallons of water an hour for makeup purposes.

6. (sense 2 a) *make-up girl, man* (later examples); (sense *2 b) *make-up kit*; (sense *2 d) *make-up mirror*; (sense 3) *make-up copy, editor, hand, man*; **make-up bed**, a bed that can be set up temporarily.

1911 A. BENNETT *Hilda Lessways* IV. i. 276, I quite forgot about the make-up bed for Florrie. **1960** G. A. GLAISTER *Gloss. Bk.* 249/1 *Make-up copy*, i.e., a set of folded sheets and plates put in the correct order as a pattern. **1903** J. RALPH *Making of Journalist* xiii. 153 Around the walls are the desks..that of the night or 'make-up' editor, and that of the managing editor. **1972** H. EVANS *Editing & Design: Newsman's English* i. 8 In the composing room ..an editorial man watches... He may be called a production editor, a make-up editor or a stone sub or stone editor. **1957** *Times* 28 Aug. (Radio & T.V. Suppl.) p. xix/2 Ordeal by Television..under the impersonal inspection of..camera-men, make-up girls. **1971** 'W. HAGGARD' *Bitter Harvest* vii. 74 A make-up girl had powdered his bald patch... Now he sat..in the sweaty studio. **1949** R. HOSTETTLER *Technical Terms Printing Industry* 122/2 Make-up hand. **1955** A. HUXLEY *Genius & Goddess* 51 Ruth..squandered a year's accumulated savings on a make-up kit and a bottle of cheap perfume. **1922** S. A. CUNEO *From Printer to President* 43 It was necessary for the owner to be a typesetter, a make-up man, a press feeder, in fact an all 'round printer. **1959** Make-up man [see *goose pimples]. **1973** W. MCGIVERN *Reprisal* (1974) 116 A part in a picture..a make-up man to fuss over her. **1964** *Harper's Bazaar* Nov. 99 The make-up mirror..in black opaline and ormolu, £27. **1966** H. NIELSEN *After Midnight* (1967) vi. 86 A make-up mirror on the bedside table.

make-work (mēⁱ·k,wɒ̄ɹk). orig. *U.S.* [f. MAKE- + WORK *sb.*] Work or activity of little or no value devised mainly to keep someone busy. Also *attrib.*

1937 *Political Q.* VIII. 608 A nation-wide organization of relief work, including..genuine public works and a host of make-work projects of questionable merit. **1947** *Yale Law Jrnl.* Dec. 182 Community development subordinated to make-work and pump-priming. **1957** [see *cost-accounted* ppl. a. s.v. *COST *sb.*² 6]. **1972** *Guardian* 13 Sept. 12/1 Still the old make-work continues, the mailbags and the excessive cleaning, which..occupy almost a quarter of the prison population.

Makhzen, -an: see *MAGHZEN.

‖ **makimono** (makimōᵘ·no). Also **emakimono** [Jap. *e* picture, painting], **makemono,** (with hyphen) **maki-mono.** [Jap., something rolled up, a scroll.] A Japanese scroll containing pictures, usually with explanatory writing, to form a continuous narrative, designed to be examined progressively from right to left as it is unrolled.

1882 G. A. AUDSLEY *Ornamental Arts Japan* I. plate 16 (*caption*), She appears to be rising out of the mist at her feet bearing a *makimono* covered with writing. **1884** SATOW & HAWES *Handbk. for Travellers Cent. & N. Japan* (ed. 2) 554/2 *Maki-mono*, a long roll graphic or pictorial. **1889** S. BING in *Artistic Japan* III. 161 All the paintings.. are executed..on rolls of silk or paper, which are known in the Japanese language as *Kakémono* (that is to say, a thing to hang up) when the subject is upright, and under the word *Makimono* when it stretches itself out in a horizontal manner. **1901** L. HEARN *Jap. Misc.* 243 The shrine contained a *makémono*, or scroll, inscribed with the spirit-names of many ancestors. **1911** L. BINYON *Flight of Dragon* x. 81 The makimono, or continuous long scroll-paintings of landscapes, admirably fulfilled the aim of Taoist art. **1926** A. WALEY tr. *Sacred Tree* 31 The first painted makimonos..were regarded merely as a succession of topographical records, joined together more or less fortuitously. **1958** Y. YASHIRO *2,000 Yrs. Jap. Art* iv. 161 The finest expression and the fullest development of *Yamato-e* are the *e-makimono* (scroll-paintings). **1966** J. ROSENFIELD tr. *Noma's Arts Japan* vi. 122 These long horizontal paintings, the *emakimono*, are sometimes said to be peculiarly Japanese in form, but similar scrolls have been made by the Chinese as well.

making, *vbl. sb.*¹ Add: **8. b.** *pl.* Paper and tobacco for rolling a cigarette. *N. Amer.*, *Austral.*, and *N.Z. colloq.*

1905 'O. HENRY' in *Everybody's Mag.* Dec. 817/1 He took out his 'makings' and rolled a cigarette. **1907** S. E. WHITE *Arizona Nights* I. ix. 161 'Well,' agreed Rogers, 'pass over the "makings" and I will.' **1910** R. W. SERVICE *Trail of '98* (1911) I. iv. 15 'Got the makings?' 'No, I'm sorry; I don't smoke.' **1912** *Collier's* 21 Dec. 23/2 A revelation to any man who doesn't know a real 'makin's' cigarette. **1930** J. DEVANNY *Bushman Burke* 26 He grinned and took out the 'makings'. **1949** *Amer. Speech* XV. 213/1 The day before payday, the camp's 'smoking' has become scarce and 'rollings' or 'makings' are at a premium. **1941** *Coast to Coast* 207 We rolled our makings, lit them and stood about waiting for someone to start talking about something. **1949** S. P. LLEWELLYN *Troopships* 7 The normal Kiwi..his clothes in a heap beside him, the 'makings' handy. **1963** B. PEARSON *Coal Flat* iv. 70 Rogers offered him a cigarette but McKenzie shook his head and pulled out the makings in a way that seemed to suggest that tailor-mades were a stigma of middle-class ideology. **1963** H. GARNER in R. Weaver *Canad. Short Stories* (1968) 2nd Ser. 30, I gave McKinnon enough money to get me a package of makings.

10. b. making-out, the action of the vbl. phr. *to make out* (*MAKE *v.*¹ 91 c (*c*)).

1957 F. KOHNER *Gidget* vii. 76 'No sweaty hands, no making out in drive-in movies.' 'Making out?' 'My God, Larry, where've you been living. I guess you still call it necking.' **1964** C. NICOLAI *Murder in Fine Arts* xxviii. 248 He had a violent aversion to necking or 'making out' as the current expression had it. **1967** 'J. H. ROBERTS' *February Plan* I. iv. 113 She had been..putting him off when it came to making out (how many evasive phrases were there for the act of sexual intercourse?). **1969** E. GOFFMAN *Where Action Is* 157 Adult males may define a female as an object to initiate a sexually potential relationship with... This action is sometimes called 'making out'. In our society there are special times and places set aside for making out.

making-up. Add: (Further examples.)

1808 C. STOWER *Printer's Gram.* 467 As soon as the first person brings him his matter, he [*sc.* the clicker] counts off the number of lines,..then gives him another taking of copy, and proceeds with the making up [of the type pages]. **1816** JANE AUSTEN *Emma* I. xii. 206 She hoped they might

now become friends again... Making-up indeed would not do. *She* certainly had not been in the wrong. **1827** L. T. REDE *Road to Stage* 40 My readers will call to mind the excellent 'making up' of Mr. T. P. Cooke, in the Monster, 'Frankenstein'. **1838** DICKENS *Let.* 15 Nov. (1965) I. 453 On the other side I forward you a copy of the making-up. **1841** W. SAVAGE *Dict. Art of Printing* 470 When a compositor in a companionship has composed his copy to within the quantity of a page of the work, he gives the overplus of the copy, after having completed his own last page, to him who is composing the copy that follows his matter... This is called *giving the making-up*. **1878** E. C. MADDISON *Speculation on Stock Exchange* 15 The process known as 'making-up' settles many bargains before the arrival of the settling-day. Making-up commences on the contango-day and is continued on the ticket-day. **1894** BEERBOHM in *Yellow Bk.* I. Apr. 73 'Making-up' is an art. **1905** J. C. LINCOLN *Partners of Tide* iv. 74 His worst quarrel with Gus and her friend, Clara Hopkins—the quarrel that lasted two weeks without a making up—came about because the new member refused to tell what the initials 'stood for'. **1913** *Trans. Bibliogr. Soc.* XII. 303 There seems to have been a good deal of very clumsy making-up of copies in the early part of last century.

b. (Earlier and later examples.)

1875 *Encycl. Brit.* I. 92/1 The price at which such transactions are adjusted is the 'Making-Up' price of the day. **1969** *Jane's Freight Containers 1968–69* 195/1 Three rail sidings are available for making-up trains.

‖ **makkoli** (mæ·kǒli). [Korean.] A popular alcoholic beverage in Korea.

1972 P. M. BARTZ *S. Korea* 73/1 Domestic production [of wheat] is one-quarter the volume of imports and is used mainly for noodles and *makkoli*, the common alcoholic beverage. **1972** E. FODOR *Japan & E. Asia* 477 These are both cloudy and light-tan colored and are known together as *makkoli*.

mako¹ (ma·ko). [Maori.] In full, *mako shark*. A large blue shark of the genus *Isurus*, esp. *I. oxyrinchus*; also called mackerel shark.

1727 J. G. SCHEUCHZER tr. *Kæmpfer's Hist. Japan* I. I. 133 *Mako* never exceeds three or four fathom in length. **1848** R. TAYLOR *Leaf from Nat. Hist. N.Z.* 14 *Mako*, a shark, peculiar to this latitude, teeth prized as ear ornament. **1872** F. W. HUTTON *Fishes N.Z.* 77 *Lamna Glauca*. Tiger Shark. Mako... The shark from which the Maoris obtain the teeth with which they decorate their ears. **1936** 'R. HYDE' *Check to Your King* xiii. 153 They wore pieces of *mako* tooth in the lobe of the ear. **1938** *Times Lit. Suppl.* 24 Sept. 619/1 Giant mako in New Zealand waters. **1952** E. HEMINGWAY *Old Man & Sea* 100 He was a very big Mako shark built to swim as fast as the fastest fish in the sea. **1959** *Manch. Guardian* 13 July 5/1 The sharks come to Cornwall..blue sharks, makos, porbeagles. **1969** A. WHEELER *Fishes Brit. Isles & N.-W. Europe* 53/1 The mako has no commercial value beyond its angling appeal. **1970** *E. Afr. Standard* (Nairobi) 2 Jan. 19/4 The big item of fishing news last week..was the capture of Kenya's first mako shark. **1972** *Shooting Times & Country Mag.* 27 May 17/1 The four British species of shark are blue, mako, porbeagle and thresher.

mako², var. *MAKOMAKO².

Makololo (makǒlōu·lo), *sb.* and *a.* Also Makalolo, Ma Kololo. **A.** *sb.* A Negro people of Africa now living in Zambia near the junction of the Zambesi and Kafue rivers; a member of this people. **B.** *adj.* Of or pertaining to this people.

1857 D. LIVINGSTONE *Missionary Trav. & Res. S. Afr.* ix. 179 Mamochisane..said she would never consent to govern the Makololo so long as she had a brother living. *Ibid.* x. 204 The Makololo chiefs pride themselves on eating with their people. **1867** [see SJAMBOK *sb.* y]. **1871** J. MACKENZIE *Ten Yrs. North of Orange River* ii. 34 Both the Matebele and Makololo countries were far beyond the territories of the Transvaal. **1871** C. M. YONGE *Pioneers & Founders* xi. 306 There was no choice but to have recourse to the Makololo, and thus let loose one set of savages against another. **1900** A. H. KEANE *Boer States* vii. 101 The Makololos and other Basutos..founded a powerful State about the middle Zambesi. **1932** C. FULLER *Louis Trigardt's Trek* 21 The foundation of the Ma Kololo nation. **1974** J. R. BAKER *Race* xx. 371 By far the largest group of houses recorded by any of the explorers was at Linyanti, in Makololo territory. *Ibid.* 389 Among the Bakuena and Makololo..there was no despotic cruelty.

makomako¹ (mā·komā·ko). *N.Z.* [Maori.] = *KORIMAKO.

1848 R. TAYLOR *Leaf from Nat. Hist. N.Z.* 8/2 Makomako, a bird. Syn. with korimako. **1873** W. L. BULLER *Hist. Birds N.Z.* 91 *Anthornis Melanura* (Bell-Bird).. Native names. Mako, Makomako..Korimako..Kopara. Of the above names, Korimako is most generally used by the northern and Makomako by the southern tribes. **1875** W. E. ATKINSON *Let.* 16 Aug. in *Richmond–Atkinson Papers* (1960) II. 399, I have also the mako mako, silvereye, [etc.].., and besides the birds a great many shells. **1911** *Encycl. Brit.* XIX. 626/2 The tui and makomako rank high as songsters. **1966** [see *KORIMAKO].

makomako² (mā·komā·ko). *N.Z.* Also mako. [Maori.] A small New Zealand tree, *Aristotelia serrata* (or *A. racemosa*), of the family Elæocarpaceæ, which bears clusters of small pink flowers and dark red berries; also called wineberry.

1848 R. TAYLOR *Leaf from Nat. Hist. N.Z.* 20/2 *Mako*, a tree; the bark used as a black dye. *Makomako*, a tree (*Friesia racemosa*). **1861** A. S. ATKINSON *Jrnl.* 24 Mar. in *Richmond-Atkinson Papers* (1960) I. 696 Just before the fireplace were a few makos which they had been sleeping on. **1866** LINDLEY & MOORE *Treas. Bot.* II. 92/1 The berries of *Aristotelia racemosa*, the Mako-Mako of the natives, are eaten. **1883** J. HECTOR *Handbk. N.Z.* (ed. 3) 130 Mako, a small handsome tree, six to twenty feet high, quick-growing, with large racemes of reddish nodding flowers. **1949** P. BUCK *Coming of Maori* (1950) II. ix. 239 The spears were formed of..rods of light *mako* wood. **1966** *Encycl. N.Z.* II. 670/1 (*caption*) *Aristotelia serrata*, makomako or wineberry, is a small tree of graceful appearance.

Makonde (măkōu·ndi), *sb.* and *a.* **A.** *sb.* A Bantu-speaking people of Tanzania and Mozambique; a member of this people. **B.** *adj.* Of or pertaining to this people.

1911 *Encycl. Brit.* I. 330/2 Bantu negroids... Ma-konde. *Ibid.* III. 359/1 The archaic *Makonde* or *Mabiha* [language] of the lower Ruvuma, and the coast between Lindi and Ibo. **1948** D. DIRINGER *Alphabet* 26 The Makonde people, an important tribe of Tanganyika Territory. **1973** *Times* 17 Feb. (Mozambique Suppl.) p. iv/3 (Advt.), The Makondes were more given to tattooing. **1974** *Times* 2 May 5/2 Mr Simon Makada, a Makonde..and a Frelimo youth leader. **1974** *Afr. Encycl.* 317/3 The Makonde are traditionally an agricultural people... In Mozambique many Makonde and Makua people are involved in war against the Portuguese administration.

makoré (makǒre·). Also makora, makori. [Native name in West Afr.] A large West African tree, *Tieghemella* (or *Mimusops*) *heckelii*, of the family Sapotaceæ; also, the dark red-brown wood produced by it.

1915 J. H. HOLLAND *Useful Plants Nigeria* III. 422 *Dumoria Heckeli*... Vernac[ular] names... Mako, Makoré, Makerou. **1936** *Nature* 9 May 791/1 Skirting and dado in specially cut logs of Makoré with small marquetry banding in the Makoré doors of maple burr. **1947** J. C. RICH *Materials & Methods of Sculpture* x. 292 Makore is also known as Makori, Makora, and African cherry. The wood is beautifully figured. **1972** *Handbk. Hardwoods* (Building Res. Establishment) (ed. 2) 121 Marine plywood of makoré is also widely used in boat-building.

maktuk, var. *MUKTUK.

makuk, var. *MOCOCK.

makumba, var. *MACUMBA.

makuta: see *LIKUTA.

makutu (măkū·tu). *N.Z.* [Maori.] Sorcery, witchcraft; a magic spell. Also as *v. trans.*, to bewitch.

1846 J. WHITE *Jrnl.* (MS.) 1 If anyone..offended us.. we should try to kill them by makutuing them to see if makutu was true. **1905** W. B. *Where White Man Treads* 41 Another decimating tool in the hands of spite and revenge was makutu (witchcraft)... Let one fear that a makutu spell had been laid upon him,..he would..die! **1938** R. D. FINLAYSON *Brown Man's Burden* 70 She was sure someone had put a makutu spell on her and the evil spirit was eating her life away. **1943** N. MARSH *Colour Scheme* i. 25 'I'll tell my great-grandfather..and he'll *makutu* you.' 'Kid-stakes! Nobody's going to put a jinx on me.' **1963** *Evening Post* (Wellington, N.Z.) 16 Dec., The true tohunga whiawhia, who had gained complete mastery of the powers of makutu, was able to project his spirit in such a manner as to kill men and women. **1971** *N.Z. Listener* 29 Mar. 11 A number of modern case histories of patients whose illness or death has been connected with makutu.

Mal, var. *MALER *sb.* and *a.*

mal-. Add: *malperformance.*

1938 R. G. COLLINGWOOD *Princ. Art* xii. 283 It is the malperformance of the act which converts what is merely psychic (impression) into what is conscious (idea). **1964** M. CRITCHLEY *Developmental Dyslexia* ix. 60 Dyslexics show only a mild tendency towards a malperformance of higher order right-left orientation exercises.

Malabar. Add: **1.** An inhabitant of the Malabar coast.

1582 N. LICHEFIELD tr. *Lopez de Castaneda's Hist. Conquest E. Indias* f. 37ᵛ They asked of the Malabars which went with him what he was? **1681** R. KNOX *Hist. Relation Ceylon* IV. ix. 159 This Plain is..inhabited by Malabars, a distinct People from the Chingulayes. **1867** C. J. BOYLE *Far Away* 72 Started on foot up the gorge, our bags on the shoulders of Malabars. **1931** M. YEO *St. Francis Xavier* xii. 155 One night his faithful Malabar..woke to the sound of blows. *Ibid.*, The Malabar told his tale.

2. The language spoken on the Malabar coast.

1801 T. MUNRO in G. R. Gleig *Life T. Munro* (1830) I. 322 From Miliserum to the Chandergeery river no language is understood but the Malabars of that coast. **1837** T. BACON *First Impr. Hindostan* I. 99 He was compelled to fall back upon his only two words of Malabar. **1872** [see TAMULIC *a.*]. **1931** M. YEO *St. Francis Xavier* x. 124 Tamil, the pre-Aryan language of southern India, which Francis, Portuguese-fashion, calls Malabar.

3. A kind of handkerchief (see quots.).

1882 CAULFEILD & SAWARD *Dict. Needlework* 340 *Malabars*, cotton handkerchiefs, printed in imitation of Indian handkerchiefs, the patterns of which are of a peculiar and distinctive type, and the contrasts of colour brilliant and striking. **1957** M. B. PICKEN *Fashion Dict.* 218/2 *Malabar*, cotton handkerchief printed in brilliant colors and designs of East Indian type.

4. *attrib.*

1696 J. OVINGTON *Voy. Suratt* 213 Many of their Women by their usual Custom in these cases..have gain'd the Name of Malabar Quills. **1778** Malabar language [see TAMIL]. **1872** tr. *St. Francis Xavier's Lett.* in H. J. Coleridge *Life & Lett. St. Francis Xavier* II. 73 Enrico Enriquez ..writes and speaks the Malabar tongue.

Hence **Malabare·se** *a.* [-ESE], of or pertaining to the Malabar coast or its inhabitants; **Malaba·rian** *a.* and *sb.*; **Malaba·ric** *a.* and *sb.*; **Malaba·rish** *a.* and *sb.*

1709 A. W. BOEHM *Propagation of Gospel in East* 17 This place [*sc.* Tranquebar] is altogether stocked with Malabarian Heathens. *Ibid.* 28, I will set down here..the Malabarick Letters. *Ibid.*, I caused..The Lord's-Prayer.. to be put into Malabarick. **1717** J. T. PHILIPPS *Acct. People Malabar* i. 2 According to the Malabarish way of Reasoning. *Ibid.* 8 The chief Reasons why the Malabarians refuse to embrace the Christian Religion. *Ibid.* v. 53 There are some things..writ in Malabarish. **1718** ZIEGENBALG & GRUNDLER *Let.* in R. Millar *Hist. Propagation of Christianity* (1731) II. viii. 505 We catechise..every Friday in Malabarian. **1788** Malabaric [see TAMIL]. **1808** C. STOWER *Printer's Gram.* Index, Malabaric alphabet. **1922** *Blackw. Mag.* May 612/1 The Moplahs..are the descendants of Arab fathers and Malabarese mothers. **1922** O. JESPERSEN *Language* ii. 39 He [*sc.* Rask] was also the first to see that the Dravidian (by him called Malabaric) languages were totally different from Sanskrit.

ma:labso·rption. *Physiol.* [f. MAL- + ABSORPTION.] Imperfect absorption (of food material by the body).

1932 DORLAND *Med. Dict.* (ed. 16) 739/2 *Malabsorption*, disorder of normal nutritive absorption; disordered anabolism. **1962** *Lancet* 2 June 1168/2 The rickets of cœliac disease is commonly attributed to malabsorption of vitamin D. **1974** PASSMORE & ROBSON *Compan. Med. Stud.* III. xix. 58/1 The term malabsorption syndrome is applied to a number of conditions that affect the gut or digestive glands and which result in disturbance of the absorption of one or more nutrients.

Malacca. Malacca cane (earlier and later examples).

1844 *Ainsworth's Mag.* VI. 501 He..struck the pavement..with the brass-shod point of his Malacca cane. **1846** A. J. H. DUGANNE *Daguerrotype Miniature* 7 He held..a musk cigar, and twirled in his right..a unique and delicate Malacca cane. **1963** J. KIRKUP *Tropic Temper* 83 There were some stalls selling..the famous Malacca Canes, stout walking-sticks with carved and decorated handles. **1965** C. SHUTTLEWORTH *Malayan Safari* vi. 88 Malacca cane grows in clumps in the jungle.

malachite. Add: **2. malachite kingfisher,** a small blue, green, and red kingfisher, *Corythornis cristata*, found in Africa south of the Sahara; **malachite sunbird,** a blue and green sunbird, *Nectarinia johnstoni*, found in parts of southern and eastern Africa.

[**1875** *Ibis* V. 68 Malachite-crested Kingfisher. This charming little Kingfisher is found invariably frequenting the small streams and ditches close to Durban.] **1903** A. C. STARK *Birds S. Afr.* III. 82 The Malachite Kingfisher is found throughout the greater part of Africa south of the Sahara. **1906** *Daily Chron.* 10 Feb. 7/7 A great rarity is a Malachite sun bird, a most wonderfully-formed bird with a bill as long as its body and as fine as a piece of wire. **1947** J. STEVENSON-HAMILTON *Wild Life S. Afr.* xxxiv. 300 The beautifully coloured malachite kingfisher (*Corythornis cristata*)..likes to sit on an overhanging branch, whence he scrutinizes the water beneath. **1966** E. PALMER *Plains of Camdeboo* xii. 197 The male malachite sunbirds would be flashing their astonishing green and gold. **1971** *Country Life* 28 Oct. 1127/2 Tiny malachite kingfishers, brilliant red and blue, sped among the tall rushes.

malacon (mæ·lăkǒn). *Min.* Also † **malacone.** [ad. G. *malakon* (T. Scheerer 1844, in *Ann. d. Physik* LXII. 436), f. Gr. μαλακόν, neut. of μαλακός soft.] A soft brown altered form of zircon.

1854 DANA *Syst. Min.* (ed. 4) III. ii. 196 Malacone. **1868** *Ibid.* (ed. 5) 275 The following tetragonal zircon-like minerals are probably altered zircon... Malacon. **1921** *Mineral. Abstr.* I. 173 The malacon of Madagascar shows a higher degree of radioactivity than is accounted for by its content of thorium. **1941** *Amer. Jrnl. Sci.* CCXXXIX. 306 The third type of [zircon] is characteristic of the younger granite in the Oxford House Area, and of the late pre-Huronian and Huronian granites of the Lake Superior region. This variety is malacon, a form of zircon with relatively low refringence, weak birefringence and a dirty, altered appearance. **1968** I. KOSTOV *Mineral.* II. v. 294 Malacon is a metamict zircon.

maladaptation. Add: Hence **malada·ptive** *a.*; **malada·ptively** *adv.*

1931 *Brit. Jrnl. Psychol.* Jan. 334 Prof. Fisher begins his study of the abnormal by considering..how maladaptive the responses of the normal individual often are, when he is faced with a difficult situation. *Ibid.* Oct. 132 Both images and symbols function maladaptively [in mental defectives]. **1957** P. LAFITTE *Person in Psychol.* v. 58 Three modes of adaptive and eight modes of maladaptive behaviour that are used in response to frustration. **1969** *Sci. Jrnl.* Nov. 70/3 Long fingers are..generally maladaptive in terrestrial primates. **1971** *Sci. Amer.* Sept. 132/3 Some aspects of what we have called progress or social evolution may be maladaptive. **1974** *Times Lit. Suppl.* 30 Aug. 923/1 Man's instincts..have become seriously maladaptive. *Ibid.* 923/5 The hypertrophied human brain has become as maladaptive as the dinosaur's armour.

‖ **malade imaginaire** (malad *imaʒinɛ̄r*'). [Fr. (after the title of Molière's play, 1673); cf. MALADE.] A person suffering from an imaginary illness.

1818 LADY MORGAN *Florence Macarthy* IV. v. 202, I trust you will not think I am playing the *Malade Imaginaire*, when I assign indisposition as an excuse for my absence. **1888** *Athenæum* 15 Dec. 811/1 A *malade imaginaire*..who sacrifices her daughter to her own comfort. **1911** G. B. SHAW *Doctor's Dilemma* Pref. p. xxviii, Doctors ..nurse the delusions of the *malade imaginaire*. **1958** M. STEWART *Nine Coaches Waiting* v. 60 Enough pills and boluses to satisfy the most highly-strung *malade imaginaire*. **1974** E. AMBLER *Dr. Frigo* II. 80 He's..inclined to worry about his health. If you mean do I think him a malade imaginaire, no I don't.

‖ **maladif** (maladif), *a.* [Fr.; cf. MALADIVE *a.*] = MALADIVE *a.*

1481 [see MALADIVE *a.*]. **1859** QUEEN VICTORIA *Let.* 8 Jan. in R. Fulford *Dearest Child* (1964) 157, I thought he was too maladif to marry. **1886** *Portfolio* 51/2 Standing in the corner..a fragile, *maladif* little figure, with a disproportionately impressive head. **1911** D. H. LAWRENCE *Let.* 30 Dec. (1962) I. 90 You'll find it [*sc.* the story], perhaps, thin—*maladif*. **1950** D. GASCOYNE *Vagrant* 55 For a maladif, mandarin-miened, mauve melody-man.

maladive, *a.* (Later examples.)

1907 R. BROOKE *Let.* Oct. (1968) 112 Lippo Lippi's girl-Madonna's, with the maladive sensuality of their tired faces. **1940** *Horizon* Mar. 171 There is the road to New-church-on-Arrow, up which Kilvert..used to stride to see his sweet but *maladive* Emmeline. **1953** *Economist* 6 June 641 The most dangerous trend in post-war Britain..the tendency..to indulge in maladive self-attention.

maladju·sted, *a.* [f. MAL- + ADJUSTED *ppl. a.*] Inadequately adjusted; exhibiting or characterized by psychological maladjustment.

1885 [see MAL-]. **1930** R. S. WOODWORTH *Psychol.* (ed. 8) xiii. 564 Ways of helping maladjusted individuals. **1931** E. WILSON *Axel's Castle* iv. 93 Only thirty at the time of his death, Tristan Corbière had been an eccentric and very maladjusted man. **1953** R. LEHMANN *Echoing Grove* 32 Where did she get this magpie streak from? Can she be maladjusted? **1957** P. LAFITTE *Person in Psychol.* vi. 75 Persistence is characteristic of the maladjusted person, who cannot change because he is unable to learn by getting to grips with his situation. **1970** R. C. CARSON *Interaction Concepts of Personality* vi. 203 The families from which maladjusted persons emerge.

maladjustment. Add to def.: *spec.* in *Psychol.*, unsuccessful adaptation to one's social environment. (Further examples.)

1909 E. T. DEVINE in *Fabian News* Dec. 94/1 Not poverty and not punishment explains the misery of our modern commercial and industrial communities, but rather social maladjustment. **1923** J. S. HUXLEY *Ess. Biologist* i. 55 Whatever overstress and maladjustment the complexity of modern civilization has brought with it. **1930** R. S. WOODWORTH *Psychol.* (ed. 8) xiii. 565 This.. picture of the situation in which the maladjustment arose is of value to the troubled adult. **1949** E. JENKINS *Six Criminal Women* 166 Cook did not take to the road through want, but rather from what the psychiatrists call 'maladjustment'. **1965** J. R. WITTENBORN in B. B. Wolman *Handbk. Clin. Psychol.* 1039/1 Evidence of periodic or constant maladjustment of varying degree from early life. **1970** R. C. CARSON *Interaction Concepts of Personality* vi. 203 Processes that appear to be implicated in the acquisition of maladjustment within the family.

† **malaëra·tion.** *Med. Obs.* [f. MAL- + AERATION.] Imperfect aeration (of the blood).

1843 R. J. GRAVES *Syst. Clin. Med.* xx. 245 Her countenance exhibits no proof of malaëration of the blood. **1908** *Practitioner* Mar. 321 Such cyanosis may..indicate lack of propelling power in the circulation, with consequent malaëration.

malagas (mæləgæ·s). *S. Afr.* Also 8 **malagos**; **malagash**, Afrikaans **malgas** (malχa·s). [Afrikaans, f. Du. *mallegas*, a. Pg. *mangas(-de-velludo)*, 'velvet-sleeves', the wandering albatross.] The Cape gannet, *Morus* (or *Sula*) *capensis*.

1731 G. MEDLEY tr. *Kolb's Present State Cape Good-Hope* II. 143 As soon as the *Malagos* 'spies a Fish under her, she pops her Head nimbly into the Water. **1906** STARK & SCLATER *Birds S. Afr.* IV. 17 *Sula capensis.* Malagash. *Ibid.* 19 The Malagash is found along the coasts of South Africa. **1936** E. L. GILL *First Guide S. Afr. Birds* 186 Malagas, Malgas, Cape Gannet; *Morus capensis*. This is the gannet of the South African guano islands. **1944** M. DE B. NESBITT *Road to Avalon* (1949) xxi. 163 The malagas seabird..is prolific here. **1964** A. L. THOMSON *New Dict. Birds* 330/1 The Cape Gannet (or Malagash) *S*[*ula*] *capensis* (with dark tail), breeding off South Africa and migrating northwards. **1970** MCLACHLAN & LIVERSIDGE *Roberts's Birds S. Afr.* (ed. 3) 21 Cape Gannet. Malgas. *Morus capensis*... These birds may be picked up at some distance by their conspicuous whiteness. **1974** *Eastern Province Herald* 7 Nov. 22 There are vast colonies of malgas (gannets) and other birds which live off the shoals of fodder fish in our waters.

Malagueña (mæləge·nyă). [Sp. (see MALAGA).] **1.** A woman of Malaga.

1845 R. FORD *Hand-bk. for Travellers Spain* I. 352/1 Teresita, the daughter, is a pretty specimen of a *Malageña*. **1868** H. O'SHEA *Guide to Spain & Portugal* (ed. 3) 312/2 The Malagueñas are considered to be the prettiest women in all Spain.

2. (Also with small initial.) A Spanish dance resembling the fandango; also, a song accompanying this dance.

1883 GROVE *Dict. Mus.* III. 599/2 The dance-songs—*fandangos*, *rondeñas*, and *malagueñas*,..have..more symmetry and more animation. *Ibid.*, Songs and dances often derive their names from the provinces or towns in which they are indigenous; thus..*malagueña* from Malaga. **1922** J. HERGESHEIMER *Bright Shawl* (1923) 69 The ceaseless playing of the guitars, strains of jotas and malagueñas. **1925** *Blackw. Mag.* Jan. 80/2 Hansson sang a queer malagueña which he had heard often in Andalucia. **1968** K. BIRD *Smash Glass Image* ix. 113 The next dance was slow, nostalgic. A *malagueña* perhaps? **1973** *Times* 6 Jan. 14/4 One typical dance [in the Canaries], the *malagueña*, reveals its peninsular origin in its name.

malaky, var. *MALARKEY.

malamute (mæ·lămiut). Also **malemut(e)**. [The name of an Eskimo tribe living on the Alaskan coast.] A large grey or black and white dog with a thick coat, pointed ears, and a plumed tail curling over its back, belonging to the spitz breed so called, which first developed in Alaska. Also *attrib.*

[**1874** *Ann. Rep. Board of Regents Smithsonian Inst.* 27 Maglemut.] **1898** *Klondike Nugget* (Dawson, Yukon Territory) 20 July 3/2 After appointing a committee to keep stray Malamoots and donkeys off the diamond, the game was called. **1898** *Yukon Midnight Sun* (Dawson, Yukon Territory) 1 Oct. 2/5, I have the first man to find in the country who owns a dog, it matters not whether he is malamute, husky,..or little mongrel. **1908** *St. Nicholas* Mar. 387/2 Few pure malamutes..are now employed in the mail service. **1913** *Outing* Feb. 521/1 Sitting among a litter of Malamute puppies. **1922** G. C. F. PRINGLE *Tillicums of Trail* 84, I first picked on a big grey-muzzled malemute named Steal as a likely fellow to lead... All malemutes are born thieves, some men think. **1934** *Times Educ. Suppl.* 15 Sept. p. iv/2 These Arctic or sub-Arctic dogs—huskies, malamutes, Samoyeds..are wonderful in their strength, powers of endurance, and stoutness of heart. **1948** *Chicago Tribune* 23 Feb. IV. 1/6 Along with the Eskimos will be a representation of the Malemute sled dogs that provide the only motive power available to Eskimos. **1952** M. K. WILSON tr. *Lorenz's King Solomon's Ring* x. 117 The purest wolf-dogs that exist are certain breeds of Arctic America, particularly the so-called malemuts, huskies etc. **1955** *Reader's Digest* (Austral.) Dec. 122/2 This malemute was bitten by a mad red fox. **1962** M. E. MURIE *Two in Far North* I. vi. 51 Long strings of Malemutes lope down the streets. **1971** F. HAMILTON *World Encycl. Dogs* 569 The Malamute must give an impression of great strength and tremendous propelling power.

malaprop, *sb.* and *a.* Add: Also as *v. intr.*, to utter a malapropism; *trans.*, to make a malapropism of (a word).

1959 I. JEFFERIES *Thirteen Days* v. 67 The usage was so wild that I thought he was malapropping. **1970** M. TRIPP *Man without Friends* iii. 27 She malaprops any word of more than two syllables.

malaria. Add: **c.** *malaria-carrying* adj.

1916 *Brit. Mus. Econ. Ser.* IV. 8 This group [of mosquitoes]..includes also several of the malaria-carrying *Anopheles*. **1946** *Nature* 10 Aug. 202/2 The experimental infection of laboratory-hatched larvæ of the malaria-carrying *Anopheles gambiæ* Giles with a fungus of the genus *Cœlomyces* Keilin.

malariologist. Delete *rare* and add further examples.

1944 *Living off Land* v. 115 Sir Ronald Ross, of the Indian Medical Service..became the world's foremost malariologist. **1966** *New Scientist* 18 Aug. 374/3 Malariologists are seeking to add to the established methods for controlling the disease. **1971** *Nature* 5 Mar. 65/1 For many years he was a 'wet-foot' malariologist in some of the most difficult countries in the world.

malariology (mălēəriǫ·lŏdʒi). [f. MALARI(A + -OLOGY.] The scientific study of malaria.

1925 *Science* 9 Oct. 320/2 In the field of malariology Dr. Carter has long held..the same position of preeminence that he enjoyed in relation to yellow fever. **1936** *Discovery* Nov. 353/1 Instruction in malariology was given to a number of medical practitioners. **1967** D. F. CLYDE *Malaria in Tanzania* p. x, Britain provided..grants with which the research units in Dar es Salaam and Tanga were enabled to lay the scientific foundations of modern malariology in this country. **1974** *Nature* 1 Feb. 318/3 His fleeting acquaintance with the discipline of malariology and with the realities of malaria control.

malarkey (mălā·ɹki). *slang* (orig. *U.S.*). Also **malaky**, **malarky**, **mullarkey**. [Origin unknown.] Humbug, nonsense, foolishness.

1929 J. P. MCEVOY *Hollywood Girl* vii. 102 It's a wonder you notice me, I told him. That's a lot of malaky, says he. **1930** *Variety* 29 Oct., The song is ended but the Malarkey lingers on. **1934** *Esquire* Dec. 49/3 Daughter of Mrs. Sally Alden, father unknown! What malarkey! All hooey, even protected by the official records of a friendly republic. **1938** *Down Beat* Mar. 5/4 We've got to say to the recording companies..'Cut out the Mullarkey and give us some down-home stuff!' **1945** J. STEINBECK *Cannery Row* xiii. 55 He knew God damn well the story was so much malarky. **1958** *Sunday Times* 20 Apr. 31/1, I will only give you the politician's malarky about imponderables and changing circumstances. **1960** G. M. WILSON *It rained that Friday* xi. 107 Somebody's passed the word round that the island's haunted. I told them it was a lot of malarkey. **1963** J. MITFORD *Amer. Way of Death* iii. 139 The malarkey that surrounds the usual kind of funeral. **1964** *Punch* 23 Dec. 964/3 Any mullarkey from ratting to potato picking. **1965** *Sunday Mail Mag.* (Brisbane) 15 Aug. 5/3 Here was a man who didn't give you the old malarky. **1971** [see *FLOPSY BUNNY]. **1973** *Observer* 25 Mar. 12/2 Tall stories..of rattlesnakes bringing up a nestful of baby robins,..or some such malarkey.

malathion (mælăþəi·ǫ̆n). [The substance is manufactured from diethyl *male*ate (an ester of MALEIC acid) and a *thio*-acid (see s.v. THIO-).

The name orig. proposed was *malathon* (see quot. 1953[2]). Later *malathion* was registered in the U.S. both as a generic (i.e. non-proprietary) name and as a trade-mark of the American Cyanamid Co.]

An organophosphorus insecticide which is relatively harmless to plants and animals; in commercial preparations it is a brownish liquid with a strong smell of garlic and is also used in the form of a powder.

1953 *Official Gaz.* (U.S. Patent Office) 14 Apr. 322/2 American Cyanamid Company... *Malathion* For Insecticide. **1953** *Substitution of Malathion for Malathon as a Coined (Generic) Name for the Insecticidal Chemical O,O-Dimethyl Dithiophosphate of Diethyl Mercaptosuccinate* (Interdepartmental Comm. Pest Control, Bureau Entomol. & Plant Quarantine, U.S. Dept. Agric.), On January 30, 1952 the Interdepartmental Committee on Pest Control approved the name 'malathon' as coined name for O,O-dimethyl dithiophosphate of diethyl mercaptosuccinate. Because of difficulty encountered in the trade-marking of the name selected at first the commercial sponsor, American Cyanamid Co., decided to change the name to 'malathion'. The American Chemical Society and the American Medical Association are agreeable to the change. Malathion has been registered with the Trade-Mark Division and released for general use. On March 27, 1953, the Interdepartmental Committee on Pest Control approved the name 'malathion' as a coined (generic) name for the chemical in question. **1955** *Sci. News Let.* 3 Sept. 157/1 The insecticides DDT, EPN, heptachlor and malathion have been tested in granular forms. **1960** *Farmer & Stockbreeder* 19 Jan. 119/3 However, as a cure [for red mite in woodwork], it is best to use a B.H.C. or malathion preparation. **1964** *Which?* Apr. 114/1 The organo-phosphorus compounds, such as dimethoate, malathion, menazon, are mainly poisonous to sucking insects, such as greenfly. **1968** M. PYKE *Food & Society* viii. 119 It is reckoned that whereas 0·5, 0·06, 9 and 1·2 micrograms of DDT, lindane, malathion and carbaryl are ingested for each kilogram of human body weight, the least amounts of these pesticides likely to be harmful are 10, 12, 14 and 20 micrograms respectively.

Malawi (mălā·wi), *a.* and *sb.* [Name of a Central African state, formerly Nyasaland.] **A.** *adj.* Of or pertaining to Malawi or its inhabitants. **B.** *sb.* A native or inhabitant of Malawi. Also **Mala·wian** *sb.* and *a.*

1960 *Economist* 15 Oct. 252/1 Dr Banda's Malawi Congress party. **1963** *Ibid.* 6 July 23/2 His [*sc.* Dr. Banda's] Malawians have lost from the absence of a Nyasa delegation. **1964** *Times* 6 July (Suppl.) 1/2 He [*sc.* Dr. Banda]..has invited the Prime Minister of Southern Rhodesia, Mr. Ian Smith, to the Malawi independence celebrations. **1964** *Observer* 12 July 13/2 The brand-new Malawi flag with a red rising sun. **1965** *Guardian* 4 Oct. 9/6 A brawl at a nightclub between a young British bank clerk and a Malawian. **1966** *Listener* 5 May 637/2 In Rhodesia..Malawis are regarded as the best employees. **1970** *Times* 26 Mar. (Malawi Suppl.) p. i/6 As for Rhodesia, it is inconceivable that the Malawians should adhere strictly to sanctions. *Ibid.* p. iv/4 At Fort Johnston we.. acquired the company of a Malawian student hitching a ride home to see his parents. **1971** *Rand Daily Mail* 4 Dec. 1/4 The tiny Malawi Defence Force. *Ibid.* 3/8 Terrorists might enter Malawi purely to embarrass the Malawian Government. **1972** *Whitaker's Almanack 1973* 756/2 In 1970 a 70-mile line was opened..linking the Malawi rail system with the Mozambique network. **1973** *Guardian* 17 Apr. 12/2 Dr. Banda..believed passionately that grammar was what the Malawians most needed.

malaxation. Add: **c.** A form of massage.

1887 D. MAGUIRE *Art of Massage* (ed. 4) 46 Malaxation is the same movement [as pétrissage], differing only on account of the flat of the hand being applied with more or less strength before bringing the fingers together to exercise the pétrissage. **1961** *Brit. Med. Dict.* 870/1 *Malaxation*, pétrissage, one of the movements carried out in massage, in which the muscles are grasped in the masseur's hands and rolled and pressed; kneading.

Malay, *sb.* and *a.* Add: **A.** *sb.* **1. b.** *spec.* in S. Afr. One of the Muslim community of Cape Town and adjoining districts (see quots. 1944 and 1972). In full, *Cape Malay*.

1785 tr. *Sparrman's Voyage to Cape of Good Hope* I. 12 The burial grounds of the Chinese and free Malays that live at the Cape. **1812** A. PLUMPTRE tr. *Lichtenstein's Trav. S. Afr.* I. I. ii. 28 This practice receives great encouragement from the natural inclination that the slaves, particularly the Malays, have to music. **1844** J. BACKHOUSE *Narr. Visit Mauritius & S. Afr.* v. 82 The religion of the False Prophet was introduced into the Colony by the importation of Malacca slaves, by the Dutch. Hence the terms Malay and Mahomedan became synonymous in the Colony. **1944** I. D. DU PLESSIS *Cape Malays* i. 1 Strictly speaking 'Malay' stands for that section of the local Muslim community in which the descendants of Malay slaves and political exiles are to be found. **1972** *Standard Encycl. S. Afr.* VII. 145/2 Coming from Java and the neighbouring Indonesian islands, the Cape Malays belong essentially to the Javanese and Balinese section of the Malay race.

B. *adj.* **c.** Of, pertaining to, or characteristic of the Cape Malays.

1881 *Cape Monthly Mag.* Mar. 192 A Malay hat. **1953** Du Plessis & Lückhoff *Malay Quarter* 9 A Malay wedding. **1974** *S. Afr. Panorama* Mar. 7 The oldest of its two gables, dated 1800, is..reputedly the work of a Malay craftsman.

Malayalam (malăyā·lăm). Also 9 **Malayalma, Malayalim.** [Native name; cf. next.] A Dravidian language, closely related to Tamil, spoken in southern India. Also *attrib.* or as *adj.*

1837 H. Harkness *Anc. & Mod. Alphabets Pop. Hindu Lang.* p. i, Under the head of Malayalma are also included the Characters of..Tuluva. **1839** F. Spring *(title)* Outlines of a grammar of the Malayalim language. **1864** A. J. Arbuthnot *(title)* Malayalam selections. **1902** [see *Dravidian A. *adj.*]. **1908** T. G. Tucker *Introd. Nat. Hist. Lang.* 136 *Malayālam*, occupying a comparatively small area of the west or Malabar coast south of Mangalore. **1911** *Encycl. Brit.* XVII. 466/1 *Malayalam*, a language of the Dravidian family, spoken on the west coast of southern India. **1960** *Universe* 14 Apr. 24/2 Malayalam, a vernacular language of Southern India, was used for the first time as the liturgical language in an ordination in the Syro-Malabar rite at Ernakulam. **1971** *Leader* (Durban) 7 May 8/4 He wrote in Malayalam, which is the mellifluous, if impossibly difficult language of Kerala... His directness and his Malayalam-accented English were always irresistible.

Malayali (malăyā·li). Also **Malayalee.** [Native name, f. Dravidian *mala* mountain + *āḷ* possess.] A member of a Malayalam-speaking people inhabiting the state of Kerala on the Malabar coast of southern India. Cf. *Malayalam. Also *attrib.*

1856 R. Caldwell *Compar. Gram. Dravidian Lang.* 491 The higher castes are styled 'Hindus', or else 'Tamilians', 'Malayâlis', &c., according to their language and nation. **1889** L. J. Frohnmeyer *Progressive Gram. Malayalam Lang.* p. xii, The Malayalees have not a few Folk Songs. *Ibid.* xvi. 133 The Malayali..prefers to divide in two or three activities, what Europeans would express by one Verb. **1928** *Chambers's Jrnl.* XVIII. 244/1 Chetwynd managed to hold the Malayalees together for another three days. **1961** P. Spear *India* vii. 91 The southern Dravidian people were articulated in four groups..the Tamils,..the Telugus or Andhras,..the Malayalis along the west coast in the modern state of Kerala; and the Kanaras. **1971** *Hindustan Times Weekly Rev.* (New Delhi) 4 Apr. p. iv/5 We celebrate both Malayali and Bengali festivals.

Malayan, *a.* and *sb.* Add: **B.** *sb.* **3.** During the existence of the Federation of Malaya (from 1948 until 1963), an inhabitant of Malaya (regardless of race or creed).

1954 V. Bartlett *Rep. from Malaya* ii. 23 A Malayan is anybody—be he Malay, Chinese, Tamil, Eurasian or European—whose home is in Malaya, whereas a Malay is a member of a large race of whom about 3,000,000 live in Malaya, and more than 70,000,000 in Java, Sumatra and the other islands of Indonesia. **1958** G. Mikes *East is East* 114 A *Malayan* is an inhabitant of Malaya, irrespective of race or creed. **1961** L. D. Stamp *Gloss. Geogr. Terms* 304/2 Since the independence of Malaya..Malayan has a political significance as a citizen of Malaya.

Malayanize (mălē̆·ănəiz), *v.* [f. Malayan *a.* and *sb.* + -ize.] *trans.* To make Malayan in character or composition. So **Mala:yaniza·tion.**

1955 *Times* 24 Aug. 5/5 With regard to Malayanization of the Civil Service, there were good men among Malayan members of the Civil Service. **1956** *Times* 22 Nov. 9/5 The Government [of Singapore] would begin to put its Malayanization scheme into effect next January. **1960** *Times* 25 Nov. 13/2 Singapore had better get ahead with 'malayanizing' its university. **1965** R. McKie *Company of Animals* i. 15 'Malayanization'—the replacement of Europeans in government services by local-born people. **1971** N. Barber *War of Running Dogs* iii. 46 Everything would change with independence and Malayanization. **1972** *Accountant* 5 Oct. 420/2 It was contended for the taxpayer that there was no evidence..that he had accepted any variation of the agreement because of the policy to Malayanize the staff.

Malayic (mălē̆·ik), *a.* *rare.* Also 8 **Malaic.** [See -ic.] = Malayan *a.*

1723 R. Millar *Hist. Propagation Christianity* II. viii. 478 Sermons..in the Malaic Tongue. **1890** D. G. Brinton *Races & Peoples* 230 The Malayic stock.

Malayo-. (Further examples.)

1876 *Encycl. Brit.* V. 288/1 Their [*sc.* the Macassars'] language..belongs to the Malayo-Javanese group. **1879** A. H. Keane in A. R. Wallace *Australasia* 607 Papûans proper in the centre; Malayo-Papûans in the Indian Archipelago. **1880** A. H. Sayce *Introd. Sci. of Lang.* II. viii. 188 The agglutinated adjuncts..may be almost wholly dispensed with, as in Malayo-Polynesian. **1887** A. Featherman *Social Hist. Races Mankind* II. i. 251 The Malayo-Melanesians are the most important branch of the Melanesian stock. **1896** A. H. Keane *Ethnol.* 285 The Negroid Malayo-Malagasy peoples of Madagascar. *Ibid.* 331 Semi-cultured and rude Malayo-African populations. *Ibid.* 333 The Philippine half-castes may be roughly classed as..Malayo-Indonesians, Malayo-Europeans, and Malayo Chinese. **1911** Webster, Malayo-Negrito. **1933** [see *Austric *a.*]. **1934** Priebsch & Collinson *German Lang.* i. ii. 35 A Creolized language, in this case a blend called Malayo-Portuguese, which was used by the whites in dealing with slaves.

Malaysian, *a.* Add: Of or pertaining to the Federation of Malaysia (formed in 1963 from the states of Malaya, Sabah, Sarawak, and (until 1965) Singapore).

1962 *Times* 9 Jan. 9/3 English is to remain as an 'international language' in the proposed Malaysian Federation. **1963** *Daily Tel.* 12 Sept. 21/7 The agreement covers the question of sovereignty for Singapore and arrangements as between the Singapore Government and the Malaysian Government for emergency security measures. **1963** *Guardian* 16 Sept. 9/4 The Malaysian Government is fully aware that recognition is not a right but a privilege. **1971** *Ibid.* 22 Feb. 3/1 About ninety bills face the Malaysian Parliament when it re-opens tomorrow after 21 months. **1973** J. M. White *Garden Game* 97 A crumpled fistful of Malaysian money.

B. *sb.* A native or inhabitant of the Malay archipelago (quot. 1625) or of Malaysia.

1625 Purchas *Pilgrimes* I. iii. xiv. 321, I cannot imagine what the Hollanders meane to suffer these Maleysians, Chinesians, and Moores of those countries. **1955** *Times* 15 June 9/6 The population of the Malay States comprises roughly 50 per cent. Malaysians, 40 per cent. Chinese, 10 per cent. others. **1965** *Guardian* 24 July 8/6 His efforts to overrun the Malaysians in Borneo. **1970** *Daily Tel.* 16 June 2/8 *(heading)* Malaysian jailed for blackmail. **1974** 'G. Black' *Golden Cockatrice* v. 93 You are as good a Malaysian as I am a Taiwanese.

malaysianite (mălē̆·ziănəit). *Geol.* [f. Malaysian *a.* + -ite[1].] Any tektite from the tektite field of the Malay peninsula.

1940 *Pop. Astron.* XLVIII. 45 Malaysianites tend to show irregular and heavily etched surfaces. **1964** *New Scientist* 16 Jan. 160/2 The widespread Australasian strewn field..consisting of the australites, the javanites, the malaysianites, billitonites and philippinites.

maldesce·nded, *a.* *Med.* [f. Mal- + Descended *ppl. a.*] Of a testis: not having descended all the way into the scrotum from the abdominal cavity during development of the fœtus, or having descended ectopically.

1908 *Ann. Surg.* XLVIII. 321 *(heading)* Treatment of the undescended or maldescended testis. **1933** *Post-Graduate Med. Jrnl.* IX. 248 There is a widespread.. belief that if a young boy with a mal-descended testis is left alone the organ will drop..at puberty. **1936** H. Bailey *Dis. Testicle* ii. 11 A maldescended testis is one which cannot be made to touch the bottom of the scrotum. **1962** *Lancet* 19 May 1059/1 A few weeks ago we attempted to evaluate the dangers of malignancy arising in undescended and maldescended testes.

maldesce·nt. *Med.* [f. Mal- + Descent.] The state (of a testis) of being maldescended; incomplete or ectopic descent.

1908 *Ann. Surg.* XLVIII. 324 The different types of maldescent of the testis. **1948** L. Martin *Clin. Endocrinol.* viii. 159 In cryptorchidism the testes remain in the abdomen, in maldescent they lie in the inguinal canals or unduly high in the scrotum. **1954** G. I. M. Swyer *Reproduction & Sex* vi. 65 Sometimes maldescent is present on one side only, the testicle on the other side being situated in the normal position. **1964** *Arch. Dis. Childhood* XXIX. 607/1 Any testis not in the scrotum, that is, 4 cm. or less from the pubic crest in infants and boys is undescended. If it is more than this distance but not as low as it should be it is incompletely descended. The terms mal-descent and imperfect descent have no useful meaning.

maldistribution (mæ:ldistribiū·ʃən). [f. Mal- + Distribution.] Faulty distribution. Hence **ma:ldistri·buted** *ppl. a.*

1895 *U.S. Dept. Agric. Farmers' Bulletin* xxxiii. 22 This ruinous state of affairs is not attributable to over-production, but to maldistribution. **1928** *Britain's Industr. Future* (Liberal Industr. Inquiry) iii. xix. 243 We agree with the Socialists in thinking that a distribution so uneven as is at present found is maldistribution. **1931** *Times Trade & Engin. Suppl.* 24 Jan. 431/2 We are suffering from maldistribution of gold. **1933** *Planning* 6 June 1 Unemployment has grown..to a world-wide problem of maldistributed leisure. **1935** *Discovery* Jan. 14/1 Poverty persists and populations become maldistributed. **1957** *Economist* 23 Nov. 694/2 The chronic maldistribution of wealth. **1969** *Listener* 6 Mar. 318/1 The story which began in the wilderness ends..in automated (if maldistributed) affluence. **1971** *Daily Tel.* 3 July 12 Summer is the time when maldistribution of business at the start of the session catches up with the Lords.

Maldivian (mǫldi·viăn), *sb.* and *a.* Also 9 **Maldivan.** **A.** *sb.* A native or inhabitant of the Maldive Islands in the Indian Ocean; their language. **B.** *adj.* Of or pertaining to the Maldive Islands or their inhabitants.

1836 *Trans. Bombay Geogr. Soc.* I. 77 The Maldivans have a written, as well as an unwritten law. **1841** *Jrnl. R. Asiatic Soc.* VI. 42 *(title)* Vocabulary of the Maldivian language. **1959** *Times* 19 Mar. 6/3 He was able to learn something of the Maldivian language. **1970** *Trans. Philol. Soc.* 148 The Maldivian numerals are lexically related to the Indic numeral systems. **1972** *Guardian* 15 Mar. 13/5 The Maldivians are hopefully extending the runway. **1972** *Language* XLVIII. 464 The only language closely related to Sinhalese is Maldivian, spoken in the Maldive Islands and on the island of Minicoy, which is part of India.

‖ **mal du siècle** (mal dü syękl'). [Fr.] World-weariness, weariness of life, deep melancholy because of the condition of the world.

In French with specific reference to the early 19th-c. Romantic poets.

1926 A. Huxley *Essays New & Old* 38 The *mal du siècle* was an inevitable evil. **1932** *Times Lit. Suppl.* 16 June 439/1 We have the sentimental and practical romanticism, the *mal du siècle*. **1957** G. Smith *Friends* ii. 36 A bijou house in Chelsea, premature obesity, *mal du siècle* and incipient gout. **1963** R. Wellek in N. Frye *Romanticism Reconsidered* 109 Little has been accomplished by calling familiar states of mind—*Weltschmerz, mal du siècle*, pessimism—'negative' romanticism.

male, *a.* and *sb.*[2] Add: **A.** *adj.* **1. e.** Also used, not jocularly, in referring to professions that are usually considered to be predominantly female, as *male midwife, model, nurse, prostitute.*

1878 Trollope *John Caldigate* (1879) II. iv. 45 He took the child very gently... He had already assumed for himself the character of being a good male nurse. **1915** Mrs. Belloc Lowndes *Diary* 12 Mar. (1971) 58 It is very difficult to get the right type of man to be a male nurse. **1948** A. Kinsey et al. *Sexual Behavior in Human Male* vi. 216 Some male prostitutes ejaculate five, six, or more times per day with regularity over long periods of years. **1961** S. Baker *Visual Persuasion* ii. 47/2 Male model agencies and actors' guilds always have a few personalities on hand. **1972** 'W. Haggard' *Protectors* vi. 71 The man in the chair..was kept alive by two male nurses. **1974** *Mother & Baby* Feb. 44 *(heading)* Would you like a male midwife? **1974** H. Waugh *Parrish for Defence* (1975) xix. 321 He is presently serving as a male prostitute for other males. **1975** *Times* 11 Mar. 4/8 It would be wrong to rule out male midwives as a matter of principle. **1975** 'G. Black' *Big Wind* vii. 114 He looked like a male model in one of those ads for expensive men's knitwear.

2. a. male-sterile *a.*, (of a hermaphrodite plant) incapable of producing fertile pollen; so **male-sterility.**

1921 *Jrnl. Genetics* XI. 269 *(heading)* Male-sterility in flax, subject to two types of segregation. *Ibid.* 271 In the breeding work it was not thought necessary to emasculate the male-sterile flowers. **1946** *Nature* 21 Sept. 422/2 Further tabulation of male-sterility genes in varieties of the onion is given. **1959** *New Biol.* XXVIII. 75 Certain willow-herb crosses which produce male-sterile progeny.

B. *sb.* **4.** Comb. *male climacteric, menopause, pill, supremacist* (also *attrib.*), *supremacy*; *male-determining, -dominated* adjs.; **male chauvinism,** an attitude attributed to men of excessive loyalty to members of the male sex and of prejudice against women; hence **male chauvinist,** one who adopts this attitude; also *attrib.*, esp. in phr. *male chauvinist pig*; **male impersonator,** a female who impersonates a male on the stage.

1970 *Time* 17 Aug. 23 European women have accepted their lot much more readily than their American counterparts. Recently, however, growing numbers..have launched their attack on male chauvinism. **1973** O. Lancaster *Littlehampton Bequest* 84 Their marriage has always been a completely unselfish relationship, both taking an active part in the struggle against Imperialism, Neo-Colonialism and Male Chauvinism. **1970** *New Yorker* 5 Sept. 27/1 Hello, you male-chauvinist racist pig. *Ibid.*, Repent Male Chauvinists. **1972** *Southerly* XXXII. 75 The male chauvinist aspects of mateship have come in for considerable discussion since the spread of women's liberation critiques. **1972** *Punch* 1 Mar. 289/1, I know, I know; me male chauvinist pig, you Jane. But the exercise has finally woken me up to ask—why should there be separate magazines for men and women at all? **1974** J. Heller *Something Happened* 333, I enjoy fucking my wife. She lets me do it any way I want. No Women's Liberation for her. Lots of male chauvinist pig. **1966** G. B. Mair *Kisses from Satan* vii. 78 I've got a male climacteric and I don't like it. **1972** *Daily Colonist* (Victoria, B.C.) 8 Feb. 2/1 Men may experience a certain slackening in sexual interest that may be related to what medical literature calls 'male climacteric' (a retrogression of the sex glands). **1931, 1957** Male-determining [see *female B. *sb.* 3]. **1958** W. J. H. Sprott *Human Groups* 65 The home..is in certain important respects male-dominated. **1964** W. McCord in I. L. Horowitz *New Sociol.* xxv. 434 The city is a male-dominated area (more men enter the city seeking jobs than women). **1973** I. Singer *Goals of Human Sexuality* i. 33 She submits to the relationship as a way of conforming to the demands of a male-dominated society. **1895** Stuart & Park *Variety Stage* 222 Serio-comics, sisters, dancers, male impersonators, and ballad and character vocalists. **1930** *Bulletin* 14 May 5 That popular male impersonator and pantomime principal boy, Miss Nora Delany. **1972** *Times* 29 Sept. 16/8 To the connoisseurs of the music hall there have been only two great male impersonators, one of whom was Vesta Tilley, the other Hetty King. **1949** Ernst & Loth *Sexual Behaviour & Kinsey Report* viii. 93 Another reason which has sometimes been given is that many men reach in middle age a climacteric which is dubbed a male menopause. **1963** E. Lanham *Monkey on Chain* xii. 195 You think dirty, you act dirty—like a dirty old man. What is it? Male menopause? **1971** J. Wainwright *Last Buccaneer* ii. 187 Middle-aged men get odd ideas. It's a sort of male menopause—a change of life. **1966** *New Statesman* 27 May 767/1 Techniques like the 'male pill', tying of the spermatic cords..are in use or under investigation. **1971** *Black Scholar* Dec. 7/2 Excepting the woman's role as caretaker of the household, male supremacist structures could not become deeply embedded in the internal workings of the slave system. **1973** J. Jones *Touch of Danger* xxviii. 167 You just don't want to understand Jane... She's a threat to all you male supremacists. **1908** G. K. Chesterton *Man who was Thursday* i. 12 Most of the women were of the kind vaguely called emancipated, and professed some protest against male supremacy.

Male, var. *MALER *sb.* and *a.*

malease. Restrict † *Obs.* to sense 2 and add later examples of sense 1.

1923 *S.P.E. Tract* XIII. 35 All French loan-words that are sufficiently naturalized to be considered as English should be treated as English... We should be glad if London editors would..print as follows:..*malease* for *malaise.* **1929** R. BRIDGES *Testament of Beauty* I. 231 [St.] Francis climbed—rather his gentle soul had learn'd From taste of vanity and by malease of the flesh. **1930** *Times Lit. Suppl.* 4 Dec. 1022/2 Yet her achievement was muted by excess of ardour and by a subtle, fundamental malease. **1938** L. P. SMITH *Unforgotten Yrs.* vi. 165 My tutor gave it unusual praise, in which praise I was conscious of the mingling of a curious malease.

maleate (mǣlĭ·ēit). *Chem.* [f. MALE(IC *a.* + -ATE[4].] A salt or ester, or the anion, of maleic acid.

1853 H. WATTS tr. *Gmelin's Hand-bk. Chem.* VIII. 153 The Salts of Maleic acid, the Maleates, are all soluble in water. **1925** *Jrnl. Amer. Chem. Soc.* XLVII. 1073 First, association occurs between permanganate ion or molecule with maleate or fumarate ion. **1970** R. W. MCGILVERY *Biochem.* xi. 220 Fumarate is a *trans* compound (maleate is the corresponding *cis* isomer), and hydrates to yield the L-enantiomorph.

maledictive (mælĭdi·ktiv), *a.* [f. L. *maledict-* (see MALEDICTION) + -IVE.] Characterized by cursing or curses; uttering maledictions.

1865 S. FERGUSON *Lays of Western Gael* 54 Daily in their mystic ring They turn'd the maledictive stones. **1905** K. MEYER *Cáin Adamnáin* p. vii, A poem on the maledictive psalms selected by Adamnan. **1922** JOYCE *Ulysses* 326 Seats of learning and maledictive stones.

maleesh (mā·lī∫), *int.* Also **ma(a)lesh.** [ad. colloq. Eastern Arab. *mā 'ale-š* no matter.] No matter! never mind! Also as *sb.*, indifference, slackness.

1913 'S. ROHMER' *Mystery of Dr Fu-Manchu* iv. 44 '*Ma 'alesh!*' came her soft whisper; 'but I am afraid to trust you—yet.' **1919** W. H. DOWNING *Digger Dial.* 33 *Maleesh*, it doesn't matter. **1925** FRASER & GIBBONS *Soldier & Sailor Words* 151 *Maleesh*: Never mind. It doesn't matter. Used colloquially on Eastern Fronts. **1946** *Happy Landings* (Air Ministry) July 12/1 The manpower problem will solve itself in time, but there is no excuse for the *maleesh* attitude. **1947** *Landfall* I. 162 Not so much of the *ma lesh!* **1958** L. DURRELL *Mountolive* xvi. 315 *Ma-a-lesh!* Let it be forgiven! Nothing avails our grief! **1971** *Guardian* 22 June 3/3 The general air of 'malesh', Arabic for 'never mind', or 'forget it', continues to hang over the police force.

maleic, *a.* Add: Also † **malæic. maleic anhydride**, the anhydride, $C_4H_2O_3$, of maleic acid which is a crystalline compound that forms addition compounds with substances containing conjugated carbon–carbon double bonds; *maleic* (*anhydride*) *value*, a measure of the number of conjugated double bonds in a substance (e.g. an oil) obtained by reaction with maleic anhydride.

1857 W. A. MILLER *Elem. Chem.* III. v. 335 Hydrated malæic acid when maintained in a state of fusion at 300°, is converted into a crystalline mass of fumaric acid. If distilled by a temperature suddenly elevated to 460°, malæic anhydride is formed. **1898** *Jrnl. Chem. Soc.* LXXIV. I. 177 Maleinoid chlorobromosuccinic acid is prepared by saturating with chlorine a solution of bromine in chloroform, adding maleic anhydride, again passing chlorine into the liquid, which is then exposed to bright sunlight. **1936** ELLIS & JONES in *Analyst* LXI. 814 The calculation of the 'maleic anhydride value' (M.A.V.) or, more shortly, 'maleic value' is given... At the moment the term 'maleic value' is suggested for this figure in preference to 'diene value'. **1944** H. G. KIRSCHENBAUER *Fats & Oils* v. 46 The theoretical Maleic Anhydride Value of trielaeostearin is 87·2. **1950** K. A. WILLIAMS *Oils, Fats & Fatty Foods* (ed. 3) iii. 116 The maleic anhydride value is given by the expression: 12·692 × ml. of alkali used ÷ weight of sample taken in grams. **1964** N. G. CLARK *Mod. Org. Chem.* xix. 389 A purely aliphatic compound, maleic anhydride, an intermediate for alkyd resins..is obtained from benzene by passing its vapour, mixed with air, over a vanadium pentoxide catalyst at 450°. **1972** *Materials & Technol.* IV. xiii. 465 The peculiar structure of maleic anhydride, in which a C=C double bond is in conjugation with a C=O double bond, makes it the most important and widely used dienoph[i]lic component in the Diels–Alder reaction with 1,3-dienes to produce non-aromatic six-membered ring compounds.

maleinoid, obs. var. *MALENOID *a.*

‖ **mal élevé** (mal eləve), *adj. phr.* Also fem. **mal élevée.** [Fr., lit. 'badly brought up'.] Of a person: bad-mannered, ill-bred. Of an object or situation: lacking in refinement.

1878 H. JAMES *Europeans* II. v. 198 Even that *mal-élevée* little girl..makes him do what she wishes. **1924** A. D. SEDGWICK *Little French Girl* III. v. 263 It was odd.. but not *mal élevé.* **1949** E. BOWEN *Encounters* p. xi, If I was *mal élevée*..so were my betters. **1964** A. WILSON *Late Call* 24 She echoed her mother's horror at all things *mal élevées.* **1974** E. AMBLER *Dr. Frigo* I. 34 The wives of certain French officials have expressed disapproval [of her]. *Mal elevée* is their verdict.

malemut(e, varr. *MALAMUTE.

maleness. a. Delete † (*obs.*) and add later examples; also = virility.

1925 *New Yorker* 27 June 17/2 Her strongest reason was the fascination of St. Mawr's terrific 'maleness'. **1929** D. H. LAWRENCE *Pansies* 126 So it is with Englishmen. They are all double roses And their true maleness is gone. **1937** *Discovery* Oct. 315/1 His [*sc.* the stag's] maleness reigns supreme. **1975** A. FRASER *Whistler's Lane* xi. 173 His jacket smelt of horses and tobacco and general maleness.

malenoid (mæ·lĕnoid), *a. Chem.* Formerly also **malei·noid.** [f. MALEIN(IC *a.* + -OID.] Resembling maleic acid in having a *cis* configuration in geometrical isomerism.

1895 [see *FUMAROID *a.*]. **1898** [see *MALEIC *a.*]. **1907** [see *CIS- 3]. **1938** [see *FUMAROID *a.*]. **1964** *Internat. Encycl. Chem. Sci.* 709/2 *Malenoid form*, the *cis* form of geometrical isomerism.

Maler (mā·ləɹ), *sb.* and *a.* Also **Mal, Male, Moler, Muler.** [Native word = 'hillmen', ult. f. Dravidian *mala* mountain.] **A.** *sb.* **a.** A Dravidian people living in the Rajmahal hills of northern India; a member of this people. **b.** The language spoken by this people (also called *MALTO, *RAJMAHALI). **B.** *adj.* Of or pertaining to the Maler people or their language.

1811 F. BUCHANAN *Jrnl. Survey Bhagalpur* (1930) 133 The Not Pahariyas..eat and intermarry with the Moler... Many of the men speak the Moler language. *Ibid.* 138 The interpreter tribe is here called Desi Moler... Many of them speak the Muler language, and they eat and can intermarry with the Muler of the hills. **1853** J. R. LOGAN in *Jrnl. Indian Archipelago* VII. 50, I infer that the Male and Kol resemble the coarser Binua tribes of the Malay Peninsula more than the Burmans. **1872** E. T. DALTON *Descriptive Ethnol. Bengal* viii. 264 The Málers were the first of the aboriginal tribes of Bengal that were prominently noticed by the officers of the East India Company. **1873** E. BALFOUR *Cycl. India* III. s.v. *Male*, The Male or Rajmahali are described as mostly very low in stature, but stout and well proportioned. **1885** G. C. WHITWORTH *Anglo-Indian Dict.* 262/1 *Rájmaháli*, the name of a tribe called also Pahári. Also the name of their language, which is Dravidian. These people call themselves Maler. **1892** H. H. RISLEY *Tribes & Castes Bengal: Ethnogr. Gloss.* II. 54 In 1782..one of the archers murdered a Málé woman, and in order to punish this..Mr. Cleveland proposed the formation of a district tribunal. **1906** G. A. GRIERSON *Ling. Survey India* IV. 446 In former days the Maler made frequent raids on the plains. **1915** *Encycl. Relig. & Ethics* VIII. 344/2 *Māl, Mālē, Māl Pahāriā*, a non-Aryan tribe, containing various groups... The inter-relations of the North and South groups have not been clearly ascertained, but they seem to be, to a large extent, pure Dravidians, and those in the Rājmahāl Hills in Bengal are closely allied to the Orāons. **1930** C. E. A. W. OLDHAM in F. Buchanan *Jrnl. Survey Bhagalpur* 138 Here we find Bhuiyās still speaking the Maler or Malto language. **1938** S. S. SARKAR *Mālérs of Rajmahal Hills* i. 8 The dress of the womenfolk of the Mālérs and the Orāons differs greatly from one another. *Ibid.* 15 The Mālér country is bounded by the Ganges in the north. **1963** L. P. VIDYARTHI *Maler* i. 11 To a Maler, the pleasure or wrath of spirits and supernatural powers controls the nature of happenings in the Maler family, village,..field or..forests.

‖ **malerisch** (mā·ləri∫), *a.* [G., 'painterly', f. *maler* painter.] After H. Wölfflin's use (1915 *Kunstgeschichtliche Grundbegriffe*): of or pertaining to a manner of painting characterized more by the merging of colours than by the more formal linear style; painterly.

1933 *Burlington Mag.* Dec. 269/2 Ruskin somewhere draws a distinction between drawing with a brush and painting with a brush—a distinction which in our time has been further elaborated by Heinrich Wölfflin. In Wölfflin's sense, the English water-colourists are always linear, and never malerisch. **1937** *Ibid.* Oct. 168/1 The most splendid examples of Raphael's draughtsmanship... They are '*malerisch*'. **1955** *Times* 2 Aug. 10/2 This is..a resuscitation of the great malerisch tradition, which was rejected by those who thought they were following Cézanne. **1961** *Times* 1 Mar. 15/3 The *malerisch* flow and swirl of the paint itself.

malfunction (mælfʌ·ŋk∫ən), *sb.* [f. MAL- + FUNCTION *sb.* 3.] Faulty functioning. So **malfu·nction** *v. intr.*; **malfu·nctioning** *vbl. sb.* and *ppl. a.*

1928 E. BAGBY *Psychol. of Personality* xi. 154 Conditions of this sort are usually found to be *symptoms* of a malfunctioning of fundamental bodily processes. **1941** JOHNSON & HAVEN *Automatic Arms* 128 The slide on an automatic pistol may fail to remain open after the last shot, due to a malfunction of the catch... The use of the term 'malfunction' conveys nothing unless we know *what malfunctioned.* **1957** *New Scientist* 9 May 38/2 As an ophthalmic optician I was entertained by 'Geminus' (25 April) on his visits to his optician and his own experiments at correcting the malfunctions of his extra-ocular muscles. **1957** *New Biol.* XXII. 83 They [*sc.* psychosomatic disorders] come to the attention of patient and physician through some malfunctioning of an organ. **1958** *Times* 14 Mar. 10/1 Through 'mechanical malfunctioning', a B-47 bomber aircraft dropped what is described as 'an unarmed nuclear device'. *Ibid.* 17 Oct. 15/2 Eyes whose tear-ducts were malfunctioning because of the absence of gravity. **1961** *New Scientist* 7 Dec. 617/1 Some tiny valves in the spaceship's plumbing system failed to function properly... This malfunction has been brushed off in the newspapers. **1966** T. PYNCHON *Crying of Lot 49* i. 14 A dented, malfunctioning version of himself. **1972** *Daily Tel.* 22 Jan. 17/2 An investigation was being made to discover why the warm-air heating system at the house ..had malfunctioned. *Ibid.*, Recommendations would be made to the house builders when the cause of the malfunction had been discovered. **1973** *Sci. Amer.* Oct. 69/3 An instrumental malfunction at the crucial time can spoil the results of months of preparation.

malgas, var. *MALAGAS.

‖ **malgré.** Add: Freq. followed by a pronoun, as **malgré lui** (lüi), in spite of himself or herself; also **malgré elle, eux, moi,** etc., in spite of herself, themselves, myself, etc. Also **malgré tout**, despite everything.

1830 C. C. F. GREVILLE *Mem.* (1874) II. xi. 38 This was my first dinner at Dudley's, brought about *malgré lui* by Lady Glengall. **1843** THACKERAY *Confessions of G. Fitz-Boodle: Mr. & Mrs. Berry* in *Fraser's Mag.* Mar. 359/2 We obliged the Frenchman to drink *malgré lui.* **1852** GEO. ELIOT *Let.* 24–25 July (1954) II. 50, I congratulate you on your ability to be cheerful *malgré tout.* **1883** G. BLOOMFIELD *Reminisc.* II. xiii. 45 They say that, *malgré eux*, they cannot yield. **1904** WODEHOUSE *Gold Bat* xiii. 142 He could imagine their feelings when the prodigal strolled into their midst—an old Wrykinian *malgré lui.* **1929** A. HUXLEY *Holy Face* 26 That too, too merry laughter of clergymen who want to prove that, *malgré tout*, they can be good fellows. **1932** *Mind* XLI. 24 He [*sc.* Callicles] stands revealed as a moralist *malgré lui.* **1933** *Times Lit. Suppl.* 26 Jan. 56/2 The Bulpington as a warrior *malgré lui*, whose conduct in action might..have brought him to the execution squad. **1943** WYNDHAM LEWIS *Let.* 15 Aug. (1963) 363 As you know I am here malgré moi; but I attempt to put to some serious use my prolonged immersion in this N. American civilisation. **1950** A. HUXLEY *Let.* 11 Aug. (1969) 629 One likes him, *malgré tout.* **1963** *Economist* 28 Dec. 1318/1 These central bankers..have created, almost *malgré eux*, a code of practice. **1970** *Guardian* 11 Dec. 10/6 The weight of the acting fell mostly on Anna Cropper as the fertility goddess *malgré elle.*

mali, var. MALLEE[1].

1908 C. SORABJI *Between Twilights* xii. 150 While my *Mali* and I did tidyings in the Garden, I spoke to him gently about the plant. **1934** 'G. ORWELL' *Burmese Days* ii. 20 A nearly naked mali, watering-can in hand. **1971** *Hindustan Times Weekly* (New Delhi) 4 Apr. 10/7 The groundsmen and malis were being paid from the University Sports Fund.

Mali (mā·li), *a.* and *sb.* Also **Melle, Melli. A.** *adj.* Of or pertaining to Mali, an ancient empire (of the 13th and 14th centuries) and a modern republic (founded in 1960) in west Africa. **B.** *sb.* A native or inhabitant of Mali. So **Ma·lian** *a.* and *sb.*

1906 H. H. JOHNSTON *Liberia* II. xxvii. 896 The Melli.. empire..arose and flourished in Nigeria before the foundation of Timbuktu. **1911** *Encycl. Brit.* XVII. 565/1 It is not known by whom the Melle (Mali) state was founded... The first king whose name is preserved was Baramindana, believed to have reigned from 1213 to 1235. **1960** *Times* 28 Mar. 6/1 The Mali folklore is less unfamiliar to Parisians than that of its sister republic. **1960** *Daily Tel.* 24 Aug. 1/1 The Mali force..was due to be withdrawn from the Congo. *Ibid.*, Irish troops of the U.N. were to have taken over from the Malis. **1960** *Economist* 31 Dec. 1367/2 The Malians themselves (or Soudanese, as they used to call themselves) have only lately emerged from black Africa's first working experiment of a sovereign federation. **1967** S. KNIGHT *Window on Shanghai* xv. 65, I especially like the beautifully robed Malians... They are all members of the Malian government. **1970** P. OLIVER *Savannah Syncopators* 106 Mali lutes, Senegal *kora.* **1973** *Times* 15 Oct. 8/8 Police today charged a 31-year-old Malian with illegal entry into Italy after the deaths yesterday of three young Africans believed to have been involved in illegal traffic of African labourers to Europe. **1974** *Black World* Feb. 56 West African elements, in particular the Malians, were installed in America before the arrival of the Europeans.

Malibu, malibu (mæ·libū). Chiefly *Austral.* and *N.Z.* [The name of *Malibu* Beach in California.] In full, *Malibu board.* A short lightweight surf-board.

1962 *Austral. Women's Weekly* Suppl. 24 Oct. 3/3 *Malibu*, type of surfboard made from foam, balsa, or fibreglass and under 10 ft. long. **1965** *N.Z. Listener* 17 Dec. 4/4 Australia had its first look at the Malibu board when film star Peter Lawford took one 'down under' in 1954. **1969** *Times* 25 July 5/2 Worried by the number of thefts of malibu boards, police have issued leaflets in the surfers' own language. **1970** *N.Z. News* 8 Apr. 16/3 A. Griffin won both the ski and malibu board races.

malic, *a.* Add: Applied to enzymes whose substrate is malic acid, as *malic dehydrogenase*; *malic enzyme* (see quot. 1951).

1937 H. TAUBER *Enzyme Chem.* vii. 170 Malic dehydrogenase may be prepared by washing frog or ox muscle with *M*/15 phosphate buffer. **1948** *Jrnl. Biol. Chem.* CLXXIV. 997 There might be a mechanism for fixation of CO_2 by pyruvate other than that involving the 'malic' enzyme. **1951** *Physiol. Rev.* XXXI. 86 Enzymes catalyzing the reversible oxidative decarboxylation of *l*-malic acid are widely distributed. These enzymes are distinct from malic dehydrogenase, which catalyzes the reversible oxidation of *l*-malic acid, and are referred to as 'malic' enzymes. The majority of the known malic enzymes func-

tion specifically with TPN as coenzyme. **1972** *Biochem. Genetics* VII. 303 Polymorphic variation of the human mitochondrial malic enzyme was detected in Caucasians and Negroes.

malihini (mālihī·ni). [Hawaiian *malihini* stranger.] In Hawaii, a stranger, a newcomer; a beginner, a novice.

1914 *Outing* LXIV. 26/1 A couple of canoes are launching..where the neophytes, the 'malihini', are learning their first lessons in riding the rollers. **1966** *Surfer* VII. 39 Hawkshaw rode tandem with two malihinis (beginners) on his shoulders. **1967** J. SEVERSON *Great Surfing* Gloss., *Malihini*, a newcomer to the Hawaiian Islands. Newcomers to the sport of surfing are also referred to as malihinis.

Malines (mălī·n). [The name of a town (also called MECHLIN) in Belgium.] **1.** In full *Malines lace* = Mechlin lace. In full *Malines* (also *Maline*) *net*, a net made for millinery or veils.

1833 CARLYLE *Sart. Res.* I. iv. in *Fraser's Mag.* Nov. 590/2 To Teufelsdröckh the highest Duchess is respectable ..but nowise for her pearl bracelets, and Malines laces. **1842** THACKERAY *Fitz-Boodle's Confessions* in *Fraser's Mag.* June 713/1, I thought she would not let the evening pass without talking of her Malines lace. **1850** *Harper's Mag.* Aug. 431/2 Another pattern is..embroidered and trimmed with *malines*. **1897** *Sears, Roebuck Catal.* 318/1 A 27 inch Maline net veiling..in black, brown, cream or navy blue. **1909** *Daily Chron.* 4 Mar. 4/5 Lady Anne Lambton was the wearer of Malines net, the skirt panelled with lace. **1911** J. MASEFIELD *Jim Davis* iii. 30 It contained a dozen yards of very beautiful Malines lace. **1912** *Queen* 13 Apr. 613/1 This coat..had long sleeves slit up at the wrist, and edged with white net bordered with Malines. **1964** MRS. L. B. JOHNSON *White House Diary* 12 Mar. (1970) 89, I dressed early this morning, in solid black, with my mantilla draped over my maline hat, and set out..for the Requiem Mass for King Paul.

2. A Belgian breed of the domestic fowl. Also *attrib.*

1906 E. BROWN *Races Domestic Poultry* viii. 117/1 The birds which are known as *poulets* and *poulardes de Bruxelles* are entirely Malines. **1910** *Encycl. Poultry* II. 295 The Malines fowl is of the Asiatic type, and is large in size... There are two varieties—the Coucou and the white. **1938** T. NEWMAN *Princ. & Pract. Poultry Husbandry* i. 23 The Maline..was the result of a cross between the Langshan and Campine, and the Antwerp Brahma.

Malinke (măli·ŋke). The name of a people of western Africa and their language. Also *attrib.* or as *adj.* Cf. *MANDINKA *sb.* and *a.*

1883 *Encycl. Brit.* XV. 475/2 *Mandingoes*, otherwise known as *Wangawara, Malinkes*, or *Wakore*..are one of the most widely distributed and important peoples of Western Africa to the north of the equator. **1911** F. W. H. MIGEOD *Lang. W. Afr.* I. i. 33 Among the tribes whose languages furnish evidence of the extent of Mandingo influence are the Malinke, Bambara, Susu, [etc.]. *Ibid.* viii. 202 Malinke, Susu, and Soninke take suffixes to the verb. **1913** *Ibid.* II. xxi. 332 The Malinke held in the past a less leading position than many other branches of the Mandingos. **1950** D. JONES *Phoneme* xxviii. 206 Variphones consisting of r-like and l-like sounds would also appear to occur in some languages of Africa, for instance, in Bambara and Malinke. **1970** P. OLIVER *Savannah Syncopators* 106 Lobi and Malinke xylophones. *Ibid.* 112 *Malinke*, extensively distributed tribe occupying large areas of Senegal, Guinea and western Ivory Coast. **1970** *Western Folklore* XXIX. 241 Among the Kissi and Malinké of Liberia..*banga* has the specialized meaning of a children's instrument of several strings.

Malinois (malinwa·). [Fr., f. *Malinois* of or from Malines in Belgium.] A wire-haired variety of the Belgian Sheepdog.

1947 C. L. B. HUBBARD *Working Dogs of World* 104 The Malinois forms one of the three main groups of Belgian Sheepdogs... The breed takes its name from the district of Malines, where it probably originated. **1948** B. VESEY-FITZGERALD *Bk. Dog* 564 The Malinois represents the wire-haired Belgian Sheepdog. **1971** F. HAMILTON *World Encycl. Dogs* 56 The Malinois is short-haired,.. generally fawn in colour, with dark tips to the hairs on back and sides, giving a 'blackened' or shaded effect, and with a black mask.

Malinowskian (mæːlinǫ·fˌskiăn), *a.* [f. the name of Bronislaw Kasper *Malinowski* (1884–1942), Polish-born anthropologist + -AN.] Of, pertaining to, or characteristic of Malinowski and his works.

1954 *Amer. Anthropologist* Oct. 915 A fascinating personality—a Malinowskian anthropologist and a classical Confucian scholar rolled into one. **1955** HOMANS & SCHNEIDER *Marriage, Authority & Final Causes* 15 We may also call it Malinowskian functionalism. **1956** L. A. FALLERS *Bantu Bureaucracy* 129 It is rather in the nature of a 'mythical charter', in the Malinowskian sense. **1960** *Guardian* 19 Feb. 6/2 Malinowskian methods of field investigation. **1968** *Listener* 9 May 614/3 Interminable guest-shows communicated nothing (though even that laughing, wisecracking phatic stuff has its Malinowskian place).

mal-inse·rtion. *Anat.* [f. MAL- + INSERTION.] Abnormal insertion (INSERTION 3).

1904 E. H. FENWICK *Handbk. Clin. Electr.-Light Cystoscopy* xxi. 439 Some form of ureteric obstruction—either an acute bend of the ureter, due to adhesion or mal-insertion in movable kidney,..or a stone impacted low down in the ureter. **1964** S. DUKE-ELDER *Parsons' Dis. Eye* (ed. 14) xxix. 460 It occurs chiefly in cases of congenital origin—probably mal-insertion of the muscles—but has been met with after interference with the pulley of the superior oblique in frontal sinus operations.

Malkite, var. MELCHITE.

1909 A. S. LEWIS *Codex Climaci Rescriptus* p. xiii, As this version was adopted by the Malkite Church, it cannot be older than the Council of Chalcedon (A.D. 451).

mall[1]. Add: **4.** Now usu. pronounced (mæl). **b.** (Further examples.) Also, a shopping-precinct.

1914 JOYCE *Dubliners* 24 All the branches of the tall trees which lined the mall were gay with little light green leaves. **1963** *Observer* 15 Sept. 23/6 The central paved avenue, or 'mall' [in a shopping-centre], wider than any street, with booths in the middle. **1969** *Daily Tel.* 19 Aug. 13/2 Basically, the housewife is demanding more comfort and convenience in shopping. This means covered and heated 'malls' with car-parking facilities adjacent. **1974** *Economist* 21 Dec. 47/1 The developers have discovered an even more potent device for generating sales: the rigidly controlled 'shopping environment' of the enclosed malls... Woodfield Mall, near Chicago..includes 235 stores in a roofed-over area of 191 acres. **1975** *Times* 19 Feb. 4/8 Malls smoke danger. Special fire precautions are needed in single-storey shopping malls.

Mallaby-Deeley (mæːlăbiˌdī·li). [f. Harry *Mallaby-Deeley* (1863–1937), an English clothing manufacturer.] A cheap suit of clothes (see quots.). Also *transf.*

1920 *Punch* 10 Mar. 196 Oo, Lumme! Wot price Reginald in 'is Mallaby-Deeleys? **1937** *Evening Standard* 5 Feb. 3/1 In 1920 he [*sc.* Mallaby-Deeley] became the leader of cheap mass-production tailoring... A 'Mallaby-Deeley' soon became another name for a suit. **1959** R. POSTGATE *Every Man is God* xxiii. 218 'You don't know what a Mallaby Deeley is?' said his one-time Major... David Roddman learned that a Mallaby Deeley was a cheap mass-produced suit invented by a smart M.P. Ex-officers, out of work, for the use of. **1962** GRANVILLE *Dict. Sailors' Slang* 74/2 *Mallaby-Deeley's*, plain clothes worn by Naval officers and men on shore leave.

‖ **mallam** (mæ·lăm). [ad. Hausa *mālam(i)* (often used as a title).] A learned man, scribe, teacher.

1932 J. CARY *Aissa Saved* viii. 44 The white mallam put his hand on her head. *Ibid.* x. 53 She went to all the priests and mallams and juju men for a hundred miles round and commanded them to give the baby medicine. **1936** —— *Afr. Witch* xxii. 329 The old *mallam* went into his own room, which was the late Emir Aliu's office. **1939** —— *Mister Johnson* 82 He has been described..as a hamfish or *mallam* judge—that is, an office keeper. **1965** A. NICOL *Truly Married Woman* 88 'What foolishness is this?' the Mallam said sternly.

mallard. Add: **2. c.** *mallard call, decoy, duck, -shooting.*

1852 R. GLISAN *Jrnl. Army Life* (1874) ix. 102 A fine mallard duck suddenly flew up. **1874** J. W. LONG *Amer. Wild-Fowl Shooting* xiv. 186 Morning and evening mallard-shooting. *Ibid.* xix. 214 They decoy exceedingly well to mallard decoys, and come readily to the mallard call.

mallee[2]. Add: (Later examples.) **mallee root** *slang* (see quot. 1941).

1911 E. M. CLOWES *On Wallaby* ix. 249 On the Wimmera Plains is massed the dwarf eucalyptus known as the Mallee Scrub, the roots of which make such ideal firewood. **1936** I. L. IDRIESS *Cattle King* ii. 10 They passed through the mallee belt, then out on to plain country. **1941** BAKER *Dict. Austral. Slang* 45 *Mallee root*, a prostitute. **1944** A. RUSSELL *Bush Ways* xxii. 104, I think of the mallee scrubs and red gum fringes of the lower Murray River. **1958** E. O. SCHLUNKE *Village Hampden* 127 'They're going to lynch you, Regerson,' Harry told him, grinning. 'You'd better take to the mallee before they come for you.' **1963** *Times* 12 Mar. p. x/7 The mallee fowl is one of the megapodiidae or mound-building birds of the dry interior. **1966** G. DURRELL *Two in Bush* v. 166 Mallee scrub consists of a small species of eucalyptus between six and twenty feet high, and in places the trees grow very close together, their branches entwining and forming a continuous canopy. **1973** *Sun-Herald* (Sydney) 26 Aug. 85/2 *(caption)* A mallee fowl on its mound.

mallein (mæ·liˌin), *v.* [f. the sb.] *trans.* To inoculate (a horse or mule) against glanders.

1915 *Punch* 4 Aug. 101/2 All mules on joining units will in future be malleined.

mallet, *sb.*[1] Add: **1. f.** *Mus.* A light hammer used for playing the vibraphone, xylophone, or similar instrument.

1930 *Melody Maker* Jan. 69/2 You should use at least three different 'hardnesses' of mallets for solo playing. **1968** *Ibid.* 23 Nov. 18 Having started with four mallets right from the beginning, I found myself playing the instrument in piano style.

6. mallet finger *Med.*, a condition in which a finger is permanently flexed at the distal joint, usu. resulting from a blow to the tip of the extended finger, which ruptures the extensor tendon; a finger so affected; **mallet-headed** *a.*, (*b*) applied to a chisel made to be struck with a mallet; (*c*) having a head shaped like that of a mallet.

1894 GOULD *Dict. Med.* 472/2 *Mallet finger*, a deformity of a finger characterized by deficient extension or undue flexion of the terminal phalanx. **1934** KEY & CONWELL *Managem. Fractures* xx. 718 (*heading*) Drop or mallet finger (baseball finger). **1956** *Jrnl. Amer. Med. Assoc.* 21 July 1135 (*heading*) New technique for treatment of mallet fingers and fractures of distal phalanx. **1967** *Punch* 29 Mar. 458/3 Less heroically, women can contract Mallet Finger by 'tucking the bed-clothes under the mattress when bed-making'. **1906** E. JOHNSTON *Writing & Illuminating* xvii. 396 The chisels are either *Hammer-headed* or *Mallet-headed*. **1909** *Westm. Gaz.* 26 Oct. 5/2 The announcement made by the Rules of Golf Committee on the subject of mallet-headed clubs will have far-spreading consequences.

Malling (mǭ·liŋ). The names of two villages, East and West *Malling*, in Kent, used to designate: **1.** English pottery of the late sixteenth century in the form of tin-enamelled jugs, one of which was found at West Malling; = *tiger-ware.*

[**1903** *Times* 11 Feb. 10/6 The West Malling Elizabethan jug..will be sold [on]..February 19th.] **1933** W. B. HONEY *Eng. Pott. & Porc.* iii. 36 A 'Malling jug' of 1550.. was sold for five hundred and sixty guineas. **1968** A. RAY *Eng. Delftware Pott.* xi. 91 The 16th century 'Malling' jugs are the earliest tin-glazed pottery.

2. A rootstock for fruit trees developed at the East Malling Research Station. Also *attrib.*

1927 *Gardeners' Chronicle* 19 Mar. 199/2 Present-day planters have the advantage of being able to buy trees on the East Malling stocks. *Ibid.* There is a very strong demand amongst market growers for dessert Apples on Jaune de Metz (Type IX), the most dwarfing of the Malling selections. **1928** A. H. HOARE *Eng. Grass Orchard* v. 73 It is good news for orchard planters that it has been found possible to select and propagate by layering the most desirable of the seedling crabs and the very vigorous types of 'Paradise' stocks, as they are called. These are known as Malling Types XII., XIII. and XVI., and Bristol No. 5... They are not yet plentiful. **1936** H. V. TAYLOR *Apples Eng.* p. iii (Advt.), Selected trees on Malling stocks. **1966** A. G. BROWN in *Fruit Present & Future* (R. Hort. Soc.) 18 East Malling has continued to work with rootstocks and has recently introduced a new dwarfing stock Malling 26. **1973** *Pears Encycl. Gardening: Fruit & Vegetables* 23 Trees on Malling IX, which are planted closer than those of other rootstocks..will ensure the largest weight of fruit from a small garden, in the quickest possible time.

Mallorcan (mălǭ·ɹkăn, mălʸǭ·-), *sb.* and *a.* [ad. Sp. *Mallorca* Majorca + -AN.] = *MAJORCAN *sb.* and *a.* Also, the language of the Mallorcans.

1868 H. O'SHEA *Guide to Spain & Portugal* (ed. 3) 341/1 The inhabitants, especially the Mallorcans, are an honest, interesting..people. *Ibid.* 342/2 There is great similarity between Mallorcan and the Languedocian patois of Montpellier. *Ibid.* 343/1 The learned Scaliger expatiates on the excellence of the Mallorcan pottery. **1927** N. L. DURYEA *Mallorca* i. 6 Oriental eyes brood in Mallorcan faces. **1934** *Scottish Geogr. Mag.* L. 136 A great proportion of the Mallorcan trees are exceedingly old. **1937** W. FORTESCUE *Sunset House* ix. 162 A little red Mallorcan sausage. **1954** T. MAYNARD *Long Road of Father Serra* (1956) i. 13 Not all Mallorcans were so pious as the Serras. *Ibid.* 17 The beauty of the Mallorcan scene. **1972** A. LOWE *Catalan Vengeance* 140 The *Carta Catalana*, the commercial map of oriental trade drawn in 1375 by the Mallorcan Jew Abraham Cresques.

Mallorquin (mălǭ·ɹkin, mălʸǭ·-), *sb.* and *a.* Also -quine. [Sp. *Mallorquín*, f. *Mallorca* Majorca: see *MAJORCAN *sb.* and *a.*] = *MAJORCAN *sb.* and *a.* Also, the language of the Mallorquins.

1839 *Penny Cycl.* XIV. 339/1 In character the Mallorquines somewhat resemble the Catalans. **1868** H. O'SHEA *Guide to Spain & Portugal* (ed. 3) 342/2 The 'Mallorquin' is a corruption of the Catalan dialect. **1869** H. W. BATES *Illustr. Trav.* I. 267/2 The women of Soller are..by no means so plain in their appearance as the majority of the Mallorquine females. **1875** *Encycl. Brit.* III. 277/2 A railway is in course of construction from Palma by Inca to Alcudia, and the stock is all held by Mallorquins. **1926** R. MACAULAY *Crewe Train* I. i. 4 As..his knowledge of the Mallorquin idiom improved..he discovered that Mallorquins are almost the kindest and most sociable people in the world. **1929** D. H. LAWRENCE *Let.* 26 May (1932) 806 The Mallorquin servants cooked Spanish rice over a fire. **1952** [see *IBIZAN *a.*]. **1954** T. MAYNARD *Long Road of Father Serra* (1956) i. 2 They have their own language, Mallorquin, even if this is no more than a dialect of Catalan. **1973** *Times* 3 Mar. 26/2 *Mallorquin*, the local dialect of the native Catalan language, runs a poor second. **1974** R. JEFFRIES *Mistakenly in Mallorca* iii. 24 A Mallorquin inlaid sideboard. *Ibid.* v. 34 She was not..a Mallorquin or a Spaniard.

malnou·rished, *a.* [f. MAL- + NOURISHED *ppl. a.*; cf. MALNUTRITION.] Suffering from or provided with insufficient nutrition or nourishment; undernourished.

1928 *Daily Tel.* 11 Dec. 17/1 He [*sc.* Lord Eustace Percy] had emphasised the importance of local authorities making adequate provision for mal-nourished children. **1963** *Economist* 29 June 1348/1 Half the world's population is still hungry or malnourished or both. **1972** *Lancet* 22 July 143/1, 200 randomly selected malnourished children under the age of five years.

malnou·rishment. [f. MAL- + NOURISHMENT.] = MALNUTRITION.

1932 *N.Y. World-Telegram* 16 June 22/7 The inroads of starvation, diseases and malnourishment. **1936** E. P. O'DONNELL *Green Margins* 222 Many of them were tuberculous from malnourishment. **1969** N. W. PIRIE *Food Resources* iii. 99 There will be protein malnourishment unless

food, averaged over a day, contains a reasonable percentage of protein.

mal-observation. (Earlier and later examples.)

1843 MILL *Logic* II. v. iv. 387 It is mal-observation, when something is not simply unseen, but seen wrong; when the fact or phenomenon..is mistaken for something else. **1895** A. LANG in R. M. Dorson *Peasant Customs* (1968) II. 444 If he denies it, if he says with Lord Kelvin that hypnotism is all imposture and malobservation, I am silenced. **1922** *Encycl. Brit.* XXXII. 199/2 Repression of the truth would have to be added as a third to mal-observation and forgetfulness, as a very subtle source of error in testimony to the occurrence of the supernormal.

maloca (mălōᵘ·kă). Also 9 malocca. [Pg., a large hut, f. Amer. Sp., raid, attack, f. Araucanian *malocan* to fight (Webster).] A large hut in certain Indian settlements in South America.

1860 MAYNE REID *Odd People* 122 The Mundrucus build the *malocca*..only in their case it is not used as a dwelling, but rather as a grand arsenal, a council-chamber,..and, if need be, a fortress. *Ibid.* 47 Three or four hundred individuals not unfrequently assemble under the roof of a single *malocca*. **1944** S. PUTNAM tr. *E. da Cunha's Rebellion in Backlands* II. iii. 175 The ruins of the *malocas*, or native villages. **1951** J. C. FENNESSY *Sonnet in Bottle* III. v. 81 The village consisted only of three large malocas, with palm-thatched roofs reaching nearly to the ground. **1962** N. MAXWELL *Witch-Doctor's Apprentice* xiv. 171 In the Colombian Amazon, a maloca is the traditional dirt-floored, round or oval Indian house whose walls are made of the same thatch as its roof.

malocclu·sion. *Dentistry.* [f. MAL- + OCCLUSION.] Faulty occlusion (of the teeth).

1888 J. N. FARRAR *Treat. Irregularities Teeth* I. lv. 563 (*heading*) Mal-occlusion of the anterior teeth.—Treatment. **1937** *Times* 22 Nov. 9/4 A constant stream of visiting dentists..inspected their malocclusions. **1968** *New Scientist* 12 Sept. 538/2 Malocclusion of the jaws, with resulting pyorrhoea, was the pharaohs' biggest dental problem.

malonate (mæ·lǫnēit). *Chem.* [f. MALON(IC *a.* + -ATE[4].] The anion, or an ester or salt, of malonic acid.

1862 W. A. MILLER *Elem. Chem.* (ed. 2) III. v. 367 The malonates of potash and ammonia are deliquescent, but uncrystallizable. **1898** J. WADE *Introd. Study Org. Chem.* xxv. 153 Ethyl malonate, $CH_2(COOEt)_2$, is a heavy, colourless liquid, which has a pleasant aromatic odour, and boils at 198°. **1951** A. GROLLMAN *Pharmacol. & Therapeutics* xxix. 676 Both malonate and succinate of sodium are absorbed only slowly from the intestine, and act as saline cathartics. **1962** *Times* 1 May 4/1 (Advt.), They'll be available later in an attractive bound volume scented with perfumes based on certain allyl esters such as salicylate and malonate. **1962** H. A. KREBS in A. Pirie *Lens Metabolism Rel. Cataract* 351 The effects of malonate on the oxidation of succinate.

malonic, *a.* Add: *malonic ester*, the diethyl ester, $CH_2(COOC_2H_5)_2$, of malonic acid, which is a liquid widely used in synthesis, as of carboxylic acids $RR'C(COOH)_2$ or RR'CH-COOH by alkylation with alkyl halides (*malonic ester synthesis*).

1881 *Chem. News* 28 Jan. 47/1 (*heading*) Syntheses by means of malonic ester. **1906** J. J. SUDBOROUGH *Bernthsen's Text-bk. Org. Chem.* (rev. ed.) x. 238 This so-called 'malonic ester' synthesis is an important method for the preparation of higher dibasic acids. **1968** R. O. C. NORMAN *Princ. Org. Synthesis* x. 330 The use of malonic ester considerably increases the versatility of this general method [of amino-acid synthesis]. **1971** N. ALLINGER et al. *Org. Chem.* xxiv. 665 In the malonic ester synthesis, diethyl malonate is converted by sodium ethoxide into its sodium salt, which is then allowed to react with an alkyl halide.

Hence **ma·lonyl**, the radical —CO·CH_2·CO— derived from malonic acid by removal of the two hydroxyl groups.

1889 G. M'GOWAN tr. *Bernthsen's Text-bk. Org. Chem.* 282 Barbituric acid, malonyl urea, $C_4H_4N_2O_3$, is a dibasic acid. **1931** *Jrnl. Chem. Soc.* 273 The Friedel-Crafts reaction has now been extended to the coupling of malonyl chloride..with methyl ethers of resorcinol. **1970** R. W. McGILVERY *Biochem.* xvi. 317 The butyryl group can be displaced onto the neighboring cysteinyl group by an incoming malonyl group. **1971** *Nomencl. Org. Chem.* (I.U.P.A.C.) (ed. 2) C. 313 Malonyl (preferred to propanedioyl) —CO·CH_2·CO—.

Malo-Russian (mēilo͵rɒ·ʃiăn), *sb.* and *a.* [f. Russ. *Malorossiya* Little Russia, or ad. *Malorós(s)*, *-rús* or *Malorossiyánin* Little Russian.] **A.** *sb.* A member of the Little Russian race inhabiting the south of Russia; their language. **B.** *adj.* Of or pertaining to the Little Russians, Ruthenian.

1862 [see RUTHENIAN *sb.* 2]. **1880** W. R. MORFILL *Russia* 74 The Malo-Russian is very rich in Skazki (national tales) and in songs. *Ibid.* 75 The Malo-Russian philologists. **1923** E. A. ROSS *Russ. Soviet Republic* 58 Between Great Russia and the Black Sea live the Ukrainians or Little Russians (Malo-Russians).

malpais (malpa͵ī·s). *U.S.* [Sp., f. *malo* bad + *país* country, region.] Rugged or difficult country of volcanic origin.

1844 G. W. KENDALL *Narr. Santa Fé Expedition* II. 384 We had crossed the *mal pais*, or bad country, as it is called. **1847** G. A. F. RUXTON *Adventures Mexico & Rocky Mts.* xi. 79 The tract of country known as the *Mal Pais*, a most interesting volcanic region. **1896** *Nat. Geogr. Mag.* VII. 295 Bench mesas may be classified by structure into bolson mesas, stream-terrace mesas, talus-fan mesas, and malpais mesas. **1918** C. E. MULFORD *Man from Bar-20* xvii. 178 Slipping on the treacherous malpais and loose stones. **1942** KEARNEY & PEEBLES *Flowering Plants Arizona* 17 Some of these are limestone areas, whereas others are volcanic, locally known as 'mallapy' (*mal pais*).

malpresentation. (Earlier and later examples.)

1852 *Lancet* 2 Oct. 299/2 The proportion of mal-presentations is increased in cases in which labour comes on at the full term. **1962** R. H. SMYTHE *Anat. of Dog Breeding* v. 104 There is always the possibility of mal-presentation or malformation of an individual puppy.

malrotation (mælrotēi·ʃən). *Med.* [f. MAL- + ROTATION.] Faulty or abnormal rotation of a part of the body, esp. of the intestines during development.

1932 *New Eng. Jrnl. Med.* CVI. 280 At operation a distended stomach was found... There was no evidence of mal-rotation. **1961** *Lancet* 9 Sept. 598/1 There was also malrotation and severe mesenteric lymphadenitis.

malt, *sb.*[1] Add: **3.** (Further examples.) Now usu. = *malt whisky*.

1925, etc. [see *BALL *sb.*[4]]. **1967** A. DIMENT *Dolly Dolly Spy* iv. 39 He..poured himself a big shot of the finest Malt. **1972** A. ROSS *London Assignment* 32, I had put plenty of Malvern water into the malt, figuring to make it last. **1974** *Times Lit. Suppl.* 11 Jan. 38/5 Ross Wilson ignores the religious divisions of the trade ('malts' are the Catholic whiskies). **1975** *Scottish Field* Jan. 13/2 Hugh MacDiarmid, a whisky drinker for 60 years, expounds on the great malts.

4. a. *malt whisky* (further examples).

1968 *Scottish Field* Nov. 56 (Advt.), Chivas Regal is blended with the softest Glenlivet malt whiskies. **1970** SIMON & HOWE *Dict. Gastron.* 389/1 About a hundred years ago it became the custom to blend straight malt whisky with neutral grain whisky.

b. *malt (tea-)loaf*.

1901 B. S. ROWNTREE *Poverty* viii. 288/2 Malt loaf. 3d. **1969** E. GÉBLER *Shall I eat you Now?* 98 They drank tea and ate slices of a sticky malt tealoaf.

5. malt shop *U.S.*, a shop where malted milk is sold.

1943 D. BAKER *Trio* II. 88 She was out of the gate and into a little section of bright lights—college clothes,.. malt shops. **1949** *Time* 26 Sept. 25/1 The word was relayed through the drive-ins, malt shops and garages.

Malt (mǭlt), *sb.*[2] *slang.* = MALTESE *sb.* 1 a.

1959 C. MACINNES *Absolute Beginners* 40 A sickly simper,..that she turned on like a light for the two beefo Malts. **1969** *Sunday Mail* (Brisbane) 16 Mar. 10 A new and frightening power is suddenly emerging in the Sydney underworld. It is called by those who know about it 'The Malts'. Police fear it is taking the form of a Maltese 'Mafia'. **1971** *Guardian* 6 July 11/6 The 'Malts', as one used to refer to them, or sometimes 'yellow-bellied bastards'.

maltase. Substitute for def.: Any enzyme which hydrolyses maltose and other α-glycosides. (Add earlier and later examples.)

1890 *Jrnl. Chem. Soc.* LVIII. 998 The author starts with the assumption that the diastase of malt is composed of a mixture of two enzymes—maltase and dextrinase. **1946** *Thorpe's Dict. Appl. Chem.* (ed. 4) VII. 481/2 Maltase also hydrolyses..α-glycosides but not β-glycosides. **1964** N. G. CLARK *Mod. Org. Chem.* xvi. 327 Hydrolysis with dilute hydrochloric acid yields two molecular proportions of glucose, and the glycosidic linkage is established as α by the fact that similar hydrolysis occurs with the enzyme maltase (which is specific for α-glycosides). **1968** A. WHITE et al. *Princ. Biochem.* (ed. 4) xviii. 387 Maltases IV and V account for about two-thirds of the total maltase activity.

malted, *ppl. a.* **2.** (Earlier and later examples.)

1887 *Official Gaz.* (U.S. Patent Office) XLI. 358 Trade-Marks..Food preparation for infants and invalids.—Horlick's Food Company, Mount Pleasant and Racine, Wis.,..'The words *Malted Milk* and the letters "M.M."' **1920** [see *BEEZER 2]. **1930** BELLOC *New Cautionary Tales* 41 He gave him medicine by the pail And malted milk, and nutmeg ale. **1960** A. E. BENDER *Dict. Nutrition* 82/1 Malted milk—liquid separated from mash of ground barley malt and wheat flour mixed with milk and the mixture dried. **1974** *Times* 16 Mar. 11/6 My palate has reverted to childhood and adores American food—sandwiches, malted milk,..jello.

malted (mǭ·ltėd), *sb.* A drink of malted milk (MALTED *ppl. a.* 2).

1945 *Newsweek* 8 Jan. 84 The couple..went into a Walgreen drugstore for ice cream. There, high above the ads for malteds, they noticed Vedovelli's paintings. **1949** A. MILLER *Death of Salesman* II. 117 Let's go downstairs and get you a malted. **1953** *Manch. Guardian Weekly* 13 Aug. 7 The soda fountain serves such luxuries as candy and malteds. **1969** GISH & PINCHOT *Lillian Gish* xiv. 202 Order her a malted and a cheese sandwich.

Maltese, *a.* and *sb.* Add: **A.** *adj.* **2. Maltese cross,** (*b*) *Philately,* name given to the post-mark used on British postage stamps from their introduction in 1840 until 1844; (*c*) *Cinemat.* = *Geneva *mechanism*; **Maltese dog,** substitute for def.: = sense *B. 4 (later example); **Maltese terrier** = sense *B. 4.

1881 PHILBRICK & WESTOBY *Postage & Telegr. Stamps Gt. Brit.* 291 Several obliterating marks are found: 1. The Maltese cross, or *croix patée*, as then in use. **1909** J. G. HENDY *Hist. Postmarks Brit. Isles 1840–76* 9 The Maltese Cross or *croix patée* obliterator—the latter is really the correct term to apply to it from a heraldic point of view—varied a good deal in shape in different places. **1917** C. N. BENNETT *Guide to Kinematogr.* ix. 127 Modern Maltese cross movements are descendants of the 'Geneva stop' by which overwinding of watches is prevented. **1934** J. B. SEYMOUR *Stamps Gt. Brit.: Line-Engraved Issues 1840–53* 9 The design generally used for obliterating the British stamps from 1840 to 1844 has been called, incorrectly, a Croix Patée or Maltese Cross; it is neither one nor the other. But it is so well known as the Maltese Cross that it is deemed advisable to call it so for the purpose of this work. *Ibid.* 102 The stamps from the first forty plates [*sc.* of the one penny red imperforate] are usually obliterated with the Maltese Cross. **1949** P. C. LITCHFIELD *Guide Lines to Penny Black* 16 Stamps with the red Maltese Cross are more likely to have come from one of the early plates. **1953** Maltese cross [see *GENEVA[2] b]. **1963** *Gt. Brit.: Specialised Stamp Catal.: Queen Victoria* (Stanley Gibbons Ltd.) 23 The Maltese Cross is a valuable plating aid for collectors of the Penny Red imperf. Its presence on a stamp is strong evidence that that stamp is from a plate put to press before 1845. **1913** V. SHAW *Encycl. Kennel* 130 Many people persist in calling the delicate little Maltese dog a terrier, whereas he is nothing of the kind, but a fragile member of the toy family. **1880** H. DALZIEL *Brit. Dogs* III. viii. 430 Whether the dog we now call a Maltese terrier be a descendant more or less pure from the breed Strabo wrote of, it is now impossible to say. **1954** M. K. WILSON tr. *Lorenz's Man meets Dog* iv. 42 They [*sc.* two large dogs] nearly pulled a Maltese terrier in half.

B. *sb.* **4.** A very small, long-coated, white dog of the breed so called, formerly known as *Maltese dogs* or *Maltese terriers* (sense A. 2 in Dict. and Suppl.).

1867 MRS. F. LEHMANN *Let.* 22 Jan. in Geo. Eliot *Lett.* (1956) IV. 336 The Lewes's were enchanted with Chang. They say he is a real Maltese. **1950** A. C. SMITH *Dogs since 1900* 318 The Maltese. This, one of the oldest of the toy breeds in Europe, at one time had 'Terrier' added to its name. **1972** *Country Life* 10 Feb. (Suppl.) 21/1 'Floriana Maltese'..good straight white coats, with black points.

malthoid (mæ·lþoid). *Austral.* and *N.Z.* [f. MALTHA + -OID.] The proprietary name of a bituminous material made from wood fibre and used as a roof- or floor-covering or for covering other surfaces.

1936 *Patent Office Jrnl.* (N.Z.) 3 Dec. 367/1 *Malthoid.* Pabco Products (Australia), Limited... Paints, varnishes, coatings, and paint compounds, [etc.]. **1959** *Numbers* IX. 9 The malthoid roof. **1960** B. CRUMP *Good Keen Man* 76 When all the boards were on [the hut] we covered the whole structure with malthoid and tacked it into place. **1960** J. FINGLETON *Four Chukkas to Austral.* 7 An odd sort of trial upon a malthoid pitch.

Malto (mæ·lto), *sb.* [Native word = 'language of the Maler': see *MALER *sb.* and *a.*] A Dravidian language spoken by the Maler people living in the Rajmahal hills of northern India. Also called *RAJMAHALI. Also as *adj.*

1884 E. DROESE *Introd. Malto Lang.* p. i, Malto is the language of one of the aboriginal races of India who call themselves Maler *i.e.* men, and go among their Aryan neighbours by the name of Paharias (Hill people). **1906** G. A. GRIERSON *Ling. Survey India* IV. 446 Malto is almost exclusively spoken in the Rajmahal Hills in the north-east of the Sonthal Parganas... Malto is the name used by the people themselves in order to denote their language. The word simply means 'the language of the Maler', and *maler* in Malto means 'men' and is the name the people apply to themselves... It is..probable that Malto like Malayāḷam is derived from the common Dravidian *mala*, mountain, so that the original meaning of 'maler' would be 'hillmen'. *Ibid.* 447 Malto does not possess a literature of its own... The Malto language very closely agrees with Kurukh. **1938** S. S. SARKAR *Mālérs of Rajmahal Hills* i. 18 The Mālérs speak *Mālto*. **1955** T. BURROW *Sanskrit Lang.* viii. 387 The Dravidian languages Kurukh and Malto are preserved even now in Northern India, and may be regarded as islands surviving from a once extensive Dravidian territory. **1963** L. P. VIDYARTHI *Maler* iv. 57 The Maler..call themselves 'Male' in their native Malto language which means hill-man. **1972** W. B. LOCKWOOD *Panorama Indo-European Lang.* 224 Malto, the vernacular of 100,000 tribesmen, is found in the Rajmahal Hills.

maltol (mǭ·ltǫl). *Chem.* [a. G. *maltol* (J. Brand 1894, in *Ber. d. Deut. Chem. Ges.* XXVII. 810): see MALT *sb.* and -OL.] A crystalline compound, $C_6H_6O_3$, which occurs in larch bark and chicory and is formed by roasting malt; 3-hydroxy-2-methylpyran-4-one.

1894 *Jrnl. Chem. Soc.* LXVI. I. 271 Beer, prepared from caramel malt, gives a violet coloration with ferric chloride; this is not due to salicylic acid, but to the presence of a compound termed maltol, which is distinguished from salicylic acid by giving no reaction with Millon's reagent. **1945** *Jrnl. Amer. Chem. Soc.* LXVII. 2276 Hydrolysis of streptomycin chloride with *N* sodium hydroxide...yields a weakly acidic substance, m.p. 161–162°, which has been characterized as maltol. **1972** *Sci. Amer.* Mar. 16/2 In re-

cent years the use of maltol, which can intensify or modify the flavor of preserves, desserts, fruit, soft drinks and foods generally high in carbohydrates, has expanded greatly.

maltreater (mæltrī·təɹ). [f. MALTREAT *v.* + -ER[1].] One who maltreats or ill-uses.

1902 O. WISTER *Virginian* iv. 57 A maltreater of hawsses [horses]. **1906** B. VON HUTTEN *What became of Pam* I. ii, Tyrants,..drunkards, maltreaters [of women]. **1965** M. SPARK *Mandelbaum Gate* iii. 55 Much as the timid spinsters of the old days, while abroad, would be moved to violence against the maltreater of the donkey.

‖ **malum in se** (mæ·lə̆m in sī). Pl. **mala in se.** [med.L.] Something intrinsically evil or wicked. Also as *adj. phr.*

1623 J. WILLIAMS *Let.* 30 Aug. in J. Hacket *Scrinia Reserata* (1693) I. 157 But to grant a Pardon even for a thing that is *malum in se*. **1811** *Edin. Rev.* Feb. 275 That corruption is not..a *malum in se*, as Mr Windham has been pleased to assert. **1826** *Ibid.* Feb. 331 Whether there be..any solecism which is a *malum in se*, as distinct from a *malum prohibitum*. **1856** *Sat. Rev.* 26 July 290/1 It is the bargaining intention, and this is *malum in se*. The *malum prohibitum* is the contract. **1893** [see *HYPERTENSION 1 a]. **1959** JOWITT *Dict. Eng. Law* II. 1130/1 *Mala in se*, acts which are wrong in themselves, such as murder, as opposed to *mala prohibita*. **1961** *Times* 18 Mar. 12/6 That part of the criminal law which covered offences *mala in se*.

malva (mæ·lvă). [L. *malva* mallow; adopted by Linnæus in his *Genera Plantarum* (1737) 308 as the name of a genus.] = MALLOW.

[**1548** W. TURNER *Names of Herbes* sig. E3 Malva is called in greeke Malache, in englishe a Mallowe or a Mallo.] **1883** W. ROBINSON *Wild Garden* (ed. 3) xiv. 150 Some of the Malvas are..vigorous-growing plants. **1959** W. STRACHE *Forms & Patterns in Nature* 35 (*caption*) Malva flower. **1966** E. PALMER *Plains of Camdeboo* xvii. 277 The early settlers... used..the Malva to bathe sore eyes.

Malvern (mǭ·lvəɹn). The name of a town in Hereford and Worcester, used *attrib.* and *ellipt.* to designate alkaline mineral water obtained from springs there.

1757 J. WALL *Exper. & Observations Malvern Waters* (ed. 2) App. 68 She was last Year perswaded to try Malvern Water,..and..the Water has been constantly sent to London all the Winter for her Use. **1907** *Yesterday's Shopping* (1969) 27 Malvern water... Bots. 6/0 [per doz.]. **1930** A. BENNETT *Imperial Palace* lxiv. 525 She watched over his flowers and his Malvern water. **1965** *New Statesman* 14 May 753/1 One of the lackeys will carry a 10-day supply of Malvern water. **1967** *Observer* (Colour Suppl.) 28 May 38/2 Malvern. The one British mineral water that is sold on a national scale. **1974** J. STUBBS *Painted Face* iv. 70 A picnic basket, complete from cold capon..to Malvern water.

Malvernian (mǭlvə̄·ɹniăn), *a. Geol.* [f. the name of the *Malvern* Hills, a range in England between Hereford and Worcester: see -IAN.] Of, pertaining to, or characteristic of the Malvern Hills; *spec.* (*a*) applied to a Pre-Cambrian series of plutonic rocks that forms most of the hills; also *absol.*; (*b*) applied to a north–south orientation like that of the hills.

1879 *Q. Jrnl. Geol. Soc.* XXXV. 654 The contained pebbles..consist of quartzite, quartz, gneiss, mica-schist, red felspar, and granitoid rock. This assemblage strongly suggests derivation from the Malvernian series represented at Primrose Hill. **1899** *Proc. Geologists' Assoc.* XV. 426 The strike of the axes of the main folding of the country [around Stourbridge] is first north and south, in continuation of the main axes of the Malvern ridge (Malvernian folding), but at Abberley Hill it swings round almost at right angles to this direction, the axes now striking from west to east (Hercynian or Mercian folding). **1948** L. J. WILLS *Palaeogeogr. Midlands* ii. 7 The distribution of the Malvernian away from Malvern itself is quite unknown. **1969** BENNISON & WRIGHT *Geol. Hist. Brit. Isles* iii. 68 The Malvernian is composed predominantly of metamorphosed igneous rocks, diorites and gabbros. *Ibid.* x. 248 (*heading*) Structures of Malvernian trend.

malversate (mælvə̄·ɹseit), *v.* [Back-formation from MALVERSATION.] *trans.* To use (funds) for purposes other than those for which they were intended.

1881 S. BUTLER *Family Lett.* (1962) 198 If I malversated these funds or lost them, my co-trustee might come down on the company for having regarded the order of one trustee to the disregard of a joint order. **1928** G. B. SHAW *Intelligent Woman's Guide Socialism* 417 The public school (meaning a very exclusive private school malversating public endowments).

Malvi (mā·lvi). Also **Malwi.** A dialect of Rajasthani.

1883 *Census of Central Provinces 1881* (India Census) II. 91 (*table*) Languages and dialects amalgamated therein... Urdū, Mālvi, Nimāri, [etc.]. **1901, 1957** [see *JAIPUR]. **1968** B. WALKER *Hindu World* I. 586 Other Rājasthāni dialects are *Mārwāṛi*.., *Jaipuri*.., *Mālvi*.., *Mewāri*.., *Udaipuri*.

‖ **mal vu** (mal vü). [Fr.] Held in very poor esteem, or in no esteem, looked down upon. Also *attrib.*

1904 H. O. STURGIS *Belchamber* iii. 42 There is nothing so easy as to get rid of me. I am horribly *mal vu* by the authorities. **1958** L. DURRELL *Mountolive* ii. 62 He is.. rather an old-fashioned reactionary in his outlook, and is consequently rather *mal vu* by his brother craftsmen. **1958** *Times Lit. Suppl.* 21 Nov. 672/3 Her daughter Elsie's marriage to a clever but socially *mal vue* [*sic*] research scientist.

‖ **mamaku** (ma·maku). *N.Z.* [Maori.] A tree fern, *Cyathea medullaris*, or the starchy food formerly prepared from its pith.

1846 C. HEAPHY *Jrnl.* 15 May in N. M. Taylor *Early Travellers in N.Z.* (1959) 232 Encamped in order to collect and bake *mamaku*, the stem of the fern tree, which was to constitute our provisions. **1882** W. D. HAY *Brighter Britain!* II. 152 The inner stems of mamaku or tree-fern. **1905** W. B. *Where White Man Treads* 16, I have forgotten 'mamaku' (the tree fern)—fanning itself in the mid-heat of summer. **1949** P. BUCK *Coming of Maori* (1950) I. iii. 34 Tree fern pith (*mamaku*), and fern root (*aruhe*) were placed before them. **1966** *Encycl. N.Z.* II. 785/1 Mamaku or black tree fern (*Cyathea medullaris*) was an important source of starch food... The pith [of the trunk] was steamed for about two days..and the resulting sago-like substance could be eaten cold or dried for future use.

‖ **mamaliga** (məmæli·gə). [Rumanian *mămăligă*.] = POLENTA c; maize porridge: a staple food in Rumania.

1878 J. W. OZANNE *Three Years in Roumania* 121 Maize forms the staple food of the lower classes. Every day a portion is boiled for the use of the family. It is called *mamaliga*, and is usually eaten alone; a little milk or a piece of salt fish being, however, sometimes added. **1925** J. A. HAMMERTON *Countries of World* XXXIV. 3425/1 The peasants livè for the most part on mamaliga. **1970** *Sat. Rev.* (U.S.) 12 Sept. 107/3 In Rumania, unfermented grape juice or must is sold at wooden stalls..with slices of hot *mamaliga*, the national dish of of cornmeal mush.

mamaloi (ma·maˌlwa). Also **mamanloi.** Pl. **mamaloi, mamalois.** [ad. Haitian Creole *mamalwa*, f. *mama* mother + *lwa* *LOA[2].] A voodoo priestess.

1884 S. ST. JOHN *Hayti, or Black Republic* v. 194 The Haytians have corrupted the compounds Papa Roi and Maman Roi into Papaloi and Mamanloi. **1935** R. A. LOEDERER *Voodoo Fire in Haiti* The priests are called 'Papaloi' by their followers, and the priestesses 'Mamaloi', both words being Creole corruptions of 'Papa Roi' and 'Mama Roi'.

‖ **mama-san** (mamaˌsan). Also **mamasan.** [Jap., f. *mama* mother + *san* honorific title.] In Japan and the Far East, a matron in a position of authority: *spec.* one in charge of a geisha-house; the mistress of a bar.

1949 L. H. CROCKETT *Popcorn on Ginza* xvi. 218 Mamasans of some of the better Tokyo houses become well informed on all sorts of political intrigue. **1958** G. MIKES *East is East* 56 '*Mamasan*' is not surprised if someone wishes to linger late in one of those tiny little Japanese houses where the parties take place. **1962** A. CAMPBELL *Heart of Japan* iv. 113 The mama-san wanted us all to go home... A geisha party isn't supposed to go on more than three hours. **1968** *Manch. Guardian Weekly* 4 Jan. 10 We were visited by two enormous Sumo wrestlers, with their equally large Mama-San. **1971** *Nat. Geographic* Oct. 571/2 The representative bars have an institutional figure called 'mama-san', a matronly, amiable, garrulous, and straightforward woman who permits the sailors to fraternize with any of a covey of young ladies.

mamba (mæ·mbă). Also 9 **momba.** [ad. Zulu *imamba*.] A large venomous African snake of the genus *Dendroaspis* (family Elapidæ), esp. the *green mamba* (*GREEN *a.* 12 b), *D. angusticeps*, and the black mamba, *D. polylepis*. Also *attrib.*

1862 J. S. DOBIE in *S. Afr. Jrnl.* (1945) 44 He called it a green mamba and was about 9 feet long. **1878** P. GILLMORE *Great Thirst Land* xxix. 346 A black mamba—a description of snake common in Natal, and reported to be very deadly. **1897** J. BRYCE *Impressions S. Afr.* iii. 23 The black *momba*, which is nearly as large as a rattlesnake, is a dangerous creature. **1910** J. BUCHAN *Prester John* iv. 80 A black mamba might appear out of the tangle. **1912** F. W. FITZSIMONS *Snakes S. Afr.* (new ed.) 194 There are two varieties of the Mamba. One is vivid leaf-green, the other is olive or brownish-black. **1921** *Chambers's Jrnl.* 26 Feb. 203/2 It was a mamba snake, eight feet long. **1939** S. CLOETE *Watch for Dawn* 62 With the bite of a mamba or a ringhals the heart sometimes beat even after life had gone. **1958** *Listener* 23 Jan. 154/1 Black mambas..have the unattractive habit of lurking in trees and dropping down on to the unwary. **1965** A. NICOL *Truly Married Woman* 96 A poisonous one, a mamba, its middle still rippling slowly. **1969** A. BELLAIRS *Life of Reptiles* I. v. 191 The deadly mambas (*Dendroaspis*) have fangs which are relatively a little shorter and thinner than those of the average cobra.

mambar, var. *MIMBAR.

mambo (mæ·mbo). [Amer. Sp., 'prob. fr. Haitian creole (voodoo priestess)' (Webster).] **1.** A kind of rumba, a ball-room dance (and its music) of Latin-American origin.

1948 *Call-Bulletin* (San Francisco) 17 Sept. 11/1 Tony De Marco predicts the new dance fad will be 'The Mambo', which was introduced..last week. A zingier form of rhumba. **1950** *Newsweek* 4 Sept. 76 The difference between the rumba and the mambo is the difference between the regular foxtrot and the jitterbug. **1951** R. CHANDLER *Let.* 19 Apr. in *R. Chandler Speaking* (1966) 213, I doubt if he knows the new dance called a mambo, because it seems to be only recently discovered or developed. **1952** *Down Beat* 25 Jan. 2/2 Prado, who says he introduced the mambo in Mexico City in 1948, claims it is merely Afrocuban rhythm with a dash of American swing. **1955** *Caribbean Q.* IV. II. 102 Some St. Lucians..patronize the several clubs which have jukeboxes stocked largely with mambos of the Perez Prado school. **1957** J. KEROUAC *On Road* (1958) 93 Mambo blasted from jukeboxes. **1959** *Listener* 24 Sept. 473/1 Innumerable folk-dance sources, ranging from the square dance to Latin American mambos and the rest. **1964** W. G. RAFFÉ *Dict. Dance* 299/1 *Mambo* (Haiti), ritual dance of Voodoo; an initiation ceremonial which follows the ancient *Danse Shalame* (Salome) in its symbolic-realism. 'Mambo' is the official name for the chief priestess. **1966** *Crescendo* Dec. 27/1 Only bossa novas and mambos seem to be played with anything like enthusiasm by these bands. **1972** *Village Voice* (N.Y.) 1 June 4/3 Now the pop-music business, having scraped the hillbilly barrel and blown the froth off the mambo craze, has taken over R[hythm]-and-B[lues].

2. A voodoo priestess.

1964 R. SEVERN *Blood & Gold* x. 102 She must be a *Mambo*.., a *Voodoo* priestess. **1964** [see sense 1 above]. **1966** *Daily Tel.* 11 Aug. 18/6 The author and his herbalist friend became close companions with a girl who was often thus possessed, but had to be initiated and trained by an expert sorceress or *mambo*.

mamillary, *a.* Add: **2.** *mamillary body* [prob. tr. mod.L. *corpus mamillare*], either of a pair of small white hemispherical structures lying side by side between the tuber cinereum and the posterior perforated substance in the interpeduncular fossa on the ventral surface of the brain.

1832 J. QUAIN *Elem. Anat.* (ed. 2) viii. 642 A thin lamella of white substance,..called *locus perforatus*,..is triangular, the sides being formed by the crura cerebri, the base by the mammillary bodies. **1921** TILNEY & RILEY *Form & Functions Cent. Nervous Syst.* xxxiv. 613 The mammillary body serves as a relay station in the olfactory tract. **1942** O. LARSELL *Anat. Nervous Syst.* xviii. 249 The mammillary bodies are two elevations..just rostral to the posterior perforated substance. **1967** G. M. WYBURN et al. *Conc. Anat.* vii. 190/2 The depressed area between the peduncles, the interpeduncular fossa, has the following structures from behind forwards: the posterior perforated substance, the paired mamillary bodies, the tuber cinereum and infundibulum..and the optic chiasma.

mamma[1], mama. Add: **c*.** *Mam(m)a mia!* [It., lit. 'mother mine!']: an exclamation expressing surprise or astonishment.

1848 MRS. GASKELL *Mary Barton* II. iii. 47 The little hopeless stranger..spoke in some foreign tongue, with low cries for the far distant 'Mamma mia!' **1969** G. GREENE *Trav. with my Aunt* I. vii. 72 There came a strange grating noise. '*Mamma mia*,' the nurse said, 'what's that?' **1971** R. FALKIRK *Chill Factor* x. 94 'It rain every day?' asked the Italian. 'Every day,' I said. '*Mama mia*,' he said.

d. *mamma's boy*, a boy who has been pampered and spoiled; one who is excessively timid; also applied to a man. *colloq.*

1850 C. M. YONGE *Henrietta's Wish* xiii. 183, I would not give a farthing for Fred if he was always to be the mamma's boy you would make him. **1861** —— *Young Step-Mother* xxiii. 336 It might be no great harm if Maurice were a tame mamma's boy. **1929** W. FAULKNER *Sound & Fury* 141 Yah..go on then, mamma's boy. If he goes swimming he'll get his head wet and then he'll get a licking. **1967** A. M. STEIN *Executioner's Rest* vi. 100 Who was this Erridge? He was mama's boy, and if you don't know the kind of trouble mama's boy tourists go looking for when they're loose on the shores of the Mediterranean, you just haven't travelled.

mammaplasty (mæ·măplæsti). *Surg.* Also **mammo-.** [f. MAMMA[2] + -PLASTY.] Alteration of the shape or size of a breast by plastic surgery. Hence **mammapla·stic** *a.*

1938 *Revue de Chirurgie Structive* VIII. 39 (*heading*) Review of 80 cases of mammaplasty. **1947** H. MAY *Reconstructive & Reparative Surg.* xvii. 397 (*heading*) Mammaplastic procedures in the female. **1968** *N.Y. Times* 4 Apr. 26 He said the mammoplasty in the first case involved the transplant of adipose (fatty) tissue. **1969** C. ALLEN *Textbk. Psychosexual Disorders* (ed. 2) xii. 296 The procedures included..construction of a pro-vagina and mammoplasty.

mammer, *v.* (Later examples of *mammered* ppl. a.)

1861 T. HUGHES *Tom Brown at Oxf.* III. vii. 127, I be that mad wi' myself, and mammered, and down, I be ready to hang myself. **1883** W. H. COPE *Gloss. Hampshire Words* 56 *Mammered*, perplexed. **1888** B. LOWSLEY *Gloss. Berks. Words* 108 *Mammered*, amazed, confused, puzzled.

mammering, *vbl. sb.* **1.** and **2.** (Later examples.)

1941 E. R. EDDISON *Fish Dinner* (1972) vii. 108 Arquez, seeing..Clavius wounded and in a mammering whether to fly or fight: threw another chair. **1945** A. L. ROWSE *West-Country Stories* 17 The innumerable mammering of bats' voices. **1947** M. LOWRY *Let.* 13 Aug. (1967) 151, I am all of a doodah. I am in a mammering.

mammo- (mæ·mo), comb. form of MAMMA[2], used in various medical and biological terms, as **mammoge·nic** *a.* [*-GENIC], stimulating the growth of the breasts, esp. at puberty; of or pertaining to this activity; so **ma·mmogen,** any substance which has or is supposed to have mammogenic activity; **mammoge·nesis,** the stimulation of the growth of the breasts,

esp. at puberty; **mammo·graphy** *Med.* [-GRAPHY], a technique or procedure for diagnosing and locating abnormalities of the breasts by means of X-rays; an examination by this technique; hence **ma·mmogram, ma·mmograph,** a radiograph taken by this technique; **mammogra·phic** *a.*

1940 *Endocrinology* XXVII. 892 Only mammogen 1 (the duct growth factor) is present in ether-soluble extracts of the AP. Work is now progressing on the concentration of mammogen 2, the lobule-alveolar growth factor, and also on the perfection of a suitable technic for the assay of this hormone. **1958** *Proc. R. Soc.* B. CXLIX. 306 Oestrogen may resume its role as a mammogen. **1971** COWIE & TINDAL *Physiol. Lactation* iii. 115 Although the concept of *specific* mammogens of pituitary origin was never widely accepted..the 'Mammogen' theory rightly centred attention on the role of the anterior pituitary in mammogenesis. **1958** *Proc. R. Soc.* B. CXLIX. 312 The placenta may contribute as much to mammogenesis as the pituitary and ovaries combined. **1971** COWIE & TINDAL *Physiol. Lactation* iii. 117 Only in the rat and mouse have such detailed analyses of the hormones concerned in mammogenesis been made. **1938** *Proc. Soc. Exper. Biol. & Med.* XXXVII. 608 This new pituitary principle will be called the 'mammogenic hormone'. **1940** *Endocrinology* XXVII. 888 (*heading*) Evidence for the presence of a second mammogenic (lobule–alveolar) factor in the anterior pituitary. **1958** *Proc. R. Soc.* B. CXLIX. 304 Mammogenic activities of the ovarian hormones. **1971** COWIE & TINDAL *Physiol. Lactation* iii. 122 There is..a vast literature on the mammogenic potencies of ovarian steroids. **1937** N. F. HICKEN in *Surg., Gynecol. & Obstetr.* LXIV. 594/1 The procedure utilizes contrast fluids which are injected directly into the milk ducts, thus giving an accurate roentgenographic pattern of the ductal and secretory system of the mammary gland. The terms 'mammography' and 'mammograms' have been coined to describe these examinations. *Ibid.*, Gentleness, persistence, and patience are requisite in obtaining good mammograms. *Ibid.* 594/2 These mammographic visualizations afford an excellent method of studying both the physiological and pathological changes of the breast. **1969** *New Scientist* 13 Mar. 570/3 Preliminary designs for a commercial version of the system for producing mammograms. **1968** *N.Y. Times* 25 Mar. 25 This image Dr. Wolfe and many other radiologists agree is far clearer and more detailed than film mammographs. **1970** *Daily Tel.* 23 Oct. 17/4 The mammograph is another X-ray machine. Each breast is X-rayed individually, rather as though it were under a microscope. **1973** M. J. BRENNAN in Holland & Frei *Cancer Med.* xxvii. 1776/2 Combined clinical and mammographic screening detected breast cancer at a rate of 2·72 per 1,000 initial examinations. **1969** *New Scientist* 8 May 276/1 Thermography can detect presymptomatic breast cancers even when they are not palpable nor shown up by mammography. **1971** *Daily Colonist* (Victoria, B.C.) 26 Nov. 2/2 If you are still worried, you could have a mammography done—an X-ray technique commonly used in women with breast lumps that have to be identified.

mammoplasty, var. *MAMMAPLASTY.

mammoth, *sb.* and *a.* Add: **B.** *adj.* (Earlier and later examples.)

Freq. in American usage before 1850. The reference in quots. 1802² and 1803 is to a large cheese presented to Jefferson.

1802 *Port Folio* (Philadelphia) II. 31 (Th.), A baker in this city offers Mammoth bread for sale. **1802** *Balance* (Hudson, N.Y.) 19 Oct. 331 (Th.), No more to do with the subject than the man in the moon has to do with the mammoth cheese. **1803** J. DAVIS *Trav. U.S.A.* ix. 329 Its extraordinary dimensions induced some wicked wag of a federalist to call it the Mammoth Cheese. **1813** *Niles' Reg.* IV. 32/2 The Mammoth bank bill passed the senate this day on a third reading. **1924** W. R. INGE *Lay Thoughts* (1926) III. ii. 192 The new journalism, with its 'mammoth combines', is good business, but bad democracy. **1956** *Hansard Commons* 10 May 1450/2 The coal industry today is having to undertake this mammoth reorganisation because of the failures of hon. Members opposite in the years between the wars. **1966** AUDEN *About House* 39 He offered Mammoth-marrow And, perhaps, Long Pig. **1974** *Economist* 21 Dec. 65/1 Britain's mammoth current account deficit.

mammotrophic (mæmotrō͡ᵘ·fik), **-tropic** (-trō͡ᵘpik, -trǫ·pik), *a. Physiol.* [f. *MAMMO- + *-TROPHIC, *-TROPIC.] Stimulating or having the ability to stimulate the breasts, *esp.* in relation to growth or milk secretion.

1935 *Proc. Soc. Exper. Biol. & Med.* XXXII. 1049 The hypophyseal mammotropic hormone. **1942** *Ibid.* LI. 308 (*heading*) The direct mammotrophic action of lactogenic hormone. **1970** *Sci. Jrnl.* June 47/1 All males normally produce small quantities of mammotrophic hormone, but to what end remains a mystery. **1973** *Nature* 8 June 349/2 To further define the relationship between the mammotrophic and sebotrophic hormones we have studied the effect of suckling on sebum secretion.

So **mammotro·phin, -tro·pin** = *PROLACTIN.

1935 *Proc. Soc. Exper. Biol. & Med.* XXXII. 1049 (*heading*) Detection of mammotropin in the urine of lactating women. **1952** [see *lactogen* s.v. *LACTO-]. **1958** *Proc. R. Soc.* B. CXLIX. 309 By adding mammotrophin (*MH*) to these steroids, incomplete lobulo-alveolar growth was induced. **1961** *Lancet* 7 Oct. 792/1 The demonstration of mammotrophin activity.

mammy¹. Add: **1. b.** (Earlier example.)

1826 DISRAELI *Viv. Grey* I. I. iii. 14 'Mammy-sick!' growled Barlow *primus*.

2. (Earlier example.)

1837 *Southern Lit. Messenger* III. 744/1 [Aged Negro domestics] were greeted always by the kind appellatives of 'daddy and mammy'.

mammy². *W. Afr.* [Of obscure origin.] Used *attrib.*, as **mammy boat, mammy chair,** a (wicker) basket or chair used on ships for conveying persons to and from surf-boats on the West African coast; **mammy-cloth** (see quot. 1971¹); **mammy lorry, wagon,** a small open-sided vehicle in West Africa; **mammy trader,** a market woman in West Africa.

1904 *Chambers's Jrnl.* 3 Dec. 15/1 You may elect to travel over the side in the 'mammy-chair', a huge barrel with part of its side cut away slung in the air by the steam-winch. **1909** MOORE & GUGGISBERG *We Two in W. Afr.* 16 So I found myself sitting in the 'Mammy chair', an ordinary basket-chair with ropes slung to the arms and back, ..and in a moment I was whisked off the deck, swung over the side at the end of a long derrick, [etc.]. **1920** *Blackw. Mag.* June 848/1 A mammy chair was lowered, and we made the usual undignified ascent to the main deck. **1928** *Daily Express* 27 Jan. 6/3 A 'mammy' boat, which is simply a wicker basket with seats, is slung over the ship's side by crane. **1935** L. G. GREEN *Great Afr. Mysteries* xv. 192 The 'mammy-chair' is like a swingboat at a fair; just a wooden box with two seats facing each other. **1957** *Times* 17 Dec. 9/6 As we drove on to the ferry a 'mammy-waggon' full of them [*sc.* Ghanaian students] was pushed on behind us. **1959** *Times* 9 Nov. (Ghana Suppl.) p. iv/7 Coordination of the activities of the vigorous 'mammy' traders. **1959** *Listener* 31 Dec. 1156/2 The car-park [in Ghana] with its taxis and mammy-lorries. **1961** G. GREENE *Burnt-Out Case* I. i. 7 When there were no European visitors there were always the old women,..their bodies wrapped in mammy-cloths. **1961** *Listener* 2 Nov. 697/1 The mammy-wagons are the friendly little open-sided buses which ply, always crowded, between towns and villages, and which have their names painted in bright colours. **1962** *Ibid.* 22 Feb. 335/1 A mammy-lorry had stopped just outside, and was disgorging its contents. **1965** W. SOYINKA *Road* 19 Goes into the mammy-waggon stall through hidden entrance up-stage. **1970** P. OLIVER *Savannah Syncopators* 59 (*caption*) Hausa women... One wears a 'mammy-cloth' printed with portraits of Queen Elizabeth the Second and Prince Philip. **1971** A. BAILEY *In Village* (1972) vii. 56 One man I knew used to dress in the evenings in a mammy cloth, the colorful cotton robe the Africans swaddled themselves in. **1971** *Reader's Digest* (U.S. ed.) Oct. 30/1 [In Jiddah] West African 'mammy traders' hawk cocoa beans, salves for arthritis and gaily colored cloth.

mamootie (mæ·mūti). Also **mammotie, mamooty, mam(m)oty, mamuty, mometty.** [ad. Tamil *mammaṭṭi*, altered form of *maṇveṭṭi*, f. *maṇ* earth + *veṭṭi* spade.] A digging tool used mainly in India, shaped like a hoe with the blade at an acute angle to the helve.

1782 C. SALMON in G. W. Forrest *Sel. Lett. Govt. India* (1890) III. 855 He marched..with two battalions of sepoys, leaving the cavalry..who were ordered to make a show of entrenching themselves by digging with mamuties. **1852** F. A. NEALE *Narr. Residence Siam* viii. 138 By means of a mometty or hatchet..this fellow dug..a reservoir. **1858** P. L. SIMMONDS *Dict. Trade Products* 238/1 *Mammotie*, a road hoe, used in Ceylon. **1881** W. W. GREENER *Gun* 587 For shooting on the plains nothing but a mamoty, a crowbar, a mallet, and a couple of axes are required, and these can all be had in India. **1920** *Blackw. Mag.* Oct. 467/2 A company of pioneers each man with pick or shovel or mamootie slung in leather slings on his back. **1934** 'G. ORWELL' *Burmese Days* (1935) vi. 83 He..swung his mamootie aloft again and hacked at the dry ground. **1940** *Nature* 20 July 91/2 The scraping is effected with an ordinary *mammoty* (like a pointed spade with a recurved handle), removing about ⅓ in. of soil.

mampus (mæ·mpŏs). *dial.* [Of obscure origin.] A great number, a crowd.

c **1730** *Dorset Vocab.* in *N. & Q.* (1883) 21 July 45/1 A mampus, multitude. **1857** *Gloss. Provincial Words Dorset* 6 *Mampus*, a great number. **1880** HARDY *Trumpet-Major* I. ii. 32 The mampus of soldiers that have come upon the down. **1904** —— *Dynasts* I. II. iv. 46 What a mampus o' folk it is here to-day!

‖ **mamur** (mamūᵊ·ɹ). [Arab. *ma'mūr.*] An Egyptian official governing a district.

1836 E. W. LANE *Account* I. iv. 152 The whole of Egypt is divided into several large provinces, each of which is governed by an 'Osma'nlee (or a Turk); and these provinces are subdivided into districts, which are governed by native officers, with the titles of *Ma-moo'r* and *Na'zir.* **1899** A. S. WHITE *From Sphinx to Oracle* 108 Shortly afterwards I received the Mamur, who was accompanied by the officer commanding the police. **1900** G. BELL *Let.* 2 May (1927) I. 86 The Mamur (the Sultan's land agent). **1901** F. W. FULLER *Egypt* 259 Each mamurieh is under the charge of a Mamur, or Sub-Governor, who has in most cases been selected from among the native officers of the Egyptian army. **1902** *Encycl. Brit.* XXVII. 691/1 The provincial police is under the direction of the local authorities, the *mudirs* or governors of provinces, and the *mamurs* or district officials. **1958** L. DURRELL *Mountolive* ii. 43 Today, with British rule, the Copt is debarred from holding the position of Governor or even of *Mamur* —the administrative magistrate of a province. **1962** E. E. EVANS-PRITCHARD *Ess. Social Anthropol.* vii. 145 A Zande Prince went through the ceremony of blood-brotherhood with a *mamur* (Egyptian or Sudanese official) to whom he was bitterly hostile.

mamzer. Delete † *Obs.* and add later examples. Also **momser, momza, momzer.** Pl. **mamzeri·m.** Also in extended uses as a term of abuse or familiarity.

1955 H. KURNITZ *Let.* Dec. in G. Marx *Groucho Lett.* (1967) 250 When the momzerim in the aisle seats have finished clubbing me I will come to California. **1960** WENTWORTH & FLEXNER *Dict. Amer. Slang* 342/1 *Momzer, momser*, one who borrows frequently, or who expects much attention and many favors; a sponger... Any disliked person; a bastard. **1963** 'R. L. PIKE' *Mute Witness* (1965) ii. 23 Johnny Rossi? The west-coast hood?.. And we're keeping *momsers* like that alive, now? **1964** W. MARKFIELD *To Early Grave* (1965) iv. 86 That mass man, that totalitarian type, that *momza*. **1968** L. ROSTEN *Joys of Yiddish* 254 *Momzer*..is often used to describe a very bright child, a clever or ingenious person, a resourceful, gets-things-done, corner-cutting type. **1970** L. M. FEINSILVER *Taste of Yiddish* 47 *A Mamzer*..(a bastard, a thief; hence a dirty crook). **1972** *Guardian* 10 Oct. 4/2 The problem of Mamzerim, the Jewish bastard outcasts. **1973** *Jewish Chron.* 19 Jan. 1/4 Hanoch and Miriam Langer are a brother and sister declared by a rabbinical court in Petach Tikva more than seven years ago to be *mamzerim* (children of an adulterous union). *Ibid.* 2 Feb. 23/4 The husband could not be given permission to remarry in an Orthodox synagogue, so he married in a Reform synagogue. Incidentally, any child from this marriage is not a mamzer.

man, *sb.*¹ Add: **2. b.** With a qualifying word, applied to prehistoric types of man, as *Cro-Magnon Man, Neanderthal Man, Peking Man,* etc. (see under the qualifying words).

4. c. Colloq. phr. *to separate* (or *sort out*) *the men from the boys*: to distinguish which persons in a group are mature, manly, expert, etc.

1962 J. BRAINE *Life at Top* ii. 39 Every day one was tested, the men were separated from the boys. **1967** *Listener* 16 Feb. 239/1 It is always quite a pleasure to see some really professional jazz players and hear their sounds and one of the best examples is *Jazz Goes to College*..which certainly sorts out the men from the boys. **1968** *House & Garden* May 36/4 The Dry Martini..is a drink that will quickly separate the men from the boys and the girls from their principles. **1972** *Listener* 17 Aug. 201/3 The ability to memorise a whole [chess] game within a few minutes is.. what separates the men from the boys.

e. (Further examples.) Now in more general use as a form of address to both men and women, as a meaningless expletive, or as an interjection expressing surprise, delight, deep emotion, etc.; esp.: (*a*) in *S. Afr.*; (*b*) among Negroes; (*c*) among jazz musicians and enthusiasts.

1874 A. BATHGATE *Colonial Experiences* ix. 110 Man! they all looked as if they had been shot, and would hardly believe me. **1896** H. A. BRYDEN *Tales S. Afr.* i. 29 'Man!' he said, 'if I had not not been *shamed* into following you, I would never have come across that place.' **1901** M. FRANKLIN *My Brilliant Career* (1966) ii. 7 Here,..with splendid roads, mail thrice weekly, and a railway platform only eight miles away, why, man, my fortune is made! **1933** *Metronome* Aug. 23 Trum's greeting was in the Negro dialect he usually employed: 'Man! How is you?' **1952** M. TRIPP *Faith is Windsock* i. 21 The Jamaican stood up and stretched himself. 'Glad you woke me, man,' he said. **1958** *Observer* 14 Dec. 7/7 The coloured boy..doesn't like the English. 'I'm nineteen, man, and when I go into a public house, they all look at me.' **1959** *Star* (Johannesburg) 17 Dec. 17/1 His second play captures a South African atmosphere in flashes—his policeman begins almost every sentence with 'Man!' and ends it with 'Hey!' **1960** *Monthly Rev.* May 27 Negroes habitually call each other 'man' in reaction to a lifetime of being addressed by white folk as 'boy'. **1961** 'B. WELLS' *Day Earth caught Fire* ix. 145 'Cut that out, man,' the beatnik said. **1966** *Evening Standard* 1 Feb. 8/1 'I like to speak the truth, man,' he said addressing me [*sc.* a woman] with the universal Jamaican appellation of 'man'. **1969** C. F. BURKE (*title*) God is beautiful, man. **1971** *Black Scholar* Jan. 43/2 Man, this would make these fighters so mad. **1971** *Black World* June 54/2 Hey, only the squares, man, only the squares have it to keep. **1972** *New Nation* (Singapore) 25 Nov. 8/5 Close-cropped Charlie continued: 'Oh, you live in Bukit Timah... I used to visit my uncle there, man.' **1973** *Caribbean Contact* Feb. 4/3 'No, man,' the St. Lucian replies.

h. *man to man* (further examples). Also as *adj.* or *adv. phr.* (freq. hyphenated), straightforward(ly), frank(ly). Hence (*nonce-wds.*) **man-to-man-ness, man-to-mannish** *a.*

1901 E. A. ROSS *Social Control* 29 So long as the struggle is man to man..a conscience is a handicap. **1902** E. NESBIT *Five Children & It* ix. 239 The best 'man to man' tone at his command. **1908** *Daily Chron.* 11 Aug. 4/5 Another form of suasion is the 'man-to-man' talk. **1940** N. MARSH *Surfeit of Lampreys* (1941) x. 141 Mike gave Alleyn a man-to-mannish look. **1943** J. B. PRIESTLEY *Daylight on Saturday* xxi. 167 'e remembered..an' stood me a pint. Now that's what I call man-to-man style. **1948** *Dublin Rev.* II. 11 The [Chinese] character for 'jen' is made up of 'man' and 'two'... I translate it 'man-to-man-ness'. **1952** S. KAUFFMANN *Philanderer* (1953) ix. 146 Perry spread his palms wide. 'Why don't you ask her?' Confidentially, man-to-man. 'I'd like to do it just to show her our gratitude for that week-end.' **1955** *Times* 5 Aug. 7/3 Talks man to man can serve the great international peace settlement. **1958** E. HYAMS *Taking it Easy* 49 Bachelor had a brisk, man-to-man style [of writing] which was immensely popular. **1973** 'M. INNES' *Appleby's Answer* xv. 128 A confidential and man-to-man note will be in order. **1974** A. PRICE *Other Paths* I. iii. 30 We must talk man-to-man now—if you would leave us for a moment, Mrs. Mitchell.

k. *spec.* One's representative or envoy *in* a specified place.

1958 G. GREENE (*title*) Our man in Havana. **1961** I. FLEMING *Thunderball* xiv. 154 Seems to me your President is taking all this a bit more seriously than his Man in

Nassau. **1963** L. DEIGHTON *Horse under Water* vi. 33 'Welcome to Gibraltar,' said Joe MacIntosh, our man in Iberia. *Ibid.* xxxix. 154 Through the twilight 'our man in Cardiff' lifted a finger at the crooked castle of Caerphilly.

m. *man John*: delete 'nonce-substitutions' and add earlier examples.

1838 [see JOHN 1 b]. **1845** DISRAELI *Sybil* III. VI. vi. 214 My missus says that not a man John of them is to be seen.

p. (*a*) *spec.* One who is a specialist in or is expert in a specified subject; a supporter or adherent of a specified person; one who favours a specified product. See also **cruelty man.*

1921 T. S. ELIOT *Let.* 26 Oct. in *Waste Land Drafts* (1971) p. xxii, I have wondered whether he is quite the best man for me as he is known as a nerve man and I want rather a specialist in psychological troubles. **1938** A. HUXLEY *Let.* 12 Apr. (1969) 435 The cancer-man..had hit on something very fundamental. **1958** *Listener* 25 Sept. 449/2, I am therefore wholeheartedly a Galbraith man... Professor Galbraith is the first writer to attempt a systematic economic analysis of such a society. **1960** *Ottawa Citizen* 25 Mar. 1/8 Pearkes 'Bomarc Man' Despite U.S. Cutbacks... Defence Minister Pearkes today denied the Bomarc-B missile is a 'dead pigeon' and affirmed he still retained full confidence in it as an air defence system. **1964** *College Composition & Communication* XV. iv, The program of English studies was in the hands, not of the wise dean who encouraged the variousness of my undergraduate program, but of several gentlemen called 'the Malory man', 'the Restoration drama man', and 'the *Paradise Lost* man'. **1969** *Listener* 24 July 102/1, I had been the *Daily Telegraph*'s main German man for some time. **1973** J. WAINWRIGHT *Touch of Malice* 89, I wouldn't have thought..you were a beer man. **1974** *Country Life* 25 Apr. 1008/1 A wonderful cruising ground for the yachtsman, be he a power or sail man. **1974** P. LOVESEY *Invitation to Dynamite Party* ii. 25 'Is it the hard stuff that you've taken a fancy to?' 'Not me, Sarge. I never was a whisky man.'

r. *every* (or *each*) *man for himself*: applied to a situation in which each person is preoccupied with his own safety or advancement.

c **1386** CHAUCER *Knight's Tale* (1894) 1182 At the kinges court, my brother, Ech man for him-self. *c* **1515** BARCLAY *Ecologues* (1928) I. 1009 Eche man for him selfe, and the frende for for all. **1562** J. HEYWOOD *Dialogue of Proverbs* II. ix, in *Works* sig. k4 Every man for him selfe, and god for us all. **1629** T. ADAMS *Workes* 422 That by-word, Euery man for himselfe, and God for vs all, is vncharitable, vngodly; and impugneth directly the end of euery good calling, and honest kinde of life. **1825** J. NEAL *Bro. Jonathan* III. xxix. 90 'Forward! Forward!' were the cries, on every side of our hero. 'Forward! forward! every man for himself!' **1922** H. WALPOLE *Cathedral* I. i. 14 They had been troublous times. It had been every man for himself.

s. *the man* (also *the Man*): a person in authority; such persons collectively; *spec.* (*a*) a prison governor; (*b*) a policeman or detective; the police; (*c*) one's employer, 'boss'; (*d*) (*Negro slang*) a white man; white people collectively; (*e*) a drug-pusher. *U.S. slang.*

1918 G. M. BATTEY *70,000 Miles in Submarine Destroyer* (1919) 302 Any body in authority is 'the man'. **1928** R. FISHER *Walls of Jericho* 306 *The man*, designation of abstract authority. He who trespasses where a sign forbids is asked: 'Say, biggy, can't you read *the man's* sign?' **1933** *Amer. Speech* VIII. III. 29/2 Unuther goddam word out o' you-all, an' Ah'll send ev'ry goddam one of ye up t' the Man. **1953** W. BURROUGHS *Junkie* (1972) ix. 87 When I first hit New Orleans, the main pusher—or 'the Man', as they say there—was a character called Yellow. *Ibid.* 159 '*The Man*', junk seller. 'The Man' is a New Orleans expression, and can also refer to a Narcotics Agent. **1962** *Amer. Speech* XXXVII. 270 *Man*, a policeman. A word used by teen-age drivers. 'When I heard the siren, I knew it was the Man.' **1962** J. BALDWIN *Another Country* (1963) II. ii. 243 One of the musicians came to the doorway, and said, 'Ida, honey, the man says come on with it if you coming.' **1963** *N.Y. Times* 18 May 12/2 A well-educated Negro said today: 'The demonstrations, I think, suggested to "The Man" that tokenism won't make it and that he has to come to grips with the problem right now.' 'The Man', in Negro parlance, is the white man. **1965** *Times Lit. Suppl.* 25 Nov. 1035 *Man* is the title by which one Negro addresses another... *The Man* is the way in which he speaks of the enemy, of the white. **1968** *Blues Unlimited* Nov. 8 They were sharecroppers but the last crop put them so deeply in debt with 'the man' that they plan to quit farming. **1970** *Guardian* 3 Nov. 10/1 'The Man is repressive. The Man is fascist...' To the bombers and kidnappers the Man is authority. He is every policeman. He is President Nixon. He is Prime Minister Trudeau. **1972** J. MILLS *Report to Commissioner* 106, I heard you were the man, and if I really believed you were the man, you'd be dead now. **1972** *Guardian* 12 Aug. 9 Rus is not Uncle Tomming it around Harlem with 'the Man'. He has brought a foreign visitor. **1973** *Black World* Nov. 92/2 Their writing mainly concerns the street life—the pimp, the junky, the forces of drug addiction, exploitation at the hands of 'the man'. **1974** R. THOMAS *Porkchoppers* xi. 98 They'll be on my back for telling them something that they don't think the man needs to know.

18. *man of sense* (earlier example); **man of action,** a man whose life is characterized by physical activity or deeds rather than by thoughts and ideas; **man of destiny,** a man looked upon as an instrument of destiny; *spec.* Napoleon I; **man of distinction,** a person who is distinguished in his looks, manners, and bearing; **man of the moment**: see *MOMENT *sb.* 1 c; **man of the people,** a man who comes from or identifies himself with the common people; a working-class man.

1597 Man of Action [see ACTION 1 a]. **1828** SCOTT *Fair Maid of Perth* in *Chron. Canongate* 2nd Ser. I. vii. 140 Our neighbour Proudfute..is of course a man of action. **1853** C. BRONTË *Villette* II. xxiv. 193 Dr. John *could* think, and think well, but he was rather a man of action than of thought. **1937** *Discovery* July 226/1 The outdoor man of action and the indoor man of thought. **1963** AUDEN *Dyer's Hand* VII. 435 It was inevitable that..a dramatist would ask himself if the artist-genius could be substituted for the traditional man-of-action as a dramatic hero. **1827** SCOTT *Life Napoleon Buonaparte* IX. 329 The great plans which the Man of Destiny had been called upon earth to perform. **1909** *Westm. Gaz.* 26 Aug. 5/1 His man-of-destiny characteristics made him an interesting study to the newspaper correspondents. **1921** G. B. SHAW *Back to Methuselah* IV. ii. 178 *Napoleon* (*impressively*). I am the Man of Destiny. **1699** M. LISTER *Journey to Paris* 40 It is ..much more pleasing to see..a dead Friend, or Relation, or..a Man of Distinction, Painted as he was. **1954** 'P. QUENTIN' *Wife of R. Sheldon* xix. 167 He'd never been so innocent, so the man of distinction. **1971** D. LEES *Rainbow Conspiracy* vii. 111 He had a nervous apprehensive look that contrasted strangely with his man-of-distinction appearance. **1680** ROCHESTER *Poems* 12 Dares chide at Kings, and raile at Men of sense. **1849** C. BRONTË *Shirley* III. ii. 36 Mrs. Pryor..wondered how her daughter could be so much at ease with a 'man of the people'... She felt as if a great gulf lay between her caste and his. **1885** H. JAMES *Little Tour in France* xxiii. 151 A man of the people,..extremely intelligent,..yet remaining essentially of the people. **1971** W. J. BURLEY *Guilt Edged* vii. 116 'You have the most revolting habits, Jimmy.' 'A man of the people, that's me!' **1973** P. MALLOCH *Kickback* vii. 47 He was a man of the people. He'd been born in the Gorbals and had left school at fourteen.

19. (Further, esp. *poet.*, examples.) **a.** *man-eye, -flesh* (later example), *-life, -management, -mark, -meat, -monster* (later example), *-seed, -sex, -shape, -smell, -soul.*

1932 W. FAULKNER *Light in August* i. 23 She traverses the ranked battery of maneyes and enters the store. **1923** R. GRAVES *Whipperginny* 25 And frozen music dulls their need Of drink and man-flesh greed. **1918** D. H. LAWRENCE *New Poems* 43 The man-life north-imprisoned, shut in the hum of the purpled steel. **1967** A. BATTERSBY *Network Analysis* (ed. 2) xv. 271 If the senior executives of a company really feel that the risk is great, they might do better to shelve network analysis and continue with existing methods until better man-management relations have been forged. **1971** *Mod. Law Rev.* XXXIV. VI. 680 The principle of an employer's responsibility for the results of 'teamwork by his team' goes to the centre of all thinking upon the techniques of organisation of groups and 'man-management' in large organisations. **1971** C. BONINGTON *Annapurna South Face* i. 7 The smaller the party, the closer you can get to the mountains uncluttered by all the ..complications of man-management caused by a larger expedition. **1888** G. M. HOPKINS *Poems* (1967) 105 Squadroned masks and manmarks treadmire toil there. **1962** W. STEGNER *Wolf Willow* III. ii. 148 'What's a windigo?' 'What the Crees used to call an Injun that made use of man-meat.' **1971** B. MALAMUD *Tenants* 207 The sweaty youths, holding long spears, leaped and yelped as they danced, their man-meat swinging like grapes in bunches in their loincloths. **1928** BLUNDEN *Jap. Garland* 16 Clawtendrils reach, man-monsters glare. **1934** DYLAN THOMAS *18 Poems* 27 The growing bones, the rumour of manseed Within the hallowed gland. **1971** G. M. BROWN *Fishermen with Ploughs* 4 Hoof-fast Njal bore his manseed wombfurled waveward. *c* **1879** G. M. HOPKINS *Poems* (1967) 82 Breathing bloom of a chastity in mansex fine. **1888** *Ibid.* 105 Manshape, that shone Sheer off, disseveral, a star, death blots black out. **1922** JOYCE *Ulysses* 368 Perhaps they get a man smell off us. **1938** M. K. RAWLINGS *Yearling* xi. 113 I'm jest lonesome for boy-smell and mansmell. **1961** R. P. HOBSON *Rancher takes Wife* viii. 118 She [*sc.* a cow moose] would trot over to the timber, lick her calf to its feet, and lead it off—away from the contaminated area of man-smell. **1682** J. BUNYAN *Holy War* (1905) 190 For here lay the excellent wisdom of him that builded Mansoul, that the Walls could never be broken down. **1929** R. BRIDGES *Testament of Beauty* IV. 1391 From this dilemma..Man-soul made glad escape in the worship of Christ.

b. *man-friend.* Cf. sense 22 a below.

1736 LD. HERVEY *Mem.* (1952) 182 The King's letter to the Queen about this affair was an extraordinary one, asking her, as he would have done a man-friend, what she thought of all this business. **1893** *Ladies' Home Jrnl.* Apr. 39/1 There is no impropriety in a man friend writing to you without having asked your permission. **1922** D. H. LAWRENCE *Fantasia of Unconscious* xi. 204 The woman..will have a new man-friend, if nothing more.

d. *man-picker, -tamer, -tracker*; *man-carrying, -lifting, -loving, -stopping, -tracking* vbl. sbs. and ppl. adjs.; *man-shy* adj.

1909 *Westm. Gaz.* 25 Feb. 4/1 The latter..achieved for the first time in history a man-carrying machine propelled by its own motive power. **1961** *Times* 28 Apr. 3/6 The placing in orbit of a man-carrying satellite. **1846** *Pract. Mechanic* June 235/1 The man-lifting engine erected at United Mines, Gwennap..for lowering and raising the miners. **1899** *Rep. Brit. Assoc. Adv. Sci.* 948 Man-lifting kites might be used instead of a balloon. **1927** C. L. M. BROWN *Conquest of Air* 122 By 1905 Cody had attracted official attention to his man-lifting kites. **1895** W. JAMES in *Internat. Jrnl. Ethics* Oct. 8 The old warm notion of a man-loving Deity. **1939** W. B. YEATS *Last Poems* 17 Man-picker Niamh leant and sighed By Oisin on the grass. **1931** F. D. DAVISON (*title*) Man-shy. **1899** *Kynoch Jrnl.* Oct.–Nov. 15/2 The manstopping powers of the..bullets appear to be considerable at short ranges. **1905** *Ibid.* Apr.–June 96 Man-stopping bullets are not allowed. **1973** *Guardian* 17 Mar. 13/2 Both guns increase the 'man-stopping' effectiveness of police marksmen. **1922** JOYCE *Ulysses* 526 Master! Mistress! Mantamer! **1931** D. RUNYON *Guys & Dolls* (1932) i. 32 Nip and Tuck go back to Georgia..with a big reputation as man-trackers. *Ibid.* i. 17 They is man-tracking bloodhounds from Georgia.

e. *man-filled, -gripped, -measured, -powered, -propelled* ppl. adjs. Also *MAN-MADE *a.*

1909 E. POUND *Personae* 30 A bustling man-filled place. **1921** D. H. LAWRENCE *Sea & Sardinia* vi. 215 How old the real Italy is, how man-gripped, and how withered. **1943** D. GASCOYNE *Poems 1937–42* v. 60 In the pure ray shed by the loss Of all man-measured value. **1959** *Times* 27 July 7/6 A purely private effort..to achieve a man-powered 'ornithopter'. **1962** *Listener* 10 May 812/2 A man-powered flight. **1937** *Sunday Times* 10 Jan. 27/5 All man-propelled or horse-drawn traffic would automatically be relegated to the service roads.

f. *man-centred, -faced, -headed, -high* (later examples), *-smelling, -stale, -tall, -visaged* adjs.

1959 D. COOKE *Lang. Mus.* ii. 54 A proud, man-centred existence, in which the emphasis was on personal happiness. **1877** G. MACDONALD *Marquis of Lossie* II. x. 116 There's mair poetry in auld man-faced Miss Horn nor in a dizzen like them. *a* **1930** D. H. LAWRENCE *Etruscan Places* (1932) iv. 123 Some acts..the man-faced bull accepts calmly. **1855** J. GOTT *Lett.* (1918) 81 Rows of sphinxes man-headed and god-headed. **1941** L. MACNEICE *Poetry of Yeats* v. 98 The hero of this poem..is a man sailing through faerie seas haunted by man-headed birds. **1932** AUDEN *Orators* II. 44 After the death of their proud master, who Stood man-high in his socks and paid his debts. **1954** J. R. R. TOLKIEN *Two Towers* 171 Man-high, but with goblin-faces. **1973** C. BONINGTON *Next Horizon* xiv. 209 We..had reached the grass-line—great tussocks of coarse, man-high grass. **1932** W. FAULKNER *Light in August* ii. 44 The house unpainted, small..mansmelling, manstale. **1938** S. SPENDER *Trial of Judge* I. 15 Electric advertisements In city squares—those man-tall golden letters. **1920** R. GRAVES *Country Sentiment* 39 Sing then of ringstraked manticor, Man-visaged tiger.

20. man-boy, a youth, an immature man; **man-crazy** *a.* = **man-mad* adj.; **man-hair,** a man's pubic hair; **man-hungry** *a.*, desirous of a man; **man-in-space** orig. *U.S.*, an astronaut; freq. *attrib.*; **man-load,** a load such as one man can carry; **man-machine,** (*b*) a man who acts mechanically; an automaton (cf. quot. 1904 s.v. 22 a below); (*c*) used as *adj.* to denote a relationship or communication between a man and a machine; **man-mad** *a.*, madly desirous of a man or men (cf. *man-wood* adj. in Dict.); **man-mountain** (further examples); now applied esp. to a wrestler; **man-pack, manpack,** a compact package containing equipment or supplies, designed to be carried easily by one man; also *attrib.*; **man-power,** (*a*) the power or agency of man in work; (*b*) used as a unit of power or rate of working; (*c*) the number of persons available for a purpose, esp. for military service; also *attrib.*; **man-riding** *Mining*, the vehicular transport of miners underground; freq. *attrib.*; so **man-rider,** a train of vehicles designed for this; **man-rope (knot)** (see quot.); **manself** [after HIMSELF *pron.*] *nonce-wd.*, man's self; **man-shift,** (the amount of work done in) a single shift worked by one man; **man-size(d)** *a.*, of the size of a man; large, full-size; large enough to occupy, suit, or satisfy a man; **man-starved** *ppl. a.*, suffering from the lack of a man or men; desirous of a man; **man-strength** = **man-power* (*c*); **man-tailored** *a.*, of women's clothes: tailored after the fashion of men's clothes; **man-wise** *adv.* and *pred. a.*, in the fashion or way of men; in respect of a man; concerning individual men.

1927 W. DEEPING *Kitty* ix. 115 This husband of hers, this man-boy, what was he? **1945** S. SPENDER *Citizens in War* iv. 35 Tolerance defeated the religious man-boy who expected at least to be persecuted. **1923** G. ATHERTON *Black Oxen* xlii. 262 The young women would say, in their nasty slang, that I was probably man-crazy. **1967** H. VAN SILLER *Biltmore Call* 128 Never liked the woman... Man crazy and two-faced. **1972** A. AMIN tr. *Ahmad's No Harvest but Thorn* xi. 115 Let them call her bold... That Jeha was man-crazy. **1928** Man-hair [see *MAIDENHAIR 5 b]. **1951** J. CORNISH *Provincials* 220 Douglas fell..to a girl described by Bunty as twenty-eight and strictly man-hungry. **1959** *Daily Tel.* 21 Nov. 1/2 Capsule recovery is a crisis point in our man-in-space programme. **1962** *Amer. Speech* XXXVII. 43 Before April 12, 1961, the concept expressed by *cosmonaut*..was rendered..by such terms as ..*man-in-space*. **1968** *Economist* 28 Dec. 11/2 The man-in-space programme has earned itself enemies in powerful reaches of the scientific establishment. **1878** H. M. STANLEY *Through Dark Continent* I. xiv. 376 Suna commanded his Katekiro to make up 300 man-loads of hoes and old iron. **1951** M. MCLUHAN *Mech. Bride* (1967) 18/1 There is a wide range of mental states engendered in the same man–machine relationship. **1953** R. LEHMANN *Echoing Grove* 240 He was now an automaton, a man-machine. **1967** COX & GROSE *Organiz. Bibliogr. Rec. by Computer* IV. 99 This is what is meant by man–machine dialoguing. **1904** Man-mad [in def. of *man-wood* adj. in Dict.]. **1928** R. MACAULAY *Keeping up Appearances* vii. 62 If a woman went on that way about men you'd call her man-mad. **1959** *News Chron.* 28 Aug. 6/3 The man-mad duchess.. picks up the young peasant painter. **1942** BERREY & VAN DEN BARK *Amer. Thes. Slang* § 429/1 Corpulent person,.. *man mountain*. *Ibid.* § 707/2 *Man mountain*, a large wrestler. **1956** J. SYMONS *Paper Chase* XXX. 240 He was trying desperately to establish some kind of grip that would move

this man mountain. **1960** E. W. Hildick *Jim Starling & Colonel* xii. 105 'Are you—er—Mr Thimble?'.. 'Well, I'm not Man-Mountain Dean.' **1972** J. Mosedale *Football* viii. 105 A man-mountain for his time, he played tackle for the Giants and Packers. **1967** *Electronics* 6 Mar. 52/2 The jungle..absorbs and deflects transmissions from man-pack radio sets. **1970** *Islander* (Victoria, B.C.) 8 Feb. 5/3 Transportation was all by man-pack, pack-horse, canoe and raft. **1862,** etc. Man-power [in Dict., sense 19 a]. **1893** *Eng. Mechanic* Dec. 332/2 Maxim's early trials gave ..about 1 lb. per man-power. **1917** W. S. Churchill in *World Crisis 1916–18* (1927) II. 378 It is not possible to settle the question of man-power without a clear idea of the plan of campaign. **1919** *Brit. Manufacturer* Nov. 25/1 One of these man-power ploughs, adapted for small holdings and for use on terraced land, is driven by a cable. **1926** A. Bennett *Lord Raingo* xii. 60 Biggest piece of political camouflage ever attempted, the Man-Power bill is. **1972** *Accountant* 28 Sept. 386/2 The popular vogue of 'manpower planning'..must be more competently compiled where new relevant facts and figures are fed back from the human resource accounting system. **1972** *Daily Tel.* 28 Nov. 16 A great deal of manpower was being wasted before the merger. **1967** *Gloss. Mining Terms* (*B.S.I.*) x. 11 *Manrider*, a manriding train. **1950** H. F. Banks in E. Mason *Pract. Coal Mining* II. xxxv. 530/2 Where locomotives and large mine cars are in use, they serve also as a means of man riding. *Ibid.* 531/1 Fig. 78 illustrates one type of man-riding car. **1952** T. Bryson *Mining Machinery* (ed. 3) xiv. 381 The train..comprises six man-riding carriages with seating accommodation for 18 persons, two brake cars.., and one tool car. **1972** (*title*) Specification for cars for manriding in mines (B S.I.). **1973** *Times* 2 Mar. (Wales Suppl.) p. iii/3 The coal board is now concentrating on increasing 'manriding'—trains from pit bottom to coalface—wherever the geology makes it possible. **1883** *Man. Seamanship for Boys' Training Ships R. Navy* (Admiralty) (1886) 121 A double-wall, double-crowned.. is used for man-ropes, stopper-knots, &c., also called a man-rope knot. **1880** G. M. Hopkins *Note-bks. & Papers* (1937) 271 He..would raise man..infinitely above manself to the divine justice. **1930** *Engineering* 3 Jan. 23/3 Variations in the standard of living..are reflected in the average output per man-shift. **1946** *Nature* 17 Aug. 226/2 In 1938..the Ruhr coal miner produced 30·5 cwt. per man-shift; in the same year the British miner produced 23 cwt. per man-shift. **1913** R. W. Service *Rhymes of Rolling Stone* 103 The man-size mountains palisade us round on every side. **1928** *Publishers' Weekly* 16 June 2441 Since writing is a man-size job, he would have his hands full. **1963** *House & Garden* Mar. 130/1 (Advt.), Fourpenn'orth of Phurnacite 'eggs' will heat enough water for a man-size bath. **1975** *Times* 13 Jan. 8/1 We would..drink whisky out of mansize glasses. **1920** J. Gregory *Man to Man* (1921) xvii. 209 He was trying to hide a pair of man-sized feet behind his table. **1920** S. Lewis *Main St.* xxiii. 277 A regular man-sized pair of pants. **1954** 'N. Shute' *Slide Rule* vii. 167 These woodworkers, accustomed as they were to man-sized factories, regarded Airspeed Ltd as a joke. **1972** F. Durbridge *Bat out of Hell* v. 174 Thelma..blew her nose on a tiny handkerchief which seemed ridiculous in her man-sized hand. **1961** *Times* 24 Oct. 13/2 Beautiful, man-starved women. **1931** *Ann. Reg. 1930* I. 23 The United States was greatly adding to its man-strength. **1922** Joyce *Ulysses* 153 Molly had that elephantgrey dress with the braided frogs. Mantailored with selfcovered buttons. **1970** *Women's Wear Daily* 23 Nov. 31 (Advt.), Man-tailored jeans by Anvil Brand are now available. **1901** Man-wise [see *group-wise* adv. s.v. *group *sb.* 6]. **1930** D. H. Lawrence *A propos Lady Chatterley* 39 Men experience the great rhythm of emotion man-wise, women experience it women-wise.

b. With a period of time, as *man-day, -hour, -minute, -month, -week, -year*, a day, hour, etc., of one person's work (or life). Also in extended use. Cf. *man-load, -shift* (sense 20 above).

1925 E. O. Shebbeare in E. F. Norton *Fight for Everest, 1924* III. vi. 364 Each case would contain a sufficient ration of all kinds of food for a given number of 'men-days'. **1957** M. Swan *Brit. Guiana* I. iv. 83 The doctor told me that before the conquest malaria accounted for about 55,000 hospital man-days a year. **1972** D. Haston *In High Places* vi. 74 As for food.. Some dried meat, bacon, nuts, chocolate and a few hot drinks per man-day. **1972** M. D. Papagiannis *Space Physics & Space Astron.* 280 In less than 10 years from the first manned flight we have accumulated more than a year of man-days in space. **1917** *Anti-Submarine Rep.* (Admiralty, R. Naval Air Service) Dec., Many air stations have large complements, and a comparison of the number of 'man hour's' work carried out with the the hours of flying on anti-submarine service will be found of interest. **1964** H. H. Emsley *Factory Costing* 76 The number of productive 'man-hours' in each department during each 'cost period'. **1951** R. A. Knox *Stimuli* III. xxii. 131 Experts are uncomfortably reckoning out what chances..we are throwing away in terms of man-hours. **1971** *Nature* 29 Oct. 625/1 Countless man-hours have been spent on 'measuring' such allegedly useful entities as 'IQ' and 'reading age'. **1973** D. Westheimer *Going Public* ix. 133 How many man-hours do you spend actually executing an assignment? **1934** Webster, Man-minute. **1947** Crowther & Whiddington *Science at War* ii. 111 The actual working-time was only 53 man-minutes. **1969** J. Argenti *Managem. Techniques* vii. 42 This package cuts out nearly all the hard, highly skilled man-months of programming. **1973** *Computers & Humanities* VII. 190 The preparation of the double transcription of the Vulgate text took seven man-months. **1945** *Times* 19 Jan. 2/4 About 1,300,000 man-weeks remained to be consumed by March 31 if the labour force remained the same. **1961** *Jrnl. Oil & Colour Chemists' Assoc.* XLIV. 296 With proper planning fifty paints can be fully investigated in approximately two man weeks. **1928** A. S. Eddington *Nature Physical World* ix. 180 We must describe the amount of humanity in it [*sc.* Great Britain] as 400 million man-years. **1956** J. Masters *Bugles & Tiger* ii. 71 All my family's hundreds of man-years of work now focused on me. **1969** J. Argenti *Managem. Techniques* vii. 41 Linear Programming..might take two man-years to develop an 'LP Model' of a company. **1973** *Times* 12 Feb. (Anchor Project Suppl.) p. i/5 This level is likely to be little more than half the output a man-year that will be expected from single, integrated works of more than seven million tonnes capacity.

21. man's man, a man whose qualities are appreciated by other men; a man who is popular with other men; so **man's woman** (see also quot. 1905).

1897 G. Du Maurier *Martian* 214 He had been essentially a man's man hitherto, in spite of his gay light love for lovely women; a good comrade par excellence, a frolicsome chum, a rollicking boon-companion, a jolly pal! **1902** J. Buchan *Watcher by Threshold* v. ii. 277, I know he's supposed to be a man's man..but I'm honest enough to own to detesting him. **1960** Man's man [see *dig *v.* 6 c]. **1972** P. Newton *Sheep Thief* v. 39 He had had comparatively little to do with women. Essentially a man's man he had been wrapped up in his calling. **1905** A. Bennett *Sacred & Profane Love* II. vi. 191, I was at last a man's woman. I had a protector. **1930** W. S. Maugham *Writer's Notebk.* (1949) 232 She is what is called a man's woman, and exchanges chaff across the dining-room with the other guests. **1968** E. McGirr *Lead-Lined Coffin* iii. 108 Jeanie's a man's woman, you know, not a woman's woman.

22. a. (Further examples.)

1904 *Westm. Gaz.* 22 Nov. 12/1 Nowadays the Kaiser's men-machines take the best part of the pavement from anyone whom they may safely elbow off. **1907** A. C. Benson *Diary* 31 Jan. (1926) 157 Yet I do not squabble with my men-friends. **1910** F. Barclay *Rosary* ii. 10 But of men friends she had many. **1923** D. H. Lawrence *Birds, Beasts & Flowers* 172 Men-peasants from jungle villages dancing and running with sweat and laughing. **1952** S. Spender *Shelley* ii. 9 Hogg..was the first in a series of rather earth-bound men-friends. **1973** J. Burrows *Like an Evening Gone* i. 12 How many attendant men friends?

c. men-only *a.*, designating a place, etc., restricted for the use of men.

[**1935** (*magazine-title*) Men only. **1955** H. W. Allen in *Stag Party with 'Men Only'* 12 The *Sporting Times*, affectionately known from the colour of its paper as the *Pink 'Un*, that spicy and distinctly *Men Only* weekly of Victorian days.] **1965** 'S. Ransome' *Alias his Wife* vi. 57 Without discouraging women as customers, it had become a men-only place. **1967** N. Fitzgerald *Affairs of Death* ii. 34 It's a men-only bathing place. **1972** G. Beare *Bee Sting Deal* x. 123 There was one hotel..rigidly dry and rigidly men-only.

23. Men's Liberation, Men's Lib. orig. *U.S.* [after **Women's Liberation, Women's Lib.*], a movement aimed at freeing men from traditional views of their character and role in society; **men's room** orig. *U.S.*, a lavatory for men; also (ellipt.) *men's*; **men's wear, menswear,** clothes for men.

1957 S. Beckett *All that Fall* 24 *Mrs. Rooney.* 'Where were you all this time?' *Mr. Rooney.* 'In the men's.' **1972** R. Lockridge *Preach No More* iii. 43 This friend of his had..gone to the men's, or something. **1970** *New Yorker* 19 Dec. 101 We recently read in the *Times* about a group called Men's Liberation, Inc., whose aim is to free men from their traditional role of 'all-powerful provider' and embolden them to cry, complain, feel sorry for themselves, and change their minds. The members of Men's Lib say they are tired of 'having to prove our masculinity twenty-four hours a day' and believe that if their cause should prevail 'outmoded concepts would disappear in the face of reality'. **1971** *N.Y. Times* 17 June 41 To the Women's Liberation Movement the sex-role distinctions mean pressure to conform to separate and unequal rewards for being a woman. To the Men's Liberation Movement they mean pressure to conform to the 'ego ethic'—or conform to perform. **1972** 'J. Melville' *Ironwood* ix. 154 Three months of Tessa and they [*sc.* her male assistants] must have been heading for freedom and Men's Lib. **1929** 'E. Queen' *Roman Hat Mystery* iii. 31 Search the lounge downstairs. The men's room, the ladies' room. **1947** Auden *Age of Anxiety* (1948) ii. 51 Malin excused himself and went to the men's room. **1962** J. Wain *Strike Father Dead* 138 He's in the men's room. He's been wanting to go all evening, but as long as you were playing he didn't want to miss a note. **1947** *Partisan Rev.* XIV. 364 Seymour's taste in clothes and men's wear was loud, practically spectacular. **1972** P. Flower *Cobweb* II. 58 Among the heaps of flowers a wreath from the Menswear Dept. **1973** D. Robinson *Rotten with Honour* 35 [He] looked at Hale as if Hale were modelling menswear. **1974** *Radio Times* 28 Feb. 4/3 The family textile and menswear business.

man, *v.* Add: **4.** Also with *up*; *spec.* to supply with the full number of workers required.

1947 *Times* 6 Feb. 5/5 Must industries be fully 'manned up' rather than 'manned'? Must the strong, simple transitive verb..become as obsolete in England as it appears to be in America? **1947** *Hansard Commons* 18 Dec. 1895/1 Mining and agriculture are the two most vital industries which we must man-up. **1951** E. A. G. Robinson in D. N. Chester *Lessons Brit. War Econ.* iii. 52 Their most urgent jobs were not in fact manned-up as they would have liked. **1955** *Times* 20 May 11/6 The need to 'man up' undermanned industries 'in the national interest' might justify higher wages. **1969** *Times* 6 Mar. 23/1 'We're manned up again,' came a voice of relief... Superstitious members..now have the satisfaction of seeing their numbers rise from 13 to 20.

mana (mā·nă). [Maori.] Power in general, authority, prestige; *spec.* in primitive religion, an impersonal supernatural power which can be associated with people or with objects and which can be transmitted or inherited.

1843 E. Dieffenbach *Trav. N.Z.* II. III. ix. 371/2 Mana—command, authority, power. **1855** R. Taylor *Te Ika a Maui* 279 The natives..feel..that with the land, their *mana*, or power, has gone likewise. **1858** *Richmond-Atkinson Papers* (1960) I. 367 The most loyal reverence for the Queen's name and 'mana'..[is] to be found in Ngapuhi. **1877** R. H. Codrington *Let.* in Max Müller *Lect. Orig. & Growth Relig.* (1878) 54 There is a belief in a force altogether distinct from physical power, which acts in all kinds of ways for good and evil, and which it is of the greatest advantage to possess or control. This is Mana. *a* **1910** W. James *Some Probl. Philos.* (1911) i. 17 What made things act was the mysterious energy in them, and the more awful they were, the more of this *mana* they possessed. **1920** *Times Lit. Suppl.* 29 Apr. 264/2 Notions of the type of mana or orenda are of 'a nascently philosophic order'. **1937** R. H. Lowie *Hist. Ethnol. Theory* xii. 204 It is not merely spirits and deities that loom as sacred, but also the impersonal force Melanesians call 'mana'. **1951** R. Firth *Elem. Social Organiz.* vii. 215 The data accumulated on the character and functions of.. principles of mana and taboo..have enabled large regions of human religious experience to be mapped out on a comparative basis. **1959** *Chambers's Encycl.* IX. 47/2 It is this rudimentary concept of a mystic, quasi-impersonal force connected with anything mysterious and arresting that finds expression in *mana.* **1965** *Listener* 2 Dec. 920/2 Warhol has always provided a good example of the kind of *mana* which emanates from certain chosen individuals in modern society. **1975** H. McCloy *Minotaur Country* v. 53 He has *mana*... The thing most people think they're talking about when they say charisma.

attrib. and *Comb.*

1924 W. B. Selbie *Psychol. Relig.* 208 A fearful cringing before some mysterious mana-charged object. **1937** *Brit. Jrnl. Psychol.* Oct. 197 Their religious beliefs centre round a concept of magic of the 'mana' type i.e. vague, abstract, impersonal power. **1949** Koestler *Promise & Fulfilment* II. v. 274 He has a *mana*-circle in Tel Aviv.

manage, *v.* **11. b.** (Earlier examples.)

1854 M. L. Charlesworth *Ministering Children* iv. 47 Rose was..wondering how William would manage about getting some logs for Mercy's fire. **1873** 'S. Coolidge' *What Katy Did* xi. 195 I've been thinking how we are to manage about the housekeeping. **1895** 'G. Mortimer' *Like Stars that Fall* viii. 108 'How will you manage about your hair?' 'I shall cut it short, I think.'

managed, *ppl. a.* Add: **2. managed bond** (see quot. 1972); **managed currency,** a currency system which is not tied to the gold standard but is regulated by the government of the country concerned; **managed economy,** an economy in which the framework and general policies are regulated or controlled by the government.

1923 J. M. Keynes *Tract on Monetary Reform* 166 This is what is meant by saying that gold has 'intrinsic value' and is free from the dangers of a 'managed' currency. *Ibid.* 167 Gold itself has become a 'managed' currency. **1924** W. F. Spalding *Eastern Exchange Currency & Finance* (ed. 4) p. v, India and one or two other Eastern nations have found defects in a 'managed' currency. **1929** G. D. H. Cole in *New Leader* 8 Nov. 16/3 A plea for a 'managed currency'..a currency that is regulated not automatically by the supply of gold, but deliberately. **1941** G. N. Clark *Holland & War* 9 In September 1936 ..France and Switzerland gave up the gold standard and Holland too went over to a managed currency. **1969** *Adv. Sci.* XXVI. 64/2 The first objective of a managed economy..was originally stability. *Ibid.* 66/2 In considering the problems of a managed economy it is well to begin by recognizing that management is by no means the same as control. [**1971** *Investors Chron.* 2 Apr. 22 (Advt.), It's called the Abbey Selective Investment Bond, and it's issued and managed by Abbey Life Assurance.] **1972** *Observer* 8 Oct. 18/2 In theory a managed bond is an ideal investment. The investor buys units in a special bond fund which the managers can invest in property, shares or fixed-interest stock according to their expert appraisal of the investment scene.

management. Add: **1. e.** *spec.* The administration of a commercial enterprise. Also in phrases designating specific methods of business administration, as *management by exception, by objectives.*

1906 Dicksee & Blain (*title*) Office organisation and management. **1962** A. Battersby *Guide to Stock Control* x. 95 They [*sc.* the junior staff] are the instruments of 'management by exception', filtering out the run-of-the-mill cases from the few unusual ones which call for the personal attention of the Materials Controller. **1962** H. O. Beecheno *Introd. Business Stud.* ii. 17 Trade union development and legislation on conditions of work, plus more enlightened management have eradicated most forms of unfair treatment of employees. **1965** H. I. Ansoff *Corporate Strategy* (1968) 9 Management of a business firm is a very large complex of activities which consists of analysis, decisions, communication, leadership, motivation, measurement, and control. *Ibid.* iii. 36 Their potential pervasiveness is such that objectives have been used as a basis for an integrated view on the entire management process which has become known as 'management by objectives'. **1968** Johannsen & Robertson *Managem. Gloss.* 81 *Management by Objectives*, setting targets within an organisation..as a basis for achieving greater efficiency and providing motivation and an incentive to managers. **1969** J. Argenti *Managem. Techniques* 146 Management by Exception..simply says, 'don't tell someone if everything is O.K.—only tell him if something has gone wrong'. **1970** *Lebende Sprachen* XV. 11/2 Operational research is an integral part of good management.

6. *spec.* That group of employees which administers and controls an industry in contradistinction to the labour force in that industry or in industry in general. (Further examples.)

1912 F. W. Raffety *Modern Business Pract.* II. II. i. 197

Management..deals with the three sources of force or energy—capital, labor and land... The management should never lose sight of their important influence. **1940** W. TEMPLE *Hope of New World* i. 61 If there is to be tension at all, let it be between the financial interests of Shareholders and the productive interests of Management and Labour in co-operation. **1959** [see *BOARD *sb.* 17]. **1965** H. I. ANSOFF *Corporate Strategy* (1968) i. 20 Management from top to bottom continually seeks to improve efficiency, to cut costs, to sell more, to advertise better. **1968** *Lebende Sprachen* XIII. 4/2 It has been part of management philosophy to encourage and support the self-development of its employees. **1969** J. ARGENTI *Managem. Techniques* 150 In every company there are two or three dozen absolutely vital ratios that must be watched and checked by the management.

7. *management accounting, consultancy, consultant, game, science.*

1963 BROAD & CARMICHAEL (*title*) A guide to management accounting. **1967** *Oxford Computer Explained* 32 *Management accounting*, the provision of a continuous and up-to-date check and control on income and expenditure. **1958, 1966** Management consultancy [see *CONSULTANCY]. **1972** *Accountant* 19 Oct. 487/1 The rapid development of management consultancy services has resulted in the profession extending its activities far beyond its traditional role of auditor. **1961** *Times* 14 July 2/2 Management consultants..must also have..experience in personnel management. **1969** *Times* 6 Mar. 23/2 This brings the number of management consultants on the commission up to three. **1964** M. ARGYLE *Psychol. & Social Probl.* x. 133 There has been a swing away from traditional teaching methods towards group discussion, joint report-writing by syndicates, case-studies and the management game. **1965** H. I. ANSOFF *Corporate Strategy* (1968) ix. 148 Management science can offer only partial assistance to the decision maker. **1969** *Times* 2 May 34 (Advt.), Post-graduate studentships in management sciences.

managerial, *a.* Add: In more recent use esp. of a manager of a commercial enterprise.

1912 F. W. RAFFETY *Modern Business Pract.* II. II. i. 204 Management..involves not only the forces of production but careful consideration of the results to be obtained... It is this latter purpose which distinguishes the man with managerial ability from the purely technical man. **1924** J. STAMP *Stud. Current Probl. Finance & Govt.* ii. 43 It [*sc.* the Excess Profits Duty Act] conferred quite a considerable number of discretions to the Commissioners of Inland Revenue, such as..the amount to be allowed as managerial remuneration. **1940** H. G. WELLS *Babes in Darkling Wood* IV. iii. 379 They would soon draw plenty of recruits and assistants from the managerial class in the big trade machines. **1941** J. BURNHAM *Managerial Revolution* vi. 70 The theory of the managerial revolution asserts.. the following: Modern society has been organized through a..set of major economic, social, and political institutions which we call capitalist... At the present time these institutions..are undergoing..transformation... Within the new social structure a different social group..—the managers—will be the dominant..class. **1955** P. F. DRUCKER *Pract. Managem.* xxii. 268 Opportunities for participation that will give him [*sc.* the worker] a managerial vision. **1958** *Listener* 30 Oct. 685/1 The salaried middle class of professional, technical, and managerial people. **1973** *Amer. Speech 1969* XLIV. 268 Managerial positions are unquestionably the highest occupational level of the three.

Hence **manage·rialism,** belief in or the art of conducting or planning business or other enterprises by the use of managerial techniques. Also **manage·rialist,** an adherent of managerialism; also *attrib.* or as adj.

1946 'G. ORWELL' *James Burnham* 5 According to Burnham..'managerialism' has reached its fullest development in the U.S.S.R. *Ibid.* 6 He describes the New Deal as 'primitive managerialism'. [Burnham did not use the word *managerialism* in *The Managerial Revolution.*—Ed.] **1952** K. R. POPPER *Open Society* (ed. 2) I. 4 A lapse into totalitarianism (or perhaps into 'managerialism'). **1965** H. I. ANSOFF *Corporate Strategy* (1968) iii. 40 A 'managerialist' point of view came into being which..subjected the microeconomic theory to thorough criticism. *Ibid.*, The managerialists have offered a number of substitute explanations of the behaviour of the firm. **1966** *Harper's Mag.* June 67 Many remained caught in the irrelevancies of such questions as whether the Soviet Union was a 'degenerate workers' state' or a 'managerialist bureaucracy'. **1970** *Guardian Weekly* 14 Feb. 8 No doubt some cynics and managerialists will deride them [*sc.* local city councils] as 'mere talking-shops'. **1973** *Human World* Feb. 7 The anxiety Mr Maddox senses in the environmentalists comes to no more than a yearning for a universal poeticized prosperity. This they find compatible with a beneficent world-wide managerialism.

managing, *ppl. a.* Add: **3.** *managing clerk* (CLERK *sb.* 6 b); *managing director* (DIRECTOR 1 b); *managing editor* (earlier U.S. example).

1799 *Times* 1 June 1/3 (Advt.), Wanted..a managing clerk; he must understand well the Business of Conveyancing. **1861** MILL *Repr. Govt.* v. 91 Even a joint-stock company has always in practice, if not in theory, a managing director. **1865** A. D. RICHARDSON *Secret Service* 18, I found the Managing Editor in his office. **1866** MRS. H. WOOD *Elster's Folly* II. x. 230 The lawyer laughed. 'Hopkins did not know you; and strangers are generally introduced to..our managing clerk.' **1922** JOYCE *Ulysses* 484 They are immediately appointed to positions of high public trust..as managing directors of banks. **1940** W. TEMPLE *Hope of New World* i. 61 The great Managing Directors tend to rule the Boards of which they are at once both members and servants. **1972** M. GILBERT *Body of Girl* xiv. 128 She started here as my secretary. Then..she took on a number of jobs herself. I suppose you'd have called her a managing clerk by that time. **1972** J. MCCLURE *Caterpillar Cop* iv. 47, I would have you know that the managing director of your paper is a personal friend of mine. **1974** L. MEYNELL *Fairly Innocent Little Man* xiv. 180, I had a good job with a law firm. In time I daresay I would have become managing clerk.

‖ **manaia** (manəi·ă). [Maori.] A motif in Maori carving with a bird-like head and a human body.

1896 A. HAMILTON *Art Workmanship of Maori Race* 12 The thin board-like central piece with a human figure between two *pitau* spirals is called *Manaia* by the Arawas. **1910** J. COWAN *Maoris of N.Z.* xii. 165 Some of the wall slabs are carved into fantastic figures of fabulous water-monsters..others represent the mythical creatures known as the *manaia* and *wheku* with bird-like beaks and snaky tails all coiled in endless spirals. **1916** [see *bird-headed* (*BIRD *sb.* 8)]. **1924** E. BEST *Maori* II. xxi. 574 A common design in the carved work of superior houses and elevated storehouses is that known as the *manaia*..a figure composed of a long, slim body, a birdlike head, and an indefinite number of legs. **1959** FREEMAN & GEDDES *Anthropol. in South Seas* 117 The important symbol in Maori carving termed the *manaia* I believe is basically avian in origin. **1963** T. BARROW *Life & Work Maori Carver* 23 The most fascinating [mystery] is the origin and nature of a small creature called a *manaia*. There are many explanations; that it represents a malignant spirit, that it is merely a human image seen in profile, that it is a bird that attacked man in ancient times, or that it represents the *mana* or spiritual power of the human figure it is with. **1966** *Encycl. N.Z.* II. 410/2 Apart from the naturalistic figure, every type of full-faced figure has a *manaia* to match... The head of the *manaia* can, in each case, be recognised as half of the head of the appropriate matching figure divided down the middle of the face.

‖ **mañana** (mæ̃nʸā·nă), *adv.* and *sb.* [Sp., tomorrow, morrow, f. *cras mañana* lit. tomorrow early, f. pop.L. **maneana* early, f. L. *māne* in the morning.] **A.** *adv.* Tomorrow, on the day after today. **B.** *sb.* Tomorrow, the day next after the present. Often taken as a synonym of easy-going procrastination as said to be found in Spanish-speaking countries: the indefinite future. Phr. *land* (or *kingdom*) *of mañana*: sometimes applied *spec.* to Mexico.

1845 R. FORD *Hand-bk. for Travellers Spain* I. ii. 144 Andalucia... Nowhere will the stranger hear more frequently those talismanic words which mark national character..the Manaña [*sic*], [etc.]. **1879** J. W. BODDAM-WHETHAM *Roraima & Brit. Guiana* xviii. 208 With an Indian the morrow is as indefinite a period as 'mañana' with the Spaniards. **1885** *Harper's Mag.* Jan. 217/2 Is Cedar Keys just on the borderland of that vast region known as the kingdom of *Mañana*? **1889** E. RIPLEY *From Flag to Flag* 165 Their *mañana* never came, never was intended to come. **1903** A. ADAMS *Log of Cowboy* 138 Flood had had years of experience in dealing with Mexicans in the land of *mañana*, where all maxims regarding the value of time are religiously discarded. **1910** *Daily News* 27 Sept. 4 The 'manana' boys didn't work quick enough for him, so he put the crew on. **1927** D. H. LAWRENCE *Mornings in Mexico* 59 *Mañana*, to the native, may mean to-morrow, three days hence, six months hence, and never. **1938** 'G. ORWELL' *Homage to Catalonia* i. 12 A promise that there should be machine-gun instruction *mañana*. Needless to say *mañana* never came. **1961** *Guardian* 23 Jan. 6/7 'Mañana' is a concept that exists far outside the Spanish world. **1973** C. BONINGTON *Next Horizon* xiv. 201 The elaborate etiquette and principle of mañana (leave everything until tomorrow, in the absolute confidence that tomorrow will never arrive), which dominates all dealings in South America. **1973** *Nat. Geographic* May 658/1 With a dispatch that put the lie to those who claim this [*sc.* Mexico] is the land of *mañana*, the orders went out to build a subway.

mananosay (mænănǭᵘ·sēi). *U.S.* Also **mananose, maninose.** [prob. ad. Algonquian name.] The soft-shell clam, *Mya arenaria*.

[**1709** J. LAWSON *New Voy. Carolina* 162 Man of Noses are a Shell-Fish commonly found amongst us.] **1843** J. E. DEKAY *Zool. N.Y.* V. 240 *Mya arenaria*. .in some districts ..still retains its ancient aboriginal appellation of *Maninose*. **1859** BARTLETT *Dict. Amer.* (ed. 2) 84 The Soft Clam or Mananosay (*Mya arenaria*), obtained from the shores of tidal rivers by digging one or two feet in the loose sand. It has a long, extensible, cartilaginous snout, or proboscis, through which it ejects water; whence it is also called Stem-clam. **1870** *Putnam's Monthly Mag.* May 525/1 Even to the toothsome Manonosays that squirted water up through the sand what time the tides were out. **1895** *Sun* (N.Y.) 30 July 9/1 Mananosay, maninose (Maryland), man-of-noses (North Carolina), names for the round clam, from an Algonquian word meaning 'shellfish that one gathers by hand'. **1967** L. S. TAWES *Coasting Captain* xiii. 443, I used to take my launch and go fishing, sometimes digging mananoses.

manasseite (mănæ·se,oit). *Min.* [f. the name of E. *Manasse* (see quot. 1941) + -ITE¹.] A hydrated carbonate and hydroxide of magnesium and aluminium that is polymorphous with hydrotalcite and occurs as soft, foliated, whitish masses having a pearly lustre and a greasy feel.

1941 C. FRONDEL in *Amer. Mineralogist* XXVI. 310 These facts indicate with reasonable certainty that the mineral is identical in composition with hydrotalcite. The name manasseite is proposed for this mineral in honor of Ernesto Manasse (1875–1922), Italian chemist, mineralogist and petrographer,..who made important contributions to our knowledge of hydrotalcite and pyroaurite. **1962** W. A. DEER et al. *Rock-Forming Min.* V. 63 Spinel may alter to talc, mica, serpentine, or corundum: Struwe (1958) has also recorded its alteration to diaspore..and manasseite, $Mg_6Al_2CO_3(OH)_{16}.4H_2O$.

mancala (mæ̆·nkā·la). Also **mankalah, munckalah.** [ad. colloq. Arab. *manḳala*, f. *naḳala* to move.] A board game, originally Arabic but now common throughout Africa and Asia, played by two players on a special board (see quot. 1952) the object of which is the capture of the opponent's pieces. Also used as a generic term for regional variations of the basic game.

[**1813** J. GALT *Lett. from Levant* xxix. 242, I saw there today a game... The Idriots call it Mandoli, or the Almonds, and it is played at a board by two persons.] **1836** E. W. LANE *Acct. Manners & Customs Mod. Egyptians* II. iv. 46 One of the games most common among the Egyptians is that of the *munckalah*. **1877** *Encycl. Brit.* VII. 726/2 They [*sc.* the Egyptians] are acquainted with.. other games, among which is one peculiar to themselves, called Mankalah, and played with cowries. **1952** H. J. R. MURRAY *Hist. Board-Games* vii. 158 Anthropologists use the term *mancala* for any similar game played on a board in which the pattern..usual for board-games is replaced by two, three, or four rows of holes deep enough to contain a number of pieces at the same time. **1969** R. C. BELL *Board & Table Games* II. iv. 72 Ba-awa played by the Twi people of Ghana, is one of the simpler forms of mancala and appears to be extremely ancient.

Manchegan (mantʃē·găn), *a.* and *sb.* [ad. Sp. *manchego, -ga*: see -AN.] **A.** *adj.* Of or pertaining to La Mancha, a region (formerly a province) of central Spain. **B.** *sb.* A native or inhabitant of La Mancha.

[**1779** H. SWINBURNE *Trav. Spain* xxxvi. 319 The Manchegos have a pretty song about these eyes of the Guadiana.] **1841** BORROW *Zincali* I. II. ii. 245 Conde instantly unclasped one of those terrible Manchegan knives which are generally carried by contrabandistas. **1846** R. FORD *Gatherings from Spain* xxi. 296 The Manchegan bull, small, very powerful, and active, is considered to be the original stock of Spain. *Ibid.* xxiii. 326 Sancho, a true Manchegan,..maintained that for a *zapateo*, a knocking of shoes, none could beat him. **1897** A. F. JACCACI *On Trail of Don Quixote* iv. 96 It is arid, savage La Mancha which makes the Manchegan peasants shy, taciturn, and sombre. **1959** R. CROFT-COOKE *Quest for Quixote* i. 63 He was proud of being a Manchegan, a country-bred Spaniard. **1966** H. YOXALL *Fashion of Life* xxv. 239 Seven glasses were set in front of each of us, with a small piece of Manchegan cheese between each glass.

Manchester. Add: **1. Manchester terrier,** a small, short-coated, black and tan terrier of the breed so called, once particularly popular in the Manchester area. Also *absol.* Cf. *Black and tan* (BLACK *a.* 14).

1894 R. B. LEE *Hist. & Descr. Mod. Dogs Gt. Brit. & Ireland: Terriers* iv. 75 The Kennel Club acknowledged it as the 'Manchester' terrier, as well as by its own name of the black and tan. **1943** 'C. DICKSON' *She died a Lady* v. 37 A so-called Manchester terrier sprang on the front of the chair. **1971** F. HAMILTON *World Encycl. Dogs* 461 The only acceptable color for a Manchester Terrier is black-and-tan. *Ibid.*, Manchesters are very attractive little dogs equally at home in town or country.

b. (Further examples.)

1885 [see *BISMARCK 1]. **1957** *Encycl. Brit.* II. 828/2 Bismarck brown (Manchester brown), prepared by the action of nitrous acid on *m*-phenylene diamine, contains triaminoazobenzene.

Manchesterian (mæn,tʃestīᵊ·riăn), *a.* and *sb.* Also 8 **Manchestrian.** [f. MANCHESTER + -IAN.] **A.** *adj.* Of or pertaining to Manchester. **B.** *sb.* An inhabitant of Manchester; also, one of the Manchester School of politicians. Cf. *MANCUNIAN *sb.* and *a.*

1778 J. WEDGWOOD *Let.* 3 Mar. (1965) 218 Nothing but half a score Highland, Manchestrian, and Liverpool regiments amongst us will raise their malignant spirits again. **1821** *Kaleidoscope* 3 July 423/3 Professing myself to be a plain Englishman and a Manchesterian. **1837** *Times* 5 Oct. 3/2 The engine went its way to Whitmore with the Liverpool passengers..and returned to fetch the unlucky Manchesterians. **1879** W. T. ARNOLD *Let.* 15 Aug. in D. Ayerst *Guardian* (1971) xxi. 206, I like the work very much, and strange to say like Manchester or at all events the Manchesterians. **1897** *Essays in Liberalism* 70 'Sordid inhuman wretch', 'brutal Manchesterian', are the terms applied to those who demonstrate the national loss of wealth which must result from the substitution of 'Fair' for Free Trade.

Hence **Mancheste·rianism** = MANCHESTERISM.

1897 *Essays in Liberalism* 33 A sneer at Cobden, a contemptuous allusion to Manchesterianism and the 'dismal science'.

Manchesterize (mæ·n,tʃestərəiz), *v.* [f. MANCHESTER + -IZE.] *trans.* To make representative or typical of Manchester. Hence **Ma:nchesteriza·tion.**

1925 E. T. SCOTT Let. 27 Dec. in D. Ayerst *Guardian* (1971) xxix. 452 The policy, both as to popularising and Manchesterising the paper..will be determined outside the Room. **1964** *Economist* 19 Dec. 1370/3 They do not want to see their [cotton] industries 'manchesterised'. **1965** *Ibid.* 23 Oct. 416/3 The [cotton] industry has argued ..that the unrestricted entry of imported textiles from

low-cost Commonwealth countries is largely to blame for the state of the industry. (The Continentals have a word for it: 'manchesterisation'.) **1971** D. Ayerst *Guardian* xxix. 452 The policy of 'Manchesterisation' continued.

Manchu (mænˌtʃū·), *sb.* and *a.* Also **Manchew, Manchoo, Manchow, Mantcheou, Mantchoo, Mantchu,** etc. [Manchu, 'pure', the name of a tribe descended from the Nü-chên Tartars.] **A.** *sb.* **1.** A member of a Tungusic race inhabiting Manchuria, which conquered China in 1644 and was the ruling class until the Revolution in 1912.

[**1655** A. Semedo *Hist. China* iii. 292 He used to cry out in their Language *Hoo Manzu.*] **1697** L. Le Compte *Mem. Journey through China* i. i. 17 One of the Petty Kings of the Eastern Tartary..whose subjects called Mouantchéou ..entered the Province of Leauton with a numerous Army. **1736** R. Brookes tr. *Du Halde's Gen. Hist. China* IV. 86 The places belonging to the Mantcheoux have Mantcheou Names. **1759** *Universal Hist., Mod.* IV. 278 Here the present empire of the eastern Tatars, or Manchews..had its beginning. **1821** G. Staunton tr. *Narr. Chinese Embassy* 152 The Mantchoos and the Mongals bear a great resemblance to each other. **1883** S. W. Williams *Middle Kingdom* (new ed.) I. i. 44 The Manchus are an agricultural or a hunting people. **1940** E. Pound *Cantos* lviii. 77 Tai Tsong..Forbad manchus marry their sisters.

2. The language of the Manchus.

1822 G. Staunton *Misc. Notes China* 95 Table of Contents of a Chinese and Mantchoo-Tartar Dictionary. **1888** H. E. M. James *Long White Mountain* 132 Yet, so wonderful are the ways of men, the Court and the people alike are now abandoning Manchu for the cumbrous and barbarous Chinese. **1920** *Contemp. Rev.* Apr. 526 Ferdinand Verbiest ..to please Kang-hi had learnt Manchu.

B. *adj.* Of or pertaining to the Manchus, their country (Manchuria), or their language.

1736 R. Brookes tr. *Du Halde's Gen. Hist. China* IV. 90 A great Number of Mantcheou Mandarins. **1770** W. Guthrie *New Geogr. Gram.* 472 The Chinese went to war with the Manchew Tartars. **1844** C. Fox *Jrnl.* 22 Aug. (1972) 153 They gave him a hymn to translate into the Manchow language. **1848** S. W. Williams *Middle Kingdom* II. 562 Out of a Manchu population of four thousand ..not more than five hundred survived. **1882** *Encycl. Brit.* XIV. 96/1 Tobacco..grown in the province [*sc.* Manchuria] being greatly prized throughout the Chinese empire under the name of 'Manchu leaf'. **1898** *19th Cent.* Jan. 163 The Manchu dynasty is the cement that holds the heterogeneous components of the Chinese Empire together. **1948** N. Whymant *China Manual* i. 16 The Manchu leader..mounted the throne and in 1644 the Ch'ing or Manchu dynasty began. **1972** T. Shabad *China's Changing Map* ii. 45 The criteria used by the Chinese Communists in distinguishing a Manchu ethnic group are not entirely clear. **1972** *Mainichi Daily News* (Japan) 6 Nov. 17/6 The authors have no acquaintance with Korean or Manchu grammar.

Manchurian (mænˌtʃūə·riăn), *a.* [f. *Manchuria*, the country of the Manchus, now a dependency of China + -an.] **1.** Of or pertaining to Manchuria.

1876 A. R. Wallace *Geogr. Distribution Animals* I. 220 Japan and North China, or the Manchurian Sub-region. **1899** J. F. Fraser *Round World on Wheel* xxxi. 395 In five minutes down swooped several Manchurian officers. **1911** *Encycl. Brit.* XVII. 554/1 Eventually a Manchurian convention was arranged between China and Russia. **1937** *Discovery* Jan. 12/2 A candle copied from an old Manchurian pattern. **1972** W. B. Lockwood *Panorama Indo-Europ. Lang.* 154 The Manchurian languages are dispersed over an immense tract of the Soviet Far East.

2. Manchurian crane, a crane found in eastern Asia, *Grus japonensis*; **Manchurian ermine** (see quot.); **Manchurian roe, sika, wapiti,** local races of deer, *Capreolus capreolus bedfordi*, *Cervus nippon mantchuricus*, and *C. canadensis xanthopygus*; **Manchurian tiger,** a subspecies of the tiger, *Panthera tigris longipilis*, found in Manchuria and Siberia, and distinguished by its large size and shaggy fur; also called Siberian tiger.

1869 *Proc. Zool. Soc.* 628 Mantchurian Crane. *Grus montignesia.* **1898** R. Lydekker *Deer of all Lands* 102 The Manchurian wapiti is said to be smaller than the (?typical) American race. *Ibid.* 115 (*caption*) Buck and Doe of Manchurian Sika in winter pelage. *Ibid.* 231 (*heading*) The Manchurian Roe—*Capreolus Manchuricus.* **1899** R. Ward *Rec. Big Game* (ed. 3) 458 Lastly, we have the Manchurian tiger (*F. tigris longipilis*), characterised by its large size, heavy build, short limbs, and the great length and thickness of the fur. **1931–4** J. D. D. La Touche *Handbk. Birds E. China* II. 298 The Manchurian Crane breeds in Manchuria, Corea, and Eastern Siberia, and passes through Japan on migration. **1957** M. B. Picken *Fashion Dict.* 219/1 *Manchurian ermine*, fur of Chinese weasel. **1964** A. L. Thomson *New Dict. Birds* 162/1 Another species that has become alarmingly scarce is the Manchurian Crane *G[rus] japonensis*, a large white bird with black wings, a dark grey face, and a broad streak of the same colour running downwards at either side of the neck. **1964** R. Perry *World of Tiger* i. 8 A Manchurian tiger does in fact tire quickly and rest often when traversing deep snow. **1972** G. K. Whitehead *Deer of World* v. 74 The Manchurian Wapiti is similar to the North American animal. *Ibid.* 77 The principal distribution of the Manchurian Sika deer is in the central and southern parts of Manchuria. [*Ibid.* 84 Throughout the greater part of the Korean Peninsula the Roe is the Chinese or Manchurian race, *C[apreolus] c[apreolus] bedfordi.*]

Manchu-Tungus (mænˌtʃū·ˌtu·ŋgus). [f. *Manchu *sb.* and *a.* + *Tungus.] Name given to a language family comprising Manchu and Tungus.

[**1933** L. Bloomfield *Lang.* iv. 69 The Tunguse-Manchu family lies to the north of the Mongol, dividing Yakut from the rest of the Turco-Tartar area.] **1955** *Times* 15 Aug. 7/3 There are the peoples, often semi-nomad, who are in contact with civilization but only slightly affected by it: Indians and mestizos in Bolivia and Peru, the many groups, amounting in 1941 to nearly 25,000,000 souls, whom the Republic of India classifies as adivasis, the Paleoasiats and the Manchu-Tungus of the Soviet Far East. **1956** Jakobson & Halle in Saporta & Bastian *Psycholinguistics* (1961) 349/2 In Manchu-Tungus and in Paleosiberian languages. **1964** *Language* XL. 301 Coordinate with Turkic, Mongolian, and Manchu-Tungus.

mancia (mæ·ntʃia). [It.] A gratuity, a tip.

1951 [see *have *v.* 15 d]. **1963** T. Pynchon *V.* xiv. 409 Guides: there to do any bidding, to various degrees of efficiency, on receipt of the recommended baksheesh, pourboire, mancia, tip.

Mancunian (mænˌkiū·niăn), *sb.* and *a.* [f. L. *Mancunium* Manchester + -an.] **A.** *sb.* A native or inhabitant of Manchester. **B.** *adj.* Of or pertaining to Manchester.

1904 H. Beswick *Last Karkawbar* 134 'Th' Owd Rivvur' —as some old Mancunians dub the Irwell. **1908** *Westm. Gaz.* 22 Oct. 2/3 How strangely provincial—may we even say Mancunian?—is the very recent theory that Mr. Cobden invented Free Trade. **1926** *Glasgow Herald* 2 Oct. 8 In the Manchester docks..lies the real secret or the industrial trick, as the Mancunians choose to phrase it, which is at the foundation of the city's greatness. **1931** *Daily Tel.* 6 Jan. 10/3 The Mancunians who wish to play bowls on Sunday might surely be allowed their simple pleasure. **1947** H. Miles tr. *Maurois's Disraeli* (ed. 2) ii. iv. 124 A truly Mancunian rain had drowned the enthusiasm. **1963** *Times* 2 Feb. 9/3 Any middle-aged Mancunian.. can remember posters drawing attention to celebrity concerts. **1973** P. Geddes *Ottawa Allegation* ii. 18 Still the Mancunian accent, true, yet fading fast. **1973** *Guardian* 16 Mar. 13/2 Michael Croft, the beaming Mancunian who founded the National Youth Theatre.

mand (mænd). [Final element of *com*)*mand*, *de*)*mand*, etc.] B. F. Skinner's term for an utterance aimed at producing an effect or result, etc. Cf. *tact.

1957 B. F. Skinner *Verbal Behavior* ii. iii. 35 The term 'mand' has a certain mnemonic value derived from 'command', 'demand',..and so on... A 'mand', then, may be defined as a verbal operant in which the response is reinforced by a characteristic consequence and is therefore under the functional control of relevant conditions of deprivation or aversive stimulation. **1959** *Anthropol. Ling.* I. i. 41 It is interesting to speculate how far the program for the acquisition of mands and tacts will account for all verbal behavior. **1968** D. Lawton *Social Class, Lang. & Educ.* iv. 56 For Skinner, language behaviour is an example of learning by operant conditions... Requests, demands or commands (mands) tend to be reinforced by satisfaction of needs. Another kind of utterance is termed a '*tact*', which is a response to a situation rather than a response to a need (e.g. 'this apple is red'). **1972** *Language* XLVIII. 482 Beneath the linguistically questionable trappings (cf. Chomsky 1959) of mands, tacts, and echoic responses—..is there a brilliance which linguists in general have been prevented from seeing? **1973** *Archivum Linguisticum* IV. 52 'The ethnography of communication'—contains the item 'mands'.

mandala (mæ·ndălă). [Skr. *máṇḍala* disc, circle.] A symbolic representation of a magic circle usually with symmetrical divisions and figures of deities, etc., in the centre, used by Buddhists in meditation and found in many cultures as a religious symbol; *spec.* in *Jungian Psychol.*, an image of a similar magic circle visualized in dreams and symbolizing the dreamer's striving for unity of self and completeness. Also *attrib.*

1859 Max Müller *Hist. Anc. Sanskrit Lit.* i. 218 The division of the Sanhitâ which is adopted in the Brihaddevatâ, is that of Maṇḍalas, Anuvâkas, and Sûktas. **1882** *Encycl. Brit.* XIV. 228/1 Their practical belief..busied itself almost wholly with obtaining magic powers (*Siddhi*), by means of..magic circles (*Maṇḍala*). **1927** W. Y. Evans-Wentz *Tibetan Bk. Dead* 136 (*caption*) The Great Mandala of the Knowledge-Holding and Wrathful Deities. **1931** C. F. Baynes tr. *Wilhelm & Jung's Secret of Golden Flower* 97 For the most part, the *mandala* form is that of a flower, cross, or wheel, with a distinct tendency toward four. *Ibid.*, I have come across women who did not draw mandala symbols but who danced them. **1933** E. J. Thomas *Hist. Buddhist Thought* xv. 193 The great spell.. should be inscribed in a circle (maṇḍala) made of certain substances with appropriate divisions and figures. **1938** C. G. Jung *Psychol. & Relig.* iii. 96 Historically..the mandala served as a symbol in order to clarify the nature of the deity philosophically. *Ibid.* iv. 109 Since modern mandalas have..close parallels in ancient magic circles, in the centre of which we usually find the deity, it is evident that in the modern mandala man—the complete man—has replaced the deity. **1941** A. Huxley *Grey Eminence* iii. 66 An elaborate circular diagram, curiously like one of those symbolic *mandalas*, into which the Buddhists contrive to cram such a wealth of doctrinal significance. **1949** K. Raine *Pythoness* 17, I piece the divine fragments into the mandala Whose centre is the lost creative power. **1966** P. White (*title*) The solid mandala. **1973** *Jrnl. Genetic Psychol.* CXXII. 168 The complete, circular form of the Ufor is reminiscent of the mandala or 'magic circle': i.e., totality. **1974** *Time* (Canada) 18 Mar. 56/1 The appetite of the young for religious experience is leading along exotic paths these days—demons and gurus, mandalas and myths.

Mandan (mæ·ndăn), *a.* and *sb.* Also **Mandane, Mandano, Mandon.** [ad. Dakota *Matani.*] **A.** *adj.* Of, pertaining to, or designating a Siouan Indian people of North Dakota. **B.** *sb.* This people; a member of this people; also, their language.

1794 in *Mass. Hist. Soc. Coll.* (1810) 1st Ser. III. 24 The tribes of Indians which he passed through, were called the Maskego Tribe..Mandon tribe, Paunees, and several others. **1806** M. Lewis in *Deb. Congress U.S.* (1852) 9th Congress 2 Sess., App. 1065 The bridlebits and blankets I have seen in the possession of the Mandans. **1806** [see *berdache]. **1831** J. M. Peck *Guide for Emigrants* 21 At the Mandan villages, 1600 miles from the Mississippi, it [*sc.* the Missouri] is said to be nearly as wide..as at St. Charles. **1877** L. H. Morgan *Anc. Society* ii. vi. 158 In intelligence and in the arts of life the Mandans were in advance of all their kindred tribes. *Ibid.* iii. iii. 440 In Mandan my brother's wife is my wife. **1911**, etc. [see *Hidatsa]. **1933** L. Bloomfield *Lang.* iv. 72 The Siouan family includes many languages, such as..Winnebago, Mandan, Crow. *Ibid.* xvii. 283 A Mandan Indian sent the ..picture to a fur-trader. **1971** S. E. Morison *European Discovery Amer.: Northern Voy.* iv. 86 Eventually the Mandan become the most favored tribe.

mandarin[1]. Add: **1. b.** (Earlier and later examples.)

1791 Boswell *Johnson* I. 5 From a man so still and so tame..conversation worth recording could no more be expected, than from a Chinese mandarin on a chimney-piece. **1845, 1855** [see Niddle-noddle *v.*].

c. *transf.* A person of much importance, a great man. Often used *colloq.* of Government officials, leading politicians or writers, etc.

1907 *National Rev.* Aug. 838 Our Parliamentary Mandarins are ineffably shocked at the impiety of an independent Radical. **1908** *New Age* 6 June 112/2 The chams, lamas, and mandarins of London letters are doubtless devising adjectives for it [*sc.* a book]. **1919** B. Ruck *Disturbing Charm* ii. ix. 234 If you let it get known..that you've got a view like that, you'll have some of the Mandarins snaffling that office of yours for themselves. **1925** Fraser & Gibbons *Soldier & Sailor Words* 151 The Mandarins of the War Office. **1947** *Oxf. Univ. Handbk.* 261 If he is an athlete of any distinction, the mandarins of his particular game will know all about him long before he arrives. **1961** *Listener* 9 Nov. 782/3 Mr. Thody, who has written a book about Sartre no less brilliant than his two books on Camus, makes comparisons between the two *mandarins.* **1971** P. Loraine *Photographs have been Sent* v. iii. 164 The Medical Mandarins maintained stony silence.

2. (Later examples.) Also *transf.*

1959 V. Cronin *Pearl to India* xiii. 188 Some philologists claimed Mandarin to be derived from Hebrew. **1963** *Listener* 17 Jan. 140/1 BBC Mandarin, or Announcers' English, was devised as a refined product, based on so-called 'southern educated' English. **1964** *Amer. Speech* XXXIX. 26 Home's own writings..are written in a kind of middle-class international Victorian Mandarin which defies analysis. **1971** K. Hopkins *Hong Kong* 235 Cantonese is very much the predominant language but there are minorities who speak..Mandarin.

4. *mandarin language* (earlier example); **mandarin blue** (see quot. 1949); **mandarin coat** (see quot. 1957); **mandarin collar,** a narrow collar standing up from a close-fitting neckline.

1912 *Home Chat* 13 Apr. 112/2 In flamingo red, Mandarin blue or wood-violet mauve linen. **1949** *Dict. Colours Interior Decoration* (Brit. Colour Council) 17/1 *Mandarin blue*, a descriptive name for one of the blues specially produced for China by British dyers at the beginning of the twentieth century. **1911** *Daily Colonist* (Victoria, B.C.) 22 Apr. 7/1 (Advt.), Mandarin Coats. In exquisite hand-embroidered silks and silk lined. **1957** M. B. Picken *Fashion Dict.* 67/1 *Mandarin*, long, loose, richly embroidered silk coat with wide sleeves. **1972** *Vogue* June Special 94 Mandarin coat and slit dress of matching print. **1952** C. Howard *Compl. Dressmaking* 104 The collar is a mandarin collar. [**1953** *News Chron.* 2 June 7/1 You can spot him [the Sultan of Selangor] by his yellow knee-length baju (jacket) with mandarin-type collar.] **1967** G. B. Mair *Girl from Peking* vi. 69 I'll go Chinese. Gold and blue brocade with high mandarin collar and short sleeves. **1971** P. Loraine *Photographs have been Sent* iii. i. 91 A white silk suit with a mandarin collar. **1697** L. Le Compte *Mem. Journey through China* i. v. 134, I acquainted her that I spake the Mandarin language..which they constantly use at the Court.

b. *attrib.* or quasi-*adj.*, in *transf.* sense of 'superior, esoteric, "highbrow"'; applied esp. to literary productions or style: 'ornate, refined; high-flown' (often in derogatory use).

1916 H. G. Wells *Mr. Britling* i. i. 16 The conservative classes whose education has always had a mandarin quality—very, very little of it, and very old and choice. **1947** J. Hayward *Prose Lit. since 1939* vii. 47 If literature..is not to become the arcane cult of a mandarin class, it must impose its values. **1952** *Times Lit. Suppl.* 29 Aug. (Suppl.) p. xii/2 The influence that delivered the English novel from Mr. Bennett and Mrs. Brown turned out to be D. H. Lawrence and not his mandarin contemporaries. **1959** *Ibid.* 1 May 257/2 In reaction from Victorian pompousness, bureaucratic jargon, *fin de siècle* poetic prose, and 'mandarin English', a go-as-you-please attitude has crept into the language. **1962** *Listener* 13 Sept. 406/2 The conventionally acceptable accents and Mandarin prose we learn at school. **1973** *Times Lit. Suppl.* 6 July 787/2 M

Bourdieu's style has, from the first paper onwards, been growing increasingly mandarin. *Ibid.* 787/3 The mandarin observer, 'freed from the constraints and urgencies of practice'.

mandarin². **1.** (Earlier and later examples.)

1771 J. R. Forster tr. *Osbeck's Voy. China* I. 307 Here are two sorts of China oranges (*Citrus sinensis*). The first is that called the *Mandarin-orange*, whose peel is quite loose. **1926** H. H. Hume *Cultivation Citrus Fruits* xxix. 477 The other mandarin or kid-glove oranges are attacked [by citrus rust] but not often severely. **1969** *Oxf. Bk. Food Plants* 86/2 Tangerine (*Citrus reticulata*). The fruit is also known under several other names, one of which is 'mandarin', denoting its origin in the Far East.

mandarinship. (Earlier example.)

1697 L. Le Compte *Mem. Journey through China* I. i. 12 Executioners..ready to bind and cudgel whom his Mandarineship should think fit.

‖ **mandat** (mandā). [a. F. *mandat* (see Mandate *sb.*).] **1.** A paper money (in full *mandat territorial*) issued by the French Revolutionary Government from 1796 to 1797, replacing the Assignat.

1858 P. L. Simmonds *Dict. Trade Products* 238/2 *Mandats*, a national paper-money, issued..in France to replace the assignats which had become wretchedly depreciated. **1902** J. R. Moreton-Macdonald in Carlyle *French Revolution* (ed. C. R. L. Fletcher) III. 339 The Directory.. destroyed the die of the *Assignats*, but immediately replaced them by *Mandats Territoriaux* which rapidly followed the same course. **1930** S. E. Harris *Assignats* ix. 225 The Assignats were to be exchanged for Mandats which were to be supported by a special security. **1955** E. Pound *Section: Rock-Drill* lxxxviii. 45 Willing to see a currency of hard money..as France since the time of mandats and assignats. **1974** *Encycl. Brit. Micropædia* I. 594/3 In early 1796 the assignats were replaced by the mandats territoriaux (land warrants) at the rate of one mandat for 30 assignats. The failure of the mandat to gain public confidence forced the Directory to return to a metallic currency (Feb. 4, 1797).

2. In France, a money-order.

1896 E. Dowson *Let. c* 15 Mar. (1967) 345, I enclose a mandat for the price & postage, & shall be much obliged if you can get them [*sc.* newspapers] & post them here. **1939** E. Ambler *Mask of Dimitrios* xii. 251, I received here a letter from him enclosing a *mandat* for the three thousand francs.

mandate, *sb.* Add: **2.** (Earlier example.)

1501 Douglas *Pal. Hon.* (*c* 1553) II. sig. F1 Submyttand me..ȝour plesour and mandate till obeysyng.

4. (Further examples.)

1886 *Hansard Commons* 9 Apr. 1244, I am perfectly aware that there exists in our constitution no principle of the mandate... But..I maintain that there are certain limits which Parliament is morally bound to observe, and beyond which Parliament has morally not the right to go in its relations with the constituents. **1936** R. C. K. Ensor *England, 1870–1914* i. 25 Gladstone (who ten months earlier had been telling the queen that his work was done, his mandate exhausted, and he himself in need of a long rest) declared on 24 January [1874] his intention of dissolving parliament. **1968** *Daily Progress* (Charlottesville, Virginia) 11 July C14/4 We need to win only 36 [seats], which I am sure we can do, and that will be an overwhelming mandate for Scottish freedom.

b. *spec.* A commission issued by the League of Nations (1919–1946) authorizing a selected power to administer, control, and develop a territory for a specified purpose; the territory so allocated. Also *attrib.*

1919 *League of Nations Charter* Art. xxii, The character of the mandate must differ according to the stage of the development of the people, the geographical situation of the territory, its economic conditions, and other similar circumstances. **1920** *Glasgow Herald* 7 Aug. 9 It will still be necessary for the Council to set up a permanent Mandate Commission. **1921** *Spectator* 12 Feb. 189/2 The draft mandates for Palestine and Mesopotamia, which are to come before the Council of the League of Nations on February 21st, were published unofficially last week. *Ibid.* 2 Apr. 419/1 They apparently look upon mandate-making as a kind of old-fashioned diplomacy. **1924** *Brit. Weekly* 30 Oct. 98/4 The Mandate Section of the General Secretariat of the League of Nations. **1937** F. P. Crozier *Men I Killed* xii. 277 Are the British Mandates..a success? **1946** *Ann. Reg. 1945* 166 The Trusteeship System, replacing the Mandate System of the League, will cover a wider range of backward territories. **1972** *Whitaker's Almanack 1973* 951/2 Syria, which had been under French mandate since the 1914–18 war, became an independent Republic during the 1939–45 war. **1974** *Encycl. Brit. Micropædia* VI. 557/3 Both the territories and the authority to administer them were called mandates. Among them were Britain's mandates in Palestine and Tanganyika. *Ibid.* 558/1 The Mandate System was replaced by the UN Trusteeship System in 1946.

c. *doctor's mandate*: a mandate from the people empowering the government to take extreme measures in the national interest.

1931 *Times* 7 Oct. 14/1 Mr. MacDonald would issue a manifesto as the head of the National Government appealing for what is called a 'doctor's mandate'. **1961** I. Jennings *Party Politics* II. vii. 291 The Government appealed to the people on a 'doctor's mandate'. **1965** A. J. P. Taylor *Eng. Hist. 1914–45* x. 324 MacDonald asked for 'a doctor's mandate'—a blank authority for the National government to do whatever they could agree on. **1973** *Times* 17 Dec. 15/1 Some of the substantial voices that now call for a doctor's mandate from the people stand close enough to the Prime Minister for him to feel the full cogency of their persuasions. **1974** *Observer* 13 Jan. 1/3 The Prime Minister's main demand would be for a 'doctor's mandate' to enable him to take the measures he considers necessary to make the pay-and-prices policy effective.

mandate, *v.* Add: **3.** To assign (territory) under a mandate of the League of Nations. Cf. *Mandate *sb.* 4 b. So **manda·ted** *ppl. a.*

1919 J. M. Keynes *Econ. Consequences Peace* 248 The Mandated States should be compelled to adhere to this Union for ten years. **1920** *Glasgow Herald* 7 July 11 The Island of Nauru in the Pacific (which is mandated to the British Empire). **1922** *Weekly Dispatch* 5 Nov. 8 We were authorised to raise local native forces to protect the mandated area. **1922** *Times Lit. Suppl.* 23 Nov. 756/3 The result of the late war has been to eliminate Germany from the map, her territories being mandated to the British and other nations. **1944** J. S. Huxley *On Living in Revolution* xii. 119 Crown colonies, protectorates, condominiums, mandated territories of various categories. **1958** A. R. Radcliffe-Brown *Method in Social Anthropol.* I. iii. 90 Cadets who are selected for the administration of the Mandated Territory are sent to the territory for one or two years to make acquaintance with the kind of life and work they will have. **1970** *Internat. & Compar. Law Q.* XIX. 218 When this section was enacted, New Guinea was a Mandated Territory of the League of Nations.

4. To give a mandate to, to delegate authority to (a representative, group, organization, etc.). Freq. as **manda·ted** *ppl. a.*, permitted to act on behalf of a group, etc., approved by means of a mandate.

1958 *Spectator* 20 June 191/1 A delegate conference was called, and garages invited to mandate their representatives to vote for or against continuance [of a strike]. **1967** *National Observer* (U.S.) 3 July 13 Mr. Reagan must raise the money to pay off that deficit and to pay for mandated new programs. **1968** Smith & Zurcher *Dict. Amer. Politics* (ed. 2) 231 *Mandated expenditure*, an expenditure which a State requires a municipal government to make, often from locally collected funds, and often without reimbursement from State funds. **1969** D. Widgery in Cockburn & Blackburn *Student Power* 126 Universities with a strong and democratic union came to Council with an elected delegation fully briefed and mandated on all issues by general meetings. **1972** *Daily Tel.* 29 Apr. 14 The [union] delegates are elected by, and frequently mandated by, those members who attend branch meetings. **1973** *Black World* May 35/2 The Committee mandated its current chairman..to visit all O.A.U. member states. **1973** *Black Panther* 21 July p. B, Their annual salary increases exceed the nationally-mandated rate. **1974** *Daily Tel.* 25 May 6/5 Mr Thorne, a member of the national executive, said he was mandated to vote for industrial action.

mandatory, *a.* and *sb.* Add: **A.** *adj.* **a.** (Further examples.)

1966 *Listener* 15 Dec. 880/1 Mr. George Brown..puts Britain's case for mandatory sanctions to Security Council. **1972** *Soviet Weekly* 26 Feb. 1 Each delegation has one vote, and only unanimous decisions are mandatory. **1972** *Incorporated Linguist* XI. 36 For further education, postgraduate training is not mandatory, but there is much to be said for it.

c. *spec.* Designating a power or state in receipt of a mandate from the League of Nations, or the system of rule by mandate. Cf. *Mandate *sb.* 4 b.

1921 *First Assembly* (League of Nations Union) 260 The Commission shall examine the annual reports of the Mandatory States and advise the Council as to the execution of the terms of the Mandates. **1922** *Encycl. Brit.* XXX. 509/1 Under the Peace of Versailles a new form of colonial possession came into being... The 'mandatory' system was..evolved. **1930** [see *Incident *sb.*¹ 1 b]. **1946** *Ann. Reg. 1945* 167 The compromise eventually adopted required the Mandatory Powers to express their willingness to place the territories for which they were responsible under the Trusteeship system. **1950** M. Hay *Foot of Pride* ix. 269 'It will be interesting,' wrote C. R. Ashbee, civil adviser of the mandatory administration, in 1922, 'to watch..the inevitable failure of the Rutenberg scheme.' **1958** *Listener* 21 Aug. 273/1 An underground organisation [in Palestine]..directed against Britain, the mandatory power. **1974** *Encycl. Brit. Micropædia* VI. 558/1 Exercise of the mandates was supervised by the League's Permanent Mandates Commission, but the commission had no real way of enforcing its will on a mandatory power.

B. *sb.* **b.** *spec.* A power or state in receipt of a mandate from the League of Nations to administer and develop a territory (in quot. 1927, the territory assigned in this way).

1919 *League of Nations Covenant* Art. xxii, The wishes of these communities must be a principal consideration in the selection of the Mandatory. **1927** *Daily Express* 24 May 3 A memorandum issued by the Arab Executive (Nationalists)..accuses Great Britain of ignoring the covenant principle to assist mandatories to become self-governing. **1928** *Manch. Guardian Weekly* 8 June 443/3 He adopts quite frankly the very contestable position that sovereignty over the mandated territory belongs solely to the mandatory. **1936** V. Margueritte *League Fiasco* ii. 83 The Mandates Commission, consisting of nine members, would have nothing to do but examine the annual reports submitted by the mandatories. **1937** H. F. Angus *Probl. Peaceful Change Pacific Area* iii. 155 It was assumed that whichever of these countries acted as mandatory would do more for the interests of native populations than had been done by their predecessor.

M and B (em ănd bī·). Also M & B, and with points. A registered trade mark of the *M*ay & *B*aker Co. Ltd., applied to pharmaceutical preparations marketed by them, esp *M & B 693*, sulphapyridine tablets.

A symbol incorporating the letters M and B was registered as a trade mark in 1935 (*Trade Marks Jrnl.* (1935) 30 Oct. 1349).

1938 *Lancet* 28 May 1210/2 For experimental infections in mice the effective dose of M. & B. 693 varies from 0·25 mg. per g. to 2 mg. per g. **1943** J. B. Priestley *Daylight on Saturday* i. 3 With ultra-violet rays and radiant heat and *M. & B. 693* to be had for the asking. **1951** W. S. Churchill *Second World War* (1952) V. 373 The admirable M and B, from which I did not suffer any inconvenience, was used at the earliest moment, and after a week's fever the intruders were repulsed. **1953** *Trade Marks Jrnl.* 18 Feb. 139/1 M & B... Chemical products used in industry, science and photography; [etc.]... May & Baker Limited, Dagenham, Essex; manufacturing chemists. **1957** F. S. Taylor *Hist. Industr. Chem.* xvi. 250 Sulphapyridine (M & B 693) revolutionized the treatment of pneumonia. **1968** *Listener* 19 Dec. 815/3 One pocket stuffed with quinine and the other with M and B tablets.

Mande (mā·nde), *sb.* and *a.* = *Mandingo *sb.* and *a.*

1883 R. N. Cust *Sk. Mod. Lang. Afr.* I. xi. 179 The Mande-nga occupy a mountainous Region... The final syllable is a Suffix, which conveys the meaning of the people themselves, while their language should properly be called Mande. *Ibid.* 186 The Mende are Pagans and turbulent. Care must be taken to distinguish the Mende from the Mande. *Ibid.* 186 They [*sc.* the Vei] belong to the Mande Cluster. **1911** *Encycl. Brit.* XVII. 564/2 Delafosse divides the Mandingo group linguistically into three main sections: (1) the *Mande-tamu*, (2) the *Mande-fu*, and (3) the *Mande-tā*, according as they use for the numeral 10 the root *tamu*, *tā* or *fu*. *Ibid.* 565/1 The manati was the totem of the Mande group. **1930** C. G. Seligman *Races Afr.* iii. 59 The Mandingo—more correctly the Mendi or Mande—constitute one of the most important groups of French Senegal. **1952** Westermann & Bryan *Lang. W. Afr.* ii. 31 The Mande languages are spoken over a vast area extending from the Atlantic coast to the Black Volta. **1955** P. Strevens *Papers in Lang.* (1965) ix. 114 Within the area..are spoken Temne and Mande languages in Sierra Leone, [etc.]. **1968** G. Jackson *Let.* 6 Mar. in *Soledad Brother* (1971) 152 The oldest language is one spoken in Africa: Mande. **1970** P. Oliver *Savannah Syncopators* 112 *Mandingo.* Mande-speaking peoples of which the Malinke are the largest.

Mandingo (mændi·ŋgo), *sb.* and *a.* Also **Manding, Mundingo.** **A.** *sb.* **a.** A large group of Negro peoples of the upper Niger in West Africa; a member of these peoples. **b.** The language or languages of these peoples. **B.** *adj.* Of or pertaining to these peoples.

1623 R. Jobson *Golden Trade* 27, I take my beginning from the mouth of the River, whereat our first entrance, we find the Black men called Mandingos. **1757** [see *Ibo *sb.* 1 a]. **1798** *Proc. Afr. Assoc.* 4 The inhabitants are chiefly Mandingoes, and seem to be a well disposed and peaceable race. *Ibid.* 9 Of the other wild animals in the Mandingo countries, the most common are the hyæna, the panther, and the elephant. *Ibid.* 13 By the Niger, is here undoubtedly meant, the river of Senegal; which in the Mandingo language is called *Bafing*, or the Black river. **1888** L. A. Smith *Music of Waters* 329 Another very rhythmical air is the following Mandingo one. **1925** P. Radin tr. *Vendryes' Lang.* II. ii. 112 A West African language, Mandingo, distinguishes *a fa* 'his father', from *a-ta kursi* 'his breeches'. **1930** C. G. Seligman *Races Afr.* iii. 60 The typical Mandingo are described as tall and slender in build. **1936** G. Greene *Journey without Maps* II. i. 99 Some Mandingo traders whom he caught smuggling goods over the border from French territory. **1948** *Caribbean Q.* I. i. 11 Of these 101 were Mandingoes from Senegambia and the upper Niger. **1969** *Times* 19 July 9/5 Many of these slaves were..conversant with the two main languages of Senegambia: Wolof and Mandingo. **1972** *Times* 29 June 16/2 The term 'Manding' embraces a number of West African peoples who speak related forms of the same language and share a similar culture. The Manding language, in a variety of dialects.., is spoken by some 10 million people. *Ibid.* 16/5 The pious Manding who made a famous pilgrimage to Mecca in 1324. *Ibid.*, The Manding have always been natural travellers.

Mandinka (mǎndi·ŋkǎ), *sb.* and *a.* = *Malinke.

1957 M. Banton *W. Afr. City* iv. 62 Tribes largely resident in Freetown or the Colony area, for example, Kru, Sherbro and Mandinka. *Ibid.* vii. 122 The Kissi..speak a separate language similar to that of the Bulom but now much influenced by Mandinka. *Ibid.* 127 There are about 125,000 Mandinka in West Africa, from Senegal to the Ivory Coast.

mandolin, -ine. Add: **2.** *transf.* A kitchen utensil fitted with cutting blades and used for slicing vegetables. Usu. spelt *mandoline*.

1951 E. David *French Country Cooking* 19 A vegetable slicer which goes by the charming name of *Mandoline*. **1959** *Times* 16 Nov. 15/4 Slice the peeled potatoes evenly and thinly (a slicing device known as a *mandoline* makes this task a matter of moments). **1961** *Spectator* 25 Aug. 270 With the aid of that blessed instrument called a mandoline the cucumber is thinly and evenly sliced. **1969** *Daily Tel.* 16 Jan. 17 Arrange a chopping board, sharp knife, grater and cucumber slice (or mandoline) around the colourful basket of raw vegetables. **1975** *Habitat Catal.* 68 Mandolin... Wood frame stainless steel slicer and crinkle cutter.

mandor (mæ·ndōəɹ). Also **mandore, mandur.** [Malay *mandor* (*mandur*), ad. Pg. *mandador* one

who gives orders.] A foreman or overseer in Malaysia or Indonesia. Cf. *KANGANY.

1889 S. J. HICKSON *Naturalist in North Celebes* 65 The coolies were under the supervision of two mandūrs or foremen. **1926** *Blackw. Mag.* Apr. 508/1 A Malay 'mandor' is told that at a certain time on that day he must bring so many men. **1928** *Ibid.* Apr. 473/1, I remember a Malay mandor of mine laughing aloud when he was told that another Malay and two children had died..from exposure. **1958** GINSBURG & ROBERTS *Malaya* ix. 333 In the managerial class the labor foremen, *kanganies* or *mandors*, are a combination of labor boss and patriarch depending on personality factors and on the strength of the trade-union organization. **1962** B. HARRISSON *Orang-Utan* iii. 119 We heard..through one of the road engineers..that one of his Malay mandors had been asked to look for a baby gibbon which somebody wanted to keep as a pet. **1965** C. SHUTTLEWORTH *Malayan Safari* iii. 41 An Indian *mandor* (foreman) was taken from the veranda of his house whilst sleeping. **1969** K. S. SANDHU *Indians in Malaya* iii. 114 *Mandurs* (overseers)..and railway porters were classified as skilled workers and allowed to return to Malaya [from India]. **1970** T. LILLEY *Projects Section* xv. 192 Raja Gopal's house..stands..about a hundred yards from the labour lines..of which Raja Gopal is..the Mandore in charge. **1972** *Sunday Times* (Kuala Lumpur) 30 Apr. 3/2 Tin mine mandore Yaacob bin Abdul Wahab had to master more than the course.

Mandrax (mæ·ndræks). *Pharm.* A proprietary name for tablets containing methaqualone and diphenhydramine hydrochloride, used as a sedative.

1963 *Trade Marks Jrnl.* 10 Apr. 485/1 Mandrax... Hypnotics, being pharmaceutical preparations and substances. Roussel-Uclaf,..Paris. **1967** *Scottish Med. Jrnl.* XII. 63/1 Mandrax..is a hypnotic preparation, which has been actively marketed in Great Britain since Autumn 1965... It has become commonly prescribed as a non-barbiturate hypnotic. **1970** L. LEECH in *Drug Dependence* (U.S. Nat. Inst. Mental Health) 22 Another factor of importance has been the increased use of non-barbiturate hypnotics, particularly methaqualone and diphenhydramine in the form of Mandrax, by young people within the 'pill scene'. **1972** *Police Rev.* 17 Nov. 1505/1 He admits taking Mandrax tablets obtained on prescription.

mandur, var. *MANDOR.

mandy, Mandy (mæ·ndi). Colloq. abbrev. of *MANDRAX (*tablet*).

1970 *Daily Tel.* 8 Sept. 2/3 Dr Tylden says that hypnotic tablets of methaqualone and antihistamine known as 'Mandies' to addicts, had been mentioned to her by youngsters from all parts of Britain. ..The favourite mixture was four 'Mandies' and half a pint of cider, which could lead to sudden unconsciousness. **1971** *Frendz* 21 May 11/2 Avoid dealing while tripping on Acid, Speed or Mandies—you'll goof on the action. **1973** *Daily Tel.* 11 July 2/8 Addicts, who call the white tablets [of methaqualone] 'mandies', 'mainline' by crushing the tablets and injecting themselves.

mane, *sb.* Add **1. a.** *fig.* (Later examples.)

1893 F. THOMPSON *Hound of Heaven* in *Poems* 49 To all swift things for swiftness did I sue; Clung to the whistling mane of every wind. **1927** JOYCE *Flood* in *Pomes Penyeach*, A waste of waters ruthlessly Sways and uplifts its weedy mane. **1936** R. CAMPBELL *Mithraic Emblems* 38 The World put down its lovely mane.

4. *mane-flinging* ppl. adj.

1945 P. LARKIN *North Ship* 19 As some vast seven-piled wave, Mane-flinging, manifold, Streams at an endless shore.

‖ **maneaba** (mane·abă). [Native name.] In the Gilbert and Ellice Islands, a meeting-house.

1944 G. H. EASTMAN *Front Line Islands* 5 Landing at Nui Island we proceeded as our custom was to the public *maneaba* (meeting-house), where the Resident Commissioner spoke to the people. *Ibid.* 10 Our people at Hull Island..have recently erected a large new *maneaba*, which is now used as school house and for women's meetings and various other community gatherings. **1952** A. GRIMBLE *Pattern of Islands* ii. 58 Every Gilbertese village of any size had its own maneaba, or speak-house, in those days. **1970** A. COATES *Western Pacific Islands* viii. 63 In the absence of any king, the wise men conducted affairs in their council house—*manéaba*—their jurisdiction extending just as far as was acceptable, which usually meant to the limits of the land occupied by the clans whose senior members had a reserved place in the *manéaba*, which is somewhat like a hereditary parliament, with the important—and very Pacific—exception that all decisions must be taken on the basis of unanimity. **1974** *Nat. Geographic* Dec. 753/2 Once ashore, I was escorted to the large meetinghouse, the *maneaba*, with thatched eaves that stood only four feet above the ground and a roof that soared upward to a crisscross of massive beams a full forty feet overhead.

man-eater. Add: **2.** (Further examples.)

1922 BLUNDEN *Bonadventure* xvi. 95 To sleep there was to be slowly suffocated, let alone the folly of sleeping among man-eaters [*sc.* mosquitoes]. **1957** R. CAMPBELL *Portugal* iv. 61 Aulus Fedeus had another [moray]..a man-eater.

4. *fig.* Of a person (see quots.). *colloq.*

1906 E. DYSON *Fact'ry 'Ands* xi. 136 To Spats' Beauties she was always Porline or The Man-Eater. **1928** A. HUXLEY *Point Counter Point* xiv. 264 Marjorie isn't the only bore. Nor Lucy the only man-eater. **1929** F. C. BOWEN *Sea Slang* 88 *Man Eater*, a particularly tough officer under sail. **1944** T. RATTIGAN *While Sun Shines* II. 209 Aw, she's no man-eater. You don't get real man-eaters this side of the Atlantic. **1968** D. GRAY *Died in Red* xx. 122 'She 's pretty, you said?'.. 'Very, sir.' 'And a man-eater?' 'I'd say so, yes, sir.' **1974** J. MONTGOMERIE *Implosion* xiii. 97 A womaniser, to use an old-fashioned term. Was a woman ever described as a maniser? No, but I'd heard the designation man-eater.

man-eating *ppl. a.* Also *fig.*

1954 T. S. ELIOT *Confid. Clerk* II. 61 Between a couple of man-eating tigers like you and Lizzie, he's got to have protection. **1958** *Times Lit. Suppl.* 26 Dec. 749/4 He develops an obsession for a fearful man-eating television actress. **1959** *Times* 28 May 15/5 *The Affair in Arcady* has everything—a man-eating young heroine..a sinister step-father, [etc.]. **1974** K. BENTON *Craig & Tunisian Tangle* xi. 158 That sadistic bitch... She's got her man-eating eye on you.

maned, *ppl. a.* **c.** (Later examples.)

1924 R. CAMPBELL *Flaming Terrapin* iv. 68 A fierce train, maned like a ramping lion With smoke and fire, thunders on rolling iron. **1925** E. SITWELL *Troy Park* 66 Whinnying, neighed the maned blue wind.

manège. Add: **2. b.** *transf.* and *fig.*

1825 T. MOORE *Mem. Life R. B. Sheridan* II. xxi. 493 Had his talents, even then, been subjected to the *manège* of a profession. **1955** E. POUND *Classic Anthol.* IV. 214 In the cars' manège war-skill appears. **1973** *Times* 12 Jan. 10/6 She has given up even attempting the fouettés in the ballroom scene; but if the manège she substituted was slightly tame, Nureyev made up by the electrifying speed of his pirouettes.

maneton (mantoṅ). *Aeronaut.* [F. *maneton* crank-pin.] (See quot. 1949.)

1919 *Gloss. Aeronaut. Terms* (R. Aeronaut. Soc.) 44 *Maneton*, the small end of the crankshaft of a rotary engine. **1939** *Times* 30 Mar. 9/3 One simple device for assembling the maneton end of the crankshaft. **1949** *Gloss. Aeronaut. Terms* (*B.S.I.*) II. 11 *Maneton*, the detachable short end of a crankshaft in a rotary or radial engine.

ma·n-folk. *poet.* [MAN *sb.*[1]] People, human beings, men.

1875 W. MORRIS tr. *Virgil's Æneid* XII. 825 Let not that manfolk shift their tongue, or cast their garb aside. **1887** —— tr. *Homer's Odyssey* III. 252 Amid other dwellings of manfolk. *Ibid.* I. 393 Of all that befalleth manfolk dost thou deem it the evillest thing?

Manga. 1. (Earlier example.)

1824 W. BULLOCK *Six Months' Residence Mexico* xvii. 216 An elegant manga or cloak, of velvet, fine cloth, or fine figured cotton.

manganese. Add: **3. manganese purple** = *manganese violet.*

1937 *Burlington Mag.* Dec. 277/2 A large jar of early Florentine maiolica..of the class painted in manganese—purple and green, the only pigments at that time known to the maiolica painter. **1963** *Times* 25 May 11/5 An unpleasant manganese-purple tinge.

manganoan (mæŋgănōu·ăn), *a. Min.* [f. MANGAN(ESE + *-OAN.] Of a mineral: having a (small) proportion of a constituent element replaced by bivalent manganese.

1930 W. T. SCHALLER in *Amer. Mineralogist* XV. 571/2 Manganese—manganoan. **1944** C. PALACHE et al. *Dana's Syst. Min.* (ed. 7) I. 777 Mossite is..reported also (manganoan) from Yinnietharra, Western Australia. **1968** I. KOSTOV *Mineral.* II. ix. 498 Luckite is a manganoan melanterite.

manganous, *a.* **b.** Delete 'with its lower valency' and substitute 'with a valency of two'.

mange, *sb.*[1] Add: **3. mange mite**, a parasitic mite of the family Sarcoptidæ, causing mange in various mammals.

1873 A. S. PACKARD *Our Common Insects* xi. 125 (*caption*) Mange mite. **1911** *Encycl. Brit.* XXVIII. 13/1 The dermatozoa..are lice, fleas, ticks, acari or mange mites. **1950** *N.Z. Jrnl. Agric.* Jan. 68/1 Two types of mange mites affect pigs. **1962** METCALF & FLINT *Destructive & Useful Insects* (ed. 4) xx. 973 When hogs are scratching and rubbing vigorously and their hair is standing erect,.. it is probable that the animals are infested with mange mites.

mangeao (mæŋge,au·, mæŋgī·o). Also 9 mangi, mangiao, 9—mangeo. [Maori.] A New Zealand tree, *Litsea calicaris*, of the family Lauraceæ, with tough, light brown wood.

1848 R. TAYLOR *Leaf from Nat. Hist. N.Z.* 20/2 *Mangiao*, a tree; the ash of this country. **1867** J. D. HOOKER *Handbk. N.Z. Flora* II. 766/1 Mangeao, *Tetranthera calicaris*. **1873** in E. E. Morris *Austral Eng.* (1898) 282/1 Mangi—remarkably tough and compact, used for ship-blocks and similar purposes. **1882** W. D. HAY *Brighter Britain!* II. 187 The perfumy mangiao. **1960** [see *FIVE-FINGER 1 d]. **1963** POOLE & ADAMS *Trees & Shrubs N.Z.* 42 L[*itsea*] *calicaris*... Mangeao. Tree reaching 15m. Bark smooth, dark greyish brown... L[owland] Forest. North of North Island to lat. 38°.

manger (mē̆i·ndʒəɹ), *v.*[2] *rare.* [f. MANGER *sb.*[1]] *trans.* To fasten (an animal) to a manger.

1905 W. HOLMAN HUNT *Pre-Raphaelitism* II. 72 An old ram mangered by a halter.

mange-tout (mañʒtū). [Fr., lit. 'eat-all'.] In full, *mange-tout pea.* A variety of pea producing pods which are eaten with the seeds they contain; = *sugar-pea* (SUGAR *sb.* 5 c).

1928 *Daily Express* 18 July 5/2 It [*sc.* a variety of pea] is largely grown in France, where it goes by the name of 'mange-tout'..and is eaten, shell and all. **1951** *Good Housek. Home Encycl.* 591/1 The seeds [*sc.* peas] are contained in a green pod, which is not usually eaten (except in the case of the sugar or mangetout variety). **1966** *Sunday Times* (Colour Suppl.) 27 Nov. 50/3 A bowl of *mangetout* peas. **1970** *Harrod's Summer Food News* 5/1 Whether you need..a pound of potatoes, or..mange tout peas, the quality is of the best at Harrods. **1972** *Country Life* 4 May 1121/3 From the French we are learning to enjoy the *Mangetout* or sugar pea. **1974** *Observer* (Colour Suppl.) 15 Sept. 12/3 Asked with impious briskness precisely when to sow mange-touts, divide artichokes or prune plums.

mangi, var. *MANGEAO.

mangle, *sb.*[3] Add: **b. mangle-board** [Da. *manglebræt*], a board with which linen and cotton may be pressed and smoothed.

1892 E. ROWE *Hints on Chip-Carving* iii. 47 The border ..may be seen on a mangle-board from Jutland, dated 1708. **1928** *Daily Express* 22 June 12/6 The exhibits include various examples from Denmark, Sweden, Norway and Holland... Dates on the mangleboards go back as far as 1590.

c. *fig.* A bicycle. *Austral. slang.*

1941 BAKER *Dict. Austral. Slang* 45 *Mangle*, a bicycle. **1965** G. MCINNES *Road to Gundagai* viii. 122 'Where's the grid?' 'My bike!' 'Yeah, the old mangle.'

mangosteen. Add: **4.** A name used in Barbados for the jujube, *Zizyphus mauritiana.*

1750 G. HUGHES *Nat. Hist. Barbados* v. 134 The Dunk-tree, or Mangustine. This is a middle-sized Tree. **1859** BARTLETT *Dict. Amer.* (ed. 2) 263 *Mangosteen*, in Barbadoes this name is given to the Jujube (*Ziziphus jujube*). **1965** E. G. B. GOODING et al. *Flora Barbados* 272 (*heading*) *Zizyphus mauritiana..Z. jujuba* (L.).. Mangustine.. Shrub or small tree, 2–4·5 m., young stems tomentose.

mangy, *a.* **3.** (Later examples.)

1896 J. K. SNOWDEN *Web of Old Weaver* x. 127, I cannot see that it much benefits any man to tell him all these mangy quaverings. **1922** JOYCE *Ulysses* 735 We have to be thankful for our mangy cup of tea. *Ibid.*, The old mangy parcel he sent at Xmas. **1930** R. CAMPBELL *Poems* 10 The poet wags his mangy stump of rhyme. **1942** BERREY & VAN DEN BARK *Amer. Thes. Slang* § 30/4 Poor; mean; contemptible..*mangy.*

Manhattan (mænhæ·tăn). Also **manhattan.** [The name of the island on which the older part of New York is situated.] Used *ellipt.* for **Manhattan cocktail**, a cocktail made of vermouth and whisky with a dash of bitters.

1890 B. HALL *Turnover Club* 16 This order was as follows ..the Actor, 'A Manhattan cocktail'. **1895** C. D. WARNER *Golden House* v. 43 He and old Fairfax sipped their five-o'clock 'Manhattan'. **1906** *Mrs. Beeton's Bk. Househ. Managem.* xlix. 1511 *Manhattan.* Ingredients: ½ a wineglassful of vermouth, ½ a wineglassful of whisky, 30 drops of green syrup, 10 drops of Angostura bitters, 6 drops of Curaçoa, [etc.]. **1909** [see *BRONX 1]. **1937** M. SHARP *Nutmeg Tree* viii. 84 If I could have one [a cocktail], I'd have a Manhattan. **1955** W. GADDIS *Recognitions* II. iv. 474 The dumpy woman was drinking a manhattan. **1963** C. D. SIMAK *They walked like Men* xii. 70 The bartender set my drink before me and began fixing her Manhattan. **1972** D. BLOODWORTH *Any Number can Play* x. 80 Larry returned with soda-water for Max and a manhattan for himself.

Manha:ttane·se, *sb.* and *a.* [f. prec. + -ESE.] **A.** *sb.* A native or inhabitant of New York or Manhattan Island; usu. *collect.*; also, the dialect of New York. **B.** *adj.* Of or pertaining to New York or Manhattan Island.

1828 J. F. COOPER *Notions Amer.* I. 200 The New Yorkers (how much better is the word Manhattanese!) cherish the clumsy inconvenient entrances. **1842** —— *Wing-and-Wing* I. 11 Hundreds collected on the spot, which, in Manhattanese parlance, would probably have been called a battery. *Ibid.* 193 This gentleman was an American, and a native Manhattanese; his near relatives, of the same name, still residing in New York. **1844** *Knickerbocker* XXIII. 586 The sound of India-crackers and the pleasant smell of lobsters is already perceptible to the senses of the awakening Manhattanese. **1875** W. WHITMAN in *Gentl. Mag.* Dec. 706, I was Manhattanese, friendly, and proud. **1904** *Forum* (N.Y.) Jan.–Mar. 410 'Her Own Way'..brings together a number of highly piquant Manhattanese types of to-day, sketched with captivating drollery. **1908** S. FORD *Side-Stepping with Shorty* vi. 91 He drops the imitation society talk that he likes to spout, and switches to straight Manhattanese. **1909** *Nation* (N.Y.) 9 Sept. 238/3 Perhaps the most amusing thing in the book is an interpolated story based on a difference of opinion between New Englanders and Manhattanese on the subject of doughnuts and crullers. **1942** BERREY & VAN DEN BARK *Amer. Thes. Slang* § 181/5 *Manhattanese*, language peculiar to New Yorkers.

manhood. 7. manhood suffrage (earlier examples).

1859 DISRAELI in *Hansard Commons* 31 Mar. 1245 Why, Sir, I have no apprehension myself that if you had manhood suffrage tomorrow the honest, brave, and good-natured people of England would resort to pillage, incendiarism, and massacre. **1864** *Q. Rev.* CXVI. 262 If Mr Gladstone is generally supposed to have taken up the battle-cry of manhood suffrage, he has only himself to

thank for it. **1867** JOHN 1st EARL RUSSELL *Let.* 27 Mar. in B. & P. Russell *Amberley Papers* (1937) II. 24 Dizzy must know that, & I believe means 'Manhood suffrage'.

‖ **mani**² (mā·ni). [Tibetan *máṇi*, f. Skr. *maṇi* precious stone (as in the jewel-lotus prayer *om maṇi padme hum* 'Oh the lotus-jewel, Amen').] In full, *mani wall.* A Tibetan 'prayer wall', covered with stones piously inscribed (see also quots.)

1863 E. SCHLAGINTWEIT *Buddhism in Tibet* xiii. 196 Mani, originally a Sanskrit word meaning 'a precious stone',..is used to designate walls of about six feet in height and four to eight feet in breadth. **1882** *Encycl. Brit.* XIV. 197/2 It [*sc.* the palace at Lé] is surrounded by poplar plantations, with manis and ch'hordtens beyond. *Ibid.*, 'Mani', a long stone wall, several feet wide, running along the roadside, covered with loose stones deposited by the passers-by, inscribed with the prayer or ejaculation, 'Om mani padme hom'. **1925** B. BEETHAM in E. F. Norton *Fight for Everest, 1924* I. viii. 171 The mani-walls (prayer-stones) had once been of an unusually imposing nature. **1952** H. W. TILMAN *Nepal Himalaya* iv. 39 The longest mani wall I have ever seen—nearly three hundred yards of it... On each side are flat stones with carved Buddhas or religious texts for the benefit of passers-by. **1953** TSUNG-LIEN SHEN & SHEN-CHI LIU *Tibet* v. 118 The approach to a village or monastery is marked by a *Mani* wall or by a pagoda. **1959** *Times* 23 May 7/6 The people here are Buddhist and there is abundant evidence of their faith—*mani* (or prayer) walls.

mania. 1. Add to def.: Now a more general term for a condition of over-excitement and restless activity, usually denominated according to its severity (see quot. 1971). Cf. **hypermania*, *HYPOMANIA.

1925 J. RIVIERE et al. tr. *Freud's Coll. Papers* IV. 164 The most remarkable peculiarity of melancholia, and one most in need of explanation, is the tendency it displays to turn into mania accompanied by a completely opposite symptomatology. **1969** ULLMANN & KRASNER *Psychol. Approach Abnormal Behavior* II. xxi. 417/1 A person may gradually progress from hypomania to delirious mania over time, or the delirious mania may, in rare instances, be emitted without a 'warm-up' period. **1971** T. ROBERTS *Handbk. Psychiatric Nurses* II. 62 *Mania.* There are four main types:—Hypomania... Acute mania, producing a wild frenzied aggressive attack of excitement and over activity. Chronic mania sometimes called Scott's mania. Hypermania: delirious or Bell's mania. **1973** *Sci. Amer.* Sept. 117/3 Mania is manifested by psychic elation, increased motor activity, rapid speech and the quick flight of ideas. The stigmata of depression are melancholia, the slowing of thought, unusual thought content (for example overwhelming guilt over imagined transgressions and delusions of rotting away), motor retardation, sleep disturbances and preoccupation with bodily complaints.

manic (mæ·nik), *a.* [f. MANIA: see -IC.] Of, pertaining to, affected with, or resembling mania. Also as *sb.*, a person affected with mania.

1902 *Buck's Handbk. Med. Sci.* (rev. ed.) V. 124/1 She showed a typical picture of a manic excitement with great exhilaration, flight of ideas, and distractability. **1921** R. M. BARCLAY *Kraepelin's Manic-Depressive Insanity & Paranoia* 54 The conspicuous contrasts between manic and depressive attacks. **1922** R. S. WOODWORTH *Psychol.* xi. 259 In the excited insane condition known as 'mania' or the 'manic state', the patient is excessively distractible. **1957** P. LAFITTE *Person in Psychol.* vi. 75 The manic hopelessly flees the devil wherever he goes. **1957** *Observer* 6 Oct. 18/7 That manic transatlantic zing which is part of the fascination of the Marx Brothers. **1964** *New Statesman* 6 Mar. 367/1 Entirely faithful as expositor, Dr. Segal brings to bear her own contributions, particularly in regard to what she calls manic reparation.

2. *Comb.* **manic depression**, the condition of manic-depressive illness; **manic-depressive** *a.*, characterized by or affected with alternating periods of elation and mental depression; also *fig.*; hence as *sb.*, a person so affected.

1958 M. ARGYLE *Relig. Behaviour* ix. 108 The upper and middle classes have higher rates for manic depression and neurosis. **1964** —— *Psychol. & Social Probl.* vi. 78 Schizophrenia is thought by some to be inherited by two or more recessive genes, manic depression via two or more dominant ones. **1973** *Nature* 16 Feb. 480/1 A disproportionate number of patients with schizophrenia or manic-depression were born in the early months of the year. **1902** A. R. DEFENDORF *Clin. Psychiatry* 282 Manic-Depressive Insanity. This term is applied to that mental disorder which recurs..throughout the life of the individual and in which a defective hereditary endowment seems to be the ..prominent etiological factor. **1931** E. WILSON *Axel's Castle* iii. 92 The modern psychologists would probably diagnose him as introverted, narcissistic and manic depressive. **1934** P. BOTTOME *Private Worlds* xxi. 206 A gland experiment which would help them to get a certain physical reaction from manic depressives. **1943** J. S. HUXLEY *Evolutionary Ethics* ii. 13 Complete alternation of conflicting moods is exemplified in manic-depressives. **1959** R. GRAVES *Coll. Poems* 315 Have seen two parallel red-ink lines drawn Under their manic-depressive bank accounts. **1961** J. HELLER *Catch-22* (1962) xxvii. 298 Greed depresses you. Crime depresses you. Corruption depresses you. You know, it wouldn't surprise me if you're a manic-depressive! **1961** L. MUMFORD *City in Hist.* xv. 520 It was the manic-depressive rhythm of the market, with its spurts and stoppages, that made the large urban centre so important to industry. **1970** *Jrnl. Gen. Psychol.* LXXXIII. 76 A study of the neurotic tendencies shown in dementia praecox and manic depressive insanity. **1973** *Sci. Amer.* Sept. 117/3 Manic-depressive psychosis is marked by severe disturbances in mood that are self-limited in time but are recurrent and frequently cyclic.

Manichæistic (mæːniki,i·stik), *a.* Also **Manicheistic.** [f. as MANICHÆIST: see -ISTIC.] Of the nature of Manichæism.

1924 O. LODGE *Making of Man* ii. 49 A Manichæistic conception of existence can never have been really satisfying. **1932** *Times Lit. Suppl.* 3 Mar. 148/3 With something of Manicheistic fury Miss Leader tracks down the sense of physical abjection and inferiority.

Manichæism, Manicheism. Add: Also *transf.*

1894 W. ARCHER *Theatr. 'World' 1893* 224 The time is past for the elementary Manicheism on which *The Tempter* is based. **1959** B. & R. NORTH tr. *Duverger's Political Parties* (ed. 2) p. xv, The elementary Marxist opposition of middle class to working class will also often be used... There are many more shades of social stratification than this rough manicheism suggests.

‖ **manicou** (maniku). [Fr.] An opossum of the genus *Marmosa*, found in Central and South America.

1953 P. L. FERMOR *Violins of St.-Jacques* 28 The most remarkable [pets] were a family of manicous, the mother of which carried her dozen young about by twisting her tail parallel to her spine in order that they might loop their own round it and secure their positions on the parent back. **1968** E. LOVELACE *Schoolmaster* xi. 171, I will go late and headlight in the forest for manicou.

manicure, *sb.* Add: **2.** attrib. *manicure case, department, girl, parlour, scissors, set, stick.*

1895 *Montgomery Ward Catal.* 255/3 Combination Toilet and Manicure Case..contains complete set of 12 white Florence toilet and manicure fittings. **1967** 'K. O'HARA' *Unknown Man* ii. 10 There was a chip out of one nail, so that she would need the manicure case. **1887** *Mod. Society* 23 July 749/2 A young lady employed in the manicure department of one of our most popular establishments. **1922** S. LEWIS *Babbitt* xviii. 219 Young women who had recently been manicure girls. **1946** *Vogue* June 35/1 The manicure-girls stare contemptuously. **1912** *Collier's* 9 Nov. 11/3 Jack Zelig was a daily patron of a manicure parlor. **1893** *T. Eaton & Co. Catal.* Spring & Summer 35/3 Scissors, manicure, 25 c. **1913** J. WEBSTER *Daddy-Long-Legs* 194 Sawing off picture wire with manicure scissors. **1952** M. NORTON *Borrowers* ii. 17 Homily.. unhooked the blade and handle of half a pair of manicure scissors from a nail on the wall. **1973** H. NIELSEN *Severed Key* i. 14 Keith..located the cosmetic case... 'Women usually carry a manicure scissors in these things,' he said. **1897** *Sears, Roebuck Catal.* 435/2 Manicure and Buttonhook set, fancy, Solid Sterling Silver handles. **1945** E. BOWEN *Demon Lover* 72 A manicure-set in a purple box; all the objects..lay in grooves on white velvet. **1962** *Guardian* 5 Dec. 6/4 A really complete manicure set..for 22s 6d. **1909** E. BANKS *Mystery F. Farrington* 162 Orange-wood manicure sticks.

manicure, *v.*, **manicured,** *ppl. a.* Add: Also *transf.* and *fig.* **manicuring** *vbl. sb.* (earlier example).

1892 G. & W. GROSSMITH *Diary of Nobody* xviii. 230 I'm going in for manicuring. It's all the fashion now. **1922** M. ARLEN *Piracy* III. vi. 192 Even her soul was manicured. *c* **1926** 'MIXER' *Transport Workers' Song Bk.* 97 You would make a good oil-painting if your face was manicured. **1936** F. CLUNE *Roaming round Darling* viii. 68 The only prisoner in sight was a 'lifer' manicuring the garden. **1957** J. BRAINE *Room at Top* i. 10 Big houses with drives and orchards and manicured hedges. **1964** M. MCLUHAN *Understanding Media* II. xxii. 217 This shift from the mobile open road to the manicured roots of suburbia may signify a real change in American orientation. **1972** *Times* (Jamaica Suppl.) 7 Aug. p. vi/3 Manicured and well-watered fairways of tourist golf courses. **1973** A. MACVICAR *Painted Doll Affair* xiv. 164 A tractor-powered gang-mower was manicuring the last of the fairways. **1975** *New Yorker* 19 May 115 (Advt.), Your day may be occupied..testing the exquisitely manicured golf course.

‖ **maniéré** (manyere), *a.* [Fr.] Affected or characterized by mannerism; = MANNERED *a.* 3.

1743 H. WALPOLE *Let.* 14 Aug. (1857) I. 263 The Sasso Ferrati you sent me..is not so *manière* [*maniéré*, in *Corr.* (1955) XVIII] as the Dominichin. **1764** S. FOOTE *Patron* I. 2 But the figures are all finish'd alike. A maniere, a tiresome sameness throughout. **1813** A. ROMILLY in S. H. Romilly *Romilly–Edgeworth Lett.* (1936) 64 Her little maniéré airs are with difficulty supported for a few hours. **1839** THACKERAY in *Fraser's Mag.* June 749/1 You will see here a large drawing..which will shew at once how clever that young artist is, and how weak and maniéré. **1908** *Westm. Gaz.* 14 Nov. 19/1 The suit for outdoor wear delights in a daring *maniéré* simplicity.

‖ **manière criblée** (manyēr' krible). [Fr., f. *manière* MANNER *sb.*¹ + *criblé* CRIBBLED *ppl. a.*] The cribbled style of engraving. Cf. CRIBBLED *ppl. a.* and *CRIBLÉ *sb.* (and *a.*)

1903 *New Internat. Encycl.* XI. 834/2 Manière criblée. Probably the oldest process of engraving upon metal for the purpose of printing. It derives its name from the white dots with which the dark ground of the print is covered, resembling the holes of a sieve. **1960** H. HAYWARD *Antique Coll.* 174/1 *Manière criblée*, the name is derived from a group of dots made on the plate with a punch to break up otherwise black areas of background. Prints of this type were made in the late 15th and early 16th cent., especially in Florence. **1965** ZIGROSSER & GAEHDE *Guide to Collecting Orig. Prints* iv. 50 Those early prints known as dotted prints (*manière criblée, Schrotblatt*), made with various goldsmith's punches on metal.

manifest, *sb.* **2.** Delete † *Obs.* and add later examples.

1915 A. HUXLEY *Let.* Dec. (1969) 87 Meanwhile all is forgiven and forgotten if you subscribe to the *Palatine*.. vide multicoloured manifest thus conceived, which you had better distribute. **1922** *Glasgow Herald* 12 Apr. 11 The annexation itself had been proclaimed by a personal manifest of the Emperor King.

3. Also *transf.* Also, a similar list of freight or passengers carried by a train or aeroplane. Also, a fast freight train (chiefly *U.S.*).

1869 'MARK TWAIN' in *Buffalo Express* 21 Aug. 1/3 The doctor is not done taking inventory. He will make out my manifest this evening. **1872** in I. M. TARBELL *Hist. Standard Oil Co.* (1904) I. 286 The party..covenants and agrees..to make manifests or way-bills of all petroleum or its products, transported over any portion of the railroads. **1929** *Amer. Speech* IV. 342 *Manifest*, a fast merchandise freight train. **1931** G. IRWIN *Amer. Tramp & Underworld Slang* 127 *Manifest*, a fast freight train, from the 'manifest' of the goods carried. **1934** *Amer. Ballads & Folk Songs* 24 The manifest freight Pulled out on the stem behind the mail. **1936** MENCKEN *Amer. Lang.* (ed. 4) 582 A fast freight is a *manifest* or *red-ball.* **1956** W. A. HEFLIN *U.S. Air Force Dict.* 315/1 *Manifest*, a document that lists in detail the passengers or other items carried in one aircraft for a specific destination. **1959** R. COLLIER *City that wouldn't Die* ix. 143 Watching Schied initial the bomb manifest and hand it down to the chief armourer. **1969** *Jane's Freight Containers 1968–69* 128/1 Daily containers move in expedited Piggy-back trains and transcontinental manifest trains. **1971** *Sunday Australian* 8 Aug. 11/2 He came to my office with..samples of passenger manifests.

manifest, *a.* Add: **1. b.** *manifest destiny* (often written with capital initials), *Polit.* 'The doctrine of the inevitability of Anglo-Saxon supremacy. A phrase used by those who believed it was the destiny of the United States or of the Anglo-Saxon race to govern the entire Western Hemisphere' (*D.A.E.*). Also *transf. U.S.*

1845 J. O'SULLIVAN in *U.S. Mag. & Democratic Rev.* July & Aug. 5 Our manifest destiny to overspread the continent allotted by Providence for the free development of our yearly multiplying millions. **1856** *Spirit of Times* 13 Dec. 235/2 He was a 'manifest destiny' man. **1858** *Economist* 6 Feb. 139/2 What reasons can be shown for the manifest destiny to whip Africans which do not apply with equal force to prove the manifest destiny to subdue half-caste Spaniards into conformity with their will? **1867** J. R. LOWELL *Biglow Papers* 2nd Ser. p. vii, The incarnation of 'Manifest Destiny', in other words, of national recklessness as to right or wrong. **1927** J. W. PRATT in *Amer. Hist. Rev.* XXXII. 795 One can hardly read a work on the history of the United States in the two decades before the Civil War without meeting the phrase 'manifest destiny', widely used as a convenient statement of the philosophy of territorial expansion in that period. **1959** *Listener* 18 June 1048/2 The long and stern struggle by which Canada had maintained its separateness against American 'Manifest Destiny'.

c. *manifest function.* Sociol. (See quots.)

1949 R. K. MERTON *Social Theory* I. i. 51 *Manifest functions* are those objective consequences contributing to the adjustment or adaptation of the system which are intended and recognised by participants in the system; *Latent functions*, correlatively, being those which are neither intended nor recognised. **1957** M. BANTON *W. Afr. City* ix. 168, I shall describe..how the companies fulfil their explicit functions of providing mutual aid and entertainment—what R. K. Merton has termed the manifest functions.

manifold. Add: **C.** *sb.*¹ **4. b.** Short for *manifold-paper.*

1897 B. STOKER *Dracula* xvii. 229, I began to typewrite from the beginning of the seventh cylinder. I used manifold, and so took three copies of the diary. **1926** *Paper Terminol.* (Spalding & Hodge) ii. 16 *Manifold*, slightly waxed tissue or other thin interleaving paper made for employment with carbon paper. Also an extremely thin typewriting made for the multiplication to as many as ten or twelve carbon copies of typewritten letters. **1954** *Ibid.* 38 *Manifold*, papers similar in character to Bank, although thinner. They range in substance from 16½ × 21 in. 4½ lb. 500's to 8 lb. 500's and are used when a large number of carbon copies is required. **1967** KARCH & BUBER *Offset Processes* xi. 485 *Manifold*, thin, strong, [for] duplicate copies, sales books, etc.

5. Substitute for '(See quot.)': Any pipe that splits into a number of branches; *spec.* the one running from the carburettor of an internal-combustion engine to the cylinders, and the one from the silencer to the cylinders. (Earlier and later examples.)

a **1884** KNIGHT *Dict. Mech.* Suppl. 579/2 *Manifold*, the chambers with nozzles into and from which the pipes of a radiator lead. **1919** [see *exhaust-manifold* s.v. *EXHAUST *sb.* 3]. **1948** '*Motor*' *Manual* (ed. 33) v. 99 The induction manifold of a modern engine generally is heated by the exhaust. This..can be easily and neatly arranged in most engines because the exhaust manifold usually is close to the inlet manifold. **1961** *Economist* 30 Dec. 1306/1 Ford provides only the carburettor, inlet manifold and camshaft for the Classic [motor car]. **1971** *Sci. Amer.* Sept. 222/3 All gases are admitted through needle valves to a manifold that connects to the laser.

manifolder (mæ·nifōᵘldəɹ). [f. MANIFOLD *v.* + -ER¹.] A machine for multiplying copies of a document, etc., or a person using this. Also used of a typeface (see quot. *c* 1961).

1903 in *Funk's Stand. Dict.* Suppl. **1911** WEBSTER (citing G. H. Putnam), He seems to have added to his employment that of a manifolder and seller of manuscripts. *c***1961** *Imperial Type Faces* (Imperial Typewriter Co.), Pica Gothic type is an exceptionally good manifolder.

manifolding, *vbl. sb.* (s.v. MANIFOLD *v.*). Add: Also *concr.*, = MANIFOLD *sb.*¹ 5 (in Dict. and Suppl.).

1938 *Times* 9 Aug. 8/7 To adjust the tappets it would be best to lift the manifolding. **1963** BIRD & HUTTON-STOTT *Veteran Motor Car* 52 Internal manifolding and clean-cut architectural appearance were all in marked contrast to most contemporary engines.

manilla², manila. Add: **2.** Also, = *manilla paper* (now used of various papers of a light yellow-brown colour: see quots.).

1926 *Paper Terminol.* (Spalding & Hodge) ii. 16 *Manilla*, a superfine tough quality of wrapping and label paper made from Manilla hemp. The term is now loosely applied to cheap imitations made from wood pulp. **1954** *Ibid.* 38 *Manil(l)a*, a coloured paper. . not necessarily containing Manila fibre. **1959** *Gloss. Packaging Terms* (*B.S.I.*) 67 *Manilla*, an imitation manila made in a wide variety of qualities. The term is now generally used to indicate the characteristic colour.

b. The light yellow-brown colour of manilla paper.

1934 in WEBSTER. **1954** P. HIGHSMITH *Blunderer* (1956) viii. 71 He put on old manila trousers.

manipulability (mănipiu̇lăbi·lĭti). [f. MANIPULAB(LE *a.*: see *-BILITY.] The quality of being manipulable.

1947 *Partisan Rev.* Sept.–Oct. 473 Every idea is judged in terms of its political manipulability. **1957** B. F. SKINNER *Verbal Behavior* v. 124 The increasing separability and manipulability of response elements in a minimal unit repertoire is a step toward ideal conditions. **1957** L. EISELEY *Immense Journey* (1958) 6 As I tapped and chiseled there in the foundations of the world, I had ample time to consider the cunning manipulability of the human fingers. **1967** *Punch* 11 Oct. 546/2 Doctors are no more gullible than the rest of us, but they are a captive audience, and the extent of their manipulability can be observed on a firm's local sales charts. **1971** J. B. CARROLL et al. *Word Frequency Bk.* p. vi, Only the Kučera-Francis work is of sufficient size and manipulability to yield a substantial word list and citation base for lexicography. **1974** *Time* 7 Jan. 60/3 His recommendations that society change its 'system of production, ownership and consumption' depend on faith in man's manipulability and desire to change.

manipulable, *a.* Delete *rare* and add later examples.

1957 B. F. SKINNER in Saporta & Bastian *Psycholinguistics* (1961) 233/1 Suffixes such as *-ness* or *-hood* are usually readily manipulable as separate elements in composing new terms. **1963** *Punch* 2 Jan. 21/1 A swiftly manipulable key-board. **1965** J. FEINBERG in M. Black *Philos. in Amer.* 154 It would be an oversimplification. . to identify 'the cause' of an infelicitous condition with *any* manipulable necessary condition. **1971** *Nature* 12 Feb. 445/3 As well as being easy to learn and formally manipulable, [computer languages]. .should be thought-provoking. **1971** *Human World* Nov. 14 Is sovereignty something that can be arranged like this? Is it so infinitely manipulable?

manipulatable (măni·piu̇lēⁱ:tăb'l), *a.* [f. MANIPULAT(E *v.* + -ABLE.] = MANIPULABLE *a.* (in Dict. and Suppl.).

1934 in WEBSTER. **1964** E. A. NIDA *Toward Sci. Transl.* ix. 204 One must expect to find numerous and subtle distinctions, which cannot easily be reduced to readily manipulatable rules. **1970** *Computers & Humanities* IV. 327 These three considerations are separable and individually manipulatable.

manipulate, *v.* Add: **3. b.** *Finance.* To cause (stocks) to rise or fall by affecting the market in other ways than those arising out of ordinary business; to influence (the market) in such ways.

1870 J. K. MEDBERY *Men & Mysteries Wall St.* 188 The stock. .was most admirably manipulated, until it finally touched 152. **1903** S. S. PRATT *Work of Wall St.* 147 A market is rigged when it is manipulated.

4. *trans.* To stimulate (the genitalia); also *refl.*, to masturbate.

1949 O. SCHWARZ *Psychology of Sex* ii. 31 The large majority of these children simply manipulate their genitals in a purely playful manner. **1953** A. C. KINSEY et al. *Sexual Behavior Human Female* v. 161 The female may stimulate them [*sc.* the breasts] with her hand. .while she simultaneously manipulates her genitalia. **1965** MASTERS & JOHNSON in J. Money *Sex Research* iv. 107 It is a rare woman who directly manipulates the clitoris, or, if she does, maintains this type of stimulative activity for any significant length of time. **1971** 'V. X. SCOTT' *Surrogate Wife* 134 At one point he began manipulating himself.

manipulated *ppl. a.* (example).

1903 S. S. PRATT *Work of Wall St.* xi. 147 A deal is the operation resulting from a secret combination or agreement among Wall Street men to effect a certain purpose, generally of a manipulated character in the market.

manipulation. 4. Add examples of use in finance.

1888 *Nation* (N.Y.) 9 Aug. 107/2 Manipulation signifies a common understanding and design on the part of a clique of operators to raise or depress values in order to get other people's money. **1908** *Westm. Gaz.* 26 Aug. 2/2 The opportunity for market manipulation is obvious.

manipulative, *a.* (Later examples.)

1909 *Westm. Gaz.* 8 Sept. 11/4 The powerful manipulative interests are watching events closely. **1947** M. M. LEWIS *Lang. in Society* i. 24 The manipulative and the declarative are the twin incentives by which the development of language is fostered in the child, and remain the essential functions of language in society. **1966** *New Statesman* 22 Apr. 581/2 The cause was won by the politicians' desire to appear manipulative about almost any issue, regardless of its suitability for manipulation. **1968** R. KYLE *Love Lab.* ix. 125 Lillian had just completed a manipulative session and was wearing only a wrapper. **1971** *Nature* 30 Apr. 578/2 For they are also clearly pre-adaptive to efficient use of the hands as manipulative organs, in such activities as food gathering and transport. **1972** *Maclean's Mag.* Mar. 61/1 Spicer is strong, attractive and manipulative. 'He's good at persuading people to do things they might not want to do.'

Hence **mani·pulativeness.**

1949 M. MEAD *Male & Female* ii. 26 Greater awareness does not always mean greater manipulativeness. **1975** *N.Y. Times* 4 Mar. 31 You pity their failings—their determination to 'advance' their children as if life were a relay race,. . their manipulativeness and insularity.

manipulator. Add: **1. c.** One who controls the price of stocks by specially contrived methods.

1888 *Economist* 17 Nov. 3/3 If the people are apathetic it is utterly useless for the manipulators to undertake to push prices up. **1903** S. S. PRATT *Work of Wall St.* 146 A professional may or may not be a manipulator, but a manipulator is always a professional. *Ibid.* 256 By false tips and matched orders or wash sales the manipulators endeavored to establish fictitious quotations for their stocks. **1904** *N.Y. Tribune* 15 May 4 Manipulators desperately endeavoring to bring back recessions which will permit them to 'get even'.

2. f. A device for handling radioactive material, operated by remote control from behind a protective shield.

1952 *Nucleonics* Nov. 41/1 They have been named master-slave manipulators because all the seven degrees of freedom of the tongs are slaved to the single master handle. **1955** *Reactor Handbk.: Engin.* (U.S. Atomic Energy Comm.) 859 A general-purpose manipulator is considered to be a remotely-controlled mechanical arm capable of gripping diverse objects. . . All movements of the manipulator arm are controlled by a human operator. . . The manipulator may have a lower or higher load capacity than the human arm. **1958** *New Scientist* 24 Apr. 21/1 A manipulator believed to be the only one manufactured in Europe that is operated by electrical remote control will be displayed at next week's Hanover Fair. . . The power manipulator is equipped with interchangeable grasping units. .and can lift and position objects weighing up to 750 lbs. **1962** *Newnes Conc. Encycl. Nucl. Energy* 488/2 These manipulators fall into three classes: 1. Handling tongs and sphere units. . . 2. Master-slave manipulators. . . 3. Rectilinear power manipulators. **1969** *IEEE Trans. Nucl. Sci.* XVI. 594/2 The geometry of the Brookhaven AGS and of other synchrotrons requires a larger degree of remoteness than is possible with mechanically-connected master-slave manipulators.

Manipuri (mænipūᵊ·ri), *a.* and *sb.* [Native name.] **A.** *adj.* Of or pertaining to Manipur, a state in the region of Assam in north-east India; *spec.* used of a style of dancing (also *ellipt.*). **B.** *sb.* The people of Manipur; a member of this people; also, the Tibeto-Burman language of the Manipuri.

1906 E. A. GAIT *Hist. Assam* viii. 195 The Manipuri Raja was mindful of the services rendered him a few years previously. **1911** [see *KHASI]. **1918** W. PETTIGREW *Tāngkhul Nāga Gram. & Dict.* 4 In Manipuri, there are two noticeable changes in intonation in TN, a high and low tone to a great number of words which to the ignorant sound the same. **1927** *Blackw. Mag.* June 817/1 The Manipuris. .became such strict Hindus as even to 'out-Brahman' the Brahmans. **1948** D. DIRINGER *Alphabet* II. vi. 365 The Oriya, Maithili and Early Manipuri characters seem also to be somewhat connected with the Bengali script. **1957** G. B. L. WILSON *Dict. Ballet* 178 *Manipuri*, in Hindu dancing, the style of north-east India. The dances are in the form of dance-drama (supported by dialogues and songs) and many dancers participate. It is mainly lyrical and lighter than the other Indian styles. **1968** *Encycl. Brit.* XIV. 790/2 About 60% of the population [of Manipur] speak Manipuri. *Ibid.* XV. 118/2 *Meithei*, also known as Manipuri, the dominant population of the valley of Manipur. **1969** *Femina* (Bombay) 26 Dec. 53/1 Kishori also left an imprint as a noted Manipuri dancer in the early dance dramas produced by the Indian National Theatre. Her rhythmic grace is still remembered. **1971** *Ceylon Observer* (Mag. Ed.) 19 Sept. 4/8 (Advt.), New silver motive white Manipuri saree.

‖ **ma nishtana** (mā niʃtā·nā). *Judaism.* Also **mah nishtan(n)ah.** [Heb., 'Why (is this night) different (from all other nights) ?'] The opening words of the four questions in the Passover Haggadah, traditionally asked by the youngest member of a Jewish household on Seder Night; hence used to designate this part of the Passover celebrations.

1902 *Jewish Chron.* 18 Apr. 20/1 After the sanctification (*Kiddush*) with which our Haggadah begins. .the four questions *Ma nishtana* are read. *Ibid.* 25 Apr. 20/2 In olden times the children were provided with small nuts and chestnuts to give more zest to the question, 'Ma nishtana'—'why is this night different from all other nights?' **1904** *Jewish Encycl.* VI. 141/2 Its initial words, 'Mah Nishtannah', are used as the name of the Haggadah, as in the question: 'What has Korah. .to do in the Mah Nishtannah?' **1960** *Jewish Chron.* 8 Apr. 27/5 There was for me, the youngest boy, the important task of re-learning the Ma Nishtana. **1972** C. RAPHAEL *Feast of Hist.* iii. 90 The spirit of *ma nishtana*—the Four Questions in the Haggadah.

manism (mēⁱ·niz'm). [f. MANES *sb. pl.* + -ISM.] The worship of the *manes* or shades of the dead; ancestor-worship. Hence **mani·stic** *a.*

1904 G. S. HALL *Adolescence* II. xii. 179 Culture developed through the four stages of manism, when each [*sc.* the moon, sun, planets, etc.] was regarded as only the sensuous object it seemed, [etc.]. **1933** J. D. UNWIN *Sexual Regulations & Human Behaviour* i. 1 Uncivilised peoples . . Manistic—these do not erect temples but they pay some kind of post-funeral attention to their dead. **1937** A. HUXLEY *Ends & Means* xv. 311 All human societies are in one or another of four cultural conditions: zoistic, manistic, deistic, rationalistic. **1950** *Funk's Stand. Dict. Folklore* II. 673/1 Manism, the general term for the worship of the spirits of the dead, and, more specifically, for ancestor worship, is widespread in the world. **1956** E. E. EVANS-PRITCHARD *Nuer Relig.* xiii. 311 Many such origins have been propounded: magic, fetishism, manism, animism.

manitoka (mænitōᵘ·kă). *S. Afr.* Also **manotoka.** [Perhaps a name fabricated by the botanist P. Macowan.] The South African name of a large shrub, *Myoporum insulare*, of the family Myoporaceæ, native to Australia and bearing small white flowers followed by edible blue berries.

1906 F. BLERSCH *Handbk. Agric. S. Afr.* xiii. 267 Hedge shrubs and trees. . . Manotoka (*Myoporum insulare*). **1948** H. V. MORTON *In Search of S. Afr.* ii. 48 The old buildings and houses of former occupants. .were standing roofless and deserted in a jungle of manitoka trees. **1956** *Cape Times* 1 Mar. 8/6 The English myrtle hedge. .is far more interesting, is greener and less likely to dry out. This can also be said of the manitoka and tecoma hedges. **1973** M. PHILIP *Caravan Caravel* 19 A tarred road circled the middle of the thickly grassed park, and the caravans were standing in rows on four different levels, with hedges of fleshy, narrow-leaved manitokkas [*sic*] bushing out between the caravan sites.

mankalah, var. *MANCALA.

mankey, var. *MANKY *a.*

man-killer. Add: Also *transf.* and *fig.*

1929 F. C. BOWEN *Sea Slang* 89 *Man-killer*, a hard-working sailing ship in which accidents were frequent. Some ships earned extraordinary reputations in that way. **1957** R. CAMPBELL *Portugal* v. 86 They rechristened her [*sc.* a mare], Garota, or 'dear little girlie-wirlie', in order to . .give the impression that this man-killer was as sweet-tempered and innocent as she looked. Actually she had already killed two men. **1964** MRS. L. B. JOHNSON *White House Diary* 24 July (1970) 183 This was a man-killer of a day for Lyndon.

manky (mæ·ŋki), *a. local.* Also **mankey.** [f. MANK *a.* + -Y¹.] Bad, inferior, defective; dirty.

Possibly influenced by Fr. *manqué*.

1958 F. NORMAN *Bang to Rights* iii. 124 He would have to have all his teeth out as it seems that they were all mankey. **1971** B. W. ALDISS *Soldier Erect* 121 Have you chucked out that dirty manky bee you poisoned me with last time I came? **1973** A. GARNER *Red Shift* 14 That's your manky palate, lad. The dressing and the wine have to balance. **1973** 'J. PATRICK' *Glasgow Gang Observed* 231 *Clatty*, 'stourie', dirty, 'manky'. **1974** *Jrnl. Lancs. Dial. Soc.* XXIV. 28 [Westhoughton]. *Manky*, naughty.

manless, *a.* Add: **1. b.** Of a woman: lacking the company of men, *spec.* having no husband or suitor. Hence **ma·nlessness**, the state or condition of being manless.

1924 *Public Opinion* 7 Nov. 460/2 We find girls robbed of wholesome excitements. .by the loneliness and manlessness of their lives. **1942** E. PAUL *Narrow St.* xix. 161 Like so many manless women, Thérèse was extraordinarily sensitive and hostile to the masculine touch. **1962** K. ORVIS *Damned & Destroyed* xxv. 189 Fear of living out her life as a manless woman. **1970** O. NORTON *Dead on Prediction* i. 5 I'd just been going through a pretty manless period. **1972** *Guardian* 16 Feb. 13/2 The 24-year-old, man-less office worker.

manling. Delete † *Obs.* and add later examples.

1895 KIPLING *Second Jungle Bk.* 184 A Manling with a knife threw stones at my head. **1922** A. S. M. HUTCHINSON *This Freedom* 276 Her baby boy, her tiny manling.

man-made (mæ·n,mēⁱd), *a.* Also (occas.) as two words and (more freq.) **manmade.** [f. MAN *sb.*¹ + MADE *ppl. a.*] Made by man; made or devised by human effort, i.e. not existing in nature; artificial: applied esp. to fibres and fabrics manufactured from chemi-

cals of natural or synthetic origin. Also *ellipt.* and *fig.*

a **1718, 1839** [in Dict. s.v. MAN *sb.*[1] 19 e]. **1921** W. DE LA MARE *Mem. Midget* xxxiii. 237 There was nothing man-made in Fanny; and if there are women-shaped mermaids I know what looks will be seen in their faces. **1939** G. B. SHAW *In Good King Charles's Golden Days* I. 29, I tell you that from the moment you allow this manmade monster called a Church to enter your mind your inner light is like an extinguished candle. **1948** *Sci. News* VII. 86 When..the country is small and the civilisation old, one finds that the landscape is eventually almost entirely man-made. **1955** *Times* 5 July 16/3 Man-made fibres, by which I mean those made by the viscose and acetate processes and the various synthetic fibres. *Ibid.* (Suppl.) p. ii/1 The first man-made forest of such a size to be used for large-scale paper-making will provide the raw material for the 300-acre combined pulp, newsprint and timber mill. **1960** *Farmer & Stockbreeder* 1 Mar. 62/1 Yet another Welsh valley is to be flooded. In time, another man-made lake. **1966** *McGraw-Hill Encycl. Sci. & Technol.* V. 242/1 Rayon is a man-made fibre but not a synthetic fiber. Nylon is a synthetic fiber. **1968** *Daily Tel.* 4 Nov. 2/1 Still no let-up is visible in the prodigious progress of man-made fibres... This year's man-made production at the ninth-month mark was more than 26 p.c. above last year's level at the same stage. *Ibid.*, Manmades now have a quarter of the total world fibre output. **1969** D. C. HAGUE *Managerial Econ.* II. iv. 90 A large proportion of output in a modern economy is accounted for by..large firms. In the United Kingdom, this happens in the..manmade fibre industries. **1969** *New Yorker* 12 Apr. 85/1 In order to avoid capturing one of their own microflora or gathering any of the other manmade contaminants on the surface of the moon, the astronauts will have to take the sample for the exobiologists from underground. **1974** *Country Life* 3–10 Jan. 54/2 Coats and dresses in ultrasuede, a man-made, washable material.

manna[1]. Add: **9. manna-gum**, a species of *Eucalyptus*, *E. viminalis*.

[**1834** G. BENNETT *Wanderings in N.S.W.* I. xvi. 319 The elegant drooping manna-trees..were numerous.] **1884** A. NILSON *Timber Trees New South Wales* 74 *E*[*ucalyptus*] *viminalis*—Manna Gum;..Flooded Gum.—An elegant tree, attaining a height of 150 feet and a diameter of 8 feet. [**1887** Manna-drooping Gums: see *GUM *sb.*[2] 5]. **1937** *Discovery* Dec. 364/2 The Greater Gliding 'Possum..feeds also on several other eucalypts, particularly manna-gum and long-leafed box. **1940** H. ELLIS *My Life* iv. 102 The curious variety of manna gum I knew only there [*sc.* in Australia]. **1961** *Coast to Coast 1959–60* 60 Before me was a track running between walls of manna-gum, casuarina, tea-tree in full blossom, and wedding-bush even whiter.

mannan (mæ·næn). *Chem.* [f. *MANN(OSE + *-an*, after *GLUCOSAN.] Any of a group of polysaccharides that are composed chiefly of mannose residues and occur widely in plants, esp. as reserve foods.

1895 *Jrnl. Chem. Soc.* LXVIII. II. 128 (*heading*) Mannan as a reserve material in the seeds of Diospyros Kaki. **1931** [see *FRUCTOSAN]. **1965** *New Scientist* 6 May 381/1 The cell-walls of the [coffee] bean consist of a mannan which is an insoluble polysaccharide..and protein.

manned, *ppl. a.* (s.v. MAN *v.*). Add examples relating to aviation and space travel.

1906 *Nature* 8 Nov. 35/1 (*title*) The first 'manned' flying machine. **1907** *Ibid.* 4 Apr. 538/2 During the course of the last few years very rapid strides have been made in investigating the upper air by means of manned and unmanned balloons and kites. **1936** G. HEARD *Exploring Stratosphere* 18 As it was obviously impossible to obtain sufficient data by manned balloons, small sounding-balloons were released bearing a light cage containing self-recording instruments. **1946** H. HARPER *Dawn of Space Age* 4 It is intended to develop manned and instrument-carrying rockets capable of being projected in and beyond the earth's atmosphere. **1957** *Observer* 28 July 6/3 In the present phase of manned bombers, which will last into the mid-1960s, the United States Strategic Air Command has some 1,500 B47 medium bombers capable of attacking the Soviet Union from bases around its periphery. **1960** *John o' London's* 7 Apr. 395/1 Manned entry into interplanetary space is inevitable. **1968** *Times* 16 Oct. 8/7 The probe seemed to be a trial for an imminent manned flight to the moon. **1971** *Guardian* 3 July 1/3 The indication of a technical failure rather than a human failure..should be encouraging both to the Russian and the US manned space programmes.

mannequin (mæ·nikin, mæ·nəkwin). [Fr.] A woman (or occas. a man) employed in the showrooms of dress-makers, costumiers, etc., to wear and show off garments. Also, a model of a human figure for the display of clothes, etc. Also *attrib.*

1902 *Pall Mall Mag.* XXVII. 119 Another salon..ornamented with tall mirrors in which were reflected the slender elegant figures of several mannequins, most of them exceedingly pretty and all arrayed in magnificent dresses. **1919** BEERBOHM *Seven Men* 11 Then came 'Stark: *A Conte*', about a midinette who, as far as I could gather, murdered..a mannequin. **1924** [see *film super* s.v. *FILM *sb.* 7 c]. **1927** *Sunday Express* 7 Aug. 3/6 Bogus mannequin schools.., of which there are several in London, promise to train girls to become expert mannequins. **1930** *Daily Express* 6 Oct. 13/5 Autumn Mannequin Parades will be held on Tuesday and Wednesday this week. **1939** M. B. PICKEN *Lang. Fashion* 97/2 *Mannequin*.., model of human figure for display of garments, hats, furs, etc. **1940** D. MCCARTHY *Drama* 217 The *mannequin* show illustrates the 'moral' and commercial exploitation of sex interest. **1951** M. MCLUHAN *Mech. Bride* (1967) 99/1 Her mannequin past is in the way. **1960** S. BECKER tr. *Schwarz-Bart's Last of Just* III. iii. 108 The mannequin and its one unscrewed foot. **1966** J. S. COX *Illustr. Dict. Hairdressing* 95/1 *Mannequin*.., an artificial head used to display a hair style, or on which to create a hair style, or work hair for a postiche.

Hence **ma·nnequining** *vbl. sb.*, **ma·nnequinism**, the business of mannequins.

1927 *Sunday Express* 15 May 5/3 'Mannequining is a serious business now,' said the head of a mannequin school to me. **1928** *Daily Express* 2 June 4/4 More and more..distinguished women..have recently joined the ranks of teachers of mannequinism.

manner, *sb.*[1] **2. b.** Delete *Obs.* and add later examples.

1907 G. B. SHAW *How he lied to her Husband* 142 Henry places himself on guard in the manner of a well taught boxer. **1967** E. SHORT *Embroidery & Fabric Collage* iii. 60 The coverlet tells the story of Tristan, in a series of scenes showing different incidents, in the manner of a strip cartoon.

mannerism. Add: **a.** *spec.* (Freq. with capital initial.) Applied to a style of art which originated in Italy *c* 1520 and preceded the Baroque, characterized by stylistic exaggeration in figure and composition, etc.

Apart from the generalized use already illustrated in the Dict., the term has been used (*a*) of the followers of Michelangelo, Raphael, etc., as Bronzino, Pontormo, the Zuccari, etc. (mainly a 19th-c. use), (*b*) from *c* 1920 under the influence of M. Dvořak and W. Friedländer applied without pejorative associations to Italian art, in particular, from *c* 1520 to *c* 1590. Sense (*b*) is first found in English in the 1930s.

1845 A. JAMESON *Mem. Early Italian Painters* II. vii. 203 Those faults which have rendered many of his [*sc.* Parmigiano's] works unpleasing, by giving the impression of effort, and of what in art is called mannerism. **1851** tr. *Kugler's Schools of Painting in Italy* (ed. 2) II. v. ix. 469 Many of the painters in question would, fifty years earlier, have done great things; now they fell into repulsive mannerism. **1891** tr. *J. Adeline's Art Dict.* 249 Mannerism may be defined as *manner* in a bad sense. Qualities of treatment which when moderately displayed mark individuality of style, when carried to excess and too often repeated degenerate into mannerism. **1937** E. K. WATERHOUSE *Baroque Painting in Rome* 1 From 1535 until 1590 the history of painting in Rome is the history of Mannerism. **1940** A. BLUNT *Artistic Theory in Italy 1450–1600* v. 76 Those, like Dolce and Aretino..unable to follow Michelangelo as he moved on into Mannerism. **1943** *Art Bulletin* Mar. 87/2 The word mannerism..is currently used either to designate the period between the High Renaissance and the Baroque or else as a name for the anti-classical movement in sixteenth-century art. **1947** D. MAHON *Stud. Seicento Art & Theory* 59 Though the relatively recent understanding of Mannerism as a quite different artistic language from Baroque has somewhat curtailed the original scope of the latter (involving the secession of such figures as Tintoretto and El Greco) the use of the expression Baroque as a general term in its widest sense (such as Gothic), seems to have come to stay. **1961** J. D. ROSENBERG *Darkening Glass* (1963) v. 88 What we study as Mannerism he [*sc.* Ruskin] dismissed as vapidity and affectation. **1962** *Listener* 12 July 54/1 It is to move out of the serene and classical harmony of High Renaissance portraiture into the contrivance of the style that is known as Mannerism. **1965** G. SHEPHERD in P. Sidney *Apology for Poetry* 66 In the history of the pictorial arts, Lommazo and Zuccaro are spoken of as theorists of a phase of late mannerism. **1972** F. GARVIE tr. *Wundram's Art of Renaissance* 42 Architecture in the age of Mannerism played a major part historically by overcoming the static in favor of the movemented.

mannerist. Add: *spec.* An exponent or adherent of Mannerism in art (see prec.).

1695, 1716 [in Dict.]. **1833** J. CONSTABLE in C. R. Leslie *Mem. Life J. Constable* (1843) xii. 135 A certain set of painters who, having substituted falsehood for truth, and formed a style mean and mechanical, are termed mannerists. **1845** A. JAMESON *Mem. Early Italian Painters* II. x. 250 In the middle of the sixteenth century Italy swarmed with painters: these go under the general name of the mannerists, because they all imitated the manner of some one of the great masters who had gone before them. **1864** R. N. WORNUM *Epochs of Painting* 303 Hosts of copyists and mannerists arose,..with a mania for representing the naked human figure, [who] sacrificed almost every beauty, quality, and motive, to the paramount desire of anatomical display. **1907** B. BERENSON *N. Italian Painters of Renaissance* 156 The Mannerists, Tibaldi, Zuccaro, Fontana, thus quickly give place to the Eclectics. **1926** [see *ACADEMISM 2]. **1951** A. HAUSER *Social Hist. Art* I. v. 388 The antitheses of 'Gothic' and 'Renaissance'..are still..irreconcilable in the outlook of the mannerists. **1956** A. HUXLEY *Adonis & Alphabet* 229 There is not the slightest reason to believe that Catholic fervour was less intense in the age of the Mannerists than it had been three generations earlier.

2. In appositive use, passing into *adj.*

1934 R. WITTKOWER in *Art Bulletin* XVI. 216 The Laurenziana belongs to a..group of buildings arranged on similar principles, common between 1520 and 1580/90 and to be called Mannerist. **1939** *Handbk. Drawings & Watercolours Dept. Prints & Drawings Brit. Mus.* 38 The leading figure of this mannerist movement, which is largely occupied in elaborate decorative schemes in palaces and churches, was Francesco Salviati. **1944** *Archit. Rev.* XCVI. 187 The author is, it seems, of the generation to which what we now define as Mannerist is nothing but a late phase of the Renaissance. **1964** *English Studies* XLV. 98 The transition from the ambiguities of Mannerist expression to that of Baroque realism. **1972** *Guardian* 17 Nov. 12/3 It was the influence of Raphael that informed the Mannerist artists whose work clusters round that of the giants.

mannerize, *v.* (Later examples.)

1910 A. C. BENSON *Silent Isle* xv. 103 Tennyson..became solemn, mannerised, conscious of responsibility. **1956** *Archit. Rev.* CXIX. 161/2 The forms which have developed from the rationale and the initial ideology of the modern movement are being mannerized and changed into a conscious imperfectionism.

manness. Add: **2.** = MALENESS.

1921 W. J. TURNER *Music & Life* p. ix, You are not concerned with their..brains..but with something which we may call their 'manness'. **1947** J. STEINBECK *Pearl* (1948) v. 64 The quality of woman..could cut through Kino's manness.

mannie. Add: (Further, incl. non-*Sc.*, examples.) In Jewish use: see quot. 1909.

The Jewish use is perhaps a contraction of *Emanuel*.

a **1689** W. CLELAND *Poems* (1697) 105 A puffie cheek'd red bearded mannie. **1909** J. R. WARE *Passing Eng.* 173/2 *Manny* (Jewish E. London), term of endearment or admiration prefixed to Jewish name, as 'Manny Lyons'. **1914** JOYCE *Dubliners* 103 My little man! My little mannie! **1916** 'BOYD CABLE' *Action Front* 262 'My manny here was good enough,' said Macalister, 'to tell me he wouldna' bandage my eyes.' **1922** D. H. LAWRENCE *England, my England* 154 There's too much of the little mannie about him. **1971** M. WEST *Summer of Red Wolf* vi. 125 What do you want me to pack for the poor mannie?

manning, *vbl. sb.* Add: **1.** Also, in more recent use: the action of furnishing a factory, an industry, etc., with men.

1955 *Times* 22 Aug. 7/4 He refers to the dockers' insistence on full manning, with the implication that this is a restrictive practice.

3. (Further examples.)

1953 *Britannica Bk. of Year* 638/2 Other compound nouns were *manning requirements* (the number of men required by an industry). **1962** *Listener* 1 Mar. 377/1 On the labour side there are..rules about manning-scales (that is, how many men to a job). **1975** *Times* 14 Apr. 12/2 We put them there, those too many men... Manning levels were never changed. **1975** *Times* 5 June 18/4 The stoppage is by 80 door hangers and welders, who are protesting about management plans to reduce manning scales.

mannitol. Add def.: A sweet crystalline hexahydric alcohol, $CH_2OH(CHOH)_4CH_2OH$, known in three optically isomeric forms, which is found in many plants (such as sugar cane, celery, and larch) and is used in aqueous solution in kidney function tests. (Now the usual name.) (Earlier and later examples.)

1879 *Jrnl. Chem. Soc.* XXXVI. 1034 Mannityl-hexsulphuric acid is obtained as an uncrystallisable liquid by dissolving mannitol in sulphuric monochloride. **1939** *Jrnl. Amer. Chem. Soc.* LXI. 761/2 To prepare the *l*-glyceraldehyde in an analogous way from *l*-mannitol was much more difficult, since the *l*-mannitol..is not yet obtainable commercially. **1951** A. GROLLMAN *Pharmacol. & Therapeutics* xxxii. 750 Mannitol, a hexahydric alcohol sugar is filtered through the glomeruli but is neither reabsorbed nor excreted by the tubules. **1957** *Technology* July 187/2 Mannitol, which also comes from seaweed, is used by the chemical, explosive, pharmaceutical and electrical industries. **1970** H. MCLEAVE *Question of Negligence* (1973) xxvii. 208 'Intravenous saline and mannitol,' he murmured. His registrar injected the drug to shrink the brain and relieve the compression.

Mannlicher (ma·nliχəɹ). [f. the name of *Mannlicher* (see below).] A firearm of a type invented by Ferdinand Ritter von Mannlicher (1848–1904), esp. a type of sporting rifle. Also *attrib.*

The umlauted *ä* in the Kipling example is erroneous.

1884 in H. Cholmondeley-Pennell *Smoke of Battle* (ed. 2) 16 (Advt.), The Mannlicher Rifle is the one of all the specimens of Repeating Arms..which seems to us the best arm for our soldiers. **1896** T. F. FREMANTLE *Notes on Rifle* xi. 175 The ·256 Mannlicher is capable of making very fair shooting at these long ranges. **1902** KIPLING *Traffics & Discov.* (1904) 20 My gun was too good, too uniform—shot as close as a Männlicher [Mannlicher, 1902 magazine publ.] rifle. **1922** J. BUCHAN *Huntingtower* xiv. 267 McGuffog, who was a marksman, was also given a sporting Mannlicher. **1935** E. HEMINGWAY *Green Hills Afr.* (1936) I. ii. 46 There was the short-barrelled explosion of the Mannlicher. **1970** I. V. HOGG *Military Pistols & Revolvers* 41/2 The Mannlicher uses a form of delayed blowback action.

mannose (mæ·nōus, -ōuz). *Chem.* [a. G. *mannose* (Fischer & Hirschberger 1888, in *Ber. d. Deut. Chem. Ges.* XXI. 1805), f. *mann(it)ose* MANNITOSE.] A crystalline sugar, $C_6H_{12}O_6$, which is known in three optically isomeric forms which are epimers of those of glucose, and whose dextrorotatory form is obtained by the hydrolysis of mannans.

1888 *Jrnl. Chem. Soc.* LIV. 934 Mannose..is obtained by dissolving the above phenylhydrazone in four parts of hydrochloric acid..cooled with ice and salt. **1911** [see *EPIMER]. **1949** M. A. JENNINGS in H. W. Florey et al. *Antibiotics* II. xxxi. 975 The series included strains known to vary in such properties as..fermentation of carbohydrates (mannite, trehalose and mannose). **1968** A. SOLS in F. Dickens et al. *Carbohydrate Metabolism* I. iii. 71 Mannose can be efficiently metabolized by most tissues because it is a very good substitute for hexokinase.

‖ **mano** (mā·no). *Anthropol.* [Sp. *mano* hand.] A primitive stone implement, held in the hand and used for grinding cereals and other foodstuffs.

1901 *Ann. Rep. Board of Regents Smithsonian Inst. 1899* 37 The grinding-stone concordantly changes from a simple roller or crusher to a mano (or muller), and finally to a pestle, at first broad and short, but afterwards long and slender. **1911** W. K. MOOREHEAD *Stone Age N. Amer.* II. xxvii. 103 The stones used on these [mortars] are flat, or oval water-worn stones and not finished, like mano stones common to the Cliff Dweller country. **1944** G. C. VAILLANT *Aztecs Mexico* (1950) i. 35 The flat grinding-stones and mullers, still used in Mexico and called *metates* and *manos*, prove that the people relied on corn as their principal food. **1959** E. TUNIS *Indians* 119/2 The grinding was done by rubbing the grains across it with another stone, the *mano*, held in the hands. **1960** C. WINICK *Dict. Anthropol.* 342/2 *Mano*, a cylindrically shaped grindstone slightly tapered at both ends. It was held in the hand (whence its name handstone) and used as the upper stone in milling. **1964** A. D. KRIEGER in Jennings & Norbeck *Prehist. Man in New World* 32 The most important new trait, however, is that of food-grinding with stone implements: basin-shaped milling stones and manos. **1971** [see *INDIGENIZATION]. **1972** *Sci. Amer.* May 89/3 From the Maya Mountains came the metamorphic rock used to make not only axe heads of stone but also the *manos*, or stone rollers. **1974** *Encycl. Brit. Macropædia* XI. 936/2 They [*sc.* villagers of the Ocós and Cuadros phases of Meso-American civilization] were productive corn farmers as well, raising a small-eared race of maize called Nal-Tel, which their wives and daughters ground on *metates* and *manos* and cooked in globular jars.

‖ **manoao** (ma·noau). Also monoao. [Maori.] A New Zealand evergreen tree, *Dacrydium kirkii*, of the family Podocarpaceæ; formerly applied to another species of *Dacrydium, D. colensoi*; also called *silver pine*.

1867 J. D. HOOKER *Handbk. N.Z. Flora* II. 766/1 Manoao, *Dacrydium Colensoi*. **1889** T. KIRK *Forest Flora N.Z.* 191 (*heading*) The manoao. *Ibid.* 192 The wood of the manaoa [*sic*] is of a light-brown colour. **1950** *N.Z. Jrnl. Agric.* Feb. 115/2 The open pumice country, clothed in a tangled mass of manuka and manoao. **1951** *Post-Primary School Bulletin* (Wellington, N.Z.) V. xii. 274 The manoao (*Dacrydium kirkii*)—a tree related to the rimu but having its young leaves more than an inch long and its old leaves only an eighth of an inch long. **1963** POOLE & ADAMS *Trees & Shrubs N.Z.* 26 Monoao. Tree reaching 25m. Bark light brown.

Manoeline, -lino, varr. *MANUELINE *a.*

manœuvrability (mănū:vrăbi·lĭti). Also (*U.S.*) **maneuverability.** [f. *MANŒUVRABLE *a.*] Capacity for being manœuvred.

The spelling with medial *-e-* in quots. 1942 and 1954 is unusual.

1923 *Rep. & Mem. Aeronaut. Res. Comm.* No. 851. 1 (*heading*) The comparison of the manœuvrability of aeroplanes by the use of a cinematograph camera. **1927** *Daily Express* 24 Sept. 8 Much will depend on the skill of the pilots in taking the corner, and also on the manœuvrability of the machines. **1930** C. J. STEWART *Aircraft Instruments* p. xvii, The manœvrability and the adequacy of the various control surfaces of an aircraft. **1942** *Tee Emm* (Air Ministry) II. 85 A compromise between stability and manœuvreability would not be difficult. **1954** *Encounter* June 13/2 The European national economies..are peculiarly dependent upon world trade balances, and the area of manœuvreability is limited. **1968** *Encycl. Brit.* II. 874/1 Large steering gear ratios make high-speed maneuverability more difficult. **1972** *Drive* Summer 88/1 We were glad of the boat's manoeuvrability when the current increased under the bridge at Arundel.

manœuvrable (mănū·vrăb'l), *a.* [f. MANŒUVRE *v.* + -ABLE.] Capable of being manœuvred, used esp. of aircraft and motor vehicles.

The spelling with medial *-e-* in quot. 1942 is unusual.

1921 *Aëronautical Jrnl.* XXV. 520 Getting off across wind..is only attempted with relatively high-powered or manœuvrable aeroplanes. **1942** *Tee Emm* (Air Ministry) II. 86 The aircraft will become more stable, but it will be less manœuvreable. **1972** *Motor* 8 Apr. 21/1 (Advt.), There are other things that we've done to our cars which would make any size of car more manoeuvrable. **1973** J. DRUMMOND *Bang! Bang! You're Dead!* xxiv. 118 'What do you need?' 'A reasonable strike-force. Manoeuvrable.'

manœuvre, *v.* Add: **2. b.** Earlier examples of **manœuvring** *ppl. adj.*

1801 M. EDGEWORTH *Belinda* II. xvi. 122 This manœuvring lady represented this report as being universally known and believed, in hopes of frightening her niece into an immediate match with the baronet. **1822** —— *Let.* 9 Feb. (1971) 346 Mrs. Lock was one of the manoeuvring mothers who wanted to draw him in for her daughter.

manœuvring, *vbl. sb.* (Earlier example of *attrib.* use.)

1814 JANE AUSTEN *Mansf. Park* I. v. 93 Speaking from my own observation, it [*sc.* marriage] is a manœuvring business.

man-of-war. Add: Also **man-o'-war. 2. c.** (Earlier and later examples.)

1774 J. ANDREWS *Let.* 30 Dec. (1866) 79 Partaking of the extreem ill qualities of a soldier as well as that of a man-of-war's man. **1931** *Times Lit. Suppl.* 19 Feb. 124/4 'Matelot' is undoubtedly the French for sailor, but we are not told that it is the English man-of-war's-man's name for himself.

3. *man-of-war bird.* Delete † and add later examples.

1906 W. L. SCLATER *Birds S. Afr.* IV. 495 The 'Cape Sheep', 'Great Albatros', 'Man of War Bird' and 'Goney' are all names which are sometimes applied to this bird [*sc.* the wandering albatross]. **1949** M. LOWRY *Let.* May (1967) 178, I think he [*sc.* Melville] is confusing it with his man-of-war bird, the frigate bird. **1952** E. HEMINGWAY *Old Man & Sea* 30 He saw a man-of-war bird with his long black wings circling in the sky. **1962** *Times* 6 Apr. 7/2 (Advt.), Some of the country's most spectacular birds live here [*sc.* in the Florida Everglades]. The snowy egrets, cranes, water turkeys, man-o-war birds, scarlet ibis, [etc.].

6. Used *attrib.* to designate a boy's garment resembling that worn by a sailor, a sailor suit. *Obs.* exc. *Hist.*

1883 in L. de Vries *Victorian Advts.* (1968) 49 Man-o'-war suit. Complete 10/9. **1911** *Daily Colonist* (Victoria, B.C.) 5 Apr. 2/5 (Advt.), Stylish summer hats for little boys and girls... Duck man-o-war hats tams. **1922** JOYCE *Ulysses* 341 His little man-o'-war top and unmentionables were full of sand. **1965** CUNNINGTON & BUCK *Children's Costume in Eng.* 183 There was the man-o'-war suit..complete with lanyard, knife and good conduct stripes.

‖ **manoir** (manwār). [a. F. *manoir* MANOR.] A French manor-house; a country house built in this style.

1853 C. BRONTË *Villette* II. xviii. 136 This house..is rather a manoir than a chateau. **1885** A. EDWARDES *Girton Girl* I. v. 107 The look of the old manoir was cheery. **1926** V. HUNT *Flurried Yrs.* I. 76 We would walk among high hedges..to this or that old ruined *manoir* that would not let. **1954** V. SACKVILLE-WEST *Let.* 31 Aug. in H. Nicolson *Diaries & Lett.* (1968) 264 We can think back on that lovely country with the poplars..and the castles and the *manoirs*. **1968** F. WHITE *Ways of Aquitaine* II. 32 The château of Meillant is a perfect example of the high Renaissance *manoir*.

‖ **manoletina** (manolĕtī·nă). [Sp., f. *Manolet(e*, the professional name of the Spanish bullfighter Manuel L. R. Sánchez (1917–47) + *-ina*.] In bullfighting, a decorative pass popularized by Manolete, in which the muleta is held behind the back in the left hand. Also known as the *orteguina*.

1952 J. MARKS *To the Bullfight* v. 67 We may watch him [*sc.* the matador], at short range, ignoring it [*sc.* the bull] in imitation of *Manolete's* most imperious yet least estimable manner, as it rushes by under his right arm and the muleta that skims its back in a *manoletina*. **1957** A. MACNAB *Bulls of Iberia* xv. 193 Three *manoletinas* (very exciting with such big horns, which come out under man's armpits each time). **1959** V. J.-R. KEHOE *Aficionado!* xvi. 201/2 This pass is called an *orteguina* or, more commonly today, a *manoletina*—after Domingo Ortega who revived it out of an old school, and Manolete who popularized and refined it to a high degree... it is another adorno. **1961** —— *Wine, Women & Toros!* x. 129/1 His faenas include ..*manoletinas* looking at the crowd and then—surprise—he kills very well! **1971** J. LEIBOLD *This is the Bullfight* xvii. 204 The manoletina is probably the most popular of all the decorative passes and is utilized by bullfighters of every degree of experience. The manoletina is always performed as a right-handed pass with the sword extending the cloth and while it is a very spectacular pass it is not nearly as dangerous as it appears. **1974** *Aiken* (S. Carolina) *Standard* 18 Apr. 4-c/4 Then the grandstand falls silent as Diaz prepares to execute a 'manoletina', a pass rarely seen in bullfighting. The matador must not turn his head as the bull comes pounding across the sand, but only feels the rush of wind as the animal charges by.

manometer. Add: Hence **mano·metry,** the use of manometers.

1923 GLAZEBROOK *Dict. Appl. Physics* III. 191/1 (*heading*) Medium-precision manometry. **1961** *Lancet* 12 Aug. 349/1 Articles on..manometry.., chromatography, and electrophoresis.

manometrically (mænome·trikăli), *adv.* [f. MANOMETRIC, -METRICAL *adjs.*: see -LY².] In a manometric way; by means of a manometer.

1899 *Nature* 2 Feb. 321/1 The arc light cannot be used manometrically, nor..is it probable that the magnesium flame could be thus employed. **1936** *Biochem. Jrnl.* XXX. 2319 Acetoacetic acid was usually determined manometrically by the aniline citrate method. **1974** PASSMORE & ROBSON *Compan. Med. Stud.* III. xix. 97/1 Propulsive activity [of the colon] is more difficult to study manometrically and detect radiographically.

manool (mænō͝u-ǫl). *Chem.* Also **manoöl.** [a. G. *manool* (Hosking & Brandt 1935, in *Ber. d. Deut. Chem. Ges.* LXVIII. 1311): see *MANOAO and -OL.] A bicyclic diterpenoid alcohol, $C_{20}H_{34}O$, which occurs in the oil of *manoao* wood and is used as a base for perfumes.

1935 *Chem. Abstr.* XXIX. 6591 The red resin extd. with alc. from *D. biforme* yields..a neutral light yellow viscous oil.., giving on fractional distn. about 90% of a very viscous colorless liquid (II) solidifying to crystals of the compn. $C_{20}H_{34}O$... II is therefore a bicyclic diterpene alc. with 2 double bonds, for which the name *manoöl* is proposed. **1969** *N.Z. News* 23 July 4/3 Manool, an ambergris-like product which is extracted from trees that take hundreds of years to grow, may provide New Zealand with a new export market.

manor. Add: **3.** (Further example of *fig.* use.)

1874 A. J. MUNBY *Diary* 20 Apr. in D. Hudson *Munby* (1972) 366, I was 'struck all of a heap' by seeing..a picture of Wigan wenches working at brow. What right had this artist to poach on my manor..?

e. *slang.* A police district; a local unit of police administration. Also *transf.*, one's home ground, one's own particular territory.

1924 S. SCOTT *Human Side Crook & Convict Life* vii. 107 There are straight crooks and crooked crooks on the 'Manor' of a detective, and he gets to know them apart. **1928** E. WALLACE *Gunner* xii. 93, I wouldn't advise you to break in on Gennett's 'manor'—he's rather touchy, and he's got charge of the case. **1945** M. ALLINGHAM *Coroner's Pidgin* xxiii. 202 Do you realize who the Coroner is for those parts?.. It's Montie Forster's manor. **1959** *Observer* 1 Mar. 10/1 This 'manor'—a tenement neighbourhood in North London—is theirs by right of birth and conquest. **1961** C. WITTING *Driven to Kill* 24 If anything's happened to Pearce, it's in my manor, so I'm interested. **1962** R. COOK *Crust on its Uppers* iv. 47 'Then they whipped him down to the nick on the hurry-up.' 'Which manor?' 'The local nick.' *Ibid.* 49 'Where to for the next one?' says he. 'Well off the manor, if you like.' **1970** P. LAURIE *Scotland Yard* 287 Every non-policeman knows that detectives call their working-area their 'manor' or 'patch'... What they actually said was 'ground'. **1974** *Times* 23 Nov. 2/6 Mr Buck is trying to alter that situation by appealing to everyone in his 'manor' (with a population one million higher than that of Northern Ireland) to dial 999 at the slightest sign of suspicious activity.

manorial, *a.* (Later example of **manorializing** *vbl. sb.*)

1918 *Eng. Hist. Rev.* Jan. 70 The king..must forestall the lord's manorializing tendency by adding these thegns and freemen to his own estates.

mano:rializa·tion. [f. MANORIAL *a.* + -IZATION.] The process of making or becoming manorial. Also **mano·rialize** *v. trans.*, 'to conform or subject to the tenure of the manorial system' (Webster 1909).

1896 C. M. ANDREWS in R. H. I. Palgrave *Dict. Pol. Econ.* II. 684 Economic life had become manorialised but not feudalised. **1907** *Q. Rev.* July 147 Varieties occurred in the process of manorialisation. **1927** J. J. HOGAN *Eng. Lang. in Ireland* 15 Manorialization was in full progress at the beginning of the thirteenth century in Leinster. **1939** *Antiquity* XIII. 22 Villages which were but partially manorialized.

manorship. Delete † *Obs.* and add later example.

1920 *Public Opinion* 6 Aug. 127/3 Both names..are.. deeply associated with the neighbourhood of Old Jordans, its homesteads, and churches and manorships.

manostat (mæ·nostæt). [f. *mano-* (in MANOMETER) + *-STAT.] Any device for automatically maintaining a constant pressure in an enclosed space. Hence **manosta·tic** *a.*

1900 *Jrnl. Physical Chem.* IV. 546 (*heading*) On a manostat. **1923** GLAZEBROOK *Dict. Appl. Physics* III. 191/2 The majority of manostats are designed on the broad principle that whenever the pressure departs from the desired constant value, the manometer itself, through the change in liquid level in one of its limbs, automatically actuates either a supply or removal of gas..or else some equivalent means of restoring the desired pressure. **1936** *Jrnl. Amer. Chem. Soc.* LVIII. 1703/1 The new manostatic technique. **1966** *Encycl. Industr. Chem. Analysis* I. 617 As a general rule, manostats controlling four fixed pressures of 10, 50, 100, and 200 Torr, and accurately adjusted to these pressures, provide a range of operating pressures quite adequate for every distillation situation. Below 50 Torr, pressure regulation is unsatisfactory when mercury is used as the manostatic fluid.

manotoka, var. *MANITOKA.

‖ **manque** (maṅk). [Fr., f. *manquer* to fail, lack: see quot. 1903.] In roulette, the name of one section of the cloth covering the numbers 1 to 18; a bet placed on this section.

1850 *Bohn's Handbk. Games* 348 The manque wins, when the ball enters a hole numbered eighteen, and all those under that number. **1885** CAPT. PALMER *Monte Carlo & Rouge et Noir* 8 The space for Manque is so marked on the table, and the ball stopping in any of the compartments containing any number up to 18 makes Manque win. **1903** 'L. HOFFMANN' *Card & Table Games* (ed. 3) 626 If he places his money on *Manque* (so called because in this event the ball 'fails'..to fall into a higher number than 18), he is considered to wager that the ball will fall into one of the numbers from 1 to 18 inclusive. **1923** L. H. DAWSON *Hoyle's Games Modernized* II. 279 To bet on both *Passe* and *Noir* or *Rouge* and *Manque* at the same time, two separate stakes would be required. **1953** T. KING *21 Games of Chance* 31 In addition to the central strip of numbers, there are outer spaces marked *Passe, Manque, Pair, Impair, Noir* and *Rouge*. **1969** J. BINSTOCK *Casino Administration* vi. 72 This [*sc.* roulette] is played on a table with 37 numbers from zero to 36, the so-called 'even chance' bets being *pair* and *impair, passe* and *manque, rouge* and *noir*.

‖ **manqué** (maṅke), *a.* Fem. **manquée.** [Fr., pa. pple. of *manquer* to miss, be lacking.] After its noun: that might have been but is not, that has missed being. Also occas. *pred.*

1778 F. BURNEY *Diary* Aug. (1904) I. i. 54 Dr. Johnson's favourite is Mr. Smith. He declares the fine gentleman *manqué* was never better drawn. **1895** G. B. SHAW in W. Archer *Theatr. 'World' 1894* p. xxvi, A villain if you

like..a kicked, cuffed, duped pantaloon by all means; but a hero *manqué*, never. **1898** C. R. ASHBEE *Cellini's Treatises on Goldsmithing & Sculpture* p. xi, There is about his figures always something *manqué*. **1913** tr. *Gleizes & Metzinger's Cubism* i. 15 People have tried to present Cézanne as a sort of genius *manqué*. **1927** *Sat. Rev.* 17 Sept. 370/2 'The History of Anthony Waring' is a poem manqué. **1942** W. STEVENS *Let.* 29 July (1967) 4/4 That such a person [*sc.* a poet] is to be visualized as..an eccentric or a person somehow manqué is nonsense. **1948** F. R. LEAVIS *Great Tradition* ii. 61 Casaubon..is an intellectual *manqué*. **1960** V. BRITTAIN *Women at Oxf.* v. 86 Published memories of Miss Maitland..suggest that she was a hospital matron *manquée*. **1962** *Listener* 12 July 73/2 A clever, unhappy young writer *manqué*. **1974** *Listener* 26 Sept. 408/3 Was Lady O a courtesan manquée?

b. In other uses: defective, spoilt, missing, lacking, etc.

1773 H. WALPOLE *Let.* 27 Mar. (1904) VIII. 262 Dr. Goldsmith's *She Stoops to Conquer*... The author's wit is as much *manqué* as the lady's. **1793** F. BURNEY *Let.* 3 May (1972) II. 98 Our party was manqué in every way;—I came early, but with a head ache; your melancholy Note did not relieve it. **1841** THACKERAY in *Fraser's Mag.* June 724/1, I never yet had a good dinner in my life at Véfour's; *something* is always *manqué* at the place. **1876** C. M. YONGE *Womankind* i. 6 The single woman ceases to be *manquée*, and enjoys honour and happiness. **1881** H. JAMES *Notebks.* (1947) 31 He used to talk to me about Spain, about the East..till it seemed to me that life would be *manquée* altogether if one shouldn't have some of that knowledge. **1894** R. FRY *Let.* 27 Mar. (1972) I. 158 Millais..is the most *gifted* man we ever had, but somehow he's *manqué*, never done what he might have done. **1940** W. STEVENS *Let.* 9 Aug. (1967) 362 Thus, one's chords remain *manqué*; still there they are.

man-rate (mæ·nrēit), *v.* [f. MAN *sb.*¹ + RATE *v.*¹] *trans.* To make (a rocket, spaceship, etc.) suitable for manned flight; to certify as safe for manned flight. So **man-rated** *ppl. a.*; **ma·n-rating** *vbl. sb.*

1963 E. STUHLINGER et al. *Astronautical Engin. & Sci.* iv. 68 Manrating is a new term. To manrate a space vehicle means to make it suitable for carrying a manned payload. **1967** *Technology Week* XX. 23 Jan. 29/2 (Advt.), McDonnell testing and development facilities range from man-rated space chambers to Mach 28 wind tunnels. *Ibid.* 30/1 (Advt.), Their man-rated lunar descent engine is one of a family of small throttleable engines. **1968** *New Scientist* 21 Mar. 631 After it [*sc.* a new Soviet booster] has been man-rated, however, and used in orbital rendezvous and docking missions, the USSR will have achieved a major platform for further advance. **1971** *Sci. News Let.* 19 June 416 The general question of the reliability of unmanned spacecraft has always been a thorny problem for NASA. Manned spacecraft have redundant systems—back-up systems in case one fails. This method, called 'man-rating a spacecraft', is costly.

mansard. Add: **c.** *Comb.*, as *mansard-roofed* adj.

1887 J. E. TAYLOR *Tourist's Guide Suffolk* 31 The Tower Ramparts, where the red-tiled, mansard-roofed cottages have been built on the very top. **1915** E. ATKINSON *Johnny Appleseed* 80 From there he saw the white mansard-roofed mansion.

Also **ma·nsarded** *a.*

1903 *Westm. Gaz.* 11 Feb. 2/1 Handsome little hôtels, *mansarded* and *œil de bœuf'd*. **1951** W. SANSOM *Face of Innocence* viii. 100 Each pantiled or mansarded or beamed façade. **1962** *Listener* 5 Apr. 592/1 Why should we have to suffer tall mansarded roofs?

manscape (mæ·nskēip). [f. MAN *sb.*¹, formed in imitation of LANDSCAPE; see also SCAPE *sb.*³] A view or picture of a sea of faces in a crowd. (Fanciful.)

1927 *Sunday Express* 24 Apr. 1/1 A manscape of a hundred thousand souls is a moving spectacle. **1948** *Archit. Rev.* CIV. 11/1 But this is landscape. What of manscape?

manse, *sb.* Add: **3.** Also in phr. *son* (*bairn, child, daughter*) *of the manse*: the son (daughter) of a Protestant minister, *esp.* in the Church of Scotland.

1855 MRS. OLIPHANT *Lilliesleaf* III. ix. 116 To think that this was our Mary, a bairn of the Manse. **1903** G. W. BALFOUR in M. C. Balfour *From Saranac to Marquesas* p. xix, One of the few survivors left of the happy company of 'children of the manse'. **1962** *Glasgow Herald* 8 Oct. 7 Dr McIntyre..is a son of the manse, always a good step on the high road to fortune in Scotland. **1965** *Listener* 9 Sept. 372/2 Albert Schweitzer, a son of the manse, was born an Alsatian and brought up in the village of Günsbach. **1976** A. RICHARDS *Former Miss Merthyr Tydfil* 52 Dorothea was a daughter of the manse, a history graduate.

-manship, *suffix.* [f. MAN *sb.*¹ 4 p + -SHIP after CHURCHMANSHIP, CRAFTSMANSHIP, SPORTSMANSHIP, etc.] Used with prefixed sb. (occas. vb.) to denote skill in a subject or activity, esp. now so deployed as to disconcert a rival or opponent.

This traditional terminal element underwent a profound change of meaning after 1947 under the influence of *GAMESMANSHIP. Cf. also **brinkmanship*, *LIFEMANSHIP, **oneupmanship*.

1821 [see *bullmanship* s.v. BULL *sb.*¹ 11 a]. **1880** [see BUSHMANSHIP]. **1894** *Pall Mall Gaz.* 23 Oct. 4/3 Parisiennes continue to witch the world with noble bikemanship in their graceful kilted knickerbockers. **1909** M. B. SAUNDERS *Litany Lane* I. iii. 34 Otherwise the allegory—and the good-humoured clubmanship—sufficed. **1925** L. O'FLAHERTY *Informer* vi. 78 We can imagine him perfecting himself in the arts of gunmanship, deceit, [etc.]. **1939** *Amer. Speech* XIV. 80/1 Professor Kenneth B. Haas ..inserted a short paragraph concerning 'Consumer Vocabulary' in an article entitled 'Buymanship as an Economic Prophylaxis'. **1950** *Sunday Times* 9 July, Many gamesmen find a specious field for the exercise of their knowledge in the allied craft of queuemanship. **1951** C. D. MILNER *Dolomites* 81 Many fine climbers who were.. developing British cragmanship. **1959** *Evening Standard* 13 June 4/3 His hobbies..include farming, motoring.. and general do-it-yourself-manship. **1962** *Economist* 28 July 338/2 Connoisseurs of conferencemanship will be happy to find resolutions calling for the abolition of indirect taxation, [etc.]. **1973** *Nature* 24 Aug. 526/1 He has some useful and pointed things to say on 'grantsmanship'.

mansion, *sb.* **3. e.** (Earlier and later examples.)

1876 A. TROLLOPE *Prime Minister* II. iv. 67 He had been to look at a flat,—a set of rooms,—in the Belgrave Mansions, in Pimlico. **1892** A. W. PINERO *Magistrate* II. 105 *Messiter.* Where at, sir? *Vale.* Albert Mansions, Victoria Street. **1955** *Times* 15 July 10/3 The process happens more often in the case of a mews, a yard, or a court, and is almost frequent in the case of a 'mansions'. **1972** *Mainichi Daily News* (Japan) 7 Nov. 6/6 The earnings of the real estate division, including those obtained through sales of mansions (high class apartments) and lots for villas, will increase by 33 per cent.

mansion-house. b. (Earlier examples of U.S. sense.)

1679 *Public Rec. Colony of Connecticut* (1859) III. 42 He shall build upon his sayd accomodations a good sufficient mansion house. **1745** E. KIMBER *Itinerant Observations Amer.* (1878) 37 A Negro Quarter, is a number of Huts or Hovels, built at some distance from the Mansion-House. **1812** *Niles' Reg.* III. 9/2 The majority then retired to the Mansion house. **1837** W. JENKINS *Ohio Gazetteer* 162 A large and elegant Mansion house has been erected on the ground with numerous smaller cottages and out buildings. **1844** in C. Cist *Cincinnati Misc.* (1845) I. 68/1 The mansion house of E. S. Haines..and various single buildings are observable for their fine appearance.

manslaughter (mæ·nslǭtəɹ), *v. colloq.* [f. the sb.] *trans.* To kill (a person) without malice aforethought.

1920 R. MACAULAY *Potterism* III. ii. 133, I had left the house morally certain that Arthur Gideon had murdered (or anyhow manslaughtered) Oliver Hobart. **1922** A. A. MILNE *Red House Mystery* ix. 81 'Murdered him?' 'Well, manslaughtered him, anyway.'

manslaughterer. Add: (Later examples.) Also, one who commits manslaughter (sense 2).

1885 A. EDWARDES *Girton Girl* I. iii. 71 As a physician, I consider him a manslaughterer. **1912** E. A. PARRY *What Judge Saw* xvii. 297, I regarded the doctor as a manslaughterer at the time. **1965** *Lancet* 20 Nov. 1070/2 With cyclists, children, and old people safely tucked in bed, I do not have to feel a potential manslaughterer just because I sit behind the steering-wheel.

‖ **manso** (ma·nso). [Sp.] A meek, tame, or cowardly person or animal. Also *attrib.* or as *adj.* Cf. **Indio manso*.

Used esp. of 'cowardly' bulls in *Bullfighting*.

1836, 1860 [see *INDIO]. **1912** A. CONAN DOYLE *Lost World* viii. 115 'Yes sir, war drums,' said Gomez, the half-breed. 'Wild Indians, bravos, not mansos; they watch us every mile of the way; kill us if they can.' **1932** E. HEMINGWAY *Death in Afternoon* 298 *Manso*, tame, mild and unwarlike; a bull which does not have the fighting blood is *manso*, as are also the steers called *cabestros* when they are trained. **1952** J. MARKS *To the Bullfight* v. 58 He [*sc.* the president] has also a green and a red one [*sc.* handkerchief], which he holds over the edge of the box:..the red to condemn a cowardly *manso* to the stigma of black banderillas. **1957** A. MACNAB *Bulls of Iberia* vii. 73 Since 1951, in Spain the 'firing' of *manso* bulls has been symbolical only;..the sticks have no fireworks. **1967** MCCORMICK & MASCAREÑAS *Compl. Aficionado* ii. 30 He could pick out the *mansos* with eighty per-cent accuracy, which is better than most toreros can do.

mansonia (mænsōu·niă). [mod.L. (J. R. Drummond 1905, in *Jrnl. Linn. Soc. Bot.* XXXVII. 260), f. the name of F. B. *Manson* (fl. 1905), a forester in Burma who collected the first specimens of *M. gagei*.] A large tree of the genus so called, belonging to the family Sterculiaceæ, esp. the West African *Mansonia altissima* or the hardwood obtained from it. Also *attrib.*

[**1934** W. D. MACGREGOR *Silviculture Mixed Deciduous Forests Nigeria* iii. 29 *Mansonia* seedlings 4–9" in height appear to be 1932 regeneration.] **1936** *Nature* 6 June 954/2 The Mansonia (*Mansonia altissima*)..occurs in the deciduous forests of west tropical Africa. **1958** *Archit. Rev.* CXXIV. 191/2 The floors are of mansonia wood blocks, the staircase and fittings of sapele and the ceilings gaboon plywood. **1969** B. J. RENDLE *World Timbers* I. 134 Mansonia was introduced to the world market from Nigeria, as a substitute for walnut, in the 1930s.

manta. 2. Substitute for def.: [Amer. Sp. *manta*, adopted as a generic name by E. B. Bancroft in 1829: see quot.] In full, **manta ray.** A very large ray (RAY *sb.*²) of the genus so called, found in tropical seas; also called devil-fish. (Later examples.)

1829 E. N. BANCROFT in *Zool. Jrnl.* IV. 454 The Manta has, I believe, been generally supposed to belong to the Ray family. **1905** D. S. JORDAN *Guide to Study of Fishes* I. 448 The devil rays or mantas of the Tropical seas, *Manta* and *Mobula* being the most specialized genera. **1958** *Listener* 14 Aug. 247/2 The huge manta rays..opening their gills to let in the tiny cleaner-fish. **1972** *Islander* (Victoria, B.C.) 9 Apr. 7/1 A pair of manta rays making black silhouettes in the midday sun.

mantel, *sb.* Add: **3. d.** *mantel-clock* (earlier and later examples), *-mirror*; **mantel-place** *southern U.S.* = MANTELPIECE.

1870 W. M. BAKER *New Timothy* 25 The mantel-clock strikes six sharp insisting blows as she exclaims. **1963** *Times* 18 May 6/5 Fabre paid £1,200 for a bronze and ormolu elephant mantel clock, also in the Caffieri manner. **1865** MRS. STOWE *House & Home Papers* 86 Now come the great mantel mirrors for four hundred [dollars] more. **1842** W. G. SIMMS *Last Wager* in *Gift 1843* (Philadelphia) 286 You have a very singular ornament for your mantle-place.

mantelshelf. Add: *transf.* (Later examples from *Mountaineering*.) Also *attrib.*

1941 C. F. KIRKUS *Let's Go Climbing!* iv. 60 Half-way up is a ledge..with no holds for some distance above... This is known as a mantelshelf. **1955** M. E. B. BANKS *Commando Climber* xii. 230 A little higher he was stopped by a rock wall capped by an icy mantelshelf. **1963** 'G. CARR' *Lewker in Norway* viii. 161 A firm right foothold, a smooth 'mantelshelf' movement, and he was up and standing on the rock bridge. **1968** P. CREW *Encycl. Dict. Mountaineering* 81 The mantelshelf technique has three main steps as follows: a pull up to raise the body as high as possible; changing one arm, and then the other, into a press-up position; cocking one leg up onto the ledge and slowly standing up.

man-tiger. (Later examples.)

1872 *Nature* 29 Feb. 343/1 The analogous belief in man-hyenas, man-tigers, &c. **1941** J. MASEFIELD *Gautama* 35 Man-tigers dragged the white form nearer As victim on that stone to lie.

Mantinean (mæntinī·ăn), *sb.* and *a.* Also 6 Mantynyan, 9 **Mantineian.** [f. Gr. *Μαντίνεια*, L. *Mantinea* Mantinea.] **A.** *sb.* A native or inhabitant of the ancient city of Mantinea in Arcadia. **B.** *adj.* Of or pertaining to Mantinea or its inhabitants.

1550 T. NICOLLS tr. *Thucydides' Hystory* [*Peloponnesian War*] v. fol. 145 That the Argiues shulde make allyance wyth the Lacedemonyans, forsakinge the same, whyche they had concluded wyth the Athenyans, the Mantynyans and the Elyans. **1629** HOBBES tr. *Thucydides' Peloponnesian War* v. 335 A thousand Athenians..being come after the Battell to ayde the Mantineans. **1753** W. SMITH tr. *Thucydides Hist. Peloponnesian War* II. v. 180 Three thousand heavy-armed Eléans, as auxiliaries to the Mantinéans, came up. **1808** W. MITFORD *Hist. Greece* II. xvii. 263 The Tegeans, and all those other Arcadians who had not, with the Mantineians, renounced the Lacedæmonian alliance. **1846** G. GROTE *Hist. Greece* II. II. viii. 586 Sparta..drove back the Mantineians within their own limits. **1877** L. H. MORGAN *Anc. Society* II. xiv. 349 Bachofen has collected and discussed the evidence of female authority..among the..Mantineans. **1951** J. B. BURY *Hist. Greece* (ed. 3) 327 The Mantineans..were never ready to join hands with their Tegeate neighbours. *Ibid.*, The new synoecism of the Mantinean villages. **1968** V. EHRENBERG *From Solon to Socrates* vii. 284 Sparta.. made..an expedition to free the Parrhasians in Arcadia from Mantinean rule. **1970** *Oxf. Classical Dict.* (ed. 2) 644/2 After the peace of 387 the Spartans obliged the Mantineans to dismantle their walls and live in villages.

mantistic (mænti·stik), *a.* [f. Gr. *μάντις* prophet + -ISTIC.] Pertaining to divination or prophecy; prophetic, mantic.

1876 A. WILDER *Knight's Symbolical Lang. Anc. Art & Mythol.* 141 An idea of peculiar spiritual or mantistic qualities supposed to be peculiar to the female sex.

mantle, *sb.* Add: **2. b.** (Later examples: cf. sense 10*.)

1949 A. G. TANSLEY (*title*) Britain's green mantle. **1962** *Listener* 1 Mar. 376/1 Since..the upper part of the atmospheric mantle is rich in carbon dioxide, advanced life-forms on the surface of Venus seem unlikely.

10*. One of the three major layers composing the earth, extending from the bottom of the crust (at a depth of about 30 km.) for about 2,900 km. to the boundary with the region beneath (the core), and differing from the crust and the core in physical properties (esp. density) and in chemical composition.

Orig. not distinguished from the crust (see quots. 1940, 1955).

1940 R. A. DALY *Strength & Struct. Earth* i. 1 The earth contains a spheroidal core... The rest of the planet, beneath ocean and atmosphere,..may be distinguished as a whole by the name 'mantle'. *Ibid.* 21 At the depth of about 2,900 kilometers..there is..an interface or rapid transition between the earth's silicate mantle and its 'iron' core. **1955** *Sci. Amer.* Sept. 58/3 All the earth outside the core is called the mantle. The whole of the mantle (apart from the oceans and pockets of magma in volcanic regions) is now known to be essentially solid. **1958** *Nature* 13 Sept. 692/1 The Mohorovičić discontinuity is the boundary between the mantle and the assorted surface rocks of the earth, and it marks a very sharp change in the velocity with which earthquake waves travel. **1962** *Listener* 30 Aug. 304/1 Geophysicists are preparing to drill a hole six kilometres deep through the earth's crust to the mantle. **1969**

New Yorker 12 Apr. 96/2 If the structure of the moon proves to be similar to the earth's—that is, to have a core, a mantle, and a crust—then geologists may be able to learn a good deal about the structure of the earth. **1973** *Sci. Amer.* Apr. 24/2 Outside the liquid outer core is a mantle of solid rock some 2,900 kilometers thick, which approaches to within 40 kilometers of the earth's surface under the continents and to within 10 kilometers under the oceans. The thin rocky skin surrounding the mantle is the earth's crust. No drill has penetrated the earth's crust deeper than a few kilometers.

11. mantle-cavity, the space between the mantle (sense 6) and the body of a mollusc or brachiopod; **mantle fibre** *Cytology*, any spindle fibre which is attached to a chromosome.

1853 *Phil. Trans. R. Soc.* CXLIII. 37 It [*sc.* the heart] lies parallel to the rectum, with the auricle forwards at the base of the mantle-cavity. **1958** *New Biol.* XXV. 100 The visceral mass (of Cuttlefish) is closed all round by a muscular mantle in such a way that below and to the sides of it there is a cavity—the mantle cavity. **1896** E. B. Wilson *Cell* ii. 74 The daughter-chromosomes are dragged apart solely by the contractile mantle-fibres, the central spindle-fibres being non-contractile. **1920** L. Doncaster *Introd. Study Cytol.* iii. 31 In some animals these fibres are said to be of different thickness, those attached to chromosomes being thicker and called 'mantle fibres' (from their appearance at a later stage). **1966** D. M. Kramsch tr. *Grundmann's Gen. Cytol.* iii. 149 We are dealing with a central spindle, on whose exterior aspect the chromosomal spindle fibres are attached as mantle fibres.

Mantoux (maṅtū, mæ·ntū). *Med.* The name of Charles *Mantoux* (1877–1947), French physician, used *attrib.* with reference to a method, introduced by him in 1908, of testing for past or present tuberculous infection by intradermal injection of diluted tuberculin.

1931 R. J. E. Scott *Gould's Med. Dict.* (ed. 3) 764/1 Mantoux test. **1932** *Observer* 28 Feb. 11/2 The Mantoux test has a definite though limited application in the diagnosis of tuberculous disease. **1956** *Nature* 25 Feb. 367/2 A study was made of the interrelationships of the Mantoux and Lepromin reactions. *Ibid.* 368/1 The Mantoux-negative individuals. **1971** D. Lambert in C. Bonington *Annapurna South Face* App. G. 290 Immunity [from tuberculosis] is tested first by the Mantoux Test, and this is examined after three days.

mantra. Add: (Later examples.) Also *attrib.* and *fig.* Also, a holy name, for inward meditation.

1900 W. Maxwell in W. W. Skeat *Malay Magic* v. 116 Numerous *mantra*, or charms..are in use among the Pawangs. **1931** G. B. Sansom *Japan* iii. xii. 222 Recitation of the formulae known as *mantra*. **1956** E. Wood *Yoga Dict.* 93 *Mantras*, forms of speech which carry a material effect upon the mind, emotions or body, or even on things... The scriptures contain many great *mantras*, of which the greatest is the word *Om*. *Ibid.*, If these [sounds] are arranged by some person competent in this matter, words..and sentences of power can be formed. Such a person was called a mantramaker (*mantrakāra*) in ancient India. **1962** Brahmacharini Usha *Ramakrishna-Vedanta Wordbk.* 47 *Mantra*,..also mantram... The particular name of God... The mantra, regarded as one with God, represents the essence of the guru's instruction to his disciple, who is enjoined to keep it sacred and secret, and to meditate on the aspect of God which it symbolizes for the rest of his life. **1964** V. S. Naipaul *Area of Darkness* x. 249 The Tibetans..were suffering because they had forgotten the *mantras*, charms, which might have repelled their enemies. **1965** *New Statesman* 16 Apr. 616/3 He is less happy when defending the mantra, or holy names on which one must meditate. **1967** Singha & Massey *Indian Dances* iv. 56 The priest lit the sacred fire, recited the mantras (sacred texts), and tied the tali round the girl's neck. **1969** *Enactment* (Delhi) Nov. 18/1 You used to chant his name like a *mantra*. **1971** *Daily Tel.* 19 Aug. 10/4 People who ever have dinner in English country hotels know the *mantra*, or holy formula: 'Coffee will be served in the lounge.' **1972** *Language* XLVIII. 174 Secondly, the Brahmanas cannot be regarded far removed in time from the mantras, and therefore their authors might not render a particular mantra word.. which..was not altogether unintelligible in their times. **1972** *Village Voice* (N.Y.) 1 June 76/3 The birds were placed in cardboard boxes..and rushed to a building where teams of hippies, chanting the Hare Krishna mantra, worked into the dawn of the next day to save their lives. **1973** *Times* 22 Jan. 20 The Maharishi uses a technique based on a mantra, a sound which each meditator is given to intone inwardly.

man-trap. *transf.* and *fig.* (Further examples.)

1857 W. Chandless *Visit to Salt Lake* ii. xi. 330 The planks (of the streets) worn out and broken through, leaving large holes, popularly known as 'man-traps'. **1903** G. B. Shaw *Man & Superman* iii. 121 You know better than any of us that marriage is a mantrap baited with simulated accomplishments. **1922** Joyce *Ulysses* 425 You never seen me in the mantrap with a married highlander. **1929** W. Faulkner *Sartoris* (1932) v. ii. 365 Some new kind of mantrap [*sc.* an aeroplane] that flies fine—on paper. **1965** H. Sheppard *Dict. Railway Slang* 7 *Man trap*, catch points to prevent unauthorised entry from siding. **1974** P. M. Hubbard *Thirsty Evil* i. 9 She was no man-trap, but she did not miss much.

man-trap, *v.* [f. the sb.] *trans.* To beset with man-traps. Also *fig.* and as **ma·ntrapping** *ppl. a.*

1911 J. London *Son of Sun* (1913) iv. iv. 159 Besides, the runs are all man-trapped—you know, staked pits, poisoned thorns, and the rest. **1952** Dylan Thomas *Let.* 8 Oct. (1966) 378 Every lane was mantrapped for me. *c* **1953** —— *Ibid.* 416 And eel up wheezily..from all the claws and bars and breasts of the mantrapping seabed. **1957** A. Clarke *Later Poems* (1961) 61 Discharge, excrete, their centuries, Man-trapped in concrete.

‖**mantri** (mæ·ntri). Also 8 mantree. [Hindi, f. Skr. *mantri*, f. *mantrin* wise, eloquent, skilled in sacred texts or spells, f. *man* to think; cf. Mantra.] **a.** In India, etc.: a minister, counsellor. **b.** In Indonesia (including the former Netherlands East Indies): a minor official or subordinate functionary vested with some authority.

1783 W. Marsden *Hist. Sumatra* 287 The officers next in rank to the *Sultan* are called *Mantree*, which some apprehend to be a corruption of the word *Mandarin*, a title of distinction amongst the Chinese. **1814** T. S. Raffles *Substance of Minute on Land Rental on Island of Java* 218 In each division there shall be fixed a station of police, to which shall be appointed a competent officer, with such number of inferior *Mantris, Peons*, &c. as shall be deemed necessary. **1873** E. Balfour *Cycl. India* III. 146/2 *Mantra*, Sans. Counsel, hence mantri, Sans. a counsellor. **1896** Carey & Tuck *Chin Hills* I. i. 3 The elders of the village, called..by the Lushai officers 'Kharbari' and 'Mantri', surround the person of the Chief. **1917** Coomaraswamy & Duggirala tr. *Mirror of Gesture* 15 *The Ministers* (mantri)—Those who shine as royal ministers are men of their word. **1965** I. Southall *Indonesia* xxiii. 227 If the villager ever does get to the hospital, he will find an outpatient clinic with a mantri in charge. It is the duty of this mantri to treat all simpler problems and refer the difficult to the doctor.

Mantuan. Add: **A.** *adj.* (Earlier and later examples.)

1538 King Henry VIII *Epistle* sig. B2 We moste hartely desyre you, that ye wol vouchesafe, to rede those thynges, that we wrote this laste yere, touchynge the Mantuan Councille. **1940** G. F.-H. & J. Berkeley *Italy in Making* III. viii. 141 The Mantuan volunteers..gave a very creditable account of themselves.

B. *sb.* (Later examples.)

1842 K. H. Digby *Mores Catholici* xi. i. 6 Mezentius is never named by the great Mantuan without the epithet 'contemtorque Deûm'. **1953** T. F. Murray tr. *Dal-Gal's Pius X* v. 91 He had not spent long among the Mantuans before his people..were charmed by his meekness and won by his charity.

manual, *a.* Add: **1.** Also, as opposed to *automatic*, applied to hand-operated devices, systems, etc.

1921 *Conquest* Jan. 124/1 Consider what happens in an ordinary 'manual' telephone exchange when a subscriber makes a call. **1923** *Bell Syst. Techn. Jrnl.* Apr. 56 The system most commonly employed today for connecting [telephone] subscribers' lines together is the so-called 'manual' system; that is, a system in which operators.. make the actual connections. **1959** *Gramophone* Sept. 82 (Advt.), The 'Conquest' Automatic Record Changer for stereophonic and monophonic play... Provision for manual operation. **1966** *McGraw-Hill Encycl. Sci. & Technol.* XIV. 43/2 There are two general types of transmission, manual shift and automatic. Manual-shift transmissions..are used in conjunction with a clutch.

Manueline (mæ·niuĕləin), *a.* Also **Manoeline, Manoelino, Manoellian, Manuelline.** [f. the name of *Manuel* I (b. 1469, reigned 1495–1521), King of Portugal.] Of or pertaining to a style of Portuguese architecture developed during the reign of Manuel I and characterized by its ornate elaborations of Gothic and Renaissance styles.

1908 W. C. Watson *Portuguese Archit.* x. 145 Nearly all these churches and palaces were built or added to in that peculiar style now called Manoelino. *Ibid.* 147 The Jesus College at Setubal..is the best example in the country of a late Gothic church modified by the addition of certain Manoelino details. **1911** *Encycl. Brit.* XXII. 144/2 In architecture the name of King Emanuel was given to a new and composite style (the Manoeline or Manoellian), in which decorative forms..were harmonized with Gothic and Renaissance designs. **1931** S. Sitwell *Spanish Baroque Art* ii. 50 There is always an imaginary Orient at the back of their ideas... In the Manoeline there are Moghul, Persian, Moroccan influences. **1937** *Archit. Rev.* LXXXII. 129/2 The Manoeline style of architecture is as distinct from what is termed Italian 'Renaissance' as Romanesque is from Gothic... In this respect by 'Manoeline' is meant Portuguese Renaissance. **1948** G. Kubler *Mexican Archit. 16th Cent.* II. viii. 382 In Portugal, the period before *ca.* 1525 was dominated by Manueline ornament. **1960** J. Lees-Milne *Baroque in Spain & Portugal* ii. i. 144 The Manoeline style—if style it may be called—has a very positive bearing upon the last phase of Portuguese Baroque. **1968** *Encycl. Brit.* III. 271/2 The Capellas Imperfeitas ('unfinished chapels') are one of the most marvellous examples of Manuelline architecture.

manufacturing, *ppl. a.* (Earlier and later examples.)

1722 Defoe *Jrnl. Plague Year* 257 The Manufacturing Trade in England suffer'd greatly. **1789** H. More *Lett.* (1925) 165, I have written to different manufacturing towns for a [school] mistress. **1892** *Rep. Vermont Board Agric.* XII. 140 As these manufacturing centers increase in size, so do the farm lands in like ratio increase in value. **1942** *Short Guide Gt. Brit.* (U.S. War Dept.) 7 The great 'midland' manufacturing cities of Birmingham, Sheffield and Coventry. **1959** *Chambers's Encycl.* IX. 51/1 The manufacturing industries of Manchester are much more varied than in a specialized manufacturing town.

manuka. (Earlier and later examples.)

1832 G. Bennett in *London Med. Gaz.* 18 Feb. 750/1 This tree..is probably a species of Leptospermum. It is found abundantly at New Zealand,..and is named Kaetatowa, or Manuka, by the natives. **1882** W. D. Hay *Brighter Britain!* II. 195 The Manuka or Manukau..is the 'ti-tree' of settlers. **1920** *Nature* 22 July 667/1 The most abundant foods [for trout] were the green manuka-beetle,..the larvae of caddis-flies..and a small mollusc. **1936** 'R. Hyde' *Passport to Hell* ii. 47 The brown and white manuka blossoms. **1948** *Coast to Coast 1947* 76 Johnny put up a manuka shelter around the pool. **1959** *Tararua* XIII. 47 We may find on the topographical maps such New Zealand terms as..'teatree' in Auckland, 'manuka' further south. **1960** *New Scientist* 4 Aug. 330/1 Sheep farmers were beginning to get worried by manuka, which showed signs of investing large tracts of country. And then, suddenly the coccid appeared and started to destroy the weed.

manure, *sb.* Add: **1.** Also, other substances, esp. various chemicals, used as fertilizers.

1794 R. Kirwan in *Trans. R. Irish Acad.* V. i. 137 The substances principally used as manures, are chalk, lime.. gypsum, [etc.]. **1824** J. C. Loudon *Encycl. Gardening* (ed. 2) 243 Saline and calcareous substances form the principal fossil manures. **1904** T. W. Sanders *Roses & their Cultivation* 70 It is of no use applying manure that has been allowed to decay naturally, because nearly all the essential salts have been washed out or evaporated. **1922** Joyce *Ulysses* 698 James W. Mackey..agent for chemical manures. **1951** *Dict. Gardening* (R. Hort. Soc.) III. 1248/2 Manures may be classified into Organic Manures which are substances of animal or vegetable origin, and Inorganic Manures which are of mineral origin. **1971** L. D. Hills *Grow your own Fruit & Vegetables* ii. 27 There is a clear distinction between organic and inorganic manures and fertilizers.

3. *manure-spreader.*

a **1884** Knight *Dict. Mech.* Suppl. 580/2 *Manure Spreader*, a cart having a bed of traveling slats..to distribute the load while the vehicle is moving over the surface of the ground. **1915** J. London *Let.* 26 Jan. (1966) 445 My plan still holds of using litter-carriers to dump manure..into..waiting manure-spreaders. **1943** J. S. Huxley *TVA* vi. 49 He insisted on buying a mechanical manure-spreader and using it with a tractor. **1969** K. M. Wells *Owl Pen Reader* i. 46 The uphill clatter of Farmer Jim's manure-spreader as he drove it over the stubbles.

Hence **manu·r(e)y** *a.*, splashed or littered with manure.

1890–3 E. M. Taber *Stowe Notes, Lett. & Verses* (1913) 29 The stable-yard repulsive, muddy and manury. **1932** *Sunday Express* 3 July 17/4 Many's the time I've seen him all mud and manurey.

manuscript. B. *sb.* **1. b.** Add to def.: Also applied to an author's typed copy.

1967 R. A. Waldron *Sense & Sense Devel.* vi. 116 *Manuscript* is no longer something necessarily 'written by hand' but is usually the author's original copy of the text of a printed book, etc. **1967** *Anglo-Amer. Catal. Rules: Brit. Text* 267 *Manuscript*, a writing made by hand. (Original typescripts are generally treated as manuscripts in libraries.) **1967** *Listener* 2 Mar. 282/3 Perhaps you are going to transcribe the tape-recording into typewritten manuscript.

man-woman. a. Delete † *Obs.* and add later examples.

1920 D. Lindsay *Voy. Arcturus* xviii. 240 'What do you call men-women?' 'Persons of mixed sex, like yourself.' **1975** P. G. Winslow *Death of Angel* iv. 109 The new man-woman, emerging from the chaos that is matter.

Hence **man-womanly** *a.*, having the characteristics of both sexes.

1929 V. Woolf *Room of one's Own* 148 It would be well to test what one meant by man-womanly.

Manx, *a.* and *sb.* **B.** *sb.* **2.** Add to def.: Now extinct. (Further example.)

1970 B. M. H. Strang *Hist. Eng.* ix. 402 One IE language (Manx) has become extinct since the Second World War.

Manxwoman (example).

1974 J. Mann *Sticking Place* viii. 132 I'm a Manx-woman.

manxome (mæ·ŋksə̆m), *a. poet. nonce-wd.* [Invented word; cf. -some[1] (as in *fearsome, gruesome, loathsome*, etc.).] ? Fearsome.

1871 'L. Carroll' *Through Looking-Glass* i. 22 Long time the manxome foe he sought.

many, *a.* and *sb.* Add: **A.** *adj.* **5. e.** Also used of something that is repeated to excess.

1941 H. L. Mencken *Newspaper Days* (1942) xii. 193 The poor old man..nursing a hangover from a Bar Association banquet, had thrown in one too many quick ones, and so got himself plastered. **1956** A. Wilson *Anglo-Saxon Attitudes* i. ii. 43 Some people have made one imaginative leap too many and show little sign of being able to return to the realm of reason.

6. a. *many-angled* (later example), *-antlered, -centuried, -corridored, -faceted, -fingered, -hearted, -minded, -mooded, -mouthed* (later example), *-pleated, -splendoured, -twined, -volumed* adjs. Also *many-dimensional* adj.

1892 W. B. Yeats *Countess Kathleen* iii. 57 Heaven's many-angled star reversed. **1930** Blunden *Poems* 48 Bronze noonlight domes the dim blue gloom Where

many-antlered oaks immure A hush. **1848** J. R. LOWELL *Columbus* in *Poems* 2nd Ser. 11 Many-centuried shade Of some writhed oak. **1931** BLUNDEN *To Themis* 53 Beneath the accustomed dome Of this chance-planted, many-centuried tree. **1859** TENNYSON *Vivien* in *Idylls of King* 132 The myriad-room'd And many-corridor'd complexities Of Arthur's palace. **1905** W. JAMES in *Mind* XIV. 196 Satisfaction is a many-dimensional term that can be realized in various ways. **1933** A. N. WHITEHEAD *Adventures of Ideas* xi. 242 And space is many-dimensional. *a* **1963** C. S. LEWIS *Poems* (1964) 102 The many-dimensional timeless rays. **1909** *Daily Chron.* 7 Sept. 4/4 A many-faceted diamond. **1947** *Mind* LVI. 291 The many-faceted problem of perception soon came to dominate the epistemological scene. **1909** E. POUND *Personae* 36 All tremulous beneath the many-fingered breath. **1935** W. EMPSON *Poems* 19 Crossing and doubling, many-fingered, hounded. **1882** in *Eng. Dial. Dict.* (1903) IV. 33/1 (s. Dev.), He was always many-hearted [= 'soft-hearted']. **1904** W. DE LA MARE *Henry Brocken* 193 Yonder fine many-hearted poplar. **1895** *Funk's Stand. Dict.*, *Many-minded*, showing changes of mind; changeable in opinion; fickle; versatile. **1932** W. B. YEATS *Words for Music* 37 Even Cicero And many-minded Homer were Mad as the mist and snow. **1920** *19th Cent.* Aug. 272 To know him [*sc.* Stephen Phillips] was to realise how many-mooded and complex a man he was. **1935** C. DAY LEWIS *Time to Dance* 50 You shall recall one open as the day, Many-mooded as the light above English hills. **1917** D. H. LAWRENCE *Look! We have come Through!* 18 The spouse all full of increase Moiled over with the rearing of her many-mouthed young. **1927** —— *Mornings in Mexico* 81 The many-pleated, noiseless mountains of Mexico. *a* **1907** F. THOMPSON *Kingdom of God* in *Sel. Poems* (1908) 131 'Tis ye, 'tis your estrangèd faces, That miss the many-splendoured thing. **1962** *Sunday Times* (Colour Suppl.) 25 Nov. 29 (*title*) The many-splendoured fisherman. **1971** *Nat. Geographic* Oct. 548/1 The Ocean Terminal and nearby Harbour Centre in Kowloon offer a dazzling promenade past 150 or more stores selling jewelry, watches, ginger jars, television sets.., pearls, and other many-splendored items. **1909** E. POUND *Personae* 35 What should avail me the many-twined bracelets? **1857** J. R. LOWELL *Orig. Didactic Poetry* in *Atlantic Monthly* Nov. 112 Many-volumed thunder. **1927** W. B. YEATS *Senate Speeches* (1961) 138 This many-volumed ancient history.

b. (ii) *attrib.* phrases consisting of *many* with a sb. in sense 'having, consisting of, many of the things named', as *many-course*, *-electron*, *-interest*, *-particle*, *-volume*, *-word*.

1955 D. CHAPMAN *Home & Social Status* xi. 172 The many-course dinner with wines. **1929** *Trans. Faraday Soc.* XXV. 672 We use this system of energy levels for the many-electron problem just as was done in atoms. **1970** G. K. WOODGATE *Elem. Atomic Struct.* i. 5 In many-electron atoms the electrostatic interaction with the nucleus is summed over all the electrons. **1955** M. GLUCKMAN *Custom & Conflict in Afr.* v. 135 They [*sc.* rituals] are inappropriate in the family, our single many-interest group. **1955** W. PAULI *Niels Bohr* 135 The states formed in the reaction are states of a many-particle system. **1941** *Mind* L. 141 That these naïve beliefs [*sc.* about ambiguity] are false is easy to realise in this age of many-volume dictionaries. **1924** R. M. OGDEN tr. *Koffka's Growth of Mind* v. 329 Transference from a one-word to a many-word sentence is carried out. **1940** A. H. GARDINER *Theory of Proper Names* ix. 29 In some of my many-word names (e.g. Edgar Allan Poe) the coherence of the parts is much slighter than in others. **1973** A. QUINTON *Nature of Things* v. 127 Many-word sentences have to be used to guard against the misunderstandings.

c. many-body, pertaining to or involving three or more bodies or particles; applied *spec.* to the problem of predicting their positions and motions at any future time given their present values and the way the bodies interact; **many–many** *a.* (see quots.); **many–one** *a.*, applied to a correspondence or relation such that two or more members of one set are associated with or related to each member of a second set; hence **many–oneness**; **many-valued** *a.* [cf. G. *mehrwertig*] *Philos.*, 'possessing three or more truth-values in place of the customary two of truth and falsehood' (Webster 1961); **many-worded** *a.*, of a term or description involving the use of several words.

1927 FISHER & HARTREE tr. *Born's Mech. Atom* iv. 248 The analytical difficulties of the many-body problem. **1962** W. B. THOMPSON *Introd. Plasma Physics* i. 2 The microscopic dynamics of a plasma must be understood as a study in many-body physics. **1964** L. WILETS *Theories Nucl. Fission* iv. 56 The first quantitative attempt to apply many-body techniques to finite nuclei was performed by Brueckner, Lockett, and Rotenberg... The results of the infinite many-body problem were used to obtain the K-matrix as a function of density. **1922** W. E. JOHNSON *Logic* II. vii. 156 Here the denominating correlation is not one–one but many–many, and yet the names and the things happen to be numerically equal. **1933** *Mind* XLII. 53 In this third use of 'term' the total situation located by 'Tom fears Francois' is not two-termed but many-termed, and the total situation located by 'England fears France' many-many-termed. **1965** *Language* XLI. 44 Transformational relations are one–one, but expansion relations are many–many. **1910** WHITEHEAD & RUSSELL *Principia Math.* I. II. 438 Thus many–one relations are the converses of one–many relations. *Ibid.* 575 The transition from series generated by one–one or many–one relations of consecutive terms to series generated by transitive relations of *before* and *after*. **1936** *Jrnl. Philos.* 17 Dec. 706 The relation of tokens to their type..is consistently many–one: a type can have many tokens, but a token only one type. But the relation of type to word is many–many. A word can be represented by many types; but so can a type represent many words. **1955** A. N. PRIOR *Formal Logic* 279 A 'many–one' relation, *Cls*→1, is an *R* such that if *x* is an *R* of any given thing then it is not an *R* of anything else... The null relation is many–one for the same sort of reason as it is one–many. **1959** E. M. PATTERSON *Topology* (ed. 2) iv. 82 A homomorphism between a group G_1 and a group G_2 is a many–one transformation. **1971** *Language* XLVII. 8 This overwhelming predominance of many–one mapping over one–many, as we move from semantics to phonetics, can then be seen as further evidence of language's directionality. **1966** S. BEER *Decision & Control* xvii. 441 The effect of that Act..was to provide a richer mapping, to reduce the many–oneness of the homomorphic transformation. **1934** *Philos. of Sci.* I. 118 A many-valued system of logic is a code of inference which endows propositions with truth values intermediate between true and false. **1936** *Mind* XLV. 273 His [Reichenbach's] probability logic is a many-valued logic. **1940** W. V. QUINE *Math. Logic* 222 Common mathematical usage..countenances so-called many-valued functions as well as single-valued ones. **1965** *Philosophy* XL. 172 Languages based on a many-valued logic are artificial constructs. **1969** N. RESCHER (*title*) Many-valued logic. *a* **1832** BENTHAM *Chrestomathia* App. 9. § 2 in *Works* (1843) VIII. 188/1 In the many-worded appellative, part of speech, the word *part* is instructive. **1843** MILL *Logic* I. I. ii. 30 A mixed term belongs to the class of what have been called many-worded names. **1901** A. SIDGWICK *Use of Words in Reasoning* v. 143 Description ..is more often than not many-worded. **1957** G. RYLE in M. Black *Importance of Lang.* (1962) 151, I am still not quite sure why..every possible grammatical subject of a sentence, one-worded or many-worded, stands to something.

manyatta (mænyæ·tă). Also **manyat.** [Bantu.] Among certain African peoples, particularly the Masai, a group of huts forming a unit within a common fence.

1905 A. C. HOLLIS *Masai* 292 Meat may not be eaten in the manyat, or warriors' kraals. **1921** *Blackw. Mag.* Jan. 118/1 The Manyatta, a rambling collection of dome-shaped huts surrounded by a straggling zeriba, seemed to have settled down for the day. **1964** *Listener* 30 July 163/2 He returned to the family *manyatta*—a thorn-fenced cluster of low mud hovels shared with the beasts. **1971** *E. Afr. Standard* (Nairobi) 13 Apr. 9/1 A gang of Borana tribesmen attacked a Samburu manyatta at Shaba Hills.

man-year: see *MAN *sb.*[1] 20 b.

manyfold (me·nifōuld), *adv.* Also **many-fold, many fold.** [a mod. re-formation from MANY *a.* + -FOLD (after *three-*, *fourfold*, etc.), etymologically identical with MANIFOLD, though this was rarely used in this sense (MANIFOLD *adv.* 1 b).] In the proportion of many to one.

1879 [see -FOLD]. **1916** D. S. KIMBALL in *Mod. Business* (Alexander Hamilton Inst.) VII. II. vi. 293 If this difference is reflected many-fold in the product of a large and costly machine the difference in output might very well be marked. **1920** S. S. HUEBNER *Marine Insurance* p. v, The tonnage of vessels under the American Flag was, within a brief period, increased many fold. **1961** M. HYNES *Med. Bacteriol.* (ed. 7) x. 126 Urinary infections with resistant bacteria may respond to antibiotics that are concentrated many-fold by renal excretion. **1969** *Sci. Jrnl.* 36/1 If any nation can find..all the major ingredients to produce unlimited supplies of energy, fertilizer, fresh water and other necessities, then the useful part of the Earth will be increased manyfold.

many-headed, *a.* **b.** (Further example.)

1934 WODEHOUSE *Right Ho, Jeeves* xv. 181 We might have been a rather oversized greyhound and a somewhat slimmer electric hare doing their stuff on a circular track for the entertainment of the many-headed.

manyogana (manyō·gană). Also **manyokana.** [Jap., f. *Manyō(shū* 'collection of a Myriad Leaves', name of an 8th-cent. anthology of Japanese poetry + *-gana* combining form of *KANA (phonetic) letters, script.] A system of writing in use in Japan in the 8th century, found *spec.* in the Manyōshū, in which Chinese characters are used to represent Japanese sounds.

1868 J. J. HOFFMANN *Japanese Gram.* 6 The running-hand form was used in the old Japanese Bundle of Poems ..*Man-you-siu* or the Collection of the Ten Thousand Leaves, compiled about the middle of the eighth century. The first *Kâna*-form was, consequently, called *Yamáto-kána*.., the other *Man-you-kána*. **1909** tr. *S. Okuma's Fifty Yrs. of New Japan* II. i. 2 We also used these [Chinese] characters merely as symbols for our own sounds. This latter method..we find..generally used in our old works like the '*Kojiki*' and the '*Manyōshū*', whence these symbols came to be called the *Manyō-kana*. **1928** G. B. SANSOM *Hist. Gram. Japanese* i. 23 The name of this anthology was the *Manyōshū*, or 'collection of a Myriad Leaves', and the characters thus used were known as *Manyōgana*. **1934** S. YOSHITAKE *Phonetic System of Ancient Japanese* i. 7 It was that great philologist Motowori Norinaga who first discovered how strictly certain Man-yō-gana were differentiated. **1948** *Introd. Classic Japanese Lit.* (Kokusai Bunka Shinkokai) (1956) p. x, The choice of subject for ballads ranged much more widely..encouraged by the popularization of new methods of writing, by the introduction of the Japanese syllabary (*kana*) in the primitive form known as *man'yōgana* (*Man'yōshū* style *kana*) where the Chinese ideographs were used with their phonetic value. **1951** J. K. YAMAGIWA in Reischauer & Yamagiwa *Transl. Early Japanese Lit.* 277 In the eighth and ninth centuries, abbreviations and simplifications of the *Man'yōgana* resulted in the creation of the two syllabic scripts, the *katakana* and the *hiragana*. **1959** *Chambers's Encycl.* VIII. 58/2 Two [writing] systems gradually developed: one an elaborate distortion of Japanese into Chinese forms (*kambun*); the other a phonetic adaptation of Chinese characters for the reproduction of Japanese sounds (*manyōgana*). **1965** D. KEENE *Manyōshū* p. xviii, The so-called '*Manyō-gana*' are the Chinese characters which were commonly used as phonograms in the *Manyōshū*, from which the present system of *kana* was evolved. **1974** *Canad. Jrnl. Linguistics* XIX. 217 Taken together, the *ongana* and *kungana* comprise the *man'yōgana*, the eighth-century precursors of the later *kana* syllabaries.

manzanilla. Add: **2.** A variety of olive, distinguished by small thin-skinned fruit.

1911 *Daily Colonist* (Victoria, B.C.) 13 Apr. 6/1 (Advt.), Your Easter Sunday menu will demand the luscious, healthful Olive. We carry a big stock, all kinds..Manzanillas—Small Olives. **1964** *Economist* 8 Aug. 547/2 Special varieties [of olive]..like the Manzanilla and the Goodal in Spain. **1974** *Observer* (Colour Suppl.) 8 Sept. 66/3 The country around Seville in Spain is green olive country, both for the manzanillas and the huge queen olives.

manzanita. Add: Also **manzanito.** (Earlier and later examples.)

1848 E. BRYANT *California* xviii. 236 We have met occasionally with a reddish berry called by the Californians manzanita (little apple). **1869** C. L. BRACE *New West* xi. 138 Around her were..dishes of the manzanita seed. **1888** B. HARTE *Drift from Redwood Camp* in *Phyllis of Sierras* 227 A bent manzanito-bush..flew back against his breast. **1918** C. E. MULFORD *Man from Bar-20* xvii. 178 He pushed through matted thickets of oak brush and manzanito. **1928** A. BIERCE *Can Such Things Be?* i. 8 Unable in the darkness to penetrate the thickets of manzanita and other undergrowth. **1971** *Black Scholar* Apr.–May 47/2 Our job is to clear out 10 miles of oak trees, manzanita shrubs and sagebrush on both sides of the highway. **1972** *Village Voice* (N.Y.) 1 June 76/1 A sign next to a luxuriant manzanita plant welcomes you to God's land.

manzello (mænze·lo). [Origin uncertain.] A musical instrument resembling a soprano saxophone.

1962 *Melody Maker* 7 July 7/3 The manzello, which he uses frequently in solos, sounds rather like a soprano while the stritch is somewhere in the tenor range. **1966** *New Statesman* 4 Nov. 677/1 On manzello he [*sc.* Roland Kirk] echoes some of Sidney Bechet's canary-yellow flights. **1969** *Daily Tel.* 15 Feb. 15/1 Kirk's solo ability on flute, tenor saxophone, manzello and stritch.

Mao (mau). [f. *Mao* Tse-Tung; see *MAOISM.] Used *attrib.* of a simple style of clothing based on dress in Communist China, as *Mao cap*, *collar*, *jacket*, *trousers*, *etc.*

1967 *Guardian* 1 Aug. 5/5 A close-fitting standing collar to which Paris is now giving the name Mao. **1968** *N.Y. Times* 22 May 50 'Extravagances' such as the Mao jacket. **1968** *Punch* 24 July 107/2 Out, apparently, are Mao caps, Guevara beards, Maharishi gowns and Zapata moustaches. **1969** A. SINCLAIR *Last of Best* ix. 231 Silk Mao jackets. **1972** *Daily Tel.* 3 Mar. 14 The blue-clad men and women, all in Mao jackets and trousers. **1973** *Sunday Express* (Trinidad) 1 Apr. (Suppl.) 7/3 From the East was Madame Sung Chih-Kuang, 50, wife of the first Red Chinese Ambassador to Britain, who wore a grey cotton Mao suit. **1974** J. MITCHELL *Death & Bright Water* iii. 19 Mao boiler suit to show he was one of the righteous, but hand-sewn and made of silk.

b. Mao 'flu, Hong Kong influenza (see *HONG KONG 2).

1968 *Guardian* 14 Dec. 1/1 Hongkong or Mao 'flu now sweeping the United States, is likely to reach Britain next month or in February. **1973** 'G. ASHE' *Life for Death* v. 49 He's had the damned Mao flu and it's put him right out.

Maoism (mau·iz'm). [f. the name of *Mao* Tse-Tung (1893–), Chairman of the Central Committee of the Chinese Communist Party + -ISM.] The Marxist-Leninist theories of Mao Tse-Tung developed and practised in China. Hence **Mao·ist** *sb.*, a follower of these theories; also *attrib.* or as *adj.*, of or pertaining to these theories.

1951 B. I. SCHWARTZ *Chinese Communism & Rise of Mao* xiii. 189 The essential features of Maoism. *Ibid.* 190 Another peculiar feature of the Maoist strategy..is the preference for 'border area' bases. **1961** *Listener* 23 Nov. 886/2 Maoist Marxism. **1962** *Ibid.* 18 Jan. 112/1 There are several kinds of communism in the world—Titoism, Khrushchevism, Maoism in China. **1964** *New Statesman* 17 Apr. 592/3 The Maoists are blind not to see this and to identify their cause with a nostalgia for the Stalin epoch. **1967** *Guardian* 15 May 6/1 The demonstrators have been conducting their affairs in Maoist style—little red books of quotations and all. **1968** *Listener* 28 Nov. 736/1 The awful children..are now revealed as a tiny Maoist cell at the heart of the family. **1969** *N.Y. Rev. Bks.* 16 Jan. 6/2 Many of the good facets of Maoism, such as participation in social and political life and the linking of practice and theory in education. **1970** G. GREER *Female Eunuch* 22 The most telling criticisms will come from my sisters of the left, the Maoists, the Trots. **1970** *New Scientist* 19 Mar. 539/2 Neither Tories nor Labourites can be blamed for sounding like Maoists, desperately looking for a Little Red Book. **1971** *Peace News* 5 Nov. 5/1 His blend of religious fervour and Maoist rhetoric does not endear him either to pacifists or to liberals. **1973** *Listener* 2 Aug. 147/2 This year Mao will be 80, so we may assume that the Maoist era is coming to its end.

Maoize (mau·əiz), *v.* [f. *Mao* (see *MAOISM) + -IZE.] *trans.* To imbue with the doctrines of Maoism. So **Maoiza·tion.**

1970 *Guardian* 18 Sept. 11/2 The guerillas' growing ideological dependence on China..could lead to the 'Maoisation' of the Middle East. **1971** *Time* 12 July 22 Mao demolished..others who did not share his own mystical concept of the revolution. He hoped to replace them with freshly radicalized, totally Maoized youth who would be prepared to spend their lives in permanent struggle.

maomao (mau·mau). *N.Z.* [Maori.] A blue-skinned marine food fish, *Scorpis violaceus* or *S. æquipinnis*, found in New Zealand and Australian waters.

1886 R. A. A. SHERRIN *Handbk. Fishes N.Z.* 67 The delicious little maomao may be caught at the Rurima Rocks in immense quantities. **1949** P. BUCK *Coming of Maori* (1950) II. viii. 215 The longest bag net..was used to catch *maomao* (*Scorpis violaceus*), a deep-sea fish which travelled in shoals. **1966** *Encycl. N.Z.* II. 408/2 The blue maomao also occurs in Australia, where it is known as the hardbelly.

Maori, *sb.* (*a.*) Add: **1. b. Maori bug** (see quot. 1966); **Maori dog,** a type of dog, which is now extinct, first introduced to New Zealand by the Maoris; also in *fig.* use, *cunning as a Maori dog,* a phrase of vulgar abuse; cf. *KURI. **c. Maori oven** = *COPPER MAORI; **Maori P.T.** *N.Z. slang,* taking it easy and doing nothing.

1944 *Mod. Jun. Dict.* (Whitcombe & Tombs) 251 *Maori bug,* a strong-smelling, dark-coloured beetle. **1959** *Numbers* IX. 8 We..shook Maori bugs out of the blankets. **1966** *Encycl. N.Z.* I. 269/1 *Bug, Maori* (*Platyzosteria novae-zelandiae*). Maori bug is the commonly accepted name for the largest endemic cockroach of New Zealand... This species is capable of liberating a characteristic, unpleasant odour when disturbed. **1947** D. M. DAVIN *For Rest of our Lives* 103 Cunning as a Maori dog, you know him. **1950** *N.Z. Jrnl. Agric.* Feb. 136/1 Pastoralists..[in the early days] had their problems, too. Maori dogs were troublesome. **1953** M. SCOTT *Breakfast at Six* iii. 30 'The professional charmer,' jeered Larry... 'Cunning as a Maori dog,' supplemented Sam vulgarly. **1966** *Encycl. N.Z.* I. 491/2 The Maori dog (kuri)..was probably introduced during the period of the Great Migration (c. 1350 A.D.)... It became extinct some years after the arrival of the European settlers. **1849** Maori oven [see *go-ashore* s.v. *GO *v.* VIII]. **1905** [see *COPPER MAORI]. **1961** PARTRIDGE *Dict. Slang* Suppl. 1179/1 *Maori P.T.,* 'taking it as easily as possible, i.e. resting when one should be undertaking physical training'..: New Zealand soldiers': 1939–45. **1966** G. W. TURNER *Eng. Lang. Austral. & N.Z.* vi. 135 In New Zealand the word *Maori* sometimes enters into slang with contemptuous connotation, but there is a good-natured tolerance, even tinged with envy for an admirable adjustment to life's problems, in a term like *Maori P.T.*.. to mean lying down and doing nothing. **1967** *Listener* 2 Mar. 299/3 *Maori P.T.* is New Zealand *dolce far niente.* **1969** *Pocket Oxf. Dict.* (ed. 5) 1035/2 *Maori P.T.,* (sl.) loafing, doing nothing.

3. *black Maori, white Maori* (N.Z.) (see quots.).

1883 *Illustr. Guide Dunedin* 169 (Morris), Tungstate of lime occurs plentifully in the Wakatipu district, where from its weight and colour it is called White Maori by the miners. **1965** G. J. WILLIAMS *Econ. Geol. N.Z.* xiii. 190/2 This hard ferro-manganese material forms the pebbles known to the early alluvial miners as 'black Maori' (as contrasted with 'white Maori'—scheelite).

Maoridom (mauᵊ·ridəm). Also **Maori-dom.** [f. MAORI *sb.* (*a.*) + -DOM.] The Maori world; Maori culture.

1882 W. D. HAY *Brighter Britain!* I. 19 In the very heart of recent Maori-dom. *Ibid.* 278 Auckland city people know little or nothing of Maoridom. **1955** W. J. PHILLIPPS *Maori Carving Illustr.* 8 The tapu system of ancient Maoridom. **1974** *N.Z. Listener* 20 July 11/2, I told him the *Listener* should have an authentic Maori voice speaking in it, a voice that was recognisable throughout Maoridom.

Maoriland (mauᵊ·rilænd). [f. MAORI *sb.* (*a.*) + LAND *sb.*] A name for New Zealand. **Ma·orilander,** a white man born in New Zealand.

1863 F. E. MANING *Old N.Z.* i. 15, I prepared to make my *entrée* into Maori land in a proper and dignified manner. **1881** *Every Boy's Annual* 657/2 Our goose-wing pen bears us lightly down upon the Maori-land. Captain Abel Tasman, a Hollander, in 1642 discovered New Zealand. **1884** K. NICHOLLS (*title*) The King Country, or Explorations in New Zealand: a narrative of 600 miles of travel through Maoriland. **1896** *Melbourne Argus* 22 July 4/8 (Morris), Always something new from Maoriland! **1896** *Melbourne Punch* 9 Apr. 233/2 (Morris), Norman is a pushing young Maorilander. **1915** *Morning Post* 16 June 9/6 The Maorilanders gave 'Hakas' till their voices failed them. **1933** *Bulletin* (Sydney) 4 Jan. 11 A Maoriland youth.

Maoriness (mauᵊ·rinės). [f. MAORI *sb.* (*a.*) + -NESS.] = *MAORITANGA.

1963 *Times* 6 Feb. (Suppl.) p. ii/5 The failure of humanitarianism when confronted with Pakeha land hunger and Maori determination to hold fast to their *Maoritanga* (Maoriness) bred conflict. **1974** *N.Z. Listener* 20 July 10/3, I have a curious kind of status which derives from my work, from the fact of my Maoriness,—such as it is.

‖ **Maoritanga** (mauᵊrita·ŋă). [Maori.] The culture, traditions, and heritage of the Maori people; the individuality of the Maori; Maoriness.

1940 I. L. SUTHERLAND *Maori People Today* v. 176 What then..is meant by *Maoritanga*? It means an emphasis on the continuing individuality of the Maori people, the maintenance of such Maori characteristics and such features of Maori culture as present day circumstances will permit. **1948** N. SMITH *Maori People & Us* ii. 37 He [*sc.* the Maori] is very sensitive about the honour and standing of his tribe, his ancestry, and his *Maoritanga. Ibid.* xi. 218 An improved mode of living among the Maori people can be developed side by side with their *Maoritanga.* **1966** G. W. TURNER *Eng. Lang. Austral. & N.Z.* viii. 171 Should the Maori preserve his separate identity, his *maoritanga,* or should he become Europeanized as much as possible? **1968** B. BIGGS in E. Schwimmer *Maori People in Nineteen-Sixties* 76 Maori are remaining distinctively Maori without their language, often regarded as the *sine qua non* of Maoritanga. **1971** *N.Z. Listener* 8 Mar. 46 Pakehas who try to give Maoris a bad conscience about their knowledge of Maoritanga. **1974** *Ibid.* 20 July 10/4 The old man did the speaking and it gave me considerable pleasure to hear these men, these koruas, steeped in their Maoritanga, steeped in the tribal values and tradition of Tuhoe.

Mao tai (mau tai). Also **Mao Tai, mao-tai, Mao-T'ai, Maotai.** [*Maotai,* name of a town in south-west China.] A mellow and strong pot-stilled spirit produced in Maotai.

1965 O. A. MENDELSOHN *Dict. Drink* 211 Maotai, Chinese strong pot-stilled..spirit as celebrated in the Far East as is cognac in the Western world. **1967** D. BLOODWORTH *Chinese Looking Glass* xxiii. 239 The famous Chinese white wines—Mao-T'ai, Mei-Kuei-Lu, Pai-kan..—have the mule-kick of a bath-tub gin. **1970** *Observer* 10 May 8/4 A glass of *mao-tai,* the potent Chinese equivalent of vodka. **1972** *Guardian* 22 Feb. 24/2 Mr Nixon..consumed little Mao Tai, a potent Chinese drink distilled from sorghum. **1973** *Times* 13 Sept. 16/6 Mao tai, the Chinese national spirit, had increased almost ten-fold in price on the Hongkong market since President Nixon set his lips to it.

map, *sb.*[1] Add: **1. e.** *fig.* In recent phrases: (*a*) *off the map*: out of existence; into (or in) oblivion or an insignificant position; of no account; obsolete; also (with hyphens) as attrib. phr.; (*b*) *on the map*: in an important or prominent position; of some account or importance; in existence (see also quots.); so *to put on the map*: to establish the position or vogue (of someone or something).

(*a*) **1904** W. H. SMITH *Promoters* ii. 54 When she [*sc.* Carthage] wouldn't let up, the only thing left was to wipe her off the map. **1911** R. D. SAUNDERS *Col. Todhunter* vii. 99 A good set-to is the best way..to put a stop to quarrelin'. It just wipes the whole thing off the map. **1914** *Grand Mag.* Jan. 429/2 [He] had been so harried by the Federal officers that he had faded off the map. **1915** *War Illustr.* II. 328/1 One of the curious off-the-map incidents of the war was brought to notice the other day. **1922** *Tatler* 6 Sept. 386/1 A man who owns a lot of coaches..said that the big stuff..was off the map as far as he was concerned. **1924** W. M. RAINE *Troubled Waters* xiii. 143 'Anything new, Matson?'..'Don't forget we've been off the map 'most three weeks.' **1928** *Weekly Dispatch* 13 May 2/6 Cochineal insects, except for making tinctures to colour jellies, are practically off the map today. **1938** E. BOWEN *Death of Heart* I. i. 19 An off-the-map, seedy old family friend. **1973** E. LEMARCHAND *Let or Hindrance* xi. 131 We're a bit off the map up here.

(*b*) **1913** C. E. MULFORD *Coming of Cassidy* viii. 122 Cowan had just put Buckskin on th' map by buildin' th' first shack. **1916** *Munsey's Mag.* June 146/2 'The Fortune Hunter', the play that put Winchell Smith on the dramatists' map. **1918** E. POUND *Let.* 4 June (1971) 138 He [*sc.* Henry James] certainly has put America on the map. Given her a local habitation and a name. **1919** WODEHOUSE *Damsel in Distress* vii. 93 What I mean to say is, you are on the map. You have a sporting chance. **1924** W. M. RAINE *Troubled Waters* xix. 205 Didn't know you knew I was on the map. You're sure honouring me. **1926** A. BENNETT *Lord Raingo* I. xii. 60 Some say if there's two members of the War Cabinet, it isn't Andrew Clyth and Tom Hogarth—it's Andrew Clyth and Andrew Clyth... But that isn't so. Tom's on the map all right. **1934** *B.B.C. Year-Bk.* 74 Weekly Chamber Concerts..further helped to put the Hall 'on the map'. **1944** F. CLUNE *Red Heart* 2 The war has put the Red Heart on the map. **1971** *Daily Tel.* 27 Nov. 12 Nepal is very much on the tourist map today, with many tours to the Far East including a few days there. **1973** *Times* 24 Apr. (São Paulo Suppl.) p. i/7 The exhibition was so successful that in one weekend São Paulo put Brazil firmly on to the export map.

f. A diagram representing the spatial distribution of anything or the relative positions of its components.

1881 *Phil. Trans. R. Soc.* CLXXI. 653 The research..on a method of photography by which the least refrangible end of the solar spectrum could be mapped has reached such a stage that it seems desirable that I should..present a map of the solar spectrum between wave lengths 7600 and 10,750. **1926** *Encycl. Brit.* III. 622/1 An excellent photographic map of this spectrum has been given by T. R. Merton. **1950** W. L. BRAGG *Rev. Recent Adv. X-Ray Analysis* ii. 41 (*caption*) Electron density map of the phthalocyanine molecule (left) and key to the structure (right). **1973** *Nature* 21–28 Dec. 509/1 The ability to record activity in many cells at once would allow the construction of a detailed map of the functional connections within a ganglion.

g. *Genetics.* A diagram which represents the linear order and relative distance apart of the known genes of (part of) a chromosome.

1915 T. H. MORGAN et al. *Mechanism Mendelian Heredity* iii. 64 In the construction of the chromosome maps shown in the frontispiece the distance taken as a unit is that within which 1 per cent. of crossing over will occur. **1935** *Genetics* XX. 317 (*heading*) Cytological and crossover maps. **1935** L. H. SNYDER *Princ. Heredity* xv. 160 (*caption*) Linkage map for *Drosophila melanogaster.* **1939** *Jrnl. Genetics* XXXIX. 335 There is now evidence for the existence of seven sex-linked genes, and for these he has furnished a tentative map. **1954** *Adv. Genetics* VI. 1 (*heading*) Map construction in *Neurospora Crassa.* **1970** AMBROSE & EASTY *Cell Biol.* x. 338 (*caption*) Linear genetic map of *Drosophila* showing the four linkage groups corresponding to the four chromosomes.

2. (Examples.)

1782 COWPER *Hope* in *Poems* I. 171 He draws upon life's map a zig-zag line, That shows how far 'tis safe to follow sin. **1899** W. E. H. LECKY (*title*) The map of life.

d. *slang.* A person's face.

1908 [see *HANG *v.* 25 f]. **1922** WODEHOUSE *Clicking of Cuthbert* ix. 205 The portrait..was that of a man in the early thirties... 'What a map!' exclaimed the young man. **1935** —— *Luck of Bodkins* xv. 178 It's mostly a case of having a map that photographs well. **1936** J. CURTIS *Gilt Kid* xiv. 144 What d'you want to sit there staring at me for? I'm not a bloody oil-painting. You ought to know my map by now.

3*. *Math.* = *MAPPING *vbl. sb.* 2.

1949 [see *INCLUSION 3]. **1966** SZE-TSEN HU *Introd. Gen. Topology* ii. 27 Continuous functions will be called mappings or maps. *Ibid.* 28 A map $f: X \to Y$ from a space X into a space Y. **1971** G. GLAUBERMAN in Powell & Higman *Finite Simple Groups* i. 8 The main tool in investigating this property is the transfer homomorphism of G into S/S'. Unfortunately, we do not have time to define this map.

4. *map-board, -case, -light, paper, reference, -roller*; *map-drawing* vbl. sb.; *map-like* adj. (examples); **map-fire,** artillery-fire in which maps are used for laying the guns; **map-net** = *GRATICULE 2; **map projection** = PROJECTION *sb.* 7; **map-reading** *vbl. sb.,* the inspection and interpretation of a map; so (as a back-formation) **map-read** *v.,* to consult and interpret a map; **map square,** one of several squares (sense 6) drawn on a map for ease of reference.

1947 D. M. DAVIN *Gorse blooms Pale* 192 The G.I. and the A.D.C. vaulted from their perch in the back of the jeep and then bent over it again to get their map-boards. **1916** H. G. WELLS *Mr. Britling* I. v. 181 He..turned over the map in the map-case beside him, and tried to find his position. **1940** 'GUN BUSTER' *Return via Dunkirk* II. xx. 250 The A.C.P.O. and I had indulged ourselves in two expensive rain-proof map-cases. **1948** W. S. CHURCHILL *Second World War* I. II. xxii. 365 A few feet behind me, as I sat in my old chair, was the wooden map-case I had had fixed in 1911, and inside it still remained the chart of the North Sea. **1943** J. S. HUXLEY *Evolutionary Ethics* i. 6 This business of map-drawing. **1971** *Guardian* 25 Feb. 2/4 Israel's formal reply to Cairo's offer is..likely to include the first tentative attempt at 'map drawing' since the six-day war. **1922** *Encycl. Brit.* XXX. 252/2 The precision with which 'map fire' could be carried out. **1963** *Times* 13 Mar. 10 Standard equipment includes two-speed screen wipers and washers—operated from the steering wheel—anti-dazzle mirror, reversing lights, map light and a heating and ventilation system. **1966** L. COHEN *Beautiful Losers* (1970) I. 92 His cufflink gleamed in the maplight. **1920** E. SITWELL *Wooden Pegasus* 60 Our map-like cheeks are painted red. **1935** AUDEN & ISHERWOOD *Dog beneath Skin* 11 Meadows where browse the Shorthorn and the maplike Frisian. **1932** J. W. CAMERON *Maps & Map-Work* iii. 30 A map projection is any definite system of drawing meridians and parallels, the network of lines thus formed being called a *map-net* or *graticule.* **1954** FISHER & LOCKLEY *Sea-Birds* p. xvi, One of these is on a mapnet invented by the late Professor C. B. Fawcett and is used with his permission and that of the Royal Geographical Society. **1942** H. A. MADDOX *Dict. Stationery* (ed. 2) 68 *Map paper,* a specially made smooth cartridge or strong printing paper—opaque, strong and free from atmospheric influence. **1963** R. R. A. HIGHAM *Handbk. Papermaking* vii. 202 Chart and map papers. The best grades are produced from rag pulps, although sulphite and sulphate mixtures are also used. **1890** Map-projection [see TRAPEZIFORM *a.*]. **1905** [see PROJECTION *sb.* 7 b]. **1961** L. D. STAMP *Gloss. Geogr. Terms* 308/1 *Map-projection,* the representation of part or whole of the spheroidal surface of the earth on a plane-surface. **1960** *Lebende Sprachen* V. 166/2 The pilot is flying too high and too fast to map-read his way across country. **1965** D. MACKENZIE *Lonely Side of River* 176 She map-read accurately, giving him plenty of time to respond to her directions. **1968** F. WHITE *Ways of Aquitaine* xii. 161 When one looks at a really fine map..it is easy for anyone who can map-read to see the whole shape of the landscape. **1919** H. SHAW *Text-bk. Aeronaut.* xviii. 208 *Map Reading.*—It is above all necessary for the pilot of a machine to be able to understand a map. **1937** *Discovery* June 192/1 Map-reading classes. *Ibid.,* More maps and yet more maps, is the author's demand..; and more map-reading, too, we must add. **1971** M. MCCARTHY *Birds of America* 10 At a very early age he became a whizz at map-reading. **1954** J. MASTERS *Bhowani Junction* I. vi. 53 This is the map reference the Wimpy gave..where it spotted those men. **1955** E. WAUGH *Officers & Gentlemen* I. ix. 107 The assault of the island was rehearsed..scrambling inland to objectives which in Mugg were merely map-references, but, in the Mediterranean, were gun-emplacements. **1969** M. PUGH *Last Place Left* iii. 18, I..then gave him some of the facts and the map references. **1851** C. CIST *Sk. Cincinnati in 1851* 245 Shade and map-rollers, turning in ivory, done in a superior style. **1917** 'CONTACT' *Airman's Outings* 272, I looked overboard to make certain of the map square.

map, *v.*[1] Add: **1. e.** *trans.* To establish the relative positions, or the spatial relations or distribution, of (the components of).

1881 [see *MAP *sb.*[1] 1 f]. **1950** *Adv. Genetics* III. 117 With linked loci which are closely spaced the recombination value *y* may itself be used as a conventional measure of distance..in which to map the chromosome. **1969** *Times* 13 Feb. 10/3 Professor Jacobson has inverted an eye from young toads..and then mapped the connexions made between the retina and the brain. **1974** *Sci. Amer.* Mar. 122/3 Conformational analysis is the completion of the old program for mapping molecules in space. *Ibid.* 94/2 One laborious method for mapping wave forms consisted in noting a series of voltmeter readings and the corresponding angular positions of the alternator shaft.

f. *Math.* To associate with each element of (a set) one or more elements of another set in accordance with a mapping (sense *2); occas., to associate (an element) similarly. Const. *into, to*; also const. *onto* for a certain kind of mapping (see *ON TO, ONTO *prep.*).

1939 M. H. A. NEWMAN *Elem. Topology of Plane Sets of Points* i. 12 A (1, 1)-correspondence is set up between the set of all positive integers, *I*, and the set of positive even integers, *E*, by mapping *n* of *I* on 2*n* of *E*. *Ibid.* iii. 57 A circle can be mapped continuously on a square region. **1941**, etc. [see *HOMOMORPHICALLY *adv.*]. **1965** PATTERSON & RUTHERFORD *Elem. Abstr. Algebra* ii. 57 The correspondence is one–one and maps G_1/H onto Im *f*. **1971** *Sci. Amer.* Aug. 94/3 The symbolism $f:S\to\mathbf{R}$ expresses the fact that *f* causes each point of *S* to be assigned a value in **R**; the expression is usually read as '*f* maps *S* to **R**' or, more formally, as '*f* is a function from *S* to **R**'.

2. map out. a. (Later example.)

1910 *New Mag.* Nov. 204/2 A new country was mapped out by those two men.

b. (Further examples.)

1853 MRS. GASKELL *Ruth* I. xii. 262 Don't let us perplex ourselves with endeavouring to map out how she should feel, or how she should show her feelings. **1955** *Times* 9 May 10/1 The suggestion was made..to set the ball rolling and map out the times in which later discussion should proceed. **1972** *Daily Tel.* 15 Nov. 1/1 A political plan mapped out by President Lanusse.

3. *intr.* To fall into place on a map or plan.

1893 HARKNESS & MORLEY *Theory of Functions* 338 Show that..lines parallel to the axes map into unipartite Cartesians.

Mapai (mapəi·). [mod. Heb.] A Left-wing party in the State of Israel. Also *attrib.*

1949 KOESTLER *Promise & Fulfilment* II. v. 275 As he does not belong to the inner circle of Mapai,..he can't get a job. **1950** THEIMER & CAMPBELL *Encycl. World Politics* 236 The largest party is the Labour Party known as Mapai..similar in programme to West European labour parties. **1956** *Ann. Reg. 1955* 283 A State trial which had prejudicial consequences for Mapai. **1964** *Ann. Reg. 1963* 297 He had settled in Palestine in 1924 and become editor of a daily Hebrew newspaper of the Mapai Party. **1971** W. LAQUEUR *Dict. Politics* 268 The most powerful party in the *Knesset* is the Israel Labour Party made up of *Mapai*, [etc.].

Mapam (mapā·m). [mod. Heb.] A political party of the far Left in the State of Israel. Also *attrib.*

1950 THEIMER & CAMPBELL *Encycl. World Politics* 236 Mapam..based on the communal agricultural settlements which are a feature of Israel. **1955** *Times* 9 May 9/3 The election should show the relative strength of the..Mapam. **1956** *Ann. Reg. 1955* 284 The extreme Left, Mapam,.. increased their representation. **1972** *Guardian* 27 Mar. 4/2 A meeting between Mrs Meir and Mapam leaders.

mapau (mā-pau). *N.Z.* Also **mapou.** [Maori.] A name for several New Zealand trees, esp. *Myrsine* (or *Suttonia*) *australis*, of the family Myrsinaceæ, an evergreen bearing clusters of white flowers and black berries. Cf. *MATIPO.

1868 *Trans. N.Z. Inst.* I. 37 White Mapau or Piripiriwhata (*Carpodetus serratus*)... Red Mapau (*Myrsine Urvillei*). **1882** W. D. HAY *Brighter Britain!* II. 198 The Mapau..affords good material for fencing. **1889** T. KIRK *Forest Flora N.Z.* 75 By the settlers it is frequently called 'black mapou' on account of the colour of the bark. **1949** P. BUCK *Coming of Maori* (1950) I. iv. 57 The canoe also brought..a *mapau* (*Myrsine urvillei*) named Ateateahenga to be used in planting ceremonies. **1951** *Dict. Gardening* (R. Hort. Soc.) IV. 2057/2 *S*[*uttonia*] *australis*. Mapou. Evergreen tree 10 to 20 ft., or a tall shrub. **1963** POOLE & ADAMS *Trees & Shrubs N.Z.* 166 *M*[*yrsine*] *australis*... Mapou.

maphrodite, aphetic f. HERMAPHRODITE *a.* 4 b.

1849 N. KINGSLEY *Diary* (1914) 33 She is to appearance a bark or maphrodite brig. *Ibid.* 35 Was rousted early this morning to see a ship close along side...she is a Maphrodite Brig.

maple. Add: **1. b.** hedge maple, *Acer campestre.*

1906 *Westm. Gaz.* 13 Nov. 12/2 Every lane is aflame with hedge-maples. **1957** M. HADFIELD *Brit. Trees* 376 Common Maple. *Acer campestre* Linnaeus. Hedge maple, field maple. Usually a small tree..but also seen in hedgerows as a pollard or, owing to repeated cutting, a shrub.

2. b. The colour of maple.

1853 *Heal & Son Catal.* 60/1 Wardrobes, japanned maple, or any colour for gentlemen's use. **1926–7** *Army & Navy Stores Catal.* 297/2 Oil Varnish stains..in the following colours..Mahogany, Rosewood, Maple, Satinwood. **1967** [see *DUCK'S EGG c].

3. *maple forest, timber*; *maple-leaved, -timbered* adjs.; **maple beer,** a beverage made from maple sap; **maple candy,** a sweet made from maple sap; **maple leaf,** a representation of the leaf of the maple tree (as an emblem of Canada); **maple molasses** (examples); **maple pea,** a variety of garden pea with wrinkled seeds; = *maple rouncival*; also *absol.*; **maple sugar** *N. Amer.* (earlier and later examples); **maple swamp,** a swamp in which maple is the prevailing tree; **maple syrup** (examples); hence **maple-syruping** *vbl. sb.*; **maple syrup (urine) disease,** a rare condition which is usu. fatal at a very early age or (if the infant survives) leads to mental deficiency, and is caused by the absence of an enzyme which decarboxylates various metabolites of the amino-acids leucine, isoleucine, and valine, so that these substances are present in high concentrations in the blood and urine and impart a characteristic smell of maple syrup to the latter.

1788 *Amer. Museum* IV. 350/1 *Maple beer.*—To every 4 gallons of water (while boiling) add a quart of maple melasses. **1857** 'PORTE CRAYON' *Virginia Illustr.* I. 23 The table was spread with the best in the house—cold bread and meat..maple beer. **1973** L. RUSSELL *Everyday Life Colonial Canada* viii. 103 Spruce beer, made from the tender twigs of that tree, and maple beer, from the late, weak sap fermented with hops. **1840** *N.Y. Mirror* 4 Apr. 37/2 Your great dealers in Newtown pippins and maple candy. **1879** *Morning Chron.* (Halifax, Nova Scotia) 2 July 1/8 The average boy and a good sized lump of maple candy, form the materials from which we might deduct self-evident conclusion regarding the facility with which attachments are formed in early life. **1975** *Times* 22 Apr. 6 The Prince of Wales samples maple candy while visiting a sugar camp near Ottawa. **1840** *Knickerbocker* XVI. 267 A small and beautiful lake [with]..a rich tract of maple forest on one side. **1910** KIPLING *Rewards & Fairies* 146 Still autumn sets the maple-forest blazing. **1860** *Trans. Lit. & Hist. Soc. Quebec* IV. 20 The Mayflower..I am told is the emblem of Nova Scotia, as the Maple leaf is of Canada. **1900** [in Dict.]. **1964** *Globe & Mail* (Toronto) 29 Oct. 1/9 A single maple leaf on a white field flanked by red bars will be recommended to the House of Commons today as Canada's new flag. **1967** *Canadian Antiques Collector* Jan. 25/1 At least three different Maple leaf forms have been found in the pressed glass patterns of Canada. **1785** H. MARSHALL *Arbustrum Americanum* 77 Maple-leaved Liquidamber Tree or Sweet Gum. **1813** H. MUHLENBERG *Catal. Plant.* 32 Maple-leaved Mealy Tree (*Viburnum acerifolium*). **1930** Maple-leaved [see *London plane*]. **1804** T. G. FESSENDEN *Orig. Poems* 29 The lips of my charmer are sweet, As a hogshead of maple molasses. **1863** 'G. HAMILTON' *Gala-Days* 225 A land flowing with maple molasses and sugar. **1897** C. DURAND *Reminisc.* 83 We made our household sugar, and luscious maple molasses, not mixed as it is now too often with water and common Muscovado sugar. **1733** W. ELLIS *Chiltern & Vale Farming* xxxii. 219 The Maple is a larger and sweeter Pea for the Hog. **1744** —— *Mod. Husbandman* Mar. vi. 53 (*heading*) The Nature and Culture of the common and rouncival Maple Pea. **1960** *Farmer & Stockbreeder* 23 Feb. 4/2 For maples interest is mostly restricted to seed lots. **1969** *Times* 14 Jan. 8/6 One pigeon, encouraged by occasional rewards of maple peas fed to it..learnt to glide in a stationary position in a wind tunnel so that its performance could be measured. **1720** *Phil. Trans. R. Soc.* XXXI. 27 Maple Sugar is made of the Juice of Upland Maple, or Maple Trees that grow upon the Highlands. **1852** A. CARY *Clovernook* 74 Everyday in winter she used to feed them [*sc.* the bees] maple-sugar if she had it. **1885** 'MARK TWAIN' in *Century Mag.* XXXI. 195/2 We occupied an old maple-sugar camp. **1907** *Springfield* (Mass.) *Weekly Republ.* 9 May 16 The Holyoke canoe club opened the river year with a maple-sugar eat at their club-house. **1921** *Daily Colonist* (Victoria, B.C.) 30 Mar. 3/6 Up to the present the weather has not been favourable for the manufacture of maple sugar in the district of Quebec. **1931** W. CATHER *Shadows on Rock* v. i. 204 The country people had been coming..bringing maple sugar, spruce beer. **1969** E. H. PINTO *Treen* 94/1 Maple Sugar Moulds...early 19th-century, carved wood moulds for maple sugar, from Quebec Province, Canada. **1974** *Country Life* 3–10 Jan. 28/3 Maple sugar was..often the only source of sugar available to pioneers in the backwoods. **1667** *Early Rec. Providence, Rhode Island* (1894) V. 317 Standing on the west Side of a Maple Swampe. **1789** J. MORSE *Amer. Geogr.* 143 One species generally predominating in each soil has originated the descriptive names of..maple, ash and cedar swamps. **1855** *Knickerbocker* XLVI. 225 Cutting hoop-poles in the maple swamps. **1849** in *Glimpses of Past* (Missouri Hist. Soc.) (1933) I. 5 At the different houses they received sugar, coffee, lard, candles, flour, maple syrup, [etc.]. **1885** *Outing* Oct. VII. 77/1 A moment later, all smoking and puffy and swimming in maple sirup, it disappears. **1905** CALKINS & HOLDEN *Art of Mod. Advertising* 113 Maple-sirup is a product to which justice has never been done. [**1954** J. H. MENKES et al. in *Pediatrics* XIV. 462 (*heading*) A new syndrome: progressive familial infantile cerebral dysfunction associated with an unusual urinary substance... A characteristic feature of their illness was the passage of urine with an odor strikingly similar to that of maple syrup. **1957** *Amer. Jrnl. Dis. Children* XCIV. 571/2 (*heading*) Maple sugar urine disease.] **1959** *Brit. Med. Jrnl.* 10 Jan. 90/1 (*heading*) 'Maple syrup urine disease.' An inborn error of the metabolism of valine, leucine, and isoleucine associated with gross mental deficiency. *Ibid.* 92/2 A disease which may be related to 'maple syrup disease'. **1967** MRS. L. B. JOHNSON *White House Diary* 11 June (1970) 527 We went in to breakfast..., including blueberry pancakes, and, naturally, Vermont maple syrup. **1968** PASSMORE & ROBSON *Compan. Med. Stud.* I. xi. 23/1 Maple syrup disease, so rare as to be a clinical curiosity, is an inborn error of metabolism. **1969** *New Scientist* 3 July 10/1 Prevention of postnatal brain damage by dietary treatment has been reported in a number of other inborn errors of metabolism. Examples include galactosaemia, tyrosinosis, maple syrup urine disease and possibly homocystinuria. **1973** J. DRUMMOND *Bang! Bang! You're Dead!* xv. 39 A pretty girl, with a small cute body the colour of maple syrup. **1975** *Budget* (Sugarcreek, Ohio) 20 Mar. 3/8, March 17—Very damp on the outside again. Ideal weather for maple syruping. **1845** C. M. KIRKLAND *Western Clearings* 3 He had purchased fine farming land and maple timber. **1849** *Ex. Doc. 31st U.S. Congress 1 Sess. House* No. 5. II. 631 At 7½ a.m., went over good maple-timbered land to corner.

maple tree. (Further examples.)

1660 *Early Rec. Warwick, Rhode Island* (1926) 322 Bounded by a mapell tree on the Northwest corner. **1700** *Early Rec. Providence, Rhode Island* (1893) IV. 139 The maple tree is the north east Corner bound. **1810** F. A. MICHAUX *Hist. Arbres Forestiers de l'Amérique Septentrionale* I. 28 Red flowering maple,..Swamp maple,..Soft maple..[ou] Maple tree..dans Pensylvanie, la Virginia, et l'Ohio. **1867** J. N. EDWARDS *Shelby* xx. 337 To send the blood coursing through his veins like the sap in the maple-trees. **1974** *Country Life* 3–10 Jan. 28/1 One of the earliest..signs that the winter freeze is coming to an end is the sight of buckets hanging on the trunks of maple trees.

mapling (mē·pliŋ), *sb.* [f. MAPLE.] A ripple-like figure in wood, characteristic of maple.

1909 W. BATESON *Mendel's Princ. Heredity* 144 A damasked pattern showing where the mapling would have been if the plant had been a coloured one.

mappable (mæ·păb'l), *a.* [f. MAP *v.*[1] + -ABLE.] That may be represented on or by a map.

1920 A. S. EDDINGTON *Space, Time & Gravitation* vi. 106 Hurdle-counts will no longer be accurately mappable on a plane sheet of paper, because they do not conform to Euclidean geometry. **1969** BENNISON & WRIGHT *Geol. Hist. Brit. Isles* i. 14 A bed of particular lithology, and mappable as a recognizable stratigraphic unit. **1974** *Nature* 8 Feb. 344/2 In area 105 a mappable disconformity has been recognised at a stratigraphic level just above the KBS Tuff.

Hence **mappabi·lity.**

1969 *Proc. Geol. Soc.* Aug. 145 Vertical and lateral boundaries should be based on the lithological criteria that provide the greatest unity and practical utility (i.e. essentially, mappability).

mapping, *vbl. sb.* Add: **b.** *Genetics.* The making of a genetic map (*MAP *sb.*[1] 1 g); the process of determining the chromosomal position of a gene in relation to other genes.

1935 L. H. SNYDER *Princ. Heredity* xv. 153 (*heading*) The mapping of chromosomes. **1965** *Genetics* LI. 157 (*heading*) Mapping of temperature-sensitive mutants in bacteriophage T5. **1967** *Jrnl. Molecular Biol.* XXVII. 163 (*heading*) Genetic mapping in *Bacillus subtilis*. **1969** A. M. CAMPBELL *Episomes* i. 7 Of special interest was the mapping of the Hfr character itself. **1970** AMBROSE & EASTY *Cell Biol.* x. 334 (*heading*) Gene mapping with *Drosophila*.

2. *Math.* A correspondence by which each element of a given set has associated with it one element (occas., one or more elements) of a second set. (Some topologists use *transformation* in this sense and *mapping* in the narrower sense of a continuous transformation.)

1931 H. P. ROBERTSON tr. *Weyl's Theory of Groups & Quantum Mech.* iii. 110 A mapping or correspondence *S*.. is determined by a law which associates with each point *p* of the field a point *p'* as image. **1935** [see *HOMOMORPHIC *a.* 2]. **1958** G. T. WHYBURN *Topological Analysis* ii. 24 A continuous transformation will be called a mapping. **1964** W. J. PERVIN *Found. Gen. Topology* i. 10 Other terms for mapping are 'function', 'transformation', and 'operator'. **1966** F. M. HALL *Introd. Abstr. Algebra* I. ix. 156 If the mapping θ is between the object space *A* and image space *B* we write $\theta:A\to B$ (a mapping θ of *A* into *B*). **1968** M. BRUCKHEIMER et al. *Math. for Technol.* ii. 17 An example of a one–many mapping is the mapping $a\to\pm\sqrt{a}$ of the set of non-negative real numbers to the set of all real numbers. **1971** *Nature* 17 Dec. 396/2 The ideal transducer..neither stores nor dissipates energy; viewed as a mapping from input space, (e_1, f_1), to output space (e_2, f_2), $e_1f_1+e_2f_2=0$.

‖ **maquereau** (makəro). Pl. **-eaux.** [Fr.] = MACKEREL[2].

In quot. 1920 the form with final *-o* is idiosyncratic.

1898 A. M. BINSTEAD *Pink 'Un & Pelican* xi. 256 His head was pounded like a Hamburg steak, and sixty-five dollars rolled into the basket, principally contributed by the females who had been accustomed to support the maquereau during his life. **1919** C. MACKENZIE *Sylvia & Michael* i. 21 The officer..called him a *maquereau*. **1920** E. POUND *Hugh Selwyn Mauberley* 14 Bewildered that a world Shows no surprise At her last maquero's Adulteries. **1922** F. M. FORD *Let.* 15 Aug. (1965) 144 It is really too much to expect the very mildest of men to aid in sharpening a pen whose sole occupation is the describing of himself as, let us say, maquereau. **1933** 'G. ORWELL' *Down & Out* x. 78, I counted the number of times I was called *maquereau* during the day. **1939** E. AMBLER *Mask of Dimitrios* xi. 214 The clientèle began to change... We had ..more *maquereaux* and fewer gentlemen, more *poules* and fewer *chic* ladies. **1971** D. WALLIS *Bad Luck Girl* I. iii. 30 No girl..goes on ship these days. They..lead you to some place where her *maquer*[*e*]*au* can slug you.

maquette (măke·t). [Fr. (1752), ad. It. *macchietta* speck, little spot, dim. of *macchia* spot, f. *macchiare* to spot, stain, f. L. *maculāre*;

cf. MACULATE v.] A small preliminary model, in wax or clay, etc., or a preliminary painted sketch, from which a work in sculpture is elaborated. Also *transf.* and *fig.*

1903 *Athenæum* 24 Jan. 122/3 M. J. B. E. Detaille has, after a long delay, executed four *maquettes*, each comprehending three large panels. **1926** W. J. LOCKE *Stories Near & Far* 78 The maquette or model in clay. **1951** H. READ *Meaning of Art* (ed. 3) II. 240 The sculptor's maquette, or model, was reproduced, generally by other hands, either by being cast in bronze, or by being reproduced to scale by mechanical methods in marble. **1958** *Times* 8 Oct. 6/4 One might describe his art as a prolonged *maquette* for some ultimate synthesis or other. **1965** ZIGROSSER & GAEDHE *Guide to Collecting Orig. Prints* ii. 16 In some instances, the artist has actively collaborated in the adaptation of his own *maquette*, or sketch, by working on the plates or stones, and by 'proving' and approving the color separations. **1970** *Country Life* 31 Dec. 1280/3 This was the noble terra-cotta of a mourning woman..the maquette for the figure of the wife on the Westminster Abbey monument to the poet Nicholas Rowe. **1972** P. MARKS *Collector's Choice* iii. 181, I don't know why you had to go out and buy those Carpeaux maquettes last week. **1973** *Times* 11 Apr. 6/4 (*caption*) A maquette of Henry Moore's 'Family Group'.

‖ **maquillage** (makiyāʒ). [Fr., f. *maquiller* to make up one's face, f. OF. *masquiller* to stain, alt. of OF. *mascurer* to darken.] The action of applying make-up to one's face; also, make-up, cosmetics; also *transf.* Hence **maquilla·ged** *a.* made up.

1892 *Ladies' Home Jrnl.* Dec. 8/2 All this is..thrown away upon the devotees of maquillage. **1921** M. SADLEIR *Privilege* vi. 82 It was a relief to find Anthony innocent, at least, of maquillage. **1929** D. H. LAWRENCE *Pansies* 55 The caged mind..leaves a rind Of maquillage and pose and malice to shame the brutes. **1938** E. AMBLER *Cause for Alarm* iii. 47 The edge of a heavy and clumsily applied *maquillage*. **1941** 'R. WEST' *Black Lamb* (1942) II. 417 Doubly dazzling with the radiance of a Slav blonde and the maquillage of her profession. **1957** S. GAINHAM *Cold Dark Night* iv. 49 Her voice did not rise and there seemed no change in the beautifully maquillaged face. **1959** R. GRAVES *Coll. Poems* 304 Confirming hazardous relationships By kindly maquillage of Truth's pale lips. **1972** *Daily Tel.* 25 Sept. 7/3 Plastering the players all over with visual and aural *maquillage* in the form of endlessly changing lights and phonic effects.

maquis (ma·ki). Also **macquis**, (erron.) **maqui.** [Fr., 'brushwood, scrub', ad. Corsican It. *macchia* thicket, *MACCHIA, f. L. *macula* spot.] **1.** The dense scrub characteristic of certain Mediterranean coastal regions, esp. in Corsica, often used as a refuge by fugitives. Also applied to similar areas of scrub or brushwood elsewhere.

1858 T. FORESTER *Rambles Corsica & Sardinia* viii. 65 There are also..several lagoons on the coast, of which the Stagna di Biguglia, near which we turned off into the *maquis*, is the largest. **1900** 'H. S. MERRIMAN' *Isle of Unrest* xxii. 246 It is..usual for a man to take to the macquis the moment that he finds himself involved in some trouble. **1906** CONRAD *Mirror of Sea* xlii. 259 Dominic's brother had to go into the *maquis*, into the bush on the wild mountain-side. **1913** A. HUXLEY *Let.* 30 July (1969) 52 The maquis..is thicker than anything I've ever seen before, oak, hazel, maple, wild cherry and a pine or two in the more open spaces. **1923** *Nature* 24 Feb. 268/2 These types of vegetation, like the Mediterranean 'maqui', develop in regions of winter rains and long dry summers. **1932** *Forestry* VI. 173 The nature of the undergrowth—dense shrubby maquis. **1945** G. MILLAR *Maquis* xi. 226 Boulaya met us with a long face in the Maquis. **1957** J. BRAINE *Room at Top* xv. 136 The village ends abruptly.. beyond it is nothing but the moors..and a solitary farmhouse a mile west. That too has a military air; the moors are Gilden's maquis and behind its walls are planned the sudden raid..the ambush. **1966** J. BERRISFORD *Wild Garden* 167 The Jerusalem Sage..may be used to form a ground-smothering *maquis* in conjunction with cistuses, lavenders, rosemary and other sun-loving shrubs. **1973** *Daily Tel.* 13 Oct. 9/6 We were..standing in a hillside garden in the Alpes Maritimes. Around us spread the maquis for unending miles. **1975** *Islander* (Victoria, B.C.) 9 Feb. 5/2 Most of the vegetation [in Corsica] is not forest as we know it..but a tangled growth called maquis.

2. *transf.* A secret army of patriots in France during the German occupation in the war of 1939–45, so named from their being conceived as hiding in country of this kind; also, a member of this army. Also in extended use (applied to similar groups) and *attrib.*

1944 *Ann. Reg. 1943* 230 The patriots of the 'maquis' fought with admirable courage. **1944** *New Statesman* 27 May 346/2 The Italian *Maquis*, whose guerrilla operations ..are now being co-ordinated and encouraged by the Allied Command. **1944** *Hutchinson's Pict. Hist. War* 12 Apr.–26 Sept. 523 (*caption*) Field-Marshal Montgomery stops his car to have a word with a Maquis guard. **1945** W. S. CHURCHILL *Victory* (1946) 7 The tributes which are paid to the heroic French or Belgian Maquis. **1951** N. ANNAN *Leslie Stephen* iv. 160 Victorian thinkers..appeared to be unaware of the spiritual maquis burrowing underground in Europe. **1965** B. SWEET-ESCOTT *Baker St. Irreg.* vii. 205 If it had still been considered important to raise a maquis in Hungary, it might well have been worth exploring. **1966** M. R. D. FOOT *SOE in France* xi. 365 A large group of maquis known to exist in the Auvergne mountains.

3. *attrib.* and *Comb.*

1937 *Brit. Birds* Sept. 98 Small parties were seen.. flying about the maquis-covered slopes. **1944** *Times* 24 Apr. 5/6 The *maquis* country is usually thought of as confined to Haute-Savoie. It is in fact much more extensive. **1971** *Homes & Gardens* Sept. 89/1 Panoramic vistas of maquis-covered foothills merging into the stark blue inland peaks of over 2,500 feet. **1974** J. THOMSON *Long Revenge* ii. 22 The Maquis radio operator..contacted us.

Hence **maquisard** (makizār), a member of the maquis. Also *transf.* and *attrib.*

1944 *Times* 24 Apr. 5/7 Often enough the *maquisards* have had to fight against heavy odds... Today..the situation is better. Arms are reaching the *maquis* in growing volume. **1945** G. MILLAR *Maquis* v. 85 The grey-headed Maquisard, a local railway worker in peace-time. **1959** *Economist* 3 Jan. 23/2 He has always insisted that, except for a tiresome band of *maquisards* in the eastern extremity of the island [Cuba], everything was under control. **1963** N. FREELING *Gun before Butter* II. 103 During the war presumably, he had got acquainted with the border. Maquisard formation, doubtless. **1967** 'E. PETERS' *Black is Colour* viii. 152 The moustache that would have done credit to a Corsican *maquisard*. **1973** *Times* 18 Jan. 19/6 The German onslaught..was disastrous to the maquisards who stayed and fought.

mar, *sb.* Add: **3.** *Comb.*: **mar resistance**, resistance to loss of gloss by abrasion; so *mar-resistant* adj.

1942 L. BOOR in *Mod. Plastics* Sept. 80/2 Depending on the type of plastic under consideration, various methods of evaluating the optical degradation of the test areas may be used... The particular aspect of hardness of which this test is a measure has been given the tentative designation 'mar resistance'. **1969** C. O. RASPOR in W. R. R. Park *Plastics Film Technol.* iv. 87 The gloss of the marred area is measured and compared to the unabraded film to determine the mar resistance. **1973** *Washington Post* 13 Jan. C3/4 (Advt.), Seven-drawer kneehole desk..with mar-resistant top.

Mar[2] (māɹ). [Aramaic.] An honorific title for saints and higher clergy, chiefly in the Nestorian and Jacobite churches.

1694 M. GEDDES tr. *Hist. Church of Malabar* 11 Their Bishop at that time..was one Mar Joseph, who..had been sent thither by Mar Audixa, Patriarch of Babylon. **1864** G. B. HOWARD *Christians of St. Thomas* iv. 154 In the year 1856 a certain Mar Athanasius Stephanos made his appearance,..claiming to be the rightful Metropolitan of the Christians of St. Thomas. **1892** G. M. RAE *Syrian Church in India* xix. 304 The first native of Malabar that ever received consecration..was Mar Athanasius Matthew. *Ibid.* 309 The pretensions of Mar Koorilos were finally disposed of; Mar Dionysius resigned his dignity..; Mar Athanasius was by royal proclamation declared metropolitan. **1933** *Downside Rev.* LI. 399 Fr Hugh Conolly was editing a number of Texts and Studies consisting of a translation of certain Syriac liturgical homilies of Mar Narsai, a fifth century Nestorian writer. **1956** N. ZERNOV *Christian East* ix. 103 In 1665 a Monophysite bishop, Mar Gregorius, arrived in South India from Palestine. *Ibid.* 105 The Bishops Mar Mathew Athanasius and Mar Thomas Athanasius formed a separate Church, now known under the name of the Mar Thoma Church. **1964** P. F. ANSON *Bishops at Large* 27 They have given themselves impressive ecclesiastical titles,..Hierarch, Mar, Metropolitan.. and so on.

mar, *v.* Add: **2. b.** Also *absol.*

c **1420, 1542** [see MAKE *v.*[1] 46 b]. **1853** MRS. GASKELL *Ruth* III. i. 43 For the present she would neither meddle nor mar in Ruth's course of life. *c* **1865** G. M. HOPKINS *Poems* (1967) 121 So be it; I must maim and mar. **1889** [see MAKE *v.*[1] 46 b].

mar-. *mar-feast* (further examples) (*arch.*).

1887 W. MORRIS tr. *Homer's Odyssey* XVII. 446 What God this plague, this mar-feast, hath hither sent to us? **1922** JOYCE *Ulysses* 710 Superannuated bailiff's man, marfeast, lickplate, spoilsport, [etc.].

marabou[1]. Add: **3.** (Further *attrib.* examples.)

1929 *Times* 31 Oct. 11/6 An attractive bridge coat..in artificial silk velvet finished with a marabout collar. **1975** *Lady* 1 May 801/1 Marabou cap and muff.

marabunta (mærăbʊ·ntă). [Native name.] In Guyana, a name used for several social wasps. Also *attrib.*

1883 E. F. IM THURN *Among Indians Guiana* v. 150 The wasps vary much more in general appearance and size, some of them being large and beautifully coloured insects. The forest-dwelling social species are indiscriminately called by the colonists marabuntas. **1898** H. KIRKE *25 Yrs. Brit. Guiana* iii. 76 A large brown wasp, called a marabunta, builds his pretty paper combs under the eaves and galleries of our houses; his sting is severe. **1918** C. W. BEEBE *Jungle Peace* (1919) iv. 81, I listened to the buzzing of a *marabunta* wasp. **1934** E. WAUGH *Handful of Dust* v. 267 A marabunta had left a painful swelling on his left hand. **1958** J. CAREW *Black Midas* i. 12 Marabuntas built clay nests in the thatch. *Ibid.* vi. 141 Tonic and Woody Sam removed spiders, cobwebs, marabunta nests ..from the roof.

maraca (măræ·kă). Also **maracca.** [Pg. *maracá*, prob. from Tupi (Webster).] Usu. *pl.* A Latin-American percussion instrument made from the dried shell of a gourd or other material with beans or beads, etc., inside to produce a rattling sound; a gourd rattle. Also *attrib.*

1824 H. E. LLOYD tr. *Spix & Martius's Travels in Brazil* II. IV. ii. 226 The *Maracá*, a longish gourd shell, filled with maize, fastened to a handle, with which in their dancing, they make a rattling as with castanets. **1928** *Vanity Fair* (N.Y.) Nov. 72 A fashionable evening event along the Havana water-front is a concert by black boys with their primitive African instruments, the bongo, timbales, guiro, maracas, and claves. **1933** *Punch* 4 Jan. 6/3 It [*sc.* the rumba] may be recognised by a number of taps produced in rapid succession... They are made by a couple of maraccas in the orchestra... Maraccas..are the dried husks of the calabash fruit. **1952** [see *ELLINGTONIAN *a.* and *sb.*]. **1954** J. STEINBECK *Sweet Thursday* ii. 16 An orchestra took shape—two guitars, a guitarón, rhythm and maraca men. **1966** *Melody Maker* 23 July 10/5 Alan Haven mentioned maracca sticks and jingle-sticks. **1971** 'E. ANTHONY' *Tamarind Seed* i. 13 A coal-black barman ..rattling a shaker as if he were playing the maraccas. **1972** *Jazz & Blues* Sept. 5/1 The almost African rhythms with much maracca shaking.

marae. Add: Now usu. with pronunc. (mæ·rəi). The sense in Dict. is now only *Hist.* (Later examples.) Now, among Polynesian peoples, a space in front of a meeting-house or among the houses of a village, set apart for social functions. Also *fig.*

1877 RANKEN in *Jrnl. R. Anthrop. Inst.* VI. 236 The *marais*, or terraced enclosures for sacred purposes, are exactly like those of Mexico and Peru. **1905** W. B. *Where White Man Treads* 276 Every order and tribal regulation had to be decided in meeting-house convened, and proclaimed in the marae (village green) to the whole people. **1910** J. COWAN *Maoris N.Z.* xxxi. 338 We fall in on the river bank for the parade up to the village *marae*. **1910** C. G. SELIGMANN *Melanesians Brit. New Guinea* xx. 223 Each local group of each clan has..at least one *marea* [sic], which serves as the meeting place for the men of the local group, and is their clubhouse in the fullest sense of the term. **1924** R. W. WILLIAMSON *Social & Pol. Syst. Cent. Polynesia* I. x. 350 This *male* was, I presume, a *malae* or open space where meetings..were held, as in Samoa and Tonga. *Ibid.* II. xv. 60 In some islands the *marae* or *malae* was merely an open space..along with a special wooden house erected in it. **1934** *Nature* 10 Nov. 740/2 The turtle.. was the food of the gods [in Tahiti], eaten only by chiefs and keepers of the marae. **1943** N. MARSH *Colour Scheme* ix. 166 They were hangin' about the Marae in groups. **1949** P. H. BUCK *Coming of Maori* (1950) IV. iii. 480 Turning to New Zealand, it is a curious fact that the two fundamental features of the central Polynesian temples were not combined but remained as distinct entities. Thus the open court, distinguished by the term *marae*, is retained as a secular feature in front of the tribal or family meeting houses. **1959** A. MCLINTOCK *Descr. Atlas N.Z.* 72 In the country proper [i.e. rural districts] the Maori has retained his traditional mode of life which is symbolised in the *marae*. In a literal sense the term means the open courtyard in front of the communal meeting house; today, however, it embraces all aspects of community life—community buildings, tribal gatherings, church activities, and recreation. **1959** TINDALE & LINDSAY *Rangatira* iii. 32 The open-air marae temple, floored with slabs of basalt. *Ibid.* x. 93 They entertained their guests on the open marae ground among the houses. **1963** *Weekly News* (Auckland) 1 May 6/6 Dominating the marae was a cross 40 feet high illuminated with coloured lights. **1969** *Islander* (Victoria, B.C.) 6 July 5/2 The design [of a hotel in Tahiti] is reminiscent of ancient Tahitian outdoor worshipping temples (marae). **1974** *N.Z. Listener* 20 July 10/3 There was a group being welcomed on to the marae as I arrived.

marage (mā·rēidʒ), *v.* *Metallurgy.* [f. MAR(TENSITE + AGE *v.*] *trans.* To allow (a maraging alloy) to cool slowly in the air so that it develops great strength without significant changes in dimensions as a result of the transformation of austenite to martensite and subsequent age-hardening of the martensite.

1962 *Trans. Amer. Soc. Metals* LV. 524/2 Specimens were initially maraged at one temperature, and then maraged for various times at a second temperature. **1963** *Engineering* 24 May 715 When homogenized and maraged it [*sc.* steel] is claimed not to be notch sensitive despite its exceptional strength.

So **ma·raged** *ppl. a.*, **ma·raging** *vbl. sb.*, esp. in *marag(e)ing alloy, steel*, steel that has been or may be hardened by maraging, generally containing up to 25 per cent nickel and smaller amounts of titanium, cobalt, molybdenum, or other elements.

1961 *Engineering* 24 Mar. 407/3 The original American release says that the steel develops its high strength by means of a remarkably easy heat treatment involving age-hardening of martensite. For this they have invented a term 'mar-aging'. **1962** *Trans. Amer. Soc. Metals* LV. 61/2 Maraged hardness increased linerly [*sic*] as the product, cobalt times molybdenum, increased. *Ibid.* 529/2 In annealing of 18% Ni maraging steel, temperatures in the range 1100 to 1300 F should be avoided to prevent retained austenite. **1968** R. KUMAR *Physical Metall. Iron & Steel* xi. 292 In marageing alloys, the role of interstitial carbon in raising the strength of steel is taken over by substantial amounts of nickel, cobalt, and molybdenum. *Ibid.*, Maraged steel is hardened without as much sacrifice of ductility. **1969** *Times* 2 May (Suppl.) p. iv/8 The Deep Quest, which has reached 8,350 ft., the deepest point yet attained by a submersible, has a hull of maraging steel of high strength allied to exceptional toughness and weldability. **1970** *McGraw-Hill Yearbk. Sci. & Technol.* 348/2 Hardening by maraging does not produce distortion or surface softening..so that no machining is necessary after hardening. **1972** T. H. G. MEGSON *Aircraft Struct.* vii. 204 Maraging steels have been used as: aircraft arrester hooks, rocket motor cases, in helicopter undercarriages, gears, ejector seats and various structural forgings.

marahuana, marajuana, varr. *MARIJUANA, MARIHUANA.

Maranao (mæ·rănau). Also **Maranaw.** [ad. Maranao *Maranáw*, f. *ranaw* lake.] **a.** A Moro people inhabiting the province of Lanao del Sur and parts of central Cotabato province in the island of Mindanao (in the Republic of the Philippines), and some areas of northern Borneo. **b.** The Austronesian language of these people.

1957 [see *ILLANO]. **1962** H. C. CONKLIN in J. A. Fishman *Readings Sociol. of Lang.* (1968) 429 Pronoun systems in Tagalog, Ilocano.., Maranao.., and some other Philippine languages. **1963** H. OSTELIUS *Islands of Pleasure* xiii. 78 There are also the inland Moros. The Maranao and Magindanaw are farmers... Because their main home is located around Lake Lanao on the island of Mindanao the Maranaos are commonly called the Lake Moros. **1968** J. KIRKUP *Filipinescas* viii. 154 The noble movements.. portrayed a Maranaw warrior. **1969** J. COCKCROFT *Philippines* 55 About 87 different languages and dialects are spoken in the Philippines... Tagalog, spoken in Manila,..Maranao, in Lanao. **1974** *Encycl. Brit. Micropædia* VI. 595/1 Like other Filipino Muslims, the Maranao differ markedly from the Christians. **1975** *Language* LI. 365 At the opposite extreme is a language like Maranao, in which there seems to be a specific Voice morpheme for each possible realization of a verb's subcategorization feature.

Maranatha. (Further examples.)

1846 W. F. HOOK *Church Dict.* (ed. 5) 598 *Maranatha* could not be any part of the form of excommunication, but only a reason for pronouncing *Anathema* against those who express their hatred against Christ, by denying His coming. **1913** F. B. MACNUTT *Advent Certainties* vi. 97 To the Corinthian Christian and to St. Paul alike 'Maran atha' was the expression of a supreme reality..which is the keynote of the New Testament. **1926** A. CHAMBERS tr. *Arseniew's Mysticism & Eastern Church* II. vi. 123 And, finally, the closing cry quivering with joyous awe: *Maranatha* ('Come, our Lord!'). This appeal in Aramaic takes us back to the earliest period of the primitive Church in Jerusalem. **1961** NEW ENG. BIBLE *1 Cor.* xvi. 22 *Marana tha*—Come, O Lord! **1964** E. A. NIDA *Toward Sci. Transl.* viii. 170 Such expressions as 'Abba Father', *Maranatha*, and 'baptized into Christ' could be used with reasonable expectation that they would be understood.

maraschino. Delete || and add: **1. b.** Also, **maraschino cherry,** a cherry preserved in real or imitation maraschino.

1905 'O. HENRY' in *N.Y. World Mag.* 22 Jan. 2/1 The world seemed no larger than the seed of a Maraschino cherry in a table d'hote grapefruit. **1918–19** *T. Eaton & Co. Catal.* Fall & Winter 385/1 Luscious Whole Red Maraschino Cherries in a semi-liquid cream, coated with fine chocolate. **1961** [see *CRÈME 1 b]. **1964** J. DRUMMOND *Welcome, Proud Lady* xxi. 96 Maraschino cherries, olives, sliced lemon, salted nuts were arranged in small crystal bowls.

marasmus. Delete || and add to def.: esp. in undernourished children. (Further examples.)

1902 W. G. THOMPSON *Pract. Dietetics* (ed. 2) VIII. 564 Marasmus is a form of starvation occurring chiefly in artificially fed infants, but also in those at the breast, in whom there is great wasting of the muscular and other soft tissues. **1951** R. W. B. ELLIS *Dis. in Infancy & Childhood* vii. 254 Marasmus (Infantile atrophy). This is a condition of extreme and chronic malnutrition, and whilst it often arises simply from underfeeding, it may also be due to a variety of other causes, e.g. congenital syphilis ..or parasitic infection. It is not therefore a disease *sui generis* but a clinical picture of which it is first necessary to determine the etiology. **1968** MENEGHELLO & RIZZARDINI in A. Dorfman *Child Care in Health & Dis.* iii. 42 Almost all children in Chile suffer from so-called caloric-protein malnutrition, or marasmus, and this form of malnutrition is the major problem in Chile... The other form, protein malnutrition or kwashiorkor, is the most common type in other countries of the region. **1971** *Sci. Amer.* Oct. 14/3 They have advanced the understanding of the starvation disease called marasmus, which is increasing in many developing countries because mothers are giving up prolonged breast-feeding and their infants are not receiving an adequate substitute diet during a critical time in development.

Maratha, var. MAHRATTA.

1858 [see MAHRATTA 3]. **1886** KIPLING *Departmental Ditties* (ed. 2) 7 Rajah Rustum..Roused his Secretariat to a fine Maratha fury. **1913** E. M. FORSTER *Let.* 1 Jan. in *Hill of Devi* (1953) 21 Cocked rakishly over one ear was a Maratha Turban of scarlet and gold. **1925** S. N. SEN *Administrative Syst. Marathas* (ed. 2) p. vii, The Marathas ..engaged in a life and death struggle. **1942** *R.A.F. Jrnl.* 13 June 4 The Maratha heirs of Sivalji. **1971** R. RUSSELL tr. *Ahmad's Shore & Wave* i. 10 The Mughal Empire fell and the Marathas overspread the land. **1973** *Times* 16 Jan. 12/2 For years..the cry of economic exploitation by the dominant Maratha caste to the south has been raised.

Marathi. Delete 'obs.' and add examples.

1827, 1868 [see MAHRATTI]. **1875, 1880** [see *KANARESE *a.* and *sb.*]. **1908** T. G. TUCKER *Introd. Nat. Hist. Lang.* 187 Marāthi in the north-west Deccan. **1925** S. N. SEN *Administrative Syst. Marathas* (ed. 2) 2 Next in importance, are the *bakhars* or Marathi prose chronicles. **1933** L. BLOOMFIELD *Lang.* iv. 63 Such great languages as Marathi. **1949** 'G. ORWELL' *Note-Bk.* in *Coll. Ess.* (1968) IV. 513 We always had difficulty with the Marathi newsletter. **1953** E. M. FORSTER *Hill of Devi* 41 He could recall his father reciting in Marathi the ballads and epics of their race. **1958** A. TOYNBEE *East to West* xxxii. 99 If the city [*sc.* Bombay] had been merged in a separate Marathi-speaking state, [etc.]. **1967** 'W. HAGGARD' *Conspirators* ii. 20 His parents had spoken Marathi, beautiful Brahmin's Marathi. **1971** *Illustr. Weekly India* 25 Apr. 21/2 The personal feelings of eminent Marathi poet P. S. Rege. **1971** *Femina* (Bombay) 30 Apr. 16/2 (Advt.), In four languages: English, Hindi, Gujarati and Marathi. **1971** H. R. F. KEATING *Inspector Ghote goes by Train* II. ix. 211 He ordered in Hindi. He ordered in Marathi. He ordered in crude English.

marathon (mæ·răþǫn). Also **Marathon.** [The place-name *Marathon* (Gr. Μαραθών) on the north-east coast of Attica: see MARATHONIAN *a.*] **a.** The name first given on the occasion of the revived Olympic Games held in Athens in 1896 to a long-distance foot-race (now usu. of 26 miles 385 yards), with allusion to the run of Pheidippides at the time of the battle at Marathon in 490 B.C., as recorded in Herodotus and later sources. Also *attrib.*

Herodotus records that Pheidippides ran from Athens to Sparta to secure aid before the battle, but the race instituted in 1896 was based on a later less sound tradition that Pheidippides ran from Marathon to Athens with news of the Persian defeat.

1896 *Fortn. Rev.* June 950 We now come to the great glory of the Greeks—the victory in the Marathon Race. **1905** *Programme of Olympic Games Athens 1906* 3 Flat Races..e. Marathon Race, 42 kilometres. From Marathon to Athens on the road. **1908** T. A. COOK *Olympic Games* 82 The whole of Hellas seemed concentrated at Athens to see the result of the great Marathon Race in the stadium. **1908** *Westm. Gaz.* 22 July 1/3 There are two things which no one who wishes to win the Marathon can ever afford to forget. **1936** *Discovery* Feb. 48/2 Never speak to me again about a snail's pace except with reference to a Marathon runner or a racing car. **1955** J. H. PETERS *In Long Run* viii. 71 On July 21st..the A.A.A. Marathon Championship was due to be run at Birmingham on a roughly circular out-and-home course. **1964** M. WATMAN *Encycl. Athletics* 108/1 Owing to the disparity in the nature, if not distance, of various courses, marathon times should not be taken too seriously. *Ibid.*, The only woman on record as having completed a full marathon is Dale Greig. **1966** J. HOPKINS *Marathon* 11 British runners are to be found among the leaders in almost every international Marathon.

b. In extended uses, applied to other long-distance races or competitions calling for endurance. Also *attrib.* (and as quasi-*adj.*).

1908 *Daily Chron.* 5 Nov. 1/2 A competition..under a title of 'The Murphy Marathon' was decided last night... It was intended that the contestants should..peel a quarter of a hundredweight of potatoes. **1928** *Daily Express* 2 July 11/5 The dance marathon here ended at midnight, nine couples left in the competition stopping together after twenty days of continuous dancing. **1932** G. MORTON *Mystery of Hermit's End* ii. 19 The latter was taking intensive training for marathon swimming. That form of sport had caught on of late. **1932** *Times Lit. Suppl.* 26 May 393/1 His friend Cap Bridges, the marathon swimmer. **1968** *Radio Times* 28 Nov. 8/3 The London–Sydney Motor Marathon. Progress Reports. **1969** *New Yorker* 20 Dec. 64/2 One of the phenomena of America's Depression days was the marathon dance. **1975** *Ibid.* 10 Mar. 100/2 It's an album of pictures: line dancing, marathon dancing, the Lindy.

c. Other *transf.* and *fig.* uses. Esp. an event or activity of long duration.

1915 'BARTIMEUS' *Tall Ship* x. 185 'That was a bit of a Marathon, wasn't it?' He measured the distance across the lawn with a humorous eye. **1951** *N.Y. Herald-Tribune* 29 Nov. 3 The House of Commons finally went home ..after sitting through a marathon session of 20 hours and 20 minutes. **1953** C. DAY LEWIS *Italian Visit* iii. 39 After a marathon walk through the Vatican galleries. **1955** W. GADDIS *Recognitions* II. vii. 613 There's been somebody tagging around after me all day, this marathon walker, I met him in a bar. **1971** *Britannica Bk. of Year 1970* 779/2 *Marathon, specif.*, a group session in which members remain together for an extended period (as 24 hours) and interact openly and responsively so as to increase self-understanding. **1972** *Daily Tel.* 2 June 2/3 The question whether a judge and special assessors should replace the conventional jury in complicated and marathon criminal cases.

Hence **ma·rathon** *v. intr.*, to run as in a marathon race (*rare*); **ma·rathoning** *ppl. a.* (*rare*).

1920 *Chambers's Jrnl.* Aug. 519/2 Do I have to marathon ten miles and back? **1964** M. WATMAN *Encycl. Athletics* 107/2 He [*sc.* Kolehmainen] won by less than 13 sec...the closest result in Olympic marathoning history.

marble, *sb.* Add: **4. b.** Phr. *to pass in one's marble* and varr., to die, to give up. *Austral. slang.*

1908 *Austral. Mag.* 1 Nov. 1250 Instead of dying you can 'chuck a seven', 'pass in your marble', or 'peg out'. **1918** A. WRIGHT *Over Odds* 102 'I suppose the old pot knew y'old man before he passed in his marble,' ventured Dick. **1924** *Truth* 27 Apr. 6 *Throw in the marble*, to relinquish. **1951** D. STIVENS *Jimmy Brockett* 304 I'm not going to pass in my marble just yet.

c. Phr. *to make one's marble good*: to make a good impression (on a person), to ingratiate oneself, to improve one's position. *N.Z.* and *Austral. slang.*

Quot. 1938 illustrates a similiar *S. Afr.* use.

c **1926** 'MIXER' *Transport Workers' Song Bk.* 31 Some tap the boss before they join,..By this they make their marble good. **1938** A. M. BROWN *Let.* 15 Apr. in Partridge *Dict. Slang* (1961) Suppl. 1179/1 A word I have heard used in the Cape [Province], mostly from people attending Rhodes University College, Grahamstown, is *marble*. Examples are: 'His marble is high'—he is 'well-in' (with such-and-such a person). 'He is polishing his marble with so-and-so' = he is trying to ingratiate himself. **1944** J. H. FULLARTON *Troop Target* iii. 26, I was making my marble good. **1947** D. M. DAVIN *Gorse blooms Pale* 206 The crowd.. wanted to see if he could make his marble good with us. **1963** D. CRICK *Martin Place* 223 Take my tip, if you wanter make your marble good: say nothing.

5. c. (See quots.) Also *marble crust.*

1924 *Tourist* Winter Sports No. 12/2 *Marble*, a snow-crust formed by alternate freezing and thawing. Found on Southern slopes. **1948** P. LUNN *Ski-ing Primer* xviii. 90 Marble crust is so slippery that it is almost impossible to obtain a purchase on it with the skis. **1969** M. HELLER *Ski* xiv. 185 *Marble crust* looks like its name and is formed by the wind. The snow is dull and extremely hard... It is very common at high altitude in early winter.

6. c. As (false) transl. of F. *meubles*: furniture, movables, personal effects; 'the goods'. *slang.*

1864 HOTTEN *Slang Dict.* 176 *Marbles*, furniture, movables; 'money and marbles', cash and personal effects. **1867** TROLLOPE *Claverings* II. vi. 67 She won't get any money from me, unless I get the marbles for it. **1896** FARMER & HENLEY *Slang* IV. 280/1 *Marbles*,.. furniture; moveables. *Money and marbles* = cash and effects. [From Fr. *meubles*]. Hence, any substantial *quid pro quô*. English synonyms. Belongings; household gods; lares and penates; moveables; sticks; sprats, slows; traps. **1923** J. MANCHON *Le Slang* 190 *Marbles*,..des meubles (corrupt. du français). **1937** PARTRIDGE *Dict. Slang* 509 *Marbles*, furniture; moveables: somewhat low..; ob[solescent].

d. *pl.* Mental faculties; brains; common sense. *N. Amer. slang.*

1927 *Amer. Speech* II. 360 *Marbles, doesn't have all his* (verb phrase), mentally deficient. 'There goes a man who doesn't have all his marbles.' **1935** A. J. POLLOCK *Underworld Speaks* 75/1 *Marbles*, the brain. **1957** M. MILLAR *Soft Talkers* i. 7 She's a fattish little *hausfrau* with some of her marbles missing. **1958** WODEHOUSE *Cocktail Time* xvii. 148 Do men who have got all their marbles go swimming in lakes with their clothes on? **1967** M. L. ROBY *Cat & Mouse* i. 19 He ain't right in the head. Got a few marbles missing. **1969** J. WAINWRIGHT *Take-Over Men* i. 8 You lost your goddam' marbles? You gone completely crazy, you nutty slob? **1973** *Ottawa Jrnl.* 6 Feb. 9/4 'I still have most of my marbles,' he said cheerfully. **1973** R. PARKES *Guardians* xi. 204 Crazy bastard... I think he's blown his marbles.

7. b. *marble-hearted* adj. (earlier and later examples).

1605 SHAKS. *Lear* I. iv. 283 Ingratitude! thou Marble-hearted Fiend. **1927** R. GRAVES *Poems (1914–26)* 203 Not marble-hearted but your own true love.

8. a. *marble chips, saw* (earlier and later examples); **c.** *marble-built, -flagged, -slabbed, -stoppered* adjs.; **d.** *marble-still, -tall* adjs.

1791 W. BLAKE *French Revolution* I, in *Compl. Writings* (1972) 138 Shall this marble built heaven become a clay cottage..? **1926** H. CRANE *Let.* 19 Aug. (1965) 273 Examining pebbles and cinders and marble chips through the telescope. **1946** *Happy Landings* (Air Ministry) July 1/2 White stone or marble chips spread out and rolled into the macadam surface form an excellent substitute. **1889** W. B. YEATS *Wanderings of Oisin* 53 A marble-flagged, pillared room. **1839** URE *Dict. Arts* 801 The marble saw is a thin plate of soft iron, continually supplied..with water and the sharpest sand. **1890** *Cent. Dict.*, *Marble-saw*,.. a machine for cutting marble... Such machines will cut a block of marble into several slabs simultaneously, or can be arranged to cut out pyramidal blocks, or to shape a cylinder or a frustum of a cone. **1864** *Harper's Mag.* Dec. 40/1, I..had a snug marble-slabbed brick house. **1933** 'R. CROMPTON' *William—the Rebel* viii. 162 Lay his catch upon the marble-slabbed hat-stand in the hall of the inn. **1904** W. DE LA MARE *Henry Brocken* xiii. 168 He stood, thus, marble-still. **1972** *Country Life* 30 Nov. 1481/3 The screw-topped or marble-stoppered lemonade bottles of long ago. **1938** BELLOC *Sonnets & Verse* 196 The Islands have received it, marble-tall.

9. marble bone *Path.* [tr. G. *marmorknochen*], (*a*) (also *pl.*) = *OSTEOPETROSIS; also called *marble bone(s) disease*; (*b*) an affected bone in a person with osteopetrosis; **marble cake** orig. *U.S.*, a cake made of light and dark sponge, having a mottled appearance suggestive of marble; **marble orchard** *U.S. slang*, a cemetery; **marble-player, marbles-player,** one who plays the game of marbles; **marble-top** usu. *attrib.*, designating a piece of furniture the top of which is covered with marble; also *marble-topped* adj.; **marble town** *U.S. slang* = *marble orchard*.

1922 *Arch. Surg.* V. 462 In 1921, Schultz discussed the nature of the disease of marble bones (Albers-Schönberg). **1922** *Jrnl. Amer. Med. Assoc.* 2 Dec. 1955/2 A patient.. was found, on roentgen-ray examination, to have a pathologic fracture as the result of a rather obscure bone condition which has been termed osteosclerosis fragilis generalisata, Marmorknochen (marble bone), or Albers-Schönberg disease. **1947** *Arch. Path.* XLIII. 75 Marble bone disease is due to..an unknown agent which damages the bone-forming blastema at the beginning of the second period of development of each individual bone. *Ibid.* 73 Fractures in marble bones, for the most part, do not splinter. **1961** R. D. BAKER *Essent. Path.* xxi. 560 In osteopetrosis (Albers-Schönberg's disease; marble bones) the bones are abnormally hard and thick, but also easily fractured. **1973** FORFAR & ARNEIL *Textbk. Paediatrics* xxiii. 1525/1 (*heading*) Albers-Schonberg disease (osteopetrosis, marble bones disease). **1871** MRS. T. J. V. OWEN *Illinois Cook Bk.* 202 Marble Cake...White part... Three teacupsful white sugar,..Dark part... Three teacupsful

brown sugar, One teacupful molasses, [etc.]. **1878** N. A. Donnelley *Lakeside Cook Bk.* 29/1 Marble Cake. **1903** K. D. Wiggin *Rebecca* xxvi. 290 She began to stir the marble cake. **1971** M. McCarthy *Birds of America* 74 My husband used to like a marble cake. **1929** M. A. Gill *Underworld Slang* 8/1 *Marble orchard*, cemetery. **1941** J. M. Cain *Mildred Pierce* 155 You'll get your names in this marble orchard soon enough. **1973** B. Broadfoot *Ten Lost Years* x. 110 A couple more punches and it would have been the marble orchard for him. **1910** A. Bennett *Clayhanger* I. i. 9 Six men playing the noble game of rinkers... They were celebrated marble-players. **1955** *Publ. Amer. Dial. Soc.* xxiii. 7 Marble players are not imaginative as far as their terminology is concerned. **1959** I. & P. Opie *Lore & Lang. Schoolch.* xi. 228 Young marbles players..easily become prey to strange thoughts. *Ibid.*, In some places marble players are addicted to charms. **1883** *Heal & Son Catal.* Sept. 200/2 Hall Table,..St. Ann's Marble Top. **1891** 'O. Thanet' *Otto the Knight* 60 [She was] a woman of property,..owning two marble-top bureaus and a sewing-machine. **1963** *House & Garden* Feb. 1 Marble top coffee table, 36″ × 15″, £38.10.0. **1849** Marble-topped [see Longfully *adv.*]. **1864** Mrs. Gaskell *French Life* i, in *Fraser's Mag.* Apr. 435/2 The 'guéridon' (round, marble-topped table)..the one indispensable article in a French drawing-room. **1886** 'Mark Twain' *Let.* 7 Aug. (1920) 257 They never used a stove, but cooked their meals on a marble-topped table. *a* **1941** V. Woolf *Captain's Death-bed* (1950) 181 There are marble-topped tables at the corner. **1959** W. Golding *Free Fall* iv. 85 When we were sitting at the marble-topped table my plans began to come apart. **1971** M. Lee *Dying for Fun* xlii. 203 Would he have to change the décor of his flat.., those marble-topped café tables? **1975** *Times* 6 Sept. 1/4 The bomb..was thought to have been placed under one of the marble-topped tables in..the [hotel] lobby. **1945** L. Shelly *Jive Talk Dict.* 29 *Marble town*, a graveyard. **1970** C. Major *Dict. Afro-Amer. Slang* 80 *Marble town*, (1940's) a cemetery.

marbleize, *v.* (Further, including U.K., examples.)

1909 Galsworthy *Fraternity* vii. 60 She had before her ..two little books. One of these was bound in marbleized paper. **1974** *State* (Columbia, S. Carolina) 3 & 4 Mar. G 13/6 She was more than happy to pay the extra baggage fees on two dozen heavy gold-and-white marbleized candles.

marbling, *vbl. sb.* Add: **2. b.** In meat: the quality or state of having the lean streaked with thin layers of fat. Cf. Marbled *ppl. a.* 2 c.

1925 W. H. Tomhave *Meats & Meat Products* xvii. 203 Marbling is always present in ribs, loins, and chucks. **1929** *Daily Express* 7 Nov. 3/4 There are certain indications by which the official graders can detect clearly whether or not there is 'marbling' in the beef while it is in the side. **1963** *New Yorker* 22 June 21 Marbling is the most important thing in a steak. **1972** T. McHugh *Time of Buffalo* xxiii. 311 Despite the greater cost, buffalo meat is not overpriced, for its marked leanness entails less fatty marbling and less trimming.

marbling (mā·ɹbliŋ), *ppl. a.* [-ing².] = Marbled *ppl. a.* 2 c.

1958 *Times* 8 Dec. (Suppl.) p. viii/3 Tender beef can be produced..from older animals that are well-finished, i.e., in which there has been considerable deposition of 'marbling' fat between the muscle bundles. **1971** *Country Life* 9 Sept. 643/3 The older mature animal that is well finished can still provide meat of a high quality, due in part to the intimate penetration of 'marbling fat' into the deep muscle tissue.

marc. Add: = *marc brandy.*

1934 O. Sitwell *Let.* 15 Aug. in Mrs. Belloc Lowndes *Diaries & Lett.* (1971) 126 We settled them with a glass each of the strongest Marc-de-Bourgoyne. **1946** G. Millar *Horned Pigeon* xvi. 252 Ramon and Alban sat inside, drinking marc. *Ibid.* 253 Ramon ordered three more marcs. **1956** J. Baldwin *Giovanni's Room* ii. 44, I ordered black coffee and a cognac, a large one. Giovanni was far from me, drinking *marc.*

marcato (māɹkā·to), *adv.* and *a.* *Mus.* [It., pa. pple. of *marcare*, to mark, accent, of Gmc. origin: cf. Mark *v.*] (With each note) emphasized. Also *transf.*

1840 Busby & Hamilton *Dict. 3,000 Mus. Terms* (ed. 3) 109 *Marcato*, a term implying a strong and marked style of performance. **1842** J. F. Warner *Universal Dict. Mus. Terms* 56/1 *Marcato*, marked, distinguished, rendered prominent, as e.g. Ben marcato, well marked, in a clearly marked, distinct manner... This term is sometimes used over such passages or individual notes, as the composer may wish particularly to have heard. **1922** Joyce *Ulysses* 214 He read, *marcato.* **1961** *Times* 6 Dec. 17/7 Mr. Spaić got exciting results with tense 'marcato' arrangements.

Marcel (maɹse·l), *sb.* Also with small initial. [f. the name of François *Marcel* Grateau (1852–1936), French hairdresser who invented the method.] In full, *Marcel wave.* A kind of artificial wave of the hair produced by using heated curling-tongs. Also *fig.*

1895 in *N. & Q.* (1941) 6 Sept. 129/1 (Advt.), Experts in the Marcel and Last Vienna Wave. **1908** *Smart Set* Sept. 86/1 And when she 'comes to', her Marcelle wave is straight as a shad. **1909** 'O. Henry' *Roads of Destiny* 62 Man, what do you suppose she did? Loosened up like a Marcel wave in the surf at Coney. **1926** *Glasgow Herald* 25 Sept. 9 It began to rain... Many a beautiful marcel was sacrificed to save a masterpiece of millinery. **1930** R. Macaulay *Staying with Relations* xvi. 226 Little marcel waves lapped at the Eugenia's white sides as she lay at anchor in the San José harbour. **1934** E. Sitwell *Aspects Mod. Poetry* i. 11 Mr. Austin Dobson, and his Marcel Waves, the wriggling, giggling horrors of his Triolets and other imitations of French forms. **1964** L. Hairston in J. H. Clarke *Harlem* 285 The waves in my hair done unstrung... I..called Sonny for an appointment; I *had* to have a marcel!

b. *Comb.*, as *Marcel-waved, -waver, -waving.*

1908 'O. Henry' *Gentle Grafter* ii. 71 A combination steak beater, shoe horn, marcel waver. **1923** *Chambers's Jrnl.* Sept. 568/1 She could lie without turning one of her exquisitely marcel-waved hairs. **1925** *Daily Tel.* 13 May 20/5 (Advt.), Expert Marcel Waver and Manicurist. *Ibid.*, Marcel and water waving. **1927** *Daily Express* 30 Nov. 13 Miss Aylwin has been earning her living..doing shingling and marcel waving. **1932** [see *finger-waving vbl. sb.]. **1968** *Times* 30 Jan. 9/7 Your head is frizzed or Marcel-waved. **1974** *Daily Tel.* 7 Aug. 11/2 This drawing-room comedy of 1931 has been carefully resuscitated..with wind-up gramophone, a marcel-waved heroine and snip-snap jokes. **1974** *Observer* 24 Nov. 29/6 There's a lady in Wellington, New Zealand, who was still doing marcel waving from the first time round when it came back again.

marcel (maɹse·l), *v.* [f. prec. sb.] *trans.* To wave (hair) in the 'Marcel' fashion. Also *fig.*

1906 B. von Hutten *What became of Pam* I. x. 71 A gentleman who *marcelled* heads in an Oxford Street shop. **1926** Kipling *Debits & Credits* 155 The wind marcelling the grasses. **1928** *Daily Express* 28 Dec. 11/1 Her unbobbed hair is marcelled in broad waves from a high forehead. **1951** E. Paul *Springtime in Paris* iv. 81 Word and figures may be dyed, marcelled or manoeuvred like veils around a dancer. Behind them, the nakedness is there.

Hence marce·lled *ppl. a.*; marce·lling *vbl. sb.* Also *fig.*

1909 'O. Henry' *Options* 103 A stone house with an engraving of an idol with marcelled hair, playing a flute, over the door. **1922** F. Courtenay *Physical Beauty* 42 If you want that 'marcelled' look, there are comb sets (mounted on springs) which will give it. **1926** *Daily Colonist* (Victoria, B.C.) 17 Jan. 6/2 (Advt.), Swan-Marinello perfect marcelling. Home appointments made. **1927** *Daily Express* 14 Oct. 6 Women's heads in the late Roman period..are represented not only with distinct marcelling, but also with elaborate jewellery to emphasise the waves. **1930** R. Macaulay *Staying with Relations* xvi. 228 The rippling, marcelled sea. **1932** L. C. Douglas *Forgive us our Trespasses* (1937) xi. 219 Victor..calmly continued his monologue in a marcelled, affected baritone. **1936** [see *bobby pin]. **1938** D. Baker *Young Man with Horn* (1939) i. 20 Even marcelling hadn't gained any real ground. **1971** K. Wheeler *Epitaph for Mister Wynn* (1972) xxvii. 350 The halo of silver hair..was in marcelled good order.

marcescent, *a.* (Later examples.) marcescence (later example).

1904 J. C. Willis *Man. Flowering Plants* (ed. 2) 77 If it [*sc.* the perianth] remains unwithered round the fruit, persistent, withered, marcescent, enlarged as in Physalis, accrescent. **1964** *Acta Phytogeographica Suecica* XLIX. 51 (*caption*) Around the stem..there is a dense insulating mantle of marcescent dry leaves. **1974** *Kew Bull.* XXIX. 536 The stems of forest species of Giant Lobelia are usually bare of marcescent foliage. **1974** *New Phytologist* LXXIII. 981 Mature pachycauls..exhibit several characteristics often associated with the 'juvenile' stages of trees, e.g. wide pith, presence of starch-sheath, unbranched axis and marcescence.

March, *sb.*² Add: **2. a.** *March-bloom*; *March-hatched* adj.

1877 G. M. Hopkins *Poems* (1967) 67 Look! March-bloom, like on mealed-with-yellow sallows! **1921** F. M. Ford *Let.* 15 July (1965) 135 March hatched cockerels. **1960** *Farmer & Stockbreeder* 5 Jan. 103/1 My February- and March-hatched pullets started to lay.

b. **March fly,** (*a*) *U.S.*, a dark-coloured, hairy fly of the family Bibionidæ; (*b*) *Austral.*, a blood-sucking horse-fly of the family Tabanidæ.

1895 J. H. & A. B. Comstock *Man. Study of Insects* xix. 450 They [*sc.* Bibionidae] are most common in early spring, which has suggested the name March-flies; but some occur later in the season. **1907** W. W. Froggatt *Austral. Insects* 294 They [*sc.* Tabanidæ] are popularly known in Australia as 'March Flies'; in England and America they usually go under the name of 'Horse or Gad Flies'. **1908** E. J. Banfield *Confessions of Beachcomber* i. vii. 221 The sluggish 'march' fly..goes about the business of blood-sucking in a lazy..style. **1947** I. L. Idriess *Isles of Despair* viii. 58 A vicious March fly with threatening buzz dived at her. **1970** Colless & McAlpine in *Insects of Australia* (Commonwealth Sci. & Industr. Res. Organization) xxiv. 701/2 Tabanidae (March flies, horse flies;..). In Europe and North America, the term 'March fly' is applied to the Bibionidae. **1972** Swan & Papp *Common Insects N. Amer.* 603 March flies appear in large numbers early in the spring. **1973** *Islander* (Victoria, B.C.) 12 Aug. 2/1 Many a March-fly-bitten mango packer..longs to pick peaches where there are no March flies to worry about, only wasps.

march, *sb.*³ Add: **4.** *march shire.*

1917 *Eng. Hist. Rev.* Oct. 483 The Warden..had simply taken over certain duties hitherto discharged by the sheriff in the March shires.

march, *sb.*⁴ Add: **1. a.** Also, a procession organised as an expression of (esp. political) dissent, or to draw attention to a particular problem, etc. Cf. **hunger-march.*

1908, etc. [see *hunger-march* s.v. *hunger *sb.* 4 e]. **1952** *Ann. Reg. 1951* 105 In May the Commando arranged a symbolic 'march' to Capetown to present a formal petition to Parliament. **1962** [see *Aldermaston]. **1970** K. Giles *Death in Church* ii. 29 He's a crank and a fire-brand... Not a 'march' goes by without him carrying a banner. **1973** *Black World* Nov. 42/2 Perhaps the most arresting result of the thousands of 'sit-ins' and 'marches' by Afro-Americans in the early Sixties..has been the obligation and opportunity of the entire world to re-evaluate the contributions of the Black American to world society.

d. *march past.* (Examples of non-military use.)

1924 O. W. Campbell *Shelley & Unromantics* ii. 10 Telling them [*sc.* Shelley's friends] over is like calling for a march past of the Seven Deadly Sins. **1928** *Manch. Guardian Wkly.* 10 Aug. 101/1 The march past of the pilgrims in the Grand Place of Ypres. **1961** *Times* 5 June 3/5 The teams [of swimmers] risked a premature ducking by a carefully routed march-past.

2. d. (Earlier examples.)

[**1775** Burke *Speech moving Conciliation with Colonies* 51 The march of the human mind is slow.] **1818** Keats *Let.* 3 May (1931) I. 157 It proves there is really a grand march of intellect. **1821** Lady Morgan *Italy* I. viii. 170 Impediments are now thrown in the march of mind... To retrograde, not to advance, is the order of the times.

3. b. *to steal a march* (further examples).

1771 Smollett *Humph. Cl.* I. 127 She yesterday wanted to steal a march of poor Liddy. **1844** Poe *Oblong Box* in *Godey's Lady's Bk.* Sept. 133/1 He evidently intended to steal a march upon me, and smuggle a fine picture to New York, under my very nose. **1950** T. S. Eliot *Cocktail Party* ii. 93 He's quite triumphant Because he thinks he's stolen a march on her.

march, *v.*² Add: **1. f.** To engage in a protest, etc., march (see *march *sb.*⁴ 1 a).

1967 *Freedomways* VII. 102 Where is the Federal Government today as civil rights workers in Louisville face screaming mobs, throwing rocks and bottles at them as they peacefully march to end housing discrimination? **1969** *New Yorker* 14 June 76/3 He has repeatedly been asked to march and picket. **1972** *Times* 19 Oct. 5/7 (*heading*) Doctors march in Vienna.

‖ **märchen** (mēə·ɹχʸən). Also **Märchen.** [G., fairy-tale, f. MHG. *merechyn* short verse narrative, f. OHG. *mārī*, MHG. *mære* news, tale (f. OHG. *mārī*, MHG. *mære* famous, Mere *a.*¹) + the dim. suffix OHG. *-chīn* -kin.] A folk-tale or story. Also *attrib.*

1871 L. M. Alcott *Good Wives* x. 130 You and I will read these pleasant little Märchen together. **1885** *Athenæum* 22 Aug. 230/2 The Punjaub tales..are, naturally, rather modern and civilized..more so than Servian and Romaic *Märchen.* **1902** A. Lang in *Folk-Lore* XIII. 359 Mr. J. G. Frazer..starts from the idea so common in *Märchen*, of the person whose 'soul', 'life', or 'strength', is secretly hidden in an animal, plant, or other object. **1908** *Mod. Philol.* V. 402 There is no doubt..that the story of the shadowy Anglian king Offa, blended with *märchen* elements, was well known in England in the time of Cynewulf. **1928** W. W. Lawrence *Beowulf & Epic Trad.* 166 Study of *märchen*, both for their own sake and for the light that they throw upon sophisticated literature. **1950** H. L. Lorimer *Homer & Monuments* viii. 515 Outside the apologoi the poet of the *Odyssey* prefers to eliminate elements of the *märchen* type. **1963** Brown & Foote *Early Eng. & Norse Stud.* 189 The French märchen-material. *Ibid.*, Oriental märchen-motives. **1964** C. S. Lewis *Discarded Image* vi. 135 The Gnomes are closer to the Dwarfs of *märchen.*

marcher². Add: **1. b.** *spec.* A person who takes part in a protest, etc., march (see *march *sb.*⁴ 1 a).

1908, 1922 [see *hunger-marcher* s.v. *hunger *sb.* 4 e]. **1939** C. Day Lewis *Child of Misfortune* iii. ii. 334 He had hoped, perhaps, for..a feeling of community with his fellow marchers. **1960** *Times Lit. Suppl.* 10 June 362/4 We observe its [*sc.* war's] direct and unquestioned influence on 'marchers' and others whom most people consider wrong-headed. **1960** *Guardian* 28 Oct. 7/4 Many bright remarks about French politics, anti-bomb marchers..and the like. **1961** *Ibid.* 7 Mar. 8/6 Marchers of all kinds protested beside the Holy Loch. **1969** *New Yorker* 14 June 78/2 I'm not a marcher. I'm not a sign carrier.

marching, *vbl. sb.* Add: **d. marching money** (later examples); **marching order** (earlier and later examples); also *fig.*

1941 Baker *Dict. Austral. Slang* 46 *Marching money*, money to travel. **1962** R. Cook *Crust on its Uppers* (1964) ii. 18 There were no wages—hardly marching money, even. **1780** W. Heath *Let.* 31 July in *Mass. Hist. Soc. Coll.* (1905) 7th Ser. V. 93 George Washington has put the main army under marching orders. **1837** *King's Regulations Army* 32 General Officers are to cause the Troops..to be frequently paraded, and exercised at least once a week in Heavy Marching Order. **1848** A. H. Clough *Let.* 26 Feb. in T. Arnold *N.Z. Lett.* (1966) 78, I anticipate considerable trouble in getting any Constitution into Marching Order. **1850** J. J. Hort *Horse Guards* 24 In many garrisons the greater part of his time thus employed is in heavy marching order. **1918** L. E. Ruggles *Navy Explained* 127 If the stew is covered over with a crust..they call it stew in heavy marching order. **1937** B. de Holthoir tr. *Duhamel's Pasquier Chron.* 88 The barometer, too, nearly had its marching orders, but mother said: 'Oh, for what it will fetch it might as well stay where it is.' **1961** S. Chaplin *Day of Sardine* vi. 132 He was never any good to you. It makes no difference to me if you give him his marching orders...and hitch up with the Lodger. **1974** 'M. Innes' *Appleby's Other Story* x. 79 An eye should be kept on him, to my mind. Given his marching orders, he ought to be.

marching, *ppl.a.*[2] Add: **1. b.** *marching band*, a band that marches; *marching girl* (*Austral.* and *N.Z.*), a girl trained to march in formation, a drum-majorette.

1952 *Here & Now* (N.Z.) July 9 Not for a long time have I observed such a symptom of our *malaise* as the business of 'marching girls'. **1954** *N.Z. Listener* 10 Dec., Preceded, of course, by marching girls to provide just that touch of military pageantry so dear to us all. **1955** KEEPNEWS & GRAUER *Pict. Hist. Jazz* ii. 19 Laine's music was distinctively that of the marching bands and of ragtime. **1956** M. STEARNS *Story of Jazz* (1957) vii. 72 The New Orleans jazzbands, with their marching-band tradition, did not use a piano in the early days. **1961** *N.Z. Listener* 24 Nov. 36/4 Visitors from America say that as a major attraction, our marching girls are much superior to their Drum Majorettes. **1963** *Sunday Mirror* (Sydney) 27 Jan. 2 (*caption*) In gay, colorful uniforms marching girls were cheered by city crowds as they strode through city streets during the Australia Day celebrations. **1974** *Fiji Times* 3 July (*caption*) Marching girls parade through Lautoka during the Salusalu Festival at the weekend. **1974** P. DE VRIES *Glory of Hummingbird* i. 4 The sousaphone tuba he played in the local marching band.

Ma·rcobru:nner. Also Marcobrunn, Markbrunner, Markobrunn, Markobrunner. [G., f. the name of a vineyard in the Rheingau.] A Rhenish white wine.

1825 T. HOOK *Sayings & Doings* 2nd Ser. I. 48 Ruydersheimer and Markbrunner. **1851** C. REDDING *Hist. Mod. Wines* (ed. 3) viii. 224 Marcobrunner is an excellent wine, of a fine flavour. **1862** C. TOVEY *Wine & Wine Countries* 201 The landlord, pitying his condition, pressed upon him a bottle of his Marcobrunner. **1884** *Encycl. Brit.* XVII. 238/2 s.v. *Nassau*, By far the most valuable product of the soil is its wine, which includes several of the choicest Rhenish varieties (Johannisberger, Marcobrunner, Assmannshauser, &c.). **1918** H. A. VACHELL *Some Happenings* xvi. 280 Let us drink your health in some Marcobrunner. **1924** 'SAPPER' *Third Round* i. 33 An excellent bottle of Marcobrunner followed by a glass of his own particular old brandy. **1967** A. LICHINE *Encycl. Wines* 432/2 The alternative [name] Marcobrunner will be found on the labels of two estates,.. which own the best parts of the district. *Ibid.* 434/2 *Markobrunn*, sometimes written Marcobrunn.

Marconi. Insert after 'inventor': , Guglielmo, Marchese *Marconi* (1874–1937).

2. Used *attrib.* to designate a type of rig used on sailing vessels, or the various parts of such a rig.

1912 *Yachting Monthly* XIII. 256/2 Istria, Mr. Allom's 'Marconi' boat, promptly installed herself as the yacht of the year. **1915** *Ibid.* XIX. 151/1 Mr. Charles Nicholson, whose 'Marconi' topsail, first used on Istria in 1912, created such a sensation. **1916** *Rudder* 421/1 In the coming races for the Manhasset Bay Challenge Cup, Nahma will use a Marconi rig. **1921** *Ibid.* 28 [They] will carry 125 square feet of canvas in one sail on a so-called Marconi mast. **1940** W. MARTYR *Wandering Years* 14 That eighty-foot Marconi mast was held in place by a network of steel wire shrouds. **1956** A. F. LOOMIS *'Hotspur' Story* ii. 14, I expressed to Rigg my preference for a fast, marconi-rigged, windward-working cutter. **1961** F. H. BURGESS *Dict. Sailing* 142 *Marconi rig*, a sailing rig with a jib-headed mainsail set to a tall curved mast with an elaborate staying system; so named because it resembles a wireless mast. **1975** *Motor Boating & Sailing* Jan. 136/1 This little cruiser has a very attractive appearance in either Marconi or gaff configuration.

Also **marco·nigraph** *v. trans.* and *intr.*, to send a message by marconigraphy (to); **marco·nigraphing** *vbl. sb.*; **marconi·graphy**, Marconi's system of radiotelegraphy; radio. (All now *disused.*)

1903 *Nature* 23 Apr. 583/1 The history of the series of inventions and discoveries which have culminated in Transatlantic Marconigraphy. **1907** *Daily Chron.* 27 Sept. 5/2 The Lusitania was marconigraphed at 5.30 p.m. yesterday 200 miles west of Fastnet. **1909** G. STRATTON-PORTER *Girl of Limberlost* xxiv. 453 If..I want you..I'll cable, marconigraph, anything. **1911** R. BROOKE *Let.* Mar. (1968) 284 It is..cleverer and queerer than the telephone, though not so clever as Marconigraphing.

marconi (māɹkōᵘ·ni), *v. Disused.* [f. the sb.] **1.** *trans.* and *intr.* To send a message by radio (to).

1912 C. N. & A. M. WILLIAMSON *Heather Moon* I. iv. 47, I marconied her an hour after he'd said that he would come. **1919** *Times* 25 June 13/6 Messages were signalled to the coastguards requesting them to marconi to the Fleet.

2. *trans.* To transmit by radio. Also *fig.*

1908 *Isle of Man Weekly Times* 12 Sept. 9/4 An author sometimes dreams of the ideal actress who shall 'Marconi' across the footlights the puppet he has given birth to. **1922** *Glasgow Herald* 2 Nov. 6/2 These figures represent a code which can be wired, cabled, or marconied anywhere. **1926** P. BOTTOME *Old Wine* xi. 104 Marconiing the news.. across space.

Marconist (māɹkōᵘ·nist). *Disused.* [f. MARCON(I + -IST.] The operator of a Marconi radiotelegraphy system.

1900 in *Encycl. Dict.* (*c* 1904) Suppl. s.v., Then the Marconists began to pull the enemy's leg by sending what our Marconist calls 'Rot'. **1933** *Jrnl. R. Aeronaut. Soc.* XXXVII. 628 On board of the machine, an increase of the crew to probably three pilots, two Marconists and one mechanic.

marcottage (maɹkǫtā·ʒ, maɹkǫ·tėdʒ). *Hort.* Also **marcotting.** [Fr. *marcottage* layering.] A method of propagating trees or shrubs in which a ring of bark is removed from a branch, and the wound covered with a thick layer of soil, moss, etc., into which new roots grow, before the plant is cut from its parent. Hence (as a back-formation) **marcot**, the wound from which new roots grow, or the new plant formed. Also as *v. intr.*, to use this method of propagation.

1926 F. M. ESGUERRA in *Philippine Agriculturist* XV. 63 Marcottage is the term applied to the process of reproduction by which a branch of a plant is 'girdled' and wrapped with soil or other media in order to induce rooting while still attached to the mother plant. A marcot is the branch so treated... Planting marcots instead of seeds has several advantages. *Ibid.* 64 Time for marcotting. It is preferable to marcot during the rainy season. **1934** [see *air-layering* (*AIR *sb.*[1] B. II)]. **1955** R. C. M. WRIGHT *Plant Propagation* xv. 99 'Air layering', 'Chinese layering' or 'marcotting' is believed to have been used by gardeners for thousands of years. **1958** R. J. GARNER *Grafter's Handbk.* (rev. ed.) iii. 60 Marcotting..is variously known as air layering, Chinese layering, circumposition, or, in India and elsewhere, as gootee. *Ibid.*, An ingenious method of securing a continuous supply is to suspend a vessel containing water above the marcot. **1959** HARTMANN & KESTER *Plant Propagation* xiv. 406 The ancient Chinese gootee or marcottage method consists of plastering a ball of clay or other soil mixture about the ring or girdle, which is then covered with moss or fiber. **1969** *Gloss. for Landscape Work* (*B.S.I.*) v. 12 Marcotting. A form of air layering in which a soil-based rooting medium is used.

Marcusian (maɹkū·ziăn), *a.* and *sb.* [f. the name of Herbert *Marcuse* (1898–), American writer.] **A.** *adj.* Of, pertaining to, or connected with Marcuse or his political views. **B.** *sb.* One who holds the political views of Marcuse.

1968 *Economist* 20 July 25/3 In Italy, as elsewhere, it has brought to the surface a number of groups who are more articulate than the mass and can variously and very approximately be classified as maoist, trotskyist, castroist, marcusian and so forth. **1968** *Listener* 31 Oct. 594/2 (*heading*) Marcusians. *Ibid.*, The boring old proletariat is unrepresented in this Marcusian world. **1969** *Guardian* 2 Sept. 9/6 Marcuse, and the hippie generation who represent Marcusian premature antifascists, herald a radical shift towards the sensory, the imaginative and the quietist. **1969** *Pacifist* Oct. 5/2 A Marcusian analysis of the developed world shows the system beginning to transcend itself where it is most successful. **1970** G. GREER *Female Eunuch* 309 The Red Stockings..concentrate on consciousness-raising in the Marcusian sense. **1970** A. MACINTYRE *Marcuse* iv. 53 The whole recapitulation thesis in its Marcusean form [is] untenable. **1971** *Guardian* 19 Jan. 10/1 It will be asked whether the Guevarist or Marcusian infection is beginning to take effect in this country.

mard (māɹd), *a.* = MARRED *ppl. a.* b. *dial.*

1903 in *Eng. Dial. Dict.* **1911** D. H. LAWRENCE *White Peacock* vii. 493 The little devils are soft, mard-soft. **1913** —— *Love Poems* 53 Eh, tha'rt a mard-'arsed kid. **1959** I. & P. OPIE *Lore & Lang. Schoolch.* x. 187 Elsewhere the weak one may carry the label..mard 'un.

mard (māɹd), *v. dial.* [Cf. prec. and MAR *v.* 3 c.] To 'spoil' (a child).

1874 in *Eng. Dial. Dict.* (1903). **1911** D. H. LAWRENCE *White Peacock* vii. 493 She marded 'em till they were soft.

Mardi gras (mardi gra). [Fr., lit. 'fat Tuesday'.] Shrove Tuesday; the last day of carnival, esp. in France. In U.S. esp. as celebrated in New Orleans. Also *attrib.*

1699 M. LISTER *Journey to Paris* (ed. 3) 177 My Lord Ambassador was at a Ball at Monsieur de Montargis mardy Gras. **1780** T. BLAIKIE *Diary Scotch Gardener* (1931) 161 Went to Versailles..this being Mardi gras saw the people masked. **1832** *Boston Even. Transcript* 13 June 1/3 Yesterday was '*Mardi Gras*'—the last day of the reign of Folly. **1848** H. GREVILLE *Diary* 8 Mar. (1883) I. 236 This motley crew..dressed more ludicrously than any masks on a *Mardi-gras*. **1883** 'MARK TWAIN' *Life on Mississippi* xlvi. 416 The largest annual event in New Orleans is..the Mardi-Gras festivities. **1900** ADE *Fables in Slang* 148 His Father was too Serious a Man to get out in Mardi Gras Clothes. **1909** 'O. HENRY' *Options* 184 The reception they were going to put up would make the Mardi Gras in New Orleans look like an afternoon tea in Bury St Edmunds with a curate's aunt. **1924** *Blackw. Mag.* Nov. 709/2 There are those to whom Mardi-Gras is yet a religious festival. **1931** *Times Lit. Suppl.* 9 Apr. 285/3 The Mardi Gras irresponsibility..excuses the daring prank of a naughty youth. **1931** H. CRANE *Let.* 12 Dec. (1965) 392 It isn't any sort of Mardi-Gras mood at all that the Indians express, despite the flamboyant colors of their costumes. **1941** *Sat. Even. Post* 15 Mar. 14 Mardi Gras at Coney. **1972** *Guardian* 29 Dec. 12/1 Russell Harty took an 'Aquarius' [TV] team to Mardi Gras, the great New Orleans Shrove Tuesday freak-out.

mardy (mā·ɹdi), *a. dial.* [f. *MARD *a.* + -Y[1].] 'Spoilt', sulky, whining. Also as *sb.*, a spoilt child.

1903 *Eng. Dial. Dict.* IV. 34/1 A boy who cries with pain is called by his fellows a 'mardy baby'. **1913** D. H. LAWRENCE *Sons & Lovers* vi. 127 'Now, Miriam,' said Maurice, 'you come an' 'ave a go.' 'No,' she cried, shrinking back. 'Ha! baby. The mardy-kid!' said her brothers. **1915** —— *Rainbow* i. 12 Young Tom, whom he called a mardy baby. *a* **1930** —— *Phoenix II* (1968) 170 As for Harold, he was all right. He was very respectable and a bit of a mardy, perhaps..but he was all right. **1959** J. BRAINE *Vodi* i. 22 'Don't be so bloody soft, man,' Tom said. 'I don't want to go.' 'You're mardy. You're dead mardy.' **1961** J. I. M. STEWART *Man who won Pools* 35 'E were a mardy one as a nipper, our Phil. **1975** D. CLARK *Premeditated Murder* v. 83 'You can get all mardy about it if you like,' said Green, unabashed.

mare. Add: **1. c.** (Later examples.)

Not always 'contemptuous'.

1590 SHAKES. *Mids. N.* III. ii. 463 The man shall have his mare again. **1922** JOYCE *Ulysses* 231 She's a gamey mare and no mistake. **1953** C. W. OGLE in *Caribbean Anthol. Short Stories* 43 Forgot her keys! Bah! These mares give me the creeps.

mare[4] (mā·re, mā·ri, mæ·ri). *Astr.* Pl. **maria** (mā·riă), occas. **mares.** [L., = 'sea': used in 17th-c. L. works (e.g. J. Hevelius *Selenographia* (1647) vi. 133); the proper names (which are still current) given to the various regions were taken into Eng. often without translation.] Any of the extensive areas of flat land ('seas') on the surface of the moon, which appear dark and were once thought to be seas; also, any of the dark areas visible on Mars.

[**1765** R. TURNER *View of Heavens* 11 The Oceans, Seas, and Lakes are, *a* Mare Hyperboreum, [etc.].] **1860** *Monthly Notices R. Astron. Soc.* XX. 69 Whatever force might have broken down the portion of the wall towards the mare. **1876** E. NELSON *Moon* iii. 25 Although water is absent from the lunar surface, the Mares present in many places the appearance of alluvial deposits. **1895** T. G. ELGER *Moon* 6 The Maria are only level in the sense that many districts in the English Midland counties are level, and not that their surface is absolutely flat. **1901** G. P. SERVISS *Pleasures of Telescope* ix. 167 The precipitous Mount Hadley..rises more than 15,000 feet above the level of the Mare. **1938** *Ann. Reg. 1937* 356 The 'maria' are regarded as lava fields from fissure eruptions. **1962** F. I. ORDWAY et al. *Basic Astronautics* iii. 74 Other conspicuous features on Mars are the so-called maria, dark areas easily distinguished from the surrounding, desert-colored, lighter expanses. **1964** D. H. MENZEL *Field Guide Stars & Planets* vii. 251 Mares are rolling plains, generally somewhat darker than the surrounding territory. **1967** *Punch* 28 June 936/1 The maria are plains with low hills and scattered craters. Nearly half of the moon's surface which we see is covered with these maria. **1970** *Sci. Jrnl.* Mar. 83/3 A catastrophic event hit both the Earth and the Moon, melting the lunar surface—or at least surfaces of the mares. **1970** *Nature* 6 June 925/1 The form and magnitude of the mascon anomalies can be accounted for by sheets of mare volcanic rock denser than the rock of the adjacent highlands.

marechal. (Later examples of *maréchale.*)

1863 MRS. GASKELL *How First Floor went to Crowley Castle* in *All Year Round* Extra Christmas No., 3 Dec. 16/2 Her hair delicately powdered and scented with maréchale. **1905** *Smart Set* Sept. 113/1 Liszt was interpreted as ylang-ylang, myrrh, and maréchale.

‖ **maréchal** (mareʃal). Also 7 **Marishal**, 8 **Mareschall**, *Sc.* **Marichal.** [Fr.] The French word for 'marshal' or 'field-marshal' used occas. in English.

1699 M. LISTER *Journey to Paris* (ed. 3) 207 The Marishal his Father..embraced me, and saluted me. **1745** M. W. MONTAGU *Let.* 27 Jan. (1966) II. 349 It is reported here that the takeing of Mareschall Bell lisle will make the residence of France very unsafe to all the English. **1783** T. BLAIKIE *Diary Scotch Gardener* (1931) 187 At St Germains the Marichal de Noel..has a very curiouss gardin. **1919** J. BUCHAN *Mr. Standfast* xx. 355 They will not pass. Your Maréchal will hold them. **1921** W. J. LOCKE *Mountebank* xiv. 170 Were British Generals real, like French Generals, Lyautey and..Foch before he became *maréchal*?

Maréchal Niel (mareʃal nīl). Also anglicized **Marshal Niel.** [Fr., f. the name of Adolphe *Niel* (1802–69), Marshal of France: see prec.] A climbing Noisette rose of the variety so called, introduced in 1864, and bearing large, well-formed, fragrant, yellow flowers.

1864 *Gardeners' Chron.* 17 Dec. 1202/2 First-class Certificates have been given to a Tea Rose called Maréchal Niel, produced by M. Eugène Verdier, of Paris... This variety appears to be one of the noblest of the yellows. **1867** T. RIVERS *Rose Amateur's Guide* (ed. 9) 136 The rose to which I allude is Marshal Niel. **1898** H. KIRKE *25 Yrs. Brit. Guiana* iv. 81 Gardens in British Guiana are as a rule, disappointing... Roses, except the strong tea-scented ones like Maréchal Niel, will not flower successfully. **1899** O. WILDE *Importance of being Earnest* II. 67 *Algernon.* Might I have a button-hole first?.. *Cecily.* A Maréchale [*sic*] Niel? **1905** *Smart Set* Sept. 157/2 You had a great bowl of Maréchal Niels on the piano. **1928** [see *GLOIRE DE DIJON]. **1955** G. S. THOMAS *Old Shrub Roses* I. ix. 82 'Cloth of Gold' was the parent of the famous 'Maréchal Niel'. **1971** N. YOUNG *Compl. Rosarian* v. 76 Chromatella (also known as Cloth of Gold) became the parent in 1864 of Maréchal Niel which was the most esteemed of all yellow roses until well into this century.

‖ **mare clausum** (mā·ri klǭ·zŏm). [L., closed sea, from the title of a Latin work

(1635) by John Selden (1584–1654), English jurist, written in answer to *Mare liberum* (1609) by Grotius.] A sea under the jurisdiction of a particular country.

This term and *mare liberum* originated during the struggle between England and the Netherlands in the 17th century.

1652 M. NEDHAM tr. *Selden's Of Dominion of Sea* sig. g1 Mare Clausum is the Sea possessed in a private manner, or so secluded both by Right and Occupation, that it ceaseth to bee common. **1849** J. ALLEN *Navigation Laws Gt. Brit.* iv. 34 Although at one time the professed admirers of Mare Liberum, the Dutch began to consider that Mare Clausum possessed more substantial charms. **1856** *Newsp. & Gen. Reader's Compan.* I. § 1013 The Yellow Sea, which for ages has been, with few exceptions, a *mare clausum*, is now a *mare liberum* to all the world. **1911** *Encycl. Brit.* XVII. 698/2 *Mare clausum* and *mare liberum*..in international law, terms associated with the historic controversy which arose out of demands on the part of different states to assert exclusive dominion over areas of the open or high sea. **1949** *Canad. Jrnl. Pol. & Social Sci.* XV. 344 The old theory of mare clausum, under which coastal waters were sometimes fixed at sixty miles, one hundred miles, two days' journey, etc., from the shore, and under which claims were also made by agreement between two or more countries over an ocean common to them. **1973** [see *MARE LIBERUM].

Maree, var. *MARIA *sb.* and *a.*

Marek (ma·rek). The name of Dr. Josef *Marek*, Hungarian veterinary surgeon, used in the possessive in **Marek's disease** to designate *fowl paralysis* (*FOWL *sb.* 5 c), first described by him in 1907.

1961 *Brit. Vet. Jrnl.* CXVII. 332 It is suggested that this complex be termed Marek's disease, a term which has some precedence and which implies a disease and not a pathological entity. **1964** *Black's Vet. Dict.* (ed. 7) 353/1 Fowl paralysis itself (Marek's disease) has of recent years become more common. **1970** *Q. Poultry Bull.* Dec. 12 The control of Marek's Disease by vaccination is at present very topical. **1972** *Country Life* 3 Feb. 284/1 No sooner had a vaccine for Marek's Disease been found than Fowl Pest swept through our poultry flocks.

‖ **mare liberum** (mā·ri ləi·bĕrŏm). [L., free sea, from the title of a Latin treatise (1609) by Hugo Grotius (1583–1645), Dutch jurist.] A sea open to all nations. Cf. *MARE CLAUSUM.

1652 M. NEDHAM tr. *Selden's Of Dominion of Sea* sig. a2 This People [the Netherlanders]..carried out their design ..by..a daily intrusion upon the Territorie by Sea, that in time they durst plead and print *Mare Liberum*..to defie the Dominion of England over the Sea. **1806** J. RANDOLPH in *Abridgm. Deb. Congress U.S. 1789–1856* (1857) III. 428/2 Again: Is the *mare liberum* any where asserted in this unnamed book, that free ships make free goods? No, sir; the right of search is acknowledged; that enemy's property is lawful prize, is sealed and delivered. **1849**, etc. [see *MARE CLAUSUM]. **1973** *Times* 9 May 16/2 Should we discover that we too might benefit from wider zones of national jurisdiction, we should after all only be returning to the philosophy prevailing before Grotius' idea of *Mare Liberum* took hold, to John Selden's equally respectable *Mare Clausum.*

maremma. Add: **2.** *attrib.*, as *maremma sheep-dog*. Also **mare·mman** *a.*

1924 A. HUXLEY *Little Mexican* 283 The old gentleman ..taking his big maremman dog for a walk [in Tuscany]. **1945** C. L. B. HUBBARD *Observer's Bk. Dogs* 102 Maremma Sheepdog. **1948** —— *Dogs in Brit.* III. xviii. 202 Common in central Italy from Tuscany to the Abruzzes, the Maremma Sheepdog is also called the Cani da Pastor Maremmani, Abruzzi Sheepdog and Maremmes Sheepdog. The breed is centuries old and has been bred pure by Tuscan farmers for herding sheep and cattle; lately the race has been in more general use, particularly as a guard dog. **1972** *Country Life* 2 Nov. 1186/3 Maremma (Italian) Sheep Dog.

Marengo (mare·ŋgo). [See def.] The name of a village in northern Italy, the scene of Napoleon's victory over the Austrians in 1800, used in the name of the dish *chicken, fowl, poulet à la Marengo*, said to have been served to Napoleon after the battle of Marengo.

1861 MRS. BEETON *Bk. Househ. Managem.* 464 (*heading*) Poulet à la Marengo... Fowl à la Marengo. **1877** E. S. DALLAS *Kettner's Bk. of Table* 121 (*heading*) *Chicken à la Marengo*,—the chicken ..is fried in oil. **1959** *Good Food Guide* 169 Chicken Marengo and tournedos.

mareogram (mæ·ri,ogræm). [f. L. *mare* sea + -O + -GRAM.] A graphical record of variations in sea level.

1904 *Publ. Earthquake Investigation Comm. Foreign Lang.* (Japan) XVIII. 24 The following table..gives the mean monthly values of the distance between the sea surface and the datum line in the mareogram at each of the two places. **1931** C. DAVISON *Japanese Earthquake of 1923* xii. 104 The mareogram at Toba is reproduced in Fig. 25. Here, the first movement occurred at 0.57 p.m., the maximum amplitude (of 4 ft. 1½ in.) being reached with the fifth wave at 3.37 p.m. **1949** GUTENBERG & RICHTER *Seismicity of Earth* 95/1 Tsunamis are frequently recorded on mareograms written by tide gages.

Hence **mareogra·phic** *a.*

1939 *Jap. Jrnl. Astron. & Geophysics* XVII. 121 The tunamis that were associated with earthquakes..left conspicuous records on some of our mareographic stations. **1956** *Jrnl. Earth Sci. Nagoya Univ.* IV. 5 Some of these after-shocks were strong,..but no tunamis were observed, even on the mareographic records.

Marezine (mæ·rĕzīn). *Pharm.* Also **marezine.** [f. *mare-* + PIPER)AZINE.] 1-Methyl-4-α-phenylpiperazine hydrochloride, $C_{18}H_{22}N_2$.-HCl, used in the form of tablets as an anti-emetic, esp. for the prevention and treatment of motion sickness. In the *British Pharmacopœia* called *cyclizine hydrochloride.*

Marezine is registered as a proprietary name in the U.S.

1952 *Official Gaz.* (U.S. Patent Office) 23 Dec. 1007/1 Burroughs Wellcome & Co... *Marezine* for medicinal preparations intended for use in the prevention or treatment of allergies, motion sickness, nausea and vomiting in pregnancy, or nausea due to other causes. **1954** *Jrnl. Pharmacol. & Exper. Therap.* CXII. 297 (*heading*) Pharmacologic properties of cyclizine hydrochloride (marezine). **1965** *Economist* 6 Nov. 615/2 The Food and Drug Administration announced last week that three anti-histamines—Bonine, Marezine and Cyclizine—which are used to combat nausea, including morning sickness, must carry a warning on their labels that, if taken by a pregnant woman, they may harm her unborn child. **1969** *Guardian* 21 July 9/2 Each [astronaut]..carries..45 milligrams of marezine for motion sickness.

marezzo (mĕre·tso). [It., f. *marezzare* to water (silk), marble.] A kind of artificial marble (see quots.). More fully *marezzo marble.*

1876 *Encycl. Brit.* IV. 508/1 Marezzo marble is made of cement mixed with fibre for strength and to resist a blow. **1901** *Notes on Building Construction* (ed. 5) III. iii. 250 The basis of Marezzo marble, as well as of Scagliola, being plaster of Paris, neither of them is capable of bearing exposure to the weather. *Ibid.*, The Artificial Marble now manufactured in London is made on the same principle as the Marezzo, but differs from it in the character of the cement used. **1958** F. S. MERRITT *Building Construction Handbk.* XII. 9 *Marezzo*, an imitation marble formed with Keene's cement to which colors have been added. **1964** J. S. SCOTT *Dict. Building* 201 *Marezzo marble*, an artificial marble like *scagliola*, which differs from it mainly in having no chips of added coloured material. When precast, it is cast on a smooth sheet of plate glass or slate to give a polished surface.

marg, var. *MARGE².

margarine. Add: Also commonly with pronunc. (mā̆ɹdʒărī·n). For def. read: A substance made from edible oils and meat fats with water or skimmed milk, used as a spread on bread, etc., and as a cooking fat. (Further examples.)

1890 [see FILLED *ppl. a.* 1 b]. **1907** *Act 7 Edw. VII* c. 21 § 13 For the purposes of the Sale of Food and Drugs Act and this Act the expression 'margarine' shall mean any article of food, whether mixed with butter or not, which resembles butter and is not milk-blended butter. **1960** A. E. BENDER *Dict. Nutrition* 79/1 Margarine... Compulsorily fortified in many countries (and voluntarily in most) with vitamins A and D, so that nutritionally equal to butter. **1963** *Which?* July 211/1 Margarine is made from a selection of vegetable oils, sometimes whale or fish oil, and often lard, usually with skimmed milk, and water. **1975** *Listener* 16 Jan. 80/3 Sheep's head..mixed..with minced onion and margarine.

b. *margarine works*; **margarine-cheese** (see quots.).

1899 *Act 62 & 63 Vict.* c. 51 § 25 The expression 'margarine-cheese' means any substance, whether compound or otherwise, which is prepared in imitation of cheese, and which contains fat not derived from milk. **1902** *Encycl. Brit.* XXV. 93/2 From America cheese has come into the English market, made from skim-milk which has again been provided with fatty matter, generally emulsified margarine—hence the term 'margarine cheese' or 'filled cheese'. **1909** *Chambers's Jrnl.* Jan. 24/1 Margarine works are equipped with cooling machinery.

Hence **margari·ne** *v. trans.*, to smear or spread (bread) with margarine; **margarined** *ppl. a.*

1918 *Punch* 15 May 315 She knows which side her bread's margarined. **1924** GALSWORTHY *White Monkey* III. iv. 243 'Well,' he said, over their cocoa and margarined bread: 'I must see Mr. Mont, that's certain.' **1960** D. STOREY *This Sporting Life* II. i. 159 She..began to margarine the bread.

Margarita (māɹgărī·tă). Also **margarita.** [f. a woman's name.] **1.** A Spanish wine.

1920 G. SAINTSBURY *Notes on Cellar-Bk.* ii. 21 My cellars ..have seldom for fifty years been without a certain 'Margarita'. **1924** *Trade Marks Jrnl.* 17 Dec. 2876 Very superior very pale dry sherry. Margarita... Sherry wine, the produce of Spain. John Harvey & Sons, Limited,.. Bristol; wine and spirit merchants.

2. A cocktail made with tequila and citrus fruit juice.

1965 O. A. MENDELSOHN *Dict. Drink* 212 *Margarita*, mixed drink made from tequila and citrus juice, drunk from vessel whose rim has been dipped in salt. **1969** *Sat. Rev.* (U.S.) 8 Feb. 32/3 You'll learn how to make..mixed drinks, ranging from Margaritas and Mai-Tais to Irish Coffee and Moscow Mules. **1969** *Guardian* 4 July 7/4 Serve as an appetizer with..if you happen to have both limes and *tequila*—margaritas. **1969** A. GLYN *Dragon Variation* ix. 288 She handed the telephone back to the bartender and sipped her margarita. **1971** C. FICK *Danziger Transcript* (1973) 44 Her husband moved past us into..the bar... 'I'm dying for a margarita.'

marge² (māɹdʒ), **marg** (maɹg, maɹdʒ). Colloq. abbrevs. of MARGARINE, as pronounced (māɹdʒărī·n) or (mā·ɹgărīn).

1922 JOYCE *Ulysses* 150 Potatoes and marge, marge and potatoes. **1933** 'G. ORWELL' *Down & Out* xxiv. 179 'No butter, only marg,' she said, surprised. **1937** E. GARNETT *Family from One End Street* iv. 82 Fetch me a bit of marg. Lily Rose—I can't waste butter on him. **1939** N. MONSARRAT *This is Schoolroom* viii. 197 Living on the dole.. bread-and-marge, and meat once a month. **1960** J. BETJEMAN *Summoned by Bells* vii. 70 In quieter tones we asked in Hall that night Neighbours to pass the marge. **1974** W. FOLEY *Child in Forest* II. 161 The remembered slice of marge-spread toast.

margin, *sb.* Add: **2. b.** *spec.* Profit(s), profit margin (further examples).

1851 C. CIST *Sk. Cincinnati in 1851* 319 We are in the enjoyment of a clear margin, of at least, half a cent per pound, over our eastern neighbors. **1890** *Congress. Rec.* 25 June 6499/2 When an employer feels that his margin is slipping away from him, the first thing done is to scale down the price of wages. **1940** *Economist* 31 Aug. 291/1 Fixed margins, which were established..to check an incipient boom, are now..the subject of some controversy. **1971** *Daily Tel.* 21 Oct. 23 (*heading*) Doubled margins work wonders for Spillers. **1972** W. A. PANTIN *Oxf. Life* iv. 48 The estates allotted to the support of chairs were in some cases left in the hands of the university, which paid out of them the appropriate salary to the professor, and sometimes made a profit out of the margin. **1972** *Times* 16 Oct. 4/6 Wheat..is grown as much for the straw as for its £57 an acre gross margin. *Ibid.* 4/7 Bulbs ..give easily the biggest margin to the acre.

c. (Earlier and later examples.)

1848 W. ARMSTRONG *Stocks* 10 The purchaser then hands over this margin to the person with whom he hypothecates the Stock. **1870** J. K. MEDBERY *Men & Mysteries Wall St.* 62 Seven per cent a year is generally allowed on all margins advanced by customers. **1880** *Harper's Mag.* Oct. 782/2 All speculated, but they did not speculate on margins. **1934** S. S. HUEBNER *Stock Market* xxiii. 434 If the customer purchases stock worth $100 and deposits $20 as margin,..he has a margin of 20 per cent. **1971** *Investors Chronicle's Beginners, Please* (ed. 5) 310 The latter [*sc.* the broker] makes an interest charge..and receives from his client..sufficient to maintain an adequate 'margin' to protect the broker against fluctuations in the value of the collateral.

e. *margin of safety*: an allowance made for safety, *spec.* a number equal to the factor of safety (*FACTOR *sb.* 8) minus one.

1888 R. S. BALL *Exper. Mech.* (ed. 2) ii. 33 So great a margin of safety is necessary on account of the jerks and other occasional great strains that arise in the raising and the lowering of heavy weights. **1905** *Trans. Inst. Naval Archit.* XLVII. II. 203 One hears, both in the lecture theatre and drawing office, much talk of 'margins of safety'. **1941** N. H. ANDERSON *Aircraft Layout* vii. 179 If the margin of safety comes out a negative quantity, the design is not satisfactory; in all cases a positive margin of safety is required. **1968** F. K. TEICHMANN *Fund. Aircraft Structural Analysis* 78 In general, the designer of aircraft structures selects structural elements with a margin of safety of zero. This does not mean that safety is not built into the craft..since the loads, or load factors actually imposed on the craft are determined rather precisely.

5. margin call, a demand by a broker that an investor deposit further cash or securities to guarantee the margin (sense 2 c) on his investment; **margin clerk,** one who records dealings in margins (sense 2 c); **margin release, marginal release,** the mechanism on a typewriter which enables the typewriting to run into the set margin; hence **margin release key,** the key on the machine which operates this mechanism.

1961 R. E. BADGER et al. *Investment Princ. & Pract.* (ed. 5) iv. 84 If the market value of the securities in an account declines, the broker issues a 'margin call' to the customer, requesting the deposit of additional cash or securities to protect against loss on the loan. **1963** PHILLIPS & LANE *Personal Finance* vii. 180 If a stock declines in market price, a margin call may be issued by the broker who must require the required margin coverage at current market prices, else he must sell the stock to protect the interests of the creditors who have supplied the previously borrowed funds. **1972** *N.Y. Law Jrnl.* 14 Nov. 2/2 The deficit arose after defendant was unable to meet margin calls. **1886** *Harper's Mag.* July 213/2 Speculative sales of land..are also made in the Call Room ..the caller of provisions and margin clerk presiding. **1973** *N.Y. Law Jrnl.* 30 July 4/6 The regulation should be..in the language of the brokers and margin clerks who must work under it. **1913** *Pitman's Commercial Encycl. & Dict. Business* IV. 1620/2 Note what a wonderful improvement there is..in all the minor parts, such as..margin release keys. **1914** *Pitman's Commercial Self-Educator* I. 163/1 Closely connected with these Marginal Stops is the Margin Release, which in the latest models takes the form of a key marked 'Marginal Release' or 'M.R.' **1939** F. A. FAUNCE *Secretarial Efficiency* II. vi. 87 Notice the location of..the backspacer, the margin release, and the ribbon shift. **1962** J. B. PRIESTLEY *Margin Released* p. viii, Typewriters..have a key labelled 'Margin Release', frequently needed by hasty and careless typists like myself. **1967** J. HARRISON *Secretarial Duties* (ed. 3) viii. 106 When erasing, move the carriage fully to the left or right, using the margin-release key.

margin, *v.* **4.** (Later examples.)

1902 H. L. WILSON *Spenders* xxxiv. 408 As the stock fell, the banks requested the brokers to margin up their loans, and the brokers, in turn, requested Percival to margin up his trades. **1973** *N.Y. Law Jrnl.* 30 July 4/2

Once a margin account has been properly margined, the regulation imposes no further requirements respecting the status of the account in the absence of a subsequent transaction.

marginal, *a.* and *sb.* Add: **A.** *adj.* **2.** (Further examples.)

1892 *Photogr. Ann.* 229 The lenses are of special optical glass, constructed with the nicest precision of curvature, so maintaining good marginal definition. **1925** J. LAIRD *Our Minds & their Bodies* ii. 31 For scientific purposes the marginal or borderline cases are usually the most instructive. **1934** H. C. WARREN *Dict. Psychol.* 159/1 *Marginal contrast*, an accentuated type of simultaneous contrast, which occurs in regions close to the boundary between two contrasting areas. **1950** tr. *Mountaineering Handbk.* (Assoc. Brit. Members Swiss Alpine Club) ix. 88 Marginal crevasses..run diagonally upwards and towards the centre of the glacier. **1957** R. G. COLLOMB *Dict. Mountaineering* 52 The changing course of a glacier causes marginal crevasses (i.e. splits at the edges)..; the changing angle of slope over which it flows causes marginal crevasses and transverse crevasses in mid-stream. **1962** BLAKE & TROTT *Periodontology* v. 49 Marginal gingivitis involves only the free gingiva. **1962** M. L. HASELGROVE *Photographers' Dict.* 141 (*caption*) A beam parallel to the principal axis will not be brought to a focus at the principal focus; marginal rays will converge to *M* while axial rays converge to *A*. **1965** G. Y. SHEVELOV *Prehist. of Slavic* 74 As in many other cases this columnal final stress was replaced by the marginal final stress.

c. *Psychol.* Of, on, or pertaining to the edge of the field of consciousness.

1894 C. L. MORGAN *Introd. Compar. Psychol.* i. 17 We.. pay attention solely to focal consciousness, omitting all reference to the great body of marginal subconsciousness. **1899** W. JAMES *Talks to Teachers* ii. 18 The expressions 'focal object' and 'marginal object', which we owe to Mr. Lloyd Morgan, require, I think, no further explanation. **1903** [in Dict., sense 3]. **1927** W. E. COLLINSON *Contemp. Eng.* 108 The field of consciousness with its focal and marginal presentations.

3. Add to def.: Freq. in *Econ.*; esp. of or pertaining to goods produced and marketed at a small margin of profit; *spec.* in phrases *marginal cost, man, utility.* Cf. quots. 1887 and 1890 in Dict. (Further examples.)

1890 A. MARSHALL *Princ. Econ.* I. p. x, The term 'marginal' increment I borrowed from von Thünen, and it is now commonly used by German economists. **1909** J. A. HOBSON *Industr. Syst.* v. 109 So with the case of the 'marginal shepherd', the tenth man whom a farmer calculates it is just worth his while to employ because he can get him for the price of twenty sheep a year, and he will just save that number by his work. *Ibid.*, Marginal productivity of labour..the productivity of any single man, 'marginal' or other. **1920** A. MARSHALL *Princ. Econ.* (ed. 8) VI. i. 517 The farmer's interests are equally served by hiring 10 or 11 men; but..the eleventh man (supposed to be of *normal* efficiency) is the marginal man, when the markets for labour and sheep are such that one man can be hired..for the price of 20 sheep. **1925** J. M. KEYNES in A. C. Pigou *Memorials A. Marshall* 22 It undoubtedly gave Jevons priority of publication as regards the group of ideas connected with 'marginal' (or, as Jevons called it, 'final') utility. **1930** *Economist* 28 June 1441/1 The proposals were based upon marginal cost on full-time running. **1931** *Encycl. Social Sci.* V. 366/1 In 1871.. W. Stanley Jevons coined the phrase final utility, Carl Menger spoke of marginal utility and Léon Walras used the term rarity. **1934** *Punch* 17 Oct. 424/1 People babble cheerfully about the Marginal Man, the law of Diminishing Returns and so on. **1957** *Times* 21 Dec. 5/2 The weather at Idlewild international airport was reported to be 'marginal', and the captain had to ensure that sufficient fuel remained to divert to an alternative base. **1958** *Listener* 25 Sept. 447/1 The ordinary American citizen enjoys amenities which not even the rich enjoyed a century ago, and marginal output consists of goods that by any standards are patently inessential. *Ibid.* 448/1 Marginal production in affluent America today..is in general much less urgent..than was marginal production 100 years ago. **1963** *Times* 16 Apr. 13/1 At any point of time there are some who would buy less coal if the price went up, either economizing in fuel or switching to some alternative. We economists call these the 'marginal' users. **1969** J. ARGENTI *Managem. Techniques* 155 Marginal cost calculations can be extremely complex in a large multi-product company... Unless marginal costing is used, the answer given to the question 'will it pay us to meet this order or should we turn it down?' will be wrong. **1973** *Black Panther* 8 Sept. 12/3 In Southern Appalachia, Black Appalachians are 'marginal' (just above the poverty level).

b. Applied to land, ore, etc., barely worth developing. Also applied to a person working such land, etc. (Cf. MARGIN *sb.* 2 a, quot. 1863.)

1910 P. H. WICKSTEED *Common Sense of Pol. Econ.* II. vi. 571 'Marginal land'..is not land..considered with reference to the volume of supply. **1935** *Economist* 30 Nov. 1095/2 Huge quantities of marginal ore which, unattractive at the old price of gold, are attractive at the new. **1943** J. S. HUXLEY *TVA* i. 7 Reafforestation and the proper use of marginal lands. **1944** *Ann. Reg. 1943* 283 Policy..of aiding the thousands of inefficient marginal farmers to raise their standards of farming. **1954** M. BERESFORD *Lost Villages* x. 346 Derbyshire... There seems to have been surprisingly little retreat of settlement from marginal lands in the Peak. **1975** *Times Lit. Suppl.* 2 May 471/3 The bringing back into production of marginal agricultural land..formed part of his [*sc.* Keynes's] vision.

c. *Sociol.* Of an individual or social group: partly belonging to two differing societies or cultures but not fully integrated into either.

1928 R. E. PARK in *Amer. Jrnl. Sociol.* May 881 (*heading*) Human migration and the marginal man. *Ibid.*, One of the consequences of migration is to create a situation in which the same individual..finds himself striving to live in two diverse cultural groups. The effect is to produce an unstable character... This is the 'marginal man'. *Ibid.* 893 It is in the mind of the marginal man—where the changes and fusions of culture are going on—that we can best study the processes of civilization. **1937** E. V. STONEQUIST (*title*) The marginal man. **1957** V. W. TURNER *Schism & Continuity in Afr. Society* iv. 108 Sandombu was from many points of view..an atypical, marginal man in Mukanza Village. **1963** *Rev. Eng. Stud.* XIV. 258 A homosexual, he regarded himself as a marginal man, out of step with society, yet contemptuous of its hypocritical standards. **1964** GOULD & KOLB *Dict. Social Sci.* 407/1 Sociologists wrote of the second generation immigrants as the most distinctively marginal group, measured by their relatively high index of crime. **1964** R. D. HOPPER in I. L. Horowitz *New Sociol.* 324 The Creole marginal group constituted about 10 per cent of the population at the time of the revolution. **1964** L. A. COSTA PINTO in *Ibid.* 471 In a marginal society it is possible to find strong support..for quite opposite decisions.

d. Of minor importance, small, having little effect; usu. const. *to*.

1929 *New Statesman* 1 June 232/1 For the 'marginal' voter—he who is at the point of indifference whether he comes to the poll or not—is unlikely..to be induced to do so by any really important consideration. **1954** M. BERESFORD *Lost Villages* vii. 261 The lands marginal to medieval corn-growing. **1955** *Times* 11 June 9/6 Most of the changes are..shifts of emphasis rather than reversals of previous policy; they are important but they are marginal. **1959** *Times* 14 Jan. 3/6 There is no major writer who uses the stage as his preferred medium of creation... Mr. Graham Greene and Mr. Angus Wilson, for example, still seem marginal to the drama. **1959** *Times Lit. Suppl.* 29 May 321/3 Twenty-six changes of punctuation, of which four or five seem..to be improvements, fourteen almost certainly wrong, and seven or eight marginal. **1964** [see *MARGINALITY]. **1969** *Listener* 16 Jan. 92/3 The lack of a character with which we can identify—..the soldiers.. remain uncharacterised and marginal—soon stills our wish to be emotionally involved.

e. *Pol.* Pertaining to a constituency, etc., in which an election or issue is likely to be closely contested and the majority very small. Also *ellipt.* as *sb.*

1951 *Times* 25 Oct. 6/3 (*heading*) Marginal seats... A significant feature of today's General Election polling is the substantial number of constituencies which may be described as marginal, and where the result of the voting is problematical. **1955** *Times* 7 June 7/4 A marginal constituency is one where the retiring member, having won the last election by a small majority, stands a sporting chance of being defeated at the next one. **1960** BUTLER & ROSE *Brit. Gen. Election 1959* xi. 135 Despite the concentration on marginal seats, the Conservatives managed to put on a full-scale campaign almost everywhere. **1965** *Listener* 24 June 921/1 It was difficult for him to give a lead on this particular topic directly after such a marginal vote in his favour. **1966** *New Statesman* 25 Feb. 246/1 For Labour MPs in 'marginals'..it means that their perilous positions could be secured. **1970** *Guardian* 16 June 10/4 Three of the four Labour-held marginals theoretically at risk would be lost only on a swing against Labour of between 4 and 5 per cent. **1974** *Times* 13 Feb. 4/6 Redistribution can make a safe seat marginal.

4. *Stock-broking.* Pertaining to, of the nature of, margins (sense 2 c).

1870 J. K. MEDBERY *Men & Mysteries Wall St.* 59 Nor is there any dissimilarity between the conditions of purchase in complete and in marginal transactions. *Ibid.* 62 The broker..demands of his customer either solid deposit of money or stocks, or marginal deposit of money. **1930** *Economist* 22 Mar. 653/1 Dominion and colonial stocks.. attracted only the 'marginal' business of the market. **1936** *Ibid.* 15 Feb. 368/2 The Great Western, whose 'marginal' security is an ordinary stock. **1938** J. B. WILLIAMS *Theory Investment Value* iii. 21 To the marginal investor, it will be indifferent whether he invests in stock or in promissory notes. **1954** B. GRAHAM *Intelligent Investor* ii. 34 Marginal trading—a potent cause of financial ruin to many—has been held within strict limits and at times suspended entirely.

B. *sb.* **2.** *Zool.* A feather on the edge of a bird's wing.

1887 *Proc. Zool. Soc.* 347 They [*sc.* feathers along the posterior border of the wing] are best termed marginals (*tectrices marginales*). **1898** F. E. BEDDARD *Struct. & Classification Birds* 9 The patagium is mainly filled up with several rows of feathers, which are collectively termed the marginals.

marginalism (mā·ɪdʒinăliz'm). *Econ.* [f. MARGINAL *a.* + -ISM.] An economic analysis which gives prominence to marginal factors in the economy. Hence **ma·rginalist** *a.*, of or pertaining to marginalism; also *sb.*, an adherent of marginalism.

1926 J. A. HOBSON *Free-Thought in Social Sci.* iii. 118 The recent extension of Marginalism treats 'doses' as infinitesimal quantities, applies them to the demand as well as the supply side of the economic equation..and to all economic activities. *Ibid.* 119 Our modern Marginalists commit a..mistake in affecting to treat economic material in general as being..other than it actually is. **1929** —— *Wealth & Life* II. iii. 119 The development of a marginalist doctrine, representing the movements of minutely divisible units of capital and labor into businesses and trades. **1951** J. O. KAMM *Econ. Investment* ii. 33 (*heading*) Marginalism and investment policy. **1956** R. F. HARROD in A. Pryce-Jones *New Outl. Mod. Knowl.* 470 Such were the Austrian school of marginalists and their counterpart in England, Jevons. **1969** P. ANDERSON in Cockburn & Blackburn *Student Power* 220 Alfred Marshall, father of marginalist economics. **1973** K. MENGER in Hicks & Weber *Carl Menger* iii. 38 Austrian marginalism and mathematical economics. *Ibid.*, The Austrian marginalists and the mathematical economists agree in most of their fundamental economic views.

marginality (māɪdʒinæ·liti). [f. MARGINAL *a.* + -ITY.] The quality or state of being marginal (in various senses of the adj.).

1929 *Pitman's Econ. Educator* III. 1352/1 The exchange value of commodities determines their marginal utility and itself expresses their marginal cost. The notion of marginality in this way sheds light upon the economic conflict. **1951** M. S. RIX *Investment Arithmetic* xii. 117 Priority percentages are also sometimes used to compare the gearing, or marginality, of one company's equity with another. **1955** *Times* 21 June 11/7 The region now has 28 Conservative to 15 Labour marginal seats. Conservatives also have the larger share of 'marginality' in the South and West. **1961** S. R. HERMAN in J. A. Fishman *Readings Sociol. of Lang.* (1968) 508 The choice of language at the various stages in the above case history reflects the passage from a position of marginality..to a position of adjustment as a member of Israel society retaining the elements of identity derived from socialization in another culture. **1963** L. TRILLING in N. Frye *Romanticism Reconsidered* 96 And the converse of what explains Nietzsche's relative marginality explains Dostoevsky's position at the very heart of the modern spiritual life. **1964** R. D. HOPPER in I. L. Horowitz *New Sociol.* 19 Marginality here means that, in pre-revolutionary societies, there is formed a group that is marginal to the structure of political power and social prestige. **1971** *World Archaeol.* III. 146 All of these facts combine to form a general picture of marginality in resources. **1974** R. JESSOP *Traditionalism, Conservatism & Brit. Polit. Culture* ii. 42 A marginal [social] class..is more likely to become class-conscious than one that is relatively secure and unexploited. Marginality in turn can be due to adverse market conditions, to technological change, to political action, to bad luck, or some other factor.

marginally, *adv.* Add: **a.** (Later example.)

1970 M. JONES *Ducal Brittany* ii. 47 The Breton version of the homage, transcribed..at the back of the *Livre des Ostz*, is marginally glossed as simple homage.

b. Round or about the margin or edge of anything; in a way that is close to the limit or margin; by a small margin, slightly.

1909 H. G. WELLS *Tono-Bungay* III. ii. 250 Wandering marginally through distinguished gatherings, I would catch the whispers: 'That's Mr. Ponderevo!' **1931** *Brit. Jrnl. Psychol.* Jan. 226 Attention is directed to locating the proper box for response rather than to picking up a card (because this is such a very common process and everyone can do it 'sub-consciously' or 'marginally'). **1965** *New Statesman* 30 Apr. 672/1 The situation in Britain is only marginally less alarming. **1972** *Accountant* 17 Aug. 191/1 The law will be applied strictly..where schemes differ marginally from the prescribed conditions. **1974** 'A. GARVE' *File on Lester* xxxvi. 128 The papers are terrible this morning—the *Star* marginally the worst, but only marginally.

margination. Add: **2.** Annotation with marginal notes. *rare.*

1874 SWINBURNE *Let.* 13 July (1959) II. 308, I quite agree with you that the Homeric margination ought to be most carefully preserved.

maria, *pl.* of *MARE[4].

Maria (ma·riă), *sb.* and *a.* Also Maree. **A.** *sb.* A member of a jungle-dwelling Dravidian people of central India; also, the native (Dravidian) language of this people. **B.** *adj.* Of or pertaining to this people or their language.

1827 R. JENKINS *Rep. Territories Rajah of Nagpore* ii. 33 The wildest of these Gonds are the Marees. They generally go in a state of complete nudity, and even their women have no covering, but aprons of leaves. *a* **1863** S. HISLOP in G. Smith *Stephen Hislop* (1888) 22 Moria Gonds..are more civilized than the Márias. **1863** *Sel. Rec. Govt. India Foreign Dept.* No. 39. 14 The language in this talook is Teloogoo and Maria. The population is composed mainly of Marias and Telingas. **1882** H. B. ROWNEY *Wild Tribes India* I. i. 5 The Máree Gonds..live in the wildest parts of the province of Nágpore. **1938** W. V. GRIGSON *Maria Gonds of Bastar* iii. 49, I divide the so-called Marias into two divisions, the Hill Marias of the Abujhmar mountains, and the Bison-horn Marias. **1944** I. SINGH *Gondwana & Gonds* ii. 22 The Marias formerly roamed about in a state of nature and then..adopted leaves and barks as their garments. **1962** *Listener* 29 Nov. 893/1 Every young member of Indian jungle tribes like the Maria. **1971** [see *GOND *sb.* and *a.*].

‖**mariachi** (mariă·tʃi). [Mexican Sp. *mariache, mariachi.*] A group of itinerant Mexican folk musicians; also, a member of such a group. Also *attrib.*

1941 *Time* 19 May 97 There are stacks of records by the omnipresent Mexican street bands, the *mariachis*. **1948** 'P. QUENTIN' *Run to Death* xiii. 106 The *mariachis* had started to play. Over the frenzied twang of guitars a deep, chesty baritone was extolling Guadalajara. **1964** *Listener* 16 July 90/3 The *mariachis* personify all the robust colour of Mexico... They have the looks and the swagger of brigands and the dress-sense of toreadors, and they make jarring, irresistible music in the convulsive patterns of Latin-American rhythms. **1966** [see *CHARRO]. **1967** S. BLANC *Rose Window* (1968) viii. 79 The breeze carried snatches of *mariachi* music from the terrace where the guests were dining. **1970** W. APEL *Harvard Dict. Mus.* (ed. 2) 526/2 Characteristically Mexican is the *mariachi*,

the typical band that serves to entertain people in cafés and at village and country dances and celebrations. **1971** *Islander* (Victoria, B.C.) 19 Dec. 2/2 A mariachi band was ordered and two bottles of tequila to make their evening's work more pleasurable.

‖ **mariage blanc** (mariaʒ blañ). [Fr., lit. 'white marriage'.] An unconsummated marriage.

1926 *Irish Statesman* 13 Nov. 234 It is improbable, and yet quite possible, this story of a *mariage blanc.* **1931** *Times Lit. Suppl.* 17 Sept. 702/2 One must admire the tact with which Mr. Church handles the painful theme of the full-blooded Norah's revolt against the frustration of a *mariage blanc.* **1958** *Observer* 23 Feb. 14/2 We get a hint that Evan's and Cherry's is really a *mariage blanc.* **1958** G. MITCHELL *Spotted Hemlock* xi. 214 'The autopsy revealed that the girl was a virgin.'.. '*Un mariage blanc?* Good Lord!' **1975** *Listener* 21 Aug. 253/3 Opal..suggested a *mariage blanc* between Natalie and Bosie that would have enabled Opal and Bosie to have a lasting liaison.

‖ **mariage de convenance** (mariaʒ də kõñvənañs). [Fr., lit. 'marriage of convenience'; cf. CONVENIENCE *sb.* 6.] A marriage arranged or contracted from motives of convenience (sense 6) or expediency. Also *fig.* Cf. *marriage of convenience* (*MARRIAGE 8).

1854 THACKERAY *Newcomes* I. xxviii. 275 What the deuce does a *mariage de convenance* mean but all this. **1864** TROLLOPE *Small House at Allington* I. ix. 83 I'm only a half sort of lover, meditating a mariage de convenance to oblige an uncle. **1912** I. NITOBÉ *Jap. Nation* vi. 163 The sorrows of *mariage de convenance* in Europe. **1923** J. S. HUXLEY *Ess. Biologist* vii. 295 Some men are pragmatic and utilitarian in regard to Truth; by others she is worshipped as fanatically as any goddess. So some men deliberately make *mariages de convenance.* **1955** *Bull. Atomic Sci.* Mar. 97/3 History suggests that the evil partnership between Communist China and the Soviet Union may yet develop the brittle quality of a mariage de convenance. **1957** L. DURRELL *Justine* IV. 235 Someone trapped into a *mariage de convenance.* **1974** M. CECIL *Heroines in Love* iv. 91 The fashionable world, with its ill-bred ideas about money and *mariages de convenance.*

mariahuana, var. *MARIJUANA, MARIHUANA.

Marial (mēə·riăl), *a.* [F. *marial* = MARIAN *a.*[1] 1; cf. MARIAL[2].] = MARIAN *a.*[1] 1.

1904 *Catholic Herald* 23 Dec. 8/4 On the initiative of the Archbishop of Leopol [*sic*], a grand Marial Congress was organised and held in his Cathedral city. **1952** D. M. J. LANGDON *Our Lady of La Salette* v. 30 Montserrat in the mountains of Spain, and hundreds of other centres of Marial devotion. **1966** *Approaches* Nov. 123 The Marial Congregations for men, which are now actively organising their lay apostolate in all fields of public life.

Marian, *sb.*[2] Add: **2.** (Later examples.)

1969 A. FRASER *Mary Queen of Scots* II. xxii. 433 The castle of Edinburgh, so long held by Kirkcaldy and Maitland on behalf of the Marians..was at last effectively besieged. *Ibid.*, Maitland..had died a loyal Marian. **1974** G. DONALDSON *Mary Queen of Scots* v. 122 Kirkcaldy and Maitland did not emerge as open Marians until much later and were at first numbered among 'secret favourers of the Queen'. *Ibid.* 134 Balfour of Pittendreich became a Marian, though he was not at Langside.

3. An English Catholic of Queen Mary's reign (1553–8).

1868 H. H. MILMAN *Ann. S. Paul's Cathedral* xi. 256 The Primate Pole was in his grave, Heath of York a strong Marian. **1899** F. W. MAITLAND *Coll. Papers* (1911) III. 130 Canon MacColl laboured under the misfortune of knowing something about the votes that these Marians gave in Parliament. **1904** W. H. FRERE *Eng. Church 1558–1625* ii. 23 The champions of the Marians..were to dispute with the champions of the exiles. **1955** C. READ *Mr. Secretary Cecil* iv. 101 He abandoned flight and decided to throw in his lot with the Marians.

Marianne (maria·n). Also in anglicized form (*rare*) **Mary Anne.** [Fr.] The name of a Republican Secret Society formed in France after the coup of 1851 to restore a Republican Government; hence a familiar name for the Republican form of Government and, by extension, a personification of the French Republic.

1870 DISRAELI *Lothair* I. xi. 100 Our refreshment at council is very spare..but we always drink one toast... It is to one whom you love and whom you have served well. Fill glasses. brethren, and now 'To *Mary-Anne*'. **1890** BARRÈRE & LELAND *Dict. Slang* II. 45/2 'La Marianne' ..was the name of a secret Republican Society in France. **1933** KIPLING *Souvenirs of France* ii. 53, I asked a friend, an Alsatian General, whence the flood of material had come. 'From Marianne,' was the reply. 'She has all sorts of things like these in her stocking—when she needs them.' **1934** H. G. WELLS *Exper. Autobiogr.* II. ix. 747 (*caption*) Marianne asks Dadda to tell her all about it. **1940** —— *Babes in Darkling Wood* IV. iii. 374 Nor will Marianne be in a position to act the vindictive hostess this time... France and Britain had their chance of making a world peace in 1918, and they muffed it. **1958** H. J. GREENWALL *When France Fell* II. i. 66, I went to the *Marianne* office in the Avenue des Champs Elysées. **1962** *Listener* 12 July 57/2 Had Daumier wished to treat a similar theme we can be almost certain he would have selected Marianne or the Gallic cock as an impersonal national emblem. **1971** *Guardian* 3 Apr. 3/5 There is no official model for the bust of Marianne, the incarnation of the Republic, found in every Mairie in France.

Mariavite (mēə·riăvəit). [Pol. *Mariawita*, f. L. phr. *qui Mariæ vitam imitantur.*] A member of a Polish Christian sect which flourished in the early 20th century; also *attrib.*

[**1906** *Daily Chron.* 23 Apr. 5/5 The church at Leschno.. had been occupied by the sect of Marianites. **1906** *Times* 28 May 5/3 The *Osservatore Romano* publishes to-day an Encyclical..condemning the doctrine of the so-called Marianisti, and definitely suppresses the Marianisti congregation.] **1906** *Tablet* 9 June 897/2 Some priests..had founded, without permission from their lawful superiors, a kind of pseudo-monastic society, known as the *Mariavites* or *Mystic Priests. Ibid.* 898/2 The so-called Mariavite priests who are in good faith may no longer be led astray. **1949** D. ATTWATER *Catholic Encycl. Dict.* 306 *Mariavites*, a sect in Poland originating in 1906 with a number of apostate clergy. **1957** *Oxf. Dict. Chr. Ch.* 857/2 *Mariavites*, a Polish sect, founded in 1906 by J. Kowalski, a priest of Warsaw, and Felicia Kozlowska, a Tertiary sister,..on their excommunication from the RC Church.

‖ **mari complaisant** (mari kõñplęzañ). [Fr.] A husband who tolerates his wife's adultery.

1898 W. J. LOCKE *Idols* xv. 211 You are three outstanding people... Hang it all—the *mari complaisant*—and Merriam is the last man in the world—it beats me altogether. **1933** *Times Lit. Suppl.* 5 Oct. 673/1 Without being the *mari complaisant* he has hitherto stood aside, probably seeing much more than he could admit. **1937** MRS. BELLOC LOWNDES *Diary* 20 Jan. (1971) 145 The unfortunate Mr Simpson was..regarded as *un mari complaisant.* **1950** D. AMES *Corpse Diplomatique* ix. 72, I don't understand English women. In France there is such a thing as a *mari complaisant,* but I've never heard of an *amant complaisant*! **1958** L. DURRELL *Justine* I. 29 She was reputed to have had many lovers, and Nessim was regarded as a *mari complaisant.* **1972** P. M. HUBBARD *Whisper in Glen* xii. 115 If you see him as the *mari complaisant*, you'd better think again... If he knew I was carrying on with you..he'd fling me out.

mariculture (mæ·rikɒltiŭɹ, -tʃəɹ). [f. L. *mari-, mare* sea + CULTURE *sb.*] The cultivation of the resources of the sea, esp. of fish for food. So **maricu·ltural** *a.*, of or pertaining to mariculture; **maricu·lturist**, one who engages in or specializes in mariculture.

1903 *Science* 9 Oct. 461 Such maps would be purely agricultural and maricultural, dependent upon the harvests of the land and sea. **1909** *Cent. Dict.* Suppl., *Mariculture*, the development of the resources of the sea, especially with respect to food-fish; coined in distinction from *agriculture.* **1969** *Sci. Jrnl.* Dec. 30 The man who studies agriculture stands in a different place from the man who studies mariculture. There are other differences between the two fields but not so basic as the need for the mariculturist to swim. **1970** *New Scientist* 20 Aug. 378/1 The first step in an effort to use the deep ocean water for mariculture, the generation of electrical power and the production of fresh water. **1971** *McGraw-Hill Yearbk. Sci. & Technol.* 23 If we are very optimistic and assume for a moment that the yield of the traditional fishery will not change, mariculture could perhaps lead to an increment in the crop produced from the sea from the present 1% to 1.1%. **1973** *Daily Colonist* (Victoria, B.C.) 12 Apr. 12/4 Some areas should be left wild; others should be utilized for recreation; others might be developed and employed for mariculture; and still other areas might be exploited or used as dumping grounds. **1974** *Victorian* (Victoria, B.C.) 5 Apr. 2/1 The federal-provincial governments have allotted $38,000 to two companies involved in oyster mariculture in a cost-sharing program to improve and develop the oyster industry in British Columbia.

Marie (mā·ri). Also **marie.** A female Christian name used *attrib.* of a type of plain sweet biscuit.

1878 *Official Guide & Album Cunard Steamship Co.* 186/3 (List of Biscuits) Marie. **1888** *Mrs. Beeton's Bk. Househ. Managem.* ii. 31/2 Biscuits..Marie..1s. 9d. per tin. **1906** E. NESBIT *Railway Children* ii. 27 There were biscuits, the Marie and the plain kind. **1919** D. ASHFORD *Young Visiters* vi. 50 He swollowed his tea and eat a Marie biscuit hastilly. **1947** E. TAYLOR *View of Harbour* xii. 203 A jug of cocoa and a plate of Marie biscuits. **1966** B. KIMENYE *Kalasanda Revisited* 43 Though they sipped their tea, they simply could not bring themselves to touch a marie biscuit. **1972** C. DRUMMOND *Death at Bar* i. 10 The old tea lady..slopped the fluid over on to the marie biscuits in the saucer.

Marie Antoinette (ma·ri antwane·t). The name of the Austrian queen consort (1755–1793) of Louis XVI of France, used *attrib.* to designate various styles of dress, decorative art, etc., characteristic of her or her reign (see quots.).

1925 F. SCOTT FITZGERALD *Great Gatsby* v. 110 We wandered through Marie Antoinette music-rooms. **1950** '*Mercury*' *Dict. Textile Terms* 337 *Marie Antoinette*, a curtain, having appliqué sprays, flowers and leaves of cord and tape. **1960** CUNNINGTON & BEARD *Dict. English Costume* 133/1 *Marie Antoinette skirt*,..a day skirt with 7 gores, 1 in front, 2 on each side, and 2 behind, box-pleated. **1966** J. S. COX *Illustr. Dict. Hairdressing* 96/1 *Marie Antoinette chignon*, a full globular low dressed chignon. *Marie Antoinette coiffure*, hair styles similar to those worn by Marie Antoinette.

Marie Louise (ma·ri lu,ī·z). The name of *Marie Louise* (1791–1847), second wife of Napoleon I, used to designate a variety of yellow-skinned pear. Also *attrib.*

1817 *Trans. Hort. Soc.* II. 406 A box of Pears, sent to the Society by Dr. Van Mons, of Brussells, was examined. .. They are stated, by Dr. Van Mons, to be seedlings raised by himself: 1, Napoleon..; 2, Marie Louise: in shape and size resembling a small Bon Chrétien; yellow, with bright red next the sun; very rich, and ripe about the middle of October. **1820** *Ibid.* IV. 519 Specimens of the Marie Louise Pear were received. **1860** R. HOGG *Fruit Manual* 200 Marie Louise... One of our very best pears. Ripe in October and November. **1894** 'MRS. ALEXANDER' *Choice of Evils* I. ii. 34 Not even the Mervyn gardens could produce finer pears than the solitary 'Marie Louise' tree. **1929** E. A. BUNYARD *Anat. Dessert* 104 Marie Louise, cannot be overlooked,..being named after that most acquiescent of Empresses, Napoleon's second wife, and, like her, it needs the support of a strong arm to stay its languishing growth. **1958** [see *DOYENNE[1]].

marigold. Add: **8.** The colour of the marigold flower; hence *attrib.* passing into *adj.*, of this colour, bright yellow.

1774 Marigold colour [in Dict., sense 7]. **1839** [see *café au lait* (*CAFÉ 3)]. **1872** G. M. HOPKINS *Let.* 22 Mar. (1956) 55, I am jaundiced all marigold under the eyes. **1916** D. H. LAWRENCE *Amores* 49 Cluck, my marigold bird, and again Cluck for your yellow darlings. **1923** *Daily Mail* 28 Feb. 1/3 (Advt.), Shades of..Jade, Silver Grey or Marigold. **1975** *Country Life* 20 Mar. 744/2 Their clothes are matched to a limited number of colours...there are cornflower/ cool cornflower, mint/cool mint, and marigold/cool marigold.

marijuana, marihuana (mærihwā·nă). Also **mara-, maria-; mariguan(a.** [Amer. Sp.] **1. a.** A preparation of the hemp plant, *Cannabis sativa* (see *CANNABIS), for use as an intoxicating and hallucinogenic drug; usu. applied to a crude preparation of the dried leaves, flowering tops, and stem of the plant that is generally smoked.

1894 *Scribner's Mag.* May 596/2 [The] 'toloachi', [and] the 'mariguan',..are used by discarded women for the purpose of wreaking a terrible revenge upon recreant lovers. **1918** *Jrnl. Amer. Med. Assoc.* 21 Dec. 2094/1 The symptoms mentioned.. as being produced by smoking Mara Huiwane or marajuana are similar to those produced by the mescal plant. **1923** W. SMITH *Little Tigress* 102 The cockroach is unable to stagger around any more because he has no more marijuana to smoke. *Marijuana* is a form of drug that brings false heart to the user. **1927** *Amer. Speech* III. 37 The tobacco of the Turkish coffee-houses has been replaced in Mexico by marihuana, the native variety of hashish. **1928** *Daily Express* 11 Oct. 3 What is Marijuana? A deadly Mexican drug, more familiarly known as 'Mary Jane', which produces wild hilarity when either smoked or eaten. **1935** J. STEINBECK *Tortilla Flat* xiv. 246 His eyes were as wide and pained as the eyes of one who smokes marihuana. **1939** [see *DAGGA[1]]. **1944** R. A. MOORE *Textbk. Path.* lix. 657 After long-continued use of marihuana there is mental deterioration. **1952** M. MCCARTHY *Groves of Academe* (1953) ii. 19 On one occasion, even, marijuana had been smoked on the steps of the gymnasium. **1960** N. POLUNIN *Introd. Plant Geogr.* ix. 267 Cannabis consumption as hashish, marijuana, etc., causes states of ecstasy and stupefaction. **1968** P. OLIVER *Screening Blues* ii. 83 The song *Weed Smoker's Dream* referred to the hallucinations induced by marijuana. **1968** *Times* 19 Dec. 4/6 Basic findings are that.. subjects who have not smoked marihuana before do not have strong subjective experiences, even after strong doses.

b. *fig.*

1948 *Sat. Rev.* (U.S.) 19 June 24/3 One of the most cogent reasons for the success of the comics, is namely, that they are the marijuana of parents as well as of their offspring. **1965** *New Statesman* 10 Dec. 916/2 The politician who gave the Beatles the MBE..knows that if he suddenly cut off about 20 million young addicts from their supply of aural marijuana the withdrawal effects could produce unpleasant political side-effects.

2. The hemp plant; = *CANNABIS 1.

1907 A. B. LYONS *Plant Names* (ed. 2) 511 (Cannabis) a. Add Syn[onym] Marihuana (Mex.). **1934** R. E. CARRADINI *Narcotics & Youth Today* 1 In this classification [of narcotic drugs] should be included..*Cannabis Indica*, popularly known as Indian hemp or hashish, and the native plant, *marihuana.* **1934** *Jrnl. Amer. Med. Assoc.* 21 July 212 On appeal to the Supreme Court of Utah, Navaro contended that the term 'mariguana', as used in the statute, signified a plant, not a drug. **1959** *Encounter* Oct. 56/2 The land where the marihuana grows. **1973** *Daily Tel.* 4 July 4 Nepal is to ban the growing of marijuana and poppies and the production of cannabis and opium.

3. *attrib.* and *Comb.*, as *marijuana addict, cigarette, habit, -smoker, -smoking* vbl. sb. and ppl. adj., *weed.*

1936 *Amer. Speech* XI. 12 Argot of narcotic addicts... *Twister*,..one who rolls his own twists, or marajuana cigarettes or, by extension, a marajuana addict. **1938** *Manch. Guardian Weekly* 2 Sept. 188/3 Some [swing players] are 'mugglers' (Marijuana addicts). **1933** *Jrnl. Amer. Med. Assoc.* 28 Oct. 1398/1 The first person to be convicted in Hillsborough County [in Florida] of selling marajuana cigarets..was sentenced..to a year in the county jail. **1966** T. PYNCHON *Crying of Lot 49* iii. 64 Leonard the drummer..produced a fistful of marijuana cigarettes. **1953** W. BURROUGHS *Junkie* (1972) x. 107, I told them you were sick and that you needed a shot of morphine, and they said, 'Oh, we thought it was just a question of a marijuana habit.' **1951** E. PAUL *Springtime in Paris* xi. 202 Narcotics addicts and marihuana smokers are infiltrating the cafés. **1935** *Amer. Mercury* Aug. 426/1 Such practices as adultery, marihuana smoking, gambling, ..and rowdyism seldom worry the investigator. **1957** P. FRANK *Seven Days to Never* iii. 102 She married..a marijuana-smoking drugstore cowboy. **1958** *Times* 3 Dec. 6/6 Unauthorised clubs..were a great moral danger to young people. The marihuana weed was smoked.

marimba. Substitute for def.: A kind of deep-toned xylophone, originating in Africa and consisting of wooden keys on a frame with a tuned resonator beneath each key. Hence, a modern orchestral instrument evolved from this. Also *attrib.* (Further examples.)

1923 A. H. NEWBOLD *Bamboo Curtains* 27 You and I on a polished floor, And a big marimba band. **1924** S. SITWELL *13th Cæsar* 58 Loud is the marimba's note Above these half-salt waves. **1927** *Melody Maker* Aug. 732/3 (Advt.), The Rage To-Day.—'Foote' Xylophones and Marimbas. **1934** A. HUXLEY *Beyond Mexique Bay* 119 The visitor of 1933 may think himself lucky if he hears a *marimba* orchestra discoursing tangos. **1957** WODEHOUSE *Over Seventy* iii. 42 You can dance nightly to the strains of somebody's marimba band. **1958** A. JACOBS *New Dict. Mus.* 226 Milhaud wrote a concerto (1947) for marimba and vibraphone. **1961** *Guardian* 22 May 5/5 Her company of 75 dancers, singers, and marimba players presented us with authentic reconstructions of the Aztec ritual dances. **1970** J. BLADES *Percussion Instruments* xvi. 425 In *Vision of St. Augustine* Tippett writes for marimba.

marimbaphone (mărɪ·mbăfōᵘn). [f. prec. + Gr. φωνή sound, voice.] = prec.

1921 *Daily Colonist* (Victoria, B.C.) 9 Oct. 23/2 The instrumentation will be as follows: 25 Violins, 6 Pianists.., 4 Marimbaphones, [etc.]. **1923** *Weekly Dispatch* 11 Mar. 5 The marimbaphone or Mexican xylophone..depends for its depth of tone on a number of tubes of varying lengths filled with liquid. **1926** A. HUXLEY *Jesting Pilate* IV. 263 Organ chimes, giant marimbaphone, vibraphone. **1962** *Listener* 22 Nov. 885/3 A marimbaphone and six chimes.

marina[1]. Add: **2.** A dock or basin with moorings for yachts and other small craft. Also *attrib.* orig. *U.S.*

1935 *Yachting Monthly* LIX. 223/2 Fees for keeping a yacht in a municipal 'marina' (trick name for basin) are modest. Yachts are tied up in slips in these marinas. **1959** *Manch. Guardian* 15 Aug. 5/2 Everywhere in the United States the outboard motor, the cabin cruiser, the 'marina' (a little dock for pleasure craft) are to be seen. **1960** *Sunday Times* 3 Apr. 37/5 But what about entering and leaving this well-dammed basin, or marina—the American word? **1961** *Times* 28 Apr. 6/3 (*heading*) Hayling Island marina plan to be pressed. **1963** R. I. MCDAVID *Mencken's Amer. Lang.* 264 Spanish may share with Italian the credit for the current vogue of *marina*, as a de luxe designation for a yacht basin. **1969** *Daily Tel.* 11 Jan. 19/3 It will include two hotels, flats, 'boatels', yacht clubs, restaurants, two public houses and a 'marina drome'. **1971** *N.Z. Listener* 25 Oct. 7/1 In 1928 boat-owners added another word to their vocabulary, 'marina'. Coined in the United States to describe a new kind of luxury boating facility..it has altered the style and living of an increasing number of New Zealanders.

Marina[3] (mărī·nă). [f. the name of H.R.H. Princess *Marina*, Duchess of Kent (1906–68).] Used *attrib.* in *Marina green*, a shade of green.

[**1934** *Times* 29 Nov. (Suppl.) p. iii/2 The going away *ensemble* [of Princess Marina] will be in almond-green tweed.] **1935** *Discovery* Aug. 231/1 There is a popular shade of green at present in vogue, termed 'Marina green'. **1935** *Times* 18 Nov. 21/4 Cleverly designed dinner gowns in satin and lace in rust, Marina green, and royal blue. **1958** M. DICKENS *Man Overboard* iii. 46 That sickly colour which was once foisted on to a loyal public as Marina green when the Duchess of Kent was married.

marinate, *v.* Add: **1. a.** (Further examples.) Also *absol.*

1960 *Times* 18 Jan. 15/5 Fillet [steak] is exceptionally tender and should not need to be marinated or beaten. **1970** *Daily Tel.* (Colour Suppl.) 30 Oct. 62 It is..absolutely in order to make the 'gamey' flavour less pungent by marinating.

marinated, *ppl. a.* **2.** (Further example.)

1969 *Daily Tel.* 14 Jan. 15 Spicy marinated pork.

marine, *a.* and *sb.* Add: **A.** *adj.* **1.** *marine band*: a geological horizon containing fossils of marine origin situated between horizons of freshwater origin.

1920 W. GIBSON *Coal in Gt. Brit.* xxii. 277 With the exception of the marine fauna of Skipsey's Marine Band and of that above the Slaty Band Ironstone, the invertebrate fauna is not of much variety. **1939** RAISTRICH & MARSHALL *Nature & Orig. Coal Seams* ii. 33 The remains of fresh-water or marine shells are less common, forming when they occur in quantity 'mussel bands' and 'marine bands'. **1969** BENNISON & WRIGHT *Geol. Hist. Brit. Isles* ix. 224 The marine horizons (called marine bands) are sometimes of great lateral extent.

6. marine biology, the study of plants and animals living in the sea; hence **marine-biological** *a.*; **marine biologist,** one engaged in this study; **marine iguana,** a large lizard, *Amblyrhynchus cristatus,* found on the Galapagos Islands; **marineland,** a type of zoological garden, designed to exhibit and preserve marine animals.

1884 in *Jrnl. Marine Biol. Assoc.* (1887) I. 22 Report of the Foundation Meeting of the Marine Biological Association. **1959** D. A. BANNERMAN *Birds Brit. Is.* VIII. 119 The expedition..was mainly to investigate some of the marine-biological and agricultural problems of the Tristan da Cunha group. **1963** T. A. SEBEOK in J. A. Fishman *Readings Sociol. of Lang.* (1968) 30 Aristotle was also the first marine biologist who accurately classed the dolphin with the mammals. **1887** *Jrnl. Marine Biol. Assoc.* I. 1 It is not proposed to limit the contents of this journal to formal reports..but to include within its pages..brief records of observations relating to the marine biology and fisheries of the coasts of the United Kingdom. **1936** *Discovery* June 166/2 M. Paul Lemoine..referred to his [*sc.* Sir Robert Mond's] work on behalf of marine biology. **1967** *Oceanogr. & Marine Biol.* V. 111 Of all the different facets of marine science, marine biology is perhaps the oldest in India. [**1839** DARWIN *Jrnl.* in Fitzroy & Darwin *Narr. Voy. H.M.S. Adventure & Beagle* III. xix. 453 (*heading*) Marine lizard feeds on sea-weed.] **1924** C. W. BEEBE *Galapagos* v. 111 The sea or marine iguana is as good a name as could be desired. **1962** C. J. & O. B. GOIN *Introd. Herpetology* viii. 136 *Amblyrhynchus cristatus*, the Marine Iguana of the Galápagos Islands, feeds on marine algae at low tide. **1972** *Country Life* 6 Apr. 842/3 In addition to the giant tortoises..there are the marine iguanas. **1963** *Times* 17 Apr. 12/5 Southsea Castle committee agreed today to open negotiations with Billy Smart's Circus for the proposed establishment of a marineland in the castle grounds. **1968** *N.Z. News* 16 Oct. 6/2 Complete plans and specifications have been drawn up and a tender accepted for a marineland on Windsor Reserve at Devonport, Auckland.

B. *sb.* **4. c.** Phr. *tell that to the marines* (earlier and later examples): an expression of incredulity. Cf. quot. 1892 s.v. HORSE-MARINE[2].

1806 J. DAVIS *Post Captain* v. 29 He may tell that to the marines, but the sailors will not believe him. *c* **1829** D. JERROLD in M. R. Booth *Eng. Plays of 19th Cent.* (1969) I. 179 No palaver; tell it to the marines. What, tacking and double tacking! Come to what you want to say at once. **1902** J. CONRAD in *Blackw. Mag.* Dec. 802/2 'You shall get nothing from me, because I have nothing of mine to give away now.' 'Tell that to the marines!' **1928** *Times* 21 July 17/5 He said that I should..most likely be shot. I ventured to suggest that he should tell that to the Marines. **1933** E. O'NEILL *Ah, Wilderness!* (1934) IV. ii. 145 And I suppose you just sat and let yourself be kissed! Tell that to the Marines! **1944** W. S. MAUGHAM *Razor's Edge* vii. 279 '*A d'autres, ma vieille,*' I replied, which I think can best be translated by: 'Tell that to the marines, old girl.' **1967** D. FRANCIS *Blood Sport* xiv. 172 'When this is over you can sleep for a fortnight.' 'Yeah?' he said sarcastically. 'Tell it to the marines.'

6. b. marine blue, a dark blue, the colour of the uniform worn by the Royal Marines; freq. *ellipt.* as *marine.*

1873 *Young Englishwoman* IV. 78/1, I should suggest.. one polonaise of black cashmere..and one of deep marine blue vigogne. **1895** *Montgomery Ward Catal.* 3/1 Cashmere... All the fashionable colors..black, marine blue, light blue. *Ibid.* 12/3 Plain China silk..navy, marine, gray. **1910** *Encycl. Brit.* VIII. 746/2 The following is a list of the more important basic colours derived from coal-tar.. marine blue, indoïne blue, [etc.]. **1925** E. SITWELL *Poor Young People* 2 The colours most in favour are marine Blue,..myrtle green. **1930** MAERZ & PAUL *Dict. Color* 168/1 In the early nineteenth century there became popular in the general textile field a color adapted from the uniforms of sailors. This color seems first to have been called *Marine Blue*, followed shortly by the name *Navy Blue*. The color was long dyed with indigo. **1934** *Times* 30 Nov. 20/2 The Queen of Denmark's dress and..coat were both of deep marine-blue velvet. **1961** H. E. BATES *Now sleeps Crimson Petal* 43 The marine blue thorns of sea-thistle were touched with sepia rose.

‖ **marinera** (marinē·ră). [f. Sp. *marinero, -a* marine, seafaring.] = *CUECA.

1926 D. L. JOSEPH in J. F. Dobie *Rainbow in Morning* (1965) 54 Play for him a *Marinera* While they whip him. **1964** W. G. RAFFÉ *Dict. Dance* 305/1 Of Spanish extraction, the *Marinera* came to Peru from Chile and was originally called *Cueca Chilena*, or *Chilena*, the name being changed to *Marinera* during the 19th century when Peru and Chile were at war (1879–1883). The new name honoured the Peruvian Navy. **1973** K. BENTON *Craig & Jaguar* v. 53 They even succeeded in making me dance a *marinera* with one of the—er—very nubile young women. **1974** *Encycl. Brit. Macropædia* I. 669/1 This uncertain major–minor tonality pervades the Andean music. It appears in the *chinguinada* for church festivals, with a bass ostinato (repeated melodic-rhythmic pattern); in the mestizo *yaraví* serenade and in the mestizo *marinera* couple dance, with its metre alternating $\frac{3}{4}$ and $\frac{6}{8}$ patterns.

marinescape (mărī·nskēɪp). [f. MARINE *a.* and *sb.* + SCAPE *sb.*[3], after LANDSCAPE.] A picturesque view or prospect of maritime scenery. Cf. SEA-SCAPE.

1928 *Daily Express* 13 Jan. 11 The Mediterranean was like a sheet of sapphire... Everywhere the marinescape was dotted with rowing boats and other vessels. **1969** J. W. MAVOR *Voy. Atlantis* v. 112 It was the most awesome marinescape that I had ever seen.

marine store(s. Add: **1. b.** (Earlier example.)

c **1829** D. JERROLD in M. R. Booth *Eng. Plays of 19th Cent.* (1969) I. 184 Go into the mercantile line—take a shop for marine-stores.

2. (Earlier example.)

1837 BARHAM *Legend H. Tighe* in *Ingol. Leg.* (1840) 1st Ser. 158 In Ratcliffe Highway there's an old marine store.

3. (Further examples.)

1836 DICKENS *Sk. Boz* 1st Ser. I. 91 The marine-store dealer at the corner of the street. **1844** *Ainsworth's Mag.* VI. 112 A marine-store keeper of the pilfered orts and ends of literature.

Mariological (mēᵊriǫlǫ·dʒikăl), *a.* Also with small initial. [f. MARIOLOG(Y + -ICAL.] Of or pertaining to Mariology. So **mariolo·gically** *adv.*

1954 *Theology* LVII. 90 A mariological interpretation. *Ibid.*, Interpret the text mariologically. **1967–8** H. R. MCADOO in Clark & Davey *Anglican/R.C. Dialogue* (1974) vi. 93 There are..similarly differences as between Roman Catholics and Anglicans, and Anglicans would add Mariological definitions. **1969** E. L. MASCALL in A. Richardson *Dict. Christian Theol.* 208/1 By a small majority it was decided by the [Second Vatican] Council not to issue a separate Mariological document. **1971** *Catholic Dict. Theol.* III. 264/1 The most notable event in the Mariological deliberations of the Vatican Council was the vote taken on 29 October 1963 to decide whether the schema *de Maria matre ecclesiae* should be taken as a final chapter of the decree on the Church or as a decree by itself. **1974** *Encycl. Brit. Macropædia* XI. 563/1 The extravagances of Marian cult and Mariological thought that have sometimes tended to go beyond the limits both of biblical foundation and of ecclesiastical regulations.

marionettish (mæriǒne·tiʃ), *a.* Also **marionetish.** [f. MARIONETT(E + -ISH[1].] Suggestive of a marionette in appearance or movement.

1921 E. O'NEILL *Emperor Jones* v. 184 There is something stiff, rigid, unreal, marionettish about their movements. **1930** *Observer* 18 May 26/2 'Intimate Snapshots' was fresher and rounder in conception than in execution... I thought the liftman unclear in his explanation, and the journalists marionetish. **1963** A. ROSS *Australia 63* x. 196 If fast, short-pitched bowling induces an initial, marionettish jerkiness he soon settles down to more convincing methods. **1969** E. WILKINS *Rose-Garden Game* viii. 192 Their marionettish aspect encourages the impression that at any moment the gilded mandorla might begin to turn on its axis and spin.

marione·ttist. Also **marionnettist.** [f. MARIONETT(E + -IST.] One who operates marionettes.

1918 *Marionnette* (Florence) Jan. 98 The Marionnettist has put his dolls in their box...his wife is counting the pennies. **1924** *Glasgow Herald* 10 May 8 It was here the man of so many quarrels..fought the mock duel with.. the marionettist's monkey. **1936** R. S. SIBBALD *Marionettes in North of France* I. 44 M. Delannoy..gives a list of the marionettists who applied to the city of Lille..for permission to show their dolls.

Mariotte (mæ·riǒt). Also erron. **Marriotte.** The name of Edme *Mariotte* (*c* 1620–84), French physicist, used in the possessive and *attrib.* to designate apparatus he devised and a principle he enunciated: **Mariotte('s) bottle** or **flask,** a bottle with an outlet near the bottom and an adjustable glass tube passing through a cork in the neck, which if filled to above the bottom of the tube gives a flow of constant head equal to the height of the bottom of the tube above the outlet; **Mariotte's law,** Boyle's law (see LAW *sb.*[1] 17 c (*b*)); **Mariotte's tube,** a U-tube having one arm short and sealed at the end and the other elongated and open to the air.

1845 E. WEST tr. *Peschel's Elem. Physics* I. v. iii. 220 On the same principle Mariotte's flask acts. *Ibid.* iv. 228 In such a case it is more convenient..to use..a Mariotte's tube.., which being graduated according to Marriotte's [*sic*] law, will show the amount of pressure. **1898** J. C. P. ALDOUS *Elem. Course Physics* 171 (*heading*) Boyle's (or Marriotte's [*sic*]) law. *Ibid.* 172 (*heading*) Boyle's (or Mariotte's) tube. **1930** DOUGALL & DEANS tr. *P. P. Ewald's Physics Solids & Fluids* v. 217 The experiment is conveniently carried out by using the so-called Mariotte's bottle. **1966** *McGraw-Hill Encycl. Sci. & Technol.* II. 313/1 The phenomenon was discovered independently by Edme Mariotte about 1650 and is known in Europe as Mariotte's law. **1974** *Nature* 26 Apr. 798/1 Continuous flow of fluid..was maintained relatively constant by means of gravity flow from a Mariotte flask. **1975** WILLIAMS & WILSON *Biologist's Guide to Princ. & Techniques Pract. Biochem.* iii. 93 This can be overcome by the use of a Mariotte flask which will keep the operating pressure constant.

‖ **mariposa** (maripo·să). [Sp., lit. 'butterfly'.] In *Bullfighting*, a movement in which the bullfighter draws the bull by flapping the cape behind his own back. Also *fig.*

1932 [see *FAROL]. **1936** R. CAMPBELL *Mithraic Emblems* 143 If you would lepidopterize These mariposas that I fling. **1957** A. MACNAB *Bulls of Iberia* xv. 169 The bull.. is attacking what looks like a giant butterfly... The butterfly is Estudiante himself, and he is doing the famous *quite* of the *mariposa*... The matador holds the cape behind him,..as he holds out his arms sideways to form the 'wings' with the cape... As the bull turns and goes for one wing, he drops his arm and that wing folds up. **1967** MCCORMICK & MASCAREÑAS *Compl. Aficionado* iii. 92 Like all beginning novilleros, Domingo longs to learn the adornos first, the *revolera*, the *serpentina*, the *mariposa* with the cape.

mariposa lily. Add: Also **mariposa tulip.** Substitute for def.: A bulbous plant of the genus *Calochortus*, belonging to the family Liliaceæ, and native to the Pacific coast of North America and Mexico. Also *absol.* (Earlier and later examples.)

1868 A. WOOD in *Proc. Acad. Nat. Sci. Philadelphia* 169

This splendid flower [sc. *Calochortus venustus*]..has long been known to the native Californians by the name of *Mariposa* (Spanish for butterfly). **1869** J. Muir *Jrnl.* 9 June in *My First Summer in Sierra* (1911) 43 The grasses and flowers in glorious array,..monardella, Mariposa tulips, lupines. **1920** B. M. & R. Rice *Pop. Stud. Calif. Wild Flowers* 27 It would probably be more correct to say Mariposa Tulip than Mariposa Lily, for botanists place them in the tulip family. **1925** J. L. Cotter *Culture of Bulbs* 108 The name Calochortus now embraces the Mariposa Lily proper, and the Star Tulip. **1934** S. E. White *Folded Hills* 198 Here also were..mariposas. **1971** P. M. Synge *Collins Guide to Bulbs* (ed. 2) 71 It is in..the Mariposa lilies or Mariposa tulips that we chiefly find the most outstanding horticultural plants [of the genus *Calochortus*]. *Ibid.* 73 The leaves of this section are..more conspicuous than those of the Mariposas.

mariposite (mæripōᵘ·zəit, -səit). *Min.* [f. *Maripos-a*, the name of the county in California, U.S.A., where it was first found + -ite¹.] A variety of muscovite that contains a relatively high proportion of silica and up to one per cent. chromic oxide and is found as green or greenish-yellow crystals.

1868 B. Silliman in *Proc. Calif. Acad. Sci.* III. 381 The mineral is probably new, and must be referred to the mica section of an hydrous silicate. Should it..prove to be new, I would suggest the name *Mariposite* as an appropriate name for it, as it was on the Mariposa estate that it first attracted my attention, and where it exists in great abundance. **1916** *Bull. U.S. Geol. Survey* No. 610. 139 A comparison of the two analyses of mariposite made by Hildebrand with Penfield's analysis of alurgite shows that the two minerals are probably identical. **1946** *Amer. Mineralogist* XXXI. 1 Chrome micas, classed variously as fuchsite, mariposite, and chromiferous muscovite are of wide distribution throughout gold-bearing districts of the Canadian Shield. **1965** G. J. Williams *Econ. Geol. N.Z.* x. 149/2 The majority of overseas occurrences of fuchsite (and mariposite) seem to have a direct ultramafic association.

maritime, *a.* and *sb.* Add: **A.** *adj.* **6.** **maritime pine**, the cluster pine, *Pinus pinaster*, a southern European tree distinguished by cones in clusters, often planted in coastal areas to bind sandy soil.

1894 H. M. Ward *Laslett's Timber & Timber Trees* (ed. 2) xxxi. 349 The Cluster Pine..much used in the south and west of France, where it is known as the Maritime Pine from the extensive planting on the coasts, yields a highly resinous reddish wood. **1914** W. J. Bean *Trees & Shrubs Hardy in Brit. Is.* II. 187 Cluster Pine, Maritime Pine..is, as its common name implies, admirably adapted for maritime localities. **1969** T. H. Everett *Living Trees of World* 54/1 Of all two-needled pines, the species with the longest leaves,..is the cluster pine or maritime pine..a southern European tree that thrives in coastal areas.

B. *sb.* **1. b.** In *pl.*, with capital initial. The eastern provinces of Canada adjoining the Atlantic Ocean (Nova Scotia, New Brunswick, and Prince Edward Island).

1926 *Daily Colonist* (Victoria, B.C.) 24 July 1/2 Continuing his Maritime tour, Premier Meighan in an address here tonight again stressed his policy for the Maritimes. **1934** W. M. Whitelaw (*title*) The Maritimes and Canada before Confederation. **1938** L. M. Montgomery *Anne of Ingleside* viii. 58 The July night was unreasonably cold as even a summer night in the Maritimes sometimes is. **1947** G. Taylor *Canada* xvi. 385 The three small provinces linked as the Maritimes..together only amount to 1.5 per cent of the area of the Dominion. **1956** C. R. Fay *Life & Labour in Newfoundland* viii. 134 Schooners come from the Maritimes with much needed provisions and lumber. **1960** *Times* 21 Nov. (Canada Suppl.) p. v/6 The salty Maritimes or the wide-open Prairies. **1970** M. M. Orkin *Speaking Canad. Eng.* vii. 186 Nova Scotia is *The Mayflower Province*, and New Brunswick *The Loyalist Province*. Together with Prince Edward Island, they are collectively known as the *Maritime Provinces* or, more familiarly, the *Maritimes.*

‖ **Marivaudage** (marivodaʒ). [Fr., f. the name of P. C. de *Marivaux* (1688–1763), novelist and dramatist.] The expression of affected language and exaggerated sentiment in the style of Marivaux; an overdone attempt at refinement, affectation.

1765 H. Walpole *Let.* 19 Nov. in *Corr.* (1948) XIII. 144 Crébillon is entirely out of fashion, and Marivaux a proverb: *marivauder*, and *marivaudage* are established terms for being prolix and tiresome. **1882** G. Saintsbury *Short Hist. French Lit.* iv. ii. 410 All the work of Marivaux, dramatic and non-dramatic, is pervaded more or less by a peculiarity which at the time received the name of Marivaudage. This peculiarity exists partly in the sentiment, and partly in the phraseology. The former is characteristic of the eighteenth century, disguising a considerable affectation under a mask of simplicity, and the latter (sparkling with abundant, if somewhat precious wit) is ingeniously constructed to suit it and carry it off. **1894** Beerbohm in *Yellow Bk.* II. 284 The qualities that I tried ..to travesty—paradox and marivaudage. **1930** *Mod. Lang. Rev.* XXV. 71 *Marivaudage*..to quote Faguet.. 'consists much more in analysing to excess a just thought than in decking out to excess an empty one'. **1959** *Oxf. Compan. French Lit.* 455/2 The term *marivaudage*, coined from his name, is used to signify the analysis of the delicate sentiments of the heart and the subtle, affected style used by Marivaux to this end in his comedies. **1969** *Observer* 12 Jan. 26/5 It [*sc.* Lesbianism] is a tricky subject, poised on the brink of either tiresome *marivaudage* or tasteless titillation.

mark, *sb.*¹ Add: **7. d.** (Earlier and later examples of *slang* sense.) Also, *a soft* or *easy mark* (cf. *easy *a.* 13 b), a person who is easily persuaded or deceived (*slang* (orig. *U.S.*)); also (*Austral. slang*), *a good* (or *bad*) *mark* (see quot. 1941).

1845 R. Howitt *Impressions Australia Felix* 233, I heard it casually from the lips of apparently respectable settlers as they rode on the highway, 'Such and such a one is a good mark!'—simply a person who pays his men their wages, without delays or drawbacks; a man to whom you may sell anything safely. **1860** F. &. J. Greenwood *Under a Cloud* II. xiv. 332 'There's a mark!' exclaimed one to the other, looking towards the spot where Hatcher was standing. **1883** J. Greenwood *Tag, Rag & Co.* iii. 24 Publicans..are usually the unfortunate tradesmen fixed on as a mark. **1896** Ade *Artie* xvi. 150 He was the wise guy and I was the soft mark. *Ibid.* xviii. 173 When that kind of a mark comes in they..get ready to do business. **1904** G. H. Lorimer *Old Gorgon Graham* 288 He was too easy a mark to succeed in Wall Street. **1922** Joyce *Ulysses* 75 Didn't catch me napping that wheeze. The quick touch. Soft mark. **1929** 'E. Queen' *Roman Hat Mystery* xiii. 187 For a shrewd man, he certainly was an easy-mark for the wiseacres. **1941** Baker *Dict. Austral. Slang* 46 *Mark, good* (*or bad*), a general term of approval (or disapproval) for a person. **1956** H. Gold *Man who was not with It* (1965) i. 6, I floated down..to kick the smaller mark where it would tell on him. **1962** J. Ludwig in R. Weaver *Canad. Short Stories* (1968) 2nd Ser. 255 He was repulsive, old, a mark, a fool—his nerve went. **1966** 'J. Hackston' *Father clears Out* 93, I was a bit nervous and an easy mark to bamboozle. **1968** B. Turner *Sex Trap* xv. 148 You thought I might like to turn myself into an ugly mark! A square with a loud voice and a shopping-bag! Marriage! **1971** *Frendz* 21 May 11/2 In 90% of all rip-offs the naive mark hands over his capital to some virtual stranger who never returns. **1973** E. McGirr *Bardel's Murder* ii. 31 In the twenties it was the Yanks who was the suckers, but now..it's us who are the marks.

11. g. Also *fig.* in phr. *full marks* used as an expression of considerable praise or commendation. Also *top marks*.

1934 D. L. Sayers *Nine Tailors* ii. v. 175 That is well observed. Yes, Bunter, you may have full marks for that. **1941** H. Nicolson *Let.* 27 Mar. (1967) 154 It is a fine show and I give Ronnie Campbell full marks. **1945** W. de la Mare *Scarecrow* 22 'Full marks, my dear,' said Mr. Bolsover, squeezing her hand. **1966** *Listener* 29 Sept. 472/3 Full marks for the deadly opening sentence. **1973** *Times* 2 June 9/4 Full marks as always, to this hard-up, persevering, resourceful and imaginative museum. **1973** J. Thomson *Death Cap* xiii. 177 He gave Holbrook top marks for finding such a delightfully sharp and acid old lady.

12. c. Add examples with prefixed figure representing a limit or total, or an approximation of this.

[**1860** Thackeray *Roundabout Papers* vi, in *Cornh. Mag.* Aug. 256 The *Cornhill Magazine*..having sold nearly a hundred thousand copies, he (the correspondent) 'should think forty thousand was now about the mark'.] **1929** *Star* 21 Aug. 18/2 Dennis Brothers' 1s. shares can usually be regarded as a reasonable purchase under the £3 mark. **1946** *R.A.F. Jrnl.* May 170 The membership already exceeds the twenty-five hundred mark. **1948** D. Ballantyne *Cunninghams* iii. 15 Around the forty mark. **1965** N. Paul *Cine-Photogr.* ii. 19 There is a tremendous range of models on the market today, especially in the 8 mm. gauge, where they can..soar up to the £300 mark. **1973** *Times* 14 Apr. (Nepal Suppl.) p. ii/9 If the present trend continues, the 25 million mark may be reached before the end of the century.

d. Also *Austral. Rules Football* (see quots. 1968). Cf. *mark *v.* 15 d.

1965 *Sun-Herald* (Sydney) 4 July 51 Geelong Rover, Terry Farman, won a trophy for the best mark taken by his team. **1967** *Ibid.* 16 Apr. 67 Ryan's first kick struck the back of the Collingwood man on the mark, but Perkins ruled he had moved back over the mark. **1968** Eagleson & McKie *Terminol. Austral. Nat. Football* ii. 22 *Mark*,.. the catching of the ball on the full directly from the kick of another player. *Ibid.* 23 *Mark*,..the spot at which a player caught the ball ('took a mark'), and behind or over which he must make his kick. **1969** *Sun-Herald* (Sydney) 13 July 48/1 Close took a beautiful one-handed mark, his tenth for the game,..but kicked only a point.

e. *Athletics.* A line drawn to indicate the starting-point. Also in phrases (lit. and fig.), as *on your mark*(*s*), (*get set, go*), the instructions given to competitors at the start of a race; *to be first off the mark*: to gain an initial lead over one's opponents; *to be quick off* (or *on*) *the mark*: to lose no time in starting, to waste no initial advantage; *to be slow off the mark*: to start slowly or sluggishly; to waste time in starting; *to get* (or *be*) *off the mark*: to start (well); *to overstep the mark*: to infringe the rules by placing one's foot over or beyond the mark; so *fig.*, to go beyond a fixed limit or standard, to 'go too far'; cf. the phr. *overshoot the mark* (Overshoot *v.* 2 b, and Mark *sb.*¹ 7 a, e); *to toe the mark* (see Toe *v.* 2).

1887 M. Shearman *Athletics & Football* 65 It requires, however, much skill and practice not to 'take off' before the mark [in jumping]. *Ibid.* 198 Nothing was said until the men got upon their marks. **1905** *Pearson's Mag.* Sept. 290/2 He..beat his field by a yard or two off the mark. **1912** E. H. Ryle *Athletics* 91 This method..assists a runner to keep steady on the mark while awaiting the report of the pistol. **1917** E. Pound *Let.* 12 Aug. (1971) 114, I have been a bit slow getting the *Little Review* off the mark. **1919** E. P. Oppenheim *Strange Case J. Thew* i. xiii. 112 'Did he make any trouble?' 'He had no chance ..I was first off the mark.' **1921** *Daily Colonist* (Victoria, B.C.) 24 Mar. 13/3 It was felt that the Parent–Teachers' Associations were in some cases overstepping the mark in regard to requests. **1928** *Observer* 5 Feb. 23/5 When you really wish to get going you have a second, a third and a top speed change which will get the car off the mark, in the old phrase, in an inspiriting manner. **1929** F. N. Hart *Hide in Dark* i. 25 All set? On your mark! **1930** L. W. Olds *Track Athletics* iv. 26 On Your Marks... Get Set... Go or Gun. **1931** *Oxford Mail* 29 Aug. 8/3 G. Fisher and L. Rogers were quickly off the mark, 20 runs being scored in the first ten minutes. **1934** Wodehouse *Right Ho, Jeeves* i. 9 Get off the mark..like a scalded cat, and your public is at a loss. **1938** R. Warner *Professor* x. 227 Now he appeared like a person who fears that he has in some way overstepped the mark, has involuntarily wounded another's feelings, or alluded to some subject that were better left unmentioned. **1943** *Endeavour* Apr. 74/2 The dog-breeder and poultry farmer were comparatively quick off the mark in using the new therapy. **1946** B. Marshall *George Brown's Schooldays* v. 22 On your marks, go. The thing was to lob them [*sc.* rissoles] out like fives pills. **1947** 'G. Orwell' *Eng. People* 24 With all their political ignorance the English people will often show surprising sensitiveness when some small incident seems to show that 'They' are overstepping the mark. **1954** G. Mitchell *On your Marks* xv. 172 'On your marks,' said the starter. The swimmers were poised and ready. 'Go!' **1958** J. Wain *Contenders* v. 102 Ned was off the mark at once... Blue Seal Pottery seemed to become a vogue overnight. **1970** Marlow & Watts *Track Athletics* ii. 18 It is recommended that the shoulders should be forward when the athlete settles into the blocks on the command 'On your marks'. **1971** *Morning Star* 19 Oct. 2 The Institute of Teachers and the Association of Science Teachers were quick off the mark, followed by the more orthodox national trust. **1972** R. Adams *Watership Down* xxvii. 208 The pursuit was a bit slow off the mark..because poor old Bugloss wasn't there to give the orders. **1972** W. A. Pantin *Oxf. Life* iv. 50 Dr. William Buckland..was very quick on the mark with putting in plans for the future use of the building. **1973** *South Wales Echo* 30 June (Suppl.) 1/2 Then the whole Burke Special team can get off their mark. **1973** *Guardian* 8 Oct. 10/2 Beatrix Potter..wrote about Tommy Brock (the badger) and Mr. Todd (the fox) living on terms of toleration—until Tommy badly overstepped the mark.

13. b. (Earlier and later examples.)

a **1847** T. Chalmers in Bartlett *Dict. Amer.* (1860) 262 Men..called out to make and leave their mark upon the world. **1854** *Harper's Mag.* Sept. 561/2 There was a time when Jacob made his mark upon the stock-brokers and money-changers of that monetary locality. **1905** L. Strachey *Characters & Commentaries* (1933) i. iv. 34 Whether he himself [*sc.* Walpole] might not have made his mark in politics is perhaps a futile speculation. **1921** R. Macaulay *Dangerous Ages* xi. 208 Why dream wistfully of doing one's bit, making one's mark, in a world already as full of bits..as a kaleidoscope? **1927** C. Bell *Landmarks 19th Cent. Painting* 147 They have not failed to leave a mark on history. **1952** A. J. Cronin *Adventures in Two Worlds* i. 15 In medicine, or some other field, I believe that you will make your mark. **1973** *Observer* (Colour Suppl.) 5 Aug. 18/2 Woolton..making his mark as Civilian Boot and Shoe Controller in World War I. **1974** *Radio Times* 3 Jan. 49/4 Pop music has produced many trendsetters—we pick three who've made their mark in the 70s.

e. *Telecommunications.* Each of a succession of marks on paper whose relative duration and separation are used to convey information in telegraphy; hence, any kind of signal that conveys information by its presence or absence (rather than by its magnitude). Opp. *space*: hence **mark–space** *attrib.*

1837 *Amer. Jrnl. Sci. & Arts* XXXIII. 187 [*Describing Morse's telegraph.*] To read the marks; count the points at the bottom of each line. **1859** T. P. Shaffner *Telegr. Manual* xxxiv. 469 The length of the mark or of the space upon the ribbon paper will be precisely the same as the length of the contact made with the key. **1891** C. L. Buckingham in C. F. Brackett et al. *Electr. in Daily Life* 143 In 1846 Bain proposed to employ perforated strips of paper to effect automatic transmission in connection with an electro-chemical process for recording, in which marks upon a moving band of paper are made by discoloration attending the passage through it of signalling currents. **1938** *Admiralty Handbk. Wireless Telegr.* II. K. 59 When the key is pressed, the valve oscillates and we have the mark period. *Ibid.*, During mark, the oscillating circuit constitutes the load. **1953** *Electronics* July 183/2 Mark–Space Phototubes. As the perforated tape passes through the keying head, pulses of light from the exciter lamps pass through the holes and alternately strike the tone-on (mark) and tone-off (space) phototubes. The phototubes conduct and produce alternate pulses of current. **1958** P. E. K. Donaldson et al. *Electronic Apparatus for Biol. Res.* xv. 234 The circuit performs oscillations with a mark–space ratio of approximately unity, the waveforms having the form of Figure 15.14. **1969** J. J. Sparkes *Transistor Switching* iii. 52 A circuit capable of producing rectangular waves with very sharp rising and falling edges, at mark–space ratios of between 1:1 and 500:1,..is shown. **1972** *Sci. Amer.* Dec. 16/3 The computer's input element is a photoelectric paper-tape reader that handles 1,000 'marks' (punched holes) per second.

15. b. Also, freq. followed by a numeral, a designation of the stage of development in design and construction of a manufactured product or piece of equipment, as a weapon, an aeroplane, etc. Abbrev. Mk. Also *transf.* and *fig.* *Mark I*: first class (*slang*).

1888 *Treat. Mil. Small Arms & Ammunition* 52 Enfield Revolver Pistol, Mark II. **1899** *Kynoch Jrnl.* Oct.–Nov. 12/1 Despite the unfortunate failures at Edinburgh and

Bisley of the bullet known as Mark IV. **1914** *Times Bk. Navy* vii. 99 The gun has progressed through successive stages, or 'marks' as they are technically known. Marks 3, 4, 5, and 5w were 'built' guns. **1916** T. E. LAWRENCE *Let.* 22 Dec. (1938) 214 Will you please wire for 4 locks complete for Gun Maxim Converted Mark II to be sent to Yenbo? **1926** L. NASON *Chevrons* 120 This is going to be a real, old issue, Mark I scrap. **1942** W. S. CHURCHILL in *Second World War* (1951) IV. 768 There should be no difficulty in sparing 1,000 tanks and 1,000 anti-tank and A.A. guns. No doubt older marks might form the bulk. **1946** *R.A.F. Jrnl.* May 180 No fewer than 26 different 'Marks' were built and put into service... In accordance with Service custom they merited and received the bestowal of a special Mark number. **1948** 'N. SHUTE' *No Highway* i. 7 The Mark I model [*sc.* an aeroplane] which went into production first had radial engines. **1959** *Listener* 19 Mar. 514/1, I trust the Ministry of Supply is making sure that all senior naval, military, and air force officers are supplied with Mark II* crystal balls. **1973** P. JOHNSON in Johnson & Gale *Highland Jaunt* I. i. 13 Time's winged chariot is hurrying near, powered by the latest mark of internal combustion engine. **1973** J. WAINWRIGHT *Devil you Don't* 5 It was a great car—a Jag Mark II. **1974** *Economist* 21 Dec. 29/3 They are calling him [*sc.* Helmut Schmidt] Kissinger Mark II. **1975** J. SYMONS *Three Pipe Problem* xv. 129 For his white clients Riverboat often played the role of American Negro, Mark One.

22. *a mark at*, a good hand at.

1881 *Punch* 3 Dec. 263/2 Till my chummy Scholard Mike, who's a mark at A.B.C., Read me Littler's little tale.

23. (sense 11 g) *mark-sheet, system*; **mark sensing**, the process by which a machine 'senses' or reads data in the form of electrically conducting marks made by hand on cards with a lead pencil; so **mark-sense(d** *a.*, marked in this way and for this purpose.

1965 *Math. in Biol. & Med.* (Med. Res. Council) I. 10 They used 'mark-sense' cards for the details of the investigation and for the results of calculations. **1971** *Computers & Humanities* VI. 16 A newer approach employs mark-sense cards upon which musical symbols have been printed. This allows the person doing the encoding to accomplish it in a single step, quietly, and without the need for cumbersome equipment. **1964** T. W. MCRAE *Impact of Computers on Accounting* i. 14 Figure 1.8 illustrates a mark sensed card. The mark sensed positions are in columns 70–78 and the holes punched from these..are in columns 31–33. **1959** E. M. GRABBE et al. *Handbk. Automation, Computation, & Control* II. v. 19 Mark sensing uses special electrical conducting marks placed in various positions on punched cards. **1970** O. DOPPING *Computers & Data Processing* iii. 55 Information can also be recorded in a card with a pencil, and in a subsequent operation, 'mark sensing', the markings are translated to punched holes in the cards. **1961** *Oxf. Local Exam.* (*Latin, Paper 1*) p. 3 The total mark..is to be halved before it is entered on the marksheet. **1964** *Oxf. Mag.* 12 Mar. 254/1 Now that the dust has settled on the marksheets of the January Part II examination. **1885** *Encycl. Brit.* XIX. 754/2 He devised an ingenious system of recording the convicts' daily industry by marks... The mark system had already been tried with good results in Ireland.

mark, *sb.*[2] Add: **4. b.** Also, now the name of the unit of German currency.

1911 E. SYKES *Banking & Currency* (ed. 3) viii. 61 The Imperial Bank of Germany can issue notes to the value of 550,000,000 marks against the deposit of securities. **1932** J. W. ANGELL *Recovery of Germany* (rev. ed.) ii. 19 Mark prices fell... In..1921..two things happened which definitely sealed the fate of the old mark currency. *Ibid.* 21 Everyone who was unfortunate enough to possess mark currency was in danger of having it lose half its value in his pocket overnight. *Ibid.* 56 The mark notes, bank deposits, and securities became practically worthless. **1933** E. ROLL *Spotlight on Germany* i. 39 The function of the mark as a medium of exchange had disappeared almost as completely as its ability to form a standard of value. *Ibid.* 41 The mark was finally stabilized at one million-millionth of its pre-war value. **1964** M. MCLUHAN *Understanding Media* (1967) II. xiv. 156 The depreciation of the citizen went along with that of the German mark.

mark, *v.* Add **2. c.** *to mark down* (earlier and later examples); hence *marked-down* ppl. adj., also *ellipt.* as *sb.*; cf. *MARK-DOWN *sb.*; *to mark up*: to label (goods) with a higher price; to raise in price.

1859 *N.Y. Herald* 5 Jan. (Advt.), Mark every article Way Way Way down To some price which will make it.. Sell and go quick. **1870** *Amer. Naturalist* III. 3 The prices of venison and other game was so far 'marked up' that gold..was charged for salmon. **1902** G. H. LORIMER *Lett. Merchant* iv. 52 The clerks all knocked off their regular work and started in to mark up prices. **1908** *Sat. Even. Post* 24 Oct. 13/1 At another store there is a marked-down sale of parasols. **1910** 'SAKI' *Reginald in Russia* 43 They have turned instead to the muddy lanes and cheap villas and the marked-down ills of life. **1913** F. H. BURNETT *T. Tembarom* vi. 67 A remnant of crimson stuff secured from a miscellaneous heap at a marked-down sale at a department store. **1923** E. O'NEILL *Moon of Caribbees* 18 Don't you boys forget to mark down cigarettes or tobacco or fruit, remember! Three shillin's is the price. **1942** M. SCHLAUCH *Gift of Tongues* (1943) vi. 135 'Marked-downs' (overheard in a department store for 'reduced dresses'). **1962** E. GODFREY *Retail Selling & Organization* xvi. 164 A minority of firms..have abandoned them [*sc.* fixed profit margins] in favour of marking-up each item on its merits. **1965** A. CHRISTIE *At Bertram's Hotel* xii. 113 She also availed herself of some marked down lines in furnishing fabrics. **1974** *Times* 22 Oct. 12/6 Exclusive goods can be marked up to carry a full, and I suspect..very high, profit margin.

e. *to mark off* (Engin. and Shipbuilding): to mark (an object) with lines to serve as a guide for subsequent cutting, machining, alignment, etc.; to represent (a dimension or detail) on an object in this way.

1894 W. J. LINEHAM *Text-bk. Mech. Engin.* vi. 185 If the work is too large to mark-off on a table it should be levelled, and all lines be drawn by reference to an ideal horizontal or vertical plane. **1895** J. DONALDSON *Drawing & Rough Sketching for Marine Engineers* (ed. 6) 87 When the forging of a crank shaft, or other part of an engine, is delivered..it is essential..that it be accurately marked off for machining. *Ibid.*, The throw of the vertical crank is marked off from the horizontal line. **1925** F. J. DROVER *Marine Engin. Repairs* xix. 120 The cheeks are marked off for thickness. **1966** J. H. DIXON tr. *Dormidontov's Shipbuilding Technol.* i. 15 Hull details are marked off from the full-size or scaled down lofting data and from working drawings. *Ibid.* vi. 127 When the metal is being marked off, the outlines of the components are drawn full size, with an indication of the allowances and tolerances for machining.

f. To mark the ears of (a lamb, or less commonly a calf); also, to dock and geld. Cf. *MARKING *vbl. sb.* 1 a. *Austral.* and *N.Z.*

1933 *Press* (Christchurch, N.Z.) 4 Nov. 15/7 *Mark*, to ear-mark. Now a frequent euphemism for *cut and tail*. **1941** BAKER *Dict. Austral. Slang* 46 *Mark*,..to geld lambs. **1950** *N.Z. Jrnl. Agric.* Sept. 197/1 Lambs are usually marked at between 1 to 6 weeks of age; 3 weeks is probably the ideal age.

6. a. Also with *down*.

1894 'R. ANDOM' *We Three & Troddles* xxii. 210 The demon dyspepsia had marked him down.

d. Also with *out from*.

1888 MRS. H. WARD *R. Elsmere* I. viii. 222 The even gentleness which always marked her out from others. *Ibid.* III. xxxii. 34 The reasoning faculty..which marks us out from the animal. **1905** T. E. HARVEY *Rise of Quakers* ii. 10 Her son's serious ways, by which he was marked out from his other brothers and sisters.

7. f. *to mark down*: to make a note of; to set down in writing.

1881 J. FOTHERGILL *Kith & Kin* II. ix. 241 More than one matron then present had silently marked him down.. in her book of 'eligibles'. **1936** *Discovery* May 145/1 An exhaustive search was not feasible, but 51 nightingales were marked down in Devon.

g. In phr. *to mark (someone's) card* [CARD *sb.*[2] 6 e]: (from the practice in horse-racing) to provide (someone) with information; to tip (someone) off; to 'put (someone) right'. *slang.*

1961 PARTRIDGE *Dict. Slang* Suppl. 1179/2 *Mark (someone's) card*, to give him the information he needs; to put him right: barrow-boys': since ca. 1945. Ex the racecourse. **1962** R. COOK *Crust on its Uppers* ii. 34 They'd marked my card there was a new dance-hall been opened over at Peckham. **1970** P. LAURIE *Scotland Yard* 291 *Mark X's cards, to*, to brief X discreetly. **1970** G. F. NEWMAN *Sir, You Bastard* 282 The third was to phone the insurance assessor and mark his card.

13. Delete 'Now *poet.*' and add later examples.

1832 DISRAELI *Contarini Fleming* II. III. v. 241, I looked up, I marked the tumultuous waving of many torches. **1849** C. BRONTË *Shirley* II. xii. 278 She smiled, well pleased to mark the delight of her pupil. **1860** THACKERAY *Four Georges* i, in *Cornh. Mag.* July 5 Lift up your glances respectfully, and mark him eyeing Madame de Fontanges. **1893** KIPLING *Many Inventions* p. viii, The children wise of outer skies Look hitherward and mark A light that shifts. **1901** G. B. SHAW *Caesar & Cleopatra* v. 199 Rufio, satisfied, nods at Cleopatra, mutely inviting her to mark that. **1922** C. BELL *Since Cézanne* 11 They babble in the Burlington Fine Arts Club—where nobody marks them. **1972** 'M. INNES' *Open House* II. xi. 99 He paused to mark this [*sc.* a compliment] going home.

15. d. *Austral. Rules Football* (see quot. 1968). Cf. *MARK *sb.*[1] 12 d.

1968 EAGLESON & MCKIE *Terminol. Austral. Nat. Football* II. 23 *Mark*, catch the ball on the full directly from the kick of another player. **1969** *Sun-Herald* (Sydney) 13 July 48/1 Hudson marked 35 yards out, but a bad kick fell well short of the goal.

16. Also, *mark you* (or *me*, etc.). Cf. *look you* s.v. LOOK *v.* 4 a.

1837 E. HOWARD *Old Commodore* I. v. [*sc.* vi] 210 Mark you me, Mr. Alsop, mark you me. We have done our duty, sir. **1862** MRS. H. WOOD *Channings* II. ix. 137 'Impudence,' shortly answered Yorke. 'Mark you, Miss Channing! I have not done with you.' **1867** A. J. EVANS *St. Elmo* xvii. 232 It remains to be seen whether a grand success is not destined to crown it. Mark you! The grapple is not quite over. **1903** G. B. SHAW *Man & Superman* I. 23 For mark you, Tavy, the artist's work is to shew us ourselves as we really are. **1922** JOYCE *Ulysses* 139 It was the speech, mark you, the professor said, of a finished orator. *a* **1953** E. O'NEILL *Touch of Poet* (1957) III. 94 Provided, mark you, that you and your daughter sign an agreement I have drawn up. **1966** *Listener* 17 Feb. 240/1 Well, mark you, I wouldn't be the inveterate optimist I am, if I didn't live in the belief that the year of my life is yet to come.

Markan (mā·ɹkăn), *a.* [f. *Mark* + -AN.] = MARCAN *a.*

1909 B. W. BACON *Beginnings Gospel Story* p. xxviii, Let the reader simply subtract mentally the Markan element from Luke. **1926** V. TAYLOR *Behind Third Gospel* v. 130 Again the Markan stripe is characterized by unity of subject-matter. **1930** A. G. HEBERT tr. *Brilioth's Eucharistic Faith & Pract.* i. 5 An exegetical analysis of the texts leads him to the conclusions that the Markan narrative is alone authentic and original, [etc.]. **1971** *Novum Testamentum* XIII. 187 In general the changes made by Matthew and Luke to their Markan source reveal primarily a Matthean and Lukan redaction history and not a Markan one.

mark-down (mā·ɹk,daun), *sb.* [f. *to mark down* s.v. MARK *v.* 2 c.] A reduction in price; an article the selling price of which has been reduced. Also *attrib.*

1880 in *Dict. Amer. Eng.* (1942) III. 1486/2 The success of our mark-down sales. **1962** *Economist* 2 June 891/1 Specialists found it difficult to absorb shares without drastic markdowns in price. **1962** E. GODFREY *Retail Selling & Organization* ii. 16 Goods are bought in specially or are mark-downs from other sections of the store. **1972** *Oxford Times* 27 Oct. 9 To show a false mark-down price in a sale is a definite offence. **1974** *Oxford Mail* 10 Jan. 2/1 (Advt.), Gigantic genuine mark-down Fashion Sale.. Headington.

marked, *ppl. a.* Add: **1. b. marked cheque** (see quots. 1907 and 1951); **marked transfer** (see quots.).

1896 R. H. I. PALGRAVE *Dict. Pol. Econ.* II. 695/2 Marked cheques are payable in the first clearing of the next day, and cannot be refused for any reason. **1907** W. G. CORDINGLEY *London Commercial Dict.* 115 *Marked cheque*, a cheque marked by the banker on whom it is drawn, stating that it is 'good' for the amount named upon it. **1930** HUTCHINSON & LOVELL *Short Dict. Legal, Commercial & Econ. Terms* 77 *Marked cheques*,..cheques initialled by a banker as an indication that he holds sufficient balance to meet such cheque when presented. **1951** R. W. JONES *Thomson's Dict. Banking* (ed. 10) 395 *Marked Cheque.* Marking cheques takes one of two forms —marking for clearing purposes and marking at the request of the drawer. **1901** W. G. CORDINGLEY *Dict. Stock Exchange Terms* 59 *Marked Transfers.* The company..then issue a fresh Certificate to him for the part unsold, and endorse the Transfer that they hold Certificates to cover the number of shares sold, when the Transfer is said to be 'Marked' or 'Certified'. **1961** WEBSTER, *Marked transfer*, an instrument for transferring a portion of the shares of a stockholder's certificate after being certified as good by a proper official on the London stock exchange.

c. Of a linguistic construction, form, etc.: distinguished or determined by a particular feature; distinguished as intrinsically unnatural (see also *MARKER 7; opp. **unmarked*).

The corresponding Russian word was used by Trubetzkoy before Bloomfield: see R. Jakobson *Selected Writings* (ed. 2, 1971) I. 734 ff.

1933 L. BLOOMFIELD *Lang.* xvi. 268 A phrase consisting of the preposition *to* and an infinitive expression belongs to the special form-class of *marked infinitive phrases*, whose function differs from that of unmarked infinitive expressions. **1953** C. E. BAZELL *Ling. Form* ii. 19 The Latin marked construction here can be uniquely derived from the unmarked in every case. **1959** R. QUIRK in Quirk & Smith *Teaching of English* i. 44 It seems likely that this structural notion of marked and unmarked members of opposing pairs can be applied cautiously but with profit to many of the binary choices in usage at more complex linguistic levels than the lexical. **1963** *Canad. Jrnl. Ling.* VIII. 92 Whenever a demonstrative system is reduced to a binary one, the first member which can be correlated with the first person always remains and thus becomes the marked member. **1965** *Amer. Speech* XL. 175 There are certain marked forms [of the verb] which are past and future respectively. **1968** CHOMSKY & HALLE *Sound Pattern Eng.* 402 Certain aspects of this general problem can be dealt with if we incorporate the Praguian notion of 'marked' and 'unmarked' values of features into our account in some systematic way, and if we then revise the evaluation measure so that unmarked values do not contribute to complexity. *Ibid.* 404 A major difference between the Praguian conception of markedness and our own is that in the former the marked coefficient of a feature was assumed always to be + and the unmarked coefficient always −. **1972** M. SHAPIRO in *Language* XLVIII. 345 In my concept and utilization of the terms marked and unmarked, the former is to be understood as denoting relative complexity and differentiatedness, the latter as denoting the absence of these relative attributes.

markedness. Add: *spec.* in *Linguistics*: the quality or state of being marked (*MARKED *ppl. a.* 1 c).

1968 [see *MARKED *ppl. a.* 1 c]. **1968** *Language* XLIV. 714 The notion of markedness as developed within Praguean phonology..allows phonological segments to be differentiated. **1972** *Sci. Amer.* Sept. 78/3 Any syntactic structure is a member of a transformational chain and any two partially synonymous constructions display an interrelation of markedness and unmarkedness. **1973** A. H. SOMMERSTEIN *Sound Pattern Anc. Greek* iii. 82 The Markedness theory holds that phonological features are not in general symmetrical: that for each feature in each environment, one of its possible values is more normal, more 'unmarked', than the other.

marker. Add: **1. b.** One who records prices on the stock exchange.

1870 J. K. MEDBERY *Men & Mysteries Wall St.* 21 The 'marker' or black-board clerk writes off the prices upon the tablet.

f. (Later examples.)

1907 S. E. WHITE *Arizona Nights* I. viii. 149 In the meantime the marker was engaged in his work. First, with a sharp knife he cut off slanting the upper quarter of one ear [of a calf]. **1928** *Collier's* 29 Dec. 6/2 There was a lull in the stream of lumber. The marker turned for a look at the order board.

j. *U.S.* In surveying: a person who makes the marks on trees to indicate boundaries or lines of survey.

1743 *New Jersey Archives* (1883) 1st Ser. VI. 154 You are to employ..an assistant surveyor..& also proper

chainbearers & markers. **1843** *Amer. Pioneer* II. 379 In running the back line of the survey..I was about one hundred yards in advance of the chainmen and marker.

3. b. A monument, memorial stone, etc., marking a place of special interest.

1906 *Springfield* (Mass.) *Weekly Republ.* 15 Feb. 16 The committee appointed to investigate the matter of a marker for the Washington elm reported in favor of a granite marker. **1959** A. G. WOODHEAD *Study of Greek Inscriptions* iv. 45 The commonest types of monument were the small cylindrical marker (*columella*), seldom more than two feet high, [etc.].

c. A flare, distinctive sign, or object of any kind used as a guide to a pilot of an aircraft seeking a particular area, obstruction, etc.; *spec.* a flare dropped from an aeroplane to illuminate or mark a target. Also with defining word, as *ground marker, sky-marker*, etc. (see these sbs.).

1936 M. B. GARBER *Mod. Mil. Dict.* 195 *Marker*, a symbol, letter, or figure on the ground, visible from aircraft, by means of which the operators are able to determine their position. **1944** *Times* 22 Mar. 4/5 The leading aircraft then dropped markers right across the middle of the target. **1944** R. C. K. ENSOR *Miniature Hist. War* iv. 53 Accuracy was also greatly improved by the system of 'pathfinders' dropping 'markers' to guide the rest. **1951** *Gloss. Aeronaut. Terms* (*B.S.I.*) III. 24 *Markers*, objects of approved shape or colour indicating specific areas and obstructions.

4. (Earlier and later examples.)

1888 *Congress. Rec.* 12 Dec. 202/2 The waving of the bloody shirt would not have been a marker. **1904** W. H. SMITH *Promoters* xxv. 366 What little I've told you isn't a marker to other things he said.

5. a. In various games such as bridge or whist, a scoreboard or card, or other implement used to record the score. (See also *bridge-marker*, *BRIDGE *sb.*² c.)

1907 *Army & Navy Stores Catal.* 198/2 Whist marker, inlaid, pair 2/7. *Ibid.* 375/2 Playing card table..with drawer divided to take cards and bridge scoring blocks, whist cards and markers. **1960** R. C. BELL *Board & Table Games* I. vi. 157 Little bone sticks marked with..dots are used to keep the score... Usually each player [at Mah Jong] starts with..2 markers with 10 red dots [etc.].

b. *U.S. slang.* A promissory note; an I.O.U.

1887 F. FRANCIS *Saddle & Mocassin* xii. 225 Before half the deal was over, the whole bank of checks was gone, and Cuff was giving markers for hundreds as hard as he could go it. **1931** D. RUNYON *Guys & Dolls* (1932) vii. 147 Now I am going to pay my landlady, and take up a few markers here and there, and feed myself up good. *Ibid.* xiii. 279 He is willing to take Charley's marker for a million if necessary to get Charley out.

6. *Genetics.* Any allele (usu. one which is easily recognized phenotypically and whose gene has been located on a specific chromosome) which is used in genetic experiments to identify a chromosome or to locate less well-known genes on a genetic map.

1930 *Genetics* XV. 219 There is a certain expected amount of crossing over between the two mutant genes treated as markers of a given point. **1938** *Ibid.* XXIII. 291 In order to obtain Notch deficiencies, normal males carrying yellow (y—0·0) as a marker..were mated with females homozygous for cherry (w^{ch}—1·5) and wavy (wy—40·7). **1940** *Nature* 10 Aug. 199/2 It is..possible to recognise, by means of the markers used, what combination of chromosomes is present in the pseudo-backcross progeny. **1961** *Proc. Nat. Acad. Sci.* XLVII. 378 (*heading*) Transformation studies on the linkage of markers in the tryptophan pathway in *Bacillus subtilis*. **1969** A. M. CAMPBELL *Episomes* ii. 22 Phage resulting from DNA infection is distinguished from progeny of the helper phage itself by genetic markers.

7. *Linguistics.* A word, affix, etc., which distinguishes or determines the class or function of the form, construction, etc., with which it is used. Also *attrib.*

1933 L. BLOOMFIELD *Lang.* xvi. 269 Our determining adjectives, our prepositions, our co-ordinating conjunctions, and our subordinating conjunctions, may be viewed as markers. **1953** C. E. BAZELL *Ling. Form* v. 67 *And* [in 'hot and cold'] may be described as a 'marker', after which no question of constituents arises. **1960** E. DELAVENAY *Introd. Machine Transl.* vii. 110 Those strictly linguistic markers sought in the sentence by the programmers of automatic translations. **1961** R. B. LONG *Sentence & its Parts* iii. 65 The marker pronouns and adverbs are not themselves usable in declaratives ordinarily, but the marker verb forms are. **1964** *Amer. Speech* XXXIX. 53 The German plural marker *-er* is historically a derivational suffix. **1968** P. M. POSTAL *Aspects Phonol. Theory* i. 13 By the 'markers' of a linguistic level I refer to the formal structures which the rules of that level assign to sentences as part of their total structural description. **1972** HARTMANN & STORK *Dict. Lang. & Ling.* 137/1 Markers may indicate the category of a linguistic unit at any level of analysis. **1973** *Archivum Linguisticum* IV. 32 The remaining forms are sufficiently distinguished for person, i.e. in the absence of specific person markers, by differing marks of gender-cum-number.

8. *attrib.* and *Comb.*, as (sense *3 c) *marker burner*; *marker flag, light*; **marker beacon** (see *BEACON *sb.* 6 d); **marker bomb,** a bomb emitting a coloured light, dropped in an air-raid to serve as a point of direction.

1929 Marker beacon [see *BEACON *sb.* 6 d]. **1934** *Jrnl. R. Aeronaut. Soc.* XXXVIII. 828 When a pilot had to maintain height, to observe instruments to ensure that he did not get into difficulties, and had also to listen for the marker beacon. **1935** *Times* 19 Oct. 9/5 The installation will consist of a main beacon at one corner of the aerodrome and two marker beacons 300 yards and 3,000 yards away respectively. **1971** *Gloss. Electrotechnical, Power Terms* (*B.S.I.*) III. vi. 24 *Marker beacon*, in aviation, radio beacon which radiates a signal to define an area above the beacon. **1944** *Hutchinson's Pict. Hist. War Oct. 1943–Apr. 1944* 84 (*caption*) Different stages in the lighting up of a target by a marker bomb. **1947** *Shell Aviation News* No. 113. 7/3 These marker burners would give a clear patch in bad weather that would provide the pilot with actual visual contact with the ground. **1945** *Penguin New Writing* XXIII. 9 Dan buoys appeared..their marker flags drowned and bedraggled. **1959** *Listener* 12 Feb. 278/2 Among the maze of wheel tracks and hoof marks, I noticed a red marker flag. **1943** *Chambers's Techn. Dict.* Suppl. 964/1 *Marker light* (Signalling), an indicating light on a signal post, to indicate the position or aspect of the main signal should its light have failed. **1960** O. SKILBECK *ABC of Film & T.V.* 82 *Marker light*, device giving synch. between picture and sound film by simultaneous photographic exposure instead of the Clapper board. Outmoded by the use of Magnetic film for Direct recording. **1971** M. TAK *Truck Talk* 104 *Marker lights*, the small lights that serve to outline a truck's length and width at night and in bad weather.

market, *sb.* Add: **1, 3.** (U.S. examples.) Also, now, = *SUPERMARKET.

1888 *Ladies' Home Jrnl.* June 2/2 Cherries..should be avoided when..sold in city markets. **1895** *Funk's Stand. Dict., Market*,..a private store for the sale of provisions; as, a meat-*market*. **1905** *Delineator* Mar. 498/3, I patronize a small market..kept by an old Frenchman and his son. They are experts on cutting and trimming meat. **1911** *Woman's Home Compan.* Apr. 4/2, I have used inadequately filtered water, uninspected milk and shopped in markets where inspection of sanitary conditions was never dreamed of. **1967** 'D. SHANNON' *Rain with Violence* (1969) i. 19 She's pretty sure Mrs. Gerner usually shopped at the nearest market up on Marengo. **1972** *Jrnl. Social Psychol.* LXXXVII. 78 Markets were chosen which served a relatively large number of black customers.

1. b. *to go to market*: also *fig.*, to behave in an angry manner, to become angry. *Austral.* and *N.Z.*

a **1925** F. S. ANTHONY *Follow Call* (1936) 17 Peter came home drunk once every week, and made his poor wife milk the herd of twenty-four cows by herself; and then about 8 p.m. he'd arise from the sofa and go to market because the poor woman hadn't cooked a hot tea for him. **1945** BAKER *Austral. Lang.* 121 A man in a temper is said..*to go to market*.

7. a. *to be in* (or *on*) *the market*: also *fig.*

1908 M. DIVER *Great Amulet* x. 115, I don't feel called upon..to advertise the fact that I am not..'on the market'. **1929** *Amer. Speech* V. 123 A widow who was ready for another husband was said to be..'in the market'. **1936** L. C. DOUGLAS *White Banners* x. 212 She was in the market for diversion. **1955** 'A. GILBERT' *Is she Dead Too?* vii. 136 When I'm in the market for trouble of that kind I'll tip you the wink. **1955** *Times* 30 Aug. 3/1 This..is an important match with third place in the County table still in the market.

b. *black market* (see as main entry), *buyer's market* (see *BUYER 3), *common market* (see *COMMON *a.* 21), *seller's market* (see *SELLER).

c. In Horse Racing, the kind or amount of business done in bets, the state of betting.

1886 EARL OF SUFFOLK & BERKS. et al. *Racing & Steeple-Chasing* v. 85 On arriving at the rails, which separate the private stands' enclosure from the ring, he finds the market well set. **1897** E. H. COOPER *Mr. Blake of Newmarket* xxvi. 255 'I've missed the market!' My friend..explained..that he had not got the best bet against the horse which he might have got. **1972** J. MITCHELL *Betting* ii. 34 Because of..the shortness of the period..for which the betting market on a race is active, racecourse bookmakers keep their betting as simple as possible.

10. a. *market-boat* (earlier examples), *-boy, -net, -people, -sloop, survey, -wagon*; also *market-made* adj.

1780 *New Jersey Archives* (1914) 2nd Ser. IV. 401 Mrs. Roker, and one other woman, were going in a market boat from Philadelphia. **1853** 'P. PAXTON' *Stray Yankee in Texas* 278 [He] bought a market-boat, and tried trading upon the bayou. **1863** A. D. WHITNEY *Faith Gartney's Girlhood* v. 44 The market-boys, and the waiters, and the confectioners' parcels. **1947** AUDEN *Age of Anxiety* (1948) ii. 44 You will soon Not bother but acknowledge yourself As market-made, a commodity Whose value varies. **1922** JOYCE *Ulysses* 219 She passed out with her basket and a market net. **1696** *Mass. Bay Acts & Laws* 162 Hucksters and Traders of the Town, shall not..Buy of any of the Market People there. **1830** J. F. COOPER *Water Witch* I. xi. 259 The rogues will pass the pennant like innocent market people. **1873** 'VIEUX MOUSTACHE' *Boarding-School Days* 36 He had been a hand on a New York market-sloop. **1885** *Outing* VII. 206/2 A big market-sloop came along bound west. **1967** C. BERNERS-LEE in Wills & Yearsley *Handbk. Managem. Technol.* 4 Do the conclusions of this market survey stand up? *Ibid.* 13 Useful programs for planning advertising campaigns have been written, based partly on market survey data. **1973** J. GOODFIELD *Courier to Peking* vii. 92, I don't think any market surveys have been done. **1802** *Deb. Congress U.S.* (1851) 18 Mar. 1027 In the state of New Jersey five hundred and forty two [of the carriages taxed] are..principally market-wagons. **1895** C. D. WARNER *Golden House* i. 9 Here and there [was] a lumbering market-wagon from Jersey.

b. market basket (earlier examples); **market economy,** a system of economy which is subject to free competition; **market gardener** (earlier and later examples); **market gardening,** keeping a market garden; **market hunter,** one who hunts game for the market; so **market-hunting** *vbl. sb.*; **market mammy** *colloq.*, an African woman stallholder; **market master** (examples); **market money,** money for buying things in a market (see also quot. 1891 in sense 10 a in Dict.); **market potential** (see quots.); **market reporter,** one who records the market rates of goods or stocks; **market research,** the systematic investigation of the demand for particular goods, a branch of marketing research; also *attrib.* and as vb. (to carry out market research); so *market-researched* ppl. adj., **market researcher,** a person engaged in this activity; **market shooter,** one who shoots game for the market; **market socialism,** an economic system in which a country's resources are publicly owned but production is geared to the private customer; hence **market-socialist** *attrib.*; **market square,** an open square in which a town market is held; also *fig.*; **market stall** (earlier example); **market value** (earlier examples); **market work,** also, the work connected with selling goods in a market.

1807 *Salmagundi* 27 June 247 Particular description of market-baskets, butchers' blocks and wheel-barrows. **1853** DICKENS *Bleak Ho.* xxxiv. 333 Her market-basket..is a sort of wicker well with two flapping lids. **1951** R. FIRTH *Elem. Social Organiz.* iii. 117 The other frame of organization consists of a market economy where a man lives largely by selling his produce or his labour in competition with others. **1966** *Listener* 24 Nov. 755/2 A market economy is an arrangement by which people, by their purchases, make clear what they want or do not want. Their market behaviour, in turn, is an instruction to producers as to what they should produce or not produce. **1968** *Ibid.* 4 July 7/2 In the market economy of classical capitalism the interests of the working class ran clean counter to those interests which relied upon the smooth working of the economic system. **1972** *Accountant* 5 Oct. 409/1 In a market economy, in which prices of goods and services are ultimately determined by the forces of supply and demand, any intervention by government in the form of fixing or holding prices and incomes cannot for long be effective. **1826** *Westm. Rev.* V. 20 The fruit and vegetables of a market gardener, on which his subsistence depends. **1832** *Chambers's Edin. Jrnl.* 7 Apr. 76/2 An industrious but rather unsuccessful market-gardener..from Kirkcaldy. **1963** *Times* 22 Feb. 10/3 Sir Thomas Playford, orchardist and market gardener, has all the assurance even in the uncertain world of politics of a man who knows that he will reap what he sows. **1875** *Encycl. Brit.* I. 384/1 *Market Gardening*... The growth of fruits and of culinary vegetables is in various parts of Great Britain an important department of farming. **1958** HAYWARD & HARARI tr. *Pasternak's Dr. Zhivago* I. vii. 218 It is not for the sake of market gardening that we are going all this enormous distance. **1874** J. W. LONG *Amer. Wild-Fowl Shooting* 185 Blue-winged teal..are much sought for by market-hunters. **1940** M. B. TRAUTMAN *Birds Buckeye Lake, Ohio* 170 According to former market hunters and old sportsmen, the Eastern Least Bittern was the most numerous transient and summering species between 1860 and 1900. **1897** *Outing* XXX. 293/1, I had little dreamed that Michigan would ever so far forget herself as to encourage market-hunting in preference to sportsman like methods. **1962** A. LEJEUNE *Duel in Shadows* vii. 91 There were two Africans, a small man..and his wife, fat as a Market Mammy. **1966** *Punch* 21 Sept. 457/1, I stared at..this old market-mammy who had lost her 'touch' and was clinging so stubbornly to the last shreds of her trading reputation. **1972** *Daily Tel.* 21 Jan. 4/3 About 7,000 white-clad market mammies—women stallholders—with drummers and horn blowers yesterday demonstrated through Accra in support of last week's military coup against the Busia regime. **1851** C. CIST *Sk. Cincinnati in 1851* 87 A city treasurer, a marshal, a wharf and three market masters are elected. **1913** J. W. SULLIVAN *Markets for People* 104 The Pennsylvania markets usually get along with a single market-master. **1633** G. HERBERT *Church Porch* in *Temple* 13 Think heav'n a better bargain, then to give Onely thy single market-money for it. **1868** *Putnam's Mag.* Jan. 40/2 Strawberries are down to ten cents a box..but you didn't leave a cent of market-money. **1962** S. STRAND *Marketing Dict.* 436 *Market potentials*, determining the marketability of a product. **1969** J. M. RATHMELL *Managing the Marketing Function* v. 200 *Market potential* is an expression of a market's absorption of a total industry's production in units or dollar sales... The major operational value of market potential is its usefulness in determining spatial rather than temporal objectives. **1854** B. J. TAYLOR *Jan. & June* 83 And so, as Market Reporters have it, 'we have movements to note'. **1926** *Market Res. Agencies Guide to Publ.* (U.S. Dept. Commerce) p. iii, With large sums of money being spent for market research..the necessity of having an inventory of accomplishments becomes obvious. **1927** *Ibid.* p. iv, Market research is the study of all problems relating to the transfer of goods from producer to consumer, involving relationships and adjustments between production and consumption, preparation of commodities for sale, their physical handling, wholesale and retail merchandising, and financial problems concerned. **1931** R. SIMMAT *Market Res.* i. 7 Reputable agencies will not accept the advertising for a product which market research has revealed to be unsuitable. **1937** *Discovery* Feb. 47/2 Another field for psychological investigation in many parts of the Special Areas is in market research, where methods of sale and customers' psychology need to be examined side by side. **1951** M. MCLUHAN *Mech. Bride* (1967) 31/2 As market-research tyranny has developed, the object and ends of human consumption have been blurred. **1956** *Planning* XXII. 19 Individual pub-

lishers and individual booksellers continue to do what they can for themselves in the way of market research and sales promotion. **1964** M. Argyle *Psychol. & Social Probl.* xiii. 162 One of the earliest pieces of market research discovered that coffee had an unfavourable image of being connected with tiredness and strain. **1965** *Spectator* 1 Jan. 3/1 The *Sunday Times*..claimed that £100,000 was to be spent on market research. **1969** P. Dickinson *Pride of Heroes* 58, I commissioned a little firm in Chicago to market-research the American idea of what English beer ought to taste like. **1970** *New Scientist* 1 Jan. 4/2 A 'hard sell' is necessary and this must be preceded by market research. **1973** *Times* 1 Feb. 8/2 (Advt.), Some market research experience would be an advantage. **1964** *Economist* 17 Oct. 276/3 The 1800 is as much a challenge to orthodox market-researched motoring as the Mini was five years ago. **1951** M. McLuhan *Mech. Bride* (1967) p. vi/2 Today the tyrant rules not by club or fist, but, disguised as a market researcher, he shepherds his flocks in the ways of utility and comfort. **1969** J. Argenti *Managem. Techniques* 157 Market Researchers rely heavily on the analysis of statistics—a notoriously difficult subject—and on answers to questionnaires—also notoriously unreliable. **1975** *Country Life* 2 Jan. 51/2 Editors have been convinced by accountants, market-researchers and computers that stories don't help to sell their products. **1880** *Golden Days for Boys & Girls* 6 Mar. 3/2 He knew very well that the ambitious and high-spirited Oscar was not a market-shooter from choice. **1897** *Outing* XXX. 293/2 The market-shooter, with no dogs to take care of, can sneak through the known haunts of the quail. **1965** *Listener* 15 Apr. 547/2 The new methods involve a form of market socialism, on the Yugoslav model... Production would be largely guided by the market. **1969** *Guardian* 3 July 12/5 The effect of the Czechoslovak events has been to discredit, in the eyes of the official [Russian] Establishment, the idea of 'market socialism'. **1972** D. Collard *Prices, Markets & Welfare* iv. 41 Where preferences are private but the ownership of resources public we have a market-socialist system. *Ibid.* xiii. 119 In the early 'thirties..Lange, Lerner and Dickinson..suggested a series of devices known as 'market socialism'. **1794** *Mass. Hist. Soc. Coll.* 1st Ser. III. 254 Besides the lower floor of Faneuil hall being used as a flesh market, a number of stalls are erected on Market square..and let to the market men. **1836** D. B. Edward *Hist. Texas* 148 A block shall be designated for a market square. **1963** *Times* 14 Feb. 8/5 The scientist who refuses contact with the people and opts for the Ivory Tower rather than the Market Square is a traitor to himself and to humanity. **1827** Drake & Mansfield *Cincinnati in 1826* vi. 55 The Revenue of the Corporation is derived; From..Rent of Market-stalls. **1691** Locke *Money* in *Wks.* (1824) IV. 99 According to the market value. **1791** *Deb. Congress U.S.* (1834) 1st Congr. App. 1993 The rapid increase that has taken place in the market value of the public securities. **1887** H. H. Jackson *Between Whiles* iv. 226 Donald liked slow cruising and the market-work best.

market, *v.* Add: **3.** To 'trade *on*', to take advantage of.

1906 Hardy *Dynasts* II. I. i. 10 These cloaked visitors of every clime That market on your magnanimity To gain an audience.

marketeer. Add: **3.** A supporter of Britain's entry into the Common Market (cf. *common *a.* 21).

1962 *Listener* 15 Nov. 799/2 The Marketeers within the Labour Party. **1969** *Guardian* 29 Aug. 16/8 The TUC General Council is trying to avoid an embarrassing public debate on the Common Market... Pro- and anti-Marketeers united in angry condemnation of Mr. Jenkins's attempts to force the issue on to the agenda. **1970** *Times* 4 May 8/2 Mr. Douglas Jay..leads his all-party group of anti-Marketeers, under the banner of the new Common Market Safeguards Campaign. **1971** *New Scientist* 27 May 522/1 The Paris summit has made the marketeers a little bolder. **1975** *Times* 25 Feb. 14/2 A keynote of the marketeers' case is..that Britain is in Europe and that the decision is..whether to come out.

marketing, *vbl. sb.* Add: **3.** *attrib.* and *Comb.*, as (sense 1) *marketing advantage, agent, conference, day, director, policy, problem, revolution, strategy, survey*; (sense 2 a) *marketing bag, basket*; **marketing mix** (see quot. 1969); **marketing research,** the systematic study of all the factors involved in marketing a product (see quot. 1963); so **marketing researcher.**

1919 A. Marshall *Industry & Trade* App. J. 800 The low grade industries which congregate in London owe comparatively little to the marketing advantages which are to be found there. **1951** M. McLuhan *Mech. Bride* (1967) 92/1 The marketing agents reciprocate by using still more applied science. **1934** T. S. Eliot *Rock* ii. 65 Enter Mrs. Ethelbert with marketing bag, hilariously. **1925** W. de la Mare *Two Tales* 20 A small, old, spectacled lady with a large marketing-basket, was..issuing out from behind the shop. **1970** *Brit. Printer* June 57 The BFMP's fourth marketing conference in London served to emphasise the urgent need for printers to understand the term 'marketing' let alone employ its principles. **1619** Marketting day [in Dict., sense 1 a]. **1961** *Times* 14 July 2/2 Marketing Director to organize and direct the Sales Organization. **1969** D. C. Hague *Managerial Econ.* III. xiv. 293 One of the major issues in all business is how to arrive at the correct 'marketing mix'—the correct balance of product design, price, advertising and other promotional expenditure, spending on the sales force, and so on. **1972** *Lebende Sprachen* XVII. 46/1 *Marketing mix.* **1930** G. R. Collins *Marketing* v. 78 The process of formulating marketing policies should recognise the fact that consumers' demands are the origins of economic impulses. **1920** P. T. Cherington *Elem. Marketing* 3 Increase of the scale of production alone introduces maladjustments between producing and consuming conditions with regard to quantity, quality, time, and place, which it becomes part of the marketing problem to correct. **1951** E. S. Bradford *Marketing Res.* p. xi, Marketing research is coming to be recognized as essential to a successful development of marketing. **1956** G. R. Collins *Marketing* (rev. ed.) v. 78 Marketing research..must..have for its major objective the minimizing of errors in marketing judgment. **1963** *Gloss. Managem. Terms* (Brit. Inst. Managem.) (Typescript), The distinction between market research and marketing research is important but is not yet as widely used and understood in the U.K. as in the U.S.A. One is a study of the market for the product and the other is a study of the marketing of the product. **1967** G. Wills in Wills & Yearsley *Handbk. Managem. Technol.* 175 Marketing research began in the second decade of the century as a commercial tool for the collection of facts for a better direction of sales effort. *Ibid.* 178 The analysis of territorial sales potential..is within the marketing research function of the business. *Ibid.* 179 Any marketing problem has three certain dimensions which marketing manager and researcher ignore at their peril—time, cost, and resources. **1963** *Times* 5 June 17/4 Today we [*sc.* the British] are lagging behind in a..transition that might be described as the Marketing Revolution. **1969** D. C. Hague *Managerial Econ.* III. xiii. 288 Dr Rothschild was impressed by the ease with which military terminology insinuates itself into discussions of oligopoly. We talk of price wars, sales campaigns, marketing strategies, industrial espionage and so on. **1974** *Times* 18 Feb. 12 Many hoteliers now regard conferences as an integral part of the marketing strategy for their establishments. **1941** 'Balbus' *Reconstruction & Peace* 58 Marketing surveys and campaigns for increasing consumption.

market-place. Add: Also *fig.*

1958 J. Barzun in Caplow & McGee *Academic Marketplace* p. v, The observers' point of departure was the current problem of mobility within the academic marketplace. **1975** *Times* 10 Apr. 16/1 Pension schemes..tied to the earnings-related inequalities of the market-place.

marking, *vbl. sb.* Add: **1. a.** (*Austral.* and *N.Z.* examples.) Cf. *mark *v.* 2 f.

1891 R. Wallace *Rural Econ. Austral. & N.Z.* ii. 43 Lamb-tailing and marking were on at this time—the end of June. **1946** F. Davison *Dusty* iv. 45 He handled lambs at marking time..as gently as if he owned them. **1950** *N.Z. Jrnl. Agric.* Sept. 197/1 Lamb marking consists of three different operations: the placing of a distinguishing mark in one or both ears, the amputation of tails, and the castration of male lambs.

c. With advs., freq. in *attrib.* uses.

1726 [in Dict., sense 1 a]. **1894** W. J. Lineham *Text-bk. Mech. Engin.* vi. 183 (*heading*) Marking-off, machining, fitting and erecting. **1909** *Westm. Gaz.* 24 Mar. 10/3 A marking-down process was also indulged in in anticipation of selling by speculators and profit-taking. **1917** [see *assembly 1 b]. **1948** R. de Kerchove *Internat. Maritime Dict.* 451/2 Marking-off platers work to drawings supplied from the drawing office and information given from the mold loft. **1964** S. Crawford *Basic Engin. Processes* i. 36 A typical marking-out table is shown. *Ibid.* 39 This mild-steel clamp is machined to length, width, and thickness prior to marking-out. **1966** J. H. Dixon tr. *Dormidontov's Shipbuilding Technol.* v. 115 A template workshop..fitted with optical marking apparatus and a marking-off table.

d. *Stock Exchange.* The recording of prices at which bargains are made.

1903 *Pitman's Business Man's Guide* 305/1 *Marking,..* on the Stock Exchange this signifies the recording of the prices at which actual business has been done in any security between the hours of eleven and three. **1930** *Economist* 22 Mar. 653/1 Dealings begin, the marking of bargains is effected in one or other of the Stock Exchange Daily Lists, [etc.]. **1934** F. E. Armstrong *Bk. Stock Exchange* iii. 52 The marking of bargains in the *Official* and *Supplementary Lists* is..the record of business actually transacted, and provides an index to an established price level. **1959** *Times* 7 Apr. 10/6, 20,451 separate bargains were recorded. This is the highest total reached since the 'marking' of bargains was inaugurated. **1971** T. G. Goff *Theory & Pract. Investment* v. 53 A symbol beside a marking may indicate that there is some unusual feature about the underlying deal.

4. *marking brush, pencil*; **marking stitch** (earlier example).

1855 'Q. K. P. Doesticks' *Doesticks, what he Says* xxii. 198 A dry-goods box with a marking brush sticking out of the top of it. **1882** M. H. Foote *Led-Horse Claim* xvii. 228 He..swept, with one stroke of his marking-brush, a black circle around the figures. **1886** Marking pencil [see *B, BB, BBB* (*B III)]. **1961** *Lebende Sprachen* VI. 70/1 Marking pencil. **1861** Mrs. Stowe *Pearl of Orr's Island* I. xvii. 152, I was going to begin and teach her some marking stitches.

markka (mā·ɹkā). Also marka. [Finn.] **a.** The principal monetary unit of Finland, equal to 100 penniä. **b.** The name of the coin equal to this amount. (Cf. Mark *sb.*[2] 4 b.)

1903 *Finland by the 'Nord' Steamers* 11 The standard coin is the Marka, equal to 10d. of our money, divided into 100 Penni. **1911** G. Renwick *Finland Today* 336 Finnish coinage presents no difficulties, the Finnish markka (plural, markkaa) being equal to the French franc. **1963** *Economist* 1 June 925/3 Some forest owners are speculating on a rise in prices, possibly via a devaluation of the [Finnish] markka. **1972** *Daily Tel.* 3 Aug. 19/4 Your pound's worth in London... Finland..9·95 markkas.

Markov (mā·ɹkǫf). *Math.* Also **Markoff.** [The name of Andrei Andreevich *Markov* (1856–1922), Russian mathematician, who investigated such processes.] *Markov process*: any stochastic process for which the probabilities, at any one time, of the different future states depend only on the existing state and not on how that state was arrived at. *Markov chain*: a Markov process in which there are a finite or countably infinite number of possible states or in which transitions between states occur at discrete intervals of time; also, one for which in addition the transition probabilities are constant (independent of time). Also *Markov property*, the characteristic property of Markov processes.

1939 *Jap. Jrnl. Math.* XVI. 47 (*heading*) Markoff process with an enumerable infinite number of possible states. **1942** *Trans. Amer. Math. Soc.* LII. 37 Then $p_{ij}(t)$ can be considered a transition probability of a Markoff chain: A system is supposed which can assume various numbered states, and $p_{ij}(t)$ is the probability that the system is in the *j*th state at the end of a time interval of length *t*, if it was in the *i*th state at the beginning of the interval. **1950** W. Feller *Introd. Probability Theory* I. xv. 337 A Markov process is the probabilistic analogue of the processes of classical mechanics, where the future development is completely determined by the present state and is independent of the way in which the present state has developed. *Ibid.* 337 A definition of the Markov property. **1953** J. L. Doob *Stochastic Processes* v. 170 A Markov chain is defined as a Markov process..whose random variables can (with probability 1) only assume values in a certain finite or denumerably infinite set. The set is usually taken, for convenience, to be the integers 1,.., *N* (finite case) or the integers 1, 2,... (infinite case). *Ibid.* 186 The problem of card mixing is a good example of the application of Markov chains. **1953** J. B. Carroll *Study of Lang.* iii. 85 A Markoff process has to do with the different 'states' into which a phenomenon can get, and the statistical probabilities which govern the transition of the phenomenon from one state to another. **1956** *Nature* 4 Feb. 207/1 The most simple case is when all the atoms of the assembly are supposed to have no volume and no interactions (such as in an ideal gas). In that case it can be treated as a Markov process. **1960** Kemeny & Snell *Finite Markov Chains* ii. 25 A finite Markov chain is a finite Markov process such that the transition probabilities $p_{ij}(n)$ do not depend on *n*. **1962** J. Riordan *Stochastic Service Syst.* iii. 28 The simplest infinite-server system is unique among its fellows in the possession of the Markov property that future changes are independent of the past. **1966** S. Karlin *First Course in Stochastic Processes* ii. 27 A discrete time Markov chain $\{X_n\}$ is a Markov stochastic process whose state space is a countable or finite set, and for which $T = (0, 1, 2, \ldots)$. *Ibid.*, The vast majority of Markov chains that we shall encounter have stationary transition probabilities. **1968** P. A. P. Moran *Introd. Probability Theory* iii. 140 Thus a Markov chain observed in the reverse direction of time will be a Markov process. However, it will not in general be a Markov chain because the observed transition probabilities will not be independent of *t*. **1973** *Manch. Sch. Econ. & Social Stud.* XLI. 401 (*heading*) A Markov chain model of the benefits of participating in government training schemes.

Markovian (mɑɹkōᵘ·viăn), *a.* [f. prec. + -ian.] Having the Markov property.

1950 W. Feller *Introd. Probability Theory* I. xv. 338 Examples of non-Markovian processes... Let $X^{(n)}$ equal 1 or 0 according to whether the *n*th drawing [from the urn] results in a black or a red ball. The sequence $\{X^{(n)}\}$ is *not* a Markov process. **1965** N. Chomsky *Aspects of Theory of Syntax* ii. 89 A derivation involving only phrase structure rules (rewriting rules) has a strict 'Markovian' character. That is, in a derivation consisting of the successive lines $\sigma_1, \ldots, \sigma_n \ldots$, the rules that can be applied to form the next line σ_{n+1} are independent of $\sigma_1, \ldots, \sigma_{n-1}$ and depend completely on the string σ_n. **1972** *Nature* 3 Mar. 20/2 To render the process Markovian, we have assumed exponential distributions of division times for both normal and abnormal cells.

Marks and Sparks (mɑ̄ɹks ǣnd spɑ̄ɹks). Also **Marks.** Colloq. name for the merchandising company of Marks and Spencer Ltd. or any of the stores owned by this firm. Freq. *attrib.* of clothes bearing the firm's trademark.

1951 Partridge *Dict. Slang* (ed. 4) Add. 1106/2 *Marks*, a Marks & Spencer store. **1964** *Sunday Times* 5 Apr. 41/5 In their Marks and Sparks' woollies and living in what looks like a remarkably nice housing estate, Topsy and Tim clearly stand in for classless society. **1966** A. Prior *Operators* i. 8 His Marks and Sparks shirt. **1971** 'D. Halliday' *Dolly & Doctor Bird* xi. 141, I sat there in my Marks and Sparks knickers and brassière. **1972** R. Quilty *Tenth Session* 104 The girls get just about all their odds and ends in Marks and Sparks or the bargain basement at C & A.

marksman. **5.** (Earlier example.)

1887 M. Shearman *Athletics & Football* 57 The starter is helped by a 'marksman', who places the men on the scratch.

ma·rk-up. [f. *to mark up* s.v. *mark *v.* 2 c.] The amount added by a retailer to the cost price of goods to cover overhead charges and provide profits.

1920 P. I. Carthage *Retail Organization & Accounting Control* ii. 44 The mark up of merchandise refers to the percentage or the amount of money added to the cost in order to obtain the selling price. **1931** J. F. Pyle *Marketing Princ.* xx. 518 *Mark-up* is..the difference between the marked price of the merchandise, at retail, and the cost of merchandise bought. Thus the mark-up represents the gross margin that is *hoped for.* **1936** *Economist* 22 Feb. 422/1 The 'mark up' (retailers' margin) is evidently adequate to provide relatively stable earnings on a stabilised capital investment. **1957** *Times* 19 Aug.

9/2 Shops often add to the price which they pay for their merchandise to manufacturers and wholesalers a percentage 'mark up' of 30 or 40 per cent. **1965** *Spectator* 22 Jan. 116/3 A big, new market for poor-quality materials and an even larger mark-up where the garments are supplied ready-made. **1972** M. WOODHOUSE *Mama Doll* xiii. 175 The estimated value of the items on the inventory is somewhere around fifty-five million pounds... Allowing a hundred per cent markup on sale, that would make their wholesale value some twenty-seven million pounds. **1974** *Times* 7 Feb. 20/8 The exorbitant mark-up imposed by European booksellers.

marl (mɑ̄ɹl), *sb.*⁴ [Reduced form of MARBLED *ppl. a.* 2.] A yarn made from two different coloured threads twisted together so as to produce a mottled effect; the fabric produced from this yarn. Usu. *attrib.*

1892 *Queen* 5 Mar. p. xi (Advt.), Ladies write for Patterns of the entirely new designs in..Marls, Tweeds,..and Beiges. **1922** *Daily Mail* 18 Dec. 1 (Advt.), Knitted sports suit in rich Marl mixtures and plain colours. **1926** *Illustr. Official Jrnl.* (Patent Office) 20 Oct. 1668 Spinning marl or multi-ply yarns. **1968** E. GALE *From Fibres to Fabrics* iv. 45 Two marl threads are sometimes twisted together to form one yarn. **1970** A. M. COLLIER *Handbk. Textiles* iv. 88 A marl yarn is produced by combining two yarns of uneven thickness, with uneven rates of delivery so that there is excess material at intervals.

marlberry. Substitute for def.: A small, evergreen tree, *Ardisia paniculata*, of the family Myrsinaceæ, bearing clusters of pink flowers and dark red berries, and found in the West Indies and tropical America. (Examples.)

1884 C. S. SARGENT *Rep. Forests N. Amer.* 100 *Ardisia Pickeringia* Marlberry-Cherry. **1897** G. B. SUDWORTH *Nomencl. Arborescent Flora U.S.* 316 *Icacorea paniculata.* Marlberry. **1917** *Rep. Board of Regents Smithsonian Inst.* 384 In addition to these are the paradise tree or bitterwood; soapberry tree;..marlberry; [etc.]. **1924** J. A. THOMSON *Sci. Old & New* v. 27 Even the names transport us into a land of pure delight—the paradise tree, the myrtle-of-the-river, the marlberry, and the bois-fidèle.

marler (mɑ̄·ɹləɹ). [f. MARL *v.*² + -ER¹.] A marline-spike.

1929 J. MASEFIELD *Hawbucks* 15 A strong sheath knife with a marler at the back.

marlin (mɑ̄·ɹlin), *sb.*² [App. abbrev. of MARLINSPIKE, from the shape of the beak.] A large, marine, game fish belonging to the genera *Makaira* or *Tetrapterus* of the family Istiophoridæ, having the upper jaw elongated to form a beak.

1917 *Vanity Fair* (N.Y.) July 62/1 The marlin—*Tetrapterus mitsukurii*—is sometimes called the Japanese swordfish. **1923** D. K. TRESSLER *Marine Products of Commerce* 737/1 The marlin (*Tetrapterus mitsukurii*)..is also called spikefish. **1926** *Glasgow Herald* 24 June 4/5 The extract concerning the loss of a black marlin swordfish, estimated to weigh 600 lb., is one of the most dramatic passages. **1931** *Times Lit. Suppl.* 16 Apr. 301/1 Since then marlin have been taken, on heavy tackle, of 372 lb. **1937** *Discovery* Nov. 357/1 One [swordfish], a black marlin, has been recorded in New Zealand weighing 976 lbs. **1940** *Nature* 6 Apr. 555/2 The black marlin differs from the striped and the blue marlin in the fact that the pectoral fin, when adducted, remains in the horizontal position, whilst in the others it can be brought up flat against the side of the body. **1959** *Angling Times* 13 Mar. 6/3 Madeira has them: the white marlin and the blue marlin. **1970** M. SLATER *Caribbean Cooking* 11 *Marlin*, one of the most sought-after game fish, found in rocks and reefs.

marm (mɑːm, mæm). [Var. of MA'AM, freq. in U.S. writers.] **1.** = MA'AM I.

1837 R. M. BIRD *Nick of Woods* I. 120 Say the word, marm. **1845** C. M. KIRKLAND *Western Clearings* 17 'Massy no, marm!' said Jane, with a giggle. *Ibid.* 18 No, Marm; but—this 'ere is something about the team, I guess.

2. = MA'AM 2.

1837 [see MA'AM 2]. **1887** M. E. WILKINS *Humble Romance* 107 Marm Lawson was not a duchess; but she was Marm Lawson. The 'Marm' itself was a title. *a* **1922** T. S. ELIOT *Waste Land Drafts* (1971) 59 line 50 The pleasant violin At Marm Brown's joint, and the girls and gin.

3. = MA'AM 3.

1865 S. HALE *Lett.* (1919) 16 The silk is seven dollars a yard, and the marm that makes it asks a great deal. **1872** *Congress. Globe* 42nd Congress 2 Sess. App. 632/3 It will be seen that in the great race thus far the English and American marms are about 'nip and tuck'.

b. Used for 'mother'. (Also in address.)

1835 J. F. COOPER *Monikins* II. i. 35 He could scare one by threatening to tell his *marm* how he behaved. **1838** —— *Eve Effingham* II. xvi. 168 Who taught you to call me marm!..Say 'ma' this instant. **1845** S. JUDD *Margaret* I. 37 'Has your marm got that done?' asked Martha Madeline. **1890** S. O. JEWETT *Strangers & Wayfarers* 9 You've got real nice features, like your marm's folk.

marmalade, *sb.* Add **3. c.** quasi-*adj.*: of the colour of marmalade (so *marmalade-coloured* adj.).

1926 S. T. WARNER *Lolly Willowes* III. 184 Jim was..a mottled marmalade cat. **1938** K. HALE (*title*) Orlando, the marmalade cat. **1951** 'C. CARNAC' *It's her Own Funeral* iv. 38 James, the marmalade cat, was sitting disapprovingly outside. **1957** *Times Lit. Suppl.* 15 Nov. p. xvii/2 Miss White's account of how a fierce little Siamese and an unsnubbable marmalade kitten learnt to live amicably together. **1961** *Guardian* 20 Jan. 9/7 A magnificent dark marmalade-coloured Persian cat. **1965** G. MCINNES *Road to Gundagai* ii. 29, I faced a crowd of blonde giants with marmalade fuzz on their chests. **1972** J. AIKEN *Butterfly Picnic* iii. 55 The local marmalade-coloured rock. **1973** 'E. PETERS' *City of Gold & Shadows* iii. 47 A very austere dress in a dark russet-orange shade that touched off the marmalade lights in her eyes.

ma·rmalade, *v.* [f. the sb.] *trans.* To spread with marmalade. Hence **ma·rmaladed** *ppl. a.*

1967 D. PINNER *Ritual* x. 107 David..selected a piece of toast, marmaladed it, and munched it. **1968** C. NICOLE *Self Lovers* i. 18 Brice marmaladed toast. **1975** J. WOOD *North Kill* vii. 106 Eating steamed haddock along with marmaladed toast.

marmalady, *a.* Delete *rare*⁻¹ and add later examples.

1920 JOYCE *Let.* 3 Jan. (1957) I. 135 *Nausikaa* is written in a namby-pamby jammy marmalady..style. **1960** P. COLERIDGE *Running Footsteps* 59 A clipped marmaladey moustache.

marmite (marmīt). [F. *marmite* pot or kettle: see MARMIT.] **1. a.** An earthenware cooking-vessel; a stockpot.

1805 C. JAMES *New Mil. Dict.* (ed. 2), *Marmite*,.. porridge-pot, kettle; a machine in which soldiers boil their victuals. **1882** C. M. YONGE *Unknown to Hist.* II. xxi. 294 The French suite, every one of whom liked to have his own little arrangements of cookery, and to look after his own *marmite* in his own way. **1919** B. RUCK *Disturbing Charm* I. xi. 107 The door into the huge French kitchen stood open, giving a glimpse of marmites, burnished copper pans, crocks, and five-decker cookers. **1955** L. WOOLLEY *Alalakh* vi. 218 'Marmite', Type 154, of normal cooking-pot ware, black clay reddened on surface. **1960** *Home & Garden* Oct. 150/2 A range of ovenware..5s. 6d for a marmite.

b. *slang.* A bomb or shell resembling a pot.

1915 G. ADAM *Behind Scenes at Front* 48 The graves in the churchyard have been torn open by 'marmites'. **1919** [see *BLACK MARIA 2].

2. (mɑ̄·ɹmait.) (Properly with capital initial.) The proprietary term for an extract made from fresh brewer's yeast.

1907 *Yesterday's Shopping* (1969) 18/1 Marmite (Vegetable Ext.)... Marmite Bouillon, in tubes. **1920** *Trade Marks Jrnl.* 25 Aug. 1588 *Marmite*... A Concentrated Culinary Preparation, being an Article of Food. The Marmite Food Extract Co., Limited. **1923** *Nature* 12 May 626/2 In the prevention of beri-beri the addition of oatmeal and dhall to the British ration, the addition of marmite, and later, the issue of bread containing 25 per cent. of atta, were found valuable. **1925** D. H. LAWRENCE *Let.* 17 Dec. (1962) II. 871 So Sonya will never cook us another goose, only marmite pie and nut-cutlet. **1928** R. MACAULAY *Keeping up Appearances* i. 5 Doctors..prefer that one should breakfast..on marmite, Ry-Vita biscuits, and an apple. **1934** *Nature* 20 Oct. 623/2 The yeast extract 'Marmite' has long been recognised as a source of the vitamin B complex. **1947** T. H. WHITE *Mistress Masham's Repose* i. 7 She had..brown eyes the colour of marmite, but more shiny. **1966** A. E. LINDOP *I start Counting* xviii. 208 He knocked me up a Marmite sandwich.

maro. (Later examples.)

1833 A. SMITH in M. D. Frear *Lowell & Abigail* (1934) 63 Many others wear nothing but a narrow strip of tapa about their loins, called a *maro.* **1860** MAYNE REID *Odd People* 213 A coarser and scantier pareu is to be seen among the poorer people,..and not unfrequently this is only a mere strip wrapped around the loins; in other words, a 'malo', 'maro', or 'maso'—as it is indifferently written in the varied orthography of the voyagers. **1898** [see TAPA]. **1969** R. T. WILCOX *Dict. Costume* (1970) 201 *Malo*, the Hawaiian man's girdle or loincloth. Originally of tapa cloth which was made from tree bark, but now of cotton dyed in brilliant colors.

marocain (marŏkẽⁱ·n). [f. F. *maroquin*: see MAROQUIN *a.* and *sb.*] A dress fabric of ribbed crêpe. Also, a garment made from marocain.

1922 *Glasgow Herald* 28 June 8/6 For her going away dress the bride had a three-piece suit of grey wool marocain. **1922** *Tatler* 30 Aug. 354/2 An evening frock of black crêpe marocain. **1923** *Weekly Dispatch* 14 Jan. 15 A new evening model..had a trailing skirt with narrow draperies of black panne, while the upper part..was in white marocain. **1926** C. SIDGWICK *Sack & Sugar* xi. 126, I wore an embroidered marocain. **1957** M. B. PICKEN *Fashion Dict.* 88/1 *Marocain*.., ribbed crepe of silk or wool or combination.

maroodi (mărū·di). Also **maroudi.** [ad. Arawak *marodi.*] In Guyana, any of several birds included in species of guan belonging to the genera *Penelope* or *Pipile.*

1825 C. WATERTON *Wanderings S. Amer.* 23 The forest contains an abundance of..maams, maroudis and waracabas. **1876** C. B. BROWN *Canoe & Camp Life Brit. Guiana* 345 Maroodies of two kinds (the common and white-headed)..were also numerous. **1883** E. F. IM THURN *Among Indians Guiana* 62 Now and then a maroodi (*Penelope*) cried shrilly from among the trees. **1922** *Blackw. Mag.* Apr. 535/1 A quail and a maroodi rewarded their zeal.

maroon, *sb.*¹ Add: **3.** Used as an air-raid warning, etc., in the war of 1914–18.

1918 *Flying* 6 Feb. 90/1 Clearly, the authorities ought to have posted notices..explaining that the maroons are warnings to take cover. **1918** *Daily Mirror* 12 Nov. 2/1 London went wild with delight when the great news came through yesterday... Bells burst into joyful chimes, maroons were exploded, bands paraded the streets, and London gave itself up wholeheartedly to rejoicing. **1934** E. WHARTON *Backward Glance* xiii. 358 Four years of war had inured Parisians to every kind of noise connected with air-raids, from the boom of warning maroons to the smashing roar of the bombs.

maroon, *sb.*² **2.** (Further examples.)

1785 in *South Carolina Hist. & Geneal. Mag.* (1912) XIII. 188 On Monday we form a maroon party to visit some saw mills. **1838** C. GILMAN *Recoll. Southern Matron* xxxii. 223 Feeling the necessity of refreshment, we alighted for a while beneath a tree by the roadside, for a *maroon.*

maroon, *v.* Add: **2. b.** *transf.* To place or leave in a position from which one cannot escape. Also *fig.*

1910 *N.Y. Even. Post* 6 Jan. (Th.), Train No. 4.., due here from Los Angeles on January 1, is marooned in the desert. **1912** *Ibid.* 15 July 1/7 Rescue parties found dazed families..marooned on roofs. *Ibid.*, The torrent rushed.. through the [station] yard,..marooning several hundred passengers. **1916** W. OWEN *Let.* 19 June (1967) 395, I am marooned on a Crag of Superiority in an ocean of Soldiers. **1946** *Sun* (Baltimore) 10 Aug. 4/1 It comes out for..direct assistance and encouragement to farmers marooned in declining or unproductive lines. **1973** *Jewish Chron.* 29 June 16/2 Marooned in the decaying house, she hears voices and sees the ghosts of the family. **1974** *Sunday Tel.* 7 July 26/2 Living a few miles out [of a city] is all very well in itself, but it often involves two cars—one for an otherwise marooned wife and family.

marooner. Add: † **4.** = MAROON *sb.*² 1. *Obs. U.S.*

a **1738** W. BYRD *Hist. Dividing Line* in *Writings* (1901) 37 We were told that on the South Shore, not far from the Inlet, dwelt a Marooner that Modestly call'd himself a Hermit.

‖ **maror** (mārō̆ə·ɹ). Also **moror.** [Heb. *mārōr.*] A dish of bitter herbs eaten as part of the Jewish Passover *seder.*

1893 [see *CHAROSET(H)]. **1903** W. ROSENAU *Jewish Ceremonial Institutions* viii. 122 A dish is placed, on which are put three unleavened cakes... On the top of them are put..the 'Charoseth' (a mixture of scraped apples and almonds, 'Moror' (bitter herbs), parsley and salt water... The bitter herbs, usually consisting of horseradish, stand, on account of their pungent taste, for the hard work of the Israelites in Egypt. **1905** *Jewish Encycl.* XI. 146/1 None has done his duty on that night [*sc.* Passover] until he has given voice to the three words 'pesaḥ' (pascal lamb), 'maẓẓah' (unleavened bread), and 'maror' (bitter herb). **1959** [see *CHAROSET(H)]. **1968** A. MATTS tr. *Sperling's Reasons for Jewish Customs* 188 The best choice for *maror* is a piece of horseradish, because horseradish has a particularly sharp and bitter taste. **1972** C. RAPHAEL *Feast of Hist.* ii. 37 Passover..was instituted with three binding ceremonies: (1) *Pesach*—a special sacrifice at the Temple... (2) *Matzah* (unleavened bread)... (3) *Maror* (bitter herbs) —eaten at the Seder to remind us of the bitterness of the Egyptian slavery.

maroudi, var. *MAROODI.

‖ **marouflage** (maruflāʒ), *sb. Art.* [f. F. *maroufler* to attach (a painted canvas to a wall) with *maroufle*, a strong adhesive (also, a lining or layer of such adhesive): see -AGE.] **1.** The act or process of pasting a painted canvas to a wall, traditionally using an adhesive made of white lead ground in oil. Hence **marouflage** *v.*, **marouflaging** *vbl. sb.*

1883 J. W. MOLLETT *Illustr. Dict. Art & Archæol.* 205/2 *Marouflage*, a method of house-painting in France, upon a lining of prepared canvas fixed upon the surface to be decorated. **1909** *Cent. Dict.* Suppl., *Marouflage*, this device allows mural paintings to be in oil colors, and also allows the work to be done at a distance from the building for which it is intended. **1934** H. HILER *Notes Technique Painting* iv. 265 *Marouflage* as the different methods of gluing the canvas to the wall are called, was very popular throughout the nineteenth century, and most modern European wall decorations were executed by this method. *Ibid.*, A paste of rye flour, to which two or three heads of garlic were added, was the commonest way of marouflaging on the Continent. **1969** R. MAYER *Dict. Art Terms & Techniques* 235/1 Traditionally, the adhesive used in marouflage is commercial white lead in oil.

2. [Transf. sense of *maroufle* a lining, layer (of glue): see prec. sense.] In ironwork, a piece of leather or other material used as a backing to show off decoration.

1957 R. LISTER *Decorative Wrought Ironwork* 55 This decoration was called *Marouflage.* Examples of door plates backed with leather are to be seen in King's College Chapel, Cambridge. **1960** H. HAYWARD *Antique Coll.* 175/2 *Marouflage*, a scarlet cloth backing to pierced lock plates.

marque² (mɑːk). [Fr., = mark, sign.] = *MARK *sb.*¹ 15 b. A model or brand esp. of motor vehicle.

1906 C. JARROTT *Ten Yrs. Motors & Motor Racing* x. 174 Half-way to Bordeaux, and out of the first four cars two were Dietrich—this seemed a good record for the *marque.* **1956** *Road & Track* Oct. 5 (Advt.), The marque of Mercedes-Benz. *Ibid.* 14 The firm and marque has not actively participated in competition. **1958** *N. & Q.* Feb. 86/1 'Marque' is surely a recent borrowing from the French

language where it is in general use to denote a particular type of variety of a product, e.g. Frigidaire, Hoover, etc... The channel whereby the word has passed from French to English is doubtless international motor-racing. **1960** *Times* 4 July (Suppl.) 1/1 Sixty years is long..also in the reign of a branded product—particularly in the reign of a *marque* of cigarette. **1972** *Daily Tel.* 28 Jan. 6/8 The Renault 5 has all the comfort associated with the marque, despite its lack of size. **1973** *Times* 5 Oct. (Safety Suppl.) p. iv, But it should be emphasized that both marques are in the executive/luxury category and that to make a small family saloon as safe as a Mercedes or a Volvo would involve problems of weight and cost that are probably insuperable.

‖ **marquesa** (maɹke·zä). [Sp.; cf. MARCHESA.] In Spain: a marchioness.

1846 R. FORD *Gatherings from Spain* xviii. 249 We well remember the death of a kind and venerable Marquesa at Seville. **1966** H. YOXALL *Fashion of Life* vii. 63 The *marquesa* of the great neighbouring house was interested. **1968** A. BROWN *Slay me Suddenly* ix. 131 A *marquesa* may have dignity because she belongs to one of the oldest lineages in Spain.

Marquesan (maɹkē·sǎn, -z-), *a.* and *sb.* [f. *Marquesas* Islands in the Pacific + -AN.] **A.** *sb.* One of the Polynesian aborigines of the Marquesas Islands; also, the language spoken by them. **B.** *adj.* Of or pertaining to the Marquesas Islands.

1799 J. WILSON *Missionary Voy. S. Pacific* 138 Several of the Marquesans were continually plaguing the captain to take them to Otaheite. **1837** *Evangelical Mag.* Aug. 395 The spiritual enemies, which the Marquesan islanders have to encounter. **1845** J. COULTER *Adventures Pacific* xii. 155 Any liability to capsize is counteracted by the outrigger that all the Marquesan canoes have attached to them. *Ibid.* xiv. 211 Eight or ten nuts (commonly known as the candle-nut, from their emitting a bright flame, and being used by Marquesans as a substitute for candles) are strung on a piece of reed. **1896** R. L. STEVENSON *In South Seas* I. ii. 13 The alarms and sudden councils of Marquesan chiefs. **1919** F. O'BRIEN *White Shadows South Seas* iii. 28 Hence descended the Marquesans, vikings of the Pacific, in giant canoes, and sprang upon the fighting men of the Tahitians. *Ibid.* ix. 96 The Catholic chants sung thus in Marquesan took on a wild barbaric rhythm that thrilled the blood. **1936** V. A. DEMANT *Christian Polity* xi. 192 In regard to..Oceania..mention need only be made of..the effigies of chiefs among the Marquesans. **1969** J. H. VANCE *Deadly Isles* (1970) xvi. 118 A massive white-haired Marquesan with a face carved from teak. **1974** *Listener* 21 Nov. 679/2 The pathetic dependence of the Marquesans on imported foodstuffs. *Ibid.*, Curiosity about ancient Marquesan culture.

marquis. Add: **5.** A North American variety of spring wheat. Also *attrib.*

1906 C. SAUNDERS in *Bull. Canad. Dept. Agric.* No. 57. 29 *Chelsea* and *Marquis* are new cross-bred sorts produced at the Central Experimental Farm. **1924** J. A. THOMSON *Sci. Old & New* xliii. 253 Marquis is a hard, red spring wheat with excellent milling and baking qualities; it is now the dominant spring wheat in Canada and the United States. **1936** DENTON & LORD *World Geogr. for Canad. Schools* 85 Dr. Charles E. Saunders, the Dominion cerealist, had been experimenting for several years, trying to produce a new wheat which would ripen earlier than Red Fife. In 1903 his efforts were crowned with success. The new wheat was named 'Marquis'. **1960** D. E. BUBLITZ *Life on Dotted Line* 51 Marquis wheat was chosen as their crop that first year. **1965** I. REEKIE *Along Old Melita Trail* x. 150 Marquis wheat, developed from a cross of Red Fife, was released in 1911.

marquise. Add: **3. b.** *Archit.* (See quot. 1891.)

1891 tr. *J. Adeline's Art Dict.* 251/2 The term *marquise* is applied to a light roof which projects from the façade of a building. It is generally placed over a flight of steps. On the outside of theatres marquises of considerable length are not infrequently to be seen. Almost invariably they have a glass roof. **1904** B. VON HUTTEN *Pam* v. i. 237 A moment later, she stood in the door, under the little 'marquise'. **1924** 'L. MALET' *Dogs of Want* i. 7 [She] stood under the glass marquise, at the top of the flight of steps. **1930** A. BENNETT *Imperial Palace* vii. 28 On the steps under the marquise she took off her cloak.

marquisette (maɹkize·t). [Fr., dim. of *marquise* MARQUISE.] (See quots. 1968.)

1908 *Tatler* 6 May (Suppl.) p. iv, A simple house gown of black marquisette. **1909** *Daily Chron.* 12 Apr. 7/1 The soft marquisettes and satin-faced foulards. **1913** [see *FOURREAU]. **1928** *Times* 9 May 11/3 A picture gown of fine gold embroidered marquisette, over peach georgette. **1930** *Times* 13 Mar. 11/6 Lovely ankle-length frocks in flowered and plain chiffons, lace, satins, and marquisettes. **1957** *New Yorker* 5 Oct. 110/1 Its dazzling décolletage veiled in black marquisette. **1968** E. GALE *From Fibres to Fabrics* xii. 132 Some marquisettes are not woven, but are produced on a simple type of lace machine. **1968** J. IRONSIDE *Fashion Alphabet* 240 *Marquisette*, a leno-weave gauze fabric made of cotton, rayon, silk or synthetic fibres.

Marrano. (Later examples.) Also *attrib.*

1941 G. G. SCHOLEM *Major Trends Jewish Mysticism* vii. 240 The beginning of the persecution of the Jews in Spain and the appearance of Marrano Judaism after 1391. **1942** L. B. NAMIER *Conflicts* 133 More logical were those who attempted amalgamation: but even this, as a mass movement, merely produces Marranos. **1960** L. P. GARTNER *Jewish Immigrant* i. 16 The mid-seventeenth century, when the earlier flight of Marranos from Spain and Portugal was no longer important. **1973** *Jewish Chron.* 2 Feb. 3/5 The 90 members of the tribe near the town of Pachuca..claim that some of their ancestors were Marranos (baptised Jews suspected of secret adherence to Judaism) who were burnt at the stake in Mexico during the 16th century. **1973** *Publishers Weekly* 3 Sept. 44/1 The term 'Marranos' originally denoted those Spanish Jews who, during the Inquisition, or long before it, converted to Catholicism but continued secretly to practice their Jewish faith; loosely it denotes all secret Jews.

Marranism (further example). Also **Marra·nic** *a.*, **Marra·noism.**

1924 *Glasgow Herald* 25 Sept. 6 In most Latin American countries, the arrivals find no organized Jewish life—only Marranoism. **1941** G. G. SCHOLEM *Major Trends Jewish Mysticism* vii. 254 The descendant of a Marranic family. *Ibid.* viii. 311 The conception of a voluntary Marranism.

marri (mæ·ri). [Aboriginal name.] A Western Australian red gum tree, *Eucalyptus calophylla*, or its timber.

1920 R. GRIMWADE *Anthography of Eucalypts* plate 75 *E[ucalyptus] calophylla.* Marri. Western Australian Red Gum... A tall, sturdy tree, well distributed over the coastal regions of Western Australia. **1934** W. F. BLAKELY *Key to Eucalypts* 84 *E. calophylla*, R.Br. 'Marri' or 'Red Gum'... A medium-sized to large tree. Bark rough, flaky, persistent on trunk and branches. **1938** A. W. D'OMBRAIN *Gallery of Gum Trees* 48 In Western Australia ..there are two distinctive and beautiful red flowering gums, the Scarlet Flowered Gum,..and..the much larger Pink Flowered Marri. **1963** *Times* 12 Mar. (Austral. Suppl.) p. v/7 Marri and gimlet and grey-barked tuart, and..other valuable timbers. **1969** T. H. EVERETT *Living Trees of World* 269/1 The marri or red gum (*E. calophylla*) has its home in southwestern Australia. It becomes 150 feet tall with a trunk 5 feet in diameter... Its flowers, in large decorative terminal clusters, are cream-colored or pink; they produce abundant nectar. This is a good ornamental and shade tree. Its lumber is used for boxes and light construction.

marriage. Add: **8.** *marriage contract* (examples), *-day* (later examples), *-hall, manual, market* (earlier and later examples), *mart, -tie* (later examples), *-vow* (later examples); **marriage broker**, (*b*) in cultures in which arranged marriages are the norm, one who arranges marriages for a fee; **marriage bureau**, an agency which arranges introductions with a view to marriage; also *fig.*; **marriage certificate**, a copy of the record of a legal marriage which is given to the contracting parties; **marriage counselling, guidance**, the giving of advice on problems connected with marriage, usu. as a form of social service; also **marriage counsellor, marriage guidance counsellor**; **marriage of convenience** = *MARIAGE DE CONVENANCE; **marriage payment** *Anthropol.*, payment of a traditional kind made in many tribal societies to a bride or her parents by the bridegroom or his parents; cf. *BRIDE *sb.*[1] 5; **marriage rate**, the ratio of the number of marriages per year to the population (usually expressed per thousand); **marriage-ring** (earlier and later examples).

1892 I. ZANGWILL *Childr. Ghetto* I. 18 The same mould covers them all—..the marriage-brokers repose with those they mated. **1932** L. GOLDING *Magnolia Street* I. ii. 32 She didn't marry again, though she was only in the middle thirties when he died and the marriage-brokers got busy. **1968** L. ROSTEN *Joys of Yiddish* 325 A wisecrack defines a *shadchen* as 'a marriage broker who knows the perfect girl for you—and married the wrong girl himself'. **1942** OLIVER & BENEDETTA *Marriage Bureau* 19 How much better it would be if there were an organization that could arrange the actual match-making and see that suitable people met each other. And this was my idea for the Marriage Bureau. **1953** 'H. JENNER' *Marriage is my Business* i. 19 The story has often been told of the two exdebs and how they coped with opening a marriage bureau. **1960** N. EPTON *Love & English* vi. v. 355 The marriage bureau..lists all your assets for the calm perusal of registered clients. *Ibid.* 356 This modern matchmaker, the marriage bureau, is middle-class and eminently respectable. **1972** *Accountant* 5 Oct. 411/3 Its aim would be the establishment of a 'marriage bureau' for the smaller businesses of Europe. **1848** MRS. GASKELL *Let.* 11 Nov. (1966) 62, I wish I had five sisters, who were bound to love me by their parents' marriage certificate. **1860** E. EDEN *Semi-Attached Couple* II. xviii. 225 He had seen too much of life, to believe in these sudden discoveries of marriage certificates. **1911** G. B. SHAW *Doctor's Dilemma* III. 61 She carried her marriage certificate in her face and in her character. **1945** MENCKEN *Amer. Lang.* Suppl. I. 475/1 *Marriage lines* is confined to the vulgar. On higher levels *marriage certificate* is used. **1967** 'G. NORTH' *Sgt. Cluff & Day of Reckoning* xi. 101 Brittle where it had been folded, the marriage certificate held his gaze. **1824** MILL in *Westm. Rev.* I. 537 Plato is represented as exceedingly wicked, for having expounded, in his Republic, the footing upon which he thought that the marriage contract could most advantageously be placed. **1961** NEW ENG. BIBLE *Matt.* i. 19 Joseph desired to have the marriage contract set aside quietly. **1945** Marriage counselling [see *COUNSELLING *vbl. sb.*]. **1959** HERBERT & JARVIS (*title*) A modern approach to marriage counselling. **1970** *Guardian* 31 July 18/6 In the 30 years the marriage counselling movement has been in existence the lack of specific privileges for marriage counsellors has never come to a showdown. **1946** Marriage counsellor [see *COUNSELLOR 1 b]. **1970** G. GREER *Female Eunuch* 19 The revolutionary woman must know her enemies, the doctors, psychiatrists,..marriage counsellors. *a* **1640** MASSINGER et al. *Old Law* (1656) v. 69 As I am Lord of the day (being my marriage day the second) I doe advance bonnet. **1852** M. ARNOLD *Tristram* I, in *Empodocles on Etna* 115 That her lord and she Might drink it on their marriage day. **1907** W. B. YEATS *Deirdre* 36 Although her marriage-day had all but come. **1935** *Time* 13 May 28/2 Old Stone Church is one of an increasing number whose pastors run 'marriage guidance bureaus'. **1945** *Times* 25 July 5/5 Groups of people in the provinces have recently been setting up their own local marriage guidance councils. **1948** D. R. MACE *Marriage Counselling* iii. 18 Marriage guidance..falls into three natural divisions. The first is education for marriage... The second is marriage preparation..intensive preparation of engaged couples... The third is marriage counselling..offering help to married people who are confronted with difficulties. **1965** HALL & HOWES *Church in Social Work* iii. 63 Started in 1938 and revived and reconstituted on a national basis in 1943, the National Marriage Guidance Council..quickly became established. **1967** O. WYND *Walk Softly, Men Praying* xii. 186 About all that was available to me was the kind of noise that might have come from a junior apprentice marriage-guidance counsellor. **1970** G. GREER *Female Eunuch* 17 Women are not happy even when they do follow the blueprint set out by sentimental and marriage guidance counsellors and the system that they represent. **1924** W. J. LOCKE *Coming of Amos* xvi. 204 Of the marriage in the bleak marriage-hall of the Mairie, she remembered little. **1936** H. M. & A. STONE (*title*) A marriage manual. **1965** MASTERS & JOHNSON in J. Money *Sex Research* iv. 109 If the suggestions of the marriage manuals are followed, the male develops the concept that he is to find the clitoris and stay with it. **1969** 'J' *Sensuous Woman* (1970) xix. 121 Don't let any marriage manual talk you into missing that moment when he explodes in you. **1973** I. SINGER *Goals of Human Sexuality* vi. 149 The fifteen popular marriage manuals..all treat sexual response as if it were work. **1850** *Punch* 3 Aug. 54/2 If..the Duke of Cambridge were permitted to take his coronet into the home marriage-market. **1942** E. BOWEN *Seven Winters* 46 The ulterior designs of the marriage market. **1971** R. RUSSELL tr. *Ahmad's Shore & Wave* iv. 45 The oldest, it was true, was married to a prosperous consultant engineer, but the other two were still in the marriage market. **1823** BYRON *Don Juan* XII. xlvi. 7 The Smithfield Show Of vestals brought into the marriage mart. **1972** *Village Voice* (N.Y.) 1 June 70/3 For all our talk about being liberated, most of my friends are too shy, or perhaps just too snobby, to show up at marriage marts. **1711** Marriage of convenience [see CONVENIENCE *sb.* 6]. **1949** G. B. SHAW *Buoyant Billions* IV. 53 The proportion of happy love marriages to happy marriages of convenience has never been counted. **1972** C. DRUMMOND *Death at Bar* ii. 64 Reg and June are a bit peculiar in that it was simply a marriage of convenience... They went their own way. **1975** *Listener* 16 Jan. 84/3 The co-ordinators had..paired each of the piano sonatas with each of the string quartets. Was this just a marriage of convenience..for numerical rather than musical reasons? **1924** W. H. RIVERS *Social Organisation* iii. 46 Marriage by exchange..may co-exist with marriage by purchase, and ..in some cases, it is only a means of avoiding..the marriage payments. **1951** *N. & Q. Anthropol.* (ed. 6) II. iv. 111 In either case the settlement of a marriage-payment.. may be the custom. **1957** V. W. TURNER *Schism & Continuity in Afr. Society* ix. 265 He..affected to take umbrage because the marriage-payment..he had made for her in cloth was not returned. **1963** W. J. GOODE *World Revolution & Family Patterns* iv. 167 The marriage payment or groom service points to the great concern with the legal possession of children. **1859** Marriage rate [see *birth-rate* (*BIRTH *sb.*[1] 13)]. **1891** G. B. LONGSTAFF *Stud. in Statistics* iii. 14 Speaking generally, the birth-rate corresponds to the marriage-rate, but with marked exceptions. **1970** W. D. BORRIE *Growth & Control World Population* iv. 62 There was a suggestion of a considerable degree of rationality in the reactions of these populations to the food situation, with marriage rates rising in good times and falling in bad times. *a* **1631** DONNE *Jeat Ring Sent* in *Poems* (1633) 292 Marriage rings are not of this stuffe. **1878** O. WILDE *Ravenna* 5 A moon of fire Round-girdled with a purple marriage-ring. **1913** J. MASEFIELD *Daffodil Fields* 82 She dropped her marriage-ring upon the table. **1865** G. M. HOPKINS *Note-bks. & Papers* (1937) 54 The Frenchman said the marriage-tie was in every case a bad thing. **1951** R. FIRTH *Elem. Social Organiz.* ii. 59 The marriage-tie is made the basis of service as a cook. **1935** B. MALINOWSKI *Coral Gardens* II. VI. v. 234 Whether the marriage vows are treated as a sacrament or as a mere legal contract. **1965** A. CHRISTIE *At Bertram's Hotel* vii. 79 The walls of Jericho seemed to be a symbolical way of referring to a certain lady's marriage vows... They tumbled down.

marriageability. (Examples.)

1895 in *Funk's Stand. Dict.* **1910** *Encycl. Relig. & Ethics* III. 345/2 The karōḥ (lit. 'seclusion'), or declaration of marriageability of girls, is celebrated with great solemnity. **1944** G. B. SHAW *Everybody's Pol. What's What?* viii. 61 Equality of income and complete touchability and marriageability exist at present at different levels in the trades, the professions, the ranks, and the classes. **1974** *Sci. Amer.* Sept. 113/1 According to Oriental astrology, girls born that year may murder their husbands, which tends to reduce their marriageability.

marriage-bed. (Later examples.)

1913 D. H. LAWRENCE *Love Poems* 5 The low-built shed Where hangs the swallow's marriage bed. **1922** JOYCE *Ulysses* 458 He felt it his mission in life to urge me, to defile the marriage bed, to commit adultery at the earliest possible opportunity.

married, *ppl. a.* Add: **1.** *married couple*, a husband and wife; often in contexts where they are acting jointly as domestic servants.

a **1817** JANE AUSTEN *Persuasion* (1818) III. viii. 147 Admiral and Mrs. Croft..among the married couples. **1871** *Monthly Packet* Oct. 388 The grandmother had at that time as lodgers a married couple and a single man. **1890**

W. Booth *In Darkest Eng.* II. vi. 209 We shall be confronted with married couples who..demand that we should provide for them lodgings. **1962** *Times* 22 Oct. 1/3 Mr. and Mrs. G. K. require a married couple—chauffeur house-parlourman and cook-housekeeper. **1965** J. S. Gunn *Terminol. Shearing Indust.* II. 35 s.v. *Twins.* Two shearers who travel and work together, neither being prepared to 'take a pen' unless his mate gets one too. These inseparable mates are sometimes referred to as a 'married couple'. **1971** C. Whitman *Death Suspended* iv. 80 The staff..consisted of..a married couple employed as manager and housekeeper. **1972** *Listener* 21 Dec. 861/2 Up-and-coming young married couples who..are the people on whom the future of society depends. **1973** *Times* 7 Apr. 26/3 (Advt.), Young married couple needed. See domestic situations.

b. *fig.* (Later example.)

1973 *Times* 23 May 19/1 The..happily married Paternoster pedestrian precinct and the extended churchyard to the north-east.

3. Special collocation: *married print* Cinemat., a positive film carrying both pictures and a sound track.

1953 K. Reisz *Technique Film Editing* 276 From this cut negative and the negative of the re-recorded composite sound-track, a married print is prepared which is ready for projection to cinema audiences. **1959** F. Chagrin in Halas & Manvell *Technique Film Animation* xix. 238 Sound and vision have equal importance; they are equal partners, aiming at an ideal married-print status and preparing for it scrupulously by synchronizing their moods and their movements. **1965** P. Wayre *Wind in Reeds* ix. 135 From this original the first 'married' print was produced with an optical sound track down one side of the film.

B. *sb.* A married person; also *collect.* Freq. in phr. *young marrieds.*

1890 A. James *Diary* 30 Nov. (1964) 159 The married, however, thro' their ignoble state are doomed to shatter all the ideals of the soaring spinster. **1934** J. O'Hara *Appointment in Samarra* i. 8 The kids home from boarding-school and college, and the younger marrieds, most of whom she knew by their first names, and then the older crowd. **1938** *Time* 5 Dec. 8/3 No representative letter can be chosen from such heterogeneous applications—from men and women, from youngsters, young marrieds, middleaged, and oldsters. **1939** [see *cut-in *sb.* 1]. **1958** *Times* 22 Nov. 7/7 These teeming 'young marrieds' are very different from those less numerous in the Depression, a generation ago. **1959** *House & Garden* June 8 Smart young marrieds go 'natural' with Irish Linen. **1963** A. Heron *Towards Quaker View of Sex* i. 11 Among the married, faithfulness may be achieved by 'working to rule'. *Ibid.* 57 Free heterosexual relations between the young unmarried or between the married. **1965** *New Statesman* 30 Apr. 672/2 Wealthy parents, who are subsidised by the bachelors and the childless married. **1970** K. Giles *Murder Pluperfect* ii. 14 Victorian marrieds, of a certain class, used to sleep around. **1972** J. Casson *Lewis & Sybil* ix. 192 Our life together as young naval marrieds was to begin in Alexandria.

Marriotte, erron. var. *Mariotte.

Marrism (mā·riz'm). [f. the name of N. Ya. *Marr* (1865–1934), Russian linguist and archæologist + -ism.] The linguistic theories advocated by Nikolai Yakovlevich Marr, in which language is regarded as a phenomenon of social class rather than of nationality; the advocacy of such theories. Hence **Ma·rrist** *a.*

1950 *Archivum Linguisticum* II. 116 The quintessence of Marrism, he [*sc.* B. Serebrennikov] tells us, resides in four fundamental theses, viz. the four elements as the source of the world's vocabularies, linguistic growth by hybridisation, stadial evolution, and the semantic transformation of primitive totem-names. *Ibid.* 118 It is he [*sc.* V. Vinogradov] who summarises the three existing attitudes to Marr among Soviet scholars, viz. (1) that Marrism is Marxism in linguistics, [etc.]. *Ibid.* 8 Her [*sc.* R. Šor's] articles are perhaps the first reasoned statement of the Marxist standpoint that is not at the same time Marrist. **1960** [see *hybridization 2]. **1963** V. Kiparsky in *Current Trends in Ling.* I. 94 From 1925 to World War II, when the only officially accepted linguistic school in Soviet Russia was Nikolaj Marr's 'Japhetology', later simply called 'Marrism', there was no interest..in Slavic languages. **1965** H. Kučera in *Language* XLI. 118 The rehabilitation of comparativist techniques—another by-product of the 1950 renunciation of Marrism. *Ibid.* 125 The reader will find many brief references to the Marrist controversy of 1950. **1966** B. Collinder in Birnbaum & Puhvel *Anc. Indo-European Dial.* 199 Marrism, which was officially encouraged in Russia for political reasons, has raged as a kind of Asiatic flu in some European universities west of the Iron Curtain.

marrite (mā·rəit). *Min.* [f. the name of John Edward *Marr* (1857–1933), British geologist + -ite¹.] A sulphide and arsenide of lead and silver, $PbAgAsS_3$, which is found as grey monoclinic crystals in dolomite at Lengenbach, Switzerland.

1904 [see *lengenbachite]. **1905** R. H. Solly in *Mineral. Mag.* XIV. 76 The colour of marrite is lead-grey to steel-grey, but the crystals are usually tarnished with iridescent colours... The name marrite is proposed in honour of Dr. John Edward Marr, F.R.S., of Cambridge. **1967** *Zeitschr. für Kristallogr.* CXXV. 459 Marrite, a rare sulfosalt from the Binnatal, Switzerland, has been shown to have composition $PbAgAsS_3$. The phase is monoclinic, space group $P2_1/a$.

‖ **marron glacé** (maroṅ glase). [F. *marron* chestnut + Glacé *a.*] A sweetmeat consisting of a chestnut preserved in syrup.

1871 *Leisure Hour* 23 Sept. 600/1 'Marrons glacées' appeared at the confectioners'. **1875** *All Year Round* 2 Jan. 279/2 Old women are..preparing chestnuts for their ..destinies as 'marrons glacés', &c. **1880** G. A. Sala *Amer. Revisited* (1882) I. 57 Did my stock-in-trade comprise a few *marrons glacés*, so much the better for my youthful patroness. **1904** A. Bennett *Great Man* v. 45 'A pound of marrons glacés.'..'What are they?'..'Taste.'.. 'It's like chestnuts,' Harry mumbled through the delicious brown frosted morsel. **1906** Kipling *Actions & Reactions* (1909) 210 Oranges, bits of banana, and *marron[s] glacés.* **1925** C. Sidgwick *Humming-Bird* xviii. 188 Behind the loaded counter the proprietor and his assistants were weighing chocolates and marrons glacés. **1967** 'L. Black' *Two Ladies in Verona* ii. 18 A low table garnished with.. an enormous box of marrons glacés. **1973** *Times* 1 Dec. 14/1 Marrons glacés. 14 oz. tins. 2 for £5.20... Marrons in syrup. Large whole chestnuts in extra heavy syrup.. 18 oz. tins. 3 for £5.25.

marrow, *sb.*¹ Add: **5.** *marrow-freezing* adj. (examples); **marrow kale** = **marrow-stem* (*kale*); **marrow oil,** a dressing for the hair (cf. *marrowfat 2); **marrow scoop** = *marrow-spoon*; **marrow-stem (kale)** = *chou moellier (see quot. 1925); also *marrow-stemmed kale.*

1847 C. Brontë *Jane Eyre* I. xv. 295 A marrow-freezing incident enough. This was a demoniac laugh. **1900** *Sketch* 21 Feb. 191/2 A play..of a rather marrow-freezing kind. **1872** R. Hogg in *Jrnl. Roy. Hort. Soc.* III. 174 Marrow Kale..is the *Chou moellier* of the French, a form of the Jersey kale which produces a long, thickly swollen stem like a gigantic cigar, the swollen part being filled with a mass of tender pith. **1855** F. Duberly *Let.* 29 Jan. in E. E. P. Tisdall *Mrs. Duberly's Campaigns* (1963) iv. 124, I want you to write to Savory & Moore, Bond St. for 2 Large Bottles Marrow Oil, 4 Bottles of Bandoline. **1864** Trollope *Can You forgive Her?* I. xl. 310 All his apparatus for dressing,—his marrow oil for his hair, [etc.]. **1969** E. H. Pinto *Treen* 79 The marrow scoop and toothpick are missing. **1970** *Canad. Antiques Collector* Mar. 23/1 There were numerous objects..such as soup ladles..marrow scoops. **1972** *Collector's Guide* Aug. 10/2 (Advt.), Fine Marrow Scoop (crested), by Wm. Chawner, 1763, £40. **1920** *Conquest* Apr. 256/3 In place of grass it is possible to grow crops such as cabbage, vetches, rape, marrowstem kale, [etc.]. **1925** Malden & Nisbet in W. G. R. Paterson *Farm Crops* II. 191 The Marrow-stem Kale is what is known as a 'variety-hybrid'. That is, it is the result of crossing two distinct varieties—the kohl-rabi and the Thousandhead Kale, each a variety of *Brassica oleracea. Ibid.* 194 Mildews and moulds do less damage to the marrow stem than to turnips. **1960** *Farmer & Stockbreeder* 8 Mar. 131/2 Marrow-stem kale goes fibrous and woody very quickly after Christmas, and loses most of its feeding value. **1961** I. Molnar *Man. Austral. Agric.* 214 The Marrow Stemmed Kale (chou mollier) is a kale with a swollen axis. **1972** D. H. Robinson *Fream's Elem. Agric.* (ed. 15) x. 281 Marrowstem Kale is capable of producing very large quantities of greenstuff greatly relished by stock.

marrow, *sb.*² **1.** (Later examples.)

1935 A. J. Cronin *Stars look Down* I. ii. 20 His dad had gone with the marrows in his set. *Ibid.* xxii. 205 Jack Reedy..and his marrow, Cha Leeming, worked their shift in the Scupper Flats.

marrowfat. Add: **2.** *N. Amer.* A tallow-like substance prepared by boiling down marrow.

1717 J. Knight *Jrnl.* 16 Aug. (1932) 164 These Indians gave me..2 pretty bigg bladders of Marrow fatt. **1791** in *Publ. Champlain Soc.* (1934) XXI. 528 They broke the Bones of the Buffalo & made marrowfatt. **1841** G. Catlin *Lett. on N. Amer. Indians* I. 116 'Marrow-fat' is collected by the Indians from the buffalo bones which they break to pieces, yielding a prodigious quantity of marrow, which is boiled out and put into buffalo bladders. **1846** R. B. Sage *Scenes Rocky Mts.* viii. 79 Marrow-fat, an article in many respects superior to butter. **1888** *Century Mag.* XXXVI. 898/1 Then he slicked his hair with marrow-fat from a horn. **1947** *Beaver* Dec. 21 Clean Marrow fat rendered down like white butter.

†**3.** *U.S. slang.* (See quot.) *Obs.*

1903 A. B. Hart *Actual Govt. Amer. Conditions* 75 The 'marrow-fat' fraud consists in a voter's putting in more than one ballot, while the clerk puts down fictitious names to cover the extra ballots.

marrowsky (mărau·ski). Also **marouski, Marowsky, morowski, mowrowsky.** [Asserted to have been derived from the name of a Polish count, doubtfully identified with Count Joseph Boruwlaski. See *N. & Q.* 13th Ser. I. 331, 437, 467.] **a.** A variety of slang, or a slip in speaking, characterized by transposition of initial letters, syllables, or parts of two words. Also *marrowsky language.*

1863 R. Nicholson *Autobiogr. Fast Man* xviii. 200 Fanny King, or as Bill Leach, in the interesting language called *Marouski*, termed her, Kanny Fing. **1883** G. A. Sala *Living London* 491 The vocabulary of Tim Bobbin, Josh Billings,..and the 'Marowsky' language.

b. An instance of this.

1923 in *N. & Q.* 27 Oct. 331/2 In my childhood..an old cousin used to entertain me with what we now call *spoonerisms*, but which she termed *morowskis.* **1962** V. Nabokov *Pale Fire* 185, I remember one perfect evening when my friend sparkled with quips, and marrowskies, and anecdotes.

Hence **marrow·skyer,** one who uses marrowsky language or makes marrowskies in his speech; **marrow·skying** *vbl. sb.*, the intentional or accidental transposition of initial letters, etc.

1860 Hotten *Dict. Slang* (ed. 2) 173 s.v. *Medical Greek.* At the London University they have a way of disguising English..which consists in transposing the initials of words... This disagreeable nonsense is often termed *marrowskying.* **1912** *Brit. Med. Jrnl.* 22 June 1443 It would be interesting if 'marrowskyers'' blunders could also be classified. *Ibid.*, All actors live in dread of 'marrowskying', that curious transposition of syllables. **1922** O. Jespersen *Lang.* viii. 150 'Marrowskying' or 'Hospital Greek' transfers the initial letters of words, as *renty of plain.*

Marrucinian (mærūsi·niăn), *sb.* and *a.* Also **Mar(r)ucine, Marucian, Marusian.** [f. L. *Marrucini* + -an.] **A.** *sb.* **a.** A member of an Oscan-Umbrian people living near Teate in ancient Eastern Italy. **b.** The language of this people. **B.** *adj.* Of or pertaining to this people or their language.

1578 tr. *Appian's Auncient Historie of Romanes Warres* I. 25 The Marsians, the Malinians, the Vestinians, the Marucians,..and the Samnites, whiche people before had euer bin enimies, and hurtfull to the Romaines. *Ibid.* 31 A little Marusian aunswered hym, and kylled hym. **1600** P. Holland tr. *Livy's Rom. Hist.* VIII. 302 Every one of them, namely, the Marsians, the Pelignians and Marucines, were in feats of armes comparable and egall to the Samnites every way. *Ibid.* XXVII. 660 Hee dispatched likewise messengers before, through the territories of the Larinates, Marrucines, Ferentines, and Pretutians. **1601** —— tr. *Pliny's Nat. Hist.* II. lxxxiii. 39 Medowes and olive rowes.. in the Marrucine territorie. **1863** W. P. Dickson tr. *Mommsen's Hist. Rome* III. IV. vii. 235 The small but hardy confederacies in the Abruzzi—the Pælignians, Marrucinians, Frentanians, and Vestinians. *Ibid.* 237 The territory of the Pælignians, situated in the centre of the Marsian, Samnite, Marrucinian, and Vestinian cantons. **1888** J. Wright tr. *Brugmann's Elem. Compar. Gram. Indo-Germanic Lang.* I. 9 Of the Volscian, Picentine, Sabine, Aequiculan, Vestinian, Marsian, Pelignian and Marrucinian dialects we have only very scanty remains. **1933, 1939** [see *Marsian *sb.* and *a.*]. **1966** M. S. Beeler in Birnbaum & Puhvel *Anc. Indo-European Dial.* 51 The so-called minor dialects such as Paelignian, Volscian, and Marrucinian. **1974** R. A. Hall *External Hist. Romance Lang.* 48 The Sabellic dialects..: Sabine..; Paelignian, Marrucinian, Vestine, and Marsic in the central Apennines east of Rome; and Volscian.

marry, *v.* Add: **1. c.** *marry up* (earlier example). Also *fig.* (const. *with*).

1698 J. Collier *Short View Immorality Eng. Stage* iv. 154 This Spark..makes a lucky Hand on't at last, and marries up a rich Lady. **1942** *Tee Emm* (Air Ministry) II. 97 They already have had the idea of taking photos of the countryside and marrying them up with similar areas on a map. **1958** *Times* 15 Feb. 7/3 Now that poverty-stricken Jordan is married up with a rich relation. **1970** Bakewell & Garnham *New Priesthood* iv. 44 If a writer..is not ripe for TV drama, then we would certainly sit down with him, pull his script to bits, send it away, come back, try again, try it on an editor, marry them [*sic*] up with an editor if possible.

2. b. With *off.*

1860 Queen Victoria *Let.* 18 Dec. in R. Fulford *Dearest Child* (1964) 292, I do wish somebody would go and marry her off—at once. **1865** M. C. Harris *St. Philip's* viii. 59 If the young girls did not mind being.. finally married off to some of her *protégés*, it was all very well. **1894** V. Hunt *Maiden's Progress* i. 2, I sincerely hope you will be married off before *I* come on, or I shall have no peace. **1908** *Smart Set* June 14/1 Mr. Hardcastle was insisting upon marrying off Aunt Ella to Señor Dominguez y Aguirra. **1973** 'E. Ferrars' *Foot in Grave* viii. 150 I've worked quite hard at trying to get you married off.

3. b. To obtain (something) by getting married. Esp. on phr. *to marry money*: to marry a rich spouse.

1858 Trollope *Doctor Thorne* I. xiv. 297 He must marry money, or he will be a ruined man. **1911** L. J. Vance (*title*) Marrying money. **1914** Joyce *Dubliners* 98 There'll be no mooning and spooning about it. I mean to marry money. **1934** *Harrap's Stand. French & Eng. Dict.* I. 329/1 *Épouser*..*une grosse dot*, to marry money. **1936** Herzog & Blooah *Jabo Proverbs from Liberia* 180 If you marry a beautiful woman, you marry trouble.

5. a. (Later examples.)

1908 *Daily Chron.* 19 Aug. 4/7 By 'marrying' or blending the wine from different vineyards he discovered that there resulted an effervescing wine. **1919** Kipling *Years Between* 63 With a thin third finger marrying Drop to wine-drop domed on the table. **1925** Belloc *Mr. Petre* vi. 150 A genius who could marry the commonest tricks to unheard rapidity and daring. **1942** L. Bennett *Jamaica Dial. Verses* 44 Pumpkin? yuh wi Haffe buy cho-cho wid i, Dem married, same like 'ow cassada Married to yampi. **1952** M. Kerr *Personality & Conflict in Jamaica* 59 Soap and rice are popular gifts, as the shopkeepers in the country tend to 'marry them'. **1958** *Times Lit. Suppl.* 3 Oct. 567/4 It is always something of a problem with a heavily illustrated book to know how best to marry a long text with the illustrations relating to it. **1960** O. Skilbeck *ABC of Film & TV* 82 *Marry*, to combine related mute and sound negatives in printing, or different picture negatives in optical work. **1963** *Times* 24 Apr. 12/7 Rolls-Royce believe that their success with a combination of silica and aluminium opens up the possibility of 'marrying' different types of ceramics and metals. **1967** Cassidy & Le Page *Dict. Jamaican Eng.* 294/1 *Marry*, to couple something in short supply (and much in demand) with something not much wanted, so that one must purchase the latter in order to have the former. **1969** *Daily Tel.* 11 Nov. 6/7 Scientists are 'marrying' strains, such as the

Hongkong virus, to other influenza viruses that are known to reproduce and spread faster.

d. *Stockbrokers' slang.* To set (one transaction against another).

1931 *Economist* 10 Oct. 675/1 The shareholders..can do nothing, for the Trust only agrees to 'marry' buying orders for clients against selling orders. **1959** *Ibid.* 21 Mar. 1099/1 The brokers in these shares then find it convenient to 'marry' the buying and selling orders.

6. a. Also *to marry into*: to enter (a family, etc.) by marrying; to obtain by getting married. (See quot. 1662 in Dict.) Also *to marry well*: to have a successful marriage (in terms of harmony, material gain, or social standing).

1604 [see WELL *adv.* 6 c]. **1871** GEO. ELIOT *Middlem.* (1872) I. I. iv. 61, I wish you to marry well; and I have good reason to believe that Chettam wishes to marry you. **1876** C. M. YONGE *Womankind* xxxi. 281 Mothers.. cherish wishes that their girls may 'marry well'; *i.e.* richly. **1899** O. WILDE *Importance of Being Earnest* I. 39 You can hardly imagine that I and Lord Bracknell would dream of allowing our only daughter..to marry into a cloak-room, and form an alliance with a parcel. **1904** H. O. STURGIS *Belchamber* i. 10 They both married, and married what is called 'well', while many of their fairer..sisters were left ungathered on the stem. **1905** A. BURVENICH *Eng. Idioms* 224 *Marry...* To—into a fortune; *épouser une fortune, een rijk huwelijk doen.* **1923** R. MACAULAY *Told by Idiot* I. xiii. 50 What chances does a girl want, except to marry well? **1931** *Daily Express* 21 Sept. 19/1 He married into money, so that I find it difficult to credit that his contemplated return is for the purpose of restoring his balance at the bank. **1933** R. H. LOWIE in *Encycl. Social Sci.* X. 146/2 No Masai of good standing marries into a blacksmith's family. **1946** [see *BROUHAHA]. **1963** *Listener* 14 Feb. 274/1 A socialist politician who has married into a farm. **1974** 'J. MELVILLE' *Nun's Castle* i. 19 Among the other luxuries life provided for Lady Dorothy were kindred on the eastern seaboard of the United States... Probably she had someone married 'well' into the Kremlin if the truth were told.

c. *fig.* (Later examples.) Also, (of wine, etc.) to mature. Now esp. *to marry up with*, to link with.

1960 T. MCLEAN *Kings of Rugby* xi. 170 Risman began to bear to the left to marry up with the outside backs. **1963** *Harper's Bazaar* Aug. 26 Blended..the whisky must now 'marry' another year before bottling. **1969** *New Yorker* 27 Sept. 120/2 The juices are the foundation for a generous gravy, in which blanched vegetables like carrots, onions..are heated and then allowed to marry for an hour or more. **1969** [see *GAZPACHO]. **1971** C. BONINGTON *Annapurna South Face* App. C. 257 Even though there were indications that the British mask used on Kanchenjunga and the American mask used on Everest were superior in design, I preferred to keep things as simple as possible, eliminating any risk of parts failing to marry up.

d. *to marry above, below* or *beneath*, (oneself): to marry a person of higher or lower social position.

1721 J. KELLY *Compl. Coll. Scottish Proverbs* 252 Marry above your Match, and you get a Master. **1741** RICHARDSON *Pamela* (1742) III. 4 For who will offer to reproach me for marrying, as the World thinks, below me. *Ibid.* IV. 246 A Man, who..marry'd beneath him. **1860** A. J. MUNBY *Diary* 21 Feb. in D. Hudson *Munby* (1972) 51 Saw Mrs Lock (herself considerably reduced in the world, being in fact a *lady* who married beneath her). **1876** TROLLOPE *Prime Minister* III. xx. 336 He had married much above himself in every way. **1895** A. W. PINERO *Second Mrs. Tanqueray* IV. 160 All my family have chucked me over... Jus' because I've married beneath me.

e. *to marry out*: to marry a person of a different clan, group, religion, etc.

1842 *Southern Lit. Messenger* VIII. 331/2 'Marrying out', as the Friends call one of a different faith, is regarded by them with especial horror. **1923** C. ROTH *Hist. Marranos* xii. 316 His son, Jacob Israel Bernal, married out of the faith and left the community. **1954** E. E. EVANS-PRITCHARD *Inst. Primitive Society* vi. 68 The rule of exogamy—the rule of marrying-out—which required that a man must not marry inside a defined set of his own kin. **1957** V. W. TURNER *Schism & Continuity in Afr. Society* ix. 287 Most women marry out at least once. **1959** F. M. WILSON *They came as Strangers* III. iv. 212 When his daughter married a Gentile..he never reproached her for marrying 'out'. **1964** E. HUXLEY *Back Street New Worlds* ii. 20 Jewish women stick much closer to their own kind, with only between one-tenth and one-fifth marrying 'out'. **1973** *Jewish Chron.* 19 Jan. 23/4 The smugness..may be one of the reasons for the apathy among Orthodox Jews which leads to marrying out.

marrying, *vbl. sb.* Add: **1.** *transf.* and *fig.* Also **marrying-in, -out.**

1917 B. GRIMSHAW *Nobody's Island* v. 61 Such greens, such blues, such marryings of both, not brush and colour, nor pen and ink, could paint. **1940** *Chambers's Techn. Dict.* 528/1 *Marrying*, the process of lashing poles together in scaffold erection. *Ibid.*, *Marrying* (*Cinema*), the printing of the mute negative and the negative soundtrack on the release print. **1952** *Economist* 8 Nov. 401/1 The marrying of reactors with power generators. **1964** GOULD & KOLB *Dict. Social Sci.* 239/2 Endogamy and exogamy are processes of marrying-in and marrying-out. **1973** *Times Lit. Suppl.* 6 July 775/2 A drama of 'marrying out' (a painful process which one does not have to be Jewish to experience).

Mars. Add: **2*.** The proprietary name of a chocolate-covered bar with a toffee-like filling. Usu. in form *Mars bar.*

1932 *Trade Marks Jrnl.* 5 Oct. 1273 *Mars,..* a sweetmeat. Mars Confections Limited. **1943** *Penguin New Writing* XVI. (verso front cover, Advt.), Mars are made from the finest available materials—including chocolate.., glucose.., separated milk. **1948** C. DAY LEWIS *Otterbury Incident* ix. 112 Toppy gave the errand boy half a Mars bar he had in his pocket. **1963** L. DEIGHTON *Horse under Water* xi. 45 He did that twenty years ago when you were wearing a Micky Mouse gas-mask and saving your coupons for a Mars bar. **1973** J. WHITE *Norfolk Child* 176 But there were peppermints,.. and, of course, Mars. We..cut them into slices to make them last longer; first we bit the toffee off the top of the slice, then we nibbled the chocolate round the edges, and last of all..the delicious honey-sweet centre. **1973** C. BONINGTON *Next Horizon* iii. 57 'I've got a can of sardines and two Mars Bars,' I said. **1973** *Times* 20 Sept. 18/8 Getting an overweight patient to regulate his eating habit (using a knife and fork to eat a Mars Bar).

Marsa, Mars(e, varr. MAS, MASSA. Also with small initial.

Freq. in Black English contexts.

1874 'H. CHURTON' *Toinette* xxviii. 301 He gave Toinette to young Marse Geoffrey. **1880** A. W. TOURGÉE *Bricks without Straw* 408 The old time 'Marse' was now almost universally used, and few 'niggers' presumed to speak to a white man..without removing their hats. **1884** 'MARK TWAIN' *Huck. Finn* xxxviii. 391 Why, Mars Tom, I doan' *want* no rats. **1890** *Century Mag.* Nov. 65 Suit you, marsa? **1901** B. T. WASHINGTON *Up from Slavery* 12, I recall the feeling of sorrow among the slaves when they heard of the death of 'Mars' Billy'. **1909** 'O. HENRY' *Roads of Destiny* ii. 39 Marse Robert robbing the bank! *Ibid.* xxi. 350 I'm not going back on Mars' Jeff. **1949** [see *LINE *sb.*² 17 b]. **1950** R. AMES in A. Dundes *Mother Wit* (1973) 488/1 The old time darky's..love for 'ole marse' and 'ole mist'ess'. **1955** E. POUND *Classic Anthol.* I. 8 Thaar's where ole Marse Shao used to sit.

Marseillais, *a.* (*sb.*). Add: **1.** *adj.* (Later examples.)

1896 C. M. YONGE *Release* II. xxi. 294 Rumours reached us of the arrival of the Marseillais tigers. **1966** M. R. D. FOOT *SOE in France* xi. 377 He..sank himself without effort into the marseillais underworld.

2. *absol.* and *sb. pl.* **a.** (Later examples.) Also in *sing.*, an inhabitant of Marseilles.

1939 E. AMBLER *Mask of Dimitrios* i. 12 The other guests were a very noisy pair of Marseillais. **1951** E. PAUL *Springtime in Paris* ix. 159 Auvergnats, Catalans, Basques, Normans, Bretons, Marseillais. **1966** M. R. D. FOOT *SOE in France* ix. 248 The marseillais Basset and his Burgundian mate, Jarrot.

Marseilles. Add: **3.** Applied *attrib.* to a type of pottery produced in Marseilles during the seventeenth and eighteenth centuries.

1870 C. SCHREIBER *Jrnl.* (1911) I. 101 Bought..cover of Marseilles ware,..two Marseilles plates with Chinese figures. **1960** R. G. HAGGAR *Conc. Encycl. Cont. Pott. & Porc.* 302/2 The subsequent history of Marseilles faience is one of great trade expansion and the multiplication of factories... The death blow was given to the industry by the increased demand for earthenware of English type, and the French Revolution. **1974** *Times* 29 Oct. 19/4 A fine Marseilles *Veuve Perrin* soup tureen.

marsh. Add: **1. b.** *local.* A meadow; a stretch of grassland near a river or the sea.

1787 W. MARSHALL *Rural Econ. Norfolk* I. 320 The upper sides [of the fens] being frequently out of the water's way, afford a proportion of grazable land: hence, probably, they are provincially termed marshes. **1852** L. A. MEREDITH *My Home in Tasmania* I. 163 (Morris), A marsh here is what would in England be called a meadow, with this difference, that in our marshes, until partially drained, a growth of tea-trees..and rushes in some measure encumbers them; but, after a short time, these die off..and a thick sward of verdant grass covers the whole extent. **1892** J. E. TAYLOR *Tourist's Guide Suffolk* (ed. 2) 23 Some of the larger river-valleys, such as the Stour, Orwell, Deben, Alde, Blyth, and Waveney, have these soils laid down in grass, forming rich and well-known grazing land, or 'marshes' as they are locally termed.

4. a. marsh hay, hay made from marsh grasses; **marsh spot,** a deficiency disease of garden peas, caused by a lack of manganese.

1742 W. ELLIS *Mod. Husbandman* (1750) IV. 101 Curing coarse Marsh-Hay. **1839** *Cultivator* VII. 33 The common marsh hay is no better than the 'bog meadow hay' of the east. **1852** *Trans. Mich. Agric. Soc.* III. 132 They feed well at the straw stack and thrive on marsh hay. **1895** A. PATTERSON *Man & Nature on Broads* 50 A sack of sweet 'mesh' hay an' a blanket or tew to tuck yerself in. **1924** *Beaver* Sept. 460/2 There is every indication of a poor [hay] crop... The Indians who depend upon the marsh hay have the same cry. **1961** J. W. ANDERSON *Fur Trader's Story* iii. 24 Marsh hay was used at these posts to feed the cattle. **1931** J. BRYCE in *Essex Farmers' Jrnl.* X. 71/1 Marsh-Spot disease of peas..is carried in the seed. *Ibid.*, Marsh-Spot is usually brought on to a farm in the seed peas. **1934** *Jrnl. Ministry of Agric.* Dec. 833 From time to time complaints are raised concerning a defect in pea seeds to which the name Marsh Spot has been given. The term appears to have originated from the fact that the trouble is most common in seeds from crops grown in low-lying marsh land... The defect..shows itself mainly in the form of a dark, often slightly sunken spot..on the face of each seed-leaf. **1959** *New Biol.* XXX. 91 Diseases such as..'marsh spot' of peas are caused by the low availability of manganese in the soil.

b. marsh fritillary, a tawny butterfly, *Euphydryas aurinia,* formerly called the *greasy fritillary* (GREASY *a.* 9); **marsh quail** (earlier and later examples); **marsh tacky** *U.S.*, a small pony bred in marshy districts; **marsh treader** *U.S.*, a water bug of the family Hydrometridæ.

1890 C. W. DALE *Hist. Brit. Butterflies* 202 The Marsh Fritillary varies more generally than any other British butterfly. **1958** *Listener* 24 July 125/2 A series of observations on the Marsh Fritillary butterfly. **1750** J. BIRKET *Some Remarks Voy. N. Amer.* (1916) 32 Killd some Squirrels and some very pretty birds called Marsh quails something bigger than a field fare. **1935** J. C. LINCOLN *Cape Cod Yesterdays* 137 The Cape Cod market gunner of yesterday also shot upland birds for the market—quail, partridge, snipe,..'marsh quail' and an occasional pheasant. **1838** C. GILMAN *Recoll. Southern Matron* xix. 131 An accident happening to my horse, I was obliged to hire one of the little animals called 'marsh tackies' to carry me over a creek. **1937** D. C. HEYWARD *Seed from Madagascar* 118 He could..gallop his 'marsh tackey' through thickets so dense that a rabbit could scarcely get through them. **1895** J. H. & A. COMSTOCK *Man. Study of Insects* xiv. 124 The Marsh-treaders, family Limnobatidæ. **1902** L. O. HOWARD *Insect Bk.* 282 The Marsh Treaders (*Hydrometridæ*). **1972** SWAN & PAPP *Common Insects N. Amer.* 115 Marsh treader; *Hydrometra martini.*

c. marsh grass, pennywort, rosemary (later examples).

1868 *Putnam's Mag.* May 592/1 Clumps..begin to make their appearance above the reeds and tall marsh-grass. **1936** D. MCCOWAN *Animals Canad. Rockies* xix. 169 His supper was often of coarse marsh grass. **1972** *Islander* (Victoria, B.C.) 23 Jan. 6/1 Acres of marsh grass where animals and birds feed. **1885** *Outing* VII. 179/1 All the ground about is carpeted with the light-green leaves of the marsh-pennywort. **1960** *Oxf. Bk. Wild Flowers* 46/2 Marsh Pennywort or White-rot (*Hydrocotyle vulgaris*). This small, creeping or floating plant..differs from other Umbellifers in having undivided round leaves, with the leaf stalk attached at the centre of the leaf blade. **1861** MRS. STOWE *Pearl Orr's Island* I. x. 82 'Marsh rosemary is a very excellent gargle.' Said Mr. Sewell. [**1960** *Oxf. Bk. Wild Flowers* 118/2 Bog Rosemary or Marsh Andromeda (*Andromeda polifolia*). This small evergreen shrub up to 1 foot high has leaves which are shiny above and covered with a white bloom below.]

Marsh². The name of James *Marsh* (1794–1846), British chemist, used in the possessive and *attrib.* to designate a sensitive test for the presence of arsenic in a substance (published by him in 1836), in which the substance is subjected to the action of nascent hydrogen so that any arsenic in it forms the gas arsine, which may be detected by decomposing it (e.g. by passing it through a heated glass tube) and looking for a dark stain of arsenic (distinguishable from a similar stain given by antimony by its solubility in sodium hypochlorite solution).

1855 J. SCOFFERN *Elem. Chem.* 479 Arseniuretted hydrogen thus employed, as a means of removing and discovering arsenic, is called Marsh's test, from its inventor, Mr. Marsh. **1930** D. L. SAYERS *Strong Poison* xx. 265 In a small apartment usually devoted to Bunter's photographic work..stood the apparatus necessary for making a Marsh's test of arsenic. **1968** *Materials & Technol.* I. ix. 399 Very minute quantities of arsenic can be detected by means of the Marsh test.

marshal, *sb.* Add: **3. d.** Designating an officer of high rank in the Royal Air Force, as *Marshal of the Royal Air Force, Air Chief Marshal, Air Marshal, Air Vice-Marshal*; also †*Marshal of the Air* (obs.).

1919 *Times* 4 Aug. 12/6 His Majesty..has approved of new titles for the commissioned ranks of the Royal Air Force. These are..Marshal of the Air, Air Chief-Marshal, Air Marshal, Air Vice-Marshal... It will probably be some time before we have a Marshal of the Air, as at present there is no officer of the rank of either Air Chief-Marshal or Air Marshal. *Ibid.* 7 Aug. 14/6 Air Vice-Marshal Trenchard.. made the Air Force become the powerful and formidable fighting machine that it was. *Ibid.* 19 Aug. 10/4 The King has been pleased to approve the promotion of Air Vice-Marshal Sir H. Trenchard, K.C.B., to Air-Marshal. **1922** *Man. Seamanship* (Admiralty) I. 11 Marks of Rank... R.A.F. Marshal of the Air. R.N. Admiral of the Fleet. **1943** W. S. CHURCHILL *End of Beginning* 141 Most of the air-marshals, the leading men in the Air Force, think little of dive bombers. **1947** *Whitaker's Almanack* 461 (*heading*) Marshals of the Royal Air Force. **1968** *Who's Who* 1331/2 (*heading*) Harris, Marshal of the Royal Air Force Sir Arthur Travers.

marshalate. Add: **1. b.** The order of Marshal in the French army.

1945 R. HARGREAVES *Enemy at Gate* 80 Commanders.. ear-marked..for ultimate promotion to the Marshalate of France. **1973** *Times Lit. Suppl.* 16 Nov. 1390/4 A slighter but handsomely produced and welcome book on the marshalate. *Napoleon's Marshals* is partly [etc.].

2. *U.S.* The office of a marshal (cf. MARSHAL *sb.* 9 a).

1954 W. FAULKNER *Fable* 159 After some months under the threat of the full marshalate, he compromised with his father on the simple deputyship.

Marshall (mā·ɪʃăl). The name of George C. *Marshall* (1880–1959), Secretary of State in the U.S.A. from 1947 to 1949, used *attrib.* to designate a plan initiated by him in 1947 to supply financial assistance to certain Western European countries to further their recovery

after the 1939–45 war. Also applied to the aid so given or the nations receiving it.

1947 *N.Y. Times* 28 Dec. vi. 24/3 If at the end of the first year of the Marshall plan, Europe is not showing dividends, you will see what a collapse there will be. **1948** *Observer* 18 Apr. 4/6 The Paris conference of the 16—now, with the accession of the Western zones of Germany, 17—Marshall nations has made history. **1950** *Times* 6 July 5/2 Marshall aid authorizations for Britain during the month were..the second largest sum earmarked in May. **1952** R. Knox *Hidden Stream* vi. 54 Almighty God never goes in for Marshall plans, he always gives us more than we ask for. **1958** *Listener* 24 July 117/2 It looks..as though the United States are now beginning a new sort of Marshall Aid policy towards their southern neighbours. **1958** *Spectator* 15 Aug. 233/3 The Marshall-planned reconstruction of Europe. **1959** *Political Sci. Q.* LXXIV. 240 The principal object of the Marshall plan was to assist Europe to rehabilitate its factories and workshops so that its citizens would once again find employment and make their contributions to the channels of trade. **1975** *Sat. Rev.* 25 Jan. 16/3 The United States is back in the business of propping up Europe, although by more sophisticated mechanisms than the straight-aid programs of the Marshall Plan. **1975** *Times* 9 May 16/7 In the postwar period most West Germans regarded America as the great good place, the magnanimous victor whose Marshall Aid raised them from the ruins.

marshaller. Delete † *Obs. rare* and add later examples.

1718 J. Trapp tr. *Virgil's Aeneid* I. p. xlix, He [*sc.* Dryden] was the great Refiner of our English Poetry, and the best Marshaller of words. **1910** *Westm. Gaz.* 11 Apr. 8/3 The marshallers were everywhere, watching and directing. **1960** *Times* 6 Aug. 4/2 Manchester airport marshallers, who are responsible for manoeuvring airliners on the tarmac.

Marshallese (mɑ̄ɹʃălī·z), *sb.* and *a.* [f. the *Marshall* Islands in the Pacific Ocean + -ese.] **A.** *sb.* **a.** The language of the inhabitants of the Marshall Islands. **b.** The inhabitants themselves. **B.** *adj.* Of or pertaining to this language.

1945 *Language* XXI. 267 (*heading*) Notes on Marshallese consonant phonemes. *Ibid.*, The orthography of Marshallese was devised by American Protestant missionaries in the middle of the last century. **1964** E. A. Nida *Toward Sci. Transl.* iii. 54 In Marshallese, a language of Micronesia, a number of psychological states are described in terms of the throat. **1970** *Language* XLVI. 672 He [*sc.* Bender] claims that the mid-high vowels of the surface representations of Marshallese are not present in the underlying representations. **1971** *Ibid.* XLVII. 734 The glossary ..differentiates between some Marshallese words which are semantically and phonemically distinct but tend to be spelled alike by previous European students of the language—and by most Marshallese. **1972** J. L. Dillard *Black English* iv. 161 In the case of Melanesian Pidgin,..he also recognizes the influence of a similar structure in Marshallese.

marshalling, *vbl. sb.* Add: Used *attrib.*, esp. in *marshalling yard*, a railway yard in which goods trains are assembled and distributed.

1889 G. Findlay *Working & Managem. Eng. Railway* xi. 172 At certain important places throughout the country ..schemes of marshalling sidings of elaborate construction and great extent have been laid down. **1906** *Railway Mag.* XVIII. 180/1 On one side of the line is seen the recently constructed sorting and marshalling yard. **1940** *Times* 25 Sept. 4/1 One of the aircraft which bombed a marshalling yard only a few miles from the heart of Berlin. **1955** *Times* 12 July 3/4 He had just heard from the commission that they had approved new works at Perth, including the construction of a fully mechanized hump marshalling yard. **1967** G. F. Fiennes *I tried to run a Railway* v. 56, I started to draw a double direction marshalling yard.

marshite (mɑ̄·ɹʃəit). *Min.* [f. the name of its discoverer, C. W. *Marsh*, 19th-cent. Australian mineralogist + -ite[1].] Native cuprous iodide, CuI, found as colourless to pale yellow isometric crystals that redden when exposed.

1893 A. Liversidge in *Jrnl. & Proc. R. Soc. New South Wales* XXVI. 328 Mr. Marsh forwarded to me a small specimen of the copper iodide, and I have verified the principal characteristics as given in his description; as the mineral appears to be a new one, I suggest that it be named Marshite. **1939** *Amer. Mineralogist* XXIV. 629 Marshite, the natural cuprous iodide, was discovered by C. W. Marsh (1893) in the oxidized zone of the lead, zinc, and silver deposit at Broken Hill... In 1937, some crystals intimately associated with atacamite were found at the south end of the oxidized ore body at Chuquicamata [in Chile]. **1964** *Mineral. Abstr.* XVI. 491/2 The fluorescence of the halides sylvine, halite, marshite, and calomel is described.

marshlander. Add: **b.** An inhabitant of marshland.

1896 W. A. Dutt *George Borrow in E. Anglia* v. 46 Farther away the marshlanders have seized upon any slight piece of rising ground.

marshmallow. Add: **a.** *attrib.* (Further example.)

1755 *New & Compl. Dict. Arts & Sci.* IV. 3023/2 Sydenham recommends..a posset drink, in which two ounces of marsh-mallow roots have been boiled.

b. Also *fig.*, esp. something or someone that is soft at the centre, 'gooey', sentimental.

1935 A. Woollcott *Let.* 19 Dec. (1946) 126 It is the substance of this editorial that as a recommender of books over the radio, I take advantage of a nation-wide network to further the sale of soft, sentimental works. 'Marshmallows' was the term employed. **1962** *Listener* 20 Sept. 452/1 The result was a marshmallow. The production [of a radio play], the music, and the story pulled apart. **1966** *Punch* 1 June 817/3 The situations are witty, the songs as true, her eyes as mistily, romantically happy as I remembered. Perhaps it is just that I am more of a marshmallow than I was as a teenager. **1971** *Guardian* 10 May 10/5 Nine tenths of what actually goes on in schools is emotional marshmallow. **1973** M. Yorke *Grave Matters* I. ii. 14 So tough, you'd like us all to think, but inside you're a veritable marshmallow. **1974** *Times* 30 Apr. 9/3 Andy Williams might seem like marshmallow on television but ..has a superb flair.

c. *attrib.* and *Comb.* (also in *fig.* sense of 'soft, delicate; sticky, cloying, excessively sweet'); **marshmallow roast**, a party at which marshmallows are served.

1906 *Amer. Illustr. Mag.* Mar. 562/1 Girls assemble shreds and patches, buttons and marshmallow boxes. **1914** *Nation* 27 Aug. 242 A lady of the very highest fashion had been that evening entertaining at a 'marshmallow roast'. **1918** in C. B. de Mille *Autobiogr.* (1959) x. 209 The photoplay is breaking away from the marshmallow school of drama. **1926** *Hutchinson's Best Story Mag.* Nov. 109/1 Chocolate marshmallow ice cream. **1930** E. Pound *XXX Cantos* xxix. 137 Languor has cried unto languor about the marshmallow-roast. **1934** T. Wilder *Heaven's my Destination* 43 A campfire sing and marshmallow roast. **1936** M. H. Bradley *Five-Minute Girl* 235 It was to be a marshmallow roast, with coffee. **1959** *Times* 14 Feb. 9/7 His [*sc.* a pianist's] exquisite, marshmallow-fingered touch. **1973** *Washington Post* 13 Jan. A. 18/3 (Advt.), Refined, traditional sleep sofa..84" with deep tufted back and marshmallow front loose seat cushions. **1973** L. Hellman *Pentimento* (1974) 188, I never heard his name through the marshmallow English syllables. **1973** *N.Y. Law Jrnl.* 4 Sept. 4/7 A prosecutor in his summation is not required to hit the defendant with marshmallow blows, but his attack must be fair and within recognized limits of law.

Marsi (mɑ̄·ɹsī). *Hist.* [L.] A Sabine people who lived near the Fucine Lake in ancient Central Italy.

1578 tr. *Appian's Auncient Hist. Romanes Warres* I. 29 (*marginal note*) Marsi a valiant people in Latio. **1764** N. Hooke *Roman Hist.* III. vii. viii. 110 The Marsi, a people renowned for bravery,..gave their name to this war, because they were the first in the revolt. **1949** [see next].

Marsian (mɑ̄·ɹsiăn), *sb.* and *a.* [f. prec. + -an.] **A.** *sb.* **a.** One of the Marsi. **b.** The language of the Marsi. **B.** *adj.* Of or pertaining to the Marsi or their language. Also **Ma·rsic** *a.*

1578 tr. *Appian's Auncient Hist. Romanes Warres* I. 29 C. Marius did followe valiantly the Marsians that lay against them. **1632** J. Vicars tr. *Virgil's Aeneid* vii. 972 Herbs that grow on Marsian mountains high. **1697** Dryden tr. *Virgil's Georgics* ii. 230 Hence rose the Marsian and Sabellian Race. **1764** N. Hooke *Roman Hist.* III. vii. viii. 108 (*heading*) The war called the Marsic, the Social, the Italic war. **1882** *Encycl. Brit.* XIV. 327/1 Oscan or Samnite..the language of the Sabines, the Marsians, and the Volscians, of which but scanty traces remain. **1883** C. C. Perkins *Hist. Handbk. Italian Sculpture* I. i. 21 The ruins of the old Marsian city of Alba. **1890** *Cent. Dict.*, Marsic. **1897** R. S. Conway *Italic Dial.* I. 288 The Marsian, Aequian and Faliscan inscc...vary from the normal urban Latin of their time. **1933** C. D. Buck *Compar. Gram. Greek & Latin* 24 The Oscan–Umbrian group..includes also the minor dialects of central Italy, as Paelignian, Marrucinian, Vestinian, Volscian, Marsian, Sabine, [etc.]. **1939** L. H. Gray *Foundations of Lang.* 334 The third group, conventionally termed *Sabellian*, occupies a position midway between Oscan and Umbrian, but its remains are lamentably scanty. Here belong Paelignian, Marrucinian, Vestinian, Volscian, Marsian, Aequian, and Sabine. **1940** E. H. Warmington *Remains Old Latin* IV. 59 Dialect-Latin or mixed Marsian and Latin. *Ibid.*, A sacred gift to Angitia on behalf of Marsian legions. **1949** *Oxf. Classical Dict.* 541/2 The Marsi..took the initiative in demanding Roman citizenship in the Social War (hence often called Marsic War). *Ibid.*, Marsic magicians were famous for miraculous snake-bite cures. **1974** [see *Marrucinian *sb.* and *a.*].

Marsilid (mɑ̄·ɹsilid). *Pharm.* Also **marsilid.** A proprietary name for iproniazid phosphate.

1952 *Trade Marks Jrnl.* 7 May 393/2 Marsilid... All goods included in class 5... Roche Products Limited. **1953** *Internat. Jrnl. Leprosy* XXI. 64 The actions of Nydrazid and Marsilid on mouse leprosy were studied. **1965** J. Pollitt *Depression & its Treatment* iv. 56 The monoamine oxidase inhibitors include several members, among them phenelzine (Nardil), iproniazid (Marsilid), [etc.]. **1972** *Acta Histochem.* XLII. 246 After application of marsilid a strong decline of the neurosecretion..can be watched.

marsokhod (mɑ̄·ɹzŏkǫd, -χǫd). Also **Marsokhod.** [a. Russ. *marsokhód*, f. *Mars* Mars (after *lunokhod).] A type of Russian self-propelled vehicle for transmitting information about the planet Mars as it travels over its surface.

1970 *Sci. News Let.* 21 Nov. 397/3 In addition to discussing future Lunokhod explorations of the moon, the Soviets also described similar automated stations and robots for Venus, Mars and Mercury. These they call 'planetokhods' or 'marsokhods'. **1973** *Nature* 23 Mar. 219/2 The possibility of a 'Marsokhod' seems to have reached the stage of constructive planning... The lunokhods are controlled from Earth—a Mars vehicle would have to be self-controlling at least as far as such vital commands relating to its motion as 'start' and 'stop' are concerned.

martelé (mɑ̄·ɹtəle), *a.* *Mus.* [Fr., pa. pple. of *marteler* to hammer.] = *martellato *a.*

1876 in Stainer & Barrett *Dict. Mus. Terms* 281/1. **1961** D. D. Boyden in A. Baines *Mus. Instruments* vi. 124 The new bow..was more powerful, and its strength and the quicker take-up of the hair permitted *sforzando* effects such as *martelé*, which had been rare previously. **1962** *Punch* 28 Nov. 804/3 The martelé string chords of the first subject.

‖**martellato** (mɑ̄ɹtĕlā·to), *a.* *Mus.* [It., pa. pple. of *martellare* to hammer.] Lit. 'hammered'; said of notes which are heavily accented and left before their full time has expired. Also *transf.* Hence as *adv.* and *sb.*

1876 in Stainer & Barrett *Dict. Mus. Terms* 281/1. **1928** G. B. Shaw *Let.* 6 Feb. in *B. Shaw & Mrs. Campbell* (1952) 267 Such music as your [dramatic] pupils may have must come from within them; all you can teach them is the value of your..*martellato molto.* **1928** *Daily Express* 27 Aug. 3/2 The notes in small type preceding the long B. flat..must be played *martellato* and with clearness. **1931** G. Jacob *Orchestral Technique* v. 50 The martellato in the left-hand part of the original. **1959** *Listener* 8 Oct. 596/2 One was put instantly in mind of William Walton's *martellato* style. **1969** *Times* 7 Nov. 13/1 His *martellato* octaves sounding like sharp cracks of a gun. **1973** *Times* 28 Mar. 11/8 Verne Reynolds's Sonata, composed last year and proving to be no more than an impersonal essay in virtuoso keyboard devices, all sound and no real fury, despite an excess of *martellato* in the outer movements.

martemper (mɑ̄·ɹtempəɹ), *v.* *Metallurgy.* [f. Mar(tensite + Temper *v.*] *trans.* To treat (steel) so as to reduce its tendency to crack or distort by quenching rapidly to a temperature just above that at which martensite begins to form, allowing the temperature to equalize throughout, and then cooling slowly. So **ma·rtempered** *ppl. a.*, **ma·rtempering** *vbl. sb.*

1943 B. F. Shepherd in *Iron Age* 28 Jan. 50/1 Martempering is a term used to describe a heat treating operation whereby martensite is produced with a minimum of residual hardening strains. **1943** —— in *Metal Progress* July 105/2, I have coined the term 'martempering' to describe this operation of hardening by cooling quickly. **1947** *Steel Processing* XXXIII. 103/2 Steel was more susceptible to cracking when martempered than when treated by the more conventional method. **1953** Aitchison & Pumphrey *Engin. Steels* iii. 115 The properties of a martempered steel are in no way inferior to those of the same steel quenched and tempered in the traditional manner. *Ibid.* 116 Martempering is unlikely to supplant the direct quenching of normal, commercial steels. **1956** *Jrnl. Iron & Steel Inst.* CLXXXIII. 447/1 Warpage was least on martempered specimens. **1968** E. R. Petty *Physical Metall. Engin. Materials* xi. 206 Quench stresses and attendant distortion or cracking may be reduced by.. an interrupted quench (martempering).

Martenot, shortened form of *Ondes Martenot.

1931 *Electronics* July 18/1 As an example of a very fully developed [electronic musical] instrument..the 'Martenot' may be cited, named after its inventor. **1932** *19th Cent.* May 606 The Martenot instrument..looks like a small portable harmonium, from which connexions run to one or more loud-speakers. *Ibid.* 607 Anyone already able to play the piano can make a fair showing on a Martenot after a few hours' practice. **1936** *Discovery* July 222/1 The Martenot instrument... Honegger, Milhaud, Ibert are among the composers who have scored for it, and Stokowski has made use of it in his orchestra. **1938** *Oxf. Compan. Mus.* 287/2 The instrument known as Ondes Musicales..or the Ondium Martenot, or the Martenot.. is purely melodic.

martensitic (mɑ̄ɹtenzi·tik), *a.* *Metallurgy.* [f. Martensit(e + -ic.] Pertaining to or containing martensite; resembling the structure or mode of formation of martensite.

1909 in *Cent. Dict.* Suppl. **1915** *Chem. Abstr.* IX. 437 A martensitic structure is produced in 0·28% C steel without increase in hardness by heating to white heat and then cooling slowly. **1937** *Discovery* May 153/2 Carbon is mainly responsible for the characteristic martensitic mode of hardening. **1950** J. Osborne *Dental Mech.* (ed. 3) xii. 222 Two types of stainless steel find application in dentistry, Martensitic and Austenitic steels. **1967** A. H. Cottrell *Introd. Metall.* xvii. 265 An important example of a shear transformation occurs when steel is quench-hardened. The F.C.C. austenitic structure then transforms by shear, with some dilatation, into martensite, the distorted form of B.C.C. iron... In recognition of this, shear transformations are often referred to as martensitic transformations.

Hence **martensi·tically** *adv.*, in a martensitic manner.

1972 *Physics Bull.* Dec. 712/1 The difficult areas of x ray crystallography, such as in the study of martensitically transformed materials,..can be opened up by an electron microscope technique.

Martha (mɑ̄·ɹþă). **a.** The name of the sister of Mary and Lazarus in Bethany; hence used with allusion to Luke x. 40, 41 for one much

concerned with domestic affairs. In Christian allegory a symbol of the active life, opp. *MARY 4.

a **1225** *Ancrene Wisse* (1962) f. 112a/8 Husewifschipe is marthe dale. Marie dale is stilnesse & reste of alle worldes noise. **1907** [see *MARY 4]. **1907** M. HALL *Woman's Trek from Cape to Cairo* ix. 133 My host was equally busy.. while his wife, 'Martha like', busied herself in seeing a chicken cooked. **1909** *Westm. Gaz.* 30 July 2/1 The domestic servant problem..could never have become just what it is had this generation of mistresses followed in the steps of that ancestry which accorded the Marthas of the homes a certain amount of appreciation for services rendered. **1910** S. R. CROCKETT *Dew of their Youth* II. xviii. 140 You are of the tribe of Marthas, Jen, and you certainly work hard enough for everybody. **1938** E. GOUDGE *Towers in Mist* x. 277 She belonged to that noble army of Marthas who cook the dinners that the Marys gobble up to keep them going between their visions and their dreams. Grace was the best kind of Martha. **1953** G. GREENE *Living Room* I. i. 8 In this household she is obviously the anxious Martha; the weaker character intent on carrying out orders. **1962** J. D. SALINGER *Franny & Zooey* 158 For all I know, I may be a little jealous... It may very well be that I hate like hell to play Martha to someone else's Mary. **1962** *Friend* 3 Aug. 951/1 The Marthas and Marys are both essential. There is no division between the Mystical and the Practical. **1967** MRS. L. B. JOHNSON *White House Diary* 10 Aug. (1970) 553 The 'Mary' and the 'Martha' in my life have an eternal war.

b. Martha-coloured *a.*, used *transf.* (see quot. 1936) by the poet Edith Sitwell.

1924 E. SITWELL *Sleeping Beauty* xiv. 50 The Martha-coloured scabious Grew among dust as dry as old Eusebius. **1936** —— *Sel. Poems* Pref. 25 'The Martha-coloured scabious'..is the result of a personal memory... As a child, I had a nursery maid called Martha, who always wore a..gown..exactly the colour of a scabious. **1937** —— *I live under Black Sun* II. x. 296 The Martha-coloured scabious waved aimlessly.

Martha Gunn (mā·ɹþă gʊn). *Pottery.* (See quot. 1957.) Also *attrib.*

1922 R. K. PRICE *Astbury, Whieldon & R. Wood Figures & Toby Jugs* 86 Another rare Ralph Wood Toby jug in the collection is Martha Gunn. **1957** MANKOWITZ & HAGGAR *Conc. Encycl. Eng. Pott. & Porc.* 141/2 *Martha Gunn*, a female Toby jug, modelled in the likeness of Martha Gunn (1727–1815) the celebrated Brighton bathing-woman who is alleged to have dipped the Prince of Wales in the sea. **1960** R. G. HAGGAR *Conc. Encycl. Cont. Pott. & Porc.* 135/2 A large number of jugs called *Jacquelines*..are comparable to the English 'Martha Gunn' toby jugs made by Ralph Wood and others.

martial, *a.* and *sb.* Add: **A.** *adj.* **1. b.** *martial art* (usu. *pl.*), any of various fighting sports or skills mainly of Japanese origin, such as judo, karate, and kendo.

1933 *Official Guide to Japan* (Japanese Government Railways) p. clxxxvi, Contests [of kendo] take place nowadays at the annual meetings of the Butoku-kai, or Association for Preserving the Martial Arts, in Kyōto. **1955** E. J. HARRISON *Fighting Spirit of Japan* (ed. 2) x. 97 Of that branch of Japanese esoterics which belongs to what may generically be styled *bujutsu*, literally 'martial arts', though the Japanese terminology has a far wider and more comprehensive scope than its English equivalent, I may justly claim to know something. **1966** [see *KENDO]. **1968** [see *KUNG-FU]. **1974** *Isle of Wight County Press* 23 Nov. 31 Mr. Singleton, who holds a Kendo black belt, a brown belt in Karate, and has just taken up Ju-Jitsu, said he had no intention of 'cashing in' on the current martial arts boom.

Martian, *a.* and *sb.* Add: **A.** *adj.* **1. b.** Also *transf.*

1950 A. HUXLEY *Themes & Variations* 256 Man's Martian aggression against himself. *Ibid.*, The Martian forces of overpopulation and erosion. **1953** *News Chron.* 2 June 1/1 Step by step, in Martian clothing, the two figures move forward, pursuing their race against time and the mountain in the slowest of slow motion.

B. *sb.* (Earlier and later examples.)

1883 W. S. LACH-SZYRMA *Aleriel* III. iii. 109 He.. brought with him another Martian, differently attired. **1901** G. B. SHAW *Three Plays for Puritans* Pref. p. xvii, He feels concerned about the..destruction of the human race by the Martians. **1949** [see *EARTHLING *sb.*[2] 1]. **1951** R. BRADBURY *Silver Locusts* 108 From the back of the machine a Martian with melted gold for eyes looked down at Tomás. **1967** MRS. L. B. JOHNSON *White House Diary* 13 May (1970) 519 What will I remember about Camp David? The two 'Martians' in their silver suits..firefighters on hand for any emergency.

martin[1]. Add: **3. martin-box** *U.S.* (earlier and later examples); **martin bug**, a blood-sucking bug, *Oeciacus hirundinis*, whose principal host is the house-martin; **martin-cage**, a cage for holding martins; **martin-house** = *martin-box*.

1828 *Farmer's Almanac 1829* (Wendell, Mass.) sig. F3v Whose house is that with white capped chimnies, black sashed windows, and a nice little marten [*sic*] box just an epitome of the State House? **1854** B. F. TAYLOR *Jan. & June* 60 A martin-box of a cottage scuds round the corner of the Meeting House. **1871** MRS. STOWE *Oldtown Fireside Stories* 108 Your questions tumbles over each other thick as martins out o' a martin-box. **1946** J. STUART *Tales Plum Grove Hills* 85, I know what Mom is thinking when she looks at the martin boxes. **1923** E. A. BUTLER *Biol. Brit. Hemiptera-Heteroptera* 322 By most authors the martin bug is considered to be generically distinct from the rest of our British Cimicina, and is referred to the genus *Oeciacus*. **1935** *Brit. Birds* XXVIII. 278 The martin bug is rarer and resembles the much-disliked bed-bug which infests human habitations. **1959** SOUTHWOOD & LESTON *Land & Water Bugs Brit. Isles* vii. 187 The martin bug is recorded from most English counties south of a line from the Wash to the Bristol Channel. **1844** *Knickerbocker* XXIII. 442 Like a superannuated old man with a martin-cage upon his crooked back. **1826** 'A. SINGLETON' *Lett.* 74 The tasteful slave makes, perchance a martin-house, by erecting a high pole having a number of hollow calabashes hung around the top of it. **1835** R. M. BIRD *Hawks of Hawk-Hollow* I. iii. 44 Here's..the identical old Folly, with..the pot in the chimney, and the martin-house on a pole. **1854** B. P. SHILLABER *Life & Sayings Mrs. Partington* 101 He heard Gruff scolding Ike for throwing snowballs at his new Martin-house. **1884** 'C. E. CRADDOCK' *In Tennessee Mts.* I. 40 There was a lofty martin-house whence the birds whirled fitfully.

Martin[4]. Add: **4.** *Martin ware, Martinware*, a type of brown, salt-glazed, freq. elaborately modelled pottery, made by the Martin brothers in the late 19th and early 20th centuries. (See quot. 1897.)

1897 F. LITCHFIELD *Chaffers's Marks Pott. & Porc.* (ed. 8) 870 *Martin Ware.* The four brothers Martin carry on a small pottery at Southall. The initiator of the business was Robert Wallace Martin... He was joined by his three brothers..to produce the ware which now bears their name... A great point with the Martins is that the decoration of a specimen is never repeated. **1918** E. CLARKE *Story of My Life* xxxi. 411 On the top of the low book-shelves stand a few choice bronzes..and some fine specimens of my favourite Martin-ware. **1922** J. F. BLACKER *ABC Eng. Salt-Glaze Stoneware* xxv. 219 The best period of Martin ware. **1937** *Times Lit. Suppl.* 25 Sept. 696/3 The four brothers Martin responsible for the production of the nineteenth and early twentieth century pottery known as Martinware. **1957** MANKOWITZ & HAGGAR *Conc. Encycl. Eng. Pott. & Porc.* 142/1 A large collection of Martinware is exhibited at the Public Library and Museum, Southall, Middlesex. **1966** G. A. GODDEN *Illustr. Encycl. Brit. Pott. & Porc.* 214 (*caption*) A selection of Martinware birds with loose heads. **1973** *Times* 16 Feb. 21/5 A Martinware bird of exceptional size was sold at Sotheby's..for £1,250.

martin[5]. (Examples.)

1856 P. THOMPSON *Hist. Boston* 714 A twin-heifer is called a martin, and is said to be incapable of bearing young. **1903** *Rep. Kansas State Board Agric. 1901–2* II. 211 Pure-bred steer, spayed or martin heifer, two years old and under three.

martineta (māɹtinē·tă). [Amer. Sp., prob. f. Sp. *martinete* night heron.] A species of tinamou, *Eudromia elegans*, found in southern Argentina. Also *attrib.*

1872 W. H. HUDSON in *Proc. Zool. Soc.* 546 The Martineta frequents the elevated tablelands. **1892** W. R. KENNEDY *Sporting Sk. S. Amer.* 7 The 'Martinetas', or large Partridge (*Rhynchotus rufescens*), are generally found in pairs, and if one rises the other is probably not far off. **1925** L. E. ELLIOTT in J. A. Hammerton *Countries of World* VI. 4140/2 On the great undulating plains [of Uruguay] are thousands of..the double quail or martineta. **1961** G. DURRELL *Whispering Land* iv. 94 The commonest bird we saw was undoubtedly the martineta, a species of tinamu. It is plump, a partridge-shaped little bird, about the size of a bantam. Its plumage is a rich array of autumn browns, speckled and streaked with golds, yellows and creams... On its head there is an elongated crest of dark feathers, which curves like a half-moon over its head. **1964** A. L. THOMSON *New Dict. Birds* 822/2 The Martineta Tinamou *Eudromia elegans* is earth-coloured and adorned with a long slender crest which the bird when excited carries directed forwards.

Martini[1]. Substitute for def.: In full, *Martini–Henry* (*rifle*). A rifle used in the British army from 1871 to 1891, combining a breech-mechanism invented by Friedrich von Martini with a ·45-calibre barrel devised by Benjamin Tyler Henry (see *HENRY[1]). So *Martini–Henry carbine*. (Add further examples.)

1890 KIPLING *Barrack-Room Ballads* (1892) 11 We sloshed you with Martinis. *Ibid.* 48 When 'arf of your bullets fly wide in the ditch, Don't call your Martini a cross-eyed old bitch. **1892** R. CHURCHILL *Men, Mines & Animals S. Afr.* vii. 115 A good magazine is probably a better weapon than a Martini–Henry. **1900** [see *DANE GUN]. **1915** OMMUNDSEN & ROBINSON *Rifles & Ammunition* iii. 59 Another arrangement..was to make the grooves deeper at the breech than at the muzzle. The principle was adopted for the Enfield and retained in the Martini–Henry. **1962** H. L. PETERSON *Bk. Gun* 182/1 From 1871 until after the adoption of smokeless powder, the Martini served as the principal British single-shot weapon. **1967** ROBERTS & WATERS *Breech-Loading Single-Shot Match Rifle* i. 28 Martini–Henry rifles chambered for the various large British hunting cartridges were.. popular in Africa and India.

Martini[2] (māɹtī·ni). [f. the name of *Martini* and Rossi, Italian wine-makers.] The proprietary name of a type of vermouth; a cocktail consisting of gin and vermouth; *dry Martini*, such a cocktail containing more gin than vermouth, sometimes with the addition of orange bitters. Also *attrib.*

1894 *Puck* (U.S.) 28 Nov. 238/2 (Advt.), The Club Cocktails Manhattan, Martini, Whisky, [etc.]. **1896** *Crescent* (Brooklyn, N.Y.) 1 Aug. 11/2 As he sipped his martini and inhaled its seductive bouquet, a far-away look came into his baby-blue eyes. **1903** ADE *People you Know* 20 It was an actual mystery to him that any one could dally with a Dry Martini while there was a Hydrant on every Corner. **1906** *Mrs. Beeton's Bk. Househ. Managem.* xlix. 1511 Martini cocktail. **1909** [see *BRONX 1]. **1919** C. MACKENZIE *Sylvia & Michael* v. 203 What are you going to have? Ordered a Martini here the other day. **1930** WODEHOUSE *Very Good, Jeeves!* ii. 57 A nicely-balanced meal, preceded by a couple of dry Martinis, washed down with half a bot. **1953** D. A. EMBURY *Fine Art of Mixing Drinks* 36 Martinis, Manhattans, and other cocktails containing wine can be stirred with a rod or long spoon. *Ibid.* 106, I have already referred to the Martini as the most perfect of apéritif cocktails. **1958** *Times Lit. Suppl.* 19 Dec. 733/4 The sham, artificial life of all-night martini parties. **1962** 'E. MCBAIN' *Like Love* (1964) vii. 100 A tray with a Martini shaker and two iced Martini glasses. **1967** A. LICHINE *Encycl. Wines* 542/1 The Italian Cinzano may be red or white, sweet or fairly dry—as also may Martini and Gancia. **1968** [see *GIBSON[2]]. **1972** J. MOSEDALE *Football* vii. 100 People tend to think of us professionals as guys who spend all their time around the swimming pool with a blonde in one hand and a martini in the other... A lot of us don't like martinis.

Martiniquan (māɹtinī·kăn), *a.* and *sb.* Also **Martinican, Martiniquian, Martiniquen.** [f. *Martinique* (see below) + -AN.] **A.** *adj.* Of or pertaining to Martinique, an island of the West Indies. **B.** *sb.* A native or inhabitant of Martinique. So **Martiniquais** *a.* and *sb.* [Fr.].

1890 L. HEARN *Two Yrs. French W. Indies* 358 In Louisiana an almost similar dish is called *jimbalaya*: chicken cooked with rice. The Martiniquais think it..a delicacy. **1891** W. F. HUTCHINSON *Under Southern Cross* vi. 58 The Cuban becomes twice a Spaniard, a Barbadian three times an Englishman, and a Martiniquien four times a Frenchman. *Ibid.* 69 (*caption*) A fair Martiniquienne. **1907** A. E. ASPINALL *Pocket Guide W. Indies* xiv. 255 St. Pierre..was for all the world like a small French provincial city, with its cabarets and cafés, at the tables of which the Martinicans passed their leisure hours. **1926** A. BELL *Spell of Caribbean Islands* xvi. 256 The outstanding features of Martinican life. **1942** N. SMITH *Black Martinique* (1943) iii. 26 A wild-eyed youth.., brown-skinned, a true Martiniquais, came bursting toward us through the crowd. **1953** *Caribbean Q.* III. i. 28 Trinidadian patois has more faithfully retained truly Creole words which the Martiniquan has lost. *Ibid.* 29 The Martiniquan humour of M. Gratiant. **1955** *Ibid.* IV. i. 13 Another example of this poem of solidarity with Africans is the Martiniquais Paul Niger's *Je n'aime pas l'Afrique*. **1964** *Sat. Rev.* (U.S.) 10 Oct. 75/1 Lafcadio Hearn..wrote so poignantly of the 'little' Martiniquans. **1967** D. LOWENTHAL in R. D. Abrahams *Positively Black* (1970) iii. 75 A black or colored man from Jamaica or Martinique is simply a Jamaican or Martiniquian. **1970** J. BROWN *Un-melting Pot* vii. 99 '*Peau noir, masque blanc*.' The old Martiniquan saying sums up as well as any the central predicament of West Indian man. **1972** F. WARD *Golden Islands Caribbean* ii. 47 (*caption*) The Creole costume remained in vogue with Martinican women. *Ibid.* 48 A Martinican is unequivocably [*sic*] and irrevocably a Frenchman. **1973** *Nation* (Barbados) 23 Dec. 32/4 The Barbadians..will be allowed to fish freely in Martiniquan waters. *Ibid.* 32/5 Martiniquans do not eat flying fish. **1975** *New Yorker* 31 Mar. 54/3 We're all here by accident, and a Haitian and a black American could just as easily have been a Martinican or a Jamaican.

martyr, *sb.* Add: **4. a.** (Further examples.)

c **1862** E. DICKINSON *Poems* (1955) II. 417 The Martyr Poets—did not tell—But wrought their Pang in syllable—.. The Martyr Painters—never spoke. **1870** *Brewer's Dict. Phr. & Fable* 558/2 *The Martyr King*, Charles I. of England, beheaded January 30th, 1649. **1876** G. M. HOPKINS *Wreck of Deutschland* xxi, in *Poems* (1967) 58 Thy unchancelling poising palms were weighing the worth, Thou martyr-master. **1908** L. DAWSON *Nicknames & Pseudonyms* 194 *Martyr King*.., Charles i..King of England. *Ibid.* 195 *Martyr President*.., Abraham Lincoln. **1939** R. CAMPBELL *Flowering Rifle* IV. 117 The Press then bills him as a martyr-hero. **1942** BERREY & VAN DEN BARK *Amer. Thes. Slang* § 184/14 The Martyr President,.. Uncle Abe, *Abraham Lincoln*.

b. *martyr-habit, -spasm*; **martyr complex**, an exaggerated desire to sacrifice oneself for others and to have the sacrifice recognized.

1931 *Times Lit. Suppl.* 22 Jan. 58/4 In Rachel, we are asked to believe they fix a 'martyr-complex', or give her a taste for unnecessary self-sacrifice. **1902** W. JAMES *Varieties Relig. Experience* iv. 98 The 'misery-habit', the 'martyr-habit', engendered by the prevalent 'fearthought'. **1916** BLUNDEN *Harbingers* 66 Marble writhed to martyr-spasm.

martyrion (māɹti·riǫn). Also in L. form **martyrium.** Pl. **martyria.** [Gk. μαρτύριον, L. *martyrium* martyr's tomb or shrine.] = MARTYRY 2.

1711 J. BINGHAM *Origines Ecclesiasticæ* (ed. 2) III. VIII. i. 110 (*heading*) Why some Churches called *Martyria*. *Ibid.*, Such [Churches] as were built over the Grave of any Martyr, or called by his Name to preserve the Memory of him, had usually the distinguishing title of *Martyrium*, or *Confessio*, or *Memoria* given them. **1884** ADDIS & ARNOLD *Cath. Dict.* 553/1 The name 'martyrium' (μαρτύριον)..at first meant the church built over a martyr's remains. **1931** D. ATTWATER *Catholic Encycl. Dict.* 328/1 *Martyrion*, a primitive name for the place of burial of a martyr, for a church built over a martyr's tomb, and then for any church. **1931** *Times Lit. Suppl.* 23 July 584/1 The second is the largest church at Korykos and perhaps a 'martyrion'. **1960** *Antiquity* XXIV. 131 In the course of the 4th century a Christian cemetery grew up round this martyrion. **1965** *Virtue's Catholic Encycl.* II. 659/2 The original name for a church was a *martyrium*, since it was often built upon the actual site of martyrdom. **1974** *Times Lit. Suppl.* 8 Nov. 1267/1 Those of Syria and Mesopotamia were largely intended as cathedrals (rather than 'martyria').

marula (mărʊ·lă). Also **maroela** (Afrikaans), **maroola, meroola, merula, -ley, -li, morala, morula.** [Afrikaans, ad. Tswana and North Sotho *morula.*] A tree, *Sclerocarya caffra*, of the family Anacardiaceæ, found in central and southern Africa, and bearing an oval yellow fruit about two inches long that is used locally for making an intoxicating drink; also, the fruit of this tree. Also *attrib.*

1857 D. LIVINGSTONE *Missionary Travels & Researches in S. Afr.* viii. 165 Another tree, the 'Morala'.. has never been known to be touched by lightning. **1868** D. OLIVER *Flora Trop. Afr.* I. 449 S[*clerocarya*] *Caffra*,.. Mozamb. Distr. Lake Nyassa and other localities in Zambesi-land. Native name 'Morula'. **1877** T. BAINES *Gold Regions S.E. Afr.* i. 9 The Marula, as large as a peach and with a kernel almost like one, has a pleasant flavour. **1881** E. E. FREWER tr. *Holub's Seven Yrs. S. Afr.* II. 391 We passed some more of the morula-trees. **1888** P. GILLMORE *Days & Nights by Desert* vii. 47 A ridge..here and there studded with meruli and mimosa trees. **1890** —— *Through Gasa Land* 296 The meruley tree..seems to be a cross between a green plum and a walnut or hickory. **1907** *Transvaal Agric. Jrnl.* Jan. 411 The Meroola or Marula..a few specimens of the whole fruit of this tree were obtained. **1910** J. BUCHAN *Prester John* ix. 168 Tied up to a merula tree, were two of the finest beasts I had seen in Africa. **1920** *Nature* 6 May 298/2 The palms and morula-trees yield wine. **1932** C. FULLER *Louis Trigardt's Trek* x. 124 With him came three Indunas who brought a calabash of 'appel bier' (Morula wine). **1939** S. CLOETE *Watch for Dawn* xxix. 430 The wagon was jacked up by a big marula tree. **1950** *Cape Argus* 17 July 7/7 The maroela, a plant found in the Transvaal. **1955** T. V. BULPIN *Ivory Trail* (ed. 2) ii. 27 Native-made maroela beer. *Ibid.* xi. 116 September..when the maroela trees show their first flowers. **1972** *Daily Colonist* (Victoria, B.C.) 4 Apr. 21/1 Johannesburgh—The tempting marula fruit is ripe once more in South Africa's Kruger National Park and thousands of happy elephants are on their annual spree... The berry is green and about the size of a plum... The fruit ferments in the big beast's belly and the elephant acts as a ponderous four-legged still.

Marut, var. *MURUT.

marvel (mā·ɪvĕl), *sb.*² Also **marvil.** Common Eng. and U.S. dial. var. of MARBLE *sb.*

a **1734** J. COMER in *Rhode Island Hist. Soc. Coll.* (1893) VIII. 17 A little lad..was playing marvils..near the Old North Meeting House, Boston, and a cart laden passing by, a marvil rolling under the cart he stept to get it. **1743** W. ELLIS *Mod. Husbandman* July 27 A Worm,..bred in them, which raised a Wart as big as a Marvel on them. **1823** E. MOOR *Suffolk Words & Phr.* 221 *Marvels*, boys' marbles. **1845** J. J. HOOPER *Some Adventures Simon Suggs* xi. 136 Sometimes..I play marvels. **1867** P. KENNEDY *Banks of Boro* i. 5 In the season we shot marvels on the road. **1876** 'MARK TWAIN' *Tom Sawyer* ii. 13 Jim, I'll give you a marvel. **1929** *Amer. Speech* V. 19 *Marvels*,..marbles. 'Th' young-uns has got some o' these hyar store-boughten marvels.' **1942** BERREY & VAN DEN BARK *Amer. Thes. Slang* § 665/2 *Marble*, ivory, marb, marvel, man, mig, miggle.

marvellous, *a.* (*sb.*), and *adv.* Add: **A.** *adj.* **e.** Weakened use of sense a; also in affected use; also as *Comb.*

1924 E. O'NEILL *Welded* I. 94 You're going to be marvelous!.. It's going to be the finest thing we've ever done! *Ibid.* 97 The play was such a marvelous success! **1927** L. MAYER *Just between Us Girls* ii. 13, I had no iDEA you were going, my dear—how SIMply MARvelous! **1931** *Amer. Speech* VI. 181 No reviewer is fluent without adjectives..; 'marvelous power'; 'quiet beauty'. **1933** M. LINCOLN *Oh! Definitely* v. 57 'You write, don't you.'.. 'Yes.'.. 'Marvellous!' she said with enormous sincerity, whilst her blue eyes shouted, 'What piffle!' *Ibid.* 58 'You must let me get you seats,' I said. 'Marvellous of you,' said Ursula. **1950** M. LOWRY *Let.* 1 Mar. (1967) 190, I feel another million thanks are in order to..the Book Club for the marvelous-looking book.

marvellously, *adv.* Add: **b.** In affected use; see *MARVELLOUS *a.* e.

1926 E. O'NEILL *Great God Brown* 16 He can paint beautifully and write poetry and he plays and sings and dances so marvellously.

marvelry (mā̆ɪ·vĕlri). *poet.* [f. MARVEL *sb.* + -RY.] A marvellous thing.

1874 A. O'SHAUGHNESSY *Mus. & Moonlight* 12 And the moon's pallid taper fingers played With all the scarce-seen marvelries that stayed In the strange fitful glimmer.

Marwari (mā·ɪwarī), *sb.* and *a.* Also **Marvari, Marwaree, Marwarry.** [Hindi, f. Skr. *maru* desert, wilderness.] **A.** *sb.* **a.** A native or inhabitant of Marwar, a region in the state of Rajasthan in India. **b.** The dialect of Hindi used in Marwar. **B.** *adj.* Of or pertaining to the Marwar region.

1815 J. R. CARNAC *Let.* Feb. in *Trans. Lit. Soc. Bombay* (1819) I. 297 The failure of rain in Marwar, and the ruin by the locusts of the products of the land..drove the inhabitants of that unfortunate country into..Guzerat... Miseries seemed to follow the footsteps of the Marwarees. **1826** W. B. HOCKLEY *Pandurang Hari* II. iii. 70, I.. implicated by name..Sewchund the Marwarry, and many others. **1832** J. TOD *Ann. Rajast'han* II. III. ii. 234 The wealthy bankers and merchants of these regions scattered throughout India, are all known under one denomination, *Marwari*, which is erroneously supposed to apply to the Jodpoor territory. **1855** H. H. WILSON *Gloss. Judicial & Revenue Terms* 332/2 *Márwárí* bankers are mostly of the Jain religion. **1880** [see *BUNNIA]. **1885** G. C. WHITWORTH *Anglo-Indian Dict.* 199/2 Márwárí is also the name of the language of Márwár. **1899** KIPLING *From Sea to Sea* I. xiv. 129 A black, flamboyant Marwari stallion. **1908** G. A. GRIERSON *Ling. Survey India* IX. II. 16 Standard Mārwāṛī varies but little from Jaipuri. **1926** A. HUXLEY *Jesting Pilate* I. 72 These houses..are the palaces of the Marwari merchants, the Jews of India. **1960** 'S. HARVESTER' *Chinese Hammer* xxv. 202 A cluster of Marwari women was achingly brilliant in rainbow-coloured saris. **1964** S. K. CHATTERJI in D. Abercrombie et al. *Daniel Jones* 412 In Rajasthani,..the passage will be as follows (in the Marwari dialect). **1971** R. RUSSELL tr. *Ahmad's Shore & Wave* viii. 92 Money-lenders..in their Marwari turbans.

Marxian (mā·ɪksiăn), *a.*¹ and *sb.*¹ [f. the name of Karl *Marx* (1818–83), German-born socialist writer + -IAN.] **A.** *adj.* Of or pertaining to the socialist doctrines or theories of Karl Marx. Also *Marxian-Soviet* adj., of or pertaining to the type of socialism found in the U.S.S.R.

1887 G. B. SHAW *Let.* 17 May (1965) 169 Your notion that he is getting the best is a Marxian illusion. **1896** B. RUSSELL *German Social Democracy* 71 The 'honourable' Social Democrats, as they called themselves, the party of thorough-going Marxian Communism. **1902** B. KIDD *Princ. Western Civilisation* 87 [Spencer] really has in view, like the Marxian socialists, a state of society in which [etc.]. **1919** J. SPARGO *Psychol. Bolshevism* iii. 12 Only an infinitesimal minority of those who call themselves Marxian Socialists have ever studied Marx at first hand. **1920** M. BEER *Hist. Brit. Socialism* II. III. i. 21 He [*sc.* Harney] stood much nearer to O'Brien and Louis Blanc than to the Marxian policy. **1930** T. OKEY *Basketful of Memories* vii. 61 The Marxian revolutionary social teaching was slow in penetrating this country. *Ibid.*, Indications were obvious..that the Marxian bible..had begun to leaven English democratic thought. **1948** J. TOWSTER *Political Power in U.S.S.R.* i. 4 (*heading*) The Marxian-Soviet view of state and law. **1949** KOESTLER *Promise & Fulfilment* II. v. 281 The marxian dictum that man is a product of his environment. **1959** C. MACKENZIE *Lunatic Republic* xi. 190 We also regard revisionism as treachery to Marxian ideology. **1966** E. A. CARLSON *Gene* ix. 95 'Morganism', to this rival school, represented 'reactionary' and 'idealistic' tendencies which ran counter to the 'materialist' attitudes expressed by Marxian and Leninist (later Stalinist) outlooks on science. **1966** P. HEATH tr. *Wetter's Soviet Ideology Today* III. x. 294 The Marxian theory of value and surplus value has encountered its most serious troubles over the question of the average rate of profit. **1971** Z. A. JORDAN *Karl Marx* 20 Recent contributions concerning the concept of alienation..follow the Hegelian rather than the Marxian path.

B. *sb.* One who holds or supports Marxian views; a follower of Marx. Cf. *MARXIST *sb.*¹

1896 B. RUSSELL *German Social Democracy* 89 Although this programme showed, on the whole, a victory of the Marxians, Marx protested against it. **1918** E. B. BAX *Reminisc.* 138 The question of Internationalism was indeed one of the great bones of contention between them and the Marxians. **1923** E. A. ROSS *Russ. Soviet Republic* 394 Even though it fell in partly with the program of the extreme Marxians, the expropriation of the landlords and capitalists was not really a thing planned. **1935** D. FAHEY *Mystical Body Christ* ix. 199 Marxians will take account of circumstances, in order to get their programme accepted.

Hence **Mar·xianism,** adherence to Marxian doctrines or theories. Cf. *MARXISM¹.

1896 B. RUSSELL *German Social Democracy* 93 The new philosophy of life which Marxianism had introduced. **1905** J. R. MACDONALD *Socialism & Society* iv. 99 Marxianism, however, is a product of German thought during the second and third decades of the nineteenth century. **1912** *Eng. Rev.* June 413 The British workman will never take up the theoretics of orthodox Marxianism. **1926** *Spectator* 22 May 871/2 It was Western Europe which gave Marxianism to Russia.

Marxian (mā·ɪksiăn), *a.*² and *sb.*² [f. the name of the *Marx* Brothers (Chico, Harpo, Groucho and Zeppo), American comedians + -IAN.] **A.** *adj.* Of or pertaining to the Marx Brothers. **B.** *sb.* An admirer of the Marx Brothers. So **Ma·rxism²**, (*a*) the type of comedy performed by the Marx Brothers; (*b*) a witticism typical of the Marx Brothers. Also **Marxist** *a.*² and *sb.*²

1933 *Cherwell* 25 Feb. 131/2 No one who disliked *Monkey Business* will be converted to Marxism by *Horse Feathers*. **1940** G. MARX *Groucho Lett.* (1967) 47 Don't come out bluntly and say, 'How much dough have you got?' That wouldn't be the Marxian way. **1946** *Times* 6 July 5/4 There will be something like mourning among Marxists in London next week. **1951** K. CRICHTON *Marx Brothers* xv. 196 They opened on Thursday night and closed on Saturday. The post-mortem was short and typically Marxian. They had gambled, they had lost, and there would be no lamentations. **1962** *Sunday Times* 1 Apr. 32/8 Dr McCabe asked Groucho for a few words. The resultant Marxism is very much to the point. **1962** *Oxford Mail* 21 July 6/2 There are only one or two Marx Brothers comedies left in circulation now, so I recommend this..to Marxians. **1965** *Oxf. Mag.* 29 Apr. 303/2 We might not have been so much amused if there had not been a grain of zany probability—almost Marxist, in the Bros. sense—in it. **1966** A. EYLES *Marx Brothers* xvii. 156 'It made sages out of screwballs and accused wise men of being fools.' A perfect description of comedy's Marxism. We could be in *Duck Soup*, but this was American politics. **1969** *New Yorker* 25 Jan. 104/3 *The Marx Brothers at the Movies*... The book is the work of dedicated Marx fans, and its ideal readers are the nation's equally dedicated Marxists.

‖ **Marxisant, marxisant** (mārksizaṅ), *a.* Also (*erron.*) **marxisan.** [Fr., f. *Marxis*(*te* + -*ant* pr. pple. ending.] With Marxist leanings.

1961 *New Left Rev.* May–June 31/2 The Marxist and *marxisan* tradition. **1966** G. LICHTHEIM *Marxism in Mod. France* iii. 89 It took the full-scale assimilation of contemporary German philosophy after 1945 to render Existentialism popular, even fashionable, among *Marxisants* intellectuals. **1967** *Philosophy* XLII. 287 The Dialectical Laws..are seen as some *Marxisant* positivists saw them in the thirties. **1968** *Listener* 18 July 81/2 Malcolm X's abandonment of black racism, his conversion to Islam, his *Marxisant* tendencies.., all meant a move in a direction incompatible with that taken by the present-day Black Power movement. **1969** J. MANDER *Static Society* iv. 118 Almost the entire Latin American intelligentsia is *marxisant*. **1970** *New Society* 5 Mar. 406/3 Marxists, marxisant or radical, the New Past men exemplify the ambiguities of Plumb's inevitably conditioned 'rationality'.

Marxism¹ (mā·ɪksiz'm). [f. *Marx* (see *MARXIAN *a.*¹ and *sb.*¹) + -ISM, or ad. F. *Marxisme*, G. *Marxismus*.] The political and economic theories of Marx, esp. that, as labour is basic to wealth, historical development, following scientific laws determined by dialectical materialism, must lead to the violent overthrow of the capitalist class and the taking over of the means of production by the proletariat. Cf. *DIALECTICAL *a.* 1 b.

1897 *Social-Democrat* Dec. 365 Marxism, as generally conceived, is a catastrophic theory rather than a theory of development. **1903** *Social Democrat* Feb. 88 Both ultra-revolutionaryism and opportunism..rest in contradistinction to Marxism on an ideological or quasi-ideological basis. **1908** H. G. WELLS *New Worlds for Old* xi. 251 It seemed to me, that fatalistic Marxism crumbled down to dust. **1920** *Q. Rev.* Apr. 477 M. Millerand..was throwing sops to the Cerberus of unchained Marxism. **1935** F. A. VON HAYEK *Collectivist Econ. Planning* I. 18 It is essentially in this form that Marxism has been interpreted by the social-democratic parties on the Continent. **1959** OVERSTREET & WINDMILLER *Communism in India* II. xx. 488 But according to Marxism, the prime movers of history were not nations but classes. **1968** J. H. KAUTSKY *Communism & Politics of Devel.* iv. 76 Leninism is an adaptation of Marxism, a product of the industrialized West, to the conditions of an underdeveloped country.

So **Marxism-Leninism,** the doctrines of Marx as interpreted and put into effect by Lenin; Leninism; official communist interpretation of the doctrines of Marx as implemented by Lenin developed as a set of principles to guide policy and behaviour. Cf. *LENINISM.

1932 (*title*) The Marxist Library: works of Marxism-Leninism. **1934** [see *DIALECTICAL *a.* 1 b]. **1936** J. STRACHEY *Theory & Pract. Socialism* IV. xxviii. 356 The science [*sc.* Marxism] is now sometimes referred to as 'Marxism-Leninism'. **1946** tr. *Lenin's Sel. Works* Pref. 13 The revolutionary theory of Marxism-Leninism 'gives practical workers the power of orientation,..faith in the victory of our cause' (*Stalin*). **1948** [see *LENINISM]. **1966** P. HEATH tr. *Wetter's Soviet Ideology Today* 328 The struggle against the various revisionist tendencies gave birth to Marxism-Leninism. **1970** D. JAMES *Ché Guevara* xv. 312 But it is revolutionary thought *outside* Marxism-Leninism with which Ché Guevara appears to have most in common. **1973** *Listener* 26 July 118/2 The Chinese leadership..still has this notion of China as the homeland of Marxism-Leninism.

Marxist (mā·ɪksist), *sb.*¹ and *a.*¹ [f. as prec. + -IST or ad. F. *Marxiste*, G. *Marxist*.] **A.** *sb.* A follower of Marx's theories or doctrines; a member of a political organization with international affiliations which is based on Marxism.

1886 [see *GUESDIST]. **1889** E. SIMCOX *Diary* 18 Sept. in K. A. McKenzie *Edith Simcox & George Eliot* (1961) 56 The Anarchists [were] bestowing most of their attention on the Marxists. **1908** H. G. WELLS *New Worlds for Old* xv. 350 Those 'class war' ideas of the Marxist that have been superseded in English socialism. **1918** B. MIALL tr. *Hamon's Lessons of World-War* vii. 206 They [*sc.* German Social Democrats] professed to be Marxists..and they were acting as supporters of the capitalist class in the war which was then commencing. **1928** E. & C. PAUL tr. *Stalin's Leninism* 210 Comrade Trotsky is apparently unmindful of the fact that Lenin (who was surely a Marxist!) ..was writing of 'the need for an immediate transfer of all power into the hands of the revolutionary democracy'. **1938** J. F. SCANLAN tr. *Mauriac's Communism & Christians* 209 Marx himself was a person in revolt against the world, but Marxists can no longer be such. **1947** HENDERSON & PARSONS tr. *Weber's Theory Social & Econ. Organization* ii. 199 There is the type, which includes especially the Marxists, which is evolutionary. **1964** D. CAUTE *Communism & French Intellectuals* IV. i. 263 The first generation of communist intellectuals in France were conspicuously immature Marxists.

B. *adj.* Of or pertaining to Marxism. Freq. in *Comb.*

1897 *Social-Democrat* Dec. 367 It [*sc.* the Italian Socialist party] is gradually losing the catastrophic character with which the Marxist teachings have stamped it. **1928** E. & C. PAUL tr. *Stalin's Leninism* 349 In other words, Leninism includes all that Marx taught, with the addition of Lenin's contribution to the Marxist treasury. **1938** J. F. SCANLAN tr. *Mauriac's Communism & Christians* 209 In such a case judgements and condemnations of the moral kind take the place of psychological theses, and

this is the defect of the whole Marxist theory of man. **1949** J. LINDSAY *Marxism & Contemporary Sci.* ix. 223 One brief example will serve to show how essential Marxist method has beaten against the Hegelian dualism. **1957** J. S. HUXLEY *Relig. without Revelation* (rev. ed.) iii. 63 Marxist Communism is much better organised and more competent [than Nazism], but its purely materialist basis has limited its efficacy. **1957** *Times Lit. Suppl.* 25 Oct. 645/3 What had been the house of the local Marxist-Socialist party, who had left it filthy. **1959** *Encounter* Jan. 20/1 In the West, where thought tends to be either Marxist-materialistic or Christian-supernatural..it is difficult to envisage a religion not based on transcendental hopes and promises. **1964** *Daily Tel.* 15 Jan. 14/2 It is not sufficient to make Marxist-sounding speeches,..or even to embrace Mr. Khruschev. All these things Dr. Castro has done before. **1969** R. C. TUCKER *Marxian Revolutionary Idea* vi. 213 The history of radical movements, Marxist ones included, suggests that Mao's fear of the coming deradicalization of Chinese communism is well founded. **1973** *Times* 28 June 16/7 A Labour Party led by Mr Wilson and controlled, to the extent that it already is, by its Marxist wing.

So **Ma·rxist-Le·ninism,** = **Marxism-Leninism*; **Ma·rxist-Le·ninist** *a.*, of, pertaining to, or characteristic of Marxism-Leninism; cf. **Leninist-Marxist.* Also **Marxi·stically** *adv.*

1933 in K. Marx *Critique Gotha Programme* Introd. 8 The successes of socialist construction are the result of a revolutionary Marxist-Leninist policy. **1937** J. M. MURRY *Necessity of Pacifism* iii. 49 Those Socialists who imagine that Marxism, or Marxist-Leninism will either supply, or stiffen it, imagine a vain thing. **1938** *New Statesman* 15 Jan. 87/1 The wretched Mensheviks were Marxistically correct in supporting the Provisional Government.., but they found their attitude difficult to explain to hungry workers and mutinous sailors. **1940** tr. *Stalin's Leninism* 653 There is hardly need to dwell on the cardinal importance of Party propaganda, of the Marxist-Leninist training of our people. **1945** KOESTLER *Yogi & Commissar* III. ii. 173 A question which automatically cropped up in every marxistically trained mind. **1948** J. TOWSTER *Political Power in U.S.S.R.* 9 Interests of the Soviet Union cannot be deduced only from a study of the..Marxist-Leninist Ideology. **1957** *Times Lit. Suppl.* 6 Dec. 731/2 The Titoists regard Stalinism as the negation of Marxist-Leninist principles. **1963** Z. A. JORDAN *Philos. & Ideology* III. xi. 228 By denying that knowledge is relative to the mind, Marxist-Leninist thinkers put reality beyond the reach of the mind. **1966** *Listener* 20 Oct. 559/3 Marxist-Leninist philosophy is a dark room in which you're looking for a black cat, and there is no cat, but every so often you shout: 'I've got it! I've got it!' **1970** *New Society* 5 Mar. 408/1 Marxist-leninist theory has tended to play down the specific nature of agricultural production, which limits its applicability to developing countries. **1973** *Denver Q.* VIII. ii. 94 The long-term goal is the elimination of the capitalist bourgeois society, and within the universities, the gradual replacement of conservative professors with Marxistically trained and oriented scholars. **1975** *New Yorker* 21 Apr. 141/1 The Hanoi Communists are not, as far as is known, dogmatic Marxist-Leninists.

Marxite (mā·ɹksəit), *a.* and *sb.* [f. as *MARXIAN *a.*[1] and *sb.*[1] + -ITE[1].] = *MARXIST *sb.*[1] and *a.*[1]

1895 *New Age* 12 Sept. 377/3 Mutual concessions on the part of Catholic Socialists on the one hand and revolutionary Marxite Socialists on the other, would..result in a great and victorious movement for the regeneration of society. **1902** *Amer. Jrnl. Sociol.* July 68 This idea is implicit in the position of the 'orthodox' Marxite. **1914** A. CLUTTON-BROCK *William Morris* viii. 153 Mr. Hyndman..was, and still is, a Marxite. *Ibid.* 154 His aim was to make and keep the Federation a Marxite body.

Marxize (mā·ɹksəiz), *v.* [f. as *MARXIAN *a.*[1] and *sb.*[1] + -IZE.] *trans.* To form, adapt, etc., in accordance with the doctrines of Karl Marx; to follow or advocate Marxism. Hence **Marxiza·tion; Ma·rxizing** *vbl. sb.* and *ppl. a.*

1940 'G. ORWELL' *Inside Whale* 163 By being Marxised literature has moved no nearer to the masses. **1951** *Scrutiny* XVIII. 49 The days of Public School Marxising and Fellow-travelling had begun. **1972** J. WAIN in Cox & Dyson *20th-Cent. Mind* II. x. 346 During the Marxizing decade, poets whose imaginative world was subjective rather than objective..had tended to be crowded out of the centre of the stage. **1975** *Times* 15 Apr. 15/5 The 'Socialist' fixation that the Marxization of the West will be hindered with Britain in the EEC.

Mary. Add: **1. c. Mary Ann** *Taxi-drivers' slang*, a taximeter; **Mary Queen of Scots cap**, a Mary Stuart cap (*MARY STUART).

1939 H. HODGE *Cab, Sir?* 218 It [*sc.* the taximeter] has other names... 'Mary Ann'. **1813** M. EDGEWORTH *Let.* 1 May (1971) 44, I may venture to praise Angelica..with a lace Mary Queen of Scots cap. **1966** J. S. COX *Illustr. Dict. Hairdressing* 96 Mary Queen of Scots cap.

d. In various names, as *Mary Ann, Mary Warner*, etc., used as slang substitutes for *MARIJUANA. Cf. also *MARY JANE 2.

1925 *Writer's Monthly* June 487/1 Laughing-weed, Mary Ann—A Mexican 'dope' rag-weed. **1935** A. J. POLLOCK *Underworld Speaks* 75/2 *Mary and Johnny*, marihuana. **1938** *New Yorker* 12 Mar. 36/2 Marijuana cigarettes..are sticks, reefers, Mary Anns. **1938** *Detective Fiction Weekly* 8 Jan. 47/2 He found plenty of marijuana. As always it came in cigarettes, called 'reefers', 'muggles',..or sometimes, playfully, 'Mary Warners'. **1949** PARTRIDGE *Dict. Underworld* 433 *Mary Ann*, a Mexican drug—the 'loco weed'... An alteration of *Mary Jane*, the English of the folk-lore interpretation of marijuana... *Mary Warner*, a marijuana cigarette. **1971** E. E. LANDY *Underground Dict.* 129 *Mary Ann*,..marijuana... *Mary Warner*,..marijuana.

2. (Earlier and later examples.) Also *white Mary*, in Pidgin, a white woman.

1817 J. L. NICHOLAS *Narr. Voyage to N.Z.* I. vii. 201 The sister of one of our New Zealand sailors, a damsel who dispensed unlimited favours among our people, to whom she was well known by the name of Mary. **1882** A. J. BOYD *Old Colonials* 234 They [*sc.* the 'Australian blackfellows'] also fail to comprehend how it is that a Chinaman who is 'baal white fellow' can get a white woman for a wife. They say, 'Chinaman got 'im white Mary; black fellow get 'im white Mary.' **1931** V. PALMER *Separate Lives* 68 White mary no walk about all day. She belonga one boss, sit down longa one house. **1956** T. RONAN *Moleskin Midas* v. 326 Harness up the buggy and take this Mary back to town. **1962** *Coast to Coast 1961–2* 54 Some of the older marys did not remove frayed or dirty skirts. They put new ones on over the old.

4. The sister of Martha and Lazarus in Bethany; hence used with allusion to Luke x. 39, 42, for a contemplative or intellectual person, opp. Martha (see *MARTHA a).

a **1225** [see *MARTHA *a*]. **1907** KIPLING *Twenty Poems* (1918) 1 The Sons of Mary seldom bother, for they have inherited that good part; But the Sons of Martha favour their Mother of the careful soul and the troubled heart. **1929** C. MACKENZIE *Gallipoli Memories* xv. 272 She was the Mary of the household, sitting back and entertaining the guest with tales of a cosmopolitan life. **1938**, etc. [see *MARTHA a].

5. *Little Mary*: see *LITTLE *a.* 13.

Mary Jane (mēə·ri dʒē̆in). The female Christian names *Mary* and *Jane* used in *transf.* senses: **1.** [Proprietary name.] A type of low-heeled shoe with a strap round the ankle or across the instep, worn chiefly by young girls. Also *attrib.*

1921 *Amer. Wholesale Corporation* (*Baltimore*) *Catal.* 341 Infants' first step Mary Janes. *Ibid.*, Infants' soft sole 'Mary Jane' slippers. **1938** D. BAKER *Young Man with Horn* II. iii. 115 The little girl..was wearing pink cotton half socks and black patent leather Mary-Janes. **1967** J. J. PARETI *How to sell Footwear Profitably* xi. 130 Bell bottom trousers and mini skirts..are complemented by low-heeled barebacks, Mary Janes, T-strap sandals and boots. *Ibid.* xv. 159 *Mary Jane.* The classic party shoe previously for little girls, now for adults as well. Black leather patent pump with instep strap and bow. **1968** *Guardian* 26 July 1/5 Soft-soled Mary Jane shoes or supple white boots. **1969** R. JAFFE *Fame Game* (1970) i. 21 She had on white stockings and black patent Mary Janes. **1973** *Washington Post/Potomac* 30 Dec. 4/1 Massey's shoe store ..had the low-heeled Mary Janes made for her.

2. Also **Mary J, maryjane.** = *MARIJUANA. *slang.* Cf. *MARY 1 d.

1928 *Daily Express* 11 Oct. 2/7 What is Marijuana?.. A deadly Mexican drug, more familiarly known as 'Mary Jane', which produces wild hilarity when either smoked or eaten. **1940** *Amer. Speech* XV. 336 The cigarettes are usually called reefers, but other names are:..Mary Anns, Mary Janes. **1959** N. MAILER *Advts. for Myself* (1961) 245, I had marijuana. Mary-Jane..was the door back to sex. **1965** F. SARGESON *Mem. of Peon* vii. 254 He..returned with the news that the backyard was all overgrown with a harvest of Mary Jane. **1967** *Boston Sunday Herald* 26 Mar. IV. 1/1 Marijuana..is better known..as 'pot', 'grass' and 'Mary J'. **1967** *Punch* 26 July 123/2 He probably wouldn't even need the pot, grass, boo or maryjane. **1970** 'D. SHANNON' *Unexpected Death* (1971) x. 146 'What did they buy?' asked Mendoza. 'Oh, Mary Jane. Twenty reefers,' said Callaghan. **1971** D. HEFFRON *Nice Fire & Some Moonpennies* i. 11 'You Indians were onto this kinda stuff long before we were.' 'Onto *what*?' 'Mary Jane, Maizie, Mary *Jane*!' **1972** *Sunday Sun* (Brisbane) 2 July 14/3 Detectives from the CIB Drug Squad in Brisbane are becoming quite familiar now with words like..mezz, Mary Jane.

Maryland (mēə·rilænd). **a.** The name of one of the eastern states of North America (named in 1632 after Queen Henrietta *Maria*) used *attrib.* in **Maryland chicken**, a piece of chicken covered in breadcrumbs and fried, and served with sweet corn and bacon; also **chicken (à la) Maryland; Maryland end, parson** (see quots.); **Maryland yellow-throat**, a ground warbler, *Geothlypis trichas*, found in the eastern United States.

1906 A. FILIPPINI *Internat. Cook Bk.* 125 *Chicken Maryland*... Arrange six thin slices fresh broiled bacon on top of the chicken and, lastly, place six freshly prepared crisp corn fritters..around the dish and serve. **1929** *Amer. Speech* IV. 499 Can any reader of *American Speech* give me any information concerning the origin of the expression 'chicken à la Maryland', or the dish? **1935** M. MORPHY *Recipes of all Nations* 610 Maryland chicken... Young chickens are jointed.., coated with..egg and fine breadcrumbs, and sauté in clarified butter. **1941** F. M. FARMER *Boston Cooking-School Cook Bk.* (ed. 7) 376 Maryland Chicken... Season chicken with salt and pepper, dip in flour, then in 1 egg, beaten slightly with 2 tablespoons cold water, then in soft bread crumbs. **1959** *Good Food Guide* 76 Occasionally Maryland chicken and veal escalop appear. **1969** B. SIAS *Chicken Cookbk.* 48 Chicken à la Maryland..is said to have originated in St. Clement Island and was later introduced into Maryland by Lord Baltimore. **1975** *Times* 26 Sept. 16/6 Maryland chicken with corn fritters. **1859** BARTLETT *Dict. Amer.* (ed. 2) 265 *Maryland end*, said of the hock of the ham. The other is the Virginia end. **1903** S. CLAPIN *New Dict. Amer.* 270 *Maryland end*, in Maryland and Virginia, the curious name given to the hock end of a ham. **1811** A. GRAYDON *Mem.* 292 Mr. L— seemed in all respects to be what was then called in Pennsylvania a Maryland parson; that is, one who could accommodate himself to his company. **1702** PETIVER *Gazophyl.* I. 10 *Avis Mary-Landica gutture luteo.* The Mary-Land Yellow-Throat. **1839** J. J. AUDUBON *Ornith. Biogr.* V. 75 The Maryland Yellow-throat..keeps near the ground in low bushes. **1948** *N. & S. Dakota Horticulture* July–Aug. 106/1 From a nearby coulee came the odd but musical notes of a Maryland Yellow Throat.

b. Used *attrib.* or *ellipt.* of tobacco from Maryland.

1867 P. L. SIMMONDS *Dict. Trade* (rev. ed.) Suppl. 445/1 *Maryland*, a mild kind of tobacco. **1930** KIPLING *Limits & Renewals* (1932) 324 He exhaled the smoke through his finely-cut nostrils. 'Yes, it *is* Smyrna.... Good! And Monsieur appreciates our "Marylands" also? Hmm. *I* remember the time when our Government tobaccos were a national infamy.' **1933** *Discovery* Mar. 74/1 Experiments were carried out..by Garner and Allard as a result of difficulties they experienced in making a variety of tobacco (Maryland Mammoth) produce flowers. **1953** J. E. BROOKS *Mighty Leaf* ix. 207 By the early thirties the culture of the Maryland Broadleaf began in the Valley and this type, of fine texture and subtle odor, soon supplanted other local kinds.

Ma·rylander. Also **Marilander.** [f. prec. + -ER[1].] A native or inhabitant of the state of Maryland in the United States; also, something characteristic of Maryland.

1665 in *Mass. Hist. Soc. Coll.* (1849) 3rd Ser. X. 55 A forbearance of such hostility..may prevent the destruction of divers dutch or English of the hither parts, or Marilanders. **1678** *Rec. Court of New Castle on Delaware* (1904) 234 They had gott out of Maryland for old debts due for Cattle sold to the Marylanders. **1755** L. EVANS *Geogr. Ess.* 14 The Sasquehannocks, after the great Defeat by the Marilanders, were easily exterminated by the Confederates. **1838** J. F. COOPER *Homeward Bound* I. xii. 298 This beef is not indigestible, and here is a real Marylander, in the way of a ham. **1860** O. W. HOLMES *Prof. at Breakfast-Table* ii. 57, I am a Marylander. **1931** *Times Lit. Suppl.* 7 May 359/2 Naturally, a book dealing with Maryland houses is of the greatest interest to the owners of the houses, and next to other Marylanders. **1948** *Chicago Tribune* 9 May 3/2 Marylanders, used to disappointments, are keeping their fingers crossed. **1949** B. A. BOTKIN *Treas. S. Folklore* IV. i. 552 Marylanders grow lyrical over Brunswick stew, diamond-back terrapin. **1967** *National Observer* (U.S.) 3 July 12/2 Captain Kusel admits that the Marylanders look and sound better in drill. **1974** *Times* 6 Nov. (Maryland Suppl.) p. i/3 He spoke for a lot of Marylanders when he added: 'I like our provincialism.'

Mary Stuart (mēə·ri stiū·ăɹt). Also **Marie Stuart.** The name of Mary, Queen of Scots (1542–87), used *attrib.* and *ellipt.* to designate styles of clothes, hair, etc., similar to those she wore, *spec.* headwear with a central dip or peak over the forehead.

1852 E. RUSKIN *Let.* 26 Jan. in M. Lutyens *Effie in Venice* (1965) II. 254 A coiffure I have made for myself... It is a piece of scarlet velvet with a fringe of large and small pearls all round; a point à la Marie Stuart comes in front. **1873** *Young Englishwoman* Mar. 130/1 A Marie Stuart bonnet of rice straw lined with blue silk. **1880** in *American Mail Order Fashions* (1961) 18 *The Mary Stuart.* Jetted lace bonnet..$6.50. *a* **1913** F. ROLFE *Desire & Pursuit of Whole* (1934) x. 93 The kind of female liable to wear Mary Stuart caps by night. **1965** *Listener* 20 May 743/3 Then came the Mary Stuart cap, worn both with and without a veil. **1965** J. LAVER *Contini's Fashion* 231/1 The return of the Royal family to Paris brought the first signs of romanticism... Then the first Mary Stuart belts appeared, which tended to lower the waist. **1966** J. S. COX *Illustr. Dict. Hairdressing* 96/1 *Marie Stuart Coiffure*, (1) a coiffure similar to that worn by Mary, Queen of Scots..; (2) a woman's hair style of *circa* 1865 based on that worn by Mary Queen of Scots.

marzacotto (mā:ɹtsăkǫ·to, -z-). *Ceramics.* [It. (Florio, 1598, 'an instrument or toole that potters use').] A transparent glaze used by Italian majolica workers (see quots.).

1873 C. D. E. FORTNUM *Descr. Catal. Maiolica* 152 Glazing it with 'marzacotto', a mixture of oxide of lead, sand and potash. **1885** *Encycl. Brit.* XIX. 625/1 The white enamel, 'bianco', was composed of thirty parts of 'marzacotto' to twelve of oxide of tin. **1960** R. G. HAGGAR *Conc. Encycl. Cont. Pott. & Porc.* 304/1 *Marzacotto*, a silicate of potash..used as the basis of the tin-enamel or tin-glaze of the maiolica potter. **1972** J. SCOTT-TAGGART *Italian Maiolica* 56 *Marzacotto*..is a potassium silicate made by fusing a mixture of sand and calcined wine-lees. *Ibid.*, This *marzacotto* provides the 'glassy' element.

Marzine (mā·ɹzīn). A trade name in the U.K. for *MAREZINE.

1954 *Trade Marks Jrnl.* 24 Mar. 297/1 Marzine... All goods included in class 5 [pharmaceutical, veterinary, and sanitary substances, etc.]. The Wellcome Foundation Limited,..London,..manufacturing chemists. **1956** *Approved Names* (Brit. Pharmacopœia Commission) Suppl. Aug., Cyclizine, 1-Methyl-4-α-phenylbenzylpiperazine. Marzine is the hydrochloride. **1958** *Martindale's Extra Pharmacopœia* (ed. 24) I. 1112 Marzine (known in U.S.A. as Marezine Hydrochloride) (Burroughs Wellcome). Cyclizine hydrochloride. **1959** *Lancet* 25 Apr. 853/1 Cyclizine hydrochloride ('Marezine', 'Marzine') in doses of 50 mg. daily was also found effective [in motion sickness].

‖ **mas** (ma), *sb.*[2] [Fr. dial.] A farm or cottage in the South of France; a house.

1921 *English* May 495 We see the flocks returning to the 'mas' after having spent the long summer in the mountains. **1924** R. FRY *Let.* 2 July (1972) II. 555 Two peasant

proprietors who live in a little Mas. **1932** R. CAMPBELL *Taurine Provence* 48 The 'Mas' is a mixture between a manor and a huge farm-house. **1942** 'A. BRIDGE' *Frontier Passage* xii. 221 The peasant's rough-and-ready method of defending his *mas*. **1964** F. WHITE *West of Rhone* iv. 51 The *mas*, the farms, were devoted to stock-raising. **1966** 'R. STANDISH' *Widow Hack* vi. 69 The villa was a well-faked *mas provençal*, but instead of the conventional rounded Roman [roof] tiles, they were flat.

Masai (mā·səi, măsəi·). [Bantu.] **A.** *sb.* **a.** A pastoral people of mixed Hamitic stock inhabiting parts of Kenya and Tanzania; a member of this people. **b.** The Nilotic language of this people. **B.** *adj.* Of or pertaining to this people or their language.

1857 ERHARDT & KRAPF (*title*) Vocabulary of the Enguduk Iloigob, as spoken by the Masai-tribes in East Africa, in two parts (Masai–English, and English–Kimasai, with a song of the Masai). **1873** [see *KAVIRONDO]. **1894** [see *KIKUYU]. **1898** E. CLODD in R. M. Dorson *Peasant Customs* (1968) I. 384 Among the Masai..while it is bad form to kiss a lady, it is *comme il faut* to spit on her. **1902** *Encycl. Brit.* XXV. 140/1 The Masai east of Lake Victoria..are undoubtedly Hamites, mixed..with negro elements. **1933** L. BLOOMFIELD *Lang.* iv. 67 Among the languages of this region..we may mention..Nuba,.. Dinka, and..Masai. **1947** *E. Afr. Ann. 1946–7* 41/2 The Samburu..are closely associated with the Masai and are called from the Masai word 'Samburer' which means 'butterfly'. **1955** *Times* 12 July 9/7 The Mau Mau gangs must be leading a life not altogether unlike that which their grandfathers led in the struggles with the Masai over 60 years ago. **1962** *Listener* 6 Sept. 343/2 No one lived there and even Masai cattle seldom came. **1967** M. J. COE *Ecol. Alpine Zone Mt. Kenya* 1 The retention in the Masai language of many words that refer to Mt. Kenya. **1969** *Reporter* (Nairobi) 13 June 36/4 This new spirit of the Masai is exemplified by 700 Masai families who migrated from their motherland some years ago. **1973** *Sunday Express* 11 Mar. 23/2 She has just come back from Kenya .., where she has been photographing the Masai.

Masarwa (māsā·ɹwă). *S. Afr.* [Native name.] **A.** *sb.* The name given to the Bushmen distributed over the Northern Kalahari desert. **B.** *adj.* Of or pertaining to this group.

1871 J. MACKENZIE *Ten Yrs. North of Orange River* viii. 128 The other subject race is that of the Bushmen, called Barwa by the Bechuanas in the south, and Masarwa by those in the north of the country. **1896** H. A. BRYDEN *Tales S. Afr.* ii. 42 You may never..see a Masarwa Bushman..who does not show marks of fireburn upon the nether limbs. **1905** G. W. STOW *Native Races S. Afr.* xiv. 265 Bushman speaking peoples as the Masarwa. **1928** E. H. L. SCHWARZ *Kalahari & its Native Races* viii. 172 The term Masarwa..is used for all Bushmen in the Northern Kalahari. *Ibid.* 174 There were several Masarwa women about the palace precincts. **1931** [see *game-land* (*GAME *sb.* 16 a)]. **1971** *Sunday Times* (Johannesburg) (Mag. Section) 28 Mar. 3/3 The people of Dilepe..are not prepared to receive a Masarwa in their midst.

mascal, var. MESCAL.

1850 W. R. RYAN *Personal Adventures Upper & Lower Calif.* I. 193 The usual beverages, besides water, are wine, *mascal*, and *aguardiente*. **1887** F. FRANCIS *Saddle & Mocassin* iv. 68 The Mexican..reduced himself to a state of complete intoxication with *mascal*.

mascara (mæskā·rä). Also (*rare*) mascaro. [It. *mascara, maschera*, Sp. *máscara* MASKER *sb.*[1]] A preparation for colouring the eyelashes and eyebrows.

1890 *Cent. Dict.*, *Mascaro*, a kind of paint used for the eyebrows and eyelashes by actors. **1922** I. & H. KLUMPH *Screen Acting* 59 You will have your own make-up..cold cream, mascara for the eyelashes. **1927** N. MARTIN *Constant Simp* (1928) vi. 101 No black globules of mascara hung from the tips of her long lashes. **1930** H. RUBINSTEIN *Art Feminine Beauty* xvi. 250 My mother had brought us up to use a little powder on our faces but would have been horrified at the thought of rouge or lipstick, or mascara for the eyes. **1938** M. ALLINGHAM *Fashion in Shrouds* xvi. 267 Her long eyelashes thick with mascara. **1958** E. DUNDY *Dud Avocado* I. vii. 121 My eyes, which stung and swam from the running mascara. **1966** T. PYNCHON *Crying of Lot 49* v. 125 She knew she looked terrible—knuckles black with eye-liner and mascara from where she'd rubbed.

Hence **masca·ra** *v. trans.*, to treat with mascara. So **masca·raed** *ppl. a.*

1935 S. LEWIS *It can't happen Here* xxxviii. 407 A lady with mascaraed eyelashes. **1938** N. MARSH *Death in White Tie* iii. 36 Our hostess's mascaraed eyes. **1944** W. S. MAUGHAM *Razor's Edge* ii. 68 They had the same heavily mascaraed eyelashes, the same brightly painted lips, the same rouged cheeks. **1961** M. HOWARD *Surgeon's Dilemma* viii. 247 Adelia, frantically mascaraing her eyelashes.

‖ **mascaret** (maskare). [Fr. (16th c.), f. Gascon *mascaret* spotted cow, f. *mascara* (cf. Pr. *mascarar*, OF. *mascurer*, F. *mâchurer*) to daub, to black the face: app. arising from the resemblance of the tidal bore to the movement of running cattle.] A tidal bore in an estuary in France.

1841 W. A. BROOKS *Treat. Improvement Navigation of Rivers* xi. 127 The mascaret of the Dordogne consists of two, three, and sometimes four lofty waves, which follow each other rapidly, damming back the whole breadth of the river. **1900** P. DEARMER *Highways & Byways in Normandy* xii. 315 At high tides there is the spectacle of the famous *mascaret* or bore. **1902** *Encycl. Brit.* XXXII. 508 The tide begins to make itself felt at Poses, 11 miles above Elbeuf, and between Caudebec and Villequier the *mascaret*, or bore, has its greatest development. **1959** *Listener* 5 Feb. 248/1 The *mascaret* is to the Seine what the bore is to the Severn. **1971** S. E. MORISON *European Discovery Amer.: Northern Voy.* viii. 256 The navigation of the Seine is more hazardous..and even dangerous when a tidal bore, the *mascaret*, sweeps up the river unexpectedly.

‖ **mascaron** (maskaroṅ, mæ·skărǫn). [Fr., = grotesque mask (1603 in Robert), ad. It. *mascherone*, f. *maschera* MASK *sb.*[3]]. In decorative art: a grotesque face or mask (cf. MASK *sb.*[3] 4 a).

1664 EVELYN tr. *Fréart's Parallel Antient Archit. with Mod.* Pref. 3 They produce nothing save Mascarons, wretched Cartouches, and the like idle and impertinent Grotesks. **1883** J. W. MOLLETT *Illustr. Dict. Art & Archaeol.* 207/1 *Mascaron*,..the face of a man or animal employed as an ornamentation for decorating the keystones of arches or vaults, or the stones of an arch, &c. **1926** R. GLAZIER *Man. Hist. Ornament* (ed. 4) II. 169 The Italians from about 1480 favoured elaborate borders [in MSS.]..composed of classical columns,..mascarons, etc.

mascon (mæ·skǫn). *Astr.* [f. *mass concentration.*] One of the concentrations of denser material thought to exist under some lunar maria, discovered as a result of the variations they produce in the speed of an orbiting satellite; also, a similar region on another planet.

1968 MULLER & SJOGREN in *Science* 16 Aug. 680/1 The Urey–Gilbert theory of lunar history has predicted such large-scale high-density mass concentrations below these maria, which, for convenience, we shall call mascons. **1969** *Times* 22 Feb. 7/7 Exactly what the mascons are has puzzled selenologists since the discovery last year, and one explanation is that they are the remnants of enormous meteorites. **1969** *Sci. Jrnl.* May 61/1 The so-called mascons extend laterally for 50 to 200 km, are about 5 km thick and lie at a depth of between about 50 and 100 km. **1971** *Nature* 26 Nov. 168/2 The following findings were announced... Gravitational anomalies which may be caused by martian mascons. **1973** J. STRONG *Search the Solar Syst.* x. 104 Density anomalies, or 'mascons' on the Moon were located by their disturbance of the lunar orbiters.

mascot. Delete '*slang*' and add earlier and later examples.

1881 FARNIE & REECE *Mascotte* I. 4 Ah! blest their lot whom fate shall send A true Mascotte, a fairy friend!.. Luck's his for ever! **1918** E. M. ROBERTS *Flying Fighter* 328 Each man had his own little fetish. It was known as the pocket-piece or mascot. In some cases it might be a dice or a playing-card... In other cases it might be a locket, then again a medal, while many of us carried little wooden dolls. **1921** R. HICHENS *Spirit of Time* vi. 106 'She says you brought her luck.'..'I didn't know I was a mascot,' he remarked. **1955** *Halsbury's Statutory Instruments* II. 2276 No mascot shall be carried by a motor vehicle..where it is likely to strike any person with whom the vehicle may collide. **1975** *Times* 6 June 17/4 Christie's ..launched a new collecting field yesterday with a sale of motoring mascots, the figurines mounted on car bonnets. *attrib.* **1898** *Speaker* 31 Dec. 783/2 His mascot snakes that were kept, buried in flannel, in an oblong glass-topped box.

ma·scotism. [-ISM.] = next.

1924 W. J. LOCKE *Coming of Amos* viii. 94 If there is anything in luck, in mascotism or anti-mascotism, one might have reason to believe that Amos..had the most maleficent of influences.

mascotry (mæ·skǫtri). [f. MASCOT + -RY.] Attachment to or belief in mascots; the use of mascots.

1916 *Church Times* 7 Apr. 332/4 Mascotry,..the growing superstition with regard to mascots. **1923** *Sunday at Home* May 504/3 There is a worse aspect of mascotry than mere folly,..for mascotry is, in its essence, simply idolatry.

masculinism (mæ·skiŭliniz'm). *rare.* [f. MASCULINE *a.* + -ISM.] **a.** Tendency to masculine physical traits in a woman. **b.** Advocacy of the rights of men.

1895 [see *INFANTILISM]. **1916** H. ELLIS *Essays in War-Time* viii. 88 The advocates of Woman's Rights have seldom been met by the charge that they were unjustly encroaching on the Rights of Man. Feminism has never encountered an aggressive and self-conscious Masculinism.

masculinist (mæ·skiŭlinist). [f. MASCULINE *a.* + -IST.] **1.** An advocate of men's rights, opp. *FEMINIST *sb.* Cf. *HOMINIST.

1918 V. WOOLF *Writer's Diary* (1953) 6 He [*sc.* Milton] was the first of the masculinists. **1967** *Times* 13 Oct. 8 No militant masculinists stooped to conquer; indeed almost the only men to be seen on the premises, apart from the staff, were male journalists invited to help celebrate the occasion.

2. A person of the female sex who adopts or affects characteristics or qualities usually thought of as masculine.

1928 *Daily Express* 11 July 5/3 The suffragists modelled their appearance, their manners, and their education on that of boys and men... They were, in short, thorough-going masculinists.

3. *attrib.*

1951 R. CAMPBELL *Light on Dark Horse* xvii. 257 Bloomsbury still awaits its 'masculinist' Messiah.

masculinization (mæ:skiŭlinəizē¹·ʃən). [f. next: see -IZATION.] The action of *MASCULINIZE *v.* (in either sense); the process of becoming masculine; also, a masculine state or condition.

1895 H. JAMES *Notebks.* (1947) iv. 196 There is a big comprehensive subject in the *avènement*, or rather in the masculinization of women. **1922** F. H. A. MARSHALL *Physiology of Reproduction* (ed. 2) xv. 696 (*caption*) Masculinisation of guinea pig. **1924** *Glasgow Herald* 24 Dec. 4 The masculinisation of woman deprives society of a 'precious asset'. **1927** *19th Cent.* Aug. 266 We find him throwing all his authority against the masculinisation prevalent in our schools. **1952** SRB & OWEN *Gen. Genetics* xiv. 287 Freemartins are sterile, and show considerable masculinization in a number of traits. **1970** *Sci. Jrnl.* June 50/2 They are of course normal genetic and anatomical females on whom the male sex hormones from their adrenals have imposed a false masculinization. **1971** *Daily Tel.* (Colour Suppl.) 10 Dec. 18/2 In the production of millions of children a year, it is not surprising that occasionally nature's complex technology should break down to produce an imbalance of hormones with masculinisation of the female foetus or feminisation of the male.

masculinize (mæ·skiŭlinəiz), *v.* [f. MASCULIN(E *a.* + -IZE.] *trans.* **a.** To render masculine or more masculine in nature, form, or character.

1912 MME MORET tr. *A. Moret's Kings & Gods Egypt* i. 29 She even tried to change the very name she had received at her birth and to masculinise it by omitting the feminine ending. **1927** C. C. MARTINDALE *Relig. of World* 19 The first way in which Brahmā could be '*thought*', was, as sufficiently 'masculinised' (Brahmā) to be a god, supreme, yet to that extent specified.

b. *Biol.* To induce male sexual characteristics in.

1924, 1962 [see *FEMINIZE *v.* 2]. **1971** *Daily Tel.* (Colour Suppl.) 10 Dec. 21/3 The amount of androgen required for normal masculinizing of the brain is greater than that required to masculinize the genitalia.

Hence **ma·sculinized** *ppl. a.*, **ma·sculinizing** *ppl. a.* and *vbl. sb.*

1927 *Daily Express* 28 Sept. 8/7 The second type of masculinised female is the politically-minded woman. **1928** *Sunday Express* 19 Aug. 5 'The Cinderella Man'.. was a masculinised version of the old story. **1936, 1939** [see *ANDROGEN]. **1961** M. F. A. MONTAGU *Genetic Mechanisms in Human Dis.* xii. 113 Completely masculinised genetic females are almost common, forming something like 1 in 40 of the masculine population. **1970** *Nature* 3 Oct. 94/2 In the glow-worm *Lampyris* the apical cells of the testis produce a masculinizing hormone.

masculinoid (mæ·skiŭlinoid), *a.* [f. MASCULIN(E *a.* + -OID.] Masculine (but not male); of male form or appearance.

1921 [see *ADRENAL *a.* and *sb.* A]. **1923** J. S. HUXLEY *Ess. Biologist* iv. 145 The 'masculinoid' woman (to use the current jargon) tends physically also to be less feminine.., while the 'feminoid' man shows the reverse tendency.

Masdeu (masdǭ). [See quot. 1851.] A sweet firm-bodied wine of a dark colour and mellow flavour produced at a vineyard in the South of France.

1851 C. REDDING *Hist. Mod. Wines* (ed. 3) vi. 154 This wine is not a factitious French port from the harbour of Cette... It is a genuine production called Masdeu, from the vineyard which produces it, between Perpignan and Collioure. **1903** *Whitaker's Almanack* 453 Of wines imported in casks the following are the usual measurements: Pipe of Port or Masdeu = 115 gallons, [etc.]. **1958** A. L. SIMON *Dict. Wines* 108/1 *Masdeu*, red, fortified wines of Roussillon, very popular in England in early Victorian days. Also written *Masdu* and *Masdieu*. **1965** O. A. MENDELSOHN *Dict. Drink* 214 *Masdeu*, French (Roussillon) red dessert wine.

masdevallia (mæsdĭvæ·liă). [mod.L. (H. Ruiz Lopez & J. Pavon *Floræ Peruvianæ et Chilensis Prodromus* (1794) 122), f. the name of Jose *Masdevall* (d. 1801), Spanish physician and botanist + -IA[1].] An epiphytic orchid of the large genus so called, belonging to the family Orchidaceæ and native to the cool, mountainous regions of South America.

1845 *Curtis's Bot. Mag.* LXXI. 4164 Windowed Masdevallia... is one of the very curious productions of nature. **1896** F. H. WOOLWARD *Genus Masdevallia* 1 The first *Masdevallia* known to science was..discovered by the Spanish botanists, Ruiz and Pavon, in the Andes of Peru, during their residence in that country from 1777 to 1794. **1911** *Encycl. Brit.* XX. 172/1 *Masdevallia* is common in cultivation and has often brilliant scarlet, crimson or orange flowers. **1970** B. & W. RITTERSHAUSEN *Pop. Orchids* ix. 211 The flower [of *Masdevallia muscosa*] is of a translucent yellow colour, the lip being somewhat large for Masdevallias.

mase (mē¹z), *v.* [Back-formation from next, the ending *-er* being treated as the suffix -ER[1] of agent nouns.] *intr.* To *LASE, esp. in the microwave part of the spectrum. Hence **ma·sing** *vbl. sb.*

1962 *Engineering* 2 Feb. 191 The device 'mases' 30 per cent of the time. **1962** *New Scientist* 1 Mar. 486 One knows when the alignment is good enough only by the fact that the device starts to 'mase'. **1964** *Encycl. Sci. Suppl.* (Grolier) 308/1 Many substances have been made

to 'mase' and 'lase'—that is, to behave like masers or lasers. **1966** Smith & Sorokin *Laser* vii. 369 At this point the stage was nearly set for the actual achievement of an injection maser. The main remaining question was: in what sort of a structure could masing action be achieved? **1973** *Nature* 21/28 Dec. 468/1 Since none of the CH lines have so far been seen in absorption, irrespective of the nature of the source where they have been found, one is led to believe that all transitions are masing weakly.

maser (mē̆i·zəɹ). [An acronym: see quot. 1955[2].] A laser, esp. one that emits microwaves.

The first masers emitted microwaves. Later ones emitted in other parts of the spectrum, and these were also called masers for a time until *laser* came to be adopted as the general name for all such devices.

1955 *Sci. News Let.* 5 Feb. 83/1 Scientists can, for the first time, generate microwaves of extremely high frequency by tapping directly the energy of molecules, Dr. Charles H. Townes of Columbia University's physics department reported in New York. His device for doing so is known as the 'maser'. *Ibid.*, Work on the maser began three years ago. **1955** Gordon, Zeiger, & Townes in *Physical Rev.* 15 Aug. 1264/1 The device utilizes a molecular beam in which molecules in the excited state of a microwave transition are selected. Interaction between these excited molecules and a microwave field produces additional radiation and hence amplification by stimulated emission. We call an apparatus utilizing this technique a 'maser', which is an acronym for 'microwave amplification by stimulated emission of radiation'. **1958** Schawlow & Townes in *Ibid.* 15 Dec. 1940 (*heading*) Infrared and optical masers. **1960** *Times* 17 Oct. 2/2 (Advt.), Development work on existing long range programmes in: solid-state millimetre and optical masers, parametric amplifiers, [etc.]. **1960, 1962** [see *laser[2]]. **1962** *Engineering* 2 Feb. 190/2 The basic type of maser, from which the principle of *optical* masers is derived, is a quite recent electron device... Research later extended the upper frequency range of this technique of low-noise signal amplification, until it eventually reached the visible region—giving rise to the optical maser, otherwise known as the laser. **1967** T. P. Melia *Introd. Masers & Lasers* iv. 34 The power output of the ammonia maser is very small (about 10^{-10} watt) but the frequency stability is of the order of 1 in 10^{12} over a 1 minute period and 1 part in 10^{10} over very much longer periods. **1968** *Nature* 30 Mar. 1237/2 (*heading*) Is interstellar hydrogen capable of maser action at 21 centimetres? **1969** S. G. & H. Lipson *Optical Physics* xi. 369 A maser is, of course, a very-narrow-band amplifier; it is because of its narrow band that the noise-level achieved is very low, since there is a theoretical minimum noise-level per unit band-width. **1972** *Sci. Amer.* Sept. 136/3 The greatest contributor..to the receiver's ability to handle Telstar's faint signals (about 10^{-12} watt) was a maser amplifier that combined very high gain with extremely low noise.

mash, *sb.*[1] Add: **3. d.** *slang.* Mashed potatoes; esp. in the phr. *sausage(s) and mash.*

1904 A. E. W. Mason *Truants* xxii. 213, I..go into a public-house..and have a sausage and mash and a pot of beer. **1939** W. S. Maugham *Christmas Holiday* i. 7 They could drop in..and eat kedgeree and sausages and mash. **1973** 'H. Carmichael' *Too late for Tears* vi. 85 He..ordered sausage and mash with peas. **1974** *Woman* 4 May 18/1 Sizzling sausages and tasty mash.

mash, *sb.*[3] Add: **2.** (Earlier and later examples.) Also, *to make* (or *have*) *a mash* (*on*).

1884 E. W. Nye *Baled Hay* 135 Two Laramie girls on horseback yanking a fly drummer along the street..because he tried to make a mash on them. **1909** 'O. Henry' *Roads of Destiny* iv. 61, I certainly seemed to have a mash on her. **1912** D. Canfield *Squirrel-Cage* III. xxix. 319, I thought it would be fun to tease Paul about the mash you made on old What's-his-name.

Comb. **mash note**, a love-letter.

1890 B. Hall *Turnover Club* 134 He is greatly afflicted by that dreadful bane of fine-looking actors, yclept the 'mash note' in the profession. **1899** *Chicago Record* 7 Jan. 4/6, I was writin' mash notes to myself. **1913** R. W. Chambers *Gay Rebellion* i. 6 That poem seemed to deal a direct blow at this suffragette strike. Several women subscribers sent in mash notes. **1930** W. R. Burnett *Iron Man* 85 He gets mash notes by the ton. **1970** *New Yorker* 14 Nov. 87/2 (Advt.), A pen that roared through the Twenties and Thirties writing checks, letters, autographs ..jazz and mash notes.

mash, *sb.*[5] Eng. and U.S. dial. variant of Marsh.

1671 *Coll. S. Carolina Hist. Soc.* (1897) V. 336 About ye rivers mouth & up the river beyond ye mashes. **1840** *Knickerbocker* XVI. 210, I reckon you won't get nothing for him without you turn him out on the mash. **1843** 'R. Carlton' *New Purchase* I. ix. 58 They had been sufficiently fortunate as to..learn the nature of 'mash land'. **1876** W. Whitman *Specimen Days* (1882–3) 94 The sedgy perfume..reminded me of 'the mash' and south bay of my native island. **1892** P. H. Emerson *Son of Fens* iii. 23, I went back to the sheep... I used to drive 'em down to mash along with the cows.

mash, *v.*[4] *U.S.* Var. of Mesh *v.* 3 b.

1850 *Rep. Comm. Patents 1849* (U.S.) 155 What I claim as new..is..the shaft H, with the pinions i, mashing into racks H. **1860** Bartlett *Dict. Amer.* (ed. 3) 265 In machinery, one wheel is said to *mash* into or with another, i.e. to 'engage' with it.

‖ **masha** (mæ·ʃă). [Hindi *māshā.*] An Indian weight, equivalent to about fifteen grains troy or eight rattis, originally based on the weight of a seed of the bean *Phaseolus mungo* var. *radiatus.*

1848 J. H. Stocqueler *Oriental Interpreter* 148/2 Masha, a weight of fifteen grains troy. Used by native goldsmiths and jewellers, and in the native evaluation by assay of the precious metals. **1855** E. Acton *Mod. Cookery* (rev. ed.) xxxii. 612 Five eggs, two tolahs of milk, one masha of salt, two mashas of cayenne pepper. **1969** *Daily Tel.* 1 Oct. 19/8 Customers had their purchases weighed in tolas, mashas and ruttees by a Pakistani shopkeeper.

Masham (mæ·ʃăm). The name of a small town in the northern part of Yorkshire, used to designate a breed of sheep produced by crossing Wensleydale or Teeswater rams with Blackface or Swaledale ewes.

1951 A. Fraser *Sheep Husbandry* (ed. 2) ii. 68 The Wensleydale..is pre-eminently a crossing breed... It provides sires to cross with the hill breeds of sheep indigenous to the North of England... The cross lambs thus produced are variously known as 'Mashams'—Half-breds—or Greyfaces, and are very useful lambs for feeding on low ground. **1971** *Farmers' Weekly* 19 Mar. 43/3 Certain wool types such as Blackface..have met a better market demand than..Masham.

mashed, *ppl. a.* Add: Hence as *sb.*, mashed potatoes (esp. in the phr. *sausage and mashed*). *slang.*

1923 in J. Manchon *Le Slang.* **1926** G. B. Shaw *Translations & Tomfooleries* 225 One [*sc.* a public-house] had a placard up 'Sausage and Mashed'. **1934** T. S. Eliot *Rock* i. 40 Restaurants where you can get..sausage and mashed or toad-in-the-'ole for twopence. **1963** H. Garner in R. Weaver *Canad. Short Stories* (1968) 2nd Ser. 52, I ate a lunch of meat pie, mashed and gravy.

mashie-niblick. *Golf.* [f. Mashie, mashy + Niblick.] An iron club combining the features of the mashie and the niblick, now called the number 7 iron.

1907 W. M. Butler *Golfer's Manual* 5 The marriage of different pairs of clubs has produced such implements as mashie-niblicks and putting-cleeks. **1912** H. Vardon *How to play Golf* vii. 146 Nowadays tools called mashie-niblicks are popular. **1929** Wodehouse *Mr. Mulliner Speaking* vi. 196 How bitterly he regretted now those raking drives, those crisp flicks of the mashie-niblick of which he had been so proud ten minutes ago. **1931** *Times* 28 Feb. 4/6 A little bullet-headed mashie niblick..was also highly efficient. **1964** J. Stobbs *A.B.C. of Golf* 61 Out have gone..the tried and proved regular favourites... Among these..the mashie niblick, a large round-shaped-faced lofted mashie (modern equivalent the 7-iron). **1972** T. Scott *Club Golfers' Handbk.* 127 *Mashie-niblick*, another name which has been replaced by a number.

Mashona (măʃō̆u·nă), *sb.* and *a.* Pl. **Mashona, Mashonas.** [Native name.] **A.** *sb.* **a.** A group of Bantu peoples inhabiting parts of Rhodesia and Mozambique; a member of one of these peoples. **b.** Any of the languages of these peoples. **B.** *adj.* Of or pertaining to these peoples.

1835 A. Smith *Diary* (1940) II. 222 The Bakalaka and the Mashoona speak a different language to the Bechuanas. **1846** H. H. Methuen *Life in Wilderness* vi. 143 To the north-east the land becomes mountainous, and the Mashona, a tribe possessing guns, inhabit it. **1893** A. M. Hartmann (*title*) A grammar of the Mashona language. **1894** —— (*title*) English–Mashona dictionary. **1895** G. W. H. Knight-Bruce *Memories Mashonaland* ii. 41 The Mashona..are very fond of meat, but they hardly ever get it. To give him meat is the one way that will nearly always ensure a wild Mashona working well. **1896** *Scientific African* 78 (Pettman), The careful workmanship displayed in the crude musical instrument known as the Mashona piano. **1900** A. H. Keane *Boer States* vii. 101 Mashonas..and several other smaller groups for whom there is no collective national or racial designation, except the all-comprehensive 'Kaffre'. **1911** *Encycl. Brit.* XVII. 837/2 The name Mashona has been derived from the contemptuous term *Amashuina* applied by the Matabele to the aborigines owing to the habit of the latter of taking refuge in the rocky hills with which the country abounds... The Mashona..are in general a peaceful, mild-mannered people. **1911** J. G. Frazer *Golden Bough: Magic Art* (ed. 3) I. vi. 352 The king of the Matabeles..prays..: 'O great spirits.., I thank you for having granted last year to my people more wheat than to our enemies the Mashonas.' **1928** C. Bullock *Mashona* iii. 12 The word Mashona is used *faute de mieux*; nor need we look for its etymological derivation, because it has none. It is simply one of those British bowdlerisations..a race name to cover numerous clans. **1936** J. Buchan *Island of Sheep* iv. 68 They are Mashonas and are timid as rabbits. **1959** *Chambers's Encycl.* II. 107/2 In the Shona (Mashona) group [*sc.* of Bantu languages] there are about 40 dialectal forms. **1972** *Police Rev.* 24 Nov. 1521/1 Cecil John Rhodes..began negotiating..for rights to explore the mineral wealth of the regions east of the royal kraal at Bulawayo, at that time inhabited by the Mashona tribe.

mashwa (ma·ʃwă). Also **machwa, mashua, mashuwa.** [Marathi, 'fishing-boat', f. Skr. *matsya* fish.] A kind of small open boat (see quots.).

1885 G. C. Whitworth *Anglo-Indian Dict.* 184/1 The machwás of different ports vary slightly in build. They are considered to be amongst the swiftest sailing-vessels known; they are very sharp in the bows, with hollow keel, well rounded in the stern, and the mast slopes a little forward; these vessels are chiefly made of teak, and cost from Rs. 300 to Rs. 400; they last about forty years. **1906** H. W. Smyth *Mast & Sail in Europe & Asia* ix. 310 A smaller class of Zanzibar vessel is the *mashuwa*, or open fishing-boat worked by the Arab of the neighbourhood. They are generally dilapidated little crafts with the usual long bow and transom-stern. **1929** *Ibid.* (ed. 2) x. 359 The term Mashwa, or Mashuwa on the African coast, is applied apparently to any small round-stern vessel, meaning originally a fishing-boat. The larger seagoing craft all carry a small 'mashwa' on deck. **1942** *Mariner's Mirror* XXVIII. 21 The *Mashwa* or *Machwa*. The larger Arab fishing boats, the *mashwas*, are built after the design of the *sambuk* and the *jehazi* in their respective home ports. At Zanzibar they are employed also for the transport of coral rag and firewood. All are fitted with a single mast and are undecked save at the ends; the stern is of the square transom type; the tack of the sail is extended by means of a bowsprit as in the *jehazi*. **1948** R. de Kerchove *Internat. Maritime Dict.* 453/1 *Mashuwa, mashwa*, generic name in the Persian Gulf and in Southern Arabia for an open ship's boat with straight or curved stem and transom stern, usually propelled by oars, but also rigged with one mast on occasion... This name also refers to a small open boat with raking stem and rounded stern of Deccan used for fishing and local trading on the Gujarat coast between Bombay and Cam-Bay.

mask, *sb.*[3] Add: **1. b.** Also = *gas mask.

1915 H. W. Wilson *Great War* IV. 331 A Highlander wearing a mask. **1918** *Ibid.* XI. 454 French soldiers wearing the masks, fitted with goggles and respirators, that rendered them immune to noxious gases. *Ibid.* 455 Special masks were devised for the horses.

4. b. Also, the head-skin of any 'game'; the face or muzzle of a dog.

1894 C. Phillipps-Wolley et al. *Big Game Shooting* II. xv. 417 Peel off the whole mask from the antlers downwards to the muzzle. **1928** C. S. Stockley *Big Game Shooting* 88 Skins..should..be..hung on a frame to dry, the mask being filled with dry grass or paper. **1945** C. L. B. Hubbard *Observer's Bk. Dogs* 214 A light Cairn may have a dark mask. **1972** *Daily Tel.* 8 Apr. 17/4 Six more dog pelts, all complete with masks—the head of the dog—have been found..at Nuneaton... Mr Horner, whose firm exports between 40,000 and 50,000 dog skins a year, commented: 'I am baffled as to why someone should prepare pelts with masks.'

g. A cosmetic preparation, a face-pack.

1931 H. G. Wells *Work, Wealth & Happiness of Mankind* I. v. 221 She has her face put under a 'mask', an affair of beaten-up eggs and other ingredients which tightens on the face. **1934** M. Verni *Mod. Beauty Culture* I. v. 28/2 The foundation for a general type of mask is fuller's earth made into a paste with liquid. *Ibid.*, If the operator has neither given nor received a mask treatment before, she should give herself one. **1955** C. Hart *Handbk. Beauty* 29 Masks serve the purpose of stimulating the circulation, thus improving your complexion color... You can buy a mask ready-made or concoct one at home. Buttermilk all by itself is a good mask; so is oatmeal..so is an egg. *Ibid.*, Cover your hair.., because the mask stuff is sticky.

h. *Electronics.* In the manufacture of microcircuits, a thin surface layer that is removed in parts so as to permit selective modification of the underlying material.

1956 *Bell Syst. Techn. Jrnl.* XXXV. 25 For the emitter, a film of aluminium approximately 1,000 Å thick was evaporated onto the surface through a mask which defined an emitter arc of 1 × 2 mils. **1957** *Jrnl. Electrochem. Soc.* CIV. 549/1 A SiO_2 surface layer provides a selective mask at high temperatures against the diffusion of some donors and acceptors into Si. **1967** *Electronics* 6 Mar. 60/2 Faster IC's can be built with the dimensional resolutions possible in present diffusion masks. **1973** *Sci. Amer.* Apr. 65/2 Masks can be made from various types of material, for example insulators such as silicon dioxide,..or metals such as aluminum, molybdenum and gold. To expose the regions in which ion implantation is desired the mask is removed by chemical etching.

5. mask jug, a jug with a lip or front shaped like a face; also *masked jug.*

1910 Downman & Gunn *Eng. Pott. & Porc.* (ed. 5) 58 (*caption*) Masked jug in Fulham brown stoneware of the 18th century. **1963** *Times* 1 May 15/5 A Worcester yellow-ground mask jug fell to Tilley at £700. **1970** *Canad. Antiques Collector* Jan. 30/1 Mask jugs, in which a face, or even a figure, formed the shape of the front of the jug, opposite the handle, had been made for centuries in most European countries.

mask, *v.*[4] Add: **1. c.** To provide with a gas mask.

1916 *War Illustr.* IV. 607 Machine-gun section masked, ready for the enemy. **1918** H. W. Wilson *Great War* XI. 455 French soldier with one of the French army dogs, both masked against enemy gas attack.

2. g. To disguise the real character of or diminish the effect of.

1922 W. G. Kendrew *Climates of Continents* 18 The south-east trades..are now at their greatest strength, but sea breezes mask them on the immediate littoral. **1931** *Times* 18 Feb. 6/5 It was this late stroke, masked, into the left corner which defeated the game of Joshua Crane.

h. Of a sound or other object of perception: to diminish or prevent the perception of (another stimulus, usu. one affecting the same sense).

1923 *Physical Rev.* XXI. 706 When the masking tone is loud it masks tones of higher frequency better than those of frequency lower than itself. **1949** McCord & Witheridge *Odors* xvii. 190 The opportunity for masking objectionable textile odors by..impregnating the goods with a definitely noticeable perfume seems to be negligible. **1960** *Lang. & Speech* III. 160 The low-frequency noise masks the voicing of a consonant. **1966** *Jrnl. Exper. Psychol.* LXXII. 233/1 Backward masking refers to the power of certain stimuli, the masking stimuli, to disrupt or mask the processing of other stimuli, the target stimuli, which have been presented *earlier.* **1973** D. L. Richards *Telecommunication by Speech* iii. 113 Room noise that masks

speech from the other station will make conversation more difficult. **1974** *Encycl. Brit. Macropædia* XVI. 555/1 The substantially greater intensity of one odour may mask another.

i. *Chem.* To prevent (a substance or ion) from taking part in a certain reaction by causing it to undergo another preliminary reaction.

1934 in WEBSTER. **1936** *Industr. & Engin. Chem.* (*Analytical Ed.*) 15 Nov. 409/1 A characteristic example in the analysis of anions is that..in which sulfite is masked by the addition of formaldehyde. **1970** D. D. PERRIN *Masking & Demasking Chem. Reactions* i. 2 Silver is masked by ammonia against precipitation as the hydroxide or chloride.

masked, *ppl. a.*² Add: **2. c.** Of a sound or other stimulus (see *MASK *v.*⁴ 2 h, *MASKING *vbl. sb.*² 2 b).

1924 *Physical Rev.* XXIII. 270 The frequency of the masked tone is indicated on each curve. **1965** T. S. LITTLER *Physics Ear* vii. 134 We usually determine the level at which a sound has to be maintained in order to be just audible in the presence of another. This is known as the masked threshold of the masked or maskee sound in the presence of the masking or masker sound.

d. *Chem.* Of a substance or molecular group: prevented from taking part in a certain reaction by being in a bound form, esp. as a result of another preliminary reaction.

1932 *Discovery* Mar. 96/2 The first traces of the masked iron indicative of haemoglobin appear in the nuclei of certain cells. **1940** R. E. OESPER tr. *Feigl's Specific & Special Reactions for Qualitative Analysis* iv. 49 This fact was used..to release the cationically masked sulfate groups in the green complex chronic sulfate solutions. **1974** *Angewandte Makromolekulare Chemie* XXXIV. 111 Tertiary aliphatic amines containing masked methylol groups, e.g. methylolalkylether.., prove efficient catalysts in the production of polyurethane foams.

maskelynite (mæ·skĕlinəit). *Min.* [ad. G. *maskelynit* (G. Tschermak 1872, in *Sitzungsber. d. K. Akad. d. Wissensch.* (*Math.-Natur. Cl.*) LXV. 131), f. the name of Nevil Story-*Maskelyne* (1823–1911), English mineralogist): see -ITE¹.] A colourless aluminosilicate of calcium and sodium which has a composition near to that of andesine and is found in some kinds of meteorite.

1875 E. S. DANA in J. D. Dana *Syst. Min.* (ed. 5) App. II. 37 Maskelynite. **1921** *Bull. Geol. Soc. Amer.* XXXII. 402 The name maskelynite..was first given by Tschermak to an isotropic constituent of the habit and composition of a labradorite feldspar occurring in the stone of Shergotty. The name has since been extended to cover a colorless interstitial substance, sometimes quite isotropic and sometimes faintly doubly refracting, of like appearance and habit, and a common if not universal constituent of the chondritic meteorites. **1971** *Physics Bull.* Oct. 578/2 It appears that intense shock disorders the lattice to produce the isotropic mineral maskelynite.

masking, *vbl. sb.*² **2.** Delete *Photogr.* and add to def.: Obscuring or covering (wholly or in part) by the interposition or overlaying of something. Also *masking-out.* (Add further examples.)

1933 E. MOLLOY *Mod. Motor Repair* III. 980/1 Where a line is required or a clear finished edge, this is obtained by masking. *Ibid.*, Any upholstery will require masking..if the whole car is going to be sprayed. **1949** C. E. CHAPEL et al. *Aircraft Maintenance & Repair* xxi. 361/1 Figure 6 illustrates the masking of an airplane wing in order that the wing may be finished in two colors. **1951** *Electronics* Feb. 109/1 In color photography a technique known as 'masking' has been developed in which a negative image is combined with a positive image in printing, thus effectively introducing negative light in the final result. **1956** *Bell Syst. Techn. Jrnl.* XXXV. 334 If part of the work is coated with an insulating varnish, electrolytic etching will take place only on the uncoated surfaces. This technique, often called 'masking', has the limitation that the etching undercuts the masking if any considerable amount of material is removed. **1967** E. CHAMBERS *Photolitho-Offset* iv. 39 Additional equipment should include an airbrush, for use in connection with continuous tone negatives and positives complete with frisket-paper for masking-out and vignetting. **1972** L. LAMB *Picture Frame* i. 16 Adhesive tape was used for temporary masking-out so that a colour could be given a straight, hard-edge.

b. The action of one stimulus in diminishing the sensitivity of a subject to another (cf. *MASK *v.*⁴ 2 h).

1923 *Physical Rev.* XXI. 706 For tones introduced into the same ear, except when the frequencies are so close as to produce beats, the masking is greatest for tones nearly alike. **1949** MCCORD & WITHERIDGE *Odors* xvii. 186 Masking is an effect produced at the point of sense perception in the respiratory passages together with the final interpretation in the brain and does not constitute an aromatic correction of the aerial components. **1962** A. NISBETT *Technique Sound Studio* x. 170 A second reason for holding effects back..is the masking that is caused by even moderately quiet background sound. **1967** *Science* 15 Sept. 1335/3 Visual backward masking consists in the retroactive interference with the perception of one visual stimulus, the target, by another visual stimulus, the mask, closely following the target in time. **1974** *Encycl. Brit. Macropædia* IX. 243/2 Some dentists use auditory analgesia (a 'masking' of pain by sound).

c. *Chem.* The prevention of a substance or ion from taking part in a certain reaction by causing it to undergo another preliminary reaction.

1936 F. FEIGL in *Industr. & Engin. Chem.* (*Analytical Ed.*) 15 Nov. 409/1 The masking of certain reactions of mercury, copper, nickel, and cobalt by cyanide and thiocyanate has been known for a long time. **1963** P. W. WEST in E. W. Berg *Physical & Chem. Methods of Separation* xviii. 343 The term *masking* was introduced many years ago by Prof. Fritz Feigl, who utilized this technique in making specific or highly selective spot tests when the available reagents were general. **1971** *Nature* 19 Mar. 194/1 Generally speaking 'masking' has come to mean the prevention of the normal reaction of an ion upon addition of a reagent with which it reacts.

4. *Comb.* **masking board** *Photogr.*, the board on which the printing paper is fixed in an enlarger; **masking frame** *Photogr.* (see quot. 1940); **masking tape,** adhesive tape used for masking, esp. to protect certain areas of a surface before applying paint.

1958 *Newnes Compl. Amat. Photogr.* 319 The paper is removed from the masking board, and the next negative lined up in position. **1972** G. L. WAKEFIELD *Exposure Control in Enlarging* viii. 110 As a good masking board for the enlarger easel is expensive..it is worth making one. **1940** F. J. MORTIMER *Wall's Dict. Photogr.* (ed. 15) 441 *Masking frame*, an accessory used with vertical enlargers to hold the paper flat and provide a white border. **1958** *Newnes Compl. Amat. Photogr.* 318 The sheet of bromide paper is then placed in the masking frame. **1972** G. L. WAKEFIELD *Exposure Control in Enlarging* viii. 107 It had been intended to build the microammeter and associated electronics into a masking frame. **1936** BRIMM & BOGGESS *Airplane & Engine Maintenance* 282 After the numbers or letters have been outlined by pencil, they should be blocked in with masking tape. **1962** *Which? Car Suppl.* Oct. 138/1 Marks had been left by masking tape on the right rear body panel. **1971** D. E. WESTLAKE *I gave at the Office* (1972) 53 Someone had fairly recently put strips of masking tape over some sort of company name on the doors [of the trucks].

masking, *ppl. a.*³ (Further examples.)

1923 [see *MASK *v.*⁴ 2 h]. **1969** T. C. THORSTENSEN *Pract. Leather Technol.* viii. 115 In the study of masking agents it was established very early in chrome tanning research that the anions could be listed in order of increasing affinity for the chromium tanning complex. **1970** D. D. PERRIN *Masking & Demasking Chem. Reactions* i. 1 A masking reagent..is one that lowers the concentration of a free metal ion or a free ligand to such a level that certain of its chemical reactions are prevented. **1970** *Jrnl Gen. Psychol.* LXXXII. 37 An exhaust fan provided masking noise.

masochism. Now usu. with pronunc. (mæ·sŏkiz'm). Substitute for def. A form of sexual perversion in which a person finds pleasure in abuse and cruelty from his or her associate (cf. SADISM). Recently applied more generally to a form of perversion in which a sufferer derives or is believed to derive pleasure from pain or humiliation. (Later examples.)

1930 W. R. INGE *Christian Ethics & Mod. Probl.* iii. 109 Modern psychology has invented the word masochism for that perversion of the sex-instinct which takes the form of self-torture. **1943** H. READ *Politics of Unpolitical* ii. 18 Masochism is the unconscious impulse to dissolve oneself in the power of another person and to participate in his annihilating power. **1963** A. HERON *Towards Quaker View of Sex* 71 *Masochism*, obtaining pleasure (usually sexual) through suffering pain, subjugation or humiliation. **1974** *Listener* 21 Nov. 679 That Johnson had masochistic fantasies..was first mooted 20 years ago... That Johnson's masochism did not stop at fantasy seems to be indicated by..entries in Mrs Thrale's diary.

masochist (mæ·sŏkist). [f. as MASOCHISM + -IST.] One who is given to masochism.

1895 tr. *M. Nordau's Degeneration* v. i. 538 Masochists or passivists..clothe themselves in a costume which recalls, by colour and cut, feminine apparel. **1917** C. R. PAYNE tr. *Pfister's Psychoanal. Method* 78 Very many tormentors of animals are..sadists, consequently also, more or less masochists. **1957** *London Mag.* Jan. 75 Psychologically her affinities were with the more heroic type of masochist, such as Saint-Exupéry, T. E. Lawrence, and Orwell. **1974** 'J. MELVILLE' *Nun's Castle* iv. 88 'Are you telling me Lynnet was some sort of masochist?'..'I think she associated love and pain.'

masochistic (mæsŏki·stik), *a.* Also (*erron.*) masso-. [f. prec. + -IC.] Of, pertaining to, resembling or characterized by masochism.

1904 G. S. HALL *Adolescence* II. 112 Women may acquire a Massochistic love of violence and pain for the ideal of pleasure. **1928** *Music & Lett.* July 125 The almost masochistic melancholy of the average fox-trot. **1958** *Essays & Stud.* XI. 65 The very energy of the style is masochistic—a tormenting awareness of its own impotence to do, or change, anything. **1959** *Times* 30 Sept. 13/5 Eighteenth-century patrons seemed to take a masochistic delight in seeing themselves lampooned on the stage. **1974** [see *MASOCHISM].

Hence **ma:sochi·stically** *adv.*, in a masochistic manner.

1936 *Times Lit. Suppl.* 18 July 597/2 Minor Canons speak of themselves masochistically as 'mere' minor canons. **1947** S. J. PERELMAN *Westward Ha!* (1949) vii. 87 Masochistically allowing chickens to peck at our bare tootsies.

Mason (mē¹·s'n), *sb.*³ orig. *U.S.* [f. the name of John *Mason*, who was granted the patent for such jars in 1858.] *Mason jar*: a wide-mouthed glass jar with an airtight screw top widely used in home bottling; also *Mason fruit-jar.*

1885 *N.Y. Weekly Tribune* 6 Aug. 13/2 The Illinois Agricultural Society calls attention to the fact that Mason fruit-jars have been sent to that State packed in straw foul with Canada thistle. **1888** L. HARGIS *Graded Cook Bk.* 472 Quince and apple butter... Put a little of the mixture in a plate and invert, if it adheres the butter is done. Fill Mason jars and seal. **1947** *Nat. Geogr. Mag.* June 822/1 His annual cherry crop amounted to one forlorn little cherry which he covered with a mason jar. **1950** *N.Z. Jrnl. Agric.* Jan. 51/3, 2-pint mason jar feeders..were placed in the group of hives. **1972** H. C. RAE *Shooting Gallery* ii. 80 Landscapes evolved in his mind, like smoke in a Mason jar. **1973** J. JONES *Touch of Danger* xxvii. 162, I began to swish the martini mixture in the big Mason jar.

Mason and Dixon. *U.S.* = *Mason's and Dixon's line*: see LINE *sb.*² 17 b. Now usu. **Mason-Dixon.**

1779 in W. B. Reed *Life & Corr. J. Reed* (1847) II. 134 The Virginia gentlemen offer to divide exactly the 40th degree with us... Perhaps we [of Penna.] would be as well off with Mason and Dixon's line continued. **1834** C. A. DAVIS *Lett. J. Downing* 36 And he tell'd me Georgia would go for me, arter the Gineral, as soon as any north of mason and dickson. **1843** *Knickerbocker* XXII. 185 The writer, who dwelleth near Mason and Dixon, descants upon the awful climate. **1948** *Downers Grove* (Illinois) *Reporter* 21 Oct. 3/2 Two Dixiecrats, out of their element north of the Mason-Dixon, nevertheless registered their convictions on the States' Rights issue. **1969** I. KEMP *Brit. G.I. in Vietnam* vii. 155 You're crazy, Limey! You couldn't keep me here for all the girls south of the Mason-Dixon Line. **1975** *Times* 20 Aug. 12/3 The tortured condition of the Jewish middle-class intellectual seems..the dominant subject of novels written north of the Mason-Dixon line.

Also *transf.*

1948 *Sat. Even. Post* 30 Oct. 124/4 This same little band has long since adopted three war-ruined families in the old country—two in Bizonia, one on the other side of Europe's bitter Mason and Dixon's line. **1970** *New Yorker* 22 July 4/3 Sub-Mason-Dixon dining.

Masonite³ (mē¹·sŏnəit). Also **masonite.** The proprietary name of a type of fibreboard made from wood-fibre pulped under high steam pressure.

1926 *Official Gaz.* (U.S. Patent Office) 23 Nov. 802/1 Mason Fibre Company, Laurel, Miss. Filed July 24, 1926. *Masonite. Particular description of goods.*—Fiber Board, Insulating Board, Composite Construction Board, Synthetic Lumber, or Artificial Lumber. **1933** *Sci. Amer.* Jan. 39/1 Floors will be of Masonite cushioned flooring. **1948** *Archit. Rev.* CIII. 270 (*caption*) The walls are covered with masonite sheeting fixed with broken recessed joints and slightly rounded corners, and painted grey-white. **1950** in W. Schack *Man. Plastics & Resins* 279 *Masonite* (trade name) refers to a series of headboards having considerable structural strength and resistance to abrasion and moisture. **1970** *Jrnl. Gen. Psychol.* LXXXII. 58 A five-digit counter, a speaker, two lights, and two standard Gerbrands rat levers were mounted on the lower panel (the unused lever was concealed by a masonite mask). **1970** *Southerly* XXX. 186 His blunted thumb jerked over the hump of his shoulder, pierced the masonite lining, pierced the weatherboards, rode the thirty odd miles of train-tracks and arrived in Sydney. **1973** *Jrnl. Genetic Psychol.* CXXII. 19 The stimuli used for pretraining and oddity training were multidimensional common household items and toys mounted on 4 × 4 inch brown-masonite squares.

masonry, *sb.* Add: **3.** Also *transf.*

1926 J. BLACK *You can't Win* xv. 202 George..took no pains to hide himself, feeling sure that the masonry of the road..would protect him against the common enemy—the law.

b. (See quot. 1896.) *slang.*

1841 LYTTON *Night & Morning* (ed. 2) II. III. viii. 178, I was one of them, and know the masonry. **1896** FARMER & HENLEY *Slang* IV. 289/1 *Masonry*, secret signs & passwords.

mass, *sb.*¹ Add: In the use of Roman Catholics freq. with pronunc. (mɑs). **7.** *mass-time* (earlier and later examples); **mass rock** *Hist.*, a rock at which persecuted Irish Catholics would gather to celebrate the mass in secret.

1914 W. P. BURKE *Irish Priests in Penal Times* p. vii, The 'Mass Rock'.., the 'Priests' Hollow',..and many a similar name..are witnesses..to a hunted priesthood. **1932** H. CONCANNON *Blessed Eucharist in Irish Hist.* xix. 389 He was often placed on the summit of a high rock, to signal the approach of the 'priest hunters', while around a great stone, 'a Mass rock',..the parishioners were assembled for Mass. **1933** FATHER AUGUSTINE *Ireland's Loyalty to Mass* x. 166 Carraig an Aifrinn, (the Mass Rock). **1959** D. D. C. P. MOULD *Peter's Boat* vi. 79 There are, in fact, an enormous number of known Mass rocks in this country, and that is to be expected, for they were in use whenever persecution was hot, and in fact, come almost into living memory. **1483** in *N. & Q.* (1973) Apr. 125/1 His Highnes wyth a sword in his hand berying yt upright all the masse tyme. **1845** 'C. MALONE' in S. J. Brown *Poetry of Irish Hist.* (1927) 258 At Mass-time once I went to play. **1922** JOYCE *Ulysses* 279 And once at masstime he had gone to play... A boy. A croppy boy.

mass, *sb.*² Add: **4. a.** Also freq. in pl. (Further examples.)

1958 Observer 18 May 16/4 If you weren't a poor little rich girl, or very pretty or exciting socially, there were still masses of fun to be had. 1974 A. Morice Killing with Kindness viii. 56 I'm sure you've got masses to do.

e. (Earlier example.)

1873 E. Atkinson tr. Helmholtz's Pop. Lect. Sci. Subjects 1st Ser. 101 Although we are not usually clearly conscious of these beating upper partials, the ear feels their effect as a want of uniformity or a roughness in the mass of tone.

g. *Psychol.* (See **apperceiving mass, *apperception mass.*)

1907 W. James in Jrnl. Philos. 18 July 397 My statements may seem less obscure if surrounded by something more of a 'mass' whereby to apperceive them.

10. *attrib.* and *Comb.*, passing into *adj.* Examples, of which a selection is listed below, are very numerous in the 20th century. Used to mean: of, involving, composed of masses of people (or things) or the majority of people (or a society, group, etc.); done, made, etc., on a large scale.

mass-appeal, art, audience, behaviour, circulation, communication (hence *mass communicator*), *consciousness, consumer* (hence *-consuming, consumption*), *cult, culture, deportation, education, emotion* (hence *emotional* adj.), *entertainment, fear, grave, hypnosis* hence *-hypnotized* adj.), *hysteria, immigration, literacy, migration, mind* (hence *-minded* adj., *-mindedness*), *movement, murder* (hence *mass murderer*), *party, persuasion, propaganda, psychology, public, society, suggestion, suicide, unemployment*; *mass-made* ppl. a.; *mass-advertising, -buying, -merchandising* (also *-merchandised* ppl. a., *-merchandiser*), *-selling, -thinking* vbl. sbs. **b.** spec. *Mil.*, as *mass attack* (also as vb.), *formation, raid*; *mass-bombing* vbl. sb. **c.** *Physics*, as *mass-flow, transport.*

1958 New Statesman 20 Dec. 881/2 Not all the spice goes into the thick wedges of Christmas pudding; and surely, as we sink deeper and deeper in the treacle of mass-advertising, we deserve this one tiny life-saver? 1944 L. MacNeice Christopher Columbus 14 To assert..that all art should have mass-appeal is like asserting that all mathematics should be 'for the million'. 1962 Rep. Comm. Broadcasting 1960 16 in Parl. Papers 1961–2 (Cmnd. 1753) IX. 259 It has been said that in fact people watch these items; that the justification lies precisely in the fact that they are mass-appeal items. 1962 S. Strand Marketing Dict. 441 In marketing, a product is said to have *mass appeal* when it is desired by the multitudes in all income levels. 1938 Current Hist. Feb. 54 (caption) A Mass Art. 1959 M. McCarthy Sights & Spectacles p. xiv, Some of the editors felt that the theatre was not worth bothering with, because it was neither a high art, like Art, nor a mass art, like the movies! 1964 Hall & Whannel Pop. Arts iii. 68 Mass art often destroys all trace of individuality and idiosyncrasy which makes a work compelling and living. 1970 I. C. Jarvie Towards Sociol. of Cinema vii. 99 Cinema is in a real sense a mass art, not only in that it appeals to the mass audience, but also in that the individual is lost in the darkness of the continuous performance. 1947 Crowther & Whiddington Science at War 101 When convoys of merchant ships were mass-attacked by U-boats in 1942, they were liable to suffer heavy losses. 1959 Chambers's Encycl. XIV. 733/1 On 8 August a mass attack was launched on a convoy near the Isle of Wight. 1960 L. L. Snyder The War 1939–45 vi. 117 August 6, 1940. From his country home..Goering issued orders for the first great mass attack on England. 1938 Time 21 Nov. 53/1 Hitchcock pictures..are often too intricately built and written to appeal to mass audiences. 1957 R. Hoggart Uses of Literacy vi. 147 Genuine controversy..alienates, divides and separates, the mass-audience. 1957 P. Martineau Motivation in Advertising xiv. 169 The 'mass-audience' housewife. 1967 M. McLuhan Medium is Massage 22 The mass audience..successor to the 'public'. 1974 B.B.C. Handbk. 261/2 Opera, so obviously appropriate to television but with a limited appeal to the mass audience. 1940 Harrisson & Madge War begins at Home i. 21 When hundreds of those replies show similar attitudes, we know we are on to something really important in terms of mass behaviour. 1941 E. C. Shepherd Mil. Aeroplane 4 Anti-aircraft fire can..break up the formations so that mass bombing or pattern bombing becomes impossible. 1929 Mass buying [see *mass selling* below]. 1950 B. Schulberg Disenchanted (1951) v. 61 Occasionally appearing in mass circulation magazines with stories increasingly ordinary. 1957 F. Williams Dangerous Estate: Anat. Newspapers xviii. 284 The tabloids and mass-circulation Sunday newspapers. Ibid. 291 The great mass-circulation newspapers..command their millions. 1963 Times Lit. Suppl. 26 Apr. 298/4 The mass-circulation magazines. 1941 Beals & Brody Lit. Adult Educ. v. 139 Concentration of power in the agencies of mass communication is vicious. 1946 J. S. Huxley Unesco ii. 25 The spread of information through all media of Mass Communication—in other words, the press, the cinema, the radio and television. 1954 J. B. Priestley Magicians ii. 47 Mass communications become stronger in their effects every year. 1968 P. Oliver Screening Blues 9 Mass communication through recording, and later through radio, spread the culture of the blues beyond the local definition until the whole Negro world was its habitat. 1971 B. Mafeni in J. Spencer Eng. Lang. W. Afr. 100 The great potentialities of the language [sc. Nigerian Pidgin] as a medium of mass communication. 1965 Punch 9 June 858/1 One way and another Lord Thomson is quite a mass communicator. 1967 Ibid. 4 Jan. 23/2 The delusion you are suffering from usually attacks columnists, commentators and other mass communicators. 1922 D. H. Lawrence Aaron's Rod x. 139, I want to get myself awake, out of it all—all that mass-consciousness. 1947 Koestler in Partisan Rev. XIV. 141 Structural changes in economy without functional changes in mass-consciousness, must always lead to a dead end. 1931 A. Huxley Music at Night iv. 208 A man who has no interest in the things of the mind..is the ideal consumer, the mass consumer. 1971 G. Steiner In Bluebeard's Castle iv. 87 The informational energy required by a mass-consumer society is being transmitted pictorially. 1954 Encounter Mar. 5/2 Those who accept conformity do not challenge the existence of a mass-producing, mass-consuming society, even though they refuse its values. 1969 R. B. Fuller Operating Man. Spaceship Earth viii. 117 As we study industrialization, we see that we cannot have mass production unless we have mass consumption. 1963 Spectator 14 June 783 Mr. Macdonald's target is 'mass culture' and its nauseating child 'Midcult', which, if anything, is worse than 'Masscult'. 1971 M. W. Young Fighting with Food in Massim Society i. 11 Cargo beliefs are still held by many individuals, however, and a fresh catalyst could well provoke another mass cult. 1939 Life 24 July 65/2 The State of Texas..has never been properly recognized for its contributions to U.S. mass culture. 1957 R. Hoggart Uses of Literacy i. 23 We are moving towards the creation of a mass culture. 1957 Economist 5 Oct. 45/1 Whether the reader turns to Shakespeare or to Mr Erle Stanley Gardner for solace may depend less on his psyche and the state of 'mass culture' than on the thorny economics of the book business. 1975 Listener 9 Jan. 40/2 The mass culture which is everyone's hope..depends upon everyone sharing what has previously been the preserve of a privileged few. 1952 C. P. Blacker Eugenics 146 Since these words were written, we have witnessed the inhumanities of concentration and extermination camps, of labour camps and mass deportations, which have scarcely been surpassed by previous tyrannies. 1955 Koestler Trail of Dinosaur 160 The mass-deportations in the 'thirties produced new waves of the plague. 1927 A. Huxley Proper Stud. 113 The ordinary system of mass education. 1940 Graves & Hodge Long Week-End iv. 50 The terms 'thriller' and 'shocker'..had been in use since the Eighties—an early by-product of mass-education. 1964 C. Barber Ling. Change Present-Day Eng. ii. 20 The influence of mass-media and of mass-education. 1927 A. Huxley Proper Stud. 183 Periodic revivalism and the evoking of great mass-emotions on such occasions as pilgrimages provide the necessary emotional excitement. 1961 A. O. J. Cockshut Imagination of Charles Dickens v. 78 Mingling with the crowd he is untouched by mass emotions. 1963 Economist 3 Aug. 445/2 Everyone interested in political, mass emotional, historical causes should read it. 1933 Radio Times 14 Apr. 71/1 A music-hall or other large centre of mass-entertainment. 1960 20th Cent. Dec. 557 The huge metropolitan machines of mass entertainment. 1932 H. Nicolson Public Faces xii. 324 There is only one human emotion stronger than mass-hatred, and that is mass-fear. 1952 Pankhurst & Holder Wind-Tunnel Technique i. 31 The rate of mass flow per unit cross-sectional area (the mass velocity) is given by [etc.]. 1957 Times 4 Oct. 11/7 In the by-pass engine a given thrust is obtained by a greater mass-flow of air at reduced velocity, the engine being both bigger and heavier than the 'straight jet'. 1917 A. G. Empey Over Top 299 *Mass formation*, a close order formation in which the Germans attack. 1948 E. Pound Pisan Cantos (1949) lxxvii. 49 By getting me onto the commission To inspect the mass graves at Katin. 1972 New Statesman 28 Jan. 109/3 The communists..murdered several thousand political prisoners, whose bodies were later discovered..in three separate mass graves. 1974 Times 4 Sept. 8/1 Turkish troops today uncovered more bodies from the mass grave at the Turkish Cypriot village of Maratha. 1951 M. McLuhan Mech. Bride (1967) 10/2 Power, glitter and mass hypnosis engendered by regular ranks. 1967 G. Playfair Prodigy iii. 82 There was..an element of mass-hypnosis in Bettymania, as there is in all such manifestations of idolatry. 1946 R. Campbell Talking Bronco 61 Mass-hypnotized, dinned drunken by the tireless Mechanic repetition of the wireless. 1934 A. Huxley Beyond Mexique Bay 276 The mindless mass hysteria of howling mobs. 1954 Economist 22 May 611/1 Yet Mr Graham does not produce mass hysteria, although he is certainly dramatic. 1969 Milgram & Toch in Lindzey & Aronson Handbk. Social Psychol. (ed. 2) IV. xxxv. 507 Such diverse phenomena as 'collective excitement, social unrest.., riots.., mass hysteria, [etc.]'. 1973 Times 7 Dec. 19/4 There is an argument for introducing rationing in London where some form of mass hysteria seems to have occurred. 1949 Koestler Promise & Fulfilment vii. 69 The next transformation came after the First World War when mass immigration started in earnest. 1973 Times 5 Dec. 18/2 Israel was founded on..mass immigration as the dynamic of growth. 1937 C. Madge in C. Day Lewis Mind in Chains 147 A fact of to-day which is so near to us that it is hard for us to see it is mass-literacy. 1967 Economist 15 Apr. p. i/3 The Franklin Book Programs Inc..uses all kinds of techniques from mass-literacy and mass-distribution schemes to training programmes. 1934 T. S. Eliot Rock i. 46 Those whose souls are choked and swaddled In the..new winding sheets of mass-made thought. 1959 V. Packard Status Seekers (1960) i. 3 They can dine on mass-merchandised vichyssoise. Ibid. 4 Everybody could enjoy the good things of life—as defined by mass merchandisers. 1962 S. Strand Marketing Dict. 442 *Mass merchandising*, a large-scale selling method, appealing to the population as a whole with convincing advertising. 1972 R. H. Buskirk et al. Concepts of Business xii. 169 The mass-merchandising specialty store..frequently calls itself a discount house. 1901 E. A. Ross Social Control xxix. 396 The common perils of war or mass migration may call for stricter corporate discipline. 1935 Huxley & Haddon We Europeans ix. 273 Mass-migration and military conquest. 1932 H. J. Massingham World without End x. 264 A man or woman who deserts his or her distinctive colour of being and joins the mass-mind. 1936 G. M. Young Victorian Eng. xxviii. 158 The propagandist, the advertiser and all other agents of the mass-mind. 1955 Koestler Trail of Dinosaur iii. 242 An unexpected mutation of the mass-mind may occur. 1964 M. McLuhan Understanding Media xi. 107 Creating the paradox of the 'mass mind' and the mass militarism of citizen armies. 1934 Webster, Mass-minded. 1942 D. Powell Time to be Born (1943) xii. 280 The masses of women..too mass-minded in their ambitions to be even faintly understood by her. 1939 H. J. Massingham Countryman's Jrnl. xxxiii. 143 It is good for a man..to converse with his own spirit or what mass-mindedness has left of it. 1961 Ann. Reg. 1960 430 The first of these was Eugene Ionesco's Rhinoceros, a savage satire on mass-mindedness. 1897 Amer. Jrnl. Sociol. Nov. 344 They are cultivating mass sympathies and drilling themselves in mass movements. 1927 D. H. Lawrence Let. 11 July (1932) 684 They [sc. the Germans] are capable of mass-movement. 1935 Discovery Oct. 292/1 Occasional mass-movements, like those of the lemmings of Scandinavia, were not to be confused with true migration. 1939 Encycl. Brit. Bk. of Year 19/2 In the United States there is taking place what may roughly be termed a mass movement towards Adult Education. 1967 H. Arendt Orig. Totalitarianism (new ed.) x. 313 The decisive differences between nineteenth-century mob organizations and twentieth-century mass movements are difficult to perceive. 1931 S. Nearing (title) War: organized destruction and mass murder by civilized nations. 1945 R. A. Knox God & Atom vi. 79 Democracy labours for breath, when the power of mass-murder is concentrated..in the hands of a few. 1958 Times Lit. Suppl. 13 June 334/3 His solution for the whole problem of mass-murders is 'family-love'. 1967 H. Arendt Orig. Totalitarianism (new ed.) xii. 421 The bulk of the armed SS served at the Eastern front where they were used for 'special assignments'—usually mass murder. 1952 B. Wolfe Limbo (1953) vii. 80 Look at this baby-faced mass murderer. 1960 Sunday Express 25 Dec. 10/2 A reprieved mass-murderer in Dartmoor. 1947 'G. Orwell' Eng. People 22 The Communist Party [in Britain]..has never shown signs of growing into a mass party of the kind that exists in France. 1954 B. & R. North tr. Duverger's Pol. Parties i. ii. 63 The mass-party technique in effect replaces the capitalist financing of electioneering by democratic financing. 1956 C. W. Mills Power Elite xiii. 310 The increased means of mass persuasion that are available. 1960 J. B. Priestley Lit. & Western Man ii. 16 The time of vast urban masses and all our techniques of mass persuasion. 1950 Koestler et al. God that Failed 65 Independent of the mass-propaganda methods of the Münzenberg enterprises. 1967 H. Arendt Orig. Totalitarianism (new ed.) viii. 264 Entirely new and complicated forms of mass propaganda were adopted by all parties. 1900 Amer. Jrnl. Sociol. Jan. 521 This is the reason why ethnology is finding its most promising developments today in the line of ethnic or folk-psychology, which is only a cross-section of mass-psychology. 1916 B. Russell Princ. Social Reconstruction ii. 60 Even the few questions which are left to the popular vote are decided by a diffused mass-psychology. 1929 Chesterton Thing xxii. 166 The abandonment of individual reason, in favour of press stunts and suggestion and mass psychology. 1937 Koestler Spanish Testament ii. 308, I could wish that everyone who talks of mass psychology should experience a year of prison. 1960 H. Read Forms of Things Unknown iv. xi. 179 A resort to mass psychology is evasive. 1938 Times Lit. Suppl. 17 Sept. 598/1 The mass-public does not want opinion, it wants news. 1960 New Left Rev. May–June 65/2 Personalities..with an existence quite different in tone from the mass public. 1939 War Weekly 25 Oct. 1313/1 First night mass raid on London... On the Tuesday night, a night mass air attack was tried for the first time. 1929 Publishers' Weekly 19 Oct. 1928/1 Our shop, like other small shops, is not geared for mass selling or mass buying. 1968 Listener 29 Aug. 285/3 There is now hardly a significant publication, from the weekly reviews to the mass-selling dailies, which does not have equity in one or other of the programme-contracting companies. 1948 T. S. Eliot Notes Def. Culture ii. 40 This gives it [sc. 'bourgeois' society] a difference in kind from the aristocratic society which preceded it, and from the mass-society which is expected to follow it. 1950 Antioch Rev. X. 382 Mass society is no more stable under dictatorship than it is under democracy. 1957 F. Williams Dangerous Estate: Anat. Newspapers xviii. 285 The straits to which an industrial mass-society has brought millions of its members. 1967 G. Steiner Lang. & Silence 69 The possibility that..certain elements in the technological mass-society..have done injury to language is the underlying theme of this book. 1901 E. Ross Social Control 148 In public opinion there is something which is not praise or blame, and this residuum is mass suggestion. 1920 W. McDougall Group Mind ii. 42 A proposition which voices the mind of the crowd..and so comes with the power of a mass-suggestion. 1924 W. B. Selbie Psychol. Relig. 116 We have here to reckon with the influence of mass suggestion. 1947 Mind LVI. 60 There can be mass suggestion, there are methods of group persuasion, but reasoning is carried on by each of us not only for himself but by himself. 1937 M. Covarrubias Island of Bali (1972) vii. 199 The famous krisses of the kings of South Bali taken by the Dutch as war booty at the time of the great mass-suicide of Den Pasar in 1906. 1959 Manch. Guardian 9 July 6/6 A..policy of mass suicide masquerading as a policy of defence. 1924 Public Opinion 30 May 528/3 Our modern saints of co-operative mass-thinking. 1958 R. Williams Culture & Society iii. 298 Mass-thinking, mass-suggestion, mass-prejudice would threaten to swamp considered individual thinking and feeling. 1953 Phil. Trans. R. Soc. A. CCXLV. 535 The mass-transport velocity can be very different from that predicted by Stokes on the assumption of a perfect, non-viscous fluid. 1957 G. E. Hutchinson Treat. Limnol. I. v. 347 The small deepwater waves of negligible amplitude..produce virtually no mass transport of water. 1974 A.I.Ch.E. Jrnl. XX. 88/1 One of the potential advantages of slurry reactors is reduction of intraparticle mass transport resistances. 1937 'G. Orwell' Road to Wigan Pier viii. 153, I wanted to see what mass-unemployment is like at its worst. 1965 J. L. Hanson Dict. Econ. 387 Mass unemployment is the most serious type since it is due to a general deficiency of demand. 1974 Times 5 Nov. 15/3 The monetarists fear that some unemployment may be the necessary price of avoiding mass unemployment.

d. mass action, (*a*) *Chem.*, the effect which the concentration of a reactant has on the rate of a chemical reaction; (*b*) the action of a mass of people; **mass balance** *Aeronaut.*, a

state in which inertial coupling between the angular movement of a control surface and other degrees of freedom of the aircraft is eliminated, so avoiding flutter of the surface; also, a mass attached to a control surface to bring about such a state; also as *v. trans.*; so **mass-balanced** *ppl. a.*, **mass-balancing** *vbl. sb.*; **mass concrete,** concrete which is not reinforced; **mass defect,** a deficiency of mass; *spec.* in *Nuclear Physics*, the sum of the masses of the constituent particles of a nucleus, as free individuals, less the mass of the nucleus (a quantity which effectively represents the binding energy needed to disperse the particles of the nucleus); **mass distribution,** the distribution of goods in bulk; **mass-effect,** (*a*) (see quot. 1902); (*b*) *Metallurgy*, the effect of size and shape in causing different rates of cooling, and so different hardnesses, in different parts of an object following heat treatment; (*c*) (usu. in *pl.*) a total or 'grand' effect; (*d*) an effect due to or dependent on mass; **mass-energy,** (*a*) the property of which mass and energy are regarded as different but interconvertible manifestations, being related by the equation $E = mc^2$ (propounded by Einstein in *Ann. d. Physik* (1905) XVIII. 641), where E is the energy equivalent of a mass m and c is the speed of light; (*b*) *attrib.*, relating to (the equivalence of) mass and energy; **mass man,** a hypothetical average man; one typical of mass society, characterized by a lack of individuality and a tendency to be manipulated by stereotyped ideas from the mass media; **mass market,** the market for mass-produced goods; also (with hyphen) as *vb.*; hence **mass-marketed** *ppl. a.*, **mass-marketing** *vbl. sb.*; **mass meeting** (earlier and later examples); also *transf.* and *fig.*; **mass noun,** a noun which in common usage lacks a plural form (opp. **count-noun*); **mass number** *Nuclear Physics*, the total number of protons and neutrons in an atomic nucleus; **mass phenomenon** (see quot. 1968); **mass-point** *Physics*, an entity conceived as having mass and (like a geometrical point) occupying a position but lacking spatial extension; **mass radiography,** radiography of the chests of large numbers of people by a quick routine method; **mass-ratio,** the ratio of the masses of two things; *spec.* in *Aeronaut.*, the ratio of the mass of a rocket with full fuel tanks to that of the same rocket with empty fuel tanks; **mass-reflex** *Physiol.*, (in patients who have suffered gross injury to the spinal cord) a reflex which may involve all parts of the body innervated from the part of the spinal cord below the lesion; **mass spectrograph,** a type of mass spectrometer (in the broader sense) in which deflected ions are made to strike a photographic plate so as to produce a photographic mass spectrum; hence *mass-spectrographic* adj.; **mass spectrometer,** any instrument in which material in a vacuum is ionized and the resulting ions are formed into a beam, separated according to the ratios of their mass to their net electric charge (e.g. by deflecting them in a magnetic field or accelerating them in an electric field), and then detected; *esp.* one in which the detection is done electrically rather than photographically; so **mass spectrometry;** also *mass-spectrometric* adj., *-spectrometrically* adv.; **mass spectroscope** (*rare*), an instrument for producing a mass spectrum; a mass spectrometer (in the broader sense); **mass spectroscopy,** the art of using the mass spectrometer or mass spectrograph; that branch of science which involves the use of these instruments; so *mass-spectroscopic* adj.; **mass spectrum,** a record obtained with a mass spectrometer or mass spectrograph, in which ions from a sample material are represented as dispersed according to their mass-to-charge ratio; **mass transfer** *Chemical Engin.*, movement of one substance through or into another on a molecular scale; **mass unit** = *atomic mass unit* (s.v. *ATOMIC *a.* and *sb.* A. 1); **mass wasting** *Geomorphol.*, movement of rock, soil, fallen snow, or the like under the influence of gravity; **mass-word** = **mass noun.* See also *MASS MEDIUM, *MASS OBSERVATION, *MASS PRODUCTION.

1891 G. M'GOWAN tr. *E. von Meyer's Hist. Chem.* 461 Berthollet..deduced precisely the opposite from his own assumption—that mass-action comes into play in chemical processes. **1903** H. C. JONES *Princ. Inorg. Chem.* xxviii. 346 If these crystals are redissolved in more water, and the solution evaporated to crystallization, the neutral salt will separate, showing a further splitting off of sulphuric acid due to the mass action of the water. **1924** W. B. SELBIE *Psychol. Relig.* 73 It is not only that mass action has a marked effect upon the will, but that [etc.]. **1958** R. WILLIAMS *Culture & Society* III. 298 The derived ideas have arisen from urbanization..from the working class, mass-action. **1970** PASSMORE & ROBSON *Compan. Med. Stud.* II. iii. 1/2 Whatever the nature of a receptor, its reaction with a drug is presumably chemical and can be described by the Law of Mass Action. **1974** *Daily Tel.* 17 Sept. 6/3 He went on to justify the disruption of academic life during student campaigns, and said that mass action in support of student policies would go ahead. **1931** *Flight* 11 Sept. 906/1 The control surfaces have been mass-balanced in order to reduce the risk of flutter. **1935** PIPPARD & PRITCHARD *Aeroplane Struct.* (ed. 2) xii. 238 A bob weight used to give mass balance to an aileron should be placed as far outboard of any point of wing support as possible. **1959** J. L. NAYLER *Dict. Aeronaut. Engin.* 168 The mass balance may be a single lump of metal or be distributed along the span of the control surface and connected to it by a series of links. **1966** F. G. IRVING *Introd. Longitudinal Static Stability Low-Speed Aircraft* viii. 82 Full mass-balance..may not be required as an anti-flutter measure on slow-speed aircraft. **1934** *Jrnl. R. Aeronaut. Soc.* XXXVIII. 76 Aeroplanes employing mass-balanced ailerons. *Ibid.*, Those [aeroplanes] in which the anti-flutter device of mass-balancing is incorporated. **1947** C. F. TOMS *Introd. Aeronaut.* v. 195 There can arise cases in which dynamic mass-balancing with a single mass is not possible and two masses are required. **1972** T. H. G. MEGSON *Aircraft Struct.* xiii. 468 The position of the inertia axis may be adjusted by a redistribution of wing weight, a process known as mass-balancing. **1930** *Engineering* 25 July 101/2 After the completion of the mass concrete foundation, the reinforcement was erected for the columns. **1924** J. G. A. SKERL tr. *Wegener's Orig. Continents & Oceans* xi. 160 Subterranean mass-defect and mass-excess above the sea-level..mutually counterbalance, isostasy thus prevailing in mountain masses. **1927** F. W. ASTON in *Proc. R. Soc.* A. CXV. 510 There would have been no loss of energy, that is mass defect, in the latter [*sc.* alpha particles] to represent the binding forces holding the four particles together. **1962** H. D. BUSH *Atomic & Nucl. Physics* iii. 69 According to the principle of the equivalence of mass and energy, the mass defect is equivalent to the energy necessary to separate the constituent particles: $\Delta E = c^2.\Delta M$. This relation shows that a mass defect of one a.m.u. is equivalent to a binding energy of 931×10^6 eV (931 MeV). **1936** J. F. PYLE *Marketing Princ.* (ed. 2) xviii. 575 Mass distribution, the corollary of mass production, is made possible through the effective use of sales-promotional methods and devices. **1951** C. W. MILLS *White Collar* I. ii. 26 What good would your mass production be without our mass distribution? **1967** *Economist* 15 Apr. p. i/3 One of the most effective spearheads of American book publishing..uses all kinds of techniques from mass-literacy and mass-distribution schemes to training programmes. **1902** HILLEBRAND & PENFIELD in *Amer. Jrnl. Sci.* CLXIV. 217 The alkalies and lead play so small a rôle, and the remaining constituents so prominent a part in the complex chemical molecules, that the latter control or dominate the crystallization by virtue of what may be called their mass-effect. **1925** *Jrnl. Iron & Steel Inst.* CXII. 473 (*heading*) Initial temperature and mass effects in quenching. **1934** WEBSTER II. 1510/2 Arranged in or involving masses, as a mass effect. **1936** *Mind* XLV. 226 It may be true that macroscopic phenomena involve—or, if we like to say so, are mass-effects of—large quantum numbers. **1939** CARPENTER & ROBERTSON *Metals* II. xvi. 1362 To discover whether duralinium was subject to mass-effect in the same way as steel, Teed quenched 5 in. diam. and 0·564 in. diam. bars of the same material from 490°C. into water. **1945** H. D. SMYTH *Gen. Acct. Devel. Atomic Energy Mil. Purposes* iv. 35 It was found that the total absorption of neutrons by such spheres could be expressed in terms of a 'surface' effect and a 'mass' effect. **1947** A. EINSTEIN *Mus. Romantic Era* xvi. 248 The rhythmic piquancy and the mass-effects of Auber. **1968** D. R. CLIFFE *Technical Metall.* v. 112 The actual cooling rate depends upon several factors, including the diameter of the bar or thickness of section (i.e. mass effect). **1970** G. K. WOODGATE *Elem. Atomic Struct.* ii. 28 This is an example of isotope shift arising from the normal mass effect. **1935** *Proc. R. Soc.* A. CXLIX. 415 The data..afford strong evidence of the validity of the laws of conservation of mass-energy, and of momentum, in some atomic transmutations. **1938** EINSTEIN & INFELD *Evolution of Physics* 208 According to the theory of relativity, there is no distinction between mass and energy... Instead of two conservation laws we have only one, that of mass-energy. **1942** J. D. STRANATHAN *'Particles' of Mod. Physics* ix. 374 According to the mass-energy equivalence concept, the rest mass of an electron represents an energy $V = ..0{\cdot}511 \times 10^6$ EV. **1968** M. S. LIVINGSTON *Particle Physics* i. 6 The released energy [in fission and fusion] comes from the excess mass which is transformed into energy... We can compute the energy release through the Einstein equivalence relation $E = mc^2$. This mass energy was stored in the heavy nuclei and in the very light nuclei in the form of excess mass at the time our galaxy was formed. **1928** A. HUXLEY *Point Counter Point* v. 76 They were armed to protect individuality from the mass man, the mob. **1945** H. READ *Coat Many Colours* lxxi. 348 Screwed-up tissue papers, cigar butts, all the characteristic droppings of Mass-man. **1966** D. JENKINS *Educated Society* ii. 70 They will become increasingly dependent on the public media..on the way to becoming mass-men. **1973** *Black World* May 8/1 Black community newspapers and talk shows on Black radio stations are other avenues for reaching our mass man. **1959** *Times* 9 Mar. (Britain's Food Suppl.) p. vii/7 The housewife who has an outside job now forms an important factor in the mass-market. **1959** *Time* 16 Mar. 61/1 An ultrasonic dishwasher for the home is already technically feasible but too expensive to mass-market. **1962** *Guardian* 7 Feb. 8/1 The mass-market furniture designers. **1971** *Engineering* Apr. 41/3 For which their whole mass-market philosophy had prepared them. **1960** *New Left Rev.* Sept.–Oct. 3/2 Mass-marketed commodities. **1945** B. NASH *Developing Marketable Products* ii. 23 This relationship between the large-volume manufacturer, the many different users, and the mechanisms of mass marketing is typified by the activities of every manufacturer using mass-marketing methods. **1733** B. LYNDE *Diary* (1880) 39 Our mass meeting at which the village intend to urge their being a township. **1851** A. O. HALL *Manhattaner* 4 We steamed..by mass meetings of democratic looking logs and snags. **1880** A. E. HOUSMAN *Let.* 10 May (1971) 20 They were chairing Harcourt from the station to a mass-meeting at the Martyrs' Memorial. **1904** WODEHOUSE *Gold Bat* viii. 90 They would never run the risk involved in holding mass-meetings in one another's studies. **1960** R. CAMPBELL *Coll. Poems* III. 73 In the mass-meeting of the waves. **1970** *Daily Tel.* 17 Apr. 2 Their 10-man executive committee would be calling a mass meeting of the 2,000-strong student body. **1933** L. BLOOMFIELD *Lang.* xii. 205 Mass nouns never take *a* and have no plural. **1963** *Language* XXXIX. 209 The mass noun *blood* in the singular takes *the* and *some* but not numerical quantifiers. **1965** [see *COUNT *sb.*[1] 9]. **1970** *Archivum Linguisticum* I. 24 There is no special class of mass-nouns in Portuguese marked by the absence of metaphony. **1923** F. W. ASTON in *Phil. Mag.* XLV. 945 These integers are provisionally called 'mass-numbers'. The mass-number may be taken to represent the number of protons in the atom. **1946** *Electronic Engin.* XVIII. 153/2 The separation of the uranium isotope of mass number 235..from that of mass number 238..constituted one of the major investigations in the development of the atomic bomb. **1962** H. D. BUSH *Atomic & Nucl. Physics* iii. 63 A nuclide is indicated by the chemical symbol with the mass number as a superscript and atomic number as a subscript, the latter often being omitted. For example, $_7N^{14}$ or N^{14} refers to one of the isotopes of nitrogen ($Z = 7$), namely the one which has mass number 14. **1936** J. R. KANTOR *Objective Psychol. Gram.* iii. 32 Comparative grammar deals with auditory–vocal mass phenomena. **1954** R. W. BROWN in G. Lindzey *Handbk. Social Psychol.* II. xxiii. 833/2 Social scientists have not been content to define mass phenomena as collective misbehavior. **1967** H. ARENDT *Orig. Totalitarianism* (new ed.) ix. 277 Statelessness, the newest mass phenomenon in contemporary history. **1968** A. F. C. WALLACE in *Internat. Encycl. Social Sci.* X. 55/2 'Mass phenomenon' signifies that class of social event in which a large number of people at the same time behave in a way which constitutes a notable interruption of their routine, socially sanctioned role behavior. **1911** J. WARD *Realm of Ends* xii. 255 The mass-points of the modern physicist.. Leibniz held to be only phenomenal. **1956** E. H. HUTTEN *Lang. Mod. Physics* vi. 243 Newtonian mechanics..treats only of such phenomena as can be described in terms of a few concepts, e.g. masspoint, force, etc. **1971** *Amer. Jrnl. Physics* XXXIX. 484/2 Consider a finite one-dimensional mass-point lattice in which nearest neighbors are joined by massless ideal springs. **1943** *Electronic Engin.* XVI. 108 Equipment for mass radiography installed in a large industrial concern for examination of the workers. **1954** E. JENKINS *Tortoise & Hare* x. 114 These mobile X-ray units for mass radiography. **1971** *Brit. Med. Bull.* XXVII. 93/2 Of the people screened by mass radiography..a large number have disabilities that warrant referral to a medical practitioner. **1946** A. S. EDDINGTON *Fund. Theory* ii. 32 (*heading*) Mass-ratio of the proton and electron. **1949** W. LEY *Conquest of Space* (1950) i. 26 The mass-ratio is 2·7:1 —that is,..the rocket at take-off weighs 2·7 times as much as its empty hull, machinery and payload. **1958** *New Scientist* 9 Jan. 19 To obtain an intercontinental range of 2,500 miles requires a mass ratio of 12:1, to achieve a satellite orbit requires a ratio of 25:1, and to escape to the Moon needs a ratio of 100:1... The German V2 had a mass ratio of only 3·2:1. **1968** R. A. LYTTLETON *Mysteries Solar Syst.* i. 42 The Earth and Mars can be paired together satisfactorily as components resulting from a single rotationally unstable planet since their mass-ratio is as high as 9:1. **1917** HEAD & RIDDOCH in *Brain* XL. 233 It is evident, therefore, that under certain conditions the spinal cord below the level of the lesion may show signs of diffuse reflex activity. Scratching the sole of the foot may not only evoke a flexor spasm, but may cause premature evacuation of the bladder and an outburst of excessive sweating. This we have spoken of as a 'mass-reflex'. **1970** M. HOLLANDER tr. *Monnier's Functions Nervous Syst.* II. xii. 242 A mass reflex is an irradiation phenomenon consisting of flexion of the legs with visceromotor reflexes: sweating, micturition and defecation. **1920** F. W. ASTON in *Phil. Mag.* XXXIX. 611 The Positive Ray Spectrograph or, as it may be more conveniently termed, Mass-Spectrograph. **1945** H. D. SMYTH *Gen. Acct. Devel. Atomic Energy Mil. Purposes* x. 109 Kellex, whose mass spectrograph methods of isotope analysis were sufficiently advanced as to become of great value to the project, as in analyzing samples of enriched uranium. **1963** J. B. FARMER in C. A. McDowell *Mass Spectrometry* ii. 8 The primary, although not the exclusive, task of mass spectrographs is..mass comparison... Mass spectrometers are primarily useful for work involving abundance determination. **1935** *Proc. R. Soc.* A. CL. 253 The masses which we have suggested give a much closer fit with the observed transmutation data than do the mass-spectrographic values. **1957** G. E. HUTCHINSON *Treat. Limnol.* I. iii. 215 The more modern mass spectrographic determinations..indicate very clearly that..the D and O^{18} contents [of water] vary concomitantly. **1932** *Physical Rev.* XL. 429 A new type of mass spectrometer..in which no magnetic fields are used. **1955** *New Biol.* XVIII. 66 It is possible by using a mass-spectrometer to determine the proportions of heavy nitrogen, N^{15}, and the normally more abundant isotope, N^{14}, in a given sample. **1963** Mass spectrometer [see *mass spectrograph* above]. **1966** A. J. AHEARN *Mass Spectrometric Analysis of Solids* i. 2 In the past, the term mass spectrometer was reserved for electrical detection. However, the term mass spectrometry is now the generally accepted designation for this mass analysis technique regardless of the type of detection employed. **1969** PRICE & WILLIAMS *Time-of-Flight Mass Spectrometry* p. ix, There are now about 300 time-of-flight mass spectrometers in use throughout the world. **1966** D. G. BRANDON *Mod. Techniques Metallogr.* iii. 124 We shall also consider the possi-

bility of ion-bombarding a specimen to sputter a thin layer from the surface, followed by a mass-spectrometric analysis of the atoms in this layer. *Ibid.* 172 The surface of the sample is bombarded by positive ions, and the sputtered ions are collected and analysed mass-spectrometrically. **1952** (*title*) Mass spectrometry (Inst. Petroleum, London). **1974** *Nature* 29 Mar. 458/1 The first fraction..was evaporated to dryness and subjected to mass spectrometry... Molecular ions at m/e 420 and m/e 448 are consistent with the presence of a mixture of palmitic and stearic aldehyde 2,4-dinitrophenylhydrazones. **1958** H. E. DUCKWORTH *Mass Spectroscopy* 204 Mass spectroscopes. **1963** J. B. FARMER in C. A. McDowell *Mass Spectrometry* ii. 7 The term mass spectroscope is applied to any device which has the ability to separate gaseous ions according to mass–charge ratio. **1938** R. W. LAWSON tr. *Hevesy & Paneth's Man. Radioactivity* (ed. 2) xix. 178 Mass-spectroscopic investigations. **1968** M. S. LIVINGSTON *Particle Physics* vi. 120 The results of mass-spectroscopic measurements have been summarized from time to time to deduce by least-squares analysis the best values of atomic masses. **1926** R. W. LAWSON tr. *Hevesy & Paneth's Man. Radioactivity* xviii. 135 Not until the method of mass-spectroscopy had been devised and developed was it possible to establish that many of the ordinary elements are..mixed elements. **1958** H. E. DUCKWORTH *Mass Spectroscopy* i. 10 For many years photographic plates had served as the standard ion detectors in mass spectroscopy, but in the early 1930's these began to be supplanted by systems of electrical detection. **1920** F. W. ASTON in *Phil. Mag.* XXXIX. 611 (*heading*) The mass-spectra of chemical elements. *Ibid.* 625 A positive ray spectrograph capable of giving a focussed mass-spectrum is..described. **1966** *Encycl. Industr. Chem. Analysis* II. 465 Mass spectra are related in a direct and simple way to molecular structure, thereby providing a unique and characteristic spectrum for each molecule which can be vaporized in the ion source. **1937** W. H. WALKER et al. *Princ. Chem. Engin.* (ed. 3) xiv. 447 The mass transfer from the main body of the gas to the interface can be visualized as meeting two resistances in series, that of the turbulent main body of gas and that of the gas film. **1962** J. C. WRIGHT *Metall. in Nucl. Power Technol.* ix. 169 Mass transfer between ferrous constructional materials and a sodium coolant circuit is accelerated if the oxygen content exceeds 30 p.p.m. by weight. **1971** R. HARDBOTTLE tr. *Grassman's Physical Princ. Chem. Engin.* ix. 553 A typical feature of mass transfer is the slowing down of transfer of the migrating components by components not participating in mass transfer. **1942** POLLARD & DAVIDSON *Appl. Nucl. Physics* v. 74 If a positron is emitted it must be treated as costing 0·0011 mass unit or 1 Mev extra. **1953** BARNETT & WILSON *Inorg. Chem.* iv. 28 There has been a loss of 0·0184 mass units. **1966** GUCKER & SEIFERT *Physical Chem.*(1967) ii. 25 Prior to 1961 two different mass units were used: the physical mass unit.. and the chemical mass unit. **1951** *Ohio Jrnl. Sci.* LI. 299 (*heading*) Mass wasting, classification and damage in Ohio. **1968** R. W. FAIRBRIDGE *Encycl. Geomorphol.* 697/2 Frequently the immediate cause of mass wasting can be related directly to changes in shearing stress brought about by (1) increase in the weight of materials, (2) withdrawal of support, or (3) earth tremors. **1914** O. JESPERSEN *Mod. Eng. Gram.* II. v. 115 Words which represent 'uncountables'..are here called mass-words; they may be either material..such as *silver, quicksilver, water, butter*,..or else immaterial, such as *leisure, music, traffic, progress*, [etc.]. **1935** *Jrnl. Eng. & Germ. Philol.* XXXIV. 429 Masswords (like *gold, embers, knowledge*). **1954** PEI & GAYNOR *Dict. Ling.* 133 *Mass-word*, Jespersen's term for words denoting concepts, properties or things which ordinarily cannot be separated into distinct component units.

Mass, *sb.*[4] Var. MAS, *MARS(E.
1837 *Southern Lit. Messenger* III. 174 Mass Phil been very uneasy about you.

Massa. For def. read: Representing *master* in the written form of Negro speech. Also **massa.** (Add further examples.)
1821 P. EGAN *Life in London* II. v. 289 But the black *slavey*, who is entering the room, is singing out, '*Massa*, you ought to be shamed.' **1935** in Z. N. Hurston *Mules & Men* (1970) I. i. 25 It was night and Ole Massa sent John, his favorite slave, down to the spring to get him a cool drink of water. **1953** *Caribbean Q.* III. III. 157 As one writer put it:..It has ever been their practice, to prevent the extension of useful practical knowledge, other than the hewing of cane fields, and feeding the mill, to the Negro lest he may one day rise to the rank of an Overseer, and supersede Massa Busher (Overseer). **1973** *Sunday Express* (Trinidad & Tobago) 8 Apr. 13/3 Day after day he sat glued to the t.v. and behaved generally as though he didn't know 'massa day is done'. **1973** J. RYDER *Trevayne* (1974) xi. 94 'I'll set up interviews.' Bonner looked at Andrew and laughed. '*Your* interviews, massa.'

massage, *sb.* Add: Now usu. with pronunc. (mæ·-). (Further examples.) Also *fig.*
1907 *Yesterday's Shopping* (1969) 538/3 Massage Rollers, for the face..13/0. **1929** H. WALPOLE *Hans Frost* II. iii. 143 Then with that by now practised and customary spiritual massage she set to work on herself. **1963** E. H. EDWARDS *Saddlery* xxii. 168 A convenient and efficient massage pad..can be made from leather stuffed with hay. **1966** J. S. COX *Illustr. Dict. Hairdressing* 97/1 *Massage oil*, an oil which is applied to the scalp to aid the process of massage and increase its beneficial effect. **1969** E. H. PINTO *Treen* 17 The massage roulette..is English, of mahogany, and was advertised for sale between 1880 and 1890. The three rollers revolve independently. **1973** *Times* 8 Aug. 7/1 At present £52m is spent annually on pills and low calorie foods, then there are health hydros, sauna baths, massage parlours, exercising machines, gymnasiums and slimming clubs.

b. Used *euphem.* for: sexual activity.
The expressions *massage establishment, parlour*, etc., used as signs outside a building, are frequently alleged to mean 'brothel' (see quots.).
1913 *Collier's* 25 Jan. 7/1 Along with them go the announcements of 'massage parlors' (an all-too-obvious euphemism), free whiskies, and other agencies of public injury. **1921** E. WEEKLEY *Etym. Dict. Mod. Eng.* 1416 *Stew*[1]..Brothel... The public hot-air baths acquired a reputation like that of our massage establishments some time ago. **1966** *Economist* 3 Sept. 894/2 The American authorities..allow their free-spending men to attract the usual proliferation of bars, night-clubs and 'massage parlours'. **1971** *Sunday Tel.* (Brisbane) 16 May 42/5 A sheriff's deputy herds a group of women arrested in raids last month on 22 'massage parlors' in Los Angeles. **1972** D. BLOODWORTH *Any Number can Play* ix. 66 The imitation opium den and the model massage parlour. **1972** *Screw* 12 June 33/3 (Advt.), A totally dominant English massage by a lovely female, in your home or office. **1972** *Times* 4 Nov. 9/1, I noticed a few discreet establishments that looked as unauthentic, or as authentic according to your viewpoint, as New York's massage parlours. **1973** *Publishers Weekly* 8 Jan. 66/2 There is a difference between what a massage used to be, and what it has come to be a euphemism for lately. **1973** *Listener* 5 Apr. 439/2 The bars and massage parlours are..to re-open. But where are the clients now?.. The Americans have gone. **1974** *Publishers Weekly* 29 Apr. 45/1 The 'massage parlors' which have mushroomed in America's big cities. *Ibid.*, Massage parlor prostitutes in New York. *Ibid.*, 'Massage parlor' prostitution is considered by many to be 'glamorous' therapy.

massage, *v.* Add: Now usu. with pronunc. (mæ·-). Also *transf.* and *fig.*. Hence **massa·ging,** *vbl. sb.*
1924 R. HICHENS *After Verdict* III. § 1. 314 Arabs were washing sacks below the dam and massaging them with persistently stamping bare brown feet. **1931** *Times Lit. Suppl.* 30 Apr. 340/2 'Shellacking', 'massaging'.., euphemisms which cover the long ordeal of beating, pounding..by which the detective learns the truth. **1936** F. CLUNE *Roaming round Darling* viii. 68 In the outer courtyard were several straw-hatted inmates in cover-alls massaging the lawns. **1966** *Aviation Week & Space Technol.* 5 Dec. 23/2 The interim has permitted an overall massaging of the initial reports, which resulted..in the revision that last week amounted to a major change in design philosophy for post-Apollo. **1974** *Globe & Mail* (Toronto) 23 Sept. 7/5 The Japanese government's efforts to massage the press coverage of the visit have been substantial. It offered to pay the fares of Canadian journalists to go to Tokyo for the interview and is bringing 30 Japanese journalists with the Prime Minister.

massager (mæ·sāʒəɹ). [f. MASSAGE *v.* or *sb.* + -ER[1].] **a.** One who practises massage, = MASSEUR, MASSEUSE.
1921 E. G. LOWRY *Washington Close-Ups* 85 He is..a politician to his finger tips and a strong josher; a real handshaker and an elbow massager.

b. A massaging machine.
1940 *Life* 4 Nov. 54 Wooden barrel massager with rollers like clothes wringers is designed for action on the hips and buttocks. **1969** E. M. BRECHER *Sex Researchers* (1970) x. 291 Dr. Dickinson was responsible..for the introduction into American gynecological practice of the electrical vibrator or massager. This device, applied to the mons area near the clitoris, produces intense erotic stimulation. **1969** 'J' *Sensuous Woman* (1970) iii. 29 Since the machine is advertised as a facial massager, you can purchase it without embarrassment.

Massagetæ (mæsagī·təi). Also **Massagetes.** [L. *Massagetæ*, Gr. *Μασσαγέται*, perh. f. native name *Masakata* Great Sakas.] An ancient Scythian people that lived to the east of the Caspian Sea.
1601 HOLLAND tr. *Pliny's Nat. Hist.* VI. xvii. 123 The principall nations of Scythia, bee the Saræ, Massagetæ, [etc.]. **1709** I. LITTLEBURY tr. *Herodotus' Hist.* I. I. 134 The Massagetes resemble the Scythians in their Habit and Way of Living. **1874** G. GROTE *Hist. Greece* III. II. xvii. 329 The Scythians, originally occupants of Asia, or the regions East of the Caspian, had been driven across the Araxês, in consequence of an unsuccessful war with the Massagetæ. **1911** J. G. FRAZER *Golden Bough: Magic Art* (ed. 3) I. i. 15 The Spartans, Persians, and Massagetae sacrificed horses to him [*sc.* the sun]. **1926** *Cambr. Anc. Hist.* IV. i. 15 Cyrus died fighting... His opponents were the Massagetae, a savage race who occupied the great plain to the East of the Caspian. **1967** C. A. ROBINSON *Anc. Hist.* (ed. 2) xxi. 410 The first business of the Greek king of Bactria was to protect this land, the gateway of Iran, from the semibarbarism of the north, and in particular to guard against the strong confederacy of the Massagetae, who were massed across the Oxus and Jaxartes rivers. **1969** J. CONWAY tr. *Bengtson's Greeks & Persians* xv. 318 Alexander was unable to capture him [*sc.* Spitamenes], but the Scythians beyond the Jaxartes, the Massagetae, to whom Spitamenes had fled, cut off his head and sent it to Alexander as a gift. **1973** G. WIDENGREN in D. J. Wiseman *Peoples Old Testament Times* xiii. 320 When Cyrus..again turned to the east, he ultimately suffered a defeat in a battle against some nomadic northern people of Iranian origin, either..the Massagetae ..or the Danae.

Massaliot(e: see *MASSILIOT *sb.* and *a.*

massasauga. Delete ‖ and for Latin names substitute: *Sistrurus*, esp. *S. catenatus*. Also *attrib.* (Earlier and later examples.)
1835 C. BRADLEY in *Ohio Archaeol. & Hist. Soc. Publ.* (1906) XV. 257, I learned that my conquered enemy was the massassagua, the Michigan rattlesnake. **1941** *Amer. Midland Naturalist* XXV. 659 (*title*) Habit and habitat studies of the massasauga rattlesnake. **1954** R. C. STEBBINS *Amphibians & Reptiles Western N. Amer.* 464/1 The massasauga is usually unaggressive, but the venom is dangerous.

massecuite (mæskwī·t). Also **masse cuite.** [Fr., lit. = cooked mass.] In sugar-making, the juice of the sugar-cane after concentration by boiling.
1882 *Spons' Encycl. Industr. Arts* v. 1927 The *massecuite* is quickly let out of the pan into a tank. **1886** *Harper's Mag.* June 88/2 After the *masse-cuite* has left the pan, the crystallization is completed by cooling. **1921** [see *box-hand* (*BOX *sb.*[2] 24)]. **1925** *Chambers's Jrnl.* June 368/2 This dark-looking mass of semi-liquid substance is called masse-cuite. **1968** *Encycl. Brit.* XXI. 379/2 The cycle ..varies from 2 minutes for very high-test massecuites to 15 minutes or more for low grades.

massed, *ppl. a.* Add: **1.** (Earlier example.) spec. *massed entry*: see quot. 1964.
1881 'MARK TWAIN' *Prince & Pauper* ix. 84 The massed world on the river burst into a mighty roar of welcome. **1955** W. W. GREG *Shakes. First Folio* v. 157 In *The Winter's Tale*..there are massed entries in all but two scenes, but some individual entries are repeated later on. **1964** F. BOWERS *Bibliogr. & Textual Crit.* v. i. 137 A massed entry is the notation at the start of a scene of the entrance in a group of all the characters, although some will make their entrances later at different points in the scene.

2. In reference to carved or written inscriptions, having the words arranged to form a solid column of lettering.
1906 A. E. R. GILL in E. Johnston *Writing & Illuminating* xvii. 392 In that space set out the Inscription, either 'Massed' or 'Symmetrical'. **1940** G. HEWITT *Lettering* xvi. 163 Italics..are not often successful when massed.

3. massed practice, training, trials *Psychol.*, a method of conditioning or training in which practice is concentrated with hardly any rest between repetitions.
1938 *Jrnl. Exper. Psychol.* XX. 201 The method of distributed practice should, therefore, yield relatively less accumulated inhibition than the method of massed practice. **1940** HILGARD & MARQUIS *Conditioning & Learning* vi. 148 Spaced practice favors conditioning over massed practice. **1949** B. J. UNDERWOOD *Exper. Psychol.* xi. 366 Several studies have shown that conditioning takes place more rapidly by distributed than by massed trials. *Ibid.* 631 *Massed training*, training in which trials are given in rapid succession with little if any time intervening between successive units of work. **1953** C. E. OSGOOD *Method & Theory Exper. Psychol.* III. xii. 504 The empirical law that 'distributed practice is superior to massed practice' has been found to hold under nearly all conditions. **1960** H. J. EYSENCK *Behaviour Therapy & Neuroses* i. 17 The extinction of 4 tics in a female patient by..repeated voluntary repetition of the tic by massed practice. **1969** W. MAYER-GROSS et al. *Clin. Psychiatry* (ed. 3) 186 The optimal technique was massed practice..followed by prolonged rest to permit the dissipation of reactive inhibition.

Massic (mæ·sik), *a. Obs.* exc. *Hist.* [ad. L. *Massic-us* the name of a mountain in Campania.] Designating an ancient wine produced in Campania, Italy. Also *ellipt.*
1638 T. HAWKINS tr. *Horace's Odes* I. i. 19 Some others use Old Massique wines to ply. **1653** B. HOLYDAY tr. *Horace's Odes* I. i. 19 In Massic Wines some bouze their time away. **1751** J. STIRLING tr. *Horace's Odes* I. i, in *Horace's Works* I. II. 2 Cups of old Massic. **1833** C. REDDING *Hist. Mod. Wines* 8 The Falernian..grew upon the volcanic Campania near Naples, where also the Massic was produced. **1920** *Punch* 15 Sept. 209, I raise my cup of massic Not to the earlier but the later 'classic'. **1961** H. W. ALLEN *Hist. Wine* v. 10 Massic appears to mean, not an individual wine, but any really fine Campanian wine. Virgil, Horace and Martial all use it in this rather general sense. **1965** O. A. MENDELSOHN *Dict. Drink* 214 *Massic*, a wine from Campania, Italy, mentioned in classical writings.

massif. a. Delete '?' and '(*obs.*)' and add later examples.
1966 *New Statesman* 13 May 701/2 Martin proposes to remove everything in favour of his uniform *massif* of offices. **1973** *Times* 9 Jan. 12/7 There must, dear God, be something between slums and concrete massifs.

massify (mæ·sifəi), *v.* [f. MASS *sb.*[2] + -IFY.] *trans.* To form into a mass, *spec.* a mass society. Also **massifica·tion; ma·ssified** *ppl. a.*
1954 W. G. PECK *Christian Econ.* i. 20 We shall further massify and denature our people. *Ibid.* x. 162 He has been calling for security through the further 'massification' of his society. **1961** R. WILLIAMS *Long Revolution* III. 350 What the Americans call the 'massification' of society can only happen..if a majority of the people whom they regard as 'the masses' accept this version of themselves. **1966** D. JENKINS *Educated Society* ii. 59 The Nazis carried to its ruthlessly logical conclusion the attitude of those who wish to massify society for their own ends. *Ibid.* iv. 176 [A] society suffering from a dull uniformity..is because people have become massified or because those in positions of privilege have become listless. **1967** D. COOPER *Psychiatry & Anti-Psychiatry* ii. 45 Human motivation in courts of law and also in massified political judgements. **1969** G. S. JONES in Cockburn & Blackburn *Student Power* 42 Although there has been a substantial increase in the number of students, there has been nothing like the same process of massification that has occurred in the USA or Japan.

‖ **mässig** (mę·sixʸ). *Mus.* [G.] = MODERATO *adv.*
1884 F. NIECKS *Conc. Dict. Mus. Terms* 171 *Mässig* (Ger.), Moderate. **1938** *Oxf. Compan. Mus.* 545/2 *Mässig* (Ger.), (a) 'Moderate', 'moderately'; (b) 'in the style of' (e.g. *Marschmässig*, 'in march style').

Massiliot (mæsi·liǫ̆t), *sb.* and *a.* Also **Massaliot, Massaliote, Massilian.** [f. L. *Massilia*, Gr. *Μασσαλία* Massalia.] **A.** *sb.* A native or inhabitant of Massalia (or Massilia, mod. Marseilles), a Greek colony founded *c* 600 B.C. to the east of the mouth of the Rhône on the Mediterranean coast of southern France. **B.** *adj.* Of or pertaining to Massalia or its inhabitants.

1601 P. HOLLAND tr. *Pliny's Nat. Hist.* III. iv. 55 Townes in the other parts..namely, Agatha, in times past belonging to the Massilians. **1856** GROTE *Hist. Greece* XII. II. xcviii. 614 In an age when piracy was common, the Massaliot ships and seamen were effective in attack and defence. *Ibid.* 615 Except the Phenicians and Carthaginians, these Massaliots were the only enterprising mariners in the Western Mediterranean. **1873** G. W. KITCHIN *Hist. France to 1453* I. ii. 23 The whole seaboard from Var to Rhone was given to the Massiliots. **1898** A. HASSAL *Jervis's Hist. France* (rev. ed.) i. 7 Pompey was beaten, and Cæsar's hand fell heavily on the Massiliots. **1932** *Times Lit. Suppl.* 8 Sept. 617/2 The voyage of the Massilian Pytheas. **1945** *Proc. Prehist. Soc.* XI. 56 Massilian coins have been obtained from the archaeological strata. **1949** *Oxf. Classical Dict.* 543/2 Massiliot seamen played an important part in the Second Punic War. **1957** *Encycl. Brit.* XIV. 965/1 The Massaliots made their way by prudence and by vigilant administration of their oligarchical government. *Ibid.*, In the 4th century B.C. the Massaliot Pytheas visited the coasts of Gaul. **1963** CARY & WARMINGTON *Anc. Explorers* (rev. ed.) ii. 36 Syracusan and Massilian traders could join hands in the ports of Rome. **1964** J. BOARDMAN *Greeks Overseas* v. 227 In the sixth century the Marseilles route is vouched for by the Massaliot and Phocaean pottery found at Mt Lassois. **1970** *Oxf. Classical Dict.* (ed. 2) 654/1 Massaliote ships helped Rome in the Second Punic War.

massily, *adv.* Delete '† *Obs.*' and add later example.

1922 E. R. EDDISON *Worm Ouroboros* vii. 75 Benches of green jasper massily built and laden with velvet cushions.

Massim (mæ·sim). Also **Misima.** The eastern Papuo-Melanesian people of the Territory of Papua New Guinea; also, a member of this people; the language of this people. Also as *adj.*

[**1889** E. T. HAMY in *Revue d'Ethnogr.* VII. 504 La plupart des Mélanésiens de la mer d'Entrecasteaux sont aujourd'hui appelés collectivement *Massims*.] **1893** S. H. RAY in *9th Internat. Congr. Orientalists* II. 760 Of these, the Misima is the same as the New Guinea Melanesian, whilst the Nada forms..show the pronouns usual as possessive suffixes. **1894** A. C. HADDON *Decorative Art Brit. New Guinea* 184 Following Dr. E. T. Hamy, I adopt the term Massims as a collective name for the mixed people inhabiting the archipelagoes off the south-east of New Guinea... The term Massim..originally arose from an imperfect knowledge of the island of Misima, but I employ it solely as a convenient conventional name. **1910** C. G. SELIGMANN *Melanesians Brit. New Guinea* 9 The most characteristic cultural feature of the Massim is the existence of a peculiar form of totemism with matrilineal descent. **1936** R. FIRTH *Art & Life New Guinea* 22 The Massim area, in the south-east, is particularly famous for the wealth of carving with which its spatulæ are embellished. **1961** B. A. L. CRANSTONE *Melanesia* 42 The prow-boards of Massim canoes..are always carved by specialists. **1971** M. W. YOUNG *Fighting with Food in Massim Society* iii. 54 Unlike in many areas of the Massim, men do not attribute malevolent supernatural powers to women.

massive, *a.* Add: **2. a.** (Further examples.) Now freq. used in weakened senses, 'large, great, far-reaching'.

1958 [see *AIR-LIFT 2]. **1958** G. KENNAN *Russia, Atom & West* v. 77 The Marxists claim, of course, that colonialism invariably represented a massive and cruel exploitation of the colonial peoples. **1958** *New Statesman* 6 Sept. 306/2 The tendency to make *massive* a substitute not merely for *enormous, immense* and *huge* but even for *large* and *extensive* as applying to all sorts of phenomena, social, financial, political and psychological. **1963** *Daily Mail* 25 Feb. 16/6 Cowdrey again showed massive good form to make 86 in 163 minutes. **1965** R. & D. MORRIS *Men & Snakes* ix. 201 We required a massive sample of the population. **1973** *Word 1970* XXVI. 119 He died suddenly of a massive heart attack.

e. massive retaliation, name given to a military strategy, inaugurated in the U.S.A. by J. F. Dulles in the 1950s, which uses the threat of a punitive response with thermonuclear weapons to deter aggression.

[**1954** *N.Y. Times* 13 Jan. 2/3 [Speech of J. F. Dulles] Local defense must be reinforced by the further deterrent of massive retaliatory power.] **1954** *Times* 29 Mar. 5/5 The plan of 'meeting any aggression with massive retaliation in places of our choosing'. **1955** *Bull. Atomic Sci.* Jan. 29/1 We believe that the announced concept of massive retaliation contains the elements of adequate military support to arrest the expansive aims of communism. **1959** *Times Lit. Suppl.* 25 Sept. 542/2 Mr. Dulles's 'massive retaliation' speech of January 1954..could hardly be read in the Soviet Union otherwise than as a threat. **1971** E. LUTTWAK *Dict. Mod. War* 128/1 Massive retaliation was never central US policy, and was in any case associated with the diplomatic technique of brinkmanship.

3. Also *Zool.*, applied to organisms which are compact in structure.

1888 ROLLESTON & JACKSON *Forms Animal Life* (ed. 2) 250 There appear to be two fresh-water Sponges in Great Britain... The former is branched, the latter massive and lobate.

massively, *adv.* (Later examples.)

1959 *Times Lit. Suppl.* 20 Feb. 97/2 The road of elaborate verbal analysis of a poem which the trained reader immediately and massively *feels* to be wrong. *Ibid.* 27 Feb. 113/3 We must have massively responded..to a poem..before we can usefully talk about it. **1962** *Listener* 29 Mar. 540/1 The Administration was never crystal-clear on exactly how we would massively retaliate with nuclear weapons. **1974** *Physics Bull.* Apr. 132/3 Past CEGB technological choices and commercial practices have resulted in massively unproductive investments.

massivity (mæsi·vĭti). [f. MASSIVE *a.* + -ITY.] The fact or condition of being massive.

1908 W. H. DAWSON *Evolution Mod. Germany* 13 Everywhere one sees the worship of massivity, the striving after crude, imposing effects—in the modern monuments, the public buildings, the bridges. **1921** S. GRAHAM *Europe* xiv. 186 A mighty stone structure, of great height and massivity. **1953** E. BARKER *Age & Youth* iv. 72 But New College had a massivity, if I may coin that word—an invisible massivity which matched the visible physical massivity of its chapel and hall and cloisters and tower—that captured my spirit and stretched my powers.

Mass-John: see MAS 2.

massless, *a.* Add: (Further examples.) Also **ma·sslessness.**

1947 *Mind* LVI. 50 Consider a weight of mass *m* hanging downwards under gravity on a (massless) elastic strand. **1963** K. W. FORD *World of Elementary Particles* 115 One necessary condition for masslessness seems to be the absence of charge. Every charged particle has mass, although not every neutral particle is massless. **1971** *Guinness Bk. Records* (ed. 18) v. 70/1 Of all sub-atomic concepts only the neutrino calls for masslessness. **1972** *Sci. Amer.* June 53/1 Massless uncharged particles that interact so little with other particles that the outer layers of the sun and solid bodies such as the earth are virtually transparent to them.

mass medium (mæ:s mī·dĭə̆m). [f. MASS *sb.*[2] + MEDIUM *sb.*] A medium of communication (such as radio, television, newspapers, etc.) that reaches a large number of people; usu. in pl. *mass media.*

The *pl.* form *mass media* is sometimes erroneously construed as *sing.*

1923 S. M. FECHHEIMER in N. T. Praigg *Advertising & Selling* v. 238 (*title*) Class appeal in mass media. *Ibid.*, The several million readers of a big mass medium. G. SNOW in *Ibid.* 240 Mass media represents the most economical way of getting the story over the new and wider market in the least time. **1942** D. WAPLES *Print, Radio & Film* 19 Radio (which, according to German propaganda theory, is the 'real' mass medium). **1946** J. S. HUXLEY *Unesco* ii. 58 The media of mass communication—the somewhat cumbrous title (commonly abbreviated to 'Mass Media') proposed for agencies, such as the radio, the cinema and the popular press, which are capable of the mass dissemination of word or image. *Ibid.* 60 The use of the mass media to foster education, science and culture... Regarded from this angle, the mass media fall into the same general category as the libraries and museums—that of servicing agencies for man's higher activities. **1957** R. HOGGART *Uses of Literacy* ii. 27 A great deal has been written about the effect on the working-classes of the modern 'mass media of communication'. **1964** M. ARGYLE *Psychol. & Social Probl.* vii. 101 Propaganda over the mass media may be intended to change behaviour, beliefs or feelings, or all three. *Ibid.* xiii. 157 Mass media such as TV, radio, newspapers and posters. **1966** N. TUCKER (*title*) Understanding the mass media. **1968** P. OLIVER *Screening Blues* 3 For the Negro in Tuscaloosa, Alabama.., the blues record afforded the first real opportunity of contact through a mass medium with others of his social status. **1971** *New Scientist* 18 Mar. 610/1 The department's trendy, mass-media sounding title is a historical accident. **1974** *Black World* Dec. 5/1 Nevertheless, the mass media continues to emphasize the attitudes, beliefs and rhetoric of a minority of the Black community.

mass observation (mæ:s ǫbzəɹvē·ʃən). [f. MASS *sb.*[2] + OBSERVATION.] The study and record of the social habits of people (taken in the mass); also (with capital initials) the name of an organization established for this purpose. Also *attrib.* So **mass-observationist, -observer; mass-observe** *v. trans.*

1933 L. BLOOMFIELD *Lang.* ii. 38 The observer..by this mass-observation, gives us a statement of the speech-habits of a community. **1937** MADGE & HARRISSON *Mass-Observation* 8 If after reading the pamphlet you should wish to co-operate by becoming a Mass-Observer, send a card. *Ibid.* i. 10 A group of people started *Mass-Observation*, which aims to be a scientific study of human social behaviour, beginning at home. **1937** JENNINGS & MADGE (*title*) May the twelfth: Mass-Observation day-surveys 1937. **1938** *Times* 10 Mar. 15/4 Nor are they mass-observationists..testing the movements of public opinion with cold curiosity. **1939** 'N. BLAKE' *Smiler with Knife* xvi. 233 'I thought..you wur one of them Mass Observers..' 'No. I'm just one of the mass-observed.' **1948** J. BETJEMAN *Coll. Poems* (1958) 229 The Mass-Observer with the Hillman Minx. **1951** 'A. GARVE' *Murder in Moscow* ii. 34 He's supposed to have an assignment..but he spends all his time doing his own private mass observation. **1967** G. WILLS in Wills & Yearsley *Handbk. Managem. Technol.* 184 The two other major quantification techniques are the consumer survey..and the mass-observation study. **1970** *Guardian* 10 Dec. 8/4 The Mass Observers..mass observed blind drinkers. **1974** *Daily Tel.* (Colour Suppl.) 19 Apr. 23/3 The Mass-Observation method..is the absolute opposite of interviewing.

mass-priest. (Later examples.)

1902 J. BUCHAN *Watcher by Threshold* II. 109 The family changed its faith, and an Episcopal chaplain took the place of the old mass-priest in the tutoring of the sons. **1922** JOYCE *Ulysses* 379 She said that he had a fair sweet death through God His goodness with masspriest to be shriven, holy housel and sick men's oil to his limbs.

mass production. [f. MASS *sb.*[2] + PRODUCTION.] The production of manufactured articles in large quantities by a standardized process. Also *transf.* and *attrib.*

1920 *Teacher's World* 19 May 283/2 (Advt.), Mass production. High class..chairs. **1922** TURNER & WOOD *Man. Up-to-Date Organisation* 110 Mass Production is a continuous replica of a standardised master-pattern or design. **1923** J. M. SCOTT-MAXWELL *Costing & Price-Fixing* 31 Factories on a mass production basis will have all material most carefully specified, examined, and tested. **1929** W. DEEPING *Roper's Row* xxxii. 353 The new world of smudged faces, mass-production man in the making. **1930** G. B. SHAW *Apple Cart* I. 25 Don't forget our racing motor boats and cars, sir: the finest on earth, and all individually designed. No cheap mass production stuff there. **1944** W. TEMPLE *Church looks Forward* x. 82 The problems due to mass-production press upon us. **1946** J. S. HUXLEY *Unesco* i. 18 A mass-production system can indirectly destroy creative initiative and aesthetic appreciation. **1947** J. HAYWARD *Prose Lit. Since 1939* 26 Literary and historical biography was already a flourishing industry. What particular..forces were concerned in its mass-production cannot be investigated here. **1948** [see *conveyor belt* s.v. *CONVEYER 4 c]. **1962** H. O. BEECHENO *Introd. Business Stud.* x. 86 Mass-production methods have called for mass-selling methods. **1967** M. MCLUHAN *Medium is Massage* 50 Printing..provided the first uniformly repeatable 'commodity', the first assembly line—mass production.

Hence **ma:ss-produ·ce** *v. trans.* and *intr.*, to manufacture (articles) by mass production; also **ma:ss-produ·ced** *ppl. a.*; **ma:ss-produ·cer; ma:ss-produ·cing** *ppl. a.*; **ma:ss-pro·duct.**

1922 JOYCE *Ulysses* 661 They drank..Epps's massproduct, the creature cocoa. **1923** *Daily Mail* 22 Jan. 5 All cars made in the United States are not necessarily mass-produced. **1929** E. GILL *Art-Nonsense* 318 The ordinary person..says, what is to hinder him from having..mass-produced pots and pans designed by artists to look artistic? **1929** A. HUXLEY *Do what you Will* 90 The mass-producers will do their best to make everybody more and more prosperous. **1930** —— *Vulgarity in Lit.* vii. 45 Asceticism is not popular in this mass-producing age. **1938** *New Statesman* 23 July 143/2 Trades which mass-produce luxury or semi-luxury goods. **1940** *Life* 9 Dec. 84/2 U.S. now mass-produces. **1950** M. HAY *Foot of Pride* iii. 74 St. Vincent Ferrer and other preachers sent thousands of panic-stricken people to the font where a priest mechanically turned them into Christians. Theologians..decided that these mass-produced Christians had been validly baptized. **1954** *Encounter* Mar. 5/2 A mass-producing, mass-consuming society. **1958** Mass-produce [see *BATTERY 12* c]. **1967** E. SHORT *Embroidery & Fabric Collage* iii. 68 There is no way of mass-producing patchwork. **1973** *Country Life* 15 Mar. 718/1 This is our 18th Century style bedroom suite. Not for everyone because it is not mass-produced.

massula (mæ·siŭlă). *Bot.* [mod.L., dim. of L. *massa*: see MASS *sb.*[2]] (*a*) In heterosporous ferns of the genera *Azolla* and *Salvinia*, the tissue surrounding the maturing microspores; (*b*) in certain orchids, a cluster of pollen grains developed from a single cell.

1856 J. S. HENSLOW *Dict. Bot. Terms* (ed. 2) 105 Massula (a little lump). One of the smaller fragments which ..compose the pollen mass in Orchidaceæ. **1882** S. H. VINES tr. *F. G. J. von Sachs's Text-bk. Bot.* II. 454 In the microsporangia [of *Azolla*] the mucilage looks like a large-celled tissue, and forms from two to eight separate clumps (*Massulæ*), each of which encloses a number of microspores. In some species..these massulæ have their surfaces covered with hair-like appendages. **1894** S. H. VINES *Students' Text-bk. Bot.* I. III. 410 In *Azolla* the microspores are likewise embedded in this substance, but in more than one group or massula according to the species. **1895** —— *Ibid.* II. III. 564 The pollinium may consist..of larger groups of cells, termed *massulæ* (e.g. Orchis). **1938** G. M. SMITH *Cryptogamic Bot.* II. ix. 358 The functional macrospore lies in the large massula at the base of a sporangium. *Ibid.* 360 A microspore remains embedded within a massula during the entire course of its development into a gametophyte. **1959** WIRTH & WITHNER in C. L. Withner *Orchids* v. 157 In some genera, such as *Peristylus*, there is a variation on the normal mode of development. All the cells resulting from the divisions of an archesporial cell remain attached to each other, eventually forming a small cluster of tetrads known as a massula. **1965** BELL & COOMBE tr. *Strasburger's Textbk. Bot.* 582 *Azolla* is of interest for the arrangements which ensure fertilization. After liberation from the microsporangium the sixty-four microspores are aggregated into 5–8 roundish floating balls (massulae) formed of the frothy periplasmodium. Arising from the surface of each massula are a number of stalked, barbed hooks.

massy, Eng. and U.S. dial. var. of MERCY *sb.* 4.

1817 A. ROYALL *Lett. from Alabama* (1830) ix. 22 Massy upon me! **1867** W. F. ROCK *Jim an' Nell* 31 Law! massy, Jim. **1884** J. C. EGERTON *Sussex Folk & Ways* 41 'Massy!' she said, 'the girls nowadays don't know naun about work!' **1905** *Dialect Notes* III. 17 *Massy sakes! sakes alive!* interj. All feminine exclamations. **1944** H. WENTWORTH *Amer. Dial. Dict.* 380/1 Massy = mercy.

mast, *sb.*[1] Add: **3.** Also used in various special senses (see quots.).

1910 *Flying in Bournemouth* (Souvenir Wallisdown Flying Whit-Week) 13 (*caption*) Mast with supporting wires. **1914** R. STANLEY *Text-bk. Wireless Telegr.* xiv. 189 The aerial to be supported by ten tubular steel masts each 300 feet high. **1918** E. S. FARROW *Dict. Mil. Terms* 371 *Mast*, in aëronautics, the upright part, usually extending upward from the center of a monoplane for support of controls and guy or truss wires; a vertical upright in the main or supplementary planes. **1920** [see *HORN *sb.* 21 h (i)]. **1924** *Harmsworth's Wireless Encycl.* II. 1409 *Mast*, term used in wireless work to describe generally any structure used to raise and support the aerial wires. **1931** D. ROSE *J. de la Cierva's Wings of Tomorrow* 110 A sort of whipping action of the rotor blades [of a helicopter] which jerked at the mast as they turned in their circle. **1956** W. A. HEFLIN *U.S. Air Force Dict.* 317/1 *Mast* n., 1. A spar for the support of an antenna. 2. A rotor mast... 3. In certain early airplanes, any of various vertical members used to hold guy wires or struts. **1966** *Listener* 1 Dec. 799/2 The German pavilion..is made of a semi-transparent plasticized fabric supported on a network of cables slung between a very few slender steel masts.

mast, *sb.*[2] **4. mast year** (add definition, and earlier and later examples): a year in which forest trees produce a good crop of fruit.

1744 W. ELLIS *Mod. Husbandman* (1750) VI. II. 89 Under these Trees, the Hogs generally get Pork in a Maste-Year. **1927** *Forestry* I. 28 The rarity of full mast years and heavy weed growth are often held responsible for the failure of most attempts at natural regeneration of oak. **1953** H. L. EDLIN *Forester's Handbk.* ii. 30 But with many kinds [of trees] full seed crops are only found at intervals of three or four years—the *mast* years.

‖ **mast** (mɑst), *sb.*[6] [Pers.] (See quots.)

1819 W. OUSELEY *Trav. East* I. vi. 268 Here also was abundance of *mâst*,.. coagulated milk or clotted cream, slightly sour, which when diluted with water forms *âb i dúgh*..a beverage in warm weather equally grateful and salubrious. **1933** *Discovery* Sept. 284/1, I was given *mast* or sour milk [in Persia]. **1963** *Times* 6 Feb. 12/6 Quantities of tea served in glasses and drunk, at any rate by the Iranians, with lots and lots of sugar and the local yoghourt, known as *mast*. **1968** C. RODEN *Bk. Middle Eastern Food* 60 Yoghourt is an essential part of the Middle Eastern diet... In Iran today it is known as *mâst*.

mastaba(h. Add: **2.** (Further examples.) Also *attrib.* and *Comb.*

1883 *Encycl. Brit.* XX. 122/2 They have been extended upwards and around into a great stepped mass of masonry .., the successive faces of which rise at the characteristic mastaba angle of 75°. **1931** G. A. REISNER *Mycerinus* i. 3 Some of the mastaba tombs also belonged to members of the royal family. **1932** *Times Lit. Suppl.* 26 May 389/1 The concession of the area of that pyramid and of large areas in the vast mastaba-field of Giza. **1936** *Ibid.* 13 June 501/1 Around the three great pyramids..are grouped.. the *mastaba*-tombs of the nobles. **1952** E. B. GARSIDE tr. *Ceram's Gods, Graves, & Scholars* II. x. 120 A mastaba is an oblong structure with sloping sides containing cult rooms and connected by a shaft with a burial chamber in the rock beneath. **1964** W. L. GOODMAN *Hist. Woodworking Tools* IV. i. 160 The only tool shown in use on mastaba reliefs. *Ibid.*, This method of constructing the cabin or house with overlapping vertical boards may explain why the walls of the early mastaba tombs..show the deep recesses.

mastectomy (mæste·ktŏmi). *Surg.* [f. Gr. μαστ-ός breast + *-ECTOMY.] Excision or amputation of a breast.

1923 in STEDMAN *Med. Dict.* (ed. 7). **1935** *Jrnl. Med. Assoc. Georgia* XXIV. 119 (*heading*) The seasponge as a postoperative dressing following radical mastectomy. **1973** M. J. BRENNAN in Holland & Frei *Cancer Med.* xxvii. 1777/1 Since skillful biopsy followed by a short wait before definitive treatment does not penalize results, there is no reason for immediate mastectomy when the frozen section does not give certain diagnosis.

master, *sb.*[1] Add: **I. 4. b.** *his* (or *her, my,* etc.) *master's voice*, a catch-phrase, originating from the trade name of a gramophone record company, denoting, freq. ironically, the voice of authority.

[**1910** *Trade Marks Jrnl.* 5 Oct. 1604 His Master's Voice. .. Talking machines, talking machine needles, talking machine records and other talking machine accessories,.. The Gramophone Company, Limited,..London,..manufacturers.] **1922** M. A. VON ARNIM *Enchanted April* xviii. 297 'Francesca!' shouted Briggs. She came running... 'Her Master's Voice,' remarked Mr. Wilkins. **1922** JOYCE *Ulysses* 465 My master's voice. **1969** 'H. PENTECOST' *Girl with Six Fingers* (1970) I. iv. 68 'He—he'd hesitate to do anything that would displease Angela.' 'Not when he hears his master's voice,' said Jericho. **1972** R. QUILTY *Tenth Session* 42 Bank's personal secretary..announced.. that the doctor would like to see Angus in his office... 'His master's voice,' he informed Norman.

9*. a. An original disc († or cylinder) with grooves cut by a stylus during recording. **b.** (Also *master matrix.*) A disc with ridges in place of grooves that is made from the plating of an electroplated original and is used as a stamper or (more usually) to make a 'mother'.

1904 S. R. BOTTONE *Talking Machines & Records* 69 With the master running in the phonograph, the trained ears of the specialists enable them to detect the most minute imperfections. **1908** *Daily Chron.* 29 Oct. 7/1 A special room is devoted to recording, or making the master from which copies are to be taken. **1918** H. SEYMOUR *Reproduction of Sound* 68 The original master is recorded by means of a feed thread... This is thereupon electrotyped—that is, a metallic negative is grown upon it, and this is called the master matrix. A small number of casts in wax are made from this... These are similarly electrotyped, and become the working matrices. **1935** H. C. BRYSON *Gramophone Record* vi. 130 (*caption*) Stripping copper masters from the wax. *Ibid.* 142 The wax is positive, the copper master is negative, the mother is positive, the stamper is negative, and the record produced from it is therefore positive and will play on a gramophone. **1952** GODFREY & AMOS *Sound Recording & Reproduction* v. 139 Only one master can be prepared from a wax original.., but more than one master can sometimes be made from a lacquer-coated disk. **1962** A. NISBETT *Technique Sound Studio* 259 The master has ridges instead of grooves. In half processing (when only a small run is required) the master is also used as a stamper. **1972** *Jazz & Blues* Oct. 29/2 The final batch of King Jazz recordings were done on 12″ masters.

c. (See quot. 1958.)

1930 W. DESBOROUGH *Duplicating & Copying Processes* iii. 21 The master is produced in negative or mirror form by placing the face of a special hekto carbon at the back of the sheet of paper on which the master is to be made. **1957** G. W. W. STEVENS *Microphotogr.* xi. 213 The time and care expended on a master negative give it considerable value ..therefore..it is advisable to make at least two masters, once the camera has been set up. **1958** T. LANDAU *Encycl. Librarianship* 204/2 *Master*, the original plate or stencil in duplicating processes from which copies are made. In photocopying, the negative from which a positive print is made. **1971** R. BUSBY *Deadlock* iv. 39 Could you make that four copies?.. You'll need two for the index apart from this master.

II. 15. *the master* (or *Master*): further examples (see quot. 1870 in Dict.); *old master* (further examples).

1869 'MARK TWAIN' *Innoc. Abr.* 260 Who painted these things? Why, Titian..Raphael—none other than the world's idols, the 'old masters'. **1889** G. B. SHAW in *Hawk* 13 Aug. 172/2 Behind the Master's house is the Master's grave; for Wagner..is 'buried in the back garden, sir, like a Newfoundland dog'. **1908** *Pop. Mechanics* Nov. 741/2 A Munich artist and inventor has devised an electric machine by which the famous paintings of the 'old masters' can be renewed. **1937** H. G. WELLS *Camford Visitation* v. 58 All his fancied novelties of criticism were fully foreseen by the Master [*sc.* Karl Marx]. **1959** *Times* 20 Aug. 9/5 In calling the anonymous hero of *The Aspern Papers* 'H. J.' I may have misled a few people into thinking that I have attempted to make 'the publishing scoundrel' into a portrait of 'The Master'. **1962** *Listener* 14 June 1043/3 The style, a pastiche of Nabokov's..is a style less functional, more baroque, than the Master's.

b. (Further examples.) *The Old Masters*: the name given to the annual Winter Exhibition of the Royal Academy from the name of the first exhibition (1870), 'Exhibition of the Works of the Old Masters'.

1824 J. FISHER *Let.* 18 Jan. in C. R. Leslie *Mem. Life J. Constable* (1845) viii. 130, I am shut up in lodgings here,—the walls covered with *old masters*. **1861** G. MEREDITH *Let.* 19 Nov. (1970) I. 111 He is in new chambers full of pictures, Old Masters, we hear. **1870** *Times* 3 Jan. 5/1 Exhibition of old masters at the Royal Academy. The noble new rooms of the Royal Academy..the place of exhibition of a selection from the finest works of the old masters in English private galleries, opened..for the public today. **1880** GEO. ELIOT *Let.* 5 Feb. (1956) VII. 248 If you had come to town you would have liked to see ..the Old Masters at the Academy but perhaps you may yet come before they are removed. **1890** G. B. SHAW *London Music in 1888–89* (1937) 284 My ticket for the Press view at the Old Masters on Friday! **1908** *Outlook* 19 Dec. 848/2 The disappointment at the prospect of no Old Masters exhibition this winter is barely mitigated by the *menu* of the banquet provided by the McCulloch collection. **1968** S. C. HUTCHISON *Hist. R. Acad.* xiii. 141 The Old Masters Exhibition of 1879 was conceived on a much larger scale than its forerunners and occupied nine galleries. **1975** *Times* 23 June 12 The value of Old Masters is perhaps more subjectively determined than in any other field... The Old Master market has been very strong in the 1970s.

c. *spec.* in Chess. Cf. *chess-master, *GRAND MASTER 3*.

1852 H. STAUNTON *Chess Tournament* p. l, To reward the ability of first-rate masters throughout the world, they offered..prizes. **1910** *Encycl. Brit.* VI. 104/1 The terms *master* and *amateur* are not used in any invidious sense, but simply as designating, in the former case, first-class players, and in the latter, those just on the borderland of highest excellence. **1969** *Times* 25 Jan. 17/7 There are three types of F.I.D.E. master title: international grandmaster, international master, and international woman master. **1973** *Daily Tel.* 25 Apr. 16/3 After six of the 11 rounds of the Birmingham International Chess Tournament, Tony J. Miles, 18, the Birmingham schoolboy, still leads the mixed concourse (one grand master, several international masters, candidate masters and others). **1973** *Sci. Amer.* June 93/2 Kalme is a senior master with a rating of 2,455 on the International Chess Federation scale, on which 2,200 denotes a master and Fischer's rating is 2,785.

IV. 22. *young master* (later examples).

c **1874** D. BOUCICAULT in M. R. Booth *Eng. Plays of 19th Cent.* (1969) II. 201 Did you see the young master? **1923** WODEHOUSE *Inimitable Jeeves* i. 9 He had been clearing away the breakfast things, but at the sound of the young master's voice cheesed it courteously.

b. Prefixed, with disparaging implication, to the name of an adult.

1885 C. M. YONGE *Nuttie's Father* II. ix. 105 I'm not going to have a *tête-à-tête* with Master Mark. **1959** *Listener* 22 Jan. 155/2, I never liked Jinnah... I thought a great deal of his ambition was for Master Jinnah rather than anything else. **1975** T. HEALD *Deadline* vii. 151, I think you'll find Master Wimbledon will do very well at anything if he thinks it will further his career. He's an exceedingly ruthless and ambitious young man.

V. 24. d. *master carpenter* (later examples), *clockmaker*.

1824 R. HUMPHREYS *Mem. J. Decastro* 76 He calls for his scene-painter, composer, master-carpenter, property-man. **1933** *Burlington Mag.* Nov. 239/2 A master-clockmaker of the class of Thomas Tompion. **1936** *Ibid.* Aug. 54/1 At nineteen he was..a master-carpenter and a painter. **1964** W. L. GOODMAN *Hist. Woodworking Tools* II. vii. 78 The wide-ranging migrations of the master-masons and master-carpenters of the Middle-Ages.

e. (Further examples.)

1930 *English Jrnl.* XIX. 628 The Minnesota *Quarterly* is at present running a series of tales about a master criminal. **1932** WODEHOUSE *Louder & Funnier* 72 The psychology of the Master Criminal is a thing I have never been able to understand. **1939** T. S. ELIOT *Old Possum's Pract. Cats* 33 He's the master criminal who can defy the Law. **1968** D. M. SMITH *Mod. Sicily* lv. 505 That notorious character Don Calogero Vizzini,..master criminal and boss of Villalba,..made a fortune out of wartime shortages. **1975** L. DEIGHTON *Yesterday's Spy* vi. 54 Champion was some kind of master spy.

f. *Chess.* Designating play or players of the highest class at national or international level. (Cf. *15 c.)

1894 J. MASON *Princ. Chess* 186 In the case of master players, a slight initial error..will permeate the remainder of the game. **1938** P. W. SERGEANT *Champion Chess* 191 The *Benoni Counter-Gambit* had for years been out of favour in master-play. **1958** *Listener* 13 Nov. 803/1 It is really only in master chess..that knowledge of the latest variations and finesses becomes important. **1959** *Ibid.* 5 Nov. 794/1 You need not go as slow as the sixteen moves an hour customary in master practice.

25. a. *master bathroom, bedroom, dish, list, pattern* (also *fig.*), *star, switch, tape*.

1959 *Sunday Times* 3 May 19/4 The kitchen and master bathroom. **1926** *New Republic* 7 Apr. p. iii (Advt.), Large living-room and dining-room opening on court, four master bedrooms. **1937** M. HILLIS *Orchids on your Budget* ii. 35 Crisp white argentine curtains in the master bedroom. **1945** NELSON & WRIGHT *Tomorrow's House* ii. 12/2 The discussion continued in the privacy of the master bedroom. **1972** *Country Life* 5 Oct. (Suppl.) 32d/2 Master bedroom suite with dressing room, bath and shower rooms. **1960** AUDEN *Homage to Clio* 26 Doomed to observe Beauty peck at a master-dish. **1962** Y. MALKIEL in Householder & Saporta *Probl. Lexicogr.* 9 Fragmentary master-lists of the items. **1967** *N.Y. Times* (Internat. ed.) 11–12 Feb. 9/6 Master list of investment and speculative stocks—key lists for both the conservative and more speculative investor. **1948** H. HALL *Home Dress-Making Simplified* xxxiii. 311 The safe plan, when remodeling, is to fit a master pattern in muslin... This pattern is then used as a guide for fitting the section when cutting. **1960** R. LISTER *Decorative Cast Ironwork* 230 *Master pattern*, a pattern from which a production work is cast. **1962** W. NOWOTTNY *Lang. Poets Use* vi. 138 It is Eliot's peculiar insight..to have..expressed the longing for the master-pattern that will free us from the fret of a world in which there are too many equipollent patterns. **1904** W. DE LA MARE *Henry Brocken* vi. 62 The master-stars shone earlier here. **1907** A. HAY *Introd. Course Continuous Current Engin.* xvi. 284 A small switch which is arranged to control simultaneously a number of larger switches is spoken of as a master switch. **1943** *Gloss. Terms Electr. Engin.* (*B.S.I.*) 52 *Master switch or circuit-breaker*, a switch or circuit-breaker to which the operation or function of one or more other switches is subservient. **1975** P. ORGAN *House on Cheyne Walk* i. 1 The night is going. Soon someone somewhere will throw a master switch..and the lights will go out..all over London. **1954** Master tape [see *FILE *sb.*[2] 4 b]. **1962** *Times* 5 July 15/6 In a disc-cutting room at Decca's London studios, a master tape of a recent recording of music by Prokofiev and an ordinary commercial pressing of a disc made from it were started simultaneously. **1967** *Lebende Sprachen* XII. 137/2 *Master tape*, original recording by informant of a language laboratory drill. **1973** *Daily Tel.* (Colour Suppl.) 12 Oct. 29/2 The signals..from the master tape are then fed into the recording head that drives the cutting stylus.

b. *master-coup, -dream, -fulcrum, plan, -power, -voice.*

1939 R. CAMPBELL *Flowering Rifle* VI. 148 The cynic master-coup of propaganda. **1928** BLUNDEN *Jap. Garland* 21 Sleep's master-dream there stands alone: The tower of East and West! **1957** T. HUGHES *Hawk in Rain* 11 And I..strain towards the master-Fulcrum of violence where the hawk hangs still. **1935** Master plan [see *FREEWAY]. **1939** H. M. LEWIS *City Planning* xii. 128 A master plan.. may be defined as a general plan for the future layout of the city. **1957** L. F. R. WILLIAMS *State of Israel* 77 The bulk of the population is being systematically spread out in accordance with a master plan drawn up by the Government. **1960** *Washington Post* 16 Nov. A.16 The Friends, who have retained consultants to study the Zoo's problems and form a master plan, found that the institution has almost never received adequate funds. **1971** B. DE FERRANTI *Living with Computer* ix. 82 He therefore ..gives them names so that they can be filed and described on the master plan. **1821** HAZLITT *Table-Talk* I. v. 96 His mind grappled with that which afforded the best exercise to its master-powers. **1910** W. DE LA MARE *Three Mulla-Mulgars* xiii. 174 Of its calm authority the master-voice said, 'So shall it be.'

29. master-batch, a concentrated mixture employed in the production of synthetic rubbers and plastics; hence as *v. trans.*, to mix in a master-batch; **masterbatching** *vbl. sb.*; **master-brain**, = *MASTER-MIND *sb.* b; **master**

card, (*a*) *Bridge* (see quots.); (*b*) a record card which summarizes the information recorded on a number of other cards; **master class,** (*a*) the most powerful or influential class in society; (*b*) a class receiving instruction from a 'master' (a person of distinguished skill), esp. in *Music*; **master clock,** a clock which transmits regular pulses of electricity for controlling impulse dials or computer operations; **master-craftsman,** a craftsman thoroughly conversant with his trade; one who employs workmen; also *transf.*; hence *master-craftsmanship*; **master number** = *matrix number* (*MATRIX 7); **master oscillator,** an oscillator used to produce a constant frequency, esp. the carrier frequency of a radio or television transmitter; **master race,** a race of people considered to be pre-eminent in greatness or power; *spec.* the Germans or 'Aryans' (see *ARYAN *sb.* 2) regarded as a superior people (cf. *HERRENVOLK) during the Nazi period; **master rod,** in a rotary or radial engine, a rod which connects one of the pistons to the crankshaft and carries the wrist pins to which the link rods are connected; **master-scene, shot** *Cinematography*, (see quots.); **master–slave manipulator,** a type of manipulator (sense *2 f) which reproduces at the handling end the positions and motions of the operator's fingers.

1937 H. BARRON *Mod. Rubber Chem.* vii. 79 Certain fundamental ingredients such as accelerators, antioxidants and sulphur are always added in small quantities... It is now common practice to add them as a 'masterbatch'. **1953** N. L. CATTON *Neoprenes* 32 A convenient method of making sure that mixing operations are carried out in the elastic phase is through the use of concentrated masterbatches. **1959** *Times* 13 Mar. 10/2 The Cariflex range consists of hot and cold polymers, oil masterbatches, carbon black masterbatches and hot and cold latices. **1964** *Amer. Speech* XXXIX. 272 Most stocks..in a tire are mixed in two stages. The masterbatch is the first stage, in which all the rubbers and pigments are mixed except for the curing agents. **1953** *Industr. & Engin. Chem.* May 1059/2 Copolymers of butadiene and styrene..have been extended with various rosin-type acids in a manner similar to that employed in extending with petroleum oils (latex masterbatching). **1971** CROWTHER & EDMONDSON in C. M. Blow *Rubber Technol. & Manuf.* viii. 269 It is generally accepted that masterbatching improves the physical properties of those compounds where a high degree of carbon black dispersion must be achieved. *Ibid.* 270 The curing ingredients themselves may be masterbatched. **1923** E. WALLACE *Missing Million* xiv. 112 The master-brain who took his pick of the cleverest criminals at large. **1905** R. F. FOSTER *Compl. Bridge* 316 *Master card*, the best left in play of any suit which has already been led. **1937** *Times* 13 Apr. p. iv/3 A..tabulator, which ..can collate, record and analyse 900 production facts a minute, as well as produce master cards summarizing the figures it tabulates. **1961** T. LANDAU *Encycl. Librarianship* (ed. 2) 236/2 *Master card*, a main entry in a card catalogue bearing tracings indicating all the added entries, [etc.]. **1964** COHEN & BARROW *A.B.C. of Contract Bridge* 282 *Master card*, a card that can be beaten only if it is trumped. **1970** O. DOPPING *Computers & Data Processing* iv. 72 If the machine has only one card feed, data are transferred from a master card to the following cards which are often called detail cards. **1861** MILL *Repr. Govt.* ii. 38 Slavery is..corrupting to the master-class when they once come under civilized influences. *c* **1926** 'MIXER' *Transport Workers' Song Bk.* 47 Note the constant drop in wages..Endorsed by every rag-time press That the master-class command. **1930** J. DOS PASSOS *42nd Parallel* I. 104 Big Bill talked about..sticking together in the face of the masterclass. **1963** *Ann. Reg. 1962* 446 Pablo Casals conducting a master class. **1965** *Listener* 10 June 873/2 Master-class exercises in comparative semantics and applied imagery. **1970** *Times* 26 Feb. 16/1 Old singers don't forget—they teach. And the best of them conduct master classes. **1973** *Times* 17 Apr. 32/4 Crash course on British Portraiture... Contact: Master Classes. **1973** *Ms.* Nov. 46/3 Ms. Rosenberger has worked out a variety of exercises like the one she suggested to the tense master-class student. **1904** Master clock [see *JOURNEYMAN 3 b]. **1922** G. L. OVERTON *Clocks & Watches* x. 108 If the master clock should have gained or lost at all, the arrangements provided for putting it right again are such that all the connected dials are at the same time automatically set to the right time. **1951** Master clock [see *impulse clock* s.v. *IMPULSE *sb.* 5 b]. **1967** H. JACOBOWITZ *Electronic Computers made Simple* xiii. 261 Unless the computer is asynchronous.., all its operations are controlled by a series of equally spaced timing pulses from a master clock oscillator. **1937** G. B. BROWN *Arts in Early Eng.* VI. II. xi. 215 We are in almost complete ignorance as to the personalities of the master craftsmen who created the schemes of enrichment. **1952** C. DAY LEWIS tr. *Virgil's Aeneid* II. 36 That master-craftsman of crime, Ulysses. *Ibid.* VIII. 177 Now there is need for Your strength, your speediest work and your master-craftsmanship. **1969** *John Edwards Mem. Foundation Q.* V. IV. 146 Such documents are of great importance to the discographer who is trying to assemble the usual discographic data of master number, recording date..and release number. **1973** in B. Holiday *Lady sings Blues* 208 In the era of 78 rpm records most companies assigned a number to each recording they made for the sake of handy reference, called the 'master' number. **1928** STERLING & KRUSE *Radio Manual* viii. 305 The tuning of this type of circuit consists fundamentally of setting the master oscillator at the desired wavelength and then resonating the antenna circuit for maximum antenna current. **1951** W. E. PANNETT *Radio Installations* vii. 177 The quartz crystal..has largely superseded valve circuits as a master oscillator for controlling the frequency of a transmitter. **1971** M. G. SCROGGIE *Found. Wireless & Electronics* xv. 244 The function of what is usually called the master oscillator is to define the frequency of the station at least as accurately and constantly as the now very narrow international regulations require. **1942** J. S. HUXLEY in *South Atlantic Q.* XLI. 354 The [German] nation is formidably united behind its own ideal of an 'Aryan' Master-Race. **1945** D. THOMSON et al. *Patterns of Peacemaking* iii. 118 Her expansionism has been due to a triple convergence of forces: the economic greed and lust for power of her ruling classes, the primitive and tribal nationalist and imperialist sentiments of her people, and hatred of the foreigner which takes the form of theories of Japanese being a 'master-race'. **1949** D. MACARDLE *Children of Europe* xiv. 212 Boys and girls who had been impregnated with the teaching of Nazi schools..shared the overwhelming pride of the 'Master Race'. **1953** P. ABRAHAMS *Return to Goli* vi. 215 Imperceptibly, a 'master race' mentality is in the making [in Kenya]. **1974** *Times* 21 Oct. 3/4 To suggest that I [*sc.* Sir Keith Joseph] was arguing for a 'master race'..is..very wrong. **1922** *Encycl. Brit.* XXX. 36/2 Connecting-rods of rotary and radial engines consist usually of one master rod, ball or roller-bearinged, with the big-end enlarged to form circular lugs to secure wrist pins carrying the plain or auxiliary type of rod of the remaining cylinders. **1928** Master rod [see *link rod* s.v. *LINK *sb.*[2] 7]. **1946** J. W. VALE *Aviation Mechanic's Engine Manual* iii. 87 Constructing the crankshaft in sections permits use of the one-piece master rod. **1960** O. SKILBECK *ABC of Film & T.V.* 83 *Master scene*, usually an establishing shot; the basic scene from which a sequence is edited by intercutting or adding closer shots. A master scene script is an optional stage in writing..in which only the above appear. **1960** D. WILSON *Television Playwright* 16 The plays in this book are printed in 'Rehearsal Script' form, that is to say, the manuscript as the author wrote it. In the Cinema this would be called a 'Master-scene Script'. **1953** K. REISZ *Technique Film Editing* 280 *Master shot*, single shot of an entire piece of dramatic action taken in order to facilitate the assembly of the component closer shots of details from which the sequence will finally be covered. **1959** P. BULL *I know Face* v. 94 We started..with a 'master-shot', which means that the actors go through the entire scene from rather far off and only portions of the shot are likely to be used in the final film. **1972** R. MANVELL *Internat. Encycl. Film* 356 *Master shot*, the main shot of a complete piece of dramatic action, which facilitates the assembly of the component shots of which it will finally be composed. **1952**, etc. Master–slave manipulator [see *MANIPULATOR 2 f]. **1960** *Times* 24 May 20/4 Closed-circuit stereoscopic television combined with a light-duty master–slave manipulator.. enables an operator to see the articles which he is moving in a solid radiation-proof container.

VI. 30. As a suffix forming compounds (mostly proprietary names) designating articles, appliances, etc., that are held to be supreme or superior in the field denoted by their first elements.

1935 *Vogue* 1 Dec. 110 Rainbow Matchmaster. **1937** *Amer. Speech* XII. 265 Then there are the *Buffet-Master*, a 'combination grill and waffle iron', *Menu-master*, *Kook-master*, and *Grill Master*, all electric grills. **1947** J. BERTRAM *Shadow of War* 334, I glanced across the lighted interior of the big Skymaster. **1955** M. MCCARTHY *Charmed Life* (1956) ii. 52 The combination waffle iron and sandwich grill, the roto-broiler, the mixmaster. **1960** *Times Lit. Suppl.* 1 July 414/2 The shops were filled with goods and buyers..in the houses washers, dryers..Mixmasters. **1972** M. CRICHTON *Terminal Man* I. v. 41 Robert Morris was sitting in the hospital cafeteria..when his pagemaster went off... He..went to the wall phone to answer his page.

masterate (mā·stərĕt). [f. MASTER *sb.*[1] + -ATE[1]; cf. DOCTORATE *sb.*[1]] The degree or dignity of a master (see MASTER *sb.*[1] 13).

1902 *Science* 17 Oct. 612 The masterates should, of course, be permanent, and should not involve financial relations with the Institution. **1961** *Press* (Christchurch, N.Z.) 23 Mar. 10/8 There was not enough incentive for the best students to proceed to masterate degrees. **1966** *New Statesman* 16 Sept. 411/2 (Advt.), The Department [in Massey University, New Zealand] offers courses leading to the masterate level in Arts and to the Diploma in Education. **1971** *Commonwealth Universities Yearbk.* 1408 There is no uniformity among either universities or faculties as to the stage at which honours are awarded but they are frequently deferred to the masterate.

master-key. (Further *fig.* examples.)

1821 HAZLITT *Table-Talk* I. xvi. 376 Affectation is the master-key to both. *a* **1930** D. H. LAWRENCE *Phoenix II* (1968) 101 And he, she knew to her anguish and mortification, he was still the master-key to almost all life, for her. **1934** *Planning* II. XL. 2 Self-government for industry may prove to be the master key to many of our..problems.

masterless, *a.* Add: **1. c.** *transf.* Of unknown authorship or provenance.

1899 A. LANG *Homeric Hymns* 6 The conventional attribution of the Hymns to Homer..is merely the result of the tendency to set down 'masterless' compositions to a well-known name. **1903** *Library* IV. 397 It has become possible to assign to..Peter von Olpe a small group of books hitherto masterless.

ma·ster-mi·nd, *sb.* [MASTER *sb.*[1] 24, 25 b.] **a.** An outstanding or commanding mind or intellect; a person with such a mind. Also *transf.*

1720 [in Dict. s.v. MASTER *sb.*[1] 25 b]. **1821** HAZLITT *Table-Talk* I. ix. 198 He shews the marks of a great moving intellect, so that we trace the master-mind, and can sympathise with the springs that urge him on. **1839** POE *William Wilson* in *Gift 1840* (Philadelphia) 235 The despotism of a master mind in boyhood over the less energetic spirits of its companions. **1841** —— *Colloquy Monos & Una* in *Graham's Mag.* Aug. 52/2 At long intervals some master-minds appeared, looking upon each advance in practical science as a retro-gradation in the true utility. **1857** DICKENS *Dorrit* II. xxiv. 529 The master-mind of the age ..became mute again. **1909** WODEHOUSE *Mike* xxxii. 183 You can't expect two master-minds like us to pig it in that room downstairs. **1930** H. G. WELLS *Autocracy of Mr. Parham* III. viii. 220 This immediate personal recognition of the new régime by the master mind of Britain. **1949** E. JENKINS *Six Criminal Women* 11 Hers was one of the earliest master-minds in advertising. **1961** *Observer* 19 Feb. 5/4 An electronic master-mind called the 'Honeywell Data Centre'.

b. *spec.* Such a mind, or a person, directing a criminal enterprise.

1872 TROLLOPE *Eustace Diamonds* (1873) III. lxix. 203 The police thought that I had been the master-mind among the thieves. **1913** 'D. D. CARTER' in *Hearst's Mag.* July 137 (*title*) The master mind. **1920** 'SAPPER' *Bull-Dog Drum.* v. 121 A gang of international criminals..controlled by a master-mind. **1936** E. AMBLER *Dark Frontier* v. 80 From now on, he, Carruthers, would be the master mind. **1959** [see *crime-writing* s.v. *CRIME *sb.* 4]. **1960** *Observer* 24 Jan. 5/2 These were recognised prop-men or putters up of jobs, what the mugs called master minds.

Hence **ma·ster-mi·nd** *v. trans.*, to be the master-mind behind (an enterprise, a crime, etc.); to plan and direct; also occas. *intr.*; so **ma·ster-mi·nding** *vbl. sb.* and *ppl. a.*

1941 *Time* 26 May 24/2 The *Telegram* hired a series of detective storytellers to mastermind the Hess case. **1941** *True Detective* June 18/3 Often suspected but never convicted of masterminding some of the plots hatched in his grog shop. **1945** *Sun* (Baltimore) 30 Nov. 8 Baseball owes him nothing much but an opportunity to retire from the strenuous side of the competition and take over the job of master-minding. **1949** R. CHANDLER *Little Sister* xxi. 151 Somebody had to master-mind this deal. **1956** W. H. WHYTE *Organization Man* (1957) vi. 75 What they mean by sales is..master-minding the work of those who do the helping. **1957** 'B. BUCKINGHAM' *Boiled Alive* xxxiii. 249 She master minded it all right, but..Pepe is not without blame. **1973** *Guardian* 29 June 15/7 A ruthless master-minding conspirator. *Ibid.* 15/8 It was possible he was.. capable of master-minding a vast conspiracy. **1973** A. HUNTER *Gently French* viii. 74 Quarles has master-minded for several of the gangs. **1974** D. RAMSAY *No Cause to Kill* II. 132 Hy Goldman..was..sceptical of her master-minding potential.

masterpiece. Add: (Further examples of orig. sense.)

1940 *Burlington Mag.* Sept. 93/2 Who could have ordered a cabinet made in this, apparently, needlessly expensive way? I think the only solution is that it must have been made as a 'master-piece', a test of workmanship to gain admission to a trade guild. **1951** *Oxf. Jun. Encycl.* VII. 143/2 The apprentice..was also at times required to provide a sample of his work, or 'masterpiece'. **1965** *Listener* 11 Nov. 761/1 The Mud Bath was another young man's 'masterpiece' (I am using the word 'masterpiece' in its original sense—as a test of a young painter's professional skill).

1. c. *colloq.* A person, thing, or action to be admired for being remarkable, singular, etc.

1906 KIPLING *Puck of Pook's Hill* 249 Ah, he was a masterpiece!..he never winked an eyelid. **1933** W. S. MAUGHAM *Sheppey* I. 20 It was a masterpiece the way I kidded him. **1963** N. MARSH *Dead Water* (1964) vii. 178 She spotted it [*sc.* sex] everywhere... She was a masterpiece. *Ibid.* viii. 223 He'm a masterpiece for holding his liquor.

master-stroke. 1. (Further examples.)

1690 in E. Waller *Poems* II. Pref. sig. A5, Some Painters will hit the chief Lines, and master strokes of a Face so truly, that [etc.]. **1867** EMERSON *May-Day* 108 And in their vaunted works of Art, The master-stroke is still her part.

mast-fed, *a.* [MAST *sb.*[2]] Fed on mast.

1566 [in Dict s.v. MAST *sb.*[2] 4]. **1843** 'R. CARLTON' *New Purchase* II. lvi. 246 It was *mast* fed, i.e. fed on acorns and beech nuts. **1851** C. CIST *Sk. Cincinnati in 1851* 284 Much the larger share of this, is..made of mast-fed and still-fed hogs.

mast-head, *sb.* Add Now usu. **masthead** (without hyphen). **1. c.** In newspapers, journals, etc., the title, colophon, motto, etc., printed in some conspicuous position, usually immediately preceding the editorial matter or at the top of the first page. orig. *U.S.*

1838 *Hennepin* (Illinois) *Jrnl.* 22 Dec. 1/1 Many of our Whig friends..were anxious that the Journal should.. carry Whig colors at the mast-head. **1923** O. G. VILLARD *Some Newspapers* iii. 43 The vision of its purpose..which it now daily carries under its 'mast-head' on the editorial page. **1932** P. VAN D. STERN *Introd. Typogr.* 198 *Masthead*, the heading on the first page of a newspaper. **1937** *Amer. Speech* XII. 13 About 35 dailies use the word *Telegram* in their masthead. **1952** S. KAUFFMANN *Philanderer* (1953) ix. 141 She was a young, bright, snub-nosed, bobbed-hair cartoon character, to appear in the masthead and all institutional advertising. **1959** *Manch. Guardian* 22 Aug. 4/1 The masthead on page one will follow the style adopted..above our principal comment of the day. **1967** *Bucks Examiner* 3 Feb. 1/7 This week the 'Bucks Examiner' has a new masthead—the name given by newspaper men to the title at the top of page one. **1973** *Guardian* 28 Feb. 13/3 Varsity, the Cambridge University newspaper.. will appear next term under the mast head of its brasher rival Stop Press.

3. masthead cutter, -sloop (see quot. 1961);

masthead genoa, a Genoa jib which is attached to the topmost part of the mast.

1949 *Yachting Monthly* LXXXVII. 235/2 Her rig is a masthead cutter—that is to say the working jib sets to the masthead. **1961** F. H. Burgess *Dict. Sailing* 144 *Masthead cutter* or *sloop*, a cutter or sloop whose fore stay, on which the luff of the foresail is set, reaches up to the masthead. **1962** J. A. S. Russell in *Roving Commissions 1961* 147 Her masthead cutter rig, with the mast well inboard and a boomed staysail, is snug and versatile. **1958** *Yachting World Ann.* 115 *Springtide* has 900 sq. ft. in her working rig of main, mizzen, and boom staysail. The area may be increased by 400 sq. ft. with the masthead genoa. **1967** J. Howard-Williams *Sails* vii. 102 A bending mast..will mean abandoning ideas of a masthead genoa. **1954** D. Phillips-Birt *Rigs & Rigging of Yachts* 49 The masthead sloop—the sloop in which a headsail may be set on a forestay from the masthead. **1958** *Yachting World Ann.* 102/2 For some reason, yachtsmen appear shy of the masthead sloop rig; yet it is difficult to see what a yacht like this would gain by the lower fore-triangle.

mastika (mæstĭ·kă). Also **mastica, masticha.** [ad. mod.Gr. μαστίχα mastic.] = Mastic *sb.* 6.

1926 P. M. Shand *Bk. Wine* x. 264 Chios is also the home of the Mastic plant, whence a horrible liqueur, very popular in the Levant, called Chio-Mastica-Raki..is made. **1930** E. Waugh *Labels* vi. 148 He said if one ever drank *mastika* one returned to Greece. **1966** 'S. Harvester' *Treacherous Road* ix. 85 They were drinking mastica, the local brandy. **1967** A. Lichine *Encycl. Wines* 346/2 *Mastika* (or *Masticha*), a favourite Greek aperitif, made on the island of Chios, from a brandy base with gum mastic added. **1968** L. Durrell *Tunc* iii. 114 He poured me a glass of fiery mastika. **1969** *Listener* 2 Jan. 31/2 The aniseed-flavoured mastika. **1974** *Times* 21 Feb. 14 The guide maintained that, while Bulgarians were indeed virile, this was due more to drinking slivovice and mastika than to anything they ate.

mastitis. Add to def.: (in man or other mammals). (Further examples.)

1950 *N.Z. Jrnl. Agric.* Mar. 265/1 Milk from cows suffering from mastitis may be dangerous to public health. **1970** *Black's Vet. Dict.* (ed. 9) 531/2 When penicillin became available for veterinary use, it began to change the bacteriological picture of mastitis in our dairy herds.

ma·stman. *U.S.* [Mast *sb.*[1] 1.] (See quot. 1890.)

1839 C. F. Briggs *Adventures Harry Franco* I. xxii. 236 All hands call him dismal Jerry, except Mike, the mast man, and he calls him Sergeant Longshanks. **1890** *Cent. Dict.*, *Mastman*, a seaman stationed at a mast in a man-of-war to keep the ropes clear and in order. **1901** A. M. Knight *Mod. Seamanship* 382 Caution the mastmen to keep fast the weather sheets until the yards are down.

mastodon. *fig.* (Later examples.)

1851 C. Cist *Sk. Cincinnati in 1851* 187 There are five other tubs, which in the aggregate, contain as much as the great mastodon just described. **1936** [see *blue-print, blueprint *sb.* 1 a]. **1965** *Listener* 2 Sept. 337/2 It is high time we..began to inquire more coolly how we can expect this mastodon in our midst to behave.

mastoidectomy (mæstoide·ktŏmi). *Surg.* [f. Mastoid *a.* and *sb.* + *-ectomy.] Any operation for the relief of inflammation of or within the mastoid process (esp. within the cavities, i.e. the mastoid cells and mastoid antrum, inside this process), as by penetrating into and cleaning out these cavities; excision of the mastoid process.

1898 *Laryngoscope* IV. 365 But the now perfected mastoidectomy, even with its tympanic communication, established under the best antiseptic measures,..left more to be desired. **1909** *Practitioner* Nov. 695, I have of late reserved the operation of mastoidectomy for cases of mastoid abscess in the acute stage with local signs. **1956** *A.M.A. Arch. Otolaryngol.* LXIII. 248/1 The surgery included both mastoidectomies (endaural and postauricular approach) and fenestrations.

masturbate, *v.* For def. read: To produce an orgasm by stimulation of the genitals, not by sexual intercourse. (Add further examples.) Also *fig.* and as *v. trans.*, to cause (another person) to have an orgasm by stimulation of his or her genitals.

1934 R. Campbell *Broken Record* vi. 125 A bankclerk has to masturbate his mind all day: when he comes home he has no strength to mount the muse. **1964** H. Montgomery Hyde *Hist. Pornography* i. 19 He [*sc.* Pepys] finished the book the same evening, and we now know that it excited him to masturbate. **1966** L. Cohen *Beautiful Losers* (1970) i. 36 She wanted to see me masturbate for the last time. **1968** M. Courtenay *Sexual Discord in Marriage* vi. 61 He..had masturbated with heterosexual fantasies. **1970** B. W. Aldiss *Hand-Reared Boy* 62 During this miserable period I masturbated myself for consolation, and Ann also did it to me. **1974** *Daily Tel.* 3 Oct. 3/1 Clients at the parlour..paid £15-plus to be masturbated by young women in various stages of undress.

masturbator, masturbatory: further examples. Also **masturba·torily** *adv.*

1868 *Index Expurgatorius of Martial* 90 Titius was a masturbator. **1924** J. Riviere et al. tr. *Freud's Coll. Papers* I. 100 The tendency to anxiety in masturbators. **1932** *Jrnl. Amer. Med. Assoc.* 24 Dec. 2201/2 Mechanical masturbators. **1948** A. C. Kinsey et al. *Sexual Behavior Human Male* ii. v. 170 Many pre-adolescents take a good many years to discover masturbatory techniques. **1960** *Spectator* 3 June 809 The prose background to his [*sc.* Swinburne's] violent, cerebral, masturbatory poetry. **1963** *Listener* 24 Jan. 163/2 To be sexually attractive was one thing, but to become a sexual fetish was another. Marilyn Monroe became a pair of lips, a walk, a set of numbers, 38-24-36. The artificiality of the unresolved tension I have described finds a parallel here in this ersatz, masturbatory sex stimulus. **1967** B. Bross *Pleasures of Love* vii. 98 These magazines are being bought by masturbators, male ones and lesbians. **1973** S. Fisher *Female Orgasm* xii. 338 If a woman wants to escape restriction and explore the new she is particularly positive toward masturbatory gratification. **1973** M. Seymour-Smith *Guide Mod. World Lit.* 225 One senses Williams hanging masturbatorily over his nasty, midcult images of evil.

masturbation. For def. read: The action or practice of masturbating; deliberate erotic self-stimulation. (Add further examples.) Also *attrib.* and *fig.* Also **mutual masturbation,** stimulation of the genitals of one person by another in order to produce an orgasm without sexual intercourse.

1897 H. Ellis *Stud. Psychol. Sex* I. 117 The sexual relationship rarely goes beyond close physical contact, or at most mutual masturbation. **1924** J. Riviere et al. tr. *Freud's Coll. Papers* I. 90 Neurasthenics whose potency has already been seriously diminished by masturbation. **1929** D. H. Lawrence *Pornogr. & Obscenity* 32 The masturbation self-enclosure produces idiots. **1948** A. C. Kinsey et al. *Sexual Behavior Human Male* iii. xiv. 497 As more usually employed, the word 'masturbation' refers to any self stimulation which is deliberate and designed to effect erotic arousal. *Ibid.* xxi. 616 Mutual masturbation between two males may be dismissed, even by certain clinicians, as not homosexual. **1949** M. Mead *Male & Female* xiii. 271 The attempts of some child specialists to break down the masturbation taboo. **1951** R. Campbell *Light on Dark Horse* xxiii. 346 The libcraloid mentality that they had acquired from reading the masturbations of ..Rousseau. **1954** W. Faulkner *Fable* (1955) 59 That sort of masturbation about the human race people call hoping. **1961** R. F. C. Hull tr. *Jung's Coll. Works* IV. 212 She had induced a number of girls of her own age to perform mutual masturbation. **1967** E. Lea in R. E. L. Masters *Sexual Self-Stimulation* 325 The Dresden Criminal Museum..houses an elaborate..masturbation machine that the user operates with a foot pedal. **1968** *Listener* 14 Mar. 350/3 It contains..many, many accounts of adventures with women, masturbation phantasies, [etc.]. **1968** M. Courtenay *Sexual Discord in Marriage* vi. 68 He became worried about the possible harmful effects of masturbation. **1972** *Daily Tel.* 28 Nov. 17/3 Lines such as 'I like to play with my ding-a-ling' and 'Most of all with your ding-a-ling' are intended as deliberate stimulation to self and mutual masturbation. **1974** *Ibid.* 3 Oct. 3/3 For the £15 massage—with masturbation—the girls received £3 commission. *Ibid.*, He had first set up massage facilities.., but clients had wanted masturbation.

masurium (măziūə·riŏm). *Chem.* [mod.L. (W. Noddack et al. 1925, in *Sitzungsber. d. Preuss. Akad. d. Wissenschaften* 409), f. G. *Masur-en* name of a region in NE. Poland + -ium.] A name proposed for the element of atomic number 43 (later named *technetium), which was claimed to have been discovered spectroscopically in certain platinum ores.

1925 *Glasgow Herald* 16 June 6 These new elements have been named by their discoverers 'Masurium', after the Masurian Lake region, and 'Rhenium', after the Rhineland. **1941** *Chem. & Industry* 11 Oct. 729/2 Japanese investigators have studied the decay curves of the chemically separated masurium fraction from molybdenum after bombardment with slow neutrons and they distinguished the two masurium isotopes 99 and 101. **1947** [see *illinium]. **1962** J. H. White *Inorg. Chem.* xxv. 480 Technetium..has been called masurium, and it has not yet been isolated from natural minerals.

masut, var. *mazut.

mat, *sb.*[1] Add: **1. e.** *N.Z.* A type of cloak or cape worn by the Maori (cf. quot. 1777 under sense 1 a in Dict.); also used allusively to refer to the Maori way of life.

1807 J. Savage *Some Acct. N.Z.* viii. 50 The dress of the natives consists in a mat finely wove of the native flax. **1832** A. Earle *Narr. Residence N.Z.* (1966) 59 They were clothed in mats, called Ka-ka-hoos. **1840** W. Deans *Let.* 29 Mar. in J. Deans *Pioneers of Canterbury* (1937) 23 Two New Zealanders, clad in a native mat. **1849** W. T. Power *Sketches in N.Z.* xvii. 146 New habits are rapidly modifying the old ones... In throwing off the mat and the blanket, they also dispense with shark oil and red ochre. **1874** J. C. Johnstone *Maoria* i. 16 The rough *pureki*..when seen upon the men in the canoes which boarded the first vessels that visited the Island, was not inappropriately called 'a mat', and the ugly name came to be applied to any description of garment worn by the Maoris. **1905** W. B. *Where White Man Treads* 54 He is a warrior; and at any moment may cast off his mat and defend his privileges. **1947** 'A. P. Gaskell' *Big Game* 92 She must have been somewhere to a Maori High School and then come back to the mat. **1970** D. M. Davin *Not Here, Not Now* iii. vi. 197 All a man can do is go back to the mat and cry, or laugh.

f. *Bowls.* = Footer *sb.*[1] 4.

1892 J. Brown *Man. Bowling* (ed. 2) 69 The mat shall be placed by the lead of the party who lost the previous head. **1910** *Encycl. Brit.* IV. 347/2 The bowler delivers his bowl with one foot on a mat or footer, made of india-rubber or cocoanut fibre, the size of which is also prescribed by rule as 24 by 16 in. **1959** *Times* 12 Aug. 4/6 Their No. 3..went to the mat. **1962** *Bowls* ('Know the Game' Series) 4 At the beginning of the first end the mat is placed lengthwise on the centre line of the rink, the back edge to be four feet from the ditch.

g. Phr. *on the mat*, orig. in army use (see quot. 1919); in trouble with some authority. Cf. *on the carpet* (s.v. *carpet *sb.* 1 b).

1898 *Pearson's Mag.* Oct. 372/2 The sergeant..shouts with military brevity: 'On to the mat, John Smith.' [*ante*, Close to the medical officer's desk is a thick padded carpet about a yard square.] **1917** A. G. Empey *Over Top* 302 *On the mat*, when Tommy is haled before his commanding officer to explain why he has broken one of the seven million King's regulations for the government of the Army. His 'explanation' never gets him anywhere unless it is on the wheel of a limber. **1919** *Athenæum* 1 Aug. 695/1 'He 's on the mat' means the same [as 'He's for the high jump']; the pre-war orderly room was furnished with a piece of carpet, in the exact centre of which the accused stood. **1925** Fraser & Gibbons *Soldier & Sailor Words* 154 *Mat, on the*: up for trial. In trouble. **1935** A. J. Pollock *Underworld Speaks* 92/2 *Put on the mat*, a thorough questioning, usually by the police. **1949** J. R. Cole *It was so Late* 62 Then I was on the mat again. Now it seems a wonder I kept out of trouble as long as I did. **1973** J. Thomson *Death Cap* x. 136 Mrs Holbrook had been given the impression that she was on the mat in front of her husband's superior officer.

h. A piece of padded material, canvas, etc., used as a floor covering in gymnastics, wrestling, etc. Hence *fig.*, in phr. *to go to the mat*: to engage in a struggle or controversy; to argue.

1903 P. Longhurst *Wrestling* i. 5 Ordinary gymnasium mats covered with canvas or sail-cloth form the best surface for this style of wrestling. **1924** Wodehouse *Leave it to Psmith* i. 28, I..heard..you and Aunt Constance going to the mat about poor old Phyllis. **1937** D. Aldis *Time at her Heels* i. 26 She just didn't have time at the moment to call him in and go to the mat with him about it. **1950** *Oxf. Jun. Encycl.* IX. 489/1 In this type of wrestling a 'fall' is gained by bringing the opponent's two shoulders simultaneously into contact with the mat. **1967** V. L. Drehman *Head over Heels* i. 3 Wide mats must be used for the learner in tumbling. **1970** *New Yorker* 12 Dec. 131/1 These senators felt that the President had handed them two lemons, had gone to the mat for his choices when he didn't have to.

2. b. (Earlier examples.)

1800 M. Edgeworth *Parent's Assistant* (ed. 3) V. 32 These here half dozen little mats, to put under my dishes. **1852** Mrs. Gaskell *Let.* Dec. (1966) 217 The little ones had worked mats, & gathered flowers &c &c for her dressing-room.

3. a. (Later examples.)

1898 Pound & Clements *Phytogeogr. Nebraska* iii. 53 This group is composed of acaulescent or low-stemmed plants which grow aggregated into dense cushion-like mats. **1916** B. D. Jackson *Gloss. Bot. Terms* (ed. 3) 224/1 *Mat*, a closely intertwined vegetation, with roots and rhizomes intermixed. **1930** *Forestry* IV. 70 A 'mat' of actively growing mycelium of the parasite was present in the watering flasks of many of the cultures. **1971** *Nature* 30 Apr. 599/1 At Kariba..where the lake took 4–5 yr to fill, extensive mats of *Salvinia auriculata* and *Pistia stratiotes* accumulated over much of the lake. **1972** *Science* 27 Oct. 403/1 Microbial mats occur in Yellowstone at temperatures up to about 70°C. **1973** *Nature* 4 May 12/1 The meeting concluded with a field trip to the algal mats at the north shore of the Great Salt Lake.

8. a. *mat-house, -shed* (examples), *-skirt, -work*. **c.** *mat-forming, -making* (examples). **d. mat-man** *slang*, a wrestler.

1951 *Dict. Gardening* (R. Hort. Soc.) IV. 1878/1 [*Saxifraga*] Section 2. Hirculus. Mat-forming plants with undivided, deciduous, oval leaves. **1971** D. Bartrum *Rock Gardens* vii. 162 The 'Cheddar Pink' is another very tough mat-forming plant that doesn't mind being walked upon when not in flower. **1898** W. C. Scully *Between Sun & Sand* 18 (Pettman), On either side of it stood respectively, a mat-house and a square tent. **1854** Thoreau *Walden* 283 Might not the basket, stable-broom, mat-making, corn-parching, linen-spinning, and pottery business have thrived here? **1890** Ld. Lugard *Diary* 21 Feb. (1959) I. ii. 111 The Banga reed grows by the river here, but very poorly, and useless for building and mat-making. **1923** *N.Y. Times* 11 Feb. i. ii. 1/4 (*heading*) Navy matmen on top. In a finely contested wrestling match..the Naval Academy won. **1930** *Ibid.* 16 Feb. xi. 3/5 It was..the first time in four seasons that the Midshipmen have been able to take the measure of the matmen from South Bethlehem. **1942** Berrey & Van den Bark *Amer. Thes. Slang* § 707/2 Matman. **1968** *Globe & Mail Mag.* (Toronto) 17 Feb. 8/3 He became one of the best known mat men in Canada. 'Wrestling always fascinated me,' he says now. **1971** *Soviet Weekly* 8 May 14 A popular group exercise among the matmen. **1926** M. Leinster *Dew on Leaf* i. iii. 41 Warehouses, mat-sheds, and hovels. **1939** 'A. Bridge' *Four-Part Setting* ii. 8 To sit in a mat-shed on the sand and drink cocktails. **1908** *Daily Chron.* 15 Aug. 1/6 A Maori chief..saying..he was to fasten the native mat-skirt about his body. **1944** *Horizon* Jan. 48 P.T. exercises ..mat work, track work.

mat, *sb.*[2] **3.** Substitute for def.: A sheet of cardboard placed on the back of a print or drawing and then covered by a mount which forms a margin round the area of the print; also used for the mount itself. Cf. Mount *sb.*[2] 3 a. Also *attrib.* (Add later examples.)

1909 F. Weitenkampf *How to appreciate Prints* xiii. 291 Sometimes mat and mount are fastened together on all four sides, forming what is known as a 'sunk mount'. **1932** —— *Quest of Print* xii. 270 Some collectors place a sheet of celluloid, cellophane, or similar material..over the print

and under the mat. **1965** ZIGROSSER & GAEHDE *Guide to Collecting Orig. Prints* vii. 100 Quality of Mat Board. Only 100 percent rag-fiber mat stock is to be used. **1967** *Boston Sunday Globe* 23 Apr. B. 58/7 Sometimes prints come with a mat (white space around the art), but the framed picture is much better if the mat is made from a mat board. **1973** F. TAUBES *Painter's Dict. Materials & Methods* 149 Made, as a rule, from cardboards of various colours, mats serve in the framing of watercolors and all kinds of prints... The width of a mat..should be equal on top and at the sides but somewhat greater at the bottom, or the picture will have a tendency to 'droop'. **1974** P. HIGHSMITH *Ripley's Game* v. 50 He needed more mat paper.

mat, *sb.*[5] Colloq. abbrev. of MATINÉE.
1914 G. ATHERTON *Perch of Devil* I. viii. 55 Although Mr. Compton won't take me to any balls, there are the movin' pictures and the mats—matinées. **1940** *Amer. Speech* XV. 204/2 *Mats,* matinees.

mat, *sb.*[6] Abbrev. of MATRIX 4.
1923 M. V. ATWOOD *Country Newspaper* 20 Just a word should be added about matrices, or 'mats' as they are always called. **1937** E. J. LABARRE *Dict. Paper* 172/1 This matrix or 'mat' is then baked and used for making a metal plate for flat or roll printing. **1942** F. BROWN *Angels & Spaceships* (1955) 38 The cost of getting special Linotype mats cut would be awfully high. **1967** V. STRAUSS *Printing Industry* v. 225/2 Matrices, called mats by the industry, are intermediate elements in the production of stereotypes but they are also independent items of commerce. *Ibid.* 226/1 During mat-making an intaglio replica of the original relief material is produced. **1975** *Printing Historical Soc. Newslet.* No. 28. 3 A few large display matrices of the Caslon series (original founders' mats) are offered to PHS members.

mat (in Cinematography): see *MATTE[3].

-mat (mæt), *suffix.* [abbrev. of *-MATIC *suffix.*] A terminal element in sbs. (usu. proprietary names) denoting a device that works automatically, as *ROTISSOMAT, or a business that contains automatic or self-service equipment, as *AUTOMAT, *LAUNDROMAT. orig. *U.S.*
1935 [see *-MATIC *suffix*]. **1951** *Amer. Speech* Oct. 166 Probably the 'Automat', a self-serving institution supplying food, gave special impetus to the extension of the suffix *-mat.* A 'Mail-O-Mat' is available in the Reception Section of the Pentagon building at Washington. **1971** *Amat. Photographer* 13 Jan. 78/1 (Advt.), Nikkormat FTN f2 Nikkor, £80.

mat (mæt), *v.*[4] [f. *MAT *sb.*[2] 3.] *trans.* To mount a print on a cardboard backing, or to provide it with a border. So **ma·tted** *ppl. a.*; **ma·tting** *vbl. sb.*
1965 ZIGROSSER & GAEHDE *Guide to Collecting Orig. Prints* vii. 100 The collector or owner who will have to rely on commercial framers to have his prints matted is cautioned to insist on the following points. *Ibid.* 104 If the matted print belongs to a study collection and is stored horizontally, hinging at the side is preferable because it makes for easier and safer handling. **1967** *Boston Sunday Globe* 23 Apr. B. 58/7 Oil paintings, on the other hand, do not take glass or matting. **1968** P. NUTTALL *Picture Framing* ii. 24 Different papers can be used to surface the mounting (matting) boards before the window is cut.

Matabele (mætăbī·li). Also 9 **Matabeli, Matabili.** [Native name.] **1.** A people of Zulu stock living in Rhodesia; also, a member of this people. Also *attrib.* or as *adj.* Cf. *NDEBELE. (See also quot. 1925.)
1823 R. MOFFAT *Jrnl.* 27 May in I. Schapera *Apprenticeship at Kuruman* (1951) iv. 84 Several men from the Barolongs had just passed them on their way to Mahumapeloo to request their assistance..to endeavour to make the Matabeles retreat. **1835** A. SMITH *Diary* 16 June (1940) II. 75 Most of the people appeared to be the original inhabitants of the country, having a different look to the Matabeli. **1839** W. C. HARRIS *Wild Sports S. Afr.* iv. 22 The country of Moselekatse, king of the Abaka Zooloos, or Matabili. *Ibid.* xiv. 111 Numerous Matabili villages. **1854** R. MOFFAT *Matabele Jrnls.* (1945) I. 319 Scarcely a child is to be seen in a real Matabele town. **1894** *Jrnl. Anthrop. Inst.* XXIII. 83 As soon as a Matabele is dead his relations tie the corpse in a blanket. **1896** F. C. SELOUS *Sunshine & Storm Rhodesia* viii. 64, I should not be at all surprised to see it stated that the rebellion was caused by the inhuman behaviour of the white men in Rhodesia, who, it will be said, were in the habit of shooting down the poor, meek, inoffensive Matabele. **1919** H. H. JOHNSTON *Compar. Study Bantu & Semi-Bantu Lang.* I. v. 798 Tebele (Sindebele). This dialect of the Matabele (Amandebele) Zulus [etc.]. **1925** A. WERNER in J. A. MacCulloch *Mythol. all Races* VII. II. vii. 246 There are various tribes of ogres having only one arm and one leg, while others..have not this peculiarity. The Basuto call the former class of beings 'Matabele'—probably from having come to look on their dreaded enemies, the Zulu tribe of that name, as something scarcely human. **1936** *Discovery* June 172/1 The Xulu-Xosa (including the so-called 'Kaffirs', and the Matabele). **1967** T. O. RANGER *Revolt in S. Rhodesia* i. 38 While the Company made use of the missionaries for its own ends, employing them to obtain a favourable press for the Matabele war, Company officials themselves shared these missionary beliefs. **1972** *Police Rev.* 24 Nov. 1521/1 Cecil John Rhodes..began negotiating with Lobengula, king of the Matabele.

2. Matabele ant, a large, black, stinging ant, *Megaponera foetens,* found in Rhodesia.
1924 E. STEP *Go to Ant* xiii. 193 One of these [stink ants] is the Stink Ant proper (*Paltothyreus tarsatus*) and the other is the Matabele Ant (*Megaponera foetens*). **1932** *Discovery* July 225/2 The big black Matabele ant, *Megaponera foetens,* often marched through our camp in military formation. **1953** S. H. SKAIFE *Afr. Insect Life* xxii. 361 The Matabele ant, *Megaponera foetens,* is one of the largest and best-known members of this sub-family [*sc.* the Ponerinæ].

matador. Add: **1. b.** *fig.*
1930 R. CAMPBELL *Adamastor* 8 The matador of truth, he trails his scorn Before their lowered horns and bloodshot eyes. **1944** AUDEN *For Time Being* (1945) 118 George, you old matador, Welcome back to the Army.

c. Used *attrib.* to designate garments resembling those worn by a matador. Cf. TOREADOR C.
1959 M. SHADBOLT *New Zealanders* 217 She was..clad in black, in tight sweater and matador slacks. **1960** *Tamarack Rev.* XIV. 137 The girls dress mostly in matador pants and bright blouses. **1962** C. ROHAN *Delinquents* 144 She used to sit on the top of the front steps, clad in her matador pants and skin-tight sweater.

‖ **matadora** (mæ·tădǭ·ră). [Sp.] A woman matador.
1955 *People* (Austral.) 11 Jan. 20/2 In Mexico the girls are invading the bullrings. Pretty matadoras with flashing swords and whirling red capes are taking much of the limelight. **1956** P. MCCORMICK *Lady Bullfighter* i. 30 The words..are particularly welcome when someone substitutes the word '*matadora*' for '*señorita*'. **1968** C. CINTRON *Torera: Mem. Bullfighter* II. 70 Since they barely tolerated the idea of a gringa rejoneadora, they wouldn't even consider the possibility of an American matadora. **1974** *Publishers Weekly* 24 June 54/2 The cast includes a nervous novice matador, an ace matador,..an aspiring gypsy matadora.

matagouri. Add: (Also with pronunc. (-gau·ri).) Also **matagory, -gowry**; = *IRISHMAN 2. Also *attrib.* (Later examples.)
1934 *Bulletin* (Sydney) 16 May 39/1 Her [*sc.* an old ewe's] long wool became entangled in the thorns of a stunted matagory bush. **1939** C. BRASCH in A. E. Currie *Cent. Treas. Otago Verse* (1949) 100 Alone on the parched rise, inhuman matagowry Dry-green and fibrous. **1958** *Landfall* XII. 18 My hands were thorned with the matagauri from pulling off the finer neck wool. **1962** J. FRAME *Edge of Alphabet* xxx. 164 He remembers his last visit up Central..where the matagouri, the 'spiked plant that does not cry' grows on the hills among the snow-grass. **1963** *Times* 6 Feb. p. vii/3 What were once harsh, unlovely *matagouri* flats are now green with lucerne.

Mata Hari (ma·ta hā·ri). [f. Malay *mata* eye + *hari* day.] The name taken by Margaretha Gertruida Zelle (1876–1917), used *fig.* to signify a beautiful and seductive spy; also *attrib.* and as *vb.*
1936 E. WAUGH *Waugh in Abyssinia* iii. 96 Patrick's spy..was soon known to the European community as Mata Hari. **1947** 'N. BLAKE' *Minute for Murder* vii. 163 He's got it into his thick head that I'm a male Mata Hari. **1948** 'P. QUENTIN' *Run to Death* iii. 25 Why don't you come out from behind the Mata Hari and tell me the truth? **1962** M. CARLETON *Dread Sunset* vii. 122, I somehow can't see Miss Gantry as Jaspar's Girl Friday, let alone a Mata Hari. **1963** H. SLESAR *Bridge of Lions* (1964) i. 19 'She?' Shortlake grinned. 'Ah. Mata Hari stuff.' **1970** T. LILLEY *Projects Section* xix. 257 She was beginning to look haggard; the strain of Mata-Hari-ing was sure to tell. **1973** 'A. HALL' *Tango Briefing* xiv. 183 You wouldn't have to frisk this pint-sized Mata Hari: you could see she was armed half a mile away.

‖ **matai** (mata,i). [Samoan.] In a Samoan extended family, the person who is chosen to succeed to a chief's or orator's title and honoured as the head of the household.
1928 M. MEAD *Coming of Age in Samoa* (1929) iv. 40 The *matai* exercises nominal and usually real authority over every individual under his protection, even over his father and mother. **1934** F. M. KEESING *Mod. Samoa* i. 30 In general the *matais,* or titled men,..engage mostly in ceremonial activities while the work as the white man views it is done by the rest of the community. **1956** F. M. & M. M. KEESING *Elite Communication in Samoa* ii. 17 The community is made up of a series of households of 'extended family' or 'multiple family' type, each under the authority of a 'head' or '*matai*'. **1974** *Sunday Advocate-News* (Barbados) 16 Dec. 21/2 The matais usually deal out justice to law breakers in the Samoan spirit of 'forgive and forget' before the matter ever reaches the ears of the authorities. **1974** *Encycl. Brit. Macropædia* XVI. 205/2 Within the villages, close kinship ties have traditionally bound individuals into a sternly collectivist society. Elected family leaders called *matai* (titled chiefs or orators) form village or district councils to administer group affairs.

matapo, var. *MATIPO.

Matara, var. *MATURA.

matata (ma·tătă). *N.Z.* [Maori.] = *fern-bird* (*FERN *sb.*[1] 2 b).
1835 W. YATE *Acct. N.Z.* (ed. 2) ii. 60 Matata—A small dusky-coloured bird, with a white and brown spotted breast. **1863** A. S. ATKINSON *Jrnl.* 29 Sept. in *Richmond-Atkinson Papers* (1960) II. 64 The korimakos in the bush and the larks and matatas in the open about us. **1882** [see *fern-bird* (*FERN *sb.*[1] 2 b)]. **1966** R. A. FALLA et al. *Field Guide to Birds N.Z.* 205 Fernbird. *Bowdleria punctata.* Other names: Matata, Tataki Thrush.

Matawila, var. *METAWILEH.

match, *sb.*[1] Add: **7.** (Earlier example of use in Cricket.)
1700 *Post Boy* 30 Mar. 2/1 A Match at Cricket, of 10 Gentlemen on each side, will Be Play'd.

12. match ball, a ball of the quality and dimensions specified by the laws of the game; also, in lawn tennis, a ball that may decide a match; **match-book,** (*b*) *Cricket* (see quot. 1934); **match-card** *Cricket* (see quot. 1934) (= *score-card* (a)); **match-fit** *a.*, in good physical condition for a match; also *transf.*; hence **match-fitness; match-play, player** (add examples of lawn tennis usages); so *match-playing* vbl. sb.; **match-point,** (*a*) the state of a game when one side or player needs only one point to win the match; also, the point itself; (*b*) in *Bridge,* a unit used in scoring in tournament play; so *match-pointed* ppl. a.; **match race,** a race run as a competition; **match-winner,** one who, by his skill, makes a major contribution to the winning of a match; hence **match-winning** *ppl. a.*
1849 in 'Bat' *Cricketer's Manual* (Advt.), Dark's and Duke's Match Balls. **1895** KIPLING *Day's Work* (1898) 344 In the black jersey..of the First Fifteen, the new match-ball under his arm. **1927** *Daily Express* 5 July 2/1 They.. retrieved two successive match balls in the third set. **1928** *Daily Tel.* 26 June 11/7 On the tenth game, the American had three match balls. The first time he smashed out of court. **1934** W. J. LEWIS *Lang. Cricket* 8 A match ball is one of superior quality for match-play, of the size and weight specified in the Laws. **1961** *Amer. Speech* XXXVI. 44 With a lob Fraser lifted the deciding matchball out of bounds. **1969** M. BRADY *Lawn Tennis Encycl.* 129 Match Balls. The following championships were won after the winner was match point down. **1845** W. DENISON *Cricketer's Compan.* p. iv, The Compiler feels it necessary to offer his thanks to the Presidents and Secretaries..for ..allowing him to make extracts from their match-books. **1900** W. A. BETTESWORTH *Walkers of Southgate* II. vii. 253 In the [Harrow] Sixth Form match-book Mr. Tremlett's score..is given as follows. **1934** W. J. LEWIS *Lang. Cricket* 161 *Match book,* a book containing the scores or tabulated records of the matches played by a club or an eleven. **1901** H. BLEACKLEY *Tales of Stumps* iv. 96 Match-cards with the 'order of going in' had been printed and eagerly purchased by the spectators. **1908** *Westm. Gaz.* 20 Oct. 11/2 The Jam Sahib of Nawanagar, who, however his name may be printed on the match-cards, will always be known to the cricket-loving public. **1934** W. J. LEWIS *Lang. Cricket* 162 *Match card,* a card giving the names of the players in the order of going in to bat, and a summary of the score up to the time of issue. **1960** V. JENKINS *Lions Down Under* xii. 179 Terry Davies, Tony O'Reilly and Jeff Butterfield..were still far from match-fit. **1962** *Times* 1 Aug. 3/1 J. G. Willcox..is still not match-fit. **1967** *Listener* 24 Aug. 241/2 It took me about three months of being back in the theatre to feel match fit. **1960** V. JENKINS *Lions Down Under* xvi. 251 He..failed to reach match-fitness in time. **1961** *Times* 1 July 3/1 It was more than the flesh and blood of a man below physical and match-fitness could stand. **1920** W. T. TILDEN *Art Lawn Tennis* 67 Match play, where both men are in the same class as tennis players, resolves itself into a battle of wits and nerve. **1909** E. H. MILES *Lessons Lawn Tennis* (ed. 3) 50 The ideal match player. *Ibid.*, Hints on Match-playing. **1921** A. W. MYERS *20 Yrs. Lawn Tennis* 48 In the end he won the match, Dixon, after lazily reaching match point some eight or nine times,..retiring at two sets all. **1928** *Daily Express* 22 June 1/6 The British doubles team held match point twice in the fourth set with Eames serving. **1936** E. CULBERTSON *Contract Bridge Complete* xxxiv. 371 In duplicate Contract with match-point scoring, the unit of play is not a game or a rubber, but an individual deal. **1940** *Ibid.* (ed. 2) xxxiv. 369 Top-score (7 match-points) went to the North-South pair that fulfilled a six-spade contract. **1955** *Times* 6 July 8/5 The British [bridge] team continued to disappoint ..although they beat Finland to-day by 53 match points. **1965** *Listener* 30 Dec. 1091/1 Except at match-point scoring. It can be argued that at this method of scoring One No Trump is almost certain to give East-West a very good score. **1969** *New Yorker* 14 June 61/1 Pasarell can drive Graebner out of his mind, because he sometimes waits until Graebner has him at or near match point. **1973** *Country Life* 13 Dec. 2048/1 This was a good match-point result, for many pairs reached Six Diamonds. **1958** *Listener* 30 Oct. 709/2 Match-pointed Pairs. Game All. Dealer West. **1974** *Guardian* 25 Mar. 24/7 Match-pointed pairs events require an entirely different approach from team competitions. **1804** M. CUTLER in W. P. & J. P. Cutler *Life & Corr. M. Cutler* (1888) II. 172 It was a match race of two two-year-old colts for $1,000. **1854** W. G. SIMMS *Mellichampe* xviii. 157 If by..a match-race on foot with an Indian runner, I could do the creature a service, I could go to work cheerfully. **1874** B. F. TAYLOR *World on Wheels* 105 The train..ran a match race with a train on the Michigan Central, and reached Chicago twenty-five minutes ahead. **1948** *Chicago Daily News* 1 Nov. 13/3 He whipped Sir Barton, a 4-year-old, in a memorable match race. **1955** *Amer. Speech* XXX. 22 The term match or match race in common acceptance encompasses any specially arranged two-horse race. R. [Rules of the N.Y. State Racing Commission] 159, however, applies the term to such a race only when the track management has added 'no money or other prize'. **1961** F. C. AVIS *Sportsman's Gloss.* 166/2 *Match Race Conditions,* those normally applied to a cycle race, and affecting the number of competitors; their positions; the start, etc. **1908** *Westm. Gaz.* 21 Aug. 3/1 If you..should encounter as keen a match-winner as yourself [at golf]. **1964** J. MERCER *Great Ones* x. 69 At Wembley nothing happened to upset matters. Reg

Lewis was undoubtedly our match-winner. **1908** *Westm. Gaz.* 21 Aug. 3/1 And if you, match-winning disciple, find yourself placed in this delicate position [etc.]. **1909** *Ibid.* 12 June 16/1 In the indefatigable Mr. Brearley they have a match-winning bowler on fast wickets. **1958** *Times* 20 Sept. 2/6 Without Wardle they have no match-winning spinner. **1960** V. Jenkins *Lions Down Under* xii. 173 The accepted New Zealand pattern for match-winning rugby. **1972** G. Ross *Hist. Cricket* i. 16 Mynn was the greatest match-winning cricketer the game produced before W. G. Grace.

II. The state of being matched. **11*.** *Electr.* An equality of impedance between two coupled devices (cf. *match *v.*¹ 5 c).

1931 *Proc. IRE* XIX. 725 By introducing capacitative elements,..a match can be obtained. **1952** D. D. King *Measurement at Centimeter Wavelength* ii. 51 No assurance of match exists without prior knowledge of the impedance to be matched. **1962** Simpson & Richards *Physical Princ. Junction Transistors* v. 89 The condition of conjugate match can be obtained quite readily when tuned transformer coupling is used as in many radio-frequency applications.

match, *sb.*² Add: **5.** *match-point*; **match-book,** a 'book' containing (safety) matches; **match-box,** (*c*) *slang* a very small house; also *attrib.*, esp. in phrases *match-box skirt* (see quot. 1968), *match-box toy*, a toy small enough to fit into a match-box; **match-pot,** a small vessel for holding matches; **match-stand,** a stand for holding matches; **match-stick,** also (*b*) *slang*, a nickname for a thin person; (*c*) *attrib.*, esp. designating simple drawings in short straight lines.

1951 C. Armstrong *Black-Eyed Stranger* (1952) iv. 31 The old match-books in the gutter. **1966** H. Waugh *Pure Poison* (1967) xxiii. 140 The counter..boasted a ledger..a postcard rack and a basket of matchbooks advertising the motel. **1968** Mrs. L. B. Johnson *White House Diary* 7 Feb. (1970) 628 One table asked me for my autograph and I wrote it for them on White House matchbooks. **1905** *Pearson's Mag.* July 103/2 Few fingers are too old and few too tiny to help the match-box maker. **1920** Joyce *Let.* 29 Sept. (1957) I. 148 Got notice to quit this match-box and am..looking for a flat. **1946** A. J. Cruse (*title*) Match-box labels of the world. **1962** *Harper's Bazaar* Oct. 134/2 A matchbox skirt. A flipover belt ties on the hips. **1964** *New Statesman* 10 Apr. 579/1 *Lesney Products* (matchbox toys) has reported an accelerated increase in exports, turnover and profits. **1968** J. Ironside *Fashion Alphabet* 45 *Match-box*, a skirt given a squared box-like look by outside stitched seams back and front, introduced by Dior. **1969** E. H. Pinto *Treen* 211/1 A large range of German 'matchbox' wooden toys was made at that time [1930]. **1929** W. Faulkner *Sartoris* v. 351 The thick cables along the veranda eaves would be budding into small lilac match-points. **1856** J. C. Robinson *Inventory of Objects Mus. Ornamental Art* 37 Wedgwood Match-pot... Pair of Match-pots. **1882** *Hamilton Palace Collection Catal.* No. 600 A two-handled Chinese Vase and Cover, of rock crystal, with a matchpot at the side. **1873** *Young Englishwoman* July 357/2 This match-stand is made of pasteboard, covered with velvet. **1909** *Chambers's Jrnl.* Aug. 506/1 One lot tells us of '4 silver-mounted match-stands..and a quantity of imitation jewellery'. **1959** I. & P. Opie *Lore & Lang. Schoolch.* ix. 169 Thin people inspire almost as many names and jokes as fat people..match-stick (sometimes abbreviated to 'matchy'), needles, [etc.]. **1959** Halas & Manvell *Technique Film Animation* 14 In France, Emile Cohl began to make his little white match-stick figures jump about against a black background as early as 1908. **1963** *Times* 22 May 3/3 One man mastered it, little Harmer, of the matchstick legs and the cool footballer's brain. **1966** *Guardian* 22 Apr. 6/5 Matchstick men—taught by adults, copied by infants—can be death to child art. **1967** J. Wainwright *Worms must Wait* i. 5 They were wasted, emaciated men... They were match-stick men... They were men who should have died, but who refused to die.

match, *a.* Add: **1. match dissolve** [cf. *dissolve *v.* 7 b] *Cinemat.* (see quots. 1959, 1970); also *matched dissolve*; **matchmark** (see quots.).

1953 K. Reisz *Technique Film Editing* II. xi. 172 When diagrams *are* used, it is most important to make exactly clear what they refer to... This is accomplished most simply by the matched dissolve. **1959** W. S. Sharps *Dict. Cinematogr.* 110/1 *Match dissolve*, the overlapping of two *shots* so that, because of the identical positions of their subjects, only one person or object appears to be seen about the point of overlap. **1970** W. Wager *Sledgehammer* (1971) ix. 39 Match dissolve. That's a film term for a standard motion-picture transition, say, from the face of a clock in a police chief's office to the face of another clock in the senator's bedroom. **1918** Webster Add., *Match-mark*.., a mark placed on the contiguous separable parts of any device to aid in the proper reassembling of any of those parts. **1962** *Gloss. Terms Glass Industry* (*B.S.I.*) 41 *Match mark*, a line or seam on glassware formed at the join of two mould parts.

match, *v.*¹ Add: **5. c.** *Electr.* To equalize (two coupled impedances) so as to bring about the maximum transfer of power from one to the other; to make (a device) equal in effective impedance *to*.

1929 E. Mallett *Telegr. & Telephony* vii. 162 Where the impedances cannot be matched transformers may be introduced to give the same effect. **1931** *Proc. IRE* XIX. 725 At high frequencies a transformer consisting of primary, secondary and mutual inductances cannot be constructed to match a generator effectively to a resistive load. **1938** Q. P. Harnwell *Princ. Electr. & Electromagn.* iv. 114 When resistances are matched, half the power developed is delivered to the load and half is lost in the source. **1959** R. L. Shrader *Electronic Communication* xiii. 371 The requirement is to match a 4-ohm speaker to a 4,000-ohm power tube. **1966** R. C. Hansen *Microwave Scanning Antennas* III. ii. 186 The sinuous feed and couplers..terminated in radiating elements which are matched to free space.

8. b. *to match up to*: to equal; to be comparable with.

1958 *Times* 18 Sept. 13/3 But Blanche can match up to Emily, indeed she surpasses her in the end. **1958** *Listener* 13 Nov. 800/2 This musical image..cannot match up to the breadth and immediacy of 'Mars'. **1964** M. Gowing *Britain & Atomic Energy* v. 163 Britain's manpower resources did not match up to her programmes.

matchableness. (Later example.)

1857 C. M. Yonge *Let.* 1 Oct. in C. Coleridge *C. M. Yonge* (1903) viii. 214 A most perfect marriage..as to the matchableness of the two people.

matched, *ppl. a.* Add: **3.** *matched orders*: the name given to systems of manipulation on the Stock Exchange, which involve artificial treatment of orders to buy and sell. Also occas. *sing.* Also *matching orders*. orig. *U.S.*

1903 S. S. Pratt *Work of Wall St.* 146 The Syndicate may be washing sales by matched orders through curb brokers in order to market watered stock. **1908** *Westm. Gaz.* 26 Aug. 2/2 An order to buy is given to one broker and an order to sell to another, and an arrangement is made that the two brokers shall only deal with one another... The opportunity for market manipulation is obvious, and 'matched orders' have led to grave scandals. **1920** A. C. Pigou *Econ. of Welfare* II. vi. 178 It should be observed that the device of 'matched orders' may be made difficult by a rule forbidding offers and bids for large amounts of stock on the terms 'all or none'. **1930** J. E. Meeker *Work of Stock Exchange* (rev. ed.) xvi. 455 A..subtler evil consists of 'matching orders'... Instances where there is danger of matched orders..deserve brief explanation. **1941** Dice & Eiteman *Stock Market* (ed. 2) 467 When a trader gives one broker orders to buy a given stock and another orders to sell a like amount of stock in a manner to either advance or depress the price artificially, such a trader is said to be giving matched orders. **1951** G. L. Leffler *Stock Market* xx. 327 Artificial market activity was accomplished..through matched orders and ..without matched orders... Matched orders were in violation of state law and the rules of the New York Stock Exchange... The same effect as the matched order could be obtained without its actual use. **1964** P. Wyckoff *Dict. Stock Market Terms* 163 *Matched orders.* 1. Orders to buy or sell a particular stock which are placed simultaneously with different brokers by the same person... 2. Buy and sell orders matched legitimately by the specialist in a stock in order to arrange an opening price as closely as possible to the previous close.

4. Designed to match in colour, style, etc.; matching.

1972 A. Roudybush *Sybaritic Death* (1974) vii. 70 Clare's status-conscious matched luggage. **1974** P. de Vries *Glory of Hummingbird* iii. 49 A matched set of luggage. **1975** P. G. Winslow *Death of Angel* vi. 142 He presented her with a set of matched luggage..for the weekends.

mate, *sb.*² Add **1.** (Further, esp. Austral., examples.)

1845 C. Griffith *Present State of Port Philip* 79 Two [bushworkers] generally travel together, who are called mates; they are partners, and divide all their earnings. **1890** 'R. Boldrewood' *Miner's Right* 136 We have been firm friends and true mates all this time. **1901** M. Franklin *My Brilliant Career* i. 3 Daddy's little mate isn't going to turn Turk like that, is she? **1908** E. J. Banfield *Confessions of Beachcomber* I. v. 174 With a mate he had been for many months, bêche-de-mer fishing, their station ..a lonely islet in Whitsunday Passage. **1911** C. E. W. Bean *'Dreadnought' of Darling* xxxv. 311 Perhaps the strongest article in the out-back code is that of loyalty to a mate. **1942** C. Barrett *On Wallaby* iv. 75, I told my mates some of these facts on returning. **1966** *Observer* 17 Apr. 30/1 A 17-year-old boy..said, 'I haven't got a real mate. That's what I need.' **1968** K. Weatherly *Roo Shooter* 109 Old Sam, born and reared in the bush, a good mate and bushman. **1973** *Parade* (Melbourne) Sept. 34/1 An obelisk in the Jewish section of the Melbourne General Cemetery records the names of those who fought for Australia in the 1914 War. Many of them trained in the Faraday Street School cadets. They assimilated the lessons of patriotism and were great mates.

b. (Austral. examples.)

1852 R. Cecil *Diary* 31 Mar. (1935) 36 When the diggers address a policeman in uniform they always call him 'Sir', but they always address a fellow in a blue shirt with a carbine as 'Mate'. 'Mate' is the ordinary popular form of allocution in these colonies. **1862** A. Polehampton *Kangaroo Land* 99 A man, who greeted me after the fashion of the Bush, with a 'Good day, mate'. **1974** *Sydney Morning Herald* 14 Feb. 7, I asked a station attendant (attired in a dirty open-necked shirt and trousers, recognizable only by a dirty cap) if the train was the North-West Mail. 'I wouldn't have a clue, mate,' was the reply.

d. Also *to be mates with*.

1880 H. Lapham in D. M. Davin *N.Z. Short Stories* (1953) 57 At this time I was mates with a young fellow called Jim Smith, a good enough lad as a mate, and would do just as big a day's labour as any man.

e. (See quot. 1904 and cf. 4 b.)

1881 H. & C. R. Smith *Isle of Wight Words* 21 *Meyat*, a mate; the carter's assistant. **1884** J. C. Egerton *Sussex Folk & Ways* ii. 26 [A] carter-boy credited with the following..advice to his father, whose 'mate' he was. **1904** Goodchild & Tweney *Technol. & Sci. Dict.* 384 *Mate*, an assistant or subordinate who assists a more skilled workman. **1951** *Engineering* 9 Mar. 296/3 It is claimed by the strikers that a new electrician's mate..should resign. **1963** *Times* 9 Mar. 9/5 The Scottish chimney sweep..always has a mate.

3. d. *spec.* A point on tramway lines which is cast solid and pairs or 'mates' with the movable tongue or switch on the other rail; an 'open' or 'fixed' point. orig. *U.S.*

1909 in Webster. **1922** *Glasgow Herald* 3 Oct. 8 The weight of the inserts varies from about 100 to 300 lb., depending on the angle of the crossing or mate.

mate, *v.*² Add: **1.** Delete ? *Obs.* and add later examples.

1874 Swinburne *Bothwell* I. i. 4, I might sleep well and laugh and walk at ease, With none to mate me. **1891** W. Morris *Poems by Way* 129 *Fig-tree.* I who am little among trees In honey-making mate the bees.

6. a. *intr.* Of an engineering part: to make a good or proper fit *with*.

1909 in Webster. **1956** S. Parker *Drawings & Dimensions* vii. 52 When considering the application of 'Go' and 'Not Go' gauges..the questions 'Will *like* mate with *like*?' and 'How much force may be used when gauging?' inevitably arise. **1959** *Motor Manual* (ed. 36) v. 132 The end of the axle hub is threaded and extends outside the wheel to take a large eared nut, which is coned internally to mate with a cone on the edge of the wheel hub. **1967** *Electronics* 6 Mar. 15/3 (Advt.), Push-pull coupling mates easily.

b. *trans.* To fit or join *with* or *to*.

1959 *Nat. Geographic* Feb. 159/1 High on skeletal service towers, we watched engineers mate, or couple, rocket stages and gingerly install the payloads containing custom-built miniaturized instruments. **1962** V. Grissom in *Into Orbit* 119 On 1 July the capsule was taken from the hangar..to be mated to the Redstone. **1970** N. Armstrong et al. *First on Moon* iii. 55 By mid-May it was time to 'mate' the electrical systems of the rocket boosters with those of the spacecraft.

mated, *ppl. a.*² Add: **b.** Fitted or fitting together.

1958 V. H. Watson *Rover Cars* xiv. 230 Wash and examine all parts, renew as necessary, bearing in mind that the crown wheel and pinion are 'mated' parts and must be replaced as such.

matelot (mæ·tlo). [Fr., sailor; cf. *matlo(w.] **1.** A sailor. *Naut. slang.*

1911 'Guns' & 'Theeluker' *Middle Watch Musings* 8 You've just got two old and respected matelots well scrubbed for nuffing. **1915** *Blackw. Mag.* July 89/1 We invite the matelots to lie on their backs on the upper-deck. **1947** *Landfall* I. 283 What time we had left was spent on fruitless errands for the Pommie matelots. **1955** *Times* 10 Aug. 3/3 The Navy was there once more and so were the two matelots of Monday. **1970** [see *Jock¹ 1 b]. **1974** *Listener* 21 Nov. 672/1 Our screen matelots..should be as reticent as..*Captain Horatio Hornblower*.

2. Applied to a shade of blue.

1927 *Daily Tel.* 26 Apr. 13/5 (Advt.), Fawn, Rose, .. Almond, Matelot. **1928** *Daily Express* 27 July 5/4 A lovely deep blue known as 'matelot'.

mater. 1. (Later examples.)

1905 *Sci. Amer.* 12 Aug. 120/2 The Astrolabe of Regiomontanus... *Mater* is the name given to the large disk divided into degrees. **1974** *Ibid.* Jan. 101/1 Each plate being engraved on both sides and all being stacked in the mater, or main body, of the astrolabe.

Mater Dolorosa (mē¹·təɹ dǫlǒrōᵘ·să). [med. L., lit. 'sorrowful mother'.] A title of the Virgin Mary, emphasizing her role in the Passion of Christ; a representation, in painting or sculpture, of the Virgin Mary sorrowing. Also *transf.*, a woman who has the attributes of the sorrowful mother.

The term probably originated in the medieval Latin hymn beginning 'Stabat mater dolorosa Iuxta crucem lacrimosa'.

1800 J. Dallaway *Anecdotes of Arts in England* 516 He has a mater dolorosa and a boy playing on a lute by Guido. *c* **1869** Taylor & Dubourg in M. R. Booth *Eng. Plays of 19th Cent.* (1973) III. 308 Crosses her hands on her bosom, à la Mater Dolorosa. **1872** Geo. Eliot *Middlem.* IV. viii. lxxx. 283 Dorothea's face..had the pale cheeks and pink eyelids of a *mater dolorosa*. **1888** *Cycl. Painters & Paintings* III. 220/2 Mater Dolorosa.. By Murillo, Madrid Museum... Companion to Ecce Homo. **1892** *Servite Manual* (Servite Fathers) 200 (*heading*) Via Matris Dolorosæ or, The Stations of the Way of the Seven Dolours of Mary. **1895** *Yellow Bk.* IV. 280 A vast cape that might have enshrouded the form of a Mater Dolorosa hung by the side of a jauntily-striped Langtry-hood. **1904** G. Gronau *Titian* vii. 147 We can follow exactly the history of this picture and of its companion, the 'Mater Dolorosa', which Titian sent off to Charles V in 1555. **1917** M. G. Segar *Some Minor Poems Middle Ages* xxi. 48 Old English poems on the Mater Dolorosa are always wonderfully full of feeling. **1923** M. Innes *Ten Florentine Painters* 117 This group of the 'Mater Dolorosa' and her dead Son is called a *Pietà*. **1936** R. Lehmann *Weather in Streets* iv. ii. 398 Mrs. Cunningham stood in the double doorway..receiving with a smile of the lips, but not of the hollowed *mater dolorosa* eyes, congratulations upon Amanda. **1938** *Times Lit. Suppl.* 11 June 415/3 Patricia is the picture of the *mater dolorosa* of all time. **1942** G. D. Carleton *Mother of Jesus* xiv. 68 The Mother of Jesus is indeed the *Mater Dolorosa*, the Sorrowful Mother. **1951** L. MacNeice tr. *Goethe's Faust* I.

120 In a niche on the wall is an image of the Mater Dolorosa. **1955** W. Smith tr. *Mieggé's Virgin Mary* viii. 171 All this conforms with..medieval piety..and the more recent veneration of the *Mater dolorosa.*

material, *a.* and *sb.* Add: **A.** *adj.* **2.** (Further examples.)

1685 tr. *Arnauld & Nicole's Logic* III. xiii. 65 The truth of a Consequence..is only propounded conditionally, and separated from the material Truth, as I may so say, of what it contains. **1883** F. H. Bradley *Princ. Logic* 471 If 'material' is a name for what transcends mere 'concepts' and commits itself to truth, then of course all logic must be material. **1889** J. Venn *Princ. Empirical Logic* Pref., In such a province..as that of Material or Inductive Logic the case is very different. **1936** *Mind* XLV. 442 Wisdom.. gives the name *Material Analysis* to the substitution, for sentences about wholes, of sentences mentioning the individual parts of the whole, where the parts are of the same order of ultimacy (as previously defined) as the whole. *E.g.*, material analysis of sentences about awe will be in terms of fear and admiration. **1937** A. Smeaton tr. *Carnap's Logical Syntax of Lang.* IV. 237 We will..assign to the material mode of speech any sentence which is to be interpreted as attributing to an object a particular property, this property being quasi-syntactical, so that the sentence can be translated into another sentence which attributes a correlated syntactical property to a designation of the object in question. **1946** *Mind* LV. 321 If we follow the material logicians in holding that universal propositions are existential as to individuals also [etc.].

b. *material implication*: a relationship which holds between two propositions, irrespective of content, save only when the first is true and the second false.

1903 B. Russell *Princ. Math.* ii. 14 How far formal implication is definable in terms of implication simply, or material implication as it may be called, is a difficult question. **1932**, etc. [see *formal *a.* and *sb.* 1 d]. **1965** Hughes & Londey *Elem. Formal Logic* iii. 17 A material implication is always true when its antecedent is false, and also when its consequent is true. That is, a false proposition materially implies any proposition; and a true proposition is materially implied by any proposition. **1974** *Encycl. Brit. Macropædia* XI. 40/2 Reading $p \supset q$ as 'If p, q'..is made convenient by the fact that 'if' is often used in English in a 'material-implication' sense (someone who asserted 'If it isn't raining, it's snowing' would usually be held to have spoken truly *unless* the antecedent were true but the consequent false; i.e., unless it was neither raining nor snowing).

3. e. Philos. *material object, thing*: an object considered as a physical existent independent of consciousness; hence *material objectness,* the state of existing as a material object.

1605 Bacon *Adv. Learning* I. i. § 3 View and inquiry into these sensible and material things. **1649** tr. *Descartes' Discourse* 59 Imagination..is a particular manner of thinking on materiall things. **1713** Berkeley *Three Dialogues* 61, I wou'd, therefore, fain know, what Arguments you can draw from Reason, for the Existence of what you call *real Things,* or *material Objects.* **1737** A. Baxter *Inquiry Human Soul* (ed. 2) II. 204 He supposes that from the surfaces of all material things there are continually flying off thin membranes. **1865** Mill *Exam. Hamilton's Philos.* i. 6 We at first limit ourselves to the case of physical, or what are commonly called material objects. **1899** W. James *Talks to Teachers* vii. 58 The result of all this is that intimate familiarity with the physical environment, that acquaintance with the properties of material things, which is really the foundation of human consciousness. **1912** B. Russell *Probl. Philos.* iv. 58 Common sense regards tables and chairs and the sun and moon and material objects generally as something radically different from minds. **1920** A. N. Whitehead *Concept of Nature* ii. 43 Thus colour is not part of the reality of the material object. **1932** H. H. Price *Perception* ii. 52 'Material-objectness' cannot be defined without mention of it. **1933** *Mind* XLII. 291 On the phenomenalistic view of material-objectness, there *is* evidence that material objects exist. **1940** A. J. Ayer *Found. Empirical Knowl.* i. 1 It does not normally occur to us that there is any need..to justify our belief in the existence of material things. **1941** *Mind* L. 282 The puzzle is this: if sense-data are all that we are directly aware of in perception, how have we ever acquired the concept of 'material-objectness' at all? **1959** J. L. Austin *Sense & Sensibilia* (1962) ii. 7 'Material thing' is not an expression which the ordinary man would use. *Ibid.* x. 107 The material-object language *must somehow* be 'reducible' to the sense-datum language. **1964** *Philos. Rev.* LXXIII. 324 A corpse, like a material object, is non-conscious, rather than merely unconscious.

4. c. *material culture*: the physical objects (tools, articles of domestic and religious use, dwelling-places, etc.) which give evidence of the type of culture developed by a social group.

1929 *N. & Q. Anthropol.* (ed. 5) 187 The study of the artefacts and material culture of a people should not be viewed solely from their material aspects. *Ibid.* 188 The investigator of socio-religious matters may find that he cannot get information, and he will then find that a study of material culture provides him with a convenient avenue of approach. **1931** *Encycl. Social Sci.* IV. 622/1 Material equipment of culture is not, however, a force in itself... Material culture requires a complement less simple, less easily catalogued or analyzed, consisting of the body of intellectual knowledge. **1937** R. H. Lowie *Hist. Ethnol. Theory* iii. 27 Evolution is a positive fact in material culture. **1971** *World Archaeol.* III. 119 Most items of material culture will have been removed.

d. Gram. *material noun,* = **mass noun.*

1892 [see *class-noun* (*class *sb.* 10)]. **1892** H. Sweet *New Eng. Gram.* I. 56 When a material noun is used to express an individual object of definite shape, it is no longer a material noun, but a class-noun. **1925** Grattan & Gurrey *Our Living Lang.* xviii. 110 A material-noun is a word which stands for the whole mass of matter possessing the qualities implied by the word, or for an indefinite quantity of that matter—for example, *water, iron, veal, butter.* **1969** R. Kingdon *Palmer's Gram. Spoken Eng.* (ed. 3) II. 61 Common nouns..are subdivided into Material nouns and Class nouns. Material nouns..name substances.

B. *sb.* **6*.** Preceded by a qualifying word, as *officer material,* a person who has (or persons who have) qualities thought of as suitable for an officer; similarly *headmaster material,* etc.; also with non-animate qualifier, as *football material,* a person or persons potentially suitable as footballers; *grammar-school material,* a person or persons suitable for admission to a grammar school.

1892 *College Index* (Auburn, Alabama) Nov. I. i. 23 He still kept a sharp lookout for football material. **1927** *Officers Training Corps Gaz.* Apr. 59/1 The sorely needed officer material caused by the early casualties. **1946** *Amer. Speech* XXI. 238 *Officer material,* an enlisted man short in mentality. **1951** H. Wouk *Caine Mutiny* xi. 123, I regard both those men as excellent officer material. **1964** 'E. Peters' *Flight of Witch* i. 9 Tom Kenyon, confident, clever and ambitious, was obvious headmaster material. **1968** L. Berg *Risinghill* 86 The inspector who denounced the school the first time was a man who was interested in grammar-school 'material'. **1969** M. Pugh *Last Place Left* xxvii. 194 It was difficult recruiting men... 'Some of them, well, they're not leadership material.' **1969** B. Weil *Dossier IX* ii. 4 His secretary came in. She was a tall fair girl with a tendency to stride. Wren officer material, Asher thought. **1970** 'J. Melville' *New Kind of Killer* i. 8 Her report..was, on the whole, a favourable one: 'This officer is good promotion material.' **1971** D. Eden *Afternoon Walk* viii. 109 Aren't all top executives ulcer material?

7. *materials technology, material(s testing*; **material(s control** (see quot. 1959); hence *materials controller*; **material(s handling,** the movement and storage of materials in a factory; **material(s science,** that branch of science which treats of the structure and properties of materials, esp. in so far as they are relevant to their usefulness and potential applications; so *material(s scientist.*

1918 C. E. Knoeppel *Organization & Administration* xv. 252 The material control sheet takes care of pieces ordered, pieces rough, pieces in progress, and pieces finished. **1938** W. B. Cornell *Business Organization* xvi. 318 The other important duties of the standards and methods section include..development of stores and material control and production control methods. **1959** *Gloss. Terms Work Study* (*B.S.I.*) 33 *Material control,* procedures and means by which the correct quantity and quality of materials and components are made available to meet production plans. **1962** A. Battersby *Guide to Stock Control* 123 The Materials Control office calculated that the increase in the first-grade stock would have to be 200 items to preserve the same risk level as before. *Ibid.* x. 90 The Finance Director..will then need a subordinate who can translate his general decisions on policy into detailed instructions. The subordinate would be the Materials Controller: this title is better than the more usual 'Stock Controller' because, as we have seen, he controls the *flow* of materials rather than the stocks themselves. **1921** E. T. Elbourne *Factory Administration & Cost Accounts* (new ed.) 807 A form of production service having special reference to material handling and custody. **1932** S. J. Koshkin *Mod. Materials Handling* i. 2 It is of the greatest importance that the materials-handling methods and devices should be sufficiently worked out at the time the plant is designed so as to make them an integral part of the design. **1966** A. Battersby *Math. in Managem.* vii. 163 A recent paper dealing with steel fabrication showed that an extra crane costing £15,000 would not be needed in a new materials-handling system. **1961** (*title of periodical*) Progress in materials science. **1966** P. Feltham *Deformation & Strength of Materials* p. v, One of the effects of the unprecedented advance in the synthesis and use of new materials in the last few decades..has been the widespread introduction of 'materials science' into curricula of university courses. **1974** *New Scientist* 9 May 349/1 (Advt.), Applicants should have a degree in physics or a material science discipline. **1974** *Nature* 16 Aug. p. vii (Advt.), A vacancy exists for a Materials Scientist to study basic factors concerned with lubrication, wear, fatigue and corrosion of plastics and metals used in the manufacture of orthopaedic implants. **1962** *Technology* June 129/1 The course on materials technology will draw on the methods of physics, chemistry, metallurgy and engineering. **1972** N. J. Parratt *Fibre-Reinforced Materials Technol.* p. ix, Much of industry is concerned with making materials or with turning them into useful hardware, so that it cannot safely ignore any advances in materials technology. **1924** *Trans. Amer. Soc. Mech. Engin. Index* 124/2 (*heading*) Materials testing. **1950** *Chem. Engin. Progress* XLVI. 110/3 Materials Testing Reactor which..will be used in studies of material to be employed in building reactors. **1969** R. F. Lang tr. *Henglein's Chem. Technol.* 315 The so-called technical laboratories..carry out the routine analyses..as well as material testing.

materialistical, *a.* (Further example.)

1973 C. & R. Milner *Black Players* v. 115 There's too much paranoia, too much greed... And suspicion, and too much materialistical fear.

‖ **materia prima** (mătīə·riă prəi·mă). [L., 'first matter'; cf. Gr. *ἡ πρώτη ὕλη* (see Hyle).] = *first matter* (Matter *sb.*¹ 6 c).

1551 S. Gardiner *Explication True Catholique Fayth* 137 If we agree with the Philosophers that there is (*Materia prima*)..the same (*Materia prima*) beyng as it were (substancia) that altereth not. [*a* **1586** Sidney *Apol. Poetrie* (1868) 55 The quiddity of..*Prima materia* will hardely agree with a Corslet.] **1603** Holland tr *Plutarch's Morals* xvi. 229 The substance or matter that hath neither forme nor any colour, which they call *Materia prima,* is a subject capable of all formes. **1665** J. Locke *Let.* in P. King *Life of Locke* (1829) 20 Poor *materia prima* was canvassed cruelly. *Ibid.*, The young monks..dispute as eagerly for *materia prima,* as if they were to make their dinner on it. *a* **1721** Prior *Locke & Montaigne* in *Dialogues of Dead* (1907) 240 When he [*sc.* Descartes] gave Us his subtil matter, he only new Christened Aristotles *Materia prima.* **1905** W. James in *Jrnl. Philos.* 25 May 281 'Pure experience'..was the name I gave to the *materia prima* of everything. **1961** *Times* 28 Dec. 11/4 A continuum of active or quiescent energy which..would reintroduce a *materia prima* to the satisfaction of metaphysicians.

‖ **mater lectionis** (mēⁱ·təɹ lekti,ōᵘ·nis). *Gram.* Pl. **matres lectionis.** [mod.L., lit. 'mother of reading'.] A letter which has the function of a diacritical mark; *spec.* in Hebrew writing, a sign indicating a vowel sound.

1846 B. Davies tr. *Gesenius's Hebrew Gram.* I. i. § 8 The vowel-letters are also called by grammarians, *matres lectionis* (since they partly serve as guides in reading the unprinted text). **1925** P. Radin tr. *Vendryès's Lang.* v. i. 328 In the Greek alphabet the principle of the *matres lectionis* was skilfully used for the creation of a special sign for each vowel. **1962** Davidson & Mauchline *Introd. Hebrew Gram.* (ed. 25) 13 Thus ו would come in time to stand for long *o* and *u*, י for long *e* and *i*. ה likewise came to have a vocalic usage and the three letters are often termed vowel-letters or vocalic consonants (also *matres lectionis*).

maternity. Add: **3.** *maternity leave*; **maternity benefit,** a welfare service payment made to women, under specified conditions, after the period of confinement; **maternity home** = *maternity hospital*; **maternity jacket** *slang* (see quot. 1925); also *ellipt.* as *maternity.*

1911 *Q. Rev.* Oct. 561 When both husband and wife are insured, they are to be entitled, in case of the wife's confinement, to both sickness and maternity benefit. **1911** [see *benefit *sb.* 3 d]. **1945** *Release & Resettlement* (H.M. Govt.) xii. 40 The benefits of the National Health Insurance Scheme include..maternity benefit. **1957** Brudno & Bower *Taxation in U.K.* 523/1 Maternity benefits. **1970** *National Insurance: Maternity Benefits* (Dept. Health & Social Security, NI 17A) I. i. 6 There are two maternity benefits—maternity grant and maternity allowance. Both benefits may be paid for a confinement provided the conditions are satisfied. *Ibid.* III. xxiii. 18 Any question about contributions, including whether the contribution tests for maternity benefit..are satisfied, is reserved for the Secretary of State for Social Services. **1922** *Encycl. Brit.* XXX. 652/1 The supervision of midwifery, including the establishment of maternity homes. **1926** *Act* 16 & 17 *Geo. V* c. 32 § 12 The expression 'maternity home' means any premises used or intended to be used for the reception of pregnant women or of women immediately after childbirth. **1967** *Encycl. Brit.* XV. 66/1 Increasing grants have been made by some governments for the construction of free maternity homes or maternity wards in general hospitals. **1925** Fraser & Gibbons *Soldier & Sailor Words* 154 *Maternity jacket,* the name given the double breasted tunic, worn formerly in the Royal Flying Corps. **1958** 'N. Shute' *Rainbow & Rose* ii. 66 A very young man in the double-breasted 'maternity' jacket of the Royal Flying Corps. *Ibid.* iii. 91 She insisted on giving me a buttonhole..but my maternity hadn't got a buttonhole to put it in. **1970** *Guardian* 21 May 13/2 At present, maternity leave is based on the custom and practice of either individual companies or sections of industry. **1973** *Times* 17 Mar. 2/2 Mrs Christine Page.. said: 'Because of the economic uncertainty of some families, we are asking for this maternity leave to be negotiated.'

b. Used *attrib.* of garments spec. designed for pregnant women.

1893 *Ladies' Home Jrnl.* Apr. 28/2 Summer maternity gowns. **1907** *Dress* Jan. p. xx, My Maternity corsets are recommended by physicians everywhere. **1951** I. Shaw *Troubled Air* x. 164 She was wearing one of her shapeless tent-like maternity dresses. **1962** M. Drabble *Summer Bird-Cage* vi. 92 She would wear pretty maternity dresses and be an excellent mother. **1963** 'G. Bagby' *Murder's Little Helper* (1964) ii. 14 What kind of a burglar is it that swipes maternity clothes? *Ibid.*, She hadn't splurged on maternity garments. **1964** M. Drabble *Garrick Year* i. 11 Three years of child-bearing and modelling maternity clothes. **1966** *Guardian* 5 Aug. 8/4 The wide coats and dresses have the ease of maternity wear. **1971** B. Malamud *Tenants* 211 Under a short maternity skirt her stomach is in flower. **1971** C. Storr *Thursday* vi. 63, I can just see myself in maternity smocks for the next ten years.

mateship. Add: (Austral. examples.)

1905 H. Lawson in B. Stevens *Bush Ballads* (1910) 76 The College Wreck..Tramps West in mateship with the man Who cannot write his name. **1930** W. H. Hancock *Australia* x. 199 Thwarted individualism found consolation in the gospel of mateship. **1960** J. Fingleton *Four Chukkas to Austral.* xviii. 158 Benaud knew, too, that he had to cultivate mateship. **1962** *Guardian* 14 Aug. 6/5 A beery sense of 'mateship' among the men. **1968** *Courier-Mail* (Brisbane) 20 July 2/2 When I was..Prime Minister ..he gave me not only his personal co-operation, understanding and loyalty but also his mateship, often in the most difficult circumstances, even when we disagreed.

matey. (Further examples.)

1859 H. Kingsley *Recoll. G. Hamlyn* II. xiv. 277, I took him for a flash overseer, sporting his salary, and I was as thick as you like with him. And 'Matey,' says I, (you see I was familiar, he seemed such a jolly sort of bird),

'Matey, what station are you on?' **1909** S. WATSON *Wops the Waif* i. 2 'I say, Tickle matey, wot's all them a-readin' of on that bill over there?' interrupted Wops. **1916** 'TAFFRAIL' *Pincher Martin* ii. 16 A gray, cigar-shaped vessel lying in a dry dock, with dockyard 'maties' swarming on board her. **1931** KIPLING *Limits & Renewals* (1932) 197 Polyphemus damned back at Jemmy like a Chatham matey. **1958** E. HYAMS *Taking it Easy* I. ii. 72 The dockyard 'mateys' who had been sent us to do the work were all Bretons from the Arsenal at Brest. **1973** J. DRUMMOND *Bang! Bang! you're Dead!* xxv. 86 Right, matey, 'oo told you? **1974** 'M. HEBDEN' *Pride of Dolphins* III. iii. 232 Many of the lights in the control room were missing, probably stolen by dockyard mateys.

matey (mē̆i·ti), *a.* [f. MATE *sb.*[2] + -Y[1].] Like a mate or mates; friendly and familiar (*with*); sociable, companionable. Hence **ma·teyness** = *MATINESS.

1915 T. BURKE *Nights in Town* 50 You are all so—what is the word?—matey, isn't it? Yes, that's the note of the London [music] hall—mateyness. **1919** WODEHOUSE *Damsel in Distress* xv. 172 After the game he took me off to his cottage and gave me a drink... We got extremely matey. **1926** *Contemp. Rev.* June 682 The *British Worker*, an equally deplorable organ produced by *intelligentsia* trying to be 'matey'. **1929** W. DEEPING *Roper's Row* xxi. § ii, Elizabeth would..want to be matey with people. **1946** WODEHOUSE *Joy in Morning* i. 4, I..continued to tut-tut a bit at having missed the young pipsqueak, with whom my relations had always been of the matiest. **1958** *Times Lit. Suppl.* 20 June 347/3 When the implied mateyness is further established by such otiose asides..one stirs uncomfortably to ask why a writer who has so much that is interesting to say should waste our time with these lazy transcriptions. **1967** *Listener* 24 Aug. 244/2 Continuous pop and advertisements, presented with that bogus trans-atlantic mateyness which apparently 'sends' teenagers. **1974** V. GIELGUD *In Such a Night* ix. 82 She would throw a party. And in the ensuing haze of drink and mateyness grievances would..disappear.

math[1]. (Later examples.)

1917 MOTHER ST. JEROME *Garden of Life* 18 You feel as you lie in the math The watching unseen of his eyes. **1968** R. E. ZUPKO *Dict. Eng. Weights & Measures* 103 *Math*,.. in Herefordshire equal to approximately 1 acre..or to the amount of land that a man could mow in a day.

math[2]. Add: (Earlier and later examples.) Also **matha.**

1828 H. H. WILSON in *Asiatick Researches* XVI. 103 The disciples, who are domesticated in the several *Maths*, profess also perpetual celibacy. *a* **1851** M. M. SHERWOOD *Hist. Little Henry & his Bearer* (1866) 84 This sahib..had himself built a mutt. **1877** M. WILLIAMS *Hinduism* 224 *Yatis*, monks or ascetics,..often congregate in Maṭhas or 'monasteries'. **1913** 'A. AVALON' tr. *Tantra of Great Liberation* p. xvii, Kedarnath... A *matha* and temple dedicated to Shrī Sādāshiva. **1956** R. REDFIELD *Peasant Society & Culture* iii. 81 Some sweet-voiced, gifted expounder sitting in a temple, *mutt*, public hall or house-front.

math[3] (mæþ). *U.S. colloq.* = *MATHS.

Math. is used as an abbreviation in written English in the U.K. but not in speech, the normal form being *Maths.*

1890 in *Cent. Dict.* **1895** W. C. GORE in *Inlander* Nov. 64 *Math.* n. Mathematics. **1899** J. LONDON *Let.* 24 Oct. (1966) 62 She's well up in the higher math. **1916** [see *my guess is* (*GUESS *sb.* 1)]. **1938** I. GOLDBERG *Wonder of Words* x. 200 He [*sc.* a student] says *math* and *ec.* **1961** C. WINSTON *Hours Together* (1962) vii. 139 There was Morton Kersh, with the math book propped against the milk bottle on the kitchen table. **1971** *Black World* June 80/2 T. J. failed Math and English. **1973** *Jrnl. Genetic Psychol.* CXXIII. 163 The follow-up results with the math-science boys. **1974** *State* (Columbia, S. Carolina) 8 Mar. 19-B/5 Parents who have children in a Title I reading, math or kindergarten program are also invited to attend.

mathematical, *a.* and *sb.* Add: **A.** *adj.* **1. b.** *mathematical model*: see *MODEL *sb.* 2 e.

e. *mathematical linguistics*: a branch of linguistics concerned with the application of mathematical models and procedures to the analysis of linguistic structure; so *mathematical linguist*; *mathematical logic*: logic that is mathematical in its method, using symbols and following definite and explicit rules of derivation; modern logic; symbolic logic; so *mathematical logician*; *mathematical philosophy*: that branch of philosophy concerned with the nature of mathematics.

1951 *Language* XXVII. 221 There is a growing cleavage between the mathematical linguists, or metalinguists, and the physical linguists, whom I should call just plain linguists. **1956** J. WHATMOUGH *Lang.* xi. 220 The development of mathematical linguistics is opening a new field of inquiry, and may rightly be expected to bring greater order into a subject, which..has been and still remains chaotic. **1961** C. MOHRMANN et al. *Trends European & Amer. Ling.* 21 In his report to the 1957 Congress, Professor Joshua Whatmough mentioned the initiation of the Seminar in Mathematical Linguistics at Harvard University two years previously—the first appearance of the subject in an academic curriculum. **1964** E. BACH *Introd. Transformational Gram.* vii. 145 At several universities.. courses in 'mathematical linguistics' are offered. **1968** J. LYONS *Introd. Theoret. Ling.* ii. 71 What one might refer to loosely as 'mathematical' linguistics is now a very important part of the subject. **1972** HARTMANN & STORK *Dict. Lang. & Ling.* 137 Mathematical linguistics may be said to begin with the counting of linguistic units such as phonemes, graphemes, or vocabulary items. **1858** A. DE MORGAN *On Syllogism* (1966) 78 This *mathematical* logic.. will commend itself to the educated world. **1880** J. VENN in *Princeton Rev.* 248 What with the logicians who hate mathematics, and the mathematicians who despise logic, a theory of so-called mathematical logic does not find many friends. **1908** B. RUSSELL in *Amer. Jrnl. Math.* XXX. 222 (*title*) Mathematical logic as based on the theory of types. **1940** W. V. QUINE (*title*) Mathematical logic. **1941** O. HELMER tr. *Tarski's Introd. Logic* ii. 18 Logic..has undergone a complete transformation with the effect of assuming a character similar to that of the mathematical disciplines; in this new form it is known as mathematical or deductive or symbolic logic. **1967** J. VAN HEIJENOORT *From Frege to Gödel* p. vii, Mathematical logic is what logic, through twenty-five centuries and a few transformations, has become today. **1850** A. DE MORGAN *On Syllogism* (1966) 58 There is no occasion for the mathematical logician to pay the least deference to the Christian followers of Aristotle; the master himself was a mathematician. **1883** F. H. BRADLEY *Princ. Logic* 360, I may suggest to the mathematical logician that [etc.]. **1903** B. RUSSELL *Princ. Math.* iii. 457 But now, thanks mainly to the mathematical logicians, formal logic is enriched by several forms of reasoning not reducible to the syllogism. **1879** W. JAMES *Coll. Ess. & Rev.* (1920) 141 Clifford's..chapters on the 'Philosophy of the Pure Sciences'..form as luminous an introduction to mathematical philosophy as was ever written. **1897** B. RUSSELL in *Mind* VI. 112 The problems of mathematical philosophy. **1901** *Mind* X. 30 It is..imperative, in the interests of mathematical philosophy, to supply the defect. **1919** B. RUSSELL (*title*) Introduction to mathematical philosophy.

mathematicism (mæþĭmæ·tisiz'm). *Philos.* [f. MATHEMATIC *a.* + -ISM; cf. G. *mathematizismus.*] The opinion that everything can be described ultimately in mathematical terms, or that the universe is fundamentally mathematical.

1933 *Mind* XLII. 107 Russell..is dismissed on the grounds that his subjectivism rests on a surreptitious basis of realism, that his mathematicism ignores qualities, and that his neutral monism leaves no room for mind in its indefeasible quality of awareness. **1962** L. J. COHEN *Diversity of Meaning* i. 19 Forgotten principles, like the mathematicism of Plato's *Timaeus.*

mathematicization (mæþĭmæ:tisəizē̆i·ʃən). [f. MATHEMATICIZ(E *v.* + -ATION.] = *MATHEMATIZATION.

1952 F. X. MEEHAN in *Proc. Amer. Catholic Philos. Assoc.* XXVI. 19 Philosophy became for them a mathematicization of nature under the impetus given by Descartes and Newton. **1962** *Technology* May 12/3 The 'mathematicization' of science and technology.

mathematico-. (Further examples.)

1857 *Encycl. Brit.* XIII. 578/2 Now the mathematico-logical theories tend..to convert logical study into a mere cramming of the memory with formulae. **1865** MILL *Auguste Comte* 119 The sciences, all..except the mathematico-astronomical couple are still..in a very early stage. **1890** W. JAMES *Princ. Psychol.* II. xxxviii. 669 Take any other mathematico-mechanical theory and it is the same. **1908** C. S. PEIRCE in *Monist* XVIII. 463 This would be very far from establishing the idea of certain mathematico-logicians that a line consists of points. **1937** [see *CENTRIFUGE *sb.*]. **1940** C. L. HULL et al. (*title*) Mathematico-deductive theory of rote learning. **1965** *Math. in Biol. & Med.* (*Med. Res. Council*) IV. 135 We feel more secure when we have the guiding influence of a mathematico-physiological model in our experiments. **1973** *Nature* 6 July 60/2 Economic theorists take fairly naturally to the set-theoretic and mathematico-logical underpinning of mathematical methods.

mathematization (mæ:þĭmătəizē̆i·ʃən). [f. MATHEMATIZ(E *v.* + -ATION.] Mathematical treatment; the state of being mathematized.

1936 W. F. R. HARDIE *Study in Plato* v. 38 In the *Philebus* Plato refers to the discovery of the musical intervals (17[d]), and pays tribute to the inspiration derived from this example of successful mathematization. **1952** G. SARTON *Hist. Sci.* I. xvi. 416 His [*sc.* Plato's] mathematization of political thought. **1956** E. H. HUTTEN *Lang. Mod. Physics* ii. 37 There is no part of physics that can be said to be completely formalised as a system. At best, we find a 'mathematization'. **1962** L. J. COHEN *Diversity of Meaning* i. 19 He may too easily ignore what was contributed to the mathematization of science by medieval influences like Roger Bacon's stress on the need for a strictly mathematical treatment of optics. **1973** *Sci. Amer.* Dec. 101/1 In the Copernican system the planets are harmoniously ordered out from the sun so that the shorter the period, the closer the distance. It is this pattern that opened the way to the mathematization and mechanization of the universe.

maths, colloq. abbrev. MATHEMATICS *sb. pl.*

1911 W. OWEN *Let.* 14 Sept. (1967) 81 The Answers to Maths. Ques. were given us all this morning. **1917** *Wireless World* Sept. 385 Extremely 'rusty' in 'maths'. **1931** [see *DUB *sb.*[6]]. **1956** A. S. C. ROSS in N. Mitford *Noblesse Oblige* 32 The U equivalent is *master, mistress* with prefixed attribute (as *maths-mistress*). **1960** M. SPARK *Bachelors* x. 155 I've got a pile of homework to do. Maths papers.

-matic (mæ·tik), *suffix.* [f. AUTO)MATIC *a.*] A terminal element in words (usu. proprietary names) designating devices which work automatically or mechanically, as *Hoovermatic, traffomatic.* orig. *U.S.*

1935 *Amer. Speech* Feb. 35/1 In Providence, Rhode Island *traffomatic* signals turn red lights to green as cars approach them. *Adjustomatic* and *Ceomatic* also occur, and there is a *Nickel-mat* restaurant. **1938** S. CHASE *Tyranny of Words* xiv. 173 Dial-a-matic. **1941** *Word Study* Nov. 7/1 This year bids fair to be the *-matic* year of all years. **1957** *Journal des Traducteurs* II. 50 Admen all over the continent have coined hundreds of magic brand names with this productive adaptation suffix, exploiting to the full the suggestion of 'minimum effort' it connotes..: *Accumatic* watch, *Ajustomatic* pipe, *Coffeematic* percolator. **1959** *Amer. Speech* Oct. 237 English trade names.. such as *Hoovermatic* (an automatic washer and dryer) or *Sensimatic* (a Burroughs bookkeeping machine). **1966** L. COHEN *Beautiful Losers* (1970) III. 238 The Bowl-a-Matic habitually divided every strike between First and Second Player regardless of who or how many threw. **1971** *Amat. Photographer* 13 Jan. 92/2 (Advt.), Pakmatic.., Easymatic,.. Instamatic. **1972** *House & Garden* Feb. 79 'Brush-o-matic', to clean upholstery.

‖ **matière** (matiẹ̄r'). [Fr.] The quality given to his pigment by an artist. Also *fig.*

1915 W. H. WRIGHT *Mod. Painting* xiv. 320 De Vlaminck has a rich and compelling *matière* and an art sense which is almost coquettish. **1921** R. FRY *Lett.* (1972) I. 62 In the *Nature Morte*..he [*sc.* Picasso] has gained a certain plastic quality by the extraordinary contrasts of *matière.* **1936** *Burlington Mag.* July 35/1 Though the *matière* is still heavy, the paint is applied in parallel oblique strokes. **1960** *Times* 12 May 10/5 Dubuffet has experimented with the potentialities of *matière* in his paintings. **1963** *Guardian* 29 Feb. 9/2 Kossoff struggles with his grotesquely sensual matiere like a Vietnamese trooper slurping in the mud of a rice paddy. **1971** *Guardian Weekly* 7 Aug. 19 Lecture Four. The matiere of verse demonstrated further in Wallace Stevens; who isn't my poet.

Matilda (mătildă). *Austral. slang.* Also **matilda.** [A female Christian name.] = SWAG *sb.* 10. So *to walk* or *waltz Matilda*: to carry one's swag, to travel the road (cf. *WALTZ *v.*); *Matilda-waltzer*, a tramp, traveller.

1893 *Bulletin* (Sydney) 18 Nov. 20/3 A swag is not generally referred to as a 'bluey' or 'Matilda'—it is *called* a swag. *Ibid.*, No bushman thinks of 'going on a wallaby' or 'walking Matilda'..he goes on the track. **1916** J. B. COOPER *Coo-oo-ee* i. 3 Somehow things appear different to a man on a coach to a swaggie padding the hoof along the same road with 'Matilda' slung from his shoulders. **1917** A. B. PATERSON *Waltzing Matilda* in *Saltbush Bill* (1924) 24 And he sang as he looked at his old billy boiling, 'Who'll come a-waltzing Matilda with me?' *c* **1926** 'MIXER' *Transport Workers' Song Bk.* 139 That night he packed up his 'Matilda'. **1933** *Bulletin* (Sydney) 3 May 20/2 Matilda-waltzers with one black (or brown) shoe or boot are an everyday sight. **1934** *Ibid.* 12 Dec. 25/2 He chucks Matilda into a corner and is rummaging for tucker when Old Dave comes back. **1962** MARSHALL & DRYSDALE *Journey among Men* xii. 116 It was a beautiful place for a camp. It was good to stretch out in the arms of Matilda at the end of the day, and slowly smoke a cigarette. **1965** J. S. GUNN *Terminol. Shearing Industry* II. 29 In the days of itinerant workers and wanderers the swag had many names, including 'matilda', 'bundle', [etc.].

matildite (măti·ldəit). *Min.* [a. It. *matildite* (A. D'Achiardi *I Metalli* (1883) I. 136), f. the name of the *Matilda* mine (near Morococha in the department of Junín) in central Peru: see -ITE[1].] A sulphide of silver and bismuth, $AgBiS_2$, occurring as brittle, grey to black, orthorhombic crystals that are opaque with a metallic lustre.

1892 E. S. DANA *Dana's Syst. Min.* (ed. 6) 115 Matildite. **1900** *Mineral. Mag.* XII. 313 A description is given of 128 mineral species found in Japan... The occurrence of the rare mineral matildite is recorded. **1969** *Canad. Mineralogist* IX. 655 A characteristic feature of matildite in most of its occurrences from widely separated regions of the world is its intergrowth in galena which form [*sic*] Widmanstätten-like structures.

matily (mē̆i·tili), *adv.* [f. *MATEY *a.* + -LY[2].] In a friendly, familiar, or companionable fashion.

1973 *Daily Tel.* 10 Mar. 17/1 A squirrel chattered matily at me as I climbed the stile. **1974** *Listener* 21 Nov. 674/3 *The Hammers*..is jolly, warm-hearted,..matily naive.

matinée. Add: **1.** (Further examples.) Also one in a cinema.

1858 *Boston Even. Gaz.* 6 Mar., A dramatic matinee is a novel idea. **1879** *Dramatic Notes* 23, I have given 379 *Matinées*, equal to one year and a quarter of night performances. **1973** P. EVANS *Bodyguard Man* i. 13 A child raised on Saturday matinée soap-operas at the local cinema.

2. A woman's lingerie jacket.

1896 *Woman's Life* 11 July 178/2 The pretty summer matinée of white cambric or lawn that accompanies this petticoat is made with full bell sleeves edged with lace. **1908** A. BENNETT *Old Wives' Tale* III. iv. 338 She sat up and managed to drag her *matinée* from a chair and put it round her shoulders. **1960** CUNNINGTON & BEARD *Dict. Eng. Costume* 134/2 *Matinee* 1851.., a hooded pardessus made of jacconet or muslin and worn outdoors over a morning dress.

3. *attrib.* and *Comb.*, as *matinée actor, girl, public, ticket*; **matinée coat,** a baby's short outer garment; **matinée hat,** a lady's hat worn at matinées; **matinée idol,** a handsome actor of a type supposed to be especially attractive to matinée audiences.

1895 W. ARCHER in *World* 13 Feb. 25/2 He will learn next to nothing from matinée actors and audiences. **1929** *Treasure Cot Catal.* Nov. 31 Very pretty Matinee Coat in

good quality Crepe-de-chine. **1957** W. RODWELL *Cutting & Designing Juvenile Outerwear* I. 2 Basic draft for infant's matinée coat... This draft is for the earliest type of coat worn by children. **1899** H. VAN DYKE *Fisherman's Luck* 101, The matinée girl is not likely to have a very luminous or truthful idea of existence floating around in her pretty head. **1894** *Million* 10 Feb. 223/2 The disappearance of the *matinée* hat would be seriously felt by the writer of jokes. **1898** [in Dict.]. **1905** G. B. SHAW *How to become Mus. Critic* (1960) 256, I once, in Drury Lane Theatre, sat behind a *matinée* hat decorated with two wings of a seagull. **1902** 'H. MCHUGH' *Back to Woods* vii. 107 Mrs. John..you should be proud of this matinee idol husband of yours. **1909** 'O. HENRY' *Roads of Destiny* xiii. 210 Being conspirators from the cradle and matinee idols by proclamation. **1924** J. BUCHAN *Three Hostages* iv. 54 He's not in the least the ordinary matinée idol. He is.. adored by women and also liked by men. **1952** GRANVILLE *Dict. Theatr. Terms* 116 A perfect example of the matinée idol was the late Owen Nares. **1973** *Times* 26 Mar. 12/5 In the heyday of the matinee idol he had commanded.. a sober, serene and loyal admiration. **1919** F. HURST *Humoresque* 206 It was just their always playing in the same pictures, and that silly matinée public..got to linking their names together. **1904** 'A. DALE' *Wanted: a Cook* 208 What do you say to mentioning matinée tickets once a week?

ma·tiness. [f. *MATEY *a.* + -NESS.] Friendly quality or character.

1928 *Evening News* 28 Dec. 8/3 There is the same expansive geniality, the same note of unassumed 'matiness'. **1950** *Landfall* IV. 345 The defensive bar-room and backfence matiness of New Zealand life.

mating, *vbl. sb.*[1] Delete † *Obs.* and add later *attrib.* examples.

1908 *Westm. Gaz.* 12 Aug. 7/3 Mackenzie ran into a mating net with Gunsberg in a lively game. **1968** S. MORRISON *Chess* vi. 52 Black would reply 10..K–R3 and..escapes the mating net.

mating, *vbl. sb.*[2] Add further *attrib.* examples.

1888 W. DAY *Horse* xviii. 239 The management of mares at the mating season, and during the period of gestation, is a subject requiring more than mere passing notice. **1905** E. WHARTON *House of Mirth* II. xiii. 500 The blind motions of her mating instinct. **1919** T. S. ELIOT *Hippopotamus* in *Poems*, At mating time the hippo's voice Betrays inflexions hoarse and odd. **1936** *Brit. Birds* XXIX. 307 The 'mating rite' is performed only on the nest. **1936** *Discovery* Oct. 307/2 During the mating season, its call is startling. **1938** *Proc. Amer. Philos. Soc.* LXXXIX. 412 As conjugation takes place usually or only between individuals of diverse types, these types will be referred to as mating types. **1953** D. A. BANNERMAN *Birds Brit. Isles* I. 78 The mating-call..can be heard all this time. **1960** G. BLANCHET *Search in North* xi. 142 The nesting season..was already ended, the mating songs were no longer heard and the young..on the wing. **1962** *Times* 30 Mar. 15/4 The mating-call or whistle of the juvenile 'wolf'. **1973** *Country Life* 29 Nov. 1848/2 The condition of the ewes by the end of mating time should be at least maintained for the first half of pregnancy.

mating, *ppl. a.* (Further examples, corresponding to *MATE *v.*[2] 6.)

1941 N. H. ANDERSON *Aircraft Layout* iv. 99 Dural mating parts should not be used in bearings. **1967** M. CHANDLER *Ceramics in Mod. World* iv. 129 Yet another method is to fire the rings separately, then grind the mating surfaces and join them with an epoxy resin adhesive.

matipo (mæ·tipo). *N.Z.* Also **matapo.** [Maori.] Either of two New Zealand evergreen trees, *Pittosporum tenuifolium*, of the family Pittosporaceæ, which is also called black matipo and bears clusters of purple flowers, or *Myrsine australis*, the red matipo (see *MAPAU).

1866 M. A. BARKER *Let.* in *Station Life N.Z.* (1870) 94 Varieties of matapo, a beautiful shrub, each leaf a study, with its delicate tracery of black veins on a yellow-green ground. **1879** J. B. ARMSTRONG in *Trans. N.Z. Inst.* XII. 329 The tipau or matipo, Pittosporum tenuifolium.. makes the best ornamental hedge I know of. **1921** H. GUTHRIE-SMITH *Tutira* vii. 51 Later, appeared slender matapo (Pittosporum tenuifolium). **1960** N. HILLIARD *Maori Girl* II. xiii. 152 Henry commented on the legs of the girls: 'Too thin! Like *matipo*.'

matless (mæ·tlės), *a.* [f. MAT *sb.*[1] + -LESS.] Not furnished with a mat or mats.

1880 J. ROSS *Hist. Corea* x. 318 The dead body..is not, like the Chinese, put on a matless floor.

matlo(w (mæ·tlo). *slang.* [Phonetic ad. F. *matelot* sailor.] A sailor. Cf. *MATELOT.

1903 KIPLING *Traffics & Discov.* (1904) 58 Simultaneous it hits the Pusser that 'e'd better serve out mess pork for the poor matlow. **1908** *Westm. Gaz.* 31 July 2/1 Evolutions and exercises to keep the modern 'matlow' busy and happy. **1914** 'BARTIMEUS' *Naval Occasions* xxii. 200 In less formal surroundings..he is wont to refer to himself as a 'matlow'. **1916** 'TAFFRAIL' *Pincher Martin* ii. 16 Matloes, Pincher, the same as you an' me. **1946** *News Chron.* 27 June 2 (R.N. Advt.), It's a good life and a good job, too! I'm a Matlo—Able Seaman to you. **1974** S. E. MORISON *European Discovery of America: Southern Voyages* xiii. 316 Magellan was always a sailor's sailor, and *os rudos marinheiros*, as Camoëns called the common 'matlow' of that era, always stood by him in his contests with officers.

matoke (mato·ke). [Local name.] A preparation of the flesh of bananas, used as food in Uganda; also, the fruit itself. Also *attrib.*

1959 N. W. SIMMONDS *Bananas* ix. 261 In Uganda.. the unripe fruit is peeled, wrapped in banana leaves and.. steamed... The product is called 'matoke' and it was the basic food of the Baganda people. **1962** *Lancet* 5 May 942/1 The excretion of 5-hydroxyindolacetic acid (5-H.I.A.A.) increases after the ingestion of matoke bananas, a normal article of diet of the Baganda people of Uganda. **1966** B. KIMENYE *Kalasanda Revisited* 17 The gleaming vehicle..was only on the road when they needed fresh supplies of matoke from the market. *Ibid.* 33 Kibuka had to resort to collecting matoke peelings in an old bucket. **1969** *Reporter* (Nairobi) 16 May 39/1 For large areas of Uganda the staple food crop is bananas, or as it is known locally, matoke.

matra (mā·trā). [Skr.] In Indian music, a beat, or a subdivision of one, within a rhythmic phrase.

1898 B. A. PINGLE *Indian Mus.* (ed. 2) v. 161 The number of Mátrás in a Tála is fixed. **1971** *Shankar's Weekly* (Delhi) 4 Apr. 24/3 The tabla player has to go through a cycle of matras, each of which is divided into a number of beats. **1972** P. HOLROYDE *Indian Mus.* v. 199 Tala (= palm of the hand) is a complex organization of rhythms or differing beats..in multiple groupings or thekas which are again subdivided by the individual components of the beat, the fractional matras. *Ibid.* 200 Matras are the smaller individual beats, each matra being determined in length by the pace of the overall rhythm.

‖ **matraca** (matrā·kă). Also **mattraca.** [Sp.] In Spain: a kind of mechanical wooden rattle used instead of church bells on Good Friday.

1910 C. B. LUFFMANN *Quiet Days in Spain* i. 14 A singular contrivance in the high towers takes the place of bells on Good Friday; this is the 'mattraca'—three long boxes of heavy wood arranged round a spindle, with several roughly fashioned hammers with rings in their handles, through which a rod is run to keep them in place. At short intervals during the whole of Good Friday the mattraca is turned round, grindstone fashion, and creates a most awful din... As I can find no clue to the origin of the mattraca, I fall back on the belief that it was intended to inform the multitude of the building of, or nailing of Christ to, the cross. **1974** S. E. MORISON *European Discovery of America: Southern Voyages* v. 92 Holy Week in Seville... The supreme Passion on Good Friday when one heard the clacking of the *matraca* in place of cheerful bells.

matral (mæ·trăl, mē̆ⁱ·trăl), *a. rare.* [f. *MATR(I- + -AL.] = *MATRICENTRED *ppl. a.*

1956 [see *MATRICENTRED *ppl. a.*].

matri- (mæ·tri, mē̆ⁱ·tri), used, esp. in *Anthropol.* and *Sociol.*, as the combining form of L. *māter* (*mātr-is*) mother, in various words denoting aspects of social organization defined by relationship through women. Some examples are given below as main words. Cf. also MATRIARCH, MATRIARCHAL, etc., in Dict.

Matric. Add: Also **matric.** (Later examples.)

1936 AUDEN & ISHERWOOD *Ascent of F6* (1937) I. i. 18 The Crowthers' pimply son has passed Matric. **1937** A. S. NEILL *That Dreadful School* ii. 38 My staff and I have a hearty hatred of all examinations, and to us the Matric. is anathema. But we cannot refuse to teach children their Matric. subjects. **1948** [see *INTER., INTER]. **1965** W. SOYINKA *Road* 83 To have served in Burma was to have passed your London Matric. **1967** D. P. CAREW *Many Years, Many Girls* vii. 135 Sixth formers took the School Leaving Certificate... Matric could be achieved on this same exam. **1971** *Sunday Express* (Johannesburg) 28 Mar. (Home Jrnl.) 14/2 My daughter is writing Matric this year. **1971** R. RUSSELL tr. *Ahmad's Shore & Wave* iv. 31 Their parents were only concerned with seeing that somehow or other they passed their matric. **1971** *Southerly* XXXI. 100 Not to mention the Matric next term. **1972** *Nature* 1 Dec. 267/2 He got a first in the London Matric, and became a 'temporary laboratory assistant' at Bradford Technical College.

matric (mē̆ⁱ·trik), *a. Math.* [f. L. *mātrīc-*, stem of *mātrix* MATRIX.] Of or pertaining to a matrix or matrices.

1921 *Proc. Nat. Acad. Sci.* VII. 84 The notion of a norm or numerical value of a complex quantity.., as it arises in algebra, has a more or less immediate generalization to more extensive matric systems. **1941** *Mind* L. 273 The total matric algebra of order sixteen over the field of complex numbers. **1952** *Electronic Engin.* XXIV. 264 The application of matric theory to networks containing thermionic valves. **1958** R. V. ANDREE *Sel. Mod. Abstr. Algebra* v. 107 The Pauli matrices form a closed set under matric multiplication. **1972** *Computer Jrnl.* XV. 228/2 Pairwise interactions..may be used to define a distance function without requiring the qualitative data themselves to constitute a matric space.

matricentred (mætrise·ntəɹd), *ppl. a.* [f. *MATRI- + CENTRED, CENTERED *ppl. a.*] Centred on the mother. Hence **matrice·ntric** *a.*, **matricentri·city.**

1956 R. FIRTH *Two Stud. Kinship in London* 41 We might speak then of South Borough kinship as being *matri-centred* or *matral*. **1957** M. BANTON *W. Afr. City* xi. 205 The composition of tribal and Creole matricentric households does not differ significantly. **1957** V. W. TURNER *Schism & Continuity in Afr. Society* p. xix, Another consequence of virilocal marriage making for instability in residential structure is the measure of autonomy it confers on the matricentric family. *Ibid.* iii. 76 The transition from matricentricity to matriliny as the basis for local groupings must always be hazardous. **1963** J. J. HONIGMANN *Understanding Culture* v. 85 Matricentric households are a 'natural' solution that arises in any social system..when people occupy a very low ranking, economically hazardous position.

matriclan (mæ·triklæn). [f *MATRI- + CLAN *sb.*] A matrilineal clan.

1950 D. FORDE in Radcliffe-Brown & Forde *Afr. Syst. Kinship & Marriage* 309 All members of a matriclan within a village..regard one another as kin. **1957** *Jrnl. R. Anthrop. Inst.* LXXXVII. 92 But wealth, that is money and livestock, is vested in the matriclan... The matriclan, holding only moveable property, is a non-localized descent group. **1959** G. D. MITCHELL *Sociol.* 69 Tribal offences include sexual relations between a man and a woman of the same matri-clan.

matriculability (mătri:kiŭlăbi·lĭti). [f. MATRICUL(ATE *v.* + -AB(LE + -ILITY.] Ability or fitness to matriculate.

1927 *Cambr. Univ. Reporter* 11 Oct. 142 The name of every candidate for matriculation on November 1 or 2, together with evidence of matriculability..must be sent to the Registry. **1963** *Statutes & Ordnances Univ. Cambr.* Suppl. 710 The Matriculation Registration Form when completed, together with any necessary evidence of matriculability, shall be submitted to the Registry.

matriculand (mătri·kiulæ:nd). [f. MATRICUL(ATE *v.* + *-AND[2].] = MATRICULANT.

1975 *Times Lit. Suppl.* 23 May 556/3 In the sixteenth century Salamanca had about 5,000–7,000 matriculands a year.

matrifocal (mæ·trifōᵘkăl), *a. Sociol.* [f. *MATRI- + FOCAL *a.*] Applied to a family in which the mother is left with the responsibility for and authority over the household; mother-centred. Hence **matrifoca·lity**, the condition of a family which depends on the mother.

1952 *Internat. Afr. Inst. Memorandum* XXVI. 12 These matrifocal cells of the compound family. **1956** R. T. SMITH *Negro Family Brit. Guiana* ix. 221 We maintain that the matri-focal system of domestic relations..can be regarded as the obverse of the marginal nature of the husband–father rôle. **1969** O. LEWIS in D. P. Moynihan *On Understanding Poverty* vii. 198 For example, matrifocality, a high incidence of consensual unions, and a high percentage of households headed by women, which have been thought to be distinctive characteristics of Caribbean family organization or of Negro family life in the United States, turn out to be traits of the culture of poverty. **1969** J. & S. BARATZ in T. Kochman *Rappin' & Stylin' Out* (1972) 11 This assumption left social scientists with no other alternative than to wrongly describe..the matrifocal family unit so prevalent in lower-class black society as 'evidence of male emasculation'.

matrilateral (mætrilæ·tĕrăl), *a.* [f. *MATRI- + LATERAL *a.*] Of or pertaining to relationship involving the mother's brother or sister, used esp. of cross-cousin marriage.

1951 *Jrnl. R. Anthrop. Inst.* LXXXI. 24/2 Matrilateral cross cousin marriage (father's sister's son—mother's brother's daughter). **1957** V. W. TURNER *Schism & Continuity in Afr. Society* viii. 254 Ndembu men appear to marry their patrilateral and matrilateral cross-cousins with equal frequency. **1963** *Brit. Jrnl. Sociol.* XIV. 23 From the point of view of this hypothetical individual, whom anthropologists for many years have called *Ego*, his non-lineage kin are *patrilateral* and *matrilateral* as the case may be. **1971** *World Archaeol.* III. 191 It is probable that this alliance..continues today due to prescribed matrilateral cross-cousin marriage.

matriline (mæ·triləin). [f. *MATRI- + LINE *sb.*[2] 24.] The matrilineal line of descent.

1957 *Jrnl. R. Anthrop. Inst.* LXXXVII. 11 As Evans-Pritchard's analysis of the distribution of bride-wealth shows..there is explicit recognition of both the bride's patriline and matriline. **1963** W. J. GOODE *World Revolution & Family Patterns* v. 221 The marriage of a mother's brother's daughter to a father's sister's son repeats the relationship of deference and respect which is due from the matriline. **1965** I. M. LEWIS in M. Banton *Relevance of Models for Social Anthropol.* 109 The functional implications of descent are often much more significant than whether descent is traced in the patri- or matri-line. **1971** R. NEEDHAM *Rethinking Kinship & Marriage* i. 20 It is conceivable, and may in one alleged case be so in fact, that a terminology composed of matrilines should govern the affairs of a society that was preponderantly patrilineal. **1972** P. LASLETT *Household & Family in Past Time* 22 The daughter, not the son, brings her working class spouse into the family circle... This..occurs within a matriline, not a patriline.

matrilineage (mætrili·nĭĕdʒ). [f. *MATRI- + *LINEAGE] 2 c.] Matrilineal lineage.

1949 M. FORTES *Social Struct.* 60 Membership of the matrilineage is *ipso facto* membership of a widely dispersed exogamous clan. **1951** B. Z. SELIGMAN in *N. & Q. Anthropol.* (ed. 6) II. ii. 89 A matrilineage consists of all the descendants through females of a single ancestress. **1957** *Jrnl. R. Anthrop. Inst.* LXXXVII. 93 It is this group, a dispersed, basic matrilineage, which defines the extent of the lateral inheritance of wealth. **1957** V. W. TURNER *Schism & Continuity in Afr. Society* iii. 80, I regard a *minimal* matrilineage as a group consisting of the descendants through women of a common grandmother,

a *minor* matrilineage as the matrilineal descendants of a common great-grandmother. **1963** W. J. GOODE *World Revolution & Family Patterns* iv. 194 The father is increasingly able to assert new rights against the traditional rights of the matrilineage.

matrilineal (mætrili·niăl), *a.* [f. *MATRI- + LINEAL *a.* 2.] Of, pertaining to, or based on (kinship with) the mother or the female line; recognizing kinship with and descent through females.

1904 N. W. THOMAS in *Man* LIII. 84 Mr. Hill-Tout argues that totemism originates in a patrilineal just as much as in a matrilineal state of society. **1906** —— *Kinship Organisations & Group Marriage Austral.* 30 Membership of a phratry depends on birth and is taken *directly* from the mother (matrilineal descent) or father (patrilineal descent). **1914** W. H. R. RIVERS *Kinship & Social Organisation* ii. 40 The people of Buin still practice matrilineal descent. **1921** *Edin. Rev.* July 163 His discovery of matrilineal institutions in Europe. **1946** *Nature* 28 Sept. 457/2 It is clear that the ancient Chamorro had an elaborate social organisation with matrilineal clans and village chiefs whose power was based mainly on inherited wealth and monopolies. **1951** E. E. EVANS-PRITCHARD *Social Anthrop.* ii. 29 According to Bachofen, there was first everywhere promiscuity, then a matrilineal and matriarchal social system, and only late in the history of man did this system give way to a patrilineal and patriarchal one. **1969** *Times* 22 Oct. (Ghana Suppl.) p. vii/3 The women have legal rights which would be the envy of any Englishwoman. They own property absolutely and the matrilineal system—inheritance through the women—means that the children belong to the mother's family.

Hence **matrili·neally** *adv.*

1907 *Athenæum* 20 Apr. 477/1 The method of reckoning descent matrilineally. **1937** *Nature* 20 Feb. 328/1 The husband in such a group, finding property to descend matrilineally, would try to provide for his portionless sister's family. **1964** GOULD & KOLB *Dict. Social Sci.* 367/1 In a patrilineally organized society a man must also have kinship relations through his mother, and mutatis mutandis in a matrilineally organized society.

matrilinear (mætrili·niăɹ), *a.* [f. *MATRI- + LINEAR *a.*] = *MATRILINEAL *a.*

1910 *Manch. Guardian* 8 Aug. 5 It is said that they [*sc.* the Choctaw Indians] were governed by chiefs who succeeded by matrilinear descent. **1913** B. S. PHILLPOTTS *Kindred & Clan* 275 Kindreds organized on matrilinear or on patrilinear lines. **1926** *Contemp. Rev.* Apr. 528 That these powers are related to a previous system of matrilinear descent there can be no doubt. **1950** DARLINGTON & MATHER *Genes, Plants & People* v. 57 The historic change from matrilinear to patrilinear inheritance has also led to important conflicts.

matriliny (mæ·trilini). [f. *MATRI- + LIN(E *sb.*[2] + -Y[3].] The observance of matrilineal descent and kinship.

1906 N. W. THOMAS *Kinship Organisations & Group Marriage Austral.* ii. 19 We may now examine the relation of matriliny to the seat of authority in the family. **1927** [see *bien entendu*]. **1937** *Nature* 20 Feb. 328/1 Though most of the tribes of Assam are now patrilineal, yet an earlier stratum of matriliny should not be overlooked. **1955** [see *father-right* (*FATHER *sb.* 12)]. **1965** I. M. LEWIS in M. Banton *Relevance of Models for Social Anthropol.* 109 The lumping together of societies on the basis of patriliny or matriliny alone can only lead to confusion.

matrilocal (mætrilō^u·kăl), *a.* [f. *MATRI- + LOCAL *a.*] Applied to the custom in certain social groups for a married couple to settle in the wife's home or community.

1906 N. W. THOMAS *Kinship Organisations & Group Marriage Austral.* iii. 30 When the husband removes and lives in his wife's group the marriage is *matrilocal*. **1927** *Contemp. Rev.* July 84 The clan is held together by matrilocal marriage. **1933** *Times Lit. Suppl.* 8 June 390/2 Marriage is matrilocal, or, in other words, the man goes to live with his wife. **1949** M. FORTES *Social Struct.* 70 Households with female heads can be..'matrilocal', that is, made up of a woman and her dependants by marriage and motherhood. **1956** R. PIERIS *Sinhalese Social Organization* VI. i. 203 In the *binna* (matrilocal) marriage, the husband lived in his wife's parental home. **1956** J. WHATMOUGH *Lang.* 250 But the Apache 'great family', with matrilocal residence after marriage, has its special terminology. **1966** NYE & BERARDO *Emerging Conceptual Frameworks in Family Analysis* ii. 26 The extended family is a group founded on kinship and locality, and resulting from the rules of patrilocal or matrilocal marriage.

Hence **matriloca·lity**, the custom of matrilocal residence; **matrilo·cally** *adv.*, in a matrilocal manner.

1935 *Geogr. Jrnl.* LXXXVI. 262 The increasing amount of patrilocal marriages instead of the former pure matrilocality of the people. **1938** *Jrnl. R. Anthrop. Inst.* LXVIII. 301 The Hopi also transmit functions, such as priesthood and office, from male to male, without renouncing their matrilocality. *Ibid.*, Matrilocality here means, fundamentally, the succession of female descendants each one of whom remains her whole life in one spot. **1941** *Sudan Notes & Rec.* XXIV. 55 In a few cases the Shilluk settle matrilocally. **1963** *Economist* 13 Apr. 157/2 A mass of theorising about 'matrilocality' and the Cockney Mum.

matrimonial, *a.* and *sb.* Add: **A.** *adj.* **3. b.** *matrimonial agency, bureau* = *marriage bureau* (see *MARRIAGE 8); *matrimonial agent*, one who works in a matrimonial agency.

c **1888** C. E. MORLAND *Matrimonial Agency* (1902) 3, I have always expressed myself shocked at the indelicacy of marriages arranged by Matrimonial Agencies. *Ibid.* 4 A letter of introduction from a certain matrimonial agent. **1890** W. BOOTH *In Darkest Eng.* II. vi. 233 *A matrimonial bureau*... In London at the present moment how many hundreds..of young men and young women..are practically without any opportunity of making the acquaintance of each other! **1895** [see *CO-ED *a.*]. **1908** A. BENNETT *Buried Alive* ii. 51 I've been thinking for years of getting married again... And what is there except a matrimonial agency? **1917** N. DOUGLAS *South Wind* ii. 18 He..resembles a broken-down matrimonial agent. **1925** E. H. YOUNG *William* xxxvi. 308, I hope the matrimonial bureau will be a great success. **1966** K. WHITE *Lett. from Gourgounel* 40 He approaches Matrimonial Bureaux to try and find a wife. **1967** C. WATSON *Lonelyheart 4122* iii. 33 A matrimonial bureau. Well, what else could be meant by 'Handclasp House. Are you weary of the solitary path?' *Ibid.* v. 46 He has the traditional English middle-class attitude to matrimonial agencies. Terribly *infra dig.*

matrix. Add: The normal pronunc. of *matrices* is now (mē^i·trisīz).

4. c. A (positive or negative) copy of an original disc recording that is used in the making of other copies; *spec.* one used as a stamper.

1904 S. R. BOTTONE *Talking Machines & Records* 86 A copper matrix is first made from it [*sc.* the original disc] by electrotyping... From the copper matrix thus produced any number of duplicates can be moulded out of ebonite by hot pressure. **1918** H. SEYMOUR *Reproduction of Sound* 175 A stamper is a working matrix for pressing records, and as such is merely a duplicate of the master matrix. *Ibid.* 310 To get an exact replica of a master matrix, an intermediate process is necessitated, in the production of a 'mother' matrix, which is a facsimile in metal of the original record..from which the subsequent negatives can be obtained. **1922** O. MITCHELL *Talking Machine Industry* vi. 69 Several matrices are formed,which are then nickel-plated, polished and receive a strong backing of heavy steel as a support. They are then ready for the presses. **1929** *Melody Maker* Apr. 375/2 For sale. Matrices by leading U.S.A. Records Company, containing latest and biggest American successes. **1935** H. C. BRYSON *Gramophone Record* vi. 142 Negative matrices, i.e., master and stamper, may be made to reproduce by means of a special needle, the end of which is split into a tiny fork which just fits over the ridge. **1952** [see *MOTHER *sb.*[1] 10*]. **1964** P. J. GUY *Disc Recording & Reproduction* vi. 76 When the third shell—which is called the Matrix or Stamper—is stripped off, its ridges are nickel plated.

d. *Photogr.* A dyed print in relief used for transferring colour to a final colour print.

1947 *Van Nostrand's Sci. Encycl.* (ed. 2) 917/2 Dyed relief films or differentially hardened films are generally called matrices when used in an imbibition process. **1957** R. W. G. HUNT *Reproduction of Colour* v. 44 The matrix film is..then washed with hot water to leave a hardened gelatin relief image. **1970** C. B. NEBLETTE *Fund. Photogr.* xxii. 312 After drying, the films, now termed matrices, are dyed in the proper colours.

6. b. *spec.* in *Logic.* An array of symbols representing truth-values, giving the result of all possible assignments of truth-values to components of a propositional form or proposition; = **truth-table*. Also, that part of a truth-table which is an array of the total truth-possibilities (see quot. 1965). Also, a set of basic truth-tables for a particular system of logic (see quot. 1973). Also *attrib.*, as *matrix method*, etc.

1914 C. I. LEWIS in *Jrnl. Philos., Psychol. & Sci. Methods* XI. 600 The matrix algebra for implications is useful as an instrument for investigating the interrelations of necessity, truth, possibility, falsity. **1932** —— & LANGFORD *Symbolic Logic* vii. 201 That any principle, expressible in the symbols of the system, holds or does not hold can be determined by investigating its truth-status for all combinations of the truth-values of the elements. This is the matrix method. **1955** A. N. PRIOR *Formal Logic* 243 In the other matrices, the corner values are the usual ones for the corresponding two-valued operators. **1965** HUGHES & LONDEY *Elements of Formal Logic* iii. 21 The array of possible combinations of truth-values of the variables (always set out on the left) will be called the matrix. **1973** J. J. ZEMAN *Modal Logic* v. 89 What we refer to may be called the matrix method... A truth-value system, or matrix, may be thought of as a set of tables, one for each of the primitive operators of the system, which may be used in computing a 'truth table' for any wff of the system.

c. *Logic.* An expression that would become a statement if its variables were replaced by constants, i.e. by names of individuals or classes or statements, as appropriate; = either **propositional function* or **statement-form*, depending on which type it is; *esp.*, in predicate calculus, a quantifier-free part of a formula (see quots. 1954, 1971).

1908 B. RUSSELL in *Amer. Jrnl. Math.* XXX. 238 Then p/a, which we will call a matrix, may take the place of a function. **1910** WHITEHEAD & RUSSELL *Principia Math.* I. 262 Let us give the name of matrix to any function, of however many variables, which does not involve any apparent variables. **1932** LEWIS & LANGFORD *Symbolic Logic* ix. 267 Such functions as $f(x)$ and $p \vee q$..we may call matrices. **1954** I. M. COPI *Symbolic Logic* ix. 298 In any *wff* in prenex normal form $(Qx_1)(Qx_2)..(Qx_n)$ G the group of quantifiers $(Qx_1)(Qx_2)..(Qx_n)$ is the prefix and the quantifier-free formula G is the matrix. **1971** G. HUNTER *Metalogic* 252 A formula A is in prenex normal form iff it is of the form $Qv_1..Qv_nB$, where each Q is either $\wedge$ or $\vee$, $n \geq 0$, B is a wff, and no quantifiers occur in B. The B..is called the matrix of A, and the part of A (if any) that precedes the matrix is called the prefix.

d. *Computers.* An interconnected array of diodes, cores, or other circuit elements that has a number of inputs and outputs and somewhat resembles a lattice or grid in its circuit design or physical construction.

1948 *Gloss. Computer Terms* (Mass. Inst. Technol. Servomechanisms Lab. Rep. R–138) 7 *Matrix switch*, a multi-position switch used in computers for decoding binary numbers. By mixing the output of flip-flops holding a binary number in an array of crystal rectifiers or resistors, it permits selection of one or a group of output lines. **1952** *RCA Rev.* June 185 The selected core will be magnetized in the desired direction while all other cores in the matrix will remain unaffected. The read-out is obtained by applying read-in current pulses. **1955** R. K. RICHARDS *Arithmetic Operations in Digital Computers* iii. 75 In other applications the matrix is used to 'gate' an external signal (such as a series of pulses) onto one of a multiplicity of signal lines. **1969** P. B. JORDAIN *Condensed Computer Encycl.* 315 Such a diode matrix will encode decimal into binary. **1970** O. DOPPING *Computers & Data Processing* x. 136 Cores are usually built together to form square or possibly rectangular matrices in which each matrix contains as many cores as there are words in the memory bank. Most matrices nowadays contain (64 × 64 =) 4,096 cores.

e. *Television* and *Broadcasting.* A circuit designed to accept a number of inputs and produce outputs that are linear combinations of them in different proportions. Freq. *attrib.*

1953 *Proc. IRE* XLI. 842/1 We show the pickup system giving information in the form of three channel voltages... All three of these voltages are fed to the inputs of three separate matrix or mixing units. **1954** *Ibid.* XLII. 201 (*heading*) Matrix networks for color TV. *Ibid.* 201/2 In a 3-tube video matrix with R_L and r_b equal to 5000 ohms, the gain per tube will be one third of the gain of a one-tube amplifier. **1961** CARNT & TOWNSEND *Colour Television* vii. 185 The matrix circuits, in effect, solve the three equations $R' = Y' + 0{\cdot}96\ I' + 0{\cdot}62\ Q'$, $G' = Y' - 0{\cdot}27\ I' - 0{\cdot}65\ Q'$, $B' = Y' - 1{\cdot}11\ I' + 1{\cdot}70\ Q'$, and derive their name from the matrix notation used in algebra as a form of shorthand for writing and solving such equations. **1970** *Jrnl. Audio Engin. Soc.* XVIII. 627/1 (*caption*) One form of resistive matrix employed in four-channel stereo receiver or adapter to provide electrical separation of front and rear signals in left and rear stereo channels if transmission matrix of Fig. 4 is utilized at FM broadcast transmitter. **1971** D. J. SEAL *Mazda Bk. Pal Receiver Servicing* i. 7 Two colour difference signals (R–Y and B–Y) are fed from the decoder to the matrix, where they are combined with the luminance signal (Y) to form the three primary colour signals red, green and blue. **1973** *Sat. Rev. Arts* (U.S.) 1 Apr. 49/2 *Matrix system*, the quadraphonic disc system in which four signals are fed into a circuit (matrix) that mixes (encodes) them into two signals that are inscribed on the walls of a record groove... If the disc is played on a properly equipped quad system, the signals are fed into a complementary matrix, which restores (decodes) them back to the original four, and the disc is heard quadraphonically.

7. *matrix algebra*; **matrix mechanics** *Physics*, a form of quantum mechanics developed by W. Heisenberg in which the operators corresponding to physical co-ordinates (position, momenta, etc.) are represented by matrices with time-dependent elements; **matrix number**, a number assigned by a record company to a matrix in the manufacture of gramophone records; **matrix printer**, a printer in which each printed character is made up of dots printed by the tips of small wires selected out of a rectangular array; **matrix sentence** *Linguistics* (see quot. 1967[1]).

1930 RUARK & UREY *Atoms, Molecules & Quanta* xvii. 577 (*heading*) The laws of matrix algebra. **1969** D. C. HAGUE *Managerial Econ.* i. 24 With complex decision problems..calculus and matrix algebra may have to be used. **1926** P. A. M. DIRAC in *Proc. R. Soc.* A. CXII. 666 In Heisenberg's matrix mechanics it is assumed that the elements of the matrices that represent the dynamical variables determine the frequencies and intensities of the components of the radiation emitted. **1966** *McGraw-Hill Encycl. Sci. & Technol.* VIII. 181/2 Matrix mechanics is disadvantageous for obtaining quantitative solutions to actual problems; because it is concisely expressed in a form independent of special coordinate systems, however, matrix mechanics is advantageous for proving general theorems. **1974** G. REECE tr. *Hund's Hist. Quantum Theory* xiii. 171 First Heisenberg showed in the language of matrix mechanics that two identical coupled systems always behaved like the two oscillators. **1965** G. MELLY *Owning-Up* xi. 129 He was a record collector who knew the matrix number..of every record in his immaculately filed collection. **1968** LEADBITTER & SLAVEN *Blues Records 1943–66* 7 All matrix numbers where known are given for completeness sake, even though they may only be the issue number with A or B suffixes or numbers allocated by pressing plants. **1958** GOTLIEB & HUME *High-Speed Data Processing* iii. 59 IBM has matrix printers for use with the 702 and 705 data processors. **1964** T. W. MCRAE *Impact of Computers on Accounting* i. 17 The 'matrix' printer and the 'chain' printer can reach speeds of up to 1200 lines a minute. **1964** Matrix sentence [see *CONSTITUENT B. 5]. **1967** D. STEIBLE *Conc. Handbk. Ling.* 77 *Matrix sentence*, in transformational grammar, a basic sentence, known in traditional grammar as an independent clause, into which other structures may be embedded. **1967** *Word* XXIII. 338 The ultimate fate of an included-sentence construction, of course, is to become so thoroughly embedded in the matrix sentence as to be no longer distinguishable. **1968** *Canad. Jrnl. Ling.* XIII. 83 Infinitive phrases have

a wide range of function within the matrix sentence. **1972** HARTMANN & STORK *Dict. Lang. & Ling.* 138 Matrix sentences often coincide with what is known in traditional grammar as main clauses.

b. Applied to precious stones (see quot. 1909).

1909 *Cent. Dict.* Suppl., *Matrix-gem*, an opal, turquoise, ruby, or other gem intimately mixed with the matrix material and cut with it. **1921** *Brit. Mus. Return* 157 in *Parl. Papers* XXVII. 651 A suite of specimens of sapphire ..comprising two matrix specimens.

matrix (mēⁱ·triks), *v.* [f. prec. sb. (Orig. formed as the vbl. sb.)] *trans.* To combine (signals) in different proportions so as to obtain one or more linear combinations of them.

1969 CARNT & TOWNSEND *Colour Television* II. iii. 106 Matrixing *R–Y* and *B–Y* produces *G–Y*. **1971** D. J. SEAL *Mazda Bk. Pal Receiver Servicing* i. 7 The decoder accepts the PAL chrominance signal.., demodulates it and produces two colour difference signals to be matrixed and amplified by the colour difference amplifiers. **1972** H. F. OLSON *Mod. Sound Reproduction* ix. 188 The four inputs *LF, LR, RF*, and *RR*, representing the left front, left rear, right front, and right rear respectively, are matrixed and encoded to the left, *L*, and right, *R*, channels of the conventional two-channel stereophonic recording system. Each of the two channels *R* and *L* contains a mixture of the four channels in such a manner that the four channels can be reconstituted in reproduction by means of the decoder and matrix. **1972** *Gramophone* Jan. 1412/1 The extra channels of information intended for feeding to the back loudspeakers are simply mixed (or matrixed) with the front channel signals prior to the cutting of the disc.

So **ma·trixed** *ppl. a.*, **ma·trixing** *vbl. sb.*

1951 *Proc. IRE* XXXIX. 1158/2 All that is required is the addition (or subtraction..) of fractions of the camera currents to derive the currents required to control the receiver. [*Note*] This operation has been called 'matrixing' in some discussions. The analogy to the matrix operation, which is used in vector algebra to change from one system of co-ordinates to a second, is obvious. **1955** J. W. WENTWORTH *Color Television Engin.* iv. 125 Matrixing can be used to improve color fidelity only when camera signals are produced by linear devices; if the camera signals are nonlinear functions of red, green, and blue, the linear equations of the matrix process cannot be worked out properly unless the matrix circuit is preceded by linearity correctors. **1971** D. J. SEAL *Mazda Bk. Pal Receiver Servicing* v. 89 Since the luminance signal (– Y) is applied to all three cathodes, the tube performs the final matrixing, and the three gun currents are proportional to the original red, green and blue separation signals from the colour cameras. **1972** H. F. OLSON *Mod. Sound Reproduction* ix. 189 The performance, as exemplified by..spatial effects, of a two-channel-to-four-channel coded and matrixed system is inferior to that of four discrete channels. **1972** *Observer* (Colour Suppl.) 22 Oct. 54/4 Not all the matrix systems are compatible with each other, though a machine like the Pioneer QX-8000 *is* capable of dealing with all forms of matrixed four-channel.

matroclinous (mætroklǝi·nǝs), *a.* *Biol.* [f. L. *mātr-, māter* mother + Gr. κλίν-ειν to lean + -OUS.] Resembling the female rather than the male parent; involving or possessing a tendency to inherit a character or characters from the female parent only. So **ma·trocliny**, matroclinous inheritance.

1913 *Jrnl. Exper. Zoöl.* XV. 587 Morgan has explained the case of criss-cross inheritance on the ground that the *X*-chromosome is the carrier of all sex linked factors. The sons are matroclinous because they receive their unpaired chromosome directly from the mother, and must show all the sex linked characters which she showed. **1917** *Genetics* II. 247 But even if one hybrid should be judged to indicate patrocliny in one cross, the same hybrid appears in the reciprocal cross where it would be a case of matrocliny for the same hybrid. **1925** C. C. HURST *Exper. in Genetics* xxxviii. 535 Gametic chromosomes, male and female, are either equal with 7–14–21 or 28 each, or unequal and matroclinous with a maternal bias in the ratio of 1·5–2–3–4 or 5 : 1. **1939** *Nature* 14 Jan. 81/2 To account for the purely matroclinous inheritance, the following explanation is suggested. The eggs of *M. formosa* are fertilized by the other two species, but the paternal chromosomes remain inactive. **1961** A. MÜNTZING *Genetic Res.* xxvi. 257/1 F. von Wettstein..observed that this matrocliny was clearly noticeable also in [the] F_2. **1968** R. C. KING *Dict. Genetics* 149 In *Drosophila* the daughters produced by attached-X females are matroclinous in terms of their sex-linked genes.

matron. Add **1. d.** A female dog or horse used for breeding.

1931 A. C. SMITH *About our Dogs* vi. 67 When the matrons have been purchased..the question of finding mates for them is uppermost. **1948** C. L. B. HUBBARD *Dogs in Brit.* xxi. 365 Brood matrons were sent to Welsh Hound studs. **1966** *Telegraph* (Brisbane) 22 Jan. 5/1 King's Daughter could have been an above average stud matron. **1971** *Country Life* 11 Nov. 1267/1 The breeding of hounds ought not to be merely a question of appearance and dash... They should also be the offspring of stallions and matrons of time-honoured residence in the kennels.

4. b. matron of honour, a chief bridesmaid who is married.

1903 *N.Y. Tribune* 20 Sept., Her only attendant, as matron of honor, wore pale blue crepe de chine. **1948** *Daily Oklahoman* (Okla. City) 9 June 13/3 The bride and I wonder whether I should be called matron of honor or maid of honor. **1961** A. BARNES *Mod. Wedding Etiquette* vii. 61 There is never more than one matron of honour and she wears, not the usual youthful style bridesmaids' dresses, but an afternoon gown with hat and gloves. Her duties are exactly the same as those of the chief bridesmaid. **1963** *Listener* 14 Mar. 473/3 The groom's brother ..has to listen to the indignant and delightfully comic complaints of the matron-of-honour. **1969** EDWARDS & BEYFUS *Lady Behave* 268 If the bridesmaid is married she is known as a Matron of Honour.

matronize, *v.* **1.** (Earlier example.)

1741 S. RICHARDSON *Familiar Lett.* 187 Childbed matronizes the giddiest Spirits.

matso, var. *MATZAH.

matsu. Substitute for def.: A local name for several pine trees, especially the two native to Japan, *Pinus densiflora*, the Japanese red pine, and *P. thunbergii*, the black pine, both valuable ornamental and timber trees. (Earlier and later examples.)

1727 J. G. SCHEUCHZER tr. *Kæmpfer's Hist. Japan* I. I. 118 The common Fir, which they call *Matzuoki*, will come to the age of a thousand. **1884** tr. *J. J. Rein's Japan* I. vii. 151 The Aka-matsu or red pine..and the Kuro-matsu or black pine..are the commonest conifers in the country. **1916** E. H. WILSON *Conifers & Taxads Japan* 25 The Japanese Red Pine, or Aka-matsu, is very widely distributed in Kyushu. *Ibid.* 27 This Black Pine, or Kuro-matsu, is found in Japan. *Ibid.* 28 Another name for this pine [*sc.* Black Pine] in Japan is O-Matsu (Male Pine). **1923** DALLIMORE & JACKSON *Handbk. Coniferæ* 466 *Pinus Thunbergii*,..Black Pine,..Kuro-matsu. **1938** D. T. SUZUKI *Zen Buddhism & its Influence on Jap. Culture* II. iii. 247 The Japanese species of the pine known as *matsu* generally spreads its branches irregularly and the trunk is gnarled. **1965** J. OHWI *Flora Japan* 115/2 *Pinus thunbergii*... Kuro-matsu, O-matsu. **1971** S. ELIOVSON *Gardening Jap. Way* 86 Pine (*Matsu*). This is the symbol of longevity, being hardy and evergreen during cold winters.

‖ **matsuri** (mætsu·ri). [Jap.] A solemn celebration or festival held periodically at every Shintō shrine in Japan in order to deepen the consciousness of the gods in the daily lives of the worshippers.

1727 J. G. SCHEUCHZER tr. *Kæmpfer's Hist. Japan* I. III. 223 It is a custom which obtains in all cities and villages, to have two such Matsuri's celebrated every year with great pomp and solemnity in honour of that God, to whose more particular care and protection they have devoted themselves. **1841** *Manners & Customs of Japanese* iii. 65 Many and..various peculiarities belong to the *Matsuri* festival. **1883** E. G. HOLTHAM *Eight Yrs. Japan* viii. 194 The Kiyōto matsuri, specially connected with the 'Gion' quarter of the city, inhabited by singing and dancing girls and such like,..was well worth seeing. **1928** F. A. LOMBARD *Outl. Hist. Jap. Drama* iii. 62 *Matsuri*..have from ancient times in Japan been occasions of great popular rejoicing. **1964** *Asia Mag.* 20 Sept. 9 (*caption*) The winding festival or *matsuri*.

matt, *a.* Now the usual spelling, esp. in *Photogr.*, of MAT *a.*

1876 *Encycl. Brit.* V. 170/1 Water gilding..is finished either 'matt' or burnished... Matt-work is protected with one or two coats of finish-size. **1892** *Photogr. Ann.* II. 76 The metal separates in a matt grey form. **1925** *Morris Owner's Manual* 79 The operation is finished when the valve face has a clean, even, matt-surfaced ring around it. **1933** *Archit. Rev.* LXXIII. 265 To treat plastic materials without humbug so as to bring out their..pleasant matt texture. **1944** L. MACNEICE *Springboard* 32 The matt-grey iron ship, Which ought to have been the Future. **1953**, **1958** [see *EGG-SHELL c]. **1967** E. CHAMBERS *Photolitho-Offset* iii. 27 Some smooth, semi-matt prints give fair results, but, in general, sepia tone prints, matt-surface prints and hand-coloured prints should be avoided.

matte³ (mæt). *Cinemat.* Also mat. [Fr.] A mask (MASK *sb.*³ 4 e) used to obscure or shade (part of) the image shown. Also *attrib.*

1938 *Motion Pict. Sound Engin.* (*Acad. Motion Pict. Arts & Sci.*) 39 A more recent procedure is to use a W-type mat which reduces the track width from the center as well as from both..edges. **1948** MENCKEN *Amer. Lang.* Suppl. II. 699 *Matte shot*, a film made with a section blocked out, to be filled later on another set. **1949** W. H. OFFENHAUSER *16-Mm. Sound Motion Pict.* xii. 382 A traveling matte..is merely a film interposed at the gate between the light source and the image-bearing film that alters the light intensity in the manner of a neutral density film. *Ibid.* 549/2 Matte rolls are a pair of film rolls used as light modulators. **1959** W. S. SHARPS *Dict. Cinematogr.* 110/2 *Matte box*, a box fitted to the front of a camera to hold mattes. The matte box frequently combines the functions of a lens hood and filter holder as well. **1960** O. SKILBECK *ABC of Film & TV* 84 *Matte*, a specially photographed Mask which..leaves blanks which can be correspondingly filled with something else at a second printing; e.g. adding a false Background as though seen through a window. **1972** L. D. GIANNETTI *Understanding Movies* 73 Mattes are used to block out certain areas of the real scene where the animated drawings will appear in the finished print.

matte, var. *MATT *a.*

1897 [see *GLOSSY *a.* a]. **1909** *Chambers's Jrnl.* Oct. 684/1 Taken altogether, it cannot compare with the 'matte' appearance of the flatted enamel which is so extensively used in French decoration. **1969** *Sears Catal.* Spring/Summer 6 Uniquely styled in matte-finished vinyl. **1973** *Sci. Amer.* Oct. 128/1 For those who wish a definite opaque matte appearance, talc is cut to a third, and rice starch or particularly fine precipitated chalk is added to improve absorption.

matter, *sb.*¹ Add: **26. matter wave** *Physics*, a de Broglie wave (see *DE BROGLIE).

1930 RUARK & UREY *Atoms, Molecules & Quanta* xxi. 722 When electrons impinge on polycrystalline metal surfaces the fraction scattered at an angle θ with the normal to the surface does not decrease uniformly as θ increases... The results seemed likely to remain unexplained, until Einstein discussed de Broglie's matter waves, in 1924 and 1925. **1972** *Sci. Amer.* Oct. 106/3 The bombarding particles have the properties not only of particles but also of waves. Such 'matter waves' are called de Broglie waves (after Louis de Broglie, who first suggested that the wave-particle duality observed for electromagnetic radiation might also exist for matter). **1974** G. REECE tr. *Hund's Hist. Quantum Theory* xi. 141 The intuitive theory of matter waves and of fields of matter is modified to the point where there is room for the idea of particles.

matter, *v.* Add: **2.** Examples with personal subject.

1909 H. W. C. NEWTE *Sparrows* xl. 505 With your appearance and talents you should be a great social success with people who matter. **1926** G. B. SHAW *Translations & Tomfooleries* II. 49 Well, what about Edith? Doesn't she matter? **1933** E. A. ROBERTSON *Ordinary Families* x. 233 Wives still matter politically, if a man's to be offered a comfortable Conservative seat.

mattery, *a.* **1.** Delete 'Now *rare*' and add later examples.

1955 W. W. DENLINGER *Compl. Boston* I. 152 Small mattery spots on the inside of the thigh..are often the first indication that a dog is suffering from distemper. **1961** S. CHAPLIN *Day of Sardine* i. 8 This was a sick kitten. Thin as a rake, mattery eyes, scabby eyes.

Matthew Walker. *Naut.* In full *Matthew Walker knot*, a multi-stranded rope end knot, prob. named after its originator.

[**1808** D. LEVER *Young Sea Officer's Sheet Anchor* 5 Matthew Walker's knot.] **1841** R. H. DANA *Seaman's Manual* vii. 37 A Matthew Walker knot,..unlay the end of a rope [etc.]. **1856** C. NORDHOFF *Man-of-War Life* xii. 212, I practised..and was soon master of long and short splices, manrope knots, turks-heads, and Matthew Walkers. **1860** *All Year Round* 28 July 382/1 'Which knot?' asked Toby... 'Matthew Walker, spritsail-sheet, stopper or shroud?' **1883** *Man. Seamanship for Boys' Training Ships R. Navy* (Admiralty) (1886) 105 A Matthew Walker knot is used for the standing part of the lanyards of lower rigging. **1953** *People* (Austral.) 26 Aug. 47/3 Mason will talk by the hour about Matthew Walker knots, bell ropes ..and cross-pointing if he encounters a pair of sympathetic ears. **1961** F. H. BURGESS *Dict. Sailing* 144 *Matthew Walker*, a knot, single or double, used to make a collar on a rope; the strands may be relaid when formed (a development of the wall knot). **1968** E. FRANKLIN *Dict. Knots* 20 *Matthew Walker* and *Double Matthew Walker*, probably the best and most useful of the multistrand rope end knots. It is claimed that the unknown Matthew Walker is the only man to have a knot named after him. **1971** I. IMRIE tr. *Svensson's Handbk. Seaman's Ropework* 79 The Mathew Walker knot on a three-stranded rope is the simplest of all knots with a rope's own end.

mattraca, var. *MATRACA.

mattress¹. Add: **3. b.** *U.S.* A bed of sugar-cane. Hence **mattress** *v. trans.*, to form (sugar-cane) into 'mattresses'.

1829 A. SHERWOOD *Gazetteer Georgia* (ed. 2) 255 The stacks or banks in which seed cane is preserved during winter, are called mattresses. **1833** B. SILLIMAN *Man. Sugar Cane* 12 They are cut near the ground, and carted to the vicinity of the fields where they are to be planted; being formed..into long beds about fifteen feet wide, which are called *mattresses*. **1850** *Rep. Comm. Patents: Agric. 1850* (U.S. Dept. Agric.) 423 It was..supposed that the cane was spoiled in the mattress by the continued warm weather after it was mattressed.

4. b. mattress antenna, array = *BILL-BOARD, BILLBOARD 2, also *ellipt.*; **mattress-jig** *slang*, sexual intercourse.

1947 D. G. FINK *Radar Engin.* iv. 247 The power efficiencies of properly adjusted mattress arrays vary from 80 to 95 per cent. *Ibid.* 249 The gain of a paraboloid is generally lower than that of a mattress of the same area expressed in square wavelengths. **1950** Mattress antenna [see *BILL-BOARD, BILLBOARD 2]. **1961** R. L. MATTINGLY in H. Jasik *Antenna Engin. Handbk.* xxv. 26 A common transmitter-receiving antenna can be implemented with a mattress array. **1896** FARMER & HENLEY *Slang* IV. 290/2 *Mattress-jig*, copulation. **1922** JOYCE *Ulysses* 418 Smutty Moll for a mattress jig.

Matura (mā·tǒră). Also Matara. [Name of a town (now called *Matara*) in Sri Lanka.] *Matura diamond*: a colourless variety of zircon used as a gem. Cf. JARGON *sb.*²

1880 *Encycl. Brit.* XIII. 532/1 The Singalese variety [of pale jargoons], found chiefly at Matura, has been termed 'Matura diamond'. **1936** L. J. SPENCER *Key to Precious Stones* xvii. 189 Much of the colourless zircon..is known as 'Matura diamond'. **1962** R. WEBSTER *Gems* I. vii. 118 The colourless stones..were..called by the misnomer 'Matara diamonds', a term which should now be forgotten.

maturation. Add: **5. a.** Also in *Psychol.*, the physical growth which, together with learning, leads to full development. Also *transf.* Hence **matura·tional** *a.*, of or pertaining to maturation.

1921 *Psychol. Rev.* May 196 The process runs along

parallel with the process of maturation and it is not clear in any case just what is contributed by heredity and what is due to learning. **1929** A. Gesell in C. Murchison *Found. Exper. Psychol.* 651 (*heading*) Maturational correspondence in identical twins. *Ibid.* 658 Maturational factors preserve his native endowment. **1938** R. S. Woodworth *Exper. Psychol.* xxix. 764 Maturation consists largely in development of the ability to learn. **1943** C. T. Morgan *Physiol. Psychol.* vii. 124 Many experiments have been carried out on the general problem of the relative importance of maturation and learning. **1953** *New Biol.* XIV. 27 Clearly this 'setting' of the perceptual and behavioural pattern in the third and fourth years must have as its base important maturational changes in the physiology and anatomy of the brain. **1958** K. Lovell *Educ. Psychol. & Children* vii. 103 In studying the effects of maturation on learning in children, use has been made ..of identical twins. **1961** J. Berko in Saporta & Bastian *Psycholinguistics* vi. 372/1 Throughout childhood, girls are perhaps from a maturational point of view slightly ahead of the boys who are their chronological age mates. **1968** M. Bunge in Lakatos & Musgrave *Probl. Philos. Sci.* 134 Scientific Research can pass through several phases of maturation, the degree of maturity attained depending on the depth and the logical organization of the ideas involved. **1970** D. S. Wright et al. *Introducing Psychol.* iv. 70 There is still some value in contrasting maturation and learning... This is simply a convenient way of classifying different antecedent conditions of the single process of development.

b. Add to def.: *spec.* of their gametes. (Further examples.)

1896 E. B. Wilson *Cell* 338 *Maturation*, the final stages in the development of the germ-cells. More specifically, the processes by which the reduction of the number of chromosomes is effected. **1972** Balin & Glasser *Reproductive Biol.* v. 319 (*heading*) Maturation of epididymal spermatozoa.

7. *attrib.*, as **maturation division** *Biol.*, either of the two divisions of meiosis.

1896 E. B. Wilson *Cell* v. 185 It is plain that the nature of the maturation-divisions can only be approached through a study of the origin of the tetrads. **1966** *Chromosoma* XIX. 99 (*heading*) The maturation divisions of the parthenogenetic stick insect *Carausius morosus* Br.

mature, *a.* Add: **1. d.** Of a soil: having a fully developed profile. Of a soil profile or its parts: fully developed.

1926 C. F. Marbut in Tansley & Chipp *Study of Vegetation* vii. 131 Mature soils..owe their essential characters to the nature of the climate in which they are developed. **1927** [see *immature *a.* 2 e]. **1954** W. D. Thornbury *Princ. Geomorphol.* iv. 76 A mature soil profile exhibits well-developed horizons. **1971** E. A. Fitzpatrick *Pedology* vii. 249/2 Marbut placed great emphasis on mature freely drained soils.

2. d. *mature student*: an adult who undertakes a course of study at a later age than normal.

[**1924** L. G. E. Jones *Training of Teachers in Eng. & Wales* xiv. 352 The sprinkling of more mature students is a great help.] **1953** C. A. Richardson et al. *Educ. of Teachers in Eng., France & U.S.A.* iii. 59 The mature student is one who..wishes to embark on a course of training as a teacher at an age considerably later than the normal age of entry to college. **1969** H. C. Dent *Educ. Syst. Eng. & Wales* (ed. 4) x. 205 From 1962–63 the Minister of Education ceased to give State scholarships (except to mature students). **1969** *Guardian* 16 Sept. 5/3 The formation of a new union for mature students has given fresh hope to people who are taking up teachers' training courses late in life. **1970** *St. Hilda's College (Oxf.) Rep. 1968–69* 21 One mature student was accepted to read for the B.A. in English. **1971** *Mod. Law Rev.* XXXIV. 652 A better solution to the problem of democratising recruitment would be to facilitate the attendance at law school of mature students.

6. b. Of a progressive cataract: characterized by complete opacity.

1850 [see *immature *a.* 2 d]. **1904** L. W. Fox *Dis. Eye* xii. 310 Operations should not be performed on both eyes at the same time, even though both cataracts are mature. **1970** A. H. Keeney *Ocular Exam.* ix. 143/1 A mature cataract is one that has developed complete opacification throughout.

maturely, *adv.* **3.** Delete *rare*$^{-1}$ and add later examples.

1902, 1965 [see *dissected *ppl. a.* 2 b]. **1965** M. Spark *Mandelbaum Gate* iv. 108 The rest were Arabs and Jews, most of whom were maturely sixteen years of age and upward.

matzah (ma·tsa). Also **matso** (ma·tso), **-za, -zho, -zo, -zot, -zoth, mazzot, -oth, motso, -za, mozza.** Pl. **matzoth, -os.** [Yiddish *matse*, f. Heb. *maṣṣāh*.] (A wafer of) unleavened bread, eaten by orthodox Jews during the Passover.

1846 *Jewish Manual, or Pract. Information Jewish & Mod. Cookery* p. xiv, *Matso*, Passover cakes. **1871** E. Levy *Jewish Cookery Bk.* 32 Soak two matzos, or crackers, in cold water. **1891** M. Friedländer *Jewish Relig.* ii. 380 The head of the family..who reads the [Passover] Service has before him on the table..three unleavened cakes (*matsoth*). **1893** I. Zangwill *Childr. Ghetto* (ed. 3) xxii. 202 Now is the national salutation changed to 'How do the *Motsos* agree with you?' **1904** *Jewish Encycl.* VIII. 393/1 The eating of *maẓẓot* during the seven days of the Passover festival is intended to recall the hurried departure from Egypt. **1922** Joyce *Ulysses* 79 Something like those mazzoth: it's that sort of bread: unleavened shewbread. **1927** *Daily Express* 16 Apr. 9 The command concerning unleavened bread, known as 'Matzos' is strictly observed. **1950** G. Mikes *Milk & Honey* 152 On the feast day..matzot is eaten instead of bread. **1952** S. Spender *Learning Laughter* xi. 159 This night we eat *matza* and no leavened bread. **1963** *Ann. Reg. 1962* 374 In March the Soviet Government banned the making of *matzot* (unleavened bread) required for Passover observances. **1965** M. Spark *Mandelbaum Gate* ii. 33 The unleavened bread, crisp *matzho* that made crumbs everywhere, was uncovered. **1970** L. M. Feinsilver *Taste of Yiddish* iii. 323 Even the Air Force..has a pretty good idea of what matzo is, for a New Jersey woman reported an Unidentified Flying Object as looking like a big matzo. **1973** *Jewish Chron.* 2 Feb. 23/2 This particular hechsher only applies to matzot manufactured in Britain.

attrib.

1846 *Jewish Manual, or Pract. Information Jewish & Mod. Cookery* i. 9 *Matso soup*... Take half a pound of *matso* flour. **1906** *Mrs. Beeton's Bk. Househ. Managem.* lv. 1574 Take up a little of the motza paste..roll lightly in the motza meal. **1921** *Dict. Occup. Terms* (1927) 433 *Matzo* (or *matzoth*) *baker*..expeditiously removes circular matzo bread i.e. Jewish passover bread. **1953** W. P. McGivern *Big Heat* ix. 111 He liked Jewish food..mozza ball soup. **1970** S. J. Perelman *Baby, it's Cold Inside* 208 The exhibit you see here..was first believed by the coroner to be a fossilized matzo ball. **1971** M. McCarthy *Birds of America* 36 She should be making *gefüllte* fish and matzoth balls. **1973** *Times* 3 Feb. 13/5 You can try the kneidlach soup (with matzo-meal dumplings).

mauby (mǭ^u·bi). Also **mawby.** [See Mobbie, mobee.] In Barbados, a drink made from the diluted extract of the bark of a tree or shrub of the genus *Gouania* or related plants; cf. Mobbie, mobee 1.

1790 J. B. Moreton *Manners & Customs West India Islands* 105 Cool drink or mauby is a delicious nectar to them in the morning. **1954** S. M. Sadeek *Windswept & Other Stories* (1969) 25 He drank, at first sipping the tall mauby slowly. **1957** I. Bayley in F. A. Collymore *Notes for Gloss. Words & Phr. Barbadian Dial.* 56 Mauby is made from bark, boiled in water for about an hour, and concentrated to a basic extract. When making the drink, some of the stock is diluted with water; sugar and vanilla essence are added... The result is a bitter-sweet drink, with a frothy head, popular for quenching the thirst, and for 'cooling' the blood. **1958** J. Carew *Black Midas* i. 17 One Friday Tanta Moore invited him in for a drink of mauby. **1962** *Listener* 16 Aug. 248/2 A man stands beside his handcart dispensing mawby or snowball, which consists of shaved ice covered with scarlet syrup. **1965** *Ibid.* 8 Apr. 523/3 Constant chatter is punctuated with the high-pitched, rather doleful cry of the 'mauby' girl: she..carries a two-gallon tank on her head, with a tap on it that she manipulates to dispense cold tea to her customers; a special kind of cold tea, brewed from the bark of the mauby plant. **1968** E. Lovelace *Schoolmaster* i. 8 Fruit wines from cashew and guava, and sorrel and mauby. **1973** *Advocate-News* (Barbados) 15 Dec. 8/1 In short, it is like serving mauby and ginger beer in a cocktail glass. **1974** *Sunday Advocate-News* (Barbados) 10 Mar. 14/1 Formerly, mauby women walked the streets with their load on their heads, and a bench in hand. But today, some of them drive or are driven.

maucherite (mau·χ-, mau·k-, mau·ʃərəit). *Min.* [ad. G. *maucherit* (F. Grünling 1913, in *Centralbl. f. Min., Geol. u. Paläont.* 225), f. the name of W. *Maucher* (1879–1930), mineral dealer of Munich; see -ite[1].] A nickel arsenide, approximately $Ni_{11}As_8$, occurring as brittle, reddish grey tetragonal crystals that are opaque with a metallic lustre and tarnish on exposure.

1913 *Jrnl. Chem. Soc.* CIV. ii. 516 Maucherite, a new nickel mineral from Thuringia... This new mineral, which was at first mistaken for rammelsbergite, occurs..in veins..in the copper-shales..at Eisleben, Thuringia. **1940** *Mineral. Mag.* XXV. 570 A physical, chemical, and preliminary structural study of maucherite..from Eisleben, Thuringia, and Sudbury, Ontario, and temiskamite ..from Elk Lake, Ontario, shows that these minerals.. represent a single mineral species. **1963** *Mineral. Abstr.* XVI. 263/1 Syntheses from nickel and arsenic were carried out by means of dry thermal procedures... At arsenic vapour pressure, Ni_5As_2, maucherite, niccolite, rammelsbergite or paramelsbergite [*read* pararammelsbergite], are formed depending on the temperature.

maul, *sb.*[1] **4.** (Later examples.)

1960 *Times* 7 Dec. 17/1 The ability to start attacks from line-outs and loose mauls. **1973** *Times* 9 Feb. 11/2 We did not do well in the rucks and mauls against Wales.

‖ **Maulana** (maulā·nă). Also **Maulanah, Mawlana, Mulana.** [Arab. *maulānā* our Lord: cf. Moolvee and Mullah.] A title given to a learned Muslim.

1832 H. H. Wilson *Relig. Sects of Hindus* in *Asiatick Researches* XVII. 297 Maulana Rum observes—'What is the world? forgetfulness of God, not clothes, nor wealth, nor wife, nor offspring.' *a* **1846** G. Ouseley *Biogr. Notices Persian Poets* 112 The author of this sublime poem on Divine Love and the Súfi Philosophy, was Mulánà Jeláluddin. *Ibid.* 116 The Mulánà was sixty-nine years of age when he closed his earthly career in Koniah. **1855** H. H. Wilson *Gloss. Judicial & Revenue Terms* 335/2 *Maulánà*,..the title of a person of learning or respectability, teacher, doctor: in the Maratha countries, the usual designation of the Mohammadan village schoolmaster. **1888** *Encycl. Brit.* XXIII. 656/1 Ottoman literature may be said to open with a few mystic lines, the work of Sultán Veled, son of Mauláná Jelál-ud-Dín, the author of the great Persian poem the *Mathnawí*. **1895** *Jrnl. Asiatic Soc. Bengal* LXIII. iii. 54 When sixteen years of age, he studied under Maulánáh 'Abd-ul-'Azíz of Delhi. **1902** E. A. Gait *Rep. Census India 1901* VI. iv. 174 Other reformers were spreading the doctrines of the Patna School, the most successful of whom was Mauláná Karámat A'li of Jaunpur. **1936** *Encycl. Islām* III. 417/2 Allāh is often called *Mawlānā* 'our Lord' in Arabic literature. *Ibid.* 418/2 Peace was negotiated..by Mawlānā Ḥamza. **1962** *Economist* 9 Mar. 889/1 The maulanas want..the kind of obscurantist stranglehold on the [Pakistani] nation..the president is determoned to resist. **1975** *Bangladesh Times* 18 July 2/1 Maulana Abdur Rab.. breathed his last recently at his village home due to heart attack... The late maulana was renowned for his social services, community developments and preaching the ideals of Islam.

mauler. Add: **2.** *slang.* A hand; a fist. Cf. Mauley.

1820 'W. T. Moncrieff' *Mod. Collegians* 18 The Old Gentleman wishes to know how to put his maulers in action. **1936** 'F. Gerald' *Millionaire in Memories* vii. 193 To a young fellow who fancied himself with his 'maulers' the proposition was attractive..plenty of fighting. **1960** S. H. Courtier *Gently dust Corpse* xii. 170 Wait till I get my maulers on Lew Boston. **1973** J. Rossiter *Manipulators* viii. 92 You keep your big maulers off this.

maum, mawm, varr. Ma'am or Mam[1]. *U.S.*

1826 A. Royall *Sk. Hist., Life & Manners U.S.* 121 Yes mawm, no mawm. **1835** A. B. Longstreet *Georgia Scenes* 110 'Aunt' and 'mauma', or 'maum', its abbreviation, are terms of respect commonly used by children, to aged negroes. **1881** *Harper's Mag.* Apr. 728/2 Maum Dulcie, is my habit ready? **1928** J. Peterkin *Scarlet Sister Mary* ii. 14 Mary had grown up in Maum Hannah's old house in the Quarters. **1950** *Publ. Amer. Dial. Soc.* xiv. 46 Maum' Dinah.

mauma, maumer, maumie, varr. *mamma*, = Mammy 2.

1835 W. G. Simms *Partisan* 141 You have told me nothing of old mauma. **1838** C. Gilman *Recoll. Southern Matron* xv. 101 Who does not remember his youthful Christmas; the reiterated charge to his *maumer* to awaken him first? **1881** *Harper's Mag.* Apr. 737/2 Maumie, how I should like to see a Hoodoo meeting! **1890** *Ibid.* July 232/1 Respectable colored 'maumas', ample of girth, in spotted white aprons. **1895** *Century Mag.* May 155/2 Only a few, a very few, of the faithful old 'maumers' and loyal house- and body-servants remain. **1950** *Publ. Amer. Dial. Soc.* xiv. 46 *Mauma*,..name by which elderly Negro women were called by the children of the family with which they were connected.

Mau Mau (mau·mau). [Kikuyu.] Name of an African secret society originating among the Kikuyu, having as its aim the expulsion of European settlers and the ending of British rule in Kenya. Also *attrib.*

1950 *E. Afr. Standard* 16 June A/5 We have arrived at a state of dissatisfaction and insecurity, bitterness and delusion which has given rise to the formation of such societies as the 'Dini ya Mswambwa' and the 'Mau Mau Association'. **1952** L. S. B. Leakey *Mau Mau & Kikuyu* xi. 96 The Kikuyu regard the Mau Mau Association as nothing more than the old Kikuyu Central Association under another name. **1952** *N.Y. Times* 26 Oct. i. 3/2 Large groups of natives fled today to lofty mountain hideouts to escape the Government drive..against Mau Mau terrorists, who have sworn death to the white man. **1955** *Times* 13 July 6/5 Further evidence of the infiltration of Mau Mau into tribes other than the Kikuyu, Embu, and Meru was revealed here to-day. **1960** F. D. Corfield *Hist. Survey Orig. & Growth Mau Mau* 78 On 21st September [1948] the Director of Intelligence and Security reported..that a new movement, the *Mau Mau*..had appeared in Naivasha. **1971** *Sunday Nation* (Nairobi) 11 Apr. 12/5 Events beyond human control—famine, Mau Mau, the changing environment.

Hence **mau·-mau** *v. U.S. slang*, to threaten, terrorize; so as *sb.*; **mau·-mauer; mau·-mauing** *vbl. sb.*

1970 T. Wolfe *Radical Chic & Mau-mauing Flak Catchers* (1971) 97 Going downtown to mau-mau the bureaucrats got to be the routine practice in San Francisco. *Ibid.* 124 In public you used the same term the whites used, namely, 'confrontation'. The term '*mau-mauing*' was a source of amusement in private. The term *mau-mauing* said, 'The white man has a voodoo fear of us, because deep down he still thinks we're savages. Right? So we're going to do that Savage number for him.' *Ibid.* 148 And it was here that Bill Jackson proved himself to be a brilliant man and a true artist, a rare artist of the mau-mau. **1971** *Harper's* June 9 His [*sc.* Norman Mailer's] demonstration of the inadequacies and distortions of Kate Millett's *Sexual Politics* is convincing and indicates that the English Department of Columbia University had been mau-maued by that termagant of Women's Lib. **1974** *Maclean's Mag.* Dec. 108/1 We've had a belly full of Indian rhetoric. After a threat is made for the fifth, twelfth or fortieth time, the excitement wears off; boredom becomes contempt when we find out that each hollow boast brings more government money tinkling into the Indian organizations' pockets. American writer Tom Wolfe calls the technique 'mau-mauing'; it's no accident that the most successful mau-mauer, Harold Cardinal, runs one of the strongest Indian organizations in Canada.

maumet. Add: **2. c.** A baby, child. *dial.*

1932 S. Gibbons *Cold Comfort Farm* v. 69 Far from those that loves her and cowdled her in their bosoms when she was a mommet. **1949** *Antiquity* XXIII. 42 The poor mommet whose father was 'in trade' is discernible even on its tomb as 'a really vulgar babe'.

maund, *sb.*[2] **1.** (Later examples.)

1909 *Chambers's Jrnl.* Oct. 665/2 The import of dyeing materials into Kashmir in one year was: Indigo, fourteen maunds, or one thousand one hundred and twenty pounds. **1955** *Times* 12 May 12/5 Throughout the Himalaya the unit of weight for barter is the load a man can

carry—a maund, or 80 pounds. **1969** *Commerce* (Bombay) 26 July 188/1 Raw jute arrivals in the last week remained static at the previous level of 30,000 maunds a day. **1972** *Nat. Geographic* Oct. 532/2, I harvested about 33 maunds an acre. At a fraction more than 82 pounds to the maund that is roughly 2,700 pounds. **1975** *Bangladesh Observer* 21 July 7/3 On July 4 Bangladesh Rifles personnel chased an alleged smuggler near the border, but he fled away leaving one maund thirty seers of fertilizer.

maunderingly (mǭ·ndəriŋli), *adv.* [f. Maundering *ppl. a.*[2] + -ly[2].] In a maundering manner; inconsequently.

1909 I. Zangwill *Melting-Pot* iii. 172 *David.* (..he picks up the violin, and as his fingers draw out the broken string he murmurs) I must get a new string. (He resumes his dragging march toward the door, repeating maunderingly) I must get a new string. **1915** F. M. Hueffer *Good Soldier* iv. vi. 282 Edward..believed maunderingly that some essential attractiveness in himself must have made the girl continue to go on loving him. **1955** J. Slotkin in *Perspective* Autumn 152 He raised his head maunderingly, like a jackal from a lion's kill no longer warm.

maundful. [f. Maund *sb.*[1]] The amount contained in a maund.

1828 W. Carr *Dial. Craven* (ed. 2) I. 314 *Maund-ful*, a basket full. **1924** *Chambers's Jrnl.* 20 Sept. 673/2 Two maunfuls at a time, the pilchards are tipped out of the baskets.

maundy. Add: **4. maundy money**, now usu. distributed by the reigning monarch at Westminster Abbey.

1967 *Everyman's Encycl.* VIII. 293/1 In 1833 ..the dole was replaced by a money payment ('Maundy money') distributed by the sovereign in person or through a royal almoner.

maureeyah, var. *moya.

Mauritanian (mǫritēⁱ·niăn), *a.* and *sb.* Also Mauretanian. [f. *Mauretania* (see below) + -an.] **A.** *adj.* Of or pertaining to the ancient country of Mauretania in North Africa, or the modern independent republic of Mauritania on the west coast of Africa, formerly a French colony. **B.** *sb.* A native or inhabitant of Mauritania. Also **Maurita·nic** *a.*

1594 Marlowe & Nashe *Dido* iv. iv. 215 And will my guard with Mauritanian darts, To waite vpon him. **1607** Topsell *Four-f. Beasts* 247 That same herbe (called *Doronicum*)..[is] highly esteemed among the Arabians[,] Graecians, and Mauritanians. *Ibid.* 461 These also are the Epethets of lions, wrathfull, maned..stout, great, Masilian, Mauritanian, Parthian, [etc.]. **1652** J. Taylor *Rule of Holy Dying* (ed. 2) iii. 95 Masinissa the Mauritanian. *a* **1680** Evelyn *Diary* an. 1645 (1955) II. 467 There were kept in it two Eagles, a Crane, a Mauritanian Sheepe, a stag, and sundry foule. **1776** [see Moor *sb.*[2] 1]. **1895** [see *Afro-European adj. and sb.]. **1911** 'I. Hay' *Safety Match* xiv. 221 Algiers—that curious combination of Mauretanian antiquity and second-rate French provincialism. **1959** *Times* 7 Jan. 11/7 The Mauritanian trader is a common sight in the markets. **1964** *Times* 29 Sept. 10/7 An attack by a gang of white youths on Mr. Youssouf Gueye, the First Secretary of the Mauritanian delegation. **1967** *Oceanogr. & Marine Biol.* V. 450 Two regions of the Atlantic Ocean, namely the Lusitanian..and the Mauritanian extending from Gibraltar to Cape Blanc, and including the Canary Islands and Madeira. **1968** *Encycl. Brit.* XIV. 1124/2 Mauretanian history really begins with the Punic Wars... Mauretanians were good military material and were used by the Romans in both Africa and other parts of the empire. **1972** *Guardian* 8 Feb. 13/1 A couple of Mauritanians selling silver spoons.

Mauritian (mǫri·ʃăn), *sb.* and *a.* [f. Mauritius + -an, -ian.] **A.** *sb.* A native or inhabitant of the island of Mauritius in the Indian Ocean. **B.** *adj.* Of or pertaining to Mauritius.

[**1835** J. Jeremie *Recent Events at Mauritius* i. 5 The Mauriciens are to set an example 'au monde entier'.] **1865** *Chambers's Jrnl.* Sept. 546/2 To Mauritians..this droll little Mauritian journal..may very probably appear a most influential exponent of public opinion. **1884** H. W. Little *Madagascar* xiii. 280 Cheap rum..is often used.. for the purchase of bullocks for the Mauritian markets. **1896** B. Burleigh *Two Campaigns* 60 Fiery Mauritian rum. *Ibid.* 111 The place was under a Mauritian named Hemming. **1918** L. Huxley *Life J. D. Hooker* II. xxviii. 12 The Mauritian Herbarium was to go back, as soon as the assistant had revised the lists. **1926** *Chambers's Jrnl.* Apr. 212/1 The Mauritian Creole is a crafty fellow. **1963** *Guardian* 26 Feb. 4/2 A young Mauritian said he would now shave off his beard. **1966** M. R. D. Foot *SOE in France* xi. 380 The Mayer brothers,..Mauritians by origin. **1967** R. I. McDavid in G. V. Bobrinskoy *Lang. & Areas* 86 A viable language in its own right—like.. Haitian or Mauritian Creole. **1971** *Leader* (Durban) 7 May 1/2 Officials of the sports body..have already had negotiations with Mauritian football authorities. **1972** *Guardian* 8 Mar. 13/3 Ramgoolam would have to decide whether to..find a Mauritian for the top job, or (swallowing Mauritian pride..) find a suitable Englishman. **1973** *Times* 5 Mar. (Mauritius Suppl.) p. i/3 Warmed by the sun and Mauritian friendliness we relaxed. **1974** *Times* 14 Mar. 16/4 The Mauritians invited me to their binge.. celebrating the sixth anniversary of their independence.

Maurya (mau·riă). [Skr., f. the name of Chandragupta *Maurya*, who founded the dynasty.] The name of a dynasty that ruled northern India from 321 to *c* 184 B.C.; a member of this dynasty. Also *attrib.* Hence **Mau·ryan** *a.*

1870 *Jrnl. R. Asiatic Soc.* IV. 96 The celebrated Mauryan king..was not only sovereign of the valley, but of the whole of Northern India. *Ibid.* 122 (*heading*) Maurya dynasty, 130 years. **1886** *Encycl. Brit.* XXI. 272/2 The oldest hitherto known specimens of Indian writing are five rock-inscriptions, containing religious edicts in Pāli..issued by the emperor Aśoka..of the Maurya dynasty. **1910** *Ibid.* XIV. 399/1 After Asoka the Mauryas dwindled away, and the last of them..was treacherously assassinated in 184 B.C. **1935** *Times Lit. Suppl.* 4 July 434/4 The interest that the Mauryan State took in preventing famine and in relieving distress appears to have been more vigorous than in modern days. **1956** A. Toynbee *Historian's Approach to Relig.* vii. 90 In the age of the Maurya Emperor Açoka. **1959** *Chambers's Encycl.* VI. 553/2 About 185–175 King Demetrius conquered the Mauryan empire in north India up to Patna on the middle Ganges. **1968** I. W. Mabbett *Short Hist. India* v. 61 The Mauryan dynasty, like the rest of them, eventually became a line of kings jostling with others, a principality in the north-east. **1973** *Times* 14 Apr. (Nepal Suppl.) p. ii/2 The oldest monuments found on Nepalese soil are contemporaneous with the Mauryan empire of North India.

mauryah, var. *moya.

‖ **mauvais coucheur** (movę kūʃör). [Fr., lit. 'bad bedfellow'.] A difficult, uncooperative, or unsociable person.

1959 *Times* 19 Nov. 15/2 Brecht at best was a *mauvais coucheur*. **1960** C. P. Snow *Affair* iv. 45 The moral roughneck, the *mauvais coucheur*, often seemed to her to have a dignity and elevation not granted to the rest of us. **1963** *Times Lit. Suppl.* 26 Apr. 297/3 Goddard was a man of talent but he was obviously a *mauvais coucheur*.

‖ **mauvaise langue** (movęz lāṅg). [Fr., lit. 'bad tongue'.] An evil or venomous tongue; a vituperative gossip; a scandal-monger.

1888 C. M. Yonge *Beechcroft at Rockstone* II. xiii. 14 The foreboding that the *mauvaises langues* would get hold of it. **1924** A. D. Sedgwick *Little French Girl* iv. i. 304 Marigold is a wretched gossip, and worse. She's a *mauvaise langue*; I would not trust her story. **1936** 'R. West' *Thinking Reed* i. 18 In another moment that couple of *mauvaises langues* would have something to wag about. **1939** C. Beaton *My Royal Past* ix. 101 A lady..with a very *mauvaise langue*. **1974** *New Society* 11 Apr. 58/2 We are told that all Europe is at a standstill, until it knows who has been elected president (and those who are *mauvaise langue* will add that if it is Chaban-Delmas, there will be a further delay whilst he acquaints himself with foreign affairs).

‖ **mauvais pas** (movę pā). *Mountaineering.* [Fr., lit. 'bad step'.] A place that is dangerous or difficult to negotiate.

1816 Shelley *Let.* 25 July (1964) I. 500 The one [mule] which I rode fell, in what the guides call a *mauvais pas*. **1843** J. D. Forbes *Trav. through Alps of Savoy* iv. 67 The spot has acquired the name of the *Mauvais Pas*, which it bears more frequently than its proper one of La Roche de Moré. **1871** L. Stephen *Playground of Europe* v. 315 As a mere gymnast upon the mountains..in overcoming *mauvais pas* of all descriptions—the guide is incontestably superior. **1907** G. D. Abraham *Compl. Mountaineer* iv. 56 The leader can retie himself on the end and scramble safely up the *mauvais pas*. **1940** F. S. Chapman *Helvellyn to Himalaya* vii. 166 We decided to return once more to the couloir..thus short-circuiting the *mauvais pas* we had seen in our reconnaissance. **1971** N. Tennent *Islands of Scotl.* i. 30 The northern section of the ridge..has some fine situations, including a tricky descent on the Iorsa side to the 'impassable' 'mauvais pas'.

‖ **mauvais quart d'heure** (movę kār dōr). [Fr., lit. 'bad quarter of an hour'.] A short period of time which is embarrassing and unnerving; a brief but unpleasant experience.

1864 M. B. Chesnut *Diary* 8 Jan. (1949) 353 General Preston rushed in to the breach... But Mr. Willie Mountford had his *mauvais quart d'heure*. **1871** M. Arnold *Friendship's Garland* 95 You must needs have..a *mauvais quart d'heure*. **1883** Ld. Saltown *Scraps* II. iii. 77 My modesty was severely tried, and I do not remember to have often spent a more *mauvais quart d'heure*, which was actually about the length of time that my martyrdom endured. **1897** J. McCabe *Twelve Yrs. in Monastery* iv. 64 We gave him many a *mauvais quart d'heure* by running to the door when we saw his shadow near it, and chasing him through the convent. **1905** E. M. Forster *Where Angels fear to Tread* ii. 47 He takes it so well. But you must have had a *mauvais quart d'heure*. **1920** *Punch* 18 Feb. 138/3 Last week's programme had its *beaux moments*, but it had also at least two *mauvais quarts d'heure*. **1924** P. C. Wren *Beau Geste* i. i. 25 At the end of ten minutes, a very *mauvais quart d'heure*, I beckoned the Sergeant-Major. **1960** *Guardian* 21 Sept. 8/6 The long-term effects of a transitory *mauvais quart d'heure*. **1965** *Economist* 5 June 1125 John Kennedy had his *mauvais quart d'heure* between April and June, 1961.

mauvais sujet. (Earlier and later examples.)

1793 T. Fremantle in *Wynne Diaries* (1952) xix. 251 Find the surgeon to be a mauvais subjet [*sic*], talk much to him. He crys, and promises to amend. **1813** A. Romilly *Let.* 12 Aug. in S. H. Romilly *Romilly–Edgeworth Lett.* (1936) 56 The youngest son, who was a very mauvais sujet, has just been killed in a duel. **1825** H. Wilson *Mem.* I. 179, I will lay my life, you two desperate mauvais sujets came here together! **1897** E. A. Bartlett *Battlefields Thessaly* viii. 171 These *mauvais sujets* had maltreated their own countrymen and women. **1945** R. Hargreaves *Enemy at Gate* 56 Rome had failed to save one of its children, and even if that *mauvais sujet* had been guilty of recusancy, in the offspring's downfall the parent was no less undone. **1953** *Essays in Crit.* III. 217 The things in my criticism that he shakes his head over..endorsing the charges of..'bad form' and '*mauvais sujet*', *are* the effort to win that recognition. **1975** A. Christie *Curtain* v. 46 The *mauvais sujet*—always women are attracted to him.

mauve, *a.* Add: **b.** *Comb.* Also with other colours, as *mauve-pink*, *-red*.

1899 B. W. Warhurst *Colour Dict.* 44 Lilac-rose is a dull rose..which..as a tint will appear as..Mauve-pink. **1917** D. H. Lawrence *Look! We have come Through!* 57 Their mauve-red petals on the cloth. **1952** A. G. L. Hellyer *Sanders' Encycl. Gardening* (ed. 22) 92 *Catalpa Fargesii*..with its fine var. *Duclouxii* with large mauve-pink flowers.

maven (mēⁱ·vən). *U.S. colloq.* Also **mavin, mayvin.** Pl. **-im.** [ad. Heb. *mevin* understanding.] An expert or connoisseur.

1965 *Hadassah News Letter* Apr. 30 (Advt.), Get Vita at your favorite supermarket, grocery or delicatessen. Tell them the beloved *Maven* sent you. It won't save you any money: but you'll get the best herring—Vita. **1968** L. Rosten *Joys of Yiddish* 223 *Mavin* was recently given considerable publicity in a series of newspaper advertisements for herring tidbits. 'The Herring *Mavin* Strikes Again!' proclaimed the caption. The picture showed an empty jar. A real advertising *mavin* must have thought that up. **1969** *Time* 12 Sept. 78 Much of the credit for the Cinderella publishing story goes to Robert Gottlieb, then the editorial genie in residence at Simon & Schuster, now the mavin at Alfred Knopf. **1970** L. M. Feinsilver *Taste of Yiddish* iii. 323 Canada Dry has been touting its product as 'Maven's Choice' in American Jewish weeklies, where Switzerland Emmentaler cheese announces itself with: 'Calling all Mayvinim!' **1972** *Publishers Weekly* 10 July 22/1 If Shawn is not exactly a boxing *maven*, he knows even less about baseball. **1973** *Milwaukee Jrnl.* 4 Mar. V. 4/1 Miss Decter (no Ms., please) is one of the culture 'mavins' of New York, to use a newly chic term borrowed from the Hebrew. **1973** *N.Y. Times* 8 July X. 31/4 Mama, who had managed to support herself by becoming a local real estate *maven*, negotiated the purchase.

maverick, *sb.* [Etym. note: read 'Samuel A. *Maverick* (1803–1870), a Texas cattle-owner who left the calves of his herd unbranded'.]

1. (Earlier and later examples.)

1867 in J. G. McCoy *Hist. Sk. Cattle Trade* (1940) 83 The term maverick which was formerly applied to unbranded yearlings is now applied to every calf which can be separated from the mother cow. **1942** S. Kennedy *Palmetto Country* 223 Most likely candidates for rustling are unbranded calves and cattle, called 'mavericks' in the West. **1974** G. Jenkins *Bridge of Magpies* xv. 229 Cowpunchers riding herd and trying to rope the most bloody-minded maverick that ever cut loose on the plains of Texas.

2. a. Add to def.: An independent person; an individualist; also applied *spec.* in the U.S. to a politician who will not affiliate with a regular political party. Also *attrib.* in sense 'independent, unattached'.

1886 *Calif. Maverick* (San Francisco) 13 Feb. 4/1 People would say, 'He holds maverick views', meaning that his views were untainted by partisanship in the matter. **1901** *McClure's Mag.* Dec. 147 Occasionally they found a maverick legislator, or traded for one. **1948** *Manch. Guardian Weekly* 8 Jan. 4/1 A few maverick liberals. **1948** *Chicago Daily News* 11 June 16/7 One Republican Senator, and not by any means a conspicuous maverick, pointed out that the Senate might have acted. **1954** *Manch. Guardian Weekly* 30 Dec. 8/3 His fellow 'maverick' ..also appeared to have gone into not uncomfortable shadows. **1957** *Times Lit. Suppl.* 8 Mar. 1/3 A contrast of Maverick with Movement verse will illustrate this... To Mavericks, Movement verse expresses 'antagonism towards sensibility and sentiment'. **1957** *Oxf. Mag.* 17 Oct. 22/2 The story is not just of local boy making good, but also, and more significantly, of maverick making friends. **1963** *Listener* 17 Jan. 115/1 Neither the novelists of the central tradition of English writing, nor the great Mavericks of the nineteenth century, whose strong apprehension of evil forced them to break through the domestic web in which they wished to remain, had any clear theological pattern in which to embody their sense of evil. **1968** P. Oliver *Screening Blues* 18 Maverick lines that move from blues to blues are given new rhymes and new meanings by their juxtaposition with other ideas, while they retain the quality of surprise. **1973** *Radio Times* 4–10 Aug. 8 Ruth Inglis met the 77-year-old maverick zoologist at his Oxford base.

maverick, *v.* (Examples.)

1883 in *Amer. Speech* (1958) May 141 The Indians stole them..and the Texans 'mavericked' the unbranded. **1948** J. K. Rollinson *Wyoming Cattle Trails* 139 The artful practice of burning or working over brands was resorted to, with honest mavericking as a side line.

b. *intr.* To stray or wander like a maverick.

1910 W. M. Raine *Bucky O'Connor* 203 It hadn't penetrated my think-tank that this was your hacienda when I came mavericking in.

mavrodaphne (mævrodæ·fni). [mod.Gr., f. late Gr. μαῦρος dark (Gr. ἀμαυρός) + δάφνη laurel.] A dark-red sweet Greek wine made from the grape of the same name.

1911 in Webster. **1935** A. L. Simon *Wines & Liqueurs from A to Z* 36 *Mavrodaphne*, a sweet dessert wine from Patras (Greece). **1945** E. Waugh *Brideshead Revisited* i. ii. 52 Neither the mixture of wines, nor the Chartreuse, nor the Mavrodaphne Trifle..explains the distress of that

hag-ridden night. **1958** R. Liddell *Morea* II. ii. 52 The sweet wine, *Mavrodaphne*..reminds me too often of the Looking-glass precept: 'Come fill up your glasses with treacle and ink.' **1960** M. Stewart *My Brother Michael* vi. 82, I sipped the wine. It was dark as mavrodaphne. **1972** *Times* 10 June 9/1 Mavrodaphne, the only Greek wine apart from retsina to be well-known outside its homeland, comes from the Peloponnese.

mavrone (mǎvrōᵘ·n), *int.* Anglicized form of Irish *mo bhrón* my grief (f. *brón*), used as an exclamation of sorrow.

1892 W. B. Yeats *Countess Kathleen* iii. 64 The treasure-room is broken in—mavrone, mavrone The door stands open, and the gold is gone. **1922** Joyce *Ulysses* 197 He wailed:—And we to be there, mavrone, and you to be unbeknownst. **1939** —— *Finnegans Wake* II. 232 Stop up, mavrone, and sit in my lap.

maw, *sb.*¹ **3.** (Earlier and later *fig.* examples.)

1818 Keats *Endymion* II. 272 Weary, he sat down before the maw Of a wide outlet. **1931** F. Hurst *Back St.* xxxi. 277 The small vestibule where stood a row of these iron men of chance. Occasionally one of the guests, feeding coins into these metal maws, staked her. **1955** *Times* 5 Aug. 9/7 The grim realities of economics are rapidly driving the stubbornly 'independent' man into the insatiable maw of large combines.

mawby, var. *Mauby.

Mawlana, var. *Maulana.

mawley, var. Mauley.

maw-wormy, *a.* [f. Mawworm².] = *mawwormish* adj.

1885 in J. R. Ware *Passing Eng.* (1909) 174/2 Without being mawwormy, I fail to see why a wreath should be presented to any man who makes a business of giving opera.

maxi- (mæ·ksi), combining form of Maximum 5 denoting things, esp. articles of clothing, which are very long or large of their kind. Also as *sb.* Cf. *Midi-, *Mini-.

1961 *Spectator* 30 June 965 If you get into a maxi-taxi after midnight with a companion, there is 3/3d on the clock before you start. **1966** *Times Educ. Suppl.* 24 June 2015/2 There will be Lady X in Rutland realizing with a gasp of horror that she is wearing the same maxi-skirt as Lady Y. **1966** *Daily Tel.* 24 Oct. 11/1 The maxi-bag must be the next thing. And by the natural sequence of bag fashion psychology, the manufacturers are now designing bags on briefcase lines. **1967** *Punch* 3 May 624/1 The clampdown in Greece..may shut up those tireless critics, in our own land of the free, of mini-skirt girls and maxi-hair boys, now banned by the Greek Minister of the Interior. **1967** *Evening Standard* 7 Dec. 9/1 You're in a black crêpe maxi-skirt... If everyone is wearing maxi's, you're all right. **1968** *Daily Tel.* 18 Jan. 15/3, I doubt if we'll see the Queen in a real maxi yet awhile, but the belted emerald maxi coat sketched was certainly the Royal dressmaker's newest looking garment in the collection he showed yesterday. **1968** *Guardian* 2 May 7/4 Here are expensive clothes from 30 to 70 guineas. They are not for youngsters who wear maxis for kicks. **1970** R. Lowell *Notebk.* 167 The girl's maxi-coat, Tsar officer's, dragged the snow. **1970** *Time* 16 Nov. 67 To relieve the sterile monotony of nurses' uniforms, Fashion Designer Pierre Cardin recently unveiled three new creations at a London showing. Two of his designs—nunlike wimples with white maxidresses—were harmless affairs that might make ward nurses look functional if not fashionable. **1971** 'V. X. Scott' *Surrogate Wife* 230 He was wearing a great big olive green maxicoat. **1971** *Ink* 12 June 1/2 'Have a whiff' was released by Pye on a maxi-single (two tracks on each side). **1973** S. B. Jackman *Guns covered with Flowers* vi. 98 Marija slipped off her tweed maxi-coat. **1975** *Daily Tel.* 4 Jan. 16 This figure is quite impressive until it is compared with the 1974–75 budget of £1,325 million, which means that it is only a 1½ per cent. mini-reduction in what promises to be a maxi-budget.

maxim, *sb.*¹ Add: **3.** *spec.* Used of precepts of morality or prudence occurring in Old English verse.

1883 H. Kennedy tr. *B. ten Brink's Hist. Eng. Lit.* I. 64 The poet is fond of beginning a new maxim or a chain of them with the second half of a verse. **1892** S. A. Brooke *Hist. Early Eng. Lit.* II. 277 The *Gnomic Verses*..consist of folk-proverbs, maxims, short descriptions of human life, [etc.]. **1902** *Jrnl. Eng. & Germ. Philol.* IV. 477 The *Wife's Complaint*..closes with a general maxim deduced from the sad experiences of the once happy couple. **1966** S. B. Greenfield in E. G. Stanley *Continuations & Beginnings* 143 The diction of secular gnomes or maxims.

maximal, *a.* (Later examples.)

1955 *Bull. Atomic Sci.* Apr. 107/2 The tradition of an insistence on maximal loyalty—the tradition of hyper-patriotism—is an old one in the United States, and it becomes very demanding in periods of crisis. **1958** E. Winter in Middleton & Tait *Tribes without Rulers* 140 What is termed the maximal lineage consists of all the descendants in the male line of a single eponymous ancestor. **1960** P. Suppes *Axiomatic Set Theory* viii. 244 *A* is a maximal chain in *B* if and only if *A* is a chain in *B* and there is no chain *C* in *B* such that $A \subset C$. **1963** W. V. Quine *Set Theory* x. 231 There are notable equivalents of the axiom of choice... One is Hausdorff's law that every partial ordering harbors a maximal ordering. **1964** E. Mendelson *Introd. Math. Logic* 10 A maximal ideal is a proper ideal which is included in no other proper ideal. **1971** D. Crystal *Ling.* 199 The investigation of grammatical models in terms of maximal units. *Ibid.* 201 The sentence is the maximal unit of grammatical analysis. **1972** *Language* XLVIII. 264 The present delayed publication is intended especially to permit me to acknowledge that before today the only adequate publication of the principle of maximal redundancy has been in the Presidential Address of December 1969.

maximally *adv.* (later examples).

1969 *Daily Tel.* 11 Jan. 5/3 The answer, as with the short-term gain.., is to tax yourself maximally. In this case you would assume that £700 would be left to you after 30 p.c. had been deducted. **1970** *Nature* 30 May 804/1 The enzyme was assayed in maximally activated conditions. **1971** *Jrnl. Gen. Psychol.* LXXXIV. 88 It has been found that the same manners of input timing that maximally increase brightness also act to affect hue and desaturation maximally. **1971** D. Crystal *Ling.* 175 Phonology deals with sounds and contrasts between sounds only within the context of some language (maximally, in any language). **1973** *Nature* 2 Mar. 68/1 Histamine is synthesized maximally in the hypothalamus.

maximalism (mæ·ksimăliz'm). [f. Maximal *a.* + -ism or ad. Russ. *maksimalizm.*] The policy or theory of a 'maximum' programme of some kind. Cf. *Maximalist.

1920 *Glasgow Herald* 11 May 10 Bologna is undoubtedly to-day one of the chief Italian strongholds of Maximalism. **1951** N. Gorodetzky *St. Tikhon Zadonsky* ix. 189 The tendency of many Russians to seek extremes, maximalism, paroxysms, even in spiritual matters. **1967** J. M. Cammett *Antonio Gramsci* iv. 88 Thereafter, the break between *Ordine Nuovo* and maximalism widened, eventually contributing heavily to the Socialist schism at Livorno. **1967** C. Seton-Watson *Italy from Liberalism to Fascism* xii. 524 Maximalism..provided only revolutionary talk as a substitute for revolution.

Maximalist (mæ·ksimălist). Also **maximalist.** [f. Maximal *a.* + -ist or ad. Russ. *maksimalíst*, f. L. *maximum*, or ad. F. *maximaliste.*] A member of the more extremist 'fraction' of the Russian Socialist-Revolutionary Party which split off from the main body of the party in 1904 and which used and advocated terrorist methods. Later regarded as a translation of Russ. *bol'shevik* and used as an alternative name for a Bolshevik. Also, a member of any similar group outside Russia. Also *attrib.* or as *adj.*, of or pertaining to a policy or theory of maximum demands (of some kind specified in the context).

1907 I. Zangwill *Ghetto Comedies* 408 'Ah, you're a Maximalist,' said the beadle. 'No, I am only a Minimalist.' **1909** *Westm. Gaz.* 23 Dec. 7/4 He is said to have joined the 'Maximalists' in 1907. **1921** tr. *Trotsky's Defence of Terrorism* ix. 173 Plekhanovists, Maximalists, Anarchists... Absolutely all the 'shades of Socialism'. **1921** *Glasgow Herald* 14 Oct. 9 Forty out of 100 Deputies are Reformists..headed by some of the best brains in the country, like Signore Turati..and Modigliani. To them are opposed an equal number of Maximalists. **1933** M. Eastman tr. *Trotsky's Hist. Russ. Revolution* II. xiii. 309 While on the right the 'democracy' was competing with the Bolsheviks, on the left too there were the anarchists, the Maximalists, the Left Social Revolutionaries, trying to crowd them out. **1933** *Mind* XLII. 181 The rule..of always acting so as to produce the greatest amount of good, which latter rule the 'Maximalists' say we ought always to follow. *Ibid.*, The 'Maximalist' Theory (this designation suggests quantity better than 'Optimific') concentrates generally upon the consideration, not of individual situations, but of what happens when a general practice, custom or institution is dropped and replaced by another. **1954** *Ann. Reg. 1953* 153 There were the 'maximalists'..who wanted a real surrender of sovereignty, and the 'minimalists'. **1955** D. W. Treadgold *Lenin & his Rivals* IV. xi. 212 They were bitterly denounced by orthodox SR's, who took fright..at 'their own reflection in the Maximalist mirror'. **1962** R. R. Abramovitch *Soviet Revolution* i. 30 This concept shocked the Russian Marxists..they considered it a betrayal of scientific Socialism, a reversion to the old, utopian, Bakuninist, maximalist-anarchist ideas. **1966** *Economist* 5 Nov. 568/1 We have moved from a position of protest to one of responsibility and have put behind us the old maximalist dreams and illusions. **1967** C. Seton-Watson *Italy from Liberalism to Fascism* xii. 511 The [Italian Socialist] party elected a 'maximalist' executive at its Rome congress in September 1918 and proclaimed the dictatorship of the proletariat to be its goal. **1969** D. M. Smith *Italy* (ed. 2) VII. xxvii. 216 The maximalists were made strong and uncompromising by the belief that history was on their side.

maximality (mæksimæ·lĭti). [f. Maximal *a.* + -ity.] The property of being maximal.

1964 A. P. & W. Robertson *Topological Vector Spaces* i. 4 This would contradict the maximality of μ. **1971** D. Gorenstein in Powell & Higman *Finite Simple Groups* i. 102 But $[Q_1, Z] = Q_1$, so $Q_1 = Q$ by the maximality of Q.

maximed, *a.* [f. Maxim *sb.*¹] Expressed as or in a maxim.

1883 J. C. Van Dyke *Bks. & how to use Them* i. 19 There is another maximed truth in this connection..: 'Knowledge is a two-edged sword.'

maximin (mæ·ksimin), *sb.* and *a.* [f. Maxi(mum + Min(imum *sb.* and *a.*, after *minimax.*] The largest of a set of minima; usu. *attrib.* (passing into *adj.*), *spec.* designating a strategy that maximizes the smallest gain that a participant in a game or other situation of conflict can guarantee himself. Cf. *minimax *sb.* and *a.*

1954 Blackwell & Girshick *Theory of Games & Statistical Decisions* i. 27 ξ_0 is called a maximin strategy for player I. **1957** Luce & Raiffa *Games & Decisions* iv. 81 A strategy which dictates choices *c* and *g* on moves 2 and 4, respectively, cannot be maximin for this game. **1958** *Engineering* 21 Mar. 369/2 Player A will thus determine the smallest value in each row and choose the largest of these minima, the 'maximin'. **1968** G. Owen *Game Theory* vii. 140 Though it is of course impossible to determine how a person will act.., we can nevertheless set a minimum to the amount that a player will accept for himself. This is the amount that he can obtain by unilateral action, whatever the other player does. This is, of course, the maximin value of the game for that player. **1970** Beveridge & Schechter *Optimization* xii. 656 This result represents the mini-max theorem of von Neumann and Morgenstein [*sic*] (1953), which states that *A*'s expected gain is at least *P*, and *B*'s expected loss is at worst *L*, where $P = L$... The value of *P* (and *L*) lies between the row maxi-min and the column mini-max. **1972** J. Rawls *Theory of Justice* § 26. 152 The maximin rule tells us to rank alternatives by their worst possible outcomes.

maximize, *v.* Add: **1. a.** (Further examples.) Also *spec.* in *Economics*.

1943 E. R. Walker *From Econ. Theory to Policy* v. 93 He [*sc.* the businessman]..is frequently engaged in exploratory action, designed to discover methods of maximizing profit. **1968** *Listener* 28 Mar. 403/1 The evidence is not inconsistent with the hypothesis that peasants act as if they maximised profit. **1970** *Jrnl. Gen. Psychol.* LXXXII. 15 The adversarial system of justice, which demands that each litigant do whatever is necessary to maximize the probability of a favorable result. **1970** T. Lupton *Managem. & Social Sci.* (ed. 2) i. 11 So arranging spells of work and rest that output would be maximized. **1971** *Daily Tel.* 12 June 20/7, I wish to maximise my after tax income. Do you consider an investment in Guaranteed Income Bonds is a safe way of doing this? **1971** J. Z. Young *Introd. Study Man* xxv. 361 Difficulties of adjustment will be maximized by ignorance and uncertainty. **1972** *Jrnl. Social Psychol.* LXXXVI. 57 These groups were selected so as to maximize the variety of occupational areas included.

Hence **ma·ximized, ma·ximizing** *ppl. adjs.*

1920 A. S. Pringle-Pattison *Idea of God* (ed. 2) 356 Eternal, not in the sense of a maximized consciousness of time, but as an apprehension different in type. **1927** N. P. Williams *Ideas of Fall & Orig. Sin* 395 The maximising and minimising versions of the Fall-Doctrine. **1949** *Mind* LVIII. 195 The concept of a maximising individual, the famous 'Economic Man', has arisen. This maximising assumption is usually held to be the fundamental assumption of Economics. **1968** *Listener* 28 Mar. 403/1 Time enough, if the peasant is already a maximising Economic Man in the Henry Ford mould.

3. *intr.* To attain a maximum value.

1972 *Physics Bull.* Oct. 587/3 Photons of energy $h\nu$ greater than satisfies equation (1) suffer absorption while at some energy $h\nu_{max}$ the gain maximizes. **1973** [see *minimize v. 3]. **1974** *Globe & Mail* (Toronto) 21 Oct. 4/3 If emissions were curtailed now, the resultant ozone destruction would maximize around 1990 and would remain significant for several decades.

maximum. Add: **4.** (Later example.)

1941 R. R. Palmer *Twelve who Ruled* x. 239 The Maximum of September 29 caused trouble from the start.

5. b. Also in *Comb.*, as *maximum-security* (used *attrib.*).

1966 *Punch* 28 Dec. 962/2 The family wing of every prison enjoyed maximum security arrangements. **1969** E. Ambler *Intercom Conspiracy* (1970) ii. 27 The special maximum-security passes that would be needed to gain admittance. **1972** *Guardian* 29 Jan. 9/5 Albany, the new maximum security prison on the Isle of Wight.

maxixe (maʃī·ʃə, mæksī·ks). [Pg.] A round dance of Brazilian origin resembling the two-step.

1914 *Maclean's Mag.* Nov. 82/2 The Maxixe comes to us from Brazil. **1922** C. Bell *Since Cézanne* xx. 227 Sportsmen at the bar who like a fox-trot or a maxixe. **1925** *Chambers's Jrnl.* July 427/1 They sang..and danced the *maxixe* until cockcrow! **1954** *Ballet Ann.* VIII. 102/1 Ready to seek consolation..to the rhythm of the *maxixe.* **1969** F. Rust *Dance in Society* x. 82 In the early months of 1914, the general craze for the tango in England helped to popularize another South American dance—the Brazilian maxixe.

Maxwell¹ (mæ·kswel). The name of Charles *Maxwell*, 19th-century English soldier and explorer, used in the possessive to designate **Maxwell's duiker**, a small brown West African antelope, *Cephalophus maxwelli*, brought back from Sierra Leone by him.

[**1827** E. Griffith et al. tr. *Cuvier's Animal Kingdom* IV. 267 Maxwell's Antelope. (*A. Maxwellii.*) A specimen somewhat inferior in size was brought home from Sierra Leone by Colonel Charles Maxwell.] **1905** Sclater & Thomas *Bk. Antelopes* I. 182 Maxwell's Duiker appears to extend from Senegal and Gambia all along the west coast of Africa to the mouths of the Niger. **1960** *Times* 29 Sept. (Nigeria Suppl.) p. xxi/4 The little Maxwell's duiker..is everywhere abundant.

Maxwell² (mæ·kswel). *Physics.* [The name of James Clerk *Maxwell* (1831–79), Scottish physicist.] **1.** Used in the possessive and *attrib.* to designate various concepts originated by him, as **Maxwell('s) demon,** a being imagined by Maxwell as allowing only fast-moving molecules to pass through a hole in

one direction and only slow-moving ones in the other direction, so that if the hole is in a partition dividing a gas-filled vessel into two parts one side becomes warmer and the other cooler, in contradiction to the second law of thermodynamics; **Maxwell('s) distribution**, the distribution of molecular velocities predicted by Maxwell's law, the number with a velocity between v and $v+dv$ being proportional to $\exp(-\frac{1}{2}mv^2/kT)v^2dv$ (where m is the mass of a molecule, k is Boltzmann's constant, and T is the absolute temperature); **Maxwell('s) equation**, each of a set of four linear partial differential equations (first proposed by Maxwell in 1864) which summarize the classical properties of the electromagnetic field and relate space and time derivatives of the electric and magnetic field vectors, the electric displacement vector, and the magnetic induction vector, and also involve the electric current and charge densities; usu. *pl.*; **Maxwell('s) law**, a law in classical physics giving the probabilities of different velocities for the molecules of a gas in equilibrium.

1879 W. THOMSON *Pop. Lect. & Addresses* (1889) I. 137 Clerk Maxwell's 'demon' is a creature of imagination.., invented to help us to understand the 'Dissipation of Energy' in nature. **1885** *Science* 31 July 83/1 (*heading*) Maxwell's demons. **1956** E. H. HUTTEN *Lang. Mod. Physics* iv. 152 It would require a Maxwell demon..to select the rapidly moving molecules according to their velocity and concentrate them in one corner of the vessel. **1971** *Sci. Amer.* Sept. 182/2 Maxwell's demon became an intellectual thorn in the side of thermodynamicists for almost a century. The challenge to the second law of thermodynamics was this: Is the principle of the increase of entropy in all spontaneous processes invalid where intelligence intervenes? **1899** R. E. BAYNES tr. *Meyer's Kinetic Theory of Gases* 370 If the number of particles is limited..Maxwell's distribution cannot exist at every moment, but will occur with exactness only when the changing states which succeed each other in the course of a sufficiently long period are all taken into account together. **1955** FRIEDMAN & WEISSKOPF in W. Pauli *Niels Bohr* 138 The spectrum of neutrons and protons emitted from nuclei bombarded with neutrons of 14 Mev or with protons of similar energy fits approximately the predicted Maxwell distribution of an evaporating compound nucleus. **1907** *Sci. Abstr.* A. X. 1295 The principle of relativity in conjunction with Maxwell's equation leads to the conclusion that the inertia of a body changes in a quite determinate manner with its energy-content. **1962** CORSON & LORRAIN *Introd. Electromagn. Fields* iii. 101 If the symmetry of the [electrostatic] field is simple and if the charge density ρ is zero, as it often is, we can usually integrate the Maxwell equation $\nabla\cdot\mathbf{D}=\rho$ to find the displacement vector **D**. **1964** E. A. POWER *Introd. Quantum Electrodynamics* i. 4 Maxwell's equations are not invariant under Galilean invariance and thus are not valid in all inertial frames. Historically this was a most important result leading to special relativity. **1899** R. E. BAYNES tr. *Meyer's Kinetic Theory of Gases* iii. 48 That this extension of Maxwell's law to compound molecules is admissible was first recognised by Boltzmann. **1943** MARGENAU & MURPHY *Math. Physics & Chem.* xii. 432 The Maxwell law for the distribution of velocities in an ideal gas.

2. (Usu. written **maxwell.**) The unit of magnetic flux in the C.G.S. system, equal to the flux through an area of one square centimetre normal to a uniform induction of one gauss.

In the International System of Units the unit of magnetic flux is the weber (= 10^8 maxwells).

1900 *Nature* 30 Aug. 414/1 The Commission proposes to assign to the unit of magnetic flux, of which the magnitude will be subsequently defined, the name of Maxwell. **1924** A. STILL *Elem. Electr. Design* iv. 68 It is desired to estimate the total flux in maxwells carried by a closed circular iron ring. **1959** R. L. SHRADER *Electronic Communication* iii. 72 The gauss is the flux density in maxwells per square centimeter.

Maxwell-Boltzmann (mæ·kswel,bǫ·ltsmăn). *Physics.* The names of J. C. *Maxwell* (see prec.) and L. *Boltzmann* (see *BOLTZMANN), used (in some cases as an alternative to *Maxwell* or *Boltzmann* alone) to designate concepts arising out of their work on the kinetic theory of gases.

1901 O. LODGE in *Phil. Mag.* II. 241 Any rotational energy possessed by a dumbbell about its longitudinal axis could have no influence on smooth collisions, and accordingly could not be transferred or altered in amount; therefore such rotation ought not to be included in the partition of energy within the meaning of the Maxwell-Boltzmann law when properly stated. **1927** R. C. TOLMAN *Statistical Mech.* iv. 53 In a system containing a large number of molecules appreciable deviations from the Maxwell-Boltzmann distribution will have a very small probability of occurrence. **1951** D. BOHM *Quantum Theory* i. 16 For a perfect gas..we obtain the familiar Maxwell-Boltzmann distribution of velocities. **1968** M. S. LIVINGSTON *Particle Physics* iii. 58 In classical mechanics the distribution of thermal velocities and energies among the molecules of a gas, in thermal equilibrium due to the exchange of energy in random impacts, is described by Maxwell-Boltzmann statistics.

Maxwellian (mækswe·liăn), *a. Physics.* Also **maxwellian.** [f. *MAXWELL[2] + -IAN.] Of, pertaining to, or originated by J. C. Maxwell; in accordance with Maxwell's theory.

1886 *Electrician* 26 Mar. 386/2 The Maxwellian stress. **1914** L. SILBERSTEIN *Theory of Relativity* ii. 48 In using the Maxwellian stress..in his theory, Lorentz considers it ..as a system of 'merely fictitious tensions'. **1939** *Brit. Jrnl. Psychol.* XXIX. 253 The light from an electric bulb, rendered nearly parallel by a condenser, filled a large lens at whose principal focus the eye was placed. This lens appeared uniformly illuminated by the 'Maxwellian view'. **1958** H. J. GRAY *Dict. Physics* 318/1 The Maxwellian view refers to the method of making a lens apparently flooded with a uniform brightness: a real image of a source of light is formed by a lens in the pupil of the eye. An extended area of bright white light or coloured light is produced and has wide application in photometry and colorimetry. **1968** R. A. LYTTLETON *Mysteries Solar Syst.* i. 32 For a whole group of individual stars, these relative speeds are distributed rather like the maxwellian distribution of velocities for the particles of a gas.

May, *sb.*[3] Add: **5. a.** (sense 1) *May-glad* adj., *-hope*, *-mess*; *May-time* (earlier, later, and *attrib.* examples).

1911 E. POUND *Canzoni* 4 No poppy in the May-glad mead. *a* **1889** G. M. HOPKINS *Poems* (1967) 38 May-hope of our darkened ways! **1877** —— *Poems* (1967) 67 Look, look: a May-mess, like on orchard boughs! *c* **1350** *Will. Palerne* (1881) 823 Alle freliche foules þat on þat friþ songe, for merþe of þat may time þei made moche noyce. **1633** P. FLETCHER *Purple Island* XII. lxxxii. 179 More fruitfull then the May-time Geminies. **1930** T. S. ELIOT *Ash-Wednesday* 14 The broadbacked figure..Enchanted the maytime with an antique flute. **1963** A. CLARKE *Coll. Plays* 161 Who will wash them by the river's edge, Hang them unseen upon as white a hedge In Maytime?

c. May-blob, the marsh marigold, *Caltha palustris*; also applied to other plants (see *Eng. Dial. Dict.*); **may-haw** (examples); **may-pop** (earlier example).

1863 May-blob [see **granny's nightcap*]. **1881** S. EVANS *Evans's Leicestershire Words* (new ed.) 192 *May-blob*, the marsh-marigold. **1908** *Pacific Monthly* XX. 94/2 Could they or their children after them pick out a May-blob from a May-pop? **1916** D. H. LAWRENCE *Amores* 38, I can smell the gorgeous bog-end, in its breathless Dazzle of may-blobs. **1960** *Oxf. Bk. Wild Flowers* 4/2 Marsh Marigold (*Caltha palustris*)... The plant has many other names such as Kingcup and May Blobs. **1868** *Amer. Naturalist* II. 468 They [*sc.* deer] visit the ponds in which the May-haw grows, the fruit of which is juicy with the flavor of the apple. **1938** M. K. RAWLINGS *Yearling* xi. 112 He concentrated on light bread and mayhaw jelly. **1851** *De Bow's Rev.* XI. 49 May Pop, Passion Flower, is also abundant here.

may (mē̆i), *sb.*[4] [f. MAY *v.*[1]] An utterance of the word 'may'; a possibility.

1897 G. SAINTSBURY *Flourishing of Romance* ii. 30 These 'mays' are not evidence. **1935** G. K. ZIPF *Psycho-Biol. of Lang.* (1936) 303 From the great number of.. *mays* of today are taken those which are to belong to the matrix of *musts* of tomorrow.

may, *v.*[1] Add: **B. 9. d.** In † *be as be may*, *be that* (or *it* or *this*) *as it may*, *that is as may be*, and similar expressions: whether that is so or not, that may well be so: phrases used to indicate that a statement or act, etc., is perhaps true or right from one point of view but not from another, or that there are other factors to be taken into consideration.

c **1386** CHAUCER *Man of Law's Tale* (1894) 1012 Be as be may, ther was he at the leste. **1470–85** MALORY *Works* (1967) I. 73 Be as hit be may. **1530** [see MAY *v.*[1] 8 d (*b*)]. **1593** SHAKS. *3 Hen. VI* I. i. 194 But be it as it may: I here entayle The Crowne to thee. **1796** [see MAY *v.*[1] 9 a]. **1820** R. SOUTHEY *Let.* 17 Nov. in *N. & Q.* (1975) Sept. 400/1 Be that as it may, I wish you would let me know what books of mine you have not received from Longmans. **1834** M. EDGEWORTH *Tour in Connemara* (1950) i. 10 There goes a story, you know that no woman must ever appear at Ballinasloe Fair... Be this as it may, we were suffered to drive very quietly through the town. **1875** TROLLOPE *Way we live Now* I. xlix. 311 'Good news?' she asked... 'That's as may be,' he said. **1883** A. DOBSON *Old-World Idylls* 211 Rose kissed me to-day. Will she kiss me to-morrow? Let it be as it may, Rose kissed me to-day. **1910** GALSWORTHY *Motley* 168 'Yu'le tak' the ole 'arse then?' 'That's as mebbe—waal, gude naight.' **1928** F. HURST *President is Born* 14 Be that as it may, the circle of giving in Centralia was anything but a vicious one. **1935** G. HEYER *Death in Stocks* iv. 41 'That's as may be, and if it's true you couldn't say but what it's a judgment. **1939** G. M. GATHORNE-HARDY *Fourteen Points & Treaty of Versailles* 14 The Fourteen Points..has been described, by Mr. Winston Churchill, as 'certainly an accommodating document'. Be that as it may, it was presumably what the President had actually meant. **1949** F. MACLEAN *Eastern Approaches* I. viii. 133 If the authorities..had received no instructions regarding my journey it could only be due to a most regrettable omission... To this he answered that this was as it might be; but without explicit instructions.. he could not allow me to remain on Chinese territory. **1949** H. PAKINGTON *Young W. Washbourne* vi. 51 'But if it was used as a sitting-out place it wouldn't be secluded,' said Mrs. Harbottle. That was as it might be, retorted Mrs. Wilkins. **1958** *Economist* 1 Nov. 387/2 There have been reports of some exchange of views between these two formidable figures. Be that as it may, the manner in which their views have been made known shows a wide and characteristic difference. **1975** T. HEALD *Deadline* ii. 23 'I shall have to liaise with the police.' 'That's as may be,' said Lord Wharfedale.

Maya (mā·yă, məi·(y)ă, mē̆i·ă), *sb.*[2] and *a.* Also 9 **Maye.** [Sp.] **A.** *sb.* **a.** A member of an ancient Indian people of Yucatan and Central America; these people collectively. **b.** The language of this people. **B.** *adj.* Of, pertaining to, or designating this people.

1825 J. CONDER *Mod. Traveller Mexico & Guatimala* I. 191 The number of these [Mexican] languages exceeds twenty, of which fourteen have grammars..tolerably complete; viz. the Mexican or Aztec, the Otomite,..the Maye or Yucatan. **1832** J. BELL *Syst. Geogr.* V. 584 In the space between the Rio del Norte and the American frontier, are the following tribes: 1. The *Tawakenoes*, on the *Rio Brassos*, 200 warriors, 800 souls;..5. *Mayes*, at the mouth of the Guadaloupe river, 200 warriors, 800 souls. **1845** *Trans. Amer. Ethnol. Soc.* I. 252 *K* has in the Maya a different sound from our *c* before *a*, *o*, *u*. **1875** H. H. BANCROFT *Native Races Pacific States* II. 117 This Maya culture. *Ibid.* 118 Yucatan was occupied in the sixteenth century by the Mayas proper. **1877** [see *CHIBCHA]. **1914** T. A. JOYCE *Mexican Archæol.* viii. 202 Both divisions of this people originally spoke Maya. *Ibid.* 203 The Maya language as a whole exhibits certain points of similarity to that of the Mixtec and Zapotec. *Ibid.* xi. 282 Of the land system among the Maya we know very little. **1928** T. GANN *Discoveries Cent. Amer.* 89 The old man..knew no word of any language but Maya. *Ibid.* 206 In none of them [*sc.* cities] is the Maya arch found. **1959** E. TUNIS *Indians* 21/2 The Maya of Mexico were the only Indians who achieved a written language, with symbols that stood for individual words. **1974** *Nat. Geographic* Nov. 661 In Guatemala's lofty highlands..Maya Indians dwell amid the cloud-ripping hulks of dead and dormant volcanoes. *Ibid.*, Here live Maya-speaking Indians in villages that garland the lakeshore with a litany of saints' names.

Hence **Ma·yan** *a.*, of, pertaining to, or designating the Mayas; *sb.*, one of the Mayan people; their language; **Ma·yanist,** an expert in, or student of, Mayan culture.

1889 S. HALE *Mexico* viii. 82 The Mayan legends..tell of nothing but wars and conquests, struggles and defeats. **1911** *Encycl. Brit.* XVIII. 335/2 These Pipils..migrated into territories previously occupied by an older race of Mayan origin... The easternmost limit of prehistoric Mayan civilization, on the Pacific coast of Central America is Fonseca Bay. **1923** H. I. PRIESTLEY *Mexican Nation* ii, In the modern oil region along the Pánuco River and the coast, was a segregated group of Mayans. **1926** *Blackw. Mag.* Nov. 647/2 This man..was of pure Maya blood, and was filled..with old Mayan lore and tradition. **1933** E. PINCHON *Viva Villa!* x. 135 The craftsmanly and aristocratic Mayans and Tehuans of the south. **1950** *Caribbean Q.* II. II. 27 Later that year Dr. Linton Satterthwaite, Associate Curator of the Pennsylvania University Museum and a Mayanist of note, was put in touch with the writer. **1961** T. PROSKOURIAKOFF in L. Deuel *Conquistadors without Swords* (1967) xxvii. 384 We Mayanists spend an inordinate amount of time deciphering half obliterated hieroglyphic texts. **1962** L. KEMP tr. *Leon-Portilla's Broken Spears* iii. 31 By the time Cortes ransomed him from the natives eight years later he spoke Mayan fluently. **1965** B. ROSS *Mexico* i. 21 They asked him where he had obtained the cloth and the pottery? The Mayan said that it came from a land not very far away. **1968** *Listener* 11 July 53/3 They describe the attempts of Olson, newly arrived in Yucatan, to come to terms with Mayan culture. *Ibid.* 54/1 He takes off for Yucatan unprepared for his task, learning Mayan as he goes, and from inadequate books. **1973** *New Yorker* 24 Mar. 116/2 He got the word in Mayan for 'road' or 'journey'. *Ibid.* 116/3 One can thus understand the interest among Mayanists when..it was announced that a wholly unknown fourth codex had come to light. **1973** *Listener* 7 June 746/1 The Mayans..invented essentially the same way of writing large numbers as a sequence of digits that we use.

may-be, maybe, *adv.* Delete *arch.* and *dial.* and add later examples. Also phr. *and I don't mean maybe*: I am positive (*colloq.*).

1897 KIPLING *Capt. Cour.* vii. 147 Don't want nothin', 'less, mebbe, an anchor that'll hold. **1926** MAINES & GRANT *Wise-Crack Dict.* 5/1 And I don't mean maybe, jazz form of putting one's self on oath. **1930** JOYCE *Anna Livia Plurabelle* 23 I'll make it worth your while. And I don't mean maybe. **1931** E. LINKLATER *Juan in Amer.* v. v. 401 When a guy..tries to get fresh..a girl's justified in giving him the razz—and I don't mean maybe! **1933** E. CALDWELL *God's Little Acre* viii. 110 We've sunk a hole twenty feet since this morning, and I don't mean maybe, either. **1953** *Manch. Guardian Weekly* 20 Aug. 7 Except maybe a guy had been there two years. **1968** B. FOSTER *Changing Eng. Lang.* i. 30 Some years ago a song popular in this country bore the title 'Maybe', and on consulting the *O.E.D.* one finds this word described as archaic and dialectal! Yet by now it is in everyday use in Britain. **1968** *New Society* 29 Aug. 305/1 The *Oxford English Dictionary* describes 'maybe' as archaic and dialectal. But within the last generation it has been re-instated in England, obviously as a result of its popularity in the American vocabulary, where 'perhaps' is a very rare bird. Yet all this time 'maybe' (or 'mebbe') has been thriving in northern England, Scotland and Ireland. **1975** *New Yorker* 13 Jan. 36/1, I wanted to think maybe she was different now.

May-butter. (Later U.S. example.)

1812 J. J. HENRY *Accurate Acct. Heroes Campaign against Quebec* 23 We gave salted pork, and they returned two fresh beaver tails, which when boiled, renewed ideas, imbibed with the May-butter of our own country.

May-day[1]. Add: **c.** *attrib.*, *spec.* of political processions, celebrations, etc., on the first day of May.

1906 [see *COMMUNISM 1 b]. **1930** I. LOW *His Master's*

Voice x. 120 Scaffolding began to appear in the Red Square for May Day celebrations. **1939** [see *hunger-march]. **1973** *Listener* 9 Aug. 184 In 1890, during the first of the big May Day demonstrations, we read of trade-union branches assembling from every quarter of London.

May-day[2]. Also **Mayday, mayday.** [Phonetic repr. of F. *m'aider* imper. inf. 'help me!', or shortening of *venez m'aider.*] An international radio-telephone signal of distress. Also *transf.* and *attrib.*

1927 *Internat. Radio Telegraph Convention* 51 Rules apply to the radio telephone distress call which consists of the spoken expression MAYDAY, (corresponding to the French pronunciation of the expression 'm'aider'..). **1929** *Times* 18 June 16/1 The pilot, after wirelessing the S.O.S. of the Air Service 'May Day'..endeavoured to return to Lympne aerodrome with the power still at his disposal. **1930** *B.B.C. Year-Bk.* 399 *Aircraft and Wireless*... In case of distress, due to engine failure over the sea, the word 'Mayday'—equivalent to the S.O.S. used by ships—transmitted through the microphone, will summon immediately all possible help. **1951** O. BERTHOUD tr. *Clostermann's Big Show* I. 30 If you can't get back to the coast, bale out after calling 'May Day' on frequency D. **1962** *Listener* 1 Mar. 370/2 With the onset of lambing time the farmers' 'Mayday' signal begins to hum along the network of telephone wires. **1962** *Sunday Express* 5 Aug. 1/2 Her first 'Mayday' distress message came soon after midday. **1971** *Islander* (Victoria, B.C.) 16 May 13/1 When her topmast chains snapped, she radioed a mayday signal. **1971** *Daily Tel.* 23 Aug. 1/5 The radio operator sent a Mayday distress call before the sea rushed into the cabin.

may-duke. (Later U.S. examples.)

1841 *Knickerbocker* XVII. 154 The air is impregnated with the fragrances..of the blossoming may-dukes. **1874** *Rep. Vermont Board Agric.* II. 359 This variety, and the.. May Duke, Late Duke, and other Dukes,..are hardly less hardy than plums.

Mayfair (mēi·fēəɹ). [MAY *sb.*[3] + FAIR *sb.*[1]] **a.** A fair held in May, esp. that held annually from the 17th century until the end of the 18th century in Brook fields near Hyde Park Corner. **b.** The district of London, very fashionable since the 19th century, between Oxford Street and Piccadilly, occupying the site of the old fairground. Also as quasi-*adj.*

1701 B. FAIRFAX in *Tatler* (1786) I. Notes 418, I wish you had been at May-fair, where the rope-dancing would have recompensed your labour. **1709** *Tatler* 24–26 May, The Crowd of the Audience are fitter for Representations at May-fair, than a Theatre-Royal. **1748** H. WALPOLE *Let.* 3 Sept. (1903) II. 336 A chosen committee waited on the faithful pair to the minister of May-fair. **1754** *Connoisseur* 17 Oct. 227 Catalogue of Males and Females to be disposed of in Marriage to the Best Bidder, at Mr. Keith's Repository in May Fair. **1848** THACKERAY *Van. Fair* li. 453 Yesterday, Colonel and Mrs. Crawley entertained a select party at dinner at their house in May Fair. **1874** H. C. PENNELL (*title*) The Muses of Mayfair: selections from *vers de société* of the nineteenth century. **1933** J. BUCHAN *Prince of Captivity* II. i. 146 Clothes slightly astray from the conventions of Mayfair. **1953** A. CHRISTIE *Pocket Full of Rye* i. 8 Miss Grosvenor..wailed in a voice whose accent was noticeably less Mayfair than usual.

c. *attrib.* and *Comb.*

1752 H. WALPOLE *Let.* 27 Feb. (1903) III. 85 They were married with a ring of the bed-curtain..at Mayfair chapel. **1843** CARLYLE *Past & Present* III. ix. 252 Patent-Digester, Spinning-Mule, Mayfair Clothes-Horse. **1866** M. MACKINTOSH *Stage Reminisc.* vi. 74 So elegant and comfortable that even luxurious west-enders might have fancied themselves at home in their own May-Fair drawing-rooms. **1940** N. MARSH *Surfeit of Lampreys* (1941) ii. 31 The twins were saying..that..the only thing..was for them to turn crooks and be another lot of Mayfair boys. **1943** I. BROWN *Just Another Word* 24 'She got terribly akimbo'..a species of Mayfair slang for what was earlier called 'high horse'. **1957** R. W. ZANDVOORT *Handbk. Eng. Gram.* v. ii. 225 It's such a bore, don't you know. In the..example (which really represents 'Mayfair' English) the tag practically ceases to be a question. **1962** J. D. SALINGER *Franny & Zooey* 155 He was still for a moment. Then, in an almost unintelligibly thick Mayfair accent: 'I'd rather like a word with you, Miss Glass.' **1967** K. GILES *Death in Diamonds* i. 21 He's insolent, smooth and tough, very hip in his talk. Like the Mayfair boys in the thirties. **1970** C. DRUMMOND *Stab in Back* iv. 88 They 'ad a saying when we were young about 'Mayfair Boys', meaning gentlemen crooks.

Hence **May·fairish** *a.*, of the nature or character of Mayfair.

1938 G. ALLIGHAN *Sir John Reith* iv. 235 The B.B.C. organisation..is too isolated from the common people. There is a West End outlook, a Mayfairish idea of the elite, an everlasting implication of superiority. **1967** [see **ideal home*].

mayo (mēi·o), colloq. abbrev. of MAYONNAISE.

1960 WENTWORTH & FLEXNER *Dict. Amer. Slang* 335/1 *Mayo*, mayonnaise. Common lunch-counter use since *c* 1930. **1969** L. HELLMAN in *Atlantic* Apr. 118 Run down to the corner and get me a ham and cheese on rye and tell them to hold the mayo. **1971** *New Yorker* 10 July 20 We were sitting at a luncheonette counter the other day, just about to bite into a b.l.t. down, with mayo, when a familiar voice addressed us from an adjacent stool.

Mayologist (māyǫ·lŏdʒist). [f. *MAYA *sb.*[2] + -OLOGIST (see -OLOGY).] A student of Maya antiquities.

1926 *Glasgow Herald* 18 May 9 Mr. Joyce, perhaps the ablest of living Mayologists, has been sent..on a mission of inspection.

mayonnaise. For etym. read: [F. *mayonnaise*, also *magnonaise*, *mahonnaise*, the latter being prob. fem. of *mahonnais* of Port *Mahon*, capital of Minorca, taken by the duc de Richelieu in 1756.] Also with defining word, as *egg, fish, lobster, salmon mayonnaise.*

See quots. s.v. *LOBSTER[1] 5.

1861 MRS. BEETON *Bk. Househ. Managem.* 225 For a fish Mayonnaise, this sauce may be coloured with lobster-spawn, pounded. **1910** *Encycl. Brit.* VII. 74/2 The mayonnaise (originally *mahonnaise*) is ascribed to the duc de Richelieu. **1975** D. BLOODWORTH *Clients of Omega* xvi. 153 The partners..began to eat salmon mayonnaise off the altar.

2. *Contract Bridge* = *GOULASH 2.

1927 M. WORK *Contract Bridge* 138 *Mayonnaise*, old name of Goulash.

Hence **mayonnai·sed** *a.*

1968 C. DRUMMOND *Death & Leaping Ladies* i. 7 A hearty trencherman himself, a victor over many a mayonnaised lobster. **1972** P. A. WHITNEY *Listen for Whisperer* vii. 130 An array of tiny mayonnaised shrimps.

mayoress. 2. Delete '*nonce-use*' and add earlier and later examples. *U.S.*

1884 *Chicago Tribune* 5 May 4/3 She cannot under the laws monopolize the holding of nice special offices like Mayoress. **1947** *Chicago Sun* 4 Nov. 16/5 The dish..will be delivered..by Mrs. Margaret Craig, mayoress of Twickenham.

3. A person appointed to assist a female mayor.

1932 *Times* 10 Nov. 8/6 Mrs. Emily F. George, the Labour Mayor of Bermondsey, has appointed her daughter..to be Mayoress.

Mazahbi, var. *MAZHABI. **Mazal tov,** var. *MAZEL TOV.

Mazatec (mæ·zătek), *sb.* and *a.* **a.** (A member of) an Indian people inhabiting northern Oaxaca in southern Mexico. **b.** The language of this people. Also *attrib.* or as *adj.* Hence **Mazate·can** *a.*

1909 WEBSTER, *Mazatec*, one of a tribe of Zapotecan Indians of northeastern Oaxaca, Mexico. They raise silk and are noted for gorgeous silken fabrics. **1949** E. A. NIDA *Morphol.* (ed. 2) II. 24 Mazatec, a language of Mexico. **1957** *Encycl. Brit.* V. 138/2 *Mazatec* (Guerrero, Puebla, Oaxaca; includes *Trique* and *Chocho*). **1958** J. BERRY in J. A. Fishman *Readings Sociol. of Lang.* (1968) 751 One of the Mazatec dialects. **1962** D. H. HYMES in *Ibid.* 111 The Mazatecs of Mexico. *Ibid.* 129 Neighboring dialects may differ, as when one group of Mazatec abstract the tones of their language for a whistled code, while the Soyaltepec Mazatec do not. **1963** *Times* 27 April 9/7 Land where heron live at peace with primitive Mazatecan Indians. **1967** S. C. GUDSCHINSKY *How to learn Unwritten Lang.* ii. 19 Transitive relationship is expressed in Mazatec by a transitive verb followed by a noun object and a noun subject. *Ibid.* 22 Mazatec possessive phrases are quite different from English. **1974** *Encycl. Brit. Micropædia* VI. 728/1 The Mazatec language is most closely related to Chocho, Ixcatec, and Popoloca. *Ibid.*, The Mazatec are Roman Catholic with syncretistic elements.

Mazbi, var. *MAZHABI.

Mazdaist (mæ·zdă,ist). [f. as MAZDAISM + -IST.] An adherent of Mazdaism.

1920 in WEBSTER. **1932** *Antiquity* VI. 277 Where Mazdaists and Christians were found together, there must certainly have been adherents of the Manichæan creed. **1941** *Burlington Mag.* Aug. 59/1 Mohammedans..Mazdaists..Christians, Buddhists and perhaps Jews as well had their own temples.

maze, *sb.* Add: **4. a.** *spec.* in *Psychol.*, a device, consisting of a correct path concealed by blind alleys, used to study human and animal intelligence and learning. Also *attrib.* and *Comb.*

1901 W. S. SMALL in *Amer. Jrnl. Psychol.* XII. 228 The process of learning the way through this maze is adequately described as a gradual establishment of direct associations by profiting by chance experience. **1914** F. A. C. PERRIN (*title*) An experimental and introspective study of the human learning process in the maze. **1921** *Lancet* 19 March 597/2 The..Porteous maze tests which, testing as they do the foresight, the capacity to plan, the practical judgment and concentration of the child, supply a marked lack of the Binet scale. **1940** *Brit. Jrnl. Psychol.* Jan. 191 Many maze workers have noted the fact of variability in performance from day to day. **1951** G. HUMPHREY *Thinking* viii. 257 Verbal instruction improves the score in stylus-maze running. **1958** *Spectator* 8 Aug. 201/1 The obsessional maze-running experiments of the American rat-psychologists. **1964** M. ARGYLE *Psychol. & Social Probl.* v. 67 [Areas in which delinquents differ from non-delinquents] Impulsiveness, weakness of 'ego-control', tendency to cut corners in maze tests.

‖ **mazel tov** (ma·zel tōv, tǫf). Also **mazal tov, mazzel tov,** etc. [ad. mod.Heb. *mazzāl ṭōḇ* good luck, f. Heb. *mazzālōth* pl., constellations.] As a salutation: good luck, congratulations.

1862 *Once a Week* VII. 192/2 Whereupon all present wish him *mazal tov* (good speed), and the ceremony is at an end. **1892** I. ZANGWILL *Childr. Ghetto* I. 37 There was a hubbub of congratulation ('*Mazzoltov, Mazzoltov*', 'Good Luck'). **1932** L. GOLDING *Magnolia St.* III. iv. 520 The air pattered like hail with their good luck wishes..*Mazel tov, mazel tov!* **1957** L. STERN *Midas Touch* III. xx. 149 '*Mazeltof*, father,' he said. **1959** B. KOPS *Hamlet of Stepney Green* II. ii, Going to have another one?..Mazeltoff, darling. **1970** *New Yorker* 19 Sept. 32/1 'Uri is going to be a father.' Yigael..said, 'He told me. *Mazel tov*.' **1972** 'H. HOWARD' *Nice Day for Funeral* x. 138, I said, 'Mazeltov. I hope you're both very happy.' **1973** *Jewish Chron.* 2 Feb. 19/3 Mother and baby..are..doing well. A hearty mazzeltov to them!

Mazhabi (mʋ·zhabi). *India.* Also **Maz(ah)bi, Muzbi, Muz(hu)bee.** [Hindi, f. Arab. *mazhab* religion.] A convert to the Sikh religion from Islam, *spec.* in the Punjab; a converted Chuhra or member of the sweeper caste.

1849 J. D. CUNNINGHAM *Hist. Sikhs* 379 *Muzhûbee*, converts from Mahometanism are so called. **1858** R. TEMPLE *Let.* 25 May in Yule & Burnell *Hobson-Jobson* (1886) 464/1 To the same destination (Delhi) was sent a strong corps of Muzhubee (low-caste) Sikhs, numbering 1200 men, to serve as pioneers. **1908** KIPLING *Lett. of Travel* (1920) 162 A fair sprinkling of Punjabis—ex-soldiers, Sikhs, Muzbis, and Jats—are coming in on the boats. **1917** *Encycl. Relig. & Ethics* IX. 608/2 Such converts may form new castes, like the Mazbi or Mazhabi Sikhs, who were by origin Chūhṛās, or scavengers, outside the Hindu pale. **1923** *Chambers's Jrnl.* 20 Jan. 113/1 He was not going to give his daughter in marriage to a *Muzbee.* **1965** SHER SINGH *Sansis of Punjab* ix. 188 If a Sansi takes food from a Choohra, Mazahbi, Chamar or other lower castes, he is outcast and fined.

mazout, var. *MAZUT.

mazuma (măzū·mă). *U.S. slang.* Also **mazume.** [Yiddish.] Money, cash.

1904 G. V. HOBART *Jim Hickey* i. 15 We're a sad bunch ..when we haven't a little mazume in the vest pocket. **1906** 'O. HENRY' *Four Million* (1916) 131 Burn a few punk sticks in the joss house to the great god Mazuma. **1907** C. E. MULFORD *Bar-20* viii. 90 When th' mazuma is divided up it won't buy a meal. **1913** —— *Coming of Cassidy* xii. 191 'What's this?' he demanded... 'Money,' replied Hopalong. 'It's that shiny stuff you buy things with. Spondulix, cash, mazuma.' **1926** *Amer. Speech* May 456/1 How many of those using the word *mazuma* know its meaning? As originally used by the Jewish people it is '*m'zumon*' and is a Chaldean word meaning in literal translation the 'ready necessary'. It is employed in the Talmud which is written in Chaldean and not Hebrew. **1941** *Amer. Mercury* May 615/1 When you die, you have to leave your mazuma behind. **1943** W. H. CHASE *Sourdough Pot* xvi. 97 A sign tacked on a tent pole, informed the public, that 'No Credit—You must produce the mazuma. We are not in business for our health.' **1972** *Times Lit. Suppl.* 29 Sept. 1154/3 Likewise piling up its mazuma by legerdemain.

mazut (măzū·t). Also **masut, mazout.** [Russ. *mazút*, ad. Arab. *makhzulat* refuse, waste.] The viscous liquid left as residue after the distillation of Russian petroleum, used as fuel oil and a coarse lubricant.

1897 *Chambers's Jrnl.* 19 June 393 Masut, the new substitute for coal. **1907** *Times Engin. Suppl.* 16 Oct. 4/2 Among liquid fuels which may be employed that known as 'masut' will help to supply the increasing demand. **1924** J. A. HAMMERTON *Countries of World* II. 1277/1 'Crude oil'..is refined into benzine, petrol and kerosene, the refuse or 'mazout' being consumed for common fuel and furnaces. **1924** *Blackw. Mag.* Feb. 152/1 They caught the sickly sweet smell of half-burnt 'Mazut' fuel. **1951** R. CAMPBELL *Light on Dark Horse* xx. 288 The oil, or mazout, has also spoilt the quality of the red-mullet. **1974** P. HIGHSMITH *Ripley's Game* v. 47 He tackled with broom and dustpan the exterior of the pipes and the floor around their *mazout* furnace.

mazzel tov, var. *MAZEL TOV.

Mazzinian (mætsī·niăn), *sb.* and *a.* [f. the name of Giuseppe *Mazzini* (1805–72), Italian patriot and revolutionary + -AN.] **A.** *sb.* An adherent of Mazzini. **B.** *adj.* Of, pertaining to, supporting, or resembling Mazzini or his policy. So **Mazzi·nianism, Mazzi·nism,** the principles or methods of Mazzinians; **Mazzi·nist** = *MAZZINIAN A.

1850 J. MILEY *Hist. Papal States* III. VIII. iv. 644 They ..have loaded the memory of Gregory XVI., just as much as the Mazzinians, with every species of libellous invective. **1860** *Illustr. London News* 7 Jan. 18/3 Even the Mazzinists claim him at times as their own. **1861** tr. *A. Bresciani's Jew of Verona* p. iv, Misrepresentation which had been so assiduously thrown around the recent events by the Mazzinian press. **1862** *Dublin Rev.* Feb. 203 The universal dread which Mazzinism inspired. **1866** H. E. MANNING in S. Leslie *Life H. E. Manning* (1921) xiii. 195 Mazzinianism and Fenianism are one in principle. **1875** P. K. O'CLERY *Hist. Italian Revolution* v. 165 The Mazzinian programme was the establishment of a single republic... The literary propaganda of Mazzinianism. *Ibid.* 187 They were no less revolutionists than the Mazzinians. **1932** G. F.-H. BERKELEY *Italy in Making* I. xiv. 209 Aurelio Saffi, the well-known Mazzinian, who lived in Forlì. **1937** *Times Lit. Suppl.* 1 May 322/4 Meredith's attack..was a satire of social extravagances tinged with Mazzinian idealism. **1965** C. HIBBERT *Garibaldi & his Enemies* I. x. 140 Louis Napoleon could not free himself so easily..from the indiscretions of the Mazzinians. *Ibid.*, The Mazzinian *L'Italia e Popolo* of Genoa. **1967** C. SETON-WATSON *Italy from Liberalism to Fascism* xi. 422 The militant irredentists from Istria and Dalmatia..cared nothing for the Mazzinian dream of Italo-Slav friendship.

mazzot, mazzoth, varr. *MATZAH.

‖ **mbongo** (mˌbǫ·ŋgo). *S. Afr.* Also **imbonga, imbongo, mbonga, mbongi.** [Zulu.] An official who sings the praises of the (Zulu) king; hence applied to any flatterer of a high personage or institution.

1839 W. C. HARRIS *Wild Sports S. Afr.* xiv. 116 We.. were accordingly preparing to start when a herald, called, in the Matabili language, *Imbongo*, a proclaimer of the king's titles, suddenly made his appearance outside the kraal. **1871** in T. Baines *Northern Goldfields Diaries* (1946) III. 687 His *Imbonga*, or court flatterer..recounted the battles of the Matabele. **1945** *Cape Times* 29 May, Municipal mbongo... The Mayor made quite a good case for the appointment of an official who would be a sort of professional praiser. **1948** *Cape Argus* 16 Sept. 7 Government supporters have danced around their Ministers like dutiful, adoring and disciplined mbongos. **1957** *Ibid.* 15 June 1/7 They were..a lot of mbongas to hymn the praises of the incompetent Nationalist hierarchy. **1973** *Drum* 8 Mar. 53 The mbongis..climb up his ancestral tree singing the praise poems of Vorster's illustrious forebears.

Mbret, var. *MPRET.

Mc. All words of Scottish or Irish origin beginning with *Mc* (e.g. *MCCARTHYISM, *MCCOY) are placed alphabetically as if spelt *Mac-*.

Mdlle: see MADEMOISELLE 1.

Mdme: see MADAME 1.

me, *pers. pron.* Add: **4.** (Later examples.)

1814 JANE AUSTEN *Let.* 2 Mar. (1932) II. 92, I am to call upon Miss Spencer: Funny me! **1895**, etc. [see *little me* s.v. *LITTLE *a.* 13]. **1961** 'P. DENNIS' (*title*) Little me: the intimate memoirs of that great star..Belle Poitrine. **1973** 'D. HALLIDAY' *Dolly & Starry Bird* viii. 111 'As Timothy would say, silly me,' Johnson said in a voice as hard as his bifocals.

5. For 'Now chiefly *arch.* and *poet.*' read 'Freq. in U.S. colloq. usage', and add further examples.

1821 W. SEWALL *Diary* (1930) 75 Purchased me some linens. **1874** *Rep. Vermont Board Agric.* II. 512 In 1861 I built me a horse barn, twenty-eight by forty. **1916** 'B. M. BOWER' *Phantom Herd* iii. 42 I'm going to make me one. **1972** '*Gramophone*' *Pop. Record Catal.* Dec. 129/2 (*song-title*) I'm gonna get me a gun. **1974** M. HASTINGS *Dragon Island* xv. 129 I'll grab me the first-aid box and..see how my patients are doing.

6. (Later examples.)

1903 *Dialect Notes* II. 320 *Me and you*,..almost universal for 'you and I'. **1905** *Westm. Gaz.* 11 Nov. 3/1, I can foresee..that unless me and Ellen advise you, you'll become simply ——. **1936** MENCKEN *Amer. Lang.* (ed. 4) ix. 457 Him and me are friends. **1966** 'J. HACKSTON' *Father clears Out* 50 Me an' me mate's eyes was dancin' out of our 'eads.

7. e. Now somewhat more commonly used intensively like French *moi*.

1923 *Dialect Notes* V. 244, I am not going to-day, *me*. **1963** *Listener* 20 June 1041/3 Me, I like fighting, too.

9. With the verb *to be*: suited to or representative of my tastes, ability, personality, etc.; appropriate for me; my real self.

1899 J. LONDON *Let.* 29 July (1966) 47 This is me all the time and all over. **1905** A. BENNETT *Sacred & Profane Love* I. v. 83 But that poor little book isn't *me*... I shall never write another like it. **1925** R. HALL *Saturday Life* vii. 79 Nothings, just nothings, they didn't count; this is the thing that's *me*. **1938** J. CARY *Castle Corner* 557 The house has got to be contemporary, it's got to be art..and it's got to be me. **1949** R. CHANDLER *Little Sister* xxviii. 209, I don't like the script... It just isn't me, if you know what I mean. **1957** P. WILDEBLOOD *Main Chance* 56 Cardigans are not..particularly *me*. **1963** F. T. VISSER *Hist. Syntax Eng. Lang.* I. iii. 240, I like this dress, it's me!

II. 10. Used *colloq.* and *dial.* (also *Austral.* and *N.Z.*) as a poss. adj.

Treated in Dict. s.v. MY *poss. adj.*, e.g. in 19th-cent. representations of Irish speech.

1862 G. MEREDITH *Let.* 23 June (1970) I. 152 B. Wyse came the other day..and hoped for forgive *miss*: 'Me deer Mardith', etc.! **1901** M. FRANKLIN *My Brilliant Career* x. 84 Now it's your turn, me fine lady. *Ibid.* xxvi. 220 A couple of letters..stuffed in me pocket. **1911** W. OWEN *Let.* 20 Sept. (1967) 83 Love to Mary and me brethren twain. **1946** K. TENNANT *Lost Haven* (1968) i. 20 Me own mother sent me word he wants to see me! *Ibid.* ii. 39 Me granddaughter's coming to stay with me. **1960** G. SLATTER *Gun in my Hand* ii. 21 An' it ran like a hairy goat an' I did me chips. **1966** F. SHAW et al. *Lern Yerself Scouse* 20 *Me dollypegs*, my legs... *Me webs*, my feet. **1968** K. WEATHERLY *Roo Shooter* 21 'Cost you a night's shooting, me backside,' roared the driver. **1972** *Southerly* XXXII. 6 Me motorbike's out at the station. **1973** *Sunday Express* (Trinidad & Tobago) 1 Apr. (Suppl.) 13/1 Ah on de road, Putting out me hand Like a mas in a band.

meach, var. *MEECH *v.*

meachin(g), varr. *MEECHING *ppl. a.*

‖ **mea culpa** (mē̆·ā ku·lpā, mī·ā kv·lpā). [L., lit. 'through my own fault'.] A phrase from the prayer of confession in the Latin liturgy of the Church; used *lit.* and *transf.* as an exclamation of repentance, and as the name of such an exclamation; also *mea maxima culpa*. See CONFITEOR.

c **1374** CHAUCER *Tr. & Cr.* (1894) II. 525 Now, *mea culpa*, lord! I me repente. **1602** W. WATSON *Decacordon* 40 Shall lay their hands a little heavier on their hearts with *Mea maxima culpa*. **1818** LADY MORGAN *Florence Macarthy* IV. v. 208 Mingled a broken *ave-maria* and *mea-culpa*, in utter consternation and superstitious fear. **1891** E. DOWSON *Let.* 7 Feb. (1967) 184 Today, mea culpa, mea maxima culpa, I have done nothing. **1922** JOYCE *Ulysses* 279 He beat his hand upon his breast, confessing: *mea culpa*. **1948** R. BUTLER *Words of Mass* I. 10 The striking of the breast at the *mea culpa* is an emphatic recognition of guilt and expression of sorrow. **1958** *Times* 17 Oct. 17/1 Eisenstein made a public *mea culpa* at the time in the form of an open letter to the Committee. **1960** [see *guilt-complex]. **1974** 'D. SHANNON' *Crime File* (1975) v. 79 *Mea culpa*... We all do stupid things sometimes.

mead¹. Add: **c. mead-bench, -hall**: later examples.

1959 A. G. BRODEUR *Art of Beowulf* 16 A mead-bench is a seat in a royal hall, where the dispensing of good drink symbolizes the warm relationship between lord and retainer. **1903** L. F. ANDERSON *Anglo-Saxon Scop* 36 Personal valour and prowess on the field of battle, courage.., hardihood.., these were the all-absorbing topics of conversation in the mead-hall. **1968** E. B. IRVING *Reading of Beowulf* v. 242 The clustering of the clan family in the lighted mead-hall.

meadow, *sb.* Add: **4. a.** *meadow-down, -farmer.*

1877 G. M. HOPKINS *Poems* (1967) 71 Meadow-down is not distressed For a rainbow footing it. **1742** W. ELLIS *Mod. Husbandman* II. III. 109 There are two Sorts of Farmers, who carry on this Business..*viz.* the Grass, or Meadow-farmer, and the Plough-farmer. **1884** R. JEFFERIES *Life of Fields* 139 The meadow-farmers, dairymen, have not grubbed many hedges.

b. meadow brown (butterfly), for Latin name substitute '*Maniola jurtina*' and add examples of absol. use; **meadow-hen** (earlier examples); **meadow-lark** (earlier and later N. Amer. examples).

1930 *Times Educ. Suppl.* 4 Oct. p. iv/4 The meadow-brown's heavy, indolent flight. **1974** *Lady* 1 Aug. 169/1 Butterflies abound..from the innumerable brown ringlets, 'gate-keepers', speckled woods and meadow browns, to various beauties like the common blues. *a* **1841** W. P. HAWES *Sporting Scenes* (1842) I. 18 The principal inhabitants are gulls, and meadow-hens. **1863** 'G. HAMILTON' *Gala-Days* 97 You know you didn't scare a little meadow-hen. **1775** B. ROMANS *Conc. Nat. Hist. E. & W. Florida* 114 Meadow larks, fieldfares, rice birds, &c. are very frequently had. **1948** H. JACOBS *We chose Country* 161 Birds were everywhere, first killdeers, making a din in the fields at dusk, then meadowlarks, caroling in the morning sun. **1963** G. H. THOMSON *Crocus Country* xx. 131 The bird we loved most..was the meadow lark. **1969** N. W. PARSONS *Upon Sagebrush Harp* viii. 42 There were many birds, but the meadowlark moved me most.

c. *meadow pea* (examples), *trefoil* (earlier example); **meadow lily,** a common lily of the eastern U.S., *Lilium canadense*; also, formerly used for lily-of-the-valley, *Convallaria majalis*.

1832 W. D. WILLIAMSON *Hist. State Maine* I. 125 [We have] two varieties of meadow-lilies,..May-lily, or 'lily of the valley'; and nodding-lily. **1894** *Jrnl. Amer. Folk-Lore* VII. 102 *Lilium Canadense*,..meadow lily, nodding lily. **1946** E. HODGINS *Mr. Blandings builds his Dream House* (1947) viii. 104 When the bluebells and the columbine faded, the meadow lilies and the wild geranium took up the torch... August was well along. **1896** G. HENSLOW *How to Study Wild Flowers* 98 *Lathyrus pratensis*, Meadow Pea. This genus resembles vetches, but has fewer leaflets. **1960** *Oxf. Bk. Wild Flowers* 22/2 Meadow Vetchling or Meadow Pea (*Lathyrus pratensis*). Although this Pea has thin, rather weak stems, it may reach up to 3 feet in height by scrambling over other plants. **1629** J. PARKINSON *Parad.* I. lxxix. 341 The Medica's are generally thought to feede cattell fat much more then the Medow Trefoile, or Clauer grasse.

meady (mī·di), *a. rare.* [f. MEAD¹ + -Y¹.] Resembling or suggestive of mead.

1887 G. MEREDITH *Ballads & Poems Tragic Life* 102 Yellow flamed the meady sunset. **1900** *Sydney Mail* 31 Mar. 777 If you simply let it stand it will usually work up into the meady beverage.

meal, *sb.*¹ Add: **3. a.** *meal-bag, -drift*; *meal-dusty, -white* adjs.

1644 *Essex County, Mass. Probate Rec.* (1916) I. 46 Too meal baggs. **1738** *New Hampsh. Probate Rec.* (1914) II. 622 He knows of no meal Bag that his son had but what he borrowed of him. **1876** *Wide Awake* 72/1 She was bundled up so you would hardly have known her from one of the meal-bags. **1968** E. R. BUCKLER *Ox Bells & Fireflies* ii. 34 Father puts three basketsful [of potatoes] into each meal bag. **1877** G. M. HOPKINS *Poems* (1967) 70 What lovely behaviour Of silk-sack clouds! has wilder, wilful-wavier Meal-drift moulded ever and melted across skies? **1951** W. DE LA MARE *Winged Chariot* 40 Meal-dusty polls, glossed plumage. **1938** —— *Memory* 95 This meal-white snow.

meal, *sb.*² Add: **2. b.** *meals-on-wheels*: a service, usually provided by a women's voluntary organization, whereby meals are taken by car to old people, invalids, etc. Also *attrib.*

1961 *Times* 17 Jan. 7/1 Of those who get meals-on-wheels, less than 10 per cent have adequate meals on week days when there is no delivery. **1961** *Guardian* 19 Apr. 2/5 The need for an extension of the meals-on-wheels schemes as a contribution to the care of the home-bound. **1966** 'O. MILLS' *Enemies of Bride* xii. 106 Having just completed a tour with a Meals-on-Wheels van to less fortunate old ladies, she was dressed in a green, shirt-waister dress of the Women's Voluntary Services. **1966** 'K. A. SADDLER' *Gilt Edge* i. 22 I'm on National Assistance. I get Meals-on-Wheels twice a week. **1970** J. FLEMING *Young Man, I think you're Dying* ii. 25 On weekday mornings the meals-on-wheels service would bring hot food for the invalid.

d. *to make a meal of* (further examples); also, to treat in an over-fussy or laborious manner.

1961 C. WILLOCK *Death in Covert* iv. 93 Dyson..was making a meal of everything. He had carefully paced the distance... He had stuck sticks in the ground. **1968** *Guardian* 22 Aug. 7/2 When university people get on to fashion they make a meal of it. **1970** *Ibid.* 5 Dec. 8/5 He had as one of his guests Inia Te Wiata, whose name has been pretty familiar to radio listeners for some years now but Mr Murray still made a meal, if not a light snack, of promoting it. **1970** *N.Z. News* 21 Jan. 16/4 New Zealand scored 325 for six wickets declared—everyone except M. G. Burgess and G. E. Vivian making a meal of University bowlers. **1971** M. POLLAND *Package to Spain* vii. 95 His small sharp face was full of righteous outrage... Henry was making a meal of it. **1972** J. EASTWOOD *Henry in Silver Frame* xxiii. 191, I wouldn't want the gutter-press to make a meal of me.

4. *meal-break*; **meal ticket** *orig. U.S.*, (*a*) a ticket entitling a person to a meal; (*b*) *fig. slang*, a source of income or livelihood (esp. a husband or wife regarded as such).

1958 *Guardian* 20 Aug. 1/1 The central committee's advice to busmen..was to insist on full meal breaks. **1971** 'H. CALVIN' *Poison Chasers* ix. 112 Ronnie Samson had to stop me to let the boys off for a meal break. **1870** O. LOGAN *Before Footlights* 248 The rather scrubby party who occasionally purchases..a 'Meal Ticket', and thus gets entrance to the festive dining hall. **1899** 'J. FLYNT' *Tramping with Tramps* 395 *Meal-ticket*, a person 'good' for a meal. **1912** *Collier's* 23 Nov. 38/2 I've been doin' a lot for her—a regular meal ticket an' ticket agency for her. **1926** [see *GOOD A. *adj.* 1 f]. **1929** T. WOLFE *Look Homeward, Angel* (1930) xxvii. 377 She can't bear to give him up... He's her meal-ticket. **1939** ADE *Let.* 7 July (1973) 214 The play remained at the Garden until the following summer and next year it was being played by three companies. It turned out to be my meal ticket. **1972** 'H. HOWARD' *Nice Day for Funeral* iii. 40 He was her meal-ticket. Why should she want him sent to the pen? **1972** *Lebende Sprachen* XVII. 34/1 US meal ticket—BE [*sc.* British English] luncheon voucher. **1973** *Jewish Chron.* 2 Feb. 23/5 Our young women do not look for 'meal-ticket' marriages.

meal, *v.*² **1.** (Earlier and later examples.)

1628 O. FELLTHAM *Resolves* (ed. 3) lxxvi. 236 With Earthen Plate, *Agathocles* (they say) Did vse to meale. **1891** H. C. BUNNER *Zadoc Pine* 201 A lodging-house for those who 'mealed' at the hotel. **1918** *Jrnl. Friends' Hist. Soc.* 7 John Lecky..generally arranged to meal at Friends' houses. **1960** A. POWELL *Casanova's Chinese Restaurant* 113 'Doesn't Carolo ever eat himself?'.. 'He often meals with us as a matter of fact.'

mealie. Add: (Further *attrib.* examples.) Cf. *MIELIE.

1855 W. C. HOLDEN *Hist. Natal* x. 282 The consumption of mealie (maize) meal in D'Urban has increased. **1884** E. P. MATHERS *Glimpse of Gold Fields* 29 At one of our camps I tried to get some mealie porridge made. **1925** P. SMITH *Little Karoo* 18 Just outside the door was the worn mealie-stamper, cut out of a tree-trunk and shaped like an hour-glass, in which the mealies were pounded into meal. **1928** R. CAMPBELL *Wayzgoose* i. 27 Your notice boards like mealie-stems are stripped. **1929** D. REITZ *Commando* xiv. 129 Rations were chiefly game and mealie-meal. **1944** M. DE B. NESBITT *Road to Avalon* (1949) xiv. 113, I sit on the mealie planter, control the levers and see that the hoppers are well filled as they drop mealies in the furrows. **1956** N. GORDIMER *Six Feet of Country* 9 The girl catching her stockings on the mealie-stooks. **1962** *Cape Times* 13 June 1/4 A Harvard aircraft..crashed in a mealie land near Dunnottar. **1971** *Sunday Times* (Johannesburg) 28 Mar. 12/5, I made all sorts of things like mealie bread to make a bit of money for my poor old husband to buy a piece of industrial ground. **1973** *Times* 28 Nov. 8/7 Mealie-meal, the staple food, was..in short supply. **1974** G. JENKINS *Bridge of Magpies* iii. 51 A slovenly breakfast of half-burnt mealie-meal porridge and boiled penguin eggs.

2. mealie-cob, a corn cob; **mealie-cob worm,** the caterpillar of *Heliothis armigera*, a noctuid moth; **mealie-pap** = *mieliepap* (*MIELIE).

1859 R. J. MANN *Natal* 137 (Pettman), The young mealy-cob is generally preferred to bread. **1932** S. ZUCKERMAN *Social Life Monkeys* xii. 195 The meally cobs and fruit it [*sc.* chacma] plunders from cultivated lands. **1911** J. D. F. GILCHRIST *S. Afr. Zool.* 150 (Pettman), The Mealie-cob worm..does extensive damage to mealies, peas, tomatoes, and lucerne. **1880** E. F. SANDEMAN *Eight Months in Ox Waggon* xxvii. 273 Guinea fowls..form a very relishing change from the never-varying *menu* of bôk or mealie pap. **1902** J. H. M. ABBOTT *Tommy Cornstalk* 28 A few Kaffir transport drivers..are boiling their 'mealie-pap' in three-legged pots. **1903** J. Y. F. BLAKE *West Pointer with Boers* iii. 49 We had to come down to straight mealie pap (corn meal mush), and fresh beef. **1922** J. BUCHAN *Bk. Escapes* vi. 120 For food he had to trust to mealie-pap at Kafir kraals. **1966** D. VARADAY *Gara-Yaka's Domain* xii. 135 Mealie-pap—maize-porridge—the bush substitute for bread was cooking.

mealy, *a.* Add: **2.** *mealy pudding* = *white pudding* (WHITE *a.* 11 e).

1914 F. B. JACK *Cookery for every Household* 517/1 *Mealy Puddings.* 1 lb. oatmeal. ½ lb beef suet... When

the puddings are required, toast them a few minutes in front of the fire. **1946** F. M. McNeill *Recipes from Scotland* 65 *White* or *Mealie Puddings*... The puddings will keep for months if hung up. **1951** *Good Housek. Home Encycl.* 550/1 *Mealy Pudding*, an oatmeal pudding which is served with grilled sausages, bacon, herrings, etc.

4. b. mealy-bug. Substitute for def.: a scale insect of the family Pseudococcidæ, esp. one of the genus *Pseudococcus*; (further examples).

1927 *Chambers's Jrnl.* Aug. 502/1 The mealybug, so called from its white waxy or mealy coating, belongs to the big family of scale insects known as the Coccidae. **1953** S. H. Skaife *Afr. Insect Life* xi. 122 Mealy bugs are small insects, the largest being only about one-eighth of an inch long, pink or purplish in colour but appearing to be white because their bodies are covered with a waxy powder. **1971** *Daily Colonist* (Victoria, B.C.) 5 May 27/5 The Comstock Mealybug, also known as the Pseudococcus Comstocki, is a serious threat to citrus, sugar beets, grapes, apples and other crops.

mealy-mouth (mī·liˌmauþ). [Mealy *a.* 8; cf. Mealy-mouthed *a.*] **1.** A mouth which never utters plain terms; a soft, indirect, or reticent manner of speaking; hence a mealy-mouthed person. Also ironically: see quot. 1941. *slang.*

1600, 1828, 1862 [see Mealy *a.* 8]. **1898** B. Kirkby *Lakeland Words* 100 *Mealy-Mooth*,..eny body 'at's mealy-moothed's o' that sooart. **1919** J. C. Snaith *Love Lane* xlvii. 254 It was no use having a divided mind, it was no use having a mealy-mouth. **1941** J. Smiley *Hash House Lingo* 37 *Mealy mouth*, fault finding customer. **1942** *Scrutiny* X. 400 Iudushka, the chief character, is the apotheosis of the mealy-mouth.

2. *dial.* Applied to various birds, as the willow warbler, *Phylloscopus trochilus*, or the whitethroat, *Sylvia communis*.

1885 C. Swainson *Provincial Names & Folklore Brit. Birds* 26 Willow Warbler..Mealy mouth (Craven). **1961** *Countryman* LVIII. 468 A missel thrush is a 'greybird'.. the whitethroat a 'mealymouth' [in S. Pembrokeshire].

mean, *sb.*[2] Add: **10. g.** *means-end(s)* (used *attrib.*): of or pertaining to the ways of achieving a result considered together with the result.

1933 *Psychol. Rev.* XL. 60 The 'means-end-readiness' Tolman defined as a certain selectivity as regards stimuli, and as regards the responses..to such stimuli. **1951** R. Firth *Elem. Social Organiz.* iii. 85 Structural change implies that there was some imperfection in the previous means-ends schedule of a substantial number of members of the society. **1958** *Listener* 5 June 931/2 We must look at the contexts where the means-end model *is* appropriate. .. The second means-end context is that of making or producing things. We mix the flour in order to make a cake. **1963** A. Kaplan in P. A. Schilpp *Philos. R. Carnap* 840 If there were a final end it could not have the derived cognitive meaning of a means-end implication. **1965** H. I. Ansoff *Corporate Strategy* ii. 24 The two sets of rules have a means-ends relationship; objectives set the goals, and strategy sets the path to the goals. **1965** *Language* XLI. 80 Aiming towards a means-ends model of language.

15. means test, an official inquiry into an applicant's private resources, determining or limiting a grant or allowance from public funds; also (with hyphen) as *vb.*; hence **means-testable** *a.*; **means-tested** *ppl. a.*; **means testing** *vbl. sb.*

1930 *Economist* 7 June 1263/2 We should not cavil greatly at the principle of granting, on the basis of a means test, maintenance allowances for children compelled to attend school. **1935** *Planning* II. 11 A system of Transitional Payments was introduced..subject, however, to a household 'Means Test' administered by the local Public Assistance Committees. **1940** *Manch. Guardian Weekly* 23 Feb. 153/3 Non-contributory pensions, to which alone the household means test was to apply, had been conditioned by the applicant's means ever since 1908. **1957** *Times* 31 Dec. 11/5 Provision should be made in the new scholarship scheme for giving adequate assistance to students who would be debarred under 'means tests' from accepting scholarships offered by the State and other sources. **1963** *Economist* 1 June 882/2 All university awards are means-tested now. **1966** *Ibid.* 29 Jan. 388/1 The genuinely poor long-term sick should be generously treated, preferably through generous means-tested national assistance. **1970** *Guardian* 29 Oct. 13, 1971 is going to be a record year for means-testing... Millions of new means-test forms will have to be designed. .. More people..will..make the sudden move from means-tested exemption from Health Service charges to paying the full rate. **1970** *Daily Tel.* 12 Dec. 2/6 Many of them are now living on fixed private incomes or with the aid of supplementary benefits which are means-tested. **1972** *Times* 30 Sept. 15/4 The poorest being supported by means testable benefits. **1973** *Times* 13 Feb. 16/7 Means-testing over a wide range of social benefits has been introduced on a scale unprecedented since the war.

mean (mīn), *sb.*[3] *colloq. rare.* [*sb.* use of Mean *a.*[1] 5.] A mean person; = *meany.

1938 E. Bowen *Death of Heart* ii. iv. 241 You *are* a mean, Dickie!

mean, *a.*[1] Add: **2. f.** *U.S. colloq.* In low spirits or poor state of health; poorly, not quite well.

1857 'Dow, Jr.' *Dow's Patent Sermons* 1st Ser. 7 As mean..as a rooster in a thundershower. **1911** H. S. Harrison *Queed* vii. 90 Mebbe you could do better writing and harder writing if only you didn't feel so mean. **1911** J. F. Wilson *Land Claimers* i. 21 'Feel pretty mean,' the packer asked him kindly.

3. a. Of domestic animals or things in general: poor in quality or condition; comparatively worthless; unpleasant, disagreeable.

1817 in *Trans. Illinois State Hist. Soc. 1910* 148 Hogs in this Country are the meanest that I have ever seen... I do not believe you ever see half so mean hogs as we have here. **1823** W. Faux *Memorable Days Amer.* 219 The horses here are nearly all mean,..dwarfish things. **1842** C. M. Kirkland *Forest Life* I. 140 You've had a pretty mean time, I reckon. *a* **1890** in Barrère & Leland *Dict. Slang* (1890) II. 49/1 The night was dark and stormy, about as mean a night as was ever experienced in Washington. **1936** Ade *Let.* 29 Apr. (1973) 192 We arrived home on the 17th without mishap and almost immediately ran into mean weather including one snow fall which completely covered the ground. **1948** 'N. Shute' *No Highway* ix. 245 Eight handles it [*sc.* a coffin] had, for carrying, but gee, that was a mean load. **1973** *Kingston* (Ontario) *Whig-Standard* 11 Aug. 7/5 That was just about the meanest electric storm I ever sat through.

5. b. (Later examples.)

(*a*) **1841** 'Dow, Jr.' *Short Patent Sermons* 78 [One girl] thought me real mean for uttering such super-diabolical sentiments. **1891** R. T. Cooke *Huckleberries* 14 It would be awful mean of me to leave you here alone.

(*b*) **1862** R. H. Newell *Orpheus C. Kerr Papers* 1st Ser. ii. 21, I see he felt powerful mean, so I walked up to him. **1884** 'Mark Twain' *Huck. Finn* xli. 421 [She] tucked me in, and mothered me so good I felt mean.

d. *colloq.* (orig. *U.S.*). Remarkably clever, adroit, etc.; excellent; formidable.

1920 H. C. Witwer in *Collier's* 15 May 6/3 Everything was jake until K. O. Krouse shook a mean dice and win $28 from Battlin' Lewis on the way to Toledo. *Ibid.* 57/2 You never heard tell of Kane Halliday?.. The big..football star, the weights thrower..what they call a round-about athalete? *You* know, one of them bimbos which flings a wicked spear and hurls a mean hammer and that there stuff, get me? *Ibid.* 62/2 Your wonder child may pack a mean wallop. **1924** *Ladies' Home Jrnl.* Feb. 21/1 'That Lucy Layman sure does shake a mean foot,' began Edmond airily. **1931** D. Runyon *Guys & Dolls* (1932) iii. 64 She swings a very mean skillet, and gets me up some very tasty fodder. **1963** *Economist* 23 Nov. 775/2 Mr Ronnie Scott..plays a mean saxophone. **1968** *Globe & Mail* (Toronto) 13 Jan. 34/7 He blows a mean trumpet and sings well, too. **1973** *Observer* 9 Sept. 30/3 Does a mean goulash, taught him by his grandmother and perfected in Hungary. **1973** *Listener* 25 Oct. 578/2 Jack Palance smokes a mean cigar in *Oklahoma Crude*.

7. *mean-faced* adj.

1918 Mrs. Belloc Lowndes *Out of the War?* 211 Thin, mean-faced, yet sharply intelligent-looking man. **1953** E. S. Grenfell in C. K. Stead *N.Z. Short Stories* (1966) 69 A shiftless, mean-faced fellow.

B. *adv.*[1] (Later U.S. example.)

1861 O. W. Norton *Army Lett.* (1903) 26 Virginia has acted meaner than South Carolina.

mean, *a.*[2] and *adv.*[2] Add: **A.** *adj.* **7. a.** *mean square*: the (arithmetical) mean of the squares of a set of numbers; *mean-square deviation* (*mean-square error*, † *error of mean square*): the mean of the squares of the differences between a set of numbers and some fixed number; usu. identical with the variance; formerly, † the square root of this (usu. identical with the standard deviation).

1845 *Encycl. Metrop.* II. 460, k' and k'' are approximately found by taking the actual mean, and the actual mean square, of a large number of observed durations. Again, the mean risk of error in estimating a single duration is $\cdot 39894\sqrt{[(k''-k'^2)\div s]}$. **1894** Error of mean square [see *deviation 2 d]. **1956** A. A. Townsend *Struct. Turbulent Shear Flow* iii. 44 The contributions to the mean-square rate of strain of the eddies larger than $1/k$ come mostly from values of $E(k')$ for k' near k. **1968** R. A. Lyttleton *Mysteries Solar Syst.* vii. 245 This regrouping of the equations of condition..results in a further reduction of the number of unknowns at the price..of increasing the mean-square error associated with each equation. **1970** S. Brandt *Statistical & Computational Methods* vi. 83 A sum of squares..divided by the number of degrees of freedom is called the mean square or more explicitly the mean-square deviation... Its square root (which has the dimension of the measured quantity, i.e. the mean) has the lengthy name root-mean-square deviation.

mean, *v.*[1] Add: **1. f.** *to mean well* (used ironically).

1813 Jane Austen *Pride & Prej.* III. v. 108 Perhaps she *meant* well, but, under such a misfortune as this, one cannot see too little of one's neighbours. **1889** F. Anstey in *Granta* 17 May 9/2 Still, with all their presumption, they meant well, poor fellows! **1910** R. Brooke *Let.* 9 Jan. (1968) 206 He *is* a silly man... Yet he means well. **1961** G. Smith *Business of Loving* ix. 206 Felix obviously meant well. **1973** S. B. Jackman *Guns covered with Flowers* x. 159 He smiled apologetically, 'He means well'. Stevens grinned. 'And you can't say worse than that about anyone.'

2. b. (Earlier and later examples.)

1854 Thackeray *Newcomes* I. xxix. 287 What the devil do you mean about your Chimène and your Rodrigue? **1930** G. B. Shaw *Apple Cart* i. 16 What do you mean? Isn't it what I have always said?

c. (*if*) *you know, see, understand, what I mean,* i.e. 'have I made it clear?'

1846 G. E. Jewsbury *Sel. Lett. to Mrs. Carlyle* (1892) 203 There would be a want of reverence in it, if you understand what I mean. **1968** *Guardian* 24 Apr. 9/8 If I thought..he was going to back-chat me like he does now ..I'd half-kill him now, you know what I mean? **1968** *Listener* 30 May 711/3 A braying Brooklyn accent studded with 'You know what I means'. **1974** *Sunday Times* 20 Jan. 12/4 [He'll] be only too keen to get back to his boat, if you see what I mean.

3. b. Of a person or thing: to be of some account or importance, to 'matter' *to* (someone); to be a source of benefit, or an object of regard, affection, or love *to* (someone).

1888 Mrs. H. Ward *R. Elsmere* II. iii. xxvi. 279 It was only by a great effort that he could turn his thoughts from the Squire, and all that the squire had meant to him during the past year. **1912** *Red Mag.* 1 Mar. 515/1 It came over me how much she meant to me and how hard a wrench it was going to be to live along without her. **1914** *Times Lit. Suppl.* 8 Jan. 12/1 Comprehension of what Lady Gregory has meant to him and to others who worked with her. **1922** Joyce *Ulysses* 356 He would never understand what he had meant to her.

c. *pass.* To be destined (by providence); to have special significance.

1897 Kipling *Captains Courageous* viii. 169 It couldn't have been *meant*. It was only the tide. **1956** M. Stewart *Wildfire at Midnight* i. 16 So *handy* having that address. It's as if it were *meant*. **1962** M. Allingham *China Governess* (1963) xii. 151 That's miraculous! That's what people mean when they say a thing is 'meant'. **1974** I. Murdoch *Sacred & Profane Love Machine* 239 When I need you, you are here. You must see how *meant* it all is.

mean, *v.*[3] Restrict †*Obs. rare* to senses in Dict. and add: **3.** *trans.* [f. Mean *a.*[2] 7 or *sb.*[2] 8.] To calculate the arithmetical mean of. Also with *up*.

1882 W. J. L. Wharton *Hydrogr. Surveying* 210 We need not mean up each column of times. *Ibid.* 213 When working several sets, calculate them simultaneously as far as this, and mean the results. *a* **1888** P. F. Shortland *Naut. Surveying* (1890) 64 The permanent errors will destroy each other in the results of all..observations so meaned.

meander, *v.* Add: **4.** *U.S.* To pass or travel deviously along or through (a river, etc.).

1821 in *Missouri Hist. Soc. Coll.* (1906) II. 61 We still continued meandering the Arkansas. **1831** J. O. Pattie *Personal Narr.* 13 We crossed the Missouri..and meandered the river as far as Pilcher's fort. **1839** Z. Leonard *Adventures* (1904) 69 We separated, each party to meander the rivers that had been respectively allotted to them. **1839** in *Trans. Mich. Agric. Soc.* (1856) VII. 360 Branches of Swan creek meander this track in such manner as to facilitate drainage.

me-and-you. *slang.* [Jocular adaptation of colloq. pronunc. (mī·niū) of Menu.] = Menu 2.

1932 P. P. *Rhyming Slang* 23 Me and you..Menu. **1943** N. Marsh *Colour Scheme* iv. 68 Come on, Beautiful. Let's have a slant at the me-and-you.

meanie, var. *meany.

meaning, *vbl. sb.*[1] Add: **6.** *attrib.* and *Comb.*, as *meaning-analysis, -area, -change, -content, -relation, -relationship, -unit*; *meaning-bearing, -carrying* adjs.

1936 Wirth & Shils tr. *Mannheim's Ideology & Utopia* i. 46 There are..vast possibilities of precision in the combination of meaning-analysis and sociological situational diagnosis. **1966** C. G. Hempel *Philos. of Nat. Sci.* viii. 103 The characterization of these substances by their molecular structure is arrived at, not by meaning analysis, but by chemical analysis. **1958** C. Rabin in *Aspects of Translation* vii. 124 The object in question has to be assigned either to the meaning-area of *watch* or to that of *clock*. **1957** N. Chomsky in Saporta & Bastian *Psycholinguistics* (1961) 266/2 We have counter examples to the suggestion.. that morphemes be defined as minimal meaning-bearing elements. **1972** *Archivum Linguisticum* III. 83 Generativists have attempted to remove all meaning-bearing elements from transformations into the deep structure. **1965** H. A. Gleason *Ling. & Eng. Gram.* 192 We might have had the meaning-carrying verb *washed*. **1954** F. G. Cassidy *Robertson's Devel. Mod. Eng.* (ed. 2) ix. 232 The various types of meaning-change. **1968** M. Black *Labyrinth of Lang.* vii. 163 A reasonably adequate account of the nature of such meaning-changes..is bound to be very complicated. **1946** Priebsch & Collinson *German Lang.* (ed. 2) ii. iii. 234 In several Indo-European languages are types of compounds in which the meaning-content or 'determination' is left unexpressed. **1948** *Mind* LVII. 80 Each separately is intelligible by itself and has its own meaning-content independently of the other. **1934** Priebsch & Collinson *German Lang.* ii. iii. 208 From the point of view of the meaning-relation of their component words compounds fall into several well-marked classes. **1963** J. Lyons *Structural Semantics* ii. 28 The only meaning-relation that is relevant in the case of phonemes is sameness and difference of meaning. **1961** R. B. Long *Sentence & its Parts* i. 11 Meaning relationships are obviously varied. **1966** *English Studies* XLVII. 256 We find the same meaning-relationship between the adjunct clause and its verb. **1938** I. Goldberg *Wonder of Words* xvi. 323 The smallest meaning-unit of a word is called a semanteme. **1962** W. Nowottny *Lang. Poets Use* vii. 162 What we call the 'same word' is not a single meaning-unit.

meaningful, *a.* Add: (Later examples.) Also, amenable to interpretation; having a recognizable purpose or function; *spec.* in *Logic*, resulting from the application of the rules of a language or sign system; able to function as a term in such a system.

1922 *Times Educ. Suppl.* 29 Apr. 200/2 The pupils see at once that their studies are meaningful. **1934** Cohen & Nagel *Introd. Logic* ix. 185 It has been said that to the two alternatives *true* and *false*, there is a third, the *meaningless*... The question of what constitutes a

meaningful expression is a large one. **1940** W. V. Quine *Math. Logic* iv. 164 Under Russell's scheme an abstraction prefix..can be applied outright to any meaningful formula. **1942** T. C. Pollock *Nature of Lit.* ix. 192 If the charge is made that a particular work..is..'meaningless'..a good critic may be able to discriminate privately..that it is..highly meaningful. **1952** C. P. Blacker *Eugenics* ix. 203 It is a different matter to test the tests and to prove them to be meaningful and workable. **1953** *Mind* LXII. 8 We often ask what a word means, but we do not ordinarily ask whether a word is meaningful or not. If it were not meaningful we would not call it a word. **1954** *Essays in Crit.* IV. 349 Tragedy affirms a cosmos of which man is a meaningful part. **1959** B. Wootton *Social Sci. & Social Path.* iii. 92 Meaningful conclusions are, moreover, inhibited by the inadequacy of the available evidence. **1970** O. Dopping *Computers & Data Processing* i. 18 We can add the information contents from different parts of the message and obtain a meaningful result from the addition. **1971** *Sat. Rev.* (U.S.) 18 Dec. 59/1 All of us..see a need to be related in a meaningful way to the black experience. In our case, this means teaching black people. **1973** *Times* 9 Feb. 24/4 Federation met again last month to try to get meaningful talks going again on a new disputes machinery. **1973** *Physics Bull.* May 281/3 The phoneme is the smallest meaningful unit of sound a listener can perceive.

meaningfully, *adv.* (Later examples.)
1937 *Mind* XLVI. 385 The finitist must hold..that of 'the sequence of time intervals' also, it cannot meaningfully be supposed that it denotes an infinite extension. **1955** *Sci. Amer.* Aug. 84/2 We cannot meaningfully look for any further sense of 'rational'. **1961** J. McCabe *Mr. Laurel & Mr. Hardy* (1962) vi. 122 He must arrange the sequence of action clearly, meaningfully, dramatically.

meaningfulness (mī·niŋfŭlnės). [f. Meaningful *a.* + -ness.] The fact or quality of being meaningful.
1919 R. H. Fisher *Outside of Inside* 105 In mystical trance he discerned the meaningfulness of the third heaven **1922** J. Y. Simpson *Man & Attainment of Immortality* xiv. 320 The exquisite sensitivity of their minds to the meaningfulness of his language. **1935** *Mind* XLIV. 426 'Redness' is a concept which has application in experience, and this is all that is required for meaningfulness. **1940** W. V. Quine *Math. Logic* iii. 147 The meaningfulness of an expression—the eligibility of an expression to occur in statements at all, true or false—is a matter over which we can profitably maintain control. **1941** A. D. Woozley in T. Reid *Ess.* p. xxix, He is far more interested in..universals as related to words—*i.e.* in the meaningfulness of language. **1951** *Trans. Philol. Soc.* 43 Here also the fundamental argument is meaningfulness. **1953** *Essays in Crit.* III. 107 Verification of meaningfulness in literature must lie, in the last analysis, outside literature. **1959** *Cambr. Rev.* 30 May 567/2 Whether or not the verifiability criterion is a criterion of the meaningfulness of a statement or of the scientific character of a statement, the defects which it has in either case can be reproduced *quid pro quo* for the falsifiability criterion. **1959** H. Gardner *Business of Crit.* II. iii. 131 Our first step towards making it [*sc.* a play or poem] meaningful to us is to be aware of the meaningfulness of the images to men of its own day. **1971** *Human World* Nov. 40 The question of the meaningfulness of religious utterances.

meaningless, *a.* Add: (Later examples.) Also, not 'meaningful' (cf. *meaningful *a.*).
1890 W. James *Princ. Psychol.* I. xvi. 676 He learned lists of meaningless syllables by heart. **1934, 1942** [see *meaningful *a.*].

mean while, meanwhile. Add: **A.** *sb.* **1.** (Later examples.)
1908 H. G. Wells *First & Last Things* III. viii. 123 The organized state..has not arrived..and in the meanwhile they must act like its anticipatory agents. **1960** G. Sanders *Mem. Professional Cad* II. viii. 170 In the meanwhile the boat..evidently decided to end it all. **1972** *Listener* 1 June 705/2 In the meanwhile sanctions would be continued.
2. After '*Obs.*' add 'exc. *arch.*'
1922 Joyce *Ulysses* 381 This meanwhile this good sister stood by the door.

meany (mī·ni). *colloq.* Also **meanie.** [f. Mean *a.*[1] + -y[6], -ie.] A mean-minded or stingy person.
1927 H. C. Brown *In Golden Nineties* iii. 107 It was whispered by some old meanies that many of the five-foot floral offerings were purchased by the actors themselves and sent to the theatre with fictitious names attached. **1928** J. P. McEvoy *Showgirl* xiii. 212/1 This old meany..last night..found himself, much to his aged surprise, in the Klaw Theatre. **1936** L. C. Douglas *White Banners* xiv. 315 Colonel Livingstone was an old meanie. **1951** J. B. Priestley *Festival at Farbridge* II. i. 34 He was at heart, she felt, a cunning old meanie. **1974** *Times* 15 Feb. 4/4 A bunch of local 'baddies' reinforced by 'meanies'.

mearing: see Mering *vbl. sb.* in Dict. and Suppl.

measle, *sb.* **1.** (Later examples of *sing.*)
1924 Galsworthy *White Monkey* I. iii. 21 Fleur knew how catching the word was; it would run like a measle round the ring. **1948** Mencken *Amer. Lang.* Suppl. II. 383 False singulars, made by back formation, are numerous, *e.g.*,..*measle*, nor are they confined to the untutored.

measle, *v.* Add: **4.** *fig.* To be full of or teem *with* (objectionable things). *rare.*
1856 C. Reade *Never too Late* II. xxv. 245 All this..in thieves' cant, with an oath or a nasty expression at every third word. The sentences measled with them.

measly, *a.* **4.** (Earlier and later examples.)
1864 M. E. Braddon *Henry Dunbar* II. xi. 212 The audacity to offer a measly hundred pounds or so for the discovery of a great crime! **1905** *Dialect Notes* III. 14 *Measly*,..poor. 'I don't want that *measly* stuff.' **1919** E. O'Neill *Ile* in *Moon of Caribbees* (1923) 13 Did you ever hear o' me pointin' s'uth for home with only a measly four hundred barrel of ile in the hold? **1973** J. Porter *It's Murder with Dover* vi. 55 Ten measly years in the nick doesn't worry anybody. **1974** *Sunday Tel.* 9 June 34/4 A spineless exhibition by the early Yorkshire batting—they have mastered only a measly five batting points all season—put them on the rack yet again.

measurability. Delete '*rare*' and add further examples.
1955 W. Pauli *Niels Bohr* 71 Measurability of electromagnetic fields. **1957** *Times Lit. Suppl.* 18 Oct. 620/2 A chapter on 'Illusionism and Perspective' deals with..measurability in quattrocentro compositions. **1969** *Nature* 14 June 1033/1 Though a physical quantity is considered primarily an attribute of the object under investigation, the need for measurability implies that the characteristic features of the relevant instruments of observation are an integral part of the quantity. **1975** *Times* 26 May 6/2 The main cause of this domination is measurability. Money provides an incontrovertible unit of measurement.

measure, *sb.* Add: **2. a.** *made to measure* (later example). Also *transf.* and *fig.*: fashioned to fulfil specified requirements; appropriate for a particular purpose; chiefly *attrib.*
1928 *Punch* 11 July p. xix/1 (Advt.), It is to give all the benefits of made-to-measure shoes..that these Lotus Bespoke Models have been created. **1937** *Evening News* 5 Feb. 8/2 We shall have made-to-measure houses..with provision for adding rooms as families grow. **1958** *Listener* 9 Oct. 563/2 The new knowledge..may ultimately enable us to produce made-to-measure mutant viruses. **1959** *Ibid.* 2 Apr. 608/1 The Boat Race..made to measure for television.
16. *spec.* Applied to Old English verse.
1774 R. Henry *Hist. Gt. Brit.* II. 432 The kinds and measures of their [*sc.* Saxon and Danish poets'] verses. **1802** J. Sibbald *Chron. Scottish Poetry* IV. p. lviii, In the same kind of measure [as the Fragment of the genuine Cædmon] are almost all the popular rhymes which still continue to be repeated by children in their ring-dances. **1873** H. Morley *First Sk. Eng. Lit.* 20 There is one measure for Beowulf, Cædmon's Paraphrase, and all subsequent First English poems. **1877** H. Rehrmann *Ess. Anglo-Saxon Poetry* 10 A foot or measure is made up..of one accented syllable and its connected unaccented syllable, or syllables. **1942** J. C. Pope *Rhythm of Beowulf* 44 According to Heusler, alliteration must introduce the first measure in the second half-line.

measure, *v.* Add: **2. c.** *transf.* and *fig.* uses.
1824 R. Humphreys *Mem. J. Decastro* 156 Mr. Cross..when he wrote a character for a person, measured the extent of his genius the same as a tailor does the body for a garment, and was generally very successful in making a *good* fit. **1859** B. Jerrold *Life D. Jerrold* vi. 94 The pig was to be measured for his part. *a* **1890** in Barrère & Leland *Dict. Slang* (1890) II. 49/1 He had been measured for a funeral sermon three times, he said, and had never used either one of them. **1896** Farmer & Henley *Slang* IV. 296 *To have been measured for a new umbrella*..(American), —(1) To appear in new but ill-fitting clothes; whence (2) to pursue a policy of doubtful wisdom. **1942** Berrey & Van den Bark *Amer. Thes. Slang* § 117/16 Be buried,..be measured for a new overcoat.
4. b. Also, to be comparable *with.*
1904 G. Parker *Ladder of Swords* vi. 61 Her words for the great cause had measured well with her deeds. **1907** *Smart Set* Mar. 126/2 The dog moved a cat-like step forward, making up the interval, and the man made a mental note that its single stride measured with his.
c. fig. *to measure up to*: to be equal (in ability, etc.) to; to match (cf. *match up to* s.v. *match *v.*[1] 8 b); to have the necessary qualifications for. orig. *U.S.*
1910 *N.Y. Even. Post* 16 Dec. 8 A man should be found for Senator who in ability and character will measure up to the just demands of such a situation. **1930** J. W. Johnson *Black Manhattan* xiv. 177 These plays..made a high demand on the versatility of the company... The demand was fully measured up to. **1931** G. T. Clark *Leland Stanford* xii. 405 Stanford..had in mind the problem of selecting some one who measured up to his ideal. **1958** *Spectator* 7 Feb. 181/2 The later period, however, does not measure up to the earlier in the originality or interest of its political literature.

measured, *ppl. a.* Add: **2. a.** *measured mile*: a distance of one mile carefully measured, esp. such a distance used for determining the speed of a ship; also *attrib.*
1608 J. Chamberlain *Let.* 15 July (1939) I. 262 A gentleman wan a great wager for riding five measured miles..twenty times over in lesse than five howres. **1666** [in Dict.]. **1720** *Britannia Depicta, or Ogilby Improved* (title-page), Wherein are..Engraven, All y[e] Cities..scituate on or near the Roads, with their respective Distances in Measured and Computed Miles. **1843** *Pract. Mechanic* June 358/2 The *Mermaid* then..performed the measured mile at the rate..of above thirteen miles through the water per hour. **1901** *Trans. Inst. Naval Archit.* XLIII. 23 The whole idea of the design has been, not so much to procure a very high measured-mile speed for a few hours, as to assure a good, continuous ocean speed. **1950** *Engineering* 10 Feb. 147/1 Measured-mile posts were in existence at Hartley..prior to 1884.

measurely, *adv.* (Later U.S. example.)
1878 J. H. Beadle *Western Wilds* xiv. 222 It is measurely free from winter storms.

measurer. 1. (Examples of special use.)
1636 *Early Rec. Dedham, Mass.* (1892) III. 36 We doe order yt all high wayes..he orderly set out by our Measurer. **1641** *Rec. Colony & Plantation New Haven* (1857) I. 51 Bro: Pecke chosen measurer for the towne to fill and strike all the corne. **1706** *Rec. Early Hist. Boston* (1882) VIII. 37 Allexander Seers, Samuell Bridge,..to serve as Measurers of board, Timber, and Plank. **1827** Drake & Mansfield *Cincinnati in 1826* vi. 51 The council have power to appoint..Measurers of wood and coal. **1841** in C. Cist *Cincinnati in 1841* (Advt.), George Warren, Measurer of Stone-work, Birch-work, and Plastering. **1916** Blunden *Harbingers* 24 The binman found the measurer pleased, For hops were clean and work was through. **1972** *Classification of Occupations* (Dept. of Employment) III. 408/2 Workers in this group weigh and otherwise measure materials, goods and products,..for example:..Measurers.

measuring, *ppl. a.* **b.** measuring-worm (earlier and later examples).
1843 J. E. DeKay *Zool. N.Y.* VI. 41 It walks after the manner of some caterpillars called Measuring worms. **1903** W. J. Holland *Moth Bk.* 323 The larvæ, which are commonly known as 'measuring-worms', 'span-worms', or 'loopers', have the power in many cases of attaching themselves by the posterior claspers to the stems and branches of plants, and extending the remainder of the body outwardly at an angle. **1939** Duncan & Pickwell *World of Insects* x. 172 Certain large measuring-worms, of the family Geometridae, have the ability, when danger threatens, to stiffen themselves out at angles to the stem on which they have been feeding or crawling, and thereafter for several minutes or hours to resemble perfectly bare and lifeless twigs. **1956** W. R. Bird *Off-Trail in Nova Scotia* viii. 215, I saw some of those long 'loopers' or 'measuring worms' that I hadn't seen since a boy.

meat, *sb.* Add: **1. c.** (Later examples.)
1853 Mrs. Gaskell *Cranford* xv. 296 After that she acknowledged that 'one man's meat might be another man's poison'. **1902** J. Conrad *End of Tether* xiv, in *Youth* 370 One man's poison, another man's meat. **1905** A. Burvenich *Eng. Idioms* 240 It is nuts to him; meat and drink to him, viz. the very sort of thing he likes. **1914** G. B. Shaw *Misalliance* 17 Whats one woman's meat is another woman's poison. **1929** J. B. Priestley *Good Companions* I. iii. 82 She had a trick of repeating phrases, raising her voice the second time, that had been meat and drink to mimics at Washbury for years. *a* **1930** D. H. Lawrence *Phoenix* (1936) 701 In the free, spontaneous self, one man's meat is truly another man's poison. And therefore you *can't* draw any average..unless you are going to poison everybody. **1937** Partridge *Dict. Slang* 515 *Meat, the nearer the bone the sweeter the*, a..low catch-phrase applied by men to a thin woman. **1939** F. Thompson *Lark Rise* i. 20 In spite of their poverty and the worry and anxiety attending it, they were not unhappy, and, though poor, there was nothing sordid about their lives. 'The nearer the bone the sweeter the meat', they used to say. **1939** N. Marsh *Overture to Death* xxii. 254 I'm no psycho-analyst, but I imagine she'd be meat and drink to any one who was.
3. Also, *local U.S.*, confined to certain types of meat, usu. pork.
1832 J. K. Paulding *Westward Ho!* I. 124 Nothing is called meat in these parts but salt pork and beef. **1845** C. M. Kirkland *Western Clearings* 93 Venison is not 'meat' to be sure, in our parlance; for we reserve that term for pork, *par excellence.* **1891** *Fur, Fin & Feather* 182 A bearskin is worth $5 to him..besides, he likes the flesh if meat (i.e. pork) is 'skeerse'. **1902** *Dialect Notes* II. 239 *Meat*, bacon always understood. **1903** *Ibid.* 320 *Meat*,..pork. Not often applied to beef, mutton, etc. **1927** *Ibid.* V. 469 *Meat*,..ham; —used only of the hog.
c. (*b*) Also, matter of importance or substance; the gist or main part (of a story, situation, etc.). Cf. Meaty *a.* 1 b.
1901 Kipling *Kim* xv. 390 At evening time..she won to the meat of the matter, explained low-voicedly by the lama. **1937** *Jrnl. R. Aeronaut. Soc.* XLI. 1025 There was so much real meat in this paper that it was impossible to enter into any long discussion about it. **1942** *Tee Emm* (Air Ministry) II. 129 Delving into detail, digging out the meat, and giving your advice. **1951** in M. McLuhan *Mech. Bride* (1967) 36/4 It is not only full of meat, but so interestingly written that I am going to loan it around the store. **1955** *Bull. Atomic Sci.* June 226/3 But the real meat of the book is in the depiction of the moral conflicts keenly felt by these men. **1960** *Times* 23 June 3/4 This makes the meat of Wimbledon. **1970** *Nature* 12 Sept. 1092/2 Shift registers..perform the meat of a computer calculation.
d. *transf.* Delete example in Dict. and add:
1872 'Mark Twain' *Roughing It* I. 357 Come along—you're my meat *now*, my lad. **1907** S. E. White *Arizona Nights* I. vii. 136 'Whew!' I whistles, 'That's a large order —But I'm your meat.' **1917** A. G. Empey *From Fire Step* xvi. 103, I gleefully fell in with the scheme, and told Cassell I was his meat. **1922** A. Bennett *Let.* 14 Nov. (1966) I. 319 It was not everybody's meat, but it was in my opinion somebody's meat. **1922** E. O'Neill *Hairy Ape* (1923) iii. 29 Say, dis is a cinch! Dis was made for me! It's my meat, get me! **1942** W. E. Johns *Biggles sweeps Desert* v. 66 The way you snaffled my Hun! I call that a bit thick... He was my meat, absolutely, yes by Jingo. *Ibid.* 67 'You were jolly nearly his meat,' Biggles pointed out, coldly. **1956** B. Holiday *Lady sings Blues* (1973) iv. 46 'I Cried' was my damn meat, just like 'Rhythm' was Lester's. **1972** *Dict. Contemp. & Colloq. Usage* (Eng.-Lang. Inst. Amer.) 19 *Meat*,..one's field of interest;..as: Math, that's my *meat.*

e. *coarse slang.* The penis; the female genital organs; the human body regarded as an instrument of sexual pleasure; a prostitute.

1595 GOSSON *Pleasant Quippes* sig. B2 That you should coutch your meat in dish, And others feele, it is no fish. **1597** SHAKS. *Henry IV: Part Two* (1623) II. iv. 83/1 Away you mouldie Rogue, away; I am meat for your Master. **1611** L. BARRY *Ram-Alley* v. sig. H4ᵛ Faith take a maide, and leaue the widow, Maister. Of all meates I loue not a gaping oyster. **1664** T. KILLIGREW *Parson's Wedding* v. ii, in *Comedies & Tragedies* 142 Your bed is big enough for two, and my meat will not cost you much. **1860–1** W. WHITMAN *Leaves of Grass* (ed. 3) 301 Feeling with the hand the naked meat of his own body. **1923** J. MANCHON *Le Slang* 192 *A bit of meat*, une putain. **1967** G. DAVIS in W. King *Black Short Story Anthol.* (1972) 341 Maxine's mother was never home on Saturday mornings, so I kept Maxine's three younger brothers outside while Teddy slipped the meat to her in the bedroom. **1970** G. GREER *Female Eunuch* 265 It would be unbearable, but less so, if it were only the vagina that was belittled by terms like *meat*. **1971** B. MALAMUD *Tenants* 31 I'm not saying I don't appreciate her company, especially when my meat's frying, but not when I have something I got to write. *Ibid.* 136 Sam wanted the brothers to beat up on you and crack your nuts for putting the meat to his bitch. *Ibid.* 143 I got you in bed with nothin on you You gonna eat my meat. **1971** *Black Scholar* Sept. 36/1 She was in his arms..and gabbing his erect meat. **1973** D. BARNES *See Woman* (1974) 94 I've tried the white meat..so I can understand why you might be wondering if the dark meat isn't better.

f. The centre (of a cricket bat, of the head of a golf club, etc.), esp. in phr. *to hit* (a ball) *on* or *with the meat*. *slang*.

1909 *Westm. Gaz.* 15 Jan. 4/2 If you did not take the gutta-percha ball right in the middle of the club (right 'on the meat', according to the modern abominable phrase) it declined to go at all. **1922** WODEHOUSE *Clicking of Cuthbert* ix. 203 You think..that lovely woman loses in queenly dignity when she fails to slam the ball squarely on the meat? **1925** *Country Life* 11 July 48/2 It is easy to drive a lob bowler..on the 'meat' or drive of the bat. **1959** R. FULLER *Ruined Boys* II. ix. 143 Wilkes hit the second ball of the over with the meat of the bat. **1963** *Times* 28 Jan. 4/3 It was apparent that here was the severest and purest hitter in the game at the pinnacle of his form, tuning up as though the ball were tied to the meat of his racket by a string of elastic. **1974** *Guardian* 6 Aug. 23/2 Kitchen was well held, full off the meat, by Younis at forward short leg in Arnold's first over.

5. a. *meat can, -platter, -tin, -trough, -tub* (earlier example), *vat*. **b.** *meat-chopper, -eating* sb. and adj. (examples), *-freezer, -freezing* (examples of *attrib.* use), *-packer, -packing, -producer, -producing* adj., *rationing, -tenderizer*. **d.** similative, as *meat-faced, -pink* adjs.

1897 *Outing* XXX. 284/1 For active service..the two regiments would need to be supplied with..meat cans. **1868** *Mich. Agric. Rep.* VII. 348, 1 lightning meat chopper. **1922** JOYCE *Ulysses* 302 In the course of the argument..meatchoppers..were resorted to. **1956** *Amer. Speech* XXXI. 87 Back-formations from nouns in *-er* indicating agents, such as..*meat chopper*. **1853** *Trans. Mich. Agric. Soc.* IV. 154 The Americans are notoriously a meat eating people. **1905** *Vegetarian Messenger* Jan. 14 Vegetarianism *v.* meat-eating. **1921** G. B. SHAW *Back to Methuselah* II. 77 One of his sons invented meat-eating. **1939** DYLAN THOMAS *Map of Love* 24 Sewing a shroud for a journey By the light of the meat-eating sun. **1958** A. R. RADCLIFFE-BROWN *Method in Social Anthropol.* I. v. 115 The two chief meat-eating birds. **1922** JOYCE *Ulysses* 33 The meatfaced woman, a butcher's dame. **1909** *Daily Chron.* 2 Nov. 5/4 Australian globe-trotters, meat-freezers, financiers. **1908** *Westm. Gaz.* 14 Dec. 2/1 The meat-freezing works employ over 3,000 men. **1909** *Chambers's Jrnl.* Jan. 23/1 Argentina..had in 1884 the first meat-freezing works established. **1903** E. JOHNSON *Amer. Railway Transportation* 131 The large meat-packers..own their own cars. **1921** *Daily Colonist* (Victoria, B.C.) 7 Apr. 8/1 The strike situation between the meat packers and their employees remained unchanged this morning. **1973** *Guardian* 23 Feb. 18/1, I finally got a job as a meat packer on £18 a week. **1873** *Rep. Iowa Agric. Soc. 1872* 175 The panacea for all these ills is to be found in tanneries..meat packing and curing houses, [etc.]. **1891** J. J. FLINN *Chicago* 330 Meat packing is the oldest of Chicago's industries. **1907** G. B. SHAW *Major Barbara* Pref. 179 Who chips a corner of the veneering from the huge meat packing industries of Chicago. **1974** *Daily Colonist* (Victoria, B.C.) 28 July 16/8 Meatpacking companies have reaped most of the benefits of the present subsidy while producers received very little. **1939** AUDEN & ISHERWOOD *Journey to War* i. 31 Hairy, meat-pink men. **1863** 'G. HAMILTON' *Gala-Days* 75, I decided upon a meat-platter. **1916** *Daily Colonist* (Victoria, B.C.) 2 July 7/1 (Advt.), Large Meat Platters, regular value 60 c. July Clearance each 35 c. **1909** *Westm. Gaz.* 14 Dec. 2/1 The consumer is called upon to pay £5,600,000, in order that..the Colonial meat-producer may receive the negligible gift of £350,000. **1932** J. S. HUXLEY *Probl. Relative Growth* vi. 202 Animals cannot show their full potentialities as meat-producers if kept in unfavourable nutritive conditions. *Ibid.* iii. 90 Meat-producing animals. **1918** *Times* 7 Feb. 3/1 Should the currency coupon become the basis of meat rationing, it is probable that [etc.]. **1969** *New Yorker* 27 Sept. 122/2 Unite, slaves of the steam kettle and the shakers of meat tenderizer and MSG. **1970** M. SLATER *Caribbean Cooking* 12 The pulp [of pawpaw] contains pepsin and the skin and seeds are useful as meat tenderisers. **1889** *Century Mag.* Apr. 909/2 They say that he sometimes fills an old meat-tin with water in anticipation of a long march. **1902** E. BANKS *Autobiogr. Newspaper Girl* 64, I would have been capable of going into the street and knocking down any little butcher's boy who refused peaceably to deliver up to me the contents of his wooden meat-trough. **1779** E. PARKMAN *Diary* (1899) 171 We are unhappily low in ye Meat Tub. **1847** *Rep. Comm. Patents 1846* (U.S.) 310 The mode by which I obtain a vacuum in meat vat A. for curing meat.

6. meat-ant, a name used in Australia for an ant of the genus *Iridomyrmex*, esp. *I. detectus*, a large copper-coloured ant; **meat ball** (see quot. 1970); also *fig.*; also used *attrib.* to designate a type of landing system for aircraft (*U.S. slang*); **meat-block,** a block of wood on which meat is cut up; **meat-breakfast,** a breakfast that includes a meat dish; **meat card,** a card entitling the holder to a ration of meat; **meat coupon,** one of the coupons of which a meat card is made up; **meat cube,** a small cube of concentrated meat extract; **meat-grinder,** a mincing machine; also *fig.*; **meat-head** *slang* (chiefly *U.S.*), a stupid person; so **meat-headed** *a.*, stupid; **meat hog,** a hog intended for food (*U.S.*, *rare*); **meat-hook,** (*a*) in Dict., sense 5 a; (*b*) an arm or hand *slang*; **meat-house,** (*a*) a house in which meat is hung; (*b*) *dial.*, 'a larder; *fig.* a house where a liberal allowance of good food is given' (E.D.D., *q.v.*); (*c*) *slang*, a brothel; **meat jelly,** a jelly prepared from meat; **meat loaf** = *LOAF *sb.*¹ 2 e; **meat man,** (*c*) (examples); (*d*) a man responsible for supplying meat to a camp; **meat-market,** (*c*) *slang*, a rendezvous for prostitutes, homosexuals, etc.; **meat rack** = **meat-market* (*c*); **meat ticket,** (*a*) *Mil. slang*, an identity disc; (*b*) = **meal ticket* (*b*); **meat tool** *coarse slang*, the penis; **meat train,** the men, horses, etc., conveying meat to a party; **meat-wagon** *slang* (chiefly *U.S.*), (*a*) an ambulance; (*b*) a police van, 'black Maria'; (*c*) a hearse; **meat-works** chiefly *Austral.* and *N.Z.*, an establishment where meat is processed and packed; also, a slaughterhouse.

1907 W. W. FROGGATT *Austral. Insects* 95 Most of them [*sc.* ants of the genus *Iridomyrmex*] are small, except our 'Mound Ant', sometimes known as the 'Meat Ant', *Iridomyrmex detectus*, which is the commonest and most widely distributed ant in Australia. **1952** *Coast to Coast* 101 The ant-lion had seized the meat-ant by one leg. **1970** BROWN & TAYLOR in *Insects of Australia* (Commonwealth Sci. & Industr. Res. Organization) xxxvii. 958/1 The meat ants (*Iridomyrmex* spp.) can be a serious pest around homes and food-processing plants. *c* **1838** C. MATHEWS in M. R. Booth *Eng. Plays of 19th Cent.* (1973) IV. 138 You must be content with pâté or forced meat ball. **1877** *Cassell's Dict. Cookery* 413/1 *Meat Balls, Minced, Fried.*—Take some roast mutton, some chestnuts, and neck of veal boiled in water with salt and vinegar. **1941** P. GALLICO in *Sat. Even. Post* 14 June 110/2 As for that revolting meatball, I never wish to see him again. **1957** *Economist* 31 Aug. 688/2 The mirror reflects a bright light astern and upward into a beam which the pilot follows straight to a landing by keeping the 'meatball' light precisely centred in the mirror. **1957** *New Yorker* 5 Oct. 82/3 I'll polish off a meatball sandwich. **1960** *Aeroplane* XCIX. 65/1 The equipment evaluated by the F.A.A. included the U.S.A.F. 'Meat Ball' system, the U.S. Navy mirror system. *Ibid.* 401/1 The pilot aligns the 'meatball', or blob of reflected light, in the centre of the deck-landing mirror. **1962** *Flight Internat.* LXXXII. 100/1 A steady descent at 250kt to 1,000 ft..would be followed by a further descent to 600 ft, with the talkdown continuing until the pilot picked up the 'meatball' light of the mirror sight. **1969** R. AIRTH *Snatch!* iv. 36 He looked a very tough meatball. **1970** SIMON & HOWE *Dict. Gastron.* 262/2 *Meat balls*, any combination of meat, raw or cooked, shaped into balls. **1838** E. FLAGG *Far West* II. 59 Mr. W...was on the stump, in shape of a huge meat-block at one corner of the market-house. **1857** GEO. ELIOT *Scenes Clerical Life* (1858) I. 105 The unpleasant circumstances..together with heavy meat breakfasts, may..have contributed to his desponding views. **1910** *Bradshaw's Railway Guide* Apr. 1149 *Hotel Bedford—Paris*... Room, meat breakfast, electric light.., from 6s. **1870** *Food Jrnl.* 1 Dec. 622 The restaurateurs are compelled to ask for their customers' 'meat card'. **1918** *Times* 6 Feb. 8/2 (*heading*), The London meat card. *Ibid.* 25 Feb. 9/5 Only three coupons each week of a meat card can be used for butcher's meat. *Ibid.*, You must not tear off meat coupons yourself. This duty rests with the retailer. **1919** 'I. HAY' *Last Million* 97 'Got my meat coupons?' They shook their heads... 'Better have bacon and eggs,' announced Hebe. 'They're not rationed.' **1951** *Good Housek. Home Encycl.* 392/2, 1 meat cube, or 1 tsp. meat extract. **1971** *Guardian* 19 May 8/2 Make stock with a meat cube, sieve in left-over vegetables and you have an economical soup. **1951** M. MCLUHAN *Mech. Bride* (1967) 128/1 That man..whose school training wins him the privilege of getting at once into the technological meat grinder. **1969** R. & D. DE SOLA *Dict. Cooking* 150/1 *Meat grinder*, utensil or attachment for grinding meat, usually provided with a variety of cutting blades for different grinds. **1970** W. BURROUGHS JR. *Speed* vii. 145 I'd be sucked right into the actual meatgrinder of another reel. **1972** *Listener* 17 Aug. 199/1 The North Vietnamese.. managed to tie down South Vietnam's strategic reserve.. in a gruesome 'meat-grinder'. **1945** H. I. PHILLIPS *Private Purkey's Private Peace* i. 8 'Harriet!' mocked a battered buddy. 'Honey bunch! Lissen to the meathead.' **1967** *Boston Globe* 18 May 27/3 It seems to this meat-head that the building of a branch of the state university..gives all of us a great chance to upgrade some area which needs a little up-grading. **1971** *Newsweek* 29 Nov. 52/1 Archie Bunker, the middle American hero of 'All in the Family'.. sees himself menaced by a rising tide of spades,..meat-heads,..fags and four-eyes. **1949** W. R. BURNETT *Asphalt Jungle* (1950) vi. 72 Some meat-headed tart. **1856** G. N. JONES *Florida Plantation Rec.* (1927) 169, I doe not see but verry few of the shoats that I turned out for meat hogs this year. **1919** W. H. DOWNING *Digger Dial.* 33 *Meat-hook*, arm. **1932** *Amer. Speech* VII. 334 *Meat hooks*, hands. **1945** L. SHELLY *Jive Talk Dict.* 29 *Meat hooks*, the hands. **1805** W. CLARK in Lewis & Clark *Orig. Jrnls. Lewis & Clark Expedition* (1905) III. 284 Had the Meet house covered and the Meat all hung up. **1831** J. M. PECK *Guide for Emigrants* II. 126 Around it [*sc.* the cabin] are put a meat or smoke house [etc.]. **1862** R. HENNING *Let.* 28 Aug. (1966) 95 The woolshed, meathouse..and dwelling-house are so very well put up. **1896** FARMER & HENLEY *Slang* IV. 296/2 *Meat-house*, a brothel. **1906** *Dialect Notes* III. 146 *Meat-house*,..smoke-house; a wooden shed in which smoked and preserved meats are kept. **1923** J. MANCHON *Le Slang* 192 *Meat-house*,.. maison publique. **1937** PARTRIDGE *Dict. Slang* 515/1 *Meat-house*, a brothel. **1381** *Forme of Cury* (1780) xxxvi. 103 For to make mete Gelee that it be wel chariaunt. **1865** MRS. STOWE *House & Home Papers* 248 Those fine, clear meat-jellies which form a garnish..palatable to the taste. **1965** V. HOLLAND tr. *A. Escoffier's Ma Cuisine* 67 Beef tea and meat jelly for invalids. **1932** E. CRAIG *Cooking with E. Craig* 58 (*heading*) Banana and meat loaf. **1939,** etc. Meat loaf [see *LOAF *sb.*¹ 2 e]. **1831** R. COX *Adventures Columbia River* II. x. 222 The meat-men did not return until nine this morning..but at eleven the hunters' signal drew us to the shore, and the meat-men were despatched. **1910** *Dialect Notes* III. 445 *Meat-man*,..butcher, or driver of a butcher's wagon. **1920** *Ibid.* V. 83 *Meat man*, for butcher. **1896** FARMER & HENLEY *Slang* IV. 296/2 *Meat-market*,..any *rendezvous* of public women. **1937** PARTRIDGE *Dict. Slang* 515/1 *Meat-market*, a rendezvous of harlots. **1957** J. OSBORNE *Entertainer* i. 18 Every tart and pansy boy in the district are in that place... It's just a meat-market. **1973** *Amer. Speech 1970* XLV. 58 *Meat market* n., street on which homosexuals gather, cruise, and pick up tricks. **1972** B. RODGERS *Queens' Vernacular* 132 *Meat rack*, outdoor setting..where homosexuals gather to parade their wares. **1919** W. H. DOWNING *Digger Dial.* 33 *Meat Ticket*, (or Dead Meat Ticket)—an identification disc. **1925** FRASER & GIBBONS *Soldier & Sailor Words* 154 *Meat ticket*, the identity disc. **1929** *Papers Mich. Acad. Sci., Arts & Lett.* X. 307 *Meat-ticket*, wrist-tag for purposes of identification; 'dog-tag'. **1936** P. BOTTOME *Level Crossing* xvi. 192 He'd better not try to settle too much on my meat ticket! **1948** PARTRIDGE *Dict. Forces' Slang* 117 *Meat ticket*, identity disc. **1971** B. MALAMUD *Tenants* 88 What do you do..with your meat tool? You got no girl, who do you fuck other than your hand? **1845** J. C. FRÉMONT *Rep. Exploring Expedition* 234 The meat train did not arrive this evening, and I gave Godey leave to kill our little dog. **1925** J. H. TABER *Story of 168th Infantry* I. xvi. 189 By this time all of the old members of the regiment..cheerfully referred to the ambulance as the 'meat wagon'. **1939** *Forum* (N.Y.) July 42/1 He must have pulled his rip cord because he woke up in the meatwagon. **1942** BERREY & VAN DEN BARK *Amer. Thes. Slang* § 81/13 *Hearse*, meat cart, -crate, or wagon. **1943** R. CHANDLER *Lady in Lake* (1944) xvi. 95 Murder-a-day Marlowe, they call him. They have the meat wagon following him around to follow up on the business he finds. **1954** *Britannica Bk. of Year* 637/1 The meat-wagon was the police-van in which the criminal rode to captivity. **1956** S. LONGSTREET *Real Jazz* 7 The band would march out behind the meat-wagon, black plumes on the hearse horses. **1964** *Listener* 31 Dec. 1055/2 The bogeys..bundle us into the back of a meat-wagon. **1971** 'E. MCBAIN' *Hail, Hail, Gang's all Here* i. 15 We'll need a couple of meat wagons. The minister and two other people were killed, and..there're a lot of injured. **1973** 'H. HOWARD' *Highway to Murder* xiii. 153 She hadn't deserved to become a parcel of broken flesh and bone in the meat wagon. [**1895** T. A. COGHLAN *Wealth & Progress New South Wales* I. 367 All the cattle killed, except 27,891 treated in the meat-preserving works, were required for local consumption.] **1934** WEBSTER, *Meat works*. **1948** V. PALMER *Golconda* ii. 9 Driving them across country to the meatworks at Wyndham. **1960** B. CRUMP *Good Keen Man* 46 The hut stank like a meat works. **1968** *Times* 23 Jan. (Austral. Suppl.) p. xiv/3 In one year before the meatworks opened a large property shot 10,000 scrub bulls (not branded or castrated).

meater. Restrict † *Obs.* to sense in Dict. and add: **2.** *rare.* One who eats (butcher's) meat; a meat-eater.

1920 *Contemp. Rev.* Dec. 819 The 'meater' lives at higher pressure and exhausts his energy quicker than the non-meat-eater.

meatless, *a.* Add: **2.** (Further examples.) *spec.* Of foods specially prepared or supplied for vegetarians: containing no butcher's meat.

1909 C. H. SENN (*title*) Meatless fare and lenten cookery. **1909** *Daily Chron.* 2 Nov. 7/3 Even that anomaly—to most people—'the meatless meal' is included. **1969** *Daily Tel.* 9 Oct. 16/4 The era of meatless meat, chickenless chicken and cheeseless cheese is already dawning in America. **1972** *Guardian* 8 June 7/5 Some of them [*sc.* countries] had their meatless days. *Ibid.* 31 July 2/4 The city's three big department stores..decreed meatless menus.

Hence **mea·tlessness.**

1918 *Punch* 27 Mar. 206/2 If he [*sc.* our butcher] were removed we should be plunged into absolute meatlessness.

me·bbe, me·bby, *colloq.* and *dial.* variants of MAY-BE, MAYBE (see *E.D.D.*).

1844 'J. SLICK' *High Life N.Y.* I. vi. 65 Mebby I'll mention where I got them. **1886** H. BAUMANN *Londinismen* 106/2 Mebbe. **1906** W. CHURCHILL *Coniston* I. x. 119 Mebbe I be, and mebbe I hain't. **1910** R. BROOKE *Let.* 8 June (1968) 240 Jacques'll be here about then, mebbe. **1948** E. POUND *Pisan Cantos* (1949) lxxxi. 110 A vacant lot where you'd occasionally see a wild rabbit Or mebbe only a loose one. **1961** S. CHAPLIN *Day of Sardine* vii. 148 'We're goin' to the pictures and mebbe afterwards we'll fill up with some fish and chips. **1972** *Last Whole Earth*

Catalog (Portola Inst.) 152/1 I read in *Newsweek* or somewhere that this is the New Renaissance—Mebbe so.

mebos (mī·bǫs, *Afrikaans* mē·bǫs). *S. Afr.* Also **meebos.** [Afrikaans, prob. ad. Jap. *umeboshi*, a dried, preserved plum.] A confection made from apricots dried, flattened or pulped, and preserved in salt and sugar.

1793 tr. *C. P. Thunberg's Trav. Europe, Afr. & Asia* III. 120, I saw several kinds of fruit, the produce of this country [*sc.* Japan], either dried or preserved in yeast, in a mode which is, I fancy, only practised at Japan or China. The fruit that was only dried, such as plumbs and the like, was called *Mebos.* **1899** *Answers* 18 Nov. 7/2 The best sort of preserve is called *mebos*, and is made of stoned and sun-dried apricots, flattened out, and pickled with salt and sugar. **1912** *Northern Post* 27 Sept. (Pettman), I have now come to the conclusion that our old navigators became acquainted with this delicacy in Japan, learned to like it, and afterwards at the Cape attempted to imitate it, but used the fruit of apricot trees.., and that the word *Meibos* or *Meebosje* had its origin in [Jap.] *Umeboshi.* **1939** S. Cloete *Watch for Dawn* iii. 39 He had mebos and raisins and sun-dried peaches. **1954** M. Kuttel *Quadrilles & Konfyt* i. 9 Have a jar of mebos handy on board..in case of sea-sickness. **1959** J. Collier *Stellenbosch Revisited* ii. 45 A delicacy called 'mebos' which consisted of apricots dried, flattened and treated with salt and sugar. **1974** *Eastern Province Herald* 27 Nov. 37 Mevrou Van Niekerk..fed them on mebos and honey cakes in her big farm kitchen.

Mebyon Kernow (me·byǫn kǭ·ɹno). [Cornish.] 'Sons of Cornwall', the name of a Cornish party of independence.

1962 *Rep. Comm. Broadcasting 1960* 224 in *Parl. Papers 1961–2* (Cmnd. 1753) IX. 259 We note..a submission entered by Mebyon Kernow (Sons of Cornwall) advocating a service of broadcasting for Cornwall. **1963** *Guardian* 8 Apr. 3/6 Mebyon Kernow, the Cornish home rule movement. **1967** *Ibid.* 5 Dec. 3/2 Mebyon Kernow (Sons of Cornwall) are to put forward candidates in the next general election. **1975** *Isis* 17 Oct. 9/3 Mebyon Kernow (The Sons of Cornwall), the nationalist organisation, has never demanded autonomy but the more reasonable 'self-government in domestic affairs' within the United Kingdom.

mecamylamine (me:kămai·lămīn). *Pharm.* [f. Me(thyl + **cam*(*phane* + -yl + Amine.] A potent ganglion-blocking drug, 3-methylaminoisocamphane, $C_{11}H_{21}N$, which is used in treating hypertension.

1955 *Sci. News Let.* 29 Oct. 281/1 A nerve-blocking drug called mecamylamine. **1956** *Arch. Internal Med.* XCVII. 561/1 Such side effects as constipation were just as prominent with the small completely absorbed doses of mecamylamine as with the relatively large poorly absorbed doses of other ganglion-blocking agents. **1968** L. Gyermek in A. Burger *Drugs Affecting Cent. Nervous Syst.* I. iv. 290 Mecamylamine depresses the vasomotor center independently of its ganglionic blocking action. **1971** *Nature* 17 Sept. 207/1 Previous work in this laboratory with monkeys trained to puff cigarette smoke showed that mecamylamine, a nicotinic-blocking agent, reduced their smoking. **1974** M. C. Gerald *Pharmacol.* viii. 159 Ganglionic blocking agents such as mecamylamine (Inversine)..prevent cholinergic transmission at the autonomic ganglia.

Meccano (mĭkā·no). Also **meccano.** The proprietary name of a set of metal pieces, nuts, bolts, etc., and tools, specially designed for constructing small models of buildings, machines, or other engineering apparatus; any portion of such a set. Also *attrib.* and *fig.*

1907 *Trade Marks Jrnl.* 23 Oct. 1893 Meccano... Constructional toys. Frank Hornby,..Liverpool; manufacturer of constructional models. **1908** (*title*) Meccano (mechanics made easy): manual of instructions for the whole series of models. **1924** H. De Sélincourt *Cricket Match* iii. 56, I shall make a prison cell of meccano, and pretend you're locked..inside. **1927** *Sunday at Home* Aug. 675/1 There was meccano in the goldfish bowl. **1928** *Television* May 20/1 String, cardboard, and pieces of rough wood with Meccano parts;..all combined to make the television machine. **1928** 'R. West' *Strange Necessity* ii. 199 The complete meccano set for the mind that is in The First Men in the Moon. **1930** J. B. Priestley *Angel Pavement* vi. 307 It seemed only yesterday when he was..putting the Meccano set by the boy's bedside. **1934** *Amer. Speech* IX. 167/1 An economy may be made for the foreigner by presenting to him the elementary words only, thereby substituting a linguistic Meccano for the expense of ready-made models. **1945** J. Betjeman *New Bats in Old Belfries* 45 Pressed 'neath the box of his Meccano set. **1957** *New Scientist* 25 Apr. 9/2 The vocabulary is largely a 'Meccano' vocabulary; it is built up from bits and pieces which can be stuck together in twos, threes and fours. **1960** S. R. Ranganathan *Colon Classification* (ed. 6) 13 The Meccano feature makes it necessary to give, in addition to the unit-schedules, a set of Rules for constructing Class Numbers with the aid of the unit-schedules. **1965** *Listener* 23 Sept. 464/3 In crisp Technicolor images and prose painstakingly constructed on a Meccano-like principle. **1970** J. A. Howard *Aerial Photo-Ecol.* xi. 122 The mechanical or spider templates are provided by 'meccano' type strips. **1972** R. Perry *Fall Guy* iii. 48 The suspension bridge was still standing, its graceful lines making Sydney harbour bridge look like a clumsy piece of Meccano. **1972** *Guardian* 14 Oct. 3/2 The Eiffel Tower..is quite a piece of Meccano: there are more than 18,000 structural components in the 985 ft high tower. **1973** *Ibid.* 10 Feb. 10/2 He's the sort of uncle who'd give you a Meccano set for Christmas and then stay all afternoon and tinker with it. **1974** *Trade Marks Jrnl.* 30 May 939/2 Meccano Multikit... Toys and playthings, all sold in kit form. Meccano Limited,..Liverpool,..manufacturers and merchants.

mech (mek), colloq. abbrev. of Mechanic *sb.* 3.

1951 Partridge *Dict. Slang* (ed. 4) 1107/2 *Mech*, mechanic; esp. in the old *air mech* of the R.F.C. and the current *flight mech* of the Air Force: coll.: since ca. 1912. **1968** J. Sangster *Touchfeather* xvi. 191 Bud carries a heater, the mechs don't. **1973** A. Hunter *Gently French* iii. 23 Hanson called over a mech. The mech started it for us and drove it out.

mechanic, *a.* and *sb.* Add: **B.** *sb.* **2.** *Mechanics' institute*: see also Institute *sb.*[1] 4.

d. One who cheats at gambling games, *spec.* cards; a card-sharp. *U.S.* and *Austral. slang.*

1909 in *Cent. Dict.* Suppl. **1944** D. Runyon in *Collier's* 12 Feb. 12/4 What I must know is are you a mechanic at gin? **1949** J. Scarne *On Cards* i. 1 To the average card player the man who makes his living by cheating at cards is a sharper, sharp or shark, but to card hustlers and house men he is known as a *mechanic. Ibid.* ii. 10 Some mechanics keep two fingers curled around the long edge of the deck and two around the short upper edge. **1953** Baker *Australia Speaks* v. 121 *Mechanic*, a person who cheats at cards, especially a professional card sharp (Americans use *mechanic* for a dishonest player at faro). **1966** K. Giles *Provenance of Death* v. 146 The games were straightish, no real mallarky, though Jack himself was a 'mechanic' with the cards if necessary. **1966** *Daily Tel.* (Colour Suppl.) 30 Sept. 27/2 As croupier..always on guard for the sharps—the mechanics. **1970** R. & J. Paterson *Cranberry Portage* vii. 40 He was what other gamblers called a 'mechanic', an expert manipulator of playing-cards.

mechanical, *a.* and *sb.* Add: **A.** *adj.* **3. e.** *mechanical* (*wood*) *pulp* (see quot. 1926).

1888 Cross & Bevan *Text-bk. Paper-Making* vi. 105 Mechanical Wood Pulp.—A very large quantity of pulp is used in the commoner kinds of paper, such as cheap news, etc., which is obtained by disintegrating wood by mechanical means alone. **1890** A. Watt *Art of Paper-Making* x. 113 Mechanical wood pulp is also used in a moderate degree. **1926** *Paper Terminol.* (Spalding & Hodge) ii. 17 *Mechanical wood*, the lowest grade of wood pulp prepared by the purely mechanical process of grinding. **1936** *Economist* 8 Feb. 304/1 Of sulphate as well as of mechanical pulp, both annual production and stocks have been sold out. **1937** [see *ground *ppl. a.* 4]. **1953** *Economist* 26 Sept. 883/1 Mechanical pulp, from which newsprint is made, is about 10s. a dry ton higher [than chemical pulp]. **1963** R. R. A. Higham *Handbk. Paper-Making* v. 129 Mechanical pulp is an important cheap grade used in the manufacture of papers such as newsprint, wallpaper, [etc.].

f. *mechanical twin* (Metallurgy): a twinned crystal produced by mechanical deformation; so *mechanical twinning.*

1913 *Engineering* 10 Oct. 510/3 There is now good reason to doubt that mechanical twinning ever occurs in metals. **1923** Glazebrook *Dict. Appl. Physics* V. 344/1 These internal stresses cause internal straining of the metal, which in turn causes the formation of numerous mechanical twins. **1935** G. E. Doan *Princ. Physical Metall.* iii. 77 In mechanical twinning, each atom moves a certain distance relative to the neighboring plane. **1966** *McGraw-Hill Encycl. Sci. & Technol.* VIII. 293/1 Typical phenomena observable are...effects of deformation—strain markings,..mechanical twins, and microcracks. **1966** W. J. McG. Tegart *Elem. Mech. Metall.* v. 121 Another important mode of deformation is that of mechanical twinning.

5. a. *mechanical equivalent of heat*: see Equivalent *sb.* 2 c.

8. c. *mechanical advantage* (of a machine): the ratio of the load to the force applied to the machine; *mechanical zero* (see quot. 1971[2]).

1894 W. J. Lineham *Textbk. Mech. Engin.* ix. 481 The first is the principle of virtual velocities, and the second mechanical advantage. **1962** A. Nisbett *Technique Sound Studio* v. 94 A reversed-reading instrument is used: it has its mechanical zero at the right-hand end of the scale and is deflected back to the scale zero (its 'electrical zero') by a steady current. **1971** B. Scharf *Engin. & Its Lang.* ix. 68 To calculate the efficiency of a machine we divide the real mechanical advantage by the ideal mechanical advantage and multiply the result by 100%. **1971** *Gloss. Electrotechnical, Power, Terms* (*B.S.I.*) i. iv. 9 *Mechanical zero*, equilibrium position which the index will approach when the measuring element..is de-energized.

10. *Comb.*, as *mechanical-minded* adj.

1947 J. Steinbeck *Wayward Bus* xvii. 223, I suppose people really think they are mechanical-minded.

B. *sb.* **1.** (Later examples.)

1963 *Times* 20 Apr. 4/1 The play scene is omitted and the rest of the mechanicals, a couple of fellows boldly designated on the programme as 'Bottom's Friends', are left deliberately vague. **1968** *Listener* 1 Feb. 148 Frivolity seems to me the only, precarious excuse for this novel—a let-out, for instance, for treating the income-earning group as characters and the rest as 'mechanicals'.

3. *Printing.* The artwork and 'copy' as finally assembled. Also *transf.*

1967 V. Strauss *Printing Industry* xi. 744/2 At its simplest, the mechanical is a piece of artists' illustration board, somewhat larger than the final size of the printed piece. To this board are attached, by cementing or pasting.., a number of line images, all in the same focus and, of course, of inspected quality. This board bears, furthermore, all notations that will enable it to serve as the blueprint of the job. **1967** Karch & Buber *Offset Processes* iii. 47 This final assembly of reading matter and artwork for the printer is called a *mechanical.* **1967** *Britannica Bk. of Year* (U.S.) 66 Many regulations, particularly in relation to TV, prevented advertisers from using international campaigns if the basic mechanicals—artwork, films, and so on—were not produced in Italy by Italians. **1973** *Publishers Weekly* 12 Mar. 38 The layout [of an advertisement] was changed at the last minute, and the mechanical bearing [the publisher] Quadrangle's name either was not replaced, or it fell off.

mechanicalization (mĭkæ:nikălaizē·ʃən). [f. Mechanicalize *v.* + -ation.] The being or becoming mechanical in character or in means of operation; *esp.* in military terminology.

1922 *Glasgow Herald* 5 Jan. 4 A record of experimental progress towards mechanicalisation of wireless telegraphy in as simple and portable a form as possible. **1924** *Westm. Gaz.* 26 Mar., Colonel Rudkin..proved himself an expert on mechanicalisation—the new word to indicate army tendencies. **1924** *Times Lit. Suppl.* 16 Oct. 654/4 The mechanicalization of the army. **1926** *Glasgow Herald* 27 Aug. 11 Military minds turn to 'mechanicalisation', an ugly word but an indication of the abolition of what Tommy Atkins terms 'foot-slogging'. **1927** *Sunday Times* 6 Mar. 20/3 The real benefits that result from a mechanicalisation of industry.

mechanicalize, *v.* Add: (Later examples.) Hence **mecha·nicalized** *ppl. a.*

1924 *Army Q.* Oct. 39 The first step suggested is that the divisional transport should be mechanicalized. **1926** *Glasgow Herald* 9 Sept. 9 One of the problems studied..was the landing of a mechanicalised force on an open beach in the face of opposition.

mechanically, *adv.* Add: **7.** *Comb.*, as *mechanically-minded* adj.

1922 *Guardian* 19 May, Any mechanically-minded person can make a simple receiving set for a pound or two. **1937** B. H. L. Hart *Europe in Arms* xvii. 231 Some doubt must remain..as to the ability of horse-minded soldiers to become mechanically minded. **1972** G. Durrell *Catch me a Colobus* ii. 45 Oscar the orang-utan,..the most mechanically-minded of all the apes.

mechanicism. Delete *Obs. rare*[−1] and add further examples.

1962 W. Stark *Fund. Forms of Social Thought* ii. xii. 176 A fresh high-water mark of mechanicism was reached in the eighth decade of the nineteenth century. **1971** *Archivum Linguisticum* II. 115 But if to avoid the limitations of Kuryłowicz's method, we have to admit that a form passes arbitrarily from one function to another, not taking into account the facts of polarization, attraction, etc., then we fall into mechanicism.

mechanicist (mĭkæ·nisist). [f. Mechanic *a.* and *sb.* + -ist.] = Mechanicalist.

1934 *Mind* XLIII. 248 'Mechanical' is a highly ambiguous term, and many who call themselves mechanicists would not deem it inconsistent with their principles to recognise in the molecule a different unit from the atom, with different properties. **1936** *Nature* 4 Apr. 559/2 Haldane asserts that the real universe is a universe of personality and the manifestation of God... No doubt materialists and mechanicists would take exception to some of the arguments. **1939** *Ibid.* 8 July 52/2 Controversies about the philosophy of animate Nature..keep alive the old feud between vitalists and mechanicists. The latter favour the view that life is a by-product of blind processes of dead matter.

mechanico-. Add: *mechanico-acoustic*, *-material* adjs.: **mechanico-morphic** *a.* = *mechanomorphic *a.*; **mechanico-morphism** = **mechanomorphism*; **mechanico-physical** *a.*, of or pertaining to the philosophy which explains all phenomena as the outcome of the physical laws of the motions and interactions of matter.

1964 Y. R. Chao in D. Abercrombie et al. *Daniel Jones* 39 The mechanico-acoustic set-up for recording speech on wax masters. **1920** D. H. Lawrence *Touch & Go* 9 The strike situation..is a mechanico-material struggle, two mechanical forces pulling asunder from the central object, the bone. **1937** *Mind* XLVI. 176 We wish to stress here what we conceive to be the inadequacy of all 'mechanico-morphic' representations of concrete becoming in nature. **1935** J. Murphy tr. *Schrödinger's Sci. & Human Temperament* Introd. 19 We must..abandon the mechanical structure. We must turn to the statistical concept... In other words, Schrödinger pleads for the abandonment of what may be called mechanico-morphism in the pursuit of natural science,..the casting aside of all models and the wholesale employment of mathematical formulas in their stead. **1890** W. James *Princ. Psychol.* II. xxviii. 666 The modern mechanico-physical philosophy..which..includes the nebular cosmogony, the conservation of energy, the kinetic theory of heat and gases, etc.,..begins by saying that..the only laws [are] the changes of motion which changes in collocation bring.

mechanics. Add: **3.** *transf.* The procedural or operational details (*of* something).

1925 E. B. Wilson *Cell* (ed. 3) ii. 172 This fact is fundamentally important for the mechanics of mitosis. **1930** *Writer* Sept. 265/2 Is the playwright perpetually making references in his dialogue to the mechanics of his craft? **1932** *Punch* 13 Jan. 55/1 Miss E. B. C. Jones is well up in the mechanics of psycho-analysis. **1940** *Punch* 10 Apr. 407/3 It is a pity the mechanics of the story take up so much of the time. **1960** L. Picken *Organization of Cells* viii. 373 (*heading*) The mechanics and energetics of changes in cell shape. **1974** *Nature* 22 Mar. 280/3 Speakers at current meetings in the field generally give little information on how their results are actually obtained, that is, the pure mechanics of the business.

mechanism. Add: **2.** (Later examples.) Also used, esp. *Psychol.*, of the means or agency by which mental processes and bodily actions are caused to take place (cf. quot. 1885 in Dict.).

1910 G. N. Calkins *Protozool.* i. 29 Bodies closely associated with the mechanism of nuclear division and of locomotion. **1913** J. S. Haldane *Mechanism, Life & Personality* i. 9 Descartes, in his writings about the nervous system,..suggested nervous mechanisms. *Ibid.* ii. 58 The real difficulty for the mechanistic theory is that we are forced..to postulate that the germ-plasm is a mechanism of enormous complexity and definiteness, and..that this mechanism..can divide and combine with other similar mechanisms. **1921** H. C. Miller *New Psychol. & Teacher* 161 This mental mechanism [*sc.* the complex] lies at the root of all bias, all injustice, and all inability to think clearly. **1924** *Brit. Weekly* 28 Aug. 471/3 He will see strange recesses in human personality and unsuspected mechanisms fashioning religious beliefs. **1929** K. S. Lashley (*title*) Brain mechanisms and intelligence. **1941** *Psychosomatic Med.* July 227/1 The adaptive mechanisms by means of which the organism strives to achieve this goal. *Ibid.* 233/1 By 'cognitive field' or 'practical insight' we mean a mechanism capable of registering and integrating stimuli. **1958** *Amer. Jrnl. Psychiatry* Sept. 204/2 The brain, unlike a machine into which any mechanism can be set, appears to have mechanisms of its own. **1964** Cofer & Appley *Motivation* xi. 573 Conceptions of learned drive basically assert that responses which produce strong stimuli are the mechanisms of such drives. **1968** M. Bunge in Lakatos & Musgrave *Probl. Philos. Sci.* 128 Something mediating between inputs and outputs, i.e. a mechanism triggered by the inputs and which has the required outputs. **1972** *Physics Bull.* Mar. 141/1 Furthermore some mechanism must be found for judging the quality of the work done by the chief scientist and the controller.

6. Delete † *Obs.* and add earlier and later examples.

1690 Locke *Hum. Und.* i. iii. 22 Thereby making Men no other than bare Machins... And upon that ground they must necessarily reject all Principle of Vertue, who cannot put Morality and Mechanism together. **1902** Baldwin *Dict. Philos. & Psychol.* II. 59/1 In biology: mechanism is opposed to vitalism, and in more recent controversy to neovitalism. **1909, 1917** [see *finalism 2]. **1956** O. L. Zangwill in A. Pryce-Jones *New Outl. Mod. Knowl.* 170 *Mechanism* has sought to account for all behaviour in terms of the quasi-automatic activities of the central nervous system.

mechanist. **3.** Delete † *Obs.* and add later examples. Also as *adj.*

1913 J. S. Haldane *Mechanism, Life & Personality* i. 6 The constant controversies..between mechanists and non-mechanists. **1919** G. B. Shaw *Heartbreak House* p. xv, Their mechanist theory taught them that medicine was the business of the chemist's laboratory, and surgery of the carpenter's shop. **1925** C. D. Broad *Mind & its Place* 43 One feels that the disputes between Mechanists and Vitalists are unsatisfactory. **1931** *Brit. Jrnl. Psychol.* Oct. 137 Those whom their opponents call 'vitalists' can see in the relationship an attribute of something living. Those whom their opponents dub 'mechanists' can see in the relationship [between association processes and neuronic excitation] a property they attribute to mechanism. **1965** *Listener* 19 Aug. 286/2 Pain due to emotional disturbance..arises in the mind (or in the brain if you tend to be a mechanist).

mechanistic, *a.* Add: (Later examples.) Also, pertaining to or holding mechanical theories in psychology and linguistics.

1915 B. Holmes in *Chicago Med. Recorder* Mar. 2 (*heading*) The Mechanistic view of Dementia Precox. **1923** W. McDougall *Outl. Psychol.* i. 30 All the varieties of psychology which propose..to replace the hypothesis of a mind, a soul, a self, [etc.].., by that of a brain or a bodily organism working on strictly mechanical or physical principles..may be conveniently classed together as mechanistic psychologies. **1924** W. B. Selbie *Psychol. Relig.* 278 On the negative side they have adduced evidence of a kind which makes a merely mechanistic explanation of the universe impossible. **1933** L. Bloomfield *Lang.* 33 The *materialistic* (or, better, *mechanistic*) theory supposes that the variability of human conduct, including speech, is due only to the fact that the human body is a very complex system. **1939** *Ann. Reg. 1938* 301 The Government's revenue would be so great that extinction of the debt would be automatic. This 'mechanistic' theory was severely ridiculed. **1952** J. Drever *Dict. Psychol.* 163 *Mechanistic theory*,..the interpretation of psychological processes on a mechanical basis, and denial of the reality or efficacy of ends and purposes. **1963** Marx & Hillix *Syst. & Theories Psychol.* ii. ix. 203 One man, Gustav Fechner, seems to have shared the mechanistic-romantic conflict with Freud. **1966** M. Pei *Gloss. Ling. Terminol.* Mechanistic theory,..an approach to language and linguistics based on objective methodology in recording and classifying language phenomena. **1967** R. A. Waldron *Sense & Sense Devel.* ix. 201 The rather more austere and mechanistic tendency of twentieth-century linguistics has given such phraseology a quaint, old-fashioned air. **1968** M. Bunge in Lakatos & Musgrave *Probl. Philos. Sci.* 128 The first approach can be called phenomenological or global, the second mechanistic or atomistic.

mechani·stically, *adv.* [f. Mechanistic *a.*] In a mechanistic manner; on mechanistic principles.

1923 W. McDougall *Outl. Psychol.* vi. 189 One attempt to explain mechanistically this fundamental type of profiting by experience has been widely accepted. **1925** C. D. Broad *Mind & its Place* ii. 77 The attempts which have been made..to treat mental phenomena mechanistically. **1935** *Mind* XLIV. 88 If you show that mental activity has independent causal powers, and that it works purposively and not mechanistically, surely [etc.]. **1947** J. C. Rich *Materials & Methods of Sculpture* xi. 350 Metal negative molds..are used commercially for mechanistically manufacturing papier mâché reproductions in large quantities. **1961** *N. & Q.* June 237/2 Mr. White's method is usually to utter a few simple principles about the art of fiction.. and then test them rather mechanistically against his author's four novels. **1971** *Nature* 25 June 495/2 This situation looks unlikely to change, unless there is more collaboration in the design of mechanistically meaningful experiments. **1974** Frith & McLauchlan in R. K. Harris *Nucl. Magn. Resonance* III. xii. 393 CIDNP is normally most useful mechanistically when performed in the high field of a normal spectrometer.

mechanization. (Later examples.)

1915 A. W. Gough *God's Strong People* 32 A tyranny built..on a degradation and mechanization of the personal power. **1928** *Daily Mail* 7 Feb. 7/5 The 'mechanisation' of the army. **1937** *Daily Express* 11 Jan. 10/2 Mechanisation has come to the farmer. **1954** [see *automation]. **1960** *Post Office Electr. Engineers' Jrnl.* LIII. ii. 75/2 The mechanization of the trunk service, involving the installation of automatic trunk exchanges..is now well advanced.

mechanize, *v.* **1.** Add to def.: To change (an industry, etc.) to a mechanical form of working; to provide with machines; spec. *Mil.*, to equip with mechanical weapons and vehicles, as tanks, armoured cars, etc.

1942 E. Waugh *Put out More Flags* i. 21 The yeomanry ..had recently been mechanized, in the sense that they had had their horses removed; few of them had ever seen a tank. **1952** *Oxf. Jun. Encycl.* VI. 286/2 The spreading of farmyard manure and other winter jobs have been mechanized. **1957** *Encycl. Brit.* II. 412/2 The Germans had broken abruptly with the past by mechanizing their artillery.

mechanized, *ppl. a.* Add further examples, esp. in *Mil.* sense: of, pertaining to, equipped with, or using mechanical vehicles and weapons.

1928 *Daily Mail* 8 Feb. 7/5 The fast two-seater tanks of the mechanised army. **1939** *Punch* 8 Nov. 504/1 Their plan..was to attack..the Maginot line..along the whole extent from North to South, at the same time executing a turning mechanized movement through..Switzerland. **1941** *Picture Post* 3 May 19/1 Mechanised warfare and careful preparation have again defeated flesh and blood. **1941** *Punch* 16 July 59/2 Enemy mechanized units penetrated our defences. **1942** *Times* (Weekly ed.) 7 Jan. 4 The conscience of humanity is still a factor of which even the lords of mechanized war may have to take account. **1942** *R.A.F. Jrnl.* 16 May 9 A vital means of countering the German Panzer and mechanised troops. **1968** R. M. Ogorkiewicz *Design & Devel. Fighting Vehicles* i. 30 Some of the new ideas were explored in a series of experiments which began with the Experimental Mechanised Force assembled in 1927 on Salisbury Plain. **1970** Macksey & Batchelor *Tank* 33/1 It is one of the paradoxes of early mechanised warfare that the technologists not only produced the machines but also foresaw their tactical possibilities ahead of the soldiers.

mechano- (me·kăno), repr. Gr. μηχανο-, comb. form of μηχανή Machine *sb.*, and used in the senses (*a*) 'machine(s)'. as in Mechanology, (*b*) 'mechanical (and)', as in Mechanotherapy, *mechanochemical *a.* Also **me:chanoca·loric** *a. Physics* [*caloric *a.*], applied to the phenomenon by which a flow of the superfluid form of liquid helium (helium II) generates a difference in temperature between the sending and receiving ends; **me:chano-ele·ctric, -ele·ctrical** *adjs.*, pertaining to or producing a conversion of mechanical movements into corresponding electrical effects; also **me:chano-electro·nic** *a.* (*rare*).

1939 Mendelssohn & Daunt in *Nature* 29 Apr. 720/1 The mechano-caloric effect is evidently the reverse of the 'fountain phenomenon', for whereas the latter means that the setting up of a temperature difference results in a flow of liquid helium II, the mechano-caloric effect shows that a flow of liquid helium II is accompanied by a development of heat (or cold). **1964** *New Scientist* 24 Sept. 773/1 Shortly after the discovery of this 'thermo-mechanical' effect the complementary 'mechano-caloric' phenomenon was observed. **1958** *Jrnl. Gen. Physiol.* XLI. 1245 (*heading*) The sites for mechano-electric conversion in a pacinian corpuscle. *Ibid.* 1263 The simplest interpretation of our results would seem to be that the entire mechanoelectric transducer lies in the membrane of the nonmyelinated ending. **1974** *Nature* 1 Mar. 69/2 Isometric tension was measured with two RCA 5734 mechanoelectric transducers. **1961** M. L. Gayford *Acoustical Techniques & Transducers* vi. 279 Trying to obtain a perfect electrical copy of the groove excursion by the mechano-electrical groove-following means provided by a gramophone pick-up. **1974** *Nature* 20–27 Dec. 728/1 The muscle fibre was..mounted horizontally with one of its tendons hooked to the anode of a RCA 5734 mechanoelectrical transducer tube. **1950** *18th Internat. Physiol. Congr. Copenhagen* 171 The movements of the membrane ..are communicated to the plate of a mechano-electronic transducer (R.C.A. 5734), a triode which by means of a pivoted anode translates mechanical movements into electric current variations.

mechanochemistry (me:kănoke·mistri). [f. prec. + Chemistry.] The study or phenomenon of mechanochemical processes.

1928 P. M. Travis *Mechanochemistry* 3 This new science of mechanical dispersion, involving the principles of physical chemistry, I am calling 'Mechanochemistry', because it involves dispersion or deflocculation by mechanical means rather than by chemical. **1951** *Jrnl. Polymer Sci.* VII. 407 A simplified model which discloses the principles of the mechanochemistry of polyelectrolytes will be shown here. **1961** *New Scientist* 2 Mar. 548/3 In the USSR ..the field of investigation has been aptly named 'mechanochemistry', in line with 'electrochemistry' and 'photochemistry'. **1972** *Science* 3 Nov. 460/2 A complete understanding of the sliding filament model for generating flagellar bending waves must include an understanding of the mechanochemistry of the active sites at the molecular level.

Hence **me:chanoche·mical** *a.*, pertaining to both mechanics and chemistry; *spec.* able to convert chemical energy directly into mechanical energy; **me:chanoche·mically** *adv.*

1949 W. Garner *Textile Laboratory Manual* i. 14 (*heading*) Mechano-chemical methods for single fibres. **1949** A. Katchalsky in *Experientia* V. 320/1 In the phenomena discussed here the chemical ionization energy is transformed directly into mechanical energy. We may therefore regard them as the first synthetic examples of mechanochemical systems. **1961** *New Scientist* 2 Mar. 549/2 The action of an internal combustion engine causes substantial changes in lubricating oil viscosity due to mechanochemical breakdown of the polymer being sheared between the narrow clearances. *Ibid.* 550/3 Mechanochemically initiated polymerization has been found to occur with a large variety of polymerizable substances using substrates other than rubber. **1964** *Oceanogr. & Marine Biol.* II. 198 Takata suggested that in *Acetabularia* there may be an ATP sensitive protein that forms a mechanochemical system controlling protoplasmic streaming. **1972** *Science* 3 Nov. 460/2 The basic mechanochemical process by which energy from ATP dephosphorylation is used to produce mechanochemical work may be very similar to the active sliding process. **1974** *Nature* 31 May 475/2 Exergonic band cleavage would therefore occur in the mechanochemically coupled step.

mechanomorphic (me:kănomǭ·ɹfik), *a.* [f. *mechano- + Gr. μορφή form + -ic.] Having the form or qualities of a machine or mechanism; of or pertaining to the Deity regarded as a mechanical force. Hence **me:chanomo·rphism**, the concept of something (esp. the Deity) as mechanomorphic.

a **1885** D. D. Whedon *Ess., Rev. & Discourses* (1887) 265 A still more curious notion of dignity..rejects the *anthropomorphic* and substitutes therefor a *mechanomorphic* theory. **1926** B. H. Streeter *Reality* i. 2 Materialism pictures the Universe as an Infinite Machine; this by analogy may be called mechanomorphism. *Ibid.* 22 Mechanomorphic materialism. **1937** A. Huxley *Ends & Means* ix. 124 They have felt the effects of mechanomorphism. **1950** —— *Themes & Variations* 197 Cubists, who liked to paint machines or to represent human figures as though they were parts of machines..representation of human beings in a mechanomorphic guise.

mechanoreceptor (me:kănorĭse·ptǭɹ). *Physiol.* Also **mechano-receptor.** [f. *mechano- + Receptor.] A sensory receptor which responds to mechanical stimuli, such as pressure changes resulting from touch or sound.

1927 J. H. Parsons *Introd. Theory Perception* i. 7 Receptors which are found in animals may be classified into three groups..chemo-receptors, mechano-receptors, and radio-receptors. *Ibid.* 9 Mechano-receptors can be divided into two classes, contact and distance receptors. **1951** *Sci. Amer.* Jan. 17/2 Among these mechano-receptors are the receptor organs for rotatory and translatory motion in the inner ear, the receptors responsible for the pressure sense of the skin, the muscle spindles imbedded in all muscles that fix and move bodily masses, and the so-called Pacinian or Vater's corpuscles found throughout the connective tissues. **1970** *Nature* 28 Mar. 1263/2 These passive movements are perceived by mechanoreceptors of the pedicel.

Hence **me:chanorece·ption,** the process by which a mechanical stimulus is converted by a mechanoreceptor into a nervous impulse; **me:chanorece·ptive** *a.*, capable of performing mechanoreception.

1951 *Jrnl. Physiol.* CXV. 16 The mechanoreceptive area was localized by touching the tongue with a thin wire while listening to the pressure impulses in the loudspeaker. **1958** *Jrnl. Gen. Physiol.* XLI. 1249 (*heading*) Mechanoreception after excision of capsular structure. **1968** R. T. Verrillo in D. R. Kenshalo *Skin Senses* vii. 139 (*heading*) A duplex mechanism of mechanoreception. **1974** *Nature* 26 Apr. 740/2 Neuromas in man must..contain mechanoreceptive endings since they are always tender when gently palpated.

meclozine (me·klǒzin, -īn). *Pharm.* Also **meclizine.** [f. Me(thyl + C(h)lo(rine *sb.* + Pipera)zine.] A piperazine derivative, $C_{25}H_{27}N_2Cl$, which is an antihistamine drug used mainly as an anti-emetic, esp. in preventing motion-sickness, and is usu. given as the dihydrochloride, a white crystalline compound.

Meclozine is the name in the *British Pharmocopœia*, *meclizine* that in the *Pharmacopeia of the U.S.A.*

1955 *Jrnl. Pharmacol. & Exper. Therap.* CXV. 483 From a perceptual-motor viewpoint there would seem to be no valid reason why operating personnel could not take advantage of the beneficial effects which cyclizine, meclizine and promethazine have upon motion sickness. **1957** *Brit. Pharmaceut. Codex 1954* Suppl. 39 Meclozine

hydrochloride has the properties of the anti-histamine drugs. **1959** *Which?* July 69/1 The 1 mg. of hyoscine protected over 80 per cent of the subjects from sea-sickness, and..this dose, for one hour, was significantly more effective than the cyclizine and meclozine. **1963** *Times* 27 May 18/4 (Advt.), The thalidomide tragedy did not directly affect your Company, but one of our most widely prescribed products, which contains meclozine, is for use in pregnancy sickness... Near the end of the year meclozine itself came under criticism. **1965** *New Scientist* 4 Nov. 328/2 Anti-histamines, containing meclizine, cyclizine and chlorcyclizine must now carry a strong warning label. **1971** J. J. BURNS in B. N. La Du et al. *Fund. Drug Metabolism & Drug Disposition* xvii. 361 Although large doses of chlorcyclizine and meclizine can induce malformations in laboratory animals, no evidence of harm to the human fetus has been reported.

Mec Vannin (mek væ·nin). [Manx, lit. 'sons of (the Isle of) Man'.] Name of a Manx nationalist party.

1966 *Isle of Man Weekly Times* 7 Jan. 8/2 (*heading*) Mec Vannin... Manx Nationalists could not be fully convinced by the argument that..the banks and the houses ..are still Manx..even though their ownership and administration is increasingly passing out of native hands. *Ibid.* 8/3 The man who comes to open a shop, or a boarding-house or a factory, which will be run by himself in the Island, is a candidate for Mec Vannin. **1974** *Times* 8 Apr. 4/6 Mec Vannin..intends to field candidates for all the Tynwald seats at the next general election.

med.[1], **med** (med). (*a*) Abbrev. of MEDIC *sb.* or MEDICAL *sb.* 1; (*b*) abbrev. of MEDICAL *a.*; (*c*) abbrev. of MEDICINE *sb.*[1]

(*a*) **1851** [see MEDIC *sb.*]. **1853** in Farmer & Henley *Slang* (1896) IV. 298/1 Take..Sixteen interesting meds, With dirty hands and towzeled heads. **1899** A. H. QUINN *Pennsylvania Stories* 19 The Meds waited till the visitors were opposite them. **1942** [see (*b*) below].

(*b*) **1933** PARTRIDGE *Slang To-day & Yesterday* III. iii. 190 Of the 'plural' variety [of abbreviation] is *med. lab.*, medical laboratory. **1942** BERREY & VAN DEN BARK *Amer. Thes. Slang* § 529/2 Doctor; physician,..*med*,..*med man*. *Ibid.* § 529/5 Medical student,..*med*. *Ibid.* § 530/9 Medical college,..*med college* or *school*. *Ibid.* § 534/1 *Med business*, the medical profession. **1955** in *Amer. Speech* (1956) XXXI. 233 The law students began the boress by storming the Medical Building singing about the evils of the med students. **1974** *Spartanburg* (S. Carolina) *Herald* 18 Apr. A3/2 The lawmakers from Charleston County, site of the existing med school, are opposed to the move.

(*c*) **1942** BERREY & VAN DEN BARK *Amer. Thes. Slang* § 531/8 Medicine; drugs, *dope*, *med*. *Ibid.* § 831/22 *Courses of study*... Medicine, *med*. **1962** 'E. MCBAIN' *Like Love* (1964) xi. 158 A page out of a textbook, elementary stuff, we had this in first-year med. **1973** H. MCCLOY *Change of Heart* vii. 71, I want to study psychiatry when I get through med.

Med[2] (med). Abbrev. of MEDITERRANEAN *sb.* 1. Also *attrib.*

1948 in PARTRIDGE *Dict. Forces' Slang*. **1955** G. FREEMAN *Liberty Man* I. i. 14 We went all round the Med., Istanbul, Capri, Gib. **1960** 'S. HARVESTER' *Chinese Hammer* ii. 26 He is off-course over the Med heading for Turkey. **1962** *Punch* 3 Oct. 486/1 Hoardings are turning Med-blue. **1971** *Guardian* 6 July 11/5 The summer cruise of the Med Fleet was a grand affair.

‖ **médaillon** (medaiyoṅ). [Fr., lit. = medallion.] A small, flat, round or oval-shaped cut of meat or fish.

1900 [see *ESCALOPE]. **1921** W. J. LOCKE *Mountebank* xvi. 207 A *médaillon de veau périgourdine*, a superimposition of toast, *foie gras*, veal and truffles. **1964** L. JOYCE-COWEN *Million Menus* 90 a Lobster médaillons with Gruyère cheese soufflé topping. **1971** *Guardian* 4 June 11/4 Medaillons of Pork Tenderloin.

medal, *sb.* **1.** Delete '† *Obs.*' and add later examples.

1922 JOYCE *Ulysses* 622 A pious medal he had that saved him. **1972** *Sci. Amer.* Feb. 57/2 (Advt.), Medals are recognized as a beautiful medium for artistic expression, as will be exemplified in this fine art series.

2. b. Freq. with a defining word indicating the degree of excellence attained, as in *gold medal* (see *GOLD[1] 1 b), *silver medal* (see *SILVER *sb.* and *a.* IV. 21), *bronze medal*.

1852 C. FOX *Let.* 29 Sept. in *Jrnls.* (1972) 207 They have not hesitated to give Anna Maria two bronze medals. **1908** T. A. COOK *Olympic Games* i. 16 For all these gold, silver, and bronze prize medals have been allotted. **1973** P. O'DONNELL *Silver Mistress* vii. 133 That may not be a hundred percent right, but do I get a bronze medal for trying?

4. medal chief *U.S.*, an Indian chief who received a medal from the Colonial or U.S. authorities; **medal ribbon**, a ribbon of specific colours and design for attaching a particular medal or for wearing without a medal; **medal round** *Golf*, a round of medal-play.

1772 D. TAITT *Let.* in N. D. Mereness *Trav. Amer. Colonies* (1916) 518 [Letter] To the Great and Small medal chiefs. **1813** *Niles' Reg.* V. 270/2 At this moment a medal chief of the Choctaw nation is soliciting to be employed. *a* **1816** B. HAWKINS *Sk. Creek Country* (1848) 27 He is one of the great medal chiefs. **1909** *Westm. Gaz.* 4 Oct. 1/3 The medal-ribbon which a soldier tore off his tunic. **1944** *R.A.F. Jrnl.* Aug. 286, I did not recognize his medal-ribbon, so asked what it was. **1971** *Daily Tel.* (Colour Suppl.) 16 July 5/3 The steward..looked too distinguished with his medal ribbons to be tipped. **1898** W. A. MORGAN '*House*' *on Sport* I. 180 It does not at all follow that the man who can play a match can also play a medal round. **1909** *Westm. Gaz.* 27 Aug. 12/3 It was arranged to play a medal round in the forenoon.

medallist. 3. (Later examples.)

1968 *Times* 18 Oct. 12/1 Tommie Smith, together with the bronze medallist, John Carlos, has made sporting history. **1973** M. MACKINTOSH *King & Two Queens* xvi. 220 Don't be a heroine. I didn't choose an Olympic gold medallist.

medarsa, var. MADRASAH.

1920 *Blackw. Mag.* Dec. 750/1 The 'universities'—'Medarsas'—of Fez and Marrakesh..are now open once more to the Christian visitor.

meddlesome, *a.* Add: *Meddlesome Matty* (or *Mattie*): a nickname for a meddlesome person (allusively, from quot. 1814).

1814 A. & J. TAYLOR *Orig. Poems* (ed. 11) II. 3 (*title*) Meddlesome Matty. [Not in 1805 ed.] [**1923** D. H. LAWRENCE *Kangaroo* xi. 230 Jaz is a meddlesome-Patty.] **1927** *Times* 17 Aug. 11/5 My warning was addressed to those who would make of the League 'a kind of international Meddlesome Matty'. **1938** A. G. MACDONELL *Autobiogr. of Cad* xxi. 259 Every reformer finds his obstructionists... In both cases Meddlesome Matties were to blame. **1960** D. HOLMAN-HUNT *My Grandmothers & I* iv. 92 Good gracious, child, what a meddlesome matty you are.

Mede, *sb.* **1.** (Further examples.)

c **1384**, **1526**, **1880** [see *ELAMITE *sb.* and *a.*]. **1930** J. D. DUFF tr. *Rostovtzeff's Hist. Anc. World* (ed. 2) viii. 123 The Iranian tribes of Medes and Mannai..grew stronger by degrees, and their pressure upon Assyria steadily increased. **1969** J. CONWAY tr. *Bengtson's Greeks & Persians* i. 5 Cyaxares the Mede seized the last, ephemeral Assyrian kingdom. *Ibid.*, Greek tradition mentions the Medes and the Assyrians in one breath.

medersa, var. MADRASAH.

1923 G. CASSERLEY *Algeria To-Day* iii. 58 There is a finely-built Medersa or theological college for Mahommedans. **1935** *Times Lit. Suppl.* 3 Jan. 4/3 President of a *medersa*—that is, an Arabic University—and commandant of the neighbouring fort of Gouridam. **1968** *Vogue* 15 Apr. 124/2 Fès, the ancient university city of Morocco ..this crowded ancient place of mosques and medersas.

medevac (me·dĭvæk). *U.S.* Also **medivac.** [f. MED(ICAL *a.* + EVAC(UATION.] A military helicopter for transporting wounded soldiers to hospital. Hence **Medevac, Med-Evac** *v. trans.*, to transport by medevac.

1966 [see *HELI-]. **1967** *Harper's Mag.* Jan. 77 The two wounded Aid Men continued to crawl about and administer care. There would be no medevac; there was no landing zone for it. **1969** *Time* 28 Nov. 23 At My Lai, Ridenhour reported, one soldier shot himself in the foot so that he would be Medevacked out of the area. **1973** *Washington Post* 13 Jan. A. 3/3 You look at an NLF (National Liberation Front) soldier who can't get Med-Evac'ed in 20 minutes. **1973** *Maclean's Mag.* July 17/3 While McCoy attended his patients, and the nurses and Thomas stood by, Logozar and Hartwell debated who would fly the medivac.

medi- (mī·di). *Zool.* = MEDIO-.

1903 *Amer. Anthropologist* V. 627 The meditemporal [fissure] consists of a segment in the cephalic region of the lobe, 6 cm. in length. *Ibid.* 631 The medifrontal [fissure] springs from the orbitofrontal.

media. Add: Esp. as pl. of *MEDIUM *sb.* 5. Also erron. as sing. in same sense (cf. *MASS MEDIUM note). Also *attrib.* or as *adj.*

1923 [see *MASS MEDIUM]. **1927** *Amer. Speech* III. 26 It was finally decided to allot a definite media to each member. *Ibid.*, One of the best advertising medias in the middle west. **1929** E. O. HUGHES *Outl. Advertising* v. 82 The advertising *media* to which reference will be made.. are newspapers, journals, magazines and such-like printed publications. **1958** *Times Lit. Suppl.* 5 Dec. 698/5 The media which appeal to our visually conscious age call for organizing ability as well as individual talent. **1962** M. MCLUHAN *Gutenberg Galaxy* 246 Is not the essence of education civil defence against media fall-out? **1966** K. AMIS in *New Statesman* 14 Jan. 51/3 The treatment of *media* as a singular noun..is spreading into the upper cultural strata. **1966** *Economist* 10 Dec. 1166/1 In any recession, media buyers, never a very adventurous lot, stay with the safest bets in any advertising medium. **1968** *Sun* (Baltimore) 4 July A16/3 Then there is 'media coordinator', that is, a tape recorder operator. **1969** T. PARSONS *Politics & Social Struct.* III. x. 250 Different media (or often the same media) carry qualitatively different content. **1971** *Daily Tel.* 4 Nov. 17/4 Decrees laid down in 1965 formally forbid direct contact between the [Dutch] Royal House and the publicity media. **1971** *Radio Times* 18 Nov. 82 The media have an ambiguous relationship with the radical left. **1972** *Guardian* 16 May 16/6 McGovern..occasionally stages a 'media event' which uses the unwitting people as props for TV news footage. **1972** *Times* 19 July 13/6 Miss Allen seems to be under the impression that the media is confined to newspapers. **1973** *Black World* Mar. 80 The theme of the poem deals with the white backlash, a media term describing the hostile reactions of white folks to civil-rights activities. **1973** 'R. MACDONALD' *Sleeping Beauty* i. 9 'You from a media?' 'No, I'm just a citizen.' **1974** *Listener* 28 Feb. 260/1 The impartial experts and media-men. **1975** *Atlantic Monthly* Jan. 29/2 'Media' is itself a code name for a stereotype. *Ibid.*, Enemies of journalism..refer to the profession as the 'media' in disdain.

medial, *a.* **2.** *medial line*: delete † (*obs.*) and add later example; also *medial area* (see quot.).

1908 T. L. HEATH tr. *Euclid's Elements* III. x. 50 A medial straight line..is so called because it is a mean proportional between two rational straight lines commensurable in square only. *Ibid.* 55 It is in the Porism that we have the first mention of a medial area. It is the area which is equal to the square on a medial straight line.

median, *a.*[1] and *sb.*[1] Add: **A.** *adj.* **1. c.** *median strip*, a strip of ground, paved or landscaped, dividing a street or highway. *N. Amer.*

1954 J. C. INGRAHAM *Mod. Traffic Control* ii. 31 Choice of the type of median strip—solid concrete, grass and curbing or grass alone. **1967** *Boston Sunday Herald* 7 May 1/1 A fence erected on the median strip to discourage the road-crossings. *Ibid.*, The need for the closing of dangerous, life-taking crossovers in the median strip. **1968** *Globe & Mail* (Toronto) 3 Feb. 31/4 A street of exceptionally broad sidewalks and a median strip for trams. **1971** *Fremdsprachen* XV. 67/1 The city of Lawndale, Calif., recently installed nearly two miles of man-made turf on its traffic median strips.

3. a. (Earlier and later examples.) *median dose*, a dose which is effective in half of those receiving it.

1882 F. GALTON in *Rep. Brit. Assoc. Adv. Sci. 1881* 245 The Median, in height, weight, or any other attribute, is the value which is exceeded by one-half of an infinitely large group, and which the other half falls short of. **1929** KELLEY & SHEN in C. Murchison *Found. Exper. Psychol.* 838 Some investigators have often preferred the median to the mean as a measure of central tendency. **1947** *Radiology* XLIX. 302/2 Most of the following data were obtained after median lethal and lower doses of radiation. **1973** *Daily Tel.* 30 Jan. 7/1 The Statistical Office report shows the median wage for Northamptonshire as £1,260.

B. *sb.* **3.** Substitute for def.: A line drawn from a vertex of a triangle to the midpoint of the opposite side. (Earlier example.)

1883 *Encycl. Brit.* XVI. 15/1 If *a*, *b*, *c* be the three sides of a triangle, and *α*, *β*, *γ* the three medians, i.e., the lines drawn from the angles to the middle points of the opposite sides.

Median, *a.*[2] and *sb.*[2] Add: **B.** *sb.* **2.** The language of ancient Media, a dialect related to Old Persian; = *MEDIC *sb.*[2]

1813 [see *KURD]. **1841** R. G. LATHAM *Eng. Lang.* I. i. 3 The Ossetic, a language spoken by an insulated tribe of Mount Caucasus, and a supposed remnant of the Ancient Median, is Indo-European. **1848** *Trans. R. Irish Acad.* XXI. II. 241 In Median..sounds were sometimes confounded. *Ibid.* 244, I..observed some Median words transcribed in one of the inscriptions, and a few other words that, though altered, appeared to be of Persian or Median origin. **1908** T. G. TUCKER *Introd. Nat. Hist. Lang.* 189 It has, however, been argued strongly that the Avestic language is in reality Old Median. **1939** L. H. GRAY *Foundations of Lang.* 32 From the New Testament ..we know that in the first century A.D. Parthian, Median, Elamite, Cappadocian, Pontic, Phrygian, Pamphylian, Cretic.., and Arabic were spoken. **1950** R. H. KENT *Old Persian* I. i. 6/2 Among the less known Old Iranian languages the most important was Median.

mediate, *a.* Add: **2. c.** Also *Psychol.* (See quot. 1897.)

1897 C. H. JUDD tr. *Wundt's Outl. Psychol.* iii. 239 'Mediate recognition'..consists in the recognition of an object, not through its own attributes, but through some accompanying mark or other. **1912** *Amer. Jrnl. Psychol.* Jan. 106 The cases of true mediate association found in these experiments.

mediate, *v.* Add: **5.** (Further examples.) Spec. in *Psychol.*, to bring about (a result) by acting as a mediating agency between an idea, intention, etc., and its realization; to act as such a mediator.

1931 G. STERN *Meaning & Change of Meaning* xiv. 388 The comprehension of *Buchmacher* was mediated by the English word. **1942** COFER & FOLEY in *Psychol. Rev.* XLIX. 522 Behavioral generalization in children was found to be mediated by verbal responses. **1957** B. F. SKINNER in Saporta & Bastian *Psycholinguistics* (1961) 67/2 Instead of going to a drinking fountain, a thirsty man may simply 'ask for a glass of water'... The consequences of such behavior are mediated by a train of events no less physical or inevitable than direct mechanical action. **1958** B. BERNSTEIN in J. A. Fishman *Readings Sociol. of Lang.* (1968) 227 The working-class child has to translate and thus *mediate* middle-class language structure through the logically simpler language structure of his own class to make it personally meaningful. **1968** M. BUNGE in Lakatos & Musgrave *Probl. Philos. Sci.* 128 [A] theory that takes the risk of hypothesizing something mediating between inputs and outputs. **1971** SUTHERLAND & MACKINTOSH *Mechanisms Animal Discrimination Learning* I. ii. 5 The behaviorists in general have denied the existence of the process of selective attention in animals except where the process could be mediated by overt orientation responses. **1972** *Jrnl. Social Psychol.* LXXXVII. 129 Of particular interest to the present investigators was the extraction of the dimensions actually used by individuals in mediating similarity. **1974** *Nature* 1 Mar. 73/1 Cholera enterotoxin mediates specific biochemical events in both intestinal and non-intestinal tissues by stimulating adenyl cyclase and cyclic AMP. **1974** *Author* Summer 89/2 People wanted direct, authentic communication that had not been mediated by sub-editors or script writers. The tape recorder made this new authenticity possible.

mediated, *ppl. a.* Add: Also *Psychol.*, arrived at by mediation; involving mediation (*MEDIATION 3 b).

1942 COFER & FOLEY in *Psychol. Rev.* XLIX. 514 A theoretical analysis of mediated generalization as a specific conditioned response phenomenon. **1950** KELLER & SCHOENFELD *Princ. Psychol.* v. 161 (*caption*) Mediated generalization in the conditioning of the galvanic skin response to verbal stimuli. **1971** A. PAIVIO *Imagery & Verbal Processes* ix. 319 Mediated transfer studies generally involve the learning of two or more lists.

mediating, *ppl. a.* Add: **2. b.** *Psychol.*, interposing between an idea, intention, etc., and its result; acting as a mediator (sense *6).

1953 C. E. OSGOOD *Method & Theory Exper. Psychol.* III. ix. 401 Certain stimulus patterns..are variably associated with systems of mediating reactions. **1963** W. W. GRINGS in M. H. Marx *Theories Contemp. Psychol.* xxxi. 517 The lack of a clear-cut basis for deducing the nature of the mediating response. **1966** W. N. RUNQUIST in J. B. Sidowski *Exper. Methods Psychol.* 503/2 A common mediating association ('army–ocean', mediated by 'navy'). **1968** K. DUNCKER in Wason & Johnson-Laird *Thinking & Reasoning* ii. 34 The final form of a solution is typically attained by way of mediating phases of the process. **1971** SUTHERLAND & MACKINTOSH *Mechanisms of Animal Discrimination Learning* IX. ii. 309 The nature of the 'mediating processes' possibly available to children but not to animals.

mediation. Add: **3. b.** *Psychol.* (See quot. 1934.) Also *attrib.*

1912 *Amer. Jrnl. Psychol.* Jan. 102 The occurrence of associations whose mediation does not come into consciousness in any recognizable manner is certainly an interesting and well-attested phenomenon. **1934** H. C. WARREN *Dict. Psychol.* 162/1 *Mediation*, the interposition of one or more ideas or acts between an initial stimulus or idea and a given end result whose genesis is under investigation. **1953** C. E. OSGOOD *Method & Theory Exper. Psychol.* III. ix. 395 Short circuiting enters into all behavior, and its most important role lies in formation of those representational mediation processes. **1963** ERVIN & MILLER in J. A. Fishman *Readings Sociol. of Lang.* (1968) 91 While there is overlap..with American studies in verbal mediation, the experimental questions have been quite different. **1970** *Jrnl. Gen. Psychol.* LXXXIII. 53 Osgood..developed it [*sc.* the Semantic Differential] and rationalized it in terms of mediation theory. **1971** A. PAIVIO *Imagery & Verbal Processes* ix. 320 The experimental and language-habit approach to the investigation of mediation paradigms.

mediational (mīdiēi·ʃənăl), *a.* [f. MEDIATION + -AL.] Of or pertaining to mediation; mediating.

1951 PARSONS & SHILS *Toward Gen. Theory Action* III. i. 280 One can assume, within reasonable limits (without, that is, detailed psychophysiological, 'mediational' investigation), what potential 'perceptions' are possible. **1953** C. E. OSGOOD *Method & Theory Exper. Psychol.* III. ix. 404 Mediational modification is indicated..by a single asterisk. **1956** *Scottish Jrnl. Theol.* IX. 228 The leading mediational theologian [*sc.* J. Baillie] of our time. *Ibid.* 234 That supreme sensitivity and mediational quality which have always marked his thought and outlook. **1964** *Language* XL. 211 'Operant' is one of those psychological terms (together with 'latency' and 'mediational') which recur frequently in psycholinguistics. **1968** M. BLACK *Labyrinth of Lang.* vii. 158 Causal theories..insist upon the importance of the 'mediational process' induced by perceiving the sign. **1971** *Jrnl. Gen. Psychol.* LXXXV. 125 A mediational process involving colour cues.

mediator. Add: **6.** That which effects a transition between one stage and another; *spec.* in *Psychol.*, that which acts as an agent in mediation (sense *3 b). Also *attrib.*

1953 C. E. OSGOOD *Method & Theory Exper. Psychol.* III. ix. 402 The self-stimulation produced by mediators. *Ibid.* 404 (*caption*) A change in the instrumental sequence elicited by a mediator. **1965** *Language* XLI. 139 Such words as *istorik*, *istorija*.., which appear already in Old Russian literature, are justly regarded by her as direct borrowings from Greek or Latin, and not as mediated by other languages... On the other hand, the more detailed data obtained on foreign words have enabled Mrs. Worth to correct and to define more precisely the role of the mediator languages, especially that of Polish. **1967** *Word* XXIII. 14 Among the numerous 'mediator' languages suggested so far those based on the symbols of mathematical logic are of especial interest to modern interlinguistics. **1969** [see *E.S.T.* (*E. III)]. **1970** N. E. SPEAR in M. R. D'Amato *Exper. Psychol.* xii. 604 S's consequential use of potential mediators for learning. **1970** *Jrnl. Gen. Psychol.* LXXXIII. 5 Rhine also furthers his analysis to the affect-arousal components that certain verbal mediators may eventually elicit. **1971** A. PAIVIO *Imagery & Verbal Processes* ix. 319 Potential mediators are either inferred from association norms or are 'built in' experimentally.

‖ **media vuelta** (mē·diă vue·ltă). Also **media-vuelte.** [Sp., lit. 'half turn'.] In bull-fighting, a method of killing the bull by approaching from behind (see quot. 1962).

1932 [see *BANDERILLA *v.*]. **1934** R. CAMPBELL *Broken Record* viii. 183 Don Simao uses a *media-vuelte* in sticking in his banderillas from horseback; that is, he takes the bull while it is turning, citing it from behind. **1962** B. CONRAD *Encycl. Bullfighting* 163/1 *Media vuelta*... A way of placing *banderillas* in which the *torero* comes at the bull from behind, forcing the animal into a *media vuelta* as the man approaches. **1967** MCCORMICK & MASCAREÑAS *Compl. Aficionado* iv. 121 Once in a great while..you will see an aging matador, green with fear, killing *a la media vuelta.*

medic. B. *sb.* Delete '*Obs.* exc. as U.S. college slang' and add further examples.

1895 W. C. GORE in *Inlander* Nov. 64 *Medic*, a student in the medical department. **1902** W. W. HALL *Appl. Relig.* I. 22 For ages medics have been laying down rules for the regimen of diseased people. **1925** FRASER & GIBBONS *Soldier & Sailor Words* 154 *The Medics*, R.A.M.C. [Royal Army Medical Corps]. **1945** *Finito! Po Valley Campaign* 61 (*caption*) Our medics treat German wounded. **1968** MRS. L. B. JOHNSON *White House Diary* 17 Jan. (1970) 618 He was a Medic and, although twice wounded, he had gone on..to save life after life, crawling across the battlefield. **1970** *Oxford Mail* 21 Feb. 12/3 (*heading*) The 'medics' are fast movers. **1973** *Black Panther* 3 Mar. 6/2, I was a member of the U.S. Army from 1967 to 1970. During the Tet offensive of 1968, I served as a combat medic with the 101 ABN. Div. at Hue, South Vietnam. **1974** *Evening Standard* 1 Mar. 48/3 Dr Brian Warren, Mr Heath's personal physician, called to see him at Downing Street—but as a friend, not as a medic.

Medic (mī·dik), *a.*[2] and *sb.*[2] [ad. L. *Mēdic-us*, Gr. *Μηδικός* Median.] **A.** *adj.* = MEDIAN *a.*[2]

1888 G. BERTIN *Abridged Gram. Lang. Cuneiform Inscriptions* 81 Medic Grammar. **1889** *Jrnl. Anthrop. Inst.* Aug. 31 The Medic language is not the same as the Akkadian, though in syntax and in vocabulary it presents a very marked connection. **1912** H. G. RAWLINSON *Bactria* ii. 25 A treaty was made between the rival nations, and ratified by a marriage between the Medic king and a Lydian princess. **1933** C. DAWSON *Enquiries Relig. & Culture* ii. 80 Assyria was at the height of her power..but her pitiless militarism was gradually ruining..Asia and prepared the way for a new series of barbarian invasions—Cimmerian, Scythian and Medic.

B. *sb.* = *MEDIAN *sb.*[2] 2.

1894 A. H. SAYCE *Primer of Assyriology* ii. 20 The script and language of Elam—sometimes, but incorrectly, called Scythian, Medic, or Protomedic.

Medicaid (me·dikēid). Also **medicaid.** [f. MEDIC(AL *a.* + AID *sb.*] Name given in the United States to a scheme making available state and federal funds for the use of persons judged to require assistance with medical expenses, and provided for under Title XIX of the Social Security Act, 1965. Also *attrib.*

1966 *Life* 29 July 4/1 The word we are going to be hearing a lot more is something called 'Medicaid'—also known as Title 19. **1967** *Economist* 2 Dec. 960/2 The states have until 1970 to set up their Medicaid schemes, but 33 have already done so, attracted by the generous federal contribution. **1972** *Daily Colonist* (Victoria, B.C.) 6 Jan. 1/7 Nearly $1 billion in medicaid payments 'went down the drain' in New York City through medical malpractice. **1973** *Interfaces* May 44 The launching of the Medicare and Medicaid programs..created a need for new technical words. **1974** *Spartanburg* (S. Carolina) *Herald* 22 Apr. B4/6 If you can be paid you will also be eligible for Medicaid provided through the South Carolina Department of Social Services.

medical, *a.* and *sb.* Add: **A.** *adj.* **1. a.** (Further examples.)

1753 *Phil. Trans. R. Soc.* XLVII. 399 Every body has consider'd what the Italians printed..upon the subject of medical electricity, as too hasty a publication. **1776** T. PENNANT *Tour in Scotl. & Voy. Hebrides 1772* II. 247 The number of medical students are now annually reckoned at about 300. **1777** T. CAVALLO *Compl. Treat. Electr.* x. 287 *Medical Electricity*, a practical method of applying Electricity to the human body, when affected with different distempers. **1814** G. J. SINGER *Elem. Electr.* III. iv. 286 Mr. Partington, whose experience as a medical electrician is considerable. **1835** F. D. MAURICE *Let.* 6 Oct. in J. F. Maurice *Life F. D. Maurice* (1884) I. xiii. 186 If I could get any influence over the medical students, I should indeed think myself honoured. **1864** MRS. GASKELL *Wives & Daughters* (1866) I. iii. 26 He went very steadily to work ..advertising in medical journals, reading testimonials, sifting character and qualifications. **1878** W. JAMES in R. B. Perry *Tht. & Char. W. James* (1935) II. IV. liii. 29 The degrading sophistries of medical materialists. **1885** *Househ. Words* 20 June 155 (Farmer), Medical students have liberally assisted in the formation of slang, their special department thereof being known as medical Greek. **1902** W. JAMES *Varieties Relig. Experience* i. 13 Medical materialism finishes up Saint Paul by calling his vision on the road to Damascus a discharging lesion of the occipital cortex, he being an epileptic. **1935** *Economist* 7 Sept. 456/2 The [National Health Insurance] scheme provided for the payment of cash benefit in time of sickness, for medical benefit..and sanatorium benefit. **1945** *Release & Resettlement* (H.M. Govt.) xii. 40 The benefits of the National Health Insurance Scheme include medical benefit (i.e. free treatment by an insurance doctor and medicine). **1966** I. JEFFERIES *House-Surgeon* ii. 20 'I know you've *graduated*,' she interposed, 'but at heart you're still a medical student.' **1975** 'M. DUKE' *Death of Holy Murderer* i. 15, I put aside the medical journal I'd been trying to read.

d. medical board [BOARD *sb.* 8 b], a body of medical men responsible for the medical examination of soldiers, the maintenance of public health, etc.; hence *medical-board* vb. trans., to refer for consideration by a medical board (*rare*); **medical certificate**, a certificate from a doctor, attesting the state of a person's health, etc.; **medical examiner,** (*a*) a doctor who carries out an examination for physical fitness; (*b*) *U.S.*, a medically qualified public officer whose duty is to investigate deaths that occur under unusual or suspicious circumstances, to perform post-mortems, and sometimes to initiate inquests; hence **medical examination,** an examination to establish the degree of a person's physical fitness, etc.; **medical garden** (earlier example); **medical hall** *Ireland*, a pharmacy, a chemist's shop; **medical jurisprudence,** the law as it relates to the practice of medicine; also = *forensic medicine*; **medical officer,** a doctor appointed by a public authority or company to attend to matters relating to health (in Gt. Britain in the public sphere the post of 'medical officer of health' was abolished on 1 Apr. 1974); **medical register,** a register, in Britain kept by the General Medical Council, of all doctors legally in practice; so *medical registration*; also *attrib.*; **medical school,** (a school or faculty of) a college or university in which medicine is studied.

1814 *Niles' Reg.* VI. 36/2 A Medical Board is now sitting at the city of Washington, by order of the secretary of war. **1843** *Times* 29 Nov. 4/3 Two distinct medical boards have declared themselves satisfied as to his sound state of health. **1922** *Encycl. Brit.* XXXI. 898/2 Every medical board paper was a kind of forecast. **1947** L. HASTINGS *Dragons are Extra* iii. 63 He was then medical-boarded and sent to the nursing-home in England. **1973** 'R. MACLEOD' *Burial in Portugal* i. 18 The last medical board had cut his army pension, reckoning his back was improving. **1838** DICKENS *Nickleby* (1839) xv. 131 A very little more and it [*sc.* a back comb] must have entered her skull. We have a medical certifiket that if it had, the tortershell would have affected the brain. **1853** C. SCHREIBER *Jrnl.* (1952) 12 The medical certificate would be quite sufficient, and..without his appearing the fellowship was safe. **1914** KIPLING *Lett. of Travel* (1920) 210 One could eat..in one's cabin without a medical certificate from the doctor. **1971** J. CLEGG *Dict. Social Services* 96 A medical certificate (on the official form) must be sent to the local social security office. **1973** E. MCGIRR *Bardel's Murder* ii. 35 'Did you get a medical certificate?' 'That and pain killers.' **1974** *Times* 23 Sept. 2/3 She had attempted suicide five years ago..but she had medical certificates that said she was now all right. **1898** F. DE H. HALL (*title*) Medical examination for life assurance. **1916** *Brit. Med. Jrnl.* 26 Aug. 300/2 (*heading*) Medical examination of recruits. **1935** S. G. LEIGH *Guide to Life Assurance* (ed. 4) viii. 92 Many people have an aversion from the medical examination. **1848** *Risks of Life Assurance* 5 Dr. Ingleby..then the medical examiner for the Norwich Office. **1877** *Acts & Resolves Gen. Court of Massachusetts 1877* 580 The governor shall nominate..able and discreet men, learned in the science of medicine, to be medical examiners. **1889** POLLOCK & CHISHOLM *Med. Handbk. Life Assurance* p. viii, Plain instructions for the guidance of the medical examiner, to afford him a ready handbook of reference on insurance rules. **1928** *Bull. Nat. Research Council* LXVI. 13 Only in New York City and Boston, where the medical examiner's system prevails, is the bulk of the work done in the properly equipped morgues. **1937** T. A. GONZALES et al. *Legal Med. & Toxicol.* ii. 9 The coroner has investigative and judicial powers; the medical examiner can conduct only an investigation. **1973** *Times* 5 June 6/4 No official ruling on the cause of death has yet been given by the medical examiner, the equivalent of the coroner. *a* **1706** J. EVELYN *Diary* an. 1658 (1955) III. 217, I went to see the Medical Garden, at Westminster, well stored with plants, under Morgan, a very Skillful Botanist. **1922** JOYCE *Ulysses* 669 Purchased by him at 10.20 a.m. on the morning of 27 June 1886 at the medical hall of Francis Dennehy. **1938** J. CARY *Castle Corner* 279 Ah, ye dirty devil, and what sort of a drip are ye to be dropped in a medical hall. **1788** S. FARR (*title*) Elements of medical jurisprudence. **1845** [see FORENSIC *a.*]. **1937** T. A. GONZALES et al. *Legal Med. & Toxicol.* p. vii, The section on legal medicine is concerned with the principal pathologic conditions encountered in cases of forensic importance,.. and medical jurisprudence or that part of the law which deals with the practice of the physician. *Ibid.*, The subjects which are considered a part of medical jurisprudence, such as the corpus delicti,..malpractice, insanity, and insurance. **1835** *Times* 2 Nov. 7/1, I have only heard of two unions, in which the number of medical officers is equal to the number employed before the formation of these unions. **1841** DICKENS *Let.* 29 Oct. (1969) II. 414 With regard to the Medical officers it will be best to say that I am going out of town. **1860** F. NIGHTINGALE *Notes on Nursing* i. 10, I have known a medical officer keep his ward windows hermetically closed. **1916** W. OWEN *Let.* 10 Feb. (1967) 379 The Medical Officer says I should get them removed. **1964** *Times* 22 Feb. 6/2 Medical officers of health should be more closely concerned with the functions of their local authority that had a bearing on health in any way. **1974** *Daily Tel.* 1 Apr. 6/6 Regional hospital boards, executive health councils and local authority departments with health responsibilities will disappear. So too will medical officers of health, some of whom will now become 'community physicians'. **1886** *Act* 49 & 50 *Vict.* c. 48 § 14 The medical register shall contain a separate list of the names and addresses of the colonial practitioners. **1926** *Brit. Med. Jrnl.* II. 430/1 A few years ago the Government of the Irish Free State announced that it had decided to establish a separate Medical Register. **1973** *Times* 26 July 2/4 Dr —— was suspended from the medical register yesterday for professional misconduct in prescribing drugs for other than bona-fide treatment. **1886** *Lancet* 10 July 85/2 The great importance of due medical registration. **1926** *Brit. Med. Jrnl.* II. 322/2 A decision on the medical registration question has not yet been reached. **1765** in J. Carson *Hist. Med. Dept. Univ. of Pennsylvania* (1869) 55 The institution of Medical Schools in this country has been a favorite object of my attention. **1841** *Southern Lit. Messenger* VII. 550/2 We had lighted upon the University, in the act of organizing an extensive

Medical School. **1909** J. S. FLETCHER in H. Greene *Crooked Counties* (1973) 228 He was anxious to see one or two experiments..being carried on in some of the medical schools. **1973** *Guardian* 25 Jan. 15/6 The shortage of doctors in some regions is directly related to the absence of a regional medical school.

B. *sb.* **3.** A medical examination for fitness.

1917 'TAFFRAIL' *Sub* i. 27 It was neither the *x* and *y* part of the business nor the 'medical' which caused me qualms. It was the dreaded interview. **1938** N. MARSH *Death in White Tie* x. 103 He wanted me to go to Edinburgh to take my medical... I wanted to go to Thomas's. **1946** H. WAYNE *Two Odd Soldiers* i. 7 The Recruiting Officer welcomed and encouraged us..and told us to present ourselves on the following Tuesday for our 'medical'. **1968** *Listener* 8 Feb. 187/3 Mr Scannell's adolescence appeared to be no more remarkable than a hundred others. He coughed at his RAF medical; he spouted Yeats to a literal-minded girl. **1973** *Times* 1 June 5/6 (*heading*) Medicals for drivers urged.

Medicare (me·dikɛ̄ᵊɹ). Also **medicare.** [f. MEDI(CAL *a.* + CARE *sb.*[1] 4.] **a.** Name given in the United States to a scheme of health insurance for the elderly, provided for under Title XVIII of the Social Security Act, 1965; cf. *MEDICAID. **b.** Name of a similar scheme in Canada. Also *attrib.*

1962 *Economist* 16 June 1099 Ailing Medicare. **1963** *Times* 25 Feb. (Canada Suppl.) p. vi/6 The Canadian medicare problem must be seen against Canada's geographical, economic and political background. **1963** *Punch* 16 Oct. 577/3 The cost of providing Medicare.. would be less than the annual cost of burying them. **1965** *New Statesman* 6 Aug. 177/1 Last week he [*sc.* President Johnson] signed the medicare bill. **1968** *Globe & Mail* (Toronto) 13 Feb. 1/7 Under the federal medicare legislation starting July 1, Ottawa will pick up half the average per capita cost. **1970** *Ibid.* 28 Sept. 17/1 A meeting of the Quebec Cabinet in Montreal tonight to discuss the possibility of passing emergency legislation to implement medicare. **1971** *Maclean's Mag.* Oct. 65/3 However he discharges his other campaign promises from abolishing deterrent fees for users of Medicare to renegotiating the pulp-mill deal, [etc.]. **1971** *Optometry Today* (Amer. Optometric Assoc.) 22 At present, optometrists..cannot provide optometric services to American senior citizens under the Medicare program. **1973** [see *MEDICAID]. **1974** *Globe & Mail* (Toronto) 2 Mar. 8/3 Saskatchewan, which introduced medicare amid stormy and turbulent summer days in 1961, is embarking on a denticare programme.

Medici (me·ditʃi), *a.* [It. surname: cf. MEDICEAN *a.*] = MEDICEAN *a.*, esp. *Medici collar* (see quot. 1968); *Medici lace* (see quot. 1969), *Medici porcelain* (or *china*), a type of porcelain produced under the patronage of Francesco de' Medici; *Medici print, reproduction,* etc., one produced by the Medici Society, Ltd., London. Also *ellipt.*

1799 N. W. WRAXALL *Mem. Courts* II. xxi. 114 A broad Medicis of Dresden lace surrounded her bosom and shoulders. **1868** J. MARRYAT *Hist. Pott. & Porc.* (ed. 3) xiv. 456 (*caption*) Brocca of Medici Porcelain, 15 inches high. **1873** *Young Englishwoman* May 234/1 The Medici's collarette..is..becoming only to those ladies who have a slender swan-like neck. **1890** *Amer. Mail Order Fashions* (1961) 13 [Drawers] Cambric, ruffle of Medici lace, 75 c. **1900** F. LITCHFIELD *Pott. & Porc.* ii. 18 It was of soft paste, is extremely rare, and is known as 'Medici china'. **1902** JOURDAIN & DRYDEN *Palliser's Hist. Lace* (rev. ed.) iv. 56 The Medici collars were supported by fine metal bars called 'verghetti'. **1906** *Burlington Mag.* Oct. 47/1 If their quality can be maintained the *Medici* prints now being issued by Messrs. Chatto and Windus, of which the first three plates now lie before us, will undoubtedly represent a great advance upon anything which has yet been done in colour reproduction. **1908** BEERBOHM in *Around Theatres* (1924) II. 405 Nor was I embarrassed by the hoop and Medici collar that Dalila wore. **1936** *Catal. Medici Prints* 3 This Series has now attained a world-wide reputation under the title of 'Medici Prints'. **1940** *Burlington Mag.* May p. x/2, Medici porcelain. *Ibid.*, A 'Medici' plate, marked with the letter F and the dome of the Cathedral of Florence. **1949** F. TOWERS *Tea with Mr. Rochester* 24 The study with its Axminster carpet and Medici prints and rows of encyclopædias. **1957** J. BRAINE *Room at Top* vi. 60, I was..looking at the Medici reproduction of Olympe. **1960** R. G. HAGGAR *Conc. Encycl. Cont. Pott. & Porc.* 306/1 With one exception, all the known pieces of Medici porcelain are painted in blue, or blue and manganese purple. **1963** A. GERNSHEIM *Fashion & Reality* ii. 79 Many capes had a small Medici collar. Such upstanding collars were worn on evening dresses, 1888–92..and fur Medici collars on coats and jackets during the winter of 1889–90. **1964** M. CLIVE *Day of Reckoning* iv. 42 There was a gap between those large, pale, repellant Victorian Arundel prints and the neat Medici reproductions which took their place. **1968** J. IRONSIDE *Fashion Alphabet* 51 *Medici collar*, a stiffened collar usually of lace, fan-shaped; high at the back of the neck and tapering away at the sides. **1969** R. T. WILCOX *Dict. Costume* (1970) 206/1 *Medici lace*, French bobbin-lace similar to Cluny lace, but of finer thread. Woven closely and open in intricate pattern with one edge scalloped.

medicine, *sb.*[1] Add: **2. f.** *to take one's medicine*, to submit to or endure something disagreeable; to learn a lesson; *a dose, taste,* etc., *of one's own* (*kind of*) *medicine*, repayment or retaliation in kind; 'tit for tat'.

1865 A. D. RICHARDSON *Secret Service* v. 75 The leaders refused to take their own medicine. **1894** P. L. FORD *Hon. Peter Stirling* xxvii. 150 'He snubbed me..,' explained Miss De Voe, smiling slightly at the thought of treating Peter with a dose of his own medicine. **1903** *N.Y. Times* 21 Sept., Canada can do nothing—she must take her medicine and make the best of it. **1904** 'O. HENRY' *Cabbages & Kings* xvii. 299 You go back and take your medicine like a man. **1939** T. S. ELIOT *Family Reunion* I. i. 18 Make him feel that what has happened doesn't matter. He's taken his medicine, I've no doubt. **1941** V. PERDUE *Singing Clock* (1945) viii. 52 It was only fair for them to get a taste of their own medicine. **1961** L. VAN DER POST *Heart of Hunter* I. vii. 111 Giving him some of his own medicine, I said: 'How very charming of you!' **1961** C. WILLOCK *Death in Covert* xii. 217, I set the spring-guns, sir... I'm willing to take my medicine for that... If it's found out..it'll make the other things look black for me. And them I did not do. **1968** E. GAINES in A. Chapman *New Black Voices* (1972) 102 He ain't the first one they ever beat and he won't be the last one, and getting in it will just bring you a dose of the same medicine.

4. Also *colloq.* in phr. *bad medicine*, something or someone sinister or ill-fated.

1825 G. SIMPSON *Jrnl.* in *Fur Trade* (1931) 136 Some of them have it that I am one of the 'Master of Life's Sons' sent to see 'if their hearts were good' and others that I am his 'War Chief' with bad medicine if their hearts were bad. **1869** *Harper's Mag.* Jan. 151/2 Will Comstock was sure that it was bad 'medicine' (luck) to camp on the Stinking Water. **1945** P. CHEYNEY *I'll say she Does!* ii. 38 I'd like to talk to him. He's bad medicine. **1964** 'E. PETERS' *Flight of Witch* i. 25 'Did you know that outcrop of rock is known locally as the Altar?'..'So that's it,' he said. 'Just bad medicine.' **1969** 'J. MORRIS' *Fever Grass* xxiii. 214 When people like me..get together we can be bad medicine fer anybody from outside. **1973** P. O'DONNELL *Silver Mistress* xiii. 216 Momma's gotta go redundant. She's a great kid..but she's gonna be bad medicine on the run.

6. a. *medicine bottle* (earlier example), *cabinet, chest* (earlier and later examples), *cupboard*; **medicine ball,** a stuffed leather ball which is thrown and caught to provide exercise; **medicine glass,** a small drinking-glass graduated for use in measuring medicines; **medicine show** *N. Amer.*, a travelling show, in which entertainers attract customers to whom medicine can be sold.

1895 *Crescent* (Brooklyn, N.Y.) 1 Nov. 14/1 While Charlie Notman opines that the 'gym' needs more medicine ball, the few inoffensive ones now on hand are kicking for more 'gym'. **1903** W. L. SAVAGE in *Athletics & Outdoor Sports for Women* 49 The illustrations below show two of the methods for passing medicine balls. **1930** *Bulletin* 13 Feb. 8/2 The Prince of Wales..instead of indulging in ..tennis and quoits, preferred to devote the time after tea to throwing the medicine ball. **1965** G. MCINNES *Road to Gundagai* x. 156 Down the middle of the hall three teams were competing at medicine ball. **1974** J. HELLER *Something Happened* 314 It was a relay race, and he was ten yards ahead,..carrying a heavy medicine ball. **1852** DICKENS *Bleak Ho.* (1853) v. 35 Quantities of dirty bottles: blacking bottles, medicine bottles, [etc.]. **1899** *Montgomery Ward Catal.* 576/2 Medicine cabinet, made of oak. **1922** S. LEWIS *Babbitt* i. 14 Above the set bowl was a.. medicine cabinet. **1955** W. GADDIS *Recognitions* II. vii. 572 Esther set off with her to the bathroom, where they interrupted someone who was looking through the medicine cabinet. **1974** M. BABSON *Stalking Lamb* xiv. 93 The sleeping tablets..in the bathroom medicine cabinet. **1731** in E. Singleton *Social N.Y. under Georges* (1902) 85 A very fine Medicine Chest with great variety of valuable Medicines. **1957** P. KEMP *Mine were of Trouble* i. 6, I remember a bulky 'medicine chest' which seemed to contain chiefly iodine, quinine and cascara. **1907** *Yesterday's Shopping* (1969) 131/3 Fumed oak Medicine Cupboard..4/7. **1966** A. E. LINDOP *I start Counting* xiii. 151, I fled to the bathroom. I yanked open the medicine cupboard so hard that the mirror came off its hinges. **1853** Medicine glass [see *bed table* s.v. *BED *sb.* 19]. **1938** H. ASBURY *Sucker's Progress* 355 Minnie and Colorado Charley then organized a medicine show with which they traveled through Mexico and Central America. **1958** P. GAMMOND *Decca Bk. Jazz* ix. 117 Thelonious Monk, passing through with a travelling medicine show, was once heard as an uncomplicated swing stylist there. **1962** E. LUCIA *Klondike Kate* 7 They travelled with medicine shows, carnivals, [etc.]. **1970** P. OLIVER *Savannah Syncopators* 96 With the demise of the work song, the blues became the song vehicle to accompany labour and, in earlier years, for the medicine show or the barber shop.

b. *medicine bag* (earlier and later examples), *bundle, lodge* (earlier and later examples), *pipe, sack*; **medicine line,** a name given by American Indians to the border between Canada and the United States; **medicine man** substitute for def.: a magician or shaman among American Indians and other peoples (earlier and later examples); hence *colloq.*, a doctor (cf. sense 2 a in Dict.); also *transf.* and *fig.*; **medicine murder,** murder committed to obtain parts of the body for 'medicine'; ritual murder; **medicine wolf** *U.S.* = COYOTE; **medicine woman,** an Indian woman dealing in magic.

1797 C. CHABOILLEZ *Jrnl.* in B. C. Payette *Northwest* (1964) [I] made him consent to go for his Medicine Bag. **1801** A. HENRY *Jrnl.* in E. Coues *New Light Hist. Greater Northwest* (1897) I. 162 The fellow came accordingly with his drum and medicine bag. **1865** MILTON & CHEADLE *N.W. Passage by Land* iv. 66 The chief..dressed in a spangled shirt, a cap covered with many-coloured ribbons, and an elaborately-worked medicine-bag, rose and made an oration. **1971** J. MCDOUGALL *Parsons on Plains* xix. 180 With their medicine-bags in hand they stood like statues. **1936** *Canad. Geogr. Jrnl.* XII. 98/2 Wherever they went they carried with them a medicine pipe and bundle upon the back of a milk-white steed. **1952** *Beaver* Sept. 27 Medicine bundles, both personal and tribal, were of great importance. **1969** *Ibid.* Summer 49/1 Each member had his own medicine bundle containing various items. **1910** A. L. HAYDON *Riders of Plains* 95 The Indians..called the International Boundary the 'Medicine Line', assuming that in the absence of any agreement between the two Governments relative to this crime, they were perfectly safe on one side of the line with regard to what had been done on the other. **1913** L. V. KELLY *Range Men* 143 In their own tongue they [*sc.* Indians] called it the 'medicine line', and were very well pleased with the condition of affairs. *Ibid.* 162 The Canadian Indians were not entirely disappointed at the results of their own forays south of the 'medicine line'. **1962** W. STEGNER *Wolf Willow* II. vii. 96 By that time Crow and Gros Ventre and Sioux and Blackfoot and Assiniboin would already know that the 'Medicine Line', as they called it, was something potent in their lives. **1970** *Beaver* Winter 28/1 In 1801 he was.. just across the North Dakota medicine line, the magical boundary between Canada and the States. **1973** R. D. SYMONS *Where Wagon Led* I. vii. 110 The various ranch outfits would make up big trail herds and move them across the Medicine Line. **1808** C. MACKENZIE in L. R. Masson *Les Bourgeois* (1889) I. 354 The women were directed to go into the woods for branches to cover the Medecine lodge. **1901** F. H. GIDDINGS *Inductive Sociol.* 207 Religious Societies—..In North American Indian tribes, they are known as Medicine Lodges. **1944** *Beaver* June 35 At the end of the medicine lodge inside, Moanday erects two poles, a cross-bar between. At the foot of each pole he lays the body of a dog he has killed. **1801** A. HENRY *Jrnl.* in E. Coues *New Light Hist. Greater Northwest* (1897) I. 162 An Indian who pretended to be a medicine man was employed by Maymiutch to cure his sick brother. **1890** E. DOWSON *Let.* 10 Oct. (1967) 170 In spite of my rooted aversion to the genre I shall have to call in a medicine-man. **1898** G. B. SHAW *Doctors' Delusions* (1932) 107 Out of sheer credulity as to the infallibility of the medicine man, we are drifting into a legal procedure which relieves them from all necessity to gain our confidence by the good they do us. **1922** JOYCE *Ulysses* 16 She bows her old head to a voice that speaks to her loudly, her bonesetter, her medicine-man. **1939** J. DILLARD in A. Dundes *Mother Wit* (1973) 278/2 Medicine men..falsify their experience..in order to qualify for their craft. **1947** AUDEN *Age of Anxiety* (1948) iii. 72 The medicine men who keep this body Politic free from fevers, Cancer and constipation. **1961** *Listener* 20 Apr. 683/2 He [*sc.* a foreign correspondent] has, like a medium or a circus medicine man, simply to go into a trance to pronounce what '*the*' American people feel about it all. **1965** R. & D. MORRIS *Men & Snakes* ii. 46 A double-sexed two-headed snake named Sachan..was the typical emblem of the Near Eastern and Mediterranean medicine man. **1966** B. KIMENYE *Kalasanda Revisited* 92 The medicine man at Nakivubo bus park had a fresh supply of snuff. **1974** WODEHOUSE *Aunts aren't Gentlemen* iii. 17, I was a bit early for my appointment, and was informed on arrival that the medicine man was tied up for the moment with another gentleman. [**1947** *Times* 25 Oct. 3/5 Seventeen Africans were sentenced to death in two cases..here today for committing murder for 'medicine'.] **1952** *Basutoland 1951* (H.M.S.O.) ix. 57 During 1951 fourteen trial cases..were heard by the High Court. Two of these cases dealt with the crime known as Medicine Murder. **1966** *New Statesman* 25 Feb. 265/1 A chapter..on the abominations of 'medicine murder'. **1833** G. CATLIN *N. Amer. Indians* (1841) I. 111 At that hour.., with medicine-pipes in his hands and foxes tails attached to his heels, entered Mah-to-he-hah (the old bear). **1971** J. MCDOUGALL *Parsons on Plains* xii. 110 First, the oldest conjuror took the big medicine pipe with the long stem. *a* **1831** J. SMITH *Jrnl.* in M. S. Sullivan *Trav. J. Smith* (1934) 5 You observe at the door [of the Indian Lodge] three straight and handsome poles set up in a triangular form and joined together at the top, on which is suspended the medicine sack of the owner, consisting of such things as he fancies to possess a certain undefined charm. **1883** 'MARK TWAIN' *Life on Mississippi* 613 See his medicine-sack and my war club tied to it. **1837** W. IRVING *Capt. Bonneville* II. xv. 147 This little, whining, feast-smelling animal, is..called among Indians the 'medicine wolf'. **1846** [see *CAYEUTE, CAYOTE]. **1860** E. J. LEWIS in *Colorado Mag.* (1938) XV. 30 Went up town and saw a young grizzly bear, a young swift or medicine wolf much resembling a fox. **1834** *Knickerbocker* IV. 372 The mother evinced her sagacity, as a diviner or medicine woman. **1836** *Ibid.* VIII. 152 It was at the wigwam of an old Indian 'medicine-woman' that I stopped.

medick. (Later examples.)

1912 W. SOMERVILLE *Agric.* iii. 69 Species standing wide apart, like beans and medick, have no mutual interest in any particular organism. **1960** *Oxf. Bk. Wild Flowers* 20/2 Spotted Medick or Calvary Clover... The leaflets are much bigger than those of other Medicks.

medico. Add: **1.** (Later examples.) Pl. **medicoes, medicos.**

1915 A. CONAN DOYLE *Valley of Fear* I. iv. 53 The medicos will have a word to say before we finish. **1923** A. BENNETT *Riceyman Steps* I. x. 46 Dr. Raste would sometimes say with a dry, brief laugh, 'we medicoes'. **1943** A. HUXLEY *Let.* 7 May (1969) 489 One can only.. pray that the army doctors aren't merely pumping him full of toxic sulfanilamide..which is what so many medicos do. **1951** E. PAUL *Springtime in Paris* xv. 284 Leaving Hortense to the medicos, young and old, I went with Busse to the Gare de Lyon. **1971** *Lancet* 23 Oct. 919/1 We really need a new word for doctor. Perhaps the Common Market will insist on a common term—medico perhaps? **1973** *Nature* 6 Apr. 377/2 The twenty thousand or so scientists, engineers, medicos and so on on the staff of British universities.

medico-. Add: *medicosocial* adj.

1961 *Lancet* 29 July 259/1 (*heading*) Medicosocial aspects. **1967** *Times* 20 Feb. 13/4 Everything is to be gained by the widest publicity being given to these serious medico-social problems affecting all sections of the community.

medina (mĭdī·nă). Also **Medina.** [Arab., 'town'.] The non-European section of a North African town.

1906 D. SLADEN *Carthage & Tunis* II. i. 330 Inside, these great houses of the Medina are just as stately. **1935** G. GORER *Africa Dances* I. vii. 76 The dispossessed negroes went to live in the Medina, a geometrical ghetto of one-room stone huts. **1950** R. LANDAU *Invitation to Morocco* iii. 28 Leaving the native *medina* surrounded by its ancient walls untouched, he erected outside it an entirely new town. **1961** J. ANTHONY *About Tunisia* i. 28 My favourite walks were in the residential quarters high in the Medina. **1972** *Country Life* 13 Jan. 86/2 The crowded Medinas of Islamic cities. **1972** W. MCGIVERN *Caprifoil* (1973) x. 174 He never made the mistake of pretending he understood Arabs. He had grown up with them..listened in the *medinas* to the rise and fall of the wise men's prayers.

Medinal (me·dinăl). *Pharm.* Also **medinal.** A proprietary name for the sodium salt, $C_8H_{11}N_2O_3Na$, of barbitone; it is a hypnotic of similar action to barbitone.

1908 *Trade Marks Jrnl.* 12 Aug. 1319 Medinal... Medicines for human use. Chemische Fabrik auf Actien (Vorm. E. Schering),..Berlin, Germany, manufacturers. **1922** *Daily Mail* 16 Dec. 7 The verdict was Death from an Overdose of Medinal taken by Misadventure. **1946** J. B. PRIESTLEY *Bright Day* vii. 217 As I undressed I chewed two tablets of medinal... I knew that medinal acts slowly with me, but it was all I had there. **1965** J. POLLITT *Depression & its Treatment* v. 66 As these patients are already retarded it is rarely necessary to give tranquillisers or sedatives during the day, but barbitone sodium (Medinal) at night is often most effective in preventing early waking.

‖**medio** (me·dio). Also **medio real.** [Sp. *medio* half.] An obsolete Mexican coin, also used in Cuba, worth half a *real fuerte* or 6¼ *centavos*.

1824 J. R. POINSETT *Notes on Mexico* 141 A *medio*, the sixteenth of a dollar. **1844** G. W. KENDALL *Santa Fé Expedition* II. xii. 239 One of the lads [handed] each of the unfortunate prisoners a medio. **1845** T. J. GREEN *Jrnl. Texian Expedition* 246 One medio would buy a leaden rivet. **1859** R. H. DANA *To Cuba* 47 As there is no coin in Cuba less than the medio, 6¼ cents, the musicians get a good deal or nothing. **1897** T. A. JANVIER *Mexican Guide* vii. 81 Medio real = 6¼ centavos. **1909** 'O. HENRY' *Roads of Destiny* xxi. 358 I've got one Chili Dollar, two *real* pieces, and a *medio*.

medio-. Add: **1.** *medio-laterally* adv.

1971 *Nature* 20 Aug. 542/2 The nucleus is crescent shaped in cross section and extends 1·4 mm rostro-caudally and mediolaterally.

2. In *Philol.*, as **medio-palatal** *a.*, articulated with the tongue against the middle part of the hard palate; **medio-passive** *a.*, of the voice of a verb, intermediate between active and passive (cf. MIDDLE *a.* 4 a); also as *sb.*; hence *medio-passivization*.

1902 E. W. SCRIPTURE *Elem. Exper. Phonetics* xvii. 297 Roof articulations are indicated by the names..pre-, medio-, postpalatal. **1942** BLOCH & TRAGER *Outl. Ling. Analysis* 15 Different points of articulation are designated by the terms prepalatal, mediopalatal, and postpalatal, indicating that the front [of the tongue] touches or approaches respectively the anterior, the middle, or the posterior part of the hard palate. **1949** R.-M. S. HEFFNER *Gen. Phonetics* vi. 148 In Midwest American pronunciations of English there is an open *r* sound, which is formed by raising the middle region of the dorsum of the tongue towards the mediopalatal junction between the hard palate and velum. **1962** CHAVARRIA-AGUILA & PENZL in Householder & Saporta *Probl. Lexicogr.* IV. 241 A contrasting pair of voiced and voiceless medio-palatal fricatives occur. **1921** E. SAPIR *Lang.* iv. 74 Of the seven suffixes..*-o(ht)-* indicates activity done for the subject (the so-called 'middle' or 'medio-passive' voice of Greek). **1933** E. H. STURTEVANT *Compar. Gram. Hittite Lang.* vi. 250 Hittite has a medio-passive, which has the same uses as the Gk. middle voice. It most frequently represents the subject as acting upon or in respect of himself. **1934** PRIEBSCH & COLLINSON *German Lang.* II. vi. 296 Germanic retained in Gothic an inflected medio-passive present from Indo-European. **1952** O. R. GURNEY *Hittites* vi. 118 The verb has two voices—active and medio-passive. **1968** *Encycl. Brit.* XI. 558/1 Besides the active there survives a medio-passive voice [in Hittite] characterized in the present by a somewhat loose *-r(i)* attached to the old middle endings. **1972** *Language* XLVIII. 393 A reflexive—hence, by ergative criteria, mediopassive—form of the verb. *Ibid.* 395 In keeping with the ergative focus, the object (non-ergator) is retained formally in an intransitive, mediopassive form, there being no external agent of the action described. **1973** A. H. SOMMERSTEIN *Sound Pattern Anc. Greek* ii. 13 The infinitive ending in all medio-passive senses is /-sthay/. **1975** *Language* LI. 97 Ambiguity between reflexive and medio-passive constructions is possible (e.g. 'I got out' vs. 'I cut myself'); but in practice this is not much of a problem, since many verbs do not undergo medio-passivization.

Mediterranean, *a.* and *sb.* Add: **B.** *sb.* **1. b.** Also, pertaining to the lands or countries in or around the Mediterranean Sea; spec. *Mediterranean anæmia* or *disease*, thalassæmia, esp. thalassæmia major; *Mediterranean climate*, the climate of lands around the Mediterranean Sea, characterized by hot, dry summers and mild, wet winters; also applied to any similar climate in other regions, as parts of California, Chile, South Africa, and southern Australia; *Mediterranean pine = maritime pine* (*MARITIME *a.* 6), or STONE-PINE.

1760 G. WASHINGTON *Diaries* (1925) I. 145 Planted 4 nuts of the Mediterranean Pine in the Pen. **1896** *Jrnl. R. Microsc. Soc.* 324 (*heading*) Influence of the Mediterranean climate on plants. **1908** R. DE C. WARD *Climate* v. 124 The sub-tropical belt is exceptionally wide... The fact that the Mediterranean countries are so generally included in this belt has led to the use of the name 'Mediterranean climates'. **1924** *Scottish Geogr. Mag.* XL. 150 (*heading*) The Mediterranean climates of Eurasia and the Americas. **1933** Mediterranean pine [see *CORONILLA]. **1936** WHIPPLE & BRADFORD in *Jrnl. Pediatrics* IX. 279 (*heading*) Mediterranean disease—thalassemia (erythroblastic anemia of Cooley). *Ibid.*, This interesting disease presents three important abnormalities together characterizing a syndrome which may be designated 'Mediterranean disease'. *Ibid.* 292 The clinical diagnosis was Mediterranean anemia, pericardial effusion, bronchopneumonia terminal. **1953** A. SMITH *Blind White Fish in Persia* iii. 51 Truly the Elburz mountains divide the arid heat of Tehran from the Mediterranean climate of the Caspian. **1954** *Blood* IX. 648 The term Mediterranean anemia is used in this paper to encompass the entire group of diseases characterized by microcytosis, hypochromia, ovalocytosis, anisocytosis and poikilocytosis, and, most prominently, targeting, together with certain familial hereditary patterns and clinical features. It is recognized that this group covers the spectrum from the most benign to the most severe forms clinically, and the range from hypochromic polycythemia to the severe Cooley's anemia hematologically. **1961** R. D. BAKER *Essent. Path.* xviii. 494 In thalassemia (Cooley's or Mediterranean anemia) there is an inherited anomaly of the red blood corpuscles consisting of flat 'target' cells. **1969** NEUBERGER & CAHIR *Princ. Climatol.* vi. 81 Climates having dry summers and wet winters as a result of the shifts of the subsidence belts are said to be 'Mediterranean' or 'California' climates. **1971** F. A. WARD *Primer of Haematol.* vi. 54 If,..in Mediterranean anaemia, it can be shown that excessive destruction of red cells is taking place almost exclusively in the spleen, then splenectomy will relieve but, of course, not cure the condition.

3. A racial type found especially in countries bordering on the Mediterranean sea; a person of this racial type. Also *attrib.* passing into *adj.* (Cf. *EURAFRICAN *a.* and *sb.*)

1888 C. MORRIS *Aryan Race* i. 13 The hair of the Mediterraneans is not so long or so cylindrical in section as in the Mongolians. **1899, 1910** [see *EURAFRICAN *a.* and *sb.* 1]. **1921** *19th Cent.* May 896 It would be difficult to deny that the latinised 'Mediterraneans' are the most finely tempered peoples of Europe. **1921** *Man* CVII. 180 The brown dolichocephals called Mediterraneans. **1928** [see *EURAFRICAN *a.* and *sb.* 1]. **1935** HUXLEY & HADDON *We Europeans* iv. 137 The Nordic, Eurasiatic, and Mediterranean types which are now scattered through the European population. *Ibid.* vi. 172 The Mediterranean type is much more widely distributed than the Mediterranean area. **1939** C. S. COON *Races of Europe* iv. 83 Some Mediterraneans were probably white skinned, and others brown. *Ibid.*, The Mediterranean group seems to be of purely *sapiens* ancestry, without Neanderthaloid or other mixture. **1959** *Chambers's Encycl.* XI. 433/1 Caspians.. are taller and less glabrous than the European Mediterraneans. **1960** J. COMAS *Man. Physical Anthropol.* ix. 602 This is the Dinaric race, which seems to be a Mediterranean type brachycephalized by some non-Mediterranean agency. **1962** C. S. COON *Orig. Races* (1963) i. 19 Races like the..Mediterranean, East Baltic, and Dinaric, which loom large in the Europe-centred literature of anthropology, are neither subspecies nor, in a strict sense, local races. **1971** J. C. KING *Biol. of Race* vi. 114 For the European populations one began to hear of Nordic, Alpine, Mediterranean..and God alone knows how many other races and subraces. **1974** N. FREELING *Dressing of Diamond* 11 He didn't look the part... A round Mediterranean head, and coarse black hair... A slightly Slav face. **1974** I. MURDOCH *Sacred & Profane Love Machine* 288 He ..looked into the big dark eyes..Mediterranean eyes, African eyes.

Mediterra·neanize, *v.* [f. MEDITERRANEAN *a.* + -IZE.] *trans.* To make Mediterranean in character or attributes. So **Mediterra:neaniza·tion.**

[**1896** T. COMMON tr. *Nietzsche's Case of Wagner* iii. 9 *Il faut méditerraniser la musique*: I have reasons for using this formula. The return to nature, to health, to gaiety, to youth, and to *virtue*!] **1915** *Nation* (N.Y.) 6 May 485/3 The Greeks are Mediterraneanized Slavs whose only heritage is a language which Demosthenes could neither have pronounced nor understood. **1921** *19th Cent.* May 894 The ancient Alpine race has been mediterraneanised, latinised, slavonised, and teutonised in Europe, and the Teuton in his turn has undergone mediterraneanisation, latinisation and slavonisation. **1947** N. CARDUS *Autobiogr.* III. 244 He mediterraneanises Wagner, to use Nietzsche's term.

medium, *sb.* and *a.* Add: **A.** *sb.* **5.** *spec.* of newspapers, radio, television, etc., as vehicles of mass communication. Also *attrib.* and in *pl.* (see *MEDIA).

1967 M. MCLUHAN (*title*) The medium is the massage. **1968** *Listener* 28 Mar. 394/3 My recent visits to the theatre, together with my colour television set, have convinced me that McLuhan has it wrong. The medium *impedes* the message.

7. For 'gas-jet' in def. substitute 'source of light'. (Later example.)

1933 P. GODFREY *Back-Stage* vii. 90 'Two more floods up-stage, Bill,' says the stage-manager. 'What mediums, sir—amber or pink?'

9. c. (Earlier example.)

1777 in *Essex Inst. Hist. Coll.* (1906) XLII. 319 There cargo is Salt..37 bales, cases, hhds of mediums [etc.].

10. A medium-dated security.

1968 [see *medium-dated* adj., sense B. 3 below]. **1974** *Daily Tel.* 25 May 20/6 The popularity among high tax-payers of low coupon mediums such as Treasury 3 p.c. 1979 is not all that difficult to comprehend. **1975** *Times* 25 Apr. 24/7 'Shorts', after being ⅛ point higher at one stage, ended mixed... 'Longs' and 'mediums' were up to ⅛ point up.

B. *attrib.* and *adj.* **1. d.** Of sherry, wine, etc., having a flavour intermediate between dry and sweet. So *medium dry, medium sweet* adj. phrs.

1906 *Hatch, Mansfield Price List* 11 *First Quality*, Extra or Medium Dry. *Ibid.* 20 *Light*, Medium Sweet. **1933** H. W. ALLEN *Sherry* iii. 46 This medium wine is likely to find its way into a blend of Amoroso. **1951** R. POSTGATE *Plain Man's Guide to Wine* iii. 57 Their labels contain nothing more informative than 'Best South African Sherry: Medium Dry', or some such phrases. **1960** I. JEFFERIES *Dignity & Purity* i. 18, I expect you'd like sherry, wouldn't you? Medium? **1961** *Twining Bros. Wine List* 2 Amontillado Rico (Medium Dry)... Ancient Browne Rednutt (Medium Sweet). **1969** *Guardian* 13 Feb. 9/1 The medium dry white wine. **1972** A. HUNTER *Vivienne* viii. 101 The waiter..remembered the Major's buying Mrs. Selly a drink, a medium sherry. **1972** *Country Life* 23 Mar. 673/3 One can make it [*sc.* mead] very dry or quite sweet... I intended to make mine medium sweet. **1973** J. PORTER *It's Murder with Dover* v. 45 He sipped his medium sweet cider. **1974** 'A. GILBERT' *Nice Little Killing* iv. 61 Maybe a Dubonnet or a medium sherry—spirits never.

e. The designation of meat cooked between 'well done' and 'rare'. So *medium done, medium rare* adj. phrs. (cf. RARE *a.*[2] b).

1939 P. K. NEWILL *Good Food* iv. 72 Beef..medium.. 22–25 [minutes per pound]. **1953** J. & M. ROBERSON *Meat Cookbk.* ii. 47 Beefsteaks...medium 1 in. 7 min. on each side. **1968** L. O'DONNELL *Face of Crime* (1969) vii. 104 His own steak was just as ordered: medium rare and delicious. **1972** 'E. MCBAIN' *Sadie when she Died* iv. 45 Carella ordered prime ribs, medium rare. **1972** *House & Garden* Feb. 111/1 Steak au poivre was ordered *bleu*..but arrived medium done. **1975** M. KENYON *Mr Big* xix. 176, I never saw myself..tellin' Jeeves to do the steak medium.

3. *Comb.* **a.** *medium-haul, -heel, -range, -rise, -term, -weight* adjs. **b.** *medium-powered, -priced* adjs.; **medium-dated** *a.* (see quots. 1958 and 1968).

1948 *Financial Times* 5 May 1/6 Among medium-dated stocks War Loan 3½ per cent was a good spot. **1953** *Economist* 25 July 287/3 In the gilt-edged market interest at first was concentrated upon the 'shorts' and the medium dated issues. **1958** 'NEDLAW' *Your Guide to Stocks & Shares* III. 78 *Medium dated*, a gilt-edged security having more than five years but less than ten years to run to its final maturity or redemption date. **1968** P. A. S. TAYLOR *Dict. Econ. Terms* 70 *Medium-dated, 'mediums'*. Securities with a life of between five and fifteen years. **1963** *Punch* 4 Sept. 352/3 The new medium-haul Trident. **1965** 'W. HAGGARD' *Hard Sell* iii. 31 SAGA was building a medium-haul aircraft. **1974** *Times* 14 Mar. 5/4 The new dishes now being served on all medium-haul flights. **1973** A. ROY *Sable Night* iii. 24 Dark red suède medium-heel shoes. **1963** BIRD & HUTTON-STOTT *Veteran Motor Car* 41 Georges Richard himself was more interested in the medium-powered, medium-priced car. **1895** *Montgomery Ward Catal.* 15/3 The most satisfactory medium-priced cottons on the market. **1972** E. HARGREAVES *Fair Green Weed* v. 67 They were booked in at a medium-priced hotel. **1943** *Sun* (Baltimore) 24 Aug. 2/6 But it could be of real value to medium and short-range planes. **1974** 'F. CLIFFORD' *Grosvenor Square Goodbye* II. 166 The provision of a medium-range aircraft at Heathrow. **1968** *Guardian* 19 June 3/3 'Medium-rise' housing—flats going up to only four or five stories. **1972** *Times* 17 June 8/8 Aaron Wallis lived in Battersea, in a medium-rise block of no great character. **1958** *Spectator* 15 Aug. 216/3 A high credit rating for medium-term loans. **1965** *McGraw-Hill Dict. Mod. Econ.* 321 A medium-term forecast made in July, 1963, could cover the period from January, 1965, through 1967. **1969** *Times* 5 May 22/2 The Midland Bank Finance Corporation..specialises in medium-term credit. **1971** *Jrnl. Gen. Psychol.* LXXXIV. 243 Span memory is distinct from medium-term memory in the case of semantic material. **1895** *Montgomery Ward Catal.* 282/3 Men's medium weight, natural wool color undershirts. **1964** *McCall's Sewing* i. 11/1 Select medium-weight fabrics which drape nicely and add roundness. **1968** M. S. LIVINGSTON *Particle Physics* i. 5 Medium-weight nuclei are the most tightly bound and the most stable.

c. *attrib.* and *Comb.* examples of sense 8 b of the sb.

1872 SCHELE DE VERE *Americanisms* 245 A Circle is held for Medium Developments and Spiritual Manifestations at Bloomfield-street every Sunday. **1886** W. JAMES in *Proc. Amer. Soc. Psychical Res.* 105 Her pupils contract in the medium-trance. **1919** J. M. KEYNES *Econ. Consequences Peace* iii. 37 Mr. Lloyd George's unerring, almost medium-like, sensibility to every one immediately round him. **1972** A. FORD *Life beyond Death* i. 49 'I'm willing to go along with this stuff,' a medium baiter said one time, 'if you'll positively guarantee to bring me Socrates.'

d. Special collocations: **medium bomber,** a bomber intermediate between the heavy and the light; **medium close-up** *Cinematogr.*, a cinematographic or television shot intermediate between a medium shot (see below) and a close-up; also called *medium-close shot*; **medium frequency,** an intermediate frequency

(of oscillation); *spec.* in *Broadcasting*, a frequency of a medium wave, viz. one between 300 kilohertz and three megahertz; **medium shot** *Cinematogr.*, a cinematographic or television shot intermediate between a close-up and a long shot; **medium wave** *Broadcasting*, a radio wave with wavelength between a hundred metres and a kilometre (see quot. 1929 for former limits); freq. *attrib.* (usu. hyphenated).

1935 *Flight* 22 Aug. 204*a*/2 The specialized light bomber ..may..be supplanted eventually by the very fast medium bomber. **1938** *Encycl. Brit. Bk. of Year* 161/1 A medium bomber can carry enough incendiary bombs to start 150 separate simultaneous fires. **1956** *U.S. Air Force Dict.* 321/2 *Medium bomber*,..currently (1956), a bomber having a gross weight, including bomb load, of between 100,000 and 250,000 pounds..; a medium bomber is thought of as having medium range, and as being best used at medium altitudes, as well as having a medium gross weight. **1971** E. LUTTWAK *Dict. Mod. War* 45/2 'Medium' bombers and 'light' bombers retain a residual role in 'tactical' situations. **1957** MANVELL & HUNTLEY *Technique Film Music* ii. 34 Long track, mostly in medium or medium-close shot, with one large pull-back during the market-place scene. **1933** A. BRUNEL *Filmcraft* 147 Scene 168. Medium close up. The slave-driven father looks desperately round again. **1948** E. LINDGREN *Art of Film* v. 82 A medium close-up of his body on which shadows of the prison bars form a pattern. **1950** E. E. BRODBECK *Handbk. Basic Motion-Pict. Techniques* 103 *Medium close up*... Such a scene shows the most vital part of the subject plus some of that part's surrounding area. **1969** W. RUTHERFORD *Gallows Set* vi. 77 David in medium close up came on the monitor screens. **1920** *Whittaker's Electr. Engineer's Pocket-Bk.* (ed. 4) 348 The result..has been the adoption of two frequencies, a medium frequency for general power and lighting, and a low frequency for systems supplying rotary converters. **1946** *Happy Landings* (Air Ministry) July 9/1 The radio compass, when tuned to any medium frequency, was seriously affected by thunderstorms... The compass pointer did not point towards the M/F station selected. **1966** *McGraw-Hill Encycl. Sci. & Technol.* I. 363/2 European medium-frequency (mf) broadcasting channels are assigned at 9-kc intervals rather than the 10-kc intervals used in the Western hemisphere. **1933** A. BRUNEL *Filmcraft* 150 Scene 488. Medium shot. The waiter pouring out champagne into the glasses on Pauline's table. **1937** *Discovery* Nov. 330/2 The [television] cameras are also fitted with lenses of suitable focal length for getting long-shots, medium-shots and close-ups as desired. **1953** K. REISZ *Technique Film Editing* ii. 81 In a long-lasting shot (33) Bill slows down as he approaches the camera and finally comes to rest in medium shot. **1966** H. P. MANOOGIAN *Film-Maker's Art* vi. 219 In traditional editing the scene is established, usually in a long shot, and as the action within the scene proceeds a number of medium shots and close-ups are taken to relate that action. **1975** *New Yorker* 26 May 32/3, I think we can get around the full lotus by having a stunt man do it, and using medium and long shots in a half-lit room. **1928** *Wireless World* 7 Nov. 626/2 It will..be best to concentrate on maximum efficiency in medium-wave transformers. **1929** *Jrnl. Inst. Electr. Engin.* LXVIII. 22/2 The definitions were fixed as follows [by the International Radio Technical Committee]... Medium waves: kilocycles/sec 1500 to 100; m 200 to 3000. **1938** D. H. SURGEONER *Aircraft Radio* iii. 23 Medium waves are..suitable for both communications and direction-finding and these can be transmitted over reasonable distances. **1961** *Radio Times* 6 Apr. 9/1 The Network Three transmitters, both medium-wave and VHF, will be used for one channel..and the BBC's television sound transmitters for the other. **1974** Medium wave [see *long wave* s.v. *LONG *a.*[1] 18].

mediumistic, *a.* (Earlier and later examples.)

1868 *Harper's Mag.* July 193/2, I should think they were both highly mediumistic. **1920** D. H. LAWRENCE *Lost Girl* xv. 344 The terror, the agony, the nostalgia of the heathen past was a constant torture to her mediumistic soul. **1941** L. A. G. STRONG *John McCormack* xiv. 217 That almost mediumistic quality which enabled the singer to surrender to the song and yet keep his own individuality. **1954** A. HUXLEY *Let.* 5 Dec. (1969) 717 Huene's reactions were wholly aesthetic; Gerald's mainly verbal and mediumistic—with other personalities talking through him from a variety of mental levels. **1974** *Times Lit. Suppl.* 27 Sept. 1046/3 What relation do they bear to mediumistic trances?

mediumly (mī·diəmli), *adv.* [f. MEDIUM *a.* + -LY[2].] Moderately; to a medium or average extent.

1909 *Nation* (N.Y.) 16 Dec. 598 An excellent anthology, for old as well as for the 'mediumly' young. **1958** *Times Lit. Suppl.* 30 May 301/4 Well-known names and personalities even to the mediumly informed. **1961** A. WILSON *Old Men at Zoo* iv. 213 I'm wedged as hell and mediumly happy there.

medivac, var. *MEDEVAC.

medjelis, medjliss, varr. *MAJLIS.

Medo- (mī·do), combining form of MEDE *sb.* (L. *Mēdus*, Gr. *Μῆδος*), used parasynthetically with terms denoting other peoples or countries, esp. *Medo-Persian* adj.

1769 J. BROWN *Dict. Bible* II. 381/2 The three kingdoms..conquered by Cyrus and his Medo-Persian troops. **1835** J. B. ROBERTSON tr. *Schlegel's Philos. of Hist.* I. vii. 272 The Assyro-Babylonian empire which preceded the Medo-Persian. **1869** G. RAWLINSON *Man. Anc. Hist.* II. 9 A revolution in the Medo-Persian capital. **1875** *Encycl. Brit.* I. 604/2 The name for God in Medo-Scythic is *Annap.* **1899** *Captain* Apr. 96/2 There are certain Medo-Persian laws pertaining to a successful stamp collection. **1938** *Times Lit. Suppl.* 1 Jan. 14/2 For a long period the technique of American journalism has been almost Medo-Persian in its rigidity.

medulloblastoma (mĭdʌ:loblæstōᵘ·mă). *Path.* Pl. **-blastomas, -blastomata.** [f. MEDULL(A + -O + BLAST(O- + *-OMA.] A malignant tumour of the central nervous system that usually occurs in the cerebellum of children.

1925 BAILEY & CUSHING in *Arch. Neurol. & Psychiatry* (Chicago) XIV. 193 We shall adopt for our cases the term *Medulloblastoma* as appropriate to the particular tumors to which we independently wish to call attention. **1926** —— *Classification Tumors of Glioma Group* 118 Medulloblastomas..are rapidly growing, soft, malignant tumors which not infrequently, when they reach the leptomeninges, disseminate themselves through the subarachnoid spaces. **1974** PASSMORE & ROBSON *Compan. Med. Stud.* III. xxxiv. 75/1 Medulloblastomata usually arise from the inferior vermis and involve the flocculus and nodule. Hence the presentation is often difficulty in walking, truncal ataxia and a tendency to sudden falls.

mee (mī). [ad. Chinese *mien* flour, noodles, dough, prob. via the Hokkien pronunc. (mīⁿ).] A Chinese dish popular in Malaysia, consisting basically of noodles, with a variety of other ingredients.

1935 A. DIXON *Singapore Patrol* xiii. 107 We were confronted by a large dish piled with a startling mixture of spaghetti, bamboo shoots, sliced prawns, and tiny cubes of pork. The concoction was well seasoned with garlic, chillies, and soya-bean sauce. Its name..was *mee. Mee* is a favourite dish of the Chinese, and is on sale at all hours of the day and night. **1955** P. ANDERSON *Snake Wine* II. vi. 163 A Chinese cook tosses a handful of bean-sprouts, a bundle of pale yellow *mee.* **1963** J. KIRKUP *Tropic Temper* viii. 82, I had some nice fried mee at a Chinese stall. **1965** C. SHUTTLEWORTH *Malayan Safari* v. 72 They sit.. wrestling manfully with knives and forks over English lamb chops, with their stomachs clamouring for Chinese *mee* or *kuay teow.* **1966** D. FORBES *Heart of Malaya* ii. 31 One could get a plate..of the noodles called *mee*, for a few cents.

meech, *v.* Chiefly *U.S.* Also **meach.** [Dial. var. of MICHE *v.*] (Examples of sense 2 of MICHE *v.*)

1857 'DOW, JR.' *Dow's Patent Sermons* 1st Ser. 203 When you fall short of the object for which you jump, you go meechin off, like a cat that has missed her mouse. **1833** S. SMITH *Life & Writings J. Downing* 176 The old man hauled in his horns and meeched off looking shamed enough. **1902** H. L. WILSON *Spenders* xxxi. 366 I'd hate to have you come meachin' around after that stock has kited.

meeching, *ppl. a.* Also **meaching, meachin, me(e)chin.** [var. of MICHING *ppl. a.*; now dial. and the preferred spelling in the U.S.] Skulking, furtive; mean.

1610 BEAUMONT & FLETCHER *Scornf. Lady* (1616) v. i. 9 Sure shee has some Meeching raskall in her house. **1792** *Mass. Spy* 22 Mar. 1/1 There is a kind of meaching souls in the world. *a* **1800** *Spirit of Farmer's Museum* (1801) 287 We observed, however, that he had lantern jaws and a meaching look. **1836** T. C. HALIBURTON *Clockmaker* 1st Ser. (1837) xv. 140 Father goes up to him, lookin as soft as dough, and as meechin as you please. **1844** 'J. SLICK' *High Life N.Y.* II. 219, I gin her hand a leetle mechin shake. **1869** *Harper's Mag.* 193/2 Of old the contrast between the Southerner's proud self-assertion and the Northerner's meeching humility was inexpressibly mortifying to every thoughtful inhabitant of the free States. **1884** W. D. HOWELLS *Rise S. Lapham* (1885) ix. 153 I'm not going to have you do anything that will make you feel meeching afterward. **1944** H. WENTWORTH *Amer. Dial. Dict.* 383/1 *Meech*,..1926, Maine, 'He was so meechin' that butter wouldn't melt in his mouth.' Common.

meek, *a.* Add: **4.** *meek-faced, -mild, -swarded* adjs.

1871 J. G. WHITTIER *Miriam* 29 That lean, fierce priest ..Meek-faced, barefooted. **1933** W. DE LA MARE *Fleeting* 92 Meek-faced, they snuff the air. **1951** —— *Winged Chariot* 23 Meek-mild as chickweed. **1953** C. DAY LEWIS *Italian Visit* I. 24 Immortal landscape of a day..Meek-swarded, comely pastoral.

meemies (mī·miz), *sb. pl. slang.* [Origin obscure.] In full, *screaming meemies.* **1.** Hysterics; a hysterical person. (See also quot. 1927.)

1927 *New Republic* 9 Mar. 72 The following is a partial list of words denoting drunkenness now in common use in the United States... To have the screaming meemies [etc.]. **1942** *Ibid.* 19 Jan. 78 If the mother gets the screaming meemies every time the siren growls, this deep and damaging fear is reflected and associated with all sirens, and all talk of bombs. **1946** MEZZROW & WOLFE *Really Blues* (1957) xvii. 323 The jangled nerves, the reefer flights, the underworld meemies. **1970** *N.Z. Listener* 12 Oct. 13/3 Thunderclap. Gets the screaming meemies. I couldn't help hearing her shouting, in the next room. **1973** GAGNON & SIMON *Sexual Conduct* (1974) v. 151 We've got a nice circle of friends that aren't a bunch of screaming meemies.

2. Also *sing.* **meemie, mimi.** (See quots.)

1944 *Infantry Jrnl.* Sept. 23 In Sicily it was the Nebelwerfer mortar, nicknamed the 'woof-woof' or 'screaming mimi'. **1945** *N.Y. Herald Tribune* 4 Feb. 3 The nebelwerfer is a six-barreled projector firing six-inch rockets... The rockets, not very accurate, are variously called 'screaming meemies' and 'moaning Minnies', but, like most Army slang terms, these names are also applied to other enemy explosives. **1945** *Sat. Rev. Lit.* 3 Nov. 7 The Screaming Meemie is a German multi-barreled rocket-mortar (so named for the sound it makes going off).

meer, var. *MIR *sb.*[1]

meet, *sb.* Add: **1. b.** *slang.* A meeting; an assignation or appointment, esp. a meeting with a supplier of drugs; a meeting-place, esp. one used by thieves.

1879 *Macm. Mag.* Oct. 503/1 At six I was at the meet (trysting-place). **1889** 'MARK TWAIN' *Lett.* (1917) II. 512 We'll manage a meet yet. **1893** L. W. MOORE *His Own Story* xxxvii. 460 Where he could see the 'meet'. *Ibid.* 461 He made a 'meet' for the following day. **1916** C. J. DENNIS *Songs Sentimental Bloke* 23, I dunno 'ow I 'ad the nerve ter speak, An' make that meet wiv 'er fer Sundee week! **1929** *Chicago Tribune* 11 Oct. 14/3 The [drug-] peddler takes his stock to a point on the street or possibly a pool hall. The place where he meets his customer is called a 'meet' or a 'stand'. **1930** *Amer. Speech* VI. 118 Coast dental meet set for July 8–12. **1938** D. RUNYON *Take it Easy* xv. 291 He finally arranges a personal meet with the Judy. **1944** [see *GROUSE *a.*]. **1955** W. GADDIS *Recognitions* II. v. 490 I'm going to make a meet, he answered..—I'm going out to meet a passer, to hand this stuff over to him. **1962** K. ORVIS *Damned & Destroyed* xxv. 183 Your man made a meet... No drugs changed hands. **1967** J. MORGAN *Involved* 26 I've made the meet with Alfie Stride for twelve-thirty. **1970** G. F. NEWMAN *Sir, You Bastard* vi. 180 Manso was considering trying to make a meet with you.

2. a. *Geom.* A point, line, or surface of intersection.

1893 J. W. RUSSELL *Pure Geom.* 156 The meets of opposite sides of a hexagon..inscribed in a conic are collinear. *Ibid.* 236 Given five points on each of two conics, to construct the conic which passes through the four meets of these conics and also touches a given line. **1958** A. BARTON *Introd. Coordinate Geom.* viii. 147 (*heading*) Meet of two tangents. *Ibid.* x. 213 Find the equation of the lines joining O to the meets of $4x-3y=10$ and $x^2+y^2+3x-6y-20=0$.

b. *Algebra.* The intersection of two or more sets; also, the infimum of two or more elements of a lattice.

1933 G. BIRKHOFF in *Proc. Cambr. Philos. Soc.* XXIX. 441 Let Π be any collection of subalgebras S_k... By the meet $\Delta\{\Pi\}$ of Π we mean the set of elements in every S_k of Π. **1933** H. F. BAKER *Princ. Geom.* VI. ii. 70, [*h*] and [*k*] have a common space [*m*], which we may call their meet. **1938** T. G. ROOM *Geom. of Determinantal Loci* i. 6 The join of two spaces is defined as the space of least dimension which contains all the points of each of them, and the meet (or intersection) of the two spaces as the space of least dimension containing all points common to both of them. **1965** D. E. RUTHERFORD *Introd. Lattice Theory* i. 3 We frequently call the l.u.b. of a subset the union of the elements which compose the subset, and correspondingly we call the g.l.b. of the subset the intersection or meet of its elements. **1972** A. G. HOWSON *Handbk. Terms Algebra & Analysis* xv. 76 Every two elements of *P* have a meet and a join, e.g. $12 \wedge 30 = 6$, $3 \vee 5 = 15$, and so *P* is a lattice.

meet, *v.* Add: **2. e.** *more than meets the eye*: greater significance than is at first apparent.

1853 'P. PAXTON' *Stray Yankee in Texas* 308 There might be more in it than at first met the eye. **1906** GALSWORTHY *Man of Property* III. viii. 368 There's more here, sir, however,..than meets the eye. I don't believe in suicide, nor in pure accident, myself. **1911** BEERBOHM *Zuleika D.* xvi. 247 Quick in more than meets the eye, John. Spiritually quick. You saw me putting on my hat; you did not see love taking on the crown of pity. **1923** WODEHOUSE *Inimitable Jeeves* ii. 21 'There is more in this than meets the eye,' I said. 'Why should your uncle ask a fellow to lunch whom he's never seen?' **1943** F. W. CROFTS *Affair at Little Wokeham* ii. 21 There's more in most things than meets the eye.

g. Naut. *to meet* (*her, the ship*): see quots. 1776 and 1948.

1776 W. FALCONER *Universal Dict. Marine* (Phr. French Marine), s.v. *Rencontre!* The order to the helmsman, to meet the ship, right the helm, or put it towards the opposite side, in order to check the ship's sheer. **1841** R. H. DANA *Seaman's Manual* 183 If the order is..'Ease her!' 'Meet her!' or the like, the man should answer by repeating..the order. **1856** C. NORDHOFF *Merchant Vessel* 233 The obstinate craft takes a mighty, almost resistless sweep to the other side, and 'meet her', is the cry, while poor Jack tugs desperately at the heavy-moving wheel. **1902** B. LUBBOCK *Round the Horn* 187 Occasionally he says sharply, 'Meet her! Meet her!' and sometimes he jumps to the wheel and gives us his powerful aid in grinding it up and down. **1948** R. DE KERCHOVE *Internat. Maritime Dict.* 461/1 *Meet her*, an order given to the helmsman to shift the rudder so as to check the swing of the vessel's head in a turn. **1968** H. F. CHASE *Boatswain's Manual* (ed. 3) xi. 255 If given too much wheel,..her head may start to fall off to port. When this is about to happen the helmsman will 'meet her' by putting the wheel to starboard for a few minutes.

4. Freq. used in the imperative as part of a formula of introduction.

1920 C. E. MULFORD *Johnny Nelson* vi. 37 'Meet th' Doc, Nelson,' said Dave. Johnny turned. 'Glad to meet you, Doctor.' **1926** A. A. THOMSON (*title*) Meet Mr. Huckabee. **1933** 'HAY' & 'ARMSTRONG' *Orders are Orders* II. 46 Waggermeyer (*breezy as ever*) Good morning, boys! Meet Miss Marigold, my secretary and continuity girl. **1961** T. HUGHES (*title*) Meet my folks!

12. Sc. *to meet in with*, to encounter (a person); = sense 4.

1825 JAMIESON Suppl., *To meet in wi'*, to meet with. S. B. **1828** D. M. MOIR *Mansie Wauch* xi. 96, I..advised him to take a step in at his leisure to St. Mary's Wynd, where he would meet in with some merchants in scores. **1878** R. CUDDIE *Corstorphine Lyrics* 18, I met my auld frien' Tam. Wha had met in wi' some guid chiel' and tasted half a dram. **1889** R. L. STEVENSON *Master of Ballantrae* ix. 247, I was not always as I am today; nor (had I met in with a friend of your description) should I have ever been so.

13. *to meet up with*: to overtake or fall in with; to meet, encounter; to become acquainted with. *colloq.* (orig. *U.S.*). Also *absol.*, *to meet up*.

1837 A. SHERWOOD *Gazetteer Georgia* (ed. 3) (Provincialisms), *Met up with*, for overtook. **1889** K. MUNROE *Golden Days* ix. 96 They'd meet up with you somewheres along Coloma way. **1905** *Dialect Notes* III. 87 He started before I did, but I met up with him before we got to town. **1919** F. HURST *Humoresque* 297 Tell him his little Sid is here with thirty minutes before she meets up with the show on the ten-forty. **1935** [see *GET *v.* 66 c]. **1949** G. DAVENPORT *Family Fortunes* I. i. 10 It was better than staying at home and they would probably meet up with friends. **1955** E. HILLARY *High Adventure* vi. 104 We..there met up with Evans and his two Sherpas. **1959** *N.Z. Listener* 12 June 5/4 It was there that I met up with Lowry again. **1972** D. HASTON *In High Places* xi. 116 Everyone met up on Pokhara airstrip. **1972** *Daily Tel.* 13 May 20/8 The Sun Life is a very competitive office and would seem to meet up with your requirements. **1973** C. BONINGTON *Next Horizon* v. 92, I met up with Mick Burke in the camp site.

14. Comb. *meet-the-people*: phr. used *attrib.* to describe a tour, etc., made by an eminent person to meet members of the general public (in quot. 1943 of a hamburger with 'popular' appeal). orig. *U.S.*

1943 *Amer. Speech* XVIII. 148 *Meet-the-People burger* (musical comedy 'Meet the People' Los Angeles 1940). **1959** *Economist* 30 May 820/2 Their 'meet-the-people' tours of factories and shipyards. **1959** *Punch* 16 Sept. 160/2 His colleagues mysteriously disappeared during a 'meet the people' tour of the Isle of Wight. **1975** *Times* 2 July 6/2 The Belgian Prime Minister..continued his meet-the-people tour in Edinburgh yesterday.

meeterly, *a.* and *adv.* **b.** *adv.* (Further examples.)

1847 E. BRONTË *Wuthering Heights* I. xiii. 321 They's a pack uh corn i' t' corner, thear, meeterly clane.

meeting, *vbl. sb.* Add: **7.** *meeting bonnet, clothes, coat, -day, gown, hat, -time*; **meeting seed** (see quot. 1851).

1867 J. R. LOWELL *Biglow Papers* 2nd Ser. p. lxxix, Her new meetin'-bunnet Felt somehow thru' its crown a pair O' blue eyes sot upon it. **1775** in O. E. Winslow *Amer. Broadside Verse* (1930) 141/2 He got him on his meeting clothes. **1867** 'T. LACKLAND' *Homespun* I. 63 The 'meetin clothes' of the children are laid away for another week, and the old ones got out again. **1887** M. E. WILKINS *Humble Romance* 139 An thar was Israel in his meetin coat, an' me in my best gown. **1644** *Early Rec. Portsmouth, Rhode Island* (1901) 32 It is..ordered that the businesse of such metinge dayes shal be specified. **1686** S. SEWALL *Diary* (1878) I. 146 Mr. Moodey exercises at our House being our meeting-day. **1776** T. PENNANT *Tour in Scotl. & Voy. Hebrides 1772* II. 364 After three market-days or meeting-days within the town of Halifax. **1856** M. J. HOLMES *'Lena Rivers* 30 Nobody'd think any better of them for being rigged out in their very best meetin' gowns. **1887** M. E. WILKINS *Humble Romance* 300 Hatty in her meeting-gown of light-brown delaine, and her white meeting-hat..was not pretty. **1851** *Knickerbocker* XXXVIII. 372 (Th.), Some people call it 'caraway' and 'aniseseed', but we call it 'meetin'-seed', 'cause we cal'late it keeps us awake in meetin'. **1889** R. T. COOKE *Steadfast* xxxix. 414 Mothers of young families distributed fragrant bunches of dried 'meetin' seed' among their flocks. **1905** E. U. VALENTINE *Hecla Sandwith* 25 [He] sat contentedly munching 'meeting seed' which Molly Tucker..had given him. **1940** E. EARLY *New England Sampler* 319 In old New England gardens there grew three plants called *Meetin' Seed*—Fennel, Dill, and Caraway. **1639** *Rec. Colony & Plantation New Haven* (1857) I. 26 On the Lords Day in the meeting time. **1881** MRS. STOWE *Sam Lawson's Oldtime Fireside Stories* 200 We were in disgrace, we boys; and the reason of it was this: we had laughed out in meeting-time!

meeting-house. Add: **2.** (Earlier and later examples.)

1632 *Rec. Cambridge, Mass.* (1901) 4 Every person.. shall [be]..within [the] meeting-house in the Afternoone. **1634** *Rec. Watertown, Mass.* (1894) I. 1 The charge of the Meeting House shal be gathered by a Rate justly levied. **1910** *Dialect Notes* III. 445 *Meeting house*,..church. Older generation. **1959** *Amer. Speech* XXXIV. 9 Around the turn of the nineteenth century, Baptists,..and others began dropping the term *meetinghouse* and replacing it with *church*.

b. *Polynesia.* A tribal hall (see quot. 1949).

1865 L. ANDREWS *Dict. Hawaiian Lang.* 144/1 *Ha-le-ha-la-wai*, *s. Hale* and *halawai*, to meet; assemble. A meeting house; a synagogue; a place of meeting. **1897** A. HAMILTON *Maori Art* (1901) II. 112 *Whare-matoro*, a large meeting house. **1944** D. STEWART in D. M. Davin *N.Z. Short Stories* (1953) 267 The young Maori..led me over to the meeting-house, a long, low, gusty barn of a building. **1949** P. BUCK *Coming of Maori* (1950) III. iv. 374 The meeting houses formed the social focus of the tribe, hence they were generally named after tribal ancestors. When the people assembled within its walls for tribal discussions, the orators were justified when they said, 'We have gathered together within the bosom of our ancestor.' The carved meeting houses were a source of pride to the people and they gave an atmosphere to the village that nothing else could equal. **1960** N. HILLIARD in C. K. Stead *N.Z. Short Stories* (1966) 239 There I go walking into the meeting-house with my shoes on. **1974** *N.Z. Listener* 20 July 10/4 They are clustered, the kuia, around the tent in which the body lies alongside the meetinghouse.

3. *meeting-house chamber, ground, land, lot, post, rate, yard* (earlier example).

1651 *Official Rec. Springfield, Mass.* (1898–9) I. 200 The above mentioned bargain about the meeting house chamber. **1689** S. SEWALL *Diary* (1878) I. 286 Paid 40£..for the Releases of Meetinghouse Ground. **1690** *Ibid.* 334 Mrs. Judith Winthrop's Deed of the Meeting-house Land in Boston. **1735** *New Hampsh. Probate Rec.* (1914) II. 523, I give to my son..a lot of land lying in the Meeting house lot. **1647** *Rec. Watertown, Mass.* (1894) I. 11 A wrighting shall be sett upon the meting-house-post, to give Warning [etc.]. **1656** *Ibid.* 48, 2ly [that] ye give acompt of the meeting howse rate. **1712** *New Hampsh. Probate Rec.* (1907) I. 687 Northerly on the fence by the metinge house yard.

mefeesh, var. *MAFEESH *a.* and *int.*

‖ **méfiance** (mefiãns). [Fr.] Mistrust.

1876 H. JAMES *Let.* 8 Feb. in R. B. Perry *Tht. & Char. W. James* (1935) I. 366 Touches that are too raffiné, words and phrases that are too striking, or too complete, inspire him with an instinctive *méfiance*. **1921** D. H. LAWRENCE *Sea & Sardinia* vii. 285 Partly it is barbaric *méfiance*. **1938** E. BOWEN *Death of Heart* II. vi. 280 'Oh, did you,' said Dickie, with a certain *méfiance*.

Meg[3]**:** see *MEGGER.

mega-. Add: **me·ga-city,** a very large city; **megaco·lon** *Path.* [COLON[1]], gross dilatation and hypertrophy of the colon; a colon in this condition; **megaka·ryocyte** (also **-caryo-**) *Biol.* [KARYO- + -CYTE], any of the giant cells with large multilobar nuclei which are found in small numbers in normal blood marrow and which are believed to give rise to blood platelets by their fragmentation; so **me:gakaryocy·tic** *a.*; **me·ga-machine,** a social system dominated by technology and functioning without regard for specifically human needs; **mega-millionaire,** a multi-millionaire; **mega·phyllous** *a. Bot.* [Gr. φύλλον leaf], having large leaves; **me·garipple** *Geol.*, an extensive undulation of the surface of a sandy beach or sea bed that is typically tens of metres from crest to crest and tens of centimetres in height, but may be much larger; **me·gashear** *Geol.* [SHEAR *sb.*[2]], a trans-current fault in which the displacement is very large (of the order of a hundred kilometres); **megaspore,** substitute for def.: the larger of the two kinds of spores in heterosporous cryptogams; later, extended to the homologous structure in seed plants (i.e. the immature embryo sac); (further examples); **megasporophyll,** substitute for def. of senses (*a*) and (*b*): any leaf or modified leaf which bears megasporangia; **megate·chnics,** the extensive mechanization of a society with a highly developed technology; **megavi·tamin** *attrib.*, based upon the administration of large doses of vitamins.

1968 *Harper's Mag.* Feb. 61 The noisy, ugly, chaotic, increasingly dangerous and ever-spreading mega-cities. **1975** *N.Y. Times* 20 Aug. 37/2 Or, as the Mailer–Breslin platform said, 'New York will become the first insane asylum of the megacity.' **1906** DORLAND *Med. Dict.* (ed. 4) 419/2 Megacolon. **1908** *Practitioner* Sept. 459 True congenital idiopathic megacolon, or Hirschsprung's disease. **1949**, etc. Megacolon [see *HIRSCHSPRUNG]. **1890** W. H. HOWELL in *Jrnl. Morphol.* IV. 118, I shall speak of them hereafter as megakaryocytes, or large nucleated giant cells. **1938** H. DOWNEY *Handbk. Hematol.* I. vii. 449 (*heading*) Blood platelets and megacaryocytes. **1966** *Lancet* 24 Dec. 1416/1 There was virtual absence of erythroid precursors in the bone-marrow, with normal myeloid series and megakaryocytes. **1938** H. DOWNEY *Handbk. Hematol.* I. vii. 482 Many of the blood platelets of the peripheral blood were rather large megacaryocytic fragments. *Ibid.*, Wuyts produced a marked megacaryocytic reaction in rabbits. **1972** *Nature* 7 Apr. 293/3 Erythroid, granulocytic or megakaryocytic cells. **1967** L. MUMFORD *Myth of Machine* i. 12 Cosmic order was the basis of this new human order. The exactitude in measurement, the abstract mechanical system, the compulsive regularity of this 'megamachine', as I shall call it, sprang directly from astronomical observations and scientific calculations. **1967** *Harper's Mag.* Oct. 110 The megamachine was 'invisible' because its tens of thousands of interacting parts were human. **1970** L. MUMFORD in *New Yorker* 31 Oct. 85 What is needed to save mankind from the megamachine—or whatever controls the megamachine—is to displace the mechanical world picture with an organic world picture, in the center of which stands man himself. **1973** *Physics Bull.* Jan. 5/2 The sophisticated industrial megamachines of the present century are also based on system centred technology, and the troubles they have led us into are only too clear. **1968** *Time* 8 Mar. 21 Nelson Aldrich Rockefeller, 59, a megamillionaire via the Rockefellers, a political patrician through the Aldriches. **1973** *Observer* 12 Aug. 11/1 He has managed to reach the near top of the mega-millionaire league table. **1904** *Science* 21 Oct. 529/1 The pteridophytes..may be disposed according to the prevalent size of their leaves in a series, leading from microphyllous to megaphyllous types. **1909** D. H. SCOTT in A. C. Seward *Darwin & Mod. Sci.* 203 A large proportion of the higher plants are microphyllous in comparison with the highly megaphyllous fern-like forms from which they appear to have been derived. **1953** L. M. J. U. VAN STRAATEN in *Geol. en Mijnbouw* XV. 3/1 Initial stages of transverse megaripples covered with the common small scale current ripples are frequently seen on the large, sandy tidal flats. **1968** *New Scientist* 18 Apr. 113/1 The strange features that have come to be known as megaripples—regularly formed giant undulations, measured by echo sounders, that straddle the ocean floor with distances of three to four miles between crest and crest. **1954** S. W. CAREY in *News Bull. Geol. Soc. Austral.* July 1 The known megashears, where orogens are displaced hundreds of km., were next examined. **1971** *Nature* 2 July 23/1 We regard these two [American] plates as distinct entities separated mainly by the Cayman–Puerto Rico megashear. **1900** *Jrnl. R. Microsc. Soc.* 605 The division of the megaspore of *Erythronium* is..essentially the same as in *Lilium philadelphicum*. **1965** K. ESAU *Plant Anat.* (ed. 2) xviii. 563 The ovule developing from the placenta of the ovary is the seat of formation of the megaspores (or macrospores). **1967** L. MUMFORD *Myth of Machine* ix. 189 When all the components, political and economic, military, bureaucratic and royal, must be included, I shall usually refer to the 'megamachine': in plain words, the Big Machine. And the technical equipment derived from such a megamachine thence becomes 'megatechnics'.. At its inception no inferior chief could organize the megamachine and set it in motion. **1967** *Harper's Mag.* Oct. 108 Under the impulsion of unprecedented 'megatechnics'—'nuclear energy, supersonic transportation, cybernetic intelligence, and instantaneous distant communication'—the far-flung settlement patterns of Megalopolis are resistlessly expanding in many parts of the world, transforming man and the earth. **1970** *New Yorker* 10 Oct. 76/2 The idea of universal mechanization (megatechnics) was established in the megamachine of Egypt. **1970** L. PAULING *Vitamin C & Common Cold* 70 The use of very large amounts of vitamins in the control of disease has been called megavitamin therapy. Megavitamin therapy is one aspect of orthomolecular medicine. It is my opinion that in the course of time it will be found possible to control hundreds of diseases by megavitamin therapy. **1972** *Daily Colonist* (Victoria, B.C.) 20 Feb. 19/2 Dr. Abram Hoffer, a Saskatchewan psychiatrist who pioneered megavitamin therapy for schizophrenia. **1975** *Nature* 14 Aug. 529/3 Efforts of the FDA to regulate megavitamin promotion, however, were set back by a court decision and by the passage last year of a bill in the US Senate that specifically prevents the FDA from classifying high-potency vitamin preparations as drugs.

b. *megabar* [*BAR *sb.*[6] 1, 2], *-bit* [*BIT *sb.*[4]], *-byte*, *-curie*, *-dalton* [*DALTON[2]], *-hertz*, *-newton*, *-parsec*, *-rad*, *-volt* (examples; hence *megavoltage*), *-watt*; also **me·gabuck** *colloq.* [*BUCK *sb.*[8]], a million dollars; **me·gacorpse,** a million dead bodies, a term used in estimating the possible effects of nuclear warfare; **me·gadeath,** the death of a million persons, as a unit in estimating the possible effects of nuclear warfare; **megaunit** (me·găyūnit) *Biol.* and *Med.*, a million international units.

1903 RICHARDS & STULL *New Method determining Compressibility* 43 The pressure of a megadyne per square centimeter would be called a megabar. **1925** J. JOLY *Surface-Hist. Earth* iii. 55 The megabar is one million dynes per sq. cm. It is nearly one atmosphere. **1969** *New Scientist* 9 Jan. 81/3 The pressure needed to produce metallic hydrogen may well be less than a megabar. **1957** *Electronics* 1 Oct. 163 (*heading*) High-speed computer stores 2·5 megabits. **1972** *Sci. Amer.* Sept. 139/2 A broadcast-quality color-television signal in digital code calls for 90 megabits per second. **1946** *Picture Post* 7 Dec. 10/1 Atomic research is so expensive that American scientists have ceased to use the dollar as their unit. They have laughingly coined the term 'megabuck'—one megabuck equals a million dollars. **1952** *Galaxy* June 16/2, I had already pencilled in a tentative campaign in the budget well under a megabuck. **1968** *Amer. Anthropologist* LXX. 608/2 He certainly had no megabuck research grant. **1973** *Nature* 12 Jan. 86/1 The diamond project was not cheap (I think I first heard the word 'megabuck' in connexion with diamond synthesis). **1973** Megabyte [see *kilobyte* s.v. *KILO- b]. **1958** *Tuscaloosa* (Alabama) *News* 4 Sept. 4/5 The eeriest new word coined in the space age is 'Megacorpse'. **1968** *Economist* 13 Apr. 29/2 Dr. Kahn, a controversial figure best known for his calculations on thermonuclear war and his invention of the term 'megacorpse', has begun to broaden the institute's scope. **1947** *Radiology* XLIX. 326/1 The amount of radioactivity from these fission products with moderately long half-lives was in the range of hundreds of megacuries. **1957** *New Scientist* 10 Oct. 28/3 Large amounts of radioactivity can be measured in megacuries: one megacurie is the equivalent of one [metric] ton of radium. **1960** *New Biol.* XXXI. 121 The weight of 1 per cent of the particle [*sc.* T2 phage] is 1·2 Md. [*Note*] Md = megadaltons or 1,000,000 molecular weight units. **1973** *Sci. Amer.* Apr. 22/2 The molecular weight of the *E. coli* chromosome is 2,500 megadaltons. **1953** *Birmingham* (Alabama) *News* 21 June E3/1 He does not deal in numbers of atomic bombs or precise methods of delivery, in kilotons or megadeaths. **1959** *New Statesman* 21 Nov. 693/3 Mr Krushchev's announcement that a single Soviet factory is producing 250 megadeath weapons a year is a timely reminder of the risks of delay. **1962** R. E. LAPP *Kill & Overkill* viii. 100 '55 megadeaths' does not sound as bad as 55 million Americans dead. **1971** *Islander* (Victoria, B.C.) 5 Dec. 15/4 The brain that was good enough to produce the skilled hunter was also good enough to produce huge empires, noble causes to die for, vast armies, and megadeath. **1941** *Chem. Abstr.* XXXV. 2159 (*heading*) Molecular changes following irradiation with hertzian waves of a frequency of 1875 megahertz. **1966** *Electronics* 3 Oct. 171 Transatlantic airliners will

communicate with the satellite on the 118 to 136 Megahertz band. **1971** D. W. SCIAMA *Mod. Cosmol.* iv. 52 The revised 3C catalogue gives a virtually complete list of the [radio] sources between declinations −5° and +90° that are brighter than 9 flux units at 178 megahertz. **1970** *Sci. Jrnl.* June 16/1 It is possible to transform maraging steels with a high content of embrittling components..into fine wire having a tensile strength of about 5200 meganewtons per square metre. **1975** *Physics Bull.* Apr. 165/1 Traditionally, standard forces up to meganewtons are produced on deadweight machines. **1933** *Proc. Nat. Acad. Sci.* XIX. 1001 At the distance of three megaparsecs, the largest galaxies in the Virgo group have linear diameters of approximately six kiloparsecs. **1938**, etc. Megaparsec [see *HUBBLE]. **1973** *Physics Bull.* Nov. 674/1 There is evidence for an intergalactic [magnetic] field of order 10^{-18} T which seems to be uniform over scales of several thousand megaparsecs. **1958** *Times Rev. Industry* July 25/3 For many applications the megarad (one million rads) is more suitable. **1960** A. CHARLESBY *Atomic Radiation & Polymers* iv. 65 A reactor running at 100 megawatts power output could provide 30 megarads to 1 ton of material. **1953** *Economist* 31 Jan. 307/2 During last summer, British production [of penicillin] fell below the 1951 weekly average of 1,216,000 mega units. **1970** *New Scientist* 19 Mar. 543/1, 2.4 megaunits of long acting benzathine penicillin can maintain a treponemicidal blood and tissue level for three weeks or more. **1924** C. R. UNDERHILL *Magnets* i. 11 The volt per microcoulomb or the megavolt per coulomb. **1957** *Technology* July 181/1 A research physicist at work on the 450 megavolt synchro-cyclotron. **1961** *Lancet* 16 Sept. 616/2, 3 patients with a recurrent infiltrating neoplasm after megavoltage therapy were included. **1961** D. W. SMITHERS in Tanner & Smithers *Tumours Oesophagus* xxi. 265 The next step forward came with the introduction of megavoltage [X-ray] apparatus. **1900** WEBSTER, Megawatt. **1955** *Times* 16 July 6/4 The first atomic stations of the Central Electricity Authority will have two nuclear reactors each, together providing a net output of electricity of 100 to 200 megawatts. **1969** P. W. McDANIEL in D. Z. Robinson et al. *Nucl. Energy Today & Tomorrow* (1971) II. iv. 210 In 1962 the largest U.S. power reactor was 180 megawatts.

megacycle (me·găsəik'l). [f. MEGA- b + CYCLE *sb.*] **a.** One million cycles (of an oscillation or other periodic phenomenon). **b.** *ellipt.* One million cycles per second; = *megahertz* (*MEGA- b).

1928 STERLING & KRUSE *Radio Manual* 45 The frequency of 1,000,000 cycles can then be expressed as 1,000 kilocycles or 1 megacycle. **1936** A. HUND *Phenomena High-Frequency Syst.* ii. 56 It may be assumed from the theory of the ionized layer that for waves below 10 m in length (above 30 megacycles/sec) the sky wave passing toward this layer will never be returned. **1955** *Radio Times* 22 Apr. 3/1 The BBC decided..to build..short-range V.H.F. stations operating on frequencies around 90 megacycles per second. **1959** [see *KILOCYCLE]. **1971** C. BONINGTON *Annapurna South Face* iii. 38 Kelvin plunges into details of frequencies, megacycles and all the other gibberish of technical experts.

megagametophyte (megăgæ̆mī·tofəit). *Bot.* [f. MEGA- + *gametophyte* (s.v. GAMETE).] A gametophyte that develops from a megaspore; a female gametophyte.

1933 *Amer. Jrnl. Bot.* XX. 217 (*heading*) Morphology of the megagametophyte and the embryo sporophyte of *Isoetes lithophila*. **1964** H. J. DITTMER *Phylogeny & Form Plant Kingdom* xxi. 487 A single megagametophyte may contain several archegonia with ripe eggs.

megalithic, *a.* Add: **2.** Special collocations, as **megalithic fathom**, a name given to a measure of length equal to 5·44 ft., used in the construction of certain British megalithic monuments; **megalithic yard**, half a megalithic fathom (2·72 ft.).

1961 A. THOM in *Math. Gazette* XLV. 83 The unit of length used was the same from Land's End to John o' Groats... This unit was 5·44 ft... Half of this, 2·72 ft., might be called the Megalithic Yard, but whether this or the Megalithic Fathom (5·44 ft.) was the length of the standard rod carried about the country it is not possible to say. **1962** —— in *Jrnl. R. Statistical Soc.* A. CXXV. 243 In an earlier paper (Thom, 1955) it was shown that in a statistically significant number of cases the diameters of stone circles were multiples of 5·44 ft. This might be called the megalithic fathom. *Ibid.* 246 About 55 per cent. of all circles have the diameter an even number of fathoms. In setting out a circle it is the radius rather than the diameter which has to be measured out on the ground, so that where the diameter is an odd number of fathoms, that is, in about 45 per cent. of all circles, the constructors used a half fathom. Thus for our present purpose it seems better to take as the unit a length of half a fathom (2·72 ft) and for convenience call it the megalithic yard. **1967** —— *Megalithic Sites in Britain* v. 36 We first demonstrate that there is a presumption amounting to a certainty that a definite unit was used in setting out these rings. It is proposed to call this the Megalithic yard (MY). Two of these might be called the Megalithic fathom... It will appear that the Megalithic yard is 2·72 ft and so the Megalithic fathom is 5·44 ft. **1975** *Country Life* 16 Jan. 134/2 The megalithic yard of 2·72 ft that Professor Thom has recently so convincingly shown to have been used by the builders of Stonehenge, Avebury, Carnac.

megalo-. Add: **me·galopod** *a.* and *sb.* [Gr. πούς foot], (*a*) *adj.* having large feet, megalopodous; (*b*) *sb.* a person with large feet.

1909 *Cent. Dict.* Suppl., Megalopod, *a.* and *n.* **1951** AUDEN *Nones* (1952) 40 The basalt Tombs of the sorcerers shatter And their guardian megalopods Come after you pitter-patter.

megalomaniac, *a.* (Examples.)

1899 *Pall Mall Gaz.* 14 Feb. 2/3 A megalomaniac world is always apt to regard a waistcoat-pocket community as a joke. **1929** W. J. LOCKE *Ancestor Jorico* 29 They had to attribute the great fortune to the megalomaniac dreams of a dying man. **1974** J. POPE HENNESSY *R. L. Stevenson* xii. 226 A project emanating from Fanny's now megalomaniac brain.

megalopolis (megălǫ·pŏlis). [f. Gr. μεγαλο- great + πόλις city; see MEGALO-, -POLIS.] Used (freq. with capital initial) as a designation of a very large city or its way of life; also, the practice of building large cities. Also *attrib.* Cf. † MEGAPOLIS.

The normal Eng. pl. (after METROPOLIS) would be *megalopolises*, but the irregular formation *megalopoli* occurs occasionally.

1832 WEBSTER, Megalopolis. **1869** M. COLLINS *Ivory Gate* II. 211 Paul and his wife are back in the precincts of Megalopolis. **1945** *Archit. Rev.* XCVII. 5/1 Normal impulses, suppressed and frustrated in Megalopolis, return in the form of collective aggressions. **1951** M. MCLUHAN *Mech. Bride* (1967) 38/2 Megalopolis is both humanly and economically wasteful. **1959** *Economist* 25 Apr. 330/1 The dream of a massive shift of the American economy to the Great Lakes, and the growth of a vast new megalopolis along their shores. **1964** *Economist* 12 Sept. 1010/2 'Megalopolis'—or excessive urbanisation resulting from modern technology. **1968** C. A. DOXIADIS *Between Dystopia & Utopia* 4 The city turned into a metropolis, which has now grown into a megalopolis. **1969** *Daily Tel.* 29 May 16/3 Los Angeles..is a vast megalopolis of over 10 million, not so much a city as an endless sprawling suburb without a centre..and criss-crossed with multi-lane freeways. **1970** *New Scientist* 5 Feb. 259/1 From the mud hut level of Indian villages and towns to the concrete towered megalopoli of Europe and North America. **1972** *Listener* 9 Mar. 293 Big money is unlikely to be made except perhaps in a very few megalopolis centres.

So **megalopo·litan** *sb.* and *a.*, (*a*) *sb.* an inhabitant of a megalopolis; (*b*) *adj.* of or pertaining to a megalopolis or the way of life characteristic of large cities.

[**1633** E. GRIMSTONE tr. (*title*) The History of Polybius the Megalopolitan.] **1926** *Brit. Weekly* 29 July 355/3 Follows the winter season, with its dawning of 'megalopolitan civilization', its extinction of spiritual creative force. **1930** E. WAUGH *Labels* i. 15 After the exaggerated cleanliness and sparkle of the preceding country, this exaggerated sombreness and squalor, called up..all the hatred and weariness which the modern megalopolitan sometimes feels towards his own civilisation. **1946** *Theology* XLIX. 94 The report deplores the sprawl of houses but not that of megalopolitan culture. **1957** R. HOGGART *W. H. Auden* 15 Auden's interest is in men in urban societies, in men now living through their perennial moral and metaphysical problems in megalopolitan settings. **1971** *Daily Tel.* 30 Nov. 10/4 The same international, megalopolitan forces, rolling over everything in their path, threaten Welsh and English alike. **1974** *Listener* 10 Jan. 53/2 Megalopolitan life brings with it anonymity and bewilderment.

Meganthropus (megæ·nþrǫpŏs). [mod.L. (G. von Koenigswald, 1942), f. Gr. μεγα- great + ἄνθρωπος man.] A large fossil hominid of the genus so called, esp. *Meganthropus palæojavanicus*, fragments of whose remains were first discovered by G. von Koenigswald in Java in 1941. Also *attrib.*

1942 G. VON KOENIGSWALD *Let.* 15 Jan. in *Anthropol. Papers Amer. Mus. Nat. Hist.* (1945) XL. 16/1 *Meganthropus* is a newly discovered fossil hominid perhaps related to *Australopithecus*. **1944** *Science* 16 June 480/2 The *Meganthropus* jaw is much too large and massive. **1959** J. D. CLARK *Prehist. S. Afr.* iii. 73 It has been suggested that the *Meganthropus* form living in Java at this time is another early hominid of the Australopithecine group. **1967** M. H. DAY *Guide to Fossil Man* (ed. 2) 238 (*caption*) The Meganthropus II mandibular fragment.

megaphone. Add: **2.** Also *attrib.* and *fig.*

1905 'O. HENRY' *Trimmed Lamp* (1907) 180 The megaphone man roars out at you to observe the house of his uncle. **1909** *Daily Chron.* 7 June 5/1 They felt sure that the British Press were not the paid megaphones of financial buccaneers. **1951** M. MCLUHAN *Mech. Bride* (1967) 138/1 Is there any role left for the individual in a world of collective megaphone personalities? **1960** V. NABOKOV *Invitation to Beheading* xvi. 162 The director..examined a piece of paper, and in a megaphone voice addressed Cincinnatus. **1968** *Listener* 20 June 803/1 Tell Joanna she must stop being a megaphone for a negative tendency in a parent–child participating democracy.

megaphone (me·găfōun), *v.* [f. the sb.] *intr.* and *trans.* To speak or utter (as) through a megaphone. Hence **me·gaphoned, me·gaphoning** *ppl. adjs.*

1901 *Daily Colonist* (Victoria, B.C.) 30 Oct. 1/7 The Cufic..megaphoned the lightship asking to be reported. **1901** R. C. LEHMANN *Anni Fugaces* 70 The air grows blue with loud reproaches Hurled at the crews by megaphoning coaches. **1912** J. H. MOORE *Ethics & Educ.* 97 Long ago she [*sc.* a dog] and her associates were accustomed to megaphone to each other in this way. **1920** *Glasgow Herald* 21 Apr. 8 The captain megaphoned an invitation to come on to the flag deck. **1927** H. G. WELLS in *Sunday Express* 2 Oct. 12/7 The impressive gatherings.., the megaphoned and broadcast speeches. **1963** A. SMITH *Throw out Two Hands* iv. 46 Aldermanic individuals had to be given captive ascents on a long rope while they megaphoned their impressions to the gaping faces down below. **1967** *Punch* 26 July 121/2 The compere's megaphoned voice could be heard from the concert hall.

me·gaphonist. [f. MEGAPHONE 2.] One who speaks through a megaphone.

1906 'O. HENRY' *Four Million* 203 'What's eatin you?' demanded the megaphonist. **1949** *Box Office* 5 Nov. 20 Elliot Nugent is the megaphonist and William H. Wright the producer. *Ibid.* 21 As the month began, no megaphonist had been set for 'Jet Pilot'.

megapolis. (Later example.)

1855 I. C. PRAY *Mem. J. G. Bennet* 450 Capital alone is wanting to make this city in point of influence..the megapolis of the world.

Megarian, *a.* Add: Also applied to a type of bowl of the Hellenistic period, usu. hemispherical and with relief ornament.

[**1874** A. DUMONT *Peintures Céramiques* vi. 50 On leur a donné en Grèce le nom de Mégare, parce qu'elles se rencontrent..sur le territoire de cette ville.] **1905** H. B. WALTERS *Hist. Anc. Pott.* I. xi. 499 A series of vases known as Megarian or Homeric bowls, of hemispherical form, without handles. **1960** R. M. COOK *Greek Painted Pott.* vii. 215 The so-called 'Megarian' bowls, commercially the most successful relief ware of the Greeks, extend through most of the Hellenistic world and age. The shape is roughly hemispherical with or without a low ring foot. **1961** *Oxf. Univ. Gaz.* 10 Mar. 832/2 A 'Megarian' bowl with figures of Pan and (?) Heracles and Auge.

‖**megaron** (me·gărǫ̆n). [Gr. μέγαρον hall.] The great central hall of a type of house characteristic esp. of the Mycenæan period. Also *attrib.*

1877 *Architect* 4 Aug. 54/2 Palace of Ulysses at Ithaca... Within was another portico and a stately doorway, admitting to the *megaron*; this was a large apartment, unfloored, but lofty, roofed, and used as a dining hall by the men. **1906** *Ann. Brit. Sch. Athens* XII. 253 A fixed central hearth was introduced into the megaron to suit the needs of a more rigid climate than the original Africo-Aegean one. **1907** T. D. SEYMOUR *Life Homeric Age* vi. 188 The great hall or *megaron* is the centre of the life of the household—not unlike the baronial halls of the old English castles. **1928** C. DAWSON *Age of Gods* iii. 58 They brought with them a new type of house, with a pillared porch opening into a single large room or hall. This is the so-called Megaron house, which was characteristic of the early Greeks. **1950** H. L. LORIMER *Homer & Monuments* i. 6 A form of the megaron house, rectangular, with a single entrance to the main room and a more or less central hearth standing clear of the walls. **1963** *New Scientist* 9 May 301 Evidence which strongly suggests that the 'megaron' was an Anatolian rather than a Greek invention.

megascopically, *adv.* (Examples.)

1894 H. S. WASHINGTON *Volcanoes Kula Basin* 21 Megascopically it is much more frequent and prominent than either the augite or the olivine. **1909** J. P. IDDINGS *Igneous Rocks* I. II. iii. 445 Coarse-grained rocks..must be measured megascopically on the surface of proper-sized specimens. **1938** A. JOHANNSEN *Descr. Petrogr. Igneous Rocks* IV. 377 Megascopically, laths of black pyroxene up to 2 cm. in length are seen. **1943** *Amer. Mineralogist* XXVIII. 499 The material under the botryoidal surface is also megascopically crystalline. **1970** K. C. JACKSON *Textbk. Lithology* iv. 214 Epidote..is difficult to recognize megascopically because of small grain size and masking by associated micaceous minerals.

megasea (megæ·siă). [mod.L. (A. H. Haworth *Saxifragëarum Enumeratio* (1821) 6), f. Gr. μέγας large, in reference to the large leaves of the plants.] A perennial herb of the genus formerly so called; = *BERGENIA.

1886 [see *BERGENIA]. **1914** G. JEKYLL *Colour Schemes for Flower Garden* (ed. 3) 96 The Megaseas persist the whole year round. **1962** R. PAGE *Educ. Gardener* I. iv. 135 The bergenias which we used to call saxifrage or megasea are handsome through the twelve months of the year with their bold leathery leaves.

megastructure (me·găstrɒ:ktiŭɹ), *sb.* [f. MEGA- + STRUCTURE *sb.* 5.] A massively large construction or complex, esp. one consisting of many buildings. Hence **me:gastru·ctural** *a.*

1965 *Life* 24 Dec. 146 Other planners foresee skeletal Megastructures of enormous, light-weight 'space frames'—grid-works towering high in the air. **1967** *Listener* 6 July 12/2 Those temporary heavens of exhibition and transport—the Victorian megastructures—..have acquired a permanence in people's minds out of all proportion to the functions they originally housed. *Ibid.* 20 July 73/3 The megastructural schemes by Corbusier's followers in Japan. **1968** *Daily Tel.* (Colour Suppl.) 13 Dec. 30/1 Rudolph's design..truly qualifies as a 'megastructure', a city-within-a-city. **1973** *Observer* (Colour Suppl.) 2 Dec. 33/3 An early attempt to blend housing, commerce and townscape in one huge building—the lumpish description, 'urban megastructure', has been much used.

megathermic (megăþɜ̄·ɹmik), *a.* [f. MEGATHERM + -IC.] Pertaining to, connected with, or consisting of megatherms.

1903 W. R. FISHER tr. *Schimper's Plant Geogr.* 226 The megathermic flora is already perceptibly impoverished.

megaton (me·gătɒn). [f. MEGA- b + TON[1].] **a.** A unit of explosive power, equal to that of one million tons of T.N.T. Freq. *attrib.*

1952 *N.Y. Herald-Tribune* 18 June 23/7 The first true super-bomb to be detonated is expected to have a power of two megatons. **1955** *Times* 30 May 7/7 The Pacific tests in 1952 and 1954 showed that a hydrogen bomb equivalent to 10 to 15 million tons of T.N.T. (commonly called 10–15 megatons) dropped on the centre of an ordinary city would cause total destruction within a circle of four to five miles. **1957** *Oxford Mail* 20 Aug. 1/5 Britain, he said, was concentrating on ballistic missiles because aircraft were unable to have 100 per cent success against an enemy equipped with megaton bombs. **1959** *Listener* 2 Apr. 613/3 The force of each detonation is believed to have been in the kiloton rather than the megaton range. **1962** *Newnes Conc. Encycl. Nucl. Energy* 48/1 A Bikini-type megaton bomb would destroy completely most ordinary buildings in an area of 84 square miles. **1965** *New Statesman* 21 May 810/2 Six megatons were used in the whole of the Second World War. **1972** [see *MAGNITUDE 2 c].

b. *fig.*

1957 M. SHULMAN *Rally round Flag, Boys!* (1958) vi. 74 A broth of a woman..filled with energy in the megaton range. **1963** *Daily Tel.* 9 July 1 Another British spy scandal of 'megaton proportions' was forecast yesterday. **1969** N. COHN *AWopBopaLooBop* (1970) ix. 86 Music splintering and feet shuffling, butts twitching by the megaton.

Hence **me·gatonnage**, explosive power of nuclear weapons, as expressed in megatons.

1963 *Economist* 23 Nov. 746/2 Nato is probably much closer to equality with the Warsaw alliance, in numbers of footsloggers as well as in nuclear megatonnage, than used to be thought. **1967** *Listener* 9 Feb. 186/2 The Russians have not been very explicit..about doubling the megatonnage of their warheads. **1971** *Guardian* 3 Aug. 11/5 The deliverable megatonnage of nuclear weapons. **1971** *Nature* 24 Dec. 493/2 The Soviet Union has already substantially overtaken the United States in numbers of ICBMs, in megatonnages, and in underground tests of large nuclear devices.

Megger (me·gəɹ). The proprietary name of apparatus designed esp. for measuring electrical insulation resistance. Also **megger**. Also **Meg**³, a type of Megger.

1903 *Trade Marks Jrnl.* 2 Sept. 962 Megger... Electric testing apparatus..and scientific instruments..Evershed and Vignoles, Limited,..London,..manufacturers. **1920** *Whittaker's Electr. Engineer's Pocket-Bk.* (ed. 4) 282 *Evershed's Megger.* The Megger insulation testing set contains in one case a hand-driven magneto generator and a direct reading moving coil ohmeter. **1923** *Nature* 13 Jan. 63/2 The 'Meg' insulation tester.., a remarkably light and cheap megger running to 10,000 mgo. which should prove a boon to linemen. **1923** [see *insulation tester*]. **1924** *Trade Marks Jrnl.* 28 May 1189 Megger... All goods included in class 6 [Machinery of all kinds, and parts of machinery, except agricultural and horticultural machines]. Evershed & Vignoles, Limited,..London,..electrical engineers. **1928** *Naval Electr. Manual* (Admiralty) I. ix. 204 The 'Megger' is a direct-reading ohmmeter for the measurement of high resistances, such as the insulation resistance wiring, etc. **1930** *Engineering* 31 Jan. 129/3 A demonstration model of their megger earth tester. **1936** *Discovery* July 220/2 This instrument [*sc.* the Timber Humidity Meter]..has the appearance of a Megger. **1942** *Trade Marks Jrnl.* 11 Nov. 468/1 Meg... Electrical apparatus for testing insulation resistance and electrical apparatus for testing earth resistance, each comprising an electric generator and an electric measuring instrument. Evershed & Vignoles Limited,..London,..electrical and mechanical engineers. **1942** *Tee Emm* (Air Ministry) II. 84 Always remember the importance of megger-testing the insulation. **1950** *Engineering* 14 Apr. 404/1 The same firm were showing a new pattern of Megger insulation tester. **1957** G. CLARK *Archæol. & Society* (ed. 3) ii. 63 By using a 'Megger' Earth Tester, and measuring resistivity at intervals, it is possible to contour degrees of resistivity and so to detect areas of ancient disturbance, in the form of ditches.

Megillah (mĕgi·lă). Also † **meghillah, megilla(h), megille.** Pl. **megil(l)oth, megil(l)a(h)s.** [Heb. *megillah* roll, scroll.] **a.** Each of five books of the Old Testament, namely S. of S., Ruth, Lam., Eccles., and Esther, appointed to be read by adherents of the Jewish faith on certain feast days; freq. with particular reference to the book of Esther, read at the feast of Purim. Also, a copy of any one, or all, of these books.

1650 E. CHILMEAD tr. *Leon Modena's Hist. Rites of Jews* III. x. 165 They read..the whole book of Esther; which they have..in a long Roll:..and this they call..*Meghillah*, that is to say, *Volumen*, a Volume, or Roll. **1652** E. BARGISHAI *Brief Compendium Vain Hopes of Jews Messias* 17 In the same *Talmuth* and book *Megilla*..saith *Chennina*, when the *Messias* shall appear, then shall God ..shew great honours to the Jews. **1818** *Jewish Preceptress* 85 After the usual service, the Megilla, or book of Esther, is read. **1836** *Nethiboth Olam (Old Path)* 26 Feb. 27/1 We request the attention of our readers to the reason given why the reading of the Megillah is more important than any of the commandments. **1857** C. D. GINSBURG *Song of Songs* p. vii, The following is an exposition of the first of the five books called Megilloth. *Ibid.* 2 This Song is the first of the..five Megiloth, or books which are annually read in the Synagogues. **1926** 'R. LEARSI' tr. *Ash's Kiddush Ha-Shem* 89 Young men drew artistic designs in colors for..*Megillahs*. **1932** A. Z. IDELSOHN *Jewish Liturgy* 391 Mĕgilla chanting. **1957** *Oxf. Dict. Chr. Ch.* 882/1 *Megilloth* (Heb..., 'rolls'), the name given to five Books in the OT, all of them in the third and latest section of the OT canon known as the 'Hagiographa', which were read by the Jews on certain feast days. **1968** L. ROSTEN *Joys of Yiddish* 230 *Megillah*... Hebrew: 'scroll'. 1. *Megillah* usually describes the Book of Esther..; also the Book of Ruth. (There are five *megillahs* in all.) **1973** *Synagogue Light* Sept. 12/2 We read in Megilas Ruth [etc.]. **1974** *Jewish Chron.* 13 Sept. 17/1 A megilla in an engraved casket..was presented to the Brighton and Hove Hebrew Congregation.

b. *slang.* With allusion to the length of the Megillah: a long, tedious, or complicated story; freq. in phr. *a whole Megillah* (Yiddish *a gantse Megillah*).

1957 L. M. FEINSILVER in *Chicago Jewish Forum* Summer 228/1 *A gantse Megillah* or 'a whole *Megillah*' has been thrown around by a number of TV personalities..presumably with little idea of the origin of the phrase. **1968** L. ROSTEN *Joys of Yiddish* 230 *Megillah*... 2. Anything very long, prolix; a rigmarole... 3. In popular parlance: Anything complicated, boring, overly extended, fouled up. **1968** *Punch* 1 May 626/1 Feeding all the *megillah* to the papers about his family of Irish Polacks who came over with the Pilgrim Fathers. **1970** L. M. FEINSILVER *Taste of Yiddish* i. 28 The *Megille*, or scroll, of Esther which is read aloud on Purim, and which takes some time to read, gave rise to the humorous description of a long story as *a gantse megille* (a whole *megille*). **1970** S. SHELDON *Naked Face* (1971) x. 110 'Do you know the most peculiar thing about this whole megillah?' queried Moody thoughtfully.

mehari (mĕhā·ri). Also **maharee, mahari, maherry, mehara, meheri,** etc. [F. *méhari*, f. Algerian Arab. *mehrī*, Class. Arab. *mahrī*, of Mahra, a province in South Arabia.] An Arabian, single-humped camel, used for riding.

1738 T. SHAW *Travels or Observations relating to Barbary & Levant* 240 That species of the Camel-kind, which is known to us by the name of the *Dromas* or Dromedary, is here called *Maihāry*; though it is much rarer in Barbary than in the Levant. **1821** G. F. LYON *Narr. Trav. N. Afr.* i. 23 A small Kafflé passed us, consisting of ten or twelve camels, and amongst them one or two Maherries. **1826** DENHAM & CLAPPERTON *Narr. Trav. & Discoveries in N. & Cent. Afr.* i. 22 A marauding party was sent out to plunder some maherhies. *Ibid.*, Nine camels of the maherhy species were brought in. **1848** J. RICHARDSON *Travels in Great Desert of Sahara* I. iii. 87 The two races, the coast-camel, and the Maharee or desert-camel... The most fierce and dominant was the Maharee. **1854** J. R. MORELL *Algeria* 480 The mahari supports fatigue better than the camel, and never betrays an ambuscade. **1857** H. BARTH *Trav. N. & Cent. Afr.* I. viii. 178 Riding my own méheri, I was quite at liberty to go before or fall behind. **1863** J. HUTTON tr. *Daumas's Horses of Sahara* II. 342 Fetoum remounted her *mahari* and gave the signal for retreat. **1904** R. HICHENS *Garden of Allah* II. viii. 113 'He who smokes the keef is like a Mehari with a swollen tongue,' he rejoined. **1921** M. W. HILTON-SIMPSON *Among Hill-Folk Algeria* 120 In the great desert he rides the 'mehari', or trotting camel. **1923** G. CASSERLY *Algeria To-Day* 235 A Targui's *mehara* (riding camel) is usually white, is speedy and full of endurance. **1926** *Contemp. Rev.* Oct. 425 Captain Domèvre of the Spahis..after being severely wounded in action with his *méhari*, is transferred to the military intelligence section at Beyrout.

Meiji (mē̆i·dʒi). [Jap., 'enlightened government'.] The name given to the period of the rule of the Japanese emperor Mutsuhito (1868–1912), which was marked by the modernization and westernization of Japan. Freq. *attrib.*

1873 E. M. SATOW tr. *Kinsé Shiriaku: Hist. Japan* 125 The chronological period was also changed to Meiji (Enlightened Government), and an imperial proclamation was published making it a rule for all time that there should be only one chronological period for each reign. **1894** D. MURRAY *Japan* xv. 378 The year-period, which from January 1865, had borne the name of Keiō, had been changed to *Meiji* (Enlightened Peace), and was fixed to begin from January, 1868. **1901** C. LOWE tr. *A. von Siebold's Japan's Accession to Comity of Nations* p. vi, The writer..felt particularly called upon to contribute to an appreciation of the magnificent achievements of the statesmen and diplomatists of the *Meiji* Era. **1931** I. NITOBÉ *Japan* iv. 225 The two great reforms of Japanese history—those of the Taika and Meiji eras. **1936** J. A. B. SCHERER *Three Meiji Leaders* i. 1 Hirobumi Ito..became Japan's first Premier under the new Meiji government. *Ibid.* xiv. 133 The three Meiji leaders differed widely from one another, but each was of a classic grandeur. **1957** *Encycl. Brit.* XII. 967/1 During the first years of the Meiji period, when western ideas were being adopted in the newly reopened Japan, the European style of painting was more cultivated than any other. **1961** A. M. CRAIG *Chōshū in Meiji Restoration* i. 6 Chōshū and Satsuma, han whose samurai were subsequently to carry out, as the dominant center of the new Meiji government, the revolution of the early Meiji period. **1972** M. KOCHAN tr. *P. Akamatsu's Meiji 1868* II. ii. 258 As far as government accounts in the early years of Meiji can be known, nine and a half million *yen* are said to have been devoted to military expenditure in the period between November 13, 1871, and December 31, 1872. **1974** G. JENKINS *Bridge of Magpies* xiii. 206 My grandfather..lived at the time of the Meiji Revolution which made Japan into a modern state.

‖ **mein Gott** (məin gǫt), *int.* [G., = my God.] Used as a typically German exclamation corresponding to *My God* (GOD 7).

c **1838** C. J. MATHEWS in M. R. Booth *Eng. Plays of 19th Cent.* (1973) IV. 130 Oh mine Got, mine Got, ven I tink of zat bewitching Miss Parker! **1867** TROLLOPE *Claverings* I. xix. 239 'Yes, yes;—mein Gott, yes,' said Schmoff. **1891** KIPLING *Life's Handicap* 261 Mein Gott! I would sooner collect life red devils than liddle monkeys. **1924** 'SAPPER' *Third Round* vi. 142 And think—five, ten minutes more and I also to pieces would have been blown. *Mein Gott!* it makes me sweat. **1968** R. SAWKINS *Snow along Border* iv. 33 Oh, mein Gott, I've just remembered something odd.

‖ **mein Herr** (məin hēr). [G., = my lord.] Used in a jocular or ironic tone in addressing a German man; so as *sb.*, a male German.

1922 JOYCE *Ulysses* 202 The gross virgin who inspired *The Merry Wives of Windsor* let some meinherr from Almany grope his life long for deephid meanings in the depth of the buckbasket. **1967** [see *HERR]. **1975** J. BLACKBURN *Mister Brown's Bodies* xxii. 185 Very clever, *mein Herr*, though the real prize will excape you.

meinie. 5. (Later example.)

1970 J. WAIN *Winter in Hills* IV. 361 A speech was now made by McAlister, the Scotch poet in whose ostensible support this meinie was assembled.

meiobenthos (məi:obe·nþǫs). [f. Gr. μείων smaller + *BENTHOS.] The section of the benthos that includes animals neither small enough to be grouped with the microfauna nor large enough to be grouped with the macrofauna. So **mei:obe·nthic.**

1942 M. F. MARE in *Jrnl. Marine Biol. Assoc.* XXV. 519 A new terminology is needed, and these groups are here designated the macrobenthos, meiobenthos, and microbenthos. The macrobenthos is equivalent to the macrofauna of the bottom... The meiobenthos here comprises the fauna of intermediate size, such as small crustacea (copepods, cumaceans, etc.) small polychaetes and lamellibranchs, nematodes and foraminifera. The microbenthos comprises all the small organisms. **1967** *Oceanogr. & Marine Biol.* V. 522 The number of individuals given by Kiseleva has the great merit of taking into account the meiobenthos. **1969** *Nature* 15 Nov. 720/2 Nematodes are among the commonest meiobenthic animals. **1971** *Ibid.* 28 May 260/1 (*heading*) Deficiency of gravity corers for sampling meiobenthos and sediments. **1973** *Ibid.* 30 Mar. 324/1 Where hydrodynamic conditions and bottom configuration are so subdued that meiobenthic bioturbation becomes a locally prominent sedimentological process.

meiofauna (məi·ofǭnă). [f. Gr. μείων smaller + FAUNA.] = *MEIOBENTHOS. So **mei:ofau·nal** *a.*

1967 M. L. WASS in Olson & Burgess *Pollution & Marine Ecol.* vi. 272 Benthic animals under stress may be meiofaunal in size. *Ibid.*, An extensive study has been done..on a group of protozoan meiofauna. **1973** *Nature* 30 Mar. 323/2 Ostracods and nematodes were the most widely distributed and active members of the meiofaunas. *Ibid.* 324/1 Data confirming..the complete disappearance of some meiofaunal groups, in sediments of the deeper seafloor.

meiosis. Add: Pl. **meioses. 3.** *Biol.* (Formerly also **maiosis.**) The division of a diploid cell nucleus into four haploid nuclei, which offsets a doubling of chromosome numbers at a subsequent fertilization and normally comprises a reduction division (meiosis I) followed by an equational division (meiosis II); commonly used to include also the accompanying division of the cytoplasm.

1905 FARMER & MOORE in *Q. Jrnl. Microsc. Sci.* XLVIII. 489 We propose to apply the terms Maiosis or Maiotic phase to cover the whole series of nuclear changes included in the two divisions that were designated as Heterotype and Homotype by Flemming. **1907** *Rep. Brit. Assoc. Adv. Sci.* 689 There is reason to believe that a sorting of the chromosomes, analogous to that seen in meiosis, takes place in the third division of the ascus. **1925** E. B. WILSON *Cell* (ed. 3) vi. 576 Meiosis brings about two additional results... One is to establish new haploid combinations of the original maternal and paternal chromosomes in the germ-cells... Not less important is the reorganization of the chromosomes, individually considered, that takes place during meiosis, by means of 'crossing-over'. **1934** L. W. SHARP *Introd. Cytol.* (ed. 3) xvi. 254 Meiosis involves two nuclear divisions but only one chromosomal division. **1949** DARLINGTON & MATHER *Elem. Genetics* i. 34 Since crossing-over can probably take place between any two chromomeres, it will be rare indeed for two identical haploid nuclei to be produced from different meioses. **1971** *Sci. Amer.* Aug. 56/3 Without mitosis there could be no meiosis, the type of cell division that gives rise to eggs and sperm.

meiotic (məiˌǫ·tik), *a.* [f. Gr. μειωτικ-ός diminishing (see MEIOSIS).] **1.** *Rhet.* That represents things as less than they really are; characterized by meiosis or litotes.

1907 *Westm. Gaz.* 17 June 2/2 Is there not..a good deal to be said for the meiotic method [of portraying the Caesars] preferred by Sir Lawrence Tadema? **1915** *Oxf. Mag.* 18 June 38/2 We have occasionally mentioned in mild meiotic terms that the Oxford roads do not wholly satisfy our ideal of perfection.

2. *Biol.* (Formerly also **maiotic.**) That is characterized by meiosis (sense *3); of, pertaining to, or occurring at meiosis.

1905 [see *MEIOSIS 3]. **1913** W. BATESON *Mendel's Princ. Heredity* (rev. ed.) 270 This differentiation will come about at this reduction, or meiotic division, as it is called. **1952** SRB & OWEN *Gen. Genetics* vii. 119 The period between the two meiotic divisions is designated by the special term interkinesis. It may be rather long, but typically it is very short. **1962** *Lancet* 15 Dec. 1270/1 Three types of meiotic non-disjunction have been recognised. **1973** *Nature* 5 Oct. 261/2 For spermatozoa and meiotic preparations, ripening testes were removed.

Hence meio·tically *adv.*

1676 R. MEGGOTT *Sermon preached on St. Paul's Day* 6 This is that which according to the Hebrew way of speaking is here meiotically expressed by *It is not good.* **1959** *Times* 7 Oct. 4/1 To put it meiotically, the match was rather one-sided. **1966** *Times* 28 Mar. (Austral. Suppl.) p. xiv/5 A γ chromosome might..be attached to another meiotically driven chromosome. **1968** R. RIEGER *Gloss. Genetics & Cytogenetics* 274 Thus, the zygotic (diploid) chromosome number is meiotically reduced to the gametic (haploid) number. **1973** *Nature* 5 Oct. 259/1 When the brandspore germinates its nucleus divides meiotically to re-establish the haploid sporidial phase.

‖ **mei p'ing** (mē̆i piŋ). Also **mei ping** and with capital initials. [Chin., lit. = prunus vase.] A Chinese porcelain vase with a narrow neck designed to hold a single spray of flowers.

1915 R. L. HOBSON *Chinese Pott. & Porc.* v. 79 A vase of the form known as *mei p'ing* with green Imperial dragons in a yellow ground and the Wan Li mark. **1953** S. JENYNS *Ming Pott. & Porc.* iv. 39 Other blue and white pieces.. are the *mei ping* vases decorated with sages. **1968** J. UPDIKE *Couples* ii. 152 An empty but perfect blue vase of *mei ping* form. **1972** *Country Life* 21 Dec. 1715/3 The Mei Ping (a vase designed with an aperture to hold a single flower). **1973** *Ibid.* 2 Aug. 290/1 A Mei-P'ing, literally 'plum blossom vase', a shape which first appeared in the 10th century..small mouth, wide shoulders and tapering body. **1974** *Times* 3 Apr. 1/5 She paid £160,000 for an early Ming blue-and-white *mei p'ing* and cover.

meisie, meisje (mēⁱ·si). *S. Afr.* [Afrikaans *meisie*, f. Du. *meisje*, cogn. w. Eng. MAIDEN *sb.*] Girl; young lady or woman.

1890 *Digger's Doggerel* 27 Romeo Troilus Giddy McSmack Has been granted, secure from all legal attack, The sole right to practise and use osculation On the 'meisjes' and 'vrauws' of the Transvaalsche Nation. **1895** H. A. BRYDEN in *Blackw. Mag.* July 131/1 A little wizened Hottentot has been..making coffee for the *baas* and *meisje.* **1910** *Cape Times* 7 Oct. 10 There is enough to be done before nightfall for an idle meisje to bestir herself without waiting to be called. **1927** W. PLOMER *I speak of Afr.* 47 He was stared at, especially by fat meisjes here and there, flappers with matronly figures. **1934** 'N. GILES' *Ridge of White Waters* II. ii. 207 That child of Isaak Prinsloo's grows into a pretty meisie. **1953** J. COLLIN-SMITH *Locusts & Wild Honey* II. iv. 146 The lass loves you; which is more than can be said for me of that wilful 'meisjie' your sister. **1965** *Economist* 17 Apr. 339 Milling about in front as well as behind the open counters are the attractive *meisies*, known as hostesses.

Meissen (məi·sĕn). The name of a town near Dresden used *attrib.* or *absol.* to designate a hard-paste porcelain made there since 1710; Dresden porcelain (*DRESDEN). Also *fig.*

1863 W. CHAFFERS *Marks Pott. & Porc.* 176 *Dresden.* Meissen. The two swords crossed..; used about 1730. **1882** 'OUIDA' *Bimbi* 50 A lovely little lady..made of the very finest and fairest Meissen china. **1938** *Burlington Mag.* Dec. p. xvii/2 Pieces of Meissen and other porcelains. **1951** 'J. TEY' *Daughter of Time* i. 11 People wouldn't send you a lot of fool nonsense when you were flat on your back, and bossy bits of Meissen wouldn't expect you to read them. **1951** [see *CHANTILLY 1]. **1961** J. WADE *Back to Life* xiv. 195 Her face..had the smooth, pleased prettiness of Meissen. **1964** MRS. L. B. JOHNSON *White House Diary* 5 June (1970) 156, I recognize it as Meissen from Germany. **1968** *Michelin Guide N.Y. City* 52 German stoneware, faience and porcelain (Meissen, Nymphenburg and Hochst). **1970** *Canad. Antiques Collector* May 29/1 Meissen was the first true porcelain made in Europe. It was produced in a factory at Meissen, about 10 miles from Dresden, from about 1710 onwards.

Meissner effect (məi·snəɹ). *Physics.* [named after Fritz Walther *Meissner* (1882–1974), German physicist, who with R. Ochsenfeld published an account of the phenomenon in *Naturwissenschaften* (1933) XXI. 787.] The existence of zero, or very low, magnetic induction in a superconducting material even in the presence of a magnetic field; esp. the (partial or complete) expulsion of magnetic flux when the material becomes superconducting in a magnetic field.

[**1935** *Proc. R. Soc.* A. CXLIX. 73 Equation (6) says more than (2), so far as it includes Meissner's effect.] **1935** *Ibid.* CLII. 10 The magnetization curve for decreasing fields is in striking contradiction to the classical electromagnetic description of a Supraconductor, and provides an independent confirmation that B = 0 is characteristic of the ideal supraconducting state (Meissner effect). **1953** C. F. SQUIRE *Low Temperature Physics* vii. 116 The complete Meissner effect (B = 0) is difficult to obtain experimentally. *Ibid.* 117 (*heading*) A permanent magnet floats above the superconducting tin dish because of the Meissner effect. **1968** C. G. KUPER *Introd. Theory Superconductivity* iii. 44 It is rather unusual in physics for purely topological properties of a body to be important, but superconductivity provides an example. In a multiply-connected superconducting body, although the Meissner effect ensures that the magnetic flux will be expelled from the material of the body, flux may be trapped in the holes.

Meistersinger (məi·stəɹzi:ŋəɹ, -s-), *sb. pl.* and *sing.* [G.: cf. MASTER-SINGER.] German lyric poets and musicians in the 14th to 16th centuries organized in guilds and having an elaborate technique; (*sing.*) a member of such a guild.

1845 LONGFELLOW *Poets & Poetry of Europe* (1847) 373/2 These Chambers [of Rhetoric] were to Holland, in the fifteenth century, what the Guilds of the Meistersingers were to Germany. [**1854** A. G. HENDERSON tr. *Cousin's Philos. of Kant* i. 5 The poetry of this period is to be found in the songs of the *Minnesängers* and the *Meistersängers.*] **1954** *Grove's Dict. Mus.* (ed. 5) VII. 912/2 The Meistersinger were either preoccupied with the observance of rules or were rarely visited with inspiration. **1968** *Encycl. Brit.* XV. 118/2 The *Meistersinger* were not popular figures, as Wagner's opera *Die Meistersinger* suggests; they were largely ignored by professional men.

fig. **1924** R. CAMPBELL *Flaming Terrapin* iv. 56 Across the night with dismal hum The hurricanes, your meistersingers, come.

mejliss, var. *MAJLIS.

mekometer. Add: **b.** Also **Mekometer.** A device for the accurate measurement of distances in which light elliptically polarized at a microwave frequency is beamed at a reflector at the distance to be measured and the polarization of the reflected light analysed to find the amount by which the distance of the reflector exceeds a whole number of modulation half-wavelengths.

1961 FROOME & BRADSELL in *Jrnl. Sci. Instruments* XXXVIII. 458/1 The paper describes an experimental equipment (known as the 'N.P.L. Microwave Mekometer') using elliptical polarization modulation of a light beam at 9·4 Gc/s (9400 Mc/s) and intended for the accurate measurement of distances of the order of 50 m. **1962** *New Scientist* 26 July 207/2 At the NPL the Mekometer is to be used for the verification of surveyors' precision tapes. **1964** *Trans. Soc. Instrument Technol.* XVI. 31 By September 1960 patents had been filed and in early 1961 the mekometer had become a reality using the Pockels effect at 9·375 G c/s in a device for the accurate measurement of distance. **1970** *Physics Bull.* Aug. 349/2 Prof R G Mason and his collaborators at Imperial College used a new electromagnetic distance measuring instrument, the mekometer, developed by Dr K D Froome..and in the course of nearly two years detected movements of a few centimetres.

mel (mel). *Acoustics.* [f. MEL(ODY *sb.*] A unit of subjective pitch, defined so that the number of mels is proportional to the pitch of a sound, and the pitch of a 1000-hertz note (often, one forty decibels above the listener's threshold of hearing) is 1000 mels.

1937 S. S. STEVENS et al. in *Jrnl. Acoustical Soc. Amer.* VIII. 188/1 The numbers on the pitch scale are related to each other as the subjective magnitudes of the pitches. A pitch of 1000 units (mels) is subjectively twice as high as a pitch of 500 units... The name *mel* was chosen as a name for the subjective pitch unit. **1957** J. L. HUNTER *Acoustics* viii. 249 A tone having an apparent pitch twice as high has a pitch of 2,000 mels..regardless of its frequency. **1962** P. LADEFOGED *Elem. Acoustic Phonetics* vi. 79 Frequency data about speech sounds are often converted into mel units before being presented graphically. **1966** R. L. SURI *Acoustics* I. ii. 21 The unit of pitch has been given the name 'mel' such that the pitch at 1000 cycles is 1000 mels.

melamed (mĕlā·mėd). Also **melammed.** Pl. **melamdim.** [Heb.] A teacher of elementary Hebrew.

1892 I. ZANGWILL *Childr. Ghetto* II. 16 A *Melammed*, or Hebrew teacher. **1902** H. HAPGOOD *Spirit of Ghetto* i. 19 He is carried by his father to the school and received there by the 'melamed', or teacher. **1968** L. ROSTEN *Joys of Yiddish* 232 Pitying, even derogatory, tales about *melamdim* abound among Jews. In all of them, the *melamed* is not the hero but the goat—hapless, unlucky, unresourceful. **1970** L. M. FEINSILVER *Taste of Yiddish* ii. 233 Where the melamed used the ruler and threatened with his strap, the modern Hebrew teacher takes all he can and then sends the kid to the office. **1972** F. B. MAYNARD *Raisins & Almonds* 163 A world peopled by rabbis, starving *melameds* (teachers), matchmakers, [etc.].

melamine. Now usu. pronounced (-īn). Add: **2.** Also **Melamine.** Melamine resin, or a plastic derived from it.

1940 *Plastics* IV. 162/3 The Westinghouse panels for refrigerators making use of the new plastic were made, initially at least, with a white 'Melamine' coating over phenolic laminated sheet. **1943** *Jrnl. Oil & Colour Chem. Assoc.* XXVI. 187 There has been some tendency to regard melamine and melamine resin as meaning the same thing. **1958** *Spectator* 26 Sept. 406/3 Much of the tough new plastic tableware is made of melamine. **1972** *Daily Tel.* 6 June 13/4 Young couples usually eat in the kitchen, and kitchen/dining tables with white melamine tops are attractive. **1973** 'D. HALLIDAY' *Dolly & Starry Bird* ii. 20 Charles.. poured him a noggin..into a yellow Melamine cup.

3. *attrib.* and *Comb.*: *melamine-formaldehyde, -surfaced* adjs.; **melamine resin**, any of the synthetic resins made by the condensation of melamine with an aldehyde, used in making tableware, as coatings for working surfaces, in adhesives, and for treating cloth and paper.

1941 *Industr. & Engin. Chem.* June 771/2 In order that melamine-formaldehyde resins are to be of use to the paint and varnish industry. **1962** J. T. MARSH *Self-Smoothing Fabrics* vi. 81 Melamine-formaldehyde finishes suffer little loss in strength on chlorination but the fabric becomes yellow. **1967** *Times Rev. Industry* June 74/3 No kitchen interior is acceptable to-day without its melamine-formaldehyde laminated surfaces. **1939** *Brit. Plastics* June 28/2 (*heading*) Creaseless fabrics containing melamine resin. **1943** *Jrnl. Oil & Colour Chem. Assoc.* XXVI. 192 The American paint industry is showing a great interest in melamine resins. **1966** *McGraw-Hill Encycl. Sci. & Technol.* XIV. 216/2 Melamine resins are especially valuable as adhesives for laminates of paper or fabrics. **1960** *Times* 16 Mar. (Canberra Suppl.) p. viii/5 Bulkheads and deckheads..will be covered in either melamine-surfaced laminated plastic, or the softer material commonly known as P.V.C. **1971** *Woman's Own* 27 Mar. 53/3 Elegant shelves can be made from white melamine-surfaced Contiplas.

melampyre (me·læmpəiəɹ). [f. mod.L. *Melampyrum*, the generic name of cow-wheat: see MELAMPYRIN.] = COW-WHEAT.

1905 E. PHILLPOTTS *Secret Woman* III. v. 244 The melampyre's lemon blossoms and the orange stars of the woody loosestrife mingled close at hand.

Melanesoid (melănī·zoid), *a.* [f. *Melanes(ia* (see MELANESIAN *a.* and *sb.*) + -OID.] Similar in racial type to the Melanesian; resembling a Melanesian.

1932 *Man* Dec. 283 The term Melanesoid was used to indicate the offspring of tribes from Southern China (Yunnan) and Northern Indo-China (Tonkin). **1939** F. WEIDENREICH in *Peking Nat. Hist. Bull.* XIII. 170 The morphological analysis of the three skulls..led to the result that they typify three different racial elements, best to be classified as primitive Mongoloid, Melanesoid and Eskimoid types. **1943** —— *Skull of Sinanthropus Pekinensis* 251 Skull of a female... The female, B, shows the greatest similarity to the Melanesians of today. For this reason I have designated the type as 'Melanesoid'. **1946** [see *ESKIMOID *a.*].

mélange, *sb.* Add: **3.** (See quot. 1935.)

1922 JOYCE *Ulysses* 245 I'll take a *mélange*, Haines said to the waitress... He sank two lumps of sugar deftly longwise through the whipped cream. **1935** H. SIMPSON *Cold Table* 264 Café Mélange. Ingredients: Coffee, milk; water; whipped cream; castor sugar. **1971** *Guardian* 27 Feb. 7/4 The famous Viennese coffee houses where you can sip your *melange* (or a dozen other varieties of coffee).

melanic, *a.* Add: **2.** Esp. in reference to the darker varieties of moths and other animals that have developed in certain industrial areas. (Later examples.) Also as *sb.*, an animal characterized by melanism.

1915 R. C. PUNNETT *Mimicry in Butterflies* viii. 101 In some parts of England the common peppered moth, *Amphidasys betularia*, has been almost entirely supplanted by the darker melanic form *doubledayaria.* **1940** H. B. COTT *Adaptive Coloration in Animals* I. i. 17 The distribution of such melanic varieties, coinciding as it often does with industrialism, is very significant. So is the fact that the melanic forms have not..become established, even though they are present, in rural districts. **1958** H. B. D. KETTLEWELL in *New Scientist* 3 July 298/2 New theories were evoked to account for the rapid spread of species [of moths] changing from light coloration to black—the 'industrial melanics'. **1970** *Nature* 12 Sept. 1155/1 The murk of nineteenth century Manchester fostered the melanic form *carbonaria* of the peppered moth, *Biston betularia* (L.). **1971** *Ibid.* 29 Oct. 586/3 The value of smoke abatement is demonstrated by the almost immediate decline in the frequency of the melanics where smoke control zones are introduced. **1973** *Ibid.* 21/28 Dec. 535/1 Intensive selective predation by birds on moths, which largely accounts for the presence of melanics in both industrial and some non-polluted rural areas. **1975** *Sci. Amer.* Jan. 90/2 The first [problem] is the question of why there is a difference in the proportion of melanics found among populations of various moth species that share the same environment. *Ibid.* 95 (*caption*) Frequency of melanic form is different in various species.

melanization (melănəizēⁱ·ʃən). [f. MELANIZ(E *v.* + -ATION.] The process or result of becoming melanized.

1945 W. M. KROGMAN in R. Linton *Sci. Man in World Crisis* 47 A possible exception may be found in the 'protective' melanization or skin coloring of tropic-dwelling peoples. **1954** *Sci. News* XXXIV. 94 The pink and brown colour of insectorubin is completely obscured by the melanization of the outer cuticle. **1974** *Nature* 10 May 187/1 The epidermal cells..showed progressive granulation and melanisation.

melano (mĭlā·no). [f. Gr. μελαν-, μέλας black: after ALBINO.] An animal distinguished by an abnormal development of black pigment in the epidermis, hair, feathers, etc.; opposed to ALBINO.

1902 *Ann. & Mag. Nat. Hist.* IX. 59 Spotted tiger-cats of the *F. Macrura* group. The small specimen is a melano, but shows indications of the normal spotted condition.

melano-. Add: **melanoblast** (me·lăno-, mĭlæ·noblast) *Zool.* [a. G. *melanoblast* (S. Ehrmann *Das melanotische Pigment* (1896) viii. 20): see -BLAST], a cell that produces melanin; also, a precursor of a melanin-forming cell; **melanocra·tic** *a. Petrol.* [ad. G. *melanokrat* (W. C. Brögger *Eruptivgesteine des Kristianiagebietes* (1898) III. 263), f. Gr. κρατ-εῖν to rule, prevail)], (of a rock) dark-coloured; rich in dark-coloured minerals; **me·lanoderm** (also

Melano-) *sb.* and *a.* [Gr. δέρμ-α skin], (of, pertaining to, or being) a person of a dark-skinned (negroid) race; **melanodermic** *a.*, (*b*) (naturally) dark-skinned, negroid; **melanoge·nesis** *Physiol.* [-GENESIS], the formation of melanin; **melanophore** (me·lăno-, mĭlæ·nofōəɹ) *Zool.* [ad. G. *melanophor* (R. Keller 1895, in *Arch. f. Physiol.* LXI. 141): see -PHORE], a cell containing melanin; esp. such a cell in the lower vertebrates which is contractile and confers the ability to change the depth of colour (see quot. 1953); **me·lanosome** *Physiol.* [*-SOME[4]], a particle in the cytoplasm of melanocytes in which melanin is thought to be formed from tyrosine (see quot. 1961).

1902 *Encycl. Medica* XI. 182 Ehrmann.., from his investigations of amphibians and reptiles, concludes that the epithelial colouring matter is elaborated in special connective tissue corpuscles (chromatoblasts or melanoblasts), from material derived from the red blood corpuscles. **1942** G. H. BOURNE *Cytol. & Cell Physiol.* viii. 329 A spread of melanin formation from the melanoblasts to similar but non-pigmented dendritic cells of the white area of the skin. **1953** *Science* 5 June 640/1 The term melanoblast is used by medical investigators for the mature cell elaborating melanin, whereas in biology the term melanoblast refers to an immature pigment cell during its migration from the neural crest. *Ibid.* 640/2 The term melanoblast for the mature pigment-forming cell as originally suggested by Bloch is objectionable. *Ibid.* (*table*) Recommended terminology of pigment cells. Immature melanin-forming cell: Melanoblast. **1968** H. HARRIS *Nucleus & Cytoplasm* i. 11 Enucleate fragments of prospective pigment cells (melanoblasts) from the developing neural crest of urodele embryos also survive for long periods *in vitro*. **1909, 1954** Melanocratic [see *leucocratic* adj. s.v. *LEUCO-]. **1963** D. W. & E. E. HUMPHRIES tr. *Termier's Erosion & Sedimentation* 411 *Peridotite*, an ultrabasic (melanocratic) crystalline rock. **1924** A. C. HADDON *Races of Man* (ed. 2) 13 Among the xanthoderms and melanoderms the irides are almost uniformly dark brown in colour. **1927** H. H. WILDER *Pedigree of Human Race* vi. 345 The Melanoderm Race has developed several moderately high civilizations, especially on the west of the Sahara. **1935** *Jrnl. R. Anthrop. Inst.* LXV. 123 The three main divisions of mankind—Leukoderms (Caucasians), Xanthoderms (Mongolians) and Melanoderms (Western and Eastern Negroes)—did not prove to have a blood-group factor of their own. **1924** A. C. HADDON *Races of Man* (ed. 2) 144 A tropical jungle may have been a refuge for an indigenous melanodermic folk from fairer intruders into the country. **1928** *Funk's Stand. Dict.*, Melanogenesis. **1964** *Oceanogr. & Marine Biol.* II. 409 An interesting feature of melanogenesis in the ophiuroids is that in light-coloured individuals which are regenerating arm-tips the regenerate is dark, suggesting that under conditions of wound-healing and repair the normal inhibitor of melanogenesis..is overcome or absent. **1903** *Proc. Amer. Acad. Arts & Sci.* XXXIX. 261 The conspicuous black bodies of Anolis..well buried in the derma and sending branching processes outward toward the epidermis, correspond to the melanophores described by Keller. **1946** *Nature* 7 Sept. 344/1 The pigmentary hormone of *Dixippus*, the regulator of colour change in this animal, activates the melanophores of frogs..by causing expansion of them. **1953** *Science* 5 June 640/1 Investigators in biology and medicine at the present time are using different terms for the same cell. For example, the term melanophore which has long been used by biologists refers to certain dendritic-shaped cells in the skin of fish, amphibians and reptiles which have 'contractile' properties. The melanin contained in the melanophores may, in response to certain stimuli, disperse into the dendrites or concentrate in the perikaryon, thus accounting for the color change. In human cytology and pathology the term melanophore is a macrophage. *Ibid.* 640/2 (*table*) Recommended terminology of pigment cells. 'Contractile' cell: Melanophore. **1965** LEE & KNOWLES *Animal Hormones* x. 128 A characteristic feature of hormonally controlled melanophores is that colour change takes hours to occur, whereas this is achieved in minutes if there is nervous control. **1961** M. SEIJI et al. in *Jrnl. Investigative Dermatol.* XXXVI. 251/2 Because the melanin granule has been shown by electronmicroscopy to be structurally distinct from mitochondria, to be unique in its localization within the cytoplasm of mammalian melanocytes, and to contain a specialized metabolic pathway that converts tyrosine to melanin, we would like to suggest that during its enzymically active stages it be called a melanosome... The term 'melanin granule' could be reserved for the mature, fully melanized particle which has lost its tyrosinase activity and is no longer confined to the cytoplasm of the melanocyte. **1973** *Nature* 26 Oct. 436/3 The melanocyte's contribution [to pigmentation] begins with the synthesis of melanosomes, and the oxidation of tyrosine to melanin.

melanocyte (me·lăno-, mĭlæ·nosəit). *Zool.* [f. MELANO- + -CYTE.] A mature melanin-forming cell; also, a melanophore.

1890 in BILLINGS *Med. Dict.* II. 128/1. **1935** *Chem. Abstr.* XXIX. 8125 Melanocyte reaction of the preparations of pituitary body and the urine of cancer patient. **1953** *Science* 5 June 640/2 (*table*) Recommended terminology of pigment cells. Mature melanin-forming cell: Melanocyte. **1957** *Times* 4 Oct. 5 There are 500 to 2,000 melanocytes per square millimetre of skin surface, except on the face, forehead and behind the ears, where there are 1,500 to 4,000 per square millimetre. **1971** *New Scientist* 12 Aug. 366/1 It is difficult to understand why MSH is still secreted by the pituitary gland of birds and mammals, when these animals have lost the capacity for varying the colour of their body through the movements of pigment granules in melanocytes.

Hence **melanocyte-stimulating hormone**, a hormone that stimulates melanocytes or melanophores and causes darkening of the skin; abbrev. *MSH.

1953 LERNER & FITZPATRICK in M. Gordon *Pigment Cell Growth* 329 There are many indications that the pituitary gland produces a melanocyte-stimulating hormone (MSH) Rattner *et al.*). **1954** A. B. LERNER et al. in *Jrnl. Clin. Endocrinol. & Metabolism* XIV. 1465 We have called the pituitary factor which darkens skin the melanocyte-stimulating hormone or MSH, a term first suggested by W. H. Rattner. Names used previously include melanophore hormone, melanophore-dilating principle, intermedin, and others. **1956** *Jrnl. Biol. Chem.* CCXXI. 958 Two distinct melanocyte-stimulating hormones (α- and β-MSH) are present in hog pituitary gland. **1964** [see *INTERMEDIN]. **1971** *New Scientist* 12 Aug. 365/2 Melanocyte-stimulating hormone and corticotrophin..are two of the many polypeptide hormones secreted by the pituitary gland.

melanotekite (me:lănotī·kəit). *Min.* [ad. Sw. *melanotekit* (G. Lindström 1880, in *Öfversigt af K. Vetenskaps-Akad. Förhandl.* XXXVII. VI. 56), f. Gr. μελανο- MELANO- + τήκ-ειν to melt, dissolve: see -ITE[1].] A black to dark grey silicate of lead and iron (see quot. 1962).

1882 *Jrnl. Chem. Soc.* XLII. 291 Melanotekite, so called from its behaviour before the blowpipe (fusion to a black bead),..is a black to blackish-grey mineral, often with a bluish tinge. **1962** *Arkiv för Mineral. och Geol.* III. 143 Kentrolite and melanotekite are isostructural. They form a series with the end-members $Pb_2Mn_2Si_2O_9$ and $Pb_2Fe_2Si_2O_9$... Kentrolite can be defined as those members of this series which contain more than 50 mol per cent $Pb_2Mn_2Si_2O_9$, and the others are called melanotekite. **1968** *Amer. Mineralogist* LIII. 1278 The synthesis of melanotekite ($Pb_2Fe_2Si_2O_9$), kentrolite ($Pb_2Mn_2Si_2O_9$) and of intermediate members of this complete solid solution series has been reported elsewhere (Ito and Frondel, 1967). Using similar procedures, we have synthesized the Sc, Ga and Cr analogues of these compounds.

melanovanadite (me:lănovæ·nădəit). *Min.* [f. MELANO- + VANAD(IUM + -ITE[1].] A black opaque oxide of calcium and vanadium that occurs as bunches of acicular monoclinic crystals.

1921 W. LINDGREN in *Proc. Nat. Acad. Sci.* VII. 249 In 1920 Mr. W. Spencer Hutchinson, Consulting Engineer for the Vanadium Company of America, brought to my attention three specimens of a mineral collected by him at Mina Ragra, Peru. He suspected that it was a new mineral, and this opinion was proved correct by chemical and optical examination. The formula is $2CaO.3V_2O_5.2V_2O_4$ and I wish to propose for it the name of melanovanadite, in allusion to it being practically the only vanadium mineral of a deep black color. **1956** *Science* 1 June 990/3 Along fractures in the ore-bearing sandstone there is commonly a thin massive coating of an undescribed vanadium oxide. On this coating duttonite occurs as crusts and coatings... Associated minerals are melanovanadite and abundant crystals of hexagonal native selenium. **1968** I. KOSTOV *Mineral.* II. 470 Simplotite and melanovanadite have perfect {010} cleavage.

melatonin (melătōᵘ·nin). *Biochem.* [f. Gr. μέλα-ς black + *SERO)TONIN.] An indole derivative, $CH_3O{\cdot}C_8H_5N{\cdot}CH_2{\cdot}CH_2{\cdot}NH{\cdot}CO{\cdot}CH_3$, which is formed in the pineal gland in various mammals (principally from serotonin) and may be concerned with the regulation of certain physiological activities, esp. the reproductive cycle.

1958 A. B. LERNER et al. in *Jrnl. Amer. Chem. Soc.* LXXX. 2587/1 We wish to report isolation from beef pineal glands of the active factor that can lighten skin color and inhibit MSH. It is suggested that this substance be called melatonin. *Ibid.* 2587/2 In preventing darkening of frog skin by MSH, melatonin..was at least..5,000 times as active as serotonin. **1965** *Sci. Amer.* July 60/3 The ability of melatonin to modify gonadal function suggests, but does not prove, that its secretion may have something to do with the timing of the estrus and menstrual cycles. **1968** PASSMORE & ROBSON *Compan. Med. Stud.* I. xxiv. 36/1 Evidence from experiments in rats has led to the discovery that the pineal produces a hormone named melatonin, capable of antagonizing the effects of gonadotrophic hormones, slowing the oestrous cycle and reducing the weight of the ovaries. Production of melatonin falls when a rat is in a constantly lit environment... How far these findings relate to man is uncertain; but secreting tumours of the pineal in children lead to delayed sexual development, as if too much melatonin were being released. **1970** *Nature* 30 May 804/1 Melatonin controls diurnal and seasonal adjustments of activity in many species. **1974** *Sci. Amer.* June 62/3 The pineal..makes a hormone called melatonin that inhibits the activity of sex glands.

Melba (me·lbă). The stage name Nellie *Melba* (adopted from *Melbourne*, Australia, by Helen Mitchell (1861–1931), an Australian operatic soprano): used to designate certain foods, etc., named in her honour, as **peach Melba** (also **melba, pêche à la Melba, pêche Melba** (pẽʃ me·lbă)), a confection of ice-cream and peaches flavoured with raspberry sauce, etc.; **Melba sauce** (see quot. 1951); **Melba toast** (or **toast Melba**), thinly-sliced bread toasted to crispness.

1905 [see *COUPE[1]]. **1907** G. A. ESCOFFIER *Guide Mod. Cookery* xx. 778 *Pêches Melba.* Poach the peaches in vanilla-flavoured syrup. Dish them in a timbale upon a layer of vanilla ice-cream, and coat them with a raspberry purée. **1907** *Yesterday's Shopping* (1969) 33/2 *Sauces*.. Melba (Escoffier's)—1/6. [**1909** A. G. MURPHY *Melba* xxiii. 141 Melba's..tour for 1898–99. By this time innumerable soaps and sauces, ribbons and ruffles, had been named after her.] **1909** W. J. LOCKE *Septimus* iii. 40 The spoonful of peach Melba which she was going to put in her mouth. **1923** *Mrs. Beeton's All about Cookery* 418/1 Peach Melba... Halve and peel the peaches... serve them piled around a mould of vanilla ice cream... pour over a rich raspberry syrup. **1925** I. C. B. ALLEN *Mrs. Allen on Cooking* xii. 222 Patti Bread or Melba Toast. **1926** KIPLING *Debits & Credits* 28 Filet béarnaise, Woodcock and Richebourg '74, Pêches Melba, Croûtes Baron. **1928** D. L. SAYERS *Unpleasantness at Bellona Club* xviii. 214 You're as cold as a *pêche Melba.* **1938** *Times* 19 Aug. 7/3 Future generations may want more chickens and more peach melbas and less bread and cheese. **1938** M. L. RITZ *César Ritz* xiv. 204 Toast thin slices of bread once, then cut it through again, and again toast it... The result was Escoffier's justly famous *toast Melba*... During that year [*sc.* 1897] Melba had returned from America very ill... I had heard Escoffier discuss her *régime*. Dry toast figured on it... 'Call it *toast Melba*,' I said. **1951** *Good Housek. Home Encycl.* 552/1 *Melba Sauce*, a bright-red sweet sauce made from fresh raspberries and served with fruit sundaes, peach melba and similar desserts. **1953** E. TAYLOR *Sleeping Beauty* ix. 161 Sundaes, shakes, parfaits, whips, melbas. **1964** A. LAUNAY *Caviare & After* 137 *Melba*, large or small cuts of meat garnished with truffles, mushrooms, [etc.].. and served with a Port-flavoured sauce. *Also* fruit served with vanilla ice-cream and thick raspberry syrup. **1970** SIMON & HOWE *Dict. Gastron.* 292/2 The peach is historically associated with ice-cream because when Dame Nellie Melba, the great Australian singer, gave a party at the Savoy Hotel in London in 1892, Escoffier, who was then the chef at the Savoy, created the famous *Pêche Melba* in her honour. **1972** S. ATTERBURY *Waste Not—Want Not* 142 The Slow Cooking Method is ideal for Melba toast. **1972** *Vogue* June Special 128/3 *Melba sauce.* Blend 8 oz. fresh raspberries and pass through a sieve. Mix in 4 tablespoons icing sugar and add Kirsch to taste.

meld, *v.*[2] and *sb.* Add: Also in other card games, esp. canasta and rummy. Also as *v. intr.* Hence **me·lding** *vbl. sb.* (Further examples.)

1952 *Times Rev. Year* 1 Jan. p. v/2 Canasta has begun to influence the language, if slightly. It has spread the use of natural..as a noun, and figurative jobs have been found for meld, a combination of three or more cards of the same rank. **1958** 'J. WELCOME' *Run for Cover* iv. 83 He melded several more times—small melds which did not look dangerous from a canasta point of view. **1964** A. WYKES *Gambling* vii. 163 In most card games, players aim either to make specific card combinations (or 'melds') as in rummy, or to take tricks, as in whist. *Ibid.* 164 Games in which 'melding' (making specific combinations of cards) is a basic principle. These are the *rummy* games, which include all forms of *poker*.

meld (meld), *v.*[3] orig. and chiefly *U.S.* [perh. a blend of MELT *v.*[1] and WELD *v.*; but cf. E.D.D. *melder* entanglement, mental confusion; *meldered*, mixed, entangled.] *trans.* and *intr.* To merge, blend; to combine, incorporate. Hence as *sb.* and **me·lding** *vbl. sb.*

1939 *New Yorker* 23 Sept. 31 (Advt.), Schenley's exclusive process—melding—which 'marries' the whiskey blend so perfectly that it retains its rich flavor. **1952** *N.Y. Times* 18 Jan. 4/6 (*citing W. S. Churchill's Address to U.S. Congress*) What matters most is not the form of fusion, or melding—a word I learned over here. **1952** *Time* 29 Dec. 37/1 Taylor hopes to remodel the entire museum... He has plans to meld his eleven departments into five. **1959** M. STEEN *Tower* I. iii. 50 Our small..existence couldn't meld with his design for living. **1960** S. PLATH *Colossus* (1967) 14 Then I was seeing A melding of shapes in a hot rain. **1971** *Nat. Geographic* Oct. 560/2 Then clouds and gray sea melded and a steady rain slanted across the dry sides of the island. **1973** *Times Lit. Suppl.* 3 Aug. 911/5 The craft..of melding brisk jollity with real death. **1974** *Spartanburg* (S. Carolina) *Herald* 21 Apr. A6 (Advt.), A lovely cushioned group that offers a compatible meld of Ivy Leaves and light scrollwork. **1975** *New Yorker* 19 May 12/3 Jones' meld of traditional techniques with radical conceptions is in itself a radical conception, and gives the photographs their special, quiet interestingness.

melded (me·ldĕd), *ppl. a.* [Blend of MELT *v.*[1] and WELDED *ppl. a.*: cf. prec.] Formed from or using man-made fibres that have an outer sheath which has been melted to bind the fibres together into a fabric.

1969 *Sci. Jrnl.* July 77 (*caption*) New possibilities have now been opened up by side by side or core/sheath bi-component fibres which, when heated enough to melt one component, result in 'melded' (melt welded) fabric. **1970** *Cabinet Maker & Retail Furnisher* 23 Oct. 174/1 The most recent development of durable non-woven fabrics for upholstery is the production of melded fabrics. **1972** *Guardian* 5 Apr. 9 Melded fabrics have arrived from ICI Fibre.

Melean, var. *MELIAN *sb.* and *a.*

mêlée. Add: Also **melée, melee. 2.** [perh. a different word.] Small diamonds less than about a carat in weight.

1911 L. COHEN *Reminisc. Kimberley* 267 (Pettman), On a certain day I had entrusted him with two or three hundred carats of melée—small stones—to sell. **1920** *Daily Tel.* 22 June 1/2 Stones of various weights from 1⅞ carats downwards, and a quantity of melee. **1962** R. WEBSTER *Gems* I. ii. 39 Farther down the scale are mêlée

which are crystals less than 1 carat in weight. **1972** *Daily Tel.* (Colour Suppl.) 30 June 10/2 Stones under one carat, known as Melée, are divided into fewer categories, but with subdivisions of these main ones according to colour, quality.., and of course size, there are well over 2,000 kinds.

Melian (mī·liăn), *sb.* and *a.* Also Melean. [f. *Melos* (Gr. Μῆλος), the name of an island in the Ægean Sea + -IAN.] **a.** *sb.* An inhabitant of Melos. **b.** *adj.* Of or pertaining to the island of Melos.

1550 T. NICOLLS tr. *Thucydides' Hystory* [*Peloponnesian War*] v. xi. sig. Bb3ᵛ The Meliens..refused to be under the obeissaunce of the Athenyans. **1629** T. HOBBES tr. *Thucydides' Peloponnesian Warre* v. 341 Dialogue betweene the Athenians and Melians. **1709** I. LITTLEBURY tr. *Herodotus' Hist.* II. VIII. 300 The Hermionians..were ejected by Hercules and the Melians out of that Country which is now call'd Doris. *Ibid.* 302 The Melians..arriv'd in Gallies of fifty Oars. **1832** J. BELL *Syst. Geogr.* II. 513 Marbles of many varieties are abundant in Greece... Another variety was..the Melian. **1887** L. E. UPCOTT *Introd. Greek Sculpture* viii. 110 The statue of Aphrodite in the Louvre, called the 'Melian Venus' (Venus de Milo), found in 1820 in the island of Melos. **1910** W. JAMES *Mem. & Stud.* (1911) 270 The Meleans say that sooner than be slaves they will appeal to the gods. **1936** *Discovery* Oct. 325/1 One of the finest Egyptian masterpieces in the world, a royal portrait, was actually executed in Melian obsidian. **1946** G. MURRAY *Euripides & his Age* v. 128 The Melians..answer as best they can. **1968** *Encycl. Brit.* XV. 132/1 The Melian earth was employed as a pigment by ancient artists. *Ibid.* 132/2 In 416 B.C. the Athenians attacked the island and compelled the Melians to surrender.

melibiose (melibəi·ōᵘz, -s). *Chem.* [a. G. *melibiose* (Scheibler & Mittelmeier 1889, in *Ber. d. Deut. Chem. Ges.* XXII. 1684), f. G. *meli-tose* MELITOSE: see BI-² and -OSE².] Glucose-6-α-galactoside, $C_{12}H_{22}O_{11}$, a crystalline sugar obtained from raffinose.

1889 *Jrnl. Chem. Soc.* LVI. 953 This disaccharide is, therefore, not lactobiose (lactose), which it closely resembles, but a new carbohydrate, for which the author proposes the name *melibiose*. **1948** [see *DIOSE]. **1970** G. C. WHITING in A. C. Hulme *Biochem. Fruits* I. i. 8 Kliewer..detected trace amounts of maltose and melibiose in the grape. **1975** *Sci. Amer.* Jan. 82/3 The molecule bears a close resemblance to two common plant galactosides: melibiose, a disaccharide (two-sugar compound), and raffinose, a trisaccharide.

Hence **melibi·ase** [a. G. *melibiase* (A. Bau 1895, in *Chemiker-Zeitung* 16 Oct. 1874/1): see *-ASE], an enzyme which brings about the hydrolysis of melibiose.

1899 J. R. GREEN *Soluble Ferments* ix. 136 Barr [*sic*] has extracted the enzyme from low fermentation Froberg yeast but he attributes it only to the final stage in the hydrolysis, the conversion of melibiose into glucose and galactose, and he has named it melibiase in consequence. **1943** H. TAUBER *Enzyme Technol.* i. 28 Ale yeast does not contain melibiase, whereas lager yeast does. **1956** *Nature* 25 Feb. 383/1 (*heading*) Complementary action of melibiase and galactozymase on raffinose fermentation.

melik, var. MALIK.

1920 *Blackw. Mag.* Nov. 669/1 Each hilla, or village, has its sheik, each group of hillas is under a melik.

melioidosis (me:li͵oidōᵘ·sis). *Path.* [mod.L., f. Gr. μηλί-ς a distemper of asses, prob. glanders + -OID + -OSIS.] An infectious disease similar to glanders which is caused by the bacterium *Pseudomonas pseudomallei*, is endemic in rodents in certain (chiefly tropical) regions, and is occas. transmitted to man (in whom it is usu. fatal) and to other animals.

1921 STANTON & FLETCHER in *Trans. 4th Congr. Far Eastern Assoc. Trop. Med.* 197 The Greek physicians described under the name 'Melis' a variety of conditions resembling glanders. We propose for this disease of such varied form the name 'Melioidosis'. **1925** —— in *Lancet* 3 Jan. 10/2 Melioidosis..apart from one case in Singapore, has been recognised nowhere except in the towns of Rangoon and Kuala Lumpur. **1939** *Nature* 11 Nov. 801/1 The great plague of Athens in 430 B.C. may, Scott believes, have been melioidosis. **1952** M. E. FLOREY *Clin. Applic. Antibiotics* I. viii. 237 Five West African soldiers employed in Burma were found to be suffering from melioidosis. **1970** JUBB & KENNEDY *Path. Domestic Animals* (ed. 2) I. iii. 162/2 Outbreaks of melioidosis, as well as isolated cases, occur in sheep, goats, and pigs.

meliorant (mī·liŏrănt). [ad. late L. *meliorantem* pr. pple. of *meliōrāre*: see MELIORATE *v.*] Something that makes better; an improver.

1920 G. SAINTSBURY *Notes on Cellar-Bk.* 102, I am afraid that the 'whets' of our ancestors were rather stimulants to drinking..than meliorants of appreciation.

meliorative, *a.* Delete † *rare* and add: *spec.* in *Linguistics*, giving or acquiring a more favourable meaning or connotation (opp. *pejorative*). (Later examples.)

1902 *Encycl. Brit.* XXXI. 678/1 The so-called meliorative and pejorative developments in word-meaning. **1916** F. SWINNERTON *Chaste Wife* xvii. § 2. 254 Its note had been meliorative rather than optimistic. **1933** G. A. VAN DONGEN *Amelioratives in Eng.* I. 146 A meliorative sense-development can be shown to have taken place in a far greater number of words than is generally supposed. **1954** PEI & GAYNOR *Dict. Ling.* 134 *Meliorative suffix*, a suffix which gives a word a more favorable or flattering connotation. **1967** R. A. WALDRON *Sense & Sense Devel.* vii. 159 *Shrewd* is certainly most often a term of praise nowadays, though it comes from ME *shrewede* 'wicked, vicious' ..and passes through the 'cunning, crafty' stage before reaching its present mainly meliorative sense. **1971** *Archivum Linguisticum* II. 36 Not only is *silly old* — recognizably an example of a 'meliorative-pejorative' adjectival compound in English but, more generally, the example has..been shown to be ambiguous. **1973** *Times Lit. Suppl.* 8 June 647/3 His qualities were British, in the meliorative sense.

b. As *sb.* A word which has had a meliorative sense-development.

1933 G. A. VAN DONGEN *Amelioratives in Eng.* I. 115 The delimitation of the scope of content displayed by those words..may result in the word becoming a meliorative or a pejorative.

melisma. Add: Pl. **melismata, melismas.** Also, in singing, the prolongation of one syllable over a number of notes. (Further examples.)

1938 *Oxf. Compan. Mus.* 557/1 The melisma is a feature of eighteenth-century vocal music, often used merely for display purposes but also descriptively and for emotional expression (Handel, 'Rejoice greatly' and 'Thou shalt break them' in *Messiah*; Bach in such words as 'wept' and 'scourged' in his Passions). **1957** *Times* 22 Oct. 3/1 Some of the tunes were of considerable interest, varying from oriental melismata to a modal melody like an English folksong. **1959** *Listener* 8 Jan. 80/2 The opening cantabile theme..continuously flows into more ornate melismata. *Ibid.* 15 Jan. 145/2 Little arabesques and melismas. **1962** A. HUXLEY *Island* xiv. 242 Long-drawn, almost bird-like melismata on a single vowel sound. **1963** *Times* 27 Dec. 4/7 The melismas with altered vowels ('I saw her yesterday-ee-ay') which have not quite become mannered. **1965** *Observer* 5 Sept. 24/8, I enjoy the graceful vocal melisma of the improvisations. **1971** *Daily Tel.* 25 June 10/4 The melismata of Boulez' 'Pli selon Pli' are wearing well. **1972** E. T. SITHOLE in T. Kochman *Rappin' & Stylin' Out* 70 The black man..appreciates the rhythm of his speech and retains it in his songs by avoiding the melisma (many notes to one syllable of a word), as most of the Negro spirituals illustrate.

melismatic, *a.* (Examples.)

1909 C. H. H. PARRY *J. S. Bach* 99 A recitative for soprano with a beautiful melismatic close. **1936** *Jrnl. Theol. Stud.* XXXVII. 165 Does that mean that these sequences were originally intended to be sung as they stand, and that afterwards the melismatic form was combined with the syllabic? **1971** *Daily Tel.* 6 May 14/6 The English performances..entirely lacked the minute melismatic ornaments..that gave the Greek singers' performances their idiomatic character. **1972** *Times* 29 May 5/4 The sopranos, soaring effortlessly through melismatic phrases like 'music', 'praise' and 'rejoice'.

melkbos (me·lkbǫs). *S. Afr.* Also **melkbosch.** [Afrikaans, f. *melk* milk + *bos* bush.] A deciduous shrub or small tree, *Diplorhynchus condylocarpon*, of the family Apocynaceæ, which has a milky latex; also = *milk-bush* (*d*) s.v. *MILK *sb.* 10 b. Also *attrib.*

1862 'A LADY' *Let.* 23 Apr. in L. G. Ross *Life at Cape* (1963) ix. 100 Here also you find tufts of reed called the 'melkbosch', which are full of a milky fluid, only grateful to goats, for sheep will not touch it. **1898** in T. R. Sim *Forests & Forest Flora Cape Good Hope* (1907) 316 The local name of the plant [*sc. Euphorbia cervicornis*] is Olifant Melkbosch. **1939** 'D. RAME' *Wine of Good Hope* I. vii. 92 They camped below melk-bosch trees. **1951** L. G. GREEN *Grow Lovely* xxiv. 199 An even more historic landmark..is the gnarled melkbos tree known as 'the old slave tree'. **1957** *Cape Times* 18 Feb. 2/3 Seedlings from the old Melkbos tree at Mossel Bay should be cultivated. *Ibid.* 12 Sept. 2/4 The Board decided to give a melkbosch tree for an afforestation scheme. **1973** PALMER & PITMAN *Trees S. Afr.* III. 1911 One of the features of the tree [*sc. Diplorhynchus condylocarpon*] is its milky latex which when 'dry' is soft, sticky and rubber-like and which gives it the common names of 'rubber tree' or 'melkbos'.

Melkite (me·lkəit), var. MELCHITE.

1902 *Encycl. Brit.* XXVII. 237/2 The emperor appointed a new bishop of Alexandria, whose adherents the Copts styled Melkites or Imperialists. **1927** B. J. KIDD *Churches Eastern Christendom* xviii. 460 Originally a 'Melkite' meant a Christian who accepted the Emperor's religion. **1933** *Times Lit. Suppl.* 14 Dec. 890/2 They [*sc.* Christians] actually tended to welcome the Moslem conquest as releasing them from the persecution of the Melkite Church. **1947** G. EVERY *Byzantine Patriarchate* xii. 158 In Palestine..most Syrian Christians were Melkites. **1961** N. ZERNOV *Eastern Christendom* ii. 68 The official hierarchy.. was nicknamed *Melkites* (King's men).

melktert (me·lktēᵊrt). *S. Afr.* [Afrikaans, f. *melk* milk + *tert* tart, pie.] A kind of pie with a cinnamon-flavoured custard filling.

1944 I. D. DU PLESSIS *Cape Malays* 42 Many old Cape dishes such as *melktert*..are still to be found in the Malay home. **1947** *Cape Argus* 22 Feb. 2 Melktert, which the Queen enjoyed at Paarl this week, is one of those old Cape afternoon tea dishes which are as popular to-day as they were two centuries ago. **1949** L. G. GREEN *In Land of Afternoon* iv. 61 She was able to bake a cake and prepare *melktert* and *poffertjies* for Queen Mary. **1958** *Cape Argus* 1/2 Dr. and Mrs. Verwoerd gave them tea, melktert and sandwiches. **1972** *Good Housek. World Cookery* 406/2 (*heading*) Melktert (Dutch Milk Tart).

mell, *v.*² For 'Now *arch.* and *dial.*' substitute 'Now chiefly *arch.* and *dial.*' **1.** (Further examples.)

a **1889** G. M. HOPKINS *Poems* (1967) 185 May Mells blue and snowwhite through them, a fringe and fray Of greenery. **1959** *Encounter* Aug. 60/2, I published an excerpt from *Road* (melling it with parts of *Visions of Neal*).

7. Delete † *Obs.* and add later example.

1941 E. R. EDDISON *Fish Dinner* (1968) vii. 92, I find close harbours of discontentment:..foolish and furious designs. Go, I'll mell me with no flirtations but them as end in bed.

mellah (me·lă). [Etym. unknown.] The Jewish quarter in a Moroccan or Turkish city; cf. GHETTO.

1874 tr. *G. Rohlfs's Adventures Morocco* vi. 105 There is a Jew's quarter (Mälha) or Ghetto, for there is no town in Morocco, and scarcely an oasis in the desert where Jews are not to be found. **1893** S. BONSAL *Morocco* xvii. 315 In the large towns the Jews are obliged to reside in a separate quarter called the Mellah, the gates of which are closed and placed under guard at night. **1925** P. GUEDALLA *Napoleon & Palestine* v. 41 Old men in Turkish *mellahs* muttered the undying *Esperança de Israel*. **1963** *Guardian* 17 July 8/6 The mellahs, as the ghettoes of Morocco are called. **1972** *Country Life* 17 Feb. 414/3 The different quarters of the town: the kasba or quarter of government officials and Europeans; the Medina or Moorish quarter and the Mellah or Jewish town.

Melle, Melli, varr. *MALI *a.* and *sb.*

mellophone (me·lofōᵘn). Chiefly *U.S.* [f. MELLO(W *a.* + *-PHONE.] A type of brass instrument similar to the orchestral horn; an alto or tenor horn.

1927 *Melody Maker* May 491/1 The Mellophone has a distinct tone of its own; mellow, as its name implies. In colour I can only liken it to a cross between the tone of the French horn and trombone. In looks the instrument.. closely resembles a French horn. **1929** *Ibid.* Apr. 369/3 A mellophone is used and scored for..as part of the brass section. **1946** R. BLESH *Shining Trumpets* (1949) vii. 166 The brass section was rounded out by Isidore Barbarin on mellophone (alto horn). **1958** P. GAMMOND *Decca Bk. Jazz* xix. 229 He was mainly featured on an E-flat tenor horn, which produced a mellophone-like sound. **1966** *Crescendo* Sept. 35/2 Roy Fox's *Whispering* (with Nat himself soloing on mellophone).

Hence **mello·phonist**, one who plays a mellophone; **mellopho·nium**, a mellophone.

1962 *Melody Maker* 7 July 9 The Stan Kenton–Tex Ritter Capitol album soon to be released, has mellophoniums, trombones, and rhythm only, plus the hawaiian guitar. *Ibid.* 21 July 5 Two odd instruments currently in London. Above,..the skoonum... Below, Jimmy Deuchar with his new mellophonium. **1975** *New Yorker* 5 May 7/1 (Advt.), Mellophonist Don Elliot's quartet is on hand Wednesday and Thursday.

Mellotron (me·lŏtrǫn). *Mus.* [f. *mello*w + *electron*ic.] (See quots.)

1969 *Britannica Bk. of Year* (U.S.) 800/2 *Mellotron*, an electronic musical instrument programmed to imitate the sounds of orchestral instruments. **1970** *Times* 22 Dec. 11 The cold, windswept string tone of the Mellotron, a keyboard instrument which simulates—but not quite—the sound of an orchestra. **1974** *Melody Maker* 20 Apr. 46 The Mellotron, which was first introduced in 1963, cannot be slotted into any known category, but is best described as a series of controlled tape machines manipulated by a single keyboard. Each key relates to a tape on which has been pre-recorded a single note of an orchestral instrument. When the key is depressed the tape is played.

mellow, *a.* Add: **5. b.** *U.S. slang.* Satisfying, attractive, skilful, pleasant.

1942 Z. N. HURSTON in A. Dundes *Mother Wit* (1973) 224/2 If they's white, they's right! If they's yellow, they's mellow! If they's brown, they can stick around. **1944** D. BURLEY in *Ibid.* 207/1 The whole town's copping the mellow jive. **1945** L. SHELLY *Jive Talk Dict.* 15/1 *Mellow* (adj.) superlative. *Ibid.* 29/1 *Mellow fellow*, a satisfactory person. *Mellow mouse*, attractive female. **1960** WENTWORTH & FLEXNER *Dict. Amer. Slang* 336 *Mellow*,.. skillful; sincere, heart-felt; said of a jazz performance. **1970** C. MAJOR *Dict. Afro-Amer. Slang* 81 *Mellow*, gentle, sincere, satisfying; cool. **1973** *To our Returned Prisoners of War* (Office of U.S. Secretary of Defense) 7 *Mellow*, pleasant or satisfied. Just good.

6. b. *U.S. slang.* (See quot.)

1946 MEZZROW & WOLFE *Really Blues* (1957) 376 *Mellow*: feeling good, especially after smoking marihuana.

7. b. *mellow yellow* (*U.S. slang*), banana peel used as an intoxicant; also as *adj.*

1967 *Boston Sunday Herald Mag.* 30 Apr. 28/3 So I offered him—grass, acid, speed, magic—mushrooms, DMT, hash, and mellow yellow. **1968–70** *Current Slang* (Univ. S. Dakota) III–IV. 82 *Mellow yellow*, intoxicated from smoking a banana peel.

mellow (me·loᵘ), *sb.* *U.S. slang.* [perh. *catachr.* f. MELODY *sb.*] (See quots.)

1942 BERREY & VAN DEN BARK *Amer. Thes. Slang* § 568 *Mellows*, spirituals or religious songs. **1958** P. GAMMOND *Decca Bk. Jazz* i. 21 There were sustained 'mellows'—hollers in which a single idea or phrase might be repeated with numerous variations until the singer tired of it or thought of another.

melo (me·lo), colloq. abbrev. of MELODRAMA.

1889 E. DOWSON *Let.* 24 Mar. (1967) 54, I could no more go *twice* than I could to an Adelphi *melo.* *Ibid.* 24 Dec. 121

Even bad melo doesn't cause me to vomit as it did of old. **1920** A. Huxley *Let.* 23 Apr. (1969) 183 What one wd call a West End melodrama as opposed to a Lyceum melo. **1971** *Radio Times* 26 Aug., True life was *melo* about the first woman to win the George Cross. (As a stump word, '*melo*' is short for '*melodrama*'.) **1973** *Ibid.* 20 Dec. 18/4 *The Roots of Heaven*..John Huston's melo about elephant conservation.

melodeon, melodion. **1.** (Earlier and later examples.)

1847 W. G. Hammond *Jrnl.* 30 Sept. in G. F. Whicher *Remembrance Amherst* (1946) 183 Under the lead of Goodale with his melodeon [they] sing 'Sparkling and Bright'. **1850** *Rep. Comm. Patents 1849* (U.S.) 278 Improvement in Melodeons. **1964** *Amer. Folk Music Occasional* I. 39 As a youngster he heard his father's fiddle and listened to his mother's singing of the old songs to the strain of a wheezy melodeon.

3. Delete ? from ? *U.S.* and add examples.

1840 *Boston Transcript* 1 Jan. 3/1 A grand vocal and instrumental concert will be given by Mr. John Bartlett, at the Melodeon, Washington street, on Saturday evening. **1861** E. Cowell *Diary* (1934) 283 Hattie James..was burned to death, lately at the Gayities or Melodeon. **1948–9** *Northwest Ohio Q.* Winter 19 Parker occupied Cleveland's Melodeon again on June 12, 1854, when he delivered 'The Progress of Mankind' to a 'crowded house'.

melodicon (mĭlǫ·dikǫn). [ad. Gr. μελῳδικόν neut. of μελῳδικός pertaining to melody, f. μελῳδία: see Melody *sb.*] (See quot.) *Psalm melodicon*: see Psalm *sb.* 3.

1876 Stainer & Barrett *Dict. Mus. Terms* 285/2 *Melodicon*, an instrument made of steel bars in different lengths tuned to the diatonic scale, struck with hammers held in the hand. **1938** *Oxf. Compan. Mus.* 789/1 Grenié's invention, the *Orgue Expressif*, became the parent of a progeny including the..Melodicon.

melodramatics (melodrămæ·tiks), *sb. pl.* [f. Melodramatic *a.*] Melodramatic behaviour, action, or writing.

1915 *Nation* (N.Y.) 11 Feb. 161/2 We do not know when we have witnessed so disgusting a misuse of Federal authority, heightened as it was by the melodramatics with which Dr. Allen took the stand on his own behalf. **1929** J. C. Powys *Meaning of Culture* 374 No tricky affectations or morbid self-consciousnesses, no melodramatics with regard to art or with regard to one's own originality. **1959** *Economist* 7 Feb. 493/1 The melodramatics of 'massive resistance'. **1959** *Times* 19 Oct. 6/7 Then it [*sc.* a film] falls back defeated, although the melodramatics are exciting enough. **1963** *Guardian* 18 Sept. 20/4 No melodramatics had followed Mr. Macmillan's receipt of the Denning report.

melody, *sb.* **6.** (Later examples.)

1934 S. R. Nelson *All about Jazz* i. 27 In his melody section, Whiteman had a complement of violins, 'cellos, saxophones, trumpets and trombones. *Ibid.* ii. 56 The more attractive section in the orchestra, in which we have the melody instruments. **1955** L. Feather *Encycl. Jazz* (1956) 64 The slide trombone was at first considered no less a rhythm than a melody instrument in jazz.

melomaniac. (Further examples.)

1921 W. J. Turner *Mus. & Life* 18 It seems characteristic of that bogus science rampant among us to call persons fond of music 'melomaniacs'. **1926** C. Gray in Gray & Heseltine *Carlo Gesualdo* I. 46 This musical education and culture was by no means confined to the male sex... Lucrezia d'Este, afterwards Duchess of Urbino, was a veritable melomaniac. **1973** *Times Lit. Suppl.* 17 Aug. 955/5 A silent musical feast, this one, but a must for all connoisseurs and melomaniacs.

melon[1]. Add: **1. c.** *to cut the melon*, to decide a question.

1911 H. Quick *Yellowstone Nights* xii. 308 The O.M. as usual cuts the melon with a word.

d. Abundant profits to be shared among a number of people. Esp. in phr. *to cut the melon*. Hence **melon-cutting** *vbl. sb.*, in Stock Exchange and Betting slang, the dividing up or sharing of profits.

1908 *Daily Report* 24 Aug. 2/4 The theory that any prospective melon-cutting will be postponed until next year. **1909** *N.Y. Even. Post* (Semi-Weekly ed.) 7 Oct. 2 A purse of $25,000 will be distributed among employees. About 8,000 men will participate in the cutting of the melon. **1911** *Daily Colonist* (Victoria, B.C.) 11 Apr. 14/2 The Suez Canal..has been earning a gross revenue of upward of $20,000,000 a year, forming one of the juiciest melons every year anywhere in the world. **1927** C. A. & M. R. Beard *Rise Amer. Civilization* II. xx. 203 All went well until The Credit Mobilier in 1868 'cut a melon' in the form of dividends composed of the stocks and bonds of the Union Pacific. **1927** *Sunday Express* 24 July 6/4 As the company distributed some Preference shares only a short while ago we should think it unlikely there will be any further melon-cutting yet. **1928** *Weekly Dispatch* 24 June 6/4 The Union Pacific's portfolio [of outside investments] is one of the biggest potential 'melons' on the American horizon. **1939** *New Statesman* 7 Jan. 7/1 The enemy could practically destroy our commerce and industry... Every nation of the world would have an incentive to have a free cut at the melon. **1941** Dice & Eiteman *Stock Market* (ed. 2) 462 *Cutting a melon*, the declaration of a large extra dividend. **1942** Berrey & Van den Bark *Amer. Thes. Slang* § 734/6 *Melon cutting*, the division of heavy winnings by a group of bettors. *Ibid.* § 745/7 *Melon cutting*, the division of heavy winnings by a group of gamblers. **1948** *Aurora* (Illinois) *Beacon News* 7 Nov. (Suppl.) 39/2 This year, a record number of your friends and neighbors will split a record 'melon' in our 1948 savings clubs. **1964** P. Wyckoff *Dict. Stock Market Terms* 163 *Melon*, slang expression referring to the sum total of extraordinary profits waiting to be divided.

e. = *melon pink* below.

1930 Maerz & Paul *Dict. Color* 199/1 Melon... *Melon Yellow.* **1975** *Harper's & Queen* June 172/3 Striped swimsuit... Cassis, citron, melon,..chocolate.

4. melon pink, a yellowish-pink colour.

1949 *Dict. Colours for Interior Decoration* (Brit. Colour Council) III. 17/2 *Melon pink*,..a descriptive colour name, from the fruit, used in the textile trade. **1975** *Country Life* 6 Mar. 561/2 Daylilies..provide a show of yellows, melon pinks and apricots.

melongene (me·lǫ̆ndʒīn). [ad. F. *mélongène* aubergine.] A West Indian name for the aubergine, *Solanum melongena*, or its fruit; = Melongena.

1939 *Nature* 29 July 178/1 The very general use to which the [Trinidad Low Temperature Research] Station could be put was recognized..and..work was..extended to tomatoes, limes,..melongenes, cucurbits of various kinds, and to the assortment of vegetables that can be grown in the tropics. **1952** S. Selvon *Brighter Sun* ii. 37 Lettuce taking good... But ochro and melongene would take good. **1969** G. Sims *Sand Dollar* iv. 50 We might..fry some jacks and melongene, that's a kind of egg-plant. **1973** *Express* (Trinidad & Tobago) 26 June 3/6 Outside of the same building melongene is offered at 20 cents a pound.

melon-hole: see Melon[3].

melopœic (melopī·ik), *a.* [f. Melopœ(ia + -ic.] Of, pertaining to, or characterized by melopœia.

1927 *Contemp. Rev.* July 73 Wagner..turned to the melopœic chant, dramatised but not lyricised, for the expression of the words. **1940** *Burlington Mag.* Oct. 109/2 This melopoeic pattern is the chief beauty of Augustan verse.

melos (me·lǫs, mī·lǫs). *Mus.* [a. Gr. μέλος song, tune.] Song, melody; *spec.* the succession of tones considered apart from rhythm; an uninterrupted flow of melody.

1740 J. Grassineau *Mus. Dict.* 129 *Melos*, is no more than a song or piece of melody. **1811** Busby *Dict. Mus.* (ed. 3), *Melos*, a term applied by the ancients to the sweetness of any melody; or to that quality or character by which a melody was rendered agreeable. **1876** Stainer & Barrett *Dict. Mus. Terms* 286/2 Melos... A succession of musical sounds as opposed to *noises*. A tune. A song. **1887** E. Dannreuther tr. *Wagner's On Conducting* 18 He [*sc.* a conductor] found the right tempo whilst persistently fixing the attention of his orchestra upon the *melos* of the symphony. The right comprehension of the *melos* is the sole guide to the right tempo. **1903** A. W. Patterson *Schumann* 205 The tasteful *melos* or *arioso* which, throughout, takes the place of recitative. **1947** *Penguin Music Mag.* II. 13 The 'melos' by which he [*sc.* Wagner] means the unifying thread of line that gives a work its form and shape. **1963** *Times* 5 June 15/4 Size and melos and purposeful rhythm are the chief characteristics of Professor Josef Krips's Beethoven readings. **1964** C. Howell tr. *Gélineau's Voices & Instruments Christian Worship* i. 20 By means of melos he lets the words take on the colors of the prism of sentiments which illuminates them.

melt, *sb.*[3] Add: **2.** (Further examples.) Also *fig.*

1962 Simpson & Richards *Physical Princ. Junction Transistors* iii. 39 A small single crystal, known as the seed crystal, is inserted in the melt and withdrawn slowly in the vertical direction... A large single crystal having the same orientation as the seed is thus formed. **1966** *New Statesman* 22 Apr. 591/2 Pan American has now chucked a large, expected crystal into the melt by ordering 25 jumbo-jets from Boeing. **1971** *Nature* 8 Jan. 80/3 In the Vale of York, the most densely populated area liable to flooding discussed in the report, the chief culprits are snow melt..and violent thunderstorms. **1971** I. G. Gass et al. *Understanding Earth* i. 17/1 The composition of the olivine formed by crystallization from a silicate melt is of course a function of the availability of the two elements.

5. Special Comb.: **melt spinning**, the process of extruding a substance (esp. a polymer) which has been softened by heat through a spinneret so as to form a fibre; hence (as back-formations) **melt-spin** *v. trans.*, **melt-spun** *ppl. a.*; **melt-water** *Geol.*, water resulting from the melting of ice or snow, esp. that of a glacier.

1950 R. W. Moncrieff *Artificial Fibres* xvii. 197 Nylon is melt spun. **1973** *Materials & Technol.* VI. iv. 325 The molten polymer produced is melt-spun directly. **1939** W. W. Triggs *Brit. Pat. 528,455* 27 Apr., In melt spinning, the spinneret is generally placed so that the filaments fall vertically from the spinneret. **1963** A. J. Hall *Textile Sci.* ii. 75 With the introduction of nylon an entirely new method of fibre-spinning was established—so-called melt-spinning in which the polymer..is melted in a novel device above the spinneret so that it can by means of a pump be extruded through the multi-holed spinneret into cold air to ensure the immediate solidification of the issuing fluid streams into filaments. **1973** *Materials & Technol.* VI. iv. 297 Melt spinning is used for the majority of thermoplastic man-made fibre-forming materials. **1948** Schmidt & Marlies *Princ. High-Polymer Theory & Pract.* viii. 340 Nylon, polyvinylidene-vinyl chloride (e.g. saran), and Fiberglas are commercially important examples of melt-spun fibers. **1962** *Economist* 20 Jan. 241/1 Part of the industry where there was overlapping of effort, namely the melt-spun fibre field. **1934** *Geogr. Jrnl.* LXXXIII. 79 The amount of melt-water is so great that temporary rivers and lakes form. **1970** *Nature* 24 Oct. 352/1 Because most of the volcano is covered by glaciers, a great deal of melt-water has caused floods. **1973** C. Bonington *Next Horizon* x. 144 The face of the Pillar was sheer, clean and dry, but the slabby flanks were dotted with snow patches and running with melt water.

melt, *v.*[1] **2. d.** (Later examples.) Also const. *away*.

1934 A. Thirkell *Wild Strawberries* vi. 118 David..melted from the room. **1957** C. MacInnes *City of Spades* I. viii. 58, I could see no sign of Hamilton, and hoped he'd melted. **1959** M. Dolinsky *There is no Silence* iv. 61 What friends?.. They melted with the first headline. **1970** 'D. Halliday' *Dolly & Cookie Bird* vii. 72 People had started to melt, walking fast round the side of the house. **1975** P. Somerville-Large *Couch of Earth* iii. 48 Otway came bursting out... The girl melted away immediately.

meltdown (me·ltdaun). [f. vbl. phr. *to melt down* (Melt *v.*[1] 8 c).] **a.** The process of melting.

1937 *Ice Cream Trade Jrnl.* Mar. 36/1 The Sod. Alg. ice cream melts down cleanly in the mouth... Due to the clean melt-down..a cooler sensation results in the mouth than with gelatin ice cream. **1965** *New Scientist* 15 Apr. 161/3 Overheated fuel may result in 'meltdown' and general contamination of the reactor system. **1975** *New Yorker* 12 May 98/2 He was worried about loss-of-coolant accidents, core meltdowns, and breaches of containment walls.

b. A melted mass.

1973 *Sci. Amer.* Aug. 114/2 They recycle..bottles into gemlike necklaces, the meltdown fanned by the bowl bellows of ancient Egypt.

meltemi (melte·mi). Also **meltem.** [a. mod. Gr. μελτέμι, Turk. *meltem.*] A wind experienced in the north-eastern Mediterranean; etesian wind.

1921 *Handbk. Macedonia* (Admiralty, Naval Intelligence Div.) ii. 50 At the coast of the Aegean Sea, and at Constantinople, the northerly and north-easterly winds (the 'Etesian' winds of the Greeks and the 'Meltemi' of the Turks) become more definitely the prevailing wind. **1942** *Turkey* (Admiralty, Naval Intelligence Div.) I. v. 196 The west coast also has north-west (*etesiae* or *meltemi*) winds in summer. **1957** L. Durrell *Bitter Lemons* 73, I will take you to a special place of mine to taste the *meltemi* wind. **1958** *Times* 20 Sept. 9/6 In Aegina the *meltemi* will be blowing, a fresh salty breeze which tempers the noonday heat. **1959** *Chambers's Encycl.* VII. 775/2 The prevailing wind [in Istanbul]..in summer..is the *meltem*, a refreshing breeze. **1967** J. Rathbone *Diamonds Bid* xx. 171 The gusty dry wind, which the Turks call 'meltemi', sending clouds of dust down the boulevards.

Meltonian, *a.* (Example.)

1901 *Edin. Rev.* Jan. 100 The red evening coat in which fox-hunters dine may be traced to the Meltonian dandies.

melusine (meliūsī·n). Also **Melusine.** [a. Fr. *mélusine*, a kind of felt. Connection w. *Mélusine*, the name of a fairy in French folk-lore, is likely.] A silky, long-haired felt, used for making hats. Also *attrib.*

1908 *Westm. Gaz.* 24 Oct. 19/2 The Parisienne's latest love in millinery is the hat of silky beaver felt that she calls melusine. **1952** C. W. Cunnington *Eng. Women's Clothing* ii. 62 Toques in Melusine beaver. **1959** *Housewife* June 98 My white melusine hat is now a little soiled. **1962** A. Southern *Millinery* ii. 29 Melusine is a high-grade fur felt which is made in a range of beautiful colours.

mem, var. Ma'am. (Further examples.)

1854 B. P. Shillaber *Life & Sayings Mrs. Partington* 47 'This is grand weather, mem, for poor people' said Mr. Tigh, the rich neighbor of Mrs. Partington. **1867** *Goodwife at Home* i. 5 Eh! Dear be here, mem, is this you, In sic a byous day? **1876** E. B. Ramsay *Reminisc. Scottish Life & Character* (ed. 21) iv. 78 Then I canna engadge wi' ye, mem; for 'deed I wadna gie the crack i' the kirkyard for a' the sermon. **1877** G. Macdonald *Marquis of Lossie* III. ix. 161 But, mem,..I canna lee.

mem: see *Mem-sahib.

mem, *v.* [f. the sb.] *trans.* To note or write down as a memorandum.

1915 W. J. Locke *Jaffery* v. 61 Once having 'mem-ed' an unpleasant thing in my diary, the matter is over.

member, *sb.* Add: **1.** Also *virile member*: see Virile *a.* and *sb.* 3.

b. Delete *Obs.* and add later example.

1966 L. Cohen *Beautiful Losers* (1970) I. 24 This member of mine rigid as a goal post.

4. b. (Later examples.)

1888 J. Runciman *Chequers* 187 You're a red-hot member! **1891** *Sporting Life* 28 Mar. 3/5 But, warm a member as our hero was, standing in front of a blazing furnace for hours..was too hot even for Jem's *sanguinary* temperament. **1922** Joyce *Ulysses* 298 Gob, he's a prudent member and no mistake. *Ibid.* 228 Hot members they were all of them, the Geraldines.

d. Usu. *attrib.*, applied to a country, nation, state, etc., belonging to an international organization.

1931 *Times Lit. Suppl.* 28 May 429/4 Common action by a society of States against a member-State. **1959** *Ibid.* 13 Feb. 79/2 The member-nations' extra-European commitments. **1959** A. H. ROBERTSON *European Institutions* iv. 93 The Member States would consult together. **1962** *B.S.I. News* June 11/2 Copies of the national standards.. would go to each member-country. **1971** W. LAQUEUR *Dict. Politics* 361 Departmental ministers of member countries. *Ibid.* 362 Representatives of the member states' Chiefs of Staff. *Ibid.* 525 All member nations have one voice and one vote.

e. *U.S. slang.* A Negro.

1964 L. HAIRSTON in J. H. Clarke *Harlem* 290 Three more, one of 'em a member,..sailed over. **1970** H. E. ROBERTS *Third Ear* 10/1 Member, a fellow black person.

12. member bank *U.S.*, a bank which holds shares in, and has representation on the board of directors of, a Federal Reserve Bank (see also quot. 1930); **member-mug** *slang* and *dial.* (see *E.D.D.*) [f. sense 1 b + MUG *sb.*[1]], a chamber-pot.

1914 *Federal Reserve Act* § 1 The term 'member bank' shall be held to mean any national bank, state bank, or bank or trust company which has become a member of one of the reserve banks created by this Act. **1923** E. A. SALIERS *Accountants' Handbk.* 865 Member banks may rediscount short-time commercial notes with federal reserve banks. **1930** J. M. KEYNES *Treat. Money* I. 9 The typical modern Banking System consists of a Sun, namely the Central Bank, and Planets, which, following American usage, it is convenient to call the Member Banks. **1948** G. CROWTHER *Outl. Money* (ed. 2) ii. 43 The banks other than the Central Bank are usually called 'joint-stock banks' in Great Britain and 'member banks' in the United States (i.e. members of the Federal Reserve System). **1699** B. E. *New Dict. Canting Crew*, *Member-mug*, a Chamber-pot. **1785** GROSE *Dict. Vulgar T.*, *Member Mug*, a chamber pot. **1932** AUDEN *Orators* III. 104 The war-memorials decorate with member-mugs.

member, *v.* Add: **2.** Aphetic form of REMEMBER *v.* Freq. written as 'member.

1899 KIPLING *Stalky & Co.* 254 'Member the snow all white on his eyebrows, Tertius? **1936** M. MITCHELL *Gone with Wind* lxi. 1009, I gave him to you, once before—'member?—before he was born. **1945** 'O. MALET' *My Bird Sings* II. x. 167 '*I* remember Papa!' shouted out Amaryllis... 'So do I 'member Papa!' said Acanthus. **1971** *Black World* June 72/2 You member the day I left, Carrie Jean? **1973** *Amer. Speech 1970* XLV. 76 'Member the day I saw you on Broad Street?

memberess (me·mbərĕs). Also **membress.** [f. MEMBER *sb.* + -ESS[1].] A female member; *spec.* a female member of Parliament. (Not in freq. use.)

1867 J. MACGREGOR *Rob Roy on Baltic* x. 126 It would ..be worth while being an M.P...to see the Chancellor of the Exchequer badgered..by Dr. Emma Blew, Memberess for Honiton. **1876** C. M. YONGE *Three Brides* I. xix. 338 You proved yourself the fittest memberess for the future parliament. **1933** H. BELLOC in *G. K.'s Weekly* 7 Dec. 212/1 Your member, or membress, of Parliament is all for what he or she will call temperance.

‖ **membra disiecta, disjecta,** varr. DISJECTA MEMBRA *Lat. phr.*

1957 N. R. KER *Catal. Manuscripts containing Anglo-Saxon* p. liv, One volume of **29** belonged to Cotton, as well as *membra disiecta* of **22, 83** [etc.]. *Ibid.* p. lxii, The *membra disiecta* have come into existence for various reasons and especially because one part of a manuscript seemed more important than another part or had a different sort of interest. **1963** A. E. ELSEN *Rodin* 175 Vitrines filled with the sculptor's arsenal of membra disjecta. **1970** *Times Lit. Suppl.* 23 July 787/1 As they fed wanly on their ration of membra disjecta, they had scant hope of introduction to the more invigorating study of the specifically human phenomenon of language as a whole.

membrana·ceously, *adv.* [f. MEMBRANACEOUS *a.*] With membranaceous material.

1821 W. P. C. BARTON *Flora N. Amer.* I. 14 Stem erect, ..four-sided, membranaceously winged on the angles, smooth, nearly naked.

membrane. Add: **3. membrane filter,** any of various filters made of cellulosic material and capable of retaining objects as small as bacteria; so *membrane filtration.*

1951 *Jrnl. Amer. Water Works Assoc.* XLIII. 975/1 It appears reasonably certain that membrane filters have approached a degree of refinement that suggests their extended application. **1969** *Methods in Microbiol.* I. vii. 207 Membrane filters, as manufactured by the Millipore Corporation. **1951** *Jrnl. Amer. Water Works Assoc.* XLIII. 945/2 Recent German development in the field of membrane filtration. **1957** G. E. HUTCHINSON *Treat. Limnol.* I. ix. 646 The probability..that seston collected by membrane filtration or centrifugation is very largely detritus.

membranophone (membrē·nŏfōun). [f. MEMBRANO- + *-PHONE.] A musical instrument which employs a stretched membrane to produce the sound.

1937 *Times Lit. Suppl.* 17 Apr. 288/2 Those [instruments] which employ a stretched membrane (membranophones), such as drums. **1958** *Oxf. Univ. Gaz.* 10 Mar. 772/1 Membranophones, instruments with taut membranes made to vibrate by percussion, friction, or sympathetically. **1960** *Times* 18 Mar. 4/6 But aerophones, idiophones, membranophones..are universal and they are the concern of organology. **1971** *Sci. Amer.* Dec. 90/3 A drum is a membranophone.

‖ **membrillo** (membrī·lyo). [Sp. *membrillo* quince.] A preserve of quinces.

1920 A. E. W. MASON *Summons* viii. 75, I..made money..by selling dulces and membrilla and almond rock. **1935** M. HUXLEY *Let.* 4 May in A. Huxley *Lett.* (1969) 393 Cherries..have been preserved in all ways possible. Bottled, made into jams, made into queso, like membrillo, under alcohol. **1947** M. LOWRY *Under Volcano* vii. 239 There were big green barrels of jerez, habanero, catalán, parras, zarzamora, malaga, durazno, membrillo, raw alcohol at a peso a litre. **1966** P. V. PRICE *France: Food & Wine Guide* 263 A thick quince jelly, like the Spanish *membrillo.* **1970** *Guardian* 20 Nov. 11/1 *Membrillo*..is the famous Spanish quince cheese.

memento. Add: **6.** ‖ **memento vivere** [L. = 'remember (that you have) to live' (used in conscious opposition to *memento mori*): a reminder of life; a reminder of the pleasure of living.

1928 BLUNDEN *Undertones of War* ii. 17 Sitting in the headquarters dugout with 'La Vie Parisienne' as a *memento vivere.* **1931** A. HUXLEY *Cicadas* 8 Rosy among the funeral black (*Memento Vivere*) a naked girl. **1966** *Punch* 19 Oct. 603/2 A *memento vivere* from an asylum sought, found, but ultimately rejected.

memoirist. (Later examples.)

1889 G. W. CABLE *Strange True Stories Louisiana* ii. 48 Carlo was beginning to swear 'fit to raise the dead', writes the memoirist, at the tardiness of the Norman pair. **1907** *Daily Chron.* 11 Jan. 3/2 In almost every section of the volume he advances, as a memoirist, a moralist,..or a translator.., someone whose name deserves to be re-written over a faded tomb. **1914** *N.Y. Times* 31 May, These memoirists are as frankly revealing as any that described the daily life of the Grand Monarch's Court. **1970** *Daily Tel.* (Colour Suppl.) 13 Nov. 54/4 Hack memoirists often describe [Greta] Garbo as 'lonely' or 'loveless'.

memomotion (me·momōuʃən). [f. *memo* (? repr. L. *memor* mindful, and derived words) after *MICROMOTION.] A term used (usu. *attrib.*) in place of *MICROMOTION when time-lapse photography is used in place of ordinary cinematography.

1950 M. E. MUNDEL *Motion & Time Study* xiii. 253 Memomotion study is the name given to the special form of micromotion study in which the pictures are taken at unusually slow speeds, one frame per second being the most common. **1961** *Engineering* 6 Oct. 449 Both memomotion and micromotion filming have developed into very useful study aids. **1967** G. WILLS in Wills & Yearsley *Handbk. Managem. Technol.* x. 183 With techniques from work study using memo-motion cameras and a variety of other photographic techniques, an accurate picture of behaviour can be deduced. **1970** R. HAMMELL in D. Baker et al. *Physical Design Electronic Syst.* I. xi. 507 A highly precise form of activity sampling, called memomotion study, employs a motion picture camera.

memorandize (memŏræ·ndəiz), *v.* [f. MEMORAND(UM *sb.* + -IZE.] *trans.* and *intr.* To make memoranda (of).

1881 W. WHITMAN *Specimen Days* (1882–3) 178 Now he is sitting on the limb of an old tree..—seems to be looking at me while I memorandize. **1912** G. MALLORY *Boswell* ix. 246 Miss Burney has left us an admirable account of Boswell's deportment when in the act of 'memorandising' Dr. Johnson's conversation.

memorandum, *sb.* **6.** *memorandum-book* (earlier example).

1748 S. RICHARDSON *Clarissa* V. xlii. 301 On which she observes in her memorandum-book as follows.

memorial. A. *adj.* **3. a.** (Later examples.)

1891 S. W. MITCHELL in *Century Mag.* Dec. 287/2 The man thus imprisoned within himself recovers by effort a vast amount of memorial property presumed to have been lost. **1920** *Times Lit. Suppl.* 20 May 320/2 A link of material transmission..which..puts the theory of simple memorial piracy definitely out of court. **1959** F. BOWERS *Textual & Lit. Crit.* iii. 71 A memorial lapse, but not a misreading, must be posited. **1963** *Medium Ævum* XXXII. 23 It is often impossible to be sure whether scribal or memorial transmission has produced a given cluster of variants.

memoried, *a.* **2.** (Further example.)

1951 N. M. GUNN *Well at World's End* i. 9 She had a rosy wrinkled face like some memoried moony fruit.

memorist. 2. (Later example, not U.S.)

1920 H. G. WELLS *Outl. Hist* 115/2 Here we have..the medicine-man, the shrine-keeper, and the memorist, developed, with the development of the community.

memory, *sb.* Add: **1.** In *Psychol.* freq. subcategorized according to its manifestation or the bodily process with which it is believed to be connected. (Further examples.)

1883 F. GALTON *Inquiries into Human Faculty* 106 One favourite expedient was to associate the sight memory with the muscular memory. **1897** tr. *T. Ribot's Psychol. of Emotions* 153 Others..recall the circumstances *plus* the revived condition of feeling. It is these who have the true 'affective memory'. **1899** *Amer. Jrnl. Psychol.* XI. 7 He found that recollection could be mediated..(1) through visual images, (*a*) successive in time or space, or (*b*) grouped..*plus* motor memory. **1906** C. S. SHERRINGTON *Integrative Action Nervous Syst.* ix. 330 The relative haste with which an animal when hungry approaches food.. suggests that conation attaches to the visual reaction by association through memory with affective tone. **1921** B. RUSSELL *Analysis of Mind* ix. 157, I shall attempt the analysis of memory-knowledge..because memory, in some form, is presupposed in almost all other knowledge. **1955** H. E. GARRETT *Gen. Psychol.* x. 381 The phenomena of memory may be classified under the four headings *fixation* or acquisition, *retention, recall*, and *recognition*... Each of these four processes is a necessary part of memory. **1961** F. H. GEORGE *Brain as Computer* viii. 280 The hippocampus and hippocampal gyrus are therefore important features in recent memory. **1967** M. B. ARNOLD in Appley & Trumbull *Psychological Stress* 139 How intensely we experience stress may depend on the strength of this affective memory. **1969** T. FREEMAN *Psychopathol. of Psychoses* viii. 134 Sometimes the patient appears to have no capacity for short-term recall and yet at other times this function is quite intact. Similar inconsistencies of performance affect long-term and immediate memory.

c. The capacity of a body or substance for manifesting effects of its previous state, behaviour, or treatment; the effects themselves.

1887, etc. [see *magnetic memory* (*MAGNETIC *a.* and *sb.* A. 5)]. **1935** *Proc. R. Soc.* A. CXLIX. 72 The [magnetic] field..is to be regarded as 'frozen in' and represents a permanent memory of the field which existed when the metal was last cooled below the transition temperature. **1949** *Proc. Internat. Congr. Rheology 1948* i. 5 In the usual form of the theory of viscosity it is assumed that the rate of deformation is so slow compared with the relaxation process, that only slight deviations from the equilibrium state will be found... When the relaxation-time is large and the rate of deformation high..the deviation from the equilibrium state will then show traces of a more distant past. Here we see manifested a kind of 'memory' on the part of the flowing medium. **1950** *Physical Rev.* LXXVIII. 341/2 (*heading*) Memory in simple ferromagnetic domain crystal. **1964** J. M. BLATT *Theory Superconductivity* ix. 332 Since the supercurrent acts in such a direction as to make the total flux approach more closely to an integral number of flux quanta, this initial value of m_0 remains unchanged..and preserves a 'memory' for the initial, external flux. **1971** *Nature* 5 Mar. 28/1 The palaeomagnetic memory of most igneous rocks resides in grains of magnetite and titanomagnetite which are chemically unstable. *Ibid.* 30/2 Titomagnetite retains a memory of its original magnetization after oxidation.

d. The capacity of a body or substance for returning to a previous state when the cause of the transition from that state is removed.

1956 *Chem. Abstr.* L. 4577 The conversion of a naturally occurring twinned quartz crystal to single crystals by torsion often results in the formation of an unstable state, and the crystal reverts to its original twinned state. Natural crystals exhibiting 'memory' usually contain large amounts of impurities. **1961** *Chem. & Industry* 12 Aug. 1261/2 [This] could have accounted for that part of the diameter increases observed when the polymer solution flowed out of a capillary, which could not be attributed to memory of the convergent flow at the entrance to the capillary. (This memory could not account for all the diameter increase because as the length of the capillary was increased, the diameter increase decreased, but did not tend to zero.) **1964** A. S. LODGE *Elastic Liquids* x. 236 'Bouncing putty'..may be said to have a 'memory' of a few seconds in the sense that if a sample is first rapidly elongated and then held at constant length for a few seconds, no recovery occurs on release; whereas, on immediate release following the initial elongation, appreciable recovery (i.e. decrease in length..) occurs.

2. d. A device (usu. part of a computer) in which data or program instructions may be stored and from which they may be retrieved when required. Freq. *attrib.* (see *12).

1946 *N.Y. Times* 15 Feb. 16/4 Numerical values covering a wide range of scientific 'constants' are interjected as and when they are needed. There are four kinds of 'memory' in the Eniac to accomplish this. **1946** *Nature* 20 Apr. 527/2 The units in which addition is carried out provide a 'memory' with a capacity of about twenty numbers. **1948** *Math. Tables & Other Aids to Computation* III. 123 The instructions governing the routine operations that the machine is to perform can be stored in the memory in exactly the same manner in which the numbers on which the machine is to operate are stored. **1959** *Listener* 25 June 1109/1 In a typical ferrite-core memory several thousand tiny ferrite rings..are threaded on to thin copper wires. **1959** *Times* 13 Oct. 11/7 Data are stored in an electronic 'memory' or 'information bank', using digital techniques. **1962** F. I. ORDWAY et al. *Basic Astronautics* iv. 137 When a particle traverses the two scintillators..the pulse height from one of the counters is processed by a channel analyzer. Data are accumulated in the analyzer's magnetic core memory and then read out serially. **1970** O. DOPPING *Computers & Data Processing* x. 134 A secondary memory..cannot exchange data directly with any unit other than primary memory. .. In an external memory..the information contents can be changed not only by programmed operations, but also by manual operations... However, many people use the word external memory for what has been called secondary memory in this book.

12. (sense 1) *memory-bowed, -lit, -masking, -moving, -sweet* adjs.; *memory-cell, hole, -idea, -image, -judgement, -knowledge, lane, -mirror, -process, sketch, -trace, work*; (sense *2 d) *memory device, disc, element, store, unit*; **memory bank,** the memory device of a computer; also *fig.* of the human memory; **memory-belief,** the faith, probably unverifiable, that a person has in the truth of his memories; **memory book** *U.S.*, a blank book in which cuttings from newspapers and the like are pasted for preservation; a scrap-book; me-

mory cycle *Computers*, (the time taken by) the process of replacing one unit of data in a memory by another; **memory drug,** a drug supposed to improve the memory; **memory drum,** (*a*) *Psychol.*, a revolving device on which material to be learnt appears; also *transf.*; (*b*) a drum-shaped memory device in a computer; **memory effect,** an effect arising from 'memory' (senses *1 c, d); **memory span** *Psychol.*, the amount of material learnt under controlled conditions which is capable of being recalled; so *memory-span test*; **memory trace** *Psychol.*, a trace hypothetically left in the nervous system by the act of memorizing.

1955 *Astounding Sci. Fiction* Jan. 56 The memory banks of the computers would still contain all data pertaining to the course set for the EDS. **1970** E. Tidyman *Shaft* (1971) i. 16 Every face that passed him on the street became a deposit of his memory bank. **1971** J. H. Smith *Digital Logic* vi. 119 A shift register is a memory bank in which the numbers may be moved. **1972** J. D. Buchanan *Professional* v. 63 He ran the last two or three assignments through his memory bank to see whether or not they bore a residual potential for violence. **1921** B. Russell *Analysis of Mind* ix. 159 Everything constituting a memory-belief is happening *now. Ibid.*, It is not logically necessary to the existence of a memory-belief that the event remembered should have occurred. **1925** C. D. Broad *Mind & its Place* v. 233 Memory-beliefs..are not reached by inference. **1948** *Mind* LVII. 17 According to this theory a memory-belief has an 'intrinsic' probability; it carries its evidence, as it were, on its face. **1931** *Publishers' Weekly* 14 Feb. 843/1 Another demand..is that for inexpensive memory books used by grammar school children. **1925** Blunden *Eng. Poems* 28 And to my spirit memory-bowed The world with all its wars and wails Seems turning slow. **1892** Van Liew & Beyer tr. *Ziehen's Introd. Physiol. Psychol.* 156 These numerous sensory cells transmit their excitation further to one other ganglion-cell, a memory-cell. **1964** *Ann. N.Y. Acad. Sci.* CXV. 655 Most of the linc's instructions require from one to four memory-cycle times of eight microseconds each for execution. **1970** O. Dopping *Computers & Data Processing* x. 136 In a memory cycle, the computer can either erase the contents of a cell and write new information into it, or read the content of a cell and re-write it. **1959** *Times* 9 Oct. 7/4 On a memory device within the machine are stored details of the votes going to each candidate in each constituency in 1955. **1969** J. J. Sparkes *Transistor Switching* v. 118 The commonest memory device nowadays is the ferrite magnetic core. **1961** *Flight* LXXIX. 464/1 The equipment contains 10,000 diodes, 1,500 transistors, 3,500 resistors, 670 capacitors and a memory disc. **1965** M. Spark *Mandelbaum Gate* v. 129 Are these the memory drugs? **1966** *New Scientist* 4 Aug. 249/3 The new memory drug..is said to increase brain RNA production by 30 to 40 per cent. **1951** E. R. Hilgard in S. S. Stevens *Handbk. Exper. Psychol.* 547 (*caption*) Memory drum... The material to be memorized appears in the small aperture as the drum revolves. **1953** C. E. Osgood *Method & Theory Exper. Psychol.* iii. xii. 502 Lists of 12 nonsense syllables..are learned in constant order on a memory drum. **1962** [see *fish-finder* (*fish *sb.*[1] 7)]. **1964** C. Dent *Quantity Surveying by Computer* iii. 22 The memory drum of a Pegasus computer. **1971** *Jrnl. Gen. Psychol.* LXXXV. 137 Whether the results would be similar to those found with the use of the more..traditional memory drum. **1957** *Jrnl. Chem. Physics* XXVII. 93/2 'Memory' effects..can occur particularly in nucleation processes involving condensed phases. **1971** *Physica* LXII. 393 (*heading*) Memory effects and dynamical correlations in liquid argon and sodium. **1972** *Sci. Amer.* Nov. 40/2 Hysteresis arises because of memory effects in the magnetic materials surrounding the coil. **1958** *Electronic Engin.* XXX. 1/1 Although considerable research on switching and memory elements is still proceeding the basic design of the digital and analogue computer is fairly well established. **1949** 'G. Orwell' *Nineteen Eighty-Four* i. 40 When one knew that any document was due for destruction, or even when one saw a scrap of waste paper lying about, it was an automatic action to lift the flap of the nearest memory hole and drop it in, whereupon it would be whirled away on a current of warm air to the enormous furnaces which were hidden somewhere in the recesses of the building. **1894** Creighton & Titchener tr. *Wundt's Lect. Human & Animal Psychol.* xix. 282 Memory-ideas are aroused by sense-perceptions, and again interrupted by new impressions. **1890** W. James *Princ. Psychol.* I. xv. 620 He thinks it is almost entirely the amount to which the memory-image of the first impression has faded when the second one overtakes it, which makes us feel how wide they are apart. **1895** R. P. Halleck *Psychol. & Psychic Culture* 106 Memory images are those which most nearly represent existing things. **1904** G. S. Fullerton *Syst. Metaphysics* iii. 37 He may easily introduce into the memory-image elements..not present..in the original. **1921** B. Russell *Analysis of Mind* 207 A memory-image of a particular occurrence. **1964** M. Critchley *Developmental Dyslexia* viii. 52 Orton believed that during the normal processes of early visual education, storage of memory-images of letters and words takes place in both hemispheres. **1896** L. T. Hobhouse *Theory of Knowl.* i. i. 35, I substitute for the memory-judgment proper..the apprehension of the content of the memory judgment as an idea. **1937** *Mind* XLVI. 211 The only natural interpretation is to take it as questioning not the accuracy of memory-judgments but the worth of clear and distinct perception itself. **1931** *N. & Q.* 5 Sept. 180/1 The position is illustrated and supported by comparison of our knowledge of the physical world with our memory-knowledge. **1943** *Mind* LII. 192 We do possess both knowledge of the past generally and memory knowledge in particular, even though we may be mistaken in particular cases. **1954** Dannett & Rachel (*title*) Down memory lane. **1958** *Times* 5 June 16/6 *Liberty Hall*, an unhappily managed trip down memory lane. **1967** A. Wilson *No Laughing Matter* iv. 422 You were all down Memory Lane, no doubt, judging by the laughter. **1970** R. Hill *Clubbable Woman* vii. 203, I don't live down memory lane. What this photograph says to me is not that happiness is gone for ever, but that it's repeatable. **1973** *Ottawa Jrnl.* 5 Feb. 11/3 It was a journey down memory lane, full of anecdotes of the good old days. **1933** W. de la Mare *Fleeting* 72 Those eyes that, memory-lit, Now ponder on my own. **1923** Blunden *To Nature* 37 I'm not rejected then, my mind's delight Was not a play of memory-masking fancy. **1938** R. Graves *Coll. Poems* 163 Where port in Limerick glasses Glows twice as red reflected In the memory-mirror of the waxed table. **1908** Hardy *Dynasts* III. v. v. 212 Amid no memory-moving urgencies. **1897** C. H. Judd tr. *Wundt's Outl. Psychol.* 241 The process that arises under such circumstances is a memory-process. **1906** *Daily Chron.* 16 Apr. 3/5 Some clever memory sketches of the Franco-British Exhibition. **1925** R. Fry *Let.* 7 Sept. (1972) II. 581, I managed to do one picture... This is a memory sketch of the composition. **1917** H. J. Humpstone (*title*) Some aspects of the memory span test. **1930** R. S. Woodworth *Psychol.* (ed. 8) iii. 76 If the list of numbers to be memorized exceeds the memory span, several readings are necessary before it can be recited. **1951** E. R. Hilgard in S. S. Stevens *Handbk. Exper. Psychol.* 547/2 Related to what has sometimes been called the span of attention or the span of apprehension is the immediate memory span—the number of items that can be learned in one trial when they are presented serially at a controlled rate. **1955** H. E. Garrett *Gen. Psychol.* x. 386 One of the simplest ways of determining the efficiency of immediate memory (fixation) is to test the memory span. **1969** C. N. Coffer in Talland & Waugh *Path. of Memory* 219, I would anticipate that the first locus of pathology would lie in the memory span, that is, the size of the core of actually retained list members. **1964** C. Dent *Quantity Surveying by Computer* iii. 19 For the computer's main memory store, magnetic core storage is now frequently used. **1938** W. de la Mare *Memory* 3 Still memory-sweet its old decoy. **1924** J. Rivière et al. tr. *Freud's Coll. Papers* I. 63 Both the memory-trace and the affect attached to the idea are there once and for all. **1951** C. T. Morgan in S. S. Stevens *Handbk. Exper. Psychol.* 781/1 Learning problems in which memory traces had to last some time in order for the animal to make the correct choice. **1953** C. E. Osgood *Method & Theory Exper. Psychol.* iii. xiii. 588 The gestalt theory..must make two predictions: (1) The modifications within the memory trace for visual forms must be in the direction of reducing the stresses present in the original perception. **1967** Hilgard & Atkinson *Introd. Psychol.* (ed. 4) xii. 321/2 This particular hypothetical construct means that the memory trace does exist and that we may some day discover its nature... Hydén has proposed the theory that ribonucleic acid (RNA) might well be the complex molecule that serves as a chemical mediator for memory. **1959** *Science* 16 Oct. 957/1 Although tables of probabilities..containing over 300 items were used in the present study, they did not exhaust the capacity of the computer's memory unit. **1966** C. R. Tottle *Sci. Engin. Materials* vi. 141 Application of ferroelectrics includes memory units in computers and in capacitors. **1939** F. J. Brown *Sociol. Childhood* 456 It has..encouraged or even compelled him to do 'memory work'.

Mem-sahib. Add: Also **memsahib** and abbrev. **mem.** Also, one who behaves like a European woman. (Further examples.)

1873 C. M. Yonge *Pillars of House* III. xxxii. 205 She.. heard that 'it was but a few steps, and the Mem Sahib was waiting'. **1884** Kipling *Plain Tales from Hills* (1888) 236 The half-caste woman that we call the *Mem Sahib*... The *Mem Sahib* looks very old now. **1939** 'N. Blake' *Smiler with Knife* i. 19 Snug little billet, this. How does the Mem like country life? **1971** N. Barber *War of Running Dogs* xi. 124 The mems met at tea-parties to roll bandages. **1971** R. Dentry *Encounter at Kharmel* iii. 45 'Memsahib!' he exclaimed incredulously. 'Correct,' said Pepper. 'One memsahib, two memsahibs.' She held up two fingers. *Ibid.* 47 Respectfully, mem, you are tired. You come to the rest-house. **1971** R. Russell tr. *Ahmad's Shore & Wave* ii. 23 These nawabs are turning their daughters into mem-sahibs. **1971** *Femina* (Bombay) 30 Apr. 23/1 The shopkeeper is all smiles at having produced something exactly that the *mem-sahib* wanted. **1972** A. Christie *Elephants can Remember* x. 151 You are speaking of what you might call the memsahib days..when there were Service communities in Malaya. **1972** 'J. Ross' *Here lies Nancy Frail* ix. 114 The room was a monument to a long-dead British Raj... She had the demeanour of a mem sahib in the making.

menace, *sb.* Add: **f.** *colloq.* Applied to a person.

1936 D. Carnegie *How to win Friends and influence People* 63 A few doors down the street lived a 'menace', as they say out in Hollywood—a bigger boy who would pull the little boy off his tricycle and ride it himself. **1942** Berrey & Van den Bark *Amer. Thes. Slang* § 583/16 *Villain*..menace. *Ibid.* § 636/23 *Formidable opponent*.. menace. **1944** J. H. Fullarton *Troop Target* iii. xiii. 95 That B.S.M.'s a bloody menace.

menadione (menădəi·ǭun). *Pharm.* orig. *U.S.* [f. Me(thyl + Na(phthalene + *-dione.] 2-Methyl-1,4-naphthoquinone, $C_{11}H_8O_2$, a yellow crystalline powder which is a synthetic analogue of vitamin K and is used, often in the form of its sodium bisulphite compound, in treating hæmorrhage due to hypoprothrombinæmia. In the *British Pharmacopœia* called *menaphthone.

1941 *Jrnl. Amer. Med. Assoc.* 15 Mar. 1054/1 The Council has adopted the term 'menadione'..and has authorized its use as a nonproprietary name to describe the substance 2-methyl-1,4-naphthoquinone. **1942** T. Sollmann *Man. Pharmacol.* (ed. 6) 496 Various other naphthoquinone derivatives have the same action, for instance..'menadione', N.N.R. (menaquinone),..which is three or four times more potent than the K vitamin. **1955** J. G. Davis *Dict. Dairying* (ed. 2) 566 It has been claimed that feeding menadione..to lactating cows will increase the keeping quality of the milk. **1968** J. H. Burn *Lect. Notes Pharmacol.* (ed. 9) 83 Menaphthone (menadione or methylnaphthoquinone) is a substance which..increases the production of prothrombin in those deficient. It is commonly given to mothers a day or two before the baby is born.

ménage. Add: **4.** ‖ **ménage à trois** [Fr., lit. 'household of three'], an arrangement or relationship in which three people live together, usually consisting of a husband, his wife, and the lover of one of these. Also *transf.* and *fig.* Cf. *à trois. Hence ‖ **ménage à deux,** an arrangement of two people living together.

1891 G. B. Shaw *Quintessence of Ibsenism* 116 An elderly gallant who quite understands how little she cares for her husband, and proposes a *ménage à trois* to her. **1911** —— *Getting Married* 114 Nelson..formed a *menage à trois* with Sir William and Lady Hamilton. **1929** D. H. Lawrence *Lovely Lady* (1932) 106 The scheme of a *ménage à deux* with her mother had not succeeded. **1933** *Times Lit. Suppl.* 19 Oct. 713/3 He meets, and marries.. a highly sexed waitress, who inevitably tires of..the mother's dominance of the *ménage à trois*. **1944** H. G. Wells *'42 to '44* 102 They [*sc.* a Roman Catholic husband and wife]..submit to a domestic *ménage à trois*, with the priest as controlling intervener. **1958** P. Kemp *No Colours or Crest* xii. 249 That curious *ménage à trois*, the Anglo-American honeymoon with Russia. **1959** N. Mailer *Advts. for Myself* (1961) 285 A *ménage-à-trois* was completed—the bohemian and the juvenile delinquent came face-to-face with the Negro, and the hipster was a fact in American life. **1959** *Times* 28 Dec. 3/6 This happy *ménage-à-trois*—the errant wife, the lover and the unsuspecting husband. **1960** *Times* 30 Apr. 9/2 Primarily it [*sc.* a song] is a marriage of voice and verse, but since an instrument is soon added it turns the relationship into a *ménage à trois*. **1973** *Country Life* 14 June 1768/3 Pauline Viardot..the opera singer who with her husband and Turgenev formed a *ménage à trois*.

Menangkabau, var. *Minangkabau *a.* and *sb.*

menaphthone (mĕnæ·fþǭun). *Pharm.* [f. Me(thyl + Naphth(alene + *-di)one.] The name of *menadione in the *British Pharmacopœia.*

1943 *Brit. Pharmacopœia 1932* Add. vi. 19 Menaphthone should be kept in a well-closed container, protected from light. **1954** *Thorpe's Dict. Appl. Chem.* (ed. 4) XI. 369 Menaphthone, B.P.,..has outstanding activity, being several times as active as the natural vitamin-K. **1962** J. H. Burn *Drugs, Med. & Man* v. 60 It is fortunately possible to restore the prothrombin in the blood by giving vitamin K, or, as an alternative, a synthetic substance menaphthone, which is allied to vitamin K in composition. **1968** [see *menadione].

menarche (mĕnā·ɹkī). [a. G. *menarche* (E. H. Kisch 1895, in *Berl. klin. Wochenschr.* 30 Sept. 848/1), f. Gr. μήν month + ἀρχή beginning.] The first appearance of menstruation.

1900 in Dorland *Med. Dict.* **1905** *Index-Catal. Library Surg.-General's Office* X. 670/1 (*heading*) Menarche. *See* Menstruation (Commencement of). **1910** M. E. Paul tr. *Kisch's Sexual Life of Woman* i. 83 The diseases of the female genital organs at the time of the menarche are very various. **1949** E. B. Hurlock *Adolescent Development* ii. 41 It may be only a few days or it may be nearly a year after the menarche before the pubescent girl menstruates again. **1949** M. Mead *Male & Female* iii. viii. 178 In Samoa, there is no social stress on menarche. **1966** *Lancet* 31 Dec. 1453/2 No significant association was found between cervical cancer and abstinence from intercourse during or shortly after the menses; median age at menarche; regularity of the menstrual cycle, [etc.].

menazon (me·năzǫn). [f. Me(thyl + *n* (in *amino-)+Az(o-+*thi*)*on*(*ate*(s.v.*thio-1).] An organophosphorus compound, $(CH_3O)_2PS{\cdot}S{\cdot}CH_2{\cdot}C_3N_3(NH_2)_2$, which is used as an insecticide for aphides (see quot. 1961).

1961 A. Calderbank et al. in *Chem. & Industry* 13 May 630/1 A new class of heterocyclic thiophosphate ester has been prepared which combines outstanding aphicidal properties with low toxicity to other insect species and to mammals... One of the most active members is *S*-(4,6-diamino-1,3,5-triazin-2-ylmethyl)*O,O*-dimethyl phosphorothiolothionate.., which has been given the common name 'menazon'. **1964** *Which?* Apr. 114/1 The organophosphorus compounds, such as dimethoate, malathion, menazon, are mainly poisonous to sucking insects, such as greenfly. **1972** *Bull. Entomol. Res.* LXII. 177 In order to ensure protection from secondary spread of rosette virus on the sprayed plots, menazon was applied five times at weekly intervals.

mench: see *mensh.

mend, *v.* Add: **5. a.** *to mend up*: delete (? obs.) and add later examples. Phr. *to mend one's fences*: see *fence *sb.* 5 c.

1747 in *Amer. Speech* (1940) XV. 228/2, I went to mamacock & Crossman Lot & mended up fence. **1833** S. Smith *Life & Writings J. Downing* lvi. 192 They've got their clothes pretty much mended up, and they look quite tidy. **1854** M. L. Charlesworth *Ministering Children* ii. 19 Mamma is going to give me all Edward's old warm stockings, if I mend them up quite neat!

d. *to mend a pen* (earlier example).
1820 KEATS *Lett.* (1958) II. 262, I have been writing with a vile old pen the whole week... The fault is in the Quill: I have mended it.

6. b. Also *to mend up*.
1877 A. SEWELL *Black Beauty* (c 1878, ed. 5) xliv. 217 The farrier said he [*sc.* a horse] might mend up enough to sell for a few pounds.

10. c. To recover from, get better *of*, grow out *of*.
1881 J. FOTHERGILL *Kith & Kin* III. ii. 43 He had always trusted that the boy would mend of such outlandish indifference.

mendang (mendæ·ŋ). Also **mendong, mendung.** [Tibetan.] A sacred wall composed of flat stones carved with Buddhas or religious texts. Also *attrib.*
1925 J. A. HAMMERTON *Countries of World* VI. 3946/2 The mendangs—long walls in the middle of the road composed for the most part of inscribed stones. **1939** M. PALLIS *Peaks & Lamas* vi. 65 Each entrance to a village is marked by a *mendong* or *Mani* wall, a low cemented breastwork upon which innumerable flat stones carved with sacred texts in low relief have been laid, the accumulated offerings of local piety. **1952** H. W. TILMAN *Nepal Himalaya* I. iv. 39 These walls or 'mendongs', which are seven or eight feet high, must be passed on the left. **1960** 'S. HARVESTER' *Chinese Hammer* x. 94 A *mendang* wall in the town, the sacred wall. **1972** J. & R. GODDEN *Shiva's Pigeons* II. 88 Mendungs—low stone walls—carved..are built beside mountain tracks and along the trade routes of the north-eastern passes. *Ibid.*, It is reverent to pass a mendung on the right-hand side.

Mende (me·ndi), *sb.* and *a.* Also **Mendi. A.** *sb.* **a.** A group of Negro peoples inhabiting Sierra Leone and Liberia; a member of this group. **b.** The language of the Mende. **B.** *adj.* Of or pertaining to the Mende or their language.
1887 *Encycl. Brit.* XXII. 44/2 The following are the more important races [of Sierra Leone] that can be distinctly classified..Mendis, 3088. **1908** T. G. TUCKER *Introd. Nat. Hist. Lang.* 147 *Mende*, of Upper Guinea, including dialects of Mandingo, Bambara, etc. **1911** *Encycl. Brit.* XVI. 542/1 Some of the Krumen are coarse and ugly, and this is the case with the Mende people. **1936** G. GREENE *Journey without Maps* I. iii. 62 He could speak Mende; he was picking up Buzie. **1948** —— *Heart of Matter* I. I. i. 7 His Mende sergeant clicked his heels. **1957** C. MACINNES *City of Spades* 216 Mr. Karl Marx Bo.. planned to send..a tendentious report on the trial to the Mendi newspaper of which he was part-time correspondent. **1970** P. OLIVER *Savannah Syncopators* 112 *Mende*, Sierra Leone tribe situated near the coast. **1971** E. JONES in J. Spencer *Eng. Lang. W. Afr.* 68 The official news bulletin put out daily over the Sierra Leone Broadcasting Service by the Ministry of Information, as well as other important government statements, are broadcast in Krio as well as English, Mende and Temne. **1972** J. L. DILLARD *Black English* iii. 130 There will probably never be any reliable evidence as to whether the slaves themselves differentiated between the Vai-Hausa forms and the Mende form in pronunciation. **1974** *Times* 4 May (Suppl.) p. i/6 Typically a [Sierra Leonean] minister will be a Mende or a Temne with a Creole permanent-secretary.

mendelevium (mendělī·viŏm, -ēi·viŏm). *Chem.* [f. the name of Dmitri Ivanovich *Mendeleev* (1834–1907), Russian chemist + -IUM.] An artificially produced transuranic element, the longest-lived isotope of which has a half-life of two months. Atomic number 101; symbol Md (formerly Mv).
1955 A. GHIORSO et al. in *Physical Rev.* XCVIII. 1519/2 We would like to suggest the name mendelevium, symbol Mv, for the new element in recognition of the pioneering role of the great Russian chemist, Dmitri Mendeleev. **1967** *New Scientist* 21 Sept. 598/2 The new mendelevium isotope, with 101 protons and 157 neutrons, falls into the odd-odd class... The long half-life will enable quite large quantities of mendelevium to be made. **1971** C. KELLER *Chem. Transuranium Elements* II. ix. 596 Six isotopes of mendelevium are known with mass numbers 252 and 254–258... They can be produced by the bombardment either of uranium or plutonium with heavy ions, or of einsteinium with α particles. *Ibid.* 597 Since ^{258}Md can only be obtained by nuclear reactions with accelerated ions, it is impossible to produce weighable quantities. Consequently, the chemical investigation of mendelevium is restricted to tracer work.

Mendelian, *a.* Add: **B.** *sb.* One who adheres to or supports Mendel's principles of heredity.
1903 K. PEARSON in *Phil. Trans. R. Soc.* A. CCIII. 57 If we were 'pure Mendelians' we should for the purpose of character classification make *v*=*w*. **1907** *Nature* 23 May 73/1 It would be regarded as a demonstration of the falsity of the doctrine of gametic purity by everyone who was not a Mendelian. **1925** A. HUXLEY *Let.* 25 Feb. (1969) 242 You Mendelians have made all that..philosophy look.. dubious. **1941** J. S. HUXLEY *Uniqueness of Man* ii. 82 Twenty-five years ago..the field of heredity was still a battle-field. The Mendelians and the Biometricians were disputing for its possession. **1972** *Science* 12 May 623/3 The Mendelians, with their insistence upon large mutations as the agent of evolutionary change, undercut the Darwinian assumption of insensibly graded variation.

Mendelianism (mendī·liăniz'm). *Biol.* [f. MENDELIAN *a.* + -ISM.] = *MENDELISM.
1903 K. PEARSON in *Biometrika* II. 215 Mendelianism fails also for skin-colour in crosses between the black and white races of man. **1906** *Mem. & Proc. Manch. Lit. & Philos. Soc.* L. XI. 11 What is the essential feature of that which is called Mendelism by those who believe in it, and Mendelianism by those who do not? **1947** JACOBS & STERN *Outl. Anthropol.* 309 *Mendelianism*, the theory regarding the process of inheritance of characters, first published by Gregor Mendel in the 1860's and rediscovered about 1900. **1965** J. D. WATSON *Molecular Biol. of Gene* i. 27 All four wrote major works, each showing..how Mendelianism and Darwinism were indeed compatible.

Mendelism (me·nděliz'm). *Biol.* (now chiefly hist.). [f. the name *Mendel* (see MENDELIAN *a.*) + -ISM.] The theory that discrete bodies (now called genes) control the inheritance of any particular character and that these are inherited in accordance with certain simple laws first propounded by Mendel; the body of knowledge (forming the basis of the modern science of genetics) founded on the experiments performed and laws propounded by Mendel.
1903 *Science* 20 Mar. 451/2 The breeder wants to preserve the desirable characters or traits and eliminate the undesirable ones, but under the strict interpretation of Mendelism this is difficult. **1905** R. C. PUNNETT (*title*) Mendelism. **1906** L. H. BAILEY *Plant Breeding* (ed. 4) 168 Already so many adjustments have been made of the Mendelian principles that it is becoming difficult to determine what Mendelism is. **1920** *Edin. Rev.* July 135 Mendelism promises to furnish the stock-breeder with better and more certain means of increasing the economic value of his stock. **1927** HALDANE & HUXLEY *Animal Biol.* ii. 62 The comparatively new science called Mendelism. **1942** [see *BIOMETRY 2]. **1966** E. A. CARLSON *Gene* ii. 11 If Weldon had stopped here he might have won the battle and delayed the inevitable victory of Mendelism for more years than it took.

Mendelist (me·ndělist). *rare.* [f. as prec. + -IST.] = *MENDELIAN *sb.*
1910 H. WALKER *Lit. Victorian Era* I. iii. 230 There are Mendelists and Mutationists as well as Darwinians. **1951** *Biol. Abstr.* XXV. 657/1 The author opposes what he describes as the 'theories of the Mendelists and the Morganists' that the origin of life on earth is an extraordinarily rare occurrence.

Mendelize (me·ndělaiz), *v.* Also **mendelize.** [f. as prec.: see -IZE.] *intr.* To behave or be transmitted in accordance with Mendel's laws of inheritance.
1906 L. H. BAILEY *Plant Breeding* (ed. 4) 171 We do not know what plants will Mendelize until we try. **1913** M. HARTOG *Probl. Life & Reproduction* vii. 190 He found the characters thus acquired behaved as unit ('allelomorph') hereditary characters to the normal ones, and Mendelised just as do the unit characters which have arisen spontaneously, or have been transmitted for generations. **1924** E. W. MACBRIDE *Introd. Study Heredity* viii. 212 'Sports'.. which breed true when crossed with their like, but which 'mendelize' when crossed with the type. **1973** *Sci. Amer.* Apr. 8/2 Mendel repeated Nägeli's work with seeds supplied by him and to his disappointment found that they did not Mendelize.

Hence **Me·ndelizing** *ppl. a.*
1918 BABCOCK & CLAUSEN *Genetics Rel. Agric.* 286 Those changes in specific factors which result in the appearance of new Mendelizing characters. **1952** *Amer. Scientist* XL. 89 The differences between subspecies are hereditary and they are based upon mendelizing differences. **1969** *Nature* 14 June 1101/2 Their results..constitute the first thorough genetic analysis of a maternally determined Mendelizing character.

Mendelssohnian (mendělsōu·niăn), *a.* [f. the name of the German composer Felix *Mendelssohn*-Bartholdy (1809–47) + -IAN.] Of, pertaining to, or characteristic of Mendelssohn, or his musical productions.
1887 G. B. SHAW *How to become Mus. Critic* (1960) 132 The modern Mendelssohnian 'culture', with all its refinement, its elegance, its reticence, and its 'chastity'. **1900** *Musical Standard* LIX. 283/1 The second movement was rendered with a Mendelssohnian elegance. **1909** H. G. WELLS *Ann Veronica* iii. 60 The organ..was, in its Mendelssohnian way, as glad as ever it could be. **1928** *Observer* 29 Jan. 14/4 A clearly conceived and agreeable piece of music with Mendelssohnian orchestration. **1974** *Daily Tel.* 28 Oct. 11/1 Helen Donath's singing of the consolatory, very Mendelssohnian soprano solo gained in security after a nervous opening.

Also **Mendelsso·hnic** *a.*
1889 G. B. SHAW *London Music 1888–89* (1937) 164 Her Mendelssohnic sense of form in composition. **1890** *Ibid.* 300 This Mendelssohnic curse of speed for speed's sake. **1928** *Observer* 4 Mar. 14/5 Ask yourself what are the real Beethoven touches in the Mendelssohnic finale.

mending, *vbl. sb.* Add: **1. c.** Also *attrib.*
1856 C. M. YONGE *Daisy Chain* I. vii. 63 Ethel had to fetch her mending-basket. **1863** 'G. HAMILTON' *Gala-Days* 41, I find myself in a mending-basket. **1867** A. D. WHITNEY *Summer in L. Goldthwaite's Life* viii. 165 What should we do without our mending-day? **1899** A. NICHOLAS *Idyl of Wabash* 18 Taking his hose from the mending basket and darning them. **1966** *Olney Amsden & Sons Ltd. Price List* 28 Mending cotton, white only. **1974** J. STUBBS *Painted Face* vii. 107 Bessie..opened her mending basket.

2. a. (Also in *sing.*)
1891 *Harper's Mag.* Sept. 579/1 Mrs. Dorset was on the bench in the porch, the basket of mending by her.

mendong, var. *MENDANG.

mendopo, var. *PENDOPO.

mendung, var. *MENDANG.

meneer, var. MYNHEER.
1939 S. CLOETE *Watch for Dawn* i. 5 What are these questions that you torment me with, meneer? **1946** *Cape Times* 16 Nov. 4 Meneer is a strange man. **1948** *Cape Argus* 9 Aug. 9/5 The meneer found those spoons... Mr. Erlank swung back to the constable. 'Did you find spoons there?' he asked. **1970** G. CROUDACE *Scarlet Bikini* vii. 79 I'm listening, *meneer.*

‖ **mengkuang** (meŋkwæ·ŋ). [Malay.] A tree belonging to one of the larger species of *Pandanus*, providing leaves that can be woven into matting, etc. Also *attrib.*
1900 H. N. RIDLEY in *Jrnl. Straits Branch Roy. Asiatic Soc.* XXXIII. 170 *Pandanus atrocarpus* Griff. 'Mengkuang'. The biggest species here, often 40 feet high with very long leaves. **1908** L. WRAY in A. Wright *20th Cent. Impressions Brit. Malaya* 235/3 Of late years a fairly large industry has sprung up in Negri Sambilan in the manufacture of mat hats... The finer are of *Pandan* leaves, and the coarser of *Mengkuang* leaves. **1935** I. H. BURKILL *Dict. Econ. Products Malay Peninsula* II. 1644 Such species [of *Pandanus*] as are used for matting are called by the Malays 'mĕngkuang'. **1947** R. O. WINSTEDT *Malays* 175 Dish covers are sometimes made of this mad plait, or they are made of strips of the white inner sheath of bamboo..stuck over a conical *meng-kuang* lining shaped like Chinese hats. **1954** R. E. HOLTTUM *Plant Life Malaya* ii. 23 The big swamp Pandan called Mengkuang, with trunks sixty feet or more high and leaves twenty feet long, rivals most palms in bulk. **1965** C. SHUTTLEWORTH *Malayan Safari* ii. 29 A patch of earth near the cooking fires was swept clean and laid with broad *mengkuang* leaves. **1972** M. SHEPPARD *Taman Indera* 158 Coarser matting for everyday household use and sacking are made of *mengkuang*. Pandan is frequently dyed and woven into elaborate patterns. *Mengkuang* is more often used in its natural form.

mengkulang (me·ŋkulaŋ). [Malay.] A timber tree belonging to the Malaysian genus *Tarrietia*, esp. *T. simplicifolia*, or its wood.
1940 E. J. H. CORNER *Wayside Trees Malaya* I. 622 The species of Tarrietia are mostly timber-trees known to Malays as Mengkulang. **1956** *Handbk. Hardwoods* (Forest Prod. Res. Lab.) 150 Locally, mengkulang is used for interior construction, flooring and furniture. **1972** *Timber Trades Jrnl.* 13 May 39/2 Mengkulang is not easy [to obtain], presumably because of the competition from the plywood mills.

Ménière (‖ meniḗr). *Path.* The name of Prosper *Ménière* (1799–1862), French physician, used in the possessive to designate a disease of the membranous labyrinth of the ear associated with dizziness, tinnitus, etc., and causing progressive deafness in the ear affected (described by Ménière in 1861).
Accentuation of the name varies. The forms *Menière*, used by the physician himself, and *Ménière*, used by many writers about him and now by his descendants, are both common. The unaccented form *Meniere* is used in some modern English works.
1876 *Edin. Med. Jrnl.* XXI. 716 (*heading*) Case of Menière's disease. **1885** *Encycl. Brit.* XIX. 39/1 A diminution of the power of co-ordinated action, as in Menière's disease. **1907** *Brit. Med. Jrnl.* 11 May 1107/2 Ménière's disease..is a rare disease, while cases exhibiting Ménière's symptoms are not by any means uncommon. **1938** *Proc. R. Soc. Med.* XXXI. 1317 (*heading*) Observations on the pathology of Ménière's syndrome. **1955** W. GADDIS *Recognitions* III. i. 732 If it is Ménière's syndrome, we'll have you up staggering around in no time. **1968** HARRISON & NAFTALIN (*title*) Menière's disease. **1968** J. L. PULEC (*title*) Meniere's disease. **1971** *Daily Tel.* 30 Jan. 3/2 Grounded by Ménière's syndrome, a malady of the inner ear which was causing increasing deafness, he secretly went into hospital.

meningioma (menindʒiōu·mă). *Path.* Pl. **-omas, -omata.** [mod.L., f. by shortening *mening(othel)ioma*, f. MENINGO- + *ENDO)-THELIOMA.] A tumour, usu. benign, arising from the meninges (esp. those of the brain).
1922 H. CUSHING in *Brain* XLV. 282 (*heading*) The meningiomas (dual endotheliomas): their source, and favoured seats of origin. *Ibid.* 285 The term *meningothelioma* was first proposed, but it has, on further consideration, been shortened to *meningioma.* This word, consequently, will be used to indicate the entire group of tumours which appear to arise from the pachymeninx. **1961** *Lancet* 16 Sept. 656/2 Of particular interest was the activity of the cells comprising the whorls of a meningioma. **1974** PASSMORE & ROBSON *Compan. Med. Stud.* III. xxxiv. 110/2 About 18 per cent of intracranial tumours are meningiomata.

meningo-. Add: **meni:ngococ·cal, -coc·cic** *adjs.*, of, pertaining to, involving, or caused by a meningococcus; **meni:ngo-ence·phalocele** [ENCEPHALOCELE], the protrusion of brain substance and meninges through a hole in the skull; the mass so protruded; **meni:ngo-ence:phalomyeli·tis** [*encephalomyelitis* s.v. *ENCEPHALO-], inflammation of the meninges,

brain, and spinal cord; **meningo-myelocele** (examples); = *MYELOMENINGOCELE.

1907 *Edin. Med. Jrnl.* LXIV. 227 One case..associated with tubercular meningitis..clearly falls..into line with meningococcal arthritis. **1949** H. W. FLOREY in H. W. Florey et al. *Antibiotics* I. i. 23 Meningococcal carriers were successfully cleared of micro-organisms. **1966** *Jrnl. Amer. Med. Assoc.* 2 May 391 (*heading*) Meningococcal disease, 1965. **1907** *Jrnl. Med. Res.* XVII. 229 Seven different antigonococcic serums and a meningococcic serum. **1950** *Amer. Jrnl. Med.* VIII. 468 (*heading*) Cause of death in meningococcic infection. **1891** F. P. FOSTER *Med. Dict.* III. 2277/1 *Meningo-encephalocele*, a tumour of the head analogous to hydro-myelocele. **1901** *Brit. Med. Jrnl.* 22 June 1542/1 (*heading*) Case of meningo-encephalocele treated by excision of the mass. **1964** S. DUKE-ELDER *Parsons' Dis. Eye* (ed. 14) xxxiii. 529 Clinically they [*sc.* dermoid cysts of the orbit] may be mistaken for meningo-encephaloceles, protrusions of the cerebral contents, which usually occur at the upper and inner angle where there are most sutures between bones. **1900** DORLAND *Med. Dict.* 381/1 Meningo-encephalomyelitis. **1966** WRIGHT & SYMMERS *Systemic Path.* II. xxxiv. 1199 Myalgic Meningoencephalomyelitis. An extensive epidemic of a benign myalgic encephalomyelitis occurred among the staff of the Royal Free Hospital in London, in 1955. **1885** *Trans. Clin. Soc.* XVIII. 340 Protrusion of the membranes together with the spinal cord and its appertaining nerves, meningo-myelocele. **1966** WRIGHT & SYMMERS *Systemic Path.* II. viii. 1234/2 In its least serious form, spina bifida occulta, there is incomplete closure of one or more of the vertebral arches... In a more serious and commoner variety, meningomyelocele, the spinal cord is involved, and portions of its posterior columns may be stretched out in the wall of the subcutaneous cystic swelling.

Mennecy (me·nəsi), *a.* Also **Menecy.** [Name of a town in France, near Paris.] The designation of a soft-paste porcelain made at Mennecy. Also *absol.*

1863 W. CHAFFERS *Marks Pott. & Porc.* 203 Menecy, marked in blue on a soft paste egg cup, of very early manufacture. **1869** C. SCHREIBER *Jrnl.* Aug. (1911) I. 32 Mennecy china box. **1870** *Ibid.* 71 We found a..Mennecy basket and cover with coloured flowers in relief. **1874** *Ibid.* 255 A small piece of Mennecy at Van Houtum's. **1957** *Encycl. Brit.* XVIII. 351/2 At its best, Mennecy porcelain is of unsurpassed quality, mellow in tone and texture and of a warm white colour. **1960** R. G. HAGGAR *Conc. Encycl. Cont. Pott. & Porc.* 314/1 The Mennecy porcelain manufacture originated in the rue de Charonne, Paris..in 1734. **1960** H. HAYWARD *Antique Coll.* 181/2 Mennecy porcelain, soft-paste porcelain..made at Mennecy, Ile-de-France, between 1735 and 1785. **1972** *Country Life* 8 June (Suppl.) 58/1 An ormolu birdcage with Mennecy flowers.

Mennist (me·nist). *U.S.* [irreg. f. *Menno* (see MENNONITE) + -IST.] = MENNONIST, MENNONITE. Also *attrib.*

1771 G. TAYLOR *Voy. N. Amer.* 170 In the City of Philadelphia you see Churchmen, Quakers, Lutherans, Calvinists, Moravians, Catholics, Menists, [etc.]. **1869** *Atlantic Monthly* Oct. 474/1 The Mennists in many outward circumstances very much resemble the Society of Friends. *Ibid.*, In the interior of the Mennist meeting, a Quaker-like plainness prevails.

meno (me·no), *adv. Mus.* [It.] Less; used in musical directions, as *meno mosso*, rather slower, less animated (lit. 'less moved').

1876 STAINER & BARRETT *Dict. Mus. Terms* 286/2 *Men, meno*... Less; as *meno forte*, not so loud. **1880** GROVE *Dict. Mus.* II. 311/2 *Meno mosso*, a direction, which, like Più lento, generally occurs in the middle of a movement. *Ibid.* 312/1 Beethoven uses 'Meno mosso e moderato' in the Fugue for strings in B♭, op. 133, and 'Assai meno presto'—'very much less quick'—in the Trio of Symphony No. 7.

menologist (mėnǫ·lŏdʒist). [f. MENOLOGY: see -IST.] A compiler of a menologium.

1895 F. TUPPER in *PMLA* X. 224 The Menologist (*Cælendcwide*, 56) ushers in Easter thus: 'Aprelis monað on þam oftust cymð [etc.]'. **1948** K. MALONE *Middle Ages* I. 35 For sources the menologist presumably used church calendars and the like... In any case the menologist was no mere clerk, learned in Church Latin only. He was steeped in classical Old English poetry, as his style and choice of words reveal.

menology. Add: In sense 1 b now usu. in form *menologium.* (Earlier and later examples.)

1709 E. ELSTOB tr. *Ælfric's Homily on St. Gregory* App. 26 The Original MS. of the Menologium is in the Cottonian Library. **1735** M. SHELTON tr. *Wotton's Short View G. Hickes's Anc. Northern-Lang.* 20 The first of these is a Poetical Calendar, translated into Latin, wherein it is observable, that this Menology, wrote at the Command of some Anglo-Saxon Bishop, or King, who reigned after the Dissolution of the Heptarchy, makes mention of no Saints except Pope Gregory, and Austin the Monk. **1807** S. TURNER *Hist. Anglo-Saxons* (ed. 2) II. 280 The elegant Menology in the Cotton Library. **1830** B. THORPE tr. *Rask's Gram. Anglo-Saxon Tongue* 138 Another remarkable instance of this [lack of strophic or stanzaic divisions] is the conclusion of the *Menologium Saxonicum.* **1905** E. D. HANSCOM in *Jrnl. Eng. & Germ. Philol.* V. 441 The *Menologium* preserves the popular names of October and November, *Winterfylleð* (184) and *Blotmonað* (195). **1932** CHADWICK & KERSHAW *Growth of Lit.* I. 380 The *Menologium* or metrical calendar at the beginning of MS. C of the *Saxon Chronicle.*

Menominee (mėnǫ·minī). *U.S.* Also **Menomini, -onee.** [ad. Ojibwa *manōminī*, lit. 'wild-rice people'.] **1.** The name of a tribe of Algonquian Indians first discovered near the mouth of the Menominee River in Michigan and Wisconsin; also *attrib.*; also applied to the language spoken by this people.

1762 T. HUTCHINS *Jrnl.* 26 June in *Mich. Hist. Mag.* (1926) X. 369, I delivered the same Message to the Meynomeneys that I had done to the Sax and Reynard Nations. **1830** [see *HALF-BLOOD 4]. **1835** C. F. HOFFMAN *Winter in West* II. 3 The Mè-nó-mé-nê, or wild-rice-eaters, is a broken band that served with effect against the Sauks and Foxes in the Indian difficulties of 1832. **1920** L. BLOOMFIELD in C. F. Hockett *Leonard Bloomfield Anthol.* (1970) 90 Have been writing down Menominee words and stories. They are a delightful people, of good culture: it must have been an elaborate and beautiful culture 200 years ago. **1922** —— in *Ibid.* 99 These stems are a living (freely formed) derivation in Menomini. **1953** A. HUXLEY *Let.* 17 Aug. (1969) 683 The Menomini are Indians in a reservation in Wisconsin. **1964** E. BACH *Introd. Transformational Gram.* i. 2 To learn Greek or Menomini..it is not enough to read through a compact presentation of paradigms or rules. **1975** *Times* 8 Jan. 6 Troops of the Wisconsin National Guard were called out today to deal with a group of Menominee Indians occupying a large estate... The Menominees have a reservation near by.

2. In full, *Menominee whitefish.* The round whitefish, *Prosopium cylindraceum*, found in lakes of northern North America.

1884 G. B. GOODE *Fisheries U.S.: Nat. Hist. Aquatic Animals* 541 *Coregonus quadrilateralis.* The only name which I have heard applied to this fish is that of 'Menomonee White-fish'. **1902** *Rep. U.S. Comm. Fisheries 1901* 653 Table showing, by States, the products of the fisheries of the Great Lakes in 1899..White-fish (Menominee) fresh ..White-fish (Menominee) salted. **1944** G. L. NUTE *Lake Superior* 186 Menominees, a kind of whitefish, are listed at 14,940 pounds, all caught in American waters.

menopausal (menŏpǭ·zăl), *a.* [f. MENOPAUSE + -AL.] Of, pertaining to, or connected with the menopause. Also *fig.*

1910 *Practitioner* June 787 Permanent cessation of the menses, so long as the ovaries have been conserved, is not associated with so-called 'menopausal' symptoms. **1964** L. MARTIN *Clin. Endocrinol.* (ed. 4) vii. 233 If human menopausal gonadotrophin units (HMG) are used, the average normal result is 30 units and values above this may be found in cases of malignant testicular tumours. **1969** D. WIDGERY in Cockburn & Blackburn *Student Power* 126 It was inevitable that students would eventually come to revolt against the menopausal leadership of NUS and its flaccid policies. **1974** M. SPARK *Abbess of Crewe* iii. 83 She is behaving in a most menopausal way, and she claims there is a plot against her to prevent her being elected Abbess.

menopause. Add: (Further examples.) Also *fig.*

1954 W. FAULKNER *Fable* 69 It was winter again now, the long unbroken line from Alps to sea lying almost quiescent in mud's foul menopause. **1962** J. H. BURN *Drugs, Med. & Man* xv. 152 Stilboestrol is also used at the menopause when menstruation ends. **1970** JENNER & SEGAL *Men & Marriage* 144 In the nineteen-fifties a spate of 'popular medicine' articles flooded the press bearing the news that men, too, suffered from the Change of Life and middle-aged men found themselves swamped with sympathy over their newly recognised menopause. **1972** F. WARNER *Lying Figures* III. 19 Having your mental menopause?

menorah (mĕnōᵘ·ră, -ǭ·ră). [Heb. *mĕnōrāh* sabbath or festival candelabrum.] A holy candelabrum having seven branches used in the ancient temple in Jerusalem; also a candelabrum having any number of branches used in modern synagogues.

1888 (*title*) Menorah monthly. **1936** *Jews in Palestine Campaign* (Menorah Club) 41 A Club under the name of Menorah (seven branched candlestick)..was established. **1958** B. MALAMUD *Magic Barrel* (1960) 128 Don't those peaks..look like a Menorah?.. Like a seven-branched candalabrum..? **1966** L. DAVIDSON *Long Way to Shiloh* ii. 31 The great seven-branched lamp, the Menorah, has been the symbol of Judaism for some thousands of years; of..Israel, for the past fifteen or so... Titus took the lamp when he destroyed the Temple in August of 70. **1970** L. M. FEINSILVER *Taste of Yiddish* 247 The Sabbath menorah has seven holders, to accommodate a candle for each day of the week. The Chanuka menorah has nine holders. **1973** *Jewish Chron.* 2 Feb. 16/5 The Mayor of Hackney..was presented with an Israeli-made menorah. **1973** *Country Life* 20 Sept. 784/2 The symbol of the Menorah, the seven-branched candelabrum, was originally placed in the tabernacle in the Sinai Desert and in the First Temple in Jerusalem, and was carried away by Titus. Today the Menorah, framed by two olive branches, is the emblem of the modern state of Israel.

men's: see *MAN *sb.*[1] 23.

mensa. Add: **3.** (With capital initial.) Adopted as the name of an organization of people with above-average intelligence quotients. Also *attrib.*

Members qualify by passing a test equivalent to an I.Q. of 148 or more on the Cattell scale.

1962 *Mensa Register* p. ii, The Mensa Register is published to satisfy members' curiosity as to who the other members are, and to allow such individual contact to be made as is desired. **1968** *Brit. Mensa* Dec. 6/2 Mensa is essentially a social organisation, designed to bring mutually congenial people together. *Ibid.*, Examination of the Bulletin will show thriving Mensa groups in every geographic region. **1971** *Sear* (Manch. Branch Brit. Mensa) Nov., Mensa is a social club with the entry requirement that members have an IQ higher than 98% of the general population. **1972** *Times* 2 Nov. 9/4 All participants have mensa minds that have read Wittgenstein. **1972** W. GARNER *Ditto, Brother Rat!* vi. 46 Mensa is a sort of high IQ élite. Anyone can try their tests. Very few pass.

‖ **mensch** (menʃ). Also **mensh.** [Yiddish, a. G. *mensch* person.] A person of integrity or rectitude; one who is morally just, honest, or honourable.

1953 S. BELLOW *Adventures A. March* 43, I want you to be a *mensch.* **1959** H. PINTER *Birthday Party* III. 55 You'll be a mensch... You'll be a success. **1968** L. ROSTEN *Joys of Yiddish* 234 The key to being 'a real *mensh*' is nothing less than—character: rectitude, dignity, a sense of what is right, responsible, decorous. Many a poor man, many an ignorant man, is a *mensh.* **1970** *New Statesman* 30 Oct. 556/1 Mr Nixon is seen as an essentially decent man,..but not as a *mensch* on the scale of Roosevelt, Eisenhower, Kennedy. **1972** *New Yorker* 24 June 26 What is a *mensch*?.. It means you're a substantial human being.

mensh (menʃ). Also **mench.** Colloq. abbrev. of MENTION *sb.* and *v.*; freq. in phr. *don't mensh*, = *don't mention it* (see MENTION *v.* 1 c).

1937 in PARTRIDGE *Dict. Slang* 517/1. **1955** 'G. CARR' *Corpse at Camp Two* iii. 40 'Pray forgive my tactlessness.' .. 'Don't mench, sir.' **1961** J. DAWSON *Ha-Ha* ii. 31 'I'm sorry to hear it.' 'Thank you, not at all, don't mensh.' **1968** C. WATSON *Flaxborough Crab* iii. 35 'Thank you very much.' 'Don't mensh.' **1973** *Times* 27 Apr. 4/3 One little boy asked if we could 'have a mensh [mention] for Aunty Dora who fell down the stairs and broke her leg'. **1974** F. NOLAN *Oshawa Project* iii. 24 'Thanks, Lucky.' 'Don't mensh, don't mensh,' Luciano said.

Menshevik (me·nʃĭvik), *a.* and *sb.* [a. Russ. *men'shevík*, f. *mén'she*, compar. of *málÿĭ* little. The Russ. pl. *men'shevikí* has been used by some English writers.] **A.** *adj.* Of, pertaining to, or characteristic of, the Mensheviks or Menshevism.

1907 [see *BOLSHEVIK B. *adj.*]. **1919** J. REED *Ten Days that shook World* iii. 47 Said the Menshevik *Dien*, 'The Government ought to defend itself and defend us.' *Ibid.* iv. 91 Raising his voice to a shout he [*sc.* Khintchuk] read the Menshevik declaration. *Ibid.* viii. 204 The familiar faces of the Menshevik and Socialist Revolutionary intellectuals. **1920** *Glasgow Herald* 14 Oct. 9 Martov (Zederbaum), who headed the Menshevik opposition when Lenin broke up the Russian Social Democratic Party in 1903. **1923** E. A. ROSS *Russ. Soviet Republic* 323 The imprisonment of the Menshevik members of the Moscow printers' union. **1971** D. SMITH *Russia of Tsars* viii. 128 The Petrograd Soviet was equally hesitant... Alexander Kerensky, its Menshevik vice-president,..used his influence. **1975** *Times Lit. Suppl.* 4 July 740/5 When accused..of holding menshevik positions, he replies..that revolutionary virginity is not worth preserving at the price of inaction.

B. *sb.* A member of the political group or party forming the smaller part of the Russian Social-Democratic Party after the split with the Bolsheviks in 1903 and denounced as counter-revolutionaries after the 'October' Revolution of 1917. Cf. *BOLSHEVIK *sb.* Also *transf.* and *fig.*

1917 [see *BOLSHEVIK *sb.*]. [**1919** J. REED *Ten Days that shook World* p. xiv. *Russian Social Democratic Labour Party.* Originally Marxian Socialists. At a party congress held in 1903, the party split, on the question of tactics, into two factions—the Majority (Bolshinstvo) and the Minority (Menshinstvo). From this sprang the names 'Bolsheviki' and 'Mensheviki'—'members of the majority' and 'members of the minority'.] **1923** E. A. ROSS *Russ. Soviet Republic* 322 The Mensheviks can get no paper, which is a government monopoly, for pamphlets or leaflets at election time. **1926** *Contemp. Rev.* Sept. 274 He was an outsider—a 'menshevik' (the 'minority' man). **1935** N. MITCHISON *We have been Warned* I. 67 Idlers, parasites, mensheviks, defeatists. **1973** *Listener* 1 Feb. 135/3 The Provisionals..by playing the Bolsheviks to the Officials' Mensheviks—though not in ideology of course—have indeed become the party of the majority.

Menshevism (me·nʃĭviz'm). [a. Russ. *men'shevízm*: see *MENSHEVIK *a.* and *sb.*] The doctrines and practices of the Mensheviks.

1920 *Glasgow Herald* 14 May 9 Communism as it is offered to Trans-Caucasia has assumed the form of Menshevism. **1926** *Contemp. Rev.* Sept. 275 Marx would prove it: but that would be 'Menshevism'. **1928** *Observer* 1 July 9/2 Comrade Trotsky's theory of permanent revolution is a variety of Menshevism.

Menshevist (me·nʃĭvist). [a. Russ. *men'shevíst* (now disused) *MENSHEVIK *a.* and *sb.*] A Menshevik; a supporter of Menshevism. Also *attrib.* or as *adj.*

1919 *Times Lit. Suppl.* 14 Aug. 432/3 A pleasing description of the Menshevists. **1926** *Contemp. Rev.* Sept. 274 He was known to return in all intricate cases to his menshevist fallacies. **1931** *Times* 7 Mar. 12/2 The Menshevists had always been opposed to the violent overthrow of the Bolshevists. *Ibid.*, Documentary evidence of the alleged Menshevist propaganda all, strangely enough, got destroyed.

Men's Lib.: see *MAN *sb.*[1] 23.

‖ **mens rea** (menz rī·ă). *Law.* [mod.L., lit. 'guilty mind'.] The criminal state of mind accompanying an act which condemns the perpetrator of the act to criminal punishment; criminal intent.

1861 LEIGH & CAVE *Crown Cases Reserved* (1866) 53 The *mens rea* is an essential ingredient in every offence. **1914** D. A. STROUD *Mens Rea* i. 14 There is no real contradiction in describing a mere absence of mind as a *mens rea* or guilty mind. **1955** *Times* 15 July 11/6 If the customer used it to apply to some other dress she would be guilty of fraud. One is not anxious to multiply criminal offences in which there is no *mens rea.* **1959** *Chambers's Encycl.* IV. 241/1 Drunkenness may render the accused incapable of forming the specific intent necessary to commit the crime —when *mens rea* will not be present and the accused must be acquitted. **1965** *Listener* 16 Dec. 1006/2 The compulsory death penalty for murder, which led to a special interpretation of *mens rea,* has been abolished. **1972** *Police Rev.* 10 Nov. 1446/3 The prosecution has failed to adduce sufficient evidence of the presence of *mens rea* (or guilty knowledge).

men's room: see *MAN *sb.*[1] 23.

‖ **mens sana in corpore sano.** Lat. phr. (occurring in Juvenal *Satires* x. 356): a sound mind in a sound body, esp. regarded as the ideal of education. Also *ellipt.*, as *mens sana.*

c **1605** J. HARINGTON or S. DANIEL *Prayse of Private Life* in J. Harington *Lett. & Epigrams* (1930) iii. 329 Desyrynge of God noe more than the Satericke Poet wished, *Mens Sana, in Corpore Sano.* **1629** in *Camden Misc.* (1854) III. 10 To beare *mens sana in corpore sano,* a valient heart in such a bodie..w[ch] hath never bene debilitated. **1749** CHESTERFIELD *Let.* 2 Oct. (1932) IV. 1415 *Mens sana in corpore sano,* is the first and greatest blessing. **1824** J. WIGHT *Mornings at Bow Street* 55 The General angrily declared he was altogether *mens sana in corpore sano.* **1851** GEO. ELIOT *Let.* 11 Sept. (1954) I. 359, I am really strong and healthy and hope to bring a mens sana in corpore sano to London. **1966** 'K. NICHOLSON' *Hook, Line & Sinker* xiii. 159 Cold bath first thing: *mens sana,* and all that. **1967** S. JOHNSON *Gold Drain* ii. 22 [They] accused him of suffering from the effects of a public-school education, from the *mens sana* approach. **1973** *Listener* 23 Aug. 260/1 One lady, supporting *mens sana in corpore sano* against Jo Grimond, wrote that Christ must have kept himself fit.

‖ **mensur** (me·nsūr). [G.] In Germany, a fencing duel between students fought with partially blunted weapons.

1911 L. KNOWLES *Day with Korps-Students in Germany* (ed. 2) 6 My visit was not to admire Heidelberg, but to see my *Korps*-student friends,..for on the morrow there was to be a *Mensur,* or fighting-bout. *Ibid.* 4 Even to Germans, these *Mensuren,* or lighter student-duels,..have their humorous side. **1960** *Times* 17 Sept. 9/7 The *Mensur* or duel..is, however, frowned upon by officialdom. **1967** A. ARENT *Gravedigger's Funeral* xiii. 221 That final accolade of Teutonic narcissism, the face scars or *Mensur* marks of the military caste. **1970** 'M. HEBDEN' *Mask of Violence* (1971) xxv. 219 Anarchical young men of..the older universities, with the *Schmisse*—the duelling scars—on their cheeks, were already shouting the old *Mensur* wish before the commencement of a fight: '*Waffenschein!*' **1972** *House & Garden* May 142/4 Over the river, Hirchgasse where the 'mensor' [*sic*] duel is still fought.

mensuralist. Add: **2.** An advocate of a style of plainsong in which the rhythm depends on using notes of fixed length. Also *attrib.*

1905 *Grammar of Plainsong* I. i. 3 The 14th century brought a further falling off in the chant. At that time.. the harmonists and mensuralists were making their mark even on the Church's song, and destroying its rhythm. **1911** *Catholic Encycl.* XII. 147/1 The mensuralists.., with Decheurens as their principal representative, hold that the notes of plain chant are subject to strict measurement. **1929** *Music Q.* XV. 18 Even the mensuralist.. expressed the opinion that the Gregorian composers probably were not clearly conscious of writing metric arrangements. **1954** *Grove's Dict. Mus.* (ed. 5) VI. 820/1 The Mensuralists, in so far as they agree among themselves, hold that the notes in early medieval manuscripts are not..of approximately equal duration, but that they represent longs and shorts, the longs always being twice the duration of the shorts. **1959** *Times Lit. Suppl.* 13 Feb. 83/4 For more than fifty years many books and articles have been published expounding the 'mensuralist' view with great ingenuity. **1964** E. CARDINE *Is Gregorian Chant Measured Mus.?* 10 The *a priori* mensuralist appears perfectly clearly from the Introduction [of Vollaerts' book] onwards.

men's wear, menswear: see *MAN *sb.*[1] 23.

mental, *a.*[1] and *sb.* Add: **A.** *adj.* **1.** (Further examples.)

1843 MILL *Logic* II. vi. iv. 506 These differences of mental susceptibility..may be consequences of the previous mental history of those individuals. **1874** J. SULLY *Sensation & Intuition* i. 7 To understand fully all the facts of a single mental history. **1879** W. JAMES *Coll. Ess. & Rev.* (1920) 139 Ever some vital factor of our mental life will rebel and refuse to be dragged the same way with the rest. **1883** F. H. BRADLEY *Princ. Logic* 182 If we say, 'I wish S–P were a fact',..the judgment..is concerned with nothing but my mental attitude. **1890** W. JAMES *Princ. Psychol.* I. ii. 48 A most interesting effect of cortical disorder is *mental blindness.* This consists not so much in insensibility to optical impressions, as in *inability to understand them. Ibid.* II. xx. 205 Sounds certainly play a far more prominent part in the mental life of the blind than in our own. **1897** C. H. JUDD tr. *Wundt's Outl. Psychol.* 326 The law of mental growth is as little applicable to all contents of psychical experience as any other psychological law of development. **1919** L. M. TERMAN *Measurement of Intelligence* i. 6 The large majority of these belong to the moron grade; that is, their mental development will stop somewhere..between 9 and 12. **1921** B. RUSSELL *Analysis of Mind* i. 25, I should say that images belong only to the mental world. *Ibid.* iii. 68 Since Kant it has been customary to recognize three great divisions of mental phenomena, which are typified by knowledge, desire and feeling. *Ibid.* vi. 109 When you realize that you are glad to meet him, you acquire knowledge of a mental fact. *Ibid.* viii. 141 The sensation, as a mental event, will consist of awareness of the colour. **1932** *Mind* XLI. 137 A man whose whole life had been devoted to thought, and whose intense mental energy came out all the more clearly as his bodily powers declined. **1936** *Discovery* Jan. 22/2 Only in this way is it possible to render intelligible the mental attitude of the Chinese to other peoples. **1949** G. RYLE *Concept of Mind* i. 16, I shall probably be taken to be denying well-known facts about the mental life of human beings. *Ibid.* vi. 163 The argument, then, that mental events are authentic..must be rejected. **1949** R. G. SIMPSON *Fund. Educ. Psychol.* ii. 22 Growth of mental functions is not as easily traced as that of physical abilities, primarily because mental growth is composed of many characteristics. **1958** K. LOVELL *Educ. Psychol. & Children* x. 127 The effects of training would be transferred from one mental function to another of the same type. **1966** *Guardian* 16 May 3/7 The students at Lancaster confess to a mental block about using nuclear weapons in any circumstances. **1968** J. A. SHAFFER *Philos. of Mind* i. 5 The only evidence we have for the existence of these faculties is the existence of the very mental phenomena they were intended to explain. **1969** C. HODDER-WILLIAMS *98·4* iv. 41 Having a mental block about one's past is all right... Security work makes a virtue out of forgetting things. **1970** K. CAMPBELL *Body & Mind* vi. 113 The new view allows, indeed requires, that mental states be causes. *Ibid.* 125 Mental objects such as images and dreams..resist being brought within the fold of Materialism. **1973** A. KENNY *Wittgenstein* viii. 142 When we hear a sentence in a language we know, there are mental events—feelings, images, etc.

b. (*a*) *mental breakdown, deficiency, derangement, disease, disorder, handicap, illness, incapacity, retardation, subnormality,* etc.: general terms indicating temporary or permanent impairments of the mind, due to heredity, birth injury, environment, or accident, which usually need special care; *mental health,* health of mind as distinct from physical health; *mental hygiene,* mental health; measures directed towards the preservation or improvement of mental health;

(*b*) *mental case, defective, incapable, patient,* etc.: persons suffering from some kind of mental impairment; persons under medical care for mental illness;

(*c*) *mental home, hospital, institution, ward,* etc.: places where those with mental disorders are confined or treated;

(*d*) *mental nurse, specialist,* etc.: persons specializing in the treatment or care of those with mental disorders.

(*a*) **1794** H. L. PIOZZI *Brit. Synonymy* II. 6 Phrenzy, madness and distraction are the poetical expressions of what we call mental derangement, or disordered spirits, in elegant conversation. **1833** MILL *Lett.* (1910) I. 38, I..am so far from being in better mental health than yourself, that I need sympathy quite as much. **1839** POE *Fall House of Usher* in *Burton's Gentleman's Mag.* Sept. 150 And now, some days of bitter grief having elapsed, an observable change came over the features of the mental disorder of my friend. **1848** GEO. ELIOT *Let. c* 14 May (1954) I. 261 Study *mental hygiene*—take long doses of 'dolce far niente'. **1856** *Educ. of Imbecile* (Home for Invalid & Imbecile Children, Edinburgh) 11 His appearance and bearing gave evidence of great mental deficiency. **1869** GEO. ELIOT *Let.* 21 Sept. (1956) V. 56, I have such a horror of a mental breakdown. **1902** B. RUSSELL *Let.* in A. Wood *B. Russell* (1957) viii. 79 Since I finished my book, I have devoted myself to what you [*sc.* Beatrice Webb] would call mental hygiene, with good results so far. Beyond reading a mathematical MS. of Whitehead's, I have done no work for the last fortnight, but have spent my whole days out of doors basking in the return of summer. **1904** *Lancet* 27 Aug. 598/2 Scientific views regarding mental disease have..been undergoing great changes. *Ibid.* 17 Sept. 838/1 Those cases of mental incapacity arising from incipient or oncoming insanity. **1907** [see *BREAK-DOWN 1 c]. **1908** *Lancet* 12 Sept. 812/2 It was difficult..to secure effective treatment for early undeveloped cases of mental disorder. **1913** *Act* 3 & 4 *Geo. V* c. 28 (*title*) Mental Deficiency Act. **1914** W. B. DRUMMOND tr. *Binet & Simon's Mentally Defective Children* ii. 16 Some heads of schools..have fixed to almost a year the mental retardation of the child as compared with normal children of the same age. **1921** C. BURT *Mental & Scholastic Tests* ii. 163 The central problem of this memorandum —the line of demarcation for mental deficiency. **1946** C. P. BLACKER (*title*) Neurosis and the mental health services. **1946** *Amer. Jrnl. Psychiatry* CIII. 323/1 At the present time it cannot be said that we *cure* any of the more important and more fixed mental diseases. **1957** S. H. KRAINES *Mental Depressions* xv. 422 The goal of such mental hygiene is to remove and correct those unhealthy attitudes which add to the physically based tension. **1960** *Guardian* 16 Mar. 4/6 The most important change in terminology made by the new Act [*sc.* Mental Health Act, 1959] is that the expressions 'mental deficiency' and 'mental defectives' should be abolished... 'Mental disorder' is introduced as a new term covering all forms of mental ill health. **1962** E. CLEAVER in A. Dundes *Mother Wit* (1973) 10/2 The continued application of these judgments is the cause of an untold amount of mental illness and frustration. **1964** J. TIZARD *Community Services for Mentally Handicapped* I. ii. 18 There is a statutory obligation placed upon the local authorities in Britain to ascertain cases of mental subnormality..and to make provision for them. **1970** 'T. COE' *Wax Apple* (1973) vi. 50, I automatically *had* felt superior. After all, I'd never had a mental breakdown. **1970** L. J. KARMEL *Measurement & Evaluation in School* III. vii. 182 Some states will use 75 or even 80 as the cut-off point for mental retardation. **1971** *Rand Daily Mail* 4 Sept. 2/1 Nothing he had heard in court suggested that Muller has ever had a mental disorder. **1971** *Guardian* 18 Oct. 10/3 Mental illness is an *illness* needing therapeutic treatment... Mental handicap..is an innate condition for which there is no cure. **1972** R. QUILTY *Tenth Session* 58 A lifetime in mental-health nursing. **1973** *Black World* May 7/1 A crucial matter here is the role The Black Church can play in our mental hygiene and group advancement. **1974** *Guardian* 28 Jan. 6/7 The patient is no longer suffering from mental illness and..[should] be discharged.

(*b*) **1899** *Pop. Sci. Monthly* Apr. 747 (*title*) Mental defectives and social welfare. **1904** *Lancet* 17 Sept. 838/1 The Home Secretary..has at last been impressed with the total inadequacy of the provision made for..mental incapables. **1908** *Ibid.* 12 Sept. 813/2 Dr W. C. S. Clapham ..had many suspected mental cases sent to his outpatient department. **1913** E. MEYNELL *Life F. Thompson* 279 Many a time I've asked him to have his bit of lunch with me and the other 'mental'—O yes, she's a mental case, as I may have told you. **1922** W. R. INGE in *Edin. Rev.* July 34 The Eugenics Education Society..actively supported the Act for the compulsory segregation of mental defectives. **1938** *Brit. Jrnl. Psychol.* July 37 The implications of Wiersma's results obtained from mental patients have therefore been shown to hold for normal subjects. **1944** H. G. WELLS *'42 to '44* 182 The highly bred dogs are mostly physical and mental defectives. **1970** 'T. COE' *Wax Apple* (1973) iv. 33 The majority of mental patients who have been hospitalized once will be hospitalized several times more. **1973** 'D. SHANNON' *No Holiday for Crime* (1974) iv. 61 If you're going to say a mental patient, I don't think it was that kind of hospital.

(*c*) **1898** H. MORTEN *Compl. Syst. Nursing* 249 A year's training in a general hospital, and two years' training in a mental hospital, would be the proper scheme to turn out the best mental nurse. **1908** *Lancet* 26 Dec. 1943/1 (*heading*) Mental observation wards in Glasgow Parish Hospital. **1928** *Daily Mail* 25 July 8/3 One in ten of the people who reach the age of 40 in the State of New York will already have passed some time in a mental home or institution. **1932** KIPLING *Limits & Renewals* 151 They pushed him into a Mental Home, And that is like the grave. **1958** 'N. SHUTE' *Rainbow & Rose* v. 182 He had three young children and disliked the thought of bringing them up in the surroundings of a mental home. **1964** *Penguin Bk. Austral. Ballads* 18 The discharged mental-hospital patient..with a certificate to *prove* that he was sane. **1970** 'T. COE' *Wax Apple* (1973) ii. 17 The Midway was a haven for people recently out of mental institutions. **1972** R. BLOCH *Night-World* (1974) viii. 49 The mental wards were like a prison, only worse. **1974** N. FREELING *Dressing of Diamond* 74 We're looking at every affair..linked to mental homes, prison releases..psychopathic anything. **1974** *Guardian* 24 Jan. 15/8 The 'oriental girl'..had been led down from her ledge and taken off to mental hospital.

(*d*) **1898** [see sense 1 b (*c*) above]. **1922** *Lancet* 5 Aug. 290/1 The two duties of mental nurses. **1932** *Daily Tel.* 25 Apr. 9/3 Dr. Caton, the eminent mental specialist,.. has completed his findings of the state of Lt. Massie's mind at the time.

c. *colloq.* Mentally disordered or defective. Also in phr. *to go mental,* to become mentally disordered.

1927 D. L. SAYERS *Unnatural Death* iv. 41, I gather she was a little queer towards the end—a bit mental, I think you people [*sc.* nurses] call it? **1930** J. B. PRIESTLEY *Angel Pavement* ii. 68, I don't care if Mr. Dersingham goes mental, we're going to be lucky. **1958** 'N. SHUTE' *Rainbow & Rose* iv. 151 Everybody goes a bit mental in a war. **1959** S. GIBBONS *Pink Front Door* iv. 48 They had the same round eyes, only his hadn't got that almost mental look. **1973** 'J. PATRICK' *Glasgow Gang Observed* iii. 34 They must be mental... Shit-bags the lot o' them. **1974** N. FREELING *Dressing of Diamond* 65 There's somebody mental floating about.

2. Also, taking place in the mind. (Further examples.)

1676 LOCKE *Jrnl.* 26 Aug. in *Ess. Law Nature* (1954) 278 The thing to be believed was a proper object of faith and not of sense, a mental proposition, viz. that the God of the three children was the true God. **1843** MILL *Logic* I. I. iii. 66 His mental image..of the sun, and his idea of God, are thoughts. **1865** —— *Exam. Hamilton's Philos.* vi. 72 The belief is without understanding, for we form no mental picture of what we believe. *c* **1873** W. JAMES in R. B. Perry *Tht. & Char. W. James* (1935) I. 499 Under each and all of these formulations lurks the same mental act, that of insisting that things do not exist, so to speak, only once, but are in a manner duplicated. **1880** —— *Coll. Ess. & Rev.* (1920) 161 This complex aggregate of afferent feelings..renders absolutely precise and distinctive our mental image of the exact strength of movement to be made. **1882** L. STEPHEN *Sci. of Ethics* vi. 231 And thus the same words may call up the mental images which would be generated in the most and in the least sympathetic witness. **1889** Mental arithmetic [see *GUESSING *vbl. sb.*]. **1921** B. RUSSELL *Analysis of Mind* i. 19 The whole question of the relation of mental occurrences to objects grows very complicated. *Ibid.* vi. 109 'Introspection' is supposed to furnish data for knowledge of our mental processes. **1925** J. RIVIERE et al. tr. *Freud's Coll. Papers* IV. 14 In the psychology which is founded on psycho-analysis we have accustomed ourselves to take as our starting-point the unconscious mental processes. **1932** *Mind* XLI. 37 There are four corresponding 'mental ex-

periences' (παθήματα ἐν τῇ ψυχῇ, 511 D). **1935** C. Burt *Subnormal Mind* i. 41 The reading test and the mental arithmetic test..will yield a fair estimate of the child's educational level. **1944** J. S. Huxley *On Living in Revolution* iv. 56 The deliberate 'mental operation' of psycho-analysis or other form of psychotherapy. **1949** G. Ryle *Concept of Mind* 8 The logical categories in terms of which the concepts of mental..operations have been co-ordinated have been wrongly selected. *Ibid.* vii. 200 Stomach-aches ..have physiological attachments which threaten to sully the purity of the brook of mental experiences. *Ibid.* viii. 254 In short, there are no such objects as mental pictures. **1963** R. Carnap in P. A. Schilpp *Philos. R. Carnap* 8 All mental processes are intimately connected with the brain. **1971** P. A. Chilton tr. *Piaget & Inhelder's Mental Imagery in Child* p. xiii, Having attempted to analyse some of the characteristics of perceptual development, it was necessary to go on to tackle the question of the evolution of mental images. **1972** W. C. Coe *Challenges Personal Adjustment* iv. 76 Mental telepathy is the transfer of thought from one person to another without overt communication.

5. Special collocations: **mental age,** the degree of mental development of a person, expressed as the age at which a similar level is attained by an average person; **mental chemistry** *Psychol.*, J. S. Mill's term for the psychological processes by which complex ideas, sensations, etc., are formed from an aggregate of simple ones; **mental cruelty,** conduct which inflicts suffering on the mind of another person, esp. *U.S.* as constituting grounds for legal separation or divorce; **mental healing,** healing effected solely by the mind of the healer; so *mental healer*; **mental ratio** = *intelligence quotient* (s.v. *Intelligence *sb.* 8); **mental set,** the set (Set *sb.*[1] 12) or predisposition of the mind which governs reactions to stimuli; **mental test** = **intelligence test*; so *mental tester, testing*; **mental year,** the average mental attainment of each year of growth, used as a unit of measurement of mental development.

1912 *Pedagogical Seminary* XIX. 189 Table I. Mental Ages..showing the chronological and mental age distribution of the two thousand public school children graded by the Binet tests. **1919** L. M. Terman *Measurement of Intelligence* iii. 40 A mentally defective child of 9 years may have a 'mental age' of only 4 years, or a young genius of 9 years may have a mental age of 12 or 13 years. **1937** 'M. Innes' *Hamlet, Revenge!* III. iii. 259 His mental age 's about eight. **1972** J. Aiken *Died on Rainy Sunday* 88 Really Ellie *is* a child, she thought; in some ways her mental age can't be more than twelve or thirteen. **1843** Mill *Logic* II. vi. iv. 503 These therefore are cases of mental chemistry: in which it is proper to say that the simple ideas generate, rather than that they compose, the complex ones. **1890** W. James *Princ. Psychol.* II. xx. 202 Discrimination, association, [etc.]..are quite capable of giving us all the space-perceptions we have so far studied, without the aid of any mysterious 'mental chemistry'. **1929** W. McDougall *Mod. Materialism* v. 119 J. S. Mill's use of the expression 'mental chemistry' had suggested some analogy between such mental and such physical syntheses. **1948** R. S. Woodworth *Contemp. Schools Psychol.* (ed. 2) iii. 44 This idea of a 'mental chemistry' reappeared from time to time in later psychological theories. **1928** *Harper's Mag.* July 159/1 The Nevada laws..necessitate a minimum of fraud... The judges demand very slight evidence to prove mental cruelty. A woman may obtain her freedom on the ground that her husband has..told her to go to hell once too often. **1936** M. Allingham *Flowers for Judge* vii. 125 Not a care in the world except Mr. Brande's neglect and mental cruelty to her. **1967** R. S. Master *Elem. Psychiatry* xx. 398 The petitioner has to prove..that the spouse can differentiate between right and wrong and understand the nature of the mental cruelty. **1968** *Globe & Mail* (Toronto) 17 Feb. 29/1 The third wife of wealthy playboy John Jacob Astor III was granted a divorce yesterday on grounds of mental cruelty. **1920** in Webster, Mental healer. **1957** O. Nash *You can't get there from Here* 67 The characters in many of our popular songs are fair game for the nearest mental healer. **1970** T. S. Szasz *Ideology & Insanity* (1973) xiii. 240 The precise activities of the various 'mental healers' are rarely defined by their practitioners. **1888** L. E. Whipple (*title*) Mental healing. **1902** W. James *Varieties Relig. Experience* iv. 121 Their savage and primitive philosophy of mental healing. **1924** Galsworthy *White Monkey* I. xii. 100 No need of any of these vitamins, false teeth, mental healing. **1921** C. Burt *Mental & Scholastic Tests* ii. 151 If a child's mental age be divided by his chronological age, the quotient will state what fraction of ability the child actually possesses... This fraction may be termed..the child's 'intelligence quotient' or, more euphoniously.., his 'mental ratio'. **1927** A. Huxley *Proper Stud.* 67 A mental ratio is obtained by dividing the child's mental by his chronological age. **1934** *Brit. Jrnl. Psychol.* Jan. 312 Not all candidates with high mental ratios succeed. **1913** E. L. Thorndike *Educ. Psychol.* II. xii. 356 In the case of alternative systems of bonds there is then often an inhibition for a time, reducing to zero as the two systems of bonds get organized in connection with two systems of mental sets. **1922** R. S. Woodworth *Psychol.* iv. 72 Much used also are 'adjustment' and 'mental set', the idea here being to liken the individual to an adjustable machine which can be set for one or another set of work. **1934** H. C. Warren *Dict. Psychol.* 164/2 *Mental set*,..the attitude or determination of an individual before receiving an expected stimulus or with reference to a problem or general situation. **1953** *Jrnl. Exper. Psychol.* XLVI. 50 The aspect of directed thinking commonly called 'mental set'. **1963** J. Lyons *Structural Semantics* ii. 35 He [*sc.* the hearer] must be thought of as being in a certain state of 'expectancy' (or 'mental set'), in which he is disposed to hear certain units rather than others. **1890** J. M. Cattell in *Mind* XV. 373 Psychology cannot attain the certainty and exactness of the physical sciences, unless it rests on a foundation of experiment and measurement. A step in this direction could be made by applying a series of mental tests and measurements to a large number of individuals. **1934** H. C. Warren *Dict. Psychol.* 165/1 Mental test. **1958** M. Argyle *Relig. Behaviour* vi. 58 A child's mental age is the average chronological age of children showing the same degree of intelligence, as measured by mental tests. **1972** L. S. Hearnshaw in Cox & Dyson *20th-Cent. Mind* I. vii. 234 Francis Galton..attempted.. to devise techniques for measuring intelligence. These techniques were christened 'mental tests' by the American psychologist, J. M. Cattell, in 1890. **1952** *Brit. Jrnl. Psychol.* Feb. 23 When the subjects are in full sympathy.. but the mental tester rarely has such a favourable situation. **1959** *Chambers's Encycl.* XII. 655/1 Mental testing began with the testing of intelligence (i.e. of general intellectual capacity). **1921** C. Burt *Mental & Scholastic Tests* ii. 147 The estimate for the intelligence of every child has been converted into terms of mental years. **1942** F. J. Schonell *Backwardness in Basic Subjects* iv. 74 Rene C. was, in arithmetic, almost two mental years ahead of her achievements in reading.

B. *sb.* Restrict † *nonce-uses* to senses in Dict. and add: **c.** *colloq.* A mentally-deranged person; a mental patient.

1913 [see 1 b (*b*) above]. **1937** Partridge *Dict. Slang* 517/1 *Mental*, a person mentally deranged, mad. **1942** Berrey & Van den Bark *Amer. Thes. Slang* § 529/16 Mental, nut, psycho, psychot, *a psychopathic case.* **1973** F. De Felitta *Oktoberfest* (1974) xiv. 162 'What's to prevent him from going?' 'He is a mental.'

mentalism. Restrict *rare* to sense 1 in Dict. and add: **2.** Esp. the theory that physical and physiological phenomena are ultimately only explicable in terms of a creative and interpretative mind.

1917 A. S. Pringle-Pattison *Idea of God* xx. 392 The position is open..to the general objections which have been brought against Monadism and Mentalism. **1932** *Times Lit. Suppl.* 28 Apr. 314/4 Scientists who repudiate mechanism only to involve themselves in thoroughpaced mentalism. **1954** *Essays in Crit.* IV. 235 But MacNeice has tried mentalism and so raged against it..that he nearly knocked his brains out with rhyme. Therefore we must settle for monadism. **1964** *Language* XL. 124 Linguists who conceive of their science as a discipline.. often pride themselves on their freedom from mentalism. But freedom from mentalism is an inherent feature of the taxonomic conception of linguistics. **1972** *Ibid.* XLVIII. 418 Writing grammars..was motivated for Boas by a theoretical concern, a 'mentalism' derived partly from the German tradition of Herder, Humboldt, [etc.]. **1973** *Word 1970* XXVI. 93 We can arrive at a knowledge of the *signifié* independently of the particular *signifiant* under study, yet still avoid mentalism.

mentalist. Restrict *rare* to sense 1 in Dict. and add: **2.** (Further examples.) Also *attrib.* or as *adj.*

1927 B. Russell *Outl. Philos.* xxvii. 303 Idealists in the technical sense, or mentalists, as Dr. Broad more appropriately calls them. **1933** L. Bloomfield *Lang.* ix. 142 For the mentalist, language is the expression of ideas, feelings, or volition. **1966** *Philos.* XLI. 141 We must give a sense to this mentalist and substance vocabulary. **1972** *Language* XLVIII. 418 A mentalist tradition more recent than the 'Cartesian'.

mentalistic (mentăli·stik), *a.* [f. Mentalist + -ic.] **1.** Of or pertaining to the processes of the mind or to processes of a similar nature. *rare.*

1962 *Listener* 29 Mar. 568/3 Other practitioners may turn it [*sc.* treatment of insanity] into a purely mentalistic and verbal technique, letting slip all the gains which psycho-analysis has achieved by its attention to physical processes.

2. Of or pertaining to mentalism (sense *2). Hence **mentali·stically** *adv.*

1917 A. S. Pringle-Pattison *Idea of God* x. 191, I feel it to be important..to free the position I am defending from any supposed dependence on the Mentalistic doctrines which have often been used to support it. **1925** C. D. Broad *Mind & its Place* xiv. 611, I class these two alternatives together under the name of 'Mentalistic Neutralism'. **1927** *Mod. Philology* Nov. 225 This theory.. makes the hitherto otiose mentalistic factors play an actual part in linguistic change. **1950** D. Jones *Phoneme* vii. 23 This is evidence in favour of a mentalistic view of the phoneme. **1965** N. Chomsky *Aspects of Theory of Syntax* i. 4 Hence, in the technical sense, linguistic theory is mentalistic, since it is concerned with discovering a mental reality underlying actual behavior. **1967** [see *identity theorist* (*Identity 10 b)]. **1971** D. Crystal *Ling.* 95 Very little of language..can be tested in the same way as material objects.., as mentalistically-inclined linguists have been quick to point out. **1973** *Word 1970* XXVI. 150 The chapter on Syntax gives a traditional mentalistic statement of the function of the cases and moods.

mentality. Add: **3.** Mental character or disposition; outlook; kind or degree of intelligence.

1895 *Funk's Stand. Dict.*, *Mentality*..cast or habit of mind. **1911** Beerbohm *Zuleika D.* viii. 132 Your words show up your good heart... Your mentality, too, is bully, as we all predicate. **1922** Joyce *Ulysses* 132, I speak the tongue of a race the acme of whose mentality is the maxim: time is money. **1926** Fowler *Mod. Eng. Usage* 348/1 'The mentality of the politician is a constant source of amazement to the engineer.' Twenty years ago, no-one would have written that. **1931** L. Watt *Future of Capitalism* ii. 23 It is useless to pretend that there will be anything but hostility between the partners in industry so long as this mentality persists. **1958** R. F. C. Hull tr. *Jung's Coll. Works* XI. vii. 480 Something of the kind happens as soon as we are confronted with the Eastern mentality.

mentalize, *v.* Add: In nonce-uses: **b.** To stimulate the mind. **c.** To realize mentally or invest with mental qualities. So **me·ntalized** *ppl. a.*, **me·ntalizing** *vbl. sb.*

1807 T. Campbell *Let.* 6 July in W. Beattie *Life & Lett. T. Campbell* (1849) II. iv. 110, I sometimes call on the satirical Gifford..who *mentalises* me for a few moments, but the impression lasts too short. **1837** H. Smith *Let.* 2 Oct. in A. Mathews *Mem. Charles Mathews* (1839) IV. xviii. 447 While others satisfied themselves with endeavouring to *embody* their originals, he made it his study to *mentalize* them. I am obliged to coin a word, but my meaning is, that while he surpassed all competitors in the mere mimicry of externals, he was *unique* in the subtlety, acuteness, and truth with which he could copy the *mind* of his prototype. **1927** D. H. Lawrence *Let.* 28 May (1962) II. 981 One emerges with a body all right— but a different one, perhaps, not so mentalised. **1935** W. de la Mare *Early One Morning* ii. 404 Seeming stupidity may be due to a highly individualised way of mentalizing things. **1936** *Downside Rev.* LIV. 551 The body continues to produce its own characteristic actions, but along with these it produces a new action—thought. Body becomes mind, or rather mentalised. **1936** J. R. Kantor *Objective Psychol. Gram.* v. 66 We react to printed words..as though they were words heard in conversation. .. It is precisely the mentalizing procedure that produces the confusion of responses to language activity. **1973** D. Ramsay *Deadly Discretion* 76 Want to try mentalizing? .. First empty your mind... Then wait for me to send you the message.

mentally, *adv.* **b.** (Further examples.)

1894 *Psychol. Rev.* I. 425 It is..the mission of the mentally defective to give us..object lessons in psychology. **1934** H. S. Sullivan in H. S. Perry *Fusion of Psychiatry & Social Sci.* (1964) 9 Disorder of the emotional life of the mentally deranged is too striking to be ignored. **1964** J. Tizard (*title*) Community services for the mentally handicapped. **1970** L. J. Karmel *Measurement & Evaluation in School* iii. vii. 182 The lowest 2 per cent of the population..could be justifiably described as mentally defective.

menthol. Add: *menthol cigarette*, a cigarette flavoured with menthol.

1952 M. Tripp *Faith is Windsock* i. 10 He threw a packet of American menthol cigarettes across the hut. **1962** L. Deighton *Ipcress File* xx. 131 She offered me one of those menthol cigarettes that taste like paint remover. **1969** O. Hesky *Sequin Syndicate* xi. 114 She..might have been an advertisement for some brand of menthol cigarette.

mentholated (me·nþǫlēⁱtėd), *ppl. a.* [f. Menthol + -ate[3] + -ed[1].] Treated or impregnated with menthol; containing menthol.

1933 *Tobacco World* 1 May 13 (Advt.), And now say 'hello' to KOOL, B & W's mild mentholated new cigarette. **1962** P. Moyes *Death on Agenda* ix. 149 He was lighting up yet another mentholated cigarette. **1970** G. Greer *Female Eunuch* 259 One vaginal deodorant is..flavoured with peppermint... Others are mentholated.

menthone (me·nþōᵘn). *Chem.* [f. L. *menth-a* mint + -one.] 3-Methyl-6-isopropylcyclohexanone, $C_{10}H_{18}O$, an optically active cyclic ketone whose lævorotatory form is a liquid with an odour of peppermint and occurs in American peppermint, geranium, and other oils.

1889 Roscoe & Schorlemmer *Treat. Chem.* III. v. 470 Menthone, $C_{10}H_{18}O$, is formed by heating menthol with sulphuric acid and potassium bichromate. **1929** *Org. Syntheses* IX. 53, *l*-Menthone can be prepared by the oxidation of rhodinol with a chromic-sulphuric acid mixture. **1969** W. Templeton *Introd. Chem. Terpenoids & Steroids* iii. 53 Menthone..is found in oils of peppermint, geranium and pennyroyal, mainly in its (−)-form. **1970** [see *isovaleraldehyde* (*iso- b)].

menticide (me·ntisəid). [f. L. *menti-*, *mens* mind + -cide 2.] A word coined by J. A. M. Meerloo to designate the undermining or destruction of a person's mind or will by 'psychological intervention and judicial perversion'; also in extended use. Cf. *brain-washing.

1951 J. A. M. Meerloo in *Amer. Jrnl. Psychiatry* Feb. 595/1 Such an organized system of psychological intervention and judicial perversion, in which a powerful tyrant synthetically injects his own thoughts and words into the minds and mouths of the victims he plans to destroy by mock trial, may well be called menticide. **1957** —— *Mental Seduction & Menticide* Pref., The modern words 'brainwashing', 'thought-control', and 'menticide' serve to provide some indication of the..methods by which man's integrity can be violated. **1973** *Black Panther* 20 Oct. 17/1 No treatise on prisons in 1973 can possibly be complete and up-to-date without dealing with the scientifically modernized versions of these conditions and practices as they are manifested in the forms of menticide and genocide.

mention, *sb.* Add: **2. f.** *Mil.* A commendatory reference made to a person in an official military dispatch (abbrev. of *mention in dispatches*).

1915 A. N. LYONS *Kitchener Chaps* 81 No, sir, there's no particular cop about these 'mentions'; only something for your pals to read. **1921** S. C. JOHNSON *Medal Collector* viii. 180 No more than one leaf, however, may be fixed to the ribbon even though the wearer may have been the subject of several mentions. **1958** M. DICKENS *Man Overboard* iii. 35 Other people came out of the war with Mentions and worthwhile gongs. **1964** T. WHITE tr. *Leulliette's St. Michael* 221 I've got the Médaille Militaire, the Croix de Guerre and seven mentions.

mention, *v.* Add: **1. a.** *to be mentioned in dispatches*: to receive a 'mention' (see *MENTION *sb.* 2 f). Also *transf.*

1915 A. HUXLEY *Let.* June (1969) 73 Poor Bob Gibson is killed. He was as good a soldier as he was a don. He was mentioned in dispatches. **1922** JOYCE *Ulysses* 449, I fought with the colours..and was disabled at Spion Kop and Bloemfontein, was mentioned in dispatches. **1961** PARTRIDGE *Dict. Slang* Suppl. 1182/2 *Mentioned in despatches.* To have one's name appear in a newspaper, a parish magazine, or even on a notice board: jocular. **1975** *Times* 27 Aug. 20/3 In proud and loving memory of Captain Jocelyn Fulke Dalrymple Radice, The Queen's Bays, mentioned in British and French Army dispatches, ..who died of wounds on August 27, 1944.

b. (Later examples.)

1863 G. MACDONALD *D. Elginbrod* III. III. ix. 158 He mentioned to Miss Talbot that he had been his guest that night. **1929** C. K. S. MONCRIEFF tr. *Proust's Cities of Plain* I. II. ii. 268, I mentioned to him that I had thought I heard him come upstairs.

c. (Earlier example.)

1841 LYTTON *Night & Morning* I. II. ii. 264 'I am going to leave your house, ma'am; and I wish to settle any little arrears of rent, &c.' 'Oh! sir! don't mention it,' said the landlady.

mento-. **mento-meckelian,** also as *sb.*, a small bone formed by the ossified end of Meckel's cartilage.

1892 J. A. THOMSON *Outl. Zool.* 449 The mento-meckelians seem to arise from two lower labial cartilages. **1925** J. S. KINGSLEY *Vertebr. Skeleton* 71 The other cartilage bone is a mentomeckelian, best known in Anura, at the symphysis of the lower jaw.

menton (me·ntǫn). *Anat.* [a. F. *menton* chin:— L. *mentum.*] = *GNATHION.

1937 *Amer. Jrnl. Physical Anthrop.* XXII. 483 Menton. .. By all authors, this is designated as the lowest point on the lower border of the mandible in the median plane. **1954** T. C. WHITE et al. *Orthodontics* ix. 165 The Mandibular Plane passes from the menton (lowest point on the cross-section of the mandibular symphysis)..to the lowest point on the angle of the mandible. **1968** [see *GNATHION]. **1974** *Nature* 8 Mar. 165/1 Six bilateral and four single roentgenographic landmarks were delineated. The single landmarks were: sella; anterior nasal spine; incisal point; menton.

‖ **mentri** (me·ntri). Also 9– **mantri.** [Mal. *mentri*, ad. Skr. *mantri* *MANTRI.] A title used in the Malay states for a minister. Also **mentri besar,** a title for the chief minister of a Malay state.

Mentri was used *spec.* of a Perak territorial chief in the 19th century.

1839 T. J. NEWBOLD *Pol. & Statistical Acct. Straits of Malacca* I. v. 239 The Mantris were the privy councillors to the Panghúlus, two in number. **1880** F. A. SWETTENHAM *Some Acct. Independent Native States Malay Peninsula* i. 7 He had..got the Mĕntri to assist him in farming the revenues of Krïan, a Province claimed by the Mĕntri. **1900** W. E. MAXWELL in W. W. Skeat *Malay Magic* iii. 65 The grave was discovered..by workmen employed by the Mĕntri of Perak. **1907** F. A. SWETTENHAM *Brit. Malaya* vi. 118 The Malay chief of the Lârut district was styled the Mantri, and he was one of the four high officers of state. **1955** *Times* 1 Aug. 6/6 They would be the symbol of loyalty of all classes and of all races loyal to Malaya. 'I only hope that in a short time their highnesses will see fit to appoint as their mentris besar (chief ministers) elected members of state councils.' **1958** J. SLIMMING *Temiar Jungle* ii. 27 *Mentri* is a Malay title superimposed on the Temiar system of leadership. **1972** *Straits Times* (Malaysian ed.) 4 May 6/4 Malaysia and Indonesia will be closer, and grow better in education when a common spelling system is used by both governments, Mentri Besar Inche Ja'afar bin Hassan said yesterday.

menu. Add: **2.** (Further *transf.* examples.) Also *menu card* (earlier example).

1881 C. C. HARRISON *Woman's Handiwork* II. 124 A menu card, with gilded edge and lettering. **1922** JOYCE *Ulysses* 161 Maul her a bit. Then the next thing on the menu. **1940** H. G. WELLS *Babes in Darkling Wood* II. iii. 206 All the intelligent ones feel baffled at the menu of these degree courses. **1971** *Computers & Humanities* VI. 104 The musical symbols at the top of the workscope are the 'menu'. **1974** *Some Technical Terms & Slang* (Granada Television), *Menu*, a list of items read out at the start of a magazine programme.

‖ **menus plaisirs** (mənü plęzīr), *sb. pl.* [Fr., lit. 'small pleasures'; pocket-money.] Simple pleasures; small personal expenses or gratifications; fanciful or trifling objects bought with one's pocket-money. Also *attrib.*

1697 VANBRUGH *Relapse* I. ii. 8, I shall see you stand in damnable need of some Auxiliary Guineas, for you[r] *Menu Plaisirs.* **1779** H. WALPOLE *Let.* 14 Jan. (1904) X. 363 My *menus plaisirs*, a few sprinkled visits of charity from a few friends that remained in town. **1814** JANE AUSTEN *Mansf. Park* II. v. 114 He will have a very pretty income ..and as..he will still live at home, it will be all for his *menus plaisirs.* **1883** M. E. BRADDON *Golden Calf* II. xi. 293 Whatever honorarium he received for his work was expended upon his *menus plaisirs.* **1915** F. M. HUEFFER *Good Soldier* III. v. 193 He may have had five hundred pounds a year English, for his menus plaisirs. **1966** 'M. INNES' *Change of Heir* v. 40 'It's in her letter. The bit about..*menus frais.*' 'What's that?' 'The same as *menus plaisirs.* Pocket-money on the scale appropriate to an English gentleman.'

Meo (mī·o). Also 9 **Mewoh.** [Native name.] An Indian people of Rajasthan and the Punjab, whose religion is a blend of Hinduism and Islam; a member of this people. Also as *adj.* Cf. *MEWATI *sb.* and *a.*

1832 J. TOD *Ann. Rajast'han* II. 393 At this period.. the mountainous region, called Méwat, was inhabited by a daring and ferocious banditti, called Mewohs, who pillaged in gangs. **1855** H. H. WILSON *Gloss. Judicial & Revenue Terms* 339/2 *Meo*, (?) H. A class of cultivators in the province of Dehli. **1873** E. BALFOUR *Cycl. India* (ed. 2) III. s.v., Meo, cultivators in the Delhi province, are a tribe of people inhabiting the low hills about Gurgaon. **1880** P. W. POWLETT in *Rajputana Gazetteer* III. 201 Meos do not marry into their own pál, or clan, but are lax about forming connections with women of other castes, whose children they receive into the Meo community. **1885** G. C. WHITWORTH *Anglo-Indian Dict.* 204/2 *Mewáti*, the name of a branch of the Jádon Rájputs;..they rule in Alwar, and are connected with the Meo tribe of the same country. **1896** W. CROOKE *Tribes & Castes N.-W. Provinces & Oudh* III. 487 Whatever their connection with the Mînas may be, the Meos themselves pretend to be of Râjput descent. **1916** R. V. RUSSELL *Tribes & Castes Cent. Provinces India* IV. 235 Abu Fazl writes that the Meos were in his time famous runners, and one thousand of them were employed by Akbar as carriers of post. **1970** D. G. MANDELBAUM *Society in India* II. xxix. 558 This intensified Islamization is shown by the Meos, the dominant jati in some two thousand villages on the borderlands of Rajasthan and Punjab. *Ibid.* 559 The Meos have adopted more of Muslim practices in the last 17 years than they had in the previous 450 years.

Meo, var. *MIAO *sb.* and *a.*

meow (miau), var. MIAOW *int.* and *sb.*

1873 *Young Englishwoman* May 217/2 'Meow!' And an enormous cat came out. **1947** M. LOWRY *Under Volcano* vi. 166 Provocative nocturnal meows. **1956** H. G. DE LISSER *Cup & Lip* vii. 81 'What you really mean is that but for the help of the coolie..you couldn't have had Miss Ludford over here.' 'Meow, meow,' laughed Arthur.

mepacrine (me·păkrin, -īn). *Pharm.* [perh. f. ME(THYL + PA(LUDISM + A)CR(ID)INE.] A tricyclic base, $C_{23}H_{30}N_3OCl$, derived from acridine and usually administered in the form of its dihydrochloride dihydrate salt, which is a yellow crystalline compound formerly widely used in the treatment of malaria and now used mainly as an anthelmintic. Cf. *ATEBRIN, *QUINACRINE.

1943 *Lancet* 29 May 699/1 The only synthetic antimalarial compound of any real value so far in general use is mepacrine. **1956** W. SLIM *Defeat into Victory* xvi. 352 The jaundice yellow of all our complexions as a result of the daily dose of mepacrine. **1962** *Lancet* 29 Dec. 1387/2 A related drug, chloroquine, has proved superior to mepacrine in the suppressive treatment of malaria, rheumatoid arthritis, lupus erythematosus, and light eruptions. **1971** B. W. ALDISS *Soldier Erect* 74 The site where hundreds of BORs had pretended to swallow the morning mepacrine tablet and instead had ground it underfoot, happily risking malaria in the exercise of their own free will.

meperidine (mĕpe·ridīn). *Pharm.* Chiefly *U.S.* [f. ME(THYL + PI)PERIDINE.] = *PETHIDINE.

1947 *Jrnl. Amer. Med. Assoc.* 25 Jan. 243/2 In this country only 1 case of spontaneous addiction to meperidine hydrochloride is reported. **1962** J. H. BURN *Drugs, Med. & Man* x. 104 The disadvantage can however be countered by choosing one of the substitutes for morphine which have been made in the laboratory in the last twenty years. The first of these was meperidine (in Britain called pethidine). **1971** J. J. BURNS in B. N. La Du et al. *Fund. Drug Metabolism* xvii. 343 The rhesus monkey and the dog metabolize..meperidine and antipyrine much more rapidly than does man.

mephenesin (mĕfe·nĕsin). *Pharm.* [f. ME(THYL + PHEN(YL + CR)ES(OL + -IN[1].] A colourless crystalline compound, $CH_3{\cdot}C_6H_4O{\cdot}CH_2CH(OH)CH_2OH$, which is used as a muscle-relaxant in the treatment of spastic, hypertonic, and hyperkinetic conditions, and as a tranquillizer.

1952 *Brit. Pharmaceutical Codex 1949* Suppl. 40 Mephenesin consists of 3-(2-methylphenoxy)propane-1:2-diol. **1955** *Sci. News Let.* 16 July 40/3 In the great majority of 109 cases [of cerebral palsy] treated before dental surgery with mephenesin,..the drug produced feelings of well-being and relaxation, and nervousness diminished or disappeared. **1962** J. H. BURN *Drugs, Med. & Man* xii. 127 Another study was made by other workers to test the claim that the drug mephenesin exerts a specific effect on subjective anxiety and feeling of tension, and also on objective manifestations of this state. **1972** *Neuropharmacology* XI. 733 Amino-oxyacetic acid did not protect rats against the audiogenic seizures that constitute the barbiturate abstinence syndrome whereas mephenesin ..did provide protection.

mephitical, *a.* Delete † and add later examples.

1930 D. L. SAYERS *Strong Poison* viii. 95 In one corner an anthracite stove, glowing red and mephitical, vied with a roaring gas-oven in another corner. **1933** *Punch* 6 Dec. 641/3 In the sphere of things political An atmosphere malign, mephitical, Infects the universe.

meprobamate (meprōu·bămēit). *Pharm.* [f. ME(THYL + PRO(PYL + *car*)*bamate* (s.v. CARBAMIDE).] A colourless crystalline compound, $CH_3CH_2CH_2C(CH_2O{\cdot}CO{\cdot}NH_2)_2CH_3$, which is a mild tranquillizer used in the treatment of motion sickness, neuroses, and insomnia.

1955 *Dispensatory U.S.A.* (ed. 25) 1861/1 Meprobamate. Equanil (Wyeth). Miltown (Wallace).—This is 2-methyl-2-*n*-propyl-1,3-propanediol dicarbamate. **1962** A. HUXLEY *Island* xiii. 201 Mass opiates in the form of television, meprobamate, positive thinking and cigarettes. **1965** J. POLLITT *Depression & its Treatment* iv. 48 When tension is more prominent than depression, chlordiazepoxide, meprobamate or even amylobarbitone in average doses will help tide the patient over difficult phases. **1965** *Evening Standard* 13 Sept. 10/3 He had an envelope full of pep pills—amphetamine—in his left coat pocket and an envelope full of Equanils—meprobamate—in his right pocket. **1967** *Martindale's Extra Pharmacopoeia* (ed. 25) 391/2 Suicide attempts with meprobamate are not infrequent... There is a serious addiction risk. **1969** *Punch* 5 Mar. 340/3 The classic example was the test of the tranquilliser meprobamate, sold here under the brand names Miltown and Equanil. It had been one of the most profitable drugs ever marketed—but in the trials, the placebo proved just as effective.

mepyramine (mepi·rămīn). *Pharm.* [f. ME(THYL + PYR(IDINE + AMINE.] A crystalline substituted amine, $C_{17}H_{23}N_3O$, or its maleate, which is an antihistamine drug used in treating allergic conditions.

1949 *Lancet* 9 July 47/2 The histamine antagonist, N(2-dimethylaminoethyl)N(*p*-methoxybenzyl)2-aminopyridine maleate..later known on the continent as 'Neo-antergan' and in this country as 'Anthisan' or mepyramine maleate..was soon recognised as the most powerful and specific of the histamine antagonists. **1964** W. G. SMITH *Allergy & Tissue Metabolism* v. 61 One of these was histamine whose actions could be blocked by mepyramine. **1972** *Nature* 21 Apr. 369/1 Certain responses..are not antagonized by the classical antihistaminic drugs, such as mepyramine.

mer (mɔɹ). *Chem.* [f. POLY)MER.] The repeating unit of a polymeric molecule.

1936 W. O. CAROTHERS in *Trans. Faraday Soc.* XXXII. 49 Assume that the weight of the mer or unit is 100. **1947** R. L. WAKEMAN *Chem. Commercial Plastics* xx. 554 The word 'mer'..has..been used by Carothers to designate the individual unit of repetition in both addition and condensation polymers (as distinguished from the monomeric substances themselves from which the polymer is produced). **1952** *Jrnl. Polymer Sci.* VIII. 258 The slight variability in composition and chemical structure permitted..for high polymers results from the presence of end groups, occasional branches, variation in orientation of the mers (monomeric units), irregularity in the sequence of different types of mers (in copolymers), and sometimes other irregularities. **1967** MARGERISON & EAST *Introd. Polymer Chem.* i. 3 As soon as more than one mer is involved, a wide diversity of polymer structure and type becomes possible.

-mer (mɔɹ), terminal element repr. Gr. μέρος part, occurring in various chemical terms: orig. in *polymer* and *isomer*, and usu. in words denoting particular kinds of polymer (as *dimer*, *elastomer*) or isomer (as *epimer*).

meranti (mĕræ·nti). [Malay.] A hardwood timber produced by trees of the genus *Shorea*, belonging to the family Dipterocarpaceæ, and native to Malaya, Sarawak, and Indonesia; also, a tree yielding this wood.

1783 W. MARSDEN *Hist. Sumatra* 130 *Maranti maracooly* and *murbow*, are in much estimation for building. **1839** T. J. NEWBOLD *Pol. & Statistical Acct. Straits of Malacca* I. vii. 442 The trees chiefly in use for purposes of house and ship are the Chingei,..the red and white Meranti for planks, etc. **1900** W. W. SKEAT *Malay Magic* 109 The *mĕranti* is a fine hard-wood forest tree. **1935** I. H. BURKILL *Dict. Econ. Products Malay Peninsula* II. 2002 Red Mĕranti is the commonest Malayan timber. **1955** *Nomencl. Commercial Timbers* (*B.S.I.*) 74 For the light to medium-weight timbers it should be noted that *meranti* is the group name for species of *Shorea* in Malaya, Sarawak, Brunei and Indonesia. **1956** *Archit. Rev.* CXX. 117 All windows and doors are framed in red meranti hardwood. **1956** *Handbk. Hardwoods* (Forest Prod. Res. Lab.) 150 In Malaya this timber is commonly classified for export mainly on the basis of colour and weight as light red meranti (the most important), dark red meranti, yellow meranti and white meranti. **1966** D. FORBES *Heart of*

Malaya x. 113 Their box-like wooden houses..are dull and plain in contrast with the charming thatched cottages of red meranti wood, in which the Malays live. **1971** *Timber Trades Jrnl.* 14 Aug. 42/2 Malaysian and Singapore plywoods, of which meranti and mengkulang are the most important, accounted for 11·9% of deliveries of 102 500m³.

merbau (mə·ɹbōu). Also **marbow, merabau, murbow.** [Malay.] A hardwood timber obtained from *Intsia bijuga* or *I. palembanica*, of the family Leguminosæ, trees native to Malaysia and Indonesia; also, the tree itself.

1783 [see *MERANTI]. **1836** J. Low *Diss. Soil & Agric. Penang* v. 202 *Marbow*—this is a high tree, affording large planks. **1911** *Encycl. Brit.* XVII. 472/2 Good hard-wood timber is found in plenty, the best being the *merabau*, *penak*, *rasok* and *chengal*. **1935** I. H. BURKILL *Dict. Econ. Products Malay Peninsula* II. 1243 Mĕrbau is used for all kinds of high-grade construction on land, for furniture, and for sleepers. **1940** E. J. H. CORNER *Wayside Trees Malaya* I. 396 This small genus [sc. *Intsia*] includes the well-known timber-tree *Merbau*. **1958** J. SLIMMING *Temiar Jungle* iv. 60 The children play with spinning tops, made of *Merbau* wood. **1965** C. SHUTTLEWORTH *Malayan Safari* i. 16 There are heavy hardwoods such as merbau, balau and chengal. **1972** *Timber Trades Jrnl.* 13 May 39/2 Of the lesser species merbau and kapur are readily available.

Mercalli (məɹkæ·li). *Seismology.* The name of Giuseppe *Mercalli* (1850–1914), Italian geologist, used *attrib.* to designate an arbitrary 12-point scale he devised (in 1897) to express the intensity of an earthquake at any place.

1921 C. DAVISON *Man. Seismol.* iii. 45 The Mercalli scale..is suitable for strong earthquakes and is adopted in Italy. **1927** —— *Founders Seismol.* vi. 106 Mercalli found that the higher degrees of the Rossi-Forei scale were insufficient... His modification of that scale contains the germs of the Mercalli scale now so widely used. **1972** *Times* 28 Nov. 5/2 The tremor (eight on the 12-point Mercalli scale) damaged many buildings in the old part of the city. **1973** *Daily Colonist* (Victoria, B.C.) 8 Apr. 10/5 An earthquake can have only one magnitude but it can have several intensities and these are registered on what is known as the modified Mercalli intensity scale.

mercapto(-) (məɹkæ·pto). *Chem.* [f. MERCAPT(AN + -O.] **a.** As an inseparable formative element in chem. names indicating the presence of the radical —SH, as *mercapto-acetic* adj., *mercaptoethanol*; **mercaptopu·rine** *Pharm.*, any of the monomercapto derivatives of purine, *spec.* 6-mercaptopurine, $C_5H_4N_4S$, which is a yellow crystalline powder and is a cytotoxic agent used chiefly in treating leukæmia in children.

1971 *Nomencl. Org. Chem.* (I.U.P.A.C.) (ed. 2) C. 211 When —SH is not the principal group, the prefix 'mercapto-' is placed before the name of the parent compound to denote an unsubstituted —SH group.

1884 ROSCOE & SCHORLEMMER *Treat. Chem.* III. II. 88 Thioglycollic acid, or mercapto-acetic acid, $CH_2(SH)CO_2H$, is obtained by the addition of chloracetic acid to an aqueous solution of potassium hydrosulphide. **1947** *Biochem. Jrnl.* XLI. 49/2 BAL is also effective in detoxicating this arsenical, whereas a concentration of 2-mercaptoethanol equivalent to twice that of BAL is almost completely inactive. **1965** PEACOCKE & DRYSDALE *Molecular Basis Heredity* vii. 73 By inhibiting nuclear division in sea urchin eggs with mercaptoethanol, Mazia provided evidence that the prophase chromosome contains at least four strands. **1954** *Amer. Jrnl. Med. Sci.* CCXXVIII. 376/2 We have in mercaptopurine a new type of agent which has demonstrated activity against experimental tumors and leukemia in the mouse and against leukemia in man. **1961** *Lancet* 7 Oct. 821/1 Methotrexate..and mercaptopurine..are folic-acid antagonists, which..interfere with nucleic-acid synthesis by inhibiting folic-acid reductase. **1965** Mercaptopurine [see *immunosuppressant* s.v. *IMMUNO-]. **1973** *Arthritis & Rheumatism* XVI. 139 Thirteen patients with psoriasis and arthritis were treated with 6-mercaptopurine in dosages ranging from 20 to 150 mg/day.

b. As an independent word, usu. *attrib.* and sometimes joined by a hyphen to the second element: the radical —SH, present in mercaptans; sulphydryl.

1896 *Jrnl. Chem. Soc.* LXX. I. 412 Unsymmetrical homologues of thiodiglycollic acid..are prepared by the interaction of the neutral sodium salts of mercapto-acids and those of haloid fatty acids. **1930** *Chem. Rev.* VII. 511 Mercapto acids may be made in the same way as hydroxy acids. **1957** R. H. BARRY in E. Sagarin *Cosmetics* xx. 468 These inventors obtained coverage also in Great Britain for other organic mercapto compounds which function in alkaline-reacting media as depilatories.

mercapturic (məɹkæptiūə·rik), *a.* *Chem.* [ad. G. *bromphenyl)mercaptur(säure* bromophenylmercapturic acid (Baumann & Preusse 1879, in *Ber. d. Deut. Chem. Ges.* XII. 807), f. *mercapt(an* MERCAPTAN + *ur(in* URINE *sb.*¹: see -IC.] *mercapturic acid*: any of the acids of the formula $RSCH_2CH(NH{\cdot}CO{\cdot}CH_3)COOH$ (where R is an aryl radical), some of which are excreted in the urine, probably as detoxication products of aromatic compounds.

1879 *Jrnl. Chem. Soc.* XXXVI. 803 An examination of the urine of a dog, to which 3 to 4 grams of bromobenzene had been daily administered for six months, showed... The urine contains bromophenyl-mercapturic acid. **1884** *Ibid.* XLVI. 1395 A body strongly lævorotatory, which on treatment with acids yields mercapturic acid. **1934** *Times Lit. Suppl.* 9 Aug. 555/2 Naphthalene is detoxicated in the rabbit partly by conjugation with cysteine and subsequent excretion as the mercapturic acid. **1971** H. G. MANDEL in B. N. La Du et al. *Fund. Drug Metabolism* x. 168 Acetylation takes place in the liver..and the resulting mercapturic acid is then excreted in the urine.

Mercator (məɹkēi·tǒɹ). Also **mercator.** [L., = 'merchant'.] **a.** The name of Gerhardus *Mercator* (= L. equivalent of Gerhard Kremer) (1512–94), Flemish cartographer, used *attrib.* and in the possessive with reference to the orthomorphic cylindrical map projection first used by him in 1568, in which meridians are represented by equidistant straight lines at right angles to the equator and any course that follows a constant compass bearing is represented by a straight line.

1669 Mercator's projection [see PROJECTION *sb.* 7 b]. *a* **1877** KNIGHT *Dict. Mech.* II. 1419/2 *Mercator-chart*, a mode of projection invented by Gerald Mercator, in which the meridians and parallels are straight and parallel lines. **1883** *Encycl. Brit.* XV. 520/2 By 1601 Mercator's projection was in use for all sea charts. **1908** G. R. PUTNAM *Naut. Charts* 9 The Arcano del Mare, 1646, was the first marine atlas in which all the maps were drawn on the mercator projection. **1912** A. R. HINKS *Map Projections* iii. 29 The great distortion in the north and south makes Mercator's projection altogether unsuitable for a land map. **1938** L. M. MILNE-THOMSON *Theoret. Hydrodynamics* v. 138 An illustration of conformal mapping is afforded by an ordinary map on Mercator's projection. **1960** C. ECKART *Hydrodynamics of Oceans & Atmospheres* 280 The vertical co-ordinate, μ, on a Mercator chart of the Sphere is defined by $d\phi = \cos\phi d\mu$.

b. *absol.* (A map drawn on) Mercator's projection.

1879 *Encycl. Brit.* X. 208/2 The meridian Mercator drawn as described in the last paragraph..may be made to serve the important purpose of enabling one to trace on the ordinary Mercator's chart the track of a great circle joining any two places. **1953** A. H. ROBINSON *Elem. Cartogr.* iii. 43/1 The poles cannot be represented for they are 'at' infinity on the conventional Mercator.

Mercatorial (məɹkătōə·riăl), *a.*² Also **mercatorial.** [f. prec. + -IAL.] Of, pertaining to, or derived from Mercator or Mercator's projection or chart.

a **1888** P. F. SHORTLAND *Naut. Surveying* (1890) 144 Their Mercatorial meridians will be inclined to each of them respectively about 1'·2. *Ibid.* 346 To reduce a plane sheet to a Mercatorial projection proceed as follows. **1942** *Jrnl. R. Aeronaut. Soc.* XLVI. 21 It is..possible to include these scales in certain navigational devices, so that rhumb lines and mercatorial bearings may be projected if required without the aid of an actual graticule.

merchandise, *v.* Restrict *arch.* to senses in Dict. and add: **3. a.** To put on the market; to promote the sale of (goods, etc.).

1926 *Publishers' Weekly* 22 May 1687/2 When an author suddenly springs into prominence with a best seller.. I would make that best seller work retroactively and I would merchandise all of his preceding books. **1959** I. Ross *Image Merchants* (1960) xv. 270 A new breakfast food or a new form of aspirin can easily be merchandised. **1970** R. LOWELL *Notebk.* 43 This typing paper..only merchandised in Maine. **1971** *Daily Tel.* 9 June 5/3 Books can be merchandised like other products.

b. *transf.* To advertise (an idea or person); to publicize; to 'put over'.

1973 J. RYDER *Trevayne* (1974) xxxix. 309 Andrew Trevayne could be merchandised with extraordinary effect. He has all the qualifications. **1974** *Radio Times* 20 Jan. 9/3, I was never merchandised in my career as any kind of symbol. **1974** *Saturday* (Charleston, S. Carolina) 20 Apr. 1-A/3 Paul said the effect of trouble will depend on how the 'unfortunate situation' is merchandised.

merchandiser. Delete *Obs.* except *arch.* and add later examples.

1965 F. SARGESON *Mem. Peon* iv. 68 A merchandiser of building material. **1971** *Daily Tel.* 10 June 25 (Advt.), We are seeking to appoint Merchandisers who will be responsible within a Sales Team for maximising the Company's sales in cash and carries and supermarkets. **1973** *Ibid.* 3 Jan. 19 (Advt.), A vacancy exists for a Merchandiser to develop fashion ranges of men's shirts.

merchandising, *vbl. sb.* Delete † and add later examples. Also, the promotion of sales (of goods, etc.) by advertising and publicity; the process of selling goods (see *MERCHANDISE *v.* 3).

1922 S. LEWIS *Babbitt* iv. 39, I guess that'll show Chan Mott..something about modern merchandizing! **1940** *Economist* 11 May 860/1 The distinctive feature of the chain stores' success is the wedding of efficient merchandising with the control of production from the retail end. **1958** *Ibid.* 18 Oct. 200 (Advt.), Merchandising..means following up your advertising. It means getting retailers on your side, and giving them all they need to help you sell. **1968** *Globe & Mail* (Toronto) 17 Feb. B 6 (Advt.), Must be experienced in all areas of supermarket operations and merchandising. **1971** *Daily Tel.* 10 June 25 (Advt.), Candidates should be in their twenties with good education and preferably have experience in selling or merchandising in the Grocery field. **1973** *Times* 10 Mar. 14/6 In the past two decades the merchandizing of Disney's cartoon creations in a plethora of T-shirts, key-rings and assorted trivia may have obscured their creator's rightful claim to be regarded as one of the most original film producers in cinema history.

attrib. (Later examples.)

1926 *Publishers' Weekly* 16 Jan. 171/1 His frank criticism of 'price-cutting for bait' indicates that he has found other merchandising practices of more value in business building. **1930** *Daily Express* 9 Sept. 2/6 A wide assortment of issues rose from 1 to 3 points, with utilities, merchandising stocks, coppers, and specialities prominent.

merchant, *sb.* and *a.* Add: **A.** *sb.* **1. d.** (Further examples.)

1704 S. KNIGHT *Jrnl.* (1825) 56 [The Indians] give the title of merchant to every trader. **1784** J. F. D. SMYTH *Tour U.S.A.* I. 99 Linen-drapers, grocers, stationers, &c. are not known here; they are all comprehended in the single name and occupation of merchant, or store-keeper. **1809** 'D. KNICKERBOCKER' *Hist. N.Y.* II. VII. x. 251 If peradventure some straggling merchant of the east, should stop at his door, with his cart load of tin ware or wooden bowls, [etc.]. **1818** in *Trans. Illinois State Hist. Soc. 1910* 162 Dry goods are geting very cheap, the country is full of them; we have more merchants than any thing else. **1853** *Harper's Mag.* Aug. 425/1 The subject, we take it, is the 'merchant' of a country-store; quite a different variety from the big bugs of the trade in the Great Metropolis. **1871** R. SOMERS *Southern States since War* 129 Few are able at the end of the year to square accounts with 'the merchant'. **1897** J. L. ALLEN *Choir Invisible* i. 5 A heavy roll of home-spun linen, which she was taking to town to her aunt's merchant as barter for queen's-ware pitchers. **1924** *Scots Mag.* Aug. 342 The merchan's in an awfu' ill teen the day, swearin' like a' that. **1961** *Buchan Observer* 6 June 5 (Advt.), For Sale, by Private Bargain, this well-sited General Merchant's Business, at the junction of the main Fraserburgh and Peterhead Roads. **1975** 'E. LATHEN' *By Hook or by Crook* xiii. 129 An ancient panama..part of the summer uniform demanded of city merchants.

f. merchant of death, one who makes a profession of war; *spec.*, a dealer in armaments; a mercenary soldier.

1934 ENGELBRECHT & HANIGHEN *Merchants of Death* xviii. 261 The business of the arms industry is steadily increasing..and governments are everywhere drawing closer the ties which bind them in a virtual partnership with the merchants of death. **1956** C. W. MILLS *Power Elite* viii. 189 Top generals..lived through the general anti-militarist peace of the 'twenties and 'thirties, begging for appropriations, denying the merchants-of-death charges. **1959** E. AMBLER *Passage of Arms* ix. 233 Nowadays..we don't hear the phrase 'merchants of death' very much. **1963** *Guardian* 11 Jan. 8/1 A mist of superstition and loathing of the trade in arms, of the 'Merchants of Death'. **1974** D. SEAMAN *Bomb that could Lip-Read* xi. 98 Inflation would hit a merchant of death as much as any working man.

3. Delete † *Obs.* and add later examples. Now usu. with a qualifying word, as *speed merchant*, denoting one who has an interest in or partiality for the thing specified. *slang.*

1886 *Referee* 17 Oct. 2/3 The success of 'Indiana' mainly depends upon the extravagant humours of the chief low-comedy merchant. **1909** J. R. WARE *Passing Eng.* 175/2 The theatre coming to be called the 'shop', actors dubbed themselves 'merchants', qualified by their line. **1914** *Automotor Jrnl.* 246/2 It may be that when the new road has been built the speed merchant and the road-hog..may pay their money and betake themselves to their favourite seaside haunt at any speed they like. **1919** J. BUCHAN *Mr. Standfast* ix. 176 Some movie-merchant had got a graft with the Government, and troops had been turned out to make a war film. **1923** *Daily Mail* 15 Feb. 6 The chauffeur of a motor-car has a rain-blurred wind-screen, and the goggled 'speed-merchant' cannot see so well as usual. **1929** A. CONAN DOYLE *Maracot Deep* 244 Storr, the googlie merchant, had a better showing with four for ninety-six. **1933** D. L. SAYERS *Murder must Advertise* xviii. 316 He was now faced by the merchant with the off-break. The first two balls he treated carefully. **1957** *Railway Mag.* Nov. 752/2 One wonders how many drivers, other than the confirmed speed merchants, will even attempt to run the 8.20 a.m. from Kings Cross from Hitchin to Huntingdon in 24 min. **1963** *Pix* 28 Sept. 63 Being a good weather 'merchant' is one of the finest refinements in surfing. **1970** D. FRANCIS *Rat Race* vi. 83 Here is this bloody bomb merchant running around loose with no one knowing what he'll do next. **1971** *Guardian* 24 Sept. 13 Anthony Tucker on America's leading doom merchant Mister Catastrophe. **1971** G. SIMS *Deadhand* II. iii. 97 Sorry to be such a gloom merchant. But..we're broke, you see.

4. Delete † *Obs.* and add later examples.

1899 KIPLING *Five Nations* (1903) 8 The pot-bellied merchant foreboding no wrong With headlight and side-light he lieth along. **1905** J. MASEFIELD *Mainsail Haul* 65 There's a fat merchant on the coast... We're going out for her.

6. a. *merchant shipper.*

1912 *Pitman's Commercial Encycl. & Dict. Business* II. 822/1 We will take as an example an indent for cotton goods, such as a large firm of merchant shippers would receive. **1919** *Brit. Manufacturer* Nov. 16/2 Orders may.. be distributed by the merchant shipper of this country.

b. merchant prince (earlier and later examples); hence **merchant-princely** *a.*

1843 L. M. CHILD *Lett. from N.Y.* viii. 53, I sometimes ask whether the age of Commerce is better than the age of War? Whether our 'merchant princes' are a great advance upon feudal chieftains? **1961** NEW ENG. BIBLE *Rev.* xviii. 23 Your traders were once the merchant princes of the world. **1967** *N.Y. Times* (Internat. ed.) 11–12 Feb. 4/1 Prince Philip, describing himself as a merchant prince working to increase British exports, told 500 businessmen

yesterday that no matter where he traveled he was questioned about Britain's financial woes. **1874** TROLLOPE *Way we live Now* (1875) I. x. 59 He..had twice dined.. amidst all the magnificence of merchant-princely hospitality in Grosvenor Square. **1928** *Daily Express* 20 Dec. 6 Even the final figure, the three million dollar trade, is nothing breath-bereaving nor merchant-princely.

merchantability (mɜ̄ːɹtʃăntăbi·lĭti). [f. MERCHANTABLE *a.*: see -ITY.] The condition or state of being fit or prepared for market; the ability to be bought or sold.

1939 *Credit Manual of Commercial Laws* (Nat. Assoc. Credit Men) 31 *Merchantability*. Where goods are bought by description from a dealer in goods of that kind..there is an implied warranty that they shall be of a merchantable quality. **1961** *Listener* 21 Sept. 417/1 This condition, unlike the condition of merchantability, may be expressly excluded. **1972** *N.Y. Law Jrnl.* 31 Oct. 17/6 The findings on such issues..constitute a breach of the implied warranty of merchantability. **1973** *Ibid.* 1 Aug. 4/6 The issue is whether the pacemaker was fit for the ordinary purpose for which pacemakers were used (merchantability).

merchant bank (mɜ̄·ɹtʃănt bæŋk). [MERCHANT *a.* 1 + BANK *sb.*[3] 7.] A bank whose main business is the providing of long-term credit and the support and financing of trading enterprises. So **merchant banker**, a member of such a bank (also *pl.*, the bank as a firm); **merchant banking** *vbl. sb.*, the activity undertaken by a merchant bank.

1904 H. T. EASTON *Hist. Banks* xxi. 215 The chairman of the London and Westminster Bank stated some time ago that 'acceptances drawn by mercantile firms abroad is [*sic*] part of the business that ought to be carried on by a merchant or merchant-banker'. **1924** L. LE M. MINTY *Eng. Banking Methods* ii. 51 The Merchant Bankers..are a class of large importing and exporting firms that, in addition to their regular business in trade, carry on an accepting business... Many firms referred to as 'merchant bankers' are merchants no longer. **1926** W. LEAF *Banking* vii. 184 Several of the great merchant banking houses of the Continent found it worth their while to transfer their international offices to London. **1928** *Daily Mail* 25 July 18/1 Dr. David Jochelman... Merchant Banker. **1930** S. E. THOMAS *Princ. Banking* ii. 18 In a sixth class [of banks] are the various concerns in the City which are known as 'merchant bankers' or 'merchant banks'. Most of these function mainly as 'accepting houses'. **1933** B. ELLINGER *This Money Business* ii. 16 Merchant Bankers or Accepting Houses, whose business it is to accept bills for other people and earn a commission by doing so. **1940** T. S. ELIOT *East Coker* iii. 10 They all go into the dark.. The captains, merchant bankers, eminent men of letters. **1959** *Chambers's Encycl.* II. 100/2 Mention may also be made of the London merchant bankers. Their traditional function has been to facilitate the finance of international trade by 'accepting' (guaranteeing) bills of exchange. **1961** M. SPARK *Prime of Miss Jean Brodie* vi. 161 A successful business man who varied in his line of business from canned goods to merchant banking. **1965** J. L. HANSON *Dict. Econ.* 276/1 Many foreign merchant bankers found it convenient to transfer their headquarters to London—hence the number of merchant banks in England with foreign names. **1965** PERRY & RYDER *Thomson's Dict. Banking* (ed. 11) 375/1 Merchant bank. The great merchant banking houses of today have evolved from the merchants who, coming to this country in the early or middle years of the eighteenth century, built up their business by lending their names to bills financing particular transactions and by accepting such bills made them first-class bills freely discountable. **1966** *Times Rev. Industry* Oct. 99/1 When I became chairman of Lazards last year I was able to put down my occupation as 'merchant banker' instead of the less reputable 'company director'... I certainly was not a 'merchant' and not really a 'banker'. **1972** *Accountant* 19 Oct. 500/2 The work of an accountant in the field of merchant banking or taxation are [*sic*] worlds apart from the work in manufacturing industry or in practice.

merchanting, *vbl. sb.* Add: (Further examples.) Also *attrib.*

1957 *Listener* 28 Nov. 876/1 There is London as a merchanting centre... I have in mind the work done by the commodity markets and the large merchanting houses in buying and selling throughout the world. **1963** *Times* 16 Feb. 6/1 The merchanting trade has a considerable processing element, about a third of the 9m. tons of compound feed produced in the United Kingdom being manufactured by country compounders. **1967** *Economist* 28 Oct. 420/2 Lord Cromer, when still Governor of the Bank of England, put a figure of £200 million on the overseas earnings from all of Britain's insurance, merchanting, brokerage and banking services in 1965. **1971** *Timber Trades Jrnl.* 21 Aug. 13/1 The merchanting and retail side of the timber trade. **1973** *Daily Tel.* 31 July 17 (Advt.), More depots have been acquired in the merchanting and retailing section where we now have 87 outlets.

merchanting (mɜ̄·ɹtʃăntiŋ), *ppl. a.* [f. MERCHANT *v.* + -ING[2].] Engaged in trade as merchants.

1930 *Observer* 9 Feb. 18/1 The merchanting body itself is in no greatly better case. **1957** *Times* 23 Dec. 11/2 Two main divisions—the producing subsidiary companies with their mills and the merchanting subsidiaries in Manchester and London.

merchant mill. *U.S.* ? *Obs.* [f. MERCHANT *a.* 1.] A mill engaged in the grinding of grain for the purpose of trade.

1774 P. V. FITHIAN *Jrnl.* (1900) 111 Mr. Carter's Merchant Mill begins to run to-day—She is calculated to manufacture 25,000 Bushels of Wheat a Year. **1816** U. BROWN *Jrnl.* in *Maryland Hist. Mag.* (1915) X. 273 He has a Merchant Mill, a Saw Mill,..all on the Waters of Bath. **1837** W. JENKINS *Ohio Gazetteer* 68 The village contains..1 large merchant mill,..with four run of stones. **1851** C. CIST *Sk. Cincinnati in 1851* 194 It proposes to perform in a small compass..the work of a merchant mill. **1877** W. A. JOHNSON *Hist. Anderson County, Kansas* 252 In the spring of 1874 Chris. Bouch..commenced the construction of a first-class merchant mill.

merchant navy (mɜ̄·ɹtʃănt nēi·vi). [MERCHANT *a.* 2 + NAVY[1].] A fleet or number of ships used in trade and not for purposes of war.

In 19th-cent. official sources called 'merchant shipping', 'merchant service', 'mercantile marine', 'mercantile navy', but not 'merchant navy'.

1875 T. FARRER in A. Hurd *Merchant Navy* (1921) I. 80 The actual increase of our Merchant Navy is a most remarkable fact. **1921** A. HURD *Merchant Navy* I. 2 Within a few months of the opening of hostilities, the King, in a message of appreciation of the services of the merchant seamen, referred to 'his Merchant Navy',..and the Prime Minister..described the Merchant Navy as 'the jugular vein of the nation'. **1928** *Times* 14 Feb. 14/6 The King has appointed the Prince of Wales Master of the Merchant Navy and Fishing Fleets. The announcement will appear in the *London Gazette* to-night. **1929** *Ann. Reg. 1928* I. 10 On February 13 the King paid a graceful compliment to the British seafaring population outside the ranks of the Royal Navy by creating the Prince of Wales 'Master of the Merchant Navy and the Fishing Fleets'—a new title for which there was no exact precedent in British history or usage. **1937** *Discovery* June 165/1 Seamen, whether of the Royal Navy, the Merchant Navy, or the Fishing Fleet. **1965** S. J. HARLAND (*title*) The dustless road: a career in the Merchant Navy.

merchant-tailor. Delete *Obs.* etc. and add further examples.

1653 *Rec. Early Hist. Boston* (1886) X. 1, I Robert Keayne, Cittizen and Merchant Taylor of London by freedome,..now dwelling at Boston. **1818** H. B. FEARON *Sk. Amer.* 33 Taylors are numerous: they are denominated, (in conformity with the accustomed vanity of the country), 'Merchant Taylors'. **1889** *Kansas City* (Missouri) *Times & Star* 13 Nov., Call on Ed. Howe, the artistic merchant tailor. **1922** JOYCE *Ulysses* 717 The establishment of George Mesias, merchant tailor and outfitter. **1975** *Times* 5 July 14/7 The following were elected officers of the Merchant Taylors' Company for the year beginning July 14.

mercurate (mɜ̄·ɹkiūᵊrēit), *v. Chem.* [f. MERCUR(Y *sb.* + -ATE[3].] *trans.* To convert into a mercury derivative, esp. by replacing a hydrogen atom in an aromatic ring by a group containing mercury.

1923 *Org. Syntheses* III. 14 Phenol has been mercurated in water solution. **1942** FUSON & SNYDER *Org. Chem.* xxxi. 430 Hydrocarbons are mercurated by treatment at 90–160° for one or more hours. **1967** I. L. FINAR *Org. Chem.* (ed. 5) I. xx. 583 Aromatic compounds containing almost all the common functional groups have been mercurated.

So **me·rcurated** *ppl. a.*; **mercura·tion**, the process of mercurating or of becoming mercurated.

1921 *Jrnl. Amer. Chem. Soc.* XLIII. 621 The 3 mercurated phenols were boiled with aqueous potassium iodide. **1923** *Org. Syntheses* III. 100 p-Tolylmercuric chloride has been prepared..by the direct mercuration of toluene with mercuric acetate. **1965** PHILLIPS & WILLIAMS *Inorg. Chem.* I. xi. 420 Mercuration of aromatic systems occurs very rapidly, presumably through a similar intermediate. **1967** I. L. FINAR *Org. Chem.* (ed. 5) I. xx. 584 The position of the acetoxymercuri-group can be found by treating the mercurated compound with halogen.

Mercurey (‖merküre, mɜ̄·ɹkiŭri). Also **mercurey.** [Fr., name of a vineyard of the Côte Chalonnaise.] A Burgundy wine produced in the Chalonnais district of France.

1907 A. BENNETT *Grim Smile of Five Towns* iii. 225 It was a bottle of mercurey, a wine which has given me many dreadful dawns, but which I have never known how to refuse. **1928** P. M. SHAND *Bk. French Wine* iv. 173 Mercurey is the only real 'name' of the Côte Chalonnaise. *Ibid.*, Mercurey owes its classical name to a former temple of Mercury. **1958** A. L. SIMON *Dict. Wines* 110/1 Most of the *Mercurey* wines are red, and they are also of better quality than the few white wines of that district. **1972** D. MCLACHLAN *No Case for Crown* xiii. 165 The wine was his favourite *Mercurey*, which he ordered himself from France.

mercurial, *sb.* **3.** Add. to def.: Also more widely, any compound that contains mercury. (Further examples.)

1971 *Sci. Amer.* May 18/3 Among other inorganic mercurials, some of the oxides, such as the red oxide used in antifouling paint for ship bottoms may be potentially hazardous. **1971** *Nature* 23 July 222/1 The build-up of alkyl mercurials in the environment and their toxicological properties was the subject of many of the contributions.

mercurochrome (mɜ̄ɹkiūᵊ·rokrōum). *Pharm.* Chiefly *U.S.* [f. MERCUR(Y *sb.* + -O + Gr. χρῶμ-α colour.] A mercury derivative, $C_{20}H_8O_6Br_2HgNa_2$, of fluorescein which forms greenish iridescent scales, dissolves in water to give a red solution, and is used as a weak antiseptic. (Orig. given a wider meaning: see quot. 1919.)

1919 H. H. YOUNG et al. in *Jrnl. Amer. Med. Assoc.* 15 Nov. 1484/1 To the substance obtained by substituting one atom of mercury in the molecule of dibromfluorescein we have given the name 'mercurochrome-220'. [*Note*] The name 'mercurochrome' will be applied generally to all the mercury-bearing dyes that we are investigating, the individual being distinguished by the laboratory number following the name. **1942** W. SIMPSON *One of our Pilots is Safe* iii. 63 They left my face uncovered, painted with scarlet mercurochrome. **1951** R. BRADBURY *Illustr. Man* (1952) 178 He smelled the cutting odours of iodine, raw adhesive, and pink mercurochrome. **1960** O. NASH *Boy is Boy* (1961), It's easy to spot a boy... He smells of licorice, he smells of mice, Of Mercurochrome, and vanilla ice. **1960** E. GURR *Encycl. Microsc. Stains* 1. 262 Mercurochrome is an excellent substitute for eosin, as unlike the latter it is extremely fast to light and preparations stained with it do not fade even when exposed to strong sunlight for a very considerable time. **1961** J. HELLER *Catch-22* (1962) xiv. 100 Give me a minute or two to put some mercurochrome on these cuts.

mercury, *sb.* Add: **11. mercury arc lamp** (also *ellipt.* as *mercury arc*) = **mercury vapour lamp*; **mercury arc rectifier**, a rectifier consisting of one or more graphite or iron anodes and a mercury pool cathode enclosed in an envelope from which the air has been pumped out; **mercury fulminate**, fulminate of mercury; **mercury gilding** (see quot. 1960); **mercury lamp** = **mercury vapour lamp*; **mercury pool**, a mass of liquid mercury, esp. one used as an electrode; **mercury vapour lamp**, a lamp in which light (rich in the ultra-violet) is produced by an electric discharge through mercury vapour, the envelope being often coated with a fluorescent substance so as to produce more visible light (cf. **fluorescent lamp*); **mercury vapour pump**, a pump for producing high vacua which works by entraining molecules of the gas to be evacuated in a jet of mercury vapour; **mercury vapour rectifier** = **mercury arc rectifier*.

1906 *Trans. Amer. Inst. Electr. Engin.* XXIV. 372 The constant current mercury arc rectifier system, as used for operating..mercury arc lamps..is sketched diagrammatically. **1916** F. B. PIDDUCK *Treat. Electr.* ix. 363 The absence of strong lines in the red unfits the mercury arc for certain purposes. **1936** TEAGO & GILL *Mercury Arcs* ii. 13 Steel containers are used for demountable mercury arcs of large output. **1971** *New Scientist* 3 June 564/1 The conventional sources of infrared radiation are hot bodies (the globar or mercury arc lamp). **1906** Mercury arc rectifier [see *mercury arc lamp* above]. **1930** *Engineering* 24 Jan. 109/3 A 650-volt direct-current supply from mercury arc rectifiers. **1966** G. F. ALLEN *Brit. Rail after Beeching* v. 133 In the Eastern Region's multiple-units.. the resultant distortions in the electrical circuitry were aggravated by serious failures of the mercury-arc rectifiers. **1904** *Kynoch Jrnl.* Oct.–Dec. 199 The flame from the mercury fulminate..ignites the charge of explosive contained in..the case. **1973** L. RUSSELL *Everyday Life Colonial Canada* xii. 150 The hammer [of a gun] was reduced to a simple head, designed to strike the top of the copper [percussion] cap. Under this top was a pinch of mercury fulminate, a compound so unstable that a moderate impact causes it to explode. [**1910** R. L. HOBSON *Worcester Porc.* xii. 100 A radical change came over the ware about 1780, when the cheaper process of mercurial gilding came into use... This later gilding has a more metallic and brassy appearance.] **1957** MANKOWITZ & HAGGAR *Conc. Encycl. Eng. Pott. & Porc.* 95/2 Mercury gilding was introduced about 1785. **1960** R. G. HAGGAR *Conc. Encycl. Cont. Pott. & Porc.* 207/1 s.v. *Gilding*, Mercury-gilding came in about 1780, and consisted of a mixture of gold with mercury which could be painted onto the ware, the mercury being driven off as a vapour during the firing process. **1971** *Country Life* 10 June 1419/2 This mercury gilding was harder, longer wearing and more brilliantly lustrous than honey gilding, but tended to display a brassy tinge. **1904** *Trans. Amer. Inst. Electr. Engin.* XXII. 73 Hewitt's investigations..are.. pioneer work in the field of the mercury lamps. **1966** HEWITT & VAUSE *Lamps & Lighting* xviii. 276 Mercury lamps are used for street lighting and to a limited extent in industrial installations. **1907** FRANKLIN & ESTY *Elem. Electr. Engin.* II. ix. 172 The mercury-arc rectifier consists essentially of a highly exhausted glass bulb..with two iron or graphite electrodes..and the mercury-pool electrode. **1956** *Nature* 11 Feb. 267/2 Industrially, the polarograph is finding an ever-increasing application as a continuous service indicator. For such purposes, the mercury-pool anode is unsatisfactory. **1970** J. SHEPHERD et al. *Higher Electr. Engin.* (ed. 2) xxv. 799 The connexions apply equally to 3- and 6-anode mercury-arc rectifiers in which case all the 'cathodes' are common and are in fact the mercury pool. **1904** *Brit. Pat.* 3657 2 The light given out is similar to that which is given out by an ordinary mercury vapour lamp. **1909** *Westm. Gaz.* 6 Mar. 3/2 A 'new' process of sterilising milk by exposing it to the ultra-violet rays of a mercury-vapour lamp. **1943** J. B. PRIESTLEY *Daylight on Saturday* i. 2 The factory inside is..lit with innumerable mercury-vapour lamps that produce a queer greenish-white mistiness of light. **1955** E. B. FORD *Moths* i. 15 Owing to the high power and surface-brightness of a mercury-vapour lamp, such a source may provide a more efficient means of collecting than an ordinary light. **1972** *New Yorker* 26 Aug. 20/3 In the glare of mercury-vapor street lamps, the Bronx presents a

silent, bland, greenish face. **1926** J. H. SMITH tr. *Dunoyer's Vacuum Practice* i. 42 In mercury vapour pumps the size of the orifice through which the vapour is driven is..of secondary importance. **1966** ADAM & EDWARDS tr. *Diels & Jaeckel's Leybold Vacuum Handbk.* I. vi. 90 Special forms of cold traps with maximum practicable conductivity have been designed for large mercury vapour pumps. **1908** M. SOLOMON *Electr. Lamps* xi. 283 This property of the mercury-vapour arc has led to the invention and development of mercury-vapour rectifiers. **1966** R. G. KLOEFFLER *Electron Tubes* ix. 194 The mercury-vapor rectifier diode uses a hot cathode and mercury vapor under a low pressure.

mercy, *sb.* Add: **8.** For *Obs.* read *Obs.* exc. *arch.* or *Hist.* (Later examples.)

1890 W. P. BAILDON *Sel. Civil Pleas* I. 44 Let them have their seisin thereof, and James is in mercy for the unjust detention. **1895** POLLOCK & MAITLAND *Hist. Eng. Law* II. II. iv. 512 At first the declaration that a man is in the king's or the lord's mercy implies that the king or lord may, if he pleases, take all his goods. **1914** G. F. DEISER *Year Bks. of Richard II: 12 Richard II* 161 The judgment was that the plaintiffs take nothing by their writ, but be in the mercy for their false plaint.

10. *attrib.* passing into *adj.* (orig. *U.S.*): now esp., administered or performed out of mercy or pity in order to terminate or relieve pain or distress (cf. *mercy-stroke* in Dict.), as *mercy flight, mercy killing* (so *mercy killer; mercy-kill* v. nonce-wd.), *mission, murder,* etc.

1927 *Daily Express* 24 Mar. 3/6 The 'mercy bullet'.. contains a chemical which is released on striking the animal. The fluid in the blood will cause temporary unconsciousness. **1969** *Listener* 23 Jan. 111/3, I had representatives in touch with both sides to get the mercy corridor working, to try and get flights in by day as well as by night. **1933** *Meccano Mag.* Mar. 195/2 Never a month passes without a 'mercy flight' being carried out. **1944** *Beaver* Dec. 40/2 The aeroplane..is proving of the greatest value as a means of conveying medical assistance. .. Such 'mercy flights' are increasing annually. **1973** *Guardian* 14 Feb. 4/4 Two American prisoners of war freed by the Communists were making mercy flights home tonight to be with their families. **1957** *Observer* 8 Dec. 14/3 This [melodrama], with its brilliant young scientist strangling his wife and volunteering for deep freeze and being mercy-killed by his boss. **1935** *Amer. Speech* X. 120/2 On the trail of the..mercy killer..the public follows day by day. **1951** J. D. SALINGER *Catcher in Rye* xxi. 194 He feels sorry for it [a child]..sticks this blanket over her face..and makes her suffocate... He was a mercy killer. **1935** A. A. BRILL in *Vital Speeches* 16 Dec. 165 (*title*) Is 'mercy killing' justified? **1952** J. CARY *Castle Corner* Pref. 6 Think of Oates' suicide in the Antarctic, or thousands of 'mercy killings', which are technically murder. **1974** *Times* 6 Feb. 6/1 A Long Island doctor who was accused of a 'mercy killing' of a dying cancer patient, was acquitted. **1972** *Reader's Digest* Mar. 76/1 (*heading*) Their mercy missions reach new heights of skill and ingenuity. **1974** *Times* 23 Apr. 4/6 An Army convoy of 20 four-ton lorries left Lyneham..yesterday on the start of a 3,000-mile mercy mission to Niger. **1930** *Commonweal* (N.Y.) 16 July 293 Mercy murders once more: euthanasia. **1943** S. M. EMERY *Commander of Clouds* 7 He turned the nose of his own kite toward the mercy ship and thrust on more power. **1944** F. CLUNE *Red Heart* 8 On an average, Doctor John Grieve Woods travels over 17,000 miles annually by air on mercy-trips.

merd. Delete † *Obs.* and add later examples, freq. in Fr. form *merde.* Also as *adj.*

1920 T. S. ELIOT *Ara Vos Prec* 11 The goat coughs at night in the field overhead; Rocks, moss, stonecrop, iron, merds. *a* **1930** D. H. LAWRENCE *Phoenix* (1936) 13 Don't you see, in his [*sc.* a rabbit's] very immobility, how the whole world is *merde* to him? **1960** 'A. BURGESS' *Doctor is Sick* xv. 111 Lurching from one delightful street-smell to another—merds, garlic, mutton-fat, urine, food-tins. **1962** *Listener* 26 July 141/1 It's still evasion to ignore the new tragedy of what might be called the *merde* world. **1968** J. UPDIKE *Couples* ii. 167 'Janet, you disgust me,' Harold said. 'How can you unload this *merde* on three people who adore you?' **1970** *New Yorker* 7 Mar. 36 We cannot have that kind of pornographic *merde* in this majestic and high-minded sentence.

b. As *int.* (in Fr. form *merde*). *coarse slang.*

1920 E. E. CUMMINGS *Let.* 14 Oct. (1969) 74, I am *not* self-sufficient do I hear you say? Merde! **1924** D. H. LAWRENCE *Let.* 9 Aug. (1932) 606 A great *merde!* to all latter-day Joan-of-Arcism. **1933** 'G. ORWELL' *Down & Out* iii. 25 '*Merde!*' he used to shout, '*you* here again?' **1961** I. JEFFERIES *It wasn't Me!* x. 132 'Oh, well, Merde!' He stuck out his hand and I shook it. 'Merde to you.' **1974** N. FREELING *Dressing of Diamond* 78 He never lost his temper or said merde.

‖ **merdeka** (mɜɪdē·kă). [Malay.] Freedom, independence; *spec.* independence for Indonesia or Malaya.

1954 N. EPTON *Islands of Sunbird* iii. 58 South-west of the capital to the distant cocoanut palms and freedom, 'Merdeka', at last! Merdeka... An Indonesian official once told me that Merdeka is still a rousing rallying cry for many Indonesians. **1955** *Times* 16 Aug. 6/7 A banner bearing the word merdeka ('liberty'). **1961** P. KEMP *Alms for Oblivion* ii. 85 The nationalists did not spare their prisoners, whom they usually put to death by hewing in pieces to the greater glory of *Merdeka*. **1969** *Guardian* 2 Sept. 10/3 Tunku Abdul Rahman's Alliance Party..the old guard who had 'won' Merdeka. **1972** 'G. BLACK' *Bitter Tea* iii. 36 *Merdeka*..is how the Malays label their national sovereignty. The word means freedom.

mere, *sb.*[1] Add: **2.** Freq. used of Grendel's abode in the Old English poem *Beowulf.*

Beowulf [in Dict.]. **1849** A. D. WACKERBARTH tr. *Beowulf* 53 It is not far,—a Mile from here, Where stands the Monster's sluggish Meer. **1855** B. THORPE tr. *Beowulf* 107/2 Departed home thence the gold-friend of men,.. and on the mere they gaz'd. **1898** G. SAINTSBURY *Short Hist. Eng. Lit.* I. i. 5 Beowulf..soon hears from the King that his adventure is not done, and determines to finish it in the mere itself. **1912** *PMLA* XXVII. 208 (*title*) The haunted mere in *Beowulf.* **1951** *Speculum* XXVI. 33 Grendel's mere has other attributes... The hart pursued by hounds chooses rather to give up its life than to hide its head in the grove surrounding the pool. **1957** *Rev. Eng. Stud.* VIII. 6 All this radiance is eclipsed when under cover of darkness Grendel's mother carries off Æschere to her retreat below the mere.

mere, mear, *sb.*[2] **1, 1. b.** (Later examples.)

1956 G. E. EVANS *Ask Fellows who cut Hay* xxv. 227 Robert Savage recently used it [*sc.* the word *mere*] to indicate the division between the *yards* on the Common. 'They called them *meres*: they were usually made wide enough so that each man could have a load o' muck taken to his yard.' **1972** *Parl. Debates Commons: Rep. Standing Comm. D: Local Govt. Bill, 18th Sitting* 27 Jan. 1043 A 'mere' is, in fact, a boundary.

mere, *a.*[2] Add: **5. c.** Esp. in *predic.* use: insignificant, ordinary; foolish, inept.

1732 SWIFT *Let.* 19 Feb. in *Corr.* (1965) IV. 4, I..am as meer a Monk as any in Spain. **1893** BEERBOHM *Lett. to R. Turner* (1964) 64 She is still very mere but not quite so mere—in the strict sense of the word—as she was four weeks ago. **1919** D. ASHFORD *Young Visiters* v. 46 Peaple who have got something funny in their family and who want to be less mere if you can comprehend. **1942** M. DICKENS *One Pair of Feet* ix. 191 Sissons, who didn't count, because she was the Junior and mere. **1955** T. H. PEAR *Eng. Social Differences* viii. 182 In such situations American and Dominion soldiers have always felt less 'mere' than the English.

mere, *v.*[2] Delete 'exc. *dial.*', restrict *Obs.* to sense 2, and add: **1.** (Further examples.) Also, to record the position of (a boundary) by specifying its relation *to* a visible feature on the ground.

1925 A. S. GREEN *Hist. Irish State to 1014* xiii. 241 On all sides fertile soil was reclaimed for tillage, partitioned, mered, and fenced. **1932** *Instructions to Field Revisers* (Ordnance Survey) App. A. 47 Revision of Boundaries... It often happens that detail is placed on the actual boundary and the original fence entirely obliterated. Before mereing the new detail it is usual to consult the owner or tenant, and not mere on the supposed custom of the district. *Ibid.* 48 Fences to woods..are, as a rule, maintained by the owner or occupier of the wood,..and are, therefore, mered accordingly on Ordnance maps. **1971** *House of Commons Bill 1971–2, No. 2: Local Govt.* Sched. I. III. 192 The boundaries of the new local government areas shall be mered by Ordnance Survey. *Ibid.* 193 Any such boundary defined on the map annexed to any order under..the Local Government Act 1958 by reference to proposed works shall..be mered as if the boundary had not been so defined. **1975** J. B. HARLEY *O.S. Maps* i. 12 The surveyor who completes the map detail also..perambulates and meres administrative boundaries. *Ibid.* iii. 39 Because boundaries are invisible..their precise location in relation to visible ground features is recorded by perambulating the boundary line and 'mereing' it to those features.

‖ **mère** (mɛ̄r). [Fr., mother.] An identifying word appended to a name (usu. a surname) to distinguish her from others of the name.

1862 Q. VICTORIA *Let.* 12 Nov. in R. Fulford *Dearest Mama* (1968) 130 All you say about poor Marie Leiningen Mère interests me. **1881** TROLLOPE *Ayala's Angel* I. xviii. 222, I am told by Tringle mère that I am less acceptable than old Traffick. **1947** M. LOWRY *Under Volcano* i. 23 Taskerson mère had taken a fancy to the French boy. **1967** J. FLEMING *No Bones about It* 98, I have never known Borgan *père* and *mère* attend a point-to-point. **1968** J. HAYTHORNE *None of us cared for Kate* 15 Prentice *mère* has been bombarding the Secretary of State with letters. **1973** *Listener* 1 Nov. 607/3 The execution of Hugo *mère*'s lover.

-mere (mɪᵊɹ), terminal element repr. Gr. μέρος part, occurring with the sense 'part', 'segment' in various biological terms, as *centromere, genomere, hyalomere, metamere.*

Meredithian (meridi·þiăn), *a.* and *sb.* Also **-ean.** [f. the proper name *Meredith* + -IAN.] **A.** *adj.* Of, pertaining to, or characteristic of George Meredith (1828–1909), English novelist and poet, or his works. **B.** *sb.* An admirer of Meredith.

1889 E. DOWSON *Let.* 7 July (1967) 89 Excuse me for straining after the Meredithian but I have been reading 'Diana' until I am pink and my brain quavers. **1891** *Lit. World* 29 May 510/3 Even the girl-actress catches the infection, and swathes her thought in Meredithean phrase. **1892** *Review of Reviews* Jan. 95/2 Meredithians owe a debt of gratitude to the publishers. **1909** *Daily Chron.* 22 Jan. 3/4 The bookseller, an enthusiastic Meredithian. **1910** *Westm. Gaz.* 9 Apr. 13/2 Your crazy Meredithian will tell you that this is because it is the least worthy of the master's works. **1928** *Daily Tel.* 5 June 12/7, I was never initiated into the inner Meredithian cult, though I have always been a great admirer of his poetry. **1935** J. AGATE *More First Nights* (1937) 123 One or two of my colleagues have dismissed this piece as 'Meredithian', as though that were a term of disparagement. **1936** CHESTERTON *As I was Saying* xvi. 100 In a score of ways, the modern world has followed the Meredithean model for the world. **1968** *Listener* 18 July 91/3 Inevitably, little of the Meredithian style remains.

mereness. Restrict † *Obs.*[-0] to sense in Dict. and add: **2.** The state or quality of being merely something or of being small or insignificant.

1960 *Times Lit. Suppl.* 25 Mar. 193/3 Your reviewer.. and others have made something of the fact that Bevin used to refer to Lord Attlee as the Little Man. Lloyd George's colleagues used exactly the same phrase about him: both Prime Ministers lacked inches. Is it wise to see a value judgment in this statement of physical mereness? **1966** W. V. QUINE in *Jrnl. Philos.* LXIII. 658 The word 'concept', which Russell applied to these nonexistents, connotes mereness.

merengue (mĕre·ŋge). Also **meringue** (mĕræ·ŋ). [f. Haitian Creole *méringue* and Amer. Sp. *merengue* (Webster).] A dance popular in Dominica and Haiti. Also *attrib.*

1936 L. A. HUDSON tr. *Possendorf's Damballa Calls* iv. 48 Dancing a second Merinque with Diane. **1956** M. STEARNS *Story of Jazz* iii. 25 The Haitian *meringues* sometimes sound a little like our ragtime without the force and drive. **1957** *New Yorker* 26 Oct. 166/2 In the cafés and restaurants one hears everything from Vivaldi to Afro-Cuban merengues. **1964** W. G. RAFFÉ *Dict. Dance* 318/2 The *Merengue* folk dance is very popular in the Dominican Republic as a favourite example of Caribbean rhythm. **1965** *Evening Standard* 17 Sept. 8/6 The kid who danced was doing the merengues... The solo merengue kid was dervishing around. **1972** *New Yorker* 21 Oct. 34/2 They danced tangos, merengues..to the strains of the Nagy Hungarian band. **1973** *Sunday Advocate-News* (Barbados) 18 Mar. 14/4 [Haiti] Now cruise ships are calling once more and holiday-makers from the United States, Canada and Europe come by the planeloads to a festive welcome by meringue bands at the airport.

mereology (merɪǫ·lŏdʒi). *Logic.* [ad. F. *meréologie*, irreg. f. Gr. μέρος part + -OLOGY.] (See quots. 1946, 1962.)

[**1937** A. TARSKI in J. H. Woodger *Axiomatic Method in Biol.* App. E. 161 The general theory of the concept 'part of' has been developed by S. Leśniewski under the name of *Meréologie*.] **1946** *Mind* LV. 368 The attempt to provide a foundation for mathematics in logic led Lesniewski to formulate a system consisting of 'Protothetic'..'Ontology' ..and 'Mereology' (which is formally similar to the Boolean algebra except for the exclusion of the null class). **1956** J. H. WOODGER tr. *Tarski's Logic, Semantics, Metamath.* ii. 25 The geometry of solids is based upon mereology, in the sense that the relation between part and whole is included in the system of primitive notions of the geometry of solids. **1962** W. & M. KNEALE *Devel. of Logic* vi. 426 An extended system of Boolean algebra in which there are two operations of a non-finitary character, namely that of taking the logical sum or union of all the elements of some specified set..and that of taking the logical product or intersection of all the elements of some specified set... This extended system is closely related to ..'mereology'. In fact the difference is simply that Leśniewski's system excludes the possibility of a null element included in every other element. **1967** H. SKOLIMOWSKI *Polish Analytical Philos.* iv. 106 In mereology the word 'part' is given the meaning it has in everyday usage, i.e. by a 'part' is understood a section of a given object, and such a section as is not identical with the object itself.

merese (mĕrī·z). [Etym. unknown.] A rib, flange, or collar, on the stem of a glass vessel. Also *attrib.*

1923 H. J. POWELL *Glass-Making in Eng.* iii. 44 *Merese*, a sharp-edged button between bowl and leg of wine glass, or connecting sections of stem or in place of step. **1935** *Burlington Mag.* Oct. 150/1 The two mereses and the foot-stem cast are of kinds which occur repeatedly. **1949** W. A. THORPE *Eng. Glass* (ed. 2) vi. 170 Meantime..the foot merese is moving up the stem, regardless of its use as camouflage and boundary mark. **1960** H. HAYWARD *Antique Coll.* 182/1 *Merese knop*, a knop or protuberance in the stem of a drinking glass or other glass vessel of sharp-edged, flattened form. **1968** O. N. WILKINSON *Old Glass* vi. 100 'Mereses' (flat discs) and knopping appear, more commonly at the top and bottom of stems to disguise welding than as a decorative feature.

meresman. (Earlier and later examples.)

1828 R. GRIFFITH *Let.* 26 Sept. in C. Close *Early Yrs. Ordnance Survey* (1969) 112 Any casualty among the meresmen or expense incurred by calling back the boundary surveyors from distant parts..must be charged to the Ordnance. **1935** *Rep. Progress Ordnance Survey* I. 6 In 1841..the Survey Act of that year authorized the appointment, by Justices of the Peace in England..and by Sheriffs in Scotland, of 'meresmen' to aid the surveyors in identifying and locating the parish boundaries. *Ibid.*, The legally appointed meresmen often disagreed. **1972** *House of Commons Rep. Standing Comm. D: Local Govt. Bill* 27 Jan. 1043 A 'meresman' is someone whose job it is to ascertain.. boundaries.

merestone. (Later examples.)

1970 H. BRAUN *Parish Churches* xx. 235 Let it [*sc.* the church] rise from the land untroubled by fencing. Its yard can be kept from the plough by mere-stones. **1972** *Parl. Debates Commons: Rep. Standing Comm. D: Local Govt. Bill, 18th Sitting* 27 Jan. 1044 A 'merestone' is a boundary stone.

merge, *v.* Add: **3. b.** Of firms or trading companies: to combine or amalgamate; to combine *with* another.

1926 *Office Appliances* Feb. 49/1 With regard to merger reports..two propositions had been received—one to sell out; the other to merge with another company. **1930** J. B. PRIESTLEY *Angel Pavement* ii. 54 That's the way things are going all the time now,..big combinations—merging away till you don't know where you are. **1965** NEWMAN & LOGAN *Business Policies & Cent. Managem.* (ed. 5) xiv. 353 Poor health or old age makes them [*sc.* large stockholders] willing to merge at an attractive price. **1965** J. F. BRADLEY *Administrative Financial Managem.* xxviii. 577 If Company A and Company B are to merge, Company A might take over Company B.

Hence **merged** *ppl. a.*

1965 NEWMAN & LOGAN *Business Policies & Cent. Managem.* (ed. 5) xiv. 356 The character and the operating policy of the merged firms may differ..sharply.

mergee (məɹdʒī·). [f. MERGE *v.* + -EE[1].] One who takes part in a merger.

1964 *Punch* 30 Dec. 989/2 Mergees are going to need twice the stuff. **1967** *Time* 24 Nov. 60 Royal Little, retired founder of Textron, Inc., counsels..students on the pitfalls of getting together [in mergers]. These include such dangers as whether the mergee's inventory is all he says it is. **1971** *Atlantic Monthly* Oct. 85 Elsewhere in the motel—we learn later—the rival corporation, Penta, has chosen a more ingenious method: they tell their mergees that it seems important only that the change be comfortable for everyone.

merger[1]. 1. b. For '*U.S.*' read 'orig. *U.S.*' and add: Also *transf.* (Further examples.)

1915 E. WALLACE *Man who bought London* vi. 54 The Shearman Anti-Trust Law which..drove what is known on the other side of the Atlantic as the 'mergers' out of business. **1928** *Manch. Guardian Weekly* 10 Aug. 104/2 Washington..is shown by the dispatches to suspect something like an Anglo-French alliance or merger or pooling behind the text of the naval compromise. **1930** J. B. PRIESTLEY *Angel Pavement* ii. 55 Along comes a big merger—a bit of syndicate and trust work—and up they go. **1931** CHESTERTON in *London Mercury* Feb. 342 The great moral institutions of modern times, the Straddle, the Wheat Corner, the Merger, and the rest. **1949** I. DEUTSCHER *Stalin* iii. 79 A merger between Mensheviks and Bolsheviks was the main item. **1949** WODEHOUSE *Uncle Dynamite* ii. 24, I have always hoped that you and Sally would eventually form a merger. **1961** *Listener* 16 Nov. 834/3 Theology seems to have made a 'merger' with philosophy for three centuries. **1970** T. LUPTON *Managem. & Social Sci.* (ed. 2) iv. 103 If an organization is being created *de novo*, as the result, say, of a merger. **1971** *Farmer & Stockbreeder* 23 Feb. 18/3 The crunch comes when we look at the most important reason for industrial mergers—marketing. **1974** WODEHOUSE *Aunts aren't Gentlemen* ii. 10, I had once asked her to marry me... In due season I suggested a merger. But apparently I was not the type, and no business resulted.

3. *attrib.* and *Comb.*

1914 W. H. LOUGH *Corporation Finance* (rev. ed.) xiv. 231 The average merger bond should prove a safe investment. **1926** *Office Appliances* Feb. 49/1 With regard to merger reports..two propositions had been received. **1928** *Daily Mail* 3 Aug. 18/2 There is no compulsion on the Preference shareholders to accept an offer from the merger company. *Ibid.* 18/3 The merger shares issued to ..shareholders may bring a bigger income than the.. Preference shares. **1964** G. G. FISCH *Organization for Profit* x. 140 The merger-acquisition specialist is the official corporate professional 'wheeler-dealer'. **1967** H. B. MAYNARD *Handbk. Business Administration* ix. xi. 125 The SEC's financial statement requirements in 'merger proxies' are..similar to those of Form S-1. *Ibid.*, In the merger situation, the acquired company will attempt to obtain SEC approval to terminate its reporting requirements.

meri[2]. Add: Now usu. in the spelling *mere.* (Earlier and later examples.) Also, a miniature greenstone version.

1829 J. F. ATKINS in R. McNab *Hist. Rec. N.Z.* (1908) I. 692 The chief..shot him through the head, and with his *maree* (a short stone club, with a sharp edge) he split his skull. **1833** in R. McNab *Old Whaling Days* (1913) 48 An instrument made of a beautiful blue or green marble stone, which they call a Mary. **1874** A. BATHGATE *Colonial Experiences* xviii. 258 The Maories used them [*sc.* stone implements] to kill the Moriories rather than..degrade their own meres. **1905** W. B. *Where White Man Treads* 134 He yearned to take the taiha and mere from his hand, and substitute the axe and spade. **1921** *Outward Bound* June 46/2 The valuable greenstone from which the Maoris fashion all their meres, their tikis, canoe-chisels, brooches and other articles. **1938** R. FINLAYSON *Brown Man's Burden* 10 In the clear space by the flagpole old Tamarua is delivering a speech of welcome, mere in hand. **1942** N. MARSH *Death & Dancing Footman* ix. 158 It hung on the wall there... It came from New Zealand... It's called a mere. **1956** M. DUGGAN *Immanuel's Land* 15 The chipped greenstone *mere.* **1957** *N.Z. Listener* 22 Nov. 4/2 We know what a 'mere'..or a 'hangi' is, but they remain essentially Maori in idea. **1975** D. BAGLEY *Snow Tiger* iv. 53 The greenstone *mere*—the Maori war axe.

meridianal, var. MERIDIONAL *a.*

1900 *Geogr. Jrnl.* XV. 540 The great meridianal systems, *e.g.* the Urals and the Rocky mountains. **1936** *Discovery* Mar. 69/2 The endeavour of the continents themselves to rotate is generally in a different direction from that of the poles of the earth, so setting up meridianal directed forces acting westward.

meridionality. Add to def.: the state of having an alignment or direction along a meridian (i.e. north or south). (Later example.)

1973 *Nature* 30 Mar. 295/1 During the present period of meridional global circulation the specific tendency over the European Arctic and sub-Arctic seas has been towards northerly meridionality and climatic deterioration... The increased northerly airflow has been held responsible.. for the extension of sea ice to the north Icelandic coast.

mering, mearing, *vbl. sb.* Also **mereing.** Restrict *Obs.* to sense 1, delete 'exc. *dial.*' and add: **2.** (Further examples.) (See also quot. 1975.) Also *fig.*

1900 *Century Mag.* Feb. 605 Billy starts up an' lifts the tether to lead the goat to the mearin' of the parishes. **1920** E. POUND *Umbra* 113 At midnight mirk, In secrecies I nurse My served make In heart; nor try My melodies At other's door nor mearing. **1925** W. B. YEATS *Early Poems & Stories* 449 Some world out of sight and misty, that has for its mearing the colours that are beyond all other colours. **1932** *Instructions to Field Revisers* (Ordnance Survey) App. A. 46 When boundaries have been surveyed, the initials of mereings are shown in ink along the surveyed features. *Ibid.* 48 Mereings on O.S. maps show to which field or inclosure the boundary fence..belongs, whether or not the land on both sides is owned or occupied by one and the same person. **1975** J. B. HARLEY *O.S. Maps* iii. 39 The term mereing has also been extended to apply to the written statement indicating the precise relationship of a boundary to the adjacent detail (for example, 4 ft RH = 4 ft from root of hedge)... Where space permits, mereings in this sense are placed parallel to the boundary, and when the type of mereing changes (as from the edge of a curb to the face of a wall) a special symbol.. indicates the point of change.

3. *mering-fence, -hedge, -stone, -wall.*

1846 T. KEIGHTLEY *Notes Bucolics & Georgics of Virgil* 9 On this side is the meering or boundary-hedge of sallows between you and your next neighbour. **1911** J. CAMPBELL (*title*) Mearing stones: leaves from my note-book on tramp in Donegal. **1928** R. A. S. MACALISTER *Archæol. of Ireland* i. 26 A mearing-wall (as boundary-walls are called in Ireland). **1933** *Irish Press* 10 Nov. 1/4 A huge earth bank which serves as a mearing fence between the lands.

meringue[1]. Add: **b.** *meringue* (*à la*) *Chantilly*: a meringue filled with Chantilly cream; also *fig.*

1901 C. H. SENN *New Cent. Cookery Bk.* xxvii. 561 *Meringues à la Chantilly*... Fill the shells with whipped cream sweetened with vanilla sugar. **1949** *New Statesman* 15 Oct. 422/2 The food in the cafeteria is excellent, but it is in the dining-room that you get the Meringues Chantilly. **1959** *Listener* 2 July 39/1 For the meringues Chantilly take 3 egg whites. **1962** K. O'HARA *Double Cross Purposes* i. 5 An incredible figure wearing fly-leg heels, a meringue-chantilly hat and a pint of perfume. **1970** SIMON & HOWE *Dict. Gastron.* 264/1 (*heading*) Meringue Chantilly.

meringue[2], var. *MERENGUE.

merino. Add: **1. b.** *fig.* **pure merino** *Austral. slang,* an early immigrant to Australia with no convict origins; a member of a leading family in Australian society; a person of fine breeding or good character. Hence as *attrib. phr.*, first-class; well-bred; excellent.

1827 P. CUNNINGHAM *Two Yrs. New South Wales* II. xxiv. 116 The *legitimates*..such as have *legal* reasons for visiting the colony; and the *illegitimates*, or such as are free from that stigma. The *pure Merinos* are a variety of the latter species, who pride themselves on being of the *purest blood* in the colony. **1827** *Monitor* 13 Jan. 2 It operates greatly to the credit of the Pure Merino Bank. **1936** M. FRANKLIN *All that Swagger* vii. 69 It was too early to regard Delacy as a deserter,..he was a pure merino who would not abscond from a fine young wife. **1941** BAKER *Dict. Austral. Slang* 46 *Merino, pure,* originally, a free settler. Later, members of the alleged 'leading families'. Also (adj.) first-class, superlative in quality. **1954** T. RONAN *Vision Splendid* 113 'Old Mentmore,' he explained, 'is one of your pure merino sportsmen: member of all the big racing clubs down south.' **1966** G. W. TURNER *Eng. Lang. Austral. & N.Z.* i. 9 These sterling characters were also known as *pure merinos* when the sheep industry began to be based on imported merino sheep.

2. (Earlier examples.)

1818 M. EDGEWORTH *Let.* 29 Oct. (1971) 130 Tell me which you prefer the Merino or the Queens cloth... The Merino looks much the best in the piece. **1820** G. KEATS *Let.* in Keats *Lett.* (1958) II. 357 We will send Miss Brawn an india Crape dress or merino shawl or something scarce with you, but cheap with us.

b. (Earlier examples.) Also, a merino shawl.

1845 M. M. NOAH *Gleanings* 16 Thin kid shoes and gloves [are worn by the lady of fashion]; a fine merino over her arm. **1848** MRS. GASKELL *Mary Barton* I. iv. 44 She put on her pretty new blue merino, made tight to her throat. **1849** C. BRONTË *Shirley* II. ii. 46 These fine sunny days began to make me ashamed of my winter merino; so I have furbished up a lighter garment.

4. A variety of potato.

1849 E. EMMONS *Agric. N.Y.* II. 41 Merino Potato... Not highly esteemed for the table. **1853** *Trans. Mich. Agric. Soc.* V. 208 A great many varieties of the potato are cultivated in Europe and America. Some of the more approved kinds are..the Merino [etc.]. **1887** A. W. TOURGÉE *Button's Inn* 178 He picked up the potatoes,.. —delicate white 'Kidneys',..and coarse red 'Merinoes'.

merisis (me·risis). *Biol.* [mod.L., f. Gr. μερίς part (cf. MERIS) + *-sis*, Gr. suff. of action.] (See quot. 1962.)

1940 [see *AUXESIS 2]. **1962** R. RUGH *Exper. Embryol.* (ed. 3) 486/2 *Merisis,* growth by cell multiplication (in plants).

meristele (meristī·l, -stī·li). *Bot.* [f. Gr. μερίς part + STELE.] A strand of vascular tissue made up of xylem surrounded by phloem. Hence **meriste·lic** *a.*

1894 S. H. VINES *Student's Text-bk. Bot.* I. 153 When the stem is monostelic, each leaf receives a portion, termed a meristele, of the stele of the stem. **1902** A. G. TANSLEY in *Encycl. Brit.* XXV. 413/1 Such a leaf-bundle contains parts of all the tissues of the stele, and is hence called a meristele. *Ibid.* 414/2 (*caption*) Meristelic arc of collateral bundles, united by conjunctive. **1911** [see *DICTYOSTELE]. **1956** *Nature* 4 Feb. 218/1 There is a reduction in the number of meristeles in the axis and in the leaves [of *Dryopteris aristata* under conditions of starvation]. **1964** A. J. BROOK *Living Plant* xxxv. 441 Each vascular strand or meristele, consists of a central core of xylem surrounded by a ring of phloem.

meristem. (Later examples.) **meristematic** *a.* (later examples).

1908 W. R. FISHER *Schlich's Man. Forestry* (ed. 2) V. I. i. 9 The widening of the cells of the meristem, or primary growing tissue of the yearling shoot, is caused by the water taken from the plasmic contents of the nascent organs. **1954** *Biol. Rev.* XXIX. 62 If the development is delayed, the bud appears as a 'detached meristem' in the sense that it is separated from other meristematic tissues by enlarging vacuolating cells. **1961** F. A. L. CLOWES *Apical Meristems* xi. 110 The primary meristem mantle..is prominent in some monocotyledons. **1967** *Times* 15 Mar. 7/1 The revolutionary method of propagating orchids by 'meristem' cuttings aroused great interest yesterday... This new method consists of cutting a tiny piece from the centre of the stem of an orchid..and placing it in a tube of culture solution. In two months this meristem cutting proliferates, producing as many as 20 tiny plants. **1974** *Nature* 2 Aug. 382/2 All divisions within the apical meristems of the shoots give rise to daughter cells with different fates: some remain meristematic.

merit, *sb.* Add: **5. b.** In Buddhism (and Jainism), the good actions in one of a person's successive states of existence which help determine his fate in the next; esp. in phr. *to acquire merit.*

1832 C. COLEMAN *Mythol. Hindus* xiii. 220 Like the Buddhas, they [*sc.* the Jains] believe that there is a plurality of heavens and hells; that our rewards and punishments in them depend upon our merit or demerit. **1834** *Jrnl. Asiatic Soc. Bengal* III. 383 These attributes appertain to persons subject to mortal births and deaths, of which the series is as little limited as is that scale of cumulative merits to which it expressly refers. **1853** R. S. HARDY *Man. Budhism* ix. 450 Let him who has the opportunity of acquiring merit, by being born when the precepts of Budha are taught, be careful not to let his privileges pass away without improvement. **1863** E. SCHLAGINTWEIT *Buddhism in Tibet* iv. 25 Emancipation takes place either instantaneously, on account of the merit accumulated in previous existences, or by assiduous attention to the various exercises prescribed. **1876** *Encycl. Brit.* IV. 433/1 This seed of existence Buddhism finds in 'Karma', the sum of merit and demerit. **1901** KIPLING *Kim* xiv. 380 'She has acquired merit beyond all others,' said the lama. 'For to set a man upon the way to Freedom is half as great as though she had herself found it.' 'Umm,' said Kim thoughtfully, considering the past. 'It may be that I have acquired merit also... At least she did not treat me like a child.' **1909** W. J. LOCKE *Septimus* xv. 225 I've done little enough in the world..! Give me this chance of —the Buddhists call it, 'acquiring merit'. **1920** —— *House of Baltazar* iv. 43 'A strong man keeps temptation at his elbow in order to defy it.' 'In that way, honourable master, is merit acquired.' **1935** *Chambers's Encycl.* II. 527/2 According to Buddhist belief, when a man dies he is immediately born again, or appears in a new shape; and that shape may, according to his merit or demerit, be any of the innumerable orders of being composing the Buddhist universe—from a clod to a divinity. **1967** D. T. KAUFFMAN *Dict. Relig. Terms* 309/2 Buddhism sees merit as the result of selfless love. **1972** 'E. PETERS' *Death to Landlords!* xi. 162 The easiest way to peace of mind is to give. It is a fairly cheap way to acquire merit. **1974** *Encycl. Brit. Micropædia* VIII. 303/2 Merit making involves *dāna* (giving, such as offering food and robes to monks or donating a temple or monastery); *sīla* (the keeping of the moral precepts); and *bhāvanā* (the practice of meditation).

9. merit increase, an increase in pay resulting from **merit rating*; **merit money,** the money awarded in a merit increase; also *attrib.*; **merit rating,** the assessment of an employee's ability to do his job; a measurement of this ability; also *attrib.*; hence *merit rate.*

1952 *Federal Register* (U.S.) 15 Feb. 1466/1 The type of increase (such as 'ten percent increase', 'merit or length of service increase', 'inter-plant inequity'). **1959** J. H. TAYLOR *Personnel Administration* vii. 146 The descending line of authority should have a systematic basis for consideration of merit increases. **1961** R. LIKERT *New Patterns Managem.* ii. 15 Motivational forces..are involved in reactions to rating systems linked to merit increases. **1967** H. B. MAYNARD *Handbk. Business Administration* XI. x. 109 Generally, merit increases are granted for improved performance. **1973** *Daily Tel.* 10 Mar. 2/5 The inquiry found considerable support for general changes in salary levels to be clearly distinguished from individual 'merit' increases. **1947** O. DE R. FOENANDER *Industr. Regulation Austral.* ix. 84 'Merit money', whether purely voluntary, or under pressure from the Court in profitable industries, had, too, expanded. **1963** *Times* 11 Feb. 7/2 On the question of 'merit money' a spokesman said the title was misleading, and though theoretically such payments were at the discretion of supervisory staff they were not always based on merit and were sometimes virtually automatic. **1964** *Daily Tel.* 16 Jan. 23/1 (*heading*) Teachers' merit money urged by Bow Group. **1967** *Economist* 15 Apr. 278/2 The company's previous merit-money system has

proved both unfair and inflationary. **1946** F. H. Johnson et al. *Job Evaluation* xiii. 264 Experience has shown that merit rating's principal effect is to control the flow of newer workers as they go up the ladder. **1947** Gilbreth & Cook *Foreman in Manpower Managem.* xiv. 183 Requests for detailed discussion of the foreman's merit-rating sheet with executives will furnish a series of points of view ..which should be invaluable. **1954** *Merit Rating* (Brit. Inst. Managem.) ii. 6 An employee's merit rating history is invaluable for promotion purposes. **1959** *Gloss. Terms Work Study* (*B.S.I.*) 26 *Merit rating*, the systematic assessment of the behaviour and/or ability of workers in their work... *Merit rate*, the wage increment for a worker's merit. **1967** Coulthard & Smith in Wills & Yearsley *Handbk. Managem. Technol.* 206 Regrettably, the merit-rating forms usually place the emphasis on personality traits rather than performance... A more limited group have taken the merit-rating report to the next logical stage and set up a system of annual feedback meetings at which the manager and the subordinate carry out a post-mortem on the past year's work.

meritable, *a.* Delete ?*Obs.* and add later examples.

1927 *Observer* 20 Feb. 13/1, I should still have some meritable pieces left over in case the visitor wished to go to a few matinées. **1928** *Ibid.* 15 Apr. 8 What an odd yet meritable set of people.

meritocracy (meritǫ·krăsi). [f. Merit *sb.* + -ocracy.] Government by persons selected on the basis of merit in a competitive educational system; a society so governed; a ruling or influential class of educated people. Hence **me·ritocrat** *sb.* and *a.*; **me:ritocra·tic** *a.*

1958 M. Young *Rise of Meritocracy* iv. 71 Before the meritocracy was fully established, age-stratification as a substitute for the hereditary order may have been necessary for the sake of social stability. **1958** *Economist* 1 Nov. 407/1 Mr Young's meritocratic Britain, though described with ostensible enthusiasm, is an odious place. **1960** *Guardian* 28 Apr. 10/4 If it [*sc.* Oxbridge] adopts purely intellectual criteria it..is accused..of creating an isolated meritocracy. **1960** *20th Cent.* Apr. 358 They teach their future rulers, oligarchic or meritocrat, how to acquire and wield power. **1961** *Harper's Bazaar* Feb. 56/1 The grammar schools..have given birth to a new class, the meritocracy. **1961** D. Jenkins *Equality & Excellence* vi. 110 One of [Michael] Young's most unlikely prognostications is that the best public schools will be taken over by the meritocrats. **1964** M. Argyle *Psychol. & Social Probl.* xi. 146 Selection in Britain is not only producing a meritocracy, but is perpetuating a class system. **1966** *Guardian* 9 July 4/3 The lobby which says the independent schools produce 'insensitive meritocrats'. **1967** *New Scientist* 10 Aug. 308/1 Public subsidy of the future meritocrat elite is efficient, but inequitable. **1969** *Sci. Jrnl.* June 9 Pronouncements on the issue by scientists alone might appear to be the jabberings of a meritocracy. **1973** *Guardian* 21 Apr. 13/8 The monarchy..is, perhaps, our last stronghold..against the relentless advance of the meritocracy. **1973** *New Statesman* 28 Sept. 410/3 On the surface his background was impeccable for a rising Labour politician in the meritocratic Forties and Fifties. **1975** *Times Lit. Suppl.* 2 May 471/2 Keynes..was a meritocrat —not a democrat.

merkin. Add: **b.** Also, an artificial vagina. (Further examples.)

1886 R. F. Burton tr. *Arabian Nights' Entertainments* X. 239 For the use of men they have the 'merkin', a heart-shaped article of thin skin stuffed with cotton and slit with an artificial vagina. **1962** E. Wilson *Night Thoughts* 203 Said Philip Sidney, buttoning his jerkin 'Allow me, darling: you have dropped your merkin.' **1967** G. Legman *Fake Revolt* 31 A sort of ice-cold dildo-and-merkin combination. **1972** *Variant* I. vi. 54 *Variant* reporters interviewed a French pubic wig maker, the head of one of the world's most important firms making merkens and other 'intimate wigs'.

merle (mɜ̄ɹl), *a.* [f. dial. *mirlet, mirly* speckled.] Of a dog, especially a collie: having blue-grey fur speckled or streaked with black. Also as *sb.*, a dog coloured in this way. Cf. Marled *ppl. a.*², Mirled *ppl. a.*

1905 C. H. Wheeler in J. Watson *Dog Bk.* v. 351 The remainder of the litter [of collies] were blue merles. **1936** A. W. Meyer *Dogs* 262 Merle—Bluish-gray with some black, as seen in certain collies. **1948** C. L. B. Hubbard *Dogs in Brit.* xviii. 193 The eyes [of collies] are medium in size, almond in shape, and coloured brown except in merle dogs when they are 'wall' (a blue-and-white or china shade). *Ibid.* 463 Merle.—The term applied to a blue-grey mixture flecked or streaked with black, uncommon except in working sheepdogs. **1968** J. F. Gordon *Beagle Guide* 240 *Merle*, bluish-grey color marbled with black, seen in working sheepdogs. **1971** F. Hamilton *World Encycl. Dogs* 67 (*caption*) Blue merles provide an extra challenge for Collie breeders, because of the difficulty of producing correct markings and a good color. Silva Gale from Shiel was not only a lovely merle but certainly lost no points in head.

mermaid. Add: **5. b.** A vigorous climbing rose with single yellow flowers, produced by crossing *Rosa bracteata* (**Macartney rose*) with a yellow tea rose and introduced in 1918 by William Paul & Son.

1918 *Rose Annual* 148 The most sensational Rose among Climbers of the year was undoubtedly that fine Hybrid, Mermaid. The huge golden lemon single flowers charmed everyone who saw it. **1922** T. G. W. Henslow *Rose Encycl.* xix. 409/2 Mermaid..Wm Paul & Son 1918: —Flower sulphury yellow,..of great size, single, produced continuously from early summer till late in autumn. **1965** G. S. Thomas *Climbing Roses* iv. 62 A few old roses.., and some newer varieties like 'Mermaid' and 'New Dawn', show that grace and recurrence of bloom can be combined. **1974** *Times* 26 Oct. 12/4 Plant a fast-growing rose like Mermaid or Albertine to cover the pergola.

mero-¹. Add: **me·rocrine** (-krəin) *a. Physiol.* [ad. F. *mérocrine* (L. Ranvier 1887, in *Jrnl. de Micrographie* XI. 9), f. Gr. κρίν-ειν to separate], of, pertaining to, or designating a gland in which secretion is unaccompanied by any substantial change in the secreting cells; **merocy·anine** *Chem.* [so called from having part of the structure of cyanine dyes], any of a class of neutral dyes (many of which are used as sensitizers for photographic emulsions) in which a nitrogen atom (usu. part of a basic heterocycle) is linked to a carbonyl group (usu. part of an acidic heterocycle) by a conjugated chain of carbon atoms; freq. *attrib.* in *merocyanine dye*; **meromi·ctic** *a.* [ad. G. *meromiktisch* (I. Findenegg 1935, in *Internat. Rev. d. ges. Hydrobiol.* XXXII. 377), f. Gr. μικτός mixed], applied to a lake in which, when overturn occurs, water below a certain depth does not take part in it owing to its high density (usu. the result of a high salt concentration); so **meromi·xis** [Gr. μίξις mixing], the state of being meromictic; **meromy·osin** *Biochem.*, either of the two fractions obtained from myosin by the action of enzymes, of which the lighter fraction consists of long rod-shaped molecules from the 'tail' of the myosin molecule and the heavier one consists of molecules having a short rod-shaped portion attached to a globular 'head'; **meropla·nkton** *Biol.* [back-formation from the adj.], a collective term for aquatic organisms that are meroplanktonic; **meroplankto·nic** *a.* [ad. G. *meroplanktonisch* (E. Haeckel *Plankton-Studien* (1890) iii. 25)], passing only part of the life-cycle drifting or swimming weakly in water; **merozo·ite** *Zool.* [ad. F. *mérozoïte* (P. L. Simond 1897, in *Ann. de l'Institut Pasteur* XI. 551): see *-zoite], (in many sporozoa, esp. in the orders Coccidia and Hæmosporidia) any of the spores produced by multiple fission (schizogony) of a schizont.

1905 Gould *New Med. Terms* 358/1 Merocrine. **1928** E. V. Cowdry *Special Cytol.* I. ii. 36 The sweat, or sodoriferous glands, are of distinctly different nature... Ranvier speaks of these glands as 'merocrine'. **1958** *Gray's Anat.* (ed. 32) 1302 Most of the sweat glands are merocrine in nature, i.e. produce their thin watery secretion without demonstrable changes in the gland epithelium. **1965** Lee & Knowles *Animal Hormones* v. 91 [In the thyroid gland] the colloid is secreted from the surface of the epithelium into the lumen of the acinus (merocrine secretion). **1937** L. G. S. Booker *U.S. Pat. 2,078,233* 27 Apr. 6/1 It has recently been proposed to call the dyes of this new and very large class, merocyanine dyes. **1955** D. Graham in H. A. Lubs *Chem. Synthetic Dyes & Pigments* xii. 676 The λ max. of a strongly polar merocyanine dye shifts to a shorter wavelength with an increase in polarity of the solvent. The λ max. of a weakly polar merocyanine shifts to longer wavelengths. **1956** K. M. Hornsby *Basic Photogr. Chem.* iii. 34 While these merocyanines are..useful sensitisers, those containing a >C=S grouping..can be converted to more complex dyes. **1973** *Nature* 21–28 Dec. 508/1 This was achieved in a giant axon using a merocyanine dye; in a stained axon a single action potential gave rise to a fluorescence increase which was detectable with a signal-to-noise ratio greater than 10:1. **1937** *Trans. Connecticut Acad. Arts & Sci.* XXXIII. 74 The lake is in fact meromictic, to use Findenegg's (1935) useful term. **1970** *Limnol. & Oceanogr.* XV. 363 (*heading*) Physicochemical limnology and geology of a meromictic pond on the Red Sea shore. **1955** *Mem. Ist. Ital. Idrobiol. de Marchi* VIII. Suppl. 141 (*heading*) Längsee: a history of meromixis. **1970** *Limnol. & Oceanogr.* XV. 363 The meromixis is described of a small (140 × 50 m) coastal pond on the Sinai shore of the Red Sea. **1952** A. G. Szent-Györgyi in *Federation Proc.* XI. 297/1 The fraction with the lower sedimentation constant (meromyosin-L), has the peculiar solubility of myosin... The fraction with the higher S_{20} (meromyosin-H), is soluble at any KCl concentration at $_{p}$H 7 and precipitates at $_{p}$H 5·1. **1966** *McGraw-Hill Yearbk. Sci. & Technol.* 258/2 These experiments have shown that the myosin molecules aggregate in an antiparallel, overlapping fashion, the straight L-meromyosin forming the backbone of the filament and the H-meromyosin constituting the cross bridges. **1909** Groom & Balfour tr. *Warming's Oecol. Plants* xxxviii. 161 These terms 'neritic' and 'pelagic' or 'oceanic' plankton approximately correspond to Haeckel's 'meroplankton' [*printed* 'neroplankton'] and 'holoplankton'. **1942** H. U. Sverdrup et al. *Oceans* xvii. 814 This temporary element, or meroplankton as it is sometimes called, is especially abundant in the neritic waters. **1967** *Oceanogr. & Marine Biol.* V. 241 The results are summarized and brought together in a voluminous thesis on the larvae of Crustacea Decapoda of the meroplankton of the Gulf of Marseilles. **1973** *Nature* 16 Feb. 475/2 There are few comparable estimates of growth efficiencies for meroplankton species. **1893** G. W. Field tr. *Hæckel's Planktonic Stud.* in *Rep. U.S. Comm. Fisheries 1889–91* 583 The meroplanktonic organisms..are found swimming in the sea only for a part of their lives, passing the other part vagrant or sessile in the benthos. **1903** *Amer. Naturalist* XXXVII. 516 The meroplanktonic stage..was apparently suppressed even in the earliest species of Fulgur. **1963** J. E. G. Raymont *Plankton & Productivity in Oceans* xiv. 371 Even with coastal or neritic plankton it is not the meroplanktonic species which cause the main seasonal fluctuations. **1900** *Jrnl. R. Microsc. Soc.* 336 In the author's nomenclature this process of asexual multiplication is known as schizogony, the mother-cells are schizonts, and the daughter-cells merozoites. **1940** L. H. Hyman *Invertebrates* I. iii. 144 The growing vegetative parasite is called a trophozoite. When this..undergoes multiple fission directly into agametes, it is called a schizont or agamont, the multiple fission is termed schizogony or agamogony, and the agametes are known as merozoites. **1967** J. H. Wilmoth *Biol. Invertebr.* ii. 40/2 Among the Coccidia, multiple division occurs during both asexual and sexual phases. *Eimeria schubergi* parasitizes the intestinal cells of the centipede, *Lithobius*. Infective sporozoites invade epithelial cells of the host. Schizogony produces many merozoites which are freed to invade new cells.

Meroitic (mero,i·tik), *a.* and *sb.* [f. *Mero-ē*, the name of the capital of an ancient Nubian kingdom in north-east Africa, + *-itic*.] **A.** *adj.* Of, belonging to, or pertaining to an ancient Nubian kingdom (see above), its language, or its inhabitants. **B.** *sb.* The language of this kingdom.

1852 tr. *C. R. Lepsius's Discoveries in Egypt* xx. 227 Three royal personages..had built the principal temples in Naga, Ben Naga and in Wadi Temêd, and belonged..to the most shining period of the Meroitic Empire. **1902** E. A. W. Budge *Hist. Egypt* VIII. 169 The Meroïtic inscriptions have not as yet been deciphered. **1911** F. L. Griffith *Karanòg* vii. 83 It may be that, while Meroitic was the official language for writing, Nubian was the mother-tongue of Lower Nubia. **1911** A. H. Sayce in J. Garstang et al. *Meroë* ix. 50 Whether *u*ᶜ was actually the word for 'land' in Meroitic is..uncertain. *Ibid.* 51 The destruction is more complete even than that of the Meroitic temples at Kerma and Kawa. **1934** A. Toynbee *Study of Hist.* II. 117 This Meroitic Power lived on, as a politically independent embodiment of the Egyptiac Society, until the third century of the Christian Era. **1955** A. J. Arkell *Hist. Sudan* vii. 160 The Meroitic hieroglyphic..script seems to have been invented on the basis partly of the Meroitic cursive script, and partly of Egyptian hieroglyphs. **1967** P. L. Shinnie *Meroe* v. 133 There is also just a hint that Meroitic may be related to the little-known group of languages known as Koman, now spoken in a limited area up the Blue Nile and around Jebel Gule. *Ibid.* vii. 156 The numerous finds of glass vessels imported as containers for oils and unguents as well as the mirrors show that Meroitic ladies, at least of the richer classes, took considerable trouble over their appearance.

meroola, var. *marula.

merrily, *adv.* Delete 'Somewhat *arch.*' and add further examples.

1912 G. B. Shaw *John Bull's Other Island* Pref. p. vi/2 He chalks up No Surrender merrily, and puts up one of the famous fights of history. **1926** W. R. Inge *Lay Thoughts* iii. i. 185 The process [*sc.* increase of population] went on merrily at first because the new countries produced far more food than they needed for themselves. **1939** Joyce *Finnegans Wake* iii. 615 On the top of the longcar, as merrily we rolled along, we think of him looking at us yet. **1966** *Listener* 17 Feb. 247/1 Frontier wars ..continue as merrily in our own nuclear age as ever they did before 1914. **1972** R. Adams *Watership Down* xxxiii. 261 Why not a water-rabbit? I shall float merrily along—. **1974** *Observer* 3 Mar. 34/3 McKenzie merrily complained that the Battleground machine wasn't telling him anything.

merry, *a.* Add: **1. b.** Also *Merrie England*, freq. in ironic or satirical use; so *Merrie Englander*.

1839 G. Daniel in *Bentley's Misc.* v. 98 (*title*) Merrie England in the olden time. *c* **1882** (*title*) Merrie England its kings & queens..with pictures and stories from English history. **1893** *Ladies' Home Jrnl.* Feb. 13/1 The old Roman custom..was transplanted to merrie England. **1902** Hood & German (*title*) Merrie England: a new and original comic opera in two acts. **1912** A. Huxley *Let.* 16 June (1969) 43 It [*sc.* a monument] is made of a peculiar grey stone, which looks just like that horrible papier-mâché stone of which ruined castles are made in exhibitions of Merrie England. **1930** E. Waugh *Labels* 22 The Merrie-Englanders have so eloquently upheld the cause of freedom that a subdued but smouldering resentment is now one of our national characteristics. **1946** J. B. Priestley *Bright Day* x. 301 The war was over, democracy saved, and here was Merrie England. **1970** H. Braun *Parish Churches* xx. 236 The happy breed of the wool-rich yeomen followed in that Merrie England which was later to turn to mourning for Englishmen clubbed to death by neighbours in the Great Rebellion. **1971** B. Inglis *Poverty & Industr. Revolution* iv. 197 Cobbett.. was far from being a Merrie Englander, in the sense of seeing the past bathed in a romantic glow. **1973** *Radio Times* 13 Dec. 27 (*caption*), The redoubtable Dr Who returns..to fight *The Time Warrior* in not-so-merrie England: 5.10. **1974** *Punch* 23 Oct. 654/1 Mecca had planned to build a Merrie Englande entertainment complex to rival Disneyland.

3. e. *merry hell*: see *hell *sb.* 10 q.

f. *the more the merrier* (later examples).

1614 Jonson *Barth. Fair* (1631) i. vi. 83, I, and Salomon too, Win, (the more the merrier) Win, we'll leaue Rabby Busy in a Booth. **1811** Jane Austen *Sense & Sens.* II. iii. 38 The more the merrier say I, and I thought it would be more comfortable for them to be together. **1874** Trollope

Way we live Now (1875) I. xxxiii. 208 The more the merrier. Ruby'll have enough for the two o' you, I'll go bail. **1922** E. O'Neill *Hairy Ape* (1923) v. 47 De more de merrier when I gits started. **1928** A. Huxley *Point Counter Point* xi. 168 The more the merrier was her principle; or if 'merrier' were too strong a word, at least the noisier, the more tumultuously distracting. **1952** 'M. Cost' *Hour Awaits* 28 The more the merrier,..for with her cousins also crowding the Hotel, additional 'cover' would be afforded. **1974** D. Fletcher *Lovable Man* ii. 120, I moved over to features. More the merrier. I'm free-lance now.

merry-go-round. Add: **2.** Also **merry-go-rounder**, a cause of astonishment.

1838 Dickens *O. Twist* II. xxv. 81 Oh, my eye! here's a merry-go-rounder!—Tommy Chitling's in love!

3. Used *attrib.* or as *adj.* of a railway system, whereby a train of coal hoppers runs perpetually on a circular route between consignor and consignee.

1963 *Mod. Railways* Jan. 23 Some of the desirable characteristics of the 'Merry-go-round' railway..are found in the Tyne Dock–Consett iron ore traffic of the N.E.R. **1966** G. F. Allen *Brit. Rail after Beeching* viii. 255 Inauguration of 'merry-go-round' coal supply by rail, one of the outstanding concepts of the Beeching era. **1970** *Railway Mag.* Oct. 552/1 Wagons, each capable of carrying up to 32 tons, are permanently coupled into 'Merry-go-round' trains, making 'non-stop' journeys between collieries and generating stations. *Ibid.*, The fully-automated 'Merry-go-round' system works efficiently. *Ibid.* 584/2 Merry-go-round workings in the Knottingley area have seen a variety of motive power recently. **1972** P. Levy *Spotlight on Trains* 32 British Rail came up with the idea of the 'merry-go-round' train..a long train of coal hoppers running in a circular route between the coal mine and the power station. **1973** *North Berks Herald* 13 Dec. 1/2 Sixteen merry-go-round coal trains have been arriving at Didcot power station each week.

merry-maker. (Earlier example.)

1827 G. Griffin *Holland-Tide* iii. 236 Music..was constantly in high request..among the merry-makers.

merry man, merryman. Add: **1.** *pl.* Also *colloq.* (somewhat jocular): followers, subordinates.

1873 Trollope *Phineas Redux* (1874) I. i. 2 Moderate Liberals had been glad to give Mr. Daubeny and his merry men a chance. **1921** *Daily Colonist* (Victoria, B.C.) 8 Apr. 4/3 The result of their round robin was equally effective;..it took the place of the robber's mask so that no one could tell the leaders from their merrymen. **1932** D. L. Sayers *Have his Carcase* xvi. 205 It's Umpelty and his merry men. Pass me the field-glasses, Bunter. **1939** Joyce *Finnegans Wake* I. 48 *Hurleyquinn* the zitherer of the past with his merrymen all. **1960** N. Mitford *Don't tell Alfred* ii. 24 He will keep Bouche-Bontemps and his merry men in a state of chronic perplexity. **1970** *Punch* 17 June 890/1 The Tories, according to Harold Wilson and his merry men, are dishonest, heartless, reckless and dangerous. **1973** *Times* 24 Nov. 11/4 Tomorrow night Miss Laine, Mr Dankworth and his three merry men will be in concert in Glasgow. **1973** R. Perry *Ticket to Ride* iv. 61 Abbott and his merry men still weren't on my trail.

Merry Widow. a. The English name of Franz Lehár's operetta *Die Lustige Witwe* (first produced (in German) in Vienna, 1905, and (in English) in London, 1907) used allusively, freq. joc., of an amorous or designing widow.

1907 *Times* 10 June 4/3 The fame of *Die Lustige Witwe* must have preceded the coming of the opera, for the appearance of the composer was greeted with thunders of applause... *The Merry Widow*..is a genuine light opera. .. Perhaps, in the original, Sonia..is a 'merry' widow. **1922** Joyce *Ulysses* 209 Woos and wins her, a whoreson merry widow. **1942** H. C. Bailey *Dead Man's Shoes* xxvii. 105 Randolph also found the marriage in the paper that morning... He burst out laughing..'Queen Caroline! The merry widow!' **1961** *Studies in Eng. Lit.* (Houston, Texas) I. iv. 23 (*heading*) *Lady Susan*: Jane Austen's character of the Merry Widow. **1965** J. M. Cain *Magician's Wife* (1966) iv. 31 She'll be a Merry Widow, that we know for sure, but not with your help.

b. Used *attrib.* and *absol.* to designate a type of ornate, wide-brimmed hat.

1908 *Daily Chron.* 9 July 1/4 The women in the galleries took off their 'Merry Widow' hats, and waved them frantically. **1909** *Ibid.* 21 Jan. 7/3 A huge Merry Widow of the approved Occidental pattern from China. **1922** Joyce *Ulysses* 554 Under the umbrella appears Mrs. Cunningham in Merry Widow hat and kimono gown. **1956** C. H. B. Kitchin *Secret River* i. 61 Mrs Ashworth in a Merry Widow hat, in which she thought she had looked ravishing. **1966** *Times* 15 June 15/5 When *The Merry Widow* music echoed across Europe, Lily Elsie wore *the* hat every night at Daly's. It caught on. From the opening night, June 8, 1907, everybody wore the Merry Widow hat.

mersalyl (mɜ̄·ɹsălil). *Pharm.* [f. Mer(cury *sb.* + Sal(ic)yl.] The sodium salt, $C_{13}H_{16}NO_6HgNa$, of *o*-[(3-hydroxymercuri-2-methoxypropyl)carbamoyl]phenoxyacetic acid, which is a powerful diuretic formerly used in the treatment of œdema.

1936 *Brit. Pharmacopœia 1932* Add. I. 46 (*heading*) Mersalyl. **1940** *Jrnl. Amer. Med. Assoc.* 23 Nov. 1786/1 (*heading*) The effect of mersalyl (Salygran) on plasma volume. **1958** *Times* 23 Apr. 15/4 He had referred to ammonium chloride as a diuretic normally used in conjunction with mersalyl. **1972** *Nature* 7 Apr. 301/2 Mersalyl, a potent inhibitor of myofibrillar ATPase, was without effect on the contraction induced by calcium.

Mersenne (mɜ̄ɹ-, ‖ mɛrse·n). *Math.* The name of Marin *Mersenne* (1588–1648), French mathematician and musician, used *attrib.* and in the possessive to designate numbers of the form $2^p - 1$ (where p is a prime number).

1892 *Messenger of Math.* XXI. 40 The riddle as to how Mersenne's numbers were discovered remains unsolved. **1911** *Encycl. Brit.* XIX. 863/1 Similar difficulties are encountered when we examine Mersenne's numbers, which are those of the form $2^p - 1$, with p a prime; the known cases for which a Mersenne number is prime correspond to $p = 2, 3, 5, 7, 13, 17, 19, 31, 61$. **1939** Uspensky & Heaslet *Elem. Number Theory* iv. 82 Numbers of the form $2^p - 1$ are called Mersenne's numbers because of a statement made concerning them in the preface to his 'Cogitata physico-mathematica', published in 1644. **1966** Ogilvy & Anderson *Excursions in Number Theory* ii. 22 The Mersenne number $2^{11} - 1$ is composite (it equals 23×89). **1974** *Nature* 16 Aug. 610/3 The largest known Mersenne prime, by 1971, is $2^p - 1$ where $p = 19937$.

Mersey (mɜ̄·ɹzi). The name of the river *Mersey*, on which stands the city of Liverpool, applied *attrib.* in **Mersey beat, Mersey sound,** to the kind of popular music associated with 'The Beatles' [*Beatle].

1963 *Meet the Beatles* 12/2 The Beatles, undoubted monarchs of the Mersey Beat scene. **1965** S. Jepson *Third Possibility* v. 36 The Mersey sound banged and twanged into the night. *a* **1966** M. Allingham *Cargo of Eagles* (1968) iv. 60 The adenoidal moan of the Mersey beat: '*I wanna be your rave...*' **1969** C. Booker *Neophiliacs* viii. 203 The 'Liverpool phenomenon' and the 'Mersey Sound' were now [*sc.* in 1963] arousing interest far beyond circles normally interested in pop music.

Merseysider (mɜ̄·ɹzisəidəɹ). [f. *Mersey side* (Side *sb.*[1] 7 a) + -er[1].] A dweller on a bank of the river Mersey in England, *spec.* within the area of Liverpool. Cf. *Clydesider.

1943 *Bombers over Merseyside* (Liverpool Daily Post) 25 (*caption*) It was spectacles of destruction, such as this, that steeled the Merseysiders' resolution to defeat the Luftwaffe's brazen challenge. **1963** *Times* 17 Apr. 3/6 Everton took root in Birmingham territory, yet..the Birmingham defensive covering was such that there were serious doubts about the Merseysiders' ability to create the vital chink. **1966** 'L. Lane' *ABZ of Scouse* Foreword, A Scouser is a Merseysider who conducts his ordinary, everyday conversations in Scouse. **1971** N. Fisher *Rise at Dawn* vi. 95 This was driven by Lance-Corporal Simmonds ..a taciturn Merseysider. **1973** *Guardian* 4 June 16/4 The peculiar inspirational quality of the city..laughs at the rest of the world who has never known the magic of being ..a Merseysider.

Merthiolate (mɜ̄ɹþəi·ŏlēⁱt). *Pharm.* Also **merthiolate.** [f. *mer*curi*thio*salicy*late*, f. Mercuri(co- + Thio- + Salicylate *sb.*] A proprietary name (in the U.S.) for thiomersal, sodium ethyl mercurithiosalicylate.

1928 *Official Gaz.* (U.S. Patent Office) 6 Nov. 14/2 Eli Lilly and Company... *Merthiolate* for medicine or pharmaceutical preparation—viz., sodium mercurithiosalicylate or organic mercury compound solution useful in antisepsis. **1931** *Amer. Jrnl. Hygiene* XIII. 310 Merthiolate is found to have certain unusual properties..which makes it well adapted to tissue antisepsis. **1957** F. & R. Lockridge *Tangled Cord* (1959) xii. 150 Hilda Graham.. had found merthiolate in a medicine cabinet in the bathroom and poured it on Ferris's foot. **1973** *Nature* 21/28 Dec. 521/2 The supernatant was decanted, a sample removed for protein estimation by the method of Lowry, and stored at 4° C with the addition of 1/10,000 merthiolate as preservative.

Mertonian (mɜ̄ɹtǭu·niǎn), *sb.* and *a.* [f. the name of *Merton* College (founded by Walter de Merton in 1264) + -ian.] **A.** *sb.* A member of Merton College, Oxford.

1883 *Fortn. Rev.* XXXIX. 34 Another Mertonian, John Tatham,..was elected Rector of Lincoln College. **1899** B. W. Henderson *Merton College* 172 Not a few Mertonians have been appointed to University Chairs. **1954** *Postmaster* (Merton College, Oxf.) Sept. 13 The only other Mertonian to appear in New London was Louis MacNeice. **1961** D. Knowles *Eng. Mystical Trad.* iii. 41 In mathematics and kindred sciences the series of great Mertonians at Oxford, Thomas Bradwardine, Richard Swineshead, William Heytesbury and Ralph Strood were the masters of the academic world of their day. **1971** E. Grant *Physical Sci. in Middle Ages* iv. 25 The Mertonians arrived at a precise definition of uniform acceleration.

B. *adj.* Of or pertaining to Merton College or its members; used *spec.* with reference to a school of mathematics and astronomy that existed there in the 14th century.

1899 B. W. Henderson *Merton College* 278 The society ..entertained a large Mertonian company at a dinner in Hall. **1947** G. Sarton *Introd. Hist. Sci.* III. i. 116 Our knowledge of the early Mertonian scientists is very insufficient, because a good part of the Merton library and archives was sold as waste paper about the middle of the sixteenth century. **1959** A. C. Crombie in M. Clagett *Critical Probl. Hist. Sci.* 91 In finding expressions for rates of change, they [*sc.* Oxford mathematicians] formulated sophisticated concepts like those of acceleration and instantaneous velocity..and reached important results like the Mertonian Mean Speed Law. **1974** A. J. Pomerans tr. *Clavelin's Nat. Philos. Galileo* ii. 80 This proof.. remained indirect, as did all the Mertonian attempts to prove the mean-speed theorem.

Meru (me·ru), *sb.* and *a.* Also **Mweru.** [f. the name of a town and district in central Kenya.] **A.** *sb.* **a.** A Bantu tribe inhabiting the Meru region of Kenya; also, a member of this tribe. **b.** The language of this people. **B.** *adj.* Of or pertaining to the Meru people or their language.

1883 R. N. Cust *Sk. Mod. Lang. Afr.* II. xii. 342 A little to the North of the Ma-Konde dwell the Wa-Mwera, not a large tribe, but..they have a separate language. **1909** J. H. Patterson *In Grip of Nyika* xxviii. 350 They approached, decked out in all the finery of the Meru belles, and each with a broad smile..selected a favourite warrior. **1910** C. W. Hobley *Ethnol. of A-Kamba* vi. 156 Mweru is the name of a very large tribe living on the North and N.E. slopes of Kenia and on the Jombeni range. **1919** H. H. Johnston *Compar. Study Bantu & Semi-Bantu Lang.* iii. 112 The Meru dialect..is said to be markedly distinct. It is spoken in the north-east portion of the Kikuyu area. **1942** *Man* XLII. 58/1 To the north of the Mwimbi and Tharaka, near neighbours also of both the Kikuyu and Kamba peoples, are to be found the Meru-speaking peoples, numbering roughly some 150,000. *Ibid.* 59/1 The most significant feature of the Meru tribal organization is the intricate system of age grades which cuts across family and clan loyalties. **1944** W. H. Laughton *Meru* 8 The Meru live in families in small groups of huts built on the numerous hillsides. **1953** J. Middleton in *Ethnogr. Survey Afr.: E. Cent. Afr.* (Internat. Afr. Inst.) v. 40 The Meru have a system of age-sets based on circumcision. **1963** *Times* 25 May 8/7 Fighting broke out when..Somalis surrounded the polling station..intent on preventing Turkana and Meru tribes people from voting.

merula, var. *marula.

mesa. Delete ‖ and *South. U.S.*, and add further examples.

1948 C. A. Cotton *Landscape* (ed. 2) x. 139 (*caption*) The Schlern mesa, of dolomite, South Tyrol. **1951** Wodehouse *Old Reliable* v. 68 There he was..under the dressing-table, with his fanny sticking up like a mesa in the Mojave desert. **1963** A. Lubbock *Austral. Roundabout* 73 The descent on the northern side of the plateau winds down, between table-top mesas and rugged bluffs. **1970** R. J. Small *Study of Landforms* iii. 72 To the east of Lyme Regis..very broad valleys are separated in interfluves occasionally surmounted by butte-like hills..and mesa-like plateaus developed in the near horizontal Upper Liassic sandstones. **1974** H. MacInnes *Climb to Lost World* x. 163 Only the proud tops of the neighbouring mesas stood out above the swirling clouds. *Ibid.* xii. 217 We saw a magnificent panorama of mesas: a weird contorted skyline of grotesque sandstone figures towards the Venezuelan part of the summit.

fig. **1963** V. Nabokov *Gift* iii. 150 Out of the total of five hundred copies printed, four hundred and twenty-nine still lay, dusty and uncut, forming a neat mesa in the distributor's warehouse.

2. *Electronics.* In some transistors and semiconductor diodes, a raised, flat-topped portion of *n*- or *p*-type semiconductor surrounded by an area from which the upper layer has been etched away to expose the underlying *p*- or *n*-type material (respectively). Usu. *attrib.*, as *mesa diode, transistor.*

1958 C. H. Knowles in *Electronic Industries* (Philadelphia) Aug. 55 Recent developments at several locations have resulted in a new line of VHF–UHF Transistors... We will refer to this new line of transistors as Mesa Transistors. *Ibid.*, The Mesa Transistor gets its name from its physical configuration... A basic part of its structure is the 'Mesa', (Spanish name for 'table'), which is the active region of the transistor. **1962** Simpson & Richards *Physical Princ. Junction Transistors* viii. 169 Following construction of the device the germanium surrounding the electrodes was etched away to form the table-like area or 'mesa'. **1966** *McGraw-Hill Encycl. Sci. & Technol.* VII. 316/1 Silicon mesa diodes are also used for high-speed, low-power applications. **1972** Boylestad & Nashelsky *Electronic Devices & Circuit Theory* iii. 137 The diffusion technique is employed in the production of mesa and planar transistors, each of which can be of the diffused or epitaxial type. **1973** *Nature* 12 Jan. 92/3 Improved cut-off frequency..and noise performance result in useful performance up to 4 GHz with promise of extending this to at least 8 GHz by reverting to an improved version of the old 'mesa' design.

mesarch (me·zāɹk), *a.* [f. Mes(o- + Gr. ἀρχή beginning.] **1.** *Bot.* [a. G. (H. zu Solms-Laubach *Einleitung in die Paläophytologie* (1887) xi. 263).] Of the development of the primary xylem, spreading in two or more directions from the earliest parts formed.

1891 [see *exarch *a.*]. **1902** A. G. Tansley in *Encycl. Brit.* XXV. 414/2 (*caption*) Typical siphonostele (represented as mesarch) with internal phloem. **1954** *Biol. Rev.* XXIX. 63 Such studies resulted in the recognition of the now well-known centripetal and centrifugal patterns of differentiation, the exarch, endarch, and mesarch types of xylem. **1965** K. Esau *Plant Anat.* (ed. 2) xv. 378 In the third [type of xylem] the differentiation progresses in two or more directions from the first mature xylem elements. The resulting primary xylem is called mesarch.

2. *Ecology.* (See quot. 1923.)

1923 G. E. Nichols in *Ecology* IV. 171 A third type [of succession] is here suggested, *viz.*, mesarch... Mesarch series are those which originate in mesophytic habitats such as are afforded by moist, rich soils, and in which the vegetation likewise becomes progressively more and more advanced. **1960** [see *hydrarch *a.*].

mesatipellic (me:sătipe·lik), *a.* *Anthrop.* [f. Gr. μέσ(σ)ατ-ος midmost (superl. of μέσος

middle) + -I- + πέλλ-α wooden bowl (taken in sense PELVIS) + -IC.] Characterized by an index of the pelvic brim between 90 and 95.

1886 W. TURNER *Rep. Crania* in *Rep. Sci. Results Voy. H.M.S. Challenger* XVI. 40 In the males the same index was at or about 91, so that they were mesatipellic. **1924** *Proc. Soc. Antiquaries Scotl.* LVIII. 34 An index of 93·22 is mesatipellic, and considerably higher than that of the average European male. **1966** B. J. ANSON *Morris's Human Anat.* (ed. 12) iv. 282/2 Pelves with an index below 90 are platypellic; from 90 to 95, mesatipellic; and above 95, dolichopellic.

mesaxon (mesæ·ksǫn). *Anat.* [f. MES(ENTERY (see quot. 1955) + *AXON.] In a nerve fibre, a structure composed of a pair of parallel membranes contiguous with the plasma membrane of the Schwann cell, forming in an unmyelinated fibre a channel leading from the outside of the cell to the axon it surrounds and in a myelinated fibre a spiral round the axon that constitutes the myelin sheath.

1955 H. S. GASSER in *Jrnl. Gen. Physiol.* XXXVIII. 713 The membrane sharply visible on the outside of the Schwann tubes may be taken as the starting point. To this membrane..the axons are in continuous attachment. On account of the analogy with the mesentery the attachments have been designated mesaxons. **1961** *Lancet* 16 Sept. 656/1 H. F. de Webster..in a study on the demyelination which occurs in experimental diphtheritic neuritis found that the earliest changes amount to focal fragmentation of the mesaxons. **1970** J. PICK *Autonomic Nervous System* v. 127/1 According to Gasser.., an unmyelinated nerve fiber usually consists of several axons which are placed in the infoldings of their Schwann cell. The plasma membrane of this sheath cell doubles up and together with the intervening channel forms the mesaxon. Upon reaching the axon, the membranes of the mesaxon separate and surround the axolemma.

mescal. Add: Also 8–9 **mascal, mescale, mixcal, muscal(e. 1.** (Further examples.)

1833 B. LUNDY *Jrnl.* 16 Oct. in *Life B. Lundy* (1847) x. 61 They have a kind of whiskey here, called muscal, which is distilled from a plant called Maguey. **1854** in *Southwestern Hist. Q.* (1931–2) XXXV. 235 About one dozen men came over, bringing..muscal liquor... This Liquor has a tast between whiskey and brandy, and considerable intoxicating power. **1926** D. H. LAWRENCE *Plumed Serp.* iv. 80 The fiery white brandy distilled from the maguey: mescal, tequila. **1947** M. LOWRY *Under Volcano* x. 319 There had been until recently several drinks of mescal (why not?—the word did not intimidate him, eh?) waiting for him outside in a lemonade bottle. **1974** *Encycl. Brit. Macropædia* X. 972/2 The alcoholic liquor mescal is distilled from pulque.

2. Substitute for def.: Any of several plants of the genus *Agave* found in Mexico and the southwestern United States that are used as sources of fermented liquor, food, or fibre, esp. the American aloe or maguey, *A. americana*, a stemless plant having long spiny leaves. (Earlier and later examples.)

1743 J. LOCKMAN tr. *Trav. Jesuits* I. 399 On the Mountains grew Mescales, a fruit peculiar to the Country, and is gathered all the year round. **1759** [see *2 b]. **1808** W. SHALER *Jrnl. Voy. between China & Amer.* (1935) 53 They also have a plant called the mixcal. **1848** W. H. EMORY *Notes Mil. Reconn.* 59 This afternoon I found the famous mezcal, (an agave,) about three feet in diameter, broad leaves, armed with teeth like a shark. **1891** *Century Mag.* Mar. 653 Along deserts bristling with spines of the cactus, spanish bayonet, mescal and palo verde. **1914** C. F. SAUNDERS *With Flowers & Trees in Calif.* 139 The mescal buds are capable of making by distillation one of the fieriest intoxicants known. **1951** KEARNEY & PEEBLES *Arizona Flora* II. 192 The names century-plant and mescal are applied to the large, paniculate species, and some of the small species are known as lechuguilla and amole.

b. The cooked root of the mescal as an article of food.

1759 tr. *Venegas's Nat. & Civil Hist. Calif.* I. 44 The mountains and forests yield the mezcal,..the root of which boiled is a principal ingredient of the mexcalli. **1831** J. O. PATTIE *Personal Narr.* 63, I afterwards ascertained that it was a vegetable called by the Spanish mascal (probably maguey). **1844** J. GREGG *Commerce Prairies* I. 290 Those [Apaches] that are found east of the Rio del Norte are generally known as Mezcaleros, on account of an article of food in use among them, called mezcal. *Ibid.*, Mezcal is the baked root of the maguey. **1881** *Amer. Naturalist* XV. 875 The 'mescal' of the Arizona Apaches, that is, the baked head of the *Agave palmeri* and *Agave parryi*. **1951** KEARNEY & PEEBLES *Arizona Flora* II. 192 The name 'mescal' is applied also to the food obtained by roasting the caudex and emerging flower stalk. *Ibid.* 193 Even at the present time a small quantity of mescal is made by the Papagos.

3. a. A small desert cactus, *Lophophora williamsii* (formerly *Anhalonium lewinii*, etc.), found in northern Mexico and southern Texas and having a soft, segmented body a few inches high in the form of a flattened globe. Cf. *PEYOTE.

1885 [see *mescal head* in *4]. **1895** *Therapeutic Gaz.* XI. 579/2 In connection with the physiological action of the mescal, its use by the Indians is of great interest. **1896** *Ibid.* XII. 8/1 The exercises open with a prayer by the leader, who then hands each man four mescals, which he takes and eats. **1911** *Encycl. Relig. & Ethics* IV. 736/1 The Nahuatl *peyotl*..under the incorrect title of *mescal*.. is well known to the whites. **1920** *Sci. Amer.* 14 Feb. 157 The peyote, often popularly miscalled 'mescal' through confusion with the maguey cactus from which a fiery intoxicant is prepared, is a species of small cactus widely used for both medicinal and ceremonial purposes by the Indian tribes of the southwestern U.S. **1937** J. BORG *Cacti* 209 Lophophora Williamsii (*Lem.*) *Coulter*... This is the famous mescal or peyotl of the ancient Mexicans.

b. A preparation of the cactus for ingestion.

1896 *Brit. Med. Jrnl.* 5 Dec. 1625/2 The history of the use of mescal by the Indians of New Mexico is very well known in the United States. **1899** *Jrnl. Physiol.* XXX. 83 'Mescal' never gives rise to merriment, but rather to a condition of ideal content, and produces wakefulness. **1937** J. BORG *Cacti* 209 The dried tops of the plant made into bunches or wreaths used to be sold as mescal.

4. *attrib.* and *Comb.*, as *mescal-eater, intoxication*; *mescal-inspired* adj.; **mescal button**, a dried disc-like top of the cactus *Lophophora williamsii*, eaten or drunk as a decoction for its intoxicating and hallucinogenic effects (cf. *MESCALINE); also, the plant itself, = sense *3 a; **mescal head** = **mescal button*.

1888 *Therapeutic Gaz.* IV. 232/1, I undertook to experiment with a drug..which they had received from Mexico. In its own country the drug is said to be called 'Muscale Buttons', and is used as a narcotic, food, or relish. *Ibid.*, *Anhalonium Lewinii*, nov. spec., Mexico. Local name, 'Muscale Buttons'. **1896** *Brit. Med. Jrnl.* 5 Dec. 1625/2, I took fully 1½ drachm of an extract of which each drachm represented one mescal button. **1913** *Jrnl. Nervous & Mental Dis.* XL. 427 We endeavoured further to extend knowledge of pathological mental states by producing mental conditions nearly allied to generally recognized types of insanity... For this purpose we used the Mexican drug [*printed* drag] pelotte—the mescal button. **1959** O. & M. LEESE *Desert Plants* iv. 41 There are too the Lophophoras or Anhaloniums, known as the Mescal Button or Peyote, which are devoid of spines and look somewhat like a denizen of the sea. **1934** R. HAMER in R. Skelton *Poetry of Thirties* (1964) 88 The mescal-eater's almost heard Omnipotent transcendental word. **1885** *Outing* Oct. 24/2 The old and young squaws..had brought down from the hillsides donkey-loads of mescal-heads. **1933** L. SPIER *Yuman Tribes* 55 The mescal heads were baked in a pit. **1946** in M. Lowry *Let.* 2 Jan. (1967) 61 The mescal-inspired phantasmagoria, or heebie-jeebies, to which Geoffrey has succumbed. **1897** *Lancet* 5 June 1541/2 It cannot be said (from my experience) that the pleasure of mescal intoxication lies in any resultant passive emotional state such as is produced by tea or alcohol, but strictly in enjoyment of the colour visions produced.

mescaline (me·skălin, -īn). Also **mescalin**, † **mezcaline.** [ad. G. *mezcalin* (now *mescalin*) (A. Heffter 1896, in *Ber. d. Deut. Chem. Ges.* XXIX. 222), f. Sp. *mezcal* MESCAL: see -IN[1], -INE[5].] **a.** The alkaloid 3,4,5-trimethoxyphenethylamine, $(CH_3O)_3 \cdot C_6H_2 \cdot CH_2CH_2NH_2$, which is the chief active principle of mescal buttons, producing effects similar to those of LSD but much less strongly.

1896 *Jrnl. Chem. Soc.* LXX. I. 267 Alkaloïds of *Anhalonium Lewinii*, Hennings (*Lophophora Lewinii*, Rusby).—The dried 'discs' (Scheiben) of this cactus are used by the Indians of N. Mexico for the preparation of an intoxicant, and are brought into commerce under the name of 'Muscale buttons'... They were extracted with 70 per cent. alcohol, and the residue obtained by evaporating this extract was extracted with ether and then with chloroform. The chloroform dissolved an alkaloïd which was named mezcaline. **1899** *Jrnl. Physiol.* XXV. 82 Mezcaline, whilst agreeing precisely with the other alkaloids as regards cardiac and respiratory action, etc., appeared more effective in the production of colour visions. **1900** DORLAND *Med. Dict.* 384/1 Mescalin. **1936** *Mind* XLV. 68 My first experience of a similar kind was during an experiment with mescaline. **1956** A. HUXLEY *Heaven & Hell* i. 11 The soul is transported to its far-off destination by the aid of..mescalin. **1958** M. ARGYLE *Relig. Behaviour* ix. 112 A number of drugs produce quasi-mystical experiences, the best-known being mescaline. **1962** *Q. Rev.* XVI. 136 The outstanding result of mescaline ingestion is visual hallucination, but depersonalisation and time distortion frequently occur. **1966** T. PYNCHON *Crying of Lot 49* i. 17 The experiment he was helping the community hospital run on effects of LSD-25, mescaline, psilocybin, and related drugs on a large sample of suburban housewives. **1974** *Sci. Amer.* June 66/1 Other hallucinogenic agents such as mescaline and amphetamine, on the other hand, are related in structure to noradrenaline.

b. *attrib.*, as *mescaline hallucination, psychosis*.

1913 *Jrnl. Nervous & Mental Dis.* XL. 432 A mescalin hallucination is felt to be much more objective than a mere idea such as a visual image. **1941** *Arch. Neurol. & Psychiatry* (Chicago) XLV. 130 (*heading*) Mescaline hallucinations in artists. **1940** *Jrnl. Mental Sci.* LXXXVI. 36 The feeling of unreality, both as regards the self and the external world, so often found in schizophrenics, is one of the typical features of the mescaline psychosis. **1958** M. ARGYLE *Relig. Behaviour* ix. 114 It is acute schizophrenia which most resembles 'mescaline psychosis', and Andis has described a number of psychotic patients whose reported experiences resembled mescaline psychosis more than the classical type of psychosis.

mescalism (me·skăliz'm). [f. MESCAL + -ISM.] **a.** The practice of taking mescal buttons. **b.** The state of intoxication produced by them.

1902 *Amer. Anthropologist* Oct.–Dec. 789/1 Through mescalism one seems almost to 'attain an objective knowledge of one's own personality'. **1936** *Mind* XLV. 70 Like the starry and bejewelled scenes observed in mescalism, spots of light or their relatives seen in hypnagogic images have also a retro-retinal origin.

mese, var. *MEZE.

‖ **meseta** (mĕse·tă). [Sp., dim. of *mesa* MESA, f. L. *mēnsa* a table.] A plateau; *spec.* the high plateau of central Spain. Also *attrib.*

1904 T. H. HOLDICH *Countries of King's Award* xiii. 366 The moraines streak the surface of the 'mesetas', which here represent the beds of ancient lakes and are disposed more or less in the form of terraces. **1905** *Spectator* 28 Jan. 112/2 The region of the Patagonian Andes..presents a jumble of mountains, rivers, 'mesetas', 'pampas', forests, and glaciers. **1958** FISHER & BOWEN-JONES *Spain* I. ii. 20 By far the largest proportion of Spain is occupied by the Meseta, which, however, is far from being a uniform mass. It is best regarded as comprising two enormous tablelands, or upland basins, which are separated by a diagonally-running fold mountain series. **1962** R. WAY *Geogr. Spain & Portugal* xiii. 257 The peasants..have long journeys to make by mule or ox before they begin their day's work, and then have to endure the vagaries of the meseta climate, particularly strong winds. **1963** *Guardian* 13 July 6/4 The regions of the high *meseta*—the Castiles, Aragon, Leon, and Estremadura. **1969** J. MANDER *Static Society* ii. 81 The landscape resembles..the *meseta* of Spain.

mesh, *sb.* Add: **1. c.** *Electr.* A closed loop of windings or other impedances connected in series.

1881 J. C. MAXWELL *Treat. Electr. & Magnetism* (ed. 2) I. II. vi. 374 If the conducting wires form a simple network and if we suppose that a current circulates round each mesh, then the actual current in the wire which forms a thread of each of two neighbouring meshes will be the difference between the two currents circulating in the two meshes. **1892** S. P. THOMPSON *Dynamo-Electr. Machinery* (ed. 4) xxiv. 709 The three coils may be joined..in a closed mesh joined with the three lines at its corners. **1970** J. SHEPHERD et al. *Higher Electr. Engin.* (ed. 2) ii. 47 Circuits involving multiple meshes may be solved by considering either the meshes (mesh analysis) or the junctions (node analysis).

d. With prefixed numeral, e.g. *50 mesh*, designating a screen with that number of square openings per unit length (e.g. per inch), and applied to materials which will pass through such a screen (but, usually, not through the next finest screen).

1930 *Engineering* 22 Aug. 223/2 The dust cloud which it would encounter would consist..of particles ranging from 60 mesh to beyond 200 mesh. **1932** RILEY & JOHANNSEN *Med. Entomol.* xvii. 264 A 16-mesh screen is ordinarily employed. **1933** W. T. READ *Industr. Chem.* vii. 65 This relationship has been established by the United States Bureau of Standards for 200-mesh screens so that the wire has a diameter of $2 \cdot 1 \times 10^{-3}$ in. and each opening a width of $2 \cdot 9 \times 10^{-3}$ in., thus giving 200 openings per linear inch. **1948** PIERCE & HAENISCH *Quantitative Analysis* (ed. 3) v. 63 The usual sample for analysis should pass a screen of 80–100 mesh or smaller. **1971** *Nature* 25 June 524/2 Samples of powder were first ground to 400 mesh and then briquetted.

3. c. *Building.* A steel network used as reinforcement in concrete.

1904 C. F. MARSH *Reinforced Concrete* ii. 44 The ribs on the Cottançin system are considered as N-girders, of which the joints are absolutely fixed, the mesh forming the tension bracing and the concrete the compression bars. **1936** E. PROBST *Princ. Plain & Reinforced Concrete Construction* ii. 97 Ready-made reinforcements are often used for slabs and also for beams and columns. An example of this is the triangular mesh, made from interwoven round steel bars. **1948** L. J. MURDOCK *Concrete Materials & Pract.* xvii. 251 Expanded-metal (steel) reinforcement..is made by cutting slits in blank steel plate and sheets and then expanding them into diamond-shaped meshes. **1971** B. P. HUGHES *Limit State Theory for Reinforced Concrete* 397 The fabric in sections is indicated by heavy dashed lines—for oblong mesh, long or short dashes according to whether the section is parallel or at right angles to the main wires.

4. b. *In*, or *out of, mesh.* Of gearwheels or their teeth: engaged, or not engaged, with each other. So *into mesh*.

1904 A. B. F. YOUNG *Compl. Motorist* 78 When the top gear is engaged, none of the other gears are in mesh, although they rotate. **1905** R. T. SLOSS *Bk. Automobile* 207 The gears must be thrown into mesh sharply or not at all. **1921** [see *COASTING *vbl. sb.* 4 c]. **1948** *Motor Manual* (ed. 33) vii. 126 If one wheel has 20 teeth and another has 40, the two being in mesh, then the larger one will turn exactly half as fast as the smaller one. *Ibid.* 129 At one time it was common to slide one gear along splines on its shaft..so that its teeth came into mesh with those of its mate. **1972** 'J. & E. BONETT' *No Time to Kill* xi. 143 The gears of his brain, he reflected, were not in mesh. A walk before breakfast might re-engage them.

6. *mesh-bag*; (sense *1 c) *mesh-connected* adj., *-connection*.

1911 *Daily Colonist* (Victoria, B.C.) 25 Apr. 6/4 (Advt.), Solid Gold Mesh Bags, nothing more intrinsically beautiful in the category of Hand Bags. **1920** *Edin. Rev.* Oct. 349 The mesh-bag in which the Mexican hunters carried their arrow heads. **1960** L. HELLMAN *Toys in Attic* I. 27 Gives Anna a large gold mesh bag. **1896** D. C. & J. P. JACKSON *Alternating Currents* viii. 395 In a three-phase machine, if the armature is mesh-connected, the pressure between any two collector rings is equal to the pressure developed in one coil. **1954** E. HUGHES *Fund. Electr. Engin.* vi. 221 (*caption*) Conventional representation of a mesh-connected winding. **1896** D. C. & J. P. JACKSON *Alternating Currents* xiii. 552 The arrangements are either of the star or mesh

connection. **1971** *Gloss. Electrotechnical, Power Terms (B.S.I.)* II. i. 7 *Mesh connection*, in a polyphase device or system of devices. The arrangement in which the end of each phase is connected to the beginning of the next in sequence so as to form a ring, each point of connection being connected to a terminal.

mesh, *v.* Add: **3. b.** (Further examples.) Also *trans.*, to cause (gears, esp. those of a motor vehicle) to become engaged; to put into mesh.

1890 *Cent. Dict.*, *Mesh*, to engage (the teeth of wheels or the teeth of a rack and pinion) with each other. **1907** C. Wheeler *Bicycles in Making* 78 Small pinion wheels.. also mesh with what is called a fulcrum pinion. **1913** R. Kennedy *Bk. Motor Car* II. 194 Then..gear wheels which are revolving have to mesh with gear wheels which are stationary. **1926** J. A. Moyer *Gasoline Automobiles* (ed. 2) vii. 237 The rod *A*..meshes the gear wheel *B* with the flywheel *C*. **1935** M. M. Atwater *Murder in Midsummer* xx. 192 He meshed the gears and the old car moved slowly away. **1957** *Laboratory Investigations* VI. 562 Racks are mounted on the sides of the blades to mesh with the idling gear in each plate. **1961** L. Gribble *Wantons die Hard* i. 15 He meshed the gears and the car headed out of.. Tyler Place. **1972** H. Buckmaster *Walking Trip* 58 Norman..meshed the gears noisily as he watched for an entrance into the traffic.

d. *intr.* (occas. *trans.*). To fit in; combine. Also const. *with*. (Cf. sense 3 b.)

1944 H. G. Wells *'42 to '44* 65 Such perplexities and failures to mesh are by no means confined to Anglo-Russian relationships. **1951** *Good Housek. Home Encycl.* 291/2 The units are generally designed to 'mesh' together. **1963** *New Society* 7 Nov. 19/1 Many young people are bewildered by school and unable to mesh with it. **1964** I. L. Horowitz *New Sociol.* 15 The general theory of action is really a general theory of how the parts mesh to form a whole. **1967** *Listener* 9 Nov. 609/3 What has always meshed best in his verse is precisely the neat machinery of ideas which he shared with half a dozen contemporaries, such as Mr Alvarez and Miss Jennings. **1968** *Economist* 17 Feb. 54/4 The difficulties of meshing management and staff at Holland's Amro bank, four years after that merger. **1971** *Nature* 12 Nov. 61/1 The TXE-4..cannot mesh with the pulse code modulation digital transmission systems which the Post Office is installing.

meshing, *vbl. sb.* Add to def.: a meshed structure; mesh-work.

1907 *Daily Chron.* 25 Sept. 8/4 Splash! go the dredges, small scoops of steel meshing. **1926** *Brit. Weekly* 26 Aug. 430/2, I had a copper frame constructed with a panel of copper meshing to which the letters were fixed. **1968** J. Arnold *Shell Bk. Country Crafts* 300 While the Honiton makers worked the pattern first and then 'grounded' it with meshing,..in the East Midlands pattern and ground were made in a single process.

meshuga, meshugga (mĕʃu·gă), *a. slang.* Also **mash-, meshuggah, meshuger, mishugge,** etc. [ad. Yiddish *meshuge*, f. Heb. *mĕshuggāʿ* part. of *shāgag*, to go astray, wander; cf. G. *meschugge* crazy.] Mad, crazy; stupid. The adj. has the form **meshugener, meshugenah,** etc., when it precedes its noun. This form is also used as *sb.*

1892 I. Zangwill *Childr. Ghetto* I. 156 She's *meshuggah*—quite mad! **1900** *Atlantic Monthly* LXXXVI. 108/2 'Meschugener,' leered the banker. **1922** Joyce *Ulysses* 157 Meshuggah. Off his chump. **1930** *Amer. Mercury* Dec. 455/1 Me broad gets caught in a snow-storm [= becomes drugged with cocaine] an' goes meshuga. **1952** V. Gollancz *My Dear Timothy* xii. 110 My father probably murmured to my mother.., 'The boy's *meshuggah* (which means cracked).' **1959** B. Kops *Hamlet of Stepney Green* II. ii. 44, I don't like saying this, Bessie, but your boy is meshuger. **1961** B. Vawter *Conscience of Israel* i. 22 The 'son of *nabi*' sent by Elisha to anoint Jehu is called by Jehu's companions 'this madman'—*meshugga*. **1962** J. Baldwin *Another Country* (1963) III. i. 377 We finally got that *meshugena* of a broken-down movie star in town. **1968** L. Rosten *Joys of Yiddish* 237 A crazy man is a *meshuggener*. A crazy woman is a *meshuggeneh*. That *meshuggener*! Has he gone yet? **1971** *Sunday Times* (Johannesburg) 28 Mar. 4/3 Going steady!.. What kind of a meshugenah idea is this? **1972** *Listener* 24 Aug. 243/3 My favourite speaker was known to us all as Meshuggener Moishe. *Ibid.* 244/1 That Moishe, bless him, is he a meshuggener! **1973** *Jewish Chron.* 19 Jan. 24/1 The kids at school call me meshugga. That means crazy.

meshugaas (mĕʃu·gās). *slang.* Also **mishugas.** [ad. Yiddish *meshugaas* f. Heb. *mĕshuggāʿ* (see prec.).] Madness, craziness; nonsense, foolishness.

1907 I. Zangwill *Ghetto Comedies* 59 'Hannah, will you explain to me what this *meshuggas* (madness) is?' cried S. Cohn, lapsing into a non-Anglicism. **1970** L. M. Feinsilver *Taste of Yiddish* i. 59 Everyone has his own wackiness—often heard as 'We all have our own mishugas'. **1971** *Sunday Times* (Johannesburg) 28 Mar. 4/2 He is so well-acquainted and up-to-date with genes and other anthropological meshugaas.

meshumad, meshummad (mĕʃu·mād). Pl. **-im.** [Yiddish, f. Heb. *mĕshummādh*, lit. one who is destroyed.] An apostate from Judaism.

1892 I. Zangwill *Childr. Ghetto* I. 14 The new-fangled Jewish minister..rigged out like the Christian clergyman, has been mistaken for..a *Meshumad*, and pelted with gratuitous vegetables. **1903** R. T. Herford *Christianity in Talmud & Midrash* II. ii. 336 'Meshummadim' are those who wilfully transgress some part of the ceremonial law, and thereby proclaim their apostasy. **1938** *Vallentine's Jewish Encycl.* 45 The Heb. words for apostate are *min*,.. *mumar*,..*meshumad* (one who has renounced his religion or, perhaps, one who has become baptized), and *apikoros*... The terms *mumar* and *meshumad* are often used indiscriminately... The *Meshumadim*, from early Middle Ages, developed a super-zeal for their new religion. **1962** *Stand. Jewish Encycl.* 1308 *Meshummad* (Heb.): a convert to Christianity; an apostate (used opprobriously). **1968** L. Rosten *Joys of Yiddish* 238 Jews distinguish forced converts, or *anusim*, from those who joined another faith of their own volition, *meshumadim*.

mesic (me·sik, mī·sik), *a.*[1] *Ecology.* [f. Gr. μέσ-ος middle + -ic.] Having, or characterized by, a moderate amount of moisture.

1926 [see *hydric *a.*[2]]. **1967** M. E. Hale *Biol. Lichens* vii. 91 The curves of frequency show the relative abundance of lichens in oak-dominated woods and their rarity ..in mesic climax forests. **1974** *Environmental Conservation* I. 60/1 A small tracked vehicle..was employed to establish a series of repetitive passes in a level mesic 'meadow'.

mesic (mī·zik, me·zik), *a.*[2] *Nuclear Physics.* [f. *mes(on[3] + -ic.] Of, pertaining to, or being a meson; applied *spec.* to a system analogous to an atom in which a meson takes the place of either an orbital electron or the nucleus.

1939 *Physica* VI. 877 'Mesic' charges. **1952** R. E. Marshak *Meson Physics* iv. 153 There are also selection rules for radiative and mesic absorption. **1956** S. Tolansky *Introd. Atomic Physics* (ed. 4) xix. 328 Since mesons only exist virtually within unexcited nuclei and are only made free to exist alone by collision processes, there are no mesic atoms in normal unexcited materials. **1969** *Sci. Jrnl.* July 44/1 The pion can be used to prepare mesic atoms in which a π^- replaces an electron in the atom. **1972** *Physics Bull.* Mar. 148/2 The meson then cascades down first by Auger transitions and, as it reaches lower orbits, increasingly by radiative transitions, emitting mesic x rays.

mesmerize, *v.* Add: **a.** Also *transf.* and *fig.*, to fascinate, spellbind.

1936 G. B. Shaw *Simpleton* I. 50 *Vashti*... Would you not die for me? *Iddy.* (*mesmerized by her eyes*) Oh DEAR!!! Yes: your eyes make my heart melt. **1940** W. Faulkner *Hamlet* II. i. 113 She seemed to be momentarily mesmerised by a complete inert soft surprise. **1955** *Economist* 26 Mar. 1068/1 Members seemed to be mesmerised by an uncouth demagogue sitting with his acolytes in the public gallery. **1975** *Times* 24 July 4/7 Sir G. Howe said..Labour ministers..had been mesmerized by their own verbal fantasies.

meso-. Add: Now usu. with pronunc. (mī·zo) or (mī·so). **me:saorti·tis** (also **mesoaortitis**) *Med.*, inflammation of the middle layer of the aorta; **mesaxo·nic** *a. Zool.* [Gr. ἄξων, ἀξον- axis], of the feet of certain ungulate mammals: having the axis in the central toe; **mese·cto·derm** *Embryol.* [ad. G. *mesektoderm* (J. B. Platt 1894, in *Archiv f. mikrosk. Anat.* XLIII. 913)], (*a*) that part of the mesenchyme which is derived from ectoderm rather than from mesoderm; (*b*) (see quot. 1956); **mese·ndoderm, mese·ntoderm** *Embryol.* [ad. and a. G. *mesentoderm* (J. B. Platt 1894, in *Archiv f. mikrosk. Anat.* XLIII. 913)], (*a*) that part of the mesenchyme which is derived from endoderm rather than from mesoderm; (*b*) (see quot. 1957); **Meso-Ame·rica, Mesoamerica** [f. Sp. *Mesoamérica* (P. Kirchhoff in *Acta Americana* (1943) I. 92)], the central region of America, from northern Mexico to Nicaragua, which was civilized in pre-Spanish times; **Meso-Ame·rican** *a.*, of or pertaining to Meso-America; also as *sb.*, an inhabitant of Meso-America; **mesoaortitis,** var. *mesaortitis* above; **me·soconch** (-kǫŋk), **mesoconchic** (-kǫ·ŋkik), **-conchous** (-kǫ·ŋkǝs) *adjs. Anthropol.* [Gr. κόγχ-ος eye-socket], having orbits of moderate height in relation to their width, as expressed by the orbital index (see quots.); so **me·soconchy** (-kǫŋki), the property of being mesoconchic; **me·soform** *Physical Chem.* = *mesophase* below; **mesoku·rtic** *a. Statistics* [Gr. κυρτ-ος bulging], applied to (a graph of) a frequency distribution having the same kurtosis as the normal distribution; hence **mesokurto·sis** [*kurtosis], the property of being mesokurtic; **me·sopause,** the boundary between the mesosphere and the thermosphere, at an altitude of about 80 km. (50 miles), where the temperature stops decreasing with height and starts to increase; **me·sophase** *Physical Chem.* [a. G. *mesophase* (Zocher & Birstein 1929, in *Zeitschr. f. physikal. Chem.* A. CXLI. 415)], a mesomorphic phase; **mesophi·lic** *a. Biol.* [*-philic], (of an organism, esp. a bacterium) flourishing at moderate temperatures; so **me·sophile,** a mesophilic organism; **meso-sa·lpinx** *Anat.* [Salpinx 2], an upper fold of each of the broad ligaments of the uterus which contains and supports the Fallopian tube; **mesosa·probe, mesosapro·bic** *adjs.* [ad. G. *mesosaprobe* (Kolkwitz & Marsson 1908, in *Ber. Deutsch. Bot. Ges.* XXVI. 507): see *saprobe], of running water: partially polluted; **me·soscaph(e** [ad. F. *mésoscaphe* (J. Piccard): cf. *bathyscaph(e], a submersible vessel designed for exploration of the sea at moderate depths; **mesosco·pic** *a. Geol.* [after *micro-, macroscopic*], large enough for examination with the naked eye but small enough for examination as a single entity; **me·sosphere,** the layer of the earth's atmosphere between the stratopause below and the mesopause above; hence **mesosphe·ric** *a.*; **mesotarsal** *a.* (example); **mesothelium,** delete entry and see *mesothelium; **mesothe·rmal** *a. Petrol.*, of, pertaining to, or designating mineral and ore deposits formed by hydrothermal action at intermediate temperature and pressure.

1909 *Cent. Dict.* Suppl., Mesaortitis. **1910** *Practitioner* Apr. 422 A large proportion of all cases of aneurysm in young and middle-aged men are due to a syphilitic mesaortitis. **1962** *Lancet* 28 Apr. 889/2 The response to the mesoaortitis of syphilis is primarily an endarteritis. **1898** A. S. Woodward *Outl. Vertebr. Palæont.* 319 They [*sc.* Perissodactyla] are all digitigrade quadrupeds, with the axis of both feet passing through the digit No. iii (hence mesaxonic). **1933** A. S. Romer *Vertebr. Paleont.* xvi. 300 In the majority of ungulates..the third toe was the longest, and the axis of symmetry of the foot lies through this digit (mesaxonic). **1974** *Nature* 8 Mar. 174/2 In the development of a mesaxonic foot perissodactyls have reduced the astragalo-cuboid contact. **1894** *Jrnl. R. Microsc. Soc.* 544 Miss J. B. Platt has studied the ontogenetic differentiation of the ectoderm in *Necturus*. The 'mesoderm' in the head is differentiated by the yolk spherules which it contains into two sharply separable layers—mesectoderm and mesendoderm. **1921** *Jrnl. Compar. Neurol.* XXXIII. 4 In 1894 Miss Platt elaborated the idea..introducing the terms mesectoderm and mesentoderm for mesenchyme derived from the ectoderm and endoderm, respectively. **1938** *Nature* 23 Apr. 754/1 The mesectoderm..normally migrates ventrally over the mesentoderm. **1956** C. H. Waddington *Princ. Embryol.* xii. 256 'Mesectoderm'..is also used for the epiblast of a blastoderm before the mesoderm has invaginated and thus become separated from the ectoderm. **1965** L. B. Arey *Developmental Anat.* (ed. 7) ii. 22 Mesenchyme is predominantly derived from the mesoderm,..but some of it comes from the ectoderm and this contribution is often called mesectoderm. **1894** Mesendoderm [see *mesectoderm* above]. **1964** H. W. Manner *Elem. Compar. Vertebr. Embryol.* v. 50 The morphological result of this invagination [of the blastula] is a cup-like structure, composed of two layers of cells, an outer ectoderm and an inner mesendoderm, so called because it contains the presumptive material for both the mesoderm and endoderm. **1921, 1938** Mesentoderm [see *mesectoderm* above]. **1957** *Dorland's Med. Dict.* (ed. 23) 818/2 *Mesentoderm*, the inner layer of an amphibian gastrula not yet separated into mesoderm and entoderm. **1948** A. L. Kroeber *Anthropol.* (rev. ed.) xviii. 793 We have seen that native Meso-America..consisted of most of what now is Mexico and of Guatemala and that it constituted the North American half of prehistoric Nuclear America. **1952** tr. *P. Kirchhoff's Mesoamerica* in S. Tax *Heritage of Conquest* 23 We include these tribes in Mesoamerica, because of the very considerable number of..Mesoamerican cultural traits. **1967** L. Deuel *Conquistadors without Swords* xv. 189 The close parallels between the formative cultures of Mesoamerica and the Central Andes became evident. **1974** *Encycl. Brit. Macropædia* XI. 934/2 About half of Mexico; all of Guatemala, British Honduras, and El Salvador; and parts of Honduras and Costa Rica are included in Meso-America. **1948** A. L. Kroeber *Anthropol.* (rev. ed.) xviii. 786 The term 'South Mexican–Central American' would.. be more accurate..but it is cumbersome; and *Meso-American* has been suggested and employed as a convenient coinage that runs no risk of being confused. **1956** R. Redfield *Peasant Society & Culture* 74 Those Meso-American peoples. **1965** *Canad. Jrnl. Ling.* Spring 101 Jicaque, a Mesoamerican language. **1967** L. Deuel *Conquistadors without Swords* xv. 189 Its importance as a prototype of Mesoamerican architecture may well be compared to the step pyramid of Zoser in early dynastic Egypt. **1969** J. Mander *Static Society* ii. 83 What is true of the Aztecs is true of the Meso-American and Andean civilisations. **1974** *Encycl. Brit. Macropædia* XI. 935/1 The only linguistic groups that played any great part in Meso-American civilization were the Mixtec and Zapotec. *Ibid.*, The Meso-Americans reached stages of development unknown away from those areas. **1909** *Cent. Dict.* Suppl., Mesoconch. **1920** H. H. Wilder *Lab. Man. Anthropometry* i. 67 Chamaeconch..below 76. Mesoconch..76–85. **1960** M. F. A. Montagu *Introd. Physical Anthropol.* (ed. 3) 606 Mesoconch..[Orbital index of] 76·0–84·9. **1909** *Cent. Dict.* Suppl., Mesoconchic. **1960** J. Comas *Man. Physical Anthrop.* vii. 409 Mesoconchic..[an orbital index of] 83·0 to 88·9. **1885** *Jrnl. R. Anthrop. Inst.* XIV. 71 Mesokonchous..[orbital index of] 80·1 to 85·0. **1904** *Biometrika* III. 214 (*table*) Mesoconchy. **1933** *Trans. Faraday Soc.* XXIX. 1008 For a mesoform to appear, it is necessary for these [binding] forces to persist in either one or two dimensions after loosening of the third. **1946** *Thorpe's Dict. Appl. Chem.* (ed. 4) VII. 350/2 Some substances show only one of these mesophases; some show both, in which case the smectic is always the lower-temperature form. The matter is somewhat complicated, however, by the existence of substances which show three, four, and even five mesoforms. **1905** Mesokurtic [see *leptokurtic *a.*]. **1972** R. B. Cain *Elem. Statistical Concepts* xix. 159 Any curve which has the same degree of kurtosis as the standard normal curve is said to be mesokurtic. **1905**

K. Pearson in *Biometrika* IV. 173 The mesokurtosis of the Gaussian curve is not a universal characteristic of frequency distributions. **1943** M. G. Kendall *Adv. Theory Statistics* I. v. 129 [For the normal distribution] we also have $\beta_2 = 3$, $\gamma_2 = 0$, which accounts for the standard adopted for mesokurtosis. **1950** S. Chapman in *Jrnl. Atmospheric & Terrestrial Physics* I. 121 The..upper boundary..would be the stratopause, and the mesosphere would extend from this level to the mesopause. **1963** *New Scientist* 25 July 169/2 At a height of some fifty miles there is a sudden drop in the temperature of the atmosphere from freezing point to about −80°C. It is here, in the 'mesopause', that the so-called 'noctilucent' clouds occur. **1972** *Nature* 28 Jan. 215/1 A sounding rocket was launched..chiefly to study the ion composition around the cold summer mesopause. **1929** *Brit. Chem. Abstr.* A. 870/1 Mesophases occupy an intermediate position between crystals and purely amorphous substances. **1937** O. B. Darbishire tr. *A. von Buzágh's Colloid Syst.* vii. 135 Mesophases only show a symmetrical arrangement in certain given directions, and not in all three directions of space. **1972** *Physics Bull.* May 279/1 The characteristic anisotropy of the mesophase is now known to result from the strong tendency of the constituent molecules to lie with their long axes parallel. **1928** P. H. Foster in C. M. Hilliard *Text-bk. Bacteriol.* viii. 95 Mesophiles..may be further subdivided to distinguish organisms which have as their optimum temperature 37°C.. and those growing best below this, usually between 20° and 30°C. **1969** *New Scientist* 27 Nov. 450/2 Mesophiles (organisms with a maximum temperature for growth of 37°C and a minimum less than 20°C) multiply rapidly. **1897** Lehmann & Neumann *Atlas & Essent. Bacteriol.* 98 Mesophilic bacteria: minimum at 10°–15°, best at 37°, maximum at about 45°. **1964** *New Scientist* 12 Nov. 445/2 The method of the Microalgae Research Institute is to separate its algal strains into high-temperature or 'thermophilic', normal temperature or 'mesophilic', and low-temperature or 'psychrophilic' varieties. **1890** *Syd. Soc. Lex.*, *Mesosalpinx*, the fine fold of peritonaeum which continues the mesovarium to the Fallopian tube in the foetus. **1901** *Gray's Anat.* (ed. 15) 1013 The Fallopian tube is contained in a special fold of the broad ligament, which is attached to the part of the ligament near the ovary, and is known by the name of the mesosalpinx. **1970** L. J. A. DiDio *Synopsis Anat.* 297/2 The position of the ovarian ligaments divides each broad ligament into an upper mesosalpinx and a lower mesometrium. **1927** *Glasgow Herald* 11 June 4/2 Investigators distinguish a.. meso-saprobe zone which carp, tench, sticklebacks, and the like can endure. **1925** *Bull. Illinois Nat. Hist. Survey* XV. 441 The polluted or mesosaprobic zone represents the next step towards purification of the waters. A variety of higher water-plants may exist..and there may be considerable amounts of dissolved oxygen present. **1970** tr. *J. Schwoerbel's Methods Hydrobiol.* 8 This self cleansing of running water..leads from the poly-saprobic zone through the meso-saprobic zone to the oligo-saprobic zone with only small residues of pollution. **1955** *Britannica Bk. of Year* 490/1 *Mesoscaphe*, an underwater helicopter designed by Auguste Piccard. **1963** *Observer* 13 Jan. 14/4 The mesoscaphe, a cylindrical steel shell sealed at each end, will be lighter than water even when fully loaded with passengers. **1969** *New Scientist* 19 June 626/1 The submersible..is a direct descendant of the *Auguste Piccard*—the 'mesoscaph' that, carrying 40 passengers at a time, gave thousands of visitors..a glimpse of the depths of Lake Geneva. **1973** *Times Lit. Suppl.* 13 July 815/4 Twenty years ago Auguste Piccard..conceived the idea of a mesoscaphe or exploratory vessel that could operate at intermediate depths. In 1964 his son Jacques.. launched the first mesoscaphe. **1957** Weiss & McIntyre in *Jrnl. Geol.* LXV. 577/2 The different kinds of mesoscopic structures found in the area. [*Note*] The use of the terms 'microscopic', 'mesoscopic', and 'macroscopic' in this paper accords with the definitions suggested elsewhere by one of the writers (Weiss, 1957 [='at press': *published* 1958]), as follows:..2. *Mesoscopic*: This covers fields ranging in size from a single hand specimen to a single continuous exposure (generally, but not always, of small size) in which data can be measured with sufficient accuracy and continuity to allow determination of its over-all structural geometry. **1965** G. J. Williams *Econ. Geol. N.Z.* vi. 66/1 Grindley (1963) noted that post-metamorphic folding in southern Westland was accompanied by axial-plane cleavage on mesoscopic shear folds. **1969** *Nature* 22 Nov. 827/1 Attention is to be confined to structures on what is called the mesoscopic scale, that is, visible in anything between hand specimen and outcrop. **1950** S. Chapman in *Jrnl. Atmospheric & Terrestrial Physics* I. 121, I propose the name *mesosphere* for the layer between the top of the stratosphere and the major minimum of temperature existing somewhere below 100 km. **1961** *New Scientist* 30 Nov. 568/3 Winds at heights of 80 to 100 km in the Earth's atmosphere—in the so-called mesosphere. **1973** *Physics Bull.* Dec. 727/1 The fifth experiment aboard Concorde concerned emission from the stratosphere and mesosphere arising from the electronic transition between the metastable $^1\Delta_g$ and the ground $^3\Sigma_g^-$ states of molecular oxygen. **1960** *Meteorol. & Geoastrophysical Abstr.* XI. 1535 Mesospheric temperatures. **1972** *Nature* 28 Jan. 194/1 It is, perhaps, of interest to enquire whether the low mesospheric temperatures existing at the time of the flight render the weakly-bound cluster ions more stable. **1897** Parker & Haswell *Text-bk. Zool.* II. 366 The ankle-joint of the bird is a meso-tarsal joint. **1922, 1969** Mesothermal [see *hypothermal* adj. c s.v. *hypo- II].

2. *Chem.* (Often italic.) **a.** [app. first used in *mesotartaric*.] As an inseparable formative element in chem. names denoting the meso isomer (see below), as *meso-erythritol*, *-inositol*; *mesotartaric* adj. (in Dict.).

1936 *Chem. Abstr.* XXX. 7625 While *meso*-inositol can serve as a part of the bios complex, it has never been isolated from yeast. **1937** F. C. Whitmore *Org. Chem.* 385 Since the liquid 1,4-dibromide gives *meso*-erythritol it must be the *cis* form of configuration (A). **1968** I. L. Finar *Org. Chem.* (ed. 4) II. vii. 231 On oxidation, D-erythrose gives *meso*-tartaric, and on reduction gives *meso*-erythritol. **1971** *Biochim. & Biophys. Acta* CCXLI. 204 Pea chloroplasts are also impermeable to the six-carbon cyclic polyhydroxy alcohol, *meso*-inositol.

b. Used as quasi-*adj.* (either as a separate word, usu. *attrib.*, or joined by a hyphen to a following sb.) to denote an isomer which has one or more pairs of enantiomorphic structural units so arranged that the molecule as a whole is optically inactive; as *meso form*, *isomer*.

1896 *Jrnl. Chem. Soc.* LXX. I. 412 It is impossible to say which is the racemic acid and which the meso-form. **1907** J. B. Cohen *Org. Chem. Adv. Students* I. ii. 94 Ordinary inositol from beans and flesh is a meso compound. **1937** F. C. Whitmore *Org. Chem.* 53 These are stereoisomers of the same type as the tartaric acids, one being meso and the other racemic. *Ibid.* 371 Usually the meso-form can be separated from the *dl*-form by patient application of fractionation. **1956** *Nature* 11 Feb. 281/1 When it [*sc.* the filtrate] was acidified..the meso-isomer precipitated. **1968** R. O. C. Norman *Princ. Org. Synthesis* v. 154 As with other examples of diastereoisomers, the properties of *meso* forms are different from those of the isomeric mirror-image pairs.

mesocephal (mesǝse·făl, mīzo-). [f. Meso-cephali *sb. pl.*] One who has a mesocephalic skull.

1900 [see *dolichocephal]. **1901** [see *brachycephal]. **1935** Huxley & Haddon *We Europeans* vi. 185 In South Arabia..they [*sc.* the Jews] are preponderantly dolicocephals, and in North Africa dolicocephals or low mesocephals. **1957** C. G. Seligman *Races Afr.* (ed. 3) iv. 78 They are essentially mesocephals, perhaps reaching the lower grades of brachycephaly.

mesocratic, *a.* (In Dict. s.v. Mesocracy.) Add: **2.** *Petrol.* [after *leuco-*, *melanocratic*.] Of a rock: intermediate between a leucocratic and a melanocratic rock.

1904 *Amer. Geologist* XXXIV. 134 The main body of the boss is made up of a coarsely crystalline, mesocratic, hornblende gabbro. **1954** [see *leucocratic* adj. s.v. *leuco-].

mesolithic, *a.* **2.** (Earlier and later examples.)

1866 *Jrnl. Anthropol. Soc.* IV. p. clxxxiv, The author [*sc.* H. M. Westropp] described in some detail the characteristic forms of the gravel drift, flint implements of Ireland, and polished stone implements. The following terms were proposed by the author to distinguish them—Palæolithic, Mesolithic, Kainolithic. **1932** *Jrnl. R. Anthrop. Inst.* LXII. 257 Until recently the true Mesolithic was unknown in Palestine, although it was the custom among local archaeologists to describe as such the industry containing small unpolished axes or adzes which is found so abundantly on the surface all over the country. **1936, 1970** [see *epipalæolithic *a.*]. **1975** *Guardian* 21 Jan. 6/3 The Mesolithic or Middle Stone Age. *Ibid.* 6/7 Mesolithic man achieved partial domestication of the red deer.

mesomerism (mesǫ·mĕriz'm). *Chem.* [(in sense a) ad. F. *mésomérie* (A. Cornillot 1927, in *Ann. de Chim.* VIII. 267), f. *meso-* Meso- after *tautomérie* Tautomerism.] † **a.** A kind of tautomerism (see quot.). *Obs.*

1928 *Chem. Abstr.* XXII. 2155 The term *mesomerism* is proposed to designate affinitive tautomerism and distinguish it from structural tautomerism (or desmotropism) and activation tautomerism (or tautomerism proper).

b. The property exhibited by certain molecules of having a structure which cannot adequately be represented by a single structural formula but can only be said to be intermediate between two or more graphical structures which differ in the distribution of electrons; resonance.

1934 *Nature* 23 June 947/1 Mesomerism and tautomerism are different concepts. **1951** I. L. Finar *Org. Chem.* I. ii. 15 Heisenberg (1926), from quantum mechanics, supplied a theoretical background for mesomerism; he called it resonance, and this is the name which is widely used. **1973** B. J. Hazzard tr. *Organicum* III. iv. 147 The capacity of a substituent for entering into mesomerism with a neighbouring double bond is defined as the mesomeric effect, and its sign is determined..by the polarization of the substituent accompanying the mesomerism.

So **mesome·ric** *a.*, exhibiting or arising from mesomerism (sense b).

1933 C. K. Ingold in *Jrnl. Chem. Soc.* 1124 The permanent polarisation associated with the tautomeric effect was originally distinguished by the name 'electronic strain', but this term has not proved convenient and, on account of considerations indicated later, the designation *mesomeric* effect is now substituted. **1956** E. de B. Barnett *Mechanism Org. Chem. Reactions* i. 5 Neither the double-bonded formula nor the dipolar formula is a true representation of the molecule, which must be regarded as a mesomeric hybrid to which both structures contribute. **1973** B. J. Hazzard tr. *Organicum* III. iv. 146 A mesomeric system may involve not only double and triple bonds between the various bond partners but also free electron pairs conjugated with them.

mesomorph (me·somǫɹf, mī·zo-). [f. Meso- + Gr. μορφ-ή form.] **1.** *Anthropometry.* A person with a powerful, compact body-build in which the physical structures developed from the mesodermal layer of the embryo, i.e. the bones, muscles, and connective tissues, predominate: one of W. H. Sheldon's three constitutional types (cf. *ectomorph, *endomorph 2).

1940 W. H. Sheldon *Varieties Human Physique* iii. 35 Bones, muscles, connective tissue..predominate overwhelmingly in the variants of type 2. We therefore call these variants mesomorphs. **1944** A. Huxley *Let.* 19 July (1969) 508 The football team entirely composed of big-boned, large-faced mesomorphs. **1951** Auden *Nones* (1952) 56 Behold the manly mesomorph Showing his splendid biceps off. **1971** J. Z. Young *Introd. Study Man* xxxix. 573 In mesomorphs muscle and bone predominate, ..and they are adventurous, aggressive, extroverted, and dominating.

Hence **me·somorphy**, the mesomorphic body-build; the quality of being mesomorphic.

1940 W. H. Sheldon *Varieties Human Physique* i. 5 Mesomorphy means relative predominance of muscle, bone, and connective tissue. **1944** [see *endomorphy]. **1962** [see *ectomorph]. **1969** Downs & Bleibtreu *Human Variation* vii. 248 A football player, for example, would be high in mesomorphy.

2. *Physical Chem.* = *mesophase* (s.v. *meso-). *rare.*

1969 [see *mesomorphism].

mesomorphic (mesomǭ·ɹfik, mī·zo-), *a.* [f. Meso- + Gr. μορφ-ή form + -ic.] **1.** *Physical Chem.* [ad. F. *mésomorphe* (G. Friedel 1922, in *Ann. de Physique* XVIII. 273).] Existing in, pertaining to, or designating the state of a liquid crystal, intermediate between the ordered state of matter in crystals and the disordered state in ordinary liquids.

1923 *Chem. Abstr.* XVII. 3267 (*heading*) The mesomorphic states of matter. **1938** [see *liquid crystal* s.v. *liquid *a.* 7]. **1940** Glasstone *Text-bk. Physical Chem.* vii. 506 Mesomorphic behavior is restricted to substances having long chains. **1962** [see *liquid crystal* s.v. *liquid *a.* 7].

2. Characteristic of or resembling a mesomorph; of or pertaining to mesomorphy.

1940 W. H. Sheldon *Varieties Human Physique* i. 5 The mesomorphic physique is normally heavy, hard, and rectangular in outline. **1944** A. Huxley *Let.* 19 July (1969) 508 The ectomorph and his endomorphic wife in the museum, looking at the mesomorphic ideal of Greek sculpture. **1959** *Chambers's Encycl.* XI. 335/2 Correlation coefficients as high as 0·8 have been obtained..between the somatotonic component and extreme mesomorphic physique. **1963** *Punch* 25 Dec. 935/3 Mesomorphic McCarthies.

mesomorphism (mesomǭ·ɹfiz'm, mīzo-). *Physical Chem.* [f. *mesomorph(ic *a.* + -ism.] The state of being mesomorphic.

1933 [see *lyotropic *a.* 2]. **1969** J. S. Dave et al. in G. H. Brown et al. *Liquid Crystals 2* II. 229 The authors have investigated mixed mesomorphism in the binary mixtures wherein one of the components is a pure smectic mesomorph and the other a non-liquid crystalline Schiff's base.

mesomorphous (mesomǭ·ɹfəs, mīzo-), *a.* *Physical Chem.* [f. as prec. + -ous.] = *mesomorphic *a.* 1.

1930 *Engineering* 7 Nov. 575/3 The so-called liquid crystals of Lehmann, which he regards as mesomorphous crystals. **1972** P. A. Winsor in Brown & Labes *Liquid Crystals 3* I. 66 An idealized phase diagram showing the relationships between the amorphous solution phase and the succession of fused mesomorphous solution phases found in binary amphiphile/water system[s] is shown.

‖ **meson**² (mesǫ·n). [a. Sp. *mesón* an inn.] A type of inn in Mexico (see quot. 1861).

1824 J. R. Poinsett *Notes on Mexico* iv. 32 We entered the town..and drove through it to the meson. **1847** G. A. F. Ruxton *Adventures Mexico & Rocky Mts.* viii. 52 The meson was better than usual, being the stopping place of the diligencia to Fresnillo. **1861** E. B. Tylor *Anahuac* 209 The *meson* of Mexico is a lineal descendant of the Eastern Caravanserai... It consists of two courtyards, one surrounded by stabling and the other by miserable rooms for the travellers, who must cook their food themselves, or go elsewhere for it. **1910** A. Santleben *Texas Pioneer* 164 Meson means an inn or hostelry. **1955** *Amer. Speech* XXX. 258 *Meson*, an inn.

meson³ (mī·zǫn, me·zǫn). *Nuclear Physics.* [Alteration of the earlier name *mesotron: see *-on¹.] **a.** Any of a group of unstable subatomic particles (first found in cosmic rays) that are intermediate in mass between an electron and a proton; the name is now commonly restricted to particles that are strongly interacting and have zero or integral spin (cf. *muon), certain of which occur in atomic nuclei as transmitters of the binding force between the nucleons.

1939 H. J. Bhabha in *Nature* 18 Feb. 276/2 The name 'mesotron' has been suggested by Anderson and Neddermeyer..for the new particle found in cosmic radiation with a mass intermediate between that of the electron and proton. It is felt that the 'tr' in this word is redundant, since it does not belong to the Greek root 'meso' for middle; the 'tr' in neutron and electron belong, of course, to the roots 'neutr' and 'electra'... It would therefore be more logical and also shorter to call the new particle a meson instead of a mesotron. **1942** Pollard & Davidson *Appl. Nucl. Physics* ii. 13 The positive and negative

mesotrons or mesons should be mentioned here. **1947** *Sci. News* IV. 125 Mesons are the most penetrating component of cosmic rays. **1948** *Times* 10 Mar. 4/7 Other scientists spoke of mesons as the 'cosmic cement' which is believed to hold together the nucleus of the atom. **1963** S. Tolansky *Introd. Atomic Physics* (ed. 5) xxiii. 391 They [*sc.* muons] were once called mu-mesons but it was recognised that they were not in fact mesons since they had different spins. They are fermions, not bosons, and now the name meson is reserved for bosons only. **1971** *Sci. Amer.* Oct. 42/3 Such high-energy cosmic ray collisions produce a shower of secondary particles, principally kaons (*K* mesons) and pions (pi mesons), which in turn decay spontaneously into muons. *Ibid.*, The detector, a 2,000-ton array of concrete water tanks, light-collecting tubes and gas-filled cylinders, was designed to record the arrival of muons, or mu mesons.

b. Special Comb.: **meson factory** *colloq.*, an establishment having a high-energy accelerator for producing an intense beam of mesons and the equipment for making experimental use of such a beam.

1966 *Physics Today* Dec. 21/1 Meson factories, which will produce beams of nucleons and mesons thousands of times more intense than those presently available, can be expected to take us to our next level of understanding of nuclear structure... By meson factory I mean a complete nuclear-physics installation based on an accelerator of 500–1000 MeV, which is capable of providing at least 100 microamperes of high quality external beam. All ancillary facilities for performing high precision experiments with the primary and secondary beams are included: targeting, beam transport, data-handling equipment and beam dumps for the residual beams. **1972** *Physics Bull.* Mar. 148/3 With the completion of high intensity proton accelerators, meson factories, around the world.., it will soon be possible to produce muonic atoms and molecules copiously.

mesonic (mī-, mezǫ·nik), *a. Nuclear Physics.* [f. *Meson[3] + -ic.] = *Mesic *a.*[2]

1939 *Nature* 8 July 78/1 The most important problem is the construction of a classical model of the heavy mass by means of a mesonic field in the same manner as the electronic mass is built up from an electromagnetic field. **1953** *Physical Rev.* XCII. 801/2 The use of the μ^- meson as a nuclear probe is possible because the mesonic orbits are much closer to the nucleus than the corresponding electron orbits. **1954** *Ibid.* XCVI. 1145 The effects of vacuum polarization on the energy levels of π and μ mesonic atoms are computed. **1959** *Chambers's Encycl.* XIII. 241/2 The measurement of mesonic mass is very difficult. **1968** M. S. Livingston *Particle Physics* vi. 122 The first estimate of the mass of the muon came from studies of the ionization density of the tracks of mesonic particles in cloud chamber photographs of cosmic rays.

mesonomic (mesonǫ·mik, mī·zo-), *a. Law.* [f. Meso- + Gr. νόμ-ος law + -ic.] In the terminology of A. Kocourek: 'a jural relation which does not directly affect the natural physical freedom of a human being with the support of the law but yet has legal consequences in its evolution'. Opp. *zygnomic *a.*

1927 A. Kocourek *Jural Relations* v. 69 Compared with zygnomic relations, mesonomic relations are inferior in legal potency. A zygnomic relation directly constrains the servus of the relation with the support of the law, but a mesonomic relation either does not constrain the servus directly or lacks the support of the law. **1930** —— *Introd. Sci. of Law* iv. 294 Put broadly, the function of mesonomic relations is to initiate or destroy zygnomic relations. *Ibid.*, Mesonomic relations have many different forms and functions... The power to commit a tort is mesonomic. The duty to pay damages for the tort is zygnomic. The power to pay damages for the tort is zygnomic. The power to violate a contract is mesonomic. The duty to pay damages is zygnomic... A duty owed by a subject to the sovereign not to commit a crime is mesonomic. The power of a prosecutor to prosecute a criminal offender is zygnomic. **1964** J. Stone *Legal Syst. & Lawyers' Reasonings* iv. 148 Kocourek's mesonomic–zygnomic distinction is no doubt a valuable one, even if we shrink back at the neologisms. *Ibid.* 149 For citizens' counsellors, as well as for citizens .., it is predominantly in the range of alternative courses left open by privileges and powers, the mesonomic relations, that attention and concern mainly moves.

mesopelagic (mesopĭlæ·dʒik, mīzo-), *a. Biol.* [f. Meso- + Pelagic *a.*] Of, pertaining to, or designating the intermediate depths of the sea, *spec.* those between 200 and a thousand metres down.

1951 Allee & Schmidt *Hesse's Ecol. Animal Geogr.* (ed. 2) xiv. 312 The eyes of many mesopelagic animals are especially large. **1957** *Mem. Geol. Soc. Amer.* LXVII. I. 643 Among the typical animals of the mesopelagic zone..are such well-known fishes as *Idiacanthus, Chauliodus, Stomias*, and the lantern fishes. **1964** *Oceanogr. & Marine Biol.* II. 367 The photophores of most mesopelagic animals shine downwards (if the creature swims with its ventral surface downwards), and the colour of the light they emit is approximately that of..transmitted sun- and sky-light. **1970** [see *dysphotic* adj. s.v. *Dys-]. **1975** *Nature* 5 June 452/2 The mesopelagic migrants, spending the daytime at depths down to perhaps 1,000 m and rising to within 200 m or so of the surface at night, show an increased respiratory rate not only with increased temperature but also with increased pressure.

Mesopotamia. For 'A country between two rivers' read 'A tract between two rivers' and add later examples.

1886 *Pall Mall Gaz.* 23 June 13/2 Every Oxford man has known and loved the beauties of the walk called Mesopotamia. **1944** G. B. Cressey *Asia's Lands & Peoples* xxvi. 401/2 The land between the rivers, that is, the true 'Mesopotamia', is thus capable of easy irrigation from either side. **1963** A. R. Woolley *Clarendon Guide Oxf.* 130 A path continues between the river and a mill-race and this is known as Mesopotamia.

b. = *Belgravia.

1864 E. Yates *Broken to Harness* (ed. 3) xv. 271 A house in Great Adullam Street, Macpelah Square, in that district of London whilom known as 'Mesopotamia'.

2. As the type of a word which is long, pleasant-sounding, and incomprehensible; used allusively for something which gives irrational or inexplicable comfort or satisfaction to the hearer (see quots.).

1827 Scott *Chron. Canongate* 1st Ser. I. v. 109 She resembled exactly in her criticism the devotee who pitched on the 'sweet word Mesopotamia', as the most edifying note which she could bring away from a sermon. **1870** *Brewer's Dict. Phr. & Fable* 572/1 *The true 'Mesopotamia' ring..i.e.*, something high-sounding and pleasing, but wholly past comprehension. The allusion is to the story of an old woman who told her pastor that she 'found great support in that comfortable word *Mesopotamia*'. **1886** 'M. Gray' *Silence of Dean Maitland* III. iii. iv. 94 It was said of the Bishop of Belminster that he could pronounce the mystic word 'Mesopotamia' in such a manner as to affect his auditors to tears; but of the dean it might be averred that his pronunciation of 'Mesopotamia' caused the listeners' hearts to vibrate with every sorrow and every joy they had ever known, all in the brief space of time occupied by the utterance of that affecting word. **1906** F. M. Parsons *Garrick & his Circle* 245 Whitefield possessed the inborn gift of preaching to the nerves, and there is an edifying, though probably fallacious, report of Garrick's having remarked that he could pronounce 'Mesopotamia' in such a way as to move any audience to tears. **1908** G. B. Shaw *Platform & Pulpit* (1962) 47 There are people who will swallow as inspired revelation any sort of stuff that, so to speak, has the word Mesopotamia in it. **1924** L. Parks *What is Modernism?* p. xviii, The reaction to words is a curious psychological—I suspect pathological—phenomenon. The oft-told tale of the good woman who found 'Mesopotamia' a soothing word is one example.

Mesopotamian, *a.* Add: (Further examples.) Also as *sb.*, a native or inhabitant of Mesopotamia (the larger part of which is now Iraq).

1616 T. Coryat *Traveller for English Wits* 42 Your generosities most obliged Countreyman,..the Hierosolymitan - Syrian - Mesopotamian - Armenian - Median.., Thomas Coryate. **1673** A. Woodhead *Guide to Controversies Relig.* (ed. 2) iii. viii. 283 The Assyrians, Persians, and Mesopotamians, are ranged also under a new Patriarch. **1935** Huxley & Haddon *We Europeans* vi. 175 A North Syrian group which received accretions from Mesopotamian, Egyptian, Hittite, Amorite, and perhaps other sources. **1952** Gerth & Martindale tr. *Weber's Anc. Judaism* i. i. 6 The rise to political prominence of Babylonian power at the end of the third millenium and the continuous ascendancy of Babylon..constituted later aspects of Mesopotamian influence. **1954** H. Frankfort *Art & Archit. Anc. Orient* p. xxv, The Mesopotamians congregated in cities. *Ibid.* 6 The Mesopotamian deeply felt the enormity of the presumption that man should offer residence to a deity. **1974** *Encycl. Brit. Micropædia* VI. 820/1 Because religion provided the only total view of existence in ancient Mesopotamian civilization, religious themes, attitudes, and presuppositions were frequently included in quasi-secular writings.

mesorrhine, mesorhine, *a.* Add: **B.** *sb.* A person or skull having a nasal index intermediate between leptorrhine and platyrrhine. Hence **me·sorrhiny**, the state or quality of being mesorrhine.

1904 *Biometrika* Mar.–July 214 Nasal Index. Mesorrhiny. **1953** Beals & Hoijer *Introd. Anthropol.* iv. 98 Mesorrhines, like the Polynesians, who live in tropical regions.

mesoscale (me·soskēil, mī·zo-). *Meteorol.* Also **meso-scale.** [f. Meso- + Scale *sb.*[3]] An intermediate scale, between that of high- and low-pressure systems on the one hand and that of microclimates on the other, on which such phenomena as storms occur. Freq. *attrib.*

1956 T. Fujita *Mesoanalysis of the Illinois Tornado of Apr. 9, 1953* (Univ. of Chicago Dept. Meteorol. Technical Rep. to U.S. Weather Bureau, Contract No. Cwb 8613) 2 A method of analyzing mesoscale charts. **1959** *Modernizing the Aviation Weather Service* (U.S. Weather Bureau) 39 This meso-scale is considered a necessary link between the present synoptic scale and local weather events. **1969** *Britannica Bk. of Year* (U.S.) 518 Basic research continued into cyclonic storms and other aspects of the mesoscale or so-called secondary circulation of the atmosphere, including tropical cyclones (hurricanes and typhoons), mid- and high-latitude lows, and tornadoes. **1970** *Nature* 15 Aug. 646/2 Is there any sense in seeking to understand the effects of, say, major afforestation schemes on climate in the surrounding region without knowing much more about the behaviour of the atmosphere on the mesoscale? **1971** *Sci. News Let.* 30 Jan. 81 Dr. H. A. Panofsky.. pointed to weaknesses in the knowledge of mesoscale meteorology, the meteorology of areas 10 to 20 miles in diameter. **1974** *Times Lit. Suppl.* 13 Sept. 982/3 Given the 3 to 5 kilometre photographic resolution, satellite data are most usefully applied to macroscale phenomena such as the major global wind patterns, or to mesoscale phenomena ranging in scale from 10 to 100 kilometres.

mesosiderite (mesosi·dĕrəit, -səidiə·rəit, mī-zo-). *Geol.* [ad. G. *mesosiderit* (G. Rose 1865, in *Amtlicher Bericht 39. Versammlung deutscher Naturforscher und Ärzte, Giessen 1864* 111); see Meso- and Siderite[1].] Any of the stony-iron meteorites in which the silicates are principally present as pyroxene and plagioclase.

1868 *Geol. Mag.* V. 76 Meteorites have long since been arranged under two great divisions, the irons and the stones... In examining a certain number of these masses it has been thought convenient by some to establish a third, or intermediate division, to which the names of *Mesosiderites, Lithosiderites*, or of *Siderolites*, have been given. *Ibid.* 78 For these meteorites M. Rose has proposed a special name, that of *mesosiderites*. **1918** G. T. Prior in *Mineral. Mag.* XVIII. 151 In the Rose–Tschermak–Brezina classification of meteorites the intermediate class of stony-irons, in which iron and stony matter occur in approximately equal amounts and to which Maskelyne gave the name siderolites, is divided into (1) siderolites proper..and (2) lithosiderites, comprising the groups of the mesosiderites, grahamites, and lodranites. Mesosiderites are defined as consisting of iron and crystalline olivine and bronzite... As seen in the following pages, chemical and microscopic examination of typical members of these two groups fails to reveal any real distinction between them based on the amount of felspar they contain. For the combined group, all the members of which contain abundant felspar, it is proposed to retain the earlier name of mesosiderite. **1962** B. Mason *Meteorites* viii. 120 The stony-irons are a minor group of meteorites... They are divided into two major groups according to the nature of the silicate minerals, the pallasites (olivine stony-irons) and mesosiderites (pyroxene-plagioclase stony-irons).

mesosoma. Add to defs.: Also, the central part of the body of certain other invertebrates. (Later examples.)

1932 Borradaile & Potts *Invertebrata* xv. 450 The lung books are found on segments 3–6 of the mesosoma. **1962** D. Nichols *Echinoderms* xiv. 174 The lophophore itself is borne by the mesosome, and there is a strong partition between this division of the body and the metasome.

2. *Bacteriology.* (Used in the form **mesosome.**) A cytoplasmic structure in many bacteria which is principally composed of membranes, probably being formed by invagination of the cell membrane, and may be a site of active respiratory activity and the place of attachment of the bacterial genome.

1960 P. C. Fitz-James in *Jrnl. Biophysical & Biochem. Cytol.* VIII. 508/2 This [*sc.* 'dense body'] is probably an unsuitable name. Certainly they are not always electron dense... Since they appear to be attached to the surface membranes of the cell, one should adopt the suggestion of Robertson..for such membrane-attached cytoplasmic structures and use the term 'mesosomes'. Henceforth in this paper this term will be used. **1968** H. Harris *Nucleus & Cytoplasm* vi. 123 The loss of the ability to form the cell wall appears to be associated with the disappearance from the cytoplasm of the cell of specific membranous structures, known as 'mesosomes', which appear to be essential for the formation of the wall. **1974** *Nature* 1 Feb. 303/1 These properties together with the possession of fimbriae and the absence of mesosomes are commonly shared by Gram-negative, but generally absent in Gram-positive bacteria.

mesothelioma (me:sopīliōu·mă). *Path.* Pl. **-omas, -omata.** [f. next + *-oma.] A tumour of mesothelium; formerly, † a tumour composed of cells derived from the embryonic mesothelium.

1909 J. G. Adami *Princ. Path.* I. 647 Of mesothelial origin: Tumors (mesotheliomas) whose characteristic constituents are cells derived in direct descent from the persistent mesothelium of the embryo. (*a*) Typical.—Adenoma of kidney, testicle,..'mesothelioma' of pleuræ, peritoneum, etc. *Ibid.* 746 If a convenient term is required for all this order of tumors, the transitional adenocarcinomas of adrenal, kidney, ovary, and testis, we have, from embryogenetic considerations, suggested the term mesothelioma. **1921** *Lancet* 23 July 173/2 The true nature of these tumours has been the subject of much controversy as is seen by the variety of names given to them—e.g. endothelial cancer,..mesothelioma, and so on. **1966** Wright & Symmers *Systemic Path.* I. i. 6/1 Primary tumours of the pericardium..are very rare: most of those that have been described appear to have arisen from mesothelial cells, and may in consequence be termed 'mesotheliomas'. **1971** *Brit. Med. Bull.* XXVII. 71/2 Wagner.. discovered the first of a large group of pleural and peritoneal tumours—mesotheliomata—apparently related to exposure to crocidolite. **1973** *Nature* 8 June 352/2 Mesotheliomas of the pleura and peritoneum have been linked with the inhalation of asbestos fibres.

mesothelium, delete entry in Dict. (s.v. Meso-) and substitute:

mesothelium (meso-, mīzopī·liǒm). *Embryol.* and *Histology*. Pl. **-thelia.** [f. Meso- + Epi)thelium.] In a vertebrate embryo, epithelium that forms the surface layer of the mesoderm and lines the body-cavity; in a post-natal organism, the tissue derived from this that forms the lining of the pleuræ, peritoneum, and pericardium (by some writers, esp. pathologists, not regarded as epithelium).

1886 C. S. Minot in *Buck's Handbk. Med. Sci.* III. 176/1 The whole of the mesoderm..does not go through this metamorphosis, but..a part remains closely compacted; but ultimately it is only the single layer of cells immediately bounding the cœlom, and the cells constituting the myotomes.., which remain thus close together. These cells, therefore, have all the characteristics of an epithelium, so that the cœlom is limited by an epithelium of cuboidal cells, for which I have proposed the name *mesothelium*. *Ibid.* 176/2 Derivatives of the mesothelium (epithelial mesoderm). **1945** W. J. Hamilton et al. *Human Embryol.* vi. 80 The mesoderm bounding the coelom [of the embryo] will persist throughout life as an epithelium (so-called mesothelium) which forms the visceral and parietal linings of the peritoneal, pleural and pericardial cavities. Parts of the peritoneal mesothelium become specialized to form the germinal epithelium, the paramesonephric ducts..and the cortex of the suprarenal gland. **1950** A. W. Ham *Histol.* xi. 140/1 Endothelium and mesothelium, structurally, are both typically epithelial... Nevertheless, pathologists usually prefer to consider endothelium and mesothelium as apart from ordinary epithelium because endothelial and mesothelial cells behave differently from ordinary epithelial cells. **1960** F. D. Allan *Essent. Human Embryol.* xvii. 165 The cells of the cortical primordium are derived from the coelomic mesothelium. **1968** Passmore & Robson *Compan. Med. Stud.* I. xvii. 3/2 Endothelia and mesothelia arise only from mesoderm.

Hence **mesothe·lial** *a.*

1892 C. S. Minot *Human Embryol.* (1897) vii. 159 Although the pancreas, ovary, and spinal cord all contain connective tissue, we do not call them mesenchymal, but respectively entodermal, mesothelial, and ectodermal. **1946** B. M. Patten *Human Embryol.* xv. 469 In the case of a part of the gut tract which lies within the body cavity, the corresponding connective-tissue layer will be supplemented by an epithelial layer derived from the mesoderm which lines the coelomic cavities... This mesothelial layer provides a smooth, moist surface which permits the viscera within the body cavity to change shape and position with a minimum amount of friction. **1950** [see above]. **1968** Passmore & Robson *Compan. Med. Stud.* I. xvi. 5/2 (*heading*) Mesothelial or serosal sac membranes.

mesotherm. Add: (Later example.) Hence **mesothe·rmic** *a.*

1903 W. R. Fisher tr. *Schimper's Plant-Geogr.* 236 The most important family of the north temperate zone among the *Polycarpicae*, that of the Ranunculaceæ, is mesothermic and microthermic. **1960** N. Polunin *Introd. Plant Geogr.* x. 201 Examples [of climatic relics] are the mesothermic plants to be found in some boreal areas that have cooled at least since the 'postglacial optimum' when such plants presumably migrated to these areas. *Ibid.* 285 The great world vegetational zones..depend primarily on temperature, and we find it convenient to distinguish between megatherms (plants favouring warm habitats), microtherms (plants favouring cold habitats), and the intermediate mesotherms.

mesothorium (mesoþō·riŏm, mīzo-). *Chem.* [mod.L. (O. Hahn 1907, in *Ber. d. Deut. Chem. Ges.* XL. 1469): see Meso- and Thorium.] Either of two radioactive nuclides in the thorium decay series: *mesothorium I* (symbol MsThI), the isotope of radium with mass number 228, produced by the alpha decay of thorium 232, or *mesothorium II* (symbol MsThII), the isotope of actinium with mass number 228, produced by the beta decay of mesothorium I.

1907 *Jrnl. Chem. Soc.* XCII. ii. 359 The suggestion is made that thorium is not directly transformed into radiothorium, but into an intermediate product, 'Mesothorium', which then yields radiothorium. **1935** *Jrnl. R. Aeronaut. Soc.* XXXIX. 857 The mesothorium preparation produces a point source of gamma radiation suitable for the inspection of thick metal objects for which X-ray investigation becomes very expensive. **1937** *Nature* 21 Aug. 318/1 *Lemna* [duckweed] accumulates mesothorium I and concentrates it a hundredfold as compared with its content in the water. **1969** R. F. Lang tr. *Henglein's Chem. Technol.* 546 Mesothorium is present in monazite to the extent of 1 mg per t, and serves as a substitute for radium.

mesotron (mī·-, me·zotrǫn, me·sotrǫn). *Nuclear Physics.* Now *rare* or *Obs.* [f. Meso- + *-tron.] The name orig. given to the meson (*meson³).

1938 Anderson & Neddermeyer in *Nature* 12 Nov. 878/2 The existence of particles intermediate in mass between protons and electrons has been shown in experiments on the cosmic radiation... We should like to suggest..the word 'mesotron' (intermediate particle) as a name for the new particles. It appears quite likely that the appropriateness of this name will not be lost, whatever new facts concerning these particles may be learned in the future. **1939** *Ibid.* 13 May 796/2 The meson or mesotron was first introduced by Yukawa to serve as the connecting link between β-ray disintegration and the forces responsible for nuclear binding. **1942** *Endeavour* Jan. 22/2 Skobeltzyn..has argued against the theory of Heisenberg and Euler that the spontaneous disintegration of mesotrons is the mechanism responsible for the formation of the electronic component observed in the lower layers of the atmosphere. **1949** Koestler *Insight & Outlook* x. 136 The so-called 'elementary particles'—electrons, photons, neutrons, mesotrons, and so forth.

Mespot (me·spǫt). Also Mess-pot. Slang abbrev. of Mesopotamia.

1917 *To-Day* 6 Jan. 246/3 *Mesopotamia.*—So you call it the 'Mess-pot', do you? **1920** *Sat. Rev.* 3 July 4/1 The 'Messpot' madness. **1933** J. Buchan *Prince of Captivity* I. iii. 107 What front were you on—the Western, Palestine, Mespot? **1943** C. S. Forester *Ship* viii. 48 Mr. Whipple.. had gone off and joined the army and had done his bit in Mespot.

mesquite, mesquit². Add to forms: **masketo, moscheto, musqueto, mus-, mesquito; musquet, -quit, -kit; muskeete. 1.** (Earlier and later examples.)

1759 tr. *Venegas's Nat. & Civil Hist. Calif.* I. 100 Their most usual device was to hold up in their hands some little tablets of wood made with great labour, for want of iron tools of mesquite. **1806** M. Lewis in *Deb. Congress U.S.* (1852) 9th Congress 2 Sess., App. 1083 A bean that grows in great plenty on a small tree resembling a willow called masketo. **1838** 'Texian' *Mexico v. Texas* 70 Even where a tree appears it is sure to be a mesquite (*Mimosa nilotica*). **1838** C. Newell *Hist. Revolution Texas* 147 Live oak,.. black walnut, cypress, and musquit prevail. **1909** 'O. Henry' *Roads of Destiny* viii. 129 Near the store, scattered among the mesquite and elms, stood the saddled horses of the customers. **1948** *Reader's Digest* Jan. 70/1 Anywhere in America has its particular hearth perfume—..mesquite floating out of desert chimneys in the Southwest. **1969** T. H. Everett *Living Trees of World* 201/1 The mesquite..[is] a native of the southwestern United States, Mexico, Central America and the West Indies.

b. A thicket of mesquite trees.

1834 A. Pike *Prose Sk. & Poems* 63 We emerged from the broken hills into the musquito. **1910** W. M. Raine *Bucky O'Connor* 224 The Irishman..kept his party in the mesquit till the headlight of an approaching train was visible. **1945** *New Yorker* 25 Aug. 26 A railroad bull came walking along the tops of the cars and kicked me into the mesquite. **1974** *Sci. Amer.* Apr. 104/1 The particular dung beetles concerned would colonize only pads dropped in open pastures, however, and not those dropped in the dense growth of mesquite, where the cattle sought shelter from the heat of the day.

2. (Earlier examples.)

1823 W. B. Dewees *Lett. from Early Settler Texas* (1852) 35 The musquit grass grows very thick and about three feet high, and looks very much like a blue grass pasture. **1831** M. Holley *Texas* (1833) vi. 69 The pasturage here.. called Muskit grass, (pronounced Muskeet) bears a strong resemblance to the blue grass.

3. (Earlier and later examples.)

1806 M. Lewis in *Deb. Congress U.S.* (1852) 9th Congress 2 Sess., App. 1103 Some small cultivated fields, fenced round with small cedar and moscheto brush. **1831** J. O. Pattie *Personal Narr.* 59 We found the river skirted with very wide bottoms, thick set with the musquito trees. *Ibid.* 83 There is here little timber, beside musqueto wood, which stands thick. **1834** A. Pike *Prose Sk. & Poems* 56 The valley was..full of small hills interspersed with mezquito bushes. **1846** J. A. Quitman *Diary* 13 Aug. in J. F. H. Claiborne *Life & Corr. J. A. Quitman* (1860) I. 239 The steamer purchases muskeet-wood at $2.50 per cord for dry, $2.25 green. **1867** A. D. Richardson *Beyond Mississippi* xix. 226 Another waiting coach was soon rolling us forward among mesquite groves. **1905** A. Adams *Outlet* 16 The horses had run idle during the winter in a large mesquit pasture. **1957** J. Kerouac *On Road* (1958) 166 Tucson is situated in beautiful mesquite riverbed country.

mess, *sb.* Add: **1. c.** (Earlier and later U.S. examples.)

1697 S. Sewall *Diary* (1878) I. 455 Betty gets her Mother a Mess of English Beans. **1775** B. Romans *Florida* 12 (Th.), He told me that his mother had an inclination to eat fish, and he was to come to get her a mess. **1842** *Knickerbocker* XIX. 557 Sally couldn't hardly bring in the pail, she gave such a mess. **1861** O. W. Norton *Army Lett.* (1903) 26 H. and I got enough [potatoes] for a mess, and some parsnips. **1872** *Rep. Vermont Board Agric.* I. 197, I tested their milk by weighing every mess for a month. **1877** *Ibid.* IV. 54 We took off what cream arose on the night's mess, and churned it. **1883** J. C. Harris *Nights with Uncle Remus* iii. 30 Brer Rabbit, he hop in, he did, en got 'im a mess er greens, en hop out ag'in.

e. *N. Amer.* A quantity or number *of* something. See also quot. 1970.

1830 *Mass. Spy* 23 June (Th.), We saw yesterday a large mess of early potatoes. **1834** C. A. Davis *Lett. J. Downing* 40 With that, he out with his wallet, and unrolled a mess on 'em. **1854** *Knickerbocker* XLI. 502 There was wolves in the Holler—an unaccountable mess of 'em. **1872** *Rep. Vermont Board Agric.* I. 634 They will dress a mess of ore to any required per cent. **1939** L. M. Montgomery *Anne of Ingleside* xxxviii. 300 Tell Susan Baker I'm much obliged for that mess of turnip greens she sent me. **1956** B. Holiday *Lady sings Blues* (1973) xix. 154 Just before I was set to go on for the second set a big mess of gardenias arrived backstage. **1966** W. T. E. Kirkeby *Ain't Misbehavin'* v. 51 This is Fats Waller, the baby who plays that mess of organ over at the Lincoln. **1970** C. Major *Dict. Afro-Amer. Slang* 81 *Mess*, large quantity;..someone ..[who] is remarkable or puzzling.

3. d. *colloq.* Excrement, esp. of an animal; usu. in phr. *to make a mess.*

1903 in *Eng. Dial. Dict.* s.v. Mess, *sb.*² 4. **1928** Kipling *Limits & Renewals* (1932) 50 It [*sc.* a dog]'s made a mess in the corner. **1937** V. Woolf *Years* 245 The pigeons were a nuisance, he thought, making a mess on the steps. **1939** A. Huxley *After Many a Summer* I. x. 138 A lovely stinking little baby who still made messes in its bed. **1940** N. Mitford *Pigeon Pie* ix. 144 Perhaps, she thought, the bird wants to go out... It made a mess on her skirt. **1960** *Woman's Own* 6 Aug. 49/2 It's the dog. It made a mess on the carpet. **1972** *New Yorker* 30 Sept. 44/2 Happy..had helped them unpack by..pulling one of Mrs. Webster's dresses from a hanger and then making a mess on it.

e. *slang.* An objectionable, ineffectual, or stupid person.

1936 M. Mitchell *Gone with Wind* I. vi. 122 'Oh,' thought Scarlett...'To have that mealy-mouthed little mess take up for me!' **1938** E. Bowen *Death of Heart* I. ii. 40 From what you say, her mother was quite a mess. **1965** M. Spark *Mandelbaum Gate* iv. 104 These were lapsed Jews, lapsed Arabs, lapsed citizens, runaway Englishmen, dancing prostitutes, international messes.

4. b. Also, the place where food is served (see quot. 1886 in Dict.). Phr. *to lose the number of one's mess* (earlier and later examples).

1807 in A. Paget *Paget Papers* (1896) II. 314 If we are going against Copenhagen many of us will lose the number of our mess. **1911** C. E. W. Bean *'Dreadnought' of Darling* xxx. 260 That meant a ride out to the blacks' camp and some of them losing the number of their mess. It did not matter who was shot. **1934** G. B. Shaw *Too True to be Good* II. 76 The conversation in the officers' mess doesnt suit me. *Ibid.* III. 81 *Sweetie.* Well, of course. Youre in the sergeants' mess. **1969** D. Hay *Man in Hot Seat* vi. 60 At the Aldershot end of the airfield..stood the long blue-carpeted Mess of the Empire Test Pilots' School.

7. (sense 3) *mess-maker*; (sense 4) *mess-bag, -basket, -bill, -chest* (earlier examples), *-cloth, -dinner, -fire, fund, -gear, -hall, -man, -pan, -pork* (earlier examples), *-pot, -table* (earlier and later examples), *-tent* (later example); **mess-boy** *Naut.*, one who waits at table in a mess-room; **mess-jacket** (add definition): a short tailless jacket reaching just below the waist-line (further example); **mess-kit,** (*a*) utensils for cooking or handling food; (*b*) (military) uniform designed to be worn at meals.

1885 *Outing* VII. 55/1 From some dark corner of the messbags, or petacas, he unearthed a handful of dried apples. **1839** *Knickerbocker* XIII. 211 Tell Margaret to prepare the mess-basket. **1916** F. M. Ford *Let.* 29 Nov. (1965) 78 Also I have found a considerable portion of my Mess Bill out of Auction. **1917** W. Owen *Let.* 24 May (1967) 464 There have been a number of Mess Bills, & other cheques drawn lately. **1934** E. Bowen *Cat Jumps* 67 If mess-bills ran up..was John to blame? **1963** *Times* 24 May 14/7 Chits were signed, which sooner or later found their way to the Mess and appeared on one's mess-bill. **1818** 'A. Burton' *Adventures J. Newcome* II. 74 The Mess-boy to the Coppers dragged it [*sc.* a pudding]. **1955** C. S. Forester *Good Shepherd* 116 A big pot of coffee. And a sandwich. Tell the mess-boy I want one of my specials, **1964** O. E. Middleton in C. K. Stead *N.Z. Short Stories* (1966) 210 The messboy's discreet ropesoles pad patiently to and fro. **1970** *Islander* (Victoria, B.C.) 22 Feb. 5/1 The American trading schooner Nanook arrived. Its messboy had hanged himself for some unknown reason. **1830** J. F. Cooper *Water Witch* III. ix. 258 The smaller booms with the mess-chest and shot-boxes were all that lay between the group..and the depths of the ocean. **1858** T. Vielé *Following Drum* 15 A camp-kettle, mess chest, bundle of canvas, and set of tent poles. **1839** C. F. Briggs *Adventures H. Franco* I. xxiii. 250 Throwing down my knife..I leaped on to the messcloth, and gave him a blow in the eye. **1803** Scott *Let.* 10 July (1932) I. 195, I can proceed no further being alarmed by the Bugle Call not indeed to summon to battle but to the less hazardous task of a Mess Dinner where our Society tho' somewhat noisy is very good humoured. **1825** H. Wilson *Mem.* II. 116 The mess-dinner at Lewes..must more resemble a..private party than a mess-room, as they seldom mustered more than seven or eight persons together at table. **1885** A. Edwardes *Girton Girl* I. xiv. 283 The usual guest-night at mess. Curious how precisely alike all mess dinners are. **1837** W. Irving *Capt. Bonneville* (1895) I. 24 The various mess-fires were surrounded by picturesque groups. **1850** L. H. Garrard *Wah-to-Yah* xii. 180 He..walked to a messfire. **1850** J. J. Hort *Horse Guards* 70 He cannot act otherwise than by occasionally adding to the mess and the band funds. **1876** Voyle & Stevenson *Mil. Dict.* (ed. 5) 254/1 Married men pay one half if they do not regularly attend the mess, but they pay all contributions to the mess fund. **1970** V. Canning *Great Affair* xii. 216 Ex-pilot officer Robinson, cashiered for fiddling the mess funds. **1890** *Cent. Dict.*, Mess-gear. **1918** L. E. Ruggles *Navy Explained* 98 *Mess gear*, the tableware, plates, cups, saucers, food containers and implements used by mess cooks. **1862** G. C. Strong *Cadet Life at West Point* 66 We were as unfortunate in the mess-hall as out of it. **1958** *Listener* 6 Nov. 717/1 Food eaten at the communal mess-hall [in China]. **1905** A. M. Binstead *Mop Fair* i. 10 A tall blonde in a heel-tipping skirt and mess-jacket of blue herring-bone. *a* **1877** Knight *Dict. Mech.* II. 1421/2 *Mess-kit*, that portion of camp equipage consisting of cooking utensils. **1953** J. Masters *Lotus & Wind* vii. 89 His mess-kit was grey and black with silver facings. **1954** W. Faulkner *Fable* (1955) 343 Bottles, old messkits. **1929** D. H. Lawrence *Pansies* 89 It is hard.. to put up with the clever mess-makers. **1850** *Punch* 20 July 33/1 Messman wanted for a Cavalry Regiment. **1920** *Chambers's Jrnl.* May 285/2 Understanding the messman to have come off from the Colon with plenty of oysters. **1813** *Niles' Reg.* III. 295/2 [List of Military Supplies] Mess pans. **1846** R. B. Sage *Scenes Rocky Mts.* xxvii. 227 A large tin mess-pan, and a tin-cup and plate for each of its number. **1861** O. W. Norton *Army Lett.* (1903) 35 New knapsacks, canteens..mess pans and a complete outfit. **1832** *Louisville* (Kentucky) *Public Advertiser* 10 Mar., Mess and Prime Pork in barrels and half barrels, for sale. **1848** *Rep. Comm. Patents 1848* (U.S.) 527 The finest and fattest [hogs] making clear and mess pork. **1857** R. Glisan *Jrnl. Army Life* (1874) viii. 86, I shall be able to say good bye to the messpots of Uncle Sam. **1819** J. A. Quitman *Diary* 15 Nov. in J. F. H. Claiborne *Life & Corr. J. A. Quitman* (1860) I. 42 Mrs. and Miss Griffith, charmed with our mess-table, became our boarders. **1895** M. A. Jackson *Mem. Stonewall Jackson* xi. 191, I took my meals with him and the staff at their mess-table. **1916** in 'Contact' *Airman's Outings* (1917) 266 A great wind..whines past the mess-tent.

mess, *v.* Add: **4.** Examples of *to mess about in boats.* Also const. *around.*

1908 K. GRAHAME *Wind in Willows* i. 7 There is *nothing*—absolutely nothing—half so much worth doing as simply messing about in boats. **1932** *Amer. Speech* VII. 334 Mess around, to 'kill time'; to interfere; to meddle. **1957** D. ROBINS *Noble One* iv. 41, I can't see the attraction of messing around with a lot of sick animals. **1962** J. CANNAN *All is Discovered* iv. 87 What he enjoyed was messing about in boats and sitting in the sun. **1964** *Evening Post* (Wellington, N.Z.) 4 Jan., A few audible reminders to himself to 'stop messing around' failed to help matters. **1970** H. E. ROBERTS *Third Ear* 10/1 Mess around, to engage in a great deal of purposeless activity. **1973** *Times* 18 Apr. 3/2 (Advt.), And if you ask the Chancellor of the Exchequer what a company like ours is doing 'messing about in boats' he'll tell you we're the world's largest manufacturer of quality inflatable leisure craft.

b. *to mess with*: to interfere or get involved with; to make a mess of; to trouble or annoy. *U.S. colloq.* or *dial.* Cf. sense 7 in Dict.

1903 *Dialect Notes* II. 299 *Mess with*, to meddle with; also, to make a mess of. 'Don't mess with your food.' **1913** *Ibid.* IV. 5 *Mess with*, to associate with. 'We don't mess with those people.' **1955** S. WHITMORE *Solo* 27 And what little lady is going to mess with you. **1955** SHAPIRO & HENTOFF *Hear me talkin' to Ya* 374 The really good musicians are too smart to mess with it. **1956** B. HOLIDAY *Lady sings Blues* (1973) iv. 46 This talk about a big tone messed with Lester for months. **1968** E. GAINES in A. Chapman *New Black Voices* (1972) 101, I never messed with a woman I didn't love. **1971** *Black World* Apr. 66 You hit her with a chair leg. You didn't have no right to mess with that poor girl.

c. *to mess up*: to make a mess or muddle of a situation; to get into trouble; to become mixed up or involved. *U.S. colloq.*

1933 *Amer. Speech* VIII. III. 29/2 Boy, I ain't a-goin' t' mess up no more from now on. **1938** M. K. RAWLINGS *Yearling* xxiii. 290 If she's nothin' but one o' them leetle ol' chipperdales, why do he mess up with her? **1956** B. HOLIDAY *Lady sings Blues* (1973) iii. 33 When the time came to take those bills off the table, I was always messing up. **1969** H. KOHL in T. Kochman *Rappin' & Stylin' Out* (1972) 110 He wanted to learn badly, they told me, and was messing up by memorizing the signs in the neighborhood and thinking that's all there was to reading.

5. (Further examples.) Also, to spoil, ruin.

1909 *Dialect Notes* III. 349 The house is all messed up. **1919** G. B. SHAW *Heartbreak House* II. 85, I get my whole life messed up with people falling in love with me. **1959** I. FLEMING *Goldfinger* xiv. 194 Bond only prayed that she hadn't got some private plot involving him or Goldfinger that was going to mess up his own operation. **1966** *Word Study* Dec. 3/2 There's no real point in worrying anyhow. It just messes you up.

6. Change '*vulgar*' to '*colloq.*' and add further examples. Also, to inconvenience or annoy. Also with *around*.

1934 A. P. HERBERT *Holy Deadlock* 276 Why *should* our private lives be spied upon—and messed about in a Court like this? **1955** *Times* 20 May 14/6 If industry is once again going to be messed about by Government interference—more nationalization, more controls. **1957** M. SPARK *Comforters* v. 110 Her great desire to travel by train was dispersed by the obvious necessities of going to Mass, and of not messing Laurence around any further. **1973** *Time Out* 2–8 Mar. 14/1 My impression is that when the surge of violence was on—at its height, two years ago—quite a few teachers got messed about. It was somewhere beyond extreme rudeness, but short of your actual NAS physical assault.

‖ **messa di voce** (me·sā dī vō·tʃe). Pl. **messe di voce.** [It., lit. 'placing of the voice'.] In singing, a gradual crescendo and diminuendo on a long-held note.

1801 in BUSBY *Dict. Mus.* **1876** STAINER & BARRETT *Dict. Mus. Terms* 286/2 *Messa di Voce (It.)*, the swelling and diminishing of the sound of the voice upon a holding note. **1938** *Oxf. Compan. Mus.* 567/2 [In the eighteenth century] every long note (irrespective of the sense of the words) was expected to bear a *messa di voce*. **1958** *Listener* 14 Aug. 250/3 The tenor's wonderful *messa di voce* at the cadence leading to the reprise. **1964** *Conc. Oxf. Dict. Opera* 259/1 *Messa di voce*.., the art of swelling and diminishing tone on a single note.

message, *sb.*[1] Add: **1. b.** (Further *transf.* examples.) Now esp., the broad meaning (of something); a view expressed in a piece of writing, etc., esp. one communicating a criticism of a social or political matter.

1936 *Time* 17 Feb. 46/2 In *Modern Times*, the 'message' has been underlined rather than, as in the old days, subconsciously implied. **1940** 'G. ORWELL' *Inside Whale* 156 It will be seen that once again I am speaking of these people as though they were not artists, as though they were merely propagandists putting a 'message' across. **1949** H. NICOLSON *Diary* 7 Sept. (1968) 174 T. S. Eliot.. is off to lecture in Germany. He asked me whether they would expect a 'message'. I said the only thing to do was to treat them as ordinary members of cultured society. **1955** *Times* 12 May 13/4 Mr. Kauffmann resembles other talented American novelists in that his real gifts for storytelling and satirical observation are somewhat obscured by too heavy an insistence on the 'message' implicit in the plot. **1969** J. ARGENTI *Managem. Techniques* ix. 54 If the chairman of the company shows an informed interest in techniques just occasionally, this should be enough for the message to get through to all levels. **1970** *Guardian* 17 Aug. 6/2 David Halliwell is..the black sheep of the student militants... 'Do you approve?' asked a nicely-dressed teenager, identifying the shock with the message. **1975** *Broadcast* 23 June 17/1 The medium may not be the message, but undeniably the characteristics of the medium shape the message.

c. (Earlier example.) Also, a communication from Parliament to members of the royal family, or between the two houses of Parliament themselves.

1566 *House of Commons Jrnl.* 30 Sept. (1742–62) I. 73/1 At which Thirtieth Day of September, 1566,..Mr. Comptroller..with a convenient Number, went up to the Lords with that Message. **1621** *Ibid.* 13 Feb. (1742–62) I. 520/1 Having faithfully discharged themselves in their Message to the King. **1701** *Ibid.* 20 June (1742–62) XIII. 638/1 A Message was sent to the House of Commons, by Mr. Baron Tracy and Mr. Baron Berry. **1818** *Ibid.* 6 June LXXIII. 424/1 Resolved, *Nemine Contradicente*, That a Message be sent from this House to congratulate their Royal Highnesses the Duke and Duchess of Cambridge, on their happy nuptials. **1820** *House of Lords Jrnl.* 15 Aug. LIII. 367/2 Ordered, *Nemine Dissentiente*, That a Message of Condolence be sent from this House to His Royal Highness The Duke of York..and that The Duke of Wellington and The Earl Graham do attend His Royal Highness with the said Message. **1844** ERSKINE MAY *Law of Parl.* xvi. 249 A message is the most simple and frequent mode of communication; it is daily resorted to for sending bills from one house to another [etc.]. *Ibid.* xvii. 268 Messages are frequently sent by both houses to members of the royal family, to congratulate them upon their nuptials ..or other auspicious events..or to condole with them on family bereavements. **1950** *Times* 21 Oct. 3/5 Before 1855 ..messages were always carried to the Lords by members of the Commons themselves, and from the Lords to the Commons by Masters in Chancery or judges.

2. c. Phr. *to get the message*: to understand a position stated or implied.

1964 'C. E. MAINE' *Never let Up* xv. 149 'Let's go in and have a drink anyway.' 'Now you're getting the message,' he commented. 'Lead the way.' **1967** O. WYND *Walk Softly, Men Praying* viii. 134 They didn't ask me in for a drink... Richard..realized it would only be postponing the inevitable. He had got the message at last. **1972** D. LEES *Zodiac* 90 They don't seem able to make up their minds whether to warn me off or knock me off but I do get the message loud and clear and..I'm going. **1974** *Times* 9 Jan. 14/8 (*heading*) Will Nato get the message?

4. *message bag*; **message-lad** = *message-boy*; **message-stick**, also used in Norway.

1917 'CONTACT' *Airman's Outings* vii. 184 The contact patrol buses..by means of message bags dropped over brigade headquarters report progress to the staff. **1948** 'N. SHUTE' *No Highway* xi. 289 Stubbs came back with the message bag. **1836** DICKENS *Sk. Boz* (1837) 2nd Ser. 101 The mother had got the boy a message-lad's place in some office. **1860** *Leisure Hour* 3 May 287/1 To this day the people in Norway are called together for the despatch of public business, in a somewhat similar manner. A bud-stick, or message-stick..is painted and stamped with the royal arms.

messageless (me·sėdʒles), *a.* [f. MESSAGE *sb.*[1] + -LESS.] Without a message; having no message to communicate.

1925 *Brit. Weekly* 18 June 268/2 He lost his faith in the Bible..and (to use his own significant words) 'I became a messageless man'. *a* **1930** D. H. LAWRENCE *Last Poems* (1932) 283 The dark and gleaming beauty of the messageless gods.

‖ **messagerie** (mesaʒri). [Fr.: see MESSAGERY.] Usu. *pl.* The transportation or delivery of goods, messages, or people; a conveyance for these. Also *attrib.* So **messageries maritimes,** the transport of goods, etc., by sea; the name of a shipping-line.

1792 A. YOUNG *Tra. France* I. 11 In ten miles we met not one stage or diligence; only two messageries, and very few chaises. **1878** LADY C. SCHREIBER *Jrnl.* 29 June (1952) 150 We took our passage in the French Messageries boat. **1907** G. B. SHAW *John Bull's Other Island* p. x, Many Englishmen like Frenchmen better than Englishmen, and never go on board a Peninsular and Oriental steamer when one of the ships of the Messageries Maritimes is available. **1931** E. WAUGH *Remote People* 12 French colonial officials, their wives and disorderly children..make up the bulk of a normal Messageries Maritimes passenger list. **1934** A. CHRISTIE *Murder on Orient Express* II. xiv. 169 He saw me on board a French Messagerie boat for Smyrna. **1974** S. COULTER *Chateau* II. vi. 286 She had come down by the Messageries coach.

Messalina (mesălī·nă). The name of Valeria *Messalina*, third wife of the Roman emperor Claudius, used allusively for a licentious and scheming woman.

1887 *Athenæum* 8 Oct. 467/1 His heroine is a New York Messalina who fastens herself upon a villain of the worst type. **1925** W. J. LOCKE *Great Pandolfo* xx. 257 I'm not either a Messalina, or one of the *grandes amoureuses*. **1931** G. J. RENIER *The English* iv. 85 Messalinas are exceptions. A woman needs only one partner. **1946** KOESTLER *Thieves in Night* 146 Particularly Gaby, our red-haired Viennese Messalina who, having a year ago left Max for Mendl, has now left Mendl too. **1975** 'J. LYMINGTON' *Spider in Bath* ii. 39 'Unfaithful bitch!' he cried. 'Messalina! Medusa! Gorgon!'

messaline (me·sălīn). [Fr., = *Messalina* (see prec.).] A soft, lightweight, and lustrous twilled-silk fabric. Also *attrib.*

1909 *Public Ledger* (Philadelphia) 26 June 7/7 Sale of Pongee & Messaline Dresses (title). *Ibid.*, Beautifully made of extra fine natural pongee silk and messaline. **1920** *T. Eaton & Co. Catal.* Spring & Summer 1/2 This delightful Frock of Messaline Silk. **1921** *Daily Colonist* (Victoria, B.C.) 11 Oct. 5/3 (Advt.), Black Messaline Silk, a beautiful heavy quality for making skirts and dresses. *Ibid.* 23 Oct. 16/4, 36-Inch Black Messaline, in an exceptionally good dye. A well woven silk in which you will realize the best wear. **1968** J. IRONSIDE *Fashion Alphabet* 241 *Messaline*, named after the wife of the Emperor Claudius (Messalina) this is a lustrous..satin-weave silk fabric.

Messapian (mĕsēi·piăn), *sb.* and *a.* Also **Messa·pic.** [f. L. *Messāpi-us* + -AN.] **A.** *sb.* **a.** A native or inhabitant of the ancient district of Messapia (now Apulia and Calabria) in southern Italy. **b.** The language of the Messapians. **B.** *adj.* Of or pertaining to the Messapians or their language.

1773 [see *IAPYGIAN *a.* and *sb.*]. **1876** *Encycl. Brit.* IV. 650/2 The inhabitants [of Calabria] were Sallentines and Calabrians or Messapians, both probably of Pre-Hellenic or Pelasgic race. **1880, 1882** [see *IAPYGIAN *a.* and *sb.*]. **1932** W. L. GRAFF *Lang.* 375 Venetic of Northeastern Italy and the South Italian Messapic. **1932** *Times Lit. Suppl.* 21 July 530/4 The three groups of Apulian vases, Messapian, Peucetian and Daunian. **1948** D. DIRINGER *Alphabet* II. viii. 471 The Messapic or Messapian was the earliest European offshoot of the Greek language. **1949** *Oxf. Class. Dict.* 560/2 The Apulian Peucetii..and Daunii ..also spoke Messapic. **1966** M. S. BEELER in Birnbaum & Puhvel *Anc. Indo-European Dial.* 52 The undoubtedly Illyrian Messapic of the southeastern end of the peninsula.

messeigneurs, pl. of MONSEIGNEUR.

messenger. Add: **1. e.** Used as the name of a newspaper, periodical, etc.

1834 (*title*) Southern literary messenger. **1886** *Encycl. Brit.* XXI. 109/2 Many excellent literary journals and magazines..among these..the time-honoured *Viestnik Yevropî* ('Messenger of Europe'). **1922** JOYCE *Ulysses* 460 *Messenger of the Sacred Heart* and *Evening Telegraph* with Saint Patrick's Day Supplement. **1975** (*title*) Kent Messenger.

f. *Biol.* A molecule or substance that carries genetic information. Freq. *attrib.* (cf. *messenger RNA* in *7).

1961 BRENNER, JACOB, & MESELSON in *Nature* 13 May 576 The paradox..can be resolved by the hypothesis, put forward by Jacob and Monod [in *J. Mol. Biol.* (in the press)], that..ribosomes are non-specialized structures which receive genetic information from the gene in the form of an unstable intermediate or 'messenger'. **1962** *Listener* 8 Mar. 413/2 'Messenger' molecules of RNA. **1969** A. M. CAMPBELL *Episomes* ix. 116 The genes of one operon are all transcribed onto the same messenger molecule. *Ibid.* 117 The rate of messenger synthesis. **1971** *Nature* 2 July 12/1 Where there are no operons messengers are evidently monocistronic.

4. Also, 'any line sent ahead by which a larger line is run to a dock, buoy or similar use' (G. Bradford *Gloss. Sea Terms* 1927).

5. b. A device which may be sent down a line in order to trip some mechanism attached to it.

1929 *Jrnl. du Conseil* IV. 193 When a messenger is sent down the line it first hits the arm holding the stop. By the blow the stop is forced away, the messenger below is set free. **1959** H. BARNES *Oceanogr. & Marine Biol.* iii. 113 When the required depth has been reached, the bottle is allowed to remain there for 3 to 5 minutes, so that the thermometer may reach equilibrium and a 'messenger' is then sent down the wire. The hook is released and the springs contract closing the bottle. **1963** H. F. P. HERDMAN in M. N. Hill *Sea* II. vi. 124 When the messenger hits this catch, the lids are immediately closed and the bottle falls away through 180°.

7. *messenger boy* (examples); **messenger cable,** a cable used to support a power cable or other conductor of electricity; a suspension cable or wire; **messenger RNA** *Biol.*, RNA which, after being synthesized in a cell nucleus in accordance with the genetic information carried by a gene ('transcription'), passes out of the nucleus and carries this information to a ribosome, where it determines which particular protein is synthesized there ('translation'); abbrev. *mRNA* (*M 5); **messenger wire** = **messenger cable.*

1876 J. S. INGRAM *Centenn. Exposition* 713 The messenger boys were seen everywhere conspicuous in their neat uniforms. **1886** *Pall Mall Gaz.* 26 Aug. 11/1 A Wall-street banker..sent a note by a district messenger boy to the office of his broker. **1922** JOYCE *Ulysses* 84 Messenger boys stealing to put on sixpence. **1959** N. MAILER *Advts. for Myself* (1961) 208, I was amateur agent for it, messenger boy, editorial consultant..and I made a hundred mistakes. **1916** *Stand. Rules Amer. Inst. Electr. Engin.* § 778 A messenger wire or cable is a wire or cable running along with and supporting other wires, cables or contact conductors. **1948** *Building, Estimating & Contracting* (Amer. Techn. Soc.) IX. 48 A stranded steel messenger cable is strung over the chord of the trusses. **1961** BRENNER, JACOB, & MESELSON in *Nature* 13 May 577/1 Model III implies that a special type of RNA molecule, or 'messenger RNA', exists which brings genetic information from genes to non-specialized ribosomes. **1961** JACOB & MONOD in *Jrnl. Molecular Biol.* III. 350 A small fraction of RNA, first observed by Volkin & Astrachan (1957) in phage infected *E. coli* and recently found to exist also in normal yeasts..and coli.., does seem to meet all the qualifications listed above. This fraction (which we shall designate 'messenger RNA' or M-RNA) amounts to only about 3% of the total RNA. **1970** AMBROSE & EASTY *Cell Biol.* iii. 113 Three types of RNA are involved in protein synthesis

in the cytoplasm—messenger, transfer, and ribosomal RNA. **1973** *Sci. Amer.* Aug. 21/1 Some of the RNA (messenger RNA) determines the structure of the proteins (primarily enzymes) that constitute or manufacture all the tissues of the organism. **1898** E. J. Houston *Dict. Electr. Words* (ed. 4) 849/2 Messenger wire of aerial cable. **1916** Messenger wire [see *messenger cable* above]. **1948** *Man. Uniform Traffic Control Devices* (U.S. Pub. Roads Admin.) III. 117 All overhead cable shall be supported by a suitable aerial messenger wire whenever there is a span of more than 30 feet.

Messenian (mesī·niăn), *sb.* and *a.* [f. L. *Messenius*, Gr. Μεσσήνιος Messenian + -AN.] **A.** *sb.* **a.** A native or inhabitant of Messenia, a region in the south-west Peloponnese bordered on the east by Laconia. **b.** The dialect of this region. **B.** *adj.* Of or belonging to Messenia.

1579 North tr. *Plutarch's Lives* 674 The Lacedæmonians brake of from this general peace, and..made warre, in hope to recouer the Messenians contrie. **1600** Holland tr. *Livy's Romane Hist.* XXXVI. 936 But the Messenians.. sent the embassadors away. **1794** T. Taylor tr. *Pausanias' Descr. Greece* I. IV. iv. 346 A disagreement, for the first time, took place between the Messenians and Lacedæmonians. **1826** *Kaleidoscope* 14 Feb. 261/2 Ephemerus, the Messenian, advanced this paradoxical opinion. **1830** W. M. Leake *Trav. Morea* I. 366 Andhrússa..is advantageously situated, overlooking the rich Messenian plain. **1910** C. D. Buck *Introd. Study Gk. Dial.* 10 The Doric Group... 2. *Messenian.* There is scarcely any material until a late period, when the dialect is no longer pure. **1911** *Encycl. Brit.* XXV. 610/1 Under Alcamenes and Theopompus a war broke out between the Spartans and the Messenians, their neighbours on the west. **1958** R. Liddell *Morea* II. 95 Currants from the rich Messenian vineyards lay everywhere. **1960** A. R. Burn *Lyric Age Greece* ix. 182 A Messenian hero, Aristomenes..gained fame in song. **1968** V. Ehrenberg *From Solon to Socrates* ii. 33 The kings Polydorus and Theopompus, the contemporaries of the First Messenian War. *Ibid.* vii. 275 The place was held by Messenians from Naupactus. **1969** A. Toynbee *Some Probl. Greek Hist.* III. ii. 164 It is probable that the Laconians and Messenians..were of mixed origin. **1972** A. Bartoněk *Classification West Gk. Dial.* 91 In principle..Messenian produces the impression of representing an archaic form of Laconian. **1974** *Encycl. Brit. Micropædia* VI. 822/3 Many modern historians believe that there were only two early Messenian wars; the first (*c.* 735–*c.* 715) was the Spartan conquest of Messenia; but a Messenian revolt precipitated a second war, in which the Spartans were ultimately successful.

messer[2] (me·səɹ). *colloq.* [f. Mess *v.* + -ER[1].] One who makes a mess; a muddler, bungler (see also quot. 1951).

1937 E. Pound *Let.* July (1971) 296 The respectable and the middle generation, illustrious punks and messers, fakes like Shaw, stew like Wells, nickle cash-register Bennett. **1949** F. Sargeson *I Saw in my Dream* xiii. 131 Though of course he's an old messer. **1951** Partridge *Dict. Slang* (ed. 4) 1108/2 *Messer*,..a 'near' prostitute; an amateur not above taking money or a present... A man, or a woman, that does not keep to one lover. **1966** 'J. Hackston' *Father clears Out* 69 Where money and accounts were concerned she was the greatest messer living.

Messerschmitt (me·səɹʃmit). Also (erron.) **Messerschmidt.** [f. the name of Willy *Messerschmitt* (b. 1898), German aircraft designer.] Any of several types (esp. fighters) of German military aircraft used in the 1939–45 war. Also as *adj.*

1940 I. Halstead *Wings of Victory* I. ii. 52 The Messerschmitts attacked us from the rear. **1948** A. M. Taylor *Lang. World War II* (rev. ed.) 130 *Messerschmitt*, twin-engined German fighter monoplane, especially adapted to bomber escort work. **1955** E. M. Hull in G. Conklin *Sci.-Fiction Adventures in Dimension* 12 If a flight of Messerschmitts attack us in the next forty minutes, our machine-guns won't be much good. **1957** L. G. S. Payne *Air Dates* 276 Munich, where Messerschmitt 262 jet fighters were being built. **1969** *Listener* 1 May 595/3 A wartime Spitfire chasing about after Messerschmidts over Kent. **1971** L. Deighton *Declarations of War* 155 Above them the Messerschmitts and Spitfires were now only a mile apart.

messor. Restrict *Obs.*⁻⁰ to sense in Dict. and add: **2.** *Ent.* [mod.L. (A. Forel 1890, in *Ann. Soc. Ent. Belg. Bull.* p. lxviii).] A member of the genus of harvesting ants so called. Also *attrib.*

1924 J. A. Thomson *Sci. Old & New* xii. 68 In the case of the Messor ants of the Sahara there are deep and spacious underground galleries, in which food is accumulated for the dry season.

mess-up. *colloq.* [f. *to mess up* (Mess *v.* 5).] = Mess *sb.* 3.

1902 C. J. C. Hyne *Mr. Horrocks, Purser* 111, I should say he feels this mess-up more than any of us. **1920** W. J. Locke *House of Baltazar* xxii. 274 It is ruin to your career and a mess up of your whole life. **1929** *Star* 21 Aug. 12/3, I am afraid there has been a bit of a mess-up.

messy, *a.* Add: **b.** *colloq.* Immoral; unethical.

1924 Lawrence & Skinner *Boy in Bush* xxi. 299, I can't bear to think of Monica messy with Easu. **1928** D. H. Lawrence *Woman who rode Away* 198 He was a perfectly decent boy, and there would never have been anything messy to fear from him. **1960** Wentworth & Flexner *Dict. Amer. Slang* 337/1 *Messy*,..immoral; unethical.

mestang, var. Mustang.

1834 A. Pike *Prose Sk. & Poems* 74 Lewis & Irwin obtained young and unbroken wild horses, (or, as the hunters call them, mestangs). **1837** W. Irving *Capt. Bonneville* II. xix. 28 She was mounted on a mestang or half wild horse.

mestizo. Add: (Further examples.) Also applied to other persons of mixed blood, or to a Central or South American Indian who has adopted European culture.

1878 C. Hallock *Amer. Club List & Sportman's Gloss.* p. vii/2 *Mestizo* (Sp.), a cross between an Indian and a negro. **1909** Webster *Mestizo*... In Spanish America and the Philippines, a person of mixed blood; esp., the offspring of a European or person of European stock and an (East) Indian, Negro, Malay, or other person of dark, non-European stock; often specif., *Phil. I.*, a person of Chinese and native blood. **1930** R. Macaulay *Staying with Relations* vi. § 1. 75 They [*sc.* the Spaniards] go mestizo sooner or later, and are the better for it; a little Indian blood gingers them up. **1941** R. Humphreys *Latin Amer.* 6 In Brazil..half the population is white, but Indians predominate in the interior, mestizos in the north, and the negro element is strong in Bahia. **1959** [see *Cholo, cholo]. **1962** N. Maxwell *Witch-Doctor's Apprentice* v. 52 Cholo means mestizo, half-breed. Seems it's more polite to call a man a half-breed than an Indian. **1967** Webster, *Mestizo*... 2: a completely acculturated Central or So. American Indian. **1969** *Time* 14 July 14/2 *Mestizo*, person of mixed Spanish and Indian blood, as are most Mexican Americans. **1973** *Nat. Geographic* May 642/1 Juan himself is a mestizo, part Indian, part Spanish. **1974** *Encycl. Brit. Micropædia* VI. 824/3 In some countries—*i.e.*, Ecuador—the word has acquired social and cultural connotations; a pure-blooded Indian who has adopted European dress and customs is called a mestizo (or cholo).

b. *mestizo labourer, town.*

1970 L. Grebler et al. *Mexican-Amer. People* xiv. 322 A leisured 'Spanish' *hidalgia* and a mass of *mestizo* and Indian laborers. **1887** L. Oliphant *Episodes* (ed. 4) vi. 118 There was absolutely nothing to see in the sleepy little *mestizo* town.

‖ **mesto** (me·sto), *a.* *Mus.* [It., f. L. *maestus* sad.] As a direction in music: sad, mournful.

1811 in Busby *Dict. Mus.* (ed. 3). **1880** Grove *Dict. Mus.* II. 315/2 *Mesto*, 'sadly'; a term used three times by Beethoven, in the pianoforte sonatas, op. 10, no. 3, and op. 59, and in the slow movement of Quartet op. 18, no. 7. The slow movement of the first of these is called Largo e mesto, and of the second and third Adagio molto e mesto. It is also used by Chopin in the Mazurkas, op. 33, nos. 1 and 4. **1938** *Oxf. Compan. Mus.* 568/1 *Mesto* (It.), 'mournful', sad. **1959** *Collins Mus. Encycl.* 424/1 *Mesto*.., sad.

mestranol (me·străn*ǫ*l). *Pharm.* [f. Me(thyl + *(œ)stra(diol + -*n*- + -ol.] The 3-methyl ether, $C_{21}H_{26}O_2$, of ethinylœstradiol which has actions similar to, but more potent than, those of œstradiol and is used in treating disorders of menstruation, fertility, and pregnancy, and (together with a progestational agent) as a contraceptive.

1962 *Approved Names* (Brit. Pharmacopœia Comm.) 15 Mestranol. **1963** *Federation Proc.* XXII. 481 A 2-year.. test was conducted..to determine the safety of Ortho-Novum, an oral contraceptive preparation containing norethindrone..and mestranol..in a ratio of 1,000 to 6. **1968** *Times* 21 Dec. 13/8 Most of the young quail fed on mestranol became sterile. **1971** *Brit. Med. Bull.* XXVII. 26/1 No difference could be detected between the risks associated with two different types of oestrogen (mestranol and ethynyloestradiol [*sic*]) when used in the same dose.

Mesvinian (mesvi·niăn), *a.* and *sb.* *Archæol.* [ad. F. *mesvinien*, f. *Mesvin* in Belgium: see -IAN.] **A.** *adj.* Belonging to the middle palæolithic period or culture of Belgium. **B.** *sb.* The Mesvinian period.

1911 W. J. Sollas *Anc. Hunters* 109 The Mesvinian, now accepted as the oldest of the Palaeolithic horizons. *Ibid.* 111 The Mesvinian implements are ruder than the Chellean, and the characteristic boucher is lacking. **1922** *Proc. Prehist. Soc. E. Anglia* III. 602 The Mesvinian Industry..might well be the precursor of the Mousterian Industry. **1948** [see *eolithic *a.*].

met.[1], **met,** colloq. abbrev. of Metropolitan *a.* (as in *Metropolitan Railway, Metropolitan Opera House, Metropolitan Police*, etc.). In *pl.*: stocks or shares in the London Metropolitan Railway.

1886 H. Baumann *Londinismen* 107/2 *Mets*, Aktien der unterirdischen (Metropolitan) Eisenbahn. **1896** Farmer & Henley *Slang* IV. 305/2 *Met.* 1. A member of the Metropolitan (or New York) Base-Ball Club. 2. in *pl.* (Stock Exchange), Metropolitan Railway Shares. 3. *The Met* (London), the Metropolitan music-hall. **1908** *Daily Report* 7 Feb. 1/4 Both 'Mets.' and 'Districts' have moved in contrast with the Railway market generally. **1926** [see *metroland]. **1937** 'C. McCabe' *Face on Cutting-Room Floor* iii. 18 Then I was suddenly in the crowd of clerks and typists rushing towards King's Cross Met station. **1944** 'D. Hume' *Toast to Corpse* ix. 91 You haven't had thirty years in the Mets for nothing, and you've been about a bit. **1946** L. Baker *Out on Limb* viii. 85 She walked like a queen,..sang like head bird at the Met, and had a brilliant career. **1953** *Manch. Guardian Weekly* 1 Oct. 2/4 There is very little Wagner at the Met this year. **1968** 'M. Underwood' *Man who killed too Soon* xiv. 120 Inspector Drew's colleagues in other forces, especially those in the Met. **1971** [see *firm *sb.*[1] 2 c]. **1972** P. Marks *Collector's Choice* i. 15 The crowds came to ogle the Van Goghs and the multi-million-dollar Rembrandts—the Met had thirty-seven. **1973** *Radio Times* 26 Feb. 7 It is no longer cheap to travel to and from London on the Met. **1973** 'S. Harvester' *Corner of Playground* III. iv. 202 An operatic mezzo-soprano, who had sung at the Met, La Scala, Covent Garden. **1974** S. Gulliver *Vulcan's Bulletins* 112 Something or other might be found to interest the Mets or the Home Office... Your trading days would be over. **1974** D. Ramsay *No Cause to Kill* II. 147 The television set blared baseball. The New York Mets were playing the Los Angeles Dodgers.

met.[2], **met,** colloq. abbrev. of Meteorological *a.* or of *Meteorological Office(r)*. Freq. with capital initial.

1940 *War Illustr.* 26 Jan. 19/2 One of the 'Met. men' studying the big thermometer attached to one of the interplane struts of his 'Gladiator'. **1942** T. Rattigan *Flare Path* I. 113 What's the met. report like? **1943** L. Cheshire *Bomber Pilot* iii. 45 The latest 'met' forecast came in... Navigation should be easy. **1943** Hunt & Pringle *Service Slang* 45 *Met.* or *Mets.*, the Meteorological Officer. [R.A.F.] **1943** *R.A.F. Jrnl.* Aug. 32 The Met. Officer has sent his obs. through each hour. **1958** *New Scientist* 15 May 9/2 The met. observations become meaningful only when compared with the observations made by the other parties all over the continent. **1964** *Punch* 7 Oct. 527/1 Metmen ask each other. **1970** *New Scientist* 24 Dec. 569/1 It is almost inevitable..that the Met Office will come in for derision over their latest idea. **1972** K. Campbell *Thunder on Sunday* 9 He picked up the blue weather folder that the Met Officer at Keflavik had given him. **1973** W. M. Duncan *Big Timer* i. 14 The met men promise a hard winter. **1974** L. Lamb *Man in Mist* viii. 50 The Superintendent turned..to ask what the met. report had been.

me·ta[2], **Meta,** abbrevs. of Metaldehyde. *Spec.* a block of metaldehyde used (*a*) as fuel for cooking and heating, (*b*) for killing slugs. Also *attrib.*

Registered as a proprietary term by Lonza Elektrizitätswerke, Switzerland, in 1924 *Trade Marks Jrnl.* 26 Mar. 717 (as a fuel) and in 1938 *Ibid.* 18 May 603 (slug-killer).

1925 E. F. Norton *Fight for Everest 1924* v. 102 Our loads..comprise one 10-lb. tent, two sleeping bags, food and 'meta' (solid spirit). *Ibid.* 706 The meta cooker doing its indifferent best to produce half a pot of warm water. **1938** *Times* 26 Nov. 15/6 Tablets of Meta crushed and used by itself or mixed with bran, may be put about among plants before dark and the victims collected in the morning. **1947** F. Smythe *Again Switzerland* vi. 120 He carries with him a packet of 'meta' fuel. **1952** E. R. Janes *Flower Garden* 119 Metaldehyde (Meta) is a very fine slug killer... Under some conditions in the dead of winter it is hardly possible to apply Meta. **1955** P. Bauer *Kanchenjunga Challenge* IV. iv. 196 We went on travelling light with perhaps the Zdarsky sack and a small meta-tablet cooker.

meta (me·tă), *a.* *Chem.* Now usu. italicized. [f. Meta- *prefix.*] Characterized by or relating to (substitution at) two carbon atoms separated by one other in a benzene ring; at a position next but one *to* some (specified) substituent in a benzene ring. Also as *adv.*

1876 *Jrnl. Chem. Soc.* XXIX. 237 The author places the sulpho-acids obtained by the action of sulphuric acid on.. iodobenzene in the meta (1:3) series. **1924** E. J. Holmyard *Outlines Org. Chem.* xix. 367 The *para* isomer $C_6H_4X_2$ can yield only *one* trisubstitution product $C_6H_3X_3$, while the *ortho* can give *two* and the *meta* can give *three.* **1938** L. F. Fieser in H. Gilman *Org. Chem.* I. ii. 146 There is..no such enormous difference in reaction rate.. as there is between the ortho-para directing amines and the meta orienting ammonium salts. **1949** [see *orient *v.* 4 a]. **1968** R. O. C. Norman *Princ. Org. Synth.* xi. 357 Position *a*, which is *ortho* to acetamido and *meta* to methyl, is more reactive than position *b*, which is *meta* to acetamido and *ortho* to methyl.

meta-. Add: **1. meta-e·thics,** a name applied to the study of the foundations of ethics, esp. of the nature of ethical statements; hence **meta-e·thical** *a.*; **meta-hi·story,** inquiry into the principles governing historical events; so **meta-histo·ric(al** *adjs.*, transcending history, controlling the course of history; **meta-philo·sophy,** inquiry into the problems ulterior to philosophy or philosophical theories; so **metaphiloso·phical** *a.*; **metasocio·logy** (see quot. 1970); so **metasociolo·gical, meta-sociologi·stic** *adjs.*; **meta-theo·logy,** (*b*) the philosophical study of the nature of religious language or statements; hence **meta-theolo·gian, meta-theolo·gical** *a.*

1949 A. J. Ayer *Philos. Ess.* (1954) x. 246 All moral theories..are neutral as regards actual conduct. To speak technically, they belong to the field of meta-ethics, not ethics proper. *Ibid.*, Expounding my meta-ethical theory. **1957** D. M. MacKinnon *Study in Ethical Theory* i. 10 The moral philosopher is..preoccupied with..problems of meta-ethics, with the question of where ethical language belongs on the language-map. *Ibid.* 11 This problem of the relation of duty and good is in some sense meta-ethical. **1966** G. C. Kerner *Revolution in Ethical Theory* 1 The problems of ethical theory are thus..problems..of moral language;..they are 'meta-ethical'. *Ibid.* ii. 70 Meta-ethics is conceived to be a purely theoretical and ethically neutral enterprise. **1973** *Nature* 26 Jan. 249/2 With someone who prefers an incoherent picture of nature, I have no idea how to proceed—just as in meta-ethics, one is powerless to proceed with someone who

regards a universe without sentience as possessing greater intrinsic value than one with sentience. **1929** R. HUGHES tr. *Deissmann's New Testament in Light of Mod. Res.* vi. 172 The holy is pre-historic and metahistoric. **1945** G. DIX *Shape of Liturgy* ix. 264 These meta-historical facts of the resurrection and ascension. **1949** *Mind* LVIII. 411 The value of morals as 'meta-historical reason' controlling history and determining the future. **1969** P. A. ROBINSON *Freudian Left* 148 The typical practicing psychoanalyst carefully distinguished the discrete precepts and techniques of his therapeutic science from the ambitious metahistorical adventures in which Freud had indulged. **1957** *Times Lit. Suppl.* 27 Dec. 782/2 Metahistory (which stands in much the same relation to history as metaphysics does to physics). **1964** C. S. LEWIS *Discarded Image* viii. 175 What Virgil puts forward in a mythical form is precisely meta-history. **1942** *Mind* LI. 284 'Why are no philosophical disputes ever settled?' It is with this 'metaphilosophical' problem..that Professor Ducasse's book..is concerned. **1964** *Philos. Rev.* LXXIII. 554 Blakeley.. proposes an original and provocative metaphilosophical thesis. **1970** M. LAZEROWITZ in *Metaphilosophy* I. 91 Metaphilosophy is the investigation of the nature of philosophy, with the central aim of arriving at a satisfactory explanation of the absence of uncontested philosophical claims and arguments. **1959** R. BIERSTEDT in L. Gross *Symposium Sociol. Theory* 137 The distinction between methodological (or metasociological) theory on the one hand and substantive (or sociological) theory on the other. **1964** P. MEADOWS in I. L. Horowitz *New Sociol.* 448 Formulations which phrase a meta-sociologistic model, that is, the theme that beyond the teeming and changing varieties of social life and differentiated functions there are social patterns generating and guiding the social work life. **1958** W. STARK *Sociol. of Knowl.* I. iv. 197 A metasociology which would be..a study of man as he appears in all societies, of man *as such.* **1970** G. A. & A. G. THEODORSON *Mod. Dict. Sociol.* 254 *Metasociology*, the branch of sociological theory that is concerned with the methods and logic of sociological inquiry, rather than with propositions, principles, and generalizations about social life. **1967** *Philosophy* XLII. 197 The meta-theologian..claimed that Christian discourse, as it stands, is incoherent. **1969** R. S. HEIMBECK *Theol. & Meaning* i. 20 Since 1955, the quantity of metatheological literature has multiplied many times over. **1957** I. M. CROMBIE in B. Mitchell *Faith & Logic* ii. 77 It is from reading theology, not meta-theology, that one can come to understand how theological statements work. **1959** P. MUNZ *Probl. Relig. Knowl.* 12 The meta-theology which I have put forward neither stands nor falls with any one particular theological opinion which I have expressed or implied. **1967** *Philosophy* XLII. 195 One piece of meta-theology which has won wide acceptance..is that 'God' is not a substance-word.

b. Prefixed to various classificatory words to designate concern with the ulterior or underlying principles peculiar to that classification, as *metacriterion, metacriticism*, (hence *metacritical* adj., *-ally* adv.), *metasystem, metatheorem, metatheory* (so *metatheoretic, -ical* adjs.).

1953 C. E. BAZELL *Ling. Form* v. 63 Universality of application is only one meta-criterion for the choice of criteria. **1954** C. F. HOCKETT in *Word* X. 233 Neither any existing version of IA nor any existing version of IP meets all the metacriteria. **1963** *Listener* 3 Jan. 21/1 They [*sc.* the techniques of modern criticism] could make exciting sense (if not in strictly critical terms, then in metacritical ones) of works which would have seemed absurd if taken literally. **1970** A. RODWAY *Truths of Fiction* i. 9 Concentrate, metacritically, on what the text refers to... Study of form is purely critical, of content either critical or metacritical; of what the work leads to, whether in the way of causes or effects or general topics, purely metacritical. **1966** *Philosophy* XLI. 320 The aesthetician..is concerned (among other things) with metacriticism. **1970** A. RODWAY *Truths of Fiction* i. 6 The logical primacy of intrinsic criticism suggests that extrinsic criticism might also be called *metacriticism.* **1956** J. H. WOODGER tr. *Tarski's Logic, Semantics, Metamath.* 116 It is possible to construct a particular science, namely the 'metasystem', in which the given system is subjected to investigation. **1964** P. MEADOWS in I. L. Horowitz *New Sociol.* 452 Meta-system or general systems theory. **1969** *New Scientist* 4 Sept. 461/1 What Professor Beer is asking for is that we approach the problem at a higher level—the level of the 'metasystem'. **1940** W. V. QUINE *Math. Logic* ii. 89 We establish theorems wholesale, by arguments which show that the appropriate sequences *could* be found for each particular case. Such principles, describing general circumstances under which statements are theorems, will be called metatheorems. **1943** *Mind* LII. 267 Closely connected with the distinction between use and mention is that between a theorem and a metatheorem, the latter being, as the name suggests, a theorem *about* theorems, wherein symbols are mentioned and names of symbols used. **1971** G. HUNTER *Metalogic* p. xii, Complete proofs for metatheorems (theorems *about* a system) are..more laborious for natural deduction systems than for axiomatic ones. *Ibid.* I. 11 A theorem about a theorem (also called a metatheorem) is a true statement about the system expressed in the metalanguage. **1965** B. MATES *Elem. Logic* viii. 128 We are now in a position to..give informal proofs of a number of metatheoretic generalizations about the theorems of logic. **1953** *Mind* LXII. 557 The metatheoretical problems of logical calculi, such as independence of axioms, completeness, and decision methods. **1956** E. H. HUTTEN *Lang. Mod. Physics* iii. 81 When we want to explain how scientific theories are constructed ..we must speak *about* them; and this requires a suitable terminology. This meta-theory, or methodology, is as necessary to science as grammar is to ordinary language. **1963** *Language* XXXIX. 208 A metatheory for semantics must also exhibit the relations between semantics and other areas of linguistics. **1974** *Sci. Amer.* May 122/3 He outlines a metatheory in which the universe at every micromicroinstant branches into countless parallel worlds.

4. me·tacneme [Gr. κνήμη tibia; cf. CNEMIAL *a.*], a secondary mesentery which develops in some Zoantherians; so **metacne·mic** *a.*; **metanephri·dium** [a. G. *metanephridium* (B. Hatschek *Lehrbuch der Zoologie* (1889) II. 162): see NEPHRIDIUM], in certain invertebrates, a nephridium with a ciliated opening into the coelom; so **metanephri·dial** *a.*; **metaphase**, delete **metaphasis** and substitute for def.: [a. G. *metaphase* (E. Strasburger 1884, in *Arch. f. mikrosk. Anat.* XXIII. 260)], the stage in mitotic or meiotic nuclear division which follows prophase and precedes anaphase, during which the chromosomes become arranged with their centromeres on the equatorial plate; a dividing nucleus at this stage; (later examples); **metaphlo·em**, a constituent of primary phloem which is formed after the earliest development of the shoot; **metatra·cheal** *a. arch.*, usu. in phrase *metatracheal parenchyma*, describing the structure of wood in which concentric bands of parenchyma independent of the vessels are formed; **metaxy·lem**, a constituent of the primary xylem which is formed after the earliest development of the shoot.

1900 J. E. DUERDEN in *Johns Hopkins Univ. Circular* XIX. 47/2 The first six pairs of mesenteries are found to differ so essentially in their mode of origin and significance from the mesenteries appearing later that I find it convenient to have some word which will include them either as a whole or individually. I therefore propose for them the term 'Protocnemes', and shall refer to the mesenteries subsequently developed as 'Metacnemes'. **1902** *Ann. & Mag. Nat. Hist.* IX. 397 The different fundamental types of metacnemic sequence now known within the Actiniaria and Madreporaria. *Ibid.*, The metacnemes arise as unilateral pairs at one, three, seven, etc. regions within all the six primary exocoeles. **1940** L. H. HYMAN *Invertebrates* I. vii. 589 In most forms [of sea anemone] additional septa called metacnemes arise in pairs. *Ibid.* ii. 37 The nephridial system of the coelomate invertebrates is of the metanephridial type, i.e., the nephridial tubules begin as coelomic openings. **1963** R. P. DALES *Annelids* v. 98 The metanephridial funnels or postnephridial solenocytes lie in the coelomic fluid. **1930** W. R. COE in *Biol. Bull.* LVIII. 208 This type of excretory organ may be designated a metanephridium in order to distinguish it from the more usual type, protonephridium, found in nemerteans. **1967** E. J. W. BARRINGTON *Invertebr. Struct. & Function* xii. 236 The nephridium occurs in two main forms, the protonephridium and the metanephridium. **1924** E. W. MACBRIDE *Study of Heredity* ii. 42 The formation of the equatorial plate and of the spindle is known as the metaphase. **1961** *Lancet* 26 Aug. 489/1 Metaphases in freshly aspirated sternal and iliac crest marrow were analysed. **1962** *Ibid.* 26 May 1098/2 Rich crops of cells in metaphase were obtained twice. **1969** *Times* 20 June 7/3 Shortly before ovulation the oocyte goes through the process of cell division and then starts to divide a second time, a stage known as metaphase 2. **1973** *Nature* 1 June 290/2 Well-spread metaphases were photographed with a 95 × fluoride objective. **1902** *Encycl. Brit.* XXV. 413/1 In many cases external protophloem..can be distinguished from metaphloem. **1965** K. ESAU *Plant Anat.* (ed. 2) xii. 292 The sieve elements of the metaphloem are commonly longer and wider than those of the protophloem. **1908** BOODLE & FRITSCH tr. *Solereder's Systematic Anat. Dicotyledons* II. 1143 The wood parenchyma generally forms tangential bands (known as the 'metatracheal' parenchyma in contrast to the 'paratracheal' parenchyma, aggregated round about the vessels). **1933** *Tropical Woods* XXXVI. 9 *Metatracheal parenchyma*, aggregated wood parenchyma forming concentric laminae, mostly independent of the vessels and vascular tracheids. **1970** WILSON & WHITE *Jane's Struct. Wood* (ed. 2) vi. 116 Apotracheal parenchyma may occur as..tangentially arranged sheets of cells..or in more extensive tangential bands... The two latter types are sometimes referred to as metatracheal parenchyma but this term is better avoided. **1902** *Encycl. Brit.* XXV. 415/1 Sometimes..the centre of a bulky root stele has strands of metaxylem..scattered through it. **1965** K. ESAU *Plant Anat.* (ed. 2) xi. 243 The metaxylem, which appears after the protoxylem, is in the process of differentiation while the shoot is elongating.

5. b. Prefixed to the names of rocks or of classes of rock to indicate that they have undergone metamorphism, as *metadiorite, metadolerite, metagranite, metasediment* (hence *metasedimentary* adj.), *metasyenite, metavolcanic*; also *metaigneous* adj.

1876 J. D. DANA in *Amer. Jrnl. Sci. & Arts* XI. 121 The rocks are..*Metamorphic doleryte, metamorphic diabase*, and *metamorphic melaphyre*... To distinguish these metamorphic rocks from the igneous of the same composition, they are named, on my suggestion, *metadoleryte, metadiabase*, and *metamelaphyre*. The examples are part of a long series of rock species which have representatives both among igneous (or intrusive) and metamorphic rocks. Other kinds are *dioryte* and *metadioryte, syenyte* and *metasyenyte, felsyte* and *metafelsyte*, etc. **1920** A. HOLMES *Nomencl. Petrol.* 154 *Meta-*, a prefix used before the names of igneous rocks to signify that the mineral and chemical composition of the latter have been modified by alteration. **1942** M. P. BILLINGS *Struct. Geol.* xii. 215 Metasediments, metavolcanics, and meta-igneous rocks are metamorphic rocks derived, respectively, from sedimentary, volcanic, and igneous rocks. **1961** J. CHALLINOR *Dict. Geol.* 126/1 *Meta-(rock).* A metamorphosed rock which was originally of the kind or type included in the name. Thus 'metasediment' or 'metasedimentary rock', 'meta-igneous rock', 'metadolerite', &c. **1973** *Nature* 21 Sept. 120/1 The metasediments occur in a (refolded) syncline among granitic gneisses. *Ibid.* 139/2 The lithology of some of these enclaves strongly suggests that they were originally supracrustal rocks similar to those that occur at Isua, including metasedimentary ironstones.

6. a. metapro·tein, an intermediate product in the hydrolysis of a protein which is soluble in acids and alkalis but insoluble in water.

1909 *Cent. Dict.* Suppl., Metaprotein. **1911** *Encycl. Brit.* XIX. 922/1 The first result of the action of this secretion on protein matter is to render it soluble—a metaprotein or acid albumin (syntonin) being formed. **1949** G. B. BACHMAN *Org. Chem.* xviii. 220 Primary derivatives: proteins, metaproteins, and coagulated proteins.

7. a. Add to def.: *spec.* denoting (partial) dehydration.

b. Delete entry in Dict. and see sense *5 b.

metabio·logy. Also **meta-biology.** [f. META- 1 + BIOLOGY.] A hypothetical or postulated science dealing with phenomena of living organisms beyond the scope of conventional biology, or treating them in a more fundamental way. Chiefly in non-scientific use, freq. with allusion to Shaw.

1921 G. B. SHAW *Back to Methuselah* Pref. p. lxxxv, As the conception of Creative Evolution developed I saw that we were at last within reach of a faith which complied with the first condition of all the religions that have ever taken hold of humanity: namely, that it must be, first and fundamentally, a science of metabiology. **1936** *Scrutiny* Mar. 377 And Keats's genius..is not really illuminated by the procedure of *Keats und Shakespeare* or, except as another of Metabiology's cloudy trophies, exalted. **1945** K. R. POPPER *Open Society* I. v. 72 Plato's idealist historicism ultimately rests..upon a kind of meta-biology of the race of men. **1962** A. HUXLEY *Let.* 1 Mar. (1969) 929 He would radiate a kind of religious enthusiasm—about Dostoevsky and his ideas, about 'metabiology', about Lawrence as 'The Son of Man', the 20th-century Messiah. **1968** *New Scientist* 21 Nov. 415/2 They will be searching for a new integral approach to biology, in which organisms will be described *as a whole*, rather than simply in the terms of the molecules from which the organisms are constructed... Monod offered to these members of a future biological avant-garde the term 'meta-biology'.

So **me:tabiolo·gical** *a.*

1921 G. B. SHAW (*title*) Back to Methuselah: a metabiological pentateuch. **1935** *Theology* XXX. 89 The metabiological reality which Mr. Murry would substitute for Deity. **1960** C. S. LEWIS *Four Loves* v. 125 A theory [of the love of lovers] more likely to be accepted in our own day is what we may call Shavian—Shaw himself might have said 'metabiological'—Romanticism. According to Shavian Romanticism the voice of Eros is the voice of the *élan vital* or Life Force. **1967** *Listener* 3 Aug. 141/2 Belonging to this period was the spirited exchange of letters between Bernard Shaw, Julian Huxley and others which lasted from the beginning of November 1942 to well into March 1943—referred to in the office as the metabiological marathon.

metabiosis (metăbəiōu·sis). *Biol.* [f. META- + Gr. βίωσις mode of life, but formed as back-formation from the adj.] A type of symbiosis in which one of the organisms modifies the environment before the second is able to live in it. So **metabio·tic** *a.* [ad. G. *metabiotisch* (C. Garré 1887, in *Correspondenz-Blatt für Schweizer Aerzte* 1 July 390).]

1899 *Knowledge* July 151/2 It [*sc.* the yeast organism] is dependent upon its predecessor for its particular action—that is to say, we have here a condition of metabiosis. *Ibid.* 152/1 This implies nothing more or less than metabiotic relationships between the different kinds of the bacteria concerned. **1966** F. H. MEYER in S. M. Henry *Symbiosis* I. iv. 172 The nitrite bacteria are dependent on ammonia-producing organisms, while the nitrate bacteria are again dependent on the activity of the nitrite bacteria. For such direct living 'one after another', Garré gave [*sic*] the name metabiosis.

metabolic, *a.* Add: **5.** *Biol.* Of unicellular organisms, exhibiting metaboly.

1906 M. HARTOG in *Cambr. Nat. Hist.* I. v. 125 Such movements, permissible by the perfectly flexible but firm pellicle, are termed 'metabolic' or 'euglenoid'. **1926** G. N. CALKINS *Biol. Protozoa* vi. 254 In all cases of amoeboid and metabolic forms the cell symmetry is variable. **1955** *New Biol.* XIX. 116 Change in shape in unicellular organisms is referred to by the somewhat confusing term 'metaboly' and organisms which exhibit it are termed 'metabolic'.

Hence **metabo·lically** *adv.*, in, or as regards, metabolism.

1913 *Jrnl. Amer. Med. Assoc.* 18 Oct. 1465/1 The total metabolically active tissues of the body. **1928** *Biochem. Jrnl.* XXII. 1049 Patients, suffering from various complaints, though presumed to be metabolically sound. **1964** *Oceanogr. & Marine Biol.* II. 178 This classification is important metabolically. **1967** [see *GUANASE].

metabolism. 1. (Further examples.) Add to def.: The rate at which the body functions over all; the sum of the chemical changes undergone in the body by any particular substance.

1951 A. GROLLMAN *Pharmacol. & Therapeutics* iii. 77 Metabolism of alcohol..proceeded at about the same rate irrespective of whether the subjective was at rest or engaged in muscular activity. **1962** A. PIRIE (*title*) Lens metabolism in relation to cataract. **1966** WRIGHT & SYMMERS *Systemic Path.* II. xxxi. 1098/1 Thyroid hormone stimulates metabolism, increases oxygen consumption, and causes a rise in heat production. **1968** PASSMORE & ROBSON *Compan. Med. Studies* I. xxxi. 1/1 The liver holds a key place in the metabolism of the body. **1969**

J. H. GREEN *Basic Clin. Physiol.* xvii. 96/1 If the thyroid gland is underactive (hypothyroidism),..there will be a reduction in the body's metabolism. **1971** B. N. LA DU et al. (*title*) Fundamentals of drug metabolism and drug disposition. **1972** *Internat. Jrnl. Biochem.* III. 294 (*heading*) An anti-anabolic role of adenosine 3′, 5′-cyclic monophosphate in the control of liver metabolism.

metabolite. Substitute for def.: **a.** Any substance formed from another by metabolism. **b.** A substance necessary to metabolism or to a particular metabolic process. (Further examples.)

1923 *Jrnl. Physiol.* LVII. 248 The increased combustion of sugar is immediately followed by the physiological oxidation of the accumulated fatty acid metabolites. **1946** P. H. MITCHELL *Textbk. Biochem.* xii. 322 The modern view of typical cases of biological oxidation is that enzymes catalyze the transfer of H_2 from a fuel food (the metabolite) to another substance. **1951** M. ABERCROMBIE et al. *Dict. Biol.* 159 Most metabolites are made by the organism in the course of metabolism; others must be taken in from the environment... Autotrophic organisms need to take in only inorganic metabolites, e.g. water, carbon dioxide, nitrates... Heterotrophic organisms need ..a wide range of organic metabolites from the environment. **1965** LEE & KNOWLES *Animal Hormones* iv. 76 Progesterone appears to be an intermediary metabolite in the formation of adrenal cortical hormones. **1967** [see *FUSIDIC *a.*]. **1967** M. E. HALE *Biol. Lichens* iv. 58 Nitrogen is an essential metabolite for synthesizing proteins in both the alga and fungus. **1970** G. R. TAYLOR *Doomsday Bk.* vi. 130 In the body..DDT tends to convert into similar substances known as DDE and DDD, the three being known..as 'DDT and its metabolites'.

metabolizable (metæ·bŏləizăb'l), *a.* [f. META-BOLIZ(E *v.* + -ABLE.] Capable of being metabolized: applied to (*a*) substances that can be utilized by the body, and (*b*) energy that can be made available or produced by metabolic processes.

1905 *Bull. Bureau Animal Industry, U.S. Dept. Agric.* No. 74. 7 The metabolizable, available and utilizable energy of the hay. **1957** G. E. HUTCHINSON *Treat. Limnol.* I. ix. 617 Metabolizable material derived from the mud. **1961** *Ann. Rev. Physiol.* XXIII. 17 The metabolizable energy supplied by a feed. **1968** *New Scientist* 28 Nov. 496/1 They have investigated the possibility of obtaining metabolizable sugars from sawdust on a commercial basis.

Hence **meta:bolizabi·lity,** capability of being metabolized.

1929 MITCHELL & HAMILTON *Biochem. Amino Acids* vii. 360 The experiments..demonstrate the ready metabolizability of histidine, as compared..with..imidazole lactic acid. **1949** *Jrnl. Agric. Res.* LXXVIII. 487 The digestibility and metabolizability of two rations by sheep are reported.

metabolize, *v.* Add: **2.** *intr.* To perform metabolism.

1934 in WEBSTER. **1943** *Bacteriol. Rev.* VII. 139 The animal tissue cell is formed and metabolizes in an environment which is stabilized within narrow limits compared with the wide range of..conditions to which bacteria are subjected. **1971** *Sci. Amer.* Dec. 36/3 The anoxybiotic species does not stop metabolizing as soon as it encounters anaerobic conditions; it continues to metabolize for as long as six days, even though the new metabolic end product is unusual and potentially harmful.

†**metabolon** (mĕtæ·bŏlǫn). *Physics. Obs.* [ad. Gr. μεταβόλον, neut. of μεταβόλος changeable, f. μεταβάλλειν to change.] A radioactive atom produced in the process of radioactive disintegration.

1903 RUTHERFORD & SODDY in *Phil. Mag.* V. 586 At each stage [of disintegration] one or more α 'rays' are projected, until the last stages are reached, when the β 'ray' or electron is expelled. It seems advisable to possess a special name for these now numerous atom-fragments, or new atoms, which result from the original atom after the ray has been expelled, and which remain in existence only a limited time... We would..suggest the term *metabolon* for this purpose. **1904** E. RUTHERFORD *Radio-Activity* x. 324 The various metabolons from the radio-elements are distinguished from ordinary matter by their great instability and consequently rapid rate of change.

metaboly (metæ·bŏli). Substitute for entry: *Biol.* [ad. G. *metabolie* (M. Perty *Zur Kenntnis kleinster Lebensformen* (1852) 127), f. Gr. μεταβολή change.] The changes of shape characteristic of certain unicellular organisms; euglenoid movement.

1926 G. N. CALKINS *Biol. Protozoa* vi. 254 Metaboly may still be observed. **1969** F. E. ROUND *Introd. Lower Plants* ii. 13 A characteristic of *Euglena* is the spirally striate pellicle which is pliable and allows the cell to assume a variety of shapes—metaboly—an unfortunate term.

metacentric, *a.* Add: **2.** *Cytology.* [*-CENTRIC 2.] Of a chromosome: having the centromere in or near the centre.

1939 C. D. DARLINGTON in *Jrnl. Genetics* XXXVII. 357 Two sister chromatids would become the concurrent arms of a new metacentric chromosome. **1945, 1946** [see *ACROCENTRIC *a.*]. **1962** *Lancet* 2 June 1158/1 The 46 chromosomes..in the cultured cells of the blood of their patient included an unpaired metacentric chromosome. **1970** *Nature* 5 Dec. 938/2 Somatic mouse cells have forty acrocentric and telocentric and no metacentric chromosomes.

Hence as *sb.*, a metacentric chromosome.

1945 M. J. D. WHITE *Animal Cytol. & Evolution* iv. 56 Whether such a metacentric could pass through an indefinite number of mitoses without being frequently disrupted is open to doubt. **1961** *Lancet* 26 Aug. 463/2 The usual human Y..is normally about the same length as the smallest metacentric..or very slightly longer. **1971** *Nature* 15 Oct. 481/2 The karyotype presented as typical by Kao and Puck was interpreted by them as having three hamster telocentrics replaced by two human metacentrics.

metachromasia (metăkrōᵘmē̆ⁱ·ziă). *Biol.* Also in anglicized form **metachromasy** (-krōᵘ·măsi). [mod.L., f. META- + Gr. χρῶμα, χρώματ- colour: see -IA¹.] The property exhibited by certain biological materials and structures of staining a different colour from that of the stain used; also, the corresponding property of certain stains of changing colour in the presence of certain biological materials and structures.

1903 *Lancet* 18 July 177/1 The cells which contain granules contain also a store of ferment (zymogen), whilst the cells that are destitute of granules exhibit the reaction of mucin (metachromasy). **1956** *Nature* 3 Mar. 428/1 Anaphylactic shock brought out..degranulation and decrease of the metachromasia of the remaining granules in most of the cells. **1960** L. PICKEN *Organization cf Cells* x. 481 The amoebae..are found to become metachromatic.. in increasing numbers as aggregation approaches... The appearance of metachromasy seems, however, to precede sensitivity to acrasin. **1964** W. G. SMITH *Allergy & Tissue Metabolism* iii. 33 Both tissue and blood mast cells are characterised by a coarse granular cytoplasm possessing a strong affinity for basic dyes, some of which change colour (exhibit metachromasia) as staining occurs. **1967** *New Scientist* 2 Feb. 275/2 These fragments are then encapsulated by a high polymer (producing the green metachromasia) and enter some kind of 'spore' stage. **1971** E. GURR *Synthetic Dyes* I. ii. 63 The significance of the dimer spectra in terms of theories of metachromasy is discussed.

metachromatic, *a.* Add: **2.** *Biol.* Exhibiting or involving metachromasia.

1897 MUIR & RITCHIE *Man. Bacteriol.* i. 11 It is..very probable that the occurrence of metachromatic granules in a bacterium indicates the onset of degenerative changes. **1902** *Jrnl. R. Microsc. Soc.* 89 (*heading*) Metachromatic granules in sporiferous bacteria. **1925** C. H. BROWNING *Bacteriol.* ii. 29 Sometimes with methylene-blue these beads stain of a different tint from the rest of the bacillus (metachromatic staining). **1957** *New Biol.* XXIV. 52 Structures which change the colour of the stain in this way are said to be metachromatic. **1964** W. G. SMITH *Allergy & Tissue Metabolism* iii. 36 Metachromatic staining of the faded granules began.

Hence **metachroma·tically** *adv.*

1908 *Anatomical Rec.* II. 106 Sections from such material stained in toluidene blue show the mucous secretion metachromatically stained, but no metachromatism is visible in the demilune cells. **1957** *New Biol.* XXIV. 54 Polysaccharides of high molecular weight other than heparin stain metachromatically. **1971** *Nature* 24 Sept. 264/2 The lipid mass was stained metachromatically pale orange-brown with cresyl violet..and thionin.

metachromatism. Add: **b.** *Biol.* = *METACHROMASIA.

1893 *Jrnl. R. Microsc. Soc.* 563 (*heading*) Metachromatism of parasitic sporozoa and carcinoma cells. **1904** [in Dict.]. **1908** [see *METACHROMATICALLY *adv.*]. **1917** C. E. MARSHALL *Microbiol.* (ed. 2) ii. 43 These bodies..are stained violet-red by most of the basic dyes, aniline blue or violet... By reason of this property of metachromatism, they have been called metachromatic granules.

metachrome. Add: **B.** *adj. Dye Chem.* Designating mordant dyes and their mordants that may be applied simultaneously in the same bath, and the method of dyeing by this process.

1901 *Jrnl. Soc. Dyers & Colourists* XVII. 66/1 Metachrome Brown B Paste: This colour is the first of a new series of (metachrome) dyes which have the property of dyeing in the single bath with metallic salts. *Ibid.*, With less than 3 per cent. dyestuff, 3 per cent. metachrome mordant must be used, but with larger amounts of dyestuff an equal amount. **1927** HORSFALL & LAWRIE *Dyeing Textile Fibres* ix. 263 The meta-chrome process as originally introduced..was confined to a comparatively small number of dyestuffs derived from picramic acid. **1963** A. J. HALL *Textile Sci.* iv. 184 The third (metachrome) method enables both dye and bichromate to be applied at the same time and it depends on the fact that no appreciable combination occurs between the bichromate and the wool or the dye under alkaline conditions, but this holds only for a limited number of dyes. **1971** R. L. M. ALLEN *Colour Chem.* iv. 45 In 1900 the Berlin Aniline Company devised the metachrome method whereby selected dyes can be applied simultaneously with a chroming agent.

metachronism. Add: **2.** *Biol.* The coordination of the movement of parts, esp. cilia, into a progressive wave.

1905 *Jrnl. Exper. Zool.* II. 408 It is the principal object of this paper to discuss the cause of metachronism in ciliary action. **1928** J. GRAY *Ciliary Movement* vii. 117 Any particular cilium is slightly in advance of the cilium behind it in the series and slightly behind the one just in front of it. This regular sequence is known as metachronism. **1972** M. S. GARDINER *Biol. Invertebr.* IV. xi. 189/1 In Metazoa, the cilia on adjacent cells may exhibit a similar coordination in metachronism.

So **metachro·nal** *a.*, exhibiting or characteristic of metachronism (sense *2); **metachro·nally** *adv.*

1905 *Jrnl. Exper. Zool.* II. 407 The cause of metachronal action is..to be sought..in the mechanical effect of one cilium on another. *Ibid.*, These swimming plates are arranged in rows and the members of each row, like ordinary cilia, beat metachronally, not synchronally. **1928** J. GRAY *Ciliary Movement* vii. 118 Although the direction of the metachronal wave..differs in different tissues, it is remarkably constant in each particular case. **1940** G. S. CARTER *Gen. Zool. Invertebr.* viii. 359 Metachronal rhythm is not confined to metazoan cilia; it can be well seen in such ciliate protistans as *Opalina*. **1962** D. NICHOLS *Echinoderms* viii. 99 In at least one urchin, *Diadema*, the spines show metachronal rhythm during locomotion, and they move the animal across the ocean floor with considerable speed. **1971** *Nature* 12 Feb. 491/1 The cilia of these last two cell types beat metachronally.

metacommunica·tion. [META- 1.] Communication that takes place with, or underlies, a more obvious form of communication; principles or theories about communication derived from the study of communication. Hence **metacommunica·tional, metacommu·nicative** *adjs.*

1951 RUESCH & BATESON *Communication* vi. 152 He is, also,..making implicit metacommunicative statements about his own position and stock of information. *Ibid.* vii. 203 (*heading*) Communication between two persons and metacommunication. **1963** T. A. SEBEOK in J. A. Fishman *Readings Sociol. of Lang.* (1968) 28 The metacommunicative messages used by rhesus monkeys, enabling them to distinguish between play and nonplay, have received particularly careful attention. **1967** J. A. MEERLOO in L. Thayer *Communication* 54 We cannot, of course, recover man's contemplations about himself from fossil remains, and data from living nonliterate men are lamentably deficient in metacommunicational material. **1967** P. WATZLAWICK et al. *Pragmatics Human Communication* i. 40 When we no longer use communication to communicate but to communicate *about* communication, as we inevitably must in communication research, then we use conceptualizations that are not part of but *about* communication. In analogy to metamathematics this is called metacommunication. **1974** *Publishers Weekly* 29 Apr. 47/3 The author is one of the students of 'metacommunications' or body language—Gregory Bateson and Raymond Birdwhistell are the two best-known names in this field, though their work derives from anthropologists such as Lorenz.

metacone (me·tăkōᵘn). *Zool.* [f. META- + CONE *sb.*¹] An external cusp on the outer back corner of a mammalian upper molar tooth. Hence **metaco·nal** *a.*

1888 H. F. OSBORN in *Amer. Naturalist* XXII. 1072 Proposed terms... Metacone. **1896** *Proc. Zool. Soc.* 570 The dental germ presenting the appearance of a high cone with a large posterior heel (metaconal region) and a slight internal extension. *Ibid.*, The posterior extension representing the metacone. **1933** A. S. ROMER *Vertebr. Paleont.* xii. 248 Inside the metacone [there is often] a smaller one [*sc.* cusp], the metaconule. **1971** P. HERSHKOVITZ in A. A. Dahlberg *Dental Morphol. & Evolution* viii. 103 In the first molar of *Potamogale*, the first indication of the metacone is a wedgelike indentation. *Ibid.* 129 In cercopithecoids, crista V is transverse and meets the buccal and metaconal portion of the plagiocrista.

metaconid (metăkōᵘ·nid). *Zool.* [f. *METACON(E + *-ID⁵.] A cusp on a mammalian lower molar tooth corresponding to the metacone on an upper molar.

1888 H. F. OSBORN in *Amer. Naturalist* XXII. 1073 Only the paracone and metaconids and hypoconids [of *Amphitherium*] have been observed heretofore. **1904** *Ann. & Mag. Nat. Hist.* XIII. 409 The antero-internal cusp not or scarcely divided into its constituent paraconid and metaconid. **1919** [see *HYPOCONID]. **1933** A. S. ROMER *Vertebr. Paleont.* xii. 248 The lower teeth tend also to square up..so that the four definitive cusps are the protoconid, metaconid, entoconid, and hypoconid. **1968** R. ZANGERL tr. *Peyer's Compar. Odontol.* 186 In the lower jaw..paraconid and metaconid are lingual. **1975** *Nature* 31 July 402/2 Paraconid and metaconid were clearly separated at their bases on the medial face of the tooth.

metacontrast (metăkǫ·ntrast). *Psychol.* [ad. G. *metakontrast* (R. Stigler 1910, in *Arch. f. ges. Physiol.* CXXXIV. 386), f. Gr. μετα- META- + *kontrast* CONTRAST *sb.*] A change, esp. a diminution, in the after-effect of a visual stimulus as a result of a second stimulus following shortly afterwards.

1950 *Jrnl. Optical Soc. Amer.* XL. 796/1 An investigation of the effect of variation of the luminance, exposure asynchrony, and spatial separation of the stimuli on the magnitude of metacontrast. **1971** *Jrnl. Gen. Psychol.* LXXXIV. 86 Masking and metacontrast studies do, however, demonstrate that a second stimulus may impair the perception of the first stimulus. **1972** *Science* 13 Oct. 179/3 They suggest that temporally backward and spatially lateral inhibition (metacontrast) occurs when the duration of the flash is long enough.

metaconule (metăkōᵘ·niul). *Zool.* [f. *METACON(E + *-ule.*] An intermediate cusp between the hypocone and the metacone of a mammalian upper molar tooth.

1888 H. F. Osborn in *Amer. Naturalist* XXII. 1074 The Bunodont series are universally characterized by the initial or advanced development of the proto- and metaconules in the upper molars. **1905** *Amer. Geologist* XXXV. 244 The intermediate cusps (protoconule and metaconule) are both well-defined. **1968** R. Zangerl tr. *Peyer's Compar. Odontol.* 187 Intermediate cusps occurred.., a metaconule between protocone and metacone. **1971** W. D. Turnbull in A. A. Dahlberg *Dental Morphol. & Evolution* ix. 163 (*caption*) Specimen consists of the protocone and metaconules.

metacryst (me·tăkrist). *Petrol.* [f. Meta- + *-cryst* after Phenocryst.] A large crystal formed in a metamorphic rock by recrystallization.

1913 W. Lindgren *Mineral Deposits* xi. 158 An individual in another may be briefly called a metasome; if the metasome develops strongly with crystal outlines it may be called a metacryst. **1932** F. F. Grout *Petrogr. & Petrol.* 365 Metacrysts commonly have abundant inclusions..and in some the inclusions are oriented so as to show that the metacrysts grew by replacement. **1963** D. W. & E. E. Humphries tr. *Termier's Erosion & Sedimentation* xvii. 339 Dolomite is present in limestones as rhombic 'metacrysts' which can cut across original structures (for example, oolites) and fossils.

metadyne (me·tădəin). *Electr.* [ad. F. *métadyne* (J. M. Pestarini 1930, in *Rev. gén. de l'Électr.* XXVII. 355/1), f. Meta- + Gr. δύναμις power.] A rotary direct-current generator in which the output voltage can be varied by a small signal applied to a control field perpendicular to the main field and which is used in position- or speed-control systems.

1930 *Sci. Abstr.* B. XXXIII. 376 The 'Métadyne' is a direct-current machine having more than two brush axes per pole-pair. **1945** [see *Amplidyne]. **1951** F. J. Teago in P. Kemp *Electr. Engin.* III. 89/1 One of the chief reasons for using metadyne control is that the alternating current may be kept constant. **1970** J. Shepherd et al. *Higher Electr. Engin.* (ed. 2) xiv. 496 Metadyne generators are uncompensated or undercompensated cross-field generators.

metagalaxy (metăgæ·lăksi). *Astr.* [f. Meta- 1 + Galaxy *sb.*] The entire system of galaxies (see quot. 1930); also, a cluster or group of galaxies. So **metagala·ctic** *a.*

1930 H. Shapley *Flights from Chaos* xiii. 141 Corresponding to individual stars, multiples, and star clusters we have galaxies, multiple galaxies, and clusters of galaxies... To designate the system including all of these I propose to use Lundmark's term, the Metagalactic system—or, more briefly, the Metagalaxy. **1951** *Astron. Jrnl.* Apr. 47/2 (*heading*) Differential rotation of the inner metagalaxy. **1957** H. Shapley *Inner Metagalaxy* p. v, The terms 'Metagalaxy' and 'metagalactic' refer to the total recognized assemblage of galaxies. The Metagalaxy includes also whatever there may be in the way of gas, particles, planets, stars, and star clusters in the spaces between the galaxies. It is essentially the measurable material universe. **1965** *Rev. Mod. Physics* XXXVII. 654/1 In principle there may be several condensations of the initial plasma so that there may be other metagalactic systems in the universe. *Ibid.* 663/2 According to Klein there may be other metagalaxies in the universe. **1965** J. D. North *Measure of Universe* ii. 20 His prediction of a high collision rate between the nebulae of a single metagalaxy. *Ibid.* App. 408 The galaxies assigned to the Local Group increased in number and the 'local metagalaxy' took its place with the other known clusters. **1970** *Nature* 12 Dec. 1069/1 According to this scheme, an initial contraction of the metagalaxy (containing equal amounts of matter and antimatter) resulting from its self-gravitation was turned into an expansion by the pressure of radiation produced by annihilation reactions. *Ibid.*, Although the gravitational and radiation fields in this case are metagalactic, the scale of the matter–antimatter separation is determined by the magnetic field and is likely to be much more local.

metagenesis. 1. For 'generation' read 'generations' in both cases.

metageometry. Add: Also **me:tageometri·cian** = Metageometer.

1903 *Science* 16 Jan. 106/2 Our metageometricians tried to derive the basic geometrical principles from pure reason but failed.

metagnomy (metæ·gnŏmi). *Psychics.* [ad. F. *métagnomie* (Boirac, 1917), f. Meta- + Gr. γνώμη thought.] The acquisition of information by supernormal means; divination. So **me·tagnome,** one who has the power of metagnomy; a medium; **metagno·mic** *a.*, of or pertaining to metagnomy.

1919 W. de Kerlor tr. *Boirac's Psychol. of Future* xi. 232 Clairvoyance, or 'metagnomy'. *Ibid.* 256 It is especially in the somnambulistic state, natural or provoked, that metagnomic manifestations occur. *Ibid.* 257 The mesmerist or hypnotist..evokes the metagnomic faculty. **1933** T. Besterman tr. *Driesch's Psychical Res.* I. i. 2 The subject of the investigation, the sensitive, the medium, the metagnome, or whatever one likes to call him. **1960** *New Scientist* 28 July 306/2 Prosopopesis, metagnomy, telergy and teleplasty: if these are accepted, what remains of the 'laws' of physics, chemistry, biology and psychology? **1965** *Listener* 29 Apr. 639/3 With the existence of such phenomena as telepathy, metagnomy, precognition, etc., now well established,..there is surely a possibility that some astrologers may be psychically gifted individuals.

metagon (me·tăgǫn). *Biol.* [f. Meta- + Gr. γόν-ος offspring.] (See quot. 1968.)

1962 Gibson & Beale in *Genetical Res.* III. 25 As a provisional hypothesis..we proposed that the cytoplasm of mate-killer paramecia contained, in addition to the visible mu particles, certain other factors, here denoted 'metagons', which are assumed to be formed only in the presence of one or other of the genes M_1 and M_2. **1964** *New Scientist* 6 Aug. 322/2 Particles of RNA called 'metagons'. **1968** R. Rieger *Gloss. Genetics & Cytogenetics* 285 *Metagon*, presumably, a primary, gene-initiated product in *Paramecium* which is RNA (complementary to the DNA of a specific gene) in nature, conditionally stable, infectious (capable of transmission from one *Paramecium* to another through the cytoplasm and the external medium), and capable of replication under certain conditions.

metake (me·take). [Japanese.] A tall slender Japanese bamboo, *Pseudosasa* (or *Arundinaria*) *japonica.*

1896 A. B. Freeman-Mitford *Bamboo Garden* 69 *Arundinaria japonica* or Métaké... The word Métaké, or, more correctly, Médaké, means in Japanese 'female Bamboo', but there is no scientific reason for using the word 'female' in connection with this species. *Ibid.* 72 The Japanese gardeners consider Ya-daké and Mé-také to be two different plants. **1966** F. A. McClure *Bamboos* 293 *Pseudosasa japonica* (*Arundinaria japonica*; *Sasa japonica*). Metake; Yadake; arrow bamboo. **1971** *Country Life* 18 Nov. 1371/1 The common Metake, *Arundinaria* or *Pseudosasa japonica*..[is] a particularly fine species [of bamboo] with slender canes quite 10 ft. high and glossy green leaves that are glaucous beneath.

metakinesis (metăkəinī·sis). Now *rare.* Pl. **-kineses.** [mod.L., f. Meta- + Gr. κίνησις motion.] **1.** *Cytology.* [coined (in Ger.) by W. Flemming in *Zellsubstanz, Kern und Zelltheilung* (1882) xx. 268.] **a.** (See quot. 1968.)

1888 [see *homœotypical* adj. (*homœo-)]. **1899** *Jrnl. R. Microsc. Soc.* Apr. 168 Karyokinesis in the Root-tips of Allium... Anaphase. (5) After the longitudinal segmentation of the chromosomes, which, as a general rule, does not begin until the chromosomes are in the equatorial plane, the daughter chromosomes are gradually pulled apart... This stage is known as metakinesis. **1903** *Bot. Gaz.* XXXV. 251 Heuser ('84) seems to have been the first to call attention to the double character of the daughter chromosomes in the diaster stage of *Tradescantia virginica*, but he interpreted the separation of the daughter segments during metakinesis of the first mitosis as a transverse division. **1968** R. Rieger *Gloss. Genetics & Cytogenetics* 286 *Metakinesis*, the separation of the two chromatids of each chromosome and their movement to opposite spindle poles during anaphase of mitosis.

b. [given this sense by F. Wassermann 1926, in *Zeitschr. f. Anat. u. Entwicklungsges.* LXXX. 399.] (See quot. 1968.)

1948 W. Andrew tr. *E. D. P. de Robertis's Gen. Cytol.* viii. 182 The prometaphase generally begins with the disintegration of the nuclear membrane... When the nuclear membrane has disintegrated, a more fluid zone is noted in the center of the cell in which the chromosomes..begin to be displaced in apparent disorder toward the equator. This mechanism of equatorial arrangement was called metakinesis (Wassermann). **1968** R. Rieger *Gloss. Genetics & Cytogenetics* 286 *Metakinesis*,..chromosome congression to the spindle equator.

2. A manifestation of consciousness or mental phenomena.

1890 C. L. Morgan *Animal Life* xii. 467 We call manifestations of energy 'kinetic' manifestations, and we use the term 'kinesis' for physical manifestations of this order. Similarly, we may call concomitant manifestations of the mental or conscious order 'metakinetic', and may use the term 'metakinesis' for all manifestations belonging to this phenomenal order. *Ibid.* 488 When, in man, the metakineses associated with these neural kineses assume the form of hypotheses, theories, interpretations of nature, moral ideals, and religious conceptions, these are..no longer subject to the law of natural selection. **1892** K. Pearson *Gram. Sci.* ix. 401 This metakinesis does not appear to be more than a metaphysical name for nonconscious life, for there is no sense-impression that we have of such life that we can describe as metakinetic. **1903** L. F. Ward *Pure Sociol.* 156 Morgan's metakinetic energy is therefore the same as my conative energy or form of causation, and the difference between kinesis and metakinesis is the difference between motion produced by physical or ordinary efficient causes and motion produced by psychic or conative causes.

Hence **metakine·tic** *a.*

1890, etc. [see 2 above]. **1925** *Glasgow Herald* 11 July 4 Who can be sure that there is not a psychical or metakinetic side to the mountain and the precious stone, the waterfall and the great sea?

metal, *sb.* Add: **11.** (Earlier and later examples.)

1782 in *Sc. Nat. Dict.* (1965) VI. 259/3 The mettle for the road is not to be got but at the south end of the road. **1815** T. Telford *Life T. Telford* (1838) 483 The metal to be of the best blue or red whin. *c* **1906** P. C. Cowan *Making & Maintenance Roads* 17 The old macadam surface was first carefully levelled up and solidly rolled with any necessary amount of new metal. **1970** *N.Z. Listener* 21 Sept. 14/3 The lush pastures gave way to upland scrub country; the road metal became pumice and then clay merely.

13. b. *metal-detector*; *metal-clattering, -cutting, -using* adjs. **c.** *metal-bushed, -clad, -faced, -lustred, -rimmed, -studded* adjs. **d.** similative, as *metal-blue, -cold* adjs.

1930 Blunden *Poems* 309 The metal-blue cucumber slices. **1883** *Man. Seamanship for Boys' Training Ships R. Navy* (Admiralty) (1886) 14 *Spindle*..passes through a metal bushed hole in the partners, up through the centre of the barrel. **1926** *Gloss. Terms Electr. Engin.* (*B.S.I.*) 87 *Metal-clad*, a qualifying term applied to apparatus to denote that the conducting parts are entirely enclosed in a metal casing. **1931** *Flight* 22 May 461/1 So gradually..the general theory of the metalclad airship was mathematically and experimentally proved. **1956** *Proc. Inst. Electr. Engin.* CIII. A. 82/1 When closing a metalclad switch I have observed..sparks jumping from one metal part to another. **1932** D. Gascoyne *Roman Balcony* 12 A metal-clattering cavalcade Advanced Across the beach. **1918** D. H. Lawrence *New Poems* 47 Is it all nought? Cold, metal-cold? **1934** Webster, Metal-cutting *adj.* **1961** *Times* 29 Dec. 12/4 Metalcutting machines. **1971** B. St. J. Wilkes *Nautical Archaeol.* vi. 120 Metal detectors are sold quite extensively in the US and Canada to amateur 'prospectors' to aid their hunt for gold. **1975** *Guardian* 1 Oct. 2/1 Chicago police will be using hand-held metal detectors on all crowds who come near President Ford. **1934** *Archit. Rev.* LXXV. 34/1 There are various metal-faced papers on the market. **1967** *Jane's Surface Skimmer Systems 1967–68* 60/2 The float table's conveying surface is of metal-faced plywood construction. **1862** G. M. Hopkins *Vision of Mermaids* (1929), Others small braids enclustered Of glassy-clear Aeolis, metal-lustred With growths of myriad feelers. **1932** C. Isherwood *Memorial* i. iii. 36 Eric's tall bony figure, with his metal-rimmed glasses and the odd pauses in his speech. **1909** *Q. Rev.* Jan. 148 Motor-cars,..having armoured or metal-studded tires damage the surface. **1928** C. Dawson *Age of Gods* iii. 50 What we term the neolithic age in Europe was really the first stage in the diffusion of the higher metal-using culture of the Near East. **1964** T. L. Kinsey *Audio-Typing & Electr. Typewriters* vii. 77 A large proportion of the remainder are at work in the engineering and other metal-using industries.

14. metal age *Archæol.*, the period or stage of development in the human race in which copper and bronze were used for making weapons and tools; **metal arc welding,** arc welding in which the melting of a metal electrode provides the joining material; **metal fatigue,** fatigue (sense 1 b, in Dict. and Suppl.) of metal; **metal Mike** *Naut. colloq.* (see quot. 1961); **metal rectifier** *Electr.*, a rectifier in which rectification takes place at the junction of a metal and another solid substance (such as copper oxide or selenium); **metal thread, yarn** = *metallic thread, yarn* (*metallic *a.* 1 f); **metal-to-metal** *a.*, used of a contact or connection; **metal-works,** a factory where metal is produced.

1927 Peake & Fleure *Hunters & Artists* vii. 112 The dawn of the Metal Age. **1951** *Proc. Prehist. Soc.* XVII. 1 The beginnings of a Metal Age in the Middle East are known to go back before the earliest written documents. **1963** H. N. Savory in Foster & Alcock *Culture & Environment* iii. 33 We can no longer think of a Secondary Neolithic element in south Wales as something introduced only a short while before the dawn of the Metal Age. **1926** *Jrnl. Iron & Steel Inst.* CXIV. 611 Metal arc welding can also be used for this purpose. **1952** Fuchs & Bradley *Welding Pract.* II. v. 107 One of the characteristic features of metal arc welding..is the highly localised intensity of heat input. **1968** J. Giachino et al. *Welding Technol.* iv. 70 Gas metal-arc welding was considered a high current density, small diameter filler wire process. **1954** *This Week's Listening* 30 Dec. 18 *No Highway* is about metal fatigue, which one of the characters describes as 'a disease of the metal'. **1958** *Economist* 11 Oct. 169/2 The Comet should, by rights, have been in service on the North Atlantic four years ago: the lapse of time is a measure of the work needed to stiffen its skin against metal fatigue that sent two of the original Comets in quick succession to the bottom of the Mediterranean. **1973** P. Dickinson *Green Gene* ix. 180 It's like metal fatigue. You stand the stresses OK for years, so you think you'll stand them for ever. Then you snap, under no load at all. **1929** *Yachting* June 41/2 While in the act of setting 'Metal Mike' on the new course, we sighted a small ship's boat a point on the starboard bow. **1961** F. H. Burgess *Dict. Sailing* 145 *Metal Mike*, the 'automatic helmsman'. **1927** *Wireless World* 30 Nov. 733/1 (*heading*) Battery charging rectifier incorporating the new dry 'metal' rectifier. **1971** B. Scharf *Engin. & its Lang.* xx. 276 Three important types of rectifier are diode rectifiers, mercury arc rectifiers and metal rectifiers. **1959** *Times* 28 Apr. 20/6 A Chinese silk and metal-thread carpet. **1967** E. Short *Embroidery & Fabric Collage* ii. 49 Gold and silver threads couched by hand, or synthetic metal threads (Lurex) used on the machine. **1906** Metal-to-metal [see *leather-faced* adj. s.v. *leather *sb.* 5 c]. **1910** *Daily Chron.* 2 Feb. 5/1 The surface where the wheel had been on the axle showing a bright metal-to-metal contact. **1922** *Encycl. Brit.* XXX. 36/2 The head of steel being secured to the liner with a plain metal-to-metal joint by bolts from the head to the crank-case. **1971** *Flying* Apr. 5/1 Aluminium honeycomb panel construction and metal-to-metal bonding. **1908** *Westm. Gaz.* 3 Oct. 10/1 On the hours of work in foundries and metal-works generally the Committee felt itself still imperfectly informed. **1913** J. M. Matthews *Textile Fibres* (ed. 3) i. 12 Bayko metal yarn is a textile product recently introduced.

metalanguage (metălæ·ŋgwėdʒ). [See Meta- 1, *1 b.] A language which supplies terms for the analysis of an 'object' language; a system of propositions about other propositions.

[**1935** A. Tarski in *Studia Philosophica* I. 282 Die Namen der Ausdrücke der ersten Sprache und der zwischen ihnen bestehenden Relationen gehören schon zu

der zweiten Sprache, der sog. Metasprache (welche übrigens die Grundsprache als Fragment enthalten kann).] **1936** *Mind* XLV. 486 The concepts *analytic* and *contradictory* in the language *L*, for instance, cannot be defined in *L*, as Carnap has shown. In order to escape from these restrictions one must build up a new language (a so-called *meta-language*) disposing of more means of expressing thoughts than the former. **1947** H. REICHENBACH *Elem. Symbolic Logic* i. 9 We say that signs of signs constitute a language of a higher level, which we call *metalanguage*. **1948** L. HJELMSLEV in *Studia Linguistica* I. 75 This would mean, in logistic terms, that linguistics is a metalanguage of the first degree, whereas phonetics and semantics are metalanguages of the second degree. **1954** A. J. AYER *Philos. Ess.* 12 Particulars, considered as occasions, would be referred to only at the level of the meta-language; when it was a question not of using the language, but of talking about its use. **1959** *Listener* 1 Oct. 520/1 We can then avoid the clumsy term 'meta-language'—the name for the language in which we talk about the terms of any formalized language. **1960** E. DELAVENAY *Introd. Machine Transl.* vii. 110 Between metalanguage and pure poetry, from the clear and distinct expression of a scientific representation to the synthetic expression of the vibrations of the poet's ego at the centre of his individual universe, there exists a whole vast range of untranslatables. **1962** *Times Lit. Suppl.* 13 Apr. 252/5 Machine translation research may be of value..in that, because one of its basic techniques is the establishment of a metalanguage or intermediate language of ideas, it is in principle capable of constructing automatically an abstract. **1964** C. CHERRY in *Endeavour* Jan. 13/2 A meta-language is a formal language-system for describing language or a linguistic source. Strictly, a book of grammar is written in a meta-language—it defines a syntax but is itself not literature. **1973** *Computers & Humanities* VII. 223 Each segment is analyzed as to content and translated into a 'meta-language', which allows unambiguous comparisons among the variant readings.

Hence **me·ta-me·tala:nguage**, a language used in the description of another language which is itself a meta-language; the universal linguistic or symbolic system from which a particular metalanguage derives.

1954 I. M. COPI *Symbolic Logic* App. B. 341 The first of these is the meta-metalanguage's synonym for the name relation in the metalanguage. **1957** N. CHOMSKY *Syntactic Struct.* vi. 54 Linguistic theory will thus be formulated in a metalanguage to the language in which grammars are written—a metametalanguage to any language for which a grammar is constructed. **1963** H. B. CURRY *Found. Math. Logic* ii. 31 In that case we use a third language, L_3, customarily called the metametalanguage. **1967** *Encycl. Philos.* VII. 352/2 A proof of adequacy..requires an inductive argument of the meta-metalanguage.

metalation (metălē¹·ʃən). *Chem.* [f. METAL *sb.* + -ATION.] The introduction into an organic compound of an atom of a metal in place of one of hydrogen (usu. one attached to an aromatic ring).

1934 GILMAN & YOUNG in *Jrnl. Amer. Chem. Soc.* LVI. 1415/1 The term metalation is proposed for reactions involving replacement of hydrogen by a metal to give a true organometallic compound. *Ibid.*, Metalations were effected by metals, organometallic compounds and salts. **1937** F. C. WHITMORE *Org. Chem.* 724 The aniline sulfate solution contains the strongly positive group —NH_3 and consequently gives *m*-substitution. The 'metalation' of benzine apparently offers an exception to this generalization. **1957** E. G. ROCHOW et al. *Chem. Organometallic Compounds* iii. 54 Metalation reactions occur only with the derivatives of the strongly electropositive alkali and alkaline earth metals and, rarely, magnesium. **1968** R. O. C. NORMAN *Princ. Org. Synthesis* xi. 392 Electrophilic metalations by metal salts should not be confused with the metalation of aromatic compounds with metal.

Hence (as a back-formation) **me·talate** *v. trans.*, to bring about metalation in; **me·talated, me·talating** *ppl. adjs.*

1939 *Jrnl. Amer. Chem. Soc.* LXI. 109/2 Phenyl ether was not metalated by triphenylmethylsodium. **1954** *Organic Reactions* VIII. vi. 260, *n*-Butyllithium metalates thiophene in the 2 position. *Ibid.* 261 The usual metalating agents..yield volatile acids which are easily separated from the acids of higher molecular weight obtained from the metalated products themselves. **1966** *McGraw-Hill Encycl. Sci. & Technol.* IX. 402/2 The most commonly used 'metalating agent'..is *n*-butyllithium in ether solution.

metalaw (me·tălǭ). [f. META- 1 + LAW *sb.*[1]] A hypothetical legal code based on the principles underlying existing legal codes and designed to provide a framework of agreement between diverse legal systems (orig. conceived as between terrestrial and possible extra-terrestrial beings); so **metale·gal** *a.*, of questions, etc.: pertaining to the basic principles underlying legal systems or upon which laws are formulated.

1956 *N.Y. Times* 20 Sept. 12/3 Andrew G. Haley.. sought to codify some general principles of space law or 'metalaw' as he called it, by analogy to metaphysics. **1956** A. G. HALEY (*title*) The present day developments in space law and the beginnings of metalaw. **1957** *Observer* 20 Oct. 14/4 Still more tricky are the laws which should govern our relations with any extra-terrestrial intelligent beings we may meet. Here, something which Mr. Haley [an American lawyer] calls 'Metalaw' must prevail. **1959** BENN & PETERS *Social Princ. & Democratic State* iii. 58 What criteria must a rule satisfy to be a valid law?.. How are legal rules related to particular decisions..? These questions..involve analysis of the formal structure of a legal system, and of the relation between norms of different levels of generality; they might be termed metalegal questions. **1969** *New Scientist* 2 Jan. 36/3 The legal aspects of space—what is now called 'metalaw'—a subject that has an interest of its own. **1971** G. SCHWARZENBERGER *Internat. Law & Order* iv. 29 Alleged rules of international *jus cogens* which are based on no other evidence than postulates of natural law or other metalegal norms must be ignored on the level of *lex lata*.

metaldehyde. Add: (Later examples.) Cf. *META².

1949 *New Biol.* VI. 29 The most usual and one of the most successful methods of killing large numbers is to put out heaps of bran mixed with metaldehyde—the bran attracts the slugs which feed on the mixture, while the metaldehyde causes them to slime so profusely that they remain on the surface of the soil in close proximity to the bait. Here they die partly as the result of the metaldehyde acting as a stomach poison and partly owing to desiccation. **1963** *Which?* Mar. 88/2 A comparatively 'safe' poison is metaldehyde, now the most generally used for killing slugs. **1974** *Country Life* 24 Oct. 1228/1 Work at the Terrington EHF has compared metaldehyde and methiocarb [slug] pellet baits.

metalimnion (metăli·mniǫn). Pl. **-limnia.** [f. META- + Gr. λιμνίον, dim. of λίμνη lake.] The layer of water in a stratified lake which lies beneath the epilimnion and above the hypolimnion and in which the temperature decreases rapidly with depth. So **metalimne·tic** *a.* [cf. Gr. λιμνήτης living in marshes], of or within the metalimnion.

1935 P. S. WELCH *Limnol.* II. iv. 54 The term *thermocline* was first used by Birge in 1897... Since then, the terms *transition zone, mesolimnion*, and *metalimnion* have been proposed. **1957** G. E. HUTCHINSON *Treat. Limnol.* I. vii. 428 It is convenient to define the widely used term *metalimnion* to designate the whole of the region in which the temperature gradient is steep. *Ibid.* 464 In general, the smaller lakes..showed very striking metalimnia at depths of between 3 and 10 m. **1957** Metalimnetic [see *EPILIMNION]. **1960** *Limnology & Oceanogr.* V. 216 (*heading*) The cause of a metalimnetic minimum of dissolved oxygen. **1974** *Nature* 8 Feb. 393/2 During the summer, in the metalimnion of Lake Kinneret, the photosynthetic, green sulphur bacterium, *Chlorobium phaeobacteroides* can reach concentrations as high as 10^7 cells ml^{-1}.

metalingual (metăli·ŋgwăl), *a.* [f. META- + LINGUAL *a.*] = *METALINGUISTIC *a.*

1950 *Mind* LIX. 490 Due..to the common confusion of words and things its metalingual character has been overlooked. **1961** *Word* XVII. ii. 128 To these R. Jakobson has recently added three more functions—the poetic, phatic and metalingual. **1964** E. A. NIDA *Toward Sci. Transl.* iii. 45 In this volume the words *metalanguage* and *metalingual* refer to that part of language which is used in speaking about language itself, namely, the terms designating all the various features of language and the way these are used in describing and talking about languages.

metalinguistic (metăliŋgwi·stik), *a.* and *sb.* [f. META- + LINGUISTIC *a.* (cf. *METALANGUAGE).] **A.** *adj.* Of or pertaining to a metalanguage, or to metalinguistics (see B). **B.** *sb. pl.* Trager's term for that branch of linguistics which is concerned with the relation of language to the other elements of a culture (see also quot. 1974). Hence **metali·nguist** *sb.*, **metalingui·stically** *adv.*

1944 *Mind* LIII. 26 It cannot occur at the zero-level (it is a metalinguistic statement). **1944** H. REICHENBACH in P. A. Schilpp *Philos. B. Russell* 53 The use of a metalinguistic vocabulary is not a sufficient criterion for a more advanced state of logical analysis. **1949** G. L. TRAGER in *Studies in Ling.: Occasional Papers* I. 7 The full statement of the..relations between the language and any of the other cultural systems will contain all the 'meanings' of the linguistic forms, and will constitute the metalinguistics of that culture. **1951** TRAGER & SMITH *Outl. Eng. Struct.* 83 The metalinguist can turn it [*sc.* a datum] into a conclusion by clearly identifying out the microlinguistic characteristics of the speech. **1951** *Language* XXVII. III. 212 The discussion of linguistic research techniques is not a linguistics as we have known it, but rather a metalinguistics. **1952** R. M. HARE *Lang. Morals* I. iii. 38 A metalinguistic analysis is tempting. *Ibid.*, Some hypothetical imperatives might be analysed metalinguistically. **1953** C. E. BAZELL *Ling. Form* viii. 98 The study of microcriteria, whether phonetic or semantic, belongs to metalinguistics. **1966** J. J. KATZ *Philos. of Lang.* v. 222 S is metalinguistically true if, and only if, the semantically interpreted underlying phrase marker for its constituent sentence satisfies the condition in the reading for its metalinguistic predicate. **1967** C. L. WRENN *Word & Symbol* 4 The rather programmatic 'science' of metalinguistics recognises the need to study language and culture in intimate relationship. **1972** G. H. FISHER *Public Diplomacy* v. 119 This aspect of comparative linguistics is in its infancy. Anthropologists and linguistic scientists.. call it 'metalinguistics'. **1974** *Encycl. Brit. Micropædia* VI. 827/3 Some linguists use the term metalinguistics in reference to the study of metalanguages, languages or codes used to discuss or describe other languages.

metalled, *ppl. a.* **2.** (Earlier and later examples.)

1825 J. C. LOUDON *Encycl. Agric.* 511 In a road from a highway to a farmery, it may often be advisable to place the metalled road in the middle. **1955** *Times* 25 June 7/6 They live in this far-away valley at the end of a good metalled road that accompanied by power and telephone lines winds over the pass from Malakand. **1969** *Jane's Freight Containers 1968–69* 139/2 It has its own drinking water system, sewage, drains, metalled roads and mains.

metallic, *a.* and *sb.* Add: **A.** *adj.* **1. e.** *metallic circuit* (Telegr.), a circuit composed entirely of metal conductors, as opposed to one in which the return path of the current is through the earth; similarly *metallic return.*

1854 W. F. COOKE *Electr. Telegr.* 25 If, from the copper at one end, a piece of wire, or metallic circuit is carried.. round to the zinc..a current of electricity immediately passes through the wire. **1928** A. WILLIAMS *Telegr. & Telephony* ix. 131 The first telephone companies had a hard fight to interest the public in their services, and to keep down costs—which would have been nearly doubled by a metallic return—only one wire was used for each subscriber. *Ibid.*, The result was that lines with earth-return lines had to be converted into metallic circuits.

f. *metallic thread, yarn*: thread made from metal, or a synthetic material resembling metal.

1904 J. M. MATTHEWS *Textile Fibres* i. 4 Metallic threads are largely imitated by coating linen yarns with a thin film of gold or silver. **1963** A. J. HALL *Textile Sci.* ii. 105 Metallic yarns are made by various methods which include bonding metal. **1968** J. IRONSIDE *Fashion Alphabet* 211 Today, aluminium or plastic has been substituted for the rather heavy metals and 'metallic' yarns are now light, soft and non-tarnishing.

g. *metallic soap*: any of a class of soaps that are salts of carboxylic acids with an alkaline-earth metal or a heavy metal (instead of with an alkali metal as in ordinary soap) and are soluble in organic solvents but not in water, some of which are used in waterproofing materials, finishing textiles, and making anti-oxidants, lubricants, and fungicides.

1918 H. SEYMOUR *Reproduction of Sound* ii. 44 The metallic soaps so long in use [for the moulding and shaping of disc record blanks] have been superseded on the score of efficiency..but the [new] substance is more difficult to handle than the metallic soaps. **1940** A. WOOD *Acoustics* xviii. 504 The recording wax is a circular slab..which is composed of a metallic soap and has a highly polished plane surface. **1952** R. A. PINGREE in H. C. Speel *Textile Chem. & Auxiliaries* xx. 404 Air permeable water-resistant treatments were first obtained by depositing a metallic soap in and upon the fibers of the fabric. **1971** *Materials & Technol.* IV. ii. 70 Metallic soaps of long chain fatty acids will gell lubricating oil fractions and the properties of the grease will be governed mainly by the metallic radical.

h. *metallic arc welding* = *metal arc welding* s.v. *METAL *sb.* 14.

1927 *Jrnl. Iron & Steel Inst.* CXV. 909 The welding processes considered by the author are thermit welding, resistance welding..and metallic arc welding. **1948** F. KOENIGSBERGER in H. W. Baker *Mod. Workshop Technol.* I. ix. 181 Metallic-arc welding is the arc-welding process most frequently used in general engineering.

3. a. (Further examples.)

1936 *Discovery* Dec. 367/2 The marvellous, metallic blue *Morphos* are eminently characteristic of Tropical America. **1968** *Motor* 21 Dec. 66/3 (Advt.), Lotus Elan.. metallic blue with matching interior. **1975** G. V. HIGGINS *City on Hill* xi. 233 A metallic blue Opel.

c. Also, of the taste of tea made in a metal tea-pot.

1909 *Chambers's Jrnl.* Nov. 693/1 The objection to metal is simply that there is a danger of giving the tea what is known as a 'metallic' taste.

metallically, *adv.* Add: **1.** (Later examples.)

1909 *Physical Rev.* XXVIII. 159 The clamp *K* containing the molybdenite is metallically connected with the binding post *H*. **1913** V. B. LEWES *Oil Fuel* vi. 173 A second platinum rod also passes through the cover, being metallically connected with it.

4. In the manner of a metal or metals.

1944 *Physical Rev.* LXVI. 326/1 There are some substances such as the aniline dyes and $KMnO_4$ which reflect metallically in narrow wave-length regions.

metallization. (Further examples, corresponding to *METALLIZE *v.* 1 b.)

1876 *Chem. News* 7 July 9/2 (*heading*) Metallisation of organic bodies to render them fit to receive galvanic deposits. **1934** *Archit. Rev.* LXXV. 33/3 Metal surfaces may now be obtained by a new process called metallization, which enables any dry non-greasy surface to be sprayed with metal. **1952** J. DELMONTE *Plastics Molding* xiv. 430 In vacuum metallization, the art has been successfully developed for coating molded plastic parts. **1967** *Electronics* 6 Mar. 25 Litton engineers haven't decided whether to use a single or two-layer metalization to interconnect the circuits within the wafers.

metallize, *v.* Add: Also **metalize. 1.** (Later example.)

1912 G. B. BARHAM *Devel. Incandescent Electr. Lamp* iv. 37 When the untreated carbon filament, used as a base, is metallized, its weight is reduced by about 8 per cent.

b. To coat or cover with metal.

1911 *Engin. & Mining Jrnl.* XCI. 532/1 It [*sc.* the process] mainly consists of throwing finely distributed liquid metal..against the surface to be metallized. **1929** *Daily News* 16 Jan., Doors, window sashes, wainscotings, panel boards and panelling can be artistically metalized with one metal or another. **1952** J. DELMONTE *Plastics Molding* xiv. 431 Another technique of metallizing plastic parts..

is the chemical deposition of a silver film upon a carefully cleaned plastic surface. **1973** M. I. KOHAN *Nylon Plastics* xvii. 585 Small nylon parts can often be vacuum metallized without predrying.

metallized *ppl. a.* (further examples); also **me·tallizer,** (*a*) a machine or plant for metallizing; (*b*) a person or organization involved in metallizing; **me·tallizing** *vbl. sb.*

1905 J. C. HOWELL in *Electrician* 28 July 590/1 On account of the positive-resistance curve and physical characteristics of these filaments, they have been given the name 'metallised filaments'. **1911** *Engin. & Mining Jrnl.* XCI. 532/1 The metallizing process invented by M. U. Schoop, of Zurich, is..different from any process so far known. **1912** G. B. BARHAM *Devel. Incandescent Electr. Lamp* iv. 37 It is said that the intense temperature of the metallizing process changes the composition of the carbon filament by removal of the ash residue and by the volatilization of the hydrocarbon contained in the filament. **1952** J. DELMONTE *Plastics Molding* xiv. 429 The metallizing of plastics parts has become a popular procedure for some molded parts. **1955** *Sci. News Let.* 21 May 336/3 Game includes five metalized, full-color replicas of regulation traffic signs. **1969** W. R. R. PARK *Plastics Film Technol.* viii. 195 As the applications for metallized film continued to grow, more sophisticated continuous metallizers have been evolved. **1969** R. F. LANG tr. *Henglein's Chem. Technol.* 807 Metallizing of fabrics increases their value. **1973** M. I. KOHAN *Nylon Plastics* xvii. 585 The composition of these lacquers is proprietary with metallizers. **1974** *Sci. Amer.* Mar. 112/2 A simple measurement of the focal length can be made by standing the mirror on edge, directing a flashlight toward the metallized surface [etc.].

metallo-. Add: **meta·lloenzyme** *Biochem.*, an enzyme which is a metalloprotein; **me:tallogene·tic** *a.*, of or pertaining to metallogeny; hence **me:tallogene·tically** *adv.*; **metalloge·nic** *a.*, (*a*) (of an element) occurring in ores or as the native metal, rather than in rocks; (*b*) = **metallogenetic* adj.; **metallo·geny** *Geol.* [ad. F. *métallogénie* (L. de Launay *Sci. Géol.* (1905) ix. 263): see -GENY], (the study of) the origin of mineral deposits, esp. as related to petrographic and tectonic features; **me:tallo-orga·nic** *a. Chem.* = *organometallic* adj. s.v. ORGANO-; also (*rare*) **me:tal(l)orga·nic** *a.*; **metallophone,** (*b*) (later examples); **meta·lloprotein** *Biochem.* (see quot. 1964).

1955 *Adv. Protein Chem.* X. 321 The metalloenzyme can be isolated from its matrix, retaining all of its metal complement in the 'natural' state. **1971** WISEMAN & GOULD *Enzymes* iii. 43 It is mainly this involvement in metalloenzymes and metal-activated enzymes which is responsible for the requirement for these metal ions..in the food of animals. **1972** *Nature* 15 Dec. 417/1 Nitrogenase is a metalloenzyme containing iron and molybdenum both of which are essential for catalytic activity. **1909** *Cent. Dict.* Suppl., Metallogenetic province. **1910** *Q. Jrnl. Geol. Soc.* LXVI. 281 His [*sc.* de Launay's] object is to delineate the various regional types of ores.., the regional types being termed 'metallogenetic provinces'. **1965** G. J. WILLIAMS *Econ. Geol. N.Z.* vi. 61/2 The interplay of opinion reflecting metallogenetic fashions current from time to time. **1926** *Mineral. Abstr.* III. 133 Igneous activity was subordinate in Palaeozoic times, but very extensive and of much significance metallogenetically during the late Mesozoic in both Japan and Korea. **1920** H. S. WASHINGTON in *Jrnl. Franklin Inst.* CXC. 782 It may be as well to suggest here, and to use henceforward, two terms... We may call the 'rock elements' petrogenic and the 'ore elements' metallogenic. **1959** *Nature* 28 Nov. 1693/1 During the past few decades the problem of construction of metallogenic maps of various countries..has been discussed. **1974** *Encycl. Brit. Micropædia* VI. 828/2 Among the excellent examples of metallogenic provinces in North America are the gold province on the Canadian Shield [etc.]. **1905** *Nature* 13 Apr. 576/1 On the possible *rôle* of slipping in metallogeny. **1908** O. C. WILLIAMS tr. *L. de Launay's World's Gold* p. xiv, Those who..are interested in the manner of the concentration of metals in the earth or in what I call their 'Metallogeny'. **1959** *Nature* 28 Nov. 1693/1 Valuable contributions to the metallogeny of various ores were recently made by N. S. Shatsky. **1971** *Mineralium Deposita* VI. 404/1 This note is only intended to link some past ideas of the authors with what may emerge in the future as a key model of metallogeny. **1886** E. F. SMITH tr. *V. von Richter's Chem. Carbon Compounds* 141 Most of the metallo-organic compounds can be prepared by the direct action of the metals or their sodium amalgams upon the bromides and iodides of the alkyls. **1946** *Nature* 30 Nov. 791/1 This suggests that some of the polyvalent metal in soil exists as an insoluble metallo-organic complex with some of the organic matter. **1974** *Sci. Amer.* Oct. 75 (*caption*) Metallo-organic complexes, such as titanium diisopropoxide [Ti(OR)$_2$], also fix nitrogen under ambient conditions. **1961** K. P. WACHSMANN in A. Baines *Mus. Instruments* i. 31 Whereas the metallophones can be dated—the saron to not much before A.D. 900 and the gender to not later than A.D. 1157—the ancestry of the xylophone is quite obscure. **1961** P. KEMP *Alms for Oblivion* vi. 102 A *gamelan* of musicians invited by Le Mayeur to play us Balinese music... There were metallophones with polished bronze keys of different pitch. **1969** *Listener* 10 July 58/1 One has read a lot about the exotic Balinese gamelan orchestra with its myriad metallophones. **1972** *Where* Sept. 252/2, I was..unprepared, and unfortunately quite inequipped, for the spate of song books now also coping for xylophones, chime bars, guitars, tuned percussion, autoharps, Indian bells, metallophones, wood blocks, glockenspiels and maracas. **1940** *Biochem. Jrnl.* XXXIV. 1163 The metallo-protein compounds present in the red blood corpuscles. **1964** *Ann. Rev. Biochem.* XXXIII. 331 The term metalloprotein is used to designate those types of metal-protein complexes in which the strength of the binding is so great that a metal atom can be considered an integral part of the structure of the protein. **1971** *Nature* 10 Sept. 136/2 The ferredoxins are members of a class of metalloproteins known as iron–sulphur proteins. **1890** WEBSTER, *Metalorganic*... Written also *metallorganic*. **1965** *Polymer Rev.* VIII. p. v, The Editors invited Professor Andrianov to write a monograph on his pioneering work on metalorganic polymers—or 'elemento-organic polymers', as they are called in the Soviet Union. **1974** *Nature* 27 Sept. 307/1 The surfaces were covered with a monolayer of metallorganic soap.

metallographer. (Earlier and later examples.)

1902 *Jrnl. Iron & Steel Inst.* LX. 242 Samples cut from ..test bars have already been..microscopically examined by an eminent metallographer. **1961** *Evening Standard* 17 July 14/5 Metallographer required..for examination of ferrous and non-ferrous materials. **1966** D. G. BRANDON *Mod. Techniques Metallogr.* 3 The successful metallographer combines an understanding of the effects of specimen preparation with a knowledge of the optics of image formation.

metallographical (metălǫgræ·fikăl), *a.* [f. METALLOGRAPHIC *a.* + -AL.] = METALLOGRAPHIC *a.*

1902 *Jrnl. Iron & Steel Inst.* LX. 242 No regard has been paid to the chemical or purely metallographical alterations..connected with the process of heating or annealing any iron material with subsequent slow or sudden cooling. **1950** *Engineering* 10 Nov. 341/2 However carefully determined the mechanical and metallographical factors might be [etc.].

Hence **me:tallogra·phically** *adv.*, by metallographic methods.

1936 L. R. VAN WERT *Introd. Physical Metallurgy* ii. 23 Crystallographers distinguish six distinct crystal types. Only three of these are of any interest metallographically. **1967** A. H. COTTRELL *Introd. Metall.* xx. 373 Determining the extent of the isothermal transformation metallographically. **1969** J. A. SCOTT in A. F. Madayag *Metal Fatigue* iii. 92 Microscopic examination of a metallographically prepared sample is the usual method of inspection for inclusions.

metalloid, *sb.* **b.** Add to def.: Also (now the usual sense), an element intermediate in its properties between a typical metal and a typical non-metal. (Further examples.)

Cf. quot. 1836 in Dict. (given corrected and more fully below).

1836 W. T. BRANDE *Man. Chem.* (ed. 4) v. 318 And then, adverting particularly to the unmetallic substances, he [*sc.* Berzelius] subdivides them into three classes, namely, — 1. Permanently elastic or gaseous bodies (Gazolyta)... 2ndly. Metalloids: sulphur, phosphorus, carbon, boron, and silicon. 3rdly. Salifying substances (Halogenia). **1876** *Encycl. Brit.* V. 476/1 The non-metallic elements are also sometimes termed metalloids, but this appellation.. strictly belongs to certain elements which do not possess the properties of the true metals although they more closely resemble them than the non-metals in many respects. **1894** G. S. NEWTH *Text-bk. Inorg. Chem.* I. ii. 8 The element arsenic possesses many of the physical properties of a metal, but in its chemical relations it is more allied to the non-metals; such elements as these are often distinguished by the name *metalloids.* **1959** *Nomencl. Inorg. Chem.* (I.U.P.A.C.) 10 The word metalloid should not be used to denote non-metals. **1959** B. CHALMERS *Physical Metall.* ii. 72 In these structures, the anion is a 'metalloid', such as sulfur, selenium, tellurium, tin, or antimony, and the cation is a transitional metal, such as chromium, nickel, iron, etc. **1964** E. G. ROCHOW *Organometallic Chem.* (1965) ii. 10 There also are some elements which look like metals but are brittle and have the electrical properties of semiconductors; these are commonly called the metalloids.

metallurgic, *a.* (Earlier example.)

1778 J. C. LETTSOM *Hist. Orig. Med.* vi. 98 Metallurgic chemistry was one of the most remote inventions.

metallurgically (metălə̄·ɹdʒikăli), *adv.* [f. METALLURGIC, -ICAL *adjs.*: see -ICALLY.] From a metallurgical point of view; as regards metallurgy.

1890 in *Cent. Dict.* **1911** F. W. HARBORD in Harbord & Hall *Metall. Steel* (ed. 4) I. viii. 199 What is to all intents and purposes metallurgically the Bertrand–Thiel process is at work in the Hoesch Works in Germany. **1968** *Physics Bull.* Dec. 411/2 A metallurgically good type II superconductor shows electrical resistance in the vortex state.

metallurgist. Add: Now commonly with main stress on the second syllable (mĭtæ·lɒɹdʒist).

metallurgy. Also with pronunc. (mĭtæ·lɒɹdʒi). Add to def.: Now understood as including the scientific study of the structure, properties, and behaviour of metals. (Further examples.)

1914 W. ROSENHAIN *Introd. Study Physical Metall.* i. 1 The scope of Physical Metallurgy..brings it well over the border-land of several sister-sciences—such as chemistry .., physics.., and that branch of knowledge generally known as 'strength of materials'. **1948** R. H. HARRINGTON *Mod. Metall. Alloys* p. ix, The House of Metallurgy has, today, many rooms filled with stacks of measured data concerning heat treatments, physical properties, microstructures, and crystal lattice measurements. **1950** *Sci. News* XV. 138 Modern metallurgy borders also on physics and chemistry, mining and mineral dressing, applied mechanics and physical chemistry. **1967** A. H. COTTRELL *Introd. Metall.* i. 1 Metallurgy is now a disciplined applied science based on a clear understanding of the structures and properties of metals and alloys.

metally, *a.* **1.** Delete † *Obs.* and add later *poet.* example.

1898 G. MEREDITH *Empty Purse* in *Poems* II. 202, I can hear a faint crow Of the cock..As down the new shafting of mines, A cry of the metally gnome.

metalogic. Add: (Further examples.) See also quots. 1936, 1937.

1902 R. R. MARETT in H. Sturt *Personal Idealism* v. 232 The no-man's-land of dogmatic 'Metalogic'. **1936** *Mind* XLV. 482 If a contradiction appears at the end of a chain of inferences one at least of two cases must be realised according to a very evident theorem of metalogic: (1) either there is a fallacy in the chain..or (2) the premises are contradictory. *Ibid.* 485 Lukasiewicz, the great Polish logician, has generalised that idea by introducing what he calls *metalogic*, which has to ordinary logic the same relation as metamathematics to mathematics. **1937** A. SMEATON tr. *Carnap's Logical Syntax of Lang.* 9 The Warsaw logicians..have spoken of..*metalogic*... The word 'metalogic' is a suitable designation for the subdomain of syntax which deals with logical sentences in the narrower sense. **1955** A. N. PRIOR *Formal Logic* 64 The consideration of these deductions from outside may be called 'metalogic', and that is in fact the name now commonly applied to it. **1963** R. CARNAP in P. A. Schilpp *Philos. R. Carnap* 54 At that time I defined the term 'metalogic' as the theory of the forms of the expressions of a language. Later I used the term 'syntax' instead.

metalogical, *a.* Add: (Further examples.) Cf. prec.

1951 J. ŁUKASIEWICZ *Aristotle's Syllogistic* 103 The.. metalogical principle of traditional logic: 'utraque si praemissa neget, nil inde sequetur'. **1955** A. N. PRIOR *Formal Logic* 65 'Metalogical' demonstrations ought..to be themselves 'logical' in the sense of being cogent.

Hence **metalo·gically** *adv.*

1946 C. I. LEWIS *Analysis of Knowledge* v. 129 Analytic statements in non-logical terminology, like 'All birds are bipeds', will not be metalogically derivable from its postulates. **1955** A. N. PRIOR *Formal Logic* 132 This rule is metalogically derivable.

metalogi·cian. [f. METALOGIC: see -ICIAN.] One who is versed in metalogic.

1902 R. R. MARETT in H. Sturt *Personal Idealism* v. 237 A condition of existence which even the 'metalogician' finds it difficult to conceive. **1964** *Amer. Philos. Q.* I. 236/2 As used by grammarians, metalogicians, etc., they mention a type.

metalogue (me·talǫg). *rare*$^{-1}$. [f. META-, on model of *prologue* and *epilogue*.] A speech delivered between the acts or scenes of a play.

1956 AUDEN & KALLMAN *Magic Flute* [at end of Act I] 57 Metalogue (To be spoken by the singer taking the role of *Sarastro*.)

metamathematical (me:tămæþĭmæ·tikăl), *a.* [f. as next, after *mathematics, mathematical.*]

a. (In Dict. s.v. META- 1.) *rare.*

b. Of or pertaining to metamathematics.

1926 F. P. RAMSEY in *Mathematical Gaz.* XIII. 188 It is contended that the principles used in the metamathematical proof that the axioms of mathematics do not lead to contradiction, are so obviously true that not even the sceptics can doubt them. **1933** M. BLACK *Nature of Math.* 150 It is extremely probable that a metamathematical proof of the consistency of the whole of pure mathematics is impossible. **1952** S. C. KLEENE *Introd. Metamath.* vi. 140 In either case, the rules of inference must have the character of schemata, i.e. they must employ metamathematical variables, since infinitely many applications have to be provided for. **1971** *Nature* 8 Jan. 104/2 Hilbert's programme for demonstrating the consistency of arithmetic by metamathematical methods resulted in a new outburst of activity which culminated..with Gödel's incompleteness theorem.

Hence **me:tamathema·tically** *adv.*, by means of, or from the point of view of, metamathematics.

1937 *Philos. of Sci.* IV. 329 Gödel has proved metamathematically that there are surely theorems and problems about the natural numbers which cannot be proved or solved by elementary means. **1956** J. H. WOODGER tr. *Tarski's Logic, Semantics, Metamath.* 116 Let us now consider the situation metamathematically. **1967** S. C. KLEENE *Math. Logic* § 39. 214 Ackermann in 1924–5 thought he had proved metamathematically the consistency of N.

metamathematician (me:tămæþĭmăti·ʃăn). [f. next, after *mathematics, mathematician.*] An expert in metamathematics.

1935 *Mind* XLIV. 394 The metamathematician may use mathematical induction for the recursive definition of simple functions. **1952** S. C. KLEENE *Introd. Metamath.* iii. 64 The interpretation motivates the metamathematician in his choice of the particular formal system which he introduces by his definitions.

metamathematics (me:tămæþĭmæ·tiks), *sb. pl.* (const. as *sing.*). [f. META- 1 + MATHEMATICS *sb. pl.*] (In Dict. s.v. META- 1); *spec.*

[after G. *metamathematik* (D. Hilbert 1923, in *Math. Ann.* LXXXVIII. 153)], the field of study concerned with the structure and formal properties of mathematics and similar formal systems.

1890 in *Cent. Dict.* **1926** *Encycl. Brit.* II. 831/1 The science on which Hilbert is now (1926) engaged, which takes for its subject matter the meaningless formulae of mathematics, he calls metamathematics, and believes it to be capable of establishing many important results relating to the multiplicative axiom or axiom of selections, and to the continuum problem. **1940** *Mind* XLIX. 242 The investigation of calculi, in this light, independently of all regard for the 'meaning' of the component complex marks, was christened metamathematics. **1952** S. C. Kleene *Introd. Metamath.* iii. 63 The formal systems which are studied in metamathematics are (usually) so chosen that they serve as models for parts of informal mathematics and logic with which we are already more or less familiar, and from which they arose by formalization. **1956** E. H. Hutten *Lang. Mod. Physics* ii. 35 That we require a meta-mathematics in order to prove the consistency and completeness of mathematics..does not mean that we are confronted with the final break-down of logic and mathematics. **1963** G. T. Kneebone *Math. Logic* 381 Metamathematics began as a study of particular formal systems, and it was initially concerned with questions of consistency and completeness of given sets of axioms. But it now embraces investigations of altogether wider scope, designed to yield fundamental information about entire classes of formal systems of some particular kind. **1966** J. J. Katz *Philos. of Lang.* iii. 27 Metamathematics, as the general theory of the formal structure of the language of mathematics, was closely parallel to Carnap's idea of logical syntax, as the general theory of the formal structure of scientific and factual discourse. No wonder, then, that metamathematics appealed to Carnap as a model for his theory of logical syntax.

meta-metalanguage: see *metalanguage.

metamict (me·tămikt), *a. Min.* [ad. Da. *metamikt* (W. C. Broegger 1893, in *Salmonsens Konversationsleksikon* I. 743/2), f. Gr. μετα- Meta- + μικτ-ός mixed, blended.] Of a mineral: converted into an amorphous state as a result of the radioactive decay of atoms contained in it. Also applied to the state itself.

1927 *Phil. Mag.* IV. 525 Metamict substances like xenotime and thorite have probably been formed under very high pressure. **1950** *Science* 24 Mar. 312/2 For materials which are completely metamict, it would be possible to determine only a minimum age. **1965** G. J. Williams *Econ. Geol. N.Z.* xiii. 203/2 He suggested the red colouration occurs only in pegmatites sufficiently old for the transformation of the radioactive mineral to the metamict state. **1970** *Nature* 11 Apr. 147/2 Quartz is thus a 'metamict' mineral, like zircon.

Hence **me:tamictiza·tion**, the process of becoming, or state of being, metamict; **me·tamictness**, metamict character.

1952 *Amer. Mineralogist* XXXVII. 142 There has been some speculation as to the reasons for variations in degree of metamictness of different samples of the same mineral. *Ibid.* 154 More powerful sources of radiation..might prove useful in the study of metamictization. **1966** *McGraw-Hill Encycl. Sci. & Technol.* VIII. 296a/1 X-ray methods do not permit a close estimate of the degree of metamictness. **1970** *Science* 30 Jan. 617/1 The U and Th contents of baddeleyite are quite low, which explains the high transparency and the lack of metamictization.

metamorphic, *a.* Add: **2.** Also as *sb.* (usu. *pl.*), a metamorphic rock.

1881 King & Rowney *Old Chapter Geol. Rec.* 49 The rocks of the locality are well-bedded metamorphics. **1923** *Univ. of Toronto Studies, Geol. Ser.* xvi. 7 A few blocks of the same granite were observed along with metamorphics like those seen in the till. **1970** *N.Z. Jrnl. Geol. & Geophysics* XIII. 72 Piroutet..regarded all the metamorphics as pre-Cambrian rocks.

metamorphize, *v.* Delete † *Obs.* and add later U.S. example.

1943 W. Stevens *Let.* 29 Mar. (1967) 444 It would not help to change them to something else, any more than it would help to metamorphize this, that or the other (clouds into foam, living blossoms to blossoms without life, heat to a form of heat).

metamorphose, *v.* Add: **1. b.** *intr.* with *into*.

1927 Haldane & Huxley *Animal Biol.* ix. 180 When the tadpole metamorphoses into the frog, some of its tissues start to dedifferentiate.

metamorphosize (metămǭ·ɹfŏsəiz), *v.* [f. Metamorphos(is + -ize.] *trans.* and *intr.* = Metamorphose *v.* Hence **metamo·rphosized** *ppl. a.*

1908 *Dict. Nat. Biogr.* V. 1312/1 Dowsing's acquaintance with 'Lating'..led him to metamorphosise Dr. Billingford into a maid recommending her daughter's soul to the Virgin Mary. **1928** *Observer* 29 Jan. 9/3 It may well be found that Unwin and his biographer between them have metamorphosised the study of economic history in this country. **1969** *Daily Tel.* 4 Aug. 15/1 It [*sc.* Shaw's *As Far as Thought Can Reach*] envisages the world in A.D. 30,000, when children of 17 are hatched from eggs to spend a few years on adolescent pursuits—love, mating, music, the dance—before metamorphosising into Ancients. **1972** *Ibid.* 17 May 12/6 The parable of metamorphosised man is beautifully photographed by Walter Lassally.

metanalysis (metănæ·lisis). *Philol.* [f. Met(a- + Analysis.] Reinterpretation of the division between words or syntactic units: as *adder* < OE. *nædre* by analysis in ME. of *a naddre* as *an addre*. Hence **meta·nalyse** *v. trans.*

1914 O. Jespersen *Mod. Eng. Gram.* II. v. 141, I have ventured to coin the word 'metanalysis' for the phenomenon frequent in all languages that words or word-groups are by a new generation analyzed differently from the analysis of a former age. **1940** —— *Ibid.* V. xix. 308 A good many sentences of this type are double-barrelled and present the possibility of a 'metanalysis', by which 'It is good for a man/not to touch a woman' may come to be apprehended 'It is good/for a man not to touch a woman'. **1957** G. V. Smithers *Kyng Alisaunder* II. 138 *jker* < OE. *nicor* by a process of metanalysis in which an initial consonant is treated as the final consonant of the preceding word, or a final consonant is attracted into the beginning of the next word. **1962** R. Quirk *Use of English* viii. 127 When the French word *crevice*..was introduced into Middle English, its connexion with 'sea food' caused people to *metanalyse* the final syllable as *-fish* ('crayfish'). **1970** B. M. H. Strang *Hist. English* iv. 250 Assimilations account for the /m/ (earlier /n/) in such words as *comfort, noumpire* (later metanalysed as *umpire*). *Ibid.* 268 *For then ones* metanalysed as *for the nonce.* **1972** J. L. Dillard *Black English* iv. 162 *Metanalysis* describes the analysis of words or groups of words into new elements... *a napron* was metanalyzed to *an apron.*

metanoia (metănoi·ă). [Gr. μετάνοια, f. μετανοεῖν to change one's mind, to repent.] Penitence, repentance; reorientation of one's way of life, spiritual conversion.

1873 M. Arnold *Lit. & Dogma* vii. 196 Of 'metanoia', as Jesus used the word, the lamenting one's sins was a small part; the main part was something more active and fruitful, the setting up an immense new inward movement for obtaining the rule of life. And 'metanoia', accordingly, is: *a change of the inner man.* **1881** *Amer. Church Rev.* July 167 What a Metanoia was there, to both Jesus and John! .. And what a Metanoia had come also upon the disciples of John and upon Israel! **1918** *Encycl. Relig. & Ethics* X. 733/2 'Repentance' has an emotional tone; μετάνοια is ethical and intellectual; the former is negative—a turning away from sin; the latter is positive—an enthusiasm for righteousness. **1939** V. A. Demant *Relig. Prospect* ix. 237 If we understand St. Paul's use of the word 'spiritual', not in our misleading sense of 'non-material' but as the nature of a creature turned to God, we see how this *metanoia*, this turning about, brings a restored understanding of the order of human powers and faculties. **1945** A. Huxley *Let.* 10 Apr. (1969) 520 Virgil's *metanoia* was in the nature of a death-bed repentance. **1969** F. de Graeve in J. Kerkhofs *Mod. Mission Dialogue* p. xvi, It must reveal the Church..as the community in which the religious intentionality of all people can blossom into that newness of life that is the real metanoia. **1973** E. Powell *No Easy Answers* xii. 123 To entertain this idea and to be penetrated with it is the change of mind, repentance, *metanoia*, of which the baptist was not the announcer but the forerunner.

metaphone (me·tăfōᵘn). *Phonetics.* (f. Meta- + Phone *sb.*[1]] (See quots.)

1930 H. E. Palmer *Princ. Romanization* ii. 52 Contrasted with *monophones* we have *metaphones*, which we may define as two or more phones which serve jointly as units of meaning within the limits of a given linguistic community. **1934** Yuen-Ren Chao in M. Joos *Readings in Linguistics* (1958) 38/2 A dynamophone is a metaphone which contains two or more phones differing..in quality. **1966** M. Pei *Gloss. Ling. Terminol.* 161 *Metaphone*, a free allophonic variant chosen in preference to another because regarded as more suitable to the type of speech used (*tomahto, eyether*, used in a given situation instead of the more customary pronunciations of *tomato, either*). **1972** Hartmann & Stork *Dict. Lang. & Ling.* 140 *Metaphone*, a free variant of a phoneme, e.g. [ai] or [i:] in *neither*.

metaphony. Add: (Later examples.) Hence **metapho·nic** *a.*

1950 *Trans. Philol. Soc. 1949* 23 The name *apophony* may be retained for the quantitative alternations, and.. the qualitative alternations may be distinguished as *metaphony*. **1953** K. Jackson *Lang. & Hist. Early Brit.* 371, -ạ̄ui- > eu appears to be due to metaphony rather than to palatalisation. **1957** *Archivum Linguisticum* IX. 107 Metaphonic Spanish and Portuguese verbs. **1970** *Ibid.* I. 22 Moreover, in Lena all adjectives of the type *blanco* have three forms: one ending in -u which undergoes metaphony and is used in agreement with masc. nouns. **1973** A. H. Sommerstein *Sound Pattern Anc. Greek* ii. 76 There are three main ablaut rules—Vṛddhi, Vowel Weakening and *e/o* ablaut or metaphony.

metaphorize, *v.* (Earlier and later examples.)

1731 J. Constable *Reflections Accuracy of Style* 100, I wish too, that..the vanity of metaphorizing did not put several upon a greater stretch of thoughts than their wit will bear. **1909** *N.Y. Even. Post* 27 Nov. 5 However agitated or depressed they may be, they must go on metaphorising. **1949** Wellek & Warren *Theory of Lit.* xv. 202 We metaphorize also what we love, what we want to linger over, and contemplate.

metaphyseal, metaphysial: see *metaphysis.

metaphysic, *sb.*[1] **1. a, b.** (Later examples.)

1918 B. Russell in *Monist* XXVIII. 496 In the present lectures, I shall try to set forth..a kind of logical doctrine which seems to..result from the philosophy of mathematics..: a certain kind of logical doctrine, and on the basis of this a certain kind of metaphysic. **1968** J. M. Ziman *Public Knowl.* iii. 38 One further condition may be necessary for consensible knowledge—a common metaphysic. Those who participate in the consensus must already share many beliefs. **1969** *N.Y. Rev. Bks.* 16 Jan. 15/1 The United States, whose metaphysic, according to Lionel Trilling, is always material and practical, has much more closely fulfilled the nineteenth-century Comtean vision of the future. **1972** D. Bell in Cox & Dyson *20th-Cent. Mind* I. vi. 211 On this central point Bosanquet's metaphysic remains impenetrably obscure, sustained by a combination of piety and metaphor.

metaphysical, *a.* Add: **1. b.** Hence *absol.*

1935 E. R. Eddison *Mistress of Mistresses* x. 192 You may have a nose for metaphysicals..but here you cry out upon no trail. I know nothing. Only, I am.

c. Applied to concepts or propositions which, by relying on abstract principles, are not considered verifiable in terms acceptable to some logical positivist or linguistic philosophers. Cf. *metaphysics *sb. pl.* 1 c.

1865 Mill in *Westm. Rev.* XXVII. 344 The mode of thought which M. Comte terms Metaphysical, accounts for phænomena by ascribing them, not to volitions either sublunary or celestial, but to realized abstractions. **1922** tr. *Wittgenstein's Tractatus* 151 *Where in* the world is a metaphysical subject to be noted? **1936** A. J. Ayer *Lang., Truth & Logic* i. 31 We may accordingly define a metaphysical sentence as a sentence which purports to express a genuine proposition, but does, in fact, express neither a tautology nor an empirical hypothesis. **1950** R. Carnap *Logical Found. Probability* ii. 38, I hope that nobody will misinterpret my statement of the objectivity of logical relations as a metaphysical statement of the 'subsistence' of these relations in a Platonic heaven. **1953** G. E. M. Anscombe tr. *Wittgenstein's Philos. Investigations* § 116 What *we* do is to bring words back from their metaphysical to their everyday use.

3. d. *Christian Science.* Applied to that which transcends matter or the physical; *metaphysical healer*, one who heals physical ills through metaphysics; so *metaphysical healing*.

1876 A. B. Alcott *Jrnls.* (1938) 466 A wider acquaintance with idealism in its various phases will be serviceable to these 'Metaphysical Healers' and 'Christian Scientists' as they call their school. **1884** M. B. Eddy in *Christian Sci. Jrnl.* 2 Feb. 2 Metaphysical healing, or Christian Science, is a demand of the times. **1907** 'Mark Twain' *Christian Sci.* i. 70 Mrs. Eddy is president of the Trust's Metaphysical College in Boston, where the student of C. S. healing learns the game by a three weeks' course. **1939** M. Gregory *Psychotherapy* iv. 178 Students, intoxicated with her doctrines, came there for instruction in metaphysical 'obstetrics' and moral science. **1958** T. L. Leishman *Why I am Christian Scientist* viii. 116 Now, as then, signs and wonders are wrought in the metaphysical healing of physical disease. **1972** *Pioneers in Christian Sci.* (Mary Baker Eddy Mus., Longyear Hist. Soc.), Asa Gilbert Eddy..studied with her and began the practice of metaphysical healing.

5. Add to def.: In more recent use, of poetry which expresses emotion within an intellectual context; (further examples); also *ellipt.* as *sb.*, a metaphysical poet. Hence **metaphysica·lity**, the quality of being metaphysical.

1898 G. Saintsbury *Short Hist. Eng. Lit.* vii. ii. 412 Crashaw is perhaps the chief metaphysical, the type of the whole class. **1906** H. J. C. Grierson *First Half 17th Cent.* ix. 374 In Donne's love-poetry there is a real metaphysical strain, while the range of erudition from which he draws his imagery was something altogether new. **1921** G. Saintsbury in *Times Lit. Suppl.* 27 Oct. 698/2 [Dryden] might..so use 'metaphysics' as equivalent to 'second thoughts', things that come *after* the natural first; and, once more, this definition would, I think, fit all the poetry commonly called 'metaphysical'. *Ibid.*, I only hope that in a second edition he will add a few more 'specimens' of the lighter metaphysicality. **1936** *Essays & Stud.* XXI. 137, I use 'metaphysical' not in the Johnsonian sense of 'conceited', but as implying a certain refinement and complexity of thought—a kind of ecstasy of intellectual parturition as we find it in Shakespeare and Donne. **1947** C. Day Lewis *Colloq. Element Eng. Poetry* 21 The poets of the Romantic Movement gave an outlet to new ideas.. beneath the crust of their age, just as the Metaphysicals had done for the new ideas of their time. **1955** R. Graves *Crowning Privilege* ii. 27 Dryden's conversion from metaphysicality was not to the poetic faith of his English predecessors, but to current French theory. **1960** D. Daiches *Crit. Hist. Eng. Lit.* II. xiv. 1114 The insistence that intellect and emotion should work together in poetry and that one should seek to recover the 'unified sensibility' of the metaphysical poets. *Ibid.* 1116 But the poets who began to write in the late 1920's and 1930's saw both Hopkins and Eliot as their masters, as well as the metaphysicals..and the popular singers of the English music hall.

7. in appos. use, as *metaphysical-aesthetical, metaphysical-epistemic* adjs.

1963 *Times Lit. Suppl.* 4 Jan. 4/4 Dr. Kramrisch does not disdain any of the resources of jargon, metaphysical-aesthetical, aesthetical-theosophical. **1971** *Hist. of Sci.* X. 111 A consistent and effective metaphysical-epistemic understanding of science.

metaphysician. Add: (Later examples.)

1936 A. J. Ayer *Lang., Truth & Logic* i. 33 The metaphysician fails to see this [*sc.* 'substance' fallacy] because he is misled by a superficial grammatical feature of his language. **1956** J. O. Urmson *Philos. Analysis* vii. 110 But let us now suppose that the technical statements we are brought up against are the technical statements of metaphysicians. **1958** G. J. Warnock *Eng. Philos. since*

1900 ix. 121 Even if..the conclusion could really be drawn that the metaphysician's employment of language was without significance.

2. One who practises metaphysical healing. Cf. *METAPHYSICAL *a.* 3 d.

1881 M. B. EDDY *Sci. & Health* (ed. 3) iii. 151 Metaphysicians can heal the sick, absent from them: space is no obstacle to mind.

metaphysico-. (Further examples.)

1848 D. G. ROSSETTI *Let.* 20 Aug. (1965) I. 40 Hunt's stanzas..partook of the metaphysico-mysterioso-obscure. **1850** H. L. MANSEL *Lett., Lect. & Rev.* (1873) 12 Another metaphysico-grammatical theory. **1905** *Spectator* Suppl. 28 Jan. 119/1 One of those extremely clever and almost painfully 'up-to-date' metaphysico-theological books which America produces in such abundance. **1930** D. B. W. LEWIS *Stuffed Owl* p. xx, Verse which..crystallises the metaphysico-theologo-cosmologo-nigology to which the best modern thought..inclines. **1936** L. S. STEBBING in Day Lewis & Stebbing *Imagination & Thinking* 15 The truth of this statement is logically independent of any metaphysico-psychologist's *-ism*. **1955** H. B. ACTON *Illusion of Epoch* 3 The criticisms that apply no more to it than they do to other metaphysico-ethical systems.

metaphysics, *sb. pl.* Add: **1. a.** (Later examples.)

1951 G. J. WARNOCK in Edwards & Pap *Mod. Introd. Philos.* (1973) 781, I do not know..how the term 'metaphysics' really ought to be defined. I suspect..that it is useless to try to divide philosophy into compartments. **1959** P. F. STRAWSON *Individuals* viii. 247 If metaphysics is the finding of reasons, good, bad or indifferent, for what we believe on instinct, then this has been metaphysics. **1960** C. C. GILLISPIE *Edge of Objectivity* xi. 496 Comte had to..repudiate not only metaphysics but also ontology. Thus would he deprive science of any and every claim to deal with objective reality or with any truth deeper than consistency or efficacy. **1967** J. W. YOLTON *Metaphysical Analysis* (1968) xi. 189 The typical double level of metaphysics: the level of exposition, which is always external to the system being developed, and the level of participation in the system.

b. (Further examples.) Occas. construed as *sing.*

1859 MILL in *Fraser's Mag.* LIX. 489/2 His [*sc.* Austin's] book on the *Province of Jurisprudence* stepped at once into the very highest authority on what may be termed the metaphysics of law. **1958** W. STARK *Sociol. of Knowl.* I. iv. 197 A metasociology which would be, not a metaphysics, in so far as metaphysics is divorced from the empirical, but a study of man as he appears in all societies. **1964** A. W. GOULDNER in I. L. Horowitz *New Sociol.* 209 This.. is a metaphysics of the underworld, in which conventional society is seen from the standpoint of a group outside of its own respectable structures.

c. Used by some followers of positivist, linguistic, or logical philosophy: concepts of an abstract or speculative nature which are not verifiable by logical or linguistic methods.

1865 MILL in *Westm. Rev.* XXVII. 347 In repudiating metaphysics, M. Comte did not interdict himself from analysing or criticising any of the abstract conceptions of the mind. **1936** A. J. AYER *Lang., Truth & Logic* 30 Philosophy, as a genuine branch of knowledge, must be distinguished from metaphysics. **1937** A. SMEATON tr. *Carnap's Logical Syntax of Lang.* 8 The sentences of metaphysics are pseudo-sentences which on logical analysis are proved to be either empty phrases or phrases which violate the rules of syntax. **1956** J. O. URMSON *Philos. Analysis* vii. 106 The view of Wittgenstein that metaphysics was not merely outdated as the old positivism had it, but was a logically impossible enterprise, being excluded by the essential nature of language. **1957** S. KÖRNER in C. A. Mace *Brit. Philos. in Mid-Cent.* 126 This principle [of verification]..has dominated European thought for at least three centuries..and its acceptance does not mean, therefore, the end of metaphysics as had been believed by some logical positivists. **1966** R. STERNFELD *Frege's Logical Theory* II. iii. 55 Thus, the general problem of existence is simply replaced by arithmetical attribution, plus Frege's philosophic superstructure. And this portion of metaphysics is replaced by arithmetic.

metaphysis. Restrict *rare*$^{-0}$ to sense in Dict. and add: **2.** *Anat.* [after DIAPHYSIS, EPIPHYSIS.] The region either at one or at both ends of a growing long bone which lies between the diaphysis and the epiphysial cartilage and which is the site of advancing ossification.

1913 DORLAND *Med. Dict.* (ed. 7) 560/2 *Metaphysis*, the end of the diaphysis of a long bone where it joins the epiphysis. **1926** *Biochem. Jrnl.* XX. 380 The upper end of the tibia was isolated and slices..containing the epiphyseal cartilage, the metaphysis and a little of the shaft were made. **1947** *Radiology* XLIX. 347/1 In the rat the isotopes that seek bone come down not only in old bone but predominantly in the zone of new bone growth in the metaphysis. **1966** *Lancet* 31 Dec. 1430/1 The proximal metaphysis contained less bone than the distal metaphysis in both control and treated animals.

Hence **metaphyseal, -physial** *adjs.* (metăfi·ziăl, -fisī·ăl), of or pertaining to a metaphysis.

1913 DORLAND *Med. Dict.* (ed. 7) 560/2 *Metaphyseal*, pertaining to a metaphysis. **1931** D. M. GREIG *Clin. Observations Surg. Path. Bone* vii. 190 This slim exostosis has doubtless been one of the earliest manifestations of the metaphysial growth disturbance. **1961** *Lancet* 30 Sept. 744/2 Vertebral osteomyelitis commences in the metaphyseal region of the vertebral body. **1966** *Ibid.* 31 Dec. 1430/1 This appearance resembled the metaphysial sclerosis sometimes seen in vertebræ of patients with secondary hyperparathyroidism.

meta-political, *a.* **1.** Delete † *Obs.* and add later example.

1937 J. M. MURRY *Necessity of Pacifism* ii. 38 The deep-seated social urge towards life becomes necessarily anti-political in its manifestation. Perhaps meta-political would be a better word. It points and thrusts *beyond* politics.

metapsychic (metăsəi·kik), *a.* [ad. F. *métapsychique*; cf. *METAPSYCHICS *sb. pl.*] = next.

1905 *Westm. Gaz.* 25 Feb. 10/3 The new President [*sc.* M. Richet]..suggested the term 'metapsychic sciences' as a substitute for 'modern miracle'. **1923** S. DE BRATH tr. *Richet's 30 Yrs. Psychical Res.* 4 The terms 'supernatural' and 'supernormal' must therefore be rejected along with 'the occult'... I proposed the term Metapsychic.

metapsychical (metăsəi·kikăl), *a.* [f. META- + PSYCHICAL *a.*, after METAPHYSICAL *a.*] That is beyond the sphere of ordinary psychology; pertaining to *METAPSYCHICS.

1905 L. I. FINCH tr. J. Maxwell (*title*) Metapsychical phenomena. **1914** A. L. TEIXEIRA DE MATTOS tr. *Maeterlinck's Unknown Guest* 50 Nevertheless it may be said that these regions quite lately annexed by metapsychical science are as yet hardly explored. **1927** *Glasgow Herald* 19 Apr. 12 The author of this book was the director of the Metapsychical Institute of Paris.

metapsychics (metăsəi·kiks), *sb. pl.* [ad. F. *métapsychique* (C. Richet 1905, in *Proc. Soc. Psychical Research* XIX. 2), f. Pol. *metapsychika* (W. Lutosławski 1902, in *Wykłady Jagiellosńkie* II), after METAPHYSICS *sb. pl.*] A name applied to a science or study of certain phenomena which are 'beyond the scheme of orthodox psychology'. Cf. *PARAPSYCHOLOGY.

1905 O. LODGE in L. I. Finch tr. *Maxwell's Metapsychical Phenomena* p. xi, To emphasise the fact that these occurrences are at present beyond the scheme of orthodox psychology..Professor Richet has suggested that they be styled 'meta-psychical phenomena', and that the nascent branch of science..be called for the present 'Metapsychics'. **1922** B. MIALL tr. *Maeterlinck's Gt. Secret* xi. 249 The recent researches of Dr. W. Crawford which have made a sensation in the world of metapsychics. **1957** *Encycl. Brit.* XXI. 245/1 A group of investigators..are not prepared to accept the explanation in terms of human survival and..therefore dislike the term spiritualism, preferring to employ some noncommittal term such as metapsychics or parapsychology.

Hence **metapsy·chism; metapsy·chist,** a student of metapsychics.

1922 *Glasgow Herald* 27 Oct. 4 Modern spiritualism, under the term Metapsychism, is favourably viewed. **1922** B. MIALL tr. *Maeterlinck's Gt. Secret* xi. 216 Our occultists, who are now assuming the name of metapsychists. **1927** *Brit. Jrnl. Psychical Res.* I. VII. 207 It was said that the English spiritualists did not understand the French metapsychists. **1928** *Daily Express* 27 June 6/4 What a palpitating problem for the psychologists and the metapsychists!

metapsychological (metăsəikolǫ·dʒikăl), *a.* [f. next.] Of or pertaining to metapsychology.

1922 J. STRACHEY tr. *Freud's Group Psychol.* 63 It is much more difficult to give a clear metapsychological representation of the distinction. **1924** W. B. SELBIE *Psychol. Relig.* 295 These questions..cannot be settled on psychological or even on metapsychological grounds. **1944** *Scrutiny* XII. 137 The metapsychological stage for the poet is..an attempt..to achieve some sort of compromise between a desire for ultimate belief..and the many confused modern influences which have moulded his sensibility. **1952** E. WEISS in Alexander & Ross *Dynamic Psychiatry* 61 The history of metapsychological concepts, as they developed in the study of psychoanalysis. **1972** M. SCHUR *Freud: Living & Dying* III. xiv. 375 All these metapsychological explanations can be applied to neurotic anxiety.

metapsychology (metăsəikǫ·lŏdʒi). [f. META- I + PSYCHOLOGY.] A name given to speculative inquiry regarding the ultimate nature of the mind and its functions which cannot be studied experimentally.

1909 in *Cent. Dict.* Suppl. **1914** A. A. BRILL tr. *Freud's Psychopathol. Everyday Life* 309 We venture to explain in this way the myths of paradise and the fall of man, of God, of good and evil, of immortality and the like—that is, to transform *metaphysics* into *meta-psychology*. **1946** J. H. MASSERMAN *Princ. Dynamic Psychiatry* 285/1 *Metapsychology*, a psychological theory that cannot be verified or disproved by observation or reasoning. **1970** *Jrnl. Gen. Psychol.* LXXXIII. 71 Those who like to conceptualize their data from the point of view of psychoanalytic metapsychology. **1970** H. F. ELLENBERGER *Discovery of Unconscious* x. 754 He [*sc.* L. Daudet] also wrote nonfiction about daydreams and human personality, notably on the ego and the Self, and he called his own psychological system a metapsychology.

metapsychosis (metăsəikōᵘ·sis). Pl. **-oses.** *rare.* [f. META- + PSYCHOSIS 2.] The supposed psychic action of one mind upon another.

1885 *Proc. Soc. Psychical Res.* III. 422 It would be a grave retardation of science were it assumed that this strange metapsychosis was a medical curiosity alone. **1902** J. M. BALDWIN *Dict. Philos. & Psychol.* II. 668/2 The term metapsychosis has been suggested to designate mental stata especially of the percipient under telepathic conditions. **1945** C. WILLIAMS *All Hallows' Eve* vii. 112 The terrible metapsychosis gnawed at him.

metarhodopsin (me:tărodǫ·psin). *Biochem.* Also **meta-rhodopsin.** [f. META- + *RHODOPSIN.] Either of two interconvertible intermediates (the orange metarhodopsin I and the yellow metarhodopsin II) that are formed when rhodopsin is bleached by light, being produced from lumirhodopsin and undergoing spontaneous hydrolysis to retinal and opsin.

1950 G. WALD et al. in *Science* 17 Feb. 180/1 If the solution of lumi-rhodopsin is warmed to about −20°C, a further change occurs in darkness. The absorption band shifts another 7–9 mμ toward the blue, with little further change in height or shape... We shall call this second product meta-rhodopsin. **1970** G. S. BRINDLEY *Physiol. Retina* (ed. 2) i. 11 Figure 1.4 shows the effect of pH on the absorption spectrum of metarhodopsin at 3·2°C. Increase of temperature favours the acid form ('metarhodopsin II'). *Ibid.*, It seems that when rhodopsin is bleached by light the alkaline form ('metarhodopsin I') is always formed first, and this passes quickly into the equilibrium mixture appropriate to the pH and temperature. **1975** [see *LUMIRHODOPSIN].

metarule (me·tărūl). [f. META- I + RULE *sb.*] A convention or universal rule in a symbolic system, esp. a linguistic system.

1957 *Encycl. Brit.* XIV. 319/1 The inference schemas which make up the calculus are never confused with the meta-rules for their reduction to one another. **1966** J. R. Ross in Reibel & Schane *Mod. Stud. in English: Readings in Transformational Gram.* (1969) 289, I propose that the following metarule, or convention, be added to the theory of grammar. **1970** *Language* XLVI. 28 Then objective guidelines are needed, meta-rules, to decide on the priority of application. **1972** W. LABOV in Stockwell & Macaulay *Ling. Change & Generative Theory* 160 We can then argue for an alpha-switching meta-rule which reverses the direction of the nasality constraint.

metascience (me·tăsəiĕns). [f. META- I + SCIENCE.] (See quot. 1938.) So **metascienti·fic** *a.*, of or pertaining to metascience; **metascienti·fically** *adv.*

1938 C. W. MORRIS in *Internat. Encycl. Unified Sci.* I. I. 69 We may introduce the term 'metascience' as a synonym for 'the science of science'. **1953** *Brit. Jrnl. Psychol.* XLIV. 52 [Scientific] problems are periodically discarded ..because they are intrusions from 'meta-science' and depend, therefore, upon emotional bias for working solution. **1954** J. G. KEMENY in P. A. Schilpp *Philos. R. Carnap* (1963) 712 Degree of confirmation..is used meta-scientifically, it is applied to theories. **1965** P. CAWS *Philos. of Sci.* iv. 28 The clarification and refinement of concepts..is a metascientific activity. **1971** J. WIATR in R. Klibansky *Contemp. Philos.* IV. 308 Historical materialism, defined as philosophical meta-scientific reflection of the greatest importance for all the social sciences.

metasequoia (metăsĭ·kwoi·ă, -sĭ·koi·ă). [mod. L. (S. Miki 1941, in *Jap. Jrnl. Bot.* XI. 261), f. META- + SEQUOIA.] A deciduous, coniferous tree of the genus so called, belonging to the family Pinaceæ and known only from fossil remains until the single living species, *Metasequoia glyptostroboides*, was discovered in the Szechuan province of China in 1941; also called dawn redwood or water fir. Also *attrib.*

1948 *Science* 6 Feb. 140/2 This living *Metasequoia* is a large tree... It is deciduous, the trees being leafless in the winter months. **1948** *Jrnl. N.Y. Bot. Garden* XLIX. 204 (*caption*) The landlord of the property where the second lot of *Metasequoia* trees was discovered. **1950** *Ecology* XXXI. 262/2 The general region within which lies the home of Metasequoia is a mountainous tableland cut by deep valleys, southeast of the Yangtze River. **1960** *Times* 19 Sept. 5/3 The 'living fossil' tree, *Metasequoia*. **1971** *Country Life* 2 Sept. 553/3 This border has a backing of large shrubs that include bamboos..and is dominated by the metasequoia.

metasomatic, *a.* Add: Hence **metasoma·tically** *adv.*

1921 *Geol. Mag.* LVIII. 553 The great eastern mass of rauhaugite is metasomatically derived from sövite. **1965** *Amer. Mineralogist* L. 1485 Hibschite or hydrogrossular.. has long been known from..metasomatically altered anorthosites and pyroxenites.

metasomatize (metăsōᵘ·mătəiz), *v. Geol.* [f. METASOMAT(ISM + -IZE.] *trans.* To change as a result of metasomatism. So **metaso·matized** *ppl. a.*

1942 *Mineral. Abstr.* VIII. 242 Xenoliths of siltstone or sandstone country-rock are metasomatized to granophyre. **1955** *Mineral. Mag.* XXX. 681 The carbonatite contains abundant fragments of fine-grained phlogopite-rock, which can be shown to represent metasomatized fragments of brecciated gneiss. **1963** Metasomatized [see *JOHANNSENITE].

metastability (metăstăbi·lĭti). [f. next, after *stable, stability*.] The property or state of being metastable.

1901 *Jrnl. Physical Chem.* V. 270 (*heading*) The metastability of the Weston cadmium cell. **1914** W. Rosenhain *Introd. Study Physical Metall.* xiv. 328 The metallic state, in the conditions which prevail at the surface of the earth, is for the majority of metals a state of chemical meta-stability. **1924** *Nature* 13 Dec. 859/2 Atomic theory would suggest that these lines were connected with a faint metastability of certain possible quantum states of the atoms. **1950** *Engineering* 3 Feb. 137/3 This type of undercooling is made possible only by the metastability of iron carbide. **1968** C. G. Kuper *Introd. Theory Superconductivity* i. 4 The latter is a small and very simple device which exploits the metastability of superconducting persistent currents.

metastable (metăstēi·b'l), *a.* [Irreg. f. Meta- + Stable *a.*, as tr. of G. *metastabil* (coined in sense 1 by W. Ostwald, in *Lehrb. d. allgemeinen Chem.* (1893) II. i. 517).] **1.** Of a physical system: persisting (in its existing state) when undisturbed or subject to disturbances smaller than some small or infinitesimal amount, but passing to a more stable state when subject to greater disturbances.

1897 *Jrnl. Chem. Soc.* LXXII. ii. 309 The author gives to the above form of instability, where the change to solid can only be caused by the presence of the solid itself, the name of 'metastabile' [*sic*]. *Ibid.* 777/1 (Index), Equilibrium, metastable and labile. **1899** J. Walker *Introd. Physical Chem.* xi. 101 A supercooled liquid may be kept for a very long time without any solid appearing, but as soon as the smallest particle of the substance in the more stable solid phase is introduced, the less stable, or, as it has been called, the metastable phase is transformed into it. **1940** Glasstone *Text-bk. Physical Chem.* vi. 459 The term metastable is used to describe a definite equilibrium, which is nevertheless not the most stable equilibrium at the given temperature; a metastable system undergoes spontaneous change on the addition of the stable phase. **1941** J. H. Keenan *Thermodynamics* xxiii. 404 A system is in a state of metastable equilibrium if for all infinitesimal possible variations $\Delta S)_E < 0$, that is, $\Delta E)_S > 0$, while for some finite possible variations $\Delta S)_E > 0$, that is, $\Delta E)_S < 0$. A marble at rest at the bottom of the higher of two depressions in a continuous surface is an example of metastable equilibrium. **1954** *Electronic Engin.* XXVI. 60/1 The 11 points *a, c, e,...t, u* are the stable positions corresponding to the digits 0, 1, 2,... 9 and the reset point [of the counting tube], whereas the 10 points *b, d, f,...* are metastable. Suppose the anode current is at the point corresponding to *b* and a small disturbance shifts the beam to the left... The beam will then move farther away..and soon reach the point corresponding to *c* at which it will remain despite any small disturbances. **1968** C. G. Kuper *Introd. Theory Superconductivity* i. 11 Long-lived metastable states cannot be rejected *a priori* as impossible. Diamond at room temperature shows no tendency to graphitize, nor glass to crystallize. But in all cases like these the excess entropy is frozen in by the *immobility* of the atoms at low temperatures.

2. *Physics.* Of an excited state of an atom, nucleus, or other quantum-mechanical system: having an exceptionally long lifetime because the transitions to states of lower energy are forbidden transitions. [Introduced in this sense (in Ger.) by Franck & Knipping 1919, in *Physik. Zeitschr.* XX. 485/2.]

1922 A. D. Udden tr. *Bohr's Theory of Spectra* iii. 86 These experiments showed that the impact of electrons could bring helium into a 'metastable' state from which the atom cannot return to its normal state by means of a simple transition. **1942** J. D. Stranathan *'Particles' of Mod. Physics* xi. 455 It seems that certain nuclei can exist for considerable time in an excited state, known as a metastable state. **1961** Powell & Crasemann *Quantum Mech.* xii. 458 The ground state of the orthohelium system ..is therefore stable with respect to optical transitions of the usual kind, and has a correspondingly long lifetime. For this reason, it is frequently referred to as a metastable state. **1973** *Sci. Amer.* Feb. 93/2 The singlet and triplet metastable states have long lifetimes because they have no means of radiating their energy.

metastably (metăstēi·bli), *adv.* [f. prec. + -ly[2].] In a metastable state.

1938 A. Johannsen *Descr. Petrogr. Ign. Rocks* IV. 401 Clinopyroxesnes..may form metastably at lower temperatures. **1963** W. A. Deer et al. *Rock-Forming Min.* IV. 181 The higher temperature forms..can exist metastably below their inversion temperatures. **1973** A. D. Edgar *Exper. Petrol.* iii.61 For some compositions it may be necessary to avoid certain very reactive components, e.g. α- cristobalite, which is known to persist metastably well below its equilibrium stability field.

Metastasian (metăstēi·siăn, -ziăn), *a.* [f. the name of Pietro *Metastasio* (1698–1782), Italian poet and librettist + -an.] Of or pertaining to P. Metastasio or characteristic of his works.

1947 A. Einstein *Mus. Romantic Era* ix. 89 Canzonets on Metastasian texts. **1961** *Times* 16 Feb. 16/7 The Metastasian masterpiece, *Il Zio.* **1963** *Listener* 14 Feb. 313/2 Dissatisfied with the Metastasian libretto, he looked to Paris for an alternative. **1964** *Conc. Oxf. Dict. Opera* 259/2 It was against the abuses to which Metastasian opera lent itself—above all the halting dramatic progress, with the plot continually arrested to make way for demonstrations of vocal skill—that Gluck rebelled.

metastasize (metæ·stăsəiz), *v. Path.* [f. Metastas(is + -ize.] *intr.* Of a disease, esp. a tumour: to pass from one part or organ to another; to undergo metastasis (sense 2 a).

1907 *Jrnl. Med. Res.* XVII. 187 As might be expected the tendency to metastasize is much greater in certain tumors than in others. **1947** *Nature* 4 Jan. 15/1 Many prostatic cancers which have metastasized stand still or disappear after the removal of the patients' testicles. **1974** Passmore & Robson *Compan. Med. Stud.* III. xix. 14/2 This tumour invades neighbouring structures, advances along nerves and often recurs after local removal. It may eventually metastasize to distant organs.

metate. (Earlier and later examples.)

1834 in *Southwestern Hist. Q.* (1942) XLV. 330 Mrs. Roark had a Mexican utensil for grinding corn, called a *metate*. It was a large rock which had a place scooped out of the center that would hold a peck of corn. **1847** W. S. Henry *Campaign Sk. War with Mexico* 134 The eldest was on her knees at the medatstone, grinding corn. **1932** E. Wilson *Devil take Hindmost* xviii. 199 In the caves there are only the metates left—the big stones on which they [*sc.* the Indians] ground their meal. **1972** *Sci. Amer.* May 89/3 The *manos*, or stone rollers, and *metates*, or shallow stone troughs, that are used together to grind maize. **1975** *Ibid.* Jan. 100/3 Other fragments showed evidence of splitting, indicating that the grain had been prepared not by pounding but by being rolled back and forth on a stone *metate*.

metathesis. Add: **1. b.** (Further examples.) Also, *quantitative metathesis*, *metathesis of quantity*, a change of sequence *long vowel* + *short vowel* to *short vowel* + *long vowel*.

1891 D. B. Monro *Gram. Homeric Dial.* (ed. 2) 15 *Metathesis.* This term has been employed to explain a number of forms in which a short vowel is lost before a liquid, and the corresponding long vowel follows the two consonants thus brought together: as ξυμ-βλή-την *met*, Mid. βλῆ-το *was struck* (βαλ-, βελ-ος). *Ibid.* 51 G. Curtius.. made the counter-supposition that..the successive steps might be ὁράοντες, ὁρώοντες and (by metathesis of quantity) ὁρόωντες. **1901** H. Oertel *Lect. Study Lang.* 227 What goes under the name of 'quantitative metathesis' in Greek hardly belongs here. The 'metathesis' is confined to adjacent vowels, and the quantitative increase of the second vowel is probably compensative in its nature, going parallel with a quantitative reduction of the first. **1931** B. F. C. Atkinson *Gr. Lang.* 206 Another curious phenomenon of the metre is the metathesis of quantities or shortening of a long vowel or diphthong before hiatus. **1933** C. D. Buck *Compar. Gram. Gr. & Lat.* 93 Long vowels are shortened before other vowels in various dialects... When the second vowel is short it may be lengthened, resulting in what is known as 'quantitative metathesis'. **1959** A. Campbell *Old Eng. Gram.* 184 By full metathesis a consonant moves from immediately before a vowel to immediately after it, or the reverse. *Ibid.* 185 More usual than full metathesis is reversal of order in consonant groups, so that e.g. *sk* > *ks*, *sp* > *ps*. **1973** A. H. Sommerstein *Sound Pattern Anc. Gr.* 70 Another non-occurring vowel sequence is [ę̄ǭ]. Quantitative Metathesis can be extended without difficulty to modify this sequence by shortening the first vowel (there is no need to lengthen the second, it being already long).

metathesize (metæ·þĭsəiz), *v.* [f. Metathesis 1 b + -ize.] **a.** *intr.* To undergo metathesis. **b.** *trans.* To transpose (sounds, etc.) by metathesis; to subject (a word, etc.) to metathesis of some of its constituent sounds. Hence **meta·thesized** *ppl. adj.*

1920 H. C. Wyld *Hist. Mod. Colloq. Eng.* 300 In Received Standard we use many metathesized forms, such as *wright* O.E. *wyrhta*. **1946** E. A. Nida *Morphol.* ix. 180 A preconsonantal *y* metathesizes with the following consonant. **1951** *Traditio* VII. 411 About the second theme, *-ferth*, there can be little room for disagreement. It is obviously a metathesized form of *frith* (peace) which occurs in many Germanic names. **1959** M. Schlauch *Eng. Lang. in Mod. Times* vi. 161 There are instances [in Northern dialects] of metathesised *r*, as in *gert* for *great.* **1968** F. G. Lounsbury in J. A. Fishman *Readings Sociol. of Lang.* (1968) 52 Cayuga has many metathesized pairs [of syllables] in similar alternation, where the metatheses affect the relative order of vowels and the glottal stop. **1971** *Canad. Jrnl. Ling.* Fall 5 The only way to save the hypothesis of sibilant dissimilation would be to posit some rule metathesizing /z/ and /s/, and there appears to be no real evidence for voicing metathesis in modern Greek dialects. **1973** A. H. Sommerstein *Sound Pattern Anc. Greek* ii. 30 Send them first to /dz/; then we will need to metathesize this to [zd].

metatony (metæ·tŏni). *Linguistics.* Also **metatonie.** [ad. F. *métatonie* (F. de Saussure 1894, in *Mémoires de la Société de Linguistique de Paris* VIII. 429), f. Meta- + Tone *sb.* + -y[3].] In Baltic and Slavonic languages, one of certain kinds of substitution of one distinctive intonation for another in a given syllable; these substitutions collectively. Hence **meta·to·nic** *a.*

1936 *Trans. Philol. Soc.* 17 The long monophthongs, which have now a rising intonation, are abnormal. Except in loan words, they are due to various obscure causes, known collectively as *metatonie*. *Ibid.* 29 But *metatonie* in the Slavonic period (i.e. *nowocyrkumfleksowa*) may be present in some of these cases. **1949** Entwistle & Morison *Russian & Slavonic Languages* iv. 74 The process by which acutes change to circumflexes and *vice versa* is known as metatony. **1957** C. S. Stang *Slavonic Accentuation* 21 Thus neo-acute does not arise as a result of metatony, if by this term is implied a change of intonation within one and the same stressed syllable. *Ibid.* 23 An assumption based on the behaviour of metatonic circumflex. **1960** W. K. Matthews *Russ. Hist. Gram.* ii. 42 The Russian form *voróna*..illustrates a shift of stress forward in the word, which is known as progressive metatony and is the outcome here of the greater energy of the acute accent as compared with that of the circumflex. *Ibid.* vi. 99 The modern instances of metatony or shift of stress.. have parallels in the fourteenth century. **1965** G. Y. Shevelov *Prehist. of Slavic* xxxiii. 532 He [*sc.* Rozwadowski] called [the] whole phenomenon of their rise and all the changes associated with it metatony... The original idea of metatony as a pitch mutation resulting in the appearance of the two new intonations was a typical product of the Neogrammarian approach. *Ibid.* 533 Metatonic changes are most marked in those Sl[avic] languages or dialects which preserve distinctive (phonemic) pitch. **1973** T. Mathiassen in A. Ziedonis et al. *Baltic Lit. & Linguistics* 165, I am inclined to assume for such cases..only the working of metatony, which involves merely a shift of *intonation* from circumflex to acute.

Metatron (mĕtæ·trǫn). [Etym. uncertain.] In Jewish theology, a supreme angelic being, usually identified with either Michael or Enoch.

1865 C. D. Ginsburg *Kabbalah* 27 The Kabbalistic description of *Metatron* is taken from the Jewish angelology of a much older date than this theosophy... Metatron ..is the Presence Angel..the visible manifestation of the deity. **1904** *Jewish Encycl.* VIII. 519 *Meṭaṭron*,..name of an angel found only in Jewish literature... Meṭaṭron combines various traits derived from different systems of thought. **1914** *Encycl. Relig. & Ethics* VII. 625/1 This mediator is usually known as Meṭaṭron... Meṭaṭron appears in a praiseworthy capacity in his relations with Moses... Michael and Meṭaṭron are sometimes interchanged. **1941** G. G. Scholem *Major Trends Jewish Mysticism* ii. 66 The Metatron mysticism which revolves round the person of Enoch..who..was raised..to the rank of first of the angels. **1959** D. D. Runes *Conc. Dict. Judaism* 168/2 *Metatron*, the highest angel, identified with the archangel Michael, or with Enoch who was transformed into a heavenly being; a mystic figure. **1967** D. T. Kaufman *Dict. Relig. Terms* 310 *Metatron*, in Jewish belief, a supreme angelic being.

metatrophic (metătrōu·fik), *a. Biol.* [ad. G. *metatroph* (A. Fischer *Vorlesungen über Bakterien* (1897) v. 47), f. Meta-: see Trophic *a.*] Needing the presence of organic substances for nutrition.

1900 A. C. Jones tr. *Fischer's Struct. & Functions Bacteria* v. 48 The metatrophic bacteria..cannot live unless they have organic substances at their disposal. **1902** *Encycl. Brit.* XXV. 439/1 Some Angiosperms are persistently heterotrophic, either as saprophytes (metatrophic) or as parasites (paratrophic), and this manner of life involves some kind of symbiosis. **1930** S. Thomas *Bacteriol.* (ed. 2) v. 75 Metatrophic bacteria..include the bacteria causing fermentation, decay, and the decomposition of fatty substances.

Metawileh (metā·wile). Also **Matawila, Metawaileh, Metawala,** etc. [ad. Arab. *matāwila*, pl. of *mutawālī* one who professes to love 'Alī.] Name of a sect of the followers of 'Alī who live in Lebanon and Syria.

1799 W. G. Browne *Travels* 406 Some precaution was necessary against the *Metaweli*, Mohammedans of the sect of Ali, who once formed a powerful and ferocious tribe. **1845** *Encycl. Metrop.* XXV. 395/1 'Alí, whose followers, here called Motewális, or Mutewellís, are persecuted by the Sunnís. *Ibid.*, This word..has been variously spelt Metwalí, Motwâli, &c. **1860** D. Urquhart *Lebanon* I. xi. 94 The Metuali race... In religion..are Shiites, in race Arabs. *Ibid.* 96 The Metuali..do not exceed 60,000. **1875** *Encycl. Brit.* III. 177/1 In 1400 it [*sc.* Baalbec] was pillaged by Timur..and afterwards it fell into the hands of the Metaweli, a barbarous predatory tribe. **1888** *Ibid.* XXIII. 711/1 The present town [of Tyre] has arisen since the Metâwila occupied the district in 1766. **1900** G. Bell *Let.* 8 June (1927) I. 119 The Metawaileh (he belonged to that peculiar Muhammadan sect—please note that in the plural the accent is on the second syllable—Metāwaileh). **1909** T. E. Lawrence *Let.* 2 Aug. (1938) 68 Nabatiyeh, the Metawileh (Xtian) Headquarters in the hills. **1917** —— *Let.* 10 July (1938) 231 The Metowala [*sic*] of the Jebel Amr. **1926** —— *Seven Pillars* (1935) v. lviii. 331 On the higher slopes of the hills clustered settlements of Metawala, Shia Mohammedans from Persia generations ago. **1969** H. Z. Hirschberg in A. J. Arberry *Relig. Middle East* II. xviii. 340 A harsh judgement awaits the Mutāwila (the adherents of 'Alī).

Metaxa (metæ·ksă). Also **metaxa, -as.** In full, *Metaxa brandy.* A proprietary name for a dark Greek brandy; a drink or glass of this brandy.

1940 H. J. Grossman *Guide to Wines, Spirits & Beers* xviii. 184 A great deal of brandy is distilled in Greece... A sweet, dark, resinous brandy, which is quite popular and sells in fair quantities, is Metaxa. **1948** S. Ellin *Dreadful Summit* (1958) ix. 91 Dr Cooper said to the bartender, '..Make it two Metaxas.' **1962** K. Royce *Night Seekers* v. 69 Spurling ordered Turkish coffee..and a bottle of Metaxa. **1966** 'A. Hall' *9th Directive* xxiii. 213, I went into the bar and drank a Greek Metaxa brandy. **1967** E. Ambler *Dirty Story* i. iii. 25, I sipped Metaxa. **1974** C. Spencer *How Greeks kidnapped Mrs Nixon* x. 68 Kalvos gave them a bottle of Metaxas brandy. **1975** *Times* 6 Sept. 5/4 Metaxas is the big name in Greek brandy.

metaxenia (metăzī·niă). *Bot.* [f. Meta- + Xenia.] (See quots.)

1928 W. T. Swingle in *Jrnl. Heredity* XIX. 263/1 In order to be able to refer to this newly discovered action of

pollen on the ovarial tissues of the mother plant..I proposed at Phoenix, Arizona, in February, 1926, the term metaxenia to designate the action of the male parent on tissues of the mother plant outside of the embryo and endosperm. The term metaxenia is formed..by analogy with the term xenia which denotes the influence exerted by the male parent on the endosperm of the seed. **1949** DARLINGTON & MATHER *Elem. Genetics* 426 Xenia, the effect of more distantly related, as contrasted with more closely related, pollen on the maternal tissue of a fruit... Metaxenia has been used for true xenia. **1973** PROCTOR & YEO *Pollination of Flowers* xi. 351 The pollinations which produce larger seeds yield dates with more flesh (i.e. maternal tissue), the pollen having influenced the flesh indirectly ('metaxenia') through its direct genetic effect (xenia) on the seed.

metazoa, *sb. pl.* Add to etym.: (E. Haeckel 1874, in *Jenaische Zeitschr. Naturw.* VIII. 10). (Later examples.)

1940 L. H. HYMAN *Invertebrates* I. v. 249 Even the simplest Metazoa are two-layered or diploblastic. **1963** A. REMANE in E. C. Dougherty et al. *Lower Metazoa* ii. 26 No biologist regards *Protohydra* as the most primitive metazoön.

metazoan, *a.* and *sb.* (Later examples.)

1940 L. H. HYMAN *Invertebrates* I. v. 250 The ancestral metazoan would not have required a digestive sac or mouth. *Ibid.* 252 The three lowest metazoan phyla, the Porifera, the Cnidaria, and the Ctenophora, are commonly stated to have remained at the gastrular level of construction. **1965** B. E. FREEMAN tr. *Vandel's Biospeleol.* vii. 64 Those Metazoan groups which are almost exclusively marine are represented underground by very few species. **1971** *Nature* 28 May 260/1 Gravity corers are widely used for the collection of the smallest marine metazoans (meiofauna) from subtidal grounds.

metempsychosic (mete:mpsəikōu·sik), *a.* [f. METEMPSYCHOS(IS + -IC.] Relating to metempsychosis.

1905 W. J. LOCKE *Morals M. Ordeyne* xviii. 217, I have bemused myself with gnostic and metempsychosic speculations.

metencephalic, *a.* (Example.)

1899 *Proc. Zool. Soc.* 1024 The metencephalic fossa of the Pygopodes.

meteor. Add: **6. d. meteor bumper** *Astronautics*, a structure on the outside of a spacecraft that serves to protect it from the impacts of meteoroids; **meteor trail**, a bright streak of ionized gas formed by a meteor passing through the upper atmosphere, which can provide a reflector for radio communication.

1951 *Jrnl. Brit. Interplanetary Soc.* X. 275 For space station lifetimes of more than one year, it is concluded that either a heavily-armoured hull or a 'meteor bumper' will be required. **1960** *Aeroplane* XCVIII. 680/2 Dorsey described the space-laboratory as a double shell, three compartment, cylinder with convex end domes. The outer shell, made of beryllium, would serve as a 'meteor bumper' and thermal shield. **1962** F. I. ORDWAY et al. *Basic Astronautics* xi. 450 A double-wall meteor bumper in which the outer wall serves to break up the impacting meteor. **1930** R. H. BAKER *Astron.* vi. 246 (*caption*) Meteor trail. **1935** —— *Introd. Astron.* ix. 195 It is estimated that a single observer can see an average of ten meteor trails in the course of an hour on clear, moonless nights. **1958** *Jrnl. Atmospheric & Terrestrial Physics* XII. 329 At an early stage it became apparent that reflections from meteor trails play an important part in v.h.f. ionospheric forward scattering. **1968** *Radio Communication Handbk.* (ed. 4) xii. 17/2 There are times when the more orthodox modes of propagation fail to provide a satisfactory means of communication and one or other of the various forms of propagation by scatter may then offer a useful alternative: these include tropospheric scatter, ionospheric scatter..and meteor-trail scatter.

meteorette (mī:tĭ͵ŏre·t). [f. METEOR + -ETTE.] A small meteor.

1876 *Gentl. Mag.* XVI. 552 Specks flitting like meteorettes over the crests of the billows.

meteoric, *a.* Add: **2. a.** (Later examples.)

1965 G. J. WILLIAMS *Econ. Geol. N.Z.* viii. 94/2 Morgan (1924) had difficulty in visualizing how meteoric solutions could descend to the depth at which veins have been found. **1969** C. OLLIER *Volcanoes* ii. 17 The water emitted by hot springs is usually of meteoric origin, that is derived from rain, and only a very minor part is likely to be derived from magma.

meteorically, *adv.* Add: **b.** With the suddenness and speed of a meteor.

1916 A. S. NEILL *Dominie's Log* xiv. 154 She dons the bridal white, and at once she rises meteorically in the social scale. **1955** *Sci. Amer.* Apr. 38/3 Meanwhile they also spread through the Straits of Mackinac into Lake Michigan and increased meteorically there. **1973** *Current Hist.* May 204/1 Born in 1926, he had joined the Communist party in 1943, fought with the Partisans, and risen meteorically in the Croatian Communist party.

meteorite. Add: (Earlier example.)

1824 *Phil. Mag.* LXIV. 113, I shall..pass in review.. the principal new facts..respecting igneous meteors and meteorites, which have been made known..during the year 1823.

Hence **meteori·tical** *a.*, **meteori·tically** *adv.*

1919 BEERBOHM *Seven Men* 5 At the end of Term he settled in—or rather, meteoritically into—London. **1939** *Pop. Astron.* XLVII. 328 The Editor ventures the following suggestions relative to three..meteoritical terms. **1946** *Ibid.* LIV. 430 These amendments went into effect at the adjournment of the meeting on September 10; whereupon the name of the Society was officially changed from 'The Society for Research on Meteorites'..to 'The Meteoritical Society'. (It is hardly necessary to add that *meteoritical* is merely the adjective of *meteoritics*, defined as 'the science of meteorites and meteors'.) **1950** *New Mexico Q.* Autumn 270 The Institute of Meteoritics, the first scientific organization, at least in the English-speaking world, devoted to meteoritical research. **1974** *Geotimes* Mar. 8, Aug. 7–9 Meteoritical Society, ann. mtg, Los Angeles.

meteoritics (mī:tĭ͵ŏri·tiks), *sb. pl.* (const. as sing.). [f. METEORIT(E + -ICS, as ad. Russ. *meteoritika* (Yu. I. Simashko 1889, in *Niva* XX. 82/2).] The scientific study of meteors and meteorites.

1934 in WEBSTER. **1946, 1950** [see *METEORITICAL *a.*]. **1952** *Jrnl. Brit. Interplanetary Soc.* XI. 243 The astronomer in particular is interested in the composition of meteorites as chemical samples of the universe... The techniques of investigation are, however, not astrophysical but rather mineralogical and metallurgical, and it is hoped that the coining of the new term 'meteoritics' for the subject..may signify an increased co-operation between astronomers and the laboratory investigators. **1960** I. VIDZIUNAS tr. *Krinov's Princ. Meteoritics* i. 29 One of the most important areas of meteoritics is the study of the motion of meteoric bodies in the Earth's atmosphere and the observation of bolides. **1963** *Nature* 5 Jan. 38/1 Meteoritics is a young science. Only since around 1945 has extensive research been undertaken. **1975** *Sci. Amer.* Jan. 29/1 In recent years the discipline of meteoritics has moved beyond the taxonomic stage, and sound geochemical and physical reasoning has been applied in interpreting the masses of data.

Hence **meteori·ticist**, an expert in meteoritics.

1952 *Jrnl. Brit. Interplanetary Soc.* XI. 243 The first problems that meteoriticists (!) must tackle are the location and classification of falls, and a statistical analysis of the information so obtained. **1971** *New Scientist* 3 June 556/1 From studies of the amount of xenon present in various meteorites, meteoriticists had speculated that Pu-244 once existed in achondritic meteorites. **1975** *Sci. Amer.* Jan. 29/2 Some meteoriticists boldly construct multistage scenarios of condensation, agglomeration, accretion, heating, metamorphism and differentiation to explain the accumulated facts.

meteorogram (mī·tĭ͵ŏrŏgræm). [f. METEORO(GRAPH + -GRAM.] A record furnished by a meteorograph.

1904 *U.S. Dept. Agric. Monthly Weather Rev.* XXXII. 121/2, (1) instrumental errors, (2) errors in exposure of instruments when comparing with standards, (3) errors in reading from meteorograms. **1923** N. SHAW *Forecasting Weather* (ed. 2) v. 144 The trace given by a barometer is called a 'barogram', that by a thermometer a 'thermogram', while a trace of either the direction or force of wind is called an 'anemogram'. When two or more of these traces are all combined in one picture..the whole is called a 'meteorogram'. **1955** W. J. SAUCIER *Princ. Meteorol. Analysis* xii. 386 (*heading*) 'Meteorograms' of surface weather elements for 27 February through 3 March 1950.

meteorological, *a.* Add: **b.** *Meteorological Office, officer.*

1930 *Daily Express* 6 Oct. 2/4 Mr. M. A. Giblett, M.Sc., meteorological officer, R 101..organised the necessary meteorological services for airship flights to Canada. **1937** *Discovery* Jan. 5/1 For this a Benndorf self-registering electrometer was kindly lent by the Meteorological Office. **1967** *Ships' Code & Decode Bk.* (Meteorol. Office) (ed. 7) 66 Meteorological Officers. **1968** *Measurement Upper Winds by Pilot Balloons* (Meteorol. Office) (ed. 4) 37 The Meteorological Office has produced electric torches for use with pilot balloons. **1975** *Times* 12 Aug. 3/4 The Meteorological Office held a competition..for the best ideas for a new television presentation of weather.

meter, *sb.*³ Add: **1. d.** = **exposure meter.*

1920 *Sat. Westm. Gaz.* 22 May 16/2 The golden rule is to expose by meter on the holiday, and leave all else to the return home.

e. *U.S. slang.* (See quots.)

1940 *Music Makers* May 37/2 *Meter*, quarter, twenty-five cents. **1960** WENTWORTH & FLEXNER *Dict. Amer. Slang* 337/2 *Meter*, a quarter... From the coin which often is needed to operate a gas meter. Orig. Negro use. Never common. **1970** C. MAJOR *Dict. Afro-Amer. Slang* 81 *Meter*, twenty-five cent coin.

f. = **parking meter.*

1960 *Daily Tel.* 31 Mar. 15/1 What promises to be the most important experiment in traffic control starts next Monday, when car parking over the whole of Mayfair becomes subject to meters. **1973** *Weekly News* (Glasgow) 11 Aug. 2/2 After a search, I found a parking place in Glasgow on a Saturday afternoon. I was standing next to the meter..when a man who'd been standing on the opposite pavement came over. **1974** *Times* 21 Jan. 12/8 Since many meters in the Whitehall area have been suspended because of bomb threats, the wardens had a field day.

2. b. Special Combs.: **meter-feeder**, a motorist who illicitly extends his parking time by putting more money in the meter instead of moving away; so **meter-feeding** *vbl. sb.*; **meter maid** orig. *U.S.* (see quot. 1958); **meter-park** *v. trans.*, to park a vehicle at a parking meter; **meter-parking**, the use of parking meters; a place at a parking meter; **meter-reader**, a person responsible for reading gas or electricity meters; **meter-reading**, the reading of a meter or meters; **meter zone**, a limited area where the parking of vehicles is controlled by meters.

1965 *Guardian* 5 Apr. 8/2 The would-be meter feeder is tipped off if a hostile scout appears. **1972** *Ibid.* 8 May 9/6 Scotland Yard..was setting up a special vigilante squad whose job was to keep tabs on meter feeders in Central London. **1966** *Punch* 5 Jan. 15/1 Driving dangerously, you may think, is obviously much more criminal than meter-feeding. But meter-feeding is a deliberately calculated breach of the law, whereas dangerous driving may be accidental. **1969** *Guardian* 28 Mar. 22/4 We realize councils must do something to stop meter feeding. **1957** in *Amer. Speech* (1961) XXXVI. 282 Surveys conducted in cities using 'meter maids' have found that their meter revenue increased. **1958** *Britannica Bk. of Year* 519/2 *Meter maid*,..a woman police official with the task of patrolling metered parking-sites and reporting parking offences. **1968** *Harper's Mag.* Feb. 41 A Meter Maid was soon watching me censoriously. **1970** S. ELLIN *Man from Nowhere* xxx. 150 Some meter maid found him when she looked in the car where it was parked uptown. **1970** *Sunday Times* 3 May 28/7 Why do meter maids..never look glamorous at all? **1971** H. C. RAE *Marksman* III. iii. 212 The Mark 10 was meter-parked close to the side entrance. **1959** *Daily Tel.* 15 Dec. 1/7 In the past month, 81 motorists were convicted of contravening the existing meter parking scheme. **1963** D. B. HUGHES *Expendable Man* (1964) iv. 109 There were no meter parkings open near the courthouse. **1963** *Times* 8 Jan. 9/3 In an ideal world, everyone in uniform, from guardsmen to meter readers, would be immaculately turned out and dressed in strict conformity with the rules of their service. **1971** A. PRICE *Alamut Ambush* x. 123 A duty caller like the meter reader and the postman. **1974** *Times* 18 Apr. 14 Where the occupiers are out when he calls, the meter-reader leaves a card, inviting them to be at home next day. **1957** V. J. KEHOE *Technique Film & Television Make-Up* viii. 96 The middle of the ratio scale on a meter reading. **1959** *Daily Tel.* 15 Dec. 1/7 Larger meter zone by April. **1963** *Sunday Express* 3 Mar. 4/4, I had paid out over £220 in parking fines in the past 21 months because I lived in a 'meter zone'.

meter, *v.* (in Dict. after METER *sb.*³). Add: Also, to supply through a meter. (Further example.)

1968 *Brit. Med. Bull.* 192/2 It is meaningful to envisage computer power being metered to separate offices.

b. *trans.* To regulate the flow of; to deliver (fluid) in regulated amounts *to*.

1932 *Compression Ignition Engines* xi. 132 Injection Pump.—A mechanical device which meters the liquid fuel in controllable quantities and delivers it at a set pressure to the working cylinders. **1963** *Adv. Space Sci. & Technol.* Suppl. I. 173 In addition to atomizing and mixing the liquids, it meters the flow to the combustion chamber. **1972** *Sci. Amer.* Aug. 21/2 Oil could also be metered to the critical contact region.

2. To measure (the parking-time) of motorists, etc., by means of parking meters; to provide with parking meters. So **me·tered** *ppl. a.*

1957 *New Yorker* 26 Oct. 36/1 You can park scooters almost anywhere without getting a ticket. In a metered area, the usual thing is to park them sidewise, between two parked cars. **1960** *Guardian* 13 Jan. 6/7 When all Mayfair becomes metered..the position of the motorists will be worse than ever. **1961** *Ibid.* 27 June 5/6 A motorist ..may only park his car in a metered parking place. **1962** *Times* 16 Apr. 11/3 Brighton has proposed to meter the sea-front motorists' parking-time. **1963** 'W. HAGGARD' *High Wire* iii. 24 The comfortable little street..had recently been metered... This was a metered parking ground.

metered (mī·təɹd), *ppl. a.* In the senses of the vb. Cf. prec.

1928 M. RITTENBERG *Mail-Order made Easy* xiv. 177 'Metered' mail—where a printed impression is put on the envelope instead of an adhesive stamp. **1957**, etc. [see *METER *v.* 2]. **1968** *Listener* 27 June 851/1 The trouble is that in this country taxi-drivers who work for garages and not for themselves are commonly paid no set wages, but instead a proportion of the metered fare—say, 40 per cent.

metering (mī·təriŋ), *vbl. sb.* [f. METER *v.* + -ING¹.] Measuring; freq. *attrib.* as *metering-point, pump, station*, etc. Also in other senses of METER *v.* (in Dict. and Suppl.).

1913 *Wireless World* May 93/2 We must take a point just behind the metering-point..as the beginning of the plant essential to the particular system under consideration. **1935** *Geogr. Jrnl.* LXXXV. 538 At each metering station a sufficient number of discharge measurements is taken. **1935** *Economist* 7 Dec. 1143/1 The development of the hand-operated metering pump affixed to an underground tank at garages..revolutionised the service of distribution. **1959** *Daily Tel.* 24 Dec. 6/2 To improve off-street parking by general metering of the kerbs. **1962** *Rep. Comm. Broadcasting 1960* 264 in *Parl. Papers 1961–2* (Cmnd. 1753) IX. 259 Metering and access-barring apparatus. **1963** *Lancet* 5 Jan. 17/1 In order to do this, a multi-channel metering pump was made which consists of laminæ massaging silicone-rubber or plastic tubes. **1973** *Country Life* 20 Sept. 826/1 Full aperture metering gives you a bright clear image of the subject... The FD range consists of fully automatic metering lenses.

metestrus, -um, varr. *METŒSTRUS.

metethereal, var. METETHERIAL *a.*

1911 T. FLOURNOY *Spiritism & Psychol.* ii. 57 We participate..in a higher order of phenomena—of a metethereal world, as Myers called it. **1924** T. H. Y. TROTTER *Mus. & Mind* I. ii. 28 A metethereal world,..transcendental and spiritual. **1963** *Listener* 24 Jan. 175/3 Esoteric volumes on astral projection, crammed with words like 'metethereal'.

meth (meþ), colloq. abbrev. *METHEDRINE; also, a Methedrine tablet.

1967 *N.Y. Times* 16 Oct. 53 She was a good kid, if she hadn't been so freaked out on meth. **1968** *Guardian* 21 Nov. 20/3 The pushers passing out bombers, meths, dexes, and blues. **1972** M. J. BOSSE *Incident at Naha* i. 38 She snorted Methedrine... The Feeler offered me a snort of Meth, but I never use Speed. **1972** J. WAMBAUGH *Blue Knight* (1973) v. 74 She's a meth head and an ex-con.

meth, var. *METHS.

meth- (meþ), used as comb. form of METHYL before a vowel in a few chemical names, as **me·thacrylic acid,** 1-methylacrylic acid, CH_2:-$C(CH_3)COOH$, a colourless compound melting at 15°C, which polymerizes when distilled and which is used in the manufacture of methacrylate resins; so **metha·crylate,** (*a*) a salt of methacrylic acid; (*b*) any of the esters of methacrylic acid, some of which are used in making resins by polymerization (see *methyl methacrylate* s.v. *METHYL c); **metho·xide,** (a salt of) the anion CH_3O^-, derived from methanol.

1865 *Jrnl. Chem. Soc.* XVIII. 142 Ethylic methacrylate is readily decomposed by boiling alcoholic potash. *Ibid.*, Silver methacrylate is best obtained pure by precipitating ammonium methacrylate with nitrate of silver. **1936** *Industr. & Engin. Chem.* Mar. 269/1 The monomeric methacrylates cannot be stored or transported with safety. **1962** *Economist* 6 Oct. 74/3 An airdrying paint (based on methacrylates) has been used..for several years. **1964** G. H. HAGGIS et al. *Introd. Molecular Biol.* iv. 91 (*caption*) A thin section preparation showing T_2 bacteriophage infection of *E. coli* bacteria (osmium tetroxide fixation and methacrylate embedding technique..). **1865** *Jrnl. Chem. Soc.* XVIII. 142 Methacrylic acid is a colourless oil, which..possesses a faint odour, like pyrogallic acid. **1889** G. M'GOWAN tr. *Bernthsen's Text-bk. Org. Chem.* 166 Meth-acrylic acid..is found in small quantity in Roman camomile oil, and smells like decaying mushrooms. **1972** *Materials & Technol.* IV. xii. 428 Technical production of methacrylic acid employs the oxidation of isobutene by a mixture of nitric acid and nitrogen dioxide to hydroxyisobutyric acid, which is then dehydrated. **1885** *Jrnl. Chem. Soc.* XLVIII. 1031 Anhydrous sodium methoxide, NaOMe, was prepared by heating the solution [of sodium in methyl alcohol] at 180–200° in a current of dry hydrogen. **1934** *Ibid.* 1204 The agreement between the values for the mobility of the methoxide ion is fair. **1965** *New Scientist* 26 Aug. 513/3 Ordinary methyl alcohol is sufficiently acidic to form salts with alkali metals like sodium and potassium, the 'methoxides', whose general formula is $CH_3O^-M^+$ (where M^+ is any metal ion).

metha: see *METHO[1].

methadone (me·þădōun). *Pharm.* orig. *U.S.* Also **-on** (-ǫn). [f. METH(YL + *A(MINO- + D(I-[2] + -ONE in 6-dimethylamino-4,4-diphenyl-3-heptanone, the systematic chemical name.] A powerful synthetic analgesic, $(CH_3)_2N \cdot CH(CH_3) \cdot CH_2 \cdot C(C_6H_5)_2 \cdot CO \cdot CH_2 \cdot CH_3$, which is similar to morphine in its effects but less sedative and is used (usu. as the hydrochloride) as a substitute drug in the treatment of addiction to morphine or heroin.

1947 *Jrnl. Amer. Med. Assoc.* 23 Aug. 1483 The Council voted to recognise the word Methadon as the generic designation for 6-dimethylamino-4,4-diphenyl-3-heptanone. **1948** *Ann. N.Y. Acad. Sci.* LI. 17 It is not certain whether the Germans succeeded in the complete resolution of *dl*-methadone. **1952** W. T. SALTER *Textbk. Pharmacol.* vi. 81/1 The danger of addiction of racemic methadon and levo-methadon is about equal to that of morphine. **1962** K. ORVIS *Damned & Destroyed* xxiii. 174 A new drug, methadon, is being used successfully as a reduction treatment... The patient starts regaining strength—moral and physical strength—almost at once. **1967** *Martindale's Extra Pharmacopoeia* (ed. 25) 783/1 Symptoms of morphine withdrawal in addicts may also be mitigated by methadone substitution; addiction to methadone is easier to treat than addiction to morphine. *Ibid.* 800/2 Methadone hydrochloride may be used for the relief of severe pain of all types. **1970** *Sunday Times* 8 Mar. 1/2 She was taking big doses of heroin three times a day, together with the morphine-antagonist, methadone, ..every four hours. **1971** *Guardian* 4 June 3/3 The aim of the methadone programme is to switch the mainliner's addiction from heroin to methadone, an addictive drug.. which allows its addicts to lead a normal life... The methadone programme was begun in New York in 1965 by the Beth Israel Medical Centre. **1972** *Science* 26 May 882/2 Methadone not only reduces the hunger for heroin, it affects respiration, digestion, and sexual behavior; it also, as does any opiate, affects social and psychological behavior.

methamphetamine (meþæmfe·tămīn, -in). *Pharm.* [f. *METH- + *AMPHETAMINE.] A methyl derivative, $C_6H_5 \cdot CH_2 \cdot CH(CH_3) \cdot NH(CH_3)$, of amphetamine, used in the form of the hydrochloride, a white crystalline compound, as a stimulant of the central nervous system; its effects resemble those of amphetamine but are more rapid in onset and longer lasting.

1949 *Jrnl. Amer. Med. Assoc.* 22 Jan. 228 New and nonofficial remedies. Methamphetamine hydrochloride... *d*-Desoxyephedrine hydrochloride. **1951** A. GROLLMAN *Pharmacol. & Therapeutics* xi. 212 Methamphetamine hydrochloride..may be considered as the methyl derivative of amphetamine. It is a potent analeptic and, like amphetamine, has been used in the treatment of narcolepsy, postencephalitic parkinsonism, alcoholism, and in certain depressive states..and in the treatment of obesity. **1960** J. J. LEWIS *Introd. Pharmacol.* viii. 287 Amphetamine, dexamphetamine and methamphetamine have qualitatively similar properties but vary in potency. Methamphetamine is more potent than dexamphetamine which is in turn more potent than its racemate amphetamine. **1970** C. M. B. PARE in C. W. H. Havard *Current Med. Treatm.* (ed. 3) xv. 479 Following injection of the methamphetamine the doctor directs the interview towards topics which he thinks may be particularly stressful.

methanation (meþănē·ʃən). [f. METHAN(E + -ATION.] Conversion (esp. of carbon monoxide and hydrogen) into methane.

1956 M. GREYSON in P. H. Emmett *Catalysis* IV. vi. 506 The development of commercial methanation procedures is normally undertaken on the assumption that means exist, or will exist, for the conversion of coal to mixtures of hydrogen and carbon monoxide. **1969** R. F. LANG tr. *Henglein's Chem. Technol.* 425 This reaction is used for the production of especially high-grade fuel gases from water gas ($CO + 3H_2 - 48{\cdot}87$ kcal $= CH_4 + H_2O$) (methanation) ($CO_2 + 4H_2 - 39{\cdot}1$ kcal $= CH_4 + 2H_2O$). **1973** *Nature* 7 Dec. 326/2 It is the catalytic enrichment (a methanation) which is the key to the production of SNG [*sc.* substitute natural gas] and the Gas Board is loath to reveal the full details of its operation.

Hence (as a back-formation) **me·thanate** *v. trans.*, to convert into methane, to subject to methanation.

1963 DIRKSEN & LINDEN *Pipeline Gas from Coal by Methanation of Synthesis Gas* (U.S. Inst. Gas Technol. Res. Bull. No. 31) p. iii, This program established that a variety of nickel catalysts were capable of methanating synthesis gas to 900 Btu/SCF pipeline gas. **1974** *Sci. Amer.* Apr. 9/3 Methanating animal wastes from feed-lots in the Middle West is probably the best application of this idea.

methane. Add: Now usu. pronounced (mī·þēin).

methanol (me·þănǫl). *Chem.* [f. METHAN(E + -OL.] Methyl alcohol, CH_3OH, a colourless, volatile, poisonous liquid with a pungent odour which is produced mainly by the high-pressure reduction of carbon monoxide or dioxide with hydrogen and is used as an intermediate in the synthesis of formaldehyde, as a solvent, and as a denaturant for ethyl alcohol.

The adoption of *methanol* as the systematic name of methyl alcohol was a consequence of Resolution 15 (on alcohols and phenols) of the report of 1892 of the International Conference on Chemical Nomenclature (see *Nature* (1892) 19 May 58–9).

1894 G. M'GOWAN tr. *Bernthsen's Text-bk. Org. Chem.* (ed. 2) 87 Methyl alcohol. [*Note*] 'O[fficial] N[ame]' Methanol. **1932** *Discovery* May 165/2 Besides its important use as a methylating agent, methanol is the raw material for formaldehyde. **1958** *Times Rev. Industry* Dec. 57/2 Refueller..designed for replenishing aircraft with..methanol. **1973** *Daily Tel.* 27 July 2/7 Hawkshaw ..knew that methanol was an anti-freeze substance used on buses and for stripping paint and cleaning paintbrushes.

Hence **methano·lic** *a.*, in or of methanol.

1953 *Jrnl. Polymer Sci.* X. 375 The results of viscosity and molecular weight determination obtained in methanolic solution are presented in Figure 2. **1975** *Nature* 3 Jan. 8/1 Solvolysis of $[\{(C_5H_5)_2Ti\}_2N_2]$ with methanolic HCl yields mainly nitrogen.

methaqualone (meþæ·kwălōun). *Pharm.* [f. *2-methyl-3-o-tolyl-4(3H)-quinazolinone*, the systematic chemical name (with inserted *a*), f. METHYL + TOLYL + *quinazolin(e* (f. QUIN(OLINE + *azol(e* (f. Az(o- + *-OLE) + -INE[5]) + -ONE.] A hypnotic and sedative drug used generally in the form of its hydrochloride, $C_{16}H_{14}N_2O \cdot HCl$, a white crystalline powder with a bitter taste.

1961 *Brit. Med. Jrnl.* 21 Jan. 173/1 Methaqualone in a single dose of 150 mg. is a reliable hypnotic. **1969** *Daily Tel.* 17 Dec. 13/1 Methaqualone, a drug used by thousands of people in sleeping tablets and slimming capsules, is to be referred to the Committee on Safety of Drugs. **1973** *N.Y. Times* 10 June 1. 59/1 Nonmedical use quickly spread when users found that methaqualone can produce a tingly, relaxed, uncoordinated drunken euphoria. It also developed a reputation—some say unfounded—as a powerful aphrodisiac. **1973** *Daily Tel.* 11 July 2/8 Mandrax is the trade name for a sleeping tablet otherwise known as methaqualone and has been controlled as a potentially dangerous drug since 1971 following cases of abuse by drug addicts.

Methedrine (me·þĕdrin, -īn). *Pharm.* [f. METH(YL + *BENZ)EDRINE.] A proprietary name for methamphetamine.

1939 *Trade Marks Jrnl.* 11 Jan. 46/2 Methedrine... Pharmaceutical and veterinary preparations. The Wellcome Foundation Ltd.,..London,..manufacturing chemists. **1943** *Brit. Med. Jrnl.* 20 Mar. 348/2 Methedrine has been found to be an effective blood-pressure-raising drug. **1965** J. POLLITT *Depression & its Treatment* iv. 47 Methedrine produces euphoria, mental alertness and pressure of talk. **1967** *Economist* 11 Nov. 628/2 Their deaths were just one instance of the violent crime that is being associated with the increasing use of an amphetamine with the trade name of Methedrine and the nick-name of 'speed'. **1975** *Harpers & Queen* May 126/2 Out come..a half-dozen bottles of Methedrine.

metheglin. (Later examples.)

1789 J. MORSE *Amer. Geogr.* 197 The perry..is an agreeable liquor, having something of the harshness of claret wine, joined with the sweetness of metheglin. **1839** J. K. TOWNSEND *Narr. Rocky Mts.* v. 203 Among the rest, was some *metheglen* or diluted alcohol sweetened with honey. **1855** T. C. HALIBURTON *Nat. & Hum. Nat.* II. ix. 267 All the friends of the new married couple..did nothing for a whole month, but smoke, drink metheglin, [etc.]. **1971** J. DOXAT *Drinks & Drinking* 152 *Metheglin*, old name for mead, but probably, from its derivation, from an ancient Welsh word for 'spicey potion'.

methenamine (meþī·n-, mĕþe·nămīn). *Pharm.* [f. METHEN(E + AMINE.] The name given to *hexamethylenetetramine* (s.v. *HEXA-) in the *Pharmacopeia of the U.S.A.*

1926 *Pharmacopeia U.S.* 238 Methenamine. **1926** *Dispensatory U.S.A.* (ed. 21) 695/2 Not only are there a large number of compounds of methenamine upon the market, but the official drug is sold under an almost innumerable number of trade names. **1948** E. POUND *Pisan Cantos* (1949) lxxiv. 17 Methenamine eases the urine. **1951** A. GROLLMAN *Pharmacol. & Therapeutics* xxv. 526 Hexamethylenetetramine ($(CH_2)_6N_4$), official as methenamine (U.S.P.) and hexamine (B.P.)..is of interest from its liberating formaldehyde in the course of its excretion in the urine. **1969** J. H. THOMPSON in J. A. Bevan *Essent. Pharmacol.* xlix. 511 Methenamine mandelate is a mixture of methenamine and mandelic acid.., two old urinary antiseptic agents which today are rarely given separately.

methicillin (meþisi·lin). *Pharm.* [f. *METH- + *PEN)ICILLIN.] A penicillin, $C_{17}H_{19}N_2O_6$-$NaS \cdot H_2O$, which is especially useful for its activity against staphylococci which produce penicillinase. Also called *methicillin sodium* or *sodium methicillin*.

1961 *Brit. Med. Jrnl.* 25 Mar. 865/1 During a period of 12 weeks one ward was sprayed at regular intervals daily with 4g. of methicillin. **1963** *Brit. Pharmacopœia* 486 Methicillin Sodium is the monohydrate of sodium 6-(2,6-dimethoxybenzamido)penicillinate. **1968** *New Scientist* 18 Jan. 118/3 There were signs of bacterial infection in the lungs, and the doctors prescribed methicillin. **1970** *Daily Tel.* 23 Oct. 13/3 The second [semi-synthetic penicillin], methicillin,..was active against the resistant staphylococci and was soon accepted as a major life-saving antibiotic.

methionine (meþai·ǒnīn). *Chem.* [Blend of *METH- + THION-: see -INE[5].] A sulphur-containing amino-acid, $CH_3 \cdot S \cdot CH_2 \cdot CH_2 \cdot CH(NH_2) \cdot COOH$, which is probably a constituent of all proteins.

1928 BARGER & COYNE in *Biochem. Jrnl.* XXII. 1418 Since the amino-acid has a good title to be regarded as a constituent of protein, a shorter name than *γ*-methylthiol-*α*-aminobutyric acid seems desirable, and..we suggest for it the name *methionine*, in allusion to the characteristic grouping. **1956** *Nature* 11 Feb. 280/1 The amino-acid requirement of this organism [*sc.* a trypanosomid flagellate] could be satisfied by methionine alone. **1962** [see *ISOLEUCINE]. **1971** J. Z. YOUNG *Introd. Study Man* xxiii. 315 Old people are said to require more methionine than young. **1972** *McGraw-Hill Yearbk. Sci. & Technol.* 123/1 Since methionine is the only metabolic precursor of homocysteine in the human diet, deliberate reduction in the amount of dietary animal protein, which contains more methionine than plant protein, may prove to be effective in preventing arteriosclerosis.

methisazone (meþi·sæzōun). *Pharm.* [f. METH(YL + IS(ATIN + *THIOSEMICARB)AZONE (cf. the chemical name given in def.).] A fine orange-yellow powder that has prophylactic activity against smallpox; *N*-methylisatin *β*-thiosemicarbazone, $C_{10}H_{10}N_4OS$.

1964 *Brit. Med. Jrnl.* 5 Sept. 621/1 Methisazone breaks new ground in the rational therapy of virus infections. **1966** *New Scientist* 17 Nov. 336/3 Dr D. J. Bauer and Dr K. Apostolov..had shown methisazone ('Marboran') to be active against certain adenoviruses growing in tissue culture. **1970** PASSMORE & ROBSON *Compan. Med. Stud.* II. xx. 36/1 In man, methisazone has been shown to be effective in preventing disease in contacts of patients suffering from smallpox... Methisazone has not been shown to be effective in treating established infections.

metho[1] (me·þo). *Austral.* and *N.Z. colloq.* Also **metha** (*rare*). [f. *meth(ylated spirit* + *-O.] **1.** Methylated spirit. Also *attrib.*

1933 *Bulletin* (Sydney) 18 Oct. 10/2 A metho. drinker—a regular visitor—came into the pharmacy the other day. *Ibid.* 1 Nov. 11/1 Charged in a Melbourne court with having drunk metho., an elderly gent. at first declared [etc.].

1935 K. TENNANT *Tiburon* ii. 23 The two metho-drinkers were escorted out firmly. **1938** 'R. HYDE' *Nor Years Condemn* x. 190 They drink a lot of metha, don't they? Great names they've got for it—Phar Lap, and Johnny Gee, and White Light. **1944** W. E. HARNEY *Taboo* (ed. 3) 33 She is a 'metho' addict and, as a result, is blind and half paralysed. **1945** O. E. BURTON *In Prison* 116 A half-crazed sponge for absorbing 'metho'. **1953** A. UPFIELD *Murder must Wait* xvii. 153 The straight-out metho drinkers and city crooks. **1973** *Sunday Mail* (Brisbane) 18 Mar. 25/5 The oldtimer who'd tried to smuggle it through, by carrying it nonchalantly in his hand, surrendered it sadly. When it comes to metho spotting, Envoy Smith has the nose of a connoisseur.

2. A person who is addicted to drinking methylated spirit. See also *METHS.

1933 *Bulletin* (Sydney) 1 Nov. 11/1 A John Hop who has helped to deal with many 'methos.' tells me not a few prefer petrol. **1945** BAKER *Austral. Lang.* 166 Addicts of these noxious drinks are known as *meths, methos,* [and] *metho artists.* **1966** G. W. TURNER *Eng. Lang. Austral. & N.Z.* vi. 118 Words in *-o* are more specifically Australian, though..*metho* (a drinker of methylated spirits) and *smoko* (with the sense 'morning or afternoon tea'..) are current in New Zealand. **1973** *Brisbane City Mission* Sept. 17/2 The methos... When a man takes to drinking methylated spirits, you know..that he has no thought for betterment of his lot.

Metho² (me·þo). *Austral.* Colloq. abbrev. of METHODIST 4.

1941 in BAKER *Dict. Austral. Slang* 46. **1961** P. WHITE *Riders in Chariot* viii. 232 Only the civil servants are Roman Catholics here... Arch and me are Methoes, except we don't go; life is too short.

method, *sb.* Add: **I. 2. c.** (Further examples.)

1843 MILL *Logic* I. III. viii. 450 These two methods may be respectively denominated the Method of Agreement, and the Method of Difference. *Ibid.* 462 This method may be called the Indirect Method of Difference, or the Joint Method of Agreement and Difference. *Ibid.* 465 The Method of Residues is one of the most important among our instruments of discovery. *Ibid.* 470 The method by which these results were obtained, may be termed the Method of Concomitant Variations. **1916** H. W. B. JOSEPH *Introd. Logic* (ed. 2) xx. 434 So obvious is the difficulty of finding such instances as these canons require, that Mill, having begun by mentioning four methods (of Agreement, of Difference, of Residues, and of Concomitant Variations), adds a fifth, which he calls the Joint Method of Agreement and Difference. **1929** A. N. WHITEHEAD *Process & Reality* 6 When the method of difference fails, factors which are constantly present may yet be observed under the influence of imaginative thought. **1953** I. M. COPI *Introd. Logic* xii. 365 We may begin with an example or two in which the scrupulous use of the Methods results in a more or less conspicuous failure to discover the cause of a given phenomenon. **1965** S. F. BARKER *Elem. Logic* vii. 237 When we infer from these data that the hamburgers caused the ptomaine, we are employing what Mill called the method of concomitant variation.

e. *Theatr.* A theory and practice of acting associated with the Russian actor and director Konstantin Stanislavsky (1863–1938), in which the actor seeks the complete illusion of reality by identifying himself as closely as possible with the part he plays. Often *attrib.*, as *method-acting, actor, school,* etc. Also *method-act* vb., *method-acted* ppl. adj. Hence (not in common use) *methodic, methody* adjs.; *methodism, methodist* sbs.

1923 O. M. SAYLER *Russian Theatre* 254 'My method, though imperfect,' he [*sc.* Stanislavsky] says, 'I consider psychologically natural.' **1925** H. CARTER *New Spirit European Theatre* xviii. 225 The third movement also was a form of protest by theatrical reformers, who were sick of M. Stanislavsky's hair-for-hair actualistic method. *Ibid.* 230 Stanislavsky was unable to change his method of production and style, which were suited to a particular species of bourgeoisie play. **1954** F. M. WHITING *Introd. Theatre* vi. 136 The actor, if sufficiently sensitive to the drives and motives of the character he portrays, will 'instinctively' sense what the basic responses should be. To achieve this goal, Stanislavski devised his method. **1956** K. TYNAN in *Harper's Mag.* Mar. 63/2 This is Stanislavsky without Freud, physiological acting without the psychiatric glosses beloved of American 'method' actors. **1957** *Observer* 15 Dec. 10/4 Eli Wallach, the American disciple of the Method.., was admirably solid, but not noticeably more absorbed in his role than some of our own best actors look to be in theirs. **1958** E. DUNDY *Dud Avocado* I. vii. 114 The Method..the Stanislavsky Method: working for realism through improvisations and sense memory, and emotional recall. **1958** *Times* 11 Nov. 4/5 It was surely not for nothing that [Jackson] Pollock himself belonged to the country that has promulgated the cult of 'method' acting. **1959** *Times Lit. Suppl.* 27 Mar. 172/1 The whole 'Method' school about which so much pedantic and often absurd controversy has raged are dealt with mordantly. **1959** *Spectator* 29 May 765/1 This was a Method *Don Giovanni,* with real people caught up in a real drama. **1959** *Guardian* 15 Oct. 8/3 What emotional exercises had he done in preparation for Romeo? The real Methodist is not so much different in kind as different in degree. **1960** R. LEWIS *Method—or Madness?* i. 4 One hears that Method actors are 'mumblers'. *Ibid.* iv. 75 Another reason that some actors..seem 'Methody', or inexplicably involved, is that their approach is *too* analytical. **1960** *New Left Rev.* Sept.–Oct. 65/1 The method-acted *Tomorrow With Pictures.* **1961** *20th Cent.* Feb. 134 Other factors include the impact of Method-ism in the theatre. **1962** *New Statesman* 19 Jan. 97/1 This long film forfeits seriousness..by being..too thunderously repetitious, too Methodic, strenuous and symbolic. **1963** *Times* 17 Jan. 4/6 Even the Method groups that were flourishing in London a few years ago have now mainly vanished. **1967** *Spectator* 7 July 22/2 His method acting is not merely an attack on their academic ennui, but a mask for his own profound frustrations. **1970** J. QUARTERMAIN *Man who walked on Diamonds* xvii. 90 Method-act yourself into a super-sleuth. **1971** J. WILLETT in A. Bullock *20th Cent.* 243/1 In America..the Group Theater..applied the realistic Stanislavsky 'method' for social ends. **1972** *Daily Colonist* (Victoria, B.C.) 24 Feb. 44/1 A method actor will use his own memory to simulate an emotion for the cameras. **1973** H. MCCLOY *Change of Heart* xii. 146 If she could feel like that, maybe she would look like that. 'Method' acting. Stanislavsky.

3. e. *Campanology.* (See quot. 1901.)

1668 'CAMPANISTA' *Tintinnalogia* 2 Before I Treat of the method and diversity of Peals, I think it not impertinent to speak something of the Properties wherewith a Young Ringer ought to be qualified. **1852** B. THACKRAH *Art Change Ringing* 14 These twenty-four changes may be rung in several other methods. **1879** W. BANISTER *Art & Sci. Change Ringing* (ed. 2) 14 The Plain Bob Method—is applicable to any number of bells, but is properly an even bell method. **1901** H. E. BULWER *Gloss. Technical Terms Bells* 10 *Method,* any special way in which continuous 'changes' on five or more bells are produced by the regular and orderly movement of all, without repetition of any one 'change'. **1901, 1928** [see *EXTENT *sb.* 7]. **1962** G. E. EVANS *Ask Fellows who cut Hay* (ed. 2) xviii. 147 The old ringer answered.., 'No tunes. We allus rang the *method,* the same as we did in the steeples.' **1965** W. G. WILSON *Change Ringing* xviii. 149 We showed how variations in a method could be made in the Plain Bob type of method by means of second place.

II. 5. Phr. *method in one's madness* (also varr. of this expression, normally with allusion to quot. 1602 in Dict.): reason, orderliness, or sense lying behind one's apparent insanity or stupidity.

1843 POE *Gold-Bug* in *Dollar Newspaper* (Philadelphia) 21 June 1/7 My friend, about whose madness I now saw, or fancied that I saw, certain indications of method. **1850** F. E. SMEDLEY *Frank Fairleigh* xxix. 241 A fear of completely knocking up..induced me to preserve some little method in my madness. **1894** A. CONAN DOYLE *Mem. Sherlock Holmes* 128, I have usually found that there was method in his madness. **1911** BRERETON & ROTHWELL tr. *Bergson's Laughter* i. 2 The comic spirit has a logic of its own, even in its wildest eccentricities. It has a method in its madness. **1922** CHESTERTON *Man who knew too Much* 110 He may be mad, but there's method in his madness. There nearly always is method in madness. It's what drives men mad being methodical. **1953** A. HUXLEY *Let.* 21 July (1969) 680 There is, in the long run (at least I hope so), some kind of method in my madness.

III. 10. methods engineer, a person concerned with method study and methods engineering in a business; **methods engineering,** the organization of business methods through method study; **method(s) study,** the use of time-and-motion study and other systems to determine the most efficient methods to use in business activities.

[**1928** R. C. DAVIS *Princ. Factory Organization & Managem.* vi. 72 The methods manager or industrial engineer is concerned primarily with the efficient application of the human forces of the organization.] **1939** MAYNARD & STEGEMERTEN *Operation Analysis* i. 5 Time formulas are useful mathematical devices that the methods engineer employs. **1944** —— *Guide to Methods Improvement* ii. 9 A methods engineer secured a position in a textile mill in the South. **1953** J. R. IMMER *Materials Handling* iii. 30 This part of materials movement is.. more often the concern of the methods engineer than of the materials-handling engineer. **1960** *News Chron.* 28 July 8/8 (Advt.), Methods Engineer..experience of Time and Methods Study and Ratefixing. **1939** MAYNARD & STEGEMERTEN *Operation Analysis* i. 1 Before discussing the methods-engineering procedure in detail, it will be advisable to formulate a clear statement of what the term covers... Methods engineering is the industrial science which is chiefly concerned with increasing labor effectiveness. **1944** —— *Guide to Methods Improvement* i. 5 In order to continue to make improvements in methods, a procedure known as 'method engineering' has been developed. **1953** J. R. IMMER *Materials Handling* iv. 41 The methods-engineering department has the responsibility for 'planning the manual part of the operation'. **1932** A. H. MOGENSON *Common Sense appl. to Motion & Time Study* i. 11 More attention is being given to this phase of methods study at present. **1939** MAYNARD & STEGEMERTEN *Operation Analysis* i. 2 A methods study always begins with a careful primary analysis of existing conditions. **1955** *Furniture Devel. Council Newslet.* June 3/2 Efficient method study cannot be put into practice without a sound knowledge of the work in hand. **1959** *Gloss. Terms Work Study (B.S.I.)* 6 *Method study,* the systematic recording and critical examination of existing and proposed ways of doing work, as a means of developing and applying easier and more effective methods and reducing costs. **1969** J. ARGENTI *Managem. Techniques* i. 2 One glance round the factory is enough to reveal to an expert whether the manager there has been using Method Study, for example. *Ibid.* 167 The Method Study Officer ..analyses the purpose and function of each step in the process.

Methodee, var. METHODY (in Dict. and Suppl.).

‖ **Methodenstreit** (meto·dənstrəit). [G., lit. 'methods struggle'.] Discussion or dispute of opinions concerning the methodology of a field of study.

1958 *Spectator* 7 Feb. 173/2 In history, since the *Methodenstreit* of sixty years ago, the flood of 'scientific' research [etc.]. **1968** *Explorations in Entrepreneurial Hist.* VI. 75, I would like to narrow my comments on this twentieth-century *Methodenstreit* to three questions. **1970** *Computers & Humanities* V. 2 A literature of criticism is just beginning to emerge, but it has not yet created the type of *Methodenstreit* that has apparently debilitated scholarship in economic history.

methodic. B. *sb.* **2.** Add to def.: esp. in the teaching of languages.

1962 P. STREVENS *Papers in Lang.* (1965) v. 70 This organizational framework for arranging linguistic terms into a teachable pattern is known in Britain as *Methodics.* **1964** *New Statesman* 6 Mar. 378/1 (Advt.), Applications are invited for a post as Lecturer in the methodics of language teaching. **1964** M. A. K. HALLIDAY et al. *Ling. Sci.* x. 200 Methodics is a framework of organization for practical language teaching, in which pedagogical techniques and linguistic theory cross-fertilize each other.

Methodism. Add: **3.** The doctrines and practice of the 'methodic' school of physicians.

1896 T. C. ALLBUTT in *Classical Rev.* X. 346/2 A second school was Methodism, which was satisfied to refer all symptoms and all disease to the variations of the 'strictum' and the 'laxum'; that is, to the restriction or laxity of the secretions and other fluids of the body. **1958** D. GUTHRIE *Hist. Med.* (rev. ed.) v. 67 This theory, known as 'Methodism', was elaborated by Themison (123–43 B.C.), the pupil of Asclepiades.

methodize, *v.* Add: **1. c.** To convert into Methodists.

1846 A. WILEY in *Indiana Mag. Hist.* (1927) XXIII. 428 Some disciples who are hard cases, will be hard to methodize.

3. *Theatr.* = *method-act* vb. (see *METHOD *sb.* 2 e).

1958 *Spectator* 31 Jan. 136/3 The pouting and posturing and methodising. **1960** *Ibid.* 18 Nov. 782/3 John Dexter's production has been much condemned... Perhaps he should have varied the pace, Methodised the delivery.

methodology. Add to def.: Also, the study of the direction and implications of empirical research, or of the suitability of the techniques employed in it; also *attrib.* (Further examples.)

In some contexts weakened to mean little more than 'method'.

1932 W. E. D. ALLEN *Hist. Georgian People* vii. 91 Alp-Arslan and his commanders were tacticians who evolved a new methodology in mediæval Asiatic war. **1937** T. PARSONS *Struct. Social Action* II. v. 178 (*heading*) The methodology and main analytical scheme. **1944** F. KAUFMANN *Methodology of Social Sci.* p. vii, A reconsideration of the problem how the logical analysis of scientific procedure (methodology) is related to deductive logic. **1949** SHILS & FINCH tr. *Weber's Methodology of Social Sci.* iii. 114 The most significant achievements of specialist methodology use 'ideal-typically' constructed conceptions of the objectives. **1960** *Amer. Speech* XXXV. 212 The authors tell too little about their methodology. **1970** O. DOPPING *Computers & Data Processing* xxii. 343 So far, what we have considered is a straight simulation which does not give rise to any methodology difficulties. **1971** *World Archaeol.* III. 210 The main challenge appears to be in establishing connections that bridge the methodologies of different fields of study. **1972** *Jrnl. Social Psychol.* LXXXVII. 127 None of these methodologies have been extended into the realm of applied psychology. **1974** *Nature* 22 Mar. 294/3 The interfacing of the two techniques..is discussed in depth together with the methodology of operating them together.

methodological *a.*, **methodologically** *adv.*, **methodologist:** further examples.

1914 B. RUSSELL *Our Knowl. External World* viii. 238 It is necessary to practise methodological doubt, like Descartes, in order to loosen the hold of mental habits. **1937** T. PARSONS *Struct. Social Action* I. i. 23 These [assumptions] may lie in a number of different directions. But the ones to which special attention should now be called are the 'methodological'. **1941** J. C. RANSOM *New Crit.* ii. 208 In my mind Dante's beliefs are very bold speculations at which the accusing finger has pointed steadily for a long time now, but substantively are better grounded, and methodologically far more consistent, than Shelley's beliefs. **1942** *Economica* IX. 286 That he [*sc.* the social scientist] systematically starts from the concepts which guide individuals in their actions, is the characteristic feature of that methodological individualism which is closely connected with the subjectivism of the social sciences. **1949** SHILS & FINCH tr. *Weber's Methodology of Social Sci.* iii. 113 The professional methodologist will take umbrage at many of Meyer's formulations. **1952** K. R. POPPER *Open Society* (ed. 2) I. iii. 31, I use the name methodological essentialism to characterize the view..that it is the task of pure knowledge or 'science' to discover and to describe the true nature of things, i.e. their hidden reality or essence. **1962** F. WILLIAMS tr. *Sartre's Imagination* p. vi, This truism has some far-reaching methodological implications, however. **1964** GOULD & KOLB *Dict. Social Sci.* 425/2 The methodologist examines systematically and logically the aptness of all research tools, varying from basic assumptions to special research techniques, for the scientific purpose. *Ibid.* 471/1 Methodologically the term [*sc.* non-empirical] is used to describe all methods of acquiring belief other than those of positive science. **1965** B. B. WOLMAN *Scientific Psychol.* 18 One form of this practice is an extreme and radical methodological reductionism. Instead of developing methods and concepts derived from human life, they imitate..physical science. **1969** R. BLACKBURN in Cockburn & Blackburn *Student Power* 203 What is sometimes called 'methodological individualism' (the bourgeois doctrine that all statements about society can be reduced to statements about individuals) is a device for evading such facts as these. **1972** *Computers & Humanities*

VII. 86 When one kind of analysis is conveniently included in the package but a more methodologically sound analysis is not, inappropriate analysis may result. **1973** *Amer. Speech 1970* XLV. 124 Labov has led something of a methodological revolution.

methods-time. [f. pl. of METHOD *sb.* + TIME *sb.*] Used *attrib.*, esp. in phr. *methods-time measurement* (also with capital initials): see quots. 1948[2], 1968. Abbrev. *MTM.*

1948 H. B. MAYNARD et al. *Methods-Time Measurement* p. v, The methods-time measurement procedure eliminates the necessity for judging the performance level at which an operator works while being observed. *Ibid.* ii. 12 Methods-time measurement is a procedure which analyzes any manual operation or method into the basic motions required to perform it and assigns to each motion a predetermined time standard which is determined by the nature of the motion and the conditions under which it is made. *Ibid.* iii. 25 The desirability of having accurate methods-time data available has long been recognized by methods engineers. *Ibid.* xv. 129 A question which was uppermost all during the period when the methods-time standards were being developed. **1952** A. G. SHAW *Purpose & Pract. Motion Study* iii. 60 The Methods-Time Measurement technique analyses a movement cycle into elements. **1959** V. H. ROTROFF *Work Measurement* iii. 30 Applying the MTM technique, the analyst summarizes all motions required to perform the job properly. **1968** JOHANNSEN & ROBERTSON *Managem. Gloss.* 87 *Methods Time Measurement*, a predetermined motion time work measurement technique devised by the Methods Engineering Council (USA) which analyses manual operations and methods into basic motions required to perform them... There are nine basic MTM motions.

Methody. Add: Also 8 **-dee.** (Earlier and later examples.)

1753 J. WESLEY *Jrnl.* 8 Aug. (1913) IV. 78 As soon as we entered the town [*sc.* Mevagissey] many ran together, crying, 'See, the Methodees are come.' **1794** W. B. STEVENS *Jrnl.* 19 Mar. (1965) 140 A mighty good Methody Parson comes every day. **1834** [see *BATTLESHIP c]. **1907** T. E. KEBBEL *Lord Beaconsfield* xvi. 259 Do I not remember many a sturdy villager who was always ready with a gibe at 'the Methodies', as they were called. **1933** *Bulletin* (Sydney) 25 Oct. 20/1 You should have told him Methodies don't dance. **1962** G. LAWTON *John Wesley's English* ix. 211 Three other nicknames for 'Methodist'—'Culamite', 'Macabee' and 'Methodee' may..be considered here.

methonium (meþōᵘ·niǝm). *Pharm.* [f. *METH- + *-ONIUM.] Any of various polymethylene bistrimethylammonium cations, $[(CH_3)_3N(CH_2)_xN(CH_3)_3]^{2+}$ (where *x* is an integer), or salts of these ions, some of which are used as ganglionic blocking agents in the treatment of hypertension.

[**1949**: cf. *DECAMETHONIUM, *hexamethonium* (s.v. *HEXA-).] **1950** *Lancet* 26 Aug. 353/1 (*heading*) 'Medical sympathectomy' in hypertension. A clinical study of methonium compounds. **1952** *Pharmacol. Rev.* IV. 220 The name of 'methonium' compounds for the members of the polymethylene bistrimethylammonium series has been approved by the British Pharmacopoeia Commission, and it is under this name, preceded by the appropriate numerical prefix, that they are now known. **1969** *Jrnl. Neurochem.* XVI. 1173 Some members of the methonium series are..taken up by a saturable mechanism and..the uptakes can be described quantitatively by Michaelis-Menten type kinetics.

methotrexate (meþo-, mīþotre·ksēit). *Pharm.* [Origin unknown.] 4-Amino-10-methylfolic acid, $C_{20}H_{22}N_8O_5$, an orange-brown powder which is a folic acid antagonist and is used in the treatment of tumours, esp. cancer and leukæmia.

1955 *Sci. News Let.* 5 Feb. 88/2 The new drug is an anti-folic acid compound very similar to Aminopterin. It is called Methotrexate by its manufacturers, Lederle Laboratories, Pearl River, N.Y. **1961** [see *mercaptopurine* s.v. *MERCAPTO(-)]. **1970** *Times Lit. Suppl.* 26 Mar. 332/4 Burkett's [*read* Burkitt's] tumour..can be treated easily and successfully by dosing with methotrexate. **1971** *Nature* 22 Oct. 518/3 The Food and Drug Administration has decided to allow the controversial drug methotrexate to be used for severe cases of psoriasis. **1973** *Brit. Pharmacopœia* 300/1 Methotrexate.

methoxy(-) (meþǫ·ksi). *Chem.* [f. METHOXY(L (cf. HYDROXY-).] **a.** As an inseparable formative element in chem. names, indicating the presence of a methoxyl group, as *methoxyacetophenone, -benzoic* adj., *-pyridine, -succinic* adj.; **metho·xychlor,** a crystalline compound, $(C_6H_4OCH_3)_2CHCCl_3$, of similar chemical structure to DDT, which is used as an insecticide, esp. for veterinary hygiene.

1942 FUSON & SNYDER *Org. Chem.* xxi. 288 A remarkable instance of catalysis has been observed in the formation of *p*-methoxyacetophenone from anisole by treatment with acetic anhydride. **1964** N. G. CLARK *Mod. Org. Chem.* xviii. 479 Like the aromatic aldehydes, the ketones are frequently employed as synthetic intermediates, and as ingredients in perfumery. Some simple derivatives possess quite delightful odours, for example, *p*-methylacetophenone (hawthorn), *p*-methoxyacetophenone (heliotrope). **1895** PERKIN & KIPPING *Org. Chem.* II. xxvi. 397 The methylcresols..are oxidised by chromic acid, yielding the corresponding methoxybenzoic acids, $C_6H_4(OCH_3)\cdot COOH$. **1949** *Jrnl. Econ. Entomol.* XLII. 845/1 Ellenville line flies exhibited resistance to residues of both DDT and methoxychlor. **1959** H. MARTIN *Sci. Princ. Crop Protection* (ed. 4) x. 203 When methoxychlor was used instead [of DDT], Carter *et al.* were unable to detect the insecticide in the milk. **1969** K. A. HASSALL *World Crop Protection* II. iv. 88 Methoxychlor..shows a lower tendency than DDT to dissolve in animal fats and also possesses a much lower acute oral toxicity to higher animals. It is therefore used on and near livestock. **1973** *Globe & Mail* (Toronto) 8 Sept. 8/3 City golf courses and cemeteries were relatively mosquito-free, having been fogged all along with methoxychlor, a new insecticide that doesn't have the harmful properties of DDT. **1889** G. M'GOWAN tr. *Bernthsen's Text-bk. Org. Chem.* 486 Methoxy-pyridine and methyl-pyridone, which result from these two forms by exchange of H..for CH_3, are known. **1893** *Jrnl. Chem. Soc.* LXIII. 229 Inactive methoxysuccinic acid may be resolved into two active acids, of equal and opposite rotatory powers.

b. As an independent word, usu. *attrib.* and sometimes joined by a hyphen to the second element: = METHOXYL.

1900 PERKIN & KIPPING *Org. Chem.* (rev. ed.) xxxiii. 485 By far the greater number of alkaloids contain one or two, sometimes three or more, methoxy-groups.., united with a benzene nucleus. **1946** *Jrnl. Pharmacol. & Exper. Therap.* LXXXVIII. 413 Substitution of chlorine by a..methoxy, butoxy or amyloxy group yields ineffective compounds. **1969** *Times* 10 Feb. 10/8 Dr. Shulgin..prepared many derivatives of mescalin, differing from the parent compound in their pattern of methoxy substitution on the phenyl ring. **1971** *Nomencl. Org. Chem.* (I.U.P.A.C.) (ed. 2) C. 154 The following contractions for oxygen-containing radical names are recommended... Methoxy CH_3—O—.

meths (meþs). Also **meth.** Colloq. abbrev. of *methylated spirit(s)*. Also *attrib.*, freq. as **meth(s)-drinker,** one who is addicted to drinking methylated spirits. (See also *METHO[1].)

1933 M. MARSHALL *Tramp-Royal on Toby* 367/1 *Meth*, methylated spirit. **1935** [see *JAKE *sb.*[2]]. **1939** 'N. SHUTE' *What happened to Corbetts* i. 18 A Primus stove..and paraffin and meths. **1947** [see *HOTTIE, HOTTY *sb.*]. **1959** *Listener* 21 May 893/3 A lovely copper kettle with a meths-burner underneath. **1961** *Times* 15 Aug. 11/3 The surly greetings of the meth-drinkers. **1966** J. BINGHAM *Double Agent* x. 149 It sounds like a meth-drinkers' camp. **1968** *Daily Tel.* 12 Nov. 16/2 Young people who work at clearing slag heaps, helping meths-drinkers or cleaning canals to make them navigable. **1970** M. TRIPP *Man without Friends* i. 7 I'd seen a meths drinker spewing blood the night before. **1973** D. JORDAN *Nile Green* xxxiv. 167, I shook my head like a meths drinker.

Methuselah. Add: **2.** *transf.* A very large wine-bottle (see quots.).

1935 A. L. SIMON *Dict. Wine* 172 *Methuselah*, double Jeroboam, holding 8 reputed quarts or 6·40 litres, equal to 225·350 fluid ounces. **1951** *Bohemian Life* (Bohemian Distrib. Co., Los Angeles, U.S.A.) Apr., Out-size bottles include the..Methuselah..8 bottles or 213·30 ounces. **1959** *Gloss. Packaging Terms* (*B.S.I.*) 28 *Methuselah*, a wine bottle—capacity 9 reputed quarts. **1962** [see *BALTHAZAR]. **1972** E. MEIGH *Story Glass Bottle* 73 Wine bottlers ransacked the Old Testament for names of kings and captains to name the bottles in which their valuable liquids were confined: thus, in ascending order of magnitude are jeroboams, rehoboams, methuselahs.

methyl. Add: **c. methyl alcohol,** add to def.: = *METHANOL; **methylcellulose,** any of a range of white, tasteless compounds which are produced by etherifying cellulose with various proportions of methyl chloride or sulphate and are used as thickening, emulsifying, and stabilizing agents, esp. in the food industry, as laxatives, and in adhesives; **methyldo·pa** *Pharm.*, a whitish powder, $C_{10}H_{13}NO_4$, which is used as a hypotensive agent; **methyl ethyl ketone,** a colourless volatile liquid, $CH_3COCH_2CH_3$, which is widely used as a solvent for organic materials; butanone; **methylglyo·xal,** a yellow liquid aldehyde, CH_3COCHO, with a pungent odour, which readily polymerizes and is an intermediate in carbohydrate metabolism; **methyl isobutyl ketone,** a liquid ketone, $(CH_3)_2CHCH_2COCH_3$, which is manufactured by the hydrogenation of mesityl oxide and widely used as a solvent; hexone; **methyl methacrylate,** (*a*) the methyl ester of methacrylic acid, a volatile colourless liquid that readily polymerizes to resinous glass-like materials that are sold under trade-names such as *Lucite, Perspex,* and *Plexiglas*; (*b*) polymerized methyl methacrylate; **methyl orange,** an orange crystalline compound, $(CH_3)_2N\cdot C_6H_4\cdot N{:}N\cdot C_6H_4\cdot SO_3Na$, which is the sodium salt of an azo-dye made by coupling diazotized sulphanilic acid with dimethylaniline and is chiefly used (in dilute aqueous solution) as an acid–base indicator in volumetric analysis, giving a pink colour at a pH of 3 and a yellow colour at a pH of 4·4; **(6α-)methylpredni·solone,** a synthetic compound, $C_{22}H_{30}O_5$, which functions as a glucorticoid and is used mainly in treating rheumatoid arthritis and rheumatic fever; **methyl red** [tr. G. *methylrot* (Rupp & Loose 1909, in *Ber. d. Deut. Chem. Ges.* XLI. 3905)], a red crystalline compound, $(CH_3)_2N\cdot C_6H_4\cdot N{:}N\cdot C_6H_4\cdot COOH$, that is analogous to methyl orange (anthranilic acid being used in its preparation in place of sulphanilic acid) and is used similarly, the colour of an alcoholic solution being red at a pH of 4·4 and yellow at a pH of 6; **methyl rubber,** an early synthetic rubber made by polymerization of dimethylbutadiene; **methyl salicylate,** a colourless or pale-yellow liquid, $C_6H_4(OH)CO\cdot OCH_3$, which is the chief constituent of oil of wintergreen and sweet birch oil and is used as a flavouring material, in perfumery, and in liniments and ointments; **methyltesto·sterone** *Pharm.*, any of the methyl derivatives, $C_{20}H_{30}O_2$, of testosterone; *spec.* 17-methyltestosterone, a white crystalline powder with similar actions and uses to those of testosterone; **me:thylthiou·racil,** any compound which is a methyl and a thio derivative of uracil; *spec.* 6-methyl-2-thiouracil, $C_5H_6N_2OS$, an antithyroid substance used to control thyrotoxicosis.

1921 *Jrnl. Chem. Soc.* CXIX. I. 79 A methyl cellulose of this limiting methoxyl content can be prepared which is representative of the whole of the original cellulose. **1947** WINDING & HASCHE *Plastics* iii. 119 Water solubility plus the ability to produce viscous solutions has made methyl cellulose useful as a thickening agent in the textile, food, and adhesive industries. Since it is edible, it can be used as a base for salad dressings. **1954** *Jrnl. Pharmacy & Pharmacol.* VI. 731 Methylcellulose eye-drops..are liable to contamination by moulds. **1966** *Punch* 5 Jan. 11/1 In its survey of strawberry jam it [sc. *Which?*] found two specimens in which the composers had succeeded in soaring far above the sordid world of methyl cellulose and lecithin. **1954** *Arch. Biochem. & Biophysics* LI. 456 Two compounds, α-methyl-3,4-dopa (α-MD) and α-methyl-3-hydroxyphenylalanine, respectively, added in a low range of concentrations, accelerated, and at higher concentrations, inhibited, kidney dopa decarboxylase. **1961** *New Zealand Med. Jrnl.* LX. 569/2 Methyl dopa, like other potent hypotensive agents, produces side-effects including fatigue. **1972** *Materials & Technol.* V. xxi. 792 Methyldopa and pargyline cause the replacement of noradrenaline by a weaker transmitter. **1876** *Jrnl. Chem. Soc.* XXIX. 897 By the reduction of methyl-ethyl ketone, pinacone $C_8H_{18}O$ is obtained. **1938** H. P. STARCK *Princ. Org. Chem.* vii. 186 Methyl ethyl ketone was formerly used as a solvent in the preparation of cordite from gun cotton and nitroglycerine. **1959** *Times Rev. Industry* Aug. 98/1 Methylethylketone for removing waxy materials. **1898** *Jrnl. Chem. Soc.* LXXIV. I. 224 Methylglyoxal is formed from dihydroxyacetone..when the latter is distilled with dilute sulphuric acid. **1913, 1951** Methylglyoxal [see *GLYOXALASE]. **1962** A. PIRIE *Lens Metabolism Rel. Cataract* 431 Experiments were done in the hope of detecting methylglyoxal which Salem and Crooke (1950) stated was formed from hexosediphosphate by liver. **1888** *Jrnl. Chem. Soc.* LIV. 125 Its ketone.. is therefore identical with methyl isobutyl ketone. **1960** *Times Rev. Industry* Dec. 16/3 The chloride is dissolved in water, and then treated with an organic solvent called methylisobutyl ketone (MIBK) which extracts the iron. **1973** H. M. STANLEY in E. G. Hancock *Propylene* i. 9 The Shell Oil Company..in 1937–8 commenced the manufacture of acetone derivatives, including diacetone alcohol, mesityl oxide and methylisobutyl ketone. **1933** *Chem. Abstr.* XXVII. 4363 Thermoplastic products are obtained by polymerizing methyl methacrylate..by exposure to light or heat. **1936** *Industr. & Engin. Chem.* Oct. 1161/2 These properties make methyl methacrylate an outstanding plastic. **1964** N. G. CLARK *Mod. Org. Chem.* x. 194 Acetone cyanohydrin..is an important intermediate in the manufacture of methyl methacrylate, the material used for making the polymer 'Perspex'. **1967** *Times Rev. Industry* June 74/3 Methyl methacrylate and/or polyester reinforced glass fibre are used for hand basins, baths, complete bath room heat units, heating ducts, roof lights, &c. **1881** G. LUNGE in *Chem. News* 16 Dec. 288/1 It is in reality a salt of sulpho-benzene-azo-dimethylamin, for which long name I propose the short and sufficiently clear name 'Methyl-orange'. **1930** FIELD & WEILL *Electro-Plating* 56 The ordinary indicators used by the chemist such as litmus, methyl orange and phenolphthalein. **1969** H. A. FLASCHKA et al. *Quantitative Analytical Chem.* II. ix. 110 Methyl orange is therefore unsuited to the titration of a weak acid. **1957** *Ann. Rheumatic Dis.* XVI. 298/2 6-Methyl-prednisolone was administered under various conditions to 41 patients with active peripheral rheumatoid arthritis. **1960** *Antibiotic Med.* VII. 704 The subcutaneous injection of depot methyl prednisolone has demonstrated significant permanent relief of refractory anal pruritus in 14 patients. **1973** *Jrnl. Amer. Med. Assoc.* 19 Feb. 896/1 Large doses of methylprednisolone were used intravenously as the sole steroid agent in 44 transplants in 43 renal allografted patients for the first two to three weeks after operation. **1910** *Jrnl. Chem. Soc.* XCVII. 2490 As a means of measuring colorimetrically the concentration of hydrogen ions in a solution, methyl-red would probably be found valuable when such concentration lies between 10^{-5} and 10^{-6}. **1951** WHITBY & HYNES *Med. Bacteriol.* (ed. 5) xii. 193 When *Bact. coli* is grown for 5 days at 30° C. in the glucose phosphate medium described above an acid reaction is maintained which is sufficient to give a red colouration on the addition of 0·04 per cent aqueous methyl red as indicator. **1969** FISCHER & PETERS *Brief Introd. Quantitative Chem. Analysis* viii. 212 At pH 4·2 (and below)..methyl red is present as the red acid form and..it exists as the yellow base form if the pH becomes

6·2 (and above). **1919** *India-Rubber Jrnl.* 16 Aug. 18/2 The dye works laid themselves out for the manufacture of large quantities of methyl-rubber hot polymerisation products. **1936** *Trans. Faraday Soc.* XXXII. 91 The sharpness of the fibre pattern depends on the sample of methyl rubber investigated. **1972** *Materials & Technol.* V. xiv. 456 During the first World War the Germans worked out..the first factory-scale synthetic rubber plant which produced the so-called methyl rubber... The quality of this rubber was poor; it was only useful for the preparation of hard rubber battery boxes for submarines. **1876** *Encycl. Brit.* V. 572/2 Oil of wintergreen..contains methyl salicylate. **1948** *Jrnl. Amer. Med. Assoc.* 28 Feb. 651/2 Methyl salicylate is a potent and fairly rapidly acting poison. **1972** *Materials & Technol.* IV. xii. 448 Methyl salicylate, which is a known anti-rheumaticum, is made by the Fischer esterification of salicylic acid. **1936** *Biochem. Jrnl.* XXX. 292 Various..derivatives methylated at position 17, including methyltestosterone. **1955** W. GADDIS *Recognitions* II. v. 526 Crossing the Atlantic Ocean to get laid. He can't even get it up without a dose of methyltestosterone. **1959** *Brit. Med. Jrnl.* 31 Jan. 259/2 Methyltestosterone was introduced to clinical medicine..in 1939, and since that time must have been used for its androgenic and protein anabolic effects in thousands of cases. **1970** PASSMORE & ROBSON *Compan. Med. Stud.* II. xii. 11/2, 17α-Methyltestosterone is active by oral administration. **1974** *Nature* 13 Dec. 585/2 We have induced reversible infertility, with little effect on libido, in five healthy young men by giving them tablets containing methyltestosterone and ethynyloestradiol. **1944** *Q. Jrnl. Pharmacy & Pharmacol.* XVII. 318 Methylthiouracil produces hyperplasia of the thyroid gland of the rat. **1960** *Lancet* 19 Mar. 653/2 Professor Wayne's references..to methylthiouracil prompt me to record the long-term follow-up of 100 consecutive cases of thyrotoxicoses. **1968** *Listener* 18 July 70/1, I had recently been diagnosed as hyperthyroidic and had with remarkable benefit embarked on a course of methylthiouracil tablets.

methylate, *v.* Substitute for first part of def.: To introduce one or more methyl groups into (a compound or group). Add further examples of this use.

1861 *Jrnl. Chem. Soc.* XIII. 324 These crystals were not analysed, but there can be no doubt that they were the methylated phosphorus-urea of the allyl-series. **1917** *Ibid.* CXI. 848 Experiments have proved the wide scope of the use of formaldehyde for methylating amino-compounds. **1929** *Jrnl. Amer. Chem. Soc.* LI. 2535 We have found methyl bromide to be a satisfactory methylating agent with both malonic ester and acetoacetic ester. **1967** I. L. FINAR *Org. Chem.* (ed. 5) I. xxvi. 683 Veratrole ..may be prepared by methylating catechol with methyl sulphate in alkaline solution.

methylated *ppl. a.* (examples of *ellipt.* use, = methylated spirit).

1912 D. H. LAWRENCE *Let.* 2 Sept. (1962) I. 142 We take rucksacks..with food and methylated, cook our meals by some stream. **1938** MRS. BELLOC LOWNDES *Let.* 29 Sept. (1971) 165, I also got..rather more methylated, rice and matches than usual.

methylene. Add: **methylene chloride,** dichloromethane, CH_2Cl_2, a volatile liquid used as a solvent, esp. in paint-removers and for extractions in pharmacy, and as a refrigerant.

1880 *Jrnl. Chem. Soc.* XXXVIII. 307 Methylene chloride, CH_2Cl_2, is best obtained by cautiously adding hydrochloric acid to a mixture of alcohol, chloroform, and metallic zinc. **1953** O. E. ANDERSON *Refrigeration in Amer.* xii. 193 Other absorption machines were brought out for air-conditioning work. One of these used methylene chloride as the refrigerant. **1957** H. R. SHEPHERD in E. Sagarin *Cosmetics* xxxvi. 803 Ethyl chloride, methylene chloride, and others..among the earliest aerosol propellents, are not presently being used for cosmetic purposes. **1973** *Oxf. Univ. Gaz.* CIII. Suppl. 5. 10 The goddess has now been degreased with lustrations of methylene chloride and acetone.

methylol (me·þilǫl). *Chem.* [f. METHYL + -OL.] = *hydroxymethyl* s.v. *HYDROXY- 3.

1898 *Jrnl. Chem. Soc.* LXXIV. I. 506 Nitrobutylic alcohol..readily condenses with formaldehyde (1 mol.) to form a glycol (2-methylol-2-nitro-1-butanol). **1937** F. C. WHITMORE *Org. Chem.* 521 Formaldehyde condenses with urea to give methylol ureas, $NH_2CONHCH_2OH$ etc. The methylol groups can combine with more urea to form more and more complex molecules until a resin is formed. **1962** J. T. MARSH *Self-Smoothing Fabrics* i. 3 The fundamental basis of the process remains unchanged and depends on the application of methylol compounds within the fibre of the fabric followed by their further condensation.

methysergide (meþɪsɜ̄·ɹdʒəid). *Pharm.* [f. *METH- + *L)YSERG(IC *a.* + AM)IDE.] 1-Methyl-D-lysergic acid butanolamide, $C_{21}H_{28}N_3O_2$, a serotonin antagonist that is administered, usu. in the form of its maleate, in the prophylaxis of recurrent migraine.

1962 *Amer. Jrnl. Med. Sci.* CCXLIII. 152/1 Fifty-seven patients..were treated with antiserotonin agent, methysergide (UML-491). **1962** *Daily Tel.* 30 July 11/6 Methysergide (Deseril), is being tested as a preventive against chronic forms of migraine. **1968** J. H. BURN *Lect. Notes Pharmacol.* (ed. 9) 30 In some patients methysergide causes dizziness and nausea and produces aching in the legs.

metic. (Further examples.)

1921 *Times Lit. Suppl.* 10 Nov. 731/2 The proportion of the horrific in Poe's poetry..is entirely different; he is a metic in the land of shadows. **1936** *Ibid.* 14 Nov. 918/4 Sir Harry Preston was not Brightonian by birth—but then most of the town's great men have been metics. **1974** *Sci. Amer.* Sept. 95/1 In Athens the free immigrants called *metics*, who were permanent residents rather than passing traders, may have outnumbered the slaves.

meticulosity. (Later example.)

1972 *Country Life* 16 Mar. 657/2 The meticulosity of manners was necessary inside or outside the novels, in the villainy of a manor house character or at the tea-table.

meticulous, *a.* Add: **2.** In present usage: careful, punctilious, scrupulous, precise.

1952 W. D. JACOBS *William Barnes, Linguist* i. 9 They [*sc.* Barnes's linguistic studies] present a possible solution to mongrelized English and an alternate program of greater scale and with more meticulous plan than any previous to Barnes. **1964** *New Statesman* 8 May 710/1 Wilson is far too meticulous a constitutionalist not to appreciate the impropriety—not to mention the impossibility—of an opposition's seeking to govern a country in advance. **1973** *Times* 4 May 2/7 Dr Ramsey said in a meticulous English accent: 'Can I just say [etc.].'

meticulously, *adv.* Add to def.: In present usage: in a careful or punctilious manner. (Cf. *METICULOUS *a.* 2.)

1961 'J. WYNDHAM' *Consider her Ways* 90 He had..a black felt hat meticulously brushed. **1971** *Nature* 4 June 334/3 It is essentially a reference book, meticulously cross-referenced, with a huge bibliography and a good index. **1974** *Physics Bull.* Mar. 104/2 With the aid of a meticulously detailed account of the formal basis of quantum mechanics, Professor Scheibe has provided a precise characterization of the orthodox interpretation of the theory.

meti·culousness. [-NESS.] The quality of being meticulous; meticulosity.

1923 *Sunday at Home* Mar. 382/2 He was measured and cautious in his statements to the point of meticulousness. **1927** *Daily Tel.* 2 Mar. 5/5 Examples..handed down to posterity in paint with a meticulousness that..never fails to charm us. **1928** *Observer* 1 July 15/6 The paragraph of last Sunday did not do justice to the meticulousness of the index to Mr. Shaw's 'Intelligent Woman's Guide to Socialism'. **1937** *Discovery* Jan. 32/2 The pleasing meticulousness of a Chinese drawing.

métier. (Later examples.)

1950 T. S. ELIOT *Cocktail Party* III. 157 You understand your *metier*, Mr. Quilpe—Which is the most that any of us can ask for. **1958** *Listener* 27 Nov. 874/1 It is fashionable to regard technical and physical craft [in the theatre] as adventitious and to have no sense whatever of what the French call *métier*. **1975** *Times* 18 Sept. 36/2 The parallels started to extend from the man to the *métier*.

metis. Add: (Earlier and later examples.) Also applied to other persons of mixed blood and *transf.* to animals and plants.

1816 C. ROBERTSON in *Publ. Hudson's Bay Rec. Soc.* (1939) II. 248 Your European Servants and Metiss are in many places deserting over to the North West Company. **1949** *Amer. Speech* XXIV. 95 A common term to indicate a crossbreed between Persian lamb and other Asiatic species of lamb is *metis*, derived from the French for 'half-breed'. **1966** *Kingston* (Ontario) *Whig-Standard* 29 July 6/3 A settlement of about 1500 Cree Indians and 300 Metis. **1972** *Guardian* 4 July 16/2 The estimated 15,000 to 50,000 *métis* children in South Vietnam—children of American soldiers, either half-black or half-white. **1972** D. BLOODWORTH *Any Number can Play* v. 37 He nodded towards a plump Eurasian... 'Bonjour, les gars,' murmured the métis. **1974** *Sci. Amer.* June 115/1 In California the work has taken mainly the direction of producing new *métis* (crosses within species) by crossing Europe's temperate-climate and Mediterranean vines with a view to obtaining better grapes for the fertile but desertlike Central Valley. **1975** *Time* 3 Feb. 8/3 The oppression and mistreatment of the Indians and Métis..never become anything more than a rhetorical device.

‖ **métissage** (metisāʒ). [Fr.: cf. METIS.] Cross-breeding. Also *fig.*

1895 in *Funk's Stand. Dict.* **1959** *Times* 13 Aug. 9/7 He is, too, on historical grounds, a firm believer in the value of *métissage*—the cross-fertilization of civilizations. **1972** *Guardian* 8 July 9/1 Léopold Senghor, President of Sénégal,..is a great believer in the virtues of *métissage*, or racial mixture.

métisse (metīs). Fem. of METIS.

1895 in *Funk's Stand. Dict.* **1955** G. GREENE *Quiet Amer.* III. i. 196 Across the way a *métisse* with long and lovely legs lay..reading a glossy woman's paper. **1961** E. BRUTON *King Diamond* vi. 87 'She's not African. Not entirely anyway...She's a metisse.'..'I know he wouldn't have gone for an African.' 'He didn't exactly. She's half and half.'

metœstrus (metī·strɒ̆s). *Biol.* Also **-um,** (*U.S.*) **metestrus** (-e·strɒ̆s, -ī·strɒ̆s), **-um.** [f. MET(A- + ŒSTRUS, ŒSTRUM.] The short period following œstrus in many mammals during which sexual activity subsides.

1900 W. HEAPE in *Q. Jrnl. Microsc. Sci.* XLIV. 8 Metœstrum or the Metœstrous Period.—If conception does not take place during œstrus the activity of the generative organs gradually subsides during a definite period, which I have called the metœstrum; and this is followed..by a long period of rest. **1923** *Amer. Jrnl. Anat.* XXXII. 340 Follicular phase [of the sexual cycle]: *a*, proestrus. *b*, oestrus. *c*, metoestrus (in certain species where ovulation is separated from oestrus by an interval). **1966** *McGraw-Hill Encycl. Sci. & Technol.* XI. 476/1 After metestrus a relatively longer period of diestrus occurs before proestrus recurs... All these phases can be demonstrated in the guinea pig and rat. **1973** *Nature* 12 Jan. 129/2 When the drug was administered on other days of the cycle, metoestrus, dioestrus or pro-oestrus, it failed to increase ovulation rate.

Hence **metœ·strous** *a.*

1900 [see above]. **1956** *Nature* 4 Feb. 235/1 These groups were of pro-œstrous, œstrous, metœstrous and diœstrous rats.

metonymic, *a.* (Examples.)

1952 M. MCCARTHY *Groves of Academe* (1953) v. 85 As he had paused in the hall outside Domnar's door..he had not yet..felt the metonymic urge that would prompt him ..to substitute the effect for the cause. **1969** P. ANDERSON in Cockburn & Blackburn *Student Power* 261 'I' is no longer I in the opaque, metonymic *double-entendre* of Freud's patients.

me too (mī tū). Phr. used alone or in various collocations (see quots.) of a person who, or a course of action which, adopts or acquiesces in the views, policies, etc., of someone else, often *spec.* those of one's political or other opponents. Freq. in a derogatory sense. orig. *U.S.* Also (with hyphen) as *vb.* Hence **me-too·er, me-too·ism.**

The colloq. ejaculation 'Me too!' signifying either that the speaker shares another person's view or experience or that the speaker wants the same share as another is getting, is the basis of the modern use.

1745 CHESTERFIELD *Let.* 13 Apr. (1932) II. 596 You must mark out Lord Granville by exterminating without quarter all who belong to him... If you take this resolution,..I empower you to make what use you please of my name as quitting with you; and I say as Will Seymour did, *And me, too, sweet Jesus.* **1851** H. MELVILLE *Moby Dick* I. xxxix. 275 Me too; where's your girls? **1873** L. M. ALCOTT *Work* II. xi. 336 'Me too!' cried little Ruth, and spread her chubby hand above the rest. **1921** H. WILLIAMSON *Beautiful Yrs.* 128 'Where are you going?' 'Out.' 'Where to man?' 'Mr. Norman's.'..'Norman's, you said? Right-o. Me, too!' **1922** JOYCE *Ulysses* 459 *Mrs. Mervyn Talboys...* He implored me..to give him a most vicious horsewhipping. *Mrs. Bellingham.* Me too. *Mrs. Yelverton Barry.* Me too. **1924** A. S. NEILL *Dominie's Five* xii. 245 'I'm going to start to-day to learn to read.' 'Me too,' said Donald. **1940** H. L. ICKES *Diary* (1954) III. 312, I think that Willkie overlooked the best chance that he had by being content merely to 'me too' the President on his foreign policies and most of his domestic ones instead of striking out for himself in a bold and positive way. **1949** *Time* 7 Feb. 10/3 We [*sc.* the Republicans] suffered because we tried to me-too the New Deal. **1949** *Sun* (Baltimore) 14 Dec. 2/1 A recommendation that..the Republican party..divest itself of 'me-tooism' and go to the people with a program clearly and unmistakably in opposition to that now offered by our opponents. **1951** *Economist* 10 Nov. 1109/1 He is against any 'Me Too' procedures, by which he means opposition acceptance of Administration policy at home or abroad. **1952** *Manch. Guardian Weekly* 1 May 3 If General Eisenhower gets the Republican nomination he will have to risk the shame of me-tooing the Truman policy. **1958** *Spectator* 1 Aug. 156/3 With the collapse of doctrinaire Socialism, and the adoption instead of a modified me-tooism, the range of controversy is being still further reduced. **1959** *Guardian* 28 Dec. 6/1 Wendell Willkie, Governor Dewey, and General Eisenhower were all..'me-tooers'—men whose chief appeal was to the vague, uncontroversial idealism of the non-partisan. **1960** *New Left Rev.* Jan./Feb. 1/2 The champions of 'me-too' advance into..an 'American' future. **1960** J. R. ACKERLEY *We think the World of You* 82 The almost mad stare with which her starting eyes pierced and searched my own for the answer to the only question in the world: 'Me too?' **1962** *Sunday Times* 19 Aug. 18 'I'm a rugged individualist: I think for myself.' 'Me too.' 'Same here.' **1965** *Economist* 14 Aug. 607/2 The unions have few independent ideas to contribute to this design for a better America; they were 'me tooers' in Roosevelt's New Deal, Truman's Fair Deal and Kennedy's New Frontier. **1967** *Spectator* 13 Oct. 419/2 The usefulness of 'me-tooism' in capturing the floating voter should not be underestimated. **1975** G. V. HIGGINS *City on Hill* i. 18 Sam gets round to saying it on the floor a week later, and he's me-tooing.

Metopirone (metopi·rōᵘn). *Pharm.* Also **metopirone.** [f. 2-*meth*yl-1,2-di(*pyr*id-3-yl)-propan-1-*one*, the chemical name (see *METYRAPONE), with alteration of *y* to *i* and insertion of *o*.] A proprietary name for metyrapone.

1960 *Lancet* 17 Dec. 1332/2 Metopirone is an 11 β-hydroxylase inhibitor which presumably prevents the production of aldosterone by the adrenal gland. **1961** *Trade Marks Jrnl.* 8 Feb. 172/1 Metopirone... Pharmaceutical preparations and substances for human use and for veterinary use. CIBA Limited.., Basle, Switzerland. **1962** *Lancet* 19 May 1041/2 The duration of the action of metopirone was investigated, in order to determine the best dosage schedule in tests of pituitary function. **1973** *Arch. Internat. de Pharmacodynamie et de Thérapie* CCII. 93 Metopirone was found to provoke in normal, but not in adrenalectomized rats, a three-fold increase in blood sugar and a four-fold increase in plasma adrenaline.

metoposcopy. 2. (Later example.)

c **1886** L. HEARN in G. M. Gould *Concerning L. Hearn* (1908) 87 'Are you not a Greek?' I asked, for there was no mistaking the metoposcopy of that head. Yes; he was from Zante.

metovum. Substitute for def.: An ovum in its second stage, e.g. a meroblastic ovum after formation of the food-yolk; also called *deutovum* (DEUTO- 2).

Metrazol (me·trăzǫl). *Pharm.* Also **metrazol.** [f. *penta)me(thylenete)trazol*, its chemical name, f. PENTA- + METHYLENE + TETRA- + AZO- + -OL.] A proprietary name of *LEPTAZOL.

1928 *Official Gaz.* (U.S. Patent Office) 11 Sept. 265/1 E. Bilhuber, Inc... *Metrazol* for medicine for the heart and the vascular system. **1932** *Arch. Internat. de Pharmacodynamie et de Thérapie* XLII. 200 Cardiazol (metrazol) is pentamethylenetetrazol. **1950** *Brit. Jrnl. Psychol.* Dec. 104 Metrazol was used to induce convulsions in another unsuccessful attempt to apply therapy at a physiological level. **1973** *Physiol. & Behaviour* X. 94/2 Convulsive doses of Metrazol..may not actually prevent memory storage but rather modify the conditions under which these processes take place.

metre, *sb.*[2] Add: **a.** Now one of the base units of the International System of Units, and redefined in terms of the wavelength of a spectral line (at 605·8 nanometres) of an isotope of krypton (see quot. 1970). (Further examples.)

1961 *Nature* 21 Jan. 195/1 The eleventh General Conference of Weights and Measures was held in Paris during October 11–20... One epoch-making scientific decision was taken, namely, to redefine the metre in terms of a natural atomic standard, the wave-length of light, thus deposing the platinum–iridium bar—the International Prototype Metre—from the supremacy it has held in the field of length measurements since 1889. *Ibid.* 196/2 The specification of the conditions of excitation and observation [of the radiation] ensures a reproducibility of the new optical metre to about 1 part in 100 millions. **1970** *Internat. System of Units* (*B.S.I.*) 5 The metre is the length equal to 1 650 763·73 wavelengths in vacuum of the radiation corresponding to the transition between the levels $2p_{10}$ and $5d_5$ of the krypton-86 atom. (11th CGPM (1960), Resolution 6). **1971** *Physics Bull.* July 397/1 The definition of the metre in terms of the wavelength of the orange spectral line of a krypton discharge was internationally accepted in 1960 and brought about a new interest in interferometry for length measurement.

b. metre-angle *Ophthalm.* [tr. G. *meterwinkel* (A. Nagel, in Graefe & Saemisch *Handbuch der gesammten Augenheilkunde* (1880) VI. x. 479)], a unit of convergence equal to the angle between the line of sight of either eye and the median line passing between them when the eyes are fixating a point on that line one metre away; **metre-candle** = *LUX *sb.*; **metre-kilogramme-second,** used *attrib.* to designate a system of units in which the basic units of length, mass, and time are respectively the metre, the kilogramme, and the second, and which was taken as the basis of the International System of Units; commonly abbreviated **M.K.S.*, *m.k.s.*

1886 C. M. CULVER tr. *Landolt's Refraction & Accommodation of Eye* ii. 187 We are indebted to Nagel for the ingenious idea of rendering the mensuration of convergence so simple and..so practical. He calls this unit-angle the 'Meterwinkel' *metre-angle.* **1949** H. C. WESTON *Sight, Light & Efficiency* i. 27 The value of the metre-angle depends on the distance apart of the two eyes, but is commonly equal to about 1·75°. **1964** S. DUKE-ELDER *Parsons' Dis. Eye* (ed. 14) xxviii. 455 With an emmetropic person the amount of convergence, reckoned in metre angles, is the same as the amount of accommodation reckoned in dioptres. **1909** *Cent. Dict.* Suppl., Meter-candle. **1915** R. A. HOUSTON *Treat. Light* xx. 362 It is often necessary to measure in foot-candles or metre-candles the degree of illumination of a surface. **1939** A. W. BARTON *Text Bk. Light* ix. 197 A metre-candle is equal to a lumen per square metre,..so that there are 10,000 metre-candles in a phot. **1970** M. V. KLEIN *Optics* iv. 126 Lux are also called meter-candles. **1940** *Chambers's Techn. Dict.* 544/1 Metre-kilogramme-second (M-K-S) system of units. **1943** LEMON & FERENCE *Analytical Exper. Physics* ii. 38/1 Recently adopted by an international congress as the official system of metric units is the meter-kilogram-second (MKS) system. **1963** *Listener* 24 Jan. 156/1 The metre-kilogram-second system has been preferred by the Institute of Electrical Engineers.

metric, *a.*[1] and *sb.* Add: **A.** *adj.* **2.** (Examples.) Add to def.: *esp.* relating to, involving, or defining distance; *metric geometry* = *metrical geometry* s.v. METRICAL *a.*[1] 2; *metric space* [tr. Ger. *metrischer raum* (F. Hausdorff *Grundzüge der Mengenlehre* (1914) vii. 211)], a set together with a metric defined for all pairs of elements of the set.

1873 *Proc. Lond. Math. Soc.* IV. 387 This metric geometry is due to Prof. Cayley. **1910** VEBLEN & YOUNG *Projective Geom.* i. 12 The difference between projective and the ordinary Euclidean metric geometry. **1916** *Monthly Notices R. Astron. Soc.* LXXVI. 701 The line-element *ds* must be invariant for all transformations, and it entirely characterises the metric properties of the four-dimensional time-space. **1923** J. RICE *Relativity* xiii. 312 Space-time is a metric four-dimensional manifold. **1927** *Bull. Amer. Math. Soc.* XXXIII. 14 The following illustrations convey some notion of the scope of the concept metric space. If the aggregate *P* denotes the linear continuum of all real numbers and $(p, q) = |p - q|$, the resulting space is metric. Similarly euclidean space is also metric. **1963** R. A. ROSENBAUM *Introd. Projective Geom. & Mod. Algebra* i. 12 Note that all the items of this list of nonprojective properties involve magnitudes of lengths and angles. Such 'metric' properties are the concern of traditional elementary geometry. The situation may be loosely described by stating that metric geometry treats of more highly restricted properties than those of projective geometry. **1968** E. T. COPSON *Metric Spaces* i. 3 The study of the properties of sets of 'points' in a 'space' whose only geometrical property is the existence of a 'distance' between each pair of 'points' is called metric space topology. *Ibid.* ii. 21 Different choices of metric on a given set *E* give rise to different metric spaces. **1971** *Nature* 5 Nov. 35/1 It has the properties of a metric function in a space, the elements of which are finite non-empty sets.

B. *sb.* **1.** (Further examples.)

1892 *Mod. Lang. Notes* VII. 100 Metrics and æsthetics go hand in hand. **1952** G. SARTON *Hist. Sci.* I. xx. 521 Ancient music included not only music as we understand it but also metrics, poetry. **1970** *Jrnl. Eng. & Gmc. Philol.* LXIX. 81 Rules for syntax and metrics in *Beowulf.*

2. *Math.* and *Physics.* A metric function, i.e. one defining a distance or an abstract quantity analogous to distance (see quot. 1962).

1921 *Proc. R. Soc.* A. XCIX. 104 In the non-Euclidean geometry of Riemann, the metric is defined by certain quantities, $g_{\mu\nu}$, which are identified by Einstein with the potentials of the gravitational field. **1934** C. C. KRIEGER tr. *Sierpiński's Introd. Gen. Topology* vi. 90 In every metric space *M* a metric, which is equivalent to the given one, can be established,..such that the new distances between the elements of *M* are all ≤ 1. **1956** E. H. HUTTEN *Lang. Mod. Physics* iii. 114 Riemann gave a better representation for the multiplicity of geometries by taking space to be a three-dimensional manifold, and it is the metric given by a mathematical expression referring to distance that decides the type of geometry. **1962** B. H. ARNOLD *Intuitive Concepts Elem. Topology* viii. 138 The function of *d* is a metric in *X* if and only if the following conditions are satisfied for all points *x*, *y*, and *z* of *X*. (1) $d(x, y) \geq 0$. (2) $d(x, y) = 0$ iff $x = y$. (3) $d(x, y) = d(y, x)$. (4) $d(x, y) + d(y, z) \geq d(x, z)$. **1965** J. D. NORTH *Measure of Universe* iv. 63 In 1908 Minkowski introduced into the context of the Special Theory of Relativity the metric now known by his name: $ds^2 = dt^2 - (1/c^2)(dx^2 + dy^2 + dz^2)$. The null geodesics of Minkowski space-time represent the paths followed by light.

3. = METRE *sb.*[1] 1 a.

1933 T. S. ELIOT *Use of Poetry* ii. 38, I do not even believe that the metric of *The Testament of Beauty* is successful. **1941** R. GIRVAN in *Proc. Brit. Acad.* *1940* 331 The metric is astonishing and cannot be paralleled in Anglo-Saxon poetry. **1951** T. S. ELIOT *Poetry & Drama* ii. 20 He [*sc.* Yeats] wrote plays in verse..in a metric which..is not really a form of speech quite suitable for anybody except mythical kings and queens.

4. (See quot. 1934.)

1934 H. C. WARREN *Dict. Psychol.* 166/2 *Metric*, a system or standard of measurement in terms of which the conclusions stated hold. **1968** *Language* XLIV. 715 The simplicity metric demands that one choose the unmarked segment as the underlying one, since its choice leads to less complexity in the phonological representation. **1973** A. H. SOMMERSTEIN *Sound Pattern Anc. Greek* iii. 94 This statement does not depend on the acceptance of a feature-counting simplicity metric. P. H. Matthews, in a seminar at Cambridge, has criticized the assumption that such a metric is the appropriate evaluation measure for grammars.

metric, *a.*[2] Add: *metric ton*, 1000 kilogrammes (2204·6 lb. avoirdupois, or 0·9842 ton); = *TONNE.

1924 *Times Trade & Engin. Suppl.* 29 Nov. 238/3 The output of certain important goods has considerably increased:..sugar to 318,987 metric tons, against 270,279. **1957** G. E. HUTCHINSON *Treat. Limnol.* I. viii. 546 A quantity of salt of the order of 100,000 metric tons per year is transported. **1973** *Guardian* 25 Jan. 7/5 The Government yesterday took a hard line with newsprint manufacturers by allowing increases of only £2 a metric ton (tonne).

b. Having the metric system as the principal system of weights and measures.

1919 [see *NEWTON, 2]. **1960** *Nature* 2 July 30/2 There is no strong feeling in industry or commerce that Britain is being adversely affected..in exports to metric countries by the retention of the Imperial system. **1961** *B.S.I. News* Apr. 16/1 The controversial issue of whether this country should 'go metric'. **1971** *Sci. Amer.* Sept. 76/2 A metric America..would seem to be desirable in terms of our stake in world trade. **1974** *Times* 22 May 6 Virtually every country in the world is metric.

B. *sb.*[2] Metric measurement; metric weights and measures collectively.

1969 *Times* 21 July p. vii/5 Metric is so much easier to teach and to learn. **1970** *Daily Tel.* 21 May 10/5 Metric was so simple that a toddler could learn it, he said. And the litre was not strange to car-buyers. **1971** *Nature* 13 Aug. 439/1 The deliberate encouragement of the tendency towards metric could quite quickly create a situation in which the metric system was as widely used as the conventional system in the United States. **1973** *Country Life* 27 Dec. 2186/1 Once we get used to metric, things should be simpler for all of us.

-metric (me·trik), a terminal element of adjs. corresponding to sbs. ending in -METER or -METRY.

metrical, *a.*[1] Add: **1.** *spec.* applied to Old or Middle English verse.

1802 J. RITSON (*title*) Ancient Engleish metrical romanceës. **1807** S. TURNER *Hist. Anglo-Saxons* (ed. 2) II. 294 This poem [sc. *Beowulf*] is certainly a metrical romance in the Anglo-Saxon language. **1830** B. THORPE tr. *Rask's Gram. Anglo-Saxon Tongue* 150 The Anglo-Saxons..in many M.S.S., carefully separate the verse by metrical points. **1897** *Mod. Lang. Notes* XII. 79 This regularity of arrangement holds only for the half line, the metrical unit. **1923** G. SAINTSBURY *Hist. Eng. Prosody* (ed. 2) I. II. i. 90 The metrical romances present by far the largest section.. of earlier fourteenth-century verse-literature. **1930** FRENCH & HALE *M.E. Metrical Romances* p. v, The metrical romances are the first large body of English fiction. **1946** *Trans. Philol. Soc. 1943–6* 59 What neither Sievers nor any other writers..have ever pointed out, is that the 'five types' are language patterns not metrical patterns. **1953** *Speculum* XXVIII. 449 The discovery of..the non-existence of metrical formulas in the poetry of lettered authors. **1963** R. QUIRK in Brown & Foote *Early Eng. & Norse Stud.* 159 Metrical units in variation.

metricalization. [-IZATION.] A making metrical in character.

1924 *Glasgow Herald* 13 Nov. 10 The question of the metricalisation of our coinage.

me·trically, *adv.*[2] [f. METRICAL *a.*[2] + -LY[2].] In or with the metric system.

1969 *Daily Tel.* 5 Sept. 25/2 A builder of iron and steel plants has found his design time reduced by 15 per cent. when working metrically.

metricate (me·trikēit), *v.* [Back-formation from next: see -ATE[3].] **a.** *intr.* To change to or adopt the metric system of weights and measures.

1965 [see *METRICATION]. **1968** *Guardian* 27 July 3 It may not be practicable to metricate, except possibly over a far longer period than that suggested. **1970** *Daily Tel.* 14 May 18 Current Admiralty Tide Tables, now beginning to metricate in earnest, propose to use decimetres. **1972** *B.S.I. News* June 17/2 Did it not take..nearly a century for Britain to decide to metricate?

b. *trans.* To convert or adapt to the metric system.

1970 *Times* 28 Oct. 7 The cost of metricating road signs..would eventually have to be considered. **1972** *Daily Tel.* 13 Oct. 19/3 The Royal Navy..started to metricate Admiralty charts in 1970.

Hence **me·tricated** *ppl. a.*, made or sold in accordance with metric measurements; converted to or using the metric system.

1970 *Daily Tel.* 14 May 18 Your metricated cook cannot have, standing alongside the kitchen scales, a set of SI weights... There will be no SI weights. *Ibid.* 1 Dec. 3/2 When clothes are fully metricated, at least two things will still be recognisable in the old shapes, brassieres and shoes. **1971** *Timber Trades Jrnl.* 14 Aug. 54/3 This is the second season of metricated wood and the system is now accepted as normal practice among the merchants. **1972** *Bookseller* 18 Mar. 1642/3 Publishers have already invested hundreds of thousands of pounds in metricated editions of educational works. **1972** *B.S.I. News* June 12/1 The encouragement of the use of 'metricated' products.

metrication (metrikēi·ʃən). [f. METRIC *a.*[2] + -ATION.] The process of converting to the metric system of weights and measures; the adoption of the metric system.

1965 J. V. DUNWORTH (Director, Nat. Physical Lab.) in *Times* 29 Nov. 11/5 Earlier this year the National Physical Laboratory sought the guidance of the editor [*sc.* E. McIntosh] of the *Concise Oxford Dictionary* on this matter... His reply was as follows:—'Consider the following: Carbon(ize); decimal(ize);..methyl(ate); oxygen(ate). The modern tendency is to use -ize, -ization in forming new words rather than -ate, -ation. It seems to me that either *metrication* or *metricization* could be used.' In the light of these comments the N.P.L. and the Ministry of Technology chose 'metrication' on the grounds of brevity and euphony. The corresponding verb 'metricate' seems very satisfactory. **1966** *New Scientist* 6 Jan. 32/1 Some British scientists who have worked for years with dynes and oersteds, calories and millimetres of mercury, may think they need not share the worries of their fellow citizens about metrication. **1968** *Observer* 21 Apr. 7/1 The Board of Trade has refused to announce a programme for metrication. **1969** *Guardian* 27 Jan. 3/4 The metrication of large sections of British industry will soon be an accomplished fact. **1971** *Daily Colonist* (Victoria, B.C.) 25 Nov. 26/2 Creeping metrication is upon us and the CFL [*sc.* Canadian Football League] has taken official cognizance of the fact.

metrification. Add: **2.** = *METRICATION.

1965 *Observer* 5 Dec. 40/5 If of old measures we're forsakers..How describe it? There are cries For Metrification, Metricize. **1970** *Times* 17 Apr. 6 Now there was a threat of metrification of weights and measures. **1973** *Daily Tel.* 27 July 16 What angers us is the manner in which the Government has tried to persuade us that VAT..was to our benefit, like decimalisation, two-tier postal systems and now metrification. **1974** *Publishers Weekly* 25 Nov. 12/3 [*heading* 1980: Target Date for Metric Conversion in U.S.] Metrification has been called the non-issue of the century.

metrify, *v.* Add: **2.** *intr.* = *METRICATE *v.* a. *rare.*

1968 *Sunday Times* 31 Mar. 10 The Confederation of British Industry hopes that 75 per cent. of Britain's industries will have metrified by 1975.

metrizable (metrəi·zăb'l), *a.* *Math.* [f. as next + -ABLE, tr. G. *metrisierbar* (P. Urysohn 1924, in *Math. Ann.* XCII. 275).] Of a topological space: capable of being assigned a metric which makes it a metric space identical to the original space.

1927 *Bull. Amer. Math. Soc.* XXXIII. 25 It is therefore of interest to formulate the conditions that a space be metrizable in terms of continuous functions. **1968** E. T. Copson *Metric Spaces* ix. 142 General topology is a generalization of the theory of metric spaces since there are topological spaces which are not metrizable.

So **metrizabi·lity,** the property of being metrizable.

1927 *Bull. Amer. Math. Soc.* XXXIII. 23 Axiom 1 is a sufficient condition for metrizability. **1964** W. J. Pervin *Found. Gen. Topology* x. 158 In the case of separable metric spaces, Urysohn..found necessary and sufficient conditions for metrizability.

metrization (metrəizēi·ʃən). *Math.* [ad. G. *metrisation* (P. Urysohn 1924, in *Math. Ann.* XCII. 275): see prec. and -ation.] The process of assigning a metric to a metrizable topological space.

1927 *Bull. Amer. Math. Soc.* XXXIII. 14 The Metrization Problem. The problem is to state in terms of the concepts point, and point of accumulation the conditions that a topological space be metric. **1937** *Ibid.* XLIII. 141 This theorem gives conditions for the metrization of neighbourhood spaces and a comparatively simple method of introducing the metric. **1964** W. J. Pervin *Found. Gen. Topology* x. 158 The metrization theorem.

metro[2] (me·tro). *colloq.* [Fr., abbrev. of (*Chemin de Fer*) *Métropolitain* Metropolitan Railway.] The Metropolitan Underground Railway of Paris (usu. in form **métro**). Hence applied to the underground railway in other countries. (Applied to London trains *metro* (me·tro) is an abbreviation of Metropolitan *a.* rather than a use in English of F. *métro.*)

1904 A. Bennett *Jrnl.* (1932) I. 202 Wandering down through the Palais Royal and then taking the Métro. **1919** Mencken *Amer. Lang.* 110 In England..a subway is always a *tube*, or the *underground*, or the *Metro.* **1924** S. Story *Dining in Paris* 12 Business men, clerks, stock-brokers..have lit the eternal cigarette..before going to a restaurant for dinner or taking omnibus or 'metro' to their distant homes. **1927** W. E. Collinson *Contemp. Eng.* 66 Recently attempts have been made to put the short form metro [for the Underground railway in London] before the public. **1953** X. Fielding *Stronghold* iv. ii. 263, I realized why the ibex..smelt so strongly of the Paris *métro.* **1963** *Listener* 7 Mar. 418/1 It was in the way of a roundabout and the new metro [in Rotterdam]. **1966** *Ibid.* 1 Dec. 801/1 The underground system..is called the *métro*, but, typical of bilingual Montreal, is more often referred to as the subway. **1973** *Nat. Geographic* May 658/1 The Metro, Mexico's new subway system, is one of the wonders of the city.

Metro[3] (me·tro). *Canad.* [Abbrev. of Metropolitan *a.* 2.] The Metropolitan area of Toronto and other Canadian cities. Also *attrib.* or as *adj.*

1957 *Maclean's Mag.* 17 Aug. 3/3 Metro chairman.. said a Bloor Street subway would be a mistake; Metro would study others. **1962** *Time* (Canad. ed.) 26 Jan. 10/2 Canada's second experiment with metropolitan government... The Metro [of Winnipeg] did not follow Toronto Metro's example. **1963** J. N. Harris *Weird World Wes Beattie* (1964) xi. 138 The threat that the Metro Police would try it if the provincials didn't was sufficient to settle the matter. **1966** *Globe & Mail* (Toronto) 25 June 3/4 [He] faced an indirect challenge during the election campaign from a ginger group of eight Liberal in metro Winnipeg ridings. **1968** *Ibid.* 5 Feb. 1/9 There were 25,000 [drunks] charged in Metro Toronto last year. **1970** *Toronto Daily Star* 24 Sept. 35/2 (Advt.), This outstanding offer is good in Metro Toronto only. *Ibid.* 35/3 Metro-area delegates. **1975** *Globe & Mail* (Toronto) 11 June 3/4 A Toronto criminal lawyer says Metro police have told him some members of the Rastafarian Brethren are walking time bombs as far as violent crime in Metro is concerned.

metroland (me·trolænd). [f. Metro(politan *a.* + Land *sb.* 3.] The area surrounding a metropolis; *spec.* the district around London served by the (Metropolitan) underground railway. Also, *collect.* the people inhabiting these areas. Hence **me·trolander** *sb.*

1926 R. Macaulay *Crewe Train* iii. v. 295 That house at Great Missenden..will suit them exactly. In metroland, and such nice people all about... They *must* have a car, though; relying entirely on the Met. is too awkward, with so many strikes and so few late trains... After all, it's not London; metro-land can't be London. *Ibid.* vi. 298 Metro-landers have *pieds-à-terre* in London. **1938** J. Betjeman *Oxf. Univ. Chest* v. 102 The houses of Metroland and beechy Bucks dot the landscape. **1940** Graves & Hodge *Long Week-End* viii. 114 In 1923 the London Underground, wishing to popularize 'Metroland' ..published two guide-books. **1951** R. Hoggart *Auden* v. 137 The appropriate isolation for Auden is..isolation in a vast anonymous metroland such as New York. **1963** *Times* 24 May p. iii/3 Under that great general manager Mr. R. H. Selbie, the Metropolitan invented Metroland. **1973** *Radio Times* 26 Feb. 7 The Metro-landers who bought houses took a great pride in their gardens.

Metroliner, metro-liner (me·troləi:nəɪ). [f. Metro(politan *a.* 2 + Liner[2] 8.] A high-speed inter-city train in the United States.

1969 'O. Bleeck' *Brass Go-Between* xiv. 156 Between Washington and New York they finally got one new high-speed Metroliner running. **1970** *Guardian* 19 Jan. 4/1 The metroliner, a Government-supported experiment in fast inter-city transport..has cut the travelling time from Washington to New York..by nearly ninety minutes. **1972** *Daily Tel.* 23 Nov. 9/2 The official said that the trains at present operating as metro-liners between the three [American] cities were capable of 150 mph. **1973** J. Di Mona *Last Man at Arlington* (1974) 57 The Metroliner to Washington waited in the station.

metrologist. (Later examples.)

1969 *Physics Bull.* Sept. 365/2 A number of speakers considered that would-be metrologists would be better advised to make a broad study in science or engineering at the undergraduate level and specialize in metrology by spending a further year taking a MSc course in this discipline. **1970** *Daily Tel.* 14 May 18 For heaven's sake, exasperated metrologists explain, do try to remember that shop scales do not show the weight of apples; they show the force exercised by the apples in that particular gravitational environment.

metrology. 1. b. (Later examples.)

1969 *Physics Bull.* Sept. 365/2 A large proportion of conference participants deprecated the term 'measurement science' and the use of the term 'metrology' appeared to have a large measure of support. **1971** *Inside Kenya Today* Mar. 29/2 We might have weights manufactured to International Specifications, i.e. to specification of Legal Metrology.

metronome. Add: **b.** *fig.* Also as *v. intr.*

1959 *Listener* 2 Apr. 600/2 They..listened to the stillness of the white moonlight metronomed to the trot, trot, trot of the horse's hooves. **1962** L. Deighton *Ipcress File* ii. 21 Pin-tables metronoming away the sunny afternoon.

metronomic, *a.* Add: **b.** *fig.* Resembling the action of a metronome.

1959 *Times* 30 May 3/1 The Hungarian..is metronomic as she unwinds the rallies. **1963** *Listener* 3 Jan. 45/2 The metronomic dance music rhythm of our time. **1975** 'E. Lathen' *By Hook or by Crook* xi. 107 Miss Martineau sobbed with metronomic regularity.

metronomically, *adv.* (Later examples.)

1970 R. P. Warren *Incantations* 49 The disturbance you are so metronomically creating. **1974** *Daily Tel.* 14 Sept. 11/8 Both in the opening of the symphony and in the Adagio Mr Davis adopted and almost metronomically maintained tempi as fast as Beethoven has presumably imagined them.

me:tronomiza·tion. [f. Metronome + -ization.] The determining or indicating of the rate at which music should be played.

1923 A. Betti in *Music & Lett.* Jan. 3 Can the metronomisation of a piece be absolutely exact?

metronym (mī·tronim). [f. Gr. μητρ-, μήτηρ mother + ὄνομα, Doric ὄνυμα name.] A metronymic name.

1904 *Nature* 5 May Suppl. p. xiii/2 The acceptance of metronyms in the genealogies as proofs of female kinship, while patronyms are rejected.

metronymic, *a.* and *sb.* **a.** *adj.* Add to def.: Also applied to a people or state of society where such a system of naming prevails.

1896 F. H. Giddings *Princ. Sociol.* 158 In a metronymic group all relationships are traced through mothers; paternal relationships are ignored. **1903** L. F. Ward *Pure Sociol.* 339 The metronymic family. **1944** H. P. Fairchild *Dict. Sociol.* 192/2 *Metronymic*, deriving the personal or family name from the mother or other matrilineal relative. **1960** C. Winick *Dict. Anthropol.* 521/2 *System, metronymic*, tracing kinship exclusively through the mother.

metrop (mĭtrǫ·p). Colloq. abbrev. of Metropolis 2.

1888 [see *kilo[2]]. **1919** Wodehouse *My Man Jeeves* 216, I think we've had about enough of the metrop. for the time being. **1925** —— *Carry on, Jeeves!* v. 105 Dear old Rocky made him look like a publicity agent for the old metrop! **1974** 'A. Gilbert' *Nice Little Killing* i. 13 'Know the Metrop?' She shook her head. 'You want to be a bit careful.'

metropole. 1. Delete † *Obs.* and add later examples.

1937 A. Huxley *Let.* 3 June (1969) 422 Our nearest railway is Santa Fe, 70 miles away, and our metropole is Denver at 350 miles. **1970** *Financial Times* 23 Mar. 19/1 What Algeria lacked could easily come from the metropole. **1973** *Caribbean Contact* Jan. 10/2 The ill-defined.. countries of the Caribbean Sea are becoming states in their own right, and are slowly..severing their traditional ties with their respective European metropoles.

3. A luxury hotel.

1890 W. Booth *In Darkest Eng.* ii. vi. 209 A superior lodging-house, a sort of poor man's Metropole. **1925** E. Sitwell *Troy Park* 74 That child is the small wicked ghost Of Metropoles and oyster bars.

metropolitan, *a.* and *sb.* Add: **A.** *adj.* **2. a.** (Later examples.)

1930 H. Crane *Let.* 29 Nov. (1965) 359 In one of the many Doubleday-Doran shops in the metropolitan area. **1936** [see *hinterland]. **1958** *Listener* 11 Dec. 981/2 Black cities; white suburbs—that is how the current trend is often summarized... The pattern of 'metropolitan segregation' (as it has been called) has opened a new, and a frightening, chapter of the 'American Dilemma'. **1961** E. A. Powdrill *Vocab. Land Planning* v. 89 The 'metropolitan region' is a giant urban regional system, different less in kind than in size from that of any urban region. **1963** *Times* 7 June 3/7 It contains a detailed breakdown of the rates levied by the 83 county boroughs and 28 metropolitan boroughs. **1969** *Daily Tel.* 12 June 23/2 Three areas—Manchester, Birmingham and Liverpool—will become Metropolitan authorities, with the key functions of planning, transportation and development... These three will have below them metropolitan district authorities running education, the personal social services, health and housing. **1971** *Ibid.* 17 Feb. 9 Six new metropolitan county councils are proposed by the Government in its plans for reorganisation of local government published today. **1972** *Times* 12 Feb. 14/8 His Lordship had not failed to observe the practice in some metropolitan courts. **1973** *Times* 12 May 1/1 The 36 metropolitan district councils in England and 37 district councils in Wales created under the Local Government Act 1972, will take over in 12 months' time the statutory powers of the present bodies which they will replace. **1974** *Daily Tel.* 1 Apr. 6/4 The 45 new counties will contain 332 districts, including 36 metropolitan districts covering towns in the six metropolitan counties.

b. Of or pertaining to an underground railway serving a large city; *spec.* of the London Underground Railway, now extended overground to serve an extensive suburban area. Also *ellipt.*

1867 Trollope *Claverings* II. xix. 233 He was very keen at the present moment about Metropolitan railways. *c* **1875** 'Brenda' *Froggy's Little Brother* (new ed.) iii. 33 A Metropolitan train was just in, and a crowd of passengers, as usual, came swarming up the steps into the street. **1883** E. W. Hamilton *Diary* 13 Nov. (1972) II. 505 The proposal of the Metropolitan Railway to run an underground line from the back of the India Office to Knightsbridge, and thence across the Park to the Marble Arch and up the Edgeware Road. **1909** Chesterton *Tremendous Trifles* 244 A Metropolitan station, where I took a train home. **1934** H. G. Wells *Exper. Autobiogr.* II. ix. 817 Moscow also is making an imitative tube system... It will be the least stable 'Metropolitan' in the world. *Ibid.* 819 The constructors of the new Metropolitan. **1959** [see *district *sb.* 3 g]. **1974** M. Birmingham *You can help Me* ii. 38 The Metropolitan train from Euston Square..[to] Aldgate East.

c. Of a type of early English pottery found in or near London: (see quots.).

1891 J. E. & E. Hodgkin *Examples Early Eng. Pott.* 6 Of a less decorative character than most of the slip-decorated pieces is the ware which we have classed..as *Metropolitan Slip*, the pieces in this group having been mainly found in or near London. *Ibid.* 9 Metropolitan Slip... A Jar of elegant shape, recently dug up..near Bishopsgate Street. **1903** R. L. Hobson *Catal. Eng. Pott. Brit. Mus.* 108 Examples of Metropolitan Slip ware, made of red clay, with ornament in white slip and a transparent yellowish lead glaze. **1924** Rackham & Read *Eng. Pott.* iii. 28 Another type of ware, showing the same technical methods as the Staffordshire slipwares, has been given the name of 'Metropolitan', because it has usually been found in or near London. *Ibid.*, The earliest date on a piece of Metropolitan ware is on a jug.., inscribed..1638. **1957** Mankowitz & Haggar *Conc. Encycl. Eng. Pott. & Porc.* 149/1 *Metropolitan slipware*, the name given to a class of red earthenware decorated with white trailed slip... Examples dated from 1638 to 1659 are recorded. *Ibid.* Plate 66 (caption) Metropolitan jug. **1967** *Times* 14 Mar. 21/7 (Advt.), A Metropolitan ware silver-mounted jug.

3. Freq. with reference to France: of or pertaining to the home country (as distinct from colonial territories). (Further examples.)

1910 *Encycl. Brit.* X. 795/2 The organization of the 'metropolitan troops' [in France] by regiments. **1943** H. Nicolson *Diary* 4 Feb. (1967) 278 In Metropolitan France de Gaulle is the great symbol. **1958** *Optima* Mar. 22/1 Were peace to be restored, metropolitan France would have, within the following few years, to devote $2\frac{1}{2}$ per cent. of her national revenue to raising the Algerian standard of living. **1959** B. & R. North tr. *Duverger's Pol. Parties* (ed. 2) ii. ii. 330 The practice of alliances.. made it possible for the Centre parties to gain 61% of the seats in metropolitan France with 51·4% of the votes. **1972** *Sci. Amer.* Apr. 19/3 Back in colonial times the metropolitan countries certainly maintained peace in and among their colonies.

metroscope[2]. (Earlier example.)

1845 in C. Cist *Cincinnati Misc.* 270 A very ingenious instrument, called a Metroscope, which has been lately invented for the purpose of taking the measure of the human head so as to furnish an exact fit of hats.

metrostyle (me·trŏstəil). [f. Gr. μέτρον measure + Style *sb.*] A device for regulating the speed of a mechanical piano. (Now disused.)

1904 E. Newlandsmith *Temple of Art* 152 A totally wrong rendering of the work..is obviated in the Pianola by an apparatus called the 'metrostyle'. By means of following with the metrostyle pointer a certain line drawn on the paper music-roll [etc.]. **1907** *World* 16 July 140/2 The Model 'K' is a pianola equipped with the Metrostyle. **1909** H. G. Wells *Tono-Bungay* i. ii. 76 There was a different grand piano with a painted lid and a metrostyle pianola.

Hence **me·trostyle** *v. trans.* and *intr.*, to regulate the speed of (a mechanical piano roll) by a metrostyle; to employ a metrostyle.

1908 G. Kobbé *Pianolist* ii. 31 Grieg—here are a couple of rolls from his 'Peer Gynt' suite metrostyled by himself. **1920** E. Newman *Piano-Player* 147 The roll [of the piano-player] should be metrostyled by some artist who knows the work thoroughly. *Ibid.* 148 Careful metrostyling would no doubt do away with the necessity for most of the time signs.

|| **metteur en scène** (mɛtör aṅ sɛ̄n). [Fr., lit. 'one who puts on the stage'.] A producer of a play; a director of a film.

1911 *Proc. Musical Assoc.* Mar. 94 The producer or '*metteur en scène*' of a play draws up a plan of the whole action in every detail. **1921** CONRAD *Let.* 23 Oct. in G. Jean-Aubry *J. Conrad: Life & Lett.* (1927) II. 262 One of our most clever producers (*metteurs en scène*). **1930** *Times Lit. Suppl.* 17 Apr. 333/2 Mr Jacques Arnavon is a great *metteur-en-scène.* **1963** *Movie* Feb. 36/2 To treat *The Barber of Stamford Hill* as a tentative work is to predict that Wrede could become a notable *metteur en scene.* **1968** *Times Lit. Suppl.* 26 Sept. 1079/1 For Clair's *écriture*, as he readily admits, is primarily a matter of words on paper; from then on he is literally a *metteur en scène.* **1968** L. DURRELL *Tunc* iv. 196 But she is being directed and rehearsed by the *metteur-en-scène.* **1974** *Times* 4 Jan. 8/7 Murnau's greatness as *metteur-en-scène* is unimpaired by time.

metump (line). *N. Amer.* = TUMP-LINE.

1754 in *Coll. New Hampsh. Hist. Soc.* (1824) I. 279 The deponent sold the said Indians two shirts,..and there was next to their skin tied a number of small metump lines, not such as are usually made for tying packs. **1963** W. S. AVIS et al. *Dict. Canad. Eng., Intermediate Dict.* 561/1 *Metump*, a broad strap or headband that is passed around the forehead and attached to a load carried on the back.

|| **mettwurst** (me·tvūɹst). [G.] A type of smoked German sausage.

1895 *Army & Navy Co-op. Soc. Price List* 104/2 Mettwurst. **1911** [see *BLUTWURST]. **1966** W. S. RAMSON *Austral. Eng.* 161 Some unrecorded borrowings from German may be in local use in parts of South Australia. Price noted that..*mettwurst*,..'sausage',..had 'penetrated to the English colonists'. **1971** *Sunday Times* (Colour Suppl.) 27 June 50/1 Mettwurst can be found in the form of a small sausage ('ends') or a horseshoe-shaped 'Westphalian' ring. Very heavily smoked; lightly spiced, no garlic. Mettwurst is eaten cold, sliced, but is also very good poached, sliced fairly thickly and served with boiled potatoes and cabbage.

metyrapone (meti·-, metəiə·răpōᵘn). *Pharm.* [f. 2-*met*hyl-1,2-di(p*yr*id-3-yl)*p*ropan-1-*one*, the chemical name (f. METHYL + DI-² + PYRIDYL + PROPAN(E + *-ONE), with insertion of *a*.] A whitish crystalline compound, $C_5H_4N{\cdot}CO{\cdot}C(CH_3)_2{\cdot}C_5H_4N$, which inhibits the synthesis of cortisone and hydrocortisone and is used for testing the function of the anterior pituitary.

1962 *Lancet* 8 Dec. 1199/1 This paper reports the prevention of massive adrenal necrosis due to D.M.B.A. by the concurrent administration of metyrapone. **1970** PASSMORE & ROBSON *Compan. Med. Stud.* II. vi. 14/2 The metyrapone test depends upon the fact that the feedback control mechanism between the adrenal cortex and the hypothalamo-pituitary axis is mediated by the circulating concentration of unbound cortisol. **1973** *Clin. Pharmacol. & Therapeutics* XIV. 455 After 1 year of treatment urinary steroids and their responses to oral metyrapone were unchanged.

|| **meunière** (mönyɛ̄r), *a.* and *adv. Cookery.* [a. F. (*à la*) *meunière*, lit. 'in the manner of a miller's wife'.] Cooked in or served with hot butter (see quots.).

Usu. following the sb. qualified, as *trout* (*à la*) *meunière*, etc.

1846 A. SOYER *Gastronomic Regenerator* 102 Brill à la Meûnière. **1895** G. A. SALA *Thorough Good Cook* 155 Sole à la Meunière. **1903** C. H. SENN *Pract. Gastron.* 74 (Truite) à la Meunière (Trout, Meunière Style).—Braised trout served with burnt butter, breadcrumbs, and chopped parsley. **1958** J. GROSSINGER *Art Jewish Cooking* (1962) 34 Baked stuffed brook trout meunière. **1959** *Good Food Guide* 145 Good filleted haddock meunière. *Ibid.* 161 Rainbow trout meunière. **1974** *Times* 1 June 13/3 We..opted for a well-known Mexican delicacy, *crialladas*... Served meunière, they tasted delicious.

Meursault (mōrso). [Name of a commune in the department of Côte d'Or, France.] A white wine of Burgundy, produced near Beaune.

1833 C. REDDING *Hist. Mod. Wines* v. 99 Between Volnay and Meursault the vineyard of Santenot is situated; it..produces a celebrated white wine, called Meursault. **1907** *Yesterday's Shopping* (1969) 97/2 White Burgundy..Meursault. **1928** E. WAUGH *Decline & Fall* II. vi. 198 He dined at Basso's..off bouillabaisse and Meursault. **1963** *Sunday Times* (Colour Suppl.) 27 Oct. 51/1 Just before serving, poach stuffed trout in fish stock and Meursault. **1967** A. LICHINE *Encycl. Wines* 354/1 Most Meursault is white and the wines are soft, round and feminine in texture, with a bouquet that eludes description, bordering now on the scent of violets, now on the aroma of almonds.

mevalonic (mevălǫ·nik), *a. Chem.* [f. ME(THYL + VAL(ERIC *a.* + LACT)ON(E + -IC.] *mevalonic acid*: 3,5-dihydroxy-3-methylvaleric acid, $C_6H_{12}O_4$, a crystalline compound which is a growth factor for some lactobacilli and is a precursor of cholesterol in animals and of carotenoids in plants.

1957 D. E. WOLF et al. in *Jrnl. Amer. Chem. Soc.* LXXIX. 1486/1 The name 'mevalonic acid' is now being used to designate β,δ-dihydroxy-β-methylvaleric acid. **1962** H. A. KREBS in A. Pirie *Lens Metabolism Rel. Cataract* 351 The reaction sequence is inhibited by cholesterol itself and some of its immediate precursors by stopping an early stage, probably that giving rise to mevalonic acid. **1973** *Plant Physiol.* LI. 110/1 Mevalonic acid-2-^{14}C was readily incorporated into the free, esterified, and glycosidic sterol fractions of tobacco..seedlings.

Hence **meva·lonate**, the anion of mevalonic acid.

1959 A. WHITE et al. *Princ. Biochem.* (ed. 2) xix. 488 Mevalonic kinase..catalyzes the formation of phosphomevalonic acid and ADP from mevalonate and ATP. **1971** HUNTER & ROSE in Rose & Harrison *Yeasts* II. vi. 243 Brewer's solubles were shown to contain a compound which could replace acetate in sterol biosynthesis, and this compound was shown to be mevalonate.

Mewari (mewā·ri), *sb.* and *a.* [f. *Mewar*, a former native state of India, also known as Udaipur, now part of the state of Rajasthan.] **A.** *sb.* The language spoken in Mewar. **B.** *adj.* Of or pertaining to Mewar or its inhabitants.

1888 KIPLING *From Sea to Sea* (1899) I. 48 The Thakur ..spoke shrilly in Mewari. The Englishman replied in English-Urdu. *Ibid.* 51 Mewari [Mewarri, 1888 newspaper publ.]..is a heathenish dialect, something like Multani to listen to. **1925** A. HUXLEY *Let.* 21 Dec. (1969) 262 Bikaner [is]..inhabited..by a community which counts more millionaires to the thousand than any other population in India, perhaps in the world. These are the Mewari merchants, the Jews of India. **1958** [see *MEWATI *sb.* and *a.*].

Mewati (mewā·ti), *sb.* and *a.* Also **Mewatti.** [Native name (see def.).] **A.** *sb.* **1.** An Indian people native to Mewat, a region south of Delhi and now part of Rajasthan; a member of this people, *spec.* one professing Islam. Cf. *MEO. **2.** The language of this people, a dialect of Rajasthani. **B.** *adj.* Of or pertaining to this people or their language.

1788 J. RENNELL *Mem. Map Hindoostan* p. xlix, Of the state of the internal government of Hindoostan, a judgment may be formed, by the punishment inflicted on the Mewatti, or the Banditti tribe, which inhabit the hilly tract, within 25 miles of Delhi. **1824** J. MALCOLM *Mem. Cent. India* (ed. 2) II. xiv. 174 The Mewatties, a well-known Mahomedan tribe in Hindustan, have long resorted to Central India. **1832** J. TOD *Ann. Rajast'han* II. 393 Gírdhur..with a small but select band hunted the Mewatti leader down, and..slew him in single combat. **1855** H. H. WILSON *Gloss. Judicial & Revenue Terms* 340/2 *Mewáti*,.. a tribe of Rajputs inhabiting the province of *Mewat*, now known as *Mucheri*, and formerly notorious for their turbulent and predatory character. **1880** P. W. POWLETT *Rajputana Gazetteer* III. 170 These repeated expeditions against the Mewáttis did not render them quiet. *Ibid.* 171 Rewári is referred to as being in the hands of a Mewátti chief. *Ibid.* 174 Humayun..conciliated them..by causing his minister Bairám Khan to marry a younger daughter of the same Mewátti. **1896** W. CROOKE *Tribes & Castes N.-W. Provinces & Oudh* III. 493 Common proverbs.. mean that, in dealing with a Mewâti, you had better kick or abuse him before you do business with him. **1901** [see *JAIPUR]. **1908** G. A. GRIERSON *Ling. Survey India* IX. II. 44 Mēwātī is, properly speaking, the language of Mewat, the country of the Mēōs, but it covers a larger tract than this. It is the language of the whole of the State of Alwar, of which only a portion is Mewat. *Ibid.* 45, I am not acquainted with any literary work in the Mēwātī dialect. **1908** *Imperial Gazetteer India* XVII. 313 The Muhammadan Meos call themselves Mewātīs. **1914** H. A. ROSE *Gloss. Tribes & Castes Punjab & N.-W. Frontier Province* III. 80 In the Muhammadan historians the Meos appear to be unknown by that name, but the Mewātis were notorious throughout the Muhammadan period. **1957** [see *JAIPUR]. **1958** B. N. PRASAD in V. K. Narasimhan et al. *Lang. India* 90 The New or Modern Indo-Aryan languages... Rājasthānī (Mārwarī, Mewāri, Mālawi, Jaipuri and Mewatī). **1974** *Encycl. Brit. Micropædia* VIII. 395/1 Rajasthani's 20 dialects are classified into four main groups: the northeastern Mewati [etc.].

Mewoh, var. *MEO.

mews. Add: **2. c.** A mews converted into accommodation for people; freq. *attrib.*

1805 [in Dict., sense 2 a]. **1848** THACKERAY *Vanity Fair* xxxiv. 305 Come down with me to Tom Corduroy's, in Castle Street Mews, and I'll show you such a bull-terrier. **1885** *List of Subscribers, Brighton* (South of Eng. Telephone Co.) 4 Nye, Sons & Silverthorne—Regency-mews. **1932** *Times Lit. Suppl.* 10 Nov. 841/1 Elizabeth..lived in the inevitable mews flat. **1954** T. S. ELIOT *Confid. Clerk* I. 9 And the flat in the mews? How soon will that be ready for him? **1958** *Observer* 18 May 16/4 Those saucy, disreputable mews dwellings. **1964** D. FRANCIS *Nerve* ii. 21 The big converted mews garage which served her as sitting-room, bedroom and rehearsal room. **1974** M. BABSON *Stalking Lamb* xvii. 127 He intended to make the mews house his operational headquarters.

Mex (meks), *a.* and *sb.* **a.** *U.S.* Colloq. abbrev. of MEXICAN *a.* and *sb.*

In quot. 1913, 'Mexican money'.

1854 G. D. BREWERTON in *Harper's Mag.* Apr. 584/2, I thought it proper to consult with one of the Quartermaster's agents..which resulted in my receiving the information that the 'United States Hotel' upon the 'Plaza' provided 'chicken fixins and corn doins'—or, if a 'stranger' wanted 'Mex livin', *frijoles* and *tortillas* to boot —in better style than any other establishment in Santa Fé. **1906** *McClure's Mag.* June 121/1 'Where'd you get the coat?' I asked the Mex. **1913** *Ibid.* Mar. 119 Is that gold or Mex, dear? **1929** J. PARKER *Old Army* 246 He was evidently not one of those who looked with pleasure upon 'Mex' officers. **1934** J. M. CAIN *Postman always rings Twice* 97 Ensenada is all Mex. **1970** G. JACKSON *Let.* 22 Mar. in *Soledad Brother* (1971) 187 An Italian..killed a Mexican in Folsom because the Mex suddenly started telling everyone not to trust someone. **1974** *Times* 21 Feb. 11/6 John Wayne's *The Alamo* ('better Tex than Mex') is a Goldwater Western.

b. *U.S. Forces' slang.* Foreign currency, esp. that of the Philippine Islands.

1898 *Amer. Soldier* (Manila, Philippine Islands) I. x. 8/1 We will send a set..to any address in America for 25 cents (mex). **1907** *Army & Navy Life* (U.S.) June 679 M stands for money, which is mostly in 'Mex'. **1926** ANDERSON & STALLINGS *What Price Glory?* in *Three Amer. Plays* II. 67, I wouldn't take a hundred dollars Mex. for that. **1941** T. CRUSE *Apache Days & After* 287 The rent was $100 a month 'Mex', which translated as $50 in gold.

Mexican, *a.* and *sb.* Add: **A.** *adj.* **b.** *Mexican blanket, cotton, eagle, flycatcher, saddle, trader, wagon*; **Mexican fruit fly**, a central American insect pest, *Anastrepha ludens*; **Mexican hairless (dog)**, a small dog of the breed so called, lacking hair except for tufts on the head and tail; **Mexican hog**, the peccary; **Mexican orange (-blossom, -flower)** = *CHOISYA; **Mexican overdrive** *U.S. slang* (see quots.); **Mexican poppy** (earlier and later examples); **Mexican thistle** (examples); **Mexican War**, the war of 1846–8 between the U.S.A. and Mexico in which the allegiance of Texas was the most important issue.

1834 A. PIKE *Prose Sk. & Poems* 74 We gave him a red and gaudy Mexican blanket. **1894** *Harper's Mag.* Jan. 299/1 He had parted with Pedro for forty dollars, a striped Mexican blanket, and a pair of spurs. **1827** *Western Monthly Rev.* I. 82 The kinds of cotton which are chiefly cultivated are Louisiana, green seed, or Tennessee, and recently Mexican. **1834** R. BAIRD *View of Valley of Mississippi* xxiv. 304 Cotton is the chief staple. Three kinds are cultivated,—sea island, Mexican, and green seed. **1835** in *Southwestern Hist. Q.* (1925) XXVIII. 190 The most common birds and fowls found [in Texas] are the Mexican eagle, the hawk, [etc.]. **1836** M. HOLLEY *Texas* v. 100 The Mexican eagle, which is among the smallest of the aquiline tribe. **1870** *Amer. Naturalist* III. 473 A solitary Mexican Fly Catcher..gave a specimen of the summer group of migrants. **1924** *Monthly Bull. Calif. Dept. Agric.* XIII. 55 The Federal Horticultural Board placed a quarantine against the Mexican fruit fly in Mexico. **1947** *Jrnl. Econ. Entomol.* XL. 483/1 Neither four applications of a DDT spray nor three applications of DDT dust gave significant reductions in populations of the Mexican fruit fly, *Anastrepha ludens.* **1972** SWAN & PAPP *Common Insects N. Amer.* 627 The Mexican Fruit Fly, *Anastrepha ludens*, occurs in Central America, Mexico, and southern Texas, attacks citrus and mangoes chiefly; it is conspicuous—considerably larger than a house fly, brightly colored with attractive wing pattern. **1899** R. B. LEE *Hist. & Descr. Mod. Dogs Gt. Brit. & Ireland (Non-Sporting Division)* (new ed.) xix. 410 A peculiar looking object, and one which requires a great stretch of the imagination to call handsome, is the hairless, or, rather, the crested dog... He is mostly known as the Mexican hairless dog. **1948** C. L. B. HUBBARD *Dogs in Brit.* 296 The Mexican Hairless Dog..is recognised by the American Kennel Club and classified as a Toy Dog. **1970** *New Yorker* 28 Feb. 31/1 Larry Wolf..totally bald..plays a Mexican hairless. **1971** F. HAMILTON *World Encycl. Dogs* 537 Although not recognized by the British or the American Kennel Clubs, the Xoloizcuintli (pronounced Shollosquintly) or Mexican Hairless Dog, is one of the oldest breeds, now almost extinct. **1821** T. NUTTALL *Jrnl. Trav. Arkansa* ix. 216 The *Sus tajassu* or Mexican hog is not uncommon some distance higher up Red river. **1836** M. HOLLEY *Texas* v. 95 The Pecari or Mexican hog is even yet occasionally met with on the frontiers, in considerable gangs. **1899** G. JEKYLL *Wood & Garden* vi. 71 On the southern sides of the same gateway are two large bushes of the Mexican orange-flower (*Choisya ternata*), loaded with its orange-like blooms. **1951** *Good Housek. Home Encycl.* 115/2 Mexican Orange, a bright-leaved, white-flowering shrub. **1971** H. L. V. FLETCHER *Pop. Flowering Shrubs* viii. 176 *Choisya ternata*, an evergreen, is called the Mexican Orange Blossom. It has white scented flowers all spring and summer. It is easy in some gardens but of doubtful hardiness. **1975** *Times* 5 July 10/5 (*caption*) The Mexican orange..and *Senecio laxifolius*..both respond well to hand trimming. **1961** *Amer. Speech* XXXVI. 272 Mexican overdrive... Coasting down hill with gears disengaged. **1971** M. TAK *Truck Talk* 105 *Mexican overdrive*, the 'gear' a trucker uses when, in going downhill, he throws the transmission out of gear and lets the truck coast down in neutral. **1848** W. H. EMORY *Notes Mil. Reconn.* 13 We find in the bottoms Mexican poppy. **1936** F. CLUNE *Roaming round Darling* xxi. 211 We crossed a score of creeks in ten miles, fringed by tobacco-bush with privetlike leaves, and Mexican poppy simulating a Scotch thistle. **1965** *Austral. Encycl.* VII. 188/2 Most widespread and troublesome of introductions among the Papaveraceae is the Mexican poppy (*Argemone mexicana* and its variety *ochroleuca*), which was naturalized about Sydney more than a century ago. **1846** in *Calif. Hist. Soc. Q.* (1942) XXI. 203 Many of them [*sc.* Indians] had Mexican saddles, cartridge boxes, and different parts of the Mexican dress. **1848** *Knickerbocker* XXXI. 328 Their strong, gaunt horses were equipped with rusty Spanish bits, and rude Mexican saddles. **1865** *Atlantic Monthly* Jan. 59/2 A Mexican saddle,—out of which you can scarcely fall. **1910** J. HART *Vigilante Girl* 345 She galloped on in her high-peaked Mexican saddle. **1837** J. MACFADYEN *Flora Jamaica* I. 20 *Argemone Mexicana.* Mexican or Gamboge Thistle. **1906** F. BLERSCH *Handbk. Agric. S. Afr.* 144 Mexican poppy or yellow poppy,

usually called Mexican thistle at the cape. **1826** H. G. Rogers in H. C. Dale *Ashley-Smith Explor.* (1918) 208 He is what they term here [*sc.* in the Los Angeles area] a Mexican trader. **1862** M. D. Colt *Went to Kansas* 37 So here may be seen the huge Mexican wagon, stubborn mule, swarthy driver. **1846** *Dollar Newspaper* (Philadelphia) 27 May 3/1 (*heading*) The Mexican War. **1881** *Harper's Mag.* Jan. 258/2 The Mexican War..the Abolitionists declared..was waged to obtain new territory for the extension of slavery. **1931** E. O'Neill *Mourning becomes Electra* (1932) I. 19 He went to the Mexican War and come out a major.

c. *Comb.*, as **Mexican-American,** of or pertaining to Mexican settlers or their descendants in the U.S.A.; also as *sb.*

1953 *Jrnl. Social Issues* IX. I. 26 Another fortunate situation has been the fact that our Mexican-American membership has been the most insistent and aggressive in the fight against the illegal alien from Mexico, popularly called the wetback. **1964** S. M. Miller in I. L. Horowitz *New Sociol.* 293 This urban poor is composed of many strands:..Puerto Ricans and Mexican-Americans. **1972** *Jrnl. Social Psychol.* LXXXVII. 3 Mexican-Americans comprise one of the largest minority groups in the United States. **1973** D. Barnes *See Woman* (1974) p. i, To the north, Hollywood's own unique night life seethed... In the east, the Mexican-American community slept. **1973** *Black Panther* 21 July 14/1 The Mexican-American workers in the canneries.

B. *sb.* **2.** (Earlier examples.)

1827 J. F. Cooper *Prairie* I. v. 149 A foal that is worth thirty of the brightest Mexicans that bear the face of the King of Spain. **1836** *Knickerbocker* VIII. 580 The lad could not change the Mexican which I gave him. **1845** J. J. Hooper *Some Adventures Simon Suggs* 76 There's an old friend of mine..that's got three or four hamper baskets-full o' Mexicans.

3. A variety of sheep.

1878 I. L. Bird *Lady's Life Rocky Mts.* (1879) x. 173 The flocks are made up mostly of pure and graded Mexicans. **1887** *Scribner's Mag.* II. 511/1 The season comes for the shearing of Southdowns or rough-fleeced Mexicans.

Mexicanize, *v.* Add: Also, to subject to the influence or domination of Mexicans. (Further examples.)

1844 J. Gregg *Commerce Prairies* II. 119 To this great ball, however, no Americans were invited, with the exception of a Mexicanized denizen or two. **1872** 'Mark Twain' *Roughing It* 178, I had never seen such wild, free, magnificent horsemanship..as those picturesquely clad Mexicans, Californians, and Mexicanized Americans displayed. **1900** *19th Ann. Rep. U.S. Bureau Amer. Ethnol. 1897–98* p. xvi, These Indians, now practically Mexicanized. **1904** *Baltimore American* 15 June 6 With the prospective passing of President Diaz, of Mexico, all the world will hope that his country will not revert to that condition which once led to the invention of the word Mexicanized. **1910** *N.Y. Even. Post* 13 Oct. 8 Some object to describing the Roosevelt plan as one to Mexicanize our government. But that is precisely what it is. **1941** R. Humphreys *Latin Amer.* 23 To Mexicanize the Indian and to make the Mexican master in his own country. **1973** *Nature* 13 July 66/3 Mexico recently passed two laws, one to regulate transfer of technology into the country in an attempt to make sure that the imported technology is suited to Mexico's needs, and the other to limit foreign investment, with the long-term goal of Mexicanizing industry.

So **Me:xicaniza·tion.**

1878 *Detroit Free Press* 2 June 4/1 'Mexicanization'—Taking evidence to see whether election protests were forged, and, if so, who forged them, who connived at the forgery, or were aware of it. **1890** *Congress. Rec.* 5 June 5655/1 Gentlemen, do you know what a single silver standard means in this country? It means Mexicanization. **1938** *Newsweek* 28 Mar. 20/3 Cárdenas' swift action caught the British and American Governments off guard. Following developments in anxious silence, they feared the 'Mexicanization' campaign might next strike their mining interests. **1963** *Times* 6 July 18/5 After many months of negotiation..one of the major obstacles to the company's Mexicanisation proposals has now been cleared.

Meyerbeerian (məiˌəɹbɪə·riăn), *a.* [f. the name of the German operatic composer Giacomo *Meyerbeer* (1791–1864) + -IAN.] Of, resembling, or characteristic of the style or work of Meyerbeer.

1890 G. B. Shaw *London Music 1888–89* (1937) 359 Mr Goossens seemed to me to be imperfectly in sympathy with the electrical Meyerbeerian atmosphere. **1955** E. Dent in H. van Thal *Fanfare for E. Newman* 103 Balthazar is a typically Meyerbeerian character, and his music is more like Meyerbeer than Donizetti.

Hence **Meyerbee·riad,** something resembling the style or work of Meyerbeer; **Meyerbee·rianism** *sb.*; **Mey·erbeerish** *a.*

1947 A. Einstein *Mus. Romantic Era* xvii. 308 Serov..wrote a Biblical drama *Judith* and a grand opera *Rogneda*—both of which might be characterized as merely gaudy Meyerbeeriads. **1955** F. Toye in H. van Thal *Fanfare for E. Newman* 163 *Don Carlos* is permeated with Meyerbeerianism from beginning to end. **1962** *John o' London's* 8 Mar. 233/3 A certain amount of Meyerbeerish trafficking with 'grand opera'.

meyerhofferite (məiˌəɹhǫ·fĕrəit). *Min.* [f. the name of Wilhelm *Meyerhoff* (1864–1906), German chemist + -ITE[1].] A colourless to white hydrated calcium borate that is found chiefly as an alteration product of inyoite.

1914 [see *INYOITE]. **1951** C. Palache et al. *Dana's Syst. Min.* (ed. 7) II. 357 The meyerhofferite occurs as pseudomorphs after inyoite with a fibrous internal structure, as small transparent colorless crystals on the surface of these pseudomorphs, and as masses of interlaced glassy crystals or fibrous aggregates embedded in clay. **1967** [see *INDERBORITE].

‖ **mézair** (mezẹ̄r'). [Fr., f. It. *mezzaria* middle gait.] (See quot. 1960.)

1754 R. Berenger tr. *Bourgelat's New Syst. Horsemanship* xvii. 115 The Mezair is higher than the Action of *Terre-a-Terre*, and lower than that of *Curvets*; we may therefore conclude, that the *Terre-a-Terre* is the Foundation of the Mezair, as well as of *Curvets*. **1928** *Daily Express* 22 June 11/3 There is the 'piaffe' in which the horses keep time without advancing, and the 'mezair', that sets them mincing forward, balancing on their hind legs. **1956** L. Mins tr. *Seunig's Horsemanship* (1958) iii. 313 The *mézair* is performed by having the horse fall back on its haunches after a gallopade. **1960** A. Podhajsky *Spanish Riding School Vienna* 36 The Mézair is a series of Levades following upon each other at short intervals, after each of which the fore-legs always touch the ground for an instant, the hind-legs following in a jump and then the Levade is repeated, so that a small increase of space forward occurs.

mezcaline, obs. var. *MESCALINE.

‖ **meze** (me·ze). Also **mese, mezée, mezze, mezzeh.** [f. Turk. *meze* snack, appetizer.] A type of hors-d'œuvre served esp. with an aperitif in Greece and the Near East. Also *attrib.*

1926 *Manch. Guardian Weekly* 19 Feb. 151/2 It is taken as a habit with the dried fish and *mézés* that accompany a summer beer. **1950** E. David *Bk. Mediterranean Food* 146 Tarama is the name given to the dried eggs of grey mullet pressed and sold out of a barrel—a favourite mézé in Greece and Turkey. **1955** *Times* 16 July 1/5 It is customary, throughout Greece and the Near East, to serve Mezedes with your aperitif. **1957** L. Durrell *Bitter Lemons* 25 We..shared a stirrup-cup and a *meze*. **1958** R. Liddell *Morea* II. ii. 58 The bit of cheese or the meat ball, brought to me with a slice of tomato by way of *mézé*, when I drank my ouzo. **1966** J. Aldridge *Statesman's Game* ix. 67 He drained his martini and said 'Louise! Bring in that mezée trolley will you?' **1968** J. Cleary *Season of Doubt* xii. 216 Lucille..passed around a tray of *mezzeh*, the traditional Lebanese hors-d'oeuvre. **1974** *Times* 16 Feb. 15/2 *Mezes*—a distinctive form of eating throughout the Middle East, where the concept of hors d'oeuvres is Lucullan.

mezz (mez). *slang.* [f. the name of *Mezz* Mezzrow (1899–1972), a jazz clarinettist and drug addict.] Marijuana; **me·zzroll,** a marijuana cigarette.

1938 *Amer. Speech* XIII. 188/1 *Mezz*, marijuana. **1946** Mezzrow & Wolfe *Really Blues* (1957) 215 New words came into being..*mezzroll*, to describe the kind of fat, well-packed and clean cigarette I need to roll. **1960** *Time* 25 Jan. 87/2 In U.S. slang marijuana is called..mezz. **1972** *Sunday Sun* (Brisbane) 2 July 14/2 Detectives from the CIB Drug Squad in Brisbane are becoming quite familiar now with words like..mezz, Mary Jane.

‖ **mezzadria** (medzădrī·ă). Also **mezzeria.** [It.] A system of land tenure in Italy whereby the farmer pays a proportion (orig. half) of the produce to the landowner as rent, the landowner usually supplying the stock, seeds, etc. Also *attrib.*, as *mezzadria district, system,* etc. So **me·zzadro** (pl. **-i**), the tenant farmer of this system.

1875 *Encycl. Brit.* I. 415/1 A system..in certain provinces of Italy..called mezzeria..the halving, that is, of the produce of the soil between landowner and landholder. **1909** King & Okey *Italy Today* (new ed.) viii. 171 In the *mezzadria* districts there are comparatively few agricultural labourers and therefore less pauperism. *Ibid.*, Occasionally,..the rent is proportioned to the crop, and thus the system slides imperceptibly into *mezzadria*. **1928** L. B. Register tr. *Calisse's Hist. Italian Law* III. xx. 727 In the years following..the Germanic invasions land was not as yet capable of returning an adequate compensation for the labor required for cultivation... It was preferable to fix the return as a proportion of the profits,..sometimes it was a proportion of the harvest, a half for example, as in the 'mezzeria'. **1949** L. Olschki *Genius of Italy* (1950) i. 10 *Mezzadria* imposes hard penalties on the peasant. **1962** *Listener* 30 Aug. 309/2 He has always worked on the share-cropping system known as the *mezzadria*. **1964** *Economist* 4 July 55/2 The *mezzadri* strike, vote communist.., or leave for the cities. **1967** C. Seton-Watson *Italy from Liberalism to Fascism* viii. 303 The *bracciante* resented the *mezzadro*'s reliance upon his own family and his reluctance to employ paid labour. **1970** I. Origo *Images & Shadows* ix. 212 Our land was worked on the system which had been almost universal in Tuscany for nearly six centuries, the *mezzadria*,..the tenant—called *mezzadro*,..contributed the..labour. **1973** *Daily Tel.* 23 Jan. 17/3 Mrs Doxat has plans for her vineyards, which are run under the *mezzadria* system, whereby the Italian tenant works them and takes 52 per cent. of the profits, while all capital investment is the owner's responsibility.

mezzani (medzā·ni). [It., pl. of *mezzano* middle, medium.] A type of medium-sized macaroni.

1895 'M. Ronald' *Century Cook Bk.* II. vii. 225 The macaroni called 'Mezzani', which is a name designating size, not quality, is the preferable kind for macaroni dishes made with cheese. **1958** *Catal. County Stores, Taunton* June 17 *Naples Macaroni.* Long—Mezzani, Tagliatelle, Linguine. **1964** M. Waldo *Art Spaghetti Cookery* (1965) 9 There are larger types [of pasta] such as *mezzani*, so large that merely one, stuffed with a filling, makes a portion.

mezzanine. Add: **1. d.** In a theatre or cinema: see quot. 1961. *U.S.*

1927 Sexton & Betts *Amer. Theatres of Today* 3/2 If..the site is unusually small, or if, due to its location or to the high cost of land, the maximum number of seats are required, balconies and mezzanines are necessitated. *Ibid.* 4/2 Seats lost by reducing the length of the main balcony are obtained in a mezzanine balcony. **1933** *Radio City News* 1 May 1/3 It is now possible for patrons to reserve seats in the first smoking mezzanine for any performance of the week. **1957** *New Yorker* 29 June 22/1, I was in a movie house, fairly plush, in a sort of mezzanine, or balcony. **1961** Bowman & Ball *Theatre Lang.* 219 *Mezzanine*, a seating area just above the orchestra, or the forward part of such an area; the first balcony.

mezza voce, *adj.* Add: Also as *sb.* and *adj.*

1877 G. B. Shaw *How to become Mus. Critic* (1960) 29 The critics will fall into raptures over his exquisite management of the *mezza voce*. **1927** *Sunday Times* 6 Mar. 7/3 Though he can achieve an extraordinary *mezza voce* at times, his voice is really far too big for a small hall. **1954** C. K. Scott *Fund. Singing* iii. 163 This is the principle of *mezza voce* which gives perhaps the most appealing sound that can be made. **1955** *Times* 29 June 3/1 He does not suffer from the common fault of Italian tenors of yelling continuously; his *mezza voce* is pleasing. **1958** *Times* 10 Nov. 14/3 She..impressed upon her excellent accompanist..a similar *mezza voce* treatment. **1973** *Guardian* 12 Mar. 8/3 A clear, *mezza voce* climax.

mezze(h, varr. *MEZE.

mezzeria: see *MEZZADRIA.

mezzo, *a.* Add: *mezzo forte*, also as *sb.*

1955 *Times* 30 May 3/5 It seems a pity not to take advantage of it in place of the unblinking mezzo-forte adopted by Mr. Jones. **1967** *Times* 23 Nov. 8/8 She scarcely ever spoke at less than a shout and needs to find the occasional mezzo forte.

mezzo-brow, *sb.* and *a. colloq.* Now *rare.* [f. It. *mezzo* middle + Brow *sb.*[1]] = *middle-brow* (see *MIDDLE *a.* 6).

1925 N. Playfair *Story Lyric Theatre* i. 6, I am not a 'high-brow', but what I believe is now called in America a 'mezzo-brow', an Uncompromising Mezzo-brow! And if you imagine that to be a 'mezzo-brow' means that one has no positive opinions..I give you the lie. **1925** *Times Lit. Suppl.* 12 Nov. 751/2 (*heading*) A mezzo-brow manager: the story of the Lyric Theatre, Hammersmith. **1935** *Punch* 19 June 734/2 He deplores..the red rash of rural villadom. But, resolutely mezzo-brow, he has a good word for Blackpool beach and the roadside Lido. **1940** [see *BOOK *sb.* 13]. **1945** Mencken *Amer. Lang.* Suppl. I. 325 The search for a term to designate persons neither *high-brows* nor *low-brows* has led to the suggestion of *mizzen-brow* and *mezzo-brow*..but they have not caught on.

Mezzofanti (medzofæ·nti). The name of Giuseppe *Mezzofanti* (1774–1849), an Italian cardinal who was master of more than fifty languages, used to denote a person of exceptional linguistic ability. Hence **mezzofa·ntic** *a.*

1872 G. M. Hopkins *Let.* 3 Dec. (1956) 238 We have a half-English half-Italian young sucking Mezzofanti among us who could have written in seven languages to my knowledge. **1904** A. Vambéry *Story my Struggles* I. i. 88 The high-flown announcements of my mezzofantic perfections remained without the slightest result. **1939** Joyce *Finnegans Wake* II. 260 Long Livius Lane, mid Mezzofanti Mall. **1972** *Times Lit. Suppl.* 30 June 752/5 Misspellings are legion and mezzofantic in scope.

‖ **Mezzogiorno** (medzoˌdʒiǭ·rno). [It.] The southern part of Italy, including Sicily and Sardinia.

1932 Joyce *Let.* 13 May (1966) III. 245 You seem to be cruising in the mezzogiorno. **1952** P. H. Bonner *SPQR* (1953) vi. 54 The cities of the Mezzogiorno, like Naples and Salerno and Bari. **1960** E. & R. Chevallier *Mezzogiorno* 7 Magic is by no means a thing of the past in the Mezzogiorno. There are still witches in the land, and the people still fear the 'evil eye'. **1963** 'W. Haggard' *High Wire* viii. 92 He had..a loving little wife in Naples, but he hadn't seen her for a year. That was a long time to leave a woman in the mezzogiorno. **1972** A. Thorne *Rome & S. Italy* ii. 45 The houses of the Mezzogiorno have far more in common architecturally with those of Byzantium and the islands of the Aegean. **1973** A. B. Mountjoy *Mezzogiorno* i. 10 An abundance of children characterized the villages and towns of the Mezzogiorno.

Mganda, var. *MUGANDA.

‖ **mganga** (mˌga·ŋgă). Also **m'ganga, nganga.** Pl. **mgangas, waganga.** [Swahili *mganga*, pl. *waganga* medicine man.] In Tanzania and other parts of East Africa, the name given to a native doctor or witch-doctor. (In quots. 1864, 'an object used in magic rites, a charm'.)

1864 J. A. Grant *Walk Across Afr.* p. xvi, M'ganga or Onganga; a general term for a charm, or for a man who divines events. *Ibid.* iii. 39 The only superstitious observance we noticed was in a field at the foot of a tree; a grass model of a hut was erected for the rain-god..and called, as usual, a 'M'ganga'. **1895** H. H. Johnston *River Congo* (ed. 4) xvi. 273 Somebody is suspected of having caused

the death by supernatural means, and the horrid old *nganga* or 'medicine man' who holds the inquest..is called upon to detect the guilty person. **1930** *Discovery* Aug. 265/1 The mganga (as the native calls his medicine-man) is the surgeon, physician, neurological expert, herbalist, toxicologist, and veterinarian. **1947** *E. Afr. Ann. 1946–7* 55/1 The 'mgangas', or general practitioners..prescribe or apply remedies, and in some cases even set fractures and do simple operations. **1965** J. LISTOWEL *Making of Tanganyika* iv. 35 For thousands of years, the relationship between chiefs and witch doctors, in Swahili called *waganga*, had been a close one. **1971** N. Q. KING *Christian & Muslim in Afr.* 67 The *mganga*, wrongly but regularly translated as 'witch-doctor', is a healer and 'putter-together', with knowledge of herbal and spirit powers.

Mgr. *R.C. Ch.* Abbrev. of MONSIGNOR, -NORE. Also **Msgr.**

1853 J. R. LOGAN in *Jrnl. Indian Archipelago* VII. 53, I have received valuable assistance..from Mgr. Pallegoix, Mgr. Le Fevre and several other learned missionaries. **1858** N. P. S. WISEMAN *Let.* in M. F. Roskell *Mem. F. K. Amherst* (1903) v. 217 Mgr Searle joins me in these feelings. **1897** ADDIS & ARNOLD *Cath. Dict.* (ed. 5) 425/1 Mgr. Pap-Szilagyi has made a methodical compendium of these documents. **1922** JOYCE *Ulysses* 312 The rt rev. Mgr M'Manus. **1959** E. WAUGH *Life R. Knox* III. ii. 244 'Father Knox', a name prominent in letters since 1912 gave place to the less familiar 'Mgr Knox'. **1965** W. MITCHELL tr. *Huyghe's Relig. Orders Mod. World* p. v, Contents... What do we mean by Religious? Mgr. Gerard Huyghe... The call to holiness in the Church Mgr. Charue.

mi, abbrev. of MINOR *a.* 7.

1791 [see MINOR *a.* 7]. **1867** J. A. SYMONDS *Let.* Mar. (1967) I. 703 Our tutor lists will need to be filled up next term... I claim B mi as my own. **1932** WODEHOUSE *Louder & Funnier* 12 Faber *mi* got hold of the manuscript and refused to give it up, and Faber *ma*..hit him over the head. **1963** *Times* 5 June 14/3 Frost mi..was only allowed to shake his head.

miacid (maɪ·ăsid). *Palæont.* [f. mod.L. family name *Miacidæ*, f. the generic name *Miacis* (E. D. Cope 1872, in *Proc. Amer. Philos. Soc.* XII. 470): see -ID[3].] A small, carnivorous mammal of the family Miacidæ, known from North American fossil remains of the Palæocene and Eocene epochs. Also as *adj.*

1966 R. & D. MORRIS *Men & Pandas* viii. 191 About thirty million years ago the ancestors of all the modern carnivores appeared on the scene. These were the miacids and they were small creatures rather like present-day civets. **1972** T. A. VAUGHAN *Mammalogy* xii. 194/2 Miacids were small and perhaps mostly arboreal carnivores. **1973** R. F. EWER *Carnivores* v. 225 It is impossible to believe that any carnivore could have evolved a dentition of miacid type without some corresponding behavioural adaptations. **1973** *Nature* 14 Dec. 391/1 The earliest carnivora are the miacids *Protictis* and *Ictidopappus*.

‖ **miai** (mi·əi). [Jap., f. *mi* seeing + *ai* mutually.] The first step in a Japanese arranged marriage whereby the prospective partners meet briefly in company with their families to decide if they are mutually acceptable.

1890 B. H. CHAMBERLAIN *Things Japanese* 221 The middleman arranges for what is termed the *mi-ai*, literally, the 'mutual seeing'—a meeting at which the lovers (if persons unknown to each other may be so styled) are allowed to see, sometimes even to speak to each other. **1902** L. HEARN *Kottō* x. 90 To arrange for the *miai* ('see-meeting') tomorrow. **1966** P. S. BUCK *People of Japan* (1968) v. 62, I have a young friend who was married several months ago, who saw his wife for the first time at the miai seven weeks before the wedding.

Miao (miɑu·), *sb.* and *a.* Also **Meo.** [Native name.] **A.** *sb.* **a.** A member of the Miao, a mountain-dwelling people of China and Indo-China; the Miao people. **b.** The language spoken by the Miao. **B.** *adj.* Of or pertaining to the Miao people or their language.

1917 S. COULING *Encycl. Sinica* 4/2 There have been frequent revolts of the Miao, the last great one being during the T'ai P'ing rebellion. The Miao women wear wonderfully embroidered clothes and short, white kilted skirts. **1937** E. SNOW *Red Star over China* v. iii. 195 The Reds had a method. They had already safely passed through the tribal districts of the Miao and the Shan peoples, aborigines of Kweichow and Yunnan, and had won their friendship. **1939** L. H. GRAY *Foundations of Lang.* 390 Miao, Yao, Khamti, the extinct Ahom, etc. **1948** D. DIRINGER *Alphabet* 418 Miao spoken on the borders of northern Siam. **1948** R. A. D. FORREST *Chinese Lang.* i. 33 Miao..has indeed close relationship with Chinese; but it is a relationship of influence and not of kinship. **1955** *Times* 9 May 8/4 The Meos, or Miaos as they are more commonly known in China, are more recent emigrants from Kweichow and Yunnan provinces. **1963** *Times* 24 Apr. 10/3 According to Prince Souvanna Phouma, the Pathet Lao has also demanded the withdrawal of trained Meo tribesmen, and it is not clear whether the rightist troops mentioned are Meo, or, for that matter, whether the latter have descended from their hills. **1970** *Daily Tel.* 4 Mar. 16/4 The Meo general and his predominantly Meo hill-tribe force..form the Government's only credible shield against the North Vietnamese. **1972** *Nat. Geographic* Feb. 275 Soon Meo harvesters will scrape off the sticky sap, boil it, and sell the crude narcotic for at least $25 a pound. **1972** *Times* 4 July 16/1 Some of the Meo have succeeded in preserving themselves and their cultural identity by not taking sides in the war. **1974** R. BUTLER *Buffalo Hook* xii. 105 They're an odd bunch, the Hainanese... The island's aboriginal people are called, of all things, Miao.

Miaotse (miɑu·tsɪ). Also **Miao-chia, Meaou-tse, Miautsz', Miaotsze,** etc. = prec., sense A.

1836 J. F. DAVIS *Chinese* I. vii. 287 The Chinese law prohibits all marriages between subjects and foreigners, and even forbids any alliances between the unsubdued mountaineers, called Meaou-tse, in the interior of the empire, and its own people in the neighbouring plains. **1848** S. W. WILLIAMS *Middle Kingdom* I. iii. 147 The unsubdued Miautsz'..occupy the north-east portion of the [Western] province, in the mountain fastnesses between it and Kweichau. **1883** *Encycl. Brit.* XVI. 223/2 In figure the Miautse, both men and women, are shorter and darker-complexioned than the Chinese. **1911** *Ibid.* XVIII. 354/2 The emperor K'ien-lung..attacked the Miaotsze, who suffered a crushing defeat, and were compelled to purchase peace by swearing allegiance to their conquerors. **1917** S. COULING *Encycl. Sinica* 4/2 *Miao-chia*,..or *Miao-tzu*..is the name given by Chinese to tribes calling themselves Mhong, whose head-quarters are in Kueichou, but who are also found in south Yünnan, Ssûch'uan and Hunan. **1932** W. L. GRAFF *Lang.* 421 The Miaotse or Mautzy group, probably related to Tai.

miaow, *int.* Add: Often used to imply that the person addressed is a 'cat' (see CAT *sb.*[1] 2 a).

1937 M. IRWIN *Stranger Prince* 321 'Congratulations, sweetheart! I did not know you had secured him...' 'Miaow!' **1948** 'E. CRISPIN' *Love lies Bleeding* xii. 134 'I sometimes wonder if she has any *deep* emotions at all.' 'Miaouw,' said Fen gently. Elspeth grinned. 'All right, I *am* being catty.' **1962** E. BRADFORD *Touchstone* xi. 91 'He's always..where the bar is.' She leaned forward. 'Miaouw!' **1965** L. BRAIN *It's Free Country* xv. 146 'P'raps she just likes men,' said Howard. 'Men with money,' said Susan. 'Miaow!' **1967** 'S. WOODS' *And shame Devil* 89 'He probably has some money of his own. Otherwise, why should she have married him?' 'Miaow,' said Antony.

miaow, *v. intr.* (Further example.)

1975 J. SYMONS *Three Pipe Problem* xvii. 174 It miaowed in faint protest, arched its back.

miarolitic (mɪ̄,ăroli·tik), *a. Petrol.* [ad. Ger. *miarolitisch* (H. Rosenbusch *Mikrosk. Physiogr.* (ed. 2, 1887) II. 39), f. It. dial. *miarolo*, name of a kind of granite containing cavities + *-lit* -LITE: see -IC.] Characterized by irregular cavities into which well-formed crystals project; also applied to the cavities themselves.

1895 A. HARKER *Petrol.* ii. 31 Vacant spaces are apt to occur, into which project the sharp angles of well-formed crystals. This miarolitic or drusy structure is more or less marked in some granites (e.g. the Mourne Mts in Ireland). **1931** A. JOHANNSEN *Descr. Petrogr. Igneous Rocks* I. iii. 36 Miarolitic cavities are generally irregular and angular in form, and are seldom more than a few inches in diameter. **1970** *Nature* 28 Nov. 850/2 The nepheline gabbro..is a subangular block coated by a thin crust of MnO_2... The texture is ophitic and miarolitic.

miasmal, *a.* (Later example.)

1919 T. S. ELIOT *Hippopotamus* in *Poems*, The True Church remains below Wrapt in the old miasmal mist.

miasmatic, *a.* (Later and *fig.* examples.)

1938 M. BRINIG *May Flavin* iv. 396 An incomparable California sun pushing the miasmatic mists back into the sea. **1968** 'HAN SUYIN' *Birdless Summer* I. vi. 132 Pao and his benevolent brothers bemoaned the miasmatic disorder in which they were involved.

miasmic, *a.* Add: (Later *fig.* example.) Hence **mia·smically** *adv.*

1938 E. WAUGH *Scoop* I. v. 81 Suddenly, miasmically, in the fiery wilderness, there came an apparition. **1961** B. FERGUSSON *Watery Maze* iii. 80 The Pantellaria project and another miasmic one were abandoned.

mic, mic. (maɪk). Colloq. abbrev. of MICROPHONE. (Cf. *MIKE *sb.*[5])

1961 A. BERKMAN *Singers' Gloss. Show Business* 58 Microphone: (Abbr. mike or mic). **1973** *Sci. Amer.* Apr. 2/1 (Advt.), Eight input controls for complete mic/line mixing. **1974** *Some Technical Terms & Slang* (Granada Television), *Mic.*, microphone.

mica. Add: **2.** *water mica*, a trade name for clear, colourless mica.

1905 *Jrnl. Franklin Inst.* Sept. 200 The clear kind is known to the trade as 'water mica'.

3. *mica-packed, -scaled, -topped* adjs.; **mica flap,** the flap of a mica valve; **mica valve,** a device consisting of a flap of mica hinged at the top which is used to allow air to flow in one direction only.

1906 J. W. THOMAS *Ventilation, Heating & Lighting of Dwellings* ii. 27 There are many chimney ventilators on the market, some having mica flaps..to shut against a down current. **1934** E. L. JOSELIN *Ventilation* iii. 44 Outlets with mica flaps are frequently fitted into chimney breasts near the ceiling. **1964** J. S. SCOTT *Dict. Building* 207 Mica-flap valve. **1909** *Westm. Gaz.* 9 Mar. 4/3 A new three-point sparking-plug..which has no asbestos or mica-packed joints. *a* **1963** S. PLATH *Crossing Water* (1971) 44, I shone, mica-scaled, and unfolded To pour myself out like a fluid. **1958** A. WILSON *Middle Age of Mrs Eliot* III. 381 David banged his fist on the mica-topped table in front of him so that its little contemporary steel-tube legs rattled. **1880** S. S. HELLYER *Plumber & Sanitary Houses* (ed. 2) xxii. 262 When no convenient place can be found for leaving the mouth of the induct-pipe open to the atmosphere, a mica-valve can be fixed over it. **1909** G. B. SHAW in *Trans. Medico-Legal Soc.* VI. 217 One day on the Health Committee a question came up with regard to a mica valve not being in order.

micaceously (məikē·ʃəsli), *adv.* [f. MICACEOUS *a.* + -LY[2].] Like mica.

1933 H. G. WELLS *Bulpington of Blup* i. 18 It had walls and pinnacles of a creamy sort of rock that glittered micaceously.

Micarta (məikā·ɹtă). Also **micarta.** [perh. f. MICA + It. *carta* paper.] A laminated electrical insulating material, originally consisting of paper, mica, and enamel: now a proprietary term for one composed of layers of paper or fabrics bound by a resin and used esp. in the form of sheets and tubes.

1912 *Sci. Abstr.* B. XV. 230 The coil is wrapped with several layers of a foil termed 'Micarta Folium', consisting of paper, mica, and enamel; the whole coil is then..compressed. **1914** *Official Gaz.* (U.S. Patent Office) 10 Feb. 585/2 Westinghouse Electric & Manufacturing Co... *Micarta*..Electrical insulating sheets and tubes. Claims use since Apr. 4, 1912. **1921** *Raw Material* IV. 449/2 The method of manufacturing *micarta*..consists of impregnating the base material with a solution of the binder, evaporating the solvent and then fusing together laminations of impregnated base material by the action of heat under pressure. **1923** *Trade Marks Jrnl.* 3 Jan. 42 Micarta... Electrical insulating sheets and tubes... Westinghouse Electric and Manufacturing Company. **1938** *Jrnl. R. Aeronaut. Soc.* XLII. 9 For those engineers dealing with wooden or micarta airscrews or metal airscrews of less usual form. **1966** *Sci. & Technical Aerospace Rep.* IV. 667/1 The ablation rate of contoured Micarta (laminated plastics) specimens immersed in solid propellant exhaust gases was measured under closely controlled conditions.

Micawber (mikǭ·bər). The name of Wilkins *Micawber*, a character in Dickens's novel 'David Copperfield', applied *gen.* to a feckless optimist with a habit of 'waiting for something to turn up'. Also *attrib.* and *Comb.*, as **Micawber-like** *a.*; **Micaw·ber** *v. intr.*, to behave like Micawber; **Micawberish** (mikǭ·bəriʃ) *a.*, characteristic of a Micawber, irresponsible; **Micaw·berishly** *adv.*; so **Micaw·berism; Micaw·berite** = Micawber.

1852 GEO. ELIOT *Let.* 2 June (1954) II. 31 No good news yet, but I have a Micawber-faith that something will turn up. **1880** J. HOLLINGSHEAD *Plain Eng.* 2 Undeceived by the Micawberism of one class, or the dazzling brilliancy of the other. **1882** W. D. HAY *Brighter Britain!* I. vi. 143 A Micawber-like roll of his voice. **1920** *Glasgow Herald* 19 June 6 He was in a state of what may be described as 'Micawberish embarrassment'. **1927** *Observer* 22 May 8 Nancy's father, a sort of Micawberish Costigan. **1939** *Times Lit. Suppl.* 18 Mar. 162/3 We find a grand collection of literary people who have become household words, like..Micawber. **1948** E. GOWERS *Plain Words* 48 The present inclination of the official is in the opposite direction. He is a Johnsonian rather than a Micawberite. **1949** I. DEUTSCHER *Stalin* iii. 70 Lenin treated such Socialists contemptuously as the romantic Micawbers of revolution. **1950** *Mind* LIX. 84 An opportunistic, capricious, or Micawberish policy. **1961** *Times* 5 June 15/3 The British Government can hardly be blamed for being somewhat Micawber-like in their approach to this problem. **1963** *Punch* 24 July 126/1 Every author must spend half his life Micawbering, waiting for something to turn up. **1969** *Times* 2 May (Suppl.) p. viii/3 History has been on the side of the Micawbers. **1971** *Guardian* 16 July 10/2 Mr Wilson's social contract..will..look remarkably like the 1964 or 1966 vintage, with a dash of Micawberism added. **1972** *Ibid.* 11 Oct. 12/2 The Green Paper's hope that growth will provide comes dangerously near the Micawber tradition. **1972** 'J. & E. BONETT' *No time to Kill* x. 138 Idle men who take a job in the sunshine that leads nowhere...today's Micawbers, aimlessly awaiting what will never turn up. **1973** *Nation Rev.* (Melbourne) 31 Aug. 1463/3 Despite portraying a Micawberlike optimism, Plorn died destitute. **1974** *Times* 7 Jan. 5/5 The Micawberish disasters that threatened them so long as the father—that sad barrister without briefs—was still alive. **1974** *Times* 4 Mar. 15/3 The Liberal Party..has always Micawberishly hoped that some rich sympathizer would turn up.

micell, var. next.

micella. Add: Also **micell(e.** [ad. G. *micell* (C. Nägeli *Mikrophysik* (1877) 424.] Substitute for def.: **a.** Each of the minute ordered aggregates of macromolecules from which the microfibrils of many natural and artificial fibrous materials are made up. (Earlier and later examples.)

1881 *Encycl. Brit.* XII. 12/1 Nägeli concluded that these structures were made up of crystalline doubly refracting particles or micellæ, each consisting of numerous atoms and impermeable by water. **1937** O. B. DARBISHIRE tr. *A. von Buzágh's Colloid Syst.* vii. 133 The above structural picture of the cellulose micelle is in agreement with a number of physical and physico-chemical properties of

cellulose. Chief among them is the well-known great stability of the cellulose micelle, as shown, for instance, by the insolubility of cellulose in water. **1946** *Nature* 10 Aug. 199/2 The main component of starch..is considered to be a network of primary valency chains, which are linked in crystalline micells in which water is bound in the lattice. **1959** *Chambers's Encycl.* III. 222/1 Later evidence suggests rather that the micelles are areas in which the molecular chains are regularly arranged and crystalline; these merge into amorphous areas with possibly some of the long chains extending from one micelle to another. **1965** Micella [see *CRYSTALLITE 4].

b. An ultramicroscopic aggregate in a colloid consisting of some tens or hundreds of ions or molecules.

1901 *Jrnl. Chem. Soc.* LXXX. II. 231 A 'micelle' is used to denote the smallest quantity of a colloid which possesses all the physical properties of the colloid and is formed by the association of molecules of large size. **1926** H. S. HATFIELD tr. *Freundlich's Colloid & Capillary Chem.* 371 For the micella of the gold sol we must take into account the fact that foreign substances enter into its structure, which largely determine its chemical properties. **1927** H. S. VAN KLOOSTER tr. *Kruyt's Colloids* vi. 102 The micell is the particle plus the entire double layer. **1949** ALEXANDER & JOHNSON *Colloid Sci.* I. ii. 31 It is generally agreed that the physical properties of soap solutions, such as surface activity, conductivity, osmotic coefficients, solubilization of organic compounds, the Krafft phenomenon, etc., are due..to the occurrence of micelles. **1969** *New Scientist* 21 Aug. 379/1 The granules correspond to what are generally referred to as casein micelles, being formed by the denaturation and aggregation of the milk proteins during the manufacture of cheese. **1971** *Nature* 9 July 118/1 The bulk of DDT carried in contaminated water is probably in an organic environment, dissolved in suspended liquid fats, in soap and in detergent micelles.

micelle, now the usual form of prec.

micellization (mise:ləizēɪ·ʃən). *Chem.* [f. MICELL(A + -IZATION.] The formation of micelles.

1966 *Jrnl. Amer. Chem. Soc.* LXXXVIII. 247/1 DPI [*sc.* dodecylpyridinium iodide] was chosen because a large spectral change accompanies its micellization and thus provides a self-indicator of the micellization process. **1972** *Nature* 3 Mar. 32/2 The results further suggest that at concentrations of ganglioside above 30% the formation of membranous structures would be inhibited by lipid micellization.

Michael. Add: **4.** = *MICKEY FINN. *U.S. slang.*

1942 BERREY & VAN DEN BARK *Amer. Thes. Slang* § 509/9 Opiate; 'knockout drops'... *Michael.* **1957** B. BUCKINGHAM *Boiled Alive* xxiv. 178 He only pretended to trust me and just slipped me a Michael in my drink. I passed out in the car a few minutes after leaving the bar.

5. Slang phr. *to take the Michael* (*out of*) = *to take the micky* (*out of*) (see *MICKY[1] 6).

1959 H. PINTER *Birthday Party* I. 9 They won't come. Someone's taking the Michael... It's a false alarm. **1962** *Spectator* 23 Feb. 242/2 Like many satirists Mayakovsky takes the michael out of both sides. **1966** L. DAVIDSON *Long Way to Shiloh* xi. 157 Jesus, did we take the Michael! We used to chat 'em up, these old bats out looking for prospects.

Michaelangelesque, var. MICHELANGELESQUE *a.*

1845 R. FORD *Hand-bk. for Travellers Spain* II. viii. 635/2 Two grand subjects in *chiaro oscuro* on a gilded ground..are quite Michael-Angelesque. **1856** M. D. WYATT in O. Jones *Gram. Ornament* xix. 4 Primaticcio, a master whose style of drawing was founded upon the Michael-Angelesque system of proportion. **1864** [see MICHELANGELESQUE *a.*]. **1874** E. EASTLAKE tr. *Kugler's Handbk. Painting: Italian Schools* (ed. 4) I. IV. i. 251 In addition to his larger Michael-Angelesque peculiarities *Luca* may be known by the squareness of his forms in joints and extremities. **1886** [see MICHELANGELESQUE *a.*]. **1934** R. CAMPBELL *Broken Record* iv. 84 He looked very Mosaic in the Michaelangelesque sense of the word. **1935** *Burlington Mag.* June 278 Some Michaelangelesque drawings by Maurice Delacre.

miche, *v.* **2, 2. b.** (Further examples of the spelling *mitch*, which is now usual.)

1867 W. F. ROCK *Jim an' Nell* 6 Wan vomoon Hur mitched vro' schule. **1888** 'Q' *Troy Town* xi. 117 Turn your back, an' they'd be mitchin' in a brace o' shakes. **1907** J. M. SYNGE *Playboy of Western World* II. 42 You're pot-boy in this place, and I'll not have you mitch off from us now. **1933** DAVIES & THOMSON tr. *O'Sullivan's 20 Yrs. A-Growing* i. 6 What would you say for us to go mitching? **1939** DYLAN THOMAS *Map of Love* 14 When I whistled with mitching boys through a reservoir park. *a* **1953** —— *Quite Early One Morning* (1954) 84 He cribbed, mitched, spilt ink, rattled his desk and garbled his lessons with the worst of them. **1960** A. CLARKE *Later Poems* (1961) 84, I mitched from miracles. **1968** *TV Times* 28 Sept.–4 Oct. 69/1, I used to mitch a lot from school because I simply dreaded it.

Michelangelesque, *a.* (Later examples.)

1903 [see *CONTRAPPOSTO]. **1932** R. FRY *Let.* 10 Mar. (1972) II. 666 The cubico-Michelangelesque affair may best express the spirit of your house. **1956** K. CLARK *Nude* iv. 134 The same Michelangelesque motive is used. **1963** A. E. ELSEN *Rodin* 55 The Michelangelesque motive of the right elbow crossed over to the left thigh..pleased the artist. **1970** T. HILTON *Pre-Raphaelites* viii. 196 In such Michelangelesque subjects as *The Wheel of Fortune*, Burne-Jones's relations with the Italian masters were always to be uneasy.

Michelin (mi·tʃəlin, ‖miʃelæ̃n). The name of André *Michelin* (1853–1931) and Édouard *Michelin* (1859–1940), French manufacturers of motor vehicles, used to designate motor-vehicle tyres produced by the company they founded; freq. with allusion to the symbols included in its advertising, or to the gastronomic and touring guides produced by the company.

1902 C. L. FREESTON in A. C. Harmsworth et al. *Motors* 226 The tyre which was most favourably known abroad, i.e. the Michelin. *Ibid.*, The Michelin tyre is made in various sizes. **1921** W. J. LOCKE *Mountebank* iv. 45 The avocations that had led him to know the Inns of France with the accuracy of a Michelin guide. **1933** A. G. MACDONELL *England, their England* vii. 99 A blazer of purple-and-yellow stripes..surmounted by a purple-and-yellow cap that made him somehow reminiscent of the Michelin twins. **1934** H. MILLER *Tropic of Cancer* 18 A caricature of a man... Thyroid eyes, Michelin lips. **1951** G. GREENE *End of Affair* III. vii. 145, I can't stand twenty-four hours of maps and Michelin guides. **1954** *Observer* 18 July 10/3 The Michelin man (whose name is.. Bibendum) is..evocative of such delights as foreign travel, luscious food, the best maps in the world. **1958** E. DUNDY *Dud Avocado* I. i. 11 Baedekers and Michelins and museum catalogues..discarded as too boring and corny. **1959** *Motor Manual* (ed. 36) v. 130 The unusual Michelin X, in which three layers of steel cords are built into the cover between the casing and the tread. **1962** L. DEIGHTON *Ipcress File* 221 Joigny a Michelin-starred town a hundred kilometres south of Paris. **1968** A. DIMENT *Gt. Spy Race* viii. 125 The old charlatan has got a Michelin star to his name. **1971** C. BONINGTON *Annapurna South Face* App. B. 244 They [*sc.* down jackets] had the advantage of being quite close-fitting and did not make one feel like the Michelin tyre man. **1972** *Guardian* 20 Oct. 13/2 The spirit of the French Michelin man is quietly pacing the British byways. Michelin will bring out their first guide to British hotels and restaurants in March 1974. **1975** R. HILL *Jackdaw* 147 He opened his Michelin..and studied the list of hotels.

Michelsberg (mi·χĕlzbɐrk). [Place-name in Baden, Germany.] A Neolithic Belgo-Germanic culture illustrated by remains (esp. pottery) found at Michelsberg. Also *attrib.* Cf. *CORTAILLOD.

1929 PEAKE & FLEURE *Way of Sea* i. 12 The Michelsberg culture occurs at many sites near the Rhine between Lake Constance and Cologne. *Ibid.* ii. 21 The pottery.. was introduced from France into Switzerland..about 2200 B.C., and here this culture developed into that known as Michelsberg, with its tulip-shaped vases, about a century later. **1954** S. PIGGOTT *Neolithic Cultures* ii. 32 A similar mingling of agricultural and hunter-fisher strains is probably perceptible in the Michelsberg culture in Belgium and the Rhineland. **1970** BRAY & TRUMP *Dict. Archaeol.* 146/2 *Michelsberg*, a Neolithic culture of Belgium, north France, the Rhineland and parts of Switzerland... There are many regional sub-groups. The Belgian one has leaf-shaped arrows, antler combs, flint mines, and enclosures similar in construction to causewayed camps, and may have links with the Windmill Hill culture.

Michelson (məi·kĕlsən). *Physics.* The name of A. A. *Michelson* (1852–1931), German-born U.S. physicist, used *attrib.* and in the possessive to designate (*a*) the Michelson-Morley experiment (see next); (*b*) the type of interferometer that was used in this experiment (invented earlier by Michelson).

1902 *Encycl. Brit.* XXX. 250/1 Lodge..studied the behavior of a beam of light which was divided into two portions by a semi-transparent mirror as in Michelson's interferometer. **1956** E. H. HUTTEN *Lang. Mod. Physics* iii. 99 The theory of *special* relativity rests mainly on the Michelson experiment. **1966** Michelson interferometer [see *MICHELSON-MORLEY]. **1965** M. GARBUNY *Optical Physics* vi. 308 That such a wavetrain moving through space with a finite length has actually a physical significance..can be demonstrated by the Michelson experiment. **1972** C. MØLLER *Theory of Relativity* (ed. 2) i. 28 Michelson's experiment was only the first of a long series of attempts to determine the motion of the earth relative to the ether.

Michelson-Morley (məi:kĕlsən mōᵊ·ɹli). *Physics.* The names of A. A. *Michelson* (see prec.) and E. W. *Morley* (1838–1923), U.S. chemist and physicist, used *attrib.* to designate an experiment first performed by them in 1887 in which a beam of light is divided into two parts which are made to travel over paths at right angles to one another before being reunited, the behaviour of the resulting interference fringes (e.g. when the whole apparatus is rotated through 90 degrees) showing that the speed of light is the same in both directions, in contrast to what would be expected if the earth were in motion through an 'ether'; so *Michelson-Morley apparatus.*

1913 O. LODGE *Continuity* 20 Many forms of statement of the famous Michelson-Morley experiment are misleading. **1925** I. A. RICHARDS *Princ. Lit. Crit.* x. 71 No new facts nor any new hypotheses—no Michelson-Morley experiment, nor any widened purview—led up to the separate value theory of art. **1965** D. BOHM *Special Theory of Relativity* xxii. 107 The Michelson-Morley experiment may be regarded as an excellent confirmation of the Lorentz contraction. **1966** *McGraw-Hill Encycl. Sci. & Technol.* VII. 505/1 The Michelson-Morley apparatus..consists of a horizontal Michelson interferometer with its two arms at right angles.

michenerite (mi·tʃĕnĕrəit). *Min.* [f. the name of C. E. *Michener*, 20th-cent. Canadian mineralogist + -ITE[1].] A palladium bismuthide, $PdBi_2$, or perhaps a telluride and bismuthide of palladium and platinum (see quot. 1963), which is found as greyish-white isometric crystals.

1958 HAWLEY & BERRY in *Canad. Mineralogist* VI. 200 Two palladium bismuthides from nickeliferous ores of the Frood Mine, Sudbury, Ontario, detected and described by C. E. Michener some years ago, are re-described and named michenerite and froodite. **1963** *Mineral. Abstr.* XVI. 283/1 Michenerite associated with the moncheite and kotulskite is shown to have a composition approximating to $Pd_{0.75}Pt_{0.25}BiTe$ rather than $PdBi_2$. **1972** *Ibid.* XXIII. 316/1 Moncheite and michenerite occur as disseminations between sulphides and rock-forming silicates and as idiomorphic grains.

Michigan (mi·ʃĭgăn). **a.** The name of the State on the Great Lakes of North America, used *attrib.* to denote a thing or type found in, peculiar to, or characteristic of Michigan.

1835 C. BRADLEY in *Ohio Archaeol. & Hist. Soc. Publ.* (1966) XV. 257 My conquered enemy was the massassagua, the Michigan rattlesnake. **1838** *State of Indiana Delineated* (J. H. Colton & Co.) 26 A rail road is located from Madison to Indianapolis, and the great Michigan road through the state commences here. **1855** 'Q. K. P. DOESTICKS' *Doesticks, what he Says* xii. 97 One was afflicted with the measles, and the other had the Michigan itch. **1857** *Trans. Illinois Agric. Soc.* III. 496 For this purpose [*sc.* subsoiling] the Michigan double or subsoil plow is used. **1884** G. B. GOODE *Fisheries U.S.: Nat. Hist. Aquatic Animals* 505 The Michigan Grayling..is at present most interesting to the angler. **1900** *Atlantic Monthly* LXXXV. 102/2 Heavy horses or oxen draw a brace of huge wheels for hauling. (This is the Michigan buggy.) **1922** H. TITUS *Timber* 12 Didn't Michigan Pine build th' corn belt? **1932** *Evening Sun* (Baltimore) 9 Dec. 31/5 *Michigan roll*, a bankroll..of stage money with a genuine banknote..outside. **1955** *Publ. Amer. Dial. Soc.* XXIV. 116 If the *bundle* consists largely of small bills, it is called a *michigan bankroll*, or a *mish.* **1962** E. LUCIA *Klondike Kate* ix. 195 It proved to be a Michigan bank roll, for the only ten[-dollar bill] was on the outside, all the others being ones. **1971** M. TAK *Truck Talk* 105 *Michigan rig*, a double-bottom rig out of Michigan, where such combinations are legal.

b. *U.S.* A card game similar to Newmarket.

1944 A. H. MOREHEAD *Pocket Bk. Games* 80 Michigan is a simple game, yet rewards careful attention. **1946** 'L. FORD' *Honolulu Story* 176 'I want to play hearts. On the floor.' 'Michigan,' Mary said. 'Michigan it is.' **1952** E. KEMPSON et al. *Hoyle Up-to-Date* 215 (*heading*) Stops family. Newmarket (Boodle, Newmarket, Chicago, Saratoga, Michigan, Stops). **1972** R. HARBIN *Waddingtons Family Card Games* 110 In the USA, Newmarket is known as Michigan, or Chicago, or Boodle, or Stops; and they play it slightly differently. But I think that our name, and our rules, are better. **1974** W. B. GIBSON *Hoyle's Mod. Encycl. Card Games* 161 *Michigan*, a modern game of the 'stops' type, played with a standard fifty-two-card pack, with cards running in ascending value. *Ibid.* 164 *New Market*, the English counterpart of *Michigan*.., the only difference being that the extra hand, or 'widow', is never taken up for play but is 'dead' from start to finish.

Michigander (miʃigæ·ndəɹ). [f. prec.] A native or inhabitant of the State of Michigan.

1848 A. LINCOLN *Coll. Works* (1953) I. 509, I mean the military tail you Democrats are now engaged in dovetailing on to the great Michigander. **1865** *Harper's Mag.* May 814/1 One of the Michiganders uses the goose-quill to some purpose. **1897** *Outing* XXX. 293/1 (*heading*) Michi-gander lawmakers. **1952** *Manch. Guardian Weekly* 8 May 4/2 Jackson would like to have been known thereafter as 'The Republican City' and several boosters and patriotic Michiganders did their best to make that name take.

Michiganian (miʃigēɪ·niăn). [f. *MICHIGAN + -IAN.] = prec.

1813 *Niles' Reg.* V. 185 The Michiganians. **1835** [see WOLVERENE, -INE 3]. **1837** H. MARTINEAU *Society in Amer.* I. I. 65 The Michiganians were in the singular position of having a state government in full operation, while they were excluded from the Union.

miching, *vbl. sb.* and *ppl. a.* Add: Also **mitching.**

Examples s.v. *MICHE *v.* 2, 2 b.

Michler (mi·χləɹ, mi·k-). The name of Wilhelm *Michler* (d. 1889), German chemist, used in the possessive to denote certain compounds first studied by him, as **Michler's hydrol,** 4,4′-bis(dimethylamino)benzhydrol, $[C_6H_4N(CH_3)_2]_2CHOH$, a crystalline compound which is made by the condensation of dimethylaniline and formaldehyde or by reduction of Michler's ketone and is an important intermediate for the synthesis of triphenylmethane dyes; **Michler's ketone,** the ketone $[C_6H_4N(CH_3)_2]_2CO$ corresponding to Michler's hy-

drol, which is made by treating phosgene or carbon tetrachloride with dimethylaniline.

1910 *Jrnl. Chem. Soc.* XCVIII. I. 451 Tetramethyldiaminobenzhydrylphosphinous acid.., prepared from Michler's hydrol, occurs in colourless crystals. **1971** R. L. M. ALLEN *Colour Chem.* viii. 110 Michler's hydrol.. condenses with bases such as dimethylaniline to give triphenylmethanes which by oxidation and treatment with acids yield rosanilines. **1897** *Jrnl. Chem. Soc.* LXXII. I. 157 The author obtained crystalline leuco-bases of dyes by the condensation of Michler's ketone with various phenols. **1949** P. W. VITTUM tr. *Fierz-David & Blangey's Fund. Processes Dye Chem.* i. 140 Michler's ketone and its homologs are important starting materials for the preparation of valuable triphenylmethane dyes such as Victoria blue B and Victoria pure blue BO.

Michurinism (mitʃūᵊ·riniz'm). Also **michurinism.** [f. the name *Michurin* + -ISM.] Belief in or advocacy of the views of the Russian horticulturalist I. V. Michurin (1855–1935): = *LYSENKOISM.

1949 J. S. HUXLEY *Soviet Genetics & World Sci.* i. 23 Michurinism is..an essentially non-scientific or prescientific doctrine. **1955** *Bull. Atomic Sci.* June 210/1 Genetics seems to be the field of 'natural' science which is most abused with political and other special interests, in their attempts to fabricate theoretical bases for their practices, as in the case of Hitler's racist obsessions and Stalin's Michurinism. **1974** *Encycl. Brit. Micropædia* VI. 862/2 Michurin's theories of hybridization, labelled michurinism, which accepted completely the inheritance of acquired characteristics, were adopted as the official science of genetics by the Soviet regime.

Hence **Michu·rinist**, one who believes in or advocates Michurinism; also as *adj.*

1949 *Ann. Reg. 1948* 210 The Michurinists, who regarded environment as the chief determinant of heredity. **1949** C. ZIRKLE *Death of a Science in Russ.* vii. 174 The most advanced, materialistic, biological science is the Michurinist trend in the Soviet agrobiology. **1957** C. HUNT *Guide to Communist Jargon* xxviii. 100 In 1948 it was the turn of the biologists, and a number of them were deprived of their posts for supporting Weissmann–Morganist as opposed to Michurinist genetics.

Mick[1]**. a.** For 1882 in first quot. in Dict. read 1872, and add earlier and later examples. Also sometimes applied derogatorily. Also *attrib.* or as *adj.*

1856 *Butte Record* (Oroville, Calif.) 20 Sept. 3/3 One of the 'bucks' jerked something from his belt..and made for a Mick. **1894** P. L. FORD *Hon. Peter Stirling* lvii. 369 Fortunately it's a Mick regiment, so we needn't worry over who was killed. **1913** J. LONDON *Valley of Moon* 27 They's been too much drink, an' you know what the Micks are for a rough house. **1932** E. WILSON *Devil take Hindmost* vii. 38 The Communists..have..recruited..a considerable number of seedy unemployed—niggers, micks. **1943** [see *GEORDIE 2]. **1961** *Spectator* 12 Aug. 254 Labels such as Wop, Polack and Mick. **1970** M. KENYON *100,000 Welcomes* iv. 32 Where's Ireland, huh? Who needs Micks?

b. A Roman Catholic. Also **Mickey.** Freq. derogatory. Also *attrib.* or as *adj.*

1924 P. MARKS *Plastic Age* 201, I suppose you refer to.. my one mick friend, although he isn't Irish. **1948** P. WHITE *Aunt's Story* 258 He says that Mother is wrong to send a girl to a convent with a lot of micks. **1956** 'N. SHUTE' *Beyond Black Stump* ii. 57 Stanley and Phyllis went to Church of England schools..but all the rest of us are Micks. **1960** *Times* 28 Jan. 15/5 Religious rivalries from Salvationists to Plymouth Brethren—united in hatred of the 'Mickeys' or Catholics. **1971** *Guardian* 27 May 13/7 Curiously, in the circumstances of the Australian fondness for the 'o' suffix, a Roman Catholic is apparently never a Catho, but remains, in lower-level Protto usage, a Mick. **1973** *Times* 31 July 12/7 On this theory the Council of Ireland can be presented as a second inter-Parliamentary tier—'a place where the Micks and Prods can get together occasionally' as one Assembly member put it—built on a structure that already exists.

c. Examples of various *slang* (usu. derogatory) extended uses.

1928 F. SCOTT FITZGERALD in *Sat. Even. Post* 28 Apr. 4/2 In sordid poverty, below the bluff two hundred feet away, lived the 'micks'—they had merely inherited the name, for they were now largely of Scandinavian descent. **1937** in Partridge *Dict. Underworld* (1949) 437/2 *Mick*, a road mechanic. **1941** J. SMILEY *Hash House Lingo* 37 *Mick*, Englishman. **1958** L. A. G. STRONG *Light above Lake* 94 He's a dismal ould mick of a God. **1974** *Amer. Speech 1971* XLVI. 81 *Mexican*: greaser, spick, wetback, mick, halfbreed.

d. *mad mick*: a pick. *slang.*

1924 *Truth* (Sydney) 27 Apr. 6 *Mad mick*, a pick. **1935** A. J. POLLOCK *Underworld Speaks* 74/1 *Mad mick*, a pick (prison) **1973** F. HUELIN *Keep Moving* 78 Well, I won't buy drinks f'r any bloody ganger, just f'r a chance to swing a mad mick.

mick[2] (mik). *Austral. slang.* [Origin unknown.] The head, or sometimes the reverse, of a penny (see also quot. 1919).

1919 W. H. DOWNING *Digger Dial.* 33 *Mick*, (1) the Queen's head on a coin... (2) a queen in a pack of cards. **1938** J. ROBERTSON *With Cameliers in Palestine* xx. 198 'A pair of Micks', which means that the offerings [in the game of two-up] are not accepted. **1941** BAKER *Dict. Austral. Slang* 46 *Mick*, the 'head' of a penny. **1953** T. A. G. HUNGERFORD *Riverslake* 126 'Ten bob he tails 'em!' he intoned,.. 'I got ten bob to say he tails 'em—ten bob the micks!'

mick[3] (mik). *slang.* Also **mickey, micky.** [var. of MIKE *sb.*[3] reinterpreted as a proper name.] *to do a mick*, etc., to go away, to clear off (see *MIKE *sb.*[3]).

1937 PARTRIDGE *Dict. Slang* 519/1 *Mick, do a* [equated with *do a mike*]. **1959** I. & P. OPIE *Lore & Lang. Schoolch.* x. 192 *Sending away*,..do a mickey. **1961** S. CHAPLIN *Day of Sardine* xi. 225, I laid the ring on the notepaper and did a mickey as soon as I heard the front doorbell go.

mick[4] (mik). *slang.* [Origin unknown.] A seaman's hammock.

1929 *Papers Mich. Acad. Sci., Arts & Lett.* X. 308/1 *Mick*, an abridgement of 'face like a scrubbed hammock'. **1946** J. IRVING *Royal Navalese* 115 *Mick*, hammock. **1961** PARTRIDGE *Dict. Slang* Suppl. 1183/1 *Mick*,.. a seaman's hammock.

mick[5] (mik). *dial.* Also **mickey, micky.** [Origin unknown.] A pigeon.

1940 *N. & Q.* 3 Aug. 79/1 Mick was the usual word for a pigeon, especially the domesticated kind [in Cheshire]. **1965** *Jrnl. Lancs. Dial. Soc.* Jan. 7 Woodpigeon..Mick, Micky: Southport, Liverpool. **1966** F. SHAW et al. *Lern Yerself Scouse* 23 *De mickeys are lettin on de roof*, the pigeons are alighting on the roof. **1966** 'L. LANE' *ABZ of Scouse* 68 *Mickey-snatcher*, a person who steals municipal pigeons.

mickery (mi·kĕri). *Austral.* Also **mickerie.** [Origin unknown.] **a.** A type of well (see quot. 1934). **b.** Marshy ground; = SOAK *sb.* 2 d. Also *attrib.*

1934 *Bulletin* (Sydney) 6 June 20/2 A mickery was a timbered well-shaft sunk into the sandy bed of a creek; it was worked by means of a pole placed across a forked stick, the pole having a bucket attached to one end and a weight to the other. **1935** H. H. FINLAYSON *Red Centre* x. 98 The Wonkonguroos, themselves an offshoot of the Aruntas, occupying until recently what is known as the mickerie country, a desolation to the north-west of the Yalliyandas. **1945** BAKER *Austral. Lang.* iii. 58 *Mickery country*, country which holds moisture after rain or which is of swampy 'soak' type.

Mickey (mi·ki). *U.S. slang.* [f. *MICKEY MOUSE.] A type of radar-assisted bombsight. Also *attrib.*

1944 *News* (San Francisco) 28 Nov. 7/3 'Mickey', a sensational radar device which 'sees' through darkness, clouds and artificial smoke. **1944** *Time* 11 Dec. 24 Mickey was a British invention, freely given to the U.S. U.S. scientists later developed an improved model. It was first used by U.S. bombers just over a year ago; today every fleet of heavy bombers over Europe presumably is or will be equipped with it, on day or night raids. **1945** *News* (San Francisco) 15 Aug. 10 (Advt.), Mickey radar sends out super-high frequency radio waves which bounce back from solid targets and are picked up by the radar receiver and transformed into a radar picture on a screen like the one in a home television receiver. **1954** BERREY & VAN DEN BARK *Amer. Thes. Slang* § 819 *Mickey*, the improved American airborne radar. **1955** M. REIFER *Dict. New Words* 131/2 *Mickey*.., a radar-type bomb-sight that permits air navigation in zero visibility and pinpoint strategic bombing despite overcast or darkness. Named for the cartoon figure, Mickey Mouse, created by Walt Disney.

Mickey, var. *MICK[1] b, *MICKEY FINN, *MICKEY MOUSE.

mickey: see *MICK[3], *MICK[5], *MICKY[1].

Mickey Finn (mi:ki,fi·n). *slang* (orig. *U.S.*). Also **Mickey Flynn** and ellipt. **Mickey.** [Origin uncertain.] A strong alcoholic drink; a drink adulterated with a narcotic or purgative substance, usu. administered to a person with the deliberate intention of stupefying or greatly discomforting him; the adulterant itself; also *transf.* and *fig.* (Cf. **knock-out drops.*) Hence **mickey-fi·nn** *v. trans.*, to adulterate with a Mickey Finn; to stupefy with a Mickey Finn; also *ellipt.*

1928 M. C. SHARPE *Chicago May* xii. 99, I got a bottle of brandy... He was lit up..but I shot a few more Mickey Finns (double drinks) into him. **1931** *Amer. Mercury* Mar. 316/1 But he never slipped an obstreperous customer the croton oil Mickey Finn of the modern night club. **1934** *Cosmopolitan* Apr. 131/1 She had been mickey-finned. **1934** J. O'HARA *Appointment in Samarra* (1935) iii. 86 The cheap bastard... I'd like to give him a Mickey Finn. **1935** N. ERSINE *Underworld & Prison Slang* 53 *Mickey Finn*, a drink spiked with knockout drops. **1936** *Amer. Speech* XI. 124/1 *Mickey Flynn* or *Mickey Finn*, a knockout dose (often cigar ashes in a carbonated drink) administered to an addict or a sucker. **1938** A. J. LIEBLING *Back where I came From* 88 Mickeys..act so drastically that one may kill a drunk with a weak heart. **1951** WODEHOUSE *Old Reliable* v. 71 She had been about to suggest that the butler might slip into Adela's bedtime Ovaltine what is known as a knockout drop or Mickey Finn. **1957** P. FRANK *Seven Days to Never* iv. 118 This was no ordinary hangover... He had been expertly mickey-finned. **1960** *Guardian* 17 June 7/4 The reader cannot be sure when Mr. Colquhoun is about to slip him a Bible..and when a Mickey Finn. **1962** E. LUCIA *Klondike Kate* iv. 107 However, the dames seldom rolled the miners or slipped them a Mickey. **1966** R. W. TAYLOR *Doomsday Square* (1967) xiii. 144, I Mickey-Finned him with my little pressure syringe. Let him sleep. **1971** 'C. FRANKLIN' *Home Secretary Affair* vii. 99 Two men..had mickey-finned his drink. **1972** M. PUGH *Murmur of Mutiny* xix. 144 I'd a couple or so in the sergeants' mess... They mustaf been mickied. **1973** D. BAGLEY *Tightrope Men* xii. 93 Meyrick was probably knocked out by a Mickey Finn in his nightly Ovaltine.

Mickey Mouse (mi·ki maus). **1.** The name of a mouse-like character in a series of animated cartoons designed by the American cartoonist Walter Elias ('Walt') Disney (1901–66), used with direct or indirect reference to the character in these cartoons. Also *ellipt.* **Mickey,** a Mickey Mouse cartoon. Also *attrib.* or as *adj.*, characteristic of, resembling, or featuring Mickey Mouse. Frequently (esp. in *U.S.*) designating something small, insignificant, or worthless.

1934 R. STOUT *Fer-de-Lance* v. 66 Everybody..would be..laughing at us instead of going to a movie to see Micky Mouse. **1935** S. LEWIS *It can't happen Here* ix. 84 Dr. Goebbels..is privily known throughout Germany as 'Wotan's Mickey Mouse'. **1936** N. COWARD *To-night at 8.30* II. 49 We'll miss the Mickey. **1936** 'G. ORWELL' *Let.* 26 Aug. in *Coll. Ess.* (1968) I. 228 You have moved too much away from the ordinary world into a sort of Mickey Mouse universe where things and people don't have to obey the rules of space and time. **1937** *Cinema Arts* July 24 The light which the electrician is aiming at Mr. Gable's head is the smallest 'spot' used in the studio, and is therefore known as a Mickey Mouse. **1939** *War Illustr.* 18 Nov. 310/3 Special 'Mickey Mouse' gas-masks in various colours and having separate eye-pieces and a little nose are being made for small children who are repelled by the ordinary ones. **1941** *San Francisco Examiner* 2 Mar. Pict. Rev. 7/1 George Graham, a timid, middle-aged mickey mouse who was afraid of crowds, people, anything. **1942** N. STREATFEILD *I ordered Table for Six* 20 That little bit of the room at the top must have been a nursery once, there's some Mickie Mouses on that wallpaper. **1951** *San Francisco Examiner* 3 Feb. 1/3 (*heading*) 40th Division. Troops Lack Equipment. Woes of 'Mickey Mouse Army'. **1957** T. GUNN *Sense of Movement* 54 Bent keys, Italian grammars, Mickey Mouse caps. **1958** *Amer. Speech* XXXIII. 226 A 'Mickey Mouse course' means a *snap* course. **1962** *New Statesman* 19 Jan. 96/2 A Mickey Mouse clock ticks beside the marital bed. **1963** *Amer. Speech* XXXVIII. 176 [Kansas University slang] An assignment which is regarded as foolish and a waste of time is a *Mickey Mouse*. **1966** MRS. L. B. JOHNSON *White House Diary* 4 June (1970) 387 It [*sc.* the graduation ceremony] is such a mass production affair—'Mickey Mouse', as she calls it—not quite the sophisticated thing to do anymore. **1968** *Sunday Times* 20 Oct. 8/4 Cunningham referred to 'Micky Mouse' (unnecessary and childish) operations. **1969** C. DAVIDSON in Cockburn & Blackburn *Student Power* 329 The forms given us for our self-government are of the Mickey Mouse, sand-box variety. **1972** J. MOSEDALE *Football* ii. 25 One reason for the AFL's reputation as a Mickey Mouse league is that it gave new life to NFL rejects. **1973** R. LUDLUM *Matlock Paper* xix. 161 The average purchase of chips was $200 to $300. Hardly 'Micky Mouse'. **1974** *Globe & Mail* (Toronto) 13 Nov. 1/2 The titles kept the press and broadcast media from thinking 'it was such a Mickey Mouse operation'. **1975** *Amer. Speech 1972* XLVII. 152 You getting flew coy with the gray boys, Mickey Mouse? *Ibid.* 153 *Mickey mouse n*, white; black who 'puts on a white face'.

2. *Mus.* Inferior dance-band music, similar to that played as a background to a cartoon film; usu. *attrib.*

1938 *Down Beat* Apr. 25/2 A strictly 'mickey mouse' band is still box office. **1945** *Ibid.* 1 Sept. 15/1 Strictly mickey mouse is what they [*sc.* night clubs] advocate, and many of the truly good musicians are forced to play the tripe in order to get work. **1954** *San Francisco Chron.* 17 June 17 (*heading*) Glenn Miller's music was all Mickey Mouse. **1958** *Amer. Speech* XXXIII. 225 A mickey or Mickey Mouse band is not merely a 'pop tune' band,..but the kind of pop band that sounds as if it is playing background for an animated cartoon. **1966** *Crescendo* May 4/2 The jazzman's struggle for self-expression in a world of commercial Mickey Mouse bands. **1970** C. MAJOR *Dict. Afro-Amer. Slang* 81 *Micky Mouse* (*music*), popular, commercialized music.

3. *Air Force slang.* A name applied to an electrical device which releases bombs from aircraft.

1941 *N.Y. Times* 6 Apr. 30/5 This war is producing a new batch of army slang... Many of the words are peculiar to certain units, and very few are yet in general use... An R.A.F. pilot calls his cockpit the 'pulpit'... The instrument releasing the bombs, an electrical distributor, is called a 'Mickey Mouse'. **1943** HUNT & PRINGLE *Service Slang* 46 *Mickey Mouse.* The bomb-dropping mechanism on some types of bomber aircraft is so called because it strongly resembles the intricate machinery portrayed in Walt Disney's cartoons. **1943** L. CHESHIRE *Bomber Pilot* i. 8 If I knew how to use 'Mickey Mouse', to open and shut bomb doors, or use a bomb-sight.

Hence **Mickey-mousing** (see quots.).

1957 MANVELL & HUNTLEY *Technique Film Music* ii. 38 'Mickey-Mousing' in film musical terminology..means the exact, calculated dove-tailing of music and action. **1960** *Times* 1 Dec. 7/3 Odds and ends of Albeniz.. treated to what film composers would call 'mickey-mousing', with every detail of the music mirrored with stupefying literalness in the dancing. **1973** *New Society* 2 Aug. 288/1 What is known in the film-music trade as 'Mickey-Mousing'—the action of the film gets a simultaneous musical parody. When Tarzan swings down on his rope, a harp plays a descending glissando.

mickle, muckle, *a.*, *sb.* and *adv.* Add: **A.** *adj.* **1. d.** (Further example.)

1887 W. S. Gilbert *Ruddigore* II. 44 His gallantries were mickle.

3. muckle-mouthed *a.*, = *mickle-mouthed.*

1951 J. D. Salinger *Catcher in Rye* xi. 93 She was sort of muckle-mouthed... When she was talking and got excited,..her mouth sort of went in about fifty directions.

micky[1]. Add: Also **mickey. 1.** (Further examples.) Also **mick.**

1934 *Bulletin* (Sydney) 1 Aug. 46/3, I lifted nearly two hundred Poolpee micks on my way back and took 'em home with me. **1958** *Amer. Speech* XXXIII. 167 *Mickey, maverick*, a wild young bull. **1966** Baker *Austral. Lang.* (ed. 2) iii. 63 *Micky* or *mick*, an unbranded steer, perhaps from the Aboriginal *micky*, quick.

2. (Earlier example.)

1858 J. D. Lovett in *Harvard Mag.* July 267 While Mickey there stands, A-wringin' his hands, And Biddy is wipin' her eyes on her slave.

3. *Austral.* A honeyeater, *Myzantha melanocephala.*

1911 J. A. Leach *Austral. Bird Bk.* 173 Noisy Miner, Garrulous Honeyeater, Snake-Bird, Cherry-eater, Soldier, Micky, Squeaker, *Myzantha garrula.* **1931** N. W. Cayley *What Bird is That?* 81 Noisy Miner *Myzantha melanocephala...* Also called.. Soldier-bird, Micky, and Squeaker. In small parties, frequenting open forest country and partly cleared lands. **1971** *Courier-Mail* (Brisbane) 24 July 12/8 Mickeys, or Soldier Birds, or Noisy Miners, are great little fighters and battle the hawks, crows and goannas quite fearlessly.

4. Chiefly *Canad. colloq.* A flask of liquor.

1914 Jackson & Hellyer *Vocab. Criminal Slang* 58 *Micky*, current amongst bottle drinkers. A corruption of Michael..a flask of liquor. **1926** J. Black *You can't Win* vi. 66 A four-bit micky, a fifty-cent bottle of alcohol. **1935** A. J. Pollock *Underworld Speaks* 76/1 *Mickey*, half pint of bootleg whiskey. **1950** H. Sutton *Footloose in Canada* 5 An American pint holds 16 ounces, a Canadian 'mickey', 12 ounces of rye, or 13 ounces of Scotch. **1971** *Islander* (Victoria, B.C.) 21 Mar. 16/2 Mark, the public nuisance that he was, bought his liquor in mickeys that he hid in the woodpile around the cannery. **1972** *Regional Lang. Stud.—Newfoundland* IV. 11 *Flask* is used in the Atlantic provinces only. In central and western Canada this would be a *micky*.

5. *slang.* The penis. *rare.*

1922 Joyce *Ulysses* 765 Ill put on my best shift and drawers let him have a good eyeful out of that to make his micky stand for him.

6. Colloq. phr. *to take the micky* (*out of*) (someone): to act in a satirical, disrespectful, or teasing manner (towards). Cf. **mike sb.*[6] Hence **micky-take** *v.* and *sb.*, **micky-taking** *ppl. a.* and *vbl. sb.*

The more usual spelling of this sense is 'mickey'.

1952 'J. Henry' *Who lie in Gaol* iv. 66 She's a terror. I expect she'll try and take the mickey out of you all right. Don't you stand for nothin'. **1954** A. Heckstall-Smith *Eighteen Months* xi. 136 For a while everyone tried to take 'the Micky' out of Bobbie, but they soon gave up trying after the first foolish failure. Then their ridicule turned to admiration. **1956** A. Wilson *Anglo-Saxon Att.* II. i. 206 'You're not going to take the mickey out of me, Vin Salad, I'll spatter you,' he cried. **1957** L. P. Hartley *Hireling* 134 He had no great regard for Constance, except in so far as she sometimes took the mickey out of Hughie. **1958** *Observer* 28 Dec. 3/1 'Tonight' is not only a tough and irreverent programme, but glib and smart and anxious to take the mickey. **1959** R. Storey *Touch it Light* in *Plays of Year* XVIII. 419 You don't stop at nothing, do you? As long as you can take the mickey. Mr. Funnyman, that's you. At any price. **1959** *Oxford Mail* 13 June 6/3 This modern dress, mickey-taking version of Aristophanes. **1959** *Vogue* Dec. 101 They'd think you were a nutter and laugh and mickey-take. **1960** E. W. Hildick *Jim Starling & Colonel* ix. 76 The servers must have thought that no boy would dare to take the mickey in such circumstances. **1962** *Times* 20 July 10/6 The micky-taking ways of their own brand of insolent wise-cracking. **1965** *Listener* 25 Mar. 451/2 Those 'fruits' don't like people trying to, how do you say, take the mickey. **1967** *Spectator* 3 Nov. 535/2 One looks forward after reading this brilliant exercise in mickey-taking to Miss Tracy's next novel. **1968** J. Lock *Lady Policeman* ix. 85 He keeps up a barrage of mickey taking. **1968** *Listener* 7 Nov. 622/3 He parried Kenneth Allsop's micky-take. **1971** B. W. Aldiss *Soldier Erect* 101 Geordie looked anxiously at me, in case I thought he was taking the micky too hard. **1973** 'J. Patrick' *Glasgow Gang Observed* xiv. 127 Big Sheila indulged in the same sort of 'mickey-taking'.

micky[2] (mi·ki). *N.Z.* Also **micky-mick, miki-miki**, etc. Representing a dialectal variant (within the Maori language) of **mingimingi.*

1898 Morris *Austral Eng.* 294/2 Mingi..in south New Zealand..is often called Micky. **1907** 'G. B. Lancaster' *Tracks we Tread* Gloss., *Mic-a-mic*, scrub. **1933** *Press* (Christchurch, N.Z.) 25 Nov. 15/7 *Scrub*..The best known components in Canterbury are Manuka, Wild Irishman Miki-miki (of which the shepherds make walking sticks), and Mountain pine. **1944** *Mod. Jun. Dict.* (Whitcombe & Tombs) 258 *Micky-mick*, a corrupt form of mingi-mingi, the Maori name of a class of shrubs, one of which makes a good walking-stick. **1949** F. Sargeson *I saw in My Dream* xiv. 229 I'll make a garland for her hair. Out of micky-mick. **1963** B. Pearson *Coal Flat* vii. 122 Willows and the trees they called..mickeymick, mockamock, whiteywood, birch.

micky, var. **mick*[3], **mick*[5].

Micmac (mi·kmæk), *sb.* and *a.* [Native name, lit. 'allies'.] **A.** *sb.* **a.** An Indian people of the Maritime Provinces and Newfoundland in Canada; a member of this people. **b.** The Algonquian language of this people. **B.** *adj.* Of, pertaining to, or designating the Micmacs or their language.

1830 W. S. Moorsom *Lett. from Nova Scotia* 110 The tribe to which the Indians of Nova Scotia belong is called the Micmac. *Ibid.* 112, I am not aware that any one Indian claims authority over the whole Micmac tribe. **1877** L. H. Morgan *Anc. Society* II. vi. 174 They affiliate more closely with the Micmacs than with the New England Indians south of the Kennebeck. **1891** [see **Indian sb.* 2 b]. **1911** A. L. Pringle *Home of Evangeline* iv. 139 He taught her the Micmac, and proud she was in his absence to be catechist to the Indians. **1933** [see **Cree sb.* and *a.*]. **1964** P. K. Bock in J. A. Fishman *Readings Sociol. of Lang.* (1968) 217 A recurrent situation on the Micmac Indian Reserve studied by the author in 1961 will be used to illustrate how the method of structural description..may be applied. **1969** *Canad. Jrnl. Ling.* XV. 78 Micmac morphophonemics. **1969** *Observer* (Colour Suppl.) 18 May 25/1 The French..offered the Micmac Indians a bounty for every scalp they took from the Beothuk of Newfoundland. **1972** G. V. Higgins *Friends of Eddie Coyle* vi. 35, I get five of these Micmacs come in, real Indians, for a change.

Micoquian (mĭkōu·kiăn), *a.* and *sb.* Also **Micoquean.** *Archæol.* [ad. F. *Micoquien* (O. Hauser *La Micoque* (1916) 55), f. La *Micoque* (see below).] **A.** *adj.* Of or pertaining to a late Acheulian culture (earlier called *Moustérien supérieur*) of southern France and England, represented by the remains found at La Micoque, near Les Eyzies (Dordogne) in S.W. France. **B.** *sb.* The Micoquian culture.

1937 Garrod & Bate *Stone Age Mt. Carmel* I. 120 By far the most instructive site for comparison..is La Micoque, type-station of the Tayacian and the Micoquian. *Ibid.*, Well-made Micoquian hand-axes. **1945** *Proc. Prehist. Soc.* XI. 21 The Summertown terrace gravels were deposited contemporaneously with the Upper Acheulian or Micoquian culture stage. **1946** F. E. Zeuner *Dating Past* vi. 173 From the *base* of the Younger Loess I, a Micoquian handaxe was recovered. *Ibid.* 195 A new stage of the Acheulian cannot be recognized clearly before the advent of the Micoquian. **1957** *Encycl. Brit.* II. 238/2 The Micoquian, or Final Acheulean, is characterized by elongated hand axes. *Ibid.* 539/2 Some pieces belonging to the Micoquian..industry were excavated in 1937 in the terraces of the stream of Cubuksuyu at Etiyokusu near Ankara.

micrergate (məikrɜ̄·ɹgēit). *Zool.* [f. Gr. μικρ-ός small + ἐργάτης worker.] A small worker ant.

1907 W. M. Wheeler in *Bull. Amer. Mus. Nat. Hist.* XXIII. 56 The micrergate, or dwarf worker, is a worker of unusually small stature. It appears as a normal or constant form in the first brood of all colonies that are founded by isolated females. **1915** H. St. J. K. Donisthorpe *Brit. Ants* 41 The micrergate is a worker of unusually small size.

micrite (mi·krəit). *Geol.* [f. Micr(ocrystalline *a.* + -ite[1].] Microcrystalline calcite present as an interstitial constituent or matrix material in some kinds of limestone; a limestone consisting chiefly of this.

1959 R. L. Folk in *Bull. Amer. Assoc. Petroleum Geologists* XLIII. 17 Finally, it was decided to use a composite word, the first part of which refers to the allochem composition... Whether the rock is type I or type II is shown by the second part of the name '-sparite' for those with sparry calcite cement and '-micrite' (pronounced 'mick-rite') for those with microcrystalline ooze matrix... Type III limestones, almost entirely ooze, are designated simply as 'micrite' without any allochem prefix. **1970** K. C. Jackson *Textbk. Lithology* vi. 401 The proportion of micrite in limestone varies from a minor interstitial filling between allochems to the entire rock. **1973** *Nature* 2 Mar. 41/2 The patch reef, 13 m long and over 2 m high, tongues out to the west into 2 m of thinly bedded calcitic micrites of quiet water origin.

Hence **micri·tic** *a.*, containing a high proportion of micrite.

1962 Leighton & Pendexter in *Mem. Amer. Assoc. Petroleum Geologists* I. 37/2 Photographs *A* and *B*.. illustrate limestones composed of 90 per cent, or more, micrite. Two subtypes of these micritic limestones are recognized. **1973** *Nature* 20 July 145/2 The deep water Alpine Triassic is represented by cherty, micritic, radiolarian limestones with thin-shelled pelecypods.

micro. 1. Substitute for def.: Abbrev. of Microlepidoptera *sb. pl.*, used to refer to a moth belonging to any of several families whose members are mostly smaller than those of interest to collectors, the Macrolepidoptera. Add examples.

1869 *Rep. Comm. Agric. 1868* (U.S. Dept. Agric.) 313 The presence of 'micros' is indicated by discolored lines... It may be ascertained whether the 'micro' is at home by holding the leaf up to the light. **1907** R. South *Moths Brit. Isles* 1st Ser. 6 Possibly, when this new order of things is more generally understood the so-called 'Micros' will receive their proper share of attention. **1972** L. E. Chadwick tr. *Linsenmaier's Insects of World* 172/2 As for the 'micros', they are neither a uniform grouping nor properly to be separated from the rest of the moths.

2. *Fashion.* Short for *micro-skirt* (**micro-* 1 c).

1968 *N.Y. Times* 22 Jan. 36 Hemlines go to all lengths. In extremes, there are micros, which barely cover the buttocks; minis, maxis and the nineteen-thirties length. **1969** D. Clark *Death after Evensong* ii. 40 She's some bird... Legs just a bit skinny for a micro, but still a good shape.

micro-. Add: In some words, esp. in *Med.*, the pronunc. (mi·kro) also occurs. **1.** For 'object' read 'entity' and add: *microabscess, -aneurysm, -biota, -chromosome, -constituent, -crater, -earthquake, -environment* (hence *-environmental* adj.), *-event, -explosion* (hence *-explosive* adj.), *-fossil, -fracture* (so *-fracturing* vbl. sb.), *-fungus* (later examples), *-graver, -instability, -lens, -metazoan, -metazoon, -particle, -phenocryst, -plankton* (hence *-planktonic* adj.), *-population, -pore* (further examples, also of *-porous* adj.) (hence also *-porosity*), *-powder, -quantity, -state* [State *sb.* 30], *-system, -tektite, -vegetation, -zone*; **mi·croatoll,** a circular growth of coral a few metres in diameter and with a central depression, such as is found in intertidal areas in warm seas and on the flats inside a coral reef; **mi·crobeam,** a very narrow beam of radiation; **mi·croblade** *Archæol.*, a flake chipped from a prepared flint core; **mi·crobody** *Cytology*, one of the round or egg-shaped microscopic particles occurring in cytoplasm which are surrounded by a membrane and contain oxidases; **mi·crocapsule,** a minute capsule used to contain, and render temporarily inactive, drugs, dyes, etc.; **mi·crocirculation** *Physiol.*, circulation of the blood in the smallest blood vessels; **mi·crocolony** *Biol.*, a group of animals or plants, esp. bacteria, found in a microhabitat; a very small group of cells in culture; **mi·crocontinent** *Geol.*, an oceanic, often submarine, plateau that is thought to be an isolated fragment of continental material; so **mi:crocontine·ntal** *a.*; **mi·crocrack,** a microscopic crack; hence **mi·crocracked** *ppl. a.*, **mi·crocracking** *vbl. sb.*; **mi·croculture** *Biol.*, (*a*) culture (of tissue, micro-organisms, etc.) on a small scale; **mi·croele:ctrode,** an electrode with a very fine tip, such as one suitable for investigating the electrical properties of individual cells; **microfi·bril** *Biol.*, a small fibril in living tissue that is visible only under the electron microscope, esp. one of a group that together make up a fibril (such as a cellulose fibril in the wall of a plant cell); hence **microfi·brillar** *a.*; **microfila·ria** *Zool.*, the minute larval form of a filaria; **mi:croha·bitat** *Ecol.*, a habitat which is of small or limited extent and which differs in character from some surrounding more extensive habitat; **mi·crologic,** micro-electronic logic (**logic sb.* 3*); freq. *attrib.*; **mi·cromodule** *Electronics*, a miniaturized module, consisting of a stack of interconnected micro-elements; **micromuta·tion** *Biol.*, (an instance of) mutation that has a superficially small or trivial effect on the phenotype; **mi·cro-operation** *Computers*, a simple operation carried out in response to a microinstruction (see also sense *2 a); **mi·cro-order** *Computers*, a micro-instruction produced by a microprogram; **mi·croplate** *Geol.*, a relatively small lithospheric plate; **mi·cro-process,** a process that occurs on a minute scale; **micropro·cessor** *Computers*, a processor small enough to be accommodated on a single chip, or just a few chips, and capable of serving as the central processing unit of a computer of comparable size; **mi·cropulsa:tion,** a small oscillation in the strength of the earth's magnetic field; †**micro-ray** = **microwave* (*obs.*); **microsphere,** (*c*) any minute spherical object; *spec.* one of those obtained by the cooling of a solution of proteinoid; **mi:crostratifica·tion,** (*a*) small-scale horizontal stratification of the water of a pond or lake; **mi·croswitch,** a switch which can be operated rapidly by a small movement; **microtri·chium** *Ent.* [Gr. θρίξ, τριχ- hair], usu. in pl. **microtri·chia,** minute hair-like structures found on the wings of certain insects, esp. those of the order Diptera; **microtu·bule** *Biol.*, any of the small, relatively rigid tubules, typically about 25 nanometres in diameter, that are present in the cytoplasm of many

plant and animal cells and are thought to have a structural function and to be involved with cell motility; so **microtu·bular** *a.*; **microvi·llus** *Biol.* (*pl.* **-vi·lli**), one of a number of minute projections from the surface of some cells; any process similar to a villus but smaller; **mi·crowire,** very fine glass-coated wire; **mi·croworld,** a realm or world (World *sb.* 13) very restricted in its dimensions or variety.

1946 *Nature* 5 Oct. 487/2 Thrombo-angiitis, phlebitis and lymphangiitis with micro-abscess formation can be found on study of sections of these structures. **1962** *Lancet* 1 Dec. 1134 The kidneys showed the changes of acute and chronic pyelonephritis, with microabscesses and gross fibrosis. **1948** Parsons & Duke-Elder *Dis. Eye* (ed. 11) xvii. 371 These droplets..tend to obscure the lumen of the vessel, forming a small micro-aneurysm. **1962** H. Heath in A. Pirie *Lens Metabolism Rel. Cataract* 366 The fact that microaneurisms [*sic*] develop only in some cases of long-standing diabetes would seem to indicate a derangement in some slow metabolic process. **1933** P. H. Kuenen in *Snellius-Expedition* V. ii. iii. 64 Conditions unfavourable to coral growth above low tide level certainly favour the formation of the micro-atolls. **1963** D. W. & E. E. Humphries tr. *Termier's Erosion & Sedimentation* xiii. 286 Pools are frequently observed on the surface of the reef-flats... These pools contain micro-atolls which have overhanging margins, indicating a reaction against choking muds. **1967** *Oceanogr. & Marine Biol.* V. 488 Sometimes this calcareous worm produces small reefs fringing the piers, or even micro-atolls. **1950** *Engineering* 5 May 498/3 The Cambridge work on micro-beams was most promising. It was nearing the stage when an investigator could look down a microscope, see a particle which he had etched, and direct X-rays on to that one particle, thus obtaining its diffraction pattern and identify it. **1962** *Times* 17 May 14/4 Investigate the effects of irradiation with a microbeam of ultraviolet light. **1972** *Science* 3 Nov. 461/2 Sea urchin sperm flagella are irradiated near their base with a laser microbeam. **1968** *New Scientist* 1 Aug. 223/1 Professor James B. Lackey.. has been looking at..esturine [*sic*] habitats, concentrating on the microbiota, especially the growth and decline of algae and protozoa. **1974** *Nature* 8 Feb. 361/2 Only a selection of the diverse Bungle Bungle microbiota [from Western Australia] is presented here. **1969** *Britannica Bk. of Year* (U.S.) 101 Late in the Upper Paleolithic and during the ensuing Mesolithic, it became the fashion to make smaller and smaller bladelettes. Commonly inserted as 'side blades' into lateral grooves in antler and bone projectile points, such 'microblades' lacerated the flesh of wounded game animals and thus promoted free bleeding and rapid death. **1972** *Sci. Amer.* Jan. 51/1 Working near Telegraph Creek in northwestern British Columbia in 1969 and 1970, Jason W. Smith and his colleagues from the University of Calgary unearthed several hundred delicate obsidian 'microblades', flakes seldom more than an inch long or a fifth of an inch wide, along with eight of the 'cores' that yield such blades. **1954** J. Rhodin *Correlation Ultrastruct. Organization & Function in Tubule Cells Mouse Kidney* ii. 21 The number, size and shape of the microbodies varies from cell to cell with a mean of about 10 in each cell. **1973** *Plant Physiol.* LI. 905/2 Electron micrographs frequently show association of microbodies with the rough endoplasmic reticulum. **1961** *New Scientist* 20 Apr. 115/3 The National Cash Register Company first developed microcapsules of a dye in a colourless form, which were spread on paper. **1967** *Britannica Bk. of Year* (U.S.) 803/2 *Microcapsule*, a tiny capsule containing a liquid or solid substance (as a chemical or medicine) that is released when the capsule is broken, melted, or dissolved. **1969** *New Scientist* 3 Apr. 18 Microcapsules—tiny bags made of synthetic membrane containing enzymes or other active materials—show promise as a means of treating kidney failure. **1972** *Chem. Processing* Apr. 21/2 Wass, Pritchard have developed a dry system for the application of fragrance or flavour microcapsules during the printing process. **1905** E. B. Wilson in *Jrnl. Exper. Zool.* II. 375 Especially large or small chromosomes may be designated as 'macrochromosomes' or 'microchromosomes', irrespective of their behavior. **1958** C. P. Swanson *Cytol. & Cytogenetics* xiii. 459 Apart from accessory chromosomes, which are generally..smaller than the usual chromosomes, microchromosomes are found throughout the plant and animal kingdom. **1969** Brown & Bertke *Textbk. Cytol.* 755/1 *Microchromosome*, very small metaphase chromosome of a karyotype possessing only two sizes of chromosomes, very small ones and quite large ones; the latter are called macrochromosomes. **1959** *Angiology* X. 241/1 Pressure differences in the vessels of the microcirculation are small. **1969** *Sci. Jrnl.* Apr. 20/2 To increase an impaired microcirculation patients are commonly treated with histamine which is a strong vasodilator and rapidly relaxes the walls of capillaries. **1959** *New Biol.* XXX. 53 The fact that a large number of nests are collected each year may be attributed to birds successfully breeding in the inaccessible parts of the caves. These micro-colonies form reservoirs from which the caves are restocked annually. **1968** *Brit. Med. Bull.* XXIV. 246/1 It is often found that cells grown in culture after irradiation show a spread of colony size;..there are often micro-colonies notably smaller than those growing from unirradiated controls. **1968** L. E. Casida in Gray & Parkinson *Ecol. Soil Bacteria* 100 Many soil bacteria grow as microcolonies within the larger pores of soil aggregates. **1973** R. G. Krueger *Introd. Microbiol.* iii. 31/2 Microcolonies are formed by some photosynthetic bacteria that produce buds from the ends of filamentous outgrowths of the cell. **1901** Taylor & White *U.S. Pat.668, 269* 19 Feb., When treated with higher heats..the steel of the tools show under the microscope a distinctly larger grained structure in many cases interspersed with austenite, a micro-constituent of steel discovered by Osmond. **1930** *Times* 29 Mar. 17/1 The metallurgy of steel castings, and the discovery of about 25 micro-constituents of steel. **1966** D. G. Brandon *Mod. Techniques Metallogr.* i. 1 Micro-constituents were successfully identified. **1965** Heezen & Tharp in *Phil. Trans. R. Soc.* A. CCLVIII. 98 We may, of course, in referring to these aseismic ridges as micro-continents, infer that they are either (1) fragments of former continents, or (2) nuclei of growing continents. **1966** R. W. Fairbridge *Encycl. Oceanogr.* 373/2 Madagascar is clearly a microcontinent. *Ibid.* 874/1 In the mid-ocean there have been identified..(3) true mid-ocean plateaus, to which Heezen has applied the genetic connotation 'microcontinent'. **1970** *Nature* 13 June 1044/2 We suggest that the East Canaries block is a microcontinent or sialic continental fragment detached from the African margin. **1966** R. W. Fairbridge *Encycl. Oceanogr.* 964/2 Submarine ridges and rises in other oceans..often have foundations of 'microcontinental' blocks. **1974** *Nature* 14 Mar. 204/2 This suggests that the Rockall–Faeroe Plateau as a whole may form a single microcontinental fragment. **1950** *Welding Res.* Suppl. Sept. 473-s/2 The microcracks have produced..highly localized strain. **1960** W. D. Biggs *Brittle Fracture of Steel* v. 154 Ingot irons and spectrographically pure irons do contain quantities of iron oxide in the form of inclusions in which micro-cracks may be nucleated. **1972** *Science* 2 June 1015/1 This can be attributed to the absence of water in the lunar rocks combined with the effects of porosity and microcracks. **1970** *Times* 22 May 27 At low thicknesses the deposits of chrome thrown by the new method are microporous, while thicker coatings are microcracked. **1956** *Welding Res.* Suppl. Feb. 78-s/3 The pearlite area..showed no evidence of microcracking. **1972** *Sci. Amer.* Nov. 92/2 Concrete is an inhomogeneous mixture of materials and is subject to local microcracking. **1965** *Jrnl. Appl. Physics* XXXVI. 3701/1 From the crater fields observed at low power density irradiation it can be concluded that the formation of microcraters is an early stage in the development of laser-induced radiation damage of metal surfaces. **1970** *Daily Tel.* 7 Jan. 3 (*caption*) A grain of lunar soil highly magnified to reveal a microcrater. **1892** *Phil. Trans. R. Soc.* B. CLXXXIII. 132 (*caption*) Glass micro-culture chamber in use with gas generators. **1973** *Nature* 5 Oct. 263/2 We analysed microcultures containing small numbers of cells (10^4 to 10^5) and the antibody response could be followed for up to 40 d. **1967** *N.Y. Times* 23 May 29 Before a volcano erupts it generates micro-earthquakes, which we are able to detect on our seismographs. **1974** *Nature* 24 May 308/1 [They] used sonobuoys in an attempt ..to see if, notwithstanding the lack of large earthquakes, they could detect microearthquake (magnitude less than 4·0) or earthquake swarm activity. **1917** *Amer. Jrnl. Physiol.* XLIV. 521 The electrodes were of copper or platinum, the muscle resting on an indifferent plate and subject above to the light contact of an active needle, microscopically sharpened—the micro-electrode. **1946** *Nature* 20 July 97/2 As soon as the results of Granit's micro-electrode experiments on the retinæ of animals were published, it was clear that a method was wanted for obtaining similar information with regard to the colour vision of man. **1955** C. R. N. Strouts et al. *Analytical Chem.* II. xviii. 576 A microelectrode usually consists of a platinum wire about 0·5 mm. in diameter, sealed into the side of a glass tube. **1966** T. Pynchon *Crying of Lot 49* iii. 55 Something tidal began to reach feelers in past eyes and eardrums, perhaps to arouse fractions of brain current your most gossamer microelectrode is yet too gross for finding. **1954** *New Biol.* XVII. 7 Dr. Edney's account of the water relations of woodlice is a study in comparative physiology, within a single order, linked closely to the differences in environments—and indeed micro-environments—of the species concerned. **1962** F. I. Ordway et al. *Basic Astronautics* xiii. 515 The apparent simplicity of the concept of a microenvironment within the spaceship leaves one serious gap. **1973** *Nature* 2 Mar. 20/2 Commitment may not occur until stem cells enter the micro-environment of the thymus or bursa (or bursa equivalent). **1971** *World Archaeol.* III. 128 A village..in a different micro-environmental zone. **1974** *Nature* 27 Sept. 317/2 Oscillations of microenvironmental pO_2 in the medium overlaying attached cultures of 10^7 cells per 50 mm Petri plate were measured amperometrically with calibrated Pt/Ir micro-oxygen cathodes polarised between 0·6 and 0·8 V. **1949** A. Pap *Elem. Analytic Philos.* vii. 137 The belief in micro-events involving micro-objects which are the hidden causes of observable events. **1957** C. Day Lewis *Poet's Way of Knowledge* 14 During the last half-century, physical scientists have moved towards the study of the micro-event. **1959** K. R. Popper *Logic Sci. Discovery* viii. 196 Hypothetical and not directly observable 'micro events'. **1968** *Sci. Jrnl.* Nov. 44/2 The rate of current growth must be increased and the plasma contained in a special non-cylindrical shape—the so-called plasma focus. However, the process itself will be so brief as to resemble a strong explosion. If the dimensions of the system are not too large this can be manifested as a 'micro-explosion' which will be a good source of both fast neutrons and hard x-rays. **1971** *Jrnl. Physics D* IV. 1941 Joule heating immediately underneath an operating site raises the local temperature of the metal above its boiling point... The resulting micro-explosion..gives rise to a crater with a surrounding lip of electrode debris. **1974** *Sci. Amer.* June 24/1 Calculations were undertaken..to try to find out what would happen when tiny deuterium-tritium pellets were imploded to thermonuclear conditions by intense beams of laser light. It was also proposed that the fusion microexplosions could be applied to the generation of power. **1971** *Jrnl. Physics D* IV. 1945 The micro-explosive disruption of the layer following Joule heating of the underlying metal causes collapse of the high trapped-ion field and the quenching of local emission. **1938** *Nature* 19 Nov. 902/1 It may be observed ..that the micelles themselves are aggregated into 'micro-fibrils', separated by spaces rather larger than the usual intermicellar spaces. **1962** J. T. Marsh *Self-Smoothing Fabrics* xx. 351 It is also probable that with cotton, there is some binding or entanglement of the microfibrils and even of the growth layers. **1970** T. S. & C. R. Leeson *Histol.* (ed. 2) ii. 37/1 In many cells cytoplasmic microfibrils are present, probably consisting of elongated protein molecules. **1971** *Sci. Amer.* June 44/3 Using the electron microscope to inspect the formation of ligament and tendon during the very first stages, we found no sign of the amorphous component in the embryonic elastic fibers. At this time the fibers appeared to consist only of the 110-angstrom microfibrils. **1956** *Nature* 18 Feb. 319/1 Sikorski and Woods pointed out the difficulty of reconciling the macrofibrillar type of structure observed in the follicle of a wool fibre with the occurrence of extended microfibrillar sheets in disintegrated fibres. **1972** *Canad. Jrnl. Bot.* L. 479 The microfibrillar material transports sucrose in pulses at about 400 cm h^{-1}. **1878** *Lancet* 23 Mar. 440/2 Micro-filariae in chylous urine. **1946** *Nature* 21 Dec. 913/1 The disease [*sc.* equine dermal filariasis] is associated with the presence of microfilariæ in the skin lesions. **1966** *New Scientist* 1 Sept. 482/3 Adult worms spawn progeny called microfilariae. They are ingested by, and develop in, several varieties of mosquito. **1924** *Bull. Amer. Assoc. Petroleum Geologists* VIII. 539 (*heading*) The value of micro-fossils in petroleum exploration. **1961** J. Challinor *Dict. Geol.* 127/2 There is no definite size limit for the category of microfossil, but one recent worker..has taken 2 mm. **1969** *Times* 11 Jan. 15/8 It is..possible that the rocks may have been contaminated by chemical fossils and microfossils after they were laid down. **1939** *Amer. Mineralogist* XXIV. 73 The streaks, patches, and veinlets of coarsely crystalline kaolinite and halloysite are sedimentary in origin and appear to be related to recrystallization along the micro-fractures in the clay. **1973** *Jrnl. Biomech.* VI. 5/2 Preliminary results from our study of human materials have demonstrated evidence of healing or healed microfractures in the subchondral bone taken at autopsy from patients with early signs of degenerative joint disease. **1969** *Nature* 27 Sept. 1306/1 All the rock samples are characterized by small surface pits lined with glass, areas of spattered glass and whitish markings which are small areas of microfracturing. **1920** Microfungus [see *encroach *sb.*]. **1971** N. E. Hickin *Wood Preservation* 66 Micro-fungi... An imprecise term of no taxonomic significance, usually used to include those fungi whose classification is in doubt as no sexual process has been observed, the *fungi imperfecti*, and including also the smaller *Ascomycetes* with small sporophores. **1926** *Guide Antiquities Stone Age Dept. Brit. & Mediaeval Antiquities Brit. Mus.* (ed. 3) 90 The early sites with the angle-graver or true graver, and the later with the micro-graver as the typical implement. **1939** V. G. Childe *Dawn European Civilization* (ed. 3) i. 6 Pigmy flints or microliths, ingeniously worked into regular geometrical shapes..or into microgravers. **1933** *Ecol. Monogr.* III. 169 Niche—the microhabitat or ultimate division of the habitat including recognition of its modifying factors. **1970** *Watsonia* VIII. 93 Like several other British ferns, it shows a partiality for railway platforms, which often supply a very special moist and calcareous microhabitat. **1971** *Sci. Amer.* Sept. 105/3 All habitats—from the expanses of sea ice and open water to the microhabitats of tidal flats, leeward waters and protected valleys—are utilized [by Eskimos]. **1962** W. B. Thompson *Introd. Plasma Physics* viii. 235 Since the wavelength is so small, this instability is almost independent of the macroscopic geometry, and represents one of the 'micro-instabilities'. **1971** *Science Year 1972* 222 Fusion researchers have been trying to find magnetic-bottle configurations that will be able to reduce the microinstabilities to acceptable proportions. **1964** S. Duke-Elder *Parsons' Dis. Eye* (ed. 14) vii. 82 Micro-lenses resting on the cornea are easier to fit and to wear. **1971** *Time* 19 July 48 Walon Green..used microlenses and extreme slow motion to get awesome footage of mayflies living out their brief lives. **1960** *Electronics* 25 Nov. 107/1 (*heading*) Micrologic computer. **1965** *New Scientist* 25 Mar. 769/1 Marconi..has a pilot 'micro-logic' circuit manufacturing plant at its laboratories. **1971** J. H. Smith *Digital Logic* i. 4 The Integrated Circuit. This is often referred to as micro logic. **1972** *Sci. Amer.* Sept. 2/1 (Advt.), This revolutionary small computer lets your people use the languages which best express the problems you need to solve. Its variable micrologic processor operates efficiently with each language by instantly restructuring itself as it shifts from one program or program segment to the next. **1964** *Oceanogr. & Marine Biol.* II. 382 This remarkable interstitial fauna..consisting of protozoans and micrometazoans.. has been eagerly studied since the twenties by Kiel zoologists. **1969** *New Scientist* 3 Apr. 34/2 The dozen or so micrometazoa with which they are working. **1959** *Times* 19 Mar. 10/5 New miniature military radios, radar controls and other products of a revolutionary programme of micro-module electronics. **1965** *Listener* 1 July 6/1 I.B.M. already has 80 per cent. of the world computer market. With its micro-modules it looks like keeping it. **1940** R. Goldschmidt *Material Basis of Evolution* 324 Among these evolutionary steps there are many of a type which preclude an evolution by slow accumulation of micromutations. **1972** *Science* 12 May 623/3 In the 1930's population geneticists recognized micromutation as the raw material of evolutionary change. **1953** Micro-operation [see *microprogram]. **1970** O. Dopping *Computers & Data Processing* xii. 197 A program step, i.e. the execution of an instruction in a computer, consists of a number of micro program steps, or micro operations. **1953** Micro-order [see *microprogram]. **1972** D. Lewin *Theory & Design Digital Computers* iv. 71 The main function of the control unit is to decode the order digits of an instruction word, thereby generating the necessary sequence of control waveforms (micro-orders) to allow the instruction to be executed. **1969** *Encycl. Sci. Suppl.* (*Grolier*) 78 The search continues for facts about the similarities and differences between 'organized elements', microfossils, and microparticles formed from amino acid polymers. **1926** G. W. Tyrrell *Princ. Petrol.* v. 86 The terms *microporphyritic* and *microphenocrysts* may be used when the texture can only be made out with the use of a microscope. **1946** *Jrnl. Geol.* LIV. 27/2 Microphenocrysts of augite are set in a microcrystalline to cryptocrystalline and hyaline groundmass. **1973** *Nature* 9 Feb. 374/1 It occurs as inclusions in both the other minerals, and forms skeletal microphenocrysts about 0·05 mm across. **1903** *Jrnl. R. Microsc. Soc.* 638 Spinelli publishes a first contribution to the marine flora of Sicily... The micro-plankton of the Sicilian coast has not been included. **1969** Bennison & Wright *Geol. Hist. Brit. Isles* xiv. 319 Marine microplankton has also been found [in the Wealden area]. **1971** *Nature* 30 Apr. 562/1 Cita and Blow compared the microplanktonic succession in these stratotypes with that of the tropical zonation scheme. **1972** *Ibid.* 4 Feb. 253/2 From the point of view of plate tectonics the Mediterranean is a complicated part of the world, being a region of numerous small interacting plates (microplates)

rather than a part of one large one. **1967** *Oceanogr. & Marine Biol.* V. 543 There is a highly detailed zoning of ecological conditions and micro-populations in the supra- and the mediolittoral zone. **1956** *Nature* 17 Mar. 502/1 The same type of micro-pore structure as occurs in the coking coals. **1967** M. Chandler *Ceramics in Mod. World* iv. 133 Translucent alumina ceramics that contain no micropores. **1939** *Chem. Abstr.* XXXIII. 4099 With increasing percentages this reduction continues until with 5% of Cu_2O there is no change in vol. However, this is in part only apparent, since Cu_2O causes microporosity. **1961** A. Taylor *X-ray Metallogr.* iii. 32 For the more subtle flaws and fine detail, such as hairline cracks or microporosity, the much more sensitive photographic method must be employed. **1963** J. Osborne *Dental Mech.* (ed. 5) xiv. 325 A shrinkage develops causing a microporosity throughout the entire casting. **1955** *Sci. News Let.* 29 Jan. 67/1 Oxygen..diffuses through a microporous filter disk made of porcelain and having 800,000,000 holes to the square inch. **1970** *Times* 22 May 27 At low thicknesses the deposits of chrome thrown by the new method are microporous. **1953** *Electronic Engin.* XXV. 233/1 Micropowder magnets can be made—after the powder has been produced—in a great variety of shapes. **1965** *New Scientist* 6 May 368/1 This metal could be either in very finely divided state (micropowder) or else as a sintered iron oxide compound. **1936** *Mind* XLV. 275 Jordan's attempt to account for it in terms of an intensification of acausal micro-processes is not supported by the facts. **1962** *Times* 13 Apr. 19/7 A higher resolution..is still more attractive on account of the prospects it affords of exploring those structural details and micro-processes upon which the functioning of living matter depends. **1970** *IEEE Trans. Computers* XIX. 710 LX-1 is an integrated circuit prototype of a microprocessor which is being used as a design vehicle to study the problems associated with the design and implementation of a similar computer constructed with large-scale integrated circuits. **1974** *Computer* July 22/2 There are at least four major classifications of systems that can be designed using microprocessors: calculators, controllers, data processors, and general-purpose computers. Controllers and calculators are the most likely candidates for single-chip CPUs. **1974** *Ibid.* Aug. 34/1 The present system uses a microprocessor and a small number of other custom LSI devices to control the spark ignition timing and EGR valve position based on a number of input engine variables. **1975** *Sci. Amer.* May 34/2 In 1971..the Intel Corporation, which had undertaken to develop a calculator chip, chose to design it as a more versatile programmable, single-chip microprocessor. **1949** *Proc. Japan Acad.* XXV. ix. 24 A remarkable micropulsation of *dH/dt* at the sudden commencement [of the magnetic storm] frequently took places [*sic*] during the summer and equinox, while it is weak during the winter. **1960** *Jrnl. Geophysical Res.* LXV. 1843/1 Micropulsations belong to the family of disturbances that have been related to the arrival of solar terrestrial particles. **1968** *McGraw-Hill Yearbk. Sci. & Technol.* 241/1 The instability also generates geomagnetic micropulsations and..very low frequency radio emissions. (Micropulsations are small quasi-sinusoidal oscillations of the Earth's field having periods ranging from about 1/5 sec to several hundred seconds.) **1946** F. Schneider *Qualitative Organic Microanalysis* vi. 164 The method can be readily adapted to the use of microquantities by the use of a reflux tube. **1971** *Nature* 7 May 11/2 The microquantities of compounds or isotopes which have now become detectable can serve as tracers to distinguish between, say, older and more recent material on the surface. **1931** *Electrician* 3 Apr. 509/2 The great advance made..has opened up the range of wave-lengths between 10 cm. and 1 m. for practical use... These short wavelengths have been designated 'micro-rays'. **1934** *Discovery* Sept. 242/2 The micro-rays used have the great advantage of freedom from disturbance by other wireless transmissions. **1937** *Jrnl. R. Aeronaut. Soc.* XLI. 47 The micro-ray equipments used on the commercial Lympne–St. Inglevert and the experimental Escalles–St. Margaret's [radio] links. **1960** *Science* 22 July 204/2 A tendency to yield microspheres having diameters in a bacterial range is illustrated. *Ibid.*, Another property of the microspheres is the tendency to shrink in sodium chloride solution hypertonic to that in which they are produced. **1965** R. S. Young in S. W. Fox *Orig. Prebiological Syst.* iv. 349 It is difficult to imagine that this phenomenon of microsphere formation, so easily demonstrable in the laboratory, did not occur in nature if there were a suitable accumulation of building blocks. Whether this had anything to do with the origin of the cell is purely speculative at this stage, but it is certainly suggestive. *Ibid.* 354 The microsphere is a remarkably stable structure. **1974** *Nature* 10 May 177/1 About 100,000 microspheres 25 μm in diameter labelled with ^{46}Sc were injected into the left ventricle over 30 s. **1962** *Economist* 20 Jan. 204/1 The micro-states left behind by France—Niger, Chad, Dahomey, Togo. **1970** *Britannica Bk. of Year* (U.S.) 463 Other events included..proposals that a special UN membership category be created for 'microstates'. **1974** *Austral. Outlook* XXVIII. i. 24 No clear and universally acceptable definition of a microstate has yet emerged. **1937** *Science* 26 Feb. 224/1 (*heading*) Microstratification of the waters of inland lakes in summer. **1956** *Nature* 17 Mar. 520/1 With a small amount of plankton in such a large body of water [as Lake Tanganyika], it is possible that its distribution is uneven due to currents and microstratifications. **1957** G. E. Hutchinson *Treat. Limnol.* I. vi. 396 In very many lakes..elaborate microstratification occurred throughout the hypolimnion. **1958** *Jrnl. Exper. Analysis of Behaviour* I. 173 The *S* read from loose printed pages; every time he stuttered, *E* pressed a microswitch which activated an Esterline-Angus recorder. **1961** *New Scientist* 13 Apr. 16/1 Carbon dioxide is used for inflation, its flow being controlled..for patients with very slight residual power, by an electrical system using microswitches. **1967** E. Chambers *Photolitho-Offset* ix. 128 The exposed film enters the processor at the film feeding station, the film activating a microswitch that starts a metering pump. **1940** *Ann. Rev. Biochem.* IX. 609 Since this is exactly the field served by the widely used Warburg manometric apparatus, and since the sensitivity of the diver method is about 1500 times as great as that apparatus, many possibilities of application to the microsystem exist. **1969** *New Scientist* 27 Feb. 452 One early form of life could have been a thermodynamically open, self-assembled, proteinaceous microsystem, capable of propagating its own kind through the use of preformed polyamino acids. **1967** *Nature* 22 Apr. 374/1 It is concluded that the glassy objects [in deep-sea sediments] discussed in this report are microtektites, and that they constitute a portion of the Australasian strewn field which extends from Thailand to Tasmania. **1973** *Ibid.* 16 Feb. 431/2 Microtektites (diameters < 1 mm) are also associated with the two most recent strewn fields. **1934** C. H. Curran *Families & Genera N. Amer. Diptera* 488 Microtrichia—The smaller abundant hairs of the wing. When these are present the wing is said to be villous. **1957** Richards & Davies *Imms's Gen. Textbk. Entomol.* (ed. 9) i. 13 Microtrichia..are minute hair-like structures, found, for example, on the wings of the Mecoptera and certain Diptera. They resemble very small covering hairs. **1963** D. B. Slautterbach in *Jrnl. Cell Biol.* XVIII. 384/2 It may be generally recognized that cells possess a 'microtubular system'. **1971** *Sci. Amer.* Aug. 52/3 At the base of every eukaryotic flagellum and cilium is a distinct microtubular structure: the basal body. **1963** D. B. Slautterbach in *Jrnl. Cell Biol.* XVIII. 367 Small cytoplasmic tubules are present in the interstitial cells and cnidoblasts of hydra. They are referred to here as 'microtubules'. **1974** *McGraw-Hill Yearbk. Sci. & Technol.* 124/2 Microtubules are hollow cylinders about 250 A..in diameter which are present in a wide variety of cellular structures, including the mitotic spindle, cilia and flagella, and neural axons... They probably provide an internal 'cytoskeleton' that produces or maintains asymmetric cell structure, and they appear to be involved in the production of certain types of cell motility. **1956** *Nature* 4 Feb. 221/2 It seems quite plausible..that the stream of nutrient salts and metabolites excreted by the cuticle serves as the nutrient medium of the epiphyllic micro-vegetation. **1958** *Blumea* IX. 206 Barnacles were collected in order to get an impression of the algal microvegetation..growing on them. **1953** Borysko & Bang in *Bull. Johns Hopkins Hosp.* XCII. 259 The cell surface in contact with the allantoic fluid was consistently characterized by the presence of variable numbers of small projections..which we have named 'microvilli' to distinguish them from other types of surface projections (cilia, pseudopods, brush borders, blebs, etc.). These microvilli appeared as club-shaped projections extending into the allantoic sac. They were approximately 0·1 micron in width, ranging from 0·1 to 1·0 micron in length. **1968** *New Scientist* 28 Nov. 513/1 The skin of many tapeworms possesses a number of very small, finger-like projections. They are known as microvilli, from their resemblance to the larger, but similar, projections called villi found in the small intestine of most types of vertebrate. **1969** *Nature* 11 Oct. 116/2 (*caption*) This normal baby hamster kidney (BHK) cell is magnified about 3,300 times. The tendril-like processes are microvilli which appear at particular phases of the cell cycle, noticeably when the cell rounds up before division. **1963** *Times* 21 May 20/2 World scientists are taking their turn in a growing queue for Britain's newest export—glass-sheathed copper microwire 50 times thinner than a human hair. **1970** *New Scientist* 30 Apr. 228/3, 100 grammes of microwire, about 100 km long, would cost £1000. **1955** O. Klein in W. Pauli *Niels Bohr* 117 Einstein..may have felt that on the side of the quantum physicists the importance of the general relativity claim in the search for the laws of the microworld was usually underestimated. **1967** *New Scientist* 18 May 383/2 The pavilion [at London Zoo] is an assemblage of micro-worlds in which the jumpers can jump, the climbers climb, the burrowers burrow and the nocturnal sleepers sleep. **1973** C. Bonington *Next Horizon* ii. 46 In the micro-world of an expedition the pettiest details, like an unwashed pan or an irritating mannerism, are blown up out of all proportion. **1957** G. E. Hutchinson *Treat. Limnol.* I. ix. 609 By covering lake mud in the laboratory with oxygenated water, he was able to show that a microzone of oxygen-poor water was rapidly produced above the mud. **1964** *Oceanogr. & Marine Biol.* II. 137 Cores often exhibit a well marked horizontal stratification into the microzones of Perfiljew.

b. Other terms in which *micro-* indicates reduced size or scale, but not of what is denoted by a following sb., as *micro-distribution*; **mi·crobreccia** *Geol.* (see quot. 1972); **mi·crocamera**, a camera used in photomicrography; **mi:crocosmopo·litan**, one who regards himself as a citizen of every part of a particular society; a citizen of a defined and limited world; **mi·cro-evolu:tion**, evolutionary change within a species or smaller group of plants or animals, taking a relatively short time; hence **mi:cro-evolu·tionary** *a.*; **mi·croglossary**, a glossary or dictionary of terms in a particular subject; **microplasti·city**, plastic flow which occurs in small areas of a material at stresses below the elastic limit of the bulk material; so **micropla·stic** *a.*; **mi·crorelief** *Physical Geogr.*, small-scale relief (Relief[3] 3 b); **mi:cro-stimula·tion** *Physiol.*, stimulation applied to a very small area; **mi·crotheory**, a theory about one particular aspect or part of some subject or phenomenon.

1948 *Jrnl. Geol.* LVI. 149 (in facing Table 3), Siltstone (gritty). a. siltstone proper. b. Micro-conglomerate or micro-breccia. **1951** E. B. Knopf tr. *B. Sander's Contrib. Study of Depositional Fabric* 28 The fragments in this deformation breccia are calcitized crinkled dolomite and various sedimentary microbreccias. *Ibid.* 29 Some fragments in the microbreccia are themselves fragments of breccia. **1963** D. W. & E. E. Humphries tr. *Termier's Erosion & Sedimentation* xiii. 294 The true reefs contain several facies:..breccias and microbreccias formed of fragments of calcareous organisms; oyster limestones; [etc.]. **1972** *Gloss. Geol.* (Amer. Geol. Inst.) 449/2 *Microbreccia*, (*a*) A poorly sorted sandstone containing relatively large and sharply angular particles of sand set in a very fine silty or clayey matrix; e.g. a graywacke. It is somewhat less micaceous than a siltstone. (*b*) A breccia within fragments of a coarser breccia (Sander, 1951, p. 28). **1973** *Nature* 23 Mar. 252/2 A feldspathic microbreccia from the Descartes region of the lunar highlands contains an unusual assemblage of pyroxene fragments. **1928** *Daily Express* 21 June 12 Modern science has at its disposal, 'doctors, chemists, biologists, ultra-violet lamps, micro-cameras, and spectroscopes'. **1958** *Newnes Compl. Amat. Photogr.* xxv. 219 Apart from the micro-camera, a plate camera is perhaps the next best. **1961** A. Taylor *X-ray Metallogr.* vi. 163 Equally good resolution may be obtained with quite small cameras provided the focus of the X-ray tube is restricted and the geometry of the camera and the specimen is suitably modified, as, for example, in certain microcameras. **1938** S. Beckett *Murphy* xi. 240 It was as though the microcosmopolitans had locked him out. **1966** *Punch* 12 Jan. 50/1 Liberal Jewish New Yorkers..are cosmopolitans, but New York is their cosmos. They are really microcosmopolitans. **1964** *Oceanogr. & Marine Biol.* II. 111 The study of.. micro-distribution with reference to mixing processes in the sea. **1971** *Nature* 25 June 524/2 So far it has not been possible to study the micro-distribution of lead in materials, except by using electron microprobes or rather crude microchemical techniques which are only really valid if the lead concentration is high. **1940** R. Goldschmidt *Material Basis of Evolution* 199 Microevolution by means of micromutation leads only to diversification within the species. **1963** Davis & Heywood *Princ. Angiosperm Taxon.* ii. 72 They [*sc.* biosystematists] have gone a long way in elucidating the processes of evolution at and below the species level (micro-evolution). *Ibid.* xii. 405 The significance of ecological modifications in a micro-evolutionary context has probably been underestimated. **1974** T. Heyerdahl *Fatu-Hiva* ii. 86, I was on constant look-out for animals to save in bottles and tubes for the study of trans-oceanic migration and micro-evolution. **1955** Locke & Booth *Machine Translation Lang.* 11 The main deficiency at the present time is the absence of adequate field dictionaries for various technical fields and for all relevant languages. Preparation of these *microglossaries*..is important, though tedious work. **1956** *Nature* 7 Jan. 1/1 To solve the problem of word-order, the grammatical structure of the language must be investigated in detail and micro-glossaries—stem-ending dictionaries in the specified subject—must be compiled and coded. **1960** E. Delavenay *Introd. Machine Transl.* vi. 91 Research since 1949 has led to the provisional conclusion that in scientific texts non-grammatical polysemantic nouns and verbs do not present any great difficulty within the limits of the restricted vocabulary of any given science or technical subject. Thus special restricted dictionaries—microglossaries—should be constituted. **1960** *Mech. Engin.* July 71/3 Future investigations should be extended to a variety of materials to investigate further the validity of microplastic-strain hysteresis energy as a criterion for fatigue fracture. **1966** *Jrnl. Strain Analysis* I. 415/2 It is..a fact that plastic flow occurs in some parts of the cross-section even if the material is within the nominal elastic limit. This plastic deformation, which is of the same order of magnitude as the elastic strains, will be termed as [*sic*] micro-plastic throughout the paper. *Ibid.*, It is believed that micro-plasticity constitutes an important source of failure in the case of metal fatigue. **1972** T. Imura in G. Thomas *Electron Microsc. & Struct. Materials* 129 The microplasticity can be attributed solely to the motion of edge dislocations. **1932** Fuller & Conard tr. *Braun-Blanquet's Plant Sociol.* xi. 272 Causes of injury are..direct effect upon soil formation by stirring of the fine earth and changing the microrelief (hummocks and paths). **1938** *Geogr. Jrnl.* XCII. 271 [Articles] deal with glaciation, with melting and formation of micro-relief, and with run-off and thawing of glaciers. **1968** R. W. Fairbridge *Encycl. Geomorphol.* 795 Relief refers to relative height, while microrelief refers to small-scale differences in relief. Microrelief consists of any minor undulations on the surface of the land, usually of a scale which would not show on a normal topographic map. **1946** *Nature* 28 Dec. 947/1 Two point sources of light of about the same brightness were presented to an observer by means of the micro-stimulation apparatus. **1972** *Jap. Jrnl. Pharmacol.* XXII. 635 (*heading*) Re-examination of a centrally-induced cough in cats using a micro-stimulation technique. **1956** W. H. Whyte *Organization Man* (1957) 28 Perhaps an overall theory of behavior is..a will-o'-the-wisp. If so, our efforts may still be rewarded by the salvage of microtheories about limited areas. **1971** *Jrnl. Gen. Psychol.* LXXXIV. 155 Almost all of them have been extremely cautious about extending their data to explanatory microtheories of the perceptual phenomena.

c. *Fashion.* Denoting extreme shortness of a woman's garment, as in *micromini*, *-shift*, *-skirt* (hence *-skirted* adj.).

1967 *Word Study* Dec. 3/2 *Mini*..has undergone further compounding in the formation *micromini* denoting an exceptionally short miniskirt. **1971** 'V. X. Scott' *Surrogate Wife* 40 She wore micro-minis to show lots of leg. **1967** *Punch* 1 Mar. 308/2 The latest collection included a transparent micro-shift worn over an emaciated G-string. **1966** *Courier-Mail* (Brisbane) 29 Aug. 11 Mini-skirts, Micro-skirts, Maxi-skirts—the fashion battle rages on in London. **1967** *Punch* 21 June 893/2 Micro-skirts are designed to keep elders in their place, for no woman over forty can wear them without looking idiotic. **1969** *Guardian* 27 May 2/4 Women students of Pretoria University turned up..in ankle-length and calf-length dresses, in a campaign against 'micro-skirts'. **1973** J. Di Mona *Last Man at Arlington* (1974) viii. 73 A young blonde.. in a microskirt. **1967** *Times Educ. Suppl.* 13 Oct. 763 (*caption*) Mortar-boarded candidate..for student office at Boston's North-eastern University and his mortar-boarded micro-skirted assistant.

2. a. (*Micro-* now often implies simply a smallness of scale of the subject, rather than any use of microscopy, and so this use passes into 6. Cf. *macro- 1 e.) *microanatomy* (hence

-anatomist), *-chemistry* (in Dict.: hence also *-chemist*), *-cinematography* (so *-cinematographic* adj.), *-dissection* (hence *-dissect* vb.), *-ecology*, *-injection*, *-metallurgy*, *-operation* (see also sense *1) (so *-operative* adj.), *-palæontology* (hence *-palæontologic*, *-logical* adjs., *-palæontologist*), *-physiology* (hence *-physiologist*), *-sociology* (hence *-sociological* adj.); **mi:cromachi·ning**, the process or technique of shaping objects on a very small scale by non-mechanical means; **mi:cropinocyto·sis** *Biol.*, a submicroscopic form of pinocytosis in which material is taken into a cell as a result of the invagination and pinching off of the cell surface; hence **mi:cropinocyto·tic** *a.*

1964 G. H. Haggis et al. *Introd. Molecular Biol.* i. 1 The concentration of anatomists and microanatomists on finer and finer detail may be illustrated by four centuries of work on the structure of the vascular system and the blood. **1935** *Times Lit. Suppl.* 24 Oct. 662 What he has done is to present in a lively—almost exciting—way the more significant facts of human physiology and micro-anatomy as far as they have yet been discovered. **1946** *Nature* 26 Oct. 578/1 His researches have been mainly in the fields of micro-anatomy, embryology and the more physiological side of zoology. **1962** *Science Survey* III. 252 Her main interests have been in the micro-anatomy of the retina and its relationship to visual function in different animals. **1940** *Ann. Rev. Biochem.* IX. 610 Little used by biochemists or microchemists. **1971** *Nature* 7 May 11/1 There is also methane..in the indigenous rocks on the surface of the Moon. Is this..the remnant of the primordial gas from which the Moon was formed? That, no doubt, is a question that will preoccupy lunar microchemists for a long time to come. **1940** *Chem. Abstr.* XXXIV. 289 (*heading*) Micro tearing machine for the photomicrographic and microcinematographic examination of materials. **1962** *Lancet* 1 Dec. 1172/1 The misshapen lymphocytes may reasonably be regarded as dying cells; this view is supported by the microcinematographic studies of human blood-cells by Bessis. **1952** *Chem. Abstr.* XLVI. 13336/3 Microcinematography. **1971** *Nature* 10 Dec. 352/1 We are continuing to use single smooth muscle cells in dynamic studies of contraction recorded with microcinematography. **1973** *Ibid.* 2 Mar. 52/1 Cytoplasm was micro-dissected from salivary glands of larvae. **1915** *Science* 19 Feb. 291/1 The cells were isolated and studied by means of microdissection and vital staining in a hanging drop of the insect body fluid. **1972** *Sci. Amer.* June 95/1 A small bundle of fibers from a single receptor is separated by microdissection from the main trunk of the optic nerve and placed on an electrode. **1963** *New Society* 3 Oct. 26/1 A pioneering work in the micro-ecology of housing estates. **1969** *Nature* 29 Nov. 846/1 The microecology of the blowfly's gut has not been well explored. **1921** *Science* 28 Oct. 411/2 The microdissection and microinjection of marine ova and of animal and plant cells. **1970** *Nature* 22 Aug. 857/2 For micro-injection we used a hydraulic system of mineral oil with the micro-pipette tip filled with tracer solution. **1960** K. R. Shoulders in *Proc. Western Joint Computer Conf.* 251/2 The most highly resolved construction process that we have any control over is what we call electron beam activated micromachining. *Ibid.* 256/1 Electron-beam micromachining is the combination of certain methods of deposition, resist production, and etching. **1970** *New Scientist* 16 Apr. 101/1 Micromachining has received much publicity in the past, and forms the mainstay of Laser Associates' range of systems. **1899** *Proc. R. Soc.* LXV. 85 (*heading*) Experiments in micro-metallurgy:—Effects of strain. **1958** *Engineering* 11 Apr. 458/1 The accomplishments in micrometallurgy at the laboratory soon led to the determination of some of the properties of the new metal. **1913** *Jrnl. R. Microsc. Soc.* 207 (*heading*) Apparatus for micro-operations. **1968** *Sci. Jrnl.* Nov. 54/1 Micro-operations such as removing parts of the embryo or grafting tissues from one embryo to another. **1922** *Anatomical Rec.* XXIV. 18 Instruments for micro-operative work. **1941** *Bull. Amer. Assoc. Petroleum Geologists* XXV. 1208 The progressive multiplication of the micro-paleontologic groups studied is considered. *Ibid.* 1219 These micropaleontologic objects he called 'microzoa'. **1972** *Biol. Abstr.* LIII. 3865/2 (*heading*) Lithologic and micropaleontologic study of the Lias..of Mayorca. **1929** *Jrnl. Paleont.* III. 229 (*heading*) Micropaleontological activities. **1973** *Nature* 13 July 74/2 Theyer presented palaeomagnetic and micropalaeontological data which seemed to invalidate the timing of what was thought to be one of palaeontology's most reliable datum planes. **1928** *Jrnl. Paleont.* II. 159 This is no reflection upon the micro-paleontologist. **1972** *Daily Tel.* 31 Aug. 21 (Advt.), The palynologist should preferably have experience in the Mesozoic/Tertiary, the micropalaeontologist preferably on Mesozoic/Tertiary Foraminifera. **1883** A. H. Foord (*title*) Contributions to the micropalæontology of the Cambro-Silurian rocks of Canada. Part 1. **1928** *Jrnl. Paleont.* II. 158 Micropaleontology should, in no way, radically depart from the general field and fundamental principles of paleontology. It is merely a study of the smaller fossils whose characteristic features are studied by the aid of a microscope. **1957** *New Biol.* XXIV. 11 Micro-palaeontology, which is mainly the study of fossil foraminifera, has become an important and highly specialized profession and practically the whole of current research on these animals is devoted to this aspect of the matter. **1974** *Sci. Amer.* May 136/3 Two clever micro-physiologists have measured the power involved, and they conclude that one gliding algal filament..used about 7,300 molecules of ATP per second to move. **1954** *New Biol.* XVI. 37 We cannot expect to close the evolutionary gap preceding the establishment of cellular organisms until we know far more of intracellular histology and micro-physiology. **1956** *Jrnl. Biophysical & Biochem. Cytol.* II. Suppl. 107 The particles, possibly coated with protein, become attached to the plasma membrane. Minute invaginations of the membrane, with the adherent granules, develop. The invaginated membrane is pinched off, resulting in the formation of an intracellular vacuole. Possibly a type of micropinocytosis takes place. **1973** *Nature* 2 Mar. 57/1 Electron microscopic studies..suggest that some synaptic vesicles form by a process of micro-pinocytosis at the presynaptic terminal membrane. *Ibid.* 57/2 A micropinocytotic origin of synaptic vesicles remains uncertain. **1942** *Jrnl. Legal & Pol. Sociol.* I. 55 We will forego here any prolonged analysis of this 'micro-sociological aspect', and will concentrate all our attention on the functional relationship between democracy and types of particular groups and all-inclusive societies. **1944** *Man* XLIV. 21/1 The most valuable contribution of the social anthropologist may well still lie in this micro-sociological field. **1972** P. Sheriff tr. *Rocher's Gen. Introd. Sociol.* 1. i. 4 The microsociological plane of different types of social links. **1941** *Jrnl. Philos.* XXXVIII. 486 The problems of mass, community, and communion arise in 'microsociology'. **1944** *Man* XLIV. 21/1 Much of the anthropologist's work has lain hitherto in what may be called micro-sociology—the study of small groups or of small units in larger groups. **1959** G. D. Mitchell *Sociol.* i. 23 These two traditions may be said to be the fore-runners of the modern tendency for sociology to bifurcate into what may be called macro- and micro-sociology. **1966** P. A. Sorokin *Sociol. Theories Today* IV. xiv. 470 Micro-sociology studies the simplest manifestation of social reality—sociability, that is, 'the multifarious ways of being bound by a whole and in a whole'. **1974** *Times Lit. Suppl.* 22 Nov. 1304/1 Micro-sociology, indeed any serious sociology of an analytic kind, has to begin with a study of the most elementary social relations.

b. *micro-texture.*

1965 G. J. Williams *Econ. Geol. N.Z.* x. 157/2 The hardness and toughness of greenstone depends partly on its mineral composition, these qualities resulting from a micro-texture of very closely felted and interwoven minute fibres. **1971** *Good Motoring* Sept. 9/2 A road surface which gives grip at low vehicle speeds must incorporate roadstone of a harsh rather than a polished micro-texture.

c. *micro-slide* (examples).

1909 in *Cent. Dict.* Suppl. **1951** *Electronic Engin.* XXIII. 8/1 The combination of a television camera with a microscope makes it possible for a large group of students to watch simultaneously the events taking place on a microslide. **1971** *McGraw-Hill Yearbk. Sci. & Technol.* 359/2 A rapid detection method for the major components of cannabis..involves the use of microslides for thin-layer chromatography.

3. microgy·ria, abnormal smallness of the gyri of the brain; **microma·stia** [Gr. μαστ-ός breast], the condition in a post-pubertal woman of having an abnormally small breast; **microma·zia** [Gr. μαζ-ός breast] = prec.; **microphthalmia**: also **microphtha·lmos**, abnormal smallness of the eye; **micropsia**: also **mi·cropsy**.

1840 Billings *Med. Dict.* II. 154/1 Microgyria. **1905** *Brit. Med. Jrnl.* 28 Oct. 1100/1 In this case of microgyria the right side of the brain was less than two-thirds the size of the left. **1920** *Brain* XLIII. 26 Microgyria, which has hitherto been usually known under the name of hemiatrophy of the brain or arrested development of the nervous system, has been comparatively rarely described, and merits further study. **1961** *Lancet* 2 Sept. 513/2 Microgyria was apparent in the posterior part of both lobes. **1918** Deaver & McFarland *Breast* iii. 45 These terms are applied to conditions in which there is congenital total absence of one or both of the mammary glands, or in which one or both glands are undeveloped or rudimentary in development. To the latter condition the term 'micromastia' might more correctly be applied. **1953** *New Statesman* 5 Sept. 254/3 About 4,000,000 young American women suffer in some degree from micromastia (immature breasts). **1965** L. B. Arey *Developmental Anat.* (ed. 7) xxiii. 452 Retention of the prepubertal condition (micromastia). **1890** *Syd. Soc. Lex.*, Micromazia. **1894** W. R. Williams *Monogr. Dis. Breast* iii. 33 When the defect is less complete than in the above cases, we get a very small imperfectly-developed gland, like the normal male breast, or smaller—micromazia. **1928** F. Z. Snoop *From Monotremes to Madonna* 22 The breast may be absent, amazia; or very small, micromazia. [**1845** *Dublin Jrnl. Med. Sci.* XXVII. 29 Microphthalmus is the term applied by continental writers to that peculiar condition of the eye, when there appears to be an arrest of development of this organ at some particular period of its growth, without either atrophy or disease.] **1850** *Boston Med. & Surg. Jrnl.* XLII. 421 (*heading*) Microphthalmos, complicated with congenital cataract in both eyes. **1934** *Arch. Ophthalm.* XI. 516 It is justifiable to consider the two forms of microphthalmos as one genetic entity with the morphologic distinction between microphthalmos with external, or orbital, cysts and microphthalmos with intraocular cysts. **1971** *Amer. Jrnl. Ophthalm.* LXXI. 1128/1 In colobomatous microphthalmos, the pathogenesis of the small eye is related to faulty closure of the embryonic fissure. **1890** W. James *Princ. Psychol.* II. xix. 93 In consequence of this so-called micropsy, Aubert relates that he saw a man apparently no larger than a photograph.

4. microae·rophil(e = *microaërophilous* (s.v. Micro- 4); also as *sb.*, a microaerophile organism; **mi:croaerophi·lic** = *microaërophilous* (s.v. Micro- 4); **microce·llular**, containing or characterized by minute cells; **micro·phagous** *Zool.* [-phagous], feeding on minute particles; **microva·scular**, of or pertaining to the smallest blood-vessels.

1903 *Science* 6 Mar. 371/1 The microaerophiles will grow luxuriantly under normal conditions under diminished oxygen pressure. **1909** *Cent. Dict.* Suppl., Micro-aërophile *a.* **1957** G. E. Hutchinson *Treat. Limnol.* I. xiii. 757 It would seem that the limnetic purple bacteria are microaerophil rather than anaerobic. **1970** Passmore & Robson *Compan. Med. Stud.* II. xviii. 46/2 These micro-aerophiles often prefer a concentration of CO_2 that is higher than normal, e.g. 5–10 per cent. **1903** *Science* 6 Mar. 371 *Clostridium Pasteurianum*..is an anaerobe, but it also grows in symbiosis with aerobic forms; it is, therefore, microaerophilic. **1971** *Nature* 9 July 132/2 *Campylobacter*, a genus of microaerophilic bacteria including the organism formerly called *Vibrio fetus*. **1909** Webster, Microcellular. **1958** *Punch* 8 Oct. 476/3 Bottines have micro-cellular rubber soles and are very neat and light. **1965** *Biol. Abstr.* XLVI. 5347/1 (*heading*) Complex treatment of the microcellular bronchial carcinoma by means of the nitrogen mustard and X-rays. **1971** D. G. Jones in C. M. Blow *Rubber Technol. & Manuf.* x. 397 Microcellular soling containing minute discrete air cells and having a specific gravity as low as 0·3 is also used extensively. **1923** J. W. Folsom *Entomol.* (ed. 3) xiii. 373 According to the nature of their food, most insects may be classified as follows:..*microphagous* ([feeding] on micro-organisms, as bacteria, yeasts, etc.). **1950** Microphagous [see *chemotaxis]. **1963** R. P. Dales *Annelids* iii. 76 The evolution of the Polychaeta is thus mirrored by the evolution of feeding methods; a transition in one direction towards burrowing, tube building, sedentary life and microphagous feeding; and in the other to a more active scavenging or predatory existence. **1959** *Ann. N.Y. Acad. Sci.* LXXXII. 236 Can anything be learned about the mechanism that damages blood vessels in diabetes mellitus by studying the dynamic morphology of the superficial micro-vascular system in man? **1967** *Sci. News Let.* 9 Sept. 262 Precise formations of the microvascular system and other spaces in organs of dead animals are revealed in detail when this liquid silicone compound is injected.

5. a. *microbar* [*bar *sb.*[6] 1, 2], *-calorie*, *-curie*, *-henry* [*henry[3]], *-inch*, *-mho*, *-poise*, *-rad*, *-second*, *-watt*; **mi·crodegree**, one millionth of a degree centigrade (kelvin). Also duplicated to denote division by a million million (corresponding to the single prefix *pico-), as in *micromicrocurie*, *-farad*.

1918 Microbar [see *bar *sb.*[6] 2]. **1963** Jerrard & McNeill *Dict. Sci. Units* 22 Acoustic pressure of the order of one dyne cm^{-2} is now described by the microbar. **1971** *Nature* 1 Jan. 15/3 The figures..indicate that a pressure wave moving at 330 m s^{-1} generates a displacement of the Earth's surface of 10 to 15 nanometres per microbar with periods between 20 and 100 s. **1969** *Sci. Jrnl.* Aug. 42 Heat flow through the ocean crust is on average 1·2 microcalories/cm^2/s except in active regions such as mid-ocean ridges. **1911** *Sci. Amer.* 29 Apr. 429 The 'optimum' or most favorable dose of radiation, which developed the mold in four days, was found to be ½ microcurie per cubic centimeter of air. **1958** *Immunology* I. 29 The status of the grafts was assessed at monthly intervals after grafting by administering 5 microcuries of ^{131}I intraperitoneally. **1970** Passmore & Robson *Compan. Med. Stud.* II. vi. 8/2 When used for diagnostic purposes, radioiodine is usually given by mouth in a dose of 5–15 microcuries. **1957** *Science Progress* XLV. 415 Another..task would be the study of lattice specific heats at microdegree temperatures. **1971** *Physics Bull.* Dec. 713/1 Recent work, such as the specific heat measurement by Ahlers (1971) is characterized by temperature resolution as small as a microdegree. **1909** *Cent. Dict.* Suppl., Microhenry. **1911** *Physical Rev.* XXXII. 612 (*heading*) Inductance in microhenrys. **1964** R. F. Ficchi *Electr. Interference* iv. 39 Experience has shown that as the L exceeds 0·025 microhenries in magnitude, the effectiveness of the bond diminishes rapidly. **1941** Oberg & Jones *Machinery's Handbk.* (ed. 11) 1776 Assume that the quantities *a*, *b*, *c*, etc., equal the various profile measurements in micro-inches. **1962** *B.S.I. News* June 24/2 Another firm..even specified surface finished [? *read* finishes] in micro-inches on their drawings. **1970** *Sci. Amer.* Mar. 142/3 The rotor is driven magnetically on a superb ball-bearing axis. (The tolerances are specified to five or 10 microinches.) **1919** *Electric Jrnl.* XVI. 322 Micromhos per mile of each conductor. **1940** *Bell System Technical Publ. Monograph B-1268* 7 One interesting commercial tube in which one stage of secondary electron multiplication is added to an ordinary tetrode, has a transconductance of 14,000 micromhos. **1962** Simpson & Richards *Physical Princ. Junction Transistors* viii. 175 Present values of its mutual conductance are small (~100 micromhos). **1961** *Daily Tel.* 10 Oct. 18/3 In the past 23 days, the average amount of radioactivity in every kilogram of air has been 3·42 micro-microcuries. **1909** *Cent. Dict.* Suppl., Micro-microfarad. **1921** *Physical Rev.* XVIII. 143 This plate had coatings so small that its normal capacity was only about 0·67 micro-micro-farads. **1962** Corson & Lorrain *Introd. Electromagn. Fields* ii. 60 A sphere one meter in radius has a capacitance of about 100 micro-microfarads. **1941** *Ann. Reg. 1940* 353 For hydrogen vapour it [*sc.* the viscosity] is *c.* 10 micropoise at 14·5° K. **1963** Jerrard & McNeill *Dict. Sci. Units* 107 The viscosity of gases is frequently given in micropoises (μP); (air 181 μP at 20° C). **1969** *Times* 2 Sept. 10/4 On some of the islands of the atoll..the intensity of fall-out radiation range[s] from three to seven microrads an hour. **1906** A. E. Kennelly *Wireless Telegr.* ix. 99 If we call the one millionth part of a second one microsecond for convenience of description, then one complete wave would pass off in 1/2·5 microsecond. **1942** J. D. Stranathan *'Particles' of Mod. Physics* xii. 481 These particles are radioactive with a half life of a few microseconds. **1966** T. Pynchon *Crying of Lot 49* v. 114 'Nearly three weeks it takes him,' marvelled the efficiency expert, 'to decide. You know how long it would've taken the IBM 7094? Twelve micro-seconds.' **1909** *Cent. Dict.* Suppl., Microwatt. **1914** R. Stanley *Text-bk. Wireless Telegr.* xvii. 261 Duddell carried out experiments to find the minimum power required to produce audible signals in a telephone receiver at different frequencies, and found that, while 430 microwatts were required at 300 frequency, only 7·7 microwatts were required at 900 frequency. **1970** *Physics Bull.* Sept. 403/2 Sound power of the order of a microwatt from a dripping tap.

6. Substitute for 'Prefixed..as': Prefixed to the names of instruments and techniques with the sense 'specially designed for dealing with

or measuring small effects or small quantities of material'. (In the names of techniques this use passes into 2 a.) *microammeter, -balance, -burette* (U.S. *-buret*), *-calorimeter* (hence *-calorimetric* adj., *-calorimetry*), *-densitometer* (hence *-densitometric* adj., *-densitometry*), *-determination, -electrophoresis* (hence *-electrophoretic* adj., *-electrophoretically* adv.), *-estimation, -gasometer* (hence *-gasometric* adj., *-gasometrically* adv., *-gasometry*), *-gravimetric* adj., *-Kjeldahl* (used *attrib.* or *absol.*: cf. *KJELDAHL), *-manometer* (hence *-manometric* adj., *-manometrically* adv.), *-method, -photometer* (hence *-photometric* adj., *-photometry*), *-pipette, -respirometer* [ad. G. *mikrorespirometer* (T. Thunberg 1904, in *Zentralbl. f. Physiol.* 3 Dec. 553)] (hence *-respirometric* adj., *-respirometry*), *-spectrograph* (hence *-spectrographic* adj., *-spectrography*), *-spectrophotometer* (so *-spectrophotometric* adj., *-spectrophotometrically* adv., *-spectrophotometry*), *-syringe, -technique*; **mi·croburner,** a small Bunsen burner for giving a single small flame; **microdiffu·sion** *Chem.*, diffusion of the vapour of a substance in an open container into an adjacent container in which there is a second substance, by which the first may be detected; usu. *attrib.*; **mi·crofilter,** a filter for separating out small quantities of material or very fine particles; **mi:cro-incinera·tion,** a process by which tissue sections are heated to a high temperature so as to remove organic matter and facilitate chemical analysis *in situ* of the inorganic constituents left behind; **mi·croneedle,** a very fine needle used in micromanipulation; **mi·croprobe** = *MICROANALYSER; also as *v. trans.*, to analyse with a microanalyser.

1930 *Telegraph & Telephone Jrnl.* Dec. 47/2 The deflection on the microammeter is proportional to the speed at which the tongue of the standard relay is oscillating, and a direct speed reading is given on the microammeter scale in terms of words per minute or cycles per second. **1964** R. F. FICCHI *Electr. Interference* vii. 127 A useful indicating device for locating leaks can easily be constructed using a tuned circuit consisting of a coil and variable condenser together with a 0-100 microammeter and crystal diode detector (1N34). **1903** *Jrnl. Chem. Soc.* LXXXIV. II. 571 A micro-balance with torsional control is described, having a sensitiveness of 0·0380 mg. per scale division. **1966** *McGraw-Hill Encycl. Sci. & Technol.* II. 74/1 Microbalances, used to weigh masses of a fraction of a gram, may be of the beam or the torsion type. **1926** *Chem. Abstr.* XX. 2543 A microburet for measuring minute drops is described. **1946** *Nature* 19 Oct. 556/2 The apparatus is completed by a microburette mounted on a movable arm. **1964** Micro buret [see *BURETTE 2]. **1911** *Jrnl. Infectious Dis.* VIII. 351 Natural gas for the microburner may be improved by causing it to pass through alcohol or benzine. **1938** *Jrnl. Laboratory & Clin. Med.* XXIV. 310 Two cubic centimeter samples of unhemolyzed serum are digested in pyrex test tubes..with 1·5 c.c. of concentrated sulfuric acid... The digestion may be carried out.. rapidly by the direct flame of a microburner. **1962** *B.S.I. News* July 28 Specifies the following items of apparatus for use in micro-chemical analysis: (i) Crucible holder... (ii) Micro-burner jet for use with coal gas, giving a non-luminous flame up to about 5 cm in height. **1911** *Jrnl. Physiol.* XLIII. 261 (*heading*) A new form of differential micro-calorimeter, for the estimation of heat production in physiological, bacteriological, or ferment actions. **1959** DAWSON & LONG *Chem. of Nucl. Power* i. 9 A microcalorimeter has been developed at Harwell for the rapid estimation of small amounts of polonium. **1924** *Chem. Abstr.* XVIII. 2723 (*heading*) Utilization in biology of the microcalorimetric method. **1971** *Nature* 22 Oct. 560/2 Microcalorimetric studies of sperm whale ferri-MbCN have demonstrated a change in heat capacity (C_p) in the range 35° ± 18° C. **1924** *Chem. Abstr.* XVIII. 4483 Microcalorimetry. **1973** *Nature* 16 Feb. 473/1 For research purposes, microcalorimetry provides highly informative data regarding microbial metabolism. **1935** *Discovery* Nov. 324 Micro-densitometer for analysing sound track. **1966** *Aviation Week & Space Technol.* 5 Dec. 99/3 The CRT system will be used..as a flying spot scanner and will scan through a precision optical chain providing a high-resolution microdensitometer. **1959** *Listener* 12 Mar. 451/2 Micro-densitometric tracing of the profile of the crater. **1973** H. L. SNYDER in L. M. Bibermann *Perception of Displayed Information* iii. 89 The *X-Y* luminance patterns of any given object or area of a scene can then be determined by scanning microdensitometric measurements for a film transparency input to the television system. **1957** A. ENGSTRÖM in V. E. Cosslett et al. *X-Ray Microsc. & Microradiogr.* 32 Microdensitometry of the fine-grained photographic emulsion presents the same type of problems as does direct microspectrography of biological material. **1973** *Nature* 17 Aug. 413/1 More has been achieved from a digitized array of optical densities of the image obtained by microdensitometry. **1925** *Analyst* L. 302 (*heading*) Micro-determination of methoxyl. **1947** CHERONIS & ENTRIKIN *Semimicro Qualitative Org. Analysis* ii. 72 The Alber specific-gravity pipettes that are commercially available may be used for the microdetermination of densities. **1967** *Oceanogr. & Marine Biol.* V. 173 A colorimetric method has recently been described for micro-determination of lipids. **1939** E. J. CONWAY *Micro-Diffusion Analysis & Volumetric Error* i. 4 (*heading*) Scale and accuracy of the micro-diffusion methods described. *Ibid.* ii. 7 (heading) A standard micro-diffusion apparatus or unit. **1956** *Nature* 31 Mar. 623/2 The asparaginase activity of the extract was estimated from the ammonia formed (by the Conway microdiffusion method). **1959** *Times* 14 Oct. 14/5 Ultracentrifuge and micro-electrophoresis equipment. **1971** *Nature* 22 Oct. 567/1 Cell electrophoresis was performed with a thin walled cylindrical cell in a particle micro-electrophoresis apparatus. **1961** *Lancet* 16 Sept. 656/2 Microelectrophoretic analyses of the ribosenucleic acid formed in the neurone and in the glia. **1973** *Neuropharmacology* XII. 77 A technique has been described for stereotaxically performing microelectrophoretic studies on single brain cells in awake, non-paralyzed cats. **1963** *Federation Proc.* XXII. 625/2 Responses of neurones to microelectrophoretically applied Acetylcholine (ACh)..have been obtained. **1973** *Jrnl. Pharmacy & Pharmacol.* XXV. 309 Responses of single cortical neurons to microelectrophoretically applied noradrenaline at pH 3·1 and 5·0 and to hydrogen ions were compared in the halothane-anaesthetized cat. **1922** *Analyst* XLVII. 80 (*heading*) Micro-estimation of nitrogen and its biological applications. **1972** *Analytical Chem.* XLIV. 1879 (*heading*) Simultaneous microestimation of choline and acetylcholine by gas chromatography. **1911** *Jrnl. Chem. Soc.* C. II. 225 (*heading*) A micro-filter for the treatment of small quantities of precipitate. **1958** *Ann. Rep. Chief Inspector of Factories on Industr. Health 1957* 23 in *Parl. Papers 1958–9* (Cmnd. 558) XIII. 183 He wore a microfilter respirator. **1972** *Physics Bull.* Aug. 455/1 The difference is due to the use of a microfilter in an aircraft fuelling system. **1951** *Amer. Jrnl. Clin. Path.* XXI. 1153 (*heading*) A practical microgasometer for estimation of carbon dioxide. **1972** *Analytical Biochem.* XLV. 112 The magnetic diver microgasometer is operated at a constant pressure so that the enclosed gas bubble can contract or expand freely. **1956** *Nature* 28 Jan. 185/2 In 1937, Linderstrøm-Lang introduced a microgasometric method based on the principle of the Cartesian diver. **1967** *Internat. Jrnl. Neuropharmacol.* VI. 266 The electron microscopic–cytochemical technique has been applied directly to unfixed isolated neurons following microgasometric analysis. **1968** *Progress Brain Res.* XXIX. 41 Ultracytochemistry was then applied to individual neurons, which had been analyzed microgasometrically. **1957** G. E. HUTCHINSON *Treat. Limnol.* I. xvii. 879 A technique involving characteristically ingenious microgasometry..has been used by Krogh and Lange. **1972** *Analytical Biochem.* XLV. 115 The dimensions of the ampullas most frequently used for magnetic microgasometry. **1931** *Industr. & Engin. Chem.* (*Analytical Ed.*) III. 345 An apparatus is described for microgravimetric analyses, such as sulfate, halide, and phosphate determinations. **1966** *McGraw-Hill Encycl. Sci. & Technol.* II. 199/2 Microgravimetric analyses, in which weighings are made to ±0·002 mg on a Kuhlman beam balance. **1924** *Analyst* XLIX. 52 (*heading*) Micro-incineration applicable to histochemical investigation. **1969** BROWN & BERTKE *Textbk. Cytol.* iii. 23/1 Micro-incineration involves the ashing of tissue sections at a temperature of about 600°C. This method can provide information regarding general distribution of certain minerals. **1923** *Jrnl. Amer. Chem. Soc.* XLVI. 2069 A new micro-Kjeldahl method..has been devised. **1946** *Nature* 30 Nov. 791/1 The extract was then filtered and its nitrogen content determined by micro-Kjeldahl. **1973** *Analytical Biochem.* LIII. 36 We have developed two simple modifications which minimize, if not eliminate, the excessive foaming encountered during micro Kjeldahl digestion of biological materials. **1897** *Jrnl. Physical Chem.* I. 596 The author's micromanometer (l.c., 1895), giving measurements accurate to 0·0033 mm water or 0·00024 mm mercury was used. **1949** O. G. SUTTON *Sci. of Flight* 201 The most sensitive micromanometer in general use, the Chattock-Fry gauge, is simply a glorified U-tube. **1972** *Physics Bull.* Aug. 491/2 The new vacuum micromanometer has been designed for applications requiring sensitive differential pressure measurements at high vacuum levels. **1937** *Discovery* July 224/2 We have new micromanometric techniques which can be applied directly to small-celled animals or plants in life. **1956** *Jrnl. Laboratory & Clin. Med.* XLVII. 642 The development of the micromanometric methods described herein was undertaken because of the need for a precise but rapid method for detecting sudden alterations in acid-base balance. **1973** *Jrnl. Neurochem.* XX. 1029 The rate of oxygen consumption has been measured micromanometrically in fresh mouse neuroblastoma cells. **1920** *Jrnl. Soc. Chem. Industry* 15 Mar. 206A/1 A micro-method in which 1–2 c.c. of urine and 1·5–3 c.c. of alkali need only be used. **1946** *Nature* 10 Aug. 199/2 We have developed a new micromethod for X-ray diffraction investigation of biological objects. **1967** *Oceanogr. & Marine Biol.* V. 171 A micromethod for determination of protein in extremely small quantities by the quenching of dye fluorescence has also been described. **1974** *Nature* 3 May 37/2 Studies of lymphocyte transformation *in vitro* were carried out by our micromethod. **1921** *Science* 28 Oct. 411/2 The method of making the glass micro-needles and pipettes. **1940** C. SHERRINGTON *Man on his Nature* iv. 116 The protein coat of the fertilized egg-cell..can be cut by the 'microneedle' without loss of its rigidity. **1971** *Nature* 2 July 28/2 The microneedles are made from 1 mm 'Pyrex' or borosilicate glass rod drawn out to form a thin (~0·3 mm) shaft, ~50 mm long. **1899** J. HARTMANN in *Astrophysical Jrnl.* X. 325 The apparatus..may be designated as a microphotometer, since it is a combination of microscope and photometer. **1947** *Jrnl. Brit. Interplanetary Soc.* VI. 162 Meteor light-curves, which must be examined photographically, with the help of a recording microphotometer. **1971** *Tsitologiya* XIII. 1530 The scanning and integrating microphotometer permits to define the quantity of substance, area and the linear dimension of micro-objects. **1952** *Chromosoma* V. 341 The microphotometric evaluation of cytochemical color reactions, such as the Feulgen-reaction on desoxyribose nucleic acid (DNA), has in recent years attained increasing importance. **1960** *Jrnl. Histochem. & Cytochem.* VIII. 4/1 It is of importance in some microphotometric studies of cells and tissues to determine the protein content of a single cell, nucleus, or nucleolus. **1937** *Monthly Notices R. Astr. Soc.* XCVIII. 113 A slit ·025 mm. wide and < 0·4 mm. high was used in all the microphotometry. **1973** *Acta Cytol.* XVII. 94 It is the objective of this paper to examine the feasibility of using automated scanning microphotometry with computer analysis of the cell images for the purpose of differentiating nonmalignant from malignant cells in pleural fluid. **1918** *Biol. Bull.* XXXIV. 134 The capillary attraction in the lumen of a micropipette..is quite sufficient for the purpose. **1922** *Anatomical Rec.* XXIV. 2 With the micropipette..one can..inject substances into..a cell. **1955** *Sci. Amer.* Aug. 98/2 Deposit five thousandths of a milliliter of serum on the ruled strip with a calibrated micropipette. **1968** *Times* 14 Nov. 8/7 A few of the cells, typically about three, are sucked up into a micropipette and injected through the slit in the first embryo. **1960** *Oxf. Univ. Gaz.* 19 Feb. 743/2 X-ray Fluorescent Micro-probe. A study is being made of the possible archaeological applications of this very new technique. **1969** *Awake!* 22 Oct. 19/2 A painting that was supposedly done by a sixteenth-century painter was exposed as a forgery by this laser device, which is called a microprobe. **1973** *Nature* 12 Jan. 87/1 Six olivines (three from Venezuela and three from Ghana) microprobed at the Geophysical Laboratory in Washington showed..an extremely constant Ni content. **1974** *McGraw-Hill Yearbk. Sci. & Technol.* 291/2 The ion microprobe mass spectrometer uses primary ions of argon or oxygen..that are focused to a 1–2-μm spot before the sample is bombarded. **1905** *Jrnl. Chem. Soc.* LXXXVIII. II. 44 By means of an apparatus termed the 'micro-respirometer'..the respiratory exchanges in small objects like nerves can actually be measured. **1946** *Nature* 27 July 126/2 A Cartesian diver micro-respirometer. **1965** B. E. FREEMAN tr. *Vandel's Biospeleol.* xx. 342 The measurement of respiration is carried out in respiratory chambers or micro-respirometers. **1905** *Jrnl. Chem. Soc.* LXXXVIII. II. 44 Micro-respirometric investigations. **1970** *Acta Soc. Bot. Poloniae* XXXIX. 497 The micro-respirometric technique has been used for many research works on leaves and leaf segments. **1960** E. J. BOELL in Sasser & Jenkins *Nematology* viii. 109 (*heading*) The Cartesian diver technique in microrespirometry and enzyme assay. **1973** *Soil Biol. & Biochem.* V. 271 A new method has been developed for microrespirometry utilizing gas chromatography. **1934** *Photogr. Jrnl.* LXXIV. 518/2 The application of the microspectrograph to the identification of organic compounds. **1953** *Experientia* IX. 422/2 The transmission curves obtained with the microspectrograph were transformed into extinction curves. **1950** T. CASPERSSON *Cell Growth & Cell Function* iii. 61 There are two groups of cell substances that are more easily studied by microspectrographic procedures than any others. These are the proteins..and the polynucleotides. **1947** *Acta Path. & Microbiol. Scand.* XXIV. 417 (*heading*) Ultraviolet microspectrography as an aid in the study of the nucleotide content of bacteria. **1957** Microspectrography [see *microdensitometry* above]. **1951** *Rev. Sci. Instruments* XXII. 866/2 The electronic part of the microspectrophotometer consists of the two photocells, one above the other. **1966** *McGraw-Hill Encycl. Sci. & Technol.* II. 595/1 Such microspectrophotometers, capable of carrying out spectral analyses within the dimensions of a single cell, will play an increasingly powerful role in furthering our knowledge of cell biology. **1950** T. CASPERSSON *Cell Growth & Cell Function* ii. 45 This is a further reason for the use of high-aperture lenses in microspectrophotometric work. **1970** *Nature* 17 Oct. 255/2 Microspectrophotometric analyses of the salic particles in the visible and near ultraviolet show a continuous absorption spectrum increasing towards the ultraviolet. **1951** *Exper. Cell Res.* II. 301 In order to obtain significant data on the content of a certain absorbing substance of a whole cell the only as yet available way is to work microspectrophotometrically with photographic procedures. **1971** J. M. PAULUS *Platelet Kinetics* 330 Ploidy measurements of megakaryocytes have usually been obtained by determining microspectrophotometrically the total relative extinction of megakaryocyte nuclei. **1935** *Chem. Abstr.* XXIX. 1117 (*heading*) Ultraviolet absorption spectrum of sea-urchin eggs. Technic of microspectrophotometry. **1972** *Amer. Jrnl. Bot.* LIX. 829/1 The two-wavelength method of microspectrophotometry..was employed in the Feulgen-DNA studies. **1958** *Listener* 9 Oct. 563/1 The bacterial virus is really a tiny syringe—a microsyringe. **1973** *Internat. Jrnl. Peptide & Protein Res.* V. 208/1 All dilutions and sampling by volume were performed with a microsyringe..that delivered volumes accurate to $10^{-3} \pm 5 \times 10^{-4}$ ml. **1892** *Jrnl. R. Microsc. Soc.* 555 (*heading*) Zimmermann's botanical microtechnique. **1956** *Nature* 28 Jan. 153/1 The general climate of micro-chemistry has changed greatly in the interval. In 1949 the applications of micro-techniques were few and not very widely used, but at the present day they are ubiquitous. **1964** *Oceanogr. & Marine Biol.* II. 111 The micro-techniques described here are primarily those for small or micro-amounts of sea water.

7. Prefixed to a sb. (or used *attrib.* without a hyphen) to indicate that the object designated has been reduced in size by the use of microphotography, or is used in connection with such an object, as *micro book, edition, -record, -recording, -reproduction, -text*; **mi·croreader, -viewer,** an apparatus that produces from microfilm or microprint an image enlarged sufficiently to be readable.

1970 *New Scientist* 31 Dec. 601/1 The micro book.. opens up the prospect of vast reductions in the world's consumption of paper. **1971** *Brit. Printer* Jan. 80/1 An inventor, who has been working for two years to develop a practicable 'micro book', has come up with a solution. *Ibid.*, Microfilming was not the simplest or most economical way of producing a micro book. **1970** *New Scientist* 31 Dec. 601/2 Publishers of technical journals..could put out in micro editions some of the..specialised research material that cannot be included in their normal issues. **1971** *Brit. Printer* Jan. 80/2 PVC paper also has the advantage, for micro editions, of being durable, difficult to tear and waterproof. **1949** M. C. KEELEYSIDE in *Summary Proc. 3rd Ann. Conf. Amer. Theol. Library Assoc.* 11 The reading machines are new on the market. I am proud to say that our library has the first microreader that any library in the world ever possessed. **1970** *Publishers' Weekly* 8 June 152/1 Obviously it is not possible for people to read microfilmed material without some magnification

device, hence the microreader which you can see in most libraries. **1948** *Sci. News* VII. 90 The Airgraph scheme.. made one advantage of such micro-records obvious to the general public. **1957** J. BURKETT *Microrecording in Libraries* i. 8 Microrecording was first put on a business-like footing in 1928 when Eastman Kodak introduced its Recordak Division. *Ibid.* ii. 13 An opaque microrecord is ..a positive print made from a photographic negative. **1971** *Brit. Printer* Jan. 80/1 Davies started on the project mainly as a result of an inquiry from the American Council for Library Resources, which was interested in obtaining a small, cheap and portable method of retrieving micro-records. **1938** G. VAN ITERSON in *Trans. 14th Conf. Fédération Internat. de Documentation* I. 149 (*heading*) The preparation and reading of micro-reproductions of treatises. **1958** *Engineering* 4 Apr. 443/3 To this [*sc.* the decrease in library accommodation] there is one reasonable solution and that is micro-reproduction. **1944** F. RIDER *Scholar & Future of Research Library* II. i. 99 Why might we not combine the micro-texts of our books, and the catalog cards for these same books, in one single entity? *Ibid.* 100 A fair amount of micro-text can be put on the back of a standard-size catalog card. **1958** *Times Rev. Industry* Mar. 61/3 The United States has been a fertile ground for the spread of microtexts. **1973** *Computers & Humanities* VII. 163 Anyone who uses the subject part of an ordinary library catalog, whether in card, book, or microtext form, would benefit from this explanation. **1972** M. J. BOSSE *Incident at Naha* iii 153, I feel I'm turning into a library. I'll start dreaming I'm a card catalog or a microviewer.

8. *micro* is now freely prefixed to sbs., often resulting in trivial or nonce words; from being used as an independent word without a hyphen it passes into a quasi-*adj.* with the meanings: **a.** Microscopic, minute; small-scale, small.

The examples are arranged in chronological order.

1922 *Encycl. Brit.* XXX. 34/2 Micro-investigation of glued joints proved the value of carefully preparing the timber and glue. **1926** R. W. LAWSON tr. *Hevesy & Paneth's Man. Radioactivity* i. 2 Very small quantities of two different gases..gradually accumulate within the tube, and can be detected by the methods of micro-gas analysis. **1931** *Boys' Mag.* XLV. 157/1 Any good crystal detector will do. One with fine or micro adjustment is to be preferred. **1935** *Discovery* Nov. 320/1 Whenever it finds a patch of..dry, dusty ground, there it arrives... Such patches, for the purposes of that *Acrotylus*, are deserts. They are, in fact, micro-deserts. **1946** KOESTLER *Thieves in Night* 279 Pen-holders of olivewood with a tiny inlaid lens through which one could see a micro-panorama of Jerusalem. **1958** *Spectator* 15 Aug. 236/2 Micro, corneal and contact lenses. **1967** G. WILLS in Wills & Yearsley *Handbk. Managem. Technol.* x. 176 At the macro level, marketing management became concerned with understanding its social environment; at the micro level, the concept of the marketing mix postulated a co-ordinative and integrative activity for product distribution and communication. **1969** *Jane's Freight Containers 1968–69* 552/2 Ten models of these 1-ton micro-fork lift trucks are available for loading and unloading containers. **1970** *Globe & Mail* (Toronto) 26 Sept. 9/5 More attention will be given to the ubiquitous 'micro' problems in non-sugar sectors of the [Cuban] economy. **1973** *Physics Bull.* Oct. 626/1 Finally, going lower than micro, we might mention the HP-45, Hewlett-Packard's new pocket 'scientific' calculator, said to be the most powerful of its size and price. **1974** *Sci. Amer.* July 134/2 A computer patiently runs the long repetitive scans looking for tiny needles in microhaystacks.

b. *Chem.* Of or pertaining to microanalysis. Cf. *micromethod* in *6, *MICRO-SCALE.

1931 J. W. BROWN in C. A. Mitchell *Recent Adv. Analytical Chem.* II. xv. 306 The work of Emich inspired Fritz Pregl..to attempt to carry out organic determinations on a micro scale. **1937** *Ann. Rev. Biochem.* VI. 85 While many important studies have been made on reducing sugars in recent years, most of these have not involved the use of methods which are strictly micro. **1946** BELCHER & WILSON *Qualitative Inorg. Microanalysis* i. 1 Micro methods handle solid samples over the range of 0·1 to 1 mg., and volumes of solution ranging from 0·02 to 0·2 ml. **1955** C. R. N. STROUTS et al. *Analytical Chem.* I. xiv. 314 The economy of time afforded by many micro procedures favours their adoption even when the amount of sample available is sufficient for macroanalysis. **1971** *Nature* 19 Mar. 194/2 Any laboratory where the analysis of metals is practised at macro, micro or trace levels. **1974** *Encycl. Brit. Macropædia* IV. 79/2 Samples..can be classified as macro (10^{-1} g), semi-micro ($10^{-1}-10^{-3}$ g), micro ($10^{-3}-10^{-6}$ g), sub-micro ($10^{-6}-10^{-8}$ g), nanogram (10^{-9} g), or picogram (10^{-12} g).

microabscess, -aerophil(e, -aerophilic, -ammeter: see *MICRO- 1, 4, 4, 6.

microanalyser (məikro,æ·nǟləizəɹ). Also (chiefly *U.S.*) **-analyzer.** [f. MICRO- 6 + ANALYSER, -ZER.] An instrument in which a beam of radiation (usu. electrons) is focused on to a minute area of a sample and the resulting secondary radiation (usu. X-ray fluorescence) is analysed to yield chemical information about the area.

1944 HILLIER & BAKER in *Jrnl. Appl. Physics* XV. 665/1 Figure 1 is a photograph of the first experimental model of an electron microanalyzer. **1959** *Electronic Engin.* XXXI. 680/1 In the Hinxton Hall microanalyser the specimen surface is scanned at slow speed by an electron beam focused to a diameter of less than one micron. **1960** *Archaeometry* III. 36 During the past eighteen months the Laboratory has been engaged upon the construction of an X-ray microanalyser for archaeological applications. **1966** D. G. BRANDON *Mod. Techniques Metallogr.* 173 (*caption*) Secondary-ion emission microanalyser. **1973** *Histochem. Jrnl.* V. 176 EMMA-4 combines the full facilities of a conventional transmission electron microscope and an electron probe X-ray microanalyser.

microanalysis (məikro,ænæ·lĭsis). [f. MICRO- 2 a + ANALYSIS.] The analysis for chemical information of very small samples, or very small areas of an object; now *spec.* the quantitative analysis of samples weighing only a few milligrammes (contrasted with semimicroanalysis and ultramicroanalysis). Cf. *MICRO- 8 b.

1856, 1904 [in Dict. s.v. MICRO- 2 a]. **1937** *Discovery* Aug. 227/2 The addition..of the delicate weapon of micro-analysis to the analyst's armoury. **1966** D. G. BRANDON *Mod. Techniques Metallogr.* iii. 172 In all the methods of microanalysis discussed so far, a point-by-point determination of the x-ray emission or absorption spectrum is related to the chemical composition in order to find the spatial distribution of the components.

Hence **microa·nalyst**, one who performs or is skilled in microanalysis; **mi:croanaly·tical** *a.*, of or using microanalysis.

1924 E. FYLEMAN tr. *Pregl's Quantitative Org. Microanalysis* i. 4 He has worked out a microanalytical method for the determination of glycerine. *Ibid.* ii. 13 A watchmaker's lens..should always be in the pocket of the microanalyst. **1938** *Ann. Reg. 1937* 354 Paneth and Glückauf showed, by microanalytical methods, that when neutrons are produced by bombarding beryllium with gamma-rays the beryllium..breaks down into helium. **1964** N. G. CLARK *Mod. Org. Chem.* xxiv. 496 He later returned to Graz, where he established an international reputation as a micro-analyst.

microanatomist, -anatomy, -aneurysm, -atoll: see *MICRO- 2 a, 2 a, 1, 1.

microbalance, -bar: see *MICRO- 6, 5 a.

microbarom (məikrobæ·rǫ̈m). *Meteorol.* [f. MICRO- + BAROM(ETER.] A minute oscillation of atmospheric pressure with a period of the order of 5 seconds.

1939 BENIOFF & GUTENBERG in *Bull. Amer. Meteorol. Soc.* XX. 424/1 The waves..exhibit no relation to microseisms nor to the barometric conditions in this region. No hypothesis as to their origin has yet been suggested. We designate them microbaroms. **1953** *Jrnl. Acoustical Soc. Amer.* XXV. 796/1 Microbaroms apparently originate in ocean storms associated with low pressure areas. **1967** *Times* 21 Nov. 3/5 The detection of microbaroms depends very much on the availability of sensitive equipment.

microbe. Add: Also *fig.*

1890 in J. R. Ware *Passing Eng.* (1909) 175/2 The abdication by the Radical party of its proper functions has an unfortunate tendency to foster..the microbe of sectionalism.

microbeam: see *MICRO- 1.

microbial, *a.* Add: Also **micro·bially** *adv.*, by or with microbes.

1971 *Flying* Apr. 88 (Advt.), Microbially induced corrosion of fuel tanks. **1974** *Nature* 27 Sept. 316/2 Plants in the three microbially contaminated pots produced proteid roots.

microbiology. Add: Also **microbiolo·gic** *a.* = MICROBIOLOGICAL *a.*; **microbiolo·gically** *adv.*, by microbiological methods.

1909 *Westm. Gaz.* 9 Dec. 2/1 He is..reminded of the doctrine of the etiology of infectious diseases before the advent of the microbiologic epoch. **1942** *Industr. & Engin. Chem.* (*Analytical Ed.*) 15 Aug. 667/1 The extracted residue of dried skim milk was microbiologically inert, while the residue of alfalfa leaf meal exerted a little stimulatory action. **1956** *Nature* 4 Feb. 221/1 The relation between seven different tree-supports..and two epiphytes was examined microbiologically. **1966** *McGraw-Hill Encycl. Sci. & Technol.* IX. 620/2 Penicillin can also be chemically or microbiologically degraded and then built up to form new penicillins. **1969** WILSON & MIZER *Microbiol. in Nursing Pract.* i. 11/2 Since Leeuwenhoek's first glimpse of bacteria and protozoa, microbiologic investigations have resulted in the accumulation of a vast body of knowledge..that has lightened immeasurably the burden of human disease.

microbiota: see *MICRO- 1.

microbism (məi·krobiz'm). *Med.* [f. MICROB(E + -ISM.] Infection with microbes.

1904 *Lancet* 18 June 1724/1 The various explanations of 'return' cases were considered, including..the possibility of a relapse of the original disease, of latent microbism, or of missed cases. **1963** *Biol. Abstr.* XLI. 553/2 (*heading*) Investigations on the role of staphylococci in cutaneous microbism.

microbody, -burette: see *MICRO- 1, 6.

microburin (məikrobiūə·rin) *Archæol.* [f. MICRO- 1 + BURIN.] (See quot. 1970.)

1932 *Antiquity* VI. 364 A feature of the industry is the presence of the burin of upper Palæolithic type... The microburin is not mentioned either as occurring or as absent. **1955** [see *IBERO-]. **1957** V. G. CHILDE *Dawn European Civilization* (ed. 6) i. 6 At Parpalló in Eastern Spain even microburins occur from the Solutrian layers upward. **1958** *Man* Apr. 57/2 The ends are then shaped either by twisting off, or by retouching, and even by the microburin technique of notching and then snapping... The microburins, the 'anti-microburins' and the obliquely snapped waste..were all backed as well. **1970** BRAY & TRUMP *Dict. Archaeol.* 147/1 *Microburin*, a by-product of the manufacture of microliths. A blade is notched, and then snapped off... One piece becomes a microlithic tool, while the residue (the 'microburin') still shows traces of the original notch and fracture.

microburner: see *MICRO- 6.

microbus (məi·krobɒs). [f. MICRO- 1 + BUS *sb.*[2]] A small vehicle designed to carry passengers in seats fitted as in a bus.

1959 *Cambr. Rev.* 7 Mar. 428/2 (Advt.), Micro-buses available on continent, fitted camping facilities. Make up your own party. **1960** [see *JAMBOREE]. **1962** E. KIMBROUGH *Pleasure by Busload* ii. 17 'This is a Volkswagen Microbus,' Sophy answered... No one had told me it looked as big as a trailer and that the span from ground to floorboard was a span well over three feet. **1968** *New Scientist* 19 Sept. 596/1 Caltech relied on a less streamlined red and white 1958 Volkswagen microbus. **1971** *Telegraph* (Brisbane) 14 Sept. 22/4 Mr. Ralph Nader claimed the famous Beetle was loaded with safety hazards... He claimed the VW microbus was even worse.

microcalorie, -calorimeter (etc.), **-camera, -capsule:** see *MICRO- 5 a, 6, 1 b, 1.

microcard (məi·krokāɹd). Also **Microcard.** [f. *MICRO- 7 + CARD *sb.*[2]] An opaque card bearing microphotographs of a number of pages of a book, periodical, etc. (A proprietary name in the U.S.)

1944 F. RIDER *Scholar & Future of Research Library* II. i. 99 Why might we not combine the micro-texts of our books, and the catalog cards for these same books, in one single entity?.. I called this new concept..a 'micro-card'. **1950** *Official Gaz.* (U.S. Patent Office) 24 Jan. 907/1 The Micro Library Incorporated, La Crosse, Wis.... *Microcard* for publications in card form, reproduced by printing, photographing and otherwise. Claims use since November 1947. **1950, 1953** [see *MICROFICHE]. **1958** *Engineering* 31 Jan. 155/1 Micro-card can also be used on the reverse side for such purposes as abstracts in normal type and catalogue notations. **1958** *Times Rev. Industry* Mar. 61/1 For recording such material as technical periodicals or newspapers, the microcard system is often the better method. **1964** M. MCLUHAN *Understanding Media* (1967) iii. 49 Today with microfilm and micro-cards..the printed word assumes again much of the handicraft character of a manuscript. **1973** *Computers & Humanities* VII. 168 Few agencies even assemble material on microfiches or microcards.

So **mi·crocard** *v.*, to reproduce on microcards; **mi·crocarded** *ppl. a.*

1944 F. RIDER *Scholar & Future of Research Library* II. vii. 189 What types of material, and..what titles.. ought, therefore, to be micro-carded first. *c* **1960** *Microcards* (Microcard Foundation), Reports coming in from men in the field are collated and the completed reports are Microcarded... Literally shelves of Microcarded books and periodicals can be stored in one file cabinet.

microcellular, -chemist, -chromosome, -cinematography (and **-graphic**): see *MICRO- 4, 2 a, 1, 2 a.

microcircuit (məi·krosɜ̄ɹkit). *Electronics.* Also **micro-circuit.** [f. MICRO- 1 + CIRCUIT *sb.*] An integrated circuit or other minute circuit.

1959 *Electronics* 4 Sept. 49/3 New circuit fabrication techniques such as are used in microcircuits. **1960** *IRE Trans. Military Electronics* IV. 461/1 (*caption*) Detailed sketch of a silicon integrated microcircuit. **1965** *Economist* 25 Sept. 1228/1 A micro-circuit is no bigger than a pinhead, replacing transistor circuits as big as a large envelope knitted out of wires. **1970** *Daily Tel.* 8 May 21 Not only do they have the advantage of smaller size: microcircuits are also more reliable and faster—a vital factor for computer use. **1971** *Physics Bull.* Jan. 45/1 The chips measure ⅛ in² and contain 1434 microcircuit elements each, integrated into 128 memory and 46 support circuits.

So **mi·crocircuitry**, microcircuits collectively; the branch of electronics concerned with microcircuits.

1959 *Electronics* 4 Sept. 44/1 The microcircuitry program is concerned with the development of a circuit fabrication technique based on the combination of elementary materials rather than on the assembly of individual components. **1960** *IRE Trans. Military Electronics* IV. 459/2 Integrated microcircuitry. **1970** *Daily Tel.* 21 Sept. 19 Recent developments in microcircuitry.. have made it possible to reduce the circuitry of an amplifier to the size of an ordinary jacket button. **1974** *Country Life* 5 Dec. 1763/1 By..a brilliant piece of microcircuitry, the oscillations are translated into a constant, one second pulse.

microcirculation: see *MICRO- 1.

microclimate (məi·krokləimĕt). Chiefly *Ecol.* and *Meteorol.* [f. MICRO- 1 + CLIMATE *sb.*] The climate of a very small or restricted area, or of the immediate surroundings of any individual or object of interest, esp. as it differs from the climate generally.

1925 *Rev. Appl. Mycol.* IV. 471 Temperature, absolute

and relative humidity, aeration, insolation, &c., which prevail at various levels..are comprised by him [*sc.* L. F. Roussakov] under the term 'microclimate'. **1934** [see *MICROCLIMATOLOGY]. **1951** R. GEIGER in T. F. Malone *Compendium Meteorol.* 994/1 We shall first consider microclimate as the special climate prevailing in a layer of air about two meters in height adjacent to the surface of the ground. In this layer friction between the air and the earth's surface plays a decisive role. **1958** *Engineering* 14 Mar. 352/1 A basic item influencing the design of an air-conditioning system is the 'micro-climate'—the climate existing immediately around the structure to be air conditioned. **1967** T. J. CHANDLER *Air around Us* x. 116/1 Climates can differ from one side to the other of a hedge or garden wall, or from the base of a bush to its leafy crown. Such conditions are usually described as microclimates. **1972** *Physics Bull.* June 342/1 Cool air is introduced into the microclimate between the pilot's clothing and his skin. **1973** *Times* 17 Nov. 12 Provided the compost is kept always moist a moist 'microclimate' is created around the plants.

Hence **microclima·tic** *a.*, **-clima·tically** *adv.* **1929** *Conf. Empire Meteorologists, Agric. Section* II. 131 The actual, *i.e.* the microclimatic, conditions often bear only a very remote relation to the general conditions in the habitat. **1952** *Archit. Rev.* CXII. 323 The total site area (shaded) is over 45,000 acres but more than half of this will be devoted to forestry—for microclimatic control, for experimental purposes, and as capital investment. **1972** *Nature* 10 Mar. 64/1 The immigration and establishment of local small stands of trees in microclimatically favourable habitats. **1974** *Ibid.* 15 Mar. 261/3 The alternative explanation..relates the higher soil moisture beneath vegetation to the modified microclimatic conditions in such situations.

mi:croclimato·logy. *Meteorol.* [f. MICRO- 2 a + CLIMATOLOGY.] The study of microclimates.

1934 L. A. RAMDAS in *Current Sci.* II. 445/2 The aims of 'micro-climatology' are (1) to investigate the physical laws underlying the deviations of 'micro-climate' from 'macro-climate'..and (2) to apply the theoretical results to practical ends. **1944** V. CONRAD *Methods in Climatol.* i. 14 The layering of the air is of interest..as one of the most important features from which 'Microclimatology', and especially 'Orographic Microclimatology', makes its start. **1972** *Last Whole Earth Catalog* (Portola Inst.) 83/1 This appears to be the definitive text on microclimatology: the climatic conditions within six feet or so of the earth's surface. **1974** *Daily Colonist* (Victoria, B.C.) 28 Aug. 6/4 Principles of microclimatology and its relationship to plant growth will be discussed.

Hence **mi:croclimatolo·gical** *a.*, **-climato·logist.** **1937** *Geography* XXII. 87 (*heading*) Reality in climate: the results of recent microclimatological studies, with special references to temperatures. **1951** R. GEIGER in T. F. Malone *Compendium Meteorol.* 993/2 Location considerations in plant growth are always microclimatological in nature; whether a plant is located in an open field or at the north side of a large boulder..is a decisive factor with respect to the conditions affecting its growth. *Ibid.*, The biology of bees can be understood only if one knows the microclimate of the beehive. It is the problem of the microclimatologist to investigate these small-scale climates.

microcolony, -constituent, -continent: see *MICRO- 1.

microcopy (məi·krǫkǫpi), *sb.* [f. *MICRO- 7 + COPY *sb.*] A copy of the text of a book, periodical, etc., that has been reduced in size by the use of microphotography; *in microcopy*, in the form of a microcopy or microcopies. Also as *v. trans.*, to make such a copy of; also *absol.*; **mi·crocopying** *vbl. sb.*

1934 WEBSTER, Microcopy *n.* **1936** *Microphotogr. for Libraries* (Amer. Library Assoc.) 3 We microcopy because, by reducing the size of letters, we can reduce tremendously the cost of making copies. *Ibid.* 4 Whenever we contemplate reproducing something in microcopy for a number of users, we should give especial attention to materials cost. *Ibid.* 13 The production of microcopies is relatively easy and inexpensive. **1942** *Punch* 14 Jan. 4/2 By means of photographic 'micro-copying', miniature negatives of all kinds of documents can be taken on continuous lengths of..films. **1944** F. RIDER *Scholar & Future of Research Library* II. ii. 115 All that we have to do is to take two copies of the book that we are proposing to micro-copy. *Ibid.* vi. 170 The library can usually supply a borrower at once with a duplicate micro-copy. **1950** [see *flat film* (*FLAT *a.* 15)]. **1962** *B.S.I. News* Feb. 39 Specifies size ranges for transparent bases for microcopies—roll or strip microfilm, microfiches and unexposed rolls of sensitized film. **1972** *Computers & Humanities* VII. 46 The National Library will acquire most periodicals required in order to back up these services, as well as other references available in microcopy.

microco·smically, *adv.* [f. MICROCOSMIC *a.*: see -LY[2].] In relation to the microcosm.

1881 MAX MÜLLER tr. *Kant's Critique Pure Reason* I. ii. 363, I might call the two former [ideas], in a narrower sense, cosmical concepts (macrocosmically or microcosmically) and the remaining two transcendent concepts of nature. **1939** [see *MACROCOSMICALLY *adv.*]. **1942** *Mind* LI. 235 A microcosmic being exists microcosmically under divine reference in constitutive *communitas* with a complement that is not absolutely other; and under self-reference in indefinitely continuing commerce of co-operation and opposition with an imaginative other.

microcosmopolitan, -crack (etc.), **-crater:** see *MICRO- 1 b, 1, 1.

micro-crystal. Add: Also **microcrystal.** (Earlier and later examples.)

1886 *Jrnl. R. Microsc. Soc.* VI. 725 (*heading*) Preparing microcrystals. **1964** L. MARTIN *Clin. Endocrinol.* (ed. 4) viii. 267 Alternatively, long-acting injections of microcrystals of œstradiol monobenzoate (Ovocyclin I.M.) may be given in doses of 10 mg.

microcrystalline, *a.* Add: *microcrystalline wax*, a mixture of hydrocarbons of higher molecular weight than those in paraffin waxes and with a melting point of up to 90°C which is obtained from the residual lubricating fraction of crude oil and is used in making waxed paper, adhesives, and polishes.

1943 *Jrnl. Amer. Pharmaceutical Assoc.* (*Sci. Ed.*) XXXII. 111/2 A series of 'Petro-waxes', one of which melts at about 160°F. It is a white microcrystalline wax that is available in quantity. It was thought that due to the microcrystalline structure of this wax, it might make stable ointments containing as much as 50% water. **1944** H. BENNETT *Commercial Waxes* i. 60 The designations of microcrystalline and amorphous waxes are now being used synonymously although the former is a more accurate designation. **1957** VAN DER HAVE & VERVER *Petroleum* xi. 339 As its name implies, 'micro-crystalline wax' has a very fine crystal structure; it is a flexible and often somewhat sticky product; it has a high molecular weight (550–600) and a melting point within the same range as ceresin. **1972** *Oxf. Univ. Gaz.* CII. Suppl. No. 3. 10 They [*sc.* metal objects] are boiled to remove chlorides and after drying in an infra-red cupboard are impregnated with microcrystalline wax.

Hence **mi:crocrystalli·nity**, the property or state of being microcrystalline.

1946 *Nature* 28 Dec. 930/1 Microcrystallinity and a capacity to yield strong and pliable fibres are properties by no means confined to the linear poly-amides. **1967** *Encycl. Polymer Sci. & Technol.* VII. 207 It is possible to distinguish microcrystallinity, detectable by x-ray examination, from macrocrystallinity, visible through a polarizing microscope.

microculture, -curie: see *MICRO- 1, 5 a.

microcyclic (məikrosəi·klik), *a.* *Bot.* [f. *MICRO- 1 b + CYCLIC *a.*] Of a plant rust: having a short life cycle.

1926 [see *MACROCYCLIC *a.* 1]. **1950** E. A. BESSEY *Morphol. & Taxon. Fungi* xii. 396 These last two are properly speaking microcyclic rusts. **1970** J. WEBSTER *Introd. Fungi* 376 Some rusts have only telia, with or without pycnia, and are said to be microcyclic.

microcyte. Add: (Now freq. with pronunc. (mi·kro-).) Hence **microcytic** (-si·tik) *a.*, typical or characteristic of a microcyte; characterized by microcytes; **microcytosis** (-səitōu·sis) = MICROCYTHÆMIA.

1890 BILLINGS *Med. Dict.* II. 154/1 *Microcytosis*, production of microcytes. **1925** *Amer. Jrnl. Med. Sci.* CXXX. 684 Measurements..showed the majority of the cells to be microcytic. **1932** [see *MACROCYTE]. **1938** H. DOWNEY *Handbk. Hematol.* III. xxxi. 2286 One cannot fail to notice that the average size of the red cells is less than normal; there is a distinct microcytosis. **1962** *Lancet* 12 May 1004/2 Clinical and hæmatological examinations.. showed anæmia with anisocytosis, microcytosis, macrocytosis, and reticulocytosis. **1966** *Ibid.* 24 Dec. 1398/2 Prasad described a syndrome of microcytic anæmia.

microdegree, -densitometer (etc.), **-determination, -diffusion:** see *MICRO- 5 a, 6, 6, 6.

microdiorite (məikrodəi·ǒrəit). *Petrol.* [f. MICRO- + DIORITE.] (See quots. 1920, 1961.)

1920 A. HOLMES *Nomencl. Petrol.* 157 *Micro-*, a prefix commonly added—..(2) to the names of phanerocrystalline rocks to indicate a microcrystalline rock or groundmass of corresponding mineral composition and texture; e.g., *microgranite, microdiorite, microsyenite*, etc. **1961** J. CHALLINOR *Dict. Geol.* 127/1 *Microdiorite*, the medium-grained equivalent of a diorite, usually porphyritic (diorite porphyrite, or porphyrite). **1963** D. W. & E. E. HUMPHRIES tr. *Termier's Erosion & Sedimentation* iv. 94 (*caption*) The eroded surface of a microdiorite dike. **1965** G. J. WILLIAMS *Econ. Geol. N.Z.* x. 150/1 Positive nickel reactions are also produced by many of the less basic rocks from the 'mineral belt' such as the gabbros, leucogabbros and quartz microdiorites.

microdissect(ion), -distribution: see *MICRO- 2 a, 1 b.

microdot (məi·krodǫt), *sb.* [f. MICRO- (here merely emphasizing the smallness implied by *dot*) + DOT *sb.*[1]] **1.** A photograph, esp. of printed or written matter, reduced to about the size of a dot. Freq. *attrib.*

1946 J. E. HOOVER in *Reader's Digest* May 50/2 It was incredibly ingenious and effective, this micro-dot gadget. It perfectly counterfeited a typewritten or printed dot. The young Balkan agent, for example, had four telegraph blanks in his pocket, carrying Lilliputian spy orders that looked like periods; 11 micro-dots on the four papers. **1961** *Daily Mail* 8 Feb. 10/1 There was also a piece of glass with three microdots between the pieces of glass. These little dots are tiny pieces of film... By enlarging the dots again you can see what they contain. One microdot can contain a great deal of writing. **1964** M. GOWING *Britain & Atomic Energy* ix. 246 The communication of the message was in the best spy thriller traditions; it was by a microdot concealed in the hollow handle of a doorkey. **1965** I. FLEMING *Man with Golden Gun* viii. 108 The minor tools of espionage—codes, microdot developers, cyanide. **1968** *Listener* 1 Aug. 150/1 A house stacked with high-frequency transmitters, microdot readers.

2. A tiny capsule or tablet of LSD.

1971 *Oxford Times* 10 Dec. 1/5 Produced 2½ microdot tablets in foil which were later found to contain LSD. **1972** *Daily Colonist* (Victoria, B.C.) 5 Jan. 1/1 Called a microdot, the deceptively small, purple pill packs super-concentrated doses of the hallucinatory drug LSD. **1973** R. BUSBY *Pattern of Violence* v. 81 Gelatine micro-dots of the hallucinogenic drug LSD.

microdot (məi·krodǫt), *v.* [f. prec. sb.] *trans.* To make a microdot or microdots of. So **mi·crodotting** *vbl. sb.*

1957 *Time* 28 Oct. 22 Some messages were recorded on a film which could be softened and rolled into a ball; others were microdotted, i.e., whole pages of printing were reduced on film to pinhead size. **1961** *Daily Tel.* 22 Mar. 23/5 The wireless transmitter and equipment for microdotting at the house. **1963** J. JOESTEN *They call it Intelligence* I. vi. 61 Colonel Abel..did a brisk business in microdotting. **1969** D. LAMBERT *Angels in Snow* xix. 251 He decided to micro-dot the information and despatch it to Washington.

microearthquake, -ecology: see *MICRO- 1, 2 a.

mi:cro-econo·mics, *sb. pl.* (usu. const. as *sing.*). Also **microeconomics.** [f. MICRO- 2 a + ECONOMIC *sb.* 2 c.] That branch of the science of economics which deals with the individual (firm, product, consumer, etc.) rather than the aggregate.

1948 K. E. BOULDING *Economic Analysis* (rev. ed.) xiii. 259 There are two main branches of modern economic analysis, to which the names 'microeconomics' and 'macroeconomics' may conveniently be given. Microeconomics is the study of particular firms, particular households, individual prices, wages, incomes; individual industries, particular commodities. **1949** L. H. HANEY *Hist. Econ. Thought* (ed. 4) xxxvii. 734 The preceding chapters have mostly dealt with 'micro-economics'—economics concerned with the determination of *particular* prices or values. Now comes a chapter which deals with 'macro-economics', or national *aggregates* in the shape of total national income as affected by total spending or not-spending. **1960** A. CAIRNCROSS *Introd. Econ.* (ed. 3) ii. 23 When he is talking about the decisions made in an individual business the economist is in the realm of micro-economics. **1965** *McGraw-Hill Dict. Mod. Econ.* 324 Micro-economics deals with the division of total output among industries, products, and firms and the allocation of resources among competing uses. **1968** *Economist* 11 May 66/2 If the Government can provide the micro-economics that industry wants, then industry will willingly co-operate to help to provide the macro-economics that the Government needs. **1974** *Sci. Amer.* Jan. 27/2 A social decision, one not based entirely on microeconomics must be made on the value of the land to the society as a whole.

So **mi:cro-econo·mic** *a.*, **mi:cro-eco·nomist.** **1949** L. H. HANEY *Hist. Econ. Thought* (ed. 4) xxxiv. 692 The 'over' theories are mostly micro-economic. The 'under' theories all tend toward macro-economics, and are concerned with totals and averages, not margins. **1958** HENDERSON & QUANDT *Microecon. Theory* i. 3 Microeconomic theories are sufficiently flexible to permit many variations in their underlying assumptions. **1965** H. I. ANSOFF *Corporate Strategy* (1968) i. 16 The so-called microeconomic theory of the firm..sheds..little light on decision-making processes in a real-world firm. **1968** *Economist* 13 Jan. 46/1 Mr. Merton Peck..is mainly a 'micro-economist', interested in marketing questions and industrial problems. **1973** *Spectator* 3 Mar. 281/1 The most distinguished body of micro-economic thinkers, gathered together in one place, in the world. **1974** *Times Lit. Suppl.* 12 Apr. 398/1 Those conventional micro-economists who presume that their rather scholastic abstractions provide adequate criteria for decisions in nationalized industries.

microelectrode: see *MICRO- 1.

microelectronics (məi:kro,ĭlektrǫ·niks, -elektrǫ·niks), *sb. pl.* (usu. const. as *sing.*). Also **micro-electronics.** [f. MICRO- 2 a + *ELECTRONICS.] **a.** The branch of technology concerned with the design, manufacture, and use of microcircuits. **b.** Microelectronic devices or circuits.

1960 K. AMIS *New Maps of Hell* (1961) i. 19 Even if the problem of fitting all that machinery into a container on the human scale would require the development of a kind of micro-electronics that for the time being, one would imagine, is at a rudimentary stage [etc.]. **1967** *New Scientist* 11 May 342/2 Complete radio and TV sets have been built experimentally with 90 per cent microelectronics. *Ibid.* 342/3 There are..practical difficulties in packaging microelectronics in order to make the best use of their inherently high reliability. **1968** *Brit. Med. Bull.* XXIV. 192/2 Micro-electronics is having a profound effect on the application of computer power. **1970** *Daily Tel.* 8 May 21 Microelectronics, developed for American space and military hardware, is a way of miniaturising large circuits so that up to 100 transistors and associated components take up no more space than a pinhead. **1974** *Nature* 8 Feb. 338/2 Every week seems to bring a new idea for making use of ion implants in microelectronics.

So **mi:croelectro·nic** *a.* **1960** *Proc. Western Joint Computer Conf.* 251/1 Microelectronic data processing systems are analyzed. **1967**

New Scientist 11 May 342/1 Many ground and airborne radar systems, missiles and communications receivers for all three services are being developed in microelectronic form. **1973** *Sci. Amer.* Apr. 65/1 The size of microelectronic circuits has decreased to the point where their surface dimensions are measured in microns..and their thickness in angstroms.

micro-electrophoresis (etc.): see *MICRO- 6.

microelement (məi·kro,elĭmĕnt). [f. MICRO- + ELEMENT *sb.*] **1.** *Plant Physiol.* = *MICRONUTRIENT.

1936 *Chem. Abstr.* XXX. 1496 Yields of oats..were greatest with the doubled concn. of nutrients with a special addn. of microelements. **1950** CURTIS & CLARK *Introd. Plant Physiol.* xiii. 367 We prefer the terms trace or micro elements. **1966** F. M. IRVINE tr. *Lundegårdh's Plant Physiol.* vi. 251 Manganese takes up an intermediate position between a macro- and a microelement.

2. *Electronics.* A thin, flat, miniaturized circuit made with standardized length and width for assembly into a micromodule.

1959 *Proc. IRE* XLVII. 897 (*caption*) Micro-module, exploded view, before stacking and interconnecting. As many micro-elements as desired may be assembled to form the module... A 0·01-inch space is allowed between micro-elements. **1963** S. F. DANKO et al. in E. Keonjian *Microelectronics* iii. 142 The 0·016-in.-diameter riser wires are soldered to appropriate metallized notches in the stack of microelements.

microencapsulation (məi:kro,enkæpsiulēi·ʃən). [f. MICRO- 2 a + *ENCAPSULATION.] The process of enclosing substances in microcapsules. Hence **microenca·psulate** *v. trans.*, **-enca·psulated** *ppl. a.*, **-enca·psulating** *vbl. sb.*

1961 *New Scientist* 20 Apr. 115/2 Pre-packed flavour and aromas, contained in microscopic plastic capsules, might be added to beverages, cokes and the like—this is one of the applications envisaged for the techniques of 'microencapsulation' being developed in the United States. **1967** *Britannica Bk. of Year* (U.S.) 803/2 *Microencapsulate, vb.*, to enclose a small amount of a substance in a microcapsule (*microencapsulated* aspirin); *microencapsulation.* **1969** *New Scientist* 3 Apr. 18/1 These results led us to suggest the possibility of using microencapsulated enzymes for experimental enzyme replacement. **1970** BAKAN & ANDERSON in L. Lachman et al. *Theory & Pract. Industr. Pharmacy* xiii. 402/2 The process is capable of microencapsulating liquids and solids. *Ibid.*, By vertical stacking of the microencapsulating units, production rates of 50 pounds per hour have been achieved. **1970** *Daily Tel.* 2 Oct. 5/1 The different synthetic aromas are contained in small labels employing the technique of micro-encapsulation. **1971** *New Scientist* 15 July 122/3 The technique has the advantage over other attempts that are being made to microencapsulate enzymes for therapy that liposomes are constructed of 'natural' materials. **1971** *Reader's Digest* (U.S.) Oct. 206/1 (Advt.), Through a special microencapsulation process, hundreds and hundreds of tiny granules of pure aspirin are concentrated in each Bayer Timed-Release tablet.

microenvironment(al), -estimation, -event, -evolution(ary), -explosion, -explosive: see *MICRO- 1, 6, 1, 1 b, 1, 1.

microfauna (məi·krofǭnă). *Biol.* [f. MICRO- 1 + FAUNA.] A fauna made up of minute animals, or one found in a microhabitat.

1902 *Geogr. Jrnl.* X. 323 The average amount of Plankton (micro-fauna) contained in them [*sc.* mountain lakes] is only the tenth..part of that contained in the standing waters of..lowlands. **1910** H. F. OSBORN *Age of Mammals* iv. 254 Of the microfauna we first observe among the castroids that the genus *Chalicomys* replaces the *Steneofiber* of the Oligocene. **1924** *Bull. Amer. Assoc. Petroleum Geologists* VIII. 549 All of the evidence at hand is studied and weighed in the light of intensive study of the microfaunas of the Gulf Coast region. **1947** *Antiquity* XXI. 190 Both diggers and sieve-men became very skilful at descrying even the smallest specimen... The sieve-men would pick out tiny bones of microfauna with amazing verve. **1957** G. E. HUTCHINSON *Treat. Limnol.* I. xv. 817 This rise [*sc.* in soluble copper] may contribute to the disappearance of certain members of the microfauna and microflora from the lake. **1975** *Times* 27 May 14/7 The upper part of those river-borne sediments [at Hoxne] contains a rich microfauna of small mammals, fishes and amphibia.

Hence **microfau·nal** *a.*

1935 *Bull. Geol. Soc. Amer.* XLVI. 498 The microfaunal evidence in the Wheeler Canyon section is not quite conclusive. **1964** *Oceanogr. & Marine Biol.* II. 385 The species minimum at about 5‰ salinity..has also been found in more recent investigations on..various microfaunal groups. **1972** *Times* 11 Dec. 1/8 The microfaunal remains have shown that fishes, birds and crabs played almost as important a part in the diet of the population as that of cattle. **1973** *Nature* 7 Dec. 347/1 Experiments introducing modern lichens into the normal preparation of microfaunal samples using hydrogen peroxide failed to mineralise the plant structures.

microfibril(lar): see *MICRO- 1.

microfiche (məi·krofīʃ). Pl. **microfiche, -fiches.** [f. *MICRO- 7 + F. *fiche* slip of paper, index-card.] A flat piece of film, usually the size of a standard catalogue card, containing microphotographs of the pages of a book, periodical, etc. Also shortened to **fiche.**

1950 *Rev. Documentation* XVII. 216/1 Perhaps the French decision of reserving the word microcard for the opaque microcopy and using microfiche for the transparency may show us the way [to avoid confusion in terminology]. **1953** *Library Sci. Abstr.* 193 The translucent microfiche is considered by some people to be better than the opaque microcard. **1959** *Times* 2 Apr. 11/7 Research work..can be economically published on *microfiche*... The cost of a *fiche* is very low, about 2s. 6d., and many research reports would not need more than two or three *fiche* to cover them. **1967** J. R. U. PAGE in De Reuck & Knight *Communication in Sci.* 151 Master microfiche are made for NASA and the Space Documentation Service. **1969** *Daily Tel.* 19 Mar. 14/8 The fiches will allow universities and other institutions to have vast reference library resources in small spaces. **1970** *Library Assoc. Rec.* Mar. 97/1 The National Aeronautics and Space Administration..makes available microfiches of the documents. *Ibid.* 97/2 The bibliographic information, together with the document and microfiche copy, is sent to NASA. **1970** *Publishers' Weekly* 8 June 152/1 A typical microfiche has 72 printed pages in an area 4 by 6 inches. **1972** J. POYER *Chinese Agenda* (1973) xiv. 210 He tossed a slim creased manila envelope..to Gillon. It felt empty... 'Microfiche,' Liu explained. **1974** *Bookseller* 8 June 2600/2 Colour printing on microfiche is now being done.

microfilaria: see *MICRO- 1.

microfilm (məi·krofilm), *sb.* Also with hyphen. [f. *MICRO- 7 + FILM *sb.*] **1.** (A length of) photographic film containing microphotographs of the pages of a book, periodical, etc.

1935 *Library Jrnl.* LX. 145/1 The only way to find out how well the film, made by M. Dagron, has preserved its original qualities during its sixty-four years, was to consider it like one of our modern micro-films and try to print enlargements from it. **1936** *Science* 1 May 403/1 Bibliofilm Service copied upon 35 mm film material in the library [*sc.* U.S. Department of Agriculture library], substituting microfilm for loan of the books and journals. **1936** *Dialect Notes* VI. 528 Documents in microfilm form ..will cost approximately 1 cent a page. **1939** *Nature* 11 Mar. 392/2 The so-called micro-film..offers one means for the photographic reproduction of bulky reports. **1940** A. HUXLEY *Let.* 14 Oct. (1969) 461 All the big libraries make these micro-films now. **1948** *Times* 17 Feb. 7/4 A brochure describing the micro-film reproduction of *The Times* from its first issue in 1785 to the present day. **1957** *Listener* 24 Oct. 646/2, I should not be able to go to California or Russia. I should just have to go home and work with microfilms. **1961** L. MUMFORD *City in Hist.* xvii. 546 What is visible and real in this world is only what has been transferred to paper or has been even further etherialized on a microfilm or a tape recorder. **1972** *English Studies* LIII. 533 He reads Eckhart in Latin at the public library from microfilm.

2. Special Comb.: **microfilm reader**, a small projector used to produce a readable image from microfilm; **microfilm viewer** (see quot.).

1950 *Amer. Documentation* I. 139/2 (*caption*) Griscombe portable microfilm reader. **1962** A. GÜNTHER *Microphotogr. in Library* (Unesco) 8 A system whereby..positive microfilm strips copied from the negative master are kept near the microfilm reader offers the best advantages. **1936** *Science* 1 May 403/2 Microfilm viewer—a small monocular optical device for reading 35 mm microfilms a line at a time, suitable for inspecting film or for use while travelling.

microfilm (məi·krofilm), *v.* [f. the sb.] *trans.* To record on microfilm. Hence **mi·crofilming** *vbl. sb.*

1940 *N. & Q.* 12 Oct. 253/2 Steps are being taken to have parish registers microfilmed... Micro-filming is a very cheap as well as speedy process. **1955** *Times* 28 July 9/4 It is intended to continue the microfilming..as and when funds permit. **1955** H. VAN THAL *Fanfare for E. Newman* v. 63 The Germans, who have always held Bizet in high respect,..micro-filmed the manuscript. **1972** M. J. BOSSE *Incident at Naha* ii. 76 Any microfilming service would do the job at ten cents a page. **1973** F. DE FELITTA *Oktoberfest* (1974) xiv. 164 There are a number of sources of wartime documentation which Yad Vashem has not yet microfilmed.

microfilter: see *MICRO- 6.

microflora (məi·kroflōᵊră). *Biol.* [f. MICRO- 1 + FLORA.] A flora made up of minute plants, or one found in a microhabitat.

[**1905** *Ann. Rep. Board of Regents Smithsonian Inst. 1904* 351 Has any competent hand celebrated the mikroflora of the highest ridges, those tiny, vivid forget-me-nots and gentians.] **1932** FULLER & CONARD tr. *Braun-Blanquet's Plant Sociol.* viii. 235 The microflora of the soil..is composed of countless bacteria, fungi, and algae. **1969** *New Yorker* 12 Apr. 85/1 The exobiologists have insisted that..the astronauts' microflora—bacteria and other organisms—have all been typed and catalogued. **1974** *Nature* 8 Feb. 361/2 This previously unknown microflora of blue-green and green or red algal affinities is from ..the Bungle Bungle dolomite which outcrops in the Osmond Range of Western Australia.

microform (məi·krofǭɹm). [f. *MICRO- 7 + FORM *sb.*] Microphotographic form; a microphotographic reproduction on film or paper of a manuscript, book, etc., requiring magnification to produce a readable image.

1960 *N. & Q.* Jan. 2/1 The genealogical and heraldic material listed as being already in 'microform' includes the Huddersfield Parish Registers, 1606–1812. **1962** A. GÜNTHER *Microphotogr. in Library* (Unesco) 14 The first supplementary note [to a catalogue entry] should indicate the microform. **1969** *R. & E. Coordinator* (Res. & Engin. Council Graphic Arts Industry) Apr. 4/2 Libraries make microform reproductions of everything from rare books to technical publications. **1971** *Amer. N. & Q.* X. 11/2 A selection of the major works from this catalogue is being offered in microform by the Erasmus Press. **1974** *Reprographics Q.* VII. 85/1 The cost/benefit of issuing parts lists and maintenance manuals on microforms.

microfossil, -fracture, -fracturing: see *MICRO- 1.

microgametophyte (məikrogǣmī·tofəit). *Bot.* [f. MICRO- + *gametophyte* (s.v. GAMETE).] A gametophyte that develops from a microspore; a male gametophyte.

1907 *Amer. Naturalist* XLI. 360 In our material of Agathis the protoplasm is unfortunately very much shrunken..but this fortunately does not interfere with the understanding of the general conditions present in the microgametophyte. **1938** G. M. SMITH *Cryptogamic Bot.* II. v. 132 Microgametophytes of other genera also have but one vegetative cell. **1959** FOSTER & GIFFORD *Compar. Morphol. Vascular Plants* viii. 161 Early stages in formation of the microgametophytes [in *Selaginella*] begin while the microspores are still within the microsporangium.

microgasometer, -metric (etc.): see *MICRO- 6.

microgenic (məikrodʒe·nik), *a.* Chiefly *Journalists' colloq.* [f. MICRO(PHONE + *-GENIC b.] Of a voice: that sounds well when transmitted by microphone; well suited to broadcasting.

1931 S. GOLDWYN in *Sat. Rev.* 14 Feb. 220/1 An actor may be 'photogenic'..but that is not enough. He must also be 'microgenic', that is to say, he must have a voice that is suitable to the microphone. **1944** *Evening Standard* 5 Dec. 6/4 It seems strange that words like flak..should escape censure by the austere..while such bitter eloquence is directed against..microgenic (good for broadcasting).

microglia (məikro-, mikroglǝi·ă). *Anat.* [f. MICRO- 1 + NEURO)GLIA.] Neuroglial cells derived from mesoderm and functioning as macrophages (scavengers) in and about the central nervous system (now regarded as components of the reticulo-endothelial system); a tissue composed of such cells. Usu. const. as *pl.* So **microgli·al** *a.*

1924 *Jrnl. Nervous & Mental Dis.* LIX. 346 In 1918 del Rio-Hortega succeeded..in impregnating clearly and specifically a homogeneous group of cells... These cells he called microglia. **1929** *Amer. Jrnl. Path.* V. 452 The microglial reaction around a sterile puncture wound of the cerebrum. **1932** *Times Lit. Suppl.* 10 Nov. 843/3 The rod-cells..are in fact generally held to be a variety of microglia. **1962** *Gray's Anat.* (ed. 33) 56 The astrocytes and oligodendroglia are ectodermal in origin..whilst the microglia is of mesodermal origin. **1966** W. ANDREW *Microfabric of Man* x. 147 (*caption*) Microglia in gray matter of spinal cord. Cell bodies of these cells are often angular or elongated. *Ibid.* 148/1 The microglia..are capable of remarkable transformations. **1973** PALAY & CHAN-PALAY *Cerebellar Cortex* vi. 178/2 Often microglia laden with such inclusions can be found to have wandered even into the molecular layer. *Ibid.*, The processes of a microglial cell can even invade the confines of the myelin sheath.

microglossary: see *MICRO- 1 b.

micrograph. Add: **3.** An enlarged image of an object (as seen through a microscope) obtained either by hand drawing or (now more usu.) photographically.

1904 *Electrochem. Ind.* Mar. 88/2 This embodies..the determination of oxygen content, the preparation of micrographs, and..the planimetric measurements of enlarged micrographs, with calculation of the percentage of oxygen. **1916** *Trans. Amer. Inst. Mining & Metall. Engin.* LI. 832 A microscopic examination was made of the threaded end of each of the 108 tensile bars. The micrographs shown at the end of this report reproduce the average structure of the top and bottom tensile bars. *Ibid.* 833 All micrographs are magnified 100 diameters. **1941** R. M. ALLEN *Photomicrogr.* i. 1 The word *micrograph* used alone has had to be broadened in meaning to include pictures of minute objects either drawn by hand or produced through photographic processes. **1953** *Jrnl. Appl. Physics* XXIV. 616/1 The simplest method of obtaining x-ray micrographs is to place the specimen in contact with a photographic film of the maximum resolution type and expose it to the radiation from a normal x-ray tube. All the enlargement is obtained photographically. **1960** D. F. LAWSON *Technique Photomicrogr.* ii. 4 Drawings made from images projected from a microscope are referred to as micrographs. **1968** H. HARRIS *Nucleus & Cytoplasm* iii. 59 Some electron micrographs of isolated 'polysomes' also appeared to show the ribosomes connected by some form of strand.

micrographically (məikrogræ·fikăli), *adv.* [f. MICROGRAPHIC *a.* + -AL + -LY[2].] By means of micrography or micrographs.

1898 *Jrnl. Iron & Steel Inst.* LIV. 191 The presence of thin decarbonised outer layers..may be frequently recognized micrographically. **1908** *Analyst* XXXIII. 289 All further changes (hardening) which take place inside the B constituents cannot be followed micrographically, because B appears to be a uniform substance by reflected light.

1971 (*title*) The compact edition of the Oxford English Dictionary: complete text reproduced micrographically. **1974** *Nature* 30 Aug. 702/2 Grain growth [in metals] has been studied micrographically for many years.

micrography. Add: **1. b.** The technique of producing micrographs (sense *3), or of studying objects by means of micrographs.

1908 *Analyst* XXXIII. 289 (*heading*) The micrography of cement. **1953** *Jrnl. Appl. Physics* XXIV. 623/1 The experiments so far made support the theoretical indications that x-ray shadow micrography is a practicable technique at least up to the resolution of the optical microscope. **1973** *Jrnl. Bacteriol.* CXIV. 413 (*heading*) Electron micrography of bud formation in *Metschinkowia krissii*.

micrograver, -gravimetric: see *MICRO- 1, 6.

microgroove (məi·krogrūv). [f. MICRO- 1 + GROOVE *sb.*] A very narrow groove on a gramophone record; a record having such grooves. Freq. *attrib.*

1948 *Amer. Speech* XXIII. 252 CBS announces a new-type record—microgroove. **1948** *Electronic Engin.* XX. 333/3 The groove size, from which the name 'Microgroove' has been derived, is only 0·0027 in. to 0·003 in. **1949** *Wireless World* Apr. 146/1 What is a 'microgroove' record? It is a name given to the 7-, 10- or 12-in pressings in high-grade vinylite, with a rotational speed of 33⅓ r.p.m... As it was found necessary to reduce the groove width to about one-third the size of normal record grooves, the name 'Microgroove' was coined originally by Columbia Records, Inc., for their 33⅓ r.p.m. records, but it would now appear to be used in America as a generic term for all such fine-pitch records. **1951** SACKVILLE-WEST & SHAWE-TAYLOR *Record Guide* 715 They increased the playing time of each side by..a much narrower groove-cut known as 'microgroove'. *Ibid.* 717 Even a 7-inch 33⅓ microgroove would apparently be too long—or too expensive—to meet this case. **1957** *Times* 13 Dec. 18/2 The 78 r.p.m. record began to lose favour. On the other hand, the demand for microgroove records continued strongly and sales of both 45 r.p.m. and 33⅓ r.p.m. records increased. **1958** *Times* 13 Sept. 9/1 This old Weingartner set has now reappeared..skilfully transferred to LP microgroove by Pathé-Marconi's engineers. **1972** *Jazz & Blues* Nov. 35/2 Some microgroove reissues contain edited versions of these titles.

microgyria, -habitat: see *MICRO- 3, 1.

microhardness (məikrohā·ɹdnės). [f. *MICRO- 1 b + HARDNESS.] The hardness of a very small area of a sample, as measured by an indenter.

1921 *Trans. Amer. Soc. Mech. Engin.* XLII. 1109 If we let κ be the microhardness. **1934** *Amer. Mineralogist* XIX. 163 We have undertaken to obtain microhardness values for each of the nine minerals from talc to corundum. **1954** A. R. BAILEY *Text-bk. Metall.* xiii. 457 Micro-hardness testers make it possible to obtain comparative hardness figures for the different constituents of alloys,..and may aid in the identification of constituents and inclusions. **1966** D. G. BRANDON *Mod. Techniques Metallogr.* i. 5 In soft materials it is almost impossible to eliminate surface deformation by repeated mechanical polishing and etching... A detectable increase in microhardness can be observed up to 5 μm below the polished surface.

microhenry, -inch, -incineration, -injection, -instability: see *MICRO- 5 a, 5 a, 6, 2 a, 1.

microinstruction (məi·kroˌinstrɒkʃən). *Computers.* [f. MICRO- 1 + INSTRUCTION.] One of a sequence of instructions produced by a computer in response to some more comprehensive instruction; *spec.* one that corresponds to one of the smallest, most elementary operations that can occur in the computer and is produced in accordance with a microprogram.

1959 E. M. GRABBE et al. *Handbk. Automation, Computation, & Control* II. ii. 254 Many macroinstructions can be constructed from properly sequenced microinstructions. **1964** T. W. MCRAE *Impact of Computers on Accounting* i. 24 This problem has been solved by programmers devising ..autocodes so that a single macroinstruction written down by the programmer generates the required set of microinstructions during translation by the computer from the autocode to the absolute machine code. **1969** P. B. JORDAIN *Condensed Computer Encycl.* 318 Each microinstruction is coded as several bits, one bit for each functional unit or data path in the computer hardware. The one-for-one correspondence between bit positions and functional units allows for very simple interpretation of each microinstruction.

micro-Kjeldahl, -lens: see *MICRO- 6, 1.

Micro-lepidoptera, *sb. pl.* (Later example.) Also **microlepidopterous** *a.* (examples).

1860 *Rep. Brit. Assoc. Adv. Sci.* II. 122 (*heading*) On some peculiar forms amongst the Micro-Lepidopterous larvæ. **1972** L. E. CHADWICK tr. *Linsenmaier's Insects of World* 226/1 A number of families have been included under the collective concept of the Microlepidoptera, but today the tendency is to consider them as separate groups. *Ibid.* 226/2 The microlepidopterous families are not isolated in their phylogeny.

microlinguistics (məikroliŋgwi·stiks), *sb. pl.* (const. as *sing.*). [f. MICRO- 2 a + LINGUISTIC *sb.* b.] (See quots. 1949, 1972.) So **microlingui·stic** *a.*

1949 G. L. TRAGER in *Studies in Ling.: Occasional Papers* I. 2 The whole of the field concerned with language..we shall call Macrolinguistics. The three subdivisions we shall call Prelinguistics, Microlinguistics, Metalinguistics. *Ibid.* 4 Microlinguistics..deals with the analysis of language systems. **1953** *Internat. Jrnl. Amer. Ling.* XIX. ii. Suppl. 28 Smith presented the conceptual scheme developed at the Foreign Service Institute which divides linguistics into three main compartments:.. 'microlinguistics' deals with the analysis of linguistic systems. *Ibid.* 29 He gave an example of the sort of methodological error which Smith's separation of microlinguistic and metalinguistic levels would avoid. **1955** S. & M. T. CHASE *Power of Words* x. 101 Microlinguistics.. takes a long time to reach a unit as large as the sentence. **1963** *Amer. Speech* XXXVIII. 138 Since distinctive articulatory features form part of a system of contrastive correlations, any analysis based on this structure is micro-, not extralinguistic. **1967** D. STEIBLE *Conc. Handbk. Ling.* 78 *Microlinguistic meaning.* The term refers to the identity or difference in meaning which results when a part of a larger structure is replaced by a different part. **1972** HARTMANN & STORK *Dict. Lang. & Ling.* 141/2 *Microlinguistics*, those aspects of linguistic studies which are concerned with the direct analysis of linguistic material, e.g. phonology, grammar, lexicology.

microlite. 2. Add: Cf. CRYSTALLITE 2 in Dict. and Suppl. (Further examples.)

1926 [see *CRYSTALLITE 2]. **1954** H. WILLIAMS et al. *Petrogr.* ii. 13 Extremely minute incipient crystals..are called microlites, provided they are birefringent; if they are even smaller, spherical, rod- and hair-like isotropic forms, they are called crystallites.

microlith. Add: **2.** *Archæol.* A small stone tool with a sharpened edge used with a haft, characteristic of Mesolithic cultures.

1908 H. G. O. KENDALL in *Man* VIII. 103 Palæolithic Microliths... By microliths I mean tiny flakes or other pieces of flint which have been trimmed or used by man at some part of the edge. **1927** PEAKE & FLEURE *Hunters & Artists* vii. 96 This [Capso-Tardenoisian] industry is characterized by the presence of very small flints of geometric shapes, chiefly of trapezoid, rhomboid, and triangular forms; these are commonly known as microliths. **1932** J. G. D. CLARK *Mesolithic Age in Brit.* p. xx, By a 'microlith' we understand a narrow flake blunted on one or both edges by steep secondary chipping, but devoid of secondary work on either face. **1960** *New Scientist* 11 Aug. 418/3 Finds included 52 microliths (tiny points which must have been hafted as arrow-heads and other weapons). **1971** *World Archaeol.* III. 157 Often termed 'microliths' by Old World archaeologists, these tools fall into three formal categories.

microlithic, *a.*[2] Add: **b.** *Archæol.* Of or pertaining to microliths (*MICROLITH 2); characterized by the use of microliths.

1923 A. L. KROEBER *Anthropol.* xiv. 407 Terminal Capsian..was a local phase..with the microlithic flint industry especially conspicuous... In Africa..the development of the extreme microlithic forms..has been most clearly traced. **1937** GARROD & BATE *Stone Age Mt. Carmel* I. I. viii. 114 We there found a layer containing an abundant microlithic industry, without pottery, superimposed on an eroded breccia with flints of Levalloiso-Mousterian type. **1947** J. & C. HAWKES *Prehist. Brit.* (rev. ed.) 19 The reduction of the size of flints to a 'microlithic' scale. **1971** *World Archaeol.* III. 157 Numbers of fragmentary flakes with backed (or 'microlithic') retouch occur in many levels of the site.

micrologic: see *MICRO- 1.

micrologist. (Later example.)

1960 [see *MICRURGY].

micrology. 2. (Examples.)

1906 M. F. GUYER (*title*) Animal micrology. **1907** *Nature* 18 Apr. 582/1 The term 'micrology' has not received any general acceptance on this side of the Atlantic. **1914** (*title*) Journal of micrology.

micromachining: see *MICRO- 2 a.

micromanipulation (məi:kromănipiulēi·ʃən). [f. MICRO- 2 a + MANIPULATION.] The performance of extremely delicate operations (such as the isolation of a single yeast cell from a culture) under the microscope, usu. with the aid of a micromanipulator; an operation so performed.

1921 *Science* 28 Oct. 411/2 (*heading*) A simple apparatus for micro-manipulation under the highest magnifications of the microscope. **1931** *Chem. Abstr.* XXV. 1409 (*heading*) Micromanipulations on latex in dark fields. **1949** *New Biol.* VII. 72 Although the chromosomes of most cells are very small objects,..in a few favourable cases it has been possible to study their physical properties by micromanipulation. **1971** *Nature* 2 July 33/1 The micromanipulation of chromosomes of living human cells *in vitro* is a potential means of obtaining transplantable genetic material.

So **mi:cromani·pulator,** an instrument which is used in conjunction with an optical microscope to perform micromanipulations and which allows a microneedle, micropipette, etc., to be moved with great control through the field of view.

1921 *Science* 28 Oct. 413/1 There are two models of the micro-manipulator, a simple and a more elaborate form. **1949** A. G. SANDERS in H. W. Florey et al. *Antibiotics* II. xvi. 678 Spores from a conidium can be picked off singly with the point of a needle. Some people can do this with the needle held in the hand, others prefer to use a micromanipulator. **1968** *Sci. Jrnl.* Nov. 18 (*caption*) Integrated circuit chip is shown above being placed in its case with aid of a micromanipulator. **1972** *Nature* 4 Feb. 263 Zeiss micromanipulators were used to position micropipettes.

micromanometer (etc.), **micromastia, -mazia:** see *MICRO- 6, 3, 3.

micromesh (məi·kromeʃ). [f. *MICRO- 1 + MESH *sb.*] Material (esp. nylon) consisting of a very fine mesh. Freq. *attrib.*

1959 *Manch. Guardian* 27 July 4/4 Plaza..have..a cheap..micromesh. **1960** *Harper's Bazaar* Apr. 98 Seam-free in sheer micro-mesh. **1962** *Which?* Apr. 113/2 Two of the leading brands of seamless micromesh stockings. **1963** R. R. A. HIGHAM *Handbk. Papermaking* i. 6 Empty the contents on to a micro-mesh wire circle and carefully wash with distilled water. **1974** *Times* 26 Apr. 7/7 Initially only in micromesh, the tights..are in three sizes.

micrometallurgy, -metazoan, -metazoon: see *MICRO- 2 a, 1, 1.

micrometeor (məikromī·tĭˌǫ̈r). [f. MICRO- 1 + METEOR.] = *MICROMETEOROID.

1957 *Seattle Times* 10 Nov. 16/5 Density of micrometeors and meteoric dust, and the like. **1973** *Times* 16 May 1/1 The micrometeor shield was designed to protect the outer skin of the space station from minor damage but also played an important role in controlling Skylab's temperature.

Hence **micrometeo·ric** *a.*

1958 *Times* 30 Aug. 6/1 It also carried recording instruments to register impacts of micro-meteoric particles.

micrometeorite (məikromī·tĭˌǫ̈rəit). [f. MICRO- 1 + METEORITE.] A micrometeoroid; *spec.* one that has entered the earth's atmosphere (cf. the distinction between METEORITE and METEOROID *sb.*).

1949 F. L. WHIPPLE in *Science* 28 Oct. 438/1 The term *micrometeorite* is here defined as an extraterrestrial body that is sufficiently small to enter the earth's atmosphere without being damaged by encounter with the atmosphere. **1956** *Spaceflight* I. 27/1 The density of meteorites and micro-meteorites (interstellar dust) in space will also be of interest to the designers of manned research vehicles. **1967** *Technology Week* 23 Jan. 47/1 Unlike a terrestrial observatory, it will have to have airtight quarters, well-protected against radical temperature change, hard radiation and micrometeorite bombardment. **1971** I. G. GASS et al. *Understanding Earth* viii. 115/1 Many granules are so small that they do not offer sufficient air resistance to become incandescent; they sink to the ground as micrometeorites. **1973** *McGraw-Hill Yearbk. Sci. & Technol.* 277/2 Bodies less than about 0·1 mm can also be expected to survive, since their size permits them to radiate the tremendous heat energy due to friction with the atmosphere before it can cause vaporization. These smaller bodies are usually called micrometeorites, or while still in space, micrometeoroids.

Hence **mi:crometeori·tic** *a.*

1960 H. E. NEWELL in J. A. Ratcliffe *Physics Upper Atmosphere* iii. 123 Micrometeoritic material may account for a small portion of the *E*-region ionization. **1974** *Nature* 20/27 Dec. 669/2 Micrometeoritic craters.

micrometeoroid (məikromī·tĭˌǫ̈roid). [f. MICRO- 1 + METEOROID *sb.*] A solid particle in space, or of extraterrestrial origin, which is small enough to survive entry into the earth's atmosphere. Cf. prec.

1954 *Mineral. Abstr.* XII. 242 There may be 'micrometeorites' (? micrometeoroids..) too small to suffer ablation and falling as cosmic dust. **1961** *Daily Tel.* 26 Aug. 1/4 Another earth satellite, Explorer 13, was put into orbit to-day. It will measure dust-like particles in space known as micrometeoroids. **1968** *Awake!* 22 Sept. 30/2 The suit will be made to protect the astronaut..from tiny particles known as micrometeoroids. **1973** [see prec.]. **1974** *Nature* 6 Sept. 17/1 It sent back more than 300 pictures of Jupiter, as well as measurements of magnetic fields, energetic particles,..and micrometeoroids.

Hence **mi:crometeoroi·dal** *a.*

1972 *Science* 2 June 979/2 The scale of hypervelocity impact craters on the moon extends down to submillimeter and submicron micrometeoroidal pits on rock surfaces.

micrometeorology (məi:kromīˈtĭˌǫ̈rǫ·lǒdʒi). [f. MICRO- 2 a + METEOROLOGY.] The study of the meteorological characteristics of a small area; the study of small-scale meteorological phenomena.

1930 *Flight* 18 Apr. 442 The progress of European meteorology in the past fifteen years..is due to the introduction of micrometeorology, or detailed observations from an ever-increasing number of weather stations. **1953** O. G. SUTTON (*title*) Micrometeorology: a study of physical processes in the lowest layers of the earth's atmosphere. **1968** *New Scientist* 5 Dec. 565/1 By incorporating fluctuations of temperature and humidity, one can arrive at similar expressions for the transport of heat and water vapour. The determination of these three vertical transports is one of the central problems in micrometeorology. **1974** *Physics Bull.* Feb. 66/2 The heat balance of plants and animals and the micrometeorology of crops.

Hence **mi:crometeorolo·gical** *a.*, **-meteoro·logist.**

1942 *Univ. Chicago Inst. Meteorol. Misc. Rep.* No. 3. 1 The study of the exact nature of these more or less localized thunderstorms suggests the use of a micrometeorological network of stations. Such a network exists over the Muskingum Watershed in..Ohio where the United States Soil Conservation Service..has maintained a dense observational network. The stations are no more than 8 miles apart. **1953** O. G. SUTTON *Micrometeorol.* p. vii, I have attempted to meet the needs of meteorologists.. who require detailed information about physical processes in the regions of the atmosphere where life is most abundant. It is my hope that such an account will help to increase the number of micrometeorologists. **1960** *Times* 30 Aug. 2/2 The work will involve physical and micrometeorological problems of measurement. **1968** *New Scientist* 5 Dec. 564/2 While the micrometeorologist's most productive tools are certain statistical concepts of fluid mechanics and aerodynamics, much experimental work needs to be done before these concepts can be applied to the atmosphere.

micrometer, var. *MICROMETRE.

micromethod: see *MICRO- 6.

micrometre (məi·kromītəɹ). Also (*U.S.*) **-meter.** [f. MICRO- 5 a + METRE *sb.*²] A millionth of a metre: = MICRON, MIKRON (in Dict. and Suppl.).

The word has only recently become common (cf. quot. 1968), and now forms part of the International System of Units.

1880 *Jrnl. R. Microsc. Soc.* III. 327 The same reasoning ..leads us, however, to recommend the adoption of 'micrometre' instead of 'micromillimetre', which would secure the uniformity desired, besides being a more convenient word. **1966** KAYE & LABY *Tables Physical & Chem. Constants* (ed. 13) 2, μ is widely employed as an abbreviation of μm (10^{-6} m or micrometre) and is then called micron. **1968** *Nature* 16 Nov. 651/2 By resolution No. 7 the conference [*sc.* the thirteenth General Conference of Weights and Measures] decided to proscribe further use of the name 'micron', with the symbol μ attributed to this name, for the millionth part of the metre. The symbol μ is now the recognized prefix for the decimal sub-multiple 10^{-6} and the appropriate name for the millionth part of the metre is 'micrometre', with symbol μm. **1971** I. G. GASS et al. *Understanding Earth* xiv. 336/1 (*caption*) The amplitude..used for determining the magnitude is half the displacement between the two arrows—in this case 5 micrometres. **1973** *Physics Bull.* Nov. 662/3 They contain solid particles..with dimensions of about a tenth of a micrometre, a mass of 10^{-15} g each. **1974** *Sci. Amer.* July 45 (Advt.), Neutron radiography can resolve a few micrometers.

micromho, -microcurie, -microfarad, -mini: see *MICRO- 5 a, 5 a, 5 a, 1 c.

microminiature (məikromi·nitiŭɹ, -mi·niătiŭɹ), *a.* [f. *MICRO- 1 b + MINIATURE *a.*] Much reduced in size, as a result of microminiaturization; even smaller than a size regarded as miniature.

1958 *Electr. Manufacturing* Aug. 94/1 Intensive efforts at the Diamond Ordnance Fuze Laboratories..in the field of microminiature packaging have recently resulted in extremely small and compact assemblies. **1963** *Listener* 16 May 832/3 Microminiature integrator, for rocket guidance system. The integrator..is 100 times smaller than the conventionally built equipment it replaces. **1967** *Electronics* 6 Mar. 37 (Advt.), These microminiature relays are direct descendants of our military, aero/space designs. **1971** J. H. SMITH *Digital Logic* i. 5 Thin film circuits are often associated with microminiature components.

mi:crominiaturiza·tion. Also with hyphen. [f. *MICRO- 1 b + *MINIATURIZATION.] Extreme miniaturization; *spec.* the development or use of techniques for making electronic components and devices of greatly reduced size (smaller than those produced by 'miniaturization').

1955 *Proc. IRE* XLIII. 1897/2 The most attractive features [of opto-electronic devices] seem to be the possible microminiaturization (which, in the present state of the art, is the ultimate in miniaturization) resulting in small weight and extremely low power consumption, [etc.]. **1959** *Listener* 28 May 930/2 The most startling recent development [in transistors] is the technology of what is called micro-miniaturization. **1963** *Daily Tel.* 22 May 21 A stage of 'micro-miniaturisation' has been reached which makes many of the marvel-working components almost invisible. **1965** *Times Rev. Industry* Winter 12/1 Microminiaturization is now accepted as starting at a packing density exceeding 50 parts per cubic inch. **1971** *Nature* 10 Dec. 315/3 The new on-board computer and guidance system makes great use of micro-miniaturization. **1973** *Sci. Amer.* Dec. 24/2 Its nervous system is a miracle of microminiaturization, and some of its independently evolved behavior patterns are not unlike our own.

So **micromi·niaturize** *v. trans.*, to produce in a very much smaller version; **micromi·niaturized** *ppl. a.*

1959 J. E. SENSI in Horsey & Shergalis *Proc. Symposium Microminiaturization of Electronic Assemblies* I. v. 54 To realize fully the military and civilian potential of microminiaturized devices, optimum means of producing these devices in large quantities are necessary. **1959** *Electronics* 11 Dec. 51/2 Much of the knowledge gained in designing electronic circuits can be used directly, with only minor changes, in microminiaturizing circuits. **1963** *Listener* 16 May 832/3 Already..the sort of computer that only yesterday took up a whole room can be 'microminiaturized' so that it will go into a small suitcase. **1967** *N.Y. Times* 20 May 49 The transistorized lock..could be microminiaturized and adapted to any number of combinations. **1972** *Lebende Sprachen* XVII. 133/1 Plessey has evolved a small microminiaturized computer.

micromodule: see *MICRO- 1.

micromotion (məi·kromōᵘʃən). Also with hyphen. [f. MICRO- 1 + MOTION *sb.*] A small bodily movement made during the performance of some task, esp. when recorded cinematographically for purposes of work study. Usu. *attrib.*, esp. designating this method of work study.

1913 F. A. TALBOT *Pract. Cinematogr.* xiv. 174 (*heading*) Micro-motion study: How increased workshop efficiency is obtainable with moving pictures. **1913** *Technical World* XIX. 189/1 'This micro-motion study furnishes a means for the transference of skill from man to machine,' the general manager further stated. **1947** J. J. GILLESPIE *Dynamic Motion & Time Study* 3 Motion study..with its motion cameras, therbligs, micromotion clocks..has become a complex, unwieldy technique. **1948** *Sci. News* VII. 107 For the so-called 'micro-motion study' of repetition movements a cine-record is not necessary. Instead, small lamps can be attached to the moving parts of the operator's body, their light being recorded over one cycle of the operation by working in a dimly lit room while the camera shutter is left open. **1961** [see *MEMOMOTION].

micromutation: see *MICRO- 1.

micron, mikron. Add: The spelling *mikron* was never common and is now *Obs.* (Earlier and later examples.)

In the International System of Units the word has been replaced by *MICROMETRE.

[**1880** *Procès-Verbaux des Séances du Comité Internat. des Poids et Mesures 1879* 41 Le Comité international des Poids et Mesures adopte, pour ses publications et son usage officiel, le système suivant des signes abréviatifs pour les poids et mesures métriques... (*table*) Mesures de longueur... Micron... μ.] **1885** *Jrnl. R. Microsc. Soc.* V. 140 Proposal..(2) to use *micron* in place of *micromillimetre.* **1966** *Electronics* 14 Nov. 25 The detector..is believed to be the first photovoltaic detector of infrared radiation in the 8- to 14-micron range. **1968** [see *MICROMETRE].

microneedle: see *MICRO- 6.

Micronesian, *a.* and *sb.* Add: Also (*rare*) **Mikronesian.** (Earlier and later examples.)

1847 J. C. PRICHARD *Res. Physical Hist. Mankind* (ed. 3) V. 157 A certain difference has been noted between the Micronesians and the Polynesians in general. *Ibid.*, Micronesia, or the Micronesian Archipelago. **1877** *Jrnl. Anthrop. Inst.* VI. 392 The language of Yap..is the only Micronesian language in which the numerals are formed in the manner in question. **1884** W. TURNER *Rep. Crania* in *Rep. Sci. Results Voy. H.M.S. Challenger* X. 82 The islands of the Mikronesian group. **1890** D. G. BRINTON *Races & Peoples* 235 Some ethnographers would make the Polynesians and Micronesians a different race from the Malays. **1945** *Language* XXI. 214 In the vocabularies of the Micronesian languages..evidence of earlier use of English has remained in the form of loan-words. **1974** *Times* 21 Jan. 12/6 Some Micronesian families connected by marriage with Japanese see themselves in a strong compradore position. *Ibid.* 12/8 The High Commissioner.. expects that a Micronesian will succeed him.

micronize (məi·krŏnəiz), *v.* [f. MICRON + -IZE, or perh. a back-formation from *Micronizer* (proprietary name in U.S.).] *trans.* To break up into very fine particles. So **mi·cronized** *ppl. a.*, **mi·cronizing** *vbl. sb.* Also **microniza·tion.**

1940 *Jrnl. Econ. Ent.* XXXIII. 481/1 Good kill obtained with micronized cubé indicates that fine grinding may increase the toxicity. **1941** *Ibid.* XXXIV. 560/2 Micronization (fine grinding) of derris and cubé[4] increased kill over that obtained by the regular product. [*Note*] [4]Prepared by the Micronizing Processing Co., Moorstown N.J. **1952** M. E. FLOREY *Chem. Applic. Antibiotics* I. iii. 111 A ball mill for the production of a very finely divided ('micronized') mixture of potassium penicillin and glucose. **1958** *Vogue* July 5 This creamy-smooth makeup contains micronised powder, 2½ times finer than ordinary face powder. **1968** W. A. GRAY *Packing of Solid Particles* vii. 105 If, however, the particles are reduced in size to a few microns (micronized) and suitable pressure is applied, then a strong compact can be formed. **1968** *Materials & Technol.* I. viii. 263 Micronizing is used not only on sulphur but also for insecticides, fungicides, pharmaceutical preparations, grinding and polishing powders, iron oxide, etc. **1972** *Jrnl. Econ. Entomol.* LXV. 1446/1 Colorimetric analysis indicated that some decomposition took place during preparation and micronization of the dust.

micronutrient (məi:kroniū·triĕnt). *Biol.* [f. MICRO- + NUTRIENT *sb.*] Any of the chemical elements which are required by plants (or, less commonly, animals) in trace amounts for normal growth and development.

1943 *Ann. Rev. Biochem.* XII. 525 List of essential micronutrients.—The essentiality of boron, manganese, and zinc for higher plants is no longer open to dispute. **1953** J. RAMSBOTTOM *Mushrooms & Toadstools* viii. 80 Manganese, zinc, boron, copper, molybdenum, have been proved definitely to be micro-nutrients for certain fungi. **1970** [see *MACRONUTRIENT]. **1974** *Nature* 8 Feb. 392/1 Since 1957, selenium has been recognized as an essential micronutrient for animals.

micro-opaque (məikro,opē·k). [f. *MICRO- 7 + OPAQUE *a.* (*sb.*).] A type of microform produced on card or paper instead of film. Also *attrib.* or as *adj.*

1952 *Aslib Proc.* IV. 154 Micro-opaques have made far greater psychological appeal to the user than microfilm. **1956** *Amer. Documentation* VII. 169/1 Writers in several countries have concerned themselves with the general theme of micro-opaques. **1962** A. GÜNTHER *Microphotogr. in Library* (Unesco) 7 Micro-opaque cards have another advantage in that they do not need a protective envelope and may be readily filed. **1963** *Amer. N. & Q.* June 155/1 Original public records are being published in a micro-opaque series of 3 × 5-inch cards issued by the Public Record Office of Great Britain.

micro-operation: see *MICRO- 1, 2 a.

micro-operative, -order: see *MICRO- 2 a, 1.

micro-oven (məi·kro,ɒv'n). [f. *MICRO(WAVE + OVEN *sb.*] A microwave oven. Hence **micro-o·vening** *vbl. sb.*, cooking in such an oven.

1962 *Punch* 21 Nov. 738/2 A cooked meal that is quick-frozen and then re-heated in a matter of seconds in a micro-oven. **1965** *Economist* 22 May 941/3 Two micro-ovens could do the same work in half the time, using less space. **1971** *Daily Tel.* 26 July 15/2 Thus their formula for the Big Chance: clean up some traditional greasy cafes, manufacture centrally some basic dishes for instant micro-ovening and bounce into branded home cooking.

micropædia (məikropī·diă). [f. MICRO- + Gr. παιδεία learning.] A section of the 15th edition of *Encyclopædia Britannica* (published in 1974) in which information is presented in a condensed form. (Cf. *MACROPÆDIA, *PROPÆDIA.) Hence **micropæ·dic** *a.*

1974 *Daily Tel.* 12 Jan. 3/5 Consisting of 30 volumes, it will consist of what are described as a propaedia, a micropaedia and a macropaedia. **1974** *Times Lit. Suppl.* 11 Oct. 1120/4 About 180 writers are given biographies proper, the rest have to make do with a Micropaedic note.

micropalæontology (etc.), **-particle, -phagous, -phenocryst:** see *MICRO- 2 a, 1, 4, 1.

microphone. 2. Add to def.: Now applied to any instrument designed to convert sound waves impinging upon it into corresponding variations in voltage or current, which may then be amplified or transmitted for reconversion into sound (as in broadcasting and the telephone) or recorded; *esp.* one made as an independent unit (colloq. abbrev. *MIKE *sb.*⁵). (Further examples.)

This function is that of all telephone 'transmitters'. Hughes's instrument was simply a particularly sensitive one by the standards then current (hence the name: see quot. 1889), and modifications of it were for a time almost universally used as telephone transmitters, so that *microphone* became synonymous with *transmitter* and acquired its present more general meaning.

1889 PREECE & MAIER *Telephone* iv. 37 Hughes' Microphone... The microphone is nothing but a telephonic transmitter, but it owes its name..to its power to convert vibrations of feeble intensity into undulatory currents, which, passing through a receiving telephone, produce sonorous vibrations of much greater intensity than those of the original source. **1891** F. C. ALLSOP *Telephones* ii. 20 Prof. Hughes's microphone..forms the basis on which all the modern carbon transmitters are constructed. **1923** W. S. CHURCHILL *World Crisis 1915* 291 Already the microphone or hydrophone for detecting the beat of a submarine propeller in the distance had been discovered. **1923** E. W. MARCHANT *Radio Telegr.* vi. 76 Suppose..that the emission of waves from the transmitting aerial is controlled by means of a microphone, such as is employed in the ordinary telephone transmitter, the stream of waves given out by the antenna will be varied in accordance with the fluctuations in the current passing through the microphone. **1929** *Morning Post* 24 May 12/7 The engineer..in film-direction..has the last word as to whether the actor is speaking the line effectively for the microphone. **1935** H. C. BRYSON *Gramophone Record* iii. 59 Three main kinds of microphone are in common use: the carbon microphone, the condenser microphone, and the moving coil microphone. **1962** A. NISBETT *Technique Sound Studio* ii. 42 As an example of the sort of set-up which can be adopted in this type of studio is one where no less than six microphones were used for a quarter-hour playlet. **1970** M. L. GAYFORD in T. L. Squires *Telecommunications Pocket Bk.* iv. 36 The standard modern telephone sets now in production in most countries represent a considerable improvement over earlier sets... Improved designs of microphone and receiver give a generally better frequency response and transient response.

3. Special Comb.: **microphone boom,** a boom (*BOOM *sb.*² 1 d) with a microphone at the end.

1931 L. COWAN *Recording Sound for Motion Pict.* 377 *Microphone boom*, crane-like device for supporting and manipulating microphone. **1954** *Time* 12 July 47/3 Joan Diener, instead of being forced to stand near a microphone boom in order to be heard, was able to move at will in a TV studio by means of a tiny concealed microphone transmitter.

microphoned (məi·krǒfōᵘnd), *a.* [f. MICROPHONE + -ED².] **1.** Picked up and transmitted by a microphone.

1927 *Daily Express* 21 Sept. 11/5, I heard in Archie de Bear's room at the Vaudeville..a loud speaker carrying from the stage what was only a microphoned reproduction of a gramophone record made by the Revellers.

2. Containing or furnished with a microphone.

1933 *News Chron.* 13 June 1 At one end is a high microphoned platform for the President. **1934** *Punch* 11 Apr. 416/1 Put a commentator in a microphoned observation-car on each long-distance train. **1960** *Guardian* 20 July 5/7, I lived in a room in Moscow University which every-one..said was microphoned.

microphoneme (məi:krofōᵘ·nīm). *Linguistics.* [f. MICRO- 1 + PHONEME.] (See quot. 1935.) Hence **microphone·mic** *a.*

1935 W. F. TWADDELL in *Lang. Monogr.* XVI. v. 39 A term of an ordered class of minimum phonological differences among forms is a microphoneme. **1936** *Language* XII. 56 If one restricted one's attention to the series *kill*: *till*: *pill*: *hill*, one could arrive at alternative microphonemic classes. **1953** *Trans. Philol. Soc.* 84 All that we have.. are..certain microphonemes and greater or lesser sets of microphonemes.

microphonic (məikrofǫ·nik), *a.* and *sb.* [f. MICROPHON(E + -IC.] **A.** *adj.* **1.** (In Dict. s.v. MICROPHONE.)

2. a. Characterized by or pertaining to the production of variations in electrical potential in response to sound waves or vibrations.

1879 *Telegraphic Jrnl.* VII. 132/1 The communication of the current with the vibrating plate..is effected by means of two small springs which are lightly pressed by the membrane..which act as a weak microphonic contact. **1919** R. STANLEY *Text-bk. Wireless Telegr.* (new ed.) II. vi. 116 With some valve designs there is a microphonic effect in L.F. amplifiers so that the slightest jar given to the apparatus, such as tapping it with the finger or even walking near it, is strongly magnified. **1931** *Jrnl. Physiol.* LXXI. p. xxix, I conclude that the effect is due to some kind of microphonic action by which vibrations produce changes in the potential between different points in the inner ear. **1940** A. WOOD *Acoustics* xvii. 478 The microphonic response of the cochlea of a cat to a pure tone of 1000 cycles/sec. is amplified and analysed with a wave analyser. **1951** *Electronic Engin.* XXIII. 429/2 An attempt has been made..to determine the absolute microphonic performance of a valve by relating its electrical output to the frequency and intensity of a sound field in which it is situated. **1970** *Nature* 11 July 184/2 The microphonic response of the cochlea.

b. Of an electrical signal: generated in response to sound waves or vibrations.

1929 *Proc. IRE* XVII. 1621 Microphonic output is caused by relative motions between the various elements of the tube. **1930** ZWORYKIN & WILSON *Photocells* ix. 114 Mechanical vibration of the elements produce what are generally called microphonic noises. **1947** *Jrnl. Appl. Physics* XVIII. 242/2 A simple experiment was set up to check Eq. (7) by mechanically driving a tube and measuring the resulting 'microphonic' output signal.

B. *sb.* **1.** *pl.* (In Dict. s.v. MICROPHONE.) *rare.*

2. a. A microphonic signal generated in the cochlea.

1938 STEVENS & DAVIS *Hearing* xii. 319 When the voltage of the cochlear microphonic is plotted against the logarithm of the sound-intensity..the function appears as a sigmoid curve. **1962** *Laryngoscope* LXXII. 432 Is the reduction in amplitude of the cochlear microphonics due to an impairment of sound transmission or to a more direct effect on the organ of Corti? **1974** *Nature* 10 May 162/2 The 'poor' cochlear microphonic obtained from BALB/c mice after priming is indicative of hair cell damage.

b. *Electronics.* An undesired signal or modulation produced (e.g. in a valve) by mechanical vibration. Usu. *pl.*

1929 *Proc. IRE* XVII. 1622 The simplest test for microphonics consists of an audio-frequency amplifier of fairly high gain, the tube under test being used in the first stage. **1947** *Jrnl. Appl. Physics* XVIII. 245/2 It may well be advantageous to operate the input stage of a high gain automatic volume controlled amplifier with fixed bias to reduce microphonics. **1960** *IRE Trans. Microwave Theory & Techniques* VIII. 372/1 Waveguide under a high acoustical field can definitely contribute to microphonics via the mechanism of phase modulation. **1965** GEWARTOWSKI & WATSON *Princ. Electron Tubes* v. 152 Vibration of grid wires in grid-controlled tubes is a principal source of 'microphonics'.

microphonism (məikrǫ·fǒniz'm). *Electronics.* [f. MICROPHON(E + -ISM.] = *MICROPHONY 2.

1947 *Jrnl. Appl. Physics* XVIII. 239/1 This suggests a method of design..by which the microphonism of a tube may be reduced since..most of the microphonic difficulties encountered in tubes are caused by the mechanical movement of the grid. **1950** *Proc. IRE* XXXVIII. 529/1 The effects of microphonism are most usually encountered in high-gain amplifiers.

microphony. Restrict *rare*⁻⁰ to sense in Dict. and add: **2.** *Electronics.* [f. MICROPHON(E + -Y³.] The generation of microphonics in electrical apparatus.

1934 F. J. CAMM *Everyman's Wireless Bk.* v. 91 (*table*) Microphony: This may result in ringing, booming, or other sounds. **1946** *Electronic Engin.* XVIII. 336/2 The ruggedness which is required to give long service will normally ensure freedom from microphony. **1951** *Ibid.* 431/2 The design of a valve with low microphony is a long and tedious process. **1963** *Mullard Technical Communications* VII. 227/1 Microphony is occasionally experienced in a tape recorder when high gain a.f. valves are used in the first stages.

microphoto (məi:krofōᵘ·to), colloq. abbrev. of MICROPHOTOGRAPH 2.

1949 *Jrnl. Geol.* LVII. 370/1 The phenomenon of corrosion between crystals (Perrin and Roubault, 1939, p. 160, pl. 5, microphotos 7 and 8). **1972** K. MASTERS *Spray Drying* xiv. 518 Each microcapsule contains numerous minute droplets of perfume oil. A microphoto of an encapsulated fragrance is shown in an article by Barreto.

microphotograph. 1. (Further examples.)

1867 *Pop. Sci. Rev.* VI. 54 'Microphotograph' is a very long name, recently introduced, to denote a very small object; it refers to the minute photographic reductions of portraits or views so often shown as curiosities under the microscope. 'Photomicrograph', on the contrary, is a name given to the photographic enlargement of a microscopic object. **1878** *Jrnl. R. Microsc. Soc.* I. 300 Microphotograph.—Mr. Langenheim..has photographed the Lord's Prayer on the ten-thousandth of a square inch. **1940** A. HUXLEY *Let.* 14 Oct. (1969) 461, I would like to have..micro-photographs suitable for reading by means of a reading machine (all the big libraries make these micro-films now) of Part III of this book. **1957** *R.A.E. News* Nov. 8/2 The National Coal Board publicity office tried to excuse..an advertisement that described a picture, about four inches by six, as a 'microphotograph'. In the O.E.D. this word certainly denotes both a small photograph of a large-or-small object and a large-or-small photograph of a small object. However, the ambiguity proved such a nuisance that after international discussion between various bodies, the words 'microphotograph' and 'photomicrograph' respectively were agreed on. **1962** A. GÜNTHER *Microphotogr. in Library* (Unesco) 5 Microphotographs are photographs which are reduced to a minute or even microscopic size. **1966** M. R. D. FOOT *SOE in France* viii. 181 A microphotograph in the false bottom of a matchbox. **1969** *Proc. R. Microsc. Soc.* IV. 142 Sixth Report of the Nomenclature Committee. The Committee recommends the following names and definitions:... *Microphotograph.* A very small photograph, intended to be viewed with a microscope.

2. (Further examples.)

1927 HALDANE & HUXLEY *Animal Biol.* ii. 51 Fig. 18. Micro-photograph (× 150) of a section through the ovary of a mammal (cat). **1944** R. SOUTH *Caterpillars Brit. Butterflies* 5 Of the eggs and chrysalids, the former [illustrations] are from microphotographs by A. E. Tonge and drawings by Horace Knight. **1968** *Punch* 21 Aug. 271/3 There are blackboard diagrams, and micro-photographs of sperm and ova. **1974** *Nature* 22 Feb. 511/3 Species of pine and hardwood trees, grasses and cultivated plants, for example, are represented in the atlas of 136 microphotographs.

microphotometer (etc.), **microphthalmos**: see *MICRO- 6, 3.

microphysics (məi·krofiziks), *sb. pl.* (const. as *sing.*). Also **micro-physics.** [f. MICRO- 2 a + PHYSICS.] The part of physics that is concerned with bodies and phenomena on a microscopic or smaller scale, esp. with molecules, atoms, and sub-atomic particles.

1885 [in Dict. s.v. MICRO- 2 a]. **1956** E. H. HUTTEN *Lang. Mod. Physics* v. 175 These rules work well enough when we describe macro-physical phenomena; but their insufficiency is revealed in micro-physics. **1962** N. R. HANSON in *Quanta & Reality* v. 86 Von Neumann advanced a 'proof' that it would be impossible to reinstate a classical determinism in microphysics; it was logically pointless to look for 'hidden variables' underlying quantum processes. **1971** *Nature* 24 Dec. 433/2 Research in Britain concentrates on the fundamental microphysics of fogs.

Hence **microphy·sical** *a.*, of or pertaining to microphysics.

1902 [see *macrophysical* s.v. *MACRO- 1 e]. **1936** *Discovery* Mar. 96/2 Microphysical inquiries into which chemistry is now being absorbed. **1956** E. H. HUTTEN *Lang. Mod. Physics* v. 179 Two micro-physical events are connected in a different way from two macro-physical events. **1962** S. TOULMIN in *Quanta & Reality* 16 In the macroscopic world, all statistical statements..report the overall aggregates or averages of large numbers of individual events..; but the microphysical statements of quantum mechanics were statistical in a more absolute sense. **1973** *Nature* 14 Dec. 378/3 According to Audretsch the effect of expansion is significant for particle creation when the age of the Universe is comparable to the microphysical time scale—when the Universe is only about 10^{-21} s old!

microphysiologist, -physiology, -pinocytosis, -pipette, -plankton(ic): see *MICRO- 2 a, 2 a, 2 a, 6, 1.

microplastic(ity), -plate, -poise, -population, -porosity, -powder: see *MICRO- 1 b, 1, 5 a, 1, 1, 1.

microprint (məi·kroprint). [f. *MICRO- 7 + PRINT *sb.*] **a.** A photographic print of text reduced by microphotography. **b.** Printed matter so reduced. Hence **mi·croprinting** *vbl. sb.*, the production of microprint.

1933 *Library Jrnl.* LVIII. 913/1 With these photographic prints on sensitized paper there is no more question of fire hazard and the necessity of projection is likewise eliminated... We have, however, to overcome one difficulty, namely to make the 'micro prints' easily legible. **1951** *Amer. Documentation* II. 151/1 Microprint is delivered in labelled, cloth slip-cases ready for shelving. **1961** T. LANDAU *Encycl. Librarianship* (ed. 2) 121/1 Microfilming and the production of microprint are camera methods. **1962** A. GÜNTHER *Microphotogr. in Library* (Unesco) 5 Micro-writing and micro-printing were known centuries ago. **1970** *Brit. Printer* Jan. 80/1 Trial runs have satisfied him that micro printing to a 10th of normal size..can be done successfully on a standard offset-litho press. **1970** *New Scientist* 31 Dec. 601/2 People of all ages have found that they can read microprint without strain.

microprism (məi·kropriz'm), *a. Photogr.* [f. MICRO- + PRISM.] Applied to an area of the focusing screen of some reflex cameras which is covered with a grid of tiny prisms and which splits up the image when the subject is not in focus; also applied to such a focusing system.

1966 H. KEPPLER *Asahi Pentax Way* 319 In using the central microprism grid for focusing, you will find that it snaps images in and out of focus with medium focal length lenses more efficiently than with either wide-angle or extremely long lenses. **1968** *Newnes Compl. Amat. Photogr.* (ed. 3) iv. 67 A new alternative [to a rangefinder] is the use of a 'microprism' zone, which gives a dotted effect when the image is out of focus. **1970** *Amat. Photographer* 11 Mar. 4 (Advt.), A very advanced camera offering a 6–1 zoom ratio and microprism focusing. **1973** *Country Life* 20 Sept. 826/1 (Advt.), Microprism focusing means speedy and accurate focusing.

microprobe, -process: see *MICRO- 6, 1.

microprogram (məi·kroprōᵘgræm), *sb. Computers.* [f. MICRO- 1 b + PROGRAM, PROGRAMME *sb.*] A program that causes any machine instruction to be transformed into a sequence of microinstructions.

1953 WILKES & STRINGER in *Proc. Cambr. Philos. Soc.* XLIX. 230 The operation called for by a single machine order can be broken down into a sequence of more elementary operations... These elementary operations will be referred to as micro-operations. Basic machine operations, such as addition, subtraction, multiplication, etc., are thought of as being made up of a micro-programme of micro-operations, each micro-operation being called for by a micro-order. **1962** HUSKEY & KORN *Computer Handbk.* xvi. 32 Once a given set of instructions has been designed into the machine by the wiring of a microprogram plugboard, the machine may be used as a stored-program computer in the normal fashion. **1969** [see *MICROPROGRAMMED *ppl. a.*]. **1971** *New Scientist* 7 Jan. 27/1 This memory can hold up to 1024 words of microprogram which can be changed easily and inexpensively and tailored exactly to suit individual requirements.

microprogramming (məikroprōᵘ·græmiŋ), *vbl. sb. Computers.* [f. MICRO- 2 a + *PROGRAMMING *vbl. sb.*] The technique of making machine instructions generate sequences of microinstructions in accordance with a microprogram, rather than initiate the desired operations directly, so that by changing the microprogram the set of possible machine instructions can be varied.

1953 WILKES & STRINGER in *Proc. Cambr. Philos. Soc.* XLIX. 230 It is also necessary that provision should be made for conditional micro-orders which play a role in micro-programming similar to that played by conditional orders in ordinary programming. **1962** HUSKEY & KORN *Computer Handbk.* xvi. 32 The concept of microprogramming suggests that the machine be designed and constructed in such a way that the individual basic command steps, such as clear the accumulator or left shift one place, are accessible for alteration. **1967** P. A. STARK *Digital Computer Programming* xix. 360 Microprogramming is a technique for letting the programmer manufacture complex instructions..from small portions of instructions. **1971** *New Scientist* 17 June 685/2 ICL is understood to be taking its own steps along the microprogramming path in its next range of computers.

So **micropro·grammed** *ppl. a.*, employing microprogramming with a number of different microprograms; (as a back-formation) **micro-pro·gram** *v. trans.*; **micropro·grammer**, one who writes microprograms; a specialist in microprogramming.

1956 *Jrnl. Assoc. Computing Machinery* III. 79 One of the basic requirements of a microprogrammed computer is a means of ensuring the microprogrammer ready control of the subcommands with which he is working. It is necessary that the microprogram be physically easy to set up on the machine. **1957** *Ibid.* IV. 161 The arithmetic floating point operations of addition, subtraction and multiplication can be micro-programmed with about 70 micro-orders. **1969** P. B. JORDAIN *Condensed Computer Encycl.* 319 It is cheaper to establish a microprogram memory which can hold many microprograms and thus allow for a large set of computer instructions which can be interpreted and implemented on simple and inexpensive computer hardware. In such computers, sometimes called microprogrammed computers, each computer instruction operation code defines the beginning of the corresponding microprogram stored in the high-speed main storage. **1970** S. S. HUSSON *Microprogramming* i. 13 The user programmer tells the system or device *what to do* by placing instructions in the high-speed main storage. The microprogrammer tells the system or device *how to do it* by controlling which storage and logic elements are used and how

they are used for each operation. Thus the machine instruction which the programmer considered to be the lowest level of communication with the system can now be viewed as a closed subroutine broken down into a sequence of more elementary functions called microinstructions. Each microinstruction is designed to specify the control gates that are opened at a particular point during the machine cycle. **1975** *Sci. Amer.* May 36/3 Some multichip machines have the advantage that they can be 'microprogrammed' by the user.

microprojection (məi:kroprǒdʒe·kʃən). [f. MICRO- + PROJECTION *sb.*] The process of projecting an enlarged image of a microscopic specimen.

1904 *Jrnl. R. Microsc. Soc.* 582 The firm..manufacture an optical bench and appliances for..micro-projection, and optical lantern projection. **1932** *Ibid.* LII. 134 The microprojection of a subject for reconstruction work is best accomplished by using an apparatus affixed in the vertical position, projecting the image upon a horizontal table for ease in drawing. **1972** *Jap. Jrnl. Pharmacol.* XXII. 636 The reactive points were identified with the aid of microprojection apparatus to make the composite map from the serial sections obtained from individual animals.

Hence **microproje·ctor**, an apparatus for microprojection.

1932 *Jrnl. R. Microsc. Soc.* LII. 136 A method devised whereby a standard microprojector is altered to allow use in the vertical position. **1948** *Times* 15 June 7/5 He introduced into his lectures the latest methods of teaching, first by lantern slides, secondly by microprojector, and later by cine-films. **1957** B. M. ROVINSKY et al. in V. E. Cosslett et al. *X-Ray Microsc. & Microradiogr.* 277 The high resolution of the microprojector with its great sensitivity in distinguishing densities of microscopic areas makes it possible to use the device for examination of a wide range of objects.

micropsy: see *MICRO- 3.

micropublishing (məi·kropɒ:bliʃiŋ), *vbl. sb.* [f. *MICRO- 7 + PUBLISHING *vbl. sb.*] The publication of copies of books, periodicals, etc., in microform. Hence (as a back-formation) **mi·cropublish** *v. trans.*; also **mi·cropublished** *ppl. a.*, **micropu·blisher**.

1969 *R. & E. Coordinator* (Res. & Engin. Council Graphic Arts Industry) Apr. 4/1 According to a recent booklet ..micropublishing sales are running at an estimated $25 million a year. **1971** *Publishers' Weekly* 23 Aug. 41/1 A new company, Congressional Information Service, which collects, indexes and micro-publishes some 450,000 pages per year of government documents. **1973** *Ibid.* 19 Mar. 52/2 Many micropublished products are compilations of public domain materials. *Ibid.* 52/3 The micropublisher is particularly affected by this unofficial copyright. **1974** *Bookseller* 8 June 2600/1 The *Oxford English Dictionary* in two volumes with a magnifying glass is a significant half way stage to micro publishing.

micropulsation, -quantity, -rad: see *MICRO- 1, 1, 5 a.

microradiography (məi:krorēⁱdiǫ·grăfi). [ad. F. *microradiographie* (P. Goby 1913, in *Compt. Rend.* CLVI. 686): see MICRO- 2 a and RADIOGRAPHY.] Radiography of the fine structure of an object.

1913 P. GOBY in *Jrnl. R. Microsc. Soc.* 373 The new method of employment of X-rays, which I have the honour of introducing to you under the name of Microradiography, aims at rendering easily visible the internal structure of microscopic objects. **1944** *Jrnl. Appl. Physics* XV. 44/1 The early work on microradiography was confined chiefly to light alloys and made use of low voltage, long wave-length radiation. **1966** D. G. BRANDON *Mod. Techniques Metallogr.* 76 The two major advantages offered by microradiography as opposed to ordinary optical metallography are, firstly, the sensitivity to chemical composition and, secondly, the ability of the technique to integrate over a large volume of material. **1973** *Calcified Tissue Res.* XI. 176 This work investigated the effect of fluoride on the mineralization of rat dentine using tetracycline-labelling and microradiography.

Hence **microra·diogram**, the original image obtained on a sensitive plate or film in microradiography; **microra·diograph**, a photographic enlargement of a microradiogram; **mi:croradiogra·phic** *a.*, of or obtained by microradiography.

1913 *Jrnl. R. Microsc. Soc.* 375 Plate XVI is a reproduction of a micro-radiogram, enlarged nineteen times, of the anterior and posterior limbs of the three-toed lizard. **1944** *Jrnl. Appl. Physics* XV. 43 Investigations have been made of the various factors considered to influence the sensitivity of the microradiographic method for the examination of alloys. *Ibid.* 52 (*caption*) Microradiographs of cartridge brass with Co radiation at 20 kv at 75 ×. **1957** A. ENGSTRÖM in V. E. Cosslett et al. *X-Ray Microsc. & Microradiogr.* 32 In order to take care of the inhomogeneous distribution of the absorbing material, various types of scanning photometry of the microradiogram are now being used. **1966** D. G. BRANDON *Mod. Techniques Metallogr.* 76 The detail seen in a microradiograph is projected from a slab of metal up to 0·1 mm in thickness. **1969** HOBDELL & BOYDE in Möllenstedt & Gaukler *Internat. Symposium X-Ray Optics & Microanalysis* 611 The interpretation of the microradiographic image was found to be in good correlation with the interpretation of the scanning electron microscopic image of bone surfaces.

micro-ray, -reader, -record(ing), -relief, -reproduction, -respirometer (etc.): see *MICRO- 1, 7, 7, 1b, 7, 6.

micro-scale (məi·kroskēⁱl). Also **micro scale, microscale.** [f. MICRO- 1 + SCALE *sb.*[3]] A small or microscopic scale; *spec.* in *Chem.*, the scale of microanalysis.

Micro is freq. apprehended as an adj. qualifying *scale* (cf. *MICRO- 8).

1931 [see *MICRO- 8 b]. **1946** BELCHER & WILSON *Qualitative Inorg. Microanalysis* i. 3 This does not arise on the micro scale, because of the larger amounts of ethanol used to ensure complete precipitation. **1956** *Nature* 25 Feb. 378/2 Schindler's procedure, which was adapted to microscale working, was followed. 2–5 mgm. of vitamin B_{12} is dissolved in 500 μl. of 10 per cent aqueous ammonium chloride solution. **1961** *New Scientist* 16 Mar. 670/3 These materials are, however, crude on a microscale—they are porous and they contain impurities. **1964** N. G. CLARK *Mod. Org. Chem.* xxiv. 496 It became imperative to develop techniques demanding smaller samples. This was achieved in 1911 by Pregl, using 1–5 mg of material (micro-scale). **1966** D. G. BRANDON *Mod. Techniques Metallogr.* 103 It is now possible to perform a very large number of metallurgical operations in [*sic*] a microscale inside the electron microscope. **1968** [see *MACRO-SCALE].

microscope, *sb.* Add: **1. c.** An instrument analogous to an optical microscope in function but employing radiation other than visible light (e.g. electrons or X-rays). (Cf. *electron microscope* s.v. *ELECTRON[2] 2 b.)

1927 G. L. CLARK *Appl. X-Rays* i. 5 The ultraviolet microscope..discloses a fine structure which appears perfectly homogeneous under visible light rays. **1939** *Electronics & Television & Short-Wave World* XII. 637/3 The electron source..might be made completely independent from the microscope. **1957** DUNCOMB & COSSLETT in V. E. Cosslett et al. *X-ray Microsc. & Microradiogr.* 374 The purpose of the microscope is to form a picture of a surface by its X-ray emission and to analyze the elements in a selected volume of about one cubic micron in the surface by the characteristic lines emitted. **1964** G. H. HAGGIS et al. *Introd. Molecular Biol.* 346 Higher voltages on the microscope increase resolution, for a given section thickness, but reduce contrast. **1966** *McGraw-Hill Encycl. Sci. & Technol.* VIII. 371/2 In the electron, proton, x-ray, and β-ray microscopes, the image is usually recorded on a fluorescent screen or is photographed.

microscope, *v.* Add: So **mi·croscoping** *vbl. sb.*, examination by microscope.

1868 G. H. LEWES *Jrnl.* 10 Jan. in Geo. Eliot *Lett.* (1956) IV. 416 With him I spent the greater part of the time at Bonn, discussing microscoping etc. **1919** S. PAGET *Sir V. Horsley* II. i. 143 He..spoke his mind against that sort of pathology which hardly gets beyond the microscoping and exhibiting of diseased organs.

microsecond: see *MICRO- 5 a.

microsegment (məi·krosegmĕnt). *Linguistics.* [f. MICRO- 1 + SEGMENT *sb.*] A unit of sound enclosed between two open junctures.

1958 C. F. HOCKETT *Course in Mod. Ling.* vi. 60 Apart from stresses, a microsegment consists of segmental phonemes—that is, vowels and consonants. **1963** *Amer. Speech* XXXVIII. 55 Miss Sivertsen describes the phonological system within which she operates; phonemes are described in a framework of macro- and microsegments which, in turn, are divided into syllables. **1971** *Language* XLVII. 739 Each section of the description is..worked out in detail..; the main headings are phonemes, syllables, micro-segments, meso-segments, macro-segments, and mega-segments.

microseism. Substitute for def.: A minor earthquake; in mod. use, any imperceptible disturbance of the earth's crust which is capable of being registered on a sensitive seismometer but which is not caused by an earthquake (see quots.). (Further examples.)

1903 [see *MACROSEISM]. **1924** *Bull. Seismol. Soc. Amer.* XIV. 28 They [*sc.* earth-tremors] are now generally known as microseisms. **1959** *Observer* 6 Sept. 4/8 Another advance is the linking of 'microseisms'—minute earth tremors which constantly vibrate the recording pens of seismographs—with storms at sea. **1965** A. HOLMES *Princ. Physical Geol.* (rev. ed.) xxv. 916 As a background to the P, S and L waves and their many associates there are small irregular earth tremors and quiverings going on all the time... These microseisms..set a limit to the degree of magnification that can usefully be employed, since they only confuse the earthquake record if they are made too big. Some of the more conspicuous microseisms are caused by distant traffic, others by the pounding of breakers on rocky coasts, while others have been traced to changes of atmospheric pressure and especially to hurricanes and typhoons. But after all such regional increases of microseismic activity have been accounted for, there still remains a world-wide background of chaotic seismic 'noise'. Don and Florence Leet have suggested that these microseisms are caused by the strained condition of the crust, which 'hums' or 'sings' like a highly strained piece of steel. **1971** *Nature* 12 Feb. 452/3 Microseisms are of practical importance in predicting the onset of a storm in areas where meteorological observations are scarce.

microseismic, *a.* Add: (See also quot. 1972.) (Further examples.)

1972 *Gloss. Geol.* (Amer. Geol. Inst.) 452/2 *Microseismic data*, earthquake measurement or observation by instrumental means, as opposed to macroseismic observations. The term is not to be confused with the connotation of the term microseism. **1973** *Sci. Amer.* Apr. 31/1 It was a great thrill when we scanned along a seismogram made at Jamestown of an explosion on Novaya Zemlya and there —Eureka!—at the travel time predicted for a wave reflected seven times was an unmistakable tiny pulse nestling in the valley of microseismic background noise.

microshift, -skirt(ed): see *MICRO- 1 c.

microsleep (məi·kroslīp). [f. MICRO- 1 + SLEEP *sb.*] A transitory state of sleep, esp. in a person deprived of his normal sleep; a period or occasion of such sleep.

1945 W. T. LIBERSON in *Digest Neurol. & Psychiatry* XIII. 106 Another feature which we described is 'microsleep', a paroxysmal sleep of 1–10 seconds. **1959** *Jrnl. Amer. Med. Assoc.* 5 Sept. 14/1 Sleep deprivation brings with it an increasing burden of drowsiness..and brief lapses of awareness or 'microsleeps'. **1969** *Sunday Times* (Colour Suppl.) 16 Feb. 44/4 Tiny seizures of sleep known as microsleeps and lasting two or three seconds have occurred in people deprived of sleep. **1970** *Sci. Jrnl.* May 14/3 The subjects developed serious anomalies in brain wave pattern accompanied by 'microsleep'—a compulsive tendency to drop off unless kept constantly active. **1974** *Times* 3 Dec. 3/1 A driver can be asleep for short periods without knowing it and without anyone else being aware of it... A neurologist..described the state as 'micro-sleep'. .. They were in fact asleep for periods lasting from five to 10 seconds.

microsmatic (məi:krǫzmæ·tik), *a. Zool.* [f. MICR(O- + Gr. ὀσμ-ή smell + -ATIC.] Having poorly developed olfactory organs.

1890 W. TURNER in *Jrnl. Anat.* XXV. 106, I propose.. to arrange the Mammalia in relation to the development of the olfactory apparatus into three groups:—(*a*) Macrosmatic... (*b*) Microsmatic, where the olfactory apparatus is relatively feeble... (*c*) Anosmatic. **1891** *Proc. Zool. Soc.* 582 The olfactory bulbs and ethmo-turbinals are present, but only moderately well-developed in this animal [*sc.* the platypus]; it therefore belongs to the group named by Sir W. Turner..Microsmatic. **1962** *Science Survey* III. 260 In the microsmatic bats and in man only a very small area [of the nasal labyrinth] is olfactory. **1971** *Nature* 6 Aug. 396/2 Olfactory communication is now known to be important in determining the interaction between the sexes in a microsmatic higher primate, namely, the rhesus monkey.

microsocial (məikrosōᵘ·ʃăl), *a.* [f. MICRO- + SOCIAL *a.* and *sb.*] Of or pertaining to a small society or community.

1909 MRS. C. WEEKES tr. *Goll's Criminal Types in Shakespeare* iii. 134 Crimes committed by her..are looked upon as typical..of micro-social family assertion, arising out of her love for the little group. **1969** A. COCKBURN in Cockburn & Blackburn *Student Power* 10 Within this framework the personnel officer can bring to bear his knowledge of micro-social dynamics.

microsociological, -sociology: see *MICRO- 2 a.

microsomal (məikrŏsōᵘ·măl), *a. Biol.* [f. MICROSOM(E + -AL.] Of or pertaining to microsomes.

1897 *Jrnl. R. Microsc. Soc.* 22 The fibrils around the centrosomes have an exquisite microsomal structure. The microsomes occur in groups on the fibrils at equal distances from the centrosome. **1955** *Federation Proc.* XIV. 262/1 It appears that all the microsomal RNA is in the small particles. **1970** [see *MICROSOME b]. **1971** *Nature* 9 July 84/1 Perhaps these ribosomes also make microsomal membrane proteins.

microsome. Add: **b.** Any of the particles which constitute the lightest fraction obtained by ultracentrifugation of cell contents under specific conditions and which are believed to be formed from fragmented endoplasmic reticulum and attached ribosomes; also (esp. formerly), a ribosome in an intact cell.

1943 A. CLAUDE in *Science* 21 May 453/2 In order to differentiate the small particles from the other, already identified elements of the cell, it may be convenient in the future to refer to this new component under a descriptive name which would be specific. For this purpose the term *microsome* appears to be the most appropriate. The term microsome..was applied originally by Hanstein (1880) to any granules, as seen in living protoplasm. The use of the word was progressively narrowed down, being retained as a general term to designate any small granules of undefined nature. Under these conditions, it seems proper to suggest that the term microsome..should be restricted to designate the small particles exclusively. **1955** *Federation Proc.* XIV. 262/1 It was found that the microsomes are morphologically identical with the vesicular and tubular elements of the endoplasmic reticula (ER) of intact cells. **1957** C. P. SWANSON *Cytol. & Cytogenetics* (1958) ii. 32 (*caption*) The structure of the cytoplasm of rat liver cells as revealed by electron microscopy, showing the endoplasmic reticulum..and the attached particles (microsomes) which are between 100 and 200 A in diameter. **1960** *New Biol.* XXXI. 30 The microsomes themselves, which are obtained after the cell has been broken down, are vesicles made of two components: a membrane, which is rich in proteins and lipids, and very small granules... These small particles contain as much as 40–50 per cent RNA and..most of the cellular RNA is present in them. **1968** L. L. LANGLEY *Cell Function* (ed. 2) i. 9 The endoplasmic reticulum is seen..to form a series of small canals

through the cytoplasm... Closely associated with the membranes which line the canals are tiny granules termed microsomes. Because they contain such a high concentration of RNA, they are often referred to as ribosomes. **1970** AMBROSE & EASTY *Cell Biol.* v. 164 Microsomes are in fact small spherical vesicles formed from disrupted endoplasmic reticulum. The microsomal fraction of homogenized cells may also contain ribosomes.

microspecies (məi·krospīːʃīz, -spīːsīz). *Taxonomy.* [f. MICRO- + SPECIES *sb.*] A species differing only in minor characters from others of its group, often one of limited geographical range forming part of an aggregate species.

1916 J. P. LOTSY *Evolution by Means of Hybridization* i. 22 They have subsequently been called: mikrospecies, Jordanian species, subspecies, small species or elementary species indiscriminately. **1922** G. C. DRUCE *Flora Zetlandica* in *Bot. Exchange Club* VI. Suppl. 45 Twenty-two micro species of Hieracia are found in the Faroes. **1946** *Nature* 19 Oct. 535/2 The genus *Psalliota*..consists of 'species' or 'microspecies' extremely difficult to separate one from another. **1953** E. MAYR et al. *Methods & Princ. Syst. Zool.* ii. 39 Although conventionally referred to as races, reproductively isolated chromosomal populations are more logically designated (micro)species. **1963** DAVIS & HEYWOOD *Princ. Angiosperm Taxon.* xiii. 425 In large critical groups of species the difficulty of deciding to which species various subspecies should be subordinated encourages the taxonomist (often against his inclinations) to maintain numerous microspecies.

microspectrograph (etc.), **-spectrophotometer** (etc.), **-sphere**: see *MICRO- 6, 6, 1.

microspore. 2. Substitute for def.: The smaller of the two kinds of spores in heterosporous cryptogams; also, the homologous structure in seed plants (i.e. the immature pollen grain). (Add further examples.)

1964 E. J. H. CORNER *Life of Plants* x. 177 The male spores [in *Selaginella*, etc.], called microspores because of their small size, are produced in large numbers in microsporangia. **1965** K. ESAU *Plant Anat.* (ed. 2) xviii. 540 A microspore develops into the male gametophyte, the pollen grain.

Hence **mi:crosporoge·nesis**, the development of microspores; **mi:crosporogene·tic** *a.*

1946 *Nature* 12 Oct. 520/1 In the microsporogenesis of buckwheat autotetraploids during the first metaphase of meiosis only very rarely were exclusively quadrivalents observed. **1961** *Developmental Biol.* III. 241 Microsporogenesis in the higher plants offers an opportunity for analyzing various stages of differentiation within the essentially closed system afforded by the microsporocyte. **1973** *Nature* 6 July 35/2 The cold treatment slowed down the microsporogenesis considerably, enabling the microsporogenetic stages to be clearly recognized.

microsporidian (məikrospori·diăn), *sb.* and *a. Zool.* [f. mod.L. name of order *Microsporidia* (G. Balbiani 1883, in *Jrnl. de Micrographie* VII. 349), f. MICRO- 1 + SPORE + Gr. dim. suff. -ιδιον.] **A.** *sb.* A protozoan parasite affecting arthropods or fishes, belonging to the order Microsporidia. **B.** *adj.* Of or pertaining to a parasite of this kind.

1910 *Encycl. Brit.* IX. 386/1 The genus *Myxocystis*.. has been shown..to be a true Microsporidian. **1912** E. A. MINCHIN *Introd. Study Protozoa* xvi. 411 The existence of the polar capsule in the Microsporidian spore was discovered by Thélohan. **1930** R. R. KUDO in Hegner & Andrews *Probl. & Methods of Res. in Protozool.* xxxiii. 327 The spore is perhaps the most important stage of a microsporidian from the taxonomic standpoint. **1964** T. C. CHENG *Biol. Animal Parasites* v. 141/1 The infective form of microsporidians is the spore, which is typically covered by a keratinous membrane. **1972** SWAN & PAPP *Common Insects N. Amer.* 291 Silkworms suffer from fungus, virus, and microsporidian (protozoan) infections.

microsporidiosis (məikrosporidiōᵘ·sis). [f. *MICROSPORIDI(AN *sb.* and *a.* + -OSIS.] = *NOSEMA.

1911 FANTHAM & PORTER in *Proc. Zool. Soc.* 626 Microsporidiosis (due to *Nosema apis*) had probably been introduced from the Continent into British apiaries. **1937** W. HERROD-HEMPSALL *Bee-keeping* II. 1425 Nosema Disease (Microsporidiosis).

microstate, -stimulation, -stratification: see *MICRO- 1, 1 b, 1.

microstrip (məi·krostrip). *Electr.* [f. *MICRO(WAVE + STRIP *sb.*[2]] A transmission line for microwaves that consists of dielectric material with a metallic film forming a conducting strip along one face and a metallic coating that serves as an earth covering the opposite face; also *collect.* (without *a*), as a material.

1952 GRIEG & ENGELMANN in *Proc. IRE* XL. 1644 (*heading*) Microstrip—a new transmission technique for the kilomegacycle range. *Ibid.* 1645/1 Because of the ease of manufacture and the apparent similarity to conventional wiring, the generic name of microstrip has been given to this transmission system. **1957** *Jrnl. Appl. Physics* XXVIII. 299/1 The 'microstrip' is a strip transmission line which consists of a thin metallic strip pasted on a dielectric layer which is in turn a coating on a ground plane. *Ibid.*, Sections of microstrip are useful as microwave filters. **1967** *Electronics* 6 Mar. 251/2 The microstrip is formed on the alumina board by depositing a silver circuit pattern and ground plane. **1971** *New Scientist* 1 July 26/1 A traditional waveguide must have dimensions comparable to the wavelength of the microwave signal it is handling—a few centimetres... No such physical restrictions apply to microstrip, which has the added advantage of a constructional technique compatible with modern microelectronics. *Ibid.* 26/2 The one [earth] plate can form the second conductor for all the microstrips used in the receiver.

mi·crostructure. Also micro-structure. [f. MICRO- + STRUCTURE *sb.*] Structure on a microscopic or very small scale; = *FINE STRUCTURE 2.

1885, 1898 [in Dict. s.v. MICRO- 2 b]. **1956** *Nature* 25 Feb. 380/2 The inhomogeneous microstructure of the muscular tissue. **1959** B. WALL tr. *Teilhard de Chardin's Phenomenon of Man* I. i. 50 We owe our knowledge of the macro-structure and micro-structure of the universe far more to increasingly accurate measurements than to direct observations. **1960** E. H. GOMBRICH *Art & Illusion* viii. 274 The clue of texture..is basically also a clue of regularity and one which proves so reliable because the microstructure of things is least affected by accidents. **1962** F. I. ORDWAY et al. *Basic Astronautics* iv. 153 Some hope to learn from gravitational research more about the microstructure of the building blocks of nature, the subatomic particle. **1973** *Sci. Amer.* Feb. 65/2 It is now customary to apply the term 'microstructure' to oceanic physical processes on the scale of a few centimeters or less.

Hence **microstru·ctural** *a.*, of or pertaining to the microstructure; **microstru·cturally** *adv.*

1893 A. GEIKIE *Text-bk. Geol.* (ed. 3) 596 *Macrostructural* metamorphism, having the external structure (morphology) changed, as where an amorphous condition becomes schistose; *micro-structural*, having the internal structure (histology) wholly changed, with or without a macro-structural alteration. **1937** O. B. DARBISHIRE tr. *A. von Buzágh's Colloid Syst.* iv. 45 With increasing crystal size the microstructural composition asymptotically approaches the stoichiometric composition. *Ibid.*, The solution of this paradox is found in a 'microstructurally correct computation'. **1966** C. R. TOTTLE *Sci. Engin. Materials* x. 224 Steels are susceptible to microstructural changes at the temperatures required for stress relief, and for this reason relief is often avoided.

microsurgery (məikrosɒ̄·ɹdʒəri). [f. MICRO- 2 a + SURGERY.] Manipulation (as by injection, dissection, etc.) of individual cells with the aid of microscopy; surgery of such delicacy as to necessitate microscopy.

1927 *Protoplasma* II. 203 Micro-surgery of plant cells shows that the impression of fluidity which one gets from mere microscopic observation is illusory. **1928** E. V. COWDRY *Special Cytol.* i. 7 With the apparatus of Chambers it is feasible to isolate a cell, to take it up with a pipette, to incise part of it and to inoculate into its cytoplasm a small amount of fluid. This microsurgery has been applied to the investigation of many problems. **1941** *Bot. Rev.* VII. 355 Harder (1926), by microsurgery, isolated the penultimate cell of a growing hypha of *Coprinus sterquilinus*. **1960** *McGraw-Hill Encycl. Sci. & Technol.* IV. 571/2 As gastrulation and embryo formation proceed, microsurgery becomes more and more the instrument of choice for analysis. The defect experiment tests the effect of removal of one part or rudiment. **1971** *Nature* 2 July 28/1 The techniques of microsurgery on single cells have been applied to a variety of cell types. **1973** *Daily Colonist* (Victoria, B.C.) 10 June 28/2 Microsurgery has been used in brain operations for the last five years, beginning in Europe.

So **microsu·rgical** *a.*

1963 *Science* 5 July 46/3 (*heading*) Ruby laser as a microsurgical instrument. **1968** H. HARRIS *Nucleus & Cytoplasm* iv. 81 Nuclei which were divested of virtually all their cytoplasm by microsurgical procedures none the less retained their ability to produce specific puffing patterns. **1974** *Nature* 29 Mar. 450/1 Microsurgical removal of the root cap of *Zea* has been shown to prevent the response of the roots to gravity.

microswitch, -syringe, -system, -technique, -tektite: see *MICRO- 1, 6, 1, 6, 1.

microtelephone (məikrote·lĭfōᵘn). *Teleph.* [f. MICRO- + TELEPHONE *sb.*] **1.** Any of various modifications of the Bell telephone transmitter which were supposed to render it more sensitive.

1879 J. OCHOVOWICZ in *Nature* 27 Mar. 482/2 The microtelephone is regulated once for all, and transmits the feeblest word with a truly perfect precision. **1879** T. A. EDISON *U.S. Pat. 222,390* 9 Dec. 311/1 This invention I term the 'micro-telephone' in consequence of the same responding to minute vibrations.

2. [f. MICRO(PHONE.] = *HANDSET.

1895 A. R. BENNETT *Telephone Syst. Europe* xvii. 296 Usually the transmitter and receiver are attached to the same handle, in 'micro-telephone' form. **1930** [see *HANDSET].

microtext, -texture, -theory: see *MICRO- 7, 2 b, 1 b.

microtine (məi·krotīn, -əin), *sb.* and *a. Zool.* [f. mod.L. subfamily name *Microtinæ* (f. generic name *Microtus* (F. von P. von Schrank *Fauna Boica* (1798) I. 66), f. MICR(O- + Gr. ὠτ-, οὖς ear): see -INA[2].] **A.** *sb.* A member of the rodent subfamily Microtinæ, which includes voles and lemmings. **B.** *adj.* Of or pertaining to this subfamily.

1926 M. A. C. HINTON *Monogr. Voles & Lemmings* I. 16 Some of the most characteristic features of the Microtine skull are shown in longitudinal vertical sections. **1936** *Proc. Prehist. Soc.* II. 53 In the case of the microtine mammals—another rapidly evolving group—detailed work along these lines has been done. **1948** A. L. RAND *Mammals E. Rockies* 165 In some areas at least in Canada the scarcity of microtines seems to cause a scarcity of certain furs. **1956** *Nature* 10 Mar. 445/2 A recognizable description of an Indian mole-vole..of the genus *Ellobius*, a microtine. **1972** T. A. VAUGHAN *Mammalogy* xv. 190 (*caption*) Population densities of several species of Microtines.

mi·crotome, *v.* [f. the sb.] *trans.* To cut in sections with a microtome. So **mi·crotomed** *ppl. a.*

1893 *Brit. Med. Jrnl.* 23 Sept. 685/2 The divided roots were microtomed and examined in serial sections. **1898** *Phil. Trans. R. Soc.* B. CXC. 95 The following nerves of muscles were microtomed for detection of some fibres. **1972** *Physics Bull.* Nov. 668/1 Evidence for twisting fibrils has also been obtained from transmission electron micrographs of microtomed specimens.

microtone (məi·krotōᵘn). *Mus.* [f. MICRO- 1 + TONE *sb.*] An interval smaller than a semitone.

1920 *Outward Bound* Oct. 77/1 The ancient Greeks also recognised and used these microtones. The Greeks found twenty-four in the octave and the Indians usually recognise twenty-two. **1927** *Observer* 23 Oct. 14 But these microtones (seventy-two in the octave) give quarters of the untempered chromatic semitone. **1946** *Mod. Music* Spring 113 The Oriental sound of Hovhaness' music is realized with occidental instruments not by preparing the instruments, nor by employing microtones, but solely through the character of the melody. **1957** MANVELL & HUNTLEY *Technique Film Music* iii. 170 Volume was controlled by varying the exposure;..portamento by a rapid series of micro-tones. **1970** W. APEL *Harvard Dict. Mus.* (ed. 2) 527/1 Long a structural feature of Asian music, the use of microtones in Western music, although far from new, has been..far less extensive.

Hence **microto·nal** *a.*, of or pertaining to a microtone or microtones; employing or producing microtones; **microtona·lity**; **microto·nally** *adv.*

1942 *Scrutiny* XI. 6 The quarter-tone or *scruti* is the microtonal interval between notes of the 'scale'. **1946** R. BLESH *Shining Trumpets* (1949) v. 106 The microtonally flatted fifth also occurs. *Ibid.* x. 234 The blues scale.. gives all the opportunity needed for microtonality. **1946** *Mod. Music* Spring 113 The microtonality of Alois Haba and others presents an Oriental characteristic not found in any of the music discussed above. **1959** *Chambers's Encycl.* IX. 627/2 The microtonality of the Czech Alois Haba (1893–), who cut the scale into ¼- and ⅙-tones. **1967** *Times* 29 May 6/4 Glissandos on the microtonal harp were pure magic. **1974** *Country Life* 24 Jan. 136/1 Mozart.. as an infant..could remember microtonal differences of tuning in instruments heard weeks previously.

microtopography (məikrotǒpǫ·grăfi). [f. MICRO- 2 a + TOPOGRAPHY.] The surface features of a material, or of the earth or other body, on a small or microscopic scale.

1956 *Nature* 24 Mar. 564/1 Prof. Tolansky selected as typical subjects for examination some of his own studies on the optical testing of surface finish, of microtopography in general, the examination of micro-hardness and directional hardness [etc.]. **1962** F. I. ORDWAY et al. *Basic Astronautics* iii. 65 Photometric observations.. suggest that the microtopography [of the moon] is rough, probably being pitted. **1969** *Ecology* L. 740 Lichen cover and microtopography were positively associated.

Hence **mi:crotopogra·phic, -topogra·phical** *adjs.*

1958 *New Biol.* XXVI. 40 Even in apparently flat and uniform grassland, the distribution of the buttercup species is usually found to be associated with microtopographical features which determine slight differences in the rate of drainage and the speed with which the soil dries out during drought periods. **1960** S. TOLANSKY *Surface Microtopogr.* vi. 71 Its [*sc.* diamond's] unique hardness makes it an ideal material for microtopographic studies. **1971** *Nature* 22 Jan. 248/1, I have had occasion recently to re-read Goethe's *Theory of Colours* (1810) and have found that he described the nature of the microtopographical interference pattern given by a crystal surface.

microtrichium: see *MICRO- 1.

microtron (məi·krotrǫn). [f. *MICRO(WAVE + *-TRON.] A variant of the cyclotron for accelerating electrons by passing them repeatedly through a cavity in which they are accelerated by microwaves, the amount of the acceleration on each passage being such as to allow for the increase in their time of revolution that results from their relativistic increase in mass.

1946 *Rev. Sci. Instruments* XVII. 9/1 The microtron, suggested by J. S. Schwinger and by V. Veksler, is an electron cyclotron in which the particles slip one cycle of phase on each circuit through a constant magnetic field. **1958** *Times* 21 June 4/7 It is called the 'microtron' because the electrical pulses used in acceleration are got from a pulsed microwave oscillator. **1974** *Nature* 1 Feb. 250/3

A prototype continuous microtron (a cyclic accelerator in which the electrons are accelerated by microwaves) has been constructed in Obninsk.. Until now, it has proved possible to operate microtron accelerators in a pulsed mode only, with a relatively low repetition frequency.

microtubular, -tubule: see *MICRO- 1.

microunit (məi·kro-, mi·kroyū:nit). [f. MICRO- 5 a + UNIT *sb.*] A millionth part of a unit, esp. of an international unit (as of insulin).

1900 DORLAND *Med. Dict.* 392/1 *Micro-unit*, a unit of small measurements. **1911** STEDMAN *Med. Dict.* 533/1 *Microunit*, the millionth of an ordinary unit, such as a meter, gram, ohm, etc. **1959** *Nature* 21 Nov. 1649/2 Two to three micro-units of human insulin were detectable in the experiment depicted. **1962** *Lancet* 13 Jan. 73/2 This difference is highly significant statistically..whether the figures are considered at the level of net glucose uptake or after conversion into microunits of insulin per millilitre.

microvascular, -vegetation, -viewer, -villus, -watt: see *MICRO- 4, 1, 7, 1, 5 a.

microwave (məi·krowēiv). [f. MICRO- 1 + WAVE *sb.*] **1.** An electromagnetic wave with a wavelength between about one millimetre and 30 centimetres (corresponding to a frequency between 300 gigahertz and one gigahertz); one whose wavelength is such that it is convenient to use hollow waveguides for its transmission.

The precise figures taken as extremes of wavelength or frequency are arbitrary and vary somewhat with different writers; formerly waves much longer than the present-day maximum were described as microwaves.

1931 *Telegraph & Telephone Jrnl.* XVII. 179/1 When ..trials..with wavelengths as low as 18 cm. were made known, there was undisguised surprise..that the problem of the micro-wave had been solved so soon. **1935** *Proc. IRE* XXIII. 1503 (*heading*) Diffraction of microwaves over the curve of the Earth. *Ibid.*, Radio waves below ten meters in length, at the present time termed 'microwaves', may be received at moderate distances over the horizon from the transmitter. **1940** *Amat. Radio Handbk.* (ed. 2) xvi. 232/1 Wavelengths below 1 metre are referred to as 'micro-waves' or 'centimetre waves', and demand special treatment. **1942** J. C. SLATER *Microwave Transmission* 1 The range of waves called microwaves: wave lengths perhaps in the range from a half meter to a few centimeters. **1965** *New Scientist* 10 June 724/3 Microwaves, or waves of even shorter wavelength, must be used because it is only when such short wavelengths are employed that a highly directional beam can be produced. **1968** *Maclean's Mag.* Dec. 19/1 Signals from the satellite will be received by ground stations and relayed by microwave or cable to home receivers. **1973** *Sci. Amer.* Sept. 74/2 Electromagnetic radiation at microwave frequencies is now widely used for cooking purposes. It may also be practical to use microwaves to 'cook' agricultural pests in the soil: insects, weeds, fungi and so on.

2. a. *attrib.*

1933 *Electrician* 6 Jan. 3/1 We decided..to concentrate our efforts on the generation and efficient radiation of what may be termed a medium wavelength on the microwave scale—that is, a wavelength of the order of half-a-metre, i.e., 600 000 k.c. **1946** *Proc. IRE* XXXIV. 775/1 The extent of the microwave spectrum has been variously defined. This paper will concern itself with the range of frequencies between approximately 2000 and 30,000 megacycles per second. **1946** *Jrnl. R. Aeronaut. Soc.* L. 956/1 During the war airborne microwave radar was used to provide in the aircraft a map or picture showing the main features, e.g., towns and rivers, of the country below. **1947** *Electronic Engin.* XIX. 17 Ultra-short and microwave radio links. **1952** *Sci. News* XXV. 30 From a study of such rotational spectra of asymmetric molecules in the microwave region the distance between the atoms can be found very accurately. **1957** *B.B.C. Handbk.* 59 The vision signals from remote outside broadcast points are carried back to the main television network by BBC microwave or VHF radio links. **1959** *Daily Tel.* 18 May 12/6 The sky platform would hover in a fixed position. Helicopter type rotary wings would be turned by microwave energy beamed from stations on earth. **1964** *Ann. Reg. 1963* 163 The microwave telecommunications network linking Ankara, Karachi and Teheran. **1967** D. WILSON in Wills & Yearsley *Handbk. Managem. Technol.* iii. 44 Data transmission is concerned with the transmission of data over private or G.P.O. lines or by using microwave techniques. **1971** *Brit. Printer* Jan. 67/2 Microwave dryers are currently at an advanced stage of development. **1972** *Sci. Amer.* Feb. 13/1 Although the microwave region of the electromagnetic spectrum is not precisely defined, we use the term to describe radiation of wavelengths ranging from 30 centimeters to three millimeters.

b. Special Comb.: **microwave oven,** an oven in which food is cooked by passing microwaves through it, the resulting generation of heat inside the food making rapid and uniform cooking possible.

1965 *Economist* 22 May 941/2 (*heading*) Microwave ovens. A meal a minute. **1968** *New Scientist* 24 Oct. 175/1 The microwave oven..is now coming into quite wide use in homes in the United States. **1973** *Daily Tel.* 26 Apr. 11/8 Microwave ovens which are still in the experimental stage, would take eight minutes to produce a standard loaf, instead of 30.

microweld (məi·kroweld), *v.* [f. MICRO- 1 b + WELD *v.*] *trans.* To join by a very small weld. So **mi·crowelded** *ppl. a.*, **mi·crowelding** *vbl. sb.*

1962 *Flight Internat.* LXXXII. 1027/1 According to Aerojet-General Corporation, a micro-welding device developed by the Corporation's Astrionics Division 'will make a reliable weld in the time it takes you to dot an 'i'... But the dot of your 'i' will be 30 times bigger than the weld.' **1963** E. KEONJIAN *Microelectronics* 380 Microwelded connections. **1968** *Sci. Jrnl.* Nov. 17 (*caption*) The microwelding machine below is used to bond leads to the circuit. **1970** *New Scientist* 13 Aug. 338/2 An army of girls some 30 000 strong is employed..in micro-welding hair-sized connections from each silicon chip. **1975** *Country Life* 3 Apr. 838/1 The use of microwelding—an engineering skill put to very effective use as in a bracelet that seems to be a web of fine interlaced wires.

microwire, -world, -zone: see *MICRO- 1.

micrurgy (məi·krɜ̄ɪdʒi). [f. MICR(O- + *-urgy* after METALLURGY.] The performance of delicate manipulations under the microscope, esp. on biological material such as individual cells. So **micru·rgical** *a.*

1927 *Protoplasma* II. 189 (*heading*) The structural organization of plant protoplasm in the light of micrurgy. *Ibid.* 191 The extensive micrurgical researches that have been made on animal cells. **1935** *Industr. & Engin. Chem.* (*Analytical Ed.*) VII. 218/1 The word 'micrurgy' was coined by Peterfi..to describe biological microdissection and later expanded by Titus and Gray..to include dissection and examination under the microscope of non-biological material. Since the term, by its pure Greek derivation, means 'operations on a small scale or work with minute quantities', it can logically be used as a general term to include microchemistry, microanalysis, and chemical microscopy... It is here so used, and is suggested for general adoption. **1960** *New Scientist* 20 Oct. 1049/1 With the new technique of micrurgy the gap between the living cell and the micrologist had been bridged. **1973** *Nature* 2 Mar. 47/2 For micrurgical manipulation, two- or eight-celled eggs from superovulated BALB/c mice were deposited into a suspension of somatic cells and virus in an 'egg-well'.

mid, *a.*, *sb.*[1], and *adv.* Add: **A.** *adj.* **1. c.** (Further examples.)

1898 G. B. SHAW *Perfect Wagnerite* 34 A..melodic bogey to mid-century ears. **1906** *Dialect Notes* III. 146 The mid-term examinations will begin the last of January. **1923** D. H. LAWRENCE *Birds, Beasts & Flowers* 103 A disgusting bat At mid-morning. **1928** T. S. ELIOT *For Lancelot Andrewes* 76 Arnold turned from mid-century Radicalism. **1938** *Encycl. Brit. Bk. of Year* 700/1 There are 1,200 firms in Britain now operating such amenities as a ten-minute mid-morning break. **1951** I. SHAW *Troubled Air* xv. 248 The mid-afternoon coffee was put up in containers. **1952** C. P. BLACKER *Eugenics* 259 At about mid-pregnancy, identical twins differ more in size than do fraternal. **1953** *Manch. Guardian Weekly* 1 Oct. 1 The Administration party loses seats at the 'mid-term' elections. **1958** P. SHORE in N. Mackenzie *Conviction* 23 All over Britain a new mid-twentieth-century society is coming vigorously to life. **1959** P. TOWNEND *Died o' Wednesday* xii. 216 Chance customers who dropped in for mid-morning coffee, light lunches and afternoon tea. **1961** *Lancet* 5 Aug. 280/1 The gradual change in uterine activity begins as early in pregnancy as midterm. **1968** A. DIMENT *Gt. Spy Race* iv. 53 The obscure type faces which these mid-century tailors use to advertise their dens. **1972** J. MCCLURE *Caterpillar Cop* ix. 144 The last lesson before mid-morning break. **1973** *Guardian* 19 Apr. 14/2 The people who fear it [*sc.* the Watergate scandal] will hurt them are Republican candidates for next year's mid-term elections.

d. *mid-flight, -race, -sentence, -stride*; **mid-Atlantic,** (*a*) the middle of the Atlantic Ocean; (*b*) something that has both British and American characteristics, or is designed to appeal to both the British and the Americans; also *attrib.* or as *adj.*; **mid-band** *a. Electronics*, of or pertaining to the middle of a band of frequencies; **mid-calf,** (*b*) *attrib.* or as *adj.*, describing a garment that reaches half-way down the calf of the leg; **mid-cycle** *a.* and *sb. Physiol.*, (occurring at) the middle of the menstrual cycle; **mid-main** *poet.*, mid-ocean; **mid-square** *a. Math.*, describing a method of generating a pseudorandom sequence of digits by squaring an arbitrary large number, taking the middle digits of the result (usu. half the total number of digits, a zero being added at the left if necessary to make the total even), and using these as the first digits of the series and as the number to be squared to provide the next digits, and so on indefinitely; **mid-town, midtown** chiefly *U.S.*, the middle of a town; a central area in a town or city; freq. *attrib.*

1892 'MARK TWAIN' *Amer. Claimant* 65 Two shipments would meet and part in mid-Atlantic. **1897** *Proc. Zool. Soc.* 351 *Monachus*, the Seal of the Mid-Atlantic. **1940** G. GREENE *19 Stories* (1947) 184 Central heating gave it the stuffy smell of mid-Atlantic. **1957** M. SWAN *Brit. Guiana* i. 25 He was drowned..when the ship in which he was returning to England from the United States was wrecked in mid-Atlantic. **1958** *Spectator* 7 Feb. 164/1, I crossed swords with the redoubtable Douglas Fairbanks Jr. on whether or not his television films could justly be called 'British'..; my argument was that as they aim at the American—or 'mid-Atlantic'—market, they do not deserve the name. **1962** *Radio Times* 22 Nov. 41/2 A spell in Hollywood where he was sent by the studio to which he was under contract to acquire a 'mid-Atlantic' accent. **1970** *Observer* 8 Feb. 30/6 There's another sameness too, a mid-Atlantic look. **1956** *Nature* 25 Feb. 392/2 At a mid-band wave-length of 3·2 cm., an input-voltage standing-wave ratio of 0·9 or better can be achieved over a 10 per cent band-width. **1962** SIMPSON & RICHARDS *Physical Princ. Junction Transistors* xiii. 300 The mid-band voltage gain. **1967** *Harper's Bazaar* Sept. 45 The mid-calf hem for day. **1969** *Guardian* 30 July 7/1 Courrèges..does in fact show one or two midcalf dresses for late day. **1974** *Country Life* 24 Jan. 181/1 Slim, mid-calf dresses in tiny stripes. **1951** C. K. WEICHERT *Anat. Chordates* ix. 399 This is the condition at the time of ovulation, and the endometrium is said to be of the mid-cycle type. **1952** E. S. TAYLOR *Man. Gynecol.* iii. 19 At mid-cycle a ripened ovum is extruded from the ovary. **1965** J. H. BURN *Lect. Notes Pharmacol.* (ed. 8) 93 The function of the progestogen is to prevent 'break-through' bleeding in the mid-cycle. **1974** PASSMORE & ROBSON *Compan. Med. Stud.* III. xxviii. 33/2 These pills relieve dysmenorrhoea, premenstrual tension, midcycle pain or bleeding, and regulate previously irregular periods. **1896** Midflight [in Dict., sense A. 1]. **1932** W. FAULKNER *Light in August* v. 98 It did not vanish in midflight. **1948** R. GRAVES *Coll. Poems* 219 That sea-birds of all sorts that flock About the Bass, repeatedly Collide in mid-flight. **1969** *Listener* 6 Feb. 163/1 (*caption*) The Lunar Excursion Module (centre) after mid-flight reassembly of the spacecraft has taken place, to allow two astronauts to enter the module from the main unit. **1862** G. M. HOPKINS *Vision of Mermaids* (1929), Mermaids..ring the knells Of seamen whelm'd in chasms of the mid-main. **1959** *Times* 5 Oct. 4/7 It is easy to criticize Eldon for his wasteful short bursts in mid-race. **1901** H. G. WELLS *First Men in Moon* xiii. 104, I looked up, and stopped in mid-sentence. **1967** *Coast to Coast 1965–66* 30 She paused in mid-sentence. **1951** *Appl. Math. Ser. Nat. Bureau of Standards* (U.S.) XII. 33 (*heading*) The mid-square method of generating digits. **1968** P. A. P. MORAN *Introd. Probability Theory* i. 46 The midsquare method has, however, been shown to be unsatisfactory. **1932** W. FAULKNER *Light in August* xix. 436 The one stopped in the act of crouching from the leap, the other in midstride of running. **1957** T. HUGHES *Hawk in Rain* 51 And his foot hung like Statuary in mid-stride. **1934** WEBSTER, Mid-town (s.v. *mid-*). **1952** S. KAUFFMANN *Philanderer* (1953) ix. 157 They went to the roof garden of a midtown hotel. **1959** J. CARY *Captive & Free* 41 The mid-town terraces which can and have so easily become slum tenements. **1963** *Listener* 31 Jan. 202/2 In the very middle of mid-town, just off (and even just on) Broadway, the whole street is sometimes used as an open-air loading bay and temporary warehouse. **1974** *Times* 19 Jan. 10/1 New York is not yet on a three-day week, but.. mid-town restaurants are doing badly.

f. *mid-clavicular, -sternal, -ventral* adjs.; *mid-Victorian* (earlier and later examples); hence as *sb.*; also † *mid-Vic* sb. and adj. in the same senses; *mid-Victorianism.*

1902 H. J. STILES in D. J. Cunningham *Text-bk. Anat.* 1184 In a well-proportioned subject, the mid-clavicular line, if prolonged downwards, will be found to be continuous with the vertical Poupart line. **1961** *Lancet* 9 Sept. 573/2 A hyperactive precordium with the maximum apical impulse in the left fifth intercostal space outside the midclavicular line was noted. **1902** H. J. STILES in D. J. Cunningham *Text-bk. Anat.* 1184 The vertical lines are: the mid-sternal, the lateral sternal, [etc.]. **1963** *Lancet* 12 Jan. 111/1 She had a severe midsternal pain which continued overnight, preventing sleep. **1904** *Amer. Naturalist* Feb. 123 The median vein lies along the mid-ventral line of the swollen abdomen. **1925** J. T. JENKINS *Fishes Brit. Isles* 315 Its colour was almost black dorsally..with an irregular mid-ventral streak. **1933** E. HAMILTON *Halcyon Era* 6 The papers, over which the poor Midvics yawned in ill-concealed boredom, dealt almost exclusively with Court news. *Ibid.* 32 The studied Midvic pose. *Ibid.* 39 No one was ever allowed to take anything off in Midvic days. **1901** F. H. BURNETT *Making of Marchioness* II. xiv. 280 'She was so respectable?' 'She was even a little Mid-Victorian, dear Mary.' **1927** Mid-Victorian [see *EDWARDIAN *a.* 3]. **1965** N. ST. JOHN-STEVAS in Bagehot *Coll. Works* I. 79 Bagehot was never in the least infected by the vulgar *No Popery* of the mid-Victorians. **1969** H. PERKIN *Key Profession* iii. 81 The mid-Victorian reforms which reduced the power of the 'Heads of Houses'. **1923** *Daily Mail* 12 Feb. 13 The artist..had an eccentric taste for mid-Victorianism. **1927** W. E. COLLINSON *Contemp. Eng.* 62 The peg-top trousers of mid-Victorianism.

2. a. *spec.* (*a*) *Phonetics.* Of a vowel-sound: produced with the tongue or some part of it in a middle position between high and low. Freq. *Comb.*

1876 [see HIGH *a.* 4 b]. **1908** H. SWEET *Sounds of Eng.* 25 If the tongue stops exactly half-way, we obtain the normal 'mid' position, as in the first elements of *ei* and *ou*, which are mid-front and mid-back respectively. **1927** J. J. HOGAN *Eng. Lang. in Ireland* 60 He notices the representation of M.E. ē slack by a mid-vowel: 'They pronounce the words tea, sea, please, as if they were written, tay, say, plays; instead of tee, see, pleese.' **1935** *Harvard Stud. Philol. & Lit.* XVII. 44 A diphthong whose first element was at first a mid-front vowel, and later..low-front-slack, mid-back-tense, or possibly 'neutral'. **1961** R. B. LONG *Sentence & its Parts* xix. 415 For mid-central /ə/ the tip of the tongue is characteristically pulled back and elevated slightly. **1965** *Language* XLI. 346 Ngbaka shows only four sequences: high-mid, mid-high, mid-low, and low-mid. **1965** [see *DOWN-GLIDE]. **1965** [see *high-tone* (*HIGH *a.* 22 a)].

(*b*) Of a colour: occupying a middle position in a range of shades.

1916 *Daily Colonist* (Victoria, B.C.) 1 July 12/3 (Advt.), The colors include white, cream, .. mid-brown, lemon, [etc.]. *Ibid.* 23 July 6/1 Gowns..in navy, black, mid-blue, [etc.]. **1929** *Radio Times* 8 Nov. 439/2 (Advt.), This stylish coat... In bottle green, burgundy, dk. brown, mid brown, navy and black. **1937** *Discovery* Oct. 325/2 The complementary..of mid-yellow is violet-blue. **1971** *Vogue* 15 Oct. 8 Dress..in violet, fir green and mid grey.

b. *mid-position, -section.*

1888 J. Rose *Mod. Machine-Shop Practice* II. xxxvii. 379/1 As the eccentric is in mid-position (*e* being equidistant from B and D), the valve will be in mid-position. **1896** *Rules governing Printing of Specifications* (U.S. Govt. Printing Office) 53 Mid-position. **1953** L. T. C. Rolt *Railway Adventure* iv. 106 We succeeded after some difficulty in doing this,..locking the valve in mid-position by screwing up the spindle gland nuts dead tight. **1957** R. W. Zandvoort *Handbk. Eng. Gram.* vi. 251 Mid-position of an adverb is apt to entail a brief pause between the adverb and the object. **1971** *Engineering* Apr. 47/1 When the sensed dimension is such that the core B is in its mid-position the primary flux is [etc.]. **1961** Webster *Midsection*, a section midway or about midway between the extremes; midriff. **1969** *Publ. Amer. Dial. Soc.* LI. 5 *Midsection*, representation of the kayak's profile if intersected by a plane perpendicular to the keel-line at the mid-point of the craft. **1972** *Sci. Amer.* Sept. 136/3 A four-foot structure with a cathode at one end and a collector at the other and a large electromagnet surrounding the midsection. **1973** *Ibid.* July 24/2 Actually all the horns called conical incorporate a certain amount of cylindrical tubing in their midsection. **1974** *Plain Dealer* (Cleveland, Ohio) 26 Oct. 4D/1 He is not throwing any punches. Instead, he is permitting Williams to pound him in the midsection.

d. mid-body *Cytology* [tr. G. *zwischenkörper* (W. Flemming 1891, in *Arch. f. mikrosk. Anat.* XXXVII. 690)] (see quots.); **mid-brow** *sb.* and *a.* = *middle-brow* (*Middle A. 6); **midcrop,** a crop harvested between the main crops; **Midcult, midcult** orig. *U.S.*, middle-brow culture; also *attrib.*; **Mid-East, mid-East, Mideast** = *Middle East; also *attrib.*; **mid-European** *a.* = *Middle-European* adj. (*middle A. 6); also as *sb.*; **mid-fi,** sound-reproduction equipment of a slightly lower quality than *hi-fi; also *attrib.* or as *adj.*; **midsa·gittal** *a. Anat.* = Median *a.*[1]; **mid-shot** *Cinemat.* and *T.V.* (see quot. 1953); **mid-west, mid-West** = *Middle West* (*middle A. 6); **mid-western, mid-Western** *a.* = *Middle Western* (*middle A. 6); **mid-westerner, mid-Westerner,** an inhabitant of the Middle West; (also in form *Midwest*, etc.); **mid-wing** *a. Aeronaut.* having the main wings placed approximately halfway between the top and bottom of the fuselage.

1896 E. B. Wilson *Cell* 338 *Mid-body* ('Zwischenkörper'), a body or group of granules, probably comparable with the cell-plate in plants, formed in the equatorial region of the spindle during the anaphases of mitosis. **1969** Brown & Bertke *Textbk. Cytol.* xix. 417/1 The portions of the continuous [spindle] fibers where cytokinesis is to occur, become thickened to form the mid-body, 'stem body' of Belar, or 'Flemming body' which has been seen in cytokinesis of other animals, including *Hydra*. **1928** *Sunday Express* 1 July 12/6 Delighting the low-brow, the mid-brow, and the high-brow with equal facility. **1959** *Manch. Guardian* 10 Aug. 3/2 The dramatic policy is good average mid-brow. **1964** *Punch* 19 Feb. 268/1 When the Midbrows are first showing signs of moving in. **1966** R. A. Downie tr. *O. Del Buono's Bond Affair* 158 It is superficial, banal, *midbrow* wherever psychological analysis is attempted. **1957** *Times* 28 Dec. 10/1 Only the small West African midcrops standing in the way of an absolute Brazilian control over international cocoa offerings until the gathering of the new West African main crops in the autumn. **1973** *Times* 13 July 21/8 Henry Stephens & Sons (London) reported that whatever happened, even at best, the 1973–74 crop would be a late one and the light and mid-crops would not be sufficient to meet internal demand for local industries. **1960** D. Macdonald in *Partisan Rev.* XXVII. 592 This intermediate form—let us call it Midcult—has the essential qualities of Masscult—the formula, the built-in reaction, the lack of any standard except popularity—but it decently covers them with a cultural fig-leaf... Midcult has it both ways: it pretends to respect the standards of High Culture while in fact it waters them down and vulgarizes them. **1962** *Listener* 22 Nov. 863/1 There may seem to be phases in broadcasting history when British broadcasting..has favoured what Dwight Macdonald has called 'midcult', something which is neither for the few nor for the many. **1966** *Ibid.* 27 Jan. 142/2 Even Wilson he feels (though he admires him), has had to sacrifice to 'Midcult' values. *c* **1944** (*newspaper-title*) Mid-East Mail. **1969** *Daily Tel.* 5 Feb. 24 (*heading*) Nixon decision on Mid-East 'in few days'. **1971** R. Thomas *Backup Men* xix. 168 A juke-box blared out some Mideast music. **1972** *Newsweek* 31 July 28/1 There seemed to be some hope for a break in the Mideast diplomatic logjam. **1974** *Publishers Weekly* 7 Jan. 25 (Advt.), 3 months ago this was to be a major study of the Middle East Conflict. Today it is the first major study of the Mideast including the October War. **1960** J. Stroud *Shorn Lamb* iv. 41 Mad Mid-Europeans camping with their chattels in the office porch. **1961** *Guardian* 1 Apr. 4/7 The hall mark of mid-European free dance. **1974** 'J. Le Carré' *Tinker, Tailor* xi. 89 Toby Esterhase's faithful mid-European echo. **1970** J. Earl *Tuners & Amplifiers* 7 There is still a margin between what the audiophiles term true hi-fi and general 'domestic quality', and here an entirely new and highly popular range of equipment is emerging. Some call this 'mid-fi' equipment,..but it is noteworthy that such equipment is already rising above the basic 'domestic quality' and entering into the hi-fi fringes. **1971** *Hi-Fi Sound* Feb. 64/3 Today's hi-fi will be tomorrow's mid-fi. **1975** *Gramophone* Jan. 1389 (Advt.), Some of those 'mid-fi' stereo systems of a few years back have a good record player and good speakers. **1957** R. T. Woodburne *Essent. Human Anat.* i. 3/2 The median plane is a vertical plane through the body reaching the surface at the mid-line in front and behind. This plane is also known as the midsagittal plane of the body. **1967** G. M. Wyburn et al. *Conc. Anat.* viii. 203/2 Cut the eyeball in a midsagittal plane. **1968** Chomsky & Halle *Sound Pattern Eng.* 302 Consonantal sounds are produced with a radical obstruction in the midsagittal region of the vocal tract. **1953** K. Reisz *Technique Film Editing* 280 *Mid-shot*, shot taken with the camera nearer to the object than for a long shot but not so near as for a close-up; in relation to the human subject, a shot of the human figure approximately from the waist upwards. **1926** E. Ferber *Show Boat* v. 80 To the farmers and villagers of the Midwest..the show boat meant music, romance, gaiety. **1948, 1968** Midwest, Mid-West [see *Far West]. **1889** Farmer *Americanisms* 365/2 *Mid-Western States*, W. Virginia, Kentucky, Tennessee, Missouri, Kansas, and Arkansas. **1906** (*title*) The Midwestern (Des Moines, Iowa). **1923** *Collier's Mag.* 25 Aug. 24/3 One of the economic causes of Mid-Western discontent is the feeling that the Mid-West is the object of discrimination. **1936** *Mind* XLV. 218 After leaving Harvard, Boodin seemed for many years to be lost in the obscurity of a small mid-western college. **1972** M. J. Bosse *Incident at Naha* ii. 93 You can never wholly shed a *Midwestern* background. **1927** *Scribner's Mag.* Oct. 480/2 These midwesterners are alike unto Americans in other rural areas. **1969** I. Kemp *Brit. G.I. in Vietnam* iii. 47 A sun-tanned, crew-cut, athletic looking mid-Westerner from Green Bay, Wisconsin. **1971** *Guardian* 10 July 9/1 Stolid and conservative Mid-westerners..are..concerned about the plight of the Indians, because the Indians are part of Middle West life. **1934** *Flight* 15 Feb. 156/1 The machine is a mid-wing cantilever monoplane with the wing in three sections. **1942** *R.A.F. Jrnl.* 16 May 16 A twin-engine mid-wing monoplane of creditable modern design.

C. *adv.* **b.** *Comb.*

1876 G. M. Hopkins *Wreck of Deutschland* xxxiv, in *Poems* (1967) 62 Mid-numberèd he in three of the thunder-throne! **1960** *Farmer & Stockbreeder* 23 Feb. 69/3 The Colman-Fella tedder..can be operated in conjunction with a mid-mounted mower. *Ibid.* 8 Mar. 75/2 There is much to be said for mid-mounting of tools that need accurate steerage.

mid air. (Examples in aeronautical contexts.)

1928 R. Fry *Let.* 25 May (1972) II. 627 Reports of aeroplanes that catch fire and grill the passengers in mid-air. **1958** 'P. Bryant' *Two Hours to Doom* 58 Mid-air re-fuelling. **1970** *Guardian* 21 Aug. 5/1 If something is not done soon about these near misses, there is bound to be a mid-air collision.

Midas. Add: **1. b.** Esp. in phr. (*the*) *Midas touch.*

[**1879** C. M. Yonge *Magnum Bonum* III. xxxix. 899 He would talk of the touch of Midas.] **1883** *Authors & Publishers* (G. P. Putnam's Sons) 12 'From the authors he seized brains and from the public gold.' Certainly a most desirable result, and the picture of our publisher, in the guise of a prestidigitateur, exercising an infallible King-Midas touch on the material submitted to him, is a very fascinating one. **1938** M. Kennedy (*title*) The Midas touch. **1960** *Times* 18 July 3/4 Picasso, with his Midas touch, has at first try made the lino-cut a more dignified medium. **1970** *Observer* 29 Nov. 10/5 [Art] objects which start out as sincere personal statements are turned, by the fatal Midas touch of capitalism, into gold.

2. b. midas-fly, mydas fly, a large fly of the family Mydaidæ.

1895 J. H. Comstock *Man. Study Insects* 461 The Midas-flies rival the robber-flies in size, and quite closely resemble them in appearance. **1972** Swan & Papp *Common Insects N. Amer.* 609 Mydas flies..are elongated, moderate to very large in size, resemble wasps and.. robber flies.

mid-course. Add: **1. b.** In contexts of interplanetary flights. Also *attrib.*

1959 *IRE Trans. Military Electronics* III. 150/1 It will become apparent that no interplanetary mission even with the crudest requirements would have a reasonable probability of success unless some midcourse or terminal guidance is carried out. *Ibid.* 159/1 The midcourse corrections may also remove residual parallel components. **1964** *Times* 1 Aug. 6 The small rocket engine which can manoeuvre the space craft slightly in mid-course. **1969** *Times* 16 July 5/8 *MCC*, midcourse correction.

midder (mi·dəɪ). *Med. slang.* [f. Mid(wife *sb.* or Mid(wifery + *-er[6].] Midwifery; a midwifery case, childbirth. Also *attrib.*

1909 A. N. Lyons *Sixpenny Pieces* iii. 23 It was no good waiting breakfast for Fatty..because Fatty's 'call' was a 'midder'. **1931** 'F. Iles' *Malice Aforethought* iv. 78 Dr. Bickleigh was wishing that a call would reach him.., a midder-case even. **1937** A. J. Cronin *Citadel* II. vii. 153 We can't go! I've got a positive conviction I'm having a midder case next Sunday evening! **1948** M. Allingham *More Work for Undertaker* xxiv. 279 You've got a midder, you say, doctor? **1965** M. Polland *Thicker than Water* (1967) iii. 29 Although he..did his medicine in Edinburgh, he came here to the Rotunda for his midder.

middle, *a.* and *sb.* Add: **A.** *adj.* **2. b.** Of a colour = *mid *a.* 2 a (*b*).

1869 *Bradshaw's Railway Manual* XXI. 460 (Advt.), Brunswick Green dark middle, and pale. **1926–7** *Army & Navy Stores Catal.* 299/1 Washable water paint... Colours ..Light Stone—Middle Stone—Dark Stone. **1950** J. Cannan *Murder Included* vii. 158 A wool frock of a dull middle-blue.

6. Middle Academy, name given to the mainly sceptic school of philosophy developed in the third century B.C. by Arcesilaus (316/15–242/1 B.C.) when he was head of the Academy founded by Plato; **Middle America,** (*a*) a geographical region comprising central America, Mexico, and the Antilles; (*b*) the 'silent' majority of Americans, regarded as a homogeneous group; hence **Middle American** *a.* and *sb.*; **middle article** = Middle B. 12; **middle-brow, middlebrow,** (*a*) *sb.*, a person of average or moderate cultural interests; (*b*) *adj.*, claiming to be or regarded as only moderately intellectual; **middle common room,** a common room for graduate students; also graduate students collectively; **middle distance,** (*b*) *Athletics*, a distance for a race longer than a sprint but shorter than a long-distance race, esp. one of 440 yards, 880 yards, or a mile (or corresponding metric distances); also (with hyphen) *attrib.*; **middle distillate,** a petroleum fraction that comes off at intermediate temperatures (about 180° to 340°C) in fractional distillation, from which is obtained paraffin, diesel oil, and heating oil; **middle eight** *colloq.*, the eight bars in the middle of a conventionally structured popular tune, often of a different character from the other parts of the tune; the B section in a tune of the form A, A, B, A; the 'release'; **Middle-European** *a.*, of, pertaining to, or characteristic of central Europe or its people; cf. *Mittel-European *a.* and *sb.*; **middle game,** the part of a game of chess between the opening and the end-game; **middle ground,** (*c*) a place half-way between extremes; an area of moderation or compromise; also *attrib.*; **middle guard** [Guard *sb.* 3 b] *Cricket*, the position occupied by a batsman so that his bat defends the middle stump; **middle income,** an average income; also (with hyphen) *attrib.*; **Middle Kingdom** (later examples); (*b*) in ancient Egypt, the Eleventh and Twelfth Dynasties, which ruled from the 22nd to the 18th century B.C.; **middle lamella** *Bot.* (see quots.); **middle leg** *slang*, the penis; **middle-length** *attrib.*, (of a story, etc.) of medium length; **middle management** orig. *U.S.* (see quot. 1957); also (with hyphen) *attrib.*; **middle-middle,** (*a*) the middle or centre; (*b*) a member of the middle-middle-class; **middle-middle-class,** the class of society midway between the 'upper' and the 'lower' class; also *pl.* in the same sense; **middle name** orig. *U.S.*, (*a*) a name between one's first Christian name and one's surname; (*b*) *fig.*, the outstanding characteristic of a person; **middle-off, -on** *Cricket* = Mid-off, -on; **middle passage** (earlier and later examples); (see also quot. 1949); **middle period,** the middle phase (of a culture, artist's work, etc.); also *attrib.*; **middle rail,** (*b*) the 'live' central rail of an electric railway; **middle-range** *attrib.*, designating a thing or things that occur in the middle of a range of items; **middle-rank,** a body of things or persons of intermediate status or value; also *attrib.* or as *adj.*, of neither high nor low rank or value; hence *middle-ranking* adj. (cf. *high-ranking *a.*); **middle rib,** in beef: one of the ribs between the fore ribs and the chuck ribs; **middle-road** *attrib.*, = *middle-of-the-road; **middle school,** (*b*) the middle forms in a grammar or independent school (see quot. 1960); (*c*) a separate post-primary school within the educational system of a state for children aged between about nine and thirteen years; also *attrib.*; **Middle States** (examples); **middle-tone** = Half-tone *sb.* 2; **middle-water** *attrib.*, applied to fishing, or to ships engaged in fishing, at a medium distance from land; **middle weight,** substitute for def.: a man of average weight; *spec.* (in various sports) used to designate an intermediate weight class; esp. in professional boxing, a boxer whose weight is not more than 11 stone 6 lbs.; also *attrib.*; (add earlier and later examples); **Middle West,** the north central states of the U.S.A., as distinct from the West or Far West (see quot. 1949); so **Middle Western** *a.*; **Middle White,** a Yorkshire breed of pig; **middle wicket** (earlier examples).

1659 T. Stanley tr. *Sextus Empiricus's Pyrr. Hyp.* in *Hist. Philos.* IV. 33 Arcesilaus, Institutor and President of the middle Academy, seems to me to participate so much of the Pyrrhonian reasons, as that his Institution and ours is almost the same. **1744** W. Guthrie *Morals of Cicero* p. xiii, We are now arrived at the middle Academy, the Founder of which was Arcesilas. **1845** G. H. Lewes *Biogr. Hist. Philos.* II. viii. iv. 165 The Middle Academy and the New Academy we thus unite in one; although the ancients drew a distinction between them, it is difficult for moderns to do. **1899** M. M. Patrick *Sextus Empiricus & Gk. Scepticism* iv. 77 Sextus himself claims a close relation

between the Middle Academy and Pyrrhonism. **1970** *Oxf. Class. Dict.* (ed. 2) 95/1 The term 'Middle Academy may also derive from Antiochus [of Ascalon]. **1898** *Pop. Sci. Monthly* Nov. 1 (*title*) Was Middle America peopled from Asia? **1952** S. Tax (*title*) Heritage of conquest: the ethnology of Middle America. **1957** *Social & Econ. Stud.* (Kingston, Jamaica) VI. III. 380 (*title*) Haciendas and plantations in Middle America and the Antilles. **1966** West & Augelli *Middle Amer.* i. 1 Middle America is an arbitrary geographic expression which refers to a mosaic of people, places, and cultures. Mexico, Central America, and the West Indies, the area which the term usually defines, share a general focus on the Gulf of Mexico and the Caribbean Sea and an intermediate location between North and South America. **1968** *Sunday Times* 29 Sept. 8 What is seriously wrong with Mr Nixon's new Middle America is that it is virtually all white. **1971** *Guardian* 5 Apr. 4/1 Mr Agnew has continued to reflect the prejudices and confusions of Middle America. **1972** P. Dickinson *Lizard in Cup* x. 159 We've got to show that we can build, but..Middle America will like that even less than the bombs. **1973** *Tucson* (Arizona) *Daily Citizen* 22 Aug. 28/1 The Braunlichs will also tell you that, sad as it is, middle America is leery of things it gets for free. **1926** F. F. Blom *Tribes & Temples* I. i. 4 There are maps of most of the Middle American countries, and the greater number of them..are remarkably inaccurate. **1969** *Collier's Encycl. Year Bk.* 3 Her [*sc.* Mrs. Richard Nixon's] looks and taste are classic Middle American, even as her husband's are. **1970** *Time* 5 Jan. 9 Who precisely are the Middle Americans?.. They make up the core of the group that Richard Nixon now invokes as the 'forgotten Americans' or 'the Great Silent Majority'. **1971** *Guardian* 5 Jan. 10/6 If the chips were to come down now, the final word would undoubtedly rest with the middle Americans. **1975** *Atlantic Monthly* Jan. 28/1 The phrase 'Middle American' was first used..by Joseph Kraft in the spring of 1968, when he was writing about the municipal workers in New York City... He specifically referred to their ethnic character: Irish policemen, Italian sanitation workers, Jewish schoolteachers, and so on. *a* **1894** C. H. Pearson in W. Stebbing *Charles Henry Pearson* (1900) viii. 90 T. C. Sandars.. created the so-called middle article—the essay on social topics. **1966** *Listener* 27 Oct. 621/3 Those 'light' middle articles which used to be a feature of the highbrow weeklies. **1925** *Punch* 23 Dec. 673/3 The B.B.C. claim to have discovered a new type, the 'middlebrow'. It consists of people who are hoping that some day they will get used to the stuff they ought to like. **1928** *Observer* 17 June 26 The standard of 'middle-brow' music and plays is always rather low. **1934** C. Lambert *Music Ho!* iv. 247 Hindemith is the journalist of modern music, the supreme middlebrow of our times. **1958** Middle-brow [see *glossy *a.* a]. **1972** L. Alcock *By South Cadbury* i. 22 The onerous and unrewarding task of Secretary was filled by Geoffrey Ashe, writer of distinguished middle-brow books on the problems of the historical Arthur. **1958** *Times* 28 Oct. 12/5 Lincoln College is to be the first Oxford college to establish a special common room for postgraduate students of the college. It will be known as the Middle Common Room. **1969** *Rep. Comm. on Relations with Junior Members Univ. Oxf.* 48 One shall be a president of a Middle Common Room elected by the conference of M.C.R. Presidents. **1971** *Guardian* 21 Dec. 1/6 The ability of the junior and middle common rooms to play their essential rôle in a collegiate university. **1891** *Harper's Young People* 7 Apr. 384/2 Among middle-distance men, as among sprinters, there are various types of runners. **1901** *Encycl. Sport* I. 56/1 It is fairer to describe a Quarter Mile as one of the middle distances. *Ibid.*, The sprinter must use different tactics to the middle-distance runner. **1929** G. M. Butler *Mod. Athletics* v. 74 Speed..should be the middle-distance runner's main objective. **1960** Middle distance [see *front-runner* s.v. *front *sb.* 14]. **1956** *Nature* 10 Mar. 460/1 Prof. Morton's research work has been concerned with the constitution of petroleum, [and] with methods of separation of hydrocarbons, particularly in the middle-distillate boiling range. **1973** *People's Jrnl.* (Inverness & Northern Counties ed.) 15 Dec. 1/1 The nature of North-Sea crude oil is more suited to what we call 'middle distillates'—diesel oil, oil fuel for heating and sulphur by-products. **1966** *Melody Maker* 16 Apr. 8 Doesn't sound as though there's a middle eight. It's good, though not as good as some of their previous records. **1968** *Listener* 1 Feb. 157/3 Popular song has long been confined to an appalling eight-bar monotony. An eight-bar section, repeated; a 'middle eight' and the first eight again. **1939** M. Allingham *Mr. Campion & Others* 86 She's frightfully susceptible. It's her Middle-European blood. **1949** E. Coxhead *Wind in West* iv. 115 That's enough gloom, turn on the Middle-European gaiety. **1972** C. Drummond *Death at Bar* vi. 159 Dee had liked middle-European victuals. **1894** J. Mason *Princ. Chess* 184 No true knowledge of it [*sc.* the opening] is possible independently of a fair knowledge of..the middle game and end. **1958** *Times Lit. Suppl.* 14 Nov. 664/4 The main portion of the work.. is concerned with middle-game tactics. **1959** *Listener* 5 Mar. 434/1 Coming to middle game, it is instructive to see how a great player defends himself when he is in trouble. **1961** A. Smith *East-Enders* vi. 102 The middleground is missing... There's no common place inside the East End for everyone as there used to be. **1972** *Language* XLVIII. 278 In the case of terms like *possible* and *impossible*, there is no middle ground; but that is simply the nature of terms which permit no qualification. **1972** *Guardian* 11 Oct. 12/2 The Laureate has to be a middle-ground man, and there are very few of them around. **1973** *Ibid.* 24 Mar. 22/6 Ultimately as the Alliance leaders know, the organisation of middleground politics is of secondary importance. **1871** 'Thomsonby' *Cricketers in Council* 25 Hold your bat up straight, on the popping crease, and ask for 'middle' guard. **1941** *Economist* 12 Apr. 475/1 Direct taxation on what have come to be known as the 'middle incomes'. **1958** B. A. Smith in N. Mackenzie *Conviction* 59 The major beneficiaries of these changes were the middle-income groups. **1971** M. McCarthy *Birds of America* 54 The subspecies they belonged to—white, middle-income intelligentsia. **1848** S. W. Williams (*title*) The Middle Kingdom: a survey..of the Chinese Empire and its inhabitants. **1890** F. L. Griffith *Antiquities Tell el Yahûdîyeh* 39/1 The earliest dateable antiquities from Tell el Yahûdîyeh are of the middle kingdom. **1906** J. H. Breasted *Hist. Egypt* III. viii. 156 The stable organization, which enabled her [*sc.* Egypt] about 2000 B.C. to enter upon her second great period of productive development, the Middle Kingdom. **1928** C. Dawson *Age of Gods* viii. 173 The Middle Minoan period corresponds to the Middle Kingdom. **1969** V. G. Kiernan *Lords of Human Kind* v. 150 That China was the Middle Kingdom, the one truly civilized realm, was..an axiom to its inhabitants. **1971** J. R. Harris *Legacy of Egypt* (ed. 2) 3 Pieces of Middle Kingdom jewellery were reproduced at Byblos in the second millennium B.C. **1925** Eames & MacDaniels *Introd. Plant Anat.* ii. 25 When a pronounced secondary wall is present the primary wall is commonly called the middle lamella. **1947** *Ibid.* (ed. 2) ii. 28 The intercellular layer is the middle layer of this group of three or five layers and the term middle lamella should be restricted to this. **1965** K. Esau *Plant Anat.* (ed. 2) iii. 34 On the basis of development and structure three parts are commonly recognized in plant cell walls: the intercellular substance or middle lamella, the primary wall, and the secondary wall. **1922** Joyce *Ulysses* 443 Are you going far, queer fellow? How's your middle leg? **1935** Dylan Thomas *Let.* Feb. (1966) 151 Men should be two tooled and a poet's middle leg is his pencil. **1928** *Scholartis Press Catal.* July, A volume of five middle-length (*not* short) stories by Norah Hoult. **1946** 'G. Orwell' *Shooting Elephant* (1950) 168 The usual middle-length review. **1957** Clark & Gottfried *Dict. Business & Finance* 228/2 *Middle management*, in general, the group or class of junior executives and senior supervisory personnel in the direct line of authority and communications between the top levels of management and the first line supervisory personnel. **1966** S. Phipps *God on Monday* vi. 76 The opposite swing of the same pendulum may be seen in the groups of middle-management-type bungalows that are appearing round the fringes of English villages. **1966** *Punch* 28 Sept. 485/1 The productivity agreement says a good deal for the efficiency of the group, at least at middle-management level. **1975** *Harper's & Queen* May 101 The Saudis need to swell their middle management by 200,000. **1914** E. M. Forster *Maurice* (1971) xliii. 202 The clientele of Messrs Hill and Hall was drawn from the middle-middle classes. **1926** D. H. Lawrence *David* iii. 21 And only from the middle-middle of all the worlds, where God stirs amid His waters, can strength come to us. **1934** H. Read *Art & Industry* IV. 126/1 He..is a middle-middle-class man with a nice little house in the suburbs. **1936** 'G. Orwell' *Keep Aspidistra Flying* iii. 54 The derelict spinsters of the middle-middle classes. **1955** T. H. Pear *Eng. Social Differences* iii. 90 When 'middle-middles' become 'upper-middles' they..drop middle-class euphemisms. **1973** *Listener* 22 Feb. 249/3 Their milieux range from lower-middle to middle-middle class. **1835** *Harvardiana* II. 23 [He] then asks their middle names. **1919** Wodehouse *Damsel in Distress* ii. 31 My dad ran a Bide a Wee Home for flowers, and I used to know them all by their middle names. *Ibid.* xvi. 203 Everyone told me your middle name was Nero. **1920** Ade *Hand-Made Fables* 92, I take it that Mixer is your middle name. **1926** A. Christie *Murder R. Ackroyd* xi. 144 'Modesty is certainly not his middle name.' 'I wish you wouldn't be so horribly American, James.' **1932** *N. & Q.* 3 Sept. 177/2 There is also a proverbial saying, 'Money is his middle name', 'Art is her middle name', meaning one's forte. **1972** P. Cleife *Slick & Dead* xvii. 134 If I had a dollar for every time I've said that, my middle name would be Rothschild. **1972** J. Porter *Meddler & her Murder* i. 11 Tact was far from being the Hon. Con's middle name. **1851** W. Clark in W. Bolland *Cricket Notes* 137 The middle off, cover point, long slip, and long stop should all save one run. **1843** 'Wykhamist' *Pract. Hints Cricket* (*caption*) Short leg or middle on. **1887** F. Gale *Game of Cricket* 139 Middle-on and middle-off were.. about equal distance from either wicket, standing back some fifteen yards from the centre between the wickets, opposite each other. **1788** T. Clarkson *Essay on Slavery* (ed. 2) III. iii. 98 The captain of a ship, then on the middle passage, had lost a considerable number of his slaves by death. **1949** C. Lloyd *Navy & Slave Trade* I. i. 5 The Round Trip..was commonly divided into three 'passages'. On the outward passage the cargo consisted of textiles, hardware, alcohol and antiquated firearms. These were traded on the coast for slaves, who were shipped to America and the West Indies on the notorious Middle Passage. The principal cargoes taken on there for the homeward passage were sugar, tobacco and rum. **1969** *Listener* 22 May 713/3 Even the unsqueamish stomachs of the 18th century were turned by accounts of the Middle Passage. **1873** C. M. Yonge *Pillars of House* IV. xxxvi. 50 Here's the dining room... This is the middle period, the Stewart style part. **1894** G. B. Shaw *Music in London 1890–94* (1932) III. 157 Those features of the middle period Beethovenism of which we all have to speak so very seriously. **1930** W. S. Maugham *Cakes & Ale* i. 17 The novels of his middle period reflected..the strain. **1951** T. S. Eliot *Poetry & Drama* ii. 20 His [*sc.* Yeats's] middle-period *Plays for Dancers*. **1905** Goodchild & Tweney *Technol. & Sci. Dict.* 401/2 *Middle rail*, a heavy conductor in the form of a rail carried on insulating supports, which is laid between the running rails of an electric railway to supply current to the motors. **1964** G. F. Arnold in D. Abercrombie et al. *Daniel Jones* 17 The middle-range percentages..are provided by comparisons of phonemes. **1967** M. Argyle *Psychol. Interpersonal Behaviour* ix. 161 In the matter of price, for example, some Ss [*sc.* salesmen] show the middle-range item first, others show the most expensive. **1961** *Times* 28 Dec. 11/4 That solid middle-rank of literature. **1969** *Daily Tel.* 10 Oct. 3 Sterling, too, is a middle-rank currency these days—apparently safe from heavy selling pressure but not exactly in demand by speculators. **1972** *Guardian* 13 Nov. 2/3 Middle-rank American and Vietnamese officials in Saigon. **1959** *Encounter* Aug. 18/1 Instructions transmitted..from on high through a number of middle-ranking personages down to floor polishers. **1747, 1844** Middle rib [see *chuck *sb.*[4] 2]. **1963** A. L. Simon *Guide Good Food & Wines* 406/1 The *Middle Ribs* and *Chuck Ribs*, sometimes called *Wing Ribs*, are both uneconomical and ungainly as joints owing to the larger proportion of bone to meat. **1958** A. Wilson *Middle Age of Mrs Eliot* III. 343 A nice middle-road historian's position, he thought to himself with comforting irony. **1971** *Guardian* 14 May 1/3 With no obviously dominating candidate to step into Nasser's shoes, they chose the safe middleroad candidate —Sadat. **1914** 'I. Hay' *Lighter Side School Life* viii. 224 The occasion of his first attendance at a meeting of the Middle School Debating Society. **1933** Middle school [see *Aryan *sb.* 2]. **1960** *Where?* III. 15 *Middle school*, usually the third and fourth forms of a school (a grammar school expression). **1962** E. J. King *World Perspectives in Educ.* III. vii. 142 The new Danish two-year programme established for all twelve-year-olds in 1959..was..a nationwide formalization of what used to happen in many urban middle schools. **1971** *Guardian* 20 Oct. 1/8 Surrey.. County Council..passed a scheme providing for middle schools followed by 12–18 comprehensives. **1973** *New Society* 10 May 294/1 In 1970, the Department of Education and Science introduced a new category called 'middle schools' into its yearly *Statistics*... What is a middle school? The official version is..a school which straddles the traditional primary-to-secondary transfer age of eleven. **1784** G. Washington *Diary* 4 Oct. (1925) II. 326 The middle States with the Country immediately back of them. **1848** J. F. Cooper *Oak Openings* I. xiii. 193 Who ever heard of the 'tribe' of New England, or..of the 'tribe of the Middle States? **1912** M. Nicholson *Hoosier Chron.* 59 There had been an infusion of population from New England and the Middle States. **1909** Webster, Middle tone. **1961** M. Levy *Studio Dict. Art Terms* 59 *Half-tone*, the tone value in a painting which is halfway between the dark and the light. Sometimes called Middle-Tone. **1962** Middle-water [see *distant-water* s.v. *distant *a.* 8]. **1967** *Times Rev. Industry* May 28/2 The near and middle-water fleet consists of boats between 80 and 140 feet long which sail mainly from Grimsby, Fleetwood, Lowestoft, Aberdeen, Milford Haven and North Shields for fishing grounds around the Faroes, in the North Sea and to the west of the British Isles. **1889** Middle weight [see Feather-weight 3]. **1909** *Westm. Gaz.* 9 Feb. 12/4 Some fine wrestling has been seen, more especially in the middle-weight class. **1947** E. Gruhn *Text Bk. Wrestling* (ed. 4) 84 *Middle-weight*, up to 174 lb. (79 Kilos). **1955** J. Murray *Weight Lifting* iii. 56 The body-weight classes used in standard international lifting competition are as follows..165½ pounds—Middleweight. **1972** F. Butler *Hist. Boxing in Brit.* xix. 132 The middleweight division was started in England in 1786... The middleweights can claim more superb champions than any section outside the heavyweight. **1898** M. H. Catherwood (*title*) Heroes of the Middle West. **1909** Middle West [see *dripped *ppl. a.*]. **1917** *Nation* (N.Y.) 17 May 589/2 The personal tour of the Secretary of the Treasury through the Middle West, to speak at public meetings, is a wise arrangement. **1949** *Oxf. Jun. Encycl.* III. 452/2 The Middle West region is oddly named, because the states of Ohio, Indiana, Illinois, Michigan, Wisconsin, Minnesota, Iowa, and Missouri, which make it up, are really neither middle nor west. **1909** 'O. Henry' *Options* 310 I'm only a little Middle-Western girl. **1916** A. Huxley *Let.* 30 June (1969) 103 Merest text-book papers, such as would be set by a Middle Western College out your way. **1967** Middle-western [see *fraternity 7]. **1893** L. M. Douglas *Man. Pork Trade* p. xiv (*caption*) Small and Middle White Yorkshire Pigs. **1912** Middle White [see *fatstock* s.v. *fat *a.* 14]. **1953** A. Jobson *Househ. & Country Crafts* vi. 65 Almost every county in England has produced its own breed of pigs, and we have amongst others Large and Middle White. **1786** Middle wick't [see *bat *sb.*[2] 3 c]. **1816** W. Lambert *Cricketers' Guide* (ed. 6) iii. 42 Middle Wicket Off. This man should stand on the off side, not far from the Bowler's wicket, and about 23 yards from the Striker's wicket. *Ibid.* 44 (*heading*) To cover the Point and Middle Wicket.

B. *sb.* **1.** *to knock* (a person) *into the middle of next week*: see Week *sb.* 6 d.

b. *U.S.* A strip of unplanted ground between rows of cotton, corn, etc. Usu. *pl.*

1829 L. Covington *Diary* 28 May in *Documentary Hist. Amer. Industr. Society* (1910) I. 238 Two Ploughs breaking middles in Popular tree cut. **1907** T. F. Hunt *Forage & Fiber Crops in Amer.* 352 The field is made up into alternate beds and middles or into 'back' furrows and 'dead' furrows. **1946** *Democrat* 11 Apr. 1/5 Two and three year old kudzu stands that have not covered the middles will be greatly helped if the middles are broken out.

2. b. Delete 'Now *rare* or *Obs.*'

c. Slang phr. *in the middle*: in a difficult, dangerous, or untenable position; in trouble. *slang* (orig. *U.S.*).

1930 *Amer. Mercury* Dec. 457/1 What's the idea? Trying to put me in the middle with the law? **1943** R. Chandler *Lady in Lake* (1944) xxxiv. 179 The other guy could have knocked him out to put him in the middle. **1954** 'N. Blake' *Whisper in Gloom* II. xvi. 217, I still don't like it. How d'ya know he's not leaving us in the middle? **1972** J. Burmeister *Running Scared* x. 131, I am the man in the middle. If your note giving my location should go astray..I could quietly starve to death.

3. b. The part of a side of bacon which is left when the fore-end and the gammon are removed.

1892 P. L. Simmonds *Dict. Trade Products* (rev. ed.) Suppl. 473/2 *Middles*,..a name for sides of bacon and pork, there are long and short middles. **1917** G. J. Nicholls *Bacon & Hams* 70 These middles are cured in dry salt. **1923** R. E. Davies *Pigs & Bacon Curing* 29 The side may be cut into three parts, comprising the fore-end, the middle, and the gammon with corner.

13. *Cricket.* = *middle guard* (see *A. 6).

1866 'Capt. Crawley' *Cricket* 22 The batsman should.. after asking the umpire for middle, and taking his block at a bat's length from the stumps, stand..in the position shewn. **1904** F. C. Holland *Cricket* 1 What guard is to be chosen? Some cricketers take centre, some the leg stump, and many middle and leg. **1960** I. Peebles *Bowler's Turn* 187 He had batted on middle and off and shown a readiness to hook.

14. *colloq.* A middle-class person.

1955 T. H. Pear *Eng. Social Differences* 101 Wealthy 'middles' are now admitted to some formerly exclusive

hunts. **1967** *Listener* 21 Dec. 802/1 If a man spoke rather loudly..keeping his vowels open, then he was an Upper. If he attempted all this and just failed, then he was a Middle.

middle, *v.* Add: **9.** *Cricket.* To strike (a ball) with the middle of the bat; also with the bowler or the stroke as object.

1954 J. H. FINGLETON *Ashes crown Year* xi. 112 Hutton was in grand form. He middled Lindwall with confidence. **1955** I. PEEBLES *On Ashes* iii. 29 The batsman started by showing every sign of good form..middling his strokes with ominous regularity. **1955** MILLER & WHITINGTON *Cricket Typhoon* x. 189 May began to middle the ball.

middle age, *sb.* Add: **2.** (Earlier examples.)

a. sing. **1621** DONNE *Sermon I Tim. 1. 15* (1661) 192 It is a perplex't question in the School, (and truly the Balance in those of the middle age, very even) whether if Adam had not sinned, the son of God had come into the world, and taken our nature and our flesh upon him. **1624** WOTTON *Elem. Archit.* sig. ¶ 4 After the reuiuing and re-polishing of good Literature, (which the combustions and tumults of the middle Age had vnciuillized).

β. pl. **1616** SPELMAN *De non temerandis Ecclesiis* (ed. 2) App. 194 Thus the eldest and newest Expositors are wholly for mee, many also (& of the best of them) of the middle ages. **1699** M. LISTER *Journey to Paris* 108 It would have been some satisfaction to have seen by the Pictures, what the middle Ages, at least, had thought of them [*sc.* animals].

3. Also *attrib.* in sense 1, as *middle-age bulge, spread* (cf. next, sense b).

1937 *John o' London's* 29 Jan. 742/1 (Advt.), Join the happy throng who have learnt to control the 'middle-age spread' by wearing the..supporting belt. **1963** *Times* 6 May 9/1 The butcher wants his beef before it has developed a middle-age spread. **1972** J. PORTER *Meddler & her Murder* iii. 46 She was fighting a losing battle against the middle-age bulge.

middle-aged, *a.* Add: **1. a.** (Earlier and later examples.) Also *transf.* and *fig.*

1608 TOPSELL *Serpents* 73 The elder looke to the family, placing in due order that hony which is gathered and wrought by the middle-aged Bees. **1611** CORYAT *Crudities* 252 He was a middle-aged man, as about forty yeares old. **1918** W. OWEN *Let.* 22 July (1967) 566, I have no unused boots with me, but I left a delicate middle-aged pair in the Kitchen Cupboard. **1927** [see *ÉCLAIR]. **1940** [see *AUTO *sb.*^{2} 3]. **1950** T. S. ELIOT *Cocktail Party* I. ii. 57 Only since this morning I have met myself as a middle-aged man. **1960** M. SPARK *Ballad of Peckham Rye* vii. 150 The chief barmaid had a tiny nose and a big chin; she was a middle-aged woman of twenty-five. **1974** *Broadcast* 28 Oct. 20/2 Young men go to bed with young ladies, middle-aged men (presumably) with middle-aged ladies, and old men with very young ladies.

b. spec. *middle-aged spread*, paunchiness in a middle-aged person; also *transf.* and *fig.* Cf. *MIDDLE AGE *sb.* 3.

1931 H. G. WELLS *Work, Wealth & Happiness of Mankind* (1932) xv. 768 Impermanence is the lot of all encyclopædias, and though the Britannica..shows now these marks of advanced maturity, of 'middle-aged spread', there is no reason for supposing that the spirit of Diderot is dead. **1942** D. POWELL *Time to be Born* (1943) ii. 43 Erase that middle-aged spread. **1957** J. BRAINE *Room at Top* i. 7, I hadn't then begun to acquire a middle-aged spread. **1962** *Listener* 20 Sept. 450/1 That impish sense of the ridiculous..which..will always stop 'Tonight' from acquiring the pompous middle-aged spread that so often accompanies success.

2. (Earlier and later examples.)

1611 T. JAMES *Treat. Corruption of Scripture* Advt. to Christian Reader, sig. *2 The open or secret wrongs done vnto Fathers, auncient, middle-aged, or moderne writers, by the Papists. **1846** DICKENS *Pictures from Italy* 5 The first chapter of a Middle Aged novel.

middle-ageing, *ppl. a.* Delete *'nonce-wd.'* and add further examples. Also **middle-aging.**

1916 E. POUND *Lustra* 104 With middle-ageing care I had laid out just the right books. **1956** D. M. DAVIN *Sullen Bell* II. iv. 130 The job was getting him. If not the job..his own middle-ageing self. **1969** D. LAMBERT *Angels in Snow* v. 74 A successful middle-ageing woman. **1973** *Publishers' Weekly* 8 Jan. 62/1 They get acquainted with a pair of middle-aging Jewish bachelor doctors.

middle-ager. orig. *U.S.* [f. MIDDLE AGE *sb.* + -ER^{1}.] A middle-aged person.

1949 *Labor & Nation* Jan.–Feb. 7 Not every youngster or middle-ager..is a double dealer. **1956** *N.Y. Times Mag.* 29 July 5 (*heading*) America's unknown middle-agers. **1962** *Punch* 12 Sept. 392/3 A tough competent middleager.

middle class. Add: **a.** (Earlier examples.)

1766 QUEEN CAROLINE MATILDA OF DENMARK *Let.* 25 Dec. in *Mem. Unfortunate Queen* (1776) 21 There is no such thing here as a middle class of people living in affluence and independence. **1792** A. YOUNG *Trav. France* I. xxii. 549 Knowledge, intelligence, information, learning, and wisdom ought to govern nations; and these are all found to reside most in the middle classes of mankind; weakened by the habits and prejudices of *the great*, and stifled by the ignorance of the vulgar.

c. *middle-class morality.*

1926 F. M. FORD *Man could Stand Up* I. iii. 49 What *should* keep them apart?... Middle Class Morality? **1966** *Punch* 13 July 78/2 The tyranny of middle-class morality must be conquered, especially in the field of the homosexuality laws. **1968** A. MACLEOD *Dam* vi. 62 A concession to your middle class morality. **1975** *Times* 15 Jan. 15/5 It was refreshing to see the virtues of middle class morality applauded.

Hence **middle-classdom, -classism,** the middle class as a whole; their characteristics, interests, or position; **middle-classness** (further examples); **middle-classy** *a.*, suggestive of the middle class.

1930 *Observer* 14 Sept. 7 The secret of Denmark's somewhat stuffy middle-classdom. **1963** *Times* 2 May 18/2 Incipient middle-classdom; outward conformity. **1909** *Working Men's College Jrnl.* Apr. 77 Mr. Lupton..did not think the question before the House was one of aristocracy *v.* middle-classism. **1923** A. HUXLEY *Antic Hay* ix. 142 The dreadful middle-classness of her Art and Craftiness. **1970** *Guardian* 2 Mar. 9/1 There is nothing so guaranteed to preserve English middle classness..as being surrounded..by foreign parts. **1926** *Glasgow Herald* 21 May 8 Highly respectable, middle-classy railway clerks.

Middle East. [f. MIDDLE *a.* + EAST *sb.*] States lying between the Near and Far East, esp. Egypt and Iran and the countries between them. Also *attrib.*

The name *Middle East* has been used with considerable freedom: see esp. quot. 1958. Cf. *FAR EAST, *NEAR EAST.

1902 A. T. MAHAN *Retrospect & Prospect* 237 The Middle East, if I may adopt a term which I have not seen, will some day need its Malta, as well as its Gibraltar. **1903** V. CHIROL *Middle Eastern Question* i. 5 'The Middle East', that is to say..those regions of Asia which extend to the borders of India or command the approaches to India. **1913** *Q. Rev.* Jan. 297 The interests of Great Britain and Russia in the Middle East..are in reality irreconcilable. **1925** A. TOYNBEE *Survey Internat. Affairs 1920–23* I. i. 3 The affairs of Turkey and the other countries of the Middle East. **1944** J. S. HUXLEY *On Living in Revolution* i. 8 Organizations like the Middle East Supply Council. **1958** LD. VANSITTART *Mist Procession* vi. 82 We had [in 1909] none of the sloppy modernism which lumps everything from the Mediterranean to Bengal as Middle East... Persia, Baluchistan, Afghanistan, India were the Middle East. **1974** *Encycl. Brit. Micropædia* VI. 871/2 *Middle East*..has come to be applied to the lands around the southern and eastern shores of the Mediterranean Sea, extending from Morocco to the Arabian Peninsula and Iran and sometimes beyond.

So **Middle Ea·stern** *a.*, of or pertaining to the Middle East.

1903 V. CHIROL (*title*) The Middle Eastern question; or, some political problems of Indian defence. **1909** A. HAMILTON *Probl. Middle East* p. xi, No study of Middle Eastern politics can avoid encroaching upon those of the Near East and of the Far East. **1925** A. TOYNBEE *Survey Internat. Affairs 1920–23* I. ii. 10 The most important permanent results of this meeting of the Supreme Council in the Near and Middle Eastern field were [etc.]. **1966** *Listener* 27 Oct. 600/1 Their children look at the world from a middle-eastern not a European standpoint. **1973** A. MANN *Tiara* iii. 28 What was the rôle of the dark girl? Her first name was Middle Eastern, not Italian.

middleman. Add: **4. c.** *Mountaineering.* The middle climber of a team. Also *attrib.*, as **middleman('s) loop, noose,** etc., a knot used by a climber to tie himself on to the middle of a rope.

1892 C. T. DENT et al. *Mountaineering* iv. 102 The 'fisherman's bend', used as a middleman noose for instance, has only 65 per cent of the strength of the rope. **1909** C. E. BENSON *Brit. Mountaineering* ii. 33 The Middleman Loop is the only one that should be used for middlemen. **1951** E. COXHEAD *One Green Bottle* vi. 160 Each child was tied on with a middleman's noose. **1968** E. FRANKLIN *Dict. Knots* 21 *Middleman's knot*, also called the *Englishman's Loop*, (in America) the *Fisherman's* or *Angler's Loop*... It is a useful loop knot tied in the bight by one of at least four different methods. Once much used for the middleman on a rope in climbing, but now superseded. **1971** J. LOVELOCK *Climbing* iii. 43 The middle man can tie on to the rope in a number of ways.

5. a. (Examples.)

1870 O. LOGAN *Before Footlights* 248, I give it up, Brudder Bones, as the middle man at the minstrels always does the end man's conundrums. **1880** [see *INTERLOCUTOR^{1} c]. **1930** C. WITTKE *Tambo & Bones* iv. 136 Lively repartee between the endmen and the middleman.

c. *N. Amer.* One who paddles or rows in the middle of a canoe or boat.

1761 A. HENRY *Trav. & Adventures Canada* (1901) ii. 14 They engage..the middle-men at one hundred and fifty livres and the end-men at three hundred livres, each. **1801** A. MACKENZIE *Voy. from Montreal* p. xxviii, The canoe men are of two descriptions, foremen and steersmen, and middlemen. **1839** J. K. TOWNSEND *Narr. Rocky Mts.* xv. 355 The middle-men ply their oars; the guides brace themselves against the gunwale of the boat, placing their paddles edgewise down her sides. **1968** [see *BOWSMAN].

middleness (mi·d'lnės). *rare.* [f. MIDDLE *a.* + -NESS.] The fact or quality of being middle, average, or middle-class.

1929 D. H. LAWRENCE *Pansies* 120 Their middleness is only an unreality separating two realities. **1963** *Times* 25 May 9/5 Some few fortunates have special attributes in highest degree, the majority have varying degrees of middleness, and the tail is sadly lacking in endowments.

middle-of-the-road. Phr., often used *attrib.* or quasi-*adj.*, pertaining to or designating a person who, or a course of action, etc., which, is moderate or unadventurous, tending to avoid extremes; orig. *spec.* in *U.S.* with reference to the views of the Populist party. Hence **middle-of-the-roader.**

[**1777** P. THICKNESSE *Year's Journey* I. vi. 43 It is necessary..to keep in the *middle* of the road, so as not to be too suddenly surprised. **1892** *Rocky Mountain News* (Denver, Colorado) 17 July 1 Side tracks are rough, and they're hard to walk, keep in the middle of the road.] **1894** *Iowa State Register* (Des Moines) 5 Sept. 8/3, I am a middle-of-the-road man, but I don't propose to lie down across it so no one can get over me. Nothing grows in the middle of the road. **1896** *N.Y. Tribune* 21 July 2/2 If the Bryan faction predominates, the Middle-of-the-Roaders will bolt and nominate another candidate. **1896** *Congress. Rec.* 10 Dec. 80/2 The only honest Populist is the 'middle-of-the-road' Populist. **1927** *Amer. Speech* II. 443/1 The 'middle of the road' is the sacred path followed by compromising politicians who desire to promote their own or their party's fortunes. **1950** *Ann. Reg. 1949* 331 The Japanese press said that..efforts to establish a 'middle-of-the-road' democracy had failed. **1951** [see *FUNCTIONALISM 1]. **1959** *Economist* 10 Jan. 101/1 He has been ultra-conservative, demagogically radical, or firmly middle-of-the-road. **1971** D. E. WESTLAKE *I gave at the Office* (1972) 151 They are neither right-wing nor left-wing but middle-of-the-roaders. *Ibid.*, There are no revolutionaries on this island, not left-wing, not right-wing, and most certainly not middle-of-the-road revolutionaries. **1973** 'S. HARVESTER' *Corner of Playground* II. i. 80 [They] wanted him, the old middle-of-the-road liberal democrat, to be their first president.

middlescent (mid'le·sənt), *a.* and *sb.* [f. MIDDLE *a.* + *-escent* after ADOLESCENT *sb.* and *a.*] **A.** *adj.* Of, pertaining to, or taking place in middle age. **B.** *sb.* A middle-aged person. Hence **middle·scence,** the period of middle age.

Not current in the U.K.

1965 *N. Y. Times* 5 Dec. IV. 10/3 Middlescence, that awkward age between youth and premature grave in which the parent undergoes alarming physical and emotional change. *Ibid.* 10/5 The middlescent parent is a highly emotional creature of quixotic moods. **1967** *Woman's Day* (Sydney) 12 June 40/4 Although most middlescent romantic folly doesn't get beyond the planning or fantasy stage, there's a lot to be said for being in love, perhaps especially at 40. **1969** *Britannica Bk. of Year* (U.S.) 800/2 *Middlescent*, a middle-aged individual, *esp.* one who has just turned 40; *middlescence, sb.* **1973** *Daily Colonist* (Victoria, B.C.) 7 Nov. 5/1 If the corporation doesn't know how to deal with middlescence..it might find itself 'drained of crucial managerial resources', because the middlescent is a troubled man.

middle town. 1. The centre of a town.

1855 S. RODMAN *Diary* (1927) 324/1, I went to the middle town [of Shirley Village, Massachusetts] on two first days and heard good sermons.

2. Usu. **Middletown.** A typical middle-class community. orig. *U.S.* Hence **Middletowner,** the average middle-class person.

1929 R. S. & H. M. LYND (*title*) Middletown: a study in contemporary American culture. **1954** KOESTLER *Invis. Writing* v. 65 Another factor..is the uniform dreariness of the average Russian town and its lack of architectural character... This uniformity reminds one of the middle-towns of America. **1974** *Times* 21 Feb. 4/7 'Middletown' is bored nearly to tears by the television coverage of the [election] campaign. *Ibid.*, I have watched the coverage after pounding the streets of 'Middletown', and what I have heard from political leaders has had little to do with what is bothering the many 'Middletowners' I have met. *Ibid.* 28 Feb. 18/7 Middletowners..are not political animals... Three weeks in Middletown suggests to me that no party leader has tried to find out what bothers its people.

Middleveld (mi·d'lfelt, -velt). *S. Afr.* Also **-veldt.** [Partial tr. Afrikaans *Middelveld*, lit. 'intermediate region'.] A region in East and West Transvaal lower than the Highveld but higher than the Lowveld, between 3,000 and 4,000 feet above sea-level. Also *transf.*

1877 C. WARREN *Diary* 17 July in *On Veldt in Seventies* (1902) 225 We arrived at a settlement station in the Middle Veldt, forty miles from Worcester, 2800 feet above it. **1878** A. AYLWARD *Transvaal To-Day* 25 The nearer and more recently settled district called the 'Middleveld' of the Orange Free State. **1929** [see *LOWVELD]. **1931** *Discovery* Aug. 259/2 There are two cotton breeding stations in the Transvaal; one at Rustenberg, where problems connected with the improvement of cottons for middle-veld areas are dealt with. **1939** tr. *E. N. Marais's My Friends the Baboons* v. 55 It was in the middle-veld between the Palala and the Magalakwen. **1955** J. H. WELLINGTON *S. Afr.* I. I. iii. 72 These two regions..have important points of dissimilarity, the chief of which are the greater altitude and humidity of the highveld and the greater areas of pre-Karoo surfaces in the middleveld. **1972** *Farmer's Weekly* (S. Afr.) 21 Apr. 11 Normal dryland conditions in the Rhodesian middleveld.

middling, *sb.* Add: **1. b.** A person who or a thing which is mediocre or second-rate (cf. MIDDLING *a.* 3 b); freq. in dial. phr. *among the middlings*, of a mediocre class; also, in a moderate condition of health.

1877 *Sunday Mag.* 182 'How are you getting on, Dick?'..'Well, only among the middlings, Sir.' **1885** R. HOLLAND *Gloss. County of Chester* 226, I said to his employer, 'What sort of a man is your team-man?' The answer was, 'Well! he's just about among the middlings;' so I did not engage him. **1931** R. CAMPBELL *Georgiad* iii. 62 They're all members of the self-same school, And drilled..to enforce on all The standards of the middling and the small. **1964** R. CHURCH *Voyage Home* ii. 28 Whenever I asked after his permanently ailing wife, he beamed with benevolence and replied: 'Oh, amongst the middlings, you know, amongst the middlings.'

3. c. (Earlier and later examples.)

1743 W. ELLIS *Mod. Husbandman* IV. III. 63 Its second, or Middling, or that Meal commonly made Use of by Farmers for spending it in their Families. **1786** G. WASHINGTON *Diary* 13 Sept. (1925) III. 116 My Corn being out, or nearly so, I was obliged to have middlings and ship stuff mixed for bread. **1960** *Farmer & Stockbreeder* 12 Jan. 107/1 A balanced ration for weaner piglets is 40 parts middlings, 25 parts barley meal, [etc.]. **1969** G. E. EVANS *Farm & Village* vi. 72 The miller..used to charge us..for grinding the corn. But we got the offal as well as the flour, and the best middlings we fed to the pigs.

d. Of minerals.

1869 *Amer. Jrnl. Sci.* XCVII. 9 The amount of heavy lubricating oil was largely increased, and the 'middlings' correspondingly diminished. **1909** WEBSTER, *Middling,..pl.* The second quality of ore obtained by washing. **1965** G. J. WILLIAMS *Econ. Geol. N.Z.* ix. 135/2 Low-grade magnetic concentrates and a high proportion of middlings.

4. *U.S.* (Earlier examples. Also in *sing.*)

1777 *Calendar Virginia State Papers* (1875) I. 288 Bakin in hams, midlings, shoulders, &c. **1831** J. M. PECK *Guide for Emigrants* 172 To make bacon of hams, shoulders, and middlings or broadsides. **1834** D. CROCKETT *Narr. Life* xi. 79, I got also a large middling of bacon, and killed a fine deer. **1848** *Rep. Comm. Patents 1847* (U.S.) 527 The hog thus cut up into shoulders, hams and middlings undergoes further trimming. **1857** 'PORTE CRAYON' *Virginia Illustr.* i. 31 Fried middling and hot coffee were then served round. **1904** E. GLASGOW *Deliverance* 51 She has had to fry the middling in the kitchen, and mother complains so of the smell.

middlingness. (Further examples.)

1929 D. H. LAWRENCE *Pansies* 120 Nothing that transcends the bourgeois middlingness. **1957** *Essays in Crit.* VII. 216 The umbrella of 'moderation'—the chief of the new slogans—means too frequently that middlingness, lack of real poetic talent and ambition has found yet another cosy corner for itself in our watered-down, democratic culture.

middy¹. For etym. read: [f. MID *sb.*² + -Y⁶.] Add: (Earlier example.)

1818 'A. BURTON' *Adventures J. Newcome* 145 A Middy rudely said, He'd sell them [*sc.* prisoners] for five pounds a head.

2. In full, *middy blouse.* A kind of loose blouse, often extending below the waistline, similar to that worn by midshipmen. Also *attrib.*

1911 *Daily Colonist* (Victoria, B.C.) 13 Apr. 24/3 (Advt.), Child's Middy Dress, in white duck. Square neck and short sleeves. **1913** *T. Eaton & Co. Catal.* Spring & Summer 31/2 Plain Galatea 'middy'. Plain Galatea waist, in Norfolk 'middy' style. **1915** E. J. KIMBLE *Commercial, Industr. & Technical Vocab.* 185 Middy blouse. **1917** D. CANFIELD *Understood Betsy* (1922) ii. 37 The necktie of her middy blouse fell forward. **1929** WODEHOUSE *Mr. Mulliner Speaking* viii. 259 A sort of middy-blouse arrangement. **1952** M. MCCARTHY *Groves of Academe* (1953) ix. 172 Mary Margaret, the eldest, in middy and skirt, followed. **1957** *Observer* 24 Nov. 11/1 The middy two-piece comes near the new silhouette, with a hip-length 'blouson' worn over a skirt mounted on its underbodice. **1965** MRS. L. B. JOHNSON *White House Diary* 6 Aug. (1970) 307 Carol Channing in her white velvet bell-bottom trousers trimmed in red and a middy blouse top.

middy² (mi·di). *Austral. slang.* [f. MID *sb.*¹ + -Y⁶.] A measure of beer or other liquor (see quots.); the glass containing it.

1945 BAKER *Austral. Lang.* ix. 169 The *middy*, a beer glass containing nine ounces, is a measure used only in N.S.W. hotels. **1956** S. HOPE *Diggers' Paradise* 230 A middyglass contains ten liquid ounces. **1957** 'N. CULOTTA' *They're a Weird Mob* (1958) ii. 25 Those big glasses are called schooners and those small ones are called middies. **1968** *Southerly* XXVIII. 38 He ordered two more middies. **1970** *Observer* (Colour Suppl.) 15 Feb. 39/2 Getting 'full' on frosty 'middies' of beer is still a serious manly business. **1974** K. COOK *Bloodhouse* 79 'Middy of rum, Mick,' said the youth... Ten ounces of rum sold over the bar cost four dollars.

midear (midīə·ɹ), var. *my dear* (see MY *poss. adj.* 2 b, DEAR *sb.*²), used as a form of address.

1959 J. BRAINE *Vodi* xiv. 191 Anything you want, midear. **1967** J. AIKEN *Ribs of Death* xxv. 176 Do-ee think it *could* be true, midear?

mid feather. **1.** (Further examples.)

1905 GOODCHILD & TWENEY *Technol. & Sci. Dict.* 402/1 *Midfeather,* (*Paper Manufac.*) a partition fixed in the 'breaker' to promote circulation of the pulp. **1930** *Engineering* 22 Aug. 223/1 Numerous tests showed that, provided the midfeather was inserted at the fan end of the duct, completely uniform distribution of the dust was obtained. **1940** *Chambers's Techn. Dict.* 547/1 *Mid-feather* (*Join.*), a cross-tongue.

mid-field. Add: Also **midfield.** (Further examples.) Also as quasi-*adv.*

1897 *Badminton Mag.* IV. 422 They [*sc.* rooks] quickly shift their position to safer quarters in mid-field. **1909** *Westm Gaz.* 24 Nov. 12/2 C. Lyle shot well, but was very slow in midfield. **1956** *Times* 16 Apr. 13/1 Haynes, in spite of the presence of Evans in mid-field, showed himself one of the very few inside forwards in the British Isles with a spark of true genius. **1960** *Times* 30 Nov. 3/6 Certainly they had no penetrative midfield player. **1968** *Listener* 7 Nov. 625/3, I was aware..that Gilzean would be playing mid-field: I knew my Spurs. **1969** [see *LINK *sb.*² 3 h]. **1973** *Liverpool Echo* (Football ed.) 17 Mar. 18/1 With Hughes pushing them forward with some strong play in mid-field, Liverpool hit back. **1974** *Times* 23 Feb. 14/8 Even eight, nine and ten-year-olds these days are taught by games masters in terms of..'midfield provider', 'sweeper' and the rest. **1974** *Guardian* 19 Aug. 16/2 The midfield men preferred the easy option of overlapping fullbacks to making their own breach. *Ibid.* 16/3 The painstaking midfield play of Kendall and Campbell.

midge. **4.** (Earlier example.)

1865 C. M. YONGE *Clever Woman* I. ii. 52 One of the midges, or diminutive flies used at Avonmouth, came to the door.

midget. **2.** For 1859 read 1848.

4. A small vehicle, aircraft, etc.

1930 *Daily Express* 8 Sept. 3/7 The midgets will function as destroyers, and the heavier tanks will discharge the duties of land battleships. **1933** M. ARLEN *Man's Mortality* ii. 32 He climbed into the midget [*sc.* aircraft], and called out to the cadet: 'Altitude?'

5. *attrib.* **a.** In sense 'weak, puny', as *midget effort.* **b.** 'small, small-scale, tiny', as *midget submarine, warship,* etc.; **midget golf,** a form of miniature golf, usually played indoors; so *midget-golf course,* etc.

1908 *Daily Chron.* 7 Aug. 4/4 The spiritual intelligences ..must..laugh at our serious midget efforts to comprehend and explain the circumambient infinite. **1922** JOYCE *Ulysses* 620 Marcella, the midget queen. **1930** *Daily Express* 6 Nov. 3/7 Sydney's midget golf boom. **1930** *Daily Tel.* 1 Dec. 23/6 (Advt.), An 18-hole midget golf course complete. **1933** *Pop. Sci. Monthly* Mar. 22/1 (*caption*) Midget submarine ready for its first test. **1934** *Discovery* Nov. 324/2 The combined radio-gramophone and deaf-aid..includes..three midget valves. **1942** *Hutchinson's Pict. Hist. War* 18 Mar.–9 June 26 (*caption*) One of the Royal Navy's midget war ships, a motor gunboat, on patrol duty round the coasts of Britain. **1945** *Jane's Fighting Ships 1943–44* 316/2 At least two classes of Japanese midget submarines are believed to exist. **1966** T. PYNCHON *Crying of Lot 49* ii. 30 He and the kid follow the old regiment to Gallipoli, where the father somehow builds a midget submarine. **1972** *Mainichi Daily News* (Japan) 7 Nov. 6/3 The National Federation of Midget Automobile Manufacturers' and Dealers' Associations revealed..that a total of 78,055 new midget automobiles were registered in October. *Ibid.*, Demand for midget commercial vehicles would increase.

Midi (mi·di), *sb.* [Fr.] The south of France. Also *attrib.*

1883 H. JAMES *Little Tour in France* (1885) xvi. 110, I could not fail to flatter myself, on reaching La Rochelle, that I was already in the Midi. **1936** C. CONNOLLY *Rock Pool* i. 16 The jungle of the Midi bourgeoisie. **1964** E. AMBLER *Kind of Anger* ii. 41 She had a strong Midi accent and sounded like a maid. **1967** A. WILSON *No Laughing Matter* III. ii. 245 M. Garcin in his Midi accent asked.., 'Qu'est ce qu'elle dit?' **1973** *Guardian* 22 Feb. 4/4 For electoral purposes the Midi is usually divided into two—the Midi-Pyrénées and the Midi-Méditérranée or Languedoc-Rousillon.

midi-, comb. f. of MID *a.*, MIDDLE *a.*, in imitation of *MAXI- and *MINI-, denoting garments longer than mini- but shorter than maxi-, normally extending to mid-calf. Hence **midi** *sb.*², such a garment. So *midi-length.*

1967 *Word Study* Dec. 3/2 In contrast to the miniskirt a skirt whose hemline comes as low as midcalf has been called a *midiskirt.* **1968** *Chicago Tribune* 9 July II. 1/7 A swaggering midi-coat that gives a new proportion to the trouser costume. **1969** *Sun* 13 Mar. 8/2 The newsy midi hem-length (note midi, *not* maxi). **1969** *Internat. Herald Tribune* (Paris) 6 Nov. 6/2 Almost every designer is nervously groping for the right length; it's touch and go whether the average woman will go for the maxis and midis. **1970** *Daily Tel.* 14 Jan. 15/3 Hardy Amies proved yesterday..that the midi length only works if it is waisted or broken by a hip-belt. His spring collection was awash with midis. *Ibid.* 15/4 Midi-dresses with big ballooning sleeves, hip sashes, polo necks. **1971** *Petticoat* 17 July 23 Baggage and General midi bumper boots, £4. **1974** *Country Life* 14 Feb. 334/2 A slim-cut, midi-length trench [coat].

‖ **midinette** (mid*i*net). [Fr. Perh. orig. a portmanteau word f. *midi* mid-day + *dînette* light dinner: cf. 1922 *Larousse* s.v., les *midinettes* sont celles qui se contentent d'une *dînette à midi.*] A milliner's female assistant, esp. in Paris.

1909 *Westm. Gaz.* 7 Aug. 15/1 The Parisian..is tired of the absurd hat. The midinette and those of her kind have made it impossible. **1919** BEERBOHM *Seven Men* 11 A midinette who..murdered, or was about to murder, a mannequin. **1925** *Brit. Weekly* 19 Feb. 498/2 She was in the same class with the midinettes of Paris, with whom travelling Englishmen spend a passing hour and quickly forget. **1932** SELLAR & YEATMAN *And now All This* vi. 60 In the South, the beautiful *Midi*, one does *not* perceive the beautiful Race of the *Midinettes* (*hélas*). **1958** J. MACGREGOR *Glamour in Your Lens* 84 She'll..be prepared to transform herself on the spot into..a French midinette. **1961** R. SEARLE *Which Way did he Go?* 38 He firmly believes that the Boulevards abound with Midinettes who are dazzled with admiration for him. **1975** R. COBB *Paris & its Provinces* 3 Some story in which a *midinette* meets a *Duc.*

Midland, *sb.* and *a.* Add: **A.** *sb.* **b.** Used *ellipt.* for the names of companies or organizations, as Midland Bank, Midland Railway.

1869 *Bradshaw's Railway Manual* XXI. 86 The question was..referred to the arbitration of Captain Galton, who decided that the Midland might work the local line **1959** *Chambers's Encycl.* XI. 489/2 When the Midland and the Glasgow and South Western decided to throw in their lot together, approval was not given, and the only tangible result..was the adoption by the Scottish company of the Midland lake livery. **1972** C. DRUMMOND *Death at Bar* i. 14 His banking account, with the Midland, is divided into business and private.

c. The central area of the United States (see quot. 1896), esp. regarded as a dialectal area of American English.

1896 *Dialect Notes* I. ix. 438 Midland: a belt separating the North from the South and extending from the Atlantic to the Mississippi (including Long Island, New York City and the adjoining counties, New Jersey, Del., all but the northern strip of Penn., the upper prong of West Virginia, southern Ohio, middle Ind., middle Ill., and St. Louis county, Mo.). **1937** *Amer. Speech* XII. 316/1 For many years *Middle West*..has reigned in solitary authority..; but there seems to be a growing tendency towards the use of three other terms... *Central West,..Mid-west,..Midland.* This shorter and more picturesque title is still rare, but growing. As noun & adjective it occurs occasionally. **1963** R. I. MCDAVID *Mencken's Amer. Lang.* 405 The..'General American' area is really made up of two major dialects: one, Inland Northern..; the other, Midland, based on the speech of Pennsylvania and its derivatives. **1972** H. KURATH *Stud. Area Ling.* 44 The transition area between the North and the Midland reflects partly the complicated history of the settlement.

B. *adj.* **1. b.** (Earlier and later examples.) Also *pl.*

1756 A. BUTLER *Lives Saints* I. 45 St. Cedd..first preached to the Midland English. **1849** D. ROCK *Church of our Fathers* I. I. v. 351 The chasuble, in its graceful, true old form, and appareled albs and amices, were spread throughout the Midland district. **1922** JOYCE *Ulysses* 703 The Link line railway laid..between the cattle park, Liffey junction, and terminus of Midland Great Western Railway..in proximity to the terminal stations or Dublin branches of Great Central Railway, Midland Railway of England [etc.]. **1942** *Short Guide Gt. Brit.* (U.S. War Dept.) 7 The great 'midland' manufacturing cities of Birmingham, Sheffield, and Coventry. **1954** DARBY & TERRETT (*title*) The Domesday geography of Midland England. **1971** M. LEE *Dying for Fun* xlii. 202 Ivor Canning had made his way to Oxford but..still spoke with a well-preserved Midlands accent. **1972** M. WOODHOUSE *Mama Doll* xiii. 180 The few words he did speak emerged in a Midlands accent.

c. Of or pertaining to the Midland of the United States or the regional type of American English spoken there.

1890 *Dialect Notes* I. ii. 57 But the differences in the different sections of the country are not so great that we can properly speak of a New England dialect, a southern dialect, a midland dialect. **1900** B. B. SMYTH *Plants & Flowers Kansas* 43 This is the Midland adder-tongue, as named by Prof. Knerr of Atchison. **1944** H. KURATH in *Language* XX. 151, I hope to be able to show before long, on the basis of the Atlas materials, that we must recognize a large Central or Midland speech area in addition to the Southern, the Northern, and the Northeastern (eastern New England). **1949** —— *Word Geogr. Eastern U.S.* p. v, There is an extensive Midland speech area that lies between the traditionally recognized 'Northern' and 'Southern' areas. **1959** E. TUNIS *Indians* vi. 86 Midland Indians were farmers first, but they all..hunted buffalo.

Midlander. (Further examples.) Also, one who lives in the Midland of the United States.

1889 G. B. SHAW *London Music 1888–89* (1937) 243, I was at Leicester, delivering to the midlanders an impassioned appeal. **1912** BELLOC *Green Overcoat* x. 191 'I know you would!' said the big Midlander. **1932** *Times Lit. Suppl.* 14 Jan. 19/2 Himself a Midlander, he is very insistent on the special virtues which Shakespeare inherited from his Midland birth. **1972** H. KURATH *Stud. Area Ling.* 53 The proportion of 'Northerners' and 'Midlanders' in these two states as a whole differs little. **1972** *Country Life* 14 Dec. 1638/1 It is always with mild surprise that you recall that Dr. Johnson was a Midlander.., that he was born not within the sound of Bow Bells but of the bells of Lichfield Cathedral.

mid-line (mi·dləin). [MID *a.*] **1.** *Zool.* A median line; also, the median plane or plane of bilateral symmetry.

1868 [in Dict. s.v. MID *a.* 2 d]. **1927** HALDANE & HUXLEY *Animal Biol.* xii. 285 (*caption*) The lateral nerve-trunks have united in the mid-line. **1957** R. H. SMYTHE *Conformation of Dog* 61 Behind the base of the neck in the midline of the back. **1959** SOUTHWOOD & LESTON *Land & Water Bugs Brit. Isles* 31 The males of this genus have a patch of wax-producing glands beneath the abdomen on each side of the mid-line. **1961** *Lancet* 26 Aug. 443/1 (*caption*) Coronal section of brain of patient who survived for 6 weeks. Note that the only abnormal appearances are slight dilatation of the ventricles and a tear (arrow) on the underside of the corpus callosum to the right of the midline. **1974** *Nature* 8 Mar. 165/1 The roentgenographic landmarks were joined to form triangles on both sides of the midline.

2. The middle of a line of poetry.

1882 G. M. HOPKINS *Lett. to R. Bridges* (1955) 164 The word is *more* and is a midline rhyme to *score.*

midlittoral (midli·tŏrăl), *a.* and *sb.* *Ecol.* [f. MID *a.* + LITTORAL *a.* and *sb.*] **A.** *adj.* Designating that zone on the sea-shore which is both covered and uncovered by the neap tides. **B.** *sb.* The zone so delimited.

1948 *Austral. Jrnl. Sci. Res.* B. I. 196 (*heading*) The mid- and upper-littoral. **1949** T. A. & A. STEPHENSON in *Jrnl. Ecol.* XXXVII. 298 The most difficult zone to rename is the Balanoid. This is the middle zone on the

shore... On the whole we favour the name *midlittoral zone* as being in keeping with the other terms proposed. *Ibid.*, The word *midlittoral* is less common, though it has been used by Dakin *et al.* (1948) in their recent account of the New South Wales Coast, even if not as an exact equivalent of our Balanoid zone. **1967** *Oceanogr. & Marine Biol.* V. 469 The lowest levels of the midlittoral. **1970** R. C. NEWELL *Biol. Intertidal Animals* i. 2 The second zone recognised by Stephenson and Stephenson (1949) is the midlittoral zone, characterized by barnacles and limpets. **1974** *Encycl. Brit. Macropædia* IV. 804/1 The midlittoral of sand and mud shores is usually inhabited by several types of polychaete worms, the most typical being lugworms.

midmost, *a.* and *adv.* Add: **A.** *adj.* **1. b.** *absol.* (passing into *sb.*) (Further *poet.* examples.)

1912 E. POUND tr. *Cavalcanti's Sonnets & Ballate* 19 As though I'd won unto his heart's mid-most. **1915** —— *Cathay* 7 And within, the mistress, in the midmost of her youth. **1955** —— *Classic Anthol.* II. 142, I have held him in love so long From heart's mid-most be it song Not to be lost.

midnight, *sb.* Add: **4. a.** *midnight mass* (earlier and later examples).

1665–7 J. LAUDER *Jrnls.* in *Publ. Scottish Hist. Soc.* (1900) XXXVI. 118 The rest of our Scotsmen ware so curious as to go hear Midnight Masses. **1848** J. H. NEWMAN *Let.* 25 Dec. (1962) XII. 382 The midnight mass was a high one. **1866** G. M. HOPKINS *Lett. to R. Bridges* (1955) 16 It is not much more than an hour to Xmas day: I am sitting up for the midnight mass. **1960** A. CHRISTIE *Adventure of Christmas Pudding* 33 Who's going to brave the snow and go to midnight mass?

5. † **midnight banquet** = ***midnight feast**; **midnight black,** an intense black colour; also *attrib.*; **midnight blue,** a very dark shade of blue; also *attrib.* or as *adj.*; **midnight feast,** a feast at midnight; *spec.* a children's secret feast in a school dormitory or the like; **midnight matinée,** a special theatrical performance presented at midnight; **midnight-tide** *poet.*, midnight.

1896 C. M. YONGE in C. Coleridge *C. M. Yonge* (1903) iii. 114 She invited the other young ladies to a midnight banquet..in their night-caps and dressing gowns. **1925** J. GREGORY *Bab of Backwoods* xvi. 201 Monte made out vaguely the slim form in white, a whitish blur against a midnight-black curtain. **1922** H. CRANE *Let.* 2 Mar. (1965) 80 Pastel tinted flowers on a background of midnight black. **1916** *Daily Colonist* (Victoria, B.C.) 8 July 12/1 (Advt.), The same style [of shoe] in jungle brown, midnight blue and bronze. **1935** R. HICHENS *Afterglow* 86 A silken collar and a midnight blue tie. **1937** *Times* 10 July 15/4 Dressed in midnight-blue crêpe-de-chine. **1940** R. CHANDLER *Farewell, my Lovely* xxxviii. 289 His dinner clothes were midnight blue. **1972** *Guardian* 5 Dec. 11/2 Toga dress..in..midnight blue. **1938** A. CHRISTIE *Appointment with Death* I. vii. 52 This is rather fun... Rather like the midnight feasts we used to have at school. **1964** C. HODDER-WILLIAMS *Main Experiment* I. vi. 57 'When will you be back from London?' 'Late tonight.' 'We'll have a midnight feast, then.' **1972** *Listener* 2 Nov. 614/1 Midnight feasts, practical jokes and all the fun of the dormitory. **1952** GRANVILLE *Dict. Theatr. Terms* 118 Midnight matinée. **1963** *Daily Express* 25 Sept. 1/4, I don't honestly see why the Stationery Office have to put on a midnight matinee for the Denning Report, even if it has got a U Certificate. **1918** W. DE LA MARE *Motley* 4 At cold of midnight-tide.

mid-ocean. [MID *a.*] **a.** The middle of an ocean

1697, 1881 [in Dict. s.v. MID *a.* 1 d]. **1905** *Smart Set* Sept. 116/2 It was as surely and as irrevocably lost as though it had sunk into a thousand fathoms of midocean. **1930** S. SPENDER *20 Poems* 3 Like Icarus mid-ocean-drowned. **1938** *Times Lit. Suppl.* 3 Sept. 572/4 His repairs in mid-ocean to his small auxiliary engine.

b. *attrib.*, esp. in **mid-ocean ridge,** one of the mountainous ridges, several kilometres high and over a thousand wide, that rise abruptly from the abyssal plain in the middle of each ocean basin and form a connected worldwide system, marked along much of its length by a central rift that overlies earthquake foci.

1956 *Geophysical Monogr.* I. 75/1 Mid-ocean islands. **1961** EWING & LANDISMAN in M. Sears *Oceanogr.* I. 5 The remaining 18% [of the earth's surface]..contains parts of the mid-ocean ridge system. **1963** G. L. PICKARD *Descriptive Physical Oceanogr.* ii. 10 The Mid-ocean Ridge is probably the most extensive single feature of the earth's topography. **1968** M. J. KEEN *Introd. Marine Geol.* iii. 46 The abyssal plains may be cut..by mid-ocean canyons. **1968** *Times* 8 Oct. 7/7 Present-day oceans are marked by underwater mountain ranges, called mid-ocean ridges, along which molten material is injected upwards from the earth's mantle and spreads out on either side of the ridge. **1971** J. R. HEIRTZLER in A. E. Maxwell *Sea* IV. I. iii. 99 The Red Sea..is bisected by the mid-ocean ridge which passes south through the Gulf of Aden and the Indian Ocean.

So **mid-ocea·nic** *a.*

1961 EWING & LANDISMAN in M. Sears *Oceanogr.* I. 9 On every crossing the ridge has been found where it was expected, with its median rift accurately following the mid-oceanic earthquake belt. **1966** R. W. FAIRBRIDGE *Encycl. Oceanogr.* 506 The Mid-Atlantic Ridge is that portion of the mid-oceanic ridge system which lies within the limits of the Atlantic Ocean. **1970** L. R. A. CAPURRO *Oceanogr. for Practicing Engineers* vii. 139 The sea bottom can be divided into three major morphologic divisions: continental margin, ocean-basin floor, and midoceanic ridge.

mid-off. In etym. for 'MID *a.* 6' read 'MID *a.* 1 d'. Add earlier and later examples.

1865 J. LILLYWHITE *Cricketer's Compan.* 25 Mr. Lyttelton from a fine hit, was cleverly had by Mr. Voules at deep mid off. **1867** J. LAWRENCE *Handbk. Cricket Ireland 1866–67* 106 Harrow drive or Mid off. **1955** *Times* 9 May 15/2 He was dropped off him at mid-off when he had got to 29. **1959** [see *DEEPISH *a.*].

mid-on. (Earlier and later examples.)

1870 *Times* 20 July 10/3 At 21 Smith was caught at mid-on. **1873** J. PYCROFT *Cricket Field* (ed. 6) xii. 289 Some bowlers prefer to dispense with long-leg... In case of his removal it would be well to place him at mid-on. **1955** *Times* 12 May 4/5 Twenty-five minutes afterwards Watson lost patience with himself and mis-hit Anderson to mid-on and then Lowson, chancing his arm in the same sort of way, was well caught also at mid-on. **1959** [see *CHECK *v.*[1] 16 d]. **1974** *Observer* 9 June 24/7 He hit one excellent four..and a single, and then holed out to mid-on.

mid-ra·nge. [RANGE *sb.*[1]] **1.** *Statistics.* The arithmetic mean of the largest and the smallest values of a group, esp. a sample.

1949 *Ann. Math. Statistics* XX. 257 The significance tests investigated..are based on the quantity [(sample midrange) – (hypothetical mean)]/(sample range). **1951** DIXON & MASSEY *Introd. Statistical Analysis* xvi. 238 It is probably not advisable to use the midrange for samples of more than five observations since its efficiency drops below that of the median beyond this point. **1973** M. H. BELZ *Statistical Methods for Process Industries* ii. 22 There are four commonly employed measures of sample location, the sample mean, the sample median, the sample mode and the sample mid-range.

2. a. The middle part of the range of audible frequencies. Freq. *attrib.*

1955 E. T. CANBY *Home Mus. Syst.* (ed. 2) x. 160 The newest wrinkles in the speaker department are the tiny super tweeter, for crispness in extremely high tones, and the large mid-range tweeter, to take over the middle 'intelligence' highs. **1960** C. BROWN *Introd. Hi-Fi* iv. 89 A third speaker to handle the mid-range can be introduced if required. **1971** *Hi-Fi Sound* Feb. 68/1 The radiogram has speaker units which are..surprisingly sensitive, particularly in the mid-range. **1975** *Gramophone* Jan. 1425/1 The tweeter maintains the smooth and wide dispersion of energy as it takes over from the bass and mid-range unit.

b. A loudspeaker designed to reproduce mid-range signals with fidelity while being relatively unresponsive to those of low or high frequency.

1955 E. T. CANBY *Home Mus. Syst.* (ed. 2) x. 160 A cheap and effective alternative is an ordinary medium-sized cone speaker used as a mid-range. **1975** *Hi-Fi Answers* Feb. 68/1 It was specifically developed as a good mid-range for the new Leak 2000 series of speakers.

midrib. Add: **2.** (Later examples.)

1901 *Chambers's Jrnl.* May 301/2 The leaves are thoroughly dried. In testing their dryness the mid-rib or vein should not be overlooked. **1965** K. ESAU *Plant Anat.* (ed. 2) xvi. 434 In some large grasses the median part of the blade is thickened into a midrib. **1974** *Country Life* 7 Mar. 479/2 Gracillimus has narrow leaves with a silver midrib.

b. *Archæol.* A structure similar to the principal rib or vein of a leaf.

1929 V. G. CHILDE *Danube in Prehist.* 126 Kite-shaped daggers with rivet-holes and a rudimentary midrib. **1938** *Proc. Prehist. Soc.* IV. 283 Three flanged axes were found with a tanged spearhead with short blade and pronounced mid-rib.

midriff. Add: **1. b.** *Fashion.* (*a*) The mid-portion of the torso; (*b*) that part of a woman's garment which covers the midriff, *esp.* if cut separately from the upper bodice; (*c*) *U.S.* a woman's garment which leaves the midriff uncovered.

1941 *Fashion Digest* Fall 74 Playsuit with wide-midriff and full-pleated skirt. **1948** *Harper's Bazaar* Jan. 99 Inside the elasticized bodice is a lightly boned midriff, an uplift brassiere. **1953** P. BINDER *Muffs & Morals* i. 31 The midriff mode..came in just before the Second World War... It shocked nobody. **1964** *McCall's Sewing* 12/1 Wide sashes, contrasting belts, set-in midriffs will give a lift to the waistline. **1966** L. HALLIDAY *Fashion Makers* ii. 41 A modern girl will cheerfully bare her midriff on the beach. **1970** *Daily Tel.* 23 Feb. 13 A real Slim Jane? Then only you, one prays, will dare to wear the new bare-midriff styles. **1972** E. LARSEN *Creative Dressmaker* viii. 73 Cover the midriff with a piece of lace.

mid-season. 2. (Further examples.)

1921 WODEHOUSE *Indiscretions of Archie* xix. 210, I was just putting old Bill through it..with a view to getting him into mid-season form. **1946** —— *Joy in Morning* v. 35 Though crushed to earth..he rises again—not absolutely in midseason form, perhaps, but perkier than you would expect. **1969** *Burpee Catal.* 81/2 Sweet Corn... A midseason corn. *Ibid.* 123/2 Delicious [straw]berries in midseason.

midshipman. Add: **3. midshipman's hitch** (see quot. 1886); **midshipman's nuts** (earlier examples); **midshipman's roll** (see quot. 1857).

1808 D. LEVER *Young Sea Officer's Sheet Anchor* 9 To make a Midshipman's Hitch. **1886** *Encycl. Brit.* XXI. 591/2 *Midshipman's Hitch.*—Take two round turns inside the bight, the same as a half-hitch repeated; stop up the end; or let another half-hitch be taken or held by hand. Used for hooking a tackle for a temporary purpose. **1828** *Night Watch* II. viii. 50 'You shall have a fistful of midshipman's nuts to crack for your supper.'.. He gave me some broken biscuits. **1846** H. MELVILLE *Typee* vi. 38, I took a double handful of those small, broken, flinty bits of biscuit which generally go by the name of 'midshipmen's nuts'. **1826** W. N. GLASCOCK *Naval Sketch-Bk.* (ed. 2) I. 8 Get your hammock slung... 'Cause,..none o' your 'midshipman's rolls', you know! **1857** H. E. DAVENPORT *Rovings on Land & Sea* 280 If any of the hammocks are lashed in a slovenly manner, or merely bundled up in what is called a 'midshipman's roll', the owner is..made to secure it in a more ship-shape manner.

midstream. Add: **2.** *Med.* Used, usu. *attrib.*, to designate any portion of urine passed by an individual other than that first passed or last passed in an act of urination.

1958 *New Engl. Jrnl. Med.* CCLIX. 764 (*heading*) A comparison of bacterial counts of the urine obtained by needle aspiration of the bladder, catheterization and midstream-voided methods. **1962** *Lancet* 15 Dec. 1246/1 The urine was examined microscopically for pus cells... In men and children midstream specimens were used. **1972** *Ibid.* 2 Sept. 452/2 Specimens of midstream urine were collected in sterile universal bottles.

midsummer. Add: **3. midsummer madness** (further examples).

1914 C. MACKENZIE *Sinister St.* II. III. v. 594 The freshmen..celebrated the beauty of the season with a good deal of midsummer madness. **1921** GALSWORTHY *To Let* II. ix. 200 Come, be reasonable, Fleur! It's midsummer madness! **1922** JOYCE *Ulysses* 482 This is midsummer madness, some ghastly joke again. **1970** M. PETERS in *Midsummer Variations* 203 Midsummer madness they all said That summer day when we were wed.

midway. Add: **A.** *sb.* **3.** *U.S.* Freq. with capital initial. At an exhibition, fair, or the like: a central avenue along which the chief exhibits or amusements are placed; hence, any cheap place of amusement; *slang*, a hall. Also *attrib.*

The use originated in the inclusion of the 'Midway Plaisance' of Chicago in the grounds of the exposition held there in 1893.

1893 *Outing* Dec. 208/1 The waiters were the hardiest set on the Midway. **1901** *World's Work* Aug. 1097/2 Nowadays we frankly admit that the Midway is the strongest magnet of a big fair. **1901** *Everybody's Mag.* Oct. 424 Can I arrange with you for placing a first-class Midway on your grounds? *Ibid.* 427/1 A mile and a half of kerwhango and clash—That is the Midway show. **1927** K. NICHOLSON *Barker* 149 *Midway Confab*, news column in the *Billboard*, the weekly trade paper for outdoor showfolk. **1932** *Evening Sun* (Baltimore) 9 Dec. 31/5 *Midway*, a hall. **1949** *Sat. Even. Post* 17 Sept. 25/1, I have worked in..big-time railroad shows whose midways had the glitter of a handful of diamonds. **1956** H. GOLD *Man who was not with It* (1965) i. 3 There he is on the midway, Grack the Frenchie, talking for his Countstore.

C. *adv.* **1.** Also *U.S.* const. *of.*

1812 J. J. HENRY *Accurate Acct. Heroes Campaign against Quebec* 192 About midway of the horn [of the moose],..there is a broad flat part. **1896** [in Dict.]. **1903** *Nation* (N.Y.) 17 Sept. 234 He died midway of his 70th year. **1927** *Sat. Even. Post* 24 Dec. 44/3 She stopped midway of her sentence.

midwife, *sb.* Add: **5. midwife toad,** a European toad, *Alytes obstetricans*, the male of which cares for the eggs until they hatch.

1901 H. GADOW in *Cambr. Nat. Hist.* VIII. vi. 158 *A[lytes] obstetricans*, the 'Midwife-toad', has the general appearance of a smooth toad... The pairing and the peculiar mode of taking care of the eggs by the male..has given it the specific name *obstetricans*, the midwife. **1934** *Times Lit. Suppl.* 16 June p. iv/2 A number of interesting toads have been received lately at the London Zoo, including a collection from Germany of 20 midwife toads with their eggs. **1954** G. DURRELL *Three Singles to Adventure* viii. 180 The midwife toad of Europe, instead of leaving its eggs in the nearest water to hatch unattended, hands them over to the male, who winds them round his hind legs and carries them about until they hatch. **1971** KOESTLER *Case of Midwife Toad* i. 14 Kammerer's undoing was a grotesque amphibian creature: the midwife toad, *Alytes obstetricans*.

midwife, *v.* Add: **2. b.** (This sense not *rare*.) (Further examples.)

1959 *Times Lit. Suppl.* 4 Dec. 709/3 It also midwifed the late editor of *Commentary* himself, Elliot E. Cohen. **1971** B. MALAMUD *Tenants* 83 Lesser, dreaming of new light in his book, beheld in his dark thoughts Bill Spear, potential executioner, requesting him to midwife his bloody fable. **1972** *Sunday Tel.* 30 Apr. 7/7 As befitted the man who midwived 'That Was The Week That Was', Sir Hugh also got the best laugh at the Colonels' expense.

midwifely, *a.* Delete † *Obs.* and add to def.: also, characteristic of a midwife.

1936 'R. WEST' *Thinking Reed* i. 15 'When a woman is very tired,' he said, with a return of midwifely sententiousness, 'she does not know what is the matter with her.'

mid-year. Add: **3.** The middle of the year. Also *attrib.*

1901 *U.S. Dept. Agric. Yearbk.* 154 To teachers the series of meetings is a series of mid-year institutes. **1909** *Cent. Dict.* Suppl. s.v., Rents due at the midyear. **1932**

Irish Press 10 Mar. 5/3 This corresponded to an annual rate of 14·6 per thousand of the estimated mid-year population for the year 1931. **1973** E. TAYLOR *Serpent under It* (1974) v. 82 This may set us back months. Instead of getting our degrees at midyears, we'll probably have to wait now until next June.

Miehle (mī·lə). The name of Robert *Miehle*, 19th-century American printer, used *attrib.* or *absol.* to designate a flat-bed, cylinder printing press invented by him in 1884, or later developments of this machine.

1887 *Inland Printer* Oct. 35/1 (*heading*) The Miehle two-revolution press. **1894** *Amer. Dict. Printing & Bookmaking* 378/1 *Miehle Press*, a new press, lately devised by Robert Miehle, a pressman of Chicago. The bed is carried in harmony with the movement of the cylinder while printing, then it is gradually slowed up, carried smoothly over the centre, and returned for the back movement... Great speed is claimed for this press. **1915** *Southward's Mod. Printing* (ed. 3) II. viii. 101 As a standard machine of the very highest class, the Miehle is widely in use. *Ibid.* 102 (*caption*) Miehle Two-Revolution Press. *Ibid.* 104 Miehle presses are also used in tandem, coupling up two or more machines for the production of colour work. **1963** *Printing & Mind of Man: Catal. Display of Printing Mechanisms & Printed Materials Brit. Mus. & Earls Court* (Earls Court Section) 80/2 The Miehle machine, in several models, continues to be marketed and sold all over the world. The cylinder revolves continuously, is raised after the impression in order to clear the forme during its second revolution, and is then brought down on impression again by the action of a cam and eccentrics. **1966** BERRY & POOLE *Ann. Printing* 258/2 Cassell's were the first printers in this country to import Miehles... For many years the Miehle was in a class by itself for the new three-colour letterpress. **1973** J. MORAN *Printing Presses* xi. 159 The Miehle, which had great impressional strength, accurate register and durability..kept its lead for some eighty years.

mielie (mī·li). *S. Afr.* [Afrikaans.] = MEALIE. Also *attrib.* and *Comb.* as *mielie cob, land;* **mieliepap**, mealie meal porridge (cf. quots. s.v. *MEALIE).

1804 J. T. VAN DER KEMP in *Trans.* [London] *Missionary Soc.* (ed. 2) I. 438 There is another kind of corn, which they call *bona*, and is known in the Colony by the name of *meelis*. **1818** G. BARKER *Diary* 7 Dec. (MS.), Began to clear the beans & mielies in the garden. **1835** A. SMITH *Diary* 28 Nov. (1940) II. 285 The Hottentots..had no pumpkins, melons, mielies nor calabases. **1926** O. SCHREINER *From Man to Man* i. 78 Near the mielie lands. *Ibid.* iii. 117 The maids were lighting the evening fires with mielie cobs. **1952** *Cape Times* 11 Jan. 3/4 The nearby Vergelegen Estate with its acres of corn and mielies. **1953** P. ABRAHAMS *Return to Goli* vi. 200 It was the kind of food I had not eaten for fourteen years: a thick *mielie pap*. **1959** *Cape Times* 26 Oct. 9/4 The mieliepap..is the staple food of millions in Africa. **1971** *Cape Herald* (Bonus) 15 May 5/1 (Advt.), With mieliepap you need never fear that some of the goodness has been lost in making. **1974** *Eastern Province Herald* 23 July 13 He is wise to discard his bowler hat when crossing a field of mielies.

mien (mīn), *sb.*² [Chinese, lit. = wheat flour.] Wheat flour noodles. (Cf. *CHOW MEIN.)

1934 in WEBSTER. **1936** P. FLEMING *News from Tartary* v. ix. 235 At noon they woke me for a meal of mien and boiled vegetables. **1950** R. ALLEY *Leaves from Sandan Notebk.* 46 They gave him a meal of mien. **1956** B. Y. CHAO *How to cook & eat in Chinese* xix. 218 Wheat is eaten more than rice as the staple food... When it is eaten wet, it is in the form of *mien*, or unraised noodles. **1971** N. FROUD *Far Eastern Cooking for Pleasure* 82 *Mien*, Chinese noodle or wun tun paste. This dough is used for Chinese noodles, wun tun and various other patties and dumplings.

mierkat. = MEERKAT 2.

1901 O. SCHREINER *Thoughts on S. Afr.* (1923) 19 There was a possibility that the red African mier-kat might ultimately creep back into its hole in the red African earth. **1949** *Cape Argus Mag.* 3 Sept. 1/9 To most people it is just a 'mierkat', but in reality it is a rodent, a squirrel, and quite different from the insect-eating, slender-tailed mierkat that is to be found in the same vicinity.

miersite (məi·əɪzəit). *Min.* [f. the name of Sir Henry Alexander *Miers* (1858–1942), English mineralogist + -ITE¹.] An iodide of silver and copper, (Ag, Cu)I (with the ratio of silver to copper approximately 4:1), which is found as yellow isometric crystals at Broken Hill, New South Wales, Australia.

1898 L. J. SPENCER in *Nature* 14 Apr. 574/2 The new mineral has been named in honour of Mr. H. A. Miers, F.R.S., Professor of Mineralogy at Oxford, who first correctly determined the crystalline form of marshite, a mineral so closely resembling miersite in appearance that the two species are only distinguished by chemical tests. **1901** [see *ISOMORPHOUSLY *adv.*]. **1922** *Mineral. Abstr.* I. 305 Silver iodide and copper iodide when fused together show..specks of birefringent iodyrite in a base of isotropic miersite. **1951** C. PALACHE et al. *Dana's Syst. Min.* (ed. 7) II. 20 Both miersite and iodyrite are obtained by metathical [*read* metathetical] reaction in water solution at ordinary temperature.

Miesian (mī·ziăn), *a.* and *sb.* [Name of the German-American architect, L. *Mies* van der Rohe (1886–1969) + -IAN.] **A.** *adj.* Of, pertaining to, or characteristic of the style of architecture of Mies van der Rohe. **B.** *sb.* A devotee or follower of Mies's style.

1956 *Archit. Rev.* CXX. 238/2 The job has some obviously Miesian passages. **1958** H. R. HITCHCOCK *Archit. 19th & 20th Cent.* III. xxiii. 390 The 'Miesian' is today almost a sub-school of the new architecture. **1960** A. DREXLER *Ludwig Mies van der Rohe* 32 The measure of Mies's authority is this: it no longer seems possible to rebel against the Miesian discipline except in Miesian terms. **1963** tr. *G. Hatje's Encycl. Mod. Archit.* 194/2 Inside the enclosure there was the usual Miesian spatial continuity. **1965** M. BRADBURY *Stepping Westward* 10 The new crematorium..was designed by a devout Miesian. **1969** *Archit. Rev.* CXLVI. 313 A long, low, not quite Miesian exercise in structural and not so structural steel and glass. **1973** *Current Affairs Bull.* (Sydney) Aug. 8/2 The shell-shapes.. are of Miesian derivation.

‖ **mietjie** (mī·tʃi, mī·kʸi). Also **meitjie, michi.** [Afrikaans.] = *Klaas's cuckoo* (*KLAAS).

1853 *Edin. New Philos. Jrnl.* LV. 82 The pretty notes of the *michi* and *diedrick* further enliven the growing day. **1936** E. L. GILL *First Guide S. Afr. Birds* 108 The usual call of Klaas's Cuckoo is quite well represented by its Afrikaans name 'mietjie'. **1939** [see *DIEDERIK, DIEDRIK]. **1970** MCLACHLAN & LIVERSIDGE *Roberts's Birds S. Afr.* (ed. 3) 242 The Afrikaans name [of Klaas's cuckoo] is onomatopoeic, 'Meitjie' and gives the call pretty closely.

miff, *v.* Add: **1.** (Earlier and later examples of *transf.* use.)

1883 *N. & Q.* 6 Oct. 267/2 A curious word came under my notice of late with regard to a flower losing its strength and beauty. I was speaking to a Surrey gardener about some fading plants, and he remarked that they were 'miffing off'. **1907** R. FARRER *My Rock-garden* v. 71 Here it flowers once, then it miffs off without any apparent reason. **1960** F. C. STERN *Chalk Garden* vii. 73 We have sometimes been successful with it [*sc.* a peony], but it miffs off for no apparent reason.

2. (Earlier and later examples.)

1811 C. MATHEWS *Let.* Dec. in A. Mathews *Mem. Charles Mathews* (1838) II. 177 You give me much gratification by your explanation of the word that miffed me. **1889** *Kansas City* (Missouri) *Times & Star* 27 Nov., Dr. G. W. Fitzpatrick..is badly miffed because he wasn't appointed surveyor of the port. **1904** E. ROBINS *Magnetic North* I. 252 Don't get mifft, Colonel. **1907** *N.Y. Even. Post* (Semi-Weekly ed.) 2 Sept. 4 He is a little miffed to find that there are other lawyers in the Cabinet whose advice the President prefers to his own. **1957** *New Yorker* 26 Oct. 82/2 The feminine contingent..was..more than a little miffed, to learn that London..had got married. **1972** *Times Lit. Suppl.* 18 Feb. 173/3 Understandably, he is more than a little miffed by all this. **1973** *Daily Tel.* (Colour Suppl.) 23 Feb. 54/2 He told us a slightly improper story. The girls were not shocked but were rather miffed at his thinking they would not be.

miffish (mi·fiʃ), *a.* [f. MIFF *sb.* + -ISH¹.] = MIFFY *a.* So **mi·ffishly** *adv.*

1957 *New Statesman* 2 Nov. 572/2 For all his shyness and laconicism, he had a green heart—miffish and virginal perhaps, but seldom sentimental. **1968** E. HYAMS *Gardener's Bedside Bk.* 35 Failure with this lily was more common than success for so many years that gardeners still have the impression that it is very difficult and miffish. **1968** 'B. MATHER' *Springers* i. 5 He went on miffishly: 'Did I ask for the job?' **1973** —— *Snowline* xv. 180 There was a lot of banter..directed at the earnest ones, who received it in silent and miffish dignity.

miffy, *a.* Add: Of a plant (further examples).

1871 S. HIBBERD *Amateur's Flower Garden* 146 *M[yosotis] dissitiflora*..is a most valuable species for early flowers, but 'miffy', and therefore needing perpetual renewal. **1907** R. FARRER *My Rock-garden* i. 19 A sound perennial in one place, soil and climate, but a miffy delicate untrustworthy creature half a mile away. **1934** *Gardeners' Chronicle* 19 May 330/3 A few plants invariably become 'miffy', from no apparent reason, and die out.

Also **mi·ffily** *adv.*, in a miffy manner.

1958 'A. BRIDGE' *Portuguese Escape* 104 'All right, all right,' Melplash said, rather miffily. 'There's no rush.'

might, *sb.* Add: **7.** *dial.* A considerable quantity or amount.

1834 W. A. CARUTHERS *Kentuckian in N.Y.* I. 28 I'm 'bliged to do a might of business in Baltimore afore I can go on. **1878** J. H. BEADLE *Western Wilds* ii. 29 It took a might of time. *Ibid.* 43 It was a might o' comfort, though, to see 'em 'fore they died. **1903** in *Eng. Dial. Dict.* (Yks., Suffolk). **1955** J. MASTERS *Coromandel!* i. 20 A sleeveless leather jerkin that..hid a might of queer things.

8. A possibility as distinct from a certainty.

1901 M. FRANKLIN *My Brilliant Career* xvi. 133 'We might have both been drowned,' he said sternly. 'Mights don't fly,' I returned. **1922** JOYCE *Ulysses* 344 There was just a might that he might be out. **1961** C. H. D. TODD *Pop. Whippet* 57 You don't want any *might* about it—you need to know.

might-be. Add: **B.** *adj.* That might be; (remotely) possible.

1934 R. CAMPBELL *Broken Record* iv. 102 This was during the Douanier rage, when every painting-railway-porter was a might-be genius. **1941** L. MACNEICE *Plant & Phantom* 26 A curfew..imposed Upon their might-be-wanderings; their might-be-applications For resurrection. **1956** AUDEN *Old Man's Road*, With might-be maps of might-have-been campaigns.

might-have-been. Add: (Further examples.) Also *attrib.*

1931 R. CAMPBELL *Georgiad* iii. 63 That moonlit people of the might-have-been. **1955** A. L. ROWSE *Expansion Eliz. Eng.* 90 The might-have-beens of history are not a very profitable subject. **1956** [see prec.]. **1970** *Guardian* 11 Aug. 11/8 One of history's might-have-been mysteries. **1974** R. THOMAS *Porkchoppers* xxvi. 230 The name that symbolized the might-have-been world of Donald Cubbin. **1974** A. GODDARD *Vienna Pursuit* III. 174 Overwhelmed with horror for the might-have-been, she paused.

mighty. Add: **B.** *adv.* (Later examples.)

1931 W. G. MCADOO *Crowded Yrs.* ii. 23 That seemed to me to be mighty good pay. **1958** *Times* 16 Oct. 17/1 They left it till mighty near no-side before they got their noses thankfully in front.

migma (mi·gmă). *Geol.* [a. Gr. μίγμα mixture, f. μ(ε)ιγνύναι to mix.] A mixture of solid and molten rock.

1943 *Proc. Geol. Assoc.* LIV. 73 The migma, if the amount of its liquid portion became great enough, would flow and could intrude itself into its surroundings in typical eruptive or intrusive fashion. **1952** T. F. W. BARTH *Theoret. Petrol.* IV. xiii. 364 In the root parts of the folded mountains..a migma is formed that corresponds to the magma of the higher levels. **1974** *Encycl. Brit. Macropædia* VI. 880/1 Between these extremes is a concept of a pore fluid, or migma, generated by the differential melting or partial fusion of the root portions of mountains.

migmatite (mi·gmătəit). *Petrol.* [ad. Sw. *migmatit* (J. J. Sederholm 1907, in *Bull. Comm. Géol. Finlande* V. XXIII. 88), f. Gr. μίγμα (see prec.): see -ITE¹.] A rock composed of a metamorphic host rock with streaks or veins of a granitic rock.

1907 J. J. SEDERHOLM in *Bull. Comm. Géol. Finlande* V. XXIII. 110 For the gneisses here in question, characteristic of which are two elements of different genetic value,.. the author proposes the name of *migmatites*. **1942** *Proc. Geol. Assoc.* LIII. 77 *Pseudodioritic migmatite* is a field-term used to name a group of fairly homogeneous foliated hornblende-rich rocks having a dioritic aspect. **1965** G. J. WILLIAMS *Econ. Geol. N.Z.* xiii. 203/2 The monazites and xenotine [*read* xenotime] in migmatites of the Charleston-Fox River area, do not seem to have produced a red colour in the adjoining felspars. **1974** *Encycl. Brit. Macropædia* VI. 880/1 Many migmatites probably represent the partial fusion of the metamorphic host during extreme metamorphism.

Hence **migma·tic, migmati·tic** *adjs.*, composed of migmatite.

1926 *Mineral. Abstr.* III. 84 Three types of pegmatites are distinguished: I, normal pegmatites; II, contact-pegmatites..; and III, migmatic pegmatites. **1942** *Proc. Geol. Assoc.* LIII. 67 The region around Bettyhill on the north coast of Sutherland furnishes a splendid display of migmatitic rocks produced by the injection of granitic and pegmatitic material into the different lithological types found in the Moine series. **1968** K. R. MEHNERT *Migmatites* i. 5 It is inappropriate to burden petrographic investigations of metamorphic or migmatic rocks from the beginning with the question about the possible parent rock. **1969** BENNISON & WRIGHT *Geol. Hist. Brit. Isles* iii. 53 The Moinian rocks are generally metasediments showing little metamorphic segregation, although in the central migmatitic core..they are gneissose.

migmatization (migmătəizēi·ʃən). *Petrol.* [f. *MIGMAT(ITE + -IZATION.] The process by which a migmatite is formed.

1932 E. G. WOODS *Baltic Region* vii. 67 A great deal of migmatization having taken place has masked very effectively the relationship of these rocks to one another. **1958** *Geol. Mag.* XCV. 383 The infrastructure, although undergoing migmatization, retains the trends of the older orogenic belt from which it is largely formed. **1971** *Scottish Jrnl. Geol.* VII. 323 The frequent spatial coincidence between areas of migmatization and centres of high-grade regional metamorphism has long been recognized.

Hence **mi·gmatized** *ppl. a.*, converted into a migmatite.

1958 *Geol. Mag.* XCV. 383 During the Caledonian orogeny, both the old crystalline rocks and a low structural level of the Caledonian geosynclinal rocks themselves became migmatized and rose as diapirs. **1971** *Scottish Jrnl. Geol.* VII. 305 In central and eastern Sutherland the Moine rocks are extensively migmatized.

migniardise. Delete † *Obs.* and add: Now only **mignardise.** Also, a fancy cake or similar delicacy, usu. served at the end of a meal. (Later examples.)

1931 BELLOC in *One Hundred & One Ballades* 16 Elderly women full of Mignardises—The latest fruit of Adam's ancient sin. **1935** W. STEVENS *Let.* 19 Dec. (1967) 303 Poulenc is a beautiful instance of *mignardise* in music. **1974** S. COULTER *Château* I. xvii. 132 Their digestive systems were dealing with Brioche de foie gras, ..ananas voilé, mignardises and fruit.

2. (See quot. 1950.) Also *attrib.*

1872 *Young Englishwoman* Nov. 606/2 A band ornamented with hem-stitch and a mignardise braid. **1873** *Ibid.* June 302/1 For this larger rosette commence with the centre star by joining the ends of a length of mignardise. **1882** CAULFEILD & SAWARD *Dict. Needlework* 111/2 Mignardise is used almost entirely to form narrow edgings for underlinen and children's dresses. *Ibid.* 112/1 Scalloped edging.—Formed of two rows of Mignardise braid. **1950** '*Mercury*' *Dict. Textile Terms* 345 *Mignardise*, a variety of crochet formed by inserting narrow fine ribbons into the design as the heavy part of the pattern that would otherwise be formed of crochet.

mignonette. Add: **1. d.** A perfume derived from the flowers of the mignonette.

1897 *Sears Roebuck Catal.* 19/2 Perfumes..Crab Apple.. Mignonette..Sweet Pea. **1913** *T. Eaton & Co. Catal.* Spring & Summer 177/1 Perfumes..Jasmin Mignionette Opoponax. **1972** *Guardian* 22 Aug. 9/4 Jacksons have revived these flower perfumes..the shop plan to reintroduce other fragrancies including wallflower, mignonette, and honeysuckle.

migod (migǫ·d), *int.* ¶ Representation of a colloq. pronunc. of *my God!* (My *poss. adj.* 3).

1953 K. Tennant *Joyful Condemned* xx. 186 Migod, what they done to Trix! **1968** M. Richler *Cocksure* ii. 16 Migod, Mortimer thought. **1970** J. Cleary *Helga's Web* v. 78 Oh migod, isn't it terrible!

migraine. Delete ‖ and add further examples. Also *attrib.* and *fig.*

1892 [see *day *sb.* 19]. **1937** *Tablet* 23 Oct. 553/2 We feel quite anxious for this young man who has fierce migraine-like black-outs. **1961** R. Graves *More Poems* 5 Love is a universal migraine, A bright stain on the vision Blotting out reason. **1971** *Brit. Med. Bull.* XXVII. 33/2 The common concept of migraine is of a syndrome in which severe unilateral periodic headache is accompanied by nausea or vomiting and preceded by a warning which is usually visual. **1971** 'D. Shannon' *Ringer* (1972) ix. 149 He's not at all well. A migraine headache. **1975** J. Symons *Three Pipe Problem* x. 72 Taking a pill for a mild migraine attack.

‖ **migraineur** (migrẹnö̆r). [Fr. Cf. Migraine.] One who suffers from migraine.

1971 *Times* 25 Jan. 6/6 The migrainous subject (or migraineur). **1971** *Daily Tel.* 11 Feb. 11/3 The general and specific measures recommended for prevention and for alleviation of the acute attack will prove a disappointment to the inveterate *migraineur* in search of relief but reflect the unpredictable and individual response to treatment. **1971** *Listener* 15 Apr. 480/3 Classical migraine is (*pace* G. B. Shaw) as uncommon among migraineurs as 'normal' vision among the rest of us.

migrainous, *a.* Add: Also, subject to attacks of migraine. (Further examples.)

1971 [see prec.]. **1973** *Tucson* (Arizona) *Daily Citizen* 22 Aug. 32/1 Migrainous women seldom put on weight, and they rarely develop any serious illness. **1974** *Radio Times* 6 June 66/1 Thousands of migrainous readers who read your feature 'The biggest aspirin splitter in the world'.

migrant. Add: **B.** *sb.* **c.** *Bot.* A plant whose distribution has changed or extended.

1905 F. E. Clements *Res. Methods Ecol.* 319 *Migrant*, a plant that is migrating or invading. **1960** N. Polunin *Introd. Plant Geogr.* vi. 165 These recent migrants were aided by natural means—wind, water or animals—or by Man, through intentional or accidental importation.

migrate, *v.* Add: **1.** (Later examples, in *Chem.* (cf. *migration a).)

1899 J. Walker *Introd. Physical Chem.* xx. 210 Had no silver ions migrated from the anode, the rise in concentration would have been 32·2. **1931** J. C. Ware *Analytical Chem.* I. ii. 11 Ions move or migrate independently in a solution and at different rates. **1938** E. S. Wallis in H. Gilman *Org. Chem.* I. viii. 724 The ease with which different groups migrate within the molecule is not wholly a property of the group itself, but is dependent to a varying extent on the molecule as a whole. **1967** J. H. Richards et al. *Elem. Org. Chem.* xi. 194 A carbonium ion is produced as an intermediate, and a methyl group migrates from an adjacent carbon to the positive center.

migration. a. Add: (Further examples.) *spec.* in *Chem.*, the (non-random) movement from one place to another of an atom or group, e.g. within a molecule as part of a rearrangement of its structure, or towards an electrode during electrolysis.

1879 *Encycl. Brit.* VIII. 108/2 For fused electrolytes a W-shaped tube..is sufficient; with solutions..the separation is more difficult, owing to the 'migration of the ions' and other causes. **1894** tr. *E. Goblet d'Alviella's Migration of Symbols* 82 Is it not the Winged Circle, whose migrations I trace in another chapter? **1898** *Jrnl. Chem. Soc.* LXXIII. I. 456 One of the following initial changes may occur. (1) Migration of the OH group. (2) Migration of the O·SO_3H group as a whole. (3) Migration of a hydrogen atom of the ring, in the meta-position with regard to the side group. **1929** *Times* 13 Nov. 11/1 A serious obstacle to the work of archæologists, historians and others..is the migration of manuscripts. **1938** A. L. Raymond in H. Gilman *Org. Chem.* II. xvii. 148 The migration of the benzoyl group from position three to six in monoacetoneglucose. **1962** D. H. Calam in A. Pirie *Lens Metabolism Rel. Cataract* 439 Although the differences in migration of a group of monoamino, mono-carboxylic acids..are small, they are well separated by chromatography.

c. *Nat. Hist.* Also, of plants, change or extension of distribution.

1905 F. E. Clements *Res. Methods Ecol.* iv. 216 Migration results when spores, seeds, fruits, offshoots, or plants are moved out of their home. **1932** Fuller & Conard tr. *Braun-Blanquet's Plant Sociol.* xiii. 306 The first step in the development of vegetation is 'migration'. **1966** E. Palmer *Plains of Camdeboo* xvi. 270 White and Sloane wondering at the reasons for plant migrations. **1973** Polunin & Smythies *Flowers of S.-W. Europe* ii. 86 The sierra ..has acted as a refuge for a number of montane species, which had in all probability previously undergone migrations and recessions culminating in the last ice age.

migrationist. Add: **2.** One who emphasizes the importance of migration in the distribution of species.

1918 L. Huxley *Life J. D. Hooker* II. xxxii. 98 Darwin was a migrationist; Forbes and others pushed the extension theory to excess.

‖**mihrab** (miχrā·b). Also 9 **mehhra'b, mehrab, mehreb, mirhab.** [Arab. *miḥrāb* praying-place.] **1.** A niche, chamber, or slab in a mosque, indicating the direction of Mecca. Cf. Kiblah.

1816 H. M. Williams tr. *Ali Bey's Travels* II. xvi. 217 In the wall at the end of the nave is the mehreb or niche where the Imam places himself to direct the prayer. **1836** E. W. Lane *Acct. Manners & Customs Mod. Egyptians* I. iii. 94 In the centre of its exterior wall is the *mehhra'b* (or niche). **1839** J. Pardoe *Beauties Bosphorus* 81 The *mihrab*, or niche at the eastern extremity of the edifice. **1845** R. Ford *Hand-bk. for Travellers Spain* I. 376/1 The exquisite niche, the *Mihrab* or sanctuary, in which the Koran was deposited. **1883** E. O'Donovan *Merv* xx. 242 A large deep recess, furnished with a *mirhab*, or devotional station. **1884** F. Boyle *On Borderland betwixt Fact & Fancy* 384 The Sayyid took his station at the mihrab. **1930** E. Waugh *Labels* 141 Agia Sophia..whose whole architectural rectitude has been fatally disturbed by the reorientation of the *mihrab*. **1931** *N. & Q.* 17 Oct. 271/1 The charm of the mosque with its *mirhab*—a false door, and its arcades—which carry nothing. **1959** *Chambers's Encycl.* VII. 763/2 The *liwan* on the side nearest to Mecca was much deeper than the others and formed a sanctuary with a central niche (*mihrab*) in its back wall. **1974** *Observer* (Colour Suppl.) 24 Nov. 43/2 The focal point of a mosque is the *mihrab*, a niche in the wall nearest to Mecca to which the congregation turns in prayer.

2. A niche motif on an Oriental prayer rug, resembling the shape of a mihrab in a mosque.

1911 G. G. Lewis *Pract. Bk. Oriental Rugs* x. 121 *Niche or Mihrab*.., the name applied to the pointed design at one end of a prayer rug. **1931** A. U. Dilley *Oriental Rugs & Carpets* viii. 201 Above this field is either one large prayer niche (called a mihrab), shaped like a tent, or a row of miniature prayer niches. **1963** tr. *I. Schlosser's European & Oriental Rugs & Carpets* 28 The mihrab, at first curved, later became steep and pointed... Scrolling stems with large flowers, or small branches..fill the border, the spandrels, and the cross panel which is usually above the mihrab. **1972** P. L. Phillips tr. *Formenton's Oriental Rugs & Carpets* 93 The mihrab, the niche in the centre of the rug, is often separated by two columns.

Mikado. Add: **2. Mikado pheasant,** a pheasant native to the island of Formosa, *Syrmaticus mikado*, first described in 1906 from specimens in the Mikado's collection in Tokyo.

[**1906** W. R. Ogilvie-Grant in *Bull. Brit. Ornith. Club* XVI. 123 Among the Mikado's collection of live animals and birds, at Tokio, there are said to be a pair of Pheasants from Formosa belonging to an undescribed species.] **1922** C. W. Beebe *Monogr. Pheasants* III. 200 In appearance,.. the Mikado Pheasant resembles the tragopans and impeyans, being heavy bodied and rather thick-necked. *Ibid.* 201 Several healthy hybrids with the Elliot pheasant... strongly resemble the female Mikado. **1965** P. Wayre *Wind in Reeds* xv. 211 The beautiful Mikado Pheasant, of which the male is a deep bluish purple with red wattles and a purple and white barred tail,.. found only on..Taiwan. *Ibid.* 212 There the Mikado inhabits the bamboo and juniper thickets..above five thousand feet. **1972** *Shooting Times & Country Mag.* 1 July 19/1 Next on the list for rehabilitation in Formosa (Taiwan to most, these days) is the Mikado pheasant. The Trust is breeding this bird and hopes soon to have enough for a further transplant.

mikan (mi·kān). [Jap.] A Satsuma orange.

[**1922** T. Tanaka in *Jrnl. Heredity* XIII. 243/2 The leading orange grown in Japan is a kind of mandarin, *Unshû Mikan*, called the Satsuma orange in the United States.] **1947** J. Bertram *Shadow of War* 193 *Mikans*—the sweet, juicy mandarin oranges. **1972** *Nat. Geographic* CXLI. 672/2 Obasan offered up sliced raw fish,..and finally the Futagami specialty, *mikan*, a tangerine-like citrus. **1973** A. Broinowski *Take One Ambassador* v. 56 Drink cans, *mikan* peel..used chopsticks, everywhere.

mike, *sb.*^{3} Substitute for def.: A rest; a period of idleness; a waste of time; esp. in phr. *to do* or *have a mike* = to be idle, escape from or evade work, go away. Add further examples. Cf. *mick^3.

1899 R. Whiteing *No. 5 John St.* xxiv. 238 It was pleasant to..share the tobacco and biscuit, and make sure of a good 'mike' on this side of a life to come. **1925** Fraser & Gibbons *Soldier & Sailor Words* 155 *Mike, to* (*to do a*), to make off. To avoid duty. **1940** M. Marples *Public School Slang* 119 *To do a mike* (St Bees, 1915 +), to break bounds. **1955** 'N. Shute' *Requiem for Wren* iii. 83 That's a good mike for you, but you'll have plenty to do later on. **1958** *Times* 26 Sept. 19/1 The day of the cheerful veteran forward, gratefully relying upon opportunities for a mild 'mike', may be coming to an end.

Mike, *sb.*^{4} Add: Phr. *for the love of Mike*, see *love *sb.*^{1} 7 a.

mike (məik), *sb.*^{5} Colloq. abbrev. of Microphone 1; also *attrib.* Cf. *mic.

1927 *Melody Maker* June 579/3, I think it is more that he plays too loudly than that he is too near the 'mike'. **1928** Ade *Let.* 7 July (1973) 134 Open the act with a fake microphone all set and adjusted for broadcasting. You come out and talk into the 'mike' announcing the name of a fake station in the town..and say you have a very interesting program ahead and then you can read it into the mike. **1937** *Daily Herald* 16 Feb. 19/6 He is unlikely to be afflicted with 'mike' fright, because, in his line, he has found visible audiences in far more truculent mood than will be his unseen Midland Regional listeners. **1939** *Evening News* 7 Nov. 4/5 To follow the players about, the 'mike' is moved across the floor on a long arm called a 'mike boom', and its operator is a 'mike slinger'. **1943** J. B. Priestley *Daylight on Saturday* xi. 68 He delighted in entertainment, liked to make his little speech at the mike. **1956** B. Holliday *Lady sings Blues* (1973) iii. 38, I got to the mike somehow and grabbed it. **1962** *Listener* 12 Apr. 656/3 Robert Kee avoided..entangling his mike-cable in the mob. **1971** D. E. Westlake *I gave at the Office* (1972) 188 'I am a soldier,' he said, 'not a baseball player. No interview.' Frankly, I think he had mike fright.

mike (məik), *sb.*^{6} In slang phr. *to take the mike out of* = to take the micky out of. Cf. *micky^1 6.

1935 G. Ingram *Cockney Cavalcade* i. 14 He wouldn't let Pancake 'take the mike' out of him. *a* **1935** T. E. Lawrence *Mint* (1955) II. vi. 117 But, mate, you let the flight down, when he takes the mike out of you every time. **1940** *N. & Q.* 1 June 382/1 'Taking the mike out of' anyone means pulling his leg, having a game with him. **1956** J. Cannan *People to be Found* i. 14 They won't 'alf take the mike out of 'im. **1973** 'B. Mather' *Snowline* vi. 75 Watch it... The Swami don't dig taking the mike out of the gods.

mike (məik), *sb.*^{7} *slang.* [Abbrev. of *microgram.*] A microgram, *spec.* of lysergic acid diethylamide (LSD).

1970 N. Saunders *Alternative London* xxii. 168 Lysergic Acid Diethylamide is the most common hallucinogen—and by far the most powerful, in that you only need a few millionths of a gram (micro-grams, 'mikes') to trip for eight hours. **1970** K. Platt *Pushbutton Butterfly* (1971) vi. 58 Janet Saunders could be on acid, dropping the usual LSD tab of two hundred and fifty mikes. That's the standard trip..a penny a microgram. **1973** J. Wood *North Beat* x. 126 They wanted me to tell where I got the mikes... The acid, see?

mike, *v.*^{1} Add to def.: to avoid work; go away, escape; also with *off*. (Further examples.) Hence **mi·king** *vbl. sb.*

1894 A. Morrison *Tales of Mean Streets* 47 'I ain't settled with you yut, my gal,' he added to Lizer; 'mikin' about at 'ome an' 'idin' money.' **1930** E. Wallace *Lady of Ascot* xxii. 219, I believe in a fair day's work for a fair day's pay and no miking. **1959** B. J. Farmer *Murder Next Year* xv. 83 He knew most of the possible 'miking' holes. *Ibid.* 84 Molden was simply 'miking' on a grand scale. *Ibid.* 85 A policeman is paid to work his beat, not 'mike' with or without permission. **1959** N. Lofts *Heaven in your Hand* 145 There was nobody to send. Both my young b—s have miked off. **1974** P. Evett in J. Burnett *Useful Toil* III. 336 [He would] spy on us as we worked, and then..thunder at any one he thought was miking.

mike (məik), *v.*^{2} *colloq.* [f. *mike *sb.*^{5}] *trans.* To place a microphone in (a place) or near (a person) for recording purposes; freq. = *bug *v.*^{1} 2. So **miked** *ppl. a.*

1962 M. Procter *Body to Spare* xvi. 124 He was put in a cell with Cony, and the cell was 'miked'. **1965** D. Torr *Diplomatic Cover* v. 82 The Russian..turned a switch on the bigger recorder... Christ, they've miked us! **1968** —— *Treason Line* 19, I take it this Dean is the American Counsellor whose bungalow you're trying to mike? **1969** 'A. Hall' *Striker Portfolio* xvi. 196 My one task for the day was to find out if the room was miked because I didn't want them to hear my movements. **1969** *Rolling Stone* 17 May 12/3 What came out was a beautifully mixed and miked package of spiritual soul. **1972** *Jazz & Blues* Oct. 30/1 Mezz is too closely miked for one to be able to follow the soprano clearly at all times. **1974** *Listener* 4 Apr. 437/3 [The] film..owes a great deal to..the unobtrusive miking techniques..and the quiet manoeuvring of the crew.

miker (məi·kəɹ). *dial.* and *slang.* [f. Mike *v.* + -er^1.] = Micher *sb.*

1890 J. D. Robertson *Gloss. Words County of Gloucester* 94 *Miker* is used for a truant. **1928** *Daily Tel.* 9 Oct. 10/5 It is reported that the casual ward of Edmonton Workhouse was known far & wide over the highway as the 'Mikers' Mecca'. **1931** C. Williams *Three Plays* 29 You always saw and sneaked your profit out Like a kerchief-miker.

Mikimoto (mikimōᵘ·to). The name of Kokichi *Mikimoto* (1858–1954), Japanese pearl farmer, used *attrib.* of pearls cultured by means of a technique which he perfected.

1956 R. Eunson *Pearl King* ii. 28 At Toba Bay Mikimoto pearls are harvested by the crop and sacked up like wheat. **1959** R. Kirkbride *Tamiko* iii. 20 Diamonds and great clusters of Mikimoto pearls gleamed in the candlelight. **1969** J. Bennett *Dragon* i. 6 A string of good cultured Mikimoto pearls around her neck.

mikva (mi·kvā). Also **mikve(h, mikwe(h.** Pl. **mikvaoth.** [Heb. *miqwāh*, lit. collection, mass, esp. of water; pool of water.] A bath in which certain Jewish ritual purifications must be performed; the action of taking such a bath. Also *attrib.*

1843 De Sola & Raphall tr. *18 Treat. from Mishna* 356 Treatise Mikvaoth. (Contains laws that relate to diving baths for the cleansing of persons.) **1904** *Jewish Encycl.* VIII. 588 *Miḳweh*... Because of the use made of this word in connection with ritual purification.., it has become the

term commonly used to designate the ritual bath... The mikweh must contain sufficient water to cover entirely the body of a man of average size. 1962 B. Abrahams tr. *Life Glückel of Hameln* v. 108 Every Jewish community had its *mikveh*—ritual communal bath. 1966 *New Statesman* 6 May 648/2 All women about to marry must endure an interview with a woman in the rabbinate who issues a ticket to the ritual bath (*mikva*). 1968 L. Rosten *Joys of Yiddish* 242 Today, only very religious Jewish women observe the *mikva* custom—or attend a bathhouse for *mikvas*. 1970 L. M. Feinsilver *Taste of Yiddish* 249 *Mikve* immersion is also part of Orthodox conversion ritual. *Ibid.*, The average American Jewish couple would be surprised to learn..that the wife should then visit the *Mikve* before union. 1974 *Observer* (Colour Suppl.) 10 Nov. 37/3 By ancient Jewish teaching..a woman becomes virtually unclean by the act of menstruation and she must abstain from sexual relations during it and for seven days after it is finished. Before she recommences relations with her husband she should immerse herself in the *mikva* (ritual bath). Brides prior to marriage should also be purified in the *mikva* and also mothers after childbirth... Reform Jews do not use the *mikva*.

mil. Add: **1.** (Later example.)

1973 *Sci. Amer.* Feb. 66/3 Away from coastal areas.. the salinity of the ocean varies from 32 to 37 grams of dissolved solid per kilogram of seawater, expressed as 32 to $37\ ^0/_{00}$. (The symbol $^0/_{00}$ is read 'per mil'.)

2. (Later examples.) Also *attrib.*

1883 *Encycl. Brit.* XVI. 734/1 Another proposal starts from the present *pound* as unit. It is to be divided into 10 *florins* (2s.), which would contain 100 *mils* (or *farthings* reduced 4 per cent.). A new coin, 10 *mils* (2s. 4d.) would probably have to be introduced. 1920 *Rep. R. Comm. Decimal Coinage* 13 in *Parl. Papers* (Cmd. 628) XIII. 467 The pound and mil provides no exact equivalent of the penny. Of the nearest equivalents 4 mils is 4 per cent. less, 5 mils is 20 per cent. more than the penny. 1920 *Glasgow Herald* 10 Apr. 4 If there were any demonstrable superiority in this 'pound mil' system it might be worth while to face all.. delays. 1960 *News Chron.* 4 May 3/2 The day when we.. pay 200 mils for a packet of cigarettes has drawn a little closer. 1963 *Rep. Comm. Inquiry Decimal Currency* p. xiv, in *Parl. Papers 1962–3* (Cmnd. 2145) XI. 195 We sometimes refer to 'mil' systems..as three-place decimal systems. 1967 *Guardian* 26 Apr. 2/6 The committee..was considering an amendment to introduce the pound-florin-mil system.

3. (Examples.)

1896 F. Bedell *Princ. Transformer* xv. 306 For conductors larger than 50,000 circular mils, flat copper ribbons are always used. 1962 A. Nisbett *Technique Sound Studio* 255 *Coarse-groove*. The groove normally used for 78 rpm recordings... Width 6 mils, depth 2·5 mils. 1973 *Sci. Amer.* July 43/1 Graphite fibers, produced by the carbonization of rayon or acrylic fibers, average about a third of a mil in diameter.

5. The name of a coin whose value is a thousandth part of the unit of currency, in Cyprus (and formerly in Palestine and Egypt) and Hong Kong.

1902 *Encycl. Brit.* XXXI. 292/1 *Hong Kong*,..the denominations are..the cent and the mill in bronze. 1908 G. B. Rawlings *Coins* xi. 317 Queen Victoria's issues for Hong Kong consisted of silver dollars, half-dollars..and mils. *Ibid.*, The mil follows the Chinese fashion and is pierced in the centre. On the one side it has a crown, V.R., and the date, and Hong Kong One Mil. 1929 *Whitaker's Almanack* 447 Palestine..*Silver*—100, 50 mils. *Bronze* 2, 1 mils. 1937 M. Comencini *Coins Mod. World* 42 Palestine Mandated Territory... Currency in Mils on a decimal basis, similar to that in use in Egypt. *Ibid.* 106 Egypt... *Currency unit*:..1 Piastre of 10 Milliemes or Mils. 1956 *Whitaker's Almanack* 783 Cyprus... 1,000 mils = £1 Sterling. 1968 C. Narbeth *Coin Collectors' Encycl.* 65 Cyprus... A new currency was introduced in 1955 of 100 mils (equals 2s.). 1970 C. Wood *Terrible Hard* v. 56 'How much?' 'Forty-five mils!' 1975 G. Lyall *Judas Country* iii. 20, I served 'em a compulsory breakfast at 500 mils each.

6. A unit of angular measure equal to 1/1600 of a right angle, which is approximately the angle subtended by one metre at a distance of 1000 metres.

1907 O. M. Lissak *Ordnance & Gunnery* xiii. 507 The horizontal deflection scale..is graduated, in sights for field artillery, to thousandths of the range. These gradations are called mils. 1920 Carter & Arnold *Field Artillery Instruction* vi. 219 The angle of site scales and the deflection scales on all instruments are graduated in mils. 1920 J. K. Finch *Topogr. Maps* 138 The vertical lines of the sketching screen, being one inch apart and twenty inches from the eye, determine an angle of fifty mils. 1941 *Amer. Math. Monthly* XLVIII. 188 Most American mobile artillery units as well as many heavy railway mounts have the scales on their sights, azimuth circles, and quadrants graduated in mils. 1955 C. R. Wylie *Plane Trigonometry* i. 21 Show that on any circle a central angle of 1 mil intercepts an arc whose length is approximately 1/1,000 of the radius of the circle. 1970 *Daily Tel.* 1 June 15/7 The Services no longer measure bearings in 360 degrees but in 6,400 mills to a circle.

mil., var. *mill *sb.*[6] and *sb.*[7]

Milan[1]. Add: **2.** (See quot. 1968.) Also *attrib.*

1895 *Montgomery Ward Catal.* 131/3 Misses' or children's, Union Milan and fancy braid. 1948 K. Hardy *Costume Design* x. 209 *Milan*, finer version of leghorn. 1950 *'Mercury' Dict. Textile Terms* 345/2 *Milan hat*, a hat of fine straw, originally manufactured in the province of Milan, Italy. 1968 J. Ironside *Fashion Alphabet* 253 *Milan*, a fine, closely woven straw from Milan, Italy, used for expensive hats.

Milanese, *a.* and *sb.* Add: **A.** *adj.* (Earlier examples.)

1617 J. Chamberlain *Let.* 21 June (1939) II. 82, I met with a Milanese gentleman of some qualitie. 1753 M. W. Montagu *Let.* 10 Oct. (1967) III. 39 A Milanese lady being now proffessor of Mathematics in the University of Bologna.

2. Of a warp knit fabric made on a Milanese loom usually from silk or rayon yarns; of a garment made of this fabric. Also *ellipt.* as *sb.*

1897 *Sears, Roebuck Catal.* 231/1 The New Four-Button Pure Silk Glove... Guaranteed all pure Milanese silk. *Ibid.*, Black Milanese Silk Mitts, the softest, finest and most durable of all silks. 1916 *Daily Colonist* (Victoria, B.C.) 19 July 14/5 (Advt.), Nothing could be more appropriate for wear at the big Fete Saturday than one of these Suits, of Milanese Silk. 1922 *Tatler* 30 Aug. Advts. p. c, Ladies' exceedingly dainty Cami-Knickers, made of best quality Milanese Silk. 1922 *Ibid.* 5 July Advts. p. m, Pure Silk Milanese Vest. 1927 *Glasgow Herald* 20 Apr. 10 What your supples and your Milanese may be, you alone may care. But one takes off one's hat to the 'shimmering crepe de soie'. 1945 M. D. Potter *Fiber to Fabric* 238 Milanese has a distinctive diagonal cross effect. Originally silk, now also rayon. 1968 J. Ironside *Fashion Alphabet* 241 *Milanese*, a warp-knit fabric made on a Milanese loom, used mainly for women's underwear, very fine and lustrous.

B. *sb.* **3.** The Milanese dialect.

1642 J. Howell *Instructions Forreine Trav.* xi. 138 There is in Italy..the Milanese, the Parmasan, the Piemontese, and others..and all these have several Dialects and Idiomes of Speech. 1818 [see *Genoese *sb.*]. 1880 *Encycl. Brit.* XIII. 493/2 It may be added that the Milanese *niin*..is really a compound or reduplication in the manner of the *ni-ni*. 1966 T. G. Griffith *Migliorni's Italian Lang.* xi. 351 Porta, who gave a brilliant example of the expressive use of his own Milanese, defended dialect against Giordani.

mild, *sb.*[2] Eng. and U.S. dial. var. of Mile *sb.*[1]

1701 in *Essex Inst. Hist. Coll.* (1900) XXXVI. 83 To run the lien of mesuer from Ipswich meting howes..six mields. 1725 in *Early Rec. Lancaster, Mass.* (1884) 231 We traueled to Groten 12 milds... We marcht up the riuer about 8 milds. 1777 R. Lincoln *Diary* 7 July in *Papers* (1904) 15 They ware Engaged in Carring gun bots..over land about one mild into Lake George. 1836 *Knickerbocker* VIII. 352, I expect we are a mild and a half from the *city*. 1886 F. T. Elworthy *West Somerset Word-Bk.* 476, I count 'tis up vower mild yer-vrom. 1903 *Dialect Notes* II. 321, I haven't walked a *mild* in a year. 1927 *Amer. Speech* III. 10 Most natives [*sc.* Ozarkers] use *mile* for both singular and plural, but some of the old-timers use the plural form *mild*.

mild, *a.* Add: **5. b.** (Further examples of *absol.* use.) Also phr. *mild-and-bitter*, a mixture of mild and bitter ale or beer.

1894 A. Morrison *Martin Hewitt* ii. 63 'Had his glass o'beer, has he?'..'Has two glasses of mild a-day... Never puts on flesh.' 1933 D. L. Sayers *Hangman's Holiday* 157 Half of mild-and-bitter, please. 1944 Dylan Thomas *Let.* 21 Sept. (1966) 267 It is time for the Black Lion But there is only Buckley's unfriskly Mild. 1951 E. Hyams *Sylvester* xxiv. 121 The chaps in the local, drinking a pint of mild and bitter. 1957 J. Braine *Room at Top* ii. 22 We used to..live on onions and cheese washed down with mild-and-bitter. 1963 *Times* 25 May 9/7 'But t'brig isn't t'world', a sewing-shop overlooker says over his gill of mild. 1974 'W. Haggard' *Kinsmen* vii. 70 He went to the bar. Mysteriously four evident locals were already inside and drinking mild.

mildewed, *ppl. a.* (Later *fig.* examples.)

1923 in J. Manchon *Le Slang*. 1930 R. Campbell *Adamastor* 56 Worse than death The palsied soul, the mildewed brain. 1959 I. & P. Opie *Lore & Lang. of Schoolch.* ix. 161 Juvenile repugnance continues to be expressed by the old standbys:..mardy, mildewed, mingy, misery-making, [etc.].

mildly, *adv.* Add: Esp. in *colloq.* phr. *to put it mildly*, to express an idea without exaggeration; freq. ironical, with an implication of understatement.

1939 Joyce *Finnegans Wake* 439 What I'm wondering to myselfwhose for there's a strong tendency, to put it mildly, by making me the medium. 1949 E. E. Cummings *Let.* 9 July (1969) 191 Thank you much more than kindly for a most (putting it very mildly) luxurious gift. 1958 *Spectator* 22 Aug. 240/1 This, to put it mildly, seems improbable. 1972 *Listener* 6 Apr. 448/3 Suggestions that conditions [on Mars] may periodically change, causing torrential rainfall every 25,000 years or so, are—to put it mildly—highly speculative as yet.

mile, *sb.*[1] Add: **1. d.** (Further examples.)

1885 *Punch* 12 Dec. 281/1 The fellows generally bag his music, and make him play the '*Mikado*' which is miles better. 1919 'C. Dane' *Legend* 64 He had heard nothing... He was miles away. 1922 Joyce *Ulysses* 639 Bloom..picked it up..meaning to return it to him.. whose thoughts were miles away from his hat at the time.. 1932 'E. M. Delafield' *Thank Heaven Fasting* i. iv. 65, I should have thought he'd be miles better than no one. 1943 J. B. Priestley *Daylight on Saturday* vii. 38 Not that the boys drew back..but..not one of them came within miles of being..Mister Right. 1951 E. Paul *Springtime in Paris* xv. 287 Pierre Vautier, smiling, gesturing and talking a mile a minute to an attractive brunette. 1961 M. Kelly *Spoilt Kill* iii. 166 Freddy was miles out in alleging Corinna's coldness. 1961 Partridge *Dict. Slang* Suppl. 1184/1 *Miles away, be*, to be either day-dreaming or lost in thought. 1964 C. Willock *Enormous Zoo* viii. 133 Ken Beaton's original estimate of the elephant, buffalo and hippo population had been miles out. 1969 A. La Bern *Nice Class of People* ii. 11 Ann Corrie had to repeat the sentence... He was miles away. 1970 J. Porter *Rather Common Sort of Crime* i. 17 She *was* on the scrounge... You could spot it a mile off. 1970 *Globe Mag.* (Toronto) 26 Sept. 9/3 The meeting..is going well. Stephen has made some miles by talking about the proposed shutdown of the Garden City Paper Mills. 1973 L. Snelling *Heresy* i. vii. 52 The French technicians are all ..very Lefty... He can keep them from getting within a mile of the set. 1974 N. Freeling *Dressing of Diamond* 176 This hasn't been done cold-bloodedly for money... Makes it all miles easier. 1974 D. Gray *Dead Give Away* ii. 28 'Aunt Milly's miles out,' said Marion. 'As usual.'

5. b. *mile-consuming* ppl. adj., *-deep* (earlier example), *-high* (examples), *-wide*.

1932 W. Faulkner *Light in August* i. 8 He drove on, the wagon beginning to fall into its slow and mileconsuming clatter. 1888 J. R. Lowell *Fitz Adam's Story* in *Heartsease & Rue* iv. 151 Mile-deep the glaciers brooded here, they say. 1963 J. Lusby in B. James *Austral. Short Stories* 229 A black speck raced towards me along the rim of a mile-high blood-red cliff of cumulus. 1968 *Listener* 27 June 841/2 The ozone-drenched, mile-high city of Denver. 1866 J. G. Whittier *Snow-Bound* 22 Where Salisbury's level marshes spread Mile-wide as flies the laden bee. 1903 Kipling *Five Nations* 56, I heard the mile-wide mutterings of unimagined rivers.

c. mile-a-minute *attrib.*, travelling at a rate of a mile a minute; covering a mile a minute; **mile-eater** (cf. *eat *v.* 18 g) *colloq.*, a fast driver or traveller; **mile-heat**, a racing heat of one mile; **mile-post** (earlier and later examples); also *fig.*; hence **mile-posted** *ppl. a.*

1957 *Railway Mag.* Nov. 752/2 In view of the Eastern, North Eastern and Scottish changes, a new table of their mile-a-minute runs for the winter appears here. 1961 *Christian Science Monitor* 9 Jan., The daredevil courage needed to flash down a hard-packed track at better than a mile-a-minute speed. 1908 *Westm. Gaz.* 20 Aug. 12/1 These mile-eaters go early to bed and prefer their steam-horses to our live ones. 1957 S. Moss *In Track of Speed* i. 9 The driver himself must possess those faculties which go to make the expert mile-eater. 1802 N. Macon *Let.* 10 Sept. in J. Steele *Papers* (1924) I. 315 He says there are no regular Mile heats at that turf. 1868 H. Woodruff *Trotting Horse* vi. 70 You can tell by the way he finishes..whether he will be likely to stand the mile-heat out and to repeat it. 1768 in *Maryland Hist. Mag.* (1907) II. 317 As we returned (besides the Mile Posts) we erected Marks on the Tops of all the High Ridges. 1909 *Westm. Gaz.* 26 Mar. 12/2 Oxford paddled up to the mile-post. 1926 Ade *Let.* 29 Aug. (1973) 107 The day in 1894 when the editor put me in charge of a department was an important mile post. 1941 W. Temple *Citizen & Churchman* i. 2 It is in reality a mile-post marking the distance away from it which thought has travelled. 1954 R. D. Burnell *Oxf. & Cambr. Boat Race* vi. 116 Cambridge led at once... At the Mile Post they led by seven seconds. 1896 'Mark Twain' in *Harper's Mag.* Jan. 294/2 The road was mile-posted with English fortresses, so to speak.

mileage. Add: **1. c.** A rate per mile charged for the use of railway vehicles carrying goods or passengers over another company's line.

1837 *Penny Mag.* Suppl. 31 Mar. 115/1 Mileage on the whole mail. 1863 *Great Western Mag.* Aug. 74 The Clearing House..will debit each company on the journey with its proper amount of 'mileage'. 1873 *Cassell's Mag.* VIII. 400/1 As..the Caledonian Company will receive the fares of the passengers, they will be required to pay for the use of the carriages conveying them; in other words the.. Company will be charged 'mileage'. 1926 Huebner & Johnson *Railroad Freight Service* vii. 129 The prevailing rate of mileage paid by one railway to another for the use of foreign cars was three quarters of a cent per car per mile.

2. b. (Further examples.)

1945 N. L. McClung *Stream runs Fast* p. xi, There was good mileage in me yet. 1962 L. Deighton *Ipcress File* xxv. 158 In the Café Budapest..'kezet csokolom' (kiss your hand) had given good mileage with the younger waitresses. 1970 W. V. Quine *Philos. of Logic* v. 71 We can still get a little additional mileage by superimposing the virtual theory. 1971 *Rolling Stone* 24 June 36/1 Sam's got mileage that any PR firm might envy: front-page space in both San Francisco dailies,.. and wire service coverage. 1971 A. Price *Alamut Ambush* ix. 114 The newspapers had got very fair mileage out of the bomb explosion. 1973 *Times* 5 Feb. 19/5 When..profits began to tumble, the..senior management of the time imagined that there was no more milage in the product. 1973 *Sci. Amer.* Apr. 103/3 Mathematical notions whose foundations have been matters of continuous debate have often yielded the most mileage. 1974 T. Allbeury *Snowball* iii. 14 They'd enjoy stirring up the Canadians, and the French-Canadians would..get a lot of political mileage.

c. (Earlier and later examples.)

1869 *Bradshaw's Railway Manual* XXI. 367 Advances are made by the Italian Government, to be made good afterwards out of the mileage subventions promised... The Italian and Pontifical Governments have given mileage guarantees. 1884 J. B. Pope *Railway Rates* 22 They [*sc.* Railway Companies] shall be allowed to vary or graduate the mileage charges according to distance. 1908 *Westm. Gaz.* 14 Nov. 15/2 An instrument, made by one of the largest clock-makers in the world,..combines a time-piece, mileage recorder, speed indicator [etc.]. 1928 C. E. R. Sherrington *Econ. Rail Transport Gt. Brit.* II. vii. 98 With the coming of the Parliamentary trains,..the equal mileage basis became..stabilized. 1969 *Observer* (Colour Suppl.) 23 Mar. 31/3 The White Car is running on Shell *with* the mileage ingredient. 1970 *Motoring Which?* Oct. 151/1 Check the mileage recorder—see how long the road test has been. 1971 'J. Ashford' *Bent Copper* iv. 34 He left and went out to..his car, a battered Ford, which he ran on a mileage allowance. 1973 *Radio Times* 20–27 Dec.

19/1 (Advt.), Explore Canada for a week with Avis for £37·50, with no mileage surcharge. **1975** *New Yorker* 26 May 60 (Advt.), In mileage tests conducted by the Environmental Protection Agency, Seville got 13 miles per gallon in the city test.

mile-castle. Add: Also **milecastle.** (Later examples.)

1935 *Antiquity* IX. 92 The recent excavations at High House Turf-Wall milecastle. **1936** *Nature* 25 July 156/2 A milecastle and three quarters of a mile of the wall itself were presented to the National Trust. **1963** E. S. Wood *Collins Field Guide Archaeol.* II. ii. 177 The milecastles [of Hadrian's Wall] were about 75 by 60 feet, the turrets about 20 feet square.

mileometer, var. *MILOMETER.

miler[2]**.** Add: (Earlier and later examples.)

1889 E. Sampson *Tales of Fancy* 31, I..was in private trials one of the fastest 'milers' of my time. **1955** *Times* 31 Aug. 3/5 To-night B. S. Hewson, potentially perhaps the greatest miler in the world, is to defend the trophy against a good field. **1965** *Illustr. London News* 4 Sept. 14/4 (*heading*) The first African miler to break four minutes. **1971** L. Koppett *N.Y. Times Guide Spectator Sports* viii. 159 The miler who excited the world's track fans in the 1920s was Paavo Nurmi, a Finn.

2. *colloq.* A walk or journey of a specified number of miles.

Properly the second element of a compound.

1856 Dickens *Let.* 14 Nov. (1938) II. 811, I went out this morning for a 12-miler.

‖ **miles gloriosus** (mī·lēiz *or* məi·līz glōəri-ōu·sǒs). Pl. **milites gloriosi.** [f. L. *miles* soldier + *gloriosus* boastful, conceited.] The name of a comedy by Plautus (*c* 250–184 B.C.), used allusively to designate a braggart soldier. Also *attrib.*

1917 K. M. Westaway *Orig. Element in Plautus* ii. 28 Other plays of Plautus contain *milites gloriosi* of smaller fame. **1936** P. Fleming *News from Tartary* vii. iv. 343 One..was a glib Turki from Turfan, the shoddiest type of the *miles gloriosus.* **1950** A. Bonjour *Digressions in Beowulf* 18 In spite of Beowulf's biting allusion to Grendel's security, we should not take this as an entirely idle vaunt of some *miles gloriosus.* **1962** G. K. Hunter *John Lyly* iv. 238 The version of *miles gloriosus* habits found here is without the menace that accompanies its adult presentation, in Pyrgopolynices (*Miles Gloriosus*) or Thraso (*Eunuchus*). **1964** *Rev. Eng. Stud.* XV. 385 A typical figure in Gleig's tales in particular was the Peninsular miles gloriosus. **1969** E. Segal tr. *Plautus' Three Comedies* Introd. 8 The *miles gloriosus* is by no means a Plautine invention, although the boastful officer is one of the Roman comedian's favorite characters.

Milesian, *a.*[1] and *sb.*[1] (Earlier and later examples.)

1550 T. Nicolls tr. *Thucydides* iv. sig. Siiii verso, They had in their compaignie the succours of Milesyans, of Andryens and of Caristians. **1600** P. Holland tr. *Livy* xliii. 1159 The Milesians for their part said, That hitherto they had done nothing. **1602** I. B. in E. Beaumont *Salm. & Hermaphr.* Pref. Verses, Or wanton Nymphs in watry bowres haue woue, With fine Mylesian threds, the verse he sings. **1607** [see *Calabrian *a.* and *sb.*]. *a* **1635** Randolph *Hey for Honesty* (1651) iv. iii. 472 You told her, The Milesians were valiant in the daies of yore. **1961** L. Mumford *City in Hist.* vii. 191 Since it would be erroneous to call this Hippodamian planning, I shall follow Roland Martin and call it Milesian, after Miletus, the chief point of origin. **1968** *Encycl. Brit.* XV. 444/1 The Milesians..were already rebuilding their city on a new grid plan to the type invented..by the Milesian Hippodamus.

Milesian, *a.*[2] and *sb.*[2] (Earlier and later examples.)

1596 Spenser *State Irel.* (1633) 31 All which are in truth fables, and very Milesian lyes, as the later proverbe is: for never was there such a King of Spaine, called Milesius. **1705** M. Kennedy (*title*) A Chronological Genealogical and Historical Dissertation of the Royal Family of the Stuarts, beginning with Milesius the stock of those they call the Milesian Irish, and of the old Scotish Race. **1839** Carlyle *Chartism* iv. 28 The wild Milesian features ..salute you on all highways and byways. *Ibid.*, The English coachman..lashes the Milesian with his whip. **1910** D. Hyde in R. M. Dorson *Peasant Customs* (1968) II. 704 Some of the Scotch stories may have been bequeathed to the Gaelic language by those races who were displaced by the Milesian Conquest in the fifth century. **1921** *Edin. Rev.* Jan. 167 And lastly the Milesians. The Milesian being a literary and honorific cognomen of the Firbolgs' conquerors, the Gaels. **1971** *It* 2–16 June 24/1 The first groups of wholly human invaders to reach these shores.. were called the Milesians or 'Sons of Miledh'.

milestone, *sb.* Add: **3.** *Naut. slang.* (See quots.)

1946 J. Irving *Royal Navalese* 116 *Milestones*, the heavy, green seas which break inboard in bad weather. **1962** Granville *Dict. Sailors' Slang* 77/1 Milestones refer to the homeward trip, for, like milestones on country roads they seem to make the journey longer and harder, and one's progress slower in consequence.

milestone, *v.* [f. the sb.] *trans.* Used *fig.*, to mark (stages) as if by milestones.

1902 J. H. M. Abbott *Tommy Cornstalk* 157 And the road was mile-stoned by the parched hides and whitened bones of horses, mules, and oxen. *a* **1910** 'Mark Twain' *Autobiogr.* (1924) I. 299 You could look back over that speech and you'd find it dimly milestoned along with those commas. **1922** *Chambers's Jrnl.* Dec. 861/1 The Overland is mile-stoned with our bones. **1973** J. Cleary *Ransom* iii. 98 Malone's life was milestoned by friends he had never made. **1973** J. Wainwright *High-Class Kill* 149 The book..will make passing reference to these things—as a means, perhaps, of milestoning his climb to the rank of chief constable.

milice. Delete † *Obs.* and add: In revived use, *spec.* a force employed by the occupied French state of 1940–44 to repress internal dissent. (In quot. 1945, by substitution for *MILICIEN.)

1945 H. Nicolson *Let.* 11 Mar. (1967) 440 The *milices* had beaten him up. **1958** *Listener* 21 Aug. 277/2 The Cagoulards, who in the event became the Kernel of the Vichy Milice. **1968** A. Diment *Bang Bang Birds* vi. 98 Their disposal was left to the Gestapo and the Milice. **1974** T. Allbeury *Snowball* vi. 32 An officer..captured in Perpignan by the Milice in 1944 and handed over to the Gestapo.

‖ **miliciano** (miliþiā·no). [Sp.] A militiaman of the irregular Republican force formed during the Spanish Civil War. Also **miliciana,** a militiawoman of this force.

1938 J. Riesenfeld *Dancer in Madrid* viii. 159 A woman *miliciana* was being helped up by two *milicianos.* **1957** P. Kemp *Mine were of Trouble* ii. 23 Women, too, enlisted in the militias... They were also employed as jailers to guard female political prisoners, several of whom have told me that they suffered much worse treatment from the *milicianas* than from the men. *Ibid.* 27 The only opposition came from the *milicianos*, who fought with courage but without discipline or military training. **1962** D. A. Puzzo *Spain & Great Powers* iii. 69 Against German and Italian air power and matériel, the *milicianos* could not hope to advance. **1965** C. D. Eby *Siege of Alcázar* (1966) iii. 65 At the Plaza de Padilla they were stopped by some *milicianos.*

‖ **milicien** (milisiæ̃). [Fr.] A member of the Milice (see *MILICE above).

1945 *Tomorrow* (N.Y.) Feb. 11/1 These fellow-soldiers.. would..comb a building for Germans or the dreaded Miliciens. **1961** P. de Vomécourt *Who lived to see Day* ix. 107 Almost to a man the *miliciens* were thugs on the make. .. Many of them were convicted criminals. **1966** M. R. D. Foot *SOE in France* v. 120 Miliciens were Frenchmen who lived and worked in their home towns and villages. **1967** *Listener* 16 Nov. 640/3 He is liquidated on suspicion of being one of the *miliciens.*

milieu. Delete ‖ and add earlier and later examples.

1854 Geo. Eliot *Let.* 6 Apr. (1954) II. 149, I could no more live out of my *milieu*, than the haddocks I daresay you are often having for dinner. **1955** *Times* 19 May 13/5 Its [*sc.* a book's] understanding of the poet's *milieu.* **1958** H. A. Wilmer *Social Psychiatry in Action* i. 21 The crucial point, however, is that a milieu was created that permitted recovery, rather than driving patients deeper into insanity. **1975** J. Rossiter *Golden Virgin* i. 11 Whitehall, a *milieu* in which you could look revoltingly nude without a bowler hat.

2. *Comb.*, as **milieu therapy** *Psychol.*, a form of group psychotherapy which relies on the social environment evolved by the staff and patients in the treatment unit.

1940 *Amer. Jrnl. Orthopsychiatry* X. 905 In environmental (manipulative, external, reality, milieu) therapy, it is assumed that the child's difficulty is in the social situation... Since the difficulties in the child are resultants of the difficulties in the environment, a milieu therapy is the truly rational therapy. **1961** R. Kee *Refugee World* 1 Their [*sc.* the refugees'] removal from a filthy, over-crowded hut to shelter considered fit for human beings is disguised as 'milieu therapy'. **1963** *New Society* 5 Sept. 17/3 Community services (or milieu therapy) for young deviants. **1964** M. Argyle *Psychol. & Social Probl.* v. 71 *Milieu therapy* and *therapeutic community* treatment consists of a residential institution run on more relaxed and permissive lines than is usual. **1972** G. Sereny *Case of Mary Bell* iv. 214 There are four of these experimental units in Britain..operated loosely on Aichhorn's 'Milieu Therapy'. They are designed to provide for persistently 'asocial' children..a secure environment.

miling, *vbl. sb.*[2] [f. Mil(e *sb.*[1] + -ing[1].] The action of running a mile (as an athletic event).

1913 S. A. Mussabini *Compl. Athletic Trainer* 73 This is miling of the best sort, disdaining the waiting tactics which so many adopt. **1955** R. Bannister *First Four Minutes* ii. 21 It is this controlled tension about to break down that gives miling its great excitement for the spectators. **1963** *Times* 27 May 5/6 Miling..received a needed fillip..when A. J. Harris won the Surrey race in 4 min. 2·4 sec.

‖ **militaire** (militẹ̄r). [Fr.] A soldier. (Cf. Militare *a.*)

1746 G. Townshend *Let.* 1 Oct. in J. H. Jesse *George Selwyn* (1843) I. 114 They look upon the *militaires* with abhorrence. **1827** Disraeli *Viv. Grey* III. v. vi. 101 He was a starch *militaire*, with a blue frock coat buttoned up to his chin. **1847** Thackeray *Van. Fair* (1848) xxxvi. 328 That young woman..forgot her charge in the society of this *militaire.* **1938** *Times Lit. Suppl.* 11 June 417/2 'Strathmore' can never be matched by an age that has learned to see *les militaires* with the cold eye of the elderly Ouida.

militancy. (Further examples.)

1912 in E. Pankhurst *My own Story* (1914) iii. iii. 258 The leaders..have so often warned the Government that unless the vote were granted to women in response to the mild militancy of the past, a fiercer spirit of revolt would be awakened. **1913** L. A. Harker *Ffolliots of Redmarley* xii. 156 Eloquent forgot her militancy. **1975** D. Ramsay *Descent into Dark* ii. 56 Militancy was her bag, and..she looked like someone who spent a lot of time at the barricades.

militant, *a.* and *sb.* Add: **A.** *adj.* **1. c.** Applied to or adopted as a designation by those who seek political or industrial change by employing or advocating the use of direct action, demonstrations, etc.; freq. applied to union leaders who hold out for high wage settlements, refuse to take part in discussions, etc.

1907 M. McMillan in 'B. Villiers' *Case for Women's Suffrage* 114 *Why* did the militant Suffragette ever come to the door of the House of Commons? **1914** E. Pankhurst *My own Story* i. iii. 37 That visit was one of the contributory causes that led to the foundation of our militant suffrage organisation, the Women's Social and Political Union. **1930** *Daily Express* 6 Oct. 11/6 Mr. Maxton leads a group of I.L.P. members who have brought a militant policy with them. **1960** *Economist* 8 Oct. 120/3 Mr Ted Hill's boilermakers..are incensed at the 'more militant than thou' attitude which Mr Greene is thus able to assume. **1969** *Rep. Comm. on Relations with Junior Members Univ. Oxf.* 158 Militant students believe that..they have a special position and function. **1975** *Times* 10 Apr. 17/3 The militant left are a menace to the welfare of Europe.

B. *sb.* **c.** A person who is a militant in the senses above.

1909 *Englishwoman* Apr. 323 That bias has been greatly intensified amongst almost all classes of suffragists by the tactics of the militants. **1914** E. Pankhurst *My own Story* i, (*heading*) The making of a Militant. **1939** *Theology* XXXIX. 437 The lives of certain of the militants reveal that Jocism stands for strength through holiness and self-sacrifice. **1968** *Daily Tel.* 12 Nov. 25/1 Ultra-left militants in the Electrical Trades Union are planning another demonstration today. **1969** *New Yorker* 17 May 114/2 A mysterious black militant. **1973** *Black World* Sept. 96/2 The young militants look down upon Anna's poetry. **1975** *Daily Mirror* 29 Apr. 4 They defeated a bid by union militants for an increase which would have broken the Social Contract. **1975** *Times Lit. Suppl.* 9 May 512/5 Intransigent NUJ [*sc.* National Union of Journalists] militants who now say they will discuss no press charter with the proprietors.

militaria (militẹ̄ə·riă). [f. Militar(y *a.* and *sb.* + -ia[1].] Military articles of historical interest.

1964 *Exchange & Mart* 26 Mar. 12/4 Wanted: militaria, early model soldiers, uniforms, head-dress, accoutrements, paintings, by keen collector. **1970** *Times* 23 Dec. 10 During his last years he spent much of his time in trying to gather together writings, militaria and other possessions left by the Field-Marshal. **1973** *Inverness Courier* 31 July 8/4 A wider range of collectors items than ever before will be on show, and..there will be specialist stands featuring fine antique glass, weapons, militaria, old postcards, and early newspapers. **1974** *Country Life* 25 Apr. 1031/2 Sale of: Sporting Guns..Hand Guns and Nazi Militaria.

militarist. Add: **B.** *adj.* = Militaristic *a.*

1934 R. Campbell *Broken Record* i. 19 This form of historical instruction is no doubt at the back of the modern militarist-political unrest. **1944** J. S. Huxley *On Living in Revolution* iii. 33 Shall it be peaceful, co-operative, democratic, or shall it be militarist, totalitarian, brutal?

militarize, *v.* (Later examples.)

1922 P. N. Miliukov *Russia* 205 The climax was reached when the Bolsheviks decided to militarize labor. **1972** *Daily Tel.* 11 Jan. 9/8 Will the generals militarise the Government? **1973** *Listener* 14 June 796/3 During the Cultural Revolution..Chinese politics were again militarised.

Hence **mi·litarized** *ppl. a.*

1922 *Edin. Rev.* July 28 Appalling slaughter and suffering, patiently endured by a militarized people.., has disillusioned the Germans.

military, *a.* and *sb.* Add: **A.** *adj.* **3. b. military academy,** a place of training in the military art (cf. Academy 5); **military age,** the age at which one becomes liable for military service; **military attaché,** an army officer serving with an embassy; also, one attached as an observer to a foreign army; hence *military attachéship*; **military band** [Band *sb.*[3] 4], a band attached to a military unit; **military braid** (see quots.); **military brush** = **military hairbrush*; **military college** (cf. College *sb.* 4 e) = **military academy*; **Military Cross** (abbrev. **M.C.*), a decoration instituted in 1915 and awarded to officers for gallantry in the face of the enemy; **military hairbrush,** a hairbrush without a handle; **military honours:** see Honour, honor *sb.* 5 and 5 d; **military hospital** (earlier and later examples); **military law** (earlier example); **Military Medal** (abbrev. **M.M.*), a decoration of similar distinction to the Military Cross which was instituted in 1916 for 'other ranks'; **military-minded** *a.* [Minded *ppl. a.* 5], having a mind of a military

character; **military orchid, orchis,** a European orchid, *Orchis militaris,* with pinkish-grey, helmet-shaped flowers, now very rare in Britain; also called soldier orchid; **military police,** the body of soldiers responsible for police duty in the armed forces; hence **military policeman; Military Secretary,** an army staff officer who acts as personal and confidential secretary to the Commander-in-Chief or certain other specified officers (see quot. 1876); hence *Military Secretaryship;* **military service** (cf. SERVICE¹ 12), now, service in the armed forces (further examples); **military two-step,** in old-time dancing, a variation of the two-step.

1776 *Jrnls. Continental Congress U.S.* (1906) VI. 860 Resolved, That the Board of War be directed to prepare a plan for establishing a..Military Academy. **1802** [see ROYAL *a.* 6]. **1805** J. ORROK *Let.* 7 Aug. (1927) 79 He is.. a Lieut. although not in orders, which he cannot be untill he has been a few months at a..Military Academy. **1934** *Amer. Speech* IX. 313/1 The United States Military Academy. **1974** *Hartsville* (S. Carolina) *Messenger* 22 Apr. 2-A/7 He made the decision to earn an appointment to a Military Academy. **1920** WEBSTER, Military age. **1934** G. B. SHAW *Too True to be Good* III. 88 Had I been of military age I should have been a conscientious objector. **1941** *Manch. Guardian Weekly* 26 Sept. 194/2 It would not be fair to raise the military age..without a thorough comb-out of the younger men. **1857** *Foreign Office List* X. 18 Military Attaché to the Embassy, Lt. Col. E. L. Claremont, C.B. **1877** H. PONSONBY *Let.* 18 Nov. in A. Ponsonby *Henry Ponsonby* (1942) 167 We have dozens of Military Attachés with the Armies in the field. **1961** J. MASTERS *Road past Mandalay* vi. 76 It was Persia, and the Military Attaché was doubtful. **1882** Military attachéship [see ATTACHÉSHIP]. **1775** *Westm. Mag.* May 231/1 Three military bands, composed of fifes, drums, cymbals, etc. **1836** Military band [in Dict., sense A. 1]. **1912** G. MILLER (*title*) The military band. **1964** A. SEXTON *Sel. Poems* 7 While a military band plays a Strauss waltz. **1950** '*Mercury*' *Dict. Textile Terms* 346 *Military braid,* a broad braid such as is worn on the tunics of soldiers. **1966** *Olney Amsden & Sons Ltd. Price List* 39 Rayon Military Braid in fashion shades 66/6 gross yards. **1968** J. IRONSIDE *Fashion Alphabet* 76 *Military braid,* a flat braid with a diagonal weave. **1926** *Daily Colonist* (Victoria, B.C.) 6 Jan. 2/1 (Advt.), Gentleman's French Ivory Military Brushes. Concave back, a fine quality bristle. **1969** *H. Knowles-Brown Ltd.* (*Hampstead*) *Christmas Catal.,* Ivory backed military brushes from; per pair £19 0 0. **1809** G. L. WARDLE *Charges against Duke of York* 334 Mr. Froome came to town to settle some old accounts of mine as treasurer to the Royal Military College. **1837** W. DYOTT *Diary* 17 Jan. (1907) II. 246 Young Palmer, a candidate for the army at the Military College at Sandhurst. **1915** *London Gaz.* 1 Jan. 7/1 Royal Warrant instituting a new decoration 'The Military Cross'. **1917** W. OWEN *Let.* 9 Apr. (1967) 451, I think Capt. Green..will get a Military Cross, which he has long deserved—for 2½ years active service. **1969** S. MAYS *Fall out Officers* viii. 52 Wearing among his campaign ribbons that of the Military Cross. **1894** *Country Gentlemen's Catal.* 148 Two Ivory Military Hair Brushes, in Solid Leather Case, 57/-. **1972** J. PORTER *Meddler & her Murder* i. 7 A couple of quick passes with her silver-backed military hair brushes. **1778** *Crit. Rev.* Sept. 189 An account of military honours paid to crowned heads and to other persons. **1853** Military honours [see HONOUR, HONOR *sb.* 5 d]. **1901** Military honours [in Dict., sense A. 1]. **1975** *Times* 2 Aug. 2/2 The UVF, a Protestant paramilitary group, said they would receive full military honours. **1777** *Jrnls. Continental Congress U.S.* (1907) VII. 162 An Inspector General of the Army..[shall] visit the Military hospitals..to examine the medicines and instruments. **1789** P. THICKNESSE *Year's Journey* (ed. 3) I. iii. 25 The *Silver Lion*..is..preferable to Dessein's, as the drains from the Military Hospital run under the latter. **1860** F. NIGHTINGALE *Notes on Nursing* iii. 23 The ordinary run of military hospitals. **1969** S. MAYS *Fall out Officers* iii. 25, I was not taken to the Cambridge Military Hospital, Aldershot, as I had thought. **1737** *London Mag.* Aug. 492/2 'Tis certain the military law may be made much stricter and more severe than the common Law can be made. **1916** *London Gaz.* 5 Apr. 3647/1 Royal Warrant instituting a new medal entitled 'The Military Medal'... We do..institute and create a silver medal to be awarded to non-commissioned officers and men for individual or associated acts of bravery on the recommendation of a Commander-in-Chief in the field. **1917** A. G. EMPEY *Over Top* 300 *Military Medal,* a piece of junk issued to Tommy who has done something that is not exactly brave but is still not cowardly. **1922** *Encycl. Brit.* XXXI. 892/1 The *Military Medal.*—Instituted in March 1916 for award to non-commissioned officers and men of the army for individual or associated acts of bravery in the field. **1957** *Ibid.* XVI. 638/1 Other awards of lesser degree in this class [awarded for gallantry] are: Distinguished Service Order, instituted in 1886 and the Military Cross (1914); only officers are eligible for the award... Also the Military Medal (1916); only 'other ranks' are eligible for the award. **1910** W. JAMES *Mem. & Stud.* (1911) xi. 288 Commonwealths fit only for contempt, and liable to invite attack whenever a centre of crystallization for military-minded enterprise gets formed anywhere in their neighbourhood. **1939** *Ann. Reg. 1938* 266 The Portuguese are rapidly becoming a military-minded people. **1934** M. J. GODFERY *Monogr. & Iconogr. Native Brit. Orchidaceæ* 168 *Orchis militaris* L. Soldier Orchid, Military Orchid. **1948** J. BROOKE *Military Orchid* i. 17 The Military Orchid had taken on a kind of legendary quality, its image seemed fringed with the mysterious and exciting appurtenances of soldiering, its name was like a distant bugle-call, thrilling and rather sad. **1969** J. E. LOUSLEY *Wild Flowers of Chalk & Limestone* (ed. 2) vii. 90 The largest..was 14 inches (35 cm.) tall with no less than 26 flowers. This must be about the finest Military Orchid seen in England. *Ibid.* 91 It is the resemblance of the hood to an ancient helmet which has led to the plant being called the Soldier or Military Orchid. **1812** W. WITHERING JR. *Withering's Brit. Plants* (ed. 5) II. 29 (*heading*) Narrow-lipped Military Orchis. *O. militaris.* **1884** W. MILLER *Dict. Eng. Names Plants* 99/2 Orchis,..Military. *Orchis militaris.* **1950** G. BRENAN *Face of Spain* vii. 156 Under an olive tree I picked a specimen of that rare plant, the Military Orchis, which I knew from the plate in Bentham's Flora but had never found before. **1827** J. J. SNODGRASS *Narr. Burmese War* v. 59 In every village there appeared a small party of military police. **1933** J. BUCHAN *Prince of Captivity* I. ii. 66 The military police arrived in quest of him. **1974** J. WAINWRIGHT *Hard Hit* 52 One evening session had seen..seven full-weight smash-ups start—and end with the arrival of the Military Police. **1973** J. STRANGER *Walk Lonely Road* v. 44 My own father was a policeman. His father was a military policeman. I suppose it's like the Services. It runs in families. **1812** J. ORROK *Let.* 26 May (1927) 130 To Colonel Torrens, Military Secretary to His Royal Highness the Commander-in-Chief. **1853** J. H. STOCQUELER *Mil. Encycl.* 179/2 All military correspondence with the commander-in-chief should be sent through the military secretary. **1876** VOYLE & STEVENSON *Mil. Dict.* (ed. 3) 255/2 *Military Secretary,* an officer attached to the staff of the commander-in-chief, to governors of provinces, and to an officer commanding an army in the field. His duties to some extent are confidential, and he relieves the officer under whom he is serving of a great deal of personal correspondence. **1947** R. G. JESSEL *G, A, & Q* iii. 9 At the end of the course, a report on each student is sent to the Military Secretary at the War Office. **1778** E. DRAPER *Let.* 12 Feb. in *N. & Q.* (1944) 29 July 51/1 Report says, that Dick Sulivan is coming home, in that case, your Brother, I suppose, Steps into the Military Secretaryship. **1863** *Act* 26 & 27 *Vict.* c. 65 § 17 Her Majesty may direct the Lieutenants of Counties..to call out the Volunteer Corps..for actual Military Service. **1909** G. B. SHAW *Press Cuttings* 25 What women need is the right to military service. **1922** *Encycl. Brit.* XXXII. 39/2 Mr. Lloyd George persuaded the Supreme Council to accept the principle that all the enemy Powers should be obliged to abolish compulsory military service. **1911** *Ball Room* Mar. 4/1 (Advt.), Finnigan's,..Manchester... Inventor of the original Military Two Step. **1949** V. SILVESTER *Old Time Dancing* 49 The Military Two-step is often danced with varying distances separating the partners at different times. **1950** M. GWYNNE *Old Time & Sequence Dancing* 78 Military Two Step... A championship dance. Commence as in the Veleta. **1966** *Listener* 24 Nov. 783/3 The military two-step ended with the ripping of Freddie's entire sleeve.

c. *Comb.* with other *adjs.,* as *military-industrial, -political, -scientific, -technological* adjs.

1961 D. EISENHOWER in *N.Y. Times* 18 Jan. 22/4 In the councils of Government, we must guard against the acquisition of unwarranted influence, whether sought or unsought, by the military-industrial complex. **1973** *Times* 13 Jan. 19/5 President Eisenhower, who warned the country of the dangers of a military-industrial complex, must be twitching in his grave. **1965** H. KAHN *On Escalation* 291 The military-political outcome of a war. **1960** *Encounter* Oct. 9 Military-scientific research. **1962** *Times* 26 Feb. (Canada Suppl.) p. ii/2 The 'military-technological complex' eating into American business and politics alike.

B. *sb.* **1.** (Later N. Amer. examples.) Also with sing. verb.

1968 *Globe & Mail* (Toronto) 3 Feb. 11/5 The military use special film to photograph hidden features of the ground below. **1968** MRS. L. B. JOHNSON *White House Diary* 8 Oct. (1970) 718 I've come to have a lot more understanding of what the military puts up with and especially the wives. **1970** *New Yorker* 3 Oct. 44/3 Other branches of the military..were not impressed.

2. Delete † and add later example.

1962 *Listener* 1 Nov. 723/3 A few splendid portraits of the Austrian court nobility and of the high militaries.

militate, *v.* Add: **1. c.** To display industrial or political intransigence; to act in the manner of a militant (sense *c).

1951 E. PAUL *Springtime in Paris* xvi. 321 Busse knew all too well what happened to French Communists who showed disloyalty, or even who failed to 'militate'. **1969** *N.Y. Rev. Bks.* 30 Jan. 4/3 Simone Weil going to work in a factory and eventually starving herself to death in order to share the diet of the people of occupied France was answering the same 'call' as..Silone militating in the underground, in clandestinity.

militia. Add: **4.** In later use, *spec.* as part of the British armed forces assembled in 1939.

1939 *War Illustr.* 16 Dec. 427/3 We have taken, besides the Militia classes which have been called up, over 85,000 voluntary recruits since the war began.

militiaman. Add: *spec.* One called up in 1939 as part of the armed services at the outbreak of the war.

1939 *War Illustr.* 14 Oct. 129 (*caption*) Regular soldiers ..and the Militiamen—all have made an excellent impression at home and in France.

Also **mili·tiawoman,** a woman in a militia force; = *MILICIANA.

1936 *New Statesman* 21 Nov. 802/1 The C.N.T., since it contains a great many Murcians.., includes the most alarming of the faces met with in Barcelona and also most of the young militia-women. **1938** 'G. ORWELL' *Homage to Catalonia* iv. 47 There were three militiawomen there who did the cooking.

Milium² (mi·liǝm). The proprietary name of a type of insulating fabric. Also **milium.**

1950 *Rayon & Synthetic Textiles* June 95/1 Milium has been chosen as the trademark name to designate the new 'warmth without weight' fabric development of Deering, Milliken & Company. **1951** *Official Gaz.* (U.S. Patent Office) 4 Sept. 39/1 The Vadium Corp., Wilmington, Del. Milium. For Textile Fabrics of Cotton, Rayon, Nylon, and Mixtures Thereof Having Heat Reflective and/or Heat Retentive Properties. Claims use since Apr. 20, 1950. **1954** POTTER & CORBMAN *Fiber to Fabric* (ed. 2) vi. 110 A wool outer fabric with a milium satin lining is approximately equal in warmth to an untreated satin lining plus an 8½-ounce wool interlining with the same outer fabric. **1956** *N.Y. Times* 20 Mar. 30/6 Milium is a metal-impregnated lining material valued for its lightness and insulating quality. **1968** J. IRONSIDE *Fashion Alphabet* 241 Milium insulates against cold and allows the body to retain heat, while in summer it protects from extreme heat. **1972** *Guardian* 30 June 7 This superb new Milium Ironing Board Cover..is scorch resistant.

milk, *sb.* Add: **1. c.** *mother's milk* (further examples); also as a slang name for various liquors (see quots.).

c **1821** 'W. T. MONCRIEFF' *Tom & Jerry* (1828) III. iii. 67 *Log.* What, my lily! here, take a drop of mother's milk. (Gives black child gin out of measure he has received from Landlord.) **1846** *Swell's Night Guide* 125/2 *Mother's milk,* rum boose, good liquor. *c* **1863** T. TAYLOR in M. R. Booth *Eng. Plays of 19th Cent.* (1969) II. 156 Brandy do a man harm! It's mother's milk. **1922** G. M. TREVELYAN *Brit. Hist. 19th Cent.* xxiii. 363 Britons had sucked in fear of Napoleonic conquest with their mother's milk. **1966** 'L. LANE' *ABZ of Scouse* 71 *Mother's milk,* Guinness, a popular brand of stout. **1972** *Guardian* 22 Aug. 4/6 A six-month-old-baby..is being kept alive by mother's milk supplied by volunteers.

g. *ellipt.* = MILKMAN 1. *colloq.*

1895 W. P. RIDGE *Minor Dialogues* 79, I know *all* the comic songs..and I sing 'em whilst I'm a doing up the front steps; and the milk, *he* says he reckons it'll end in me going on the stage. **1933** A. THIRKELL *High Rising* ii. 36 The London tradesmen..called her Miss, until a fateful day when the Milk, so she told Laura, had called her Miss once too often. **1967** 'A. GILBERT' *Visitor* x. 174 She hadn't informed the postman and anyone can put out a note for the Milk. **1975** B. MEYRICK *Behind the Light* xv. 202 The disappearance of George the Milk's horse.

h. Milk-white colour. Cf. sense 11 in Dict.

1899 SWINBURNE *Rosamund* I. i. 2 White I know from red, and dark from bright, And milk from white in hawthorn-flowers.

2. b. *pure milk*: something of the purest or finest quality.

1931 *Daily Express* 15 Oct. 2/4 Men like Mr. Runciman, who hitherto represented the purest milk of the Cobdenite gospel. **1955** *Times* 6 July 11/3 Broadcasting..probably remains the most effective way, within the compass of an election campaign, of distributing the pure milk of party doctrine. **1975** 'W. HAGGARD' *Scorpion's Tail* vii. 103 For the pure milk of doctrine she cared not a damn. She saw communism as a convenient front.

c. *milk of human kindness* (further examples); *spilt milk*: see also SPILT *ppl. a.* 2 b; *to bring* (a person) *to his milk* (U.S.): to bring (him) to his senses; to compel (him) to acquiesce or submit; *to come* (or *go*) *home with the milk*: to arrive home at the time when the milkman calls, *i.e.* early in the morning.

1775 SHERIDAN *Rivals* III. iv. 57 The thunder of your words has soured the milk of human kindness in my breast! **1839** DICKENS *Nickleby* xxxviii. 377 What's come of my milk of human kindness? It turns into curds and whey when I look at him. **1857** J. G. HOLLAND *Bay-Path* 209 There ain't anything that'll bring you to your milk half so quick as a good double-and-twisted thrashin. **1857** S. A. HAMMETT *Sam Slick in Texas* iv. 22 When you cum to bring 'em down to thar milk, they'll turn out greener than Buffalo Bayou in September. **1917** WODEHOUSE *Man with Two Left Feet* 238 You talk of a man 'going home with the milk' when you mean that he sneaks in in the small hours of the morning. **1923** W. J. LOCKE *Moordius & Co.* ii. 17 The family has nothing to do with the way the governess spends her evenings..except if she comes home with the milk after her evening out. **1947** W. S. MAUGHAM *Creatures of Circumstances* 100 Every party's got to come to an end, and next day it doesn't matter much if you went home with the milk or if you left while the fun was in full swing. **1956** G. DURRELL *My Family & other Animals* xviii. 237 Overflowing with the milk of human kindness, the family had invited everyone they could think of, including people they cordially disliked.

3. c. *the milk in the coconut*: a puzzling fact or circumstance; a crux. *colloq.* (orig. *U.S.*).

1840 *Spirit of Times* 21 Mar. 25/2 All of 'vich'..fully accounts..for the milk in the cocoa-nut. **1853** *Knickerbocker* XLII. 50 The milk in the cocoa nut was accounted for. **1898** MRS. LYNN LINTON *Let* in G. S. Layard *Mrs. Lynn Linton* (1901) xxiv. 362 The Koran is very interesting—but oh, the milk in the cocoanut! It is so queerly disjointed and non-sequential, far more so than the Epistles, and they have their full share of that milk in the cocoanut. **1972** L. MEYNELL *Death by Arrangement* i. 17 'Nobody can really be christened Waveney: it's a river...' 'In East Anglia. Hence, as they say, the milk in the coconut. Rolffe's father..called his eleven children after East Anglian rivers.'

4. *milk of magnesia*: a proprietary name for a white suspension of magnesium hydroxide in water, taken as an antacid.

1880 *Trade Marks Jrnl.* 3 Mar. 95 Milk of Magnesia... Charles Henry Phillips,..New York, United States of America; manufacturing chemist... Preparations of magnesia for medical purposes, especially hydrate of magnesia, and also proprietary medicines. **1924** H. CRANE *Let.* 30 Nov. (1965) 194, I had..taken a great deal of Alkalithia and milk of magnesia. **1961** J. HELLER *Catch-22* (1962) xxvi. 282 Aarfy had a date..with a Red Cross

girl..whose father owned an important milk-of-magnesia plant.

9. a. (*a*) *milk-loaf*; (*b*) *milk-bloom, bottle, -car, carton, -churn, -ejection, -gland, -jug* (earlier example), *lorry, -pitcher, saucepan, -shop* (earlier example), *stand, tanker, truck, wagon*; *milk-boy* (earlier and later examples).

1855 Tennyson *Maud* xxi. 70 The slender acacia would not shake One long milk-bloom on the tree. **1905** G. F. M'Cleary *Infant Mortality & Infants Milk Depôts* viii. 129 (*caption*) Packing the milk bottles in ice before sending them to the city. **1957** M. Summerton *Sunset Hour* v. 67, I could hear..milk bottles being handled in and out of crates. **1959** I. & P. Opie *Lore & Lang. Schoolch.* i. 9 Cigarette cards..are being replaced in flicking games by milk-bottle tops. **1972** C. Fremlin *Appointment with Yesterday* xii. 93 '*Everything* goes down the waste-disposal!' But not dead matches. Or milk-bottle tops. **1972** J. Mosedale *Football* x. 139 He stepped on a broken milk bottle, severing all the tendons in his foot. **1847** Thackeray *Vanity Fair* (1848) vii. 59 The groom..did not care to descend to ring the bell; and so prayed a passing milk-boy to perform that office for him. **1865** A. & E. Keary *Little Wanderlin* 125 After the milk-boy came the vegetable women. **1964** F. Warner *Early Poems* 13 A milk-boy, whistling down the wind. **1890** *Railways of Amer.* 146 The different kinds of cars which are now used.. Mail car, Milk car, Oil-car [etc.]. **1916** Joyce *Portrait of Artist* ii. 69 Often they drove out in the milkcar. **1964** 'E. Lathen' *Accounting for Murder* (1965) vi. 46 He mounted the stairs..startling two typists who were precariously balancing milk cartons. **1967** R. Lowell *Near Ocean* 24 Milk cartons, kidney heaped to spoil, Two plates sheathed with silver foil. **1931** A. Uttley *Country Child* iii. 48 He was backed into the loading place, waiting for the milk-churns. *Ibid.* xxi. 278 The milk-churns were rattled and banged across the railway line. **1963** *Times* 16 Feb. 5/5 An estimated 120,000 milk churns, valued at £5 each and believed to have been taken by householders to store water, are missing from dairies. **1967** *Ibid.* 26 Sept. 1/1 He inadvertently rolled a milk churn under an oncoming express during his first day as an apprentice at Hatfield station. **1950** *N.Z. Jrnl. Agric.* June 540/3 The problems related to the process of 'milk ejection' in the cow. **1927** Haldane & Huxley *Animal Biol.* xiii. 320 The saucer-shaped depression into which the milk-glands open. **1832** F. Trollope *Dom. Manners Amer.* I. xii. 170 An intimation accompanied the milk-jug, that the milk must be fresh. **1910** *Practitioner* June 801 Milk-loaf, scones. **1939** G. Household *Rogue Male* 110, I saw..a couple of milk lorries bobbing about..to collect the cans set out on wooden platforms by the road. **1971** W. J. Burley *Guilt Edged* i. 5 The milk lorry on its way back to the factory after morning collections from farms. **1855** *Harvard Mag.* I. 420 We were..a good deal incommoded by the diminutive size of the milk-pitchers. **1907** *Yesterday's Shopping* 213/2 Milk saucepan with earthenware lining. **1975** J. Symons *Three Pipe Problem* xvii. 163 He burnt the milk saucepan dry. **1847** Dickens *Dombey* (1848) xxi. 207 A neighbouring milk-shop. **1950** *N.Z. Jrnl. Agric.* Apr. 378/3 Milk stands erected as part of the releaser room.. have given satisfactory results. **1965** in P. Jennings *Living Village* (1968) 66 The milk..is collected by a milk tanker. **1972** *Guardian* 16 Oct. 10/2 Until the rains came..villagers were collecting water in buckets from milk tankers in High Furness. **1910** *Daily Chron.* 22 Apr. 1/3 The..express ..ran into a milk truck and a guard's van. **1947** E. Hodgins *Mr. Blandings builds his Dream House* vii. 94 Her husband got run over by the milk truck. **1973** R. L. Simon *Big Fix* (1974) xx. 170 A trio of milk trucks from a dairy. **1883** *Wheelman* Apr. 28/1 A superannuated 'bus-driver, with a conveyance strongly resembling a milk-wagon. **1960** T. Hughes *Lupercal* 46 Light and birdsong come Walloping up roads with the milk wagon.

b. *milk producer, strainer*; *milk-marketing, -producing* vbl. sbs. and adjs.

1933 *Statutory Rules & Orders* No. 789. 21 This scheme may be cited as the Milk Marketing Scheme, 1933, and applies to England and Wales. **1936** Milk Marketing [see *grade *sb.* 5 c]. **1968** *Listener* 4 July 15/2 In the new milk marketing case this truth is emphasized... Under the Milk Marketing Scheme the milk producers sell their milk to the Milk Marketing Board. **1870** *Rep. Comm. Agric. 1869* (U.S. Dept. Agric.) 449 The annual meeting of the Milk Producers' Association of Massachusetts and New Hampshire. **1950** *N.Z. Jrnl. Agric.* Feb. 163/3 It is the responsibility of the milk producer to ensure..that only milk of the highest quality leaves the farm. **1946** *Nature* 12 Oct. 523/1 The recording movement may..progress to greater service to the milk-producing industry. **1975** *Country Life* 12 June 1590/1 Different cows have different milk-producing capabilities. **1686** S. Sewall *Letter-Bk.* (1886) I. 33 Five Duz. of milk strainers of the smaller sort. **1872** W. S. Jones *Let.* 20 Mar. in G. N. Jones *Florida Plantation Rec.* (1927) 199 The milk strainer is also in bad repair.

d. *milk-blue, -dim, -green, -pale* adjs.

1917 D. H. Lawrence *Look! We have come Through!* 77 The milk-blue, morning lake. **1945** W. de la Mare *Burning-Glass* 41 Pulsing beneath the silken skin The milk-blue blood rills out and in. **1955** E. Pound *Section: Rock-Drill* xc. 65 Moon's barge over milk-blue water. **1926** H. Read *Coll. Poems* 55 Oh, turn your milk dim eyes To outer things! **1912** D. H. Lawrence *Let.* 2 June (1962) I. 130 The pale, milk-green river. **1895** W. B. Yeats *Poems* 33 And at his cry there came no milk-pale face Under a crown of thorns and dark with blood. **1910** W. de la Mare *Three Mulla-Mulgars* xviii. 248 At each thorn-tip, as the flame licks near, wells out and gathers a milk-pale globe of poison.

10. milk bank, a bank (*bank *sb.*[3] 7 f) of human milk; **milk-bar,** a place where drinks made from milk (and often also other refreshments) are sold (see Bar *sb.*[1] 28); **milk-blooded** *a.*, cowardly, spiritless; **milk chicken,** a chicken that has been fed on milk and ground oats; **milk chocolate,** † (*a*) a beverage made from chocolate and milk; (*b*) eating chocolate (Chocolate 2) made with milk; (*c*) a brown colour; also *attrib.*; **milk-coffee,** coffee made with milk; white coffee; also *attrib.*, of a light brown colour; **milk factor,** a factor causing disposition towards mammary cancer which is transmitted to offspring in milk; **milk-fish,** (*a*) substitute '*Chanos chanos*' for '*Chanos salmoneus*'; (examples); (*b*) *Austral.* = Trepang; **milk-float,** (*a*) a float (Float *sb.* 14) for the conveyance of milk; (*b*) a small electrically-driven milk-cart; **milk-flour,** a preparation of desiccated milk; **milk kitchen,** a special kitchen at a maternity hospital or the like, where babies' feeds are prepared; **milk line** *Embryol.* [tr. G. *milchlinie* (O. Schultze 1892, in *Anat. Anzeiger* VII. 266)], (the line occupied by) a ridge of thickened ectoderm that appears on either side of mammalian embryos, extending from the front to the rear limb buds, on which the mammary glands later form in females; **milk-name,** the name given to a Chinese child at a ceremony held one month after birth: it is later superseded by more formal names but continues to be used in particular situations (see quot. 1911); **milk powder,** a preparation of desiccated milk; **milk-ranch** *U.S.*, a ranch producing milk; **milk ridge** *Embryol.* [tr. G. *milchleiste* (O. Schultze 1893, in *Verhandl. d. physik.-med. Ges. zu Würzburg* XXVI. 173)] = **milk line*; **milk-room** orig. *U.S.*, a room in a house or dairy in which milk is kept; **milk-round,** (*a*) = **milk-route*; (*b*) *transf.*, a regular trip or tour in which one calls at several places; spec. *R.A.F. slang* (see quot. 1945); hence *milk-roundsman*; **milk-route** orig. *U.S.*, a route on which milk is regularly collected from farmers or delivered to customers; **milk-run** = **milk-round*; **milk-shake** orig. *U.S.*, a beverage composed of milk, flavouring, etc., mixed by shaking or agitation; **milk stout,** formerly, a kind of sweet stout made with lactose; also *attrib.* and *fig.*; **milk-toast** *U.S.*, toast which is softened in milk; **milk-train,** (*a*) a railway train chiefly transporting milk, usu. very early in the morning; (*b*) *R.A.F. slang* (see quot. 1943); **milk-tube,** (*b*) a milking tube; **milk-walk** (later examples); also, a dairy business; **milk-wine,** a beverage obtained from fermented milk; **milk-woman** (later example).

1948 *Archit. Rev.* CIV. 21 (*caption*) Mothers' milk bank. **1972** *Guardian* 22 Aug. 4/6 If there should be a shortage of mother's milk, the hospital will get supplies from the National Milk Bank. **1935** *Forres Gaz.* 20 Nov. 1/2 The milk bar, or place where milk drinks are sold, is a popular institution all over Australia, and plans are on foot for installing..them in Britain. **1938** E. Waugh *Scoop* ii. iv. 200 Legend..told and retold over the milk-bars of Fleet Street. **1957** J. Braine *Room at Top* xxx. 254 A milk bar near the railway station. **1971** J. Philips *Escape a Killer* (1972) i. v. 69 There's a milk bar in the village. **1847** E. Brontë *Wuthering Heights* I. xi. 259, I wish you joy of the milk-blooded coward. **1910** *Blackw. Mag.* Feb. 183/2 The sooner we give up all this milk-blooded, blue-spectacled, pacificist talk the better. **1902** *Encycl. Brit.* XXXI. 882/2 Chickens fattened quite young..and known as *petits poussins* or 'milk chickens'. **1723** J. Nott *Cook's & Confectioner's Dict.* sig. I8 (*heading*) To make Milk Chocolate. **1752** M. W. Montagu *Let.* 16 Feb. (1967) III. 5 As soon as I am risen, I constantly take 3 cups of milk coffee, and two hours after that a large cup of milk chocolate. **1904** 'Saki' *Reginald* 101 They all sat down to play progressive halma, with milk-chocolate for prizes. **1910** *Encycl. Brit.* X. 614/2 Milk powder..is largely employed in the preparation of so-called milk chocolates. **1926** C. Beaton *Diary* 15 Apr. in *Wandering Yrs.* (1961) iv. 80, I..bought some bars of milk chocolate. **1955** *Radio Times* 22 Apr. 21/3, 14 milk chocolate caramels. **1958** S. Hyland *Who goes Hang?* xiv. 63 A large table splendidly covered with milk-chocolate-coloured leather. **1969** *Vogue* 15 Mar. 81/1 An edging of milk chocolate suede. **1974** 'E. Lathen' *Sweet & Low* xii. 124 The creamy satisfaction of milk chocolate. **1695** J. Lightbody *Every Man his own Gauger* 62 If you would make Milk Coffee, you must, to every Pint of Water, put a quart of Milk. **1752** [see *milk chocolate* above]. **1972** H. Osborne *Pay-Day* ii. iv. 42 The girl at the desk..was a milk-coffee negress. **1939** J. J. Bittner in *Public Health Rep.* (U.S. Public Health Service) LIV. 1115 The breast cancer observations ..may be explained by a theory..assuming that three 'factors' are needed... These factors are: (A) A 'breast cancer-producing influence' transferred through the milk of high-cancer stock females to their progeny. This has been designated as the 'milk factor' in the tables. **1943** C. G. Geschickter *Dis. Breast* xxxv. 800 This so-called milk-factor or milk-influence has been extracted from the mammary glands of lactating cancer-susceptible mice by Bittner and shown to increase the incidence of mammary cancer whether injected in, or fed to young mice. **1966** Wright & Symmers *Systemic Path.* I. xxviii. 990/1 There is no evidence that a milk factor plays any part in the occurrence of carcinoma of the breast in women. There is no way by which such a factor can be demonstrated. **1880** *Proc. Linn. Soc. New South Wales* V. 128 Another species [of Trepang] is the 'milk fish', or 'cotton fish', so called from its power of emitting a white viscid fluid.., which clings to any object like shreds of cotton. **1905** D. S. Jordan *Guide to Study of Fishes* II. iii. 44 The *Chanidæ*, or milkfishes, constitute another small archaic type, found in the tropical Pacific. They are large, brilliantly silvery, toothless fishes. *Ibid.* 45 The single living species is the *Awa*, or milkfish, *Chanos chanos*, largely used as food in Hawaii. **1962** K. F. Lagler et al. *Ichthyol.* vi. 203 The irregular movements of the Asiatic milkfish (*Chanos*) into and out of fresh water make it amphidromous. **1971** *Daily Colonist* (Victoria, B.C.) 30 Mar. 5/4 Taiwan and Indonesia produce much needed sea protein in traditional milkfish 'farm ponds'. **1974** *Nat. Geographic* Dec. 788/2 Across southern Asia, from the Philippines to India, commercial aquaculturists have begun to raise milkfish, a food species that subsists on plant life. **1887** Milk float [in Dict., sense 9 a]. **1935** N. Collins *Three Friends* viii. 143 A horse attached to a milk float wore a hat made of newspaper. **1951** *Engineering* 20 July 95/3 Pedestrian-controlled vehicles (such as hand-operated electric milk floats). **1974** M. Babson *Stalking Lamb* xi. 73 An electric milk float trundling down the street. **1902** *Chambers's Jrnl.* 22 Feb. 191/1 The milk-flour is completely soluble in water. **1965** *Nursing Times* 5 Feb. 181/1 In some hospitals the labour wards and the milk kitchens were each centralized. **1893** *Jrnl. R. Microsc. Soc.* 304 Prof. O. Schultze finds in the embryos of pig, rabbit, mole, fox, and cat, that the first rudiment of the mammary glands is seen as a linear epithelial thickening on each side of the body... This 'milk-line' stretches from the anterior to the posterior limb-rudiment. **1946** B. M. Patten *Human Embryol.* ix. 241 Some animals (for example, the sow and the bitch) develop a series of nipples spread over nearly the entire length of the milk line. *Ibid.*, Not infrequently supernumerary nipples may occur at other levels along the course of the milk line. **1960** F. D. Allan *Essent. Human Embryol.* xix. 179 The primordia of the [mammary] glands form thickened strips of ectoderm located bilaterally from axilla to groin which are called the milk ridges or lines. **1836** J. F. Davis *Chinese* I. vii. 288 The birth of a son is of course an occasion of great rejoicing; the family or surname is first given, and then the 'milk name', which is generally some diminutive of endearment. **1911** J. D. Ball *Chinese at Home* vii. 75 The milk name.. clings to him or her through life, being used by parents, relatives, and most intimate friends, as well as by superiors. **1931** C. L'E. Ewen *Hist. Surnames* 8 The Chinese receive a number of names..the 'milk-name' when a month old. **1975** O. Sela *Bengali Inheritance* iii. 23 His milk name had been Chan Yan-Wo, and at school he had changed it to Richard.., the first step in accepting Western ways. **1834** *India Jrnl. Med. Sci.* I. 1. 32/2 *Milk Powder*... Specimens of an article he has advertised under the designation of Pulverised Milk. **1910** *Encycl. Brit.* X. 614/2 Milk powder is manufactured under various patents. *Ibid.*, Milk powder made from skim-milk keeps well for considerable periods. **1972** D. Bloodworth *Any Number can Play* xii. 96 A big American air force general with a complexion like milk-powder. **1856** *Calif. Pathfinder* (San Francisco) 13 Nov. 2/4 The milk ranch that burned down beyond the Mission yesterday morning. **1909** Bailey & Miller *Text-bk. Embryol.* xvi. 449 In embryos of six to seven mm., or even less, a thickening of the epidermis occurs in a narrow zone along the ventro-lateral surface of the body (Strahl). In embryos of 15 mm. this thickening, known as the milk ridge, extends from the upper extremity to the inguinal region. **1960** Milk ridge [see *milk line* above]. **1836** *Knickerbocker* VIII. 706 In the rear, is quite a city of additions, in the shape of bed-rooms, bath-rooms, milk-rooms, buttery [etc.]. **1970** *Cape Times* 28 Oct. 21/1 (Advt.), Lean-to, barn for animals, dairy and milk room, 4 calf pens. **1900** *Oxford Times* 13 Jan. (Advt.), Wanted, a single man to serve a milk-round. **1927** R. B. Forrester *Fluid Milk Market Eng. & Wales* 96 Retail Delivery. Milk Rounds...no close or detailed survey of actual roundsman systems has ever been made in this country. **1945** Partridge *Dict. R.A.F. Slang* 39 *Milkround*, a run made fairly regularly by a Squadron or a Force, if it returns to its station or base in the early morning. **1952** E. F. Davies *Illyrian Venture* x. 191 We did a 'milk-round' of all the jails in Vienna, picking up and setting down prisoners at every stop. **1958** *Times* 9 Aug. 7/7 Strange though the urgent masochism of the milk round may seem, that is how the great majority of Americans still see us, from the windows of a coach. **1970** *Times* 17 Nov. 19/8 Like other business organisations, we make what is known as the annual milkround, going to every university at the recruiting time. **1972** *Guardian* 8 Feb. 13/7 Fund-raising must be..centralized, instead of the monthly 'milk rounds' by volunteers. **1972** *Accountant* 14 Sept. 327/1 'Farmer's Wife' branded goods —cream, yogurt, butter, eggs, potatoes, bread, margarine, bacon, sausages and poultry—constitute an increasingly important part of the milk division's turnover and profit. Sales are helping to maintain regular milk rounds when other industries find rising costs of such personal service a constant headache. **1940** F. Kitchen *Brother to Ox* xiii. 202, I want to say what a pleasant job it is being a milk-roundsman. **1874** *Rep. Comm. Agric. 1873* (U.S. Dept. Agric.) 246 The most economical method of managing the delivery of milk at the factory is by establishing milk routes. **1897** 'Mark Twain' *Following Equator* xliv. 464 The vested rights..are frequently the subject of sale or mortgage. Just like a milk-route. **1959** N. Mailer *Advts. for Myself* (1961) 372 The milk companies..are saved most of the costs of local distribution by delivering the orange juice on their milk route. **1943** K. Tennant *Ride on Stranger* (1968) ix. 103 Shannon did not know anyone who wanted half a milk-run. **1944** J. H. Fullarton *Troop Target* iii. 24 Isobel married that joker with a milk-run out Henderson way. **1944** T. H. Wisdom *Triumph over Tunisia* vi. 54 It was General Doolittle who organised the 'milk-run' Fortress raids on the ports of Tunis and Bizerta. **1964** *Observer* (Colour Suppl.) 11 Oct. 17/2 Similar risks must be taken by transport aircraft pilots, flying their daily 'milk runs' to supply jungle-bound positions along the 1,000-mile frontier [of Borneo]. **1969** *Daily Tel.* 11 Oct. 11/5 Another way of island hopping down to Grenada..is to catch the early morning 'milk-run' plane from Antigua, which calls in at Dominica, St. Lucia,

Martinique and Barbados, collecting and unloading passengers, mail and newspapers as it goes. **1972** *Guardian* 30 Dec. 13 Woe betide any who suddenly discovers he has to go to Brussels the next morning. The businessmen's milkrun is always booked days ahead. **1889** *Harper's Bazaar* 4 May 330/3 You needs some milk shake..an' I got some nice new w'iskey to putt in. **1911** H. S. HARRISON *Queed* vii. 85 You ain't feelin good, are you, Doc? You're lookin' white as a milk-shake. **1937** *Daily Herald* 20 Feb. 11/3 (*caption*) Mrs.—..sampling a milk shake after she had opened a milk bar in Tottenham Court-road yesterday. **1952** 'J. TEY' *Singing Sands* xii. 196, I had a coupla bananas and a milk shake in Leicester Square. **1953** E. TAYLOR *Sleeping Beauty* xiii. 200 She saw herself translated to the Corner House, but to the same sundaes and parfaits and milk-shakes. **1968** *Blues Unlimited* Sept. 10 Joe worked in the kitchens at the Cafe six nights a week, pouring cokes and milk shakes. **1942** *R.A.F. Jrnl.* 13 June 32 'There you are, gentlemen,' boomed a rich, milk-stout voice. **1959** M. GILBERT *Blood & Judgement* i. 12 A lady..[was] addressing herself to a glass of milk stout. **1965** S. M. TRITTON *Tritton's Guide to Better Wine & Beer Making for Beginners* 133 Milk Stout... Pour hot ..water over the patent malt and stir in the flaked barley. .. Boil the hops in 2 pints of water... Dissolve sugar and lactose..and add to bulk. Follow by the yeast and ferment to completion. **1974** G. MANN *Home Wine & Beer Making* 99/1 Sweet, or milk, stout dark and sweet, but still with an underlying bitter twang. **1855** J. R. BESTE *Wabash* II. 260 Large platters of milk toast. This delicacy is made of slices of toast, buttered and sprinkled with pepper and salt, and laid in a dish of warm milk, which serves as a sauce to the rest. **1903** K. D. WIGGIN *Rebecca* xxiii. 258 She's just asked me for some milk-toast. **1853** *Knickerbocker* XLII. 532 The '*milk-train*' still had the right of way. **1897** [see *HIGHBALL 2]. **1930** WODEHOUSE *Very Good, Jeeves!* ix. 251 Her intention was..to..leave by the next train, even if that train was a milk-train, stopping at every station. **1943** HUNT & PRINGLE *Service Slang* 46 *The Milk Train*, appropriate name for the modern 'Dawn Patrol' on early morning reconnaissance flights. **1955** *Railway Mag.* May 359/1 A daily milk train which was worked by the L.N.E.R. **1877** *Rep. Vermont Dairymen's Assoc.* VIII. 106 The milk must be drawn by means of a catheter, or milk tube. **1851** H. MAYHEW *London Labour* I. 435/2 My father had a milk-walk. *c* **1864** BROUGH & HALLIDAY in M. R. Booth *Eng. Plays of 19th Cent.* (1973) IV. 240, I have a horse and cart, Miss Penelope, and a first-rate milk walk. **1905** G. B. SHAW in *Grand Mag.* Feb. 111 He..had..bought an agent's business as a doctor buys a practice or a dairyman a milkwalk. **1917** WODEHOUSE *Man with Two Left Feet* 247 He was.. owner of a milk-walk in the most fashionable part of Battersea. **1911** M. I. NEWBIGIN *Mod. Geogr.* vii. 189 A milk-wine or koumiss, produced by the fermentation of milk, is the characteristic drink. **1879** F. R. STOCKTON *Rudder Grange* v. 56 She had spent the night in a wooden rocking-chair at the milk-woman's.

10. b. milk-bush, (*c*) (example); (*d*) in South Africa and Australia, a name used for several shrubby plants, often succulent, which have a milky latex, esp. various species of *Euphorbia* (cf. sense *a*); **milk-parsley** (later example); **milk-plant,** (*b*) = **milk-bush* (*d*); **milk thistle** (further examples); **milk-wood,** (*c*) add: or other Australian trees of the genus *Alstonia* (further examples); (*d*) and (*e*) (examples).

1818 C. I. LATROBE *Jrnl. Visit S. Afr. 1815–16* 133 The milk-bush (*ficus*), a tree not unlike a Portugal laurel. **1861** J. A. GRANT *Jrnl.* 27 May in *Walk across Afr.* (1864) v. 79 After we had entered the first milk-bush enclosure, there were several cleanly-swept windings. **1883** 'R. IRON' *Story Afr. Farm* I. i. 3 The milk-bushes with their long, finger-like leaves..were touched by a weird and an almost oppressive beauty as they lay in the white light. **1907** *Nature* 17 Jan. 288/1 The common milkbush of the karroo and karroid regions of the interior, viz. Euphorbia mauritanica. **1926** [see *CAUSTIC *a.* 1 e]. **1965** *Austral. Encycl.* VI. 84/1 Milkbush, a popular name for several shrubs or small trees with a milky sap, especially *Wrightia saligna* in the family Apocynaceæ. **1966** E. PALMER *Plains of Camdeboo* xvi. 259 The milk bush grows here, the *Euphorbia mauritanica* of botanists, with its long, smooth, fleshy, yellow-green stems. **1974** *Country Life* 3 Oct. 923/1 The double-brooding swallowtail..—from milk-parsley-eating caterpillar..to Britain's largest butterfly. **1965** *Austral Encycl.* VI. 84/1 Milk plant is sometimes applied to members of the genus *Euphorbia*. **1787** W. WITHERING *Brit. Plants* (ed. 2) II. 875 *Carduus marianus*... Leaves with a net-work of white veins... Milk Thistle. Ladies Thistle. **1880** BRITTEN & HOLLAND *Dict. Eng. Plant-Names* 335 Milk Thistle... *Sonchus oleraceus*, L., in allusion to its milky juice. **1883** W. ROBINSON *Eng. Flower Garden* 270/2 If a few plants are raised in the garden and planted out in rough and somewhat bare places or banks, &c., the Milk Thistle will soon establish itself permanently. **1960** *Oxf. Bk. Wild Flowers* 34/1 Corn Sowthistle or Field Milk-thistle (*Sonchus arvensis*). A perennial with a hollow stem and milky juice. *Ibid.* 150/2 Milk Thistle (*Silybum marianum*). This rather rare annual or biennial Thistle has large, solitary, often drooping, purple flower-heads. **1862** L. PAPPE *Silva Capensis* (ed. 2) 24 *Sideroxylon Inerme Lin.* (Milk-wood; Melkhout)... Wood whitish, very hard, close, and durable. **1889** J. H. MAIDEN *Useful Native Plants Austral.* 570 *Melaleuca leucadendron*... Called 'Milkwood' in the Northern Territory. **1907** T. R. SIM *Forests & Forest Flora Cape Good Hope* 252 *Sideroxylon inerme.* (White Milkwood;..). *Ibid.* 254 *Mimusops obovata.* (Red Milkwood;..). **1908** E. J. BANFIELD *Confessions of Beachcomber* I. i. 37 On Timana are gigantic milkwood trees (*Alstonia scholaris*) which need great flying buttresses to support their immense height. **1917** [see *JAKKALSBESSIE]. **1928** D. COTTRELL *Singing Gold* III. i. 191 A thin ribbon of smoke showed against great milkwood trees. **1932** [see *JAKKALSBESSIE]. **1946** L. G. GREEN *So Few are Free* (1948) x. 137 Vaillant noted a large milkwood tree growing out of a rocky crevice. **1973** PALMER & PITMAN *Trees S. Afr.* III. 1737 The wooden rails of the little railway on the Durban Bluff in the early days..were hewn out of milkwood trees.

milk, *sb.*[2] Colloq. abbrev. of MILKSOP.

1881 *Punch* 10 Sept. 110/2 Patriotic? Well, them as talks Muggins like that to our gurls must be milks. **1923** in J. MANCHON *Le Slang.*

milk, *v.* Add: **1. f.** *colloq.* To put milk into or on to.

1877 *Trans. Devon Soc. Adv. Sci.* IX. 134 Have you *milked* your tea? **1969** J. WAINWRIGHT *Big Tickle* 52 She milked and sugared both mugs of tea.

4. e. *Theatr. slang.* (See quots.).

1939 HIXSON & COLODNY *Word Ways* xvi. 142 To overplay an audience for applause is called *milking the audience.* **1942** BERREY & VAN DEN BARK *Amer. Thes. Slang* § 593/24 *Milk a scene* or *the audience*, to try to get more laughs or applause out of a part than it deserves. **1962** *Times* 15 May 13/3 Too many of the other acts, however, have no idea how to..milk a laugh. **1971** M. BABSON *Cover-up Story* ix. 107 They milked the applause for all it was worth, then Bart held up his hand again.

milking, *vbl. sb.* Add: **4.** *milking machine* (earlier and later examples), *-shed, -yoke*; **milking bail** = BAIL *sb.*[3] 5; **milking-parlour,** a shed specially equipped for milking cows; **milking shorthorn,** a type of shorthorn developed specially for producing milk.

1890 W. H. S. ROBERTS *Hist. Oamaru* 54 A stockyard and milking-bail had also been erected. **1850** *New England Farmer* II. 282 Gutta percha patent milking machines are in use on Long Island. **1945** 'G. ORWELL' *Animal Farm* v. 37 A windmill, which could..supply the farm with electrical power..and would also run..an electric milking machine. **1974** 'E. LATHEN' *Sweet & Low* xiii. 131 Shots of ..the dairies,..complete with milking machines. **1946** *Agric. Overseas Rep.* I. 8 The milking parlour arrangement is only at the experimental stage. **1952** *Blackw. Mag.* Feb. 97/1 A thoroughly sound, commonsense opinion on..a milking-parlour. **1972** *Country Life* 2 Nov. Suppl. 3 The Farm buildings include 2 milking parlours, cubicles for 120, stock yards. *a* **1930** 'H. STONE' in Murdoch & Drake-Brockman *Austral. Short Stories* (1951) 125 It was a silent milking shed that evening. **1937** *Discovery* July 214/2 The rear parts serve as tool and store sheds, the front as byre and milking-shed. **1970** *Kenya Farmer* Feb. 36/1 'Oh Gawd!' said Fred the farmer as he came stomping up the verandah steps, his boots looking more as if he had walked from Timboroa than from the milking sheds two hundred yards away. **1910** *Encycl. Brit.* V. 539/2 The non-pedigree milking Shorthorn of the north of England is an excellent cow. **1957** Milking Shorthorn [see *dairy shorthorn* s.v. *DAIRY *sb.* 4]. **1910** J. MASEFIELD *Ballads & Poems* 42 Sleepy men bear milking-yokes Slowly towards the cattle-byre.

milko (mi·lko), *sb.* and *int.* Also **milk-o, milk-oh.** [f. MILK *sb.* + O *int.*] **A.** *sb.* A milkman. *slang.*

1911 *Answers* 11 Feb. 362/3 Milk-O! on the Make... Many of the milk-o! fraternity boast [of]..their..stealings. **1933** *Bulletin* (Sydney) 31 May 12/1 It is difficult to imagine a man looking like Il Duce while filling a billycan, but I have seen our milko perform the feat. *Ibid.* 5 July 20/3 One of Sydney's milk-ohs. **1958** *Daily Mail* 25 Oct. 5/2 The milko..has become the *milk salesman.* **1968** D. IRELAND *Chantic Bird* i. 6, I remember the milk tap I turned on in old Bay Road, the milko chased me all the way home.

B. *int.* A shout made by a milkman to indicate that milk is available.

1916 'TAFFRAIL' *Pincher Martin* xii. 232 'E wus drivin' one o' these 'ere milk-carts an' shoutin' 'Milk-o!' artside th' 'ouses. **1967** L. DEIGHTON *London Dossier* 132 The milkman shouting 'milko' as he leaves milk on a doorstep.

milkstone. Add: **2. b.** A hard deposit formed in or on dairy equipment by precipitation from milk.

1949 *N. Z. Jrnl. Agric.* Nov. 487/2 Milkstone is the casein of milk which has become attached to metal in the form of encrustations. **1963** *New Scientist* 14 Nov. 387 The alloy resisted the build-up of 'milkstone' better than polished stainless steel.

milk-warm, *a.* (Later examples.)

1894 KIPLING *Seven Seas* (1896) 36 Milk-warm wi' breath o' spice an' bloom. **1918** A. HUXLEY *Defeat of Youth* 34 At your mouth, white and milk-warm sphinx. **1922** —— *Mortal Coils* 177 Shelley had been drowned in this milk-warm sea.

milkweed. Add: **1.** (Earlier and later examples.)

1598 FLORIO *Worlde of Wordes* 199/2 Lattaria, herbe Tithimale, spurge or milk-weede. **1955** G. GRIGSON *Englishman's Flora* 227 Sun Spurge... Milk-weed, Ess[ex], Herts, E[ast] Ang[lia]. *Ibid.* 392 Sow Thistle... Milkweed, Som[erset].

2. (Earlier and later examples.)

1814 J. BIGELOW *Florula Bostoniensis* 62 *Asclepias Syriaca*, Common Silk weed or Milk weed,..is used as a substitute for feathers, fur, cotton, &c. **1854** THOREAU *Walden* 252 One very calm October after noon, for such days especially they settle on to the lakes, like the milkweed down, having looked in vain over the pond for a loon, suddenly one, sailing out from the shore.., set up his wild laugh. **1923** W. CATHER *Lost Lady* 17 The silvery milkweed was just coming on. **1933** M. DE LA ROCHE *Master of Jalna* vii. 69 A milkweed pod having burst, its hoard was released and the silvery particles,..swam delicately on the light breeze. **1957** L. EISELEY *Immense Journey* 69 There dassed before my eyes the million airy troopers of the milkweed pod. **1968** *Times* 2 Oct. 12/5 Butterflies reared on the milkweed species Asclepias curassavica.

3. In names of various North American insects feeding on milkweed: **milkweed beetle,** a brightly coloured beetle, *Tetraopes tetraophthalmus*; **milkweed bug,** either of two species of bugs of the family Lygæidæ, *Oncopeltus fasciatus*, the large milkweed bug, or *Lygæus kalmi*, the small milkweed bug; **milkweed butterfly** = MONARCH *sb.*[1] 3 (in Dict. and Suppl.).

1842 T. W. HARRIS *Insects Injurious to Vegetation* 455/2 Milk-weed beetle. **1954** BORROR & DELONG *Introd. Study Insects* xxii. 398 *T[etraopes] tetraophthalmus* Forster is a common species feeding on milkweed, and is often called the red milkweed beetle. **1905** V. L. KELLOGG *Amer. Insects* x. 211 The milkweed-bug, *Oncopeltus fasciatus*, about ⅝ inch long, orange above with most of head and prothorax except the margins black, and a broad black band across the middle of the fore wings and large black blotch on their tips, is a common showy bug on various species of milkweed. **1970** *Nature* 3 Jan. 82/1 We have treated eggs of the milkweed bug, *Oncopeltus fasciatus*, with a juvenile hormone analogue. **1972** SWAN & PAPP *Common Insects N. Amer.* xii. 125 In the Small Milkweed Bug, *L[ygæus] kalmi*, the black on the pronotum is separated from the black on the front of the wings. **1974** *Nature* 12 Apr. 556/3 Experiments in this same general field carried out on the milkweed bug *Oncopeltus.* **1889** *Insect Life* I. 221 The following is a brief account of a migratory movement of enormous numbers of the common so-called Milk-weed Butterfly. **1906** R. SOUTH *Butterflies Brit. Isles* 107 The actual number of specimens of the Milkweed, or, as it is sometimes called, Monarch butterfly, seen or caught in England..does not much exceed thirty. **1972** *Country Life* 6 Apr. 846/1 The milkweed or monarch butterfly is a denizen of North America.

milky, *a.* Add: **3. b.** (Earlier examples.)

1765 G. WASHINGTON *Diaries* (1925) I. 210 Note, the [mulberry] Stocks were very Milkey. **1768** *Ibid.* 282 Some [wheat] whose straw and head was green but the grain of full size and Milky. **1789** J. MORSE *Amer. Geogr.* 52 About the time that it begins to turn from its milky state and to ripen, they run their canoes into the midst of it.

4. Also (*slang*), cowardly.

1936 J. CURTIS *Gilt Kid* ii. 18 They just talk that way to make you turn milky. **1938** G. GREENE *Brighton Rock* II. i. 62 I'm not milky... I just don't want another killing. **1954** 'N. BLAKE' *Whisper in Gloom* xvi. 217 Look at da kid. He's not milky. **1969** H. CARVIC *Miss Seeton draws Line* ix. 171 'Getting milky?' scoffed Doris.

b. Of a noise, song, etc.: soft. *poet.*

1924 E. SITWELL *Sleeping Beauty* x. 38 Goats gold as wheat With a kind white milky bleat. **1925** —— *Troy Park* 76 A white bird sang a milky song Of easy heaven and feathered rest.

5. *milky-coloured, -sapped, -toothed* adjs.

1906 W. B. YEATS *Poems 1899–1905* 268 Hold up your hands to him, that you may pluck That milky-coloured neck out of the noose. **1923** D. H. LAWRENCE *Birds, Beasts & Flowers* 19 Folded upon itself..And milky-sapped, sap that curdles milk and makes *ricotta.* **1905** E. F. BENSON *Image in Sand* i. 2 Brown-faced, milky-toothed Arabs were there.

milky (mi·lki), *sb. slang.* Also **milkie.** [f. MILK *sb.* + -Y[6], -IE.] A familiar or nursery name for: (*a*) a milkman or milk-boy; (*b*) milk.

1886 H. BAUMANN *Londinismen* 108/1 *Milky*, milkman. **1922** JOYCE *Ulysses* 363 Go home to nicey bread and milky and say night prayers with the kiddies. **1923** 'R. CROMPTON' *William Again* xii. 203 ''Ello, kids!' said the milk-boy... ''Ello, Milky!' **1946** P. H. SIMPSON *If you'd care to Know* 134 Box in which the 'milkie' places the bottled milk. **1966** 'L. LANE' *ABZ of Scouse* 68 She keeps ther milkie on ther doorstep fer ars (hours). **1975** *Evening News* 21 Apr. 4/4 He appeared his normal easy-going self and all he said to me was, 'Hullo milkie.'

milky way. Add: **2. a.** (Later examples.) Also *attrib.*

1851 H. MELVILLE *Moby Dick* I. xl. 291 Leaving a milky-way wake of creamy foam. **1916** D. H. LAWRENCE *Amores* 93 Pleiads of people are Deployed around me, and I see The street's long outstretched Milky Way.

mill, *sb.*[1] Add: **1. b.** *to go* (*pass*, etc.) *through the mill* (further examples).

1818 SCOTT *Heart Midl.* in *Tales my Landlord* 2nd Ser. III. iv. 96 Frank here won't hear of our putting her through the mill. **1837** *Knickerbocker* IX. 356, I had been 'through the mill' of a pre-concerted, artificial revival. **1840** R. H. DANA *Two Yrs. before Mast* 50 I've been through the mill. **1868** H. WOODRUFF *Trotting Horse* vi. 76 It was thought that they would be ruined for service if they were 'put through the mill'. **1887** *Contemp. Rev.* Jan. 10 Certain persons who have gone through the mill of what is known as our 'higher education'. **1903** G. GISSING *Private Papers H. Ryecroft* 138 His hardships were never excessive; they did not affect his health or touch his spirits; probably he is in every way a better man for having..'gone through the mill'. **1904** J. C. LINCOLN *Cap'n Eri* ii. 29 Jerry's the only one of us three that's been through the mill. **1940** H. READ *Annals of Innocence* II. i. 75 A boy who is destined to be a teacher, a doctor, a technician or a scientist, must go through the mill and acquire the necessary qualifications. **1959** I. & P. OPIE *Lore & Lang. Schoolch.* x. 200 *Running the Gauntlet.* Although well known by this name, the ordeal is also termed ..'Through the Mill'. **1965** *Listener* 1 July 21/1, I am a collector—and one who has gone through the mill. I started..in the basement with bus tickets.

4. (Further example.)
1919 *Brit. Manufacturer* Nov. 26/2 In the linen industry a 'mill' means the works where flax is spun into yarns, while a 'factory' means the place of the further evolution of the yarns being woven into cloth.

6. (Earlier example.)
1835 DICKENS *Sk. Boz* (1836) 1st Ser. I. 334 The mill's a d—d sight better than the Sessions.

b. *transf.* A prison or guard-house.
1851 H. MAYHEW *London Labour* I. 352/2 A few weeks after I was grabbed for this, and got a month at the mill... When I came out of prison, I went to Epsom races. **1853** WHYTE-MELVILLE *Digby Grand* I. ix. 229 The latter worthy..gave a policeman such a licking the other night, that he was within an ace of getting 'a month at the mill'. **1889** H. H. MCCONNELL *Five Years a Cavalryman* 194 Very few, indeed, are they who during their term of service can say: 'They never had *me* in the mill.' **1916** E. C. GARRETT *Army Ballads & Other Verses* 21 And they put me in 'the mill'. **1928** L. H. NASON *Sergeant Eadie* 78 Why, put 'em in the mill! **1951** J. JONES *From Here to Eternity* IV. xlii. 636 'You were here when one of the old ones was in the mill, weren't you, Jack?' 'Two,' Malloy said. 'Both of them during my first stretch.' **1960** WENTWORTH & FLEXNER *Dict. Amer. Slang* 339/1 *Mill*.., a prison; a guardhouse.

6*. *U.S. slang.* A typewriter.
1913 *Writer's Bulletin* Oct. 103/2 After I got a good idea I would hustle to my 'mill' and pound out some copy. **1922** N. A. CRAWFORD *Weavers With Words* 22 And sometimes..I'll start to say, 'Jim, got a good cigarette?' and turn toward his battered old 'mill'. **1932** C. D. MACDOUGALL *College Course in Reporting* 498 *Mill*, typewriter. **1948** MENCKEN *Amer. Lang.* Suppl. II. 717 Writers' cramp was cured..on the advent of the *mill*, i.e., the typewriter.

7. (Earlier example.)
1819 T. MOORE *Tom Crib's Memorial to Congress* 36 We who're of the fancy-lay, As dead hands at a mill as they.

b. *U.S.* A circling movement of cattle. (Cf. MILL *v.*¹ 12.)
1897 E. HOUGH *Story of Cowboy* 146 By shouts and blows he did all he could to break the 'mill' and get the cattle headed properly. **1903** A. ADAMS *Log of Cowboy* iv. 27 We soon had a mill going which kept them [*sc.* cattle] busy and rested our horses. **1942** E. E. DALE *Cow Country* 55 Those behind them would follow and a 'mill' would be established in which the animals would swim around and around in a circle until they drowned unless it were quickly broken up and the leaders again headed for the opposite shore.

8*. *slang.* The engine of an aircraft or a 'hot rod' racing car.
1918 *Atlantic* Sept. 414 Motor is 'moulin'—to start it, one 'turns the mill'. **1923** G. H. MCKNIGHT *Eng. Words & their Backgrounds* 56 *Tail* and *joystick* and *mill* (French *moulin*) were names for different parts of the airship. **1937** E. C. PARSONS *Great Adventure* vi. 60 To nurse one of the grunting old mills up to that height,..and keep it running for an hour, was in itself quite a stunt. **1948** MENCKEN *Amer. Lang.* Suppl. II. 724 There are others [*sc.* new terms] that remain the private property of the men working in automobile plants and of those who sell or repair cars. A few specimens; Bald-head. A worn tire... Mill. An engine [etc.]. **1954** R. F. & B. W. YATES *Sport & Racing Cars* ii. 24 The additional motor 'moxie' provided by a reground camshaft is truly amazing, and all of this without running too much risk of a cranky 'mill' at low idling speeds. **1954** *Amer. Speech* XXIX. 100 *Mill*,..any engine. *Ibid.* 97 *Full mill*,..an engine with all necessary speed racing accessories. **1975** B. GARFIELD *Hopscotch* xv. 152 This was an old car but it must have had a souped-up mill.

9. *mill-bag, -brook, -lot, -room* (later example), *-yard*; *mill-cut, -like* adjs.
1832 J. P. KENNEDY *Swallow Barn* I. xv. 155 With the large canvass mill-bags spread out for saddles. **1851** R. GLISAN *Jrnl. Army Life* (1874) vi. 58, I..endeavored to throw [it] in a mill-bag style over my shoulder. **1636** *Official Rec. Springfield, Mass.* (1898–9) I. 159 The lotts.. are ordered to lye adjoining to Mill Brooke. **1864** T. L. NICHOLS *40 Yrs. Amer. Life* I. ii. 20 Grist-mills which ground our corn, and saw-mills which supplied our timber, were upon a mill brook. **1866** G. M. HOPKINS *Poems* (1967) 171 The streams are full And millbrook-slips with pretty pace Gallop along the meadow grass. **1925** *Glasgow Herald* 2 Apr. 9 To import into this country a sufficient number of mill-cut houses to supply the shortage. **1854** *Poultry Chron.* I. 148 The 'mill-like motion of the gizard'. **1918** MRS. E. LIDDELL in J. Gott *Lett.* 66 Here is a man who, alike in the mill-like grinding of life in Leeds..and amid the urgent claims of a diocese, always found time to love and to remember. **1746** *Boston News-Let.* 16 Nov., Seven Acres..to be laid out to the Right of the 30 Acre Mill-Lot, granted to Thomas Richardson. **1833** B. SILLIMAN *Man. Sugar Cane* 45 The length of the mill-room A is 64 feet. **1824** *New Hampsh. Hist. Soc. Coll.* I. 246 A saw mill torn down and twelve thousand of boards in the mill-yard carried away. **1936** *Discovery* Sept. 288/1, I saw the mill cat crossing the wall from our garden to the mill yard. **1955** J. R. R. TOLKIEN *Return of Ring* 296 The low wall of the mill-yard.

10. mill band, an endless belt for the wheels of mill machinery; **mill finish,** of paper, not subjected to any extra processing after being made; **mill log** *U.S.*, a log cut at a saw mill; **mill-power,** water-power for driving a mill; also, a unit for measuring this (see quots. 1903, 1911); **mill privilege, right** *U.S.*, the privilege or right of using water for driving a mill; **mill-run,** (*d*) applied to timber sawn to the usual specifications; (see also quot. 1957); also *transf.*, of average or mediocre quality, 'run-of-the-mill'; **mill-saw** (earlier example); **mill-scale,** read: *Metallurgy*, a deposit of iron oxide formed on iron or steel during hot working; **mill-seat** (earlier example); **mill site** *U.S.* = *mill-seat*; **mill-stream** (later examples); **mill tail** (see quot. 1835); also *attrib.* and *fig.*; **mill town, village,** a town or village characterized by the presence of mills; **mill-work** (earlier example).
1858 P. L. SIMMONDS *Dict. Trade Products* 247/2 *Mill-band maker*, a manufacturer of bands for machine shops, and for driving wheels. **1869** *Bradshaw's Railway Manual* XXI. App. 103 Manufacturers of..Engine Hose, Fire Buckets, Mill Bands, &c. **1957** J. BRAINE *Room at Top* ix. 86 The smells of East Warley tugging at me for attention..—malt, burning millband, frying fish. **1907** CROSS & BEVAN *Text-bk. Paper-Making* (ed. 3) x. 270 In hand-made paper the 'mill-finish' is obtained by pressing the sheets of paper one against another. **1952** E. J. LABARRE *Dict. Paper* (ed. 2) 163/2 Mill finish is synonymous with machine finish, and merely indicates that the paper has received its finish on the paper-machine. **1795** T. B. HAZARD *Diary* (1930) 171/2, I helpt brother Robert flote mill logs to mill. **1849** D. NASON *Jrnl.* 99, I asked the guide if there were any mill-logs among it. **1833** *Chambers's Edinb. Jrnl.* II. 167/3 This stream..at some after time may be turned to account as a mill power. **1903** *Trans. Amer. Soc. Mech. Engin.* XXIV. 983 Wherever water-power is sold it is customary to use the turbines as meters. .. From tables and curves made up from..tests of.. turbines,..data are obtained from which to compute the actual discharge. This is referred to a given head and thence reduced to mill-powers, the values of which vary with the locality. **1911** *Encycl. Brit.* XIV. 92/2 A mill-power is defined as 38 cub. ft. of water per sec. during 16 hours per day on a fall of 20 ft. This gives about 60 h.p. effective. **1734** *New Hampsh. Probate Rec.* (1914) II. 508, I also give unto my son..the one half of my mill Priviledge on the southerly side of ye River at Lole-End. **1892** *Rep. Vermont Board Agric.* XII. 134 Many mill privileges with excellent water power are afforded. **1794** *Mass. Hist. Soc. Coll.* III. 147 The principal object of the original settlers being lumber, more attention was paid to mill-rights than to the soil. **1847** W. I. PAULDING *Antipathies* III. iii, in J. K. & W. I. Paulding *Amer. Comedies* 262 There's a man at Jack O'Lantern's that owns land and mill-rights **1881** *Chicago Times* 1 June, The supply of choice mill-run lumber was generally quite limited. **1928** FOY & HARLOW *Clowning through Life* 299 He thought himself far too good for the ordinary mill run of melodramas which prevailed at that house. **1957** *N.Z. Timber Jrnl.* Nov. 59/2 *Mill run*. Usually implies all saleable output of timber from a saw-mill. **1856** 'MARK TWAIN' *Let.* 14 Nov. in *Adventures T. J. Snodgrass* (1928) 25 Everybody was a bobbin up and down like a mill saw. **1880** *Encycl. Brit.* XIII. 357/1 During rolling this film [of oxide] becomes somewhat thick and peels off, forming 'mill-scale'. **1902** BREARLEY & IBBOTSON *Analysis of Steel-Works Materials* VII. 229 (*heading*) Mill scale. **1940** SIMONS & GREGORY *Steel Manuf.* xvi. 109 The charge consists of steel scrap and grey phosphoric ..to which are added millscale..or iron ore, and lime or limestone. **1968** T. H. ROGERS *Marine Corrosion* vi. 78 Steel with mill-scale either in or on the surface, when exposed to sea water, will pit very severely wherever any couple between scale and steel occurs. **1770** G. WASHINGTON *Diaries* (1925) I. 365 Mr. Ballendine and myself leveled Doeg Run in order to fix on a Mill Seat. **1831** J. M. PECK *Guide for Emigrants* 196 There are but few good mill sites in the State. **1896** C. H. SHINN *Story of the Mine* 81 Water claims and mill sites were taken up almost as soon as work had fairly begun on the Comstock. **1956** H. EVANS *Mountain Dog* 107 Earth and stones had been bulldozed to the water's edge to form a millsite. **1815** D. DRAKE *Nat. View Cincinnati* i. 58 In summer and autumn, it [*sc.* Licking River] is a moderate mill-stream. **1840** *Knickerbocker* XVI. 22 A wooden bridge which crossed a mill-stream. **1939** JOYCE *Finnegans Wake* 175 But the Mountstill frowns on the Millstream while their Madsons leap his Bier. **1975** J. B. HARLEY *O.S. Maps* iii. 44 In Ordnance Survey usage the term 'mill race' is given to the water leading to a mill, and 'mill stream' to the water leaving it. **1835** J. ABBOTT *Expos. Princ. Hydraulic Engine* 126 *Mill tail*, the water which has passed through the wheel race; or is below the mill. **1922** BLUNDEN *Shepherd* 64 No water ever ran so blithe As that same mill-tail stream, I'd say. **1925** —— *Eng. Poems* 24 Master-fish by bridges In freshened milltails leaping. **1951** E. PAUL *Springtime in Paris* ix. 171 If the priests were right, and Busse, as a card-carrying Communist, was doomed to the foulest mill tails of hell, [etc.]. **1847** D. P. THOMPSON *Locke Amsden* x. 199 [The paper] came into town all damp from the press of Mill-Town Emporium. **1902** S. E. WHITE *Blazed Trail* xxi. 155 He arrived out of breath in a typical little mill town. **1925** T. DREISER *Amer. Trag.* (1926) I. II. vi. 195 He decided to remain—later sitting down to dinner with a small group of milltown store and factory employees. **1944** *Reader's Digest* Dec. 16/1, I used to live, years ago, in a mill town in the Deep South. **1863** A. D. WHITNEY *Faith Gartney's Girlhood* xxiii. 218 It needs just such a man [as minister] among mill-villages like these, he says. **1770** G. WASHINGTON *Diaries* (1925) I. 381 Ball and his People went about 12 oclock to Framing the Mill Work.

mill, *sb.*⁵ Add: **a.** (Earlier and later examples.)
1786 in *Amer. Museum* (1789) II. 182 Mills, the lowest money of account, of which one thousand shall be equal to the federal dollar, or money unit. **1974** *News & Reporter* (Chester, S. Carolina) 24 Apr. 1-A/8 Board Chairman J. F. (Buddy) Martin told him that in 1970 the county had raised from one mill to two the amount of money that was available for the hospital from the county.

Also *attrib.*, as *mill tax*.
1848 *Indiana Hist. Soc. Publ.* (1895–1903) III. 514 The former will pay on a mill tax $200. **1853** in *Trans. Mich. Agric. Soc.* (1856) VII. 293 A mill tax is annually levied to purchase books for these libraries. **1903** *Scribner's Monthly* Oct. 486 They support the Universities by a direct mill tax levied upon the assessed valuation of the State.

mill (mil), *sb.*⁶ Also **mil.** Colloq. abbrev. of MILLIMETRE (esp. in *Photogr.*, designating a size of film).
1960 E. MORGAN *You're a Long Time Dead* 386 *Sandy*, I'll be getting pictures of you in that outfit, don't worry, as good as anyone can take—*Best Man*, What, on 35 mill? **1971** *Guardian* 25 Oct. 8/3 'Is it videotape or 35 mill?' she asks. **1974** S. GULLIVER *Vulcan Bulletins* 26 'What do you want?' 'Eighty-one mil. mortar bombs.'

mill., mill (mil), *sb.*⁷ Also **mil.** Colloq. abbrev. of MILLION.
1955 R. J. SCHWARTZ *Compl. Dict. Abbrev.* 112/3 *Mill.*, million. **1975** *New Yorker* 20 Jan. 29/1 Thanks a mil for your letter. **1975** D. LOWDEN *Bellman & True* xi. 55 'How much will he take then?' 'Anything we can give him, up to two mill.'

mill, *v.*¹ Add: **2. e.** *Soap manufacture.*
1902 *Chambers's Jrnl.* Apr. 204/1 When quite hard, this fine soap is milled, or cut into very small shreds, after which it is pressed in moulds into fancy shapes. **1967** *Everyman's Encycl.* XI. 271/2 The chips are transferred to a mixer where the dyes and perfumes are added, which are then milled to make the soap plastic and homogeneous.

f. *slang.* To send to the treadmill; to send to prison (cf. MILL *sb.*¹ 6 in Dict. and Suppl.).
1838 DICKENS *O. Twist* II. xxv. 83, I shouldn't have been milled if it hadn't been for her advice. But..what's six weeks of it?

12. Also *transf.* (of persons, vehicles, etc.) and *fig.*
1910 W. M. RAINE *Bucky O'Connor* 227, I expect you were able to make out, even if I did get the letters to milling around wrong. **1911** H. QUICK *Yellowstone Nights* v. 127 The main thing the matter was that failure o' his a-millin' through his mental facilities. **1919** L. F. CODY *Memories Buffalo Bill* 302 Indians and soldiers milled, the Indians fighting with their knives, the soldiers with their guns. **1927** H. E. FOSDICK *Pilgrimage to Palestine* 262 We look down upon the throng milling around the Chapel of the Sepulcher. **1935** *Punch* 29 May 648/2 The sergeants are milling round like madmen with last-minute instructions. **1957** J. KEROUAC *On Road* (1958) v. 33 First we milled with all the cowboy-dudded tourists..at bars. **1968** R. M. PATTERSON *Finlay's River* III. 164 To follow their wanderings in detail would be pointless. They milled around like that for the next two days, obsessed with this ridge-climbing idea.

c. *fig.* To turn *over* in one's mind.
1905 *Smart Set* Oct. 17/1 No,..I ain't buyin' no dishes. I was just kind o' millin' things over to myself. **1923** R. D. PAINE *Comrades of Rolling Ocean* xvii. 298 Judson, on guard in the cabin, was milling this problem over. **1958** 'A. GILBERT' *Death against Clock* viii. 111 Barney's milled it over and over..and we can't think of any reason. **1964** M. GOWING *Britain & Atomic Energy* ix. 250 Nor did they [*sc.* the American engineers] want to spend much time in milling over alternative approaches to problems for which they had chosen..their own solution.

millable (mi·lăb'l), *a.* [f. MILL *v.*¹ or *sb.*¹ + -ABLE.] **a.** Suitable for milling (sense 1).
1905 A. COCKAYNE in *13th Rep. Dept. Agric.* (N.Z.) Appendix x. 402 Most of the Phormium [in flax swamps] was short, but there were considerable quantities of good millable fibre... All the millable flax is being rapidly cut down, and no doubt these swamps will in time become good agricultural land. **1955** *Times* 2 May 23/5 As far as millable grades were concerned, the wheat market showed little feature during the past week. **1959** *Cape Argus* 15 Aug. 1/5 The fire..destroyed about 2,000 tons of millable cane before it could be brought under control. **1963** *Times* 23 Feb. 5/1 The millable oat championship went to a Blenda sample from Mr. W. Sharp, of Banff, Aberdeen.

b. Suitable for cutting in a sawmill.
1924 *Times Trade & Engin. Suppl.* 29 Nov. 250/2 It is proposed..to open up 500,000 acres of farming land and 1,000,000,000 feet of millable bush. **1969** *Northern Territory News* (Darwin) *Focus '69* 83/1 There is a considerable stand of timber again reaching 'millable' stage. **1972** *Country Life* 16 Mar. 653/3 Some sort of grading [of timber]..based on veneer, planking and millable butts in the case of hardwoods.

‖ **mille-feuille** (milfōy). Pl. **mille-feuilles.** [Fr., lit. 'a thousand leaves'.] A rich pastry consisting of thin layers of puff pastry filled with jam, cream, etc. Also *attrib.* and *fig.*
1895 G. A. SALA *Thorough Good Cook* xiv. 426 Mille Feuilles (Italian Pyramid). **1902** S. BEATY-POWNALL *'Queen' Cookery Bks.* XI. vi. 169 *Millefeuilles, Gâteau* (also known as *Gâteau Milfras*). **1918** A. BENNETT *Roll-Call* I. viii. 169, I should like a strawberry ice, and a lemon-squash, and a millefeuille cake. **1945** N. MITFORD *Pursuit of Love* xviii. 146 Soon Davy was falling upon *éclairs* and *mille feuilles* with all the abandon of a schoolboy. **1967** *Listener* 21 Dec. 802/2 When strangers meet, and nature calls, our society splits into a *mille-feuille* of social strata: each one of us clinging to our own euphemism. **1971** COOMBES & WAKELIN *Good Housek. Advanced Cooking is Fun* xv. 218 *Mille-feuilles*... Spread stiffly whipped cream onto the centre of the puff paste layer.

millefleurs. Add: Also **millefleur. a.** (Earlier example.)
a **1850** J. ATKINSON in A. Davis *Package & Print* (1967) plate 8 (Advt.), Essence of Millefleur, Bouquet, Marechalle.

b. (Freq. hyphenated or written as two words.) A pattern of flowers and leaves used for tapestry, porcelain, etc. Usu. *attrib.*
1908 J. F. BLACKER *Chats on Oriental China* x. 123 The colour is not nearly as brilliant as in the '*mille fleurs*' class, though the same wavy porcelain is to be noted. **1933**

Burlington Mag. July 35/1 The style of the tapestry..the particular type of *mille fleurs* pattern. **1933** *New Statesman* 14 Oct. 444/1 The two mille fleur boots, entirely encrusted with sharp microscopic forget-me-nots. **1938** *Burlington Mag.* June p. xxix/1 The fifteenth century French armorial tapestry with its typical *mille-fleurs* decoration of varied flowers and leafwork on the coveted red ground. **1960** H. Hayward *Antique Coll.* 183/2 *Mille fleurs*, decoration occurring on Chinese porcelain with panels of growing plants reserved on a flower-covered ground. **1970** *Centennial Acquisitions Mus. Fine Arts Boston* 57 (*caption*) The relatively small size of this *mille-fleurs*..tapestry suggests that it may be part of a larger hanging.

millegrain (mi·lĭgrēⁱn). Also **milligrain.** [f. L., *mille* thousand + Grain *sb.*[1] 12.] (See quot. 1951.) Also *attrib.*

1948 W. A. Jackson *Jewellery Repairing* iv. 49 If the setting be a millegraine one and the tiny beaded edge be worn down..a new edge can sometimes be brought up by the burnisher. **1951** M. Flower *Victorian Jewellery* 253 *Millegrain*, a kind of setting in which the metal gripping to stone is decorated with a line of tiny grains or beads. **1960** H. Hayward *Antique Coll.* 183 *Millegrain setting*, a means of setting a gemstone whereby the stone is held in a mount ornamented with a band of very small beads of metal. **1970** E. Bruton *Diamonds* xx. 349 In the nineteenth century many small diamonds were set in a form known as milligrain, in which the metal used to hold the diamonds was crenelated by drawing a hardened steel ring round the metal.

milleme, var. *millieme.

‖ **Mille Miglia** (mī·le mī·lya). [It., lit. 'a thousand miles'.] The name of a sports-car race run over approx. one thousand miles of roads in Italy from 1927 to 1957; also *fig.*

1933 B. Lyndon *Combat: Motor Racing Hist.* viii. 133 The entry list suggested that there would be a merciless fight between the Bugatti team and the Alfa-Romeos, which had just won the Mille Miglia. **1957** S. Moss *In Track of Speed* ii. 27 The Italians had made a real Roman holiday of the Mille Miglia and..had come to regard themselves as almost unbeatable. **1963** P. Drackett *Motor Rallying* v. 75 The galloping Gaul's remarkable record included first in the Alpine and German and second in the Mille Miglia. **1966** W. Court *Power & Glory* iii. xviii. 166/1 The Mille Miglia, run in traditional form on 23 occasions between 1927 and 1957, was a..throw back to the days that had ended with Paris–Madrid. **1969** J. Leasor *They don't make them like that any More* i. 1 The pinheaded nutters in the Minis..roared about as though they were overtaking each other in the Mille Miglia. **1970** M. O'Brine *Crambo* xvii. 77 He took a four-berth cabin..that..had cockroaches doing a Mille Miglia around the wash-basin.

millenarianism. (Earlier and later examples.)

1856 [see *Ebionitism]. **1894** J. H. Blunt *Dict. Sects* (ed. 2) 329 Millenarianism is to a certain degree not unorthodox, but..Millenarians who uphold the doctrine of a sensual or Judaic Millennium are unequivocally condemned by theologians. **1937** A. Reese *Approaching Advent Christ* 304 Millennarianism has need to pray frequently to be saved from its friends. **1957** *Oxf. Dict. Chr. Ch.* 900 In the early Church, Millenarianism was upheld principally among the Gnostics and Montanists, but also upheld by more orthodox writers... Although primitive Millenarianism lingered on..down to the end of the 4th cent., it received its death-blow from Origen. **1961** B. R. Wilson *Sects & Society* ii. ix. 189 Mrs Eddy..was unrelenting in her attacks on spiritualism, mesmerism ..and millenarianism.

millenarism. Delete †*Obs.* and add later examples.

1894 F. C. Conybeare *Apology of Apollonius* 358/1 Millenarism of Gospel. **1957** P. Worsley *Trumpet shall Sound* 232 Where millenarism survives in countries with popular secular political organizations, it is generally escapist and quietist. **1962** N. Cohn in S. L. Thrupp *Millennial Dreams in Action* ii. 32 The oldest form of millenarism of which much is known is the messianic hope of the Jews. *Ibid.* 35 Marxists have sometimes tried to interpret the millenarism of the Spirituals..as a protest by poor peasants. **1971** *Catholic Dict. Theol.* III. 280 This decision amounted to an assessment that a mitigated Millenarism..was an error in faith, even if it could not yet be called a heresy.

millenarist. Add: (Later examples.) Also *attrib.* or as *adj.*

1894 F. C. Conybeare *Apology of Apollonius* 287 They began to compromise with the world..and they laid up their old millenarist system of faith and morality. **1957** P. Worsley *Trumpet shall Sound* vii. 137 These Papuans are typical of all millenarists. **1962** M. Eliade in S. L. Thrupp *Millennial Dreams in Action* iii. 143 The millenarist movements became savagely anti-Christian. **1967** R. A. Markus in *Cambr. Hist. Later Greek & Early Medieval Philos.* 408 He had..abandoned all traces of millenarist thinking. **1971** *Catholic Dict. Theol.* III. 279 Justin ..has been cited..as a Millenarist. *Ibid.*, This is frankly Millenarist. *Ibid.* 280 In the Middle Ages Joachim of Flora revived Millenarist ideas.

millenary, *a.* and *sb.* Add: **B.** *sb.* **1. b.** A thousandth anniversay or its celebration; a millennium.

1897 F. Harrison (*title*) Millenary of King Alfred. **1955** *Times* 18 Aug. 9/6 The few simple features which moulded the town in the past govern its shape still, so that, for all that it is new, it is recognizably Kassel. (The town celebrated its millenary in 1913). **1974** E. Lemarchand *Buried in Past* vi. 114 The borough plans to celebrate its alleged Millenary in August. I say alleged, because its claim to have received a charter from King Edgar in the year 973 has been discredited for some time. **1975** *Church Times* 14 Feb. 18/3 St. John's, Little Missenden, celebrates its millenary.

mille·nnialism. [-ism.] Belief in the coming or the present existence of the millennium (Millennium 2).

1906 *Pall Mall Gaz.* 4 Jan. 1 In a spirit of fatuous millennialism the constabulary force..was being reduced. **1937** A. Reese *Approaching Advent Christ* 305 The indictment..fails to take notice of the panics that Post-millennialism provoked in the Middle Ages. **1945** D. H. Kromminga *Millennium in Church* 6 My own view I would designate as Covenantal Millenialism. **1967** J. Wilson in B. R. Wilson *Patterns Sectarianism* x. 353 The upsurge of post-adventual millennialism induced some to make comparison of their own country with the location of the forthcoming Kingdom of God.

millennialist. Add: (Examples.) Also as *adj.*

1903 D. D. Rutledge *Christ, Anti-Christ & Millennium* xi. 291 One Post-Millennialist misunderstood this view. *Ibid.* 301 The reply of the Post-Millennialists is to the effect that Revelation xx. is all symbolical and..cannot be relied on. **1932** A. Stewart *Christianity, Communism, Adventism* 5 'Jesus will soon be here' said one, an ardent pre-millennialist. *Ibid.* xi. 111 Post-millennialists..labor with abounding hope. **1967** R. Robertson in B. R. Wilson *Patterns Sectarianism* ii. 72 A more strictly millennialist belief that 'the end of all things is at hand'.

miller[1]. Add: **3*.** *Austral.* = *floury miller* (*floury *a.* d).

1896 *Rec. Austral. Museum* II. 107 The same kind of *Cicada* is known by different names in different localities, such as 'Miller', 'Mealy-back', etc. **1941** Baker *Dict. Austral. Slang* 46 *Miller*, a nickname for a cicada.

Miller[2] (mi·ləɹ). *Cryst.* The name of W. H. *Miller* (1801–80), English scientist, used *attrib.* with reference to the method for specifying the positions of planes in crystals that he used in his *Treatise on Crystallography* (1839), esp. in *Miller index* (Index *sb.* 9 c).

1890 G. H. Williams *Elem. Crystallogr.* ii. 31 To change the signs of any Miller symbol is to change the plane to its parallel and therefore equivalent plane on the opposite side of the crystal. **1900** Moses & Parsons *Elem. Mineral.* i. i. 10 The Miller Indices may be obtained from Weiss's parameters by first dividing each by the common multiple of their numerators and taking the reciprocal of the result. **1940** Glasstone *Text-bk. Physical Chem.* v. 336 The fact is represented by a bar over the Miller index, e.g., ($1\bar{1}1$) for a face which has intercepts *a*, *-b* and *c*, on the axes *OX*, *OY* and *OZ* respectively. **1966** C. R. Tottle *Sci. Engin. Materials* iii. 55 When a plane is to be described, the notation used is that of Miller indices. The plane is extended to cut the *x*, *y*, and *z* axes, and the intercepts in steps of the unit cell dimensions *a*, *b*, *c* are written down. The reciprocals of these intercepts are next obtained, and fractions cleared to give the smallest integers again. *Ibid.* 59 There are six such planes in the cell, all having the last index in the Miller notation equal to 0, since they are all parallel to the hexagonal axis.

Miller effect. *Electronics.* [named after John Milton *Miller* (1882–1962), U.S. physicist.] The effect whereby capacitance (esp. inter-electrode capacitance) in the output of a valve or transistor increases its input impedance.

1931 in S. R. Roget *Dict. Electr. Terms* (ed. 2) 209/2. **1934** J. H. Reyner *Television* x. 130 In radio practice these bypass condensers approximate to 100 or 300 $\mu\mu$F. and reduce the Miller effect considerably. **1967** *Electronics* 6 Mar. 130/1 In applying this principle, called the Miller effect, to a transistor, the equivalent base-to-emitter capacitance..becomes the rated value of the capacitor multiplied by the voltage gain of the transistor. **1971** J. H. Smith *Digital Logic* iv. 74 This feedback effect of a capacitor from the output of an amplifier to its input, is known as the Miller effect.

Millerian (milīə·riăn), *a.* *Cryst.* [f. the surname *Miller* + -ian.] Of or pertaining to W. H. Miller or his system of specifying the positions of crystal faces (cf. *Miller[2]).

1896 C. J. Woodward *Crystallogr. for Beginners* iii. 24 In the Millerian system..fractions of the parameters are taken, and the denominators of these fractions form the indices. **1944** C. Palache et al. *Dana's Syst. Min.* (ed. 7) I. 25 When the lattice is rhombohedral, Millerian three-index symbols are also given. **1964** Hartshorne & Stuart *Pract. Optical Crystallogr.* i. 9 If *hkl* are the Millerian indices, the intercepts along the axes are *a*/*h*, *b*/*k*, *c*/*l*.

Millerism. (Earlier and later examples.)

1843 *Niles' Reg.* 240/3 Millerism. Father Miller lately visited Rochester, New York, and devoted one whole week to dealing out exhortations. *a* **1852** F. M. Whitcher *Widow Bedott Papers* (1883) xii. 44 When Millerism was makin' such a noise,..the Wiggletown folks raly thought ther was something in it. **1961** B. R. Wilson *Sects & Society* iii. xii. 239 There was little organisation..of the scattered converts from Millerism and Campbellism in Britain in the 1860s, **1962** G. Shepperson in S. L. Thrupp *Millennial Dreams in Action* ii. 51 He emphasizes how the reaction against Millerism..'speeded the adoption of a fervent postmillennialism'.

millet[1]. **2.** (Further examples.)

1889 J. H. Maiden *Useful Native Plants Austral.* 97 *Panicum decompositum*,..'Australian millet', 'Umbrella grass'... One of the most valuable of the Darling Downs (Queensland) grasses. **1896** *Australasian* 14 Mar. 488/5 One of the very best of the grasses found in the hot regions of Central Australia is the Australian millet, *Panicum decompositum.*

‖ **millet**[2] (mi·let). [Turk. *millet* nation, group of co-religionists, f. Arab. *milla* religion.] A division of the subjects of the Ottoman Empire according to allegiance to a religious leader (see quot. 1902). Often used *spec.* of non-Muslims.

[**1861** G. Finlay *Hist. Greek Revolution* I. i. 9 The Greek language was the language of the Church and the law which ruled the whole assemblage of nations called by the Othoman administration, *Roum meleti*, or Roman nation.] **1900** 'Odysseus' *Turkey in Europe* vii. 296 The Turk divides the population of the Ottoman Empire into Millets, or religious communities. **1902** *Encycl. Brit.* XXX. 395/1 All Moslems..are included in the *millet*..of Islam. The Rûm, or Roman (*i.e.*, Greek) *millet* comprises all those who acknowledge the authority of the Œcumenical Patriarch,..the Bulgar *millet* comprises the Bulgarians who accept the rule of the exarchate; the other *millets* are the Katolik (Catholics), Ermeni (Gregorian Armenians), Musevi (Jews) and Prodesdan (Protestants). **1933** *Times Lit. Suppl.* 14 Dec. 890/2 The system of organization in *millets*..which existed under the Sultans goes back to the early days of Islam. **1942** *Turkey* (Geogr. Handbk. Ser. B. R. 507, Admiralty, Naval Intelligence Div.) I. viii. 290 Each *millet* had complete autonomy, under the authority and leadership of an ecclesiastical functionary. **1971** A. Mango *Discovering Turkey* i. 69 The Ottoman Empire..was a multi-national state,..the criterion of differentiation among its subjects was religion and not nationality. *Millet*..which in modern Turkish means 'nation', was until recently used to describe a religious community. **1973** *Times Lit. Suppl.* 29 June 754/2 They could coexist in the same territory under the same loose domination, as many different *millets* did in the Ottoman Empire.

millet-seed. Add: **b.** *Petrol.* Used *attrib.* to designate (grains of) sand of almost spherical shape as a result of abrasion produced by the wind.

1935 T. Eastwood *Northern Eng.* (*Brit. Regional Geol.*) 7 Thick red sandstones (Penrith Sandstone)..betray their origin as desert sand by the presence of 'millet-seed' grains. **1971** I. G. Gass et al. *Understanding Earth* xiii. 169/2 In desert sands..the quartz grains are described as 'millet-seed' sands, a reference to the almost perfect, spherical shape.

mill-horse. c. (Earlier example.)

1859 Mill *On Liberty* v. 203 The official body are under the constant temptation of sinking into indolent routine, or, if they now and then desert that mill-horse round, of rushing into some half-examined crudity which has struck the fancy of some leading member of the corps.

milli-. Add: *millibarn* [*barn *sb.* 1 d], *-calorie* (or *-calory*), *-curie*, *-gal* [*gal[2]], *-henry* [*henry[3]], *-joule*, *-kayser*, *-kelvin*, *-lambert*, *-micron*, *-mol*(*e* [*mole *sb.*[7]] (hence *-molar* adj.), *-poise* [*poise *sb.*[2]], *-rad*, *-radian*, *-rem*, *-roentgen*, *-watt*; **mi·llidegree**, a thousandth of a degree centigrade (kelvin); **mi:lli-equi·valent**, one thousandth of a gramme-equivalent; **milliosmol, -mole** (mili,ǫ·zmǫl, -mōᵘl) [f. blend of Osmotic *a.* and *mole *sb.*[7]], an amount of any osmotically effective ion in solution equal to a milligrame divided by the atomic weight of the ion; hence **milliosmo·lar** *a.*

Also combined with *micro-* to denote division by a thousand million (corresponding to the single prefix *nano-), as in *millimicro-ampere*, *-mole*, *-second*.

1955 *Physical Rev.* XCVII. 88 The cross section..has been calculated to be approximately 35 millibarns. **1958** O. R. Frisch *Nucl. Handbk.* i. 12 Nuclear cross sections are usually expressed in barns or millibarns. **1909** *Cent. Dict.* Suppl., Millicalory. **1937** *Geogr. Jrnl.* LXXXIX. 543 The cooling power of the atmosphere at 2.0 p.m...averages 6·7 millicalories per square centimetre per second. **1953** *Brit. Jrnl. Psychol.* Nov. 280 The heat intensity required to produce pain was measured with a radiometer.. the threshold being expressed in millicalories per second per square centimetre. **1910** E. Rutherford in *Nature* 6 Oct. 430/2 This matter was left for the consideration of the standards committee; the latter suggested that the name Curie should be used as a new unit to express the quantity or mass of radium emanation in equilibrium with one gram of radium (element). For example, the amount of emanation in equilibrium with one milligram of radium would be called 1/1000 Curie or one millicurie. **1947** *Sci. News* IV. 126 One millicurie of radium expels thirty million alpha particles per second. **1963** Millicurie [see *curie 1]. **1951** *Jrnl. Chem. Physics* XIX. 1161/1 The Curie temperatures are of the order of tens of millidegrees. **1974** *Physics Bull.* Mar. 93/2 The lighter isotope, ^{3}He, had until recently shown no anomalous behaviour even when cooled to temperatures of a few millidegrees. **1929** C. J. Engelder *Textbk. Elem. Quantitative Analysis* vii. 139

There is a gram-milliequivalent weight in 1 cc. of a normal solution. **1946** *Nature* 19 Oct. 556/2 The mean value for agouti mice is 121 milliequivalents per litre, and for black 124·5. **1965** *Math. in Biol. & Med.* (Med. Res. Council) I. 37 The computer prints out in milli-equivalents per litre all the major constituents of the plasma, cells and alveolar gases. **1914** Milligal [see *GAL[2]]. **1934** *Geogr. Jrnl.* LXXXIII. 446 The Bouguer anomalies are small on the coast and decrease steadily westward to about −150 milligals in Shansi. **1969** *New Scientist* 10 July 88/2 The gal is..a unit of one cm per second per second and a milligal thus approximately one millionth of the normal gravity of the Earth. **1909** *Cent. Dict.* Suppl., Millihenry. **1922** GLAZEBROOK *Dict. Appl. Physics* II. 421/1 All the coils are used in series for the higher range (9 to 105 millihenries), but only portions of each in series for the lower range (0·7 to 12 millihenries). **1950** *Engineering* 7 Apr. 398/3 In the rectifier positive lead, a 10-millihenry air-core reactor is connected. **1972** *Physics Bull.* Apr. 205/1 Methane–air can be reliably ignited by a spark discharge of only about one millijoule. **1968** *Chem. Abstr.* LXVIII. 4308/2 The Lamb shifts of the 4*S* and 3*S* levels of the II.. are, resp., 60 ± 4 millikaysers and 138·5 ± 1·6 millikaysers. **1970** G. K. WOODGATE *Elem. Atomic Struct.* i. 2 The term values T_i are written as positive numbers in units of cm^{-1}, recently re-named the Kayser (K). The new name is more commonly found when the sub-unit milli-Kayser is used; 1 mK = 10^{-3} cm^{-1}. **1972** *Physics Bull.* Feb. 85/3 Philips shows very thin metal foils between 2 and 10 μm thick being used to solve heat exchange problems at very low temperatures, a few millikelvin. **1918** WEBSTER Add., Milli-lambert. **1920** E. N. HARVEY *Nature Animal Light* iii. 64 The brightness of a surface is measured in lamberts or millilamberts... A millilambert is 1/1000 lambert. **1970** *Nature* 24 Jan. 347/2 Each pattern subtended 7° at the eye, and was projected..at an average screen illuminance of 3 millilamberts. **1956** Millimicroampere [see *COSMOTRON]. **1960** *Cambr. Rev.* 8 Oct. 21/2 The techniques developed for handling and measuring the amounts of steroids of only a few millimicromoles likely to be present in experimental samples have made steroid chromatography a leading branch of microanalysis. **1904** C. HERING *Ready Reference Tables* I. 31, 1 milli-micron (spectroscopy) or micro-millimeter (microscopy) = 10 Angstroem units. **1966** C. R. & T. S. LEESON *Histol.* ii. 22/2 One millimicron is one thousandth of a micron, i.e., 10 Å. **1956** *Proc. CERN Symposium* II. 69 (*heading*) Recent advances in millimicrosecond counting techniques. **1964** F. L. WESTWATER *Electronic Computers* viii. 127 Switching speeds of a few millimicroseconds appear possible. **1934** WEBSTER, Millimolar. **1941** *Jrnl. Physiol.* C. 61 The value of η represents the total indiffusible substance (as millimols), and of ε the difference between the total negative and positive charges on the indiffusible molecules (expressed as milliequivalents or valencies multiplied by the millimolar concentration). **1972** *Nature* 10 Mar. 57/3 Using lower than customary magnesium concentrations (in the region of millimolar), Allet finds that lithium and caesium chloride produce similar results. **1904** C. HERING *Ready Reference Tables* I. 60, 1 millimol = 0·001 mol or gram molecule. **1934** *Biochem. Jrnl.* XXVIII. 285 If we consider the titration of 1 ml. of *N*/10 acid delivered for example from a 1 ml. simple pyrex pipette..the coefficient of variation in millimols of KOH is 25 × 10^{-5}. **1937** PIERCE & HAENISCH *Quantitative Analysis* vi. 83 The choice of unit, millimole or mole, milliequivalent or equivalent, depends upon the unit of volume chosen. **1954** [see *ISOHYDRIC *a.* b]. **1970** R. W. MCGILVERY *Biochem.* xxv. 614 It requires 2·3 millimoles of H^+ to react with the hemoglobin in a liter of blood before the pH can change by 0·1 unit. **1939** J. L. GAMBLE *Chem. Anat., Physiol. & Path. Extracellular Fluid* Notes to chart 2 The term milliosmol is used to distinguish ionic from molecular concentration. The osmolal value of a solution of Na+Cl, for instance, is double the molal value. **1942** *Ibid.* (4th printing), The milliosmolar and milliequivalence values for the univalent ions are obviously identical. The chemical equivalence of the divalent ions is twice their milliosmolar value. The term milliosmolar is used instead of millimolar to make clear the additive osmotic effect of individual ions. **1959** *Pediatric Clinics N. Amer.* VI. 272 The nephritic patient who is unable to concentrate urine ..will need a water allowance..of approximately 3 ml. per milliosmol of total urinary solute. **1963** *Lancet* 12 Jan. 77/1 The last twelve patients admitted to this hospital with diabetic acidosis have had a calculated serum osmolarity greater than 300 milliosmoles per litre. **1972** *Science* 19 May 815/3 Severely disabled chicks..had plasma osmolality values (in milliosmoles per kilogram) of 335 ± 10 as compared with 309 ± 7 for controls. **1934** *Jrnl. Amer. Chem. Soc.* LVI. 998/2 We find the freezing point of our maximum density water to be 3·82°, and the viscosity at 20°, 12·6 millipoises. **1954** *Brit. Jrnl. Radiol.* XXVII. 247/1 The value is 30 millirad per week. **1973** *Times* 31 July 5/4 He said a total dose of 0·1 of a millirad —one-third of the normal background radioactive level— had been recorded during the 21 hours following the blast. **1956** *Spaceflight* I. 28/1 Despite errors caused by ionospheric refraction of the signal, the use of data from a number of stations will, it is claimed, enable the satellite's position to be established to within a fraction of a milliradian. **1971** *Sci. Amer.* June 65/1 A similar analysis of the collision kinematics indicates that the resolution in angle should be a fraction of a milliradian, which is about three minutes of arc. **1954** *Brit. Jrnl. Radiol.* XXVII. 246/1 Basic permissible weekly doses for the critical organs. Whole body exposure...0·3 millirems per week in blood-forming organs, the gonads and the eyes. **1971** *Sci. Amer.* Aug. 115/2 The U.S. Atomic Energy Commission requires that personnel working with radiation materials receive not more than 100 millirems of radiation per 40-hour week. **1955** *Sci. News Let.* 20 Aug. 116/1 A milliroentgen is one-thousandth the unit of quantity of X-rays. **1963** B. FOZARD *Instrumentation Nucl. Reactors* i. 3 It is..often necessary to measure dose rate; a convenient practical unit for this quantity is the milliroentgen per hour (mr/h). **1929** *Papers Inst. Post Office Electr. Engin.* CXXIX. 22 It is..sent to line at the power of 1 milli-watt. **1956** *Nature* 25 Feb. 392/1 This feature of existing methods [for the measurement of power] is particularly evident at low power-levels, of the order of 1 milliwatt, at wave-lengths of 3 cm. and less.

milliammeter (miliæ·mĭtəɹ). [f. MILLI- + AMMETER or MILLIAM(PÈRE + -METER.] An instrument for measuring currents of the order of milliamperes; = *milliampère meter*.

1902 G. B. MASSEY in H. R. Bigelow *Internat. Syst. Electro-Therapeutics* (ed. 2) B. 150 (*caption*) Weston milliammeter, arranged specially for medical work. **1946** *Nature* 28 Dec. 943/1 The received signal was recorded continuously on a recording milliammeter. **1966** *McGraw-Hill Encycl. Sci. & Technol.* I. 323/2 A rectifier-type ac milliammeter consisting of a small copper oxide or germanium bridge rectifier feeding a conventional dc milliammeter has low losses, good overload capacity, and adequate accuracy.

milliamp (mi·liˌæmp). Colloq. abbrev. of MILLIAMPÈRE.

1923 *Radio Times* 28 Sept. 19/2 Another [voice], 'Five milli amps. No! Sorry! I thought you were Cardiff.' **1927** *Sunday Express* 17 Apr. 8/3 (Advt.), Every milliamp of electricity is made by the dynamo. **1957** P. LAFITTE *Person in Psychol.* ii. 12 In the sciences, the fact is strictly the instrument reading..and the report of twenty milliamps..is in a sense an interpretation. **1970** D. F. SHAW *Introd. Electronics* (ed. 2) xiii. 323 Equation 13.13 (*b*) becomes $V_a = 400 - 40I_a$ where V_a is given in volts and I_a in milliamps.

milliampère. Add: Now usually written without an accent and stressed on the penultimate syllable. (Earlier and later examples.)

1885 *Jrnl. Soc. Telegr. Engin.* XIV. 465 It [*sc.* the current] was 2·632 milliampères. **1922** F. W. ASTON *Isotopes* 48 The bulb is arranged to take from 0·5 to 1 milliampere at potentials ranging from 20,000 to 50,000 volts. **1956** [see *COSMOTRON].

Hence **millia·mperage**, current expressed in, or of the order of, milliamperes.

1909 *Cent. Dict.* Suppl., Milliamperage. **1937** *Discovery* Feb. 54/1 The meter then reads to the corrected milliamperage of the total body surface-area. **1961** *Med. X-Ray Protection up to 3 Million Volts* (U.S. Nat. Bureau Standards Handbk. 76) 18 A beam monitoring device fixed in the useful beam is recommended to indicate any error due to incorrect filter, milliamperage, or kilovoltage.

Millian (mi·liăn), *a.* and *sb.* [f. the name of John Stuart *Mill* (1806–73), English philosopher + -IAN.] **A.** *adj.* Of or pertaining to Mill or his philosophical or political theories. **B.** *sb.* A follower of Mill or his theories. (See also *MILLITE *a.* and *sb.*)

1859 J. A. SYMONDS *Let.* Apr. (1967) I. 183 He has a truly *Millian* contempt for public opinion. **1950** E. NAGEL in Mill *Philos. Scientific Method* p. xlvii, There are doubtless no perfect Millians alive today. **1958** *Victorian Studies* I. 253 Later Millians,..such as Bain, Croom Robertson and Sully, were eclipsed by the bold but philosophically shallow eloquence of men like Huxley and Tyndall. **1972** *Times Lit. Suppl.* 14 Apr. 420/5 Practical criticism operated on the John Stuart Millian assumption that out of this bedlam the truth would ultimately emerge.

milliardaire (mi:liăɹdēə·ɹ). Now *rare.* [f. MILLIARD after MILLIONAIRE.] A person possessing a 'milliard of money'.

1924 *New Internat. Year Bk. for Year 1923* 270/2 A South-American milliardaire who can have all he wants. **1926** C. H. HERFORD *Mind of Post-War Germany* vii. 34 The hero, son of a milliardaire, is engaged in manufacturing a gas more powerful than all known fuels. **1927** *Spectator* 23 Apr. 720 Including..a respectable proportion of the Royal Families and aristocracy of most European countries, besides a sufficiency of 'milliardaires' from both Americas.

millibar (mi·libāɹ). *Meteorol.* [f. MILLI- + *BAR *sb.*[6]] The usual unit of barometric pressure, equal to one thousandth of a bar (*BAR *sb.*[6] 2), i.e. 1000 dynes per sq. cm.

1910, etc. [see *BAR *sb.*[6] 2]. **1914** *Q. Jrnl. R. Meteorol. Soc.* XL. 187 The megadyne per square centimetre has been adopted and called the 'bar'... The bar is less convenient for printing and conversation than the millibar, its 1/1000th part, and the latter has therefore been generally adopted; it is equivalent to the pressure produced by about three-hundredths of an inch of mercury or by three-quarters of a millimetre. **1924** *Glasgow Herald* 23 Dec. 5 So far as I can judge from the synoptic chart for December 9, 7 a.m.,..the pressure at New Pitsligo at 7 a.m. seems to have been 1016 millibars, and by noon to have risen to about 1012 millibars, equivalent to 30·12 inches. **1942** V. C. FINCH et al. *Elem. Meteorol.* v. 104, $\frac{1}{10}$ inch on a barometer or barograph is equivalent to about 3 millibars. Either inches or millibars may be used in numbering the isobars on a weather map. **1963** G. M. B. DOBSON *Exploring Atmosphere* i. 3 A scale at the side of the frontispiece gives the average pressure at different heights in millibars (mb), where 1000 mb is approximately the average pressure at sea level.

millieme (mĭ·lyēm). Also milleme, millime. [F. *millième* thousandth.] A unit of currency, equal to a thousandth of the main unit, orig. in Egypt, now in the United Arab Republic, the Sudan, and Tunisia.

1902 *Encycl. Brit.* XXVII. 700/1 The unit is the Egyptian pound, which is divided into 100 piastres, the piastre being again divided in 10 milliemes. *Ibid.*, Pieces of 20, 10, 5, 2, and 1 piastres in silver; 5, 2, and 1 milliemes in nickel. **1919** W. H. DOWNING *Digger Dial.* 34 *Milleme*, a small Egyptian coin. **1942** C. BARRETT *On Wallaby* vi. 122 His son went round with a tambourine collecting stray milliemes. **1956** E. E. EVANS-PRITCHARD *Nuer Relig.* iii. 88 A Nuer refused to accept a milleme coin ..because a boy of his family, when playing with a milleme, got it into his ear and died. **1972** *Whitaker's Almanack 1973* 987 Tunisian Dinar of 1,000 Millimes. *Ibid.*, Sudanese Pound of 100 Piastres or 1,000 Milliemes. **1973** *Country Life* 20 Sept. 805/3 [Tunisia] One morning I was offered a necklace for '800 millimes and packet fags'.

milligrain, var. *MILLEGRAIN.

millilitre. Add: Also (*U.S.*) **-liter.** (Later examples.)

1896 C. R. HONIBALL *Engin. Arithmetic & Mensuration* xli. 308 Millilitre = ·001 Litres. **1935** C. J. SMITH *Intermediate Physics* (ed. 2) ix. 172 The litre and the millilitre (ml.) are now frequently chosen as the unit of volume, burettes, flasks, etc. being marked in millilitres and fractions thereof. **1960** *Science* 22 July 204/2, 1 billion of these units result from treating 15 milligrams of the proteinoid with 2·5 millilitres of hot water and allowing the clear solution to cool. **1969** *Guardian* 28 Feb. 4/4 Every patient prescribed liquid medicine by his doctor will receive a plastic spoon which will hold five millilitres of medicine; and all prescriptions will be in five millilitre units. **1974** *Daily Tel.* 10 Oct. 2/4 [He] had 120 milligrammes of alcohol in 100 millilitres of blood, 40 over the legal limit.

millimetric (milime·trik), *a.* [f. MILLIMETR(E + -IC.] **a.** *fig.* Minute.

1909 *Milton Memorial Lect.* 194 Those millimetric distinctions by which human character declines or ascends. **1937** E. POUND *Let.* 30 Nov. (1971) 300 As I haven't yet a projector, the small but not millimetric photos would save time. **1965** *Economist* 28 Aug. 772/2 Participation in the congress and the administrative bureaucracy is to be shared with 'millimetric' equality.

b. Of the order of a millimetre in length; employing or characterized by electromagnetic waves of this wavelength.

1962 *Newnes Conc. Encycl. Electr. Engin.* 883/2 The use of waveguides of practicable size is restricted to waves in the microwave region (i.e. centimetric and millimetric wavelengths). **1969** A. L. CULLEN in F. A. Benson *Millimetre & Submillimetre Waves* i. 5 For many purposes.. microwave radar was found to possess advantages over millimetric radar. **1973** *Physics Bull.* Feb. 99/2 The properties measured include..the absorption of millimetric microwaves. *Ibid.* Nov. 651/2 These direct measurements initially suggested that the millimetric background temperature was much *more* than 2·7 K.

mill-in: see *-IN *suffix*[3].

milliner, *v.* [f. MILLINER 2.] To make up articles of women's clothing, esp. hats. Also *fig.*

1885 G. B. SHAW *Cashel Byron's Profession* (1886) iii. 34 We will go to Paris, and be millinered there. **1895** —— *Our Theatres in Nineties* (1932) I. 205 The displays of fashionable life..are now millinered and tailored ..by the artists and tradesmen who equip the real fashionable world. **1907** in C. W. Cunnington *Eng. Women's Clothing* (1952) ii. 79 A modified *cloche* 'millinered' in a light rough-surfaced cloth.

millinering, *vbl. sb.* (Earlier example.)

1857 GEO. ELIOT *Scenes Clerical Life* (1858) II. 99 It was hard for Mrs. Raynor to have to work at millinering— a woman well brought up.

millinery. Add: **3.** *millinery wire.*

1912 *Every Woman's Encycl.* VII. 4447/2 Get some dark green millinery wire covered. **1932** D. C. MINTER *Mod. Needlecraft* 174/1 *Lace Trimmings*..are always mounted on thin millinery wire. **1966** *Olney Amsden & Sons Ltd. Price List* 29 Millinery wires..Satin wire..7/- dozen.

milling, *vbl. sb.* Add: **1.** (Further example.)

1877 *Amer. Miller* Mar. 39/1 The process of milling in the United States is carried on under two different systems, namely, low milling and high, or grits, milling.

3*. The action of MILL *v.*[1] 12 a.

1874 J. MCCOY *Hist. Sk. Cattle Trade* 101 Drovers consider that the cattle do themselves great injury by running round in a circle, which is termed in cow-boy parlance, 'milling'. **1924** *Scribner's Mag.* Dec. 607 Jack..stood outside the door and watched the milling of the excited, hysterical women. **1943** C. H. WARD-JACKSON *Piece of Cake* 41 *Milling, milling around*, flying at high speed in and out across one another's path; or flying in a defensive circle, with the nose of one aircraft a few yards from the tail of another.

4. milling machine, (*a*) *Engin.*, a machine in which a work-piece fixed to a carriage is subjected to the action of rotating cutters; (*b*) a machine for fulling cloth.

1876 [in Dict.] **1888** *Encycl. Brit.* XXIV. 661/2 The cloth to be fulled is well saturated with hot soap and water ..and rubbed between rollers in the milling-machine while so heated and soaped. **1953** L. E. DOYLE *Metal Machining* xii. 266 A milling machine must hold and rotate a cutter and have means to hold a workpiece and move it uniformly in at least one direction. **1962** W. J. ONIONS *Wool* xi. 245 In the operation of milling..fabrics are thickened and shrunk to a desired width..The operation is usually carried out in the rotary milling machine.

milling, *ppl. a.* **3.** (Further examples.)

1919 L. F. CODY *Memories Buffalo Bill* xiii. 289 Here the buffalo thundered along in their milling herd, while Will and the assembled cowboys circled them. **1931** H. F.

PRINGLE *Theodore Roosevelt* I. viii. 99 The milling crowds of the cities.

million. Add: **1. a.** (*a*) (Further example.) Also in phr. *thanks a million*: see *THANK *sb.*

1934 J. B. PRIESTLEY *Eng. Journey* ix. 316 This [ship-]yard..had been a spectacular failure in which over a million of money had been lost.

b. (Further examples.) Also in phr. (chiefly *U.S.*) (*like*) *a million dollars*: excellent, splendid, magnificent (usu. prec. by *to feel* or *to look*).

1925 WODEHOUSE *Carry on, Jeeves!* iii. 55 It was one of those topping mornings, and I had just climbed out from under the cold shower feeling like a million dollars. **1933** E. E. CUMMINGS *eimi* 109 Something which might be port ..'Looks like a million dollars'—and which tastes like awfully watered vino rosso à l'américain. **1933** ADE *Let.* 13 Nov. (1973) 176 Those [farm buildings] that have been repaired..and painted look like a million dollars compared with most of the nearby so-called improvements. **1947** *Time* 17 Mar. 43 You'll go home feeling like a million dollars, rested and refreshed as never before! **1956** D. GASCOYNE *Night Thoughts* 35 You'd look a million dollars at your worst. **1969** C. ALLEN *Text-bk. Psychosexual Disorders* (ed. 2) xx. 400 If..abnormal habits are allowed to become fixed, the patient becomes a million times more difficult to treat. **1973** *Times* 23 Apr. 5/6 A formula not a million miles removed from that of BBC 2's now defunct *Late Night Line-up.* **1973** BOYD & PARKES *Dark Number* xiii. 150 Dorothy looked, as they say, a million dollars: brushed, scrubbed, wholesome and sane. **1974** WODEHOUSE *Aunts aren't Gentlemen* ix. 75 His refusal to do as Miss Cook asked was unequivocal. 'Not in a million years' was the expression he used.

2. c. *a million to one*: a million chances to one; hence, an expression indicating very low probability. Freq. *attrib.*

1761 STERNE *Tr. Shandy* IV. ix. 73 Calculate it fairly.. and it will turn out a million to one, that..the forceps should have the ill luck just to fall upon..that one part. **1900** C. H. CHAMBERS *Tyranny of Texas* I. 9 The article hasn't a million to one chance of being finished this afternoon. **1962** P. BRICKHILL *Deadline* v. 78 So I'm supposed to..roam Paris for weeks on the million-to-one chance of spotting someone. **1974** J. WAINWRIGHT *Hard Hit* 103 It might go wrong—there's a million-to-one chance.

d. *pl.* In full, *millions fish*; = *GUPPY[1].

1906 *Chambers's Jrnl.* Apr. 345/2 A tiny fish known locally by the name of 'millions'. **1908** *Science* 18 Dec. 885/2 'Millions' are among the most active natural enemies of mosquitos. **1924** *Glasgow Herald* 2 June 11/2 In Barbadoes..the natives are accustomed to keep in their rain barrels the minute fish known as 'millions'... Hence the absence of mosquitoes. **1966** D. W. TUCKER tr. *Sterba's Freshwater Fishes of World* (ed. 2) 568 *Lebistes reticulatus*... Guppy, Millions Fish. Venezuela, Barbados, Trinidad, parts of northern Brazil and Guiana.

e. (*one*) *in a million*: (a person, thing, etc.) that is very rare, unusual, or valuable.

1900 CONRAD *Ld. Jim* viii. 99 The occasion was obscure, insignificant—what you will: a lost youngster, one in a million—but then he was one of us. **1906** E. NESBIT *Railway Children* xiii. 288 Take care of your Mother... She's a woman in a million. **1925** WODEHOUSE *Carry on, Jeeves!* i. 30 You know, Jeeves, you're by way of being rather a topper... One in a million, by Jove! **1931** *Times Lit. Suppl.* 5 Feb. 96/3 Emily was, of course, a chimp..in a million.

f. *gone a million*: (having) completely lost, done for, in a hopeless state. *Austral.* and *N.Z. colloq.*

1916 C. J. DENNIS *Battle of Wazzir* in A. H. Chisholm *Making of Sentimental Bloke* (1963) 131 Fer young Bill wus gone a million, an' 'e never guessed the game. **1922** A. WRIGHT *Colt from Country* 142 What hope would you have when that came out? You'd be gone a million. **1930** K. S. PRICHARD *Haxby's Circus* xvi. 187 If it weren't for you, I'd be gone a million on the minx. **1941** *Coast to Coast* 209 No doubt about it, Sim was right. If they drop their bundles they're gone a million. **1958** *N.Z. Listener* 23 May 6/4 We scraped in in that game, only because Elvidge scored his usual try... Otherwise, we were gone a million.

3. (*b*) **million-dollar** *a.*, worth or costing a million dollars; (also, *transf.* and *fig.*) expensive-looking; magnificent, splendid; very attractive; (*c*) *million-dollared* (*absol.* in quot. = 'a person who has a million dollars'), *-footed, -pointed, -voiced,* adjs.; **millionheiress,** an heiress to a 'million of money'; **million-seller,** a gramophone record, book, etc., of which a million copies have been sold.

1892 Milliondollar [in Dict.]. **1921** *Discovery* Feb. 48/1 The water hyacinth..is a beautiful aquatic plant..but its spread in St. John's River and the enormous sums spent in attempting its suppression have earned it the name of the 'million-dollar weed'. **1932** *Amer. Speech* VII. 250 Bing Crosby plaintively croons that he has 'Found a Million Dollar Baby in the Five and Ten Cent Store'. **1959** *Listener* 5 Mar. 432/1 A man in a million-dollar suit. **1961** J. HELLER *Catch-22* (1962) xxvii. 296 I've got this million-dollar leg wound that will take me out of combat. **1972** *News & Observer* (Raleigh, N. Carolina) 30 Dec. 4/2 We don't hear much [nowadays] about..million dollar rains, and undertakers. **1857** J. G. WHITTIER *Barefoot Boy* in *Poetical Works* II. 230 Let the million-dollared ride! Barefoot, trudging at his side, Thou hast more than he can buy. **1865** W. WHITMAN *Drum-Taps* 61 When million-footed Manhattan, unpent, descends to its pavements. **1885** W. B. YEATS *Island of Statues* II. iii, in *Dublin Univ. Rev.* July 137/1 Though I be Far fleeter than the million-footed sea. **1919** W. DE MORGAN *Old Madhouse* 457 His mind took kindly to the interruption of this young man's nuptials with an American millionheiress of startling beauty. **1942** BERREY & VAN DEN BARK *Amer. Thes. Slang* § 417 *Millionheiress*, a woman who is a millionaire. **1923** Million-pointed [see *million-voiced* below]. **1969** N. COHN *A WopBopaLooBop* (1970) iii. 27 He [*sc.* Elvis Presley] has racked up twenty worldwide million sellers. **1971** *Shout* Dec.. They performed Ship of Love & of course the near-millionseller Story Untold. **1972** *Jazz & Blues* Sept. 11/2 Fats Domino cut 16 million-sellers in this town. **1894** 'MARK TWAIN' *Those Twins* 322 The two sat unconscious of the million-voiced music of the mosquitos. **1923** BELLOC *Sonnets & Verse* 149 To-night in million-voicèd London I Was lonely as the million-pointed sky.

millionaire. Add: **1. c.** *Millionaires' Row*: a street containing the residences of very rich people.

1950 'J. GUTHRIE' *Is this what I Wanted?* iii. 56 Charles drove off past the park, the Broad Walk and Millionaire's Row. **1954** 'N. BLAKE' *Whisper in Gloom* iii. 43 [The Bentley]..swept through the doorway of 'Millionaires' Row'. **1964** B. WYNNE *Spies Within* iv. 37 What about their radio, in 'Millionaires' Row'? **1972** *Guardian* 19 Dec. 11/1 My Gozan friend had ragged, empty pockets.. but he lived on millionaires' row.

2. Used *attrib.* of a town with more than a million population.

1936 C. B. FAWCETT in Salamon & Kuchar *Mélanges de Géogr. offerts à V. Švambera* 52 A 'millionaire-city' is to be understood as a conurbation which contains at least one million inhabitants. **1958** D. L. LINTON in *Geography* XLIII. 258 The emergence of millionaire cities and even five-million cities in tropical countries is now widespread and continuing. **1961** *Land Use in Urban Environment* (Univ. of Liverpool, Dept. Civic Design) 11 The great concentration of population, housing, offices and factories in the millionaire cities.

millionai·reship. [-SHIP.] The position or state of a millionaire.

1901 *Chambers's Jrnl.* Apr. 217/2 The flour industry gave the late Mr. Charles A. Pillsbury the means of millionaireship. **1930** W. O. STAPLEDON *Last & First Men* 78 For the Individual, the goal imposed by his religious teaching was continuous advance in aeronautical prowess, legal sexual freedom, and millionaireship.

millionairess. Delete *jocular* and add further examples.

1887 *Atlantic Monthly* LX. 222 Stuffs which none but an empress or a millionairess would dare to look at. **1906** L. BELL *Carolina Lee* 38 You'll have to go on being a millionairess, whether you will or no. **1958** [see *BEERAGE]. **1971** *Nature* 17 Dec. 377/1 Mrs Mary Lasker, a New York millionairess and philanthropist. **1973** *Daily Tel.* 29 Oct. 15/4 We could be millionairesses if we were concerned only with money.

Millipore (mi·lipōəɹ). Also **millipore.** [f. MILLI- + PORE *sb.*[1]] Designating membrane filters made by the Millipore Filter Corporation of Watertown, Mass., or by a foreign subsidiary of this company.

1956 *Jrnl. Bacteriol.* LXXI. 499 Direct staining procedures for microorganisms collected on the 'millipore filter'. **1962** F. I. ORDWAY et al. *Basic Astronautics* iv. 131 Air moves through the opening into the 2-cm diameter chamber at the rear of which is located a millipore filter in a removable housing. **1967** *Oceanogr. & Marine Biol.* V. 171 Filtration through fine Millipore filters removes more of the finely dispersed material. **1969** *Methods in Microbiol.* I. vii. 207 The standard Millipore filters.

millisecond (mi·lisekənd). [f. MILLI- + SECOND *sb.*[1]] One thousandth of a second.

1922 GLAZEBROOK *Dict. Appl. Physics* II. 421/1 The arrangement of the coils is astatic and the time constant is about 1·6 milliseconds at the maximum. **1929** *Papers Inst. Post Office Electr. Engin.* CXXII. 11 It would be difficult to read to an accuracy of less than about 10 milliseconds. **1960** E. DELAVENAY *Introd. Machine Transl.* vi. 82 The lexical memory of the machine should provide random access to any word in not more than 10 milliseconds. **1973** C. EGLETON *Seven Days to Killing* i. 16 The car disintegrated, and a millisecond later the blast wave shattered the windscreen in the cab of the truck.

millisite (mi·lisəit). *Min.* [f. the name of F. T. *Millis* (see quot. 1930) + -ITE[1].] A light grey or white hydrated basic phosphate of sodium, potassium, calcium, and aluminium, (Na,K) $CaAl_6(PO_4)_4(OH)_9.3H_2O$.

1930 LARSEN & SHANNON in *Amer. Mineralogist* XV. 329 The name millisite is proposed for the species after F. T. Millis who sent the original specimens to the U. S. National Museum. **1942** *Ibid.* XXVII. 294 Millisite is invariably associated with wardite as alternating layers in spherules or crusts. It is light gray to white in color, and normally is present as layers of fine fibers normal to the layering. **1965** *Jrnl. Geol. Soc. Austral.* XII. 261 Crandallite and millisite occur in the lateritic profiles derived from apatite and barrandite and the weathering, in the presence of phosphate, of the carbonate and volcanic rocks [on Christmas Island].

Millite (mi·ləit), *a.* and *sb.* [f. the name *Mill* *(see *MILLIAN *a.* and *sb.*) + -ITE[1] I a.] = MILLIAN *a.* and *sb.*

1917 J. MORLEY *Recoll.* I. iv. 52 It was, in fact, the pure milk of the Millite word. *Ibid.* vi. 87 He [*sc.* Bagehot]..was not in the least an orthodox Millite. **1949** G. B. SHAW *Sixteen Self-Sketches* x. 56 Both societies were strongly Millite.

millivolt. Add: (Examples.)

In quot. 1861 *volt* is being used for what is now called an ohm.

1861 *Electrician* 9 Nov. 3/2 The application of the French system of notation in the table, is evidently faulty, the thousandth part of a volt being one milivolt [*sic*], and not one kilovolt, as stated. **1885** *Jrnl. Soc. Telegr. Engin.* XIV. 196 Differences of potential greater than such millivolts as are concerned in thermo-electricity. **1971** *Jrnl. Gen. Psychol.* LXXXIV. 11 A sensitivity of about 60 to 200 millimetres per millivolt was used for the average preparation.

Hence **millivo·ltmeter,** an instrument for measuring voltages of the order of millivolts.

1907 H. H. NORRIS *Introd. Study Electr. Engin.* xii. 346 The instrument..usually known as a milli-voltmeter. **1971** *Nature* 15 Jan. 167/2 Screen leads connected the coils to a millivoltmeter arranged to read from −50 to +50.

millocracy. Delete *nonce-wd.* and add further examples.

1956 G. S. HAIGHT in Geo. Eliot *Lett.* VI. 286 A small boarding school for girls..drawn largely from the millocracy, rich and profoundly ignorant. **1970** R. BLAKE *Conservative Party* i. 21 Why should not the landed aristocracy join hands with the socially dispossessed..against the northern 'millocracy'?

millpond. b. Add:

The use is anticipated in, and perhaps originally suggested by, the following passages:—

1813 'H. BULL-US' *Diverting Hist. John Bull & Bro. Jonathan* (ed. 2) i. 5 He put himself in a boat, and paddled over the mill-pond to some new lands. *Ibid.* ii. 12 The tenants began to carry their grain to different parts of the great mill-pond.

Mills (milz). The name of Sir William *Mills* (1856–1932) used *attrib.*, as *Mills bomb, grenade*, etc., to designate a type of hand grenade, serrated on the outside to form shrapnel on explosion, invented by him.

1916 *War Illustr.* 30 Sept. 162/1 (*caption*) 'Lobbing' a Mills grenade. **1917** G. M. AINSLIE *Hand Grenades* 8 Grenade hand no. 5. Mark I. Mills hand grenade. **1917** A. G. EMPEY *From Fire Step* xii. 74 The standard bomb used in the British Army is the 'Mills'. It is about the shape and size of a large lemon. **1923** KIPLING *Irish Guards in Gt. War* I. 75 The Mills bomb..was not born till the autumn of 1915. **1935** C. DAY LEWIS *Time to Dance* 38 But the aeronauts, knowing iron the coinage here, had brought Mills bombs and revolvers. **1942** J. T. GORMAN *Mod. Weapons War* vii. 121 The segmented jacket of a Mills bomb or hand-grenade is not unlike that of a pomegranate's ridged outer rind. **1973** J. WAINWRIGHT *Pride of Pigs* 17 Any damn fool can work a Mills hand grenade..slip your finger through the split-ring, jerk out the pin and throw. *Ibid.*, He smuggled a Mills bomb home in..his kitbag as a memento of El Alamein. **1974** *Daily Tel.* 6 May 1/6 A fully-primed Mills bomb which had been used as a mantelpiece ornament for 56 years was handed to police at Nottingham yesterday.

Mill's Methods (milz me·þŏdz). *Logic.* The Methods of Agreement, of Difference, of Joint Agreement and Difference, of Residues, and of Concomitant Variations which form the five canons of inductive inquiry proposed by J. S. Mill (1806–73) for discovering, and establishing the validity of, causal relations between phenomena. Cf. *METHOD *sb.* 2 c.

1896 J. WELTON *Man. Logic* II. v. v. 141 (*caption*) As Mill's Methods have obtained general currency they demand some examination. **1922** W. E. JOHNSON *Logic* II. x. 217, I hold..that Mill's methods can and should be exhibited as strictly formal. **1942** D. RUNES *Dict. Philos.* (1944) 197/2 *Mill's methods*, inductive methods formulated by John Stuart Mill for the discovery of causal relations between phenomena. **1953** S. E. TOULMIN *Philos. of Sci.* i. 9 The accumulation of confirming instances, Mill's Methods and the probability-calculus: such things form the staple of most expositions. **1965** P. CAWS *Philos. of Sci.* xxxiii. 251 Mill's methods..are an elegant recipe for detecting the constant conjunctions of which Hume speaks. **1973** H. C. BYERLY *Primer of Logic* v. xiii. 423 (*heading*) Mill's methods for discovering causes: agreement and difference.

Milltown: see *MILTOWN.

millwrighting, *vbl. sb.* (Further example.) Also as *ppl. a.*

1821 A. CONSTABLE *Let.* 25 June in J. Constable *Correspondence* (1962) I. 200 Several millwrighting jobs coming in [so] that I cannot keep my money in my pocket. **1949** K. S. WOODS *Rural Crafts Eng.* II. iv. 76 Where local smiths have lost the art the bills are sent away to millwrighting firms.

millyum (mi·lyŏm), representing a colloq. pronunciation of *million. rare.*

1940 E. POUND *Cantos* liv. 40 Jobs for two millyum men. *Ibid.* lvi. 58 Thus saved several millyum lives of those chinamen. **1955** —— *Section: Rock-Drill* lxxxix. 53 And in '34 presumably will be 2 millyum.

milo (məi·lo). Also **millo, milo maize.** [ad. Sotho *maili.*] One of a group of drought-resistant varieties of the grass *Sorghum vulgare*,

introduced from Africa to suitable regions elsewhere. Also *attrib.*

1882 *Rep. Comm. Agric. Georgia 1881–82* 23 My attention was some time since called to the claims of 'Ivory wheat' and 'Millo Maize' to a place in our long list of profitable food crops. **1887** *Florida Dispatch* 10 Jan. 34/3 The head of yellow millo maize is formed in sections of smaller heads, lying very close and compact. *Ibid.* 14 Feb. 165/3 Mr. Jones recommends the substitution of Kaffir corn, Milo Maizo, etc., for a part of the corn crop. **1920** *U.S. Dept. Agric. Farmers' Bull.* No. 1147. 3 Milo has long since passed the experimental stage as a farm crop in the southwestern United States... Milo made its first appearance in this country soon after 1880. **1965** T. CAPOTE *In Cold Blood* (1966) i. 7 One of these barns.. housed a dark, pungent hill of milo grain. **1970** H. DOGGETT *Sorghum* iii. 88 The milos of the U.S.A. stem from one introduction. **1972** *Islander* (Victoria, B.C.) 12 Mar. 11/1 Milomaize is a white corn, something like wheat. We ground it in an old coffee grinder for bread, also boiled it for porridge. **1973** *Houston* (Texas) *Chron.* 21 Oct. 26 Cotton, wheat, milo, corn and soybean production can be increased tremendously.

milometer (məilǫ·mĭtəɹ). Also **mileometer.** [f. MILE *sb.*[1] + -OMETER.] An instrument which is fitted to a vehicle to record the distance in miles travelled by it.

1953 A. SMITH *Blind White Fish in Persia* 218 Every time another 1,000 miles was registered by the milometer, those in front would cheer a little. **1963** 'B. GRAEME' *Almost without Murder* xv. 170 We hit a toll road, whereupon the milometer ticked off the miles with boring rapidity. **1968** *Punch* 31 July 172/1 One army jeep being driven aimlessly around by Georg in order that its mileometer shall record that monthly mileage total considered by higher authority appropriate for army vehicles. **1974** *Times* 9 Oct. 14/1 Guilty..of..offering for sale cars whose milometers had been altered to show a lower reading. **1975** G. LYALL *Judas Country* xxi. 153 From the mileometer I'd guess she was only just run in.

milord. Add to def.: *spec.* an Englishman travelling in Europe in aristocratic style. (Earlier and later examples.) Hence **milo·rdliness, milo·rdism.**

[**1598** J. CHAMBERLAIN *Let.* 17 Sept. (1939) I. 45 Yet me thincks still I am out of my element when I am among Lords, and I am of Rabelais minde that they looke big *comme un millord d'Angleterre.*] **1758** M. W. MONTAGU *Let.* May (1967) III. 149 He brags of having done his duty in waiting on the two Milordi. **1822** L. SIMOND *Trav. Switzerland* I. 357 Accustomed to the *Milords Anglais* of former times. **1920** A. HUXLEY *Leda* 44 They behaved like English aristocrats in a French novel... I tried to imitate their milordliness. **1931** R. CHURCH *High Summer* I. i. 8 A tall young man, very shy and nervous, very English, but trying to hide these insular virtues behind the assumption of lofty milordism. **1945** E. WAUGH *Brideshead Revisited* I. viii. 185 It's not as though he lived like a Milord. **1954** [see *EDWARDIAN *sb.* 3]. **1961** A. WILSON *Old Men at Zoo* i. 9 The Zoo authorities had been very indulgent to a number of 'milord' whims that were perhaps more in keeping with an aesthetic undergraduate. **1969** *Listener* 6 Feb. 180/3 The great man scampered about, huffing and puffing, playing the magnificent milord.

Milori (milōə·ri). Also **Milory.** The name of the 19th-cent. French colour-maker A. *Milori* used *attrib.* in **Milori blue,** a particularly pure variety of Prussian blue (PRUSSIAN *a.* 2); **Milori green** = *chrome green* (CHROME 3).

1885 J. S. TAYLOR *Fields's Chromatogr. Modernized* 194 *Milory green,* syn. Chrome Green. **1899** B. W. WARHURST *Colour Dict.* 47 *Milori,* full to dark greens; also Chinese blue. **1924** F. W. WEBER *Artists' Pigments* 2 Prussian Blue..was put on the market under quite an array of names..Turnbull's Blue, Paris Blue,..Milori Blue, Chinese Blue [etc.]. **1951** R. MAYER *Artist's Handbk.* ii. 77 There is a great difference in clarity and beauty of colour as well as in permanence between the common varieties of Prussian blue and the very best, well-washed grades, such as the pure Chinese or Milori blues. **1963** *New Yorker* 8 June 20 Wool carpets only come in these colors: ..Milori Green. **1967** [see *IRON-BLUE c].

milpa (mi·lpă). [Mexican Sp.] In Central America and Mexico, a small cultivated field, usually of corn or maize; also, designating a method of cultivation practised in tropical regions (see quot. 1936).

1844 J. GREGG *Commerce Prairies* I. 150 The *labores* and *milpas* (cultivated fields) are often..without any enclosure. **1869** J. R. BROWNE *Adventures Apache Country* 164 Our houses were closely picketed in the milpas, or corn-fields, down by the river. **1934** A. HUXLEY *Beyond Mexique Bay* 216 The peasant may need only two or three acres for his *milpa.* **1936** *Nature* 26 Dec. 1090/1 The cultivation of maize..is on the milpa system; that is, a plot, after being burned off, is cultivated for two years, when it is allowed to revert to forest conditions, taking about eight to ten years to become completely re-established and ready for burning off again. **1956** R. REDFIELD *Peasant Society & Culture* iv. 118 To the Maya Indian labor on the milpa is dignified by its connections with religion and manly virtue. **1964** *Sci. Amer.* Nov. 101/1 In Central America the Mayas,..who depended greatly on the milpa system of agriculture, were forced to abandon their cities and move north into Mexico. **1974** *Environmental Conservation* I. 17/1 This is the so-called 'slash-and-burn' or 'milpa' system, as practised in the humid tropics.

Milquetoast (mi·lktōust). orig. *U.S.* Also with small initial. [f. the name of Caspar *Milquetoast,* a cartoon character created by H. T. Webster in 1924.] A timid or unforthcoming person. Also *attrib.* or as *adj.*

1938 M. FISHBACK *Safe Conduct* vi. 70 Don't be a Milquetoast either, and be afraid to add it [*sc.* the bill] up. **1939** C. MORLEY *Kitty Foyle* xxx. 305 What is it makes a man with brains so milquetoast when he gets away from the blackboard? **1961** M. BEADLE *These Ruins are Inhabited* iii. 34 American men are Milquetoasts. **1972** L. O'DONNELL *Phone Calls* vi. 73 You couldn't expect Norah to respect a Milquetoast. **1973** *Observer* (Colour Suppl.) 4 Nov. 12/3 Any of those milquetoast settings that Britten gave Wilfred Owen's poems in the 'War Requiem'. **1974** *Ottawa Citizen* 3 Sept. 71/1 I'm wondering if a judge would let me change my perfectly good but milquetoast name to something no one will forget, like—Jake Sexchamp.

milreis. Add to def.: replaced by new currency in Portugal in 1911 (see quot.); and in Brazil in 1942 (see *CRUZEIRO).

1913 *Statesman's Yearbk.* 1155 The Decree of the Provisional Government of May 22, 1911, established a new monetary system... The unit is the gold *escudo,* of 100 *centavos,* which is equivalent to the 1-milreis gold piece.

Milton (mi·ltǫn). **1.** Name of the English poet John *Milton* (1608–74) used in the phr. *mute inglorious Milton* (see quot. 1751) to symbolize the idea of native ability frustrated by lack of opportunity.

1751 GRAY *Elegy* 8 Some mute inglorious Milton here may rest. **1883** *Authors & Publishers* (G. P. Putnam's Sons) 61 We do not believe that our American prairies conceal any Charlotte Brontës to whom the opportunity for expression and fame has been denied, or that a careful search through American villages would develop any 'mute, inglorious Miltons' rusting away their undeveloped lives. **1922** H. L. MENCKEN *Prejudices* (1923) 3rd Ser. iii. 89 A genuine artist..would have thoughts and feelings of his own, and the impulse to give them objective form would be irresistible... There are no mute inglorious Miltons, save in the hallucinations of poets. The one sound test of a Milton is that he functions as a Milton. **1933** J. BUCHAN *Prince of Captivity* I. iv. 125 We've got to see that our Miltons don't remain mute and inglorious, but above all that our Hampdens are not left to rot on a village green. **1948** T. S. ELIOT *Notes Def. Culture* vi. 102 The Equality of Opportunity dogma..derives emotional reinforcement from the belief in the mute inglorious Milton. This myth assumes that a great deal of first-rate ability—not merely ability, but genius—is being wasted for lack of education.

2. [Perh. a different word.] *slang.* An oyster.

1841 THACKERAY *Professor* ii, in *Bentley's Misc.* Sept. 285 Mrs. Grampus herself operated with the oyster-knife, and served the Milton morsels to the customers. **1845** 'BON GAULTIER' *Bk. Ballads* 35 Fill me once more the foaming pewter up! Another board of oysters, ladye mine! To night Lucullus with himself shall sup, These mute inglorious Miltons are divine.

miltonia (miltōu·niă). [mod.L. (J. Lindley 1837, in *Bot. Reg.* XXIII. 1976), f. the name of Charles William Wentworth Fitzwilliam, Viscount *Milton,* later 3rd Earl Fitzwilliam (1786–1857), English politician and horticulturist + -IA[1].] An epiphytic orchid of the tropical, South American genus so called, belonging to the family Orchidaceæ and bearing brilliantly coloured flowers.

1838 J. LINDLEY *Sertum Orchidaceum* plate 21 It [*sc. Miltonia candida*] differs in the structure of its column and labellum..from the original Miltonia. **1890** W. WATSON *Orchids* xli. 315 Miltonias are easily propagated. **1930** T. W. BRISCOE *Orchids for Amateurs* viii. 120, I have found the addition of a small portion of partly decayed oak or beech leaves has had very beneficial results on all the Miltonias. **1963** *Times* 6 Feb. 12/3 One exhibit of orchids contains many beautiful cypripediums and miltonias.

Miltonian, *a.* Add: As *sb.,* an admirer or imitator of Milton.

1842 DICKENS *Let.* 19 Oct. (1974) III. 352, I have been *going,* every day, to write to you about the Miltonians. **1907** *Illustr. London News* 4 May 672/1 Nearly all Englishmen are either Shakespearians or Miltonians... Each represents something in the make-up of England. **1947** A. J. A. WALDOCK *Paradise Lost* i. 9 Grierson..observed, supervised and corrected; but not yet had England produced a New Miltonian. **1960** *Times* 22 Sept. 15/4 The most dyed-in-the-wool Miltonian.

Miltonic, *a.* (and *sb.*). Add: **2.** As *sb. pl.,* verses, or style, typical of Milton.

1928 O. BARFIELD *Poetic Diction* x. 177 No one would have dreamed of employing the stale Miltonics, which lay at the bottom of so much eighteenth-century 'poetic diction', in *prose,* however imaginative. **1944** F. R. LEAVIS in *Scrutiny* XII. 202 Johnson's disapproval of Gray's Pinderick sublimities goes with his disapproval of Miltonics.

Miltonically, *adv.* (Earlier example.)

1853 DE QUINCEY *Autobiogr. Sk.* I. i. 2, I here record the entire list of my brothers and sisters..and Miltonically I include myself.

Miltonism. Add: (Later example.) Also **Milto·nicism.**

1936 F. R. LEAVIS *Revaluation* ii. 46 A common, limply pompous Miltonicism. **1938** E. POUND *Let.* 8 May (1971) 316, I do, however, prefer your 'supreme Hippocrates' [line 137]... Miltonism tho' it may be.

Miltonize, *v.* Add: Hence **Mi·ltonizing** *ppl. a.* and *vbl. sb.*

1936 F. R. LEAVIS *Revaluation* iv. 116 The meditative-Miltonizing poetic modes. **1944** —— in *Scrutiny* XII. 189 The author of *The Vanity of Human Wishes* has, as critic, no weakness..for the Miltonizing habit of his age. **1953** H. HOUSE *Coleridge* iii. 65 This Miltonising is not a mere matter of poetical echoes..it is part of a conscious political act. **1958** *Essays & Stud.* v. 69 These larger Miltonizing politico-social pieces like *Religious Musings.*

Miltown (mi·ltaun). *Pharm.* Also (*erron.*) **Milltown.** A proprietary name for meprobamate; a tablet of this drug.

1954 F. M. BERGER in *Jrnl. Pharmacol. & Exper. Therap.* CXII. 413 2-Methyl-2-*n*-propyl-1,3-propanediol carbamate was unique in that it possessed a muscle relaxant and sedative action of an unusual kind. This compound has been named Miltown. **1956** A. HUXLEY *Let.* 20 Oct. (1969) 810 The conference on meprobamate was quite interesting and I made some pleasant acquaintances —Dr. (F. M.) Berger, the inventor of Miltown, [etc.]. **1957** *Trade Marks Jrnl.* 27 Feb. 191/2 Miltown... Pharmaceutical preparations in pill, tablet and powder form, or in liquid form for intravenous injection, all for use in the treatment of tension, as muscular relaxants and as anti-convulsants. Carter Products, Inc... New York. **1960** C. FITZ GIBBON *When Kissing had to Stop* vii. 91 All myths are to a greater or lesser extent tranquillisers in one way or another. But a government can't function on Milltown. **1964** M. MCLUHAN *Understanding Media* (1967) vii. 77 Would it not seem suddenly to be a conspiracy to make the artist a frill, a fribble, or a Milltown? **1969** [see *MEPROBAMATE].

miltsiekte (miltsi·ktĕ). *S. Afr.* Also **meltziekte, miltsiek.** [Afrikaans, f. *milt* spleen + *siekte* sickness.] = ANTHRAX 2.

1835 A. SMITH *Diary* 1 Feb. (1939) I. 241 Bloedsiekte, or anthrax. It is also known in Afrikaans as miltsiekte. **1877** *Queenstown Free Press* 1 Dec. (Pettman), The oldest and most experienced of Kurveyors confess themselves flabbergasted by meltziekte. **1947** H. C. BOSMAN *Mafeking Road* xi. 63 After making their purchases they whiled away the time in discussing politics and the mealie-crops and the miltsiekte. **1959** *Cape Times* 12 Mar. 2/2 Miltsiek has broken out in certain areas in the Bushmanland. **1972** L. G. GREEN *When the Journey's Over* (1973) v. 51 You had to guard your oxen against redwater, *meltsiekte* and lung sickness.

miltz (milts). *Cookery.* [ad. G. *milz.*] The spleen. (Cf. MILT *sb.*)

1909 *Daily Chron.* 25 Feb. 3/5 No more cooking of chleb borsch schave and stuffed miltz. I shall have a cook of my own. **1951** L. W. LEONARD *Jewish Cookery* xiv. 189 The butcher will be glad to make the incision in the side of a beef miltz as large as you desire. **1966** *Bloom's Jewish Restaurant Menu, Entree*..Stuffed Miltz.

mim, *a.* Add non-*dial.* and U.S. examples.

1891 R. T. COOKE *Huckleberries* 96 She was a mim, soft-spoken woman, but guileful and gliding as a snake. **1959** 'J. Ross' *Boy in Grey Overcoat* viii. 93 That mim curl of grey hair across the back of her head. **1960** AUDEN *Homage to Clio* 56 Before you catch it for your mim look and gnostic chirrup.

mimamsa (mīmā·msa). Also **mimansa.** [Skr. *mimāṃsā* profound thought, consideration, investigation, f. *man* to think, consider.] The name of one of the six systems of orthodox Hindu philosophy, called more fully the *Pūrva-,* or 'earlier', *mimamsa,* which was founded by Jaimini and concerns itself with the interpretation of Vedic ritual and text.

The term also occurs in the name of a closely-related school, the *Uttara,* or 'later', *mimamsa,* often called *Vedānta,* which deals with the nature of Brahma.

1788 *Asiatick Researches* I. 352 Of the Philosophical Schools it will be sufficient here to remark, that..the two Mímánsà's, of which the second is often distinguished by the name of Védánta, [seem analogous] to the Platonick. **1811** W. WARD *Acct. Writings, Relig. & Manners Hindoos* I. ii. 370 Like the schools of philosophy among the Greeks, these several systems have each originated with a single and a different head, or founder..Jŭyŭminee of the Mēēmangsa. **1841** M. ELPHINSTONE *Hist. India* I. II. v. 215 The prior Mímánsá, which teaches the art of reasoning with the express view of aiding the interpretation of the Védas, is, so far, only a school of criticism. **1861** H. H. WILSON *Ess. & Lect. Relig. Hindus* I. 12 Jaimini, by Śiva's orders, composed the Mímánsá, which is heretical, in as far as it inculates works in preference to faith. **1915** *Encycl. Relig. & Ethics* VIII. 648/2 The Mīmāṁsā teaches that the relation of word and meaning is not dependent on general agreement, but that the meaning is naturally inherent in the word. **1964** *Language* XL. 113 He did not go any further with his study of the *mimāṃsā* system. **1971** *Illustr. Weekly India* 11 Apr. 35/2 The Indian philosophical systems such as Buddhism, Nyaya, Vaisheshika, Yoga and Mimamsa.

mimbar (mi·mbaɹ). Also 9 **mambar, monbar,** 9– **minbar** (the best form). [Arab. *minbar* pulpit.] The pulpit in a mosque. Also *attrib.*

1816 *Travels of Ali Bey* II. vi. 84 El Monbar, or The Tribune of the Priest of Fridays, is on one side of the Makam Ibrahim, at fourteen feet distance, and in front of the northern angle of the Kaaba. **1836** E. W. LANE *Acct. Manners & Customs Mod. Egyptians* I. iii. 94 To the right of this [*sc.* the mihrab] is the *mim'bar* (or pulpit). **1839** T. J. NEWBOLD *Pol. & Statistical Acct. Straits of Malacca* I. v. 249 The Khatib..recites the Khatbeh..in

the mosque, from the three steps of the mimbar, a species of rostrum. **1855** R. F. BURTON *Pilgrimage* II. xvii. 141 The Mambar, or pulpit, was the invention of a Medinah man of the Beni Najjar. **1875** *Encycl. Brit.* II. 446/2 Near this was a pulpit (*mimbar*). **1885** T. P. HUGHES *Dict. Islam* 349 *Minbar*, generally pronounced *mimbar*... The pulpit in a mosque from which the khuṭbah (or sermon) is recited. It consists of three steps, and is sometimes a moveable wooden structure, and sometimes a fixture of brick or stone built against the wall. **1932** *Times Lit. Suppl.* 10 Nov. 840/1 The charming panels in the side walls of the *mimbar* steps at the Ravali Masjid. **1967** V. PRITCHARD *Eng. Medieval Graffiti* 35/1 There is a whole panel of swastika-peltae, in a simplified form, carved on a wooden mimbar in Kairwan, North Africa.

mime, *sb.* Add: **4. b.** (The art of) gesture, movement, etc. (as distinct from words) used to express emotion and dramatic action or character; dumb show; = PANTOMIME *sb.* 4.

1932 I. MAWER *Art of Mime* II. i. 125 The aim of mime is not a performance of certain physical exercises which can be welded into some kind of whole, nor is it merely 'gesture'—gesture is one branch only. **1953** *Ballet Ann.* VII. 22 There is always a great misunderstanding of the word *mime*... In ballet it means the formal gesture language used in the narration of the classics. **1967** *Listener* 13 Apr. 503/3 Some sort of research is required..to find out the best way of using mime on television.

6. Comb. *mime-ballet, -drama, -writer.*

1955 *Times* 11 May 7/6 Two mime-ballets by Rocca and Dallapiccola respectively. **1931** A. NICOLL *Masks, Mimes & Miracles* i. 78 The Oscan mime became one of the most popular divertisements there. **1968** J. WINEARLS *Mod. Dance* (ed. 2) vii. 145 There have been Masques, Dance Plays, Mime Dramas and every combination of the fundamental expressions of movement and voice. **1957** N. FRYE *Anat. Crit.* iv. 285 Classical mime-writers like Herodas.

mime, *v.* Add: **1. c.** (Later examples.)

1915 M. E. PERUGINI *Art of Ballet* xiii. 115 The two well-known dancers..mutely mimed the actions and emotions of the leading characters. **1959** W. GOLDING *Free Fall* xiv. 250 The maker they mimed for you in your Victorian slum was the old male maker, totem of the conquering Hebrews.

d. Of a singer, to present a pre-recorded song by mime, usu. on television.

1965 G. MELLY *Owning-Up* xi. 131 A weekly [T.V.] programme featuring the new releases and illustrating them visually by..the artists miming to their own records. **1966** *Crescendo* Jan. 8/1 He seems content to mime 'Tears' to a gaggle of unbelieving teen-agers on *Top Of The Pops*. **1966** *Listener* 11 Aug. 204/3 Since the singers and dancers are so expert in miming to their own recordings, it is possible to eliminate all microphones from the stage.

Also **mimed** *ppl. a.*

1910 *Daily Chron.* 9 Apr. 7/5 The marvellous power of facial expression to convey an emotion..is brought home ..by the intense interest one feels in these 'mimed' plays. **1965** *Listener* 2 Dec. 908/3 Mimed opera... It soon became painfully obvious that sound was out of synchronization with vision.

mimeo (mi·mio), *sb.* [Abbrev. of MIMEOGRAPH *sb.*] A copy of a document, newspaper, etc., reproduced by means of a mimeograph (see MIMEOGRAPH *sb.* in Dict. and Suppl.). Also *attrib.*, as *mimeo mag, newspaper, stencil.* Hence **mimeo, mimeo-stencil** *vbs. trans.*, to reproduce by means of a mimeograph; **mimeoed** *ppl. a.*

1943 J. S. HUXLEY *TVA* 139 TVA, Mimeo, 1941. **1967** KARCH & BUBER *Offset Processes* vi. 243 Within a few minutes a phototube will scan and transfer all details to a mimeo-stencil or offset plate. **1967** *Maclean's Mag.* Jan. 56 Why Sandra Peredo's patronizing attitude toward the little magazines? She states, for instance, that the mimeo mags are interested in dirty words and anti-Establishment statements as their main themes. **1969** *Harper's Mag.* May 82 We learn later that the statement was mimeoed and a few reporters were walking off with it. **1972** M. Joos in *Language* XLVIII. 260 Having mimeo-stenciled a number of text pages without the footnoting for which I was leaving room on each stencil, I was now putting the stencils through my typewriter a second time. **1973** *Times* 17 Apr. (Liberia Suppl.) p. ii/5 These tribes have their own newspapers called mimeo-newspapers.

mimeograph, *sb.* Substitute for def.: A duplicating machine for producing copies from a stencil; also *attrib.* (Add later examples.)

From 1903 to 1948 a proprietary name.

1914 [see *DUPLICATING *vbl. sb.*]. **1935** M. M. ATWATER *Murder in Midsummer* xviii. 160 Miss Marsh ran off on the mimeograph sheets of instructions all neatly tabulated. **1952** S. KAUFFMANN *Philanderer* (1953) v. 84 The mimeograph ink of the mail-room. **1963** F. C. ARCHER *Gen. Office Pract.* (ed. 2) xvii. 233 Mimeograph paper comes in a variety of colors to contrast or to harmonize with the ink. **1967** KARCH & BUBER *Offset Processes* iv. 72 Letter shops, once using mimeograph-type equipment, added the offset process..to expand..their production.

mimeograph *v. trans.* (later examples); **mimeographed** *ppl. a.* (later examples).

1912 J. C. DANA *Mod. Amer. Library Econ.* v. 6 Mimeographed copies of texts for books and printed forms for book notes are to be distributed when needed. **1937** M. L. HANLEY *Word Index to Joyce's Ulysses* p. xii, Mimeographing: Dan Marlow. **1946** *R.A.F. Jrnl.* May 152 The *Bulletin*..was an unpretentious affair of a few mimeographed sheets. **1949** SHURR & YOCOM *Mod. Dance* 3 Would you consider mimeographing this material? **1972** *Jrnl. Social Psychol.* LXXXVII. 23 Choices were to be indicated on a mimeographed answer form.

mimesis. Add: **1.** (Earlier and later examples.) Also *transf.*

1550 R. SHERRY *Treat. Schemes & Tropes* sig. E 3 Mimisis, that is a folowing eyther of the wordes or manoures whereby we expresse not onlye the wordes of the person, but also the gesture. **1593** H. PEACHAM *Garden of Eloquence* (1954) 138 Mimesis is an imitation of speech whereby the Orator counterfaiteth not onely what one said, but also his utterance, pronunciation, and gesture. **1962** S. E. FINER *Man on Horseback* xii. 240 This is to reckon without *mimesis*. Among unstable states, particularly those with a rage for innovation, military intervention has proved to be highly contagious. **1962** *Listener* 13 Dec. 1006/1 Bunyan stands with Malory and Trollope as a master of perfect naturalness in the mimesis of ordinary conversation. **1965** M. BRADBURY *Stepping Westward* vi. 292 Walker had never before heard in anyone's speech vocabulary—*mimesis, epistemology, mythopoeic.* **1965** M. COHEN in M. Black *Philos. in Amer.* 115 If Le Corbusier has encouraged the doctrine of *mimesis* in designing the chapel at Ronchamp, he has rejected it firmly at the Villa Savoie.

2. For '= MIMICRY 3' read '= MIMICRY 2'.

3. *Sociol.* The deliberate imitation of the behaviour of one group of people by another as a factor in social change.

1934 A. J. TOYNBEE *Study of Hist.* III. 245 The problem of bringing the uncreative rank and file of a growing society into line with the creative pioneers..cannot be solved in practice, on the social scale, without also bringing into play the faculty of sheer mimesis—one of the less exalted faculties of Human Nature which has more in it of drill than inspiration. **1962** *Listener* 8 Feb. 257/3 There is..an important distinction between *mimesis*, which is imitation of those above you, and solidarity, which is imitation..of those with whom you find yourself in a common situation. **1965** P. LASLETT *World we have Lost* ix. 213 Only if imitation, mimesis, is taken to constitute 'solidity' can the phrase the solid middle class be made to apply to any substantial part of the population.

mimetism. (Examples.)

1918 B. MIALL tr. *Hamon's Lessons of World-War* ix. 271 Men hide their guns..under canopies of leaves, in order to conceal them from the view of aeroplanes. Man adopts the mimetism of Nature. **1970** *Times Lit. Suppl.* 18 Dec. 1480/5 The later history of the Inca dynasty is a depressing one of mimetism and osmosis.

mimi, var. *MAIMAI.

mimic, *v.* Add: **4. b.** *Med.* Of a drug: to produce an effect very similar to (that of some other cause).

1971 *Nature* 12 Feb. 497/1, *d*-Amphetamine closely mimicked the excitatory and inhibitory effects of *l*-NA. **1974** *Ibid.* 31 May 473/1 Colchicine..has been reported to mimic the effects of denervation on mammalian skeletal muscles.

mi·micable, *a.* [f. MIMIC *v.* + -ABLE.] Capable of being mimicked.

1955 J. L. AUSTIN *How to do Things with Words* (1962) viii. 96 The phatic act, however, like the phonetic, is essentially mimicable.

mimicry. Add: **2.** Also used of similar resemblances in plants. (Later examples.)

1931 R. N. CHAPMAN *Animal Ecol.* viii. 190 It seems likely that many controversies over protective coloration, mimicry, and resemblance might find the solution if they were investigated from the viewpoint of their contributions to the maintenance of the population of the species. **1951** *Dict. Gardening* (R. Hort. Soc.) III. 1304/1 There is often such resemblance between plants which themselves possess no special protective apparatus and those that do as to suggest that 'mimicry' occurs among them in the same way as it does among insects. **1966** E. PALMER *Plains of Camdeboo* xvi. 268 Some plants are barely recognizable as plants at all, and these are the mimicry plants which are some of the most famous plants in the world. **1968** R. D. MARTIN tr. *Wickler's Mimicry in Plants & Animals* x. 100 Some insects resembling ants live within the society of ants and devour their hosts. This latter case would seem to be a case of aggressive mimicry. **1975** *Nature* 17 Jan. 191/1 Mimicry is a phenomenon of evolutionary convergence or parallelism by which an edible mimic species gains some measure of protection from predators by virtue of its close resemblance to a model species which is unpalatable (that is, distasteful or dangerous).

miming, *vbl. sb.* (See under MIME *v.*) (Later examples in sense *1 d of the verb.)

1965 *Melody Maker* 3 Apr. 16 Miming is slowly disappearing from the pop scene. **1965** *Listener* 2 Dec. 908/3 The first programme of the series was made almost unwatchable by the process of miming.

mimosa. Add: **2*.** A yellow colour resembling that of the mimosa. Also *attrib.*

1909 *Cent. Dict.* Suppl., *Mimosa*, same as thiazol yellow. **1928** A. CHRISTIE *Mystery of Blue Train* viii. 61 The little mimosa suit of crêpe de chine. **1966** *Harper's Bazaar* Sept. 41 Evening dress... In mimosa, toast or turquoise. **1971** R. BUSBY *Deadlock* xiii. 201 The immaculate coffee-coloured tussore suit..with a fresh mimosa shirt.

3. *mimosa-bush* (earlier example); *mimosa-yellow* adj.

1856 F. FLEMING *S. Afr.* xii. 264 A broad valley, covered with rich pasturage and dotted with '*mimosa*' bushes, stretched out over several acres. **1910** *Encycl. Brit.* VIII. 747/1 The following list includes the principal coal-tar colours... mimosa yellow.

mimosine (mimō^u·sīn). *Chem.* Also † **mimosin.** [ad. G. *mimosin* (J. Renz, at the suggestion of K. Suessenguth, 1936 in *Zeitschr. f. physiol. Chem.* CCXLIV. 154), f. MIMOS(A + -INE⁵.] An amino-acid, $C_5H_4O_2N{\cdot}CH_2CH(NH_2)COOH$, found in the tree *Leucæna glauca* and in *Mimosa pudica*, the sensitive plant.

1937 *Brit. Chem. Abstr.* A. III. 50/2 The sap from the tubular cells of young shoots and leaf stalks of *Mimosa pudica*, L., and *Leucaena glauca*, Benth., yield mimosin. **1949** T. A. HENRY *Plant Alkaloids* (ed. 4) 5 Kostermanns has also investigated mimosine with results indicating that it is a derivative of 3:4-dihydroxypyridine. **1971** *Toxicon* IX. 241 When animals ingest..mimosine they suffer from growth retardation, alopecia, skin irritation and cataract formation.

mimp, *sb.* and *a.* **A.** *sb.* Substitute for quots.

1786 J. BURGOYNE *Heiress* III. ii. 54, I am preparing the cast of the lips for the ensuing winter—thus—It is to be call'd the Paphian mimp. **1822** M. EDGEWORTH *Let.* 16 Jan. (1971) 321 The famous learned Mrs. Somerville..no *set* smile or prim look—no *mimps* with her mouth.

mimsey, *a.* Add: Also **mimsy.** (Further examples.)

Lewis Carroll's *mimsy*, which may be an invented word, has influenced all subsequent uses.

1855 'L. CARROLL' *Rectory Umbrella & Mischmasch* (1932) 139 All mimsy were the borogoves. *Ibid.* 140 *Mimsy*, (whence *mimserable* and *miserable*). 'Unhappy.' **1911** C. MACKENZIE *Passionate Elopement* xxi. 186 Four shillings and sixpence, ma'am, for a little mimsy book not so thick as the magick history of Jack the Giant Killer. **1920** D. H. LAWRENCE *Touch & Go* 6 Good plays? You might as well say mimsy bomtittle plays, you'd be saying as much. **1933** W. DE LA MARE *Lord Fish* 171 Treading mimsey as a cat. **1934** *Times Educ. Suppl.* 24 Mar. p. iv/2 A people unimaginative enough to accept a mimsy and scrannel 'P.R.' in place of the organ music, the soul-uplifting harmony of 'Proportional Representation'. **1936** *Punch* 10 June 650/1 'It's the glamour of it,' sighed Josephine. 'Whenever I smell a programme I go quite mimsey—honestly I do.' **1937** 'N. BLAKE' *There's Trouble Brewing* i. 24 An affected mimsy sort of voice that she reserved presumably for cultural pronouncements: Nigel preferred her normal, unmitigated boom. **1956** J. CANNAN *People to be Found* vii. 91 With horror they had seen the lawns of the Botanic Gardens torn up and replaced by a mimsy pseudo-Elizabethan rose-garden. **1963** *Times* 8 Feb. 14/3 Moreover his interpolated variation in the first act, danced to the normally unused *andante* of the *pas de trois* and consisting largely of slow *pirouettes en attitude*, looked as mimsy as the borogroves [*sic*], and could not be regarded as successful.

mimulus. Add: **1.** (Later example.)

1794 *Curtis's Bot. Mag.* VIII. 283 Mimmulus is a classical word for the Pedicularis, or Lousewort.

2. Substitute for def.: [Linnæus 1741, in *Acta Soc. Reg. Scient. Upsaliensis* 82.] An annual or perennial herb of the large genus so called, belonging to the family Scrophulariaceæ and widely distributed in America, Asia, and Africa, esp. *Mimulus luteus*, the monkey-flower, a yellow-flowered perennial, native to western North America but naturalized elsewhere. (Earlier and later examples.)

1768 P. MILLER *Gardeners Dict.* (ed. 8) s.v. Mimulus. Upright Mimulus with oblong linear leaves. **1794** *Curtis's Bot. Mag.* VIII. 283 Linnæus first gave to it [sc. *Mimulus ringens*] the name of *Mimulus*. **1900** L. H. BAILEY *Cycl. Amer. Hort.* II. 1018/1 There is nothing difficult in the culture of Mimulus. Some of the finest plants have been self-sown on a rubbish heap. **1963** *Times* 25 Apr. 14/6, I think of a turn in a wood and a solitary exquisite butterfly-orchis; of a wide green hillside and a patch of mimulus beside a grooved trickle of water. **1974** A. SCOTT-JAMES *Sissinghurst* xiii. 143 The mimulus continues as the centre-point.

min (min), *sb.*³ Shortened form of MINUTE *sb.*¹

1890 in *Cent. Dict.* **1892** *Field* 14 May 735/3 He.. 'clocked' 2 min 2 sec all the way. **1959** P. BULL *I know Face* i. 18 Miss Pereira..told me to meet her in the ABC up the street in ten mins.

Min (min), *a.* and *sb.*⁴ **A.** *adj.* Of or pertaining to the Min district or dialect in Fukien province, S.E. China. **B.** *sb.*⁴ The dialect of this district.

1902 *Encycl. Brit.* XXVII. 27/1 The Min forts at the entrance of the Foochow river. **1910** *Ibid.* VI. 202/1 The French fleet attacked and destroyed..the forts which were built to guard the entrance to the Min river. **1959** *Chambers's Encycl.* III. 488/2 The Min dialects of Fukien, with well-marked varieties in Foochow and Amoy. **1964** M. A. K. HALLIDAY et al. in J. A. Fishman *Readings Sociol. of Lang.* (1968) 146 There are six major dialects in modern China: Mandarin, Cantonese, Wu, North Min, South Min and Hakka. **1975** *Language* LI. 258 Cháozhōu, a Mǐn dialect spoken on the southeast coast of mainland China.

minable, var. MINEABLE *a.* (in Dict. and Suppl.).

Minæan (minī·ăn), *sb.* and *a.* Also **Minean.** [f. L. *Minæus*, f. Arab. *Ma'īn*, + -AN.] **A.** *sb.* **a.** A native or inhabitant of an ancient kingdom of southern Arabia. **b.** The Semitic language of the Minæans. **B.** *adj.* Of or pertaining to the Minæans, their kingdom, or their language. So **Mina·ic** *sb.* and *a.*

1601 HOLLAND tr. *Pliny's Nat. Hist.* XII. xiv. 366 There is another tract by it selfe confronting this countrye [*sc.* Arabia], wherein the Minæans doe inhabite. **1833** A. CRICHTON *Hist. Arabia* I. iv. 148 The Minæans were rich in palm-groves, flocks, and fertile fields. **1844** C. FORSTER *Hist. Geogr. Arabia* I. ii. 133 We find Carman reg., the Minæan metropolis..peopled by Pliny with the Charmæi. **1886** *Encycl. Brit.* XXI. 654/1 The other [dialect], which expresses the causative by *sa*.., is the Minaic. To this latter branch belong the numerous South Arabic inscriptions recently found in the north of the Ḥijáz, near Ḥejr where the Minæans must have had a commercial settlement. *Ibid.*, The singular manner in which districts containing Sabæan inscriptions and those containing Minaic alternate with one another. **1902** in Gottheil & Jastrow *Semitic Study Ser.* I. (Advt.), Selected Sabaean and Minaean inscriptions. **1934** L. H. GRAY *Introd. Semitic Compar. Ling.* i. 6 South Arabic is represented only by inscriptions (Minaean,..Qatabānian,..). **1936** F. STARK *Southern Gates Arabia* 5 The Arabian empires rose and fell—Minean, Sabæan, Katabanian. **1951** W. F. ALBRIGHT in H. H. Rowley *Old Testament & Mod. Study* ii. 32 The difference between Sabaean and Minaean, the former of which has an *h*-causative whereas the latter has the *s*-causative. **1974** *Encycl. Brit. Macropædia* I. 1044/1 Four main states are known to have established themselves in South Arabia—Ma'īn (of the Minaeans), Saba' (of the Sabaeans), Qatabān (Qitbān) and Ḥaḍramawt. *Ibid.* XIX. 1084/1 Yemen..was successively the centre of the Minaean (13th to 7th centuries BC), Sabaean.., and Himyaritic..civilizations.

Minamata disease (minămā·tă). *Path.* [Named after *Minamata*, the name of a town in Kumamoto prefecture, Japan, where it was first recognized.] A disease, caused by ingestion of alkyl mercury compounds, which is characterized by impairment of cerebral functions such as speech, sight, and muscular coordination and which is usually permanent and sometimes fatal.

1957 *Acta Path. Jap.* VII. 605 The so-called Minamata-disease may be recognized as a toxic encephalopathia. The toxic substances contained in fish and shell-fish have not been yet found. **1971** *Sci. Amer.* May 15 The Minamata disease, as it came to be called, produced progressive weakening of the muscles, loss of vision, impairment of other cerebral functions, eventual paralysis and in some cases coma and death. **1973** *Biol. Conservation* V. 143/2 Minamata disease first appeared in cats, which died from eating fish scraps from the village kitchens. **1975** *Times Lit. Suppl.* 19 Sept. 1042 (*caption*) Demonstrators for the victims of 'Minamata Disease', a defect of the central nervous system caused by eating fish poisoned by mercury in industrial waste.

Minangkabau (mi:næŋkăbau·), *a.* and *sb.* Also **Manikabowe, Menangkabau, Menangkabo,** 8 **Menangcabow(e),** 9 **Menangkabow, Minangkabauer.** Pl. **Minangkabau, -baus. A.** *adj.* Of or pertaining to Minangkabau, a Malay territory in the highlands of Sumatra. **B.** *sb.* A native or inhabitant of Minangkabau.

1783 W. MARSDEN *Hist. Sumatra* 279 Between the Menangcabow people, those of Rou.., and the Achenese, wars used to be perpetual. **1808** *Asiatick Researches* X. iii. 165 The Menangkábow race..seem at an early period to have ruled the whole island of Sumatra. **1821** J. LEYDEN tr. *Malay Annals* ii. 37 All the Menangcabows were surprised at his appearance. **1839** T. J. NEWBOLD *Pol. & Statistical Acct. Straits of Malacca* I. v. 200 The inhabitants [of Naning]..are always styled 'Manikábowes', or settlers from Menángkábowe, in Sumatra. *Ibid.* II. xiv. 219 The information..was derived..from various Menangkabowe chiefs of Rumbowe and Naning. **1911** J. FRAZER *Golden Bough: Magic Art* (ed. 3) I. iii. 58 The Minangkabauers of Sumatra..will call in the help of a wizard. *Ibid.* 193 The Minangkabau people of Sumatra. **1947** R. O. WINSTEDT *Malays* viii. 154 Some of the sayings of the Minangkabau tribes of Negri Sembilan rise to poetry. **1968** *Encycl. Brit.* XV. 144/1 The Menangkabau have much in common with the coastal Malay, but differ radically in social organization. **1972** M. SHEPPARD *Taman Indera* 65 The *Randai*, the Minangkabau dance drama from West Sumatra.

minasragrite (minăsrā·grəit). *Min.* [f. *Minasragra*, name of its locality near Cerro de Pasco, Peru + -ITE[1].] An acidic hydrated vanadyl sulphate, $(VO)_2H_2(SO_4)_3 \cdot 15H_2O$, found as a blue efflorescence of monoclinic crystals on patronite.

1915 W. T. SCHALLER in *Jrnl. Washington Acad. Sci.* V. 7 The following very brief notes of four new minerals are given in order to secure priority... Minasragrite is a blue hydrous vanadium sulphate from Minasraga Peru. **1934** *Amer. Mineralogist* XIX. 198 Specimens of patronite in the Harvard mineral collection..showed in places a vivid blue incrustation which proved to be minasragrite. **1968** I. KOSTOV *Mineral.* II. ix. 517 Minasragrite, found with patronite from the well known vanadium deposit of Minasragra..in Peru, is monoclinic.

minatory, *a.* and *sb.* Add: Hence **mi·natoriness,** threateningness. *rare.*

1961 J. N. FINDLAY *Values & Intentions* viii. 344 Acknowledging a God capable of such universal minatoriness.

‖ **minaudière** (minodiẹ̄r·). [Fr. fem. adj., lit. affected, coquettish.] † **1.** An affected or coquettish woman. *Obs.*

1716 M. W. MONTAGU *Let.* 21 Nov. (1965) I. 282 The Saxon Ladys..are very genteely dress'd after the French and English modes,..but the most determin'd Minaudieres in the whole world. They would think it a mortal sin against good breeding if they either spoke or mov'd in a natural manner. **1818** LADY MORGAN *Fl. Macarthy* III. ii. 93 She struck me to be a mere *minaudiere*!

2. A small case for a woman's cosmetics, jewellery, etc.

1940 *Shopping News* (Springfield, Mass.) 15 May, Rectangular in shape, the minaudiere opens to disclose a good size mirror; there are also five lidded compartments—for powder, rouge, and eye shadow, money, keys, cigarette lighter and tortoise-shell comb. **1957** A. ADBURGHAM in *Punch* 18 Dec. 728/3 Parisian tailors have been trying..to persuade their [male] clients to forgo pockets altogether and carry a *minaudière*. **1967** *N.Y. Times* 22 June 43, I found that my regular minaudière was terribly small and I always had to stuff things in my pocket. **1969** *New Yorker* 8 Mar. 17 (Advt.), Rare shells..have been fashioned into exquisite minaudières for the hand.

mince, *sb.* Add: **3.** *Rhyming slang.* = *MINCE-PIE 4. (Usu. in *pl.*)

1937 in PARTRIDGE *Dict. Slang* 522/1. **1958** F. NORMAN *Bang to Rights* 149 'I know what's on there' said the boggie looking Solie straight in the minces. **1960** *News Chron.* 16 Feb. 6/5 She gives me a double glinty butchers out of those sharp minces of hers. **1962** R. COOK *Crust on its Uppers* (1964) iii. 28 'One pack dealer's choice,' he says, minces all gleaming. *Ibid.* xi. 32 A general look of dislike in the minces, which tremble a bit in their sockets.

mince, *v.* Add: **5. a.** Also with *out.*

1862 MRS. H. WOOD *Channings* II. v. 75 'You—are—very—kind—to—take—up—Arthur Channing's cause!' they mince out. **1888** MRS. H. WARD *R. Elsmere* III. xliii. 255 'Ah—"Reculer pour mieux *faire* sauter!"'—said Sir John, mincing out his pun as though he loved it.

mincemeat. Add: **2.** Also, to beat decisively or easily in a contest.

1876 *Coursing Calendar* 193 Maniac made mincemeat of Smoker, who was so stiff that he could scarcely raise a gallop. **1955** *Times* 20 June 13/4 Thames R.C. made mincemeat of all their opponents in the Grand Eights.

mincemeaty, [f. MINCEMEAT + -Y[1].] Suggestive of mincemeat.

1870 P. BROOKS in A. V. G. Allen *Phillips Brooks* (1908) 246 Huxley's new *Lay Sermons*..is like..most books for the people that popularize science. It is patronizing and mincemeaty.

mince-pie. Add: **4.** *Rhyming slang.* An eye. (Usu. in *pl.*)

1857 'DUCANGE ANGLICUS' *Vulgar Tongue* 13 *Mince pies*, eyes. **1892** *Sporting Times* 29 Oct. 1/2 And I smiled as I closed my two mince-pies. **1893** CROOK & DALY *Jerusalem's Dead* (*song*) 5 My mince-pies are waterin' jes like a pump. **1906** E. DYSON *Fact'ry 'Ands* xvii. 229 He thinks he'll never be able t' shut his mince pies again. **1922** JOYCE *Ulysses* 418 Got a prime pair of mincepies, no kid. **1928** M. C. SHARPE *Chicago May* xxxi. 288/1 Mince pies, eyes.

‖ **Mincha** (mi·nχā). Also **Minchah, Minha(h.** [Heb. *minḥāh*, lit. gift, offering.] (See quot. 1962.)

[**1706** I. ABENDANA *Discourses Polity of Jews* iv. 118 The Captives of Babylon..sent Money to their Brethren at Jerusalem, wherewithal they might buy them Burnt-Offerings..and prepare them Manna, (for so 'tis read corruptly for Mincha a Meat-Offering).] **1819** L. ALEXANDER *Hebrew Ritual* 25 Afternoon prayers,..Tephillath Minchah... The Hebrew word..*Minchah*..signifies a gift as offering; but is generally used by Jewish ritualists for the evening. *Ibid.* 68 About two o'clock in the Afternoon they go to the Synagogue to *Mincha*, which is the Afternoon Service. **1892** I. ZANGWILL *Childr. Ghetto* I. 169 Knowest thou what, Moses?..we shall be too late for Minchah. **1957** L. STERN *Midas Touch* III. xx. 153 Israel pronounced the *Mincha* prayers and eighteen benedictions. **1962** *New Jewish Encycl.* 322/2 *Minḥah*, Hebrew term for the Jewish daily afternoon service. In Biblical times the term *Minḥah* was applied to the 'meal-offering', but it acquired its present meaning in the days of the *Misnah*. The *Minḥah* prayer is recited before sunset. **1973** *Synagogue Light* Sept. 48/2 In the early afternoon, during *Mincha* Service, the Confession is recited.

Mincing Lane (mi·nsiŋ lēⁱn). Used *absol.* and *attrib.* with reference to an auction-room for tea and other commodities which was originally situated in the London street of this name.

1913 *Times* 13 Oct. (Finance & Commerce) 18/1 The Mincing-lane Tea and Rubber Share Brokers' Association (Limited). **1914** in *Conc. Oxf. Dict.* **1923** *Westm. Gaz.* 31 Jan., You must go to Mincing-lane for an excuse for the rise [in the price of tea]. **1959** *Chambers's Encycl.* XI. 235/2 Business in rubber, tea, coffee, cocoa, sugar, spices and condiments was carried on at the offices of Mincing Lane until the destruction of the Commercial Sale Room by bombing in 1941. *Ibid.* XIII. 490/2 Requirements [of tea] are mainly obtained by purchases in the Mincing Lane auctions. **1970** *E. Afr. Standard* (Nairobi) 23 Jan. 5/5 Mincing Lane is pretty confident of higher prices for Africans by the end of the first quarter of this year.

mind, *sb.*[1] Add: **11. g.** *to pay no mind, not to pay any mind*: to pay no heed or attention (*to* someone or something); not to care or worry. *U.S. colloq.* and *dial.*

1916 *Dialect Notes* IV. 269, I pay no mind to that. **1932** W. FAULKNER *Light in August* xiii. 275, I aint never paid it no mind. **1969** *Rolling Stone* 28 June 19/2 He..doesn't pay any mind if his calf shows when he crosses his legs. **1971** *Black World* Oct. 63/2, I don't pay her no mind.

17. h. *spec.* = SENSE *sb.* 18 b.

1951 E. BARKER *Princ. Social & Pol. Theory* II. vi. 72 We sometimes speak of the 'mind' of a meeting, or the 'sense' of a meeting... We only mean that there is a common *content* of the many minds, and the many senses, which are present and active in the meeting. **1971** *Scotsman* 20 May 1/7 Mr Herron said he was not ruling the report out of order. 'I want to take the mind of the Assembly on this.'

21. a. *mind-conditioning, -content, -dependence, -doctor, -event, -force, -hunger, -searching, -wandering, -world*; *mind-altering, -changing* (later examples), *-constructed, -dependent, -destroying, -like, -made, -numbing, -stretching, -weary* adjs.

1972 *N.Y. Times* 3 Nov. 39/3 A deluge of mind-altering drugs. **1974** *Publishers Weekly* 7 Jan. 50/2 LSD..and other mind-altering drugs. **1956** A. HUXLEY *Let.* 14 Mar. (1969) 791 Soma, in India, was taken only by the priests... I dare say some of the tropical takers of mind-changing stuff may have hit upon the Indian device independently. **1973** *Houston* (Texas) *Chron. Texas Mag.* 14 Oct. 4/1 PDAP defines mind-changing chemicals as alcohol, all narcotics, marijuana and such organics as peyote, i.e., anything inducted into the body to alter the mind. **1945** R. KNOX *God & Atom* ix. 131 There is a steady policy, all over eastern Europe, of anti-religious mind-conditioning. **1930** J. LAIRD *Knowl., Belief & Opinion* xii. 284 By a mentefact, I mean that which is mind-constructed. **1940** *Mind* XLIX. 428 The word as an element in language is a very special kind of fact,..as a thought-thing or mind-constructed thing. **1936** H. MULDER *Cognition & Volition in Lang.* 163 The intellectual components of a mind-content. **1923** C. D. BROAD *Sci. Thought* viii. 251 We must distinguish a more and a less radical sense of 'mind-dependence'. **1951** *Mind* LX. 114 The mind-dependence is dependence on some mental process. **1881** A. C. FRASER *Berkeley* I. iii. 32 It is an argument for the phenomenal, and therefore mind-dependent, nature of the material world. **1927** *Aristotelian Soc. Suppl. Vol.* VII. 56 Even if sense-data and images, or presentations, are taken to be existentially and qualitatively mind-dependent, to 'inspect' them will plainly be a process very different from that of noticing or scrutinizing mental operations. **1933** *Mind* XLII. 362 Berkeley's failure to demonstrate the mind-dependent character of the secondary qualities. **1886** HALDANE & KEMP tr. *Schopenhauer's World as Will & Idea* II. 211 A mere juggling with words, of which the most shocking example is afforded us by the mind-destroying Hegelism. **1975** *Deb. Senate Canada* 20 June 6984/1 In an age when our society is becoming complex, when many of the industrial functions are becoming routine and boring, and some of them, I am told by some people on assembly lines, are becoming mind destroying, there is some advantage to that kind of thing. **1940** *Mind* XLIX. 352 It is a book worth reading..because of her power to look afresh at what is done and what should be done by the mind-doctor. **1936** AUDEN *Look, Stranger!* 37 Every tramp's a landlord really In mind-events. **1861** J. B. DALGAIRNS *Holy Communion* i. 13 It is hard to say whether we know not more of mind-force..than of the strange aggregate of wondrous forces which we call matter. **1937** R. A. WILSON *Birth of Lang.* 82 The life-force, or mind-force..works within the sensuous material of the world. **1941** V. WOOLF *Between Acts* 22 No one ventured so long a journey, without staving off possible mind-hunger, without buying a book on a bookstall. **1940** *Mind* XLIX. 414 The answer, 'Our mind can grasp the world because the world is mind-like' is a typical *idealistic* argument. **1953** J. S. HUXLEY *Evolution in Action* iv. 89 All living substance has mental, or we had better say mind-like, properties. **1912** J. H. MOORE *Ethics & Educ.* 36 Mind-made ghosts of ideas. **1957** J. PASSMORE *100 Yrs. Philos.* iii. 58 The general principle that every object of experience is mind-made. **1898** F. HIRD *Cry of Children* (ed. 2) ii. 22 The existence of this mind-numbing slavery is only proved by careful examination into individual cases. **1971** *Guardian* 28 Jan. 11/3 The cost of the gesture could be of mind-numbing proportions. **1940** W. S. CHURCHILL *Into Battle* (1941) 229 Untiring vigilance and mind-searching must be devoted to the subject. **1959** *Brno Studies in English* I. 128 That Gissing had considerable mind-searchings over this incident we cannot doubt. **1972** *Guardian* 29 Jan. 11/4 The sheer size of Bangladesh's needs is mind-stretching. **1974** *Columbia* (S. Carolina) *Record* 25 Apr. 16–D/5 Working with Kissinger is demanding, exhilarating, fascinating, exciting and even mind-stretching, according to four State Department intimates. **1890** W. JAMES *Princ. Psychol.* I. xi. 417 This reflex and passive character of the attention..never is overcome in some people, whose work, to the end of life, gets done in the interstices of their mind-wandering. **1899** —— *Talks to Teachers* xi. 114 If he wants to get ideas on any subject, he sits down to work at something else, his best results coming through his mind-wanderings. **1923** U. L. SILBERRAD *Lett. J. Armiter* xiii. 264 But—I am tired! Foot-weary as well as mind-weary. **1890** W. JAMES *Princ. Psychol.* I. vi. 154 Somewhere, then, there *is* a transformation... The question is, Where—in the nerve world or in the mind-world? **1951** W. DE LA MARE *Winged Chariot* 44 The world without; the mind-world in our head.

b. mind-bender, a person who, or thing which, influences or alters the mind; *spec.* a psychedelic drug; so **mind-bending** *a.*; **mind-**

blower *slang*, something that blows one's mind (see *blow *v.*[1] 24 j); so **mind-blowing** *a.*; (as a back-formation) **mind-blow** *v.*; **mind-blown** *a*; **mind-body** *Philos.* and *Psychol.*, usu. *attrib.*, a term used in relation to the question of whether a distinction can be made between mental and physiological events; **mind-boggling** *a.*, that causes the mind to boggle or be overwhelmed; **mind-changer,** (*a*) a person who changes his mind; (*b*) a psychedelic drug; **mind-curist** = *mind-curer* (*b*); **mind-dust,** in materialist evolution hypotheses, the particles of 'mind' or mental substance of which mind-stuff is composed; also *attrib.*; **mind-expanding** *a.* = *psychedelic *a.*; so **mind-expander**; **mind-healing** (earlier examples); **mind-read** *v. trans.*, to discern what is passing in the mind of (another person); **mind-set,** habits of mind formed by previous events or earlier environment which affect a person's attitude (cf. *mental set* s.v. *mental *a.*[1] 5); **mind-sight** (further examples); **mind-stuff** (further examples); **mind-transference,** telepathy.

1963 J. Kennaway (*title*) The mind benders. *Ibid.* xxv. 158 Oonagh has said that there were instincts in man laid too deep for the most skilful mind-bender to probe. **1966** *New Scientist* 15 Dec. 639/3 *The mind-bender*, a persuasive person who, for subversive political purposes or financial gain (often both), bends others to his will. Increasingly, he employs drugs, particularly of the hallucinogen group. **1967** *Sci. News Let.* 22 July 80 STP is a new, untested drug, resembling both amphetamine pep pills and the active ingredient in mescaline, the cactus-derived mind-bender. **1970** K. Platt *Pushbutton Butterfly* (1971) vii. 70 LSD, marijuana—any of the mind-benders. **1973** B. Turner *Hot-Foot* xvi. 122, I felt..as if I were hearing a soapy disc-jockey play the groovy zip of some discordant group of mind-benders. **1965** *Economist* 25 Sept. 1215/3 The Socialist Labour League, furious exegetes of the gospel according to Trotsky, with their mind-bending vocabulary full of 'Pabloism' and that mythical entity the 'rank-and-file'. **1966** *New Scientist* 21 Apr. 151/1 Already 'mind-bending' gases for military purposes are said to be at an advanced stage of development. **1970** *Sunday Times* 25 Jan. 29 The theoretical mathematics of the situation [*sc.* the mining of metals] are positively mind-bending. **1971** *New Scientist* 27 May 531/1 Heroin and other mind-bending agents. **1973** *Times* 25 May 4/3 Viscount Weymouth this afternoon unveiled the mind-bending paintings and sculpture-painting with which he has encrusted the walls of his stately home inches deep, acres wide and of fathomless significance. **1970** *Listener* 22 Oct. 540 It can mind-blow a long-haired GI to know he'll have to live straighter to survive in Sweden than in the Army or in America. **1968** *New Scientist* 27 June 703/1 Two chemicals with almost identical structures can have very different psychedelic properties: one might be a real mind-blower and the other as ineffective as a sugar lump. **1969** *Gandalf's Garden* vi. 11/1 *Mindblower*, an experience or idea which changes one's thought-pattern, enlivening the mind and emotions. **1967** *Jazz Monthly* Dec. 16/3 While the music lasted little of this was evident; the spectacular mind-blowing ferocity of it all simply carried the group through. **1968** *Times* 4 May 21 The poet celebrates the mindblowing effects of LSD and laments at the same time his lost childhood. **1973** *Guardian* 8 May 18/1 For the hopeful voyeur of sheer obscenity in modern urban life, Glasgow is hard to beat. 'Mind blowing', was the concise description of a former civil servant. **1974** H. McCloy *Sleepwalker* ii. 16 A mind-blowing mustard yellow for the woodwork and on the walls a psychedelic splash of magenta and orchid and lime. **1969** B. Patten *Notes to Hurrying Man* 23 Bloated We lie dreamless, mind-blown in its ruins. **1907** *Mind* XVI. 620 The essential significance of the mind-body relationship. **1920** S. Alexander *Space, Time & Deity* II. 355 The acts of its mind-body would take the place of our organic or motor sensa. **1925** I. A. Richards *Princ. Lit. Crit.* 84 The Mind-Body problem is strictly speaking no problem. **1963** A. Kaplan in P. A. Schilpp *Philos. R. Carnap* 841 The situation is like that of the attempts to soften the mind-body dualism by introducing subtle interactions. **1970** H. Feigl in C. V. Borst *Mind-Brain Identity Theory* i. 35 The crucial..puzzle of the mind-body problem, at least since Descartes, has consisted in the challenge to render an adequate account of the relation of..mental facts (intentions, thoughts, volitions, desires, etc.) to the corresponding neurophysiological processes. **1964** *Punch* 19 Feb. 257/1 A lot of mind-boggling statistics. **1973** C. Bonington *Next Horizon* x. 146 A monstrous bergschrund, a huge, mind-boggling chasm about fifteen feet across. **1931** *Punch* 4 Nov. 494/2 Things and opinions change so quickly in these days that no one is going to crow over a graceful mind-changer. **1958** A. Huxley in *Sat. Even. Post* 18 Oct. 110/3 Within a few years there will probably be dozens of powerful but—physiologically and socially speaking—very inexpensive mind-changers on the market. **1965** Mind-changer [see *hallucinogenic *a.*]. **1894** 'Mark Twain' *Lett.* (1920) 316 A patient had actually been killed by a mind-curist. **1890** W. James *Princ. Psychol.* I. vi. 146 Evolutionary psychology demands a mind-dust. *Ibid.* xiii. 492 It is the mind-dust theory, with all its difficulties in a particularly uncompromising form. **1970** *Times* 26 Mar. 7 Hallucinogenic..agents such as L.S.D., mescaline and other so-called mind-expanders. **1973** *Black World* Apr. 16/1 The play is truly a mind-expander. **1963** *News-Call Bulletin* (San Francisco) 29 May 1/6 Professors Richard Alpert and Timothy Leary..started several years ago to experiment with 'psychedelic' or 'mind-expanding' drugs. **1972** D. Bloodworth *Any Number can Play* xv. 135 This dim, suffocating chamber..was..decorated with..mind-expanding daubs in fluorescent paint. **1883, 1891** Mind-healing [see *Christian Science]. **1968** H. Waugh *Con Game* viii. 81 These psychiatrists are too damned smart. All the time I was talking to him I had the feeling he was mind-reading me. **1972** J. Quartermain *Rock of Diamond* xxiv. 156 If I mind-read you, you're looking for a fall guy to do your dirty work. **1934** *Agric. Hist.* June 86 The 'oats' motif can be traced throughout Johnson's life. As a schoolboy the young Sam was given oatmeal porridge for breakfast, and if he was like many children, this may have given him a mind-set for life. **1964** *Spectator* 6 Mar. 303/2 It was thereafter always a wonderful fight, although the mindset one brought to it made it impossible to recognise what was happening. **1971** *Amer. Benedictine Rev.* Dec. 424 The mind-set and aspirations of a vibrant hellenistic culture. **1930** Blunden *Leigh Hunt* ii. 22 The grace which the mind-sight of those merry young scholars awoke in him. **1935** —— *Edward Gibbon* 15 He felt that there was in the world actual need of a history such as I have mentioned hovering in the mindsight of his age. **1947** S. Spender *Poems of Dedication* 27 She drinks his acres of light Which..Beyond mind-sight and eye-sight Reach a womb where his rays Penetrate her night. **1930** A. D. Lovejoy *Revolt Against Dualism* viii. 272 Mind-stuff is not supposed to be the same kind of thing as either data or the awareness of them. **1937** E. Upward in C. Day Lewis *Mind in Chains* 42 A poet's images or a novelist's characters are not created out of pure mind-stuff, but are suggested to him by the world in which he lives. **1886** *Science* 17 Dec. 559/1 Mr. Hodgson is now engaged..in some experiments on the subject of mind transference, or the occasional communication of mental impressions independently of ordinary perceptions. **1897** 'Mark Twain' *Following Equator* 317 Here was a clear case of mental telegraphy; of mind-transference.

mind, *v.* Add: **5. a.** Esp. in colloq. phr. *don't mind me*: take no notice of me; do not worry about me; do as you please. Often ironical.

1867 Trollope *Phineas Finn* (1869) I. viii. 69 'It's the meanest trade going... I don't know whether you are in Parliament, Mr. Finn.' 'Yes, I am; but do not mind me.' **1901** G. B. Shaw *Devil's Disciple* ii. 39, I never care much for my tea. Please dont mind me. **1911** —— *Doctor's Dilemma* iii. 70 *B.B.* Well, what is our friend Dubedat? A vicious and ignorant young man with a talent for drawing. *Louis.* Thank you. Dont mind me. **1926** M. A. von Arnim *Introd. to Sally* ii. 16 You go a'ead, sir, when she come back, and don't mind me. **1967** S. Knight *Window on Shanghai* iii. xx. 86 Ah, how philosophic I wax (and wane?) Don't mind me. **1973** L. Koenig *Little Girl* (1974) iii. 34 'Don't mind me,' she said, dragging the chair back.. and filling its place with the table... 'But the table belongs here.'

c. *mind you* (later examples).

1959 *Listener* 22 Jan. 154/2 The Japanese—who were scattered over a very large part of Asia at that time, mind you—would have all fought it out to the death. **1969** *Ibid.* 3 Apr. 467/2 And so to the book's title. It's not, mind you, 'why we are in Vietnam', but a question.

8. a. *do you mind?*: also used to mean 'do you mind not doing that?', i.e. 'please do not do that'.

1961 J. I. M. Stewart *Man who won Pools* xvii. 167 He was trying to put a hand on Phil's arm. '*Do* you mind?' Phil had never got it out more arrogant. Moore fell back.

d. *I don't mind if I do*: a colloq. phr. of acceptance or agreement, used esp. in accepting the offer of a drink.

c **1847** J. S. Coyne in M. R. Booth *Eng. Plays of 19th Cent.* (1973) IV. 193 You *are* a regular brick, and I don't mind if I do take some of your pickles. **1849** C. Brontë *Shirley* I. vii [*sc.* viii]. 184 'Take another glass,' urged Moore. Mr. Sykes didn't mind if he did. **1870** D. J. Kirwan *Palace & Hovel* v. 65 Tell ye me 'istry, is it? Vell. I don't mind if I do. *Ibid.* 69 'I'll give you a drink, me oul wiper.'.. 'Well, Billy, I don't mind if I do.' **1926** C. Beaton *Diary* in *Wandering Yrs.* (1961) 143 Everyone 'talked common'... 'I don't mind if I do; oo-er!' **1932** A. Christie *Peril at End House* viii. 101 'Come and have a drink,' I said... 'I don't mind if I do.' **1946** T. Kavanagh *Tommy Handley in Holidayland* 5 'Bitter, sir?' interrupted the Colonel [Chinstrap].., 'I don't mind if I do.' **1967** J. Porter *Dover & Unkindest Cut* xi. 122 'Another cup of tea, Mr Dover?' 'I don't mind if I do,' said Dover, passing his cup.

10. a. *to mind one's step*: see *step *sb.* 6.

d. *to mind out*: to look out, be careful; freq. *imp. colloq.* and *dial.*

1886 R. Holland *Gloss. County of Chester* 227 *Mind out*,..to be on one's guard. **1890** *Dialect Notes* I. 65 Mind out what you are doing. **1892** *Ibid.* 233 That is the word with the bark on it; you better mind out. **1894** W. Raymond *Love & Quiet Life* xii. 136 If I don't min' out, woone o' these days..he'l vall off. **1938** J. Stuart *Beyond Dark Hills* iii. 59 John's got a bad boy. He'll go to the pen if he don't mind out—that boy will. **1946** *Amer. Speech* XXI. 56 English children whizzing around on bicycles..will warn each other to keep out of the way by shouting 'Mind out!'.

11. *spec.* To look after (a baby or child), esp. in the absence of its parents; to look after (a shop or store) (also *transf.*).

1839 G. C. Lewis *Gloss. Herefordshire* 67, I ha left Bill at home to mind the children. **1876** C. C. Robinson *Gloss. Mid-Yorks.* 84/1 Minding the bairns and the house. **1899** Kipling *Stalky & Co.* 63 Arrah, Patsy, mind the baby; just ye mind the child awhile! **1902** *Dialect Notes* II. 239 Mind the baby while I'm gone. **1953** A. Upfield *Murder must Wait* x. 93 He accused me of neglecting the baby and said he'd..let his..secretary mind it. **1957** J. Blish *Fallen Star* vi. 75 The cabin door opened and the Commodore came out... 'Who's minding the store?' I asked him. 'Hanchett. We're on autopilot and he's watching the instruments.' **1963** J. H. Harris *Weird World Wes Beattie* (1964) iii. 32 If you will just mind the shop, I'll be on my way. **1970** G. F. Newman *Sir, You Bastard* ii. 70 The CID room was quiet. DC Jones was minding the shop. **1971** *Where* Nov. 343/2 A certificate is issued specifying the number of children and the hours and days when they can be minded. **1973** P. O'Donnell *Silver Mistress* vi. 109 'Who's running your section at the moment?' 'I am. With limited authority... I'm just minding the shop.'

12. *intr.* To matter, be important. (Not in standard use.)

1915 F. H. Lawrence *Let.* 16 Mar. in T. E. Lawrence *Home Lett.* (1954) 680, I had a room without a door or a window..but that did not mind. *Ibid.* 682 Bullets really don't mind much. **1961** *Listener* 5 Oct. 500/1 (*child's composition*) You migth see a earwig gust coming out of [an apple] but that dosenet mind gust pick it of.

minded, *ppl. a.* Add: **4. c.** With prefixed sb. forming adjs. with the sense 'interested in or enthusiastic about (the thing specified)'.

1928 [see *air-minded* adj. s.v. *air *sb.*[1] B. III. 1]. **1932** *Daily Express* 27 June 11/3 Get travel-minded. **1933** *Times Lit. Suppl.* 30 Mar. 205/3 Today we are an inland-dwelling folk, car-minded and mechanical. **1949** Helicopter-minded [see *'copter, copter]. **1956** *Planning* 23 July 153 PEP is intensely research-minded, and would rather not reach any conclusion than plump for one which cannot survive searching criticism. **1966** C. Mackenzie *Paper Lives* viii. 109 You *must* get computer-minded and appreciate that with the development of automation more and more people will be out of employment. **1972** *Guardian* 18 Aug. 9/2 There is also a bowling green for the sports-minded customer.

Mindel (mi·ndĕl). *Geol.* The name of a tributary of the Danube in Bavaria, W. Germany, adopted by A. Penck (in Penck & Brückner *Die Alpen im Eiszeitalter* (1901) I. i. 110) and used *attrib.* to designate the second (antepenultimate) Pleistocene glaciation in the Alps, and in conjunction with *Riss to designate the following interglacial period. Also *absol.*

1910 [see *Günz]. **1939** [see *interglacial *a.*]. **1957** G. E. Hutchinson *Treat. Limnol.* I. i. 6 Relatively early in the Pleistocene, probably at the time of the Mindel glaciation, the Caspian was occupied by a high-level lake. **1972** *Sci. Amer.* Mar. 60/1 Deposits laid down in the subsequent interglacial period, the Mindel-Riss, contain a few fossil remains of a true cave bear. A bear skull preserved in Mindel-Riss sediments at Swanscombe in England shows the domed forehead that is characteristic of the species.

minder. Add: **3. b.** *spec.* (*a*) a machine-minder; (*b*) one who minds (see *mind *v.* 11) a baby or child; a baby-sitter.

(*a*) **1835** [in Dict.]. **1888** *Encycl. Brit.* XXIII. 709/2 If he is a machinist, he may superintend or be a 'minder' or he may be a layer-on or a taker-off of the sheets. **1938** *Amer. Speech* XIII. 271 The man who runs the presses is a *pressman* in America, but a *machinist* or a *machine minder* or simply a *minder* in England. **1970** *Financial Times* 13 Apr. 4/5 Among minders, the proportion on litho presses is forecast to go up from 20 per cent. in 1967 to 28 per cent. in 1972.

(*b*) **1863** [see *baby-minder* s.v. *baby *sb.* B. 1 b]. **1874** [in Dict.]. **1941** [see *child-minder* s.v. *child *sb.* 22]. **1957** *Times* 25 Nov. 11/4 Of course we will not worry about the children, we assure the kind minder as we blow farewell kisses. **1971** *Daily Tel.* 4 Nov. 9/3 Mothers, forced to work to make ends meet, ship their toddlers to unregistered minders, paid to keep an eye on them in 'cramped rooms, with no toys or stimulus'.

c. *slang.* A person employed to protect a criminal; a thief's assistant.

1924 E. Wallace *Room 13* xii. 61 Glancing down into the street, he distinguished one of the 'minders' his father had put there for his protection. **1928** —— *Flying Squad* xvi. 144 Whizzers..had 'minders', whose business it was to kick and disable the poor souls who found themselves robbed and attempted to recover their own. **1960** *Observer* 25 Dec. 7/6 A climbing team..was most often three-handed. Driver, minder, and climber... The minder stays at the foot of the pipe or ladder. His job is to safeguard the climber's rear and collect any gear he may sling down. **1968** C. Drummond *Death & Leaping Ladies* vi. 160 At school he was a juvenile fence and money-lender, with a couple of tough, simple-minded older boys as his 'minders'. **1973** E. McGirr *Bardel's Murder* ii. 35 Comes of a whole family of wrong 'uns... A high class 'minder' around the big gambling set.

mindlessly, *adv.* (Further examples.)

1963 *Times* 11 June 3/7 Dumitrescu worked away mindlessly like a machine at the head of the group. *a* **1966** M. Allingham *Cargo of Eagles* (1968) xv. 170 Temper and hysteria had fought mindlessly for the upper hand. **1972** *Publishers' Weekly* 21 Aug. 71/3 The result is mindlessly entertaining.

mine, *sb.* Add: **3.** In naval warfare, such a receptacle used on the high seas as well as at the entrance to a harbour. Also, a receptacle containing explosive placed in or on the ground as a weapon of war. Freq. with qualifying word indicating the kind or use: for *acoustic, land, magnetic*, etc., *mine*, see under the first elements.

1880 *Encycl. Brit.* XI. 309/2 The arrangements for exploding submarine mines or fixed torpedoes, where hostile vessels are passing close to them, are somewhat of the same character. **1889** J. T. Bucknill *Submarine Mines* xx. 219 Just as the mines themselves form a grand obstruction to the passage of large vessels..so smaller obstructions can..impede..the passage of small craft whose aims may be to attack the mines. **1890** [see *land-mine* s.v. *land *sb.*[1] 12]. **1915** W. Owen *Let.* 8 Jan. (1967)

313, I am not exposed to chances of mine or torpedo. **1942** *War Illustr.* 16 Oct. 238/1 A man can walk over a mine easily enough, but a tank or lorry'll send them up in a proper earthquake. **1968** VISCT. MONTGOMERY *Hist. Warfare* xviii. 416 In 1855, in the Baltic, Russia made the first serious use of floating mines.

5. a. *mine-dust, -head, -mouth, -slime, -stamp* (STAMP *sb.*[3] 9), *-worker*; (sense 3) *mine-crater, -warfare.*

1917 'CONTACT' *Airman's Outings* 269 Two huge mine-craters sentinel it, left and right. **1886** J. BARROWMAN *Gloss. Scottish Mining Terms* 45 *Mine dust*, the riddlings of calcined ironstone. **1923** *Daily Mail* 16 Mar. 9 The present intention is to send labour squads..to successive mine-heads. **1886** J. BARROWMAN *Gloss. Scottish Mining Terms* 45 *Mine mouth*, the point where a mine leaves the surface of the ground. **1921** *Chambers's Jrnl.* Apr. 262/1 A savage land of rocks and lakes and mine-slime and active and derelict mine-workings. **1926** J. MASEFIELD *Odtaa* xiv. 233 It is a kind of a mine-stamp, or engine of some sort. **1953** D. LESSING *Five* III. 128 The mine-stamps thudded day and night, coming loud or soft, according to the direction of the wind. **1910** *Blackw. Mag.* June 895/2 The immense development of mine warfare. **1957** *Encycl. Brit.* XV. 531/2 A self-contained continental power..has little to lose and everything to gain by unrestricted mine warfare. **1974** *Saturday* (Charleston, S. Carolina) 20 Apr. 3-A/2 Like wood, the fiberglass hull is non-magnetic and is considered good for mine warfare. **1901** *Edin. Rev.* Apr. 496 An agreement..that the mine-workers should receive an advance of 10 per cent. in their rates of wages. **1928** *Britain's Industr. Future* (Liberal Industr. Inquiry) IV. 266 The pensioning of older mine-workers. **1975** *Times* 18 Feb. 2/1 Mineworkers' leaders in the traditionally militant areas of Scotland and Yorkshire yesterday voted to back the £140m pay deal negotiated by their national union leaders with the National Coal Board last week.

6. mine-boy *S. Afr.*, a native African who works in the mines; **mine-car** (see quots.); **mine-detector**, an instrument which, by its re-action to metal, indicates the presence of mines; **mine-dump** *S. Afr.*, a pile of refuse material on the surface of a mine, esp. a gold-mine (cf. DUMP *sb.*[4] 1); **mine-field** (later examples); also, an area of land in which mines have been laid; also *fig.*; **mine-hunt** *v. intr.*, to hunt or sweep for mines; **mine-hunter** = *mine-sweeper*; **mine-hunting** = *mine-sweeping*; **mine-layer**, a ship or aeroplane equipped to lay mines; **mine-laying**, the operation of laying explosive mines; also *attrib.* or as *adj.*; **mine-sinker**, a device for keeping a mine submerged; **mine-sowing** = **mine-laying*; **mine-sweeper** (later examples); **mine-sweeping** (later examples); **mine-thrower** [tr. G. *minenwerfer*], a trench-mortar; **mine-tipple** *N. Amer.* [TIPPLE *sb.*[3]], a tip (TIP *sb.*[5] 3) at a mine.

1945 P. ABRAHAMS *Song of City* 73 The tom-tom beat of the Maraba..danced away the seething bitterness that is attendant with repression... On the morrow the house-boy would be a good..houseboy!.. And the mine-boy. **1953** P. LANHAM *Blanket Boy's Moon* I. v. 51 One Monare, a mine-boy, friend of Ntoane here, was watching. **1954** P. ABRAHAMS *Tell Freedom* III. iii. 108 Fights often flare up between mine-boys and house-boys. **1956** F. S. ATKINSON in D. L. Linton *Sheffield* 270 Diesel locomotives with large mine-cars are being used extensively underground, particularly in Yorkshire. **1967** *Gloss. Mining Terms* (*B.S.I.*) x. 11 *Mine car*, a large tub (usually spring mounted and over 60 ft..capacity) used primarily for mineral haulage underground. **1943** *Hutchinson's Pict. Hist. War* 12 May—3 Aug. 125 (*caption*) The soldier in the foreground is sweeping the ground with a mine detector and wearing earphones as he listens intently for the buzz indicating the presence of a mine. **1945** *Finito! Po Valley Campaign* 41 The glass-topped Topf mines that fooled the mine-detectors. **1955** E. S. GARDNER *Case of Glamorous Ghost* (1960) x. 121, I used what is known as a mine detector..an electronic device so designed that when it is moved over the surface of the ground it will give a peculiar squeal when it is moved over a metallic object. **1926** S. G. MILLIN *S. Africans* iii. 77 They are the mine-dumps, the refuse of stamp-mill and cyanide tank. **1956** V. JENKINS *Lions Rampant* v. 76 Dominating the land-scape..are the huge yellow-white mine dumps which mark the gold mines. **1971** *Gloss. Soil Sci. Terms* (Soil Sci. Soc. Amer.) 11/1 *Mine dumps*, areas covered with over-burden and other waste materials from ore and coal mines, quarries, and smelters, and usually with little or no vegetative cover. **1889** J. T. BUCKNILL *Submarine Mines* xiv. 168 Secrecy is essential... Any artifice which ingenuity can suggest should be undertaken... False reports concerning the mine fields should be spread. **1917** A. CONAN DOYLE *His Last Bow* viii. 298 It would brighten my declining years to see a German cruiser navigating the Solent according to the minefield plans which I have furnished. **1938** *Encycl. Brit. Bk. of Year* 432/2 Other anti-tank agencies being given consideration are mine-fields and 'catch trenches' (*i.e.* tank traps). **1942** *Times* 8 June 4/6 The 'Cauldron', an area..between..the upper and lower gaps which Rommel forced through our minefield. **1957** *Encycl. Brit.* XV. 532/2 By the end of 1914 Britain had established extensive mine-fields in the English Channel. **1963** *Times* 16 Feb. 4/6 This bold venture into the mine-fields of satire is one to be supported and preserved. **1968** VISCT. MONTGOMERY *Hist. Warfare* xxi. 512 Wavell once compared the tactics of war in the desert to war at sea; minefields were laid in the desert very much as they were in the sea. **1973** *Times* 30 Nov. 19/1 He is..operating..in a political minefield, requiring more circumspection than he has always managed. **1915** KIPLING *Fringes of Fleet* 74 He's mine-hunting, I expect, just now. **1964** *Navy News* Nov. 5/5 After refitting and converting..H.M.S. *Iveston* commissioned on October 16th as a Coastal Minehunter. **1974** *Times* 18 Apr. 1/4 It is the diver's job to locate the unexploded bomb on the canal floor after it has been picked up by the mine-hunter's sonar equipment. **1964** *Navy News* Nov. 5/5 She will join the First Minehunting Squadron in December and will be based at Port Edgar in the Firth of Forth. **1974** *Observer* 17 Mar. 8/4 Mine-hunting ships—the Navy's new name for minesweepers. **1974** *Saturday* (Charleston, S. Carolina) 20 Apr. 3-A/2 The mine-hunting vessels include two with wood hulls and one with an experimental fiberglass hull... All three mine hunting vessels have sonar to detect mines and other objects like bombs. **1909** *Q. Rev.* Oct. 575 Six second-class cruisers of the Naval Defence Act have been converted into mine-layers. **1923** W. S. CHURCHILL *World Crisis 1915* 260 The mine-layer *Nousret* had on March 18 thirty-six mines ready for laying. **1939** *War Illustr.* 16 Dec. 435 Raid by British warplanes..on the German seaplane base at Borkum. They had been looking for the mine-layers—and they had found them. **1944** *Aeronautics* July 32/3 Suitable for duties as a torpedo bomber, a dive bomber, or a mine layer, the Fairey Barracuda was first reported in action on the 3rd April 1944. **1911** *Q. Rev.* Oct. 466 The money..is now expended upon a large and increasing fleet of mine-laying and mine-sweeping ships. **1921** *Flight* 19 May 348/2 The American naval authorities are reported to have been carrying out in Chesapeake Bay experiments in mine-laying from the air. **1928** C. F. S. GAMBLE *Story N. Sea Air Station* xviii. 310 The U.C. boats were of a type designed both for mine-laying and torpedo work. **1939** *Flight* 30 Nov. 429/2 The mine-laying machines cannot behave as the enemy reconnaissance machines have been behaving of late, namely arriving at a great height and hurrying away at the first hint of defence activity. **1955** *Times* 24 May 8/4 The risk of more serious incidents, such as Egyptian minelaying and Israel retaliation, should also lessen. **1958** P. KEMP *No Colours or Crest* iii. 37 The fast mine-laying cruiser *Manxman*. **1889** C. SLEEMAN *Torpedoes* (ed. 2) vi. 119 The only practicable method of testing the efficiency of mine anchors or sinkers is to moor a buoyant mine to an anchor. **1926** *Spectator* 21 Aug. 271/1 He..produced 50,000 minesinkers at a very low cost. **1940** BARTLETT & WILLIAMS *War of 1939* II. iii. 104 The Germans..had turned to indiscriminate mine-sowing. **1940** *War Illustr.* 5 Jan. 568/3 Particular attention being paid to the favourite areas of the mine-sowing seaplanes in the Thames Estuary. **1914** *Illustr. London News* 22 Aug. 286/3 Mine-sweepers..precede the fleet to sea and clear its path of hostile mines. **1940** BARTLETT & WILLIAMS *War of 1939* II. iii. 106 Mine damage at this time was not confined to merchant vessels, the British minesweepers *Mastiff* and *Aragonite* being sunk with casualties. *Ibid.* 107 The British Admiralty were quick.. to appeal for two hundred additional drifters to act as minesweepers. **1972** *Daily Tel.* 21 Jan. 2/8 More mine-sweepers and helicopters will be used from this summer to improve coastal fishery protection. *Ibid.*, Helicopters.. will make spotter sweeps to help the minesweepers to guard the six-mile limit fishing areas against unauthorised vessels. **1915** *Chambers's Jrnl.* May 294/2 The operation of taking up mines is known as 'mine-sweeping'. **1958** *Times* 11 Nov. 9/1 Two coastal mine-sweeping flotillas.. are already under N.A.T.O. command. **1973** *Listener* 26 Apr. 535/1 Mine-sweeping operations off Haiphong. **1915** *Illustr. London News* 13 Feb. 204/2 The Germans..had actually provided..themselves with mortars of this description, the so-called *minen-werfer*—mine-throwers. **1923** *Daily Mail* 17 Jan. 7 They captured 7 Frenchmen, 15 local policemen, 3 minethrowers, and a machine gun. **1930** J. DOS PASSOS *42nd Parallel* I. 111 In the middle of squirrels and minetipples. **1974** *Beautiful Brit. Columbia* Spring 27/2 Coal is still mined there in large quantities. The highway passes underneath a portion of the mine tipple.

mine, *v.* Add: **9.** *U.S.* (See quot. 1937.)

1937 *Amer. Speech* XII. 105 They *mine* the soil; that is, they use up fertility without restoring it. **1972** *New Yorker* 25 Nov. 42/3 When they moved here, the land had been farmed out—'mined', the local phrase was—and the one undiscouraged crop was the wild strawberries.

mineable, *a.* Add mod. examples of the form **minable.**

1971 *Sci. Amer.* May 17/1 There are minable cinnabar deposits in many regions around the world, and man was attracted to its use as early as prehistoric times. **1972** *Nature* 14 Apr. 332/1 And is it likely that economically minable lead ores are equally distributed between North America and the rest of the world?

‖ **minenwerfer** (mī·nənvɛ̱rfəɹ, mī·nənwə̄ɹfəɹ). *Mil.* [G., f. *minen* (pl.) mines + *werfer*, f. *werfen* to throw.] A German trench mortar. Cf. **mine-thrower*, *MINNIE[2].

Also called *minnenwerfer* from an expansion of MINNIE[2], the British soldiers' nickname for this gun.

1915 A. D. GILLESPIE *Lett. from Flanders* (1916) 80 About Christmas time the Germans fetched up a thing called a *Minen Werfer*, a kind of trench mortar which throws 600 lb. of gun cotton. **1915** [see **mine-thrower*]. **1916** F. M. FORD *Let.* Aug. (1965) 68 The Germans seem to have nothing but minenwerfers. **1917** A. G. EMPEY *Over Top* 300 *Minnenwerfer*, a high-power trench mortar shell of the Germans, which makes no noise coming through the air... Tommy nicknames them 'Minnies'. **1923** KIPLING *Irish Guards in Gt. War* I. 101 He retaliated..along the line of seven-inch minenwerfers.

miner[1]. Add: **6. miner's right** (earlier and later examples); also *N.Z.*

1855 in *Occasional Papers Univ. Sydney Austral. Lang. Res. Centre* (1966) No. 9. 15 It shall be lawful for the Governor..to cause documents to be issued each of which shall be called 'The Miner's Right' and shall be granted to any person applying for the same upon payment of a fee of one pound. **1858** in *Ibid.* 16 It is not generally known, ..that..any one interested in the workings at the gold-fields should hold a Miner's Right which can be had at the Treasury. **1863** *Rules & Regulations Otago Gold Fields* 7 Every person residing on a Gold Field and engaged in mining for gold, shall take out a Miner's Right; such Miner's Right to be carried on the person, and produced for inspection when demanded. **1868** V. PYKE *Province of Otago* 41 The only qualification is the possession of a 'Miners' Right'. **1950** *N.Z. Jrnl. Agric.* Feb. 189/2 Exhibits [in an Arrowtown museum, Central Otago, include] ..a miner's right. **1959** BAKER *Drum* 127 *Miner's right*, a licence to dig for gold granted to a miner, orig. in the 1850s.

b. *miner's nystagmus.*

1879 [see NYSTAGMUS 2]. **1959** *Chambers's Encycl.* X. 152/2 Owing to the inadequate illumination in mines a large number of miners get a condition known as 'miner's nystagmus'. **1962** H. C. WESTON *Sight, Light & Work* (ed. 2) ix. 262 The occupational disease known as *miner's nystagmus* is so named on account of the ocular movements commonly associated with it.

mineragraphy (minĕræ·grăfi). *Min.* [f. MINERA(L *sb.* + -GRAPHY.] = *MINERALOGRAPHY.

1924 *Amer. Mineralogist* IX. 177 Mineragraphy, the study of minerals in polished section with the metallographic microscope for the purpose of determining their identity and paragenesis, has generally been carried on under vertical illumination. **1965** G. J. WILLIAMS *Econ. Geol. N.Z.* ix. 136/2 (*heading*) Mineragraphy of titanomagnetite.

So **minera·grapher**, one who practises mineragraphy; **mineragra·phic** *a.*

1931 *Amer. Mineralogist* XVI. 209 In the course of some recent mineragraphic work on the manganiferous iron ores of the Cuyana Range..it was necessary to make quick identification of the various oxides of iron and manganese. **1953** *Austral. Jrnl. Chem.* VI. 443 The most comprehensive mineragraphic report..records the presence of more than 30 mineral species. **1964** *Weekly News* (Auckland) 10 June 8/5 The mineragrapher determines the intimacy of the admixture of minerals composing the ore. **1965** G. J. WILLIAMS *Econ. Geol. N.Z.* ix. 136/2 Titanium being an embarrassment in any metallurgical process, attention has been given to mineragraphic studies with a view to locating this element.

mineral, *sb.* Add: **4. d.** = MINERAL WATER. (Usu. in *pl.*)

1885 *List of Subscribers* (United Telephone Co.) p. xv, We have had a run upon minerals, and are nearly out. *Ibid.*, We are out of minerals. Kindly send us..one gross of seltzer, one gross of soda. **1922** JOYCE *Ulysses* 597 They might hit upon some drinkables in the shape of a milk and soda or a mineral. **1927** *Glasgow Herald* 15 Apr. 11 There will be..supper with ale and minerals at Osborne's Hotel.

6. mineral dressing, treatment of ore so as to remove gangue and concentrate the valuable constituents; so *mineral dresser*; **mineral rod** (later examples).

1895 *Funk's Stand. Dict.*, *Mineral dresser*, a machine for trimming or dressing mineralogical specimens. **1957** *Sci. News* XLVI. 35 This upgrading [of ores] is the work done by the mineral dresser. **1939** A. M. GAUDIN *Princ. Mineral Dressing* i. 1 Mineral dressing is commonly regarded as the processing of raw minerals to yield marketable products and waste by means that do not destroy the physical and chemical identity of the minerals. **1957** *Sci. News* XLVI. 37 The methods of mineral dressing most in use before World War I were limited to gravitation in pulsing or streaming currents of water.., the use of magnets on ferro-magnetic ores, and such hydro-metallic processes as the cyanidation of gold and the leaching of copper. **1974** *Encycl. Brit. Macropædia* XI. 1063/2 Modern processes in mineral dressing have become increasingly directed toward using fundamental principles governed by laws of physics, chemistry, and electricity. **1849** T. L. CLINGMAN in C. Lanman *Lett. from Alleghany Mts.* 187 Travelling about the country under the guidance of *mineral rods* or dreams in search of mines. **1902** A. D. MCFAUL *Ike Glidden* xxi. 184 They've sent for Squire Blunt to come up here in the morning, with a mineral rod, to assist them.

mineral, *a.* Add: **3. b.** Esp. in *mineral spring.* Also *attrib.*

1783 S. TENNEY *Let.* 1 Sept. in *Mem. Amer. Acad. Arts & Sci.* (1793) II. 43, I mentioned some mineral springs in the vicinity of this place. **1797** [in Dict.]. **1843** W. W. MATHER et al. *Geol. N.Y.* IV. 308 In this district the only mineral springs of interest are the salines, the sulphur springs, [etc.]. **1911** *Daily Colonist* (Victoria, B.C.) 22 Apr. 1/4 Craig..was probably fatally shot by a burglar late tonight in his room at a mineral springs resort. **1972** *Gloss. Geol.* (Amer. Geol. Inst.) 456/1 *Mineral spring*, a spring whose water contains enough mineral matter to give it a definite taste, in comparison to ordinary drinking water, esp. if the taste is unpleasant or if the water is regarded as having therapeutic value.

5. mineral soil, any soil in which the organic constituents are small in proportion to the inorganic ones; **mineral teeth**, artificial teeth.

1924 F. E. BEAR *Soil Managem.* iv. 26 The tendency of mineral soils to be similar in chemical composition, irrespective of their source of origin, is very nicely shown in the following table. **1960** TEUSCHER & ADLER *Soil & its Fertility* i. 10 The fundamental distinction should be made between mineral soils and organic soils, depending upon the proportion of organic matter which they contain... In general, a soil is designated as organic when it contains 20 per cent or more of organic matter. **1851** C. CIST *Sk. Cincinnati in 1851* 220 Mineral Teeth. One factory. **1885** *List of Subscribers, Classified* (United Telephone Co.) (ed. 6) 230 Manufacturers of Mineral Teeth and every Dental Requisite.

b. mineral brown (see quot. 1930); **mineral grey** (earlier and later examples); **mineral**

violet = *manganese violet*; **mineral white** (earlier example).

1869 T. W. Salter *Field's Chromatogr.* (new ed.) xvii. 342 Under the names of Euchrome and Mineral Brown, they [*sc.* Cappah browns] have been introduced into commerce for civil and marine painting. **1930** Maerz & Paul *Dict. Color* 167/1 *Mineral brown*, this name, or its synonym, *Metallic Brown*, is occasionally found given to specific colors in paints. It has..long been used to refer to any native earth colored by iron oxide, etc. **1869** T. W. Salter *Field's Chromatogr.* (new ed.) xix. 375 Mineral gray..is obtainable from the lapis lazuli, after the blue and ash have been worked out. **1958** M. L. Wolf *Dict. Painting* 179 A substance known as gangue (vein-stone) is often offered as mineral gray, but it is not a successful substitute. **1913** B. Brown *Painter's Palette* iv. 21 Taking these paints..and making them..account for themselves in the matter of value, we find that their values fall on the value-scale thus:..O.—Burnt Sienna. Rose Madder. Mineral Violet. **1934** H. Hiler *Notes Technique Painting* ii. 132 Mineral violet (manganous metaphosphate). **1958** M. L. Wolf *Dict. Painting* 170 Manganese pigments... The violets are particularly varied, some of the shades including mineral-, permanent-, and Nuernberger violet. **1875** E. Spon *Workshop Receipts* 93/2 White Pigments ..Mineral white.—Precipitated carbonate of lead.

mineralization. Add: **1.** (Further examples.)

1898 *Q. Jrnl. Geol. Soc.* LIV. 81 The silicification, or more generally the mineralization, of these conglomerates is, in my opinion, the result of secondary processes of infiltration and crystallization. **1918** *Mining Mag.* XIX. 196/2 The supposed essential similarities between the conglomerates and ordinary lode deposits and quartz veins seem rather to have been based on ignorance of the various factors identical to formation of fissure deposits than on clear conceptions as to how the conglomerates received their mineralization. **1935** *Amer. Jrnl. Sci.* XXX. 115 'Mineralization' was shown to be a process of chemical action in which the mineralizer, HCl, was regenerated after performing transport and combination of the Fe_2O_3 with the MgO. **1971** *Nature* 24 Dec. 460/2 We intend to use this method to monitor the growth and dissolution of crystals in gels, especially in connexion with mineralization and demineralization in biological systems.

2. (Further examples.)

1970 *Daily Tel.* 24 Oct. 13/3 Two of the three drills en-encountered insignificant mineralisation. **1971** *Nature* 6 Aug. 393/2 In regions of mercury mineralization, however, up to 100 μg/kg has been reported.

mineralize, *v.* **2.** (Further examples.)

1911 *Encycl. Brit.* XVIII. 255/1 Shales, sandstones and igneous rocks may be silicified and mineralized under suitable conditions. **1973** *Nature* 7 Dec. 347/1 Experiments introducing modern lichens into the normal preparation of microfaunal samples using hydrogen peroxide failed to mineralise the plant structures.

mineralized, *ppl. a.* Add: **2.** Also of methylated spirit (see quot. 1906), and of carbon electrodes. (Further examples.)

1906 *Act 6 Edw. VII* c.20 § 4 (1) The expression 'mineralized methylated spirits' means..spirits which, in addition to being methylated..have mixed with or dissolved in them..mineral naphtha. **1915** K. Tornberg tr. *Rasch's Electric Arc Phenomena* vii. 149 The radiation from the luminous arc flame of mineralized carbons, thus, is not always sufficient to compensate for any considerable deficiency occasioned by artificial lengthening of the arc. **1967** *Martindale's Extra Pharmacopoeia* (ed. 25) 86/2 Mineralised methylated spirits is the only variety that may be sold by retail in Great Britain for general use.

mineralizer. Add: **1. b.** *Petrol.* A volatile substance dissolved in a magma which aids the formation of minerals by altering the properties of the magma but is not necessarily present in the final mineral; also, a substance which promotes the artificial synthesis of a mineral.

1909 A. Harker *Nat. Hist. Igneous Rocks* xii. 290 Mineralisers are, before all, powerful fluxes. One of their most important offices is that of reducing the viscosity of a magma. **1921** *Jrnl. Geol.* XXIX. 205 The presence of mineralizers has lowered the temperature of freezing below the inversion range of these minerals. **1943** R. D. George *Minerals & Rocks* xx. 434 When a rock is poured out of a volcano the mineralizers have a chance to escape before they have done their work. **1958** J. H. de Boer in Everett & Stone *Struct. & Properties Porous Materials* 290 We had a mixture of alumina and silica—I don't remember if it was in the right proportion—but heating at a relatively low temperature..mullite was already formed with lithium as a mineralizer. **1974** L. N. Kogarko in H. Spenser *Alkaline Rocks* vi. iv. 480/2 Mineralizers may not enter into the composition of minerals but exert catalytic action on the process of their growth.

mineralocorticoid (mi:nĕrălokǭ·ɹtikoid). *Biochem.* [f. Mineral *sb.* + -o + *corticoid.] Any of the steroid hormones produced in the adrenal cortex which are esp. concerned with maintaining the salt balance in the body; any analogous synthetic compound.

1950 H. Selye *Physiol. & Path. of Exposure to Stress* 646 Mineralo-corticoids predispose to the formation of lung edema. **1964** L. Martin *Clin. Endocrinol.* (ed. 4) v. 165 The mineralocorticoids promote the retention of salt and water and the excretion of potassium by the renal tubules. **1965** Lee & Knowles *Animal Hormones* iv. 70 The division of adrenal cortical hormones into glucocorticoids and mineralocorticoids is a convenient one. **1970** Passmore & Robson *Compan. Med. Stud.* II. vi. 12/2 Nowadays, the mineralocorticoid of choice in the treatment of defective secretion of endogenous aldosterone is the synthetic agent 9α-fluorocortisol.

mineralogic, *a.* For † *Obs.* read: Now chiefly *U.S.* (Add later examples.)

1952 G. Sarton *Hist. Sci.* I. xxi. 560 A mineralogic analysis. **1972** *Science* 3 Nov. 497/1 Approximately one-third of the book is devoted to mineralogic and petrologic attributes of sandstones.

mineralography (minĕrălǫ·grăfi). *Min.* [f. Mineral *sb.* + -o + -graphy.] The study of the physical and chemical microstructure of minerals, *spec.* of polished sections using the reflecting microscope.

1916 J. Murdoch *Microsc. Determination Opaque Minerals* p. iii, This new method [*sc.* using the reflecting microscope]..opens an entire new field of geologic science that promises to do for the ores what petrography has done for the rocks; for this the name of 'Mineralography' is proposed. **1921** H. L. Alling in *Jrnl. Geol.* XXIX. 194 The rock-forming minerals can be studied..as the end products of crystallization of melts—geophysical chemistry, or as here proposed—mineralography. **1937** *Amer. Mineralogist* XXII. 492 Attention is restricted to instrumental and manipulative procedure with the opaque minerals; no consideration is given..to those more interpretative and philosophical phases of mineralography, such as textures.. deformation, alteration etc. **1942** *Chem. Abstr.* XXXVI. 1267 (*heading*) The imprint method in mineralography.

Hence **mineralogra·phic** *a.*, of or using mineralography.

1916 J. Murdoch *Microsc. Determination Opaque Minerals* p. v, Mineralographic methods show that..the sulphide minerals tend to be microscopically mingled and intergrown in most intimate fashion. **1937** *Amer. Mineralogist* XXII. 492 Many requests..have come for description or discussion of mineralographic technique as employed at Harvard. **1971** *Daily Tel.* 29 Apr. 25 (Advt.), Mineralographic and related analyses on ores and metallurgical products.

mineralogy. Add: **2.** (A description of) the mineralogical features of a region or a specimen.

1798 R. Jameson (*title*) An outline of the mineralogy of the Shetland Islands, and of the Island of Arran. **1878** *Mineral. Mag.* II. 106 (*heading*) The geognosy and mineralogy of Scotland. **1933** P. G. H. Boswell *On Mineral. Sedimentary Rocks* p. v, Having devoted much time to a digest of the literature of the mineralogy of sediments, I published a review of the work. **1952** *Jrnl. Geol.* LX. 107 These processes..have produced significant changes in the mineralogy and textural relationships of the plutonic acidic rocks. **1971** I. G. Gass et al. *Understanding Earth* i. 27/2 Chemical weathering is very effective in producing a mineralogy which differs greatly from that of the igneous and metamorphic rocks.

mineraloid (mi·nĕrăloid). *Min.* [a. G. *mineraloid* (J. Niedźwiedzki 1909, in *Centralbl. f. Min., Geol. u. Paläont.* 662), f. *mineral* Mineral *sb.*: see -oid.] A substance that might be regarded as a mineral but is amorphous rather than crystalline.

1913 A. F. Rogers in *Proc. Amer. Philos. Soc.* LII. 608 The question of names for colloidal or amorphous minerals arises... Niedzwiedzki has proposed the term *mineraloid* for the natural amorphous substances. **1917** —— in *Jrnl. Geol.* XXV. 526 Lechateliérite is a glass and may be considered along with other natural glasses as a mineraloid. *Ibid.* 540 The hydrocarbons may be included under Niedzwiedski's term *mineraloid.* As Niedzwiedski used this term for all naturally occurring amorphous substances, this changes somewhat the original definition of mineraloid. Such substances as opal, cliachite, limonite, collophane, halloysite, etc., are definite enough to be called minerals even though they are amorphous. The term 'mineraloid' seems appropriate for the less definite mineral-like substances. **1941** C. S. Hurlbut *Dana's Man. Min.* (ed. 15) iii. 94 There are a number of mineral substances whose analyses do not yield definite chemical formulas and further show no signs of crystallinity. They have been called gel minerals or mineraloids. **1944** A. Holmes *Princ. Physical Geol.* iv. 37 Only a few non-crystalline substances are regarded, by common usage, as minerals, and these are generally distinguished as mineraloids. **1951** [see *jordisite]. **1972** G. S. Fay *Rockhound's Manual* iii. 37 Mineraloids are substances which look like and are often grouped with minerals, but mineraloids have an amorphous, or noncrystalline, structure as is evident when viewed under high-power microscopes. Opal is a mineraloid.

minestra (mine·stră). [It.] An Italian vegetable soup; = next.

1750 [see Macaroni 1]. **1871** *Monthly Packet* Sept. 362 One of the waiters here came up to me, announcing that 'la minestra' was ready. I had ordered no soup. **1907** J. Webster *Jerry Junior* xii. 184 They supped on *minestra* and *fritto misto.* **1935** M. Morphy *Recipes of all Nations* 127 This is the traditional 'minestra' served at Easter and Christmas in the province of Parma. **1941** 'M. Home' *Place of Little Birds* vi. 89 Donati..himself saw to the making of the *minestra.* **1948** E. Pound *Pisan Cantos* (1949) lxxviii. 65 'No, there is nothing to pay for that bread.' 'Nor for the minestra.' **1972** P. Eve *European's Cook Bk.* 130 *Minestra and Minestrone.* The basic difference between these two soups is that the former is all vegetable whereas the Minestrone is made with meat stock.

minestrone (minĭstrōu·ni). [It.] A thick soup containing vegetables and rice or pasta.

1891 E. Duret *Pract. Househ. Cookery* i. 63 The minestrone is a real Italian national soup. It is composed of a mixture of vegetables and rice. **1903** [see *fritto misto]. **1922** *Blackw. Mag.* Feb. 143/2 There were slices of melon, olives and tunny and a minestrone. **1936** Auden & Isherwood *Ascent of F6* ii. iii. 95 Just as you like. What about soup? Minestrone, I think? **1959** *Sunday Times* 29 Mar. 21/6 There are..dozens of versions of Minestrone, which is a really solid soup thick with vegetables and cheese and rice or pasta and intended, with bread and wine, to constitute the entire midday meal of hungry working people. **1972** N. Froud *World Bk. Soups* 26 A really good Italian minestrone should have a foundation of salt pork or gammon and white haricot beans.

minette[1]. Add: **2.** A low-grade oolitic iron ore found mainly in Luxemburg and Lorraine. Freq. *attrib.*

1902 *Encycl. Brit.* XXIX 584/2 Of these [ores] the chief is the lean but very cheap 'Minette' ore of the enormous deposits of Luxemburg and Lorraine. **1919** J. M. Keynes *Econ. Consequences Peace* iv. 90 The German Delegation made strong efforts to secure the inclusion of a provision by which coal and coke to be furnished by them to France should be given in exchange for *minette* from Lorraine. **1940** *Economist* 13 July 40/1 A new process of steelmaking ..was..applied by Continental steelmakers to the phosphoric pig-iron produced from their minette ores. **1966** P. T. Flawn *Mineral Resources* vi. 139 The famous minette iron ores of Lorraine were exploited first on the outcrop in Germany and then followed down dip into France.

Ming (miŋ), *sb.*[2] [Chinese, lit. 'bright, clear'.] The name of a dynasty which ruled in China from 1368 to 1644; a ruler belonging to this dynasty. Also *attrib.*

[**1671** J. Ogilby tr. *Montanus' Atlas Chinensis* 485 Thus ended a Prince, perhaps the greatest in the World..: Together with him, the Name of the Empire, viz. Taiming, that is, Of great Brightness, after it had continu'd two hundred sixty six Years..was utterly extinguish'd. **1676** *China & France* 19 The antient Kings of China were of the Family of Min, which signifies Light.] **1795** W. Winterbotham *Hist., Geogr. & Philos. View Chinese Empire* i. 5 The whole of their emperors, abstracting from those who are said to have reigned in the fabulous times, are comprehended in twenty-two dynasties... 21. Ming,..1368. 22. Tsing, 1645. **1836** J. F. Davis *Chinese* I. v. 185 The first Emperor of the Ming dynasty, which expelled the Mongols in 1366, had been servant to a monastery of bonzes, or priests of Budh. **1854** *Hist. China* v. 56 Houng-nan, or the first Ming, died in 1398, after a reign of thirty years. **1940** E. Pound *Cantos* lx. 91 And Japan kept peace even all through the great Ming rebellion. **1967** D. Bloodworth *Chinese Looking Glass* vii. 68 When in the 17th century the eunuchs betrayed their Ming ruler, and the Forbidden City of Peking fell to rebels, the Emperor wrote a valedictory message on his yellow robe and strangled himself with his silken girdle.

b. Used *attrib.* and *absol.* of the porcelain of the Ming period (of which the finest examples are extremely rare and valuable).

1892 J. D. Ball *Things Chinese* 309 A street hawker may be seen..ladling iced syrup out of Ming bowls, and there is hardly a butcher's shop without a large Ming jar. **1898** W. G. Gulland *Chinese Porc.* I. 3 We must also remember that a large amount of Ming porcelain must have been destroyed at the end of the Ming dynasty. **1907** E. Wharton *Fruit of Tree* ii. xiii. 209, I want to show you a set of Ming I picked up the other day. **1936** R. Lehmann *Weather in Streets* iii. iv. 318 Just because she hasn't even the guts to put her own stockings on—she's to be treated like a Ming vase. **1939** T. S. Eliot *Old Possum's Pract. Cats* 24 Down from the library came a loud *ping* From a vase which was commonly said to be Ming. **1970** *Oxf. Compan. Art* 234/2 The standard Ming porcelain body was refined and white, capable of thin potting when necessary, and covered with a fairly even, clear glaze.

c. Used *attrib.* to denote colours characteristic of Ming porcelain, as *Ming blue, green, yellow.*

1926 *Textile Mercury* 19 June 566/3 The Textile Colour Card Association's..new greens are Locarno, elfin, ming,.. and Paradise greens. **1931** B. Rackham in R. L. Hobson et al. *Chinese Ceramics* ii. 141 The blue..is quite different from the many tones of Ming blue,..and whatever may be the attractive qualities of the Ming blues in isolation, there can be no doubt that this later blue and white porcelain is far more effective. **1935** J. P. Marquand (*title*) Ming yellow. **1966** *Country Life* 30 June 1761/2 Shift-dresses.. in white, Ming-green, navy or camel. **1969** *Vogue* 1 Mar. 99 White wool tabard, edged with waves of Ming blue.

minge (mindʒ), *sb. dial. or slang.* [Origin obscure.] The female pudendum; hence, by extension, women regarded collectively as a means of sexual gratification.

1903 *Eng. Dial. Dict.* IV. 118/2 *Minge*, the female pudendum. **1925** Fraser & Gibbons *Soldier & Sailor Words* 156 *Minge*, female society (similar to Binge—*q.v.*), *e.g.*, 'His failing is Binge and yours Minge.' **1936** J. Curtis *Gilt Kid* viii. 80 I'm going to give you a kick in the minge if you don't shut up. **1974** *New Direction* IV. iv. 19/2 They've all..scented and talced their minges.

‖ **mingei** (miŋge·i). Also **Mingei.** [Jap. f. *min* people + *gei* arts.] Japanese folk-art; traditional local Japanese handicraft. Also *attrib.*

1960 B. Leach *Potter in Japan* viii. 183 Sen cha (green tea) taste, different from 'Matt cha' and certainly not 'Mingei'. **1967** H. H. Sanders *World of Jap. Ceramics* 177 The brown clay of Ryūmon-ji, when decorated with white slip..was considered..to be one of the distinctive *mingei* products of Japan. **1969** *Sat. Rev.* (U.S.) 13 Sept. 90/1 *Mingei*, or folk art, restaurants..with décor drawn from

Japan's rich folk tradition, hand-made plates and bowls by master potters.

mingily (mi·ndʒili), *adv.* [f. *MINGY *a.*: see -LY[2].] Meanly, stingily.

1958 *Listener* 6 Nov. 722/2 The most mingily ungenerous gathers backed by elastic.

mingimingi (mi·ŋimiŋi). Also **mingi.** [Maori.] An evergreen shrub, *Cyathodes acerosa* (or *C. fasciculata*) belonging to the family Epacridaceæ, native to New Zealand, Victoria, and Tasmania, and bearing tiny, green flowers and red or white berries. Cf. *MICKY[2].

1889 T. KIRK *Forest Flora N.Z.* 213 The wood of the mingi is of a light-brown colour. **1906** T. F. CHEESEMAN *Man. N.Z. Flora* 411 C[yathodes] *acerosa*... Abundant from the North Cape southwards. Sea-level to 2500 ft. Mingimingi. **1929** W. MARTIN *N.Z. Nature Bk.* II. viii. 126 The mingi-mingi..is a rigid, pungent-leaved shrub with either white or red berries. **1963** *Weekly News* (Auckland) 10 July 37/3 The small shrub called mingimingi or black teatree is as good as manuka as a source of heat. **1966** G. W. TURNER *Eng. Lang. Austral. & N.Z.* viii. 168 Another shrub *mingi* is said by Morris to have the form *micky* in the South Island. This is likely, as the South Island dialects of Maori have *k* for North Island *ng*.

Mingrelian (miŋgrī·liăn, min-), *sb.* and *a.* Also 7–8 **Mengrelian.** [f. *Mingrelia* (see below) + -AN.] **A.** *sb.* **a.** A member of the people inhabiting Mingrelia, an area of the Kutais region of the Caucasus. **b.** The language of this people. **B.** *adj.* Of or pertaining to this people.

1639 [see *CIRCASSIAN *sb.* 1]. **1690** LOCKE *Hum. Und.* I. iii. 18 The Mengrelians, a People professing Christianity. *a* **1791** [see GEORGIAN *a.*[2] 1]. **1876** *Encycl. Brit.* V. 257/2 The Mingrelians..extend from the Zenesquali on the east to the Ingur and the Black Sea on the west, while the lower course of the Rion may be considered as constituting their limit on the south. **1883** *Ibid.* XVI. 437/1 The Mingrelians (still almost exclusively confined to the Mingrelian territory, and numbering 197,000) are closely akin to the Georgians. **1921** [see *KIRGHIZ *sb.* and *a.*]. **1939** L. H. GRAY *Foundations of Lang.* xii. 375 South Caucasian.. consists of four languages: Georgian.., Mingrelian, Laz, and Svanian. **1959** *Chambers's Encycl.* VIII. 356/1 The chief languages are:..Mingrelian, Lazic, Svanetian. *Ibid.* XI. 430/1 The Georgians, Mingrelians and Armenians of the Caucasus. **1973** *Observer* 15 Apr. 39/1 The Beria Papers by Alan Williams... Brash English journalist and rip-roaring Russian defector, with linguistic help from beautiful Mingrelian.

mingy (mi·ndʒi), *a. colloq.* Also † **mingee.** [Perh. f. M(EAN *a.*[1] + ST)INGY *a.*, or a blend of MANGY *a.* and STINGY *a.*] Mean, stingy, niggardly; disappointingly small.

1911 J. W. HORSLEY *I Remember* xi. 254 'Mingee' for greedy. **1912** R. BROOKE *Let.* May (1968) 382, I called you a mingy and coprologous Oxford poetaster. **1918** W. OWEN *Let.* 19 Aug. (1967) 569, I rushed off a note in time for this evening's post, which may seem very mingy. **1926** C. BEATON *Diary* in *Wandering Yrs.* (1961) vii. 148 A mingy little tray he had picked up from heaven-knows-where. **1930** E. V. LUCAS *Down Sky* 223 It's dear, but we are not going to be mingy. **1940** [see *CLIP *sb.*[1] 2 e]. **1972** *Guardian* 30 Aug. 9/5 The opening for filling steam irons with distilled water is usually mingy, and the thing overflows.

Comb. **1959** *Times* 28 Dec. 3/1 Both..were determined ..not to let the mingy-minded weather spoil the jubilee match. **1966** 'L. LANE' *ABZ of Scouse* 68 *Mingy-arsed bastard*, a miserly person.

Hence as *sb.*, a mean person. *rare.*

1939 M. EGAN *To Love & Cherish* II. 48 Don't be a mingy, father; they only cost a shilling.

Minha(h, varr. *MINCHA.

mini (mi·ni), *sb.* **1.** Abbrev. of *minicar, minicab* (see *MINI- b); *spec.* the proprietary name of a small car made by British Leyland (formerly the British Motor Corporation). Also *attrib.* and *Comb.*

1961 *Economist* 24 June 1327/2 Taxi-men and mini-men have tested their vocabularies in London this week: the mini-men are confident of profit. **1961** *Engineering* 17 Nov. 658 The Mini's astonishing success is due purely and simply to good engineering. **1962** *Listener* 18 Oct. 634/2 The designer of the Morris Minor and the 'minis'. **1963** *Times* 19 Apr. 17/1 The company also announces the appointment of Mr. A. A. Issigonis, designer of the 'mini' range and the technical director, to the corporation's board. **1964** *Times* 11 Feb. 11/7 At present a young man who passes a test in a mini is legally entitled to drive an eight-wheeler weighing 24 tons at 60 m.p.h. on a motorway. **1970** G. F. NEWMAN *Sir, You Bastard* iii. 99 Sneed squeezed his mini on to the drive where four other cars were parked. **1971** *Times* 6 Aug. 7/6 Feeding the fantasies of mini-drivers, convincing them..that anything the film's crack stunt-drivers could do they could do.

2. Abbrev. of *mini-skirt* (see *MINI- b).

1966 *Guardian* 27 July 6/4 The new thing about the Scherrer mini is that it flares. **1967** *Punch* 4 Jan. 1/1 The lengths of female laid bare by minis. **1968** *Listener* 12 Dec. 790/3 One after another, Arab states are banning the mini. **1971** B. MALAMUD *Tenants* 42 She wore..a plain white mini with purple tights.

mini (mi·ni), *a.* [Abbrev. of MINIATURE *a.* Cf. next.] Very small, tiny.

1963 *Daily Tel.* 17 Dec. 13 A 'mini' census covering one householder in ten will be taken by the Government in 1966. **1966** *Ibid.* 14 Nov. 10/3 M. Redlus insists: 'My minis will be the most mini in Europe but they'll be decent.' **1966** *Punch* 7 Dec. 857/1 Leg make-up..gives sitting-down confidence to the wearer of the miniest skirt. **1966** *Sunday Express* 18 Dec. 23/5 Of course 25,000 cases is pretty mini. **1967** *Word Study* Dec. 3/2 There's nothing mini about their wages. **1969** *Daily Tel.* 25 Sept. 21/1 Girls prance on the longest legs, in the mini-est skirts and the kinkiest boots.

mini-, *pref.*, combining form of MINIATURE *a.* (reinforced by the first letters of MINIMUM *a.*), used to designate things that are very small of their kind.

A prefix much in vogue from the 1960s. Only a selection from the virtually unlimited number of combs. is illustrated here. The examples are arranged in alphabetical order of the combs. for convenience of reference.

1966 *Daily Tel.* 24 Oct. 11/1 The demand for a prototype female briefcase has been underlined by a strong season of mini-bag fashions—little swinging double-sided dog lead bags that made the absence of a briefcase for women all the more apparent. **1962** *Punch* 12 Dec. 878/1 A cycle firm is bringing out a mini-bike. **1970** *Time* 2 Nov. 56 Half-size (or even smaller) motor-cycles... Recession or no, minibikes seem to be all over, but nowhere are they more visible than in Los Angeles. **1960** *House & Garden* Oct. 135 (Advt.), Hygena think of details—..like built-in bread bins,..Minibins, refrigerators. **1968** *Economist* 10 Feb. 46/3 Capital investment shows no signs (yet) of re-energising—and it shouldn't, despite the miniboom. **1968** *Observer* 22 Dec. 21/7 A mini-bottle of Gala's nail polish (Little Gems 4s. 4d. a bottle). **1970** *Jrnl. Gen. Psychol.* LXXXIII. 155 Either *S* or *E* could activate the green light by depressing the button on a minibox situated in front of each of them. **1961** 'R. M. DASHWOOD' *Provincial Daughter* 55 Squalid piles of dust, marbles and minibricks. **1966** *Times Rev. Industry* Sept. 63/3 With the 'mini-budget' having withdrawn another £500m. from internal demand. **1971** *Daily Colonist* (Victoria, B.C.) 24 Nov. 1/7 The vessels were described as 'mini-bulkers', small ships..for ferrying cargoes. **1936** *Miniature Camera Mag.* Dec. 4/2 It is perhaps to be expected that all sorts and conditions of industries and businesses should have sprung up around the successful Minicamera. **1964** *Punch* 21 Oct. 592/1 Mini-holidays, mini-cameras, mini-tellies. **1971** *Author* LXXXII. 108 Outside such writer-populated districts as Hampstead or Chelsea, even minor authors may be mini-celebrities, and so news. **1968** *Economist* 27 Apr. 79/2 America..might well take chief responsibility for producing the Olivetti mini-computers as that is where chief demand lies. **1973** *Business Week* 8 Dec. 69/1 Today, a $2,000 minicomputer is more powerful, more reliable, and easier to use than the big, $100,000 machines of a decade ago. **1963** *Aeroplane* 24 Jan. 25/2 A one-man autogyro with an estimated selling price of £1000 was demonstrated recently in South Africa... This 'mini-copter' is said to be in production already. **1971** *Time* 19 Apr. 60 But, like a stabbing pain that passes quickly, the mini-crisis was a warning that the dollar faces more trouble. **1967** *Spectator* 15 Sept. 300/2 Now a new type of winter holiday is offered by several lines—the 'mini' cruise. **1969** *Daily Tel.* 13 Feb. 27/6 Results in the 'mini-elections' in India's four northern States..show the once all-powerful Congress Party to be humbled also in the Punjab and Bihar. **1969** *Times* 27 Jan. 10/8 It will have a 30-acre 'mini-farm' for practical training on its doorstep. **1973** C. BONINGTON *Next Horizon* xix. 259 There was a long pause and then we saw the green miniflare which was the signal to follow. **1954** *Sat. Rev.* (U.S.) 24 Apr. 60 The world famous Philips Minigroove 33⅓ Long Playing Records. **1968** *New Yorker* 16 Mar. 43 Armed with three 7·62-mm. machine guns, called miniguns, which could fire a hundred rounds per second. **1969** I. KEMP *Brit. G.I. in Vietnam* vi. 117 The deep sustained roar of the dragon-ships' mini-guns. **1963** *Daily Tel.* 12 Nov. 17/3 A proposal that 'mini-houses' should be built to cater for people in lower income groups. **1963** *Ibid.* 6 June 15/5 (*heading*) Mini-jet as Paris 'ferry' to air show. **1967** *Word Study* Dec. 3/1 The sphere of clothing is..well represented with ..*mini-jupe*, [etc.]. **1973** *Publishers Weekly* 18 June 35/1 Underage hopefuls in mini-jupes. **1969** *Sunday Times* 6 Apr. 53 Of course, describing these as mini-kilts makes the purist splutter in his porridge. **1974** *People's Jrnl.* (Inverness & Northern Counties ed.) 24 Aug. 3/5 Last Friday, during the great float-out, the pair donned mini-kilt outfits and became hostesses to the many guests attending the ceremony. **1963** *Daily Tel.* 13 Apr. 15/4 The mini-lifeboats..will be normally manned by a crew of two. **1963** *Aeroplane* 21 Mar. 9/2 The third D.H. 125 'mini-liner' is shortly to go into service with Bristol Siddeley Engines. **1973** *Courier & Advertiser* (Dundee) 7 Aug. 7/2 The Fred Olsen mini-liner Basel is due over the weekend with 500 tons of paper from Norway. **1972** *N.Y. Times* 4 June 4/8 The six-mile Crazylegs minimarathon. **1963** *Times* 29 May 15/2 Most of these countries have tiny internal markets—'mini-markets' Mr. Gates calls them. **1966** J. PORTER *Sour Cream* iv. 45, I must have been out of my mini-mind to let myself be manoeuvred into this ridiculous, and dangerous, situation. **1965** *Guardian* 25 Aug. 16/8 Irresponsible action by a few mini-minded strikers. **1959** *Motor Show Catal.* 497 Mini-Minor Saloon de Luxe. **1973** *Guardian* 8 May 2 (*heading*) Mini-Nuclear arms seen as 'wishful-thinking'. **1954** *Life* 29 Nov. 83 The new 'mini-pig'..is ideal for medical research, which is what he was bred for. **1970** *Daily Tel.* 29 May 5/1 The new mini pigs..at about 140 pounds are four to five times lighter than the farm variety. **1970** *New Scientist* 29 Jan. 187/1 The minipill was developed for one reason alone: because it was believed to provide safe contraception. **1967** *Sunday Times* 14 May 12/7 Expo's own minirail system passes on a slender viaduct. **1967** *Word Study* Dec. 3/2 A financial analyst reports the good news that 1967 has experienced only a mini-recession. **1970** *Times* 17 Mar. 27 Another aspect of the current apprehension is linked to the 'mini-recession' in the American motor industry. **1967** *Courier-Mail* (Brisbane) 14 Nov. 18 The collection will include mini-shifts which can double as pant tops teamed with matching slacks or shorts, or can be co-ordinated with bikinis for beach wear. **1969** *Daily Tel.* (Colour Suppl.) 24 Jan. 17/2 A girl in a mini-shift. **1971** *Time* 1 Feb. 32 In Paris, minishorts are an every-night, run-of-the-disco affair. **1973** *Times* 27 Nov. 16/2 The arrival of the mini-short in preference to the old baggy maxi-pants. **1967** *Time* 17 Mar. 36 For added balance, ski bobbers wear mini-skis fitted with braking crampons on both feet. **1974** *Maclean's Mag.* Jan. 25/3 On our GLM mini skis, we were led out to the beginners' hill, which could not have been more than 100 feet away over almost perfectly level ground. **1966** *Economist* 31 Dec. 1385/1 The 'mini-states' must, for the sake of their own reputations and the UN's, accept a system of weighted voting. **1968** *N.Y. Times* 26 Jan. 70 South Africa's economic predominance radiates from here to the three ministates of Botswana, Lesotho and Swaziland. **1973** *Nation* (Barbados) 16 Dec. 4/2 Without the eventual federation of the unit territories or a confederation of independent mini-states, the West Indies have no future. **1959** *Chambers's 20th Cent. Dict.* Suppl., Mini-sub(marine). **1966** *New Scientist* 22 Sept. 655/2 The mini-sub *Alvin* which was used for recovering the H-bomb lost off the Spanish coast. **1963** *Flight Internat.* LXXXIII. 25/1 There has been a great deal of unofficial talk about 'mini-submarines' carrying one or two Polaris apiece, and also of a larger vessel carrying eight missiles. **1973** *Reader's Digest* Apr. 58/2 To complement the divers, mini-submarines less than 20 feet long are used by the airman for underwater surveying. **1968** *Saturday Night* (Toronto) Sept. 36 Elaine Bedard, wearing a flared pink leather minisuit, awaited him in his Mercedes-Benz. **1971** 'V. X. SCOTT' *Surrogate Wife* 254 Under the coat she wore a cream-coloured mini-suit. **1967** *Times* 18 May 23 Whisky is to be exported from Scotland by pipeline and 'minitanker', the shipping firm of Christian Salvesen and Co., of Leith, announced yesterday. **1971** *New Scientist* 2 Sept. 520 Petrol is supplied free, either by the client filling up at the company's garage or from a mini-tanker which regularly visits the special parking places. **1967** *Economist* 29 Apr. 484/3 BMC has come off even worse, working short time on truck manufacturing and likely to drop its ill-fated mini-tractor. **1966** *Punch* 14 Sept. 380/3 Hardy Amies's mini-trousers Are the latest passion-rousers. **1960** *Guardian* 30 Dec. 12/1 The first of the new vehicles to be used for road patrols will be Austin Minivans. **1968** H. C. RAE *Few Small Bones* II. viii. 142 Small personal items were taken by mini-van to the new flat. **1966** *Economist* 10 Dec. 1112/2 The day may eventually come when the big powers will stand back and permit a nuclear mini-war between smaller countries.

b. Special combinations: **minicab** [CAB *sb.*[3]], a small taxi-cab; **minicam,** a miniature camera; so as *v. trans.*; **minicar,** (*a*) a small motor car (cf. *MINI *sb.* 1); (*b*) a child's toy model of a motor car; **minicell** *Biol.*, a miniature cell, without nuclear material, produced by the division of individuals of a particular strain of the bacterium *Escherichia coli;* **mini-coat,** a short coat, one not reaching to the knee; **mini-dress,** a dress with a mini-skirt; **Mini-Moke, mini-moke,** a small motor vehicle resembling a jeep; cf. *MOKE[4]; **mini-ness** = TININESS; **Minipiano,** (a proprietary name of) a small piano; also **minipiano; Miniprinter,** a proprietary name of a type of small machine for printing tickets; **mini-skirt, miniskirt,** a very short skirt; hence **miniskirted** *a.*, wearing or having a mini-skirt.

1960 *Economist* 12 Nov. 711/3 Current regulations regarding London taxis would not allow the introduction of what Mr. Dennis Vosper, speaking for the Home Office, called 'minicabs'. **1961** *Daily Tel.* 6 June 19/6 London's taxi war, between regular taximen and minicab operators, took a new turn yesterday. **1965** *Spectator* 12 Mar. 322/3, I travelled by mini-cab from Baker Street to Kensington. **1973** *Times* 29 Nov. 4/7 A mini-cab operator..was sentenced to four years. **1937** *Amer. Speech* XII. 236/2 A professor at the University of Wisconsin minicammed his students during an examination. **1939** WEBSTER Add., *Minicam*, short for *miniature camera.* **1940** GRAVES & HODGE *Long Week-End* xxv. 432 Their photographs, largely contributed by 'minicam' amateurs. **1948** C. DAY LEWIS *Otterbury Incident* iii. 28 Penknives, Minicars, balls ..the sort of oddments you keep in your pocket. **1949** *Light Car* Dec. 599/2 Three-wheelers... The 122 c.c. Bond Minicar. **1963** *Spectator* 1 Nov. 558 To say Britain came late into the minicar race is to miss the point. **1967** H. I. ADLER et al. in *Proc. Nat. Acad. Sci.* LVII. 321 A newly isolated strain of *Escherichia coli* K12 regularly produces a large number of unusually small anucleate cells during the logarithmic phase of growth. These small cells do not divide... In this report we communicate information regarding some of the basic properties of these minicells. **1971** *Nature* 3 Sept. 11/1 Although minicells, small enucleate *Escherichia coli*, have been used occasionally by molecular biologists, it seems safe to say that they became available too late in the game. **1966** *Guardian* 8 Sept. 7/3 Topcoats were mini-coats—a little more than loose jackets. **1967** *Britannica Bk. of Year* (U.S.) 338 Rabbit had been dyed in new and heady shades—orange, mauve, navy, shocking pink, bright green—to fashion double-breasted minicoats and pea jackets. **1965** *Christian Sci. Monitor* 20 Nov. 30 The fashion pages of British papers sport mini-dresses. **1966** *Daily Tel.* 17 Oct. 10/6 The skinny model girl loped down the runway at Marlborough House in her horizontally-striped mini-dress. **1962** *Ibid.* 13 Feb. 15/4 In the BMC vehicle, named Mini-Moke, the drive is confined to the front wheels. **1972** D. FRANCIS *Smokescreen* I. 10 No one had bothered to put the canvas over the Minimoke. **1974** H. MACINNES *Climb to Lost World* iii. 46 Jonathan drove a mini-moke with Greek lettering emblazoned upon it. **1964** *Punch* 21 Oct. 592/1 Car itself victim of over-exposure, flaunting its mini-ness. **1967** *New Scientist* 13 Apr. 94/1 The current preoccupation with 'mini-ness' has now extended into the realm of..microbiology. **1934** *Trade Marks Jrnl.* 4 Apr.

434/2 Minipiano... Pianos. Brasted Bros. Ltd.,..London,..piano manufacturers; and C.A.V. Lundholm Aktiebolag (a Joint Stock Company organised under the laws of Sweden),..Sweden; merchants. **1943** H. W. VAN LOON *Lives* xviii. 558 He..went over to the little minipiano which had been wished on Frits and now stood at the foot of the stairs. **1947** A. H. HOWE *Sci. Piano Tuning* (rev. ed.) xxi. 96 Tuning the 73 note minipiano is quite different from the conventional mode. **1949** *Electronic Engin.* XXI. 461/2 It is intermediate in size between a minipiano and a small upright piano. **1949** *Railway Gaz.* 6 May 510/2 The equipment exhibited by Westinghouse Garrard Ticket Machines Limited at..Olympia, includes ... The Westinghouse mini-printer,..with four or six printing units. **1958** *Times* 11 Feb. 15/3 The company also supplies rapid and mini printers, as used in booking offices of the London Transport Executive. **1965** *Vogue* Aug. 53 Mini skirt,..snakeskin belt. **1965** *Economist* 20 Nov. 862/1 The Fashion House Group of London dumbfounded the..audience of American buyers quite as much by the sight of the British aggressively selling as by their mini-skirts and kooky outfits. **1970** G. F. NEWMAN *Sir, You Bastard* viii. 243 There were more miniskirts around three o'clock on a warm May afternoon. **1971** B. MALAMUD *Tenants* 54 Had Mary Kettlesmith described his acrobatics with her miniskirt? **1966** *Listener* 30 June 955/1 The mini-skirted or levied young. **1972** F. WARNER *Maquettes* 19 Pretty, miniskirted, and attractive young lady.

miniature, *sb.* and *a.* Add: **A.** *sb.* **5. d.** Chess [tr. G. *miniatur*]. A problem involving few men, *spec.* one in which not more than seven pieces are used; a game of relatively few moves.

1903 *Brit. Chess Mag.* 91 It shows the composer's various styles better to give No. 76, which is a four-move 'miniature'. **1907** S. S. BLACKBURNE *Terms & Themes Chess Probl.* 29 Very light-weight problems are known as 'miniatures'. **1970** A. SUNNUCKS *Encycl. Chess* 309 There is no fixed number of moves which determine whether a game can be classified as a miniature, but the term is generally used to describe a game of under 20 moves.

e. Something that is much smaller than the size normal for things of its class; *spec.* (*a*) a very small bottle of spirits; (*b*) a miniature camera.

1939 *Sun* (Baltimore) 26 June 18/2 The sale of so-called 'miniatures' in Baltimore is fostering juvenile drinking. **1954** A. LEE *Round Many a Bend* vii. 68 Sunday was also the day on which we sold most 'miniatures'. (*footnote*) This is the name for the small bottles of spirits in the trade. **1955** [see *DEFINITION 5 c]. **1958** *Spectator* 1 Aug. 167/3 The miniatures are obviously going to be the fashionable gimmick. The Pye pocket portable measures only 4 × 7 × 1½ inches. **1962** 'H. HOWARD' *Double Finesse* vi. 67 Didn't I see you knock back a miniature of whisky? **1971** C. BONINGTON *Annapurna South Face* x. 123 We had plenty of whisky—over four hundred miniatures and seventy-two full bottles.

f. A short piece of music.

1958 *Listener* 18 Dec. 1051/1 This has no connexion whatsoever with the writing of miniatures or the use of short lyric forms. **1962** *Ibid.* 15 Mar. 489/2 Schumann was a master of epigram, and the epigrammatic *Einfall* was most eminently suited to his vocal and instrumental miniatures.

7. *miniature painting* (earlier example).

1765 T. H. CROKER et al. *Compl. Dict. Arts & Sci.* II. s.v. *Marbling*, The consistence of the solution should be nearly that of strong gum-water, used in miniature painting.

B. *adj.* (Further examples.) Also, designed on a small scale; much smaller than the normal size; tiny; *spec.* of a camera (see quot. 1943); hence applied to photography, films, etc., involving the use of such a camera.

1869 S. R. HOLE *Bk. about Roses* x. 151 The Miniature or Pompon Provence,..the 'baby Roses' and the 'pony Roses' of our childhood. **1887** (*title*) Payne's Miniature Scores. No. 1. Mozart Quartet in G major. **1893** G. B. SHAW *Widowers' Houses* III. 73 With photographic portrait of Blanche on miniature easel on the top. **1911** *Daily Colonist* (Victoria, B.C.) 9 Apr. 1/5 The Department of militia has issued notice of a competition at local miniature ranges to be fired between the 11th and 19th of April. **1913** A. G. FULTON *Notes on Rifle Shooting* 7 Miniature shooting teaches almost all that is necessary to make a man a good shot with the Service rifle. **1914** *Physical Rev.* Apr. 255 From them a miniature universe could be constructed exactly similar in every respect to the present universe. **1917** *Autocar Handbk.* (ed. 7) i. 13 (*heading*) The miniature car. **1921** *Sci. Amer.* 25 June 514/2 (*caption*) Miniature camera with magazine mounted for use.. and the miniature projector. **1941** J. DU MONT (*title*) 200 miniature games of chess. **1943** C. DUNCAN *Man. Miniature Camera* (ed. 2) iii. 12 When the Royal Photographic Society found it necessary to define the term 'miniature camera' they ruled that it was one designed to make negatives 'not larger than six square inches'. **1943** *Gloss. Terms Electr. Engin.* (*B.S.I.*) 144 Miniature film radiography. **1953** J. DU MONT (*title*) Chess: more miniature games. **1956** A. L. SOWERBY *Dict. Photogr.* (ed. 18) 466 The Leica, though by no means the first camera to make small pictures, was undoubtedly the camera which popularised miniature photography. **1958** *Spectator* 1 Aug. 167/2 The new miniature transistor radios. **1959** *Chambers's Encycl.* VII. 246/1 Increased use of mass miniature radiography is resulting in many suspicious cases being discovered which cannot be definitely diagnosed. *Ibid.* XIV. 778/2 The technical quality of the present-day miniature film approximates closely to that of full-sized film. **1970** *Jrnl. Gen. Psychol.* LXXXIII. 4 The more sophisticated paradigms simulating the therapy-interview situation..and miniature systems of conditioning in the mass.

b. Applied to a dog ot a breed or variety smaller than average; also as *sb.*

1902 *Daily Tel.* 13 Feb. 6/4 [Cruft's Dog Show at Royal Agricultural Hall]. In one of the annexes of the hall are shown the Griffons, the Maltese and other miniatures. **1903** R. B. LEE *Hist. & Descr. Mod. Dogs Gt. Brit. & Ireland: Terriers* (ed. 3) xv. 401 Little dogs of these colours and toy white English terriers will not have any kind of classification, unless special arrangements are made for grouping them as a section of their own, called 'smooth-coated terriers (miniature) other than black and tan'. **1904** H. COMPTON *20th Cent. Dog* I. 301 The miniature black and tan terrier—to give it its new Kennel Club title—is more familiarly known..by its original one of the 'Toy Terrier'. **1912** *Encycl. Brit.* VII. 375/2 *Non-Sporting* [Dogs].—Bulldog, bulldog (miniature)..black and tan terrier (miniature). **1924** [see *BENCH v. 3 c]. **1945** C. L. B. HUBBARD *Observer's Bk. Dogs* 53 A miniature Dachshund should be a sturdy little sportsman. **1948**—— *Dogs in Brit.* III. xx. 319 The Miniature Poodles in Britain are mostly descended from imported French dogs although many are 'bred down' from small standard Poodles. **1959** *Observer* 1 Feb. 12 The breed standard describes miniature poodles as active and intelligent... Height at shoulder should be under 15 in.

c. Applied to a version of golf played on a miniature course.

1915 F. M. HUEFFER *Good Soldier* I. i. 10 Sitting together..in front of the club house, let us say, at Homburg ..watching the miniature golf. **1930** *Glasgow Herald* 25 Sept. 17/5 Miniature Golf Course in Glasgow. What is claimed to be a real golf course in miniature is being laid out. **1930** *Daily Express* 6 Oct. 8/3 The Government's experts have been investigating the subject because of the demand the miniature golf establishments are creating for materials. **1966** J. BALL *Cool Cottontail* (1967) xi. 118 He and his date played miniature golf, had dinner, and saw a movie.

miniature, *v.* **2.** (Earlier example.)

a **1706** EVELYN *Diary* an. 1686 (1955) IV. 531 His booke of Birds, Fish: flowers, shells &c drawn & miniatured to the life.

miniaturization (mi:nit-,mi:niătiŭrəizēi·ʃən). [f. MINIATURE *a.* + -IZATION.] The process of miniaturizing; an instance of this.

1947 *Technical News Bull., U.S. Bureau of Standards* Jan. 8/1 With the end of the war and the declassification of the principle of the VT fuse, industry is manifesting interest in the program of miniaturization of electronic devices. **1950** *Engineering* 21 Apr. 447/1 The trend towards 'miniaturisation', i.e. the production of smaller components and greater compactness of layout, is continuing. **1960** KOESTLER *Lotus & Robot* II. viii. 211 That patient biding of one's time to avenge an assumed insult by a subtle twist—a miniaturization of the mediaeval vendetta. **1967** M. CHANDLER *Ceramics in Mod. World* iv. 134 If miniaturization was to proceed, clearly much higher permittivities were needed.

miniaturize (mi·nit-, mi·niătiŭrəiz), *v.* [f. as prec. + -IZE.] *trans.* To produce in a smaller version; to render small.

1946 *Jrnl. R. Aeronaut. Soc.* L. 945/1 The weight added to the aircraft by the installation is about 120 lb., but.. this weight is based on a war-time design which could be miniaturised. **1950** *Ibid.* LIV. 281/2 There has been a general move to miniaturise radio components with consequent saving in bulk and weight. **1957** *Times* 28 Aug. (Radio and TV Suppl.) p. xv/2 The printed circuit gives the designer added ability to miniaturize his equipment. **1957** *Spaceflight* I. 77/2 A single satellite would be quite unable to carry all the instruments which scientists want to send aloft, even when they are miniaturized. **1963** A. SMITH *Throw out Two Hands* xiii. 135 The camp had been miniaturised. Micro-huts had been built, with midget cooking-pots smouldering over dwarf fires. **1972** *Lebende Sprachen* XVII. 133/1 Nowadays micro-film can be miniaturized to the point where the library on the desk can be of virtually any size required.

Hence **mi·niaturized** *ppl. a.*

1951 *Electronic Engin.* XXIII. 478/2 Miniaturized components generally are becoming more and more readily available. **1967** M. CHANDLER *Ceramics in Mod. World* iv. 135 A whole new technology for the production of miniaturized capacitors. **1971** *N.Y. Times Bk. Rev.* 19 Dec. 7/4 The pages fall open easily,..four of the original appearing in each page of the miniaturized volumes.

minibus. Delete ? *Obs.* and add earlier and later examples. (The modern use is influenced by the prefix *MINI-.)

1845 *Scotsman* 15 Feb. 3/5 (Advt.), Important sale of horses, harness, and carriages... One excellent 12-inside *omnibus*, nearly as good as new... One handsome *minibus*, in good order. **1958** *Oxford Mail* 9 June 1/1 A Morris Mini-bus which could possibly save rural services threatened with extinction through high running costs went on exhibition today... It carries twelve people, including the driver, and is designed to operate without a conductor. **1960** *Guardian* 19 Nov. 5/6 The company arrived by mini-bus. **1962** [see *COMMERCIAL sb. 2]. **1965** M. MORSE *Unattached* v. 180 Transport difficulties..were largely solved when the worker secured the use of a mini-bus. **1972** *Daily Tel.* 19 Feb. 11/3 The company minibus (or coach if there are enough of you interested) is available for excursions.

minification (mi:nifikēi·ʃən). [f. MINIFY *v.* + -ATION, after MAGNIFICATION.] Diminution or reduction in size, appearance, importance, etc.

1904 *Jrnl. R. Microsc. Soc.* June 281 A magnifying power which exactly balances the ten-fold minification before spoken of. **1961** L. MUMFORD *City in Hist.* viii. 242

These are symptoms of the end: magnifications of demoralized power, minifications of life. **1974** *New Scientist* 3 Oct. 61/1 The illustrations are generous in number and in size, though, talking of size, in many cases an indication of the minification would have been instructive.

minim, *a.* and *sb.* Add: **B.** *sb.* **9.** A very small Roman bronze (or occas. silver) coin, usu. produced locally. Pl. **minimi, minims.**

1896 W. C. HAZLITT *Coin Collector* ix. 247 Minim, a term which, for want of a better one, has been assigned to a class of bronze money of Roman type, probably of the fourth or fifth century B.C., which may have been of local or provincial origin, and is of unusually small module. **1935** *Discovery* July 196/2 A hoard of 800 minims, small coins in some cases not more than 5 mm. in diameter, buried beneath the floor of the stage. **1962** C. R. JOSSET *Money in Brit.* i. 7 An attempt to overcome the shortage was made by a local production of crude bronze coins which are known as 'minimi' because of their smallness. **1971** *Daily Tel.* 13 July 9/1 Two rare British silver minims, or small coins, of the first century A.D. have been discovered during excavations taking place on a Roman occupation site in Chapel Street, Chichester.

minimal, *a.* Add: **b.** spec. *Linguistics.* (*a*) Distinguished only by a single feature; usu. applied to a pair of similar forms; (*b*) other uses (see quots.).

(*a*) **1939** *Amer. Speech* XIV. 122 Words can be distinguished by the minimal opposition of vowel nasality and [n]. **1942** C. F. HOCKETT in *Language* XVIII. 7 The term 'contrastive pair', meaning any pair between which there are differences in a context of similarity, any pair usable for the listing of features, is used here instead of the traditional term 'minimal pair'. **1950** D. JONES *Phoneme* vi. 15 When a distinction between two sequences occurring in a language is such that any lesser degree of distinction would be inadequate for clearly differentiating words in that language, the distinction is termed a 'minimal one'... Minimal distinctions are very commonly effected by the addition or subtraction of a phoneme. **1955** C. F. HOCKETT *Man. Phonol.* vi. 212 Before analysis is complete, one cannot be certain that a given pair is 'minimal' in a strict phonologic sense—that there is but a single difference, at the level of ultimate phonologic constituents. **1961** H. A. GLEASON *Introd. Descr. Ling.* (ed. 2) i. 16 In calling *bill* and *pill* a minimal pair we assume that they differ by only one phoneme. **1964** R. A. HALL *Introd. Ling.* 81 Minimal pairs are not essential to show that two sounds do not belong to the same phoneme. **1971** *Archivum Linguisticum* II. 48 In the days of 'classical' phonemics much play was made of the 'minimal pair' in order to establish throughout a language such lexical differences as those between *pin, bin, tin, din*, [etc.].

(*b*) **1930** H. E. PALMER *Princ. Romanization* 52 We may designate by the term *monophone* any phone of the first or second degrees of abstraction of which the concrete members are so similar in point of production and of acoustic effect even when observed by a competent observer, that it may be regarded as a minimal unit of pronunciation (i.e. practically insusceptible of sub-division). **1941** G. L. TRAGER in L. Spier et al. *Lang., Culture & Personality: Ess. in Memory of E. Sapir* 133 Intensity of tone is manifested as relative height of pitch: maximal intensity is *high* tone, minimal intensity is *low* tone, medial intensity is *middle* tone. **1949** J. R. FIRTH in *Trans. Philol. Soc. 1948* 142 The weak, neutral, or 'minimal' vowel. **1955** QUIRK & WRENN *Old Eng. Gram.* 129 Taking the consonants of a word as its minimal root. **1962** B. M. H. STRANG *Mod. Eng. Struct.* vi. 84 They [*sc.* central nouns] can follow directly in minimal constructions (i.e. be head-word to) a closed system of words we shall call *determiners*. **1964** R. A. HALL *Introd. Ling.* 15 Morphemes ..are the minimal units which carry meaning. **1971** D. CRYSTAL *Ling.* 187 The grammar..could be analysed in terms of identifying a set of minimal units.

c. In *Art*, used of a form of painting and sculpture which is characterized by the use of simple or primary forms, structures, etc., often geometric and massive. Hence **mi·nimalism, mi·nimalist** (also *attrib.* or as *adj.*), **minima·lity.**

[**1958** *Listener* 23 Oct. 647/2 Creating huge, minimal forms with the palette knife in a few colours.] **1965** R. WOLLHEIM in *Arts Mag.* Jan. 26 In a historic passage Mallarmé describes the terror, the sense of sterility, that the poet experiences when he..confronts the sheet of paper..and no words come to him... Why could not Mallarmé, after an interval of time, have simply got up from his chair and produced the blank sheet of paper *as* the poem which he sat down to write?.. Such a gesture ..would provide us with an extreme instance of what I call minimal art. **1967** C. GREENBERG in E. Lucie-Smith *Movements in Art since 1945* (1969) i. 13 The working out of this problem, whose solution seems to have arrived in the form of what is called Primary Structures, ABC, or Minimal Art. The Minimalists appear to have realized ..that the far-out in itself has to be the far-out as an end in itself. **1969** *Britannica Bk. of Year* (U.S.) 800/2 *Minimal sculpture,* sculpture in the idiom of minimal art. **1969** *Time* 3 Jan. 42 Minimal forms still massively demand their unrewarding space, but they are countered by weirdly eccentric shapes that are frankly frivolous, at least unpredictable. **1969** E. LUCIE-SMITH *Movements in Art since 1945* viii. 240 His sculptures have been described as 'minimal art', or as examples of the 'single-unit Gestalt'. *Ibid.* 242 Judd's colleague, Robert Morris, defends minimality in equally emphatic terms. **1969** *Manch. Guardian Weekly* 1 May 20 Call it minimalism if you like, but the real point is that the thing insists on being just itself and nothing more. *Ibid.*, Tony Smith, usually taken as the original minimalist sculptor..is well represented by large sculptures. **1971** *Rolling Stone* 24 June 36/5 It remained only for minimal sculpture to come along, with its emphasis on the self-contained object (sometimes just a log, rock, or mound of dirt). **1973** *Phaidon Dict. 20th*

Cent. Art 254/1 The immediate predecessors of the Minimalists were Ad Reinhardt and Josef Albers, who brought to their canvases the 'exclusive, negative, absolute, and timeless' quality so desired by the Minimal artists. **1973** *Times* 30 June 12/4 There will be works of American, Continental and British artists, abstract expressionism, Pop, kinetic, minimal and conceptual art. **1973** *Times Lit. Suppl.* 9 Nov. 1363/4 The pop, minimalist, new realist, and other artists who have succeeded the abstract impressionists.

minimalist (mi·nimălist). [f. MINIMAL *a.* + -IST, or (in sense 1) ad. F. *minimaliste*, tr. Russ. *men'shevík* *MENSHEVIK *a.* and *sb.*] **1.** (Also with capital initial.) = *MENSHEVIK *sb.*; more widely, a person who advocated small or moderate reforms or policies. Also *attrib.* or as *adj.*

1907 I. ZANGWILL *Ghetto Comedies* 408 'Ah, you're a Maximalist,' said the beadle. 'No, I am only a Minimalist. I merely want the minimum—that we save our own lives.' **1917** [see *BOLSHEVIK *sb.*]. **1917** *Times* 23 June 7/1 At the 'All Russia' Congress of the Workmen's and Soldiers' Delegates the 'Minimalist Socialists' have defined their programme. **1918** E. P. STEBBING *From Czar to Bolshevik* iii. 25 The Social Democrats consisted chiefly of Bolsheviks with a smaller Menshevik group. The Social Revolutionaries were subdivided into Maximalists and Minimalists. **1922** *Blackw. Mag.* June 820/2 The delegation represented not only Communists, but also Minimalists and the converted intelligentsia. **1954** *Ann. Reg. 1953* 153 There were the 'maximalists' (Germany and the Netherlands),..and the 'minimalists' (France) who wanted the E.P.C. to be little more than a system of inter-governmental association and co-operation. **1972** *Times* 19 Oct. 1/6 A minimalist summit, dealing only with well tried issues of economic integration.

2. See *MINIMAL *a.* c.

minimality (minimæ·lĭti). [f. MINIMAL *a.* + -ITY.] **1.** *Linguistics.* The quality or character of being minimal.

1953 C. E. BAZELL *Ling. Form* i. 10 The criterion of minimality is fulfilled in either case. **1963** J. LYONS *Structural Semantics* ii. 29 What can be done, however, is to apply the criterion of minimality after the establishment of the several meaning-relations between sentences in context. **1969** *Word* XXV. 235 Because of the minimality requirement in the definition of the morpheme, the second class is not equivalent to a class of bound morphemes.

2. See *MINIMAL *a.* c.

minimally (mi·nimăli), *adv.* [f. MINIMAL *a.* + -LY[2].] To a minimal extent or degree.

1935 H. F. TWADDELL in *Lang. Monogr.* XVI. 42 In American English, the forms *beet*: *bit*: *bait*: *bet*: *bat* are minimally phonologically different. **1936** *Amer. Speech* XI. 298 They generally cite only minimally different pairs. **1951** R. FIRTH *Elem. Social Organiz.* i. 35 Even minimally, their orientations are affected by its presence. **1971** *Sci. Amer.* Sept. 40/5 In order to meet not only the food requirements but also a minimally reasonable quality of life, the contributions that can be made by the use of energy in various forms are essential. **1973** *Nature* 6 July 40/2 *In vitro* methods for the short-term culture of erythrocytic forms of *Plasmodium knowlesi* and for isolating free merozoite preparations minimally contaminated with host cells. **1973** *Publishers Weekly* 13 Aug. 52/1 Such a glaring omission will surely put off some serious movie buffs. Probably, however, sales will be damaged only minimally.

minimax (mi·nimæks), *sb.* and *a.* [f. MINI(MUM *sb.* and *a.* + MAX(IMUM.] The smallest of a set of maxima; usu. *attrib.* (passing into *adj.*: see b), *spec.* designating (*a*) a strategy that minimizes the greatest loss or risk to which a participant in a game or other situation of conflict will be liable; (*b*) the theorem of game theory that states that, for a finite, zero-sum game with two players, the smallest maximum loss that a player can make himself liable to by a suitable choice of strategy is equal to the greatest minimum gain that he can guarantee himself. Cf. *MAXIMIN *sb.* and *a.*

[**1928** J. VON NEUMANN in *Mathematische Annalen* C. 307 (*heading*) Beweis des Satzes Max Min = Min Max. **1944** —— & MORGENSTERN *Theory of Games* xvii. 154 A slightly more general form of this Min-Max problem arises in another question of mathematical economics.]

1941 COURANT & ROBBINS *What is Math.?* vii. 345 (*heading*) Minimax points and topology. **1947** A. WALD in *Econometrica* XV. 282 We shall refer to an admissible decision function η for which (1·6) takes its minimum value as a minimax solution of the problem. *Ibid.* 283 An element a_0 in *A* is said to be a minimax strategy of player 1 if $\text{Inf}_b\, K(a, b)$ takes its maximum value with respect to *a* for $a = a_0$. **1949** *Ibid.* XVII. 230 Often Nature's strategy is completely unknown. In that case Wald suggests that the statistician play a minimax strategy: that is, the statistician should select that decision procedure which minimizes the maximum risk. **1951** *Ann. Math. Statistics* XXII. 466 The minimax risk is $\frac{1}{2}(1-a)$. **1957** LUCE & RAIFFA *Games & Decisions* i. 2 Although Borel gave a clear statement of an important class of game theoretic problems and introduced the concepts of pure and mixed strategies, von Neumann points out that he did not obtain one crucial result—the minimax theorem—without which no theory of games can be said to exist. **1958** *Engineering* 21 Mar. 369/2 Player B, on the other hand, will determine the largest value in each column, and the smallest of these, the 'minimax'. **1961** L. WEISS *Statistical Decision Theory* v. 89 The minimax criterion has been criticized as being too conservative. **1962** *Sci. Amer.* Dec. 114/2 Both firms were guided by the principle of the minimax, choosing the best of the worst outcomes. **1968** *Brit. Med. Bull.* XXIV. 232/2 This would be the Bayesian Strategy of decision theory.., but other strategies, such as minimax or restricted Bayes, could also be used. **1970** [see *MAXIMIN *sb.* and *a.*]. **1972** *Computer Jrnl.* XV. 277 (*heading*) On minimax solutions of linear equations.

b. Used predicatively as adj.: equal to, or resulting in, a minimax value.

1952 *Ann. Math. Statistics* XXIII. 587 For such weight functions the supremum of the risk over all $\theta \in \Omega$ is infinite for every decision function, so that every decision function is minimax. **1965** WOZENCRAFT & JACOBS *Princ. Communication Engin.* ii. 118 The decision rule which has the smallest maximum probability of error is called the minimax decision rule. Which of the eight rules is minimax? **1970** R. B. ASH *Basic Probability Theory* viii. 250 Find a minimax test, that is, a test that minimizes max (α, β). It is immediate from the definition of admissibility that an admissible test with constant risk (i.e., $\alpha = \beta$) is minimax.

minimax (mi·nimæks), *v.* [f. prec. sb.] **a.** *trans.* To make equal to a minimax value. **b.** *intr.* To adopt or employ a minimax strategy. So **mi·nimaxing** *vbl. sb.* and *ppl. a.*

1964 GOULD & KOLB *Dict. Social Sci.* 573/2 The goal may be assumed to take the form of maximizing (or, in game theory, minimaxing) the expected value, over some time interval, of a utility function. **1968** *Listener* 4 Apr. 438/1 Just like that 50–50 combination of heads and tails, the minimaxing peasant might pick a 40–60 combination of wheat and millet. **1973** *Nature* 23 Feb. 507/1 The fundamental mechanism underlying all this work [on machines designed to play games] has been a cycle of processes: lookahead, evaluation and minimaxing.

minimization. (Further examples.)

1940 *Jrnl. Obstetr. & Gynaecol. Brit. Empire* XLVII. 236 As regards anaesthesia, the minimization of shock is the main indication. **1969** *Nature* 29 Nov. 845/1 The arrangement of molecules..points to a minimization of the electric quadrupole–quadrupole interaction energy of the crystal. **1973** *Ibid.* 27 Apr. 556/1 Some potential energy calculations on β-pleated sheets have been done by Chothia.., who finds that a right-handed twist in the direction of the polypeptide chain, which corresponds to dihedral angles within one zone of the conformational map, makes for minimization of energy. **1974** *Clin. Pharmacol. & Therapeutics* XV. 444/2 The new method, called *minimization* for brevity, is compared here with randomization in regard to its vulnerability to experimenter bias and chance skewing.

minimize, *v.* Add: **3.** *intr.* To attain a minimum value.

1973 *Physics Bull.* Dec. 725/3 One of the unexpected discoveries made using HVEM is that for a particular incident electron energy the diffracted intensity may minimize rather than maximize. **1975** *Ibid.* Jan. 13 Other parameters used to measure the intensity of the solar cycle tend to minimize at this time.

minimum, *sb.* and *a.* Add: **B.** *adj.* **b.** Special collocations: *minimum rate, wage*; **minimum free form** (see quot. 1926); **minimum vocabulary** (see quot. 1944).

1926 L. BLOOMFIELD in C. F. Hockett *Leonard Bloomfield Anthol.* (1970) 130 A minimum free form is a *word*.. which may be uttered alone (with meaning) but cannot be analyzed into parts that may (all of them) be uttered alone (with meaning). **1958** C. F. HOCKETT *Course in Mod. Ling.* xix. 171 Minimum free forms and lexemes also do not meet this requirement. **1810** Minimum rate [in Dict.]. **1866** *Leisure Hour* 8 Dec. 783/2 All the workmen insist on is a *minimum* rate of wages. **1909** *Act* 9 *Edw. VII* c. 22 § 4 Trade Boards shall, subject to the provisions of this section, fix minimum rates of wages for timework for their trades. **1974** Minimum rate [see *minimum wage* below]. **1944** B. RUSSELL in P. A. Schilpp *Philos. B. Russell* 14, I mean by a 'minumum vocabulary' one in which no word can be defined in terms of the others. All definitions are theoretically superfluous, and therefore the whole of any science can be expressed by means of a minimum vocabulary for that science. **1947** *Mind* LVI. 358 Every minimum vocabulary adequate to describing the world of ordinary experience must contain at least one universal-name. **1860** *Trades' Societies & Strikes: Rep. Comm. appointed by Nat. Assoc. for Promotion of Social Sci.* 299 And so the minimum wage which the Institute stipulates for..is constantly reduced. **1908** *New Age* 18 July 223/2 A serious objection to the fixing of a minimum wage in England for employed is that it would be most difficult to make provision for the large number of incompetent, inferior, and slow workers. **1940** *Economist* 6 July 4/2 The establishment, by law or by bargaining, of a decent minimum wage in all trades is an indispensable foundation. **1974** *Encycl. Brit. Micropædia* VI. 916/1 Minimum-wage legislation or machinery for fixing minimum rates now exists in most of the nations of Latin America, Africa, and Asia, as well as in more industrialized countries.

c. In combs. used *attrib.*, as **minimum-cost,** involving the smallest possible cost; **minimum-iron,** of a garment: requiring only a small amount of ironing; **minimum-security,** of a prison: having a minimum amount of restrictions on prisoners.

1962 A. BATTERSBY *Guide to Stock Control* vi. 52 The best period may be found by a minimum-cost procedure .., that is, by minimizing the total costs of ordering and stockholding. **1959** *Harrods News* Summer 11 Little girl's sundress of minimum-iron cotton. **1963** A. J. HALL *Textile Sci.* v. 267 Very large amounts of cotton and viscose rayon materials are finished with what is now known as..'minimum-iron' finishes. **1965** G. JACKSON *Let.* 18 Apr. in *Soledad Brother* (1971) 73, I can also obtain a parole faster there or a transfer to some minimum security camp. **1970** *Globe & Mail* (Toronto) 25 Sept. 1/6 A 26-year old escaper from the William Head minimum security prison near Victoria.

mining, *vbl. sb.* Add: **3.** *mining camp* (examples), *captain, company, engineer, -man, population, recorder, town* (earlier and later examples); **mining geology,** geology as applied to mining.

1902 'MARK TWAIN' in *Harper's Monthly Mag.* Feb. 431/2 Don't you put on any exclusiveness in a mining-camp. **1966** 'E. LATHEN' *Death shall Overcome* i. 9 Wall Street is power. The talk..closes mining camps in the Chibougamou. **1853** *Harper's Mag.* Mar. 442/2 We are accompanied by Captain John Cox, the mining captain. **1859** L. SAWYER *Diary* 23 Sept. in *Way Sk.* (1926) 116 The ..river mining companies which have not already proved failures. **1872** *Vermont Board Agric. Rep.* I. 629 Captain Thomas Pollard..had formerly been mining engineer. **1897** 'MARK TWAIN' *Following Equator* 687 The mining engineers from America. **1941** R. PEELE (*title*) Mining engineers' handbook. **1906** J. PARK *Textbk. Mining Geol.* i. 1 Economic or Mining Geology, which bears more directly on mining, and the development of the mining industry. **1874** R. W. RAYMOND *Statistics of Mines* 499 He talked over the scheme with many railroad and miningmen. **1930** J. DOS PASSOS *42nd Parallel* I. 128 The bars.. were full of ranchers and miningmen. **1854** A. DELANO *Life on Plains* xxvii. 382 There is arable land enough..to supply the whole mining population with vegetables, fruit and grain. **1876** *White Pine News* (Hamilton, Nevada) 22 July 3/1 An election took place on Treasure Hill on Thursday for Mining Recorder. **1968** Mining recorder [see *FILE *v.*[3] 1 c]. **1829** DR. WILLARD in R. G. Thwaites *Early Western Trav.* (1905) XVIII. 359 The mining towns are mostly dependent on their supplies from abroad. **1856** *Hutchings Mag.* July 33/2 [We had] to.. make a 'pilgrim's progress' to the nearest mining town. **1944** N. W. ROSS *Westward the Women* 133 She appeared in the mining town of Murray.

mining, *ppl. a.* Add: **2. mining bee,** a solitary bee of the family Andrenidæ, including many British and American species which nest in tunnels in the ground, sometimes grouped in colonies.

1893 L. N. BADENOCH *Romance Insect World* iii. 72 (*caption*) Profile view of nest of a Mining Bee (Andrena vicina). **1912** SANDERSON & JACKSON *Elem. Entomol.* xvii. 268 None of the short-tongued bees live in colonies, and many of them make their nests in the ground, which has given them the name of 'mining bees'. **1974** *Country Life* 21 Feb. 351/1 The spoil-heaps excavated by mining-bees (*Andrena armata*) when they make their nests.

miniscule, erron. var. MINUSCULE *a.*

Now with stress on first syllable.

1898 J. SOUTHWARD *Mod. Printing* I. xxii. 139 Each of the text letters already named has its own lower case or 'miniscule' letters. **1948** *N.Y. Times* 12 Dec. VII. 5 Now once again these miniscule land areas have faded from our interests. **1955** *Ibid.* 10 Apr. x. 27 Upland meadows are carpeted with miniscule wild flowers. **1961** *Economist* 16 Dec. 1118/1 Many 'gardens' would be miniscule affairs. **1967** [see *INTEGRATED *ppl. a.* b]. **1970** *Daily Tel.* 24 Apr. 1/3 If these conditions were fulfilled the risk from the pill was 'miniscule'. **1973** *Orcadian* 2 Aug. 4/4 The most interesting feature of this miniscule nation..is the strength of its national culture.

minister, *sb.* Add: **3. c. Minister of State,** a government minister, now usu. regarded in the U.K. as holding a rank below that of a head of department; **Minister of the Crown,** a minister or the head of a department in the U.K. government (see also quot. 1946); **Minister without Portfolio,** a government minister who has Cabinet status but is not in charge of a specific Department of State.

1696 Minister of State [in Dict. sense 3 a]. **1735** BOLINGBROKE *Diss. upon Parties* (ed. 2) p. xxv, But This will not become a *Matter of State*, though you are a *Minister of State*. **1864** SALISBURY in *Q. Rev.* CXVI. 253 Ministers of State are case-hardened by practice. **1950** W. S. CHURCHILL in *Hansard Commons* 31 Oct. 16, I like to see this reverence and respect for the past and all we owe to those who have gone before, and to see Ministers of State shake themselves clear from the obsession into which they fall from time to time. **1957** *Act* 5 & 6 *Eliz. II.* c. 20 § 13 'Minister of State' means a member of Her Majesty's Government in the United Kingdom..who neither has charge of any public department nor holds any other of the offices specified in the Second Schedule to this Act. **1958** A. CHANDA *Indian Administration* III. i. 64 The appointment of Ministers of State to take charge of independent portfolios was an innovation [in India]... In France, a Minister of State ranked higher than a Minister and was usually entrusted with some special functions. In the UK, a Minister of State was, however, a minister of the second rank, functioning as the principal aide to a Cabinet Minister. **1963** HARVEY & BATHER *Brit. Constitution* XV. 251 When the work is particularly heavy or involved, or when it entails frequent visits abroad, Ministers of State, who act as deputy ministers, may be appointed. **1970** J. HARVEY *How Brit. is Governed* xii. 147 In departments where the work is particularly heavy, the present-day practice is to appoint Ministers of State who virtually act on behalf of the minister.

1776 J. HATSELL *Coll. Cases Priuilege Parl.* v. 196 The increase of their consequence in the state, and their influence in the management of public affairs, rendered

them more an object of the attention of the Ministers of the Crown. **1844** Erskine May *Law of Parl.* xvii. 262 Another form of communication from the Crown to either house of Parliament, is in the nature of a verbal message, delivered, by command, by a minister of the Crown to the house of which he is a member. **1848** Disraeli in *Hansard Commons* 20 June 961 Surely, the people of this country are not accustomed to wait to express their opinion, till it may chance to be elicited by some captious expression of a Minister of the Crown. **1892** W. R. Anson *Law & Custom of Constitution* II. i. 10 The present dependence of the Ministers of the Crown, for their existence as a Ministry, upon the maintenance of a majority in the House of Commons. **1937** *Act 1 Edw. VIII & 1 Geo. VI* c. 38 § 3 If and so long as any Minister of the Crown to whom this section applies is a member of the Cabinet. **1946** *Act* 9 & 10 *Geo. VI* c. 31 § 8 (2) 'Minister of the Crown' means the holder of an office in His Majesty's Government in the United Kingdom, and includes the Treasury, the Admiralty, the Board of Trade, the Army Council, and the Air Council. **1956** Abraham & Hawtrey *Parl. Dict.* 113 Ministers of the Crown... In its widest sense..it means any member of the Government, of whatever rank (this does not, of course, include parliamentary private secretaries, who have no official status at all). **1975** *Listener* 7 Aug. 183/1 A speech by a Minister of the Crown. **1915** *Hansard Commons* LXXII. p. iv, Minister without Portfolio—Rt. Hon. the Marquess of Lansdowne, K.G. **1921** H. H. Asquith in *Ibid.* 23 June 1630, I was the first Prime Minister in modern times during the last half-century or more, to have in his cabinet a Minister Without Portfolio. **1954** Ld. Templewood *Nine Troubled Yrs.* x. 136 The Law Officers at once intervened to say that a Minister with a special Portfolio could not be a Minister without Portfolio. **1955** *Times* 30 June 8/5 M. Nguyen Huu Chau, Minister without portfolio in the Government of southern Viet Nam. *Ibid.* 18 July 8/3 The Bishop of Derby will open a debate on mining subsidence in the House of Lords on Wednesday, when the Government's views will be put forward by Lord Munster, Minister without Portfolio.

7. = *horned pout* (*horned *a.* 2 b). (Earlier and later examples.)

1839 D. H. Storer in Storer & Peabody *Rep. Fishes, Reptiles & Birds Mass.* 102 The Horned Pout..is known in the interior of the state by the vulgar names of 'Horn pout', and 'Minister'. **1849** Thoreau *Week Concord Riv.* 34 The Horned Pout..[is] sometimes called Minister. **1884** G. B. Goode *Fisheries U.S.: Nat. Hist. Aquatic Animals* 628 The common 'Horned Pout', 'Bullhead', 'Bull-pout', or 'Minister' of the Northern and Eastern States is the most generally abundant and familiar representative of this family [*sc.* Siluridæ].

ministeriable (ministīə·riăb'l), *a. rare.* [f. Ministeri(al *a.* + -able.] = *ministrable *a.*

1923 J. A. Spender *Life H. Campbell-Bannerman* II. 127 His test of complete co-operation was that Lord Rosebery should be definitely within the circle of ministeriable ex-Ministers.

ministerial, *a.* **4.** (Further examples.)

1879 Gladstone *Gleanings* I. viii. 229 Ministerial responsibility comes between the Monarch and every public trial and necessity, like armour between the flesh and the spear. **1969** *Sci. Jrnl.* Sept. 6 As an example of apparent ministerial unconcern he refers to recent exchanges in Parliament on this very problem. **1973** H. Trevelyan *Diplomatic Channels* i. 16 There are the 'grey eminences' in the corridors of power, who shun the light, who learn when to feed those dangerous animals, ministers, pacing up and down their party cages, who acquire an unrivalled knowledge of how government actually works beneath the misleading surface of ministerial responsibility. **1974** *Times* 19 Sept. 1/4 In a ministerial broadcast on all channels last night Mr Wilson said [etc.].

ministering, *ppl. a.* Add to def.: esp. in phr. *ministering angel*; *spec.* a kind-hearted person, usu. a woman, who helps and comforts people in distress; freq. a nurse.

1602 Shakes. *Ham.* v. i. 263 A Ministring Angell shall my Sister be. **1808** [in Dict.]. **1912** 'Saki' *Chron. Clovis* 223 Martin Stoner rose heavily to his feet and followed his ministering angel along a passage..into a large room lit with a cheerfully blazing fire. **1922** Joyce *Ulysses* 349 A sterling good daughter was Gerty just like a second mother in the house, a ministering angel too with a little heart worth its weight in gold. **1924** A. Huxley *Little Mexican* 140 Emmy was good, was kind, a ministering angel. **1931** M. D. George *England in Transition* iv. 92 Nurses paid by the parish—creatures compared with whom Mrs. Gamp would have been almost a ministering angel. **1956** F. F. Darling *Pelican in Wilderness* i. 10 Such detached thought as I could muster was of feeling sorry for the air hostess. She remained throughout the gentle ministering angel, imperturbable as she picked her way through the shambles. **1974** W. Foley *Child in Forest* ii. 188 She came in her nurse's uniform, and I thought 'ministering angel' a very apt description.

ministrable (mi·nistrăb'l), *a.* and *sb.* [a. F. *ministrable* in the same sense: cf. -able.] **A.** *adj.* Fit or likely to become a minister; = *cabinetable *a.* **B.** *sb.* One who is likely or hopes to become a minister.

In quot. 1968 a use of the Fr. word.

1921 *Contemp. Rev.* Mar. 289 The anti-British feeling [in France]..oozes out of declarations by Ministers and Ministrable politicians. **1927** *Blackw. Mag.* Feb. 277/2 Those that are ministrables have done the best for themselves. **1968** *Economist* 9 Mar. 53/2 The *ministrables* were more inclined to vote for the government than against it.

Ministry. Add: **5. b.** The name given to certain departments of the British government.

1916 *Whitaker's Almanack* 223/2 Munitions, Ministry of, Minister, Rt. Hon. D. Lloyd George, M.P. **1942** *R.A.F. Jrnl.* 18 Apr. 24 The Ministry of Food announces that the milk ration for children will be increased. **1963** *Listener* 28 Feb. 368/1 It [*sc.* the Treasury] has also done hitherto the work of a ministry of economic affairs. *Ibid.* 7 Mar. 422/1 The Ministries of the three Services are to be reorganized under a unified Ministry of Defence. **1968** *Times* 16 Dec. 7/1 An attempt at a Ministry takeover and a threat to a much valued independence.

minitrack (mi·nitræk). Also **Minitrack.** [f. *mini*mum-weight *track*ing.] A system for tracking satellites in which a very light-weight oscillator is fixed in the satellite and its position is calculated from the phase difference between radio signals received by each of a spaced pair of fixed aerials on the ground. Usu. *attrib.*

1956 *Spaceflight* I. 27/2 A system of radio triangulation, called Minitrack, using phase comparison techniques, will establish the satellite's position and orbital path. *Ibid.* 28/1 Minitrack will enable a limited amount of research information to be telemetered to earth. **1958** *Observer* 2 Feb. 1/3 The minitrack stations have highly sensitive directional antennae which can 'focus' on the satellite. They also collect on tape recorders all the information it transmits. **1961** *Daily Tel.* 18 Jan. 20/4 One of two remote-controlled rotating aerials at the minitrack radio tracking station at Winkfield, Berks, which is now nearly ready to go into operation. **1966** *McGraw-Hill Encycl. Sci. & Technol.* VIII. 504/1 A two-axis Minitrack system was constructed so as to measure the north-south and east-west angular positions simultaneously. **1974** G. Perry in H. Miles *Artificial Satellite Observing* vii. 145 The NASA Minitrack system provides directional observations with an accuracy of about 100 seconds of arc.

mink. Add: **1.** Also, a garment made of this fur.

1951 F. Loesser in Swerling & Burrows *Guys & Dolls* (1960) ii. i. 44 (*song-title*) Take back your mink. *Ibid.* 45 Take back your mink Those worn out pelts And go shorten the slevees [*sic*] For somebody else. **1969** S. Ellin in *Ellery Queen's Grand Slam* (1971) 19 Two cars, a new mink whenever you feel like it. **1972** J. Gill *Tenant* iii. ii. 87 On their tenth wedding anniversary he had given her a silver mink.

2. Substitute for def.: A small, semi-aquatic, stoat-like mammal belonging to one of several species of the genus *Mustela*, esp.the American mink, *M. vison*, which is farmed for its dark brown fur. (Later examples.)

1914 W. T. Hornaday *Wild Life Conservation* iv. 146 In farming communities, the Mink, Weasel, Skunk, Raccoon, and even the Opossum all become so destructive to poultry as to constitute pests. **1965** D. Morris *Mammals* 282 American Mink are farmed extensively for their lustrous, rich-brown pelts, and these animals have been deliberately introduced into other parts of the world because of their economic importance... In Britain, specimens which have escaped from fur farms have set up breeding colonies that are causing some concern.

b. A dark brown colour.

1955 *Punch* 16 Mar. 349/2 Colours are black, white, mink, and blue. **1961** *Guardian* 16 Jan. 4/7 There is a new colour available in the range [of blankets]—'mink'. **1971** *Vogue* 15 Sept. 30 This exciting trouser suit..[is] available in Mink/Black and Mulberry/Dark Navy.

4. *mink coat, farm, farmer, farming, oil, ranch, ranching, skin* (earlier example), *stole.*

1928 A. Christie *Mystery of Blue Train* x. 71 Perfectly dressed in a long mink coat and a little hat of Chinese lacquer red. **1958** *Daily Mail* 21 Mar. 5/2 A mink coat for his wife? 'Good gracious, I don't think so.' **1975** 'M. Duke' *Death of Holy Murderer* 7 An inside pocket of her mink coat. **1965** in P. Jennings *Living Village* (1968) 246 On the mink farm..mating took place early in March. **1967** *Guardian* 26 Aug. 3/6 There is a mink farm near by, and..householders have been protesting..about the smell. **1961** A. Wilson *Old Men at Zoo* i. 53 A drunken failed mink farmer from Essex. **1916** *Yukon Territory* (Canada Dept. Interior) 188 The following practical hints on mink farming have been recently published. **1965** *Harper's Bazaar* June 46 To take care of cuticles, some extravagant materials are used—the latest being mink oil. **1974** *Times Herald Record* (Middletown, N.Y.) 22 Apr. 12/2 What about *mink oil*? It is close to the human lipid and helps to control the moisture balance and moisture retention. **1948** A. L. Rand *Mammals E. Rockies* 92 In Alberta the number of mink ranches has increased steadily from 35 in 1929 to 773 in 1943. **1916** *Yukon Territory* (Canada Dept. Interior) 188 Mink ranching will become an important industry. **1678** *Rec. Court of New Castle on Delaware* (1904) 349, 22 mincq skins great and smal. **1969** 'E. Lathen' *Murder to Go* (1970) 230 Mrs. Chester Brewster..in a mink stole. **1974** D. Ramsay *No Cause to Kill* ii. 111 A mink stole or a diamond bracelet.

b. *fig.* in *attrib.* and *Comb.* uses: opulent, sumptuous, wealthy.

1960 *Spectator* 4 Nov. 681 A mink-stoled Republican residential suburb of Chicago. **1966** *Radio Times* 22 Sept. 22/1 Kenton gives the mink touch to half-price electric heating.

minke (mi·nkə). [f. the name *Meincke*; see quot. 1971.] In full, *minke whale.* A small whalebone whale, *Balænoptera acutorostrata*; also called the piked whale or lesser rorqual.

1939 *Geogr. Jrnl.* XCIII. 190 Minke and killer whales were cruising quietly in all parts of the bay [*sc.* the Bay of Whales in the Antarctic]. **1970** *Islander* (Victoria, B.C.) 19 July 13/1 We watched seven killer whales kill and eat a minke whale. **1971** F. D. Ommanney *Lost Leviathan* ii. 39 It [*sc.* the piked whale or lesser rorqual] is also known to the Norwegians as the Minke whale after a whaling gunner named Meincke who accidentally shot one in mistake for a Blue and thus achieved a rather dubious immortality. **1973** *Sci. Amer.* Aug. 43/1 The danger exists that intensive hunting of sperm and minke whales could eventually reduce both species to the level of severe endangerment.

minky. Also **minky-winky.** *colloq.* Quasi-childish nonce-words for Milk *sb. rare*$^{-1}$.

1930 D. H. Lawrence *Nettles* 8 Eat your pap, little man, like a man! Drink its minky-winky, then, like a man! *Ibid.* 9 Drop of whiskey in its minky?

minne-drinking (mi·nə,dri:ŋkiŋ), *vbl. sb.* [f. G. *minne* love + Drinking *vbl. sb.*] Originally, a heathen practice among Germanic tribes at grand sacrifices and banquets, in honour of the gods or in memory of the absent or deceased. Later, a similar practice said to survive in certain localities in Germany.

1880 J. S. Stallybrass tr. *Grimm's Teutonic Mythol.* I. iii. 62 Minne-drinking, even as a religious rite, apparently exists to this day in some parts of Germany.

‖ **minnelied** (mi·nəlīt). Pl. **-lieder** (lī:dəɪ). [G., f. *minne* love + *lied* song.] A love-song written by a minnesinger, or in the style of the minnesingers.

1876 Stainer & Barrett *Dict. Mus. Terms* 292/2 Minnesingers..devoted their talents to the production of love songs (Minnelieder). **1881** *Encycl. Brit.* XII. 90/1 The first lyrical writer of Holland was John I...who practised the *minnelied* with success.

minnenwerfer: see *minenwerfer.

Minnepoesy (mi·nəpōu:ėsi). *arch. rare.* [f. G. *minne* love + Poesy *sb.*] = next.

1845 Longfellow *Poets & Poetry of Europe* 182/2 In the fresh and youthful Minnepoesy, all art has acquired the appearance of nature.

Minnepoetry (mi·nə,pōu:ėtri). *arch. rare.* [f. G. *minne* love + Poetry.] The poetry of the Minnesingers.

1887 *Amer. Jrnl. Philol.* Dec. 454 The classical representative of Minnepoetry, Walther von der Vogelweide.

Minnesong (mi·nəsǫŋ). [ad. G. *minnesang*, f. *minne* love + *sang* Song *sb.*; cf. Minnesinger.] One of the songs of the Minnesingers. Also *collect.*

1845 Longfellow *Poets & Poetry of Europe* 182/2 This is the reason that all the Minnesongs..seem still to resemble each other. **1907** F. C. Nicholson *Old German Love Songs* p. iii, English works on the subject of the German Minnesong are..scanty in number. **1915** K. Breul *Cambr. Songs* 36 Several..of the 'Cambridge Songs' may be considered as direct forerunners of the early Minnesong.

Minnesota (minĭsōu·tă). [See next.] In phr. *Minnesota Multiphasic Personality Inventory*: a personality test made up of over 500 items, the responses to which are graded for various personality traits in accordance with criteria calculated from groups of normal subjects and subjects with clinically diagnosed psychiatric disorders. (Cf. **M.M.P.I.*)

1946 *Jrnl. Appl. Psychol.* XXX. 517 The present paper presents preliminary data on the use of the Minnesota Multiphasic Personality Inventory (MMPI) with respect to differential diagnosis, with secondary findings upon the subject of overall identification of 'abnormals' from people in general. **1952** L. W. Ferguson *Personality Measurement* viii. 235 (*caption*) Classification of items in the Minnesota Multiphasic Personality Inventory. **1973** *Jrnl. Genetic Psychol.* CXXII. 65 The tasks presented to the subjects consisted of Block Counting..and the Depression scale from the Minnesota Multiphasic Personality Inventory (MMPI).

Minnesotan (mi:nĭsōu·tăn). [f. the name of *Minnesota* (see below) + -an.] A native or inhabitant of Minnesota, a State in the north-central United States.

1888 D. D. Field *Speeches, Arguments & Misc. Papers* (1890) III. 369 Nebraskan, Kansan, Arkansan, Minnesotan, are the true designations of the citizens of those flourishing States. **1939** F. Scott Fitzgerald *Let.* Mar. (1964) 53 He's a Minnesotan and seems to me an altogether admirable fellow. **1965** Mrs. L. B. Johnson *White House Diary* 20 Jan. (1970) 229 Next we visited the Shoreham, which was full of Minnesotans.

Minnie², **minnie** (mi·ni). *Military slang.* Also **minny.** [abbrev. G. *minenwerfer* trench-mortar.] A German trench-mortar, or the bomb discharged by it. Also *attrib.* Hence as *v. trans.*, to attack with such a trench-mortar.

1917 A. G. Empey *From Fire Step* 36 A German 'Minnie' (trench mortar) had exploded in the next traverse. **1927** E. Thompson *These Men, thy Friends* 116 A minnie had been established in the enemy line. **1930** Blunden *De Bello Germanico* iv. 46 He might have 'minnied' or gunned us out in a few light-hearted rounds.

Ibid. vi. 73 The German minnie-man knew how to upset our domestic programme. **1933** —— & NORMAN *We'll shift our Ground* 14 M. M. for bombing a minny-crew out. **1950** G. WILSON *Brave Company* iii. 40 That bloody moaning Minnie... It's a hell of a weapon.

minnie, minny (mi·ni), *v. Sc.* and *north. dial.* [f. MINNIE.] *trans.* To mother; to act as a mother towards (a lamb); to find (a lamb) its mother; also *refl.*, of a lamb: to find (itself) a mother.

1772 in *Sc. Nat. Dict.* (1965) VI. 283/1 Four or six lambs broke off from the flock of eild sheep..and run [*sic*] to the ewes, and minnied or mothered themselves by sucking. **1825** JAMIESON Suppl., s.v., It is given as a proof of the accuracy of a shepherd's acquaintance with his flock.. that, after the lambs have been separated from the ewes, he can *minnie ilka lamb.* **1861** F. O. MORRIS *Rec. Animal Sagacity & Character* 117 There was not a single ewe.. which did not minny her lambs—that is, assume the character of mother towards the offspring from which she had been separated.

minnow. Add: **3. minnow-twisting** *vbl. sb.*, erratic movement or behaviour, resembling that of a minnow.

1935 L. MACNEICE *Poems* 52 The minnow-twistings of the latinist who alone Nibbles and darts through the shallows of the lexicon.

minnowed (mi·nǭud), *a. poet.* [f. MINNOW + -ED².] Containing or abounding in minnows.

1889 W. B. YEATS *Wanderings of Oisin* 71 Hour by hour He ruffles with his bill the minnowed streams.

Minoan (minǭu·ăn, məin-), *a.* and *sb.* [f. L. *Mīnōs* (Gr. *Μίνως*), the name of a legendary king of Crete + -AN.] **A.** *adj.* Of or pertaining to ancient Crete, *spec.* to the Bronze Age civilization extending from the early part of the third to the end of the second millennium B.C., or to its people, culture, or language; also, to this civilization (or aspects of it) discovered elsewhere in the Aegean area. **B.** *sb.* **a.** An inhabitant of Minoan Crete or other parts of the Minoan world. **b.** The language or scripts associated with the Minoan civilization. Hence **Mino:aniza·tion; Mino·anized, Mino·anizing** *adjs.*

The precise chronology of the successive phases and of the collapse of Minoan civilization is highly controversial.

1894 A. J. EVANS in *Jrnl. Hellenic Stud.* XIV. 367 At a time when 'Minoan' Crete and Mycenaean Greece had.. evolved independent systems of writing. **1902** *Nature* 20 Nov. 58/1 The dominion of the proud Minoan thalassocrats disappeared. *Ibid.*, The hieroglyphic of their tutelary deity may have been used by the Minoans as a sort of heraldic device. **1904** *Ibid.* 15 Sept. 482/2 It was this faïence that the Minoan potters imitated. **1921** *Spectator* 5 Mar. 293/1 A hanging lamp..with a yellow and orange shade with a sort of Minoan design on it in orange, terracotta, and black. **1931** *Times Lit. Suppl.* 16 Apr. 308/1 He makes free use of his belief that the language of the Minoan script is Greek. **1939** J. D. S. PENDLEBURY *Archaeol. Crete* iv. 230 The Minoanization of the Mainland. *Ibid.*, Though superficially Minoanized, the mainland still kept a good deal of its native culture and taste. **1950** G. E. DANIEL *100 Yrs. Archaeol.* vi. 195 Perhaps a bill of lading in Egyptian and Minoan. *Ibid.*, It seems likely that the language of the Minoans was Anatolian. **1950** H. L. LORIMER *Homer & Monuments* i. 38 The strongly Minoanizing régime of LH II. **1956** *Jrnl. Hellenic Stud.* LXXVI. 1 Documents in the script known as 'Minoan Linear B' were unearthed at Knossos in Crete over fifty years ago. **1966** C. H. GORDON (*title*) Evidence for the Minoan language. **1970** BRAY & TRUMP *Dict. Archaeol.* 149/1 'Minoan' is strictly a cultural term. Surviving bones show that the Bronze Age Cretans were a racially mixed group. **1970** *Oxf. Classical Dict.* (ed. 2) 1060/2 A Minoan colony of pre-eruption days [at Thera] is being excavated.

Min of Ag (min ǫv æg), colloq. abbrev. of *Ministry of Agriculture* (, Fisheries and Food).

1946 M. DICKENS *Happy Prisoner* vi. 106 D' you know what the Min. of Ag. want Fred to do... They want him to plough up the hill field. **1962** *Observer* 6 May 21/3 A man at the Board of Trade will talk about 'those Min of Ag people'. **1972** *Guardian* 22 Mar. 13/1 'The Archers' began ..[as] a sort of broadcast Min of Ag handout.

Minol (məi·nǫl). Also **minol.** [Prob. f. MIN(E *sb.* + -OL.] A mixture of ammonium nitrate, T.N.T., and aluminium used as the explosive in depth charges.

1946 *Battle of Atlantic* (H.M.S.O.) 57 About this time [*sc.* January 1943] the shattering power of our naval depth-charge was increased by the use of a new explosive called 'Minol'. This would crack the pressure hull of a U-boat at 25 feet. **1947** CROWTHER & WHIDDINGTON *Science at War* iv. 161 From January 1943, all Mark VII depth charges were filled with Minol. **1972** *Materials & Technol.* IV. xix. 725 The ammonals..and the minols—ammonium nitrate 40%, TNT 40% and aluminium 20% —were used for commercial and military applications, but are liable to evolve gases owing to the interaction of aluminium with moist ammonium nitrate.

minor, *a.* and *sb.* Add: **A.** *adj.* **2.** *minor poem, public school, road*; *minor league* (chiefly *N. Amer.*), the lower associations of teams in baseball, etc. (opp. *MAJOR *a.* 1 e); also *attrib.* and *fig.*; hence *minor leaguer*; *minor loyalty*: adherence to an institution, church, trade union, or the like, which is subordinate to loyalty to one's country or its government; *minor piece*: in *Chess* (see quot. 1847); *minor suit*: in *Bridge*, diamonds or clubs; *minor tactics*: the tactics or handling of bodies of troops in the immediate face or expected presence of the enemy.

1819 KEATS *Let.* 2 Jan. (1958) II. 26 It is my intention to wait a few years before I publish any minor poems. **1820** J. S. BINGHAM tr. *E. Dal Rio's Incomparable Game of Chess* I. ii. 26 Two minor Pieces, for a Rook and two Pawns, may be considered an equal contract. **1847** H. STAUNTON *Chess-Player's Handbk.* I. iii. 24 The Bishop and Knight, in contradistinction to the Queen and Rook, are called *minor Pieces.* **1863** Minor piece [in Dict.]. **1875** C. CLERY (*title*) Minor tactics. **1885** A. B. LETTS *A.B.C. of Minor Tactics* 59 Minor tactics..come into use not only on the field of battle but also off it. **1889** *Sporting Life* (Philadelphia) 29 May 1/2 It will mean..the relegation of four-fifths of the men not in those leagues to the minor leagues. **1906** *Cincinnati Enquirer* 1 Apr. IV. 2/1 The Coast team is a strong aggregation, fit to cope with the best of minor leaguers. **1916** R. F. FOSTER *Auction Bridge for All* v. 23 Clubs and diamonds are called minor, or losing suits. *Ibid.*, A much larger percentage of minor suit declarations fail to make good the contract than major suits. **1927** CARR-SAUNDERS & JONES *Survey Social Struct. Eng. & Wales* 83 To discuss the 'minor loyalties' which such associations create. **1928** H. ROWAN-ROBINSON *Some Aspects Mechanization* 3 The study of the minor tactics of petrol-driven forces. **1932** *Time* 28 Mar. 29/1 After six years in the minor leagues he has become catcher for the Washington Senators. **1936** 'J. TEY' *Shilling for Candles* vii. 81 The Grammar schools..turned out a very fine type of boy. Better often..than came from the minor public schools. **1942** E. PAUL *Narrow St.* xxxiv. 304 Daladier was well along with his minor league Kampf. He had repealed the forty-hour week, reduced the wages for overtime and removed the limit of hours. **1962** *Listener* 23 Aug. 285/1 Auden in the 'thirties was no better than Osborne in the 'fifties; both operated in a very minor league. **1963** 'W. HAGGARD' *High Wire* v. 54 The junction of the minor road to Maldington with the main to London. **1967** P. ANDERTON *Play Bridge* iii. 24 One does not readily take-out from a major suit into a minor suit at the level of 'Two' unless a five-carder is shown. **1968** A. DIMENT *Bang Bang Birds* vii. 119 He knotted the tie, from a very minor public school, round his stiff collar. **1970** *New Yorker* 28 Feb. 32/1, I played minor-league baseball in Valdosta, Georgia—Class D. **1972** *N.Y. Times* 1 June 55/3 The New York Raiders of the World Hockey Association yesterday signed a smallish minor-leaguer named Alton White. **1973** E. LEMARCHAND *Let or Hindrance* xiii. 162 The accident had happened on an unfrequented minor road. **1973** D. CHANDLER *Marlborough* xv. 318 Fourth are 'minor Tactics'—the actual fighting methods employed at unit level to gain a local success.

6. d. (Earlier example.)

1820 J. SEVERN in Keats *Lett.* (1958) II. 342 Here I must change to a Minor Key—Miss C fainted..I was very ill.. Keats assended his bed.

B. *sb.* **9.** (Earlier and later examples.)

1821 P. EGAN *Real Life in London* I. vi. 92 Mr Gloss'em, who is a *shining character* in the theatrical world, at least among the minors of the metropolis. **1931** *Times Lit. Suppl.* 1 Jan. 1/2 The vast galleries of the patented theatres and the cramped benches of the 'minors' were thronged with a new audience.

10. In American universities and colleges, a subject or course of study to which less attention is given, or for which fewer credits are given, than for a major. Also, this subject seen as a qualification. (See also quot. 1969.) Cf. *MAJOR *sb.*² 6.

1890 in T. W. Goodspeed *Hist. Univ. Chicago* (1916) 142 The plan of majors and minors..has been arranged in order to meet this difficulty. **1909** WEBSTER, *Minor*,..a subject of study,..pursued by a candidate for a higher degree, less time being devoted to it than to the major subject. **1919** *Univ. Texas Bull.* No.1925. 105 The student will note that it is possible to arrange his minor... [so] as to take in effect two majors. **1926** [see *ELECTIVE *sb.* 2]. **1948** *Ada* (Okla.) *Even. News* 2 July 6/2 Alliene Pryor-Smith..will graduate at East Central in July, with a major in history and a minor in sociology. **1969** *Amer. Heritage Dict.*, *Minor*... One studying a minor: *a chemistry minor.*

11. In *Bridge*, = **minor suit*; also, a card in a minor suit.

1927 [see *MAJOR *a.* 1 d]. **1958** *Listener* 4 Dec. 965/1 Which two aces?.. They are both of the same rank, *i.e.* both minors. **1960** *Times* 16 Nov. 17/4 A two-suiter in the minors only, with Diamonds as long as, or longer than the clubs.

minor (məi·nəɹ), *v.* Chiefly *N. Amer.* [f. MINOR *a.* and *sb.*] *intr.* Of a university student: to take, or qualify *in*, a minor (see prec., sense *B. 10).

1934 in WEBSTER. **1967** *Oxf. Mag.* 10 Feb. 205/1 [Canada] They intend to major in life sciences and minor in Phys. Ed.

minorate, *v.* Delete † *Obs.* and add later examples.

1789 J. MORSE *Amer. Geogr.* 212 Their design is by quantity to depreciate the value of their bills; and lands mortgaged for public bills will be redeemed in these minorated bills. **1922** JOYCE *Ulysses* 387 Assuefaction minorates atrocities (as Tully saith of his darling Stoics).

minority. Add: **2.** (Later example of *in minority.*)

1920 *Act* 10 & 11 *Geo. V* c. 64 § 2 A husband of full age,.. whose wife is in minority, shall be her curator during her minority.

3. b. A small group of people separated from the rest of the community by a difference in race, religion, language, etc. Also in quasi-*adj.* use.

1921 H. W. V. TEMPERLEY et al. *Hist. Peace Conf. Paris* V. ii. 112 These treaties provide for the protection of racial, linguistic, or religious minorities included within the boundaries of the specified States. **1930** *Economist* 29 Nov. 1001/1 The Nazis and the Stahlhelm have been conducting reprisals against the Polish minority in Germany. **1937** *Times* 24 Feb. 13/3 The concessions made by the Prague Government to sections of the German minority.. are disconcerting to any plans..for a large-scale minorities campaign. **1945** *Ann. Reg. 1944* 26 Some broad general declaration by the United Nations deprecating the ill-treatment by a state of its minorities. **1945** L. WIRTH in R. Linton *Sci. of Man* 347 The existence of a minority in a society implies the existence of a corresponding dominant group enjoying higher social status and greater privileges. **1970** *Washington Post* 30 Sept. B. 14/4 A hard-hat worker who loses his job to a minority worker. **1973** *Black Panther* 3 Mar. 13/3 In civil rights, aid to minority business enterprises is stressed, rather than to the minority poor. **1975** *Atlantic Monthly* Jan. 29/1 By 'minority' today, we mean a disadvantaged group of citizens. *Ibid.*, Today, by a 'minority' we mean not the privileged at the top, but the underprivileged at the bottom.

5. minority carrier *Electronics*, a charge carrier of the kind carrying the smaller proportion of the electric current in a semiconducting material (cf. *majority carrier* s.v. *MAJORITY 7); **minority group,** a group forming a minority (sense *3 b); **minority language,** a language spoken by a minority group if different from that of the majority; **minority man,** one who is in a minority or tries to secure recognition of the claims of minorities; **minority member,** a member appointed to a board, committee, or the like to represent a minority; **minority movement,** a movement to secure justice or proper representation for minorities; **minority report** (examples); **minority rights,** rights granted to minorities to act as a safeguard of their interests and help prevent discrimination against them by the majority.

1951 Minority carrier [see *majority carrier* s.v. *MAJORITY 7]. **1962** SIMPSON & RICHARDS *Physical Princ. Junction Transistors* iv. 60 Another variation in charge in the vicinity of the junction arises from the injection or extraction of minority carriers under conditions of forward or very small reverse bias respectively. **1969** J. J. SPARKES *Transistor Switching* i. 3 The current from one junction to the other is carried by minority carriers. **1942** LOCKE & STERN *When Peoples Meet* I. iv. 125 Such.. inclusion of minority groups is in marked and often ironic contrast to the more normal 'divide and rule' policy..of dominant groups. **1964** M. ARGYLE *Psychol. & Social Probl.* vii. 94 Several studies show that prejudice increases with the density of the minority group in an area. **1971** R. BENDIX in A. Bullock *20th Cent.* 357/1 The citizenship of racial minorities remains an unresolved problem. Members of minority groups are denied rights which are formally theirs. **1939** L. H. GRAY *Foundations of Lang.* v. 118 Minority-languages may thus be not merely linguistic in interest, but may also constitute political problems of all degrees of importance. **1927** *Observer* 1 May 17/1 It was a curious moment..to choose for legislation calculated..to revive the power of 'minority men' and direct actionists in Britain. **1874** *Porcupine* 31 Jan. 693/2 The city of London has already conceded a minority member. **1927** *Daily Tel.* 6 Sept. 7/3 He did not agree with the Minority Movement. **1833** *Reg. Deb. Congress U.S.* 2 Mar. 1927 A new set of majority and minority reports are to be launched upon the public. **1940** B. DE VOTO (*title*) Minority report. **1958** *Everyman's Encycl.* XII. 532/2 With Sidney Webb..she [*sc.* Beatrice Webb] issued the minority report which initiated the Socialist agitation for the reform of the old Poor Law. **1924** R. W. SETON-WATSON *New Slovakia* vi. 104 Such international opinion as regards the 'Minority rights' provided for by the Peace Treaties, as a moral obligation assumed by all members of the League of Nations. **1955** I. L. CLAUDE *National Minorities* xii. 166 Whenever the issue must be squarely faced, the U.S. takes the lead..in opposing the concept of special minority rights. **1972** 'E. LATHEN' *The Longer the Thread* viii. 74 She was a Puerto Rican—yet she had never served on a commission about minority rights.

b. quasi-*adj.* Of, for, composed of, or appealing to a minority (of people); freq. with the suggestion of 'serious, intellectual, highbrow' (as opposed to *MASS *sb.*² 10).

1930 F. R. LEAVIS (*title*) Mass civilization and minority culture. **1932** Q. D. LEAVIS *Fiction & Reading Public* II. iv. § 3. 199 Enough attention has perhaps been given to the effects of minority values. **1941** *Partisan Rev.* Mar.–Apr. 111 Leisured people who have been brought up in a minority culture. **1944** L. MACNEICE *Christopher Columbus* 9, I am in favour of occasional special [radio] programmes for small minority audiences. **1958** R. WILLIAMS *Culture & Society* III. iii. 235 Those extreme forms of the idea of a 'minority culture'. **1959** *20th Cent.* Nov. 324 Serious minority programmes [on television] at peak hours. *Ibid.* 333 A place remains for it [*sc.* sound radio].. in the evenings for special minority interests and for

music. **1960** *Housewife* Apr. 10/2 The Editor..considers very few subjects indeed too 'minority' or too apparently trivial to be given a sensible airing. **1971** *Guardian* 22 Feb. 8/1 Even from the BBC..a complete diet of minority-interest programmes..would not be..acceptable. **1972** P. BLACK *Biggest Aspidistra* I. iv. 42 The heat was taken off the minority drama.

Minotaur. (Later examples of allusive use.)
1939 SPENDER & REES tr. *Büchner's Danton's Death* I. iv. 42 The people is a Minotaur that must be fed with corpses every week if it is not to eat the Committee alive. **1945** AUDEN *Sea & Mirror* ii. 51 Home to your promiscuous pastures where the minotaur of authority is just a roly-poly ruminant and nothing is at stake. **1950** T. S. ELIOT *Cocktail Party* III. 163 We talk of darkness, labyrinths, Minotaur terrors. **1964** A. W. GOULDNER in I. L. Horowitz *New Sociol.* 196 The lair of this minotaur [*sc.* Max Weber]..is still regarded by many sociologists as a holy place.

Minox (məi·nɒks). The proprietary name of a type of miniature camera.
1952 *Brit. Jrnl. Photogr.* 5 Sept. 433/1 Several miniature miniatures have already appeared on the market. One notable example is the Minox. This uses 16-mm. film.. and the negatives produced give moderate size enlarged prints of good quality. **1962** L. DEIGHTON *Ipcress File* ii. 20 Chico..would have been making time with the Minox camera. **1966** J. BINGHAM *Double Agent* v. 72 Golchenko ..took out the rolls of Minox film. **1966** *Trade Marks Jrnl.* 6 Apr. 463/1 Minox... Photographic apparatus and instruments and parts and fittings there for..Minox Gesellschaft mit Beschränkter Haftung (a Limited Liability Company organised under the laws of the German Federal Republic),..Giessen-Heuchelheim, Germany; manufacturers. **1969** K. BENTON *24th Level* vi. 116 [He] took out his Minox..and took photographs.

minstrel, *sb.* Add: **2.** *spec.* One of the Old English period.
1767 PERCY *Ess. Anc. Eng. Minstrels* 9 The privileges and honours which were so lavishly bestowed upon the northern scalds, were not wholly with-held from the Anglo-Saxon Minstrels. **1839** T. WRIGHT *Ess. Lit. & Learning under Anglo-Saxons* 2 All literary genius centres on one person, the minstrel, who equally composed and sang. **1892** J. EARLE *Deeds of Beowulf* 136 Rieger.. understands that the minstrel did not merely narrate, but improvised. **1928** W. W. LAWRENCE *Beowulf & Epic Trad.* 46 The lines at the beginning [of *Widsith*] introducing the minstrel, and those at the end glorifying his profession. **1951** D. WHITELOCK *Audience of Beowulf* 77 The poet, if he had not wished, was not forced to make the minstrel sing of the Creation. **1966** E. G. STANLEY *Continuations & Beginnings* 129 Sometimes a minstrel working in the oral-formulaic tradition coined a phrase, for every phrase must have been new before it grew old.
4. (Earlier examples.)
1843 in G. C. D. Odell *Ann. N.Y. Stage* (1928) IV. 668 The Ethiopian Serenaders, or Boston Minstrels. **1846** *Illustr. London News* 24 Jan. 61/2 The Ethiopian serenaders. A party of American minstrels..commenced..a series of concerts.
4*. *slang.* (See quots.)
1967 M. M. GLATT et al. *Drug Scene* 115 *Minstrel* (*black and white*), Durophet. **1971** E. E. LANDY *Underground Dict.* 133 *Minstrel*, 12.5 mg. capsule of an amphetamine and a sedative.
5. *attrib.* (Further examples, esp. in sense 4.)
1865 *Chicago Tribune* 10 Apr. 1 Buckley and Budd's minstrel house is in blast. **1870** O. LOGAN *Before Footlights* 414 A clever actor..who wrote a burlesque..for a minstrel show. **1885** W. B. YEATS *Island of Statues* II. iii, in *Dublin Univ. Rev.* July 139/2 He who hath the halcyon's wing As flaming minstrel-word upon his crest. **1947** A. EINSTEIN *Mus. Romantic Era* xvii. 331 Of his [*sc.* S. C. Foster's] songs, *Oh! Susanna* was one of the oldest (1848) and was most widely circulated by the 'minstrel shows'. **1949** *Radio Times* 15 July 18/3 A black-faced minstrel show with bones, tambourines, corner men, stump speech. **1975** *Listener* 3 Apr. 454/3 At the time of the Civil War, the minstrel show became less complex in its treatment of Negro life.

mint, *sb.*[1] Add: **6. mint condition** = *mint-state*; **mint par, parity (of exchange),** the ratio between the gold equivalent of the currency units of two countries; the rate of currency exchange between two countries based on this ratio; **mint-state,** also applied to books and other objects in pristine condition.
1902 *Connoisseur* May 67/2 Nothing is more marked in present day stamp collecting than the insistence..upon what is expressively termed a 'mint' condition in unused specimens. **1923** *Punch* 7 Feb. 130 Here we have Holbein's portrait of the first earl... His *chef-d'œuvre*, in mint condition. **1956** I. MURDOCH *Flight from Enchanter* i. 9 The books were chaotic, but in mint condition, since reading was not a popular activity. **1975** 'D. RUTHERFORD' *Mystery Tour* iii. 59, I did have half a dozen vintage Rolls-Royces..but..it was becoming more and more expensive to keep the cars in mint condition. **1882** Mint par [see PAR *sb.*[1] 2 a]. **1891** G. CLARE *Money-Market Primer* 74 A Mint Par can only be established between countries that employ the same standard of value. **1928** W. F. SPALDING *Dict. World's Currencies & Foreign Exchanges* 134/2 The mint par of exchange is the rate of exchange at which the standard coin of one country is convertible into that of another country according to the terms of their respective mint laws. **1965** PERRY & RYDER *Thomson's Dict. Banking* (ed. 11) 376/2 The Mint Par between two countries never varies unless one of them alters its coinage regulations. **1928** L. D. EDIE *Money, Bank Credit & Prices* iii. 52 A so-called mint parity existed between all gold standard countries. **1940** G. CROWTHER *Outl. Money* ix. 317 The 'mint parity' being $4.86\frac{2}{3}$=£1, whenever the exchange rate..fell..it became cheaper to buy gold from the Bank of England..and..sell it to the Federal Reserve Bank for dollars. **1965** SELDON & PENNANCE *Everyman's Dict. Econ.* 285 *Mint Parity of Exchange*, the exchange rate between two currencies both of which are legally convertible at fixed rates into..gold... The mint parity then expresses the ratio between the two legal rates. **1931** *Times Lit. Suppl.* 16 Apr. 305/3 Copies of 'Waverley'..are excessively rare in mint state.

mint, *sb.*[2] Add: **1. c.** = PEPPERMINT 2 b. Also a sweet, or chocolate, flavoured with or containing mint. Also as *adj.*
1894 E. SKUSE *Compl. Confectioner* 138 (*heading*) Cheap common mints. **1958** 'R. CROMPTON' *William's Television Show* v. 161 Their pockets bulged with..pear drops, mint fancies, almond delight. **1964** *Listener* 1 Oct. 498/2 Mouth mint-happy, I drift to the bed. **1966** P. V. PRICE *France: Food & Wine Guide* 95 Really good mint chocolates are..appreciated by French friends. **1970** D. MARLOWE *Echoes of Celandine* vi. 90 A bag of mints. **1973** *Harrod's Christmas Catal.* 35/1, 1 metre box of crispy mints—a special chocolate blended in our own factory. £5.25.
3. *mint-green* adj.; **mint cake** (later examples); **mint jelly,** mint-flavoured jelly, usu. eaten with roast lamb; **mint julep** (earlier and later examples); **mint rock** (example); **mint-sling** *U.S.*, a drink containing some alcoholic beverage flavoured with mint; **mint vinegar,** mint-flavoured vinegar.
1958 E. NEWBY *Short Walk in Hindu Kush* xiv. 170 Drinking some coffee and munching Kendal mint cake. **1971** D. HASTON in C. Bonington *Annapurna South Face* xvii. 211 Food level was porridge, mint cake and assorted synthetic drinks. **1971** M. THOMPSON in *Ibid.* App. D. 272 There was far too much sugar and too much fudge and mint cake. The Kendal Mint Cake really came into its own at very high altitude. **1967** MRS. L. B. JOHNSON *White House Diary* 9 Mar. (1970) 493, I wore my mint-green silk and sat..on his right. **1973** J. SHUB *Moscow by Nightmare* ix. 97 The mint-green Winter Palace. **1922** GORDON & ROHDE *Cookery* 157 *Mint Jelly*... Pick fresh young mint. Boil the sugar in the vinegar for 5 minutes. **1951** T. STERLING *House without Door* ii. 22 The lamb was tender... She ate the mint jelly separately. **1966** I. JEFFERIES *House-Surgeon* xiii. 245 There was red-currant jelly, white-currant jelly, mint jelly..and mint sauce. **1809** 'D. KNICKERBOCKER' *Hist. N.Y.* II. VII. ii. 180 The inhabitants..were notoriously prone to get fuddled and make merry with mint-julep and apple-toddy. **1853** J. G. BALDWIN *Flush Times Alabama* 81 Great was he too at mixing an apple toddy or mint julep. **1943** *R.A.F. Jrnl.* Aug. 16 When he spoke one tasted mint juleps and water melons. **1970** A. LAUNAY *Cocktails & Snacks* 64 *Mint Julep.* 6 or 7 mint leaves.., shaved ice, $\frac{2}{3}$ cocktail glass bourbon whisky. **1952** *New Statesman* 29 Mar. 370/2 The sweets are unsophisticated and long-lasting—Bottomley's mint rock, Judy Barratt's humbugs. **1804** *Balance* 15 Mar. 86 (Th.), Three Mint Slings. **1812** 'H. BULL-US' *Diverting Hist. John Bull & Bro. Jonathan* xiii. 98 The Yankeys abhor horse-racing, cock fighting, and mint-slings. **1832** J. P. KENNEDY *Swallow Barn* I. xi. 110 It is a vulgar error..to appropriate the mint sling to the morning. **1964** *Cookbk.* (Amer. Heritage) 345 The Mint Sling and Apple Toddy..are variations on the more traditional Slings and Toddies given here. **1845** E. ACTON *Mod. Cookery* (ed. 2) v. 137 *Green mint vinegar*... The mint itself,..will keep well in vinegar, though the colour will not be very good. **1957** E. CRAIG *Collins Family Cookery* 893 *Mint Vinegar.* .. Fill up jars with the mint.., then pour in mild vinegar to overflowing.

mint, *a.* *ellipt.* for *in mint condition* (see *MINT *sb.*[1] 6).
1902 *Connoisseur* Jan. p. xiv, A hitherto unknown stamp..unused (mint). **1928** *Humphris'* (Norwich) *Catal.* No. 149. 13/1 'Mint' signifies As New. **1952** J. CARTER *A.B.C. for Bk.-Collectors* 59 A cloth-bound, a boarded or a wrappered book may be called immaculate, mint, pristine, [etc.]. *Ibid.* 120 Dust-jacket defective, otherwise mint. **1968** P. OLIVER *Screening Blues* 3 Other conditions reflect the popularity of singer or song, and some [records], grey on one side and 'mint' on the other, betray hard service in a juke-box. **1975** *Deval & Muir* (Takeley, Hertfordshire) *Catal.* No. 35. 16/1 This book is one of the prettiest small publications of the period... Apart from discolouration of the free end-papers, virtually a mint copy.

mint-drop. **2.** (Earlier examples.)
1835 HAWTHORNE *Passages from Note-Bks.* in *Atlantic Monthly* (1866) Jan. 3/2 The bar-keeper had one of Benton's mint drops for a bosom-brooch! **1837** *Congress. Globe* 29 Sept. App. 339/3 [The money flowed to Mobile] by the aid of 'the far-famed Specie circular', in 'mint drops' and 'hard currency'. **1840** J. P. KENNEDY *Quodlibet* 106 [There's] Specie Circlor and Mint Drops, and the Lord knows what.

Mintech (minte·k). Also **Mintec, Min. Tech.** Colloq. abbrevs. of *Ministry of Technology.*
1967 *Guardian* 26 Aug. 6/6 A Min Tech review of the whole problem. **1967** *Spectator* 15 Dec. 750/3 The gritty 'technological' phrasemaking of you-know-who and his Mintech. **1970** *Guardian* 25 Feb. 10/3 Mintech exists... They really do give this little name..to the great big Ministry of Technology. **1970** *Punch* 17 June 920/1 Every available taxpayer's penny is needed for wasting at Min-Tech. **1971** *New Scientist* 17 June 673/1 The civilian aspects of the defence research establishments—so laboriously cultivated under Mintech auspices.

minto (mi·ntǝ). Also **Mintoe, mintoe.** [f. MINT *sb.*[2]] The proprietary name of a type of boiled sweet flavoured with peppermint.
1935 *Trade Marks Jrnl.* 16 Oct. 1298/2 Nuttall's Mintoes... Boiled sugar sweetmeats flavoured with mint. William Nuttall Limited,..Doncaster; manufacturing confectioners. **1949** DYLAN THOMAS *Let.* 13 Oct. (1966) 328 Yesterday I broke a tooth on a minto. **1953** —— *Under Milk Wood* (1954) 2 Coughing like nannygoats, sucking mintoes, fortywinking hallelujah. **1957** *Skuse's Compl. Confectioner* (ed. 13) 63 *Mintoes.* Boil the sugar, glucose and water..knead in the oil of peppermint and.. spin out and cut. *Ibid.* 64 (caption) Kiss Cutting on 'Mintoe' Machine. **1963** *Listener* 21 Mar. 501/2, I wanted to keep on sucking mintoes for ever.

Minton (mi·ntǝn). The name of Thomas *Minton* (1766–1836), used *attrib.* to designate the pottery made at Stoke-on-Trent, Staffs., from 1793 onwards, by him and his successors. Also *ellipt.*, = Minton ware.
1857 J. MARRYAT *Hist. Pott. & Porc.* (ed. 2) xii. 302 Staffordshire is now the site of the great manufactures. From among these may be mentioned Minton, Copeland, Ridgway. **1863** W. CHAFFERS *Marks Pott. & Porc.* 125 Minton's, established in 1791 by Mr. Thomas Minton... The name, indented on the ware, is generally adopted both for china and earthenware. **1888** [see TILE *sb.*[1] 1 c]. **1926** S. T. WARNER *Lolly Willowes* I. 11 An amateur of china, who had dowered all his nieces..with Worcester, Minton, and Oriental. **1960** R. COLLIER *House called Memory* iii. 44 The best silver tea-service and the Minton tea-set. **1967** 'R. RAINE' *Wreath for Amer.* ii. 30 A small silver tray bearing two Minton cups and saucers. **1972** R. PLAYER *Oh! Where are Bloody Mary's Earrings* vii. 182 A scraping of boots on the Minton tile floor.

minuet, *v.* Add examples of *fig.* use.
1881 G. M. HOPKINS *Lett. to R. Bridges* (1955) 125 The magic nib has..minuetted and gavotted into the syllables of your name. **1972** *Newsweek* 17 July 21/3 MacGregor might have to minuet with White House aides for a Presidential audience.

‖ **minuetto** (miniue·to). [It.] = MINUET.
1724 *Short Explication Foreign Words in Musick Bks.* 46 *Minuetto*, a Minuet, a French Dance so called, or the Tune or Air belonging thereunto. **1888** [see MINUET 2]. **1923** [see *GRAPE *sb.*[1] 1]. **1971** BLOM & WESTRUP *Everyman's Dict. Mus.* (ed. 5) 431/2 *Minuetto* (It.). This, not 'Menuetto', is the correct It. name for the Minuet.

minus. Add: **2.** *spec.* as part of an examiner's mark, as in *α*— (read as alpha minus).
1932 A. HUXLEY *Brave New World* iv. 75 He..called to a lounging couple of Delta-Minus attendants to come and push his machine out. **1958** [see *BETA 3]. **1962** M. DRABBLE *Summer Bird-Cage* i. 13, I..got on the train, where I read..*Tender is the Night* (beta minus).
b. *minus quantity* (later example); also *transf.*, insignificant.
1916 R. FRY *Let.* 14 Aug. (1972) II. 401, I fear my recommendation would generally prove a minus quantity. **1922** WODEHOUSE *Clicking of Cuthbert* ix. 221 He might be a pretty minus quantity in a drawing-room or at a dance, but in a bunker or out in the open with a cleek, Eunice felt, you'd be surprised. **1965** F. SINCLAIR *Most Unnatural Murder* xv. 174 Cherub and Phyl wouldn't play; Phyl's a bit of a minus quantity, anyway, from that angle.
c. Also, absent.
1853 DICKENS *Down with Tide* in *Househ. Words* 5 Feb. 483/2 Being, when called upon to answer for the assault, what Waterloo described as 'Minus', or, as I humbly conceived it, not to be found. **1858** A. MAYHEW *Paved with Gold* III. xiv. 342 If we ain't minus in less than no time, we're blowed upon.
e. Followed by the name of a colour to designate the complementary colour, i.e. that of white light from which the specified colour has been removed; so *minus colour.*
1901 CADETT & SHEPHERD *Orthochromatic & Three-Colour Photogr.* 24 [In the Sanger Shepherd process] the prints for the minus green or pink, and minus blue or yellow positives are printed together on a special film. **1901** *Chambers's Jrnl.* 4 May 366/2 The prefix 'minus' attached to a primary colour..[implies] that this particular colour is cut out of the spectrum of white light, and that the negatively-named compound is a blend of the hues remaining. 'White minus red', 'white minus green', and 'white minus blue' would be the complete expressions; they are ordinarily termed complementary colours. **1936** *Discovery* Jan. 2/1 It [*sc.* Monastral Fast Blue BS] is a true 'minus-red' pigment for three-colour printing. **1939** J. H. COOTE *Making Colour Prints* 17 The three colours which are used for 'subtraction' are described as 'minus' colours. **1970** D. L. MACADAM *Sources of Color Sci.* 130 Red, green, and blue, being the colors in positive synthesis, minus red, minus green, and minus blue, or cyan blue, bright crimson and yellow are the printing colors.

minuscule, *a.* Add: **2.** (Further examples.) Also, unimportant.
Now usu. stressed on first syllable. See also *MINISCULE.
1963 *Ann. Reg. 1962* 17 Such minuscule militants as the boot and floor polish manufacturers. **1969** *Listener* 30 Jan. 155/3 One is impressed inevitably by the intensity and concentration of human effort on a project whose rewards, however satisfying, are bound to be minuscule. **1972** *Time* 17 Apr. 24/1 The Gallup organization, in all of its national soundings, has shown McGovern running between a minuscule 3% and 6% when pitted against his rivals for the nomination.

minute, *sb.*[1] Add: **1. b.** (Further examples.) Also in phr. *up to the minute*, completely modern.
1795 tr. *C. P. Moritz's Trav.* 93 Composing a sermon.. should not thus have been put off to the last minute. **1913** *Vanity Fair* (N.Y.) Dec. 9/2 Look at your Christmas shopping in this light... Don't put it off until the last minute.

1920 F. M. Ford *Let.* 27 July (1965) 117 Does 'for a minute' = 'at present'? or that you wouldn't think for a minute of knowing our establishment? **1937** A. J. Cronin *Citadel* ix. 75 Doctor! I think you'd be interested in our new indexometer. It has a multiplicity of uses, is absolutely up to the minute..and the price is only two guineas. **1955** R. Macaulay *Last Lett. to Friend* (1962) 208 Having the two children made it fun; they loved every minute of it. **1956** E. S. Gardner *D.A. takes Chance* iii. 24 A very attractive young woman, vivacious, up to the minute, a thoroughly modern young woman. **1958** *Spectator* 22 Aug. 249/1 These ought to be worth a trial to give ballet that shake-up it badly needs. Not merely for Art's sake, but, any minute now, for the sake of the box office. **1972** *Daily Tel.* 26 Aug. 20/4 A good atmosphere helps me to do my best, and while at the minute it doesn't feel like an Olympic Games, I think I can psych myself up when the time comes.

d. A distance expressed in the number of minutes needed for it to be traversed (on foot, etc.).

1886 *Taunt's New Map Thames* (ed. 5) Advts. 45 Hotel ..Adjoining the River, 3 minutes from Railway Station. **1907** *Daily Chron.* 18 Sept. 3/7 (Advt.), St. Pancras Station..is within a few minutes of the City. **1922** Joyce *Ulysses* 224 Can you send them by tram? Now?..—Certainly, sir. Is it in the city? —O, yes... Ten minutes. **1931** R. Campbell *Georgiad* i. 17 Up-to-date minutes: breezy situation: And only twenty minutes from the station. **1934** G. B. Shaw *On Rocks* I. 203 The Isle of Cats... Down the river, Sir Arthur. Twenty minutes from your door by underground. **1962** J. G. Bennett *Witness* vii. 86, I went to his apartment, a few minutes from where we lived.

6. *minute of dissent*, a minute recording a person's disagreement with something.

1886 Kipling *Departmental Ditties* (ed. 2) 23 No longer Brown reverses Smith's appeals, Or Jones records his Minute of Dissent. **1930** *Times* 15 Mar. 7/1 All the members have signed the report, but Lord Ebbisham did so subject to a 'minute of dissent' which is attached to the main report.

7. minute-gun (earlier and later examples); **minute steak** (see quot. 1934); **minute-to-minute** *attrib.*, from one minute to the next.

1728 G. Carleton *Mem. Eng. Officer* 205 The first Guns that were fir'd from Gorge's battery were the Minute-Guns for his Funeral. **1936** H. Nicolson *Diary* 28 Jan. (1966) 241 The King's funeral. I stay in..all morning and do not hear more than the minute-guns firing dolefully in the distance. **1970** *Brewer's Dict. Phr. & Fable* (rev. ed.) 714/2 *A Minute gun*, a signal of distress at sea, or a gun fired at the death of some distinguished person. **1934** Webster, *Minute steak*, a small thin steak that can be quickly cooked. **1959** *Good Food Guide* 204 The grills..range from 6/6 (minute steak) to 9/6 (mixed grill, including vegetables). **1966** *Listener* 27 Jan. 134/3 The minute steak is the gastronomic symbol of the age. **1948** 'G. Orwell' in *Adelphi* XXIV. 249/2 One ought, apparently, to live in a continuous present, a minute-to-minute cancellation of memory. **1968** G. M. B. Dobson *Exploring Atmosphere* (ed. 2) v. 105 In practice certain precautions have to be taken to allow for the minute-to-minute changes in the general electric field.

minute, *v.* Add: **2. b.** To inform (someone) about a matter by means of a minute or memorandum.

1918 G. S. Gordon *Let.* 13 Dec. (1943) 87 Milford has minuted me about the Oxford Trivium. **1952** *Punch* 10 Sept. 353 He had minuted General Ismay. **1964** M. Gowing *Britain & Atomic Energy* v. 174 Lord Cherwell was still minuting Mr Churchill that the British diffusion method was much superior. **1974** 'J. Le Carré' *Tinker Tailor* xxvi. 221 In no case should I phone him or minute him; even the internal lines were taboo.

Minute-man. Restrict *Hist.* to sense in Dict. and add: **1. b.** In extended uses, a 'watchdog' or political activist; a member of an organization devoted to specific political issues. Also *gen.* (with small initial), a vigilant, observant, or enterprising person. (Now usu. without hyphen or as one word.)

1923 *Minute Men of the Constitution Roster* (inside front cover), The Minute Men of the Constitution is a non-partisan association, organized to obtain delegates from Illinois to the Republican and Democratic State and National Conventions... The above is a movement for good government. **1930** P. R. Leach *That Man Dawes* x. 190 Dawes called..a number of close friends and organized 'The Minute Men of the Constitution'. The purpose of the Minute Men..was to function as an open-eyed body of men throughout the state to watch elections, prevent vote frauds at the polls and counteract unfair propaganda. The society was not secret, had no passwords or meeting places and was non-political. **1952** *Manch. Guardian Weekly* 23 Oct. 3/1 An appeal went out for minute-men to tap the moneybags in their own localities. **1961** *Guardian* 25 Nov. 7/2 The Minute Men and Birchites. **1961** Webster, *Minuteman*, one who resembles a Revolutionary minuteman esp. in qualities of vigilance and readiness to take prompt action. **1964** D. Bell *Radical Right* i. 4 Three elements [in the 1960s] conjoined to attract public attention to the radical right... The John Birch Society. .. Seminars of anti-Communist 'schools'... And, third, there was the disclosure of the existence of extreme fanatic groups, such as the Minutemen, who organized 'guerilla-warfare seminars', complete with rifles and mortars, in preparation for the day when patriots would have to take to the hills to organize resistance against a Communist-run America. **1964** *Economist* 19 Dec. 1350/2 The Minutemen, a mysterious, probably negligible, vigilante group, has drawn the gloomily righteous conclusion that America has seen its last free election. **1965** T. H. White *Making of President 1964* iii. 89 Across the sky of politics there began to float new names like the John Birch Society, the Minutemen, the National Indignation Convention, [etc.]. **1970** *Peace News* 17 Apr. 8/1 It would be easy for the casual observer to link the Panthers with..the Minutemen and American Nazis.

2. (With capital initial.) A type of intercontinental ballistic missile (see quot. 1971).

1961 *Daily Tel.* 2 Feb. 1/4 The American Air Force achieved a spectacular advance today when it launched the first Minuteman missile. **1969** *Guardian* 6 Dec. 2/2 They claim that the three five-megaton warheads fitted to these missiles are unnecessarily large and accurate for use against any target but the hardened US Minuteman missile sites. **1971** E. Luttwak *Dict. Mod. War* 130/1 The Minuteman series are three-stage missiles with solid-propellant motors designed as simplified and low-cost weapons for launching from 'hard' silo sites. They need very brief pre-launch preparation.

minuter. 1. Delete † *Obs.* and add later example.

1911 *Pitman's How to take Minutes* 14 The minuter must take sufficient notes of the proceedings.

minuterie (miniū·tĕri). [Fr., = clockwork, timing mechanism, minuterie, f. *minute* Minute *sb.*[1]] **a.** A light switch incorporating a timing mechanism that automatically turns it off a short time after it has been (manually) turned on. **b.** An electric light controlled by such a switch.

1955 W. Gaddis *Recognitions* I. ii. 72 Crémer opened the door, and the light of the minuterie threw his flat shadow across the sill. **1958** E. Dundy *Dud Avocado* I. iii. 52 Racing from minuterie to minuterie to keep the stairs in a blaze of 40-watt bulbs. **1962** A. Williams *Long Run South* v. i. 160 He went up in the lift and pressed the minuterie. **1963** 'D. Rutherford' *Creeping Flesh* iii. 153 The stairs were illuminated with a tasteful glow. No penny-wise *minuterie* here. **1971** M. McCarthy *Birds of America* 302 On the second landing he found it..in the weak light of the *minuterie*.

minuting, *vbl. sb.* (See under Minute *v.*) Add earlier example.

1856 Dickens *Dorrit* (1857) II. viii. 387 The work of form-filling, corresponding, minuting, memorandum-making.

minx. 2. b. Delete † *Obs.* and add later examples.

Sense 2 a is still the more usual sense.

1939 Joyce *Finnegans Wake* 80 What are you doing your dirty minx and his big treeblock way up your path? *Ibid.* 496 There wasn't an Archimandrite of Dane's Island and the townlands nor a minx from the Isle of Woman..would come next or nigh him. **1941** J. Smiley *Hash House Lingo* 38 *Minx*, prostitute.

minxish (mi·ŋksiʃ), *a.* [f. Minx + -ish[1].] Having the character of a minx; like a minx. Hence **mi·nxishly** *adv.* Also (*rare*) **minxy** (mi·ŋksi) *a.*; (*dial.*) **mi·nxin** *a.*

1870 *Porcupine* 12 Feb. 443/3 Through a door, left slightly ajar, he..sees another minxish 'Girl of the Period' waiting the return of her companion. **1883** M. R. Lahee *Acquitted though Guilty* 55 Hoo wur a honest dacent woman: noan-like the, the minxin slut. **1919** W. De Morgan *Old Madhouse* xxv. 387, I do *not* believe that Lucy..is half as minxish as she made out. **1927** *Daily Express* 27 Apr. 3/2 The mannequin wore it minxishly, for it was a frock for a minx. **1935** *Times Lit. Suppl.* 3 Oct. 613/3 A weak, attractive, minxish child. **1939** C. Morley *Kitty Foyle* 91 We got some right minxy columbines round here.

miny, *a.* Add: Also **miney. 1.** (Later example.)

1907 *World* 16 July 113/1 What do you say to mines? No, there's nothing miney about me.

minyan (mi·nyān), *sb.*[1] Pl. **minyanim.** [Heb. *minyān*, lit. 'count, reckoning'.] The quorum of ten males over thirteen years of age required for formal Jewish worship.

1753 *Jewish Ritual* 53 This..is executed by the Priest in the Presence of ten Jews, which Number of Jewish Men, they call in Hebrew, A Minyon. **1891** M. Friedländer *Jewish Relig.* 472 Women are disqualified for forming the quorum (*minyan*) required for public worship. **1893** I. Zangwill *Childr. Ghetto* (ed. 3) I. xii. 111 There was never lack of *Minyan*—the congregational quorum of ten. **1960** L. P. Gartner *Jewish Immigrant* vii. 215 In the early 1860's [in Leeds], there were barely the ten Jews required for a minyan. **1962** B. Abrahams tr. *Life Glückel of Hameln* iv. 78 A company of more than two *minyanim*. **1973** *Jewish Chron.* 2 Feb. 10/1 After a life of almost 33 years the congregation's list of members had of late diminished to the point where a minyan had become very difficult to secure.

Minyan (mi·niăn), *a.* and *sb.*[2] [f. L. *Minyae*, Gr. *Μινύαι* Minyans + -an.] **A.** *adj.* Also 6 **Mynian,** 9 **Minyean** (mini͵ī·ăn) [Gr. *Μινύειος*, adj. f. *Μινύαι*.] **a.** Of or pertaining to the Minyans. **b.** Designating a type of very smooth grey pottery first found at Orchomenus and originally attributed to the Minyans. **B.** *sb.* A member of a possibly historical ancient people said to have inhabited parts of central Greece (chiefly Orchomenus in Boeotia and Iolchus in Thessaly), with whom the legends concerning Jason and the voyage of Argo are associated. Also with *pl.* **Minyae, Minyai.**

1598 Chapman tr. *Homer's Seaven Bookes of Iliades* 35 Those who in Aspledon dwelt, and Mynian Orchomen. **1709** I. Littlebury tr. *Herodotus' Hist.* I. iv. 416 Their Answer was, that they were Minyans, Grandsons of those Heroes who sail'd in the *Argos*. *Ibid.*, When the Lacedemonians heard they were of Minyan Extraction, they sent another Messenger. **1867** Max Müller *Chips* II. xvi. 67 The Minyans..reigned chiefly in Iolkos, in Southern Thessaly. **1881** H. Schliemann in *Jrnl. Hellenic Stud.* II. 152 A wall of unwrought stones.. which Professor Sayce holds to be the ancient Minyean city wall. **1894** tr. *A. Holm's Hist. Greece* I. vii. 65 The oldest accounts of the Minyae are to be found in Homer where the Boeotian Orchomenus is mentioned as a Minyan city. **1912** Wace & Thompson *Prehist. Thessaly* 21 Minyan Ware. This class of pottery was first found in any quantity by Schliemann at Orchomenos. **1925** V. G. Childe *Dawn European Civilization* v. 78 It is only in Central Greece that Minyan ware occurs in such quantities... True Minyan is wheel-made and has a silver-grey colour to the reduction of the iron oxides in the clay. **1928** C. Dawson *Age of Gods* viii. 190 The Greek mainland was conquered by a new people from the north, the bearers of the so-called Minyan culture. **1929** F. W. Hasluck *Christianity & Islam under Sultans* II. xxv. 366 The role of the magician-philosopher-engineer Plato..proves to be similar to that of the Minyans in Boeotia. **1958** L. Cottrell *Anvil of Civilisation* x. 138 These invaders are characterised by a certain type of plain-grey pottery called Minyan. **1964** E. Vermeule *Greece in Bronze Age* iii. 72 The tribal name Minyan must be strenuously distinguished from the archaeological label 'Minyan' for the invaders who bring the Middle Helladic Age to Greece. We have no idea at all what these newcomers called themselves. **1969** A. Toynbee *Some Probl. Greek Hist.* I. ii. 16 The Minyai were a maritime commercial people who came by sea. *Ibid.*, We shall find independent legendary evidence of a Cretan origin for..the Minyan settlements. **1970** Bray & Trump *Dict. Archaeol.* 149/2 *Minyan Ware*, a grey or yellow wheel-made ware of high quality... It was ancestral to Mycenaean pottery, and may represent a movement of new peoples into the Aegean area.

Min Yuen (min yiŭe·n). [ad. Chinese *min yuan* people's movement.] Name of an underground Communist supply organization formed during the Malayan Emergency, 1948–1960. Also *attrib.*

1951 *Communist Banditry in Malaya* (Federation of Malaya, Dept. Information) 9 During the year [*sc.* 1949] the main incidents were carried out by small gangs operating either as killer squads or as part of the Min Yuen Organization. It was the duty of this latter Organisation to arrange for the collection of food supplies and money from the local population, and for the dissemination of Communist propaganda. **1954** V. Bartlett *Rep. from Malaya* iii. 41 There is a branch of the Communist Party known as Min Yuen (literally 'the Helpers'), which collects food for the terrorists. **1966** E. O'Ballance *Malaya* iv. 92 Supporting the insurgent army was the clandestine Min Yuen, an underground organisation that provided money, food, intelligence and communications. *Ibid.*, Min Yuen is a contraction of Min Chung Yuen Thong, which has been variously translated as 'popular mass movement' or 'people's revolutionary movement'. **1970** T. Lilley *Projects Section* ii. 20 The Min Yuen—the Communist Liberation Army's supply organisation. **1971** N. Barber *War of Running Dogs* ii. 32 The Min Yuen (which means 'Masses Movement'),..consisted of ostensibly normal, innocent citizens who would in fact back up the army.

minyulite (minyū·ləit). *Min.* [f. the name of *Minyulo* Well, Dandaragan, W. Australia, near which the mineral was first found + -ite[1].] A hydrated basic phosphate of potassium and aluminium occurring as colourless to white needles and fibres similar to wavellite.

1933 Simpson & LeMesurier in *Jrnl. R. Soc. Western Austral.* XIX. 13 In examining the Minyulo outcrop there was seen to be a fibrous mineral, closely resembling wavellite, which occurred in small quantities in a hard phosphatic ironstone carrying partly altered apatite nodules. .. The mineral has been proved in the laboratory to be a well defined new species for which the authors suggest the name Minyulite. **1961** *Mineral. Abstr.* XV. 210/2 Minyulite..occurs on Visean shales and phthanites in Belgium as fine silky fibers, ranging 60 to 300 μ, often grouped together in radiating rosettes (1 to 3 mm).

miocene, *a.* (Earlier example.)

1831 [see *eocene *a.* 1].

miogeoclinal (məi:odʒī͵oklәi·năl), *a. Geol.* [abbrev. of next.] = *miogeosynclinal *a.* So **mioge·ocline** = *miogeosyncline.

1971 *Nature* 2 July 41/1 Several models..can be invoked to explain the eventual orogenic deformation of miogeoclinal continental margins. *Ibid.* 42/1 Fossil arcs.. must face away from the miogeocline in the activation model but towards the miogeocline in the collision model. **1972** [see *miogeosynclinal *a.*]. **1972** *Sci. Amer.* Mar. 33/1 The present Atlantic marine deposits closely resemble the ancient miogeoclinal foldbelts of the Paleozoic era and earlier.

miogeosynclinal (məi:odʒī͵osinklәi·năl), *a. Geol.* [ad. G. *miogeosynklinal* (H. Stille *Einführung in den Bau Amerikas* (1940) i. 15),

f. Gr. μείων less: see GEOSYNCLINAL *a.* and *sb.*] Of or pertaining to a miogeosyncline. So **mio-geosy·ncline**, a geosyncline in which the process of sedimentation appears to have been accompanied by little or no volcanism; *esp.* one situated between a larger, volcanic geosyncline (a eugeosyncline) and an area of the crust that has achieved stability (a craton).

1942 *Bull. Geol. Soc. Amer.* LIII. 1642 In contrast to the Magog eugeosyncline, the Champlain belt contains dominant carbonates of shallow-water origin, unaffected by subsequent volcanism; it is a miogeosyncline. *Ibid.* 1643 The eastern, miogeosynclinal belt has the well-described sequence of southeastern Idaho. **1951** *Mem. Geol. Soc. Amer.* XLVIII. 4 As volcanic rocks are practically absent in the orthogeosynclines that adjoin the North American early Paleozoic craton, they are thus miogeosynclines. **1969** BENNISON & WRIGHT *Geol. Hist. Brit. Isles* iii. 58 No vulcanicity is known and the succession is probably indicative of deposition on an unstable shelf at the margin of a miogeosyncline. **1971** *Nature* 24 Sept. 252/1 The West Andean geosyncline was divided into a 'eugeosynclinal' volcanic (coastal range) zone and a 'miogeosynclinal' sedimentary (longitudinal valley) zone during the Jurassic. **1972** *Sci. Amer.* Mar. 30/2 When one examines the structure of ancient folded mountains, one finds that the classic geosyncline is divided into a couplet: two adjacent and parallel structures consisting of a eugeosyncline (true geosyncline) and a miogeosyncline (lesser geosyncline), often shortened to eugeocline and miogeocline.

Miohippus (məiohi·pŭs). [mod.L. (O. C. Marsh 1874, in *Amer. Jrnl. Sci.* 3rd Ser. VII. 249), f. MIO(CENE *a.* + Gr. ἵππος horse.] A small fossil horse of the genus once so called, known from North American remains of the Oligocene period, and now included in the genus *Anchitherium*.

1877 T. H. HUXLEY in *Pop. Sci. Monthly* Jan. 294 Next [in the equine series] comes the *Miohippus*, which corresponds pretty nearly with what I spoke of as the *Anchitherium* of Europe. **1933** A. S. ROMER *Vertebr. Paleont.* xvii. 325 In *Mesohippus*..and the somewhat larger *Miohippus* we find the beginning of a series of functionally three-toed horses. **1958** C. L. & M. A. FENTON *Fossil Bk.* xxxii. 419 *Mesohippus* was followed by *Miohippus*, a larger and somewhat more horselike beast.

miombo (mio̜·mbo). Also **miomba.** [Swahili.] A tree of the tropical African genus *Brachystegia*, belonging to the family Leguminosæ; woodland composed mainly of these trees. Also *attrib.*

1864 J. A. GRANT *Walk across Afr.* vi. 88 The wands from the Miombo, a kind of banyan, afford the natives the fibre which they attach to their wool. **1910** *Encycl. Brit.* XI. 772/2 The silk-cotton tree (*Bombax ceiba*), miomba, tamarisk, copal tree..are frequent [in German East Africa]. **1934** *Jrnl. Ecol.* XXII. 220 A strip of 'Miombo' through which a narrow, fairly shallow ravine..was running. **1947** *E. Afr. Ann.* 1946–7 95/2 The considerable forests of Unyamwezi, largely miombo, provide much honey. **1959** R. W. J. KEAY in *Vegetation Map Afr.* Explanatory Notes 9/1 In these woodlands, commonly known by the vernacular name 'myombo', several species of *Brachystegia*..are dominant. **1948** *Cape Argus* 3 Dec. 5/4 Surrounded by uninhabited miombo bush. **1966** C. A. W. GUGGISBERG *S.O.S. Rhino* iii. 53 Black rhinoceroses frequent savannah country, mopane and miombo forests, bushveld and dry thornbush. **1970** A. T. SEMPLE *Grassland Improvement* i. 14 African farmers have found that their ground-water supplies improve when they extend their settlements in the 'miombo' (*Brachystegia* woodland).

miosis, also var. MYOSIS (in Dict. and Suppl.).

miotic, var. MYOTIC *a.* and *sb.* (in Dict. and Suppl.).

mipafox (mi·păfo̜ks). [f. bis(*mono-isopropyl-amino*)*f*luorophosphine *ox*ide, its chemical name.] An organic phosphorus compound, $[(CH_3)_2CHNH]_2POF$, which is used as an insecticide.

1953 *Recommended Common Names for Pesticides* (*B.S.I.*) II. 5 Mipafox: fluorobis*iso*propylaminophosphine oxide. **1956** *Nature* 28 Jan. 186/1 It has recently been found that 8×10^{-7} *M* mipafox..completely inhibits the non-specific serum cholinesterase. **1971** *Brit. Jrnl. Pharmacol.* XLI. 21 The ileum was then incubated with mipafox (10 μg/ml) for 75 min.

Mipolam (mi·pŏlæm). Also **mipolam.** A proprietary name for plastics composed of polyvinyl chloride which are used for chemically resistant piping and containers.

1936 *India-Rubber Jrnl.* 4 Nov. 19/2 Mipolam is a purely thermoplastic mass, and behaves accordingly in electrical tests. **1939** H. R. SIMONDS *Industr. Plastics* (1940) xiii. 324 A new polyvinyl chloride plastic in Germany known as Mipolam is resistant to acids and to many other chemicals and is being used for beer, alcohol and other prime containers, and also in the form of piping and pumping fixtures in chemical plants. **1943** *Jrnl. R. Aeronaut. Soc.* XLVII. 140 The group of polymerization resins includes, among others, the plastic of German production—mipolam—remarkable for its high fire resistance, toughness and elasticity. **1951** *Trade Marks Jrnl.* 24 Oct. 980/1 Mipolam... Mouldable plastics for use in manufactures. Dynamit-Actien-Gesellschaft Vormals Alfred Nobel & Co... Troisdorf, Cologne, Germany; manufacturers. **1969** R. F. LANG tr. *Henglein's Chem. Technol.* 215 Mipolam pipes can be enlarged thermally, beaded, bent and cemented with solvents.

Mir (mīəɹ), *sb.*[1] Also **meer.** [a. Hindi and Pers. *mīr*, ad. Arab. *amīr* leader, commander: see AMEER, EMIR.] = AMEER, EMIR.

1625 PURCHAS *Pilgrimes* I. III. xii. 282 The Mir of Aden sent a Boat and a Messenger aboord. **1787** C. HAMILTON *Hist. Relation Rohilla Afgans N. Provinces Hindostan* 41 Ômdat al Moolk..was at this period Meer Buchshy or Paymaster-General of the Empire. **1792** R. HERON tr. *Niebuhr's Trav. Arabia* II. xxIII. vii. 155 Mr Kniphausen had agreed with Mir Naser, Prince of Bender Rigk,..that the Dutch should..be allowed to seat their factory there. **1800** F. GLADWIN tr. *Ayeen Akbery* I. II. 231 (*heading*) The office of Meer Behry, or Admiralty. **1840** J. B. FRASER *Trav. Koordistan* I. iii. 80 The jealousy of the Meer extends only to strangers travelling in the country without apparent business. **1873** E. BALFOUR *Cycl. India* (ed. 2) III. 284/1 Mir Jaffir, in 1702, was appointed dewan of Bengal... He was of a poor brahmin family..but was..converted to mahomedanism. **1885** T. P. HUGHES *Dict. Islam* 350/1 *Mir.* A title of respect used for the descendants of celebrated Muḥammadan saints. More generally used for Saiyids, or descendants of Fāṭimah, the Prophet's daughter. **1928** *Blackw. Mag.* May 709/1 To get the savour of the Mir's table talk, you must hear a little more about its setting. **1973** C. BONINGTON *Next Horizon* xviii. 252 On my first morning I attended the Court of the Mir of Hunza... At ten o'clock, the Mir, an absolute monarch with complete control over the internal affairs of his 20,000 people, walks from his palace to the Durbah. *Ibid.* 253 The Mir sits on a small rostrum, and his Court, in strict order of precedence, squat on carpets in two lines on either side of him. **1973** *Observer* (Colour Suppl.) 30 Sept. 51/1 In some circumstances,..the Mir (ruler) of Hunza could, from personal knowledge of his State's history, verify ages.

‖ **mir** (mīəɹ), *sb.*[2] [Russ.] A village community in pre-revolutionary Russia. Also *attrib.*

1877 D. M. WALLACE *Russia* I. viii. 179 The Mir is the most peculiar of Russian institutions. **1878** E. C. GRENVILLE-MURRAY *Russians To-Day* 21 The Mir system may be summed up in a few words; it has simply caused the peasant to exchange the domination of his old master for the more grinding tyranny of many masters. **1905** J. H. ROSE *Devel. European Nations* xi. 294 The ownership of the soil of Russia by the Mirs, the communes of her myriad villages. **1916** C. E. BECHHOFER *Russ. at Cross-Roads* 71 No period is known in Russian history when the Mir did not exist. **1925** *Contemp. Rev.* Jan. 60 They pointed out that the land-holding peasant..did not cease to be a member of the *mir*. **1967** *Listener* 2 Nov. 558/3 The break-up of the *mir* and the..transition from communal to hereditary tenure. **1975** *Times* 8 Jan. 15/7 The democratic and civic traditions of Russia, from Kievian Rus to the *mirs* and the Zaporozhean Republic.

Mir (mīəɹ), *sb.*[3] [ad. *Mirabad*, the name of a town in the Sarawan district, S.W. of Arak, Iran.] A rare and fine quality Saraband rug woven in Mirabad. Also *attrib.*

1900 J. K. MUMFORD *Oriental Rugs* xi. 197 In the Sarawan district the *tereh* Mir, so called from the village where it is said to have originated, is the almost universal design. *Ibid.*, Artisans in other localities have copied the Mir Saraband, changing the borders or coloration to suit their fancy. **1931** A. U. DILLEY *Oriental Rugs & Carpets* iv. 125 All the fine Sarabands, known as Mir from the town of that name which an earthquake destroyed, were 'Farmayashti', or special-order weavings. **1953** A. C. EDWARDS *Persian Carpet* ix. 144/2 *Miri* no doubt refers to the Mir carpets of the early nineteenth century which were the prototypes of the present-day Serabands. **1972** P. L. PHILLIPS tr. *Formenton's Oriental Rugs & Carpets* 69 The botch design came from the Seraband region and..was used at the beginning in the Mir carpets. **1973** *Times* 2 Apr. 6/5 (Advt.), A superb Mir carpet in soft pastel dyes.

mirabelle. Add: **2.** An alcoholic spirit distilled from mirabelles, *spec.* those grown in Alsace, France.

1940 H. J. GROSSMAN *Guide to Wines, Spirits & Beers* xviii. 185 The brandy obtained from plums is known by several names, depending on the country of origin:..Quetsch or Mirabelle when it comes from Alsace in France. **1963** *Times* 24 Apr. 11/7 'Try that,' he said, proffering a spoon dipped into the last vat of limpid 85° Mirabelle. **1967** N. FREELING *Strike Out* 67 Bernhard's last bottle of mirabelle.

‖ **mirabile dictu** (mirā·bili di·ktu), *Lat. phr.* [L. *mirabile*, neut. of *mirabilis* wonderful + *dictu*, supine of *dicĕre* to say: cf. Virgil *Georgics* ii. 30 quin et caudicibus sectis (mirabile dictu) truditur e sicco radix oleagina ligno.] Wonderful to relate.

1831 *Athenæum* 12 Mar. 173/2 An unassuming young female relative, whom she gives in marriage to the son of her (*mirabile dictu!*) honest attorney. **1837** J. F. COOPER *Recoll. Europe* I. 318 The late king was the Miller, and, *mirabile dictu*, the Archbishop of Paris did not disdain to play the part of the Curé. **1841** DICKENS *Let.* 21 July (1969) II. 334 A man is coming here at 8, to settle (mirabile dictu) the matter of Mrs. Macrone's book. **1861** S. B. BIRCH *Constipated Bowels* ii. 15 The tradesman..is permitted to go so far as to usurp the functions of the physician, and is even encouraged (*mirabile dictu!*) to prescribe himself on the strength of the pharmacopœia. **1943** L. MARCHAL *Vichy* xiii. 195 The Marshal was anxious to save Otto Abetz, who, *mirabile dictu*, was considered in certain Vichy circles as a 'friend of France'.

miracidium (məiəːrăsi·diŏm). *Zool.* Pl. **miracidia.** [mod.L., f. Gr. μειρακίδιον, dim. of μειράκιον boy, stripling.] The ciliated, first larval form of a digenetic trematode. Also *attrib.* So **miraci·dial** *a.*

1898 A. SEDGWICK *Student's Text-bk. Zool.* I. v. 229 The miracidium generally becomes a sporocyst, rarely a redia. **1904** C. W. STILES *Illustr. Key to Trematode Parasites of Man* 18 Miracidium ciliated, develops after eggs leave the host. **1952** J. CLEGG *Freshwater Life* viii. 127 The miracidium stage [of *Bucephalus*] is passed in the freshwater Mussels *Anodonta* and *Unio*. **1962** J. D. SMYTH *Introd. Animal Parasitol.* xxxii. 388 The miracidial immobilisation test is based on the immobilisation of miracidia in immune serum. **1963** *New Scientist* 29 Aug. 441/3 Those [schistosome] eggs which reach the outside world hatch in fresh water and the microscopic miracidia which emerge swim around. **1971** *Oxf. Bk. Invertebr.* 24/1 When the pasture is damp, the first larva [of the liver fluke], the miracidium, hatches and this swims by its cilia in the film of water on the pasture until it encounters a snail. **1974** *Nature* 22 Mar. 361/2 A better understanding of the intricacies of how miracidia and cercariae find and penetrate hosts.

miracle, *sb.* Add: **2. a.** Also with defining word prefixed designating a remarkable development in some specified area.

1959 M. CROSLAND tr. *Rovan's Germany* 78 The fact that millions of new arrivals were housed and employed..is the most miraculous aspect of the 'German miracle'. **1963** *Listener* 21 Feb. 321/2 This contract production is an important factor in the Polish miracle. **1973** A. PRICE *October Men* ix. 128, I don't mind him being part of the Italian economic miracle.

5. *miracle drug, -worker* (further examples); also *miracle-bred* adj.; **miracle man,** delete † and add further examples; **miracle rice,** a modern hybrid rice seed that yields more than the traditional varieties.

1928 W. B. YEATS *Tower* 62 Even the grey-leaved olive tree Miracle-bred out of the living stone. **1953** J. RAMSBOTTOM *Mushrooms & Toadstools* xxiii. 279 Penicillin was really on the stage at last; it dwarfed other performers into insignificance. It was hailed as a 'miracle drug'. **1962** *Lancet* 2 June 1137/1 A miracle drug that will charm away any and every form of infection. **1970** P. MOYES *Who saw her Die?* xvi. 209, I got hold of the streptomycin..and the miracle drug worked. She was cured. **1914** F. L. PACKARD (*title*) The miracle man. **1926** A. CONAN DOYLE *Hist. Spiritualism* I. iii. 54 He [*sc.* Andrew Jackson Davis] was a miracle man, the inspired, learned, uneducated apostle of the new dispensation. **1951** L. MACNEICE tr. *Goethe's Faust* 185 In priestly robes and wreath a miracle-man Will now fulfil what he in hopes began. **1959** I. & P. OPIE *Lore & Lang. Schoolch.* x. 179 They are willing to acclaim anyone who habitually comes top of the class without apparent effort, naming him Genius, The Brains, Miracle Man. **1969** *Americana Ann.* 408 The introduction of U.S.-supplied 'miracle rice' notwithstanding, the country [*sc.* Laos] was still unable to produce enough rice for its own people. **1972** *Times* 8 May 14/1 Dr Norman Borlaug, the discoverer of the 'miracle' rice and wheat strains..was awarded the Nobel Peace Prize in 1970. **1923** KIPLING *Independence* 29 He was something of a magician, if not a miracle-worker. **1970** G. GREER *Female Eunuch* 277 She twice..took a little pill... She thinks they are little miracle workers.

miraculous, *a.* Add: **2. a.** (See quot. 1965.) *dial.*

1879 F. M. FETHERSTON *Oops & Doons T. Goorkrodger* 27, I say when a man's drunk, *he's miraculus and mad.* **1925** L. P. SMITH *Words & Idioms* 142 *Miraculous* has changed its meaning to 'very drunk'. **1965** *Sc. Nat. Dict.* VI. 286/1 *Miraculous*, in a stupefied or incapable condition, esp. from drink, very intoxicated.

mirador. Add: (Later examples.) Also *fig.*

1950 G. BRENAN *Face of Spain* iv. 80 We went into the house. One wing, that of the *mirador* or tower, had been set aside for our books and furniture. **1955** J. THOMAS *No Banners* xxxi. 310 The *miradors* (watch-towers) around Buchenwald were manned by *Wehrmacht* troops. **1971** *Homes & Gardens* Aug. 36/1 Spanish women were generally kept in the background, and watched the world from behind their wooden *miradors*. **1971** *Nat. Geographic* Oct. 547/1, I spent several weeks last spring in this brilliant mirador of capitalist colonialism on the edge of China.

mirage. Add: (Now usu. with pronunc. (mi·rāʒ).) **c.** A wave-like appearance of warmed air visible just above ground level. Also *attrib.*

1913 A. G. FULTON *Notes on Rifle Shooting* 18 When mirage can be seen, it provides the best means of estimating allowances for gentle but tricky winds. **1958** J. A. BARLOW *Elem. Rifle Shooting* (ed. 5) iv. 50 The effect of wind on such air disturbance is readily remarked, since the result of a cross wind is to give the impression of the mirage flowing either slowly or swiftly in the same direction as the wind, just like a clear stream of water over a pebbly bed. **1962** *Amer. Speech* XXXVII. 270 *Mirage puddle*, a heat-caused illusion which makes the road appear wet in the distance.

2. *attrib.* and *Comb.*, as *mirage dream, -water*; *mirage-bright, -lifted, -making, -reflected* adjs.

1924 E. SITWELL *Sleeping Beauty* xvii. 65 Mirage-bright It lies, that dusty gold. **1908** *Daily Chron.* 3 Aug. 3/2 It was like one of those mirage dreams which lure the gambler to his doom. **1874** J. G. WHITTIER *Sea Dream* in *Atlantic Monthly* Aug. 160 And watched the mirage-lifted wall Of coast, across the dreamy bay. **1902** J. H. M. ABBOTT

Tommy Cornstalk i. 13 And the wide rolling downs quivered and danced with the same beautiful mirage-making islands of kopjes. **1923** R. GRAVES *Whipperginny* 9 Mirage-reflected drink At the clear pool's brink. **1918** E. SITWELL *Clown's Houses* 11 Then, mirage-waters as they flow, Or dream-perfumes, they fade and go.

miraged (mirā·ʒd), *a.* [f. MIRAGE + -ED².] Seen in a mirage; of the nature of a mirage.

1920 *Blackw. Mag.* June 817/2 A dim outline of miraged date palms. **1925** *Chambers's Jrnl.* Aug. 486/2 Framed anew, in mystic space—Miraged dream past all believing —Looms the cradle of a race.

Miranda (miræ·ndă). *U.S. Law.* [f. the name Ernesto A. *Miranda* (see quot. 1966).] The name given to a set of rules specified by the Supreme Court in the U.S. whereby law enforcement officers are required to apprise a person suspected of a crime of his rights to counsel and his privileges against self-incrimination prior to his being interrogated. Also *attrib.*

[**1966** *Washington Post* 14 June A7/1 Here are excerpts from yesterday's Supreme Court opinion on the admissibility of statements obtained in questioning of a person in police custody, and on the Fifth Amendment protections such a person is to be afforded against self-incrimination. This opinion..encompasses four cases—Ernesto A. Miranda v. the State of Arizona, [etc.].] **1967** *Time* 3 Mar. 49/1 The Supreme Court's famous *Miranda* decision.. wrought vast changes in police procedure. *Ibid.* 49/2 *Miranda* does not seem to have helped Miranda and his mates. **1970** W. WAGER *Sledgehammer* xxii. 173 I've got quite a few motions—the complete kit. I'll start with *Miranda* when the trial begins. **1972** J. MILLS *Report to Commissioner* 270 Do you know what a Miranda warning is? **1973** *N.Y. Law Jrnl.* 2 Aug. 13/5 At this point Miller read to Dixon his four required warnings under Miranda.

miration (məiərē·ʃən). *U.S. regional colloq.* [Abbrev. of ADMIRATION.] An expression of admiration, wonder, or surprise; a fuss, to-do. So **mira·te** *v. intr.*, to feel or express surprise or astonishment.

1893 in H. Wentworth *Amer. Dial. Dict.* (1944) 390/2. **1903** *Dialect Notes* II. 321 *Mirate*, to wonder at; to admire. **1909** *Ibid.* III. 349 *Miration*, an expression of admiration. 'He made a great miration over the baby.' **1926** in J. F. Dobie *Rainbow in Morning* (1965) 82 He may have made *a great miration* over the place, but it's my private opinion that he has something up his sleeve. **1935** Z. N. HURSTON *Mules & Men* (1970) I. vi. 125 Aw, man, you done seen Tookie and her walk too much to be makin' all dat miration over it. **1946** *Publ. Amer. Dial. Soc.* vi. 20 *Miration*, exaggerated and pretentious wonderment, a carrying-on. 'They made a great miration about my killing that squirrel.' **1950** *Ibid.* xiv. 46 *Mirate*, to make a miration over; to express surprise, admiration over a person or thing. **1950** A. LOMAX *Mr. Jelly Roll* (1952) i. 4 This lady displayed me in saloons, setting me on the bar and..making mirations.

Mirdita (mɜ̄ɹditā). Also **Mirditë** (mɜ̄ɹditə). The name of a region on the river Drin in Albania used *attrib.* and *absol.* to designate the tribal people living there. Also anglicized as **Mirdite** (mɜ̄·ɹdəit).

1861 G. FINLAY *Hist. Greek Revolution* I. I. ii. 43 The Mirdites are considered the most warlike of the Christians. **1920** *Q. Rev.* Jan. 65 The late Mirdite Prince, Prenk Bib Doda. **1939** A. TOYNBEE *Study of Hist.* IV. 367 The present Mirdite territory would have been a natural site for the plantation of a Mardaite settlement by a seventh-century Roman statesman. **1954** M. HASLUCK *Unwritten Law in Albania* xv. 154 There had been attacks on the Montenegrins by the Mirditë, which had followed on plenary assemblies of the Mirditë tribes. **1959** *Chambers's Encycl.* I. 220/1 The Mirdita region south of the Black Drin gorge.

mire, *sb.*¹ Add: **2. d.** Dung. *rare.*

1922 JOYCE *Ulysses* 649 Bloom..with Stephen passed through the gap of the chains..and, stepping over a strand of mire, went across towards Gardiner street lower.

3. *mire-bestrowed, mire-smirched* adjs.

1908 HARDY *Dynasts* III. vi. viii. 281 Cavalry in the cornfields mire-bestrowed. **1960** S. PLATH *Colossus* 12 Common barnyard sows, Mire-smirched, blowzy.

mire, *v.*¹ **II.** *intr.* **3.** Delete † before 'Also' and add further examples.

1835 H. EVANS *Jrnl.* in *Mississippi Valley Hist. Rev.* (1927) XIV. 195 In crossing some of these creeks some of our horses and pack mules mired down. **1840** W. SEWALL *Diary* (1930) 221 The roads being soft..I mired down. **1941** *Amer. Speech* XVI. 184 *Mire down*, to stick in mud.

b. To defecate. *rare.*

1922 JOYCE *Ulysses* 48 An archway where dogs have mired. *Ibid.* 649 Slowly..he [*sc.* the horse] mired.

mired, *ppl. a.* **2.** (Later examples.)

1891 'Q' *Noughts & Crosses* 207 My mired boots played havoc with the neatly sanded floor. **1897** T. C. DE LEON *Jealous God* v, in *Novelette Trilogy* 127 Lifting tenderly the mired, limp and senseless form of a shriveled old woman, struck down by them [*sc.* 'bus horses].

mirepoix (mirpwa). *Cookery.* [f. the name of the Duc de *Mirepoix* (1699–1757), French diplomat and general.] A mixture of diced vegetables used for flavouring or served as a vegetable dish.

1877 E. S. DALLAS *Kettner's Bk. of Table* 65 Set the steak to boil,..add to it a Mirepoix of red wine, and let it simmer... As for taste it is perilous to attempt to improve upon a good Mirepoix. *Ibid.* 304 Mirepoix..is..the convenient name for the faggot of vegetables that flavours a stew or sauce. **1877** *Cassell's Dict. Cookery* 425/2 *Mirepoix*, a flavouring for made dishes. **1906** *Mrs. Beeton's Bk. Househ. Managem.* lxi. 1648 A mirepoix is the foundation for flavouring sauces, braised meats, and a number of thick soups. **1936** LUCAS & HUME *Au Petit Cordon Bleu* 173 *Mirepoix*, carrot, onion, celery, turnip, and French beans cut into very small, even dice. **1960** *Guardian* 15 June 16/4 A mirepoix..is..another interesting way of serving early vegetables..cut into dice.

mirex (məiə·reks). orig. *U.S.* [etym. unknown.] An organochlorine insecticide active esp. against ants.

1962 *Bull. Entomol. Soc. Amer.* VIII. 89/1 The Committee on Insecticide Terminology announces the following proposed common names... Mirex. Dodecachloro-octahydro-1,3,4,-methano-2H-cyclo-buta(cd)pentalene. **1963** *Jrnl. Econ. Entomol.* LVI. 296/1 The newly developed mirex..(formerly known as GC 1283) is an analog of Kepone and has exhibited excellent ant poison characteristics with low toxicity to higher animals. **1972** *Nature* 18 Feb. 353/1 'Mirex', the chief weapon used against the fire ant, has been criticized because of its persistence in the environment and its possible toxicity to animals and fish.

mirid (məiə·rid, mi·rid), *sb.* and *a.* [f. mod.L. family name *Miridæ*, f. the generic name *Miris* (J. C. Fabricius *Entomologia Systematica* (1794) IV. 183), f. L. *mīrus* wonderful, extraordinary: see -ID³.] **A.** *sb.* A leaf bug of the family Miridæ, formerly called Capsidæ (see *CAPSID *a.* and *sb.*¹), which includes a large number of insects that live on the sap of plants, often causing damage to the plants affected. **B.** *adj.* Of or pertaining to an insect of this kind.

1941 *Bull. Illinois Nat. Hist. Survey* XXII. 2/1 The eggs of most mirids hatch early in the season. *Ibid.* 3/2 A majority of mirid species produce only one generation per year. **1957** RICHARDS & DAVIES *Imms's Textbk. Entomol.* (ed. 9) III. 461 Other Mirids do considerable damage to cultivated plants. **1962** METCALF & FLINT *Destructive & Useful Insects* (ed. 4) vi. 225 Anyone who sits down in a grassy, weedy spot in early summer..can scarcely fail to make the acquaintance of some of the hundreds of kinds of mirids that crawl about over the vegetation and feed on its sap. **1972** SWAN & PAPP *Common Insects N. Amer.* xii. 117 The mirids comprise a fairly large family commonly called plant bugs or leaf bugs.

mirifically (məiri·fikăli), *adv.* [f. MIRIFICAL *a.* + -LY².] So as to excite wonder or admiration; wonderfully, superbly.

1922 W. J. LOCKE *Tale of Triona* v. 49 Into the lounge filled with mirifically vestured fellow-creatures.

mirliton. Delete ? *Obs.* and substitute for def.: A toy instrument resembling a kazoo. Add further examples.

1865 M. EYRE *Lady's Walks S. of France* xx. 217 In returning home the pilgrims unite in bands, singing;.. while others, provided with *mirlitons*, play the wildest accompaniments. **1894** G. DU MAURIER *Trilby* I. II. 155 Taffy and Jeannot and Little Billie made the necessary music on their *mirlitons*. **1938** [see *KAZOO]. **1970** P. OLIVER *Savannah Syncopators* 109 *Kazoo*, submarine-shaped tube mirliton, played in blues bands.

mirnyong, var. *MIRRNYONG.

miro¹. Substitute for def.: A large, evergreen tree, *Podocarpus ferrugineus*, of the family Taxaceæ, native to New Zealand, or the timber produced by it. Also *attrib.* (Earlier and later examples.)

1832 G. BENNETT in *London Med. Gaz.* X. 793/1 The Miro tree..is named Miro by the natives of New Zealand. **1905** W. B. *Where White Man Treads* 19 When the red miro berries were ripe..the Maori smiled. *Ibid.*, On the ranges of the interior there are certain waterless districts, where the miro is abundant. **1926** H. GUTHRIE-SMITH *Tutira* (ed. 2) 99 Black pine, miro. **1966** *Encycl. N.Z.* II. 568/2 Miro was known and cherished by the Maoris because of its fleshy covered fruit, about an inch long, on which the native pigeon feeds... Miro is found in lowland forests throughout North, South, and Stewart Islands. **1971** *Daily Tel.* 23 Dec. 3/7 [On Pitcairn Island] Henry may give Warren..a block of scarce miro wood for carving.

miro (mīə·ro), *sb.*² Also **miro-miro,** 9 **mirro mirro.** [Maori, adopted as a generic name by R. P. Lesson in *Traité d'Ornithologie* (1831) 389.] Either of two New Zealand flycatchers of the genus *Petroica*, the black-and-white tomtit, *P. macrocephala*, or the greyish-brown New Zealand robin, *P.* (formerly *Miro*) *australis*.

1843 J. E. GRAY in E. Dieffenbach *Trav. N.Z.* II. 191 *Miro Forsterorum*..Turdus minutus..Mirro mirro of the natives of Queen Charlotte's Sound. **1848** R. TAYLOR *Leaf from Nat. Hist. N.Z.* 9/1 *Miromiro*, small land bird, very tame; can be caught by the hand. **1879** *Trans. N.Z. Inst.* XII. 119 The miro-miro is the little Petroica toitoi, which runs up and down trees peering for minute insects in the cavities in the bark. **1930** W. R. B. OLIVER *N.Z. Birds* 458 *Genus Petroica*..Distinguished from Miro by its smaller size. *Ibid.* 460 White-breasted Tit. Miromiro. **1966** R. A. FALLA et al. *Field Guide to Birds N.Z.* 200 Tomtit... Other names: Miromiro (North Island).

‖ **mirrnyong** (mɜ̄·ɹnyǫŋ). *Austral.* Also **mirnyong.** [Native word.] A mound of shells, ashes, and other debris accumulated in a place used for cooking by Australian Aborigines; an Aboriginal kitchen-midden.

1878 R. B. SMYTH *Aborigines Victoria* I. 238 (*heading*) Mirrnyongs, shell-mounds, and stone-shelters. *Ibid.* 239 The sites for *Mirrn-yong* heaps appear to have been chosen generally in localities near water. **1888** R. M. JOHNSTON *Syst. Acct. Geol. Tasmania* 337 (Morris), With the exception of their rude inconspicuous flints, and the accumulated remains of their feasts in the 'mirnyongs', or native shell-mounds, along our coasts,..we have no other visible evidence of their former existence. **1896** A. H. KEANE *Ethnol.* v. 94 Australia, numerous *mirrnyongs* (ash-heaps, shell-mounds, &c.) mainly confined to the eastern and southern regions. **1964** *Mod. Encycl. Austral. & N.Z.* 666/1 *Mirrnyong Heaps or Kitchen Middens*, aboriginal cooking areas which have grown through thousands of years of use. Consist of ashes, shells and other debris; some have an area of 5,000 sq ft and are 10 ft high. Mainly found in coastal and Murray Valley areas. **1965** *Austral. Encycl.* I. 35/1 Continued use of the same cooking-place builds up enormous deposits of ashes, such as those in Riverina and Murray River districts of New South Wales, Victoria and South Australia, where the ovens or Mirrnyong heaps are up to 125 feet long, 50 feet wide, and 12 feet thick.

mirr-n'yong, var. *MURRNONG.

mirror, *sb.* Add: **7. a.** *mirror-gazer, -hall, -light, -scroll, -stand, -trick*; *mirror-topped* adj.

1937 G. BARKER *Calamiterror* 9 The mirror-gazer self-betrayed. **1923** BLUNDEN *To Nature* 10 From the mirror-lights on the dressing table. **1970** R. LOWELL *Notebk.* 207 Your wall-mirror in a mat of plateglass sapphire, mirror-scroll and claspleaves, holds our faces. **1817** J. CONSTABLE *Let.* 10 July in *Corr.* (1964) II. 228, I am glad I have not made a purchase of the mirror stand (called a Canterbury). **1960** H. HAYWARD *Antique Coll.* 187/1 *Mirror-stand*, an adjustable mirror mounted on a shaft and tripod base, resembling a pole-screen; popular at the end of the 18th cent. **1949** D. SMITH *I capture Castle* III. xiv. 260 A mirror-topped table. **1950** M. ALLINGHAM *Mr. Campion & Others* xiii. 270 He remembered Geoffrey's face at the other end of the mirror-topped table. **1940** W. FAULKNER *Hamlet* IV. i. 247 Something to be repudiated with contempt, like a mirror trick.

b. *mirror-eye, finish, -sheen*; *mirror-dark, -flat, -polished, -resembling, -scaled* adjs.

a **1955** W. STEVENS *Opus Posthumous* (1957) 51 Your gowns..came shining as things come That enter day from night, came mirror-dark. **1923** D. H. LAWRENCE *Birds, Beasts & Flowers* 98 The red-gold mirror-eye [of a fish] stares and dies. **1951** KOESTLER *Age of Longing* II. viii. 306 She felt herself reflected in their watchful mirror-eyes, and was forced to see herself as they saw her. **1897** *Sears, Roebuck Catal.* 112/3 Heavy nickel plated and polished to a mirror finish. **1926–7** *Army & Navy Stores Catal.* 199/3 Polishing wool..gives to silver, electro-plate, gold, etc., that beautiful 'mirror' finish of newly manufactured articles. **1971** *Engineering* Apr. 118/2 A second tool produces the final truly 'mirror' finish. **1923** D. H. LAWRENCE *Birds, Beasts & Flowers* 98 This red-gold, water-precious mirror-flat bright eye. **1936** J. STEINBECK *In Dubious Battle* iv. 29 One line of worn and mirror-polished rails extended ahead. **1937** *Discovery* Feb. 57/1 Pickle mirror-polished silver sheet in sulphuric acid. **1927** W. B. YEATS *October Blast* 9 All those things whereof Man makes a superhuman Mirror-resembling dream. **1934** —— *King of Gt. Clock Tower* 40 The mirror scalèd serpent is multiplicity. **1960** S. PLATH *Colossus* 22 River lapsing Black beneath bland mirror-sheen.

c. mirror drum, a scanning device, used in early television transmitters and receivers, which consists of a rotating drum with its curved surface covered with a number of equally spaced plane mirrors, there being as many mirrors as there are scanning lines in the picture; **mirror embroidery** = **mirror-work*; **mirror fugue** *Mus.*, a fugue that can be played in a reversed or inverted manner, as if read in a mirror placed at the end of or underneath the music; **mirror-glass** (later examples); also *attrib.*; **mirror image**, something that resembles an image in a mirror in having left and right interchanged or its constituent parts arranged in reverse order (but being otherwise identical); also *transf.* and *fig.*; **mirror machine** *Nuclear Physics*, a linear device in which plasma is confined by means of magnetic mirrors; **mirror nucleus** *Nuclear Physics*, a nuclide having as many neutrons as another nuclide (of the same atomic number) has protons, and as many protons as the other has neutrons; also (more correctly) **mirror nuclide**; **mirror-painting** (see quot. 1960); also, the process of such painting; **mirror-picture** = **mirror-painting*; also, a

picture as seen in a mirror; **mirror-plate** (later example); also, a type of metal plate used for fixing two things together; **mirror room,** a room with mirrors set into the walls; **mirror scale,** a scale provided with an adjacent mirror so that parallax errors may be avoided when taking readings; **mirror-script** = *mirror-writing*; **mirror-wall,** a wall entirely covered with a mirror; **mirror-work,** small rounds of mirror appliquéd on fabric; **mirror-writer** (later example); hence (as a back-formation) **mirror-write** *v.*; **mirror-writing** (earlier and later examples).

1927 *Wireless World* 20 Apr. 480/2 As the mirror drum revolves, these seven beams trace seven lines at once on the screen, and then pass over another adjacent track of seven lines until the entire screen has been covered. **1935** M. G. Scroggie *Television* iii. 22 The scanner which has been used for the last few years to transmit the B.B.C. programmes by the Baird low-definition system, and also in a large proportion of the receivers, is the mirror drum. **1968** *Brit. Med. Bull.* XXIV. 261/2 The National Biomedical Research Corporation is developing a mirror-drum scanner, of a type pioneered at Harwell. **1967** E. Short *Embroidery & Fabric Collage* i. 17 *(caption)* Indian 'Shisha' or mirror emboidery. **1931** D. F. Tovey *Compan. to 'Art of Fugue'* 61 The original edition [of Bach's 'Art of Fugue'] . . should not have printed the mirror-fugues in succession instead of in mirror-reflection. **1962** *Listener* 27 Dec. 1109/2 The fifth fugue is again for strings only, as are the rectus versions of the 'mirror' fugues XII and XIII [of Bach]. **1973** *Times* 23 Apr. 16/2 A concert-goer who can recognize a mirror-fugue merely by listening to it has no need of assistance. **1876** J. S. Ingram *Centenn. Exposition* ix. 287 Inside was an oblong square, formed of mirror-glass, which reached to the top of the case. **1934** *Heal & Son Catal.: Better Furnit.* 8 Dressing-table, . . pink mirror-glass top. **1953** *Glass for Glazing (B.S.I.)* 18 *(heading)* Mirror glass. **1885, 1929** Mirror image [see *enantiomorph]. **1937** 'G. Orwell' *Road to Wigan Pier* xii. 244 Fascism . . is a sort of mirror-image . . of a plausible travesty of Socialism. **1949** Mirror image [see *asymmetric *a.* b]. **1961** *Lancet* 26 Aug. 447/2 The hemispheres are not exact replicas but mirror images of each other. **1962** W. Nowottny *Lang. Poets Use* vi. 141 The formal correspondence between the lines . . makes 'time is setting with me' the mirror-image of 'The wan moon is setting ayont the white wave'. **1964** *Language* XL. 247 The phonological disintegration characteristic of the aphasic's linguistic regressions is a mirror-image of the child's acquisition of its sound pattern. **1966** *New Statesman* 27 May 775/3 The Black Muslim creed is the mirror image of the white racialist one. **1972** J. McClure *Caterpillar Cop* v. 68 An element of variety had been introduced by building the bungalows in pairs and making one the mirror image of the other. **1954** R. F. Post *16 Lect. Controlled Thermonucl. Reactions* (Univ. Calif. Radiation Laboratory, UCRL–4231, 2 Feb.) p. vi, A general principle involved in the mirror machine's conception was the establishing as an initial condition that the plasma should be created by injection and trapping of a space-charge neutralized energetic ion beam into an otherwise evacuated chamber. **1958** *New Statesman* 6 Sept. 266/3 In the mirror machines the molecules of heavy hydrogen are violently injected into a chamber and go spiralling along until magnetic forces at the ends of the chamber reflect them and send them spiralling back again—from one magnetic mirror to another. **1969** *New Scientist* 25 Sept. 639/1 If mirror machines are feasible, then a fusion reactor based on the system would be relatively easy to build. **1947** H. A. Bethe *Elem. Nucl. Theory* ii. 7 If the binding energies of a pair of nuclei which differ only in the interchange of neutrons and protons are compared, a difference in binding energy which increases with the charge of the nuclei is found. Examples of such 'mirror' nuclei are: $^{1}H^{3}$ $^{2}He^{3}$; $^{3}Li^{7}$ $^{4}Be^{7}$; . . $^{14}Si^{29}$ $^{15}P^{29}$. **1962** H. D. Bush *Atomic & Nucl. Physics* vi. 127 Evidence for the equality of *n–n* and *p–p* forces is provided by certain positron emitters where the parent and product of the decay are mirror nuclei. **1955** Richtmyer & Kennard *Introd. Mod. Physics* (ed. 5) x. 510 Among the many unstable nuclides . . a set of particular importance are the so-called 'mirror nuclides'. **1960** H. Hayward *Antique Coll.* 187/1 *Mirror-painting*, a type of glass picture in which the glass was first coated at the back with an amalgam of tin and mercury to make it into a mirror. The parts to be painted were then scraped away and painted in as required. **1970** G. Savage *Dict. Antiques* 275/1 Most surviving mirror-paintings are Chinese and belong to the 18th century... Mirror-painting, being on the back of a sheet of glass, meant working in reverse. **1939** *Burlington Mag.* May p. xv/1 A pair of decorative Chinese mirror-pictures in Chippendale frames. **1959** E. Pulgram *Introd. Spectogr. of Speech* v. 46 Oscillograms of repetitive waves whose half-cycles are not mirror pictures of one another. **1964** *Amer. N. & Q.* Jan. 72/1 *Mirror pictures* . . this kind of repeated or reflected picture of a picture of a picture, ad infinitum. **1940** *Chambers's Techn. Dict.* 550/1 *Mirror plate*, . . (1) Plate glass for silvering.—(2) A fixing device in the form of a small metal plate, one end being screwed . . to the object . . and the other fixed to the base. **1966** A. W. Lewis *Gloss. Woodworking Terms* 56 *Mirror plate*, small metal plate screwed to the backs of frames, etc., so that they can be fixed to a wall. **1926** A. Huxley *Jesting Pilate* I. 70 These mirror rooms at Amber. **1901** M. W. Travers *Exper. Study Gases* vi. 56 *The mirror scale* (Jolly).—In reading barometers, manometers, etc., it is usual to employ a glass scale ruled in millimetres. The scale is etched on the surface of a strip of glass about 5 mm. in thickness, which is then silvered on the second surface. **1961** M. D. Armitage *Basic Princ. Electronics & Telecommunications* xi. 290 *(caption)* Use of mirror scale. **1890** W. James *Princ. Psychol.* I. x. 399 The subjects, e.g., often write backwards, or they transpose letters, or they write mirror-script. **1964** *Listener* 20 Aug. 264/2 A prism, or perhaps tent-shaped room, some eighty feet high, whose two inclined faces are all mirror; hidden in the ridge are two film cameras... So that film image as well as the constantly moving crowd are repeated *ad infinitum* in the mirror-wall, as if it were the inside of a kaleidoscope. **1969** *Guardian* 1 July 9/2 Mirror-work is a traditional Indian craft which looks enchanting . . densely applied to a gipsy-type waistcoat or belt. **1973–4** *Oxfam Catal.* 12 Typical Gujarat embroidery and mirrorwork covers this bag. **1960** I. Bennett *Delinquent & Neurotic Children* ix. 367 Left-handed, tends to mirror-write, poor wrist coordination. *Ibid.* 370 Mirror-writer, below average in every subject. **1776** G. Campbell *Philos. Rhetoric* I. ii. iii. 420 If the analogy of the language must be preserved in composition, to what kind of reception are the following entitled . . homedialect, bellysense, and mirrourwriting? **1924** R. M. Ogden tr. *Koffka's Growth of Mind* v. § 6. 293 Certain children can read mirror-writing at first just as well as they can ordinary writing. **1969** 'E. McBain' *Shotgun* iii. 35 A blotter was the only other thing on the desk. Carella automatically checked it for any mirror writing that might have been left on it. **1970** D. Bowden tr. *Luria's Traumatic Aphasia* xiii. 332 *(caption)* Writing disturbance in visual agraphia; 'mirror writing'.

mirth, *sb.* Add: **5.** *mirth-maker* (later example), *-provoker*; *mirth-lit* adj.

1849 C. Brontë *Shirley* II. iv. 100 Lifting up her mirth-lit face to the gallery. **1969** *Daily Tel.* 15 Feb. 14/6 Kenneth Horne . . was acknowledged as one of radio's top mirth-makers. **1895** W. Archer *Theatr. 'World' 1894* iii. 341 The pun, as a 'mirth-provoker', is dead.

mirthful, *a.* Add: **1.** (Later example.)

1940 W. Faulkner *Hamlet* iv. i. 279 His constant expression of incorrigible and mirthful disbelief had left him now.

2. (Later example.)

1877 *Athenæum* 13 Oct. 475/2 The piece . . is one of the most mirthful and original that has, during late years, been seen on the stage.

mirthquake (mɔ̄·ɹþkwēᶦk). *colloq.* Also **mirthquaker.** [f. Mirth *sb.* + Quake *sb.*, after Earthquake.] An entertainment that excites convulsive mirth.

1928 *Daily Express* 24 Apr. 4/2, I found Prince George . . among the first to see Harold Lloyd's new 'mirthquake'. **1938** *N.Y. Times* 13 Jan. 19/1 Robert Benchley's new mirthquake *After 1903—What?* Always in hot water—that's Benchley, America's Mogul of Mirth. **1939** *Amer. Speech* XIV. 4 A 'screamario' is the scenario for a comedy, which proves to be a 'mirthquake'. **1942** Berrey & Van den Bark *Amer. Thes. Slang* § 281/4 Something humorous; joke... Mirthquake, mirthquaker. **1965** Leitner & Lanen *Dict. French & Eng. Slang* 90/1 *Mirthquake*, . . film, pièce, etc., très amusant.

Mirzapur (mɔ̄·ɹzăpūᵊɹ). Also **Mirzapore.** The name of a town in the state of Uttar Pradesh in Northern India used *attrib.* and *absol.* to designate a type of carpet manufactured there.

c **1882** *Cardinal & Harford's Price List Oriental Carpets & Rugs* 10 Indian carpets from Masulipatam, Mirzapore, etc... The Mirzapore can be manufactured in less time than any other. **1900** J. K. Mumford *Oriental Rugs* (1901) xiv. 264 The designs of the old Mirzapur carpets . . showed a pronounced Hindu character. **1967** *Times* 23 Feb. 24/6 (Advt.), Really superb plain off-white 'Mirzapur' carpets with 1 in. virgin wool pile.

mis-, *prefix*[3]: see Miso- (in Dict. and Suppl.).

mis (miz), colloq. abbrev. of Miserable *a.* Cf. *miz, mizz.

1886 in H. Baumann *Londinismen.* **1939** N. Monsarrat *This is Schoolroom* ii. ix. 205 'I'm mis,' she volunteered immediately, in a muted babyish voice. **1952** 'C. Brand' *London Particular* x. 121 Rosie was ackcherly utterly *mis.* about . . poor, darling Thomas. **1974** *Observer* 27 Oct. 5/5, I wouldn't care to guess what proportion of the population has some sexual problem that makes them mis.

mis', var. Miss *sb.*[2] 5 (in Dict. and Suppl.).

misact, *v.* Delete † *Obs.* and add later example.

1925 *Contemp. Rev.* Nov. 624 The wonderful scene in Pimen's cell . . was completely 'mis-acted', if I may use a non-existing word.

misadventurer (misædve·ntiŭ̆rәɹ). *rare.* [f. Misadventure *sb.* + -er[1].] One who meets with or suffers misadventures; an unfortunate person.

1886 Hardy *Mayor Casterbr.* II. xviii. 250 His mood was no longer that of the rebellious, ironical, reckless misadventurer.

misadve·rtence. *rare.* [Mis-[1] 4.] Carelessness, thoughtlessness, absent-mindedness.

1870 Tennyson *Holy Grail* 43 Once by misadvertence Merlin sat In his own chair, and so was lost.

misali·gnment. Also **misalinement.** [Mis-[1] 4.] Bad or imperfect alignment.

1924 J. F. Hobart *Tulley's Handbk.* (ed. 7) II. xv. 582 Misalignment refers either to that of the turbine and generator, or that of the rotating and stationary elements. **1937** *Marconi Rev.* May–Aug. 27 The tracking does not allow phase misalignment greater than ±5 degrees. **1947** *Brit. Jrnl. Psychol.* Dec. 57 It is easy to present a misalinement to an operator, and then screen his eyes just before he makes his corrective movement. **1963** C. R. Cowell et al. *Inlays, Crowns & Bridges* xii. 130 Difficulty is rarely encountered with cases of gross misalignment [of the teeth]. **1974** *Sci. Amer.* May 54/3 There is often a misalignment of the eyes too.

So **misali·gned** *a.*

1948 *Aircraft Power Plants* (Northrop Aeronaut. Inst.) 216 The crank extension shaft may be misaligned. **1954** S. Duke-Elder *Parsons' Dis. Eye* (ed. 12) xxix. 483 In concomitant squint, as opposed to paralytic squint, although the eyes are misaligned, they retain their abnormal relation to each other in all movements. **1962** A. Nisbett *Technique Sound Studio* iv. 81 *(caption)* Misaligned recording or reproducing head. **1973** *New Scientist* 22 Nov. 544 Directional roof aerials pointed accurately at Wrotham for optimum BBC reception are, likely as not, hopelessly misaligned for signals from Croydon.

misalloca·tion. [Mis-[1] 4.] Failure to allocate in an efficient or correct way what is to be assigned or distributed.

1950 *Jrnl. Pol. Econ.* Apr. 118 The crop-share lease has not resulted in the gross misallocation of land that would have occurred. **1961** *Ann. Reg. 1960* 474 There can be no doubt that misallocation and waste continued in 1960. **1965** H. Kahn *On Escalation* viii. 152 There has been a startling misallocation of official emphasis. **1971** *Nature* 9 July 82/2 Mondale's argument that the shuttle is a far grosser misallocation of priorities than the SST . . may carry great weight.

misandry, misarchist: see *miso-.

misappliance (misăplәi·ăns). *rare*[−1]. [f. Mis-[1] 4 + Appliance.] Placing (of oneself) amiss.

1903 H. James *Ambassadors* iii. 58 He scarce knew where to sit for fear of a misappliance.

misappropriation. (Further examples.)

1838 W. H. Prescott *Hist. Reign Ferdinand & Isabella* III. ii. xxv. 490 He made a strict inquisition into the funds of the military orders, in which there had been much waste and misappropriation. **1922** Joyce *Ulysses* 718 Forgery, embezzlement, misappropriation of public money. **1952** M. A. Elliott *Crime in Mod. Society* iii. 59 Misappropriation of funds of private character is seldom punished unless there is a glaring embezzlement.

misarticula·tion. [Mis-[1] 4.] Inability to articulate correctly.

1959 *Jrnl. Speech & Hearing Res.* II. 244 *(heading)* A phonetic study of misarticulation of /r/. **1972** *Language* XLVIII. 492 It is important that the study of misarticulation be integrated into this dependency relationship, for the mutual benefit of speech therapy and linguistic theory.

misascri·ption. Also with hyphen. [Mis-[1] 4.] False ascription.

1923 E. K. Chambers *Elizabethan Stage* II. xii. 30 He light-heartedly accuses my friend Mr. Pollard, me, and others of perpetuating an old mis-ascription. **1946** *Mod. Lang. Notes* LXI. 61 The initial and continued misascription of the fourteen line poem, 'The Muses, fairest light in no darke time', to John Cleveland. **1971** A. Kirk-Greene in J. Spencer *Eng. Lang. W. Afr.* 137 These lexical items [in West African English] consist of creation in two ways: deliberate coining and misascription.

misassimila·tion. *rare.* [Mis-[1] 4.] Incomplete or unsuccessful assimilation.

1934 E. Sitwell *Aspects Mod. Poetry* 69 Here, too, is another misassimilation of Hopkins by the same writer.

misattribu·tion. [Mis-[1] 4.] Attribution, usu. of a work of art, literature, etc., to the wrong person. Hence **misattri·butor,** one who makes a misattribution.

1873 [see Mis-[1] 4]. **1927** *Sunday at Home* Jan. 216/1 The hurried journalist is a great misquoter and a great misattributor too. **1963** *Times* 4 June 14/4 Highmore, even until recent years, has suffered from misattributions, either of his best work to others, Hogarth in particular, or of the inferior work of others to him. **1973** *Times* 3 Nov. 15/6 Misattributions of this kind should be avoided. **1975** *Sotheby & Co. Catal.* 28–29 July 4/2 Books may not be returned nor will their sale be set aside . . for possible misattribution of authorship where the authorities are in disagreement.

misbelead, *v.* Delete † *Obs.* and add *rare.*

1909 Galsworthy *Strife* ii. ii. 251 *Thomas.* I haf ears to my head... *Jago.* Your ears have misbeled you then.

misbou·nd. [f. Mis-[1] 2 + Bound *ppl. a.*[2] 6.] Of a book: badly or wrongly bound.

1802 D. Wordsworth *Jrnl.* 5 Feb. (1941) I. 107 The Chaucer not only misbound but a leaf or two wanting. **1889** [see Mis-[1] 2]. **1952** J. Carter *ABC for Bk.-Collectors* 120 When a leaf or leaves, or an entire gathering, has been wrongly folded or misplaced by the binder, it is called misbound. Provided that nothing is missing, and that the amount of matter misbound is not too great or its misplacing too glaring, collectors commonly take a more charitable view of the result than readers.

miscarriage. Add: **2. a.** (Further examples.)

1784–5 Burns *Poem on Pastoral Poetry* in *Poems & Songs* (1968) I. 191 Scarce ane has tried the Shepherd-sang But wi' miscarriage? **1880** 'Mark Twain' *Lett. to Publishers* (1967) 123 Chatto waits . . without asking a solitary question about the book, and then pitches into *me* about the miscarriage.

3. (Later examples.)

1967 M. M. Bookmiller et al. *Textbk. Obstetr.* (ed. 5) xxii. 333/2 The term early abortion refers to expulsion of the fetus up to 12 weeks' gestation. When expelled from 12 to 28 weeks it is called a late abortion and from 28 to 36 weeks it is said to be premature termination of pregnancy. Many laymen still associate the word abortion with illegal

interference and prefer to call a spontaneous termination of pregnancy a miscarriage. The nurse should be guided accordingly. **1970** *Sci. Jrnl.* June 75/2 Most hospitals regard the loss of a pregnancy before 20 weeks as a miscarriage. **1971** Rugh & Shettles *From Conception to Birth* (1972) x. 157 There are generally signs of an impending miscarriage (another term for a spontaneous abortion). **1974** Passmore & Robson *Compan. Med. Stud.* III. xlii. 1/2 Abortion may be defined as the termination of pregnancy before the fetus is viable. In Britain this is considered to be before the 28th week of pregnancy. However, fetuses expelled before the 28th week occasionally survive, and to allow for this possibility the 20th week is sometimes used as the watershed between viability and non-viability... In many North American centres abortion is defined as the expulsion of a fetus weighing less than 500 g. A precise definition is required for medicolegal purposes and in Britain abortion means the termination of pregnancy before the 28th week. Miscarriage is synonymous with abortion and is often more acceptable to the lay public.

miscast, *sb.* Restrict † *Obs.* to sense 1 and add: **2.** *Theatr.* An actor or actress who is miscast (see *miscast *v.* 4); an instance of miscasting.

1907 G. B. Shaw *Lett. to G. Barker* (1956) 81 Barker was capable of anything in the way of casting.. Miss Sterling McKinlay was.. a very obvious miscast. **1908** *Ibid.* 142 It was not her fault; it was simply a miscast.

miscast, *v.* Add: **4.** *Theatr.* In passive, of an actor: to be cast in an unsuitable rôle; of a play: to have unsuitable actors performing in it; also *fig.*

1927 *Observer* 10 July 15/1 We say that so-and-so was good or adequate or miscast or unhappy in his part. We do not appraise the acting as we appraise the play. *Ibid.* 21 Aug. 9/4 'The Climax'.. was brought to England seventeen years ago... It was then admittedly miscast. **1944** M. J. MacManus *Eamon de Valera* xiii. 288 Poor Mr. Thomas.. was sadly miscast on the diplomatic stage. **1957** *Observer* 8 Sept. 10/4 As Tigre, M. Barrault is mournfully miscast. **1972** *Daily Tel.* 9 Feb. 13/6 This was partly because John Neville was miscast in the main role.

miscasting, *vbl. sb.* Add: **3.** *Theatr.* The allotting to an actor of a part which does not suit him.

1926 *Spectator* 25 Sept. 470/2 In a long list of characters there is not one case of miscasting. **1927** *Observer* 26 Sept. 13/4 Those instances of what I thought was miscasting have made me long to try my hand at casting a play. **1946** *Weekly Rev.* 20 June 156/1 The extraordinary mis-casting of the Elder who was made up to look like an emaciated crook suffering from T.B. **1971** *Daily Tel.* 24 Nov. 10/4 Act Four [of 'Swan Lake'] suffered.. from the miscasting of Miss Mason.

misca·talogued, *ppl. a.* [Mis-[1] 2.] Erroneously or inaccurately entered in a catalogue.

1963 [see *information retrieval* s.v. *information 8]. **1974** *Times* 10 Jan. 4/6 Low-season sales are always well scrutinized by dealers looking for miscatalogued bargains.

miscegenation. (Further examples, not *U.S.*)

1927 M. M. Bennett *Christison* ii. 29 'Miscegenation' being official jargon for what Governor Bourke called 'detaining black women by force'. **1971** *Sunday Times* 20 June 29/6 [He] must inaugurate 'creative miscegenation' by marrying a Chinese girl.

miscegen (further examples); also **miscege·nic** *a.*; **misce·geny,** miscegenation.

1865 S. S. Cox *Eight Yrs. Congress* 354 A very sprightly suffragan of the miscegen stamp. *Ibid.*, The result would be an average miscegen and a superior patriot. **1941** 'R. West' *Black Lamb* I. 527 It was a fusion, lovely but miscegenic, of the Byzantine and the baroque styles. **1935** *Punch* 14 Aug. 176/1 Since miscegeny is not a bad British trouble, *Shanghai* is a film that is more likely to interest America than ourselves.

mischancing, *vbl. sb.* For *rare*$^{-0}$ read *rare* and add example.

1929 W. Faulkner *Sartoris* v. 357 A period of history which had seen brothers and husband slain in the same useless mischancing of human affairs.

mischief, *sb.* Add: **9. c.** (Further example.) Also phr. *like the mischief.*

1876 T. E. Brown *Doctor* 36 And them givin' sheet Like the mischief. **1895** *Century Mag.* June 279/2 And there's kindnesses and kindnesses, Mr. Ludovic. There's some that cost like the mischief. **1907** J. M. Synge *Lett. to Molly* (1971) 123, I am coughing away like the mischief today. **1922** Joyce *Ulysses* 354 She wished.. they'd take the.. twins and their baby home to the mischief out of that. **1942** Berrey & Van den Bark *Amer. Thes. Slang* § 20/5 Indefinite eminence in degree. (Preceded by.. 'like')... The (very) mischief.

10. mischief night, an evening, orig. 30 April, now 4 November, on which children indulge in mischievous pranks; also *attrib.*

1865 W. S. Banks *List Provincial Words Wakefield* 47 *Mischief neet.* Boys, thirty years ago, used to go about damaging property, believing the law allowed them, on this night. Happily the practice is over at Wakefield, and the time forgotten. **1871** *N. & Q.* 17 June 525/1 The eve of May Day was formerly known as 'Mischief Night' throughout South Lancashire, and prior to the epoch of the 'new policeman', many were the strange pranks, rude practical jokes, and mortifying degradations committed. **1959** I. & P. Opie *Lore & Lang. Schoolch.* xii. 255 In the nineteenth century April the thirtieth.. was.. the traditional Mischief Night... How Mischief Night has.. come to be transferred to the other end of the year is one of the mysteries of the folklore calendar. *Ibid.* 279 '20 Boys in Mischief Night Raid at Ayton.' **1969** —— *Children's Games* ii. 68 They even celebrated Mischief Night on 4 November as do their northern contemporaries. **1972** 'J. Ripley' *My Word you should have seen Us* 119 It was 'Mischief Night'—the evening before 'Bonfire Night'—and an annual happening peculiar to the northern provinces.

mischievous. ¶. Later examples of dial., vulgar, and jocular uses of *mischevious, mischievi(e)ous.* Also *mischeivious.*

1571–1747 examples in Dict. s.v. sense 3 *β*.

1847 C. M. Yonge *Scenes & Characters* xv. 194 You thought mischievous was meant in Hannah's sense, when she complains of master Reginald being very mischevious. **1861** —— *Young Step-Mother* xxxi. 476 For shame, to be so *mischievieous*; such a great boy as you. **1913** Mrs. P. Campbell *Let.* 5 Feb. in *B. Shaw & Mrs. Campbell* (1952) 81 Some mischeivious personal experience. **1952** F. Swinnerton in *Bks. of Month* Nov.–Dec. 31/1 Wells,.. friendly with everybody, mischevious, quick-thinking, nonsensically inventive.

misch-masch, var. Mish-mash *sb.*

mischmetal(l (mi·ʃmet'l). Also **misch metal.** [ad. G. *mischmetall*, f. *misch-en* to mix + *metall* Metal *sb.*] A mixture of lanthanons containing about 50 per cent cerium which is obtained usu. by electrolysis of the fused chlorides from monazite and is used in lighter flints.

1923 B. S. Hopkins *Chem. Rarer Elements* x. 168 The most important of these [cerium alloys] is the alloy called misch metal, mixed metal, commercial cerium, or simply 'cerium'. **1924** J. W. Mellor *Comprehensive Treat. Inorg. & Theoret. Chem.* V. xxxviii. 608 A. Sieverts and G. M. Goldegg studied the action of hydrogen and nitrogen on the mischmetals. **1954** H. E. Kremers in C. A. Hampel *Rare Metals Handbk.* xvi. 343 The most common ferrous alloy of the rare earths is the common lighter flint, which contains about 30 per cent iron, the balance being misch metal. **1966** Phillips & Williams *Inorg. Chem.* II. xix. 18 A particularly interesting lanthanide alloy is 'mischmetall', with 50 per cent Ce, 25 per cent La, and the rest mostly Nd and Pr. This alloy is added to partly purified iron when it preferentially removes elements such as C, O, S, N, and P into the slag as lanthanide compounds.

mischsprache (mi·ʃ,ʃpraχə). [G., 'mixed language'.] = *mixed language* (*mixed *ppl. a.* 11).

[**1885** M. Grünbaum in *Sammlung gemeinverständlicher wissenschaftlicher Vorträge* XX. 613 (*title*) Mischsprachen und Sprachmischungen.] **1930** J. T. Hatfield et al. *Curme Vol. Ling. Stud.* 12 The question as to the justification of calling this tongue German and whether it is a *Mischsprache.* **1963** *English Studies* XLIV. 9 There are cases where.. a scribe *half*-transforms his original, producing a sort of *Mischsprache.*

misch(t)y, dial. var. Mischief *sb.*

1890 S. S. Buckman *John Darke's Sojourn in Cotteswolds* xvi. 150 Er's harmless enow when he comes yereby, er 'oodn't do none mischy. **1895** Hardy *Jude* i. i. 9 Just now he's a-scaring of birds for Farmer Troutham. It keeps un out of mischty. **1896** —— *Under Greenw. Tree* ii. v. 117 Bless ye, my sonnies! 'tisn't the pa'son's move at all. That gentleman over there.. is at the root of the mischty [mischief, 1872, 1876, 1891 eds.].

miscible, *a.* Add: Usu. *spec.* of a liquid: capable of forming a true solution *with* another liquid. (Further examples.)

1960 Hamill & Williams *Princ. Physical Chem.* ix. 244 While phenol and water at this temperature and pressure are only partly miscible the addition of acetone increases their mutual solubility. **1964** G. I. Brown *Introd. Physical Chem.* xxiii. 252 Ether will dissolve a little water (about 1·2 per cent at room temperature) to form a homogeneous solution, and water will also dissolve a little ether (about 6·5 per cent at room temperature) to form a similar solution. Within these limits ether and water are completely miscible. As their mutual solubilities are limited, however, ether and water are only partially miscible.

misco·de, *v.* [Mis-[1] 1, 3.] *trans.* To code incorrectly. So **misco·ding** *vbl. sb.*

1965 *Math. in Biol. & Med.* (Med. Res. Council) ii. 54 Gross mistakes in the date are probably rare, and are due only to mispunching and/or miscoding. **1970** *Sci. News Let.* 23 May 510 The mutant DNA miscoded a single amino acid in the sequence of structural protein in the membrane. As a result.. the entire membrane was defective.

misconduct, *v.* **2.** (Further examples.)

1901 *Daily Colonist* (Victoria, B.C.) 11 Oct. 2/1 The Jacksons.. induced girls to misconduct themselves with the belief that it was a necessary part of their religious devotions. **1922** Joyce *Ulysses* 318 Belle in her bloomers misconducting herself. *Ibid.* 457 He made improper overtures to me to misconduct myself at half past four p.m. on the following Thursday.

misconstrue, *v.* **1. a.** (Further *absol.* example.)

1842 C. Lever *Jack Hinton* (1843) xlviii. 308 It is so easy, when people have no peculiar reasons to vindicate another—to misconstrue—perhaps condemn.

miscontent, *v.* Delete † *Obs.* and add later example.

1920 M. Hewlett *Light Heart* v. 33 'I have had words come by me,' she said, 'that you are beguiling my Thordis. That miscontents me.'

miscri·ticize, *v. rare.* [Mis-[1] 1.] To criticize adversely or wrongly.

1877 Swinburne *Lett.* (1960) III. 275 Attacked and miscriticized in the Saturday Review and the Academy.

mis-cue, *sb.* Add: Now usu. **miscue. b.** Hence in other sports, and *transf.* or *fig.*, an error resulting in a failure of some sort.

1883 in *Amer. Speech* (1965) XL. 130 When I escort a lady I.. have a.. Havana And puff it all the time And should she make a small miscue And knock it from my mouth, [etc.]. **1920** Ade *Hand-Made Fables* 26 It suggested that there had been a Miscue at the Christening. **1942** Berrey & Van den Bark *Amer. Thes. Slang* § 170/2 Error; mistake; blunder... Miscue. **1958** J. A. Barlow *Elem. Rifle Shooting* (ed. 5) v. 56 The idea.. is to be able to put sufficient force behind the bolt to eliminate any chance of a miscue—in other words, a failure to close the bolt. **1970** *Washington Post* 30 Sept. D1/7 One Oriole scored, another took third on the miscue and John Oates' sacrifice fly made it 2–2.

miscue *v.* (further examples); also *transf.* and *fig.* So **miscue·d** *ppl. a.*; **miscue·ing** *vbl. sb.*

1929 *Times* 1 Nov. 7/4 At the end of the last of these breaks he missed a difficult *massé* cannon, through partly miscueing. **1941** G. Heyer *Envious Casaca* xii. 219 Mathilda shied away from the thought, miscued, and straightened herself. **1941** J. Smiley *Hash House Lingo* 38 *Miscue*, make an error. **1955** I. Peebles *On Ashes* x. 100 Bailey tried to hook Johnston and miscued so that the ball bounced off his pads. **1962** *Times* 3 Jan. 3/7 His miscued strokes always went up to score disconcertingly. **1962** *Sunday Times* 25 Feb. 22/7 Miss Truman was now mis-cueing. **1970** *Sunday Tel.* 1 Nov. 32/7 Southgate went nearest to a goal when Neale cut in from the left but Walker miscued badly.

misdemeanour, *sb.*[1] **2.** All distinctions between a felony and a misdemeanour were abolished by the Criminal Law Act of 1967.

misdescriptive, *a.* (Further example.)

1938 R. G. Collingwood *Princ. Art* v. 80 Calling it by that misdescriptive name, we patronizingly license the child to go on with it.

misdi·agnose, *v.* [Mis-[1] 1.] *trans.* To diagnose wrongly, make a wrong diagnosis of (a condition); also, to diagnose wrongly the condition of (an individual).

1928 *Daily Express* 6 Oct. 8/6 Internal troubles which have been misdiagnosed are the most common. **1949** G. Ryle *Concept of Mind* iv. 107 The.. distresses of which such feelings are diagnosed, or mis-diagnosed, as signs are not themselves feelings. **1963** *Lancet* 12 Jan. 95/1 In spite of general recognition for nearly half a century that the two conditions simulate each other, nobody can say how often torsion is misdiagnosed as 'orchitis'. **1968** *Globe & Mail* (Toronto) 5 Feb. 13/6 Many children with minimal brain dysfunction are still being misdiagnosed. **1972** *Village Voice* (N.Y.) 1 June 36/3 His primary theme, however, is that far too many of the kids being drugged have been misdiagnosed.

misdiagno·sis. [Mis-[1] 4.] A wrong diagnosis.

1949 G. Ryle *Concept of Mind* iv. 105 Such misdiagnoses are more common in children than in grown-ups. **1965** J. Pollitt *Depression & its Treatment* iii. 43 Migraine, angina pectoris, and prolapsed intervertebral disc are the commonest misdiagnoses in this field. **1971** *Daily Colonist* (Victoria, B.C.) 28 Feb. 28/5 This is a depressingly high rate of misdiagnosis.

misdi·al, *v.* [Mis-[1] 1.] *intr.* To dial (usu. by mistake) a number other than that required on a telephone.

1964 W. Markfield *To Early Grave* (1965) xii. 244 You *could* have been all along misdialing. **1967** J. Gardner *Madrigal* i. 6 He misdialled, then got it right... The signal brut-brutted at the far end of the line. **1970** *Guardian* 27 Apr. 10/2 The Post Office say the numbers are similar to his, and people misdial.

misdirected, *ppl. a.* Add: Hence **misdire·ctedness.**

1965 A. Farrer in J. Gibb *Light on C. S. Lewis* 38 The primary function of mental pain, says Lewis, is to force our misdirectedness on our attention.

misdirection. Add: **1. b.** Of the action of a conjurer, thief, etc.: distraction, guidance (of a person's attention) away from (something).

1943 A. Christie *Moving Finger* x. 124 A conjuring trick... You've got to make people look at the wrong thing and in the wrong place—Misdirection, they call it. **1949** *Amer. Speech* XXIV. 40 When the performer directs your attention, by word, glance, or gesture, away from a secret function, he calls the process *misdirection.* **1955** *Publ. Amer. Dial. Soc.* xxiv. 16 The thieves can apply misdirection (verbal, kinesic, tactile) to take his mind off his wallet—if only for a few seconds—and he will be astonished to find that he has been robbed. **1971** P. O'Donnell *Impossible Virgin* iv. 71 There had been callers at the house... None of them had been genuine... It was all part of a misdirection play.

misdistribution. [MIS-¹ 4.] Wrong or faulty distribution. So **misdistri·bute** *v.*

1914 G. B. SHAW *Misalliance* Pref. p. xxxvi, Obstructing the way of the proper organization of childhood, as of everything else, lies our ridiculous misdistribution of the national income. **1920** S. ALEXANDER *Space, Time & Deity* II. III. ix. 280 Evil is misdistribution, and vice is a feature of character which wills such misdistribution. **1958** *Archit. Rev.* CXXIV. 338/1 The misdistribution of people has inevitably brought problems, chiefly that of lack of housing. **1968** *Economist* 27 July 39/1 The schools are to have another $33 million, similarly misdistributed.

misdivision. Add: **b.** *spec.* in *Cytology.* The abnormal transverse (instead of longitudinal) division of a centromere at meiosis or mitosis.

1939 C. D. DARLINGTON in *Jrnl. Genetics* XXXVII. 341 (*heading*) Misdivision and the genetics of the centromere. *Ibid.* 346 Misdivision in..107 univalents consisted of the centromere dividing into two halves, as it does normally; but to these halves the wrong chromatids were attached or no chromatids at all. *Ibid.*, The simplest misdivision is that where two short arms are carried to one pole, two long arms to the other. **1972** tr. *J. Sybenga's Gen. Cytogenetics* v. 223 It happens occasionally that the centromeric region breaks up (mis-division), which results in two half chromosomes (the arms) each with a part of the centromere. *Ibid.*, After centromere mis-division, functional telocentric chromosomes may arise.

misdraw, *v.* Add: **1.** (Later example.)

1885 *Proc. Soc. Psychical Res.* III. 427 There were also 40 diagrams..all misdrawn.

Hence **misdraw·n** *ppl. a.*, badly or wrongly drawn (up).

1867 BAGEHOT *Eng. Constitution* 268 The practical arguments and the legal disquisitions in America are often like those of trustees carrying out a misdrawn will.

‖ **mise au point** (mīzopwæ̃n). [Fr.] A focusing or clarification of an obscure subject or problem.

1946 *Word* II. 113 A general *mise au point* of the linguistic side of semantic problems is thus overdue. **1949** *Archivum Linguisticum* I. 126 The Geneva School retorted with an important *mise au point.* **1971** *Ibid.* II. 64 For a recent *mise au point*, see P. H. Matthews,..in *New Horizons in Linguistics.*

‖ **mise-en-page** (mīzɑ̃pɑʒ). [ad. Fr. *mise-en-pages* imposition.] The design of printed pages, including the layout of text and illustrations; also, the composition of pictures.

1926 R. FRY in J. M. Cameron *Victorian Photographs* 13 Here the artist has been able to control everything, the *mise-en-page*, the disposition of the drapery, and the illumination. **1930** *Times Lit. Suppl.* 3 July 556/1 More intent on realizing the volumes than on the mise-en-page. **1938** *Burlington Mag.* Sept. p. xiii/1 There is hardly a single plate..which can be considered a really satisfactory *mise-en-page.* **1939** *Ibid.* Apr. 177/1 No difference as far as the mise-en-page is concerned between the portrait said to be by Bellini and a Turkish work. **1957** *Listener* 5 Dec. 947/2 The wrapper is deplorable..and the *mise-en-page* rather poor..nevertheless a book to be thankful for. **1959** *Times* 26 Mar. 3/4 Neither the tonal harmony..nor the *mise-en-page* is always quite strong enough in these latter pictures. **1963** *Ibid.* 18 Apr. 7/6 Of special interest are the publications in which students are given the opportunity of gaining practical experience in the design of the book and the *mise-en-page.* **1968** *Listener* 25 Jan. 106/3 Television cannot emphasise in the manner of a newspaper's *mise-en-page.* **1972** *Guardian* 19 June 11/2 Aubrey Beardsley..contributed..the art of *mise en page* ..the art of making dramatic use of big blank spaces.

‖ **mise-en-scène** (mīzɑ̃sẽn). [Fr.] **a.** The staging of a play; the scenery and properties of a stage production; the stage setting.

1833 W. C. MACREADY *Diary* 14 Dec. (1912) I. 85 Saw the play, *Coriolanus*, in so disgraceful a state that it was useless to bestow a word upon the *mise en scène.* **1840** A. BUNN *Stage* II. xi. 298 More attention was paid to the *mise en scène* than to the acting. **1891** 'L. MALET' *Wages of Sin* I. III. ii. 131 Only look at the walls of our exhibitions, look at the *mise en scène* of our theatres! **1911** G. B. SHAW *Blanco Posnet* Pref. 340 The *mise-en-scène* of a play is as much a part of it as the words spoken on the stage. **1951** *Oxf. Compan. Theatre* 715/1 Perhaps Antoine..never realized the force of some of his *mises-en-scène.* **1961** K. TYNAN *Curtains* III. 391 In the newer *mises en scène* one got a feeling of dehydrated Luhtishness. **1974** *Listener* 17 Jan. 92/3 The newspaper office *mise-en-scène*..gave it [*sc.* a radio play] early vitality.

b. *transf.* and *fig.* The setting, surroundings, or background of an event or action.

1872 E. BRADDON *Life in India* i. 8 Novelists..sometimes select India as the *mise en scène* of their tales. **1894** [see *IMPRESSIONIZE *v.*]. **1901** *Q. Rev.* CXCIII. 314 She [*sc.* Queen Victoria] was unrivalled in her sense of the proper *mise en scène* of a formal ceremonial. *a* **1916** H. JAMES *Ivory Tower* (1917) 270, I manage to treat myself to some happy..mise-en-scène or exploitation of my memory of (say) California. **1924** EARL OF BIRKENHEAD *Amer. Revisited* vi. 165 She would have dictated peace, I should imagine, at Buckingham Palace; for the *réclame* of the *mise-en-scène* would, on the whole, have been greater than that of Versailles. **1940** WODEHOUSE *Eggs, Beans & Crumpets* 12 You have simply got to get your atmosphere right... Chance your arm with the *mise en scène*, and before you can say 'what ho', you've made some bloomer. **1972** J. HODGSON *Uses of Drama* xvi. 183 In certain dramatized situations 'people' are actors, and the rush of social events, mise-en-scene.

mise·mphasis. [MIS-¹ 4.] Incorrect emphasis.

1927 *Sat. Rev. Lit.* 12 Mar 651/1 The historic church has too frequently specialized in morbid and bogey-ish suggestions until the natural trend of a faith that *is* faith has been diverted to misemphasis on guilt and introspective self-analysis under the obsession of fear. **1962** R. B. FULLER *Epic Poem on Industrialization* 3 Full of fanciful misemphasis. **1965** H. KAHN *On Escalation* viii. 152 This example of past misemphasis is now widely known and is often cited by analysts.

misère. Add: **2.** = MISERY.

1897 E. DOWSON *Let.* c 10 June (1967) 385 Writing to you has somewhat cheered me, but all my misères will return in a moment. **1903** [see *GOD-FORSAKEN *ppl. a.*]. **1964** *Punch* 2 Sept. 359/3 Recommended to those who still enjoy being stunned by the grandeurs of empire with the *misères* guaranteed absent.

miserere. 4. (Earlier *attrib.* example and later *transf.* example.)

1848 B. WEBB *Sk. Continental Ecclesiol.* ii. 39 Four beautiful stalls, with miserere-seats and canopies. **1959** *Punch* 30 Dec. 675/2, I..selected a train with the longest carriages I could find... To get the full vista, I sat on the miserere at the front.

misericord, *sb.* **1.** For † *Obs.* read *Obs.* except *arch.* and add later example.

1922 JOYCE *Ulysses* 380 They had had ado each with other in the house of misericord where this learning knight lay.

misery. Add: **2. c.** *misery me!*, an interjection expressing self-pity, distress, or general wretchedness.

1888 W. S. GILBERT *Yeomen of Guard* II. 48 Misery me, lackadaydee! He sipped no sup and he craved no crumb, As he sighed for the love of a ladye! **1968** N. MARSH *Clutch of Constables* i. 15 'O misery, misery, misery me,' she wrote with enormous relish.

6. *to put* (a person or animal) *out of* (his) *misery*: see PUT *v.*¹ 48 d.

8. *misery-line, -threshold.*

1902 W. JAMES *Varieties Relig. Experience* vi. 135 The sanguine and healthy-minded live habitually on the sunny side of their misery-line. *Ibid.* v. 135 We might speak of a 'pain-threshold', a 'fear-threshold', a 'misery-threshold'.

misestimate, *sb.* (Earlier example.)

1843 MILL *Logic* II. v. iv. 398 A positive mis-estimate of evidence actually had.

misfe·lt, *ppl. a.* [MIS-¹ 2.] Felt incorrectly or imperfectly.

1935 L. MACNEICE *Poems* 42 We whose senses give us things misfelt and misheard.

misfield, *v.* Add: (Earlier and later examples.)

1870 *Times* 10 Aug. 5/5 Both of these [*sc.* hits for four] ..were unaccountably misfielded by Smith, who rarely makes mistakes. **1954** J. B. G. THOMAS *On Tour* vi. 66 Dixon..looked at the South African wing for a moment and misfielded. **1974** *Times* 8 Jan. 7/8 The new beak picks up the pill and chucks at McCallum who misfields it.

Also as *sb.*, failure to gather the ball properly.

1909 *Daily Chron.* 25 Feb. 8/4 Guy's scored after a misfield of a high kick by Batchelor.

misfire, *sb.* Add: (Earlier example.)

1839 URE *Dict. Arts* 478 A mis-fire is hardly ever experienced with the fire-arms made at the Royal manufactory.

b. The state or action of misfiring.

1966 B. C. MACDONALD *Car Doctor* iv. 45 If there is a regular or rhythmical type of misfire, together with a blackish exhaust, then the mixture is too rich. **1973** J. B. EDWARDS in Springer & Patterson *Engine Emissions* ii. 47 A significant level of misfire may exist in a poorly maintained and/or adjusted engine.

misfire, *v.* Add: **b.** Of an internal combustion engine: to fail to explode the charge, or to explode it at the wrong instant. So **misfi·ring** *vbl. sb.*

1905 *Motor Cycle* 6 Mar. 218/3 If an engine is back firing, that is, giving explosions in the silencer, it is also misfiring. Misfiring may result from a defect in the ignition system. **1928** MONTAGU & BOURDON *Cars & Motor-Cycles* III. 1244 An engine is said to misfire when the gas in one or more of the cylinders does not ignite. **1966** B. C. MACDONALD *Car Doctor* ix. 80 Other causes of misfiring are: incorrect valve timing, weak or broken valve springs, sticking valves, too much carbon in engine, [etc.]. **1974** HAYNES & WARD *Audi 100 Owners Workshop Manual* iv. 89/2 If the engine misfires regularly, run it at a fast idling speed.

c. *fig.* To fail, to be misdirected, to make a mistake. So **misfi·red** *ppl. a.*

1942 BERREY & VAN DEN BARK *Amer. Thes. Slang* § 170/6. **1949** KOESTLER *Promise & Fulfilment* xii. 132 The other after-effects of the misfired operation were in the same strain. **1974** 'J. GRAHAM' *Bloody Passage* viii. 120 'What a wonderful idea,' he said, and then the thing misfired slightly.

misfit, *sb.* Add: *transf.* and *fig. spec.* a person unsuited to his environment, work, etc.

1903 [in Dict.]. **1936** *Discovery* Sept. 280/1 The selection and training of personnel to eliminate as far as possible the misfit and (what is far more prevalent) the partial misfit who just stands the test of results but has really missed his vocation. **1939** T. S. ELIOT *Family Reunion* I. ii. 55 The very moment when you are wholly conscious Of being a misfit, of being superfluous. **1959** *Times Lit. Suppl.* 30 Jan. 57/1 He is a determined individualist, wears Afrika Korps uniform while serving in the British Army and is something of a misfit. **1975** *Times* 20 Aug. 4/8 The police..said young misfits were taking as their victims other car drivers.

attrib. **1910** *Encycl. Brit.* XIV. 223/2 The advantage of this combination is that..it..lessens the danger of making 'misfit' pig iron, *i.e.* that which, because it is not accurately suited to the process for which it is intended, offers us the dilemma [etc.]. **1961** A. MILLER *Misfits* xi. 117 Nothin' but misfit horses, that's all they are, honey.

2. *Physical Geogr.* A stream which, if its average flow in the past was at present-day levels, would be expected to have eroded a larger or a smaller valley than it has done. Usu. *attrib.* or as *adj.*

1910 LAKE & RASTALL *Text-bk. Geol.* iii. 47 In this case the lower part of valley A is left dry, or with an insignificant stream only, which appears to be too small to have eroded the valley in which it flows. Such a stream is called a misfit. **1932** *Jrnl. Geol.* XL. 486 (*heading*) Misfit streams. **1964** *Prof. Papers U.S. Geol. Survey* No. 452-A. 6/1 Streams recognized as misfit are so usually underfit that the two names are frequently interchanged. **1968** R. W. FAIRBRIDGE *Encycl. Geomorphol.* 706/2 The most commonly recognized case of a misfit stream is the underfit river.

misgotten, *ppl. a.* **1.** (Later example.)

1903 W. S. JACKSON *Nine Points of Law* vi. 171 Here was he with a trunk-load of misgotten gold wandering haphazard..over two countries.

mish² (mɪʃ). Colloq. abbrev. of MISSIONARY *sb.*

1939 J. CARY *Mr. Johnson* 164 That's wot's wrong with some of these teetotal mishes. **1946** C. S. ARCHER *China Servant* vii. 105 You've no idea what a bunch of mishs will do, when sex rears its head.

mishellene (mɪʃe·liːn). [ad. Gr. μισέλλην, f. μισ(ο)-, f. μισεῖν to hate + Ἕλλην HELLENE, after PHILHELLENE *a.* and *sb.*] One who dislikes or is opposed to Greece or the Greeks. Hence **mishelle·nic** *a.*

1958 R. LIDDELL *Morea* I. 16 Those two learned, grumpy, and extremely mishellenic travellers, Edward Dodwell and Sir William Gell. *Ibid.* 23 To the grumpy Mishellene, it is all merely boring and tiresome. **1972** W. ST. CLAIR *That Greece might still be Free* xxxi. 350 Henry Lytton Bulwer..became violently pro-Turkish in the Greek–Turkish questions later in the century. David Urquhart..also became a noted mishellene.

mishit (mi·shit), *sb.* [MIS-¹ 4.] In cricket, tennis, etc., a faulty or bad hit.

1882 *Australians in Eng.* 25 He made two mishits which fell harmless. **1898** [in Dict. s.v. MIS-¹ 4]. **1928** *Daily Tel.* 11 May 18/1 Lyon has never played a better innings... I did not notice that he made even a mis-hit. **1963** *Times* 11 June 4/6 Bear's bold effort ended in a mishit to leg slip.

So **mishi·t** (also erron. **miss-hit**) *v. trans.*, to hit (a ball) faultily. Also **mishi·tting** *vbl. sb.*

1904 P. F. WARNER *How we recovered Ashes* ix. 189 Gregory..mis-hit Braund and Rhodes caught him easily at backward point. **1930** *Times* 17 Mar. 4/4 Three minutes from the end Craig made his only mistake of the game, miss-hitting a bumping ball. **1963** *Times* 6 May 3/5 Some flashes of brilliance,..together with a good deal of mishitting,..suggests that the final next Sunday may provide an attractive game. *Ibid.* 13 June 3/2 Booth batted sensibly for an hour to claim 33 out of 47 before mishitting a towering catch to backward point. **1974** *Country Life* 21 Feb. 360/1, I wondered whether he had mishit his tee shot.

mish-mash, *sb.* Add: (Further examples.) Also **misch-masch, mish-mosh, mish-mush.**

c **1855** 'L. CARROLL' (*title*) Mischmasch. *a* **1922** T. S. ELIOT *Waste Land Drafts* (1971) 27 From such chaotic misch-masch potpourri What are we to expect but poetry? **1957** *Time* 2 Sept. 34/2 Paul Gregory's *Crescendo*, a mishmash of American music, with Ethel Merman, Rex Harrison, Louis Armstrong, &c. **1959** N. MAILER *Advts. for Myself* (1961) 335 You call this a report?.. It is nothing but a mish-mosh. **1962** *John o' London's* 18 Jan. 68/2 How did the cast make out amid the mish-mush? **1964** G. MARX *Let.* 24 Feb. (1967) 305, I suggest you learn how to pronounce 'mishmash'. It is not pronounced 'mash',..but rather as though it were spelled *mosh.* **1965** P. ZIEGFELD *Ziegfelds' Girl* i. 7 How the elegant and impeccably British Mr. Maugham had come to write this mishmash nobody could figure out. **1975** *Listener* 30 Oct. 589/2 The original *Panorama* had consisted of a mishmash of disconnected and frequently frivolous items.

Mishnaic, *a.* (Later examples.)

1953 *Jrnl. Theol. Stud.* IV. 7 St. Mark is an apocalyptic, St. Matthew is a mishnaic writer. **1973** *Jewish Chron.* 2 Feb. 22/4 The Amoraim ('interpreters'), the post-Mishnaic teachers in the great schools of Palestine..and Babylon.

mis-hook (mishu·k), *v. Cricket.* [f. MIS-¹ 1 + HOOK *v.* 8 c.] *trans.* To hook (a ball) faultily.

1955 *Times* 19 July 12/1 The new ball was losing its shine when he mishooked a bouncer gently to mid-wicket. **1963** *Times* 12 June 4/4 Bear completely mishooked a ball and was caught at 19.

So **mi·shook** *sb.*, a faulty hook.

1961 *Times* 16 May 4/1 Minney..was caught off a mishook.

misidentifica·tion. [Mis-^{1} 4.] Erroneous identification.

1902 *Encycl. Brit.* XXV. 468/1 The chief defects in practice were (1) frequent failure to identify, (2) liability to mis-identification. **1946** F. E. Zeuner *Dating Past* III. v. 132 The implications of such misidentifications..are obvious. **1968** *Listener* 27 June 828/3 Much more serious ..is..the kind of terrible events which were foreshadowed in the novel *Fail Safe*, whereby one has accidental misidentification leading to some international disaster. **1973** *Nature* 13 July 74/3 They criticize Theyer's micro-palaeontological work by giving chapter and verse on a series of supposed misidentifications and miscorrelations.

So **miside·ntify** *v.*, to identify erroneously.

1895 L. Stejneger in *Ann. Report U.S. Nat. Museum 1893* 449 The specimens so recorded which I have had an opportunity to examine have either been misidentified, or else the locality was very doubtful. **1924** *Geogr. Jrnl.* LXIV. 457 A marks the position of Camp IV. (26,700 feet) and G the point reached by Mallory, Norton, and Somervell in 1922, which was probably misidentified and placed too high in the theodolite measure of 1922, made in very difficult circumstances. **1951** *Essays in Crit.* I. 332 He [*sc.* Iago] pretends ignorance, he pretends helpfulness, he intentionally misidentifies. **1952** *Mind* LXI. 422 He misidentifies the test he is using. **1971** *Nature* 19 Mar. 149/3 This name has been widely used for specimens of the genus in the Mediterranean and northern Europe. Templeman regards them all as having been misidentified.

Misima, var. *Massim.

misinform, *v.* (Later example.)

1974 *Physics Bull.* Jan. 3/2 All the above is well known. ..Those attempting to misinform the World Scientific Community are fully aware of my real circumstances.

misinfo·rmative, *a.* [Mis-^{1} 6.] That gives wrong information. So **misinfo·rmatory** *a.*

1912 *Times Lit. Suppl.* 15 Feb. 64/3 To modify these few misinformative parts of a work which otherwise is.. valuable. **1927** *Observer* 3 Apr. 25/3 A so-called Informatory Double that does not contain top card strength is better termed 'misinformatory'.

miski·ck, *v.* [Mis-^{1} 1.] *intr.* In various sports, to fail to kick the ball properly.

1901 [in Dict. s.v. Mis-^{1} 1]. **1963** *Times* 21 Feb. 3/6 Lancaster presented Harris with an open goal, but the Watford winger completely miskicked. **1973** *Times* 24 Apr. 8/8 He miskicked and mishandled and could take pleasure only from his two successive penalty shots.

So **miski·ck** *sb.*

1973 *Times* 1 Jan. 17/6 His miskick only emphasized his mistake.

Miskito (miski·*to*), *a.* and *sb.* Also **Misskito, Mosquito, Musquito.** [f. *Misquito*, a section of the eastern coast of Nicaragua.] **A.** *adj.* Of or pertaining to an American Indian people living on the Atlantic coast of Nicaragua and Honduras. **B.** *sb.* **a.** A member of this people. **b.** The language of this people.

1789 O. Equiano *Interesting Narr. Life O. Equiano* II. xi. 172 He had a mind for..cultivating a plantation at Jamaica and the Musquito Shore... I found with the Doctor four Musquito Indians... One of them was the Musquito king's son. **1830** *Honduras Almanack* 11 The canoe, a paddle and a harpoon, are the Mosquito man's whole wealth. **1907** F. W. Hodge *Handbk. Amer. Indians* I. 948/2 *Mosquito Indians*, a tribe named from its habitat on Mosquito lagoon. **1911** *Encycl. Brit.* XVIII. 902/2 The Mosquito Coast is so called from its principal inhabitants, the Misskito Indians, whose name was corrupted into Mosquito by European settlers and has been entirely superseded by that form except in the native dialects. **1932** *U.S. Bureau Amer. Ethnol. Bull.* No. 106. 10 Ethnographical Survey of the Miskito and Suma Indians of Honduras and Nicaragua. **1959** *Chambers's Encycl.* I. 343/2 The Lenca, Xicaque,..and coastal Misquito of the Atlantic pocket of Nicaragua-Honduras missed the stream of Maya-Nahua influence. **1964** *Amer. Speech* XXXIX. 47 The Mosquitos are Caribs. **1964** E. A. Nida *Toward Sci. Transl.* ix. 194 In Miskito, a language of Nicaragua and Honduras, one encounters the following transliterations. **1966** C. F. & F. M. Voegelin *Map N. Amer. Indian Lang.* (*caption*) Misumalpan Family 1. Miskito.

misknowing, *vbl. sb.* **2.** (Later example.)

1892 F. S. Ellis *Lexical Concordance Shelley* p. viii, Well would it be for the world if no more was known of any poet's life, except through his works, than is known of Shakespeare's; how greatly should we then be delivered from misknowing!

misla·belling, *vbl. sb.* [Mis-^{1} 3.] Incorrect labelling.

1952 M. Gardner *In Name of Science* i. 5 The government charged that displays of the book [sc. *Look Younger, Live Longer* by G. Hauser] next to jars of blackstrap constituted, because of the book's sensational claims, a 'mislabeling' of the product. **1960** *Times* 20 Sept. (Pure Food Suppl.) p. i/5 There still remains..the possibility of ..mislabelling in retail shops. **1964** *Economist* 6 June 1098/2 Some American firms..have been charged with mislabelling.

misleadingness. (Earlier and later examples.)

a **1866** J. Grote *Treat. Moral Ideals* (1876) 379 An element of deceptiveness and misleadingness. **1957** *Essays in Crit.* VII. 342 The misleadingness of any implication that I was scraping the barrel for evidence. **1975** *Nature* 10 Jan. 79/2 One example of the misleadingness of demonstration must suffice.

misline (misləi·n), *v.* [Mis-^{1} 1.] *trans.* To print with lines omitted or arranged in the wrong order. So **mislinea·tion,** the result of a mistake of this kind.

1922 Joyce *Let.* 20 Mar. (1966) III. 62 Besides misprints I see..that it is in part mislined. **1964** F. Bowers *Bibliogr. & Textual Crit.* vi. iv. 182 It may be that some mislineation at the beginning of *Othello* was caused by the trouble he [*sc.* the compositor] experienced in adjusting text about the ornamental initial letter.

mislocate, *v.* Delete *rare*$^{-1}$ and add later examples.

1954 *Word* X. 239 In diagnosing the conflict between mentalism and mechanism he [*sc.* Bloomfield] mislocates the issue. **1959** P. F. Strawson *Individuals* II. viii. 244 Such an account runs the risk of mislocating the problem altogether. **1971** *New Scientist* 18 Mar. 611/1 The flash is both harder to see and it is mislocated. **1973** *Nature* 7 Sept. 12/2 Nuclear explosions fired on Amchitka are regularly mislocated by tens of kilometres.

mislocation. (Later examples.)

1874 L. Bacon *Genesis New England Churches* p. x, Every careless mislocation of words in the structure of a sentence. **1974** *Nature* 29 Nov. 369/2 All the main features are fairly well reproduced although there are some small mislocations.

mismatch, *sb.* Add to def.: A discrepancy; lack of correspondence; also, an unequal or unfair sporting contest.

1954 F. C. Avis *Boxing Reference Dict.* 71 *Mismatch*, a contest between two boxers of very different standards of ability. **1958** *Optima* Mar. 40/2 The mismatch between arisings and normal disposal methods. **1959** *New Scientist* 9 Apr. 802/3 There is a bad mismatch which will run right through the crystal. **1961** *Times* 21 Nov. 3/3 There had been suggestions that this [*sc.* a boxing match] had been a mismatch. **1971** *Daily Tel.* 28 Apr. 5/3 There is a definite mis-match between what universities are producing and what industry is wanting. **1973** *Computers & Humanities* VII. 139 The computer..compares the corresponding words..until a mismatch occurs.

mismatching, *vbl. sb.* (Later examples.)

1971 *Jrnl. Gen. Psychol.* LXXXV. 188 The interference occurs when the pictorial and linguistic symbolic representations of the color concepts are combined together with mismatching. **1974** *Nature* 7 June 566/2 This difference in thermal stability would indicate about 5% mismatching between the Mu MTV DNA and the tumour RNA.

mismate (mismēi·t), *v. rare.* [Mis-^{1} 1: back-formation from Mismated *pa. pple.* and *ppl. a.*] *intr.* and *refl.* To mate or match (oneself) unsuitably.

1891 Hardy *Group of Noble Dames* i. iii. 113 No syllable would have been breathed of how I mismated myself for love of you! **1946** *Mod. Lang. Notes* Feb. 73 This is Milton's longest account of this Biblical episode, and it is clear than here the sons of God are pious men who mismate with the daughters of him 'who slew his brother'.

mismated, *pa. pple.* and *ppl. a.* (Later examples.)

1914 F. L. Packard *Miracle Man* i. 10 Trousers..torn at the ankles where they flapped around miss-mated socks and shoes. **1931** *Weekend Rev.* 16 May 743/2 It presents him [*sc.* Bulwer-Lytton]..as the child of his mismated parents. **1952** W. Styron *Lie down in Darkness* v. 194 At that age he was clear-headed enough to understand that he was not alone in a world of mismated passions: others betrayed and were betrayed, and got tired of loving.

mismating (mismēi·tiŋ), *vbl. sb.* [Mis-^{1} 3.] Unsuitable mating or matching; *spec.* wrong assorting (of printing types).

1900 T. L. De Vinne *Pract. Typogr.: Treat. Type-Making* vi. 236 This difficulty tempts founders to make one set of small capitals serve for two or more distinct faces. An inexpert can seldom detect the mismating. **1934** *Punch* 10 Jan. 55/2 There is enough cruelty, halfwittedness, epilepsy, moral depravity and the mismating and obstetrical bungling that sometimes prelude these horrors. **1968** *Punch* 7 Feb. 205/3 Mis-matings are most common in such surroundings.

Misnagid, var. *Mitnagged.

‖ **miso** (mi·so). [Jap.] A paste, made from soya beans and barley or rice malt, used by the Japanese in preparing various foods.

1727 J. G. Scheuchzer tr. *Kæmpfer's Hist. Japan* I. I. ix. 121 Of the Meal of these Beans is made what they call *Midsu*, a mealy Pap, which they dress their Victuals withal. **1905** *Chambers's Jrnl.* 25 Mar. 270/2 Soya beans.. from which miso, soya and tofu are made. **1930** *Economist* 4 Jan. 24/1 The higher Japanese price-level is accounted for largely by such 'sheltered' goods as red beans, miso, dried bonito, [etc.]. **1966** P. S. Buck *People of Japan* (1968) xiv. 167 Chicken with *miso* paste and raw vegetables. **1970** J. Kirkup *Japan behind Fan* 104 A red lacquer bowl of rich *miso* soy (bean paste) soup.

miso-. Add: **misandry,** the hatred of males; **misarchist,** one who hates or opposes government in any form; **misogela·stic** *a. nonce-wd.* [Gr. γελαστ-ός laughable (see Agelast; cf. Agelastic *a.* and *sb.*)], hating laughter; **misosophy** (later example); so **misoso·phical** *a.*

1946 *Scrutiny* XIII. 249 In the absence of feminine precedents, she [*sc.* Beatrice] could do no better than what she very sensibly does do: follow masculine example, and answer to their affected misogyny with the affectation of misandry. **1960** B. Kaye *Upper Nankin St.* xii. 232 Such women are common in..Kwangtung Province, where there is a tradition of misandry. **1898** L. F. Ward *Outl. Sociol.* x. 228 These misarchists see the beneficent influences of natural law in the industrial world interfered with. **1877** G. Meredith *Ess. Comedy* in *New Q. Mag.* VIII. 2 It is but one step from being agelastic to misogelastic. **1937** *Philos.* XII. 332 The disposition to be convinced of ill-founded or unfounded doctrines, or unconvinced of well-founded ones, is a 'misosophical' disposition. *Ibid.* 319 A fraternity of persons of kindred credulities could only constitute a school of 'misosophy'.

misogyne. Delete *rare*$^{-1}$ and add further examples. Also **misogyn.**

1877 C. Reade *Woman-Hater* I. v. 113 Misogyn consented, but sighed. **1919** Beerbohm *Seven Men* 186 'Tis a goodly jest! The *con*firm'd misogyn a ladies' man!

misorder, *v.* **1.** (Later example.)

1909 *Daily Chron.* 24 Aug. 4/3 [He] charged the Admiralty with having so misordered the Navy as to expose the nation to the gravest jeopardy every hour.

misorienta·tion. [Mis-^{1} 4.] Variation in orientation.

1952 *Acta Crystallogr.* V. 162 When aluminium is cold-rolled, the original grains break up into smaller particles. X-ray micro-beam back reflexion photographs permit the determination of the mean particle size and misorientation. **1966** D. G. Brandon *Mod. Techniques Metallogr.* ii. 82 If two neighbouring regions differ slightly in orientation,..and if the misorientation is extensive, characteristic radiation will only image one region at a time. **1973** *Nature* 3 Aug. 276/2 The large more misorientated subgrains (misorientation normally > 5°) could be directly related to the optical subgrains.

So **miso·rient, -o·rientate** *vbs.* [Mis-^{1} 1], to orient differently or variably; also, to orient badly. (Chiefly as pa. pples.)

1951 *New Yorker* 22 Sept. 94 The result of misorienting the Secretariat and using glass so exuberantly is to create a building that functionally is often windowless on all sides. **1953** *Acta Crystallogr.* VI. 167/1 A large number of grains in which there is widely misoriented material will be irradiated. *Ibid.* 177/1 This mosaic structure consists of particles slightly misorientated with respect to one another. **1967** *Sunday Times* 9 Apr. 52 We have the uneasy suspicion that our communal sense of values has become misorientated; and so it has. **1970** *New Scientist* 8 Oct. 65/1 Adjacent grains are misoriented with respect to one another. **1973** Misorientated [see above].

mispercei·ve, *v.* [Mis-^{1} 1.] *trans.* To perceive wrongly or incorrectly; to mistake.

1924 J. E. McTaggart in J. H. Muirhead *Contemp. Brit. Philos.* (1st Ser.) 265 Consequently H will be misperceived by G as existing in time. **1953** *Mind* LXII. 207 The bedpost was not being misperceived when I dreamed that I saw the Eiffel Tower. **1973** E. Bullins *Theme is Blackness* 174 No, of course I don't think you're the bad guy but you're misperceiving me wrongly. **1974** *Sci. Amer.* Jan. 84 One might succeed in correcting the eyes shown here so that they are perceived as gazing downward and leftward, but at that very moment the mouth is uncorrected and expresses sorrow rather than pleasure. Conversely, one might correct the mouth and misperceive the eyes.

misperce·ption. [Mis-^{1} 4.] The action of misperceiving or condition of being misperceived.

1722, 1893 [see Mis-^{1} 4]. **1949** H. C. Weston *Sight, Light & Efficiency* iii. 108 One very familiar example of this mis-perception occurs in reading when we see a group of letters as the word they ought to represent, even though the printed word is mis-spelt.

misprint, *v.* Add: **b.** *intr.* Of deer: to leave foot-prints in a pattern different from the usual one.

1909 W. A. & F. Baillie-Grohman in Edward, Duke of York *Master of Game* 262 A hind..misprints, that is sometimes the hind foot will be placed beside the fore foot, sometimes inside or in front of it. **1957** F. J. T. Page *Field Guide Brit. Deer* 71 Misprint. To step irregularly; failure to register [*i.e.* to place the hind feet in the slots made by the fore feet].

mispronou·ncer. [Mis-^{1} 5.] One who pronounces words incorrectly.

1885 *Educ. Times* 1 June 207/1 Warnings more adapted to American mispronouncers than to English.

misquo·te, *sb.* [Mis-^{1} 4.] An incorrect quotation, a misquotation.

1855 J. A. Symonds *Let.* Sept. (1967) I. 61 How very kind of M. de Condolle it was to lend Mdlle the three missquotes. *a* **1953** E. O'Neill *Touch of Poet* (1957) I. 30 Disdainfully, emphasizing his misquote of the line from Byron. **1968** C. M. Vines *Little Nut-Brown Man* ix. 149 'Preferred not to' had a different nuance from 'was not well enough to'..it seemed a curious misquote. **1974** *Daily Tel.* 21 Oct. 16 Mr Heath made little attempt to correct the misquotes and inaccurate statements made by various Labour politicians.

misrecollection. (Later example.)
1922 O. Jespersen *Lang.* iii. 70 He speaks..of other linguistic changes as well. These he refers to the following causes...(1) Mishearing and misunderstanding; (2) misrecollection; [etc.].

misre·gister, *sb. Printing.* [Mis-[1] 4.] The incorrect positioning of printed matter in relation to other printed matter on the same sheet, esp. of two or more colours in relation to each other.
1931 *National Lithographer* Feb. 27/2 It was determined to study first the factors causing misregister. **1949** R. F. Reed *What Lithographer should know about Paper* (Lithographic Technical Foundation, N.Y., Technical Bull. No. 8) 50 While misregister in the ordinary sense never occurs until two or more colors have been printed, it is obvious that improper printing of the first color may be.. the real cause of register trouble. **1963** C. W. Latham *Advanced Pressmanship* xvii. 130 When the first color plate does not register with another color plate it may be termed internal misregister or misfit. **1966** R. R. Coupe *Sci. of Printing Technol.* ii. 47 The need to avoid misregister in multicolour work is usually regarded as the major reason for air-conditioning, but there are many others. **1968** *Gloss. Terms Offset Lithogr. Printing* (*B.S.I.*) 30 *Mis-register*, the appearance of the printed image out of its correct position. **1970** R. F. Reed *What Printer should know about Paper* (Graphic Arts Technical Foundation, Pittsburgh) iii. 33 Distortion due to wavy-edged paper is probably the most common and serious cause of misregister on sheet-fed offset presses.
Hence **misre·gistered** *ppl. a.*
1963 C. W. Latham *Advanced Pressmanship* xvii. 130 If the plate is at fault, the same misregistered image will show the same error sheet after sheet.

misre·gister, *v.* [Mis-[1] 1.] *trans.* To form from elements that are not properly aligned or positioned.
1969 G. L. Hansen *Introd. Solid-State Television Syst.* xi. 265 It is imperative that the optical alignment of the light paths be precise. If they are not, the reproduced color image will be misregistered. That is, each image will not be located at exactly the same point on the camera tube..and a blurred presentation will result. **1969** P. B. Jordain *Condensed Computer Encycl.* 278 If a line is misregistered irregularly, that is, if some characters are high, others low, etc., then line registration is bypassed in favor of character registration.

mi:sregistra·tion. [Mis-[1] 4.] Faulty or imperfect registration (i.e. alignment or positioning) of images, *spec.* of the three fields that compose a colour television picture.
1942 H. C. McKay *Photographic Negative* IV. x. 649 The neutralized areas will print out gray, and the lines of misregistration will print dark. **1952** *Electronics* Nov. 216/2 Color edging includes color fringing, misregistration, etc. **1960** *Electronic Engin.* XXXII. 71 Misregistration is the least favourable feature of colour television as at present conceived. **1969** P. B. Jordain *Condensed Computer Encycl.* 87 Character misregistration takes the form of character high, character low, or character skew. **1971** [see *facture 4]. **1971** H. E. Ennes *Television Broadcasting* x. 469 This beam pulling or dynamic misregistration results in colored edges.

misruling, *vbl. sb.* (Later example.)
1927 *Daily Tel.* 25 Oct. 8/5 If in refereeing I give a flagrant legal mis-ruling..the Rugby Union can send for me and say what they think about me and my mis-ruling.

miss, *sb.*[1] Add: **7. a.** An unsuccessful gramophone record. Opp. *hit *sb.* 4.
1965 *Listener* 9 Sept. 391/1 Persons invited to give their verdict..are not being asked to say whether the songs are good or bad but merely whether they will be 'hits' or 'misses'. **1966** *Melody Maker* 16 July 20 Dusty's new single may be one of her misses.
b. Examples of transf. uses of *to give a miss*; also transf. use of the billiards phrase to *give the miss in baulk*.
1907 Westbrook & Wodehouse *Not George Washington* ii. xxi. 228 And James..is actually giving this the miss in baulk! **1919** B. Ruck *Disturbing Charm* i. ii. 10 The Professor chose (as he often did) to give lunch a miss. **1923** Wodehouse *Inimitable Jeeves* iii. 31 Anyway, it never even occurred to me for a moment to give her the miss-in-baulk. **1927** A. Huxley *Let.* 17 May (1969) 286 The result of this will be that we must, alas, give Paris a miss. **1930** *Morning Post* 16 July 8/3 The leek is..among the..vegetables that are too often given a miss. **1950** J. Cannan *Murder Included* vii. 183 I'm afraid I've given church a miss this morning. **1973** Boyd & Parkes *Dark Number* ix. 91, I think the CID would be happier if you gave the whole place a miss.

Miss, *sb.*[2] Add: **2. b.** *Miss Nancy* (further and *attrib.* examples); so *to talk Miss Nancy*, to speak politely. Hence *Miss-Nancyfied*, *-Nancyish* adjs., effeminate; *Miss-Nancyism* (earlier example).
1848 A. Brontë *Tenant of Wildfell Hall* I. iii. 53 You will treat him like a girl—you'll spoil his spirit, and make a mere Miss Nancy of him. **1855** 'Q. K. P. Doesticks' *Doesticks, what he Says* 298, I could overlook the boarding-school-ism of the Miss Nancyish 'Journal'. **1863** 'G. Hamilton' *Gala-Days* 117 A man's hair is shag... Ceasing to be shag, it does not become beauty, but foppishness, effeminacy, Miss Nancyism. **1870** A. W. Drayson *Young Dragoon* viii. 61 Officers and men must be thorough soldiers—not 'Miss Nancy' sort of fellows. **1874** *Southern Mag.* XIV. 353 Poh! 'Miss-Nancyfied' men! **1916** W. Riley *Netherleigh* xv. 152 Talkin' Miss Nancy as if 'e was a dancin' master. **1928** 'Brent of Bin Bin' *Up Country* ii. 8 He actually carried sleeping attire about with him, and a tooth-brush, Miss Nancy habits derided by the men.
d. *Miss Milligan*, a kind of patience played with two packs of cards.
1899 M. W. Jones *Games of Patience* 5th Ser. x. 27 Miss Milligan Patience. **1914** C. Mackenzie *Sinister St.* II. iii. xiv. 782 She used to sit playing 'Miss Milligan'..and said ..that she had really enjoyed Patience for the first time. **1934** H. G. Wells *Exper. Autobiogr.* I. i. 29, I have played a spread-out patience called Miss Milligan for the past fifteen years. **1938** C. Morgan *Flashing Stream* ii. ii. 205 Karen, make it four and bridge. Oh, you don't play. Five and poker. (*No answer.*) Hell, I'll play Miss Milligan. **1975** J. Symons *Three Pipe Problem* xviii. 200 She played all sorts of patience games from simple single-pack patiences like Miss Milligan and the elegant Windmill to complicated double-pack games like French Blockade and Triple Line.
e. A young woman, *Miss America, Miss England, Miss Europe, Miss World*, etc., chosen for beauty, personality, etc., to represent a country, region, etc.; also *transf.*
[**1905** R. H. Davis (*title*) Miss Civilisation.] **1922** *N.Y. Times* 5 Sept. 19/6 Miss Margaret Gorman of Washington, winner of the 1921 contest, will be known as 'Miss America'. **1927** *Maclean's Mag.* 1 June 40 'Miss Toronto' wearing a stylish Aberley of the attractive 'Bird of Gladness' design in which she won the cup at the 1926 Beauty Contest at Sunnyside. **1929** *Daily Tel.* 8 Feb. 11/4 'Miss Europe' was chosen to-night..from among the seventeen girls who had been selected as the most beautiful women of their respective countries. **1935** M. Campbell *My 30 Yrs. Speed* ix. 202 Sir Henry Segrave was killed on Lake Windermere during attempts on the water-speed record with *Miss England II.* **1953** S. Spewack *Under Sycamore Tree* ii. i. 35 Attention, everybody. We now bring you the results of the beauty contest..to pick Miss Human Ant of nineteen fifty-three. **1958** *Listener* 23 Oct. 662/1 Sport, travelogues, space-rockets, Miss World.. succeed each other rapidly and effortlessly. **1962** E. Cleaver in A. Dundes *Mother Wit* (1973) 14/2 A..blue eyed 'white' girl is..proclaimed as..Miss Universe. **1968** *Radio Times* 28 Nov. 70/3 The first Miss World in 1951 measured 37-23-36. **1972** G. Bromley *In Absence of Body* iii. 27 Poised at a desk on a low dais—as though she might have been Miss Great Britain..was a ravishing receptionist. **1974** *Times* 8 Mar. 3/4 (*heading*) Miss World stripped of title.
f. *Miss Ann(e, Annie* (see quots.).
1926 C. Van Vechten *Nigger Heaven* 286 *Miss Annie*, a white girl. **1942** Z. N. Hurston in A. Dundes *Mother Wit* (1973) 224/2 Miss Anne used to worry me so bad to go with me. **1965** [see *Charley, Charlie 7]. **1966** *Publ. Amer. Dial. Soc. 1964* xlii. 45 *The Man* and *Miss Ann* refer more specifically to the boss and the fair, young white lady of the plantation... Both..are used ironically. **1970** C. Major *Dict. Afro-Amer. Slang* 81 *Miss Ann*, a white woman—carry-over from Southern terminology, but now used with a good-natured sneer or with outright maliciousness.
g. *Miss Willmott's ghost*, a large sea holly, *Eryngium giganteum*, so called in allusion to Ellen Ann Willmott (1860–1934), English horticulturist, who was responsible for the introduction of many plants.
1956 A. M. Coats *Flowers & their Histories* 89 The biennial sea-holly..has a spectral look in the twilight which might well justify its name of Miss Willmott's Ghost. It is said that when visiting gardens, Ellen Willmott used surreptitiously to drop a few seeds of this plant here and there, to surprise the owners in due course. **1963** *Oxf. Bk. Garden Flowers* 154/1 The biennial species, *E[ryngium] giganteum*, becomes quite white and desiccated after it has flowered, and is often called 'Miss Willmott's Ghost', after that great gardener Miss Ellen Willmott. **1974** R. L. Fox *Variations on Garden* 127 It [sc. *Eryngium giganteum*] is also called Miss Willmott's Ghost, Miss Willmott being a former plantswoman of the home counties with a tongue, and tastes, as sharp as a thistle's spine.
h. Occas. uses, as *Miss Lonelyhearts* (see *lonely *a.* 6); *Miss Right*, a woman who would be a perfect wife; *Miss White*, a lavatory.
1922 Joyce *Ulysses* 347 When she wanted to go where you know she said she wanted to run and pay a visit to the Miss White. *Ibid.* 640 He would one day take unto himself a wife when Miss Right came on the scene.
3. d. A pert girl.
1818 Keats *Lett.* (1958) II. 13 She is a downright Miss without one set off—we hated her. **1864** C. M. Yonge *Trial* I. vi. 100, I came down upon little Miss at last for her treatment of the doctor. **1937** M. Allingham *Dancers in Mourning* xi. 158 A sulky little miss if ever I saw one.
e. *Miss sahib*, in India, the daughter of a mem-sahib, a European girl.
1888 Kipling *Soldiers Three* (1889) 8 *Bund karo* all the Miss Sahib's *asbab* an' look slippy! **1892** —— & Balestier *Naulakha* xx. 236 'Has the miss sahib any orders,' asked Dhunpat Rai. **1971** R. Dentry *Encounter at Kharmel* iii. 46 Oh, memsahib... Is the miss-sahib unwell? **1973** 'B. Mather' *Snowline* ix. 105, I saw the sahib... He..passed close to a group of goras and dirty miss-sahibs, who called out to him.
f. A female schoolteacher; an English governess in France.
1924 A. D. Sedgwick *Little French Girl* i. vi. 51 The 'Misses' of her childhood. **1951** R. Senhouse tr. *Colette's Chéri* 21 No 'Fräulein', no 'Miss' was ever to be seen at Chéri's side. **1968** L. Berg *Risinghill* 16 Girls are caned as well as boys in Islington. 'Miss said no one should come in the class during the dinnertimes.' *Ibid.* 227 That's not a bad thing for a child to copy—to think 'Sir's mod!' or 'Miss is mod!' **1973** *Guardian* 20 Mar. 17/3, I would like to subject some of the 'misses' and some of the 'sirs' to the indignities and fears that they have heaped upon my kids.
4. (Examples of the use designating sizes and styles of clothing.)
1880 in *Amer. Mail Order Fashions* (1961) 20 A Misses' bathing costume. The pattern..is in 6 sizes for misses from 10 to 15 years of age. **1892–3** *T. Eaton & Co. Catal.* Fall & Winter 11/1 In misses' and small women's coats, we are still unexcelled. **1930** E. Wallace *Lady of Ascot* viii. 67 She catered for what they call in America the 'Miss', and had as her principal clients thousands of working girls, who, through the Carawood stores, were able to dress fashionably. **1951** *Vogue* Feb. 94/1 We pass through the Baby Linen on our way to the Misses. **1954** M. Corey *McCall's Compl. Bk. Dressmaking* 50 In junior sizes, as in misses' and women's sizes, the size that you take in a dress pattern is also the right size for your coat or your suit. **1970** *Vogue Sewing Bk.* ii. 108 The Misses' figure is considered the statistically 'average' figure. **1973** *Philadelphia Inquirer* 7 Oct. 9 (Advt.), Misses' nationally famous Separates. Coordinated sets. *Ibid.*, Every winter coat for misses, juniors, women reduced Monday only.
5. (Further examples.) Also used conventionally of a married woman in public life.
1790 N. Webster in *Gazette U.S.* 17 Nov. (Th.), The use of Miss for Mistress in this country is a gross impropriety. **1819** *Mass. Spy* 12 May (Th.), I concluded he had resolved to marry Miss Spruce, but found upon inquiry that his name was Spruce, and Miss Spruce was his wife. **1838** Dickens *Nickleby* (1839) xxv. 246 The company ..fell to, immediately: Miss Petowker blushing very much when anybody was looking, and eating very much when anybody was *not* looking. **1854** —— *Hard T.* in *Househ. Words* 12 Aug. 598/2 Miss Josephine Sleary..was then announced... 'Here 'th Jothphine hath been and got married to E. W. B. Childerth, and shee hath got a boy.. three yearth old.' **1873** M. Holley *My Opinions* 166 Miss Aster would give up her bedroom to me, or mebby she would make Mr. Aster sleep with one of the boys, and have me sleep with her. **1878** R. T. Cooke *Happy Dodd* x. 99 Mis' Potter sent that. **1888** L. D. Powles *Land of Pink Pearl* 154 No married woman, not even excepting the Governor's wife, is ever accorded the title of 'Mrs.' but all ladies, married or single, are called 'Miss' or 'Missey' indiscriminately. **1936** Mencken *Amer. Lang.* (ed. 4) 124 The vulgar American misuse of..*Mis*' (pro. *miz*) for *Mrs.*.. was so widespread by 1790 that..Webster denounced it as 'a gross impropriety'... It survives unscathed in the speech of the common people. **1937** N. Marsh *Vintage Murder* i. 6 What about Miss Dacres? Or should I say Mrs. Meyer? I never know with married stars. **1974** *Daily Tel.* 3 Oct. 10/6 Miss Blyton seems to have indulged in a few affairs before marrying her devoted surgeon second husband. **1975** *Times* 3 Apr. 14/4 Miss [Eileen] Fowler attributes her success in her unusual field partly to the fact that she started her working life as an actress... 'My husband was a bit overweight when we married,' she said. *Ibid.* 4 Apr. 1/1 Miss Ure..was found collapsed by her husband, Mr. Robert Shaw, the actor.

miss (mis), *sb.*[4] Colloq. abbrev. of Miscarriage 3.
1897 W. S. Maugham *Liza of Lambeth* x. 167, I've 'ad twelve, ter sy nothin' of two stills an' one miss. **1951** J. Cannan *And All I Learned* v. 70, I heard of a girl who'd had eleven misses. **1959** 'J. Ross' *Boy in Grey Overcoat* x. 125, I didn't care what happened either to me or the child. I hoped I would have a miss. **1971** 'D. Shannon' *Murder with Love* (1972) viii. 138 She had a miss, that time, lost the baby.

miss, *v.*[1] Add: **5. c.** [ellipt. use of 5 a.] *intr.* Of a motor vehicle or an engine: to fail to explode the mixture in a cylinder. (In quot. 1904 *transf.*) Phr. *to miss on all* (or *four*, etc.) *cylinders*: see *cylinder *sb.* 6.
1904 *Peel City Guardian* 14 May 3/2 Hargreaves was 'missing' very badly. **1917, 1932** [see *cylinder *sb.* 6]. **1953** A. Smith *Blind White Fish in Persia* x. 199 The departure from the Consulate was unceremonious, for the truck was missing badly, stalled several times and finally pulled us out through the gate. **1973** D. MacKenzie *Postscript to Dead Let.* 8 The motor started missing a few miles back..then it died completely.
d. *he* (or *she*, etc.) *never misses* (or *has not missed*, etc.) *a trick*: he, etc., never fails to seize an opportunity, advantage, etc. *colloq.*
1962 *Oxford Times* 28 Dec. 15/2 Peter Butterworth and Joe Black are pantomime professionals who never miss a trick. **1965** *Harper's Bazaar* Feb. 66/1 Fenwicks..never misses a trick when it comes to picking up a new accessory idea. **1967** 'E. Lathen' *Murder against Grain* iv. 32 You have to hand it to them. Those boys haven't missed a trick. **1967** O. Norton *Now lying Dead* vi. 109 He never missed a trick. **1973** S. B. Jackman *Guns covered with Flowers* viii. 131 Clever chap... Doesn't miss a trick.
9. c. In various colloq. phrases, as *to miss the boat*; *to miss the bus*: see *bus *sb.*[2] 1 b.
1929 F. C. Bowen *Sea Slang* 91 *Miss the boat*, to be late for anything. **1930** *Times Educ. Suppl.* 8 Mar. 106/3 Boys of average ability..often had to neglect other pursuits.. for fear that they might 'miss the boat'. **1930** *Aberdeen Press & Jrnl.* 3 Sept. 4/5 As a medium for a dull debut, 'A Devil's Disciple' by Bernard Shaw.., to use an Americanism, missed the boat by twenty years. **1931** *Time & Tide* 29 Aug. 1001 There are ten men in the Cabinet... There are three more who, by strange irony of circumstance, have missed the train. **1934** T. E. Lawrence *Let.* 18 Aug. (1938) 875, I fear I have missed the boat, for lately a viking ship came from you: so I place you in Norway. **1939** H. Nicolson *Let.* 18 July (1966) 406 But Anthony..is in fact missing every boat with exquisite elegance. **1973** *Times* 24 Mar. 2/4 Some firms were missing the boat because their managements were not prepared to be adventurous.

22. b. To fail to menstruate at the normal time, to miss a period.

1947 C. Willingham *End as Man* 9 A beautiful but wicked girl of a good Port George family missed one month. Then she missed another month. She went to a doctor and found out the truth. 1961 G. Greene *Burnt-Out Case* vi. i. 184, I think I have a baby on the way.. I've missed twice. 1971 'P. Hobson' *Three Graces* i. 8, I think I'm pregnant. This is the second time I've missed.

25. *miss out* (*on*) ——. To fail (esp. to achieve something); to make a mistake (over something); to omit; to be omitted.

1929 D. Scarborough *Can't Get Red Bird* xxvii. 405, I feel sorry for a poor sucker that misses out on any one of 'em. 1934 *Hound & Horn* VII. 393 They have a way of missing out on emotional experience, either through timidity and caution or through heroic renunciation. 1938 R. Franken *Gold Pennies* xix. 224 Morton lumbered behind her, fearful that he might be missing out on something. 1942 Berrey & Van den Bark *Amer. Thes. Slang* § 262/2 *Fail*,.. miss out (on). 1944 D. Runyon *Runyon à la Carte* 100 He will lay them according to how he figures their word..if Brandy Bottle misses out. 1952 G. W. Brace *Spire* (1953) xii. 105 It was Flanders who was planning the reception... But he missed out on Wilfred Stearns. 1959 *Listener* 15 Jan. 115/2 We had to by-pass Tippaburra and miss out on that Christmas Eve spree. 1960 S. H. Courtier *Gently dust Corpse* iii. 32 They..had missed out when prosperity hit the Mallee. 1960 I. Cross *Backward Sex* 116 You and I are going to miss out, y' know. 1961 J. Wade *Back to Life* ix. 120 Sorry I missed out on that report. 1963 A. Lubbock *Austral. Roundabout* 48 We didn't want the kids to miss out... They don't often get the chance to have a bit of fun. 1965 M. Morse *Unattached* i. 38 It's a terrible feeling missing out. 1969 *New Yorker* 12 Apr. 56/2 The motivation derives from the desire not to miss out on any information that could be essential later. 1972 *National Observer* (U.S.) 27 May 21/5 (Advt.), Don't 'miss out' on any of the fresh, new kind of reporting that makes The Observer the national newspaper for the *business of living*.

missable (mi·săb'l), *a.* [f. Miss *v.*¹ + -able.] That can be or is likely to be missed.

1924 *Glasgow Herald* 15 June 11/6 Of course it was not a record, but he holed out everything missable. 1955 [see *holeable *a.*]. 1959 *Times* 11 Sept. 5/1 [He] holed all the missable putts.

missalist. (Later example.)

1909 *Daily Chron.* 9 Oct. 4/4 The three brothers Maris might be re-incarnations of the Van Eyck brothers, or the de Limburg missalists.

missed, *ppl. a.* Add: **c.** Med. *missed abortion*: the retention of a fœtus in the womb for a period after it has died; also, the fœtus itself; *missed labour*: the retention of a fœtus in the womb beyond the normal period of pregnancy.

[1847 H. Oldham in *Guy's Hosp. Rep.* V. 109 A female carries a child in the womb to the full period of gestation; but the process of labour is literally missed, and lactation follows on completion of gestation. *Ibid.*, Cases resembling this, in its principal feature of labour being missed, have been recorded.] 1864 *Med. Times & Gaz.* 22 Oct. 449/2 Dr. Greenhalgh did not consider that Dr. Williams' cases could be placed under the head of missed labour... Dr. Oldham said that he had used the term as the most appropriate he could find. It was a case in which the time of natural labour passed by without any pains, and the child was not expelled. 1878 J. M. Duncan in *Ibid.* 28 Dec. 730/1 In a case of missed abortion..the important element of suspicion as to the real conditions may not have come into the mind either of the patient or her physician. *Ibid.*, This is a case in which you have..slight protraction of pregnancy, and then the condition of missed labour. 1936 W. Shaw *Text-bk. Gynæcol.* xii. 262 In missed abortion the signs of pregnancy disappear. 1971 E. S. Taylor *Beck's Obstetr. Pract.* (ed. 9) xxix. 436/1 Missed labor, unlike missed abortion, is extremely rare. Pregnancy continues to term in the normal manner, but near the expected date of confinement labor starts and then ceases after a time. 1972 W. Barr *Clin. Gynaecol.* xi. 148 There is a risk that, if a missed abortion is left in situ for over four weeks, defibrination of the blood can occur.

d. *missed approach* [*approach *sb.* 13], in *Aeronaut.*, an approach that is discontinued for any reason; esp. (with hyphen) *attrib.*

1951 *Gloss. Aeronaut. Terms* (*B.S.I.*) iii. 20 *Missed-approach altitude*, the minimum height at which a final approach should be discontinued if it cannot be completed. *Ibid.* 21 *Missed-approach procedure*, procedure to be followed when an aircraft cannot complete final approach. 1971 *Flying* Apr. 42/3 Sometimes, the missed-approach procedure directs you to an NDB. 1973 *Black Panther* 13 Oct. 14/2 The Aero Commander pilot requested of Midway Tower a 'missed approach' (that he be allowed to go round again and make a second landing attempt).

mi·ssense, *a. Biol.* [Mis-¹ 4.] Causing or involving the insertion of a different amino-acid at a particular point in a polypeptide or protein molecule from that which is usual.

1961 Levinthal & Davison in *Ann. Rev. Biochem.* XXX. 651 An alteration in any base pair by a mutagen raises the possibility of a class of so-called nonsense mutations, as well as a class of missense mutations... A mis sense mutation in this context is one which causes a substitution of one amino acid for another at a particular position in the protein. 1974 *Nature* 2 Aug. 412/1 The missense mutation *trpA36* results in a Gly (GGA)→Arg (AGA) amino acid substitution at position 211 of the tryptophan synthetase A protein. *Ibid.* 413/1 The anticodons of the suppressor tRNAs are complementary to the missense codons suppressed by these tRNAs.

missfire. Add: (Further example.) Also *attrib.*

1914 W. Owen *Let.* 28 Aug. (1967) 281 After your deplorable miss-fire fashion. 1933 *Times Lit. Suppl.* 2 Mar. 148/4 Narrating the missfire of a tired New York business man who hoped his wife and daughter would fly with him.

missie, var. Missy (in Dict. and Suppl.).

missile, *a.* and *sb.* Add: **B.** *sb.* **1. b.** *Mil.* A destructive projectile that during part or all of its course is self-propelling and directed by remote control or automatically.

1945 (27 Aug.), etc. [see *guided *a.* b]. 1945 *Sci. Amer.* Nov. 283/3 Communications systems between air and ground making possible the most intricate maneuvers.. by..pilotless missiles. 1946 *Aeroplane Spotter* 1 June 128/1 A rocket-propelled missile carries its oxygen internally, whereas a jet-propelled missile takes in its oxygen from the atmosphere. 1954, etc. [see *ballistic *a.* d]. 1956 *Newsweek* 7 May 19/1 The 'Nike B' is designed as an antimissile missile as well as an improved version of the anti-aircraft 'Nike' weapons. 1959 *Times Lit. Suppl.* 13 Feb. 79/2 Some of the smaller European members of N.A.T.O. have given notice that they will not allow American intermediate-range missiles to be stationed in their territory in time of peace. 1964 *Ann. Reg.* 1963 221 Another factor may have been a realization that the arms race was becoming ruinously expensive, and..a partial test ban would prevent the United States from outpacing the U.S.S.R. in research on an anti-missile missile. 1973 *Sci. Amer.* Nov. 27/2 Under the SALT I agreement the U.S.S.R. is allowed about 25 percent more offensive missiles than the U.S.

c. *attrib.* and *Comb.*, as *missile base, carrier, gap* [*gap *sb.*¹ 6 a], *silo, site, submarine*; *missile-armed, -firing, -launching* adjs.

1959 *Daily Tel.* 20 May 10/2 The nuclear-powered, missile-armed submarine offers itself as the costly major strategic weapon of the future. 1969 *New Scientist* 28 Aug. 421/2 The Royal Navy has only three fast patrol boats in service and none of these is missile-armed. 1956 W. A. Heflin *U.S. Air Force Dict.* 329/1 Missile base. 1958 *Listener* 3 July 7/2 The Soviet Union's aim is to attract Iceland out of the Nato alliance because she is fearful of the American missile bases there. 1957 *Economist* 21 Dec. 1025/2 The wheels of the missile-carriers rumble towards Europe from east and west. 1958 *Listener* 20 Feb. 303 The missile-firing nuclear-powered submarine will..prove the most potent form of nuclear attack in the future. 1959 *Economist* 13 June 1020/2 The Air Force gets an additional $170 million to help close the 'missile gap'. 1962 *Listener* 19 Apr. 697/1 The passages on the 'missile gap' are a little dated, since Mr Kennedy has now told us that it scarcely ever existed. 1958 *New Statesman* 2 May 600/1 A missile-launching site. 1965 H. Kahn *On Escalation* vii. 141 The Soviets could increase pressure on us by simultaneously stationing missile-launching submarines or ships off our coasts, by sabotaging communications, [etc.]. 1967 *Economist* 28 Oct. 371/1 Their programme includes planes and medium-range missile silos as well as three Polaris-type submarines. 1974 *Times* 24 Oct. 6/8 Under the 1972 agreements the Soviet Union was allowed to have 1,618 operational land-based missile silos. 1949 *Aviation Week* 21 Feb. 11/3 (*heading*) Defense chiefs ask guided missile site. 1962 *Listener* 29 Mar. 553/1 On-site inspections of airfields and missile-sites. 1959 *New Statesman* 3 Jan. 6/3 A similar sum, according to one estimate, will be needed for the 40 Polaris missile-submarines which the Navy says it requires. 1974 L. Deighton *Spy Story* xii. 119 They'll have one missile submarine close enough to fire.

mi·ssileman. Also **missile man, missile-man.** [f. Missile *a.* and *sb.* + Man *sb.*¹] One who is engaged in the construction, design, flying, or operation of a missile (sense *B. 1 b).

1951 [see *bird *sb.* 4 d]. 1961 *Amer. Speech* XXXVI. 234 The verb *destruct* is used by missile men to describe the push-button blowing up of a missile. 1962 *Daily Tel.* 7 Feb. 1/6 (*heading*) 300 missile men to lose jobs. 1963 *Ann. Reg.* 1962 35 The rapid development of the missile-men's craft. 1964 *Economist* 29 Feb. 803/3 The plight of the redundant missile-men.

missilery (mi·səiləri). *N. Amer.* Also **missilry.** [f. Missile *sb.* + -ery.] Missiles collectively; a collection of missiles.

1880 *Harper's Mag.* Sept. 506/1 There were in her mainmast eighteen large grape, and sixteen musket-balls, besides smaller missilery in profusion. 1957 *Britannica Bk. of Year* 512/1 In military affairs, the prominence of the guided missile as a weapon was indicated by such terms as *missilry*, a collective term for such missiles. 1959 *Life* (Internat. ed.) 13 Apr. 20/1 We do have a mass of evidence to indicate that the Soviets have gone all-out in missilery. 1973 *Daily Colonist* (Victoria, B.C.) 27 Apr. 4/7 The [transistor] devices became important foundation stones of military aviation, missilery, and space exploration, where it is vital to save space and weight.

missing, *ppl. a.* Add: **1.** (Further examples.) spec. *the missing*, soldiers (sailors, etc.) neither present after an action nor known to have been killed or wounded; so *missing, presumed dead* (in quot., *fig.*). In wider use: (*to be*) *among the missing*: to be absent, to absent oneself (*U.S. colloq.*).

1855 T. C. Haliburton *Nat. & Hum. Nat.* I. i. 10 If a person inquires if you are at home, the servant is directed to say, No, if you don't want to be seen, and choose to be among the missing. 1859 in Bartlett *Dict. Amer.* (ed. 2) 273 There comes old David for my militia fine. I don't want to see him, and think I will be among the missing. 1917 'Contact' *Airman's Outings* p. xii, Once eleven of our machines were posted as 'missing' in the space of two days. 1918 W. Owen *Let.* 8 Oct. (1967) 581 Must now write to hosts of parents of Missing, etc. 1962 *Listener* 11 Oct. 585/1 His [*sc.* Schönberg's] music seemed dead-alive on more than one occasion... Ernest Newman..reported him missing, presumed dead, just because he did not seem to have made it in time.

4. missing link, (*b*) (earlier and later examples); **missing person,** a person whose whereabouts are unknown (and who is being sought); also *attrib.* of an organization, etc., recording information about such persons.

1862 G. du Maurier *Let.* Oct. in *Young G. du Maurier* (1951) 178, I..said that if he would take the trouble to make a post mortem on the Irish roughs I intend to kill next Sunday in the Park, he might convince himself that the 'missing link' had been found. [1876 tr. *E.H.P.A. Haeckel's Hist. Creation* II. xxii. 293 Although the preceding ancestral stage is already so nearly akin to genuine Men that we scarcely require to assume an intermediate connecting stage, still we can look upon the speechless Primæval Men (Alali) as this intermediate link.] *a* 1930 D. H. Lawrence *Phoenix II* (1968) 569 One woman.. wrote to me out of the blue: 'You, who are a mixture of the missing-link and the chimpanzee, etc.'—and told me my name stank. 1936 A. O. Lovejoy *Great Chain of Being* viii. 235 By 1760 the triumphs of the missing-link hunters were being celebrated in verse. 1966 R. & D. Morris *Men & Apes* v. 126 Albertus [Magnus] made the first attempt to bridge the gap between man and the rest of the animal world by means of a kind of 'missing link' in the shape of the pygmy and the ape. 1876 Geo. Eliot *Dan. Der.* III. iii. xx. 39 There were safer means than advertising: men might be set to work whose business it was to find missing persons. 1943 R. Chandler *Lady in Lake* (1944) ii. 15 It will mean going to the Missing Persons Bureau. 1967 R. Rendell *Wolf to Slaughter* ii. 20 They didn't want to add to their Missing Persons list if they could help it. 1970 *Guardian* 7 Jan. 18/2 A 'missing person' poster for station notice boards will be issued soon. 1975 'E. Lathen' *By Hook or by Crook* xv. 147 The.. kids had been missing persons all through the war.

missiology (misiǫ·lŏdʒi). [f. Missi(on *sb.* + -ology.] The study of the methods, purpose, etc., of religious missions.

1937 *Tablet* 23 Oct. 545/1 (*heading*) The science of missiology. First principles of mission work. *Ibid.*, Missiology is a new word for a new science. 1961 A. V. Seumois in G. H. Anderson *Theol. Christian Mission* ii. 133 Practical missiology, scientifically theological, covers the study of mission spirituality and mission methodology. 1971 *Sunday Times* (Johannesburg) 28 May 30/5 (Advt.), Senior Lecturer in Ecclesiastical History and Missiology. 1975 *Church Times* 11 July 2/5 Miss Myrtle Langley is to be head of the new department of missiology..at Trinity College, Bristol.

So **missiolo·gical** *a.*, of or pertaining to missiology; **missio·logist,** one who concerns himself with missiology.

1951 *Theology* LIV. 349 The aim of missions..is.., as a distinguished Roman Missiologist has said, to 'found' the Church'. 1957 *Scottish Jrnl. Theol.* X. 300 One meets here the biblical theologian, the scientist in religions, the missionary and 'missiologist'. 1961 A. V. Seumois in G. H. Anderson *Theol. Christian Mission* ii. 123 The writing which marked the launching of the modern missiological movement. 1970 J. Power *Mission Theol. Today* p. ix, There is a lacuna that so far has not been filled either by missionaries themselves or by missiologists. 1971 N. Q. King *Christian & Muslim in Afr.* 90 Leaving aside such theological and missiological considerations, a large number of African Christians ask us to compare some of the Christians of the older generation.

mission, *sb.* Add: **2. b.** orig. *U.S.* A military operation or project; esp. the dispatch of an aircraft or spacecraft on an operational flight; also *transf.*

1929 E. W. Dichman *This Aviation Business* v. 107 Night, heavy long-distance, slow, and large all describe a certain type of airplane designed to accomplish a particular mission. 1939 *Aircraft Yearbk.* iii. 64 Many missions were flown, day and night, by participating bombardment and attack units. 1944 *Amer. N. & Q.* Apr. 15/2 *Mission*, ordered operation against the enemy, such as dropping bombs, strafing ground troops and ships, dropping parachute troops, flying diversions (missions intended to draw the enemy away from the main objective), taking photographs, etc. 1962 J. Glenn in *Into Orbit* 43 The clock is pre-set on the ground according to a timing for retro-fire which we have computed before the mission. 1968 Mrs. L. B. Johnson *White House Diary* 1 July (1970) 694 Lynda heard from Chuck... He had returned from a mission and..had only time to read two or three letters, write her.., stuff a few more into his pocket, and leave on another mission! 1969 *Times* 23 May 1/2 Twice during the critical hours before the separation of the lunar module.. from the command service module..the mission's future looked doubtful. 1971 *Daily Tel.* 19 July 7 Apollo 15, America's eighth manned flight for the Moon, is due to be launched on a 12-day mission..from Cape Kennedy a week today.

10. *mission-chapel* (earlier U.S. example), *farm, -house* (earlier U.S. examples), *land, station, style*; also *mission-bred, -trained, -ward* adjs.

1909 *Times Lit. Suppl.* 7 Jan. 3/2 He makes capital fun of the mission-bred Kaffir's misuse of book-learning. 1871 *Scribner's Monthly* I. 497 His church was only a mission chapel, supported by a richer society of the same denomination. *a* 1861 T. Winthrop *John Brent* (1883) ii. 13 He had found his early way to California, bought a mission farm, and established himself as a ranchero. 1794 C. I. Latrobe tr. *Loskiel's Hist. Mission among Indians*

N. Amer. II. xii. 166 The mission-house on the Mahony.. was..burnt. **1824** W. H. KEATING *Narr. Exped. St. Peter's River* (1825) 150 At the time we passed at the Carey mission-house, this gentleman was absent on business. **1851** *Whig Almanac 1852* 18/2 The Commissioners are required to report to the Secretary of the Interior the tenure by which the Mission lands are held. **1828** I. McCOY in *Kansas Hist. Q.* (1936) V. 243 Here we intersected a waggon road leading from the settlements on Missouri River to Harmony Mission Station. **1844** J. McDONOGH *Papers* (1898) 78 One of these young men..is now at the mission station at Settra Kroo, Liberia, keeping a school for the native youth. **1876** W. BOOTH in H. Begbie *Life W. Booth* (1920) I. xxv. 417 What is a Mission Station?.. It is not a building..; it is not even a society, but a band of people united together to mission,..to christianize an entire town or neighbourhood. **1884** LADY MARTIN *Our Maoris* i. 15 The Bishop came a day or two later, as he had to visit a mission station on the way. **1971** *Scope* (S. Afr.) 19 Mar. 31/1 The maternal grandfather.. came to take up the same mission station. **1909** WELLS & HOOPER *Mod. Cabinet Work* 257 In America there has been a similar movement, known as 'The Mission Style', which is more or less a revival of Gothic and Jacobean forms applied to modern work. **1930** J. DOS PASSOS *42nd Parallel* I. 122 I've got several magnificent mission style bungalows. **1948** A. L. KROEBER *Anthropol.* (rev. ed.) xii. 484 Since the American occupation, the buildings and ruins of the Spanish period have stood out as landmarks and have set the model for a type of architecture: the Mission style, which in essentials is nothing but Spanish Moorish architecture. **1972** M. MEAD *Blackberry Winter* x. 117 The apartment Luther had found [in 1923] was small enough for the furniture we had: a strong round folding table,..Luther's mission-style desk, [etc.]. **1965** *Listener* 27 May 766/1 The men at the top in Uganda and Tanganyika were both mission-trained teachers. **1925** T. DREISER *Amer. Trag.* (1926) I. I. i. 8 The missionward march was taken up.

b. **mission control** *collect.*, a group or organization responsible for directing a spacecraft and its crew; **mission furniture** *U.S.*, a plain, solid style of furniture said to have been modelled originally on the furniture of the Spanish missions in North America; **mission oak** *U.S.*, mission furniture made of oak; **mission stiff** *U.S. slang*, (*a*) a missionary; (*b*) one who frequents missions, esp. a tramp who is religious or who pretends to be religious so as to get free food and lodging.

1964 J. L. NAYLER *Dict. Astronautics* 165 *Mission Control Center.* The Center..is due to be operational in 1964 for *Gemini* rendezvous flights. **1969** *Times* 16 July 5/8 Key abbreviations used by mission control and the astronauts will be [etc.]. **1973** *Guardian* 21 May 2/7 After the first switch-over, mission control commanded the computer to move back to the primary coolant circuit. **1900** *Harper's Bazaar* 28 Apr. 388/1 She stumbled upon an artistic small shop filled to overflowing with what the salesman called Mission furniture. **1910** *Daily Chron.* 24 Jan. 3/5, I have often wondered why the modest designs of the mission furniture are so attractive. **1967** *Boston Sunday Herald* 9 Apr. (Show Guide) 15/1 The turn-of-the-century Mission furniture,..coming into popularity with the recent art nouveau revival. **1927** U. SINCLAIR *Oil!* 223 Inside was furniture of a style called 'mission oak'. **1973** *Washington Post* 13 Jan. F.1/8 (Advt.), Big mission oak library table. **1904** 'No. 1500' *Life in Sing Sing* 256/2 *Mission stiff*, missionary; a convert. **1931** 'D. STIFF' *Milk & Honey Route* v. 58 You may hang on to the good life for a time, while your erstwhile companions in sin dub you a 'mission stiff'. **1948** MENCKEN *Amer. Lang.* Suppl. II. 676 At the bottom of the pile are the poor wretches..who.. gravitate dismally toward the big cities, to become beggars and mission-stiffs.

missional (mi·ʃənăl), *a. rare.* [f. MISSION *sb.* + -AL.] Relating to or connected with a religious mission; missionary.

1907 W. G. HOLMES *Age of Justinian & Theodora* II. 687 Several prelates, whose missional activities brought over whole districts and even nationalities to their creed.

missionarism (mi·ʃənăriz'm). *rare.* [f. MISSIONARY *a.* and *sb.* + -ISM.] = MISSIONIZING *vbl. sb.*

1890 H. S. HOLLAND in S. Paget *Henry Scott Holland* (1921) II. iv. 197 If I believe anything at all, I believe, with it, all that missionarism involves.

missionary, *a.* and *sb.* Add: **A.** *adj.* **1.** (Further examples.)

1841 GEO. ELIOT *Let.* 21 June (1954) I. 98 We yesterday heard him preach his last Missionary sermon. **1849** [see *AU FAIT *advb. phr.*]. **1854** C. M. YONGE *Castle Builders* v. 69 The chimney-piece ornamented with missionary boxes and cards for shilling and penny subscriptions. **1854** in C. C. Richards *Village Life Amer.* (1912) 47 If we wanted to take shares in the missionary ship, *Morning Star*, we could buy them at 10 cents apiece. **1866** J. C. PATTESON *Let.* 1 Jan. in C. M. Yonge *Life J. C. Patteson* (1874) II. x. 160, I value much these memorials of the first Missionary Bishop of the Church of England. **1873** C. M. YONGE *Pillars of House* II. xviii. 150 Mrs. Shapcote sent out invitations to a missionary tea in honour of him [*sc.* a missionary]. **1932** T. S. ELIOT *Sweeney Agonistes* 23 I'll convert *you*! Into a stew. A nice little, white little, missionary stew. **1933** P. A. EADDY *Hull Down* v. 108 On some missionary hooker where they'll want to dish up two prayer meetings in the one week to all hands. **1942** A. P. JEPHCOTT *Girls growing Up* iii. 58 We redeemed ourselves..by working hard for a missionary box. **1971** J. MANTON *Sister Dora* xvi. 272 Selwyn of Lichfield..had been the first missionary bishop in Melanesia.

b. *missionary position*: the position for sexual intercourse in which the woman lies underneath the man and facing him.

1969 *Daily Tel.* (Colour Suppl.) 10 Jan. 7 In six States [in the U.S.] a woman may still be awarded a divorce if her husband makes love to her in any other than the missionary position. **1971** *Vogue* Nov. 60/2 The face-to-face 'missionary position' (so called because it is virtually unknown in primitive races) is actually said to have been invented by Roman courtesans to hinder conception. **1971** 'V. X. SCOTT' *Surrogate Wife* 54 His wife would allow only one position—male-on-top—called the Missionary position by some and the Mamma–Papa position by others.

B. *sb.* † **4.** *N.Z.* A Christian. *Obs.*

1834 E. MARKHAM *N.Z. or Recollections of It* (MS.) 32 They are all Missionaries as they call the Christians. **1840** *N.Z. Jrnl.* 5 Dec. 292/2 The natives..call themselves missionaries, having embraced Christianity. **1841** *Ibid.* 10 Apr. 87/2, I asked whether it was true, that he had given up all fighting intrigues, and become a missionary. **1854** R. E. MALONE *Three Years' Cruise Australasian Colonies* iii. 22 Mihaneri (missionaries—the universal name, in New Zealand, for Protestant Christians).

5. The sweet-brier, *Rosa eglanteria*. *N.Z.*

1881 F. LARKWORTHY *N.Z. Revisited* 30 The sweetbriar, which here [*sc.* at Tarawera] goes by the name of the 'Missionary', blocking the roads and vacant spaces. [**1898** W. P. REEVES *Long White Cloud* i. 17 The sweetbriar.. covers whole hillsides, to the ruin of pasture. Introduced, innocently enough, by the missionaries, it goes by their name in some districts.] **1912** B. E. BAUGHAN *Brown Bread from Colonial Oven* iii. 48 'Missionary', in the North Island is frequently an alternative spelling for 'sweet-brier', which is a pest. **1921** H. GUTHRIE-SMITH *Tutira* xxvii. 274 Sweet-briar..'Missionary' as it is still called, has been spread abroad by the horse.

mi·ssionary, *v.* [f. the sb.] **a.** *intr.* To act as a missionary. **b.** *trans.* To act as a missionary towards (someone).

1862 *Independent* (N.Y.) 24 Apr. 3/1 He [*sc.* the Rev. S. H. Tyng] was always fond of missionarying. *c* **1876** J. ALBERY *Man in Possession* I, in *Dramatic Works* (1939) II. 105, I know I *was* [dreadfully wicked], but I'm not now, Teddy. I've been missionaried, and preached to. **1884** 'MARK TWAIN' *Huck. Finn* xix. 183 Preachin's my line, too, and workin' camp-meetin's, and missionaryin' around. **1893** K. D. WIGGIN *Polly Oliver's Problem* (1894) vii. 87 Boys hate to be missionaried, and I'm sure I don't blame them.

missionate, *v.* (Examples.)

1828 *Richmond* (Virginia) *Enquirer* 19 Aug. 4/1 (Th.), [Mr. Weed] was next heard of in the southern tier of counties, missionating for the administration. **1896** *Home Missionary* Oct. 303 To make professional visits, or to 'missionate' to the farmer, will not serve the purpose. **1966** *Publ. Mod. Lang. Assoc.* LXXXI. II. 7/2 Their fellow linguists who are interested in..missionating to convert the National Council of Teachers of English. *Ibid.* 8/1 Our missionaries should at least know what they are talking about before they set out to missionate.

missionee (miʃənī·). *rare.* [f. MISSION *v.* + -EE[1].] One who is susceptible to the arguments of an emissary or a missionary.

1951 'J. TEY' *Daughter of Time* v. 70 George could obviously be talked into anything. He was the born missionee.

mi·ssioning, *vbl. sb.* [f. MISSION *v.* + -ING[1].] The conducting of a religious mission.

1886 in H. BAUMANN *Londinismen.* **1961** B. R. WILSON *Sects & Society* III. xiv. 293 Costly missioning in pagan lands.

missionist (mi·ʃənist). [-IST.] One who does mission work.

1909 M. B. SAUNDERS *Litany Lane* I. iii. 34 These were wood-carvers, church artists, metal-workers, window designers, architects, carpenters and missionists.

missis, missus. Add: **1.** (Earlier and later examples.)

1833 DICKENS *Let.* *c* 10 Dec. (1965) I. 34 Hint this delicately to your *Missus.* **1836** —— *Let.* *c* 20 July (1965) I. 155 My Missis furthermore desires me to say [etc.]. **1934** T. S. ELIOT *Rock* ii. 65 Lor-love-a-duck, it's the missus! **1946** K. TENNANT *Lost Haven* (1947) i. 23, I wouldn't let any missus of mine..go gallivanting with another chap. **1975** *Daily Mirror* 29 Apr. 25 If you fancy taking the missus for a day out, you take her virtually free.

2. (Earlier and later examples.) *spec.* used by N. American Negroes and in *India* and *S. Africa* of a white employer, and loosely of any (esp. a white) woman.

1790 J. B. MORETON *Manners & Customs West India Islands* 154 Then missess fum me wid long switch. **1835** DICKENS *Sk. Boz* (1837) 2nd Ser. 87 The servant..has utterly disregarded 'Missis's' ringing. **1852** MRS. STOWE *Uncle Tom's Cabin* II. xxxiv. 203 'Missis,' said Tom, after a while, 'I can see that, some how you're quite 'bove me in everything; but there's one thing Missis might learn, even from poor Tom.' **1901** M. FRANKLIN *My Brilliant Career* xiii. 107 I'll tell the missus on you as sure as eggs. **1924** E. LEWIS *Harp* II. vii. 98 Does the missis hear the young masters in the stable? **1940** in H. Wentworth *Amer. Dial. Dict.* (1944) 392/2 Mighty fine for young missus. **1942** P. ABRAHAMS *Dark Testament* II. iii. 113 As soon as she saw it was a white person she ran back into the house. 'Ma! Ma! There's a missus at the door!' **1943** 'B. KNIGHT' *Covenant* (1944) II. x. 132 He smiled at the Ayah and said, 'I will speak to the *Missis* and perhaps she will be willing to go.' **1950** L. BENNETT et al. *Anancy Stories & Dial. Verse* 48 Eee-Hee Missis, is me same one Sidung yah all de time. **1952** P. ABRAHAMS *Path of Thunder* III. i. 190, I work for old missus when I was a child. **1971** *Weekend World* (Johannesburg) 9 May 2/2 Langton told her to cook. 'When I refused, he slapped my face hard, accusing me of making myself a "missus".'

Missisauga (misisǭ·gă). Also **Messasague, Messisauger, Missasago, Missasauga, Missis(s)a(u)ga(h), Mississagua,** etc. [Ojibwa, lit. 'people of the Mississagi River' (in Ontario).] **1.** A tribe of Algonquian Indians; a member of this tribe. Also *attrib.* or as *adj.*

1703 tr. *Lahontan's New Voy. N.-Amer.* I. xxv. 230 A list of the savage nations of Canada... The Missisagues. **1749** G. CLINTON *Let.* 3 June in E. B. O'Callaghan *Docs. rel. Colonial Hist. New-York* (1855) VI. 486 To meet the Missisaque Indians at Oswego. **1772** in *14th Rep. R. Comm. Hist. Manuscripts* App. X. 85 in *Parl. Papers 1895* (C. 7883) LIX. 1 The Chippawaes and Mississagaes are by far the most numerous and powerful nation with whom we have any connection in North America. **1798** B. S. BARTON *New Views Origin of Tribes & Nations N. Amer.* (ed. 2) App. 4 The Messaugers, or Messasagues. The language of these Indians is, undoubtedly, very nearly allied to that of the Chippewas. **1831** A. S. WITHERS *Chron. Border Warfare* 299 Their force consisted of four thousand warriors, and was led on by a Missasago chief. **1838** A. JAMESON *Winter Stud. & Summer Rambles Canada* I. 16 One solitary wigwam.., the dwelling of a few Missassagua Indians. *Ibid.* 296 The scene of bloody conflicts between the Hurons and the Missassaguas. **1888** *Jrnl. Amer. Folklore* I. 151 (*heading*) Notes on the history, customs, and beliefs of the Mississagua Indians. *Ibid.* 152 These are the most advanced in civilization of the Mississaguas. **1948** *Southwestern Jrnl. Anthropol.* Spring 100 These people, particularly the Missasaugas, seem to have occupied the southern end of the Park a century ago. **1960** D. JENNESS *Indians of Canada* (ed. 5) iv. 40 The cultivation of maize had spread..to some adjacent Algonkian tribes,..the Missisauga on the north shore of lake Huron. *Ibid.* xvii. 282 Many Missisauga moved into the old territory of the Hurons between lakes Huron and Erie.

2. = MASSASAUGA.

1843 W. OLIVER *Eight Months Illinois* 150 The inhabitants recognize two kinds of rattlesnakes, to wit, the wood- and the prairie-rattlesnake, or mississauga, of which the latter is much the smaller and less dangerous. **1961** *Listener* 16 Nov. 826/1 A mississaga rattler I once knifed.

Mississippian (misisi·piăn), *sb.* and *a.* [f. *Mississippi* (see below) + -AN.] **A.** *sb.* **1.** A native or inhabitant of Mississippi, a state on the Gulf of Mexico.

1775 J. ADAIR *Hist. Amer. Indians* 93 'The ugly yellow French,' (as they [*sc.* Indians] term the Mississippians). **1867** *Harper's Mag.* June 1/1 Two of us New Englanders, and a Mississippian. **1948** *Daily Ardmoreite* (Ardmore, Okla.) 4 May 1/6, I recognize our Negroes, as do all good white Mississippians, as a part of our citizenry. **1973** A. DUNDES *Mother Wit* 37 Mississippian David L. Cohn.

2. *Geol.* The Mississippian period or system.

1910 *Encycl. Brit.* V. 310/2 It became the practice to distinguish a 'productive' [Upper]..and an 'unproductive', barren..Lower Carboniferous; these two groups correspond in North America to the 'Carboniferous' and 'Sub-Carboniferous' respectively, or, as they are now sometimes styled, the 'Pennsylvanian' and 'Mississippian'. **1969** BENNISON & WRIGHT *Geol. Hist. Brit. Isles* ix. 184 The Carboniferous System is traditionally divided into the Lower and Upper Carboniferous in Britain and western Europe. The two systems in North America, the Mississippian and the Pennsylvanian, correspond broadly to these divisions.

B. *adj.* **1.** Of, pertaining to, or peculiar to Mississippi.

1835 J. H. INGRAHAM *South-West* II. 79 Of every variety of gaited animals..the Mississippian pacer is the most desirable. **1963** *Economist* 10 Aug. 509/2 A man who, in Mississippian terms, is a relative moderate on the race issue.

2. *Geol.* [Named after the Mississippi River, on the bluffs of which in Iowa and Missouri the system is exposed.] Of, pertaining to, or designating a period and system of the Palæozoic Era in North America that succeeded the Devonian and preceded the Pennsylvanian, and corresponds more or less to the Lower Carboniferous in Europe.

[**1870** A. WINCHELL *Sk. Creation* xii. 136 The Mountain limestone, or Lower Carboniferous mass, which I have proposed to designate the Mississippi Group, because so extensively developed in the valley of the Mississippi River.] **1891** H. S. WILLIAMS in *Bull. U.S. Geol. Survey* No. 80. 135 As these formations are bound together by a common general fauna and constitute a conspicuous feature in the geology of this region, it is proposed to call them the Mississippian series. **1933** R. C. MOORE *Historical Geol.* xvii. 257 The consensus of judgment among American geologists increasingly supports the view that the Mississippian and Pennsylvanian deposits should be reckoned as independent geologic systems rather than as subordinate divisions (series) of a so-called system that combines them. *Ibid.* 260 Red shale and sandstone.. with a maximum thickness of about 3,000 feet form the upper part of the Mississippian system in much of the Appalachian region. **1967** *Oceanogr. & Marine Biol.* V. 131 Evaporite sediments of Mississippian age have caused similar uplift in nearby Nova Scotia.

Misskito, var. *MISKITO *a.* and *sb.*

mi·ss-mark. *rare.* [f. MISS *v.*[1] Cf. MARK *sb.*[1] 7 e.] A person who misses the mark, or who fails in a purpose.

1908 HARDY *Dynasts* III. VII. ix. 520 So, as it is, a miss-mark they will dub me.

Missouri (mis-, mizū°·ri). *U.S.* [The name of a river and a state in the U.S.] **1.** A member of an American Indian people of the Sioux family, first encountered by Europeans near the Missouri River; also, the language of this people.

1703 tr. *Lahontan's New Voy. N.-Amer.* I. 130 We.. arriv'd on the 18th at the first Village of the Missouris. **1807** P. GASS *Jrnl.* 26 Six of them were made chiefs, three Otos and three Missouris. **1933** L. BLOOMFIELD *Lang.* iv. 72 The *Siouan* family includes many languages, such as.. *Missouri, Winnebago,* [etc.]. **1947** *St. Louis* (Missouri) *Globe-Democrat* 16 Mar., The Missouris were a comparatively insignificant tribe.

2. Colloq. phr. *to be* (or *come*) *from Missouri*: to be very sceptical; to believe nothing until it is demonstrated. (Originally *I come from Missouri. You have got to show me.*)

1900 *Missouri State Tribune* (Jefferson City) 13 Dec. 4/1 Ex-Lieut.-Gov. Chas. P. Johnson thinks he knows the origin of the extensively-used expression: 'I'm from Missouri; you'll have to show me'; at least he can recall its use twenty years ago in Colorado. **1901** *Columbia Missouri Statesman* 13 Dec. 1/3 You gentlemen are from Kentucky, Texas, Tennessee and Arkansas and seem to trust each other, but 'I'm from Missouri and you must show me'. **1912** C. MCCARTHY *Wisconsin Idea* 291 In the words of the current slang phrase, every Wisconsin legislator 'comes from Missouri' and you have to 'show him'. **1931** *Amer. Speech* VI. 205 *I'm from Missouri,* I don't believe that; you'll have to show me, or prove it to me. **1963** J. MITFORD *Amer. Way of Death* III. iv. 132 If you suggest..that Destiny led him there, he will give you an I'm-from-Missouri look.

3. *attrib.* and *Comb.*, as **Missouri antelope** = PRONGHORN *sb.*; **Missouri Compromise** *Hist.*, an arrangement made in 1820 which provided that Missouri should be admitted to the Union as a slave state, but that slavery should not be allowed in any new state lying north of 36° 30′; also *attrib.*; **Missouri Indian** = sense 1 above; **Missouri mule**, a mule bred in Missouri; **Missouri question** *Hist.*, the question of the conditions under which Missouri should be admitted into the Union, and the connected problems regarding slavery; **Missouri skylark**, a variety of pipit, *Anthus spraguei*.

1806 LEWIS & CLARK in *Deb. Congress U.S.* (1852) 9th Congress 2 Sess. App. 1046 The Missouri antelope, (called Cabri' by the inhabitants of the Illinois). **1820** in T. H. Benton *Exam. Dred Scott Case* (1857) 102 The line is.. nominated..by its popular descriptive appellation of 'the Missouri Compromise Line'. **1847** J. K. POLK *Diary* 16 Jan. (1910) II. 335 The line of the Missouri Compromise, *viz.*, 36° 30′. **1943** E. B. WHITE *One Man's Meat* 16 The Missouri Compromise had temporarily settled the slavery question. **1949** D. S. FREEMAN in B. A. Botkin *Treas. S. Folklore* p. x, Wirt..did not issue his life of Henry until almost the time of the Missouri Compromise. **1765** R. ROGERS *Conc. Acct. N. Amer.* 194 The inhabitants on this river are called the Missouri Indians. **1817** J. BRADBURY *Trav. Interior Amer.* 41 It is customary amongst the Missouri Indians to register every exploit in war, by making a notch for each on the handle of their tomahawks. **1923** *Nation* (N.Y.) 17 Oct. 432 Then there is the Missouri mule. He it was who won the war. **1972** *Listener* 21 Dec. 858/2 Not for nothing did the idiom 'as stubborn as a Missouri mule' come into the language. **1819** J. ADAMS *Let.* 21 Dec. in T. Jefferson *Writings* (1903) XV. 236 The Missouri question, I hope, will follow the other waves under the ship, and do no harm. **1884** J. G. BLAINE *20 Yrs. Congress* I. 15 The 'Missouri question'..formally appeared in Congress in the month of December, 1818. **1858** S. F. BAIRD in *Rep. Explor. Route to Pacific* (U.S. War Dept.) IX. 234 *Neocorys Spraguei*, Sclater. Missouri Skylark. **1940** E. T. SETON *Trail of Artist-Naturalist* 299 The strictly prairie birds were gone—of the Missouri skylark, for instance, I saw not one.

Missourian (mis-, mizū°·riăn), *sb.* and *a.* [f. prec. + -AN.] **A.** *sb.* A native or inhabitant of the State of Missouri. **B.** *adj.* Of or belonging to, native or peculiar to, Missouri.

1820 *Deb. Congress U.S.* (1855) 26 Jan. 945, I cannot believe that I, or any other man or men, are better capable of governing Missourians than they are of governing themselves. **1862** *Harper's Mag.* Sept. 450/2 Teamsters, many of whom were young Missourians embarked for the first time upon a prairie trip. **1885** 'MARK TWAIN' in *Century Mag.* Dec. 201 The Masons gave us a Missouri country breakfast, in Missourian abundance. **1944** B. A. BOTKIN *Treas. Amer. Folklore* II. 318 One of the harshest of these [*sc.* slang names] is Puke, for a Missourian. **1948** MENCKEN *Amer. Lang.* Suppl. II. vii. 173 D. S. Crumb..unearthed a great deal more that was specially Missourian, *e.g.*..*buckshot land*, poor clay soil. **1957** *Encycl. Brit.* XIII. 258/2 About 1,700 armed Missourians invaded Kansas and stuffed the ballot boxes. **1973** R. ROSENBLUM *Mushroom Cave* (1974) 83 The junior diplomat, a glad-handing Missourian.

missourite (mis-, mizū°·rəit). *Petrogr.* [f. *MISSOUR(I + -ITE[1] (see quot. 1896).] A grey, granular, igneous rock composed mainly of pyroxene, leucite, and sometimes olivine.

1896 WEED & PIRSSON in *Amer. Jrnl. Sci.* II. 323 This rock is a new type, and it fills a place which has hitherto been vacant in all systems of rock classification... We have therefore called it missourite from the Missouri River, the most prominent and best known geographical object in the region where it occurs. **1927** *Ibid.* XIV. 179 These granitoid augite-leucite rocks will be called missourite, although Pirsson's original Montana missourite contained less leucite and about 15 per cent of olivine. *Ibid.* 180 The presence of olivine in missourite need not be regarded as essential. **1963** *Mineral. Abstr.* XVI. 388/1 The first missourites recorded from Russia are in an outcrop of alkaline gabbroic rocks near the Lomachan River.

mi·ss-out. [f. vbl. phr. *to miss out*: see *MISS *v.*[1] 25.] **a.** *pl.* In *Gambling*, loaded dice. **b.** In *Craps*, a losing throw: see *CRAPS b; also, the action of losing the right to throw.

1928 J. O'CONNOR *Broadway Racketeers* xiv. 157 The game keeper has all sorts of crooked ones, those known as 'Shapes', others called 'Miss-Outs'. **1936** *Detective Fiction Weekly* 21 Mar. 139/1 If the dice are cut as 'passers', the percentage in favor of the shooter is 'mild'; but cut for a banking or fading advantage (called 'miss-outs' or 'missing dice') the advantage is stronger. **1942** W. FAULKNER *Go down, Moses* 114 The spots on them miss-out dice. **1961** in Partridge *Dict. Underworld* (1968) 846/1 *Misses*... (2) Crooked dice that are gaffed to make more miss-outs than passes. **1964** A. WYKES *Gambling* v. 109 He loses if he throws a Two, Three, or Twelve (a 'crap' or 'miss-out').

mis-speak, *v.* Add: **3. b.** *refl.* To fail to convey the meaning one intends by one's words.

1890 in *Cent. Dict.* **1894** *Congress. Rec.* 19 Jan. 1051/1, I simply wanted to bring that matter out plainly... I believe he misspoke himself. **1973** *Harper's Mag.* June 38/2 'The President,' Ziegler said, 'misspoke himself.' He explained that the President had noted his error in reviewing the transcript of the press conference. **1975** G. V. HIGGINS *City on Hill* ii. 53 If I gave that impression, I misspoke myself.

mi·ss-stays. [f. as MISSTAY *v.*] Of a ship: the act or fact of failing to go about.

1878 D. KEMP *Man. Yacht & Boat Sailing* 245 A 'miss-stays' may be the consequence.

misstay, *v.* Add: (Earlier examples.) Also miss-stay.

1829 G. GRIFFIN *Collegians* (ed. 2) I. xii. 241 Ahoy! ahoy! Have an oar out in the bow, or she'll miss-stay in the swell. **1849** N. KINGSLEY *Diary* (1914) 88 We misstayed in but 11 feet of water, but the bottom is very muddy and not dangerous.

mis-step, *sb.* (Earlier and later examples.)

a **1800** *Spirit of Farmer's Museum* (1801) 205 The Squire..can sit on the sessions, and fine poor girls for natural missteps. **1837** *Yale Lit. Mag.* III. 8 (Th.), Forgetting the round door block, he made a mis-step. **1931** F. L. ALLEN *Only Yesterday* 101 The publishers of the confession magazines..concentrated on the description of what they euphemistically called 'missteps'. **1934** D. SARGENT *Thomas More* iii. 62 As in all diplomatic conferences each side spends a great deal of time waiting for the other side to make a misstep. **1949** *Sat. Even. Post* 1 Oct. 20/3 Russians..turn sick with fear if they make the slightest little misstep. **1963** J. WALSH *Shroud* (1964) vi. 47 His headlong disregard for bodily care and his courting of the injuries or death that lay only a mis-step away. **1974** *Publishers Weekly* 4 Feb. 64/2 Henry Keller..picks up a hitchhiker... For awhile, he shares her sexual favours... Becky is killed accidentally. The police don't care much; neither does Henry's wife, who forgives his misstep. **1974** *Sci. Amer.* Oct. 87/2 A misstep would not necessarily lead to a stumble or a fall.

mis-step, *v.* Delete † *Obs.* and add later U.S. example.

1869 S. BOWLES *Our New West* v. 102 Mules don't misstep, and even the top-heavy pack jacks..carried their burden and themselves unharmed to the top.

missus: see MISSIS in Dict. and Suppl.

missy, *sb.* (Later examples.)

1919 WODEHOUSE *Damsel in Distress* vii. 107 Those—them—over there are Ayrshires, missy. **1922** JOYCE *Ulysses* 733 Little chits of missies they have now singing. **1924** R. MACAULAY *Orphan Island* xv. 202 'You're very smart and proud, missie,' her uncle told her. **1967** P. ROTH *When she was Good* III. 274 Either you calm down with that bossy little voice, missy, or you get out.

mist, *sb.*[1] Add: **1.** (Example of a techn. definition.)

1972 *Meteorol. Gloss.* (Meteorol. Office) (ed. 5) 182 *Mist*, a state of atmospheric obscurity produced by suspended microscopic water droplets or wet hygroscopic particles. The term is used for synoptic purposes when..the associated visibility is equal to or exceeds 1 km; the corresponding relative humidity is greater than about 95 per cent.

e. A colour suggestive of a mist.

1926 *Daily Colonist* (Victoria, B.C.) 21 July 16/4 (Advt.), A 4-ply worsted wool in shades of pink, mist, [etc.]. **1927** *Daily Express* 12 Mar. 3/5 Mist, a subdued mauve, suggesting the atmospheric effects of sunset. **1937** *Discovery* July 217/2 Our silk stockings are..described as..sun-tan, sandalwood, mist. **1963** *New Yorker* 29 June 57 Black, mist, rust, or olive.

5. *mist-belt, -light, -magic, -mote, -pavilion, -plash, -sheet, -thread, -veil; mist-circled, -cold, -coloured, -dimmed, -green, -pale, -shrouded* (later examples), *-tracked, -veiled, -wild, -wreathed, -wrought* adjs.; **mist-blower**, a device for spraying insecticide into the tops of trees; so *mist-blowing* vbl. sb.; **mist-net**, a net made of very fine threads, used to trap birds etc. for ringing or examination and subsequent release; also as *v. intr.*, to trap in a mist-net; hence **mist-netter**, one who uses a mist-net; **mist-pond** = *DEW-POND; **mist propagation**, a method of rooting plant cuttings in which high humidity is maintained in a greenhouse by an automatic system of watering with fine spray at regular intervals; **mist propagator**, an installation for this type of cultivation.

1906 *Rep. Brit. Assoc. Adv. Sci. 1905* 594 Passing either east or west of this 'mist-belt' the rainfall rapidly diminishes. **1946** POTTS & FRIEND in *Bull. Connecticut Agric. Exper. Station* No. 501. 48 The development of a mist blower which will apply thoroughly a small quantity of a concentrated insecticide. **1969** *Nature* 9 Aug. 558/2 Only the mistblower, which is mounted on a tractor, seems feasible for large-scale applications. **1960** *Farmer & Stockbreeder* 12 Jan. 97/2 Mistblowing of fruit trees is a practical proposition. **1935** W. EMPSON *Poems* 27 Starlit, mistcircled, one whole pearl embrowned. **1889** W. B. YEATS *Wanderings of Oisin* III. 34 Came now the sliding of tears and sweeping of mist-cold hair. **1890** *Cent. Dict.*, Mist-colored. **1929** W. FAULKNER *Sartoris* 224 That 'ere mist-colored stallion. **1880** 'MARK TWAIN' *Tramp Abroad* 398 Along their mist-dimmed heights [i.e., of the Alps]. **1961** A. SILLITOE *Key to Door* IV. xxvi. 389 Green fields rolling up to..Catstone Wood, a mist-green spearblade of sky above. **1930** BLUNDEN *Poems* 40 The wolfish shadows in the eerie places Sprawl in the mist-light. **1921** R. GRAVES *Pier-Glass* 12 Cold fog-drawn Lily, pale mist-magic Rose. **1923** H. CRANE *Let.* 15 Apr. (1965) 132 The eerie speed of the shutter..catching even the transition of the mist-mote into the cloud. **1956** *Brit. Birds* L. 450 Mist nets, a traditional Japanese method of catching birds, were introduced to British ringers at a meeting of the Bird Observatories Committee in January, and by the early autumn of 1956 it is probable that over a hundred nets were in use. **1961** *New Scientist* 23 Mar. 728/1 The watchers gather with note-books, binoculars, mist nets, Heligoland traps and boxes of rings. **1971** *Daily Tel.* (Colour Suppl.) 18 June 7/1 Birds are..snared in a 'mist net' (a long net erected on poles, which is of so fine a mesh that the birds cannot see it, and so fly into it, where they are entangled). **1972** *Science* 1 Sept. 806/3 Bats are mist-netted near cattle. **1973** *Country Life* 1 Feb. 263/3 Helpers..ring large numbers of passerines, which they trap in mist-nets. **1960** *Brit. Birds* LIII. 526 The capture of rare and difficult forms..is now within the province of every mist-netter. **1849** C. BRONTË *Shirley* III. vi. 142 He would rather have appointed tryste with a phantom abbess, or mist-pale nun. **1925** C. DAY LEWIS *Beechen Vigil* 26 Now from blue mist-pavilion You may see King Silence go Royally through the forest. **1916** BLUNDEN *Harbingers* 33 So heavily drives the rain, and lashes The open pool into white mist-plashes. **1893** DARTNELL & GODDARD *Gloss. Words Wiltshire* 104 *Mist-pond*, a pond on the downs, not fed by any spring, but kept up by mist, dew, and rain... More commonly called *dew-ponds.* **1931** *N. & Q.* 22 Aug. 141/2 High up on the hills, in various parts of the country, are to be found ponds. Some call them dew ponds, but a more correct title is mist pond. [**1941** *Amer. Nurseryman* 1 May 5 (*title*) Propagation under mist.] **1953** *Ibid.* 1 Aug. 63/2 Results of some of the work we have done at Koster Nursery appear to indicate the equal value of constant mist propagation in the open. **1961** *Amat. Gardening* Suppl. 28 Oct. 34/2 A technique known as mist propagation... The main feature of this technique is the automatic provision of a fine mist spray. **1969** *New Scientist* 10 Apr. 70 (*caption*) After five weeks' mist propagation, two-leaf cuttings of Iceberg [*sc.* a rose] are well-rooted young plants. **1972** *Country Life* 1 June 1419/3 Mist Propagation equipment. Maximises health and growth of plants. **1971** 'J. FRASER' *Death in Pheasant's Eye* xxxi. 187 He'd have sufficient cash to buy a proper heating and ventilating system... Aye, and perhaps a mist propagator! **1917** D. H. LAWRENCE *Look! We have come Through!* 47 A thick mist-sheet lies over the broken wheat. **1919** V. WOOLF *Night & Day* v. 62 Lonely mist-shrouded voyagings. **1957** MANVELL & HUNTLEY *Technique Film Music* iii. 164 Calm scenes of mist-shrouded lakes and shots of dew-spangled vegetation. **1888** W. B. YEATS *Phantom Ship* in *Wanderings of Oisin* (1889) 87 Hang the mist-threads for a little while Like cobwebs in the air. **1867** M. ARNOLD *Heine's Grave* in *New Poems* 204 And mist-track'd stream of the wide. **1928** BLUNDEN *Retreat* 14 Or mist-veil brushed thee, fine as yet was wove For moonmaid's clothing. **1908** *Daily Chron.* 14 Nov. 4/4 Down the damp roadway move long lines of mist-veiled traffic. **1936** L. B. LYON *Bright Feather Fading* 48 Mist-wild you melt now, gossamer fawn. **1849** M. ARNOLD *Resignation* in *Strayed Reveller* 123 Make, whistling, towards his mist-wreath'd flock. **1909** E. POUND *Personae* 43 Slender as mist-wrought maids and hamadryads.

mistake, *sb.* Add: **1. d.** An instance of a woman's becoming pregnant unintentionally; an unplanned baby.

1957 *New Yorker* 12 Jan. 30/3 Owing to a 'mistake', Bernadette was probably 'caught'. She was beginning to 'show'. **1959** *Times* 2 Mar. 5/3 We all know the baby is a 'mistake',..but surely it is a mistake which is understandable. **1963** in *Sc. Nat. Dict.* (1965) VI. 303/1 The peer lassie was pitten awa frae hame for makin a mistak.

2. b. Also *in mistake for*.

1906 GALSWORTHY *Man of Property* I. ii. 39 Old Jolyon ..gave the driver a sovereign in mistake for a shilling. **1923** *World's Work* May 563/1, I remember looking at him and..expecting that I had been arrested in mistake for him.

c. Also *make no mistake* (*about*) (something): have no doubt about it.

1885 W. S. GILBERT *Mikado* II. 27 Ah, pray make no mistake, We are not shy; We're very wide awake. **1911** G. B. SHAW *Shewing-up of Blanco Posnet* 390 It wont make any difference to us: make no mistake about that. **1962** *Listener* 27 Sept. 463/2 But the present terms do confront us with this choice: make no mistake about it. **1963** *Ibid.* 21 Feb. 341/1 Make no mistake about Mr Bennet: we are meant to disapprove thorougly of his detachment. **1974** *Times* 22 Mar. 11/7 Make no mistake. We had a major work of television last night.

3. mistake-free *a.*

1969 F. I. DRETSKE *Seeing & Knowing* ii. 63 What we might call a mistake-free way of seeing D.

mistake, *v.* Add: **4. c.** *to mistake one's man*: to judge incorrectly, or underestimate, the capabilities, character, etc., of the person with whom one has to deal.

1794 *Mass. Spy* 16 Apr. (Th.), If he supposes I am to be frightened by his pompous accusations, he has much mistaken his man. **1841** *Congress. Globe* 18 June 75/3 Mr. G. said that he was not to be coughed or cried down; gentlemen mistook their man if they supposed he was to be affected by the machinery of the political party.

mister, *sb.*² Add: **1. e.** *Mister Big, Mister Fixit*: see *MR. 2 e; *Mister Charlie*: see *CHARLEY, CHARLIE 7.

2. b. Colloq. shortening of *Mister Mate* (MATE *sb.*² 4 a). Freq. as vocative.

1909 F. H. SHAW *Daughter of Storm* xx. 177 'All right, sir,' said the second mate to Steadman... 'West by north,' said Steadman... 'I'll go and turn in, mister.' *a* **1966** C. S. FORESTER *Hornblower & Crisis* (1967) v. 40 The mate was marking up the traverse board. 'What's the course, Mister?' asked Hornblower. **1972** *Listener* 6 Jan. 18/3 The Captain..addressed the Mate as William, except when he thought he was getting uppish, when he called him 'Mister'.

mistify: see MYSTIFY *v.*¹, *v.*²

misting, *vbl. sb.* Add: **2.** *misting-up*, the act of obscuring as with mist, the process of becoming thus obscured; also *concr.*

1964 B. GASTON *Drifting Death* ii. 22, I rinsed out the face mask against misting-up. **1966** T. WISDOM *High-Performance Driving* x. 108 A film of dirt or misting up on the inside [of the windscreen] can make the fog seem twice as thick as it is in reality. **1969** *Listener* 6 Feb. 161/1 There were no major hitches during the flight, and only a few minor ones, such as the misting-up of windows.

mistletoe. Add: **1. b.** (Earlier U.S. examples.)

1806 LEWIS & CLARK in *Deb. Congress U.S.* (1852) 9th Congress 2 Sess. App. 1142 Mistletoe, thistle, wild hemp, bulrush. **1819** E. EVANS *Pedestrious Tour* 318 In this.. country [*sc.* Louisiana] grows the celebrated plant called mistletoe. **1838** J. HALL *Notes on Western States* ii. 28 The mistletoe is seen hanging from the branches of the trees throughout the whole course of the Ohio.

3. mistletoe bird *Austral.*, a small black, white, and crimson bird, *Dicæum hirundinaceum*, which feeds on nectar, pollen, and berries; **mistletoe cactus**, a tropical American epiphytic cactus of the genus *Rhipsalis*, esp. *R. cassytha* and other species bearing white fruits resembling those of mistletoe.

1908 E. J. BANFIELD *Confessions of Beachcomber* I. iii. 96 Flower-pecker or Mistletoe Bird. **1944** A. RUSSELL *Bush Ways* iii. 19 Already there is a mistletoe-bird, with crimson breast, swaying itself on a mistletoe twig. **1965** *Austral. Encycl.* VI. 104/2 Mistletoe-bird, a small arboreal bird (*Dicaeum hirundinaceum*), the only representative in Australia of a group found throughout southern Asia.. and belonging to a family known as flower-peckers. [**1850** J. MACFADYEN *Flora Jamaica* II. 182 Rhipsalis... Pseudo-parasitic plants, growing on trees, leafless, with small flowers, and with berries white, resembling those of the mistletoe.] **1889** W. WATSON *Cactus Culture for Amateurs* 227 They [*sc.* the flowers]..are succeeded by white berries, exactly like those of the Mistletoe, whence the name Mistletoe Cactus, by which this species [sc. *Rhipsalis cassytha*] is known. **1967** ELBERT & HYAMS *House Plants* xi. 102 *R*[*hipsalis*] *cassytha*, the Mistletoe Cactus, is a hanging mass of succulent branches dripping with white berries.

mistress, *sb.* Add: **13, 14 a.** Also *W. Indies.*

1957 F. A. COLLYMORE *Notes for Gloss. Barbadian Dial.* (ed. 2) 57 The archaic nominative of address has survived in Barbados, and may be heard any day on the lips of any servant or huckster addressing the mistress of the household, as, *I want some more butter, mistress. Mistress, you want any useful limes?* **1966** *Evening Standard* 1 Feb. 8/4, I would be very glad to get out of this hard country [sc. Jamaica], mistress. **1966** *Guardian* 14 Dec. 8/4 We go..to see Mistress Gladys Walker... Here [*sc.* in Barbados], Mrs is often spoken out, in full.

mistressly, *a.* Add: **3.** Characteristic of a man's mistress. *nonce-wd.*

1939 A. HUXLEY *After many a Summer* I. xiii. 180 Flirting with him all through dinner, so that you got the old man hopping jealous of him. That was masterly. Or should one say mistressly?

mistrust, *v.* **3. b.** (Further U.S. examples.)

1840 C. F. HOFFMAN *Greyslaer* I. x. 109, I mistrust that your Injun friend there..didn't help you much..in finding out old Josie. **1861** O. W. HOLMES *Elsie Venner* vii. 73, I mistrusted he didn't mean to come. **1867** *Harper's Mag.* July 147/1 They have left the Atlantic coast, given up by physicians as in the last stage of consumption—a fact that would never be mistrusted from their present robust condition. **1898** A. NICHOLAS *Idyl of Wabash* 188 Before early apples were ripe I mistrusted what was keeping him. **1909** *Dialect Notes* III. 349, I mistrusted he was at the bottom of it. Not common.

mistrusting, *vbl. sb.* (Later example.)

1921 *Spectator* 30 Apr. 556/2 Class bitterness and the mistrusting of the employer by the employed.

mistune, *v.* (Further examples, in *Radio.*) Hence **mistu·ning** *vbl. sb.*

1914 R. STANLEY *Text-bk. Wireless Telegr.* 134 In the Telefunken transmitter the circuits are slightly mistuned, the aerial circuit having a free wave length about 2 per cent. higher than that of the primary circuit, and this mistuning is increased with the closeness of the coupling. **1970** J. EARL *Tuners & Amplifiers* iii. 73 It is possible to mistune a stereo transmission and collect a terrific amount of sideband noise. *Ibid.*, The quality of f.m. is significantly impaired by even slight mistuning.

misty, *a.*¹ Add: **3.** *misty-eyed* adj., that brings tears to the eyes; having tears in one's eyes.

1956 W. H. WHYTE *Organization Man* (1957) III. xiii. 156 He can grow as misty-eyed as the next man at the banquet honoring the Grand Old Man. **1974** M. CECIL *Heroines in Love* vi. 151 Misty-eyed emotion and passionate declarations of love.

mis-ty·ping, *vbl. sb.* [MIS-¹ 3.] A bad or false typing; a typing error.

1936 F. M. FORD *Let.* 2 July (1965) 252 The 4 being a mistyping for ', I having just changed my machine.

misuse, *sb.* **2.** Delete † *Obs.* and add later *poet.* example.

1881 SWINBURNE *Mary Stuart* I. i. 10 The Catholics naked here to all misuse Fall off in numbered force, in means and power.

misuser¹. (Later example.)

1927 *Manch. Guardian Weekly* Oct. 315/2 An exercise in most delicate raillery at the expense of all the misusers of the English language.

misvocaliza·tion. [MIS-¹ 4.] The insertion of incorrect vowel-signs in forms of writing consisting mainly or entirely of consonants.

1932 *Times Lit. Suppl.* 14 Jan. 20/2 Surely *kābhôdh* 'glory'..is a misvocalization of *kābhēdh* 'liver'. **1942** *Jrnl. Theol. Stud.* XLIII. 155 An act. verb is required by the context on Gunkel's restoration of the text; the misvocalization is due to the unusual form.

‖ **mit** (mit). *colloq.* or *jocular.* [G., with.] With (esp. with apparent ellipsis of 'me' or 'us').

1885 W. JAMES *Let.* 19 Feb. (1920) I. 241, I..suppose Mrs. Godkin will come *mit.* **1922** JOYCE *Ulysses* 505 Will some pleashe pershon not now impediment so catastrophics mit agitation of firstclass table-numpkin? **1959** D. BARTON *Loving Cup* 237 Why not come along mit.

Mitanni (mitæ·ni). Name of the people and language of Mitanni, a Hurrian kingdom centred on the Habur and Upper Euphrates which flourished in the fifteenth and early fourteenth centuries B.C. Also *attrib.* or as *adj.* So **Mita·nnian** *sb.*, an inhabitant of Mitanni; the language of Mitanni; **Mita·nnian, Mita·nnite** (*rare*) *adjs.*, of or pertaining to Mitanni, its people, or its language.

1897 A. H. SAYCE in *Proc. Soc. Biblical Archæol.* XIX. 285 Tesup was the Mitannian Air-god. **1900** —— *Ibid.* XXII. 176 The Mitannian language was highly agglutinative. *Ibid.* 182 The verb in Mitannian has hardly been differentiated from the noun. **1907** —— *Archæol. Cuneiform Inscr.* vi. 169 On the west..the Mitannians found themselves confronted by another northern population, the Hittites. **1910** *Encycl. Brit.* XIII. 539/1 Whether the Mitanni..were racially kin to the Hatti, cannot be determined at present. **1911** *Ibid.* XVIII. 182/2 From cuneiform sources we know the names of six other Mitanni rulers. *Ibid.*, The language of the Mitanni state..was neither Aryan nor Semitic. *Ibid.* 183/1 The Hittite King's interference restored the Mitannite state as a protectorate. **1933** L. BLOOMFIELD *Lang.* iv. 65 Extinct languages of an older time..Mitanni, east of Mesopotamia, from around 1400 B.C. **1939** L. H. GRAY *Foundations of Lang.* 380 Northern Mesopotamia was the home of the *Subaraean* group,.. divided into Mitannian and Khurrian (or Kharrian), which were very similar, if not identical. **1948** D. DIRINGER *Alphabet* 90 Hurrian..differs but very little from the language of the Mitanni. **1948** G. R. DRIVER *Semitic Writing* iii. 131 The proto-Elamites in the East and the Hittites and the Mitanni in the north devised their own systems of pictographic and cuneiform writing. **1952** *Trans. Philol. Soc.* 117 Chance..has also apparently left us without a *ŭ*-stem among the Indoeuropean borrowings into certain languages of the ancient Near East—Mitanni, Kassite, Lycian and the like. **1955** T. BURROW *Sanskrit Lang.* i. 28 The author..was a Mitannian called Kikkuli. **1970** [see *ELAMITE *sb.* and *a.*]. **1973** A. MALAMAT in D. J. Wiseman *Peoples Old Testament Times* vi. 149 The Aramaeans were always strongly influenced by the specific local environment, in Mesopotamia by the remnants of the Mitanni culture and by the Assyrians. **1973** H. A. HOFFNER in *Ibid.* ix. 223 It was these Mitannians who were responsible for the introduction into the Near East of scientific techniques for the breeding and training of chariot horses. *Ibid.* 224 The Hittite conqueror caught his Mitannian foes off guard and routed all opposition.

mitch: see *MICHE *v.*

Mitchell (mi·tʃěl). The name of Sir Thomas Livingstone *Mitchell* (1792–1855), Scottish-born explorer of Australia, used *attrib.* in **Mitchell grass** to designate an Australian fodder grass of the genus *Astrebla.*

1883 F. M. BAILEY *Synopsis Queensland Flora* 660 Used for food by the natives. The most valuable fodder-grass of the colony. True Mitchell-grass. **1902** *Encycl. Brit.* XXXII. 108/2 The 'Mitchell grasses' (*Astrebla pectinata*) and its varieties, viz., the Wheat (*triticoides*), the weeping (*elymoides*), and the curly (*curvifolia*),..have the most extraordinary vitality. **1909** *Chambers's Jrnl.* Dec. 809/2 Mitchell grass is said to be able to survive a rainless period extending over three years. **1927** M. M. BENNETT *Christison* v. 55 Curly Mitchell grass shimmered gold and silver. **1934** *Bulletin* (Sydney) 27 June 22/1 Bull Mitchell grass and its seed is easily the best feed we have. **1936** I. L. IDRIESS *Cattle King* xix. 178 Thudding through the Mitchell grass to the crackling of sticks and flying gravel, the mob galloped on. **1948** V. PALMER *Golconda* xix. 153 League upon league of crinkly Mitchell grass. **1965** *Austral. Encycl.* IV. 365/1 Four species of *Astrebla* (Mitchell grasses) are known. Because the dry leaves remain attached to the plant and support stock in times of drought, they have become famous as fodder plants.

mitching, *vbl. sb.* and *ppl. a.*: see *MICHE *v.*

mite¹. Add: **3.** *mite-borne* adj.; so **mite-borne typhus**, scrub typhus; also called **mite typhus.**

1939 *Brit. Encycl. Med. Pract.* XII. 347 The classical form of the disease is the Japanese river fever which bears the same relation to mite-borne typhus fevers as does Rocky Mountain fever to the tick-borne. **1974** PASSMORE & ROBSON *Compan. Med. Stud.* III. xii. 73/2 The rash spares the face in louse-borne typhus but not in the mite-borne disease. **1921** *Indian Med. Gaz.* LVI. 370/1 (*table*) Mite typhus. **1939** *Brit. Encycl. Med. Pract.* XII. 348 Scrub or rural form of tropical typhus..has been found to be mite-typhus conveyed by *T*[*rombicula*] *deliensis.* **1959** C. OGBURN *Marauders* (1960) viii. 265 He had all of the three worst scourges of the organization, in combination: mite typhus, amoebic dysentery and malaria.

mite². Add: **4.** Used adverbially.

1939 L. M. MONTGOMERY *Anne of Ingleside* i. 9 You needn't be a mite afraid to sleep in that bed. I aired the sheets to-day. **1955** H. CROOME *Mountain & Molehill* ii. 29 We were a mite surprised to see so many German names on your prospectus. **1958** *Spectator* 22 Aug. 241/2 This, to me, is a mite depressing. **1972** J. PORTER *Meddler & her Murder* viii. 107 'There was no need to go to all that expense, dear,' said Miss Jones, a mite huffily. **1972** J. WAINWRIGHT *Night is Time to Die* 66 If..the farmer buys pigs ..and wishes to move them..he must obtain such a licence... This..may seem a mite bureaucratic. **1974** WODEHOUSE *Aunts aren't Gentlemen* iii. 20 Last night..it may be that I became a mite polluted, but that rarely happens.

6. mite society, a 19th-century society whose object was to collect funds for some charitable purpose by small contributions (see sense 1 c).

1822 *Missionary Herald* (Boston, Mass.) XVIII. 21 Female Mite So[ciety] for Cher[okee] and Choc[taw] missions [gave $]25. **1823** *Baptist Mag.* IV. 133, I have also assisted in the organization of two Female Mite Societies. **1872** *Newton Kansan* 26 Sept. 3/2 The Mite Society will hold a ten cent sociable in the school room this Thursday evening. **1878** *Harper's Mag.* Jan. 203/1 By means of 'mite' societies..sufficient money was raised to inclose it [*sc.* the grave-yard]. **1883** C. F. WILDER *Sister Ridnour's Sacrifice* 262 We call upon certain poor, we attend the 'Dorcas', the socials, the festivals, and mite societies.

mitella. 2. Substitute for def.: [Adopted as a generic name by J. P. de Tournefort in *Institutiones Rei Herbariæ* (ed. 3, 1719) I. 241.] A perennial herb of the genus so called, belonging to the family Saxifragaceæ, native to North America and north-east Asia, and bearing racemes of small flowers; usually called MITRE-WORT. (Later example.)

1882 *Harper's Mag.* Nov. 853/2 Why should the starry blossom of the fringed mitella seek the snow-flake as its model?

mithan. Add to forms: **mithong, mithun.** (Later examples.)

1921 *Blackw. Mag.* Feb. 258/2 There was no rice, no water, no fences, no herds of mithun. **1923** *Ibid.* Feb. 186/2 The mithong were once more stalled beneath the houses. **1937** *Jrnl. R. Anthrop. Inst.* 15 Over the neck of the bound and trembling Mithan.

Mithraistic (miþreiˌi·stik), *a.* [f. MITHRAIST + -IC.] = MITHRAIC *a.*

1900 *Open Court* May 290 Mithraistic Cameos. Showing Mithras born from the rocks between the Dioscuri, surrounded by Mithraistic symbols, among them the cup and bread of the Eucharist. **1920** *Glasgow Herald* 1 May 4 Hymn-writing..ran too much to gloomy terrorism and Mithraistic images of wounds and blood.

mithril (mi·þril). [Invented word.] Name given by J. R. R. Tolkien to a mythical precious metal.

1954 J. R. R. TOLKIEN *Fellowship of Ring* II. iv. 331 Here alone in the world was found Moria-silver, or true-silver as some have called it: *mithril* is the Elvish name...

The beauty of *mithril* did not tarnish or grow dim. *Ibid.*, Bilbo had a corslet of mithril-rings. **1955** —— *Return of King* v. x. 165 The coat of mithril-mail that Frodo had worn wrapped in his tattered garments. *Ibid.* vi. ix. 308 On her finger was Nenya, the ring wrought of *mithril*, that bore a single white stone flickering like a frosty star.

miticide (məi·tisəid). [f. MIT(E¹ + -I- + -CIDE.] Any substance used to kill mites.

1946 TRAVIS & MORTON *Use of Insect Repellants & Miticides* (U.S. Dept. Agric., Bureau Entomol. & Plant Quarantine, E-698) 4 Benzyl benzoate is very effective as a miticide. **1955** *Sci. News Let.* 18 June 392/2 Each of the six dusts is a mixture of insecticides, miticides and fungicides, and prevents damage by aphids, leaf-hoppers, spider mites, and by the plant diseases, mildew and blackspot. **1972** *Daily Colonist* (Victoria, B.C.) 30 July 47/5 Spray thoroughly now with a good miticide such as kelthane or malathion.

mitigate, *v.* **4. a.** Delete ?*Obs.* and add later example.

1965 W. MITCHELL tr. *Huyghe's Relig. Orders Mod. World* I. 6 The mendicant Orders..while in part adopting the monastic and canonical forms of organization..plainly mitigated them to enable their members to go out and preach..in the highways and by-ways.

mitigated, *ppl. a.* Add to def.: *spec.* designating or pertaining to a religious order less austere than other orders.

1671 [in Dict.]. **1694** EARL OF PERTH *Let.* 17 Sept. (1845) 44 They are called rich Clarisses, because the poor Clarisses are of a far more rigid order..; these are far more mitigated, and they gave us an entertainment of musick. **1888** [see *CARMELITE *sb.* and *a.* 1 b]. **1948** W. S. MAUGHAM *Catalina* ix. 43 Since it was a convent of the mitigated order they enjoyed a good deal of freedom.

Mitin (məi·tin). A proprietary name for certain mothproofing agents, spec. *Mitin F.F.*, a substituted urea, $Cl_2C_6H_3{\cdot}NH{\cdot}CO{\cdot}NH{\cdot}C_6H_3$-$(Cl)O{\cdot}C_6H_3(Cl)SO_3Na$, which is used for treating woollen goods such as carpets.

1938 *Trade Marks Jrnl.* 17 Aug. 994/1 Mitin Mothproof... Moth repelling and destroying preparations. J. R. Geigy.., Basle,..Switzerland; manufacturers. **1945** *Chem. Abstr.* XXXIX. 764 A new attack based on the insecticidal activity of *p,p'*-dihalodiphenyl sulfones, sulfoxides and sulfides, and resulting in the introduction of the H_2O-sol. dye Mitin F.F. showed the fundamental toxicity of this type of compd. **1958** *House & Garden* Apr. 7/3 (Advt.), Stockwell [carpet]... All-woollen pile. Mitin-processed; guaranteed mothproof for life. **1969** *Chem. Abstr.* 18 Aug. 206/2 For the protection of wool, mohair, camel's hair, or alpaca, mixts. of 1 part dieldrin,..Mitin FF, naphthalene..or alkylyl-2-thiazolyl sulfide and 0·33–12 parts epoxide, polyamide, and (or) acrylic resins are used.

mitla (mi·tla). [Native name.] An unidentified animal said to inhabit the forests on the borders of Bolivia and Brazil.

a **1925** P. H. FAWCETT *Exploration Fawcett* (1953) xiv. 173 In the forests [of Bolivia] were various beasts still unfamiliar to zoologists, such as the *mitla*, which I have seen twice, a black dog-like cat about the size of a foxhound. **1965** *Sun* 28 Sept. 3/1 He will spend two months looking for a mitla..in the forests of Rio Abuna.

Mitnagged (mitnā·gėd). Also **Misnagid.** Pl. **Mitnaggedim.** [ad. Heb. *miṯnāggēd* opponent.] The name given by the Chasidim to their religious opponents; hence any Jew who is not a Chasid.

1904 *Jewish Encycl.* VIII. 623/1 *Mitnaggedim,* (lit. 'opponents'), title applied by the Ḥasidim to their opponents, *i.e.*, to the Orthodox Jews of the Slavonic countries who have not become adherents of Ḥasidim... 'Mitnagged' now means..simply a non-Ḥasid. **1907** I. ZANGWILL *Ghetto Comedies* 409 'Me join the *Misnagdim*!' cried the cobbler in horror. 'Never will I join with those who deny the Master-of-the-Name.' **1936** M. GOLDSTEIN *Thus Religion Grows* iii. 269 The Hasidim as well as the Mitnaggedim, both were confronted by the challenge of a new heaven and a new earth. **1964** S. BELLOW *Herzog* 139 She..seemed to be seeing the Old World—her father the famous *misnagid.*

mitochondrion (məitokǫ·ndriǫ̆n). *Biol.* Pl. **-chondria.** [a. G. *mitochondrion* (C. Benda 1898, in *Arch. f. Anat. u. Physiol.* (*Physiol. Abth.*) 397), f. Gr. μίτος thread + χονδρίον, dim. of χόνδρος granule or lump (of salt).] An organelle that is present (usu. in great numbers) in the cytoplasm of all cells with a true nucleus and primarily functions to store and release energy by the reactions of the Krebs cycle (see *KREBS).

1901 *Jrnl. R. Microsc. Soc.* 14 Meves believes that this term [sc. *Nebenkern*] should lapse, and himself employs for the separate granules Benda's term *mitochondria*, and for the *Nebenkern* which may be formed by their union, the term *mitochondrial corpuscle.* **1911, 1920** [see *CHONDRIOSOME]. **1949** *Amer. Jrnl. Physiol.* CLVII. 136 The residue..which contained only mitochondria and microsomes was transferred to a vial. **1962** *Science Survey* III. 169 Each mitochondrion is bounded by an outer limiting membrane, then there is a narrow space and then another membrane bounding an inner chamber. **1964** A. L. LEHNINGER *Mitochondrion* p. vii, It is now some fifteen years since the mitochondria were first recognized to be the 'power plants' of aerobic cells. **1970** *New Scientist* 24 Sept. 626/1 The amount of DNA in a chick liver cell mitochondrion..is only about 0·5 per cent of that in a bacterium. **1971** [see *KREBS].

So **mitocho·ndrial** *a.*, of or pertaining to a mitochondrion or to mitochondria.

1901 [see *MITOCHONDRION]. **1920** L. DONCASTER *Introd. Study Cytol.* ii. 23 Some investigators maintain..that every mitochondrial body arises only from a pre-existing one. **1962** *Lancet* 19 May 1056/1 Increased permeability of the mitochondrial membrane leads to the escape of enzymes and cofactors. **1970** *Sci. Amer.* Feb. 100/1 Heavy mitochondrial damage was followed by an almost total absence of dehydrogenase activity.

mitogenetic (məitodʒėne·tik), *a. Biol.* [f. as next + -GENETIC.] Mitogenic; applied *spec.* to a type of radiation supposed by some to be emitted by dividing cells and to stimulate mitosis in other tissues.

1927 *Biol. Abstr.* I. 1042/2 The blood through the admission of air sends out mitogenetic currents... The mitogenetic oxidation reaction is cared for through oxyhemoglobin. **1928** *Ibid.* II. 406/2 Experiments..lead the author [*sc.* A. Gurwitsch] to believe in the physical nature of what he terms mitogenetic rays. **1930** *Jrnl. Marine Biol. Assoc.* XVII. 65 Various authors have framed the hypothesis of a mitogenetic radiation emanating from cells in the act of division. Gurwitsch first of all pointed out the mitogenetic influence of cells of embryonic tissues. **1952** G. H. BOURNE *Cytol. & Cell Physiol.* (ed. 2) ii. 94 The school of Gurwitsch has..claimed that mitogenetic radiation is closely associated with many other forms of cellular activity.

mitogenic (məitodʒe·nik), *a. Biol.* [f. MITO(SIS + *-GENIC.] Inducing or stimulating mitosis. So **mi·togen,** a substance or agent which has a mitogenic effect.

1962 *Hereditas* XLVIII. 619 (*heading*) On the effect of mitogenic plant extracts (phyto-hemagglutinin) on human white blood cells cultivated in vitro. **1963** *Proc. 9th Congr. European Soc. Haematol.* II. I. 78 (*heading*) Factors stimulating cell division in cultured leucocytes. Chemical, serological and immunological studies on mitogens. **1970** *Nature* 26 Sept. 1351/1 When certain mitogenic agents are added to lymphocytes cultured in serum, the cells are activated to transform and divide. **1971** *Ibid.* 31 Dec. 508/2 Pokeweed mitogen is one of the plant lectins which..can be used to stimulate lymphocytes *in vitro.*

mitomycin (məitoməi·sin). *Biochem.* [f. *mito-* (perh. representing Gr. μίτος thread or MITOSIS, *MITOCHONDRION, etc.: the allusion is not explained by the (Japanese) authors of the name) + *-MYCIN.] An antibiotic active against some bacteria and tumour cells that is produced by the soil bacterium *Streptomyces cæspitosus*; also, any of the three (or more) slightly different molecular species (as those designated *mitomycin A, B,* and *C*) into which preparations of this antibiotic can be resolved.

1956 T. HATA et al. in *Jrnl. Antibiotics* (Tokyo) A. IX. 141 (*heading*) Mitomycin, a new antibiotic from Streptomyces. *Ibid.* 145 Mitomycins have a high antibacterial activity against gram positive and gram negative bacteria. **1958** *Antibiotics & Chemotherapy* VIII. *S*[*trepto-myces*] *caespitosus*, which produces mainly mitomycin A and B in some cultural conditions, produces mitomycin C exclusively under other conditions. **1968** [see *INDUCTION 9 d].

mitosis. Add: Pl. **mitoses** (-ō̆u·sīz). [First formed in Ger. by W. Flemming in *Zellsubstanz, Kern und Zelltheilung* (1882) xxiv. 376.] Substitute for def. of senses a and b: The process of nuclear division by which a cell nucleus gives rise to two daughter nuclei identical with the parent nucleus; an instance of this; commonly also used to refer to the whole process of mitotic cell division, i.e. division of the cytoplasm as well as the nucleus; also, a cell or nucleus undergoing this. (Earlier and later examples.)

1887 *Jrnl. R. Microsc. Soc.* 163 (*heading*) Showing mitosis in brain of tadpole. **1918** *Surg., Gynecol. & Obstetr.* XVIII. 205/2 These cells are large and mostly polyhedric...Mitoses are found, though rarely. **1937** C. D. DARLINGTON *Recent Adv. Cytol.* (ed. 2) i. 22 Nuclei divide by the characteristic process of mitosis in the course of which the whole nucleus, apart from the nucleoli, resolves itself into longitudinally split threads, the chromosomes. **1962** D. G. COGAN in A. Pirie *Lens Metabolism Rel. Cataract* 292 Although showing few mitoses normally, the lens epithelium may be activated into lively mitotic activity when stimulated by heat. **1970** AMBROSE & EASTY *Cell Biol.* i. 20 The actual process of cell division, however, known as mitosis, is remarkably similar for all cell types.

† **mitosome** (məi·tosōᵘm). *Cytology. Obs.* Also 9 **mitosoma.** [a. G. *mitosoma* (G. Platner 1889, in *Arch. f. mikrosk. Anat.* XXXIII. 199), f. Gr. μίτο-ς thread + σῶμα body.] (See quots.)

1891 *Jrnl. R. Microsc. Soc.* 461 The portion of the mitosoma which becomes attached to the nucleus becomes chromatic and wanders to the anterior end of the spermatozoon. **1895** G. W. FIELD in *Jrnl. Morphol.* XI. 237 In view of the fact that the term 'Nebenkern' has come to be applied to many sorts of intracellular structures..it seems best, since the history of the middle piece or 'Nebenkern' is now better understood, that this non-committal term..should be replaced by some term which gives a hint as to the nature of this body. Since the middle piece or 'Nebenkern' of the echinoderm spermatozoön is formed from the mitotic spindle, the term 'mitosome', introduced by Platner, has been adopted and will be used to designate the middle piece, = Nebenkern = *corpuscle accessoire* of other writers. **1920** L. DONCASTER *Introd. Study Cytol.* vii. 95 In the spermatocyte, as the cell enlarges, the mitochondrial bodies increase in size... In the young spermatid they unite to form a fairly compact mass near the nucleus at the side of the cell at which the tail will grow out. [*Note*] This mitochondrial mass ('mitosome') constitutes the 'Nebenkern' of some authors, but as the word has been used to designate the remains of the division-spindle.., the 'idiozome'..and other cell-structures, it is now dropping out of use. **1925** E. B. WILSON *Cell* (ed. 3) iv. 366 One of these [elements of doubtful nature] is the spindle-remnant, sometimes called the 'mitosome'... This body was believed by some earlier observers to play an important part in the sperm-formation, and was confused with the nebenkern or with the acroblast; but later studies seem to show that it disappears without taking any definite part in the sperm-formation. **1934** L. W. SHARP *Introd. Cytol.* (ed. 3) xiv. 218 In insects generally the chondriosomes form a single more or less compact body, the nebenkern (the mitosome of Gatenby).

mitotically, *adv.* (Examples.)

1896 *Jrnl. R. Microsc. Soc.* 494 The cells of the inner theca layer begin to divide mitotically. **1946** [see *AMITOTIC *a.*]. **1973** *Nature* 30 Mar. 299/3 The thymus is usually thought of as a staging house through which pass stem cells and their mitotically amplified products.

mitral, *a.* **2. b.** (Further examples.)

1872 *Half-Yearly Abstr. Med. Sci.* LV. 103 (*heading*) The physical signs of mitral stenosis. **1926** *Daily Colonist* (Victoria, B.C.) 14 Jan. 4/6 In 1921 the patient, a young girl, came up to the London Hospital suffering from mitral stenosis, or a gradual closing of one of the four valves of the heart. **1966** WRIGHT & SYMMERS *Systemic Path.* I. xxiv. 50/1 In mitral stenosis, two further complications may arise which still further burden the already overstressed heart:..arterial fibrillation, and..increasing incompetence of the valve with progressively greater regurgitation of blood into the left atrium during ventricular systole.

mitre, *sb.*¹ Add: **2. f.** A medieval type of woman's headwear resembling a bishop's mitre. Also *attrib.*

1877 *Encycl. Brit.* VI. 469/2 Some of the more popular of these strange varieties of head-gear have been distinguished as the 'horned', the 'mitre', [etc.]. **1906** H. DRUITT *Man. Costume* vi. 258 The next development shows the cauls curving outwards and upwards, and terminating above the head in a pair of horns. This form is called the *horned, lunar, mitre* or *heart* shaped head-dress according to the shape which it assumes. **1960** CUNNINGTON & BEARD *Dict. Eng. Costume* 136/2 Mitre head-dress.

‖ **Mitsein** (mi·tzəin). *Philos.* [ad. G. *mit* with + *sein* being.] A term used by Heidegger to express the concept of man's being in its relationship with others.

1955 J. MACQUARRIE *Existentialist Theol.* iv. 89 Thus 'being-in-the-world' implies 'being-with-others' (*Mitsein*). **1957** H. BARNES tr. *Sartre's Being & Nothingness* III. iii. 413 The very existence of this grammatical form [*sc.* the word *we*] necessarily refers us to a real experience of the *Mitsein.* **1963** *Philos.* XXXVIII. 275 The whole world of human *Mitsein* is regarded by M. Bastide as his province. **1966** A. MANSER *Sartre* vi. 97 The essence of relations between consciousnesses is not Mitsein (being together), it is conflict.

mitsumata (mi:tsuma·tă). [Japanese.] A deciduous shrub, *Edgeworthia papyrifera*, bearing clusters of fragrant yellow flowers, belonging to the family Thymelæaceæ, and native to China, although widely cultivated in Japan, where its bast fibre is used in the manufacture of paper. Also *attrib.*

1889 J. REIN *Industries of Japan* III. 402 Mitzu-mata (*Edgeworthia*) paper has also a distinctly marked yellow colour. **1891** B. H. CHAMBERLAIN *Things Japanese* (ed. 2) 334 Several plants and trees contribute their bark to the manufacture of Japanese paper... The one most easily recognised by the unlearned is the *Edgeworthia papyrifera*, which has the peculiarity that its branches always divide into three at every articulation, whence the Japanese name of *mitsu-mata*, or 'the three forks'. **1936** D. HUNTER *Papermaking Pilgrimage Japan, Korea & China* iii. 45 The so-called 'vellum'—that smooth, long-fibred, natural-toned paper sometimes used in the printing of fine books and etchings..is made largely from the bark of the mitsumata shrub. **1947** —— *Papermaking* (ed. 2) ii. 57 The origin of mitsumata (*Edgeworthia papyrifera*) as a papermaking material is uncertain, but there is a record stating that in the year 1597 a papermaking family was granted the privilege of gathering mitsumata bark in a certain locality of Japan. **1974** G. USHER *Dict. Plants used by Man* 223/2 *E*[*dgeworthia*] *papyrifera*... Cultivated for the bark fibres which are used, particularly in Japan to make a hand-made paper (Nepal Paper, Mitsumata Paper).

mitt. Add: **2. b.** *U.S.* A protective glove worn in baseball by the catcher or first baseman.

1902 *Sears Catal.* 326 Boys' Canvas Mitt, made of can-

vas throughout; a good, cheap mitt for boys; well stuffed. **1949** *Nat. Geogr. Mag.* June 738/1 On the ball field the Indians waved their mitts.

3. For *U.S. slang* read *slang* (orig. *U.S.*). Add earlier and later examples.

1896 ADE *Artie* xiii. 116, I thought them was gloves you had on. Gee, is them your mits? **1914** JOYCE *Dubliners* 74 He was also handy with the mits. **1940** R. CHANDLER *Farewell, my Lovely* ii. 12 'Freeze the mitts on the bar.' The barman and I put our hands on the bar. **1959** I. & P. OPIE *Lore & Lang. Schoolch.* x. 197 The commonest challenge is 'Put up your mitts'.

c. *the glad mitt*: a warm or friendly reception; = *glad hand* (*GLAD *a.* 4 e); *the frozen* (or *icy*) *mitt*: an unfriendly reception; rejection; the 'cold shoulder'. *slang.*

1904 'NO. 1500' *Life in Sing Sing* 255/2 *Glad mitt*, warm welcome. **1907** J. LONDON *Road* 187 The erstwhile hospitable farmers met us with the icy mit. **1925** FRASER & GIBBONS *Soldier & Sailor Words* 156 He tried to make up to me but I gave him the frozen mit. **1937** M. SHARP *Nutmeg Tree* ix. 111, I expected any number of black eyes, Julia darling, but not the frozen mitt. **1960** A. PRIOR in *Pick of Today's Short Stories* XI. 179 She'd have taken it and then handed me the frozen mitt.

d. *attrib.* and *Comb.*, as **mitt camp** *U.S. slang*, a palmist's or fortune-teller's establishment, tent, etc.; **mitt joint** *U.S. slang*, (*a*) (see quot. 1914); (*b*) = **mitt camp*; **mitt-reader** *U.S. slang*, a palmist; a fortune-teller.

1942 BERREY & VAN DEN BARK *Amer. Thes. Slang* § 466/5 *Mitt camp* or *joint*, a fortune-telling establishment. *Ibid.* § 626/7 *Mitt camp* or *joint*, a fortune teller's tent or booth. **1956** H. GOLD *Man who was not with It* (1965) i. 4 She would..take the tickets to Palmistry Pauline's mitt-camp. **1914** JACKSON & HELLYER *Vocab. Criminal Slang* 59 A 'mitt joint' is a gambling house where victims are 'steered' for fleecing by means of deceptively 'sure thing' hands. **1923** C. R. COOPER *Under Big Top* 60, I have seen a couple halt before a 'mitt joint' where a greasy Mexican or Syrian or anything else but a gypsy stands. **1942** Mitt joint [see *mitt camp* above]. **1928** *Amer. Speech* III. 414 *Mitt reader*, a palmist, or fortune teller. **1956** H. GOLD *Man who was not with It* (1965) xiv. 120 How do you know? You a mitt reader like your mother.

‖ **Mittagessen** (mi·tāge:sən). Also **Mittags-essen**, and with lower-case initial. [Ger.] In Germany: a midday meal; lunch.

1880 GEO. ELIOT *Let.* 11 July (1956) VII. 303 There is a magnificent drive to Baden which can be reached in seven hours (including time for the Mittagsessen and the rest). **1899** R. FRY *Let.* Oct. (1972) I. 174 The Galleries shut at the absurd hour of 3..in order that the officials may have some absurd meal, a *mittagsessen* or something. **1941** M. TREADGOLD *We couldn't leave Dinah* xv. 238 The heavy *mittagessen* upon which Germany nourishes young and old. **1972** *Sat. Rev.* (U.S.) 25 Mar. 72/1 The *Mittagessen* (lunch) always begins with soup.

Mittel-Europa (mi·t'l,yūᵊrōᵘ·pă). Also **Mittel Europa, Mitteleuropa.** [Ger.] Central Europe. Also *attrib.*

1918 M. J. DAVOREN tr. *Gettlich's German Grip on Russia* 24 It is in this combination of a community of the interests of Budapest with those of the financial circles of Berlin that the idea of the new politico-commercial *consortium*, known to-day by the name 'Mitteleuropa', arose. **1918** Z. N. PREEV *Russian Riddle* iii. 36 It would be worth her while to abandon..her grandiose plans of Mittel-Europa. **1931** *Times Lit. Suppl.* 9 Apr. 281/3 The glorification of the *Mittel-Europa* ideal which Frederick the Great failed to realize. **1950** A. CHRISTIE *Murder is Announced* v. 48 Very temperamental you'll find her. Mittel Europa refugee of some kind. **1956** AUDEN & KALLMAN *Magic Flute* (1957) 116 We'll never lack friends back in Mittel-Europa. **1971** C. FICK *Danziger Transcript* (1973) 29 He had a slight Mittel-Europa accent, but at Claridge's, who doesn't? **1975** J. SYMONS *Three Pipe Problem* xviii. 176 Would the totally unknown actress be able to resist the charm of Mitteleuropa?

Mittel-European (mi·t'l,yūᵊrōpī·ăn), *a.* and *sb.* [ad. G. *mittel-europäisch*, f. *mittel* middle.] **A.** *adj.* = **Middle-European* adj.

[**1937** WYNDHAM LEWIS *Blasting & Bombardiering* xii. 189 With his dramatic miteuropean accent he gave this suggestion such a rich Austrian welcome as no suggestion ever had before or since.] **1939** C. BEATON *My Royal Past* xiii. 143 The destined lot of *mittel*-European royalty. **1957** P. KEMP *Mine were of Trouble* x. 187 The sinister but intriguing personality of a Mittel-European barman known as Otto. **1959** J. DRUMMOND *Black Unicorn* xv. 110 The fringe of the fashionable area, where the big shops give way to little mittel-European establishments. **1974** *Times* 31 Dec. 7/3 The pretence of Mittel-European dilettantism.

B. *sb.* A native or inhabitant of central Europe.

1950 A. CHRISTIE *Murder is Announced* xi. 118, I expect Mitzi, our Mittel European, would love that. **1958** *Times* 24 July 5/3 A mittel-European exploding with conversation like a fire-cracker.

‖ **Mittelschmerz** (mi·t'lʃmẹ̄rts). *Gynæcology.* Also **mittelschmerz.** [G., lit. 'middle pain'.] Pain in the lower abdomen regularly experienced by some women between menstrual periods, perhaps related to the occurrence of ovulation.

1895 *Lancet* 28 Dec. 1625/1 Dr. J. Halliday Croom read a paper on So-called Mittelschmerz, sometimes called a form of dysmenorrhœa. **1942** MAZER & ISRAEL *Diagn. & Treatm. Menstrual Disorders* ix. 135 The pain undoubtedly emanates from the ovaries, since neither hysterectomy nor resection of the presacral nerve..eliminates *mittelschmerz*, but bilateral oophorectomy does. **1971** *Vogue* Nov. 60/2 Have intercourse as near ovulation as possible. This can be detected..by the pain that some women experience (Mittelschmerz). **1971** I. A. MCDONALD *Method Obstetr. & Gynaecol.* xiii. 300 Some females regularly have a spotting of blood on day 14 of the menstrual cycle... It may be associated with lower abdominal pain (*Mittelschmerz*).

mitten, *sb.* Add: **1. d.** (*c*) Handcuffs.

1880 G. WEBSTER in *Sc. Nat. Dict.* (1965) VI. 306/1 My lad was made fast an' a pair o' mittens clappit on wi' little mair adee. **1937** 'D. HUME' *Halfway to Horror* 3 'Mittens' are handcuffs; a padlock is a 'monkey'.

4. mitten crab (see quots.).

1934 *Times* 1 Feb. 17/5 If we want an English equivalent for the German *Wollhandkrabbe* it might be called the mitten crab. **1934** *Nature* 9 June 856/1 The pincer claws are clothed with long soft hair, and a writer in the *Times* has suggested 'mitten crab' as an appropriate name for it... The mitten crab must have been introduced into German rivers before 1912... In 1923 the species was found to be established in the..Elbe and was determined as *Eriocheir sinensis*. **1959** *Chambers's Encycl.* IX. 455/1 Mitten crab, a popular name applied to a greenish grapsoid crab, *Eriocheir sinensis*, with conspicuous brown tufts of long silky hairs on the pincers of the male.

Mitty[2] (mi·ti). Also **Walter Mitty.** [f. the name of Walter *Mitty*, hero of James Thurber's short story *The Secret Life of Walter Mitty* (in *New Yorker* (1939) 18 Mar.).] A person who indulges in day-dreams; one who imagines a more adventurous or enjoyable life for himself than he actually leads; the characteristics of such a person. Freq. *attrib.* or quasi-*adj.* Hence **Mittye·sque, Mi·ttyish, Mitty-like** *adjs.*

1950 B. SCHULBERG *Disenchanted* (1951) xvii. 313 I've had daydreams of how I'd come back. Walter Mitty stuff about arriving in style. **1953** *Sunday Times* 14 June 8/4 The Mitty me, I notice, will risk his life for a trifle, but never gets his hands dirty. **1958** *Times Lit. Suppl.* 16 May 274/1 Greave takes refuge from the horrid realities of life in Mittyesque fantasies, pretending he is a high-powered American salesman. **1960** *Harper's Bazaar* Apr. 125/1 The average motoring man is..a visionary, a Walter Mitty locked in a private world of fantasy... Vintage cars seldom fail to spark off the Mitty in a man. **1960** *Sunday Express* 12 June 14/5 Women..live in a dream world of their own imagining—a Walter Mitty-ish 'Other Life'. **1961** *John o' London's* 28 Sept. 363/3 I'm in the delirious position of being able to indulge my Mitty-like obsession. **1968** S. BRITTAN *Left or Right* v. 106 The whole Walter Mitty idea of a private line from Downing Street to the White House. **1972** *Guardian* 11 July 10/5 Both men are Mittyesque failures. **1974** N. FREELING *Dressing of Diamond* 33 Bernard was doing his hospitality act... This was no Mitty performance.

‖ **mitzvah** (mi·tsvā). *Judaism.* Also **misva, mitsva(h), mitzwa.** Pl. **misvot, mitswoth, mitzvot, mitzwoth.** [Heb. *miṣwāh* commandment.] A precept; something which should be done; hence a good deed done as a religious duty, without expectation of earthly reward. Cf. *BARMITZVAH.

1650 E. CHILMEAD tr. *Leon Modena's Hist. Rites of Jews* 1. i. 2 Precepts of the Written Law..they call.. *Mizuoth de Draita*, that is to say, *Præcepta Legis*, Precepts of the Law. The second sort are..*Mizuoth de Rabbanan*,..Precepts of the Wise men. **1753** *Jewish Ritual* 33 All the eight Cakes together, for the Service of both Nights, are call'd *Mitzwoth*, i.e. the Statutes. **1831** *Ascamot, or Laws & Regulations Jewish Congregation* vii. 52 If these three *Misvot* as well as the *Misva* of saying the *Zemirot*, shall have been given..it shall not be given to any other. **1893** I. ZANGWILL *Childr. Ghetto* (ed. 3) I. iii. 41 *Mitzvah* is a 'portmanteau-word'. It means a commandment and a good deed, the two conceptions being regarded as interchangeable. **1932** L. GOLDING *Magnolia St.* I. ii. 33 To break some of the less severe laws is almost accounted a *mitzvah*, a pious duty. **1959** W. L. GRESHAM *Houdini* xxi. 154 To Harry a good deed was something to be done quietly: 'So when you do a *mitzvah* you don't take along a brass band.' **1973** *Jewish Chron.* 2 Feb. 40/2 'Neither,' he adds scornfully, 'do we give out mitzvot according to money or position or influence.' **1973** *Synagogue Light* Sept. 11/1 There is great apprehension as to the meaning and message of this act of removing the shoe, which forms an essential part in the right and mitzvah of *Chalitzah*.

mivvy (mi·vi). *slang.* [Origin uncertain; perh. a corruption of MARVEL *sb.* The three senses may not be connected.] **1.** A marble.

1856 *N. & Q.* 5 Apr. 283/2 *Mivvies*, marbles. **1917** H. H. RICHARDSON *Fortunes Richard Mahony* I. iv. 33 You were always a good one at striking a bargain, my boy! What about: 'Four mivvies for an alley!'

2. A contemptuous term for a woman; the landlady of a lodging-house.

1881 *Punch* 10 Sept. 110/1 Lor' bless yer, they don't knaw the ropes, these old mivvies don't, more than a mug. **1887** *Punch* 10 Sept. 111/1 And talk about stodge! Jest you arsk the old mivvey as caters for me at the crib where I lodge. **1892** E. J. MILLIKEN *'Arry Ballads* 13/2 Bare-armed old mivvies you meet spread out pink in a theatre stall. **1923** J. MANCHON *Le Slang* 195 *Mivvy*, femme.

3. A person who is adept at something; a 'marvel'.

1906 E. PUGH *Spoilers* xv. 162 He's a mivvy at makin' things easy. **1959** 'O. MILLS' *Stairway to Murder* xi. 121 He's a mivvy with anything like that.

Miwok (mī·wǫk, məi·wǫk). [Native name.] A Penutian Indian people of California; a member of this tribe; also, the language spoken by the tribe. Also *attrib.* or as *adj.*

1877 S. POWERS in *Contrib. N. Amer. Ethnol.* III. 346 By much the largest nation in California, both in population and in extent of territory, is the Miwok, whose ancient dominion extended from the snow-line of the Sierra Nevada to the San Joaquin River, and from the Cosumnes to the Fiesno. **1916** *Univ. California Publ. Amer. Archaeol. & Ethnol.* XII. iv. 141 With the Miwok the moiety has no subdivisions. *Ibid.* 142 That totemic symptoms of one sort or another are present in the Miwok organization cannot be denied. **1949** *Los Angeles Times* 10 Apr. II. 5/2 The name Yosemite was given to this valley by the Miwoks. **1964** GOULD & KOLB *Dict. Social Sci.* 436/1 A Miwok couple about to marry endogamously. **1966** C. F. & F. M. VOEGELIN *Map N. Amer. Indian Lang.* (*caption*) Miwok-Costanoan Family 1. Sierra Miwok. 2. Coast-Lake Miwok. **1972** *Language* XLVIII. 847, 6b is given..by Sedlak for ..Miwok, Mongol (Dagor),..and Siona. **1973** *Black Panther* 28 Apr. 10/1 He had come to participate in the Tuolumne Acorn Festival, an annual traditional ceremony of his people, the Miwok Indians.

mix, *sb.*[2] Add: **1. a.** (Further examples.) Also, a number of ingredients mixed together, or intended for mixing; *spec.* the prepared ingredients of a cake, etc., sold ready for cooking; more generally, the proportion of different constituents that make up a product, plan, policy, etc.; a combination of various components into an integrated whole.

1912 L. & M. GREENBAUM *Pract. Dentistry* xxvii. 457 It is best to subject the mass to the least amount of stirring conducive to a homogeneous mix. **1922** MOJONNIER & TROY *Technical Control of Dairy Products* xiii. 276 Ice cream made from mix No. 9 will feel about 12·00 per cent warmer to the tongue than ice cream made from mix No. 1. **1938**, etc. [see *cake-mix* s.v. *CAKE *sb.* 9]. **1945** B. MACDONALD *Egg & I* (1946) 66, I could use automatic biscuit mix for the crust. **1959** *Life* (Internat. ed.) 13 Apr. 20/2 The new term is 'mix'. There is, says the Administration, an adequate 'mix' of forces to maintain our deterrent. **1962** *Listener* 29 Mar. 579/2 When the egg mix is light and foamy add it to the sauce. **1962** *Times* 26 Apr. 9/5 (*headline*) Canada may ban food mix sales. **1962** L. DEIGHTON *Ipcress File* xviii. 110 A bottle of Scotch, gin, some assorted mixes. **1964** M. MCLUHAN *Understanding Media* (1967) v. 60 Oral societies are made up of people differentiated..by their unique emotional mixes. *Ibid.* 64 Chaplin ..hit upon the wondrous media mix of ballet and film. **1966** [see *JERSEY[1] 1]. **1967** *Daily Tel.* 17 May 17/7 Without sufficient statistics on the question of socially mixed entry to public schools, the committee believes it impossible to induce artificially a 'social mix'. **1967** *Times Rev. Industry* Aug. 16/2 Retailing strategy will probably go on trying to maximize interest in stores by an optimum mix of heavily advertised manufacturer-branded lines and an increasing proportion of housebrand lines. **1970** *Daily Tel.* 9 Apr. 36/5 The mix of dancing, cabaret, drinking and gaming created an undesirable temptation to young people. **1971** *Guardian* 9 June 13/1 Alcoholic mixes like bitter lemon. **1971** M. MCCARTHY *Birds of America* 31 First a cake made with a mix and then a real one. **1972** *Publishers Weekly* 6 Mar. 25/1 In publishing, I think you have to have a good mix, and not try to reach just one segment of the population, but to cover all segments. **1972** *Guardian* 5 Aug. 11/8 By expelling the Russians he [*sc.* Sadat] has drastically altered the strategic mix.

c. Add to def.: *spec.* (*a*) a state of confusion; a mess or muddle; (*b*) a fight. (Add earlier and later examples.)

1841 S. BAMFORD *Passages in Life of Radical* I. xv. 94, I had expected being conducted to London alone, and certainly was not prepared for a mix-up with these men. **1913** *Chums* 25 Jan. 361/2 Then for a full minute the two engaged in a 'mix-up'. **1913** *Collier's* 1 Feb. 27 (*caption*) A bad mix-up. **1919** [see *GOY]. **1923** WODEHOUSE *Inimitable Jeeves* viii. 85 When the driver started making a fuss, there was a bit of a mix-up. **1932** J. C. POWYS *Glastonbury Romance* (1933) II. xxiii. 737 God! What a mix-up it all is. **1971** D. E. WESTLAKE *I gave at the Office* (1972) 139 As soon as the mix-up was brought to light I was freed.

2. *Cinemat.* and *Broadcasting.* The action or result of mixing two pictures or two sounds (see *MIX *v.* 7 a).

1922 [see *FADE *sb.*[1] 2]. **1932** *Wireless World* 16 Mar. 276/1 A sound-mix, which corresponds to a picture-mix (when the picture dissolves into another picture) is done by starting with one microphone set at its gain figure and the second microphone set at zero gain. *Ibid.*, For a smooth mix, the two knobs must be turned as nearly as possible at the same speed. **1960** [see *FADE *sb.*[1] 2]. **1961** *Listener* 2 Nov. 716/1 If phrases overlap musically the visual counterpart is a mix; and..a mix between two different angles on the same performer is usually upsetting to the viewer. **1962** A. NISBETT *Technique Sound Studio* ix. 152 It is the way that fades and mixes are carried out.. that distinguishes the polished, finished recording from the one that sounds amateur.

mix, *v.* Add: **1. g.** Colloq. phr. *to mix one's drinks*: to drink various kinds of alcoholic liquor in succession; *spec.* to become intoxicated by drinking both wine and liquor made from grain. Also *ellipt.* and *absol.*

1898 J. D. BRAYSHAW *Slum Silhouettes* 238 'E was gettin' a bit beargered—not that 'e'd 'ad so much, but 'e would keep mixin'; first one thing an' then annuver. **1933** J. B. PRIESTLEY *Wonder Hero* vii. 269 Had a thick night last night... Mixed 'em a bit. Always a mistake—mixing

'em. **1950** G. Greene *Third Man* ii. 13 If you stayed around in a hotel lounge, sooner or later..one mixed one's drinks. **1961** J. B. Priestley *Saturn over Water* iii. 35, I mixed my drinks too much last night—I feel better now.

h. Slang phr. *to mix it*: to fight or quarrel; to start fighting; freq. const. *with*; also, to cause trouble. So *to mix it up*: to fight vigorously.

1900 A. Conan Doyle *Green Flag* 165 This round must decide it. 'Mix it oop, lad; mix it oop!' the iron-men whooped. **1905** C. H. Day *Actress & Clerk* xv. 149 As Hard Knox would have himself described in the technique of the ring, the men 'mixed it'. **1906** H. Green *At Actors' Boarding House* 359 They're goin' to mix it up. The little un'll win out, see if she don't. My eye! dames is allus fightin'. **1918** E. M. Roberts *Flying Fighter* 91 He grew angry and we mixed it. I gave him a black eye. **1919** Wodehouse *Coming of Bill* (1920) II. xiv. 239, I thought I could stay around and part 'em if they got to mixing it. **1941** E. C. Shepherd *Mil. Aeroplane* 14 Many a German bomber in daylight raids over England has accepted failure rather than 'mix it' with the British fighters which came to dispute with it. **1941** *Time* 8 Dec. 22/1 The tanks ..face the approaching column... Then they begin to mix it up. **1945** *Aeronautics* Feb. 50/3 Pilots took full advantage of every opportunity of 'mixing it' with the Hun. **1950** P. Tempest *Lag's Lexicon* 136 *Mix it, to*, to put one man against another. To make trouble. **1958** F. Norman *Bang to Rights* 28 The screw who's giving evidence against you starts telling a load of bleeding lies and mixing it for you. **1973** D. Lees *Rape of Quiet Town* vi. 92 These lads don't want to fight for nothing. If they can get away without mixing it they will.

4. a. *to mix in with*: delete † and add later examples. Also *to mix in*: to start or join in a fight (*slang*). Cf. 4 c in Dict. and *1 h in Suppl.

1870 J. P. Smith *Widow Goldsmith's Daughter* vi. 69 Of course they couldn't expect to mix in with the rich children. **1895** M. Halstead *100 Bear Stories* 117 Elk killing didn't seem half so great an achievement as it had before the bear had mixed in with the proceedings. **1912** R. A. Wason *Friar Tuck* xxi. 158 'Well, what if he did shoot,' sez Slim, 'we wouldn't have to mix in, would we?' **1971** Wodehouse *Much Obliged, Jeeves* ix. 89 If you see any more gnats headed in her direction, hold their coats and wish them luck, but restrain the impulse to mix in.

d. To be sociable.

1816 Jane Austen *Emma* III. vii. 113 Mr. and Mrs. Elton..showed no unwillingness to mix, and be..agreeable. **1905** *Dialect Notes* III. 88 He doesn't mix much. **1940** A. Christie *Sad Cypress* I. vi. 83 Rather a funny crowd of people, but I don't mix much. You told me once that I wasn't a good mixer. **1965** M. Spark *Mandelbaum Gate* I. 7 He was in no great hurry for the flat, preferring hotel life where one need not mix.

7. *Cinemat.* and *Broadcasting*. **a.** *trans.* To combine (two pictures or sounds) temporarily by fading one out as the other is faded in; freq. *intr.*, to pass from one picture *to* another in this way.

1922 L. C. Macbean *Kinematogr. Studio Technique* ix. 82 On occasions..it is necessary..to fade or mix titles into a scene to which they relate. **1929** *Radio Times* 8 Nov. 389/1 The D.C. Panel..which allows a producer.. to mix and fade speech, music, and sound-effects. **1953** K. Reisz *Technique Film Editing* I. i. 25 From the scene in the present, Griffith simply mixed to the earlier scene and then mixed back again. **1961** G. Millerson *Technique Television Production* xvi. 305 Mixing opposite directions of movement can sometimes arouse feelings of expansion or impact. **1962** *Listener* 6 Dec. 983/1 Mr Cooper uses..the language and grammar of film-making in his radio plays. He will cut sharply from scene to scene; or he will mix from one scene into the next.

b. *trans.* To combine (two or more sound signals) into one, either linearly, by adding together a fraction of each in a mixer (sense *2 b), or non-linearly, by causing one signal to modulate a second in a mixer (sense *2 c).

1928 [see *balance *v.* 4]. **1931** C. Dreher in L. Cowan *Recording Sound for Motion Pict.* xxiv. 345 He also mixes the output of the microphones when several are used. **1958** W. F. Lovering *Radio Communication* viii. 172 Suppressor-grid control may be used to 'mix' two signals to produce a modulated output. **1962** J. H. & P. J. Reyner *Radio Communication* ix. 364 A pentode valve was used as an anode bend detector.., while a small triode, assembled round the same cathode, generated the local oscillation, and the two were mixed by using a common bias resistor in the cathode circuit. **1974** *Encycl. Brit. Macropædia* XII. 549/1 When several microphones are used on the set, their outputs are often mixed and reproduced on a single film or tape.

mixed, *ppl. a.* Add: **3.** (Earlier and later examples of *mixed motives*.)

1818 M. Edgeworth *Let.* 13 Oct. (1971) 114 There were mixed motives I grant... Lord Byron was distressed for money. To be sure he could have had other fortunes but then there was vanity. **1939** L. MacNeice *Autumn Jrnl.* iii. 18 None of our hearts are pure, we always have mixed motives.

6. b. *Phonetics.* Of a vowel sound = *central *a.* 1 d.

1867 [see *back *a.* 1 c]. **1890** H. Sweet *Primer Spoken Eng.* 4 In the vowels we distinguish three horizontal positions, or degrees of retraction of the tongue: back, mixed, front. **1918** D. Jones *Outl. Eng. Phonetics* 17 An example of a mixed vowel is the vowel in *bird*. **1966** M. Pei *Gloss. Ling. Terminol.* 164 *Mixed vowel*, Migliorini's term for middle vowel.

11. mixed bag, a heterogeneous collection of people, objects, items, etc.; **mixed bathing,** simultaneous bathing in the same place by people of both sexes; **mixed bed,** a flower bed containing an assortment of plants, arranged in irregular groups; **mixed blessing,** a blessing (Blessing *vbl. sb.* 4) that has unpleasant elements in it; **mixed blood,** (*a*) descent from two or more races; (*b*) a person of mixed descent; **mixed border,** in a garden, a long bed containing a mixture of hardy herbaceous plants and shrubs, hardy and half-hardy plants, bulbs, etc.; **mixed breed,** a cross-breed; **mixed-celled** *a. Path.*, involving or containing cells of more than one kind; **mixed company,** (*a*) company comprising both men and women; (*b*) company comprising people of different classes or characters; **mixed crystal** *Physical Chem.*, a homogeneous crystal formed of more than one crystalline substance; **mixed economy,** an economic system containing both private and state enterprise; **mixed farming,** farming which combines the raising of livestock and the cultivation of arable crops; so *mixed farm*; **mixed flow,** flow (in a turbine or the like) that consists of two or more types (usu. radial and axial) in succession; usu. *attrib.* (with hyphen); **mixed grill,** a dish consisting of several different grilled or fried items of food; also *fig.*; **mixed language,** a language made up of a mixture of elements from two or more languages; a creolized language; cf. *mischsprache; **mixed-manned** *a.*, pertaining to or designating a military force comprising people of more than one nationality; so *mixed manning*; **mixed marriage** (earlier and later examples); (*b*) a marriage between persons of different races; also *transf.* and *fig.*; **mixed media,** (*a*) = **mixed technique*; (*b*) an entertainment, work of art, etc., which combines various media; = *multi-media *a.*; also *attrib.* or as *adj.*; **mixed-pressure** *a. Engin.*, applied to a steam turbine powered by both high- and low-pressure steam; **mixed technique** (see quots.).

1936 C. C. R. Murphy (*title*) A mixed bag. **1943** K. Tennant *Ride on Stranger* (1968) v. 47 This mixed bag began, not ill-naturedly, to re-arrange itself in the seating. **1973** A. Behrend *Samarai Affair* i. 13 Representatives of the press, a mixed bag in age, but not in sex. **1901** *Graphic* 31 Aug. 268/3 The case against mixed bathing has passed into the academic or empty stage. **1930** *New Statesman* 27 Dec. 356/1 He..could obtain any sum he pleased for writing on any subject he pleased, from the League of Nations to the ethics of mixed bathing. **1964** M. Laski in S. Nowell-Smith *Edwardian England* iv. 167 Bexhill where mixed bathing has just [*sc.* circa 1901] been introduced, though the custom will quickly spread. **1871** W. Robinson *Hardy Flowers* iii. 13 A mixed bed, carefully arranged as to the height, and tastefully as to the quality and disposition of the contents. In this kind of bed I should have no band or circle whatever, but simply a careful following out of the mixed principle. **1873** *Young Englishwoman* May 238/1 We hope this year to see a great improvement in the bedding system—mixed beds introduced in the place of those of one sort of plant, and of one colour. **1933** *Discovery* Oct. 309/2 The introduction of European influences may prove a mixed blessing. **1960** *News Chron.* 21 Sept. 6/3 In theory it was a Good Thing... In practice it turned out a mixed blessing. **1973** *Guardian* 16 June 11/3 Mr Duggan regards Mr Bloom's twin tub machine..as a very mixed blessing; a machine..which.. uses the same lot of suds time and time again. **1817** S. Brown *Western Gazetteer* 244 About one half of the Cherokee nation are of mixed blood by intermarriages with the white people. **1858** Thoreau in *Atlantic Monthly* Aug. 306/2 The two mixed bloods..went off up the river. **1935** Huxley & Haddon *We Europeans* i. 23 If a Scottish or Irish clan is of 'mixed blood', what likelihood is there of purity of descent among the millions that make up the population of any great modern nation? **1960** *Press* (Vancouver) Dec. 13 A new and dominant element, the mixed bloods, descended from French and Scottish fathers and Indian mothers. **1963** A. Lubbock *Austral. Roundabout* 125 The largest..group of Aborigines are those, both full and mixed bloods, who have been completely detribalized... There is a fourth group of mixed-blood Aborigines. **1973** *Guardian* 20 June 11/3 The left-overs of the Korean war—the mixed-blood children fathered and then deserted by GIs... Today only 5 per cent of children placed by Harry Holt's [adoption] agency are mixed-bloods. **1868** D. Thomson *Handy Bk. Flower Garden* xii. 326 A mixed border of hardy and half-hardy plants.. would be effective anywhere. **1871** W. Robinson *Hardy Flowers* i. 5 The mixed border is capable of infinite variation as to plan as well as to variety of subjects. The most interesting variety is that composed of hardy herbaceous plants, bulbs, and alpine plants. **1899** G. Jekyll *Wood & Garden* xvi. 200, I have a rather large..mixed border of hardy flowers. **1903** W. Robinson *Alpine Flowers* (ed. 3) I. 34 The mixed-border system rightly done enables us to cultivate..many of the more vigorous alpine plants as edgings. **1957** C. Lloyd *Mixed Border* i. 11 The mixed border stands mid-way between two extremes: the shrubbery on the one hand and the herbaceous border on the other. **1970** P. Coats *Flowers in Hist.* 39 'Mixed border' is the fashionable phrase, today, for a border of herbaceous plants with a backing of shrubs. **1974** A. Scott-James *Sissinghurst* xiii. 137 At its [*sc.* a wall's] foot is a mixed border..planted with roses, shrubs, herbaceous flowers and irises. **1775** in *South Carolina Hist. & Geneal. Mag.* (1916) XVII. 99 Breakfasting with his mixed breed daughters. **1789** P. Thicknesse *Year's Journey* (ed. 3) II. xlv. 107 If a male or female of this species [*sc.* Orang Outang] were to cohabit with an European of the contrary sex, they would..produce a mixed breed. **1838** H. Colman *1st Rep. Agric. Mass.* (Mass. Agric. Survey) 53, I have had some of the full-blood and some of the mixed breed. **1908** *Practitioner* Feb. 235 Leucocythaemia..may be qualified by such descriptive titles as mixed-celled leucocythaemia..or lymphocytic leucocythaemia. **1964** S. Duke-Elder *Parsons' Dis. Eye* (ed. 14) xxv. 369 The cells [of a melanoma of the choroid] are usually spindle-shaped; they may be cylindrical or palisade-like, arranged in columns or around blood vessels, or even endothelial in appearance; most tumours are mixed-celled. **1816** Jane Austen *Emma* II. xvii. 329 Walk half-a-mile to another man's house, for the sake of being in mixed company till bed-time. **1820** Hazlitt in *London Mag.* Sept. 253 The conversation of authors..is better than any other. That of mixed company becomes utterly intolerable. **1901** G. B. Shaw *Three Plays for Puritans* 305 As far as my social experience goes (and I have kept very mixed company) there is no class in English society in which a good deal of Drinkwater pronunciation does not pass unchallenged save by the expert phonetician. **1973** A. Broinowski *Take One Ambassador* ix. 131 Nance Donnelly..objected ..to jokes about sex in mixed company. It was alright, a bit of dirt between men... But not with ladies present. **1892** *Jrnl. Chem. Soc.* LXII. I. 265 (*heading*) Solubility of mixed crystals, especially of two isomorphous substances. **1916** R. H. Rastall *Agric. Geol.* i. 4 Many of the most important rock-forming minerals are not pure chemical compounds; they are to be regarded rather as mixtures of various compounds possessing the property of isomorphism; in other words they are mixed crystals. **1952** T. L. Tippell tr. *Guinier's X-Ray Crystallogr. Technol.* viii. 207 There are substances which can never be classified; these are mixed crystals (solid solutions) whose unit cell size varies continuously with their composition. **1963** C. R. Berry et al. in J. J. Gilman *Art & Sci. Growing Crystals* xii. 229 Mixed crystals of AgCl and AgBr..have been grown. **1938** *Encycl. Brit. Bk. of Year* 171/2 Under this mixed economy there is a large and developed system of trade unionism among producers, and another..system of co-operative societies among consumers. **1949** E. Estorick *Stafford Cripps* xix. 362 Cripps' role as the 'master planner' of Britain's mixed economy' now had its international complement. **1973** *Guardian* 1 June 12/2 Neither Lonrho's shareholders nor Labour's fundamentalists provide an argument for abandoning the mixed economy. **1892** W. E. Swanton *Notes on N.Z.* ii. 89 The farm upon which, as in England, both sheep and cattle are carried and also crops are grown..is what is generally called a 'mixed farm'. **1917** C. S. Orwin *Determination of Farming Costs* ii. 13 The analytical method is probably more useful in connexion with the highly-developed mixed farms of this country. **1942** *E. African Ann. 1941–2* 128/2 Friends who own a mixed farm ask us over. The first signs of their successful management are the calves... This is also a most successful pyrethrum farm. **1973** *Country Life* 15 Mar. 713/2 In the southern region of England..the average price of mixed farms of 10–49 acres with vacant possession..rose to £915 an acre. **1872** *Trans. Illinois Dept. Agric.* IX. 66 The majority of farmers, fruit-growers or others, generally succeed best by what is called mixed farming. **1908** Kipling *Lett. to Family* vi. 52 Providence..did not intend everlasting wheat in this section [in Canada]... Are you interested in mixed farming? **1913** W. K. Harris *Outback in Austral.* xxiv. 169 The district is an ideal one for 'mixed farming' (wheat and sheep). **1959** A. McLintock *Descr. Atlas N.Z.* p. xiv, Typical of the [Canterbury] plains is the patchwork of fields, indicative of a system of mixed farming, with supplementary fodder crops being necessary for stock. **1889** Mixed-flow [see *axial *a.* 4]. **1958** *Engineering* 21 Mar. 376/1 The runner vane shape is of particular importance, especially in mixed-flow machines, where the vanes are three-dimensional surfaces. At present it is possible only in the case of axial-flow machines to define runner vane shapes in a systematic way. **1969** *Trans. Inst. Engin. & Shipbuilders Scotl.* CXII. 221 (*heading*) Mixed flow pumps and fans. **1913** W. Pett-Ridge (*title*) Mixed grill. **1922** A. Huxley *Mortal Coils* 201 'Two mixed grills,' I said..to the waiter. **1959** *Good Food Guide* 205 The best dishes are such things as sauté river trout, mixed grill and cold turkey. **1973** 'D. Halliday' *Dolly & Starry Bird* xvii. 258 The whip..was pointing to me. I was wondering, if I got marked like a mixed grill, whether Charles would still love me. **1973** *Times Lit. Suppl.* 21 Dec. 1555/3 The audience will be a mixed-grill of faculty, students, alumni, businessmen, and perhaps a few who have simply wandered in from the rain. **1888** H. Sweet *Hist. Eng. Sounds* 55 A very intimate mixture of two languages is always a prelude to the complete extinction of the weaker one, and this is why few..of these thoroughly mixed languages become permanently fixed. **1922** O. Jespersen *Lang.* xi. 224 These [pidgin] languages are not 'mixed languages' in the proper sense of that term. **1932** W. L. Graff *Lang.* II. x. 390 In several instances English used by people of an entirely different linguistic type results in a mixed or creolized language, the best known example being the so-called *pidgin English* of the Far East. **1972** R. Anttila *Introd. Historical & Compar. Ling.* xiii. 171 The various kinds of borrowing, that is, vocabulary, adstratum phonetics, and syntax, have led to the notion of a *mixed language*. **1963** *Economist* 16 Mar. 980/3 The mixed-manned, mixed-money nuclear force that Mr Merchant is..trying to create. **1964** *Ann. Reg. 1963* 28 On June 4 Admiral C. V. Ricketts..arrived in London to sell the mixed-manned fleet to a reluctant Mr Thorneycroft. **1963** *Times* 11 June 13/6, I fail to understand the fuss about mixed manning for the proposed Nato nuclear surface fleet. **1698–9** Mixed marriage [see World *sb.* 4 b]. **1829** K. H. Digby *Broad Stone of Honour: Godefridus* xviii. 212 They are the last to admit those monstrous and impious plans..which divide the children of mixed marriages, by training some to receive as truth, what others are to protest against as error. **1961** C. McCullers *Clock without Hands* ix. 178 The conditions of the Negro in the North are appalling—mixed marriages, nowhere to live and lay his head. **1962** *Sunday Times* 8 July 32/5 David Franklin's libretto reinterprets the Orpheus legend in terms of a mixed marriage between a white composer and

a coloured cabaret-star turned opera-singer. 1966 *New Statesman* 15 Apr. 548/3 In this mixed marriage, she brings her talent from the world of working-girl and art student, weds it to the dandy showmanship that goes with a certain kind of aristocracy. 1970 J. Brown *Un-melting Pot* vii. 105 Even mixed marriages between Jamaicans and Barbadians. 1972 *Listener* 21 Dec. 854/3 They understand very well the power of the Catholic Church, and the processes by which it is maintained: clerical control of the educational system, the mixed-marriage laws and the preservation of high fertility rates. 1962 R. G. Haggar *Dict. Art Terms* 214/2 *Mixed media*, painting with water colors and paste, Indian ink, oil color, crayon, or some similar combination. 1970 Burton & Lane *New Directions* iii. 66 The most extensive development of mixed media work are the Theatre Folk Ballads which Charles Parker has developed. 1972 G. F. Brommer *Drawing* iv. 49 Paul Klee experimented freely with mixed media, as did his contemporaries in the German Bauhaus. 1972 *Guardian* 24 June 9/2 The newer, mixed-media work using a lot of sound, space, smell, and participation. 1973 *Sunday Times* 28 Oct. 37/1 (Advt.), Don't miss Contemporary Dance Theatre in Robert Cohan's *Stages*! A mixed media dance production with Bob Downes open music. 1909 *Engineering* 5 Feb. 198/1 A turbine of what is called a mixed-pressure type, having high-pressure stages, in which the live steam may..keep the turbine running during the periods of insufficient supply of exhaust steam. 1929 T. M. Naylor *Steam Turbines* i. 9 Mixed pressure turbines use both high-pressure and exhaust or low-pressure steam. Often the exhaust steam supplied is intermittent, and so to obtain constant power from the turbine, high-pressure steam is admitted and it is controlled by a governor to enable the turbine to work at constant power. 1971 B. Scharf *Engin. & its Lang.* xv. 209 We may..distinguish between straight condensing turbines, pass-out turbines, back-pressure turbines, exhaust turbines and mixed-pressure turbines. 1935 E. Neuhaus tr. *Doerner's Materials of Artist* v. 240 Painting with tempera into wet resin-oil color (mixed technique). This technique is better suited to a deliberate, stylistic type of painting. 1969 R. Mayer *Dict. Art Terms & Techniques* 246/1 *Mixed technique*, in painting, the technique of combining tempera colors with paints of an oleoresinous medium... Mixed technique first became known in the U.S. and Britain in 1934.

b. In Combs. used *attrib.*

1908 J. M. Sullivan *Criminal Slang* 16 *Mixed-ale oration*, a cheap political harangue containing bad English grammar. *Mixed-ale philosopher*, a drunken know it all. 1948 *Penguin Music Mag.* June 49 The best members of these choirs..incorporated in..a secular mixed-voice choir. 1956 *Railway Mag.* Nov. 729/2 Many Drummond mixed-traffic 4-4-0 tender engines were tried on this route. 1963 *Guardian* 28 Jan. 7/4 Everyone asks Mr Morris..how mixed-ability classes affect the number of grammar school entrances. 1963 *Daily Tel.* 25 June 1/1 President Kennedy and Dr. Adenauer agreed in Bonn to-night that the proposed mixed-crew NATO nuclear force was 'a good instrument for serving all members of the alliance in combining their defence efforts'. 1964 *Economist* 17 Oct. 228/2 A.. contribution to the mixed-fleet command. 1969 *Jane's Freight Containers 1968–69* 444 A racing Mini being loaded into a mixed-traffic, British United Airways, VC 10. 1971 *Guardian* 17 Sept. 1/5 A delegation of six mixed-race Rhodesians. 1974 *Times* 21 May 3/1 Some teachers found that their brighter pupils started slacking when they were put in mixed-ability classes.

c. mixed up, mixed-up, involved, embroiled, intermingled; (mentally) confused, unbalanced, neurotic; hence **mixed-up-ness**, confusion. Cf. Mix *v.* 6.

1862 Queen Victoria *Let.* 15 Jan. in R. Fulford *Dearest Mama* (1968) 41, I only want your advice—not to get you further mixed up. 1884 'Mark Twain' *Huck. Finn* xlii. 432 Aunt Sally she was one of the mixed-upest looking persons I ever see. 1888 'R. Boldrewood' *Robbery under Arms* II. viii. 144 How were any police..to keep the run of a few men..among such a mixed-up mob? 1903 H. James *Ambassadors* vi. xv. 206 How comes Chad so mixed up, anyway? 1927 H. T. Lowe-Porter tr. *T. Mann's Magic Mountain* I. iv. 123 'A fine mixed-up state of affairs,' said Hans Castorp. 1937 *New Yorker* 23 Jan. 12/1 M. Dali, standing alone and thinking dark, mixed-up thoughts. 1939 D. Parker *Here Lies* 61 I've been all sort of mixed up to-day... Everything so strange. 1945 G. Endore *Methinks the Lady* (1947) xi. 264 Such confusion, such mental mixed-up-ness, occurs at times in all of us. 1955, etc. [see *crazy *a.* 4 f]. 1966 J. Bingham *Double Agent* x. 157 Poor damned old mixed-up queer. 1967 A. Laski *Seven Other Years* xi. 154 It wasn't even as if she had made some kind of distinction between God and Christ and seen One as protecting her and the Other being Them: just a general mixed-upness. 1973 C. Bonington *Next Horizon* xi. 157 Layton was like a big, slightly mixed-up puppy, in need of love and care.

mixer. Add: **1. b.** One who mixes drinks; a bartender. orig. *U.S.*

1858 Longfellow *Catawba Wine* in *Atlantic Monthly* Jan. 271 To the sewers and sinks With all such drinks, And after them tumble the mixer. 1919 T. K. Holmes *Man from Tall Timber* viii. 93 He..drank several insidious concoctions of the hotel's most famous 'mixer'. 1934 M. Allingham *Death of Ghost* xxiii. 262 There was too much gin in the cocktails, he decided, and reflected that the fault was a common one among unprofessional mixers. 1939 C. Isherwood *Goodbye to Berlin* 21 Bobby is a mixer at a west-end bar.

c. *Cinemat.* and *Broadcasting.* One who operates the mixer (sense *2 b) during sound recording and is responsible for balancing different signal sources and producing transitions from one source to another.

1929 F. Green *Film finds its Tongue* xiii. 186 A 'mixing booth' or monitor room had been built about 15 feet up... It had glass sides through which the 'mixer' could view everything that was going on. 1948 L. Levy *Music for Movies* iv. 35 Just before writing this I had been sitting at the control desk in a mixer's cabinet during the rehearsals for a new picture. 1957 Manvell & Huntley *Technique Film Music* iv. 183 Regular consultation with the Music Mixer is necessary to ensure that the complete intention of the composer is..being registered on the sound-track.

2. *spec.* A domestic electrical appliance for mixing foods, ingredients for cookery, etc. See also **cake-mixer*, **electric mixer*.

1957 M. Gair *Sapphires on Wednesday* xi. 134 It was a kitchen,..American style, complete with refrigerator, dishwasher, mixer, and garbage disposal unit. 1960 *Harper's Bazaar* Oct. 98/2 You must become accustomed to your oven, to your mixer, to your omelette pan. 1974 *Trafford Catal.* Spring–Summer 781/1 Three machines in one—a mixer, a liquidiser and a mincer.

b. *Cinemat., Broadcasting,* etc. A device designed to receive two or more separate signals, from microphones or other sources, and combine them (usu. in variable proportions) in a single output.

1929 F. Green *Film finds its Tongue* xi. 171 When more than one microphone was used, each of them had an amplifying dial for monitoring. A panel containing more than one such dial was called a 'Mixer'. 1935 Nilson & Hornung *Pract. Radio Communication* viii. 356 The program fed into the mixer does not always come directly from a microphone but may be fed in from a phonograph pick-up. 1962 A. Nisbett *Technique Sound Studio* ix. 152 Where no mixer is available, it may be that linking music, etc., can be cut in by editing the tape; but I would regard a simple mixer—with two faders—as the very minimum for creative programme work. 1968 C. N. G. Matthews *Tape Recording* xi. 109 To do full justice to any group of instrumentalists you need more than one microphone and also a mixer.

c. *Electronics.* A valve or circuit that produces an output signal containing frequencies equal to the sum and the difference of the frequencies of two input signals. Freq. *attrib.*, as *mixer tube, valve*, etc.

1936 *Proc. IRE* XXIV. 208 (*caption*) Typical mixer circuit using 6L7 tube. *Ibid.* 210 The conversion conductance of a mixer tube. 1938 F. E. Terman *Fund. Radio* ix. 249 The heterodyne detector.., commonly referred to as first detector, converter, or mixer, is required to develop a difference frequency..by combining the incoming radio wave with a local oscillation differing in frequency by the desired amount. 1952 E. Armitage *Wireless Fund.* xviii. 324 The frequency-changing stage of a superhet consists of two parts—(1) a beat oscillator generating a signal of constant amplitude, and (2) a mixer valve into which are fed, on to different grids, both the aerial signal and the beat oscillator signal. 1968 *Radio Communication Handbk.* (ed. 4) 48/2 Any non-linear circuit element will act as a mixer, that is to say if frequencies f_1, f_2 are combined in the element, frequencies f_1, f_2, $f_1 + f_2$ and $f_1 - f_2$ will be present in the output.

3. A person in respect of his capacity for mixing with others; a sociable person; esp. *good mixer*, one who mixes readily with others. orig. *U.S.*

1896 Ade *Artie* xii. 105 I'm a good mixer and I've kind o' got next to the live ones. 1904 W. H. Smith *Promoters* xx. 287 He was a most excellent 'mixer', told a story well [etc.]. 1917 Wodehouse *Man with Two Left Feet* 91 Some men are shy and some men are mixers. 1925 W. S. Maugham in *Good Housekeeping* Sept. 15/2 He was a good mixer, and in three days he knew everyone on the ship. 1930 R. Macaulay *Staying with Relations* xix. 281 Good plumbers, but poor mixers; that's what we are. 1937 [see *cerebrotonic *a.* and *sb.*]. 1955 *Times* 18 Aug. 4/6 A man who is a ready mixer and with a natural flair for salesmanship may make £1,000 a year. 1967 N. Freeling *Strike Out* 148 You needed to..get on well with all the murderers? A 'good mixer'—a 'good team man'. 1975 *Listener* 24 July 126/3 He is neither so astute a tactician nor so gifted a mixer with his own men.

4. A social gathering for making people acquainted with each other. *U.S. colloq.*

1916 *Dialect Notes* IV. 277 A very successful mixer was given on Charter day. 1948 *Downers Grove* (Illinois) *Reporter* 21 Oct. 1/8 The Trojan Fathers Fall Mixer will take place Tuesday, Oct. 26 at the high school auditorium.

5. A drink with which an alcoholic liquor is diluted, as soda water, fruit juice, etc.; alcoholic liquor so diluted. Also *attrib.* orig. *U.S.*

1938 D. Baker *Young Man with Horn* iii. i. 147 They worked all possible combinations of bootleg gin and mixers, orange juice, lemon juice, grapefruit juice..and.. root beer. 1948 *Sun* (Baltimore) 1 Jan. 15/1 In the case of the Tom Collins, it's largely a matter of which mixer should be used, plain soda or ginger ale. 1961 *Encounter* XVI. v. 81 Using Coca-cola as what the Americans call 'a mixer'. 1961 *Guardian* 21 Nov. 13/1 Vodka has become, like gin, an international 'mixer',..used to make martinis or to drink with tonic water. 1965 *Economist* 11 Dec. 1251/1 It [*sc.* Beechams] has just introduced a number of 'mixer' drinks to compete with Schweppes. 1968 *Daily Tel.* (Colour Suppl.) 13 Dec. 41/4 Port was traditionally enjoyed here as a mixer—mulled, say, in the way Dr Johnson liked it, with spices, orange, and cloves. 1975 T. Teal tr. *Sjöwall & Wahlöö's Cop Killer* vii. 69 'Do you drink?' 'Yes... But..not lukewarm vodka with no mixer.'

6. A trouble-maker. *slang.*

1938 Partridge *Dict. Slang* (ed. 2) 1014/1 He's a reg'lar mixer! 1964 J. Burke *Hard Day's Night* i. 21 He's a king mixer. *Ibid.* iv. 84 'The old mixer,' growled Paul. 'Come on—we'll have to put him right.' *Ibid.* v. 116 'Look,' said Paul slowly and deliberately, 'he's a mixer and a trouble-maker!' 1966 A. E. Lindop *I start Counting* xviii. 226, I knew what a mixer she was, and I knew she was not capable of keeping a secret.

7. *attrib.*, as **mixer tap**, a tap through which both hot and cold water can be drawn in various proportions; **mixer valve**, a valve by which the proportions of the fluids or gases in a mixture are regulated.

1936 *Archit. Rev.* LXXX. 325/2 Mixer taps or hand showers are worth the extra cost of £2 or £3 they entail. 1972 *House & Garden* Dec.–Jan. 85/3 Mixer taps by Trufords..gold-plated. 1904 *Electr. World & Engin.* 2 Jan. 22/1 This magnet controls a compressed air valve, and this compressed air valve in turn controls a large mixer valve.

mixing, *vbl. sb.* Add: **c. mixing valve**, a valve in which separate supplies of hot and cold water are mixed together; = **mixer tap*.

1902 R. Sturgis *Dict. Archit.* III. 977 General Morin called attention to the necessity of the 'mixing valve'. 1951 *Good Housek. Home Encycl.* 281/2 *Mixing valves*: These are used mainly for showers and baths. 1973 J. Wainwright *Pride of Pigs* 59 A corner shower with a mixing valve that really worked.

Mixmaster (mi·ksmāstəɹ). The proprietary name of a type of electrical food-mixer. Freq. *transf.* and *fig.* (see quots.).

1931 *Good Housekeeping* (N.Y.) Oct. 223/3 (Advt.), See what you get *now* in Mixmaster. A food mixer that beats everything—a juice extractor—an automatic salad oil dripper. 1935 *Official Gaz.* (U.S. Patent Office) 11 June 278/2 Chicago Flexible Shaft Co. *Mixmaster* for Food Mixers, Fruit Juice Extractor, [etc.] filed Nov. 21, 1934. 1946 *Britannica Bk. of Year* (U.S.) 832/2 *Mixmaster*, army bomber propelled by two rear counter-revolving propellers. Made by Douglas Aircraft Co., Inc. 1951 R. Malkin *Boxcars in Sky* xiii. 156 In the business, they refer jocularly to the helicopter by a number of descriptive names: 'eggbeater', 'windmill', and 'mixmaster', to mention a few. 1963 *Economist* 11 May 537/2 A 'mixmaster' force of ships with American missiles and international crews. 1967 *Punch* 22 Mar. 410/1 On all those important matters our opinions are divided, and so therefore are our teachers; the whole situation is confused in the extreme. The mix-master whirrs, the beaters rotate, but unfortunately the recipe is missing. 1971 M. Tak *Truck Talk* 107 *Mixmaster-special*, any transmission with two shift levers; so named because, in running through the gears, the trucker's hands are constantly in motien.

mixo-. Add: **mixoha·line** *a.* [Gr. ἅλιν-ος of salt], brackish; **mixonephridium, mixonephrium**, in certain annelids, an organ in which the nephridium is combined with the cœlomoduct; **mixosco·pia, mixo·scopy** *Psychol.* [ad. G. *mixoskopie* (A. Moll *Die Conträre Sexualempfindung* (1891) v. 136), f. Gr. σκοπεῖν to look at], (see quot. 1939); hence **mixosco·pic** *a.*

1959 *Archivio di Oceanogr. e Limnol.* XI. Suppl. 243 At the final session of the Venice Symposium a revised classification of marine waters according to salinity was adopted and recommended for universal application... The term 'brackish', as a classificatory term, was avoided because of its ambiguous meaning and the term 'mixohaline' was proposed to indicate diluted sea water. 1969 G. Vevers tr. *Friedrich's Marine Biol.* vii. 419 Waters with intermediate salinities are known as brackish or mixohaline. 1946 E. S. Goodrich in *Q. Jrnl. Microsc. Sci.* LXXXVI. 119 When, as in the majority of Polychaeta, the coelomostome is so completely fused to the inner end of the nephridium as to form an apparently simple large-funnelled organ..it may be called a mixonephridium... This new name is proposed to draw attention to the difference between these two kinds of organ (the metanephridium, and the compound nephromixial organ). 1963 Mixonephridium [see *cœlomo-]. 1972 M. S. Gardiner *Biol. Invertebr.* xiii. 505/2 In a mixonephridium, the nephrostome has presumably become occluded and lost. 1958 G. A. Kerkut *Borradaile & Potts's Invertebrata* (ed. 3) viii. 287 Mixonephrium. The coelomoduct is so closely associated with the nephridium that they form an apparently simple funnelled organ. 1939 G. R. Scott *Encycl. Sex* 200/2 *Mixoscopia* or *mixoscopy*, the securing of sexual orgasm or excitation as a result of seeing human beings or animals engaged in copulation. 1940 Hinsie & Shatzky *Psychiatric Dict.* 350/2 *Mixoscopia*, a form of sexual perversion, deriving pleasure from watching the act of coition between the desired one and another person. 1903 *Alienist & Neurologist* May 167 Mixoscopic. 1905 H. Ellis *Stud. Psychol. Sex* iv. 188 Founded on the sense of vision also we find a phenomenon, bordering on the abnormal, which is by Moll named mixoscopy. This means the sexual pleasure derived from the spectacle of other persons engaged in natural or perverse sexual actions.

mixolimnion (miksoli·mniǫn). Pl. **-limnia.** [f. Mixo- + *-limnion*, after *epilimnion, *hypolimnion.] The upper, freely circulating layer of a meromictic lake. Cf. *monimolimnion.

1937 G. E. Hutchinson in *Trans. Connecticut Acad. Arts & Sci.* XXXIII. 74 A meromictic lake may be regarded as consisting of an upper region capable of complete mixture at the time of the overturn, and here called the mixolimnion, and a lower region not undergoing mixture at the overturn and termed by Findenegg the monimolimnion. 1968 *Limnol. & Oceanogr.* XIII. 273 Both lakes are permanently stratified. The chemocline, separating the mixolimnion..from the monimolimnion.., lies at 18 m in Green Lake and at 24 m in Round Lake.

mixologist (miksǫ·lŏdʒist). *U.S. slang.* [f. Mix *sb.*[2] or *v.* + -ologist.] One who is skilled in the mixing of drinks; = *mixer 1 b. Hence **mixo·logy.**

1856 *Knickerbocker* XLVII. 615 Who ever heard of a man's..calling the barkeeper a mixologist of tipicular fixins? **1870** W. F. Rae *Westward by Rail* xv. 201 The most delicate fancy drinks are compounded by skilful mixologists in a style that captivates the public. **1908** W. G. Davenport *Butte & Montana* 45 Brandy and cigarettes were furnished by an expert mixologist from the Thornton Hotel. **1952** *John o'London's* 25 Jan. 82/4 There [*sc.* at Miami], it seems, a mixer of drinks at a bar is referred to as a mixologist. The art of mixing a cocktail is consequently known as mixology.

mixoploid (mi·ksoploid), *a.* (and *sb.*). *Biol.* [f. Mixo- + *-ploid.] Containing cells which are of differing ploidy or, more widely, have differing numbers of chromosomes. Also as *sb.*, a mixoploid individual.

1931 B. Němec in *Rep. Proc. 5th Internat. Bot. Congr. 1930* 233 Many plants contain under normal conditions both diploid and polyploid cells. It is easy to get experimentally plants containing a varying number of polyploid cells. The author designates such plants mixoploid. *Ibid.*, Mixoploid organs tend to eliminate the polyploid cells when they form a minority, especially when they are highly polyploid. **1939** *Hereditas* XXV. 111 As a result of the agar treatment entire plants occasionally become mixoploids. **1944** *Jrnl. Heredity* XXXV. 359/2 Mixoploid tissue resulted from colchicine treatment. *Ibid.* 361/1 Individual anthers were mixoploid. **1951** *Nature* 2 June 891/1 In many species the diploid tissue grows at the expense of the tetraploid, and such a mixoploid reverts rapidly to the diploid condition. **1967** *Current Sci.* XXXVI. 307 (*heading*) Preferential elimination of diploid cells in a colchicine-induced mixoploid tissue. **1971** J. Hamerton *Human Cytogenetics* I. vii. 224 Autosomal mosaics are less common, and about 1% of Down's syndrome patients are estimated to be mixoploids.

So **mi·xoploidy**, the property or state of being mixoploid.

1931 B. Němec in *Rep. Proc. 5th Internat. Bot. Congr. 1930* 233 (*heading*) Mixoploidy and the cellular theory. **1958** C. P. Swanson *Cytol. & Cytogenetics* ix. 300 This gradual change, if caught before the completion of the entire process of doubling, will give both tissues of mixed ploidy and cells with an uneven degree of polyteny in the individual chromosomes. Mickey (1946, 1947) has also shown this type of mixoploidy to be true for the spermatogonia in the testes of the grasshopper, Romalea. **1963** Levan & Müntzing in *Portugaliae Acta Biol.* A. VII. 10 The present writers would suggest that the term mixoploidy should include all cases in which cell populations contain more than one chromosome number irrespective of whether the numbers are euploid or aneuploid. Mixoploidy, thus, covers all cases of mosaicism and chimeric constitution in which the heterogeneity between different elements involves differences in chromosome number. Mixoploidy may originate by all kinds of mitotic irregularities, by cellular and nuclear fusions, or even by amitotic processes, provided they give rise to viable products. **1971** J. Hamerton *Human Cytogenetics* I. vii. 225 *In vitro* studies on mixoploidy should include the use of single cell clones from a mixoploid culture so that the only genetic difference is confined to a single chromosome.

mixotrophic (miksotrōᵘ·fik), *a. Biol.* [a. G. *mixotroph* (W. Pfeffer *Pflanzenphysiologie* (ed. 2, 1897) I. vii. 349), f. Mixo- + Gr. τροφικός nursing.] Living by a mixture of autotrophic and heterotrophic nutrition; pertaining to nutrition of this kind.

1900 A. J. Ewart tr. *Pfeffer's Physiol. Plants* I. vii. 364 By others [*sc.* plants] a portion only of the organic food is drawn from the external world, the rest being supplied by the imperfectly developed chlorophyll-apparatus; such may be termed 'mixotrophic' plants. *Ibid.*, All stages of transition between pure autotrophism and heterotrophism are exhibited among obligate or facultative mixotrophic plants. **1940** L. H. Hyman *Invertebrates* I. iii. 58 Nutrition [of Protozoa] is holophytic, saprozoic, holozoic, or mixotrophic. **1965** Bell & Coombe tr. *Strasburger's Textbk. Bot.* 5 Such mixotrophic organisms [*sc.* unicellular Protista] (which obtain their energy partly directly as autotrophs, and partly indirectly as heterotrophs) are regarded as the starting-point of two great developmental series which have led on the one side to the 'typical' plants and on the other to the 'typical' animals.

Mixtec (mī·ʃtek). Also **Mixteca, Mixteco.** [Sp., f. native name.] A people of central America; a member of this people; also, their language. Also *attrib.* So **Mixte·can.**

1850 R. G. Latham *Nat. Hist. Varieties Man* 409 South of Mexico we have several languages of a small..area... *Mixteca*, spoken in Oaxaca [etc.]. **1928** D. H. Lawrence *Woman who rode Away* 267 His mother was a Mixtec Indian woman. **1934** A. Huxley *Beyond Mexique Bay* 288 In the waste land..stood a church..and, beside it, the Mixtec ruins which it had been built to exorcise and sanctify. **1948** D. Diringer *Alphabet* I. vii. 123 The Zapotecs and Mixtecs..in ancient times probably played the part of cultural intermediaries between the Maya Old Empire of the East, and the Toltec 'Empire' of the West. **1952** E. Fischer-Jørgensen in E. P. Hamp et al. *Readings in Linguistics II* (1966) 307 An exception of a different kind is formed by languages of the Mixteco-type. In Mixteco the minimal utterance is cvcv or cvv, containing two syllabic bases. **1965** *Canad. Jrnl. Ling.* Spring 152 We made the first attempt with the sixteenth century Mixtec dictionary. *Ibid.* 153 We began on the Mixtec, first listing all the affix elements we knew. **1968** Chomsky & Halle *Sound Pattern Eng.* 377 In languages such as Mixtecan or Chinese, each vowel in the word may have its own distinctive prosodic features. **1972** *Language* XLVIII. 847 Otomi nasal vowels, Mixteco,..and Zoque. **1975** *Times* 24 May 10/1, I went to Mexico with only the most cursory knowledge of..the Toltecs, the Olmecs, the Mixtecs, the Zapotecs. *Ibid.* 10/5 Friezes made up of exquisitely curved geometric patterns..were Mixtec work.

mixture. Add: **3. a.** *the mixture as before*: medicine to be taken in a similar dose as on a previous occasion (as a set phrase often found on medicine bottles); freq. *transf.* and *fig.*, something that has already been encountered, used, etc.

1834 Dickens *Let.* 3 Sept. (1965) I. 40, I have taken a wine-glass full of 'the mixture as before' twice a day, varying the amusement with an occasional pill. **1920** Wodehouse *Jill the Reckless* (1921) viii. 120 There he sat, surrounded by happy, laughing young men, each grasping a glass of the good old mixture-as-before. **1959** *Listener* 26 Feb. 363/1 What special or new responsibilities do these developments place upon industry? Some will say that it is the mixture as before, but in larger and more frequent doses. **1973** R. Hill *Ruling Passion* II. iv. 113 After ten minutes, all Pascoe had was the mixture as before.

d. In an internal-combustion engine, the mixture of vaporized or gaseous fuel with air that enters the combustion chamber to form the explosive charge.

[**1848** *Chambers's Edin. Jrnl.* 6 May 303/1 What is the moving power? The answer will be heard with surprise: the successive explosions of a mixture of gas and air in the boxes at the root of the wings, by which means they will be made to flap about twelve times a minute! The balloon ..is a mere reservoir for gas. The explosion is to be effected in the four boxes by the electric spark.] **1894** B. Donkin *Text-Bk. Gas, Oil & Air Engines* I. 6 Sometimes an auxiliary pump is used for compressing the mixture. **1914** W. D. Newton *War* iii. 19 Brun shut off mixture, and, slowing down, he swung from the motor-cycle. **1943** A. P. Fraas *Aircraft Power Plants* vi. 107 The power loss resulting from mixtures 10 or 20 per cent leaner than that for best power is not large as compared with the reduction in fuel consumption. **1968** R. H. Bacon *Car* iii. 23 Modern carburettors have..cold starting devices to give very rich mixtures when starting the engine from cold. **1973** J. Leasor *Host of Extras* i. 21 The engine..was under no stress at all, with tiny valves that let it take such delicate breaths of mixture, it never grew fussed like engines of lesser breeds.

e. Petrol to which has been added a small proportion of oil, used as a combined fuel and lubricant in some two-stroke engines; = *petroil.

[**1927**: see *petroil.] **1952** *Cyclemotor Manual* ('Motor Cycling') iii. 20 Use of oil of too thick a grade may result in the mixture being too heavy to pass through the carburetter jet in sufficient quantity. **1960** J. Queenborough *Garage & Service Station Handbk.* xv. 263 Avery-Hardoll Ltd., market the *Petroiler* which can deliver a choice of two mixtures; there are tanks for petrol (13⅜ gallons) and two grades of oil (1¼ gallons each). **1967** P. E. Irving *Two-Stroke Power Units* vii. 131 As the proportion of oil is for convenience fixed at one figure, usually..six per cent, it may on occasion be necessary to add a little more oil or dilute the mixture with more petrol to obtain the proportion recommended for any particular engine. **1972** J. Stevens *Scooter* iv. 99 The first scooters had engines calling for a 6% oil content in the mixture.

mix-up: see Mix *sb.*² c in Dict. and Suppl.

mixy (mi·ksi), *a.* [f. Mix *v.* + -y¹.] **a.** Adapted for mixing. **b.** *colloq.* Sociable.

1929 R. Bridges *Testament of Beauty* ii. 41 Nor that the unwholesomeness of mixy pollen was by the flowers contrived for their own benefit. **1942** Berrey & Van den Bark *Amer. Thes. Slang* § 363/14 Sociable,..*mixy*. **1968** P. G. Hollowell *Lorry Driver* vii. 181 Lorry drivers aren't so mixy nowadays since there are so many of them.

miz (miz). [Shortening of Mistress *sb.*] **1.** Prefixed as a title to the name of a married or unmarried woman, = 'Mrs.' or 'Miss'. *southern U.S.*

1907 'O. Henry' *Heart of West* i. 5, I ain't reflectin' none on Miz Yeager—she's the finest little lady between the Rio Grande and next Christmas. **1913** H. Kephart *Our Southern Highlanders* xiii. 290 A married woman is not addressed as Missis by the mountaineers, but as Mistress when they speak formally, and as Mis' or Miz' for a contraction. **1937** M. Mitchell *Gone with Wind* xlv. 800 'Don't you question Miz Wilkes' word,' said Archie. **1952** V. Wilkins *King Reluctant* I. iii. 46, I kin' 'spicion wat Miz Fell gwine ter say about dis-yere chile, Miz Virgie! **1975** E. Berckman *Indecent Exposure* v. 53 Miz Tor is such a wonderful lady.

2. Repr. pronunc. of *Ms².

1972 *Village Voice* (N.Y.) 1 June 28/3 Cavett addressed her as Mrs. Morgan and asked her if she would rather be called a miz and she said she didn't care. **1974** J. Philips *Power Killers* (1975) III. iv. 183 Nice to have you back, ma'am... Or should I say 'Miz'? **1975** P. G. Winslow *Death of Angel* i. 48 'Smoky Angel, I believe he is called, Mrs Jones.' 'Miz,' she corrected him.

miz, mizz, colloq. abbrevs. Misery, Miserable *a.* Cf. *mis.

1918 *Chambers's Jrnl.* Mar. 156/2 He won't get any peace now we've seen him. We'll make his life a mizz. **1954** J. B. Priestley *Magicians* ii. 27 Don't look so miz. Are you hating it? **1968** *Times* 24 Feb. 21/3 We feel a teeny bit miz—reality does depress.

mizen, mizzen. 3. *mizen-staysail* (examples).

1757 in J. S. McLennan *Louisbourg* (1918) 209 Fore stay sail, Main and Mizen stay sail all blown away. **1964** R. E. Lloyd in *Roving Commissions 1963* 228 On again next day with, to our joy, a mizzen staysail breeze.

Mizo (mī·zo), *sb.* and *a.* Pl. Mizo, Mizos. [Native name, lit. 'highlander', f. *mi* person + *zo* hill.] **A.** *sb.* A native or inhabitant of the territory of Mizoram in north-eastern India, formerly the Lushai Hills District or the Mizo Hills District. **B.** *adj.* Of or pertaining to these people. Cf. *Lushai *a.* and *sb.*

1832 *Asiatic Res.* XVII. 375 *Krisong*..is esteemed as being the more martial and decided character, and his influence..with the *Mizhus*..is consequently greater. *Ibid.*, *Ruding*, a Chief of the *Mizhú* tribe. *Ibid.* 400 The *Reiga* tribe are on the western side of the great river, beyond the *Pasi* and *Mizong* tribes. **1912** J. Shakespear *Lushei Kuki Clans* v. 110 Some Mizo (natives of these Hills) who were passing through the village also heard the song of those who knew magic. **1954** *Current Indian Statutes* II. 107 The district is largely inhabited by tribes who are collectively known as 'Mizos'—'Lusei' being one of the tribes. **1968** Chapman & Clark *Mizo Miracle* 85 The pioneer missionaries Lorrain and Savidge toured the district, learning the Mizo language and reducing it to writing. **1969** S. Barkataki *Tribes of Assam* 82 Mizo is a generic term which includes several sub-tribes..Lusei, Ralte, Hmar, Pawi (Poi). *Ibid.* 83 The *lingua franca* of the Mizos which has become popularly known as the Mizo language or *Dulhian*, is the dialect of the Lusei clan. *Ibid.* 128 One can hardly imagine the difficulty with which a Mizo or Zemi Naga has to eke a livelihood out of his little patch of land. **1975** *Times* 17 May 6/1 'Hostile' Mizos have been up in arms for more than a decade. *Ibid.*, The Mizo National Front has joined hands with the underground movement of the Nagas.

Mizpah (mi·zpă). [ad. Heb. *Miṣpah* place-name in ancient Palestine (Gen. xxxi. 49).] An expression or token of association ('The Lord watch between me and thee'), esp. used *attrib.* to designate an ornament with 'Mizpah' inscribed upon it, as given by a lover.

[**1887** *Mizpah* 21 Feb. 7 A deeper, more mysteriously beautiful meaning than appears at first sight, is comprehended in the word 'Mizpah'—light within light, circle within circle, revelation within revelation. *Ibid.* 19 It is our duty to examine from the Tower of Mizpah this wonderful Advent of Divinity.] **1898** *T. Eaton & Co. Catal.* Spring & Summer 133/5, 10k Mizpah ring. **1907** B. M. Croker *Company's Servant* xv. 152 Was she wearing his presents? the sapphire brooch..the 'Mizpah' bangle. **1909** P. Webling *Story of Virginia Perfect* i. 11 The thick wedding-ring, with the heavy 'Mizpah' ring squeezed on her finger over it. **1940** H. G. Wells *Babes in Darkling Wood* I. iv. 118 Mizpah, as they say inside the engagement rings. *Ibid.*, 'Anyhow, Gemini, Mizpah!'..'Mizpah,' he responded. Like most English people they thought that was a pledge between two young lovers. **1961** M. K. Ashby *Joseph Ashby* xv. 202 The pedlars..used to bring the silver 'Mizpah' brooches. **1970** I. Origo *Images & Shadows* ii. 69 He gave me the gold Victorian locket—engraved with the word Mizpah, 'God watch between us two'—which he had given to his fiancée.

Mizrach (mi·zrăχ). [ad. mod.Heb. *mizrāḥ*, f. Heb. *mizrāḥ* east, f. *zāraḥ* to rise.] The east, the direction of Jerusalem; a sacred picture facing east; the Judaic practice of turning towards Jerusalem in prayer. Hence **Mizra·chi**, a religiously traditionalist Zionist organization, amalgamated with Hapoel Hamizrachi in 1957.

1892 I. Zangwill *Childr. Ghetto* I. 46 A crudely-coloured *Mizrach* on the east wall, to indicate the direction towards which the Jew should pray. **1911** *Zionist* Oct. 107/2 The Misrachi profess to see in such work a danger to orthodox Judaism of which they claim to be the bulwark in Zionism. *Ibid.* Nov. 123/2 The Misrachi Federation has issued a manifesto..appealing for loyalty and labour for the Zionist movement. **1922** Joyce *Ulysses* 689 His gaze turned in the direction of Mizrach, the east. **1934** M. M. Kaplan *Judaism as Civilization* III. xiv. 174 The *Mizraḥi* organization which is orthodox in its constituency, is devoid of any systematic philosophy of Judaism. **1956** *Ann. Reg. 1955* 285 The Mizrachi (Religious) Zionists of the world. **1973** *Jewish Chron.* 19 Jan. 2/1 (*heading*) Mizrachi in stormy debates. *Ibid.*, A stormy debate as a resolution about diaspora leaders..marked the closing session here.. of the 22nd Mizrachi–Hapoel Hamizrachi conference.

mizzle, *sb.*¹ (Later examples.)

a **1963** S. Plath *Crossing Water* (1971) 34 This mizzle fits me like a sad jacket. **1975** P. G. Winslow *Death of Angel* x. 204 The neighbours would not be likely to air themselves in their gardens in a steady mizzle.

mizzle, *sb.*² *rare.* [f. Mizzle *v.*²] Phr. *to do a mizzle*: to depart suddenly.

1923 J. Manchon *Le Slang* 195 *To do a mizzle*, se trotter, se barrer.

mizzle, *v.*² Add: (Further examples.) Naut. phr. *to mizzle one's dick*: to miss one's passage.

1842 Barham *Lay St. Cuthbert* in *Ingol. Leg.* 2nd Ser. 229 Come, mizzle!—be off with you!—go! **1849** Dickens *Dav. Copp.* (1850) xxii. 236 Now you may mizzle, Jemmy (as we say at Court). **1925** J. Masefield *Sard Harker* III. 134 He had broken his word..and missed his passage; 'mizzled his dick', as Pompey Hopkins called it. **1970** 'R. Llewellyn' *But we didn't get Fox* iii. 47 There was a girl with him... He fell behind the table, and she mizzled.

mizzle (mi·z'l), *v.*⁵ [Perh. f. Moan *v.* + Grizzle *v.*²; cf. Misery.] *intr.* To complain, whimper; used also of fretful children.

a **1935** T. E. LAWRENCE *Mint* (1950) I. xiv. 49 The question took a self-pitiful turn, and I mizzled gently in the white-walled silence. **1945** BAKER *Austral. Lang.* vi. 134 To complain: *to mizzle* and *to whinge* (whence come the nouns *mizzler* and *whinger*, and the verbal nouns *mizzling* and *whingeing*).

mi·zzler². *slang.* [f. prec. + -ER¹.] One who complains.

1945 [see prec.].

Mlimo (m,lī·mo). Also **Umlimo** (umlī·mo). [Bantu; see quots.] The name given by the Matabele and other East African tribes to their god. Also, one of the prophets or priests of this cult.

[**1833** S. KAY *Trav. Caffraria* I. ix. 236 A few indeed there were who seemed to have some confused notion of invisible powers, whom they designated *Mooreemo* and *Booreemo*, and of whom they were taught by their sorcerers to stand in constant dread.] **1861** E. CASALIS *Basutos* II. xiii. 248 Every being, to whom the natives render adoration, is called *Molimo*, the signification of which shows that it is by no means of heathen origin. It is evidently composed of the prefix *mo*, which belongs to almost all those words representing intelligent beings, and of the root *holimo—above, in the sky*. *Moholimo*, or the abbreviation Molimo, therefore, signifies, *He who is in the sky*. **1896** F. C. SELOUS *Sunshine & Storm Rhodesia* xxvi. 236 The Umlimos or prophets..exist among all the tribes in Mashunoland. **1928** P. NEILSON *Matabele at Home* ii. 38 Before the occupation by the white people of this country, it had become customary for many of the Matabele to go to the Umlimo's cave..at regular intervals, and there to make obeisance by presenting the Umlimo with cattle and beer. **1955** E. C. TABLER *Far Interior* iv. 112 These magicians were diviners and hereditary priests of the cult of *Mwari* (Sintabele, *Mlimo*), a deity that was believed to have made the world and therefore controlled the rain... Lobengula, who seems to have had no faith in the *Mlimo*, nevertheless refrained from wiping out this nest of tricky parasites. **1965** L. H. GANN *Hist. S. Rhodesia* iv. 128 The Matabele, having settled north of the Limpopo, transferred their allegiance from *Nkulunkulu*, the Zulu high god, to *Mlimo*, the Karanga deity. *Ibid.* 129 *Mlimo* originally appears to have been regarded as some remote *deus abscondidus*, the Ancient of Days, who took no notice of tribal affairs... But when the Matabele fell on evil days the god gained increasing political importance, and his cult..provided an effective machinery of revolt.

Mlle. [See MADEMOISELLE I.] (Examples.)

1792 F. BURNEY *Jrnl.* May (1972) I. 155 *Mlle Planta* had told her I was going to be married!..why what I had said..a week a go, should not have reached this Mlle nor her informant, is marvellous. **1820** M. WILMOT *Let.* 3 Mar. (1935) 53 Poor nurse had her share—Mlle hers—and Nanny hers. **1896** C. K. SHORTER *Charlotte Brontë & her Circle* iv. 109 Madame Héger..has been gibbeted for all time in the characters of Mlle. Zoraïde Reuter and Madame Beck. **1975** B. GARFIELD *Hopscotch* i. 13 The German folded and then it was *Mlle* Stein's turn.

mm, m'm ('m). Also mm-m, (*rare*) mn. [Imit.] Used to express a hesitating or inarticulate utterance of interrogation, assent, reflection, or satisfaction on the part of a speaker. Cf. UM *int.*

1922 JOYCE *Ulysses* 56 A sleepy soft grunt answered:— Mn. **1924** *Dialect Notes* V. 273 *M-*: —, — -m. **1966** G. N. LEECH *Eng. in Advertising* xxii. 197 By tomorrow they'll [*sc.* sandwiches] lose not a single 'M'm' of flavoursome moisture! **1967** *Boston Herald* 8 May 24/4 (*caption*) Mm... Another dud, but not bad for a dull movie. **1967** *Listener* 21 Sept. 367/2 Restraint is unnatural, mm? **1968** [see *CHASE *v.*¹ 7 c]. **1974** D. FRANCIS *Knock Down* ii. 21 'You'd thought of that, had you?'.. 'Mm,' I said.

Mme. [See MADAME I.] (Examples.)

1806 *Young Ladies' Assistant in Writing French Lett.* i. 6 In hand-written letters, *Monsieur, Madame, Mademoiselle*, before family names, are abbreviated thus: *Mr. Mde. Mlle.*; in printed ones, we find *M.* for *Monsieur, Mme.* for *Madame, Melle.* for Mademoiselle. **1860** D. G. ROSSETTI *Let.* 9 June (1965) I. 368 My best address would be: Chez Mme Houston (as above): the said Mme is English and very obliging. **1896** C. K. SHORTER *Charlotte Brontë & her Circle* iv. 102 Mme. Héger was an accomplished spy. **1975** *Listener* 7 Aug. 190/1 Mme Laure Bernardini and her companion, Mme Thérèse, are very old.

mneme (nī·mi). *Psychol.* and *Physiol.* [a. G. *mneme* (R. Semon *Die Mneme als erhaltende Prinzip im Wechsel des organischen Geschehens* (1904)), f. Gr. μνήμη memory.] The capacity which a living substance or organism possesses for retaining after-effects of experience or stimulation undergone by itself or its progenitors.

1913 M. HARTOG *Probl. Life & Reproduction* 275 The mnemic possibilities of an organism may be termed, collectively, its 'mneme'. **1921** L. SIMON tr. *Semon's Mneme* 12 The capacity for such after-effect of stimulation constitutes what I have called the Mneme. **1928** J. T. MACCURDY *Common Princ. Psychol. & Physiol.* ii. 15 The mneme and memory are thus reduced, fundamentally, to physico-chemical phenomena. **1966** E. ENG tr. *Strauss's Phenomenological Psychol.* I. iii. 61 *Mneme* must not be limited to organic substances.

mnemic (nī·mik), *a.* [f. as prec. + -IC.] Pertaining to, of the nature of, or involving mneme. Hence **mne·mically** *adv.*, **mne·micness**, the state or quality of being mnemic.

1908 *Daily Chron.* 3 Sept. 5/7 Alleging the existence of a mnemic factor in the life of plants. **1913** [see prec.]. **1921** B. RUSSELL *Analysis of Mind* iv. 78 Following a suggestion derived from Semon..we will give the name of 'mnemic phenomena' to those responses. **1921** L. SIMON tr. *Semon's Mneme* 11 Instead of speaking of a factor of memory, a factor of habit, or a factor of heredity, and attempting to identify one with another, I have preferred to consider these as manifestations of a common principle, which I shall call the mnemic principle. This mnemic property may be regarded from a purely physiological point of view, inasmuch as it is traced back to the effect of stimuli applied to the irritable organic substance. **1925** C. D. BROAD *Mind & its Place* viii. 377 Experiences which are owned in senses (2) or (3) may be said to be 'mnemically owned'. **1941** *Mind* L. 417 The only perceptible difference between conscious and non-conscious behaviour is *mnemicness*. **1943** A. M. FARRER *Finite & Infinite* xvii. 201 That already depends on the mnemic content, which disposes us to attention in one direction rather than another, because certain elements of memory are pressing closest to the gate. **1963** O. L. ZANGWILL tr. *Luria's Restoration of Function after Brain Injury* vi. 213 The patient retained the content of this particular thought, and..his difficulties were dynamic in nature rather than mnemic. **1968** S. BOGOCH *Biochem. Memory* vi. 194 That is, the glycoproteins of the nervous system represent the mnemic substances in which experiential information s encoded.

mnemon (nī·mǫn). *Psychol.* [f. Gr. μνήμ-η memory + *-ON¹.] A unit of memory (see quots. 1965, 1966).

The coiner of the term appears to be Cherkin (quot. 1966), whose forthcoming paper is mentioned by Young in 1965. Cherkin's paper was communicated to the editor of the *Proceedings* on 19 November 1965.

1965 *New Scientist* 23 Dec. 861 In the author's [*sc.* J. Z. Young's] view, memory is localized in small combinations of brain cells, which he calls 'mnemons'. **1966** A. CHERKIN in *Proc. Nat. Acad. Sci.* LV. 88 The proposed unit is defined as the minimum physical change in the nervous system that encodes one memory... The name proposed for the unit is the 'mnemon' (mneme = memory; -on = suffix denoting a fundamental particle). **1971** J. Z. YOUNG *Introd. Study Man* xix. 252 The time to begin accumulating such units of memory (mnemons) would be as soon as they are ready.

mnemonist. Add: Also, a professional entertainer who practises recollection.

1969 *Observer* 26 Jan. 28/7 Eventually he became a mnemonist or professional 'memory man'. His powers of recall were not so far from total.

mnemotechnic, *a.* and *sb.* Add: **B.** *sb.* Also as *sing. rare.*

1922 JOYCE *Ulysses* 503 See, you have forgotten. Exercise your mnemotechnic.

mnemotechnist (nīmote·knist). [f. MNEMOTECHNY + -IST.] = MNEMONIST.

1891 *Chambers's Encycl.* VII. 240/2 The mnemotechnist who has a succession of things to be remembered.. compels himself to detect some association..between each of them and one of the 'hieroglyphs' which are to serve as memorial links.

mo (mōu), *sb.*² Also mo'. Colloq. or slang abbrev. MOMENT *sb.* Chiefly in ellipt. phr. *half a mo*: wait for half a moment, *i.e.*, for a short time.

1896 in J. R. Ware *Passing Eng.* (1909) 9/2 In half a mo' —half a mo' Your pluck and perseverance you can show. **1903** [see *'ARF]. **1905** H. G. WELLS *Kipps* II. v. 234 Chitterlow hesitated. 'Half a mo', my boy,' he said. **1929** N. C. JAMES *Sleeveless Errand* 176 Well, wait a mo, while I get my tata on. **1934** [see *'ARF]. **1938** AUDEN & ISHERWOOD *On Frontier* III. i. 98 Wait a mo. Gimme a torch. **1972** J. WILSON *Hide & Seek* vi. 110 Hang on... Hang on a mo. Look, you can't pin nothing on me.

mo, *sb.*³ Austral. and N.Z. slang abbrev. MOUSTACHE, MUSTACHE *sb.*

1936 M. FRANKLIN *All that Swagger* xli. 383 Darcy was a man. He had a 'mo'. **1946** D. STIVENS *Courtship Uncle Henry* 18 'I'll warm your pants for you..' he'd warn me, the ends of his long black mo shaking. **1947** 'A. P. GASKELL' *Big Game* 17 Never mind Henry,..we'll soon shave Hitler's mo off.

mo' (mǭ), *a.* (*sb.*) and *adv.* *U.S.* Also **mo.** An abbrev. (chiefly found in written Black English) of MORE *a.* (*sb.*) and *adv.*, esp. in phr. *no mo'*.

1902 J. D. CORROTHERS *Black Cat Club* i. 23 Read dat piece o' yo's once mo' an' let me die a-listenin' to it! *Ibid.* ii. 40 Black cats is dead bad luck. Dey's hoodooed me mo' den once. **1944** C. HIMES *Black on Black* (1973) 196 Pour me some mo' of that licker. **1953** S. A. BROWN in A. Dundes *Mother Wit* (1973) 41/2 Dere ain't no mo scufflin'. **1962** N. E. WHITTEN in *Ibid.* 402/1 White folks don' put much stock in roots and the like no mo'. **1969** S. SANCHEZ in S. Henderson *Understanding New Black Poetry* (1973) III. 272 White people Ain't rt bout nothing No mo. **1973** *Black World* Sept. 35 Me an' my baby's Got two mo' ways, Two mo' ways to do de Charleston!

-mo (mo), *suffix.* The final syllable of terms derived from the abl. sing. masc. of L. ordinal numerals which are used to denote book sizes by the number of leaves into which a sheet of the paper on which the book is printed has been folded, e.g. *duodecimo*, *sextodecimo*, etc., and, by analogy, *vicesimo-quarto*, *tricesimo-secundo*, etc., which may be pronounced or written as *12mo*, *16mo*, *24mo*, *32mo*, etc., or *twelvemo*, *sixteenmo*, *twenty-fourmo*, *thirty-twomo*, etc.

c **1716** T. RAWLINSON *Let.* in T. Hearne *Remarks & Coll.* (1901) V. 178, I..would willingly know something of y^r Sylloge Epistolar., whither MSs. & unpublish'd, or a 12mo of A^o 1640. **1742** in *N. & Q.* (1855) 2 June 419 History of the Adventures of Joseph Andrews, &c., 12mo., in 2 vols., No. 1500, with alterations. **1776** in T. Harmer *Observations Divers Passages Scripture* (ed. 2) I. 484 (Advt.), The New Testament in Greek,..2 vol. 12mo. **1801** *Schedule of Presswork Prices* in E. Howe *London Compositor* (1947) iii. 98 Twelves: Pot, such as ladies and christian ladies table part, 6mo. 35 Pica ems wide, 26 long. **1810** *Scale of Prices for Compositors' Work* Art. 6, in *Ibid.* vi. 176 English and larger type, not less than 7s... English 12mo. to be paid not less than 10s. 6d. **1841** W. SAVAGE *Dict. Art of Printing* 798 A sheet of paper folded into twenty-four leaves, forty-eight pages, is termed twenty-fourmo. **1894** *Amer. Dict. Printing & Bookmaking* 548/1 *Trigesimo-secundo*, the bibliographical term for thirty-twomo; written shortly 32mo. **1927** R. B. MCKERROW *Introd. Bibliogr.* I. iv. 34 Duodecimo, sextodecimo, vicesimo-quarto, and tricesimo-secundo, but often called 'twelvemo', 'sixteenmo', 'twenty-fourmo', and 'thirty-twomo'. *Ibid.* II. ii. 167 Both in a 16mo and a 32mo the watermark is, however, often absent. *Ibid.* 170 (*heading*) Twelve-mo by cutting. **1949** F. BOWERS *Princ. Bibliogr. Descr.* v. 193 Sexagesimo-quarto—64° *or* 64mo. **1952** J. CARTER *ABC for Bk.-Collectors* 89 The principal sizes, with their common abbreviations, are: Folio... Quarto... Octavo... Duodecimo (12mo, pronounced twelvemo). Sextodecimo (16mo, pronounced sixteenmo). Vicesimo-quarto (24mo, pronounced twentyfourmo). Tricesimo-secundo (32mo, pronounced thirtytwomo). **1973** *Collins's Authors & Printers Dict.* (ed. 11) 406/2 *Sixty-fourmo*,..a book based on 64 leaves, 128 pages, to the basic sheet..abbr. 64mo (no point).

moa. Add: **b.** *attrib.*, as *moa bone.*

1875 J. VON HAAST in *Trans. N.Z. Inst.* VII. 89 The older occupants, probably the Moa-hunters, who were inhabitants, or at least frequent visitors at the Moa Bone Point Cave. **1957** J. FRAME *Owls do Cry* xiv. 61 A moa bone.

moa-hunter, Moa-hunter (mōu·ă hɒ·ntəɹ). *N.Z.* [f. MOA + HUNTER.] The name given to early Maori inhabitants of New Zealand. Also *attrib.* Hence **moa-hunting** *ppl. a.*

1870 J. VON HAAST in *Proc. Zool. Soc.* 53, I have been so fortunate as to find a large Moa-hunters' encampment, with their cooking-places and kitchen-middens. **1872** —— in *Trans. N.Z. Inst.* IV. 78 Proceeding now to an examination of the traces left by the moa-hunting population. *Ibid.* 80, I discovered a moa-hunter encampment of considerable extent. **1873** A. TROLLOPE *Austral. & N.Z.* II. xxiii. 379 From these fractures Dr. Haast draws the conclusion that there were, before the Maoris, a race of moa-hunters. **1874** A. BATHGATE *Colonial Experiences* xvii. 241 The moa was hunted and used as food by man... Were these moa-hunters the ancestors of the Maories, or some more ancient race? **1892** W. L. BULLER in *Trans. N.Z. Inst.* XXV. 92 Long after the moa-hunters had disappeared. **1950** R. DUFF *Moa-Hunter Period Maori Culture* 7 The Moa-hunter phase of Maori culture, as defined and isolated here, is in my opinion clearly distinct from pre-European Maori culture, although it is probably ancestral to it. **1962** *Antiquity* XXXVI. 169 The existence of a widespread Moa-hunter culture in both [North and South] islands inferred by Duff has indeed been demonstrated by a number of excavations. **1974** *Nat. Geographic* Aug. 196 The men who hunted *Dinornis*..were called by later Polynesians *tangata whenua*... But the name by which they are commonly known in English is the more appropriate one: moa-hunters.

Moal, Moallakat. see *MUʻALLAQAT *sb. pl.*

moan, *sb.* Add: **1. c.** A grievance, a grumble; an 'airing' of complaints. orig. *Services' slang.*

1911 'GUNS' & 'THEELUKER' *Middle Watch Musings* 12 'Guard and Steerage 'ammicks, Sir!' I wake up with a groan; Why can't I sleep till 7 a.m.? Once more I had a moan. **1927** *Daily Express* 5 Oct. 3/4 The midshipmen fling their moanful forms into chairs, and one says:— 'Come on, you chaps, let's have a moan!' **1942** 'DUGGIE' in Forbes & Allen *Ten Fighter Boys* 20 We all had a moan to the C.O. about it, and he in turn was in full agreement. **1974** *Times* 6 Apr. 14/8 It's the one moan I have about international rugby. There ought..to be referees from neutral countries.

moan, *v.* Add: **3. c.** (See quot. 1925.) orig. *Services' slang.*

a **1922** T. S. ELIOT *Waste Land Drafts* (1971) 57 line 42 So this injurious race was sullen, and kicked; Complained too of the ship... So the crew moaned. **1925** FRASER & GIBBONS *Soldier & Sailor Words* 156 *To moan*, to complain, to grumble, to be a pessimist. (Navy—equivalent to the Army 'grouse'.) **1948** *Landfall* II. 112 He felt through his pockets for a cigarette, found a butt and lit it. Why moan?

moaner (mōu·nəɹ). *colloq.* [f. MOAN *v.* + -ER¹.] One who moans; a complainer, a murmurer; a pessimist.

In quots, 1927, 1932 'a singer of blues songs'.

1927 [see *HONKY-TONK I]. **1929** *Papers Mich. Acad. Sci., Arts & Lett.* X. 308/2 *Moaner*, a pessimist. **1932** *Amer. Speech* VII. 247 Clara Smith evidently deems it a mark of distinction to be known as 'The World's Greatest Moaner'.

1942 BERREY & VAN DEN BARK *Amer. Thes. Slang* § 406/1 Gloomy or irritable person; pessimist..complainer; fault-finder..*moaner*. **1952** *Landfall* VI. 202 Anyone who questions too often is a 'moaner', yet in New Zealand the moaner is common. **1959** I. & P. OPIE *Lore & Lang. Schoolch.* x. 187 Croydon boys have twenty names for a cry-baby:..*moaner* [etc.]. **1969** I. KEMP *Brit. G.I. in Vietnam* v. 95 Burmeister..once said to me, 'Limey, you and Goad are the two biggest moaners in my squad.' **1969** F. SARGESON *Joy of Worm* iii. 87 But my boy, I did not intend to write you a letter to make myself out what our fellow countrymen call a 'moaner'.

moaning, *ppl. a.* Add: *spec.* **moaning minnie** (also with capital initials). **a.** Either of two German types of mortar (*minenwerfer* or *nebelwerfer*); also, a shell from one of these mortars. **b.** An air-raid siren. **c.** = *MOANER.

1941 R. GREENWOOD *Mr. Bunting at War* xiv. 192 'One up now,' said Chris, listening to the drone of an engine. 'Hope Moaning Minnie doesn't sound, and bring mother downstairs.' **1944** *Hutchinson's Pict. Hist. War* 12 Apr.–26 Sept. 376 (*caption*) When the Germans beat a hasty re-treat from Cagny among the material they abandoned was this multiple mortar, or 'Moaning Minnie'. **1950** [see *MINNIE², MINNIE]. **1962** *Sunday Times* 21 Jan. 32/4 Another said that she '..just didn't believe these moaning minnies'. **1972** *N.Z. News* 26 Apr. 6/5, I don't want to give the impression of being a moaning Minnie but may I ..make a special plea to the railmen to..get back to work.

moanism (mōᵘ·niz'm). *rare.* [f. MOAN *v.* + -ISM.] The practice of lamenting; emotionalism.

1916 R. FROST *Let.* 24 May (1964) 34 Moanism and swounding.

mob, *sb.*¹ Add: **1.** Also in *Social Psychol.*

1897 E. A. ROSS in *Pop. Sci. Monthly* July 390 (*heading*) The mob mind. *Ibid.*, Great mental instability marks the true mob. **1931** E. S. BOGARDUS *Fund. Social Psychol.* (ed. 2) xxv. 315 A mob is a crowd in a very high state of suggestibility. **1940** E. A. STRECKER *Beyond Clin. Frontiers* iv. 60 Lynching mobs, certain strike mobs, etc. furnish examples of positive reality-evasion action en masse. **1959** GILL & BRENMAN *Hypnosis* ix. 293 Such people are sometimes said to be hypnotized. They show regressive phenomena similar to those revealed by a mob. **1973** G. R. LESLIE et al. *Order & Change: Introd. Sociol.* xi. 289 Although scientific interest in mobs and riots as mechanisms of social change is relatively new, the phenomena themselves have existed throughout history.

4. (Further Austral. examples.) Also in New Zealand use, without disparaging implication, a crowd, a group, a gang of workmen.

1834 in R. MCNAB *Old Whaling Days* (1913) App. C. 424 A mob of natives came running into the hut where we stopped. **1845** *N.Z. Company Rep.* XIX. 70 The Pah is small, and occupied by a few Natives, the crops, as I understood, being the property of several 'mobs' in different parts of the Sound. **1852** *Austral. & N.Z. Gaz.* 10 Jan. 11/2 In Major Hornbrook's words 'the *Stedfast*'s mob is a much jollier mob than that of the *Duke of Bronte*'. **1860** G. DUPPA in S. S. Crawford *Sheep & Sheepmen Canterbury* (1949) v. 48 Commence shearing with a strong mob of shearers. **1863** F. E. MANING *Old N.Z.* iv. 66 It was 'our mob' coming to the rescue. **1907** W. H. KOEBEL *Return of Joe* 257 [He] had but a few hours ago formed one of their 'mob', and [was] the most skilful bushwhacker in the district. **1941** *Coast to Coast* 214 The mob around the bar was thinning down, with chaps grabbing their bundles and going off home. **1944** *Living off Land* viii. 155 You may meet the Abo. He may be only a poor specimen on the outskirts of a township, or he may be a 'mob' of half-wild blokes in the furthest nor' west. **1960** S. ASHTON-WARNER *Incense to Idols* 23, I know one girl from another, course you do in my mob anyway. **1968** K. WEATHERLY *Roo Shooter* 27 Hunter pushed his way through the mob, every one of whom he knew,..and sat down at the table.

b. (Later Austral. examples.) Also quasi-*adv.*

1934 A. RUSSELL *Tramp-Royal in Wild Austral.* xiii. 91 There'll be mobs of water on the track, we'll get mobs of beef at the runs, the stages'll be mobs shorter, an' there'll be mobs better camping grounds... And of course we'll be able to take it mobs easier. **1942** C. BARRETT *On the Wallaby* iii. 41 Even an offer of..mobs of tucker..failed to gain me a guide.

c. (Further examples.)

1838 T. WALKER *Month in Bush* 8, I beheld a level plain,..with..'mobs' of cattle scattered over the surface. **1843** J. COTTON *Let.* July in Billis & Kenyon *Pastures New* (1930) xiii. 227, I inspected a mob (as it is termed here) of the cattle. **1850** *Househ. Words* 6 Apr. 42/2, I was going down to Sydney with a mob of horses. **1853** R. CLOUGH *Let.* 24 Sept. in J. Deans *Pioneers of Canterbury* (1937) 295, I should like to put all the calvers in one mob. **1875** *Trans. & Proc. N.Z. Inst.* VII. 130 For about 400 birds of this large size to have been roasted in so small a compass in one mob would be a physical impossibility. **1933** *Bulletin* (Sydney) 5 July 21/3 The dog was turning the mob to work over the fallen animal. **1936** I. L. IDRIESS *Cattle King* vii. 63 A squatter was overlanding with a big mob of stock. **1940** *Geogr. Jrnl.* XCV. 242 There is now only one firm remaining which has a mob of mules. **1964** *Sunday Mail Mag.* (Brisbane) 27 Sept. 3/5 Behind him..were the ragged outriders of the mob... I knew he didn't stand a chance of clearing those terrible hooves. **1968** K. WEATHERLY *Roo Shooter* 35 A small mob of wild pigs, mostly white with black spots. **1972** P. NEWTON *Sheep Thief* ii. 20 The two men had taken out a mob of ewes.

e. *Mil. slang.* A battalion, a regiment; a military unit.

1916 J. N. HALL (*title*) Kitchener's mob. **1916** *Anzac Book* 32 Yes; some d-d gobblers thought they would catch our mob nappin' but missed the bus. **1925** FRASER & GIBBONS *Soldier & Sailor Words* 156 *Mob*, any collection or body of troops. A very old Army term. **1948** PARTRIDGE *Dict. Forces' Slang* 120 *Mob*, unit, not necessarily in a derogatory sense. 'What mob are you from, chum?' **1972** M. PUGH *Murmur of Mutiny* iv. 34 You must have heard of Sharjah and the Trucial Oman Scouts. This mob is modelled on them.

5. a. (Earlier example.) *swell mob*: see also SWELL *a.* c.

1839 H. BRANDON *Poverty, Mendicity & Crime* 164/1 *Mobs*—companions. Working with mobs. Robbing with companions.

b. *U.S.* A more or less permanent association or gang of violent criminals. *The Mob*, a supposed permanent gang controlling much of organized crime in the U.S. and elsewhere; cf. *MAFIA. Also *attrib.* and *Comb.*, amongst gangs, on behalf of a mob or 'The Mob'.

1927 *Amer. Speech* II. 385/1 Any kind of a gang was known as a push, a word credited to Australia, but I think it is a sister of the mob of the city underworld. **1930** WODEHOUSE *Very Good, Jeeves!* xi. 302 By the time he had come to the surface, a sort of mob-warfare was going on at the other side of the field. **1952** TURKUS & FEDER *Murder, Inc.* xv. 345 One mob baron..'moved in' to the extent that he had his picture taken in a friendly pose with a candidate for the vice-presidency of the United States. **1968** P. OLIVER *Screening Blues* iv. 134 Within a year control of the New York numbers racket passed into the dominion of a mob enforcer. **1969** *Guardian* 24 Jan. 7/6 The Mob from its Chicago headquarters runs the sub-continent. **1975** 'A. THACKERAY' *One Way Ticket* 23 Better watch out... It could be the Mafia, the Mob, or whatever they call it these days.

6. a. *mob action, behaviour, -condemnation, control, -culture, -emotion, -fever, -hysteria, -indignation, -madness, mania, mind, -movement, -orator* (earlier and later examples), *-oratory, -psychology, -reaction, scene, -sensation, -storm, -sycophancy, -tide, violence* (examples), *-will, -worship.* **b.** *mob-inspiring* adj.

1972 TURNER & KILLIAN *Collective Behavior* (ed. 2) iii. 49/2 Mob action is frequently nothing more than culturally sanctioned punishment carried out by unauthorized persons without 'due process'. **1973** G. R. LESLIE et al. *Order & Change: Introd. Sociol.* xi. 289 The distinction between mob behavior and riot behavior has to do with the degree to which the hostility is focussed upon a single object or class of objects. When the hostility is so directed and is concentrated on destruction of particular scapegoats, the term 'mob' is used. **1929** D. H. LAWRENCE *Pornogr. & Obscenity* 9 When it comes to the so-called obscene words,..the first reaction is almost sure to be mob-reaction, mob-indignation, mob-condemnation. **1971** D. E. WESTLAKE *I gave at the Office* (1972) 89 The gun is the primary tool in situations of mob control. **1968** L. DURRELL *Tunc* v. 269 A surrogate mob-culture. **1928** D. H. LAWRENCE *Woman who rode Away* 231 A steam of wet mob-emotions! **1929** GALSWORTHY in *Story-Teller Mag.* Aug. 597/2 Impervious by nature and training to mob-emotion Soames yet was emotionalized. Here was something that was not mere mob-sensation. **1935** A. L. JAMES *Broadcast Word* i. 5 It will have cleansed our political life of its mob-fever. **1895** W. JAMES *Let.* 24 Dec. (1920) II. 28 Three days of fighting mob-hysteria at Washington can at any time undo peace habits of a hundred years. **1934** R. CAMPBELL *Broken Record* 59 Race-feeling, mob-hysteria. **1929** Mob-indignation [see *mob-condemnation* above]. **1782** J. TRUMBULL *M'Fingal* IV. 95 And while plebeian signs ascend, Their mob-inspiring aspects bend. **1901** E. A. ROSS *Social Control* xiii. 147 Mob-madness leads men captive to the impressions of the moment. **1935** L. MACNEICE *Poems* 60 Mob mania in the air. **1897** Mob mind [see sense 1 above]. **1933** *Essays & Stud.* XVIII. 61 After half a century's work on the mob-mind psychologists are agreed that a crowd is an entirely different problem from an individual. **1964** GOULD & KOLB *Dict. Social Sci.* 433/2 The irrationality and excesses of which people are capable when acting under the influence of the 'mob mind'. **1923** D. H. LAWRENCE *Kangaroo* xvi. 338 But revolution is not a mob-movement. **1817** H. C. ROBINSON *Diary* 13 Feb. (1967) 54 One Walker spoke also—a coarse mob-orator with a stentorian voice. **1965** *Punch* 13 Jan. 55/1 Hitler the rabble-rouser, Hitler the mob-orator. **1961** *John o' London's* 9 Nov. 517/2 His [*sc.* Hitler's] megalomaniac mob-oratory. **1896** W. JAMES *Let.* 11 June (1920) II. 36 The really bad thing here is the silly wave that has gone over the public mind—protection humbug, silver, jingoism, etc. It is a case of 'mob-psychology'. **1938** R. G. COLLINGWOOD *Princ. Art* v. 91 They cannot as a whole exhibit a compact mob-psychology. **1929** Mob-reaction [see *mob-condemnation* above]. **1922** U. SINCLAIR *They call me Carpenter* vii. 20 They're a lot of studio bums, doing a real mob scene on a real location. **1937** *Printers' Ink Monthly* May 39/3 *Mob scene*, a group of performers used as a background. **1929** Mob-sensation [see *mob-emotion* above]. **1865** J. D. BURN *Three Yrs. among Working-Classes U.S.* p. xiii, A series of mob-storms would be sure to set in. **1849** MILL in *Westm. Rev.* LI. 16 One hardly expected to hear them taunted with..mob-sycophancy. **1881** 'MARK TWAIN' *Prince & Pauper* 127 The mob-tide..dashed itself against the champion. **1893** *Ladies' Home Jrnl.* Feb. 6/1, I don't approve of mob violence. **1949** LAPIERE & FARNSWORTH *Social Psychol.* (ed. 3) xxv. 471 There is a close relationship between critical social circumstances and mob violence. **1969** M. B. ARNOLD in T. Mischel *Human Action* 192 Emotions, whether mob-violence or passive love-ins, seem to have been chosen by many young people as sole guide of their actions. **1924** J. MASEFIELD *Sard Harker* 51 Never had I thought that my fellow-citizens of Las Palomas would try to impose the mob-will upon the individual. **1893** E. DOWSON *Let.* c 27 Aug. (1967) 288 'One View of the Question', a beautiful piece of satire on English mob-worship.

7. mob-man = MOBSMAN.

1747 in *New Jersey Archives* (1883) 1st Ser. VII. 428 He discoursing with several of the mobmen,..has heard them [say]..that the King himself was unable to quell mobs in England. **1835** *Maryland Hist. Mag.* IX. 160 You may see large companies of worthies marching to and fro, and a mob man, as such, cannot be seen.

mob, *v.*² Add: **1. b.** Esp. in bird behaviour, to engage in *MOBBING (*vbl. sb.*² 1 c).

1927 E. M. NICHOLSON *How Birds Live* vii. 87 An owl appears and is surrounded by a clamorous crowd of small birds which proceed to mob it. **1936** *Brit. Birds* XXX. 28 Usually when seen it was sitting in a tree, and it was much 'mobbed' by Rooks. **1938** T. H. WHITE *Sword in Stone* xvii. 250 They [*sc.* rooks] have got the courage to mob their enemies. I should think it takes some courage to mob a hawk, even if there is a pack of you. **1965** P. WAYRE *Wind in Reeds* v. 62 The falcon, sometimes.. accompanied by the tiercel, would fly out and mob us.

mobbing, *vbl. sb.*² Add: **1. b.** *Sc. Law.* (See quot. 1959.)

1800 D. HUME *Commentaries Law of Scotl.* IV. xvi. 228 A multitude may be convened for a criminal purpose without being guilty of mobbing. **1885** [in Dict.]. **1898** J. CHISHOLM *Green's Encycl. Law of Scotl.* 370 In the law of Scotland mobbing, or 'the Tumultuous Convocation of the Lieges', includes the several degrees and stages of disorder which are known in the law of England under the names of Riot, Rout, and Unlawful Assembly. **1959** *Chambers's Encycl.* XII. 327/2 Mobbing is violent or threatening action taken in an effort to obtain a definite end and this distinguishes it from rioting and breach of the peace which are disorderly conduct at large. **1973** *Observer* 4 Feb. 29/4 We almost goat ye fur mobbin' an' riotin'.

c. Esp. in bird behaviour, a type of display in which a group of small birds engages to drive off a predator, or a similar kind of display exhibited by one or two birds, in which they fly close to the object of their apparent aggression. Also *attrib.*

1919 F. FINN *Bird Behaviour* ix. 275 The mobbing of Hawks and Owls is no doubt often dictated by revenge. **1927** E. M. NICHOLSON *How Birds Live* vii. 93 Akin to fighting and play, but not identifiable with either, is the mobbing habit. **1936** *Brit. Birds* XXIX. 307 The 'mobbings' of nesting Rooks by other members of the colony.. are sexual in origin. **1949** *Ibid.* XLII. 64 This behaviour is certainly in no way analogous to the so-called 'mobbing' of predatory birds. **1961** *Behaviour* IV. 288 (*title*) The motivational organisation controlling the mobbing calls of the Blackbird.

mobbish, *a.* (Later example.)

1920 *Q. Rev.* July 166 This mobbish or, as it may be termed, 'synnomic' character of primitive mentality is well known.

mo·bbishness. [-NESS.] Tendency to mobbism; the practice of acting in groups.

1920 *Q. Rev.* July 166 The savage enjoys no privacy, but is always in some sort of a crowd,..experiencing therefore all those peculiar mental effects which mobbishness brings in its train. **1927** W. DEEPING *Kitty* xxiv. 310 You would still hope for your super-scientist..who, by pressing a button in his laboratory, could efface all mobs and mobbishness.

mobbism. (Earlier U.S. example.)

1794 *Mass. Spy* 16 Apr. 3/2 A few days since, we experienced a scene of the most unlicensed mobism.

mob-cap. (Earlier and *transf.* examples.)

1795 T. WILKINSON *Wandering Patentee* II. 137 On she came in a frock and a little mob-cap, and sang the song. **1971** *Daily Tel.* 19 Jan. 11/2 There's a whole range of Victoriana too, including washable mob-cap lamp-shades in lace and embroidered cotton.

mobese (mǫbī·z). [f. MOB *sb.*¹ + -ESE.] The cant of American professional criminals.

1955 *People* (Austral.) 19 Oct. 13/2 A few even felt.. that Dewey should be 'hit'—which is mobese for gang murder. **1965** I. FLEMING *Man with Golden Gun* xiii. 173 In mobese, he was 'going to be hit'.

mo·b-handed, *a.* *colloq.* [f. MOB *sb.*¹ + HANDED *a.* 1 b.] In considerable numbers, constituting a large body.

1934 P. ALLINGHAM *Cheapjack* xix. 254 His companions had been 'mob-handed', that is to say, working in a big group. **1966** A. PRIOR *Operators* vi. 64 Mo and his brother had returned home penniless to find the police mob-handed. **1970** *Sunday Tel.* 9 Aug. 27/7 The evergreen X class [of yachts] turned out mob-handed at 60 strong.

mo-bike (mōᵘ·baik), colloq. abbrev. of *motor bicycle.*

1925 *Punch* 22 Apr. 433/1 Just think of going out on a mo-bike in top-hats and tail-coats! **1971** *Ceylon Observer* (Mag. ed.) 19 Sept. 7/3 A Japanese mo-bike (over 180 c.c. of course!).

mobile (mōᵘ·bail), *sb.*³ [Subst. use of MOBILE *a.*] **1. a.** (Also with pronunc. (mōᵘ·bīl).) A form of decoration consisting usu. of abstract designs in metal, plastic, etc., contrived (as by suspension) so as to be mobile. Cf. *STABILE *sb.*

[**1936** P. NASH in *Archit. Rev.* LXXX. 208/3 Shadows bring us to Calder, who is..so far as I know, the original inventor of mobile sculpture and so, also, of the '*objet*

mobile'. The mobile object is not now confined to Calder's invention; both Max Ernst and Duchamp have made various pieces of this nature.] **1949** *Ibid.* CVI. 117 Alexander Calder's work on the 'stabile' is not as well known in England as is his work on the now well established 'mobile'. In fact Calder has always done 'still' sculpture, and the term stabile, given to it by Hans Arp, appears to be some months older than the name mobile, which was invented by Marcel Duchamp. **1952** *Granta* 29 Nov. 8/1 We find it agreeable..to hang pastel-tinted antlers on the wall near a mobile. **1957** *Times* 18 Nov. 11/1 Mobiles at Heal's include a life-size black cat, and a cut-out set of small figures costs from 4s. and can be set up by children of about 10 years without help. **1958** E. Dundy *Dud Avocado* I. ix. 156 He picked up a wire coat-hanger and some string and a couple of paint-brushes and a shoe, and started making them into a Mobile. **1971** D. D. Boyden *Introd. Mus.* (ed. 2) 524 Someone has aptly noted that chance music is rather like the mobiles of Calder. **1972** *Sci. Amer.* Mar. 76/1 They were shown an arrangement of three colored geometrical objects in a 'mobile'.

b. *transf.* and *fig.*, esp. in *Mus.* (see quot. 1967).

1961 *Punch* 11 Jan. 116/3 Admirers of the hard, glittering mobiles constructed..by Stan Kenton may be pleased by *Standards in Silhouette*... A big, big band, making big, big sounds, in what was once a daringly experimental manner. **1967** *Listener* 2 Feb. 176/3 The crystallization of these new formal principles was the 'mobile'. It connotes a dynamic arrangement of musical thoughts in which several patterns are possible, depending on the decision of the interpreter... A 'mobile' is made up of finite (musical) thoughts of fairly conventional dimensions... As units they remain constant; but the arrangement of their sequence varies, subject to certain pre-compositional order. **1970** 'J. Morris' *Candywine Devel.* xvi. 184 Five electric guitars and a mobile of drums were backstopping a sleek, oxblood brown singer. **1971** E. Borroff *Mus. in Europe & U.S.* xxvii. 656 Other works include..*Symphonies* (1955), for fifteen soloists; *Mobile* for two pianos 1958.

2. Short for: (*a*) mobile canteen; (*b*) (*Austral.* and *N.Z.*) mobile barrier; (*c*) mobile police.

1940 *New Statesman* 9 Nov. 466/1 Go up and have a cup of tea at the mobile. **1969** *Australian* 24 May 34/4 Fifth.. over this trip and from behind the mobile here last week. **1971** W. J. Burley *Guilt Edged* iv. 62 Control to all mobiles: keep look out for red Mini-Cooper saloon. **1974** J. Gardner *Corner Men* ii. 14 Put out a call. There must be some mobiles around. We need them here.

Mobile, *sb.*[4]: see *Mobilian *sb.*

mobile, *a.* Now usu with pronunc. (mōu·bəil) in the U.K. **1. a.** Delete † *Obs.* and add later examples.

1927 *U.S. Daily* 22 Nov. 2/3 Mobile stations must be established in such a way as to comply as concerns frequencies and types of waves, with the general provision of Article 5. **1935** *Discovery* May 151/2 The treatment of patients far removed from the well-equipped hospitals, by means of mobile units complete with laboratories. **1937** *Archit. Rev.* LXXXI. 19 (*caption*) A mobile sculpture by Alexander Calder. **1938** *Encycl. Brit. Bk. of Year* 122/1 Mobile recording vans with a new method of editing records made it possible to broadcast composite sound records of events only a few minutes after their occurrence. **1940** *Economist* 5 Oct. 422/2 Cooking facilities have been provided by the L.C.C. Some mobile kitchens are at work. **1940** *New Statesman* 5 Oct. 321/2 Feeding centres and mobile canteens. **1955** *Radio Times* 22 Apr. 11/3 Franklin Engelmannn with a BBC mobile recording unit visits Dudley to meet local people. **1959** *Economist* 14 Mar. 991/1 Mobile shops have more than doubled in number since the war, and are still taking extra trade on to the roads at the rate of perhaps fifteen a week. **1960** *Library Assoc. Rec.* Aug. 262/2 *Mobile library*, a vehicle devised, equipped and operated to provide, as far as reasonably practicable, a service comparable to a part-time branch library. **1961** L. D. Stamp *Gloss. Geogr. Terms* 258/1 *Mobile or footloose industries*, broadly those generally called 'light'. **1962** *Economist* 17 Nov. 665/3 The mobile lounges will not only provide transport..between the terminal and the parked aircraft but will also serve as waiting rooms. **1971** *Guardian* 10 June 1/1 A 22-bed mobile hospital..was among the supplies which left for Calcutta. **1974** *Camping & Caravanning* Sept. 15/1 Fees 30p per unit per night, C.C.Y. 5 p. Mobile shop. Walking distance of beach.

f. *Sociol.* Of a person: able to move into different social levels, or a different environment or field of employment. Of a society: not rigidly stratified, in which upward or downward movement between social levels can take place, and also movement between fields of employment, etc., within the same social level.

1927 P. A. Sorokin *Social Mobility* II. vii. 138 Such a type of social stratification may be styled open, plastic, penetrable, or mobile. *Ibid.* v. xvii. 427 Unskilled labor is more mobile than skilled labor. **1940** K. Mannheim *Man & Society* II. vi. 93 The significance of the mobile elements in social and cultural life. **1945** C. W. Mills in *Jrnl. Econ. Hist.* V. Suppl. v. 39 For laissez faire, the pattern of success might involve a larger proportion of upwardly mobile persons. **1959** V. Packard *Status Seekers* (1960) xviii. 256 Many socially declining or downward-mobile people turn to alcohol or drugs for support.

g. *Philol.* = *movable *a.* 7 b.

1955 T. Burrow *Sanskrit Lang.* iii. 80 The so-called mobile *s*. Indo-European *s* when it formed the first member of an initial consonant group, was an unstable sound, and liable to disappear under conditions which it has not been possible accurately to define. **1965** G. Y. Shevelov *Prehist. of Slavic* 230 The mobile consonants, i.e. consonants sometimes used, sometimes dropped on word boundaries... *n*-mobile..*s*-mobile... Problem of *k*-mobile.

h. Special collocations: as, **mobile barrier** *Austral.* and *N.Z.*, in *Trotting*, a foldable barrier designed to facilitate a flying start; **mobile home**, a large caravan permanently parked and used as a residence.

1965 *Weekly News* (Auckland) 8 Dec. 59/1 The controversy that is developing over the use of the mobile barrier in trotting. **1954** *N.Y. Herald Tribune Bk. Rev.* 13 June 12 Books pertaining to trailer houses—or mobile homes—published within the last five years. **1961** *Daily Tel.* 22 Nov. 17/4 Mobile homes for 1,200 families could be provided on 300 vacant sites in London. **1969** *Eugene* (Oregon) *Register-Guard* 3 Dec. 5D/1 Mobile homes—the things people used to call trailer houses. **1973** *People's Jrnl.* (Inverness & Northern Counties ed.) 1 Dec. 22/5 *Mobile Home*, Coats Caravans. 32 ft. × 9 ft. 6 in. Astral Mobile Home. Double End Bedroom, Bathroom, Kitchen and Lounge. Solid Fuel Fire. £895.

2. b. (Earlier example.)

1853 Mill in *Edin. Rev.* XCVIII. 432 They [*sc.* the Athenians] were not fickle, but (a very different quality, vulgarly confounded with it) mobile; keenly susceptible.. to the feeling and impression of the moment.

3. Also of police.

1938 F. D. Sharpe *Sharpe of Flying Squad* i. 11 The Flying Squad has about twenty cars, and they are very different cars to those of the Mobile Police. **1955** *Radio Times* 22 Apr. 13/3 The Police. A series of eight talks. 7. Beats and Mobile Patrols. **1967** N. Lucas *C.I.D.* vi. 78 The new mobile patrol toured the streets with the hidden detectives scanning..the crowds.

-mobile. Used freely in the 20th century as the second element in combinations: **a.** Portable, or travelling under its own power. **b.** In occas. uses of immobile objects or structures, usu. having a function pertaining to, or being an imitation of, an automobile or other form of transport. (Examples, as *bloodmobile, bookmobile, clubmobile*, are entered under the first element in this Supplement.)

Mobilian (mobi·liăn), *sb.* Also **Mobile** (mobī·l). [? f. the town of *Mobile* in Alabama + -ian.] A lingua franca or trade language used formerly in south-eastern North America (see quot. 1907). Also as *adj.*

1840 G. Bancroft *Hist. U.S.* III. xxii. 249 The whole country south-east, south, and west of the Cherokees.. was in the possession of one great family of nations, of which the language was named by the French the Mobilian, and is described by Gallatin as the Muskhogee-Chocta. **1907** F. W. Hodge *Handbk. Amer. Indians* I. 916/1 The so-called Mobilian trade language was a corrupted Choctaw jargon used for the purposes of intertribal communication among all the tribes from Florida to Louisiana, extending northward on the Mississippi to about the junction of the Ohio. It was also known as the Chickasaw trade language. **1928** W. A. Read *Indian Place-Names Louisiana* 6 The identity of *Manchac* with the Mobilian *imashaka*, 'rear entrance', is rendered more plausible by my discovery of the form *Mashake*. **1937** *Amer. Speech* XII. 212 Besides the Shawnee words one Algonquian term has slipped in through the medium of the Mobilian trade language. **1947** P. S. Martin et al. *Indians before Columbus* 68 In the Southeast a Choctaw jargon called 'Mobilian' was spoken from Florida to Louisiana and up the Mississippi River as far north as the Ohio. **1964** *Amer. Speech* XXXIX. 16 He [*sc.* Charles P. G. Scott] attempted to push *O.K.* back to the Mobile trade language, current along the Gulf of Mexico in the eighteenth century.

mobiliary, *a.* Add: **2.** *mobiliary art* = *art mobilier* (*art *sb.* VI. c).

1927 [see *home *sb.*[1] 14]. **1960** *Times Lit. Suppl.* 2 Sept. 565/4 'Mobiliary' art in the form of sculpture, carving and engraving on bone, antler, ivory and stone.

mobility[1]. Add: **1. c.** *spec.* in *Sociol.* The possibility of movement between different social levels that exists in a society (*vertical mobility*); also the possibility of movement to different fields of employment or interest, or to new areas, within the same social level (*horizontal mobility*).

1900 *Amer. Jrnl. Sociol.* VI. 377 (*caption*) Mobility of type. **1927** P. A. Sorokin *Social Mobility* II. vii. 136 The intensiveness of the vertical mobility may be measured in the same way in the field of the political and occupational stratifications. *Ibid.* 160 Horizontal mobility, in spite of the great importance of the problem, is not an object of this study. **1938** T. H. Marshall *Class Conflict* 111 The use of mobility as an excuse for inequality is usually associated with a measure of self-deception. **1956** C. W. Mills *Power Elite* xv. 349 Only if the criteria of the top positions were meritorious..could we smuggle merit into such statistics of mobility. **1965** B. B. Wolman *Handbk. Clin. Psychol.* xxxiv. 979 While mobility has been frequently related to schizophrenia, R. Freedman..failed to find positive correlation between high mobility and high hospital admission rates of schizophrenics. **1972** S. Cotgrove *Sci. of Society* (rev. ed.) vii. 230 Restricted mobility facilitates the protection of privileges by a stratum and the development and persistence of a unitary culture.

f. *Chem.* and *Physics.* [tr. G. *beweglichkeit* (given this specific sense by F. Kohlrausch 1876, in *Nachrichten von d. K. Ges. d. Wissensch. und d. G.-A.-Universität zu Göttingen* 17 May 220).] The degree to which a charge carrier undergoes movement in a definite direction in response to an electric field, now usu. expressed as the average speed (in cm. per second) in a field of one volt per cm. divided by the net number of charges on the carrier.

1895 C. S. Palmer tr. *Nernst's Theoret. Chem.* II. vii. 315 The term mobility (Beweglichkeit) or velocity of transport will mean..the velocity with which 1 g.-ion will be transported under the influence of a pull of 1, *e.g.* 1 kilogram weight. *Ibid.* 316 If we denote the mobility of the positive and negative ions by U and V, then their respective velocities will be in the same ratio as their mobilities. *Ibid.* 317 The conductivity of a solution of a binary electrolyte is greater in accordance as it contains more free ions, and according as these have a greater mobility. **1912** *Jrnl. Chem. Soc.* CI. II. 1276 The following figures..are the results of the chief researches on the mobility of the hydrogen ion... All values are expressed in terms of the reciprocal ohm. **1924** J. R. Partington in H. S. Taylor *Treat. Physical Chem.* I. xi. 539 The equivalent conductance at infinite dilution is the sum of the mobilities of anion and kation at a given temperature. **1946** [see *carrier 1 k (ii)]. **1950** W. J. Moore *Physical Chem.* xv. 434 With two exceptions, the ionic mobilities in aqueous solutions do not differ as to order of magnitude, being all around 6×10^{-4} cm^2 $sec.^{-1}$ $volt^{-1}$. The exceptions are the hydrogen and hydroxyl ions with the abnormally high mobilities of $36{\cdot}2 \times 10^{-4}$ and $20{\cdot}5 \times 10^{-4}$. **1963** B. Fozard *Instrumentation Nucl. Reactors* ii. 15 In a uniform electric field the electrons and ions may be regarded as acquiring a uniform drift velocity which is superimposed upon their kinetic motion and directed towards the electrodes [of the ionisation chamber]... The term mobility may be used to indicate the ease with which ions may be caused to drift.

mobilization. Add: **1.** (Later examples; also examples in *Surg.*: cf. *mobilize *v.* 1 b.)

1890 Law & Jewell tr. *Gruber's Text-bk. Dis. Ear* xvii. 479 (*heading*) Mobilisation of the stapes. **1901** Rose & Carless *Man. Surg.* (ed. 4) xvi. 400 A most valuable adjuvant in the treatment of fractures is massage..whilst in some cases early mobilization is also desirable. **1930** *Morning Post* 7 Aug. 11/6 The credit mobilisation in London by the Australian banks to meet Governmental commitments..was approved. **1967** *Economist* 14 Oct. 120/1 A growing number of Labour MPs are sponsoring the case for government 'mobilisation' of the £3,200 million odd of foreign shares held by private British investors. **1967** S. R. Mawson *Dis. Ear* (ed. 2) xxi. 515 Relief of conductive deafness due to stapedial ankylosis by mobilization of stapes.

b. *Sociol.* The organizing of some hitherto unused form of social energy to bring about changes within a society.

1953 K. W. Deutsch *Nationalism & Social Communication* vi. 104 The processes of mobilization and assimilation may be illustrated rather strikingly in the case of Finland. **1964** G. Germani in I. L. Horowitz *New Sociol.* 395 We understand by mobilization the 'excess'..of group participation in relation to the level defined by the old society as 'normal'. **1968** A. Etzioni *Active Society* xv. 393 Whatever the form of mobilization, whether it be direct or indirect, the process entails a shift of control and/or a shift of the usage of assets. **1972** Turner & Killian *Collective Behavior* (ed. 2) iv. 62/2 The crowding together of Negro Americans in the black ghettoes is a type of mobilization that has contributed to urban insurrections.

mobilize, *v.* Add: **1. b.** *Surg.* To restore mobility to (an ankylosed bone); to free or detach so as to render more accessible.

1894 O. Dodd tr. *Politzer's Text-bk. Dis. Ear* 318 The stapes is mobilized by means of a single or double hook inserted between the crura. **1914** Rose & Carless *Man. Surg.* (ed. 9) xxxv. 1076 If a stone is lodged behind the second piece of the duodenum, it may be possible to manipulate it up, and make it accessible above the intestine; but otherwise the duodenum must be mobilized by dividing the peritoneum on its outer edge. **1953** *N.Y. State Jrnl. Med.* LIII. 2653/1 The stapes was mobilized, and the hearing improved on the operating table. **1967** G. M. Wyburn et al. *Conc. Anat.* iv. 121/2 Next the temporal lobes [of the brain] should be mobilised from the floor of the middle cranial fossa.

c. *Sociol.* To bring into circulation (hitherto unused social assets or energies).

1953 K. W. Deutsch *Nationalism & Social Communication* vi. 100 Within any geographical setting and any population, economic, social, and technological developments mobilize individuals for relatively more intensive communication. *Ibid.*, Population mobilized for mass communication. **1968** A. Etzioni *Active Society* xv. 409 Two disparate organizations seem to mobilize a collectivity more effectively than one. **1968** G. Myrdal in W. Ewald *Environment & Change* IV. xvi. 261 Their [*sc.* the lower strata of American society's] low rate of participation in elections, when they are not mobilized and exploited by the political machines.

2. Also *fig.*

1871 L. W. M. Lockhart *Fair to See* III. xxxiii. 100 A hundred times he had paraded the line of arguments he meant to employ, and the reserve which, in case of their failure, he held in readiness, and, so to speak, mobilised. **1951** D. B. Truman *Governmental Process* ix. 271 The political party in the United States most commonly is a device for mobilizing votes.

mobilized *ppl. a.*, **mobilizing** *vbl. sb.*: further examples.

1913 in W. S. Churchill *World Crisis 1911–14* (1923) viii. 190 A very large staff would be employed at all the mobilizing centres to report upon the whole workings of the mobilization. **1953** K. W. Deutsch *Nationalism & Social Communication* vi. 101 The rate of growth of the mobilized population..and the changes in its sociological level could all be calculated. **1968** A. Etzioni *Active*

Society xv. 408 Strains and conflicts among the organizational arms of any mobilizing collectivity should be 'routine' and expected.

Möbius (mǒ·biŭs). Also **Moebius.** The name of August Ferdinand *Möbius* (1790–1868), German mathematician, used, chiefly in *Möbius band, strip*, to designate a surface having only one side and one edge, formed by twisting one end of a rectangular strip through 180 degrees and joining it to the other end.

1904 E. R. HEDRICK tr. *Goursat's Course in Math. Analysis* I. 546 Möbius' strip. **1941** COURANT & ROBBINS *What is Math.?* v. 260 If the Moebius strip is cut along this [center] line..we find that it remains in one piece. **1950** Möbius band [see *KLEIN BOTTLE]. **1960** F. LAND *Lang. Math.* xi. 171 We have in the Moebius strip the strange object which consists of one continuous surface bounded by one continuous curve. **1965** Möbius strip [see *KLEIN BOTTLE]. **1970** *New Yorker* 28 Nov. 58/3 Barbara, taking a pair of scissors..turned the clipping on fragrant Christmas gifts into a Möbius strip. **1974** *Times* 10 Sept. 14/8 If the curtain at Covent Garden three weeks hence goes up on yet another ring, circle, hoop, saucer, dish or Möbius band I shall be heard to blow my nose in an ominous falling figure..which..betokens Doom.

mobocracy. 2. (Later examples.)

1921 G. B. SHAW *Back to Methuselah* Pref. p. lxii, Bastiat had proved convincingly that Nature had arranged Economic Harmonies which would settle social questions far better than theocracies or aristocracies or mobocracies. **1949** F. L. WRIGHT (*title*) Genius and the mobocracy.

mobsman. Add: **2.** (Earlier and later examples.) Also, = next.

1846 *Swell's Night Guide* p. iii, The tophic blacklegs and swell mobsman, who can pluck a pigeon with the sang froid of a ripened friendship. **1935** A. J. POLLOCK *Underworld Speaks* 77/1 *Mobsman*, a gangster, a thug; ruffian; gunman. **1974** *Daily Tel.* (Colour Suppl.) 29 Nov. 86/4 It is doubtful if the Victorian Londoner needed warning, for the artful mobsmen, toolers and dippers, together with their stickman accomplices, were everywhere among the crowds.

mobster (mǫ·bstəɹ). *slang* (orig. *U.S.*). [f. MOB *sb.*[1] + -STER.] A member of a group of criminals; cf. *GANGSTER. Also *attrib.* and *transf.*

1917 *Lincoln* (Nebraska) *Evening News* 11 July 4 Many mobsters have left the city, it is asserted, and leaders of the mob are going to be hard to find. **1940** *New Yorker* 13 July 17/1 A mob nickname he got from the mobsters. **1947** E. HYAMS *William Medium* x. 199 South African diamond mobsters. **1947** J. MULGAN *Report on Experience* x. 125, I never lived in Chicago, but have a wide vicarious acquaintance from films and paperbacks of mobster-rule and gang-law. **1957** *Observer* 3 Nov. 19/3 Mr. [Marc] Lawrence, renowned for his portraits of flinty Hollywood mobsters. **1962** D. WARNER *Death of Bogey* I. ii. 10 A scurrying horde of spivs and pimps, fiddlers and tweedlers, tearaways, mobsters. **1964** D. VARADAY *Gara-Yaka* xviii. 159 The dead mobsters were mangy, disease-ridden outcasts of the dog world. **1972** D. E. WESTLAKE *Cops & Robbers* (1973) xvi. 251, I was afraid to think about Vigano and his mobsters.

mocamp (mōᵘ·kæmp). [f. MO(TOR *sb.* + CAMP *sb.*[2]] (See quot. 1970.)

1967 *Times* 1 Nov. (Suppl.) p. ii/1 If you're touring Turkey, stay at BP Mocamps. Here's a welcome for campers and caravanners. **1970** *Britannica Bk. of Year* (U.S.) 798/3 *Mocamp*, a camp providing tourists with a protected area for tents and trailers and offering various conveniences and services. **1972** *Maclean's Mag.* June 54/3 In Turkey camping facilities called Mocamps are found all over the country.

moccasin. Add: **1. b.** A type of shoe for informal wear, resembling those worn by American Indians.

1895 *Montgomery Ward Catal.* 513/3 Infants' Moccasins, made from soft dingola stock, with silk lace and tassel. **1944** H. MCCLOY *Panic* ii. 13 The loose sweater, kilted skirt, and flat-heeled moccasins she had put on so hastily. **1970** B. KNOX *Children of Mist* iii. 53 He wore a blue sports shirt with brown shoes, his feet were in light tan moccasins.

c. *Austral.* and *N.Z.* (See quots.)

1929 H. B. SMITH *Sheep & Wool Industry Austral. & N.Z.* (ed. 3) x. 75 The shearers..arrayed in their working clothes, with bowyangs..and moccasins on (a kind of shoe made out of wool-pack, after the style of the foot-covering of the Red Indian). **1965** *N.Z. Listener* 26 Feb. 15/2 *Moccasin*, the shearer's home-made footwear, usually made of sacking or felt.

2. moccasin flower (earlier and later examples).

1680 in J. Ray *Hist. Plant.* (1688) II. 1926/1 Helleborine flore rotundo luteo, purpureis venis striato. The Mockasine flower. **1954** C. J. HYLANDER *Macmillan Wild Flower Bk.* 65 The Lady's-slippers or Moccasin-flowers are easily recognizable by the inflated sac which forms the lip of the flower. **1970** R. T. NORTHEN *Home Orchid Growing* (ed. 3) 197/2 Cypripedium. These are the moccasin-flowers or ladyslippers of our woods and moist meadows.

3. For '*Ancistrodon*' substitute '*Agkistrodon*'. (Earlier and later examples.)

1784 J. FILSON *Discovery Kentucke* 27 The horned and the mockason snakes. **1784** J. SMYTH *Tour U.S.A.* I. vii. 54 The most noxious, virulent, and deleterious of the species, the rattle, moccasson, and horn-snakes. **1788** [see *COPPER-BELLY]. **1965** R. & D. MORRIS *Men & Snakes* iv. 80 As recently as 1943, it was claimed that moccasin venom had been used with success in the treatment of rheumatoid arthritis.

4. *attrib.*, as **moccasin telegram** or **telegraph** *N. Amer.*, a means for the rapid or surreptitious transmission of information, orig. by an Indian runner; = **bush telegraph*.

1908 A. C. LAUT *Conquest Gt. Northwest* II. 35 Word of the white woman ran before the advancing traders by 'moccasin telegram'. **1909** A. D. CAMERON *New North* 349 And now, apprised by moccasin telegraph, we are all on the *qui vive* to catch sight of a floating bride. **1927** *Sat. Even. Post* 23 July 3/3 That agency known to white men as the Moccasin Telegraph, by which odd bits of news are flashed from one isolated native camp to another. **1969** *Islander* (Victoria, B.C.) 15 June 5/1 Word of the new constable was relayed to Simon by moccasin telegraph.

moccasined, *a.* **1.** (Earlier and later examples.)

1829 J. F. COOPER *Borderers* III. iii. 89 The two chiefs left the piazza in the noiseless manner of the moccasined foot. **1951** I. SHAW *Troubled Air* viii. 138 Moving a moccasined foot gently back and forth. **1968** M. WOODHOUSE *Rock Baby* xvii. 176 She started back towards the camp, her moccasined feet leaving damp footprints.

mocha[1]. Add: **4.** A type of English pottery, made from the late eighteenth to the early twentieth century, with white or cream body decorated with coloured bands on to which moss- or fern-like patterns have been applied. Freq. *attrib.*

1837 S. SHAW *Chem. of Compounds used in Manuf. Porc.* I. v. 346 The readiness with which they combine with earths..renders them very useful in the Mocha and dipped ware. *Ibid.* II. i. 410 The peculiar kind of clay, in this neighbourhood,..veins of which are still kept open for supplying the same, fine in grain, and dark in colour, for the mocha dip. **1953** *N. Teulon-Porter Coll. Mocha Pott.* (Stoke-on-Trent Museum & Art Gallery Comm.) 1 There are a few collectors in the field and soon Mocha will vie for attention with lustre or transfer printed pottery. **1961** L. G. G. RAMSEY *Connoisseur New Guide Antique Eng. Pott., Porc. & Glass* 67 Mocha ware, so named because of its resemblance to the quartz mocha stone, was in demand for kitchen jugs and mugs and large cups and saucers after its invention about 1780. **1968** *Canad. Antiques Collector* June 17/2 What is Mocha Ware? Sometimes referred to as 'Leeds Ware' or 'banded creamware' it is a creamware decorated with seaweed or tree silhouettes. This was made from 1787 up to 1903.

mocha[2]. Add: **1. b.** Used *attrib.* of cakes, puddings, etc., flavoured with coffee, or coffee and chocolate.

1892 A. B. MARSHALL *Larger Cookery Bk.* xii. 475 *Moka Cake*... Prepare a Genoise paste mixture.., bake for an hour and a quarter, then turn out, and, when cold, mask over with Coffee glace. **1908** J. KIRKLAND *Mod. Baker* III. lxxxi. 390 A butter cream flavoured with coffee and vanilla..will be useful for flavouring and decorating the popular cakes known as *Mocha fancies*. **1963** V. NABOKOV *Gift* v. 305 Old Stupishin, whose spoon was working its way through a wedge of mocha cake. **1972** M. J. BOSSE *Incident at Naha* ii. 102 His skin was like rich mocha chocolate. **1975** *New Yorker* 3 Feb. 26/2, I sold schnecken, cookies, apple turnovers, and mocha tarts.

c. A shade or tint of the colour of mocha coffee; a dark brown colour. Also *mocha brown*.

1895 *Montgomery Ward Catal.* 274/3 Men's Fedora Hats ..Colors: Blue black, mocha brown and slate. *Ibid.* 275/1 Fedora Hats... Colors: Black, dark brown, gray, tan and mocha. **1919** T. S. ELIOT *Sweeney among Nightingales* in *Poems*, The silent man in mocha brown Sprawls at the window sill and gapes. **1971** *Vogue* 15 Sept. 15 Eye shadow in earthy wine, rose, turquoise and mocha. **1974** *Harrods Christmas Catal.* 15 Leather clutch bag... Black, mocha brown, navy, rust, or terracotta.

3. (See quot. 1968.) Also *attrib.*

1895 *Montgomery Ward Catal.* 290/2 Men's dressed mocha kid gloves. **1922** [see *BOULTON *a.*]. **1938** E. BOWEN *Death of Heart* II. iv. 235 The stitching on her brown mocha gloves. **1968** J. IRONSIDE *Fashion Alphabet* 238 *Mocha*, a fine, soft, hard-wearing leather made from sheepskin from Arabia, Africa and Persia. The chief outlet was Mocha in Arabia, hence the name.

‖ **mochi** (mǫ·tʃi). Also 7 musho. [Jap.] A cake made from pounded, glutinous rice.

In some quots. *mochi* has the honorific prefix *o-*.

1616 R. COCKS *Diary* 10 Feb. (1883) I. 109 Shezque Dono..came to the English howse and brought a present of *mushos*, wyne, and redish. **1880** I. L. BIRD *Unbeaten Tracks Japan* I. 235 *Mochi*, a small round cake of unbaked rice dough, though insipid, is not unpalatable, and is much in favour. **1891** A. M. BACON *Jap. Girls & Women* i. 5 Cakes of mochi, or rice paste. **1936** K. TEZUKA *Jap. Food* 49 *Mochi* (glutinous rice boiled and pounded) is a special New Year food. **1960** B. LEACH *Potter in Japan* ii. 62 We were taken indoors and fed on what was described to me as good country food, which included O Mochi. These are dumplings made of pounded steamed rice of a particularly glutinous variety. *Ibid.* 239 *Mochi*, steamed and dried cakes of glutinous rice. **1970** J. KIRKUP *Japan behind Fan* 106 We would sip green tea and beer and nibble peanuts and seaweed biscuits and *o-mochi*, or sweet bean cakes.

Mochica (motʃī·kă), *a.* and *sb.* Also **Mochican, Moche,** 9 **Moxa.** [Sp., f. an Indian word; cf. *Moche*, the name of an archæological site in the valley of the same name in the coastal region of northern Peru.] **A.** *adj.* Of or pertaining to the Mochica, a pre-Inca people living on the Peruvian coast, or their modern descendants, or the language spoken by them. **B.** *sb.* **a.** The name of this people or a member of it. **b.** The language of the Mochica.

1853 F. L. HAWKS tr. *Rivero & Von Tschudi's Peruvian Antiquities* v. 97 The Moxa language has strictly no declension. **1871** *Jrnl. R. Geogr. Soc.* XLI. 283 Bishop Luis Geronimo de Orè..is the only source from which we get specimens of the Puquina and Mochica languages. *Ibid.* 323 We have..the Lord's Prayer in the *Mochica*, a dialect spoken in the valleys of Runahuanac and Huarco. *Ibid.* 326 Tribes along the Peruvian coast..the *Chimus* (the *Yuncas* of Carrera); the *Mochicas* (the *Chinchas* of Garcilasso). **1877** E. G. SQUIER *Peru* viii. 128 You should have seen my Moche children forty years ago. **1927** *Geogr. Rev.* XVII. 42 The inhabitants of Chan-Chan spoke a language known as Yunga (or Yunca) or Mochica of which today vestiges survive in the vicinity of Eten. **1948** [see *BICHROME *a.* and *sb.*[2]]. **1953** A. C. KINSEY et al. *Sexual Behavior Human Female* vii. 231 The Mochican pottery of ancient Peru..depicts practically every petting and coital technique. **1959** [see *HUACO]. **1961** J. B. PRIESTLEY *Saturn over Water* v. 57 A monochrome ceramic, of the Mochica Culture, representing a warrior in ambush. **1965** A. EMMERICH *Sweat of Sun & Tears of Moon* ii. 15 The Mochica also continued the use of elaborate gold headdresses by important personages. **1967** R. PENISTON-BIRD tr. *Gallo's Gold of Peru* 15 The Mochicans of the Peruvian coast..having as their centre the pyramids of the sun and moon at Moche developed the science of metallurgy before most of the Peruvian peoples. **1971** L. A. BOGER *Dict. World Pott. & Porc.* 229/2 The decoration on Mochica pottery which is painted or modeled or a combination of both, gives a vivid picture of the life and customs of the people.

mochree, var. *MACHREE.

mock, *sb.*[1] Add: **1. b.** *to put the* (or *a*) *mock(s) on* (someone): see quot. 1943. *Austral. slang.*

1911 E. DYSON *Benno* 33 It's up t'me t'put a mock on that tripester. **1938** X. HERBERT *Capricornia* xxxii. 482 'He put the mocks on me,' roared Norman... 'What's he saying, dear?' 'He..reckons I told the police on him.' **1943** BAKER *Dict. Austral. Slang* (ed. 3) 51 *Mocks on, put the*, to upset someone's plans, to spoil a person's calculations. Also, 'put the mock on'. **1965** W. GROUT *My Country's 'Keeper* xx. 206, I hope I am not 'putting the mock' on Norm because my feelings are the same as the rest of the Australian Test players: When O'Neill is a doubtful Test starter the job always looks grimmer.

mock, *a.* Add: **1. c.** (Earlier and later examples of *mock modesty*.)

1749 J. CLELAND *Mem. Woman Pleasure* II. 12 The mask of mock-modesty was compleatly taken off. **1880** SWINBURNE *Heptalogia* 90 Thank my stars I'm as free from mock-modesty, friend, As from vulgar fatuity. **1962** I. S. BLACK *High Bright Sun* i. 8 She had..none of the island girls' self-consciousness, none of their mock modesty.

d. Designating an examination set by a school to give pupils practice for a specified public examination. Also *ellipt.* as *sb.*

1960 *Guardian* 22 June 6/4 A prefect enters... 'It was a long time ago that we did Mock.' **1960** *Where?* III. 15 '*Mock*' *GCE*, an internal examination..run by some schools as a rehearsal for the normal GCE examinations. **1964** C. DALE *Other People* iii. 71 June..had done Tennyson for mock GCE. **1967** *Guardian* 2 May 6/5 Some interviewers..asked if students had done 'mock' 'A' levels at school. **1969** C. FREMLIN *Possession* xvii. 138 How could she ever get through her Mocks next term?

2. mock auctioneer, the auctioneer at a mock auction; **mock croc**: see *CROC[2] 1 b.

1959 *Daily Tel.* 13 Mar. 23/4 The requirement that a mock auctioneer should display his name and address was still valid though it was not enforced by the police. **1959** *Listener* 9 July 72/1 The mock-auctioneer in back street or fairground.

3. a. (Further examples.)

1931 *Times Lit. Suppl.* 18 June 479/1 The sumptuous mock-Tudor mansion. **1933** L. BLOOMFIELD *Lang.* xxiii. 421 Mock-learned words, like *scrumptious, rambunctious, absquatulate*. **1936** *Discovery* Oct. 321/2 The short 'Brutus' curls of regency mock-classical beauties. **1949** KOESTLER *Insight & Outlook* vii. 105 His facial expression and whole attitude must be mock-aggressive. **1951** W. DE LA MARE *Winged Chariot* 58 Mock-solemn creatures, with our jackdaw airs. **1952** S. KAUFFMANN *Philanderer* (1953) iii. 38 Russell inquired, in customary mock-religious tones, about the state of the Street [*sc.* Wall Street] and cotton futures. **1958** *Spectator* 8 Aug. 193/1 The viewer who is sitting proudly in mock-antique splendour. **1968** *Listener* 18 July 92/3 A baron who mock-diffidently invites him to dinner. **1969** *Ibid.* 9 Jan. 43/3 We all went off to the pub: mock Tudor, phoney like the rest of us. **1975** J. HOWLETT *Christmas Spy* II. ii. 42 Her mock-Jacobean entrance hall.

mock, *v.* Add: **4. c.** *to mock up*: to make a mock-up of (see *MOCK-UP); also, to counterfeit, simulate, imitate; to contrive or improvise; freq. **mocked-up** *ppl. a.*

1911 *Encycl. Brit.* XXIV. 971/2 The shapes and sizes of the armour plates are sometimes obtained by the 'mocking up' process, in which the surface of the armour is represented in three dimensions. **1914** in W. S. Churchill *World Crisis 1911–14* (1923) 527 It is necessary to construct without delay a dummy fleet... They are then to be mocked up to represent particular battleships of the 1st and 2nd Battle Squadrons. *Ibid.* 528 The utmost secrecy must be observed, and special measures taken to banish all foreigners from the districts where the mocking-up [of the battleships] is being done. **1950** *Jrnl. R. Aeronaut. Soc.* LIV. 305/1 The first type should be used..provided that

certain sections, as for example the engine installation, are mocked up accurately, if necessary as a separate mock-up. **1952** *Archit. Rev.* CXII. 55 It consisted of fabrics and prototype furniture by Terence Conran, arranged in a room cunningly mocked-up with a couple of venetian blinds and a bamboo ceiling. **1955** A. H. N. GREEN-ARMYTAGE *Portrait St. Luke* vii. 121 Mocked-up discourses in the biography of a man whose trade it was to deliver discourses of his own. **1959** *Observer* 5 April 18/4 The fuddy-duddy diplomat whose mocked-up vicissitudes make the story. **1961** *Listener* 12 Oct. 576/3 Denis Mitchell mocked up a couple of glimpses of America. **1967** *Ibid.* 2 Feb. 175/3 Not a very good play, perhaps, with some mocked-up dialogue and sex brought in as a perfunctory afterthought.

mockage. **1.** (Later examples.)

a **1916** A. R. MACEWEN *Hist. Church in Scotl.* (1918) II. xxvii. 176 In their mockage they termed every thing that repugned to their corrupt affections 'devout imagination'. **1922** E. A. PARRY *What Judge Thought* viii. 133 It is interesting to remember that in Lewis Carroll, an ironist of a different type from Maule, we have another example of a deeply scientific mathematician revelling in the expression of ludicrous antiphrasis and quaint ridicule and mockage of commonplace humanity.

mocker¹. Add: **1. c.** *transf.*

1611 BIBLE *Prov.* xx. 1 Wine *is* a mocker, strong drink is raging. **1972** N. MARSH *Tied up in Tinsel* vii. 177 'He was a wine-bibber,' Nigel shouted. 'Wine is a mocker.'

d. Slang phr. *to put the mocker*(*s*) *on*: to thwart or bring bad luck to (a person, enterprise, etc.), to deride, mock, denigrate. Also *to have* (*got*) *the mockers on, to give* (one) *the mockers*, etc. Cf. *MOCK *sb.*¹ 1 b.

1923 C. DREW *Rogues & Ruses* 115 They'll ave to race without me to-morrow. I've got a mocker hung on me. **1949** L. GLASSOP *Luck Palmer* vii. 62 It's that sheila... She's put the mocker on us. **1970** 'B. MATHER' *Break in Line* v. 61 'He isn't bad at all.' 'Then what did you put the mockers on him for?' **1970** J. PORTER *Dover strikes Again* ii. 36 This investigation had got the mockers on it from the start. **1974** 'J. Ross' *Burning of Billy Toober* xi. 102, I tailed him... Not to do anything. Just to let him see he was being tailed. To give him the mockers.

mocker² (mǫ·kəɹ). *Austral.* and *N.Z. slang.* Also **mokker.** [Origin obscure.] Clothes; a dress. So **mo·ckered-up** *a.*, dressed up.

1938 PARTRIDGE *Dict. Slang* (ed. 2) 1014/2 *Mockered up*, dressed in one's best. **1945** BAKER *Austral. Lang.* vi. 119 *All laired up* and its synonym *all mockered up* may also be noted. **1953** —— *Australia Speaks* iv. 106 *Mocker*, clothes in general. **1959** G. SLATTER *Gun in my Hand* 51 Gives us a hand sometimes on the mixer or labourin about. Gets into his old mocker and gets stuck in. **1965** M. SHADBOLT *Among Cinders* xxv. 250 She was mockered up to the nines.

mocker-nut. (Earlier and later examples.)

1814 F. PURSH *Flora Americæ Septentrionalis* II. 638 *Juglans tomentosa*... This is known under the name of Mocker Nut, White-heart Hickory or Common Hickory. **1832** D. J. BROWNE *Sylva Amer.* 187 In the part of New Jersey which lies on the river Hudson, this species is known by the name of Mockernut Hickory. **1926** E. M. ROBERTS *Time of Man* 364, I see you dance under the mockernut tree. **1947** COLLINGWOOD & BRUSH *Knowing your Trees* 152/1 Attaining maturity at 250 to 300 years, mockernut hickory sometimes reaches a height of ninety or a hundred feet. **1969** T. H. EVERETT *Living Trees of World* 98/2 The mockernut..forms a handsome specimen that grows up to 90 feet high with a trunk up to 3 feet in diameter... Its nuts have thick, hard shells that contain a very small amount of sweet meat.

mock-up (mǫ·kʌp). [f. *MOCK *v.* 4 c.] **a.** An experimental model (often full-sized) of a projected aircraft, ship, apparatus, etc., used esp. for study, testing, practice, or display. Also *attrib.*

1920 *Flight* 19 Feb. 218/1 If the dimensions of such parts are difficult to determine on paper, the use of 'mock-ups' should be resorted to for this purpose. **1933** *Jrnl. R. Aeronaut. Soc.* XXXVII. 759 A mock-up of the eventual design was built to full scale with every instrument, lever, and fitting installed. **1944** U. SINCLAIR *Presidential Agent* (1945) IV. xv. 292 At the moment the Germans had the fastest fighter [plane], but Robbie had a new one in the 'mock-up' stage that was going to knock them all cold. **1944** [see *CONSOLE *sb.* 3 b]. **1951** R. BRADBURY *Illustr. Man* (1952) 106 It's only a mockup... When they plan a rocket they build a full-scale model first, of aluminium. **1966** T. PYNCHON *Crying of Lot 49* iv. 84 She was gazing at a mockup of a space capsule. **1968** *Daily Tel.* (Colour Suppl.) 8 Nov. 23 (*caption*) This instrument panel mock-up..resembles as closely as possible the eventual airliner. **1971** *Sunday Australian* 8 Aug. 3/3 A 747 training mock-up at Sydney Airport.

b. *transf.* and *fig.* A plan, model, conception; an imitation.

1954 G. SMITH *Flaw in Crystal* xvi. 163 These coloured sheets..were mock-ups for a new children's magazine. **1957** J. F. HORNER *Summary of Scientology* 79 Because they do not immediately alter to fit his mock-up, he is constantly failing. **1959** J. CARY *Captive & Free* xiii. 68 'What I want to know,' she said, 'is when we're going to see the mock-up of the new front page.' **1959** *Guardian* 4 Dec. 13/5 The thing is written in a half-bantering Anglicised mock-up of the Spanish idiom. **1961** L. MUMFORD *City in Hist.* Note to plate 38, 'All under one roof' may prove just a mock-up for the terminal form of the anti-city.

mocky (mǫ·ki). *U.S. slang.* Also **mockey, mockie.** [Origin uncertain; perh. f. Yiddish *makeh* a boil, sore.] A Jew. Also *attrib.* or as *adj.*

1931 D. RUNYON in *Collier's* 10 Jan. 10/3, I consider this..disrespectful, like calling Jewish people mockies, or Heebs, or geese. **1937** E. H. SUTHERLAND *Professional Thief* i. 12, I was over on the East Side and there saw this Jew who was pointed out to me as one of their best mocky cannons. **1943** I. WOLFERT *Tucker's People* xxix. 481 Love thy neighbor if he's not..a mockie or a slicked-up greaseball from the Argentine. **1955** *Publ. Amer. Dial. Soc.* XXIV. 90 Jewish organizations are referred to as *mocky mobs* or *mocky jew mobs*. 'Mocky is not a Jew. It's a Sixth Avenue Jew.'

mocock (mokǫ·k). *N. Amer.* Also **makak, makuk, mocuck, mohcock, mokuk, muccuck.** [American Indian.] (See quot. 1827.)

1779 J. LONG *Jrnl.* (1904) II. 155 We were reduced to a few fish and some wild rice, or *menomon* (which are kept in *muccucks*, or bark boxes). **1827** T. L. MCKENNEY *Sk. Tour to Lakes* 194 A mocock is a little receptacle of a basket form, and oval, though without a handle, made of birch bark, with a top sewed on with *wattap* (the fine roots of the red cedar, split,) the smaller ones are ornamented with porcupines' quills, died red, yellow, and green. **1839** C. M. KIRKLAND *New Home* xx. 138 The Indians bring in immense quantities [of whortle-berries] slung in panniers or mococks of bark on the sides of their wild-looking ponies. **1859** P. KANE *Wanderings among Indians N. Amer.* 32 My companion was cooking some fish in a moh-cock, Indian fashion (for we had lost our kettle). **1905** *N.Y. Even. Post* 6 May, An old squaw stopped to offer a small mocock, a birch-bark box, holding perhaps a pound of maple sugar. **1931** G. L. NUTE *Voyageur* 80 In the spring maple sugar was also bought by the *makuk* (a birch-bark vessel) from the squaws. **1959** E. TUNIS *Indians* iii. 53/1 By far the commonest birch-bark container was the mocuck, with a square bottom larger than its round top, that served as box or basket at need.

mod (mǫd), *sb.*² Colloq. abbrev. of MODIFICATION. Also occas. as abbrev. of MODIFY *v.*

1943 C. H. WARD-JACKSON *Piece of Cake* 43 Has this Wimpey got the new escape gear mod? **1958** 'N. SHUTE' *Rainbow & Rose* i. 17 Captain Pascoe had it modded, special. **1967** *Autocar* 5 Oct. 24/1 This Healey had all the works racing mods which brought the engine power up to 210 b.h.p. **1967** *New Scientist* 14 Dec. 654/2 If the 'mods' are minor, the production line could absorb them without much interruption. **1974** *Publishers' Weekly* 12 Aug. 54/2 A rising generation of behavioral psychologists..is fanning out into our society to do its 'behavior mod' thing... These lab-trained mod squads have begun infiltrating schools, American family life, [etc.].

mod (mǫd), *sb.*³ and *a.* Also with capital initial. [Abbrev. of MODERN *a.* and *sb.* or MODERNIST.] **A.** *sb.* A teenager who is characterized by his sophistication and tidiness; freq. contrasted with *ROCKER¹. Also *attrib.* **B.** *adj.* Modern, sophisticated, stylish, esp. in dress.

1960 *New Left Rev.* Sept.–Oct. 4/2 Teds and Mods, Beatniks and Ravers. **1963** *Guardian* 13 May 18/1 Fights between the 'mods' and the 'rockers'. **1964** *Observer* 24 May 12/2 Mods and Rockers have co-existed comparatively well for a year or so—the Mods, neatly dressed and on scooters, the Rockers in studded leather jackets and on motor-bikes. **1964** *Punch* 3 June 815/1 (*heading*) Modgirl. **1965** *Granta* Summer 10 Student activists..have taken more account of the mod image cultivated by some universities. **1966** *Punch* 5 Oct. 505/2 He is naturally anxious that your furnishings should include what that enlightened store now calls 'Mod Gear'. **1968** J. IRONSIDE *Fashion Alphabet* 22 The Mods, both girls and boys, were very clean and neat and both wore close cut hair. *Ibid.* 194 The 'Mod' hair-cut, as opposed to long-haired 'Rockers', is short, neat and close to the head. **1970** G. JACKSON *Let.* 4 Apr. in *Soledad Brother* (1971) 207 This running dog ..was transmitting the credo of the slave to our youth, the mod version of the old house nigger. **1972** *Daily Colonist* (Victoria, B.C.) 25 Feb. 4/2 The operation by the Metropolitan Police..of a 'mod squad'..whose members stroll the streets in 'mod' dress and unshorn hair. **1973** E. BULLINS *Theme is Blackness* 167 Everybody in our integrated circle of mod people is with it, man. We're the Now Crowd. **1975** *Islander* (Victoria, B.C.) 3 Aug. 4/3 Jerry, a mod young priest from San Diego.

mod (mǫd; *also read as* 'modulo'), *prep. Math.* Also **mod.** (with point). Abbrev. of *MODULO *prep.*

The notation $b \equiv c$ (mod. *a*) ('*b* is congruent to *c* modulo *a*') was introduced by Gauss (*Disquisitiones Arithmeticae* (1801) I. 2).

1854 *Cambr. & Dublin Math. Jrnl.* IX. 85 Each of these quantities must be congruent to zero, that is $A_0 \equiv 0$, $A_1 \equiv 0, \ldots A_{p-2} \equiv 0$ (mod. *p*). **1860** *Rep. Brit. Assoc. Adv. Sci. 1859* I. 230 The congruence $\phi(x) \equiv 0$, mod P, is said to be solved, when all the integral values of *x* are assigned which make the left hand number of the congruence divisible by P. **1949** USPENSKY & HEASLET *Elem. Number Theory* vi. 128 Two congruences with the same moduli can be added or subtracted, member by member, like equalities. In other words, from two congruences $A \equiv a$ (mod *m*), $B \equiv b$ (mod *m*) it follows that $A \pm B \equiv a \pm b$ (mod *m*). **1949** W. LEDERMANN *Introd. Theory Finite Groups* i. 17, $ax \equiv bx$ (mod. *m*) implies that $a \equiv b$ (mod. *m*). **1971** D. GORENSTEIN in Powell & Higman *Finite Simple Groups* ii. 67, *q* is an odd prime power congruent to -1 (mod 4).

modacrylic (mǫdăkri·lik). [f. MOD(IFIED *ppl. a.* + *ACRYLIC *sb.*] A type of synthetic fibre consisting of molecules with between 35 and 85 per cent by mass of —$CH_2CH(CN)$— units (derived from acrylonitrile), which is used for children's nightwear, dresses, and household textiles.

1959 *Federal Register* (U.S.) 10 Feb. 981/2 The following generic names for manufactured fibers..are hereby established... Modacrylic. **1964** *Which?* Aug. 253/1 Fabrics made from modacrylic are easy to wash in warm water, and require little or no ironing. **1973** *Materials & Technol.* VI. vii. 495 Materials such as Saran and modacrylics do not burn but shrink away from the flame. **1974** *Encycl. Brit. Micropædia* VI. 958/2 Wigs made of modacrylics have had good acceptance.

modal, *a.* and *sb.* **A. 4.** Add to def.: Esp. in various collocations, as *modal logic*, that branch of logic which is concerned with the study of modal propositions (see also quots.).

1932 LEWIS & LANGFORD *Symbolic Logic* vi. 153 (*heading*) Consistency and the modal functions. **1943** *Mind* LII. 265 The ideal textbook in mathematical logic would include extensive discussion of the intensional and modal logics. **1957** *Jrnl. Symbolic Logic* XXII. 176 (*title*) New foundations for Lewis modal systems. **1957** A. N. PRIOR *Time & Modality* 133 There are some modal logicians who feel that statements containing sequences of modal operators like *MM*, *MML*,..are one and all 'meaningless'. **1962** W. & M. KNEALE *Devel. of Logic* x. 613 We turn to consider the possibility of using quantifiers to operate across modal signs. **1968** HUGHES & CRESSWELL *Introd. Modal Logic* p. xi, Modal logic can be described briefly as the logic of necessity and possibility, of 'must be' and 'may be'. *Ibid.* ii. 25 Because of the non-truth-functionality of modal operators..the initial account does not lead to any obvious formal definition of validity for modal formulae. **1970** J. N. FINDLAY tr. *Husserl's Logical Investigations* I. 32 Modal distinctions play a central part in phenomenological theory, and Husserl is now contributing importantly to their own phenomenology.

5. a. *Esp.* in phr. *modal auxiliary.*

1933 E. H. GROUT *Stand. Eng.* v. 122 The modal auxiliaries *may, might, can, could, must, ought*,..give a cast to the whole sentence in which they are. **1961** R. B. LONG *Sentence & its Parts* vi. 138 A category of modal auxiliaries is often set up for modern English, to include various verbs expressing ideas of possibility, constraint, and desire.

6. a. *Statistics.* Of or pertaining to a mode (sense *7 c); occurring most frequently in a sample or population.

1897 *Proc. R. Soc.* LXII. 175 Probable error of modal frequency y_0. **1900** K. PEARSON *Gram. Sci.* (ed. 2) 383 The average value of the character is very frequently taken as determining the type instead of the modal value. **1938** A. E. WAUGH *Elem. Statistical Method* iv. 46 In the first place it is necessary to locate the modal class. By this we mean the class which contains the most items. **1954** M. BERESFORD *Lost Villages* ix. 288 In the receipts of 1377 we have only the constables' names to add flesh and blood to the averages, modal ranges and medians of statistical calculations. **1968** *Listener* 25 July 101/1 The administrators we saw..had averaged only 2·8 years in all their completed jobs in the class; in fact, the modal (most frequently occurring) period in completed jobs was two years. **1973** *Jrnl. Genetic Psychol.* CXXII. 248 The modal age of the youngsters was 13.

b. Representative, typical; *modal personality*, an imaginary personality in which each component trait or characteristic is present to an extent equal to the modal value of a particular society or group or, more widely, which is taken as in some way representative of it.

1944 C. DU BOIS *People of Alor* I. i. 3 Modal personality, then, is the product of the interplay of fundamental, physiologically and neurologically determined tendencies and experiences common to all human beings acted upon by the cultural milieu. *Ibid.* 5 On such a base line data will show central tendencies that constitute the modal personality for any particular culture. **1948** K. DAVIS *Human Society* xv. 427 The modal divorce now occurs in the third year of marriage. **1949** R. K. MERTON *Social Theory* i. 57 The characteristic (modal) pattern for handling a standardized problem. **1954** INKELES & LEVINSON in G. Lindzey *Handbk. Social Psychol.* II. xxvi. 980/2 In our opinion, 'national character' ought to be equated with modal personality structure. **1956** W. H. WHYTE *Organization Man* (1957) 281 What might be called the modal man, however, is a twenty-five-to-thirty-five-year-old white-collar organization man. **1968** *McGraw-Hill Yearbk. Sci. & Technol.* 50/1 Examples of these typical motor patterns are the deep cooing and bowing of the domestic pigeon, the butting of a billy goat, [etc.]... These motor patterns have been given a wide variety of names, such as modal action patterns..and instinctive movements. **1968** J. O. ELLEFSON in E. Norbeck et al. *Study of Personality* ix. 142 Field primatologists report impressions of the existence of modal personalities, often designated as temperament, that characterize species. **1970** E. MCGINNIES *Social Behavior* iii. 70 Linton (1945) has conceived of national character as a modal personality structure, or configuration that appears with considerable frequency in a society. *Ibid.* 71 Identification of such modal behavior configurations makes it possible to arrive at certain generalizations about any given society and to describe more succinctly the differences between one society and another.

7. *Petrol.* Of or pertaining to the mode (sense *5 b) of a rock; as indicated by a mode.

1902 W. CROSS et al. in *Jrnl. Geol.* X. 609 A Modal Variety..may be defined as a rock having a mode with a slightly different development of the quite subordinate component minerals. **1938** *Nature* 17 Sept. 495/2 The second volume includes all the rocks with more than 5 per cent of modal quartz. **1962** A. E. J. & C. G. ENGEL in A. E. J. Engel et al. *Petrologic Stud.* 48 The thin sections used for modal analyses of two-pyroxene amphibolites

were slightly thicker than is conventional, to accentuate the color difference.

B. *sb.* **2.** *Gram.* A modal verb (see A. *adj.* 5).

1959 *Rep. 10th Ann. Round Table Meeting Ling. & Lang. Stud.* (Georgetown Univ. Inst. Lang.) IV. 112 Parallel rules apply to most of the modals and conjugators. **1965** N. CHOMSKY *Aspects of Theory of Syntax* ii. 63 *May* is a verbal auxiliary..and..a Modal. **1971** J. ANDERSON in A. J. Aitken et al. *Edin. Stud. Eng. & Scots* 69 These phenomena are often well documented in grammars purporting to give an account of the modals.

modality. Add: **1. b.** In diplomacy, politics, etc.: a procedure or method; a means for the attainment of a desired end.

1957 G. F. KENNAN in *Listener* 28 Nov. 868/1 The modalities of German unification must flow from the will of the German people, expressed in free elections. **1960** *Guardian* 23 Aug. 7/6 He did hear nine members of the Council praise his statesmanship and the procedures ('modalities' is the new and foolish word) he had adopted. **1970** *New Yorker* 17 Oct. 162/2 The new word that is constantly being heard here is 'modalities'. Everyone involved in the peace talks agrees that the military modalities of a cease-fire are more easily negotiated than the political modalities.

2. b. (Later examples.)

1949 HUTTEN & REICHENBACH tr. *H. Reichenbach's Theory of Probability* x. § 80. 404 Like probabilities, the modalities must be regarded as properties not of individual propositions but of propositional sequences. **1951** G. H. VON WRIGHT *Ess. Modal Logic* 3 Related to the problems of mixed modalities are the problems of superimposed or higher order modalities.

4. *Psychol.* **a.** (See quot. 1909.)

1895 *Amer. Jrnl. Psychol.* VII. 84 *Sinn*, sense, sensibility, modality. **1909** *Cent. Dict.* Suppl., *Modality*, in Psychol.: (*a*) the nature or character of sensation or stimulus as determined by the sense-department to which it belongs or appeals: a term proposed by Helmholtz, to avoid a confusing use of *quality*... Hence (*b*) the sense-department itself: as, the sensations of different *modalities*. **1925** G. B. PHELAN (*title*) Feeling experience and its modalities. **1951** G. HUMPHREY *Thinking* ii. 57 Sensory presentations of various modalities—auditory, kinaesthetic, and so on. **1971** tr. *H. von Helmholtz's Sel. Writings* xiv. 369 The most fundamental [distinction] is that among sensations which belong to different senses, such as the differences among blue, warm, sweet, and high-pitched. In an earlier work I referred to these differences in the *modality* of the sensations. **1972** D. R. KENSHALO in Kling & Riggs *Woodworth & Schlosberg's Exper. Psychol.* (ed. 3) v. 119/1 If we insist that each primary sensory modality has its own nerve pathway, the tactile, pain, and temperature senses fail to qualify as different modalities because their nerves are intermingled.

b. A term used to denote qualitatively different attributes or traits of personality.

1946 R. B. CATTELL in *Brit. Jrnl. Psychol.* May 159 Three classes or 'modalities' of traits: (1) Dynamic traits, e.g. dispositions, sentiments, neurotic symptoms, ergs; (2) Temperament traits, e.g. general emotionality, surgency, preservation, hyperthyroidism, personal tempo; (3) Abilities or cognitive traits, e.g. native general intelligence, acquired perceptual and executive skills. **1962** E. R. HILGARD *Introd. Psychol.* (ed. 3) xvi. 452/2 Guilford.. writes of seven 'modalities of traits', indicating that the kind of trait we see depends upon the direction from which we view personality. **1964** L. J. BISCHOF *Interpreting Personality Theories* xiv. 594 Formally, Cattell proceeds to divide traits into three *modalities*: temperament, dynamics, and ability. **1972** *Jrnl. Social Psychol.* LXXXVII. 52 The conditioning events taking place during this phase leave an indelible imprint on the psychological modalities referred to as personality.

modalize, *v.* Add: (Later examples.) Hence **modali·zable** *a.*, **modaliza·tion**, **mo·dalized** *ppl. a.*

1955 A. N. PRIOR *Formal Logic* III. i. 202 'Modalization' here plays a part. *Ibid.*, Provided that no propositional variable occurring in β occurs in α unless it is 'modalized', i.e. is either immediately preceded by '*M*' or '*L*' or occurs as part of a propositional formula which as a whole is preceded by '*M*' or '*L*'. *Ibid.* 209 A similar hexagon.. could be constructed for modalized conjunctive and alternative forms. **1957** —— *Time & Modality* 137 The only modalizable forms are single variables with or without a preceding sequence of N's. **1963** A. KENNY *Action, Emotion & Will* ix. 189 Descriptions of formal objects can be formed trivially simply by modalizing the relevant verbs. **1973** J. J. ZEMAN *Modal Logic* v. 80 Systems containing only a finite number of non-equivalent modalities will.. be called 'systems of complete modalization'. *Ibid.*, A formula is completely modalized if the prefixing of modal operators to it does not change its 'modal quality'.

mod. con. (mǫ·d kǫ·n). Also **mod. cons.** Colloq. abbrev. of *modern convenience(s)* (see *MODERN *a.* 3 a). Also *transf.*

1934 *Punch* 24 Jan. 86/2 An advertisement..describing just such a house as we wanted. Just the right number of rooms, 'five minutes from the station, h. & c. in all bedrooms, all mod. cons.' **1952** A. HOCKING *Best Laid Plans* ix. 135 Four bedrooms, two sitting-rooms, k. and b., as the house agents say; every mod. con. **1963** *Times* 13 Feb. 11/4 Such a sophisticated 'mod. con.', the equivalent of a hot bath to splash in, is, generally speaking, beyond the ambition of the normal duck. **1966** 'H. MACDIARMID' *Company I've Kept* xiii. 188 We had no 'mod cons', and were getting too old to put up with really primitive conditions. **1972** G. DURRELL *Catch me a Colobus* v. 99 It's a modest little place..but it's got all mod. con. and that sort of thing.

moddam, moddom, moddum: see *MODOM.

mode, *sb.* **I. 2.** Delete † *Obs.* and add later examples. Also freq. *attrib.*

1933 L. BLOOMFIELD *Lang.* xvi. 273 In English..the unreal appears only in clauses introduced by *if* or *though*, or in combination with the phrasal mode-forms (*he would help us*, unreal of *he will help us*). **1946** H. HOIJER et al. *Ling. Struct. Native Amer.* 97 The forms of the verb [in Algonquian] fall into five *orders*. Each order consists of one or more *modes*, each with a full set of forms. **1946** C. MORRIS *Signs, Lang. & Behavior* v. 125 A third possibility ..may be called the *mode-use classification*. **1961** R. B. LONG *Sentence & its Parts* 495 Five modes are recognized here: common (or 'indicative'), subjunctive, infinitival, gerundial, participial. **1965** *Canad. Jrnl. Ling.* Spring 175 We have now considered all the verb prefixes except those for mode-aspect. The Eyak mode-aspect system is relatively well-proportioned and clear-cut.

b. *Linguistics.* (See quots.)

1954 K. L. PIKE *Lang. in Rel. Human Behavior* I. iii. 35/2 On any level of focus each..emic unit..is divided structurally into three specific kinds of complex overlapping components which I shall call *modes*. **1967** W. A. COOK *On Tagmemes & Transforms* i. 9 Every linguistic sign is defined by its meaning, form and distribution... These are included in Pike's three modes: the manifestation mode, the feature mode, and the distribution mode. *Ibid.* 10 The tagmeme can be fully defined, parallel to the phoneme and morpheme, with its own peculiar feature, manifestation, and distribution modes.

3. b. (Later examples.) Also in wider use (see quots.).

1937 A. SMEATON tr. *Carnap's Logical Syntax of Lang.* IV. § 68. 247 Some of the known examples of intensional sentences belong to the autonomous mode of speech. **1941** O. HELMER tr. *Tarski's Introd. Logic* viii. 175 The proof of Theorem 1—like any other indirect mode of inference—can be brought under the schema sketched above. **1946** C. I. LEWIS *Analysis of Knowl.* I. iii. 39 It is desirable to recognize two further modes also, which will here be called, respectively, comprehension and signification. **1965** J. O. URMSON *Philos. Analysis* 37 'Xs are logical constructions' is in the material mode of speech. **1966** W. V. QUINE *Ways of Paradox* xiii. 156 Whatever may be said about necessity may be said also, with easy and obvious adjustments, about the other modes. **1970** A. E. BLUMBERG tr. *Stegmüller's Main Currents Contemp. Germ., Brit. & Amer. Philos.* vi. 234 Two modes may *exclude* each other (necessity and impossibility). *Ibid.* vii. 308 Put in the formal mode his thesis simply states that all thing-statements can be translated into a sense-data language (a phenomenalistic language).

4. c. *Physics.* Any of the distinct kinds or patterns of vibration that an oscillatory system can sustain.

1867 J. TYNDALL *Sound* v. 188 When we make the same passage [from a fundamental tone to the first overtone] in a stopped pipe, we obtain a note a fifth above the octave. No intermediate modes of vibration are..possible. **1877** RAYLEIGH *Theory of Sound* I. vi. 141 When a string vibrates in its gravest normal mode, the excursion is at any moment proportional to sin $\pi x/l$. *Ibid.*, The production of 'harmonics' by lightly touching the string at the points of aliquot division is a well-known resource of the violinist. All component modes are excluded which have not a node at the point touched. **1911** *Encycl. Brit.* XXV. 454/1 In fig. 34 the stationary wave systems of the first four modes are represented. **1949** H. E. PENROSE *Princ. & Pract. Radar* 626 Energy may be propagated in a wave-guide in a doubly infinite series of modes analogous, to a small extent, to a singly infinite series of modes represented by a fundamental note and its harmonics. The modes are distinguished by the patterns of the lines of force traversing the fields. **1950** STEPHENS & BATE *Wave Motion & Sound* 386 In the theory of the specific heats of a solid the thermal vibrations are supposed to result from many simultaneous modes, whose phases have a random distribution. **1962** *Newnes Conc. Encycl. Electr. Engin.* 883/2 The various higher-order modes travel [along a waveguide] with different velocities. **1969** L. ALLEN *Essent. Lasers* ii. 13 The large number of modes at infrared or optical frequencies which are present in any cavity of reasonable size poses problems. This is because of the need for a high level of spontaneous emission to ensure that sufficient photons go into any one particular mode, to maintain the rate of stimulated emission.

5. b. *Petrol.* The quantitative mineral (as distinct from chemical) composition of a rock sample. Cf. *NORM 2.

1902 W. CROSS et al. in *Jrnl. Geol.* X. 604 We introduce two terms..as substitutes for the cumbrous and oft-repeated expressions, standard mineral composition (that calculated from the rock analysis) and actual mineral composition. For the first we propose the word norm, and for the second the word mode. **1932** A. JOHANNSEN *Descr. Petrogr. Igneous Rocks* II. 111 (*heading*) Table 63. Modes of sodaclase-granites. **1962** H. R. CORNWALL in A. E. J. Engel et al. *Petrologic Stud.* 361 In ash flows in cooling unit 3 of the Bullfrog Hills caldera..lithologic differences between the lower and upper parts indicate quite certainly that more than one flow is present. The differences are shown by variations in the mode. **1974** *Nature* 16 Aug. 562/2 The Clare Castle gneisses are coarse grained and weakly banded... Modes vary within the range: garnet 20–30%, sillimanite 5–20%, plagioclase 25–30%, potash feldspar 10–20% and quartz 10–40%.

II. 7. c. *Statistics.* The value or range of values of a variate for which there is a maximum number of instances in a given population.

1895 K. PEARSON in *Phil. Trans. R. Soc.* A. CLXXXVI. 345, I have found it convenient to use the term *mode* for the abscissa corresponding to the ordinate of maximum frequency. Thus the 'mean', the 'mode', and the 'median' have all distinct characters. **1906** R. H. LOCK *Rec. Progress in Study of Variations* 89 When dealing with a symmetrical curve the position of the mode is identical with that of the median. **1947** O. L. DAVIES *Statistical Methods in Res. & Production* iii. 27 In most industrial applications, however, distributions with more than one mode (multimodal) are, or should be, rare. The presence of two or more modes usually means that the sample is not homogeneous, i.e. that two or more distinct distributions have been combined. **1948** L. D. & A. CROW *Educ. Psychol.* xx. 393 The score in a given set of data that appears most frequently is called the mode. **1973** *Jrnl. Genetic Psychol.* CXXIII. 87 The Kuhlman–Anderson scores for the one group of *Ss* from a fifth-grade class yielded a mean of 93·91, a range of 46, a median of 93, and a mode of 92.

d. [Shortened form of F. *gris mode* fashion grey.] The name given to a variety of shades of grey (see quot. 1930).

1895 *Montgomery Ward Catal.* 125/3 Kid gloves... Colors: Black, brown, tan, mode, slate. **1930** MAERZ & PAUL *Dict. Color* 167/1 Mode..was a term used in the nineteenth century to indicate a *class* of colors..usually on the pale order, running from neutral grays to strongly tinted greys of all hues... The old pattern books contain hundreds of samples of different colors, of every conceivable hue, all called 'Mode'. **1957** M. B. PICKEN *Fashion Dict.* 224/2 *Mode*..,pale, bluish-gray color, sometimes drab.

14. mode-locking *Physics*, a technique by which the phase of each mode of oscillation in a laser is 'locked' to those of the two adjacent modes (so that a fixed phase relationship arises between all the modes), resulting in the emission at intervals of about a nanosecond of short trains of extremely short pulses whose duration is of the order of picoseconds; so **mode-locked** *a.*, applied to a laser in which this technique is employed and to the resulting pulses; (as a back-formation) **mode-lock** *v. trans.*, to subject (a laser) to mode-locking.

1966 *Appl. Physics Lett.* VIII. 182/1 The YAIG:Nd laser was mode locked over a frequency width of order 12·6 Gc/sec (42 × 300 Mc/sec). **1971** *Physics Bull.* Dec. 718/2 Flashlamp pumped dye lasers have been successfully modelocked to produce high power pulses of transform-limited durations of 2–3 ps. **1965** *IEEE Jrnl. Quantum Electronics* I. 16/2 The light pulses from a mode-locked laser were observed with a magnetically focussed photo-multiplier tube. **1971** *Sci. Amer.* June 24/1 As the energy in the laser cavity is built up and then decays, a string of such mode-locked pulses emerges from the partially transmitting mirror in the front of the cavity. **1965** *IEEE Jrnl. Quantum Electronics* I. 16/1 (*heading*) Effect of mode-locking. **1967** *Science* 23 June 1558/3 In the first experimental demonstration of 'mode-locking', helium-neon and argon lasers were used.

model, *sb.* Add: **I. 2. d.** *Dentistry.* A positive copy of the teeth or oral cavity, which is cast in metal, plaster, etc., from an impression (sense *2 e) and which may be used to construct dental appliances.

1839 C. A. HARRIS *Dental Art* xxi. 348 The obtaining of a model of the alveolar ridge, or ridges, when one for each jaw is required, though apparently very easy, is nevertheless often attended with some difficulty. **1857** *Brit. Jrnl. Dental Sci.* I. 579/1 Mr. Saunders thought that the plan of bending down the front part of the model could be fatal to a correct impression. **1917** F. A. PEESO *Crown & Bridge-Work* vii. 140 When the plaster for the impression has been tinted, the impression and model are easily distinguished by the difference in coloring. **1938** *Dental Rec.* LVIII. 14, I think, from a study of the original models, that there had probably been pyorrhœa for some years. **1940** [see *IMPRESSION *sb.* 2 e]. **1973** D. H. ROBERTS *Fixed Bridge Prostheses* v. 66 Only one model can be poured from each impression.

e. A simplified or idealized description or conception of a particular system, situation, or process (often in mathematical terms: so *mathematical model*) that is put forward as a basis for calculations, predictions, or further investigation.

Cf. sense 1 c.

1913 N. BOHR in *Phil. Mag.* XXVI. 1 To explain the results of experiments on scattering of α rays by matter Prof. Rutherford has given a theory of the structure of atoms. According to this theory, the atoms consist of a positively charged nucleus surrounded by a system of electrons [etc.]... Great interest is to be attributed to this atom-model. **1923** [see *BOHR]. **1938** R. W. LAWSON tr. *Hevesy & Paneth's Man. Radioactivity* (ed. 2) viii. 89 These and other fundamental facts were responsible for the introduction of the model of the atom already described. In spite of these facts, however, it was later necessary to replace the atomic model by conceptions of a less concrete nature..in order to be able to interpret more complicated spectra. **1939** H. LEVY *Mod. Sci.* xxx. 515 Models of the universe have been erected that enable us with varying degrees of definiteness to picture these earlier stages. **1940** *Econ. Jrnl.* L. 91 Previous models of the Trade Cycle..have thus mostly been based on the assumption of statically stable situations, where equilibrium would persist if once reached. **1949** *Econometrica* XVII. 193 The Mathematical Model discussed here..is a generalization of the Leontief Inter-Industry Model. **1958** *Listener* 11 Dec. 972/1, I want to discuss the cosmological theories which are generally classed as the evolutionary models of the universe. **1969** J. ARGENTI *Managem. Techniques* 170 *Any* set of mathematical equations, linking together a complexity of factors and used to study the effects of change, is a Model. **1969** *Sci. Jrnl.* Dec. 27/1 Mathematical models of the global atmosphere..can now be constructed with the aid of large, fast computers to handle the enormous quantities of data and the complex equations that represent the movements and heat balance of the atmosphere. **1970** *Nature* 21 Nov. 719/2 The equivalence of the corpuscular and wave models in the theory of optics. **1971** *Daily Tel.* (Colour Suppl.) 3 Dec.

24/3 Forrester has designed a model of the world system to try to discover the long term effects of pollution and overpopulation. The model, processed through a computer, predicts a variety of different futures. **1972** G. H. A. Cole in Cox & Dyson *20th-Cent. Mind* I. viii. 250 A system of physical concepts and quantities that describes the main features of a situation is known as a model. **1973** *Sci. Amer.* Dec. 117/1 There are many other varieties of speech error. All of them must be accounted for in a model of speech production.

f. *spec.* in *Mathematical Logic.* A set of entities that satisfies all the formulas of a given formal or axiomatic system.

1940 W. V. Quine *Math. Logic* vi. 271 The fact that such classes constitute a model of the traditional real number system was pointed out by Dedekind. **1948** *Jrnl. Symbolic Logic* XIII. 16 (*heading*) Models of logical systems. **1952** S. C. Kleene *Introd. Metamath.* ii. 25 When the objects of the system are known only through the relationships of the system, the system is abstract... Then any further specification of what the objects are gives a representation (or model) of the abstract system, i.e. a system of objects which satisfy the relationships of the abstract system and have some further status as well. These objects are not necessarily more concrete, as they may be chosen from some other abstract system (or even from the same one under a reinterpretation of the relationships). **1963** W. V. Quine *Set Theory* vi. 135 We have provided a model of arithmetic in set theory when we have provided a way of so reinterpreting arithmetical notations in set-theoretic terms as to carry the truths of arithmetic into truths of set theory. **1974** *Encycl. Brit. Macropædia* XI. 639/2 By Gödel's completeness theorem of 1930, if a formal system based on the first-order functional calculus *F* is consistent, there is a model in which the objects are the natural numbers.

II. 7. d. An article of apparel of a particular design; a specified type or design of clothing; freq. with defining word prefixed.

1880 *Queen* 12 June (Advt.), Messrs Jay import from the first houses in Paris. Models of every style. **1906** *Bazaar, Exchange & Mart* Suppl. 3 Oct. 1308/1 Great bargains in ladies' wearing apparel, new and equal to new. Paris models. **1912** *Tatler* 23 Oct. 105 The forthcoming models are more than usually extravagant and..the latest creations all seem to have been designed 'regardless of cost'. **1933** N. Coward *Design for Living* I. 22 A silly pride made me show off to you, parade my attraction for you, like a mannequin. New spring model, with a few extra flounces! **1958** [see *casualness]. **1975** *Times* 29 July 8/5 The Valentino collection is untypically small... Strikes..have dogged the production of the models.

e. A motor vehicle of a particular design; a vehicle produced in a specified year; also *transf.*, one of a series of varying designs of the same type of object; also *fig. Model T*, an early type of car produced by the American Ford Company; also allusively, of a person or thing that is outmoded, mass-produced, etc. Also *attrib.* or as *adj.*

1900 *Automobile Topics* 22 Dec. 366/1 For sale. Two-passenger Winton, 1900 model, in first-class condition. **1901** *Ibid.* 21 Sept. 848 Type No. 2. Model 'C'—12 HP. Double Cylinder Gasoline Engine. **1909** *Automobile* 7 Jan. 9/1 Henry Ford made a name for himself which will cling for all time when he handed out a replica of a full-fledged automobile of the four-cylinder type at the price of a runabout—nay, at the price of the cheapest runabouts. Model T of the Ford line is in the same class, in that it is all automobile and no price. **1909** *Westm. Gaz.* 2 Nov. 5/1 The engine of the 20-h.p. model..is of the monobloc order. **1910** *Ibid.* 4 Jan. 5/2 Mr. Huff pays a visit to Europe..to inspect the new models at Olympia. **1912** V. W. Pagé *Mod. Gasoline Automobile* xii. 618 The Ford car is one of the most popular of moderate-priced automobiles and over 100,000 of the Model 'T' are now on the road. *Ibid.* 619 (*caption*) Outlining the distinctive control system of Ford Model 'T' automobile. **1927** *Motor Cycling* 7 Dec. 102 (*heading*) Road tests of 1928 models. **1930** L. Mumford *City Devel.* (1946) 62 One might call this the model T dilemma. Mass-production..suffers..from rigidity. **1930** H. Crane *Let.* 29 Dec. (1965) 360 The middle west business man, approved panic model of 1931. **1932** A. Huxley *Brave New World* ii. 27 Twenty-three years after Our Ford's first T-Model was put on the market. **1942** E. Paul *Narrow St.* ii. 17 Mary drew from somewhere inside her waist a dog-eared American passport of a model no longer in vogue. **1945** *Amer. Speech* XX. 148/1 *Model T*, non-com technician. **1947** *Reader's Digest* Jan. 119/1 Such simple demands as wages, hours and working conditions are strictly Model T. **1955** W. Gaddis *Recognitions* III. ii. 752 The minute you get used to the goddam thing some bastard puts out a new model. **1963** R. Wolff *I, Keturah* (1964) I. vii. 47 The Model T chugged up the hill. **1966** *Economist* 26 Mar. 1251/2 A return to the one-off, custom-built job, is playing right back into Britain's hands and away from the undeveloped nations churning out marine model-Ts. **1968** *Listener* 23 May 670/1 There are still 405-line-only models, which cannot be converted, on sale. **1970** *Globe & Mail* (Toronto) 26 Sept. B 1/5 During the past model year, the trend was accelerated by the..fact that the car companies had concentrated in their Canadian plants production of the models that happened to be most successful in the marketplace.

10. b. *Biol.* An animal or plant to which another bears a mimetic resemblance.

1877 *Encycl. Brit.* VI. 127/1 Probably this beetle shared in the immunity from attack accorded to its model. **1907** *Nature* 31 Oct. 673/2 An insect thus resembled by another is spoken of as its 'model', the imitating insect is called a 'mimic'. **1930** R. A. Fisher *Genetical Theory Nat. Selection* 148 The resemblance which is favourable to the mimic will be for the same reason disadvantageous to the model. **1968** R. D. Martin tr. *Wickler's Mimicry in Plants & Animals* i. 16 (*caption*) Leaf beetles..serve as models for roaches.., which are palatable and resemble their models so closely that they are also avoided by predators. *Ibid.* iv. 43 This weed [*sc.* rye-weed]..is less demanding and tougher than its model, the wheat plant.

11. b. Substitute for def.: A person, freq. a woman, who is employed to display clothes by wearing them, or to appear in displays of other goods. (Add further examples.)

a **1911** D. G. Phillips *Susan Lenox* (1917) II. i. 7 She was dressed in the sleek tight-fitting trying-on robe of the professional model. **1958** *Woman's Own* 5 Feb. 16/2 The first lesson every model learns is to stand and walk correctly. **1959** *Guardian* 26 Oct. 7/7 If the men were only going to become part-time models, they would need to go on doing one or two lessons a fortnight. **1962, 1970** [see *fashion-model* s.v. *fashion *sb.* 13]. **1971** B. Patten *Irrelevant Song* 55 Their beauty more awkward than even the topmost models.

c. A euphemism for 'prostitute'.

1963 [see *company director* s.v. *company *sb.* 10]. **1968** J. Lock *Lady Policeman* ii. 19 There had been an increase of newsagents' notice-board ads for 'Models'. **1970** G. Greer *Female Eunuch* 195 Working as hostesses in high-class clubs, as 'models' or simply walking the streets.

13. For 'see 14' read 'see 15'.

b. *Sc. colloq.* A model lodging-house (see sense 15 in Dict.).

1899 'J. Flynt' *Tramping with Tramps* II. 233 The price..is threepence a night, and this is the common price all over Great Britain, except in the so-called 'Models', where a penny more is charged simply for the very deceitful name. **1927** [see *flop-house* s.v. *flop *sb.* 5]. **1935** MacArthur & Long *No Mean City* xix. 282 'A model' in Gallowgate—one of those buildings which are ironically termed 'Working Men's Hotels'.

15. a. (Further examples.)

1849 J. S. Buckingham *National Evils* 25 My thoughts were thus..directed to..the desirability of forming at least one Model Town. **1857** Geo. Eliot *Scenes Clerical Life* (1858) I. 109 What a hobby farming is with Lord Watling!.. It is really a model farm. **1898** E. Howard *To-Morrow* iv. 41 Another site for a model city could be purchased. **1909** *Chambers's Jrnl.* Feb. 87/1 It [*sc.* Kinlochleven] is built on the model-town system. **1967** *Boston Globe* 18 May 14/1 The new Congress..almost stopped the Model Cities program. **1970** G. E. Evans *Where Beards wag All* xi. 117 A horseman applied for a job with a farmer who had a few years before built himself a *model* farm with the most up-to-date farm buildings and all the latest equipment.

b. *model-maker* (earlier and later examples); also *model-building, -making.* Also freq. attrib. in sense 2 a, as *model aeroplane, aircraft, boat, engine, railway, soldier, train, yacht.*

1920 Model aeroplane [see *model-making* below]. **1973** *Times* 27 July (Suppl.) p. iv/4 Thousands of different hobbies and recreations: toy soldiers, model aeroplanes, cigarette cards. **1951** *Catal. of Exhibits, South Bank Exhib., Festival of Britain* 126/2 Model aircraft. **1974** *Times* 8 Feb. 15/5 Pursuits such as whippet racing and model aircraft flying. **1912** W. Owen *Let.* 2 July (1967) 147 Bournemouth Cliffs..and especially the Model-Boat-Canal were..familiar to me. **1974** *Country Life* 3–10 Jan. 56/4 Model boats wanted... Cased or uncased. **1957** B. F. Skinner in Saporta & Bastian *Psycholinguistics* (1961) 235/2 Model-building has a special status in the field of verbal behavior. **1972** *Computers & Humanities* VII. 79 His study is one of the richest we have for its methodological innovation, its model-building, and its attempt to treat the political culture of the time both as a system and as a block of evidence for larger concerns. **1906** E. Nesbit *Railway Children* i. 3 Peter had a birthday—his tenth. Among his other presents he had a model engine. **1598** Florio *Worlde of Wordes* 106/2 *Disegnante*, a map or mode maker. **1946** *Nature* 28 Dec. 928/2 He obtained a job as a model-maker to a firm of instrument manufacturers. **1965** *Math. in Biol. & Med.* (Med. Res. Council) iv. 132 Friendly model-makers from the physical sciences are tempted to construct theories of 'how the brain works' on the basis of a few isolated and easily mathematized facts. **1920** *Glasgow Herald* 29 Oct. 9 The Prince of Wales ..accepted from him a model aeroplane with which he won first prize in the junior section of a model-making competition. **1946** *Nature* 14 Sept. 361/2 The two tanks and propeller-testing tunnel were in operation, and it was possible to see every stage in the process of model-making and testing. **1963** L. Loevinger in H. W. Baade *Jurimetrics* 32 The basic elements that these procedures have in common are explication, model-making (or operational organization or programming), and the production of a testable conclusion. **1974** *Country Life* 12 Dec. 1869/1 The exhibition is divided into several sections each dealing with a different aspect of model-making. **1909** (*title of periodical*) Model railways and locomotives. **1972** *Times* 7 Aug. 2/4 A branch from an elm tree fell on to a model railway at Blenheim Palace. **1938** *Daily Herald* 21 Dec. 6/1 The collecting of model soldiers is a nursery pastime elevated into the dignity of an adult occupation by the word 'research'. **1973** *Country Life* 17 May 1385/1 Model soldiers have gone far beyond the realm of child's play and toy soldiers. **1969** D. E. Westlake *Up your Banners* (1970) xxxviii. 274 [He] never had a model train set when he was young. **1903** A. Bennett *Truth about Author* ii. 16 He sailed model yachts for us on the foulest canal in Europe. **1967** M. Waddell *Otley Pursued* viii. 64 A solitary soul wore gumboots and carried a large white model yacht.

c. model agency, an agency that supplies models (sense 11 or *11 b); **model girl** = sense *11 b; also *attrib.*; **model school**, (*a*) a school intended to be a model in organization, teaching methods, etc.; (*b*) a school where models (sense *11 b) are trained; **model theory**, the theory of models (sense *2 e or, esp., *2 f), dealing with their construction, the conditions of their validity, etc.; so *model-theoretic, -theoretical* adjs., *model-theoretically* adv.

1945 *Glamour* Nov. 166/2 First, you have an interview with one of the leading model agencies, such as Conover or Powers. *Ibid.* 260/2 The model agency rarely selects girls for a given assignment. Invariably, the photographer calls for the girls he wants. **1950** J. D. MacDonald *Brass Cupcake* (1955) iv. 41, I went down to New York City... A model agency took me on. **1956** S. Bellow *Seize the Day* (1957) i. 27, I got hold of the artist and he gave me the number of the model agency. **1972** A. MacVicar *Golden Venus Affair* vi. 62 He got me work with this model agency. **1973** *Guardian* 25 May 5/5, I mentioned reports that a model agency apparently puts men in touch with call girls. **1962** *John o' London's* 4 Jan. 20/1 Witches who are model girls gone macabre. **1973** A. Price *October Men* vii. 92 A woman in a big hat, slender like a model-girl. **1974** R. Harris *Double Snare* iii. 19 Her figure..must once have been willowy in the model girl fashion. **1854** Dickens *Hard T.* I. iii. 15 To think of these vagabonds.. attracting the young rabble from a model school. **1935** *Discovery* Nov. 342/1 The prime cause of the excavation was the announcement that a new model school was to be built on a field..which..covered part of the site of Camulodunum. **1966** A. Prior *Operators* iv. 40 Robin..said he knew some people in modelling who could help her... He had not been able to afford the so-called Model School. **1957** *Bull. Amer. Math. Soc.* LXIII. 289 (*heading*) Model-theoretic and decidability theorems concerning generalized products. **1963** A. Robinson *Introd. Model Theory* p. vi, The model-theoretic approach to set theory. **1958** *Notices Amer. Math. Soc.* V. 673 (*heading*) Some model-theoretical results concerning weak second-order logic. **1973** J. J. Zeman *Modal Logic* p. vi. The systems are studied model-theoretically. **1960** *McGraw-Hill Encycl. Sci. & Technol.* VIII. 525/2 On the basis of model theory, a small, readily modified model can be built and tested at low relative cost and the results applied to the full-scale device. **1967** S. C. Kleene *Math. Logic* § 23. 117 In the predicate calculus, proof theory has the advantage over model theory. **1969** W. A. J. Luxemburg (*title*) Applications of model theory to algebra, analysis and probability.

model, *v.* Add: **2. b.** [after *model *sb.* 2 e.] To devise a (usu. mathematical) model of (a phenomenon, system, etc.).

1965 C. H. Springer et al. *Adv. Methods & Models* ii. 57 We 'modeled' a business process with the aid of a ready-made algebraic model. **1971** *Nature* 18 June 425/1 The first attempts to model the urban system were made by traffic engineers. **1972** *Physics Bull.* Feb. 84/3 The UKAEA has modelled the diffusion of particles in a fluid acted on by buoyancy, winds, currents and turbulence. **1972** *Sci. Amer.* May 97/3 Our hope is that the maps will.. eventually be of aid to meteorologists who are modeling the present circulation in the atmosphere. **1974** *McGraw-Hill Yearbk. Sci. & Technol.* 250/2 All models [of land use] seek to allocate land-absorbing activities on some type of spatial network of subareas. The size of the subareas will, of course, vary depending on the total area being modeled.

8. *trans.* and *intr.* To act as a model (Model *sb.* 11 and *11 b); to display (clothes) as a model.

1915 W. B. Yeats *Reveries* (1916) 153 A pretty gentle-looking girl was modelling in the middle of the room. **1927** *Cleveland Press* 4 Mar., Vivian..will model Saturday in the shoe section of the Bailey Co. **1931** *Durant* (Okla.) *Daily Democrat* 29 Oct. 3/2 See them [*sc.* coats] modeled during style promenade tomorrow. **1948** 'J. Tey' *Franchise Affair* xxii. 260 A natural blonde with the clothes and figure of a girl who has 'modelled' clothes. **1957** M. Summerton *Sunset Hour* iv. 61 Lolly..had modelled bikinis and gossamer underwear before blasé camera crews. **1969** *Guardian* 30 June 7/1, I was watching this Negro modelling sleepwear.

modelling, *vbl. sb.* Add: **3. c.** The action of *model *v.* 8; the work of a fashion-model. Also *attrib.*

1949 *Chicago Tribune* 17 Feb. 10/3, I never thought of modeling as a career. **1959** 'J. Christopher' *Scent of White Poppies* iv. 55, I did do some modelling there. **1963** G. Marx *Let.* 11 Apr. (1967) 63 She is abandoning the modeling school and plans to embark upon..settlement work. **1964** [see *fashion-modelling* vbl. sb. s.v. *fashion *sb.* 13 a]. **1973** *Sun* 25 May 3 She started her modelling career when a fashion photographer spotted her on a beach near Rimini.

d. The devising or use of abstract or mathematical models (*model *sb.* 2 e).

1965 C. H. Springer et al. *Adv. Methods & Models* i. 4 The best way to untangle the confusion which many people have about mathematical modeling as a method for solving important business problems is to untangle the whole idea of model building as a way of thinking about the world we live in. **1971** J. Howlett in B. de Ferranti *Living with Computer* ii. 13 The computer has..made it possible to apply this method—mathematical modelling followed by numerical solution of the resulting equations —to problems that would be quite intractable without its aid. **1974** *Nature* 2 Aug. 450/3 It also gives the reader some feel for the vast problems involved in any worth-while quantitative modelling of climatic change.

‖ **modelletto** (mǫdĕle·to). Pl. modelletti. [It., dim. of *modello.] = *modello.

1937 *Burlington Mag.* Mar. 133/1 The other collectors ..added the bozzetti and modelletti to their bronzes and sculptures. **1938** *Ibid.* Oct. 141/2 Tiepolo has developed his theme in masterly fashion, perhaps as a 'modelletto' for an altar-piece. **1962** R. G. Haggar *Dict. Art Terms* 215/1 *Modello*... Another name is *modelletto.*

‖ **modello** (mǫde·lo). Pl. **modelli, modellos.** [It., see Model *sb.*] A sketch, often executed

in detail, for a larger painting which is prepared for a patron's approval; also, a small model for a larger sculpture. Cf. *BOZZETTO, *MAQUETTE.

1937 *Burlington Mag.* Oct. 188/1 We find the more finished *modello* replaced by the quick colour sketch. **1959** *Times Lit. Suppl.* 20 Mar. 154/5 The relation of genuine *modelli* to 'engraver's copies' is left in a state of confusion. **1964** *Listener* 12 Nov. 767/2 Vasari, on his visit to Titian's house in 1566, noticed many of these modellos propped against the wall. **1967** W. GAUNT *Compan. Painting* 63 The more detailed *modello*..gave the full conception of the painting. *Ibid.* 67 The *modelli* of the Italians. **1972** *Country Life* 6 Apr. 857/1 It is possible that the picture is a modello for a larger work, intended for a church or chapel. **1974** *Daily Tel.* 29 July 8/6 The recently acquired picture ..is the modello for the painting of 'The Senators of Florence swearing allegiance to the Grand Duke Ferdinand II'.

modelly (mǫ·dĕli), *a.* [f. MODEL *sb.* + -Y¹.] Resembling a model (*MODEL *sb.* 11 b); having the characteristics of a fashion-model.

1961 I. JEFFERIES *It wasn't Me!* vi. 70 Ghislaine was a bit too modelly to be true. **1965** *Observer* (Colour Suppl.) 5 Sept. 6/2 They wanted actresses because they thought models were too modelly.

modem (mōᵘ·dem). [f. MO(DULATOR + *DEM(ODULATOR.] A combined modulator and demodulator (such as is used in connecting a computer to a telephone line) for converting outgoing signals from one form to another and converting incoming signals back again.

1961 G. L. EVANS et al. in *Convention Rec. 5th National Symposium Global Communications* 100 A recent study of wireline data communications..has underlined the need for advancement in the field of data modulators-demodulators (modems). **1963** *Daily Tel.* 16 Dec. 15/2 The direct current (DC) signals which flow through a computer cannot be transmitted over telephone lines, so it is necessary to convert them... The black box which does this conversion at either end of the line is called a modem. **1971** *New Scientist* 7 Jan. 18/1 It is around 3.30 pm in the communications control room of Time Sharing Ltd, in London's West End. The modems are silent... Power has been off for half an hour. **1975** *Daily Colonist* (Victoria, B.C.) 13 May 27/1 They communicated over regular telephone lines, using teletypewriters connected to the lines by electronic devices known as modems.

Modena. Add: **2.** In full, *Modena pigeon.* A pigeon of the variety so called, distinguished by its stocky build and red legs.

1879 L. WRIGHT *Pract. Pigeon Keeper* xix. 220 (*heading*) Modena flying pigeons. **1936** W. A. DALLEY in *Pigeons of Today* 105 When once here the Modena..became an exhibition or fancy pigeon pure and simple. **1965** W. M. LEVI *Encycl. Pigeon Breeds* 247 The Modena is one of the most popular breeds in the United States. **1969** H. H. SHRIVES *Fancy Pigeons* 81 Modena pigeons are divided in Gazzi or Pied, Schietti or Self-coloured, and Magnani or Harlequin.

modenature. Delete *Obs. rare*⁻¹ and add later examples.

1953 *Archit. Rev.* CXIV. 91 The two outstanding features of the doctrine of Auguste Perret are the insistence on modenature—the profiling and management of projecting features—and the philosophy of the concrete frame. **1959** P. COLLINS *Concrete* ix. 197 The only modifications to this structural composition [in Greek architecture] consisted of surface modulations intended to make the forms more pleasing to the eye (namely *modénature* or profiling), and optical corrections.

Modenese (mǫdĭnī·z), *a.* and *sb.* [f. MODENA + -ESE.] **A.** *adj.* Of or pertaining to Modena or its inhabitants. **B.** *sb.* A native or inhabitant of Modena.

1813 J. C. EUSTACE *Tour through Italy* I. vi. 131 The important 'Bucket'..was carried off from a well in one of the streets of Bologna, by a party of Modenese troops. **1839** K. H. DIGBY *Mores Catholici* IX. iii. 80 Peace was then made between all the Modenese,..more than twenty thousand of the Modenese went to Reggio and Parma; and those two cities made peace with each other. **1936** G. F.-H. & J. BERKELEY *Italy in Making* II. xvi. 245 At Fivizzano, the Modenese soldiers fired on the crowd. **1957** *Encycl. Brit.* XV. 633/2 The wooden bucket captured by the Modenese from the Bolognese in the affray at Zappolino.

moderate, *a.* and *sb.* Add: **A.** *adj.* **2. b.** (Later examples.)

1924 J. T. GWYNN *Indian Politics* iii. 18 The Moderate or Co-operating party is to-day so unpopular that it takes some strength of mind to remain a Co-operator. **1954** B. & R. NORTH tr. *Duverger's Pol. Parties* I. i. 46 In the nineteenth century parties were based upon the caucus and weak articulation; today most Conservative, Moderate, and 'Liberal' parties in Europe still display these two essential characteristics. **1973** *Perthshire Advertiser* 17 Feb. 1/1 Another member of the Moderate-Independent Association of Perth town councillors, Councillor Henry Giulianotti, has resigned from the association. **1973** T. K. DERRY *Hist. Mod. Norway* x. 325 In the summer of 1934 Hjort had failed to put through a scheme for linking the Agrarian Party with the Moderate Liberals.

3. b. (Later examples.)

1949 J. D. B. WILSON *Southern Highlands* 175 Further east are two ribs beyond a shallow gully which give defined climbs..of moderate standard. **1956** A. J. J. MOULAM *Tryfan & Glyder Fach* 85 Ordinary route. About 200 feet. Moderate. **1966** M. WOODHOUSE *Tree Frog* xv. 122 If the climb had reached any level of difficulty higher than Moderate, which is the Climbers' Club's polite way of labelling a gumshoe doddle, we'd have died. **1971** N. TENNENT *Islands of Scotl.* i. 32 Arran rock offers little choice between easy to moderate scrambles and hard, strenuous routes. *Ibid.* iv. 78 *Broad Buttress*, 450 ft., Moderate.

c. Of prices, charges, etc.: not excessive, reasonable, low.

1904 *Punch* 6 Apr. p. ii (Advt.), Hotel..standing high in its own beautiful park... Moderate tariff or inclusive terms. **1923–4** *Guide to Oxf.* 19 (Advt.), Norfolk Hotel,.. Central Position. Moderate Terms. **1971** *Bibliotheck* VI. 57 The New Aldis..at the moderate price of £4.50 and with more than 1600 additional entries..will be especially welcome. **1973** *Michelin: France* 40 Good meals at moderate prices.

4. (Later examples.)

1925 V. WOOLF *Common Reader* 134 Six moderate-sized volumes. **1959** *Guardian* 9 July 5/3 The play..has a moderate-sized cast.

B. *sb.* **a.** (Later examples.)

1920 H. V. LOVETT *Hist. Indian Nationalist Movement* iii. 69 The Moderates were pushed out of a hall and assailed with stones and mud. **1924** J. T. GWYNN *Indian Politics* iii. 18 It used to be..the fashion to decry the Moderates and Co-operators as if they were a party of weak men and time-servers. **1969** *Listener* 28 Aug. 268/3 'Moderates' (who include men with a very militant record) are at present containing the extremists and hot-heads. **1975** *Times* 6 Jan. 2/3 The moderates should exercise their overwhelming strength in the trade union movement.

moderate, *v.* Add: **1. d.** *Nuclear Sci.* To slow down (a neutron); also, to provide (a reactor) with a moderator.

1956 H. SELIGMAN in A. Pryce-Jones *New Outl. Mod. Knowl.* 158 There are very few substances which can be used for this slowing-down process. There is carbon in pure form, or water which, instead of the normal hydrogen, has the 'heavy' hydrogen atom in its molecule. These substances are called moderators, as they are moderating the neutrons. **1958** O. R. FRISCH *Nucl. Handbk.* x. 4 The type of thermal neutron spectrum obtained from a reactor depends upon the conditions under which the neutrons are moderated. **1959** *Listener* 19 Nov. 873/1 They [*sc.* the reactors]..are cooled by carbon dioxide and moderated with graphite. **1966** *New Scientist* 24 Feb. 484/3 In a fast-reactor system, so called because the neutrons causing fission are not slowed down or 'moderated' but react at high energies, it is possible in theory to consume all the uranium. **1973** *Nature* 2 Feb. 317/1 In the reactors cooled and moderated by water, the reactor vessel must also be at this pressure.

3. a. (Later examples.)

1968 *N.Y. Times* 26 June 1/5 Being shown live at the time was a panel discussion on the 'underground press' moderated by Steven V. Roberts, a reporter for The New York Times. **1975** *Listener* 9 Jan. 39/1 The closed circuit at the University of Kent at Canterbury was used recently to televise a meeting whose potential participants promised to be too numerous for any of the available halls... There were two 'teams' moderated by the chaplain.

b. (Further U.S. examples.)

1766 T. CLAP *Ann. Yale-Coll.* 15 Mr. Andrew moderated at the Commencements. **1778** E. STILES *Lit. Diary* (1901) II. 311 The first Commencements were private. Rector Pierson moderated and gave Degrees till his Death.

moderated, *ppl. a.* Add: **3.** *Nuclear Sci.* Of a reactor: provided with a moderator. Of a neutron: slowed down by a moderator.

1945 [see *GRAPHITE b]. **1950** F. GAYNOR *Encycl. Atomic Energy* 114 In a moderated reactor there remain more free neutrons to sustain and propagate the fission chain reaction of U^{235}. **1962** *Newnes Conc. Encycl. Nucl. Energy* 244/2 Most of the fissions [in a thermal reactor] are produced by these moderated neutrons.

moderation. Add: **1. e.** *Nuclear Sci.* The action or process of slowing down neutrons by the use of a moderator.

1945 H. D. SMYTH *Gen. Acct. Devel. Atomic Energy Mil. Purposes* ii. 20 The process of slowing down or moderation is simply one of elastic collisions between high-speed particles and particles practically at rest. **1958** O. R. FRISCH *Nucl. Handbk.* v. 17 The moderation of fast neutrons to thermal velocities occurs by transfer of energy on elastic collision. **1969** *New Scientist* 25 Sept. 639/2 The three essential functions of a blanket are neutron moderation, tritium breeding, and heat-transfer.

moderationism (mǫdərēⁱ·ʃəniz'm). [f. MODERATION 2 + -ISM.] A policy or doctrine of being moderate or acting with moderation.

1960 [see *CENTRISM].

moderatism. (Later examples.)

1923 G. M. TREVELYAN *Manin & Venetian Revolution* iii. 49 The event resounded through Italy and Europe. It shook the somewhat self-complacent 'moderatism' of Giobertian waiters on opportunity. **1970** *Guardian* 1 Oct. 19/4 Mr. Crouch's apologia for 'moderatism'..is as unexciting in print as it was ineffective in the worst university crises.

moderator. Add: **4.** *spec.* A chairman of a television discussion (also in extended use). *N. Amer.*

1952 in A. Rothe *Current Biogr.* 433/2 Since 1946 he [*sc.* Senator Blair Moody] has also been moderator of the radio and television program *Meet Your Congress.* **1972** *Village Voice* (N.Y.) 1 June 28/3 She kept qualifying her aggression with apologies and withdrawals and cancellations..and maintaining the good will of the moderator. **1972** *Evening Telegram* (St. John's, Newfoundland) 24 June 1/2 Ron Pumphrey, moderator of an open-line program on St. John's radio station VOCM. **1973** *Guardian* 17 Oct. 12/4 The present moderators..were picked by London broadcasting to do a specific job, that of answering the phone and referring the questions to a guest expert. **1974** R. THOMAS *Porkchoppers* xxv. 212 The program's moderator..was..the syndicated political columnist who specialized in political muckraking.

7. d. *Nuclear Sci.* A substance that slows down neutrons passing through it; *spec.* one used in a reactor to reduce the speed of fast neutrons so that they cause fission more readily.

1945 H. D. SMYTH *Gen. Acct. Devel. Atomic Energy Mil. Purposes* ii. 20 The light elements are most effective as 'moderators', i.e., slowing-down agents, for neutrons. **1958** W. K. MANSFIELD *Elem. Nucl. Physics* iv. 38 If the U^{235} content exceeds about 50 per cent it is possible to achieve a chain reaction without the use of a moderator. **1961** G. R. CHOPPIN *Exper. Nucl. Chem.* viii. 115 Since it is desirable to increase the probability of capture by slowing the neutrons down, a moderator containing a low Z element with a low capture cross section surrounds the source. **1962** *Newnes Conc. Encycl. Nucl. Energy* 509/1 The most common moderators are: light water (H_2O), heavy water (D_2O), graphite, beryllium, beryllia and organic liquids. **1966** C. R. TOTTLE *Sci. Engin. Materials* x. 236 In nuclear reactors..a moderator, or slowing-down material, is used to decrease the energy of fast neutrons produced in fission until they are more readily captured in the fissile material at lower energies. **1969** BENNISON & WRIGHT *Geol. Hist. Brit. Isles* i. 18 Since carbon is a good moderator of neutrons, carbonaceous rocks are liable to give a spurious indication of porosity.

moderatorial (mǫdĕrătōᵊ·riăl), *a.* [f. MODERATOR + -IAL.] Of, pertaining to, or characteristic of a moderator or chairman.

1867 'T. LACKLAND' *Homespun* II. 155 This moderatorial edict is echoed up in the bell-tower. **1926** *Scots Observer* 13 Nov. 4/4 There was a moderatorial flavour in the eloquence of the evening. **1968** *Guardian* 19 Mar. 16/1 In his moderatorial address to the council last night, the Rev. Edward Rogers, a former president of the Methodist Church, said the ecumenical movement had reached the point where it presented a challenge. **1975** *Church Times* 27 June 14/4 The most excitingly growing church I found during my Moderatorial year was such a union.

modern, *a.* and *sb.* Add: **A.** *adj.* **2. a.** spec. (*the*) *modern Babylon*: London; *modern Greats*: at Oxford University, the school of Philosophy, Politics, and Economics.

1835 J. M. WILSON *Tales of Borders* I. 356, I proceeded to London... Months passed away, and I was still a wanderer upon the streets of the modern Babylon. **1847** DISRAELI *Tancred* III. v. v. 77 London is a modern Babylon. **1850** DICKENS *Dav. Copp.* xxxvi. 374 Bidding adieu to the modern Babylon. **1904** A. BENNETT *Great Man* viii. 79 The human tide which beats for ever on the shores of modern Babylon. [**1909** *Wanted! A New School at Oxf.* 4 It is a plan for, as it were, a modern-side Greats, based on Philosophy, but also..containing an admixture of certain other subjects.] **1922** JOYCE *Ulysses* 611 The sights of the great metropolis, the spectacle of our modern Babylon. **1925** *Times* 15 July 19/3 The examiners in the Final Honour School of Philosophy, Politics, and Economics ('Modern Greats') issued the following class list. **1935** N. MITCHISON *We have been Warned* II. 146 He was.. thinking what a rotten school Modern Greats was. **1971** D. SCOTT *A. D. Lindsay* iii. 50 A new School of Politics, Philosophy and Economics—'Modern Greats'.

c. (Examples.)

1699 M. LISTER *Journey to Paris* 108 Another Book overwritten in a small Modern Greek Hand, about 150 years ago. **1748** SMOLLETT *R. Random* I. xxx. 275, I asserted that the modern Greek was as different from that spoke and written by the ancients, as the English used now from the old Saxon spoke in the time of Hengist. **1841** BORROW *Zincali* I. II. i. 235 The number of Persian, Sclavonian, and modern Greek words with which it [*sc.* the language of the 'Gitános of Estremadura'] is chequered. **1900** CLARKE & MURRAY *Dent's School Gram. Mod. French* p. v, An attempt has been made to make this a grammar of modern French. **1927** S. JÓNSSON *Primer Mod. Icelandic* p. v, The first suggestion that I should write a text book of modern Icelandic was made to me in 1917. **1971** B. S. J. ISSERLIN *Hebrew Word-Bk.* 1 Grammatically modern Hebrew differs less from Biblical Hebrew than Old English does from Modern English. **1971** N. FISHER *Rise at Dawn* x. 169 He was in Corfu and he speaks good modern Greek.

d. (Earlier and later examples.) Cf. quots. 162. and 1706 under sense 2 a in Dict.

1821 H. C. ROBINSON *Diary* 3 Oct. (1967) 70 Sara Coleridge..has taught herself modern languages, and is said to have great talent. **1932** AUDEN *Orators* I. i. 19 The really disgusted—the teacher of modern languages. **1961** R. B. LONG *Sentence & its Parts* xvii. 377 In *modern-language teaching* what is modern is the languages; in *modern language teaching* what is modern..is the teaching of languages.

e. *modern school*, also, a secondary modern school.

1944 *Ann. Reg. 1943* 62 Three main types of secondary schools—grammar, modern, and technical. **1957** *Listener* 13 June 951/1 The 1944 [Education] Act had brought the modern school into being. **1975** *Times* 29 Aug. 10/4 When university entrance is considered there is a 47 per cent advantage of the combined grammar and modern schools over the comprehensives.

g. *Typogr.* Used to designate a group of type-faces developed in the late eighteenth and early nineteenth centuries, distinguished by flat serifs, increased contrast between the thick and thin parts of the letters, and an effect of greater precision and vertical emphasis in use. Also *modern-cut, -face(d)* adjs.

1808 C. STOWER *Printer's Gram.* Specimens of Printing Types, (*heading*) Specimens of modern-cut printing types, from the founderies of Messrs. Fry and Steele, and Messrs. Caslon and Catherwood. **1819** R. AUSTIN in A. F. Johnson *Type Designs* (1934) iii. 97 The modern or new fashioned faced printing-type at present in use was introduced by the French, about 20 years ago. **1874** G. SIMPSON in Geo. Eliot *Lett.* (1956) VI. 44 Tinted paper ought never to be used with modern faced type. It suits ancient face only. **1894** *Amer. Dict. Printing & Bookmaking* 379/2 *Modern faces*, these are those kinds of Romans which have been cut since the beginning of the century. **1902** T. L. DE VINNE *Pract. Typogr.: Treat. Title-Pages* 234 Of modern-cut types we have many varieties. **1926** S. MORISON *Type Designs* 31 The main distinguishing characteristic of the modern-face is that the serif is thinner, longer and more refined than in the old-face. The difference as between the stem and the hair-line is more marked, and the general note of 'modern' is that of extreme precision and a certain perpendicularity. **1934** A. F. JOHNSON *Type Designs* iii. 73 During the eighteenth century the design of our roman types underwent a radical change, resulting in the style which we know as modern face, the type of the nineteenth century and still the type used in our newspapers and most of our books. **1972** P. GASKELL *New Introd. Bibliogr.* 210 By the second decade of the nineteenth century English printers were using modern face almost exclusively.

h. Of a movement in art and architecture, or the works produced by such a movement: characterized by a departure from or a repudiation of accepted or traditional styles and values. Cf. *ABSTRACT A. 4 d.

[**1849** *Art Jrnl.* XI. 69/3 Between this society and one begun some years ago for the encouragement of modern Art and native artists, there should be no rivalry.] **1895** R. MUTHER *Hist. Mod. Painting* I. 10 Because this distinction between the eclectic and the personal, the derived and the independent, has not yet been carried out with sufficient strictness..it has hitherto..been found so difficult to discover the distinctive *style* of modern art. **1927** C. BELL *Landmarks 19th-Cent. Painting* 5 Géricault and then Delacroix were the new influences in France; in England the innovator was Constable. From these points of departure you can trace the whole glorious history of modern art. **1929** H. R. HITCHCOCK *Mod. Archit.* xvii. 201 There is..little to compare with the unconsciously 'modern' work of those architects who continued the English tradition. **1938** O. LANCASTER *Pillar to Post* 74 When, shortly after the War, the Modern Movement.. was first brought to public notice it led to a natural and healthy reaction against the excessive ornament..of the previous generation. **1958** S. W. CHENEY *Story Mod. Art* (rev. ed.) p. v, I have accepted here the broadest traditional usage of the term 'modern art' as covering the course of creative invention since 1800. **1972** P. M. BARDI *Archit.* xix. 117/1 The flight of refugees from the Nazis.. scattered the pioneers of the Modern movement across western Europe and America. **1973** *Times* 19 June 14/4 *A Child of Six Could Do It*, [an exhibition of] cartoons about modern art at the Tate.

i. In full, *modern first* (*edition*). A bookseller's term for the first edition of a book published after about 1900. Also *absol.* or as *sb.*

1922 M. SADLEIR *Excursions in Victorian Bibliogr.* 7 The dapper expert in ingenious moderns with his prefaces, his cancel-titles, [etc.]. **1952** J. CARTER *ABC for Bk.-Collectors* 122 *Modern firsts*, a category widely employed but.. impossible to define with any precision, since its use among antiquarian booksellers is, and probably always will be, quite unstandardised. At present (1951) it commonly extends as far back as 1900, and will often include books published before that date if their author's hey-day was after it. **1968** *Bertram Rota Ltd. Catal.* No. 158 (verso front cover), We are always pleased to receive offers of modern first editions and private press books in fine state. **1973** *Directory of Dealers Secondhand & Antiquarian Bks. Brit. Isles 1973–75* 240 E. H. Bucknall..modern first editions. **1975** *Bibliognost* Aug. 5 The chance that someone will find a simple first edition of a modern author is slim, because [John F.] Fleming's firsts are very special... Each would be priced well above the average cost of 'moderns'.

3. a. In spec. phrases: *modern convenience*, an amenity, device, fitting, etc., such as is usual in a modern house; freq. *pl.*; cf. *MOD. CON.; *modern dance*, a free expressive style of dancing distinct from classical ballet (see quots.); hence *modern dancer, dancing* vbl. sb.; *modern jazz*, jazz of a type which originated during and after the war of 1939–45.

1859 [see *dish-lift* s.v. *DISH *sb.* 10]. **1912** E. L. URLIN *Dancing Anc. & Mod.* p. xv, Modern dances..[are] derived from some primary human instinct, such as Worship, Mimicry, Love, or War... Modern dancing begins where..the art survives solely on account of the pleasure it gives to the performer, or to the spectator. **1926** *Times* 6 May 1/6 (Advt.), Superior accommodation in lady's quiet house..all modern conveniences. **1933** J. MARTIN *Mod. Dance* 2 There are as many methods and systems of modern dancing as there are dancers. *Ibid.* 3 By the modern dance we..imply by a method of negation those types of dancing which are neither classic nor romantic. **1937** E. ST. V. MILLAY *Conversation at Midnight* I. 15 Peace and Quiet poured down the sink, In exchange for a houseful of 'modern conveniences'. **1955** D. GILLESPIE in Shapiro & Hentoff *Hear Me Talkin' to Ya* xix. 300 No one man or group of men started modern jazz. **1957** G. B. L. WILSON *Dict. Ballet* 188 *Modern dance*, the term used to designate a variety of styles which are not founded on the *danse d'école* (i.e. the Classical ballet). *Ibid.* 189 Modern Dance claims to make much use of 'natural movements' and it is also a reflexion of a state of mind. **1961** *Metronome* Apr. 12 By the 1950's 'modern' jazz, as the more advanced developments were termed, had to free itself both from esoteric tendencies within jazz itself and from over-dependence on Western European classical traditions. **1968** J. WINEARLS *Mod. Dance* (ed. 2) 9 The title 'Modern Dance' distinguishes those kinds which have been invented, developed, or adapted from various sources during the past half-century and which are clearly marked by an expressive style quite different from that of other forms such as National, Folk, Musical Comedy or Ballet. *Ibid.*, Modern Dancers consider that Ballet cannot deal satisfactorily with all possible dance-subjects.

5. *modern-built* (earlier example), *-day, -minded, -style* adjs.

1811 JANE AUSTEN *Sense & Sens.* III. vi. 111 Cleveland was a spacious, modern-built house. **1909** *Westm. Gaz.* 5 July 2/3 No one can fail to be impressed by the seriousness of modern-day cricket. **1965** *Times Lit. Suppl.* 25 Nov. 1075/4 Philip Bummidge is a modern-day Hamlet. **1907** *Dublin Rev.* July 191 The author is at times betrayed into making Neri almost impossibly modern-minded. **1970** *Guardian* 15 Jan. 12 Nigeria needs to prove that it is stable, modern-minded and representative. **1883** 'MARK TWAIN' *Life on Mississippi* 427 Inviting modern-style pleasure resorts. **1927** *Melody Maker* Aug. 781/2 The voice again is heard together with trumpet and saxophones alternating in a modern-style extemporisation. **1975** *Guardian* 20 Jan. 8/3 Modern-style choreography.

B. *sb.* **1. b.** Delete † *Obs.* and add later example.

1975 *Country Life* 2 Jan. 37/2 In the visual arts the Walker Art Centre houses a world-famous collection of moderns.

moderner. Delete † *Obs. rare* and add later examples.

1926 *Brit. Weekly* 29 July 356/1 With a moderner's contempt of ailments. **1971** *Ceylon Daily News* 17 Sept. 4/6 It is psychologically impossible for a moderner to live in the same world that his predecessors lived.

modernism. Add: **3.** *Theol.* A tendency or movement towards modifying traditional beliefs and doctrines in accordance with the findings of modern criticism and research, esp. a movement of this kind in the Roman Catholic Church at the beginning of the twentieth century.

1901 G. TYRRELL *Let.* 18 Aug. in M. D. Petre *Autobiogr. & Life Geo. Tyrrell* (1912) II. ii. 52 He [*sc.* Kegan Paul] simply rants against Modernism, and glories in what ought to be our shame. **1903** —— *Let.* 19 Nov. (1920) vii. 132, I hope that the Catholicism in which we may eventually unite will be one in which all that is good and true in Modernism will be saved and sanctified. **1907** tr. *Pius X's Encyclical Let. Doctrines Modernists* 15 If we..seek to know how the believer, according to Modernism, is marked off from the Philosopher, it must be observed [etc.]. **1913** A. FAWKES *Stud. Modernism* 373 The name Modernism was given to the present phase of the liberalising movement in the Church of Rome by the *Civiltà Cattolica*. **1915** *Hastings' Encycl. Relig. & Ethics* VIII. 763/1 Modernism is the name given by the papal encyclical which condemned it to a complex of movements within the Roman Communion, all alike inspired by a desire to bring the tradition of Christian belief and practice into closer relation with the intellectual habits and social aspirations of our own time. **1923** *Edin. Rev.* Jan. 62 Between English Modernism and the now discredited Roman Modernism there is a deep cleavage. **1927** H. D. A. MAJOR *Eng. Modernism* 18 In the Roman Church Modernism is opposed to Mediævalism; in the English Church Modernism, as in Holland, is opposed to Traditionalism; in America Modernism is opposed to Fundamentalism. **1955** *Times* 17 Aug. 9/5 The mistake of modernism is to try to force a supernatural revelation into the mould of natural science and scholarship. **1972** L. F. BARMANN *Baron F. von Hügel & Modernist Crisis in Eng.* p. ix, In the sixty years following that conflict much has been written about modernism, though mostly from partisan standpoints.

4. The methods, style, or attitude of modern artists (*MODERN *a.* 2 h); *spec.* a style of painting in which the artist deliberately breaks away from classical and traditional methods of expression; hence, a similar style or movement in architecture, literature, music, etc.

1929 H. R. HITCHCOCK *Mod. Archit.* xvii. 205 A city [*sc.* New York], whose 'modernism' consists in copying the poorest French models of the New Tradition. **1934** R. BLOMFIELD *Modernismus* viii. 145, I have already called attention to the disastrous effect of Modernism on architecture, painting, and sculpture... I find the same insidious and repulsive influence at work in a good deal of contemporary music. **1946** R. WELLEK in W. S. Knickerbocker *20th Cent. Eng.* 69 The fine arts themselves and the art of literature reacted against realism and naturalism in the direction of symbolism and other 'modernism'. **1955** *Times* 1 June 8/7 Professor A. E. Richardson..foresaw a revival of the Hellenic influence in art and the decline of 'modernism'. **1961** *Listener* 23 Nov. 848/1 The American modernism introduced by Mr. T. S. Eliot, following Mr. Ezra Pound. **1971** *New Society* 25 Mar. 496/3 'Vision in Motion'..a brilliant manual, or compendium, of modernism. **1973** *Observer* 5 Aug. 28/3 Sassoon became..increasingly embittered at his neglect by the new pundits of 'modernism'. **1973** *Black World* Sept. 19/1 During the Twenties, Jorge de Lima became an important member of the literary movement known as Modernism. **1974** *New Yorker* 25 Feb. 122/1 Modernism, we are told, is passé; the Harvard English Department lists a course, 'American Modernism', that treats of 'American writing from 1900 to 1930'.

‖ **modernismus** (mǫːdəɹni·zmʊ̆s). [G.] = *MODERNISM 4.

1934 R. BLOMFIELD *Modernismus* p. v, Since the war, Modernism, or 'Modernismus', as it should be called on the German precedent, has invaded this country like an epidemic. **1934** C. LAMBERT *Music Ho!* iv. 248 Listening to his [*sc.* Hindemith's] firmly wrought works we seem to see ourselves in a block of hygienic and efficient workman's flats built in the best modernismus manner. **1948** WYNDHAM LEWIS *Let.* 18 Oct. (1963) 464 'The Waste Land', which bit of modernismus appeared a few years before. **1958** *Listener* 17 July 102/1 A city that was to be the last word in *modernismus*, a technician's 'New Jerusalem'. **1970** *Daily Tel.* (Colour Suppl.) 9 Oct. 65/2 A bale of soft material, patterned in that modernismus which was so big in the Thirties, and now survives mainly in British Rail.

modernist. Add: **4.** *Theol.* One who inclines to, supports, or advocates theological modernism. Also *attrib.* or as *adj.*

1907 tr. *Pius X's Encyclical Let. Doctrines Modernists* 6 It is one of the cleverest devices of the Modernists (as they are commonly and rightly called) to present their doctrines without order and systematic arrangement. **1918** M. D. PETRE *Modernism* v. 101 These words are not written in a spirit of hostility to the Catholic modernist position. **1920** W. SANDAY *Divine Overruling* 67, I do not disclaim the name of Modernist. The name describes justly what I aim at being. I aim at thinking the thoughts and speaking the language of my own day, and yet at the same time keeping all that is essential in the religion of the past. **1923** *Edin. Rev.* Jan. 62 Roman Modernists took Newman's doctrine of development. **1931** J. S. HUXLEY *What dare I Think?* vii. 228 Accounts of God which are as modernist as could be desired. **1970** *Times* 19 Aug. 10/8 The appointment of another avowed Modernist with a strong sense of the Church and a flair for knowing men, proved to be the eirenic answer. **1972** L. F. BARMANN *Baron F. von Hügel & Modernist Crisis in Eng.* p. ix, Modernists have been concerned to defend themselves and their aims, and anti-modernists have been equally concerned to justify the conduct of the Roman authorities and the positions of Roman theologians.

5. An artist, architect, writer, etc., whose work is characterized by modernism (see *MODERNISM 4). Also *attrib.* or as *adj.*

1927 F. J. MATHER *Hist. Mod. Painting* 372 Modernist pictures are becoming discreet, almost cautiously monotonous in colour. *Ibid.* 373 In comparison the Modernists have attained nothing of the coherence or authority of a school. **1934** R. BLOMFIELD *Modernismus* vii. 125 The Modernist seems to glory in his own obscurity. *Ibid.* 132 In these Modernist works there is no brushwork worth looking at. **1935** H. G. WELLS *Things to Come* xii. 99 One sits on a chair of modernist form. (All furniture is metallic.) **1937** S. W. CHENEY *World Hist. Art* (1938) xxviii. 862 This wing of modernists—with Cézanne as their prime exhibit—brought in the familiar studio talk about *form* as the indispensable creative force in painting. **1961** *Listener* 23 Nov. 863/1 Rosenberg, unlike the modernists, does not go in for phanopoeia or free association. **1963** *Ibid.* 21 Mar. 518/1 The writers were, in a sense, traitors in the modernist camp.

6. One who plays, appreciates, or supports modern jazz (see *MODERN *a.* 3 a). Also *attrib.* or as *adj.*

1955 J. PRENTICE in A. J. McCarthy *Jazzbook 1955* 105 As I understand that the traditional field will be covered in another article I will confine myself to the modernists. **1958** V. BELLERBY in P. Gammond *Duke Ellington* II. 143 Such extensions and developments only lead to a destruction of its [*sc.* Jazz's] real and lasting value, as has unquestionably happened with some of the more involved modernist experiments. **1962** *Sunday Times* (Colour Suppl.) 10 June 3 The strange division between the extrovert 'traditionalists'..and the very different *avant garde* 'modernists' (whose idol is the revolutionary Charlie Parker).

modernistic (mǫdəɹni·stik), *a.* [f. MODERNIST + -IC.] Of, pertaining to, or suggestive of modernism or modernists; having affinity to or sympathy with what is modern. Hence as *sb. pl.*, examples of modernistic art, music, etc.

1909 *Daily Chron.* 12 June 1/3 'L'Unione' is denounced as reeking with modernistic and kindred ideas opposed to the principles and dogmas of the Roman Church. **1924** *Public Opinion* 17 Oct. 383/1 The New Testament in relation to its own time is essentially and boldly modernistic. **1927** *Sunday Times* 13 Feb. 20/4 The audience liked its florid style as a change from more modernistic music. **1935** *Archit. Rev.* LXXVII. 82 The beautiful new dance-hall, with its modernistic sofas and lalique panels. **1958** P. GAMMOND *Decca Bk. Jazz* xv. 190 George Shearing will be remembered for his very accomplished playing in the 1940s, not for his more recent vapid modernistics. **1960** *Times* 29 Sept. 16/7 There is much to admire in this farrago of 'modernistics'. **1973** A. BEHREND *Samarai Affair* iii. 30 A modernistic portrait in oils of the latest pilot boat.

‖ **modernus** (mǫ̆dɜ̄·ɹnʊ̆s). Pl. **moderni.** [L.] A modern person; someone who is characterized by, or notable for, his modernity.

1953 W. R. TRASK tr. *Curtius's European Lit.* II. xiii. 490 He is a *modernus* and considers that the ancients had loaded down their poetic narratives with a superfluity of similes, rhetorical figures, and digressions... These *moderni* of 1175..either consciously break with the theory of *imitatio* or restrict it very considerably. **1962** M. McLUHAN *Gutenberg Galaxy* 183 Francis Bacon, PR voice for the *moderni*, had both his feet in the Middle Ages.

modesty. 3. b. (Later example.)
1910 *Westm. Gaz.* 21 Mar. 5/3 The 'modesty' and the edge of the sleeves are of golden lace.

modification. Add: **3. b.** *Biol.* The development of non-heritable changes in an organism; cf. sense *4 b.
1896 *Natural Sci.* IX. 288 In the life of a single individual it is obvious that no modification can affect variation, since this is necessarily antecedent. **1908** *Encycl. Relig. & Ethics* I. 66/2 Individuals are born different by variation; they become different during their lives by modification. **1960** N. POLUNIN *Introd. Plant Geogr.* viii. 214 (*heading*) Modification and distributions of crops (and weeds).
4. b. *Biol.* The non-heritable changes produced in an organism in response to a particular environment.
1896 *Natural Sci.* IX. 287 In a lucid paper he [*sc.* Lloyd Morgan] brought forward his useful distinction between variations, which are of germinal origin and congenital, and modifications, which are impressed on the organism by its environment. **1918** *Trans. Brit. Mycol. Soc.* VI. 221 If the organisms and their descendants when transplanted again into the original medium are again found to be red, then the change (loss of colour) is a modification. **1926** J. S. HUXLEY *Ess. Pop. Sci.* ii. 21 We can now..distinguish definitely between 'mutations', which are due to changes in the constitution of the animal—in the hereditary factors themselves—and 'modifications', which are due to changes in the environment. **1965** BELL & COOMBE tr. *Strasburger's Textbk. Bot.* 353 The modifications induced in the alpine plant [of *Taraxacum officinale*], probably due principally to the increased amount of ultra-violet light it receives, are not inherited.

modificational (mǫdifikēi·ʃənăl), *a.* [f. MODIFICATION + -AL.] Having the nature of, or arising from, modification. So **modifica·tionally** *adv.*
1908 *Athenæum* 11 July 47/2 Many of the unfit are only *modificationally* unfit. **1924** J. A. THOMPSON in *Glasgow Herald* 19 July 4 When we put aside these parasitic diseases and modificational diseases, there remain those that may be called constitutional.

modified, *ppl. a.* Add: *Modified Standard* (*English*): see quot. 1934.
1913 H. C. WYLD in *Mod. Lang. Teaching* IX. 262/2 London English is a totally different thing from Received Standard: it is merely one of the many provincialisms, such as are heard in large cities, which fall under the designation of Modified Standard. **1914** —— *Short Hist. English* ix. 236 It seems probable that the influence of *Modified Standard*, that is, of forms of English differentiated out of *Received Standard* by factors of social isolation, will have to be admitted and studied in the future. **1934** —— in *S.P.E. Tract* xxxix. 604 Thousands of persons speak a form of English which is neither a local dialect, nor what some would call 'good English'. For this latter type,..I proposed the term *Modified Standard*..to cover all the various types of English..which..while they adhere, on the whole, to the Standard, especially in accidence and syntax, are nevertheless more or less deeply affected, either by *provincialism*, or by..*vulgarism*, in pronunciation. **1940** J. H. JAGGER *English in Future* i. 15 Changes [in Standard English]..have been mainly due to the influence of the various forms of Modified Standard—to accept Professor Wyld's terms—upon each other and upon Received Standard.

modifier. Add: **b.** *Genetics.* Any gene which modifies the phenotypic expression of a gene at another locus.
1915 T. H. MORGAN et al. *Mechanism Mendelian Heredity* viii. 203 The F_2 from the crosses to self-color indicate that such modifiers are really present in the rats. **1919** *Jrnl. Exper. Zool.* XXVIII. 337 (*heading*) Specific modifiers of eosin eye color in *Drosophila melanogaster*. **1931** E. B. FORD *Mendelism & Evolution* ii. iii. 49 If, however, another mutation controlling similar characters were to arise, such an old and ineffective gene might show itself as a 'specific modifier'. **1968** R. D. MARTIN tr. *Wickler's Mimicry in Plants & Animals* ii. 33 Such modifier genes can switch the other genes on or off or alter their functional level so as to improve the correspondence of the mimic with the model. **1971** LEVITAN & MONTAGU *Textbk. Human Genetics* xvi. 595 This [*sc.* gene interaction] is a very broad term and covers everything from genes whose interaction..is so intimate that they must be considered part of the same operating unit, to genes whose activities impinge only in a most indirect manner (and so are thought of as vague 'modifiers').
2. *spec.* in *Gram.* (see MODIFY *v.* 6). **a.** A word, phrase, or clause which modifies another.
1865 [in Dict.]. **1924** H. E. PALMER *Gram. Spoken Eng.* II. 68 Possessives used as Modifiers. (Generally known as 'possessive adjectives'.) **1933** L. BLOOMFIELD *Lang.* xii. 194 A prepositional expression and an accusative expression..appearing in entirely different syntactic positions (e.g. as a modifier of verbs: *sit beside John*, or of nouns: *the boy beside John*). **1961** R. B. LONG *Sentence & its Parts* 490 In the commonest type of syntactic combination, a word-or-multiword unit, a head, combines with another or others, a modifier or modifiers, and determines the syntactic character of the total combination. **1970** G. C. LEPSCHY *Survey Structural Ling.* vi. 107 Modifiers..such as grammatical number, or article, which are centripetal..indicate the value—singular or plural, definite or indefinite—of the particular element to which they are attached.
b. A phonetic sign or symbol which modifies a character.
1899 H. SWEET *Practical Study of Languages* iii. 21 Thus, if there is a special mark or modifier to express voice, the absence of that modifier necessarily implies breath. **1911** *Encycl. Brit.* XXI. 462/1 The Organic Alphabet especially makes a large use of 'modifiers'—characters which are added to the other symbols to indicate nasal, palatal, &c., modifications of the sounds represented by italic letters in the Narrow Romic transcription; thus (l*n*) = nasalized (l).

‖ **modistæ** (mǫdi·stəi), *sb. pl.* Also **Modistæ.** [L.] The collective name given to a number of later medieval grammarians who developed and expounded a system of Latin grammar wherein Priscian's word classes and categories were integrated into the framework of scholastic philosophy.
1903 J. E. SANDYS *Hist. Classical Scholarship* I. xxxii. 642 The work in which this philosophy of grammar was first laid down was entitled *De Modis Significandi*, and its teachers were called *Modistae*. **1951** R. H. ROBINS *Ancient & Mediaeval Grammatical Theory in Europe* iii. 77 Later writers of Grammaticae Speculativae..are often referred to as a group by the name 'Modistae'. **1963** *Canad. Jrnl. Linguistics* IX. 41 This short paper will attempt to draw attention to some of the grammarians of the Middle Ages..,in particular to the group..now known as the Modistae. **1968** J. LYONS *Introd. Theoretical Linguistics* i. 15 So many works were produced with the title 'The Modes of Signifying' (*De modis significandi*) that the grammarians of the period are often referred to collectively as 'modistae'. **1971** G. L. BURSILL-HALL *Speculative Grammars of Middle Ages* 11 Martin of Dacia..was probably the first of the Modistae. **1973** *Canad. Jrnl. Linguistics* XVIII. 177 The *modistae*, linguists of the fourteenth century who developed the *grammatica speculativa* by relating the grammatical theories current during the early part of the Middle Ages to an Aristotelian framework. **1974** *Encycl. Brit. Macropædia* VIII. 267/2 Before the *modistae*, grammar had not been viewed as a separate discipline but had been considered in conjunction with other studies or skills (such as criticism, preservation of valued texts, foreign-language learning).

modiste. (Earlier and later examples.)
c **1840** LADY WILTON *Art of Needlework* xiii. 188 Mercers and milliners, haberdashers and modistes. **1936** G. GREENE *Gun For Sale* i. 13 He leant his face against a modiste's window and jeered silently through the glass.

modistic (mǫdi·stik), *a.*[1] [f. MODISTE + -IC.] Relating to fashion or fashions.
1907 *Times* 16 Nov. 9/6 The sleeves of this dress show the trend of modistic thought in this direction. **1915** *Queen* 6 Nov. 855/3 The modistic information it contains is of the most enlightening description.

modistic (mǫdi·stik), *a.*[2] [f. *MODIST(Æ *sb. pl.* + -IC.] Of or pertaining to the modistæ.
1963 G. L. BURSILL-HALL in *Canadian Jrnl. Linguistics* IX. 51 The modus essendi is the thing itself with its various properties; the thing is perceived in the mind and in the Modistic scheme this is the modus intelligendi. **1967** R. H. ROBINS *Short Hist. Ling.* iv. 77 The same distinction between form and matter recurs at various points in modistic speculative grammar. **1971** G. L. BURSILL-HALL *Speculative Grammars of Middle Ages* ii. 40 Modistic grammatical theory rests on the study of words and the properties of these words as the 'signs of things'. **1972** *Times Lit. Suppl.* 29 Sept. 1164/2 The late medieval 'modistic' grammars, which attempted to relate the traditional 'parts of speech' to postulated categories of reality. **1974** *Lang. Sciences* XXXII. 27 Moreover, special doctrines of Thomas of Erfurt are assumed to be general features of modistic theory.

modoc (mōu·dǫk). *U.S. slang.* Also **modock.** [Origin unknown.] (See quots.)
1936 ALLEN & LYMAN *Wonder Bk. Air* 312 A *modoc*, the derivation of which is obscure, is a flashy chap who goes around wearing helmet and goggles, and more than likely, leather boots and riding breeches, too, and talking about the big things he is going to do for aviation. **1942** BERREY & VAN DEN BARK *Amer. Thes. Slang* § 756/2 *Modock*, one who has taken up aviation for publicity, social, or similar reasons. **1960** WENTWORTH & FLEXNER *Dict. Amer. Slang* 341/2 *Modoc*, one who becomes an Air Force flier for publicity, social prestige, or similar reasons.

modom (mǫ·dǫm). *colloq.* Also **moddam, moddom, moddum.** An alteration of MADAM *sb.*, in imitation of affectedly refined pronunciation.
1920 GALSWORTHY *In Chancery* II. xiii. 223 Very new, modom; quite the latest thing. **1932** 'E. M. DELAFIELD' *Thank Heaven Fasting* I. i. 9 Madame Myrtle..was full of assurances about knowing exactly what Moddam meant. *Ibid.* 11, I only wished Moddam to judge the general style. **1932** WODEHOUSE *Doctor Sally* iii. 29 Did you call, moddom? **1934** H. G. WELLS *Exper. Autobiogr.* I. iv. 153 We are showing some very pretty sunshades just now Moddum. *Ibid.* 155 You haven't shown the lady the gingham at six-three! The young man has made a mistake Moddum. **1944** A. THIRKELL *Headmistress* ix. 200 A very handsome afternoon dress..but, as the dressmaker said, almost with tears, making moddom look her age. **1961** *Punch* 1 Mar. 372/1 The saleslady coughed delicately... 'It's up to you, Modom,' she said.

mods. Add: (Later examples.) Also *attrib.*
1876 O. WILDE *Let.* 5 July (1962) 15 Tonight the Mods list comes out. **1952** V. GOLLANCZ *My Dear Timothy* I. xix. 221 The Schools in question were Mods—Classical Moderations—..Mods were for the language and literature of Greece and Rome. **1955** *Times* 11 Aug. 9/2, I make a point of asking them how often they take down Aeschylus or Catullus and the usual answer is that they have scarcely opened a classical text since they got their first in Mods or won the Ireland.

modular, *a.* Add: **1. b.** Employing or involving a module or modules (*MODULE *sb.* 4 d, e, f) as the basis of design or construction; designed as part of such a system.
1936 BEMIS & BURCHARD *Evolving House* III. iv. 64 Cubical modular design..simply requires that all parts of the house..be proportioned to the same module in all three dimensions. **1945** *Archit. Rec.* Jan. 102/2 The modular system does not necessarily involve making every product come out to even multiples of 4 inches... The system does suggest, however, that the 4-in. unit be considered as an increment wherever possible. **1956** W. H. WHYTE *Organization Man* (1957) 398 Modular construction is a condition of moderate-cost housing. **1960** *House & Garden* Dec. 31/1 As the houses are based on modular units, it is relatively simple to add a wing. **1966** B. J. KARAFIN in Kuo & Kaiser *System Analysis by Digital Computer* viii. 306 Modular programming makes it possible to build a library of simulation modules in much the same way as a library of numerical function subroutines is built. **1967** M. GOLDRING *Modular Directory Building Components* p. ix, The term 'modular components' covers those components that have at least two of their co-ordinating dimensions, such as length and width, in whole multiples of the basic 4 in/100 mm module. **1969** W. V. TIPPING *Introd. Mech. Assembly* ix. 217 The length of the machine obviously could, by the modular construction, be varied to within 30 in. Making the machine one sided only was considered but finally it was agreed to use a double sided module to keep down the length of the machine. **1970** *Washington Post* 30 Sept. B.1/1 The adjustable, modular-unit, wall-hung bookcase systems. **1970** [see *MODULE *sb.* 4 d]. **1971** *Engineering* Apr. 71/1 Based on a modular construction, Denco floor consists of timber panels supported by jacks..at 610 mm or 600 mm..centres over the sub-floor... A..steel Tee section is screwed to the perimeters of the underside of each module to fix and support it on the jackheads. **1972** *House & Garden* June 76/1 So-called portable houses—modular prefabs—which come on a truck and get erected within several hours. **1973** *Computers & Humanities* VII. 144 This program is modular in design, that is, it consists of several steps each doing a simple task.
c. *spec.* Of an educational course: designed as a series of units or discrete sections. Cf. *MODULE *sb.* 4 g.
1968 *Economist* 25 May 18/2 The board has developed proposals both for the retraining of adults for skilled jobs, and for a so-called 'modular' scheme of training for young entrants to industry. **1972** *Timber Trades Jrnl.* 3 June 41/1 The courses would be modular, so that a company could send people in to be trained in any particular aspect. **1972** *Accountant* 19 Oct. 483/1 Much ingenuity has, however, been used by public sector institutions, and they have succeeded wherever possible in providing oral tuition on a modular basis, so that students of different bodies are able to share studies.

modularity (mǫdiŭlæ·rĭti). [f. MODULAR *a.* + -ITY.] The property of being modular; use of modules in design or construction.
1937 *Architectural Forum* Apr. 252/2 The unit used in this kind of modular design may be defined as the 'multiple module'. Modularity of this kind has much greater potentialities as an integrating factor for building as a whole. **1964** FISHER & SWINDLE *Computer Programming Syst.* iv. 219 A growing trend in the design and implementation of input/output control systems is the concept of modularity. **1966** L. B. ANDERSON in G. Kepes *Module, Symmetry, Proportion* 112 Modularity in architecture is no respecter of scales. **1968** *Brit. Med. Bull.* XXIV. 192/1 In 1965–66 the manufacturers introduced the so-called 'third generation computers', whose principal feature was their modularity. **1970** *Times* 7 May 35 These [digital transmitters] will be of more complex construction..and impose the need for modularity in design to ease servicing. **1975** *Sci. Amer.* Jan. 50/2 (Advt.), Pop-in modularity makes it easy to replace logic boards when needed, without tools.

modularize (mǫ·diŭlărəiz), *v.* [f. MODULAR *a.* + -IZE.] *trans.* To construct on modular principles. So **mo·dularized** *ppl. a.* Also **modulariza·tion.**
1959 *Res. Highlights Nat. Bureau of Standards Misc. Publ.* 229 (U.S.) 18 These tubes are compatible with the modularized electronic circuitry developed as part of the Project Tinkertoy program. **1962** *Maintainability Design Criteria Handbk. for Designers of Shipboard Electronic Equipment* (Federal Electr. Corp., U.S.) iv. i. 1 Modularization usually results in a decrease in fault isolation time. **1966** L. B. ANDERSON in G. Kepes *Module, Symmetry, Proportion* 110 Later Medieval architecture did not fail to provide a more disciplined modularization. *Ibid.* 111 In the end it is space itself which is modularized. **1968** F. F. MARTIN *Computer Modeling* ix. 193 We have applied modularization to the logical flow chart of a hypothetical air traffic control model. **1971** *New Scientist* 28 Jan. 196/2 Apollo 14 will also carry a modularised equipment transporter. **1973** *McGraw-Hill Yearbk. Sci. & Technol.* 357/1 Design and construction improvements, ranging from perfection of wire-winding techniques for the prestressed concrete reactor vessel to modularization of auxiliary systems, have decreased costs significantly.

modularly (mǫ·diŭlăɹli), *adv.* [f. MODULAR *a.* + -LY[2].] On modular principles.
1943 J. M. WOLFE *First Course Cryptanalysis* (rev. ed.) II. 19 The Vigenere operates on a modular addition while the Nihilist substitution does not. If the Nihilist addition were performed modularly, then all cipher numbers would be within the range of 4 from each other. **1972** *Sci. Amer.* Mar. 121/1 We live..in a world modularly constructed on

the strictest rules; every atom is a storehouse of natural units.

modulate, *v.* Add: **5.** *trans.* Chiefly *Telecommunications.* **a.** To vary the amplitude or some other characteristic of (a wave or oscillatory signal, or a beam of particles) in accordance with the variations of a second signal, usu. a wave of lower frequency; also used with the property that is varied as obj.

1908 *Trans. Amer. Inst. Electr. Engin.* XXVII. 575 For wireless telephony three things are necessary:..2. Means for modulating this stream of waves in accordance with sound waves. **1921** J. SCOTT-TAGGART *Thermionic Tubes* xiii. 354 In wireless telephony, a steady stream of waves (usually termed the carrier wave) is usually modulated by means of a microphone. **1941** *Electronic Engin.* XIV. 485/1 The direct transmission and reception of speech or music over long distances..is impractical and propagation of audio frequencies is usually accomplished by using them to modulate an R.F. wave acting as carrier. **1952** R. W. DITCHBURN *Light* x. 299 It is not possible to observe the progress of a continuous beam of light without marking or 'modulating' it in some way. Three main methods of modulation have been used: (*a*) the toothed-wheel method, (*b*) the rotating-mirror method, and (*c*) the electronic shutter. In any of these methods the transit time is derived from a measurement of the frequency of the modulator. **1959** *Chambers's Encycl.* II. 591/2 In broadcasting on long, medium and short waves it is normally the amplitude which is modulated. **1962** *Newnes Conc. Encycl. Electr. Engin.* 428/2 In the klystron..the single cavity both modulates the beam [of electrons] to provide bunching, and abstracts energy from the beam on its return. **1965** *Science* 8 Oct. 153/3 The simplest way to modulate a beam of light—that is, the simplest way to make it carry a message—is to turn the generator of light on and off. **1972** *Sci. Amer.* Sept. 132/2 The received signal is decoded into its components and used to modulate three independent electron beams, each of which is allowed to strike only the red, green or blue phosphor dots.

b. To apply a signal to (a device) that modulates its output signal.

1920 P. E. EDELMAN *Exper. Wireless Stations* (rev. ed.) xv. 238 Starting with a telephone transmitter, this may be used to grid modulate one vacuum tube which in turn is cascaded to several others. **1953** W. A. EDSON *Vacuum-Tube Oscillators* xvi. 391 Magnetrons are ordinarily modulated by applying a large negative pulse to the cathode. **1973** *Sci. Amer.* Nov. 33/2 These diodes can be modulated rapidly by simply modulating the electric current that powers them.

c. To impress (a signal) *on to* a carrier wave by modulation.

1962 A. NISBETT *Technique Sound Studio* 267 A system for distributing audio information by modulating it on to a high frequency carrier..which is then amplified..and broadcast. **1970** J. EARL *Tuners & Amplifiers* v. 118 This [signal] cannot be added direct to the L + R information fed to the transmitter. First it has to be modulated on to a subcarrier of 38kHz. **1975** *Gramophone* Jan. 1412/3, CD-4 employs a carrier tone at supersonic frequency..on to which is [*sic*] modulated the difference signals.

d. *transf.* To exert a modifying or controlling influence on; to regulate.

1964 *Science* 15 May 819/3 This explanation..places some restriction on the details of any model involving regulation by modulating transfer RNA. **1971** *Sci. Amer.* July 55/3 It seems certain that the brain can modulate the transmission of olfactory information as early as the level of the first synapse of the olfactory pathway. **1971** *Nature* 20 Aug. 550/2 Thus we conclude that magnetism may modulate climate to some degree by the ability of the Earth's magnetic field somehow to provide a shield against solar corpuscular radiation. **1973** *Ibid.* 16 Nov. 154/1 Although strychnine had no effect in our system, actin-like proteins may form structures that modulate the mobility of lymphocyte receptors. **1974** *Sci. Amer.* Nov. 39/1 The steam flow is modulated by a control valve actuated by a speed governor on the rotor.

6. *Biol.* Of a cell: to undergo modulation *into* (see *MODULATION 8).

1956 C. H. WADDINGTON *Princ. Embryol.* xvi. 361 When differentiated vertebrate cells are grown in tissue culture.., they 'modulate' into less-specialised forms which may appear to be dedifferentiated, but they do not re-acquire the ability to develop into some tissue other than the one from which they were originally derived. **1964** N. T. SPRATT *Introd. Cell Differentiation* vi. 68 Although cells of cultured tissues may undergo temporary dedifferentiation (that is, may modulate), permanent loss of basic properties which distinguish the cells as to type seems to be rare.

modulated, *ppl. a.* (Later examples.)

1919 *Proc. IRE* VII. 193 The modulated output is therefore proportional to the curvature of the characteristic. **1920** M. B. SLEEPER *Wireless Design & Pract.* viii. 133 A modulated vacuum-tube transmitter can be divided into..the radiating, oscillating, reaction, and modulation circuits. **1921** *Electrician* 21 Jan. 95/2 In modulated wave signalling it has been proposed to leave out one of the essential modulating effects.

modulation. Add: **7.** Chiefly *Telecommunications.* The process of modulating a wave or beam (see *MODULATE *v.* 5 a) in order to impress a signal upon it; the extent to which a modulated carrier wave is varied; also, the wave-form or signal so impressed. Cf. *DEMODULATION.

Freq. preceded by a sb. denoting either (*a*) the characteristic of the carrier wave that is varied (as in *FREQUENCY MODULATION), or (*b*) the method by which the modulation is applied (as in **grid modulation*).

1919 *Proc. IRE* VII. 193 (*heading*) Modulation. **1921** J. SCOTT-TAGGART *Thermionic Tubes* xiii. 355 Two general methods of modulation are used at present; either the amplitude of the continuous waves is varied by the microphone, or the wave-length is altered... Sometimes both wave-length and amplitude modulation occur at the same time. **1924** W. JAMES *Wireless Valve Transmitters* ix. 200 The strength of the note received is dependent.. on the degree of modulation—that is, on the extent to which the amplitude of the oscillations vary. **1931** *Proc. IRE* XIX. 2146 Amplitude modulation by means of vacuum tubes can be effected in two different ways: as plate modulation or grid modulation. **1932** LADNER & STONER *Short Wave Wireless Communication* v. 73 Rectification is essential at the receiver, for the purpose of extracting the modulation. **1943** F. E. TERMAN *Radio Engineers' Handbk.* VII. 581 In phase modulation, intelligence is transmitted by varying the phase of the transmitted wave. **1949** H. E. PENROSE *Princ. & Pract. Radar* xvi. 310 The klystron and the reflex klystron depend for their action primarily upon velocity modulation of the electron stream. **1952** [see *MODULATE *v.* 5 a]. **1953** W. A. EDSON *Vacuum-Tube Oscillators* xvi. 386 The presence or absence of an output signal, in conjunction with an appropriate code, permits the communication of information. Such keying represents the simplest possible form of modulation, and is applicable to all kinds of oscillators. **1962** A. NISBETT *Technique Sound Studio* vi. 107 The equipment is lined up on a standard 1,000 c/s tone sent from the studio. The standard used is 1 milliwatt in 600 ohms..and is equivalent to 40% modulation at the transmitter. **1968** *Radio Communication Handbk.* (ed. 4) ix. 5/2 Choke modulation employs a choke as the coupling impedance between the modulator and the r.f. stage. **1972** *Sci. Amer.* Sept. 101/2 The most widely used processes of modulation are amplitude modulation (AM), frequency modulation (FM), pulse amplitude modulation (PAM) and pulse code modulation (PCM).

b. *transf.* The action or result of varying the magnitude, degree, etc., of something.

1964 *Science* 15 May 816 Modulation of transfer RNA species can provide a workable model of an operator-less operon. **1970** R. W. MCGILVERY *Biochem.* xxiii. 543 (*heading*) Regulation [of metabolism] by modulation of enzyme activity. **1971** *Physics Bull.* July 388/1 An acoustic wave produces a periodic modulation of the density of the medium. **1973** *Sci. Amer.* Aug. 50/2 The conduction between them can be controlled by the modulation of the charge in a channel between them.

c. *attrib.*, as **modulation envelope**, the envelope of an amplitude-modulated carrier wave; **modulation factor** = **modulation index*; **modulation frequency**, the frequency of a wave used to modulate another wave; **modulation index**, a coefficient representing the degree of modulation of a carrier wave; *spec.* the ratio of the difference between the maximum and minimum frequencies of a frequency-modulated carrier to the frequency of the modulating signal.

1930 *Proc. IRE* XVIII. 2161 If this leakage is slower than the rate at which the modulation envelope decreases, then the condenser voltage cannot follow the modulation envelope. **1950** P. PARKER *Electronics* x. 301 In the radio frequency stages of a receiver, distortion is important only in so far as it makes the modulation envelope of the signal voltage different from the wave-form of the modulating sound. **1970** J. EARL *Tuners & Amplifiers* ii. 47 To the centre-tap..is fed the mono and subcarrier stereo components, and the action of the switching transistors..is such that a 'modulation envelope' is formed, one side carrying the left-channel information and the other side the right-channel information. **1939** *Amat. Radio Handbk.* vi. 93/1 When using a continuous pure tone (sine wave) for modulating..the percentage modulation can be obtained by the Heising formula:—If I_O = R.M.S. value of unmodulated aerial current..I_M = ditto when modulated. m = modulation factor. Then $I_M = I_O\sqrt{(1 + m^2/2)}$. **1930** *Proc. IRE* XVIII. 2162 The rate of decrease of the modulation envelope depends upon the modulation frequency f and the degree of modulation m of the signal. **1962** SIMPSON & RICHARDS *Physical Princ. Junction Transistors* xviii. 453 The carrier and modulation frequencies are applied to one or both of the input electrodes. **1930** B. VAN DER POL in *Proc. IRE* XVIII. 1200 The whole practical problem of the amount of disturbance arising from frequency modulation depends therefore upon the value of the ratio $m = \Delta\omega/p$ of the absolute frequency deviation to the imposed audio frequency p. Owing to the importance of this parameter m..it may be found useful to designate it by a special name for which we suggest the expression 'frequency modulation index'. **1931** H. RODER in *Ibid.* XIX. 2151 B. van der Pol has introduced the expression 'modulation index' for m_f. We shall use this term for both m_p and m_f [where m_p represents the degree of phase modulation in a wave $i = A_0 \sin(\omega_0 t + m_p \sin \mu t)$]. **1974** *Encycl. Brit. Macropædia* XVIII. 91/2 The larger the modulation index (and hence the wider the bandwidth required for transmission), the more effectively FM performs.

8. *Biol.* Reversible variation in the activity or form of a cell in response to a changing environment.

1939 P. WEISS *Princ. Devel.* I. 94 This physiological, strictly nonprogressive fluctuation of a cell in response to its environmental conditions may be called modulation. It provides for a certain latitude within which a cell can comply adequately with certain variable functional demands of the developed body. **1964** N. T. SPRATT *Introd. Cell Differentiation* ii. 20 We..cannot accurately draw a line between differentiations and modulations. **1970** AMBROSE & EASTY *Cell Biol.* xiii. 441 Hormones are known to affect the synthetic function and the size of certain organs. This is an example of what Weiss has called 'modulation'.

modulator. Add: **1. b.** *spec.* A device that produces modulation of a wave (*MODULATION 7). Also *transf.*, a regulator, a controlling mechanism.

1919 *Proc. IRE* VII. 193 The curvature of the characteristic..makes possible its employment as a modulator and detector. **1930** *Discovery* Dec. 398/2 The output from the subscriber's telephone is amplified in the transmitting voice frequency amplifier and passes to the low frequency modulator. **1952** [see *MODULATE *v.* 5 a]. **1964** M. BROTHERTON *Masers & Lasers* xv. 182 If we feed into a modulator a voice frequency of 256 cps along with a carrier frequency of 50,000 cps, the modulator reacts by producing two new frequencies—one the difference frequency at 49,744 cps and the other the sum frequency at 50,256 cps. **1970** R. W. MCGILVERY *Biochem.* xxiii. 547 The deoxycytidine phosphates are not modulators of any of the reductions. **1970** *Sci. Amer.* Nov. 120/1 The use of the laser for mass communication..awaits the development of a practical modulator: an apparatus for impressing multiple signals on the light beam. **1972** *Jazz & Blues* Nov. 21/1, I..checked out this new modulator which a lot of people..are now using. You put in your voice and you get another sound on it. **1974** *Nature* 17 May 250/1 Such a test might assess the role of putrescine as a potential modulator of growth in normal and neoplastic tissue.

module, *sb.* Add: **4. c.** A length chosen as a basis for the dimensions of parts of a building, items of furniture, etc., to facilitate their co-ordination, so that all lengths are an integral multiple of it; *spec.* one of 4 inches (101·6 millimetres). Also *attrib.*

1936 BEMIS & BURCHARD *Evolving House* III. iv. 64 A dimension of 4" for the module..is selected because it is the nominal greatest common divisor of the wood-frame house, which represents the bulk of American housing. **1945** *Archit. Record* Jan. 103/1 The architect can best realize the advantage of the coordination of masonry and metal window dimensions by doing preliminary building layouts on the familiar cross section paper of the module system, each grid line representing 4 inches. **1946** *Industr. Standardization* XVII. 269/1 'Module' furniture is designed on a coordinated 6-inch scale so that all pieces are interchangeable. **1949** *Architects' Jrnl.* 20 Oct. 432/1 The planning grid on which the Hertfordshire County Council structure is based was an 8 ft. 3 in. module. **1955** *Sci. News Let.* 1 Jan. 13/1 Houses of the future may all be built using a four-inch cube called a module as the structural 'atom'. **1966** L. B. ANDERSON in G. Kepes *Module, Symmetry, Proportion* 117 Now the idea of the module is again asserted, with emphasis on its ability to encompass growth and change.

d. One of a series of production units or component parts that are standardized to facilitate assembly or replacement and are usu. prefabricated as self-contained structures.

1955 *Sci. Amer.* Aug. 30 (*caption*) Assembled module consists of a stack of wafers coated with opaque plastic. Vertical wires through notches in the wafers provide electrical connections between the parts. **1959** HORSEY & SHERGAUS *Proc. Symposium Microminiaturization of Electronic Assemblies 1958* I. iv. 44 The electronic 'module'..is an individually fabricated subassembly that may be replaced *in toto* when repair becomes necessary. **1964** R. F. FICCHI *Electr. Interference* iii. 23 For circuits and components that can be grouped together, e.g., modules (a group of components mounted on a nonconducting board and wired together), and chassis drawers (groups of modules mounted in a rack), the following wiring rules should be followed. **1969** W. V. TIPPING *Introd. Mech. Assembly* ix. 240 The modules are bolted together to form a full machine ready for final trouble-shooting. **1970** J. EARL *Tuners & Amplifiers* vi. 141 The vast majority of tuner-amplifiers are now transistored, the designs being based on printed circuit boards or 'modules'. **1970** *New Yorker* 3 Oct. 28/1 In prefabrication, flat pieces of a house are built in a plant and assembled on a site. Plumbing, electrical wiring, and heating are then installed by conventional methods. Modules are larger, three-dimensional units, which are completely finished in the factory and then bolted together at the site in a much shorter time. Modular housing gives you more control in the plant. **1971** [see *MODULAR *a.* 1 b]. **1971** *Real Estate Rev.* Fall 48/2 Our housing needs in the next nine years must be met with factory-built modules, assembled on site.

e. *Astronautics.* A separable section of a spacecraft that can operate as an independent unit.

1961 *New Scientist* 4 May 241/3 To deal with its dual function, the *Apollo* craft will have three separate sections, or modules: first, a command centre module..; secondly, a propulsion module..; and finally, a so-called 'mission' module. **1963** *Ann. Reg. 1962* 400 A capsule was to be fired from the earth into orbit round the moon, when a special part of it, christened the lunar excursion module, would detach itself. **1969** *Listener* 24 July 123/1 The ITV audience was being guided..towards the first climax of the night, the landing of the module on the Moon's surface. **1970** *Sci. Jrnl.* Aug. 35/2 As additional modules are placed in orbit and docked with the first module, some could be devoted to specialized activities.

f. One of a number of distinct, well-defined units from which a computer program may be built up or into which any complex process or activity is analysed (usu. for computer simulation), each of which is complete in itself but bears a definite relationship to the other units.

1963 L. SCHULTZ *Digital Processing* xv. 340 Ideally, the total program system could be segmented into completely independent parts (called modules) that exhibit interdependence only through a central communication pool. **1964** FISHER & SWINDLE *Computer Programming Syst.*

iv. 220 Because of such varying input/output requirements among programs and among machine configurations, it is now possible with many of the new IOCS packages to specify which modules of an IOCS [*sc.* an input/output control system, a set of routines for reading input and writing output data] are necessary for the most efficient processing of input/output requirements. **1965** *Economist* 17 July 272/2 This network is split up into sections or 'modules' that can be used in block form whenever a similar network is required. Shell used the example of the construction of chemical plant which the company put up around the world. The 'modules' in this instance are the particular items of plant, such as pressure vessels, which are standard. **1968** F. F. MARTIN *Computer Modeling* ix. 193 Modules are of two types: system or auxiliary. System modules simulate a specific function in system (or operation) logic... For example, a detection routine in a radar model is a system module that simulates the detection function of the radar... Auxiliary modules are nonsystem modules and are not necessarily unique to any given model. For example, a random statistical variates generator routine is an auxiliary module that may be applied in any stochastic model to generate random numbers. **1971** B. DE FERRANTI *Living with Computer* ix. 82 The computer programmer breaks his problem down into modules and gives the modules names so that they can be handled. **1973** R. M. ARMSTRONG *Modular Programming in COBOL* v. 60 The components of an operational control information system may be delineated as follows. Logistics: 1. Raw materials. 2. Production. 3. Salable product. Physical assets: 1. Property and equipment. 2. Capital projects... Manpower: 1. Payroll. 2. Benefits. 3. Personnel administration. We might describe these components as applicational modules at the systems level. *Ibid.* 63 In applying the above [characteristics] to a module in a computer system, a more precise definition is necessary. 1. The functions of input and output are well defined. 2. The module has a single entry point and a single exit point. 3. It exits to a standard return point in the module from which it was executed.

g. A unit or period of training or education. Cf. *MODULAR *a.* 1 c.

1966 *Economist* 3 Dec. 1005/1 Eventually the sort of retraining envisaged could fit in with the notion..of periodic training 'modules', whereby skilled men would take repeated periods off productive work to renew their perhaps rusty skills and learn new ones. **1968** *Daily Tel.* 12 Nov. 19/5 A training manual for a module course on 'Repairs and Restoration' has been produced.

5. b. *Math.* [ad. G. *modul* (R. Dedekind in P. G. L. Dirichlet *Vorlesungen über Zahlentheorie* (ed. 2, 1871) Suppl. x. 442).] Orig., a set that is a subset of a ring and is closed under addition and subtraction; now usu. defined as a commutative additive group whose elements may be multiplied by those of a ring (usu. a ring with an identity element), the product being in the group and the multiplication obeying the associative and distributive laws; *left, right module* (see quot. 1970[1]). Formerly also **modul.**

1927 *Amer. Math. Monthly* XXXIV. 64 The class concept was introduced by Dedekind as follows. A set M of elements of $I(\alpha)$ which is closed under subtraction, and hence under addition and subtraction, is called a module. If M be such that, if β is any element of M, and γ is any element of $I(\alpha)$, then $\beta\gamma$ is an element of M, the module M is called an ideal. **1937** A. A. ALBERT *Mod. Higher Algebra* i. 9 An additive abelian group is frequently called a modul. *Ibid.* xi. 252 A set $\mathfrak{M}$ of elements of a ring $\mathfrak{A}$ is called a modul of $\mathfrak{A}$ if $a-b$ is in $\mathfrak{M}$ for every a and b of $\mathfrak{M}$... Thus a modul is simply an additive subgroup of the additive abelian group $\mathfrak{A}$. **1948** O. ORE *Number Theory* vii. 159 The integers $0, \pm 1, \pm 2, \ldots$ form a modul, but the natural numbers $1, 2, 3, \ldots$ do not. *Ibid.* 161 A ring is a modul that is closed under multiplication. **1970** HARTLEY & HAWKES *Rings, Modules & Linear Algebra* v. 70 A module over a ring R (or R-module) is an Abelian group M (almost always written additively) together with a map $(r,m)\to rm$ from $R\times M$ to M satisfying the conditions $r(m_1+m_2)=rm_1+rm_2$, $(r_1+r_2)m=r_1m+r_2m$, $(r_1r_2)m=r_1(r_2m)$, $1m=m$, for all $r, r_1, r_2 \in R$ and all $m, m_1, m_2 \in M$. It would be more accurate to call what we have just defined a left R-module. There is a similar definition of a right R-module in which the elements of R are written on the right. *Ibid.* 69 A module is a construct of great versatility. It turns up in many seemingly unlikely guises and has the knack of manifesting some of the quintessential features of a wide variety of mathematical structures. **1970** *Nature* 19 Dec. 1234/2 A vector space is built up linearly by means of 'scalar' multipliers from a number field. The more general concept of a module replaces the field by an arbitrary ring (with unity) related to an Abelian group so that a 'product' is defined satisfying the usual distributive and associative laws.

8. *Engin.* The pitch diameter of a gear wheel in millimetres (or inches) divided by the number of teeth.

1909 in WEBSTER. **1912** G. T. WHITE *Toothed Gearing* ii. 17 Module = D^{mm}/N = ..25·4/diametral pitch = circular pitch″ × 8·085. **1964** MORRISON & CROSSLAND *Introd. Mech. Machines* ii. 142 One set of standard proportions is that the addendum should be equal to the module m (or the reciprocal of the diametral pitch) and the dedendum.. greater than this by an amount of one-twentieth of the circular pitch or $0{\cdot}157m$.

modulo (mǫ·diŭlo), *prep. Math.* [abl. of L. *modulus.*] With respect to a modulus of. Also *attrib.*, = modular.

1897 *Bull. Amer. Math. Soc.* III. 381 Congruences irreducible modulo p (p = prime). **1903** J. BOWDEN *Elem. Theory Integers* x. 242 The statement of congruence is written $\alpha\equiv\beta$ (mod. μ), which is read 'α is congruent with β, modulo μ'. **1939** L. E. DICKSON *Mod. Elem. Theory Numbers* i. 8 Any positive integer n is congruent modulo 9 to the sum s of its digits. **1966** OGILVY & ANDERSON *Excursions in Number Theory* iv. 43 Since 8, 15, 22, 29, etc., and also −6, −13, etc. are all congruent to 1 (mod 7), they are members of the same residue class modulo 7... In arithmetic modulo 7, 8 is equivalent to 1 in many senses. *Ibid.* 44 In number theory one must often work with very large numbers. If these can be reduced to equivalent smaller numbers, much time-consuming labor can be avoided. Herein lies one of the great contributions of modulo arithmetic. **1971** J. H. SMITH *Digital Logic* vi. 115 Modulo-7 counters count normally up to six (110). The next count must reset the counter to zero. **1973** *Nature* 20 Apr. 541/3 A sufficiently dense integer sequence is well distributed in most arithmetic progressions modulo most (small enough) primes.

modulor (mǫ·diuləɹ). [Fr.] A scale with initial dimensions of 7 feet 5 inches (226 cm.) and 3 feet 9 inches (114·3 cm.), devised by the French architect Charles-Edouard Jeanneret, called Le Corbusier (1887–1965), based on the proportions of a human figure six feet tall, and intended to be used for the co-ordinated design of buildings, their contents, and their surroundings. Also *attrib.*

1948 M. GHYKA in *Archit. Rev.* Feb. 39 Le Corbusier's Modulor, and the concept of the Golden Mean... The Modulor is a linear scale in the form of a tape. Its object is to provide a means by which practical realization may be given to the need for efficiency and harmony in the dimensioning of objects and their containers, in architectural design and in town-planning... The Modulor differs from such a [conventional] scale in that the markings on it are related to each other by the principle of the Golden Mean. **1954** DE FRANCIA & BOSTOCK tr. *Le Corbusier's Modulor* 55 The necessities of language demanded that the golden rule should be given a name. Of several possible words, the MODULOR was chosen... The 'Modulor' is a measuring tool based on the human body and on mathematics. **1962** *Listener* 27 Sept. 472/1 The modulor which he [*sc.* Le Corbusier] invented..seemed to have served this purpose. It..forced him to develop the shell from the inside in several stages, starting with the modulor as the smallest unit. *Ibid.* 472/2 His faithful students soon learned to assemble their modulor units to very much the same buildings they had designed before. **1964** J. SUMMERSON *Classical Lang. Archit.* vi. 46 It was not till the early years of World War II that le Corbusier created the system..which he has called the 'Modulor'. **1972** *Times* 30 Nov. (Books Suppl.) p. ii/5 Furneaux Jordan quotes the story of how Corbusier's six foot 'modulor' was chosen because he had heard that the 'good-looking man' in English detective novels..is always six feet tall.

modulus. Add: **2. d.** (Examples.) [Introduced in this sense by Gauss in *Disquisitiones Arithmeticae* (1801) I. 1.]

1845 *Encycl. Metrop.* I. 642/2 Numbers of the same form with respect to any modulus, are all those which can be represented by the same formula. Thus, 13, 17, 21, &c. are all of the form $4n+1$; and 19, 25, 31, &c. of the form $6n+1$; 4 and 6 being the moduli. **1888** C. SMITH *Treat. Algebra* xxviii. 487 If two numbers a and b leave the same remainder when divided by a third number c, they are said to be congruent with respect to the modulus c. **1949** [see *MOD *prep.*]. **1967** J. E. SHOCKLEY *Introd. Number Theory* iii. 48 Corollary 6.2 furnishes the most efficient method for solving several systems of congruences when the same sets of moduli appear in each system.

modus. Add: **5. b.** *modus operandi* (later examples).

1935 G. POOLE *Haulage & Winding* xiii. 324 Assuming that an overwind has taken place,..the *modus operandi* is as follows:—The engine-driver at once closes his throttle and immediately he has to call an assistant to go to the overwinding device; [etc.]. **1947** *Sci. News* V. 14 The *modus operandi* of insulin was, in Sakel's original theory, upon the nerve cells and the hormones which, he believed, excited their activity especially in the 'vegetative centres'. **1949** [see *HOW *sb.*[3] 2]. **1955** *Bull. Atomic Sci.* Feb. 58/3 Their *modus operandi* against limited aggression would be simple. **1972** *Mod. Law Rev.* XXXV. 28 The modus operandi of a small claims judge should approximate more closely to that of a police detective.

d. modus ponens (*Logic*), 'mood that affirms'; the rule that from *if p then q* together with *p*, *q* may be inferred; an argument of this form. In full **modus ponendo ponens.**

a **1856** W. HAMILTON *Lect. Metaphysics & Logic* (1860) I. 344 We can always easily convert an hypothetical syllogism of one form into another,—the *modus ponens* into the *modus tollens.* **1870** W. S. JEVONS *Elem. Lessons Logic* xix. 161 The argument is said to be of the *modus ponens*, or mood which posits or affirms. **1916** H. W. B. JOSEPH *Introd. Logic* (ed. 2) xv. 335 The argument is said to be in the *modus ponens.* **1957** P. SUPPES *Introd. Logic* ii. 32 The Latin name for the Law of Detachment is *modus ponendo ponens.* **1972** *Computer Jrnl.* XV. 230/2 Applying the rule of modus ponens on the above instance.

e. modus tollens (*Logic*), 'mood that denies'; the rule that from *if p then q* together with *not-q*, *not-p* may be inferred; an argument of this form. In full **modus tollendo tollens.**

a **1856** [see **modus ponens*]. **1881** MAX MÜLLER tr. *Kant's Critique Pure Reason* II. II. i. 678 The *modus tollens* of reasoning, from consequences to their grounds, is not only perfectly strict, but also extremely easy. **1916** H. W. B. JOSEPH *Introd. Logic* (ed. 2) xv. 337 The *modus tollens* is of the form [etc.]. **1940** *Mind* XLIX. 208 An inference in the *modus tollendo tollens*..yields the contrary of the original contrary hypothesis. **1965** E. J. LEMMON *Beginning Logic* ii. 61 *Modus tollendo tollens* is the principle that, if a conditional holds and also the negation of its consequent, then the negation of its antecedent holds.

Mœbius (mō·biʊs). The name of Bernhard *Mœbius* (fl. 1884 in Mexico as a German subject), used *attrib.* to designate an electrolytic process that he devised for parting gold and silver (*Brit. Pat. 16,554* (1884)), in which anodes of bullion and cathodes of silver or stainless steel are placed in a solution of silver nitrate, so that base metals go into solution and silver is deposited on the cathode, leaving behind the gold.

1902 *Encycl. Brit.* XXVIII. 110/1 Alloy scrap containing chiefly copper with, say 5 or 6 per cent. of gold, and other metals, and up to 40 or 50 per cent. of silver, is often treated electrolytically. Obviously, with modifications, the Mœbius process could be applied. **1970** *Materials & Technol.* III. iv. 295 Electrolytic refining [of doré metal] is now widely employed. In the Moebius process the impure silver is cast into anodes which are enclosed in cotton or linen bags and dissolved electrolytically in acid silver nitrate solution.

Moebius, var. *MÖBIUS.

‖ **moederkappie** (mŭ·dəɹkapi). *S. Afr.* Also **muttercap.** [Afrikaans, f. Du. *moeder* mother + *kap, kapje* hood, in reference to the shape of the flower.] Either of two South African orchids, *Pterygodium catholicum* or *Disperis capensis*, which bear bonnet-shaped flowers.

1887 J. MACKINNON *S. Afr. Traits* 124 Here is the Pride of Table Mountain and the Muttercap, two of the twenty-five species of orchids that exist in South Africa. **1910** D. FAIRBRIDGE *That which hath Been* xxiii. 284 Orchids in inexhaustible variety, from scarlet disas to yellow moederkapjes..are still left to us. **1952** *Cape Times* 8 May 14/1 Pine trees..together with humans, have been too much for the nerines, the *moederkappies* and other veld things which used to flower there. **1971** U. VAN DER SPUY *Wild Flowers S. Afr.* 209/2 (*caption*) Moederkappie (*Pterygodium catholicum*) bears its flowers of subtle colours in spring. **1973** *Stand. Encycl. S. Afr.* VIII. 382/1 Moederkappie. Oumakappie... These names are borne by two quite distinct species: *Pterygodium catholicum*..is usually about 20 cm high, with two or three leaves sheathing the somewhat fleshy stem. The few sulphur-yellow flowers are borne in a lax spike. As the flowers fade they turn dull red. They have a strong scent... *Disperis capensis.* Common orchid, sometimes called 'granny bonnet', with magenta, greenish or cream-coloured flowers... The leaves are rather small and clasp the stem. The flowers are usually solitary.

moekul, var. *MOGGEL.

moellon[2] (mwe·lǫn). [Presumably Fr., and perh. identical with MOELLON.] The fluid obtained when fish-oils are rubbed into hides and recovered by expression, as in the manufacture of chamois leather (cf. *DEGRAS, DÉGRAS a); also, a product made in imitation of this (see quot. 1969). Also called *moellon degras.*

1897 C. T. DAVIS *Manuf. Leather* (ed. 2) 227 French moellon oil, strictly speaking, is an expressed oil from chamois tannage, French degras being a mixture of moellon and oil obtained from washing the skins in an alkaline solution. **1922,** etc. [see *DEGRAS, DÉGRAS a]. **1939** *Thorpe's Dict. Appl. Chem.* (ed. 4) III. 552 (*heading*) Analysis of moëllon-dégras. **1969** T. C. THORSTENSEN *Pract. Leather Technol.* xii. 202 Natural moellon is produced by the oxidation of raw cod liver oil in the tanning of sheep and goat chamois skins. Synthetic moellon is produced by the controlled aeration of raw cod liver oil to the desired oxidation fatty acid value; it results in more hydrophilic properties.

Mœritherium (mīᵊripīᵊ·riŏm). [mod.L. (C. W. Andrews 1902, in *Verhandlungen V. Internat. Zool.-Congress* VI. 528), f. Gr. Μοῖρις the name of a lake in Egypt + θηρίον wild beast.] An extinct proboscidean mammal of the genus so called, known from remains found in late Eocene beds of the province of Fayum in Upper Egypt.

1902 *Encycl. Brit.* XXX. 510/2 Most remarkable is a primitive proboscidean (*Mœritherium*) with a nearly full series of front- and cheek-teeth. **1924** J. A. THOMSON *Sci. Old & New* xli. 236 Millions of years ago, in the Eocene epoch..there lived in North Africa a primitive hoofed animal called Mœritherium. **1968** A. S. ROMER *Procession of Life* xvi. 265 *Moeritherium* was still a relatively small animal, of about pig size, and, except for a rather long body, of pig-like proportions.

‖ **mœurs** (mōrs, mōr), *sb. pl.* [Fr.:—L. *mōrēs*, pl. of *mos* custom.] The behaviour, customs, or habits of a people or a group of people.

1922 BLUNDEN *Bonadventure* xxi. 136 So strongly did I feel that in his hours of leisure and coallessness he was a critic of verse and *mœurs* that I almost asked him his name. **1940** H. G. WELLS *Babes in Darkling Wood* II. i. 145, I am a student of human behaviour. I am—how shall I call it?—an experimentalist in *mœurs.* **1954** I. MURDOCH *Under Net* xiv. 192, I sat..reflecting on the difference between French and English literary *mœurs.* **1957** L. DURRELL *Bitter Lemons* 34 Yet side by side with this

crude and graceless world the true Mediterranean *moeurs* lingered. **1965** *New Statesman* 14 May 774/2 Mr. Baker's evident ambition was to present us with an authentic portrait of fleeting teenage *moeurs*.

moffie (mǫ·fi). *slang* (esp. *S. Afr.*). Also **mophy.** [? ad. colloq. shortening and mispronunciation of HERMAPHRODITE *sb.* and *a.*; cf. Afrikaans *moffiedaai*, dial. var. *hermafrodiet*.] An effeminate man.

1929 F. C. BOWEN *Sea Slang* 92 *Mophy*, a term of contempt among seamen for delicate, well-groomed youngsters. **1960** D. LYTTON *Goddam White Man* i. 27 Moffies. They don't like women but they like women's clothes... But Achmed was not a proper moffie; he just liked fooling with boys. He didn't have the moffie voice. **1971** *Post* (S. Afr.) 23 May 18 The life of Edward Shadi—described as a beautiful, sexy moffie with a sweet soprano voice—was a strange affair.

mog (mǫg), *sb. slang.* [Abbrev. *MOGGY 3.] A cat; also *transf.*, fur or a fur coat.

1927 W. E. COLLINSON *Contemp. Eng.* 26 As school-boys ..Tike for *dog*, moke for *donkey*..mog for *cat* were quite usual. **1934** P. HESELTINE in C. Gray *Peter Warlock* III. i. 253 Such lovely mogs you can't imagine—including the best cat in the world, surely. **1937** *Scrutiny* V. 391 Surrounded by vast quantities of cats and mistresses, now engaged in some fantastic quest for the Ideal Mog. **1950** PARTRIDGE *Slang To-day & Yesterday* (ed. 3) III. iii. 247 Annuvver 'orse comes up, an' it's..a new mog fer the missus.

Mogadon (mǫ·gădǫn). *Pharm.* A proprietary name for nitrazepam.

1956 *Trade Marks Jrnl.* 22 Feb. 180/2 Mogadon... All goods included in class 5 [*sc.* pharmaceutical, veterinary and sanitary substances]. Roche Products Limited,.. Welwyn Garden City, Hertfordshire; manufacturing chemists. **1965** *Brit. Med. Jrnl.* 6 Nov. 1093/2 They received 15 mg. of Mogadon (nitrazepam, an analogue of chlordiazepoxide), an effective new non-barbiturate hypnotic. **1972** D. MARLOWE *Do you remember England?* ii. 32 She took a sleeping tablet (Mogadon). **1973** *Guardian* 31 May 8/5 Police found a total of 156 drug tablets including a bottle of Mogadon.

Mogen David, var. *MAGEN DAVID.

mogey: see *MOKI².

moggadored (mǫ·gădǭɹd), *a. slang.* Also **mogodored.** [Orig. uncertain.] Confused, 'at a loss'.

Moggadored could just possibly be Irish. The element *-adore-* looks very like the Irish agent ending *-adóir*, and *moggadore* would be the natural anglicization of an Irish **mogadóir*. This is not in any of the dictionaries, but it would be a regular formation from the verbal noun *magadh* 'mock, jeer, make fun of, laugh at, etc.' (A. J. Bliss).

1936 G. INGRAM *Muffled Man* ix. 146 'I don't know,' Charlie said hopelessly, 'it's got me all "mogodored".' **1945** B. NAUGHTON in C. Madge *Pilot Papers* 105 He got some of these blokes moggadored: didn't know what to think, or do.

moggel (mǫ·gəl). Also **moekul.** [Afrikaans; see quot. 1902.] A South African freshwater fish of the genus *Labeo*, esp. *L. capensis*, belonging to the family Cyprinidæ.

1838 J. E. ALEXANDER *Expedition Interior Africa* I. vi. 144 My people came back in the evening with two or three large moekul or flat heads. **1902** *Trans. S. Afr. Philos. Soc.* XI. 214 It [sc. *Barbus capensis*] is now, however, called by the Dutch 'Moggel'— a word which..may be a corruption of the Latin *Mugil*, a generic name which has been applied to this fish, or it may refer to the general appearance and shape of this fish, 'moggel' in Dutch signifying a clumsy child. **1913** [see *BAARDMAN]. **1947** K. H. BARNARD *Pict. Guide S. Afr. Fishes* 52 The Sandfish or Moggel..has a more cylindrical body-shape... Its chief character is the mouth with its thick fleshy lips; these form a sucking disc with which the fish browses on the algae and weeds on the rocks. The barbels are not prominent.

moggie: see *MOKI².

moggy. Add: **3.** *slang.* Also **moggie.** A cat. Also *attrib.*

1911 J. W. HORSLEY *I Remember* xi. 254 Cockney slang ..'moggies' for cats. **1966** *New Statesman* 27 May 788/2 He dries his hands on a moggie and uses a kitten to blot a false death certificate; 'just a fur ball, it's nothing,' he says. **1966** *New Scientist* 15 Dec. 613/3 Humans, to moggies, are but bloodheated places to sit on. **1967** *Ibid.* 4 May 257/2 In the desert, there are several little wild cats superficially indistinguishable from domestic moggies. **1972** M. BABSON *Murder on Show* v. 64 We're concentrating on the nice pretty little moggies, remember? **1973** *People's Jrnl.* (Inverness & Northern Counties ed.) 4 Aug. 4/3 Oh, and before I leave this topic of pussies, my neighbour across the lane also had a good laugh from the moggie next door to her. **1975** *Times* 7 July 5 Dodd came on wearing a shaggy red overcoat and..saying that it was genuine moggyskin and that he wore moggyskin longjohns.

mogodored, var. *MOGGADORED *a.*

mogote (mŏgōu·ti). *Physical Geogr.* [Sp. *mogote* hillock, heap, haystack.] One of the tall, steep-sided hills, approximately circular in cross-section, that occur in karstic regions in Cuba and elsewhere.

1928 *Geogr. Rev.* XVIII. 67 The Guaniguanico Mountains..rise from a smoothly undulating plain in the form of huge blocks and mesas, known as mogotes, to a maximum height of about a thousand or twelve hundred feet above the supporting floor. **1954** W. D. THORNBURY *Princ. Geomorphol.* xiii. 335 The pepino hills of Puerto Rico are much smaller than the mogotes of Cuba and hence more commonly rise to peaks rather than have flat summits. **1972** J. ROGLIĆ in Herak & Stringfield *Karst* i. 11 The karst..is characterized by isolated steep hills ('mogotes' in Cuba).

mogul, *sb.* and *a.* Add: **A.** *sb.* **2. b.** (Later examples.)

1754 R. WALL in *Trans. R. Hist. Soc.* (1932) XV. 29 Wen you wil read this scrape, the mogol will bee five or six leagues of going to Granad. **1877** *N.Y. Daily Tribune* 16 Feb. 4/4 John A. Logan is the Head Center, the Hub, the King Pin, the Main Spring, Mogul, and Mugwump of the final plot. **1902** 'MARK TWAIN' in *Harper's Weekly* 6 Dec. 1824/2 My old friend, the great mogul..the stationmaster, you know. **1928** *Dialect Notes* V. i. 69 *Mogul*, an aristocrat. 'They think they are the *moguls* of this town.' New Mexico. **1957** *Times Lit. Suppl.* 10 May 285/2 Rich but decadent, moguls and hangers-on of the film industry. **1966** T. PYNCHON *Crying of Lot 49* i. 9 One Pierce Inverarity, a California real estate mogul. **1973** *Canad. N. & Q.* Nov. 12 Those who have examined the career of Canada's first 'movie mogul', have not been able to uncover the final chapters of his life. **1974** *Times* 14 Mar. 14/7 A group of cinema moguls asked how she [*sc.* Gertrude Stein] managed to get so much publicity. 'By having a small audience' was the reply.

B. *adj.* Also, denoting works of art, jewels, etc., noted for their richness, produced in India at the time of the Mogul empire.

1921 C. H. SMITH in C. S. Clarke *Indian Drawings* Pref., The other very important Mogul drawings bequeathed to the Museum by Lady Wantage. **1931** A. U. DILLEY *Oriental Rugs & Carpets* v. 140 The Mogul animal rugs of India, equally with the flower rugs, are photographic. **1958** A. RIDLER in C. Williams *Image of City* p. xxi, He seemed so full of the energy of thought that even the most lack lustre of his listeners felt themselves, for the time being, 'mogul diamonds'. **1963** S. C. WELCH *Art Mughal India* 12 We know dozens of Mughal Old Masters by name and style... Several of the qualities we find in Mughal art (romanticism, Indian-ness, and poetry) have frequently been denied it by critics. **1963** *Times* 20 Apr. 10/4 A sabre set with emeralds, the hilt carved in seventeenth-century Moghul jade. **1969** *Cultural News from India* Nov. 30 She illustrated her theory with slides of Moghul and Rajasthani miniature painting. **1969** *Times* 25 Nov. 14/6 (Advt.), Four 17th century Mughal carpets. **1973** *New Society* 10 May 292/1 Western art influenced mughal artists.

Hence **Mo·gulship,** used ironically.

1851 H. MELVILLE *Moby Dick* III. xxii. 148 Before I saw it off..I must call his old Mogulship, and see whether the length will be all right. **1876** C. M. YONGE *Womankind* xxiii. 197 The mistress..viewing their summons to a parent's sick-bed..as an injury to her own Great Mogulship.

mogul (mōu·gǝl), *sb.*² [? ad. S. German dial. *mugel*, *mugl* in same sense.] A bump on a ski-slope. Also *attrib.* Hence **mo·guled** *a.*

1961 R. SKEPPER *Tackle Ski-ing this Way* iii. 45 Moguls are large bumps, and occur most frequently in couloirs, on shoulders, in gullies, or very steep hills. They are usually caused by the piste skier's sheep complex... There is usually a mogul passage on every difficult run. **1965** *Daily Express* 26 Oct. 23/6 Crowded pistes and modern technique (a series of closely linked turns near the fall-line) results [*sic*] in large areas of bumps, or moguls, on the steeper portions of the piste. **1969** M. HELLER *Ski* xv. 199 Closely related to mogul slopes is the heavily rutted traverse. **1970** *Times* 18 Dec. 20/2 At the crack of dawn the snowmobiles would be at work, compacting new snow and planing off exaggerated moguls (bumps). **1972** DEAN & SMITH *Wisconsin* 161/1 Every Wisconsin ski area has something unique to offer... Some even boast of 'friendly moguls'. **1975** *Friends* (U.S.) Mar. 25 'Hot' skiing over steep and moguled terrain.

Moh: see *MOHS.

mohair. Add: Also **mo·haired, mo·hairy** *adjs.*

1873 L. TROUBRIDGE *Jrnl.* 2 Oct. in *Life amongst Troubridges* (1966) viii. 63 An ancient mohairy sort of dress. **1965** *New Statesman* 15 Oct. 576/2 Part of the Piccadilly's audience..mohaired, razor-cut and agog.

Mohammed, Mohammedan. The spellings *Muhammad, Muhammadan* are now usual (except in fixed expressions like the following word).

Mohammedan. Add: **A.** *adj.* **b.** *Mohammedan blue*, a cobalt blue used as an underglaze colour on Chinese porcelain of the Ming dynasty.

1905 MRS. W. HODGSON *How to identify Old Chinese Porc.* 8 The most celebrated colour of the Ming period was 'Mohammedan Blue'. This was brought from Persia, or some neighbouring country, as tribute, and pieces decorated with it were highly valued. **1909** S. W. BUSHELL *Chinese Art* (ed. 2) II. vii. 33 A pale grey-blue of pure tint, called at the time 'Mohammedan blue'. **1954** H. GARNER *Oriental Blue & White* iii. 15 Mohammedan blue by itself tended to run and..it was mixed with the native ore to give firm outlines. **1964** *Listener* 23 Apr. 683/1 The finished powder was..a mixture of two crude cobalt ores —one a native ore, the other imported from western Asia and known as Mohammedan blue. **1971** *Country Life* 16 Sept. 666/1 The dish..is just that, a rare but reasonably familiar type painted in the brilliant so-called Mohammedan blue.

Mohave (mohā·vi). Also **Mohawa, Mojave.** [Native name, f. *aha* water + *makave* beside.] **A.** *sb.* A Yuman Indian people along the Colorado river; a member of this people; also, their language. **B.** *adj.* Of or pertaining to this people.

1831 J. O. PATTIE *Personal Narr.* 93 We resumed our march, and on the 6th arrived at another village of Indians called Mohawa. **1853** L. SITGREAVES *Rep. Expedition Zuñi & Colorado Rivers* 18 The appearance of the Mohaves is striking, from their unusual stature, the men averaging at least six feet in height. **1858** *Harper's Mag.* Sept. 463/1 When the trading was concluded, the Mojave people sauntered about the camp. **1877** *Mag. Amer. Hist.* I. 153 Languages, with a sonorous, sweet, soft, and vocalic utterance,..are the Mohave, Hualapai, [etc.]. **1949** M. MEAD *Male & Female* vi. 129 The conspicuous transvestitism of the Mohave Indians. **1949** *Word* V. 268 (*title*) Mohave voice and speech mannerisms. **1955** W. GADDIS *Recognitions* I. i. 45 The sermon, meanwhile, had progressed from vivisection to the Mojave Indians. *Ibid.* 46 Among the Mojaves, it is believed that everyone dead under the doctor's hand falls under his power in the next life. **1963** ERVIN & MILLER in J. A. Fishman *Readings Sociol. of Lang.* (1968) 85 The Mohave claim newborn children can understand speech. **1965** *Language* XLI. 305 Yuman shows various reflexes: Mohave, Cocopa, and Kiliwa have /i/. **1970** *Ibid.* XLVI. 538 There is some evidence in Mohave for contrastive pitch.

mohcock, var. *MOCOCK.

mohel (mōu·(h)ĕl). Also **Mohel.** [Heb. *mōhēl*.] A Jewish official who performs the rite of circumcision.

1650 E. CHILMEAD tr. *Leon Modena's Hist. Rites of Jews* IV. viii. 203 They also use to make choice of a Circumciser, which they call..Mohel. **1676** L. ADDISON *Present State of Jews* (ed. 2) 59 The chief Officer at Circumcision is the Mohel. **1753** *Jewish Ritual* 19 The Operator (called the Mohel) makes use of a sharp, double edged knife... To assist the Mohel or Circumciser, is counted a meritorious Office. **1903** *Jewish Encycl.* IV. 95/2 As a rule, the wife of the godfather carries the child in and hands it to the mohel. **1932** A. Z. IDELSOHN *Jewish Liturgy* xiii. 166 The *Mohel*—Circumciser—places the child upon the 'chair of Elijah' and recites. *Ibid.* 167 Then the Mohel recites the benediction over wine and another benediction. **1973** *Jewish Chron.* 19 Jan. 11/2 [Al Jolson's] father was the local mohel and he circumcised me. **1974** *Observer* (Colour Suppl.) 10 Nov. 34/1 By Jewish law, a boy should be circumcised on the eighth day after birth... The devout treat it as a religious ceremony, with a *mohel* officiating and giving a blessing. A *mohel* is a trained and registered circumciser and there are a few score of them in Britain.

Mohican, *a.* and *sb.* Add: **A.** *adj.* (Earlier examples.)

1643 *Mass. Bay Rec.* (1853) II. 46 Concerning any advice..about the Nariganset or Mohegen sachems and their people. **1648** T. SHEPARD *Clear Sun-Shine of Gospel upon Indians New-Eng.* 26 The Mohegen Counseller..is counted the wisest Indian in the Country.

b. Of a hairstyle, resembling that worn by the Mohicans, in which the head is shaved except for a strip of hair from the middle of the forehead to the back of the neck.

1960 *News Chron.* 25 Mar. 7/5 James Greenwood, of York,..had his hair cut in Mohican style for his thirteenth birthday. **1960** *Guardian* 27 Sept. 2/4 A Lowestoft boy.. had a 'Mohican' haircut on Saturday and then went back to the barber to have the remaining strip of hair cut. **1965** *Evening Standard* 29 Oct. 6/6 A man with a Mohican haircut.

B. *sb.* **3.** Phr. *the last of the Mohicans*, the title of a novel (1826) by J. F. Cooper (1789–1851), used allusively to designate the sole survivors of a noble class or race. Also *fig.*

1832 *Boston Transcript* 3 Apr. 2/1 We have seen the last of the Mohigans and the last of the cocked-hats, and we pray that we may be able to say, on the morrow we have seen the last of the snow-storms. **1894** A. LANG *Cock Lane* 136 A hundred years after the blue stockings looked on Johnson as the last survivor, the last of the Mohicans of superstition, the Psychical Society can collect some 400 cases of haunted houses in England. **1922** JOYCE *Ulysses* 644 Fourpence (the amount he deposited unobtrusively in four coppers, literally the last of the Mohicans). **1946** H. HOWE *We Happy Few* 7 You can't pay attention to a thing that John Calcott says because he is the perfect product of the school—our own special Last of the Mohicans.

Mohini-attam (mohi·ni,atam). Also (as one word) **Mohiniattam.** [f. *Mohini* the name of the supreme seductress of Hindu mythology (f. Skr. *muh* confuse, bewilder) + Tamil *attam* dance.] The name of an Indian dance for women showing the influence of the Kathakali school and noted for its gentle and graceful style.

1948 G. VENKATACHALAM *Dance in India* xii. 109 Mohini Attam..has its own style and technique, its

peculiar idioms and expressions, coloured considerably by Kathakali. **1950** K. AMBROSE *Classical Dance & Costumes India* 11 *Mohiniattam*..was prevalent in Malabar right up to the late 'twenties, and it is very largely composed of a fusion of the Tanjore temple-dance and the *Kathakali* dance style of Malabar. **1953** F. BOWERS *Dance in India* 69 Mohini Attam was performed exclusively by women and was largely used by prostitutes to attract patrons. Because of its immoral associations, Mohini Attam fell into great disfavor and declined. **1967** SINGHA & MASSEY *Indian Dances* xii. 115 Mohini came to be synonymous with the essence of feminine beauty and allurement, and Mohini Attam is a dance which displays just such qualities. It is a solo dance, reserved exclusively for women... Mohini Attam is for the most part nritta although abhinaya is by no means absent. **1969** *Cultural News from India* Nov. 13 Kanak Rele..has done deep research into South Indian dance... Her repertoire consists of three major items: Mohini-attam; Kansa-natakam and pure Kathakali. **1971** *Femina* (Bombay) 2 Apr. 11/1 She was also one of the very first women in our time to learn Kathakali and Mohini Attam.

moho[1]. Delete 'extinct' in definition. See also NOTORNIS and *TAKAHE.

Moho[3] (mōᵘ·ho). *Geol.* Also **moho.** [Abbrev. of *Mohorovičić*.] = *MOHOROVIČIĆ DISCONTINUITY.

1956 *Adv. Geophysics* III. 118 The boundary..is now called the Mohorovičić discontinuity (vulgarly 'The Moho'). **1959** *Daily Tel.* 21 Apr. 13/1 The bore must itself be several miles deep to penetrate to the mysterious 'moho' and find out what the bulk of the world is really made of. **1960** *New Scientist* 19 May 1278/3 It is..generally accepted that both the density and the seismic wave velocities change at the Moho. **1972** *Nature* 15 Dec. 383/3 The graben gives clear Moho refractions with normal upper mantle velocities.

mohonono (mohonōᵘ·no). *S. Afr.* [ad. Lozi *muHonono*.] An evergreen tree with grey-green leaves, *Terminalia sericea*, of the family Combretaceæ, native to southern Africa; also called Transvaal silver leaf and vaalboom.

1864 T. BAINES *Explor. S.-W. Afr.* xx. 441 Passing through a thick mopane and mohonono forest, [we] outspanned about 7 p.m. in a more open flat. **1878** K. JOHNSTON *Africa* xxiv. 427 The silvery mohonono..is in form like the cedar of Lebanon. **1949** K. L. SIMMS *Sun-Drenched Veld* iii. 33 There is..the cedar-spread of the mohonono.

mohoohoo (mǒhū·hū). Also **mahoohoo, mohohoo, mohuhu, monooho(o), muchocho.** [Sechuana.] The white rhinoceros, *Ceratotherium simus*, found in central Africa and Zululand.

1835 A. SMITH *Diary* 11 July (1940) II. 107 The Baquana say that two kinds [of rhinoceros] are only in this country. The black, which they call *muchli* and the white *mohohoo*. **1842** R. MOFFAT *Missionary Labours & Scenes S. Afr.* xxvii. 461 The mohohu, the largest species [of rhinoceros], has been known even to kill the elephant, by thrusting the horn into its ribs. **1849** A. SMITH *Illustr. Zool. S. Afr.: Mammalia* plate 19 Localities abounding in grass are therefore the haunts of the Mohoohoo. **1850** R. G. CUMMING *Five Yrs. Hunter's Life S. Afr.* xii. 77/2 With considerable difficulty we separated the horn of the muchocho from the skin by means of a long sharp knife. **1856** C. J. ANDERSSON *Lake Ngami* xxx. 387 The common white rhinoceros..called Monoohoo by the Bechuanas. **1866** *Chambers's Encycl.* VIII. 236/2 The White R[hinoceros]..or Muchuco, or Monooho, is the largest of the well-ascertained African species. **1875** W. H. DRUMMOND *Large Game & Nat. Hist. S. & S.-E. Afr.* 84 *Rhinoceros simus*, the mohohu of the Bechuanas. **1879** E. P. WRIGHT *Animal Life* 141 It [*sc.* the white rhinoceros] is called by the Bechuanans, Mahoohoo, and is considered by them to be one of the original animals of their country. **1884** J. MACKENZIE *Day-Dawn in Dark Places* 189 It is said the flesh of the mohuhu, or white rhinoceros is very good. **1894** R. LYDEKKER *Royal Nat. Hist.* II. 480 The individuals exhibiting this form being known to the Bechuanas by the name of mohohu.

Mohorovičić discontinuity (mohorōᵘ·vitʃitʃ). *Geol.* Also **Mohorovicic discontinuity.** [f. the name of A. *Mohorovičić* (1857–1936), Yugoslav seismologist.] The discontinuity between the earth's crust and the mantle which is believed to exist at a depth of about 10–12 kilometres under the ocean beds and 40–50 kilometres under the continents.

1936 J. B. MACELWANE in Macelwane & Sohon *Introd. Theoret. Seismol.* I. viii. 204 We shall speak of this major boundary above which the various surficial layers lie as the Mohorovičić discontinuity, after A. Mohorovičić who discovered it. **1956** [see *MOHO[3]]. **1958** [see *MANTLE *sb.* 10*]. **1971** I. G. GASS et al. *Understanding Earth* iii. 58/2 On the basis of seismic velocities, the mantle is usually divided into three regions—from the Mohorovicic discontinuity down to 400 km, from 400 to 1000 km, and from 1000 km to the core boundary.

Mohs (mōᵘz). The name of Friedrich *Mohs* (see MOHSINE), used *attrib.* and in the possessive (chiefly in *Mohs('s) scale*) with reference to a scale of hardness he devised in which ten reference minerals that include very soft and very hard ones are assigned values of one to ten in order of increasing hardness.

The ten minerals of the scale are: 1, talc; 2, gypsum; 3, calcite; 4, fluor-spar; 5, apatite; 6, orthoclase; 7, quartz; 8, topaz; 9, corundum; 10, diamond.

1879 *Mineral. Mag.* II. 265 Its density is 1·0025; hardness between 1 and 2 of Mohs's scale. **1897** *Amer. Jrnl. Sci.* CLIV. 409 We shall describe only a preliminary series of tests with the minerals of the Mohs scale. **1951** D. TABOR *Hardness of Metals* i. 2 The Mohs hardness scale has been widely used by mineralogists and lapidaries. **1962** R. WEBSTER *Gems* I. iv. 74 The hardness of beryl is 7½ on Mohs's scale. **1974** *Sci. Amer.* Aug. 64 Each material in the Mohs scale, up to Mohs 9 (corundum), is about 1·2 times as hard as the preceding material. Thus the scale is almost logarithmic from Mohs 1 through Mohs 9, a range that includes all but a few substances.

¶ Erron. written as *Moh* (or *moh*).

1903 J. E. MARR *Agric. Geol.* ii. 28 Moh's scale of hardness. **1934** J. A. PERRY *Chem. Engineers' Handbk.* xvi. 1558 The hardness of a material as measured by the moh scale is not always a criterion of its resistance to crushing. **1969** B. R. SCHLENKER *Introd. Materials Sci.* iv. 69 A Moh's hardness determination set of minerals.

mohua, mohur, var. MAHWA (in Dict. and Suppl.).

mohuhu, var. *MOHOOHOO.

Moi (mōᵘ·i), *a.* and *sb.* [Native name.] **A.** *adj.* Of or pertaining to a people of Indo-Australoid origin who were among the original inhabitants of Vietnam and are now found in the Southern mountain region (see quot. 1959). **B.** *sb.* **a.** The name of this people. **b.** A member of this people. **c.** The name of their language. Cf. *MONTAGNARD 1 b.

1845 *Encycl. Metrop.* XVI. 780/2 The southern branches of those mountains, and the long ridge which divides Anam from Kambója are inhabited by the Múóng and Moï, or Ké-moïs tribes, whose language also differs from that of the lowlanders. **1853** J. R. LOGAN in *Jrnl. Indian Archipelago* VII. 36 The Moi or Ka-moi..on the opposite side of the Mekong occupy the broad expansion of the Anam chain towards Kamboja. **1911** *Encycl. Brit.* XIV. 491/1 The population of French Indo-China falls into five chief divisions—the Annamese..the Khmers..the Chams..the Thais..and the autochthonous tribes classed by the other inhabitants as Mois or Khas ('savages'). **1928** H. HERVEY *Trav. French Indo-China* 248 Here the Moi, aboriginal tribes of ancient Chiampa, mingle with the Laotians and the Annamites. **1957** J. OLIVER tr. *Riesen's Jungle Mission* i. 14 With her to interpret, I could understand and express the most varied ideas, increasing my French–Moï vocabulary. **1959** E. BROCKETT tr. *Bertrand's Jungle People* 11 The rather vague term 'Moi Plateau' is applied to the area bounded to the north by the River Mékong, to the west by the Cambodian jungle and to the east by the mountain range of Annam. *Ibid.* 20 On the floor..a square sod of earth placed on a tin slab formed the traditional Moï hearth. **1961** D. LANCASTER *Emancipation French Indochina* 4 The Mois..are a handsome, bronze-skinned people akin to the Dyaks of Borneo and the Bataks of Sumatra. **1965** B. NEWMAN *Background to Viet-Nam* vii. 73 Clever French philologists had adapted the Moïs languages to the Latin alphabet, so that reading and writing could be taught. **1968** *Listener* 13 June 760/3 Hill tribes..whom..the Vietnamese call *Moi*..practise a primitive agriculture, live in thatched long-houses..and are much addicted to gongs, rice wine and animal sacrifice.

moiety. Add: **2. c.** Chiefly *Biochem.* and *Pharm.* A group of atoms forming part of a molecule.

1935 DORLAND & MILLER *Med. Dict.* (ed. 17) 842/1 *Carbohydrate moiety*, the non-nitrogenous residue of the amino acids resulting from deamination. **1945** *Jrnl. Biol. Chem.* CLIX. 311 The lactone moiety [of pantothenic acid] can replace pantothenic acid for growth of the above organisms. **1954** A. WHITE et al. *Princ. Biochem.* xii. 265 The other penicillins have the same type of structure but have different side chains replacing the benzyl ($C_6H_5CH_2$—) moiety. **1962** *Lancet* 29 Dec. 1381/1 A.I.C. has been shown to be a key intermediate..in the biosynthesis of the purine moiety of inosinic acid. **1970** PASSMORE & ROBSON *Compan. Med. Stud.* II. xxxii. 9/2 Species differences may vary strikingly when the compound under examination is not itself toxic but becomes metabolized to release the toxic moiety. **1974** *Nature* 13 Dec. 586/2 Its molecular structure (containing both an indole and a phenylethylamine moiety) suggests the possibility of an interaction with brain monoamines.

4. Also a type of social division found in varying forms amongst tribes in other parts of the world, though rarely in Africa. Also *attrib.*

1914 W. H. R. RIVERS *Kinship & Social Organisation* iii. 72 The dual system in which there are only two social groups or moieties. **1934** R. H. LOWIE *Introd. Cultural Anthropol.* xiv. 261 The moiety system can not explain why the Murngin and Miwok permit only one kind of cross-cousin to be married, when both belong to the proper moiety. **1936** R. LINTON *Study of Man* xii. 207 Where both moieties and clans occur, the former are ordinarily more limited in their functions and of less social importance, possibly because the larger size of the moiety makes the establishment of well-defined attitudes..more difficult. **1937** R. H. LOWIE *Hist. Ethnol. Theory* xi. 182 Some Melanesians..have totemic moieties. **1938** G. A. REICHARD in F. Boas *Gen. Anthropol.* ix. 431 One of the Toda moieties considers itself superior to the other and has definite and important religious functions. **1944** B. MALINOWSKI *Sci. Theory of Culture* vi. 162 The family, an extended kinship group, a clan, or a moiety, constitute one type. **1949** M. MEAD *Male & Female* 422 Three different forms of marriage, and several types of age-grading and moiety systems, resulted in a rich and complex form of social organization. **1952** A. R. RADCLIFFE-BROWN *Struct. & Function Primitive Society* vi. 118 Such moiety totemism..is found in a number of different varieties in Australia, and still other varieties are found in Melanesia and in North America.

Moine (moin). *Geol.* [f. *the Moine* (Gael. *A'Mhòine*), name of an area east of Loch Eriboll in northern Sutherland where rocks of the series are exposed.] Used *attrib.* and as *the Moine(s)* to denote a highly folded series of metamorphic rocks, chiefly granulites and schists, in NW. Scotland and western Ireland which are thought to have been deposited in Pre-Cambrian (possibly Torridonian) times and metamorphosed later.

1888 *Q. Jrnl. Geol. Soc.* XLIV. 425 The various stages in the production of the Moine schists. *Ibid.* 438 Other intrusive igneous rocks pierce the micaceous flagstones of the Moine series. **1931** GREGORY & BARRETT *Gen. Stratigr.* i. 27 The lower part corresponds to the British Lewisian and Moine. **1934** *Geol. Mag.* LXXI. 303 The view that the Moines are Torridonian metamorphosed in post-Cambrian time is associated with the name of Peach. **1953** *Q. Jrnl. Geol. Soc.* CVIII. 100 The problems of the age of the Moine Series, and of the relations of the series with the other Highland formations, have been a source of controversy for more than a century and the metamorphism of the series has been assigned to periods ranging from early Pre-Cambrian to Lower Palæozoic. **1961** *Science Progress* XLIX. 715 Younger Dalradian rocks..overlie the Moines and separate the Scottish and Irish outcrops. The Moines rest on a Lewisian basement and cannot accordingly be older than 1600 million years. *Ibid.* 716 The Moine Series is the last great formation of sedimentary origin in the British Isles whose stratigraphical relations remain to be established. **1969** BENNISON & WRIGHT *Geol. Hist. Brit. Isles* iii. 53 The unmetamorphosed equivalent of the lower part of the Moine may be the Greywacke Group of the Torridonian of Islay and Oronsay.

Moinian (moi·niăn), *a. Geol.* [f. prec. + -IAN.] Of, pertaining to, or designating the Moine series of rocks (see prec.). Also *absol.*, the Moine series.

1938 A. K. WELLS *Outl. Hist. Geol.* vi. 50 There is nothing inherently impossible in the suggestion that the Moinian rocks may be metamorphosed Torridonian. *Ibid.*, It is as well to remind ourselves that the great overthrusts separate an area where the succession is Lower Palæozoic rocks, on Torridonian, on Lewisian, from one..in which the succession is: Dalradian, on Moinian, on Lewisian. **1954** *Q. Jrnl. Geol. Soc.* CX. 46 Many bodies of Lewisian gneiss are marked on the Geological Survey maps of the Moine area of Ross-shire. Preliminary studies..suggest that some at least of these bodies resemble the so-called inliers of Scardroy and Fannich in being of Moinian age. **1969** BENNISON & WRIGHT *Geol. Hist. Brit. Isles* iii. 46 The Lewisian also forms the basement to the Moinian Series, a dominantly arenaceous sedimentary sequence but everywhere separated from the Torridonian by the Moine thrust. **1971** *Geol. Mag.* CVIII. 193 Moinian and Dalradian metamorphic rocks occur in the north-east extension of the Ox Mountains [in Eire]. The petrology and migmatization of the Moinian are discussed and Dalradian rocks are described for the first time from this area.

moiré, *a.* and *sb.* Add: **A.** *adj.* (Further examples.) Also applied to other materials (as paper, linoleum) having an appearance resembling watered silk.

1873 *Young Englishwoman* Apr. 199/2 The bottom is covered with moiré-paper. **1947** D. HUNTER *Papermaking* (ed. 2) 528, 1806... The commencement of the use of moiré papers, embossed by heated cylinders, used in bookbindings. **1972** J. K. P. EDWARDS *Floors* v. 69 Linoleum can be manufactured to give many different patterns and a wide variety of types, including plain, jaspé, moiré, marble and others.

b. Applied to the wavy or geometrical pattern of light and dark stripes ('fringes') that is observed when one pattern of lines, dots, etc., is visually superimposed on another similar pattern, or on an identical one that is slightly out of alignment with the first; chiefly in *moiré fringe, pattern.*

1940 *Chambers's Techn. Dict.* 553/1 *Moiré effect* (Photog.), a 'watered-silk' pattern..arising from interference between two line-screens; a defect for which occasional uses are found. **1950** *Proc. R. Soc.* A. CCI. 189 With the [diffraction] gratings made in the manner described above the moiré pattern consisted of a very complicated wavy pattern which repeated itself with great uniformity every quarter of an inch, this being the pitch of the lead-screw. **1953** H. A. CHINN *Television Broadcasting* ii. 70 The problem of a moiré pattern caused by 'beating' of the scanning lines with the lines of the target mesh does exist. **1956** J. GUILD *Interference Syst. Crossed Diffraction Gratings* p. v, Though attention was called to them by Lord Rayleigh as long ago as 1874 the fringes produced by crossed diffraction gratings, now usually termed moiré fringes, have somehow escaped mention in the textbooks of physical optics. **1963** *Sci. Amer.* May 54/3 The only general requirement for a moiré pattern is that the interacting figures have some sort of solid and open regions. The solid regions can be lines (straight, curved or wiggly), dots or any other geometric form... In the typical moiré pattern the moiré effect materializes when two sets of straight lines are superposed so that they intersect at a small angle. *Ibid.* 63/1 Moiré patterns sometimes plague the printer whenever he is obliged to print two or more halftone impressions one atop the other,

which he must do in making multicolored reproductions. **1971** J. H. SMITH *Digital Logic* i. 3 Automatic programmed machines are..made to an extremely high accuracy, e.g. 5000 steps (digits) per inch are easily realised using moiré fringe devices. **1973** *Sci. Amer.* Oct. 120/2 Two sets of concentric circles that overlap generate moiré patterns in the form of radial lines. Concentric circles that overlap a grid of comparable spacing generate ellipses, parabolas or hyperbolas, depending on the angle of inclination between the plane of the concentric circles and the plane of the grid.

B. *sb.* **1.** (Further examples.) Add to def.: A moiré pattern or effect.

1953 H. A. CHINN *Television Broadcasting* i. 27 The most objectionable moiré is probably that produced by the blanking pulses because they usually represent the greatest possible black-to-white contrast ratio. **1963** *Sci. Amer.* May 55 (*caption*) Moiré composed of beats is produced from nonintersecting parallel lines when the spacing of one set differs from that of another. **1967** E. CHAMBERS *Photolitho-Offset* xi. 160 The Agfa-Gevaert Diffusing Diaphragm is also a most useful asset in eliminating undesirable moiré and avoiding the need for excessive retouching. **1967** V. STRAUSS *Printing Industry* iv. 194/2 Moiré can also be introduced in presswork by defective overprinting.

moissanite (moi·s-, mwa·sănəit). *Min.* [f. the name of H. *Moissan* (1852–1907), French chemist: see -ITE[1].] A green (sometimes black or bluish) silicon carbide, SiC, with metallic lustre, which is known only from the meteoric iron of Canyon Diablo, Arizona, and is made artificially as *CARBORUNDUM.

1905 G. F. KUNZ in *Amer. Jrnl. Sci.* XIX. 397 As this is the first instance in which this compound [*sc.* carborundum] has been proved to occur in nature, and therefore, as a mineral, is entitled to a distinct mineralogical name, it would seem that the name of Professor Moissan himself should be associated with it. I would, therefore, propose for it the name of Moissanite. **1968** I. KOSTOV *Mineral.* 105 Artificial moissanite is called carborundum.

moist, *a.* and *sb.* Add: **8.** *moist-lipped, -nosed, -skinned, -tinged* adjs.

1962 I. MURDOCH *Unofficial Rose* xxix. 284 She was, as he looked down at her, tense, moist-lipped. **1934** DYLAN THOMAS *Let.* 9 May (1966) 120, I would have introduced a..paragraph all about her nasty little moist-nosed muse. **1957** J. S. HUXLEY *Relig. without Revelation* (rev. ed.) ix. 216 The reptiles replaced the moist-skinned amphibians. **1943** D. GASCOYNE *Poems 1937–42* 55 Obscurely still beneath a moist-tinged blank Sky like the inside of a deaf mute's mouth.

moist, *v.* Add: **3.** *intr.* To rain slightly, to drizzle. *U.S. rare.*

1916 H. L. WILSON *Somewhere in Red Gap* iii. 117 It was moisting when we started, and pretty soon it clouded up. *Ibid.* 118 It wasn't moisting any more—it was raining for fair.

moistly, *adv.* Delete † *Obs.* and add later examples.

1905 H. G. WELLS *Kipps* II. iii. 197 The bull really came at them..opened a mouth below his moistly glistening nose, and booed. **1906** B. VON HUTTEN *What became of Pam* 78 March had moistly melted into April. **1927** H. V. MORTON *In Search of England* x. 180 Three of those prim, sallow, enthusiastic, middle-aged lovers of England ..were..regarding moistly the bare rooms in which Brewster and the 'Pilgrim Fathers' were imprisoned. **1939** L. M. MONTGOMERY *Anne of Ingleside* vii. 50 Walter hated to be kissed moistly on the forehead. **1957** R. A. HEINLEIN *Door into Summer* (1960) i. 14 He shook hands moistly, sat me down,..and attempted to take my bag.

moisture, *sb.* Add: **4.** *moisture-seal; moisture-bearing, -holding, -loving* (later examples), *-proof* (hence *-proofness*) adjs.; *moisture-proofing* vbl. sb.; **moisture content,** the proportional amount of moisture in any substance; **moisture cream,** a cosmetic cream which keeps the skin moist; a type of face-cream; cf. *MOISTURIZER; **moisture lotion,** a liquid preparation for moisturizing the skin; **moisture meter,** an instrument for indicating the moisture content of a substance (commonly by measuring its electrical resistivity).

1922 W. G. KENDREW *Climates of Continents* 290 The rainfall increases steadily towards the east and south. An irregularity is caused by the Appalachians,..within range of the moisture-bearing winds from both the Gulf and the Atlantic. **1923** H. M. BUNBURY *Destructive Distillation of Wood* iii. 20 The moisture content of the limbs or branches is also greater than that of the trunk. **1936** *Burlington Mag.* Nov. 229/2 It was necessary to bring the panels to the agreed moisture-content before these repairs were put in hand. **1952** L. M. THOMPSON *Soils & Soil Fertility* x. 159 Increasing the moisture content of soils increases the uptake of phosphorus. **1971** *Materials & Technol.* II. 601 The moisture content of coke may..be high because of its high porosity. **1957** *New Yorker* 2 Nov. 61/2 (Advt.), Tussy Moisture Cream and Lotion..won't let your skin dry out. **1961** *Which?* Mar. 58/1 Basically, like other types of face cream moisture creams are emulsions of oils, fats or waxes, with water. **1952** A. G. L. HELLYER *Sanders' Encycl. Gardening* (ed. 22) 407 Culture of Pears: Soil, well drained and well supplied with humus to improve moisture-holding capacity. **1959** *Times* 7 Dec. (Agric. Suppl.) p. viii/5 The moisture-holding properties of old clay wastings. **1957** Moisture lotion [see *moisture cream* above]. **1974** *Country Life* 28 Nov. 1694/3 Their own products include moisture lotion..eye shadow and lipsticks. **1911** E. M. CLOWES *On Wallaby* x. 272 A thick grove of moisture-loving palms. **1949** V. G. CHILDE *Prehist. Communities Brit. Isles* (ed. 3) viii. 135 The land molluscs of this period are..no longer the moisture-loving woodland species found in the neolithic camps. **1974** *Country Life* 28 Feb. 443/2 The moisture-loving hydrangeas. **1952** *Sci. Amer.* Sept. 61 (*caption*) Moisture meter..senses moisture in textile yarn by electrical conductivity and controls the speed of the drying drum by feedback. **1970** *Harrods Catal.* May 20/2 Moisture meter indicates condition of soil. ..47/–. **1904** *Electr. Rev.* (N.Y.) XLV. 422/1 These transformers are mounted in moistureproof iron cases and may be operated either dry or with oil. **1929** *U.S. Patent 1,737,187* 4/1 By the term 'moistureproof'..we mean the ability to resist the diffusion of water vapor to an extent at least as great as..that displayed by ordinary waxed papers..and functioning to resist the penetration of water vapor therethrough. **1960** *Farmer & Stockbreeder* 19 Jan. (Suppl.) 27/1 The birds being vacuum packed in moisture-proof bags. **1975** *Sci. Amer.* July 123/1 The cell that supports the mirror is also made of moistureproof plywood. **1929** *U.S. Pat. 1,737,187* 4/1 A sheet or film of regenerated cellulose combined with a moisture-proofing composition. **1971** J. F. HANLON *Handbk. Package Engin.* x. 8 For moisture protection a layer of asphalt between two layers of paper is generally used. It is the least expensive moistureproofing, but in cold weather it becomes stiff. **1929** *U.S. Pat. 1,737,187* 4/1 The product..is one which has all of the desired properties of moistureproofness, flexibility,..and lack of odor. **1962** *Punch* 22 Aug. 256/1 We have improved on the moisture-proofness of Cellophane. **1960** Moisture-seal [see *CRISPER b].

moisturize (moi·stiŭrəiz, -stʃər-). *v.* [f. MOISTURE *sb.* + -IZE.] To render moist, used esp. of a cosmetic cream applied to the skin. Hence **moi·sturized** *ppl. a.*; **moi·sturizing** *vbl. sb.* and *ppl. a.*

1945 MENCKEN *Amer. Lang.* Suppl. I. 402 Verbs made of common nouns:..to moistureize. **1958** *Inside the ACD* (Amer. College Dict.) X. II. 1/1 *Moisturize*: Television advertisers have been giving this word hard use. Creams and lotions now moisturize the skin and scalp. **1958** *Times* 22 Sept. 13/5 Intended for all types of skin, it [*sc.* a cream] is said to have balancing qualities which include moisturizing and mild stimulating action. **1958** *Vogue* July 5 This make-up..is moisturized to help guard your skin against the sun's chief danger, dryness. Wear it over..exquisite moisturised foundation. **1959** *News Chron.* 14 July 6/3 A very light type of fluid foundation..with a moisturising content. **1963** *Word Study* Dec. 6/2 The word *to moisturize*, currently fashionable in cosmetic and beauty-care advertising and attacked by some linguists as superfluous and barbaric. **1965** M. FRAYN *Tin Men* i. 5 Tropical plants.. perpetually watered by invisible built-in moisturising systems. **1966** *Harper's Bazaar* Sept. 73/2, I cover my face, lips too, with Veiled Radiance—it's essential that I use a moisturised base. **1971** *Homes & Gardens* Sept. 99/2 So much for the face, but the rest of the body will appreciate a little bit of moisturising as well. **1973** *Country Life* 26 Apr. 1194/4 The creamy moisturised lipsticks are available in pinks, browns, red and tawny tones. **1974** *She* Jan. 5 Skin Tone..moisturises and conditions your skin.

moisturizer (moi·stiŭrəizəɪ, -stʃər-). [f. *MOISTURIZE *v.* + -ER[1].] A preparation that renders or keeps the skin moist; a cosmetic cream.

1957 *Daily Mail* 17 Oct. 10/3 If the face then feels uncomfortably taut use a skin moisturiser before applying a foundation. **1966** J. S. COX *Illustr. Dict. Hairdressing* 99/2 Moisturizer permanent wave. **1967** *Times* 17 Jan. 13/1 A moisturiser under the foundation is essential if the skin is dry. **1972** *Guardian* 7 Nov. 11/3 The Vichy preparations include complete ranges of cleansers, toners, moisturisers, night creams.

moit[2] (moit). *dial.* and *Austral.* [var. MOTE *sb.*[1]] A particle of wood, stick, or some other substance caught in the wool of a sheep. Hence **moi·ting** *vbl. sb.* (see quot. 1862), **moi·ty** *a.*

1862 C. C. ROBINSON *Dial. Leeds* 359 *Moiting*, a process in the manufacture of cloth, by which the wool, subsequent to being scoured..and preparatory to its passing through the 'willey', is cleansed from 'moits' or shivs. **1878** *Yorkshireman* 17 Aug. 97/2 I've a splendid lot [of wool] in just now—..not moity, and free from burr. **1878** 'R. BOLDREWOOD' *Ups & Downs* viii. 83 The 'heavy and moity' parcels were not touched by the cautious operators at any price. **1903** *Eng. Dial. Dict.* IV. 144/2 T'sliver's full o' moits an' as rough as a bear's back. **1945** BAKER *Austral. Lang.* iii. 67 Many terms used by Australian wool-traders come from old English dialect, including..*moits*, short pieces of stick and scrub, principally found in neck wool. **1959** —— *Drum* 127 *Moity* (of wool), carrying vegetable matter other than burr. **1965** J. S. GUNN *Terminol. Shearing Industry* II. 4 *Moit(s)*, pieces of stick and rubbish matted in wool, especially the neck wool.

Mojave, var. *MOHAVE.

mojo[1] (mō̆u·dʒo). *local U.S.* [Prob. of Afr. orig.: cf. Gullah *moco* witchcraft, magic, Fula *moco'o* medicine man.] Magic, the art of casting spells; a charm or amulet used in such spells. Also *attrib.* and as *vb.*

1926 N. N. PUCKETT *Folk Beliefs Southern Negro* i. 19 The term *mojo* is often used by the Mississippi Negroes to mean 'charms, amulets, or tricks', as 'to work mojo' on a person or 'to carry a mojo'. **1930** R. BASS in A. Dundes *Mother Wit* (1973) 382/2 There are a few signs that are more or less common to all mojo-workers. *Ibid.* 384/2 [Of the deepest South] Their mojo is not fakery. It is not trickery. It is magic... Mojo is making its last stand. It has retreated to the swamp-lands. **1934** B. A. BOTKIN in W. T. Couch *Culture in South* xxvi. 585 Fragments of hoodoo and conjuration, whose spells,..mojos,..goofer bags are the special province of the Negro 'root doctor' or 'hoodoo man'. **1962** N. E. WHITTEN in A. Dundes *Mother Wit* (1973) 406/1 Local names for amulets are 'mojo', 'monjo', 'lucky hand'..and 'jomo'. **1966** *Crescendo* Aug. 3/2 With his weather mojo working overtime he got four hot sunny days. **1970** R. WELBURN in A. Chapman *New Black Voices* (1972) 356 It is overdue time To mojo the demons... Now it is time for mojo. **1971** *Black World* Apr. 81 A Mojo..a Mojo workin for you. **1973** C. HIMES *Black on Black* 18 *Slick* (in a whining voice): You got the best go and the mojo.

mojo[2] (mō̆u·dʒo). *U.S.* [Orig. unknown: see quot. 1955.] An addict's name for any narcotic drug, esp. morphine.

1935 A. J. POLLOCK *Underworld Speaks* 77/1 *Mojo*, any of the poisonous habit forming narcotics (dope). **1955** *Amer. Speech* XXX. 87 *Mojo* (probably from Sp. *mojar*, 'to celebrate by drinking')..a euphemism for morphine. **1963** R. I. MCDAVID *Mencken's Amer. Lang.* 725 An addict well supplied is *on the mojo* and is said to be *in high*. **1971** E. E. LANDY *Underground Dict.* 134 *Mojo*,..morphine.

moke[2]. Add: **2.** (Examples.)

1855 D. G. ROSSETTI *Let.* 25 Nov. (1965) I. 282 He has an irreconcilable grudge against a poor moke of a fellow called Archer Gurney. **1873** J. A. MAIR *Handbk. Proverbs* 459 *Moke*, an old person, disrespectfully spoken to. **1915** *Dialect Notes* IV. 199 Terms of disparagement..*moke* about the same meaning and usage as *mutt*, or *boob*.

3. (Earlier and later examples.)

1879 in L. A. Smith *Music of Waters* (1888) 356 For many a long time he tried a Derby to win, But I was the moke to carry him in. **1888** 'R. BOLDREWOOD' *Robbery under Arms* I. viii. 105, I am regular shook on this old moke. **1901** M. FRANKLIN *My Brilliant Career* xxvi. 220 My old moke flung a shoe and went dead lame. **1928** 'BRENT OF BIN BIN' *Up Country* xiii. 210 If I lend you my mokes, the bridles are mine if you win. **1943** 'W. HATFIELD' *I find Austral.* 53 He's an old quiet moke these days.

4. (Examples.)

1856 C. WHITE *Oh, Hush!* 9 Rose, don't you interfere, I'll show dis moke a sight. **1882** G. W. PECK *Peck's Sunshine* 53 They want to hear old fashioned negro melodies, and yet these mokes will tackle Italian opera. **1901** *Cosmopolitan* Sept. 637/2 Across the stage have paraded long processions of 'musical mokes', 'knock-abouts' and 'monologists'. **1945** MENCKEN *Amer. Lang.* Suppl. I. 635 *Moke* was thrown into competition with *coon* in 1899 by the success of 'Smokey *Mokes*', a popular song by Holzmann and Lind.

Moke[4] (mō̆uk). = *Mini-Moke* (see *MINI- b).

1963 *Daily Tel.* 8 Jan. 11/1 BMC believes the twin-engine Moke could be useful to farmers and for military and industrial use. **1967** *Guardian* 26 June 5/2 The Moke, a risky, insolent-looking little vehicle..has the minute quality of a 'Dinky' car. **1969** [see *FADE *sb.*[1] 1]. **1974** A. WILLIAMS *Gentleman Traitor* ix. 135 Keys to Thackeray Mansions and the Moke.

mok-e-mok, var. *MOKI-MOKI.

moki[1]. Substitute for def.: Either of two New Zealand marine fishes, *Latridopsis ciliaris*, which is blue-grey and white, or the red moki, *Chironemus spectabilis*, which is reddish-brown, with dark brown bars on its sides; also, formerly, the blue cod, *Parapercis colias*. (Further examples.)

1845 E. J. WAKEFIELD *Adventure in N.Z.* I. iv. 93 The *moki* is also a well-flavoured fish, weighing 10 lbs. or 12 lbs. **1851** E. WARD *Jrnl.* 14 Feb. (1951) 129 A Maori brought us a fish today which he called 'Moko'—it was a very fair fish. **1960** DOOGUE & MORELAND *N.Z. Sea Anglers' Guide* 235 Red Moki... Belongs to the same family [*sc.* the Chironemidæ] as tarakihi and porae, but the stouter body form and colour distinguish it immediately. **1968** *N.Z. Listener* 15 Mar. 6/1 I've left a moki and a feed of crayfish in the outside safe. **1971** *N.Z. News* 3 Feb. 3/2 A member of the Whangarei Underwater Club..shot a six-pound red moki.

moki[2]. Add: (Earlier and later examples.) Also **mogey, moggie.**

1835 J. A. WILSON *Jrnl.* 25 Aug. in *Missionary Life & Work N.Z.* (1889) ii. 25 The moki only carries one person at a time. You sit as on horseback. **1860** W. C. *Let.* 16 Apr. in J. H. Beattie *Pioneers explore Otago* (1947) vii. 45 He started in the dead of winter, on a moggie by himself... He crossed and re-crossed the lake several times. **1884** R. C. REID *Rambles on Golden Coast N.Z.* 53 It had been used by the diggers as the keel of their 'mogey'. **1963** *Evening Post* (Wellington, N.Z.) 9 Dec., He made the journey from Kingston to Queenstown on a mokihi.

moki, var. *MOKI-MOKI.

‖ **mokihana** (mōkihā·nă). Also **mokehana.** [Hawaiian.] A Hawaiian tree, *Pelea anisata*, of the family Rutaceæ.

1888 W. HILLEBRAND *Flora Hawaiian Islands* 64 *P[elea] anisata*... Nat[ive] name: 'Mokehana'.—All parts of the tree, but particularly the capsules, when bruised, emit a strong spicy odor of anise. **1915** W. A. BRYAN *Nat. Hist. Hawaii* xv. 221 The most highly scented of all are the seed pods of the mokihana used in making leis. **1954** *Ellery Queen's Mystery Mag.* Oct. 45/1 She..hung around her neck a *lei* of *mokihana* and *maile*.

‖ **moki-moki** (mǫ·kimǫki). *N.Z.* Also **moke-mok, moki, moki-mok, mokky.** [Maori.] = *MAKOMAKO[1]; MOKO-MOKO 2.

1928 *Daily Express* 6 June 3 What is the moki-moki? **1935** E. HODGKINSON in A. E. Currie *Cent. Treas. Otago Verse* (1949) 33 The forest rings with tuis' and mokis' chiming. **1940** N. MARSH *Surfeit of Lampreys* (1941) xiv. 218 English birdsong there was pierced by the colder and deeper notes of bell-birds and mok-e-moks. *a* **1948** L. G. D. ACLAND *Early Canterbury Runs* (1951) 361 Bell-bird.—Mako-mako, or Moki-mok.. The name is still sometimes used; but the bird is now generally called a 'Mokky'.

moksha (mǫ·kʃă). *Hinduism* and *Jainism.* Also 8 **moksh,** 9—**moksa.** [Skr. *moksha* liberation, emancipation, f. *muc* tŏ loose, release.] The final liberation of the soul when it is exempted from further transmigration; the bliss attained by this liberation. Also called *MUKTI.

1785 C. WILKINS tr. *Bhăgvăt-Gēētā* xvi. 115 The divine destiny is for *Mōksh*, or eternal absorption in the divine nature. **1828** H. H. WILSON in *Asiatick Res.* XVI. 104 An important consequence of this doctrine is the denial of *Moksha*, in its more generally received sense, that of absorption into the universal spirit. **1831** V. KENNEDY *Res. Anc. & Hindu Mythol.* vi. 185 The terms employed for final beatitude, that is identification with the supreme Being..are *kaivalyam, moksha,* or *jivanmukti.* **1840** H. H. WILSON *Two Lect. Relig. Pract. Hindus* ii. 64 All the philosophical schools propose for their object the ascertainment of those means by which the wanderings of the soul may be arrested,..its emancipation from bodily imprisonment and degradation be effected for ever. This is what is termed *Moksha*, or *Mukti.* **1875** M. WILLIAMS *Indian Wisdom* vii. 131 There are three 'gems' which together effect the soul's *Moksha*..right intuition..right knowledge..right conduct. **1915** *Encycl. Relig. & Ethics* VIII. 772/1 *Mokṣa* as the supreme aspiration runs through that best known portion of the *Mahābhārata* epic called the *Bhagavad-Gītā.* **1933** J. BAILLIE *And Life Everlasting* (1934) v. 118 In the concurrent tendency to regard *nirvana*—or *moksha*..as a state not of utter annihilation but of (unconscious) blissful union with the divine, we may surely find a foreshadowing..of a positive doctrine of eternal life. **1962** A. HUXLEY *Island* ix. 136 Murugan calls it dope... We, on the contrary, give the stuff good names—the *moksha*-medicine, the reality-revealer, the truth-and-beauty pill. **1971** *Illustr. Weekly India* 11 Apr. 9/2 They are the Tirthankaras, the Finders of the ford by which to cross the Ocean of Rebirth, or the Guides that show the way to *moksha.*

mokuk, var. *MOCOCK.

mol: see *MOLE *sb.*[7]

mola[2] (mōu·lă). [Native name.] A square of brightly coloured, appliquéd cloth worn as a blouse by Cuna Indian women of the San Blas Islands, Panama. Also *attrib.*

1941 *Nat. Geogr. Mag.* Feb. 217 With the skirt is worn a short-sleeved waist called a *mola.* The mola is of true Indian manufacture. **1964** I. SALEM tr. *M. & H. Larsen's Forests Panama* viii. 99 These *molas*..are perhaps the only really interesting things produced by the Cuna. Layers of different-coloured materials are cut into various shapes and superimposed one on another to produce a very colourful raised design. *Ibid.*, Some of these *molas* still depict the rather naïve, stylized animals portrayed on pre-Columbian pottery. **1966** J. M. KELLY *Cuna* i. 26 The 'Mola' tops had been introduced by the Spaniards who didn't like the women walking around with their breasts showing. **1972** *Islander* (Victoria, B.C.) 23 July 7/3 The women are known for their 'molas'. A mola is a square of five layers of material, and each piece is cut to show the colors of the different layers underneath. **1973** M. MACKINTOSH *King & Two Queens* v. 79 'These are original Cuna Indian molas,' said Rodger, 'and the most modern things in this upper hall.' **1974** *Daily Colonist* (Victoria, B.C.) 10 July 18/5 Molas are worn by women and girls of the Cuna tribe. The rectangular panels, approximately 16 by 24 inches, are worn in matched sets on the front and back of the blouse atop wrap-around print skirts.

molal (mōu·lăl), *a. Physical Chem.* [f. *MOLE *sb.*[7] + -AL.] **a.** = *MOLAR *a.*[3] a, *MOLECULAR *a.* 1 a.

1908 GOODWIN & MAILEY in *Physical Rev.* XXVI. 49 In the fifth column we have computed the values of the fluidity *F* divided by the corresponding molecular volume ϕ of the liquid; this we have denoted by *f* and called the molal fluidity. **1923** LEWIS & RANDALL *Thermodynamics* iii. 22 If w is the molal mass of a substance (also known as molal weight or molecular weight), a mol of the substance in question is defined as w grams. **1972** *Science* 2 June 1011/2 Carbon dioxide..has a molecular weight *M* of 44 and a partial molal volume of 34·8 ml/mole.

b. Of a solution: containing one mole, or a specified number of moles, of solute per kilogramme of solvent or (now *rare*) per litre of solution. Of a concentration: expressed in terms of these quantities. Cf. MOLAR *a.*[3] b.

1923 LEWIS & RANDALL *Thermodynamics* iv. 33 When we speak of a molal or tenth molal aqueous solution.., we shall refer, not to the concentration, but to the number of mols of solute in 1000 grams of water, which we may call the molality. **1924** J. C. W. FRAZER in H. S. Taylor *Treat. Physical Chem.* I. vii. 236 Concentrations expressed in terms of 1000 cc. of solution and using the above methods of expressing the amounts of substances are known as molal, formal or normal concentrations. **1930** W. T. HALL *Textbk. Quantitative Analysis* iii. 26 A solution is said to be molal in hydrogen ions if it contains 1·008 g of H^+ per liter. **1938** LUNDELL & HOFFMAN *Outl. Methods Chem. Analysis* xxxv. 127 One author will regard a solution containing one mole of solute per liter of solution as molal, whereas another calls such a solution molar. **1965** PHILLIPS & WILLIAMS *Inorg. Chem.* I. vii. 250 The activity coefficient is then around 10^{-14} for molal solutions of these ions. **1970** [see MOLALITY below].

Hence **mola·lity,** the molal concentration of a solution.

1923 [see sense b above]. **1931** [see *MOLARITY]. **1963** W. J. MOORE *Physical Chem.* (ed. 4) v. 117 One advantage of molality is that it is easy to prepare a solution of given molality by accurate weighing procedures. **1970** *Man. Symbols & Terminol. Physicochem. Quantities & Units* (I.U.P.A.C.) 12 A solution having a molality equal to 0·1 mol kg^{-1} is sometimes called a 0·1 molal solution. **1973** [see *MOLARITY].

Molale (molā·li). Also **Molele.** [Native name.] A Penutian Indian people of Oregon; a member of this people; also, their language. Also *attrib.*

1846 H. HALE in *U.S. Exploring Expedition 1838–42: Ethnogr. & Philol.* 561 The Waiilatpu family [of languages]... Waiilatpu... Moléle. **1848** *Trans. Amer. Ethnol. Soc.* II. i. 15 These Indians [*sc.* the Waiilatpu] include two tribes, the Cayuse..: and the Molele, west of the Cayuse..in the mountainous territory about Mounts Hood and Vancouver..; probably extinct. *Ibid.* 77 Waiilatpu,..*Language*..Molele. **1891** *7th Ann. Rep. U.S. Bureau Amer. Ethnol. 1885–86* 127 Hale established this family and placed under it the Cailloux or Cayuse or Willetpoos, and the Molele... The Molále were a mountain tribe and occupied a belt of mountain country south of the Columbia River. *Ibid.* 128 There are 31 Molále now on the Grande Ronde Reservation, Oregon. **1965** *Canad. Jrnl. Ling.* Spring 124 Inland, no..Molale, or Cayuse were found. **1966** C. F. & F. M. VOEGELIN *Map N. Amer. Indian Lang.* (*caption*) Molale language isolate. **1972** *Language* XLVIII. 380 A Molale myth.

molar, *a.*[2] Add: **b.** *Psychol.* (See quot. 1932.)

1925 C. D. BROAD *Mind & its Place* xiv. 616, I will lump together all such changes under the name of 'molar behaviour', as contrasted with 'molecular behaviour'. **1932** E. C. TOLMAN *Purposive Behavior* I. i. 7 On the one hand, he [*sc.* J. B. Watson] has defined behavior in terms of its strict physical and physiological details, i.e., in terms of receptor-process, conductor-process, and effector-process per se. We shall designate this as the molecular definition of behavior. And on the other hand, he has come to recognize..that behavior..is more than and different from the sum of its physiological parts. Behavior..has descriptive and defining properties of its own. And we shall designate this latter as the molar definition of behavior. **1946** C. MORRIS *Signs, Lang. & Behavior* ii. 55 Behavioristics naturally attempts to supplement its description of behavior in molar or macroscopic terms. **1971** *Jrnl. Gen. Psychol.* LXXXIV. 157 Attention has been concentrated on those papers which do not support the notion that single cell behavior is reflected in molar behavior.

molar (mōu·lăɹ), *a.*[3] *Physical Chem.* [f. *MOL(E *sb.*[7] + -AR[1].] **a.** Of or pertaining to one mole of a substance; = *MOLAL *a.* a, *MOLECULAR *a.* 1 a.

1902 A. FINDLAY tr. *Ostwald's Princ. Inorg. Chem.* vi. 89 The ratio of the weight of a given gas to that of an equal volume of the normal gas under the same conditions, is called its molecular weight or its molar weight. Since the former name has been derived from certain hypothetical notions regarding the constitution of the gases, notions which are not essential to the actual facts, we shall give preference to the name molar weight although, at present, the other is still the one most used. **1906** [see *gramme-molecular* adj. s.v. *GRAMME b]. **1946** J. R. PARTINGTON *Gen. & Inorg. Chem.* i. 7 This is called the molar volume V_m, and Avogadro's hypothesis shows that it is the same for all substances. **1962** P. J. & B. DURRANT *Introd. Adv. Inorg. Chem.* xi. 303 If both sides of the equation are multiplied by the molecular weight *M* and divided by the density ρ, $(k-1)M/(k+2)\rho = \frac{4}{3}\pi N\alpha = P_M$ where *N* is Avogadro's number and P_M is known as the molar polarisation. *Ibid.* 307 A quantity *R* known as the molar refraction. **1967** *Oceanogr. & Marine Biol.* V. 154 Some normal calcite and a small amount of dolomite with a molar ratio of $CaCO_3$:$MgCO_3$ of 1:1:1 were also present.

b. Of a solution: containing one mole, or a specified number of moles, of solute per litre of solution. Of a concentration: expressed in terms of these quantities. Cf. *MOLAL *a.* b.

1927 C. J. ENGELDER *Textbk. Elem. Qualitative Analysis* I. 4 Thus 34·468 grams of HCl or 58·46 grams of NaCl, dissolved and diluted to one liter, are molar solutions of these compounds. **1946** *Nature* 26 Oct. 585/1 The molar concentration required to produce a given effect is approximately one third that of the preceding member [of a homologous series]. **1970** *Man. Symbols & Terminol. Physicochem. Quantities & Units* (I.U.P.A.C.) 12 A solution with a concentration of 0·1 mol dm^{-3} is often called a 0·1 molar solution. **1971** G. D. CHRISTIAN *Analytical Chem.* i. 9 A one-molar solution of silver nitrate and a one-molar solution of sodium chloride will react on an equal-volume basis.

Hence **mola·rity,** the molar concentration of a solution.

1931 J. C. WARE *Analytical Chem.* I. i. 3 Where the solubility is very small, the molarity and the molality of the solution will be approximately the same. **1951** M. A. PAUL *Princ. Chem. Thermodynamics* vii. 388 The molarity of a given solution evidently varies in general with temperature. **1970** *Man. Symbols & Terminol. Physiochem. Quantities & Units* (I.U.P.A.C.) 12 Concentration is sometimes called 'molarity' but this name is both unnecessary and liable to cause confusion with molality and is therefore not recommended. **1973** BLOCK & HOLLIDAY *Mod. Physical Chem.* ix. 203 In general, molarities cannot easily be related either to mole fraction or to molality, unless the changes in volume on dissolution are either negligible or can be allowed for.

molarization (mōulărəizēi·ʃən). *Zool.* [f. MOLAR *a.*[1] and *sb.* + -IZATION.] The assumption, during the course of evolution, of the characteristics of a molar tooth by a non-molar tooth (usu. a premolar).

1937 *Proc. Zool. Soc.* B. CVII. 104 The molarization of the premolars is a case of convergent evolution. **1953** J. S. HUXLEY *Evolution in Action* ii. 56 The so-called molarization of the pre-molars.—The gradual conversion of the front grinders, which have milk-teeth predecessors, so as to resemble the true molars, which develop later and have no 'milk' fore-runners. **1972** *Nature* 24 Nov. 236/1 A morphological complex characterizes the earliest hominids. This complex..includes..lowering of the molar cusps, molarization of the premolars, [etc.].

So **mo·larized** *ppl. a.*, showing the consequences of molarization.

1971 A. A. DAHLBERG *Dental Morphol. & Evolution* viii. 99 The more distant from the canine, the more molarized or cuspidate the tooth. **1973** *Nature* 14 Sept. 106/1 In other cretaceous eutherians P^4 is always three-rooted and partly molarized.

molasses. Add: **1. b.** *fig.*

1925 T. DREISER *American Tragedy* (1926) I. I. xvii. 127 'You're the cutest thing here,' whispered Clyde, hugging her fondly. 'Gee, but you can pour on the molasses, kid, when you want to,' she called out loud. **1972** *N.Y. Times Book Review* 26 Nov. 1/1 The mournful molasses of his [*sc.* Eisenhower's] prose.

3. *molasses barrel, cake, candy, cask, cookie, gingerbread, hogshead, jug, scone, taffy, tierce.*

1846 D. CORCORAN *Pickings* 29 Isn't that cotton bale dancing a quadrille with the molasses barrel? **1836** W. G. SIMMS *Mellichampe* II. xxiv. 192 The negro broke his molasses-cake evenly between himself and the soldier. **1863** B. TAYLOR *H. Thurston* i. 19 The distribution of wedges of molasses-cake. **1869** *Harper's Mag.* Oct. 753/1 With that penny he bought a 'bolivar'—as the huge molasses-cake was called in those days. **1809** 'D. KNICKERBOCKER' *Hist. N.Y.* II. VII. iii. 195 Each..he patted on the head..and gave him a penny to buy molasses candy. **1850** N. KINGSLEY *Diary* (1914) 103 [We] are privately enjoying ourselves over a dish of molasses candy. **1945** *This Week Mag.* 15 Dec. 2/2 Cookies, molasses candy, popcorn balls and cider were brought out. **1834** H. J. NOTT *Novellettes* I. 79 He was in a molasses cask. **1851** A. O. HALL *Manhattaner* 5 It was a modest commercial plain..with..molasses casks, and corn sacks. **1887** I. ALDEN *Little Fishers* xxi. 373 Dough-nuts, molasses cookies, and soft gingerbread. **1974** 'D. SHANNON' *Crime File* (1975) iv. 66 She asked for my recipe for molasses cookies. **1832** L. M. CHILD *Amer. Frugal Housewife* 70 A very good way to make molasses gingerbread. **1864** T. L. NICHOLS *40 Yrs. Amer. Life* I. 36 The spectators..ate molasses-gingerbread. **1849** THOREAU *Week Concord River* 198 An 'untameable fly' buzzed at my elbow with the same non-chalance as on a molasses hogshead. **1863** 'G. HAMILTON' *Gala-Days* 76 He..came back with a molasses-hogshead. **1839** *Southern Lit. Messenger* V. 65/2 Behind the bar were..a molasses jug, a bottle of vinegar, and..decanters. **1906** F. LYNDE *Quickening* 111 She went ..to fill the molasses jug. **1927** M. DE LA ROCHE *Jalna* xxii. 275, I am bringing you a molasses scone to stay you, Mamma. **1928** S. V. BENÉT *John Brown's Body* 113 An awful molasses-taffy voice Behind them yelled 'Halt!' **1946** PARTRIDGE & BETTMANN *As We Were* 13 Molasses taffy was cooked in a kettle on top of the kitchen stove and when ready for pulling was served out in gobs. **1910** *Chambers's Jrnl.* Feb. 88/2 A few rusty molasses-tanks. **1851** H. MELVILLE *Moby Dick* I. xxii. 168 Have an eye to the molasses tierce, Mr. Stubb.

Hence **mola·ssed** *a.* = MOLASSIED *a.*

1941 *Nature* 3 May 532/2 Nehring & Schramm also tested the effect..of molassed bran plus urea [on sheep]. **1960** *Farmer & Stockbreeder* 16 Feb. 128/3 Dried molassed beet pulp can replace an equal weight of oats in rations for store cattle and calves.

moldavite (mǫ·ldăvəit). [ad. G. *moldawit*, f. *Moldau*, G. name of the Vltava River in western Czechoslovakia: see -ITE[1].] A tektite from the tektite field of Czechoslovakia; formerly, the substance (considered a local variety of obsidian) of which such tektites consist.

1896 A. H. CHESTER *Dict. Names Minerals* 179 *Moldawite*, an obs. syn. of obsidian. **1909** [see *BILLITONITE]. **1915** *Bull. Geol. Soc. Amer.* XXVI. 281 The moldavites occur here and there, but never in any manner indicative of their origin. **1935** *Times* 28 Jan. 15/4 'Tektites' from Bohemia and Moravia have for more than 150 years been cut as gem stones under the names 'obsidian', 'water chrysolite' and 'moldavite'. **1964** *New Scientist* 16 Jan. 160/2 The moldavites from Bohemia and Moravia, about 14·8 million years old (Miocene). **1972** *Science* 11 Aug. 519/2 In 1970 and 1971, two noteworthy finds of double moldavites were made in the fields of southern Bohemia.

Moldo-Wallachian (mǫ:ldo,wǫlēi·kiăn), *a.* Also **Moldavo-Wallachian.** [f. MOLD(AVIAN *a.* and *sb.* + -O + WALACHIAN, WALLACHIAN *a.*] Of or pertaining to both Moldavia and Wallachia, principalities of Rumania united in 1859. Also as *sb.*

1848 [see *ANARCHIAL *a.*]. **1869** *Bradshaw's Railway Manual* XXI. 358 A promise that the whole of the Moldo-Wallachian network should be under one supervision. **1929** W. G. EAST *Union Moldavia & Wallachia* iii. 54 The alleged desire of the Moldo-Wallachians to form one national state. *Ibid.* 58 Napoleon was secretly planning a war with Austria during his advocacy of Moldo-Wallachian union. **1971** P. CLINCA tr. *Giurescu's Making of*

Romanian Unitary State 117 The twin Moldavo-Wallachian town of Focsani lying on the former border.

mole, *sb.*² Add: **6.** (Earlier examples.)
1881 H. W. NESFIELD *Chequered Career* vii. 75 We.. met men in rough flannels and dirty soil-stained moles. **1888** G. O. PRESHAW *Banking under Difficulties* xxvi. 163 These moles are 12s. a pair.

6*. A shade of grey. Also as *adj.*
1908 *Westm. Gaz.* 29 Aug. 13/2 Mole has always been recognised..as a shade universally harmonious. *Ibid.* 26 Sept. 13/2 How charming with a mole suit is a mole hat, massed with roses! **1914** [see *BEAVER¹ 2 c]. **1923** [see *BRICK *sb.*¹ 4 c]. **1971** *Vogue* 15 Sept. 49 Rich autumn colours like wine, mole and teak.

8. mole ditch = **mole drain*; so *mole-ditching* vbl. sb.; **mole drain,** a drain made by a mole-plough; **mole-drainer** = MOLE-PLOUGH.
1868 *Rep. Comm. Agric. 1867* (U.S. Dept. Agric.) 232 *Under draining* wet, heavy places, with 'mole ditches', or blind drains. **1868** *Rep. Iowa Agric. Soc. 1867* 154 Under-draining by mole-ditching has been tried. **1939** WEBSTER Add., Mole drain. **1950** *N.Z. Jrnl. Agric.* June 534/1 A number of standard mole drains was drawn with the 3 in. plug at depths of 18 to 20 in. **1957** E. BLUNDEN *Poems of Many Years* 280 Waters drawn together From gully and moledrain by contour, chance and weather. **1859** *Trans. Ill. Agric. Soc.* III. 361 Dragging the mole drainer all over our lands.

b. mole snake, a non-venomous colubrid snake, *Pseudaspis cana*, native to Southern and E. Africa, and feeding on rats and mice.
1893 J. NOBLE *Illustr. Official Handbk. Cape & S. Afr.* 84 The Colubrinæ include the large and abundant 'black' or 'mole' snake. **1911** *East London* (Cape Province) *Dispatch* 1 Sept. 7 When alarmed the mole snake is very pugnacious. **1931** *Discovery* Mar. 74/2 The South African mole snake is a non-poisonous species. It constricts its prey and swallows it whole. **1951** R. CAMPBELL *Light on Dark Horse* ii. 36 A mole-snake has not only an apparent immunity [to bites from other snakes] but also the power to strangle other snakes. **1966** E. PALMER *Plains of Camdeboo* xiii. 220 Sometimes we see a long, graceful, chinless snake in the veld, with a dark muscular body shining as if carefully polished. This is the mole snake and is harmless to man, killing its prey by constriction. **1970** [see *BOOMSLANG].

mole (mōul), *sb.*⁷ *Physical Chem.* Also **mol** (formerly as an alternative spelling, now usu. as an abbrev.). [a. G. *mol* (W. Ostwald *Grundlinien d. anorg. Chem.* (1900) viii. 163), f. *mol-ekül* MOLECULE.] That amount of any particular substance having a mass in grammes numerically the same as its molecular or atomic weight; now defined equivalently in the International System of Units as the quantity of specified elementary entities (molecules, ions, electrons, or the like) that in number equals the number of atoms in 0·012 kilogramme of carbon 12.
1902 A. FINDLAY tr. *Ostwald's Princ. Inorg. Chem.* viii. 156 When one gram-molecule or one mole (the molar or molecular weight of a substance expressed in grams) of any substance is dissolved in a litre or 1000 gm. of water, the solution produced freezes at −1·850°. **1923** LEWIS & RANDALL *Thermodynamics* iii. 22 The mol is not defined unless the chemical formula is established by universal usage or is definitely stated. **1954** *Physiol. Rev.* XXXIV. 342 Estimations of the molar concentration (mols per kilogram of water or osmols if the salts are known..). **1959** N. FEATHER *Introd. Physics Mass, Length & Time* xv. 282 A mass equal to 'the molecular weight in grammes', which we define as 1 mole of a substance, contains the same number of molecules (Avogadro's constant), whatever the substance. **1963** W. J. MOORE *Physical Chem.* (ed. 4) ix. 326 One mole of electrons would be one faraday of electrical charge. **1970** [see *MOLALITY]. **1971** G. D. CHRISTIAN *Analytical Chem.* i. 8 Each mole of silver ion will react with one mole of chloride ion. **1972** *Physics Bull.* Jan. 40/1 The 14th General conference of Weights and Measures (CGPM) met in Paris on 4–7 October 1971... Amongst the main decisions taken by the conference were the final adoption of the 'mole' (mol) as an SI base unit. **1973** BLOCK & HOLLIDAY *Mod. Physical Chem.* xi. 256 In the chemical reaction occurring in the Daniell cell..two moles of electrons are required to convert one mole of copper (II) to one mole of zinc (II).

2. *Comb.* **mole fraction,** the ratio of the number of moles of a component in a solution to the total number of moles of all components present.
1923 LEWIS & RANDALL *Thermodynamics* xxii. 261 The mol fraction of bromine in a solution containing 160 grams bromine and 154 grams carbon tetrachloride is ½ if we are considering the formula Br_2. **1973** A. W. ADAMSON *Textbk. Physical Chem.* ix. 345 The partial pressure of a component becomes proportional to its mole fraction in the limit of zero concentration.

‖ **mole** (mōu·li), *sb.*⁸ [Mexican Sp., ad. Nahuatl *mulli, molli* sauce, stew.] A highly spiced sauce made chiefly from chilli and chocolate and served with various meats.
1932 H. W. BENTLEY *Dict. Sp. Terms in Eng.* 169 *Mole* .., a sauce used in Mexican cookery in connection with the serving of meats. **1948** *Sat. Even. Post* 2 Oct. 52/3 Señora Gonzalez does her stuff on such fabulous and sustaining dishes as chicken mole—boiled chicken bathed in a sauce of exotic Mexican spices, cinnamon, chili, mashed-up peanuts and even a dash of chocolate [etc.]. **1957** 'B. BUCKINGHAM' *Boiled Alive* xviii. 121 Turkey swimming in *mole*, a hot sauce made of chilli and chocolate, stuffed sweet peppers and mounds of pink-brown beans. **1966** *Punch* 9 Mar. 364/2 We were..sated with rich turkey *mole*.

mole, *v.*² Add: **2.** *to mole out*: also, to elicit, bring to light.
1924 W. M. RAINE *Troubled Waters* vii. 70 Tait would mole out quite enough evidence against him without any additional data supplied by indiscretion. **1932** L. C. DOUGLAS *Forgive us our Trespasses* (1937) xiii. 251 Maybe I'll ask you to mole out further data.

b. *intr.* To behave in the manner of a mole.
1856 W. G. SIMMS *Eutaw* xii. 129 How he snaked, and moled, and cooned,..we need not undertake to narrate.

molecular, *a.* Add: **1. a.** *spec.* applied to numerous physical quantities that involve the molecular weight of the substance concerned in their calculation (for most of which *molar* is a more appropriate designation; see *MOLAR *a.*³ a).
1867 C. L. BLOXAM *Chem.* 515 One equivalent of each of these hydrocarbons in the state of vapour occupies four volumes. *[Indexed, p. 660, as]* Molecular volumes of olefines. **1880** *Jrnl. Chem. Soc.* XXXVIII. 294 For every substance, therefore, (A−1)/*d* is a constant... If this constant be multiplied by the molecular weight P of any body, then P.(A−1)/*d*, referred to chemically comparable quantities, is the molecular refractive index, called in the rest of this paper the molecular refraction of the body. **1886** *Ibid.* L. 294 The author [*sc.* W. Ostwald] in continuing his researches on 'Electrical Conductivity'..has examined about 130 different inorganic and organic acids in different states of dilution (gram-molecules in *n*-litres). He..expresses his results in terms of molecular conductivity. **1921** HOOD & CARPENTER *Text-bk. Pract. Chem.* vi. x. 489 The molecular conductivity is that of a solution containing 1 gram-molecule of the substance, as above [*sc.* when placed between electrodes of indefinite size and 1 cm. apart]. **1938** H. A. PERKINS *Course of Physics* xlvii. 624 The number of gram molecules per liter, or moles per liter, is called molecular concentration. **1959** N. FEATHER *Introd. Physics Mass, Length & Time* xv. 283 Equation (126) is now the equation of state for a mass *m* of an ideal gas of molecular weight, or, strictly, of molar mass, *M*. **1966** GUCKER & SEIFERT *Physical Chem.* (1967) xiii. 346 One molecular weight of the salt contains *N* ions of *each* element in the molecular volume *V*, equal to the molecular weight divided by the density.

b. Applied to the name of a science to denote a branch of it that deals with phenomena at the molecular level.
1950, etc. [see *MOLECULAR BIOLOGY]. **1960** *N.Y. Times* 3 Jan. 1F/2 The chief executive officer..disclosed that Westinghouse was actively engaged in 'molecular electronics'. **1961** R. D. BAKER *Essent. Path.* i. 6 With the electron microscope we are entering an era of molecular pathology. **1963** *Adv. Computers* IV. 141 'Integrated' circuits fabricated using 'molecular electronics' techniques. **1963** *Listener* 17 Jan. 121/2 It seemed to me that soon what Russian biology will mean will not be Lysenko, but some first-class molecular genetics. **1966** *McGraw-Hill Yearbk. Sci. & Technol.* 43/1 This view of the gene has changed considerably in molecular genetics, since the gene is now recognized as the information necessary to assemble a protein molecule. **1970** *Sci. News Yearbk.* 225 Molecular astronomy is a science only a few years old. Its purpose is to determine what chemical molecules can be found in interstellar space and, if possible, how they got there and what their being there means for theories of galactic and stellar evolution and of cosmology. **1973** *Sci. Amer.* Apr. 52/3 That was more or less the picture of the interstellar medium in 1968, the year marking the birth of molecular astronomy as we now know it. **1974** *Nature* 23 Aug. 685/1 Now it is the turn of immunochemistry, or as some would have it, molecular immunology.

† **2.** *Biol.* Of tissue: consisting, or assumed to consist, of molecules (sense *3); finely granular. *Obs.* (but the use survives in *molecular layer* (see *5)).
1826, 1851 [see *MOLECULE 3]. **1856** *Quain's Elem. Anat.* (ed. 6) III. 26 The intermediate portion, *f*, has a longitudinally-striped appearance, and is formed by the fine fibres of Müller.., which intervene between the two parts of the granular layer, together with a homogeneous molecular uniting material.

3. *Philos.* Designating a proposition, sentence, etc., consisting of simpler propositions, sentences, etc. connected by a conjunction. Also *ellipt.* as *sb.*
1892 *Mind* I. 237 The molecular proposition—which cannot be expressed as a synthesis of more elementary propositions—involves a single (absolute or relative) predication and a number of interconnected individual subjects. *Ibid.* 239 The synthesis of moleculars having the same subject is represented by a synthesis of the predications. **1914** B. RUSSELL *Our Knowl. External World* ii. 54 'Molecular' propositions are such as contain conjunctions—*if, or, and, unless*, etc.—and such words are the marks of a molecular proposition. **1933** [see *ATOMIC *a.* 2α]. **1937** A. SMEATON tr. *Carnap's Logical Syntax of Lang.* III. § 28. 88 $\mathfrak{S}_1$ is called a *molecular sentence* when $\mathfrak{S}_1$ is either an atomic sentence itself, or is formed from one or more such by means of symbols of negation and junction (and brackets). **1965** B. MATES *Elem. Logic* iii. 44 A formula that is not an atomic formula is called *general* if it begins with a universal or existential quantifier; otherwise it is called *molecular*.

4. *Psychol.* Concerned with or pertaining to an elementary unit of behaviour such as a physiological response. Cf. *MOLAR *a.*² b.
1925, 1932 [see *MOLAR *a.*² b]. **1970** F. A. LOGAN in W. S. Sahakian *Psychol. of Learning* xvi. 307 The molar response 'bar depression' includes a number of responses distinguishable at a more molecular level, such as depression with the right paw, left paw, etc. **1973** *Jrnl. Genetic Psychol.* CXXIII. 99 The continuous-recording technique did..yield a more molecular analysis in that incidence of behaviors could be subdivided into frequency and duration.

5. Special collocations: *molecular fossil*, a molecular species found in ancient rock that is regarded as evidence of the early development of life; *molecular layer* Anat., (*a*) either of the two plexiform layers of the retina; (*b*) the outermost layer of the cortex of the cerebellum and cerebrum, containing a mass of nerve fibres with many synapses but relatively few cells; *molecular orbital*, an orbital in a molecule; *molecular sieve*, a substance containing in its crystal structure pores and channels of molecular dimensions that permit the entry of certain small molecules but are impervious to others; *esp.* a zeolite used as a selective adsorbent.
1965 M. CALVIN in *Proc. R. Soc.* A. CCLXXXVIII. 443 We are going to spend much of our time tracing organic evolution back in so far as we can trace it back in terms of 'molecular fossils' from the earliest well recognized fossils of morphological form. **1969** *Sci. Jrnl.* Apr. 36 The exciting studies of Calvin, who has attempted to prove the existence of what he calls 'molecular fossils', have not, however, firmly established the biogenic nature of these substances. **1971** *Nature* 30 July 325/2 The search for geological evidence about the origin and evolution of life on Earth has led to detailed searches for morphological and molecular fossils in Early Precambrian sedimentary rocks. [**1856** Molecular layer: cf. sense 2 above]. **1867** *Quain's Elem. Anat.* (ed. 7) III. 726 The retina..exhibits a series of dissimilar strata, together with structures not confined to one stratum. (1st) Externally is the columnar layer; (2nd), in the middle is the granular layer, comprising the external nuclear, the internuclear, the internal nuclear, and the molecular layers; and (3rd) internally is the nervous layer. **1874** A. E. J. BARKER tr. *Frey's Histol. & Histochem. of Man* 593 Externally—that is, directed towards the surface of the cerebellum—these large ganglion cells send off several (generally two) characteristic protoplasm processes through the so-called 'molecular layer of Hess'. **1955** P. D. TREVOR-ROPER *Ophthalm.* i. 19 The outer molecular layer is a reticular layer in which the end-knobs of the axons of the rod and cone cells arborise with the dendrites of the bipolar cells. *Ibid.* 20 The inner molecular layer consists of the arborisations of the axes of the bipolar cells with the dendrites of the ganglion cells. **1968** PASSMORE & ROBSON *Compan. Med. Stud.* I. xxiv. 46/1 In the older parts of the [cerebral] cortex, such as the rhinencephalon, only three layers of cells may be distinguished: the superficial molecular layer of fibres, the intermediate granular layer and a deep layer of pyramidal cells. **1932** R. S. MULLIKEN in *Physical Rev.* XLI. 50 The method followed here will be to describe unshared electrons always in terms of atomic orbitals but to use molecular orbitals for shared electrons. **1965** PHILLIPS & WILLIAMS *Inorg. Chem.* I. iii. 67 The problem will be introduced by a summary of the two important wave-mechanical approximation methods, the L.C.A.O. (linear combination of atomic orbitals) molecular-orbital method and the valence-bond method. **1926** *Colloid Symp. Monogr.* IV. 11 Collander's work on the sieve structure of semipermeable membranes of copper ferrocyanide has shown that the interstices between the micelles or aggregates are about 4 Ångstrom units in diameter. I would suggest a better molecular sieve, namely such crystals as dehydrated zeolites, etc. **1949** *Discussions Faraday Soc.* VII. 135 By cation interchange and by burning out interstitial ammonium ions a diversity of modified molecular-sieve sorbents can be produced. *Ibid.*, Some natural crystalline zeolites fall into three classes of molecular-sieve sorbent each capable of separating mixtures by selective occlusion. **1965** PHILLIPS & WILLIAMS *Inorg. Chem.* I. xiv. 544 The molecular-sieve zeolites, sodium and calcium aluminosilicates, are used to fractionate noble gases and low molecular weight molecules generally. **1966** *McGraw-Hill Encycl. Sci. & Technol.* VIII. 547/1 Molecular sieves are capable of drying gases and liquids to extremely low residual water concentrations.

molecular biology. [f. MOLECULAR *a.* + BIOLOGY.] Biology at the molecular level, esp. that branch of biology which is concerned with the formation, organization, and activity of macromolecules essential to life (i.e. nucleic acids, proteins, etc.).
1950 *Harvey Lectures* XLVI. 3 The name 'molecular biology' seems to be passing now into fairly common use. .. It implies..an approach from the viewpoint of the so-called basic sciences with the leading idea of searching below the large-scale manifestations of classical biology for the corresponding molecular plan. It is concerned particularly with the forms of biological molecules, and with the evolution, exploitation and ramification of those forms in the ascent to higher and higher levels of organization. **1963** *Listener* 17 Jan. 121/2 The newest and most refined field of genetics, which deals with definite chemical substances and is known as molecular biology. **1964** G. H. HAGGIS et al. *Introd. Molecular Biol.* p. x, We may say that molecular biology is primarily concerned with the structure of proteins, nucleic acids and other large biological molecules, and with the detailed structure of myofilaments, chromosomes, ribosomes, membranes and other cell components. But the study of structure cannot be divorced from the study of function. **1970** *Nature* 4 July 13/1 The synthesis of genes *de novo* has been an aim of molecular biology since its very inception. **1974** *Daily Tel.* 3 Sept. 6 Molecular biology and genetic engineering have reached the stage where results of research could plunge the world into far deeper problems than those raised by the atom bomb.

molecularity. Add: **2.** *Chem.* The number of reacting molecules involved in a (real or postulated) single step of a chemical reaction.

1939 FOWLER & GUGGENHEIM *Statist. Thermodynamics* xii. 500 In general there is no simple connection between the molecularity of the mechanism..and the order of the reaction. **1950** K. J. LAIDLER *Chem. Kinetics* iii. 56 Whereas the order of a reaction is deduced directly from the experimental results, the molecularity can be determined only on the basis of additional arguments about which there is sometimes some uncertainty. **1970** PRETTRE & CLAUDEL *Elem. Chem. Kinetics* v. 64 If we accept that the reaction $I_2 + H_2 \rightarrow 2HI$ is a simple one, this means that it involves a molecule of iodine and a molecule of hydrogen and that consequently its molecularity is two.

molecularly, *adv.* (Further examples.) Also, on a molecular scale.

1927 L. B. LOEB *Kinetic Theory Gases* vii. 273 The surfaces are not completely molecularly rough. **1969** *Physics Bull.* June 227/1 Muscovite mica..gives molecularly smooth surfaces on cleavage.

molecule. Add: **1. c.** (Earlier example.)

1867 C. L. BLOXAM *Chem.* 515 One equivalent of each of these hydrocarbons in the state of vapour occupies four volumes. [*Note*] Or one molecule occupies two volumes (H = 1 vol.).

† **3.** *Biol.* A minute but functional particle of animal tissue that is invisible or barely visible under the light microscope. *Obs.*

1826 KIRBY & SPENCE *Introd. Entomol.* IV. xxxvii. 3 Comparative anatomists have considered the nervous system of animals as formed upon three primary types, which may be called the molecular, the ganglionic, and cerebro-spinal. The first is where invisible nervous molecules are dispersed in a gelatinous body, the existence of which has only been ascertained by the nervous irritability of such bodies, [etc.]. **1841** T. R. JONES *Gen. Outl. Animal Kingdom* 6 In animals belonging to this division, no nervous filaments or masses have been discovered... The contractile molecules of their bodies are not yet aggregated into muscular fibre. **1851** W. WILKINSON *Outl. Physiol.* 9 Molecular and granular matter consists of particles that vary in size from immeasureable minuteness to 1·10,000th of an inch in diameter; and these particles are called molecules or granules, according to the appearance they present when examined with a magnifying power of 300 diameters. *Ibid.*, Molecules are merely indistinct granules; but under a higher magnifying power molecules become granules, and new molecules appear.

moler[2] (mōᵘ·ləɹ). Also **Moler.** [a. Da. *moler*, f. northern Da. dial. *mo* loose chalky soil (= Norw., Sw. *mo* sandy heath) + *ler* loam, clay (= Norw., Sw. *ler* clay).] (See quot. 1923.) (A proprietary name.)

1910 *Chem. Abstr.* IV. 2363 'Moler' is an argillaceous diatomaceous earth found in a limited region in the fiords of Denmark. **1923** A. B. SEARLE *Sands & Crushed Rocks* I. iii. 127 Moler is a sandy material somewhat resembling kieselguhr or diatomaceous earth.., but it is less refractory and contains a considerable proportion of clay and volcanic ash, for which reason it is self-binding and can be made into bricks without any other bond. **1932** A. G. GEESON *Gen. Building Repairs* (ed. 2) I. i. 48 Plaster, terra cotta, moler and breeze slabs have the advantage that they can be sawn to size. **1936** *Times* 9 Nov. 20/1 (Advt.), An extensive deposit of Diatomite of a high quality, known as 'Moler', which is suitable for many of the above purposes, exists on the Island of Für in Denmark. **1948** *Archit. Rev.* CIV. 57 The remaining blocks will be finished in a 4½ in. external concrete-brick cladding with an internal 4 in. skin of molar [*sic*] blocks with a 2 in. cavity. **1963** *Trade Marks Jrnl.* 6 June 766/1 Moler... Insulators and insulating materials. Aktieselskabet Skarrehage Molervaerk.., Nykbøing Mors, Denmark; manufacturers; and Refractulation Limited,.. London,.. merchants.

Moler, var. *MALER *sb.* and *a.*

moleskin. Add: **4.** *moleskin trousers* (earlier example); **moleskin squatter** *Austral.* and *N.Z.* (see quot. 1941).

1941 BAKER *N.Z. Slang* v. 40 Among other terms we have derived from farm life and sheep stations are *moleskin squatter*, 'a working man who has come to own a small sheep run.' *a* **1948** L. G. D. ACLAND *Early Canterbury Runs* (1951) 387 *Moleskin squatter*... A correspondent writes: 'The last time I heard it was when the Government cut up Cheviot in 1893... Since then *m.ss.* have become too numerous to attract attention.' **1873** TROLLOPE *Harry Heathcote* (1874) i. 3 The young man.. had on a flannel shirt, a pair of moleskin trousers, and an old straw hat.

molestive (mole·stiv), *a.* [f. MOLEST *v.* + -IVE.] Tending to annoy; troublesome, interfering.

1905 *North Amer. Rev.* Nov. 657, I suppose that the stranger always finds the patriotism of a country molestive. **1929** W. DEEPING *Roper's Row* vi. 58 If the young Prossers had persecuted the son, Mrs. Prosser had been equally molestive to the mother.

moley (mōᵘ·li), *sb. slang.* [Origin obscure.] (See quot. 1950.)

1950 J. D. CARR *Below Suspicion* xi. 132 'Use the moleys when you catch 'im.' The moley was an ordinary potato, its surface jagged with the edges of safety-razor blades. They ground it into your face, twisted it, and... **1959** *Spectator* 6 Mar. 314/1, I suppose if I go on criticising him I shall end up by having the boys with the moleys call on me one dark night.

‖ **molinete** (mǫline·te). Also **molinet.** [a. Sp. *molinete*, lit. (toy) windmill, little mill.] In *Bullfighting*, a decorative pass made by a matador (see quot. 1959[2]).

1932 [see *FAROL]. **1959** V. J. KEHOE *Aficionado!* 19 Manolo then did a *derechazo*,..ending the series with a *molinete* on his knees. *Ibid.* 208 The *molinete.* Performed with either hand, this pass is started by the matador citing the toro as for a cambiado, then spinning out of the pass in the opposite direction of the toro's charge. **1971** J. LEIBOLD *This is Bullfight* xvii. 202 The molinete can be executed with either the right or left hand... Timing, grace and elegance of execution are of prime importance in accomplishing the molinete.

moll, *sb.* Add: **1. c. moll heron** (later example).

1939 F. THOMPSON *Lark Rise* v. 97 All legs and wings, like a moll-heron.

2. (Further examples.) Also, a girl, woman; a girl-friend or sweetheart, esp. of a criminal; a female pickpocket or thief. See also **gun moll. slang.*

1753 J. POULTER *Discoveries* (ed. 2) 34 To nap the Slangs from the Cull or Moll; that is,..to take the Things from the Man or Woman. **1840** H. D. MILES *Dick Turpin* xxi. 250 You might ha' knowed his moll, a spicy, swellish sort of a bit o' muslin. **1872** G. P. BURNHAM *Mem. U.S. Secret Service* 190 Doctor Blake and his 'moll' visited the town of Toms River. **1891** J. BARON *Blegburn Dickshonary* 44 'Aw'm gooin' to meet mi Moll to-neet' is a varra common sayin' wi' factory lads: some o' th' better soort say 'woman' i' th' place o' Moll, but nooan so mony. **1923** [see *DAME 2 c]. **1931** *Amer. Speech* VII. 111 *Moll.* 1. A gangster's sweetheart or mistress. 2. Any girl whether associated with the underworld or not. **1934** DYLAN THOMAS *18 Poems* 22 In this our age the gunman and his moll, Two one-dimensioned ghosts, love on a reel. **1946** K. TENNANT *Lost Haven* (1968) i. 20 He went off with that bloody moll whose name I wouldn't speak. **1955** *Publ. Amer. Dial. Soc.* XXIV. 99 A woman pickpocket is..a *moll.* **1962** N. MARSH *Hand in Glove* iii. 90, I can see you're in a fever lest slick Ben and his moll should get back..before you make your getaway. **1975** C. FREMLIN *Long Shadow* xxvi. 190 The Psychopath's Moll. I'm doing it again, thought Imogen..saving him from the consequences of his follies.

b. *attrib.* and *Comb.*, as **moll-shop** *slang*, a brothel; **moll-tooler** *slang*, a female pickpocket.

1923 J. MANCHON *Le Slang* 196 Moll-shop. **1957** M. K. JOSEPH *I'll soldier no More* (1958) 181 Pretty faces.. peered shyly into the street. 'Looks like a moll-shop,' said Connolly. **1859** HOTTEN *Dict. Slang* 63 *Moll tooler*, a female pickpocket.

moll, *v.* Add: (Further examples.) So **molled** *ppl. a.*, associating with or accompanied by a woman.

1882 *Sydney Slang Dict.* 6/1, I see yer the other night when yer was Molled up and too proud to speak. **1935** *Flynn's* 19 Jan. 87/2 With each man molled, and his moll posing as his wife, they would not attract the suspicion which would be directed against a mob of men living together.

moll-buzzer. Add: (Further examples.) See also quots.

1900 'FLYNT' & WALTON *Powers that Prey* 225 Her gift for mathematics made it clear that 'moll-buzzing' was much more remunerative than sleeping in cellars and peddling Park Row literature. **1903** Moll-buzzing [see *GRAFT *sb.*[5]]. **1910** *N.Y. Even. Post* 25 Aug., To have the country cousin clutch his arm and enquire whether that rough-looking customer coming out of a Chatham Square saloon is a dip, a yegg, a stall, a moll-buzzer, a Fagin, or a gun. **1912** A. BERKMAN *Prison Mem. Anarchist* II. xxii. 278 The 'gun'..gathers messages for their 'moll buzzers' [*f. n.* women thieves]. **1912** *Collier's* 23 Nov. 12/2 When he came out he began as a 'moll buzzer', which, you understand, means a pickpocket who specializes on the fair sex; he buzzes the 'molls'. **1936** *Evening News* 9 Dec. 8/5 Buzzers are male pickpockets who specialise in opening women's handbags; moll buzzers are the females of the species. **1955** *Publ. Amer. Dial. Soc.* XXIV. 169 The *moll buzzer* (male or female) is not strictly speaking a pickpocket. ..But the thief takes money from the purses or handbags ..carried by women. *Ibid.*, There's a reason for moll buzzing.

mollifyingly (mǫ·lifəiˌiŋli), *adv.* [f. MOLLIFYING *ppl. a.* + -LY[2].] In a mollifying manner.

1920 E. O'NEILL *Beyond the Horizon* I. ii. 44 *Mayo* (*mollifyingly*). Of course I will, boy, and be glad to. **1928** 'S. S. VAN DINE' *Greene Murder Case* ii. 25 'You understand, of course,' he added mollifyingly, 'that I shall not interfere with your activities in any way.' *a* **1953** E. O'NEILL *Long Day's Journey* (1956) 30 *Tyrone* (*impressed —mollifyingly*). I know you may have thought it was for the best.

molluscicide (mǫ̆lʊ·skisəid). Also **mollusca-cide.** [*molluscicide* f. MOLLUSC + -I- + -CIDE; *molluscacide* f. MOLLUSCA *sb. pl.* + -CIDE.] Any substance used to kill molluscs.

1947 DORLAND & MILLER *Med. Dict.* (ed. 21) Molluscacide. **1948** *Jrnl. Parasitol.* XXXIV. Suppl. 33 (*heading*) Results of screening tests on chemicals as molluscicides. **1949** *Ibid.* XXV. 475 (*heading*) Influence of some potential molluscacides on the oxygen consumption of *Australorbis glabratus.* **1965** *New Scientist* 22 Apr. 229/2 No efforts had previously been made to wipe out the snails with molluscicides. **1972** *Country Life* 2 Mar. 527/3 A new molluscicide spray is now being used..to eradicate the pest. **1974** *Nature* 22 Mar. 363/1 The widely used molluscicide sodium pentachlorophenate is a repellant to snails.

Hence **mollusciciˑdal** *a.*

1950 *Jrnl. Parasitol.* XXXVI. 152 The molluscacidal activity of a series of 42 organic compounds has been studied. **1950** *Biol. Abstr.* XXIV. 3249/2 In this series of tests alpha-chloro-esters and amides of aliphatic mono-basic acids showed a more marked molluscicidal activity than the unchlorinated derivatives. **1968** *New Scientist* 4 Jan. 24/3 Chlorinated hydrocarbons and organo-phosphates were found to have no molluscicidal activity.

molluscous, *a.* **3.** (Earlier example.)

1837 *London Med. Gaz.* XIX. 860/2 The structure of the molluscous tubercles.

molluscum. 1. Substitute for def.: Any of various disorders characterized by soft rounded tumours or nodules on the skin, *spec.* (and orig.) molluscum contagiosum. Freq. in mod.L. collocations, as **molluscum contagiosum,** a viral disorder characterized by small, smooth, pinkish nodules with a central depression, that are painless, yield a milky fluid when squeezed, and usu. occur in groups; **molluscum sebaceum,** (*a*) molluscum contagiosum (? *Obs.*); (*b*) = *kerato-acanthoma* s.v. *KERATO-. (Add earlier and additional examples.)

This use is thought to derive from the adjectival use in quot. 1793.

[**1793** C. F. LUDWIG in W. G. Tilesius *Historia Pathologica Singularis Cutis Turpitudinis* 6/1 Verum enim vero Rheinhardi visu foedum corpus tectum est verrucis mollibus sive molluscis et madidis sive myrmeciis.] **1813** T. BATEMAN *Pract. Synopsis Cutaneous Dis.* 268 Molluscum. This form of tubercular disease is noticed rather as a singularity, which occasionally occurs, and of which a few instances are recorded, than as an object of medical treatment. **1817** —— *Delineations of Cutaneous Dis.* Explan. of Plate LXI, Molluscum contagiosum. This singular eruption had not been noticed by Dr. Willan, and was unknown to myself till after the publication of two editions of my Synopsis. **1837** *London Med. Gaz.* XIX. 860/1 (*heading*) A few remarks on molluscum; with two cases of molluscum non-contagiosum. *Ibid.* 860/2 The non-contagious molluscum is characterized by tumors of various sizes, some of them as large as a hen's egg. **1868** *Jrnl. Cutaneous Med.* I. 53 (*heading*) On molluscum sebaceum. **1870** *Med.-Chirurgical Trans.* XXXV. 225 The definition of Plenck could hardly be applied to any disease but Molluscum Contagiosum; the case recorded by Tilesius appears certainly to have been one of Molluscum Fibrosum. *Ibid.* 230 The patient was covered with the tumours of Molluscum, or, as he [*sc.* Virchow] prefers to term it, Fibroma Molluscum. **1932** R. L. SUTTON *Introd. Dermatol.* xv. 280 Molluscum contagiosum. Synonyms.—Molluscum sebaceum; Molluscum epitheliale; [etc.]. **1936** MACCORMAC & SCARFF in *Brit. Jrnl. Dermatol.* XLVIII. 625 The microscopic architecture bears a resemblance to molluscum contagiosum, and it is possible that some of the recorded cases of giant molluscum contagiosum are examples of this tumour. We suggest the name 'molluscum sebaceum' as a convenient label. **1950** Molluscum sebaceum [see *kerato-acanthoma* s.v. *KERATO-]. **1960** J. MARSHALL *Dis. Skin* xxvi. 684 Molluscum sebaceum presents as a solitary lesion usually on the centre face, sometimes..elsewhere. **1961** D. M. PILLSBURY et al. *Man. Cutaneous Med.* ix. 205 Molluscum is of no more than cosmetic importance, except when the conjunctivae are involved. **1967** H. MONTGOMERY *Dermatopathology* II. xxxiv. 1036/2 Cutaneous tags or papillomas have been given many different names in the older literature, including acrochordon, fibroma molluscum, molluscum fibrosum, and soft warts. **1970** PASSMORE & ROBSON *Compan. Med. Stud.* II. xviii. 116/2 Cowpox may develop after contact with infected animals. .. In contrast, molluscum contagiosum is contracted only from human cases.

b. A soft nodule characteristic of molluscum.

1841 *Edin. Med. & Surg. Jrnl.* LVI. 216 In the 2d and 3d Figures are represented the free and attached surfaces of a tubercle, consisting of three mollusca, each with its proper aperture. **1890** J. L. MILTON *On Path. & Treatm. Dis. Skin* (ed. 3) ix. 449 A boy, twenty-two months old, was brought to St. John's Hospital with several molluscum spots on the left side of the face and neck... His mother, who had suckled him, had now a molluscum on her breast. **1960** J. MARSHALL *Dis. Skin* xv. 336 When they appear the papules [of molluscum contagiosum] are 1 to 2 mm. in diameter and the fully developed lesions are usually 5 to 10 mm.; but much larger 'giant mollusca' are sometimes seen.

c. *attrib.*, as *molluscum tumour*; **molluscum body,** † **corpuscle,** one of the characteristic ovoid bodies that are found in the core of the nodules of molluscum contagiosum and are thought to be degenerate epidermal cells; also, a cytoplasmic inclusion in a cell that is in the early stages of degeneration.

1892 *Edin. Med. Jrnl.* XXXVIII. 283 The so-called molluscum bodies..are not independent animal organisms. **1937** E. H. MOLESWORTH *Introd. Dermatol.* vii. 228 The so-called molluscum bodies are degenerate and deformed cells contained in the core of the lesion. They are not the infective agents. **1966** WRIGHT & SYMMERS *Systemic Path.* II. xxxix. 1571/2 The epidermal cells that are infected by the virus [of molluscum contagiosum] undergo premature keratinization and form the so-called molluscum bodies, which contain the virus inclusions. **1974** PASSMORE & ROBSON *Compan. Med. Stud.* III. II. xxxi. 58/1 Cytoplasmic inclusions (molluscum bodies) form in the cells of the stratum spinosum. **1886** C. H. FAGGE

Princ. & Pract. Med. II. 688 The white material seems to be made up almost entirely of characteristic oval transparent bodies..without a nucleus... These have been described as molluscum corpuscles. *Ibid.*, A molluscum tumour resembles an ordinary sebaceous cyst or steatoma, but the contents are white instead of yellow.

Mollweide (mǫ·lvəidə). The name of Karl B. *Mollweide* (d. 1825), German mathematician and astronomer, used in the possessive, *attrib.*, and *absol.* to designate a homalographic map projection in which the surface of the globe is represented by an ellipse, with lines of latitude represented by the major axis and straight lines parallel to it (spaced more closely towards the poles) and meridians represented by the minor axis and equally spaced elliptical curves.

1901 C. F. CLOSE *Map Projections* II. 22 (*heading*) Homalographic equal-area (Mollweide's). Sometimes called Babinet's. **1912** A. R. HINKS *Map Projections* vii. 73 For the whole world on a single sheet we have Mollweide, which is useful for distribution diagrams, but can scarcely be called a map. **1937** F. DEBENHAM *Exercises in Cartography* x. 118 Draw an interrupted Mollweide projection to show continental areas with the least distortion. *Ibid.*, Make an approximate graticule on the Oblique Mollweide suitable for showing the British Empire Seas. **1947** H. D. THOMPSON *Fundamentals Earth Sci.* v. 52 Mollweide's Homalographic equal-area projection (1805) shows the entire surface of the earth inside an ellipse, the major, or equatorial axis of which is twice as long as the minor axis. **1960** F. LAND *Lang. Math.* vi. 70 Mollweide's map..is an equal-area map, preserving area relations at the expense of shapes. **1971** R. W. PURTON *Let's look at Maps & Mapmaking* 14 Mollweide's projection can be drawn with any line of longitude as its centre and can be used to draw attention to one particular part of the world.

molly, *sb.*¹ Add: **4. Molly dancer** *dial.* (see quots.).

1959 I. & P. OPIE *Lore & Lang. Schoolch.* xii. 261 In north Manchester, gangs of boys calling themselves 'Molly Dancers' wear old clothes, mostly women's, and make-up their faces, and go around singing..'Spare a copper for the Molly dancers'. **1971** *Jrnl. Lancs. Dial. Soc.* xx. 8 *Molly Dancers*, performers of a traditional folk play, of which a number survived in North Staffordshire into the 1930's. I assume the phrase to be a popular etymology for *Morris Dancers.*

molly (mǫ·li), *v.* [f. MOLLY¹ or MOLLY-CODDLE *v.*] **1.** *intr.* (See quot.) *dial.*

1884 R. LAWSON *Upton-on-Severn Words* 23 *Molly*, to do woman's work indoors, being a man. ''E were a good un to molly for 'isself, were old Joe.'

2. *trans.* = MOLLY-CODDLE *v.*

1907 M. C. HARRIS *Tents of Wickedness* II. ii. 138 Paul hasn't been mollied, and I hope he's a nice fellow.

molly, var. MALLEE¹.

molly-coddler (mǫ·likǫ:dləɹ). [f. MOLLY-CODDLE *v.* + -ER¹.] One who molly-coddles.

1863 A. J. MUNBY *Diary* 31 Aug. (1972) 172 It keeps up a wholesome protest against the Mollycoddlers, to see a whole countryful of stout lasses devoted to field-labour only. **1933** J. CARY *Amer. Visitor* 213 Minnie was a molly coddler, in Bewsher's phrase, and liked to take temperatures.

mollycot. (Earlier example.)

1826 *Blackw. Mag.* XX. 846/2 What in vulgar English is called a Molly-cot.

molly-dook (mǫ:lidū·k), *a.* *Austral. slang.* [f. MOLLY¹ (or perh. MAULEY) + DUKE *sb.* 7.] Left-handed. So **molly-dooker, -hander**, a left-handed person; **molly-duked** *a.*, left-handed.

[**1926** 'J. V. MARSHALL' *Timely Tips to New Australians*, *Mauldy*, left-handed.] **1934** *Bulletin* (Sydney) 21 Mar. 11/3 Hence the trade is taboo to the molly-hander. **1941** BAKER *Dict. Austral. Slang* 47 *Mollydooker*, a left-handed person. Whence, 'mollydook' (adj.): left-handed. **1969** *Southerly* XXIX. 8 It could be being written by someone else with the same absurdly decorous aim, someone molly-duked, atheist, over-educated.

mollyhawk. (Earlier and later examples.)

1880 L. V. BRIGGS *Jrnl.* 19 Oct. in *Around Cape Horn on Bark 'Amy Turner'* (1926) 105, I caught and skinned two mollyhawks, or mollymoke, as some sailors call them. **1917** [see *John Down* (*JOHN 4)]. **1923** D. H. LAWRENCE *Kangaroo* viii. 169 A big albatross swung slowly down the surf: albatross or mollyhawk, with wide, waving wings. **1927** M. M. BENNETT *Christison of Lammermoor* i. 16 The mollyhawks and albatrosses planed and circled, keeping up with the ship with scarcely a movement of their great wings. **1969** *Landfall* XXIII. 103 In front of his house a mollyhawk was patiently taking up and dropping a pipi to break it on the hard sand by the water.

Molly Maguire. Add: **a.** (Further examples.) Now *Hist.*

1908 L. H. DAWSON *Nicknames & Pseudonyms* 202 *Molly Maguires*, young men, usually dressed in women's clothes, who formed an Irish association to resist distraint for rent in 1843. Their name was derived from Connor.. Maguire, 2nd Baron of Enniskillen, who in 1641 took a prominent part in the Catholic conspiracy. **1909** *Westm. Gaz.* 19 Feb. 2/3 There were Molly Maguires in Ireland.. long before the time of Mr. William O'Brien. **1971** E. NORMAN *Hist Mod. Ireland* iii. 57 The secret societies formed to stimulate local violence on behalf of individual tenant claims;..societies which adopted the awful names of 'Whiteboys', 'Rockites', 'Levellers', 'Whitefeet', 'Molly Maguires', 'Ribbonmen', and so on.

b. (Further examples.)

1886 P. STAPLETON *Major's Christmas* 86 There come among us some men that belonged to a band of murderers that called themselves Molly Maguires. **1970** *Guardian* 14 May 10/1 The Molly Maguires were a group of rebel miners who fought a brave and reckless losing battle with employers who stopped at nothing to destroy them.

mollymawk, mollymauk: now more usual spellings of MALLEMUCK. Cf. *MOLLYHAWK.

1913 H. K. SWANN *Dict. Eng. & Folk-Names Brit. Birds* 153 *Mallemuck*, an old Dutch-mariner's name for the Fulmar. Now corrupted into 'Molly-mawk', and applied to various other species such as the Black-browed Albatross. **1933** *Geogr. Jrnl.* LXXXI. 217 The mollymauk is a wild sea-bird which inhabits the regions of Cape Horn. **1959** D. A. BANNERMAN *Birds Brit. Isles* VIII. 193 Dr Cushman Murphy describes this mollymauk [*sc.* the black-browed albatross, *Diomedea melanophrys*] as 'the commonest albatross in the southern hemisphere, the most sociable and the most fearless of man while at sea'. **1972** M. F. SOPER *N.Z. Birds* 181 Albatrosses and mollymawks are tube-nosed birds..that, except for a few species inhabiting the North Pacific, are confined to the Southern Hemisphere. In New Zealand waters the term 'mollymawk' is conveniently applied to the smaller forms, all of which have black backs, and the term 'albatross' to the two 'great' albatrosses, the Wandering and the Royal, the adults of which have white backs.

molossic, *a.* (Earlier example.)

1864 H. BUSHNELL *Work & Play* i. 34 You distinguish ..the solemn, religious spondee, the swift trochaic run of eagerness or fear, the heavy molossic tread of grief or sorrow.

Molotov (mǫ·lǒtǫf). Also **Molotoff,** and with lower-case initial. The name of Vyacheslav Mikhailovich *Molotov* (1890–), U.S.S.R. Minister for Foreign Affairs from 1939 to 1949, used *attrib.* in **Molotov bread-basket**, a container carrying high explosive and scattering incendiary bombs; **Molotov cocktail**, a makeshift incendiary hand-grenade, consisting of a breakable container filled with inflammable liquid, and a means of ignition; also *ellipt.* as *Molotov.*

1940 *Illustr. London News* 6 Apr. 446/2 The 'Molotov Breadbasket'..appeared to consist of two types. **1940** *Hutchinson's Pict. Hist. War* 7 Aug.–1 Oct. 91 Used with success in the Finnish war, the so-called 'Molotov cocktails' are considered an effective weapon against armoured divisions and have been adopted by the Home Guard. **1940** *Flight* 26 Sept. 244/1 A Molotoff bread basket dropped some 50 incendiary bombs in a S.E. district of London. **1942** J. T. GORMAN *Mod. Weapons of War* ix. 147 Stationary tanks can be disabled by dropping grenades or Molotov cocktails through the ventilating openings. **1943** T. W. LAWSON *Thirty Seconds over Tokyo* 32 A 500-pound incendiary, something like the old Russian Molotov Breadbasket. **1951** J. CARSWELL in A. Somerville *Autobiogr. Working Man* p. xiv, Feargus O'Connor was trying to popularize the ginger-beer bottle filled with inflammable mixture (a version of the Molotov Cocktail to which Englishmen seem to turn when ammunition is short). **1969** *Oz* Apr. 5/1 Issue number three carried instructions on how to make a molotov with diagram and said where in the university to strike with same. **1970** R. JOHNSTON *Black Camels* vi. 90 Sulaiman was on the last bottle. Half fill it with petrol, drop in one end of the wick, plug the neck of the bottle and, hey presto, a Molotov Cocktail... Select a target, light the wick, throw the bottle. Bottle hits target, bottle smashes, petrol spills out, flame from wick ignites petrol. **1972** R. K. SMITH *Ransom* iv. 168 Thirty cars zooming out of the night loaded with molotovs.

† **molrowing** (mǫ·lrau,iŋ). *Obs. slang.* Also **moll-rowing.** [Perh. f. MOLL *sb.* + ROW *v.*³ + -ING¹.] **a.** (See quot. 1860.) So **mo·lrower,** a wencher or whoremonger. **b.** Caterwauling, row, noise.

1860 HOTTEN *Dict. Slang* (ed. 2) 174 *Molrowing*, 'out on the spree', in company with so-called 'gay women'. In allusion to the amatory serenadings of the London cats. **1892** E. J. MILLIKEN *'Arry Ballads* 42 A pootily piped 'Blooming Lavender',..as meller as blackbirds in June, Beats 'Andel's molrowings a buster. **1894** G. A. SALA *Things I have Seen* II. xiii. 121 The scene wound up with a great concert of practical cats on the roof, whose diabolical mollrowings still ring in my ears. **1896** FARMER & HENLEY *Slang* IV. 332/1 *Molrower*, a whoremonger.

molten, *ppl. a.* Add: **4.** *Comb.*, as *molten-blue, -crystal, -golden* adjs.

1862 G. M. HOPKINS *Poems* (1930) 132 As though some sapphire molten-blue Were vein'd and streak'd with dusk-deep lazuli. **1950** D. GASCOYNE *Vagrant* 27 Moulting molten-crystal plumes of birds of paradise. **1849** POE *Bells* in *Sartain's Union Mag.* Nov. 304/1 From the molten-golden notes,..What a liquid ditty floats.

‖ **molto** (mǫ·lto), *a.* and *adv.* [It.] (See quot. 1801.)

1801 T. BUSBY *Dict. Mus.*, *Molto*, very or much. A word used in conjunction with some other, by way of augmentation; as *Molto Allegro*, very quick, *Molto Adagio*, very slow. **1889** G. B. SHAW *London Music 1888–89* (1937) 148 The *molto sostenuto* indicated by Gounod, which is the characteristic effect of the movement, was quite lost. **1928** [see *MARTELLATO *a.*] **1959** *Times* 15 Jan. 12/6 Mr. Buckley did not play them *molto dramatico* in octaves as Rachmaninov used to do. **1970** *Times* 23 Feb. 12/3 That striking but rarely heard effect, *molto pianissimo* from a large choral body.

moly² (mǫ·li), colloq. abbrev. of MOLYBDENUM. Also used for *molybdenum disulphide* (a lubricant).

1961 in WEBSTER. **1963** R. F. WEBB *Motorists' Dict.* 155 The [lubricating] action of 'moly' has been likened to a pack of cards resting on a table. **1970** *Financial Times* 13 Apr. 27/8 Not that Amax is remaining dormant on the moly front. The bringing in of the Henderson mine..will nigh on double production capacity.

molybdenian (mǫlibdī·niăn), *a.* *Min.* [f. MOLYBDEN(UM + *-IAN 2.] Of a mineral: having a (small) proportion of a constituent element replaced by molybdenum.

1930 W. T. SCHALLER in *Amer. Mineralogist* XV. 571 Molybdenum—molybdenian. **1953** *Amer. Mineralogist* XXXVIII. 904 Prior to oxidation the rock contained..a few grains of molybdenian scheelite.

molybdenum. Add: Now usu. pronounced (mǫ̆li·bdĕnǝ̆m). **b. molybdenum blue,** a complex oxide or mixture of oxides of pentavalent or hexavalent molybdenum with a strong blue colour that is produced, usu. as a colloidal solution, when an acidic solution of a molybdate is reduced, and is used in chemical analysis and occas. as a dye; also, the colour of this substance.

1901 *Jrnl. Chem. Soc.* LXXX. II. 163 Molybdenum blue does not appear to contain the dioxide, MoO_2,..but the semipentoxide, Mo_2O_5. **1920** F. A. MASON tr. *G. von Georgievics's Text-bk. Dye Chem.* 542 Molybdenum blue.. was used experimentally for a certain time on silk and cotton materials. **1951** *Amer. Mineralogist* XXXVI. 610 Ilsemannite is soluble in water, first producing a greenish blue solution which later deepens to a typical molybdenum blue. **1952** KIRK & OTHMER *Encycl. Chem. Technol.* IX. 203 The present importance of molybdenum blue rests on the fact that several colorimetric methods depend upon it: (*1*) the determination of trace quantities of phosphorus or phosphates by the preferential reduction of phosphomolybdic acid; and (*2*) a number of other methods employing phosphomolybdic acid as a reagent (for phenols, tyrosine, tryptophan, etc.) for reducing compounds. **1965** D. ABBOTT *Inorg. Chem.* xii. 642 Molybdenum 'blue' is an oxide formed when an acidified molybdate solution is greatly reduced. It has variable composition, usually about 67–68 per cent Mo.

molybdian (mǫ̆li·bdiăn), *a.* *Min.* [alteration of *MOLYBDENIAN *a.*] = *MOLYBDENIAN *a.*

1951 C. PALACHE et al. *Dana's Syst. Min.* (ed. 7) II. 1078 Seyrigite... A molybdian scheelite, with MoO_3 24·01 per cent.

molybdophyllite (mǫ:libdofi·ləit). *Min.* [ad. G. *molybdophyllit* (G. Flink 1901, in *Bull. Geol. Inst. Univ. Upsala* V. I. 91), f. Gr. μόλυβδο-ς lead + φύλλ-ον leaf: see -ITE¹.] A hydrous silicate of lead and magnesium.

1901 *Jrnl. Chem. Soc.* LXXX. II. 664 Molybdophyllite. —This new mineral is of rare occurrence with hausmannite in granular limestone or dolomite at Långbanshyttan, in Wermland, Sweden. **1968** I. KOSTOV *Mineral.* 327 Perfect cleavage in one direction is displayed by molybdophyllite.

molysite (mǫ·lisəit). *Min.* [said by Dana, the coiner of the name, to be f. Gr. μόλυνσις stain, which was app. taken (in error for μόλυσμα) as the sb. corresp. to μολύνειν to stain, perh. by confusion with μώλυσις scalding (f. μωλύ(ν)ειν to scald, parboil): see -ITE¹.

The statement in quot. 1935 as to the origin of the name is incorrect. In *Atti d. R. Accad. d. Sci. fis. e matem.* (1874) VI. IX. 43, Scacchi attributes the name *molysite* to Dana (in *Syst. Min.* (ed. 5)), and renders it in It. as *molisite* so as to make it conform to It. orthography (as he explains in *Lo Spettatore del Vesuviano* (1887)).]

Natural ferric chloride, $FeCl_3$, formed as a sublimation product on lavas surrounding fumaroles and occurring (before being hydrated by the air) as a yellow to red film or incrustation.

1868 DANA *Syst. Min.* (ed. 5) 118 Molysite. **1935** J. W. MELLOR *Comprehensive Treat. Inorg. & Theoret. Chem.* XIV. lxvi. 41 A. Scacchi observed in recent eruptions a yellowish or brownish-red incrustation associated with the lavas of fumaroles or steam holes. The coloration was attributed to the presence of ferric chloride, $FeCl_3$, and A. Scacchi called the mineral molisite, which J. D. Dana altered to molysite—from μόλυσις, a stain. **1968** I. KOSTOV *Mineral.* II. iii. 195 Molysite $FeCl_3$.

mom (mǫm). Also **Mom.** Colloq. abbrev. (chiefly *U.S.*) of MAMMA¹, MAMA; *spec.* the typical American matriarchal mother. Also *attrib.* and *Comb.*, as *mom cult, culture*; *mom-bashing, -like*, etc.; *spec.* **mom-and-pop** *U.S.*, used *attrib.* to denote a small shop or store, etc., of a type often run by a married couple.

1894 *Dialect Notes* I. 332 *Mam, mŏm, mæ*, for mamma or mother. **1911** R. W. CHAMBERS *Common Law* v. 156 City-wearied fathers of youngsters who called their parents 'pop' and 'mom'. **1950** *Brit. Jrnl. Psychol.* June 230 The 'mom' culture in which American adolescents are often said to live. **1951** Mom-and-Pop [see *HOLE *sb.* 7 b]. **1957** *Economist* 28 Dec. 1121/2 Tin Pan Alley, Fundamentalism, and the Mom cult had it coming to them. **1958** *Manch. Guardian* 7 June 4/6 Three leading serious comedies are studies in parent-hating or mom-bashing. **1961** J. HELLER *Catch-22* (1962) i. 9 The hot dog, the Brooklyn Dodgers. Mom's apple pie. That's what everyone's fighting for. **1961** J. MCCABE *Mr. Laurel & Mr. Hardy* (1962) v. 102 The troubles of the boys in their continuing endeavour to get away from their domineering, Mom-like wives. **1962** *Listener* 20 Dec. 1053/1 These 'mom and pop' stores and the somewhat larger ones certainly have no love for the supermarkets. **1966** *Economist* 9 July p. xxi/3 'Mom-and-pop' dealers in smaller communities and suburban fringes. **1968** *Globe & Mail* (Toronto) 17 Feb. 46/8 (Advt.), A family kitchen with mom in mind boasts a.. built-in range and oven. **1972** *New Yorker* 21 Oct. 30/1 The mom-and-pop grocery store was the New York State headquarters of the McGovern campaign. **1975** *Ibid.* 13 Jan. 36/2 'Of course we will, Mom,' I said, and I patted her hand and laid it aside.

mombin (mǒmbī·n). [Amer. Sp. *mombín*, f. Caribbean native name.] A West Indian tree of the genus *Spondias*, esp. *S. lutea*, of the family Anacardiaceæ, or its yellow or purplish fruit, resembling a small plum; = HOG-PLUM a.

1837 J. MACFADYEN *Flora of Jamaica* I. 228 The fruit [of *Spondias graveolens*] is called Mombin by the French colonists. **1920** W. POPENOE *Man. Tropical & Subtropical Fruits* iv. 156 The red mombin is a small tree, often spreading in habit. *Ibid.* 158 The red mombin is abundant in Mexico and Central America. *Ibid.* 159 The Yellow Mombin..is generally considered inferior in quality to the red mombin. **1972** A. F. SIMMONS *Growing Unusual Fruit* 201 Mombin fruit... Spondias species. *Ibid.* 202 Yellow mombin or hog plum (*Spondias mombin*). The egg-shaped yellow fruits are about 1 in long and sub-acid to sweet.

mome[2]. (Later example.)

1923 E. SITWELL *Bucolic Comedies* 17 An old dull mome With a head like a pome.

mome (mōᵘm), *a.* A factitious word introduced by 'Lewis Carroll' (see quot. 1855).

Also occurs in *Through the Looking-Glass* (1871) i. 21.

1855 'L. CARROLL' *Rectory Umbrella & Mischmasch* (1932) 139 All mimsy were the borogoves; And the mome raths outgrabe. *Ibid.* 140 *Mome* (hence *solemome, solemone* and *solemn*), 'grave'. **1960** M. GARDNER *Annotated Alice* 195/1 'Mome' has a number of obsolete meanings such as mother, a blockhead,..none of which, judging from Humpty Dumpty's interpretation, Carroll had in mind. **1970** R. D. SUTHERLAND *Lang. & Lewis Carroll* vii. 149 Humpty Dumpty is reporting the generally accepted meanings... The information he imparts is 'as sensible as a dictionary'... He admits some difficulty with *mome*.

moment, *sb.* Add: **1. c.** *not for a moment*: emphatically not; *of the moment*: of importance at the time in question; esp. *man of the moment*; *never a dull moment*: a catch-phrase designating constant variety; *to have one's* (or *its*) *moments*: to be impressive, etc., on occasions; *to live for* (or *in*) *the moment*: to live without concern for the future; (*at this*) *moment in time*: now, the present instant.

1871 BROWNING *Pr. Hohenst.* 28 Well, that's my mission, so I serve the world, Figure as man o' the moment. **1889** J. K. JEROME *Three Men in Boat* ix. 85 There is never a dull moment in the boat while girls are towing it. **1926** I. MACKAY *Blencarrow* xxiii. 207 With the proper sort of company the situation might have had its moments. **1927** *Sat. Even. Post* 9 Apr. 119 Even a mailman has his moments. **1932** *Weekend Rev.* 14 May 617/1 There is never a dull moment. **1935** E. CARR *Jrnl.* in *Hundreds & Thousands* (1966) 185 The three dogs lie on the bed,.. trusting me to attend to their wants, living for the moment. **1935** *Discovery* Aug. 220/1 Land utilisation is the problem of the moment. *Ibid.* 221/1 This is the need dictated by world economic conditions *of the moment*. **1936** *Punch* 12 Aug. 170/2, I don't suggest for a moment that these are finished ideas. They are no more than artists' roughs. **1950** L. KAUFMAN *Jubel's Children* xx. 223 Jubel says there's never a dull moment. **1963** W. H. MISSILDINE *Your Inner Child of Past* xii. 127 Because they 'live in the moment', they actually tend to be blindly unaware of the feelings of others. **1970** O. NORTON *Dead on Prediction* vii. 137 That's something I *didn't* know... You have your moments! **1972** G. BROMLEY *In Absence of Body* iii. 30 What can we actually do to help at this moment in time? **1972** 'T. COE' *Don't lie to Me* (1974) xxii. 169 Hargerson had his moments; happily this was one of them. **1972** R. ADAMS *Watership Down* xx. 126 'No one hurt?' 'Oh, several have been hurt, one way and another.' 'Never a dull moment, really,' said Bigwig. **1973** *Guardian* 12 Mar. 11/2 The usual stuff about meaningful confrontations taking place..at this moment in time. **1974** C. EGLETON *October Plot* i. 11 There were five similar [flak] towers..but at this moment in time, they were only of passing interest. **1974** V. BROME *Day of Destruction* xv. 153 Here's our man of the moment... Hail the conquering hero comes.

d. *moment of truth*: the time of the final sword-thrust in a bull-fight (Sp. *el momento de la verdad*); *transf.*, a crisis or turning-point; a testing situation.

1932 E. HEMINGWAY *Death in Afternoon* vii. 68 The whole end of the bullfight was the final sword thrust, the actual encounter between the man and the animal, what the Spanish call the moment of truth. **1949** *New Statesman* 15 Jan. 61/1 A good detective story should be like a good bull-fight... The author plunges the unexpected explanation into him like a sword—the moment of truth, as the Spaniards call it. **1954** H. CASTEEL *Running of Bulls* v. 106 The Spanish call the kill the hora de la verdad (the hour (moment) of truth)... this is still the climactic second to which the whole fight has been dedicated. **1956** I. BROMIGE *Enchanted Garden* III. iii. 140 This, thought Fiona, was the moment of truth. **1957** 'D. RUTHERFORD' *Long Echo* viii. 150 This was his Moment of Truth, but there was no arena packed with spectators to give him vicarious courage. **1959** *Listener* 6 Aug. 215/2 Now comes 'the moment of truth'... The matador causes the bull to stand square..and plunges his sword between its shoulder-blades. **1965** H. I. ANSOFF *Corporate Strategy* (1968) i. 16 We shall have..very little [to say]..about the utility function applied at the ultimate 'moment of truth' in selecting the preferred alternative. **1972** H. MACINNES *Message From Malaga* i. 9 You've become a self-centred bastard, he told himself... He blamed this moment of truth on the combination of guitar, scent of flowers, night sky.

2. d. *Geol.* [a. F. *moment* (proposed in this sense by E. Renevier 1882, in *Congrès géol. internat.: Compt. Rend. de la 2me Session, 1881* 540).] A period of geological time corresponding to a stratigraphical zone (as defined by its fossil content).

1933 W. J. ARKELL *Jurassic Syst. Gt. Brit.* i. 21 Strictly speaking,..'moment' should take priority over secule, and Diener adopts it, with the variations time-moment and zone-moment. **1958** *Bull. Geol. Soc. Amer.* LXIX. 113/2 At the Congress in Bologna in 1881..the only concrete suggestion came from the Swiss delegation (Renevier, 1882), which formally proposed 'moment' for the time equivalent of a zone. *Ibid.*, The term 'moment' has priority, as was..recognized at an early date by Diener (1919). **1969** BENNISON & WRIGHT *Geol. Hist. Brit. Isles* ii. 23 A zone is defined as strata deposited during an interval of time (known as a secule or moment, though these terms are not widely used) throughout which a particular faunal or floral assemblage existed.

8. c. *Physics.* The distance between the two poles of a simple bar magnet, or the two charges of an electric dipole, multiplied by the strength of either of them (called more fully the *magnetic* and the *electric moment*, respectively); more widely, the maximum torque that any given system of poles, or charges, can experience in a uniform magnetic, or electric, field (respectively) of unit strength; more fully called (*magnetic* or *electric*) *dipole moment*. Similarly the moment of order 2 (*quadrupole moment*) is a certain tensor of rank 2, whose components are quadratic functions of the spatial co-ordinates of the poles or charges; so *octupole moment* (moment of order 3), etc. Cf. *MULTIPOLE *sb.*

1865 *Phil. Mag.* XXIX. 441 The product of the strength of the poles into the length between them is called the magnetic moment of the magnet. **1884** J. T. SPRAGUE *Electricity* (ed. 2) iii. 110 The magnetic moment of any uniformly magnetized substance is proportional to its volume. **1892** O. LODGE *Mod. Views Electricity* 445 A circuit conveying a current exactly imitates a magnet of definite moment, the equivalent moment being..μnAC where A is the mean area of the coil, n the number of turns of wire, C the current, and μ a constant characteristic of the medium inside the coil. **1903** S. J. BARNETT *Elements of Electromagnetic Theory* xi. 282 The quantity $M = mL = T/H \sin\theta$ is called the magnetic moment of the magnet (analogous to the electric moment of an electret). **1916**, etc. [see *MULTIPOLE *sb.*]. **1920** *Chem. Abstr.* XIV. 3014 Assuming the mol. to be a dipole it is possible to obtain the distance between the 2 charges from the moment of inertia and from this in turn to calc. the elec. moment by application of the quantum theory. **1934** *Physical Rev.* XLV. 761/1 We derived the magnetic moment of the deuton in the same way as the magnetic moment of the proton. **1942** J. D. STRANATHAN *'Particles' of Mod. Physics* x. 401 The magnetic moment of a neutron must be regarded as a fundamental property of the particle. **1953** *Sci. News* XXX. 7 The magnetization [of a piece of iron] is the magnetic moment per unit volume, or the pole strength per unit cross-sectional area. **1958** CONDON & ODISHAW *Handbk. Physics* IV. ii. 19/2 A quadrupole term is related to the second-order moments of the charge distribution... (Various slightly different definitions of the quadrupole moment are to be found in the literature.) *Ibid.* 20/1 The spherical-harmonic addition theorem.. permits the writing of $V_k(\mathbf{R})$ in the form

$$V_k(\mathbf{R}) = \frac{1}{R^{k+1}} \sum_{m=-k}^{+k} Q_{km} F_{km}(\Theta) e^{-im\Phi}$$

where the 2^k-pole moment is fully described by the $2k+1$ quantities,

$$Q_{km} = \frac{4\pi}{2k+1}\int \rho(\mathbf{r}) F_{km}(\theta) e^{im\phi}\, dv.$$

1962 CORSON & LORRAIN *Introd. Electromagn. Fields & Waves* v. 210 We set $\mathbf{m} = I\mathbf{S}$ as the dipole moment of the current loop, where $\mathbf{S}$ is a vector whose magnitude is equal to the area of the loop. It is perpendicular to the loop. *Ibid.*, It is possible to generalize the concept of magnetic dipole moment to any distribution of current in space... For a current distribution $\mathbf{J}$ in a volume τ, $\mathbf{m} =$ .. $\frac{1}{2}\int \mathbf{r} \times \mathbf{J}\, d\tau$. **1970** G. K. WOODGATE *Elem. Atomic Struct.* ix. 177 In order to be able to discuss departures of the nuclear charge distribution from spherical symmetry we should like to attribute to the nucleus electric multipole moments. *Ibid.* 180 The quadrupole moment Q is positive if the nuclear charge distribution is elongated along the direction of $\mathbf{I}$ [*sc.* the nuclear spin] (prolate) and negative if the distribution is flattened (oblate).

d. *Statistics.* Each of a series of quantities (*first, second,* etc., *moment*) that express the average or expected value of the first, second, etc., powers of the deviation of each component of a frequency distribution from some given value, usu. the mean (giving a *central moment*) or zero.

1893 K. PEARSON in *Nature* 26 Oct. 615/2 Now the centre of gravity of the observation curve is found at once, also its area and its first four moments by easy calculation. **1925** R. A. FISHER *Statistical Methods for Research Workers* iii. 70 The standard error of the variance is $\sqrt{[(\mu_4 - \mu_2^2)/N]}$, where N is the number of samples, and μ_2 and μ_4 are the second and fourth moments of the theoretical distribution. **1938** A. E. WAUGH *Elem. Statistical Method* vi. 114 The formula for the first moment about the mean involves $\sum x$ and..it reduces to zero, since $\sum x = 0$. We can thus say some things about the moments of all curves in advance: (1) $v_0 = 1$, (2) $v_1 = 0$, (3) $v_2 = \sigma^2$. *Ibid.*, In any symmetrical curve the odd moments, being based on the sums of odd powers of deviations, will equal zero. **1959** G. & R. C. JAMES *Math. Dict.* 257/2 $\mu_r = \int_{-\infty}^{\infty} (x-a)^r f(x)\,dx$ is the rth moment of x around the point a, where x is a random variable with frequency function $f(x)$. **1961** D. V. HUNTSBERGER *Elem. Statistical Inference* v. 102 The first moment about the origin is the mean μ of the theoretical distribution... The variance σ^2 of a random variable Y is defined as the second moment about the mean, the average value of $(Y-\mu)^2$.

10. *moment-to-moment* attrib. phr., of an immediate requirement, necessity, etc.

1934 T. S. ELIOT *Elizabethan Essays* 8 Contemporary literature, like contemporary politics, is confused by the moment-to-moment struggle for existence. **1957** A. MILLER *Coll. Plays* (1958) Introd. 23 It wanted..a kind of moment-to-moment wildness in addition to its organic wholeness.

momentaneity (mōᵘmĕntĕnī·iti, -ēⁱ·ĭti). [f. MOMENTANE(OUS *a.* + -ITY, after SPONTANEITY.] Transitory character; momentariness.

1921 D. H. LAWRENCE *Sea & Sardinia* viii. 314, I felt my sound Sardinian soul melting off me, I felt myself evaporating into the real Italian uncertainty and momentaneity. **1923** —— *Kangaroo* vii. 157 All her high moments would have this Bacchic, weapon-like momentaneity.

momentaneous, *a.* Restrict † *Obs.* to sense 3 and add: **1.** (Later examples.) **momentaneously** *adv.* (later example).

1921 H. POUTSMA *Characters of Eng. Vb. & Expanded Form* i. 2 The actions expressed by verbs..may be.. momentaneous, i.e. covering only one moment, or comprised between two closely contiguous moments, so that the beginning and the end practically synchronize. *Ibid.* 5 [Actions expressed by verbs may be] momentaneously iterative, which may be graphically represented by a succession of dots. **1921** E. SAPIR *Language* v. 108 'Cry out every now and then' or 'cry in fits and starts' is momentaneous-iterative. **1923** D. H. LAWRENCE *Kangaroo* vii. 163 Do I want this curious transparent blood of the antipodes, with its momentaneous feelings? **1926** H. POUTSMA *Gram. Late Mod. Eng.* II. § 2. 545 When distinctly verbal in nature, the attributive past participle mostly has a momentaneous or resultative aspect.

momentarily, *adv.* Add: **1.** (Later examples.)

1928 'S. S. VAN DINE' *Greene Murder Case* iii. 39 The situation probably drove everything momentarily from their minds except the two victims of the shooting. **1975** *Times* 8 Sept. 12/3 One MP..was 'growled down'... He wondered momentarily if he had wandered into the Lords by mistake.

3. (Later example.)

1899 W. J. LOCKE *White Dove* (1900) iii. 43 Sylvester.., having done all that was momentarily possible, was at last able to reflect.

4. At any moment. *N. Amer.*

1928 *Sun* (Baltimore) 13 Aug. 1/2 Arrests were expected momentarily as police continued their investigation of the fantastic murder mill. **1944** *Musical America* 25 Mar. 7/4 An addition to the family..is expected momentarily. **1970** *New Yorker* 3 Oct. 30/3 Miss Loren had been delayed in traffic but would arrive momentarily. **1970** *Daily Tel.* 22 Oct. 18 The [Canadian] captain came on the intercom. 'Please fasten your seat belts,' he said. 'We shall be taking off momentarily.' **1972** *New York* 8 May 6/2 We are expecting our first child momentarily. **1975** *Publishers Weekly* 10 Feb. 52/1 There is one woman who imagines she is in a motel and that her deceased husband will momentarily arrive to pick her up.

momento (mǒme·nto), var. MEMENTO 3.

1871 GEO. ELIOT *Jrnl.* 19 Mar. in J. W. Cross *George Eliot's Life* (1885) III. xvi. 129 My present fear is that I have too much matter—too many *momenti*. **1951** DYLAN THOMAS *Let.* 12 Apr. (1966) 356 And the London frowsty Casino, a momento of which I enclose.

momentum. Add: **6.** Special Comb.: **momentum space** *Physics*, a three-dimensional space in which each particle of a physical system is represented by a point whose three Cartesian co-ordinates are numerically equal to the components of its momentum in the directions of the three co-ordinate axes.

1948 W. HUME-ROTHERY *Electrons, Atoms, Metals &*

Alloys xx. 143 The momentum space is divided into little cells of side *h*/*L*, and volume h^3/L^3. **1970** I. E. McCarthy *Nuclear Reactions* I. v. 111 We consider the matrix element in momentum space. **1970** G. K. Woodgate *Elem. Atomic Struct.* vi. 98 Under this assumption the electrons are moving freely, with no forces acting on them, and their translational momenta can be taken to be directed isotropically in momentum space.

momie-cloth: see Mummy-cloth 2. Also *ellipt.*

1881 C. C. Harrison *Woman's Handiwork* I. 46 (*heading*) Raw silk momie cloth, for draperies,..fifty inches wide, at $3.50... Cotton momie cloth..in all the new shades for $1.10,..Basket momie cloth, in woollen, costs $3. **1895** *Montgomery Ward Catal.* 4/2 Blade Crepon.. similar to Momie or Armure. **1960** Cunnington & Beard *Dict. Eng. Costume* 264/2 *Momie cloth*,..of cotton or silk warp and woollen weft, resembling a fine crepe; usually black and used for mourning.

momism² (mǫ·miz'm). *U.S.* Also **Momism.** [f. *Mom + -ism.] Excessive attachment to, or domination by, the mother.

1942 P. Wylie *Generation of Vipers* xi. 185 Hitherto.. man has shown a considerable qui vive to the dangers which arise from momism and freely perceived that his 'old wives' were often vixens, dragons, and xanthippes. *Ibid.* 197 The mealy look of men today is the result of momism and so is the pinched and baffled fury in the eyes of womankind. **1947** *Sat. Rev.* (U.S.) 18 Jan. 19/2 Philip Wylie's latest diatribe about momism is welcome since it frankly implies that men have relinquished their duties as fathers. **1958** *Times Lit. Suppl.* 17 Oct. 595/1 The great *condottiere* of the lodes was a victim of 'momism'. His mother, it seems, made marriage impossible. **1962** R. E. Fitch *Odyssey of Self-Centred Self* iv. 129 We reject the Father God, and turn to Mother Nature. This is metaphysical Momism. **1968** 'E. V. Cunningham' *Cynthia* (1969) ix. 117 You never made a real pass at me. You suffer from reverse Momism.

momma (mǫ·mă). Add: Also **Momma.** (Earlier and later examples.) Also *attrib.* and *Comb.* Cf. *Mom.

1884 *Century Mag.* Apr. 859/1 This incident..illustrates the position of the 'momma' or 'mammy' in a Southern family in the olden time. **1929** *Amer. Speech* IV. 476 A final note may be added on the word *momma* 'negro nurse'. .. The term is associated with the negroes..but is not an example of negro dialect, but rather of American English. **1939** L. M. Montgomery *Anne of Ingleside* viii. 58 You're nothing but a sweet little girl. Momma's Pet! **1947** Auden *Age of Anxiety* (1948) v. 116 I've made their magic but their Momma Earth is His stone still. **1951** 'J. Wyndham' *Day of Triffids* ii. 43 How'd that be, Momma? **1960** G. W. Target *Teachers* 223 A real nice Yiddisher Momma. **1961** *John o' London's* 9 Nov. 519/2 Mommy is the all-American Momma-figure. **1970** G. Greer *Female Eunuch* 158 Baby-talk, even to the extent of calling..the wife 'momma'. **1972** M. J. Bosse *Incident at Naha* iii. 128 A real live trollop..the last of the red-hot mommas. **1972** *Times* 29 Sept. 20/6 How well we have seen the result of this [price-] battle in the position of the small retailer, affectionately known as the 'Momma and Poppa shop'. **1973** *Black World* Apr. 57 My momma always set more places than there was folks to eat.

momme. Add: Also with pronunc. (mǫ·me). Also 8 mome, momi. (Earlier and later examples.)

1727 J. G. Scheuchzer tr. *Kæmpfer's Hist. Japan* I. iv. vii. 349 The yearly value of the *Cobanj*..is from 55 to 59 *Mome*, or *Maas* in silver. *Ibid.* viii. 362 The highest value of the *Cobang*, as current in the country, is of sixty *Momi*, or *Maas*, of silver. **1902** L. Hearn *Kottō* vii. 58, I have already been able to put by about one hundred *mommé* of silver. **1965** *Economist* 25 Dec. 1432/1 We buy gold by the —tael in Shanghai; momme in Tokyo; tola in Karachi; hong ping tael in Macao; and kilogram in Kabul. **1974** S. Marcus *Minding the Store* (1975) ix. 184 This select 5% are not..our best customers, but..our most exacting ones. They know..the difference between a silk scarf made of twelve-momme weight and one made of sixteen-momme.

Mommy, mommy² (mǫ·mi). Chiefly *U.S.* Var. Mammy and Mummy *sb.*² Cf. *Mom, Momma.

1902 in *Dialect Notes* II. 239. **1974** Hawkey & Bingham *Wild Card* vi. 59 Mommy'll bring you a glass of water. **1975** *Listener* 18 Sept. 386/2 'You and Mommy are always with people,' she complains.

‖ **mompei, mompe** (mǫ·mpe). [Jap.] Baggy working trousers worn in Japan.

1947 J. Morris *Phoenix Cup* II. 24 Most of the women wear *mompei*, rather ugly baggy trousers normally worn only when working in the fields. **1959** R. K. Beardsley et al. *Village Japan* v. 101 For field work, women wear a surplice-cut blouse of dark cotton work cloth tucked into roomy, gathered-ankle field trousers (*mompei*) of similar material. **1960** B. Leach *Potter in Japan* v. 109 To keep moderately clean, I wear a pair of Hamada's 'mompei' (baggy overall trousers) and rubber boots. **1965** W. Swaan *Jap. Lantern* xix. 224 The bending figures in their *mompe* or baggy trousers. **1972** *Nat. Geographic* May 672/2 Groups of women in *mompe*, the traditional baggy work trousers worn in rural areas, shifted the seaweed by hand.

momser, momza, momzer, varr. *Mamzer.

Mon (mōᵘn), *sb.*² and *a.* Also **Moan, Mun, Mwun.** [Native name.] **A.** *sb.* A people of Indo-Chinese origin, also called *Talaing, now inhabiting eastern Burma and western Thailand but having their ancient capital at Pegu in southern Burma; a member of this people. Also, their language. **B.** *adj.* Of or pertaining to the Mon. Cf. *Mon-Khmer.

1798 F. Buchanan in *Asiatick Researches* V. 235 To the kingdom, the natives of which call themselves Moan, we have given the name of Pegu, a corruption of the vulgar appellation of its capital city Bagoo. **1828** J. Crawfurd *Jrnl. Embassy to Siam & Cochin China* xv. 448 Of the Mon, or Pegu, race, although the Siamese be in possession of no part of their territory, there are a considerable number in Siam. **1854** F. Mason in *Jrnl. Amer. Oriental Soc.* IV. 284 *Moan*, the name by which the Talaings now call themselves. **1873** *Jrnl. Asiatic Soc. Bengal* XLII. 34 The people of Pegu..call themselves Mun, Mwun, or Mon... The Burmese, since the conquest of Pegu..in 1757–58, had strongly discouraged the use of the Mun language. **1877** [see *Annamite *a.* and *sb.*]. **1881** C. J. F. S. Forbes *Compar. Gram. Languages of Further India* iv. 49 In three savage and more primitive dialects we find further traces of affinity with the Mon. **1907** V. C. S. O'Connor *Mandalay* IV. ii. 400 Under Binya Dala a strenuous effort was made by the Môn people to recover their ancient ascendency in Burma, and restore the glories of Pegu. **1939** L. H. Gray *Foundations of Lang.* xii. 393 *Mōn-Khmēr* has six sub-divisions: Central (Mōn or Talaing, Khmēr or Cambodian, Bahuar, etc.). *Ibid.* 394 The earliest Mōn inscription is of 1084 (?). **1948** D. Diringer *Alphabet* vii. 410 The early Mon character was not only the ancestor of the modern Mon script, but also of the Burmese and some Shan characters. **1962** *Listener* 25 Oct. 646/2 U Nu proposed to..create separate states for the Mon and Arakanese peoples. **1971** *National Geographic* Mar. 356 Masterpieces of lacquer ware... The craft may have originated in China and spread across Southeast Asia to the Mons, who brought the technique to the capital. **1972** W. B. Lockwood *Panorama Indo-Europ. Lang.* 228 The group [*sc.* Mon-Khmer] takes its name from two of its members: Mon, the vernacular of the coastal districts round the Gulf of Martaban between Rangoon and Moulmein, and Khmer or Cambodian, the state language of Cambodia.

mon³ (mʌn). Colloq. abbrev. of Money *sb.* See also *Mun.

1895 W. C. Gore in *Inlander* Nov. 64 *Mon*,..money. *a* **1911** D. G. Phillips *Susan Lenox* (1917) II. v. 119 In little old New York..you've got to have the mon. or you get..the swift, hard, kick. **1958** A. Wilson *Middle Age of Mrs. Eliot* II. 122 *I'm* only going because she's got lots of lovely 'mon' and might leave it to me. **1963** 'J. Bell' *Flat Tyre in Fulham* iii. 30 All that good 'mon' down the drain.

monact, *a.* and *sb.* (Examples.)

1885 tr. F. E. Schulze in *Rep. Sci. Results Voy. H.M.S. Challenger, Zool.* XXI. 29 It seems to me, however, that those spicules, called by Carter 'Clavulæ'..are really monacts. *Ibid.* 37 The derived nature of a monact spicule is in many cases determinable.

monad. Add: **2.** (Later examples.) Also *attrib.*

a **1914** C. S. Peirce *Coll. Papers* (1931) I. 146, I therefore divide all objects into monads, dyads, and triads; and the first step in the present inquiry is to ascertain what are the conceptions of the pure monad, free from all dyadic and triadic admixtures. *Ibid.* ii. 149 Now in order to convert that psychological or logical conception into a metaphysical one, we must think of a metaphysical monad as a pure nature, or quality, in itself without parts or features, and without embodiment. **1929** R. Bridges *Test. Beauty* i. 19 It was no flaw In Leibnitz to endow his monad-atoms with Mind. **1937** [see *Actio in distans]. **1965** *New Statesman* 18 June 942/2, I had been very impressed, wandering around housing estates, at the growth of what..seemed 'monad' politics... People didn't connect, except through mass media, but found images difficult to accept as reality.

monadic, *a.* Add: **1. b.** *Philos.* Of a proposition, fact, function, etc., or the predicate contained therein, when the predicate is non-relational and applies to only one subject term.

1897 C. S. Peirce in *Monist* VII. 167 A non-relative name with a substantive verb, as '—is a man',..has one blank; it is a *monad*, or *monadic relative*. **1921** W. E. Johnson *Logic* I. 203 The number of substantival references are respectively one, two, three and four, and the corresponding adjectives or propositions may be called monadic, diadic, triadic and tetradic. **1939** *Mind* XLVIII. 486 It appears sometimes to be assumed that the elementary statement must be monadic, *i.e.*, must have the form of a one-termed predicate, ϕx. **1946** C. Morris *Signs, Language & Behavior* iii. 78 'Black' is in this sense *monadic*... 'Deer' and 'black' are both monadic... But it would often be added that 'deer' designates an object and 'black' a quality of an object. **1956** J. O. Urmson *Philos. Analysis* ii. 17 A fact in which a particular has some absolutely simple and determinate characteristic was known as a monadic fact. **1963** W. W. Lambert in S. Koch *Psychol.* VI. 177 Most studies in general experimental psychology are carried out in terms of a monadic rather than a dyadic character. **1965** Hughes & Londey *Elem. of Formal Logic* xxxix. 274 Such a schema might contain only monadic predicate variables (e.g. 'fx ⊃ gy').

monadically, *adv.* (Later examples.)

1934 *Proc. Brit. Acad.* XIX. 71 Thus, Carnap holds, if we insist that protocol propositions must refer to content, then each protocol-language can be used only *monadically*. **1950** W. V. Quine *Methods of Logic* (1952) § 23. 130 A capital letter occurs monadically, i.e., with variables attached singly.

monadist (mǫ·nădist). Also **Monadist.** [f. Monad + -ist.] A follower of monadism; Leibniz himself.

1855 J. M. D. Meiklejohn tr. *Kant's Critique Pure Reason* 274/2 Against the assertion of the infinite subdivisibility of matter..objections have been alleged by the Monadists. **1900** B. Russell *Crit. Exposition Leibniz* § 78. 136 A Monadist must, with Leibniz, maintain the mutual independence of substances. **1932** *Mind* XLI. 518 Leibniz ..the great Monadist.

monadistic, *a.* Delete *rare* and add later examples.

1903 B. Russell *Princ. Math.* IV. xxvi. 221 Given, say, the proposition *aRb*, where *R* is some relation, the monadistic view will analyse this into two propositions.. ar_1 and br_2. **1917** A. S. Pringle-Pattison *Idea of God* ix. 179 On this monadistic theory, the organic vesture of the spirit and its environmental conditions are both resolved into innumerable quasi-spiritual centres. **1937** *Mind* XLVI. 275 He rejects a pantheist version of the Absolute in favour of a monadistic one. **1941** D. H. Parker *Experience & Substance* xvii. 348 The merits of a monadistic as opposed to a holistic interpretation of the 'wisdom of the body'.

monadnock (mǫ̆næ·dnǫk). *Geomorphol.* [The name of a mountain in New Hampshire, U.S.A., having this character.] A hill or mountain of erosion-resistant rock rising above a peneplain.

The place-name appears in Melville's *Moby Dick* (1851), 'his great, Monadnock hump'.

1893 W. M. Davis in *Nat. Geogr. Mag.* V. 70 The continuity of the plateau-like uplands [of New England] is interrupted in two ways; isolated mountains rise above it, and branching valleys sink below it. Mount Monadnock is a typical example of the former, with its bold summit more than a thousand feet above the surrounding plateau. .. It is simply an unconsumed remnant of the greater mass of unknown dimensions and form, from which the old lowland was carved... In my teaching, Monadnock has come to be recognized as an example of a distinct group of forms, and its name is used as having a generic value. A long paragraph of explanation is packed away when describing some other mountain as a 'monadnock' of greater or less height. **1900** J. E. Marr *Sci. Study Scenery* 147 The peneplain will be cut up by denudation, which may give rise to new hills, carved out of the plain, and marked at first by the possession of flat tops; to these Davis gives the name 'monadnocks'. **1935** *Geogr. Jrnl.* LXXXVI. 268 Only here and there a monadnock stands out distinctly, as for instance the Umanak Rifkol, which forms a landmark 900 feet high. **1947** Auden *Age of Anxiety* (1948) v. 108 O stiffly stand, a staid monadnock, On her peneplain. **1968** R. W. Fairbridge *Encycl. Geomorphol.* 709/1 Monadnocks may take the form of hills, ridges or ranges.

monadological (mǫ:nădolǫ·dʒikăl), *a.* [ad. G. *monadologisch*, F. *monadologique*: see -al.] Of or pertaining to monadology. So **monadolo·gically** *adv.*

1895 A. C. Armstrong tr. *Falckenberg's Hist. Mod. Philos.* vii. 278 Leibnitz's..monadological and harmonistic principles. **1897** C. H. Judd tr. *Wundt's Outl. Psychol.* 313 Matter is thought of as made up of similar [mental] atoms of a lower order (monistic, or monado-logical spiritualism). **1937** *Mind* XLVI. 503 Must we think, monadologically, of as many object worlds as there are knowing minds, though these many object worlds may have common features, in the sense of numerically diverse instances of the same universals? **1938** *Jrnl. Theol. Stud.* XXXIX. 427 It must be a matter for consideration how far it is of any profit to be familiar with (e.g.) Leibniz's monadological religious metaphysic without his doctrine of the judgement. **1943** M. Farber *Found. Phenomenology* xvi. 533 The objective world is 'innate' in the monadological world. **1957** R. Manheim tr. *Cassirer's Philos. Symbolic Forms* III. II. iv. 170 'Monadological' time is the πρότερον τῇ φύσει, and..we can only thence arrive at mathematical-physical time.

Monagasque, var. *Monégasque *sb.* and *a.*

Mona Lisa (mōᵘ·nă lī·ză). [It.] The name of a portrait painted by Leonardo da Vinci (1452–1519), used allusively and attrib. of an enigmatic smile or expression such as that of the woman in this painting. Also *fig.* See also *Gioconda.

1923 D. H. Lawrence *Birds, Beasts & Flowers* 162 She, smiling with goaty munch-mouth, Mona Lisa, arranges it so. **1930** J. Collier *His Monkey Wife* xiv. 197 She eyed Emily with what had been called, in her last year at school, her Mona Lisa smile. **1934** T. S. Eliot *Elizabethan Essays* 60 It [*sc.* *Hamlet*] is the 'Mona Lisa' of literature. **1950** A. Wilson *Such Darling Dodos* 59 She twisted her face into what she felt to be a more than usually Mona Lisa smile. **1967** J. Creasey *Famine* xii. 113 She stood in front of him with that half-smile, a Mona Lisa kind of inscrutability. **1975** G. Lyall *Judas Country* xxx. 215 Mitzi was looking at me with a little mousey Mona Lisa smile.

Mona marble (mōᵘ·nă). [f. *Mona*, Roman name for Anglesey + Marble *sb.*] A serpentine limestone from the metamorphic beds of the island of Anglesey, off the N. coast of Wales.

1816 *Repository of Arts* (Ackermann) Oct. 243 (*heading*) Mona marble chimney-piece. *Ibid.* 244/2 The beautifully

variegated tints of the mona marble. **1911** *Encycl. Brit.* XVII. 677/1 Mona marble is an ophicalcite from the metamorphic series of the Isle of Anglesey. **1971** *Country Life* 6 May 1089/1 'A chaste and elegant structure of Mona Marble', inscribed in Latin and Welsh.

‖ **mon ami** (mon ami). Also fem. **mon amie.** [Fr.] 'My friend', as a term of address.

1786 W. Cowper *Let.* 31 Aug. (1904) III. 93 Adieu, *mon ami*, yours faithfully, W.C. **1856** *Newsp. & Gen. Reader's Pocket Compan.* II. § 1564 All in good time *mon ami*—all in good time. *Ibid.* § 1788 Throughout the journal she is designated emphatically as *mon amie.* **1896** C. M. Yonge *Release* II. ii. 95 'Are you speaking of Beaudésert, *mon amie?*' said M. de Nidemerle. **1911** 'I. Hay' *Safety Match* xv. 236 Flirtation is a crooked business, and you are straight, *mon amie.* **1966** A. Christie *Third Girl* xxi. 216 'I was quite sure she *wouldn't* walk out on me.' 'Ah yes. And then, *mon ami*, she did.' **1973** 'A. Hall' *Tango Briefing* vi. 72 The desert is different from other places, *mon ami.*

monamine. Substitute for def.: = *monoamine. Add further examples.

1943 Sumner & Somers *Chem. & Methods of Enzymes* xv. 269 It is probable that all of these enzymes are one and the same... The most suitable name for the enzyme would be 'monamine oxidase'. **1969** *Times* 21 Feb. 10/7 The patients were receiving anti-depressant drugs known as monamine oxidase inhibitors. **1973** *Sci. Amer.* Sept. 121/1 It was also discovered that iproniazid acted to inhibit the enzyme monamine oxidase. (Monamines, such as serotonin, norepinephrine and dopamine, are believed to act as chemical transmitters between nerve cells in the brain.)

monarch, *sb.*[1] Add: **3.** In full, *monarch butterfly.* Substitute '*Danaus*' for '*Danais*' in def. (Earlier and later examples.)

1890 Hyatt & Arms *Insecta* 186 The monarch or milkweed butterfly..is abundant during July and August wherever the milk-weed grows. **1945** E. B. Ford *Butterflies* i. 23 The Milkweed, Monarch, or Black-veined Brown Butterfly, *Danaus plexippus*... The first specimen [in Britain] was caught by Mr. J. Stafford at Neath, South Wales, on September 6th, 1876. **1974** A. Dillard *Pilgrim at Tinker Creek* xiv. 252 Each monarch butterfly had a brittle black body and deep orange wings limned and looped in black bands. A monarch at rest looks like a fleck of tiger. **1975** *Country Life* 20 Feb. 450/1 The magnificent black-veined brown or monarch butterfly, that rare migrant to Britain.

monarch, var. *moniker.

monarcho- (mǫnā·ɹko), comb. f. Monarchic *a.*, esp. in *monarcho-fascist*, in Communist phraseology, of a fascist form of government with a king as titular head of state, such as that established in Greece after the war of 1939–45.

1947 *Times* 10 May 3/5 Marcos speaks of the 'Monarcho-Fascist régime of the British occupation'... He refers further to the 'Greek Monarcho-Fascist forces' who collaborated with the occupation forces. **1950** R. Leeper *When Greek meets Greek* xii. 195 Our critics on the Left had got so much into the habit of denouncing us as reactionaries (I myself was generally dubbed a monarcho-fascist) that perhaps they had come to believe it. **1966** *Economist* 27 Aug. 809 Aeschylus expounds what would sound today like 'monarcho-fascist' theories. **1971** W. H. McNeill in A. Bullock *20th Century* 51/2 A new guerilla movement..claimed to represent the democratic will of the Greek people against the 'monarcho-fascist' regime.

monarda. Read: (monā·ɹdă). Also 8 **monardus.** [mod.L. (Linnæus *Hortus Cliffortianus* (1737) 11), f. the name of Nicolas Monardes (1493–1588), Spanish physician and botanist, one of the earliest writers on American plants.] An aromatic herb of the North American genus so called, belonging to the family Labiatæ, esp. *Monarda didyma*, which has bright red flowers and is also called bergamot, bee balm, or Oswego tea.

1712 [in Dict.]. **1789** W. Aiton *Hortus Kewensis* I. 36 Scarlet Monarda or Oswego-tea. **1865** [in Dict.]. **1931** M. Grieve *Modern Herbal* I. 95/1 Another American swamp plant... *M[onarda] didyma*, the Scarlet Monarda, is said to yield an oil of similar composition [to that of thymol]. **1970** C. Lloyd *Well-Tempered Garden* i. 45 For plants of an intricately branching habit like *Aster acris, Salvia superba*, or monardas, peasticks are ideal [support]. **1974** A. Scott-James *Sissinghurst* xiv. 149 A charming lilac-pink monarda called Beauty of Cobham.

-monas [a. Gr. μονάς: see Monad], an ending of some mod.L. names of genera of simple organisms (chiefly bacteria, protozoa, and algæ): cf. *chlamydomonas, *leptomonas.

Monastral (mǫnæ·străl). The proprietary name of two groups of pigments having exceptional fastness: (*a*) blue and green pigments that are derivatives of phthalocyanine and are widely used esp. in paints, printing inks, and plastics; *spec.* copper phthalocyanine (Monastral Fast Blue B, or BS); (*b*) red and violet pigments that are derivatives of quinacridone.

1936 *Trade Marks Jrnl.* 2 Jan. 2/2 Monastral... All goods included in Class 1, but not including chemical photographic developers and not including any goods of a like kind to chemical photographic developers. British Dyestuffs Corporation Limited, Imperial Chemical House,..London,..manufacturers. **1936** *Discovery* Jan. 2/1 A new blue pigment, which combines fastness to light, heat, acids and alkalis with tinctorial strength, has recently been introduced by Imperial Chemical Industries, Ltd. Known as Monastral Fast Blue BS. **1952** K. Venkataraman *Chem. Synthetic Dyes* II. xxxvii. 1133 There are only three [phthalocyanine derivatives] which are extensively used for coloring printing inks, paints, varnishes, enamels, plastics, and other materials. These are metal-free phthalocyanine (Monastral Fast Blue G, ICI), copper phthalocyanine (Monastral Fast Blue B) and highly chlorinated copper phthalocyanine (Monastral Fast Green G). **1958** *Times* 4 Dec. 3/2 Some series of squares [of mosaic] were made to order in a precise shade of colour indicated by Mr. Piper himself, a rich monastral blue and a delicate pale yellow being examples. **1961** H. F. Payne *Org. Coating Technol.* II. xx. 904 At present a family of three distinctly different pigment colors is commercially available, namely: Monastral Red B: a dark, transparent, blue-shade red toner; Monastral Red Y: a yellow-shade red toner, lighter and more opaque in mass tone than red B; Monastral Violet R: a dark, transparent, red-shade violet toner. **1970** *Sunday Times* (Colour Suppl.) 22 Nov. 69/4 Monastral Blue, an incredibly powerful synthetic pigment of fairly recent origin..is sold under.. different names: Windsor Blue, Phthalocyanine Blue.

monaural, *a.* Add: (Further examples.)

1935 *Brit. Jrnl. Psychol.* XXV. 270 Differences in the time of arrival of sounds from a single source at the two ears, or differences in intensity,..are far smaller than the monaural or binaural thresholds for such time or intensity differences. **1955** *Sci. News Let.* 24 Sept. 204/3 Splitting sounds so that one ear hears it first is known as 'monaural delay'. Its use by the Air Force and airlines promises better and clearer communications in the air. **1972** L. A. Jeffress in J. V. Tobias *Found. Mod. Auditory Theory* II. ix. 360 The case where the noise is binaural and in phase at the ears and the signal is monaural..is an interesting one.

2. = *monophonic *a.* 2.

1931 *Jrnl. Acoustical Soc. Amer.* Apr. 483 The fundamental difficulty is that we are at present restricted to monaural recording. **1948** *Electronics* Aug. 88/2 A person listening to sound through a binaural system has the illusion that the sound originates in the room rather than in the [head]phones. The effect is striking to anyone used to hearing monaural sound from a headset. **1951** *Wireless World* Mar. 85/1 Current radio broadcast and recording techniques are almost exclusively monaural, using a single microphone and transmission channel. **1959** *Sci. News* LIII. 57 A discerning listener could never be deceived into believing that even the best monaural reproduction was an original performance. **1964** P. J. Guy *Disc Recording* x. 148 Two loudspeakers are better than one, even for monaural reproduction. **1968** *Times* 29 Nov. p. iv/7 In July, 1967, E.M.I. ceased to produce new classical recordings in the monaural form. **1970** [see *monophonic *a.* 2]. **1971** M. McCarthy *Birds of America* 212 Their gramophone and scratched monaural-78 records. **1974** *Encycl. Brit. Macropædia* XVII. 53/2 Stereophonic systems..produce a far greater sense of realism than single-channel (or monaural) systems.

monaurally (mǫnǭ·răli), *adv.* [f. prec. + -ly[2].] **a.** With or to one ear.

1933 *Jrnl. Acoustical Soc. Amer.* IV. 288 The observer is placed in a sound field which is substantially that of a plane progressive wave, facing the source and listening monaurally. **1948** *Psychol. Bull.* XLV. 194 He observed that a sound heard binaurally was always louder than the same sound heard monaurally. **1972** N. I. Durlach in J. V. Tobias *Found. Mod. Auditory Theory* II. x. 385 The tone is presented monaurally.

b. In a monaural (monophonic) manner; = *monophonically *adv.* b.

1958 *Manch. Guardian* 30 June 5/3 Dvořák's Fourth Symphony is first played through one speaker, then monaurally through both, and finally stereophonically through both. **1964** P. J. Guy *Disc Recording* x. 147 It was the original aim of the record manufacturers to make stereophonic records playable monaurally with an ordinary pickup.

monbar, var. *mimbar.

Monbazillac (‖ moṅbaziyak, mǫnbæ·zilæk). Also **Mont Bazillac, Montbazillac.** [Name of a village south of Bergerac in the Dordogne department of S.W. France.] A sweet, white dessert wine, similar to Sauternes.

[**1833** C. Redding *Mod. Wines* v. 158 The best wines are produced on the hills, upon the left bank of the Dordogne, in the communes of St. Laurent and Monbazillac.] *Ibid.* 404/2 (*index of wines*) Mont Basillac, 158. **1926** P. M. Shand *Bk. Wine* v. 66 Montbazillac..is a label still met, which prepares one for a rich, sweet white wine that is made from the Sémillon grape. **1935** C. W. Berry *In Search of Wine* viii. 186 We then had a bottle of 1918 Monbazillac—a trifle sweet for me. **1955** J. Thomas *No Banners* v. 39 A bottle of Montbazillac stood on the little table between their chairs. **1967** A. Lichine *Encycl. Wines* 131/2 With one exception—sweet, white Monbazillac—the wines of Bergerac are simply not in the same class [as those of Bordeaux]. **1975** *Times* 17 May 11 Montbazillac is made with grapes that have been subjected to the action of *botrytis cinerea* or 'noble rot'.

‖ **mon cher** (moṅ ʃę̄r). [Fr.] 'My dear fellow', as a term of address.

1680 Rochester *Poems* 24 But now Moncher, dear Pug, says she, adieu. **1888** 'Rita' *Vivienne* I. ii. 23 Good bye, *mon cher*, and don't overwork yourself. **1920** F. M. Ford *Let.* 30 May (1965) 100 You see, mon cher, there are plenty of other people..with the temperament of poets. **1975** A. Christie *Poirot's Last Case* xv. 162 So far, *mon cher*, this X has operated with so much ability that he has defeated me, Hercule Poirot!

monchiquite (mǫntʃī·kwəit). *Petrogr.* [a. G. *monchiquite* (Hunter & Rosenbusch 1890, in *Tschermak's mineral. u. petrograph. Mittheilungen* XI. 447), f. Serra de *Monchique*, name of a mountain range in southern Portugal where such a rock is found: see -ite[1].] A lamprophyre containing small phenocrysts of olivine and augite, and usu. also biotite or an amphibole, in a glassy ground-mass consisting of or containing analcite.

1891 *Ann. Rep. Arkansas Geol. Survey 1890* II. iv. 110 The Brazilian dikes..form an olivine-free class of the rock that Rosenbusch calls monchiquite. **1896** *Jrnl. Geol.* IV. 679 (*heading*) On the monchiquites or analcite group of igneous rocks. **1961** [see *camptonite]. **1965** [see *ferroan *a.*].

Mond (mǫnd). The name of Ludwig *Mond* (1839–1909), German-born British chemist, used *attrib.* to designate processes devised by him and the plant and products of these processes, esp. (*a*) a method of manufacturing producer gas by passing air and an excess of steam into a gas producer so that most of the nitrogen of the coal is converted into ammonia and can be recovered; (*b*) a process for obtaining high-purity nickel by decomposing by heat the volatile nickel carbonyl, which is obtained from crude nickel oxide by reduction with hydrogen followed by reaction with carbon monoxide.

1887 *Encycl. Brit.* XXII. 244/1 The Mond process, of all the many sulphur-recovery processes yet introduced, is the best. **1903** *Jrnl. Franklin Inst.* CLV. 390 The success of the Mond nickel process, as carried on in England, has been seriously hindered by the discovery that the process is dangerous to the health of the men employed. **1907** E. L. Rhead *Metallurgy* (new ed.) vi. 76 Mond gas is generated by passing into the producer air containing the maximum amount of water vapour that the heat produced is capable of decomposing. **1936** Bone & Himus *Coal* xxiv. 424 The trades using Mond Gas are diverse, including.. manufacture of motor cars and component parts, foundries.., chemical works, [etc.]. **1946** J. R. Partington *Gen. & Inorg. Chem.* xvii. 485 Mond gas is formed with a large excess of steam which keeps the temperature low. **1947** G. W. Himus *Elements Fuel Technol.* xv. 324 A number of Mond plants were installed and found to be economic. **1969** H. T. Evans tr. *Hägg's Gen. & Inorg. Chem.* xxxiv. 727 In the so-called Mond process a very fine powder is desired, and the reduction is done with water gas at 350–400°C.

‖ **mondaine** (moṅdę̄n), *sb.* (and *a.*). [F. *mondaine*, f. *mondain* worldly, ad. L. *mundānus*, f. *mundus* world: cf. Mundane *a.* (*sb.*)] A woman belonging to fashionable society. Also **mondain** (moṅdæn), a man belonging to fashionable society.

1888 Mrs. H. Ward *R. Elsmere* II. iv. xxvi. 285 He was in a mood to be impatient with a *mondaine's* languid inquiries into clerical work. **1889** E. Dowson *Let.* 24 Mar. (1967) 55 Here you have the refinement of the mondaine with the independence of the cocotte. **1902** [see *etiquette 4]. **1906** B. von Hutten *What became of Pam* xii. 192 He was a dandy and a *mondain*, who..had never done anything noteworthy. **1908** *Westm. Gaz.* 3 Oct. 13/2 The bold attempt of the milliners to coax mondaines to the smaller hat will be watched with interest. **1912** *Tatler* 23 Oct. p. vi (Advt.), Not only have the requirements of the smart mondaine been carefully considered but [etc.]. **1920** A. Huxley *Let.* 4 May (1969) 185 Cocteau is a man of fabulous cleverness, but not serious—He is just a mondain. **1920** *Q. Rev.* July 38 The provocative elegance of the Flavian *mondaines.* **1924** *Public Opinion* 7 Nov. 458/2 She was in point of fact a most accomplished mondaine. **1970** G. Greer *Female Eunuch* 266 Flatly contemptuous words like *kept-woman* and *call-girl* have taken over.. from..*courtesan, mondaine.*

b. *adj.* Attached to things of the world; worldly.

1889 E. Dowson *Let.* c 11 Jan. (1967) 23, I will free myself from the intolerable *corvée* of the *mondain* dinner. **1896** C. M. Yonge *Release* II. viii. 144 Ah! you are *mondaine*, you are Protestant, madame. **1927** H. Nicolson *Some People* 88 When I got to bed I realised that by 'worldly' he had meant 'mondaine'. **1929** L. Rea *Six Mrs. Greenes* II. 58 Lavinia, mondaine, vivid, with a delicate certainty of touch that enabled her [etc.]. **1962** *Listener* 24 May 920/3 His pleasure in the company of children and simple people—as opposed to *mondain* people.

mondanity, var. Mundanity.

1911 Mrs. H. Ward *Case of Richard Meynell* xii. 242 With her grey hair, and her plain widow's dress, she threw her sister's charming mondanity into bright relief.

Monday. Add: **3. Monday Club,** a right-wing Conservative club (cf. Club *sb.* 13) that originally held its meetings on Mondays; so **Monday-clubber,** a member of this club; **Monday-morning** *attrib.*, suggestive of lethargy

or disinclination after a busy or eventful weekend; *Monday pop* (earlier example).

1962 *Evening Standard* 12 Feb. 6 (*caption to cartoon*), Lord Salisbury has become patron of the 'Monday Club', a new group of Young Conservatives formed to 'keep the Conservative Party Conservative'. **1966** *Observer* 16 Oct. 12/5 To dismiss them simply as acts of political vengeance or as another example of 'African savagery' is Monday Club mumbo-jumbo. **1970** G. K. ROBERTS *Political Parties & Pressure Groups in Britain* i. 9 Pressure-groups *within* political parties... Recent examples in Britain are: ..the Monday Club, which tries to maintain what it chooses to regard as the basic principles of Conservatism. **1972** R. COPPING *Story of Monday Club* 5 Rebelling against Macmillan's 'Winds of Change' speech a tiny group of young conservative dissentients formed the Monday Club on 1st January 1961. **1973** *Times* 20 June 4/3 The executive of the Monday Club, the right-wing Conservative pressure group, decided last night..to expel the Essex branch of the club for its associations with the National Front. **1973** *Guardian* 27 June 1/3 Mr Enoch Powell.. banned reporters from a Monday Club meeting last night. **1972** *Times* 21 July 12/1 His successful conservative opponent, the Monday Clubber, Harold Soref. **1921** D. H. LAWRENCE *Sea & Sardinia* 261 The rather inert, narrow, Monday-morning street. **1938** R. G. COLLINGWOOD *Princ. Art* v. 95, I get back to my book with that Monday-morning feeling. **1862** Monday pop [see POP *sb.*[4]].

mondial, *a.* Restrict † *Obs.* to sense in Dict. and add: **2.** [ad. mod. F. *mondial.*] Pertaining to, affecting, or involving the whole world; world-wide, universal. Hence **mondializa·tion.**

[**1918** A. GRAY tr. *Grelling's Crime* II. iii. 175 While in this question Germany could accept the system *individuel* she could not accept the system *mondial.*] **1919** S. HUDDLESTON *Peace Making at Paris* i. 10 Chaos threatened, with the black night of a mondial revolution. **1920** *Glasgow Herald* 28 June 8 The codification of mondial commercial laws is also aimed at. **1924** *Blackw. Mag.* Aug. 280/2 They were resolved to create their 'mondial situation', and to strengthen it..against the English. **1960** R. CARPENTER *Greek Sculpture* viii. 213 Be it hoped without consequent detriment to its mondial reputation. **1961** *Economist* 11 Nov. 528/1 A vast extension of the common market—a '*mondialisation*' to use the latest jargon. **1962** *Spectator* 5 Oct. 495 Chiding the French for their fear of *mondialisation.* **1965** *New Scientist* 2 Sept. 544/1 Perhaps this capitalist-sounding manœuvre towards the 'mondialization' of a natural resource will appeal to the Afro-Asian bloc at the UN.

‖ **mon Dieu** (mon̄ dyö). [Fr.] = *My God!* (cf. GOD 7).

1768 STERNE *Sent. Journey* I. 57 The poor monk blush'd ..*Mon Dieu!* said he..you never used me unkindly. **1849** THACKERAY *Pendennis* I. viii. 80 'You may come and live down here—down here, *mon Dieu!* for ever' (said the Major, with a dreary shrug, as he thought..of Pall Mall). **1861** G. MEREDITH *Let.* 19 Nov. (1970) I. 113, I had, the truth is, a miserable walking companion; to wit, Buonaparte Wyse (son of the Minister at Athens, who will hardly own him), and of Mde Bon[aparte] Wyse (Lucien's daughter), whom he will hardly own... Mon Dieu! **1945** 'O. MALET' *My Bird Sings* I. vi. 43 *Mon dieu!* But nobody answers. **1964** *Guardian* 10 Oct. 5/4 We eat, *mon dieu,* how we eat! **1974** P. HIGHSMITH *Ripley's Game* ii. 17 *Mon dieu!*—Well, where did *he* hear it from?

Mondism (mǫ·ndiz'm). [f. the name of Alfred *Mond* (1868–1930), British politician.] The views of A. Mond, especially his advocacy of co-ordination and co-operation as bases of industrial enterprise.

1917 F. M. FORD *Let.* 5 Jan. (1965) 82 What a Ministry! Everything one has fought against all one's life. Northcliffism,.. Mondism, Balliolism! **1928** *Daily Tel.* 10 July 10 After further disorder Mr. Cook was called upon. He attacked 'Mondism', which he declared was the infant of Fascism and should be killed at birth. **1962** T. L. JOHNSTON *Collective Bargaining in Sweden* vii. 169 This labour peace conference is usually referred to as the Swedish attempt at Mondism.

‖ **mondo** (mǫ·ndo). [Jap., f. *mon* asking + *do* answering.] An instructional technique of Zen Buddhism consisting of rapid dialogue of questions and answers between master and pupil.

1927 D. T. SUZUKI *Essays in Zen Buddhism* I. vi. 256 The following 'mondo' or dialogue (literally questioning and answering) will give us a glimpse into the ways of Zen. **1960** KOESTLER *Lotus & Robot* x. 233 In its mondos and koans, Japanese ambiguity reaches its metaphysical peak. **1961** *Times Lit. Suppl.* 17 Feb. 8/3 Perhaps the most significant part of its [*sc.* a book's] contribution consists in its argument..that the zen *mondo* are full of direct, coherent, systematic and intelligible communication.

Mondrian (mǫ·ndriăn), *a.* [f. the name of P. C. ('Piet') *Mondrian, Mondriaan* (1872–1944), Dutch painter.] Resembling the geometrical abstract style of Mondrian.

1958 *Listener* 27 Nov. 888/1 A Mondrian scheme of simple primary colors. **1963** *Times* 30 Apr. 15/5 The Mondriaan-like luminous coloured panels.

Monégasque (monegask), *sb.* and *a.* Also **Monegasque.** [Fr.] **A.** *sb.* A native or inhabitant of Monaco. **B.** *adj.* Belonging to or characteristic of Monaco or its inhabitants.

1882 T. H. PICKERING *Monaco* i. 11 That which may be, and is, done in Riviera towns,..is impossible in the Monégasque metropolis on the Mediterranean. *Ibid.* vi. 96 Three harvests of four different products make up a total, according to Monégasque arithmetic, of twelve crops. *Ibid.* iii. 59 The Monégasques enjoy the privilege of being governed—and well governed—without being called upon to contribute in any way towards the expenses. **1926** MUIRHEAD & MONMARCHÉ *Southern France* 196 The inhabitants ('Monégasques') are forbidden access to the gaming tables. **1938** H. G. WELLS *Apropos of Dolores* iii. 88 She was really Monégasque. **1962** *Listener* 3 May 761/1 The population [of Monaco] is 23,000, but only 3,000 of them are real Monégasques. **1966** G. GREENE *Comedians* iii. 64, I am uncertain whether she was French—perhaps she was a rare Monegasque. **1966** S. ROSSITER *South of France* 162 The inhabitants ('Monégasques')..enjoy immunity from taxation. *Ibid.* 167 A joint-stock company, which pays an annual tribute to the Monégasque government for its 'concession' of the gambling monopoly. **1968** *Guardian* 5 Jan. 6/6 Installed as manager is Georges Penna, a Monegasque of Italian parentage. **1973** *Daily Tel.* 19 Mar. 3/2 In 1958 there was more publicity when Prince Rainier banned them from Monaco after Lady Docker tore up a paper Monégasque flag.

monekeer, monekur, varr. *MONIKER.

Monel (mōu·nĕl). Also **monel.** [(Altered form of) the name of Ambrose *Monell* (d. 1921), president of the International Nickel Company when that firm introduced the alloys.] Used as a proprietary name (usu. *attrib.*) to denote alloys composed of about 68 per cent nickel and 30 per cent copper with small amounts of other elements, which have a high tensile strength and good resistance to corrosion, particularly towards sea-water.

1909 *Trade Marks Jrnl.* 17 Feb. 286 Monel Metal... Metal alloy. International Nickel Company.., Manhattan, New York, U.S.A. **1918** *Chambers's Jrnl.* Mar. 207/1 These discs are made of monel metal. **1945** *Electronic Engin.* XVII. 384 Electrodes on the instrument consist of Monel metal cores which do not corrode in saline solution. **1970** *Motor Boat & Yachting* 16 Oct. 49/2 The original iron fastenings have been superseded by monel fastenings. **1970** W. J. PATTON *Mod. Manufacturing Processes* iv. 54 Nickel and the monels are too soft and ductile to be readily machinable, but a more machinable monel is available in R Monel (Monel R–405), containing 66% nickel, 31·5% copper, and 0·05% sulfur. **1972** T. P. MCMAHON *Issue of Bishop's Blood* (1973) xiii. 191, I was shuddering at what Meredith was going to charge. He's got a thing about always using Monel metal on what he calls 'furnishings'.

monellin (mǫ·nĕlin). *Chem.* [f. the name of the *Monell* Chemical Senses Center, in Philadelphia, U.S.A., where it was first isolated + -IN[1].] A protein with a sweet taste isolated from the berries of the tropical plant *Dioscoreophyllum cumminsii.*

1972 MORRIS & CAGAN in *Biochim. & Biophys. Acta* CCLXI. 114 We propose the name 'monellin' for the sweet material we have isolated. **1972** *Daily Colonist* (Victoria, B.C.) 27 Feb. 25/6 [Scientists] had isolated a new, low-calorie sweetener said to be 3,000 times more intense by weight than sugar. Named 'Monellin' the product is derived from a wild red berry that grows abundantly in tropical West Africa. **1973** *Nature* 27 July 196/3 Both thaumatin and monellin exhibit sweetness to a prodigious degree.

moneme (mǫ·nīm). *Linguistics.* [a. F. *monème,* f. MON(O- + *-EME.] In the terminology of some linguists, the smallest meaningful unit of language: = *MORPHEME.

1953 C. E. BAZELL *Linguistic Form* i. 9 In the modern school of Geneva,..there is a tendency to use the otherwise unknown term *moneme* for the American *morph.* **1960** H. MARCHAND *Categories Present-Day Eng. Word-Formation* x. 367 The result of blending is, indeed, always a moneme, i.e. an unanalysable, simple word, not a motivated syntagma. **1960** A. MARTINET in *Word* XVI. 4 Minimal meaningful units..have sometimes been called 'morphemes'... I will rather use..*moneme,* which has been used with that meaning by some linguists of the Geneva school. **1968** J. W. F. MULDER *Sets & Relations in Phonology* i. 47 The phonological features..do not represent moneme expressions, i.e. they are..not distinctive on the grammatical level. **1970** *English Studies* LI. 446 It is noteworthy that Anglian *ald* often becomes *old* (in *o*-areas) in ME nicknames like *Oldman* but not in Christian names like *Aldith, Aldred* etc. which are somewhat fossilized and no longer associated with the moneme. **1970** G. C. LEPSCHY *Survey of Structural Linguistics* vi. 106 A linguistic utterance undergoes a first articulation into monemes, which are the elementary grammatical units corresponding to what American linguists call morphemes.

monenergist, monenergistic, *a.*: the more correct forms of MONERGIST, MONERGISTIC *a.* (see s.v. MONERGISM).

1915 *Encycl. Relig. & Ethics* VIII. 821/2 The Monenergistic or Monothelete controversy seems at first glance to be a mere sequel to the Monophysite conflict. *Ibid.* 822/1 The Monenergists were possessed with the idea that the redemptive activity of the God-man emanated wholly and solely from His divine nature.

monetarism (mǫ·n-, mɒ·nĭtăriz'm). [f. MONETARY *a.* + -ISM.] The economic doctrine or theory of a monetarist or of monetarists.

1969 *Newsweek* 6 Jan. 48 The combination of Stansian horse-and-buggy finance with Friedmanian go-go monetarism. **1970** *Times* 13 Mar. 10 The lecture was a full-blooded onslaught on 'the new monetarism', the doctrines of the Chicago school of economists led by the celebrated Professor Milton Friedman. **1971** *Times* 2 Aug. 13/4 Professor Paul Samuelson..describes monetarism as a disease and defines it as a 'pathological belief..that only the rate of growth of the money supply can affect significantly the rate of inflation or the level of unemployment'. **1971** *Sunday Times* 8 Aug. 4 Monetarism, the belief that the state of the economy can be decisively manipulated through regulating the flow of money, became an accepted cult in the White House after Dr Burns had left it to assume the chairmanship of the Federal Reserve Board. **1975** *Times* 28 Aug. 24/5 The Treasury['s] ..distrust of 'monetarism' arises from a belief that it has only one equation, that which links the money supply and the money national income.

monetarist (mǫ·n-, mɒ·nĭtărist), *a.* and *sb.* [f. MONETARY *a.* + -IST.] **A.** *adj.* Of a monetary character or having a monetary basis.

1914 GEDDES & THOMSON *Sex* x. 239 This order of things—avowedly mechanical, militarist, and monetarist at best,..seems to many of us..the only possible form of industrial civilisation. **1971** *Times* 2 Aug. 13/4 The father of the current monetarist school of economic thought. **1972** *Times* 6 Dec. 22/8 The distinctive monetarist assertion is that inflation is attributable solely to increase in the money supply. **1973** *Times* 16 Aug. 15/2 It is not..true —even in terms of the monetarist theories on which Mr Powell relies—that the Government deficit uniquely determines the money supply. **1974** *Financial Times* 21 Oct. 16/8 The basic argument of the sadly mislabelled 'monetarist' school is that attempts by monetary and fiscal stimulation to lower the level of unemployment below a sustainable minimum, determined by underlying forces, will not bring about a lasting drop in the level of unemployment.

B. *sb.* One who places emphasis on monetary matters, *spec.* one who advocates tighter control of the money supply as an important remedy for inflation.

1963 *Economist* 27 Apr. 299/2 To control inflation by curtailment, as prescribed by the 'monetarists'. **1965** *Ibid.* 25 Sept. p. xxiv/1 The main battle was between the 'monetarists' (who..believe that screwing down the money supply is always the answer to inflations of any sort) and the 'structuralists'. **1971** *Daily Tel.* 25 Jan. 12/2 It is argued by monetarists that lower rates of interest would contribute to inflation. **1971** *Times* 2 Aug. 13/4 In a highly controversial article in today's *Washington Post* influential monetarists in the United States are compared to water diviners.

Hence **monetari·stic** *a.*

1972 *Publishers' Weekly* 6 Mar. 60/1 Nixon's two-and-a-half-year dalliance with laissez-faire and the monetaristic theories of Milton Friedman.

monetary, *a.* **2.** (Later examples.)

1936 J. M. KEYNES *Gen. Theory Employment* xv. 203 A monetary policy which strikes public opinion as being experimental in character or easily liable to change may fail in its objective. **1944**, etc. [see *International Monetary Fund* s.v. *INTERNATIONAL *a.* 2]. **1951** R. FIRTH *Elements of Social Organization* iv. 142 Even where monetary rewards for labour are largely current, he has noted that work may be undertaken for other than money symbols. **1961** *Ann. Reg. 1960* 475 The measures ranged from the traditional restraints to a new and previously untried monetary instrument. **1973** *Times* 6 July 17/1 The 'Smithsonian' agreement, which President Nixon characterized ..as 'the most significant monetary agreement in the history of the world'.

monetite (mōu·nĕtəit). *Min.* [f. *Moneta,* name of a small island near Puerto Rico: see -ITE[1].] A hydrogen phosphate of calcium, $CaH(PO_4)$, occurring as translucent, pale yellowish white crystals.

1882 C. U. SHEPARD in *Amer. Jrnl. Sci.* CXXIII. 400 The Moneta mineral, which we call monetite from its locality, is accompanied by two other species. **1968** I. KOSTOV *Mineral.* 458 Monetite and stercorite are triclinic.

money, *sb.* Add: **3. e.** Wages, salary; one's pay.

1887 PARISH & SHAW *Dict. Kentish Dial.* 103 He's getting good money, I reckon. **1916** G. B. SHAW *Pygmalion* II. 143 His proper trade's a navvy; and he works at it sometimes..and earns good money at it. **1920** E. O'NEILL *Beyond the Horizon* II. i. 85 If that's the case, you can go to the devil... You'll get your money tomorrow when I get back from town. **1963** H. GARNER in R. Weaver *Canad. Short Stories* (1968) 2nd Ser. 45 Nobody really liked working for Malloy-Harrison, but the money was better than most places.

5. big money: see *BIG *a.* B. 2; **dirty money:** see *DIRTY *a.* 6 b.

6. a. (Further examples.)

1611 BIBLE *I Tim.* vi. 10 The loue of money is the root of all euill. *c* **1645** [see FOOL *sb.*[1] 1 d]. **1681** A. BEHN *Rover* II. III. i. 43 Money speaks sense in a Language all Nations understand. **1748** B. FRANKLIN *Advice to Young Tradesman* in *Writings* (1905) II. 371 Remember that *time* is money. **1845** C. LEVER *Let.* in L. Stevenson *Dr. Quicksilver* (1939) ix. 149 You have paid your money, and you may take your choice. **1846** *Punch* 3 Jan. 17 (*caption*) You pays your money, and you takes your choice. **1853** T. T. LYNCH *Lect. Self Improvement* v. 113 Money is power —power for bread and power for tinsel. **1898** G. B. SHAW *Arms & Man* II. III. 57 A twenty leva bill! Sergius gave me that, out of pure swagger. A fool and his money are soon parted. **1903** *Sat. Even. Post* 5 Sept. 12/1 When

money talks it often merely remarks 'Good-by'. **1905** 'O. Henry' in *N.Y. World Mag.* 12 Nov. 8/1 Money talks. But you may think that the conversation of a little old ten-dollar bill in New York would be nothing more than a whisper. **1927** E. O'Neill *Marco Millions* I. ii. 36 He'll have time enough for that, but with us time is money. *Ibid.* iii. 44 Money isn't everything, not always. **1930** G. B. Means *Strange Death of President Harding* iv. 72 One can do nothing—be nothing, without money, not even in the White House. Money is power. **1952** W. G. Hardy *Unfulfilled* 199 Money isn't everything. **1956** A. Wilson *Anglo-Saxon Attitudes* II. ii. 277 Yeah, he's on the Market... You know the sort of stuff. Money talks and so on. **1965** *Times* 14 July 8/4 In the Government today were known supporters of C.N.D. Why? Because the Prime Minister put them there. Why? Because he shared their views? Because it was expedient to do so? Because he was practising some duplicity? Why? 'You pays your money and you takes your choice.'

b. *for my money* (earlier and later examples); also, in my opinion; *to have a run for one's money*: see Run *sb.*[1] 1 d.

1549 [see Go *v.* 24 b]. **1566** E. H. tr. *Erasmus's Diuersoria* sig. B2ᵛ This behauiour doth well beseme Frenchmen peraduenture, how be it the fashions of Duche lande shall go for my monye when all is done. **1589** [see Go *v.* 24 b]. **1840** *Spirit of Times* 21 Nov. 447/3 Give me the gall, I say, that *has an eye for dirt*, for she is the gall for my money. **1932** D. L. Sayers *Have his Carcase* xi. 138 Peter's the man for my money. He won't see a hardworking man lose a job for want of a good news story. **1943** *N.Y. Times* 9 May II. 5/5 Glenn was, and for my money is still tops. **1954** J. Symons *Narrowing Circle* xiv. 59 For my money, Marian was responsible..for the trouble we'd had. **1969** D. Clark *Death after Evensong* iv. 97, I wouldn't mind not finding who did Parseloe in. For my money he deserved it.

c. *to cost money*: see *cost *v.* 1 d.

e. *money burns* (*a hole*) (*in*) *one's pocket* (or † *purse*) (and similar phrases): one is impatient to spend one's money. Cf. Burn *v.*[1] 16 in Dict. and Suppl.

1529 More *Dyaloge of Ymagys* II. x. f.lxi, Hauyng a lytell wanton money whyche hym thought brennyd out the botom of hys purs. **1702** Farquhar *Inconstant* v. iii. 77 My time lyes heavy on my hands, and my Money burns in my Pocket. **1875** S. Smiles *Thrift* viii. 125 A man who has more money about him than he requires..is tempted to spend it... It is apt to 'burn a hole in his pocket'. **1943** M. Lasswell *Suds in your Eye* xiv. 103 Her money was burning a hole in her pocket. **1958** L. Durrell *Balthazar* xiii. 227 I've scraped a dowry together over the years... The money burns my pocket. **1972** A. S. Neill *Neill! Neill! Orange Peel!* II. 238 Today, I don't see the young.. saving money. It burns a hole in their pockets.

f. *your money or your life*: a formula used by highwaymen, etc., in threatening to kill a person if he does not hand over money.

1841 F. A. Burney *Jrnl.* 23 Feb. (1926) 321 Mr. Dixon attempted expostulation, upon which the Highwayman drew out a Pistol,..exclaiming, with an oath, 'Your money or your life!' **1848** J. A. Froude *Let.* 16 May in W. H. Dunn *Froude* (1961) I. 118 Nothing will open rich John Bull's understanding but a hand at his throat and 'Your money or your life'. **1864** J. Payn *Lost Sir Massingberd* II. xiii. 212 A pistol, was protruded into the carriage. 'Your money or your life!..,' said a rough voice.

g. *in the money*: among the prize-winners in a competition, show, or the like; amply or sufficiently supplied with money; rich.

1902 'D. Dix' *Fables of Elite* 48 It is True that when the Spurt is over I am generally in the Money. **1928** *Morning Post* 20 Oct. 6/1 One of them is to-day a full champion, the other three all winners, and 'in the money', as the fanciers say, whenever shown. **1945** G. Casey in *Coast to Coast 1944* 3 Shift her round like you was doin' yesterday and you'll be in the money. **1946** L. Bromfield *World we live In* 325 Being in the money at the moment, I said that of course I'd lend her any reasonable amount. **1969** T. Parker *Twisting Lane* 200 She said we could stay there rent free until I was in the money again.

h. *money for jam, money for old rope* (and similar phrases): a profitable return for little or no trouble; a very easy job; someone or something easy to profit from, beat, etc.

1919 *Athenæum* 8 Aug. 727/2 The great use of jam in the Army..originated a number of phrases, such as 'money for jam' (money for nothing). **1927** T. E. Lawrence *Let.* 22 Sept. (1938) 540 Recently I made nearly ten pounds out of reviewing eleven books. Money for jam, as the airman says. **1936** J. Curtis *Gilt Kid* xiii. 134 He would spin her a fanny about the marriage laws, tie the poor kid up. It ought to be money for old rope. **1942** E. Waugh *Put out More Flags* 150 At the moment there were no mortars and he was given instead a light and easily manageable counterfeit of wood which was slung on the back of his haversack, relieving him of a rifle. At present it was money for old rope. **1958** 'A. Gilbert' *Death against Clock* iv. 47 If he saw the wallet it must have seemed money for jam. **1966** 'L. Lane' *ABZ of Scouse* 70 *Money fer owd rope*, something for nothing. Other similar phrases are *money fer dirt*; *money fer raggety kecks*; *money fer jam*, etc., etc. **1973** A. Hunter *Gently French* iii. 24 Wasn't no risk, it was money for jam. **1974** N. Bentley *Inside Information* v. 52 I'll advance you another two hundred. Christ, that's money for old rope.

i. *not everybody's money*: not to everybody's liking.

1923 J. Manchon *Le Slang* 196 *You ain't everybody's money*, vous ne pouvez pas plaire à tout le monde. **1933** 'G. Orwell' *Let.* c 10 Dec. in *Coll. Ess.* (1968) I. 128 As to the actual writing in *Ulysses*, it isn't everybody's money, but personally I think it is superb in places.

j. *to put one's money on*: to bet on (a horse, etc.); also *fig.*, to favour or depend on; to expect the success of.

1931 T. R. G. Lyell *Slang, Phrase & Idiom* 528 If you've got any sense, you'll put your money on that horse I told you of. **1963** *Listener* 21 Feb. 341/3 She does not put all her money on love. **1969** *Ibid.* 8 May 636/1 A century hence, prophesied one critic, it would be only 'the careless glance of curiosity, or the student's all-ranging eye' that would turn upon the Little Nells and Paul Dombeys; he put his money instead on Dickens's humour.

k. *to put* (or *get*) *one's money where one's mouth is*: to produce, bet, or pay out money to support one's statements or opinions. *N. Amer.*

1942 Z. N. Hurston in A. Dundes *Mother Wit* (1973) 224/1 'Put your money where your mouth is!' he challenged. **1951** *Amer. Speech* XXVI. 99/1 *Get your money where your mouth is*, a phrase [in poker] which means, 'put up or shut up'. **1970** *Globe & Mail* (Toronto) 26 Sept. 7/3 Eventually it got to the point when he suggested that maybe I was the guy who should take it on. Sort of put your money where your mouth is. **1975** A. Price *Our Man in Camelot* v. 95 The squadron betting book the barman keeps..for guys who are ready to put their money where their mouth is.

l. *to have money to burn*: see *burn *v.*[1] 8 d.

7. a. *money-economy, -fear, -flow, -hunger, -lust, -purse, -rent, -sense, -slave, -supply, -system, -till.*

1942 L. B. Namier *Conflicts* 50 It is not easy to translate into exact figures this barter business, which is.. contrasted with the money-economy and transactions of the Western Powers. **1962** H. R. Loyn *Anglo-Saxon Eng.* iv. 159 The earliest law-codes give evidence..of the importance of a money-economy. **1927** Money-fear [see *money-lust* below]. **1953** C. F. Hockett in Saporta & Bastian *Psycholinguistics* (1961) 64/1 Money-flow (at least in one direction) is *income*. **1891** Stevenson & Osbourne *Wrecker* (1892) vii. 120 Far from the money-hunger of the West. **1965** *Times Lit. Suppl.* 25 Nov. 1047 (Advt.), A young manhood of scheming and money-hunger in Chicago. **1927** D. H. Lawrence *Let.* 18 Dec. (1962) II. 1027 They must first overthrow in themselves the money-fear and money-lust. **1930** E. Pound *XXX Cantos* xiv. 61 The perverts, who have set money-lust Before the pleasures of the senses. c **1821** J. W. Masters in *Eng. Dial. Dict.* (1903) IV. 149/2 He brought our Jack a leather cap An' Sal a money-puss. **1878** B. F. Taylor *Between Gates* 273 We stood under fig-trees hung with money-purses filled with seeds. **1966** A. R. Scammell *My Newfoundland* 33, I kept mine [*sc.* a dollar bill] for weeks in my little money-purse (we never called them purses). **1792** A. Young *Trav. France* I. iv. 340 Much the greater part of the lands of France are not let at a money-rent, but at one-half or one-third produce. **1848** Mill *Pol. Econ.* I. II. viii. 366 An attempt to introduce..a system of money rents and capitalist farmers. **1865** D. G. Rossetti *Let.* 14 Sept. (1965) II. 571 This might have been.. executed..more profitably in a money-sense than what I did do. **1963** *Times Lit. Suppl.* 25 Jan. 62/3 Their hair-dressing or their money-sense. **1929** D. H. Lawrence *Pansies* 116 He can't help being a slave, a wage-slave, A money-slave. **1878** F. A. Walker *Money* iv. 76 (*heading*) The importance of the money supply. **1975** *Times* 18 June 29/7 For this year a 15 per cent rise in the money supply and a 12½ per cent rise in gnp..would be the right interim targets. **1929** D. H. Lawrence *Pansies* 109 Why don't we do something about the money system? **1857** *Quinland* I. II. ii. 289 If the stars were extinguished, it would not disturb him, unless his money-till were upset. **1937** C. M. Arensberg *Irish Countryman* 175 His or her remittances would eventually reach his money-till.

b. *money-grabber, -loser, -raiser, -spender*; *money-changing, -earning, -grabbing, -losing, -raising, -spending, -sucking* vbl. sbs. and ppl. adjs.; *money-conscious, -directed* adjs.; **c.** *money-mad* (further examples); *money-minded* adj.

1938 G. Greene *Nineteen Stories* (1947) 76 Mr. Calloway sat on his usual seat staring out over the money-changing booths at the United States. **1933** Money-conscious [see *conscious *a.* 12]. **1963** *Times* 1 May 15/4 The parties being money-conscious to the highest degree. **1970** T. Hilton *Pre-Raphaelites* vi. 171 The destructiveness of capitalist society, its callous and money-directed disregard of culture. **1912** J. London *Let.* 7 Sept. (1966) 364 My long stuff is pretty good at money-earning. **1903** *Eng. Dial. Dict.* s.v., He's a regular money grabber. **1933** *Times Lit. Suppl.* 27 Apr. 283/3 A money-grabber, notorious in a money-grabbing age. **1920** D. H. Lawrence *Touch & Go* 9 We say it is a mere material struggle, a money-grabbing affair. **1928** *Weekly Dispatch* 6 May 15 About 30 [musical comedies] prove to be money-losers. **1963** E. Humphreys *Gift* II. iv. 239 If a reputation for being a money-loser had reached as far as Barrot's ears, there was very little hope of him ever making a film again. **1870** J. K. Medbery *Men & Myst. Wall St.* 200 It is the greatest money-making and money-losing spot on the globe. **1960** *Farmer & Stockbreeder* 16 Feb. 87/2 All your life you have heard that farming is a money-losing proposition. **1929** D. H. Lawrence *Pansies* 79 Fear of my money-mad fellow-men. **1965** G. Jackson *Let.* 16 Mar. in *Soledad Brother* (1971) 69 The shocks and strains of this money-mad society are enough to ruin the purest of minds. **1974** A. Ross *Bradford Business* 169 Money-mad property developers. **1588** W. Kempe *Educ. Children* sig. C3 One of these money minded parents. **1957** *Times Lit. Suppl.* 20 Dec. 769/4 The insistence of the more money-minded directors on its premature exploration. **1909** *Westm. Gaz.* 11 Aug. 1/3 This remarkable man began his career as a money-raiser fifteen years ago with an £8,000 collection. **1955** W. Dean in H. Van Thal *Fanfare for E. Newman* v. 61 *Don Giovanni* in Trianon's version and Nicolai's *Merry Wives of Windsor* had to be put on as money-raisers. **1960** *Farmer & Stockbreeder* 29 Mar. 105/3 The huge success of money-raising efforts. **1920** *Edin. Rev.* July 163 Meleager was always a money spender rather than a money maker. **1900** J. London *Let.* 1 Mar. (1966) 97 The habit of money spending. **1911** H. Granville Barker *Madras House* III. 91 The Middle Class Women of England form one of the greatest Money Spending Machines the world has ever seen. **1921** Galsworthy *To Let* II. v. 162 A lot of slow-fly money-sucking officials.

8. money-back *a.*, designating a system, agreement, etc., whereby a customer will be refunded the money he pays, if he is not satisfied with the goods or service provided; **money-belt** orig. *U.S.*, a belt designed for carrying money; **money bug** *U.S. slang*, a person having great wealth or financial power; **money centre** *U.S.*, a place of pre-eminent importance in the financial affairs of a region or country; *spec.* New York; **money crop** *U.S.*, a crop that is grown mainly for selling and not for the grower's consumption; = **cash-crop*; **money-gold** *rare*, gold coin; **money illusion** (orig. *U.S.*), the illusion that money has a fixed value in terms of its purchasing power; **money king** *U.S.*, a magnate in finance; a person of great wealth; **money-man**, delete † and add later examples; **money market** (earlier and later examples); (*b*) a place in which the financial activity of a region is centred; **money-order** (further examples); **money-player**, (*a*) *U.S.*, a type of gambler (see quot. 1935); (*b*) a professional, as opposed to an amateur; **money-power**, (*a*) the power to coin money, regulate its use, etc.; (*b*) the power exercised by money or by wealthy people, firms, etc.; **money-shark** orig. *U.S.*, an avaricious money-dealer; **money shop**, a shop where money can be obtained; *spec.* an establishment which performs more conveniently many of the functions of a bank, and specializes in arranging loans; **money-spinner**, (*b*) (earlier and later examples); also, a person who, or thing which, makes a lot of money; something that is very profitable; hence **money-spinning** *vbl. sb.* and *ppl. a.*

1922 *Weekly Dispatch* 12 Nov. 4 (Advt.), All our business is conducted on the 'Moneyback' principle; that is to say, if you are not perfectly satisfied with your purchase return it to us within seven days and we will refund your money in full by return of post. **1955** *Radio Times* 22 Apr. 2/3 Sisco paints are sold on a 'money back' guarantee. **1972** *Farm & Country* 19 Dec. 13/3 We are certain that you will be satisfied and offer a money back guarantee. **1846** *St. Louis* (Missouri) *Reveille* 9 Sept. 3/2 The stock consists, in part, of Shirts, Collars,..Money Belts. **1923** *Outward Bound* Mar. 408/2 Among cowboys..one might.. leave one's money-belt full of gold and notes beside the fire. **1958** P. Kemp *No Colours or Crest* viii. 174, I had a hundred gold sovereigns in my money belt. **1898** *People* 20 Mar. 4/4 The happiness or the misery of 3 millions of people wholly dependent on the whims and caprices of, say, half a dozen 'money bugs', as they are called in the States. **1922** *Public Opinion* 11 Aug. 132/2 The profiteering class, money bugs as the Americans call them. **1838** D. D. Barnard *Speeches & Rep.* 36 Composed of twenty-six local sovereignties, of all which New-York is the money centre, as London is the money centre of half the world. **1900** *Congress. Rec.* 17 Feb. 1897/2 Gilt-edged paper can be placed in the money-centers at a small per cent. **1881** *Harper's Mag.* Oct. 723/1 Cotton is the money crop. **1904** T. Watson *Bethany* 5 They never failed to make it their object to produce on the farm the necessary supplies, tobacco or cotton being merely the surplus crop, the money crop. **1974** S. Marcus *Minding the Store* (1975) xii. 243 Until about 1932, Texas had essentially an agriculturally based economy. By 1905 cotton was the money crop. **1841** *N.Z. Jrnl.* No. 32. 92 Natives talk about money-gold. **1842** *Lett. Settlers in Wellington, Nelson & New Plymouth* (1843) 137 We can get them [*sc.* pigs] from the natives for blankets, or for 'money gold' as they call it, which we call sovereigns. **1925** J. Gregory *Bab of Backwoods* xxiii. 283 Gold that had..been dull bits of ore dug from rocky hillsides; that men had taken and made into money-gold. **1928** I. Fisher *Money Illusion* (1929) i. 4 The 'Money Illusion'.., the failure to perceive that the dollar, or any other unit of money, expands or shrinks in value. **1975** *Times* 30 June 12/8 Money illusion is, as in Germany, dying..as people spend indexed wages rather than save. **1838** D. D. Barnard *Speeches & Rep.* 106 To see him [*sc.* the President] sit as a great money king over the nation. **1900** *Congress. Rec.* 7 Feb. 1610/1 Where ought control of the currency to rest?.. At present the banks and the money kings wield this power. **1928** Money man [see *date *v.* 2 d]. **1958** Money-man [see *cackle *sb.* 3 a]. **1973** *Times* 2 Feb. 14/7 New York money men have been known to quake in the knowledge that they have on deposit $1,000m of overnight money. **1791** A. Hamilton *Establishment of Mint* in *Wks.* (1810) I. 291 In Holland, the greatest *money* market of Europe, gold was to silver..as 1 to 14·88. **1816** Scott *Antiquary* II. vii. 190 In the present state of the money-market. **1883** *Century Mag.* Sept. 691/2 Wall Street..is the money market of the whole country. **1964** *Financial Times* 12 Mar. 10/2 South Africa has developed a money market which, in relation to national income, handles a larger volume of funds than the traditional London discount market. a **1861** A. H. Clough *Mari Magno* in *Poems* (1871) 320 The money-order had been cashed. **1972** *Post Office Guide* 590 Inland money orders are issued by and payable at all money order offices. **1935** A. J. Pollock *Underworld Speaks* 77/1 *Money player*, the tougher the game, this particular

gambler excels on account of having lots of nerve. **1944** *Gen* 11 Mar. 30 It is one of the die-hard notions that no money-player is fit to lead an England team. **1829** *H. R. Doc. 21st U.S. Congress 1 Sess.* No. 6. 12 The application of the money power of the Government to regulate the unequal action. **1831** T. H. Benton in *Reg. Deb. Congress U.S.* 2 Feb. 50/2 The money power of the bank is both direct and indirect. **1840** J. S. Mill in *Edin. Rev.* LXXII. 11 The additions to the 'money-power' of the higher ranks, consist of the riches of the *novi homines* who are continually aggregated to that class from among the merchants and manufacturers. **1926** R. H. Tawney *Religion & Rise of Capitalism* ii. 89 When he [*sc.* Luther] looks at German social life, he finds it ridden by a conscienceless money-power, which incidentally ministers..to the avarice and corruption of Rome. **1959** *Ann. Reg. 1958* 90 The United Party was pictured as being..dominated by jingoes and in the hands of the money-power. **1844** *Congress. Globe* 28th Congress 2 Sess. App. 37/2 Banks.. managed..by a set of irresponsible money sharks. **1972** G. F. Newman *You Nice Bastard* 347 *Moneyshark*, unlicenced money-lender (operating at especially high rates of interest). **1816** Scott *Let.* 23 July (1932) I. 502 You had better be looking out & inquiring after some money-shop, as we shall have enough of bills. **1972** *Guardian* 9 June 11 The new 'money shop' branches which are sprouting up in the High Streets... Money shops are not really banks at all... 'Loan shop'..is still the best shorthand description. **1859** G. A. Sala *Twice round Clock* 69 The clown, the dunderheaded moneyspinner who votes that books are 'rubbish'. *c* **1880** A. W. Pinero *Money Spinner* (1890) 22 Have you forgotten my father's [gaming] house... Have you forgotten what they called me then, because of my never-failing good fortune—because of my *luck*. They called me the *Money Spinner*! **1952** W. Granville *Dict. Theatr. Terms* 119 *Money-spinner*, a successful play or artiste. **1954** G. Smith *Flaw in Crystal* 87 He found he had a pretty knack of writing so that ordinary men and women could understand and feel something of the beauty he saw around him. And he turned that touch into a money-spinner. **1958** A. Wilson *Middle Age of Mrs Eliot* ii. 237 If he publishes anything it'll have every chance of being a money spinner. **1970** *Times* 23 Jan. 25/5 (Advt.), Their products range from fertilizers and basic heavy chemicals to..complex petro-chemicals..big money-spinners for Britain's export. **1936** J. Buchan *Island of Sheep* vi. 105 He's a stockbroker—a one-man firm which he founded himself. His interests? Not financial exclusively—indeed, he professes to despise the whole money-spinning business. **1973** *Courier & Advertiser* (Dundee) 1 Mar. 2/2 The money spinning lager boom already accounts for some 12 per cent. of the beer drunk in Britain.

money-grubber. (Earlier and later examples.)

1840 *Bentley's Miscellany* VIII. 449 The money-grubber, pent up in a close city. **1932** A. Huxley *Lett.* (1969) 361 It's terrifying what can be done by people who have a monopoly of means of propaganda—private money-grubbers.

money-maker. Add: **1. b.** (Later U.S. examples.)

a **1734** J. Comer in *Rhode Island Hist. Soc. Coll.* (1893) VIII. 65 This day came up ye case of ye money makers to trial. **1777** in *New Hampsh. Hist. Soc. Coll.* (1863) VII. 93 To pay Col. Sam'l Folson nineteen pounds eleven shillings for..apprehending Money makers. **1778** in *Ibid.* 149 Jn° Mac Glauglin, a money maker.

2. b. (Earlier and later U.S. examples.)

1899 Ade *Doc' Horne* 22, I expect to have an interest in the Neapolitan Dental Parlors, where I'm working now. It's a sure money-maker. **1940** E. Fergusson *Our Southwest* xix. 349 He has instead snapped up his dances as money-makers.

mong (mɒŋ), *sb.*² Austral. slang abbrev. of Mongrel *sb.*

1933 *Bulletin* (Sydney) 16 Aug. 39/1 And the mong fired him! **1934** *Ibid.* 30 May 20/3 The silliest dogs for miles around live in Warrnambool; these mongs crouch down when a car approaches and spring out at the front wheels with snappy barks. **1956** G. Casey in *Coast to Coast 1955–6* 80 Reckon Charlie Spend's having trouble with that mong of his. **1966** [see *heel *v.*¹ 4]. **1967** [see *bludge *v.*]. **1967** Partridge *Dict. Slang* Suppl., *Mong*, a mongrel dog... 2. Hence, pejorative for any dog, even of the best pedigree. **1970** J. Cleary *Helga's Web* v. 77, I can't *lose*. I backed a mong last night that had only three legs..and it finished up beating the bunny home.

mongan (mǫ·ŋgăn). *Austral.* [Native name.] A species of ring-tailed opossum, *Pseudocheirus herbertensis*, found in the rain forest of north-eastern Queensland.

1890 C. Lumholtz *Among Cannibals* 173 (Morris), Jimmy..had..found mongan.., a new and very pretty mammal, whose habitat is exclusively the highest tops of the scrubs in the Coast Mountains. **1970** W. D. L. Ride *Guide to Native Mammals of Australia* 76 Mongan, Herbert River Ringtail, *Pseudocheirus herbertensis*... Very dark brown with white under-surface; tip of tail white.

monger (mɒ·ŋgəɹ), *v.* [f. Monger¹.] *trans.* To deal or traffic in.

1928 *Observer* 5 Feb. 15/1 Both American and British opinion is laughing out of court those who monger their scares about the United States Navy. **1962** *Times Lit. Suppl.* 10 Aug. 570/3, I laughed at her and told her, that she cannot monger any money out of my pocket.

Mongo¹ (mǫ·ŋgo). Also **Lomongo.** [Native name.] A Bantu people living in Zaïre (formerly the Belgian Congo); a member of this people; the language of this people. Also *attrib.*

1906 Visct. Mountmorres *Congo Independent State* 45 East of the Launoa..the Mongo, perhaps on account of their contact with the Arabised tribes..appear to have advanced to a much higher state of civilisation than in other parts. **1910** *Encycl. Brit.* VI. 925/1 Farther north and largely occupying the valley of the Ruki are the Mongo, a large forest tribe. **1919** A. Werner *Introd. Sketch Bantu Lang.* 314 *Congo*,..the languages included under this heading are..*Lolo* (Mongo, Lunkundu)—on the Equator within the great northern bend of the Congo. **1928** E. A. & L. Ruskin *Dict. Lomongo Lang.* Introd., Lomongo belongs to the Bantu group of languages and is spoken by at least 300,000 people, dwelling in Middle Belgian Congo, north and south of the equator. **1946** *Nature* 6 July 14/2 Important monographs were produced on the Mongo, Basongo, and Bakongo. **1961** G. Greene *Burnt-Out Case* vi. i. 178 She remembered..her father teaching her the Mongo for 'bread' and 'coffee' and 'jam'. They were still the only three words in Mongo that she knew. **1961** *Listener* 16 Nov. 831/1 If the Mongo tribes had been contained within a single province..the prospect of maintaining an independent Congo as a single state would hardly have been worth considering.

mongo² (mǫ·ŋgo). [Mongolian.] A monetary unit of Mongolia, one hundred of which are equal to one tugrik.

1935 *Statesman's Year Bk.* 774 The *Tukhrik*, a silver coin equivalent to half an American gold dollar, and divided into 100 *Mongo*. **1968** C. Narbeth *Coin Collector's Encycl.* 145 The Mongolian People's Republic..first minted coins in copper and silver of Mung and Tugrik denominations. **1969** *Whitaker's Almanack 1970* 984 Mongolia (Outer), Tugrik of 100 Mongo. **1972** *Statesman's Year-Bk.* 1165, 100 *möngö* = 1 *tugrik*.

Mongol, *sb.* and *a.* Add: **A.** *sb.* **2.** (Also with lower-case initial.) A person afflicted with mongolism.

[**1866**: see *Mongolian *a.* and *sb.* A. 3.] **1896** *Brit. Med. Jrnl.* 12 Sept. 617/1 There is probably in the Mongol a more profound and general condition of intrauterine failure of development than in the cretin. **1913** *Jrnl. Nerv. & Mental Dis.* XL. 338 Mentally, mongols are as a rule quiet, good tempered, and easily amused. **1926** *Lancet* 23 Jan. 190/2 The resemblance between the Mongol and the cretin has naturally produced an endocrine theory. **1932** [see B. 2 below]. **1960** *Guardian* 29 Apr. 6/5 The number of adult mongols was likely to increase fairly steadily. **1970** Passmore & Robson *Compan. Med. Stud.* II. xxxi. 17/1 A variety of cytogenetic aberrations have been found amongst the 2–5 per cent of mongols who are neither simple trisomics nor trisomic/normal mosaics.

B. *adj.* **2.** (Also with lower-case initial.) Pertaining to or affected with mongolism; = Mongolian *a.* and *sb.* A. 3 (in Dict. and Suppl.).

1896 *Brit. Med. Jrnl.* 12 Sept. 617/1 There are at present in the Royal Albert Asylum 19 Mongol idiots in a population of 560. **1932** Shrubsall & Williams *Mental Deficiency Pract.* xiii. 206 In mongols, laxity of the joints is very characteristic, and mongol imbeciles tend in sitting naturally, to take up the crossed position of the Buddha in contemplation. **1965** [see *Down's syndrome]. **1970** Passmore & Robson *Compan. Med. Stud.* II. xxxi. 18/1 The greatly increased risk of having mongol offspring is the reason why every effort should be made to discover translocation carriers so that appropriate genetic advice may be given. **1974** G. F. Newman *Price* ii. 68 He made contributions to the maintenance of his ex-wife and her mongol son.

Mongolian, *a.* and *sb.* Add: **A.** *adj.* **1.** Also *Mongolian lamb.*

1963 *Sunday Express* 27 Jan. 9/5 A Mongolian lamb hat. **1970** *Vogue* Jan. 22/3 A helmet of white Mongolian lamb.

b. *Mongolian hot-pot* (see quot. 1971).

1967 E. Hunt *Danger Game* viii. 152 He ate oysters at Lo Fan Shan and Mongolian Hotpot. **1968** *Times* 6 Jan. 20/5 The New Hong Kong..are serving a speciality called 'bin lo'..a cross between Mongolian hotpot and Japanese *sukiyaki*. **1971** *Good Food Guide* 421 Mongolian hot-pot (a kind of Mandarin fondue bourguignonne, for which you do your own cooking at the table).

2. b. *Mongolian fold* = *epicanthus; so *Mongolian eye*, one with an epicanthus.

1913 [see *epicanthus]. **1926** H. H. Wilder *Pedigree of Human Race* v. 298 It follows that it is not the Mongolian eye that is racial. **1927** Peake & Fleure *Priests & Kings* xii. 192 The head is..relatively low and rounded with, in many individuals, flattened features and the additional or 'Mongolian' fold of the eyelid. **1935** Huxley & Haddon *We Europeans* iv. 117 A fold of skin, the 'epicanthic fold', covers the inner angle of the eye. This gives the effect known as the 'Mongolian eye'. **1964** *New Statesman* 10 Apr. 559/1 A quick and painless operation will..remove the young lady's Mongolian fold.

3. (Earlier and later examples.) Also with lower-case initial.

1866 J. L. H. Down in *Clin. Lect. & Rep.* (London Hospital) III. 260, I have for some time had my attention directed to the possibility of making a classification of the feeble-minded, by arranging them around various ethnic standards... The great Mongolian family has numerous representatives, and it is to this division, I wish..to call special attention. A very large number of congenital idiots are typical Mongols. *Ibid.* 261 The Mongolian type of idiocy occurs in more than ten per cent. of the cases which are presented to me. **1890** *Jrnl. Mental Sci.* XXXVI. 189 Mongolian imbeciles. **1965** [see *Down's syndrome].

4. *Mongolian pheasant*, a variety of pheasant, *Phasianus colchicus mongolicus*, native to southern Russia and Mongolia, introduced to other countries early in the twentieth century; also called the Kirghiz pheasant; also *ellipt.*; *Mongolian spot*, a bluish or brownish spot found, usu. singly, in the sacral region of nearly all new-born babies of Oriental races (and occas. in other races), and which usu. disappears in two or three years.

1903 W. Rothschild in *Field* 20 June 1033/3 The bird known in America as the Mongolian pheasant is not the *Phasianus mongolicus* of Brandt, but the *Phasianus colchicus, var. mongolicus* of Pallas, otherwise our common Chinese ring-necked pheasant (*Phasianus torquatus*) Linné. *Ibid.* 1033/6, I have had a number of the true Mongolian pheasant (*Phasianus mongolicus*) alive at Tring for two years. **1909** J. G. Millais *Nat. Hist. Brit. Game Birds* 104 If the pure and cross-bred Mongolians have a fault it is a tendency to stray more than other pheasants. **1921** *Daily Colonist* (Victoria, B.C.) 23 Oct. 18/1 This boy [*sc.* an old cock pheasant] looked like a Mongolian, seemed too dark for an ordinary ringneck. **1963** D. A. Bannerman *Birds Brit. Isles* XII. 338 The Kirghiz pheasant *Phasianus mongolicus* Brandt. Commonly (but incorrectly) named the Mongolian pheasant, is distinguished by the broad white-ring around the neck interrupted in front, having the mantle, chest and breast bronzy orange-red... Introduced into England for Lord Rothschild in 1900. **1965** *Observer* (Colour Suppl.) 10 Oct. 33/2 There's a Mongolian there..a fine ring neck... That old bird he always roosts in that apple tree there. **1907** *Arch. Pediatrics* XXIV. 428 His findings led him..to a special study of the morphology of the 'Mongolian' spot. **1966** Wright & Symmers *Systemic Path.* II. xxxix. 1507/1 The blue naevus..is analogous to the 'Mongolian spot', but may occur in any race and on any part of the body. **1969** *Beaver* Spring 49/1 A baby's pale Mongolian spots are patted lovingly.

Mongolianize (mǫŋgōu·liănəiz), *v.* [f. Mongolian *a.* + -ize.] *trans.* To render Mongolian in character or quality.

1923 *Contemp. Rev.* Mar. 299 The Bolshevik, striving originally to make Russia Western, has succeeded merely in Mongolianising her.

mongolism (mǫ·ŋgŏliz'm). *Med.* Also **Mongolism.** [f. Mongol *sb.* and *a.* + -ism. Cf. Mongolian *a.* and *sb.* A. 3 (in Dict. and Suppl.).] A relatively common congenital form of mental deficiency which is associated with a low expectation of life, is always accompanied by a chromosomal abnormality (usually trisomy for chromosome 21), and is marked by numerous signs, including short stature, short thick hands and feet, a large tongue, a flat face with features somewhat similar to those of Mongolians, and a friendly and cheerful disposition; Mongolian idiocy.

1900 *Lancet* 6 Jan. 23/1 (*heading*) The differential diagnosis of Mongolism and cretinism in infancy. **1924** *Psyche* V. 1 It is..well known that a certain type of mental and physical backwardness has long been described, under the name of 'Mongolism'. **1960** *News Chron.* 1 July 5/4 From a medical dictionary he learned that mongolism was a type of congenital idiocy. **1961** R. D. Baker *Essent. Path.* xxii. 615 Cases of..spina bifida and meningocele, mongolism, and cerebral palsy occur at the rate of 1 or 2 of each of these conditions per 1000 births. **1961** [see *Down's syndrome]. **1971** *Brit. Med. Bull.* XXVII. 47/1 The epidemicity of mongolism has also been studied.

Mongoloid, *a.* and *sb.* Add: **A.** *adj.* **1.** (Later examples.)

1934 Webster & Westley *World Civilization* ii. 22 These three races are generally called Negroid, Mongoloid, and Caucasian. *Ibid.* 23 The Malays, Polynesians, and American Indians are included among Mongoloid peoples. **1939** C. S. Coon *Races of Europe* i. 2 From a branch of this hyperborean group there evolved, in northern Asia, the ancestral strain of the entire specialized mongoloid family. **1967** E. A. Hoebel in Rapport & Wright *Anthropol.* 70 The most outstanding Mongoloid physical trait is the slant eye, more elegantly known to anthropologists as the internal epicanthic fold.

b. *Mongoloid eye, fold* = *Mongolian eye, *Mongolian fold.*

1931 E. A. Hooton *Up from Ape* v. 420 The Mongoloid eye characteristically fills the orbit and protrudes slightly. *Ibid.* 421 A common modification..is the inner or internal epicanthic fold, often referred to as the 'Mongoloid fold'. **1960** J. Comas *Man. Physical Anthropol.* v. 271 Generally, the eyelid opening is horizontal, but in many groups of Asia and America the so-called Mongoloid fold is found.

2. (Further examples.) Also with lower-case initial. Add to def.: characteristic of or resembling a mongol or mongolism.

1949 S. S. Sarason *Psychol. Probl. Mental Deficiency* viii. 210 Ages of the mother and father at the birth of the Mongoloid child are relatively advanced. **1961** *Lancet* 13 May 1028/2 (*heading*) 21-Trisomy/normal mosaicism in an intelligent child with some mongoloid characters. **1962** [see B. 2 below]. **1965** Rosen & Gregory *Abnormal Psychol.* xxi. 462/1 She was mongoloid in appearance, good natured, cheerful and cooperative. **1973** *Times Lit. Suppl.* 19 Oct. 1269/5 The bereaved mother peopling her flat with 'friends' via spiritualist contact with a mongoloid daughter.

B. *sb.* **1.** (Later examples.)

1964 R. T. Anderson in M. F. A. Montagu *Concept of Race* 62 The second [interpretation] holds that the Lapps represent a remnant of an ur-race that was the ancestor of both modern Mongoloids and modern Caucasoids. **1971** *National Geographic* Mar. 323/1 Like the majorities, they are virtually all Mongoloids, and often hard to tell apart.

2. (Also with lower-case initial.) = *MONGOL *sb.* and *a.* A. 2.

1949 *Amer. Jrnl. Mental Deficiency* LIV. 204 (*heading*) Case report: reproduction in a mongoloid. **1962** *Amer. Jrnl. Human Genetics* XIV. 125 Trisomy of a short acrocentric chromosome in the human complement has come to be recognized as such a common etiologic factor in mongolism..that the discovery of a forty-seven chromosome mongoloid is no longer worthy of note. Only a few cases have been described in which the mongoloid patient had forty-six chromosomes. **1974** E. TIDYMAN *Dummy* vi. 87 Its..inmates..were mongoloids and schizoids, the emotionally disturbed and the mentally incompetent.

mongoose. Add: **1.** The proper plural form is mongooses, but *mongoose, mongeese,* and other variants are occasionally used.

1896 R. LYDEKKER *Hand-bk. Carnivora* 244 (*heading*) The mungooses. Genus Herpestes. **1927** L. GASK *All about Animals* 158 Mongooses..are well known in Africa and in the warmer parts of Asia. **1927** G. JENNISON *Nat. Hist.: Animals* 82 Mongoose saved the West Indian sugar plantations from total destruction by rats. **1960** G. DURRELL *Zoo in my Luggage* 109 Young pigmy mongooses flatly refuse to feed from bottle or from fountain pen filler. **1971** F. COLLYMORE in J. Figueroa *Caribbean Voices* I. 81 The mongoose..is a troublesome sort of creature... For nobody seems to know with any degree of certainty which to choose of his plural forms—mongooses, mongeese, mongoose or mongooze.

mo·ngrelizing, *vbl. sb.* [-ING¹.] The action of the verb MONGRELIZE.

1922 *Edin. Rev.* July 36 Unchecked mongrelising destroys the symmetry of a national type.

monic (mǫ·nik), *a. Math.* [f. MON(O- + -IC.] Of a polynomial: having the coefficient of the term of highest degree equal to one.

1937 A. A. ALBERT *Mod. Higher Algebra* ii. 24 The coefficient a_n is called the leading coefficient of *f* and we shall call *f* a monic polynomial when $a_n = 1$. [*Note*] This notion occurs so frequently in algebra that the author believes it would be wise to adopt the above term. **1963** BEAUMONT & PIERCE *Algebraic Found. Math.* ix. 328 Thus, for any nonzero polynomial $g(x)$, there is a unique monic polynomial $f(x)$ which is a multiple of $g(x)$ by a nonzero element of *F*.

monica, monick(er, varr. *MONIKER.

monies, irreg. pl. of MONEY *sb.*

moniker (mǫ·nikəɹ). *slang.* Also **monarch, monekeer, monica, monick(er, monniker,** etc. [Origin unknown.] A name, a nick-name. Also (*rare*) as *v. trans.*, to apply a name to (a person).

1851 MAYHEW *Lond. Labour* I. 218/2 'What is your "monekeer" (name)?'—Perhaps it turns out that one is 'White-headed Bob', and the other 'Plymouth Ned'. **1851** [see REAM *a.*]. **1879** *Macm. Mag.* Oct. 502/1 While at the station they asked me what my monarch (name) was. **1882** *Sydney Slang Dict.* 6/1 *Monniker*, a person's name (often assumed). *Ibid.* 10/1 The padding ken of Sally Hicks, who's got a new moniker, which is Lushing Loo. **1885** M. DAVITT *Prison Diary* I. xvi. 151 Many of them having a fresh 'monicker' (name) each conviction. **1895** *Times* 11 Nov. 3/4 The van is alright; I have had the 'monnick' (slang word for name) taken off it. **1903** 'J. FLYNT' *Rise Ruderick Clowd* i. 46 In the—Ward 'monakers', or nicknames, mean more than they do in uptown communities. **1907** J. LONDON *Road* (1914) 169 His 'monica' was Skysail Jack. **1926** J. BLACK *You can't Win* ix. 111 Whether it was his appearance or his careful manner of speech that got him his monoger, 'The Sanctimonious Kid', I never knew. **1936** J. CURTIS *Gilt Kid* v. 50 Eileen, or something, that was the sister's monick. **1936** M. FRANKLIN *All that Swagger* lii. 488 'I thought it was mimosa.' 'That's its trade moniker; it's home name is wattle.' **1938** *Amer. Speech* XIII. 195, I monikered him (gave him his moniker, or tramp name). **1944** *Sun* (Baltimore) 7 Aug. 2/7 He came by the name of Omar N. (the N being for Nelson) through his father's searching for a 'distinctive' moniker for his offspring. **1959** *Times Lit. Suppl.* 13 Feb. 84/1 Henry Handel Richardson herself..was able to hide behind the male signature on her books (her maiden name wedded to two favourite family monikers). **1960** *Melody Maker* 31 Dec. 6/3 Oliver Cool is the pseudonym of singer Larry Ellis, who found he won more success when he adopted the 'far-out' monniker. **1964** *Punch* 2 Dec. 826/1 Mildly bitter moniker given to Swiss-based moneymen. **1968** L. MORTON *Long Wake* i. 18 The documents came to Jack Roberts for my 'Monica'. **1972** *Village Voice* (N.Y.) 1 June 78/3 Slim and his brother helped bail the pilot out. The Airplane Kid moniker followed.

monilia (mǫni·liă). *Bot.* and *Med.* Also **Monilia.** Pl. **monilia, -iæ, -ias.** [mod.L., f. L. *monile*, necklace, in allusion to the chains of spores.] A fungus belonging to the genus *Monilia*, which now (properly) consists only of imperfect forms of *Sclerotinia* and *Neurospora*, several of which cause plant diseases, but formerly included some species (now assigned to *Candida*) which are important human pathogens. Also *attrib.*

1751 J. HILL *Gen. Nat. Hist.* II. 69 Monilia is a genus of Fungi, consisting of a pedicle supporting a number of naked seeds, arranged in series like the beads of a necklace. The Monilia all produce distinct male and female flowers...[Micheli] has..divided this genus into two, under the names of Botrytis and Aspergillus; but the differences, this division are founded upon, are rather specific than generical; we have therefore arranged them all together under one genus. **1916** *Jrnl. Trop. Med. & Hygiene* XIX. 89/1 White, creamy, roundish colonies, characteristic of a monilia, developed within twenty-four hours. **1920** *Lancet* 17 Apr. 851/2 The 20°C. incubator in which the collection of monilias was kept. **1932** *Jrnl. Infectious Dis.* L. 75 Various types of moniliae. **1950** *Jrnl. Amer. Med. Assoc.* 13 May 215/2 A pyoderma in which Monilia may be present merely as saprophytes. **1968** J. H. BURN *Lect. Notes Pharmacol.* (ed. 9) 112 In extreme cases there may be a fatal septicaemia due to monilia. **1975** C. A. THOROLD *Diseases of Cocoa* iii. 27 Monilia disease is confined to the north-west of South America and the adjacent part of Central America.

So **moni·lial** *a.*, of, caused by, or pertaining to a monilia or moniliæ; **moni·lioid** *a.*, resembling a fungus of this type.

1928 *Mycologia* XX. 127 (*title*) The monilioid species of *Sclerotinia*. **1947** *Jrnl. Amer. Med. Assoc.* 20 Sept. 192/2 (*heading*) Iodine treatment in monilial infections. **1951** *Ibid.* 27 Jan. 207/1 (*heading*) Monilial infections complicating the therapeutic use of antibiotics. *Ibid.* 208/1 A severe monilial esophagitis. **1973** *Nature* 28 Sept. 214/1 Specimens of clinically uninflamed gingiva were cultured with the addition of nystatin..to prevent monilial overgrowth. **1974** PASSMORE & ROBSON *Compan. Med. Studies* III. xiii. 13/1 Trichomonal and monilial infections should be excluded by the examination of smears of vaginal exudate [in the treatment of vulvovaginitis].

moniliasis (mǫnilai·ăsis). *Path.* Pl. **-ases.** [f. *MONIL(IA + *-IASIS.] Infection with or a disease caused by a fungus of the genus *Candida*.

1920 *Lancet* 24 Apr. 898/2 It is probable therefore that the so-called tea-taster's cough is a moniliasis. **1925** *Jrnl. Obstetr. & Gynæcol.* XXXII. 69 (*heading*) Vaginal monilias and vaginal moniliases. **1947** *Jrnl. Amer. Med. Assoc.* 27 Dec. 1186/2 The moniliases form a group of infections. **1958** *New Biol.* XXVII. 62 Moniliasis, which is a disease or complex of diseases with diverse manifestations caused by several yeast-like fungi of which *Candida albicans* is the most important, has a world-wide distribution... The most familiar aspect of moniliasis is thrush in infants. **1964** WINNER & HURLEY *Candida Albicans* p. v, We refer to these diseases as candidosis, this being the term, which ..we have preferred to 'candidiasis', 'candidasis' and 'moniliasis'. 'Moniliasis' was the correct term when the causative agent was known as Monilia, but its continued use today leads to confusion. **1974** PASSMORE & ROBSON *Compan. Med. Studies* III. xix. 9/2 (*heading*) Candidiasis (thrush, moniliasis).

monimolimnion (mǫ:nimoli·mniǫn). Pl. **-limnia.** [a. G. *monimolimnion* (I. Findenegg 1935, in *Internat. Rev. d. ges. Hydrobiol. u. Hydrographie* XXXII. 377), f. Gr. μόνιμο-ς stable + *-limnion*, after *EPILIMNION, *HYPOLIMNION.] The lower, denser, non-circulating layer of a meromictic lake. Cf. *MIXOLIMNION.

1937 [see *MIXOLIMNION]. **1957** G. E. HUTCHINSON *Treat. Limnol.* I. vii. 464 These lakes have never fully circulated in the ordinary way, since they developed large monimolimnia. **1968** [see *MIXOLIMNION].

monish (mɒ·niʃ), *sb.* [See MONEY *sb.* 4 ¶.] (Examples.)

1846 *Swell's Night Guide* 125/2 *Monish, tip us the,* give me the money. **1848** *Sinks of London laid Open* 116/1 *Monish, tip us the,* give me the money.

monism. Add: **1. d.** In various uses indicating a theory or doctrine of a single force, source, or system from which all particular instances devolve.

1890 W. JAMES *Princ. Psychol.* I. x. 366 The contrast between the Monism thus reached and our own psychological point of view can be exhibited schematically. **1903** B. RUSSELL *Princ. Math.* I. iv. 43 The subject is important, since the issues between monism and monadism, between idealism and empiricism..all depend, in whole or in part, upon the theory we adopt in regard to the present question. *Ibid.* 44 Numerical identity and diversity are the source of unity and plurality; and thus the admission of many terms destroys monism. **1949** P. A. SCHILPP *Albert Einstein* xxiii. 591 The question is still open whether it is possible thereby to arrive at a real monism; for the conversion of Joule into *mkg* does not prove that the two forms of energy are in essence the same. **1964** GOULD & KOLB *Dict. Soc. Sci.* 440/1 Monism is the notion..that in any society there must be one supreme power or authority and this must be lodged in the state. **1970** G. A. & A. G. THEODORSON *Mod. Dict. Sociol.* 93 *Cultural monism*, a doctrine that advocates the assimilation of ethnic minorities into the dominant culture of a society to attain cultural uniformity. **1971** R. F. C. HULL tr. *Jung's Psychol. Types* in *Coll. Wks.* VI. viii. 318 The idea-oriented attitude must tend towards monism.

monist. Add: (Later examples.)

1934 F. W. COKER *Recent Political Thought* xviii. 504 The pluralist charges the monists with the error of regarding all non-political associations created by the state as dependent for their continued existence upon the will of the State. **1960** L. LIPSON *Great Issues of Politics* (ed. 2) vi. 153 The monist, too, has his problems. Desiring to provide society with an integrating focus, he must designate what this should be. **1964** GOULD & KOLB *Dict. Soc. Sci.* 439/2 In international law the monists are those who believe that international and municipal law are both parts of a single system of law. *Ibid.* 563/2 Politically, public opinion is regarded by the monists as simply the manifested general will.

Also *attrib.* or as *adj.*, of or pertaining to the doctrine of monism.

1931 *Times Lit. Suppl.* 5 Mar. 164/2 Ramanuja fought against the monist view with as intense spiritual passion as any Christian critic could have shown. **1960** L. LIPSON *Great Issues of Politics* (ed. 2) vi. 152 Both philosophies stand unequivocally against something: the pluralist, against organized unity; the monist, against anarchic diversity.

monistic, *a.* (Further examples.)

1890 W. JAMES *Princ. Psychol.* I. x. 367 For *us* it is an unpardonable logical sin,..to change the terms without warning... For monistic idealism, this is the very enfranchisement of philosophy. **1903** B. RUSSELL *Princ. Math.* IV. xxvi. 221 The monistic view..regards the relation as a property of the whole composed of *a* and *b*, and as thus equivalent to a proposition which we may denote by (*at*)r. **1926** J. C. SMUTS *Holism & Evolution* v. 108 The fundamental concept of Holism will bring us nearer to that unitary or monistic conception of the universe which is the immanent ideal of all scientific and philosophic explanation. **1957** S. AUROBINDO in Radhakrishnan & Moore *Sourcebk. in Indian Philos.* xvi. 586 In the monistic view the individual soul is one with the Supreme. **1960** L. LIPSON *Great Issues of Politics* (ed. 2) xiv. 417 There are classic instances of a monistic state combined with a controllable government. *Ibid.*, A monistic state like Britain, therefore, has its powers both centralized and integrated. **1964** GOULD & KOLB *Dict. Soc. Sci.* 563/2 The divisions..can be roughly classified as being between advocates of a monistic, organic view and holders of a pluralistic, numerical theory of public opinion. **1971** J. Z. YOUNG *Introd. Study Man* x. 124 Others [committed by] their addiction to a monistic science, try to find a system that avoids the separation of mind and matter. **1971** R. F. C. HULL tr. *Jung's Psychol. Types* in *Coll. Wks.* VI. viii. 301 Intellectualism is always monistic.

monitor, *sb.* Add: **3. b.** One who is appointed to listen to and report on radio broadcasts, esp. from a foreign country.

1939 *Times* 2 Nov. 5/3 The material, after it is taken down and translated by the monitors, is summarized by an editorial staff. **1945** *Times* 26 May 2/4 In another room monitors were listening to Morse signals. **1974** *Daily Tel.* 16 July 1/2 Radio monitors heard what purported to be a 20-second reading by the Archbishop.

c. *Broadcasting.* A device for indicating or ascertaining the technical quality of a transmission without disturbing the transmission itself; esp. (also *monitor screen, tube*) a television screen for displaying the picture from a particular camera or that being transmitted. Freq. *attrib.*

1931 A. NADELL *Projecting Sound Pictures* ii. 36 The projectionist has only to listen to the sound in his monitor and adjust the guides until the disturbance disappears. **1934** *Proc. IRE* XXII. 450 The monitors are designed for continuous operation, giving a continuous indication of the radio transmitter's frequency, and enabling the radio station operator to tell at a glance whether the transmitter is within the assigned limits. **1944** R. E. LEE *Television* 155 The video engineer clamps down one of the 'pots' on his control panel, draining the light from the monitor screen. **1958** M. DICKENS *Man Overboard* x. 155 He caught sight of himself on the small monitor screen at one side of the cameras. *Ibid.* 160, I saw myself on the monitor. **1959** *Listener* 13 Aug. 238/1 In their monitors the searchers could see the boxes televised by the camera 200 feet down beneath the surface of the lake. **1961** G. MILLERSON *Technique Telev. Production* i. 16 Above each camera's control unit is a monitor-tube on which its picture is displayed. **1961** K. R. STURLEY *Sound & Television Broadcasting* v. 338 Equipment known as a 'transmitter executive monitor' may be installed at a station to keep a watch on distortion due to overload and noise such as hum. **1969** *Times* 22 July (Moon Suppl.) p. i/1 There's a great deal of contrast in it and currently it's upside down on our monitor but we can make out a fair amount of detail. **1971** H. E. ENNES *Television Broadcasting* i. 32 On the monitor panel are located adjustments for the kinescope focus and brightness.., oscilloscope (waveform monitor) focus and brightness, and a switch to accommodate monitoring either the line waveform..or the field waveform..on the oscilloscope tube.

d. Any instrument or device for monitoring some process or quantity; *spec.* one for detecting or measuring radioactivity.

1948 *Nucl. Sci. Abstr.* I. 282 The different types of radiation distribution..and detecting devices, such as air monitors..are briefly explained. **1958** O. R. FRISCH *Nucl. Handbk.* ii. 9 A special monitor..has been designed for the use of persons leaving a laboratory; this counts α- or β-activity on both sides of the two hands. **1961** *Rev. Sci. Instruments* XXXII. 1098 (*heading*) Transmission current monitor for high energy electron beams. **1962** *IRE Trans. Audio* X. 132/1 The audio-radar monitor recorder is designed to continuously monitor and record 16 audio channels and one radar display on a single reel of magnetic tape. **1966** P. J. O'HIGGINS *Basic Instrumentation* x. 289 A monitor is an instrument that is used to measure continuously or at intervals a quantity or condition that must be kept within a prescribed limit. An example is the oil gauge in an automobile. **1973** *Biomed. Engin.* VIII. 255/3 There are situations in which a portable monitor can with advantage be replaced by a permanently-installed instrument which performs a 'watch-dog' function and gives warning if the radiation level rises above a pre-set value (or alternatively warns if any radiation is present at times when none should exist). **1973** *Daily Tel.* 10 Aug. 3 (Advt.), A foetal heart monitor..enables medical staff to tune in to the heart-beat of an unborn baby. **1974** *Rev. Sci. Instruments* XLV. VIII. p. xi (Advt.), Continuous liquid helium level monitor.

5. Substitute for first part of def.: A large

lizard of the family Varanidæ, found in Africa, Asia, and Australia. (Later examples.)

1958 [see *AGAMID]. **1965** R. McKie *Company of Animals* i. 3 Not twenty paces away was a six-foot Malayan lizard, a monitor, grey against the shingle.

9. *attrib.* (see also *3 c), as *monitor man, room, speaker*; **monitor lizard** = sense 5.

1869 P. Gillmore tr. *Figuier's Reptiles & Birds* (1870) 13 In the Crocodiles and Monitor Lizards..a mutilated part is not renewed. **1908** E. J. Banfield *Confessions of Beachcomber* i. iii. 99 There is..no iguana (rather, monitor lizard), though a fair variety of other reptiles. **1947** I. L. Idriess *Isles of Despair* xiv. 92 The great carved head of Kodal the crocodile, of Karum the monitor lizard. **1966** D. Forbes *Heart of Malaya* viii. 93 The only creature we saw was a six-foot long monitor lizard slithering across the road. **1929** *Photoplay* (Chicago) Apr. 31/2 *Monitor man*, the person who operates the volume control on talking picture production, modulating sounds as they come through the microphone so as to get a more even and natural tone. **1931** *Star* 8 May 12/1 The 'monitor room' where the sound experts listen to the conversation was moved 50 feet away. **1960** O. Skilbeck *ABC of Film & TV* 86 *Monitor speaker*, loudspeaker used as a check in dubbing, or as an alternative to headphones by recordists. **1975** *Independent Broadcasting* Aug. 11/1 The technical area with two mixing desks..and two monitor speakers.

monitor, *v.* Restrict *nonce-word* to sense in Dict. and add: **2.** To check or regulate the technical quality of (a radio transmission, television signal, etc.).

1924 [implied in *MONITORING *vbl. sb.*]. **1929** G. Allighan *Romance of Talkies* 64 During the recording, the mixer operator monitors the record through the light valves, thereby assuring himself that no record is lost. **1930** *Bell System Techn. Jrnl.* IX. 273 The..control desk provides facilities by which the attendant can monitor the incoming voice currents and the outgoing radio signal. **1934** *Electronics* May 139/2 Methods of monitoring program transmission both visually and aurally. **1958** *Times Rev. Industry* Aug. 9/3 The output from the analyser can be monitored with headphones. **1962** A. Nisbett *Technique Sound Studio* 258 The signal is monitored by the limiter and any wave which exceeds a certain volume causes a corresponding increase in feedback, which reduces the signal.

b. To listen to and report on (radio broadcasts, esp. from a foreign country); also, to eavesdrop on (a telephone conversation).

1939 *Times* 2 Nov. 5/3 About 150 news bulletins alone, in many different languages, are monitored each day. **1948** *Amer. Speech* XXIII. 219 From secret radios, constructed and hidden by British prisoners, the B.B.C.'s broadcasts were monitored. **1955** F. Swinnerton *Sumner Intrigue* xi. 85 A telephonist had illegitimately monitored a conversation. **1958** 'N. Shute' *Rainbow & Rose* i. 7 We've been monitoring their frequency. *Ibid.* 22 The constable sat down to monitor the conversations. **1971** R. Dentry *Encounter at Kharmel* v. 92 If I were running Ziauddin's operation, I'd be monitoring every newscast in Asia. **1972** D. Haston *In High Places* vi. 74 We sat for three weeks in Kleine Scheidegg, monitoring weather forecasts twice a day.

c. In more general use: to observe, supervise, or keep under review; to measure or test at intervals, esp. for the purpose of regulation or control.

1944 *Times* 20 Mar. 5/7 American and British control officers work at the same desks throughout the 24 hours, 'monitoring' the aircraft as they travel across the 3,000 miles of ocean. **1947** C. Goodman *Sci. & Engin. Nuclear Power* I. 255 We must monitor the cooling water to be sure that it contains no dangerous activities. **1957** *Listener* 3 Oct. 501/2 The Royal Observer Corps have been given the vital job of monitoring the extent of fall-out all over the country. **1958** *Observer* 9 Nov. 17/5 The phonocardiograph is useful in monitoring the [unborn] child's heart when the mother is sleeping or is over-anxious. **1959** *Daily Tel.* 14 Apr. 1/6 The committee was set up in November, 1956, to initiate and monitor a programme of research design. **1961** *New Scientist* 21 Dec. 744/1 The principle is now used..to monitor (while in service) the thickness of boiler shell and pipe walls that are subject to corrosion. **1966** *Lancet* 24 Dec. 1387/1 Pulse-rate and blood-pressure were closely monitored. **1967** S. Woodgate in Wills & Yearsley *Handbk. Management Technol.* 94 These work schedules give supervision and management the ability to monitor progress and to detect immediately if delays to schedules are occurring. **1972** *Sci. Amer.* Aug. 110/3 The radius of the mirror was monitored frequently during the grinding operation by a center-of-curvature test. **1974** *Nature* 17 May 204/2 Thirty-five inspectors monitor the 2,000-odd works registered under the Alkali Act. **1974** *Physics Bull.* Nov. 533/1 Traces of metals in air and water as low as 0·01 parts per million can be monitored with the latest instrument.

So **mo·nitored** *ppl. a.*; **mo·nitoring** *vbl. sb.* and *ppl. a.*

1924 *Proc. IRE* XII. 561 A third requirement relates to monitoring facilities. **1929** G. Allighan *Romance of Talkies* 64 Acoustic treatment of the walls of the monitoring room secures the reverberation characteristic of the theatre. **1933** *Electronics* June 160 A monitoring panel and a two-way communication system so that the operator may keep in constant communication with the pilot of a landing aircraft. **1937** *Discovery* Nov. 330/2 At the side of the studio there is a 'monitoring' television receiving set, so that the floor directors and the announcers can see the outgoing programme. **1939** *Times* 2 Nov. 5/3 Monitoring consists of listening to and recording information contained in programmes broadcast by other countries. *Ibid.*, The monitoring service [of the B.B.C.] deals with some 250,000 words every 24 hours. **1945** *Times* 7 Apr. 4/7 The Japanese Government intended to continue its efforts..according to a monitored report from the United States Office of War Information. **1949** *Atomic Energy & Life Sci.* (U.S. Atomic Energy Comm.) 61 Automatic monitoring equipment, measuring radioactivity of water ..would stop flow if radiation were above safe limit. **1961** *Lancet* 22 July 187/2 Continuous monitoring of the atrial pressure would provide early warning of a dangerous rise. **1962** *B.S.I. News* Mar. 24/2 Two types of plug are dealt with in B.S. 196: two-pole and two-pole and pilot contact, the latter being chiefly required for use with electrical interlocks or with 'monitored earth' circuits. **1971** *Hi-Fi Sound* Feb. 66/1 Systems of this standard are, or can be, of 'monitoring' class—the sort of equipment *Hi-Fi Sound* would use for examining the qualities of new recordings or evaluating new cartridges or other components. **1972** *Accountant* 17 Aug. 214/1 A period of..regulated and monitored practical training.

monk, *sb.* Add: **4.** Also *spec.* in *Printing*, a blotch or area where the ink is excessive.

1683 [in Dict.]. **1771** P. Luckombe *Hist. & Art of Printing* 500 *Monk*, when the Press-man has not distributed his balls and the ink lies in blotches, it is called a Monk. **1892** A. Powell *Southward's Pract. Printing* (ed. 4) xliv. 409 Be very careful not to let the roller 'run into the ink'.., or the roller will be 'smothered'... If not perceived, and the roller is applied to the type, there will be great blotches of ink in different places, perhaps filling it up and causing 'monks', or black patches, in the impression. **1915** *Southward's Mod. Printing* (ed. 3) II. i. 4 This is called rolling the forme... If inefficiently performed there will be too much ink on the impression, or even blotches, technically, 'monks'. **1938** *Amer. Speech* XIII. 272 A dark spot on a page is a *monk*. **1956** *Collins's Authors' & Printers' Dict.* (ed. 10) 265/2 *Monk*,..a patch of letterpress with too much ink.

5. b. monk bond *Building* (see quot. 1936); **monk's bench** = ****monk's table***; **monk's cloth** (later examples); **monk('s) shoe** (see quot. 1969); also *ellipt.* as *monk*; **monk's table,** a convertible wooden seat, the back of which is hinged to swing over and rest horizontally on the arms, thus forming a table.

1936 *Archit. Rev.* LXXIX. 241/3 Monk bond, which is a better ordered arrangement than Yorkshire or Flying bond, is popular in the North of Europe. Two stretchers are followed by one header in every course, the headers being so disposed that verticality of their axial lines is little apparent, and a striking result is obtained of diagonal lines of stretchers, which look like a series of corbels or cantilevers embedded in the wall. **1952** *Ibid.* CXII. 87 A double monk bond was adopted, the whole of the façade being set out to a large scale to ensure that the pattern over them was an even one. **1925** Brodhurst & Layton *Gloss. Eng. Furnit.* 110 Sometimes settles were treated in a similar manner and called Monks' Benches. **1950** S. Howard *Our Furnit. through Ages* viii. 162 A table-settle ..was of Cromwellian inspiration and was in consequence most uninspiring; it is sometimes called a 'Monk's Bench'. **1950** *'Mercury' Dict. Textile Terms* 352/2 *Monks' cloth*, a heavy all-cotton fabric woven in a basket weave from coarse and rough yarns. **1972** P. Marks *Collector's Choice* i. 26 The yards of monk's cloth and fawn-colored carpet lining his galley. **1938** L. MacNeice *I crossed Minch* vii. 92 Ginger-coloured monk suede shoes. **1953** J. Korn *Boot & Shoe Production* xxv. 142 The Monk Shoe... Like the Cromwell, this was formerly a quarter-over shoe. **1968** *Times* 6 Dec. 10/6 The best-selling shoes are..boots and monks (almost boots). **1969** R. T. Wilcox *Dict. Costume* (1970) 217/1 *Monk's shoe*, a low shoe of soft but heavy leather with heel and plain toe and a strap passing over the instep and buckled at the side. **1907** *Yesterday's Shopping* (1969) 130/4 Bamboo Monks' Table... This can be used either as a seat or table, the top being made so that it will slide off to form back of seat. **1972** *Country Life* 23 Mar. 723/3 The so-called monk's table, serving as seat and table..was developed during the 17th century... In shape it was a low-backed box-chair with a solid round or rectangular back, wider than the seat, and with horizontal arms.

monk (mʌŋk), *sb.*² Colloq. abbrev. of Monkey *sb.*

1843 *Spirit of Times* 1 Apr. 54/1 P. Fowler..is one and identical with the celebrated jockey of Miss Foote, in stable parlance, yceleped Monk... The word Monk in this case..is in fact an abbreviation of a noun substantive by which a certain animal is recognised, the countenance of which is said strongly to resemble that of the very jockey in question. **1901** Greenough & Kittredge *Words & their Ways* (1902) vi. 61 Slang is fond of clipped words: as, *monk* for *monkey*. **1903** A. M. Binstead *Pitcher in Paradise* xii. 285 He swore at the monkey freely, and the monk retaliated in cordial but vehement dumbshow with every bitter curse that was known to the forest. **1958** G. Barker *Two Plays* 70 That's the one. His little monk's dead.

monkey, *sb.* Add: **1. c.** (Further examples.) Also *transf.* and *fig.*

1890 Kipling *Let.* in C. E. Carrington *Rudyard Kipling* (1955) v. 157 The blandishments of the people to whom a new writer-man is as a new purple monkey on a yellow stick. **1926** W. de la Mare *Connoisseur* 317, I went bobbing over its boulders and chasms like a jack-in-a-box or a monkey-on-a-stick. **1927** W. E. Collinson *Contemp. Eng.* 8 The monkey on a stick, often used to indicate someone very fidgety and restless. **1966** G. Butler *Nameless Coffin* xii. 192 A 'monkey' is a man who has never been in prison..but is the known associate of criminals. He is a monkey on a stick and it is usually only a matter of time before his stick breaks and he's down there with his friends.

d. *three* (*wise*) *monkeys*: a conventional sculptured group of three monkeys, one with its paws over its mouth ('speak no evil'), one with its paws over its eyes ('see no evil'), and one with its paws over its ears ('hear no evil'); hence used allusively.

1926 *Army & Navy Stores Catal.* 197/3 The three wise monkeys. 'Speak no evil, see no evil, hear no evil.' Per group of three Monkeys -/4. **1969** B. Knox *Tallyman* v. 89 The three wise monkeys would be non-starters against those people. **1969** G. Mitchell *Dance to your Daddy* x. 119 Perhaps there are three other wise monkeys in this house besides yourselves. **1970** A. Draper *Swansong for Rare Bird* viii. 66, I know the score. I'm like the three monkeys. **1974** J. Stubbs *Painted Face* vii. 108 He was like those three monkeys... Neither heard, saw nor spoke evil.

2. b. (Further examples.) Also *spec.* in various *slang* uses (see quots.).

1912 A. H. Lewis *Apaches of N.Y.* xi. 225 'Did youse lobsters hear me handin' it to th' monkeys?' he asked... 'That chink, Low Foo, snakes two of me shirts. I sends him five, an' he on'y sends back three. So I caves in his block wit' a flatiron.' **1914** Jackson & Hellyer *Vocab. Criminal Slang* 59 *Monkey*, a man, used in the mildly indifferent sense of a stranger... Sometimes used to signify a 'boob'. **1928** *Amer. Mercury* Aug. 399/2 Several chorus girls from a Broadway show entered the room against the vigorous protests of the head waiter. One of the monkies, as they are called, sang and did an infinitely torrid dance. **1941** J. Smiley *Hash House Lingo* 38 *Monkey*, dish washer. **1942** Berrey & Van den Bark *Amer. Thes. Slang* § 451/2 Plebeian,..*monkey*. *Ibid.* § 460/5 *Monkey*,.. a Chinese. *Ibid.* § 511/3 (*Bridge*) *monkey*, a bridge builder. *Ibid.* § 576/22 Orchestra leader,..*monkey*. **1966** [see sense 1 c above]. **1967** G. Jackson *Let.* 2 Nov. in *Soledad Brother* (1971) 137, I am the object of the severest ridicule (coon, monkey, shoe..). **1970** P. Laurie *Scotland Yard* 291 *Monkey, a*, an unpleasant person.

c. Slang phr. *to make a monkey* (*out*) *of*: to make a fool of (someone); to deceive, dupe; to ridicule. orig. *U.S.*

1900 Ade *Fables in Slang* 164 His friends would stand and watch him make Monkeys of these anaemic Amateurs. **1900** F. P. Dunne *Mr. Dooley's Philos.* 192 'Willum Waldorf Asthor has busted th' laws iv hospitality, an' made a monkey iv a lile subjick iv th' queen,' he says. **1931** M. Allingham *Police at Funeral* viii. 101, I don't want to put up any idea that isn't useful, and if I'm making a monkey of myself you mention it. **1932** Kaufman & Ryskind *Of Thee I Sing* ii. i. in *Famous Plays* (1933) 668 The man who ought to love me Tried to make a monkey of me. **1934** J. O'Hara *Appt. in Samarra* (1935) vii. 211 So then you turn around and pay him back by.. making a monkey out of him right in his own spot. **1938** E. Bowen *Death of Heart* i. v. 97 You make a monkey of me. **1952** [see *AGIT-PROP]. **1973** 'M. Innes' *Appleby's Answer* xxi. 180 The plain fact was that Bulkington had.. made a monkey of her. It was all very mortifying.

d. orig. *U.S.* A modern dance. Hence as *v. intr.*

1964 [see *DISCOTHÈQUE]. **1965** [see *FRUG]. **1969** N. Cohn *AWopBopaLooBop* (1970) ix. 85 Dance-crazes bossed pop right up until the Beatles broke. There was the Hully Gully, the Madison,..the Monkey. **1969** *New Yorker* 11 Oct. 50/3 Gamely they tried to Frug (or was it Monkey?) to the plangent anthems of a younger generation. **1975** *Time* (Canadian ed.) 25 Aug. 49/1 The frug, the boogaloo, the monkey and similar 'hang-loose' mating rituals.

10*. *Austral.* and *N.Z.* (See quots.).

1933 *Press* (Christchurch, N.Z.) 4 Nov. 15/7 *Monkey*, a handle made by putting a strap between two dees on a saddle and rolling it round itself. It is to hold on to when riding a bucking horse. **1945** Baker *Austral. Lang.* iii. 71 A *monkey* or *monkey-strap*, a looped strap on the offside of a saddle pommel, used by inferior 'rough-riders'.

12. b. Slang phr. *cold enough to freeze the balls off a brass monkey*: extremely cold. Also in similar and allusive phrases.

[**1835** F. Chamier *Unfortunate Man* I. iv. 117 He was told to be silent, in a tone of voice which set me shaking like a monkey in frosty weather.] **1928** *Amer. Speech* IV. 123 Cold enough to freeze the tail off a brass monkey. **1937** Partridge *Dict. Slang* 528/2 Cold enough to freeze the balls off a brass monkey. **1972** *Evening Telegram* (St. John's, Newfoundland) 5 Aug. 3/1 Here's Smallwood still putting up a brass-monkey face right to the bitter end. **1973** *Guardian* 20 July 9 (*headline*) Brass monkey weather. *Ibid.*, You ought to buy yourself a brass monkey and then you will know what a freeze is.

c. *I'll be* (or *I am*) *a monkey's uncle*: a colloquial expression of surprise.

1926 Maines & Grant *Wise-Crack Dict.* 5/2 *Be a monkey's uncle*, be surprised. **1961** Partridge *Dict. Slang* Suppl. 1142/2 I'll be a monkey's uncle!

d. Slang phr. *not to give* (or *care*) *a monkey's* (*fuck*, etc.): not to care at all; to be completely indifferent or unconcerned.

Even without the last bracketed word a fairly coarse expression.

1960 G. W. Target *Teachers* 100 The Old Man's door opened and the pair of them came out, Stillwell not seeming to give a monkey's, but too casual, and poor Jimmy Taylor with his hands clenched before him like the broken forelegs of a ginned rabbit. **1961** Partridge *Dict. Slang* Suppl. 1188/1 *Monkey's f*ck, not to care a*, not to care a rap: low (esp. Naval). **1968** M. Woodhouse *Rock Baby* xii. 116, I don't give a monkey's knee if he was with the Resistance or the Mafia. **1970** *Observer* 10 May 33/5 Tony Martin has booked himself a vasectomy... 'I was brought up a Catholic,' he said, 'but I don't give a monkey's; you've got to be practical.' **1972** J. Brown *Chancer* iii. 44, I don't give a monkey's if you drop down dead. **1975** J. Wainwright *Square Dance* 26 'Not,' snarled Sugden, 'that I give a solitary monkey's toss what you wear.'

13. (Earlier examples.)

1833 B. Webster *Golden Farmer* ii. ii. 40 The Golden Farmer,..ven his monkey's up, vould go through me like a flash of lightning through a gooseberry bush. *c* **1852** J. R. Planché *Good Woman in Wood* ii. ii. 27 I'm short in

stature—that I don't deny, But put my monkey up, I'm six feet high!

b. *to have a* (or *the*) *monkey on one's back*; (*a*) to be angry or enraged (*Obs.*); (*b*) orig. *U.S.*, to be a drug-addict (see also quot. 1942); hence *monkey* = addiction to, or habitual use of, drugs. *slang.*

1860 HOTTEN *Dict. Slang* (ed. 2) 174 A man is said to have his monkey up, or the monkey on his back, when he is 'riled', or out of temper. **1942** BERREY & VAN DEN BARK *Amer. Thes. Slang.* § 509/28 *Have a Chinaman* or *monkey on one's back*, to manifest withdrawal distress. **1949** N. ALGREN *Man with Golden Arm* 60 He *wants* to carry the monkey, he's punishin' hisself..'n don't even know it. *Ibid.*, Then I got forty grains 'n went up to the room 'n went from monkey to nothin' in twenny-eight days 'n that's nine-ten years ago 'n the monkey's dead. **1960** C. L. COOPER *Scene* xii. 168 We're just little kids with the monkey and a couple bucks. Well, *our* monkey weighs just as much as yours, and it hurts just as much, and it takes the same stuff to get it off as it does yours! **1970** E. R. JOHNSON *God Keepers* (1971) vi. 61 An addict's greatest worry would not be his, since Vito would feed his monkey. *Ibid.* 68 Having a monkey on your back.. always worked out logically to be the first purpose in a junkie's life. **1972** H. C. RAE *Shooting Gallery* iii. 204, I didn't have the monkey then. That's how I got started.

14. Delete *Betting* and add further examples.

1922 E. WALLACE *Flying Fifty-Five* x. 57, I lost a monkey on the last race, and a monkey on the Coventry. That's a thousand, isn' it? **1972** *Sunday Sun* (Brisbane) 9 Jan. 18/4 Lady from pub A told lady from pub B that the boss had given her a monkey as a bonus. Lady from pub B interpreted monkey as the slang term for $500 and immediately attacked her boss for his stinginess in only handing out $100. **1973** *Times* 9 Jan. 4/8 It looks like you are going to be roped into that theft from the pub but it will be all right. It will cost you a monkey (£500).

16. *monkey fur, -god, -mischief, -people, -skin*; *monkey-fashion* adv. (earlier example).

1868 A. J. MUNBY *Diary* 7 Sept. (1972) 245 She sprang or climbed, monkeyfashion. **1920** in C. W. Cunnington *Eng. Women's Clothing* (1952) v. 160 Afternoon frock.. with..fringe of monkey fur. **1960** *Sunday Express* 23 Oct. 14/5 The latest fur coat for cult-clothes addicts is in monkey fur. **1883, 1886** Monkey-god [see *HANUMAN 1]. **1962** *Listener* 22 Feb. 350/2 The monkey-gods of Stupidity, Mediocrity, and Servility to be always defied. **1778** P. THICKNESSE *Year's Journey* (ed. 2) II. xlv. 103 All [negroes] have a degree of monkey cunning, and even monkey mischief. **1886** C. M. YONGE *Chantry House* I. xv. 142 He made no secret of his contempt for the insufferable dulness of the country, enlivening it by various acts of monkey-mischief. **1895** KIPLING *2nd Jungle Bk.* 140 Ere Mor the Peacock flutters, ere the Monkey-People cry. **1910** W. DE LA MARE *Three Mulla-Mulgars* viii. 105 Mishcha and Môha..wouldn't touch monkey-skin. **1962** E. E. EVANS-PRITCHARD *Ess. Soc. Anthropol.* v. 112 His head was covered with a monkey-skin cap.

17. a. monkey bag (see quot.); **monkey band** = **monkey orchestra*; **monkey bridge** *Naut.* (see quots.); **monkey business** orig. *U.S.*, foolish, trifling, or deceitful conduct (cf. MONKEY *v.* 2); **monkey-chaser** *U.S. slang*, (*a*) a Negro from the West Indies or other tropical regions; (*b*) (see quot. 1952); **monkey coat** = *monkey-jacket*; **monkey-doodle business** *U.S. slang* = **monkey business*; **monkey-eating eagle,** also **monkey eagle,** the largest eagle found in the Philippine Islands, *Pithecophaga jefferyi*; **monkey forecastle** *Naut.* (see quot. 1948); **monkey gland,** a gland or testicle from a monkey, grafted on to a man as a possible means of rejuvenation; also *attrib.*; **monkey-house,** also *transf.* and *fig.*; **monkey-hurdler** *U.S. slang* (see quots.); **monkey island** *Naut. slang*, a small bridge above the pilot-house; **monkey-jacket** (earlier example; see also quot. 1968); **monkey-man,** (*a*) *U.S. slang*, a weak and servile husband; (*b*) a man resembling a monkey; **monkey meat** *U.S. Army slang*, tinned meat; *spec.* tinned beef-and-potato hash; **monkey orchestra,** a group of Meissen or other porcelain figures representing monkeys playing musical instruments; **monkey** (or **monkey's, monkeys'**) **parade** *slang* (see quots.); also **monkey-parading** *vbl. sb.* and *ppl. a.*; **monkey poop** *Naut. slang* (see quot. 1929); **monkey pox,** a virus disease of monkeys (and of human beings), similar to smallpox; **monkey's fist,** a thick knot made at the end of a rope to give it weight when it is thrown; **monkey shaft** *Austral.* and *N.Z. colloq.*, a small trial shaft; **monkey-shines** (earlier and later examples); also *sing.*; **monkey's island** *Naut. slang* = **monkey island*; **monkey strap** = sense 10* above; **monkey suit,** † (*a*) a type of child's suit (see quot. *a* 1901); (*b*) *slang* (orig. *U.S.*), a uniform; a formal dress suit, evening dress; **monkey's wedding** *S. Afr. colloq.*, a situation of alternating or simultaneous sunshine and rain; **monkey-trap** *colloq.* or *dial.*, something decorative worn by women to make themselves attractive to men; **monkey trial,** the trial in 1925 of a Tennessee school-teacher, J. T. Scopes, for teaching evolutionary theories; also *transf.* and *attrib.*; **monkey trick,** a mischievous, foolish, or underhand trick or act; an antic; usu. *pl.*; **monkey-wrench,** also *fig.*, esp. in colloq. phr. *to throw* (or *hurl*) *a monkey-wrench into the machinery*, etc.: to act as an obstruction or hindrance; to 'throw a spanner into the works'; hence as *v. trans.*, to turn with a monkey-wrench.

1847 H. MELVILLE *Omoo* xxxiv. 134 A small leather wallet—a 'monkey bag' (so called by sailors)—usually worn as a purse about the neck. **1934** W. B. HONEY *Dresden China* iv. 118 Some of the best known of all Meissen figures are the *Monkey Band*.., an assemblage of more than twenty separate figures with a conductor, which is said to have been modelled in ridicule of Count Brühl's orchestra. **1927** G. BRADFORD *Gloss. Sea Terms* 115/2 *Monkey bridge*, usually above the pilot or chart house where the standard compass is commonly set. Sometimes the fore and aft bridge on a sailing ship. **1967** C. JOKSTAD *Captain & Sea* 100 We placed the body on the monkey bridge, which is the very after end or stern of the vessel. **1883** G. W. PECK *Peck's Bad Boy* 109 There must be no monkey business going on. **1902** H. HAPGOOD *Spirit of Ghetto* vii. 209 The 'monkey business' of learning had ruined the child. **1934** C. DAY LEWIS *Hope for Poetry* vi. 29 A pandemonium of slogans, national anthems, headlines..manifestos, monkey business. **1972** 'H. CARMICHAEL' *Naked to Grave* vi. 79 Because I've seen her talking with one of the neighbours isn't to say there was any monkey-business between them. **1926** C. VAN VECHTEN *Nigger Heaven* 286 *Monkey-chaser*, a Negro from the British West Indies. **1952** *New Yorker* 30 Aug. 15/3 Monkey chasers are gin and ice, with a little sugar and a trace of water. That term 'monkey chaser' comes from Georgia. **1859** *Times* 27 Jan. 9/4 Jones was at the time dressed not as he now is, but in what they call a 'monkey coat'. **1928** *Sat. Even. Post* 12 May 41/2 They ought not to go abroad with such monkey-doodle business. **1909** *Westm. Gaz.* 6 Sept. 5/3 The general plumage of the Monkey Eagle is a rich brown above and creamy white in the under parts. **1909** R. C. MCGREGOR *Man. Philippine Birds* I. 226 (*heading*) *Pithecophaga jefferyi* Grant. Monkey-eating eagle. **1966** R. & D. MORRIS *Men & Apes* vi. 204 The heavy-billed, shaggy-crested *Pithecophaga* eagle of the Philippines is popularly called the monkey-eating eagle. **1971** J. E. DUPONT *Philippine Birds* 47 (*heading*) Monkey-eating Eagle. **1873** *Rep. R. Comm. Unseaworthy Ships* 808/1 in *Parl. Papers* (C. 853) XXXVI. 315 Has a half poop and monkey forecastle. **1948** R. DE KERCHOVE *Internat. Maritime Dict.* 473/1 *Monkey forecastle*, a short low forecastle open on the after side and used solely for anchor gear (windlass, and so on). **1924** G. B. SHAW *St. Joan* p. xix, Fortified..against old age by ..weekly doses of monkey gland. *Ibid.* p. xx, Which is the healthier mind? the saintly mind or the monkey gland mind? **1929** *Encycl. Brit.* XI. 747/2 The grafting into men of testicles from apes (the so-called 'monkey glands') has been practised by Voronoff and others with resulting rejuvenation. **1971** R. DENTRY *Encounter at Kharmel* iv. 72 Stop talking like Noel Coward after a shot of monkey glands! **1914** 'I. HAY' *Knight on Wheels* (ed. 2) xxiii. 221 The rooms..were described by the agent and Timothy as 'a lovely little bachelor suite' and 'a self-contained monkey-house' respectively. **1923** A. HUXLEY *Antic Hay* xvii. 246 The world would soon be a..bear-garden..and a monkey-house. **1924** J. BUCHAN *Three Hostages* ix. 131 It's up to the few sahibs like him in that damned monkey-house at Westminster to make a row about it. **1966** J. B. PRIESTLEY *Salt is Leaving* iv. 49 'Why do you have this window thing—here along the wall?' 'So I can see what's happening in my club... Come in later one night—..when it's all lit up down there—and you're looking through a window at a monkey house.' **1936** *Amer. Mercury* May p. x/2 Monkey hurdler, organist. **1951** W. MORUM *Gabriel* II. ix. 250 Nelson's a monkey hurdler... He plays one of those Wurlitzer organs at the talkies. **1912** 'AURORA' *Jock Scott* xix. 243, I was on Monkey Island (a pet name for the upper bridge) for hours. **1963** P. J. ABRAHAM *Last Hours* xi. 134 Up on the monkey island he had realized there would be no power for the lights. **1830** N. AMES *Mariner's Sk.* 187 My wardrobe consisted of a 'monkey' jacket, bought in Gravesend, [etc.]. **1968** J. IRONSIDE *Fashion Alphabet* 37 *Monkey-jacket.* This was originally a warm, heavy, thick, jacket worn by sailors... But more usually now it refers to a shorter waist-length jacket similar to a bell-boy, middy or mess jacket. **1924** J. E. & L. MARTIN (*song-title*) Monkey man. **1927** S. A. BROWN in C. Cullen *Caroling Dusk* 132 Had a stovepipe blonde in Macon Yaller gal in Marylan In Richmond had a choklit brown Called me huh monkey man—Huh big fool monkey man. **1928** *Collier's* 5 May 36/3 A money man is a contemptuous thing among Negroes, friendless, distrusted, and generally despised. But a monkey man! Well, there's nothing lower than a monkey man. **1935** E. R. BURROUGHS *Pirates of Venus* iii. 54 Venus was inhabited! But by what?.. Were they a species of monkey-man? **1960** P. OLIVER *Blues fell this Morning* 117 The man who is proud of his sexual prowess, real or imaginary, takes pleasure in ridiculing the 'monkey men': the West Indians and other Negroes that he despises whom he compares with the apes. **1966** *Southern Folklore Q.* XXX. 230 The Monkey Man is the servile mate who without protest turns over his hard-earned money to a woman... The husband who stayed and put up with it all became a Monkey Man and a standing joke. **1968** P. OLIVER *Screening Blues* vi. 258 The 'creeping man' and the 'monkey man' are objects of contempt in the blues, but they are the lovers who succeed when the singer fails. **1918** in Cowing & Cooper *Dear Folks at Home* (1919) x. 87 He was crying pitifully, and we gave him cigarettes and some of our monkey meat and hardtack. **1919** *Red Cross Mag.* Feb. 37/1 When you hear the soldier's side of the story, his mess in camp and on the line consists of 'monkey meat' (canned beef-and-potato hash). **1929** *Papers Mich. Acad. Sci. & Arts* X. 309 *Monkey meat*, canned beef and potato-hash. **1906** R. L. HOBSON *Porcelain* xiii. 122 A Frenchman named Acier.. worked at Meissen from 1764 till he was pensioned off in 1799, and modelled the celebrated Cries of Paris..and the Monkey Orchestra. **1960** R. G. HAGGAR *Conc. Encycl. Continental Pott. & Porc.* 22/2 Monkey orchestra: a series of twenty-one porcelain figures of monkeys playing instruments with a conductor, modelled by Kändler at Meissen in 1747. **1910** H. G. WELLS *New Machiavelli* (1911) I. iii. 66 These twilight parades of young people, youngsters chiefly of the lower middle-class, are one of the odd social developments of the great suburban growths—unkindly critics..call them, I believe, Monkeys' Parades. **1914** E. PUGH *Cockney at Home* 116 If you don't know what a monkey parade is ask Anderson here... 'It's a place where the elite of the beau monde of Suburbia meet nightly, for purposes of flirtation.' **1934** J. B. PRIESTLEY *Eng. Journey* iv. 183 Elderly citizens have been protesting against this practice of promenading on Sunday nights [in Bradford]. They have always been disgusted by the sight of young people monkey-parading in this fashion... They could easily do it in a much more civilised fashion than this of monkey-parading. *Ibid.* 185 A Sabbatarian town of this kind, which could offer its young folk nothing on Sunday night but a choice between monkey-parading and dubious pubs. **1929** F. C. BOWEN *Sea Slang* 92 *Monkey poop* [misprinted *poor*], the half deck of a flush decked ship. **1959** P. VON MAGNUS et al. in *Acta Path. & Microbiol. Scand.* XLVI. 156 The isolation of a virus from the diseased animals will also be described as well as some studies on the properties of the agent which in this paper will be referred to as monkey pox virus. **1960** *Ann. N.Y. Acad. Sci.* LXXXV. 957 The etiological agent of monkey pox has been isolated from naturally infected animals by using both embryonated chicken eggs and tissue cultures. **1971** *Daily Colonist* (Victoria, B.C.) 25 Aug. 5/1 Monkey-pox, a disease very like smallpox, has been discovered for the first time in human beings in Africa. What caused the outbreak is a mystery. **1927** G. BRADFORD *Gloss. Sea Terms* 115/2 *Monkey's fist*, a complicated knot with weight enclosed, used at the end of a heaving line. **1961** K. VONNEGUT *Sirens of Titan* (1967) i. 21 The hard, ball-like knot known as a *monkey's fist*. **1974** *Islander* (Victoria, B.C.) 29 Sept. 10/2 They were so high above us that we had to crane back our necks to look at them, waiting for the lethal lead-filled monkey's fists at the end of their lines to come whistling down. **1880** G. SUTHERLAND *Tales of Goldfields* 69 They began to think they might be already too deep for it, and a small 'monkey'-shaft was therefore driven upwards from the end of the tunnel. **1828** T. D. RICE *Jim Crow* iii, I cut so many munky shines, I dance de gallopade. **1847** 'H. FRANCO' *Trippings of Tom Pepper* I. vi. 43 Let me catch him cutting up any monkey shines in this house, and I'll bea[n] him! **1932** R. FROST *Let.* 13 Dec. (1964) 231 In a way it was a monkey-shine and he needn't have minded poetry's having a little the best of it for once. **1945** Monkey-shines [see *CUT *v.* 59 o]. **1973** 'H. HOWARD' *Highway to Murder* xi. 141 Why all the monkeyshines to get rid of Lucy? He'd been divorced before and he could be divorced again. **1917** 'TAFFRAIL' *Sub* iv. 110 He kept watch on the 'monkey's island'. **1919** W. LANG *Sea-Lawyer's Log* iii. 33 Now this 'ere is called the forebridge, and that little platform above it is the Compass Platform. Monkey's island, they calls it. **1929** W. SMYTH *Bonzer Jones* i. 13 Put a monkey strap on [the buck-jumper for riding]! **1886** C. M. YONGE *Chantry House* I. i. 9 Mrs. Gooch had only to thrust her hand into the little pocket of his monkey suit to convict him on the spot. *a* **1901** —— *Autobiogr.* in C. Coleridge *C. M. Yonge* (1903) ii. 66 'Monkey suits', with jacket and waistcoat all in one, and trousers fastened over. **1920** R. LARDNER in *Sat. Even. Post* 27 Nov. 42/4, I and the Mrs. and Kate was the only ones there in evening clothes. The others had attended these functions before and knew that they wouldn't be enough suckers on hand to make any difference whether you wore a monkey suit or rompers. **1928** *Daily Mail* 7 May 6/4 *Monkey suit*, flying suit. **1950** DYLAN THOMAS *Let.* 10 Jan. (1966) 343, I..demothed my monkey-suit and borrowed some proper shoes. **1974** A. FOWLES *Pastime* v. 46 He could..hire one of those monkey-suits from Moss Bros. **1949** *Cape Times* 29 Nov. 16/3 The Peninsula had a 'monkey's wedding' rainfall yesterday with the sun shining at intervals and rain falling intermittently. **1961** *Ibid.* 8 Aug. 7 The weather was not exactly 'monkey's wedding' weather last week, sunshine alternating with a drizzle. **1931** W. DE LA MARE *Seven Short Stories* 85, I take you for an honest man's daughter with not a ha'penny to spare on fal-lals and monkey-traps. **1925** *Evening Sun* (Baltimore) 26 June 17/3 Washington is getting the reflex of increasing European interest in the so-called monkey trial. **1963** *Times* 30 Apr. 11/6 The student teachers, Miss Dori Doss and Miss Martha Powell, are apparently prepared for a second 'monkey trial' if necessary, though they realize that their determination could cost them their careers. **1969** D. F. HORROBIN *Science is God* ii. 15 It is associated more with the summer heat of the monkey-trial country of Tennessee rather than with the coolness of the dreaming spires of Oxford. **1653** W. DENTON *Let.* 13 Mar. in M. M. Verney *Memoirs* (1894) III. vi. 203 Bringe it [*sc.* a colt] with you in your coach, and then she will teach it all her Monkey tricks. **1742** RICHARDSON *Pamela* (ed. 3) III. xxxiv. 408 Hold him fast, and play over all thy monkey tricks with him, with all my heart. **1809, 1864** Monkey trick [in Dict., sense 16]. **1910** G. K. CHESTERTON *G. B. Shaw* 152 Shaw treats vengeance as something too small for man—a monkey trick he ought to have outlived. **1951** Monkey trick [see *DOT *v.*[1] 6]. **1958** C. ACHEBE *Things fall Apart* III. xxv. 184 He had warned Obierika that if he and his men played any monkey tricks they would be shot. **1904** W. N. HARBEN *Georgians* 267 He..dug down in the road whar his pipe j'ined the main, till he got to it, an' then he monkey-wrenched it off. **1920** *Everybody's Mag.* May 36/3 Don't throw a monkey-wrench into the machinery! **1931** *Daily Express* 16 Oct. 1/2 Mr. Lloyd George hurled a monkey wrench last night into the creaking and decrepit machinery of Liberalism. **1966** D. VARADAY *Gara-Yaka's Domain* xi. 126 Just as I was about to squeeze the trigger an ebb wind threw the monkey wrench into the works. The rising ill-wind struck the back of our necks, carrying our scent down to the elephant. **1971** *Black Scholar* Apr.–May 30/2 It is the black inmate who throws the monkey wrench into the works. **1975** *Jewish Chron.* 16 May 2/3 Mr Eban has thrown a monkey-wrench into the Israeli information campaign in the United States.

b. monkey fiddle, a West Indian tree or shrub, *Pedilanthus tithymaloides* or *P. angustifolius,* of the family Euphorbiaceæ; **monkey nut** (later examples); **monkey-pod (tree)** = *GUANGO; **monkey-puzzle,** substitute for def.: a large, evergreen tree, *Araucaria araucana,* native to Chile and belonging to the family Pinaceæ, whose leaves are densely arranged to cover the whorled branches; also *fig.* (later examples); **monkey-puzzler** = **monkey-puzzle*; **monkey-rope** *S. Afr.,* one of several climbing plants, esp. *Secamone alpinii,* of the family Asclepiadaceæ.

1913 *Publ. Field Columbian Museum Bot. Ser.* II. 360 The peculiar silicious ridges of the stems and branches [of *Pedilanthus bahamensis*] produce a high squeak when they are rubbed together—children play at fiddling with them, hence the local name 'Monkey-fiddle'. **1954** *Caribbean Quarterly* III. i. 6 The duppy fiddle (more often called monkey fiddle) makes a grotesque squeaking when two sticks of it are rubbed together. **1896** H. L. TANGYE *New S. Afr.* iv. 297 He brings a whole heap of sweet potatoes.. and monkey nuts, the latter being sometimes known as ground, or pea-nuts. **1916** [see *ARACHIS]. **1950** T. S. ELIOT *Cocktail Party* III. 142 *Alex.* Three of us have been out on a tour of inspection Of local conditions. *Julia.* What about? Monkey nuts? **1888** W. HILLEBRAND *Flora Hawaiian Islands* 115 *Pithecolobium Samang,* the Samang or Monkey-pod tree, enjoys great favour as a shade tree. **1937** D. & H. TEILHET *Feather Cloak Murders* ix. 156 They drove down the scented street, overshadowed by the great leafy monkey pod trees which rustled in the night breeze. **1969** T. H. EVERETT *Living Trees of World* 203/1 The rain tree, monkey pod or saman.., an evergreen or deciduous native of the West Indies and Central America now planted in many other tropical regions... has a wide-spreading, dome-shaped crown and grows up to 100 feet in height. **1923** DALLIMORE & JACKSON *Handbk. Coniferæ* II. 160 The common name of *Monkey Puzzle* is said to have originated in Cornwall... On one occasion when the owner of a plant was exhibiting it to friends a remark was passed to the effect that 'it would puzzle a monkey to climb that tree', and the owner forthwith adopted the name 'monkey puzzle'. **1938** *Times Lit. Suppl.* 14 May 342/2 The multitudinous little Careys of the future will have to be trained in mental agility on this veritable monkey-puzzle of a pedigree. **1940** [see *CHILE]. **1969** T. H. EVERETT *Living Trees of World* 24/2 The dark green leaves of the monkey puzzle are broad, stiff, leathery and sharp-pointed. They overlap each other and clothe the curious, rather brittle snakelike branches closely. **1906** J. GALSWORTHY *Man of Property* III. iii. 298 In the shade of a monkey-puzzler or in the lee of some india-rubber plant. **1936** E. WAUGH *Mr. Loveday's Little Outing* 9 The weather..had suddenly blackened into a squall. There had been a scuttle for cover;..a table-cloth lofted to the boughs of the monkey-puzzler, fluttering in the rain. **1838** W. H. HARVEY *Genera S. Afr. Plants* 221 S[*ecamone*] *Thunbergii*... known by the colonial name of 'Babianstouw' or 'Monkey-rope', is a voluble [*sic*] climbing shrub, not uncommon in our woods. **1849** [in Dict. s.v. sense 17 a]. **1876** H. BROOKS *Natal* 125 The festooned stems of evergreen twiners hang down as 'monkey ropes'. **1907** T. R. SIM *Forests & Forest Flora Cape of Good Hope* 177 Both [species of *Vitis*] form 'Monkey-ropes', which, split up, are much used by the natives for tying down the thatch on hut-roofs. **1972** *Stand. Encycl. Southern Africa* VII. 515/1 Monkey-rope... (*Secamone alpinii.*) Plant of the family *Asclepiadaceæ,* a scrambler on bushes and trees. When it grows in a forest its old stems form the well-known 'monkey-ropes' hanging down from the trees. *Ibid.* 515/2 Other climbers, also called monkey- or bush-rope, are *Rhoicissus capensis* (monkey grapes), *Cynachum obtusifolium,* and *Dalbergia* spp. ('doringtou'). The runners of most of these plants are particularly strong and are therefore used by baboons and monkeys for climbing.

monkey, *v.* Add: **2.** (Earlier and later examples.) Also, to fool or mess *about* or *around;* to waste time, or spend time aimlessly; to tamper *with.* So **mo·nkeying** *vbl. sb.* orig. *U.S.*

1881 I. M. RITTENHOUSE *Jrnl.* in *Maud* (1939) ii. 39 What with talking, running back and forth and general monkey-ing Clara slipped and fell. **1884** E. W. NYE *Baled Hay* 38 The young coyote may come and monkey o'er his grave. **1884** *Canon City* (Colo.) *Mercury* 22 Aug. 4/1 This reminds us of a sign in a Michigan planing mill, 'Dont Munkey with the Buz Saw.' **1916** *Dialect Notes* IV. 277 'What did you do after supper?' 'We just monkeyed around.' **1932** E. WAUGH *Black Mischief* v. 168 I'm not going to have any monkeying about with my men. You'll lame the whole army in a day if you try to make 'em wear boots. **1939** G. B. SHAW *Geneva* III. 98 A frontier is a frontier; and there must be no monkeying with it. **1955** *Times* 27 June 2/7 Any attempt to 'monkey about' with the powers or composition of the Upper House would destroy the balance of the constitution. **1957** *Times* 23 Sept. 11/1 Any departure from tradition form or colour would be as serious as monkeying about with the colour of an old school tie. **1972** J. W. THOMPSON in W. King *Black Short Story Anthol.* 257 Muhdear [*sc.* Mother] monkeyed with my collar again. And for what must have been the twentieth time, she smoothed my tie.

monkey-face. Add: **1.** (Further examples.) Also, a person with a monkey-like or funny face.

1936 C. SANDBURG *People, Yes* lvi. 130 Where did ja cop dat monkeyface. *Ibid.* 131 Gwan monkeyface peddle yer papers. **1946** E. O'NEILL *Iceman Cometh* (1947) I. 17 Hello, leedle Rocky! Leedle monkey-face! I did not recognise you. *Ibid.,* Laugh, leedle monkey-faces! Laugh like fools, leedle stupid peoples! **1959** I. & P. OPIE *Lore & Lang. Schoolch.* ix. 171 A funny-faced person may also be called..'Monkey Face'.

b. A grimace. *West Indies colloq.*

1943 L. BENNETT *Jamaican Humour in Dialect* 3 For wen she laugh it like she Dah meck up monkey face. **1946** E. N. BURKE *Stories told by Uncle Newton* I. 31 The boys make monkey faces at me and I return the compliment with interest. **1952** S. SELVON *Brighter Sun* iv. 58 'Pewee, come an' go to school!' but Pewee made them a 'monkey face' and ran into the shop.

3. The monkey-faced owl. *U.S. colloq.* or *dial.*

1955 *Amer. Speech* XXX. 180 The barn owl is very generally called *monkey-faced owl,* a designation often shortened to *monkey face.*

monkey-faced, *a.* (Earlier and later examples.) spec. *U.S., monkey-faced owl,* the barn-owl, *Tyto alba.*

1803 *Lett. Miss Riversdale* II. 284, I shall be so much my own enemy, as to take up with any monkey-faced battered rake. **1915** J. BUCHAN *Thirty-Nine Steps* i. 12, I went home, dressed, dined at the Café Royal, and turned into a music-hall. It was a silly show, all capering women and monkey-faced men. **1917** *Dialect Notes* IV. 426 *Hibou paille,* the American barn owl (Aluco pratincolo): also called *monkey-faced owl.* **1955** [see *MONKEY-FACE 3]. **1961** O. L. AUSTIN *Birds of World* 154/1 Barn owls differ from the typical owls in their heart-shaped facial disk, which is so simian in aspect that the birds are often called 'monkey-faced owls'.

Mon-Khmer (mōᵘ·nˌk'mēəɹ). [f. *MON *sb.*² and *a.* + *KHMER *sb.* and *a.*] The designation of a group of Indo-Chinese languages, of which the most important are Mon and Khmer, spoken in south-east Asia and considered by some philologists to belong to the Austroasian family. Also *attrib.,* with reference to the peoples who speak these languages.

1887 *Trans. Philol. Soc. 1885–86* 428 The..Indo-Chinese division and its two branches Mōn-Khmer, and Taï-Shan. *Ibid.* 435 The numerals and many words belong to the Mōn-Khmer family. **1904** G. A. GRIERSON *Linguistic Survey of India* II. 1 The Mōn-Khmēr languages are monosyllabic. **1932** [see *KHMER *sb.* and *a.*]. **1933** [see *AUSTRIC *a.*]. **1936** [see *AUSTRO-²]. **1964** S. WAVELL *Naga King's Daughter* ii. 36 The Semelairs, whose unique language is Mon-Khmer, had lived on the lake as long as they could remember.

Monmouth. 1. (Later examples.)

1777 *Maryland Jrnl.* 22 July (Th.), [He had on a] Monmouth cap, and old coarse shoes. **1938** A. L. MAYCOCK *Nicholas Ferrar* viii. 204 The three masters in their black gowns and Monmouth caps followed by the boys, two and two.

monnick, monniker, varr. *MONIKER.

‖ **mono** (mǫ·no), *sb.*¹ [Sp.] A boiler-suit, workman's overalls (see also quot. 1937).

1937 F. BORKENAU *Spanish Cockpit* ii. 123 The streets and cafés are full of militia, all of them dressed in their *monos,* the new dark-blue uniforms. **1965** C. D. EBY *Siege of Alcázar* (1966) i. 28 Many of them wore their regular overalls—loose-fitting blue boiler-suits called *monos.*

mono (mǫ·no). [The prefix MONO- abstracted from compounds in which it occurs.] **1.** Colloq. abbrev. of *MONOPHONIC *a.* 2; also as *sb.*², monophonic recording or reproduction.

1959 *Manch. Guardian* 4 Aug. 3/2 For the benefit of non-stereo collectors, most of these records have appeared also in mono. **1961** *Times* 1 July 11/5 The mono recording is fair enough. **1963** *Which?* Jan. 3/1 When a mono orchestral record..is reproduced, the sound from any one instrument generally appears to come from much the same direction as all the other instruments. **1971** M. MCCARTHY *Birds of America* 24 'Did it *have* to be stereo?' Peter groaned, homesick for their old mono set. **1972** K. BONFIGLIOLI *Don't point that Thing at Me* ii. 16 The Flying Scotsman whooped stereophonically... I competed in mono. **1974** *Listener* 14 Feb. 219/2 A radio play with a surplus of stereo trickery is not likely to be well received by listeners on mono sets.

2. Colloq. abbrev. of *MONONUCLEOSIS.

1964 *Amer. Speech* XXXIX. 120 The general student preoccupation with internal disorders and other forms of illness, especially around examination time (cf. the frequent references among students to *mono* for 'mononucleosis'). **1970** *New Yorker* 9 May 45/3 After three sleepless, cold nights..he came down with something resembling mono. **1972** F. KNEBEL *Dark Horse* (1973) vi. 88, I had a chance to meet the Yugoslav ambassador last summer, but then I came down with mono.

mono: see *MONOSABIO.

mono-. Add: **1. monoalphabe·tic** *a.,* denoting a cipher in which each letter corresponds to one letter of the normal alphabet; **mono-a·nthropism,** belief in the unity or indivisibility of mankind; **mo·noblast** *Biol.* [a. G. *monoblast* (O. Naegeli *Blutkrankheiten und Blutdiagnostik* (ed. 3, 1923) 143): see -BLAST], a cell that develops into a monocyte; **mo·no-cable,** an aerial ropeway in which a single endless rope is used both to support the loads and to move them; usu. *attrib.*; **monocau·sal** *a.,* in terms of a sole cause; **monocistro·nic** *a. Genetics,* containing as much genetic information as is carried by a single cistron; **monoclo·nal** *Biol.* and *Med.,* forming a single clone; derived asexually from a single individual or cell; **monoco·lour** = *MONOCHROME *sb.* 2 c; **monocoloured** *a.*: delete *rare*⁻¹ and substitute *rare;* (later *fig.* example); **monoconsona·ntal** *a.,* containing a single consonant; **mo·no-crystal,** a single crystal; so **monocry·stalline** *a.,* consisting of or constituting a monocrystal; **monode·ntate** *a. Chem.* [L. *dentātus:* see DENTATE *a.*], (of a ligand) having only one point of attachment to a central atom; **monodiale·ctal** *a.,* speaking only one dialect; hence **monodiale·ctally** *adv.*; **mo·nodiet,** a diet confined to one type of food; **monodime·nsional** *a.,* existing in or having only one dimension; linear; **monodispe·rse** *a. Physical Chem.,* (of a dispersed phase) present as particles all of the same mass; (of a sol) containing such a phase; **monoenerge·tic** *a. Physics,* (consisting of particles) of the same energy; emitting radiation all of one energy; **mo·nofil, mo·nofilament,** a single strand of man-made fibre; freq. *attrib.*; **monofu·nctional** *a. Chem.,* having or corresponding to a single functional group per molecule; **mo·nogerm** *a. Agric.,* (of a sugar-beet variety or seed produced by it) having or consisting of only one seed in each seed ball; (cf. *multigerm* s.v. *MULTI- 3); **monogla·cial** *a.,* applied to the theory that there was only one ice age; so **monogla·cialism,** the monoglacial theory; **monogla·cialist** *sb.* and *a.,* (of or pertaining to) a supporter of this theory; **mo·no-log** *Linguistics* (see quots.); **monomi·ctic** *a.* [Gr. μικτός mixed], applied to a lake in which there is only one overturn each year; **mono-minera·lic** *a. Petrol.,* composed of a single mineral; **mo·nopulse,** used *attrib.* and *absol.* to designate (the mode of operation of) radar in which the direction (and usu. also the range) of a target is precisely determined from a single echo pulse that is detected using two or more adjacent aerials; **mo·no-sentence** *nonce-wd.,* a brief or insufficient sentence; **mo·no-sound** *rare*⁻¹, an abrupt single sound; **mono-speci·fic** *a. Biol.,* affecting or containing only one species; **monosta·tic** *a.,* (of radar) having a single aerial as both transmitter and receiver; **monosymptomatic** *a.,* also in *Psychol.* and more general use; **monothetic** *a.,* (*b*) *Taxonomy,* (of a classification) having groups formed on the basis of a single characteristic, or a series of single characteristics; hence **monothe·tically** *adv.*; **mo·notower,** used *attrib.* and *absol.* to designate a crane whose jib is mounted on a single tower; **mono-unsa·turated** *a. Chem.,* (of a compound) saturated except for one multiple bond (usu. between carbon atoms) at which addition can normally occur; **monoxe·nic** *a. Parasitology* [Gr. ξένος stranger], applied to a culture, or the cultivation, of a parasitic organism in the presence of a single other species; **monoxe·nous** *a. Parasitology* [a. G. *monoxen* (A. de Bary 1867, in *Bot. Zeitung* XXV. 264/1), f. Gr. ξένος stranger], of a parasitic plant or animal: restricted to a single host species during its entire life-cycle.

1927 *Daily Express* 24 Nov. 13 The most simple code is the 'monoalphabetic', in which a letter is always represented by the same sign, letter, or numeral. **1950** A. HUXLEY *Themes & Variations* 259 The best antidote to nationalistic idolatry is a monotheism with its corollary (since God's fatherhood implies men's brotherhood) of monoanthropism. **1925** *Contrib. Embryol. Carnegie Inst. Washington* XVI. 241 Naegeli..derives the monocyte from the myeloblast of the bone-marrow..and terms this young cell the 'monoblast'. **1938** H. DOWNEY *Handbk. Hematol.* I. v. 386 Ehrich has taken..exception to Bloom's conclusion that monoblasts other than lymphocytes and myeloblasts do not exist. **1968** PASSMORE & ROBSON *Compan. Med. Stud.* I. xxvi. 12/2 These cells [*sc.* monocytes] are produced mainly in the spleen and lymph nodes. The parent cell, the monoblast, is like the myeloblast and lymphoblast, a cell of about 15 μm in diameter with a large nucleus, containing 2–3 nucleoli, filling much of the cell cytoplasm. **1926** H. BLYTH *Mod. Telpherage & Ropeways* xiii. 111 The mono-cable system has been developed very extensively in this country, and although formerly considered as being suitable only for light duty and small gradients, has now proved to be quite suitable for capacities up to 150 tons per hour and gradients of 1 in 2½. **1958**

I. C. F. STATHAM *Coal Mining Pract.* II. vii. 509 The Mono-Cable is the oldest and simplest, being first used in Dantzig in 1644. **1964** *Economist* 14 Nov. 745/2 Using [for bridges] a mono-cable instead of dual cable suspension. **1973** *Gloss. Terms Materials Handling* (*B.S.I.*) VII. 8 *Mono-cable trestle*, a structure supporting a mono-cable ropeway between the ropeway stations. **1957** C. HUNT *Guide to Communist Jargon* xxiv. 86 Lenin's doctrine illustrates the weakness of monocausal explanations of highly complex phenomena. **1972** R. PLANT in Cox & Dyson *20th-Cent. Mind* I. v. 161 Weber conceded that an economic interpretation of history and social life was possible, but he was not willing to accept any monocausal view in its entirety. *Ibid.* 165 Against the Marxist monocausal view of history therefore, Weber poses a far more complex picture. **1965** *Proc. Nat. Acad. Sci.* LIV. 1193 For these purposes, one would prefer a monocistronic message containing information for only one protein. **1972** *Nature* 21 Jan. 131/2 Each segment is transcribed into a single messenger RNA and at least eight of these ten molecules are translated as monocistronic messengers. **1914** W. E. AGAR in *Phil. Trans. R. Soc.* B. CCV. 422 When a population is known to have been descended asexually from a single common ancestor, it consists of a s'ngle clone and may be described as monoclonal. *Ibid.* 442 The monoclonal population was descended from 70 original ancestors, themselves all descended parthenogenetically from a single known female. **1973** *Sci. Amer.* Aug. 44/1 Are the plaque cells transformed cells, in which the genetic material has somehow become changed from that of the normal cell population? If so, the plaque cells could be expected to be monoclonal: a homogeneous population derived from a single cell, rather than a mixed population of cells as in normal human tissue. **1963** *Listener* 31 Jan. 220/2 The idea of using full orchestra was avoided... To paint a picture which should have universality of expression..the monocolour of strings seemed the only possible medium. **1955** *Times* 25 June 5/6 The parties of the extreme left and those of the right favour a 'mono-coloured' Government..since such a one-party Government..would be more or less permanently at the mercy of right or left. **1948** D. DIRINGER *Alphabet* x. 161 The consonantal principle and the selected symbols to represent mono-consonantal words were used by the Egyptians at the beginning of the third millennium B.C. **1965** *Canad. Jrnl. Linguistics* Spring 154 In other cases we find monoconsonantal roots in one language cognate with biconsonantal forms in the other. **1934** *Rev. Sci. Instr.* V. 402/2 Monocrystals with dimensions of the order of 10 cm were readily produced. **1946** *Nature* 10 Aug. 199/2 The X-ray density must be related to monocrystals, and if indeed the starch grain were a monocrystal the numbers found might be considered as a proof. **1973** *Ibid.* 16 Nov. 124/1 Of future plans perhaps the most striking was V. Braginsky's..idea of using a massive monocrystal instead of an aluminium bar with a resultant very high quality factor to look for the sort of signals astronomers expect from nearby galaxies. **1934** *Rev. Sci. Instr.* V. 402/2 The test showed the main body of the growth to be monocrystalline with the seed. **1946** *Nature* 24 Aug. 261/1 An extensive study was made by R. Jacquersson on the effect of torsion on a monocrystalline rod. **1968** C. G. KUPER *Introd. Theory Superconductivity* vi. 97 Pippard.. made measurements with a number of monocrystalline cylindrical specimens of tin. **1949** KIRK & OTHMER *Encycl. Chem. Technol.* IV. 382 Monofunctional ligand groups..are sometimes known as unidentate or monodentate groups. **1974** *Jrnl. Inorg. & Nuclear Chem.* XXXVI. 1221/1 The behaviour of ethylenediamine as a monodentate ligand has also been reported in a few other cobalt..and chromium..complexes. **1972** J. L. DILLARD *Black English* iii. 85 Reading and writing almost presuppose a certain degree of mastery of Standard English, since nothing was written for the monodialectal speaker of Plantation Creole. **1964** *Archivum Linguisticum* XVI. 73 Martinet..[distinguishes] two senses of the term *dialect*: dialect$_1$, a variety of a language..used monodialectally within a whole language area,..and *dialect*$_2$, a local dialect within a larger dialect$_1$ area. **1920** *Chambers's Jrnl.* 1 May 349/2 No matter what the advocate of a mixed-food diet may say to the contrary, there is no disputing the fact that the nearer one gets to the mono-diet the better the health will be. **1953** 'I. DEVI' *Forever Young Forever Healthy* v. 61 The mono-diet..is the kind of diet where you eat only *one* type of food. It makes no difference whether it is only milk,..or anything else. **1952** *New Biol.* XII. 100 Besides such two-dimensional layers of more or less loosely fixed molecules there certainly must exist some analogous linear phenomena along the edges of crystals, and this would make monodimensional strings or chains of adsorbed particles. **1959** *Brno Studies in English* I. 31 The monodimensional character of spoken utterances..as opposed to the..polydimensional character of written utterances. **1925** G. BARGER tr. *H. Freundlich's Elements Colloid Chem.* 132 The preparation of colloidal solutions containing particles of uniform size—so-called unidisperse (monodisperse) sols—is mostly very difficult. **1940** GLASSTONE *Text-bk. Physical Chem.* xiv. 1232 By means of the ultracentrifuge it has been found that many protein solutions are monodisperse. **1971** *Europ. Jrnl. Biochem.* XXIII. 575 The binding of human serum albumin by monodisperse latex particles was studied. **1950** GLASSTONE *Sourcebk. Atomic Energy* xi. 310/1 Another source of monoenergetic neutrons is the $Li^7(p,n)Be^7$ reaction, the energy of the incident protons being carefully controlled. **1954** *Sci. News* XXXIII. 41 If, therefore, we bombard a nucleus of a particular element with a monoenergetic beam of particles, the nuclei which are excited as a result of the collisions taking place will have a wide range of excitation energies. **1971** *Nature* 3 Dec. 261/1 This factor can be experimentally determined through the use of mono-energetic gamma-ray sources. **1916** CROSS & BEVAN *Text-bk. Paper-Making* (ed. 4) i. 10 The [cellulose] solution has been extensively applied to the production of artificial threads of high lustre, so-called 'artificial silk', and various grades of Monofil (*Crin, Crinole*). **1940** *Times* 21 Mar. 5/5 The other two factories will convert the raw material into intermediate products —monofil at the works of I.C.I. [etc.]. **1972** *Trout & Salmon* June 58/2 Nylon monofil slips more easily through the rod-rings. **1949** *Mod. Plastics* Nov. 69/1 Nylon monofilaments are well established as a material for bristles. **1960** *Aeroplane* XCVIII. 43/3 The chafer covering the bead is of monofilament nylon, as in the case of all other Firestone tubeless tyres, to prevent capillary action of the air and so assist in the maintenance of pressure. **1960** M. SHARCOTT *Place of Many Winds* vii. 115 These lures..are attached to nylon monofilament lines in varying lengths. **1973** *Sci. Amer.* Dec. 134/1 New forms of nylon rope without stretch (a braided sheath around a monofilament core) are used for the long, dark climb. **1946** *Jrnl. Amer. Chem. Soc.* LXVIII. 360/2 The monofunctional trimethylchlorosilane acts as a growth terminating agent or 'chain-stopper'. **1949** [see *monodentate* adj. above]. **1964** *Brit. Med. Bull.* XX. 91/1 The carcinogenic action of a series of monofunctional ethyleneimines. **1971** *Nature* 10 Dec. 324/1 When the number of bonds was anything less than twelve, the bifunctional reagent was able to react with only a monofunctional stoichiometry. **1974** *Analytical Chem.* XLVI. 344 (*heading*) Potentiometric titration of monofunctional bases in ion exchanger–aqueous solution medium. **1950** *Proc. Amer. Soc. Sugar Beet Technologists* VI. 156 Monogerm sugar beet varieties have not been developed in either Europe or America. Failure to develop such varieties is due to difficulties in detecting monogerm plants. **1971** *Farmers Weekly* 19 Mar. 38/3 Modern monogerm varieties mean there is less worry about bolting than before. **1972** *Nature* 21 Jan. 136/2 Larks still destroy young seedlings, spaced scientifically and grown from monogerm seeds. **1914** W. B. WRIGHT *Quaternary Ice Age* vi. 125 We are bound to take our stand on the comparatively simple monoglacial hypothesis until we can prove at least one interglacial period. **1961** L. D. STAMP *Gloss. Geogr. Terms* 323/1 The monoglacial theory considers the Pleistocene ice-sheet to have expanded and contracted in only one general movement without any substantial 'interglacial periods' of recession followed by advance. **1957** J. K. CHARLESWORTH *Quaternary Era* II. xxxvi. 920 Upholders of monoglacialism are becoming fewer, and discussion is turning more and more upon the number of the epochs rather than upon the question of their existence. **1959** F. E. ZEUNER *Pleistocene Period* ii. 54 (*heading*) Monoglacialism. **1914** W. B. WRIGHT *Quaternary Ice Age* vi. 125 The Cyprina Clays of Denmark.. were referred by Geikie..to one of the interglacial periods, but..it was very justly held by the monoglacialists that they might easily be of preglacial age. **1946** *Antiquity* XX. 10 Controversy raged with considerable acrimony between the monoglacialist and polyglacialist exponents of Pleistocene geology. **1968** R. W. FAIRBRIDGE *Encycl. Geomorphol.* 458/2 For a long time, a considerable controversy persisted between monoglacialists and polyglacialists, eventually to be conclusively won by the latter. *Ibid.* 913/1 For a long time, there was a minority belief in only one glacial epoch, the so-called monoglacialist school, and a few representatives still survive. **1929** H. E. PALMER *Rep. Res. Activities 1928–9 Inst. Res. Eng. Teaching* (Tokyo) 9 Each of these white spots is a word, that which is contained in a ring is not a *word* but a *word-family*... I propose to call the spots *monologons* and the rings *monologemes* (the termination *on* suggests the individual unit, and the termination *eme* suggests the group unit..). There are times however when..instead of the cumbrous 'monologons or monologemes' we may use the convenient common form *monologs*. **1947** H. BONGERS *Hist. & Princ. Vocab. Control* I. iii. 56 The vocabulary of a language consists of:..Units neither more nor less than single words written without a break... These have been conveniently termed '*monologs*'. **1956** *Proc. Nat. Acad. Sci.* XLII. 84 For the three categories of Forel's classification [*sc.* polar, temperate, and tropical] the terms cold monomictic, dimictic, and warm monomictic have been used by one of us [*sc.* Hutchinson]..in a forthcoming extensive work on limnology. **1957** G. E. HUTCHINSON *Treat. Limnol.* I. vii. 438 It is..proposed to use the term dimictic for any lake circulating twice a year; warm monomictic will be employed as a substitute for tropical, implying winter circulation above 4°C; and cold monomictic as a substitute for polar, implying summer circulation below 4°C. **1968** R. W. FAIRBRIDGE *Encycl. Geomorphol.* 603/2 The monomictic lake waters [of Lake Atitlán, in Guatemala] appear to be fully circulating in the dry season, but Deevey (1957) found that in August the temperature at the surface is 24°C versus 20°C at the bottom. **1917** *Jrnl. Geol.* XXV. 243 The inquiry gives considerable support to the belief that the monomineralic rocks..are generated by the process of collection of crystals under the action of gravity. **1956** *Mineral. Mag.* XXXI. 120 Specimens (24) to (28) inclusive are practically monomineralic rock specimens from which small, platey single crystals may be obtained. **1970** *Nature* 17 Oct. 258/2 The extreme composition range of the lunar sprays can be most readily explained by solar flares melting minute, essentially monomineralic particles on the lunar surface. **1955** *IRE Convention Record* VIII. 132/2 A third method for generating both positive and negative errors simultaneously..is known as monopulse radar, since all information on range and angle errors is generated from each single pulse. This very satisfactory name was proposed by Bell Telephone Laboratories engineers. **1965** D. K. BARTON in R. S. Berkowitz *Mod. Radar* vii. 603 (*heading*) Operation of amplitude-comparison monopulse. *Ibid.* 598 In return for the added complexity in the receiving and antenna system, the monopulse radar offers reduction in tracking errors caused by target scintillation, an improved data rate.., and efficiency in overcoming thermal noise errors on distant targets. **1966** *McGraw-Hill Encycl. Sci. & Technol.* VIII. 577/2 An additional advantage of monopulse tracking as compared to conical scan is that no mechanical action is required in monopulse. **1970** *Sci. Jrnl.* May 46/1 Modern radars, such as those of the chirp or monopulse types, need compression filters to convert long shallow pulses into tall brief ones and expansion filters to do the opposite. **1817** KEATS *Let.* Mar. (1931) I. 13 Your kindness affects me so sensibly that I can merely put down a few mono-sentences. **1875** *Gentl. Mag.* XV. 445 His laugh—with an abrupt, short, monosound—more like a short gasp or snort than a laugh. **1951** WHITBY & HYNES *Med. Bacteriol.* (ed. 5) xvii. 293 One such mono-specific serum thus appropriately prepared will only agglutinate *Br*[*ucella*] *melitensis*. **1964** A. L. THOMSON *New Dict. Birds* 309/2 Flocks may be monospecific or composed of several species. **1970** *Nature* 22 Aug. 779 (*caption*) *Digenea subarticulata*..belongs to a genus formerly thought to be monospecific. **1974** *Ibid.* 1 Nov. 78/2 The reactivity of the DeV reagent was abolished by previous incubation with a monospecific rabbit anti-human IgG serum. **1957** R. WATSON-WATT *Three Steps to Victory* xxii. 128 We had already erected a direction-finding hut so close to the others as to show that we were ..confidently counting on wholly monostatic working. That is to say we would obtain all the information required from a sector of our front by observations made at a single site accommodating both transmitter and receiver. **1973** *Nature* 9 Mar. 109/2 Some work has been reported in which a steerable monostatic radar has been pointed obliquely in several directions successively, so as to measure more than one velocity component. **1937** G. W. ALLPORT *Personality* (1938) p. ix, Cultural determinism is one of the monosymptomatic approaches; it has a blind spot for the internal balancing factors and structural tenacity within personality. **1965** Monosymptomatic [see **conversion hysteria*]. **1972** H. J. EYSENCK *Psychol. is about People* iii. 111 Her patients were all..suffering from serious and complex phobic anxieties; there were no monosymptomatic cases. **1962** P. H. A. SNEATH in Ainsworth & Sneath *Microbial Classification* 291 Special classifications are usually based on single characters, or on a series of single characters... Beckner..calls such groups monotypic, because the defining set of features is unique, but since monotypic has other meanings, monothetic is a better term. **1965** *Math. in Biol. & Med.* (Med. Res. Council) III. 82 (*caption*) Group Y is monothetic, and is subdivided monothetically. **1969** E. MAYR *Princ. Systematic Zool.* iv. 83 When the definition of the logicians—'individuals sharing common characters'—was replaced by 'members of a group having descended from a common ancestor', a monothetic characterization of a taxon was no longer necessary. **1938** *Engineer* 3 June 615/1 Messrs. Butters Brothers are showing..a 'Monotower' electric crane. **1953** *Dock & Harbour Authority* XXXIV. 88/2 The design of the mast for the monotower crane. **1963** *Engineering* 19 Apr. 532 During erection as a monotower up to 90 ft, the crane grows from the bottom. **1971** B. SCHARF *Engin. & Its Lang.* xvi. 230 Monotower cranes..consist of a latticed tower surmounted by a derrick crane. **1972** J. R. ILLINGWORTH *Movement & Distribution Concrete* vi. 84 With monotowers, full circle slewing is obtained, but static base operation limits coverage to the area swept out by a particular jib length. **1939** *Thorpe's Dict. Appl. Chem.* III. 241 (*table*) Fully saturated triglycerides... Mono-unsaturated-di-saturated glycerides. **1950** *Analytical Chem.* XXII. 1261/1 Extinction coefficients..are reported for seventeen pure cis and trans monounsaturated and saturated acids, esters, and alcohols. **1965** E. D. WILSON et al. *Princ. Nutrition* (ed. 2) v. 35 The quantity of the monounsaturated fatty acids in the average American diet matches that of the saturated ones, about 40 per cent. **1953** E. C. DOUGHERTY in *Parasitology* XLII. 259/2 Such an expression as 'two-membered culture' becomes 'monoxenic culture'. **1969** *Oikos* XX. 287 (*heading*) The monoxenic cultivation of some rhabditid nematodes. *Ibid.* 288/1 Some nematode species were studied under controlled conditions on monoxenic agar cultures. **1940** B. G. CHITWOOD in J. R. Christie *Introd. Nematology* II. iv. 243/2 Parasites of animals may also be classified according to the number of hosts necessary for completion of the life cycle. Species in which there is a single host are termed monoxenous. **1962** W. P. ROGERS *Nature of Parasitism* x. 219 A specific parasite (sometimes called species-specific or monoxenous) can live on or in one species of host only. **1973** N. D. LEVINE *Protozoan Parasites* (ed. 2) i. 5/1 A monoxenous parasite has only one type of host—the definitive host. *Ibid.* 5/2 The term monoxenous parasite is used by some authors for a parasite which is restricted to a single host species.

2. Also used to indicate monomeric compounds (e.g. *mononucleotide* below). **mono-ethano·lamine,** 2-aminoethanol $H_2NCH_2CH_2$-OH, a viscous high-boiling liquid used in making detergents; **monogly·ceride,** any compound consisting of glycerol esterified at only one of its hydroxyl groups; **mononu·cleotide** [ad. G. *mononucleotid* (Levene & Mandel 1908, in *Ber. d. Deut. Chem. Ges.* XLI. 1906)], any of the compounds whose molecules are formed from a single molecule each of phosphoric acid, a sugar, and a heterocyclic base, and are the units of which nucleic acids are composed; a monomeric nucleotide.

1929 *Chem. Abstr.* XXIII. 3232 If 352 parts of ethylene oxide is added to 3400 parts of 25% aq. NH_3 at 10°, monoethanolamine is obtained. **1959** *Times Rev Industry* Jan. 67/1 The CO_2 removed by scrubbing with monoethanolamine is used as a purge gas. **1972** *Materials & Technol.* IV. xv. 516 Since monoethanolamine reacts more readily with ethylene oxide than does ammonia, excess of the latter and careful control of the ethylene oxide concentration is essential for appreciable amounts of the mono-alcohol to be formed. **1860** H. DEBUS in *Q. Jrnl. Chem. Soc.* XII. 243 (*heading*) Monoglycerides. **1926** G. D. ELSDON *Edible Oils & Fats* iv. 17 The β monoglycerides have been prepared by using dichlorhydrin. **1954** E. W. ECKEY *Veg. Fats & Oils* iv. 143 An important practical application of alcoholysis of fats is the preparation of monoglycerides which are used in shortenings to improve their cake-making properties and as emulsifiers... Monoglyceride mixtures are prepared also as a first step in the manufacture of oil-modified alkyd resins, and in the preparation of certain detergents. **1972** *Lipids* VII. 433/1 Palmitic, stearic and oleic acids were the predominant fatty acids present in the monoglycerides. **1908** *Jrnl. Chem. Soc.* XCIV. I. 587 The composition of the thyminglucophosphoric acid is almost identical with that of heminucleic acid.., and may be considered to be a mononucleotide. **1956** *Nature* 11 Feb. 271/1 Preparations or fractions of ribonucleic acid were hydrolysed in *N* potassium hydroxide to mononucleotides. **1968** H. HARRIS *Nucleus & Cytoplasm* iii. 55 The mononucleotides released from this material by alkali hydrolysis are con-

taminated with other compounds. **1974** *Nature* 1 Nov. 75/2 The data show total ^{32}P c.p.m. in the RNA and in the triphosphate termini as mononucleotides and pppNps released by KOH hydrolysis of that RNA.

monoamine (mǫno,ēi·mīn). *Biochem.* [f. MONO- 2 + AMINE.] **a.** Any compound having a single (primary, secondary, or tertiary) amine group in its molecule, *spec.* one which is a neurohormone; = MONAMINE (in Dict. and Suppl.).

1951 I. L. FINAR *Org. Chem.* I. xiii. 260 Diamines may be prepared by methods similar to those for the monoamines, using alkylene halides instead of alkyl halides. **1965** J. POLLITT *Depression & its Treatment* iv. 53 Monoamines are neurohormones regarded as essential for normal activity of the brain. **1972** *Nature* 31 Mar. 225/2 There is much evidence pointing to changes in monoamine metabolism in mental illnesses characterized by alterations in mood.

b. *Comb.* **monoamine oxidase**, the enzyme or group of enzymes that brings about the oxidation (and consequent inactivity) of monoamines in the body; **monoamine oxidase inhibitor**, any of a class of drugs which inhibit the functioning of monoamine oxidase (so allowing accumulation of serotonin and noradrenaline in the brain), some of which are used as antidepressants.

[**1943**: cf. *MONAMINE.] **1951** *Proc. Soc. Exper. Biol. & Med.* LXXVIII. 157/1 Despite numerous investigations of its enzymatic function, monoamine oxidase has not been significantly purified. **1962** *Lancet* 29 Dec. 1343/1 There is a strong impression that iproniazid is clinically more effective in relieving depression than other monoamine-oxidase inhibitors. **1965** J. POLLITT *Depression & its Treatment* iv. 47 Methedrine and other amphetamines are incompatible with monoamine oxidase inhibitors. **1973** *Nature* 6 Apr. 417/1 Roulston, studying the action of chlordimeform and related compounds on the southern cattle tick, suggested that inhibition of monoamine oxidase (MAO) could be involved.

monoao, var. *MANOAO.

monobloc (mǫ·noblǫk), *a.* (*sb.*) [Fr. (1906 in Robert); cf. MONO- 1 and BLOC(K *sb.*] Made as, or contained within, a single casting. Also as *sb.*, a monobloc engine.

1909 *Westm. Gaz.* 2 Nov. 5/1 The engine of the 20-h.p. model..is of the monobloc order. **1929** *Radio Times* 8 Nov. 448 (Advt.), Batteries beyond present standards... Above is the LDG, 2v. 60 a.h... Below: the monobloc 10v. DMHG with special elements. **1930** *Engineering* 26 Sept. 401/3 The cylinders form a monobloc casting. **1944** *Jrnl. R. Aeronaut. Soc.* XLVIII. 365 In liquid-cooled engines, separate steel cylinders were generally abandoned in favour of monobloc light alloy castings. *Ibid.*, At the outbreak of the present war the monoblocs in use were still not entirely satisfactory. **1963** *Engineering* 2 Aug. 140/3 Of monobloc construction, the new pump is available in cast iron. **1972** *Shooting Times & Country Mag.* 24 June 14/2, I must confess to being disappointed that our top-flight English gunmakers..do not offer an alternative. I visualise a self-opening boxlock, with monobloc barrels, [etc.].

monocaryon, -caryotic, varr. *MONOKARYON, -KARYOTIC *a.*

monochromasy (mǫnokrōu·măsi). *Ophthalm.* Also **-chromacy**. [f. MONO- + Gr. χρῶμα colour: see -Y^3.] = *MONOCHROMATISM b.

1900 *Stud. Yale Psychol. Lab.* VIII. 15 Still another form of color-vision is found in monochromasy. All the visible objects are seen as shades of one color. What this color is, it has as yet been impossible to say. **1922** W. PEDDIE *Colour Vision* ii. 16 The most extreme condition is that of total colour blindness in which every colour in the spectrum can be matched with grey. It is not inconceivable that a case of this kind may be one of true monochromasy, the one colour extending throughout the whole spectrum. **1957** *Jrnl. Optical Soc. Amer.* XLVII. 338/2 (*heading*) 'Blue mono-cone monochromacy': a new color vision defect. **1971** *Jrnl. Physiol.* CCXII. 211 (*heading*) Colour vision in 'blue-cone 'monochromacy'.

monochromat (mǫnokrōu·mĕt), **-chromate** (-krōu·meit), *sb. Ophthalm.* [ad. L. *monochrōmat-us*, Gr. μονοχρώματ-ος: see -ATE^1.] A person who suffers from monochromatism (sense *b).

1902 J. M. BALDWIN *Dict. Philos. & Psychol.* II. 793/2 König affirmed that the vision of the faint-light 'monochromates' was in quality blue. **1915** J. H. PARSONS *Introd. Study Colour Vision* II. i. 159 Differing from all these groups there are people who apparently see all parts of the spectrum of one hue... These are the total colour-blind or monochromats. **1956** *Brit. Jrnl. Ophthalm.* XL. 463 This female 'cone monochromate' would thus have to be a compound heterozygote for protanopia and deuteranopia. **1971** *Nature* 9 Apr. 395/1 The recovery of the rod sensitivity after a long full bleach can be followed for a wider than normal range when an area of the monochromat's retina which has few cones is tested.

monochromate (mǫnokrōu·mēit), *v.* [Back-formation from *MONOCHROMATOR.] *trans.* = *MONOCHROMATIZE *v.* So **mo·nochromated, -chromating** *ppl. adjs.*

1955 G. E. BACON *Neutron Diffraction* iv. 80 For any position *XY* of the monochromating crystal there will be some particular wavelength which is at the right glancing angle θ to the crystal to undergo Bragg reflection when it is incident along *PB*. **1955** *Rev. Sci. Instruments* XXVI. 564 A bent crystal monochromator..was constructed to monochromate the specimen-reflected x-ray beam. *Ibid.*, X-ray diffraction laboratories are making increasing use of single crystal monochromated radiation for various types of investigations. **1961** J. THEWLIS et al. *Encycl. Dict. Physics* IV. 827/2 Normally, the monochromating crystal is used in conjunction with a neutron spectrometer. **1971** *Nature* 16 Apr. 436/1 The aim of our experiments was..to check that there was no large disparity between the observed and calculated flux of monochromated synchrotron radiation.

monochromatic, *a.* Add: **1.** Also applied to other radiation that is (nominally) of a single wavelength or energy throughout. (Further examples.)

1923 GLAZEBROOK *Dict. Appl. Physics* IV. 22/2 The crystal is pulverised and the powder compressed into a rod, placed in the axis of a cylindrical photographic film and subjected to 'monochromatic' X-rays. **1955** C. R. N. STROUTS et al. *Analytical Chem.* II. xxvi. 942 It is desirable to use essentially monochromatic radiation for most analytical applications of X-ray diffraction. **1967** R. CASTAING et al. in A. Septier *Focusing Charged Particles* II. iv. 289 An incident monochromatic electron beam.

3. *Ophthalm.* Exhibiting or affected with monochromatism (sense *b); completely colour-blind.

1902 J. M. BALDWIN *Dict. Philos. & Psychol.* II. 793/2 The sensations of those individuals whom they named 'monochromatic'..were dogmatically affirmed to be vision under the form of red or blue or green, it was uncertain which. **1956** *Brit. Jrnl. Ophthalm.* XL. 470 His vision is monochromatic when examined in the colour apparatus. **1974** *Sci. Amer.* Dec. 25/3 The ophthalmologist testified that the witness was actually monochromatic, which meant he could perceive no colors at all.

monochromatically *adv.*, also *fig.*; also **monochromati·city**, the condition of being monochromatic; the extent to which any radiation is concentrated at one wavelength or frequency.

1960 S. TOLANSKY *Surface Microtopography* i. 5 For two-beam work the Wratten 77A didymium glass filter gives excellent monochromaticity. **1963** G. TROUP *Masers & Lasers* (ed. 2) vii. 113 The advantages of maser optical sources are: the extreme monochromaticity, resulting in huge spectral energy-densities; [etc.]. **1972** *Daily Tel.* 31 May 10/3 Janacek's Sonata '1905'..was massively though rather monochromatically delivered. **1972** *Nature* 22 Dec. 483/1 The intensity, coherence and monochromaticity of laser light have made it an ideal radiation source for selective alteration of cell organelles.

monochromatism (mǫnokrōu·mătiz'm). [f. MONOCHROMAT(IC *a.* + -ISM.] **a.** (In Dict. s.v. MONOCHROMATIC *a.*)

b. *Ophthalm.* Complete colour-blindness, in which all colours appear as shades of one colour, probably grey.

1934 in WEBSTER. **1946** W. D. WRIGHT *Res. Normal & Defective Colour Vision* xxiv. 297 In monochromatism, all qualitative differences in stimuli disappear, so that colour matching is reduced to brightness matching. **1956** *Brit. Jrnl. Ophthalm.* XL. 462 There exist rare cases of monochromatism in which the characteristic symptoms accompanying typical total colour blindness are lacking. **1966** *Arch. Internal Med.* CXVIII. 491/2 This report describes a family with atypical congenital monochromatism.

monochromatize (mǫnokrōu·mătaiz), *v.* [f. MONOCHROMAT(IC *a.* + -IZE.] *trans.* To make monochromatic. So **monochro·matized, monochro·matizing** *ppl. adjs.*

1951 *Jrnl. de Physique* XII. 268/1 It is..necessary to 'monochromatize' the beam. *Ibid.* 268/2 The monochromatized neutrons..had de Broglie wavelengths 1·06 Å and hence velocities approximately three times thermal. **1955** G. E. BACON *Neutron Diffraction* iv. 102 Two methods of making diffraction measurements have.. been described using a neutron beam direct from the pile, without first monochromatizing. **1962** *Rev. Sci. Instruments* XXXIII. 875/1 (*heading*) Preparation of bent crystals for monochromatizing x rays. **1974** *Nature* 19 Apr. 671/2 Both structure analyses were based on diffractometer data taken with monochromatised Cu radiation. **1974** *Physics Bull.* Oct. 443/2 The three essential components of a neutron scattering spectrometer: monochromatizing crystal, material sample and crystal for analysis of the scattered beam.

Also **mo:nochromatiza·tion**, the process of making monochromatic.

1955 C. B. WALKER tr. *Guinier & Fournet's Small-Angle Scattering X-Rays* iii. 104 It might be thought that the double monochromatization and the large distance from X-ray tube to film would require a prohibitive increase in the exposure time. **1955** *Rev. Sci. Instruments* XXVI. 564 The usual method of monochromatization consists of inserting (at the required Bragg angle) a single crystal between the x-ray source and the specimen. **1967** J. LECIEJEWICZ tr. *Auleytner's X-Ray Methods in Study of Defects in Single Crystals* ii. 76 The only disadvantage of the method is the very long exposure time caused by the low intensity due to precise monochromatization of the beam.

monochromator (mǫ·nŏkrŏmēitəɹ, mǫnokrōu·mēitəɹ). *Physics.* [f. MONOCHROMAT(IC *a.* + -OR.] Any device used to select radiation of a single wavelength or energy (or, in practice, a very narrow range of wavelengths or energies).

1909 *Chem. Abstr.* III. 2074 The monochromator is a spectrometer arrangement of the Pellin and Broca or Hilger type with constant deviation of 90°, in which the eyepiece can be replaced by a second slit. **1924** E. C. C. BALY *Spectroscopy* (ed. 3) I. iv. 109 Any fixed arm spectrometer can be converted into a monochromator by replacing the eyepiece by a slit placed in the focus of the telescope lens or mirror. **1955** C. B. WALKER tr. *Guinier & Fournet's Small-Angle Scattering X-Rays* iii. 100 Bent crystals were originally introduced in X-ray spectroscopy, serving as analyzers capable of producing intense spectra; they can serve equally well as monochromators. **1969** *Nature* 11 Oct. 146/1 Changes in diffraction geometry, and more especially the use of focusing monochromators, should yield a considerably higher neutron flux, permitting the use of smaller crystals.

monochrome, *sb.* and *a.* Add: **A.** *sb.* **1. b.** *transf.*, esp. in *Photogr.* (see quots.).

1940 *Chambers's Techn. Dict.* 555/2 *Monochrome*, a photographic print in one colour of varying brightness. **1968** *Gloss. Terms Offset Lithogr. Printing* (*B.S.I.*) 8 *Monochrome*, an original or print in a single colour. **1973** D. A. SPENCER *Focal Dict. Photographic Technologies* 394 *Monochrome*, an image or picture in a single colour which is usually (but need not be) black.

2. b. *Cinemat.* and *Television.* Reproduction in black and white.

1918 H. CROY *How Motion Pictures are Made* 294 Relieving the monotony of the monochrome. **1957** *Encycl. Brit.* XV. 859/2 Monochrome.—For black-and-white photography the principal problem is to make a reasonable compromise between film grain and film speed. **1961** G. MILLERSON *Technique Television Production* 128 Colour media can employ both tonal and colour separation, to distinguish between planes. Colour separation may mean nothing when transformed into monochrome.

c. *fig.*

1962 *Listener* 10 May 828/3 A dramatic exaggeration, associated with Verdi and Puccini, inevitably crept into the gentle monochrome.

3. A paint or glaze of a single colour.

1906 S. W. BUSHELL *Chinese Art* II. viii. 40 Some of the most brilliant monochromes of the time are plain washes of one of the enamel colours used in polychrome decoration. **1933** *Burlington Mag.* Nov. 203/1 Monochromes, which may be divided into celadons and semi-celadons, brown-glazed, white-glazed, and black-glazed wares.

B. *adj.* (Further examples.) Also *fig.*

1906 S. W. BUSHELL *Chinese Art* II. viii. 35 All the new monochrome glazes introduced under his rule. **1957** *Encycl. Brit.* II. 540/1 At Mersin, the burnished and incised monochrome pottery of the Neolithic period was almost entirely replaced by the painted wares. **1959** [see *BICHROME *a.* and *sb.*^{2}]. **1970** *Daily Tel.* 13 Jan. 16 One must have balanced communities; there is nothing worse for society than a monochrome area. **1972** C. STEPHENSON *Merrily on High* xii. 181 As a curate in Cowley St. John I worked in a completely monochrome district as far as the church was concerned.

b. *Photogr.* and *Television.* Reproducing all colours as shades of grey; 'black and white'; pertaining to such reproduction.

1918 H. CROY *How Motion Pictures are Made* 290 A strip of Priezma negative differs but slightly from a monochrome film. *Ibid.* 294 Monochrome effect on the screen is varied successfully by a different process. **1958** *Newnes Compl. Amat. Photogr.* 144 The monochrome photographer who turns to colour is rather apt to think his old principles still apply. **1961** G. MILLERSON *Technique Telev. Production* 128 A further variation can arise through distinctions between techniques when making colour and monochrome motion pictures. *Ibid.* Although colourful design may delight those in the studio, it has no significance to the viewer in monochrome television. **1972** *Sci. Amer.* Feb. 117/1 Intended largely for paramedical students, nurses and technicians, it presents both in sharp monochrome and strong color photographs, all blood red and fat yellow, a review of the general structure of the body.

monochronic, *a.* Delete *rare*$^{-0}$ and add examples of the sense: Relating to a single period of time.

1905 F. E. CLEMENTS *Research Methods in Ecology* 319 *Monochronic*, arising but once. **1967** *Philos.* XLII. 140 Geography was at one time in danger of running into a dead monochronic alley by limiting itself to the visible present.

mo·nocle, *v.* [f. the sb.] *trans.* To provide with a monocle. So **mo·nocled** *a.*

1922 M. B. HOUSTON *Witch Man* xii. 154 Major Coberton monocled his eye. **1926** L. P. GREENE *Major—Diamond Buyer* 18 The monocled one coughed deprecatingly. **1940** *Horizon* Mar. 185 The monocled idiot who made good on the fields of Mons and Le Cateau. **1965** *Listener* 30 Dec. 1063/1 Colonel Creighton, monocled, and seated bolt upright in his rickshaw as though it were a Daimler. **1974** *Times* 26 Apr. 18/6 It is ironical that youth and the new guard should be represented by a 63 year old monocled cavalry officer.

monoclinal, *a.* and *sb.* Substitute for defs.: **A.** *adj.* **a.** Consisting of strata that slope in the same direction and at the same angle throughout.

In quot. 1876 in Dict. the word appears to have been used with a slightly different meaning, perh. because 'direction' was interpreted as referring to directions in a horizontal plane rather than a vertical one.

1843 W. B. & H. D. ROGERS in *Rep. 1st, 2nd & 3rd Meetings Assoc. Amer. Geologists & Naturalists* 485 While the phrases, *anticlinal dip*, and *synclinal dip*, sufficiently express the directions of the beds, due to concave and convex flexures, we propose the term *monoclinal*, to signify a sameness in the direction of the dip, and shall term a mountain or valley, in which such sameness prevails, a *monoclinal* mountain, or *monoclinal* valley. **1858** [in Dict.]. **1875** J. W. POWELL *Explor. Colorado River* xi. 160

Monoclinal valleys..run in the direction of the strike between the axes of the fold—one side of the valley formed of the summits of the beds, the other composed of the cut edges of the formation. **1930** *Compt. Rend. 15th Internat. Geol. Congress 1929* II. vi. 361, I shall consider only four major types of blocks included between bounding faults: 1. Tilted or monoclinal blocks; [etc.]. **1942** O. D. von Engeln *Geomorphology* xv. 327 Monoclinal ridges, alternating with monoclinal valleys, appear where a series of resistant and weak beds all dip in the same direction. **1957** G. E. Hutchinson *Treat. Limnol.* I. i. 111 The channel containing Lenore Lake lies in a zone of fractured basalt on a monoclinal slope.

b. Applied to a fold consisting of a single slope connecting strata that are parallel and more or less horizontal but at different levels.

1877 [in Dict.]. **1880** C. E. Dutton *Rep. Geol. High Plateaus Utah* ii. 25 The great structural features of the High Plateaus are the faults and monoclinal flexures. **1940** E. S. Hills *Outl. Struct. Geol.* v. 111 An individual normal fault may pass either laterally or vertically into a monoclinal flexure. **1969** J. Bundred *Basic Geol. for Engineers* iv. 115 A monoclinal fold..has basically a single undulation.

B. *sb.* **a.** A monoclinal fold.

1880 C. E. Dutton *Rep. Geol. High Plateaus Utah* ii. 26 So close is the homology that we are justified in calling a monoclinal in some of its aspects a modified fault. The only difference for structural purposes is that in the case of a typical fault of the simplest form the shearing is along one plane, while in the monoclinal the shearing lies between two planes. **1886** [in Dict.]. **1914** J. Park *Text-bk. Geol.* ix. 140 In sharply bent monoclinals, the strata in the middle limb are generally drawn out, compressed, or deformed.

b. A monoclinal set of strata; = *homocline.

1916 *Bull. Geol. Soc. Amer.* XXVII. 92, I welcome the suggestion of the term homocline. The need of a term for this structure has long been felt in the United States Geological Survey, where confusion has been avoided in editing by using *monoclinal* for the homocline as distinct from *monocline* or monoclinal fold.

monoclinally, *adv.* (further examples).

1880 C. E. Dutton *Rep. Geol. High Plateaus Utah* ii. 31 At East Fork Cañon the thrown beds..are turned up monoclinally. **1968** R. W. Fairbridge *Encycl. Geomorphol.* 483/2 At coastlines the same ancient cyclic landsurface may be monoclinally warped down to pass beneath marine sequences of Jurassic or Cretaceous rocks.

monocline. Add: (Further examples.)

1916 [see *monoclinal *a.* and *sb.* B. b]. **1940** E. S. Hills *Outl. Struct. Geol.* iv. 70 A monocline is a local steepening of an otherwise uniformly dipping or horizontal series, and is composed of an anticlinal bend above, followed by a synclinal bend at a lower level... In oil-field geology, however, the term is used for formations in which the dip is more or less uniform in one direction. **1942** M. P. Billings *Struct. Geol.* iii. 41 In plateau areas.. the strata may locally assume a steeper dip... Such a fold is a monocline. The beds in a monocline may dip at angles ranging from a few degrees to ninety degrees. **1962** Read & Watson *Introd. Geol.* I. viii. 487 In this way monoclines may be formed and may grade into zones of normal faulting.

b. = *homocline.

1912 E. H. C. Craig *Oil-Finding* v. 74 Oil may be obtained from monoclines, often in great quantity. In such cases the more gentle the dip, the better. **1925** A. B. Thompson *Oil-Field Exploration* I. v. 186 The term 'monocline' is here retained in its customary oil-field phraseology as representing a series of uniformly dipping beds, irrespective of the relationship they may bear to the general structure of the district. **1951** E. N. Tiratsoo *Petroleum Geol.* iv. 79 The monocline can be considered as virtually one limb of an anticline up which the migrating fluids pass, leaving well-marked layers of dynamically separated gas, oil and water.

monocoque (mǫ·nokǫk). [a. F. *monocoque*, f. *mono-* Mono- + *coque* egg-shell.] **a.** *Aeronaut.* A fuselage or other structure having an outer covering in the form of a rigid skin or shell designed to bear all or most of the stresses that arise; now esp. one without longerons or stringers (see quot. 1948). Also *transf.* Usu. *attrib.*

1914 *Sphere* 3 Oct. p. ii/1 The very speedy monocoques of the French. **1919** A. W. Judge *Elem. Princ. Aeroplane Design* vi. 98 The Monocoque Type of Body. This type of body..consists of a single shell, conforming with the outside shape of the body, and..so constructed that it can withstand all the stresses which it is called upon to bear, without the necessity for longerons or cross bracing members. **1935** C. G. Burge *Compl. Bk. Aviation* 595/1 The 'monocoque' is becoming increasingly popular for both military and commercial aeroplanes. **1938** E. W. C. Wilkins *Aeroplane Design* vii. 171 The monocoque fuselage..consists of a thin shell..built around a number of transverse rings or formers... These formers are placed at intervals of about 2 ft. or more in the case of a wooden monocoque, but are very much closer together in the case of the metal monocoque. **1948** C. E. Chapel *Aircraft Basic Sci.* ii. 84/2 Monocoques may be divided into three classes (monocoque, semimonocoque, and reinforced shell), and different portions of the fuselage may belong to any of these classes. The true monocoque has as its only reinforcement vertical bulkheads formed of structural members... All stresses are carried by the shell or skin. **1951** *Engineering* 2 Nov. 573/1 A wing of the thin-walled monocoque type. **1969** K. Munson *Pioneer Aircraft 1903–14* 123/2 Late in 1911 the ideas of the Swedish engineer Ruchonnet, for a monocoque fuselage shell of moulded plywood, were applied by Armand Deperdussin's designer, Louis Béchereau. **1970** *New Scientist* 12 Nov. 329/2 No longer would an airship need to have a metal fabric-covered skeleton. Instead it could have a 'monocoque' structure—the strength would be in a stiff lightweight outer shell. **1971** *Daily Colonist* (Victoria, B.C.) 6 June 25/6 Launched four years ago, she is of monocoque design—one shell, no ribs, no frame, smooth inside and out.

b. In a motor vehicle, an underframe and body built as a single rigid structure (or in racing cars as a number of box-like sections) throughout which the stresses are distributed. Usu. *attrib.*

1956 Molloy & Lanchester *Automobile Engineer's Ref. Bk.* xviii. 2 All-metal bodies fall into two main categories, firstly those which are used in conjunction with a separate chassis frame and secondly which are of the type known as monocoque or unit construction. The former naturally require only body structure panels, whereas the latter, in addition, require many pressings to form a unit (underframe or subframe), which although ultimately part of the body, is [a] substitute for the chassis frame and has provision made for all necessary attachment points for the various mechanical units. **1961** Costin & Phipps *Racing & Sports Car Chassis Design* v. 43 All these, plus the single transverse torsion bar and the telescopic dampers, pick up on the rear bulkhead of the monocoque. **1963** *Engineering* 1 Feb. 181/1 GT cars featuring monocoque construction of laminated wooden box sections. **1968** *Daily Tel.* (Colour Suppl.) 15 Nov. 29/2 Despite the terrible force of the impact, the integrity of the cockpit area was preserved by the immensely strong monocoque chassis of his car. **1969** 'D. Rutherford' *Gilt-Edged Cockpit* i. 15 With the whole of his body encased in the monocoque shell and no part of his face visible he was an anonymous figure... Already other cars were flashing past. **1973** Terry & Baker *Racing Car Design & Devel.* vi. 129 Although the basic space-frame is a comparatively light structure, it requires a separate body and fuel containers, all of which are integral parts of a monocoque, so this tends to nullify any hoped-for weight advantage.

monocular, *a.* Add: **2. b.** Wearing a monocle. *rare.*

1903 G. B. Shaw *Man & Superman* p. xxiii, These college passmen, these well groomed monocular Algys and Bobbies.

c. quasi-*sb.* A glass, esp. a field-glass, in the use of which only one eye is employed in viewing an object.

1936 *British Birds* XXX. 39 It was only when I turned my monocular on the bird in the water that I realized it was a Red-legged Partridge. **1959** *Chambers's Encycl.* IX. 385/2 The modern microscope usually has interchangeable bodies, making it possible to use the same stand with monocular or binocular. **1971** D. Whillans in C. Bonington *Annapurna South Face* v. 58 There was a monocular in the tent which I focused on the dark, moving shape.

fig. (Later example.)

1923 *Public Opinion* 8 June 542/3 The bane of cancer research has been its monocular myopia.

monocularly, *adv.* (Earlier and later examples.)

1880 W. James *Coll. Ess. & Rev.* (1920) 177 If under these circumstances the object thus monocularly seen were translocated outwardly, we should have a complete verification. **1972** *Sci. Amer.* Aug. 86/3 An insect disguised as a leaf may be invisible monocularly but stand out in a different depth plane from real leaves when it is viewed stereoscopically.

monoculture (mǫ·nokɒltiŭɹ). [irreg. f. Mono- + Culture *sb.* Cf. F. *monoculture* (1842 in Robert).] **a.** The cultivation or exploitation of a single crop, to the exclusion of others that are possible. Also *fig.*

1915 C. R. Enock *Tropics* xxxiii. 373 The decline of sugar 'monoculture' may have proved a blessing in disguise. Cotton and many food-stuffs are now produced. **1925** E. F. Row tr. *Demangeon's Brit. Empire* 134 This plantation system, this exploiting to the uttermost of a single valuable product, involves the dangers of all monoculture. **1948** *Times* 17 June 5 The name [*sc.* groundnut scheme] is too suggestive of monoculture and dustbowls. **1961** J. Russell tr. *Lévi-Strauss's World on Wane* iv. 39 Humanity has taken to monoculture, once and for all, and is preparing to produce civilization in bulk, as if it were sugar-beet. **1962** *Economist* 7 July 60/1 A 'monoculture' economy dependent on only one resource for most of its income. **1970** J. Ardagh *New France* vi. 206 The monoculture of cheap wine was dangerous for the region's economy. **1974** *Country Life* 28 Mar. 710/1 The replacement of broad-leaved woodland with conifer and increasing monoculture.

b. An area in which monoculture is practised or a single kind of (higher) animal maintained.

1951 *New Biol.* X. 56 Nature abhors a monoculture, and the most carefully tended orchards soon become ecological associations with distinctive flora and fauna. **1970** *New Scientist* 21 May 372/1 The transformation of habitats from virgin forests to cultivated woods, vast crop monocultures, industrial areas and big cities is the most radical change of nature that has struck Europe since the last glaciation. **1974** *Environmental Conservation* I. 17/2 Huge areas are turned into monocultures. **1974** *Nature* 24 May 307/3 One is towards the establishment of monocultures of eland, wildebeest, gazelle or kob.

c. An area in which all the inhabitants share a common culture or way of life.

1968 *Listener* 5 Sept. 298/1 Los Angeles's least endearing characteristic: the tendency to fragment into self-contained, specialised areas—social monocultures. Functional monocultures, too: in Los Angeles you tend to go to a particular place to do a particular thing.

Hence **monocu·ltural** *a.*; **monocu·lturist**, one who practises or advocates monoculture.

1928 E. R. Johnson et al. *Princ. Transportation* xxi. 243 The South from earliest colonial days has been agricultural and primarily monocultural. **1964** Gould & Kolb *Dict. Soc. Sci.* 583/1 The 'Deep South' region of U.S.A. exhibits specialized cultural, political, and economic (monocultural) features. **1965** *New Scientist* 23 July 199/1 Monocultural crop planting on totally cleared areas. **1968** W. E. Lambert et al. in J. A. Fishman *Readings Sociol. of Lang.* (1968) 479 It is of special interest to note a basically similar pattern appearing in all three of the American settings, two bicultural and one monocultural. **1973** *Country Life* 30 Aug. 586/2 The monoculturists' ideas of good yields being likely to cause any self-respecting rotational farmer to blush with shame.

monocyclic, *a.* Add: **2. a.** (Examples.)

1882 S. H. Vines tr. *Sachs' Text-bk. Bot.* 601 When the members of a series (calyx, corolla, etc.) are in one whorl, the series is said to be monocyclic. **1895** —— *Students' Text-bk. Bot.* II. iii. 501 The simplest case is that in which each series of floral organs..occupies a single whorl, or is monocyclic.

4. *Chem.* Having a molecular structure with a single ring.

1910 *Jrnl. Chem. Soc.* XCVII. 1616 From this glycol we could obtain a monocyclic terpene. **1939** *Nature* 26 Aug. 349/1 The detailed consideration of monocyclic compounds is then taken up. **1967** M. E. Hale *Biol. Lichens* viii. 105 Free monocyclic phenolic substances.

5. *Geol.* Having undergone a single cycle of erosion or (quot. 1969) of mountain-building.

1952 *Jrnl. Geol.* LX. 188/1 Four general types of landscapes, suggested by Bryan's (1943, pp. 472–473) classification of soils: (1) simple, monocyclic landscapes which can be fitted to the idealized cycle; (2) complex, multicyclic landscapes which require historical interpretation; (3) compound landscapes..; (4) exhumed landscapes. **1954** W. D. Thornbury *Princ. Geomorphol.* ii. 23 Monocyclic landscapes are less common than multicyclic and are in general restricted to such newly created land surfaces as a recently uplifted portion of the ocean floor. **1968** R. W. Fairbridge *Encycl. Geomorphol.* 286/2 Monocyclic landscapes are rarely found except in very recently formed land surfaces. **1969** Bennison & Wright *Geol. Hist. Brit. Isles* iii. 36 Within both the Caledonian and Lewisian belts there is evidence of several periods of folding and metamorphism and neither represents a simple monocyclic unit.

monocyte (mǫ·nŏsəit). *Biol.* [ad. G. *monozyt* (Pappenheim & Ferrata 1910, in *Folia Haematologica* X. i. 81): see Mono- and -cyte.] A kind of large leucocyte which has a single oval or indented nucleus and no coarse granulation in the cytoplasm, constitutes 3–8 per cent of the total leucocytes in human blood, and is the circulating form of the macrophage.

1913 Stedman *Med. Dict.* (ed. 2) 556/1 Monocyte. **1927** A. Piney *Rec. Adv. Hæmatol.* ii. 16 The large hyaline leucocyte or monocyte is not easy to place with certainty into either the granular or the non-granular group. **1970** T. S. & C. R. Leeson *Histology* (ed. 2) viii. 140/1 Monocytes migrate readily through vessel walls and develop into phagocytic cells which cannot be distinguished from macrophages already present within the connective tissues. They are effective in combating tubercle bacilli. **1974** Passmore & Robson *Compan. Med. Stud.* III. xxi. 5/1 Absence of monocytes or basophils from the blood film or reduction in their number does not have clinical significance.

Hence **monocy·tic** *a.*; **monocyto·sis** [-osis], an abnormal increase in the number of monocytes in the blood.

1914 Stedman *Med. Dict.* (ed. 3) 576/1 Monocytosis. **1934** Webster, Monocytic. **1935** Whitby & Britton *Disorders Blood* i. 18 The origin of the monocytic cells has been and still is, the subject of much controversy. **1938** H. Downey *Handbk. Hematol.* I. v. 389 Monocytes may appear in large numbers in the peripheral blood in the monocytic leucemias. *Ibid.* II. xv. 1067 In chronic malaria, the irritation of the reticulo-endothelium often leads to a monocytosis in the peripheral blood. **1972** *Nature* 4 Feb. 275/1 Cells of the monocytic series. **1974** Passmore & Robson *Compan. Med. Stud.* III. xxi. 5/1 Monocytosis is seen in the course of infectious mononucleosis and in some bacterial infections, notably tuberculosis.

monodist. 2. (Later examples.)

1916 Stanford & Forsyth *Hist. Mus.* vii. 148 There is no sudden revolution in the method of handling the musical material such as the monodists engineered in 1600. **1974** *Country Life* 14 Mar. 590/3 In the early-17th century ..the Italian Monodists..sought to find a new expressive force by abandoning the use of the contrapuntal device.

monodrama. (Later examples.) Now esp. an opera for one singer.

1954 *Grove's Dict. Mus.* (ed. 5) V. 666/2 The title part of Berlioz's 'Lélio'.., in which a single actor appears, may also be called a 'monodrama'. *Ibid.*, A work like Schoenberg's 'Erwartung', in which a single acting singer appears, is also in the nature of 'monodrama'. **1966** *Listener* 19 May 736/3 *Erwartung*,..a monodrama or 'prose opera' (Stravinsky)... This fragmentary half-hour composition..is scored for soprano (no supporting cast) and large orchestra. **1974** *New Yorker* 29 Apr. 129/1 An extravagant monodrama for singer, pianist, and orchestra.

monodramatic, *a.* (Earlier example.)

1801 *Monthly Mirror* Aug. 136 A German..has lately appeared on this stage, in an Italian mono-dramatic interlude, called Il Cazolaro.

monodromy (mŏ̃nǫ·drŏmi). *Math.* [f. as Monodromic *a.* + -y³.] (See quot. 1909.)

1897 B. Russell *Essay on Foundations of Geometry* i. 24 As regards independence of rotation in rigid bodies (Monodromy). If (*n*−1) points of a body remain fixed, so that every other point can only describe a certain curve, then that curve is closed. **1903** *Nature* 19 Feb. 382/2 It is pointed out that in the non-Pythagorean geometrics devised by Hilbert, Helmholtz's axiom of monodromy is not verified, inasmuch as it is possible by rotation through four right angles, to bring the points of a line into positions which they do not occupy before the rotation. **1909** *Cent. Dict. Suppl.*, *Monodromy*, (*a*) the characteristic property that, if the argument returns by any path to its original value, the function also returns to its original value. (*b*) The property that the curves described by a revolution or rotation through four right angles are closed. **1949** G. & R. C. James *Math. Dict.* 237/1 *Monodromy theorem*. The theorem states that, if the function *f*(*z*) of the complex variable *z* is analytic at the point z_0 and can be continued analytically along every curve issuing from z_0 in a finite simply connected domain *D*, then *f*(*z*) is a function-element of an analytic function which is single valued in *D*; in other words, analytic continuation around any closed curve in *D* leads to the original function element.

monœcism. (Further example.)

1966 Ainsworth & Sussman *Fungi* II. xx. 661 Monoecism and dioecism..are defined on a physiological basis according to whether an organism contributes one or two nuclei to the sexual process.

monœcy (mǫnī·si). *Biol.* [f. Monœc(ism + -y³.] = Monœcism.

1949 Darlington & Mather *Elem. Genetics* xii. 242 Dioecy ensures outbreeding. Monoecy only favours it. **1970** [see *Diœcy].

monogamic, *a.* Add: Hence **monoga·mically** *adv.*, in a monogamic manner.

1911 G. B. Shaw *Getting Married* 140 In our population there are about a million monogamically superfluous women.

monogamize, *v.* Restrict † *Obs.* to sense in Dict. and add: **2.** *trans.* To make monogamous in character.

1911 H. S. Harrison *Queed* xxiii. 297 Since, however, the church and the law allowed him but one [wife], he must more drastically monogamize his heart.

monogamous, *a.* Add: Hence **mono·gamousness.**

1946 Koestler *Thieves in Night* II. iv. 170 There remains the tyranny of monogamousness.

monogenean (mǫnodʒe·niăn), *sb.* and *a.* [f. mod.L. name of order *Monogenea* (J. V. Carus in W. C. H. Peters et al. *Handbuch der Zoologie* (1863) II. 477), f. Mono- + Gr. γενεά race, generation: see -AN.] **A.** *sb.* A trematode parasite of the order Monogenea, which passes its entire life cycle in one host, esp. an ectoparasitic fluke of fishes; a monogenetic trematode. **B.** *adj.* Of or pertaining to this group of parasites.

1960 *Parasitology* L. 51 (*title*) The attachment of the monogenean *Discotyle sagittata* Leuckart. **1963** J. Llewellyn in *Adv. Parasitol.* I. 287 (*title*) Larvae and larval development of monogeneans. *Ibid.*, The two studies were based on samples of monogenean larvae. **1971** *Nature* 23 July 225/1 The targets of the larvae of monogenean flukes are mostly fish of much greater size. **1972** D. A. Erasmus *Biol. Trematodes* vii. 166 Within their hosts, monogeneans generally occur on the fins, skin, gills, gill chamber and buccal cavity.

monogenesis. Add: **3.** *Linguistics.* The theory that all languages have one common origin.

[**1905** A. Trombetti *L'Unità d' Origine del Linguaggio* 56 Noi dunque consideriamo la monogenesi del linguaggio per lo meno come un argomento assai forte in favore della monogenesi dell' uomo.] **1936** *Science & Society* I. 23 At various times scholars have raised the question of monogenesis as opposed to polygenesis of human speech: whether it had a single origin at a given time and place, whence it spread over the rest of the earth, or whether it was independently evolved by different branches of the human family. **1949** *Archivum Linguisticum* I. 76 The issue of monogenesis *versus* polygenesis is likewise evaded, although a critical appraisal of Trombetti's arguments might have been useful. **1949** M. Pei *Story of Lang.* (1952) vii. 357 A few daring linguists, like the Italian Trombetti, have strenuously asserted the thesis of the 'monogenesis', or single common origin, of all the world's tongues. **1966** H. Landar *Lang. & Culture* xx. 153 His guess implicates a monogenesis of the world's languages, much as the Italian duck-hunter Trombetti supposed, but a monogenesis which occurred as recently as 30,000 years ago.

monogenic, *a.* Add: **6.** *Biol.* [cf. *Genic *a.*] Involving or controlled by a single gene.

1939 *Jrnl. Genetics* XXXVIII. 420 These results indicate that the asynaptic condition in *N. sylvestris* is determined by a difference which behaves as a monogenic recessive. **1960** *Phytopathology* L. 766 (*heading*) Dominance of avirulence and monogenic control of virulence in race hybrids of *Ustilago avenae*. **1971** *Brit. Med. Bull.* XXVII. 40/2 Conventional measurements of blood pressure are too variable to distinguish between monogenic and polygenic models of heredity.

Hence **monoge·nically** *adv.*

1970 *Plant Disease Rep.* LVI. 696 A true resistance mechanism which is monogenically controlled.

monoger, var. *Moniker.

monogram. Add: **5.** (Later example.)

1919 T. Wright *Romance of Lace Pillow* xvi. 223 Monogram Lace, in the form of medallions—the sacred monogram I.H.S. from an antique pattern being most in demand—has been made for Mr. George Smith at Olney during the last thirty years, and sent to the Continent for ecclesiastical purposes.

Hence **mo·nogram** *v. trans.*, to decorate with a monogram; **monogrammed** *a.* (later examples); **mo·nogrammist,** one who applies a monogram.

1939 'A. Bridge' *Four-Part Setting* vi. 64 I took those new pillow-cases round to be monogramed. **1939** *Burlington Mag.* Jan. 40/2 No 'monogrammist' was too petty..to be scrutinised with the same minute and untiring precision. **1951** *Good Housek. Home Encycl.* 139/2 Monogrammed handkerchiefs must be ironed on the wrong side. **1971** *Daily Tel.* 27 Jan. 11 (*caption*) Red wool suit,.. monogrammed in red with Balmain initials. **1974** *Ibid.* 30 Sept. 12 Young Conservatives have their shirts monogrammed 'Y.C.' **1974** *Ashmolean Mus. Rep. Visitors 1972–3* 38 A 19th-century woodcut by the monogrammist *H. Ch.*, *Rothenburg ob der Tauber, Rathaus.* **1975** 'E. Lathen' *By Hook or by Crook* xvii. 160 Lois..instructed Cartier to monogram a demitasse set.

monographic, *a.* **4.** (Later examples.)

1959 C. Singer *Short Hist. Sci. Ideas* vii. 274 The earliest modern scientific works of a monographic character, the great books of Belon, Rondelet, Vesalius, Gesner, are exclusively biological. **1970** *Daily Tel.* 12 Sept. 8/5 There is Waterhouse's monograph on Gainsborough..and some exhibition catalogues that are monographic in their range. **1974** *Nature* 18 Jan. 165/3 The book as a whole usefully fills an important gap in the monographic literature.

monographically, *adv.* (Later example.)

1964 R. H. Gerhard in D. Abercrombie et al. *Daniel Jones* 281 The idea of representing monographically the vowels of *go* and *gay*.

monohull (mǫ·nohvl). [f. Mono- + Hull *sb.*²] A boat with a single hull. Also *attrib.* or as *adj.* Cf. *Multihull.

1967 *Motor Boating* Oct. 135 This year the race was split into two divisions, caused by the catamaran show of superiority: one for monohulls, the other for cats. **1968** *Observer* 9 June 23/5, I would like to see two separate [single-handed Atlantic crossing] races in future,..—one for monohulls and one for multihulls. **1969** *Sunday Times* 2 Feb. 50 The design of the monohull can be improved—there is constant experiment with materials. **1971** *New Scientist* 4 Feb. 265/2 The superiority of the Planesail concept over the conventional monohull or multihull arrangement had already been amply demonstrated. **1972** *Observer* 11 June 18/7, I am confident that Three Cheers, and certainly a multihull, will win—with the radical monohull Strongbow our only serious competitor. **1973** 'A. York' *Captivator* iii. 44 She's all but thirty feet long..and being a cat, she's fourteen feet wide. That means she has about the same accommodation as a monohull.

monohybrid (mǫnohəi·brid), *sb.* and *a. Biol.* [f. Mono- + Hybrid *sb.* and *a.*] **A.** *sb.* A hybrid that is heterozygous with respect to a single gene. **B.** *adj.* Of, pertaining to, or characteristic of such a hybrid, or a cross resulting in such a hybrid. So **monohy·bridism** (*rare*).

1904 *Rep. Evolution Comm. R. Soc.* No. 2. 126 Unresolved characters in ordinary mono-hybrids. **1907** R. C. Punnett *Mendelism* (ed. 2) 34 The cases..concern only a single pair of differentiating characters, that is to say, are cases of monohybridism. **1910** *Amer. Naturalist* XLIV. 67 The crosses have all given a simple mono-hybrid ratio. **1911** Farmer & Darbishire tr. *H. de Vries's Mutation Theory* II. 585 We have given the name of monohybrids to those mongrels whose parents differ from one another in a single elementary character only. **1931** A. F. Shull *Heredity* (ed. 2) vii. 52 Offspring produced by two parents which differ in only one inherited feature are known as monohybrids. **1964** M. Critchley *Developmental Dyslexia* x. 64 The author concluded that developmental dyslexia follows a monohybrid autosomal dominant mode of inheritance. **1967** A. Müntzing *Genetics: Basic & Applied* v. 46/2 Heterozygotes for one gene pair, monohybrids,.. display monohybrid segregation in the ratio of 3:1.

monohydric, *a.* Add: **b.** Of an alcohol or phenol: containing a single hydroxyl group.

1880 *Jrnl. Chem. Soc.* XXXVIII. 28 (*heading*) Sulphates of mono- and poly-hydric alcohols. **1926** J. Read *Text-bk. Org. Chem.* xxiv. 541 Ordinary phenol, or carbolic acid,.. is a monohydric phenol. **1937** *Jrnl. R. Aeronaut. Soc.* XLI. 737 Fuels containing monohydric alcohols are rendered harmless to magnesium and its alloys by saturating such fuels with complex alkali fluorides soluble in them. **1967** I. L. Finar *Org. Chem.* (ed. 5) I. vi. 144 The monohydric alcohols form an homologous series with the general formula $C_nH_{2n+2}O$.

monoideal (mǫnoəidī·ăl), *a.* *rare*⁻¹. [f. Mono- + Ideal *a.* 3 b.] Expressing or conveying only one idea.

1922 Joyce *Ulysses* 667 The infinite possibilities hitherto unexploited of the modern art of advertisement if condensed in trilateral monoideal symbols.

monoïdeism. Add: Also **monoideism.** Hence **monoidei·stic** *a.*, pertaining to or characterized by monoideism.

1890 tr. T. Ribot's *Psychol. of Attention* iii. 96 This higher form of ecstasy may at times reach the state of complete, absolute monoideism, that is, the state of perfect unity of consciousness. **1902** W. James *Var. Relig. Exper.* 525 Philosophy, with its passion for unity, and mysticism with its monoideistic bent, both 'pass to the limit' and identify the something with a unique God who is the all-inclusive soul of the world. **1904** G. S. Hall *Adolescence* II. 50 The history of philosophy shows that the mono-ideistic thinkers..were the victims of an environment or an age itself overwrought, one-sided and extreme. **1966** D. W. Abse *Hysteria* viii. 116 It was essentially a narrowing of the attention, or a 'monoideism'.. that ushered in the hypnotic trance.

monokaryon (mǫnokæ·riŏn). *Bot.* Also **monocaryon.** [f. Mono- after *Dikaryon.] A mononuclear cell, spore, or mycelium in higher fungi that have a dikaryotic stage of the life cycle. Hence **monokaryo·tic** *a.*, containing or characteristic of a monokaryon.

1935 E. A. Bessey *Text-bk. Mycol.* xii. 323 The secondary mycelium (dicaryon phase) is of far greater importance in the life cycle, the primary mycelium (monocaryon phase) occupying but a short period of the life of the fungus. **1936** *Amer. Jrnl. Bot.* XXIII. 310/1 Throughout this paper the terms *monocaryon mycelium* and *dicaryon mycelium* will be employed instead of the older terms *haploid* and *diploid*. **1941** *Bot. Rev.* VII. 412 These give rise either to dikaryotic diploid oidia or to monokaryotic haploid oidia. **1947** F. A. & F. T. Wolf *Fungi* II. xiv. 334 The complete cycle from the monocaryotic to the dicaryotic condition. **1968** R. Rieger et al. *Gloss. Genetics & Cytogenetics* 299 *Monokaryon*, a uninucleate cell, a spore, or a tissue consisting of such cells, as opposed to a dikaryon. **1972** E. Moore-Landecker *Fund. Fungi* iv. 91 The monokaryon is at first nonseptate. *Ibid.* 92 When the monokaryotic hyphae fuse, the nuclei of one hypha flow into the other.

monokini (mǫnokī·ni). [f. Mono- after *Bikini b, with reference to Bi- *pref.*²] A one-piece beach garment, usu. one equivalent to the lower half of a bikini and worn by women.

1964 *Daily Mirror* (Brisbane) 6 July 6 Monokinis are selling in Paris like iceboxes in Alaska. **1964** *Time* 7 Aug. 36/3 Sunbathing.., she in a bikini.., he in a monokini. **1965** *New Yorker* 10 Apr. 92 He works wearing only a jet monokini, a trained canary perched on his shoulder. **1966** B. E. Wallace *Murder in Touraine* xi. 96 She was standing there near naked in her brief monokini. **1966** *N.Y. Times* 30 May 20 Hand-loomed Orlon yarn 'monokini' has top and bottom joined by a band. **1968** B. Foster *Changing Eng. Lang.* iii. 121 In France in the year 1964.. there was much talk of a topless bathing suit, immediately known as the *monokini*. **1971** *Observer* (Colour Suppl.) 9 May (recto front cover), This monokini is not a tattered pair of cut-down jeans but the latest smart, expensive one-piece swimsuit made of disguised suede. **1974** *Guardian* 4 July 2/7 The monokini is no longer the rage only at St-Tropez. French girls usually go topless in Paris open-air swimming pools.

monolayer (mǫ·nŏlēⁱəɹ). [f. Mono- + Layer *sb.*] **a.** A layer or film one molecule thick.

1933 *Biochem. Jrnl.* XXVII. 1581 The structure of proteins in bulk solution is different from that which exists when the protein is extended as a monolayer in a film. **1950** W. J. Moore *Physical Chem.* xvi. 496 The ordinary three-dimensional states of aggregation have many counterparts in the two-dimensional world of monolayers. **1972** R. G. Kazmann *Mod. Hydrol.* (ed. 2) iii. 62 Ideally this would form a film one molecule thick on the water surface—a monolayer. **1973** *Nature* 10 Aug. 328/2 In these severe conditions of lack of water (a few monolayers of water adsorbed on soil particles) some growth and metabolic activity of bacteria..does occur.

b. *Biol.* and *Med.* A culture consisting of a layer of cells one cell thick.

1952 *Proc. Nat. Acad. Sci.* XXXVIII. 748 The virus of Western Equine Encephalomyelitis, adapted to chicken embryo, will produce plaques when it is grown on a monolayer of cells obtainable from chicken embryos. **1961** *Nature* 22 Apr. 370/2 The vaccina virus was grown in monolayer cultures of monkey kidney tissue. **1973** *Ibid.* 6 Apr. 399/2 The division of most 'normal' cells in culture is inhibited after they have grown to a confluent monolayer.

monolingual (mǫnoli·ŋgwăl), *a.* and *sb.* [f. Mono- + Lingual *a.* 4 b.] **A.** *adj.* Speaking only one language; written in a single language.

1953 *Use of Vernacular Lang. in Educ.* (Unesco) ii. 50 It cannot be denied that the business of government is easier in a monolingual than in a multilingual nation. However, it does not follow that legislation or school policy requiring the use of the official language at all times will give the same results as actual monolingualism. **1954** L. MacNeice *Autumn Sequel* 54 At times she is monolingual, monotone, At others mistress of the Tower of Babel. **1968** *Amer. N. & Q.* Mar. 109/1 As a monolingual dictionary and a ready reference work..the Larousse has no parallel in any other language. **1972** *Language* XLVIII 910 The English translations do not, I think, allow the monolingual speaker of English to get any sense of how a speaker of Japanese feels when he is addressed with -*san*.

B. *sb.* One who speaks only one language.

1956 E. Haugen *Bilingualism in Americas* iv. 77 Any

kind of sampling test which adequately measures monolingual skill can be used to make comparisons between monolinguals and bilinguals speaking the same language. **1971** G. Ansre in J. Spencer *Eng. Lang. W. Afr.* 147 Essentially,..in cases of both monolinguals and bilinguals incorporating loans, the results seem similar. **1972** H. Kurath *Studies Area Linguistics* vii. 112 A few of them have even been adopted by English monolinguals of Pennsylvania.

Hence **monoli·ngualism**, the ability to speak only one language; **monoli·nguist** = *monolingual *sb.*; **monolingui·stic** *a.* = *monolingual *a.*

1928 *Observer* 8 Apr. 14/3 There is no one living.. speaking only Manx and no English. Ten years before that the monolinguists had dwindled to under half a dozen. **1942** L. B. Namier *Conflicts* 3 Union..in monolinguistic national States became in the nineteenth century the political aim of the educated, and in time of the semi-educated, classes in Europe. **1960** J. Lodwick *Asparagus Trench* 66 All the monolinguists who..would opt for Indian tea in Pekin. **1968** Y. Malkiel *Essays on Linguistic Themes* i. 6 It is..held that bilingualism and even trilingualism are more widely disseminated the world over than is strict monolingualism. **1972** H. Kurath *Studies in Area Linguistics* 124 Monolingualism prevails in large parts of the world.

monolith, *sb.* and *a.* Add: **A.** *sb.* **2.** *transf.* and *fig.* A person or thing resembling a monolith; *esp.* (after Russ. *monolit*; cf. *monolitnost'* monolithic unity of the party) a political or social structure presenting an indivisible or unbroken unity.

1934 H. Nicolson *Curzon: Last Phase* xi. 323 M. Stamboliisky, the peasant Prime Minister of Bulgaria, was also granted an audience... Curzon was attracted towards this solid, somewhat helpless, monolith. He always felt at his ease with entirely self-made people. **1940** Auden *Another Time* 117 The monolith Of State. **1953** *Manch. Guardian* 6 Apr. 4/1 The 'monolith' of Soviet power is stirring. **1957** *Economist* 7 Sept. 766/2 A growing diversity in the economic scene is liable to lead to cracks in the political monolith. **1959** P. H. Johnson *Unspeakable Skipton* xxiii. 203 If the Commissioners of Inland Revenue ever caught up with her, she would undoubtedly bring tears to their eyes, reducing them from monoliths to simple, sentimental men with mothers of their own. **1962** J. Wain *Strike Father Dead* 115 She was a woman of few words, as thick round the middle as an oak, with strong limbs and a big head and shoulders. She wasn't talkative, but..you just wouldn't expect to get a flow of words out of a monolith like that. **1966** *Listener* 12 May 700/3 His [*sc.* Bruckner's] symphonies are towering monoliths. **1975** *Times* 4 Jan. 13/3 State run monoliths whose inspiration would owe more to the opportunism of Benito Mussolini than to idealism.

B. *adj.* **2.** *fig.* = *monolithic *a.* 4.

1922 E. Blunden *Shepherd* 53 Between great monolith trees.

monolithic, *a.* Add: **1. b.** *Electronics.* Of a solid-state circuit: composed of active and passive components formed in a single chip (or thin film: see quot. 1967).

1963 E. Keonjian *Microelectronics* i. 8 (*heading*) Monolithic circuits. *Ibid.* 9 A monolithic piece of material is treated in such a way as to possess an electronic circuit function. **1965** *New Scientist* 20 May 510/2 The multi-chip assembly has some advantages over the monolithic circuit—for example, the various chips can be tested before assembly. **1967** *Encycl. Dict. Physics* Suppl. II. 173/1 *Monolithic circuit*, an integrated circuit which uses either thin film or silicon chip techniques for both active and passive devices but not a mixture of these techniques. Since true monolithic thin film circuits are not commercially available the term is more usually applied to silicon chip construction, where it implies, in particular, that any circuit capacitors do not use evaporated dielectrics. However, monolithic silicon chip circuits may use a deposited pattern of connectors between circuit elements. **1970** [see *integrated *ppl. a.* b]. **1971** *Physics Bull.* Jan. 45/1 The new computer has a main memory constructed entirely of monolithic circuits and uses silicon memory chips instead of magnetic cores for storage.

4. *transf.* and *fig.* Resembling a monolith, having one or more of the qualities of a monolith; great, massive; immovable, unwavering, unemotional; unified, homogeneous, unchallenged. *Esp.* applied to organizations, parties, governments, etc., which are autocratic or monopolistic (freq. in derogatory use).

1920 D. H. Lawrence *England, my England* (1922) 87 Maurice had a curious monolithic way of sitting in a chair, erect and distant. **1923** A. Huxley *Antic Hay* xiii. 192 His appearance is monolithic and grim. **1937** *Nation* (N.Y.) 10 July 32/1 The monolithic corporation talks loudly to the workers. **1942** *New Republic* 9 Nov. 598/2 The monolithic power structure of the totalitarian state. **1945** A. L. Rowse *West-Country Stories* 26 The Fourth Symphony of Sibelius, the most monolithic of them all. **1948** J. Towster *Polit. Power in U.S.S.R.* p. ix, The peculiarities of the monolithic Communist Party. **1952** *Economist* 22 Mar. 702/1 Herr Grotewohl and his monolithic Socialist Unity Party are democratic. **1953** *Times* 11 Apr. 7/2 Wherever there is monolithic rule the autocrat is bound to repress all views that are not his own. **1959** *Listener* 5 Mar. 423/1 There were many contradictory ele-elements in her, but they and she were static, immovable, almost monolithic. **1971** *Nature* 7 May 2/2 But would not the merging of the research councils create too monolithic a central sponsor? **1974** E. Ambler *Dr. Frigo* ii. 124 We were never a monolithic party.

monoli·thically, *adv.* [f. Monolithic *a.*; see -ically.] In a monolithic form or manner (see senses 3 and *4 of Monolithic *a.*).

1932 Kipling *Limits & Renewals* 80, I was monolithically military. **1952** Sparkes & Smith *Concrete Roads* xvii. 398 Integral kerbs are those which are constructed monolithically with the slab. **1960** *Times* 17 Feb. 5/6 Insulating concrete can be cast monolithically. **1960** *Sunday Times* 22 May 17/5 Greedy for praise and monolithically uncharitable. **1962** *Friend* 14 Sept. 1116/1 A row of intent figures... Sometimes the families, the lovers and the photographers got mixed up with these still figures. But they monolithically stood on, for three full hours. **1966** *New Statesman* 27 May 762/3 The church [in Spain] can no longer be regarded as an institution monolithically in support of the *status quo*, opposed to change at all costs. **1975** *Times* 11 July 15/4 The contention that the Liberal Party is monolithically moderate.

monolithism (mǫnǒliþiz'm). [f. Monolith *sb.* + -ism.] The quality or fact of being monolithic (see *monolithic *a.* 4); the principle of totalitarian rule.

1927 *Nation* 21 Dec. 703 The tactics..constituted a danger to the 'monolithism' of the party. **1948** J. Towster *Polit. Power in U.S.S.R.* ii. vi. 132 Cutting across both the monopoly and monolithism power principles, this act was..condemned as 'open counter-revolution'. **1957** T. Kilmartin tr. *Aron's Opium of Intellectuals* 129 The Bolsheviks have always had two slogans, one which insisted on monolithism, the other which encouraged conflicts of ideas and tendencies to sustain the vigour of the Party.

monologue, *sb.* Add: **2. c.** Used of Old English verse.

1902 W. W. Lawrence in *Jrnl. Eng. & Gmc. Philol.* IV. 462 Ebert expressed the opinion that the Seafarer should be interpreted as a monologue from beginning to end. **1905** E. Rickert in *Mod. Philol.* II. 372 They are specimens of the *giedd* or short monologue arising from a dramatic situation, such as occurs frequently in *Beowulf.* **1935** A. C. Bartlett *Larger Rhet. Patterns Anglo-Saxon Poetry* 106 Monologue and duologue, direct and indirect discourse, all are undramatic. **1943** B. F. Huppé in *Jrnl. Eng. & Gmc. Philol.* XLII. 529 The basic outline [of the *Wanderer*] has already been set, with the two contrasting and complementary pagan monologues, framed and bound together by the expository Christian introduction, conclusion and 'bridge passage'.

monomaniac. b. *adj.* (Later example.)

1849 Geo. Eliot *Let.* 24 Oct. (1954) I. 318 How does she manage to endure her life with that poor monomaniac husband.

monomaniacal, *a.* Add: (Later example.)

1971 *Eng. Studies* LII. 249 He is, in short, a soulless creature set apart from the rest of humanity by his monomaniacal devotion to pure avarice.

Hence **monomani·acally** *adv.*

1856 Dickens *Dorrit* (1857) i. xxi. 186 Young Sparkler hovering about the rooms, monomaniacally seeking any sufficiently ineligible young lady. **1972** *New York* 3 Apr. 65 Her voice adheres monomaniacally to the same pitch.

Monomark (mǫ·nomāɹk). Also **monomark.** [f. Mono- + Mark *sb.*¹] A combination of letters and/or figures used as an identification mark for goods or personal property. Also *transf.* Hence **mo·nomark** *v. trans.*, to apply a monomark to; **mo·nomarking** *vbl. sb.*

1925 *Westm. Gaz.* 10 July, The Monomark system was explained by its inventor, Mr. William Morris, at a luncheon yesterday in London. A monomark, said Mr. Morris, is the shortest officially recognised postal name and address. **1925** *Glasgow Herald* 10 July 11 The idea.. is to set up an international system whereby firms may be granted a 'monomark', consisting of a combination of symbols preceded by B.C.M. (British Commercial Monomark). *Ibid.*, Any individual, child or adult, who cares to pay a modest fee will be entitled to be 'monomarked'. *Ibid.*, The eternal enigma of the identity of Smith—in England alone there are 530,000 bearers of the name—could be kept from business intercourse by the 'monomarking' of each number of the clan. **1926** *Ibid.* 27 Feb. 10 The persistency of the Scot's mental monomarks applied also to the vocal expression of them. **1928** *Daily Mail* 14 Aug. 9/7 Bench yesterday held that a monomark on a dog's collar did not fulfil the requirements of the law in respect of the address of the animal's owner. **1975** *Times* 18 Sept. 2/1 (Advt.), A Telex at your disposal for £25 p.a... British Monomarks (Est. 1926).

monomer (mǫ·nǒməɹ). *Chem.* [f. Mono- + *-mer.] Any compound from which a polymer might be formed by the combining together of its molecules (sometimes with the molecules of another compound).

1914 *Chem. Abstr.* VIII. 1037 If released from this combination, it [*sc.* chromic acid] gives at once a polychromic acid, which goes back to the monomer only in the presence of strong bases. **1942** *Electronic Engin.* XIV. 668/3 Impurities in the monomer styrene can have a very serious effect in the electrical properties of the finished polystyrene. **1957** *Technology* July 176/2 Will these catalysts polymerize monomers other than ethylene? **1974** *Guardian* 31 Jan. 6/2 Plastics manufacturers are now mounting health hazard investigations of vinyl chloride monomer.

Hence **monome·ric** *a.*, existing in the form of a monomer.

1929 [see *dimeric *a.* 2]. **1944** *Electronic Engin.* XVI. 348/3 This 'frost'..was caused by volatile impurities and residual monomeric styrene. **1969** *Nature* 13 Dec. 1060/2 The process by which the monomeric constituents of DNA are produced from their ribose analogues is now recognized to constitute a biochemical control mechanism of the greatest importance.

monomolecular (mǫnomǒle·kiŭlăɹ), *a.* [f. Mono- 1 + Molecular *a.*] **a.** Composed of or pertaining to a single molecule or single molecules.

1877 *Chem. News* 23 Mar. 124/1 (*heading*) On the monomolecular unit of volume for gases and vapours. **1915** *Jrnl. Amer. Chem. Soc.* XXXVII. 191 The anhydride of betaine, $(CH_3)_3NCH_2CO_2$, has the structure of a salt, but no one seems to have determined whether this is monomolecular or dimolecular. **1974** *Biochim. & Biophys. Acta* CCCXLVI. 79 (*heading*) A monomolecular electron transfer chain.

b. In chemical kinetics: having or pertaining to an order or a molecularity of one. Cf. *unimolecular *a.*

1899 *Jrnl. Franklin Inst.* CXLVII. 469 Another classical case of the monomolecular reaction is the decomposition of arsine. **1935** J. N. Friend *Text-bk. Physical Chem.* II. iii. 56 Radioactive transformations..provide the only known examples of true monomolecular reactions. *Ibid.* 81 As the solvent and catalyst molecules remain virtually constant in amount, many reactions that really are polymolecular are found to conform to the requirements of the monomolecular law. **1943** Sumner & Somers *Chem. & Methods of Enzymes* i. 13 In most instances enzyme reactions classed as monomolecular are only approximately so. **1973** *Biol. Abstr.* LV. 2244/1 The monomolecular reaction equation gives a good fit to disease progress curve in the field within the primary infection period.

c. Of a film or layer: being one molecule in thickness.

1917 *Jrnl. Amer. Chem. Soc.* XXXIX. 1904 On cooling these surfaces to liquid air temperature the surfaces become covered with a monomolecular layer. **1931** *Jrnl. Physical Chem.* XXXV. 859 If a mono-molecular layer of gas is adsorbed at 300°C while the volume is kept constant the pressure increase will be about 8 mm. **1941** *Ann. Reg.* *1940* 353 The remarkable properties of monomolecular films of certain organic liquids spread over water, mercury, or gallium. **1965** B. E. Freeman tr. *Vandel's Biospeleology* xviii. 317 It is the monomolecular waxy layer which makes the integument of terrestrial arthropods impermeable to water.

monomorphemic (mǫnomǭɹfī·mik), *a.* *Linguistics.* [f. Mono- + *morphemic *a.*] Consisting of a single morpheme.

1936 *English Studies* XVIII. 160 Alongside his [*sc.* Trnka's] five 'monomorphemic' or simple phonemes..he is forced to set up a like series of 'dimorphemic' combinations. **1942** [see *bimorphemic *a.*]. **1953** C. E. Bazell *Linguistic Form* i. 5 Neither *John start-* nor *start-ed* can be replaced by a monomorphemic constituent. **1971** B. Mafeni in J. Spencer *Eng. Lang. W. Afr.* 110 By far the greater majority of Nigerian Pidgin words are invariable in form and are usually monomorphemic—that is, not divisible into smaller meaningful units. **1973** R. Harris *Synonymy & Linguistic Analysis* iii. 66 English *older* consists of two morphemes,..while *sister* is monomorphemic, since neither *sist-er* nor any other division gives units which can plausibly be identified as having 'reasonable similarity of meaning' with phonemically comparable units in other utterances.

monomorphic, *a.* Add: (Further examples.) Now *spec.* in *Genetics*, identical as regards genotype, a particular chromosome, or a part of a chromosome.

1894 W. Bateson *Materials for Study of Varieties* 37 The..case in which the whole community, grouped according to the degrees in which they display a given character, forms one Curve of Error, may conveniently be called monomorphic in respect of that character. **1957** *Cold Spring Harbor Symp. Quantitative Biol.* XXII. 397/2 A highly polymorphic population..will be able..to leave progeny of some sort in a wider range of environment than could a monomorphic one. **1960** *Proc. Nat. Acad. Sci.* XLVI. 41 The population fails to reach the level of adaptedness which it would have if it were monomorphic for a genotype with an adaptive value equal to that of the A_1A_2 heterozygotes. Suppose, then, that a mutation produces an allele A_3 such that the fitness of the homozygote A_3A_3 is equal to that of the heterozygote A_1A_2. Natural selection is expected to lead to gradual elimination of A_1 and A_2, and to establishment of a population monomorphic and homozygous for A_3A_3. **1971** *Nature* 17 Sept. 190/2 *D. simulans* is one of the three widespread species of *Drosophila* considered to be monomorphic with regard to chromosome structure. **1973** *Ibid.* 31 Aug. 574/2 Of the thirty-one loci examined eight are monomorphic in all eleven populations. **1974** *Ibid.* 11 Oct. 514/1 *T. vivax* is generally considered monomorphic, although evidence of morphological variation between strains has been reviewed recently.

monomorphism. Add: (Further examples: cf. *monomorphic *a.*)

1957 *Cold Spring Harbor Symp. Quantitative Biol.* XXII. 399/1 In nature..it is unlikely that..a reversion to monomorphism will often occur. **1960** *Proc. Nat. Acad. Sci.* XLVI. 45 The replacement of the balanced polymorphisms present in the parental races by chromosomal monomorphisms certainly proves that acquisition in evolution of a balanced polymorphic condition need not be irreversible. **1973** *Nature* 31 Aug. 575/1 Most loci tend to monomorphism in reproductively as well as geographically isolated populations.

2. *Math.* A one-to-one homomorphism.

1956 C. Chevalley *Fund. Concepts Algebra* i. 11 A homomorphism which is injective is called a monomorphism; a homomorphism which is surjective is called an epimorphism. **1969** F. M. Hall *Introd. Abstr. Algebra* II. ii. 39 In a monomorphism different objects always have different images. **1971** E. C. Dade in Powell & Higman *Finite Simple Groups* viii. 252 The diagonal map $\sigma \to \sigma \times \sigma$ is a natural monomorphism of G into $G \times G$.

Monomoy (mǫ·nomoi). The name of a peninsula (Monomoy Point) in Mass., U.S.A., used *attrib.* or *absol.* to denote a type of surfboat (see quot. 1966).

1908 *Ann. Rep. U.S. Life-Saving Service 1907* 65 The keeper..returned to the station..to..attempt to reach the steamer in the *Monomoy* surfboat. **1966** *Random House Dict., Monomoy surfboat,* a double-ended surfboat having rather full lines with high carrying capacity and seaworthiness, used by the U.S. Coast Guard. **1967** *Proc. U.S. Merchant Marine Council* Jan. 19/2 The transfer was accomplished by the *Rockaway's* boat, a 26-foot Monomoy, with a crew of 12 men.

Monongahela. (Earlier examples.)

1805 *Mississippi Messenger* (Natchez) 1 July 3/1 *From Pittsburgh*..a Quantity of best Monongahela Whiskey for sale by the barrel. **1831** J. J. Audubon *Ornith. Biogr.* I. 504 The women..soon found my flask filled with *monongahela* (that is, reader, strong whisky). **1834** W. G. Simms *Guy Rivers* I. 76 Having cleared his throat with the contents of a tumbler of Monongahela which seemed to stand permanently full by his side. **1847** W. I. Paulding *Madmen All* in J. K. & W. I. Paulding *Amer. Comedies* 192 May I never taste Monongahela again!

mononuclear, *a.* (*sb.*) **b.** *sb.* (Examples.) Add to def.: *spec.* a monocyte.

1908 *Jrnl. Infectious Dis.* V. 175 In the experiments recorded subsequently..+ + [indicates] destruction of the large mononuclears with degeneration of the lymphocytes. **1928** *Amer. Jrnl. Physiol.* LXXXV. 490 There are many forms of large mononuclears which are hard to distinguish from lymphocytes by the ordinary Wright stain. **1956** *Nature* 21 Jan. 138/2 The total leucocyte count was about double.., the mononuclears being increased by about 10,000 and the polymorphonuclears by about 6,500. **1974** Park & Good *Princ. Mod. Immunobiol.* xiii. 171 Other chemotactic substances..derive from the complement components and these influence the mononuclears, as well as polymorphonuclears.

mononucleate (mǫnoniū·kliĕt), *a. Biol.* [f. Mono- + Nucleate *a.*] = Mononuclear *a.*

1957 *New Biol.* XXIV. 30 In the primitive type, *Iridia* studied by le Calvez, there is no visible difference between the sexual and the asexual individuals until they begin to reproduce. Both are mono-nucleate. **1971** *New Scientist* 8 July 90/1, I shall be concerned with the mononucleate hybrid cells that are produced when the nuclei of two cells (and occasionally three) fuse together.

mononucleated, *a.* Add: (Further examples.) *spec.* (See quot. 1930.)

1930 W. S. Thompson *Population Problems* xvi. 279 The modern city..always has one nucleus which is far more important than any of the others and indeed as a rule it has a 'downtown' area in which are congregated most of the important offices, stores, hotels, amusements, and public buildings... Why have our modern large cities assumed this mononucleated form? **1938** L. Mumford *Culture of Cities* vii. 489 Under this mode of design, the planner proposes to replace the 'mono-nucleated city', as Professor Warren Thompson has called it, with a new type of 'poly-nucleated city', in which a cluster of communities, adequately spaced and bounded, shall do duty for the badly organized mass city. **1971** *Nature* 10 Sept. 105/1 Attached cells..were mostly mononucleated, though sometimes binucleated.

mononucleosis (mǫ:noniūklı͡ōu·sis). *Med.* [f. Mononucle(ar *a.* (*sb.*) + -osis.] An abnormally high proportion of mononuclear leucocytes (monocytes or lymphocytes), or of monocytes alone, in the blood; esp. = *infectious mononucleosis* (see *infectious *a.* 2 c).

1920, etc. [see *infectious mononucleosis* s.v. *infectious *a.* 2 c]. **1928** *Amer. Jrnl. Physiol.* LXXXV. 497 The spleen is an important factor in the production of an emotional relative mononucleosis. **1950** *Biol. Abstr.* XXIV. 1776/1 (*heading*) Exceptional hematological reactions in chronic benzene poisoning. Neutrophilic granulocytosis, lymphocytosis, and mononucleosis. **1968** *New Scientist* 25 Jan. 203/2 Suspecting that the presence of the EB virus and the girl's glandular fever were connected, the Henles..started testing blood samples from other patients who had contracted mononucleosis. **1972** T. P. McMahon *Issue of Bishop's Blood* (1973) vii. 88 I'm not too sure that mononucleosis isn't a modern-day version of the megrims of our Victorian ancestors. **1974** J. Heller *Something Happened* 333 Even people who've been out awhile with hepatitis or mononucleosis have a hard time making their way back. They lack pep.

monooho(o), varr. *mohoohoo.

monophasic, *a.* Add to def.: Applied to (a record of) a nerve impulse that is of the same sign throughout, and to experimental arrangements devised to give such records. (Earlier and later examples.)

1883 *Phil. Trans. R. Soc.* CLXXIII. 35 (*table*) Character of variation. Monophasic, −39·1. Diphasic, +11·7, −21·2. **1915** W. M. Bayliss *Princ. Gen. Physiol.* xii. 380 If electrode B is on a spot [of the nerve] which has been killed, the wave of negativity..disappears in the killed area, so that the only electrical effect seen is that due to the becoming negative of spot A and consists, therefore, of only the first half..of the diphasic response; it is..'monophasic'. **1932** *Jrnl. Cellular & Compar. Physiol.* I. 177 Local asphyxia at one of the leading-off electrodes renders a nerve potential record monophasic even more effectively than crushing does. **1950** *Jrnl. Gen. Physiol.* XXXIII. 654 The problem of obtaining a monophasic lead, by which is meant one in which no membrane changes at the distal electrode are recorded, is one of great importance in view of the complexity of the potentials to be analyzed. Crushing or heating was so unsatisfactory that keeping the distal lead on intact nerve was a preferable arrangement. **1967** L. A. Geddes in C. C. Brown *Methods in Psychophysiol.* xv. 441 As a result of the intermittent activity of a variety of cells and organs, short duration, asymmetrical (with respect to the time axis) or completely monophasic pulses are presented to the reproducing apparatus.

Hence **monopha·sically** *adv.*, by a technique yielding a monophasic record; **monophasi·city,** the property of being monophasic.

1928 *Amer. Jrnl. Physiol.* LXXXVI. 187 The size of response was measured by the action current led off monophasically..from the peroneal nerve. **1932** *Jrnl. Cellular & Compar. Physiol.* I. 178 Gerard argues that monophasicity results because the asphyxiated region of the nerve is completely depolarized, while a killed region, if supplied with oxygen, may partially repolarize to give a diphasic record. **1941** S. H. Bartley *Vision* xii. 286 The monophasically recorded optic-nerve pattern produced by a flash of light on the retina, is a complex series of oscillations. **1950** *Jrnl. Gen. Physiol.* XXXIII. 654 By the time at which the equilibrium period was completed the fibers were fully blocked. Monophasicity continued without further difficulty to the end of the experiment. **1972** *Science* 2 June 1044/1 The excitability of primary afferent terminals was tested by stimulating the fibers through a low-resistance, glass microelectrode.., and the conducted antidromic volley was recorded monophasically.

monophonematic (mǫ:nofōunĭmæ·tik), *a. Linguistics.* [f. Mono- + *phonematic *a.*] = *monophonemic *a.*

1940 *Language* XVI. 249 The argument for the monophonematic character of Dutch *ei*,.. (and the same applies to the English sounds in *bite*..) can be shown not to hold if the total structure of the syllable and the behavior of the..diphthongs are examined. **1952** A. Cohen *Phonemes of Eng.* ii. 24 The problem of how to decide whether we have to do with one or more phonemes (monophonematic or polyphonematic interpretation). **1961** *Brno Studies in English* III. 68 It is..in this medium section of the concerned sound trace that this most essential quality of the monophonematic diphthong must obtain the most obvious prominence.

Hence **monophonema·tically** *adv.*, **monophonemati·city.**

1953 C. E. Bazell *Linguistic Form* iv. 47 The absence of possibility of being on a morph-boundary..may be a criterion of monophonematicity. **1961** *Brno Studies in English* III. 68 What matters..is..the direction and the zonal extent of the monophonematically evaluated 'gliding diphthong'. **1961** F. W. Householder in Saporta & Bastian *Psycho-linguistics* 18/1 The chief metaphysical bones hassled over..concern such points as 'biuniqueness', 'monophonematicity' [etc.].

monophonemic (mǫnofonī·mik), *a. Linguistics.* [f. Mono- + *phonemic *a.*] Of or pertaining to a single phoneme; consisting of a single phoneme.

1936 *Amer. Speech* XI. 206 Over against the monophonemic words cited above are to be set the pleiophonemic words made up of two or more phonemes each. **1955** *Archivum Linguisticum* VII. 154 A distinction is drawn between monophonemic short-vowel and polyphonemic long-vowel diphthongs. **1957** S. Potter *Mod. Linguistics* ii. 42 The simplest instances of the commutation test are provided by such monophonemic forms as occur in most languages.

monophonic, *a.* Add: (Examples.)

1920 E. Walker in F. S. Marvin *Recent Devel. Europ. Thought* 286 If we exclude some monophonic conceptions that have still their value for us, it [*sc.* music] is barely five hundred years old. **1942** *Scrutiny* XI. 1. 7 The monophonic work of Léonin and Perotin. **1972** *Harper's Dict. Mus.* 206/1 Monophonic vocal music has existed since ancient times.

2. Of sound broadcasts, gramophone records, etc.: involving only one channel, so that there is only one output signal and all the sound appears to the listener to come from a single source; = *monaural *a.* 2. Opp. *stereophonic *a.*

1958 *Newsweek* 13 Oct. 102/2 Bending an ear to a single-track (monophonic, to hi-fi devotees) record is 'like listening to a concert through a crack in the door'. **1959** *Proc. Inst. Electr. Engin.* CVI. b. Suppl. No. 14. 257/1 The monophonic reproduction on two loudspeakers appears to issue from a very small source situated between them but, when operating in a stereophonic manner, the ambient studio sound appears to fill the whole space between the loudspeakers with positional accent on the individual sound sources. **1960** *New Scientist* 4 Feb. 262/2 Such a stereo system may not be 'compatible' with ordinary monophonic receivers. **1962** A. Nisbett *Technique Sound Studio* 240 In a monophonic recording..noise at a natural level will generally sound excessive. **1968** *Consumer Reports* Sept. 502/1 Only stereo discs are reviewed, since record companies have all but stopped producing classical monophonic discs. **1968** *Times* 29 Nov. (Sound of Leisure Suppl.) p. vi/4 The sound was still monophonic: that is, it still came from a single track or radio signal and could never give us any sensation of listening to real musicians spread naturally across an audio stage. **1970** *Jrnl. Gen. Psychol.* LXXXIII. 256 The pure tones..were ..recorded on magnetic tapes by a single-track monophonic Tandberg tape recorder. Subsequently, these magnetic tapes were played back to *S* through a pair of Sharpe monaural liquid-filled headphones. **1974** *Nature* 13 Dec. 535/1 Monophonic reproduction gave no explicit directional information, even when reproduced from more than one loudspeaker.

monophonically (mǫnofǫ·nikăli), *adv.* [f. prec. + -al + -ly[2].] **a.** *Mus.* As regards monophony.

1942 *Scrutiny* XI. 12 It is well that we should understand how in 'progressing' music lost much, polyphonically as well as monophonically.

b. In a monophonic (monaural) manner; as regards monophonic reproduction; = *monaurally *adv.* b.

1959 *N.Y. Times* 8 Feb. 14X/3 The disks are available stereophonically and monophonically. **1959** *Proc. Inst. Electr. Engin.* CVI. b. Suppl. No. 14. 207/1 If coincident directional microphones are employed and we add left A to right B..the resultant may well be unsuitable monophonically. **1963** *Which?* Jan. 8/2 Both these could play stereo records, without conversion, though the sound was reproduced monophonically. **1974** *Encycl. Brit. Macropædia* XVII. 53/2 A record that can be played stereophonically over stereophonic equipment or monophonically over monophonic equipment is called a compatible recording.

monophony. Add: (Examples.)

1964 W. Lovelock *Student's Dict. Mus.* 56/2 *Monophony,* music which consists simply of a melodic line without any form of accompaniment. **1968** *Encycl. Brit.* XV. 745/2 *Monody*,..a musical term that in England is often used to describe music for a single melodic line, though in the U.S. monophony is preferred for this meaning.

2. Monophonic recording or reproduction.

1959 *Proc. Inst. Electr. Engin.* CVI. b. Suppl. No. 14. 201/1 The best microphone positions for monophony and stereophony frequently differ considerably and are often quite incompatible. **1961** *Atlantic Monthly* Jan. 146/3, I am sure their transients, meaning the quick high overtones of fiddles and trumpets, are as hard to handle in monophony as in stereo.

Monophoto (mǫnofōu·to). [f. Mono(type *sb.* and *a.* + Photo.] The proprietary name of a photo-composing machine which uses a perforated paper tape produced by a keyboard unit to control filmsetting by a second unit which replaces the type-caster of a Monotype machine. Also *attrib.*

1954 [see *filmset *v.*]. **1958** *Times Lit. Suppl.* 18 Apr. 209/3 How important the correction factor is may be seen from the history of the Monophoto..which is likely to become one of the more successful photo-composing machines. **1967** Cox & Grose *Organiz. Bibliogr. Rec. by Computer* ii. 27 (*caption*) These [*sc.* trial galley proofs] were produced on a Monophoto composing machine. **1973** S. Jennett *Making of Books* (ed. 5) v. 85 The mechanical Monophoto may be called a first-generation photo-composing machine.

monophthongize, *v.* Add: (Further examples.) Also *intr.*

1914 H. C. Wyld *Short Hist. Eng.* vi. 107 In W.S. the *ea* which resulted from *æ* preceded by a front consonant was monophthongized in L.O.E. itself, and became *e.* **1927** J. J. Hogan *Eng. Lang. in Ireland* 69 *M.E. ai, ei.* These were levelled under *ai* in M.E. This was monophthongized, and converged with M.E. *ā.* **1965** W. S. Allen *Vox Latina* ii. 62 Although French has monophthongized to *o*, the *au* diphthong must have survived long enough to cause the change of *c* to *ch* in..*chose* from *causam.* **1968** —— *Vox Graeca* ii. 71 The [ẹ̄] of Boeotian was the result of monophthongizing the diphthong [ai]. **1970** B. M. H. Strang *Hist. Eng.* ii. 111 The diphthong, in either form, began to monophthongise.

monophyletic, *a.* Add: (Later examples.) Hence **mono·phyly** (see quot. 1961).

1927 N. P. Williams *Ideas of Fall* viii. 516 The 'monophyletic' theory of the origin of humanity (that is, the view which regards the whole of mankind as descended from a single pair of ancestors). **1945** G. G. Simpson in *Bull. Amer. Mus. Nat. Hist.* LXXXV. 17/1 It is not useful to set up a classification in which groups with different names cannot be distinguished morphologically, but this does happen if theoretical monophyly is too strictly demanded. **1946** *Nature* 16 Nov. 719/1 This clear distinction between the genera at so deep a level in the Palæocene is not suggestive of a monophyletic origin for the family. **1953** E. Mayr et al. *Methods & Princ. Systematic Zool.* iii. 41 One of the objects of taxonomists in the post-Darwinian period was to construct a classification of animals composed of monophyletic groups. **1961** G. G. Simpson *Princ. Animal Taxonomy* iv. 124 Monophyly is the derivation of a taxon through one or more lineages (temporal successions of ancestral-descendant populations) from one immediately ancestral taxon of the same or lower rank. **1963** Davis & Heywood *Princ. Angiosperm Taxonomy* ii. 46 It is a widely expressed principle that taxonomic groups (at least above the species level) should be monophyletic. **1969** E. Mayr *Princ. Systematic Zool.* iv. 75 The issue of monophyly has been confounded by various confusions.

monopitch (mǫ·nopitʃ), *sb.* and *a.* [f. Mono- + Pitch *sb.*[2]] **A.** *sb.* Uniformity of pitch in speaking or singing.

1939 in WEBSTER Add. **1942** A. T. WEAVER *Speech Forms & Princ.* x. 243 Monopitch, frequently miscalled monotone, results first, from unemotional speaking and, second, from a dull or inactive mind which fails to see distinctions in the meanings of the language which is being spoken. **1964** CRYSTAL & QUIRK *Systems Prosodic & Paralinguistic Features in Eng.* ii. 16 These deficiencies also mar his discussion of..pitch (including 'monopitch', step up and down, and slide).

B. *adj.* Of a roof: consisting of a single uniformly sloping surface. Of a building: having such a roof.

1941 *Archit. Rev.* LXXXIX. 47 The mono-pitch roof was employed for simplicity and to enable all the rainwater to be collected at the front of the house owing to the limited fall available for the drains. **1961** *Guardian* 25 Mar. 5/5 A simple and comely monopitch building. **1971** *Daily Tel.* 14 Aug. 7/3 The crematorium's group of monopitch grey slate roofs appear to form a large pyramid.

monoplane (mǫ·noplēⁱn). [f. MONO- + PLANE *sb.*³] An aeroplane or glider having only one 'plane' or main supporting surface on either side of the fuselage (so called because in the earliest monoplanes the wing on each side was part of a single structure extending across the fuselage); † the wing itself. Also *attrib.* or as *adj.*

1907 *Sci. Amer.* 16 Nov. 358/1 (*heading*) The latest French aeroplanes and their records. The Pelterie monoplane. *Ibid.* 358/3 One end of the monoplane (which is made in two halves) was broken. *Ibid.*, The Pelterie aeroplane resembles the monoplane machine with which M. Bleriot experimented unsuccessfully last spring. **1907** *Nature* 5 Dec. 106/2 Another aëroplane which is also attracting considerable attention at Paris is the 'monoplane' of M. Robert Esnault Pelterie. This, unlike most recent types, has only a single transverse supporting surface. **1908** *Times* 20 May 7/6 A monoplane aeroplane.. made some successful evolutions yesterday. **1908** *Sci. Amer.* 18 July 44/1 The rear half of the monoplane, at its outer ends, has movable planes for correcting the transverse stability. **1910** *Blackw. Mag.* July 4/1 The aeroplane, whether monoplane, biplane, or other. *a* **1918** J. T. B. MCCUDDEN *Five Yrs. in R. Flying Corps* (1919) 63 Two Taube monoplanes came over St. Omer. **1922** *Glasgow Herald* 8 Aug. 8 A Swiss pilot on a motorless monoplane succeeded in making a flight lasting 45 seconds. **1935** C. G. BURGE *Compl. Bk. Aviation* 123/1 Gliders are usually of monoplane type, though biplane constructions have been used. **1960** C. H. GIBBS-SMITH *Aeroplane* x. 54 The year 1907 saw the crystallisation of the two basic forms of early aeroplane—the pusher biplane and the tractor monoplane. **1969** K. MUNSON *Pioneer Aircraft 1903–14* 98/1 Levasseur's first full-size aeroplane, a bird-like monoplane tested in 1903, was an utter failure. **1973** J. DI MONA *Last Man at Arlington* (1974) xi. 84 A single engine monoplane thundering toward an ammunition ship.

monoploid (mǫ·nǒploid), *a.* (and *sb.*). *Biol.* [a. G. *monoploid* (O. F. I. Langlet 1927, in *Svensk Bot. Tidskr.* XXI. 1): see MONO- and *-PLOID.] = *HAPLOID *a.* (and *sb.*) (see quot. 1968). Hence **mo·noploidy**, the state or condition of being monoploid.

1928 *Jrnl. Genetics* XIX. 138, I do not think it necessary to replace haploid with monoploid as Langlet (1927) proposes. **1943** L. W. SHARP *Fund. Cytol.* xiv. 211 In the sporophytes of plants true monoploidy occurs very rarely. **1944** *Genetics* XXIX. 232, 16 monosomes and five trisomes were found in the 11 aberrant offspring of a monoploid pollinated by a diploid. **1952** SRB & OWEN *Gen. Genetics* xi. 215 Doubling the chromosomes of a monoploid can give rise to diploid individuals homozygous for all the gene pairs in the organism. **1955** G. F. SPRAGUE *Corn & Corn Improvement* iv. 131 Monoploid or haploid plants, which have one set of chromosomes, arise spontaneously by the parthenogenetic development of unfertilized eggs. Much less frequent are the androgenetic monoploids. *Ibid.* Genes for a high incidence of monoploidy. **1968** R. REIGER *Gloss. Genetics & Cytogenetics* 299 *Monoploid*, of cells or individuals (monoploids) having one chromosome set with the basic number of chromosomes, i.e., the lowest haploid number of chromosomes in a polyploid series.

monopode, *sb.* and *a.* Add: (Later examples of spelling *monopod.*) Also *transf.*

a **1963** C. S. LEWIS *Poems* (1964) 43 Ran till the sunrise shone upon the bouncing Monopods at their heels. **1971** C. BONINGTON *Annapurna South Face* App. F. 286 Each member of the team was also issued with a special clamp to fit on the head of an ice axe with a ball-and-socket attachment for the camera, which made a very useful and compact monopod. **1972** QUICK & LABAU *Handbk. Film Production* xiii. 100 A 'monopod' is a single fixed leg terminating in a screw base that matches the bottom of the camera.

monopodium. Add: **2.** (See quot. 1970.) Also, the support for an early 19th-century table, sideboard, etc., comprising an animal's head with a single foot. (Cf. MONOPODE *sb.* 1.)

1807 T. HOPE *Househ. Furnit.* 36 Little round monopodium or stand, of which the top..is capable of being raised or lowered at pleasure. **1948** M. JOURDAIN *Regency Furnit. 1795–1820* (ed. 2) 105 Console table supported by carved gilt lion monopodia. **1959** G. SAVAGE *Antique Collector's Handbk.* 195 The monopodium, or single leg surmounted by a human or animal head and torso, is peculiarly Regency. **1970** —— *Dict. Antiques* 275/2 *Monopodium*..is applied to certain small tables of the Regency and Empire period which have a three-sided support usually terminating in brass claws at the bottom corners. **1971** *Country Life* 22 July 225/3 From about 1815 the marble top of a console table might be supported at each front corner by an eagle monopodium with boldly outcurving breast and widespread wings.

monopolar (mǫnopōᵘ·lăɹ), *a.* [f. MONO- + POLAR *a.*] **a.** Of, having, or using a single electrode; applied esp. to techniques and apparatus (*a*) for passing electric currents through the body using two electrodes of different sizes or natures, one being usually much larger than the other, and (*b*) for measuring electric potentials in the body, where one electrode is inserted in the region to be studied and the other acts as a reference electrode.

1906 *Practitioner* Dec. 772 The patient, if the monopolar bath had to be administered, grasped a metal bar, suspended from the ceiling, and in connection with the battery swung over the bath, the other electrode remaining in the water. **1936** H. H. U. CROSS *Electr. in Therapeutics* xiii. 296 In the spark-gap system the patient may be connected to the solenoid in monopolar or bipolar fashion. **1956** S. LICHT *Some Clin. Applic. Electroneurophysiol.* i. 8 Chauveau..introduced the monopolar method of stimulation into physiology. **1962** BLAKE & TROTT *Periodontology* xiii. 135 Monopolar diathermy of this type is particularly suitable for minor oral surgery. **1973** M. SCHWARTZ *Physiol. Psychol.* i. 20 In monopolar recordings, one electrode is placed on some relatively neutral or 'indifferent' location, such as the ear, for the EEG, while the other is placed on the scalp.

b. Of or pertaining to a *MONOPOLE³.

1971 I. G. GASS et al. *Understanding Earth* xvi. 239/2 The dipolar rather than monopolar nature of the Earth's magnetic field.

monopole¹ (mǫ·nǒpōᵘl). Restrict † *Obs.* to senses in Dict. and add: **4.** [Fr., monopoly.] (See quot. 1967.)

1883 *Daily News* 31 Aug. 6/2 The familiar pop of the champagne cork being very rarely heard. Perhaps those learned authorities, Dr. Oliver and Dr. Myrtle..have 'shut down' on 'monopole' and 'extra dry'. **1885** *Christie's Catal. Wines* 14 Apr. 9 Three Dozens of Champagne, Heidsieck's Dry Monopole, 1874. **1886** *St. Stephen's Rev.* 13 Mar. 12/1 The pint of dry Monopole, with which he sustained exhausted nature. **1915** T. BURKE *Nights in Town* 399 He shouted for a half-of-bitter with the solemnity of one who commands that two bottles of dry Monopole be put on the ice. **1967** A. LICHINE *Encycl. Wines* 356 *Monopole*. This designation, frequently found on wine labels, literally means 'an exclusive'. Blank Monopole would be the proprietary brand of the wine shipper whose name would occupy the blank.

monopole³ (mǫ·nǒpōᵘl). [f. MONO- + POLE *sb.*²] **1.** A single electric charge or, esp., a single magnetic pole, having a spherically symmetric field. Freq. *attrib.* or as *adj.*

1937 J. W. T. SPINKS tr. *G. Herzberg's Atomic Spectra & Atomic Struct.* i. 63 The system gives an external electric field, which..falls off more rapidly with increasing distance than that of the dipole, which itself falls off more rapidly than that of the monopole. **1950** D. HALLIDAY *Introd. Nuclear Physics* ii. 59 A single charge at the origin is a simple monopole, with no higher moments. **1951** *Proc. Cambr. Philos. Soc.* XLVII. 196 Dirac has suggested that the quantization of electric charge could be explained by the existence of magnetic monopoles. *Ibid.* 206 The main difference of behaviour between electric particles and monopoles lies in the greater ionizing power per centimetre of the monopole, except near the end of the path. **1958** CONDON & ODISHAW *Handbk. Physics* VII. iv. 59/1 The first term of Eq. (4.6) corresponds to a monopole or simple charge, the second to the electric-dipole moment, the third to the electric-quadrupole moment, the fourth to the electric-octupole moment, etc. A similar multipole expansion is possible with magnetic interactions..leading to magnetic-dipole terms, etc. **1962** CORSON & LORRAIN *Introd. Electromagn. Fields* ii. 54 The first term is merely the potential which we would have at P if the whole charge were concentrated at the origin. It is called the monopole term and is zero only if the net charge is zero. **1967** W. R. HINDMARSH *Atomic Spectra* v. 49 We must extend the concept of the nucleus by attributing to it magnetic and electric moments (in addition to the electric monopole or nuclear charge) and a finite volume. **1969** *Physical Rev.* CLXXXIV. 1393 (*heading*) Search for magnetic monopoles in deep ocean deposits. *Ibid.* 1401/2 This work would indicate that there is less than one monopole/4000 m^2 of the earth. **1973** *Nature* 20 Apr. 527/1 The scheme..ignores all other atomic monopoles (including those on the methyl carbons and hydrogens which closely approach the negative charge) as well as all higher moments. **1974** *Ibid.* 3 May 15/1 Searches for quarks, magnetic monopoles and intermediate vector bosons have all so far proved negative. **1975** *Physical Rev. Lett.* XXXV. 489/2 We conclude that we have detected a magnetic monopole of strength $g = 137e$.

2. *Radio.* An aerial consisting of a single conducting rod with the electrical connection made at one end, the length of which is usually about a quarter of the wavelength to be transmitted or received.

1950 *Proc. IRE* XXXVIII. 1040 (*heading*) Measured directivity induced by a conducting cylinder of arbitrary length and spacing parallel to a monopole antenna. **1966** L. V. BLAKE *Antennas* iv. 176 When the quarter-wave vertical antenna (monopole) is fed at its base with the other side of the feed line connected to ground, its radiation resistance and input impedance are just half the values for the half-wave dipole in free space. **1974** *Nature* 5 Apr. 493/1 The transmitter antenna was a vertical monopole lifted to 1,000 to 1,500 m by balloon.

monopolistic, *a.* Add: (Further examples.) Spec. *monopolistic competition*, a type of imperfect competition characterized by monopolistic trading.

1903 R. T. ELY *Studies in Evolution of Industrial Soc.* iv. 196 Private favoritism monopolies are businesses not naturally monopolistic. **1933** E. CHAMBERLIN *Theory of Monopolistic Competition* iv. 69 Monopolistic competition ..concerns itself not only with the problem of an *individual* equilibrium (the ordinary theory of monopoly), but also with that of a *group* equilibrium (the adjustment of economic forces within a group of competing monopolists, ordinarily regarded merely as a group of competitors). **1937** [see *IMPERFECT *a.* 11]. **1938** E. W. SHANAHAN *Mod. Econ. Organisation* x. 235 The movement towards combination..has been successful in establishing monopolistic enterprises. **1942** W. B. TAYLOR *Financial Policies of Business Enterprise* xxxi. 750 The warp and woof of business enterprise are interwoven with ever-changing threads of competition and monopoly; and when both are found co-existing in a given enterprise, that business is said to be carrying on its functions under conditions of monopolistic competition. **1962** *Daily Tel.* 31 Jan. 10/2 The Monopolies Commission can report on monopolistic practices referred to it. **1964** GOULD & KOLB *Dict. Social Sci.* 441/1 Monopolistic competition denotes a condition of partial market control due to the exclusive possession of the trade in some commodity on the part of a seller and limited by the fact that one commodity may be substituted for another with varying degrees of ease. **1969** *Times* 27 Jan. 10/7 It is starting to match monopolistic selling power against monopolistic buying power in the grain market. **1969** D. C. HAGUE *Managerial Econ.* II. iv. 87 The first of these [kinds of imperfect competition] can be dealt with quite briefly. It is known as monopolistic competition, though the originator of the term, the American economist Professor E. H. Chamberlin intended this to be used in a slightly different sense.

Hence **monopoli·stically** *adv.*

1923 *Glasgow Herald* 30 July 6 We need no longer cry out to obstructive departmental control and monopolistically inclined private enterprise—'A plague on both your houses.' **1957** K. A. WITTFOGEL *Oriental Despotism* ii. 45 They [*sc.* industries] were for the most part either directly managed or monopolistically controlled by the hydraulic governments. **1966** *Economist* 26 Feb. 774/1 Rises in dividends are determined individually, not monopolistically.

monopolizable (mǒnǫ·pǒləizăb'l), *a.* [f. MONOPOLIZE *v.* + -ABLE.] That can be monopolized.

1898 W. J. LOCKE *Idols* xxii. I'm not a monopolisable woman.

monopolizer. Add: Also **monopoliser.**

1779 W. SMITH in *15th Rep. R. Comm. Hist. Manuscripts* App. VI. 429 in *Parl. Papers 1897* (C. 8551) LI. 1 The common people sick of the War, and think they are made a prey of by commissaries, quarter-masters, forage-masters, monopolisers, schemers, &c., &c.

monopoly. **1.** Add to def.: In U.K. law, a situation in which one supplier or producer controls over one third of the market.

1948 *Act* 11 & 12 *Geo. VI* c. 66 Prelim. Note, This Act sets up a permanent Commission to investigate conditions in industry and trade which tend towards a monopoly. **1964** *Times Rev. Industry* Mar. 16/1 The Act also laid down the definition of a monopoly that is still operative: a situation in which one company or group of companies acting together control one third of an industry. **1970** *Daily Tel.* 15 July 17/5 By law, over a third of the market is defined as monopoly.

6*. (With capital initial.) The proprietary name of a game (invented by Mr. Charles Darrow) in which the players use imitation money to engage in simulated financial dealings. Also *attrib.* **Monopoly money**, money that is not 'real', valueless currency.

1935 *N.Y. Times* 24 Nov. x. 6/2 Heading all other 'board games'..is the season's craze, 'Monopoly', the game of real estate. **1938** C. BEATON *Diary* 1 Aug. in *Wandering Years* (1961) 344 The game of 'Monopoly' wasn't very enjoyable this morning. **1939** G. GREENE *Lawless Roads* Prol. 5 A game called 'Monopoly' played with a picture-board and dice and little counters. *Ibid.*, There were 'Monopoly' parties. **1954** *Trade Marks Jrnl.* 23 June 634/2 *Monopoly*..Board games John Waddington Limited..Leeds. **1960** *Guardian* 9 Dec. 9/7 My knowledge of the world of big business..I gained entirely from playing Monopoly. **1972** K. BONFIGLIOLI *Don't point that Thing at Me* xiii. 110 Martland's word was as good as his bond, but his bond was mere Monopoly money. **1972** *Times* 8 Apr. 1/3 Private tenants in rented flats are banding together..against property speculators whom they accuse of ruthlessly playing Monopoly with their homes. **1974** *Times* 27 Apr. 10/7, I think they are playing with Monopoly money because some people say things like 'I have lost £10,000'.

7. *monopoly licence, problem, profits, -trend*; **monopoly capitalism**, a capitalist system typified by trade monopolies in the hands of a few people; **monopoly value**, the value of anything the supply of which is controlled by the holders of a monopoly; *spec.* applied to licensed premises.

1937 C. DAY LEWIS *Mind in Chains* 13 The quality of intellectual production is inevitably debased under monopoly-capitalism. **1943** H. READ *Politics of Unpolitical* i. 6 It [*sc.* the oligarchy of trade unions] is now

openly merging itself with the ascendant oligarchy of monopoly capitalism, to form what James Burnham has called 'the managerial class'. **1955** —— *Grass Roots of Art* (rev. ed.) vii. 139, I feel fairly sure that that barrack-room will have more amenities under monopoly capitalism than in the totalitarian State. **1964** Gould & Kolb *Dict. Social Sci.* 442/2 Monopoly capitalism in Marxist terminology is the stage of capitalism in which control over means of production and distribution has become highly concentrated in the hands of a small group of capitalists. **1905** J. J. Cockshott *Licensing Act 1904* 3 The State, in conferring upon me a monopoly license, had also granted me a commercial asset of great value. **1955** *Times* 15 June 5/4 The monopoly problem is discussed usually in terms of a single seller or a small group of sellers acting in concert, who are able to restrict supplies. **1931** *Economist* 26 Dec. 1222/1 The 'ring', producing a sectionalised product, will be able to exaggerate the monopoly profits already exacted from the helpless consumer. **1964** Gould & Kolb *Dict. Social Sci.* 543/1 Profits include..permanent monopoly profits, more properly termed monopoly rents. **1944** *Horizon* Jan. 67 What is valid..is no more than the good old perception of monopoly-trends in finance and industrial organization. **1883** F. A. Walker *Polit. Econ.* iii. i. 90 Here is a high degree of value..where yet no labor has been... This is an instance of what may be called 'monopoly-value', or as some prefer to call it, scarcity-value. **1904** *Hansard Commons* 20 Apr. 735 We think that when any new licence is granted the monopoly value should go to the public. **1905** J. J. Cockshott *Licensing Act 1904* 6 The monopoly value will be secured to the public instead of being 'handed over to wealthy brewery companies for the mere asking'. **1934** Dummeier & Heflebower *Econ. with Applications to Agric.* viii. 166 Monopoly value refers to exchange value for any commodity of which the supply is sufficiently under one control that the exchange value or price which prevails for it is different..than it would be under ordinary competitive conditions. **1936** Jathar & Beri *Introd. Econ.* ix. 170 In all cases of monopoly value, the monopolist must carefully weigh..the nature of the demand, and..the expenses of production per unit. **1953** B. Spiller *Innkeeping* x. 190 On the grant of a new licence the justices must exact the payment of a *monopoly value*, i.e. the difference between the value of the premises licensed and unlicensed.

Monoprix (mǫ·nopri). [Fr., lit. 'one price'.] One of a chain of multiple stores (in France) in which a cheap class of goods is sold (orig. all at the same price).

1937 W. Fortescue *Sunset House* ix. 164 Bulky goods hastily thrust into bags at the Monoprix. **1965** V. Canning *Whip Hand* v. 48, I bought six pairs of pants at a Monoprix. **1966** G. Greene *Comedians* i. i. 23 Cynicism is cheap—you can buy it at any Monoprix store. **1973** D. Orgill *Jasius Pursuit* i. 8 She had seen *Mademoiselle* in the Monoprix down in Cannes.

monopropellant (mǫnoprǒpe·lănt), *sb.* and *a.* [f. Mono- + Propellant *a.* and *sb.*] **A.** *sb.* A substance which can be used as a rocket fuel without needing an additional oxidizing agent.

1949 G. P. Sutton *Rocket Propulsion Elements* v. 115 Monopropellants are stable at ordinary atmospheric conditions, but decompose and yield hot combustion gases when heated and pressurized. **1958** C. C. Adams et al. *Space Flight* iii. 79 A monopropellant is generally unstable and delivers energy through its own decomposition, which is generally induced by a catalytic agent such as potassium permanganate (with hydrogen peroxide). **1972** *Materials & Technol.* IV. xix. 741 Hydrogen peroxide was employed as a monopropellant to provide power for the turbine-driven pumps [in the V2 rocket].

B. *adj.* Employing a monopropellant.

1949 G. P. Sutton *Rocket Propulsion Elements* v. 115 The feed system of monopropellant units is usually simple, because only one liquid needs to be supplied. **1954** K. W. Gatland *Devel. Guided Missiles* (ed. 2) i. 23 Rockets can be classified into two main types: (*a*) Bi-propellant, in which the fuel and oxygen supplies are..injected separately into the combustion chamber, and (*b*) mono-propellant, in which the fuel and oxygen are combined in a single substance. **1967** *Technology Week* 23 Jan. 28/2 Anhydrous hydrazine will fuel the liquid monopropellant engine.

monops (mǫ·nǫps), *a.* and *sb.* [f. Gr. μόν-ος Mono- + ὤψ eye.] † **A.** *adj.* One-eyed. *Obs. rare*—⁰. **B.** *sb.* A one-eyed individual. *rare*—¹.

1857 R. G. Mayne *Expos. Lex. Med. Sci.* (1860) 716/2 *Monops*, having but one eye: one-eyed. **1876** G. Meredith *Beauch. Career* III. ix. 155 He would have been a Nelson of politics, if he had been a monops, with an excuse for not seeing. **1900** Dorland *Med. Dict.* 396/1 *Monops*, a fetus having but a single eye. [And in later med. dicts.]

monopsony (mǒnǫ·psǒni). *Econ.* [f. Mon(o- + Gr. ὀψων-εῖν to buy provisions + -y³.] A condition in which there is only one buyer for the product of a large number of sellers; cf. Monopoly. Also in extended use (see quot. 1971). Hence **mono·psonist; monopsoni·stic** *a.*

1933 J. Robinson *Econ. Imperfect Competition* xviii. 219 When the market changes..to a single buying agency ..this may be described as monopsony buying. *Ibid.* 224 Just as we have price discrimination for a monopolist, so we may have price discrimination for a monopsonist. *Ibid.* xxvi. 296 Monopsonistic exploitation can also arise where..the supply of labour to each firm is less than perfectly elastic. **1941** R. Triffin *Monopolistic Competition & General Equilibrium Theory* iii. 113 Other types of interrelationships, intermediate between monopsony and pure competition, can be distinguished. **1948** *Commerce & Industry* (Pretoria) Mar. 280 The supplying of sawlogs on a contract term of 20 years..may place the sawmiller in a monopsonistic position in a particular forest region. *Ibid.* Bargaining power will be fairly evenly divided between the two parties. The dangers of monopsony..will thus be limited. **1955** *Times* 15 June 5/4 The term 'monopsonist' for a monopoly buyer was coined in the thirties—but has got little foothold in popular discussion. **1964** *Economist* 1 Feb. 434/1 Bargaining between a monopsony buyer and a suppliers' ring. **1968** *Internat. Encycl. Social Sci.* X. 464 Analogous to a seller's monopoly power, a buyer is said to have 'monopsony' power when he can significantly affect the price of what he buys by varying the quantity bought. **1969** D. C. Hague *Managerial Econ.* ii. iv. 98 When there is a single buyer in any market, he is often described as a *monopsonist*. **1971** M. Cooper in *Royal Soc. Health Jrnl.* XCI. 220/2 The main risks of the B.M.A. scheme however are not of this type. Rather they lie in breaking up the State monopsony. *Ibid.* 221/2 A monopsony is a consumer so large that it can exert pressure on price merely by the threat of withdrawing its custom. **1973** *Times Lit. Suppl.* 9 Mar. 255/2 The granting of monopsonistic concessions to wholesale merchants.

monoptic, *a.* Delete † *Obs.*—⁰ and add to def.: Pertaining to or involving vision with one eye. (Later examples.)

1960 Kolers & Rosner in *Amer. Jrnl. Psychol.* LXXIII. 4 One may distinguish at least three modes of viewing: monocular, binocular, and a third which we shall call 'dichoptic'. [*Note*] Consistency of usage would require that the first two be called 'monoptic' and 'dioptic' respectively. **1968** *Perception & Psychophysics* III. 237/2 Under the monoptic condition, both disk and ring were presented to the same eye, half the time to the left eye and half the time to the right eye. **1971** *Jrnl. Gen. Psychol.* LXXXIV. 163 Dichoptic masking was nearly as strong as under monoptic and binocular conditions.

Hence **mono·ptically** *adv.*, with one eye.

1965 *Jrnl. Exper. Psychol.* LXIX. 199/1 The extent of masking by pattern was slightly less dichoptically than monoptically. **1972** *Nature* 22 Dec. 480/1 The observer perceives a pattern which approximates very closely a square-wave distribution, just as if the two components were superimposed physically and viewed monoptically.

mono-rail. Also **monorail.** Substitute for def.: A single rail astride which or suspended from which railway vehicles or the like run; also, a vehicle that travels in this way. Also *attrib.* (Add further examples.) Hence **mo·no-railer; mo·norailing** *vbl. sb.*

1902 *Encycl. Brit.* XXXII. 143/2 In the Langen monorail the car is hung from a single overhead rail; a line on this system is worked between Barmen and Elberfeld, a distance of about 9 miles. **1949** *Sun* (Baltimore) 3 Oct. 2/7 These chutes will pull the guns out of the rear clam shell doors of the C-82 along monorails attached to the roof of the fuselage. **1958** *Daily Mail* 17 Jan. 9/4 A trip on the world's first monorail. **1960** *Farmer & Stockbreeder* 16 Feb. (Suppl.) 35/1 One is an overhead monorail down the centre feeding passage to carry a food container from which the rations may be semi-automatically fed into the troughs. **1962** R. B. Fuller *Epic Poem on Industrialization* 44 Their 1929 failure With world monopoly 'Monorailing' Was only caused by the fact that Their first trial section of single rail Was not long enough. **1963** *Punch* 7 Aug. 194/2 The monorailer slid to a halt. **1964** *Daily Tel.* 7 Jan. 15/1 A free monorail system may be built in North Buckinghamshire. **1971** *Ibid.* 16 Apr. 6/7 A French demonstration hovertrain has been running for 18 months on an 11-mile stretch of elevated monorail outside Orléans. **1973** R. Kerrod *First Look at Railways Today* 45 It is called a monorail, for it moves along a single rail.

b. monorail camera, a technical camera having as part of its stand a bar or monorail which allows considerable adjustment of the apparatus and may support additional components.

1958 D. Charles *Commercial & Industr. Photogr.* i. 10 Monorail camera..a recent, mainly metal, engineer-built construction, with a full array of 'movements'. **1971** P. D. James *Shroud for Nightingale* iii. 52 The Yard photographer manœuvred his tripod and camera—a new Cambo monorail.

monorheme (mǫ·norīm), *sb. Linguistics.* Also **monorrheme.** [f. Mono- + *rheme.] A single element or word with a phrasal meaning. So **monorrhe·mic** *a.*

1937 J. Orr tr. *Iordan's Introd. Romance Linguistics* iv. 379 Bally proceeds to view the sentence in its genetic and psychological aspects, its development from the 'monorheme' to the 'dirheme' by a process of integration or 'condensation' of two originally independent units. **1939** L. H. Gray *Foundations of Lang.* viii. 229 Another type of monorrhemic verbal sentence is seen in verbs expressing meteorological conditions, such as Latin *pluit. Ibid.* 230 A verb is the sole part of speech which can form a complete sentence, i.e., which can contain both a subject and a predicate in a single monorrheme. **1950** *Archivum Linguisticum* II. 186 The nature of the 'monorhemes' varies between a wish or request, a questioning attitude,..and.. a mere report of something perceived. **1969** tr. *Akhmanova & Mikael'an's Theory of Syntax in Mod. Linguistics* iii. 55 Phrases are called 'monorhemes' when they consist of a single element, and 'dirhemes' when the number of elements is two. **1970** *Language* XLVI. 923 In these apparent monorhemes a hic-et-nunc adverb has been deleted.

‖ **monosabio** (mǫnosā·bio). [Sp., f. *mono* monkey + *sabio* wise, trained.] A picador's assistant in the bullring. Also *ellipt.* as **mono.**

1897 *Encycl. Sport* I. 158/2 *Monos sabios*, boys and men employed in the service of the bull fight. **1924** E. Hemingway *In our Time* xii. 22 The horse's entrails hung down in a blue bunch..the *monos* whacking him on the back of his legs with the rods. **1927** —— *Men without Women* 38 The monos were leading a horse out by the bridle toward the bull. **1928** *Daily Tel.* 17 July 9/3 In another bull-ring at Vista Allegre..the matador Albageno and a 'monosabio' were dangerously wounded by bulls yesterday. **1932** E. Hemingway *Death in Afternoon* vi. 58 You will see..the picadors arriving on the horses they have ridden in from town, these horses having been ridden from the bull ring by the red-bloused monos or bullring servants. *Ibid.* xvi. 187 [The] San Sebastian monosabios should be, by rights, policemen... They carry..puntillas, broad-headed knives. **1959** V. J. Kehoe *Aficionado!* 37 The *monosabios* ..handle the picadores' horses and aid them in getting into the correct position for the charge of the toro. *Ibid.* 53 The areneros and monosabios generally wear a red shirt, and dark blue pants. **1973** J. M. White *Garden Game* 61 An image from the *corrida de toros*..the *monosabios* smoothing the cruelly trampled area.

monosaccharide (mǫnosæ·kărəid). *Chem.* Also † **-saccharid.** [f. Mono- + Saccharide.] Any sugar which cannot be hydrolysed to give simpler sugars.

1896 W. D. Halliburton *Essent. Chem. Physiol.* (ed. 2) i. 10 (*table*) Monosaccharides or glucoses. **1902** *Encycl. Brit.* XXXI. 723/2 The simplest carbohydrates constitute the group of monosaccharids, of which dextrose..is the most important. **1936** C. S. Gibson *Essent. Princ. Org. Chem.* xv. 445 The production of a ketohexose from the preliminary aldohexose may be due to the usual interconversion of monosaccharides in the presence of alkalis in aqueous solution. **1968** *Punch* 11 Sept. 356/3 'Oh, ah,' said Walter Gabriel, 'especially considering that, at the same time, she'm also producing monosaccharides, trisaccharides, and a whole perishing range of they oligosaccharides.' **1972** *Sci. Amer.* Oct. 71/1 Lactose is a disaccharide composed of the monosaccharides glucose and galactose.

monosaccharose (mǫnosæ·kărōᵘz, -s). *Chem.* [f. Mono- + Saccharose.] = *monosaccharide.

1902 J. B. Cohen *Theoret. Org. Chem.* xx. 276 The monosaccharoses possess strong reducing properties. **1919** S. B. Schryver *Introd. Study Biol. Chem.* v. 199 All the native monosaccharoses are optically active. **1951** I. L. Finar *Org. Chem.* I. xviii. 357 Monosaccharides (monosaccharoses).

monoscope (mǫ·nǒskōᵘp). *Television.* [f. Mono- + -scope.] (See quot. 1953.)

1938 C. E. Burnett in *RCA Rev.* II. 414 'Monoscope' is the name which has been given to a developmental type of tube designed to produce a video signal of a test picture or pattern enclosed in the tube. Since the picture must be enclosed in the tube, the Monoscope is not suitable for developing a video signal which represents action. **1953** Amos & Birkinshaw *Television Engin.* I. iv. 79 A monoscope is a camera tube containing a target on which a pattern or photograph is printed and which, by scanning the target, generates a picture signal corresponding to the printed image. **1955** G. M. Glasford *Fund. Television Engin.* xv. 480 A useful device for generating a video test signal is the monoscope.

monose (mǫ·nōᵘz, -s). *Chem.* [f. Mon(o- + -ose².] = *monosaccharide; (see also quot. 1948).

1892, 1903 [see *biose]. **1935** Tipson & Stiller in Harrow & Sherwin *Textbk. Biochem.* ii. 77 (*heading*) The action of alkalis on monoses. **1948** [see *diose].

monosemantic (mǫnosimæ·ntik), *a.* [f. Mono- + Semantic *a.*] Of a word or phrase, having only one meaning. Also **monosemante·mic** *a.*

1957 S. Potter *Mod. Linguistics* vii. 147 The simplest words are manifestly those which symbolize single things or concepts, like proper names. These may be described as *monosemantemic*, and therefore unambiguous. **1960** E. Delavenay *Introd. Machine Translation* vi. 97 The vocabulary is classified into monosemantic and polysemantic grammatical words. **1966** *English Studies* XLVII. 56 Such case-forms are not strictly monosemantic, but can vary in their function according to the context.

monosemic, *a.* Add: **b.** = *monosemantic *a.*

1969 *Computers & Humanities* III. 251 The verses contain a very high proportion of monosemic words and polysemic words used in their primary meaning. **1971** O. A. Wojtasiewicz tr. *Pelc's Studies in Functional Logical Semiotics of Natural Lang.* 23 The English word 'bay' has more usages... 'Orchid', on the other hand, is a monosemic word.

monosemy (mǫ·nosīmi). [f. Mono- + Sem(antic *a.* + -y³.] Of a word or phrase, the quality of having only one meaning. Cf. *polysemy.

1951 S. Ullmann *Princ. Semantics* ii. 107 Multiple meaning—which includes a number of non-lexical elements—comprises everything running counter to 'monosemy' in the language system. **1969** S. Hook *Lang. & Philosophy* iii. 255 Now on to the comments concerning polysemy and monosemy. **1972** Hartmann & Stork *Dict. Lang. & Linguistics* 144/1 *Monosemy*, when a word or phrase has only one semantic meaning, e.g. *ball-point pen*, as opposed to polysemy or multiple meaning.

monosexual (mǫnose·ksiuăl), *a.* [f. Mono- + Sexual *a.*] Of one sex, or with the attribute

of being either male or female; pertaining to one sex exclusively. (See also quot. 1970.)

1964 *Oceanogr. & Marine Biol.* II. 209 Peripheral cells of the adult thallus undergo meiosis and give rise to attached haploid leafy appendages which are monosexual and produce anisogamous male and female gametes respectively. **1966** *Listener* 23 June 918/3 A film whose monosexual character is emphasized by a sound-track which contains only three words..spoken by a female voice. **1969** *Sunday Times* 31 Aug. 47/7 The £1.8 million belonging to well over half the university's mono-sexual seats of collegiate learning. **1970** *Diogenes* LXXII. 61 Mono-sexual, in need of no deep or lasting relation with a partner of the opposite sex. **1971** *Guardian* 2 June 9/4 The Edwardian situation in which half the bachelor population were always off doing monosexual Empire-building.

So **mo:nosexua·lity**, the property or state of being monosexual.

1910 A. A. BRILL tr. *Freud's Three Contributions to Sexual Theory* 7 The conception which we gather from this long known anatomical fact is the original predisposition to bisexuality, which in the course of development has changed to monosexuality, leaving slight remnants of the stunted sex. **1958** B. MAGEE *Go West Young Man* ii. 43 Yale has female graduate students, but no female teachers or undergraduates. This monosexuality is Yale's biggest fault. **1970** *Diogenes* LXXII. 61 In Roman times this monosexuality took the form of imperialistic sex.

monosign (mǫ·nosəin). [f. MONO- + SIGN *sb.*] A 'sign' or word with only one meaning: opp. *PLURISIGN. Hence **monosigna·tion**, **mono-si·gnative** *a.*

1940 *Kenyon Rev.* II. 266 The atomic ingredient of literal language is the monosign (called in logic the 'term'); the atomic ingredient of poetic language tends to be the plurisign. *Ibid.*, I am not inquiring whether the ideal of monosignation is ever perfectly realized. *Ibid.* 267 A logician..requires monosignative clarity. **1949** WELLEK & WARREN *Theory of Lit.* xv. 190 Instead of aiming at a system of abstractions consistently expressed by a system of monosigns, poetry organizes a unique, unrepeatable pattern of words, each an object as well as a sign. **1954** P. WHEELWRIGHT *Burning Fountain* 378 The plurisign is.. distinguished from the monosign, or steno-term. **1965** *Encycl. Poetry* 760/1 The depth symbol..defies any adequate analysis into monosignative components.

monosigni·ficant, *a.* [f. MONO- + SIGNIFI-CANT *a.*] Having only one meaning. Also **monosigni·ficance**.

1940 *Kenyon Rev.* II. 503 *Monosignificance*. Mr. Wheelwright uses..in two ways, as formal logical abstraction.. and as a useful temporarily consistent selection. *Ibid.* 505 If..words are not statically and isolatedly monosignificant in the prose of science and instruction, what better sense can be made of..the realm of poetry—connotation —plurisignificance. **1947** H. JACOB *Planned Auxiliary Lang.* 20 A high degree of precision..can be attained by assigning to each element one invariable meaning, *i.e.*, each element is monosignificant. *Ibid.*, No language..has so far achieved absolute monosignificance... The principle of monosignificance is..understood to apply to the smallest but complete unit of thought, the sentence.

mono-ski (mǫ·noskī). [f. MONO- + SKI *sb.*] A ski on which a person can stand with both feet. Hence as *v. intr.*, to use mono-skis; **mo·no-skier**, one who uses mono-skis.

1953 *Austrian Information* (U.S.) 3 Jan. 9/2 Monoskis are at present being displayed in Viennese sporting goods stores. They are single skis on which beginners or below-average skiers can stand with both feet. **1963** *Water Skier* Spring 12/2 Carry out series of connected virages across wakes on mono ski (feet on front and rear bindings). **1966** *Ibid.* Sept.–Oct. 15/2 Anne and Pat are confident mono-skiers. **1968** A. DIMENT *Gt. Spy Race* viii. 129 It looked.. pretty amateur from the beach. Round here if you can't mono-ski you're not worth watching. **1971** 'D. HALLIDAY' *Dolly & Doctor Bird* xiv. 201 Dolly's launch passed with a man and a girl on monoskis.

mono-sodium. (Later examples.)

1929, etc. [see *GLUTAMATE]. **1954** A. WHITE et al. *Princ. Biochem.* xx. 588 Guanine gout has been reported in this species [sc. the pig]; this is..analogous to human gout, in which monosodium urate may accumulate in the cartilages. **1975** *Listener* 14 Aug. 205/1 Cargoes of factory food, bound for the supermarket shelves... 'The Taste of Monosodium Glutamate.'

monosome (mǫ·nŏsōum). *Cytology.* [f. MONO- + *-SOME*[4].] **1.** A chromosome in a diploid chromosome complement which lacks its homologous partner; a diploid individual having such a chromosome in its complement.

1921 [see hexasome s.v. *HEXA-]. **1944** *Genetics* XXIX. 232, 16 monosomes and five trisomes were found in the 11 aberrant offspring. **1970** *Caryologia* XXIII. 359 In this paper, we report on the rates of transmission of disomes (21 II), monosomes (20 II + 1 I), double monosomes (19 II + 2 I) and plants carrying isochromosomes and telocentric chromosomes in two aneuploid series of wheat.

2. A single ribosome attached to a molecule of messenger RNA.

1964 HASELKORN & FRIED in *Proc. Nat. Acad. Sci.* LI. 308 In a previous communication we presented evidence indicating that the addition of RNA from turnip yellow mosaic virus (TYMV) to purified *E. coli* ribosomes results in the formation of a complex containing one 70s ribosome and one molecule of RNA. We shall call such complexes monosomes. **1971** *Nature* 10 Sept. 107/2 Most ribosomes appeared as 'free' monosomes, while in the reticular cells

most of them were attached to membranes in typical 'polysome' patterns. **1972** *Ibid.* 31 Mar. 237/2 Fig. 1 shows a typical distribution of monosomes and polysomes isolated from non-infected and infected Proctor barley leaves.

monosomic (mǫnosōu·mik), *a.* (*sb.*). *Cytology.* [f. *MONOSOM(E + -IC.] Having or being a diploid chromosome complement in which one (or occas. more than one) chromosome lacks its homologous partner. Hence as *sb.*, a monosomic individual.

1926 *Univ. Calif. Publ. Bot.* XI. 61 This paper is devoted to a second form called 'fluted', which has been found on cytological examination to be a monosomic (2n−1). *Ibid.* 67 Monosomic forms may be used advantageously for a determination of linkage groups. **1932** *Genetics* XVII. 689 Comparatively few investigations have been concerned with a study of monosomics (2n−1 types) and their mode of inheritance. **1957** C. P. SWANSON *Cytol. & Cytogenetics* (1958) vi. 190 Probably the best known monosomic type is the haplo-IV Drosophila. **1961** *Lancet* 23 Sept. 723/2 The normal male is naturally monosomic for the X, and the XO-female can reach maturity in reasonably good health. **1972** *Hereditas* LXX. 132/1 A number of monosomic lines of Chinese Spring were used as pollen parents. **1974** *Nature* 19 Apr. 714/3 Monosomics and trisomics have seldom been developed in the same species.

So **mo·nosomy**, the character or condition of having a monosomic chromosome complement.

1948 *Nature* 5 June 873/1 Genetical experience shows that, like polyploidy, monosomy and polysomy in a wide range of plants and animals can characterize whole individuals. **1961** *Lancet* 16 Sept. 625/1 Both cases show monosomy and trisomy involving the X chromosome or an autosome of similar size and morphology. **1972** *Science* 5 May 518/3 Not so well documented..are the occasional observations of monosomy, trisomy and other aneuploidies.

monostable (mǫ·nostëib'l), *a.* *Electronics.* [f. MONO- + STABLE *a.*] Stable in one position or state only; characteristic of a device with this property.

1952 [see *ASTABLE *a.]. **1966** *McGraw-Hill Encycl. Sci. & Technol.* VIII. 631/2 The monostable multivibrator has frequent application in electronic circuits where timing and gating operations are required. **1974** LONG & EVANS *Electronic Princ. & Circuits* xiii. 346 Monostable and bi-stable circuits require a triggering source in order for switching to take place.

monosyllabicity (mǫnosilăbi·sĭti). [f. MONO-SYLLAB(LE *sb.* + -ICITY.] = MONOSYLLABISM. Also **monosyllabica·tion**.

1951 N. C. BODMAN in *Language* XXVII. 205 There has been no change..in the monosyllabicity of the Chinese morpheme from the most ancient times that we know of to the present. **1956** J. WHATMOUGH *Language* iii. 42 The ideal seems to be..somewhere between the extremes of monosyllabication and polysynthesis. **1957** *Archivum Linguisticum* IX. 73 Grappin might have mentioned..the monosyllabicity of *bóbr*. **1968** *Language* XLIV. 131 The simultaneous trend toward polysyllabic creations in pseudo-scientific language and monosyllabicity (*the mods, the frug*).

monosystemic (mǫnosiste·mik), *a.* *Linguistics.* [f. MONO- + SYSTEMIC *a.* 2.] Based on a single system of language analysis.

1949 *Trans. Philol. Soc. 1948* 127 Such studies I should describe as paradigmatic and monosystemic in principle. **1951** *Archivum Linguisticum* III. 130 The structural method still tends to concern itself with units evolved by a monosystemic analysis at the word-level. **1958** J. BERRY in J. A. Fishman *Readings Sociol. of Lang.* (1968) 739 The initial consonant in the Kikuyu word for 'book'..in terms of a monosystemic analysis at any rate is a phoneme contrasting with other ('original') b-sounds..but relatively rare. **1964** R. H. ROBINS *Gen. Linguistics* iv. 158 In this sense phonemic analysis is monosystemic. **1967** F. P. DINNEEN *Introd. Gen. Linguistics* x. 319 The American structuralist approach [is] 'monosystemic', whereas Firth's approach is designed to be 'polysystemic'.

monotechnic (mǫnote·knik), *a.* [f. MONO- + TECHNIC *a.*: after POLYTECHNIC *a.* and *sb.*] Dealing with or providing instruction in a single technical subject; also designating an educational institution providing such instruction. Also *ellipt.* as *sb.*, an institution of this kind.

1904 *Jrnl. Inst. Electr. Engin.* 25 Feb. 458 Many of the American schools of engineering are practically monotechnic institutes in contradistinction to the polytechnics here. **1904** G. S. HALL *Adolescence* I. 170 Thousands of our youth of late have been diverted from secondary schools to the monotechnic or trade classes. **1931** *Times Educ. Suppl.* 15 Aug. 319/4 Some of these schools are in universities, some in schools of art, some in technical colleges and polytechnics, while one forms a monotechnic. **1962** *Technology* Dec. 276 Furniture. Monotechnic... The local College of Further Education is one of only two centres offering a complete course in furniture manufacture. **1967** *Times Rev. Industry* July 82/1 Monotechnic education, all the rage 20 years ago, is out. *Ibid.* 82/3 A comparatively small monotechnic cannot keep pace with all these developments.

monothematic (mǫnopīmæ·tik), *a.* [f. MONO- + THEMATIC *a.*] Having a single dominant

theme or element, *spec.* in *Mus.* So **mono-the·matism**.

1886 F. PRAEGER tr. *Naumann's Hist. Mus.* II. 1188 The employment of *leit-motiv*..is nothing but a return to monothematism. **1907** R. BOUGHTON *Bach* 15 Monothematic music in polyphonic style was bound to result in a fugue. **1934** C. LAMBERT *Music Ho!* v. 326 The work is entirely monothematic, and..should be regarded as a continuation of the formal principles first evolved by Liszt. **1958** *Times* 13 Sept. 10/4 The basically monothematic nature of the opening movement is unusual in a symphony. **1961** *Times* 2 Nov. 16/3 Edwin Muir, a dour, almost mono-thematic poet. **1962** H. R. LOYN *Anglo-Saxon Eng.* iii. 125 These names are often..dithematic such as Wulfbold, Wulfhere, Leofric, and the like rather than monothematic.

monotocardian (mǫnotokā·ɹdiän). [f. mod.L. name of suborder *Monotocardia*, f. MON(o- + Gk. ὠτό-ς gen. of οὖς auricle + καρδία heart.] A prosobranch mollusc having only one auricle and one row of gill leaflets, belonging to the suborder Pectinibranchia, formerly called Monotocardia. Also as *adj.* So **monotoca·rdiac** *a.*

1901 *Q. Jrnl. Microsc. Sci.* XLIV. 258 It is fairly easy to derive the Monotocardian type of nervous system, radula, gill, and reproductive system from the corresponding organs of existing Diotocardia. *Ibid.* 259 In the adult Monotocardian a single kidney alone is present. *Ibid.* 261 The monotocardian kidney. **1902** *Rep. Brit. Assoc. Adv. Sci.* 630 Recent research..has resulted in proof that the dextral torsion which leads to the monotocardiac condition, does not affect all organs lying primitively to the left of the rectum. **1958** G. A. KERKUT *Borradaile & Potts's Invertebrata* (ed. 3) xv. 613 (*caption*) Heteropods..are pelagic monotocardians. **1971** *Oxf. Bk. Invertebrates* 36 Some archaeogastropods show the primitive features of paired gills within the mantle cavity... But others, the 'monotocardians',..have lost the second gill.

monotocous, *a.* **a.** (Later examples.)

1936 *Nature* 12 Sept. (Suppl.) 451/2 Conceptual thought could only have arisen in a monotocous mammalian type with an arboreal ancestry. **1937** A. HUXLEY *Ends & Means* xiv. 264 After achieving a stable inner environment, placental and, in some cases, monotocous birth, highly developed sense organs, and a well co-ordinated nervous system, all but one [sc. mammal] proceeded to specialize. **1968** *Economist* 15 June 49/2 The rest of us, monotocous individuals that we are, certainly ought to be fascinated by all the bizarre phenomena involved in multiple births.

monotone, *a.* and *sb.* Add: **A.** *adj.* **2.** *Math.* [ad. G. *monoton* (C. Neumann *Ueber die nach Kreis-, Kugel- und Cylinderfunctionen fortschreitenden Entwickelungen* (1881) ii. 26).] = *MONOTONIC *a.* 2, MONOTONOUS *a.* 3.

1905 J. PIERPONT *Lect. Theory of Functions of Real Variables* I. ii. 68 A sequence $A = \alpha_1, \alpha_2, \ldots$, whose elements satisfy the relations $\alpha_n < \alpha_{n+1}$, $n = 1, 2, \ldots$ is called an increasing sequence... If, on the other hand, $\alpha_n \leqslant \alpha_{n+1}$, $n = 1, 2, \ldots$ A is said to be a monotone increasing sequence. **1937** *Duke Math. Jrnl.* III. 489 We assume that $\phi(\rho)$ is completely monotone in $0 \leqslant \rho < \infty$. **1948** [see *MONOTONICITY a]. **1968** P. A. P. MORAN *Introd. Probability Theory* iv. 186 We say that a sequence, A_i, is monotone if we always have $A_1 \subset A_2 \subset A_3 \subset \ldots$, or $A_1 \supset A_2 \supset A_3 \supset \ldots$ [Etc.] **1970** R. B. ASH *Basic Probability Theory* viii. 255 ϕ has a monotone nondecreasing power function.

Hence **mo·notonely** *adv.* = *MONOTONICALLY *adv.* 2.

1948 BOCHNER & MARTIN *Several Complex Variables* vii. 135 If a sequence of (real) harmonic functions which are collectively bounded from above are monotonely decreasing, then either they converge uniformly to a harmonic function proper, or they diverge 'uniformly' to −∞.

monotonic, *a.* Add: **2.** Of a function or quantity: varying in such a way that it either never increases or never decreases. Of a sequence: consisting of terms that vary in this way. = *MONOTONE *a.* and *sb.* A. 2, MONOTONOUS *a.* 3.

1901 *Ann. Math.* II. 116 It follows that $f(s)$ is a monotonic function that actually decreases in parts of the interval $0 \leqslant s \leqslant l$. **1908** T. J. I'A. BROMWICH *Introd. Theory Infinite Series* i. 5 A sequence in which $a_{n+1} \geqq a_n$ for all values of n is called an increasing sequence; and similarly if $a_{n+1} \leqq a_n$ for all values of n, the sequence is called decreasing. Both increasing and decreasing sequences are included in the term monotonic sequences. **1923** *Proc. Cambr. Philos. Soc.* XXI. 633 Z shall be monotonic considered as a function of ρ. **1957** G. E. HUTCHINSON *Treat. Limnol.* I. v. 251 The velocity at any point in a fluid could be expressed as a continuous monotonic or regularly oscillating function of time. **1968** E. T. COPSON *Metric Spaces* i. 16 Every bounded monotonic sequence of real numbers is convergent. **1970** *Nature* 3 Oct. 36/2 The rate of uptake of calcium by the isolated reticulum..also displayed monotonic dependence on the concentration of free Ca^{2+} in the medium. **1973** *Jrnl. Genetic Psychol.* CXXII. 327 Young-adult responses were...even more clearly a monotonic function of actual figure age than were preschool responses.

monotonically, *adv.* Add: **2.** In the manner of a monotonic function, i.e. either without ever increasing or without ever decreasing.

1904 E. R. HEDRICK tr. *Goursat's Course in Math.*

Analysis I. iv. 148 A function $f(x)$ is said to increase monotonically in a given interval (a, b) if for any two values x', x'' in that interval $f(x') \geq f(x'')$ whenever $x' > x''$. **1934** *Amer. Math. Monthly* XLI. 421 Equation (13) defines *Y* as a single-valued, continuous, monotonically decreasing function of *X*. **1958** *Jrnl. Geol.* LXVI. 164/2 The rate of solution should increase monotonically as the fresh solvent is brought up at ever increasing rate. **1974** *Nature* 2 Aug. 451/3 These provided the dramatic highlight of the programme, which declined monotonically in interest for its final hour.

monotonicity (mǫnǒtǒni·sĭti). [f. MONOTONIC *a.* + -ITY.] The property or state of being monotonic. **a.** Of a function or variable (see *MONOTONIC *a.* 2).

1948 *Duke Math. Jrnl.* XV. 313 (*heading*) The complete monotonicity of certain functions derived from completely monotone functions. **1961** [see *ENTROPY 2 b]. **1972** *Computer Jrnl.* XV. 218/2 We now derive a monotonicity relation which will be used in Section 5 to prove convergence.

b. Of sounds (see MONOTONIC *a.*).

1971 *Nature* 23 Apr. 524/2 Speech remained unaffected except for slight slowing and slurring of words and the presence of some monotonicity.

monotonous, *a.* **3.** (Further example.)

1935 T. CHAUNDY *Differential Calculus* iii. 51 Over the whole domain we may call the function 'monotonous'.

monotonously, *adv.* Add: **2.** = *MONOTONICALLY *adv.* 2.

1938 *Physical Rev.* LIV. 948/1 $F(\alpha)$ is a monotonously decreasing function. **1954** D. TER HAAR *Elem. Statistical Mech.* 444, ln *x* is a monotonously increasing function of *x*. **1970** *Internat. Jrnl. Quantum Chem.* IV. 611 *E* decreases monotonously from $R = 10a_H$ to $R = 2a_H$. **1974** *Nature* 17 May 243/2 The torque might have been expected to decrease monotonously as the polymer dissolved.

monotropic, *a.* Add: **3.** *Physical Chem.* Exhibiting monotropy.

1897 W. D. BANCROFT *Phase Rule* iii. 32 It is probable that the substances classified as 'monotropic' by Lehmann ..are analogous to phosphorus. **1924** A. E. HILL in H. S. Taylor *Treat. Physical Chem.* I. ix. 390 In other cases it is not easy to determine whether a given form is monotropic or enantiotropic. **1955** J. ZERNIKE *Chem. Phase Theory* ii. 29 Cubic and hexagonal white phosphorus..are monotropic with respect to the violet form. **1964** G. I. BROWN *Introd. Physical Chem.* xx. 217 In monotropic substances there is no definite transition temperature, and one form of the substance is more stable than the other.

monotropism (mǫ̆nǫ·trǒpiz'm). *Physical Chem.* [f. *MONOTROP(IC *a.* 3 + -ISM.] = next.

1924 A. E. HILL in H. S. Taylor *Treat. Physical Chem.* I. ix. 390 An example of monotropism is found in the case of phosphorus. **1950** W. J. MOORE *Physical Chem.* v. 109 (*heading*) Enantiotropism and monotropism.

monotropy (mǫ̆nǫ·trǒpi). *Physical Chem.* [ad. G. *monotropie* (O. Lehmann *Molekularphysik* (1888) I. 119), f. Gr. *μονο-* MONO- + *τροπή* turning.] The existence of two polymorphs of a substance, one of which is stable and the other metastable over the whole range of their existence, so that conversion of the latter into the former can occur but not *vice versa*.

1902 A. FINDLAY tr. *Ostwald's Princ. Inorg. Chem.* 255 (*heading*) Enantiotropy and monotropy. **1932** J. N. FRIEND *Text-bk. Physical Chem.* I. xi. 181 It may..so happen that, in certain cases of presumed monotropy, the transition point lies very much below the melting point and has not been realised experimentally for this reason. **1970** CHAKRAVARTI & MITRA *Textbk. Physical Chem.* I. vi. 232 Examples of monotropy are white and violet phosphorus, diamond and graphite, silica, iodine monochloride [and] α- and β-benzophenone.

monotype, *sb.* and *a.* **A.** *sb.* **2.** Delete def. and substitute: In graphic art, a print taken from oil-colour or printer's ink painted on a sheet of glass or metal, the process being such that prints are produced singly. Also, the method of producing such a print. Also *attrib.* (Later examples.)

1926 L. BINYON *Engraved Designs of W. Blake* ii. 13 Out of such experiments may have come the idea of the 'monotype' which Blake was to use to such good purpose. **1954** *Oxford Mag.* 21 Jan., Anyone who does not know what Monotypes are can spend a profitable twenty minutes at his exhibition at Black Hall in deducing the nature of Mr. Baynes's technique. **1955** P. HERON *Changing Forms of Art* xi. 174 No English artist living excels him in this medium, especially where it involves the process known as 'monotype'. **1962** *Listener* 18 Oct. 624/2 An exhibition of monotypes and off-set drawings completed by Robert Colquhoun just before he died. **1970** *Oxf. Compan. Art* 736/1 G. B. Castiglione made monotypes on etching plates in the 17th c., William Blake's monotypes were apparently done on pieces of card.

3. Substitute for def.: (With capital initial.) The proprietary name of a composing machine consisting of two units, a keyboard which produces the perforated paper tape used to control the caster, which produces type in individual characters. (Earlier and later examples.)

1893 *Official Directory World's Columbian Exposition* (Chicago) 459/1 Lanston Monotype Machine Co., Washington, D.C. Monotype Machine. **1931** A. ESDAILE *Student's Man. Bibliogr.* iii. 58 The monotype method..involves two machines. **1959** [see *INTERTYPE]. **1965** J. MORAN *Composition of Reading Matter* vi. 65 The Monotype machine consists of two units—the keyboard and the caster. By operation of the keyboard a paper ribbon is perforated by means of compressed air. The ribbon is fed into a caster which carries a matrix-case. This moves to different positions in accordance with the perforated ribbon and molten metal is pumped into the appropriate matrix. Cast types are ejected singly and assembled in a channel until a line is completed. **1973** S. JENNETT *Making of Books* (ed. 5) iv. 79 The type produced by the Monotype is of excellent quality, and in use is indistinguishable from founders' type.

monovalent, *a.* Add: **2.** *Med.* **a.** Containing or being an antigen from a single strain of a micro-organism.

1930 H. CHILD tr. *Besredka's Immunity in Infectious Dis.* iii. 44 The same conclusion,..that the streptococcus is unique, because the monovalent serum acts against all the human streptococci. **1960** *Jrnl. Amer. Med. Assoc.* 19 Mar. 1230/1 The influenza pandemic which occurred in the United States in 1957–1958 provided an excellent opportunity to determine the efficacy of monovalent vaccines. **1968** *Amer. Jrnl. Epidemiol.* LXXXVIII. 149/1 Group B received monovalent vaccine containing 400 CCA units of B/Maryland/1/59 antigen. **1972** *Clin. Sci.* XLIII. 871 The monovalent influenzal antigen used was the strain AO/Swine (Shope) vaccine treated with desoxycholate to eliminate possible toxic effects.

b. Of an antigen or antibody: having only one site at which it can become attached to antibody or antigen, respectively.

1960 *Jrnl. Immunol.* LXXXIV. 409 The studies..were carried out with antibodies specific for two haptenic groups of dissimilar nature... It was essential for the experiments involving hapten-antibody combination *in vivo* that the haptens be molecularly dispersed, since aggregation of hapten *in vivo* would result in the hapten no longer being monovalent. **1966** *Jrnl. Exper. Med.* CXXIII. 229 Hapten-specific delayed hypersensitivity was only transiently suppressed by intravenous injections of monovalent conjugates of arsanilic acid and *N*-acetyltyrosine. **1970** J. T. BARRETT *Textbk. Immunol.* vi. 127/2 Monovalent (incomplete) Rh antibodies can be responsible for erythroblastosis. **1972** *McGraw-Hill Yearbk. Sci. & Technol.* 142/2 The agglutinin used in this experiment was a monovalent rather than a divalent agglutinin, that is, a molecule which binds to the cell surface with its one remaining active site but which cannot cause agglutination because it lacks a second active site.

3. *Cytology.* = *UNIVALENT *a.*

1906 *Rep. Brit. Assoc. Adv. Sci. 1905* 570 Whether each half of the chromosome is to be regarded as a monovalent chromosome is doubtful.

monovular (mǫ̆nǫ·-, mǫ̆nǭu·viulăɹ), *a. Biol.* [f. MON(O- + OVULAR *a.*] = *MONOZYGOTIC *a.*

1936 *Yale Jrnl. Biol. & Med.* VIII. 589 We think of human monovular twins as having identically the same inheritance and as being so similar in height, weight, build, appearance, and mentality as to confuse relatives and friends. **1962** *Biol. Abstr.* XL. 1726/1 While neonatal polycythemia in monovular twins is obviously due to intrauterine transfer of blood.., the postnatal polycythemia in single newborn infants remains unexplained. **1966** *Arch. Surg.* XCII. 865/1 The occurrence of Hashimoto's thyroiditis in a mother and her three daughters, two of whom are monovular twins.

monozygotic (mǫnozəigǫ·tik), *a.* (*sb.*) *Biol.* [f. MONO- + ZYGOT(E + -IC.] Of twins (also *rarely* of triplets, etc.): derived from a single ovum (and therefore identical). Also as *sb.*, such an individual.

1917 H. H. NEWMAN *Biol. of Twins* 3 Such twins, quadruplets, or larger sets of offspring are known as monozygotic. **1930**, etc. [see *DIZYGOTIC *a.*] **1957** *Ann. N.Y. Acad. Sci.* LXIV. 759 Because the twins were believed to be probable monozygotics, excess skin was taken from the less extensively burned twin and cross-transplanted to her sister. **1965** *Listener* 24 June 930/2 We have learnt, too, the significance of a natural freak—the monozygotic or identical twin. **1968** [see MONOZYGOSITY below]. **1970** *Sci. Jrnl.* June 30/2 Such monozygotic twins ..form only a small proportion of all twins.

Hence **monozygo·sity**, the property of being monozygotic.

1928 *Biol. Abstr.* II. 685/2 (*heading*) Value of dactyloscopic and dermatologic methods in diagnosing monozygosity in twins. **1952** *New Biol.* XII. 28 The only method at present available for diagnosing monozygosity involves comparison of as many morphological and physiological characters as possible. **1968** *Obstetr. & Gynecol. Survey* XXIII. 940 Two-thirds of monozygotic twins have a single placenta with a single chorion, and the diagnosis of monozygosity can be definitely established in this two-thirds.

Monrovia (mǒnrǭu·viă). The name of the capital city of Liberia used *attrib.* with reference to the political grouping of African states resulting from a conference which took place there in May 1961.

1962 *Ann. Reg. 1961* 304 The Monrovia Powers, which included the heirs of *Afrique noire d'expression française*,.. were more disposed to co-operate with Europe. **1962** *Listener* 18 Oct. 594/2 It [*sc.* Nigeria] is one of the leading countries of the so-called Monrovia group of African states who have sought to maintain a realistic course on international problems. **1963** HAILE SELASSIE in *Jrnl. Mod. African Studies* Sept. 285 The commentators of 1963 speak, in discussing Africa, of the Monrovia States, the Brazzaville Group, the Casablanca Powers... Let us put an end to these terms. **1965** H. LAND in C. Legum *Africa* (rev. ed.) 217 It [*sc.* Nigeria] played a major rôle in helping to eliminate the friction between the Casablanca and Monrovia groups, and in establishing the Organization of African Unity. **1971** W. LAQUEUR *Dict. Politics* 313 Tubman..sponsored the Monrovia Conference of 1961.

mons. Add: Used for *mons veneris*, usu. in phr. **mons area**, the sensitive area of the *mons veneris*.

1965 MASTERS & JOHNSON in J. Money *Sex Research* iv. 109 The concept of manipulating only the clitoris rather than the entire mons area is grossly in error. **1968** T. LIDZ *Person* xiv. 427 Stimulation of the mons area or perineal region in general can rapidly revive the arousal. **1969** 'J' *Sensuous Woman* (1970) iii. 32 It takes longer to come to orgasm with mons manipulation, but it is just as satiating an experience as direct clitoral shaft massage.

Monsieur. 4. (Later example.)

1846 H. MELVILLE *Typee* (rev. ed.) Sequel 304 Jimmy ..had a talk about the 'Wee-Wees', as the people of Nukukeva call the Monsieurs.

monsoon. Add: **4. monsoon forest** [tr. G. *monsunwälder* (A. F. W. Schimper *Pflanzengeographie* (1898) III. iii. 281)], a deciduous forest found in regions of heavy seasonal rainfall.

1903 W. R. FISHER tr. *Schimper's Plant-Geography* III. iii. 260 The monsoon forest is more or less leafless during the dry season,..is tropophilous in character, usually less lofty than the rain-forest, rich in woody lianes, rich in herbaceous but poor in woody epiphytes. **1926** TANSLEY & CHIPP *Study of Vegetation* xv. 291 Monsoon forest occurs in regions where the rainfall exceeds 180 cm..but where there is a prolonged dry season during which the forest is more or less leafless. **1960** N. POLUNIN *Introd. Plant Geogr.* xiv. 439 Widespread though variable are the monsoon forests or similar 'seasonal' forests, developed in regions enjoying abundant rainfall during the wet season, but having this alternating with a pronounced drought lasting from four to six months or sometimes longer.

monsoonal *a.* (further examples); hence also **monsoo·nish** *a.*, suggestive or characteristic of a monsoon.

1886 KIPLING *Plain Tales from Hills* (1888) 118 Not a mere hill-shower but a good, tepid, monsoonish downpour. **1913** J. MURRAY *Ocean* iv. 83 The monsoonal deflection of the tradewinds, for some distance out to sea, out of their course to westward. **1936** *Geogr. Jrnl.* LXXXVIII. 297 The arrival of the deep mass of monsoonal air. **1961** *Aeroplane* CI. 504/1 Hundreds of these birds had made their way to Australia by soaring in front of 'monsoonal fronts'. **1972** *Kent Life* July 82/2 Under the equatorial sun and monsoonal rains, two crops of rice are easily obtained. **1975** *Bangladesh Observer* 22 July 5/3 Two friends from Dacca and I were enjoying a monsoonish evening in Delhi. It had rained not torrentially but heavily enough to flood some areas and bring the temperature down.

monster, *sb.* and *a.* Add: **A.** *sb.* **5.** (Later example.)

1966 K. MARTIN *Father Figures* i. 20 Buying from the all-purposes shop bullseyes and, for a penny, 'monsters', which were big bottles of fizzy lemonade.

6. a. *monster-browed, -headed* adjs.; **b.** *monster-killing, -queller* (later example), *-quelling, -slayer, -slaying*; **c.** *monster-spouted* adj.; **d.** *monster-cloud, -machine, -mask.*

1929 BLUNDEN *Near & Far* 49 Though the full cloud Frowns monster-browed. **1934** —— *Mind's Eye* 16 A sky of freakish monster-clouds. **1869** 'MARK TWAIN' *Innoc. Abr.* xx. 147 The more immediate scenery consisted of fields and farm-houses outside the car, and a monster-headed dwarf and a moustached woman inside it. These latter were not show-people. **1966** *English Studies* XLVII. 141 Digressions..thrown in by the poet.. as the fair means by which an experienced teller of long stories overcomes the monotony of a series of monster-killings. **1970** G. JACKSON *Let.* 4 Apr. in *Soledad Brother* (1971) 211 He was giving to us all of the life force and activity that the monster-machine had left to him. **1969** L. J. CHIARAMONTE in Halpert & Story *Christmas Mumming in Newfoundland* 89 They are great favourites with little children, who beg their parents for money to buy a new monster mask. **1959** A. G. BRODEUR *Art of Beowulf* 81 Outside the climate of mutual love.., Beowulf would be little more than the monster-queller and marvelous swimmer of folk-tale. **1948** K. MALONE in *English Studies* XXIX. 167 Beowulf's mention of sea-monsters..takes us back to the swimming match with Breca, one detail of which is precisely this monster-quelling on the part of the hero. **1948** L. SPITZER *Linguistics & Literary Hist.* iii. 98 She must ask Hippolyte to resemble his father, the monster-slayer, by slaying the monster that *she* has become. *Ibid.* 95 We learn that Hippolyte has not, to his regret, equaled his father in his feats of monster-slaying. **1942** BLUNDEN *Romantic Poetry & Fine Arts* 17 Monster-spouted fountain.

B. *adj.* **1.** (Earlier and later examples.)

1837 (*title of play*) The elements—earth, air, fire water; or, The monster ballroom of 1837 (R.A.M. 15/5/1837). **1952** 'R. CROMPTON' *William & Tramp* ii. 83 Their jaws never ceased to move rhythmically around a couple of Monster Humbugs. **1961** *Guardian* 27 Sept. 8/3 Many older housewives..find great satisfaction in a monster weekly 'bake'.

‖ **monstre** (moṅstr), *sb.*[2] [Fr.] In phr. **monstre sacré** (lit. sacred monster), a striking and

eccentric public figure; a false idol, esp. in the world of entertainment.

[**1940** J. Cocteau (*title*) Les monstres sacrés.] **1959** *Manch. Guardian* 17 July 4/3 Unlike Mlle Sagan she seems vulnerable, and capable of development, not a born 'monstre sacré'. **1965** *Listener* 10 June 870/1 We must forgive Mailer because he is both exceptional *and* typical—the paradigm who is also a *monstre sacré*. **1969** *Ibid.* 9 Jan. 62/1 Compare her with the late Edith Piaf, a *monstre sacré* of a different order. **1969** *Times* 26 Nov. 9/4 That most fabulous of *monstres sacrés*, Sarah Bernhardt. **1975** *Times* 30 Oct. 8/5 Half saint, half satyr, wholly *monstre sacré*, the face [of Bertrand Russell] looks out upon us from the photographs.

monstrous, *a.* **8. b.** Delete 'now *rare* or *Obs.*' and add 'now mainly *U.S.*' (Examples.)

1848 W. T. Thompson *Major Jones's Sketches of Travel* iii. 23 Augusty's a monstrous pretty city; but it ain't the place it used to was, not by a grate sight. It seems like it was rottin off at both eends, and ain't growin much in the middle. **1884** 'Mark Twain' *Huck. Finn* 134 Behind a monstrous long raft. **1907** *Dialect Notes* III. 233 'Yes'm, I'se *monstrous* hungry.' **1942** Berrey & Van den Bark *Amer. Thes. Slang* § 20/14 *Very; exceedingly,* .. mighty, monstrous.

montage (mǫ·ntāʒ). [Fr., f. *monter* to Mount.] **1.** *Cinemat.* and *Television.* **a.** The selection and arrangement of separate cinematographic shots as a consecutive whole; the blending (by superimposition) of separate shots to form a single picture; the sequence or picture resulting from such a process.

1929 I. Montagu tr. *Pudovkin's On Film Technique* 179 It is important to gain a clear conception of the activities embraced here by the word *Editing*. The word used by Pudovkin, the German and French word, is *montage*. Its only possible English equivalent is *editing*. **1930** *Observer* 5 Oct. 20/4 Montage, or constructive cutting.. is simply the method of building up a film from broken and isolated strips of celluloid. **1936** *World Film News* July 48/3, I recall the fate of *montage* when it was adopted in England. **1939** H. G. Wells *Holy Terror* iv. ii. 398 Using the cinema in the schools to display the rapid development of the new life of mankind.. with a montage in which the Beethovenised head of Rud, the ruler and guide, was displayed in such a manner as to evoke and sustain a world-wide enthusiasm. **1959** *Punch* 10 June 787/2 Very good photography.. and montage, or editing.. in the jazz-club scene behind the credit titles. **1961** *Listener* 10 Aug. 217/1 The programme opened with a *montage* of newspapers cascading from the presses. **1974** *Some Technical Terms & Slang* (Granada Television), *Montage*, a sequence of film images cut together, usually to music.

b. *attrib.* passing into *adj.*

1948 A. Huxley *Ape & Essence* (1949) 125 A series of montage shots exhibits, in twenty seconds, the slow, hour-long advance of Loola and Dr. Poole. **1949** *Here & Now* (N.Z.) Oct. 29/3 It doesn't matter if it's [*sc.* a film is] documentary, expressionist, montage, poetic, or just plain cinematic. **1961** K. Reisz *Technique Film-Editing* (ed. 9) ii. vi. 112 The term *montage sequence*.. refers to the quick impressionistic sequence of disconnected images, usually linked by dissolves, superimpositions or wipes, and used to convey passages of time, changes of place, or any other scenes of transition. **1962** *Listener* 4 Oct. 536/2 An edgy.. musical score, perfectly geared to the montage shots of computers, drawing-boards, teleprinters. *Ibid.* 29 Nov. 909/2 The rows of cells and their inhabitants are arranged like a montage sequence from a Russian silent film. **1963** *Movie* Jan. 5/3 Montage sequence of individual crows attacking each child.

2. The act or process of producing a composite picture by combining several different pictures or pictorial elements so that they blend with or into one another; a picture so produced.

1938 A. Cooper *Making a Poster* 34 Used as 'montage' in conjunction with blue skies, or green fields, photographs of human beings appear singularly unattractive. **1938** *Times* 26 Feb. 10/3 The colours, photographs, and lettering which in the ordinary poster are brought into an effect of unity by skilful 'montage'. **1941** A. Huxley *Let.* 27 May (1969) 467 Use either the portrait of Father Joseph.. or else a montage made of the various illustrations in the book. **1958** *Observer* 18 May 16/5 They see, upon the pink and gold jacket [of a book], a *montage* of representative faces of the period. **1972** *Islander* (Victoria, B.C.) 16 July 10/2 This art [*sc.* découpage] is not, however, to be confused with either collage or montage, both of which are used as pictures rather than as a decoration for furniture.

3. *transf.* and *fig.* (The process of making) a mixture, blend, or medley of various elements; a pastiche; a sequence, miscellany.

1934 C. Lambert *Music Ho!* v. 329 The montage or pastiche of the neo-classicists. **1941** B. Schulberg *What Makes Sammy Run?* iii. 45 It [*sc.* a night club] was a montage of hot music, drunken laughter, loud wisecracks and hostesses like lollypops in red, green and yellow wrappers. *Ibid.* ix. 172 It was flashing through my mind like a montage nightmare. **1961** *Listener* 23 Nov. 863/1 It [*sc.* a poem] is certainly not modernist, if by modernist one thinks of a play of images, a montage in free verse. **1963** T. A. Sebeok in J. A. Fishman *Readings in Sociol. of Lang.* (1968) 19 When describing speech phenomena, many linguists,.. continue to employ a mixed nomenclature, drawing for their technical vocabulary now on articulatory, now on acoustic, and sometimes on perceptual phonetics; the resulting montage may show seams, but the total picture makes sense. **1973** *Guardian* 21 Apr. 10/2 She has used a montage of sound, from the throbbing ..[of] your own heart beat to various street sounds, even a street musician.

Montagnais (mo:ṅtanyē·), *sb.* and *a.* Also **Montagnois, Mountaine(e)r, Mountainier.** [a. F. *montagnais* mountaineer; hence, member of a mountain tribe.] **A.** *sb.* An Algonquian Indian people of eastern Canada; a member of this people; also, their language. **B.** *adj.* Of or pertaining to this people.

1625 Purchas *Pilgrimes* IV. viii. vi. 1607 They were three Nations when they went to war; the *Estechemins, Algoumequins*, and *Mountainers*. **1703** tr. *Lahontan's New Voy. N.-America* I. 207 He deals with the other Savage Nations, namely, the *Montagnois*, and the *Papipanachois* in Arms and Ammunition. **1792** G. Cartwright *Jrnl.* I. Explanation of frontispiece, His jacket.., sash, and rackets are Mountaineer. **1800** *Mass. Hist. Soc. Coll.* VI. 16 The ensuing vocabulary I transcribed *viva voce* from Gabriel, a young Mountaineer Indian. *Ibid.* 17 There is evidently a great resemblance between the Skoffie and Mountaineer. **1863** H. Y. Hind *Explor. Labrador Peninsula* II. xxvii. 101 The Nasquapees, like their friends and allies the Montagnais, hate the Esquimaux. **1894** *11th Ann. Rep. U.S. Bureau Amer. Ethnol. 1889–90* 267 The Indians of the Ungava district are locally known as Naskopie, a term of reproach applied to them by the mountaineers (the Montagnais of the early Jesuit missionaries). **1916** *Trans. R. Soc. Canada* X. i. 314 It.. is possibly a transition between the Ojibwa and Montagnais snowshoe. **1933** [see *Cree *sb.* and *a.*]. **1934** D. Jenness *Indians of Canada* (ed. 2) xviii. 271 The Montagnais country was a well-wooded area abounding in moose. **1941** *Beaver* Mar. 27 The Montagnais shoe is the commonest form used throughout the Labrador Peninsula. **1966** C. F. & F. M. Voegelin *Map of N. Amer. Indian Lang.* (*caption*) Algonquian Family. 1. Cree—Montagnais—Naskapi. **1973** Howat & Taylor *Dict. World Hist.* 1013/1 *Montagnais Indians*, group of Canadian Algonquian tribes, discovered (1603) at the mouth of the Saguenay by Champlain, who enlisted them in an expedition (1609) against the Iroquois.

Montagnard. Add: **1. b.** An aboriginal people living in the highlands of South Vietnam; a member of this people; also *attrib.* or as *adj.* Cf. *Moi *a.* and *sb.*

1962 *Courier-Mail* (Brisbane) 1 Aug. 2/6 Montagnard scouts report that they have seen elephants carrying artillery pieces. *Ibid.*, Whether a montagnard could distinguish between a mortar and a field piece [etc.]. **1966** *Listener* 29 Dec. 949/2 Next.. the mountains and the high plateaux where the Montagnard tribesman lives. **1968** *Ibid.* 13 June 760/3 The Highlands take up half the physical area of South Vietnam but they contain less than one tenth of its people. Moreover most of these are not ethnic Vietnamese but hill tribes of South Seas descent whom the French called Montagnards and the Vietnamese call *Moi*, meaning savages. **1972** *Times* 31 May 5/4 (*caption*) A Montagnard woman comforts her husband as he lies in Kontum hospital. **1972** *Guardian* 3 June 11/1 The name Montagnard was first given to the hill tribes of Vietnam by the French colonisers—it means simply 'the mountain people'. **1974** *Nature* 15 Mar. 186/3 The Montagnards (the highlanders) conduct much of their agriculture in cleared areas of forests, and so their fields were often sprayed during attacks on the inland forests.

‖ **montagne russe** (moṅtanʸ rüs). *Canad.* [F. *montagnes russes* switchback.] A switchback, scenic railway, roller coaster.

1838 *United Service Jrnl.* July 302 Wherever there is a hill or declivity, a '*montagne Russe*' is speedily prepared. **1885** [see *cul-de-sac 2]. **1947** *Horizon* July 32 Political excitement.. 'ran high', but.. it seems like a switchback, a *montagne russe* compared with Mount Everest.

Montagu[1] (mǫ·ntăgiu). The name of George *Montagu* (1751–1815), British naturalist, used *attrib.* or in the possessive to designate animals first described by him, as **Montagu's blenny,** a small marine fish, *Coryphoblennius galerita*; **Montagu's harrier,** *Circus pygargus*, the smallest British harrier; also *ellipt.*; **Montagu's sea-snail,** a small marine fish, *Liparis montagui*; **Montagu shell,** the shell of a small marine bivalve of the genus *Montacuta* which lives as a commensal with an echinoderm; **Montagu's sucker, sucking-fish** = *Montagu's sea-snail; **Montagu's Venus,** the shell of the marine bivalve *Venerupis pullastra*.

1836 W. Yarrell *Hist. Brit. Fishes* I. 219 (*heading*) Montagu's Blenny. **1969** A. Wheeler *Fishes Brit. Is. & N.-W. Europe* 439/1 Montagu's blenny has a very restricted distribution in the British Isles, being found only on rocky shores on the south-western coasts. **1843** W. Yarrell *Hist. Brit. Birds* I. 101 It will.. be an advantage, as well as a gratification, to call this bird in future Montagu's Harrier and *Circus Montagui*. **1880** *Encycl. Brit.* XI. 492/1 This was called by him the Ash-coloured Falcon, but it now generally bears his name, and is known as Montagu's Harrier. **1930** J. S. Huxley *Bird Watching* ii. 27, I could take a map and mark down just where I saw my first dartford warbler, my first smew, Montagu's harrier, and so on. **1954** A. W. P. Robertson *Bird Pageant* ii. 38 While hunting, the montagu usually flies into the wind. **1971** *Country Life* 20 May 1245/3 The old, wild, undrained Fens.. where the Montagu's harrier still nests in the reed-beds. **1835** L. Jenyns *Man. Brit. Vertebr. Anim.* 473 Montagu's Sea-Snail... Discovered by Montagu, at Milton, on the south coast of Devon. **1925** J. T. Jenkins *Fishes Brit. Is.* 106 The illustration shows eggs of Montagu's Sea Snail. **1969** A. Wheeler *Fishes Brit. Is. & N.-W. Europe* 505/1 Montagu's sea snail is a more littoral species, found on the shore up to mid-tide level. **1901** E. Step *Shell Life* 101 The rusty Montagu-shell (*M[ontacuta] ferruginosa*) is more oblong, greyish white in hue, but this is hidden by a rusty-looking incrustation. **1961** P. Street *Shell Life on Seashore* viii. 122 The Montagu shells attach themselves near the mouth of the urchin so that they can extract food particles. **1836** W. Yarrell *Hist. Brit. Fishes* II. 277 (*heading*) Montagu's Sucking-fish. *Ibid.* 278 Montagu's Sucker, in the adult state, is from two inches and a half to three inches long. **1925** J. T. Jenkins *Fishes Brit. Is.* 106 Montagu's Sucker is common from the north of Norway to the Channel. **1819** W. Turton *Conchol. Dict. Brit. Is.* 243 *Venus Montacuti.* Montagu's Venus.

Montagu[2] (mǫ·ntăgiu). *Naut.* [The name of Rear-Admiral Victor Alexander *Montagu* (1841–1915): see quot. 1974.] Used to designate a rig used for small boats in the Royal Navy. Hence **Montagu whaler,** a whaler carrying this rig.

1925 A. Moore *Last Days Mast & Sail* vii. 228 The Montagu whalers recently introduced into the Navy carry a standing lug. **1939** A. S. Bennett *June of Rochester* i. 12 *Hecla* was only a converted Montagu whaler with barely sitting headroom in the tiny cabin. **1948** R. de Kerchove *Internat. Maritime Dict.* 473/2 *Montagu rig*, a two-mast fore-and-aft service rig for ship's boats in the British Navy. The sail plan includes a stay foresail, standing lug mainsail, and jib-headed mizen. A centerboard is fitted to boats with Montagu rig. **1974** W. E. May in *Maritime Monogr. & Rep.* (Nat. Maritime Museum) No. 15, 18 It was not until the early years of the present century that the Montagu whaler appeared. This boat, partially following the proposals of Rear-Admiral Victor Alexander Montagu, had a fuller body aft and was rigged with a standing-lug mainsail, triangular foresail and small triangular mizen.

Montague (mǫ·ntăgiu). *Hairdressing.* Also **Montague curl.** [Origin unknown.] A flat curl, several of which were used to dress the front of the hair, often forming a fringe.

1881 *Mme. Demorest's 'What to Wear' 1881–82* Autumn & Winter 68/1 The flat Montague curls and *crève-cœur* locks are being affected. **1882** *Mme. Demorest's 'What to Wear' 1882* Spring & Summer 80/1 Montagues continue, as formerly, to please the fancy. They may be flattened or combed up; the latter is preferred. **1905** A. B. Moler *Man. Barbering* 86 Artificial curls... Montagues are made by fastening a strand of hair to a style of hairpin for this purpose. *Ibid.* 90 Montagues, or short curls, for the front of the face,.. are usually dressed on a wig block. **1960** Cunnington & Beard *Dict. Eng. Costume* 138/1 *Montague Curls*,.. an evening dress coiffure, the front hair arranged in a crescent-shaped fringe of curls gummed to the forehead. **1966** J. S. Cox *Illustr. Dict. Hairdressing* 99 *Montague*,.. a pin curl mounted on a hairpin.

Montaignesque (moṅtēⁱne·sk), *a.* [See -esque.] Characteristic of or relating to the French philosopher and essayist, Michel de *Montaigne* (1533–92), or his writings. Also **Montai·gnian** (-iăn), **Montai·gnish** (-iʃ) *adjs.* So **Montai·gnism,** the theories or ideas of Montaigne.

1831 Disraeli *Young Duke* III. v. vi. 175 In the Lords, I admire the Duke... There is a gruff, husky sort of a downright Montaignish *naïveté* about him. **1917** J. Strahan *Andrew Bruce Davidson* iv. 65 One cannot but be struck by the curiously Montaignesque style. **1959** *Jrnl. Philos.* LVI. 544 Hume.. has also affinities to the Montaignian sceptical tradition. **1964** *Philos.* XXXIX. 205 He.. found it necessary to refute Montaignism. **1965** *Amer. Philos. Q.* II. 19/1 The same scepticism, with the same Montaignian arguments.

Montana (mǫntā·nă, -tæ·nă). The name of a state in the north-west of the U.S.A. used *attrib.* in **Montana tree,** a type of saddle or saddle-tree.

1891 *Harper's Mag.* June 7/2 Their saddle is what is known as the Montana tree.

Montanian (mǫntā·niăn, -tæ·n-), *a.* Also **Montanan.** [f. prec. + -ian or -an.] A native or inhabitant of Montana.

Montanan is now the more usual form.

1870 *Montana Pick & Plow* (Bozeman) 29 July 2/2 That desire to know, so prominently a characteristic of our countrymen, is perhaps enhanced among Montanians, by reason of their comparative isolation. **1894** *Harper's Mag.* Aug. 482/1 (*caption*) The unterrified Montanians. **1932** *Frontier* (Missoula, Montana) Mar. 206/2 The better Montanan you are.. the better American. **1972** *Fairbanks* (Alaska) *Daily News-Miner* 3 Nov. 2/4 Montanans struggled for years with the question of whether to have a convention.

montan wax (mǫ·ntæ̆n wæks). Also **Montan wax.** [f. L. *montān-us* of or belonging to a mountain + Wax *sb.*[1]] A hard, brittle substance that is extracted from lignite by means of benzene or other solvents, consists mainly of higher fatty acids and their esters, and is used in making polishes and as an electrical insulator.

1908 *Chem. Abstr.* II. 2875 Montan wax is obtained by extracting brown-coal by benzene and purifying the product by repeated distillation with superheated steam. **1920** *Times* 4 Feb. 11/3 Another by-product recovered from this particular lignite.. is Montan wax... This mineral is very valuable on account of its high melting point, and for this reason it is unequalled in the manufac-

ture of high-grade boot polishes, gramophone records, and other articles. **1936** Bone & Himus *Coal* v. 55 The raw coals contain..anything up to about 7·5 per cent. of 'Montan wax' (m.p. usually 78° to 88°). **1947** *Times* 23 June 2/7 The shortage of mined coal, together with the value of montan wax, has given added value to lignite. **1969** R. F. Lang tr. *Henglein's Chem. Technol.* 411 Montan wax is obtained from strongly bituminous, dry coal by extraction with benzene or benzene-alcohol.

‖ **montaría** (mǫntarī·ă). [Pg.] A dugout canoe used in the Amazon region.

1933 P. Fleming *Brazilian Adventure* I. xvi. 132 The other two boats belonged to smaller and faster types. One was a *montaría*, also clinker-built and actually I think a more finished and substantial bit of work than the true montaría of the Amazon. **1936** *Discovery* Dec. 382/2 Whole families, with their *montarías*, the hire of which was included in the daily wage, were recruited near the collecting-grounds.

Mont Bazillac, Montbazillac, varr. *Monbazillac.

‖ **mont de piété** (mon̈ də piete). [Fr.] = *Mount of piety* (see Mount *sb.*[1] 5 b).

1854 Thackeray *Newcomes* I. xxviii. 265, I saw his guardeur when I went lately to Strasbourg, on my last pilgrimage to the Mont de Piété. **1890** W. Booth *In Darkest England* II. vi. 215 There would be no difficulty.. of instituting a private Mont de Piété. **1923** Wodehouse *Inimitable Jeeves* iv. 43 The idea of—er—pledging the pearls at the local Mont de Pieté was, you will readily understand, repugnant to us. **1967** S. Pakenham *Sixty Miles from England* ii. 31 The Mont de Piété was full of gold earrings, pawned by fishwives, for the price of fish was low. **1969** [see *hock *sb.*[7] b].

monte[1]. Add: (Earlier example.)

1824 J. R. Poinsett *Notes on Mexico* (1825) iii. 37 We found a numerous assembly of men gambling deeply, at a game called *monte*.

b. *attrib.* and *Comb.*, as *monte-banker, blanket, card, game, operator, table*, etc.; **monte-bank,** a monte table; also used as the name of the game itself.

a **1861** T. Winthrop *Life in Open Air* (1863) 128 A background of mustangs, monte-banks, and lynch-law. **1939** T. King *21 Games to play for Money* 27 To take its [*sc.* Faro's] place, Monte Bank has come into being. **1855** F. S. Marryat *Mts. & Molehills* xiv. 267, I was soon asleep, notwithstanding..the clinkings of the monté-bankers, and the noise of the crowd below. **1898** H. S. Canfield *Maid of Frontier* 78 His long and angular shadow fell across the monte blanket spread flat upon the ground. **1897** *Sears, Roebuck Catal.* 356/3 'Spanish Monte Cards', 48 cards in pack, assortment of black and colors. **1899** T. W. Hall *Tales* 276 Judge Leander Quinn was lured away from a monte game with a couple of buck Indians. **1961** J. Scarne *Compl. Guide to Gambling* xix. 520 Countless Monte operators plied their trade on the steamboats of the Ohio and Mississippi..in the 1850s. **1873** J. H. Beadle *Undevel. West* iv. 92 We take our stand near the monte table, where a considerable crowd gathers. **1889** K. Munroe *Golden Days* ii. 15 This influx of gold caused monte-tables, and other gambling layouts, to spring up.

2. (See *monty.)

Monte[3] (mǫ·nti). Colloq. shortening of *Monte Carlo. Also = **Monte Carlo rally*.

1928 P. de Ketchiva *Confessions of Croupier* xvi. 194 After her extraordinary luck at Monte,..she had lost all her winnings the following night at the Cannes Casino. **1956** R. Baxter in M. Couper *Rallying to Monte Carlo* p. v, 'Doing the Monte' is like being a dog owner. Once you start, it's difficult to stop. **1968** *Autocar* 25 Jan. 35/3 Driving genius helps, but Montes are finally won by masterly planning.

Monte Carlo (mǫ·nti kā·ɹlo). [Name of a resort in Monaco famous for its gambling casino.] **1. a.** Used *attrib.* to designate methods of estimating the solution to numerical problems that involve the random (or pseudo-random) sampling of numbers with some chosen frequency distribution.

1949 *Math. Tables & Other Aids to Computation* III. 546 This method of solution of problems in mathematical physics by sampling techniques based on random walk models constitutes what is known as the 'Monte Carlo' method. The method as well as the name for it were apparently first suggested by John von Neumann and S. M. Ulam. **1950** *Nucleonics* May 27 (*heading*) Random sampling (Monte Carlo) techniques in neutron attenuation problems. **1955** *Sci. Amer.* May 90/3 The accuracy of a Monte Carlo approximation improves only as the square of the number of trials. **1961** *New Scientist* 16 Mar. 678/3 This method of imitating the apparently random fluctuation of events in the real world which it is unnecessary or impossible to study in detail, is the crux of the Monte Carlo simulation technique. **1964** *Guardian* 19 June 6/6 (Advt.), Familiarity with Monte Carlo methods and computer programming would be an advantage. **1970** O. Dopping *Computers & Data Processing* xx. 328 An important field of application of random numbers is in the Monte Carlo methods. They are based on the repetition of a computation in a great number of cases, where one or more parameters are allowed to vary in a random fashion from one computation to the next. *Ibid.*, Monte Carlo methods can also be used for computing determined results. For instance, we can, in principle, calculate an approximation of $\pi/4$ by investigating which fraction of a number of points, chosen at random in a square, are inside the inscribed circle. **1972** *Computers & Humanities* VII. 39 Monte Carlo methods of simulation were applied to a population model for Paleolithic human populations.

b. *absol.*

1951 *Nat. Bureau of Standards Appl. Math. Ser.* (U.S.) XII. iii. 6/1 In some instances..a judicious combination of Monte Carlo applied to the physical model with analysis of the equations is indicated. **1962** D. Slayton in *Into Orbit* 23 A branch of probability mathematics which the scientists call 'Monte Carlo'—because it boils down, really to nothing more than a complex way of figuring the odds. **1969** *Nature* 15 Mar. 999/2 Monte Carlo involves, essentially, a sequence of operations on a sequence of random numbers $\{u_i\}$, where, ideally, the $\{u_i\}$ are independent and identically distributed. **1969** J. Argenti *Managem. Techniques* 172 Monte Carlo is a form of simulation..and both often require the use of a computer. It is possible, however, to use Monte Carlo with pencil and paper.

c. *Monte Carlo fallacy*: the fallacy that the probability of any particular outcome to one of a series of repeated but independent events of chance is inversely dependent upon the previous outcomes (so that, e.g., a succession of failures is thought to increase the probability of success on the next occasion).

1957 *Sci. Amer.* Nov. 136/2 In our studies of the manifestations of subjective probability in gambling we have given particular attention to the Monte Carlo fallacy; the well-nigh unanimous belief that after a run of successes a failure is inevitable, and *vice versa*. **1973** A. J. Ayer *Central Questions of Philos.* viii. 164 The notorious Monte Carlo fallacy consists in assuming that because the odds against an even number's coming up ten times in succession are over a thousand to one, there is equally little chance of the tenth spin yielding an even number, if the previous nine have done so.

2. *Monte Carlo rally*: an annual international car rally, first held in 1911, of which the final stages take place in Monte Carlo (also shortened to *Monte Carlo*).

1950 R. Lowry *Monte Carlo Rally* ix. 76 There are Rallies ideally suited to such tastes but the Monte Carlo is not one of them. **1973** *Guardian* 26 Jan. 13/1 Irate Monte Carlo Rally drivers..complained about speed traps set up by the French police... On the Monte Carlo, two reports of excessive speeding mean automatic disqualification.

‖ **monte di pietà** (mǫ·nte di pyeta). Also **monte de pietà.** Pl. **monti di pietà.** [It.] = *Mount of piety* (see Mount *sb.*[1] 5 b).

1654 J. Howell *Parthenopoeia* Epistle to Reader sig. A1[v] *Monte de pietà*, an Hospital of 60000. Duckets of yeerly Revenue. **1805** P. Beckford *Familiar Lett. from Italy* I. 231 The *Monte di Pietà* was established first at Florence, in the year 1496, to restrain the usury of the Jews. **1883** *Athenæum* 18 Aug. 218/1 The..186 first-class pictures from the Monte di Pietà, where they had been pawned ages ago by destitute aristocratic families. **1973** *Listener* 18 Jan. 81/2 These Christian pawnshops, still in existence in Italy today, were known as *Monti di Pieta* or 'funds of charity'. When they were first founded, in Umbrian towns of the mid-15th century, they charged low interest rates.

Montefiascone (mǫntefiaskōᵘ·ne). Also **Monte Fiascone.** The name of a town in Latium, central Italy, used (freq. *attrib.*) to designate the sweet white wine made there.

1673 J. Ray *Observations Journey Low-Countries* 363 Heer [*sc.* in Rome] is great variety of Wines..: as Greco, Lagrime of Naples..Monte Pulciano, di Monte fiascone. **1803** C. Wilmot *Let.* 1 Jan. in *Irish Peer* (1920) 136 The Montefiascone wine is celebrated; we found it excellent. **1833** C. Redding *Hist. Mod. Wines* ix. 240 Of the home growths..another is the Monte Fiascone, of a fine aroma, and intoxicating. It is grown near the Lake Bolsena. **1966** H. Johnson *Wine* 136 Fugger went no further, but ended his days drinking Montefiascone, and no doubt boring his boon-companions to death with the story of Est Est Est. **1967** A. Lichine *Encycl. Wines* 356 *Montefiascone*, white wine grown in the foothills of the Volsini Mountains, Italy.

Monteith[2] (mǫ̆ntī·þ). A type of coloured cotton handkerchief with a white design (see quots.).

1882 Caulfeild & Saward *Dict. Needlework* 350 *Monteiths*, a description of Cotton Handkerchiefs, which are dyed of one uniform colour, but have a pattern of white spots occurring at regular distances... These goods are known by the name of the manufacturers, at Glasgow. **1957** M. B. Picken *Fashion Dict.* 226/1 *Monteith*.., cotton handkerchief, having colored background with white design, made by discharging dye. **1958** A. & N. L. Clow in C. Singer et al. *Hist. Technol.* IV. viii. 249, 5000 looms were employed in 1796 in the neighbourhood of Glasgow making pullicates for the Turkey-red dyers. These became known throughout Europe as monteiths, after Henry Monteith, who acquired Dalmarnock from Macintosh.

monte-jus (mon̈tˌʒüs). Also **-juice.** [Fr., f. *monter* to raise + *jus* juice, liquid.] In the making of sugar, an apparatus for raising the level of the liquid by means of air or steam pressure.

1872 P. Soames *Manuf. Sugar* 133 The cane-juice runs along the gutter to the monte-jus c, where it is elevated into the clarifiers, d. **1921** *Dict. Occup. Terms* (1927) § 449 *Montejuice attendant, montejuice boy*: stands by valves of montejus apparatus. **1924** A. J. Wallis-Tayler *Sugar Machinery* viii. 147 This monte-jus should be sunk in the ground, and enclosed with brickwork or masonry in a sort of well. **1950** N. Deerr *Hist. Sugar* II. xxxiii. 578 The montejus was introduced into the industry in 1819 by Dubrunfaut.

Montelian (mǫntī·liăn), *a.* *Archæol.* [f. the name of the Swedish archæologist, Oscar *Montelius* (1843–1921) + -an or -i)an.] Applied to a system of classification and nomenclature devised by Montelius.

1937 G. E. Daniel in *Antiquity* XI. 185 The implications of the Montelian theory of the dolmen are fivefold. **1938** —— in *Ibid.* XII. 302 These modifications are not enough to make the Montelian classification a really workable typology. *Ibid.* 303, I use the word dolmen throughout here in the Montelian sense of a small single chamber. **1941** *Proc. Prehistoric Soc.* VII. 21 Archaeologists who neglect the B-Dolmens of northern Europe are destroying ..any case they might make for the defence of the Montelian sequence. **1950** G. E. Daniel *Hundred Yrs. Archaeol.* xii. 235 The Montelian periods were rendered difficult to use because of their very close linkage in typology and name with the various classes of collective tombs.

Montélimar (mǫnte·limāɹ). The name of a town in the department of Drôme in S.E. France used *attrib.* and *absol.* to designate a type of nougat made there.

1908 J. Kirkland *Mod. Baker* IV. 16 *Nougat Montélimar* is another kind of mixture in which almonds are used. **1923** R. Whymper *Manuf. Confectionery* 139 Montélimar nougat for chocolate coating should not be as hard as that which is sold in blocks. **1968** W. J. Fance *International Confectioner* 569/1 Nougat Montélimar which is very well known, originally came from the East. **1972** 'J. Melville' *Ironwood* iii. 50, I wanted to cheer him up. I had some bags of montelimar and marchpane.

Montenegrin(e, *a.* and *sb.* Add: Also **Montenegran. A.** *adj.* (Further examples.)

1939 W. B. Yeats *Statesman's Holiday* in *Last Poems & Plays* (1940) 77 Here's a Montenegrin lute, And its old sole string Makes me sweet music And I delight to sing. **1942** *R.A.F. Jrnl.* 13 June 24 The Montenegrin guerrillas attacked the hotel. **1958** P. Kemp *No Colours or Crest* x. 220 The German and Albanian forces..had started an offensive against the Montenegrin Partisans. **1970** *Internat. & Compar. Law Q.* XIX. 334 The Montenegran Code of Property. **1972** *Times* 20 Oct. 9/7 Montenegran officials and a guard of honour awaited the Queen's arrival.

Montepulciano (mǫntepultʃyā·no). The name of a town in southern Tuscany, Italy, used to designate the red wine made there.

1673 [see *Montefiascone]. **1702** Lady Verney *Let.* 25 Aug. in M. M. Verney *Verney Lett.* (1930) I. vii. 114 Mr. Cheret..has sent you a hamper of Montepunchana [*sic*]... A dozen bottles. **1817** T. Jefferson *Let.* in A. Lichine *Encycl. Wines* (1967) i. 5 There is still another wine to be named to you, which is the wine of Florence called Montepulciano. **1958** A. L. Simon *Dict. Wines* 112 *Montepulciano*, one of the better red table wines of Tuscany. **1966** C. Ray *Wines of Italy* xiv. 135 *Marsicano*..lighter in colour and in alcohol than Montepulciano and fresh to the taste when drunk young.

‖ **montera** (mǫntēᵊ·ra). [Sp.: see Montero.] The black hat worn by a bullfighter.

1838 *Quarterly Rev.* LXII. 416 He [*sc.* the matador] then throws his cap, 'montera', on the ground with peculiar action. **1932** E. Hemingway *Death in Afternoon* vi. 62 As the matadors come in front of the president's box they bow low and remove their black hats or monteras. **1967** McCormick & Mascareñas *Compl. Aficionado* iv. 130 With a single traje de luces costing the equivalent of $225, a good montera costing $30, and all the other equipment in that ratio, to launch a novillero requires capital such as Ayala does not have. **1969** A. Arent *Laying on of Hands* (1971) xi. 125 He yanked off the sombrero and replaced it with the *montera*, the black bullfighter's hat.

Monterey. **Monterey cypress** = *macrocarpa (earlier and later examples); **Monterey pine** = *insignis (earlier and later examples).

1873 J. Lester *Atlantic to Pacific* 92 Beneath the shade of a Monterey Cypress, is the sarcophagus which holds the cherished dust of Starr King. **1969** T. H. Everett *Living Trees of World* 35/2 The Monterey cypress.., restricted to a very small area on the coast of central California,.. sometimes is as much as 90 feet tall. **1874** J. S. Hittell *Resources of Calif.* (ed. 6) xi. 358 The Monterey pine (*Pinus insignis*) is extensively cultivated as an ornamental tree. **1935** *Discovery* Mar. 82/1 The Monterey Pine (*Pinus radiata*) is the tree that has proved most successful in Australia as a forestry product. **1957** [see *insignis]. **1971** *Countryman* LXXVI. iv. 184 The collared dove has.. one stronghold in the Monterey pines on the west side of Porthcressa. **1974** Hawkey & Bingham *Wild Card* xxi. 168 A patio overlooked a large garden planted with mature Monterey pines.

Montessori (mǫntĕsǭᵊ·ri). The name of the Italian physician and educationalist, Dr. Maria *Montessori* (1870–1952), used to designate her educational system or ideas for the individual development of young children through free but guided play with apparatus designed specially to encourage sense perception and mental interest; also *ellipt.* Hence **Montesso·rian** *a.* and *sb.*, **Montesso·rianism.**

1912 A. E. George tr. M. Montessori (*title*) The Montessori method. **1917** A. S. Neill *Dominie Dismissed* vii.

96 'But I thought that was your line..Montessori and all that kind of thing!' 'I don't know what Montessorianism is,' I said; 'I have forgotten everything I ever read about Froebel and Pestalozzi.' **1929** J. van Druten *After All* III. ii. 114 Even if you do succeed in turning our kids' home into a sort of..Montessori school of confidence. **1934** Webster Montessorian, adj. & n. **1949** G. B. Shaw *Let.* in *To Young Actress* (1960) 188 Montessori is all right while the children are under six, but no use afterwards. **1958** *Times Lit. Suppl.* 31 Jan. 59/4 From the first three of these it is possible to distil the essence of the Montessorian doctrine. **1958** *Times* 20 Mar. 13/4 The question is why all teachers are not Montessorians. *Ibid.*, Montessorianism is sometimes presented more like a religious cult than an educational method. **1972** 'E. Lathen' *The Longer the Thread* viii. 81, I was thinking of something much more ambitious—with preschool training, possibly Montessori teachers.

Monteverdian (mǫntɪ̆vɜ·ɹdiăn), *a.* [See -an.] Of, pertaining to, or resembling the Italian composer Claudio *Monteverdi* (1567–1643) or his music.

1947 M. F. Bukofzer *Music in Baroque Era* (1948) iii. 98 Schein adopted here the airy dialogue of the Monteverdian continuo canzonetta. **1952** K. Dale tr. *Redlich's Claudio Monteverdi* iv. 160 The realization of the Monteverdian Basso Continuo has at all times been a rock upon which many editors have foundered. **1959** *Times* 20 Mar. 16/2 The Monteverdian recitative should be compulsory training for all second-year operatic students. **1963** D. Arnold *Monteverdi* vii. 138 Whereas no one could find anything Monteverdian in the 'Gombert Mass', the vespers bear the imprint of his style.

Montezuma's revenge (mǫntɪ̆zū·măz rɪ̆ve·ndʒ). *slang.* [f. the name of *Montezuma* II (1466–1520), Aztec ruler at the time of the Spanish conquest of Mexico + Revenge *sb.*] Diarrhœa suffered by visitors to Mexico.

1962 *Western Folklore* XXI. 28 The North American in Mexico has coined a number of names for the inevitable dysentery and diarrhea: 'Mexican two-step', 'Mexican fox-trot', 'Mexican toothache', and, less directly if more colorfully, 'Montezuma's revenge', the 'Curse of Montezuma' and the 'Aztec hop'. **1969** *Daily Tel.* 11 Apr. 28/5 Prevent gippy tummy. Also known as Delhi belly, Rangoon runs, Tokyo trots, Montezuma revenge. **1970** *New Scientist* 8 Jan. 47/1 An intestinal attack known as gyppy tummy..in the Middle East;..Montezuma's revenge in Mexico. **1970** *Times* 8 May 9/3 England's World Cup football squad suffered their first casualty in Mexico on Wednesday, when 20-year-old Brian Kidd was struck down by what is known as 'Montezuma's Revenge'—a stomach complaint.

montgomeryite (mǫntgǫ·məriˌəit). *Min.* [f. the name of Arthur *Montgomery* (b. 1909), U.S. geologist + -ite[1].] A hydrated basic phosphate of calcium and aluminium, $Ca_4Al_5(PO_4)_6(OH)_5.11H_2O$, which is found as green monoclinic crystals at Fairfield, Utah, U.S.A.

1940 E. S. Larsen in *Amer. Mineralogist* XXV. 321 The name montgomeryite is proposed for this mineral after Mr. Arthur Montgomery of New York City, who.. collected the material. **1964** *Ibid.* XLIX. 1119 This apparently represents the first reported occurrence of montgomeryite from a pegmatite.

month[1]. Add: **6. a.** *month-brother, -end; month-old* adj.; **month clock**, a clock which goes for a month between windings.

a **1889** G. M. Hopkins *Poems* (1967) 37 A sister, born for each strong month-brother. **1799** *Times* 1 June 4/4 Turkey carpets, a month clock, a quantity of old china. **1884** F. J. Britten *Watch & Clockmaker's Handbk.* 268 Month Clocks have an intermediate wheel and pinion between the great and centre wheels. **1962** E. Bruton *Dict. Clocks & Watches* plate 7 (*caption*) French month clock with skeleton frame. **1929** *Times* 30 Oct. 14/2 The corporations would..withdraw funds from the call money market to meet their month-end requirements. **1909** R. Brooke *Let.* Jan. (1968) 155 On Thursday..I go..to our filthy academy in the Fens..(by a month-old engagement) with a pack of women. **1940** W. Faulkner *Hamlet* iv. 292 The month-old corn-silk beard which concealed most of his abraded face. **1960** *Farmer & Stockbreeder* 1 Mar. 150/3 Day-old pullets..chicks as hatched..month-old pullets.

monthly, *a.* and *sb.* Add: **A.** *adj.* **4. monthly boat, ship,** a ship on a long voyage on which the crew is paid by the month; **monthly nurse** (earlier examples); **monthly rose** (earlier and later examples).

1898 *Nautical Mag.* Dec. 827 She passed the ship *Libertas*, evidently a good monthly boat, jogging along the same way under close-reef topsails. **1798** E. Wynne *Diary* 9 Mar. (1952) 294 These ladies say I shall very soon be brought to bed. I am exceedingly well, had the monthly nurse in the house. **1840** Dickens *Sk. Young Couples* 21 If one of a friend's children die, the formal couple are.. punctual in sending to the house..if a friend's family be increased the monthly nurse is not more attentive than they. **1664** Evelyn *Kalendarium Hortense* in *Sylva* 75 September... Flowers in Prime, or yet lasting... Muske Rose, and Monethly Rose. **1955** G. S. Thomas *Old Shrub Roses* ix. 60 There was one ancient Rose which under favourable conditions of high culture and special pruning often produced a second crop of flowers in the autumn. This Rose was known in England as the Monthly Rose. **1893** E. I. Barra *Tale Two Oceans* 20 She was what the sailors called a good old monthly ship. **1903** H. Holmes *Life & Adventures on Oceans* 34 'I like a good monthly ship,' remarks a seaman standing by. 'In these racehorses a fellow's dead horse is hardly worked out before you think of getting into port again.'

B. *sb.* **1.** Now *colloq.* (Further examples.)

1922 Joyce *Ulysses* 361 That squinty one is delicate. Near her monthlies, I expect, makes them feel ticklish. **1960** C. MacInnes *Mr. Love & Justice* 30 'Don't go,' she said. 'I'm sorry—I'm wrought up. I always am a bit just after my monthlies.' **1963** *Observer* 29 Sept. 31/5 One mother..said she had told him most of them [*sc.* the facts of life]—'even about girls and the monthlies'.

2. (Earlier and later examples.)

1833 *Knickerbocker* I. 185 We have articles on Political Economy in the monthlys, the weeklys, and the dailys. **1849** C. Brontë *Let.* 15 Nov. in C. Shorter *Brontës: Life & Lett.* (1908) II. 83, I feel that the fiat for which I wait does not depend on newspapers... The monthlies and quarterlies will pronounce it. **1973** *Nation Rev.* (Melbourne) 31 Aug. 1464/1 The emphasis in the early days of the new monthlies and quarterlies was on strong opinion.

Montian (mǫ·ntiăn), *a. Geol.* [ad. F. *montien* (G. J. G. Dewalque *Prodrome d'une Descr. géol. de la Belg.* (1868) x. 185), f. *Mons* (L. *mons, mont-* mountain), name of a town in SW. Belgium: see -ian.] Of, pertaining to, or designating a stage of the Palæocene series that lies above the Danian (and like it is not represented in Britain) and below the Landenian. Also *absol.*

[**1882** A. Geikie *Text-bk. Geol.* 848 The most ancient Tertiary deposit of the west of Europe appears to be the limestone of Mons (Système Montien).] **1896** J. W. Judd *Student's Lyell* xv. 220 Paleocene Beds ('Montian').—In the coarse limestone of Mons in Belgium and in the Marls of Meudon in the Paris basin we have strata which are perhaps older than any in the British Islands. **1914** J. Park *Textbk. Geol.* xxx. 416 The concretionary limestone of the upper division, representing the Montian sub-stage of the Cretaceous system, has yielded..the very characteristic Danian cephalopod, *Nautilus danicus*. **1921** *Geol. Mag.* LVIII. 146 The Montian (Calcaire pisolitique) is now only found in a few isolated patches and seems to have been deposited in certain areas rather than over the whole Paris region. **1955** G. G. Woodford tr. *Gignoux's Stratigr. Geol.* ix. 473 Far from being localized in narrow grooves, the Montian sea was widespread in a large gulf bounded on the north by the Pays de Bray and Chateau-Thierry and in the south reaching Mantes..and Vertus. **1960** [see *Danian *a.*]. **1969** Bennison & Wright *Geol. Hist. Brit. Isles* xv. 336 The earliest Tertiary beds found on the continent of Europe, the Danian and Montian which together form the Palaeocene (though some authors consider the Danian late Cretaceous), were never deposited in the British area.

Montilla (mǫnti·lyă). [Name of a town in Southern Spain.] A dry sherry-type wine made in the vicinity of Montilla.

1793 D. McBride *Gen. Instructions for Choice of Wines* i. 29 Montilla is a light white wine, the chief beverage at Seville. [**1846** R. Ford *Gatherings from Spain* xiv. 155 The name of amontillado..has been given to it from its resemblance in dryness and quality to the wines of Montilla, near Cordova.] **1851** C. Redding *Hist. Mod. Wines* (ed. 3) xii. 208 At Montilla, near Cordova, they have a very fine-flavoured dry wine, called Montilla, which is generally consumed in that place. **1876** H. Vizetelly *Facts about Sherry* viii. 86 With these wines we tasted some choice Montilla of a fabulous age. **1935** Schoonmaker & Marvel *Complete Wine Bk.* iv. 96 Montilla..is, in every way, an admirable wine. **1961** *Spectator* 21 Apr. 582 Montilla is fairly rare in this country..and is not, in the very strictest sense of the word, really a 'sherry' at all for it doesn't come from the delimited area around Jerez, but from near Cordoba. **1967** A. Lichine *Encycl. Wines* 358/1 In Spain, Montillas are usually sold from the barrel and in their first year.

montmorillonite. Add: Also, any of the montmorillonoids, or these minerals collectively (see quots. 1954, 1966[2]). (Earlier and later examples.)

1854, 1934 [see *delanovite]. **1935** *Amer. Mineralogist* XX. 482 Montmorillonite, beidellite, and nontronite form an isomorphous completely miscible series. **1949** P. C. Carman *Chem. Constitution & Properties Engin. Materials* xiii. 383 The main constituent is a mineral of the montmorillonite group, either montmorillonite or beidellite. **1954** H. Williams et al. *Petrogr.* xvii. 327 By substitution of magnesium or iron for aluminum, especially in montmorillonite, the composition of clay minerals may vary considerably from the formulas given. Beidellite, for example, is essentially a magnesian montmorillonite, and nontronite is one rich in iron. **1962** *Amer. Mineralogist* XLVII. 145 Beidellites and montmorillonites should be divided at the composition at which the lattice charges from octahedral and tetrahedral substitution equal one another. *Ibid.*, The term beidellite should be used for the aluminium-rich members of the montmorillonite–beidellite series of minerals. **1966** *McGraw-Hill Encycl. Sci. & Technol.* VIII. 587/2 Montmorillonite clays have wide commercial use. The high colloidal, plastic, and binding properties make them especially in demand for bonding molding sands and for oil-well drilling muds. They are also widely used to decolorize oils and as a source of petroleum cracking catalysts. **1966** W. A. Deer et al. *Introd. Rock-Forming Min.* III. 264 The name montmorillonite..was originally applied to a clay mineral with composition similar to that of pyrophyllite except for the presence of excess water, $Al_4Si_8O_{20}(OH)_4.nH_2O$. Chemical variation of this basic formula yields a group of clay minerals which are related by a common structure and by similarity of chemical and physical properties, and are therefore classed as the 'montmorillonite group'. According to present usage one member of this group is itself called montmorillonite and has the formula $(Na)_{0.7}(Al_{3.3}Mg_{0.7})Si_8O_{20}(OH)_4.nH_2O$. An alternative term once used for this type of clay is 'smectite', and this has now been revived to describe the group as a whole (Mackenzie, 1957a), which contains the following principal members: montmorillonite, beidellite, nontronite, saponite, hectorite and sauconite. **1971** *Nature* 15 Jan. 157/2 Montmorillonite, a silicate mineral with typical expanding layers, consists of mica-like sheets that are normally separated by one or two layers of water molecules.

b. *attrib.* **montmorillonite group,** the group of clay minerals (of which montmorillonite is the type) otherwise known as montmorillonoids.

1938 *Mineral. Mag.* XXV. 153 The montmorillonite group is shown to have three end-members, montmorillonite, $Al_2Si_4O_{11}$, nontronite, $Fe_2Si_4O_{11}$, magnesium-beidellite, $Mg_3Si_4O_{11}$. **1946** *Amer. Mineralogist* XXXI. 423 The minerals of the montmorillonite group are characterized by a very wide range in the ions which can proxy Si or Al within the crystal lattice. **1949**, etc. [see above].

montmorillonitic (mǫːntmorilǫ̆ni·tik), *a. Min.* [f. prec. + -ic.] Resembling or containing montmorillonite.

1943 *Proc. Soil Sci. Soc. Amer.* VII. 134 (*heading*) The adsorption of phosphate by kaolinitic, and montmorillonitic clays. **1958** *Nature* 6 Dec. 1596/1 The montmorillonitic nature of this mineral. **1970** *New Scientist* 15 Jan. 98/1 In Mexico..the remarkable natural montmorillonitic clay itself provides the mud.

montmorillonoid (mǫntmori·lǫ̆noid). *Min.* [f. as prec. + -oid.] Any of a group of clay minerals that comprises montmorillonite together with some chemically related minerals that likewise undergo a reversible expansion on absorbing water and have a characteristic structure in which water molecules are situated between sheets composed of two layers of silicon atoms sandwiching one nominally of aluminium, the differences between the minerals consisting in the extent and nature of the replacement of silicon and aluminium by other elements. Also *attrib.* or as *adj.*

1951 *Clay Minerals Bull.* I. 195 To avoid this confusion and also the lengthy term 'minerals of the montmorillonoid group'..the term 'montmorillonoid' was suggested [by D. M. C. MacEwan] for this group of minerals. **1951** D. M. C. MacEwan in G. W. Brindley *X-Ray Identification & Crystal Struct. Clay Minerals* iv. 86 (*heading*) The montmorillonite minerals (montmorillonoids). **1953** *Jrnl. Soil Sci.* IV. 233 It is fairly simple to detect by X-ray diffraction the presence of montmorillonoids in clays using glycerol..or ethylene glycol. **1955** *Trans. Faraday Soc.* LI. 582 Considerable attention has been paid in recent years to the retention of organic molecules by clays of the montmorillonoid group. **1959** *Clay Minerals Bull.* IV. 67 The name montmorillonoid is understood as covering a continuous isomorphous series extending from montmorillonite, with ideal formula $Al_2Si_4O_{10}(OH)_2$, to beidellite, with ideal formula $(R_1H_3O)Al_2(Si_3Al)O_{10}(OH)_2$. **1966** *Canad. Jrnl. Soil Sci.* XLVI. 235 Montmorillonoid minerals are sometimes more abundant in the lower horizons of soils in which other clay minerals are more uniformly distributed. **1971** *Clay Minerals* IX. 107 Results of..analyses confirm the general montmorillonoid character of the mineral.

Montpellier (moṅpęlye). The name of a town in the department of Hérault in Southern France used *attrib.*, as **Montpellier butter,** a sauce made from butter coloured green and flavoured with herbs and anchovies; **Montpellier green** = *verdigris green* [Verdigris 2]; **Montpellier yellow** = **Cassel yellow* [*Cassel], also called *mineral yellow* [Mineral *a.* 5 b].

1889 Montpellier butter [see *green butter* (*green *a.* 12)]. **1960** E. David *French Provincial Cooking* 117 Montpellier butter is usually served with salmon and the chef's way of doing it is to have a fine piece of middle cut of cold salmon with the skin removed, and the fish thickly spread with the green butter. **1930** Maerz & Paul *Dict. Color* 185/2 An old synonym for Verdigris is 'Montpellier Green', from the name of the French city, which was a center for the color trade in the Middle Ages and during the Renaissance. **1969** R. Mayer *Dict. Art Terms & Techniques* 420/1 Other names for verdigris are Montpellier green, viride aeris..and vederame. **1835** G. Field *Chromatogr.* ix. 77 Patent Yellow, Turner's Yellow, or Montpellier Yellow..has an excellent body, and works well in oil and water, but is soon injured both by the sun's light and impure air. **1969** R. Mayer *Dict. Art Terms & Techniques* 406/2 Turner's yellow... Among its many names are..Montpellier yellow, [etc.].

Montrachet (moṅtraʃe, moṅraʃe). Name of a wine-growing district of the Côte d'Or, France, used to designate the white wine produced there.

1833 C. Redding *Hist. Mod. Wines* v. 99 The situation to the south-west of Meursault, where it joins Puligny, is noted for the delicious white wine called Mont-Rachet, of exquisite perfume, and deemed the most perfect white wine of Burgundy, and even of France. **1839** Ure *Dict. Arts* 1300 The insulated part towards the top furnishes the wine called *Chevalier Montrachet*, which is less esteemed..than the delicious wine grown on the middle

height, called *true Montrachet*. Beneath this district, and in the surrounding plains, the vines afford a far inferior article, called *bastard Montrachet*. **1841** *Fraser's Mag.* June 533 A bottle of Montrachet, similarly poured out to us, was very fair. **1875** H. Vizetelly *Wines of World* II. 24 The distinguishing characteristics of Montrachet are *finesse*, fulness, absolute homogeneity, and softness, combined with a powerful yet delicate flavour and immense richness. **1903** A. Conan Doyle *Adventures Gerard* vi. 218 But there are times when Montrachet is better than the wine of Bordeaux. **1938** W. S. Maugham *Summing Up* 310 A dozen oysters and a pint of Montrachet. **1965** O. A. Mendelsohn *Dict. Drink* 228 Dumas has said that Le Montrachet should be drunk bare-headed, on one's knees.

Montrealer (mǫntrĭǭ·ləɹ). [f. *Montreal* + -er[1].] A native or inhabitant of the city of Montreal in Canada.

1888 [see Seigneur]. **1909** *Westm. Gaz.* 1 Apr. 9/3 Dr. Macnamara..is always claimed as a Montrealer, because he was born in this city while his father..was quartered here. **1963** *Guardian* 13 Mar. 13/5 Most Montrealers find London in winter..marrow-freezing. **1967** *Times* 28 Feb. (Canada Suppl.) 31 Two out of three Montrealers speak French.

montroydite (mǫntroi·dəit). *Min.* [f. the name of *Montroyd* Sharpe (see quot. 1903) + -ite[1].] Mercuric oxide, HgO, which is found as deep red orthorhombic crystals.

1903 A. J. Moses in *Amer. Jrnl. Sci.* XVI. 262 The name Montroydite is suggested in honor of Mr. Montroyd Sharpe, one of the owners of the mines at Terlingua [in Brewster County, Texas]. **1932** *Amer. Mineralogist* XVII. 541 The mineral [*sc.* mosesite] was found in association with eglestonite, terlinguaite, montroydite and kleinite in the quicksilver mining district [of Texas]. **1958** *Prof. Papers U.S. Geol. Survey* No. 312. 71/1 Montroydite occurs as hairs and growths and as needlelike crystals along the cleavage planes of calcite. **1968** I. Kostov *Mineralogy* II. iv. 257 Montroydite is also red but has very strong birefringence.

montuno (mǫntū·no). [Amer.-Sp. *montuno* native to mountains, wild, rustic, untamed.] An improvised passage in a rumba.

1951 *Sat. Rev. Lit.* 24 Nov. 75 His modernisms grow logically from an amalgam of influences that includes Tatum, Wilson, Hines, Gillespie, and the Cuban *montuno* masters. **1956** M. Stearns *Story of Jazz* (1957) xix. 248 The *montuno*, or *ad lib* passage,..is often based on just one, or sometimes two, chords. **1957** J. Kerouac *On Road* (1958) iv. v. 287 The piano montunos showered down on us from the speaker. **1958** E. Borneman in P. Gammond *Decca Bk. Jazz* xxi. 270 Whereas the themes of the sones were usually lilting tunes of obviously Spanish descent, the montunos were unmistakably African.

monty (mǫ·nti). *Austral.* and *N.Z. colloq.* Also **monte.** [Prob. the same word as Monte[1].] A certainty: used esp. of a horse considered certain to win a race.

1894 H. Lawson *Martin Farrell* in *Coll. Verse* (1967) I. 269 Chaps, I've got a vote for Hughie—but it ain't no monte yet. **1901** *Bulletin Reciter* (Sydney) 182 It's the biggest bloomin' monte Dat 'as ever come our way. **1908** E. S. Sorenson *Squatter's Ward* xii. 122 It's a monty the little squib would let out a yell jest as I was gettin' clear. **1910** O'Brien & Stephens *Material for Dict. Austral. Slang 1900–10* (typescript), *Monte*, a take-down game of cards—a sure thing. **1930** K. S. Prichard *Haxby's Circus* iii. 41 She's the chance of a life-time... The biggest bloomin' monty ever started on a racecourse. **1933** *Bulletin* (Sydney) 29 Nov. 10/1 'And they'll take, it's a monty, an ell,' said Pat, 'if we give them an inch.' **1946** *Coast to Coast 1945* 27 He's a monty! We always were lucky. **1947** D. M. Davin *For Rest of our Lives* 297 From Christchurch this chap Sloan, for a monty, with that particular brand of New Zealand English. **1970** *N.Z. Listener* 12 Oct. 12/1 Old Jerry wouldn't think of looking for me over this way. That's for a monty. To keep going's the right thing.

monument, *sb.* Add: **4. c.** Applied, like mod.F. *monument*, to outstanding survivals of an early literature.

1852 E. A. Andrews *Copious Latin-Eng. Lex.* App. A. 1653 (*title*) Specimens of the oldest monuments of the Latin language. **1897** W. P. Ker *Epic & Romance* ii. 183 *Beowulf* is, at any rate, the specimen by which the Teutonic epic poetry must be judged. It is the largest monument extant. **1949** G. K. Anderson *Lit. Anglo-Saxons* iii. 63 Unquestionably the most important monument of Old English epic literature..is the poem *Beowulf*.

7. Monument City = *Monumental City.

1856 *Life Illustrated* 31 May 33/4 Baltimore is the 'Monument City', from the great battle monument, and several others of note, within its limits. **1906** *Springfield* (Mass.) *Weekly Republ.* 8 Mar. 4 Baltimore has been known for years as the 'Monument City', and some of these monuments are in reality works of art.

Monumental City. *U.S.* The city of Baltimore, Md. Cf. *Monument City* above.

1827 *National Gaz.* (Philadelphia) 20 Nov. 213 The brave sons of Cincinnatus at the festal board in the 'monumental city'. **1853** F. W. Thomas *John Randolph* 178 In 'the monumental city' I read law. **1882** *Harper's Mag.* June 20/2 No women..equal the fair daughters of the Monumental City. **1904** *Baltimore American* 5 Dec. 14 Detectives..of the Baltimore force, have been working there during the past week, and it is probable that they will return to the Monumental City today. **1949** *Business Week* 24 Sept. 101 'The Monumental City' is the nation's second largest seaport.

monumentalism (mǫniume·ntăliz'm). [f. Monumental *a.* + -ism.] A monumental style; building on a grand scale.

1902 *Encycl. Brit.* XXVIII. 451/2 The plain lessons of the Crimean War were unheeded, and monumentalism became the ideal of coast defences. **1970** H. Braun *Parish Churches* xiv. 174 A tower..supplies its church with the element of monumentalism, the dimension of which is height.

monumentality. (Earlier and later examples.)

1888 G. B. Shaw *Let.* 9 Feb. (1965) 184 If I had..physical monumentality, I should bring London up to the mark. **1934** J. J. Sweeney *Plastic Redirections in 20th Cent. Painting* 60 A genuinely new 'archaism'—an extreme simplicity and monumentality of form, with no necessary naturalistic association. **1937** *Archit. Rev.* LXXXII. 49/1 The proposed King George V Memorial in Old Palace Yard..epitomizes all that is implied by the hideous word 'Monumental'. And the chosen site admits of very little monumentality. **1963** *Times Lit. Suppl.* 4 Jan. 2/3 The sculptor Ivan Schadr..who among many other monumentalities has been responsible for the large moveable pink rose. **1969** R. Banham in Jencks & Baird *Meaning in Archit.* 108 According to Baird, the Thinkbelt's avoidance of showy monumentality..will lead to practically every fashionable evil in the book. **1974** *Impressionism* (R. Acad.) 37/1 The strong contrasts between simple planes of colour, and the vigorous forms of tree and house, give the painting a great monumentality.

monumentally, *adv.* Add: **3.** (Further example.)

1955 *Sci. Amer.* Oct. 118/2 The authors deserve admiration for their persistence and energy in carrying out a monumentally tedious series of experiments.

b. In a monumental way (cf. Monumental *a.* 4).

1918 E. Pound *Let.* c Apr. (1971) 134 Frazer has of course done the whole job monumentally, but good god how slowly, in how many volumes.

‖ **mon vieux** (moṅ vyö̆). [Fr.] An affectionate form of address: old friend, old man.

1913 Baroness Orczy *Eldorado* i. vii. 55 If you are not satisfied, *mon vieux*..you can send in your resignation when you like. **1917** F. M. Ford *Let.* 5 Jan. (1965) 83 Well, God bless you, mon vieux! **1919** C. Mackenzie *Sylvia & Michael* i. 12 It has been a thoroughly third-class adventure, *mon vieux*. **1924** E. Hemingway *In our Time* i. 9 I'm drunk, I tell you, mon vieux. **1959** L. Durrell in *Spirit of Place* (1969) 360 Wait till you see the menu—it is pure trigonometry, *mon vieux*.

monzonite. Add: **2.** *Petrogr.* [a. F. *monzonite* (de Lapparent 1864, in *Ann. des Mines* VI. 259).] A granular igneous rock with a composition intermediate between syenite and diorite, *spec.* one containing approximately equal amounts of orthoclase and plagioclase.

1895 A. Harker *Petrol.* iii. 44 A special type of augite-syenite is presented by the Triassic intrusions of Monzoni in the southern Tirol (monzonite of authors). **1925** *Jrnl. Geol.* XXXIII. 506 The term 'monzonite' properly will apply only to the rocks with a mixture of andesine and orthoclase. **1956** E. W. Heinrich *Microscopic Petrogr.* iii. 53 Monzonites occur as stocks, laccoliths, dikes, sills, and small plutons. **1974** *Encycl. Brit. Macropædia* IX. 222/2 In general appearance and in field relations monzonites resemble granitic rocks; they differ from granites by reason of their lower quartz content.

Hence **monzoni·tic** *a.*, (composed) of monzonite or monzonites.

1932 F. F. Grout *Petrogr. & Petrol.* 85 The plagioclase of monzonites crystallized before orthoclase, and the resulting mixture of euhedral and anhedral crystals is the typical 'monzonitic' texture. **1936** A. Johannsen *Descr. Petrogr. Igneous Rocks* III. 96 The relations between the orthoclase rocks, the plagioclase rocks, and the monzonitic series. **1974** W. C. Luth in H. Sørensen *Alkaline Rocks* vii. 514/1 The greatest effects, in terms of producing alkaline magmas would be expected of dioritic, monzonitic and andesitic magmas.

moo (mū), *sb.*[2] Shortened f. *moola.

1945 F. Fay *How to be Poor* i. 3 In the vernacular of those in the know, you have the 'moola' (sometimes abbreviated 'moo', meaning 'money'). *Ibid.* xi. 45 What Are We Gonna Do, To Get Rid of All Our 'Moo'? Catchy, isn't it?.. Later on I shall give and teach you—for free—..the lyrics and music for this our battle cry of freedom, using my well-known 'Dum-De-De-Um-Dum' method. After you have mastered 'What Are We Gonna Do, To Get Rid of All Our "Moo"?', I shall expect to hear you full-throatedly singing this chant of Truth from the housetops. **1949** W. R. Burnett *Asphalt Jungle* (1950) vii. 56 After all, as far as she knew, he was still loaded with what the boys vulgarly referred to as moo! **1975** D. Bloodworth *Clients of Omega* ix. 84 Most of my nurses..don't work for moo... But local stuff I pay.

mooch, *sb.* Add: **3.** *slang.* = *moocher 4.

1914 Jackson & Hellyer *Vocab. Criminal Slang* 60 *Mooch*,..current amongst beggars. A mendicant, an alms solicitor. **1953** W. Burroughs *Junkie* (1972) xiv. 146 Cash was a junk mooch on wheels. He made it difficult to refuse.

mooch, *v.* Add: **5.** (Examples.)

1857 'Ducange Anglicus' *Vulgar Tongue* 13 *Mouch, v.*, to go about sponging on your friends. **1975** D. Ramsay *Descent into Dark* ii. 69, I mooch these days because I've given it [*sc.* smoking] up.

6. *trans.* To beg, cadge, scrounge.

1899 'J. Flynt' *Tramping with Tramps* iv. 395 *Mooch*, to beg. **1914** *Sat. Even. Post* 4 Apr. 10/2 And State Street, Chicago, 60. He sure mooched that stem. No nickels. Dimes, buddie.. He can beg coin. **1931** 'D. Stiff' *Milk & Honey Route* iii. 33 Loan your safety razor to a bum and he will mooch you for half your blades. **1933** 'G. Orwell' *Down & Out* xxxiv. 254 Every night I mooched tanners for my kip off of the students. **1953** W. Burroughs *Junkie* (1972) xiv. 147 He would mooch junk off Old Ike, who couldn't turn down anyone sick. **1954** G. Kersh in D. Knight *100 Yrs. Sci. Fiction* (1969) 228, I came across a student, mooching drinks, an educated man with no place to sleep. **1972** D. Morrell *First Blood* i. iii. 17 First thing I know, a bunch of your friends will show up, mooching food, maybe stealing, maybe pushing drugs.

moocha (mū·tʃă). Also **moochi(e), muchi, mutsha, mutshi, umutsha.** [Bantu.] A short skirt worn as a loin-cloth by the aboriginal inhabitants of eastern South Africa before the introduction of European dress.

1878 H. A. Roche *On Trek in Transvaal* xv. 325 A wee little Kafir boy with nothing upon him but his 'moochie', or tails, drives by a herd of calves. **1885** R. Haggard *King Solomon's Mines* x. 153 He slipped off the 'moocha' or girdle round his middle, and stood naked before us. **1898** *Chambers's Jrnl.* 8 Jan. 95/2 His only dress consisted of a monkey skin *muchi*, or apron, and in his hand he carried a rifle. **1909** N. Paul *Child in Midst* 139 Presently he appeared, a tall thin native, with no clothing except a cow-hide mutshi, with flaps around his waist. **1923** *Chambers's Jrnl.* Apr. 222/1 The native kilt or *moocha* composed of strips of raw hide. **1936** *Blackw. Mag.* Mar. 304/1 All the bravery of the Zulu war-dress was there:.. the leopard-skin karosses, the embroidered *moochas*, the white goat-hide garters. **1936** Williams & May *I am Black* xviii. 181 There came before his eyes a boy of fourteen years wearing only a *moochi* of cowhide polished with pig's fat. **1948** O. Walker *Kaffirs are Lively* 30 The menfolk stride along bare-thighed, in swinging *umutshas* of monkey-tails. **1967** E. M. Slatter *My Leaves are Green* i He wore only his 'mutsha' of monkey-skin tails. **1970** *Rand Daily Mail* 29 Oct. 12 (*caption*) Beaded 'muchi'.

moocher. Add: **4.** *slang.* A beggar, a cadger; one who begs or scrounges. Cf. *mooch *sb.* 3, *v.* 6.

1857 'Ducange Anglicus' *Vulgar Tongue* 13 *Moucher*, beggar. **1899** 'J. Flynt' *Tramping with Tramps* iv. 395 *Moocher*, a beggar. This word is the generic term for tramps in England. **1925** *Amer. Speech* I. 152/1 'Mooch' is a gem of a word, with its expressive agent-noun 'moocher', the name for a person who sponges on another. **1931** 'D. Stiff' *Milk & Honey Route* ix. 96 A moocher may do all the things a panhandler does, only he draws smaller dividends because he lacks the salesman's poise. **1933** 'G. Orwell' *Down & Out* xxxii. 236 Some of the cant words now used in London... A moocher—one who begs outright, without pretence of doing a trade. **1962** K. Orvis *Damned & Destroyed* xi. 75 You moocher, you—don't you respect a lady's natural curiosity? Be nice to me. After all, I'm paying for this party.

moochi(e), varr. *moocha.

moochin (mū·χin). *Anglo-Welsh colloq.* Also **mwchin.** Anglicized form of Welsh *mochyn* pig (cf. Ir. *muc*), applied to a person, esp. a child, as a term of reproach or opprobrium. Cf. Pig *sb.*[1] 5.

1940 Dylan Thomas *Portrait of Artist as Young Dog* 58 He sat down in the road. 'I'm on a sledge,' he said, 'pull me, Patricia, pull me like an Eskimo.' 'Up you get, you moochin, or I'll take you home.' **1945** —— *Let.* 30 July (1966) 280 He said, 'Look, what they did, the moochin.' **1953** —— *Under Milk Wood* (1954) 12 Saw him in the bushes..Playing mwchins..Send him to bed without any supper.

mood, *sb.*[1] Add: **3. e.** *attrib.* and as quasi-*adj.* That is intended to suggest, induce, recall, or depict a particular mood or frame of mind.

1898 G. B. Shaw *Perfect Wagnerite* 124 Beethoven had shown how those inarticulate mood-poems which surge through men who have..no exceptional command of words, can be written down in music as symphonies. **1927** *Observer* 14 Aug. 8 On the last side of 86 is Joseph Speaight's expressive little mood-picture for quartet, 'The Lonely Shepherd'. **1940** A. Oboler *Fourteen Radio Plays* 257 *Mood music*, music as background to plant mood of scene. **1946** R. Hull in A. L. Bacharach *Brit. Music* xviii. 230 First-rate powers of argument are to the fore.. but the variations themselves admit of mood-contrasts which keep the music free from any danger of dry impersonality. **1948** L. Levy *Music for Movies* x. 111 The slicker, more expressive phrase, 'mood music', which has been imported from the United States. **1955** D. Keene *Who was Wilma Lathrop?* ii. 19 'Would you prefer mood music?'.. Wilma stacked the spindle with records. **1957** Manvell & Huntley *Technique Film Music* i. 22 To help them in this task, volumes of classified 'mood' music began to appear as early as 1913, when the Sam Fox Moving Picture Music Volumes by J. S. Zamecnik were published. **1960** *Times* 28 Sept. 15/4 The *Moon of the Caribbees* hardly more than a mood piece. **1962** *Listener* 27 Dec. 1102/2 They seem to me to be mood-poetry in a pejorative sense. **1969** J. Burmeister *Hot & Copper Sky* ii. 39 'What did you sing?'.. 'Oldies, "Body and Soul". "Smoke Gets In Your Eyes". "Blue Moon". Strictly mood.' **1970** *Daily Tel.* 20 May 16/8 It says much for Mr Wesker's delicate mood-piece that it nevertheless made an effect. **1972** H. Kemelman *Monday the Rabbi Took Off* xiv. 99 The organ had been playing mood music, a series of mournful cadenzas in a minor key.

f. *Comb.* mood swing *Psychol.*, an abrupt change of mood without apparent cause which is associated with some forms of mental instability.

1942 *Amer. Jrnl. Orthopsychiatry* IV. 715 Present methods of examining candidates for the air service are good so far as they go since they inquire into the presence of such symptoms as enuresis, somnambulism, mood swings, or phobias. **1943** J. W. Macfarlane in R. Barker et al. *Child Behavior & Devel.* xviii. 316/1 At year five, four clusters were apparent. The first included quarrelsomeness, mood swings, negativism,..and competitiveness. **1965** J. Pollitt *Depression & its Treatment* i. 5 Manic-depressive type... Commoner among those with a family history of mood swings or similar illness. **1970** H. P. Laughlin *Ego & Defenses* xiii. 201 An interesting.. application of the principles of Inversion is encountered in the area of mood and mood swings.

mood, *sb.*² Add: **2. c.** *attrib.*

1928 H. Poutsma *Gram. Late Mod. Eng.* (ed. 2) I. i. 31 Some of these verbs..are also used as modal auxiliaries, i.e. as substitutes for actually existing mood-forms. **1931** M. Callaway *Temporal Subjunctive in Old Eng.* 19 The use of the Subjunctive of Antecedent Action, in dependent clauses introduced by particles meaning 'after'..is to be accounted for..by the nature of the main clause... This theory is substantially identical with that advocated by Oskar Erdmann..and by Ernst Bernhardt.., hereafter referred to by me as the Erdmann–Bernhardt theory of mood-syntax. **1962** F. Behre *Contrib. Eng. Syntax* 59 Certain uses of the indicative that have not earlier been duly considered by writers on mood-syntax. **1965** —— in *English Studies* XLVI. 90 In both the Old English and Middle English examples the mood-form is indeterminate.

mooded (mū·dėd), *a. rare.* [f. Mood *sb.*¹ + -ed².] Formed to convey or reflect different moods.

1868 G. M. Hopkins *Jrnls. & Papers* (1959) 166 Fine, with gracefully mooded clouding.

moodle (mū·d'l), *v.* [Origin unknown.] *intr.* To dawdle aimlessly, to idle time away. Const. *about, on.*

1893 G. B. Shaw *Music in London 1890–94* (1932) 116 The literary man..hardly able to believe that the conductor can be serious in keeping the band moodling on for forty-five mortal minutes before the singers get to business. **1921** —— *Back to Methuselah* v. 223 That old one who saw you out of your shell has gone off to moodle about doing nothing. **1928** —— *Intelligent Woman's Guide Socialism* lxix. 328 Napoleon often moodled about for a week at a time doing nothing but play with his children or read trash or waste his time helplessly.

moody (mū·di), *sb. slang.* [f. the adj.] A persuasive and insidious approach adopted in order to gain confidence; any flattery or lies intended to suggest compliance. Hence, nonsense, twaddle, 'rubbish', esp. in phr. *(a lot of) old moody.* Also as *vb.*, to bluff or deceive by means of flattery, etc.

1934 P. Allingham *Cheapjack* xii. 148 'Moody' meant a bit of humbug. It is a very common word among the grafters. They would say, 'We'd better moody the landlady a bit,' when they meant that they would pay her a few compliments; and when they did not believe something you were saying they woud tell you to 'cut out the moody'. **1958** F. Norman *Bang to Rights* I. 37 'I don't think that you are as bad as you are painted, I would like you if you would to tell me a little about yourself.' This aproch [*sic*] is known as the old moody. **1960** *News Chron.* 16 Feb. 6 You trying to give me the old moody? **1962** R. Cook *Crust on its Uppers* i. 21 Trying to moody through to the royal enclosure on the knock. **1966** A. Prior *Operators* x. 142 Emmie was always giving me a lot of old moody about you having some money stashed. **1970** R. Busby *Frighteners* x. 93 The same old moody he'd heard a thousand times before.

mooey (mū·i), *sb. slang.* Also **moey, mooe.** [f. Romany *mooi* mouth, face; cf. Mow *sb.*²] A mouth; a face.

1859 Hotten *Dict. Slang* 64 Mooe. **1896** Farmer & Henley *Slang* IV. 328/1 Moey. **1955** P. Wildeblood *Against Law* iii. 148 All nylons and high-heeled shoes and paint an inch thick on their mooeys.

Moog (mōᵘg). Also **moog.** [f. the name of R. A. *Moog*, an American engineer, its inventor.] In full, **Moog synthesizer.** An electronic musical instrument (see quots. 1969 and 1971).

The word *Moog* is a registered proprietary term.

1969 *Punch* 5 Feb. 193/3 A moog synthesiser..is an electronic musical instrument capable of generating all kinds of weird sounds. **1970** *Melody Maker* 31 Oct. 9/4 'Switched-On Bach'..gave a lot of people the idea to throw Moog records on the market very quickly. **1971** *Playboy* Feb. 156/2 Says drummer Graeme Edge: 'We've got a Moog synthesizer that gives us complete control of any sound frequency that the human ear can hear, and we plan to use it to make tapes for the Mellotron. We'll use the two combined and the Mellotron will eventually be a playback machine for the Moog.' **1971** *Guardian* 5 Mar. 9/4 A Moog synthesiser.. is a computer that can provide any thing from electronic drum beats against a background of flashing psychedelic lights, to bird song..complete with country scenes. **1971** *Melody Maker* 13 Nov. 39/1 The Moog is basically a collection of electrical modules, some of which you would find in any good recording studio. **1973** *Observer* 21 Jan. 30/3 Jesus Christ Superstar: The music from the show given the full studio treatment (including moog) by an Australian line-up. **1974** *Official Gaz.: Trademarks* (U.S. Patent Office) 5 Feb. TM 21/1 Moog Music Inc., Williamsville, N.Y. Filed Dec. 1, 1972 Moog. For Electronic Musical Instruments..First use Jan. 1, 1954.

mooktee, var. *Mukti.

moola (mū·lă). *slang* (orig. *U.S.*). Also **moolah.** [Origin unknown.] Money.

1939 J. O'Hara *Pal Joey* (1940) 97, I never saw the day wherein no matter how much moola I had I could not use some more. **1944** *Penguin New Writing* 20 111 You don't like it, but you like the moola all right. **1951** *People* (Austral.) 1 Aug. 20/3 She left there, too. 'Not enough moolah.' **1968** Busby & Holtham *Main Line Kill* v. 44 Expensive though. You blokes must spend a lot of moola on that stuff. **1970** *New Yorker* 5 Sept. 40 (*caption*) Gentlemen, nothing stands in the way of a final accord except that management wants profit maximization and the union wants more moola. **1973** J. Wainwright *High-Class Kill* 154 What did he do for a living?.. Where did the moolah come from? **1975** J. Symons *Three Pipe Problem* xiv. 113 Then the only thing to be settled is the lolly, the moolah.

mooley (mū·li). *U.S.* [Var. of Moiley, Muley *sb.*] A hornless cow; a cow. Also **mooley cow.**

1838 [see Muley *sb.* 1]. **1840** *Picayune* (New Orleans) 10 Sept. 2/6 Brought to the Pound..a red and white mooley cow. **1867** 'T. Lackland' *Homespun* II. 213 They are all so fond of patient 'mooley' too. **1877** *Rep. Vermont Dairymen's Assoc.* VIII. 50 He should hope that his next beef might come from a polled cow or mooley. **1902** A. D. McFaul *Ike Glidden* i. 3, I couldn't help laughing at the sight of your Mooley slinking it for the woods with the cans and milk flying. **1946** 'Brahms' & 'Simon' *Trottie True* iv. 55 'Hortense sounds just like an old mooley cow,' she giggled, blissfully unaware that she herself had sounded exactly like a young foghorn.

moomba (mū·mba). *Austral.* [Aboriginal word.] An annual carnival or pre-Lent festival held in Melbourne.

1963 *Times* 26 Feb. 9/1 A procession of floats to mark the beginning of Melbourne's curious Moomba festival. **1965** *Austral. Encycl.* IV. 55/1 Melbourne followed in March 1954 with a fortnight of carnival that was termed Moomba. **1967** *Australian* 18 Mar. 11/1, I recall the early Moombas very well: parts of them, at least.

Moomin (mū·min). In the children's tales of the Finnish writer Tove Jansson (b. 1914), one of an imaginary race of small, shy, fat, hibernating creatures that live in the forests of Finland. Also *attrib.* and *Comb.* So **Moomin-like** *a.*, resembling or characteristic of a Moomin.

1950 E. Portch tr. *Jansson's Finn Family Moomintroll* i. 14 One spring morning at four o'clock the first cuckoo arrived in the Valley of the Moomins. *Ibid.* 22 Moomintroll..threw his eggshell into the waste-paper basket, for he was (sometimes) a well brought up Moomin. *Ibid.* vii. 162 Now you can all have a wish—the Moomin family first! **1957** M. Allingham in T. Jansson *Moomin* 1 On the Moomins themselves I find myself uncharacteristically reticent. Their appeal is so personal and so intricate that I feel chatter about them is like gossip in public about friends... When Moomin fans discover each other they.. are..likely to sit down trustingly together. **1965** G. Mitchell *Pageant of Murder* iii. 29 Kitty made an unseemly grimace behind the massive, Moomin-like back. **1967** B. W. Alderson tr. *Hürlimann's Three Centuries Children's Bks. in Europe* vi. 81 Nonsense..is perhaps found at its best in the Moomin books of this author. The Moomins..conquered children in a trice. **1971** K. Hart tr. *Jansson's Moominvalley in Nov.* xviii. 136 Let us observe half-a-minute's silence to show our appreciation of the Moomin family.

moon, *sb.* Add: **1. e.** See also Cheese *sb.*¹ 2 a.

3. b. *to be* (or *jump*) *over the moon*: to be very happy or delighted.

[*c* **1765** in *Oxf. Dict. Nursery Rhymes* (1951) 205 High diddle, diddle, The Cat and the Fiddle, The Cow jump'd over the Moon.] **1833** S. Smith *Life & Writings J. Downing* 18, I could have jumped over the moon. **1840** T. C. Haliburton *Clockmaker* 3rd Ser. viii. 109 Ready to jump over the moon for delight. **1936** M. Kennedy *Together & Apart* III. 189 She didn't know she had a brother and she's over the moon. **1944** N. Coward *Middle East Diary* 116 The Captain..is..absolutely over the moon with pleasure at having this command. **1972** J. Brown *Chancer* iv. 53 He goes back there. She's over the moon, of course, and off they go to parties.

c. Add to def.: Esp. in phr. *to ask (cry, wish) for the moon*: to ask or wish for the unattainable.

[**1550** N. Udall *Answer to Commoners of Devonshire & Cornwall* in N. Pocock *Troubles connected with Prayer Bk. of 1549* (1884) 178 They will cry to have a piece of the moon.] **1852, 1860** [in Dict.]. **1928** E. O. Winstedt tr. *Cicero's Lett. to Atticus* II. x. 293 You are asking for the moon. **1930** J. B. Priestley *Angel Pavement* vi. 307 That was not asking much, and yet..he could not help thinking it was really like asking for the moon. **1946** V. S. Pritchett *Living Novel* 44 They are grown up. They do not cry for the moon. **1965** *Listener* 16 Sept. 431/1 To turn on the telly every night for a week and expect to see what you yourself would choose to see is little short of asking for the moon. **1972** *Accountant* 5 Oct. 410/1 To hope for equity or justice in any such scheme is to cry for the moon.

5. b. *slang.* The buttocks. (Used in *sing.* and *pl.*)

1756 *Life & Mem. E. T. Bates* iii. 31 But his Moon shall never be covered by me or Buck..'till they put down the Ready—and no Brummagums. **1922** Joyce *Ulysses* 82 Or their skirt behind, placket unhooked. Glimpses of the moon. **1938** S. Beckett *Murphy* 220 Placing her hands upon her moons, plump and plain.

c. A moon-shaped mark or area; *spec.* a small area of greater translucency observable by transmitted light in some early porcelains such as Chelsea.

1855 *Poultry Chron.* III. 57 Breast. The best spangled and clearest from tipping with white at the end of the moon. **1865** *Chambers's Encycl.* VII. 535/2 An artificial fly..adorned with two moons from a peacock's tail. **1909** *Chambers's Jrnl.* Sept. 586/2 Chelsea [porcelain]..may be distinguished by..greasy-looking discs known as 'moons' in the paste. **1935** *Amer. Speech* X. 159/1 *Moons*, crescent-shaped nicks which agates [*sc.* marbles] receive from hard hits. The belief was that soaking an agate in vinegar would take out the moons. **1948** W. B. Honey *Old Eng. Porc.* (new ed.) ii. 53 The exceptionally beautiful porcelain of the red-anchor period has a very soft paste of fine grain, often showing by transmitted light the round spots of higher translucency known to collectors as 'moons'. **1959** G. Savage *Antique Collector's Handbk.* 79 From 1750 to 1753 a body noted for its 'moons', or patches of greater translucency, was employed.

8. b. *U.S. colloq.* = Moonshine 4; *spec.* whisky.

1928 *Collier's* 29 Dec. 8/2 Wherever you go in Colorado a bootlegger..says to you 'Mister, this is good stuff. It's Leadville "moon".' *Ibid.* 8/3 The art of producing sugar 'moon' and aging it in charred casks. **1950** *Sat. Even. Post* 27 May 20/1, I would buy a couple of pints of moon.

10. b. (Further examples.) Freq. with *pl.* as *moon.*

1928 E. Wallace *Gunner* vi. 50 Gunner's got three moon for bein' a suspected. **1936** J. Curtis *Gilt Kid* iv. 39, I was doing nine moon for screwing. **1953** K. Tennant *Joyful Condemned* xviii. 167, I got a twelve moon.

15. a. *moon-base, -dew, -dust, -folk, -land, -lander, -landing, -landscape, -maid, -mist, -mountain, -pull, -rising, -rock, -setting, -shadow, -sky, -stuff, -track*; **c.** *moon-bathed, -brightened, -chained, -chequered, -crazed, -dappled, -dazzled, -drawn, -drenched, -flecked, -flooded, -haunted, -horned, -locked, -mad, -misted, -parched, -rich, -shadowed, -warmed, -washed* adjs.; **d.** *moon-blue, -cold, -coloured, -cool, -grey, -pale, -white, -yellow* adjs.

1961 *Economist* 18 Nov. 676/2 Commercial services.. between New York and Moonbase Alpha in one day. **1969** *Guardian* 15 July 6/6 One of the things we shall be doing in those early lunar flights is to find a good place for a moon base. **1909** *Daily Chron.* 4 Sept. 7/4 He was looking up at the moon-bathed cliff with a rapt intense look. **1939** Spender & Gili tr. *Lorca's Poems* 51 To the sound of cold tambourines And moon-bathed cithars. **1918** D. H. Lawrence *New Poems* 33 A moon-blue moth goes flittering by. **1922** Joyce *Ulysses* 438 Her moonblue satin slipper. **1911** Moon brightened [see *image crowded* adj. (*Image *sb.* 8)]. **1946** Dylan Thomas *Deaths & Entrances* 63 The moon-chained and water-wound Metropolis of fishes. **1910** W. de la Mare *Three Mulla-Mulgars* vii. 95 The deep shadows of the moon-chequered forest. **1933** —— *Fleeting* 119 The autumnal night Hung starry and radiant.. O'er moon-cold hills. **1944** E. Sitwell *Green Song* 1 Till the fire of that sun The heart and the moon-cold bone are one. **1922** W. de la Mare *Down-adown-Derry* 20 A beaming of moon-coloured light. **1930** R. Lehmann *Note in Music* 98 The grass..foamed with the moon-coloured profusion of the flower which she called milkwort or Star-of-Bethlehem. **1969** G. Macbeth *War Quartet* 29 Staled Of heat, now moon-cool. **1921** W. B. Yeats *Four Plays for Dancers* 72 The moon-crazed heron Would be but fishes' diet soon. **1910** W. de la Mare *Three Mulla-Mulgars* xix. 252 The moon-dappled forest through which they had so heavily ascended. **1940** C. Day Lewis *Poems in Wartime* 10 All over the countryside Moon-dazzled men are peering out for invaders. **1927** Joyce *Simples* in *Pomes Penyeach*, A moondew stars her hanging hair. **1844** Emerson *Essays* 2nd Ser. viii. 243 In countless upward-striving waves The moon-drawn tide-wave strives. **1922** Joyce *Ulysses* 48 A tide westering, moondrawn, in her wake. **1929** C. Mackenzie *Gallipoli Memories* xi. 189 The grillos shrilling far and wide across that moon-drenched island. **1959** *Britannica Bk. of Year* (U.S.) 753/1 *Moon dust*, meteoric particles on the surface of the moon. **1969** *Guardian* 30 July 1/7 The first experiments of exposing germ-free mice to moon dust. **1913** W. de la Mare *Peacock Pie* 98 Those wallowing, moon-flecked waves. **1945** C. Mann in Murdoch & Drake-Brockman *Austral. Short Stories* (1951) 262 Nights... moon-flooded, starlit. **1901** H. G. Wells *First Men in Moon* xviii. 218 We have shown these moon folk violence. **1927** J. Joyce *She weeps over Rahoon* in *Pomes Penyeach*, His sad heart has lain Under the moongrey nettles. **1934** L. B. Lyon *White Hare* 34 The moon-grey barn. **1930** Blunden *Summer's Fancy* 42 Whispering their vows below moon-haunted trees. **1894** O. Wilde *Sphinx*, And did you talk with Thoth, and did you hear the moon-horned Io weep? **1960** T. Hughes *Lupercal* 60 And has shorn Summarily the moon-horned river From my bed. **1922** J. A. Dunn *Man Trap* xv. 207 Death cold the nights in this dead land that looks like moonland. **1970** *Sci. Jrnl.* May 7/1 Neil Armstrong climbing down those few fragile steps of his moonlander's ladder to the craggy lunar surface. **1962** *Daily Tel.* 5 July 26/6 A small Moon-landing capsule. **1969** *Guardian* 16 July 17/4 An American moon landing does not constitute an unchallenged lead over Russia. **1954** Koestler *Invisible Writing* iii. 43 Certain scenes..have the rugged and hostile greatness of a moon-landscape. **1943** C. Day Lewis *Word over All* 42 The earth is buoyed in Moon-locked oblivion. **1869**

W. Barnes *Early England & Saxon-English* 103/2 Moonmad. **1920** Blunden *Waggoner* 31 To hear the moonmad gypsy rave. **1928** —— *Retreat* 14 Or mist-veil brushed thee, fine as yet was wove For moonmaid's clothing. [**1910** W. de la Mare *Three Mulla-Mulgars* i. 4 Mutta-matutta's father died from sleeping in the moonmist. **1913** D. H. Lawrence *Love Poems* 13 The moonmist is over the village. **1936** L. B. Lyon *Bright Feather Fading* 17 Yet parishes moon-misted, Yet Avon, Severn, Humber His name remember. *a* **1821** Keats *Sonnet: To Nile* in *Compl. Poetical Wks.* (1907) 305 Son of the old moon-mountains African! **1927** F. B. Young *Portrait of Clare* 129 An orchard..in which moon-pale apples lay where they had fallen. **1914** C. Mackenzie *Sinister Street* II. iii. vii. 637 Most people..would obtain the finest thrill that Oxford could offer from the sudden sight of..the moon-parched High Street in frost. **1922** D. H. Lawrence *Fantasia of Unconscious* xv. 279 Her [woman's] deep positivity is in the downward flow, the moon-pull. **1925** C. Day Lewis *Beechen Vigil* 30 In a moon-rich garden. **1927** *Observer* 11 Sept. 8 A..short interval between successive moonrisings being favourable for late harvest work. **1969** *Guardian* 15 July 7/2 On July 24, if all goes well, 50 kilogrammes of moonrock will arrive on earth. **1971** *New Scientist* 24 June 766/1 The exchange in Moscow recently of a minute quantity of Apollo moonrock for an even more minute quantity of Luna 16 moonrock. **1905** E. F. Benson *Image in Sand* xviii. 290 The sublimities of the sun-rises and moon-settings were gone from her. **1925** E., O., & S. Sitwell *Poor Young People* 28 The moon-shadows Palely pass and re-pass. **1958** J. Betjeman *Coll. Poems* 270 Near your curious mausoleum Moonshadowed on the grass. **1934** Blunden *Choice or Chance* 55 To silence too that speaks angelic tongues From moon-skies and the sun's November gleam. **1929** E. H. Visiak *Medusa* (1963) xviii. 226 They are too apt already to be taken with such moonstuff. **1969** *New Scientist* 18 Dec. 607/1 We should not go 'up there'.. merely to bring back a few pounds of 'moonstuff'. **1858** Lytton *What will he do with It?* (1859) III. vi. x. 196 They were to his eyes the moon track in the ocean of history. **1899** Kipling *Five Nations* (1903) 9 The moon-track a-quiver bewilders our eyes. **1959** R. Graves *Coll. Poems* 316 A moon-warmed world of discontinuance. **1902** W. D. Howells *Literature & Life* 62 A few moon-washed stars pierce the vast vault with their keen points. **1967** *Coast to Coast 1965–66* 131 Vicky sat staring into the mysterious moon-washed night. **1885** W. B. Yeats *Island of Statues* i. ii, in *Dublin Univ. Rev.* May 82/2 Some say that all who touch the island lone Are changed for ever into moonwhite stone. **1916** Blunden *Harbingers* 5 Through the moonwhite sea. **1957** C. Day Lewis *Pegasus* 12 O moonwhite brow and milky way of flesh! *a* **1963** S. Plath *Crossing Water* (1971) 38 The moth-face of her husband, moonwhite and ill, Circles her like a prey. **1961** R. Graves *More Poems* 29 And in my dreams went chasing here and there A fugitive beacon—your moon-yellow hair.

16. **moon-bounce**, the use of the moon as a reflector of radio waves (chiefly in the UHF band) aimed at it from one ground station and detected by another; **moonbound** *a.* (orig. *U.S.*), directed or moving towards the moon; **moonbug** *colloq.*, a lunar module; **moon buggy** = **moon-car*; **moon-cake**, a round Chinese cake eaten during mid-Autumn festivities; **moon-car**, a vehicle designed for use on the moon; **mooncraft**, a spacecraft for travel to the moon; also = **moon-car*; **moon crawler** = **moon-car*; **moon-down** *N. Amer.*, the time when the moon goes down or sets; **moon-face**, a moon-shaped face; *spec.* a rounded swollen face characteristic of individuals with excessive amounts of glucocorticoids in the body, e.g. in cases of Cushing's syndrome; **moon-flight**, a flight to the moon; **moonglow**, glowing moonlight; **moonmark** (see quots.); **moon-milk** = *Milk of the moon* (see Milk *sb.* 6); **moon-penny** (examples); **moonport** [after *airport], (*a*) a place from which rockets are launched to the moon; (*b*) a landing-place for rockets on the moon; **moon probe** *Astronautics*, an exploratory space flight made towards the moon by an unmanned vehicle; also, the vehicle itself; **moon race**, competition between nations to be the first to effect a landing on the moon; **moon-rocket**, (*a*) a ride at a fun-fair consisting of rocket-shaped cars travelling round an inclined circular track; (*b*) a rocket designed for flight to the moon; **moon-shaft**, a ray of moonlight; **moon-ship**, a spaceship designed to travel to or towards the moon; **moon-shoot** = **moon-shot*; **moon-shot** (orig. *U.S.*), the launching of a spacecraft to or towards the moon; **moon-suit**, a suit designed to be worn on the moon; **moon-walk**, the action of walking on the moon; so as *v. intr.*, to walk on the moon; **moonwalker**, one who walks on the moon (see also quot. 1950); so **moon-walking** *vbl. sb.*

1960 *Aeroplane* XCVIII. 320/1 The Moon-bounce technique was a form of long-distance radio communication which could be carried out on wavelengths which were not susceptible to ionospheric or other terrestrial disturbances. **1968** *Radio Communication Handbk.* (ed. 4) xii. 20/2 Typical ground station equipment for moonbounce requires a transmitter output power exceeding 100 watts, net aerial gains of the order of 15–20 db, and receivers of 500 c/s bandwidth. **1975** *Nature* 4 Sept. 36/1 On July 7, 1974 while using a Moon Bounce technique on 1,296 MHz I observed the appearance of strange, delayed echoes. **1965** *NASA Facts* III. i. 4 The moonbound Apollo's space navigation system includes two relatively conventional units. **1968** *Guardian* 23 Dec. 1 The world last night saw..life on board the moonbound capsule. **1963** *Britannica Bk. of Year* (U.S.) 856/1 *Moon bug*, the LEM [*i.e.* lunar excursion module]. **1969** *Daily Tel.* (Colour Suppl.) 10 Jan. 21 (*caption*) Parent spacecraft (command and service modules) separates leaving lunar module ('moonbug') attached to rocket stage. **1971** *Guardian* 23 July 11 The astronauts will have a powered moon buggy called Rover. **1938** Chiang Yee *Silent Traveller in London* 38 At this time [*sc.* mid-September] all the sweet-shops produce a great variety of seasonable cakes, which we call 'Moon-Cake', and those especially which are made in Canton in South China are very famous. **1952** D. Yen Hung Feng *Joy Chinese Cooking* xii. 211 Moon cakes are seldom made at home, for the genuine type are difficult to make and require a long list of hard-to-prepare ingredients as well as special wooden forms and cooking implements. **1966** 'Han Suyin' *Mortal Flower* viii. 174 In all the markets, the mooncakes..parade their roundness in all the foodshops, light, feathery, moon-white. **1971** *Nat. Geographic* Oct. 556 (*caption*) Golden yolks,..salted and dried in the sun.. are steamed with rice or cooked in Cantonese moon cakes, served at festival time. **1965** *Sci. World* 28 Oct. 8 Would a sticky coating of dust block the window of an astronaut's 'moon car'? **1973** *Daily Tel.* 13 Mar. 19/4 The Lunokhod 2 robot mooncar has..resumed studies of Moon soil and rock and taking photographs. **1962** F. I. Ordway et al. *Basic Astronautics* v. 216 Evidence derived from stationary and mobile mooncraft will doubtless support the belief that any manned bases or outposts on the Moon will have to be underground. **1963** *Times* 31 May 19/7 Two gigantic crawler transport vehicles for use in the Apollo mooncraft launching. **1971** *Daily Tel.* 3 Aug. 1/6 Falcon, the Apollo 15 mooncraft, blasted off yesterday from the lunar surface. **1970** *Guardian* 18 Nov. 1/2 Russia is likely to try to bring its moon crawler Lunokod-I back to earth. **1797** B. Hawkins *Let.* 23 Dec. in *Georgia Hist. Soc. Coll.* (1916) IX. 276 Last evening, just before moon down, his camp had been fired on. **1863** W. B. Cheadle *Jrnl. Trip across Canada* (1931) 125 Camp at moondown in wood close to our lake. **1938** C. H. Matschat *Suwanee River* 68 Five hours till moondown. **1855** Moonface [in Dict., sense 15]. **1944** J. Hoffman *Female Endocrinology* xxxv. 574 The facial adiposity may materially alter the normal features and is responsible for the 'moon face' and 'pig-eyed' expression of the classical case. **1958** *Spectator* 11 July 60/3 Swelling of the face—'moon-face' after cortisone. **1959** J. Fleming *Miss Bones* xii. 136 Her large moon-face remained quite expressionless. **1963** *Daily Tel.* 28 Oct. 12 The Soviet Union, he says, is planning no manned moon-flights. **1975** S. Johnson *Urbane Guerilla* v. 182 The famous moonflight of Apollo 11. **1926** *Blackw. Mag.* Oct. 530/2 She could no longer see the moving shape presently lost among the vague masses of moonglow and darkling shadow which veiled the moor. **1934** W. Hudson et al. (*song-title*) Moonglow. **1965** M. West *Ambassador* viii. 181, I..woke..to a room full of moonglow. **1879** G. M. Hopkins *Poems* (1967) 80 Only I'll Have an eye to the sakes of him, quaint moonmarks, to his pelted plumage under Wings. **1879** —— *Lett. to R. Bridges* (1955) 83 By *moonmarks* I mean crescent shaped markings on the quill-feathers, either in the colouring of the feather or made by the overlapping of one on another. **1885** *Encycl. Dict.*, Moon-milk. **1965** *New Scientist* 3 June 666/2 These crystals form a colloid in water to give the substance that, in British caves, is called moonmilk. **1973** P. O'Donnell *Silver Mistress* ix. 161 They reached a huge stalactite chamber. Around the perimeter shimmered white patches of the calcite deposit called moonmilk. **1866** Lindley & Moore *Treas. Bot.* II. 754/1 Moon-penny. *Chrysanthemum leucanthemum.* **1940** F. Kitchen *Brother to Ox* ix. 152 The grass-reaper..cuts through life, sweeping down the slender moon-pennies and toppling them over. **1963** *New Scientist* 18 Apr. 138/3 NASA has acquired 87,000 acres just north of Cape Canaveral, Florida, as the site for its 'Moonport'. **1965** *New Statesman* 16 July 74/1 To have two Moonports is extravagance enough. **1967** *Britannica Bk. of Year* (U.S.) 803/3 *Moonport*, a place on the surface of the earth equipped for sending spacecraft to the moon. **1958** *Oxford Mail* 16 Aug. 1/8 Engineers are making final checks on the multiple rocket which is expected to be launched tomorrow on America's first 'Moon probe'. **1972** *Guardian* 22 Feb. 2/4 The unmanned Soviet moon probe Luna 20 made a soft landing on the moon's surface last night. **1963** *Ibid.* 17 July 1/5 It is now intended to have the whole question of the 'moon race' brought up in the International Astronomical Union. **1971** S. Cavell *World Viewed* 63 We lash ourselves to these ideas with burning coils of containment, massive retaliation, moon races, yellow perils. **1946** G. Tyrwhitt-Drake *English Circus & Fair Ground* xvii. 202 There were many..rides, such as Airways, Autodrome Aeroplanes, and Moon Rocket. **1953** Pohl & Kornbluth *Space Merchants* (1955) i. 5 The slim V-2s and stubby Moon rockets of the past. **1954** 'R. Crompton' *William & Moon Rocket* i. 20 A fair ain't a fair these days without a Moon Rocket. **1896** E. Phillpotts *Down Dartmoor Way* 201 They turned intu the black wudes all laced wi' mune-shafts. **1930** E. Pound *XXX Cantos* xxi. 98 Yellow wing, pale in the moon shaft. **1949** Moonship [see *gravity 5]. **1963** *Wall St. Jrnl.* 19 Aug. 20 North American Aviation awarded $934.4 million job... Order is for Apollo Moonship. **1970** *Universe* 30 Jan. 9/5 The horror of some future manned moonship being marooned in space is something we don't like to think about. **1958** *Oxford Mail* 14 Aug. 1/9 The United States first 'moon-shoot' has about a one-in-ten chance of success. **1958** *Washington Post* 18 Aug. A. 8/4 Yesterday's moon shot blew up 50,000 feet and 77 seconds after the launching at Cape Canaveral. **1969** *New Scientist* 9 Jan. 56/3 Much heartened by the success of the three-man Moon shot, the National Aeronautics and Space Administration is unveiling ambitious plans for the mid-1970s. **1971** R. Nesbitt *Evolution & Existence of God* 10 If the Universe were in fact a chaos, Apollo moonshots would be inconceivable. **1953** Pohl & Kornbluth *Space Merchants* (1955) xii. 131 Moon suits rented '50 Years Without a Blowout'. **1966** Webster Add., Moonwalk, Moonwalker. **1969** *Daily Tel.* 16 July 22/2 While on the moon, the astronauts will..only moon-walk for about 3½ to four hours. **1969** *Observer* 20 July 1/2 Hints that the 'moonwalk' will also be brought forward were strengthened when the astronauts' physician, Dr Charles Berry, said that he did not now expect the two men to go to sleep on the moon. **1971** *New Scientist* 11 Feb. 286/2 Physical activity exacerbated this condition and contributed to the unusually high heart-rates seen on the moonwalk. **1973** J. Wainwright *Touch of Malice* 31 It was a little like a moon-walk. A slow deliberate progression from point 'A' to point 'B'. **1950** Webster Add., *Moonwalking*, sleepwalking outdoors in bright moonlight.—*Moonwalker.* **1969** *Times* 3 June (Suppl.) p. iii/1 The two moon-walkers will be in the lunar module's upper, or ascent stage. **1966** *Punch* 31 Aug. 336/3 Machines with metal boots are being constructed for moon-walking.

Moon (mūn), *sb.*² The name of Dr. William *Moon* (1818–94), of Brighton, used *attrib.*, *absol.*, or in the possessive to designate the embossed type which he invented to enable blind people to read.

1859 *3rd Rep. Soc. for Supplying Books in Moon's Type* 7 The plan of teaching the Blind..to read by Books embossed in Moon's type has been tested. **1859** M. Fison *Darkness & Light* 19 Moon's System of Embossed Books. .. Moon's Alphabet consists of the common letters simplified, and therefore is easily learnt... By Moon's method of Stereotyping, the letters are thrown up with such sharpness and prominence, as to be felt even by fingers become dull through age. **1910** *Encycl. Brit.* IV. 63/1 A society was instituted in 1847 by Dr. W. Moon for stereotyping and embossing the Scriptures and other books in 'Moon' type. **1959** *Listener* 14 May 868/3 Books in Braille and Moon. **1973** *Times* 28 Feb. (Victoria Centre, Nottingham, Suppl.) p. ii/1 (Advt.), [Blind people] may prefer to develop a particular handcraft as a hobby, or to concentrate on mobility, braille, Moon type reading, typing. **1973** *Times Lit. Suppl.* 7 Dec. 1511/4 (Advt.), Books in Braille and Moon that are specially prepared for the Blind of all ages.

moon, *v.* Add: **1. c.** *slang.* To expose one's buttocks to (someone). Cf. *Moon *sb.* 5 b.

1968–70 *Current Slang* (Univ. S. Dakota) III–IV. 84 *Moon*,..to display one's bare buttocks as a taunt. **1974** *News & Reporter* (Chester, S. Carolina) 24 Apr. 3-A/1 The convention..was to last through Saturday afternoon, and we imagine that it did although we did hear a wild rumor that a cut-up named Fannie might pull her own version of 'the streak' during the Sunday breakfast..just to get the Sunday session off to a good start if the session started getting dull. But, Fannie has assured us that she didn't 'moon' anybody.

moo·n-blind, *sb.* [Cf. the adj.] Moon-blindness.

1668 [see Moon-blind *a.* 1]. **1877** R. I. Dodge *Plains Gt. West* v. 67 There is said to be [a] plains malady, which, however, I cannot vouch for. It is called 'moon-blind'. The idea is that the full rays of the moon affect the eyes of a man sleeping exposed to them, so that he cannot see at night.

moon-calf. Add: **3.** An animal imagined to inhabit the moon.

1901 H. G. Wells *First Men in Moon* xi. 116 We saw.. the mooncalf's shining sides... First of all impressions was its enormous size; the girth of its body was some four-score feet, its length perhaps two hundred. *Ibid.* 120 We came upon another drove of mooncalves bellowing up a ravine. **1955** *Times* 11 Aug. 7/4 It will be nice if, when we make our landfall on the moon, we find the mooncalves prodding their craters with a noiseless drill.

moondoggle (mū·ndǫg'l). *slang* (chiefly *U.S.*). [Blend of Moon *sb.* and *boondoggle *sb.*] Lunar exploration regarded as a 'boondoggle' (see *boondoggle *sb.* b). Hence moo·ndoggling *vbl. sb.*

1962 *Economist* 1 Sept. 780/1 The..taunts of 'moondoggle'..when Mr Kennedy first outlined his plans for exploring the moon. **1963** *Punch* 1 May 620/2 The vast expense of the crash programme to put a man on the moon is..open to the charge of being..economic moondoggling. **1967** *Britannica Bk. of Year* (U.S.) 803/2 *Moondoggle*, useless exploration of the moon that is wasteful of time and money.

mooner. Add: **3.** One who moons (sense *1 c).

1974 [see *mooning *vbl. sb.* 3].

moon-eyed, *ppl. a.* Add: **1. a.** (Later U.S. examples.)

1889 'C. E. Craddock' *Despot of Broomsedge Cove* vi. 105 Do ye know ennything 'bout'n a horse's eyes? I be sort'n 'feard he's moon-eyed, or suthin'. **1905** A. Adams *Outlet* 21 Tolleston took the only blind horse in the herd... At the time of his purchase, no one could see anything in the eyeball which would indicate he was moon-eyed.

b. (Later examples.)

1886 R. E. G. Cole *Gloss. Words S.-W. Lincs.* 93 Old Jane, his first wife, was moon-eyed. When folks are moon-eyed, they have to gleg at you (look askance) out of the corner of the eye. **1912** *Dialect Notes* III. 583 *Moon-eyed*, half-blind.

4. Drunk; intoxicated. *U.S. slang.*

1737 *Pennsylvania Gaz.* 6–13 Jan. 2/1 He sees two Moons, Merry, Middling, Moon-Ey'd, Muddled, [etc.]. **1940** *Amer. Speech* XV. 447/2 Sid gits moon-eyed every Saturday night.

moon-fish. Substitute for def.: A name used for several pale-coloured marine fishes having

thin, moon-shaped bodies, esp. the OPAH, *Lampris guttatus*, a sunfish, *Mola mola*, or a North American fish of the genera *Selene* or *Vomer*.

1873 [see *ANGEL-FISH]. **1878** *Proc. U.S. Nat. Museum* I. 376 *Argyriosus vomer*.—Moon-fish. *Ibid.*, *Selena argentea*.—Moon-fish... Not common. *Ibid.*, *Vomer setipinnis*.—Moon-fish; Sun-fish. **1896** JORDAN & EVERMANN *Check-List Fishes N. & Mid. Amer.* 350 *Lampris luna*... Mariposa; Opah;..Gudlax; Moonfish. **1959** A. HARDY *Fish & Fisheries* II. iv. 75 Another wanderer from warmer waters, coming right into the North Sea and occasionally being taken off the Yorkshire coast, is the most brilliantly coloured of all our fishes, the opah or moon-fish, *Lampris guttatus* (which has in turn also been called the sun-fish). **1963** P. H. GREENWOOD *Norman's Hist. Fishes* (ed. 2) xviii. 329 The order [*sc.* Lampridiformes] includes the large oceanic Opah or Moon-fish (*Lampris*). **1965** A. J. MCCLANE *Standard Fishing Encycl.* 499/1 The moonfish (*Vomer*) have a head profile that is only moderately high. *Ibid.* 499/2 Both the lookdowns and the moonfish grow to about 10–12 inches.

moon-flower. **2.** Substitute for def.: A tropical climbing plant, *Ipomœa alba*, of the family Convolvulaceæ, which bears fragrant, white, trumpet-shaped flowers opening at night; also, other closely-related plants of the genera *Ipomœa* and *Quamoclit*. (Later examples.)

1939 A. H. WOOD *Grow them Indoors* 102 Morning glory, moon flower, dawn flower—there are numerous common names for different members of this group of woody climbers. **1963** W. BLUNT *Of Flowers & Village* 110 My cobaeas and moonflowers have both already germinated. **1969** G. MACBETH *War Quartet* 28 Split tins..Leafed into fronds of moon-flowers.

3. A name used in Africa for *Datura arborea* or *D. suaveolens*, shrubs native to Central America and belonging to the family Solanaceæ, bearing fragrant, white, trumpet-shaped flowers; also called moon-lily or angel's trumpet.

1913 C. PETTMAN *Africanderisms* 325 Moon lily or Moon flower, *Datura Knightii*, which has long, pendulous, strongly scented white flowers. **1973** PALMER & PITMAN *Trees S. Afr.* III. 1976 It [*sc.* the potato family] yields foods..flowers..shrubs—such as the moonflower, *Datura arborea* L., and *Cestrum* species.

mooniness. (Later examples.)

1929 W. DEEPING *Roper's Row* xiv. 149 The other girls at Fogson and George's observed her 'mooniness'. **1929** A. HUXLEY *Do what you Will* 55 The human countenance ..of pallid mooniness.

mooning, *vbl. sb.* Add: **3.** The action of exposing one's buttocks (*MOON *v.* 1 c).

1974 *Guardian* 22 Mar. 17/8 Streaking..seems to be the mainly male equivalent of the mainly female practice that cropped up in campuses across the United States in the late fifties and early sixties. This was known as 'mooning'. .. Mooning consisted..of exposing the bottom in the general direction of whoever the mooner wanted to impress, protest to, or affront.

moonlet. Add: (Further examples.) Also, an artificial satellite.

1895 [see *impact crater]. **1955** *Sci. News Let.* 13 Aug. 107/2 The man-made moonlets will circle the earth many times every day, appearing to rise in the west and set in the east, reversing other sky phenomena. **1965** J. BLISH *Mission to Heart Stars* ii. 27 Since Phobos always kept the same face turned towards Mars, there would be no need to bother stumbling around on the dark side of the moonlet. **1971** *Sci. Amer.* Jan. 47/1 Was the heat provided by the impact of meteorites or of a larger celestial body, or by the collision of 'moonlets' to form the present moon?

moonlight, *sb.* Add: **1. c.** The colour of the light of the moon, as a shade in fabrics.

1922 *Daily Mail* 18 Dec. 1 (Advt.), In the following colours: Turquoise, Mastic, Moonlight, Silver, [etc.]. **1927** *Daily Tel.* 26 Apr. 13 (Advt.), Following shades: Sapphire, Moonlight, Bois de Rose, [etc.].

d. *moonlight and roses*: used allusively of a situation, atmosphere, etc., characterized by sentimentality or romance.

1925 BLACK & MORET (*song-title*) Moonlight and roses. **1942** *Amer. Speech* XVII. 58 The moonlight-and-roses kind of Civil War play. **1959** *Encounter* Apr. 79/1 In *Look Homeward Angel* we have the romanticised figure of Laura James, the moonlight-and-roses woven about her.

4. Ellipt. for *moonlight flit*. *colloq.*

1958 G. BELLAIRS *Corpse at Carnival* ix. 131 His bags has gone... He's packed up... Done a moonlight as likely as not. **1971** R. PARKES *Line of Fire* xvi. 149 It's no good him trying to find 'em... Done a moonlight, they did.

6. b. Add to def.: Also, the action of leaving rented accommodation without paying the rent; a stealthy, usu. nocturnal, departure. (Add further examples.)

1821 J. GALT *Ann. Parish* xxxi. 263 He was fain to make a moonlight flitting, leaving his wife for a time to manage his affairs. **1855** [see FLIT *sb.* a]. **1892** STEVENSON & OSBOURNE *Wrecker* v. 79 In the excellent Scots' phrase, I made a moonlight flitting, a thing never dignified. **1924** M. ARGO in *Sc. Nat. Dict.* (1965) VI. 364/1 Takkin' a meenlichty flittin', are ye? **1969** *Listener* 27 Mar. 424/3 Very often we were living somewhere and couldn't pay the rent, so we had to indulge in what was known as a moonlight flit with what furniture and goods were available.

c. **moonlight lustre**, a lustre glaze with a marbled effect used on porcelain in the early 19th century, *spec.* by the Wedgwood factory.

1924 H. BARNARD *Chats on Wedgwood Ware* ix. 236 Lustre ware was not made until the beginning of the nineteenth century, when some very beautiful effects were produced, including the one which has since been called 'Moonlight'. **1966** G. A. GODDEN *Illustr. Encycl. Brit. Pott. & Porc.* p. xxiv, Messrs Wedgwood introduced a decorative type of marbled pink or purple 'gold' lustre called 'Moonlight Lustre'. **1970** *Times* 7 Oct. 10/6 This type of service was first made around 1820 and only the early examples, like that sold yesterday, are splashed in a pink glaze known as moonlight lustre.

moonlight, *v.* Add: **2.** To do a 'moonlight flit'. *dial.* and *colloq.*

1903 in *Eng. Dial. Dict.* **1971** A. NIXON *Attack on Vienna* vii. 71 He moonlit out of his luxury flat..and moved into a boarding-house.

3. To do paid work, usu. at night, in addition to one's regular employment. *colloq.* (orig. *U.S.*).

1957 [implied in *MOONLIGHTING *vbl. sb.* 3]. **1960** *Economist* 12 Nov. 657/1 The firemen and police have long been supplementing their pay..by 'moonlighting', that is, by taking outside paid work. **1965** *Daily Tel.* (Colour Suppl.) 7 May 19/1 Some manage to 'moonlight' with two or three jobs—though jobs are harder to find. **1970** P. CARLON *Death by Demonstration* xvi. 175 You think I moonlight? Believe me, one job's enough. **1974** *Times Lit. Suppl.* 15 Feb. 157/4 He..—naturally for one who moonlights as the *Financial Times*'s gardening correspondent when not otherwise engaged as a Fellow of Magdalen—never misses a turn on botanical or horticultural matters.

moonlighter. Add: **2.** One who does a 'moonlight flit'. *dial.* and *colloq.*

1903 in *Eng. Dial. Dict.* **1964** *Sunday Mail* (Brisbane) 15 Nov. 12 Brisbane flat owners..estimate that moonlighters—tenants who slip away overnight without paying the rent—are costing them £100,000 a year.

3. One who 'moonlights' (*MOONLIGHT *v.* 3). *colloq.*

1957 *Times* 12 Nov. (Canada Suppl.) p. ix/4 'Moonlighters' take a second job after hours; married women take advantage of modern kitchens to do the same. **1964** *Observer* 9 Aug. 9/2 Even in America, an estimated four million workers are 'moonlighters'—that is, they take on a part-time job on top of their full-time one. **1973** C. EGLETON *Seven Days to Killing* v. 61, I employ a lot of moonlighters, blokes who take a second job at nights.

moonlighting, *vbl. sb.* Add: **3.** The act or practice of *MOONLIGHT *v.* 3. *colloq.* (orig. *U.S.*).

1957 *Reporter* (N.Y.) 8 Aug. 11/3 He takes two or three hours off and then..departs for a second job... The practice is known as 'moonlighting'. **1961** *Economist* 16 Dec. 1145/2 Several attempts have been made to ban moonlighting on the ground that it robs the unemployed of jobs. **1972** *Times* 8 Jan. 21/2 What about moonlighting? This is not the distilling of illicit liquor but the taking of a second job to keep body and soul together, or to finance one's own personal brand of extravagance.

moon-man. Restrict † *Obs.* to senses 1 and 2 in Dict., and add: **3.** (Further examples.) Also *fig.*

1958 *Spectator* 5 Sept. 305 An electronic sideshow starred Gygan, the Man from the Moon, a seven-foot creature of steel with a sixty-inch chest to keep all the transistors in. He walked spastic fashion with that curious whirring noise which all Moonmen seem to affect. **1962** A. WESKER *Chips with Everything* I. iii. 19 All right you creepy crawly nignogs, moon men that's what you are, moon men.

4. An astronaut who travels to the moon.

1965 *N.Y. Jrnl.-American* 21 Feb. 11/1 The spot where America's Moonmen are most likely to land. **1968** *Daily Tel.* 30 Dec. 1/3 (*headline*) Moonmen greeted by wives. **1970** *Observer* 19 Apr. 8/4 They were virile men, these astronauts. They were patriots, but they were moonmen.

moonquake (mū·nkwēⁱk). *Astr.* [f. MOON *sb.* after EARTHQUAKE.] A tremor of the moon's surface. (In quot. 1940 a *poet. nonce-use.*)

1940 R. GRAVES *No More Ghosts* 41 The pallid sky heaved with a moon-quake. **1953** *Jrnl. Brit. Interplanetary Soc.* XII. 66 The work which such an expedition could do is then described: amongst other things, artificial 'moonquakes' would be set off by explosives, so that seismic records could be made. **1961** *Flight* LXXIX. 427/2 Other scientific instruments aboard the Surveyor will include a sensitive seismometer to record moonquakes or meteorite impacts. **1968** *Observer* 29 Dec. 17/3 The astronauts will place on the surface an instrument to register moonquakes. **1970** *Nature* 5 Dec. 906/1 It is now clear..that tidal strain is causing moonquakes when the Moon is at its nearest to the Earth. **1973** *Telegraph* (Brisbane) 13 Mar. 14/1 A seismologist has said that for some mysterious reason almost all moonquakes occur only in two separate belts on the moon.

moonraker. **2.** (Earlier example.)

c **1829** D. JERROLD in M. R. Booth *Eng. Plays of 19th Cent.* (1969) I. 173 Now she makes more sail..mounts her royals, moon-rakers and sky-scrapers.

moonrise. Add: (Further examples.) Also (*U.S.*), the time at which the moon rises.

1877 in BARTLETT *Dict. Amer.* (ed. 4). **1884** 'MARK TWAIN' *Huck. Finn.* viii. 63 When it was good and dark, I slid out from shore about moonrise. **1913** D. H. LAWRENCE *Love Poems & Others* 26 (*title*) Red moon-rise. **1926** E. M. ROBERTS *Time of Man* (1927) x. 379 I'll be gone at moonrise. **1931** E. O'NEILL *Mourning becomes Electra* I. i. 191 You dasn't stay there till moonrise at ten o'clock. **1975** *Sci. Amer.* Feb. 70/2 A lunar day is 24·8 hours in length, the interval between successive moonrises.

moonscape (mū·nskēⁱp). [f. MOON *sb.* + SCAPE *sb.*[3]] The surface or landscape of the moon, or a scene resembling this. Also *fig.*

1926 *World's Work* May 5 It embodies all the scientific facts known to-day, and the 'moonscape' in the foreground is an actual scene as viewed through the telescope. **1960** *20th Cent.* June 509, I..took..off..on a mighty leap across the moonscape. **1961** I. FLEMING *Thunderball* xvi. 173 Now the pale moonscape changed. **1969** *Sun* 22 July 1/3 Armstrong, the first to walk, looked at the desolate moonscape and told the world: 'It has a beauty of its own ..it's very pretty up here.' **1971** D. LEES *Rainbow Conspiracy* vi. 89 The deserted moonscape terrain of Pike's Scar. **1974** V. CANNING *Mask of Memory* ii. 23 His thin, drawn face a moonscape of chalky white.

moonshine. **4.** Add to def.: In the U.S., illicitly distilled liquor, esp. whisky.

1875 E. KING *Southern States N. Amer.* 478 Producing from his pocket a flask of 'moonshine' whiskey, [he] invited us to drink. *Ibid.* 479 Would we have some more 'moonshine'? No? **1886** *Century Mag.* XXXI. 432/1 He had a moonshine apparatus over on Sweetwater. **1901** [in Dict.]. **1957** M. MCCARTHY *Memories Catholic Girlhood* vii. 157 It did not smell like the whisky my grandfather drank. It was moonshine, they said; corn whisky. **1960** A. LOMAX *Folk Songs N. Amer.* 257 I'll eat when I'm hungry and drink when I'm dry, If moonshine don't kill me, I'll live till I die. **1973** 'B. MATHER' *Snowline* i. 16 All liquor is either bootleg—smuggled—or moonshine, distilled from anything and everything.

moonshine (mū·nʃəin), *v.* [f. the sb.] **1.** *trans.* To cheat or deceive by means of 'moonshine' (MOONSHINE 2 a). *rare*⁻¹.

1824 E. WEETON *Let.* 6 July in *Jrnl. of Governess* (1969) II. 298, I visited the Diorama... I was too much gratified to think I was moon-shined out of my money.

2. *intr.* To make liquor, esp. whisky, illicitly. *U.S. colloq.*

1883 [implied in *MOONSHINING *vbl. sb.*]. **1902** W. N. HARBEN *Abner Daniel* 209 We moonshined it together two year, though he never knowed my chief hidin'-place. **1910** 'O. HENRY' *Whirligigs* xv. 173 He acknowledged no occupation save that of a squirrel hunter, but he 'moonshined' occasionally by way of diversion. **1949** *Times-Picayune Mag.* (New Orleans) 13 Feb. 6/2 Even a small operator can make fair living moonshining.

moonshiner. Delete *U.S.* and substitute for def.: **a.** A smuggler. **b.** *U.S.* A distiller of 'moonshine' (MOONSHINE 4). (Add further examples.)

1877 *N.Y. Even. Post* 16 June, Nelson County, Kentucky, is the home of the Moonshiner; that is, the manufacturer of illicit whiskey. **1927** [see *FEUDIST 3]. **1970** N. ARMSTRONG et al. *First on Moon* iv. 77 Some seven hundred people had to be moved, including quite a few moonshiners. **1973** *Guardian* 12 Oct. 1/8 Senator Sam Ervin..has made a long-playing record of his homespun Southern philosophy. The record features stories about moonshiners. **1973** *Globe & Mail* (Toronto) 9 Nov. 31/4 That same gallon, he says, costs the moonshiner only $2 to $3 to manufacture, and—if he isn't making it for his own use—he usually sells it for around $30.

moonshining, *vbl. sb.* (Earlier and later examples.)

1883 'S. BONNER' *Dialect Tales* 183 You can't stop moonshinin' 's long's there's an honest man in Old Hickory's State. **1946** G. WILSON *Fidelity Folks* 54 He stoutly maintained that a regulated open saloon was to be preferred to the evils of moonshining and boot-legging.

moonshiny, *a.* **3.** (Earlier example.)

1857 H. MELVILLE *Confidence Man* xli. 312 And moonshiny as it in theory may be, yet a very practical philosophy.

moon-up (mū·nʌp). *U.S. dial.* [f. MOON *sb.* + UP *adv.* Cf. SUN-UP.] Moonrise.

1907 S. E. WHITE *Arizona Nights* I. v. 90 'Didn't git in till moon-up last night,' he growled. **1941** *Sat. Even. Post* 1 Mar. 84/2 They'd come between first dark and moon-up.

moonward(s, *adv.* (Further examples.)

1879 G. MACDONALD *Hist. Photogen & Nycteris* xiv, in *Graphic* Christmas No. 8/2 The fountain kept rushing moonward. **1900** O. WILDE *Let.* 21 Apr. (1962) 823 He really bayed for boots, as a dog moonwards. **1918** C. W. BEEBE *Jungle Peace* (1919) xi. 270 Here and there in the jungle on each side, where a tree had fallen, or a flue of clear space led moonwards, the effect was of cold electric light seen through trees in city parks. **1959** C. MACKENZIE *Lunatic Republic* i. 21 Every sound without was so muted that the explosion which started the rocket moonwards sounded no more than the noise of one of the old railway trains of my youth.

moor, *sb.*[1] Add: **1. b.** *spec.* (Usu. with capital initial.) Dartmoor Prison (cf. *DARTMOOR b).

1869 F. HENDERSON *Six Yrs. in Prisons Eng.* xix. 228 'How long were you at the Moor, Dick?' 'Three years.' **1924** E. WALLACE *Room 13* vii. 69, I was on the 'moor' with him. **1939** [see *ISLAND *sb.* 1 d]. **1958** F. NORMAN *Bang to Rights* 1. 22 I'm doing a bleeding neves. I'll be going down the Moor soon that will be the third poxy

time. **1962** D. Warner *Death of Bogey* iv. iii. 146 A stretch in the Ville or on the Moor. **1967** C. Drummond *Death at Furlong Post* xvi. 192 There's nothing like the Moor, T.B. more or less guaranteed after fifteen years. **1968** *Guardian* 3 Jan. 5/3 One more stretch for GBH, then down to the Moor.

5. *moor-owner.*

1915 R. Lankester *Diversions of Naturalist* v. 47 One moor-owner was able to boast that he had on several occasions killed over 500 head of grouse in a single day. **1971** *Country Life* 12 Aug. 396/1 For the moor-owner grouse soon became more profitable than sheep.

moor, *v.*^{1} Add: **2. c.** With *up*: to secure a seaplane; of a seaplane, to be made secure.

1936 [see *grabbit (boat) hook]. **1942** *Times* 3 Sept. 5/7 Night was slowly mastering daylight as we..landed, to moor up near some naval patrol boats.

Moorcroft (mūᵊ·ɹkrǫft). The name of William *Moorcroft* (1872–1945) used *attrib.* and *ellipt.* to designate pottery produced by him at his workshop in Cobridge, north Staffordshire, and noted for its powdered blue effects and flambé glazes.

1910 *Pottery Gaz.* May 551/2, I cannot now do more than mention the most interesting developments in glaze effects and wonderful colour schemes revealed in the latest examples of 'Moorcroft Faïence'. **1918** *Pottery & Glass Record* Nov. p. i (Advt.), Moorcroft ware, hand-made decorative objects..W. Moorcroft, Ltd., Potters, Burslem... Works adjoining Cobridge Station. **1923** *Pottery Gaz. & Glass Trade Rev.* 2 Apr. 660/1 Baron Hayashi, the Japanese Ambassador, on purchasing two flambé vases, expressed the opinion that the Moorcroft vases were so like early Chinese work that had Mr. Moorcroft's name not been on them experts would have found it difficult to distinguish the difference. **1939** *Times* 8 Mar. 12/4 Moorcroft pottery has for some years been recognized abroad as standing in a class by itself among the modern products of ceramic art. **1946** *Pottery & Glass* June 33/1 Several American museums possess representative collections of Moorcroft ware. **1956** C. G. E. Bunt *Brit. Potters & Pottery Today* 41 The rich and generous decoration is..all hand work. To this is largely due the distinctiveness, the individuality of Moorcroft Pottery. **1972** F. MacCarthy *All Things Bright & Beautiful* 85 Blue Moorcroft Pottery and Cornish Ware were endlessly in favour [in the 1920s]. **1974** M. Kelly *That Girl in Alley* iii. 40 The Moorcroft vases, the Lalique bowl, the silk runner on top of the piano. **1975** *Times* 17 Jan. 3 Sotheby's Belgravia sale of studio ceramics..underlined the tremendous new collector interest in the art potters of about 1880–1950... Minor Moorcroft was selling like hot cakes.

Moore (mūᵊɹ, mōᵊɹ). Designating an almanac, the first edition of which, compiled by Francis *Moore* (1657–*c* 1715), was issued in 1700 under the title of *Vox Stellarum*, and which was later known as *Old Moore's Almanac*. Also *ellipt.* Hence (nonce-wd.) *Old Moore's Almanac* v. absol., to engage in predictions of the future.

1817 Keats *Let.* 10 Sept. (1931) I. 39, I know not whether you prefer..Cinderella and her glass slipper to Moor's Almanack. *a* **1821** —— *Cap & Bells* lvi, in *Compl. Poetical Works* (1907) 476 Look in the Almanack—*Moore* never lies. **1855** Geo. Eliot in *Westm. Rev.* Oct. 437 Let him..rival Moore's Almanack in the prediction of political events. **1873** C. M. Yonge *Pillars of House* IV. xl. 170 The mysteries of Moore's Almanac on the wall. **1896** G. B. Shaw *Our Theatres in Nineties* (1932) II. 124 As devoutly as any superstitious washerwoman ever read Zadkiel or Old Moore. **1916** D. H. Lawrence *Let.* 24 May (1962) I. 452 But I am afraid I bore you Old-Moore's Almanacking. **1936** *Discovery* Dec. 389/1 He published a sort of Old Moore's Almanac and told people's fortunes, and generally practised the acts of the astrologer. **1975** *Broadcast* 15 Sept. 16/3 Throw the net wide and don't always toss back the little 'uns are old Moore's words of wisdom.

mooreed, var. *murid.

mooreite (mūᵊ·rəit, mōᵊ·rəit). *Min.* [f. the name of Gideon *Moore* (1842–1895), U.S. chemist + -ite^1.] A hydrated basic sulphate of magnesium, manganese, and zinc, $(Mg,Mn,Zn)_8SO_4(OH)_{14}.4H_2O$, found as colourless monoclinic crystals.

1929 Bauer & Berman in *Amer. Mineralogist* XIV. 165 The cavities in the pyrochroite are lined, and some of the crevices are filled, with glassy white tabular crystals which, upon investigation, proved to be a new mineral, for which the name mooreite is here proposed, in honor of Dr. Gideon E. Moore, an early investigator of Sterling Hill and Franklin minerals. **1951** *Mineral. Abstr.* XI. 384 The action of salt water on the minerals of this vein in the August Victoria mine at Hüls, Westphalia, has produced the following secondary minerals:..mooreite, dickite, sericite, and blödite. **1969** *Amer. Mineralogist* LIV. 973 Mooreite..is monoclinic although the space group is not $P2_1/m$ as previously reported but rather $P2_1/a$.

moor-grass. 3. For the generic name '*Sesleria*' substitute '*Molinia*'. (Earlier and later examples.)

1749 W. Ellis *Compl. Syst. Sheep* 321 This moor-grass ..they call *Rosa-Solis*, as it is distinguished by Shepherds from other Grasses, who know it by its three-square Leaf, Rapier-like. **1950** W. H. Pearsall *Mountains & Moorlands* ix. 179 The moor-grass may be found growing on oxygen-poor peats with a moderately high salt content and low acidity. **1972** *Country Life* 13 Jan. 104/1 There was a telling use of..a cultivated form of the extremely common purple moor grass.

mooring, *vbl. sb.* Add: **4.** *mooring boat, bridle* (examples), *chain* (later examples), *hook*; **mooring mast**, a strong upright structure to which an airship is moored; **mooring-out**, used *attrib.* to denote a site at which an airship may be moored.

1957 D. G. O. Baillie *Sea Affair* xii. 227 The Arab mooring-boat crews were ready at the buoys to cast off our lines. **1967** S. Waters *Indentures Indorsed* xxvi. 153 The two ships were almost alongside each other with only a small mooring boat containing five men between them. *a* **1865** Smyth *Sailor's Word-Bk.* (1867) 484 *Mooring-bridle*, the fasts attached to moorings, one taken into each hawse-hole, or bridle-port. **1919** *Gloss. Aeronaut. Terms* (R. Aeronaut. Soc.) 58 *Mooring bridle*, a rigging passing between two points from a fitting in the length of which the mooring rope is attached. **1948** R. de Kerchove *Internat. Maritime Dict.* 474/2 *Mooring bridle*, the chains or fasts attached to permanent moorings and taken into the hawse holes. **1812** *Dramatic Censor 1811* 223 The monopoly of the East-India Company, Lord Gwydir's mooring-chain monopoly, should be all abolished. **1888** Kipling *Departmental Ditties* (1890) 68 Through the mooring-chains The wide-eyed corpse rolled free. **1907** J. Masefield *Tarpaulin Muster* viii. 97, I..cast the painter around the mooring-hook. **1919** *Gloss. Aeronaut. Terms* (R. Aeronaut. Soc.) 59 *Mooring mast*, a mast to the head of which an airship may be moored. **1929** *Times* 2 Nov. 9/4, R 101..was walked over to the mast at dawn..in 20 minutes, was at once coupled up to the mooring-mast cable and then waited patiently..for the actual mooring. **1972** *Daily Tel.* 26 June 5/1 Europa was in the air for the first time since its mooring mast snapped and the airship careered for threequarters of a mile. **1934** J. A. Sinclair *Airships in Peace & War* 190 The mooring-out station was more of a war measure. **1971** *Country Life* 6 May 1087/1 On flying from our base in Anglesey, or our mooring-out ground at Malahide, [etc.].

Moorish, *a.*^{2} Add: **1.** Also freq. used with reference to the style of furniture and architecture, popular in England in the nineteenth century, characteristic of that made by the Moors in Spain (8th–15th c.) and in Northern Africa.

1903 A. Bennett *Leonora* iii. 80 Bessie..set a Moorish stool before the Chesterfield. **1912** —— *Matador* 49 They were having tea at a little Moorish table in..the lounge. **1965** J. Aronson *Encycl. Furnit.* (1966) 410/1 The X-type chair was common.., a light Moorish type of repeated slats with inlay. **1969** M. Allingham *Case-Book* 101 Towards the [sea] port..the architecture veers towards Victorian Moorish. **1972** E. Joy *Furniture* vii. 188 Of completely different character was the imported..Moorish furniture which first made Liberty's reputation when they began in business in 1875 as an 'Oriental Warehouse'. **1975** R. Butler *Where all Girls are Sweeter* iv. 30 'Four Winds' was all Moorish, Bauschule and Odeon but it stood back in at least five acres.

moorlog. Delete '† *Obs.*' and add later examples.

1933 *Antiquity* VII. 38 In the summer of 1932 the skipper of the steam drifter *Colinda* procured another bone harpoon of Maglemose type in a sample of 'moorlog' (peat) brought up by the trawl. **1939** G. Clark *Archæol. & Society* ii. 20 Over many parts of the North Sea bed.. fishermen have found the remains of a great freshwater fen in the form of lumps of 'moor log'.

moose^1. Add: Also used *collect.*

1817 S. R. Brown *Western Gazetteer* 202 Cabree and moose are plentiful. **1849** J. Pritts *Mirror Border Life* 60 Their food was principally the entrails of moose, deer, bears. **1957** *Listener* 14 Nov. 778/2 Large wooden corrals into which their moose were driven. **1964** *Globe & Mail* (Toronto) 12 Dec. 8/7 A few point to the slow resurgence of moose, particularly in the southwest of the province.

b. *moose-hair, -hide* (earlier and later examples), *-meat* (earlier and later examples), *-skin* (further examples); **moose-bird** *N. Amer.*, substitute for def.: a name used for several birds, esp. the Canada jay, *Perisoreus canadensis* (further examples); **moose-calling** (earlier and later examples); **moose elm**, the slippery elm, *Ulmus rubra* (earlier examples); **moose fly**, one of several North American horse flies, esp. one of the genus *Chrysops*; **moose maple**, either of two small maples of eastern North America, *Acer spicatum* or *A. pennsylvanicum*; **moose shanks** (see quot. 1887); **moose tick**, a North American tick, *Dermacentor albipictus*, which infests moose and other animals; **moose warden** *U.S.*, a person employed to protect moose; **moose-wood** (earlier and later examples); **moose-yard** (earlier and later examples).

1832 W. D. Williamson *Hist. State of Maine* I. 150 The moose-bird..feeds on the berries of the moose brush. **1890** S. M. St. Maur *Impressions of Tenderfoot* 273 My friend of the woods, the moose-bird... I found his real name was the great northern shrike, *Lanius borealis*. **1941** E. T. Seton *Trail of Artist-Naturalist* 270 Presently the wailing of the moose-bird fell on my anxious ear. **1964** *Atlantic Advocate* Oct. 67/1 This time of year there were always a pair of moosebirds on the maple. **1838** *United Service Jrnl.* July 305 In moose-calling, success mainly depends on the judicious selection of a station. **1956** W. R. Bird *Off-Trail in Nova Scotia* vi. 167 The September moon is just right for moose calling. **1810** F. A. Michaux *Hist. Arbres Forestiers de l'Amérique Septentrionale* I. 39 Red elm,..Slippery elm,..Moose elm,..dans le haut de l'Etat de New York. **1832** D. J. Browne *Sylva Amer.* 311 This species of elm..bears the name of Red Elm, Slippery Elm and Moose Elm. **1834** J. J. Audubon *Ornith. Biogr.* II. 437 The musquitoes and moose flies did their best to render us uncomfortable. **1913** *Chambers's Jrnl.* Nov. 764/1 The lordly moose finds..relief from the torturing moose-fly in the cool depths of the lakes. **1953** A. R. M. Lower *Unconventional Voyages* 43 Further south, where they are never so numerous, they [*sc.* bulldog flies] are called horse-flies, or moose-flies. **1820** D. W. Harmon *Jrnl. Voy. & Trav. Interior N. Amer.* 317 From two points in this bow,..two strips of leather..are suspended, at the ends of which, tassels, composed of moose hair, are fixed. **1956** D. Leechman *Native Tribes Canada* 43 Some used moose hair for embroidery. There is a tuft of pale, stiffish hair about seven inches long, between the shoulders of the moose. **1708** J. Oldmixon *Brit. Empire in Amer.* I. 395 Every Man has commonly two Wives, whom they.. make 'em do all Slavery; as draw Sledds,..and dress Moose Hides. **1955** R. P. Hobson *Nothing too Good for Cowboy* vii. 67, I sat up, pulled my moosehide coat over my sweater, [etc.]. **1966** *Globe & Mail* (*Toronto*) 18 May 6/2 When he is racing [on snowshoes], he wears moosehide moccasins. **1839** C. F. Hoffman *Wild Scenes Forest & Prairie* 38 We would come to a sort of plateau of swampy land, overgrown with moose maple. **1904** S. E. White *Blazed Trail Stories* vi. 104 He..was holding aside the screen of moose-maples. **1952** J. Jennings *Strange Brigade* II. iii. 128 To our left lay the woodsy thickets..beech and chokecherry and moose maple. **1797** C. Chaboillez *Jrnl.* in B. C. Payette *Northwest* (1964) 163 The People returned, they brought 1 Bear skin..8 pieces Mouse Meat half Dryed. **1930** L. Munday *Mounty's Wife* iii. 48 We camped that night with some Indians [and] huge plates of moose meat were served, as good as any beef, and far better than most other meats. **1961** H. C. Dodge *My Childhood Canad. Wilderness* i. 27 We ate them fried, roasted, boiled, but we never grew tired of moose meat. **1969** in Halpert & Story *Christmas Mumming in Newfoundland* 84 This late supper might include a meal of 'bottled moose-meat', warmed-over soup..'pork-buns', [etc.]. **1887** *Harper's Mag.* Feb. 458/2 'Moose shanks' are made by peeling the skin from the hind legs of the animal. The smaller end is then sewn up to form the toe; and thus a moose-hide stocking is formed. **1952** E. Buckler *Mountain & Valley* 100 The Rothesays down the road.. wore moose shanks with the hair still on them. **1664** *Essex County, Mass. Probate Rec.* (1916) I. 458 Moose skin sute. **1775** in *Mass. Hist. Soc. Coll.* (1822) 2nd Ser. IX. 162 Donations..1 pair moose-skin breeches. **1957** C. Harris *Cariboo Trail* 174 The mooseskin-trousered [one] looked at him darkly. **1971** D. C. Brown *Yukon Trophy Trails* x. 120 Lonny Johnny, a full-blood Loucheux, was building himself a moose-skin boat... Lonny used the lateral roots of a spruce tree for ribs and two large bull moose hides for the canvas. **1868** *Amer. Naturalist* II. 559 The Moose Tick... When the cow arrived in New York, her sides and back were almost covered with adult ticks. **1853** *Maine Acts & Resolves* 24 The governor shall..appoint one county moose warden for each of the counties. **1883** G. B. Goode *Rev. Fishery Industries U.S.* 83 He had a canoe of birch, and on it he had burnt..the title 'Moose Warden', and he said he would take care of all the moose that came within the reach of his rifle. **1778** J. Carver *Trav. N.-Amer.* 507 The Moose Wood grows about four feet high, and is very full of branches. **1933** D. G. Cameron *Twigs from Oak* 129 The under-growth consisted of..moose-wood, dogwood. **1969** T. H. Everett *Living Trees of World* 222/2 Conspicuous in winter because of its white-striped bark, the moosewood (*A*[*cer*] *pennsylvanicum*) inhabits open woods throughout eastern North America. **1800** C. D. Rouso D'Eres *Mem.* 117 The animals are overtaken in their retreats (for they herd together..) which is called the Moose yard, formed by them in trampling down the snow. **1946** W. R. Bird *Sunrise for Peter* 209 Nathan plunged to join him and almost fell into a well-trodden moose-yard.

c. *transf.* and *fig.*

1925 *Dalhousie Rev.* V. 321 There is much meandering in the neighbouring woods; and..it is known as the game of 'moose'. **1941** *Amer. Speech* XVI. 187 *Moose*, a sister, notably a kid-sister, who informs her mother when her brother is playing stick-ball, shooting dice, etc. **1948** *Sat. Even. Post* 16 Oct. 130/3 Schaeffer was a moose of a man. **1963** *Amer. Speech* XXXVIII. 173 An unattractive female date:..Ugliness..ranges from such general terms as beast..to the more specific bear, cow, goose, moose, roach .., squirrel, and wet fish. **1968** *Word Study* Dec. 3/2 *Moose* is sometimes used for any large and strong person, but it is mostly widely applied to large and strong persons of Scandinavian descent.

moose^3 (mūs). *U.S. Forces' slang.* [ad. Jap. *musume* daughter, girl.] A young Japanese or Korean woman; *esp.*, the wife or mistress of a serviceman stationed in Japan or Korea.

1953 in Partridge *Dict. Slang* (1961) Suppl. 1188/2 An eligible female of Japan or Korea is known as a 'moose',..from the Japanese word 'musume'—girl. **1954** *Amer. Speech* XXIX. 302 To spell the word *mus* might be a good transcription from the Japanese but..it is the spelling *moose* that is most encountered in semiformal Army poop sheets; in signs urging Americans..to meet the best mooses in Kyoto, [etc.]. **1964** *Ibid.* XXXIX. 236 The word *moose* refers, not without some disdain, to Korean wives of Americans, often soldiers.

MOOSE (mūs). [See quot. 1968.] A contrivance for the protection of an astronaut working in outer space.

1968 *New Acronyms & Initialisms* (Gale Research Co.) 144 MOOSE, Man (or Manual) orbital operations safety equipment (Space life raft) (NASA). **1969** *Scottish Sunday*

Express 14 Dec. 12/8 American engineers have designed a space 'lifeboat'..known as MOOSE, from the initial letters of Manned Orbital Operations Safety Equipment.

moosh[1] (muʃ), var. *MUSH *sb.*[1] 3 d.
1914 JACKSON & HELLYER *Vocab. Criminal Slang* 60 *Moosh, moush*,..the human face... Also the mouth... Example: 'He's got a harp moosh,' i.e., Irish. **1953** K. TENNANT *Joyful Condemned* x. 88, I don't usually go round pushing my moosh into anyone's business. **1966** 'L. LANE' *ABZ of Scouse* 71 'Ey you wit' ther maggerty moosh. **1972** K. BONFIGLIOLI *Don't point that Thing at Me* iv. 34 You ought to see his moosh, where I hit him, it's a treat, honest.

moosh[2] (muʃ), var. *MUSH *sb.*[4] Also (*Austral.*), prison food.
1919 *Athenæum* 8 Aug. 727/2 When a man was 'run in' the guardroom he was in 'clink' or in 'moosh'. **1945** BAKER *Austral. Lang.* vii. 141 Jail food is *moosh*.

moosh[3] (muʃ), var. *MUSH *sb.*[5] Used esp. as a term of address.
1943 *Police Jrnl.* Mar. 69 *Moosh*, a person, an individual. **1950** P. TEMPEST *Lag's Lexicon* 137 'Moosh' is used more as a greeting: 'Hullo, Moosh.' **1961** J. STROUD *Touch & Go* xvii. 183 Waiter!.. Look, moosh, this is cold. **1966** *New Statesman* 23 Dec. 934/3 My old woman's gone to Paris with a black moosh. **1972** J. BROWN *Chancer* i. 12 Look, moosh, you'll strip off or I'll take them off you.

moot, *sb.*[1] Add: **5.** Delete 'Now in use only at Gray's Inn' and substitute 'Revived in the Inns of Court after falling into disuse, and introduced into universities where law is studied'.
1926 E. WEEKLEY *Words Anc. & Mod.* 70 The practice of holding at the Inns of Court moots at which law students gain experience by arguing an hypothetical case. **1962** E. MITCHELL *Business Man's Lawyer* 441/2 *Moot*, a gathering of lawyers or law students, to argue—semi-formally—interesting but academic points of law. **1973** *Univ. of Leicester Prospectus 1974–75* facing p. 33 (*caption*) A 'moot' in the Department of Law. The Department has won the national 'Observer' mooting competition twice in the last three years.

mootah, mooter (mū·tă). *U.S. slang.* Also **moota, mootie, mota, muta,** and other varr. [Origin unknown.] Marijuana.
1933 C. DE LENOIR *Hundredth Man* xiii. 220 This drug.. looked like chopped hay, or dried clover... In short, a 'muggles', 'weed', or 'mootie', cannabis indica. **1938** *Detective Fiction Weekly* 8 Jan. 47/2 He found plenty of marijuana... As always, it came in cigarettes, called 'reefers', 'muggles', 'moocahs', 'mus', 'grifos', 'mootas', or sometimes, playfully, 'Mary Warners'. **1943** *Time* 19 July 54/2 Marijuana may be called muggles, mooter, Mary Warner, Mary Jane, Indian hay, loco weed, love weed, bambalacha, mohasky, mu, moocah, grass, tea or blue sage. **1946** MEZZROW & WOLFE *Really Blues* (1957) 52 All the time he was in the asylum he kept waiting for a big train to pull in with a carload of muta just for him. **1950** H. E. GOLDIN *Dict. Amer. Underworld Lingo* 285/1 *Marijuana*... mota; muggles; stink-weed. **1956** 'E. MCBAIN' *Cop Hater* (1958) x. 92 One of the guys was on mootah. So he got a little high. **1971** E. E. LANDY *Underground Dict.* 128 *Marijuana*,..moocah, mota, mutha.

mooti, var. *MUTI.

mootness (mū·tnės). *U.S. Law.* [f. MOOT *a.* + -NESS.] Of a legal case or question: the fact or condition of being hypothetical.
1946 *Univ. Pennsylvania Law Rev.* XCIV. 127 No distinction will be made between cases where only a single issue is alleged to be moot and those in which the entire case stands or falls on a determination of mootness or its absence. **1951** WOLFSON & KURLAND *Robertson & Kirkham's Jurisdiction of Supreme Court of U.S.* xxxvi. 505 The Court may request counsel to discuss an issue as to mootness. **1955** *Univ. Pennsylvania Law Rev.* CIII. 773 Since a court is deprived of jurisdiction when a case becomes moot, the fact of mootness can be raised at any time during the judicial proceeding and, once proved, will prevent decision of the case on the merits. **1960** *U.S. Supreme Court Reports* 362 U.S. § 577 If..George Parker's five-year quest for justice must end ignominiously in the limbo of mootness, surely something is badly askew in our system of criminal justice. **1970** *Harvard Law Rev.* LXXXIII. 1674 This Note will explore a situation, labeled a mootness question, that has become a recurrent problem for the Supreme Court: where events subsequent to the judgment of the trial court have so affected the relations between the parties that the two conditions for justiciability relevant on appeal—adverse interest and effective remedy—have arguably been compromised. **1974** *Ibid.* LXXXVIII. 373 (*heading*) The mootness doctrine in the Supreme Court. *Ibid.* 376 Mootness questions arise only once a court has determined, usually implicitly, that a litigant has standing to bring the action.

mop, *sb.*[2] Add: **1. d.** *Mrs. Mop(p*: see *MRS. 2 c.

4. a. *mop-haired* adj., *-headed* (further examples); **c. mop-board**: for *U.S.* read 'orig. *U.S.*' and add earlier example; **mop-nail** (earlier example).
1854 Mop-board [see *baseboard* (*BASE *sb.*[1] 20)]. **1924** L. ECKENSTEIN *Tutankh-aten* v. 46 The..mop-haired Syrian almost daily presented himself at the gate. **1900** M. THORN in W. D. Drury *Bk. Gardening* xi. 360 Trees that are 'mop-headed', or top-heavy, should be supported by stakes. **1926** S. T. WARNER *Lolly Willowes* II. 85 She looked at the large mop-headed blossoms [*sc.* chrysanthemums]. **1934** *Times Educ. Suppl.* 3 Feb. p. iv/4 The autumn-flowering, mop-headed group of *P[rimula] capitata*. **1966** *Gloss. Landscape Work* (*B.S.I.*) IV. 15 *Mop-headed*, having naturally or induced a compact, rounded head, small in relation to the height of stem. **1972** *Guardian* 26 Jan. 9/6 Straight Jane Ltd..are now offering a Twist-n-Wring mop..with a head of the traditional type that gave mop-headed hair-dos their name. **1974** *Sunday Express* 21 Apr. 6/8 His mop-headed adventures are told in an oddly convoluted style and some will find them decidedly gooey. **1841** S. BAMFORD *Passages in Life of Radical* I. xxxvii. 216 Some had been grinding scythes, others..screw-drivers, rusty swords, pikels, and mop-nails.

mop (mǫp), *sb.*[7] and *int. U.S. slang.* [Echoic; cf. *BOP *sb.*[2]] (See quots.)
1944 in R. S. Gold *Jazz Lexicon* (1964) 208 (*tune-title*) Mop mop. **1945** L. SHELLY *Jive Talk Dict.* 15 *Mop*, the finale. **1947** *Britannica Bk. of Year* 840/2 *Mop*, slang, a word connoting surprise, anguish; a mild sort of 'hubba, hubba, hubba' (1944). **1952** B. ULANOV *Hist. Jazz in Amer.* (1958) xxv. 349 Such words as 'mop!' an exclamation of wide currency in the early forties which accurately described a musical device (the final beat in a cadence of triplets, usually bringing the release of a jazz composition to an end). **1959** *Village Voice* (N.Y.) 28 Oct. 13, I wait a while, eyes closed, and I look, mop! I'm in the bathtub, all alone. **1970** C. MAJOR *Dict. Afro-Amer. Slang* 82 *Mop*, the last beat at the end of a jazz number with a cadence of triplets.

mop, *v.*[2] Add: **1.** (Later example.)
1927 *Motor Cycling* 7 Dec. 104/2 With a successful chromium plate the finished surface is so hard that it cannot be buffed or mopped.

2. b. To wipe (perspiration, tears, etc.) *from* the face or brow.
1872 R. W. BUCHANAN *Saint Abe & his Seven Wives* i. 4 And mopping from his brow the sweat, The boy glanced round with teeth still set. **1907** *Smart Set* Apr. 18/2 She.. mopped the hot tears from her face.

3. mop up. Also *fig.* Various slang uses: To drink greedily (further examples); also with *it*; also, to eat greedily; to get hold of (profits, etc.) (further example); to make an end of, slaughter (further examples); also *Mil.*, to complete the occupation of (a district, etc.) by capturing or killing enemy troops left there (cf. quot. 1901 in Dict.); also *absol.* and *transf.*
1898 T. TROUBRIDGE in W. A. Morgan *'House' on Sport* 393 The birds..come over in one's and two's, and are 'mopped up'. **1902** WODEHOUSE *Pothunters* i. 17, I hope your first man mops you up. **1915** A. HUXLEY *Let.* Dec. (1969) 88 It is *up to you*..to roll in the Texan subscriptions, while our agents..are..to mop up other corners of the dark continent. **1917** P. GIBBS *Battles of Somme* 295 Reserve battalions..came up behind to 'mop-up' the captured ground. **1920** M. A. MÜGGE *War Diary of Square Peg* 221 The second wave going over the top; it 'mops up', 'cleans up' the enemy's dug-outs. **1921** WODEHOUSE *Indiscretions of Archie* vii. 64 'Seacliff always had a—a tendency—a—a weakness—it was a family failing—' 'Mopping it up, do you mean? Shifting it?' **1936** —— *Laughing Gas* iii. 37, I find you here, mopping up the stuff like a vacuum cleaner. **1938** *Sun* (Baltimore) 31 Oct. 4/1 Three fires..were reported to be under control with the fire-fighters 'mopping up' today. **1940** *Times* (Weekly ed.) 10 Jan. 7/4 While mopping up the ground captured, the Zouaves took five machine-guns, 2,000 rounds of ammunition, and 12 prisoners. **1942** *R.A.F. Jrnl.* 30 May 33 The enemy was still fighting behind us but they would be mopped up in time. **1962** A. NISBETT *Technique Sound Studio* 239 Membrane and vibrating panel absorbers.. readily remove sound energy from the air at their resonant frequency and this is then mopped up within the absorber by various forms of damping. **1970** *Toronto Daily Star* 24 Sept. 1/7 King's troops were pursuing the fleeing rebels, mopping up. **1971** *E. Afr. Standard* (Nairobi) 13 Apr. 1/1 Troops were reported to be mopping up remnants of the..insurgents. **1973** *Times* 30 July 18/2 He also had to mop up the ensuing threatening chaos when prices rose much further than had been predicted. **1973** *Press & Jrnl.* (Aberdeen) 7 Aug. 16/8 A perfect crossfield ball to Hay allowed the inside left to dribble to the by-line and cut it back, but Watson was on hand to mop up the danger. **1973** *Times* 27 Dec. 11/1 The Bank of England 'mopped up' a large surplus by selling Treasury bills to both houses and banks. **1974** *Times* 5 Apr. 16/4 While mopping up a Knickerbocker Glory or two we devised a new form of the old game.

mop-up *sb.*, also, an act of 'mopping-up' (further examples).
1917 P. GIBBS *Battles of Somme* 296 The honour of the new attack was given to the 'mop-up' battalions behind. **1921** *Daily Colonist* (Victoria, B.C.) 2 Oct. 1/5 Men.. known among the strikers as 'mop-up gangs' have committed depredations, beaten up a few loyal employees, and threatened and intimidated other employees. **1944** *Sun* (Baltimore) 29 Apr. 2 (*caption*) Sergt. Charles H. Wolverton..prepares to throw a hand grenade into a Japanese dugout during the mop-up of the Empress Augusta Bay area after 18 days of bitter fighting.

mopane (mopā·ni). *S. Afr.* Also **mapani, mopané, mopani.** [Bantu *mo-pane.*] **1.** A tree, *Colophospermum mopane*, of the family Leguminosæ, native to areas of low rainfall in southern Africa, and distinguished by rough, flaking, grey or brown bark, racemes of small, pale green flowers, and leaves formed of a pair of triangular leaflets joined at the base, which fold together during periods of intense heat. Also *attrib.*
1857 D. LIVINGSTONE *Missionary Trav. & Res. S. Afr.* 91 In some parts there are forests of mimosæ and mopane. *Ibid.* 162 Numbers of 'Baobab' and 'Mopané' trees abound all over this hard smooth surface [of calcareous tufa]. **1864** T. BAINES *Explor. S.-W. Afr.* xv. 422 The palms and open grassy plain had given place to thickets of mimosa.. and mopane. **1871** J. MACKENZIE *Ten Years North of Orange River* viii. 140 We at length found in a large mopane forest a well-beaten path. **1881** E. E. FREWER tr. *Holub's Seven Yrs. in S. Afr.* I. 48 The mapani-tree, with its oleaginous leaves and porous brittle wood. **1893** F. C. SELOUS *Trav. & Adventure S.-E. Afr.* 160 The fork of a mopani tree. **1906** *Chambers's Jrnl.* Mar. 213/1 Viewed across the hazy expanse of baobab and mopane bush. **1910** J. BUCHAN *Prester John* iv. 87 The mopani trees with their dull green wearied me. **1932** *Discovery* July 224/1 The mopané is a resinous tree, making good fuel. **1947** J. STEVENSON-HAMILTON *Wild Life S. Afr.* iv. 36 The Mopani belt in its extension along the Imbabate River. **1958** L. VAN DER POST *Lost World of Kalahari* vi. 110 We came down the side of the dunes on to a level plain covered with Mopani trees. **1973** PALMER & PITMAN *Trees S. Afr.* II. 842 The mopane is the dominant tree of large parts of northern South and South West Africa where great stretches of hot, arid country..are covered with it. *Ibid.* 843 Farmers in mopane veld look upon the tree as providing valuable fodder. **1975** M. HARTMANN *Game for Vultures* iii. 44 They moved..away into the black mopani bush.

2. mopane bee, beetle, fly, worm (see quots.).
1953 S. H. SKAIFE *African Insect Life* xxi. 357 The stingless bees, or Mopani bees, as they are often called, that are found in Africa belong to the genus *Trigona*. **1972** L. VAN DER POST *Story like the Wind* vi. 161 At about ten in the morning..all the billions of mopani beetles, hidden behind the butterfly leaves of the trees, began to sing their Messiah to the day. **1975** M. HARTMANN *Game for Vultures* i. 2 Mopani flies, little black squelches, were skitting around his eyes and ears. **1966** D. VARADAY *Gara-Yaka's Domain* xvii. 182 No less a find than crawling, fat, three-inch-long worms! Mopani worms—Masonja—as the Bantu call these brightly coloured insects, are regarded by them as a great delicacy. **1973** PALMER & PITMAN *Trees S. Afr.* II. 843 Large, dark, spotted caterpillars, the larvae of the moth *Gonimbrasia belina*—5 to 8 cm long and fat as a finger—feed upon the mopane leaves and are used by Africans and Bushmen as food... Mopane worms are much valued by rural Africans and are often their richest source of protein.

mope, *sb.* **1.** Delete † and add later examples.
1932 J. T. FARRELL *Young Lonigan* vi. 259 They had a lot of pep, and weren't a bunch of mopes. **1962** E. O'BRIEN *Lonely Girl* i. 8 It happens to country mopes like you, as soon as you dance with a fellow.

mope, *v.* Add: **4.** To confine or shut *up* (in a place).
1863 A. D. WHITNEY *Faith Gartney's Girlhood* xvi. 140 The child shouldn't be moped up here, all winter!

moped (mōᵘ·ped), *sb.* [Sw. (1952), f. *tramp-cykel med motor och pedaler*, pedal cycle with engine and pedals; cf. also Ger. *moped.*] A motorized pedal cycle. Also *attrib.*
1956 I. DUNLOP *Going to Britain* (ed. 2) 21 You must have a licence to drive an autocycle ('moped'). **1957** *Times* 19 Nov. 11/3 The accompanying recommendation that the minimum age limit for riding mopeds should be reduced from sixteen to fifteen will be less readily accepted. **1960** F. FARR *Mo-Peds & Scooters* i. 14 The name 'mo-ped' originated in Sweden, was popularized in Germany and is now generally accepted here. The machines are internationally defined..as cycles fitted with engines of under 50 cubic centimetres capacity and retaining the normal characteristics of bicycles. **1971** *Guardian* 4 June 22/4 Cut the minimum age for moped riders from 16 to 14. **1973** *Times* 18 May 21/7 As the rider of a single-seater moped, I am required by law to possess insurance against claims from mythical passengers. **1974** *Guardian* 25 Mar. 21/1, I bought an electric moped. It..has a range of about 20 miles.

mophy, var. *MOFFIE.

mopiness (mōᵘ·pinės). [f. MOPY *a.* + -NESS.] Mopy state or condition.
1927 *Smallholder* 26 Mar. 115/1 Ordinary Diarrhoea [in chicks]. Symptoms. Looseness of the bowels... There may or may not be mopiness but invariably there is inactivity.

mopoke, morepork. Add: **1.** (N.Z. examples.)
1849 W. T. POWER *Sketches in N.Z.* ix. 74 Among the commonest birds which frequent the forest is a small owl, generally known..by the denomination of 'More pork'. **1866** M. A. BARKER *Let.* in *Station Life N.Z.* (1870) xiv. 100 The last cry of a very pretty little owl, called from its distinctly uttered cries, the 'more-pork'. **1874** T. H. POTTS *On Recent Changes Fauna N.Z.* 8 The name.. morepork is well-known throughout the country. Australian settlers distinguish a podargus by a similar name. **1882** —— *Out in Open* 118 *Athene Novæ Zelandiæ*, morepork, ruru rarupeho of the Maoris. **1894** C. W. RICHMOND *Let.* 22 Mar. in *Richmond–Atkinson Papers* (1960) II. x. 597 Once..they had nothing to eat but a tui and a morepork. **1905** J. M. THOMSON *Bush Boys of N.Z.* iv. 59 The More-pork is the small New Zealand owl, so-called from its peculiar guttural cry. **1963** *Evening Post* (Wellington, N.Z.) 26 Oct., In the..action shots which are skilfully interwoven with Maori legends and traditions about each bird, are the morepork..fantail, bellbird, tui.

b. (Earlier and later examples.)
1845 R. HOWITT *Impressions Australia Felix* 233 'A more-pork kind of fellow' is a man of cut-and-dry phrases;

a person remarkable for nothing new in common conversation. **1946** *Coast to Coast 1945* 132 He was such a helpless sort of a poor mopoke.

2. (Later examples.)

1916, 1934 [see *BOOBOOK].

mo·pper-up. *Mil.* [f. MOP *v.*^{2} 3 + -ER^1.] A soldier who 'mops up' an enemy area (see *MOP *v.*^{2} 3). Also *fig.* (perhaps in these uses owing as much to MOP *v.*^{2} 3 in Dict.).

1917 *London Gaz.* 26 Nov. 12330/1 Pte. Dancox was one of a party of about ten men detailed as moppers-up. **1919** W. H. DOWNING *Digger Dial.* 34 *Mopper-up*, (1) One of a party of men who follow the leading waves of an attack in order to clear the enemy from the ground behind the assaulting troops; (2) a drunkard. **1920** G. K. ROSE *2/4th Oxf. & Bucks. Lt. Infty.* x. 122 The Berks came afterwards as 'moppers-up'. **1923** KIPLING *Irish Guards in Great War* I. 230 The 'mopper-up' who dealt with the débris of attacks. **1928** *Mod. Lang. Rev.* Apr. 136 His plan of attack is described on p. 174 of his *Philosophy of Grammar*; his 'moppers up' follow in the *Modern English Grammar*. **1936** *Daily Tel.* 15 Aug. 15/5 How..fascinating to know that your goods are coming to the London market by the Mopper Up.

moppet^2. **1.** (Later examples.)

1973 *Houston* (Texas) *Chron. Mag. People, Places, Pleasures* 14 Oct. 6/3 Jane Withers..made a long-delayed transition from movie moppet 'heavy' to middle-aged TV pitchlady. **1975** *Time Out* 10 Jan. 45/2 Watching the well-mannered moppets and well-groomed mums roll up in taxis and Bentleys to the Theatre Royal, Haymarket, certainly helped to set the scene.

moppie (mǫ·pi). *S. Afr.* [Afrikaans, ad. Du. *mopje* ditty.] A street-song of the Cape Malays.

1949 *Cape Times* 10 Jan. 2/6 He hoped that the Cape 'moppies' or comic songs and the *liedjies* would become a regular feature of future carnivals. **1953** DU PLESSIS & LÜCKHOFF *Malay Quarter* iii. 48 *Moppies* are little songs (often of doubtful content) sung in order to challenge, deride, or irritate the listener, or merely as foolery. When singing a moppie, the singer often includes a person's name, and if the person referred to cannot respond in similar vein, he is laughed at by all present. **1974** *S. Afr. Panorama* June 20 The 'moppie' is a comical song. The soloist uses gestures of the hands and other movements to illustrate it as he goes.

mopping, *vbl. sb.*^{2} Add: Also **mopping-up,** the action of the verb *mop up,* in various senses (also *fig.*). Also *attrib.*

1909 *Westm. Gaz.* 3 Sept. 9/4 Persistent 'mopping up' of London stocks [of silver] naturally restricts supplies for Continental and other requirements. **1918** E. S. FARROW *Dict. Mil. Terms* 394 *Mopping up trenches*, the crushing of hostile units which continue the resistances at certain parts of the trench, and the searching of the trenches and bombproofs with a view to making sure that none of the enemy are left in them. **1925** FRASER & GIBBONS *Soldier & Sailor Words* 158 *Mopping-up*, the term for the work allotted to special parties of men appointed to follow close in the track of advancing 'waves' of troops, in order to explore and clear the enemy lines and dug-outs of men remaining behind... The Mopping-up method was first adopted at the Battle of Arras in February, 1917. **1937** *Sun* (Baltimore) 12 July 5/1 Six flood-weary West Virginia communities began mopping-up operations.. today after two surging creeks flooded homes and business houses. **1940** *Economist* 20 Apr. 717/2 We must not be diverted in Narvik, which is now..a mopping-up operation. **1940** *Ibid.* 2 Nov. 552/1 In the last war, the Excess Profits Duty proved itself an excellent 'mopping-up' tax, against an inflationary background. **1940** 'GUN BUSTER' *Return via Dunkirk* II. iv. 120 Mopping-up parties of Tommies were investigating the farmhouses. **1959** *Listener* 19 Mar. 521/1 Shakespeare is naturally drawn upon very little, since he had already been the subject of 'mopping up' in every volume of this kind. **1962** W. NOWOTTNY *Lang. Poets Use* i. 24 A mopping-up of successive problems in one area after another until the whole domain of poetic language is occupied and systematized. **1967** G. F. FIENNES *I Tried to Run a Railway* i. 4 We rounded up a few volunteers to do a mopping up operation on the permanent way. **1973** I. BUTLER *Eldest Brother* xix. 339 Mopping-up operations in Gujerat.

mopstick. Add: **1. c.** = COCKALORUM 3. *colloq.*

1969 I. & P. OPIE *Children's Games* viii. 257 In Warwick, 'Mollie, Mollie Mopstick, all off! all off!' In Nuneaton: Mopstick, mopstick, bear our weight, Two, four, six, eight, ten. *Ibid.* 260 'Jack upon the Mopstick' (Warwickshire, 1892),..'Johnny on the Mopstick' (Worcester, *c.* 1930),..'Mopstick' (Kettering, *c.* 1915).

3. *slang.* **a.** A stupid man. **b.** *U.S.* (See quot. 1915.)

1886 H. BAUMANN *Londinismen* 111/2. **1915** *World* (N.Y.) Sunday Suppl. 9 May 14/3 *Mopstick*, one who loafs around a cheap saloon or barrel house and cleans up the place for drinks.

mopsy. 2. Delete ? *Obs.* and add later examples. Also *attrib.* or as *adj.* (Sense passing into that of MOP *sb.*^{4} in some examples.)

1916 A. BENNETT *These Twain* xviii. 406, I always knew that girl was a mopsy slut. **1958** J. CAREW *Wild Coast* iii. 44 He don't have juice in his back to fill up a mopsy with delight. **1958** *Times Lit. Suppl.* 14 Mar. 140/5 Poor Swann's pain and frustration..are a simpler matter, Odette de Crécy being the most commonplace of lying mopsies and a born torturer of the sensitive.

mor (mōᵊɹ). *Soil Sci.* [Da., lit. 'humus' (adopted in this specific sense by P. E. Müller 1879, in *Tidsskrift for Skovbrug* III. 7): cf. MOOR *sb.*^{1}] Humus which forms a discrete layer on top of the soil with little or no mineral soil mixed with it, which is characteristic of coniferous forests and is generally strongly acid in reaction. Cf. *MULL *sb.*^{10}

1931, 1952 [see *MULL *sb.*^{10}]. **1971** *Nature* 10 Sept. 133/1 Formation of the mor type of forest litter..has been attributed to a number of factors. **1974** [see *MULL *sb.*^{10}].

mora^1. Add: **3.** (Earlier example.)

1832 [see TIME *sb.* 10].

b. In linguistic analysis, the minimal unit of duration of a speech-sound. Also *attrib.*

1933 L. BLOOMFIELD *Language* vii. 110 In dealing with matters of quantity, it is often convenient to set up an arbitrary unit of relative duration, the *mora*. Thus, if we say that a short vowel lasts one mora, we may describe the long vowels of the same language as lasting, say, one and one-half morae or two morae. **1941** G. L. TRAGER in L. Spier et al. *Lang. Culture & Personality* 136 In many cases it will be found that an element smaller than the phonetic syllable functions as the accentual or prosodic unit; this unit may be called, following current practice, the mora... The term *mora*..is useful in avoiding confusion, even if it should turn out to mean merely phonemic syllable. **1964** E. PALMER tr. *Martinet's Elem. General Linguistics* iii. 80 Each of the segments characterized by one of the successive punctual tones is called a mora. **1964** K. L. PIKE in D. Abercrombie et al. *Daniel Jones* 425 A train of alternating stresses..clashes with a different wave train keyed into a mora count beginning from the last suffixual syllable. **1968** W. S. ALLEN *Vox Graeca* ii. 81 For diphthongs in Greek cannot strictly be distinguished as 'short' and 'long'; for accentual purposes they all have the same value of 2 'morae' (time-units), as for a long simple vowel.

mora^4. (Earlier and later examples.)

1825 C. WATERTON *Wanderings S. Amer.* i. 5 Heedless, and bankrupt, in all curiosity must he be, who can journey on without stopping to take a view of the towering mora. **1918** C. W. BEEBE *Jungle Peace* (1919) vii. 140 A house with roof of pale pink like a giant mora in full bloom. **1949** *Caribbean Quarterly* I. III. 42 Three forest areas..could be ..logged so as to yield about 3 million cubic feet of saleable timber per year, mainly Greenheart but also Mora and other hardwoods. **1956** *Handbk. of Hardwoods* (Forest Prod. Res. Lab.) 154 Mora is a dominant tree of mixed swamp forests and is found in the Guianas, Trinidad and eastern Venezuela. **1958** J. CAREW *Black Midas* vi. 109 Santos stopped under a mora tree. **1971** *Advocate-News* (Barbados) 17 Sept. Guyana Suppl. p. ii/2 Boys at work in pouring rain felling giant mora and wallaba trees.

mora^5. (Later examples.)

1907 B. M. CROKER *Company's Servant* xviii. 195 Sitting ..on a little 'morah' at her feet. **1971** *Illustr. Weekly India* 4 Apr. 22/3, I resorted to circumlocutions..which invariably produced a *mora* or a chair in the little Chandni Chowk shops.

moraine. Add: **b.** In rock-gardening, a bed, often raised, constructed of rubble covered with fine chippings, in an attempt to produce suitable conditions for alpine plants. Also *attrib.*

1907 R. J. FARRER *My Rock-Garden* i. 14 There..is my toy-garden, my baby moraine, the particular pet joy of my heart. **1914** H. H. THOMAS *Rock Gardening* 65 The moraine may be described as a bed or border of varying size, preferably situated on a slight slope, and consisting of broken stone, with which, however, a certain proportion of light, sifted soil is mixed. *Ibid.* 72 Favourite Moraine Plants. **1931** *Times Lit. Suppl.* 16 Apr. 297/2 This [*sc.* bad drainage] is..the cause of most failures and disappointments in moraine gardening. **1961** W. INGWERSEN in W. E. Shewell-Cooper et al. *Alpine & Rock Gardening* vi. 43 If one moraine is to be divided into limestone and lime-free compartments, then the limestone area must be at the bottom.

moral, *sb.* Add: **9.** Now chiefly *Austral.* (Further examples.) Also quasi-*adj.*, morally certain.

1916 C. J. DENNIS *Moods of Ginger Mick* 40 'E 'as struck it for a moral. Ginger's found 'is game at last. **1933** *Bulletin* (Sydney) 18 Jan. 20 Had been winning all over the countryside and was a moral for the big jumping event. **1934** [see *ear-biter*]. **1946** R. FRANKLYN in *Coast to Coast 1945* 221, I think we orta go home, Darky. We're a moral to get nabbed. **1957** 'N. CULOTTA' *They're a Weird Mob* (1958) v. 72 As I was sayin' this bloke says 'e's a moral. **1972** I. HAMILTON *Thrill Machine* xxvii. 124 Eric said this bloke had a new film... It's a moral to be a load of bull but you never know. **1975** L. RYAN *Shearers* 79 Andy Burns rang last night..reckons Dallas is a moral in the first.

moral, *a.* Add: **1. a.** (Further examples.)

1949 M. FORTES *Social Structure* 60 Its form derives from a paradigm..sanctioned by..moral values. **1951** R. FIRTH *Elem. Social Organiz.* vi. 200 This can be illustrated by considering the moral values attached to human personality in certain social situations. **1964** S. M. WILLHELM in I. L. Horowitz *New Sociol.* 184 The scientific ideology simply places the scientist in a moral vacuum. *Ibid.* 186 Recognizing his historical obligation to impose the very moral accountability which certain scientists seek to avoid, the intellectual insists upon his right to direct the affairs of a recalcitrant scientist.

c. (Further examples.)

1817 COLERIDGE *Biogr. Lit.* I. x. 213 My essays contributed to introduce the practice of placing the questions and events of the day in a moral point of view. **1883** W. JAMES *Let.* 23 Jan. in R. B. Perry *Tht. & Char. W. James* (1935) I. 389 Although from a moral point of view your sympathy commands my warmest thanks, from the intellectual point of view, it seems, first, to suppose that I am a bachelor [etc.]. **1951** C. DAY LEWIS *Poet's Task* 19 As an aesthetic judgement this is so bizarre that one can only take it for a moral judgement. **1972** *Jrnl. Social Psychol.* LXXXVI. 158 The mean moral judgment quotient for girls was slightly higher than that for boys.

2. c. *moral psychology*: psychology concerned with the psychological effect of rules of conduct, esp. the sense of virtue and vice, upon behaviour. Hence *moral-psychological* adj.

1859 J. MARTINEAU in *National Rev.* IX. 504 Does an author, who has so distinguished himself in Logical psychology,..doubt that there is also a Moral psychology? *a* **1865** J. GROTE *Treat. Moral Ideals* (1876) xiii. 297 Moral psychology endeavours to co-ordinate individual experiences. **1867** MILL *Exam. Hamilton's Philos.* (ed. 3) xxvi. 586 This vital truth in moral psychology, that we can improve our character if we will. **1946** *Mind* LV. 189 His interest in moral psychology and the empirical facts of the moral life remained. **1963** J. WIESENFARTH *Henry James* ii. 51 This is precisely the decision that climaxes her coming to grips with the moral-psychological problem in the novel. **1972** J. RAWLS *Theory of Justice* § 29. 181 The parties must consider the general facts of moral psychology.

3. d. *moral tutor*: a university tutor appointed to have a particular concern for the moral well-being of a student. Hence *moral pupil.*

1932 *Oxf. Univ. Handbk.* I. 130 In some colleges an undergraduate is assigned for all his time to a 'moral tutor', who is often not the tutor to whom he is going for his reading, but one who undertakes to keep in touch with him during his career and to help and advise him generally in his life. **1963** J. I. M. STEWART *Last Tresilians* xiv. 106 That's Leech, the Pro-Provost. He's my moral tutor. **1966** *Rep. Comm. Inquiry Univ. Oxf.* II. 383 Plus £1 per moral pupil other than those for whom a fellow is tutorially responsible. *Ibid.*, Paid to 16 moral tutors. **1969** V. DE S. PINTO *City that Shone* xi. 249 Jackie would continue to be my 'moral tutor', but..my 'English tutor' would be Mr Percy Simpson.

4. Also *moral code, norm, order, rule, system.*

1690 LOCKE *Hum. Und.* I. iii. 15, I think it will be hard to instance any one moral rule. **1927** *Amer. Jrnl. Sociol.* XXXII. 736 The same forces which co-operate to create the characteristic social organization and the accepted moral order of a given society or social group determine at the same time..the character of the individuals who compose that society. **1931** H. S. WALPOLE *Judith Paris* II. ii. 240 A rather blowzy red-cheeked lady, who..had a warm heart but an uncertain moral code. **1951** R. FIRTH *Elem. Social Organiz.* vi. 185 The effective standard of judgement..has appeared to be the recognition of offences against a moral code of behaviour. *Ibid.* 187 The moral rules to be found in different types of society. *Ibid.* 202 Divergence from the Western moral norms is seen much more widely in infanticide. *Ibid.* 213 A moral system.. includes the idea of an elaborate interlocking set of judgements. **1957** P. WORSLEY *Trumpet shall Sound* 250 The role of ritual obscenity as providing an occasion for the statement and reinforcement of moral norms is well known from many societies. **1958** R. C. ANGELL *Free Society & Moral Crisis* ii. 16 The most basic—though not the most tangible—aspect of the moral order is the set of common values that motivates the members of a society. **1970** G. A. & A. G. THEODORSON *Mod. Dict. Sociol.* 264 The various moral systems of the world may include many of the same moral ideas.

7. a. (Further examples.) *moral suasion*: see SUASION 1 b.

1841 THOREAU *Jrnl.* 19 Feb. in *Writings* (1906) VII. 217 It is a moral force as well as he. **1913** *Act* 3 & 4 *Geo. V* c. 28 § 1 Moral imbeciles; that is to say, persons who from an early age display some permanent mental defect coupled with strong vicious or criminal propensities. **1927** *Act* 17 & 18 *Geo. V* c. 33 § 1 Moral defectives, that is to say, persons in whose case there exists mental defectiveness coupled with strongly vicious or criminal propensities and who require care, supervision and control for the protection of others. **1951** R. FIRTH *Elem. Social Organiz.* vi. 213 It is in the capacity to generate and adapt moral force that man derives one of the most potent springs to social action. **1952** R. M. HARE *Lang. Morals* I. iv. 71 If, when we did as we were told, the total effects of our so doing.. were always such as we would not have chosen..then we should..work out our own salvation or become moral defectives. **1967** D. J. WEST *Young Offender* v. 106 A paper ..seeking to prove the moral imbecility of habitual criminals. **1968** *Listener* 26 Sept. 408/1 'Moral insanity' was superseded by 'moral imbecility'; this in turn gave way to 'psychopathic personality' (which had developed out of 'constitutional psychopathic inferiority').

c. *moral support*: support or help the effect of which is psychological rather than physical.

1885 [in Dict.]. **1921** W. S. MAUGHAM *Circle* I. 19 You were rather scared... I thought I'd come and give you a little moral support. **1926** F. M. FORD *Man could stand Up* I. ii. 37 He needed her moral support! **1968** 'M. CARROLL' *Dead Trouble* iii. 44 Where were you? Couldn't you have given me some moral support? **1973** J. BURROWS *Like an Evening Gone* i. 7 She had it all worked out. All she wanted from her husband was a little moral support.

d. Similarly *moral fibre*; esp. in phr. *lack of moral fibre,* used *euphem.* for lack of courage. Cf. *LMF* s.v. *L 7.

1884 *Boy's Own Paper* 11 Oct. 18/2 Fanshawe was a boy in whom bad instincts had been nourished by his training, and who, from constant lack of moral fibre, had gradually deteriorated. **1942** [see *GROUNDED *ppl. a.*^{1} 8]. **1960** *Times* 11 Jan. 13/6 Fail to register for the cut-price course

in foundry management and clearly you are lacking in moral fibre. **1970** L. Deighton *Events Last Flight R.A.F. Bomber* xvii. 263 The R.A.F. authorities..would stamp the words 'lack of moral fibre' across the man's documents ..and send him away..an officially recognized coward. **1973** K. Royce *Spider Underground* iii. 52 She was tough all right, of high moral fibre.

e. *moral turpitude*: conduct considered depraved; an instance of such conduct.

1879 [see Turpitude 1 a]. **1931** J. P. Clark *Deportation of Aliens from U.S. to Europe* v. 165 An alien convicted of stealing $15 in Massachusetts was held subject to deportation because of conviction of a crime involving moral turpitude.

f. *Moral Rearmament*: a religious group founded by the American evangelist Frank Buchman (1878–1961); the beliefs or practices of this group; = *Buchmanism. Abbrev. **M.R.A.* (q.v.). Also *transf.* and *fig.* So *Moral Rearmer*.

1938 *Times* 2 Nov. 6/4 Moral rearmament, which is the true basis of national fitness, is an individual responsibility. **1940** Earl of Athlone et al. *Moral Re-Armament* 3 Moral Re-Armament stands for a change of heart, for that new spirit which must animate all human relationships. **1940** N. Mitford *Pigeon Pie* iii. 55 Luke had been guided to ask a hundred people to dinner..to talk about Moral Rearmament. *Ibid.* iv. 80 If the British people had gone all out for moral rearmament and real appeasement, things need never have reached this pass. **1951** V. A. Demant *What is happening to Us?* iii. 22 The Emperor Augustus tried to save the civilization of Ancient Rome by reviving the old cults..and the poet Horace..wrote his lovely Odes to help in this older version of 'Moral Rearmament'. **1956** A. Huxley *Adonis & Alphabet* 118 For *their* campaigns, the Moral Rearmers have a whole arsenal of Christian *Oklahomas* and ethical *Cats on Hot Tin Roofs*. **1961** [see *Buchmanism]. **1969** *Guardian* 20 June 10/4 Senator Ralph Vibert, an advocate and a Moral Re-Armer. **1973** *Ibid.* 11 June 11/6 We were made to confess all our weaknesses... It was like Moral Re-Armament.

8. b. *moral welfare*: see quot. 1965.

1927 *8th Ann. Rep. Archbishops' Advisory Board Preventive & Rescue Work* 9 The League of Nations Report on the Traffic in Women and Children..has awakened an interest in moral welfare work that is bound to help in arousing the public conscience against prostitution. **1944** A. Thirkell *Headmistress* x. 211 Doing wonders with her Moral Welfare Committee. **1965** Hall & Howes *Church in Social Work* 2 'Moral welfare' is a term which..appears to have come into general use during the inter-war period to designate the social work in relation to sex, marriage and the family.

morale. Delete || and add: **3.** *attrib.* and *Comb.* uses of sense 2, as **morale-booster**, an event, occurrence, or saying which raises one's spirits; also *morale-boosting*, *-building*, *-raising* vbl. sbs. and adjs.

1943 J. B. Priestley *Daylight on Saturday* xxx. 234 Grandiose and impracticable schemes of morale-building. **1946** *Nature* 30 Nov. 777/2 Being more formally educational and only indirectly a morale-raising agent, instruction in it could be given not only by officers, but also [etc.]. **1956** C. Cockburn *In Time of Trouble* xvi. 205 The quick-firers of..controversy who..for obvious morale-building purposes prophesied that the current crisis..was the final crisis of American capitalism. **1959** *Punch* 2 Sept. 98/3 To find so many and such diverse people coming out into the open on your side is a superb morale-booster. **1960** *Harper's Bazaar* July 21/2 A beauty salon.. has become a morale-boosting relaxant centre. **1961** *Sunday Express* 12 Mar. 10/3 Another morale-boosting idea for the troops. **1961** *Guardian* 3 May 8/3 The Festival ..was a national morale-booster. **1970** C. Kersh *Aggravations M. Ashe* xi. 158 With that morale-boosting thought to end her day, my mother went to bed. **1970** 'B. Mather' *Break in Line* vi. 71 Even though it was a slip of the tongue..it was quite a morale booster. And Lord knows I needed one. **1971** A. Price *Alamut Ambush* xiii. 155 It was immensely morale-raising to see Mary floor him.

morali·stically, *adv.* [f. Moralistic *a.*: see -ically.] In a moralistic manner; by way of moral judgement.

1890 W. James *Princ. Psychol.* II. xxi. 317 The perfect object of belief would be a God or 'Soul of the World', represented both optimistically and moralistically. **1965** *New Statesman* 30 Apr. 677/2 The historical development of psychoanalysis out of medicine, from which it inherited criteria of normality and health which are much more moralistically loaded when applied to psychological than to somatic therapy. **1972** E. Lucie-Smith *Eroticism in Western Art* iii. 66 *The Golden Age* (otherwise, and more moralistically, dubbed *The Corruption of Men Before the Deluge*).

morality. Add: **8.** *attrib.*, as **morality squad**, in Canada, a municipal or provincial police unit dealing with infractions of legislation concerning prostitution, pornography, etc. So *morality officer*, etc.

1963 J. N. Harris *Weird World Wes Beattie* (1964) x. 119 He called an acquaintance on the morality squad of the Ontario Provincial Police in order to get the low-down on the obscene film racket. **1967** *Canad. News Facts* 4 Dec. 183, 18 arrested on gambling charges... Eight of the men were arrested in Montreal by the Montreal morality squad. **1970** *Toronto Daily Star* 24 Sept. 7/5 Man appears to need some censorship to protect himself from his baser tastes. I trust the morality squad will continue its good work. **1976** *Globe & Mail* (Toronto) 17 Jan. 12/4 Pasquale Zappia..died of a heart attack Thursday while being questioned by an Ottawa police morality officer outside a restaurant.

moralizable (mǫrălǝi·zăb'l), *a.* [f. Moralize *v.* + -able.] That can be rendered moral or expressed in terms of morality; amenable to moralizing.

1916 F. von Hügel *German Soul* ii. 64 They are not really moral, nor even moralisable. **1961** J. N. Findlay *Values & Intentions* ix. 399 Religion can be seen thus to be intrinsically moralizable.

morally, *adv.* **4.** (Later examples of *morally certain*.)

1869 *Bradshaw's Railway Manual* XXI. 174 It is morally certain that there will be enough net income at the end of next half-year to pay the full year's interest. **1966** 'R. Standish' *Widow Hack* ix. 97 Morally certain that I had not been seen, I returned to my car.

|| **moran** (mǫ·răn). Also **El-moran.** [Masai.] The warrior group of the Masai tribe which comprises the younger unmarried males. Also a member of this group.

1885 J. Thomson *Through Masăi Land* (ed. 3) x. 425 A certain rite, better known in Africa than in Europe, was performed; and..he was an El-moran—a warrior. **1902** H. H. Johnston *Uganda Protectorate* II. xix. 822 In former days, before the Masai warriors, called 'El Mórran', started on an expedition, they would fortify their courage with a war medicine, which was said to be the bark of *Acacia verrugosa*. **1905** A. C. Hollis *Masai* 298 Their hair is allowed to grow, and as soon as it has grown long enough to plait, they are called Il-muran (warriors). **1947** *E. African Ann. 1946–7* 43/1 The 'moran' are the warrior age-grade... In the past the 'moran' constituted a free military organization within the tribe. **1960** *Times* 8 Nov. 13/2 One Kikuyu was killed and a score were injured by Masai *moran*. **1975** *Times* 9 Apr. 12/8 The *moran* system of organized adolescence.

morassic (moræ·sik), *a.* [f. Morass + -ic.] Of, pertaining to, or characteristic of a morass; morassy.

1897 C. MacMillan in *Minnesota Bot. Stud.* (1894–8) I. 995 All of these morassic formations characterize quiet shores.

Morasthite (mǫ·răsþǝit). Also **Morascite, Morashite, Morashtite, Morastite.** [f. *Moresheth* in Gath, name of the home town of Micah.] Epithet of Micah, the Judæan prophet of the 8th century B.C.

a **1390** Wyclif *Micah* i. 1 The word of the Lord..is maad to Mycheas Morastites. **1535** Coverdale *Jer.* xxvi, Micheas the Morascite, which was a prophet vnder Ezechias kinge of Iuda, spake. *Ibid. Micah* i, This is the worde of the Lorde, that came vnto Micheas the Morastite. **1611** Bible *Jer.* xxvi. 18 Micah the Morashite prophecied in the dayes of Hezekiah king of Iudah. *Ibid. Micah* i. 1 The word of the Lord..came to Micah the Morasthite in the dayes of Iotham, Ahaz, and Hezekiah. **1839** *Penny Cycl.* XV. 172/1 Micah..is called in the title to his prophecy the Morasthite. **1845** J. Kitto *Cyclopedia Biblical Lit.* II. 334/1 It is stated that Micah the Morasthite foretold the destruction of Jerusalem in the reign of Hezekiah. **1904** *Jewish Encycl.* VIII. 533/1 Micah..was a Morasthite; that is to say, a native of Moreshethgath. **1944** G. B. Shaw *Everybody's Political What's What?* xxvi. 231 The noble God of Micah the Morasthite. **1963** Grant & Rowley *Hastings's Dict. Bible* 674 *Morashtite*,—a gentilic used in RV to designate the prophet Micah,..(AV *Morasthite*..); probably derived from Morsheth-gath.

moratorial (mǫrătō³·riăl), *a.* [f. Moratori(um + -al.] Pertaining to or payable in respect of a moratorium.

1914 *Economist* 7 Nov. 833/1 On the debts due to them and covered by the moratorium, they are entitled to a moratorial interest of 5 per cent.

moratorium. Delete || and add: Pl. **-ia, -iums.**

1932 *Sun* (Baltimore) 7 Sept. 8/2 There is little evidence that past Farm Board 'moratoriums' on sales of its commodity holdings, or its quota schemes to sift holdings into the markets in small lots, have buoyed the market for these commodities. **1956** [see sense *2]. **1972** *Times* 27 Jan. 14/4 Those who wanted to agree to moratoria to assist businesses in financial difficulties. **1973** *Nation Rev.* (Melbourne) 31 Aug. 1434/1 Will there be resolutions to the federal or sitdown moratoria in Collins street?

2. A postponement, an agreed delay, a deliberate temporary suspension (of some activity, etc.).

1932 *Sun* (Baltimore) 5 Sept. 1/2 The moratorium on picketing ordered by Milo Reno, of Des Moines, national leader of the strike, seemed virtually achieved when only on two highways near Sioux City were farmers turning back live stock and produce trucks. **1934** W. B. Wolfe *Nervous Breakdown* i. 2 In a nervous breakdown the whole personality declares a moratorium of normal activities, and both body and soul join in a cry for help. **1944** *Word Study* May 7/2 A moratorium on 'of course' sentences. **1956** *Jrnl. Amer. Psychoanal. Assoc.* Jan. 66 Societies offer..more or less sanctioned intermediary periods between childhood and adulthood, institutionalized *psychosocial moratoria*. **1957** *Observer* 25 Aug. 8/2 Their new proposal that nuclear tests should be suspended not for ten months but for two years... Under their plan, the launching of the first year's moratorium would depend on an East–West agreement to a partial disarmament plan covering several fields. **1961** I. Murdoch *Severed Head* xiii. 113 For me they [*sc.* words] constituted rather a kind of moratorium, a momentary neutral zone where I could ..absolutely rest. **1969** *Guardian* 13 Oct. 3/2 Moratorium-day on Vietnam..has so captured the attention that Wednesday is expected to see the most wide-spread political protest in America's history. **1970** *Daily Tel.* 29 Apr. 13/4 Could we not now have a moratorium on Dylan Thomas records? **1972** *Nature* 17 Mar. 94/1 A provision calling for a five-year moratorium on the killing of all ocean mammals.

Moravian, *sb.*² and *a.*² Add: **A.** *sb.* **1.** (Earlier and later examples.)

1555 [see *Lusatian *sb.* and *a.*]. **1611** Coryat *Crudities* sig. B1 A Noble Scholler..George Haunschildt of Furstenfeldt, a Morauian. **1847** [see Zechian].

B. *adj.* **2.** (Earlier example.)

1739 W. Stephens *Jrnl.* 22 Aug. in *Colonial Rec. Georgia* (1906) IV. 393 An heavy Complaint being exhibited against the Moravian Brethren.

morbid, *a.* **2.** (Further examples.)

1902 W. James *Var. Relig. Exper.* ii. 46 The athletic attitude tends ever to break down, and it inevitably does break down even in the most stalwart when..morbid fears invade the mind. *Ibid.* vi. 163 It seems to me that we are bound to say that morbid-mindedness ranges over the wider scale of experience. **1907** —— *Mem. & Stud.* (1911) 248 Dr. Janet has discussed five cases of morbid impulse. **1918** Kipling *Land & Sea Tales* (1923) 113 My Sub's a morbid-minded young animal. **1922** Joyce *Ulysses* 413 Those who are not so intimately acquainted with the minutiae of the municipal abattoir as this morbid-minded esthete. **1935** *Discovery* Nov. 346/2 The 'misfits' and perverts of morbid psychology.

morbidezza. Add: **2.** *transf.* (esp. *Mus.*): delicacy, softness, sensibility, smoothness; sometimes (degenerating into) unwholesomeness, effeminacy, sickliness.

1890 E. Dowson *Let.* c 31 Mar. (1967) 146 As for Browning!.. The subtility, the tact of omission, the Morbidezza! **1895** *Funk's Stand. Dict.*, *Morbidezza*,.. *Mus.* Extreme delicacy: a direction to the performer. **1910** G. B. Shaw *Brieux* 3 The artistic morbidezza of Byron and Victor Hugo. **1934** *Times Lit. Suppl.* 3 May 324/2 In spite of a collective morbidezza on the part of Pansy's lovers, the characterization is clear cut. **1947** C. Gray *Contingencies* 118 In spite of its *morbidezza* and romantic sentimentality it nevertheless retains the purity of line which is the hallmark of all classic art. **1960** C. S. Lewis *Studies in Words* vi. 160 But in Mrs Radcliffe *sensibility* perhaps implies a more universal *morbidezza*. **1974** *Times* 13 May 14/7 'E lucevan le stelle' and 'O dolci mani' had true *morbidezza*.

morbidity. Add: **3.** *attrib.*, as *morbidity rate*, *statistics*.

1939 Kurtz & Edgerton *Statistical Dict. Terms & Symbols* 108 *Morbidity rate*, the ratio of the number of cases of a particular disease in a year to the midyear population, usually expressed per 100,000. **1964** Gould & Kolb *Dict. Social Sci.* 445/1 Frequently suitable criteria are provided by the effects of the illness upon everyday life. This is the only possible approach to aggregating morbidity rates from all conditions. **1971** *Brit. Med. Bull.* XXVII. 11/2 The respiratory morbidity-rates were far in excess of those found in English areas with comparable levels of pollution. **1964** Gould & Kolb *Dict. Social Sci.* 445/1 The main uses of morbidity statistics relate to the study of particular conditions, public health work, the economic aspects of illness, the cost of medical care or social security systems.

morbous, *a.* Add later *literary* example.

1922 Joyce *Ulysses* 412 Organisms in which morbous germs have taken up their residence.

morceau. Add: Pl. **morceaux.**

1767 J. Beattie *Let.* 8 Jan. (1820) I. 39, I dare say Metastasio despises those little *morceaux* of sing-song. **1839** Geo. Eliot *Let.* 22 Nov. (1954) I. 34 What I could wish to have added to many of my favourite morceaux is an indication of less satisfaction in terrene objects. **1889** J. K. Jerome *Three Men in Boat* viii. 119 We played *morceaux* from the old German masters. **1960** *Times* 29 July 13/2 Surely it would be easy to intersperse congruent *morceaux* among lyric poems.

b. morceau de musée (dǝ müze): a museum piece; **morceau de salon** (dǝ salɔ̃): a well-known tune elaborated by variations, etc.

1964 *English Studies* XLV. 237 Leaving behind the artifact, the morceau de musée, 'Medallion'. **1886** F. Hume *Mystery of Hansom Cab* (1887) viii. 41 When the gentlemen entered the drawing-room a young lady was engaged in playing one of those detestable pieces of music called *Morceau de Salon*, in which an unoffending air is taken and variations embroidered on it till it becomes a perfect agony to distinguish the tune and the perpetual rattle of quavers and demi-semi-quavers. **1906** A. Bennett *Whom God hath Joined* v. 185 A *morceau de salon* of Chaminade's stood on the open piano... Not in Lawrence's house would such examples of the brilliant secondrate have been found conspicuous. **1947** A. Einstein *Mus. Romantic Era* xv. 209 From his [*sc.* Liszt's] pen there are no 'Scenes from Childhood', though there is a series—unfortunately too extensive—of *morceaux de salon*.

morcellated, *ppl. a.* Add: Also *fig.*

1953 E. L. Mascall *Corpus Christi* iii. 57 It is perfectly possible for the parish communion to result in a far more morcellated and fragmented conception of the Church and of the liturgy than can be produced in any number of 'private masses'. **1964** *Welsh Hist. Rev.* II. 52 The centrifugal tendencies inherent in Welsh tribal life and custom did more than anything else to perpetuate the severely-morcellated political system.

morcellation. Add: (Further examples.) Also *fig.*

1968 J. Howkins *Shaw's Textbk. Operative Gynæcology* (ed. 3) xvi. 306/2 The expert at vaginal hysterectomy can

convert the difficult operation into a relatively easy one.. by removing the obstructing myoma by morcellation and vaginal myomectomy. **1973** *Amer. Jrnl. Obstetr. & Gynecol.* CXVI. 258/2 Morcellation was, and is, done when indicated by the size and extent of uterine tumors and when malignancy does not exist. **1975** E. L. Mascall in *Critique 'Eucharistic Agreement'* v. 70 Merely to state the question in this way..presupposes an artificial and perverse separation between Christ and his members, a morcellation or fragmentation of the body of Christ.

morcellement. Add: **b.** *Surg.* = Morcellation (in Dict. and Suppl.).

1903 *Philadelphia Med. Jrnl.* 31 Jan. 199/1 Porcellini suggested morcellement, the danger of which consists in the subsequent necrosis of the stump of the cervix. **1919** F. E. Leavitt *Operations of Obstetrics* xi. 239 When there are tumors to deal with, like the outgrowths in the region of the buttocks and neck, their removal by morcellement must be undertaken. **1954** W. Shaw *Textbk. Operative Gynæcology* vi. 63/1 By processes of morcellement and splitting of the uterus in the midline it is possible to remove relatively large myomata by the vaginal route.

mordant, *a.* Add: **4. b.** Of a dye: becoming fixed on the fibre as a result of forming an insoluble compound with a mordant.

1902 *Encycl. Brit.* XXVII. 559/2 Employed by themselves, Mordant Colours are usually of little or no value as dyestuffs, because..either they are not attracted by the fibre..or they only yield a more or less fugitive stain. Their importance and value as dyestuffs are due to the fact that they act like weak acids and have the property of combining with metallic oxides to form insoluble compounds termed 'lakes', which vary in colour according to the metallic oxide or salt employed. **1917** Fort & Lloyd *Chem. Dyestuffs* xiii. 112 Acid mordant dyes may be first dyed on wool like acid dyes and then after-chromed. **1940** *Thorpe's Dict. Appl. Chem.* (ed. 4) IV. 127/2 Mordant dyes rank amongst the oldest dyes used by mankind for colouring purposes. **1963** [see *after-chrome *a.*]. **1965** E. Gurr *Rational Use of Dyes in Biol.* i. 115 Since sun yellow does not contain a hydroxyl group it cannot be classified as a mordant dye.

‖ **mordida** (mordi·dă). [Central-Amer. and Mex. Sp.] A bribe; an illegal exaction (in Mexico, etc.).

1940 *Life* 2 Dec. 102 In Mexico, and throughout Latin America, it is next to impossible to make headway with petty officials without constant applications of the *mordida*, which literally translated means 'the bite', or bribe. **1946** M. Lowry *Let.* 15 June (1967) 101 The defection was the original defection of my failing to pay the 'mordida'. **1967** *Punch* 18 Jan. 102/1 Just go see my friend, Sr. G., at *Gobernacion*... He's such a good friend of mine that you'll not even have to pay a *mordida*.

Mordvin (mǭ·ɹdvin). Also **Mordv, Mordvian, Mordvine, Mordvinian.** [Russ.] **a.** A member of a Finnish people inhabiting the region of the middle Volga. **b.** The Finno-Ugric language of this people. Also *attrib.* or as *adj.* So **Mo·rdva,** this people collectively.

1736 tr. *P. J. von Strahlenberg's Historico-Geogr. Descr. N. & E. Europe & Asia* xiii. 412 Morduini, Are Pagans, in Russia, who live under the Government of Nischneygorod. **1800** W. Tooke *Hist. Russia* I. i. 19 *The Mordvines*, called by themselves Moræ, and formerly by the Russians Meren. **1802** F. W. Blagdon tr. *Pallas's Trav. S. Provinces Russian Empire* I. 34 The Mordvines..are more solicitous to preserve the forests in the countries they inhabit. **1879** *Encycl. Brit.* VIII. 700/1 Finnic or Ugrian represented by..Mordvinian. *Ibid.* IX. 219/2 The Volga Finns include..the Mordvinian, divided into small communities on both banks of the Volga. **1883** *Ibid.* XVI. 45/2 Even now part of the Mordvinians (of Finnish origin) call themselves Meschers. *Ibid.* 813/2 Mordvinians, more correctly Mordva, or Mordvs, are a people numbering about one million. **1898** R. Brown *Semitic Influence in Hellenic Mythol.* iii. iii. 89 Chaïtan (= Arabic Shaitan, Heb. Satan) appears in the Mordvinian Pantheon. **1925** P. Radin tr. *Vendryès's Lang.* iii. 118 In Chermish and Mordvian, the *-t* forms both the plural of nouns and the third person plural of verbs. **1931** K. Breshkovskaia *Hidden Springs of Russian Revolution* xxiv. 287, I talked also to the Cheremisses and the Mordva. **1933** [see *Cheremis(s)]. **1939** L. H. Gray *Found. Lang.* xii. 369 The languages of the Uralic family are..*Finnish* group: Finnish proper.., Lapp.., Cheremiss, and Mordvin. **1942** K. W. Deutsch in J. A. Fishman *Readings Sociol. of Lang.* (1968) 601 Of the 13 remaining nationalities, nine have formed administrative units on a national, linguistic basis with various degrees of political self-government within the European part of the U.S.S.R.: the Bashkirs, Chuvashs, Cheremiss, Mordvins, [etc.]. **1944** B. H. Sumner *Survey Russian Hist.* i. 23 The Mordva..centred around the junction of the Volga and the Kama. **1960** E. R. Goodman *Soviet Design for World State* ix. 275 Examining any one of the languages of the Soviet Union, e.g., Mordvinian, one is shocked by the discovery that it swarms with Russian words, and that only the suffixes are Mordvinian. **1971** P. Longworth *Cossacks* ii. 55 There was a ruling class of semi-nomadic Tatars and the primitive Ostyaks, Voguls and Mordvins paid them tribute. **1972** W. B. Lockwood *Panorama of Indo-European Lang.* 152 The chief [languages] are Estonian.., Mordvin (1 m[illion], Mordva ASSR).

more, *a.* (*sb.*) and *adv.* Add: **A.** *adj.* **1. h.** (Later examples of (*the*) *more fool* followed by a pronoun.)

1917 D. H. Lawrence *Phoenix II* (1968) 69 'What have you done now?—lost more money?' 'Three thousand marks.' She was silent in deep wrath. 'More fool you!' she said. **1971** E. Fenwick *Impeccable People* iv. 25, I had to go and feel sorry for this Iversen piece, more fool me.

2. a. Phr. *more* (something) *than one cares* (or *likes*) *to think about*.

1894 Somerville & 'Ross' *Real Charlotte* I. xi. 152 He happened to have lost more money at the Galway races than he cared to think about. **1935** E. Glasgow *Let.* 12 July (1958) 188 For more years than I like to think of (a silly figure of speech, for I am not afraid of the years) I have battered my nerves against human cruelty.

3. a. Phrs. *more days, more dollars; more ships than parish churches*.

1843 J. F. Cooper *Ned Myers* II. ii. 40, I knew there were more ships than parish churches. **1898** A. J. Boyd *Shellback* xv. 258 The captain was acting on the principle of 'More days, more dollars'. **1946** W. McFee *In First Watch* i. 28 There were more ships than parish churches. **1962** Granville *Dict. Sailors' Slang* 78/1 *More days: more dollars!* American Merchant seamen's phrase of the Second World War, meaning that the more days they were at sea the more 'danger money' they would receive. The term was used sarcastically by British Naval-men whose pay compared unfavourably with the Americans'.

B. *absol.* and quasi-*sb.* **4. h.** Phr. (*there's*) *more where it* (or *that, this*, etc.) *came from*: eat or use freely, do not be sparing of (a food, commodity, etc.).

1810 J. Porter *Scottish Chiefs* II. v. 92, I..told him not to spare it, it was a chilly night, and I should get more where it came from. **1854** Mayne Reid *Young Voyageurs* xix. 250 He only looks after his lost root with an air of chagrin, and then, reflecting that there is 'plenty more where it came from', kicks up his heels, and once more plunges to the bottom. **1954** R. Bissell *High Water* xxii. 270 Plenty more where this came from.

C. *adv.* **1. c.** Esp. in phr. *I* (or *you*, etc.) *couldn't be more* ——: I, etc., am extremely ——.

1939 N. Marsh *Overture to Death* xvii. 188 'I thought,' flashed Dinah, 'that nowadays the C.I.D. was almost a gentleman's job.' 'Oh, no!' said Alleyn. 'You couldn't be more mistaken.' **1951** —— *Opening Night* vi. 139 'I couldn't be more sorry,' Percival said weakly. **1954** 'N. Blake' *Whisper in Gloom* i. iii. 49 This party couldn't be more heaven, don't you think? **1971** P. D. James *Shroud for Nightingale* i. 12 She could hardly have been more wrong.

2. *more or less*: also used *attrib.* (usu. with hyphens).

1963 *Language* XXXIX. 460 As far as the bees are concerned, it is clear that their behavior resembles that of an analog computer.., that is, a control machine of the more-or-less type, and not at all of a digital computer, of a yes-or-no type. **1964** M. A. K. Halliday et al. *Linguistic Sci.* v. 124 But this, like synonymy, is a 'more or less' not a 'yes or no' relation. **1975** *Country Life* 13 Feb. 386/2 Every more-or-less sound horse was purchased for the Expeditionary Force by Civilian Re-mount Purchasing Officers.

4. a. Add to def.: The phrase *any more* (freq. written as *anymore*) is also used in affirmative as well as negative contexts in the sense 'now, now-a-days, at the present time; from now on'. *dial.* (chiefly *U.S.*).

1898 *Eng. Dial. Dict.* I. 63/1 A servant being instructed how to act, will answer 'I will do it any more'. **1903** *McClure's Mag.* Dec. 215/1 There's just only this one any more. **1920** D. H. Lawrence *Women in Love* (1921) xiii. 159 'Quite absurd,' he said. 'Suffering bores me, any more.' **1938** J. Stuart *Beyond Dark Hills* vi. 120 They tell me this Macey plant only hires the best of men any more. *Ibid.* x. 319 You know, Jesse, any more I don't worry a great lot. **1973** *Capital Times* (Madison, Wis.) 14 Mar. 2/1 Any more, the difference between a white collar worker and a blue collar worker is simply a matter of shirt preference.

5. a. more'n, mor'n *colloq.* (orig. *U.S.*) = more than; also *ellipt.* = no more than.

1848 J. R. Lowell *Biglow Papers* 1st Ser. 23, I felt a thing go thru my leg,—'t wuz nothin' more'n a skeeter! **1885** W. L. Alden *Adv. Jimmy Brown* 142 They say that Squire Meredith and Deacon Willets are mornhalf eaten up by mosquitoes. **1886** *Harper's Mag.* July 323/2 But he (mor'n you and I with all of our might) Could not here always remain. **1903** K. D. Wiggin *Rebecca of Sunnybrook Farm* 8 We've only just started on it,..it's more'n two hours. **1952** E. Wilson *Equations of Love* 196, I know a lot more'n I did. **1973** E. Berckman *Victorian Album* 47, I don't know any more'n I've told you.

c. *Comb.* with following *adj.* or *sb.*

1923 D. H. Lawrence *Birds, Beasts, & Flowers* 99 Cats, and the Neapolitans, Sulphur sun-beasts, Thirst for fish as for more-than-water. *Ibid.* 141 Why do you arch your naked-set eye with a more-than-comprehensible arrogance? **1924** H. E. Palmer *Gram. Spoken Eng.* p. xxvii, The words *trees, towns, boys*, form an association-group through having the..meanings 'more-than-oneness' in common. **1938** R. Graves *Coll. Poems* 150 Nor could a compromise be found Between the giver's thoughtlessness And his own more-than-thanklessness. **1950** *Scott. Jrnl. Theol.* III. 367 Nyberg says it is clear from the beginning that the Servant is a more-than-individual (*överindividuell*) figure, notwithstanding that the description moves throughout on the individual plane. **1961** *Times* 24 Oct. 13/1 The Official Image of Picasso..may well be a more-than-life-size..figure.

‖ **more** (mōə·re). [L., abl. of *mos* manner, custom: see *mores.] In phrases: chiefly with *poss. adjs.*, as **more suo,** in his own fashion, **more meo,** in my own fashion; and with national *adjs.*, as **more hispanico, turcesco,** in accordance with Spanish (Turkish) customs. Also **more majorum,** in traditional manner.

1600 Holland tr. *Livy's Romane Hist.* xxvi. 585 Hee might proceed in the suite at his owne good pleasure, *more maiorum. i.* [according to the auncient manner used by their forefathers]. **1612** T. Shelton tr. *Cervantes's Hist. Don Quixote* iii. vi. 176 Hee spoke to his Lord with his Cap in his hand, his head bowed, and his body bended (*more Turcesco*). **1713** Addison in *Guardian* 3 July 2/1, I have..been drawn in to tattle of my self, *more Majorum*, almost the length of a whole *Guardian*. **1810** Southey *Let.* 27 Sept. (1856) II. 203 The preface, *more meo*, is short and explicit. *c* **1842** H. James *Let.* in R. B. Perry *Tht. & Char. W. James* (1935) I. 43 Let him try, and above all let him forgive *more suo* all my botherings. **1865** Mill *Exam. Hamilton's Philos.* xviii. 358 In a later part of his Lectures ..he, *more suo*, forgets this definition. *a* **1937** J. L. Stocks *Reason & Intuition* (1939) xiv. 212 What Mill, *more suo*, offers us in the *Logic* is a compromise or middle position. **1943** G. Brenan *Spanish Labyrinth* vii. 154 The workmen ..shot the offending mayor and, *more hispanico*, cut off his head and those of the police who had been killed in the fight and paraded them around the town.

Morea, Moria, varr. *Muria *sb.* and *a.*

moreish, *a.* (Later examples of form *morish*.)

1905 *Dialect Notes* III. 63 That tastes morish. **1971** *Times* 3 Dec. 12/4 Home-made, thin ginger biscuits are very 'morish' they slip down so easily you cannot stop munching them.

Morellian (more·liăn), *a.*[2] [f. the name of Giovanni *Morelli* (1816–91), Italian patriot and art critic, + -an.] Of, pertaining to, or characteristic of the critical method of Morelli, which introduced a new, systematic approach to art criticism, insisting esp. on the study of detail as a guide in the attribution of paintings. So **Morellian** *sb.*, a follower of Morelli's critical method; **More·llianism,** the technique of art criticism employed by Morelli.

1890 *Academy* 3 May 306/3 It would no more be possible ..for the art-historian to go back to a pre-Morellian state of things in criticism. **1916** B. Berenson *Study & Criticism of Italian Art* 3rd Ser. 34 Morellianism, surgical, pitiless, iconoclastic even as it seemed, was yet inspired by the Romantic ideal of genius. *Ibid.* 35 We Morellians fought for authenticity with the uncompromising zeal of Legitimists. **1934** *Times Lit. Suppl.* 21 June p. xv/1 The persistence of Morellianism is naturally more apparent in the strictly historical literature of art than in its criticism. **1942** *Burlington Mag.* Oct. 241/1 In this country there are small conventicles, in which foregather members of the strictest sect of the Morellians, where hard-shell elders impart to neophytes the narrow precepts of the old Morellian creed. **1968** *Encycl. Brit.* XV. 835/2 The so-called 'Morellian method' was followed in this and his later *Critical Studies*.

more'n: see *more *adv.* 5 a.

‖ **morena**[2] (morē·nă). Also **marena.** [Native name.] The title given to a chief in Lesotho; hence a respectful form of address.

1835 A. Smith *Diary* 29 Aug. (1940) II. 186 They walked boldly in though they saw the Matabeli, saluted all the white people with '*Moron*' and then went towards the Matabeli fire. **1861** E. Casalis *Basutos* ii. xii. 214 The Basutos give to the princes who govern them the title of *Morena*... *Morena*..signifies, He who watches over the public safety and welfare. **1912** J. C. Macgregor tr. *D. F. Ellenberger's Hist. Basuto* 292 One is agreeably surprised to see..so much politeness, and so many rules of etiquette ..faithfully observed... The chiefs often addressed their subjects as *marena* ('chiefs'), *benghali* ('my masters'). **1923** E. A. T. Dutton *Basuto of Basutoland* vii. 67 You meet a man on the road; he may simply say, 'Lumela, Morena' (*Good morning, Chief*), and to this the reply is a drawn-out 'Eh!' **1953** P. Lanham *Blanket Boy's Moon* i. ii. 17 The Chief is highly respected by his subjects, who call him, *Morena*. **1974** *Sunday Times* (S. Afr.) 1 Sept. 3 If it is known, call him by his name and surname and add 'mister' (Morena), particularly if you are in his homeland.

morencite (mōə·re·nsəit). *Min.* [f. *Morenc-i*, the name of a village in Arizona, U.S.A. + -ite[1].] A variety of nontronite with part of the ferric iron replaced by magnesium, $(Fe, Mg)_2Si_4O_{10}(OH)_2$, which occurs as brownish yellow seams in lime shale.

1904 Lindgren & Hillebrand in *Amer. Jrnl. Sci.* CLXVIII. 457 Considering that the mineral is not a mixture, but optically well individualized, we have..thought it best to designate it by the name morencite, derived from the locality in which it was found. **1928** *Ibid.* CCVIII. 12 There is no good reason for separating müllerite, morencite, and hoeferite from nontronite on account of their lower water content. **1935** *Amer. Mineralogist* XX. 475 Nontronites including morencite, pinguite, faratsihite, stilpnochloran and chloropal are like montmorillonite in structure.

morenosite (more·nosəit, mōərenō͡u·zəit). *Min.* [ad. Sp. *morenosita* (D. A. Casares 1851, in *Revista Minera* II. 176), f. the name of *Moreno*, 19th-cent. Spaniard: see -ite[1].] A hydrated nickel sulphate, $NiSO_4.7$(or 6·5)H_2O, which occurs as green orthorhombic crystals and is formed by the oxidation of nickeliferous sulphides.

1868 J. D. Dana *Syst. Min.* (ed. 5) 648 (*heading*) Morenosite. **1901** M. F. Heddle *Mineral. Scott.* I. 24 [Millerite

occurs] with rosettes of brilliant green Morenosite in Mesitine Spar. **1949** *Amer. Mineralogist* XXXIV. 193 On standing in the open in dry air, crystals of morenosite generally dehydrate rapidly to the tetragonal hexahydrate, retgersite. **1962** *Mineral. Abstr.* XV. 458/2 The Valtournache morenosite with 6·5 H_2O has the same structure as $NiSO_4.7H_2O$.

Morenu (morē̆i·nu). Also **morenu.** [Heb.] A title of honour conferred on rabbis and Talmudic scholars.

1650 E. CHILMEAD tr. *L. Modena's Hist. Rites of Jews* II. iii. 69 In Germany, and Italy, they are to be honoured.. with the Title..of..Morenu,..that is to say, Master... These men, that is to say, the Cacham, Rab, or Morenu, decide all Controversies concerning the Things that are either Lawful or Prohibited, and all other Differences. **1733** tr. *Picart's Ceremonies & Relig. Customs* I. II. iii. 46 The *Cacham Rau*, or *Morenu*, determines all Manner of Debates..and passes Judgement upon all Religious Concerns. **1905** *Jewish Encycl.* IX. 15/2 *Morenu*, (lit. 'our teacher'). Term used since the middle of the fourteenth century as a title for rabbis and Talmudists. *Ibid.* 16/1 It can not be determined definitely why a special title was applied to rabbis, or why the term 'morenu' was chosen. **1962** B. ABRAHAMS tr. *Life of Glückel of Hameln* ii. 18 Rabbi David Hanau, the great scholar who bore the distinguished title 'Morenu'.

mores (mōᵊ·rīz). Normally const. as *sb. pl.* [a. L. *mores* pl. of *mos* manner, custom.] **1.** Those acquired customs and moral assumptions which give cohesion to a community or social group, the contravention or rejection of which produces a reaction of shock and outrage. Also *attrib.*

1907 W. G. SUMNER *Folkways* 30 The mores are the folkways, including the philosophical and ethical generalizations as to societal welfare which are suggested by them, and inherent in them as they grow. *Ibid.* 37 The Latin word 'mores' seems to be..convenient..as a name for the folkways with the connotation of right and truth in respect to welfare, embodied in them. **1927** J. DOWD *Negro in Amer. Life* xxi. 154 The adjustment of the South to her new educational problem is only one of the many adjustments incident to her passing from the mores of slavery to the mores of freedom; and any sociologist knows that it is impossible to change the mores of a people suddenly. **1948** *Mind* LVII. 511 It frequently happens that any individual variations from cultural traits cause great indignation. When this is so the cultural traits in question are called *mores-traits*. **1958** J. K. GALBRAITH *Affluent Soc.* xviii. 200 Television and the violent mores of Hollywood and Madison Avenue must contend with the intellectual discipline of the school. **1958** *Spectator* 1 Aug. 167/1 It is surely a mistake for a nation of independent character and traditions to ape the different and often alien *mores* of another. **1967** *Ibid.* 30 June 765/1 The law, in the shape of the jury, is the custodian of our *mores*. **1970** G. GREER *Female Eunuch* 171 Perhaps the pop revolution..has had a far-reaching effect on sexual *mores*. **1975** *Verbatim* Feb. 4/2 The fact of the matter is that mores, politics, and sentiment change.

2. *Ecology.* The habits, behaviour, etc., of a group of animals of the same kind; also, occasionally, the group itself. Cf. *NICHE *sb.* 3 c. Also *attrib.*

1911 V. E. SHELFORD in *Biol. Bull.* XXI. 146 Ecological succession is based upon physiology, habits, behavior, mode of life, and the like, which I have proposed to call mores (opposed to the term form). *Ibid.* 147 It is of course recognized that within rather uncertain limits the mores of a morphological species remain, in a general way, the same throughout its geographic range. **1913** —— *Animal Communities Temperate Amer.* ii. 33 Ecology..considers physiological life histories primarily in nature, for this reason the central problem of ecology is the *mores* problem. **1954** A. M. WOODBURY *Princ. Gen. Ecol.* xi. 197 Ecologically an individual may be classified under two or more headings in which the unit is a mores. For example, an insect may pass through an egg stage, a larval stage, a pupal stage, and an adult stage, each of which would represent a mores, an ecological unit in a community. **1962** H. HANSON *Dict. Ecol.* 229 *Mores*, the general behavioural attributes of motile organisms, or groups of animals possessing particular ecological characteristics. **1973** P. A. COLINVAUX *Introd. Ecol.* viii. 117 The fish had different physiologies, habits, behavior, and modes of life, a collection of parameters which he [*sc.* Shelford] called the mores of the animals... His word mores, which has an awkward and alien sound, disappeared, but the idea he was seeking to express by it later found an outlet in Elton's 'niche' and became a central ecological concept.

moresca: see MORESCO *sb.* 3 (in Dict. and Suppl.).

moresco, *sb.* **3.** For def. read: An Italian dance to which the English morris dance is related. Add further examples of *moresca*. Cf. *MORISCA, MORISKA.

1933 E. K. CHAMBERS *Eng. Folk-Play* 150 A *Moresca* or *Morisco* first appears in the fifteenth century used as *intermedii* in the courtly *ludi* of Italy, Burgundy, and France. **1947** A. EINSTEIN *Mus. Romantic Era* xvii. 293 Even the separate regions..began to make themselves heard: in Italy around 1535, for example, the *Canzon villanesca alla napoletana*, or the *Moresca* in the south of the peninsula. **1959** *Collins Music Encycl.* 437/1 *Moresca*, ..a dance of the 15th and 16th cent., most often a sword dance in which a fight between Christians and Mohammedans was represented.

Moreton Bay (mǭ·ɹtən bē̆i). Also **Morton Bay** (only in sense b). The name of a bay in Queensland, Australia (orig. *Morton*). **a.** Used attrib. to designate several trees native to the surrounding region, esp. **Moreton Bay ash (-tree)**, *Eucalyptus tessellaris*, of the family Myrtaceæ; **Moreton Bay chestnut,** an evergreen tree, *Castanospermum australe*, of the family Leguminosæ, bearing racemes of yellow flowers; **Moreton Bay fig (-tree)**, *Ficus macrophylla* or *F. platypoda*, of the family Moraceæ; **Moreton Bay pine,** the hoop pine, *Araucaria cunninghamii*, of the family Pinaceæ.

1847 L. LEICHHARDT *Overland Expedition* 75 (Morris), The Moreton Bay Ash (a species of *Eucalyptus*)..was here also very plentiful. **1908** E. J. BANFIELD *Confessions of Beachcomber* I. i. 15 Moreton Bay ash and other eucalypts. **1944** F. CLUNE *Red Heart* 64 Here he saw a Moreton Bay ash tree blazed with the letter L, made on Leichhardt's 1846 expedition. **1884** A. NILSON *Timber Trees N.S.W.* 40 *C[astanospermum] australe*—Moreton Bay Chestnut; Bean Tree.—A beautiful tree, attaining a height of 130 feet and a diameter of 5 feet. **1908** E. J. BANFIELD *Confessions of Beachcomber* II. i. 259 One of the chief vegetable foods of the blacks is the fruit of 'tindaburra' (Moreton Bay chestnut—*Castanospermum australe*). **1947** J. C. RICH *Materials & Methods of Sculpture* x. 286 *Blackbean* is an Australian wood, also referred to as Moreton Bay Chestnut. It is hard and heavy and resembles teakwood. The color is light to dark brown with lighter colored streaks. **1969** T. H. EVERETT *Living Trees of World* 193/2 Very handsome lumber, resembling walnut and esteemed for cabinet work and furniture, is obtained from the Moreton Bay chestnut. **1883** *Encycl. Brit.* XX. 173/2 The Moreton Bay fig-tree has immense wall-like abutments. **1890** 'R. BOLDREWOOD' *Miner's Right* xliv. 380 (Morris), The..venerable church with its alleys of araucaria and Moreton Bay fig-trees. **1917** 'H. H. RICHARDSON' *Fortunes R. Mahony* IV. ix. 362 Mahony turned in and drove past exotic firs, Moreton Bay figtrees and araucarias. **1933** D. G. STEAD *Tree Bk.* xxii. 89 A species with large glossy leaves is the well-known Moreton Bay Fig, which..is so hardy. **1943** K. TENNANT *Ride on Stranger* (1968) viii. 86 She was particularly fond of the Domain... Here were great avenues of Moreton Bay figs; great bulks cold as stone with loose-wrinkled grey skin for bark and roots. **1965** *Austral. Encycl.* IV. 58/2 The Moreton Bay fig (*F[icus] macrophylla*) is extensively planted as a shade and ornamental tree, but in its wild state is not very common. *Ibid.* 59/1 The small-leaved Moreton Bay fig (*F. platypoda*) is the most widely distributed of all the Australian species. **1838** J. C. LOUDON *Arboretum et Fruticetum Britannicum* IV. 2444 The Moreton Bay pine is found, as the name imports, on the shores of Moreton Bay: it has also..a range of 900 miles..on the eastern coast of New South Wales. **1884** [see *hoop-pine* (*HOOP *sb.*[1] 13 b)]. **1911** E. M. CLOWES *On Wallaby* ix. 251 Queensland! the home of the red pine and the kauripine, the red cedar, the Moreton Bay pine, and black-bean; and nine men to guard the interests of all this wealth! **1923** DALLIMORE & JACKSON *Handbk. Coniferæ* 155 Moreton Bay Pine... A tree 150 ft. or occasionally 200 ft. high, with a girth up to 12 ft.

b. *slang.* (See quots.)

1953 BAKER *Australia Speaks* v. 134 *Morton Bay* (*fig*), any witness who lays an information, anyone who unwarrantably attends to or meddles in the affairs of others; by rhyme on *gig*,..and which may be a contraction of *fizgig*, an informer. **1966** —— *Austral. Lang.* (ed. 2) xii. 267 *Moreton Bay*, a trickster's victim or *gay*.

Morgan[3] (mǭ·ɹgən). *U.S.* The surname of Justin Morgan (1747–98), American teacher, used *attrib.* or *absol.* to designate a breed of light, thickset horse developed in New England from the progeny of a stallion owned by him.

1843 *Knickerbocker* XXI. 331 The stage generally being able to work its own way, drawn by horses of the Morgan breed. **1849** *New England Farmer* I. 314 There has never been a stock of horses in New England which has proved so generally useful as the Morgan stock of the original Morgan horse, raised by Justin Morgan, of West Springfield, Mass., in 1793. **1869** C. L. BRACE *New West* xiv. 187 Each coach well made and comfortable, with six horses, evidently picked Morgans. **1876** *Rep. Vermont Board Agric.* III. 172 You can teach a Morgan colt anything. **1884** J. HAY *Bread-Winners* v. 77 If you don't want to talk, a train of Morgan horses couldn't make you. **1906** W. CHURCHILL *Coniston* 22 The tough little Morgans of that time..have all but disappeared. **1913** J. LONDON *Valley of Moon* xxi. 516 They call her Ramona—some Spanish name: sired by Morellita out of genuine Morgan stock. **1923** R. FROST *Selected Poems* 4 A little Morgan had one forefoot on the wall, The other curled at his breast. **1934** *Dict. Amer. Biogr.* XIII. 183/1 Before the middle of the nineteenth century Morgan horses had become a distinct type or breed, famed throughout the country for their attractive appearance and their endurance, docility, and utility as driving, riding, cavalry, stage, and general-purpose horses. **1973** *Washington Post* 13 Jan. F1/7 (Advt.), Must sell this w[ee]kend.—Dark bay Morgan gelding, 15·2 h, good temperament, excel. hunter prospect.

morgan[4] (mǭ·ɹgən). *Genetics.* [named after Thomas Hunt *Morgan* (see next).] A unit of the relative distance on a chromosome between two linked genes, defined in terms of the frequency of crossing-over between them so that the distance in morgans between two genes is equal to this frequency when they are close enough together for the effect of multiple crossing-over to be negligible. (Sometimes used for one hundredth of this unit.)

1919 J. B. S. HALDANE in *Jrnl. Genetics* VIII. 305 Let x be the distance between the loci of two factors, y their cross-over value, and let the unit of distance be chosen so that when y is sufficiently small x becomes equal to y... The value of y for a given value of x is the sum of the probabilities of all odd numbers of cross-overs. $\therefore y = ..\frac{1}{2}(1-e^{-2x})$... It is suggested that the unit of distance in a chromosome as defined above be termed a 'morgan', on the analogy of the ohm, volt, etc. Morgan's unit of distance is therefore a centimorgan. *Ibid.*, The cross-over values ·412 and ·236 correspond, according to curve (*c*),.. to distances of ·549 and ·261 morgans respectively. **1965** J. A. SERRA *Mod. Genetics* I. vii. 260 Map distances between gene loci are the cross-over values expressed as percentages of recombination for small intervals. Thus, 1% of recombination is often called one cross-over unit..or a centimorgan... One morgan is equal to 100 centimorgans. [*Note*] Some authors call a cross-over unit one morgan. **1971** LEVITAN & MONTAGU *Textbk. Human Genetics* ix. 376 Each morgan is divisible into 100 centimorgans, each centimorgan corresponding to the map distance between two loci showing 1 per cent crossing over between them. For close loci the crossover percentage can be translated directly into centimorgans, but this is not possible for more distant loci, especially those more than 30 centimorgans apart. **1971** *Nature* 24 Dec. 475/1 Pedigree studies by Lawler and her co-workers established a close linkage (0·03 morgans) between *Rh*, the rhesus set of blood group loci, and one of the loci, El_1, that can lead to elliptocytosis of the red cell.

Morganism (mǭ·ɹgăniz'm). *Biol.* [f. the name *Morgan* + -ISM.] Mendelian genetics, incorporating a theory of the gene that came to be generally accepted, as propounded by Thomas Hunt Morgan (1866–1945), U.S. geneticist and zoologist. Hence **Mo·rganist** *a.*

1934 H. J. MULLER in *Pamyati V.I. Lenina* (Akad. Nauk SSSR) 572 The great bulk of the facts of real significance, subsequent to 1911, and practically all after 1913, were found by the younger workers quite independently of any guidance from him, in experiments which they had planned... Their results and interpretations were, however, later accepted by Morgan and presented chiefly by him to the scientific and lay public, so that these developments have sometimes been referred to, especially in circles farthest removed from contact with the original work, as 'Morganism'. **1950** A. HUXLEY *Themes & Variations* 167 The canonization of Lysenko and the anathema pronounced on 'reactionary Morganism'. **1966** E. A. CARLSON *Gene* xi. 95 The article [published by H. J. Muller in 1934]..dissociates 'Morganism' from the gene concept developed at the Columbia laboratory. *Ibid.*, The controversy..eventually erupted into a clear cut 'Lysenkoist' camp and a formal genetics camp, disparagingly referred to as 'Morganist'.

morganite (mǭ·ɹgănəit). *Min.* [f. the name of John Pierpont *Morgan* (1837–1913), U.S. financier + -ITE[1].] A pink lithian variety of beryl which is prized as a gem.

1911 *Amer. Jrnl. Sci.* CLXXXI. 81 Dr. George Kunz described some new and remarkable gems which had been cut from a rose-colored beryl found in Madagascar. He proposed the name morganite for them in honor of Mr. John Pierpont Morgan of New York City. **1955** BROWN & DEY *India's Mineral Wealth* (ed. 3) xv. 598 The lovely gem known as morganite is a pink or rose beryl which owes its colour to the presence of small amounts of lithium. **1959** [see *HELIODOR]. **1968** *Rocks & Minerals* XLIII. 651/2 Morganite is a pink variety of transparent beryl. A few samples of this rare type have been found at Poona but not associated with the emerald workings.

morganize, *v.* (Examples.)

1832 *Amer. Rail Road Jrnl.* I. 165/3 Let him be *Morganized*, and his work suppressed by burning. **1923** J. MANCHON *Le Slang* 197 *Morganize*, v. (amér.), faire disparaître un témoin gênant.

Hence **morganiza·tion**, the fact or process of getting rid of or destroying by secret methods.

1919 J. L. GARVIN *Econ. Foundations of Peace* 502 When there were fears about the 'Morganisation' of British vessels, he said that it would be sounder for Britain to nationalise her entire shipping.

morgue[2]. Add: **2. a.** *slang.* In a newspaper office, the collection of material assembled for the future obituaries of persons still living.

1903 E. L. SHUMAN *Practical Journalism* 103 This can be done with the aid of the 'morgue' or cabinet of biographical and obituary materials that is maintained in every wide-awake newspaper office. **1925** B. BENEFIELD *Chicken-Wagon Family* 94, I have written a column of assorted obituaries after having dug up enough material in the 'Transcript's' 'morgue' for six columns. **1951** A. C. CLARKE *Sands of Mars* xi. 136 In a score of newspaper offices, the copy culled from the Morgue began to be set up in type. **1964** *Listener* 5 Nov. 732/2 *The Raker* begins in a newspaper obituary department, usually known as the Morgue. **1971** L. M. HARROD *Librarians' Glossary* (ed. 3) 433 *Morgue*, a collection of obituary notices of famous living people kept up to date in newspaper offices. **1975** J. SYMONS *Three Pipe Problem* xviii. 187 The *Banner* morgue was unusually comprehensive, and it contained some interesting material about Haynes.

b. Hence a 'library' of cuttings, photographs, and information in a newspaper office, film studio, etc., often including sense *2 a. Also *attrib.*

1918 H. CROY *How Motion Pictures are Made* viii. 200 To make sure that the details are true, a studio has filed away in its morgue photographs of the life it wishes to depict. **1923** G. C. BASTIAN *Editing Day's News* 10 The person in charge of the newspaper files, clippings, and pictures [is] called the 'morgue librarian'. **1927** *Amer. Speech* II. 238/2 A 'morgue' is a necessary department of a newspaper... Here photographs and engravings of prominent

men, obituaries prepared in advance, pictures of buildings, ships, and even animals, and reference clippings on every conceivable subject are filed away ready for instant use. **1937** *Nat. Geogr. Mag.* Feb. 148/2 Beside his [*sc.* Jack London's] California laurel desk, with its oil burning.. lamp..is preserved his neat 'morgue', as writers call their reference library. **1942** Berrey & Van den Bark *Amer. Thes. Slang* § 606/2 Parts of Studio... *morgue*, the film filing room. **1962** *Listener* 12 July 57/1 Cartoonists in the United States rely for day-to-day material on newspaper morgues and wire-photographs. **1972** *Times* 16 May (Wall Street Suppl.) p. vii/2 Over to the *New York Times* for background material from their morgue: yes, the library is officially called that.

3. *Comb.* **morgue-like**, resembling a morgue (sense 1); **morgue-man**, the man in charge of a morgue (sense *2).

1913 *Cassell's Magazine of Fiction & Pop. Lit.* June 50/1 The long deserted tables, shrouded in black covers, would have seemed morgue-like to a casual observer. **1947** G. Greene *Nineteen Stories* 28 Her large morgue-like mouth was full of blackened teeth. **1912** *Outlook* (N.Y.) 14 Sept. 84/1 In some newspaper offices the morgue man and his assistants..work inside of steel cages. **1935** T. E. Lawrence *Let.* 4 Feb.(1938) 851 Let us now pass to the epitaph. Yes, Hogarth did the morgue-men a first sketch of me in 1920, and they are right to overhaul their stocks.

morillo (mǫrī·lyo). *Bullfighting.* Also **morrillo, murillo.** [Sp. *morrillo* fleshy part of the neck of an animal.] The muscle at the back of the bull's neck, one of the targets for the lances of the bullfighters.

1932 E. Hemingway *Death in Afternoon* xvi. 180 The morillo, or hump of muscle that rises from the back of the bull's neck to his shoulders. **1959** V. J. Kehoe *Aficionado!* i. 34 They [*sc.* the picadors] must place a *pica* (lance) into the rear part of the toro's long hump of neck muscle, known as the *morrillo* or *cerviguillo.* **1967** [see *divisa]. **1968** S. Oag *In Presence of Death* 261 They [*sc.* the picadors] should give it a minimum of three varas to test the bull's courage, weaken its powerful tossing muscle, the murillo, and lower its head. **1971** J. Leibold *This is Bullfight* ii. 31 The throwing muscle at the back of the neck (called the *morrillo*) is remarkably developed [in the fighting bull].

Moriori (mǫriō·ri). [Native word.] An early Polynesian people of New Zealand, now extinct, who preceded the Maori; associated *spec.* with the Chatham Islands, where most evidence of their culture is found; also, a member of this people.

1865 A. S. Atkinson *Jrnl.* 9 Jan. in *Richmond–Atkinson Papers* (1960) II. iii. 145, I had a long talk with a genuine Moriori..or real aboriginal of the Chatham islands & of some of the southern parts of New Zealand. **1874** A. Bathgate *Colonial Experiences* xviii. 258 The Moriori population, which, at the time of the discovery of the islands, in 1791, was estimated at over 2,000, must at one time have been very large. **1882** T. H. Potts *Out in Open* 160 The Moriori was robust in figure, tall of stature, not darker in colour, perhaps, than many a Maori, but of a dull dusky hue. **1905** W. B. *Where White Man Treads* 27 The ancient Moriori mother scooped a shallow hole in the earth, and warmed it with embers, and lined it with dry grass and well-scorched 'kohu kohu' (moss), to nestle her new-born child in. **1949** P. Buck *Coming of Maori* (1950) i. ii. 14 The Moriori became extinct as a separate people, but their blood is present in some mixed Maori families. **1950** R. Duff *Moa-Hunter Period of Maori Culture* 15 Moriori, like Maori, is a recent term probably coined to distinguish its bearers from Europeans, and was probably never used before the eighteen hundreds. *Ibid.* 20 The Maori invasion of 1835 [of the Chatham Islands]..marked the end of the culture which we know as Moriori. **1962** *Listener* 19 Apr. 676/2 The Moriori, now extinct, were a group of Polynesians who settled in the Chathams somewhere after the twelfth century. *Ibid.*, The Morioris carved birds on the front of their houses.

morisca, moriska, varr. *moresca (see Moresco *sb.* 3 in Dict. and Suppl.).

1935 *Discovery* Sept. 265/2 Miss Violet Alford's comparative study of the relation of the Morris to other seasonal dances of Europe and to the Morisca. **1938** C. Sachs *World Hist. Dance* vii. 301 The carved figures with which Erasmus Grasser decorated the Ratssaal in Munich in 1480... These so-called *maruschka* or *moriska* dancers are..beautiful. *Ibid.* 335 In Europe..the name *morisca* covers many choral dances in double file formation. **1950** L. Armstrong *Dances of Spain* II. 13 Moriscas came into being as the Moors were driven southwards.

morish, var. Moreish *a.*

morituri te salutant (mǫritūə·ri tē̆i sælu·tænt), *phr.* [L., lit. those about to die salute you (see Suetonius *Claudius* xxi. 6).] **a.** The words addressed to the emperor by the gladiators of ancient Rome on entering the arena, in anticipation of their death. **b.** This address used allusively by anyone facing danger or difficulty. Also in third person sing., **morituri te salutat,** and in first person sing., **moriturus te saluto.**

[**1606** Holland tr. *Suetonius* 165 When he [*sc.* Claudius] was about to let out the water of the mere: Ficinus he exhibited in it a navall fight before: And as they who were to fight this battaile, cryed out to him, Ave Imperator, &c. i. All haile O Emperour; They salute thee and wish thy life who are ready to dye: and he againe made answere Avete vos.] **1704** B. Kennett *Antiquities of Rome* (ed. 3) ii. iii. 269 The Naumachiæ of Claudius which he presented on the Fucine Lake before he drain'd it, deserve to be particularly mention'd, not more for the greatness of the Show, than for the Behaviour of the Emperour: who when the Combatants pass'd before him with so melancholy a Greeting as, Ave imperator, morituri te salutant, return'd in Answer, Avete vos. **1869** S. R. Hole *Bk. about Roses* i. 6 They may say as they enter the arena, with the gladiators of old to the emperor..*Morituri te salutant.* **1894** —— *More Memories* xix. 248 If the slightest ailment affects him, it is a case of *moriturus te salutat.* **1910** *Encycl. Brit.* XII. 65/1 The admirable picture of Gérome which bears the title, 'Ave, Caesar, morituri te salutant.' **1930** E. H. Young *Miss Mole* vi. 59 I'm speaking, as it were, from my deathbed. *Moriturus te saluto!* Tomorrow ..I'm moving on. **1951** N. Marsh *Opening Night* xi. 254 Moriturus, to coin as Miss G. would say, a phrase, te saluto, Caesar. **1967** M. Grant *Gladiators* iii. 73 When the combatants arrived opposite the emperor's platform, they extended their right hands towards him and cried 'Hail, emperor, greetings from men about to die!' (*Ave, imperator, morituri te salutant!*) **1972** A. Roudybush *Sybaritic Death* (1974) xx. 166 'Ave Petersen,' Per read. 'Moriturus te salutat... I killed Clare.'

Morlach (mǭ·ɹlæk), *sb.* and *a.* Also (*pl.*) **Morla·cchi, Morla·cchian, Morla·cco, Morlack, Morlak.** [f. *mavrovlachi*, f. Gr. μαῦρο-ς black + Βλάχος Vlach: cf. Vlach.] **A.** *sb.* A member of a Vlach people centred on the eastern Adriatic port of Ragusa (mod. Dubrovnik) and, from the twelfth to the fifteenth centuries, in parts of maritime Croatia and northern Dalmatia, forming the country known eventually as Morlacchia, being later incorporated with Slavic peoples. **B.** *adj.* Of, pertaining to, or characteristic of Morlacchia or its people.

1778 tr. *A. Fortis's Travels into Dalmatia* 56 The Morlacchi, in general, have little notion of domestick œconomy... Yet the Morlack is a great œconomist in the use of his wearing apparel. *Ibid.* 65 It rarely happens..that a Morlacco carries off a girl against her will... The Morlack women keep themselves somewhat neat till they get a husband. *Ibid.* 83 Simplicity, and want of order..form.. the principal character of the Morlacchian poetry. **1778** *Critical Review* Mar. 378 The Morlacchians chiefly live on milk. **1793** *Universal Mag.* Oct. 268/1 The people called Morlacks, or Morlacchi, inhabit Morlacchia, which is among the inland mountains of Dalmatia. *Ibid.* 271/2 A Morlack village. **1837** *Mirror* 9 Dec. 383/1 At the death of a Morlach..the family weep and howl... The Morlach women go every holiday to renew their lamentations. **1849** A. A. Paton *Highlands & Islands of Adriatic* II. iii. 32 The Morlack principle is to allow the man to grow as the beast of the forest. *Ibid.* 33 The Morlack is the best soldier and the worst citizen in the Austrian empire. **1877** [see *Illyric* adj. s.v. *Illyrian *a.* and *sb.*]. **1881** E. A. Freeman *Sk. Subject Lands of Venice* 184 Are we to believe that the Morlacchi used the turban as their headdress before the Ottoman came? **1904** L. Villari *Republic of Ragusa* xii. 322 The Morlachs in the Venetian service made raids into Turkish territory. **1911** *Encycl. Brit.* VII. 773/2 The name of *Morlachs, Morlaks* or *Morlacks* commonly bestowed by English writers on the Dalmatian Slavs..is an abbreviated form of *Mavrovlachi*, meaning either 'Black Vlachs', or, less probably, 'Sea Vlachs'... In northern Dalmatia the Slavs of the interior are still called *Morlacchi*; in the south this name expresses contempt. **1920** M. E. Durham *Twenty Years of Balkan Tangle* i. 12 They are known as Morlachs,..and historically are in all probability descendants of the pre-Slav native population. **1922** D. H. Low tr. *Kraljević's Ballads* p. xii, In 1775 a translation by Werthes of the Morlacchian section was published at Berne. **1957** *Encycl. Brit.* XXIII. 230/1 In the 14th century the Mavrovlachi or Morlachs extended themselves towards the Croatian borders, and a large part of maritime Croatia and northern Dalmatia began to be known as Morlacchia. *Ibid.* 230/2 The Morlachs have now become Slavonized. **1968** *Ibid.* XXIII. 93/2 There were also colonies of the Morlachs in the interior of the ancient Serbia.

Mormon. Add: **1.** (Earlier and later examples.)

1830 [see *Campbellite]. **1837** J. M. Peck *Gaz. Illinois* (ed. 2) i. 74 There are..a few Mormons..scattered through the state. **1922** *Lit. Digest* 10 June 40/1 Because a few of the inmates of the Hollywood film colony have 'married from time to time', they are less to be censured as Mormons than pitied as morons. **1928** R. Campbell *Wayzgoose* i. 26 Muses Nine, Those strapping girls whose love, to say the least, Would make a rabid Mormon of a priest. **1963** K. S. Latourette *Christianity in Revolutionary Age* V. ii. 14 In the Rocky Mountain area and on the west coast the Mormons were prominent.

2. (Later examples.)

1913 J. London *Valley of Moon* 430 He had been provost marshal when the Mormon trouble flared up. **1920** *Encycl. Relig. & Ethics* XI. 83/1 The first principle is set forth by the chief Mormon theologian, Parley P. Pratt. **1942** W. Stegner *Mormon Country* 65 He had sprung clear across the Great Basin deserts to locate the Mormon Station. **1948** [see *Mormon cricket*, below]. **1966** *Encycl. N.Z.* III. 64/2 The many similarities between Maori traditions and Mormon teachings. **1968** *Encycl. Brit.* XIII. 795/2 Space, time, matter and the universe in Mormon theology are limitless by nature. **1975** *Times* 20 Sept. 2/5 The fires at..the high school and the Mormon church [in Kirkcaldy], caused little damage.

3. Special Combs.: **Mormon battalion** (now *Hist.*), a company of soldiers from Mormon communities in Iowa enlisted for service in the Mexican war; **Mormon Bible,** the Book of Mormon; **Mormon Church,** the name by which the Church of Jesus Christ of the Latter-Day Saints is commonly known; **Mormon City,** Salt Lake City, Utah; **Mormon cricket,** a long-horn grasshopper, *Anabrus simplex*; **Mormon fly,** a hesperiid butterfly, *Atrytone hobomok*; **Mormon State,** in the U.S., a State in which Mormons are predominant, usu. applied to Utah; **Mormon trail,** the trail followed by Mormon migrants to Utah in 1847; **Mormon war,** disorders arising between Mormon communities and their neighbours, and *spec.* the fighting between Utah Mormons and the federal troops in 1857–8; **Mormon weed** (earlier and later examples); for Latin name substitute *Abutilon theophrasti.*

1848 *Santa Fé* (New Mexico) *Republican* 27 June 1/4 Capt. Hunt of the Mormon battalion, has left the Ciudad de Los Angelos for the Salt Lake. **1929** L. H. Creer *Utah & Nation* iii. 32 While crossing the Sierras, he met the returning members of the Mormon Battalion. **1838** Whittier in W. P. & F. J. Garrison *Life W. L. Garrison* (1885) II. 221 A discussion of the merits of animal magnetism, or of the Mormon Bible, would have been quite as appropriate. **1845** *Southern Lit. Messenger* XI. 476/1 These facts were withheld from the world for the nine years which intervened from the first publication of the Mormon Bible. **1882** J. W. Buel *Metrop. Life Unveiled* 349 These three men have subscribed to an oath which will be found in all Mormon bibles. **1838** *Niles' Reg.* 13 Oct. 103/3 We, and all the Mormon church,..entertain the same feelings and fears toward the Indians. **1948** *Newsweek* 12 Jan. 38/2 Once a basic tenet of the Mormon Church, the doctrine of plural marriage was formally abandoned in 1890. **1957** W. Mulder *Homeward to Zion* xi. 289 In 1887 the Edmunds-Tucker Act..disincorporated the Mormon Church itself. **1878** J. H. Beadle *Western Wilds* 39 We got to the Mormon City all beat out. **1942** Berrey & Van den Bark *Amer. Thes. Slang* § 46/1 *Mormon City*,..Salt Lake City, Utah. **1896** J. B. Smith *Economic Entomology* iv. 97 At the base of the Rocky Mountains, extending up into the foothills..the 'Mormon cricket', *Anabrus simplex*, occasionally multiplies so greatly that it migrates to the plains below, destroying everything in its path. **1934** *Sun* (Baltimore) 1 May 13/1 The devastating 'mormon' crickets, which came into prominence in 1848, when they threatened the first colonists in Utah with starvation, have appeared in a half dozen spots of Southern Idaho to carry on the destruction they started last year. Black creatures two inches long when full grown, they eat everything in sight. **1948** *U.S. Dept. Agric. Yearbk.* 274/2 The early Mormon settlers knew no satisfactory way of fighting the Mormon cricket. **1959** E. Tunis *Indians* 109/1 Grasshoppers and big mormon crickets were driven into trenches from which they could be gathered in baskets. **1972** Swan & Papp *Common Insects N. Amer.* 75 Mormon cricket: *Anabrus simplex*... Dark brown, black, or green; stout-bodied, wings absent. **1975** *Islander* (Victoria, B.C.) 26 Jan. 15/3 Densest pheasant populations occur in areas offering bonanza supplies of grasshoppers, Mormon crickets or some other..insect. **1845** N. F. Moore *Diary* 26 Aug. (1946) 46 Our boat and everything about it is now covered with Mormon flies as they are called, being, I am told, peculiar to this neighborhood. **1847** C. Lanman *Summer in Wilderness* v. 34 They are called the Mormon fly and I was told were found on these rapids alone. [**1909** *Cent. Dict.* Suppl. 828/3 *Mormon*... In *entom.*, an American hesperiid butterfly, *Atrytone hobomok*, which occurs from eastern Canada to the Mississippi valley.] **1882** C. M. Chase *Editor's Run in N. Mexico* 109 Axtell..went so far as to lay plans..to get the territory admitted into the Union as a Mormon state. **1893** L. Wagner *More about Names* 35 Utah, otherwise The Mormon State, is called by the Mormons themselves Deseret. **1920** *Encycl. Relig. & Ethics* XI. 89/1 The economic salvation of the Mormon State arose..from the money spent in Utah by the Forty-Niners. **1948** Mencken *Amer. Lang.* Suppl. II. 640 Utah calls itself the *Beehive State*,.. but the designation *Mormon State* is far more popular, and seems likely to stick. **1850** *Ann. Iowa* (1910) 3rd Ser. IX. 453 Here we struck the old Mormon trail. **1868** 'Mark Twain' in *Galaxy* May 631 The post route..changed partly to the old Mormon trail. **1949** *Kansas Hist. Q.* Feb. 39 The War Department decided..to improve the Mormon trail from Omaha as far as New Fort Kearney. **1833** in *D.A.* s.v., The Mormon War. **1834** *Knickerbocker* Aug. 159/2 *The Mormon War*... The war between the citizens of Jackson county, Missouri, and the disciples of the Book of Mormon. **1846** *Quincy* (Illinois) *Whig* 3 Feb. 2/4 He was a Major in the last '*Mormon War*'. **1857** *San Francisco Plaindealer* 10 Dec. 2/2 The Mormon war will furnish abundant material for Buncombe speeches. **1942** C. C. Rister *Land Hunger* 8 Upon the outbreak of the 'Mormon War', Dave and his older brother Jack, rode away..to join the army. **1872** *Trans. Ill. Dept. Agric.* IX. p. ix, Mr. James H. McConnell..has..prosecuted experiments with the Indian Mallow (*Abutilon Avacennae*) variously known as 'stump weed', 'velvet leaf', 'butter print', 'Mormon weed', etc. **1907** A. B. Lyons *Plant Names* (ed. 2) 8 Abutilon... American Hemp, Indian Hemp, Mormon-weed, Pie-marker, Pie-print, Sheep-weed.

Mormondom (further examples); **Mo·rmonish** *a.*, pertaining to or characteristic of Mormons or their beliefs; **Mo·rmonry** *rare* = Mormondom.

1846 *Quincy* (Illinois) *Whig* 19 Mar. 3/3 It would be desirable by all quiet citizens that they should be able to discover a complete evacuation of everything Mormonish in Nauvoo, before they hazard purchases in that place. **1852** *Oregon Statesman* (Oregon City) 6 Jan. 2/6 Your course looks as Mormonish as anything I ever saw. **1860** *Harper's Mag.* Nov. 857/2 We may be a trifle more fastidious than they are in Mormondom, but we have a notion that all the 'bad words' ought to be skipped when the ladies are around. **1873** Mormondom [see *Dixie[2] 2]. **1920** *Encycl. Relig. & Ethics* XI. 86/2 That Joseph Smith

..was the real master of Mormondom is borne out by.. accounts of him in the height of his power. **1930** *Amer. Mercury* Jan. 6/1 The next step was an accident, one of a series that has displayed God's providence to Mormonry. **1957** W. MULDER *Homeward to Zion* xi. 289 The 'iniquitous' Cullom bill..stirred Mormondom to its center.

Mormoness (mǭ·ɹmǒnė·s). [-ESS[1].] A female Mormon.

a **1861** T. WINTHROP *John Brent* (1862) ix. 99 Selecting, perhaps, a Mormoness to kidnap to-night. **1862** C. F. BROWNE *A. Ward his Book* (1865) 76 'Yes,' hollered a lot of femaile Mormonesses, ceasin me by the cote tales & swingin me round very rapid. **1906** *Out West* May 305 (*title*) The Writer Lady and the Mormoness.

Mormonism. Add: (Further examples.) Also *fig.*

1831 *Niles' Reg.* 16 July 353/1 Mormonism..a new religion. **1855** A. L. PHILLIPPS *Mahometanism* vi. 244 Socialism and Mormonism and infidelity taking the place of religion and social order. **1913** E. F. BENSON *Thorley Weir* i. 33 'They can't all be serenading me.' 'I cannot imagine why not. A Mormonism of serenading young men is not illegal.' **1929** L. H. CREER *Utah & Nation* i. 3 Herein was also established the principle of modern revelation, one of the basic principles of Mormonism. **1958** MULDER & MORTENSEN *Among Mormons* p. v, The learned journals have discovered in Mormonism a ripe field for scholarship.

Mormonist. (Further example.)

1842 DICKENS *Amer. Notes* I. v. 181, I should like to try the experiment on a Mormonist or two to begin with.

Mormonite, *sb.* and *a.* Add: **a.** *sb.* (Earlier and later examples.)

1831 *Columbian Reporter* (Taunton, Mass.) 24 Aug. 1/5 The Mormonites. We learn..that this infatuated people are again in motion. **1947** B. DE VOTO *Across Wide Missouri* 185 The 'Mormonites'..had been driven into the unsettled lands of Clay County. **1958** MULDER & MORTENSEN *Among Mormons* p. vi, Once the new church is founded the religious press is full of letters..about the Mormonites and their New Jerusalem.

b. *adj.* (Earlier examples.) Now *rare.*

1835 C. BRADLEY *Jrnl.* 24 June in *Ohio Archaeol. & Hist. Q.* (1906) XV. 269 We have, too, a company of Mormanite missionaries aboard. **1859** MILL *Liberty* iv. 164 The article of the Mormonite doctrine which is the chief provocative..is its sanction of polygamy.

mor'n: see *MORE *adv.* 5 a.

Mornay (mǭ·ɹnē). Also **mornay.** [perh. f. the name of Philippe de *Mornay* (died 1623), a French Huguenot writer.] *Mornay sauce* (also in Fr. form *sauce mornay*): a rich white sauce flavoured with cheese. Also *ellipt.*, a dish served with Mornay sauce.

1906 A. FILIPPINI *International Cook Bk.* 623 Fillet of sole, mornay. **1925** LEYEL & HARTLEY *Gentle Art of Cookery* 20 Sauce mornay, a cheese sauce. **1939** A. L. SIMON *Conc. Encycl. Gastron.* I. 39/1 Mornay, sauce. Heat the required amount of *Béchamel*... When ready to serve, add as much Parmesan cheese as desired. **1948** L. MARION *Be your Own Chef* xii. 230 Remove the vegetable marrow from the oven. Throw away the water..and pour the Mornay Sauce over the pieces of vegetable. **1963** R. CARRIER *Great Dishes of World* 62 Mornay sauce—for fish, vegetables, poultry, poached eggs, noodle and macaroni mixtures. **1965** *House & Garden* Dec. 84/2 *Mornay.* Just cheese, but the basis of some of the most wonderful recipes there are. **1974** I. MURDOCH *Sacred & Profane Love Machine* 311 Well, *oeufs* somehow? Mornay?

morning, *sb.* Add: **1. e.** *Ellipt.* for **morning paper. colloq.*

1961 [see *EVENING *sb.*[1] 2 f]. **1966** *New Statesman* 7 Oct. 503/3 Thomson already controls the *Scotsman*, three provincial mornings and nine evenings. **1970** K. GILES *Death in Church* v. 121 Did you see the mornings?..The act of killing the clergy seems to enrage English journalists.

2. b. For 'in vulgar or off-hand speech' read 'in informal speech'.

1911 G. B. SHAW *Blanco Posnet* 390 Morning, Elder. (*Passing on*). Morning Strapper. (*Passing on*). Morning, Miss Evans. **1968** G. BUTLER *Coffin Following* vi. 120 'Morning,' said the ticket collector.

3. a. *morning, noon, and night* (earlier examples).

1808 E. WEETON Let. 1 Apr. in *Jrnl. of Governess* (1969) I. 80 Your praises..have operated almost like a dose of salts, and have worked me morning, noon, and night for these two days. **1864** TROLLOPE *Can you forgive Her?* I. xx. 160 Your sitting here all alone, morning, noon, and night, won't bring him back.

c. mornings (later examples).

1936 *S.P.E. Tract* XLV. 192 A peculiar use of the plural form is illustrated in 'The operatic tenor Campanini was engaged to sing mornings'. **1938** T. WILDER *Our Town* I. 11 Quarter of nine mornings, noontimes, and three o'clock afternoon's [*sic*], the hull town can hear the yelling and screaming from those schoolyards.

g. (*the*) *morning after* (*the night before*): a morning on which the effects of the previous night's drinking or revelry are unpleasantly felt; also *attrib.* and *absol.*, these effects or a person suffering from them; also in extended use for any unpleasant aftermath of pleasure. Also *morning after*, applied to a contraceptive pill that is effective when taken some time after sexual intercourse.

1884 *Punch* 31 May 264/1 His method of inoculation for hydrophobia seems uncommonly like the old 'morning-after' remedy, when the chippy one who could 'strike matches on his tongue' was recommended to take 'a hair of the dog that bit him'. **1909** E. NESBIT *Daphne in Fitzroy St.* xvi. 256 'I'm all right,' said the girl... 'That's what we all of us says, when it comes to be the morning after,' said Mrs. Delarue. **1922** JOYCE *Ulysses* 231 It was blue o'clock the morning after the night before. **1927** KIPLING *Limits & Renewals* (1932) 157 There wasn't much doubt what Jimmy had been up to. He was altogether 'the morning after'. **1942** T. BAILEY *Pink Camellia* v. 28 She sat up and looked at herself in the mirror. 'The morning after! And my face looks like it.' **1946** 'BRAHMS' & 'SIMON' *Trottie True* vi. 152 'The Duke's got a morning-after,' she said crisply. **1947** *Sat. Rev.* (U.S.) 12 Apr. 20/1 The nation relaxes, and only the morning-after headaches and the morning-after quarterbacks remain. **1957** A. C. CLARKE *Deep Range* iv. 43 He was not pleased to find that the entire stock of 'morning-after' pills had already been consumed. *a* **1963** S. PLATH *Crossing Water* (1971) 33 Musky as a lovebed the morning after. **1967** V. C. CLINTON-BADDELEY *Death's Bright Dart* 169 One of those aristocratic men in the advertisements whose morning-after needs are ministered to by a smiling and provident butler. **1967** *N.Y. Times* 24 Aug. 35 Dr. Chang and Dr. Pincus had been working recently on a new pill, known popularly as the 'morning-after' pill. It affects the egg after ovulation. **1969** *Daily Tel.* 3 July 23/3 Trials of a 'morning after' pill had been promising. **1973** *Express* (Trinidad & Tobago) 17 Mar. 7/1 The Food and Drug Administration will approve the use of diethylstilbestrol or DES as a 'morning after' contraceptive pill for women in emergency situations such as rape. **1973** L. MEYNELL *Thirteen Trumpeters* xiv. 215 'I felt *awful*. I didn't care whether I lived or died..' 'A classic case of the morning-after-the-night-before feeling.'

7. *morning beam, gold, light* (further examples), *performance* (earlier example).

1928 E. BLUNDEN *Retreat* 33 With friends as nimble as morning-beams, Who sped with him to this playground. **1890** KIPLING *Barrack-Room Ballads* (1892) 163 He hewed the living rock with sweat and tears, And reared a God against the morning-gold. **1930** R. CAMPBELL *Adamastor* 86 With food and drink, at morning-light, The children met me at the water-side. **1827** T. J. DIBDIN *Reminisc.* I. 251 A large play bill from Dublin, announcing morning performances, on account of a partial insurrection or rebellion.

¶ (Further examples.)

1916 D. H. LAWRENCE *Amores* 125 It seemed that I and the morning world Were pressed cup-shape to take this reiver Bird. **1917** —— *Look! We have come Through!* 77 See, glittering on the milk-blue, morning lake They are laying the golden racing-track of the sun.

b. *morning coat, jacket, suit* (earlier example).

1867 *Harper's Mag.* Aug. 362/1 He got himself a new morning suit for shop use. **1912** 'C. F. BENTON' *Fairs & Fetes* 118 They should sell brushes and combs..and morning jackets. **1933** *Week-end Review* 21 Jan. 69/2 Black morning coat and waistcoat, grey striped trousers, grey tie and pearl pin. **1969** R. GODDEN *In this House of Brede* xix. 395 Japanese gentlemen in morning coats, grey waistcoats, striped trousers.

8. For 'Only *poet.*' read 'Usu. *poet.*' and add: *morning-blue, -bright* (further examples), *-cold, -fair, -gathered, -grey* adjs.

1920 D. H. LAWRENCE *Lost Girl* xvi. 366 The lovely translucent pale irises, tiny and morning-blue, they lasted only a few hours. **1922** E. BLUNDEN *Shepherd* 48 Cheeks all morning-bright. **1923** D. H. LAWRENCE *Birds, Beasts & Flowers* 76 My heart which like a lark at heaven's gate singing, hovers morning-bright to Thee. **1945** J. BETJEMAN *New Bats in Old Belfries* 43 There splashed about our ankles as we waded Those intersecting wavelets morning-cold. **1938** W. DE LA MARE *Memory* 34 Eyes blue as speedwell, tranquil, morning-fair. **1857** *Leisure Hour* 2 July 421/1 You cannot now get out of hearing of..'strawberries, morning gathered'. **1903** *Farmer & Stockbreeder* 8 June 950/3 The vegetables mostly arrive in freight trains from distant States. They are well packed, and despatched with regularity, but nothing is absolutely fresh or 'morning gathered', as London greengrocers love to shout. **1961** *Daily Mail* 15 Mar. 8/8 'Morning gathered?' (Which morning?) **1943** C. DAY LEWIS *Word over All* 15 Children look down upon the morning-grey Tissue of mist that veils a valley's lap.

9. morning caller, one who pays a formal morning call; **morning coffee,** coffee taken at mid-morning or (a less common use) at breakfast; **morning girl,** a non-resident maidservant employed during the morning only; **morning line,** a list of probable betting odds established by the bookmaker prior to a sporting event; also *attrib.*; **morning paper,** a newspaper published so as to be on sale during the morning; **morning prayer,** (*a*) (later examples); (*c*) *Mil. slang* (see quot. 1965); **morning room** (earlier example); **morning tea,** tea taken either before rising or at mid-morning; **morning visit,** (*a*) a visit made in the morning; (*b*) a formal 'afternoon' visit (cf. *morning call*); also *morning visiting, visitor.*

1848 GEO. ELIOT *Let.* in J. W. Cross *George Eliot's Life* (1885) I. 184 The bliss of having a very high attic in a romantic Continental town..far away from morning-callers, dinners, and decencies. **1863** MRS. GASKELL *Dark Night's Work* viii. 128 She allowed Fletcher to..usher him into the library just like any common visitor, any morning-caller. **1941** G. HEYER *Faro's Daughter* i. 1 While the butler went to convey this message to the morning-caller, her ladyship tidied her ruffled person. **1855** GEO. ELIOT in *Fraser's Mag.* June 705/1 The dark little bedroom, and the arm-chair where he took his morning coffee as he read. **1917** CONRAD *Shadow-Line* iv. 131 Presently Ransome brought me the cup of morning coffee. **1959** T. S. ELIOT *Elder Statesman* II. 43 When I asked about morning coffee She said 'I'm not the one for elevens's.' **1973** A. CHRISTIE *Postern of Fate* III. xv. 231, I was just going to bring your morning coffee up. **1921** *Dict. Occup. Terms* (1927) § 900 Daily servant,..morning girl; a non-resident general servant. **1935** A. J. POLLOCK *Underworld Speaks* 77/2 *Morning line,* the betting odds quoted in poolrooms on horse races. **1941** *Sun* (Baltimore) 26 Dec. 11/5 The old Louisiana Jockey Club abandoned the sport following a controversy over the..ruling eliminating the 'morning line' bookmaking. **1964** A. WYKES *Gambling* viii. 192 The day starts with the numbers of the runners in the first race posted in order, with the 'morning line' odds in lights opposite them. The morning line is the odds established by the racing officials for each horse (on the basis of its past performance) on the morning of a particular racing day. **1968** *Wall St. Jrnl.* 31 Jan. 1/1 Mr. Lewin has been track handicapper at Atlantic City, making up the 'morning line' (early odds) and picking likely winners for the official track program. **1727–41** Morning paper [see PAPER *sb.* 8]. **1768** J. WEDGWOOD *Let.* 13 June (1965) 64 That Morning Paper which is mostly taken in by People of Fashion. **1862** Morning paper [in Dict., sense 7]. **1968** R. B. HEATH *Newspapers* i. 13 National daily morning papers. **1857** TROLLOPE *Barchester Towers* III. xv. 264 Eleanor was dressed a full hour before the time fixed in the Ullathorne household for morning prayers. **1916** JOYCE *Portrait of Artist* iii. 130 Death..is a blessed moment for him who has walked in the right path..attending to his morning and evening prayers. **1965** B. SWEET-ESCOTT *Baker St. Irreg.* viii. 250 'Morning prayers' in 12th Army headquarters, the daily briefing of the staff, began with a statement of temperature and humidity. **1816** JANE AUSTEN *Emma* II. xiv. 260 That room was the very shape and size of the morning-room at Maple Grove. **1727** SWIFT *Furnit. Woman's Mind* in *Poetical Wks.* (1967) 329 Can at her Morning Tea run o'er The Scandal of the Day before. **1923** WODEHOUSE *Inimitable Jeeves* xii. 135 Sometimes when Jeeves has brought in my morning tea and shoved it on the table beside my bed, he drifts silently from the room. **1940** Morning tea [see **evening paper*]. **1948** H. V. MORTON *In Search of South Africa* iv. 123, I saw groups of storm-bound people sitting at their morning tea. **1963** A. LUBBOCK *Austral. Roundabout* 6 The meals called 'tea'. There are three... First you have 'morning tea', which consists of cups of tea and biscuits, or savouries, at eleven o'clock. **1736** Morning visit [in Dict., sense 7]. **1787** A. YOUNG *Jrnl.* 28 June in *Trav. France* (1792) I. 25 We return in time to dress for dinner, at half after twelve or one: then adjourn to the drawing-room.. as the first thing done, by every person who arrives, is to pay a morning visit to each party already in the place. **1828** Morning visit [in Dict., sense 7]. **1864** TROLLOPE *Can you forgive Her?* I. ii. 9 The old lady walked into the drawing-room one morning at eleven o'clock..these morning visits were made almost every day. **1852** C. M. YONGE *Two Guardians* xi. 195 The afternoons were less certain to be agreeable... Marian had become liable..[to] being carried forth..on a morning visiting expedition. **1777** P. THICKNESSE *Year's Journey through France* II. 234 The French never give..any refreshment..to their morning or evening visitors. **1831** M. EDGEWORTH *Let.* 6 Jan. (1971) 469 Scarcely had I taken up my pen and breathed when other morning visitors entered.

morning-glory. 1. Substitute for def.: A twining herb of the genus *Ipomœa* or closely related genera of the family Convolvulaceæ, esp. *Ipomœa* (or *Pharbitis*) *purpurea*, which is native to tropical America and bears large trumpet-shaped flowers; also *attrib.* and *fig.* (Earlier and later examples.)

1814 F. PURSH *Flora Americæ Septentrionalis* I. 146 *Ipomoea Nil*... Flowers beautiful pale blue, only open early in the morning, from which it has been called Morning-glory. **1934** E. BLUNDEN *Choice or Chance* 11 And with wonder saw The morning-glory about the bucket twined. **1947** R. P. T. COFFIN *Yankee Coast* 59 The owners..have to make guitars and banjos do. And accordions, phonographs with morning-glory horns, and, latterly, radios. **1963** W. BLUNT *Of Flowers & Village* 176 I've not been very successful with morning glories. **1964** C. WILLOCK *Enormous Zoo* v. 89 We found the DC..in a morning glory-covered bungalow up on the Sudan border. **1966** *Times* 22 Mar. 5/1 The Pharmaceutical Society is carrying out laboratory investigations to determine whether any Morning Glory seeds sold in this country could be dangerous. **1968** PETERSON & MCKENNY *Field Guide to Wildflowers Northeastern & Northcentral N. Amer.* 338 Common Morning-glory. Alien. *Ipomoea purpurea*... A twining vine; the garden morning-glory with broad heart-shaped leaves. Flowers purple, pink, blue, or white. **1970** R. LOWELL *Notebk.* 101 The jellied green creepers and morning-glories of the saurian sunset.

3. *U.S. slang.* Something which fails to maintain its early achievement; *esp.* in sporting contexts.

1904 *Outing* XLV. 170/1 Didn't I tell you he was nothing but a morning glory—why that dog couldn't beat a ferry boat. **1920** *Harvey's Weekly* 15 May 15/2 You have ..sent one more morning glory statesman to limbo. **1935** A. J. POLLOCK *Underworld Speaks* 77/2 *Morning glory,* race horse that works in fast time in the morning but fails to race well. **1938** *Amer. Speech* XIII. 30 Clubs which bloom luxuriantly early in the season, but which are expected to wilt ignominiously as the competition becomes hotter, are known as *Morning Glories.*

morningless, *a.* (Later example.)

1930 O. GOGARTY *Wild Apples* 15 Those resinous timbers immuned from decay By thunders ancestral and morningless storms.

Moroccan, *a.* and *sb.* Add: **A.** *adj.* (Earlier examples.)

a **1706** EVELYN *Diary* an. 1682 (1955) IV. 285 We had at this time in Lond together The Russian, Morrocan, & Indian Ambassador. **1869** 'MARK TWAIN' *Innoc. Abr.* vii. 69 The Spaniards built these watch towers on the hills to enable them to keep a sharper look out on the Moroccan speculators.

b. In the names of various preparations of cannabis.

1970 E. GOODE *Marijuana Smokers* i. 18 Another recipe book..has exotic Oriental dishes, such as 'Bhang Sherbet', 'Moroccan Majoon' [etc.]. **1972** J. BROWN *Chancer* iii. 38 People talk about the effects of cannabis as if there was just one kind... You smoke Moroccan Gold.. you'll just feel, like, a little drunk. But you smoke Egyptian Black, that will stone you out of your head. **1972** *Times* 14 Dec. 2/3 The changes involved 'speed'..and other drugs, referred to in the hearing as..'Moroccan black'.

morocco, *sb.* Add: **II. 3. b.** *morocco-bound*, also used *fig.*; *morocco-covered* adj.

1873 'MARK TWAIN' & WARNER *Gilded Age* II. ix. 97 A very official chair behind a long green morocco-covered table. **1886** A. HORNBLOW tr. *Normand's Splashes from Parisian Ink-Pot* 83 Plunged in a big green morocco-covered fauteuil, he began to scan over the 'dailies'. **1896** *Sat. Rev.* 12 Dec. 623/2 'Little Eyolf'..has been promoted into a full-blown fashionable theatrical speculation, with a 'Morocco Bound' syndicate in the background. **1958** *Listener* 2 Oct. 520/2 Sentences like 'I have still to see that lofty homeland of the potato and the llama'..belong to a solid, morocco-bound tradition.

moron[2] (mōᵊ·rǫn). orig. *U.S.* [f. L. *mōrus*, Gr. μωρός stupid.] **a.** One of the highest class of feeble-minded; an adult person having a mental age of between eight and twelve. Also *attrib.*

The term was first adopted and given this meaning by the American Association for the Study of the Feeble-minded in 1910.

1910 H. H. GODDARD *Let.* 29 Apr. in *Jrnl. Psycho-Asthenics* Sept.–Dec. 65 The other (suggestion) is to call them [*sc.* feeble-minded children] by the Greek word 'moron'. It is defined as one who is lacking in intelligence, one who is deficient in judgement or sense. **1912** —— *Kallikak Family* 54 The type of feeblemindedness of which we are speaking is the one to which Deborah belongs, that is, to the high grade, or moron. **1919** H. WOODROW *Brightness & Dullness in Children* iii. 45 The term *moron*..is a new term... The desirability of this new term arose from the fact that the term feeble-minded, which is used in England to designate only the highest class of mental defectives, had long been used in America to include all three classes. **1937** C. L. BURT *Subnormal Mind* (rev. ed.) ii. 102 All through their years of training, most of them [*sc.* social workers and teachers] had never, to their certain knowledge, set eyes on a moron or an imbecile. **1948** J. W. BRIDGES *Psychol.* xxiv. 352 The moron has an I.Q. of 50 to 70..and the idiot below 20. This distinction is made on the basis of intelligence test results and is consequently not very reliable. **1968** W. B. STEPHENS tr. *Inhelder's Diagnosis of Reasoning in Mentally Retarded* ii. 72 The normal child of seven, the moron of twelve, or even the imbecile assimilates an enormous number of varied experiences which are..qualitatively irreducible from one level to the other.

b. *colloq.* A stupid or slow-witted person; a fool. Also *attrib.*

1922 W. R. INGE in *Edin. Rev.* July 48 It is possible that while we are governed by high-grade 'morons' there will be no practical recognition of the dangers which threaten us. **1922** H. TITUS *Timber* iii. 37 So this backwoods moron, even, knew something about his affairs that John Taylor did not know. **1922** L. STODDARD *Revolt against Civilization* iv. 129 It is a mutilated, deformed, moron humanity which glowers or drivels at us through expressionist pictures. **1928** HECHT & MACARTHUR *Front Page* II. 91 Another one of your moron blunders. **1930** R. MACAULAY *Staying with Relations* ii. 22 'You mutt,' said young Mrs. Rickaby..'Catherine will think we're all morons.' **1959** *Punch* 10 June 780/2 It was so obvious it might have occurred to anyone but a complete moron. **1968** M. WOODHOUSE *Rock Baby* xxiii. 219 What we have here is a poxed-up, paralytic bunch of morons... They're technically incompetent..and they're pretty useless in almost every other field. **1975** G. MOFFAT *Miss Pink* xii. 169 He'd have had to be a moron not to have guessed that the killer was really after himself.

So **moro·nic** *a.*, **moro·nically** *adv.*

1926 *N.Y. Herald-Trib.* 28 Nov. VII. 4/2 A facetious account of a young girl's discovery that her brother had died of a venereal disease which has the romping moronic quality of a tabloid front page. **1931** *Churchman* 14 Feb. 15 The philosophers go home considerably enheartened when they find Socrates moronically low in his I.Q. Scores. **1957** R. A. HEINLEIN *Door into Summer* (1960) ii. 25 It was a moronically simple idea: don't repair, replace. **1957** *Times Lit. Suppl.* 18 Oct. 621/3 The psychopathic juvenile delinquent, moronically searching for 'the truth'. **1959** *Punch* 13 May 641/2 They interrupt Macbeth, they cackle at M. Hulot, they share their moronic comments with their escorts. **1975** D. BLOODWORTH *Clients of Omega* xxi. 204 Provoking desperate people into believing that they can only bring about unity among men by knocking their moronic heads together.

morone. (Earlier example.)

1808 *Examiner* 6 Mar. 157/2 Coquelicot and morone are on the decline.

moror, var. *MAROR.

morosity. Delete 'now *rare*' and add later examples.

1923 E. BOWEN *Encounters* 13 Aunt Willoughby's baffled, bearded morosity. **1965** C. H. SISSON *Christopher Homm* xxi. 162 Even to Dad Christopher's courtship was of some use, as an exercise for morosity.

morosophist. Delete † and add later example. *rare.*

1870 K. H. DIGBY *Halcyon Hours* 255 Morosophists who love to boast Are those of course who scorn the most This holy maid.

morph[2] (mǭɹf). *U.S. colloq.* and *slang* shortening of MORPHINE *sb.* (see also quot. 1912).

1912 *Collier's* 21 Sept. 20/2 White 'dope fiends', known in the vernacular of the police as 'hops', 'cokes', or 'morphs'. **1914** JACKSON & HELLYER *Vocab. Criminal Slang* 60 *M*, or *Morph*,..used by morphine fiends. Sulphate of morphia. **1926** J. BLACK *You can't Win* xii. 160 About a spoonful of water and some of their meager store of 'morph' were put in the tin box. **1956** H. GOLD *Man who was not with It* (1965) viii. 65 No morph, no! I had really kicked that one, and would do my own traveling from now on.

morph[3] (mǭɹf). *Linguistics.* [f. *MORPH(EME.] **a.** = *ALLOMORPH[2]. **b.** A phoneme or series of phonemes forming a variant or a number of variants of a morpheme.

1947 C. F. HOCKETT in *Language* XXIII. 322 Recurrent partials not composed of smaller ones (*-way*) are *alternants* or *morphs*... By definition, a morph has the same phonemic shape in all its occurrences... Morphs are not always composed of continuous uninterrupted stretches of phonemes, but they are always composed of phonemes. Every utterance is composed entirely of morphs. **1948** P. K. BENEDICT in *Jrnl. Amer. Oriental Soc.* LXVIII. 185 This nomenclature has obvious advantages from a systematic point of view, and might well be extended to morphology, with the 'morph' as the descriptive unit, and the 'allomorph' as the member of a morpheme. **1952** C. E. BAZELL in E. P. Hamp et al. *Readings in Linguistics II* (1966) 274 The term *morpheme*..was used both for the narrower modern concept and for that of the morpheme-alternant or (in American usage) the morph. **1955** *Trans. Philol. Soc. 1954* 69 *Morphemes.* Analytic classification here would obviously refer to morpheme-alternants ('morphs')... Synthetic classification of morphs is implied in the very procedure of defining their morphemic values. For it is on account of their membership in different substitution-classes (selections), that morphs are assigned their different morphemic values, or, as we say, considered to 'represent different morphemes'. **1960** *Amer. Speech* XXXV. 218 He [*sc.* Hoenigswald] believes sound change to be due to nothing but complete borrowing of morphs between only sub-phonemically differing dialects. **1962** H. M. HOENIGSWALD in Householder & Saporta *Problems in Lexicography* 105 There can be no objection to an arrangement by morphs, that is by the phonemic shape of the allomorph or allomorphs making up the morpheme. **1964** E. BACH *Introd. Transformational Gram.* vii. 147 Phonemes have been considered by some to be classes of sounds, morphemes as classes of morphs, and so on. **1965** *Language* XLI. 420 The markers of case are almost always portmanteau morphs that are also involved in expressing other categories..of the noun phrase. **1968** J. LYONS *Introd. Theoretical Linguistics* v. 184 The word *bigger* is analysable into two morphs... Each morph *represents* (or is the exponent of) a particular morpheme... Morphemes may be represented directly by phonological (or orthographical) segments with a particular 'shape' (that is, by morphs). **1972** *Hiberno-English Dialect Questionnaire* 1 Some of the principal morphs found in polysyllables are..included in the questionnaire.

c. *attrib.* and *Comb.*

1947 *Language* XXIII. 337 Intonational morphs..are found spread through such morphs or morph-sequences as *yes, I know, no, maybe*, [etc.]. **1953** C. E. BAZELL *Linguistic Form* ii. 22 The term [*sc.* morphophonemics] has also more recently been used for the study of morph-structure proper. *Ibid.* iv. 47 In many systems no morph-boundaries are found within syllables. **1962** H. M. HOENIGSWALD in Householder & Saporta *Problems in Lexicography* 107 Is it reasonable..to consider the sentence intonations of English on a par with the segmental morph-morphemes? **1964** E. BACH *Introd. Transformational Gram.* vi. 130 The P rules will operate to select the proper morph shapes and allophones. **1965** *Amer. Speech* XL. 297 Orrm's use of double consonants, which is found only in morph-final position or in morph-final clusters, indicates plus juncture rather than shortness of the preceding vowel. **1972** *Archivum Linguisticum* III. 49 There is a regular phonological rule in Nzema and Ahanta which voices certain morph-initial obstruents if they are preceded by a vowel or nasal consonant.

morph[4] (mǭɹf). [f. Gr. μορφή form.] A variant form of an animal produced by genetic differences, or (in later use) one of several forms exhibited by an animal in the course of its life cycle. Hence **mo·rphic** *a.*; **mo·rphism** = POLYMORPHISM 2.

1955 J. S. HUXLEY in *Heredity* IX. 2, I propose to introduce the term morphism and its derivatives, morphic and morph. *Ibid.* 3, I restrict the term morphism to genetic polymorphism..in which (usually sharply distinct) genetic variants or morphs coexist in temporary or permanent balance within a single interbreeding population in a single spatial region, and in such frequencies that the rarer cannot be due solely to mutation, or to the spread of selectively neutral mutants. *Ibid.* 8 The cuckoo shows a general tendency to morphism..for it shows a plumage dimorphism, barred red and unbarred grey. Among adults, the red morph is confined to a minority, all females. **1955** —— in *Proc. R. Soc.* B. CXLIV. 215 A morphic balance-mechanism must be strong enough to prevent the break-up of the morphism through the disappearance of any morph under adverse selection in periods exceptionally unfavourable to it. **1963** E. MAYR *Animal Species & Evolution* vii. 157 Natural selection may modify the dominance of such morphs. **1968** R. D. MARTIN tr. *Wickler's Mimicry in Plants & Animals* i. 14 A leaf-beetle occurring as two separate morphs is shown. *Ibid.* vi. 61 Both sexes [of *Ityraea nigrocincta*] have two morphs, a green form and a yellow form. **1970** *Nature* 26 Sept. 1368/1 In the autumn the parthenogenetic viviparous morphs of the aphid give birth to nymphs which develop into males and oviparous females. **1974** *Ibid.* 22 Feb. 572/2 The frequencies of colour and banding morphs of the dead animals were compared with those prevailing in the population. **1975** *Jrnl. Zool.* CLXXVII. 336 From considerations of morphism, modality and sex-limitation, a descriptive classification of nine categories is advanced to encompass all situations involving pattern polymorphism and sexual dimorphism in butterflies.

-morph (mǭɹf), terminal element (repr. Gr. μορφή form) of sbs. with the sense 'thing having a (certain) form or character', as ISOMORPH, POLYMORPH, *ALLELOMORPH, *ENDOMORPH.

morphallaxis (mǭɹfălæ·ksis). *Zool.* [f. Gr. μορφ-ή form + ἄλλαξις exchange.] Regeneration by the transformation of existing bodily material.

1901 T. H. MORGAN *Regeneration* i. 23 At present there are known two general ways in which regeneration may take place... In order to distinguish broadly these two modes I propose to call those cases of regeneration in which a proliferation of material precedes the development of the new part, 'epimorphosis'. The other mode, in which a part is transformed directly into a new organism, or part of an organism without proliferation at the cut-surfaces, 'morphallaxis'. **1924** G. R. DE BEER *Growth* viii. 53 In regeneration in some cases (where morphallaxis occurs), it [*sc.* material needed for growth] is derived from the other tissues of the organism which thereby undergo reduction. **1956** C. H. WADDINGTON *Princ. Embryol.* xiv. 304 Animals such as coelenterates, flatworms and oligochaetes in which morphallaxis occurs to a considerable extent. **1965** KIORTSIS & MORAITOU in Kiortsis & Trampusch *Regeneration in Animals* 259 If the anteriorly facing cut end of the nerve cord [in the polychaete worm *Spirographis spallanzanii*] is deflected, there is a morphallaxis on one or both sides.

morpheme (mǭ·ɹfīm). *Linguistics.* [F. *morphème*, f. Gr. μορφή form, after *phonème* PHONEME.] **a.** An element such as an affix, preposition, conjunction, or stress pattern considered in respect of its functional relations in a linguistic system (now little used by linguists). **b.** The smallest meaningful morphological unit of language, one that cannot be analysed into smaller forms.

1896 R. J. LLOYD in *Neueren Sprachen* III. 615 The phonetic elements of a given word are its *phonemes*. But its significant elements, be they root, suffix, prefix, inflection or aught else, are *morphemes*. **1925** P. RADIN tr. *Vendryès's Lang.* II. i. 74 By *semantemes* we understand the linguistic elements which express the ideas of the concepts..and by *morphemes* we understand those elements which express the connexions between the ideas... The morpheme is generally a phonetic element..indicating the grammatical relations between the ideas in the sentence. **1926** L. BLOOMFIELD in *Language* II. 155 A morpheme is a recurrent (meaningful) form which cannot in turn be analyzed into smaller recurrent (meaningful) forms. Hence any unanalyzable word or formative is a morpheme. **1931** *Amer. Jrnl. Philol.* LII. 78 The morpheme of the dependent element indicates merely an unspecialised dependence (gender, number, person, case). *Ibid.* 79 Nouns are semantemes susceptible of morphemes of case. **1933** L. BLOOMFIELD *Language* x. 161 A linguistic form which bears no partial phonetic-semantic resemblance to any other form, is a *simple* form or *morpheme*. Thus, *bird, play, dance, cran-, -y, -ing* are morphemes. Morphemes may show partial phonetic resemblances. **1935** G. K. ZIPF *Psycho-Biol. of Lang.* (1936) i. 15 One may view the same word [sc. *untruthfulness*] as a sequence of five units which we shall term morphemes..i.e. *un-tru-th-ful-ness*. **1948** *Word* Apr. 20 If it is a bound form, the element must—in order to be a morpheme—be active. **1953** C. E. BAZELL *Linguistic Form* i. 5 As used in Europe, it [*sc.* morpheme] answers very approximately to one of two other American terms: (i) the morphemic component, including the morpheme with only one component, or (ii) the morphemic segment or 'morph'... (The earlier distinction of morpheme and semanteme is obsolete except in non-structuralist circles.) **1959** *Archivum Linguisticum* XI. 93 In the *Prolegomena*, morphemes ('inflectional elements', not, however, to be identified with morphemes in either the Prague or American [Bloomfieldian] sense) are regarded as constituting part of the content form of language. **1962** E. F. HADEN et al. *Resonance-Theory for Linguistics* iii. 40 The word is here defined..as a free form comprising one or more morphemes, occurring in a given position relative to other words. **1967** *General Linguistics* VII. 65 Maslov discusses the shifts in meaning and utilization which the term 'morpheme' has undergone since its coinage by Baudouin de Courtenay in the 1880's. **1973** *Sci. Amer.* Feb. 57/2 Every language has a stock of several thousand morphemes: the bearers of the basic semantic and grammatical content. An expression such as 'can openers' comprises four morphemes: 'can', 'open', '-er' and '-s'.

c. *attrib.* and *Comb.*, as *morpheme-class*, *-combination*, *-configuration*, *-count*, *-sequence*, *-structure*, *-theory*, *-unit*, *-word*; *morpheme-based*, *-initial*, *-like*, *-medial* adjs.; **morpheme alternant** = *ALLOMORPH[2].

1942 *Language* XVIII. 171 We divide each expression in

the given language into the smallest sequences of phonemes which have what we consider the same meaning when they occur in other expressions... The resultant minimum parts we call not morphemes, but *morpheme alternants*. **1947** *Ibid.* XXIII. 402 Different phonemic shapes of a given base appearing before different suffixes.. are morpheme alternants of the same morpheme. **1952, 1955** [see *MORPH[3]]. **1963** J. LYONS *Structural Semantics* ii. 11 A word-based grammar seems to be more satisfactory than a morpheme-based grammar for the description of languages of the 'inflecting' type. **1947** *Language* XXIII. 81 Morphemes are assigned to *morpheme-classes* on the basis of the environments in which they occur. Each environment determines one and only one morpheme-class. **1963** ERVIN & MILLER in J. A. Fishman *Readings Sociol. of Lang.* (1968) 76 Morpheme classes can be divided into two groups, lexical and function classes. **1953** C. E. BAZELL *Linguistic Form* vii. 81 But here it is not simply a matter of sorting out incommutable morphemes, but also a case of including commutable morpheme-combinations. **1935** G. K. ZIPF *Psycho-Biol. of Lang.* (1936) iv. 136 If a morpheme-count reveals ..that accent tends to settle on morphemes of the greatest average interval..we shall have reached the very heart of the dynamics of accent. *Ibid.* 154 The crystallization of phonemes in a morpheme-configuration. **1964** *Language* XL. 35 Morpheme-initial *s* is replaced by *x* if it is preceded by a vowel or a velar and is followed by a vowel. **1962** H. M. HOENIGSWALD in Householder & Saporta *Problems in Lexicography* 107 There are, in the view of many linguists, morphemes and morpheme-like entities with so-called grammatical meanings. **1965** *Canad. Jrnl. Linguistics* Fall 36 If paralanguage is a dual system, with phoneme and morpheme-like units,..it would be difficult to imagine the primes of a more rudimentary system exceeding in number the primes of a more complex one, language. **1951** Z. S. HARRIS *Methods in Structural Linguistics* x. 129 English has morpheme-medial clusters like /rtr/ (*partridge*) but never like /trt/. **1953** *Language* XXIX. 86 The morphophonemics of a language is then a set of rules for transducing morpheme-sequences to phoneme-sequences. **1955** *Publ. Amer. Dial. Soc.* xxiv. 20 All argots spoken in America are obviously patterned on English, though their specialized morpheme structure usually renders them partially or totally unintelligible to those who speak only the language of the dominant culture. **1972** *Language* XLVIII. 372 The asymmetrical vowel-harmony rule [in Turkish] is accompanied by an accidental gap in the inventory of suffixes, and a systematic morpheme-structure constraint on polysyllabic roots. **1971** D. CRYSTAL *Linguistics* iv. 197 Proponents of the morpheme theory have been..convinced of its validity..as a general explanation for grammatical phenomena. **1942** *Language* XVIII. 171 *Am*, which occurs only in phrases with *I*, and *are*, which never occurs with *I*, are put into one morpheme unit... A morpheme unit is..a group of one or more alternants which have the same meaning and complementary distribution. **1933** L. BLOOMFIELD *Language* xiii. 209 *Morpheme-words*, consisting of a single (free) morpheme: *man, boy, cut, run, red, big.*

Hence **morphe·mic** *a.*, **morphe·mically** *adv.*; also (*rare*) **morphema·tic** *a.*, **morphema·tically** *adv.*, **morphe:miciza·tion.**

1930 J. R. FIRTH *Speech* vi. 56 Dutchmen, Danes, Swedes, and Englishmen share many similar morphemic and phonæsthetic habits. **1933** *English Studies* XV. 87 The alternating pairs..of phonemes..evidently form special units which, being conditioned by morphematic circumstances, are called *morphonemes*. **1935** G. K. ZIPF *Psycho-Biol. of Lang.* (1936) i. 15 One may..devise a morphemic alphabet to label all the different morphemes (e.g. prefixes, roots, suffixes, and endings) of a language. **1947** *Language* XXIII. 322 We must have..a set of principles on the basis of which we identify, or refuse to identify, different stretches of speech as morphemically the same. **1953** C. E. BAZELL *Linguistic Form* vii. 83 Only semantic prejudices could lead one to suppose that there was a close content-relation with the morphemically distinct *behind*. **1957** S. POTTER *Modern Linguistics* i. 26 Plural forms of [some] substantives..which happen to end in a dental (nuts, lords..). Here the inflexion -s or -z is felt by the speaker to be morphemic. **1959** R. QUIRK in Quirk & Smith *Teaching of English* i. 34 Many of the curious and amusing forms in *Finnegans Wake*..require us to make morphemic associations in unfamiliar environments. **1964** D. WARD in D. Abercrombie et al. *Daniel Jones* 390 Such a system of orthography..would strip the graphic representation of morphemes..of morphematically conditioned modifications. **1964** E. A. NIDA *Toward Sci. Transl.* v. 102 Similarly, we must be able to analyse the relationships between expressions which are grammatically and morphemically (or lexically) different, but semantically equivalent. **1966** *Amer. Speech* XLI. 116 The phonemicization of *latter:ladder* for those dialects that *clearly* have a voiced intervocalic stop would not be impossible... It would not be so much a problem..as it would be in morphemicization. **1971** *Archivum Linguisticum* II. 49 The 'ambiguity' of morphemic -*s* equally characterizes -*ing*, to name only one further flection. *Ibid.* 59 A morphemically variable noun form.

morphemics (mǭɹfī·miks), *sb. pl. Linguistics.* [f. *MORPHEM(E: see -IC 2.] The study and description of language in terms of morphemes.

1947 *Language* XXIII. 321 Morphemics and tactics are both necessarily involved in grammar. **1951** TRAGER & SMITH *Outl. Eng. Structure* II. 53 The analysis we are now going to do, the *morphemics* of the language, deals with the recurring patterned partials in utterances. **1960** T. B. W. REID *Historical Philol. & Ling. Sci.* 9 Others maintain that..phonemics and morphemics alone constitute linguistics, whereas phonetics and semantics are independent disciplines which do not interest them. **1961** D. L. BOLINGER *Generality, Gradience & All-or-None* iii. 35 There is obligatory lengthening in too many places for us to insist that English morphemics be studied in total disregard of it. **1964** M. CRITCHLEY *Developmental Dyslexia* iv. 14 The characters have to cope not only with the phonetic properties of the sound, but also with the problem of meaning. In other words, both phonemics and morphemics must be satisfied. **1966** *Amer. Speech* XLI. 116 If the first and last words in *Betty is in her beddy* are phonetically identical, then for the morphemics, one would have to.. set up an allomorph {bet} for the morpheme {bed}.

So **morphe·micist**, one who studies morphemics.

1949 KIRBY & WOOLF *Philologica: Malone Anniv. Stud.* 312 In analyzing Joyce's work, the morphemicist would be obliged to construct diagrams in layers, piled one on top of the other.

morphically (mǭ·ɹfikăli), *adv.* [f. MORPHIC *a.* + -AL + -LY[2].] In relation to or as regards shape or form; morphologically.

1893 *Proc. Boston Soc. Nat. Hist.* XXVI. 66 This is morphically a free cell.

morphism: see *MORPH[4].

-morphism (mǭ·ɹfiz'm), terminal element [f. Gr. μορφή form + -ISM] of sbs. with the sense 'condition or property of having a (certain) form or character', and in *Math.* 'a transformation or correspondence of a (certain) kind': e.g. HETEROMORPHISM, ISOMORPHISM (in Dict. and Suppl.).

morpho (mǭ·ɹfo). [mod.L. (J. C. Fabricius 1807, in *Magazin für Insectenkunde* VI. 280), f. Gr. Μορφώ, an epithet of Aphrodite.] A large South American butterfly of the genus so called, often with shiny blue wings. Also *attrib.*

1853 A. R. WALLACE *Travels on Amazon* 14 Among them [*sc.* the butterflies] were..three Morphos, those splendid large metallic-blue butterflies which are always first noticed by travellers in South America. **1863** H. W. BATES *Naturalist on River Amazons* I. 103 The splendid metallic blue Morphos..are generally confined to the shady alleys of the forest. **1925** *Glasgow Herald* 1 Aug. 4/2 In the parapet of a fine staircase in one of the Oxford colleges there is a piece of Labradorite with a bewitching blue colour that recalls the tail of a peacock and the wing of a Morpho butterfly. **1926** *Ibid.* 12 June 4 A morpho may have a million and a half scales on its four great wings. **1969** E. BISHOP *Compl. Poems* 210 Oil..like bits of mirror—no, more blue than that: Like tatters of the *Morpho* butterfly. **1973** *Sci. Amer.* Dec. 67/2 Only here [*sc.* in the tropical rain forest] are found such insects as the brilliant blue morpho butterfly of tropical America.

morphodite (mǭ·ɹfodəit). Also **morphodyke, morphodyte.** Colloq. shortening and mispronunciation of HERMAPHRODITE *sb.*

1896 *Dialect Notes* I. 421 *Morphodite*,..for *hermaphrodite*. **1951** T. CAPOTE *Grass Harp* (1952) i. 3 One of the stories he spread, that Verena was a morphodyte, has never stopped going around. **1956** H. GOLD *Man who was not with It* (1965) xix. 174 He or she waddled by. But I suppose morphodykes are likely to take it personally when people get married.

morphogen (mǭ·ɹfodʒĕn). *Biol.* [f. Gr. μορφ-ή form + -O + -GEN.] Any agent which is or might be capable of bringing about or determining morphogenesis.

1952 A. M. TURING in *Phil. Trans. R. Soc.* B. CCXXXVII. 38 The systems actually to be considered consist therefore of masses of tissues which are not growing, but within which certain substances are reacting chemically, and through which they are diffusing. These substances will be called morphogens, the word being intended to convey the idea of a form producer. It is not intended to have any very exact meaning. **1965** *Math. in Biol. & Med.* (Med. Res. Council) VI. 247 Turing considers the behaviour of two chemical substances, A and B, which he calls 'morphogens'. The significance of the name is simply that it is supposed that a high concentration of one or other of these substances can act as an 'inducer' of further differentiation. **1972** *Nature* 13 Oct. 366/1 Many theories for the mechanism of signalling in embryos have been produced; the oldest, and simplest, is that there is a concentration gradient of a 'morphogen' from the animal to vegetal poles, and that cells can measure their ambient concentration and then behave according to their position in the gradient.

morphogenesis. Add: (Examples.)

1899 *Jrnl. R. Microsc. Soc.* 469 Factors in morphogenesis. **1936** P. D. F. MURRAY *Bones* i. 16 These experiments evidently exclude all functional factors as important agents in primary skeletal morphogenesis. **1951** *Nature* 18 Aug. 301/2 Isolated terminal growing points.. afford excellent material for the investigation of the relation between nutrition and morphogenesis. **1974** *Sci. Amer.* Dec. 44/3 They [*sc.* hydras] have a strong capacity for regenerating lost parts, so that one can study morphogenesis not only in developing animals but also in regenerating ones.

b. *Geomorphol.* The formation of landscapes or land forms.

1958 *Geol. Mag.* XCV. 126 Tricart and Cailleux..claim that a 'sufficiently dense cover of vegetation' interferes very significantly with morphogenesis. **1966** J. A. MABBUTT in G. H. Dury *Essays in Geomorphol.* 102 The hillfoot zone is..very sensitive to climatically-induced changes of morphogenesis. **1968** R. W. FAIRBRIDGE *Encycl. Geomorphol.* 130/1 An allied form of morphogenesis is rather similarly planes, aggrades and deranges drainage in areas of continental glaciation.

morphogenetic *a.* (further examples, in *Biol.* and *Geomorphol.*); so **morphogene·tically** *adv.*, as regards morphogenesis.

1905 *Jrnl. Exper. Zool.* II. 155 It seemed to me scarcely possible that all of these strikingly different kinds of oöplasm, each with its own peculiar developmental history and destiny, were nevertheless morphogenetically alike. **1932** J. S. HUXLEY *Probl. Relative Growth* iv. 117 Each such region would be characterized both by the possession of its own growth-gradient and its own morphogenetic field. **1950** *Ann. Assoc. Amer. Geographers* XL. 214 Recently Büdel (1944, 1948) has suggested the recognition of 'formkreisen' or 'morphogenetic regions'. *Ibid.* 232 Within an area in which the climate is essentially homogeneous, the geomorphic effects of climate may be assumed to be similar. These areas are here called morphogenetic regions. **1954** W. D. THORNBURY *Princ. Geomorphol.* iii. 63 The concept of a morphogenetic region is that under a certain set of climatic conditions particular geomorphic processes will predominate and hence will give to the landscape of the region characteristics that will set it off from those of other areas developed under different climatic conditions. **1957** [see *FIELD *sb.* 17 c]. **1965** *Science* 29 Oct. 627/3 (*caption*) Possible relation of collagen distribution to morphogenetically active and inactive areas. **1966** SAUNDERS & FALLON in M. Locke *Major Probl. Developmental Biol.* 289 Death of cells is a normal component of most morphogenetic movements such as foldings, detachments, and the confluence of anlagen. **1969** *Oikos* Suppl. XII. 68 (*heading*) Morphogenetic aspects of the agrarian landscape of Öland.

morphogenic, *a.* (Examples.)

1904 *Science* 2 Dec. 749/2 The specific morphogenic factors are connected in some way with specific forms of protoplasm. **1958** C. P. RAVEN *Morphogenesis: Analysis of Molluscan Development* v. 186 The notion of morphogenic substances should not be taken too strictly, as if there were a rectilinear relation between a single substance and the differentiation of a certain organ. **1972** G. D. WINTER in Maibach & Rovee *Epidermal Wound Healing* iv. 104 It is thought that in the normal epidermis the morphogenic force is the pressure of mitosis.

morphogeny. Delete *Biol.* and add further examples.

1912 *Ann. Assoc. Amer. Geographers* II. 85 Some British observers have recognized levels of erosion or abrasion at several different altitudes, on which they base a more complicated scheme of morphogeny. **1929** *Jrnl. Ecol.* XVII. 374 Of fundamental importance in morphogeny and by no means to be overlooked in adaptation is the correlation of organs and parts, based upon competition within the plant for food. **1950** *Ann. Assoc. Amer. Geographers* XL. 222 Many of the ideas here expressed are explicitly stated in the lectures of Professor Kirk Bryan, whose emphasis on climatic morphogeny has led to the formulation here set forth.

morphographemic (mǭɹfogrăfī·mik), *a. Linguistics.* [f. Gr. μορφ-ή form + *GRAPHEMIC *a.*] Of or pertaining to the written form of words; spec. *morphographemic rule*, a rule of writing in transformational grammar (see quot. 1972).

1965 O. THOMAS *Transformational Gram.* iii. 59 If we were interested in how the final sentence was pronounced, rather than in how it is written, we would have a set of *morphophonetic rules* (i.e., rules of pronunciation) rather than *morphographemic rules* (i.e., rules of writing). **1968** J. LYONS *Introd. Theoretical Linguistics* vi. 265 For the written language, 'morphographemic' rules would convert the strings. **1971** F. W. HOUSEHOLDER *Linguistic Speculations* xiii. 255 The immediate output of the lexicon is correct orthography, subject to minor morphographemic adjustments. **1972** R. A. PALMATIER *Gloss. Eng. Transformational Gram.* 98 *Morphographemic rule*,..a rule, of the final section of the grammar, which converts the morphemes of a terminal string into their graphic representations as written words; a spelling rule.

morpholexical (mǭɹfole·ksikăl), *a.* [f. Gr. μορφ-ή form + LEXICAL *a.*] Of or pertaining to lexical form (cf. also *MORPHOPHONEMIC *a.*).

1939 L. BLOOMFIELD in *Travaux du Cercle Ling. de Prague* VIII. 105 It is necessary to distinguish these morphophonemic alternations from certain others, which we may call *morpholexical* variations... These morpholexical variations are quite distinct from internal sandhi. **1940** *Language* XVI. 256 Besides zero and actual element, pairs of forms as -kamy- and -ākamy-, with the meaning identical for both ('water'), are reserved for consideration as morpholexical variations. **1951** Z. S. HARRIS *Structural Linguistics* xiii. 197 It [*sc.* the procedure]..covers regular and irregular phonological alternation, sandhi, morpholexical variation, suppletion, reduplication, and other types of morpheme variants. **1962** CHAVARRIA-AGUILAR & PENZL in Householder & Saporta *Problems in Lexicography* IV. 243 The Pashto Academy..has attempted..to establish morphological and sometimes morpholexical standards for writers.

morpholine (mǭ·ɹfŏlīn). *Chem.* [ad. G. *morpholin* (L. Knorr 1889, in *Ber. d. Deut. Chem. Ges.* XXII. 2083), f. *morphin* MORPHINE *sb.* with insertion of *-ol* -OL.] A cyclic amine,

$$\underline{CH_2CH_2NHCH_2CH_2O},$$

which is a hygroscopic oil used as a solvent for resins and dyestuffs and whose fatty-acid salts are emulsifying soaps used in floor polishes.

1889 *Jrnl. Chem. Soc.* LVI. 1218 Morpholine (tetrahydroparoxazine) may be regarded as the 'inner anhydride' of dihydroxyethylamine. **1935** *Industr. & Engin. Chem.* Aug. 871/1 Of the derivatives of morpholine, one of the most extensively investigated in the medical field has been morpholine ethanol. **1955** *Sci. Amer.* Aug. 76/3 Dilute solutions of morpholine neither attracted nor repelled salmon but were detectable by them in extremely low concentrations. **1972** *Materials & Technol.* IV. xv. 516 Diethanolamine has also appreciable value as the source of the cyclic ether, morpholine, an important solvent and intermediate in the manufacture of medicinals.

morphologic, *a.* (Further examples.)
1936 *Bull. Amer. Assoc. Petroleum Geologists* XX. 859 The peculiar morphologic phenomenon of deep-sea trenches..is confined to the peri-Pacific-Malayan region. **1936** J. KANTOR *Objective Psychol. of Grammar* xi. 158 This morphologic pattern no doubt is as highly evolved as the English. **1944** *Federation Proc.* III. 231/1 An.. account of the morphologic changes in muscle following denervation. **1961** A. JUILLAND *Structural Relations* iii. 52 Morphologic segmentation has been explored especially by American structuralists. **1962** H. E. THALMANN tr. *Goguel's Tectonics* ii. 6 The use of morphologic analysis to distinguish rock types..involves great risks of error. **1967** *Word* XXIII. 380 All morphologic composites are based on the same syntagmatic pattern 'determinatum determined by determinant'. **1975** *Language* LI. 142 This fact speaks for the morphologic antiquity of all Type A infinitives cognate with those of Vedic.

morphological, *a.* Add: **5.** Of or pertaining to morphology (sense *4).
This sense can be regarded as including also the senses in Dict.
1895 N. STORY-MASKELYNE *Crystallography* i. 3 By reference to this system of planes, it is possible to establish the morphological relationship of all crystals of the same substance, whatever faces they may exhibit. **1918** *Amer. Jrnl. Med. Sci.* CLV. 70 The cardiac signs and symptoms produced as a result of hypothyroidism are not due to morphological alterations in the heart muscle. **1972** D. HERBERT *Urban Geogr.* iii. 66 A clear indication of past functional patterns can often be obtained from the morphological evidence which is left in the urban landscape. **1974** D. MCKIE *Crystalline Solids* xi. 384 Morphological studies are..applicable only to substances which form well developed crystals.

morphologist. Delete *Biol.* and add further examples.
1935 [see *CLINOGRAPHIC *a.*]. **1972** D. HERBERT *Urban Geogr.* iii. 66 The necessity to incorporate the physical fabric of towns into more general theories of urban growth has long been advocated by urban morphologists. **1974** *Nature* 13 Sept. 100/2 Although glial cells can be studied by morphologists, physiologists know very little about their function.

morphology. Add: **I. 2. b.** *Appos.*, as *morphology–syntax*. *Comb.*, as *morphology-based* adj.
1965 H. A. GLEASON *Linguistics & Eng. Gram.* vi. 118 'Preposition' is available and not needed in the morphology-based system. **1945–9** *Acta Linguistica* V. 125 A problem in morphology-syntax division. **1964** P. L. GARVIN *On Linguistic Method* 157 Morphemic analysis [is].. primarily syntactic for those languages to which the morphology-syntax division applies.
II. 4. Shape, form, external structure or arrangement, esp. as an object of study or classification.
1890 C. P. MITCHELL *Philos. Tumour-Dis.* ii. 52 Facts so varied as those comprised in the morphology of tumours. **1894** *Jrnl. Physiol.* XVII. 81 (*heading*) The morphology and distribution of the wandering cells of Mammalia. **1895** N. STORY-MASKELYNE (*title*) Crystallography: a treatise on the morphology of crystals. **1921** *Geogr. Rev.* XI. 155 (*heading*) Morphology of the Altai Mountains. **1924** A. E. H. TUTTON *Nat. Hist. Crystals* vii. 60 The 'elements' of a crystal..together with a list of the 'forms' observed, and a table of the interfacial angles, define the morphology of the crystal. **1937** *Rep. Brit. Assoc. Adv. Sci.* 373 (*heading*) A comparative study of the morphology of the North Downs and the Chiltern Hills. **1950** *Jrnl. Gen. Physiol.* XXXIII. 651 Two separate lines of approach..were required: a study of the functional behavior of the [nerve] fibers, and a study of their morphology. **1954** M. BERESFORD *Lost Villages* 23 In the study of village morphology..an opportunity of seeing a medieval village plan without any of the accretions of later building. **1964** R. C. EVANS *Crystal Chem.* (ed. 2) xi. 184 Before the discovery of X-ray diffraction, crystals could be classified only on the basis of morphology, and in terms of their symmetry were assigned to one or other of the thirty-two classes. **1965** E. GURR *Rational Use of Dyes in Biol.* I. 106 (*heading*) Possible influence of molecular morphology in staining. *Ibid.* 107 We can refer to the shape and/or size of a molecule as its morphology. **1971** W. A. PRYOR in R. E. Carver *Procedures Sedimentary Petrol.* vii. 142 Quantitative analysis of grain morphology requires measurement of particle radii, diameters, and lengths. **1974** *Nature* 29 Nov. 377/2 The morphologies found—spheroids, single or paired, filaments, segmented or nonsegmented, 'colonial' structures..—have all been described from prokaryotic groups such as the blue-green algae.

morphomaniac (mǭɹfomē̆·niæk). [Irreg. f. MORPHIA + MANIAC *sb.*] = MORPHINOMANIAC.
1906 G. K. CHESTERTON *Dickens* ii. 41 These great popular leaders..become drunkards; they become demagogues; they become morphomaniacs. **1912** L. J. VANCE *Destroying Angel* xii. 165 He's just short of a raving morphomaniac.

morphometric (mǭɹfome·trik), *a.* [f. Gr. μορφ-ή form + -O + *-METRIC.] Of or pertaining to morphometry or morphometrics; morphometrical.
1931 T. L. WOO in *Biometrika* XXII. 325 A special advantage of taking measurements on the individual bones of the skull is that we thus get some idea of the size and shape of relatively small regions,..giving us a better appreciation of local asymmetries than the run of anthropometric measurements can. I think it might be useful to distinguish the two types of measurements as ethnometric and morphometric, for both are actually anthropometric. **1934** *Geogr. Jrnl.* LXXXIV. 424 Other questions, such as the morphology of arctic regions, morphometric methods, classification and variation of climate. **1952** *Bull. Geol. Soc. Amer.* LXIII. 1117 Detailed morphometric analysis of basins in five sample areas in the equilibrium stage show distinctive, though small, differences in hypsometric integrals and curve forms. **1968** *Mineral. Abstr.* XIX. 240/1 Cumulative curves for the morphometric parameter of the grains composing a sample of sand are figured. **1970** *Evolution* XXIV. 220/2 Morphometric data from 91 crania and 123 mandibles of 2 and 3 year old male white-tailed deer from Michigan were used in this study. **1972** A. YOUNG *Slopes* i. 3 Morphometric analysis takes the river basin as the fundamental unit; this is a consequence of its origin in hydrological studies, in particular in the attempt to predict flood discharge from the landform characteristics of river catchments. **1974** *Nature* 24 May 371/1 A three-fold enrichment (as judged by morphometric analysis of electron micrographs) of synaptic junctions..was obtained.
Hence **morphome·trically** *adv.*
1937 *Trans. Connecticut Acad. Arts & Sci.* XXXIII. 67 The lake is primarily eutrophic, secondarily or morphometrically oligotrophic. **1957** G. E. HUTCHINSON *Treat. Limnol.* I. ii. 170 The number of lakes of maximum depth of over 400 m. will, however, be greatly increased when the large lakes of southern South America become known morphometrically. **1960** *Jrnl. Animal Ecol.* XXIX. 310 The parents were most probably very similar morphometrically to the fledglings.

morphometrics (mǭɹfome·triks), *sb. pl.* [f. as prec.: see -IC 2.] Morphometry (esp. of living forms); also, morphometric features or properties.
1960 *Jrnl. Animal Ecol.* XXIX. 309 The shape of an animal, of which morphometrics are a numerical expression, is dependent upon genetically transmitted characters and the modifying influence of the environment on them. *Ibid.* 310 No completely reliable evidence was obtained for either the morphometrics or the behaviour of the parents of two of the populations studied. **1971** BLACKITH & REYMENT *Multivariate Morphometrics* ii. 9 An essential problem in morphometrics is to measure the degree of similarity of two forms. **1974** *Nature* 22 Mar. 303/3 The chapters on multivariate morphometrics and optical data analysis are particularly good.

morphometry. Add: Esp. in *Geomorphol.* (Further examples.)
1957 G. E. HUTCHINSON *Treat. Limnol.* I. ii. 168 (*heading*) Morphometry of lakes over 400 m. deep. **1958** *Geogr. Jrnl.* CXXIV. 370 (*heading*) Aspects of the morphometry of a 'poly-cyclic' drainage basin. **1961** *Geomorphological Abstr.* Sept. 33 Earlier work showing the dominance of rock type in pebble morphometry is strongly supported. **1963** E. R. WEIBEL (*title*) Morphometry of the human lung. **1970** R. J. SMALL *Study of Landforms* i. 4 Quantification is applied..to landscape forms, giving rise to the branch of modern geomorphology known as 'morphometry'.
morphometrical *a.* (examples).
1935 *Geol. Mag.* LXXII. 183 Its [*sc.* the clinographic curve's] utility in delicate morphometrical determinations seems to me undoubted. **1935** *Biometrika* XXVII. 465 (*heading*) Morphometrical indices. **1953** *Anti-Locust Bull.* XVI. (*heading on title-p.*) Morphometrical studies on phases of the Desert Locust (*Schistocerca gregaria* Forskål).

morphon. Add: **b.** *Linguistics.* A term in stratificational grammar for *MORPHOPHONEME. Also *attrib.* Hence **morpho·nic** *a.*
1964 S. M. LAMB in *Rep. 15th Ann. Round Table Meeting Ling. & Lang. Stud.* (Georgetown Univ. Inst. Lang.) 105 Morphons (i.e. morphophonemes) often have alternate phonemic realizations. **1965** *Language* XLI. 200, I shall use Lamb's convenient neologism *morphon*. The syntactic component of a correct generative grammar..yields sentences as strings of morphons. **1966** S. M. LAMB *Outl. Stratificational Gram.* ii. 29 There are three separate alternation patterns, the lexonic, the morphonic, and the phononic. **1967** C. F. HOCKETT *Language, Mathematics, & Linguistics* iii. 95 Relative to the terminal subalphabet **T′(G′)**, a morphon string is a simple (linear) string. **1968** P. M. POSTAL *Aspects Phonol. Theory* iii. 41 It must be emphasized..that stratificational grammar insists that the morphophonemes, or 'morphons' in their terms, are unanalyzable symbols. **1968** *Language* XLIV. 595 Rules c & e are necessary because the objects on the higher stratum, called 'morphons', are distinct from the objects on the lower stratum, which are bundles of phonons. **1970** G. SAMPSON *Stratificational Gram.* ii. 33 The large number of neutralisations represented by almost every morphon. *Ibid.* iii. 45 In a complete description of English, there would be two further strata, each with its tactics, below the morphon level... I am not in a position..to give the morphonic realisations of the morphemes.

morphoneme (mǭ·ɹfonīm). *Linguistics.* [f. Gr. μορφ-ή form + *PHO)NEME.] = *MORPHOPHONEME. So **morphone·mic** *a.*
1933 *English Studies* XV. 87 The alternating pairs (sometimes groups) of phonemes like *i/e, f/v* evidently form special units which, being conditioned by morphematic circumstances, are called *morphonemes*. **1934** *Language* X. 335 The five Russian vowel morphonemes are very variable... The consonant morphonemes are: [p, pȷ, b, bȷ..]. *Ibid.* 340 The interchange here is morphonemic, and does not properly concern us in a purely phonemic study. **1942** *Ibid.* XVIII. 309 Summarizing briefly Trager's article '[The] Phonemes of Russian' (Language 1934, No. 4) and generally valuing its positive outlook, Reformatsky deplores his terminological unclearness connected with [his] use of [the] word 'morphoneme'. **1966** J. VACHEK *Linguistic School of Prague* iv. 81 The generativists after establishing the morphonemic make up of their strings, proceed to 'rewrite' the morphonemes by concrete sounds found in the phonetic implementations of these strings.

morphonology (mǭɹfǫ̆nǫ·lŏdʒi). *Linguistics.* [f. Gr. μορφ-ή form + PH)ONOLOGY.] A term used by the Prague school of linguists for the study of the phonology of morphemes. So **morphonolo·gic, morphonolo·gical** *adjs.*
[**1929** *Travaux du Cercle Linguistique de Prague* I. 85 La grammaire doit comprendre encore un chapitre particulier, qui étudie l'utilisation morphologique des différences phonologiques, et qui peut être appelée la '*morpho-phonologie*' ou, en abrégeant, la '*morphonologie*'.] **1933** *English Studies* XV. 87 That part of phonology which examines the phonological structure of morphemes, is called *morphonology*. **1935** *Amer. Speech* X. 252/2 Another branch of phonology, established by the Prague linguists, called *morphonology*,..examines the phonological structure of morphemes. **1936** *Ibid.* XI. 114 Morphological phonology or 'morphonology',..investigates the morphological use of phonemes or groups of phonemes, or more inclusively, for phonological means. **1949** H. SPANG-HANSSEN in *Travaux du Cercle Ling. de Copenhague* V. 69 Morphonologic or morphemic monographs have no direct bearing on this subject either, since they also presuppose that the phoneme inventory has already been established. **1950** *Lingua* II. 241 This morphonology, according to Trubetzkoy, has a threefold task: 1. the investigation of the phonological (i.e. phonematic) structure of the morphemes, 2. the investigation of the combinatorial sound-changes.., 3. the investigation of the series of sound-changes..which have a morphological function. **1966** J. VACHEK *Linguistic School of Prague* iv. 81 The other recent trend in linguistic thinking that has substantially contributed to the revival of interest in morphonology is the stratificational approach by Sydney M. Lamb and his colleagues. *Ibid.*, The first language to be characterized from the morphonological point of view was..Russian. **1971** tr. *Akhmanova's Phonology, Morphonology, Morphology* ii. 82 Professor Vachek speaks of the present state of morphonological research... The 'generativist and transformationist' morphonology is, perhaps, best described as 'codificational morphonology'.

morphophoneme (mǭɹfofōu·nīm). *Linguistics.* [f. Gr. μορφ-ή form + *PHONEME.] One of the variant phonemes which belong to the same morpheme.
1934 M. SWADESH in *Language* X. 129 Morphologically distinct phonemes are called morpho-phonemes. A morpho-phoneme is one of a class of like phonemes considered as components of actual morphemes which behave alike morphologically, i.e., have a like place in the same mutation series. **1939** L. BLOOMFIELD in *Travaux du Cercle Linguistique de Prague* VIII. 106 The morphophoneme u seems to occur in only one suffix. **1947** C. F. HOCKETT in *Language* XXIII. 323 Morphophonemic statements may involve morphophonemes—that is, the symbols used for phonemes, plus supplementary ones, with special definitions as to phonemic value under varying circumstances—or they may not. **1957** N. CHOMSKY *Syntactic Structures* iv. 33 The elements that figure in the rules can be classified into a finite set of levels (e.g. phonemes and morphemes; or, perhaps, phonemes, morphophonemes, and morphemes). **1964** E. BACH *Introd. Transformational Gram.* ii. 25 We distinguish the final morphophonemes in *laugh* and *wife* on the basis of their plural formation. **1968** *Language* XLIV. 508 The major thesis of this paper is that the most efficient description of morpheme alternants requires the use of morphophonemes, and, moreover, that these morphophonemes do in fact constitute psychologically real units. **1972** *Ibid.* XLVIII. 372 In Turkish, the target is satisfied at a level preceding the application of the first law of vowel harmony, which maps the morphophonemes *A I U* onto their respective phonetic reflexes.
Hence **morphophonema·tic** (*rare*), **morphophone·mic** *adjs.*, **morphophone·mically** *adv.*
1939 [see *MORPHOLEXICAL *a.*]. **1944** *Amer. Speech* XIX. 136 The 'neutrality' of *e* in Hungarian and Finnish is not phonetic but morphophonemic. **1951** Z. S. HARRIS *Methods in Structural Linguistics* xiv. 239 The *al* of *moral* would appear to be morphophonemically /æL/, where /L/ represents phonemic zero before *ly*, but /l/ otherwise. **1957** *Publ. Amer. Dial. Soc.* XXVIII. 58 Morphophonemically *be* behaves like an auxiliary, regardless of its complement. **1960** C. E. BAZELL in *Year's Work in Eng. Studies 1958* 47/2 Evidence for the diphthongal character of Gothic *iu* is largely morphophonemic (e.g. the alternation *triu/triwa*). **1964** D. WARD in D. Abercrombie et al. *Daniel Jones* 390 There are some departures from the morphophonemic principle in Russian, including such sporadic ones as, for example, *nozdri* 'nostrils' (cp. *nos* 'nose'). **1965** *Canad. Jrnl. Linguistics* Spring 169 Most noun stems [in Eyak] are morphophonemically invariable. **1968** P. M. POSTAL *Aspects Phonol. Theory* vi. 117 Even setting up new allomorphs like 'is', etc. does not avoid the consequence that the morphophonemic rules must appeal to categorial properties. **1970** *Bible Translator* XXI. 25 There is reason to believe that most function morphemes should be read at sight rather than 'sounded out', and this also supports the idea of writing such morphemes morphophonemically. **1971** tr. *Akhmanova's Phonology, Morphonology, Morphology* ii. 72 It is quite impossible to formulate any morphophonemic rules to explain the would-be substitution of [-a] for [-i] or [:y].

morphophonemics (mǭɹfofonī·miks), *sb. pl.* [f. prec. + -ICS.] The study and description of the phonemic aspects of the constitution of morphemes.

1939 L. BLOOMFIELD in *Travaux du Cercle Linguistique de Prague* VIII. 105 The present paper describes..the *internal sandhi* or *morphophonemics* of the language. **1953** [see **morpheme-sequence*]. **1957** S. POTTER *Mod. Linguistics* vii. 146 As we proceed from morphophonemics, and morphology proper, to syntax, so we observe a rise in the scale of semantic values. **1965** B. M. H. STRANG *Metaphors & Models* 15 The study of how a language encodes its different meanings is called *morphophonemics*. **1968** *Amer. Speech* XLIII. 233 The author includes a description of Jamaican Creole..morphophonemics. **1972** *Language* XLVIII. 805 This negative is realized from the sentence modality without going through the morphophonemics of pre-verbal location. **1973** *Computers & Humanities* VII. 218 How does one handle the unbelievably complex morphophonemics in choosing headwords?

morphophonics (mǭɹfofǫ·niks), *sb. pl.* [f. Gr. μορφ-ή form + PHONICS *sb. pl.*] = *MORPHOPHONEMICS *sb. pl.* (see also quot. 1962). Also **mo·rphophone**, a unit representing the class of phonemes occurring in dialectally different pronunciations of morphemes; **morphopho·nic** *a.*

1962 E. F. HADEN et al. *Resonance-Theory for Linguistics* iii. 30 Such sets of allophones, as expressions of morphological units, are *morphophonic expressions*. *Ibid.* 40 Morphophonics..is the intermediate area between phonology and morphology... Morphophonics is the process of transposing phonemic entities from the context of phonology into the context of morphology. **1967** H. L. SMITH in *Language* XLIII. I. 306 A three-stratum, twenty-seven level model for linguistic analysis indicates structural units—the *morphophones*—between phoneme and morpheme. Morphophones are seen as the basic units of the morphemes, and are themselves composed of dialectally different phonemic variants, which are non-contrasting in the same lexical items. *Ibid.* 311 From one point of view, the morphophone can be seen as a sort of 'holding company' or 'super-family' of different phonemes which are non-contrasting in the same words. But from another point of view, the morphophone is a unit of the language as a whole, and as a unit furnishes the basis of what might be thought of as 'higher order' or 'higher level' contrasts. *Ibid.* 323 Substitutions and interchanges are aspects of the morphophonic system. *Ibid.* 341 The donor language's morphophonics have been subject to a pretty thorough Anglicization. **1972** G. L. TRAGER *Lang. & Languages* iii. 49 The diacritic part of morphology, which examines the items of which morphemes are composed, may be called *morphophonics* (more commonly the term is *morphophonemics*, but there are good theoretical reasons for omitting the *-em-*). *Ibid.* 56 Morphemes with more than one allomorph are made up of or composed of morphophones, and it follows that morphemes with only one allomorph are also composed of morphophones... The morphophonic alternations that occur can then be considered as relations between (simple) morphophones.

morphophonology (mǭɹfofǒnǫ·lǒdʒi). *Linguistics.* [f. Gr. μορφ-ή form + PHONOLOGY.] = *MORPHONOLOGY. So **morphophonolo·gical** *a.*

1934 *Language* X. 128 Morpho-phonology includes, in addition to the study of the phonemic structure of morphemes, the study of interchange between phonemes as a morphologic process. **1938** *Trans. Philol. Soc.* 106 The morpheme in the sense of Skalička and of the Prague Linguistic Circle is a morphophonological unit, and the corresponding phonomorphological unit is the phonemic function. **1953** K. JACKSON *Lang. & Hist. in Early Britain* II. 548 The development of IE. *p* cannot be connected in any way with lenition, since it does not follow the special morphophonological rules for its occurrence. **1970** G. C. LEPSCHY *Survey Structural Linguistics* iii. 56 [One of the] main tasks of synchronic phonology [is]..to describe the morphological utilization of phonological differences (morphophonology or morphonology). **1973** *Archivum Linguisticum* IV. 47 No account is being taken here of regular, if often quite subtle morphophonological alternations, as between..viyis and vayas. *Ibid.* 50 The lengthening of the vowel of -ha in the example..belongs rather to the (morpho)phonology of the language.

morphosyntax (mǭɹfosi·ntæks). *Linguistics.* [f. Gr. μορφ-ή form + SYNTAX 2.] A branch of linguistic study which combines the study of morphology and syntax.

1961 F. W. HOUSEHOLDER in Saporta & Bastian *Psycholinguistics* 23/2 So also in morpho-syntax it should be possible to agree on definitions for terms like 'noun phrase', 'verb phrase', 'sentence', etc. **1967** *Word* XXIII. 472 In morpho-syntax the sequential chain model should perhaps not be completely disregarded. **1968** Y. MALKIEL *Essays on Linguistic Themes* i. 3 A few scholars have gone so far as to consolidate all of morphology and syntax into the single domain of 'morphosyntax', which forms the hard, inalienable kernel of linguistics. **1969** tr. *Akhmanova & Mikael'an's Theory Syntax Mod. Linguistics* ii. 26 He [*sc.* Brøndal] not only remained faithful to his conception of 'morphology' and syntax, but also developed it by introducing the notion of 'morphosyntax' to cover such phenomena as the functioning of words in sentences, the semantic modification of words in context, [etc.]. **1972** *Archivum Linguisticum* III. 89 As a final instance of the general validity of a systematic approach to diachronic morpho-syntax, let us examine a well-documented change within the verbal system of Romance.

Hence **morphosynta·ctic** *a.*, **morphosynta·ctically** *adv.*

1959 F. W. HOUSEHOLDER in *Word* XV. 232 It does not appear that languages have a semantic structure which is separate and distinct from the morpho-syntactic one. **1962** H. C. CONKLIN in Householder & Saporta *Problems in Lexicography* 119 While an 'appeal' to meaning does not improve grammatical analysis, neither does an intuitive appeal to morphosyntactic form yield the most appropriate analysis of meaning and reference. *Ibid.* 121 The compounds *firewater* and *silverfish*..are endocentric morphosyntactically. **1968** *Word* XXIV. 55 The United States dialect refers to any variety of English set off from other varieties of English, phonetically, morphosyntactically, or lexically. **1969** tr. *Akhmanova & Mikael'an's Theory Syntax Mod. Linguistics* v. 119 The *words*..had to have canonical phonemic shapes, to 'behave' morphophonemically and morphosyntactically. **1970** *Language* XLVI. 332 The proposal does not spell out how one gets from the morphosyntactic surface structure to the phonemics.

morphotactics (mǭɹfotæ·ktiks), *sb. pl. Linguistics.* [f. Gr. μορφ-ή form + TACTICS.] The study of the sequence of morphemes in a language (*MORPHEME b). Hence **morphota·ctic** *a.*; **morphota·ctically** *adv.*

1958 A. A. HILL *Introd. Linguistic Structures* vi. 68 The term 'phonotactics', now widely used, as well as other terms in -'tactics' to indicate sequences of items such as 'morphotactics' and 'logotactics', I owe to an unpublished lecture by Robert P. Stockwell delivered before the Linguistic Institute held at the Georgetown University Institute of Languages and Linguistics in 1954. *Ibid.* viii. 120 With most prebases, it is a morphotactic characteristic which identifies them. *Ibid.*, These are the 'grammatical endings' of familiar terminology. They can be defined morphotactically as morphemes which stand frequently before terminal junctures. *Ibid.* xxi. 414 Morphotactics gives us the partial predictability of morphemes and allomorphs. **1962** E. F. HADEN et al. *Resonance-Theory for Linguistics* iii. 35 Whereas in morphemics our task is to identify the form and the property of a grammatically functioning unit, in morphotactics we focus our attention on such a unit occurring in a sequence of morphemes... The morphotactic identification will be made with the same criteria for determining Form and Property as in morphemics. *Ibid.* 40 Morphotactics complements morphemics with morphology in a manner exactly parallel to phonotactics and phonemics within phonology. **1966** S. M. LAMB *Outl. Stratif. Gram.* ii. 23 When a lexonic ordering is of elements belonging to different morphotactic classes, e.g. verb stem and verb suffix, it is up to the morphotactics to determine their relative order. **1967** D. G. HAYS *Introd. Computational Linguistics* xi. 184 The morphotactic rules come to light as restrictions on sequence are found... The establishment of the morphotactics can be exceedingly simple or as complex as the development of a full syntax. **1970** G. SAMPSON *Stratificational Gram.* vi. 59 The morphotactics generates sequences of 'words' (M-Word), separated by the downward-determined element 'word-boundary'. *Ibid.* 62 The preference value of this derivation is six, one from the semotactic trace, four from the lexotactic, and one from the morphotactic.

morphotectonics (mǭɹfotektǫ·niks), *sb. pl.* [f. Gr. μορφ-ή form + -O + TECTONICS.] The branch of geomorphology concerned with the form and structure of the larger features of the earth's surface (as continents, mountain ranges, river basins); also, the morphotectonic character or features of a region.

1956 E. S. HILLS in *Jrnl. Geol. Soc. Austral.* III. 1 (*heading*) A contribution to the morphotectonics of Australia. *Ibid.*, A model of this size does in fact afford a unique basis for the study of morphotectonics, since no other medium can present a synoptic view of the topography of an area as large as [a] continent. **1961** —— in *Q. Jrnl. Geol. Soc.* CXVII. 79 What I have called morphotectonics implies, as well as structural geomorphology, something broader and applicable to regional study on a large scale, using topography as the primary criterion, but of course not neglecting all that may be known as to geology and geophysics. **1968** R. W. FAIRBRIDGE *Encycl. Geomorphol.* 734/1 The concept of 'Gondwanaland' in the southern hemisphere..evolved in the late nineteenth century..on the basis of extraordinarily similar morphotectonics, as much as from common features of stratigraphy, paleontology and paleoclimate. *Ibid.* 734/2 Up till now only one attempt has been made at a detailed world survey of morphotectonics.

Hence **morphotecto·nic** *a.*, of or pertaining to or seen from the point of view of morphotectonics.

1961 *Q. Jrnl. Geol. Soc.* CXVII. 84 A purely morphotectonic map for Egypt..shows, firstly, that it is not possible to conceive of the region as an elliptical upwarp. **1967** *Geogr. Abstr.* A. 280 The Provence foldings south-east of the Durance and the Verdon confluent give a good summary of the morphotectonic evolution of the Provence Range. **1973** *Nature* 2 Mar. 43/2 The morphotectonic features shown in Figs. 1 and 3 show a close agreement between structure and topography.

morphotropism (mǭɹfǫ·trǒpiz'm). *Cryst.* [f. as next: see -ISM.] = next.

1905 *Amer. Chem. Jrnl.* XXXIV. 104 The chapter on Morphotropism deals with the dependence of the crystal structure on the chemical constitution of the body. **1959** tr. *W. F. de Jong's Gen. Crystallogr.* 184 If a change of structure that occurs by replacement becomes so great that we no longer want to use the term 'isomorphism', we speak of morphotropism. **1966** *McGraw-Hill Encycl. Sci. & Technol.* VIII. 599/1 Organic compounds also show morphotropism.

morphotropy (mǭɹfǫ·trǒpi). *Cryst.* [ad. G. *morphotropie* (P. Groth 1870, in *Ann. d. Physik und Chem.* CXLI. 39), f. Gr. μορφ-ή form + τροπή turning.] (The study of) the progressive change in crystal structure brought about by replacing one of the species of atom or radical in a crystal by other species.

1900 *Rep. Brit. Assoc. Adv. Sci.* 1900 167 Morphotropy and isomorphism have a common cause, and..this is more likely to be discovered by the crystallographic study of substances showing morphotropic relationships than from the examination merely of materials likely to exhibit isomorphism. **1924** W. S. STILES tr. *F. Rinne's Crystals & Fine Struct. Matter* ix. 105 P. v. Groth has founded the science of morphotropy. By comparing crystalline forms, he succeeded in showing how the replacement of H by (OH), NO_2, NH_2, CH_3, Cl, in benzene (C_6H_6) manifests itself in changes of corresponding angles, and ultimately the symmetry. **1939** R. C. EVANS *Introd. Crystal Chem.* iii. 60 The structural importance of the quantitative lattice theory..lies in the light which it throws on..the problems of polymorphism and morphotropy.

So **morphotro·pic** *a.*, characteristic of or exhibiting morphotropy.

1899 *Mineral. Mag.* XII. 66 The three minerals may be members of a morphotropic series, in which the vertical crystallographic axis increases in length with an increase in the amount of lead. **1937** W. L. BRAGG *Atomic Struct. Minerals* ix. 150 The members of the chondrodite series are interesting because of the morphotropic relationships which exist between them. **1959** tr. *W. F. de Jong's Gen. Crystallogr.* 184 A morphotropic range of compounds is one in which the replacing atoms differ gradually in one property—for example, in size or polarizability. **1973** A. I. KITAIGORODSKY *Molec. Crystals & Molecules* i. 18 Morphotropic changes associated with a loss of symmetry are accompanied by an increase in the packing density.

morpion. Restrict † *Obs.* to sense in Dict. and add: **2.** (mǭ·ɹpiǫn) *transf.* Applied scornfully to a person. *rare*⁻¹.

1954 S. BECKETT *Waiting for Godot* II. 48 Moron!.. Vermin!..Abortion!..Morpion!

morrillo, var. *MORILLO.

Morris (mǫ·ris). The name of William *Morris* (1834–96), poet and craftsman, used *attrib.* of styles of furniture, wallpaper, etc., designed by him or made in his factory or at the Kelmscott Press, *spec.* as **Morris chair,** a type of easy chair with open padded arms and an adjustable back. Also **Morris-papered** *a.*, papered with Morris wallpaper.

1880 LADY JEBB *Let.* 6 Mar. in A. Adburgham *Shops & Shopping* (1964) xvi. 173, I wish you could see Mrs Sellar's drawing-room..; Morris papers on the walls, Burne-Jones' photographs. **1900** *T. Eaton & Co. Catal.* Spring & Summer 235/3 Morris chair, golden oak or mahogany finish. **1912** T. E. LAWRENCE *Let.* 20 May in *Home Lett.* (1954) 209 The piece of Morris tapestry I have. **1912** E. WORDSWORTH *Glimpses of Past* xii. 140 Those were the days of green serge gowns, and Morris papers, depicting miniature orange trees and pomegranates, daisies, and sunflowers. **1920** J. GALSWORTHY *In Chancery* III. iii. 257 On a wall, not yet Morris-papered, was a print of the Queen. **1925** G. B. SHAW *Let.* 24 Feb. in *To a Young Actress* (1960) 83 Morris made all sorts of chairs: there is no particular Morris chair that I know of. **1935** N. MITCHISON *We have been Warned* I. 107 The Morris curtains would be drawn. **1936** J. DOS PASSOS *Big Money* 248 He let himself drop into the morrischair. **1937** V. WOOLF *Years* 54 There she was among the Morris wall-papers and the cabinets. **1938** J. CARY *Castle Corner* 274 A Bible in Morris binding. *Ibid.* 303 I'm quite sure our Morris sugar sifter is far greater than Milan. **1958** *Listener* 28 Aug. 317/1 The Morris dining-room. **1961** A. MILLER *Misfits* iii. 31 The complete assortment of furniture, from the Morris chair to the studio couch. **1967** O. LANCASTER *Eye to Future* v. 123 A charming cottage, stone-walled and Morris-papered. **1972** D. MARLOWE *Do you remember England?* i. 20 The warm bottle of Malvern water by the bedside, Morris wallpaper, and a train-journey biography.

Hence **Mo·rrisan, Morri·sian** *a.*, of, pertaining to, or characteristic of William Morris or his work; also **Mo·rrisite,** a follower or adherent of the principles, etc., of William Morris.

1897 A. BEARDSLEY *Let.* 26 Dec. (1971) 413 On the art side I suggest that it [*sc.* a projected new periodical] should attack *untiringly and unflinchingly* the Burne-Jones and Morrisian medieval business. **1918** A. BENNETT *Roll-Call* I. ix. 187 A quiet, inexpensive blue dress, embroidered at the neck in the Morrisian manner. **1936** *Archit. Rev.* LXXX. 179/3 Morris's passionate campaign is famous enough, but there were true Morrisites before Morris, men such as Pugin and Semper. **1936** W. R. TITTERTON *G. K. Chesterton* I. i. 23 The S.D.F.ers had always been Marxian in theory, though revolutionary Morrisites in sentiment. **1949** G. B. SHAW *Sixteen Self Sketches* x. 57 A lady in the esthetic dress momentarily fashionable in Morrisan cliques just then. **1970** *New Society* 31 Dec. 1151/2 It seemed plausibly argued that plastic would demean all our sensations and our contact with nature... This kind of approach had wood in mind—more Morrisite than luddite, perhaps. **1972** *Listener* 6 Apr. 458/2 Ernie's father, killed just before the Armistice, had been a Morrisian socialist and preached an end to deference.

Morrison (mǫ·risən). Name of Herbert S. *Morrison*, Secretary of State for Home Affairs and Home Security (1940–5), used *attrib.* in **Morrison hour** (see quot. 1963); **Morrison shelter,** a transportable indoor steel table-shaped air-raid shelter.

1945 S. SPENDER *Citizens in War* 21 In addition to the Anderson shelters, Morrison shelters and Surface shelters were built at the time of the Blitz. **1948** *Hansard Commons* 18 Mar. 2268 Why should Anderson shelters rust more than Morrison shelters? **1952** *Oxf. Jun. Encycl.* X. 89/1 Morrison shelters, also made of steel and shaped like a rectangular dinner-table, could be set up inside a house to give protection if the house collapsed. **1963** T. & P. MORRIS *Pentonville* iv. 84 Some men complain that though at the time of joining they are told of the so-called 'Morrison Hour' they are not told about compulsory overtime. *Ibid.*, The 'Morrison Hour' is one extra hour worked at the end of the day from Monday to Friday and is compulsory. It dates from 1943... Herbert Morrison was Home Secretary at the time.

morrowless (mǫ·rouləs), *a. rare.* [f. MORROW *sb.* + -LESS.] Not subject to time; without end.

1871 W. D. HOWELLS *Suburban Sk.* 163 Sometimes this choice company sits on the curbing that goes around the terrace..and then I envy every soul in it, so tranquil it seems, so cool, so careless, so morrowless. **1954** J. R. R. TOLKIEN *Fellowship of Ring* xi. 205 Through halls of iron and darkling door, And woods of nightshade morrowless.

Morse, *sb.*³ Add: (Earlier and later examples.)

1858 in G. B. Prescott *Hist. Electr. Telegraph* (1860) xiv. 191 We work with Morse key and detector. **1916** [see *DASH *sb.*¹ 7 f]. **1931** F. L. ALLEN *Only Yesterday* 13 A mechanically inclined boy has a wireless set, with which, if he knows the Morse code, he may listen to messages from ships at sea. **1972** V. PITT *First Look At Signals* 38 The most famous distress signal is S.O.S... It may be tapped out in Morse Code.

morse *v.*, also *trans.*

1920 *Punch* 31 Mar. 245/1 It can be used for Morsing instructions about breakfast to the cook. **1944** *Jrnl. R. Aeronaut. Soc.* XLVIII. 534 Sudden load changes of 18 kw. (29 h.p. at 85 per cent. efficiency) could be thrown on and off the engine by violently 'morsing' the switch on the load panel without upsetting stability.

Morse (mǭɹs), *sb.*⁴ *Engin.* [prob. f. the name of the *Morse* Twist Drill Co., now Morse Cutting Tools, of New Bedford, Mass., U.S.A.] *Morse taper*: a taper on a shank or socket that is one of a standard series having specified dimensions and angles; also *ellipt.*

The word *Morse* is a registered proprietary term in the U.S.

1894 *Machinery* (N.Y.) Nov. p. ii (Advt.), The Standard Tool Company, Cleveland, Ohio. Manufacturers of.. Taps, Milling Cutters, Morse Taper Reamers. **1896** R. GRIMSHAW *Shop Kinks* 96 'Morse' and 'American' Tapers. There are still shops which have twist-drills and sockets of the old 'American' taper, and sometimes it is bothersome to work them in with the 'Morse', as the American is 9–16 inch to the foot, and the Morse is ⅝ inch. **1906** *Official Gaz.* (U.S. Patent Office) 28 Aug. 2956/2 Morse Twist Drill & Machine Company, New Bedford, Mass. Filed May 29, 1905. Used ten years. *Morse* [for] Drills, Reamers, Taps, ..and Milling Cutters. **1930** *Engineering* 25 Apr. 539/2 The centres, both of the workhead and tailstock..are 2½ in. in diameter. They have shanks with a No. 6 Morse taper. **1964** S. CRAWFORD *Basic Engin. Processes* v. 114 The barrel is hollow, at one end a morse-taper bore locates the dead centre, and also provides the location for drill and reamer shanks. **1971** B. SCHARF *Engin. & its Lang.* x. 87 Morse tapers which are numbered from 0 to 7 make it possible to interchange drills, sockets, etc. as required.

mort, *sb.*¹ **4.** (Later example.)

1888 H. JAMES *Let.* 31 July (1920) I. 138 You have become a beautiful myth—a kind of unnatural uncomfortable unburied *mort.*

mortadella (mǭɹtăde·la). Pl. **mortadelle.** Also **mortadel, mortadello.** [It. dim., irreg. f. L. *murtātum* (sausage) seasoned with myrtle berries.] A large spiced pork sausage; Bologna sausage.

1613 [see *CERVELAT 1]. **1732** LD. ESSEX *Let.* 26 Aug. in R. B. Peake *Mem. Colman Family* (1841) I. ii. 30 If you would let your steward buy for me a good Parmesan cheese and some Mortadellos. **1846** R. FORD *Gatherings from Spain* xi. 129 The savoury piquant *embuchados*, which are akin to the *mortadelle* of Bologna, only less hard. **1921** D. H. LAWRENCE *Sea & Sardinia* iii. 118 There is mortadella, the enormous Bologna sausage, thick as a church pillar. **1934** F. SCOTT FITZGERALD *Tender is Night* I. xiii. 76 They ate sandwiches of *mortadel* sausage. **1950** E. HEMINGWAY *Across River & into Trees* xxii. 162 People at home think *mortadella* is a sausage. **1962** G. BUTLER *Coffin in Oxford* xi. 151 A plate of mortadella. **1972** M. HOWELLS *Pop. Ital. Cookery* 13 *Mortadella.* There are many varieties of this sausage, in different sizes and shapes. **1973** E. MCGIRR *Bardel's Murder* ii. 54 If you'd seen the knife he was using to cut up the mortadella sausage, guv'nor, you'd have gone peacefully away.

mortal, *a.* Add: **2. e.** *mortal mind*: according to Christian Scientists, the source in man of all delusion and error, creating the illusion of bodily sensations, pain, and illness.

1875 M. B. EDDY *Science & Health* vii. 341 Faith is all that ever made a drug remedy the ailments of a man. Mortal mind is belief, the immortal is understanding, the latter is Spirit, the former personal sense; we must learn to hold the immortal and mortal mind or belief separate. **1881** —— *Ibid.* (ed. 3) I. ii. 108 Mortal mind, and not muscles, nerves, bones, etc., determines the condition of its own body. *Ibid.* 114 Mortal mind is the remote cause of all suffering and sickness. **1903** 'MARK TWAIN' in *North Amer. Rev.* Apr. 508 In Christian Science terminology, 'claims' are errors of mortal mind, fictions of the imagination. **1910** *Encycl. Relig. & Ethics* III. 577/2 In Christian Science this lying material sense, or sense of evil, is termed 'mortal mind'. **1970** F. S. MEAD *Handbk. of Denominations in U.S.* (ed. 5) 71/1 Certain terms are important in the exposition of Christian Science... Mortal mind is 'the flesh opposed to Spirit'.

mortality. Add: **5.** *mortality rate, statistics.*

1909 *Daily Chron.* 27 Jan. 3/3 Dr. Millsom points out that..the want of air, ventilation, and light are dangerous or injurious to the health of the residents, and that the mortality rate from all diseases (especially consumption) is very high. **1966** *Lancet* 24 Dec. 1371/1 In an attempt to reduce the mortality-rate, clinicians used ever-increasing amounts of antitetanic serum. **1970** PASSMORE & ROBSON *Compan. Med. Stud.* II. xxxiv. 10/1 The death certificate is both a legal and a statistical document. Its form has been agreed internationally to provide for worldwide comparisons of mortality statistics.

mortar, *sb.*¹ Add: **5.** (sense 3) *mortarman.*

1952 G. E. THORNTON *Hand-bk. Weapon Training* x. 109 The auxiliaries are placed in position by the mortarman's assistant, who works backwards in co-operation with the mortarman. **1965** M. W. BROWNE *New Face of War* iii. 19 They lack optical sighting devices, but good mortarmen don't need gadgets like that. **1970** *Globe & Mail* (Toronto) 25 Sept. 9/8 U.S. mortarmen mistakenly fired 36 rounds into an element of U.S. infantrymen.

mortar, *v.*² Add: Hence **mo·rtaring** *vbl. sb.*

1954 M. BERESFORD *Lost Villages* ii. 73 Packing and mortaring had been carefully executed, and both faces of the wall were regular and straight.

mortar, *v.*³ [f. MORTAR *sb.*¹ 3.] *trans.* To direct mortar fire upon; to hit with mortar shells.

1951 in *Conc. Oxf. Dict.* (ed. 4). **1967** C. CONNELL *World's Greatest Sieges* xxix. 239 The Germans followed the rearguard down to the water's edge..mortaring men and boats indiscriminately. **1974** *Times* 18 Mar. 6/6 In the towns, he said, the Arab garrisons had mortared and bombed Kurdish quarters.

Hence **mo·rtaring** *vbl. sb.*

[**1920** G. M. CHURCHER in *R. Artillery War Commem. Bk.* II. 43/2 The infantry were more than friends... Without their help trench-mortaring..would not have been the fun it was.] **1971** B. W. ALDISS *Soldier Erect* 229 All that shelling, mortaring and machine-gunning hadn't put a single bunker out of action, although it had spread the jungle about the place. **1972** L. LAMB *Picture Frame* ii. 21 Mortaring started just as he reached the Bois Mesnil lane.

mortarium (mǭɹtā·riǒm). Pl. **mortaria.** [L.] A Roman mortar (see quots.).

1842 W. SMITH *Dict. Gk. & Rom. Antiquities* 622/1 *Mortarium*, also called Pila and Pilum. **1863** W. CHAFFERS *Marks & Monograms on Pott. & Porc.* 18, Fig. 24 is a mortarium; 10¾ inches diameter, of light brown ware, unglazed... Mortaria are sometimes found of the red lustrous ware, called Samian. **1937** *Discovery* Apr. 98/1 They have unearthed..bits of a mortarium. **1938** [see *find-spot* s.v. *FIND *sb.* 4].

mortician (mǭɹti·ʃən). *U.S.* [f. L. *mors, mort-* death (cf. MORT *sb.*¹) + -ICIAN.] An undertaker; one who arranges funerals.

1895 *Columbus* (Ohio) *Dispatch* 14 Aug. (Advt.), We, Mank & Webb, are the only Morticians in the city who do not belong to the Funeral Director's Protective Association. **1915** *Literary Digest* 16 Jan. 130/3 The word 'mortician' is a recent innovation due to a need felt by undertakers for a word more in keeping with, and descriptive of, their calling. **1927** *Glasgow Herald* 1 Oct. 10/7 As the jury troop out of their boxes every tread of their heels will mean another call for the mortician. **1930** *Punch* 18 June 696 He passed me on to a mortician... His prices ..were huge, but then he was mortician to all the best movie-stars' husbands. **1948** *Christian Cent.* 4 Feb. 146/1 Give the morticians credit—their cosmetic arts are highly skilled. **1951** M. MCLUHAN *Mech. Bride* (1967) 14/2 This sentiment also fits glovelike over the mortician chapel. *Ibid.* 43/2 It is therefore ironic that the present *Life* feature..should have so mortician-like an air. *Ibid.* 62/1 Our refusal to face death at all in the mortician parlor. **1953** 'M. INNES' *Christmas at Candleshoe* i. 10 He is a bald pale person from Buffalo, where he carries on the profession of mortician. **1958** *Oxf. Mag.* 30 Oct. 49/2 Well—hush!—there it is, a thing of beauty in a mortician's parlour; embalmed but—see there!—quite conscious. **1972** *Lebende Sprachen* XVII. 34/1 US *mortician*..undertaker.

Mortlake. Restrict '*Obs.* exc. *Hist.*' to sense in Dict. and add: **2.** (Written **mortlake, mort-lake** (with hyphen).) = **ox-bow lake.*

1902 LD. AVEBURY *Scenery Eng.* ix. 303 The loop often remains as a dead river-channel or 'Mortlake'. Such looplakes are known in America by the special name of 'Oxbows'. **1937** [see *CUT-OFF *sb.* 2]. **1957** G. E. HUTCHINSON *Treat. Limnol.* I. i. 123 The term *mortlake*, presumably derived from the place name, has been used in some English works as the equivalent of *bras mort* or *Altwasser.* **1962** READ & WATSON *Introd. Geol.* iv. 172 When the loop of the meander becomes large it is liable to be cut-off across its neck, leaving an abandoned separated portion which may remain as an oxbow-lake or mort-lake. **1968** *Geogr. Abstr.* B. 112 The fish fauna of various rivers, peat hags and mortlakes was examined.

Morton's Fork (mǭ·ɹtənz fǭɹk). [f. the name of John *Morton* (*c* 1420–1500), Archbishop of Canterbury and minister of Henry VII + FORK *sb.* 1.] John Morton's method of levying forced loans by arguing that those who were obviously rich could afford to pay, and those who lived frugally must have savings. Cf. quot. 1622 *s.v.* CROTCH 7. Also *transf.*

1889 J. GAIRDNER *Henry Seventh* x. 151 One article suggested an argument familiarly known as 'Morton's fork'. **1930** SELLAR & YEATMAN *1066 and all That* xxix. 49 Henry VII was a miser and very good at statecraft; he invented some extremely clever policies such as the one called Morton's Fork. **1964** *New Statesman* 28 Feb. 318/1 The political consequence of this is that he is now—publicly at least—caught on Morton's Fork. **1965** *Listener* 16 Sept. 429/2, I don't think Mr Smith can altogether pass unscratched between the twin prongs of that Morton's fork. **1973** *Times Lit. Suppl.* 17 Aug. 957/5 A fine Morton's fork technique this—those who went were conspirators and those who stayed away were cowards. **1974** *Cosmopolitan* May 132/1 'Morton's Fork,' she laughed wryly. 'Young and torpid or old and energetic.'

||**morucho** (moru·tʃo). [Sp.] A half-breed bull reared in Spain; originally the name of a thoroughbred race of cattle in the Salamanca area.

1932 E. HEMINGWAY *Death in Afternoon* xii. 128 Half-bred bulls or bulls in which there is a little fighting blood, called moruchos in Spanish, are often very brave while calves. **1957** A. MACNAB *Bulls of Iberia* i. 8 There do exist animals of mixed race, called *moruchos*, half fighting blood and half tame blood of the Salamanca area. **1959** V. J. KEHOE *Aficionado!* iv. 67/2 Another variety of Spanish toro is the half-breed *morucho*. This type, which extends from the Salamanca area down to the Guadarrama range section, does not have animals of the fine form, perseverance of charge and nobility as do the pure breeds.

morula, var. *MARULA.

mor-yah, var. *MOYA *int.*

mosaic, *a.*¹ and *sb.* Add: **A.** *adj.* **1. c.** Resembling the colours or patterns of mosaic work.

c **1890** tr. *T. de Dillmont's Encycl. Needlework* 133 *Mosaic stitch*.., the first row consists of one short and one long stitch, alternately; the second, of short stitches only, set between the long stitches of the first row; the third row is a repetition of the first, and so on. **1900** E. JACKSON *Hist. Hand-Made Lace* 127 The Lace resembling Duchesse made in Venice in the present day is called Mosaic lace, on account of small sprigs being used to build up the pattern as the pieces of stone and glass are used in Mosaic work. **1934** M. THOMAS *Dict. Embroidery Stitches* 151 *Mosaic filling*, a drawn fabric stitch. **1960** H. HAYWARD *Antique Coll.* 191/1 *Mosaic binding*, book-binding with polychrome decoration. **1961** J. CARTER *ABC for Bk.-Collectors* (ed. 3) 136 *Mosaic bindings*, leather bindings decorated with contrasting colours, whether inlaid, onlaid or painted.

5. *Embryol.* Of, pertaining to, or characterized by that mode of development in which regions in an embryo are predetermined by the corresponding regions in that embryo at an earlier stage of development.

1893 *Jrnl. Morphol.* VIII. 579 (*heading*) Amphioxus, and the mosaic theory of development. **1904** *Jrnl. Exper. Zoöl.* I. 2 Similar views were more or less clearly expressed by Van Beneden, Flemming, Platner and others prior to the definite formulation of the mosaic-theory of development by Roux in 1888. *Ibid.* Such 'mosaic eggs' as those of mollusks or ctenophores. **1933** J. H. WOODGER tr. *L. von Bertalanffy's Mod. Theories Development* x. 143 After injury we obtain partial embryos from mosaic eggs and whole embryos from the regulative ones. **1963** J. COHEN *Living Embryos* 11 In the Annelid worms and the Molluscs, almost all of the interactions between parts of the egg occur before cleavage commences, and in consequence, if the cells are separated at the 4-cell or 8-cell stage they have already been determined in their fates and can only produce parts of animals. This kind of development is called determinate or mosaic, and is also shown by many primitive Chordates. **1970** AMBROSE & EASTY *Cell Biol.* xiii. 422 Eggs of this kind, in which the cytoplasm is clearly divided into different regions required for the development of specific regions of the embryo, are known as mosaic eggs.

6. *mosaic disease* [tr. G. *mosaikkrankheit* (A. Mayer 1886, in *Die Landwirtschaftlichen Versuchsstationen* XXXII. 453)], a virus disease affecting plants, characterized by a mottled pattern of discoloration on the leaves; also *absol.*; cf. *tobacco mosaic* (*TOBACCO 3).

1894 *Jrnl. Mycol.* VII. 382 The first symptom [of tobacco mosaic] is a geographic or mosaic coloring of the leaf surface, light and dark green... The name 'mosaic disease' was given by Dr. Mayer. **1925** *Contemp. Rev.* Dec. 753 Cuba..is finding soil depletion and mosaic disease increasingly serious matters. **1930** *Discovery* June 196/1 The first virus disease to be discovered was the 'mosaic' of tobacco, which manifests itself in a bright mottling and spotting of the foliage. **1940** *Sun* (Baltimore) 29 Jan. 5/6 First reports of a new disease spreading into Pennsylvania peach orchards have located the dread 'mosaic' in the Spring Grove section of York county. **1970** LIEBSCHER & KOEHLER tr. *Fröhlich & Rodenwald's Pests & Diseases of Tropical Crops* 39 A number of virus diseases, such as mosaic disease, infectious chlorosis, and 'heart rot', manifest themselves by retarded growth, discoloration, and leaf curl.

7. *Biol.* Having or composed of cells of two genetically different types.

1902 W. Bateson et al. *Rep. Evolution Comm. R. Soc.* I. 23 Among the large number of capsules examined, there were some of the mosaic type, in which part of the capsule was prickly and the remainder smooth. *Ibid.* 127 'Mosaic' fruits in *Datura*, where..the otherwise pure extracted recessives (thornless) showed exceptionally a thorny patch... Such a phenomenon may be taken as indicating that the germ-cells may also have been mosaic. **1926**, etc. [see *chimera, chimæra 3 d]. **1968** [see *gynandromorph* s.v. *gynandro-]. **1969** *New Scientist* 16 Jan. 133/1 Cytogeneticists have found human mosaic individuals. **1974** S. L. Robbins *Pathologic Basis Dis.* vi. 178/1 Nondisjunction after zygote formation yields a mosaic individual who has more than one chromosome count in his body cells.

8. Photogr. *mosaic screen*, a screen containing a pattern of small filters of each of the primary colours which was placed in front of the emulsion for both exposure and viewing in some methods of colour photography; so *mosaic process*.

1908 *Brit. Jrnl. Photogr.* Suppl. 3 Jan. 13 To make the Krayn mosaic screen..line-screens are again cemented together and form a block. **1935** *Discovery* July 188/2 The well-known 'screen' or 'mosaic' processes, in which the photograph is recorded through a regular or irregular pattern of coloured rulings or grains. **1942** C. B. Neblette *Photography* (ed. 4) xxxii. 786 The irregular mosaic screens are made from a mixture of small colored particles. **1957** R. W. G. Hunt *Reprod. Colour* iii. 30 In photography, the mosaic processes have had a long and distinguished career.

9. Chiefly *Aerial Photogr.* Applied to a composite photograph made up of a number of separate photographs of overlapping areas.

1920 H. E. Ives *Airplane Photography* xxvi. 316 (*heading*) Arranging prints for a mosaic map. **1930** *Air Ann. British Empire* 207 A photographic survey was made for a railway company, the mosaic strip..being produced on a scale of 130 inches to the mile. **1934** *Discovery* June 15/1 The chief photographic contribution ..is an aerial mosaic map of an area of about 200 square miles. **1972** *Sci. Amer.* Mar. 10/2 In the past six months the first complete aerial-mosaic map of Manhattan Island has been assembled, and photographic prints are being made on a scale that brings out a wealth of interesting detail.

10. *Ecol.* Applied to an area in which plant associations occur in an alternating pattern.

1930 G. E. du Rietz in *Svensk Bot. Tidskr.* XXIV. 496 Phytocoenose-complexes are vegetational units consisting of phytocoenoses with little or no relationship to each other but more or less regularly alternating. They are of several kinds. Good examples for [*sic*] mosaic complexes are furnished by the..Scandinavian bogs, maritime rocks, etc. **1970** P. Oliver *Savannah Syncopators* 41 As one moves north from the rain forest and into the tropical woodlands and savannah mosaic regions, the trees become fewer and smaller.

11. *Cryst.* Applied to (the structure of) crystals made up of small blocks of perfect lattices set at very slight angles to one another.

1934 W. P. Davey *Study Cryst. Struct. & Applic.* xii. 363 It will be of interest..to examine the various ways in which crystals may be grown in the hope of finding mechanisms of crystal growth which will lead easily to the mosaic type rather than the perfect type of structure. **1938** W. A. Wooster *Text-bk. Crystal Physics* ii. 62 The mosaic crystal was imagined to be built up of a number of small blocks of perfect crystal, of not more than some 500 A.U. side, arranged nearly parallel to each other. **1964** R. C. Evans *Introd. Crystal. Chem.* (ed. 2) ix. 206 As normally prepared, a crystal has a pronounced mosaic structure. **1970** R. A. Laudise *Growth Single Crystals* i. 17 There is a continuous series of states of order between mosaic structures and structures showing conventional low-angle grain boundaries.

12. Biol. *mosaic evolution* (see quots.).

1963 E. Mayr *Animal Species & Evolution* xix. 598 There is not a steady and harmonious change of all parts of the 'type', as envisioned by the school of idealistic morphology, but rather a 'mosaic evolution'. Every evolutionary type is a mosaic of primitive and advanced characters, of general and specialized features. **1971** J. Z. Young *Introd. Study Man* xxxiii. 457 The human character appears in some features (the gait) before others (size of brain); this is the phenomenon called mosaic evolution.

B. *sb.* **3. b.** *Biol.* An individual (commonly an animal) composed of cells of two genetically different types. Cf. *chimera, chimæra 3 d.

1902 W. Bateson et al. *Rep. Evolution Comm. R. Soc.* I. 23 These mosaics occurred as rarities both on prickly individuals and on smooth ones still more rarely. **1946** R. R. Gates *Human Genetics* I. ix. 281 Case I. 1 was an albino and it is said that two of her children were albino mosaics, the girl having half her hair white and half black, with one blue eye and one black. **1949** Darlington & Mather *Elem. Genetics* v. 112 In animals the effects of somatic mutation are slightly different [from those in plants]... The changed cells give flakes and sectors instead of layers and the product is known as a mosaic instead of a chimaera. **1968** *New Scientist* 14 Nov. 383/2 Chimaeras, or mosaics—animals containing cells from two sets of parents—have been made experimentally before. **1974** S. L. Robbins *Pathologic Basis Dis.* vi. 187/2 Approximately 2 per cent of 'mongoloids' are mosaics (trisomy 21/normal).

c. *Photogr.* = *mosaic screen* (in A. 8 above).

1911 A. Watkins *Photography* (ed. 5) xii. 227 The Thames colour plate. This is a regular mosaic, formed by three printings (each being dyed) on bichromated colloid; the pattern originating with a 200-line half-tone screen. **1957** R. W. G. Hunt *Reprod. Colour* iii. 30 The Autochrome plate, which consisted of a random mosaic of red, green and blue starch grains with the interstices filled with carbon black, came on the market in 1907. **1973** D. A. Spencer *Focal Dict. Photogr. Technol.* 395 After exposure through this mosaic the emulsion is reversal processed to a positive transparency.

d. Chiefly *Aerial Photogr.* A mosaic map or photograph (see A. 9 above).

1920 H. E. Ives *Airplane Photography* xxvi. 316 For a mosaic of any size an accurate outline map must be drawn on the surface of which the prints are to be attached. **1920** *Flight* XII. 187/2 He then showed the similarities and differences between a photographic mosaic and a map, and outlined the various difficulties that had to be contended with. **1940** *War Illustr.* 2 Feb. 45 The map-like pictures are afterwards assembled in a big mosaic..which forms a complete plan of the area photographed. **1971** R. Dentry *Encounter at Kharmel* vii. 113 The Yanks updated their U2 mosaic of the area. **1972** *Nature* 18 Feb. 391/2 Electron micrographs of the inner plexiform layer at a magnification of 25,000 times were used to construct mosaics covering the area from the ganglion cell layer to the vitreal margin.

e. An array of many small photo-emissive metal plates, each of which temporarily stores a charge dependent on the amount of light falling on it, that forms the target plate in some television camera tubes (e.g. the iconoscope); also, an array of piezo-electric transducers in a detector of ultrasound.

1928 *Discovery* Nov. 337/1 Carey's idea was to replace the mosaic of the retina by a mosaic of a large number of minute selenium cells..and, further, to replace the nerve fibres by separately insulated electric wires carrying an electric current from a battery, and to use this device to vary the light given by a number of very minute electric lamps..so placed that each lamp would correspond in position to each of the selenium cells. **1933** *Proc. Wireless Section Inst. Electr. Engin.* VIII. 220/2 The charge acquired by each element of the mosaic is released by the cathode-ray beam once in each repetition of the picture. **1953** Amos & Birkinshaw *Television Engineering* I. iv. 54 The mosaic must be of very fine construction with a number of individual cells to each element otherwise the cells show up in the reproduced image as a grain. **1961** G. N. Patchett *Television Servicing* III. vii. 197 The mosaic is composed of antimony islands which are made photosensitive with caesium. **1966** *McGraw-Hill Encycl. Sci. & Technol.* XIII. 464/2 The mosaic is electrically coupled to the signal plate by electrostatic capacitance between the two. **1969** J. S. Wood tr. *L. D. Rozenberg's Sources of High-Intensity Ultrasound* II. ii. iv. 215 The construction of ultrasonic receivers in which a kind of 'mosaic' was used, consisting of several piezoelectric cylinders mounted on a large-diameter diaphragm.

mosaicism (mozē·isiz'm). *Biol.* [f. Mosaic *a.*[1] and *sb.* + -ism.] The quality or state of being mosaic (*mosaic *a.*[1] 7).

1926 *Jrnl. Genetics* XVI. 230 No attempt to represent analytically the genetical behaviour of irregular mosaicism in plants has been altogether satisfactory. **1932** *Genetics* XVII. 39 The facts secured from the different breeding tests demonstrate that the mosaicism is due to an unstable translocation. **1947** *Nature* 11 Jan. 66/2 Chemical treatment of female embryos [of *Drosophila melanogaster*] leads to high frequency of mosaicism. **1961** [see *Mongoloid *a.* and *sb.* A. 2]. **1963** *Lancet* 13 May 1028/2 The term mosaicism, in cytogenetic usage, describes a condition in which a substantial minority of cells differ from the majority in their chromosomal content. **1971** *Nature* 11 June 388/2 We have recently had the opportunity to study the rare association of mixed gonadal dysgenesis in a female child and X/XY/XYY mosaicism in karyotypes from blood and fibroblast cultures.

Mosan (mōu·zăn), *a.* [Fr., of or pertaining to the Meuse river, f. L. *Mosa* Meuse.] Pertaining to the style of decorative art developed in the Meuse valley in the 11th to 13th centuries.

[**1882** C. de Linas *L'Art et l'Industrie d'autrefois dans les Régions de la Meuse Belge* i. 12 Le temps a pu faire surgir un art..ni rhénan, ni flamand, ni français, bien qu'il se rattache à tous les trois... Cet art,..il faudrait aujourd'hui lui donner un nom: pourquoi pas *art mosan*?] **1910** *Archaeologia* LXII. 22 The appearance of these medallions is of unusual brilliancy and richness, even for the productions of the Mosan school of enamelling. **1933** *Burlington Mag.* Apr. 198/1 The term Mosan art was introduced forty years ago by Charles de Linas, who maintained that the art of the middle, that is Belgian, section of the Meuse country was original. **1957** G. Zarnecki *Eng. Romanesque Lead Sculpture* 12 It has been generally accepted that this manuscript was influenced by Mosan art. The blending of Winchester and Mosan features found in it was probably not confined to this manuscript alone. **1972** *Times* 6 Dec. 1/6 (*caption*) The exquisitely delicate little statue..is characteristic of the Mosan style of the eleventh and twelfth centuries.

Mosan (mōu·săn), *sb.* [f. *mōs*, lit. 'four' in various N. Amer. Indian languages + -an.] The name of a North American language group comprising Chemakuan, Salish, and Wakashan.

1929 *Encycl. Brit.* V. 139/1 The following reductions of linguistic stocks which have been proposed may be looked upon as either probable or very possible:..5, *Mosan*, consisting of Salish, Chimakuan and Wakashan. **1955** H. A. Gleason *Introd. Descriptive Linguistics* xxiv. 368 The Pacific Northwest from the Columbia River Valley to southern Alaska is occupied by a number of languages... Most of the languages fall into three families which are related in one phylum known as *Mosan*. **1965** *Canad. Jrnl Linguistics* Spring 78 It was suggested by Sapir, in..1929, that Kutenai may be distinctly related to both Algonkian and Mosan. *Ibid.* 98 Algonkian–Wakashan has perhaps been more commonly known as Mosan-Algonkian. **1968** *Encycl. Brit.* I. 728/2 Tsimshian and Maidu have probably been considerably influenced by contact with Mosan.

mosasaur. (Later examples.)

1966 *McGraw-Hill Encycl. Sci & Technol.* VII. 474/1 Suborder Lacertilia... The group..includes modern lizards..and extinct marine mosasaurs (Cretaceous). **1968** A. S. Romer *Procession of Life* xi. 195 The mosasaurs.. had a long, flexible trunk and a highly developed tail, and hence were able to use body and tail undulation for forward progression in somewhat fish-like fashion. **1971** *Nature* 15 Jan. 172/1 In a great many aquatic and marine reptiles, past and present, ichthyosaurs..mosasaurs..the external nares are just in front of the eyes.

moscato (mǫskā·to). Also **moscatto.** [It.: see Muscat.] A range of sweet Italian dessert wines; also, the grape from which the wine is produced.

1903 *Consular Reports* (U.S. Bur. Foreign Commerce) July 336 For each liter of sparkling wine, as Margarita, moscatto, moselle, etc., 1 peso (36.1 cents). **1925** A. Huxley *Those Barren Leaves* iv. vi. 314 We'll have a bottle of the sweet *moscato*. **1961** *Guardian* 21 Nov. 14/2 (Advt.), *Moscato*. Semi-sweet, fragrant, sparkling..9/0. **1972** *Times* 25 Mar. 10/6 The moscato grape from which Asti Spumante is made.

Moscow (mǫ·sko, *U.S.* mǫ·skau). **1.** The name of the capital of the U.S.S.R. used allusively to describe the government, political influence, ideology, etc., of the U.S.S.R. So **Mo·scowism.**

1938 *Times Lit. Suppl.* 19 Mar. 182/1 'What Are We To Do?' is less a work of new thinking than of the application and adaptation of Moscowism. **1940** *Manch. Guardian Weekly* 17 May 388 'This book on Poland,' says Cardinal Hinsley in his foreword, 'shows that Nazism and Moscowism agree in two broad lines—Godlessness and ruthlessness.' **1957** C. Hunt *Guide to Communist Jargon* xxiii. 82 Moscow-appointed officials of a non-Russian Soviet republic. **1967** H. Arendt *Origins of Totalit.* (new ed.) xi. 371 The European Communist parties became branches of a Moscow-directed Bolshevik movement. **1971** P. O'Donnell *Impossible Virgin* ii. 46 He wants a list of our local agents in Prague. Moscow will pay him the earth for that. **1972** T. Lilley *K Section* viii. 57 A Moscow-trained and dedicated Communist. **1974** *Times* 27 Aug. 4/8 Mr Florakis leads the Moscow-orientated rump of the [Greek Communist] party.

2. *Moscow mule*, a cocktail containing vodka.

1963 *House & Garden* Mar. 114/2 A Moscow Mule (vodka, ginger beer, ice and half a lime). **1965** O. A. Mendelsohn *Dict. Drink* 229 *Moscow mule*, cocktail of vodka, ginger beer and lime. The concoction is reported to be unknown in Russia. **1969** [see *Margarita 2].

Moses. Add: **1. c.** (Earlier examples.)

1840 in *Amer. Speech* (1965) XL. 130 Oh! Moses how they opened dare eyes. **1842** S. Lover *Handy Andy* xiv. 123 O'Grady, casting a look of mingled rage and contempt on the fisherman, merely uttered the ejaculation, 'Oh Moses!' and threw himself back in his chair.

d. A derogatory appellation for a Jew.

1844 *Punch* 6 July 19/1 (*heading*) A hint for Moses... Passing by the eminent establishment of E. Aaron and Co.,..I was naturally attracted..to examine the beauteous objects of gent.'s attire, which are exhibited in their unrivalled plate-glass windows. **1858** *Ibid.* 10 July 12/2 The Jews are no more a disqualified caste, And *moses* will henceforth in Parliament sit.

2. b. (Later examples.)

1812 *Boston Gaz.* 26 Oct. Suppl. (Advt.) (Th.), On Saturday was picked up, on Dorchester Flats, a small Moses boat. **1970** *Brewer's Dict. Phr. & Fable* 731/2 *Moses boat*, a type of boat made..by a famous boat-builder, Moses Lowell, in the 18th century.

3. Moses basket, a basket used for carrying babies.

1945 N. Mitford *Pursuit of Love* x. 84 She..returned carrying a Moses basket full of wails. **1948** M. Dickens *Joy & Josephine* i. i. 13 She was trying to make out whether the young officer were the father of the baby in the Moses basket. **1949** E. Taylor *Wreath of Roses* vii. 100 Carrying the baby between them in a Moses basket. **1959** 'A. Stafford' *Custody of Anne* i. 45 She shook the moses basket so that the child stirred and whimpered. **1974** 'J. Melville' *Nun's Castle* i. 22 A display of nursery furniture, including an elegant Moses basket of natural straw lined with soft cotton.

mosesite (mōu·zizəit). *Min.* [f. the name of Alfred J. *Moses* (1859–1920), U.S. mineralogist + -ite[1].] A hydrated nitrogen compound of mercury which is found as yellow isometric crystals and has the formula $Hg_2NX.H_2O$, where X represents chiefly chloride and sulphate.

1910 F. A. Canfield et al. in *Amer. Jrnl. Sci.* XXX. 202 We propose the name *mosesite*, which name, besides perpetuating the high attainments of Professor Moses in the science of mineralogy, is particularly appropriate as it links his name with a group of minerals which he first definitely put on record. **1953** *Amer. Mineralogist* XXXVIII. 1225 Mosesite from El Doctor, Mexico, contains AsO_4 and very little MoO_4, but that from Terlingua, Texas, has only Cl and SO_4 as anions. *Ibid.* 1234 Mosesite may be easily synthesized by treating HgCl with dilute ammonium hydroxide. **1959** *Prof. Papers U.S. Geol. Surv.* No. 312. 70/1 The kleinite and mosesite..furnish direct evidence that they were formed at temperatures well above those to be expected during weathering.

mosey, *v.* **1** and **2.** (Earlier and later examples.)

1829 *Virginia Lit. Museum* 30 Dec. 459 *Mosey*, to move off. **1836** *Public Ledger* (Philadelphia) 2 Dec. (Th.), You'r not going to smoke me. So mosey off. **1870** 'Mark Twain' *Curious Republic Gondour* (1919) 57, I hain't got time to be palavering along here—got to..mosey along. **1874** —— in *Atlantic Monthly* Nov. 592/2 De way dey made dem sojers mosey roun'! **1901** 'H. McHugh' *John Henry* 42 Abie had moseyed away. **1902** W. N. Harben *Abner Daniel* 59 Now I must mosey on down-stairs. **1918** *Punch* 27 Mar. 206/1 Her funnel's caked with Cape Horn ice and blistered in the sun, She's moseyed round above a bit, and, poor old ship, she's done. **1961** C. McCullers *Clock without Hands* v. 111 While Mr Malone made up the Coca-Cola, Jester moseyed over to the scales and stood on them. **1966** T. Pynchon *Crying of Lot 49* v. 110 She was moseying along a street..when she collided with a gang of guided tourists. **1973** *Daily Tel.* (Colour Suppl.) 16 Mar. 22/3 Map in hand he moseys round the alleys and yards of Southwark. **1974** *Black World* June 70/2, I had moseyed over to see what they were yakking about. **1974** D. Ramsay *No Cause to Kill* ii. 134, I thought I'd mosey on over to the liquor store.

mosh, dial. var. Mush *sb.*[1] and *v.*[2]

1848 A. B. Evans *Leicestershire Words* 58, I thought that she would have moshed her children then and there. **1914** D. H. Lawrence *Widowing of Mrs. Holroyd* iii. 74 One of my sons..was shot till 'is shoulder was all of a mosh.

‖ **moshav** (mōu·ʃāv). Also **moshaev, moshavah.** Pl. **moshavim.** [ad. mod. Heb. *mōshābh* dwelling, colony.] In Israel: a group of agricultural smallholdings worked co-operatively. So **moshav-ovdim, moshav-shitufi** (see quot. 1950).

1931 [see *kibbutz]. **1934** *Cook's Traveller's Handbk. to Palestine, Syria & Iraq* (ed. 6) 48 The *Moshav*, in which small holdings of land are allotted to families on hereditary lease by the Jewish National Fund... The co-operative principle is applied in the purchase and sale of produce and agricultural requirements. **1944** H. F. Infield *Co-operative Living in Palestine* (1946) iii. 46 The Moshav is intermediate between individualism and the Kvutza. Here the settler lives in his own house, owns a piece of land and some cattle. *Ibid.* xi. 122 From 1936 to 1939, new Kvutzot were 26, new Moshve-Ovdim only 9. The ration of Kvutzot to Moshve established has doubled. **1950** G. Mikes *Milk & Honey* 136 Some halfway solutions have been attempted. First the *Moshav Ovdim*, in which each family has its own unit of land. The purchase of supplies and the marketing of agricultural products is on a cooperative basis. These..are smallholders' settlements in which every farmer shoulders his own risks... Then there is the *Moshav Shitufi*, in which the women have to work four or five hours a day for the community, but otherwise the family is a separate unit. No personal risk, no private enterprise but more private life. **1959** *Economist* 16 May 640/1 The *moshavim* (the farming settlements where the families rent their own land but co-operate over marketing, tractor stations, seed buying, etc.). **1969** P. Worsley in Ionescu & Gellner *Populism* 231 Since family-farming units and communitarian village life are perfectly compatible, forms resembling the *moshav*, or the Saskatchewan Group Farm, have been the favoured models. **1972** C. Raphael *Feast of History* i. 13/1 A *moshav* (small-holders' settlement) in Galilee. **1973** *Times Lit. Suppl.* 18 May 544/4 A moshav is a village devoted to agricultural pursuits and run on cooperative lines. It is not as austere as some of the kibbutzim. **1973** *Jewish Chron.* 6 July 3/2 The first families moved into the second moshav..occupying 30 of the 40 houses built.

Moshi, Mosi, varr. *Mossi.

‖ **moskonfyt** (mǫ·skǫnfėi:t). *S. Afr.* [Afrikaans, f. *mos* must + *konfyt* jam.] A thick syrup prepared from grapes.

1891 *Pall Mall Gaz.* Extra No. 58, Oct. 13/2 It was *mos-komfyt*, I found, made with grape-juice. **1905** *Agric. Jrnl. Cape of Good Hope* 483 (Pettman), The first idea in planting vines is to provide *mos confyt*, a kind of grape sugar syrup, which is given as part of their rations to the coloured labourers. **1931** T. J. Haarhoff *Vergil in Experience S. Afr.* i. 3 '*Moskonfyt*' is used, as it was by the Romans, partly as a syrup and partly to break down the acidity of wines. **1953** *Cape Times* 10 Mar. 2/4 A consignment of 600 110-gallon drums of *moskonfyt*, which will be processed into wine in Britain. **1975** *Daily Dispatch* (East London, Cape Province) 20 Sept. 5 A grape for raisins and also for the production of sweet wines, moskonfyt and even jam.

Moslem, Muslim, *sb.* and *a.* Add: The predominant form is now *Muslim.*

A. *sb.* (Further examples.) *spec.* = **Black Muslim.*

1955 *Times* 3 May 9/4 Lahore witnessed the astonishing sight of hundreds of Sikhs of all people being fêted by Muslims. **1961** [see *Black Muslim* s.v. *black *a.* 19]. **1969** *Sunday Standard* (Bombay) 3 Aug. 1/8 The promised equal opportunities to Buddhists and Muslims in Ladakh had not materialised so far. **1972** J. Mills *Report to Commissioner* 120 They [*sc.* Black Panthers] aren't like the Muslims. **1973** *Jewish Chron.* 9 Feb. 11/2 The basic credo of the Muslims is a hatred of Whites.

B. *adj.* (Further examples.)

1968 *E. African Law Jrnl.* IV. 17 The establishment of special courts to deal exclusively with Muslim law is peculiar in East Africa to Kenya and Zanzibar. **1970** *Times* 3 Apr. (Arab League Suppl.) p. iii/1 The Indians are the only large non-Muslim group, besides Christian Arabs and Europeans.

b. Moslem (or **Muslim**) **League,** in full **All India Moslem League,** a Muslim political organization founded in India in 1906 whose demands in 1940 for an independent Muslim state led to the establishment of Pakistan; so **Moslem Leaguer.**

1907 *Times* 2 Jan. 3/1 Resolved [on 30 Dec. 1906], that this meeting, composed of Musulmans from all parts of India, assembled at Dacca, decides that a political association be formed, styled the All India Moslem League. **1913** *Times* 31 Oct. 7/4 The All-India Moslem League..Mr. Ameer Ali has tendered his resignation of the presidentship of the London All-India Moslem League..and his Highness the Aga Khan..will retire from the headship of the League in India. **1955** *Times* 7 July 9/2 The Muslim League did not win a majority, but remains the largest single party. **1971** *Hindustan Times Weekly* (New Delhi) 4 Apr. 7/1 Besides the Congress (N)..it includes such disparate elements as..the Muslim League. **1972** *Guardian* 5 Feb. 11/5 Muslim Leaguers are helpless now.

Mosleyite (mōu·zli,əit). [f. the name of Sir Oswald Ernald *Mosley* (born 1896) + -ite[1].] A follower or supporter of Sir Oswald Mosley or his views; a British fascist. Also *attrib.* or as *adj.*

1932 Auden *Orators* iii. 104 The Simonites, the Mosleyites and the I.L.P. **1944** H. G. Wells *'42 to '44* 33 The Mosleyites running like the wind down Regent Street from the Jewish prizefighters. **1960** *Economist* 8 Oct. 141/2 The lunatic Mosleyite fringe. **1961** *Ibid.* 17 June 1266/1 The alliance of politicians, civil servants and 'sound' outside minds which generally rules England did not go Mosleyite. **1973** *Guardian* 10 Apr. 1/2 Mr Jonathan Guiness said: 'I am supposed to say that..it is a question between the Powellites and the Mosleyites..because I am Sir Oswald Mosley's son-in-law.'

mosquito. Add: **2. a.** *mosquito-borne, -breeding, -carried, -thin* adjs.

1961 M. Hynes *Med. Bacteriol.* (ed. 7) xxv. 392 The Venezuelan virus is also mosquito-borne, but the reservoir is uncertain. **1926** M. Leinster *Dew on Leaf* 208 Mosquito-breeding ponds. **1909** *Westm. Gaz.* 11 Feb. 2/3 The City of Rio de Janeiro, as regards mosquito-carried diseases, has ..undergone a complete transformation. **1933** R. Campbell *Flowering Reeds* 26 When to their roost the sacred ibis file, Mosquito-thin against the fading West.

b. mosquito-boot, a boot worn to protect the foot from mosquitos; **mosquito coil,** a spiral made from a dried paste of pyrethrum powder with a combustion-supporting substance, which when ignited burns slowly and produces a smoke that inhibits mosquitoes from biting; **mosquito door,** a door designed to exclude mosquitoes from a house; **mosquito-dope** *N. Amer.*, insect repellent; **mosquito hawk** *N. Amer.*, (*a*) the night-hawk, *Chordeiles minor* (earlier and later examples); (*b*) (examples); **mosquito-net** (earlier and later examples); **mosquito room,** a room from which mosquitoes are excluded; **Mosquito State** *U.S.*, a nickname for New Jersey; **mosquito trousers,** trousers designed to protect the legs from mosquitoes; **mosquito wire,** wire mesh used to exclude mosquitoes.

1774 E. Long *Hist. Jamaica* III. 884 In those places where they [*sc.* mosquitoes] are very numerous..the usual guard for the legs is the muskeeto-boot, or a kind of half-trouzer, made of linen, tied above the knee, and reaching to the shoes. **1945** *Tee Emm* (Air Ministry) V. 36 Mosquito-boots, which are issued to airmen..are meant to be worn in the evenings. This is a malaria precaution. **1956** E. Ambler *Night-Comers* i. 1 The mosquito boots and the sweat-stained hats. **1963** *Pyrethrum Post* VII. 22/2 Mosquito coils, as their name implies, are used to prevent adult mosquitoes from biting, particularly during the hours of sleep and are therefore designed to burn for about 8 hours. **1971** *Inside Kenya Today* Mar. 46/2 The prospects for a mosquito coils market [*printed* marker] in the Far East are very promising, and if this market is fully exploited, pyrethrum powder will be a more important product of the pyrethrum industry that it is now. **1972** D. Sale *Love Bite* ii. 31 There are some mosquito coils there, too. Light them at dusk..and you won't be troubled. **1967** P. M. Hubbard *Custom of Country* (1969) vi. 68 A servant who had been sitting in the veranda got up and held open the mosquito door. **1903** S. E. White *Forest* 383 Pack one, or absolute necessities for hard trip. .. Knife; mosquito-dope; compass; match box. **1948** *Chicago Tribune* 11 July 7/1 New mosquito dopes are being tested by fishermen now that the insects are buzzing. **1709** J. Lawson *New Voyage to Carolina* 144 East-India Bats or Musqueto Hawks, are the Bigness of a Cuckoo, and much of the same colour. **1737** J. Brickell *Nat. Hist. N. Carolina* 163 The Muskeetoe-Hawks, are Insects, so called, from their continually hunting after Muskeetoes, and killing and eating them. **1832** J. Pickering *Inquiries of Emigrant* 59 Thousands of long large flies, similar to the English dragon fly, but a little smaller, are flying about the fields; they are called musquito hawks, on account of their killing and living on those insects. **1851** *Southern Planter* (Richmond, Va.) July 195/2 Unlike the.. mosquito hawk of the South [the joint worm] does not make its appearance suddenly. **1866** W. R. King *Sportsman & Naturalist in Canada* 108 The somewhat rare swallow-tail or musquito-hawk,..soaring in pursuit of insects. **1938** G. Cash *I like Brit. Columbia* 187 A mosquito hawk zoomed belatedly overhead. **1967** E. B. Nickerson *Kayaks to Arctic* ix. 77 We learned..that in my father's childhood they [*sc.* dragon-flies] had been called 'mosquito hawks'. **1745** *London Mag.* Nov. 551/2 To scorn Umbrellas and Musketto-Nets, as Jamaican and Carolinean Effeminacies. **1867** M. E. Herbert *Cradle Lands* i. 3 One comfort only was wanting in this hotel, and that was mosquito-nets. **1969** I. Kemp *Brit. G.I. in Vietnam* viii. 160 The unexpected comforts of a camp bed, an air mattress, and a mosquito net. **1974** P. Dickinson *Poison Oracle* iv. 111 He had packed the medicines, clothes, mosquito net, compass. **1949** M. Mead *Male & Female* viii. 171 We asked Tomi..to..stop up the crevices between the mosquito wire and the..floor of our mosquito-room. **1923** *World Almanac* (N.Y.) 422 Nicknames of the States... N.J. 'Jersey Blues', 'Garden', 'New Spain', 'Mosquito'. **1930** in G. E. Shankle *Amer. Nicknames* (1937) 376 We get the scornful title, the *Mosquito State*, because we seem to have our share of these industrious and bloodthirsty insects. **1792** Scott *Let.* 10 Sept. (1932) I. 22 Wading through the mosses upon this errand, accoutred with the long gun, a jacket, mosquito trowsers, and a rough cap. **1828** Mrs. B. Hall *Let.* 27 Apr. in *Aristocratic Journey* (1931) 261 We got her a pair of mosquito trowsers. **1949** Mosquito wire [see **mosquito room*].

c. mosquito boat, (*a*) (see quot. 1914); (*b*) a motor-torpedo boat; **mosquito craft** (examples).

1914 *Dialect Notes* IV. 150 *Mosquito boat*, small river craft carrying light guns. **1940** *Topeka* (Kan.) *State Jrnl.* 29 Apr. 2 (*headline*) Trial run for 'mosquito boat'. **1850** H. Melville *White Jacket* II. iii. 12 All the mosquito craft of Abba Thule, king of the Pelews. **1944** in R. W. Zandvoort et al. *Wartime Eng.* (1957) 158 You always drive a boat; but do not refer to any of them as mosquito craft.

Mosquito, var. *Miskito *a.* and *sb.*

moss, *sb.*[1] Add: **3. b.** (Later examples.)

1853, 1866 [see Rolling stone 1]. **1914** G. B. Shaw *Misalliance* p. lxxxiv, We keep repeating the silly proverb that a rolling stone gathers no moss, as if moss were a desirable parasite. **1936** A. Christie *ABC Murders* xxxiv. 241 You have been the rolling stone—and you have gathered very little moss. You were bitterly jealous of your brother's wealth.

5. d. Ellipt. for **moss green.*

1897 *Sears Roebuck Catal.* 333/1 Crepe Tissue Paper.. in the following colors..Apple, Moss, Grass, Nile and Sea Green. **1923** *Daily Mail* 26 May 1 (Advt.), Superb colours, including: Rose Pink,..Moss, Tomato. **1971** *Vogue* Dec. 148/2 Jersey..colours..rosewood, oak, moss.

e. Hair. *slang.*

1942 in Berrey & Van den Bark *Amer. Thes. Slang* § 121/43. **1966** J. S. Cox *Illustr. Dict. Hairdressing* 99/2 *Moss.* (1) Head hair. Slang. (2) Pubic hair. Vulgarism.

6. a. *moss-land.*

1887 T. Darlington *Folk-Speech S. Cheshire* 264 *Moss-land*, boggy land. **1934** *Geogr. Jrnl.* LXXXIII. 425 The surviving mosslands of the Lancashire plain. **1971** *Daily Tel.* 3 July 9/2 Greater provision for visitors is planned for the Wildfowl Trust's projected reserve at Martin Mere, on the mosslands east of Southport.

7. b. *moss-bearded, -cankered, -dappled, -hung, -mantled, -shadowed* adjs.

1851 H. Melville *Moby Dick* III. ii. 26 Venerable moss-bearded Daniel Boone. **1959** D. Davie *Forests of Lithuania* iv. 37 A moss-bearded oak that bears The weight of full five hundred years. **1904** Kipling *Traffics & Discoveries* 304 The moss-cankered oak and beech. **1945** J. Betjeman *New Bats in Old Belfries* 6 The view from my bedroom of moss-dappled path. **1869** 'Mark Twain' *Innoc. Abr.* 421 Look down upon these moss-hung ruins. **1923** R. Graves *Feather Bed* 11 By falls of scree, moss-mantled slippery rock. **1931** C. Day Lewis *From Feathers to Iron* 19 The virgin spring moss-shadowed near the shore.

d. moss-agate (earlier and later examples); **moss-bag** *Canad.* (see quot. 1865); **moss crêpe** (see quots.); **moss green,** a green colour resembling that of moss; **moss horn** = **mossy horn*; **moss opal,** a variety of opal containing dendritic markings like those of moss-agate; **moss-peat,** peat formed from mosses, esp. those of the genus *Sphagnum.*

1798 G. Mitchell tr. *D. L. G. Karsten's Description Minerals in Leskean Mus.* I. 98 Milk white Moss Agate, traversed by brownish particles; from Ceylon. **1837** J. D. Dana *Syst. Min.* vi. 343 *Dendrachates*..was our moss agate. **1904** L. J. Spencer tr. *M. Bauer's Precious Stones* ii. 507 Moss-agate is characterised by the presence of green enclosures, such as are found in many specimens of rock crystal. These enclosures..have the general effect of a piece of moss; hence the term moss-agate. **1943** R. D. George *Minerals & Rocks* xix. 414 Moss agate is similar to agate, but the coloring is in arborescent or moss-like forms. **1947** J. C. Rich *Materials & Methods of Sculpture* viii. 236 Moss agate is a variety of agate whose decorative appearance militates against its use as a sculptural medium. **1962** R. Webster *Gems* I. x. 178 In England and America the term mocha stone is used synonymously with moss agate, but in European countries the green moss agate alone is known as moss agate while the black and red coloured dendritic agate is termed mocha stone. **1865** Milton & Cheadle *N.W. Passage by Land* vi. 85 The 'moss-bag' or Indian cradle. This is a board with two side flaps of cloth, which lace together up the centre. The child is laid on its back on the board, packed with soft moss, and laced firmly down, with its arms to its side, and only its head at liberty. **1960** J. J. Rowlands *Spindrift* 120 A baby whimpered in its moss bag laced to a backboard. **1963** *Beaver* Summer 37/2 The 15-day-old baby sleeping in a moss bag. **1955** E. Ostick *Draper's Encycl.* iii. 84 Moss crêpe is a dress fabric which relies for its characteristic effect on a special yarn called a moss crêpe yarn. **1966** E. Palmer *Plains of Camdeboo* ii. 20 The people of Pearston district in dark suits and moss crêpe demurely assembling for church on a Sunday. **1884** Moss green [see sense 7 c in Dict.]. **1938** R. Field *All this &*

Heaven Too (1939) xxiii. 302 She..selected her best dress, the moss-green moire with bands of russet. **1972** H. C. RAE *Shooting Gallery* iii. 210 Tight broadcloth pants in moss green. **1944** H. WENTWORTH *Amer. Dial. Dict.* 398/1 *Mosshorn, n.*, old cattle; an old cowboy. **1948** H. L. MENCKEN *Amer. Lang.* Suppl. II. xi. 742 *Mosshorn*, an old steer; also, an old cowboy. **1968** R. F. ADAMS *Western Words* (rev. ed.) 201/1 *Mossy horn*,..also called *moss horn.* **1904** L. J. SPENCER tr. *M. Bauer's Precious Stones* II. 386 Milk-opal sometimes exhibits black arborescent markings, or dendrites so-called, similar to those in certain varieties of chalcedony. Opal of this kind is known as moss-opal. It is cut so as to bring the markings..near the surface. **1966** J. SINKANKAS *Mineralogy* II. 447 If containing dendritic or mossy inclusions, it is called moss opal. **1875** S. F. PECKHAM in *Amer. Cycl.* XIII. 217/2 Moss-peat is oftenest fibrous, and when dried forms elastic masses. **1955** *Times* 21 May 10/6 Bracken..is admirable as a mulch, having all the good qualities of moss-peat, plus a high nutrition value. **1974** *Country Life* 2 May 1076/1 Moss peat can be bought from all suppliers of horticultural sundries, in bags or bales.

moss, *v.* **1.** Delete † and add later example.
1939 G. GREENE *Lawless Roads* iv. 119 Would the Cupid's bow just moss a little more as the flowers dropped?

moss-back. Restrict *U.S.* to senses 1 and 2a in Dict. and add: **2. b.** In *Canad.* and occas. *U.K.* use. (Earlier and later examples.)
1878 C. HALLOCK *Amer. Club List & Sportsman's Gloss.* p. viii, *Mossback*, a settler; a homesteader; a pioneer farmer. (Western.) **1884** *Nor'Wester* (Calgary) 3 June 4/1 The local mossback refers to the recent picking up of stones on Stephen Avenue. **1924** J. BUCHAN *Three Hostages* i. 10, I was becoming such a mossback that I had almost stopped reading the papers. **1935** E. POUND *Let.* 28 Jan. (1971) 266 With De Vechii at Ministry of Education there wd. be more chance of *action* than with some aesthetic mossback, sentimentalizing over Dela Crusca. **1937** J. D. CARR *To wake the Dead* xi. 162 Oh, Chris, you are an old mossback! **1941** J. SMILEY *Hash House Lingo* 38 *Moss back*, conservative eater. **1959** W. A. LEISING *Arctic Wings* 97, I listened to old mossbacks, prospectors, and trappers. **1973** 'TREVANIAN' *Loo Sanction* (1974) 212 The moss-backs of the National Gallery had pulled off quite a coup in securing the Marini Horse for a one-day exhibition.

moss-backed, mossy-backed, *a.* (Earlier and later examples.)
1876 *Congress Rec.* 13 Jan. 411/1 [In the cotton states] those too cowardly to fight..were known as 'mossy-backed rangers' during the war. **1881** *Harper's Mag.* Sept. 640/2 A thorough-bred, mossy-backed mountaineer. **1889** 'MARK TWAIN' *Let.* (1917) II. 520 Still mouthing empty reverence for those moss-backed frauds. **1963** *Economist* 7 Sept. 826/1 Bankers..found themselves looking hopelessly moss-backed. **1975** G. V. HIGGINS *City on Hill* vi. 148 He's mossbacked and close to a fascist, but he's perfectly sincere.

Mössbauer (mö·sbauər). *Physics.* The name of Rudolf L. *Mössbauer* (b. 1929), W. German physicist, used *attrib.* with reference to an effect he reported in 1958, in which gamma rays emitted by an atomic nucleus bound in a crystal exhibit very little Doppler line-broadening (owing to the absence of translational motion of the nucleus) and have almost all the energy released in the transition between nuclear states (owing to the entire mass of the crystal being involved in the recoil of the emitting nucleus, which is consequently very small), so that it is possible to obtain resonance absorption in another similar nucleus with a high degree of precision and hence derive information about the energies and widths of nuclear energy levels; so *Mössbauer effect, spectroscopy*, etc.
1960 *Physical Rev. Lett.* IV. 28 (*heading*) Observations on the Mössbauer effect in Fe^{57}. **1960** *Ibid.* V. 364/2 The Mössbauer spectrum was observed with an Fe absorber, enriched to 75%Fe^{57} and of equivalent thickness 2·2 mg/cm^2. **1962** *Listener* 6 Dec. 964/2 Physicists all over the world scramble to examine the 'Mössbauer effect' to find out by how much gravity makes a clock run slow. **1965** PHILLIPS & WILLIAMS *Inorg. Chem.* I. v. 146 The Mössbauer shift can then be correlated with the degree of ionic bonding. Thus the shift of the γ-ray energy from the value found in metallic Sn increases from SnI_4 through $SnBr_4$, $SnCl_4$, and SnO_2 to SnF_4. **1966** *Jrnl. Physics & Chem. Solids* XXVII. 85 The Mössbauer effect was used to measure the line shifts and electric quadrupole splittings of the 14·4 keV level of Fe^{57} in absorbers at 81°K and 300°K of the marcasite structure compounds FeS_2, $FeSe_2$, $FeTe_2$, and $FeSb_2$. **1970** *Physics Bull.* June 247/1 The Mössbauer nuclear resonance is the narrowest spectral line so far available. **1971** GREENWOOD & GIBB *Mössbauer Spectrosc.* i. 1 The Mössbauer effect has been detected in a total of 88 γ-ray transitions in 72 isotopes of 42 different elements. **1971** *Sci. Amer.* Oct. 86/2 Mössbauer-effect spectroscopy is now used extensively for studying chemical bonds, the architecture of molecules and the distribution of electronic charge around atoms. **1973** G. M. BANCROFT *Mössbauer Spectrosc.* iii. 47 In comparison to many spectroscopic experiments, the basic Mössbauer equipment is rather simple and inexpensive. *Ibid.*, A Mössbauer spectrum consists of a plot of the number of gamma ray photons transmitted through an absorber as a function of the instantaneous relative velocity of the source with respect to an absorber.

Mossi (mǫ·si). Also **Moshi, Mosi.** Pl. **Mossi, Mossis.** The name of a negroid tribe living in Upper Volta in West Africa. Also *attrib.*
1858 H. BARTH *Trav. N. & Cent. Afr.* IV. 551 The strongest among these pagan kingdoms..is that of the Mósi, although the country is split into a number of small principalities..paying only some slight homage to the ruler of the principality of Wóghodogó. **1911** F. W. H. MIGEOD *Lang. W. Afr.* I. i. 38 The powerful nation of the Moshis and other kindred tribes evidently prevented the extension of the Nta in a northerly direction. **1930** C. G. SELIGMAN *Races of Afr.* iii. 63 The Mossi are agriculturalists, with millet as the staple crop. **1959** *Chambers's Encycl.* XIV. 197/2 Upper Volta..was originally created ..in order to stimulate the economic development of the densely peopled Mossi country lying north..of the British Gold Coast. **1964** E. A. NIDA *Toward Sci. Transl.* iii. 54 The Mossis of Haute Volta in West Africa speak of most emotional states in terms of the heart.

mossie[1] (mǫ·si). *S. Afr.* [Afrikaans, f. Du. *mosje* dim. of *mos* sparrow.] The Cape sparrow, *Passer melanurus.*
1884 R. B. SHARPE *Layard's Birds S. Afr.* (rev. ed.) 479 The 'Mossie', like its cousin the English bird, is essentially a 'cit'. **1936** E. L. GILL *First Guide S. Afr. Birds* 21 The cock Mossie, with his black head, white eye-stripe and cinnamon back, is a handsome and unmistakable bird. **1959** *Cape Argus* 22 Aug. 5/6 The mossies in her neighbourhood never seem to stray more than a few blocks away. **1974** *Stand. Encycl. S. Afr.* X. 209/2 The Cape Sparrow (*Passer melanurus*) has the same size, and much the same habits as the European sparrow, but the male has a different and more handsome plumage, with a black head and throat and a white curved spot on the side. Mossies, as they are called locally, are common birds in South Africa, especially on farms, occurring in flocks during the non-breeding season.

mossie[2] (mǫ·si, mǫ·zi). Also **mozzie, mozzy.** Slang abbrev. of MOSQUITO.
1941 BAKER *Dict. Austral. Slang* 47 *Mossie, mozzie*, a mosquito. **1954** R. S. PORTEOUS in *Coast to Coast 1953–4* 117 Blast these mossies. There's more inside this net than out of it. **1964** M. DICKSON *World Elsewhere* v. 182 Sleeping bags, 'mossie' nets and other equipment. **1971** B. W. ALDISS *Soldier Erect* 167 When we were off guard, we kipped on one of the station platforms outside the RTO office, under our mozzy-nets. **1973** *Shooting Times & Country Mag.* 7 July 14/2 If it *has* chosen unwisely, then the newly-hatched mossies rise triumphantly from the surface only to hit their heads on the caterpillars' safety net and fall back into the liquid.

mossite (mǫ·səit). *Min.* [ad. G. *mossit* (W. C. Brögger 1897, in *Skrifter udgivne af Videnskabsselskabet i Christiania: Mat.-nat. Kl.* VII. 4), f. *Moss*, the name of the city in Norway near which it was found: see -ITE[1].] **a.** A mineral, $(Fe,Mn)(Ta,Nb)_2O_6$, similar to tapiolite but containing a high proportion of niobium. **b.** The end member of the series obtained by substituting niobium for tantalum in tapiolite.
1898 *Jrnl. Chem. Soc.* LXXIV. II. 387 The new mineral, mossite, occurs with yttrotantalite and columbite in a pegmatite vein at Berg in the parish of Råde, near Moss, in Norway. **1917** *Mineral. Mag.* XVIII. 120 The relationship which exists between strüverite and ilmenorutile bear to rutile, on the one hand, and to tapiolite and mossite, on the other hand, may be graphically illustrated. **1955** *Amer. Mineralogist* XL. 445 These features lead one to question the existence of mossite and of a complete tetragonal mossite–tapiolite series. **1968** I. KOSTOV *Mineralogy* II. iv. 247 Tapiolite and mossite have a rutile type of structure in which two $[(Ta, Nb)O_6]$ octahedra alternate with one $[FeO_6]$ octahedron along the tetragonal axis.

mosso (mǫ·so), *a.* [It., pa. pple. of *muovere* to move.] Of musical movement: rapid; animated.
1876 STAINER & BARRETT *Dict. Mus. Terms* 297/1 *Mosso* (It.), moved, as *più mosso*, more moved or faster; *meno mosso*, less fast. **1952** H. HUNTER *Gram. Mus.* 87 *Italian terms relating to speed...* Più mosso, Più tosto, Stretto, [etc.]. **1962** *Listener* 26 Apr. 749/3 The intense urgency of the 'Libera me', especially of the *più mosso* middle section with the threatening syncopations of the brass.

mossy, *a.* Add: **5. b.** Extremely conservative or reactionary; old-fashioned, out of date; old. *U.S. slang.*
1904 *Collier's* 20 Feb. 1 Arthur Lynch's release has the approval of all England except a few peculiarly mossy old Tories. **1932** *Amer. Speech* VII. 402 That's a mossy hat he wears. **1942** BERREY & VAN DEN BARK *Amer. Thes. Slang* § 116/6 Old; aged,..*mossy. Ibid.* § 233/12 Old-fashioned, ..*mossy.*
6. **mossy crêpe** = **moss crêpe*; **mossy horn** *U.S.*, an old steer; also, an old cowboy.
1945 M. D. POTTER *Fiber to Fabric* xii. 239 *Mossy crepe*, ..fabric with texture giving fine moss effect. **1885** C. A. SIRINGO *Texas Cow Boy* viii. 75 They were all old mossy horn fellows from seven to twenty-seven years old. **1944** R. F. ADAMS *Western Words* 101/2 *Mossy-horn*, a Texas longhorn steer, six or more years old, whose horns have become wrinkled and scaly... The term sometimes is slangily applied to an old cowman. **1955** FOSTER-HARRIS *Old West* viii. 227 Little wrinkles would begin to grow up from the bases of the horns, and the older the steer got, the more the wrinkles would show, giving rise to the term 'mossy horns', meaning old-timers. **1973** R. D. SYMONS *Where Wagon Led* I. vi. 93 It only takes one ole' mossy-horn to take fright at his own shadder to start the whole lot off.

most, *a.* (*sb.*) and *adv.* Add: **A.** *adj.* **II.** *absol.* (quasi-*sb.*) **4. b.** *slang.* The best, (something that is) extremely good, most exciting; also as quasi-*adv.*
1953 *Time* 17 Aug. 3/1 It's the most! **1954** *Time* 1 Feb. 14/1 Last week the general and even the Pentagon conceded that the bop campaign was the most, to say the least. **1958** *Sunday News* (N.Y.) 11 May 2 Of her husband, she said, 'Adam and I dig each other the most. We have a perfect understanding. It couldn't be better.' **1958** *News Chron.* 22 May 4/5 When a man is found to be attractive—he's the most. **1959** *Punch* 16 Sept. 167/2 It has in fact been voted 'The Sleeve With the Most'..by the editors of the *Beat Disc Review and Pop Chronicle.* **1960** *Guardian* 17 Mar. 4/1 American women get the *most!* **1968** *Listener* 7 Mar. 314/3, I would infinitely prefer to listen to the Kenny Everett programme—'the show that's the most with your tea and toast', as that masterly DJ himself puts it. **1969** H. WAUGH *Young Prey* (1970) 6 'So—you like the ride?'.. 'No kidding, it was the most!'
5. e. *the most of*: the greatest part of, the majority of.
1790 in *Eng. Dial. Dict.* (1903) IV. 170/2. **1843** T. WILSON *Pitman's Pay* 27 The myest of which was left below. **1862** M. D. COLT *Went to Kansas* 192, I..have taken leave of the most of my friends. **1879** STEVENSON *Travels with Donkey* iii. 96 Without doubt, the most of mankind grossly overeat themselves. **1931** H. BELLOC *Hist. Eng.* IV. i. 127 Much of the most of English wealth in 1536 came from tillage. **1963** C. D. SIMAK *They walked like Men* ix. 49 'You say all my neighbors have lost their leases or sold out?' 'The most of them.'
B. *adv.* **4.** For '*Obs.* exc. *dial.*' read 'Now *dial.* and *U.S.*'
1775 in *Essex Inst. Hist. Coll.* (1877) XIII. 198 It is so long since I saw, or heard direct from you that I most forgit you. **1800** *Farmers' Register* (Greensburgh, Pa.) 8 Nov. (Th.), And though he squeez'd me most to death, I could not help it, no, not I. **1803** *Port Folio* (Philad.) III. 97 (Th.), You know how it most makes you blind, in winter, to look on the snow. **1825** J. NEAL *Bro. Jonathan* I. 107 Most off the handle, some o' the tribe I guess. **1883** 'MARK TWAIN' *Life Miss.* iii. 26 Then they both got at it.., swelling round and round each other, and punching their fists most into each other's faces. **1901** MERWIN & WEBSTER *Calumet 'K'* i. 6, I 'most met my death climbing up just now. *a* **1911** D. G. PHILLIPS *Susan Lenox* (1917) II. iv. 87 The street girls..they 'most starve. **1935** in Z. N. Hurston *Mules & Men* (1970) I. i. 26 He moved by jerks, and he had most no tail.
b. With *all, any, every*, etc.
1770 WASHINGTON *Diary* 25 Aug. (1925) I. 395 As the Tassels of most all the Corn..was entirely dry. **1775** J. ANDREWS *Let.* 11 Apr. in *Mass. Hist. Soc. Proc.* (1866) VIII. 403, I think it exceeds most every thing of the kind. **1834** C. A. DAVIS *Lett. J. Downing* 35 Most all these southern folks are good fellows. **1854** J. E. COOKE *Virginia Comedians* I. viii. 50 'Never argues with women!' adds Kate, 'as if he was not arguing with me all the time 'most!' **1855** [in Dict.]. **1865** 'MARK TWAIN' *Celebr. Jumping Frog* (1867) 10 He was lucky,..he most always come out winner. **1894** [see *HELGRAMITE]. **1897** KIPLING *Captains Courageous* i. 5 She's 'most always sick on the ocean. **1904** *Sun* (N.Y.) 16 Aug. 5 Most everybody in the Twelfth Ward was there. **1926** *Publishers' Weekly* 10 July 117 Most any bookbinder will be glad to tell you all about du Pont Fabrikoid. **1956** *Rev. Sci. Instrum.* XXVII. 961/2 If $K > 1$, which is most always the case, then [etc.]. **1964** W. B. HUIE *Hiroshima Pilot* ii. 15 By 1923 most every surviving Confederate veteran had 'been with Pickett'. **1968** *Wall Street Jrnl.* 28 Feb. 16/1 In most any organization, the man who succeeds a reformer faces the task of consolidating the reforms while smoothing feathers the reformer has ruffled. **1968** *Amer. N. & Q.* Mar. 108/1 A book which touches most all of the high spots for the jet set.

mostest (mōᵘ·stėst), *dial.* and *joc.* var. MOST *a.* (*sb.*) and *adv.* Esp. *the mostest*, the greatest amount or degree (of something).
Regarded by many users as a double or strengthened superlative.
1885 *Indianapolis Jrnl.* 15 Nov. 10/4 We set around the kitchen fire an' has the mostest fun. **1887** PARISH & SHAW *Dict. Kentish Dial.* 104 *Mostest*, farthest; greatest distance. 'The mostest that he's bin from home is 'bout eighteen miles.' **1892** E. TERRY *Let.* 4 July in *Ellen Terry & Bernard Shaw* (1931) 9 It's mostest kind to write to me so about my young friend. **1905** *Memphis* (Tenn.) *Commercial Appeal* 14 May II. 4/6 It is one of the favorite arguments of his detractors that General Nathan Bedford Forrest, the noted Confederate cavalry leader, was an illiterate man... One [story]..gives Gen. Forrest's answer to the question, 'How do you manage to win your battles?' 'Git thar fust with the mostest men,' is the reputed reply. **1909** M. DIVER *Candles in Wind* XXXV. 360 'I'm her friend, Paul—just as much as you are...' 'No, I'm the mostest. She said so.' **1935** *Word Study* Oct. 2/2 One of their favorite games was called 'The Ten Mostest'. Each player would choose 30 words: 10 that he or she considered the most beautiful words, 10 funniest words, and 10 most descriptive words. **1940** C. BOOTHE *Europe in Spring* vii. 172 Norway of all countries was the kind of country which, if you 'got there fust with mostest men', you couldn't be got out of in a day or a year, perhaps ever. **1949** O. NASH *Versus* 68 K is for Keeler..The fustest and mostest To hit where they ain't. **1958** *Daily Herald* 25 Mar. 5/7 Here's the hostess with the mostest... Her guests all agreed Sophia was pretty good..well, pretty, anyway. **1959** *Times* 14 Sept. 3/5 A great ambition to be there firstest with the mostest. **1960** *Time & Tide* 24 Dec. 1599/1 Eddie Byrnes..he's the mostest act on scope. **1971** *Engineering* Apr. 57 But we make the mostest. **1973** A. HUNTER *Gently French* vii. 64, I reckon you admire the mostest in anything.

most-favoured-nation: see Favoured *ppl. a.*[1] in Dict. and Suppl.

mot, var. Motte.

mot[4], mott. = Mort *sb.*[4]

1773 in Partridge *Dict. Underworld* (1949) 451/1 The first time I saw the flaming mot, Was at the sign of the Porter Pot. *a* **1790** H. J. Potter *New Dict. Cant & Flash* (1795) 42 *Morts*, or *motts*, lewd women, whores, shoplifters, &c. **1796, 1812** [see Mort *sb.*[4] b]. **1821** P. Egan *Real Life in London* I. xii. 223 The Hon. Tom Dashall.. was in close conversation with his *mott*. **1837, 1851** [see Mort *sb.*[4] a]. **1846** *Swell's Night Guide* 60, I don't think as how he ever doss'd with a mott or could fake a shiver if he had it for nix. **1866** E. Sellon *Let.* 4 Mar. in 'Pisanus Fraxi' *Index Librorum Prohibitorum* (1877) 394, I! who had expected some swell mot or other, soon found myself seated beside the most beautiful young lady I ever beheld. **1922** Joyce *Ulysses* 247 He saw the image of Marie Kendall, charming soubrette... One of them mots that do be in the packets of fags. **1969** J. Blackburn *Bury him Darkly* 10 'Look at them two mots, Fergus.' Dan pointed at two mini-skirted girls.

mota, var. *mootah, mooter.

‖ **motard** (motār). [Fr.] A French motor-cycle policeman.

1963 'B. Abro' *July 14 Assassination* vi. 43 Two motards were by the door... They..kicked their machines into life. **1966** 'D. Rutherford' *Black Leather Murders* xi. 223 They were stopped by a motor-cycle patrolman... The *motard* raised a white gloved hand to his equally white helmet in salute. **1972** D. Lees *Zodiac* 136 Two blue-shirted, crash-helmeted *motards* sitting on their bikes.

‖ **mot d'ordre** (modǫrdr). [Fr. (Mot[2]), lit. 'word of command'.] A political slogan or watchword; an expression of policy; an oral directive or plan.

1855 *Newsp. & Gen. Reader's Compan.* I. § 159 'A *mot d'ordre* was given by the Legitimist leaders of the fusion'; that is to say, A watchword, &c. **1878** L. W. M. Lockhart *Mine is Thine* I. vii. 144 Another kind of success was to be procured by occasional fits of recalcitrancy against the *mots d'ordre* of the party. **1884** E. W. Hamilton *Diary* 18 Nov. (1972) II. 735 The Tory Party held their meeting at the Carlton this morning; and *Pax* was the *mot d'ordre*, much to the discomfiture of the hot-headed ones. **1905** B'ness Orczy *Scarlet Pimpernel* xii. 119 Evidently expecting to meet their chief—and perhaps to get a fresh *mot d'ordre* from him. **1930** *Observer* 13 Apr. 17/5 The official *mot d'ordre* is that Mr. Gandhi's salt campaign must be treated with a sense of humour. **1947** *Ann. Reg. 1946* 217 The sustained Soviet offensive..against Great Britain and the United States had the appearance of conformity with a *mot d'ordre*.

mote, *sb.*[1] **3. b.** Add to def.: or in cotton.

1842 in J. S. Bassett *Southern Plantation Overseer* (1925) 166 The gin dos not doo good work it draws too many motes through. **1902** W. Hannan *Textile Fibres* 102 The fragmental portions of cotton seeds carry a tuft of attached fibres on the outer membrane; this is termed a bearded *mote*, and is regarded as an imperfection or impurity.

5. *mote-laden, -like* adjs.; **mote-knife,** a knife in a carding machine for removing motes from textile fibres.

1896 W. S. Taggart *Cotton Spinning* I. 132 The cotton is no sooner taken from the feed than it is carried past one or two bars C and D with sharp edges, known as mote knives. **1951** S. Spender *World within World* iii. 123 The characters of his novels radiate round him under a glowing cloud of dirty varnish, not unlike the mote-laden lighting of Fräulein Thurau's apartment. **1956** H. Gold *Man who was not with It* (1965) xii. 102 The mote-laden rays striking guide-rope and stand. *a* **1889** G. M. Hopkins *Poems* (1967) 194 Swayed about Mote-like in thy mighty glow. **1929** W. Faulkner *Sartoris* III. 168 It oozed chaff and a sifting dust, motelike in the sun.

mote, *sb.*[2] Add: **1.** (Later examples.)

1884 G. T. Clark *Mediæval Military Archit. in England* I. ii. 27 Many of these mounds under the name of motes (motæ) retained their timber defences to the twelfth and thirteenth centuries. **1898** D. Christison *Early Fortifications Scotl.* I. i. 3 The motes of which I have to speak are..fortresses..and consist essentially of conical flat-topped mounds, which were defended by palisades. **1919** *Proc. Soc. Antiquaries Scotl.* LIII. 43 Alexander Elphinstone in 1507 took up his residence upon the old deserted Norman mote.

3. *Comb.*, as **mote-castle** = *motte-castle* (*Motte *sb.*[2] 2).

1919 *Proc. Soc. Antiquaries Scotl.* LIII. 42 Such a fortress is well represented in the mote-castles of Dinan, Hastings and Rennes, in the Bayeux tapestry.

motel (mō^u^te·l). [f. Mot(or *sb.* and *a.* + Hot)el *sb.*] A hotel catering primarily for motorists, *spec.* one comprising self-contained accommodation with adjacent parking space. Also *attrib.* and *Comb.*

1925 *Hotel Monthly* Mar. 37/2 The Milestone Interstate Corporation..proposes to build and operate a chain of motor hotels between San Diego and Seattle, the hotels to have the name 'Motel'. **1931** *Sociology & Social Research* XV. 372 The new kind of cottage hotel (e.g., 'Motel'), luxuriously furnished and served like any other hotel, but placed directly on the highway. **1947** A. Huxley *Let.* 14 Nov. (1969) 575 From the Blue Bird Motel in Little Rock, Ark, where we have been held up by torrential rains, I take this opportunity of telling you how grateful we all are. **1950** *Archit. Rev.* CVIII. 394 The motel is a new kind of hotel; like an hotel it has an attached restaurant and various services that earlier and more primitive sorts of roadside hostelries omit. **1955** *Times* 28 June 5/7 Although the 'motel' is still regarded as a novelty in the United Kingdom, an establishment of that kind was opened (and is still operating) at Boroughbridge..some time before the war. **1958** *Times* 24 Nov. (Canada Suppl.) p. viii/6 He has almost no contact with..the motel employees. *Ibid.* p. viii/7 The motel business is a field for individual..enterprise. **1962** *Listener* 25 Oct. 692/3 The vast motel-resort..now in the process of erection outside Seoul. **1970** *Homes & Gardens* June 150/1 In a motel the car is meant to be beside your room, but is not invariably. **1970** *New Yorker* 10 Oct. 141/1 A motelkeeper..was serving our breakfast. **1974** *Washington Post* 11 May E23/1 The oldest motel in America is alive and well..in San Luis Obispo, Calif. *Ibid.*, The establishment..opened Dec. 12, 1925, as the Motel Inn.

Hence **mote·l** *v. intr.*, to stay at a motel; **mote·l,land** (*nonce-wd.*), the realm of motels; **mote·lier,** the owner of a motel; **mote·lled** *a.*, provided with motels.

1959 *Guardian* 6 Nov. 8/3 He, the over-fastidious European, is dragged by her through the appalling delights of motelland. **1959** S. H. Courtier *Death in Dream Time* i. 5 A *motelier's* aspirations. **1963** *Economist* 17 Aug. 595/1 The conventional hotel trade from whose custom, as American moteliers..have found out, the growth must be drawn. **1965** *Punch* 1 Dec. 798/1, I drove through twenty-seven states with a freedom and foot-loose mobility unknown in a nation so thinly motelled as Britain. **1968** G. De Fraga *Murder at Cookout* xii. 56 They're motelling in Canberra for a night or two. **1972** *Sydney Morning Herald* 26 Aug. 37/3 Tasmanian motelier Four Seasons Motels Ltd increased profit by 14 per cent.

moteless, *a.* **2.** (Further examples.)

1876 *City-Road Mag.* 141/1 When the air was rendered moteless. **1882** *American* 19 Aug. 298/2 In this moteless air were placed test-tubes containing various organic infusions. **1932** [see *beam-blindness].

moth, *sb.*[1] Add: **1. f.** A prostitute. *slang.*

1896 in Farmer & Henley *Slang* IV. 360/1. **1935** A. J. Pollock *Underworld Speaks* 78/1 *Moth*, a female of easy virtue.

3. *moth-face, -flit, -hour, -light, -repellant, -trap*; also *moth-coloured, -hung, -resistant, -soft, -white* adjs.; *moth-like* adj. and adv. (further examples); *moth-hunting* vbl. sb.; **moth-borer,** the larval forms of various moths which damage plants by boring into stems, etc., esp. the sugar-cane borer, *Diatræa saccharalis*; **moth-miller,** substitute for def.: one of several moths with white-flecked, powdery-looking wings (earlier example); **moth spot** = *moth patch.*

1900 *Nature* 21 June 182/2 A considerable number of the eggs of the moth borer (which are laid in patches on the leaves of the sugar-cane) are attacked by parasites. **1931** *Discovery* Sept. 300/1 The attacks of the giant moth-borer..and many other pests began in comparatively recent times [in the West Indies]. **1957** *Encycl. Brit.* XXI. 525/2 The giant moth borer (*Castnia licoides*) is particularly destructive in Trinidad and the Guianas. **1974** *Encycl. Brit. Macropædia* XVII. 771/1 The moth borer, *Diatraea saccharalis*, which is widely distributed throughout cane-growing areas, is capable of causing extensive damage when out of control. **1931** V. Woolf *Waves* 254 Jinny's yellow scarf is moth-coloured in this light. *a* **1963** S. Plath *Crossing Water* (1971) 38 The moth-face of her husband, moonwhite and ill, Circles her. **1921** W. de la Mare *Veil* 68 Soundless the moth-flit, crisp the death-watch tick. **1890** W. B. Yeats *Countess Kathleen* (1892) 108 At the moth-hour of eve. **1909** E. Pound *Personae* 23 The moth-hour of our day is upon us Holding the dawn. **1933** W. de la Mare *Fleeting* 161 The secret scent of the moth-hung flower. **1910** —— *Three Mulla-Mulgars* 166 Andy's eyes was never made for moth-hunting. **1930** E. Blunden *Poems* 326 The fete grows late and dark, The King in moth-light traverses the park. **1934** T. S. Eliot *Rock* ii. 84 Moon light and star light, owl and moth light. **1804–8** Blake *Milton* I. xi, in *Compl. Writings* (1972) 492 Her moth-like elegance shone over the Assembly. **1885** W. B. Yeats in *Dublin Univ. Rev.* July 136/1 Gently shook their moth-like wings. **1904** W. H. Hudson *Green Mansions* xiii. 174 She, too, moth-like, had vanished from my side. **1934** S. Spender *Poems* (ed. 2) 36 The mothlike lips at dusk. **1865** *Harper's Weekly* 25 Nov. 747/3 If there is *one* little hole in your linen or paper, some industrious moth-miller is pretty sure to discover it. **1942** G. G. Denny *Fabrics* (ed. 5) II. 119 Dry cleaners and laundries may apply moth-repellent treatment. **1958** S. Hyland *Who goes Hang?* xli. 200 Paradichlorbenzene was sold for the first time in the shops as moth repellant in 1932. **1964** N. G. Clark *Mod. Organic Chem.* xix. 390 It [*sc.* naphthalene] has been employed in the manufacture of fire-lighters, and as a moth-repellent and insecticide. **1970** *Which?* Sept. 265/2 The carpet is moth-resistant. **1876** G. M. Hopkins *Wreck of Deutschland* xxvi, in *Poems* (1967) 60 Or night, still higher, With belled fire and the moth-soft Milky Way. **1958** L. Durrell *Balthazar* i. 17 Brightly lit up in the moth-soft darkness of the Aegean night. **1922** F. Courtenay *Physical Beauty* 26 The so-called 'moth spots', brown spots or patches which appear after middle life, are due to this tan pigment. **1890** *Cent. Dict.*, Moth-trap. **1928** Metcalf & Flint *Destructive & Useful Insects* ix. 263 Mechanical devices, such as..fly traps, moth traps, maggot traps,..have been used successfully for catching and killing a variety of insects. **1970** *Daily Tel.* 19 Oct. 11/8 A moth new to Britain, Plusia accentifera, has been caught in Mr Terry Dillon's moth-trap at Halsted. **1920** D. H. Lawrence *Lost Girl* xi. 275 Irises rearing purple and moth-white.

moth, *sb.*[2] [f. Hind. *moth* moth bean.] In full, *moth bean.* An Indian bean, *Phaseolus aconitifolius*, of the family Leguminosæ, cultivated in tropical and sub-tropical countries as food for both man and livestock.

[**1832** W. Roxburgh et al. *Flora Indica* III. 299 *P*[*haseolus*] *aconitifolius*... *Hind.* Moot. This plant I have reared from seed sent me by Dr. Hunter from the province of Oude where it is much cultivated..and used for feeding cattle.] **1840** *Penny Cycl.* XVIII. 58/1 *P*[*haseolus*] *aconitifolius*, Moth of the natives, is cultivated in the north-western provinces, and used for feeding cattle. **1884** tr. *A. de Candolle's Origin of Cultivated Plants* v. 345 Moth, or Aconite-leaved Kidney Bean... An annual species grown in India as fodder, and of which the seeds are eatable, though but little valued. The Hindustani name is *mout*, among the Sikhs *moth*. **1886** A. H. Church *Food-Grains of India* 152 The moth-bean..is found from the Himálaya to Ceylon... It is not esteemed as a food for man, for although it is rich in nutrients, it is generally thought to possess heating properties. **1923** H. C. Thompson *Veg. Crops* xxiv. 334 The term 'bean' as used in the United States includes..several species of oriental beans, including adsuki,..moth and rice beans belonging to the genus Phaseolus. **1972** G. A. C. Herklots *Vegetables in South-east Asia* 244 (*heading*) Moth bean... A slender annual with decumbent branches growing to 18 inches or a foot in length.

mo·thball, *sb.* Also **moth ball, moth-ball.** [Ball *sb.*[1]] **1.** A ball of naphthalene (sometimes mixed with other substances) used among stored fabrics to repel moths. Also *fig.*

1906 'O. Henry' in *Munsey's Mag.* Dec. 288/1 Me and Solly..prepared to shake off our moth-balls and wing our way against the arc-lights of the joyous and tuneful East. **1911** G. S. Porter *Harvester* xiii. 282 Wouldn't she like me to wear her things better than to have them lying in moth balls? **1916** M. Lees-Dods *Ideal Home* x. 161 When furs are kept by a lady in her own house, a plentiful supply of pieces of camphor, or moth-ball, should be wrapped in tissue paper and distributed amongst the folds. **1932** *Conc. Househ. Encycl.* 808 The round balls sold as moth balls consist of naphthalene, a product of the distillation of coal tar. **1958** S. Hyland *Who goes Hang?* xli. 199 Synthetic camphor wasn't used for moth-balls until 1914! **1964** *Horlicks Home Bk.* 178 In the past naphthalene (usually in the shape of moth balls) was used. **1974** 'J. Melville' *Nun's Castle* i. 10 She had conceived the idea of staging afresh the forgotten Victorian tournament.. wearing the original clothes, most of which were still packed away in mothballs.

2. orig. *U.S.* Used *attrib.* to designate armaments or installations stored away, held in reserve, or disused. Similarly *in mothballs*, laid up, put out of use or action for a long time.

1946 *Amer. N. & Q.* Apr. 7/2 '*Mothball fleet*': inactive U.S. Navy ships to be preserved for long periods by newly-developed techniques. **1946** *Newsweek* 13 May 22/2 The Navy plans to reduce yard personnel to peacetime proportions by early fall. The moth-ball laying-up program will be complete by that time. **1947** *N.Y. Times* 26 Jan. E. 6/5 The moth ball fleet consists of United States warships now undergoing preservative treatment which will enable them to be put back in use rapidly if needed. **1948** *Sun* (Baltimore) 16 Jan. 1/1 The 45,000-ton New Jersey and Wisconsin had been put in 'moth-balls' January 1. **1950** *Hansard Commons* 22 Mar. 2079 We have a 'moth-ball fleet', as it is somewhat vulgarly termed in some countries, reasonably widely dispersed.. round the United Kingdom. **1958** *Oxford Mail* 12 Aug. 1/2 The United States is to sell for cash 47 liberty ships kept in 'moth balls' since the last war. **1967** *Boston Sunday Herald* 30 Apr. I. 7/1 A..port improvement paid for by the MPA has remained in mothballs.., because no container ships have been scheduled to or from Boston. **1970** *Globe & Mail* (Toronto) 26 Sept. 6/3 Seventy-four of these fighter-bombers are going directly into mothballs as they roll off the production line at Canadair Ltd. **1972** *Guardian* 14 Jan. 1/5 Orange dust found in crater Shorty could mean..that Apollo hardware put in mothballs..could be brought out for another final journey. **1974** *Evening Standard* 15 July 11/2 (*heading*) Air fleets may be put in moth-balls.

3. *transf.* and *fig.*

1943 Baker *Dict. Austral. Slang* (ed. 3) 51 *Moth balls*, tracer bullets. **1945** L. Shelly *Jive Talk Dict.* 29 *Moth ball*, an aggravating person. **1951** *Football Record* (Melbourne) 8 Sept. 5 And now for eight teams it's mothballs until 1952. **1966** *Listener* 28 Apr. 629/1 The work..was certainly interesting to hear even if it now has to be put back in moth balls. **1971** M. Tak *Truck Talk* 109 *Mothballs*, balls of ether used by truckers to start cold diesel engines. **1974** *Guardian* 31 Jan. 1/5 The distinguished BBC cheerfully took the most improbable creations [*sc.* films] out of mothballs.

mo·thball, *v.* [f. prec.] *trans.* To place in mothballs, in the senses of the sb. Hence **mo·thballed** *ppl. a.*

1943 R. Malkin *Marriage, Morals & War* xi. 159 His civvies, all dusted off, were mothballed, and shipped back home. **1949** *Jane's Fighting Ships 1949–50* 357 *Princeton, Tarawa* and *Antietam* are also being 'mothballed'. **1957** P. Frank *Seven Days to Never* ii. 80 We've got two thousand Fifty-Twos and Forty-Sevens mothballed, lined up on every desert in Arizona. **1959** *Times* 18 May 5/3 The best service a retired general could perform 'is to turn in his tongue along with his suit and mothball his opinions'. **1959** *Time* (Atlantic ed.) 24 Aug. 52/3 Both plants..will have to be mothballed unless they can be

adapted to produce other chemicals. **1965** *New Scientist* 2 Dec. 642/1 The capability now coming on stream cannot be mothballed. We must use it or see its value erode. **1966** *Aviation Week & Space Technology* 5 Dec. 22/3 Essential consideration to the proposal is that the separately orbited satellite modules could be mothballed in space—fully equipped with all experiments, however—until ready for use. **1973** *Wall St. Jrnl.* 28 Nov. 1/2 Mobil Oil plans to 'mothball' its aging East Chicago, Ind., petroleum refinery. **1974** *Evening Standard* 15 July 11/2 There is no doubt that the Trident One may be mothballed.

mothed, *ppl. a.* (Later example.)

1930 W. DE LA MARE *Desert Islands* 39 Stuffed, glass-eyed, a little mothed and dusty.

mother, *sb.*[1] Add: **1. a.** Also used colloquially by a husband addressing or referring to his wife.

1855 DICKENS *Dorrit* (1857) I. ii. 13 Mother (my usual name for Mrs. Meagles) began to cry so, that it was necessary to take her out. 'What's the matter, Mother?' said I..'you are frightening Pet.'..'Yes, I know that, Father,' says Mother. **1898** J. D. BRAYSHAW *Slum Silhouettes* 156 'Sit yer down, mother,' said Joe, taking his seat at the head of the table. **1932** A. CHRISTIE *Peril at End House* v. 68 Mother and I..feel it's only neighbourly to do what we can. **1970** P. CARLON *Souvenir* ii. 35 Don't you *loathe* the way old folks call each other Mother and Dad?

g. (*just*) *like mother makes* (or *used to make*) (*it*): having the qualities of home cooking; exactly to one's taste; also *fig.*

1919 WODEHOUSE *Damsel in Distress* i. 18 There's a new musical comedy at the Regal. Opened last night, and seems to be just like mother makes. **1927** W. E. COLLINSON *Contemp. Eng.* 52 The notice outside some eating-houses, beef-steak pie like mother makes it! **1963** WODEHOUSE *Stiff Upper Lip, Jeeves* v. 39 Its façade, its spreading grounds..and what not were all just like Mother makes. **1975** D. CLARK *Premedicated Murder* iv. 68 Just like my old mother used to make. A bit of candied peel in a bun can't be beat.

h. Used as an exclamation of surprise, dismay, etc.; freq. *my mother!*

1869 'MARK TWAIN' *Innoc. Abr.* 52 Twenty-five cigars, at 100 reis, 2500 reis! Oh, my sainted mother! **1909** *Sat. Even. Post* 22 May 6/3 'Gee, what a peach of an idea!' 'Oh, mother!' **1959** N. MAILER *Advts. for Myself* (1961) 93 He roared with laughter now. 'Oh, my mother.' **1972** C. ACHEBE *Girls at War* 107 'Plane!' screamed his boy from the kitchen. 'My mother!' screamed Gladys.

i. *mothers and fathers*: a game in which children act out the roles of mother and father.

1903 G. R. SIMS *Living London* XXXIII. 271/1 Sometimes..they [*sc.* the boys] will join the girls in a mimic domestic drama of 'Mothers and Fathers'. **1969** [see *INFANT-SCHOOL]. **1972** J. WILSON *Hide & Seek* vii. 130 Shall we play mothers and fathers with our dolls?

j. Ellipt. for **mother-fucker. U.S. slang.*

[**1948** MANONE & VANDERVOORT *Trumpet on Wing* 70 'I'll be a motheree if I'll wear any damn bedpan intern's suit,' I screamed.] **1955** S. WHITMORE *Solo* iii. 42 Jaeger said..'He's..so weak now, he can't blow note one.' 'Hell, this mother never could,' Alfred laughed. **1959** N. MAILER *Advts. for Myself* (1961) 358 Old K, he's nothing but a mother. **1967** *Melody Maker* 14 Jan. 8 *Mother*, term of abuse. As in 'You're a mother, baby!' **1972** *Sunday Times* 7 May 10/6 'Man we must just get out of here before those mothers get us all..,' he shouted at me. **1973** *New Yorker* 17 Feb. 62/2 Out the parachute, out the radio, change the c.g., and the mother will go. **1975** *N.Y. Times* 8 Sept. 33/2 'You mothers! I ain't been out five minutes and I just got *outta* the pen this morning!' Her name is Judy, and although she is white, she talks black jive.

2. d. *spec.* in *Mother Russia.*

1966 J. BINGHAM *Double Agent* v. 71, I love Russia... Great Mother Russia. **1972** P. RUELL *Red Christmas* xv. 153 Came as quite a shock to them when they realised we weren't doing it all for Mother Russia. **1973** D. BAGLEY *Tightrope Men* xxiv. 164 'See that tower over there?'..'A Russian observation tower. That's Mother Russia.'

3. e. Colloq. phr. *to be mother*: to serve out portions of food or drink; *spec.* to pour out tea.

[**1926** G. B. SHAW *Glimpse of Reality* in *Translations & Tomfooleries* 184 Let us get to work at the supper. You shall be the mother of the family and give us our portions, Giulietta.] **1958** 'J. BROGAN' *Cummings Report* ii. 17 We'll go and have tea, and you be Mother. **1967** J. PORTER *Dover & Unkindest Cut* iv. 41 MacGregor, hearing the tea cups rattling outside..opened the door again. 'Shall I be mother, sir?' **1974** J. MITCHELL *Death & Bright Water* xx. 243 'Shall I be mother?' Callan nodded, and Blythe's strong fingers popped the cork, the champagne foamed into the glasses.

f. The female owner of a pet, esp. of a dog. *colloq.*

1924 GALSWORTHY *White Monkey* I. vi. 39 Ting was.. trying to climb a railing whereon was..a black cat.. 'Give him to me, Ellen. Come with Mother, darling!' **1940** N. MITFORD *Pigeon Pie* ix. 139 Many mothers of dogs had fetched their little ones home.

4. b. *Mother Bunch* [f. the name of a noted ale-wife of late Elizabethan times]: (*a*) *Obs. slang*, water; (*b*) a stout or untidy old woman; *Mother Hubbard* (further examples); also, a kind of loose-fitting garment (chiefly *U.S.*).

1600 DEKKER *Shoemaker's Holiday* sig. H2ᵛ Am I sure that Paules steeple is a handful higher than London stone? or that the pissing conduit leakes nothing but pure mother Bunch? **1847** C. BRONTË *Jane Eyre* II. iii. 81 You talked of going..to visit the gipsy camp;.. one of the old Mother Bunches is in the servants' hall at this moment. **1861** G. J. WHYTE-MELVILLE *Market Harborough* viii. 94, I *have* seen mammas whom the fairest of Eve's daughters might be proud to resemble; but it is sometimes hard upon the young Phœbe to have..at her side the shapeless Mother Bunch, into the *fac-simile* of which she must eventually grow. **1878** F. M. A. ROE *Army Lett. from Officer's Wife* (1909) 186, I made a Mother Hubbard apron of white paper-cambric. **1882** *Wide Awake* (Boston, Mass.) Jan. 18/2 A little girl in a sort of Mother Hubbard cap..is starting off on a journey. **1884** *Nat. Police Gaz.* (U.S.) 30 Aug. 12/3 Mattoon's Chief of Police issued an order that any woman appearing on the streets wearing a Mother Hubbard dress would be arrested and lodged in jail. **1911** *Daily Colonist* (Victoria, B.C.) 19 Apr. 24/4 Overall Aprons, of navy print with white dots, made in Mother Hubbard style. **1919** W. S. MAUGHAM *Moon & Sixpence* xlix. 212 Tiaré Johnson..was dressed usually in a pink Mother Hubbard. **1939** J. STEINBECK *Grapes of Wrath* viii. 99 Ma..wore a loose Mother Hubbard of grey cloth... The dress came down to her ankles. **1943** H. W. KRIEGER *Island Peoples of Western Pacific* 40 The native dress of the women [of the Gilbert Islands], a grass skirt extending from the waist to the knee, has been for the most part replaced by the 'Mother Hubbard', which is made of imported cotton print cloth. **1964** *Guardian* 28 Dec. 6/4 She no more looks like a Mother Bunch than sounds like one.. a fairly plump but elegant, well-dressed woman. **1966** 'R. STANDISH' *Widow Hack* viii. 87, I can persuade you to swim wearing a Mother Hubbard over your swimsuit. Then I'll be able to concentrate.

II. 10*. A disc with grooves that is made from the plating of an electrotyped master matrix and is used to make a stamper for gramophone records.

1918 H. SEYMOUR *Reproduction of Sound* 182 The obverse impressions of the original matrix are called 'mothers' in the trade, in view of their office in reproducing matrices from the 'master'. **1935** H. C. BRYSON *Gramophone Record* vi. 134 The mother, usually about ·03 inch thick, is then stripped from the master by inserting a blunt knife carefully between them and prising them apart. **1952** GODFREY & AMOS *Sound Recording & Reproduction* v. 139 A second negative copy known as the 'stamper' or 'working matrix' is obtained from the mother. **1968** *Jazz Monthly* Feb. 4/1 John Steiner..owns the rights to what remains of the Paramount company, including numerous masters and mothers, so it is likely that the actual recording quality will be a great deal better than that on most past Paramount-derived reissues.

13. c. *spec.* **mother-house,** the founding house of a religious order.

1661 *Manifest publisht to their Brethren by General Chapter of Catholick English Clergy* 3 Dr. Leyburn does calumniate us, as being Enemies to our Mother-house, the Colledge of Doway. *a* **1773** A. BUTLER *Lives Saints* (1779) III. 243 When in 1504 the abbey of Mount Cassino joined this Congregation, it took the name of this mother-house. **1840** [see *branch house* s.v. *BRANCH *sb.* 13]. **1932** C. P. CURRAN in F. J. Sheed *Irish Way* 269 In this spirit she worked for ten years in the Mother-house and novitiate. **1956** K. HUME *Nun's Story* i. 12 The Order was established at the end of the eighteenth century. How many postulants had passed through this mother house could never be guessed.

14. a. *mother-instinct, -sentiment*; *mother-centred, -dominated* adjs.

1956 FIRTH & DJAMOUR in R. Firth *Two Studies of Kinship in London* ii. 41 Some United States sociologists ..have suggested the term 'mother-centred families' for households in which the mother has the dominant role. **1965** *Observer* 4 Apr. 26/4 Pirandello..was a mother-centred man. **1963** *Times* 23 Apr. 16/4 The mother-dominated hero. **1881** 'MARK TWAIN' *Prince & Pauper* 114 Her sharp mother-instinct seemed to detect it. **1920** T. P. NUNN *Education* xi. 131 A thorough-going misogynist could make out a case for applying the adjectives 'mechanical', 'blind', 'unintelligent', even to human mother-instinct. **1920** Mother-sentiment [see *FATHER *sb.* 11 b].

15. a. mother's blessing (see quot. 1861); **mother's boy,** a boy or man who resembles or is dominated by, or excessively attached to, his mother; a sissy; **mother's darling** = **mother's boy*; **Mother's** (or **Mothers'**) **Day** orig. *U.S.*, a day on which mothers are particularly honoured: in the U.S., the second Sunday in May; in Britain = *Mothering Sunday*; also *attrib.*; **mother's help,** a person who helps a mother, mainly by looking after children; **mother's milk** (see MILK *sb.* 1 c in Dict. and Suppl.); **mother's pet** = PET *sb.*[1] 2 a; also, the youngest child of a family; **mother's ruin** *slang*, gin (cf. RUIN *sb.* 10); **Mothers' Union,** an organization for mothers to meet together regularly.

1861 MAYHEW *London Labour* (1862) Extra vol. 245/2 My husband..can't do nothink but give the babies a dose of 'Mother's Blessing' (that's laudanum, sir, or some sich stuff) to sleep 'em when they's squally. **1880** F. STEVENSON *Let.* July in J. Pope-Hennessy *R. L. Stevenson* (1974) vii. 142 Louis is, as I know, a mother's boy..and I am sure he looks like you. **1924** D. H. LAWRENCE *Phoenix II* (1968) 619 Oh, women, beware the mother's boy! **1945** 'L. LEWIS' *Birthday Murder* (1951) ii. 26 Stan's happy as he is being supported by his mother. He's a mother's boy. **1973** W. J. BURLEY *Death in Salubrious Place* ii. 42 Mother's boy—that's his trouble, but it takes all sorts. **1857** LYTTON *What will he do with It?* (1859) I. i. 7 He looked like a mother's darling—perhaps he was one. **1922** JOYCE *Ulysses* 33 That knockkneed mother's darling. **1936** 'J. TEY' *Shilling for Candles* iv. 41 Mother's darlings had those eyes; so, sometimes, had womanizers. **1908** *Congr. Rec.* 9 May 5971/1 *Resolved*, That Sunday, May 10, 1908, be recognized as Mothers' Day. **1926** A. HUXLEY *Jesting Pilate* IV. 264 In the First Methodist Church..they were going to distribute 'Mother's Day Flowers to all Worshippers'. (On Mother's Day you must wear a red carnation if your mother is alive, a white one if she is dead.) **1958** *Listener* 27 Nov. 874/1 As uniquely and inimitably American as John Foster Dulles or Mothers' Day. **1959** I. & P. OPIE *Lore & Lang. Schoolch.* xii. 242 In 1956 the majority of High Street shops [in Britain] were displaying 'Mother's Day' gifts in their windows. **1962** *Listener* 12 Apr. 628/1 Last Mother's Day—a retail selling device imported from the United States—the flower-shops were as busy as ice-cream vans during a heat wave. **1881** *Instr. Census Clerks* (1885) 30 Mother's Help. **1908** A. S. M. HUTCHINSON *Once aboard Lugger* I. vii. 41 She is not exactly my friend; she is my—my employer. I'm a mother's-help. **1961** *Evening Standard* 14 July 25/5 (Advt.), A Mother's Help..for happy family. **1824** J. MACTAGGART *Scottish Gallovidian Encycl.* 348 *Mithers-pet*, the youngest child of a family; the mother's greatest favourite; the *Tony Lumpkin* of the house. **1830** A. PICKEN *Dominie's Legacy* I. 104 He was..as raw looking, overgrown, gawky a youth, as any mother's pet of a student. **1937** PARTRIDGE *Dict. Slang* 535/1 Mother's ruin. **1955** P. JONES *Birthday Honours* I. 10, I have been to a party, darling... What would you like? 'Mother's Ruin'? **1970** *New Scientist* 23 Apr. 165/2 Gin, as shown by the old temperance demonstration of dropping earthworms into adjacent glasses of water and mother's ruin, can certainly eliminate unwanted planarians. **1888** MRS. G. SUMNER *To Mothers of Higher Classes* vi. 55 The 'Mothers' Union', now started in the Winchester Diocese, and in other Dioceses, is a very simple plan. **1972** L. LAMB *Picture Frame* xiv. 123, I shall have to run a mothers' union or something.

16. a. mother-and-baby home, an establishment serving as a maternity home for unmarried mothers, usu. with pre- and post-natal services; **mother-bomb** (see quot. 1971); **mother-cell** *Biol.*, a cell which later undergoes cell division and gives rise to daughter-cells; *spec.* a cell which later undergoes meiotic division; **mother-child** *a.*, of or pertaining to a mother and her child; **mother-city** (further example); (*b*) a city regarded as serving as a mother to someone; **mother complex,** a complex (see *COMPLEX 3) about one's mother; **mother-cult,** the worship of a mother-goddess; **mother-daughter** *a.*, of or pertaining to a mother and her daughter; **mother-feryer** *U.S. slang* = **mother-fucker*; **mother figure,** a person or thing endowed with some of the attributes of a mother; **mother fixation,** a fixation (see *FIXATION 3 b) on one's mother; **mother-fucker** *coarse slang* (orig. and chiefly *U.S.*), a base, despicable person; someone or something that is very unpleasant; hence **mother-fucking** *ppl. a.*, despicable, base; unpleasant; = BLOODY *a.* 10; **mother-grabbing** *ppl. a.* (*U.S. slang*) = **mother-fucking* ppl. adj.; **mother image, imago,** the mental or realized image of an idealized or archetypal mother; **mother-in** (or **and**)**-babe,** used *attrib.* to designate a wooden bobbin, the hollow shank of which contains another smaller bobbin; **mother-lode** *Min.*, the principal vein of ore; also *fig.*; **mother-loving** *ppl. a.*, (*a*) that loves one's mother; (*b*) = **mother-fucking* ppl. adj.; freq. used as a vague intensive; **mother mould** *Sculpture*, a rigid mould which holds casting material; **mother plane** orig. *U.S.*, an aircraft which launches or controls another aircraft; **mother-raper** *U.S. slang* = **mother-fucker*; **mother-raping** *ppl. a.* (*U.S. slang*) = **mother-fucking* ppl. adj.; **mother ship,** substitute for def.: (*a*) a ship or airship escorting or having charge of a number of other, usu. smaller, craft; also *transf.*; (*b*) an aircraft or rocket from which another aircraft or rocket is launched or controlled; = **mother plane*; **mothers' meeting** (earlier and later examples); also *fig.*; **mother-son** *a.*, of or pertaining to a mother and her son; **mother substitute, surrogate,** a person or thing that takes the place of the mother; **mother-symbol,** that which is symbolic of the mother or of motherhood; **mother tincture,** in Homœopathy, a pure undiluted tincture of a drug; **mother-to-be,** an expectant mother.

1965 HALL & HOWES *Church in Social Work* v. 90 The county council was running its own mother and baby home. **1972** *Guardian* 14 July 11/2 Miss McM will not consider going into a mother and baby home and is against adoption. **1971** *New Scientist* 21 Jan. 135/2 Shrapnel grenades..are dropped individually, or in clusters from canisters ('mother-bombs'). **1845** Mother-cell [in Dict., sense 13 d]. **1875** Mother-cell [see *ASCOMYCETES]. **1920** W. E. AGAR *Cytology* vii. 212 The diagrams start with the pollen mother-cell in the male and the embryo-sac mother-cell in the female—in each case the last cell generation of the diploid phase. **1932** C. D. DARLINGTON *Rec. Adv. Cytol.* i. 5 In a 'mother-cell' two nuclear divisions follow one another rapidly while the chromosomes only divide once. **1959** W. ANDREW *Textbk. Compar. Histol.* xii. 486 Earlier workers believed this cell to be a mother cell for the successive groups of

spermatogonia. 1937 H. Read *Art & Society* v. 191 At first these instincts are concentrated on the mother, and any being that threatens to interfere with the mother–child bond incurs the child's enmity. 1963 Auden *Dyer's Hand* 440 The mother–child relationship..stands for the kind of love that is unaffected by time. 1908 *Westm. Gaz.* 4 Aug. 5/1 Capetown..is in the truest sense the μητρόπολις of South Africa, the 'mother-city' from which the rest have sprung. 1935 L. MacNeice *Poems* 20 See Belfast... This was my mother-city, these my paps... I cannot be Anyone else than what this land engendered me. 1919 M. K. Bradby *Psycho-Analysis* v. 59 If sexual fixation takes place at the third stage, the 'mother-complex' will create an obstacle to a man's happiness in married life. 1924 *Spectator* 16 Aug. 229/1, I got a mother-complex. 1936 C. Day Lewis *Friendly Tree* I. vi. 87 He sucks a pipe constantly. The mother-complex. Infantilism. 1948 *Yearbk. Psychoanal.* IV. 172 (*title*) The mother complex in literature. 1960 R. F. C. Hull tr. *Jung's Structure & Dynamics of Psyche* in *Coll. Wks.* (1966) VIII. v. 369 Analysis shows an infantile longing for the mother, a so-called mother complex. 1909 *Westm. Gaz.* 2 Feb. 5/1 From the trend of recent writings in Hindu literature it is suggested that the Mother cult has been revived. 1969 C. Fremlin *Possession* ii. 17 The closeness of the mother–daughter relationship. 1974 —— *By Horror Haunted* 138 An ordinary, typical mother–daughter misunderstanding. 1946 Mezzrow & Wolfe *Really Blues* 4 A motherferyer that would cut your throat for looking. 1953 *New Biol.* XIV. 29 In birds, for instance, we have the astonishing phenomenon called imprinting, by which the sign stimulus of the IRM to follow a mother-figure differentiates. 1957 *Economist* 7 Sept. 821/2 The commonest illusion..is that the United Nations is a miraculous mother-figure which will give suck and shelter to all comers. 1970 *Daily Tel.* 22 Sept. 14 Mrs Meir is both a superb politician and a Jewish mother-figure which the young State [of Israel] may well need. 1971 *Ibid.* 18 Jan. 10/7 The association also says there should be a 'mother figure' in each nursing school to whom students can turn for advice. 1921 *Internat. Jrnl. Psychoanal.* II. 55 Jesus is no longer satisfied to make Joseph his ideal (a hard task for a boy with a strong Mother-fixation of love). 1954 *Scott. Jrnl. Theol.* VII. 393 Rationalism has handed the problem [of worship] over to the psychologist to explain in terms of repressions, mother-fixations, infantile-regressions and the like. 1969 C. Allen *Textbk. Psychosexual Disorders* (ed. 2) xvii. 375 Sailors usually carry..the mother's photograph... There is strong mother-fixation in their choice of prostitutes. 1956 *Amer. Speech* XXXI. 111 This linguistic vacuum is being filled by a new obscenity symbol, *mother-fucker*. 1960 J. Baldwin in *Partisan Rev.* Spring 292 You've got to fight with the elevator boy because the motherf*****'s *white*! 1970 R. D. Abrahams *Positively Black* ii. 45 I'm one motherfucker that don't mind dying. 1971 B. W. Aldiss *Soldier Erect* 142 Jock..looked up into my face. 'The bastards, the fucking mean scab-devouring mankey-minded shower of mother-fuckers!' 1971 J. Mandelkau *Buttons* xiii. 149 These mother-fuckers had been whining they had no food to sell the people—and this place was stacked! 1973 *Black Panther* 21 July 16/1 We will kill any motherfucker that stands in the way of our freedom. 1959 N. Mailer *Advts. for Myself* (1961) 351 They could smash some mother-f——ing Reds. 1968 *Rat* 13–16 May 10/2 The police were interminably long in getting into Math. Good mother-fucking barricades. 1969 P. Roth *Portnoy's Complaint* 106 You muff-diving, mother-fucking son of a bitch! 1974 S. Ellin *Stronghold* 23 'You motherfucking black clown,' Harvey says without heat, 'nothing is changed.' 1959 M. Russ *Half Moon Haven* (1961) i. 60 There isn't one item on this mother-grabbing planet that I 'like'. 1941 L. MacNeice *Poetry of W. B. Yeats* vii. 138 It would be tempting to regard Cathleen ni Houlihan, the Poor Old Woman, as a mother image and so to refer much of Irish nationalism to a mother-fixation. 1968 C. Rycroft *Crit. Dict. Psychoanal.* 93 Conceptions of the mother existing in the infant's mind formed by splitting of the mother image. 1973 J. Singer *Boundaries of Soul* iv. 91 The Mother image appeared under strange circumstances to my analysand Margaret. 1916 B. M. Hinkle tr. *Jung's Psychol. of Unconscious* v. 250 That amount of libido which unconsciously is fastened to the mother-imago. 1956 R. F. C. Hull tr. *Jung's Symbols of Transformation* in *Coll. Wks.* V. ii. v. 222 The water and tree symbolism.. likewise refer to the libido that is unconsciously attached to the mother-imago. 1919 T. Wright *Romance Lace Pillow* xiii. 126 *Mother-in-Babe Bobbins*, in the hollowed shank of which a tiny wooden bobbin rattles. 1928 G. Whiting *Tools & Toys of Stitching* 220 The Cow-and-Calf and Mother-and-Babe bobbins—they are a perfect, never-ending joy and a masterpiece of the Midlands! 1969 E. H. Pinto *Treen* xxi. 311 Collectively, they are known as church window bobbins, but those with smaller bobbins inside the windows are described as mother-in-babe types. c 1882 J. H. Beadle *Western Wilds* xxxiv. 561 What miners call a 'mother lode' is often like a tree in its upward development: below is the main trunk, above the branches diverge. 1927 B. A. McKelvie *Black Canyon* p. vi, They started up-stream in search of the mother-lode. 1960 *Encounter* XIV. iii. 74 The pages of the T.L.S. were the very mother-lode of academic inanity. 1965 G. J. Williams *Econ. Geol. N.Z.* v. 58/1 The mother-lode that had been envisaged as the source of the gold in the Bluespur 'cement'. 1972 *Times Lit. Suppl.* 25 Feb. 219/1 It is mother lode, with rich ore; but it lacks the refining that the author intended to give it. 1964 O. E. Middleton in C. K. Stead *N.Z. Short Stories* (1966) 198 We'd all be drawing the dole like every other mother-loving beachcomber. 1969 'J. Morris' *Fever Grass* i. 6 Get her out of that mother-lovin' joint an' into the cab. 1898 C. R. Ashbee tr. *Cellini's Treat. Goldsmithing & Sculpture* 116 Put them into the cavities..in the mould... Or 'mother mould' as the sculptors would call it. 1947 J. C. Rich *Materials & Methods of Sculpture* v. 100 A heavily bodied plaster mix can be applied over the agar impression to form a mother mold or casing. 1969 R. Mayer *Dict. Art Terms & Techniques* 254/1 *Mother mold*, an outer case or container for a negative mold made of gelatin, rubber, or another weak, flexible substance. The mother mold is made of a rigid material. 1936 *Sun* (Baltimore) 6 July 9/1 Progress on the pick-a-back airplane, a combination in which a 'mother' plane will carry on its back a smaller long range seaplane for 'launching' at high altitude is more secret. 1945 *Time* 19 Nov. 52/2 Everything it sees is projected by radio on a screen in the mother plane. 1962 *Daily Tel.* 10 Sept. 18/4 The 'mother' plane would carry pick-a-back a plane which would be launched at the fringe of space. 1966 C. Himes *Heat's On* iii. 30 Some mother-raper is shooting at me with water-melon seeds. *Ibid.* ii. 22 The dirty mother-raping white nigger! 1969 Mother-raping [see *cock-sucking* ppl. adj. *s.v.* *cock *sb.*[1] 23]. 1902 H. C. Fyfe *Submarine Warfare* v. 108 A wireless message..has been sent to the commander of the 'mother ship'. 1909 *Q. Rev.* Oct. 575 Depôt ships for destroyers, mother-ships for submarines, and oil-supply vessels. 1922 *Encycl. Brit.* XXX. 17/2 Scouts were flown off lighters at sea against airships, and off the decks of battleships and 'mother' ships. 1926 H. T. Wilkins *Marvels Mod. Mech.* 215 An engineer, aboard the airship, opened the telescopic apparatus which left the aeroplane swaying in space some 60 feet below the mother ship. 1938 *Flight* 8 Sept. 197/1 They [*sc.* engineers] designed for catapult launch from a mother ship;..they used diesel engines. 1946 in *Amer. Speech* (1947) XXII. 230/2 The Navy's drones will be sent into the cloud by one mother ship. 1962 J. Tunstall *Fishermen* ii. 46 The fleet of catching vessels transfers its fish..to a mother ship, which processes and freezes the fish at sea. 1967 *Times Rev. Industry* Apr. 48/3 Trailers, operating from the central plant and acting as 'mother ships' to the delivery vans, can replace the depots. 1969 *Observer* 20 July 7/3 After it has docked with the mother ship the astronauts will spend four hours going over every inch of the LEM. 1973 *Sci. Amer.* Nov. 23/1 The small 'killer' satellites in a 'mother ship' equipped with central guidance and detection devices. On command the mother ship would have oriented itself and determined when, at what rate and in what direction to launch its subsatellites. 1865 C. M. Yonge *Clever Woman of the Family* II. xxx. 312 The mothers' meetings for the soldiers' wives. 1925 Fraser & Gibbons *Soldier & Sailor Words* 159 *Mother's meeting*, an occasional name among bluejackets for the captain's address to a ship's company. 1946 D. Hamson *We fell among Greeks* xviii. 195, I noticed one particular squad which was openly idling... 'Why do you stop work and hold a mother's meeting when I go away?' 1927 B. Malinowski *Sex & Repression in Savage Society* ii. iii. 100 Not one single case of mother–son incest could be found. 1949 M. Mead *Male & Female* xvi. 326 A mother–son combination is classified as bad for the son. 1943 J. S. Huxley *Evolutionary Ethics* ii. 16 The absence in the infant's life of a mother or effective mother-substitute during the crucial period from about one to three years old. 1965 F. Sargeson *Memoirs of Peon* vi. 173 Two young sparrow-legged ruffians..engaged in selling my mother-substitute a large trolley-load of empty bottles. 1959 *Science* 21 Aug. 422/3 We took the calculated risk of constructing and using inanimate mother surrogates rather than real mothers. 1969 E. Stotland *Psychol. of Hope* viii. 126 Cloth-covered objects..appear to satisfy a need for contact and closeness; the babies cling to these mother surrogates while they do not cling to those made of uncovered wire. 1956 R. F. C. Hull tr. *Jung's Symbols of Transformation* in *Coll. Wks.* V. 301 At this stage the mother-symbol..points towards the unconscious as the creative matrix of the future. 1902 *Encycl. Brit.* XXIX. 312/2 The pure tinctures are denominated 'mother tinctures'. 1906 W. De Morgan *Joseph Vance* xvi. 149 She makes some concession to my feelings on the subject of High Dilutions, and (at great risk to myself, she says) allows me to have Mother-Tinctures. 1960 C. Dale *Spring of Love* i. 26 She would take a magazine..and re-read..Sister Jane's advice to mothers-to-be. 1973 A. Morice *Death & Dutiful Daughter* vii. 68 Has our little mother-to-be surfaced yet?

b. Mother of Commonwealths *U.S.*, Virginia; **Mother of Parliaments,** (*a*) England; (*b*) the British Parliament; **Mother of Presidents** *U.S.*, (*a*) Virginia; (*b*) Ohio; **Mother of States** *U.S.*, (*a*) Connecticut; (*b*) Virginia; **mother of thousands,** (*a*) for '*Linaria cymbalaria*' substitute '*Cymbalaria muralis*'; (earlier and later examples); (*c*) (examples); (*e*) = *helxine.

1879 *Congress. Rec.* 10 Jan. 413/2 To pour out the vials of his impotent wrath upon the 'Mother of Commonwealths'. 1865 J. Bright in *Birmingham Daily Post* 19 Jan. 5/1 We may be proud of this, that England is the ancient country of Parliaments... England is the mother of Parliaments. 1910 *Encycl. Brit.* VII. 15/1 The early date at which the principle of self-government was established in England, the steady growth of the principle, the absence of civil dissension, and the preservation in the midst of change of so much of the old organization, have given its constitution a great influence over the ideas of politicians in other countries. This fact is expressed in the proverbial phrase—'England is the mother of parliaments'. 1918 *Daily Mirror* 12 Nov. 6/2 Never has the Mother of Parliaments seen such a scene of enthusiasm as when Mr. Lloyd George read out the armistice terms yesterday. 1926 Fowler *Mod. Eng. Usage* 548/1 Mother of Parliaments (British Parliament). 1974 *Times* 24 Aug. 2/4 *France Soir*..went on to explain why in the country of the 'Mother of Parliaments' social tension has grown. 1827 A. Sherwood *Gaz. Georgia* 98 James Monroe..was born in Va., the mother of Presidents. 1897 *Chicago Record* 8 Mar. 4/1 Ohio may claim to take rank with Virginia as a 'mother of presidents'. 1904 *N.Y. Tribune* 12 June 8 Virginia concluded not to indorse any candidate. The 'Mother of Presidents' is a trifle particular. 1948 *Chicago Daily News* 21 Apr. 1/5 Ohio is the mother of Presidents, and Taft is one of her sons. 1834 W. A. Caruthers *Kentuckian in N.Y.* ii. 195 Virginia has been the mother of states. 1838 *Yale Lit. Mag.* III. 86 To thee, Mother of States! to thee, good old Connecticut, do our praises most belong. 1855 *Southern Lit. Messenger* XXI. 675/1 Virginia..[was] hailed as 'the Mother of States'. [1731 P. Miller *Gardeners Dict.* s.v. *Linaria*, The first of these Plants [*sc.* common yellow toad-flax] grows in great Plenty upon the Sides of dry Banks in most Parts of England and is seldom cultivated in Gardens, for it is a very troublesome Plant to keep within Bounds, the roots being very apt to spread under-ground, and rise at a great Distance from the Mother Plant, whereby it greatly injures whatever Plants stand near it.] 1855 A. Pratt *Flowering Plants & Ferns Gt. Brit.* IV. 126 This plant [*sc. Linaria cymbalaria*] is familiarly known to many persons by the name of Mother of Thousands. 1910 T. W. Sanders *Window & Indoor Gardening* xi. 111 Ivy-leaved Pelargoniums..make delightful basket plants... So, too, [do] Saxifraga sarmentosa (Mother-o'-Thousands or Wandering Jew). 1952 A. R. Clapham et al. *Flora Brit. Is.* 713 *H[elxine] soleirolii* Req. Mind-your-own-business, Mother of thousands... Naturalized on walls and damp banks. 1958 *N. & Q.* Sept. 411/2 Have your readers ever heard of a plant called 'Mother of Thousands' or 'Wandering Sailor'? *Ibid.* Oct. 452/1 Mother of thousands... I believe this plant is *Saxifraga sarmentosa*. *Ibid.* Nov. 488/2 'Mother of thousands'... The name is given to the Ivy-leaved Toad-flax which is also known as 'Mother of Millions'. 1961 *Countryman* LVIII. iii. 547 Mother of-thousands (ivy-leaved toadflax). 1971 K. G. Messenger *Flora of Rutland* 69/1 *S[oleirolia] soleirolii*.. Mother-of-Thousands... Pavements, Uppingham, 1961... Intrusive alien. 1975 *Times* 22 Nov. 10/5 The elegant climber..the mother of thousands..produces small plantlets on thread-like runners.

mother, *v.*[1] Add: **5.** (Further examples.) Also, to pick out from a flock the mother of (a particular lamb). Also *intr.*, *transf.*, and const. *up*.

1889 *Zealandia* I. 30 He pretended to give me every opportunity at 'mothering' (as it is called) my missing lambs, but for fifteen ewes I could find but four. 1890 *Cornh. Mag.* Oct. 386, I was shepherding for Gasgarth, and his missus said to me, 'Jem, mother that 'un,' and I went reight intill middle o' t' flock and browt out t'mother on it. 1950 *N.Z. Jrnl. Agric.* Sept. 197/3 All lambs can be properly mothered up before nightfall. *Ibid.* 202/1 Do not move the ewes until all the lambs have mothered. 1957 *New Biol.* XXII. 101 Some lambs failed to 'mother' after treatment. 1961 R. M. Patterson *Buffalo Head* iv. 134 At Bull Creek we stopped for a little while to give the calves a chance to 'mother-up'; very soon every cow had her calf. 1962 [see *hay-bale* (*hay *sb.*[1] 4)]. 1972 *Country Life* 30 Mar. 812/3 Both lambs and ewes are marked with identical letters to facilitate shepherding, particularly the mothering up, at night, which is very important with winter lambing.

mothercraft (mʌ·ðəɹkrɑft). [f. Mother *sb.* + Craft *sb.*] The 'craft' or business of a mother; knowledge of, and skill in, the care of children. Also *attrib.*

1914 *Times* 25 Apr. 10/3 The School of Mothercraft. 1917 B. Vaughan *Menace Empty Cradle* 44 How much better it would be to teach them mothercraft. 1922 *Daily Mail* 28 Oct. 7 A Mothercraft question set by the Association of Infant Welfare. 1945 [see *Karitane]. 1969 *Sydney Morning Herald* 7 June 4/2 A man wearing a white stocking mask with eye-slits stuck a pistol into the ribs of a mothercraft nurse in a $14,200 payroll robbery at the Royal Hospital for Women, Paddington, yesterday. 1970 *Globe & Mail* (Toronto) 28 Sept. 7/6 As the mother of a child in the Mothercraft nursery may I be permitted to clear the distorted view some of your..readers have.

motherhood. Add: **1. c.** *transf.* Used *attrib.* of an issue, report, etc.: protective, withholding the worst aspects. *N. Amer.*

1973 *Ottawa Jrnl.* 4 Apr. 6/2 They think public participation is such a motherhood issue in politics these days that it must be paid homage to at all cost. 1974 *Evening Herald* (Rock Hill, S. Carolina) 18 Apr. 4/4 At the meeting, officials from Kaiser, Reynolds, Southwire, Alcoa and others agreed that a 'motherhood' package concealing the dangers of aluminium wiring was the best way to deal with the hearings of the Consumer Product Safety Commission in Los Angeles. 1974 *Ottawa Citizen* 14 Nov. 37/2 Opposition spokesmen attacked him for presenting a 'motherhood' report which told nothing of the real situation of the peacekeeping forces, only that Canadian troops are loved overseas.

mothering, *vbl. sb.* [2]: see Mother *v.*[2]

mothering, *ppl. a.* Add: **2.** *U.S. slang.* = **mother-fucking* ppl. adj.

1968 L. W. Robinson *Assassin* (1969) ii. 8 We are lost in the motherin' fog. 1970 'J. Morris' *Candywine Development* xxiii. 253 What I don't see is how those motherin' hijackers expect to get away with it. 1975 *New Yorker* 23 June 40/2 I'm out there cutting that mothering grass all day!

mother-in-law. 4. mother-in-law's tongue, a tropical African herbaceous plant, *Sansevieria trifasciata* or its variety *laurentii*, of the family Liliaceæ, distinguished by a rosette of long, pointed leaves with white or yellow markings, and often cultivated as a house plant.

1958 *Times* 29 Nov. 9/5 Probably the most long-suffering house plant is the 'Mother-in-law's Tongue'. 1961 *Amateur Gardening* 11 Nov. 7/1 The sansevieria, because of its sword-like shape has received the unsympathetic name of Mother-in-Law's Tongue. 1970 'D. Halliday' *Dolly & Cookie Bird* ii. 15 The place was modern and airy and full of..mother-in-law's tongue in long boxes. 1974 *Times* 5 Oct. 12/1 The real tough ones include aspidistras, ..mother in law's tongue *Sansevieria laurentii* and the rubber plant *Ficus elastica*.

motherless, *a.*[1] Add: Also as an intensive quasi-*adv.*, esp. in phr. *stone motherless broke*. *Austral. colloq.*

1898 *Bulletin* (Sydney) 17 Dec. Red Page, To these are prefixed the adjectives *motherless* and *dead*, thus *dead motherless broke*. **1916** A. WRIGHT *Under Cloud* 35 I'm stone motherless meself an' I could do with that hundred Booth is offerin'. **1925** E. S. SORENSON *Murty Brown* 135 That leaves me stony, motherless broke again. **1945** G. CASEY *Downhill is Easter* I. 20 I'd only known Reg when we were both stone motherless broke. **1972** A. MACDONALD *Ukulele Player under Red Lamp* 147 Happy, full as a boot, and stone motherless broke.

mother of pearl. Add: **4. b. mother-of-pearl cloud** *Meteorol.* [tr. Norw. *perlemorsky* (H. Mohn 1893, in *Forh. i Vidensk.-Selsk. i Christiania* 1)], a kind of iridescent cloud occurring above the tropopause which is sometimes seen in high latitudes after sunset; cf. *noctilucent cloud* s.v. *NOCTI-.

1932 *Q. Jrnl. R. Meteorol. Soc.* LVIII. 307 The remarkable stratospheric clouds which the late Professor Mohn called mother-of-pearl clouds again appeared over Scandinavia several times during the months of January and February this year. **1957** LUDLAM & SCORER *Cloud Study* 69 Mother of pearl clouds are rare. They have been seen most often in Norway (but occasionally also in Scotland, Iceland and Alaska), and then only in the months between November and March. **1972** R. SCORER *Clouds of World* v. 74 Mother of pearl clouds are at altitudes between 19 and 30 km. where they may be brightly illuminated by the sun after sunset at the ground, and after the sun has ceased to illuminate the troposphere where most of the blue colour of the sky originates.

mother's brother. *Anthropol.* The maternal uncle, usu. with reference to his importance in kinship affairs and social customs. Also *attrib.*

1871 L. H. MORGAN in *Smithsonian Contrib. Knowl.* No. 218 12 My father's brothers and my mother's brothers, in English, are generalized into one class, and the term *uncle* is employed... The relationships to *Ego* of the two classes of persons are equal in their degree of nearness, but not of the same kind; wherefore, the Roman method is preferable, which employed *patruus* to express the former, and *avunculus* to indicate the latter. *Ibid.* 13 In Seneca-Iroquois, for example, my father's brother is my father... My mother's brother, on the contrary, is my uncle. **1934** R. H. LOWIE *Cultural Anthropol.* xiii. 251 A preponderant position of the mother's brother may occur even without matrilocal residence and is termed 'avunculate'. **1949** E. E. EVANS-PRITCHARD in M. Fortes *Social Structure* 95 It is worse with a mother's brother's daughter than with a father's brother's daughter. **1951** R. FIRTH *Elem. Social Organization* ii. 48 Reference has been made..to the importance of the mother's brother relationship in Oceanic communities. **1972** J. S. LA FONTAINE *Interpretation of Ritual* 166 While all non-agnatic kin ceremonially recognize a girl's maturity, the primary ritual figure, to the exclusion of her father or senior agnates, is her mother's brother.

moth-proof (mǫ·þ,prūf), *a.* Also **moth proof, mothproof.** [f. MOTH *sb.* + PROOF *a.*] Resistant to damage by moths.

1893 *Ladies' Home Jrnl.* May 13/4 Moth proof bag. **1907** *Yesterday's Shopping* (1969) 275/2 Moth proof Cotton underlay to go between wire bottom of bed and mattress. **1916** *Independent* (N.Y.) 15 May 248/2 Colorfast, reversible moth-proof rugs. **1922** *Sci. Amer.* 22 Oct. 260/1 Making wool moth-proof. **1924** *Ibid.* July 39/4 (*heading*) Making the closet moth-proof. **1931** *Daily Express* 21 Sept. 7/5 Hygienic, dustproof, mothproof and washable. **1959** *Times* 12 Jan. 11/3 Courlene..is..rot and mothproof, washable and quick drying. **1960** *Which?* Jan. 18/2 Wool can be made mothproof by the application of certain chemicals, and mothproof wool is available from some manufacturers and is particularly desirable for carpets.

Hence as *v. trans.*, to render moth-proof; so **moth-proofing** *vbl. sb.*; **moth-proofer,** a substance for moth-proofing clothes or textile fibres.

1925 *Chem. Abstr.* XIX. 184 (*title*) Mothproofing fibrous materials. *Ibid.* 993 (*title*) Moth-proofing fabrics. **1932** *Discovery* Oct. 321/2 Science has provided sufficient mothproofing substances and means for combating this pest [*sc.* the moth]. **1938** *Chatelaine* May 79/1 Her lovely clothes at Columbia Studios are mothproofed with *Larvex*. **1958** *Spectator* 4 July 15/3 Expert mending, dying to pattern, mothproofing. **1960** *Which?* June 130/1 For woollens that have not been mothproofed in manufacture, the consumer can use *household mothproofers*—liquids which impregnate the material and kill the larvae—or *moth repellents*. **1961** *Times* 13 Dec. 21/7 Air fresheners..mothproofers.

mothy, *a.* Add to def.: Characterized by the presence of moths; suggestive of a moth, resembling the movements of the wings of a moth.

1898 HARDY *Wessex Poems* 155 At mothy curfew-tide. **1917** —— *Moments of Vision* 255 Some nocturnal blackness, mothy and warm. **1949** E. BOWEN *Heat of Day* vi. 113 Your mothy way of blinking and laziness about keeping your eyelids open.

motif. Add: **1. b.** (Earlier and later examples.) Also in *Folklore*, a recurrent character, event, situation, or theme.

1857 KINGSLEY *Two Years Ago* I. vi. 161, I owe you a debt, sir, for having furnished me with one of the most striking 'motifs' I ever had. **1877** *International Rev.* (N.Y.) Jan. 73 Having endeavored to discover the *motif* and purpose of George Eliot's work. **1884** A. LANG in R.M. Dorson *Peasant Customs* (1968) I. 312 Turning from the Samoyeds and the Epirotes to Africa, we find the *motif* (escape of brother and sister) in a Kaffir tale. **1902** W. W. LAWRENCE in *Jrnl. Eng. & Gmc. Philol.* IV. 476 Repetition of motifs and consequent disturbance of logical arrangement is characteristic of Anglo-Saxon poetry. **1935** A. C. BARTLETT *Larger Rhet. Patterns Anglo-Saxon Poetry* 80 The conception of the hereafter clothed in definite form is, in Germanic poetry, found only in Anglo-Saxon, and..it is a favorite motif in poems not bound by Bible text. **1941** G. G. SCHOLEM *Major Trends in Jewish Mysticism* ii. 67 Some of the oldest mythical motifs are to be found..in an extremely interesting..text. **1968** P. OLIVER *Screening Blues* ii. 63 The parody sermons, as Stith Thompson shows, are one of the more popular of folk-tale motifs and they abound in Negro folk-lore. **1971** *English Studies* LII. 501 In addition to the motif of longing, the themes of former happiness and of present estrangement from friends also unify the poem.

4. *attrib.* and *Comb.*, as *motif classification, framework, research, -work*; *motif-less, -like* adjs.; **motif-index,** an index of standard folklore motifs.

1966 K. LUOMALA in M. Jacobs *Anthropologist looks at Myth* 164 Kirtley's *Motif-Index*..follows Stith Thompson's system for motif-classification. **1971** R. L. WELSCH tr. *Krohn's Folklore Methodology* iii. 31 The fact that it occurs more or less incidentally in other complexes is due to the influence of the motif framework. **1932** S. THOMPSON in *Indiana Univ. Stud.* No. 96 (*heading*) Motif-index of folk literature. **1958** T. P. COFFIN *Analytical Index to Jrnl. Amer. Folklore* 239 It was deemed advisable not to attempt a complete Thompson-style motif-index of the Journal. **1972** *Jrnl. Amer. Folklore* LXXXV. 278 One would hope this *Index* would be shelved in every library beside the Thompson Type and Motif indexes. **1973** A. DUNDES *Mother Wit* 114 These tools include various tale type indices and motif indices... By using tale type and motif indices, Dorson is able to demonstrate the European provenience of the greater portion of the tales. **1970** *Daily Tel.* 27 June 7 This work, while not..unmotivated, is entirely motif-less—introductory clinking of pebbles, toneless blowing into instruments built for lusher uses. **1964** *English Studies* XLV. 446 Two terms which characterize Christina's..reputation through their motif-like occurrence, *caprice* and *banality*, are a source of insight and confusion. **1938** P. S. WATSON tr. *Nygren's Agape & Eros: Part 2* I. 23 The answer can only be supplied by motif-research, that is, by an enquiry which detects the motif behind the formed expression. **1948** L. SPITZER *Linguistics & Lit. Hist.* v. 193 This..movement is incarnated in..the rhythm—as in the verbal motif-work.

motile, *a.* Add: **2.** *Psychol.* Of or relating to responses that involve motor imagery. Cf. *MOTOR *a.* 3. Also as *sb.*, one who responds to perceptions more readily in terms of motor or kinæsthetic imagery than in terms of auditory or visual.

1886 *Mind* XI. 415 This division of men into visuals, audiles, motiles and indifferents..is of great interest and importance. **1889** *Proc. Soc. Psychical Res.* V. 536 A 'motile' reading the above question will dimly imagine the movements of his own larynx in uttering the word elephant. **1890** W. JAMES *Princ. Psychol.* II. xviii. 61 Persons who belong to this type (*les moteurs*, in French, *motiles*, as Mr. Galton proposes to call them in English) make use, in memory, reasoning, and all their intellectual operations, of images derived from movement. *Ibid.* 62 Professor Stricker of Vienna..seems to have the motile form of imagination developed in unusual strength. **1892** —— *Text-bk. Psychol.* xix. 308 All blind persons must belong to the 'tactile' and 'motile' types of the French authors. **1909** [see *AUDILE *a.*].

Motilon (mōᵘtilōᵘ·n). Also **Motilone.** Pl. **Motilon, Motilones.** [Sp., of Amer. Ind. origin.] A Cariban Indian people of Colombia; a member of this people; also, their language. Also *attrib.*

1913 P. J. EDER *Colombia* xii. 186 The white settlers have at times been driven away by the onslaughts of the Motilones Indians, who dwell in the forests of the Eastern Cordillera to the east. **1937** T. ROURKE *Tyrant of Andes* 26 The Motilones are no myth. They..have been sending the six-foot arrows flying from the bush into the American ..geologists working for the oil companies. **1949** L. S. & E. JUDSON *Let's go to Colombia* v. 213 The Motilone Indians. Of fierce Carib origin the Motilones were never subdued by the Spaniards. **1950** J. A. MASON in J. H. Steward *Handbk. S. Amer. Indians* VI. 232 The *Cariban* affinities of *Motilón*..have always been accepted. **1957** *Encycl. Brit.* XXI. 80/1 They [*sc.* the Carib] reached the Andes on the west and small groups entered Colombia (Motilon, Opon and Carare Indians). **1964** E. A. NIDA *Toward Sci. Transl.* iii. 37 The Motilones in Colombia have borrowed the Spanish word *purísima* 'most pure' from the phrase *María purísima* 'Mary, most pure', but have given it the meaning of 'the devil'. **1965** MOSER & TAYLOR *Cocaine Eaters* IV. ii. 151 The arrow is the most treasured object a Motilon possesses. *Ibid.* iii. 157 We had been intrigued by the question of death amongst the Motilon. *Ibid.* 179 The Motilon chiefs. **1968** G. ANTHONY *Colombia: Land of Tomorrow* xiii. 160 It was left as a souvenir of a raid by the Motilone Indians... The Motilones, who live along the mountainous border between Colombia and Venezuela, are still amongst the fiercest and least-known of all Colombia's Indians.

motion, *sb.* Add: **3. b.** *to go through the motions of* (examples). Also *fig.*, to do something only perfunctorily; to pretend. Also with ellipsis of 'of' and following phr. So *going-through-the-motions*.

1816 SCOTT *Old Mortality* in *Tales my Landlord* 1st Ser. II. x. 255 She pressed her handkerchief to her face, sobbed with great vehemence, and either wept, or managed, as Halliday might have said, to go through the motions wonderfully well. **1850** 'M. TENSAS' *Odd Leaves Life Louisiana Swamp Doctor* 88 Cuss you! I was only going through the motions; the rifle ain't loaded! **1856** DICKENS *Dorrit* (1857) I. xxxvi. 316 Mr. Dorrit urbanely went through the motions of playing a game at skittles with the Collegian who was the next oldest inhabitant to himself. **1900** 'MARK TWAIN' *Man that corrupted Hadleyburg* 298 A Government cannot satisfy all these public opinions; it can only go through the motions of trying. This Government does that. It goes through the motions, and they do not succeed. **1933** AUDEN *Poems* (ed. 2) 58 Go through the motions of exploring the familiar. **1944** H. CROOME *You've gone Astray* xvi. 166 It was pleasant, undoubtedly pleasant. But both of them felt..that in some fundamental sense they were merely going through the motions. **1958** *Spectator* 22 Aug. 247/1 Her gaoler is called her secretary and in public goes through the motions of secretaryhood. **1963** *Times Lit. Suppl.* 11 Jan. 27/4 A mere exasperated going-through-the-motions. **1973** W. J. BURLEY *Death in Salubrious Place* i. 24 It's really a diplomatic mission... It would be better if we at least go through the motions of an investigation.

4. (Later examples with reference to the agitated condition of water.)

1864 DICKENS *Mrs. Lirriper's Leg.* i, in *All Year Round* Extra Christmas No., 1 Dec. 7/1 Not much motion on the whole, though me with a swimming in the head. **1971** E. R. SEARY *Place Names Avalon Penin. Newfoundland* v. 90 Petty Harbour Point, now Motion Head..derived its latest name..from The Motion, the heavy cross sea caused by the irregular and broken ground.

15. motion photography, the photographing of moving subjects, later known as *cinematography*; **motion picture,** a 'moving picture'; a cinema film; also *attrib.*; **motion sickness,** nausea induced by motion; travel sickness; **motion study,** the study of the movements necessary for the most effective and least tiring method of performing a task; also *attrib.*

1912 F. A. TALBOT *Moving Pictures* xxviii. 312 Motion photography as an educational force. **1913** *Chambers's Jrnl.* Sept. 688/1 In the early days the long exposure necessary rendered motion-photography well-nigh impossible. [**1891** *Leisure Hour* Aug. 711/1 A highly composite mechanism which is to be known as the 'kinetograph', or motion-picture.] **1896** *Boston Even. Transcript* 7 Nov. 16/4 The cinematographe motion picture programme will be augmented daily. **1913** F. A. TALBOT *Pract. Cinematogr.* 129 Plate, The first motion-pictures of an opening flower, taken at the Marey Institute. The complete opening of a convolvulus is shown in fifteen pictures. **1915** WODEHOUSE *Something Fresh* v. 117 The maiden in distress..was merely earning the salary paid her by some motion-picture firm. **1917** H. GARLAND in Ade *Lett.* (1973) 69 What a change is indicated in a few words. The motor car, the telephone,..and the Motion Picture Theater! **1923** R. D. PAINE *Comr. Rolling Ocean* vii. 112 There were a few stores, a church,..but not a solitary motion-picture theater. **1929** M. R. WERNER *Bryan* 264 Between 1916 and 1919 Bryan was engaged in negotiations for a motion picture on the curse of drink, of which he was to be the star. **1934** *Discovery* June 171/1 Fifty thousand feet of standard motion-picture film will be exposed. **1952** *Manch. Guardian Weekly* 5 June 7/2 The nine judges of the United States Supreme Court handed down a unanimous decision this week that exerts an historic restraint on the censorship of motion pictures. **1972** D. SHIPMAN *Great Movie Stars: Internat. Yrs.* p. v, The coming of Sound to the motion-picture medium killed it as a means of almost effortless international communication. **1973** L. SNELLING *Heresy* I. i. 8 This was a visual generation and the motion-picture its natural medium. **1942** *Sci. News Let.* 12 Dec. 378/1 Air sickness can be prevented or cured if you know how. So can seasickness and the other kinds of motion sickness that attack men lurching over battlefields in tanks and jeeps. **1953** A. SMITH *Blind White Fish in Persia* x. 189 We had been asked to investigate the effectiveness of Kwells pills against the motion sickness occasionally experienced in riding camels. **1971** *Jrnl. Gen. Psychol.* LXXXV. 87 (*heading*) A psychophysiological test for motion-sickness susceptibility. **1973** *Times* 1 Aug. 6/1 Still suffering from the motion sickness which has put their mission behind schedule, the three Skylab astronauts today started to tidy up the orbiting laboratory. **1911** F. B. GILBRETH (*title*) Motion study. *Ibid.* p. v, The phrase 'Motion Study' explains itself. The aim of motion study is to find and perpetuate the scheme of perfection... Standardizing the trades is the world's most important work to-day, and motion study is the first factor in that work. **1918** C. S. MYERS *Present-Day Applications of Psychol.* 17 Yet in regard to industry, the need for good method and the need for systematic training are only just beginning to be realised, as is instanced in the following illustrations of what is now technically known as 'motion-study'. **1933** M. S. VITELES *Industrial Psychol.* xx. 436 In the practical application of motion study techniques the emphasis is upon the ease of work, upon *human* and not primarily upon *economic* efficiency. **1960** M. SPARK *Ballad of Peckham Rye* ii. 15 Motion study did marvels in the factory.

motion, *v.* Add: **5.** *trans.* To impart motion to.

1929 BRIDGES *Test. Beauty* I. 24 Wisdom..choosing to be call'd Athena daughter of Zeus Motion'd the marble to her living grace.

motional, *a.* Add: (Further examples.) In *Electr.* applied *spec.* to an impedance that arises out of the motion of a conductor in a magnetic field.

1892 O. HEAVISIDE *Electr. Papers* I. 446 In general $\mathbf{h} = \mathbf{VDv} \times 4\pi$, where **D** is the displacement of the field, **v** the velocity, **h** the induced magnetic force, and V is as in equation (3). [*Note*] The force [so defined]..I now term the motional magnetic force, and its companion (21*a*) be-

low, the motional electric force. **1912** KENNELLY & PIERCE in *Proc. Amer. Acad. Sci.* XLVIII. 113 The difference obtained by subtracting the damped values from the corresponding free values may be called the motional values of resistance, inductance, etc.; since such differences are due to the motion of the diaphragm. *Ibid.* 144 This means that the impedance of the receiver has become increased, through the vibration of the diaphragm, by a motional impedance. **1957** W. FRASER *Telecommun.* xvi. 510 The movement of the speech coil in the air gap induces a back e.m.f. in the coil so that the loudspeaker has a motional impedance under dynamic conditions. **1969** F. A. BOVEY *Nuclear Magn. Resonance Spectrosc.* i. 14 In liquids of ordinary viscosity..the local variations in magnetic field strength have become so short-lived that motional averaging is complete.

motionally (mōᵘ·ʃənăli), *adv.* [f. MOTIONAL *a.* + -LY².] As regards motion.

1974 *Nature* 7 June 593/3 As the average pore radius approaches 100 Å, the amount of motionally restricted water in the Vycor glass is reduced to below 10% (v/v).

mo·tionlessly, *adv.* [f. MOTIONLESS *a.* + -LY².] Without motion, stilly; in a motionless manner.

1887 W. JAMES in *Pop. Sci. Monthly* June 170 It is the very same instinct which leads a boy playing 'I spy' to hold his very breath when the seeker is near, and which makes the beast of prey..motionlessly lie in wait for his victim.

motivate, *v.* Add to def.: To provide with a stimulus to some kind of action; to direct (a person's energy or behaviour) towards certain goals. (Further examples.)

1924 W. B. SELBIE *Psychol. Relig.* iv. 89 Freud has shown very clearly that forgetting is not the unconscious process that we think, but that it is generally motivated. **1949** *Here & Now* (N.Z.) Oct. 29/2 The vast majority of pictures are sexually motivated. **1953** 'M. INNES' *Christmas at Candleshoe* v. 53 When at fifteen he was eventually packed off to apprenticeship in the city, the action was motivated only by the plain fact that there was nothing else to do with him. **1964** M. ARGYLE *Psychol. & Social Probl.* xii. 152 A special feature of the teacher's job is the need for him to motivate the pupils—there is no wage incentive for school work, and the competitive marks system is only a partial solution. **1966** J. PARTRIDGE *Middle School* vii. 139 A Secondary Modern in which boys are poorly motivated towards their school work at the best of times. **1971** E. DICHTER (*title*) Motivating human behavior. **1974** *Daily Tel.* 2 May 22 (Advt.), Can you motivate salesmen? Not an easy task, because these people are supposed to be self-starters.

2. To serve as or provide a motive for; to justify.

1970 *Nature* 4 Apr. 44/1 The publisher motivates the slim size of these volumes by claiming it makes them more likely to be read. **1973** *Physics Bull.* Apr. 234/3 The demand for a relativistically acceptable version of momentum conservation is used to motivate the introduction of relativistic concepts of dynamics.

Hence **mo·tivated, mo·tivating** *ppl. adjs.*

1909 *Proc. Mod. Lang. Assoc.* XXIV. 175 The motivating reason is of another sort. **1928** C. J. WARDEN *Outl. Compar. Psychol.* v. 126 Punishment was introduced as a motivating stimulus. **1959** B. WOOTTON *Social Sci. & Social Path.* viii. 245 Their actions appear motiveless or strangely motivated. **1963** *Economist* 23 Nov. 767/2 Some form of sales promotion (the motivated-sell). **1968** R. WEST *Sketches from Vietnam* iii. 75 The Americans concede with regret that the Vietcong tend to be more highly motivated than the government supporters. **1973** *Jrnl. Genetic Psychol.* CXXII. 198 The majority of subjects..could be regarded as highly motivated to enter university.

motivation. Add: **1. b.** *Psychol.* and *Sociol.* The conscious or unconscious stimulus for action towards a desired goal provided by psychological or social factors; that which gives purpose or direction to behaviour.

1904 *Psychol. Rev. Monogr. Suppl.* V. II. 11 (*heading*) The egoistic and the social in motivation. **1922** R. S. WOODWORTH *Psychol.* viii. 137 The instincts are extraordinarily important in the study of motivation. **1932** W. MCDOUGALL *Energies of Men* xvi. 245 It is in relation to the problems of motivation that the postulation of subconscious activities is most urgently required. **1937** T. PARSONS *Struct. of Social Action* III. xvi. 637 Weber's work necessitated the ideal-typical formulation of systems of ideas which are relevant to concrete motivation. **1950** LUCAS & BRITT *Advertising Psychol. & Res.* II. v. 107 Lists of human wants and related advertising appeals are included in this chapter mainly for the purpose of illustrating the theory of motivation. **1954** R. F. C. HULL tr. *Jung's Coll. Works* XVII. vii. 193 The real motivations are sought and real discoveries are made. **1966** *Rep. Comm. Inquiry Univ. Oxf.* I. 69 Weight can properly be given to evidence about their motivation,..the nature of their schooling, or their non-academic interests and activities. **1972** *Sci. Amer.* Feb. 48/1 There are other important motivations for attempting to synthesize speech. One is learning how speech is produced in the human vocal tract. **1973** B. O'CONNELL *Aspects of Learning* vi. 103 Motivation may be considered as either intrinsic or extrinsic; intrinsic motives include those of exploration and curiosity, and extrinsic those of status and social approval.

2. Manner or means of movement.

1946 M. PEAKE *Titus Groan* 407 There could be no mistaking that nimble, yet shuffling and edgeways-on—that horribly deliberate motivation that was neither walking nor running. **1948** M. H. NICOLSON *Voyages to Moon* v. 195 Swift's flying chariot remains unique in the history of literature..both for its vast size..and for the plausibility of its principle of motivation.

3. *attrib.* and *Comb.*, esp. in connection with market research and advertising, as *motivation analyst, department, psychology, study*; **motivation research,** research, usu. with the object of increasing a product's sales, undertaken to discover the underlying psychological and social motives that influence people; so **motivation researcher**; cf. *MOTIVATIONAL *a.* b.

1958 A. HUXLEY *Let.* 15 Feb. (1969) 846 American advertising techniques as perfected by the Motivation Analysts. **1957** V. PACKARD *Hidden Persuaders* iii. 29 The McCann-Erickson advertising agency in New York had five psychologists manning a special motivation department. **1961** *Daily Tel.* 14 Mar. 17/2 The 'motivation psychology' that allows a driver to be placid and content at one moment and at the next makes him rush forward 'like a raging lunatic'. *Ibid.*, He described 'motivation psychology' as the study of what makes the individual road user tick. **1953** *Business Week* 5 Sept. 40/2 The publication of a..book called 'An Introductory Bibliography of Motivation Research'. **1960** *Times Rev. Industry* July p. ii/2 Motivation research and ergonomics are but two examples of new terms... The one seeks the reasons for decisions and actions; the other is devoted to the study of man and his working environment. **1967** M. ARGYLE *Psychol. Interpersonal Behaviour* ix. 153 A number of special methods are used in motivation research interviews to get at genuine feelings. **1968** M. RICHLER *Cocksure* xxii. 139 The Motivation Research boys, the pollsters, covered America for us, and came back with 20,000 completed forms. **1954** G. H. SMITH *Motivation Res.* I. ii. 23 In order to do profitable work at this level, the motivation researcher should be familiar with the major concepts of psychiatry and abnormal psychology. **1967** G. STEINER *Lang. & Silence* 45 'Motivation researchers', those gravediggers of literate speech, tell us that the perfect advertisement should neither contain words of more than two syllables nor sentences with dependent clauses. **1954** G. H. SMITH *Motivation Res.* v. xvii. 206 Perhaps the best single person to guide a motivation study is a social psychologist.

motivational (mōᵘtivēⁱ·ʃənăl), *a.* [f. prec. + -AL.] Of or pertaining to motivation.

1931 L. T. TROLAND in *Psychologies of 1930* 460 Narrowly and popularly conceived, motivational psychology would be concerned primarily with 'motives', but broadly and scientifically considered, it deals with all of the determinative functions and dynamics of mind. **1940** *Q. Rev. Biol.* Dec. 403 These conventional categories proved satisfactory only so long as each individual was looked upon as a discrete action-centre without intimate motivational connections with others of his species. **1943** *Mind* LII. 137 As to its motivational aspects, one can at least imagine that the cross connections just mentioned make it relatively easy to tap at least one of the just active hungers. **1951** G. HUMPHREY *Thinking* vi. 183 The mechanism of thinking was at least in the earlier work still associational though this was supplemented by motivational factors. **1958** M. ARGYLE *Relig. Behaviour* xii. 144 This is because the [social learning] theory shows how religion is passed on but does not show the motivational forces maintaining it. **1967** L. B. ARCHER in Wills & Yearsley *Handbk. Managem. Technol.* 131 Even in the most technical situations, motivational and aesthetic considerations have a material bearing upon performance. **1970** *Nature* 26 Sept. 1369/2 Investigations of animal learning usually include motivational components which activate and direct behaviour to relevant goals. **1974** *Ibid.* 15 Mar. 195/2 Problems of such motivational 'conflicts' are of great interest in finding out how behaviour in general is organised.

b. Special collocations: *motivational analyst, consultant, selling*; **motivational research** = **motivation research*; **motivational researcher** = **motivation researcher*.

1957 V. PACKARD *Hidden Persuaders* i. 8 These motivational analysts..are adding depth to the selling of ideas and products. **1959** *Times Rev. Industry* Nov. 4/2 The copywriter has been joined by the art director, and round them have formed phalanxes of executives and research departments and motivational consultants. **1953** *Reporter* (N.Y.) 13 Oct. 27/3 Motivational research means just what it seems to—exploration into..the real reasons why a consumer buys..a product or service. **1957** *Observer* 22 Sept. 11/6 Last week he [*sc.* Dr. Ernest Dichter] described to an audience of advertising people what motivational research—M.R. to its friends—is, and what it does. 'It takes the social sciences out of the seminar,' he says, 'and into the supermarket.' **1960** *Sunday Express* 12 June 14/5 'You are not *typical*,' say the Motivational Research boys. **1960** E. DICHTER *Strategy of Desire* (1961) 15 Often the assignment given our organization for conducting motivational research was a very sober and concrete one. **1971** —— *Motivating Human Behavior* 3 Some people begin to question the manipulative nature of motivational research. **1964** M. MCLUHAN *Understanding Media* xxii. 223 These tales from the Vienna Woods, dreamed up by motivational researchers. **1963** *Horizon* (U.S.) July 36/2 The *beau idéal* of all motivational selling is the use of language to conceal the *absence* of thought.

Hence **motiva·tionally** *adv.*, as regards or in terms of motivation.

1952 T. PARSONS *Social System* i. 4 Only in so far as his relation to the situation is in this sense motivationally relevant will it be treated in this work as action. **1967** M. ARGYLE *Psychol. Interpersonal Behaviour* iii. 52 Synchronization is necessary along a number of different dimensions for smooth and motivationally satisfying interaction to take place.

motivative (mōᵘ·tivēⁱtiv), *a.* [f. MOTIVAT(E *v.* + -IVE.] Serving to motivate; providing a reason for, or a stimulus to, action or thought.

1949 *Mind* LVIII. 37 It might be said that..commands ..are unreliable from the logical point of view, because their real function is motivative. **1963** R. CARNAP in P. A. Schilpp *Philos. R. Carnap* 45 Metaphysical theses.. often have other meaning components, e.g. emotive or motivative ones.

motivator (mōᵘ·tivēⁱtəɹ). [f. MOTIVAT(E *v.* + -OR 2 c.] Something or someone that initiates, or is a stimulus to, action or behaviour.

1943 *Mind* LII. 124 The hypothesis that the prime motivators, such as hunger, thirst, pain-avoidance, and sex, are the driving power, the source of energy behind the whole infinitely complex pattern of socio-psychological behaviour. **1956** A. HUXLEY *Adonis & Alphabet* 41 Meaningless pseudo-knowledge has at all times been one of the principal motivators of individual and collective action. **1958** *Listener* 18 Sept. 414/2 Sex is clearly vitally associated with survival and is a primary motivator. **1959** HALAS & MANVELL *Technique Film Animation* 17 Television is now the main motivator of the increased output of animation. **1972** M. ARGYLE *Social Psychol. of Work* ix. 241 Herzburg and his colleagues concluded that 'motivators' (achievement, etc.) mainly affect satisfaction.

motive, *sb.* Add: **7.** Also in extended use. (Further examples.)

1865 F. B. PALLISER *Hist. Lace* xxxv. 425 The French, by adopting what is technically termed eight 'motives', produce their lace of a finer make and more complex pattern. **1868** C. L. EASTLAKE *Hints Household Taste* ix. 201 Some of the table-china is also very good in what may be called the *motive* of its design. **1893** *Jrnl. Amer. Folklore* VI. 255 The motive that Brer Wolf seeks protection from his pursuers with Brer Rabbit..is akin to the episode in the Roman de Renart. **1928** *Daily Express* 21 Apr. 6/2 These motives are mounted in various designs on a background of satin. **1930** S. W. CHENEY *New World Archit.* i. 20 The primary 'motive' [of New York] is the repeated pier-line, the chief relieving factor the occasional terrace. **1931** A. U. DILLEY *Oriental Rugs & Carpets* plate 16 (*caption*) Vestibule of the Madrassa (college) Mader-i-Shah (Mother of Shah) Sultan Hussein (1700), Ispahan. Compare ceiling motive with rug medallion.

b. For '= MOTIVO, MOTIF 3' read '= MOTIVO, MOTIF 1 c'.

8. *motive-hunter, -pattern.*

1905 *Spectator* 28 Jan. 141/1 He is..a motive-hunter, seeking on every side for little justifications for his pride. **1941** KOESTLER *Scum of Earth* 232 No attempt to discriminate, to discover political motive-patterns.

motive, *a.* Add: **2.** *motive power* (later *attrib.* example).

1936 *Discovery* Nov. 380/1 Motive-power accessories—like electric batteries—are not required.

motivelessly *adv.* (Further example.)

1970 G. GREER *Female Eunuch* 37 When men began to grow their hair in our generation they were not acting motivelessly.

motivelessness. (Further example.)

1933 L. STRACHEY *Characters & Commentaries* IV. ix. 315 This triumphant invention of the motivelessness of Iago has been dwelt upon by innumerable commentators.

motivic (mōᵘ·tivik), *a. Mus.* [f. MOTIV(E *sb.* + -IC.] Of or pertaining to a musical motive or motives. Also *Comb.* So **moti·vically** *adv.*

1947 A. EINSTEIN *Mus. Romantic Era* vii. 67 The thematic connection of the introductory *Andante* with the *Allegro ma non troppo*, a motivic 'safeguard' that one will not as yet find so clearly stressed in the Classics. *Ibid.* xi. 144 He [*sc.* Liszt] also feels doubly strongly the need for grappling the parts of the whole together motivically. **1957** E. T. CONE in N. Frye *Sound & Poetry* I. 4 The motivic shapes..of the music. **1959** *Listener* 16 July 114/1 These processes are not entirely explained by either motivic-contrapuntal or expansive-polyphonic methods. **1961** *Times* 13 Oct. 18/6 Webern's instrumentation of the Ricercare is not..so cannibalistic as a single hearing might lead one to suppose. A letter which he wrote.. shows that his principal aim..was with its motivic coherence. **1964** *Listener* 13 Aug. 250/2 *Erwartung* is composed without proper themes, without continuity of motivic work, [etc.]. **1970** *Daily Tel.* 19 Nov. 14/5 A wealth of further motivic events in these two slowish movements.

‖ **motiviert** (motivi·rt), *a.* Also **motivirt.** [G., pa. pple. of *motivieren* to motivate.] Motivated. Also **Motivie·rung,** motivation.

1812 H. C. ROBINSON *Diary* 20 Aug. in *On Bks. & their Writers* (1938) I. 108 He [*sc.* Coleridge] thinks the character of Faust himself not *motiviert.* **1866** GEO. ELIOT *Let.* 10 Apr. (1956) IV. 237, I feel sure that there are deficiencies..in what the Germans call the *Motivirung* seen from a legal point of view. **1890** G. B. SHAW *Let.* 17 Aug. (1965) 255, I also opined that the fatalistic apathy of Christ..was inadequately motivirt.

‖ **mot juste** (mo ʒüst). [Fr., lit. 'exact word'.] The precisely appropriate expression.

1912 *Nation* (N.Y.) 14 Mar. 264 Here and throughout we have conspicuously the *mot juste*, not one too many and each where it will tell. **1915** E. POUND in Joyce *Lett.* (1966) II. 364 My head is a squeezed rag, so don't expect le mot juste in this letter. **1916** [see *DIM *a.* 4 b]. **1932** WODEHOUSE *Louder & Funnier* 8 Most of these essays were written..at a time when the wolf at the door left little leisure for careful thought and the patient search for the *mot juste.* **1955** E. POUND *Section: Rock-Drill* lxxxv. 17 Get the mot juste before action. **1966** J. DOS PASSOS

Best Times (1968) ii. 44 For years I'd been reading Flaubert: letters, short stories... I caught his obsession for the *mot juste*.

‖ **moto** (mōu·to). *Mus.* [It.] In regard to musical tempo: motion, pace; *spec.* in **moto perpetuo**, a rapid instrumental composition consisting mainly of notes of equal value.

1740 J. Grassineau *Mus. Dict.* 145 *Moto*,..is a term that has many significations in music; sometimes it means only a motion or passage from one note to another... Sometimes it regards the quickness and slowness of such motion, as a brisk, slow, lively or languid motion. **1801** Busby *Dict. Mus.*, *Moto contrario* (Ital.), an expression applied to that progression of the different harmonic parts of a composition by which they move in opposite directions. **1884** F. Niecks *Conc. Dict. Mus. Terms* 177 *Moto* (It.), (1) Motion... (2) Movement... *Moto contrario* (It.), contrary motion. *Moto misto* (It.), mixed motion. *Moto obliquo* (It.), oblique motion. *Moto perpetuo* (It.), perpetual motion. **1901** G. B. Shaw *London Music in 1888–89* (1937) 389 A light-fingered and humorous *moto perpetuo* which might have come straight out of a Mendelssohn concerto. **1969** *Times* 30 Oct. 13/4 A brief moto perpetuo (with splendidly clean, disciplined figuration) by way of conclusion.

moto-. Add: **b. moto-cross**, cross-country motor-cycle racing.

1951 *Motor Cycle Sport in Pictures* 9 (*caption*) 1950 Moto-Cross victors. Left to right, B. W. Hall (B.S.A.), G. J. Draper (B.S.A.) and H. H. Lines (Ariel), three of the British team of 12 which won the Moto-Cross des Nations in Sweden. **1960** *Motor Cycling Sports Yearbk.* 81 (*heading*) Scrambles and Moto-cross. *Ibid.*, A dark cloud which has passed over the moto-cross world. **1968** K. Bird *Smash Glass Image* vii. 85 His machine kicked over the ground as if he were taking part in moto-cross.

motoneurone (mōutoniūə·rən). *Biol.* Also **motoneuron.** [f. Moto-: see Neuron in Dict. and Suppl.] = *motor neurone* s.v. *motor *sb.* and *a.* B. 2.

1908 *Nature* 6 Feb. 333/2 The inhibition of the motoneurones is .. followed by a superactivity in them. **1943** *Jrnl. Neurophysiol.* VI. 311 Few if any extensor motoneurons could have discharged in the earlier reflex. **1964** J. Z. Young *Model of Brain* iv. 50 In a mammal the largest motoneurons of the spinal cord may have a dendrite spread of 1 m. **1973** *Nature* 3 Aug. 254/1 The authors rule out the possibility that this occurs *via* the neural feedback loop involving the sensory fibres from the muscle to the motoneurone.

Motopia (mǒtōu·piă). [f. Mot(or *sb.* + Ut)opia.] A name for an urban environment designed to meet the needs of a pedestrian society by strict limitation of the use of the motor car. So **Moto·pian** *a.*

1959 *Engineering* 18 Sept. 206 (*heading*) Motopia: where traffic and pedestrians never meet. **1961** G. A. Jellicoe *Motopia* 7 Motopia..arises..from the realization that our present physical conditions are being thrown into chaos by the advent of one car per family and even one per person. *Ibid.* 15 The English preference..fixed the shape and alignment of the Motopian rectangle. **1968** C. A. Doxiadis *Between Dystopia & Utopia* 20 Such efforts as the *Motopia* of 1961, all of whose cars were to circulate on the tops of the roofs of the buildings.

motor, *sb.* and *a.* Add: **A.** *sb.* **1. a.** Restrict † *Obs.* to senses (*a*), (*c*), and (*d*), and add later example of (*b*).

1952 G. Sarton *Hist. Sci.* I. xix. 498 God exists, for it is the necessary principle and end of everything, the first motor.

2. c. A person in whom motor representations of perceptions predominate over auditory or visual ones.

1890 W. James *Princ. Psychol.* II. xviii. 62 The young savage was a *motor*. **1902** —— *Var. Relig. Exper.* xiv. 347 The shrew-type is defined as possessing an 'active unimpassioned temperament'. In other words, shrews are the 'motors', rather than the 'sensories'. **1929** J. Adams *Everyman's Psychol.* vii. 155 Men fall into two classes of sensories and motors... Motors have to receive sense impressions, and sensories have to send out messages leading to actions. *Ibid.* 156 The motor is often on the edge of action, eager to go.

3. b. (Further examples.)

1912 E. M. Forster *Let.* 25 Dec. in *Hill of Devi* (1953) 17 The Luards..got the Maharajah of Indore's motor. **1929** M. de la Roche *Whiteoaks* xxviii. 381 They were going by motor to the lakes.

5. *motor-ambulance, -hearse, -landau, -lorry, -plough, -sledge, toboggan, -tractor, -truck, vehicle, -wagon*; also designating sea vessels, aircraft, and other devices driven or powered by a motor, as *motor-cannon, -craft, -cruiser, -launch, -liner, meter, -mower, -ship, -sloop, torpedo-boat, -vessel, yacht.*

1915 Motor-ambulance [see *joy-ride *sb.*]. **1917** W. Owen *Let.* 25 Mar. (1967) 447, I went a joy ride on a Motor Ambulance, a Daimler. **1931** *Times Lit. Suppl.* 18 June 478/4 The occasional British practice of sending on billeting-parties in motor-ambulances. **1889** F. R. Stockton *Great War Syndicate* 79 She carried one motor-cannon of large size. **1939** *War Illustr.* 9 Dec. 390 It was to a similar type of French engine that the first successful 'motor-cannon', or shell gun, firing between the arms of the 'V', was fitted. **1905** *Daily Chron.* 17 June 9/1 The latest regulation that no small boat should 'lock' with a motor-craft appears to have caused considerable surprise. **1921** *Daily Colonist* (Victoria, B.C.) 9 Oct. 23/2 The motor cruiser Speejacks was reported safe last night. **1936** *Discovery* Sept. 272/2 Charting the coast from a small motor-cruiser. **1975** *Times* 19 Sept. 4 (Advt.), A boat test on the fast 33' motor cruiser Cleopatra. **1924** P. Creswick *Beaten Path* xxxiii. 180, I see there are motor-hearses now. **1973** 'R. MacLeod' *Burial in Portugal* i. 23 An elderly motor hearse with black paintwork and tarnished chrome.. carried a polished oak coffin. **1916** 'R. Dehan' *Earth to Earth* 73 The motor-landau in waiting for him at Covertsham Station, Deershire, was destined to receive a second passenger. **1912** W. Owen *Let.* 31 Aug. (1967) 158, I was asked to accompany them & Vicar on a motor-launch-trip. **1935** *Discovery* Dec. 372/2 A little undecked motor-launch for inshore work. **1975** 'D. Rutherford' *Mystery Tour* iii. 40 The trip by motor launch through the canals. **1913** *Chambers's Jrnl.* Jan. 31/1 The motor-liner above mentioned and her two sister-ships were built. **1931** *Evening Standard* 16 Jan. 9/1 (*caption*) The new motor-liner Warwick Castle leaving Belfast for her final trials. **1902** Kipling *Traffics & Discoveries* (1904) 391 There's a heavy load of grist just in from Lamber's Wood. Eleven miles it came in an hour and a half in our new motor-lorry. **1926** *Daily Chron.* 13 May 2/6 Three men were each sentenced to three months hard labour for inciting a crowd of people to set fire to a railway motor lorry in the city. **1934** *Discovery* Apr. 94/1 In most portions of the globe explorers under the new order have the valuable aids of aeroplane and motor-lorry. **1903** L. C. Reed *Amer. Meter Practice* iii. 37 These ten watts are the input into the motor meter, and the efficiency of this motor meter will give the ratio of the torque exerted on the armature. **1971** *Gloss. Electrotechnical, Power Terms* (*B.S.I.*) I. iv. 12 *Motor meter*, meter incorporating a motor. **1923** *Punch* 15 Aug. 165 (*caption*) The motor-mower takes charge. **1959** *Oxf. Univ. Gaz.* 1 Dec. 345/2 One new motor-mower was acquired in replacement of an old one now worn out and for which spare parts are no longer available. **1972** 'H. Carmichael' *Naked to Grave* vi. 74 Through the window he saw a motor mower, cans of paint, fertilizer in paper sacks. **1901** *Chambers's Jrnl.* Nov. 764/2 Great things are anticipated of a new method of land culture by means of a motor-plough. **1916** *Daily Colonist* (Victoria, B.C.) 25 July 11/3 The motorship City of Portland..has been given her trial trip. **1929** *Times* 2 Nov. 10/2 The Tuscan Star..is the first motorship ordered by the Blue Star Line. **1955** *Times* 3 May 15/6 The construction of two motor ships of about 1,300 tons deadweight, designed to operate in our short sea services. **1910** *Chambers's Jrnl.* Aug. 546/2 The 'final dash' [to the Pole]..will be made with the help of motor-sledges. **1936** *Discovery* July 215/1 Captain Scott took motor-sledges to the Antarctic in 1910. **1931** *Times Lit. Suppl.* 15 Jan. 33/3 M. Knut Stubbendorff..chartered the motor-sloop Isbjörn. **1948** *New Deal for Saskatchewan Fisheries* 20 Motor toboggans..manoeuver in almost any kind of terrain. **1940** Motor torpedo-boat [see *E-boat]. **1928** *Punch* 29 Feb. 248/3 The world is still a stage; the ruling factors Are petrol and pink legs and motor-tractors. **1934** *Discovery* June 143/2 Although aircraft and motor tractor have been used they are in no sense in competition with the dog-sledge. **1916** *Daily Colonist* (Victoria, B.C.) 2 July 15/5 The iron-shod war horse of former days has evolved into the padded wheel motor car, motor truck, and motor cycle of 1916. **1937** *Discovery* Nov. 359/1 The sandy wastes of the Gobi are being cut to ribbons by motor-truck tyres. **1890** J. W. Quinn *U.S. Pat. 431,993*, I.. have invented certain new and useful Improvements in Motor-Vehicles. **1937** *Discovery* July 194/2 The noise from motor vehicles. **1959** P. Bull *I know Face* ix. 148 He was referring to his motor-vehicle. **1931** *Daily Tel.* 21 May 7/5 Pioneers of motor-vessels to the East. **1969** *Jane's Freight Containers 1968–69* 394/1 This service is carried out by motor-vessels of 600–1,500 tons. **1909** *Chambers's Jrnl.* June 343/2 Large warehouses have their veritable fleets of motor-wagons. **1929** J. Buchan *Courts of Morning* III. i. 320 The raiders..helped themselves..loading the loot into light motor-wagons. **1905** *Outing* May 218/2 A 90 foot motor yacht was launched late last season. **1973** 'I. Drummond' *Jaws of Watchdog* i. 31 A fast, low-profile motor yacht five miles out to sea.

b. Of, pertaining to, or designed for use in motors, motor vehicles, or motoring, as *motor accident, age, bonnet, cap, -chassis, club, -coat, -dealer, -driver, fitter, garage, -goggles, -hooter, horn, -house, insurance, lantern, licence, -mania, -mask, mechanic, oil, race, -racing, -ride, -road, run, salesman, scarf, show, -smash, -spectacles, -tour, track, traffic, transport, -travel, -travelling, trip, trouble, tyre, -veil.*

1910 'Saki' *Reginald in Russia* 17 What I had mistaken for a motor accident was evidently a case of savage assault and murder. **1972** M. Yorke *Silent Witness* vi. 123 Roy's father had been killed in a motor accident. **1937** *Amer. Speech* XII. 317/1 The influence of..the motor age. **1963** *Daily Tel.* 28 Nov. 16/2 The root of the trouble is that our cities were never built for the motor age. **1910** *Blackw. Mag.* Nov. 604/2 My wife..had been patiently sitting in the hall wearing a new motor-bonnet. **1937** J. Laver *Taste & Fashion* x. 151 The latest trimming for these motor bonnets. **1906** *Daily Colonist* (Victoria, B.C.) 5 Jan. 3/4 (Advt.), Motor Caps. 50c, 75c, $1.00 reduced to 40c. **1907** Motor cap [see *ear-flap]. **1915** *Pearson's Mag.* Jan. 25 Great lines of these old motor-chassis, mounted with a serviceable lorry body, are to be met with on all the roads of France. **1934** *Amer. Speech* IX. 111/1 Such motor clubs as the *A.A.A.*, the *A.M.A.*, and the *Automobile Club of Southern California*. **1909** W. J. Locke *Septimus* iv. 57 Shrugging himself into his motor-coat, which the chauffeur brought him. **1910** *Blackw. Mag.* Apr. 480/1 A long leather motor-coat. **1937** *Discovery* May 164/1 Motor dealers in South America..order what they need by air mail. **1902** *Pall Mall Mag.* XXVIII. 410/1 Should motor drivers be subject to an examination as to proficiency? **1968** J. H. Burn *Lect. Notes Pharmacol.* (ed. 9) 7 It is good for a motor-driver driving through the night. **1961** *Evening Standard* 26 July 22/6 Skilled..motor fitter required. **1973** *Times* 16 Oct. 6/8 Christopher Smart, aged 25, a motor fitter. **1974** P. Wright *Lang. Brit. Industry* ix. 77 He's a mechanic, but he'd rather be called a motor fitter. **1902** Motor garage [see *garage *sb.* 1]. **1922** W. J. Locke *Tale of Triona* xxiv. 273 An ex-officer..who has just set up a motor garage. **1914** Beerbohm *Seven Men* (1919) 127 He did not wear motor-goggles. **1922** Joyce *Ulysses* 483 In motor jerkin, green motorgoggles on his brow. **1911** Beerbohm *Zuleika D.* xix. 291 All along the soaked towing-path lay strewn the horns, the rattles, the motor-hooters, that the youths had flung aside. **1909** *Chambers's Jrnl.* June 401/1 The predominant sounds.. were not those of wheels or whistles or motor-horns. **1931** M. Allingham *Look to Lady* x. 105 The squawk of a motor-horn. **1970** V. Canning *Great Affair* xii. 211 A chorus of motor horns began to blow in anger at some road block. **1902** D. Salomons in A. C. Harmsworth et al. *Motors* vi. 84 A well-built motor-house should cost nothing in the up-keep. **1971** *Daily Tel.* (Colour Suppl.) 18 June 33/4 There is the medium-sized house with its own tennis court and 'motor house', as garages were first called. **1955** *Times* 3 May 16/1 Motor insurance, which constitutes a substantial portion of our Accident business. **1975** *Times* 24 Sept. 3/2 The estimated cost of motor insurance premiums in 1975 was £580m. **1914** Chesterton *Flying Inn* xxi. 248 Humphrey had hung one of the motor lanterns on to a branch. **1907** *Yesterday's Shopping* (1969) 413/2 The motor licence case. **1957** *Railway Mag.* June 392/1 The beginnings of a reaction from the worst of motor-mania are bringing the unintimidated back on to the narrow gauge. **1966** *Punch* 16 Feb. 232 The ingenuity, energy and wealth that mechanised intellectual Peter Pans devote to indulgence of their motor-mania. **1916** *War Illustr.* V. 451/3 Our goggles..are shaped like a motor-mask. **1930** *Daily Express* 6 Oct. 7/4 James Horn, aged thirty-one, a motor mechanic. **1961** *Evening Standard* 25 July 15/1 (Advt.), Motor Mechanics required. **1939** G. B. Shaw *Geneva* II. 45 Motor oil is a sanction when you withhold it. Castor oil is a sanction when you administer it. **1900** *Racing Rules & Regulations* (Motor Car Club) 11 In all Motor Races held under the Rules of the Motor Car Club it must be stated on all Entry Forms..that they are so held. **1936** J. B. Priestley *They walk in City* iii. 41 An aeroplane parade, a motor race, a parade of cadets. **1905** *Official Programme Internat. Tourist Trophy* 4 A new departure in the history of motor racing. **1956** *Nature* 11 Feb. 246/2 The establishment of a motor-racing circuit on public roads in the Peak District National Park. **1974** J. Gardner *Corner Men* ii. 19 Most of the books were..concerned with motor cars or motor racing. **1914** Chesterton *Flying Inn* xx. 241 You owe me a motor-ride, you know. **1919** G. B. Shaw *Inca of Perusalem* Prologue in *Heartbreak House* 234 Dresses, hats, furs, gloves, motor rides: one bill after another. **1909** *Westm. Gaz.* 27 Aug. 2/2 Of more dramatic interest is the second part of the Bill, with its proposal for the creation of motor-roads. **1926** T. E. Lawrence *Seven Pillars* (1935) VII. lxxxii. 457 Gilman and Dowsett..had spent months in Wadi Itm, building, like engineers, a motor road through the gorge. **1949** *Archit. Rev.* CV. 118/1 The average speed of 30 m.p.h. here allowed for the surface plan is high, but, even allowing this figure, the advantage of elevated motor-roads is obvious. **1975** *Listener* 14 Aug. 199/1 A new motor road roaring past their windows. **1936** Joyce *Let.* 18 Nov. (1966) III. 393 Perhaps you could make your suggested motor run to the school at Zug? **1936** J. B. Priestley *They walk in City* i. 17 Mysterious and vaguely amorous gentlemen friends, usually commercial travellers or motor salesmen, loom and soar and suddenly vanish. **1973** A. Behrend *Samarai Affair* vi. 65 That Bromborough motor salesman chap separated from his wife. **1899** in A. Adburgham *Shops & Shopping* (1964) xxii. 261 Motor scarves. **1911** *Daily Colonist* (Victoria, B.C.) 28 Apr. 20/6 Waterproof Motor Scarf of good size.. each 75¢. **1905** S. A. Barnett *Let.* 2 Dec. in H. Barnett *Canon Barnett* (1918) II. 194 We have been to the Motor Show, when vast Olympia was crammed by a fashionable crowd. **1965** A. Christie *At Bertram's Hotel* i. 13 He could talk racing shop, cricket..give Motor Show information. **1972** *Nature* 31 Mar. 193/1 It is difficult to believe that international motor shows are instrumental in selling cars. **1916** W. Owen *Let.* 3 July (1967) 398, I was so happy to learn that your motor-smash came to no harm. **1931** R. Lehmann *Letter to Sister* 22 Things happen to you... You have been in a motor smash. **1911** D. H. Lawrence *White Peacock* II. iii. 262 She disengaged her arms to take off his disfiguring motor-spectacles. **1909** *London Mag.* Sept. 18/2 Excursions through the sky..are to become as common as motor-tours. **1915** J. Buchan *39 Steps* iv. 90 That's the end of my Scotch motor tour. **1928** *Manch. Guardian Weekly* 19 Oct. 301/2 Motor traffic and the urbanisation of large rural stretches are producing a hideous outbreak of advertisement hoardings, petrol pumps..and gaunt new motor-tracks. **1933** G. Robey *Looking Back on Life* xxviii. 306 Lord Dewar..made the famous epigram about there being only two classes of pedestrians in these days of reckless motor traffic—the quick, and the dead. **1926** *Brit. Gaz.* 12 May 2/4 At Liverpool there have been a few cases of interference with motor transport, for which heavy sentences have been inflicted. **1936** *Discovery* June 189/1 An ever-extending network of good macadamised roads is increasingly introducing the use of motor transport. **1923** A. E. Housman *Let.* 18 Aug. (1971) 215 Blazing hot all the time while motor-travel could temper it [*sc.* the weather]. **1909** *Chambers's Jrnl.* June 342/2 Putting the accidents on railways and on the roads together, motor-travelling included. **1934** Joyce *Let.* 25 Apr. (1966) III. 304, I was swept off..to make my first motor trip. **1950** M. Laski in *Contact* May–June 26/1 It is, of course, possible to take an extended motor-trip abroad without ever coming into contact with the Art of Navigation. **1911** *Chambers's Jrnl.* Jan. 55/1 Cleaver and Latham dropped into the Mediterranean..because of motor trouble. **1907** *Nature* 14 Feb. 383/1 Chemical composition of some motor-tyre rubbers. **1937** *Discovery* June 186/1 The wayside was strewn with motor tyres and broken down cars. **1970** Y. Carter *Mr. Campion's Falcon* vii. 59 Packing-cases, old motor tyres, drums of paint. **1907** *Yesterday's Shopping* (1969) 320D/3 Motor veil. In Crêpe de Chine. **1926** W. de la Mare *Connoisseur* 70 She was a rare one for the fashions: scarves and motor-veils, and that kind of thing.

c. Instrumental, as *motor-assisted, -driven, -dusted, -infested, -mad, -paced* adjs.

1954 *Highway Code* 32 To motor cyclists and riders of motor-assisted pedal cycles..*you must not* carry more than one passenger on a two-wheeled machine. **1904** *Motor Cycle* 6 June 551 A motor-driven roundabout. **1937** *Discovery* Dec. 387/1 The motor-driven fan. **1967** Karch & Buber *Offset Processes* v. 168 Motor-driven lenses, or hit-or-miss methods involving tricky out-of-focus photographic and lighting techniques are used. **1974** H. R. F. Keating *Bats fly up for Inspector Ghote* iii. 31 A powerful motor-driven dhow. **1909** M. B. Saunders *Litany Lane* iii. xviii. 236 His eyes were fixed on the white, motor-dusted hedges. **1909** *Q. Rev.* Jan. 143 This singularly congested and motor-infested country. **1931** T. H. Pear *Voice & Personality* 43 Today's world of motor-infested 'beauty-spots'. **1922** W. J. Locke *Tale of Triona* xxvi. 292 England ran motor-mad that summer. **1938** *Encycl. Brit. Bk. of Year* 100/1 Mills also set up a new record of 2 mins. 1⅕ secs. for the mile, standing start, unpaced; while Albert Marquet did the distance in 41⅗ secs. from a flying start and motor paced. **1973** *Observer* 16 Sept. 26/6 Instead of winning a motor-paced race by 10 laps, he would come from behind in the final lap to take it on the line.

6. motor-bandit *Obs.*, a thief who uses a motor car; **motor-bicycle** *v. intr.*, to travel on a motor bicycle (*rare*); so *motor-bicycling* vbl. sb., *motor-bicyclist*; **motor-bike** = *MOTORCYCLE *sb.*; hence as *v. intr.*, to travel on a motor-bike; so *motor-biking* vbl. sb.; **motor-bus,** a motor-driven omnibus; hence as *v. intr.*, to travel by motor-bus; **motor camp** orig. *U.S.*, a place where a motorist may park his car and set up camp; **motor caravan,** (*a*) a caravan designed to be towed by a motor car; (*b*) (see quot. 1964); **motor-coach,** (*a*) a single-decker motor-bus; (*b*) (see quot. 1940); **motor-coaster,** (*a*) a motorized vessel employed in sailing along the coast; (*b*) a type of big dipper at a fun-fair; **motor cop** *U.S. colloq.* = **motor-cycle cop*; **motor court** *U.S.*, (*a*) (see quot. 1936); (*b*) a motel; **motor-drive,** (*a*) a drive or journey in a motor-car; (*b*) driving power provided by a motor or engine; **motordrome** *Obs.*, a course for motor-racing; **motor generator** *Electr.*, an apparatus consisting of an electric motor and a generator with their armature shafts mechanically coupled which may be used to change the voltage, frequency, or number of phases of a supply; **motor glider,** an aircraft constructed like a glider but having an engine (now used in training glider pilots); **motor-home** *N. Amer.*, a very large vehicle equipped as a self-contained home; **motor hotel,** a hotel designed particularly for use by motorists; a motel; **motor inn** = **motor hotel*; **motor lodge,** a motel; **motor mate** *Obs.*, one who attends to the motor of an airship; **motor park,** (*a*) *U.S.* = **motor court* (*a*); (*b*) a car-park; **motor-sailer,** a boat equipped with both sails and a motor; **motor-school,** a school where the driving of motor vehicles is taught; **motor-scooter,** a two- or three-wheeled vehicle resembling a child's scooter, propelled by a small engine; hence **motor-scooterist,** one who rides a motor-scooter.

1913 *Punch* 19 Feb. 133/3 On top of all this Motor Bandit business comes the news that two men have been charged..with breaking into a bakery and stealing a sponge-cake, value one penny. **1935** *Ibid.* 6 Mar. 253/3 Returning from a jumble sale a man was held up by a motor-bandit. **1960** J. Betjeman *Summoned by Bells* v. 49 He motor-bicycled his life away, Looking for orchids in the Wytham Woods. **1912** W. Owen *Let.* 16 Aug. (1967) 155 Captain Wigan has had a motor-bicycling accident! **1908** R. Brooke *Let.* 4 Aug. (1968) 136 Abercrombie..is a Metrical Motor Bicyclist, a mumbly Wump, but often splendid. **1903** *Work* 18 Apr. 176/3 (Advt.), Motor Bike, 1½-h-p. **1911** W. Elmhirst *Freshman's Diary* (1969) 20 He went over to Malvern yesterday on his motor bike. **1927** H. G. Wells *Short Stories* 627, I remember my wild rush on my motor-bike to London. **1944** F. Clune *Red Heart* 33 He motor-biked to Alice Springs. **1958** J. Betjeman *Coll. Poems* 224 Along the village street the sunset strikes On young men tuning up their motor-bikes. **1972** M. Gee *In my Father's Den* 27 That motor-bike gang. **1913** G. B. Shaw *Let.* 21 Mar. in *B. Shaw & Mrs. Campbell* (1952) 100 It looked like a superb stroke of motorbiking. **1901** H. G. Wells in *Strand Mag.* Dec. 623/2 'You really think such a thing *is* possible?'.. 'As possible,' said Gibberne, and glanced at something that went throbbing by the window, 'as a motor-bus.' **1914** A. D. Godley *Let.* 10 Jan. in *Reliquiae* (1926) I. 292 What is this that roareth thus? Can it be a Motor Bus? **1915** D. O. Barnett *Lett.* 39 We came on from our last stopping place, whither we motor-bused, in a car. **1972** *Daily Tel.* 24 Mar. 15/1 Trolleys were a merger of motorbus and tram. **1925** *Sat. Even. Post* 10 Oct. 98/1 The average motor camp is too well known to need any description. **1926** *Daily Colonist* (Victoria, B.C.) 4 July 1/4 Motor Camp is Winning Favor. **1970** *N.Z. Listener* 21 Dec. 8/3 Don't join a joker in a motor camp cabin for the night... Try yelling for help in a motor camp in the holiday season, mate. **1930** *Daily Express* 1 Aug. 9/2 The most modern form of holiday transport—the motor-caravan, or trailer caravan. **1959** *Motor* 7 Oct. 246 Motor Caravans as practical vehicles. **1964** *Which?* Apr. 35/1 A motor caravan is basically an ordinary van that has been fitted with windows, beds and cupboards, a table, cooker and sink. **1923** Motor coach [see *COACH *sb.* 1 e]. **1926** *Times* 6 May 3/5 Intimidation of owners and drivers of motor-cars and motor-coaches plying for public hire is reported to-day in several localities. **1940** *Chambers's Techn. Dict.* 559/2 *Motor-coach*, a passenger coach, equipped with its own motors, for use on electrified railways; it is commonly used in conjunction with trailer coaches to make up a multiple-unit train. **1958** J. Betjeman *Coll. Poems* 153 Then the mystery tour By motor-coach inland this afternoon. **1972** *Modern Railways* Sept. 334 Bob [*sc.* Berner Oberland Bahn] trains are motorcoach-hauled and not fitted for push-pull operation. **1973** J. Porter *It's Murder with Dover* v. 42 All the cars and motor coaches..streaming through the village. **1928** *Daily Express* 5 Dec. 11/4 It is feared that the London motor-coaster, Wander (82 tons), has been lost, with a crew of five. **1974** *Amer. Speech 1971* XLVI. 84 Fast-moving amusement rides on elevated rails: toboggan, high rides,..shoot the chutes, motor coasters. **1915** *Policeman's Monthly* Oct. 14/1 The motor cops were brought in on the 'carpet'. **1918** R. Wagner *Film Folk* 23 If one goes home some afternoon and finds an ambulance or a motor cop outside the door, he instinctively looks for the camera. **1936** *Pop. Mechanics* LXVI. 674/1 The motor court is a recent development of the motor age. It's not a tourist park, it's not an auto camp... It's a collection of miniature homes clustered around a central service and administration building. **1962** I. Fleming *Spy who loved Me* i. 15 'Motel' isn't a good word any longer. It has become smart to use 'Motor Court' or 'Ranch Cabins'. **1906** Beerbohm *Around Theatres* (1924) II. 221 The details of the motor-drive are quite plausible. **1936** *Discovery* Apr. 113/2 The compressor, or vacuum pump, has an independent motor drive. **1971** *Amateur Photographer* 13 Jan. 51/1 The exposure system is powered by the motor drive batteries but a bridge circuit makes it independent of their precise voltage as they run down. **1908** *Westm. Gaz.* 4 Aug. 4/3 Mr. Locke-King has spent a large fortune in building this wonderful motordrome. **1887** *Electrician* 2 Dec. 74/1 We are enabled to reproduce photographs and sectional drawings of the Paris and Scott motor generator which recently underwent some tests at the Newcastle Exhibition. **1907** Parshall & Hobart *Electr. Railway Engin.* ix. 351 The locomotive is equipped with a motor-generator set comprising a single-phase motor directly connected to a continuous-current generator. **1930** *Engineering* 28 Feb. 278/2 The electrical load is consequently divided between the steam-driven sets and motor-generator sets in accordance with the demand for heating steam. **1966** *McGraw-Hill Encycl. Sci. & Technol.* VIII. 617/1 Motor-generator sets are used for a variety of purposes, such as providing a precisely regulated dc current for a welding application, a high frequency ac power for an induction-heating application, or a continuously and rapidly adjustable dc voltage to the armature of a dc motor employed in a position control system. **1923** *Jrnl. R. Aeronaut. Soc.* XXVII. 531 One of the things that instantly occurred to most people..was that the motor glider heralded the dawn of a new era in commercial aeronautics. **1969** *Sailplane & Gliding* XX. 491/2 The flying training will be based on glider and motor glider experience. **1971** D. Piggott *Gliding* (ed. 3) i. 8 The two-seater motor glider has proved an unqualified success for all stages of training. **1966** *Economist* 15 Jan. 181/1 There is the 'motor home', especially built on a lorry or bus chassis, an elaborate 'land yacht'. **1970** *Globe & Mail* (Toronto) 25 Sept. 38/9 (Advt.), Wanted Motor home, used, good condition. **1973** *Sci. Amer.* Apr. 1/1 (Advt.), These air springs are the only ones of their kind on motorhomes. **1974** *Trailer Life* Nov. 92 Writers, editors and publishers, who formerly had only the word trailer to contend with when referring to recreational vehicles now had to wrestle with trailers, pickup campers, chassis-mounts and the few then-existing motorhomes. **1965** *Punch* 1 Dec. 798 They call themselves motor lodges, motor courts, motor hotels, even tourtels and autotels, but motel is the word that blisters the night sky of the American suburbs. **1967** *Autocar* 5 Oct. 44/1 (*caption*) New motor hotels—not motels—specially designed for motorists, are being opened by the Trust House group. **1967** *Time* 21 Apr. 25, 46 restaurants and six motor inns. **1974** *Country Life* 21 Mar. 693/2 This privately owned Motor Inn situated on the water's edge. **1965** Motor lodge [see **motor hotel*]. **1975** *Globe & Mail* (Toronto) 24 May 10/2 Judge Dunlap dismissed two charges of procuring, one of attempting to procure and a charge of keeping a common bawdy house in a motor lodge here. **1928** C. F. S. Gamble *Story N. Sea Air Station* xxii. 411 One of the motor-mates of the amidships gondola raised the black curtain. **1939** *New Yorker* 14 Oct. 72 The usual phrase for cabin colonies in California is 'auto court'; 'motor park', perhaps copied from 'trail park'. **1965** W. Soyinka *Road* i. 1 The motor-park layabouts are sprawled on the floor and on benches. **1972** C. Achebe *Girls at War* 60 Everybody, even a motor-park tout, knows what school fees are for. **1934** *Yachting* (N.Y.) Jan. 39 A consideration of the motor-sailer. **1937** [see *FIFTY-FIFTY *adv.* and *a.*]. **1971** J. R. L. Anderson *Reckoning in Ice* vi. 111 His boat was what is called a motor-sailer, which generally means..more engine than sail. **1974** *Country Life* 24 Jan. 153/1 We have pure sailing craft, motor sailers and motor yachts, excellently crewed.. from £15 to £100 per person per day. **1909** *Chambers's Jrnl.* June 342/1 The..gentleman..is now getting his country grooms trained at a motor-school. **1919** Motor-scooter [see *BULLER *sb.*[4]]. **1938** *Times* 28 Feb. 12/2 He then tears down the course on a motor-scooter. **1956** *Railway Mag.* Nov. 722/2 Goods agents..have been provided with motor scooters, to enable them to cover ground more quickly. **1957** J. I. M. Stewart *Use of Riches* 58 The age of the motor-scooter had brought little of modernity to Castelarbia as yet. **1960** *News Chron.* 22 Mar. 7/8, I saw White running behind one of the motor-scooterists. **1965** J. Creasey *Toff & Spider* ii. 22 The motor-scooterist had turned into the Square and was slowing down.

B. *adj.* **2.** (Further examples.) *motor cortex*, the part of the cerebral cortex which has a motor function; *motor neurone*, a neurone having a motor function; *motor root*, the anterior or ventral root of spinal or certain cranial nerves, containing axons of motor neurones; *motor unit*, a neuroanatomical unit which comprises a single motor neurone and the muscle fibres on which it acts.

1840 W. J. E. Wilson *Anatomist's Vade Mecum* viii. 387 There are thirty-one pairs of spinal nerves, each arising by two roots, an anterior or motor root, and a posterior or sensitive root. **1878** *Jrnl. Nerv. & Mental Dis.* V. 766 The largest nerves of the human body (sciatics) arise precisely from that point of the lumbar cord where we find the largest, so-called motor, cells. **1890** W. James *Princ. Psychol.* I. ii. 61 The motor cortex might be sensitive as well as motor. **1898** *Jrnl. Compar. Neurol.* VII. 185 The neuraxis of the motor neuron loses its medullary sheath before piercing the sarcolemma. **1925** Liddell & Sherrington in *Proc. R. Soc.* B. XCVII. 516 The experimental results suggest that a reflex maintains maximal response of the individual 'motor-unit' by a degree of central excitation which is commonly 'supramaximal'. **1926** J. S. Huxley *Essays Pop. Sci.* 286 The rest of the [spinal] cord, however, and in particular the motor areas and motor roots, show no increase in size, showing that the number of muscle-fibres to be supplied does not stimulate the growth of the supplying cells. **1942** O. Larsell *Anat. Nervous Syst.* xxiv. 326 The upper motor neuron fibers of the pyramidal tract terminate in synaptic relation to large motor cells in the anterior column of the gray matter of the spinal cord. **1970** M. Hollander tr. *Monnier's Functions Nervous Syst.* II. xxvi. 572 (*heading*) Functions of the motor cortex and pyramidal system. **1970** J. G. Chusid *Correlative Neuroanat. & Functional Neurol.* (ed. 14) ii. 76/2 The motor unit is made up of the anterior horn cell of the spinal cord and the muscle group it innervates. **1973** *Gray's Anat.* (ed. 35) 1002/2 The motor nucleus of the trigeminal nerve gives rise to the fibres of the motor root. **1974** Passmore & Robson *Compan. Med. Studies* III. xxxiv. 53/2 Motor neurone disease may present with any combination of upper and lower motor neurone signs.

3. Substitute for def.: Of, pertaining to, or involving muscular movement; based upon or received through the movement of parts of the body. (Further examples.)

1880 W. James *Coll. Ess. & Rev.* (1920) 163 Wundt says that were our motor feelings of an afferent nature, 'it ought to be expected that they would increase and diminish with the amount of inner or outer work actually effected in contraction.' **1890** —— *Princ. Psychol.* II. xix. 131 The facts shade off into the phenomena of motor automatism, trance, etc. **1899** A. G. Whyte tr. *Binet's Psychol. of Reasoning* 24 When we think of the ball, this idea must comprise the images of these muscular sensations, as it comprises the images of the sensations of sight and touch. Such is the motor image. **1925** C. Fox *Educational Psychol.* 228 Walking is not bringing into use unconscious motor-images. **1936** *Amer. Speech* XI. 88/2 Speech responses are so complex that they can hardly be considered identical with motor reflexes. **1942** A. T. Poffenberger *Princ. Appl. Psychol.* vi. 105 The fineness of motor control or coördination is..an essential factor in many forms of adjustment. **1951** A. D. Woodruff *Psychol. of Teaching* (ed. 3) xvi. 270 Motor behavior that is guided by perceptual cues, such as playing the piano. **1951** C. I. Hovland in S. S. Stevens *Handbk. Exper. Psychol.* xvii. 627/2 An important change with practice in motor learning is change in muscular tension. **1958** M. Argyle *Relig. Behaviour* v. 56 Evidence drawn from actual studies of conversion shows that people converted at public meetings are more easily hypnotized, display more motor automatisms and can therefore be classified to some extent as hysterics. **1962** *Canadian Jrnl. Linguistics* VII. 65 The assumption that the ability to speak is simply a motor-skill which can be measured by tests of imitation and reading aloud. **1969** Miller & McNeill in Lindzey & Aronson *Handbk. Social Psychol.* (ed. 2) III. xxvi. 687 At the other [extreme] would be the so-called 'motor theory' of speech, which holds that a listener can recognize speech only by imitating (at least covertly) the motor movements that would produce it. **1971** *Jrnl. Gen. Psychol.* LXXXV. 208 In the events intervening between stimulus input and motor output, there is ordinarily first the operation of cognition.

motor, *v.* Add: (Further examples.) Also (*trans.*), to traverse (a distance) in a motor vehicle.

1919 Wodehouse *Damsel in Distress* viii. 103, I motored down with a boy I know. **1928** 'S. S. Van Dine' *Greene Murder Case* xii. 141 Vance and Ada and I motored the few blocks to 18, Broad Street. **1932** J. Buchan *Gap in Curtain* i. 31 Mayot had motored to Cirencester to meet a friend. **1972** *Daily Tel.* (Colour Suppl.) 27 Oct. 86/3 From Sidmouth I walked (though most people motor) to Salcombe Regis. **1972** *Listener* 21 Dec. 849/1 If we were opening a show with a Boxing Day matinee, we should have finished rehearsing on Friday night and then have motored to our respective homes.

b. *intr.* To travel in a motor-boat; to use the engine in a sailing-boat.

1968 'D. Halliday' *Dolly & Singing Bird* xiii. 147 'You don't deny you were motoring?' Johnson kept his voice reasonable. 'We used the engine..to South Rona and back. At Portree, we changed over to sail.' **1971** P. M. Hubbard *High Tide* xiii. 134 There was no wind to sail with. I could motor down river and hope to pick up something of a sailing breeze outside.

motorable (mōᵘ·tǝrăb'l), *a.* [f. Motor *v.* + -able.] Of a road or district: suitable for motor vehicles; capable of being travelled over in a motor vehicle.

1920 A. L. Bagley *Holiday Rambles N. Wales* 178 This is certainly not a motorable road. **1953** X. Fielding *Stronghold* 93 The only motorable highway in the whole of Sphakia province. **1972** P. M. Hubbard *Whisper in Glen*

iii. 25 Roads which were a little alarming but just about motorable. **1974** *Country Life* 24 Jan. 144/2 We..thought of a certain lake. Ten hours by pony from the nearest motorable road.

Motorail (mōᵘ·torēᵻl). [Blend of MOTOR *sb.* and RAIL *sb.*[2]] A service whereby cars, with their drivers and passengers, are transported by railway. Also *attrib.*

1968 *Daily Tel.* 6 Jan. 10/6 This year British Rail will have nearly 100 more Motorail trains, giving a total carrying space for 90,000 cars. **1971** *Country Life* 25 Nov. 1463/3 British Rail unveiled their plans for 1972 Motorail... The 27 routes to be operated will have a combined capacity for 120,000 cars and over half a million passengers. **1974** *Ibid.* 18 Apr. 965/4 Excellent train service to Penzance..and Motorail links throughout Britain.

Motorama (mōᵘtǒrā·mă). [Blend of MOTOR *sb.* 3 b and *-or)ama* after PANORAMA.] An exhibition of motor vehicles.

1950 *Richmond* (Va.) *News Leader* 18 Jan. 38/1 General Motors opens its auto show here. The display which General Motors calls 'Mid-century Motorama' brings..38 of GM's 1950 model cars. **1954** *Amer. Speech* XXIX. 157 *Motorama*, an automobile exhibit. **1974** *John O'Groat Jrnl.* (Wick) 6 Sept. 2/2 *Motorama*, Wick & District Round Table present Motorama Spectacular at Ackergill on Sunday, 15th September at 2 p.m.

mo·tor-boat, *sb.* A motor-driven boat or launch.

1902 *New Liberal Rev.* Apr. 440 The paraffin motor..is ..impossible in anything but an open motor-boat. **1913** E. F. BENSON *Thorley Weir* i. 11 If I must go on the river, give me a motor-boat. **1973** A. BEHREND *Samarai Affair* ii. 24 He would..step overside into the boarding punt, a small-sized motor-boat. **1973** *Fisheries Fact Sheet* (Environment Canada Fisheries & Marine Service) No. 1. 2/2 Individual fishermen fishing near their homes from small row-boats or motor-boats.

mo·tor-boating, *vbl. sb.* Also without hyphen and as two words. [f. prec. + -ING[1].] **1.** Travel in a motor-boat.

1918 *Chambers's Jrnl.* Aug. 541/1 The water is never dangerously rough, and provides the finest possible field for motor-boating. **1961** *Guardian* 8 Feb. 10/2 The sports of motor-boating and water-skiing.

2. *Electronics.* Oscillation in an amplifier that is of such a low frequency that individual cycles may be heard, giving a characteristic sound, and caused by feedback from the output to the input of earlier stages, often through a common voltage supply.

1930 J. H. REYNER *Testing Radio Sets* vi. 84 Back-coupling with a mains unit usually takes the form known as motor-boating. The oscillation set up is of a low frequency and gives a continuous 'pop, pop, pop'. **1943** F. E. TERMAN *Radio Engineers' Handbk.* v. 409 A power supply having low internal impedance at low frequencies is also helpful in eliminating motorboating. **1945** *Electronic Engin.* XVII. 429 Regeneration may lead to low-frequency oscillation (about 5 to 10 c/s) known as 'motor boating'. **1965** G. J. KING *Radio & Audio Servicing Handbk.* iii. 78 Decoupling prevents signals which could occur in an element common to two or more stages from getting back into the input circuits and causing oscillation or motorboating.

So **mo·tor-boat** *v. intr.*, (*a*) to travel in a motor-boat; (*b*) (of an amplifier) to exhibit motor-boating.

1922 *Contemp. Rev.* Mar. 409 The scenery through which he tramped or motor-boated. **1932** F. E. TERMAN *Radio Engin.* vii. 277 Amplifiers receiving their plate voltage from a common dry battery have a tendency to motor-boat when the batteries are near the end of their useful life, particularly when the amplification is high. **1970** *Nature* 28 Nov. 797/2 Two men motor-boating on the loch collided with a large object.

motorcade (mōᵘ·tǒɪkēᵻd). orig. *U.S.* [f. MOTOR *sb.* + *-CADE.] A procession of motor vehicles.

1913 *Arizona Republican* (Phoenix) 5 June 2/4 The motorcade can make its music self supporting and donate large and salubrious gobs of melody to the natives at all points along the line. *Ibid.* 4 July 4/2 This 'motorcade' came from a suggestion thrown out by the sporting editor of the Republican. It was immediately accepted by several local automobile owners, whereupon, the sporting editor [*sc.* Lyle Abbott] became the busiest man in Phoenix and hammered away at the 'motorcade' a term which, by the way, he had invented sometime before in order that newspapers might keep pace with the developments of vehicular transportation. **1924** *N. & Q.* 19 Apr. 288/1 A parade of motor cars..was termed in the local [Florida] papers a 'motorcade'. **1928** in *Amer. Speech* (1930) VI. 155 The North Dakota farmers' motorcade started to-day on its long drive to the Republican Convention at Kansas City. **1933** *Sun* (Baltimore) 19 Aug. 3/1 The action was taken after a telegram from the Governor was read to workers who came into Mahanoy City in a motorcade. **1936** [see *-CADE]. **1942** S. L. A. MARSHALL *Armies on Wheels* vi. 99 A motor-cade in which the cars become bogged down. **1953** *Times* 13 July 3/5 The word 'motorcade'..is..no novelty. Some years before the war it was employed—and perhaps coined—by the Salvation Army in advertisements of a procession of cars which bore the Army's principal officers on a tour of the main towns of the country. **1969** *Wall St. Jrnl.* 28 Jan. 1/6 He rides in Presidential motorcades. **1972** *Guardian* 25 Oct. 2 The old-style motorcade..is hard to beat as a campaigning technique. **1974** *Northern Times* (Golspie, Sutherland) 23 Aug. 7/6 Mr. George Reid, M.P. for Clackmannan and East Stirling, accompanied by Mr. Sutherland, will be in a motorcade covering Helmsdale, Brora, Golspie, Dornoch and Bonar-Bridge.

motor car. Add: (Further examples.) Also *attrib.* Hence **mo·tor-carist,** a motorist; **mo·tor-carring,** travel in a motor car.

1899 *Motor-Car World* I. 37/2 Many of the disabilities under which motorcarists suffer in England will be removed. **1901** 'SAKI' *Let.* 17 Aug. in *Square Egg* (1924) 61 Travelling with Aunt Tom is more exciting than motorcarring. **1903** *Westm. Gaz.* 12 Jan. 10/1 The champion motor-carist of the House of Commons. **1909** *Daily Graphic* 26 July 7/4 Numbers came from all the neighbouring towns, while motor-car parties came from considerable distances. **1931** H. G. WELLS *Work, Wealth & Happiness of Mankind* (1932) 21 The motor-car 'bandit'. **1970** 'D. HALLIDAY' *Dolly & Cookie Bird* i. 4 George is a motor-car salesman. **1972** *Daily Tel.* (Colour Suppl.) 20 Oct. 52/1 The Rolls-Royce approach to making motor cars (they are never just 'cars' at Crewe). **1974** *Times* 4 Dec. 17/2 The motor-car industry..has been the most important single engine of economic development in industrial countries for the past fifty years.

mo·tor-cycle, *sb.* [MOTOR *sb.* 5.] A form of bicycle, usually larger and heavier than an ordinary bicycle, having a small (usu. petrol) motor by which it is propelled. Also *attrib.*, as **motor-cycle cop** (*U.S. colloq.*), **policeman,** a policeman who rides a motor-cycle.

1896 [see MOTOR *sb.* 5]. **1902** *Motor Cycling* 12 Feb. 24/1 In a year or two motor cycles will be as plentiful as the ordinary cycle is to-day. **1919, 1928** [see *COMBINATION 9* b]. **1927** K. EUBANK *Horse & Buggy Days* 33 There's always some fool motor-cycle cop coming along to interfere. **1928** 'S. S. VAN DINE' *Greene Murder Case* xxv. 288 On North Broadway we were forced to the kerb by a motor-cycle policeman. **1934** T. S. ELIOT *Rock* i. 21 Every son would have his motor cycle. **1958** *New Statesman* 22 Feb. 220/1 A motor-cycle policeman seized his shoulder and flung him along the pavement. **1972** C. WESTON *Poor, Poor Ophelia* (1973) vii. 39 All those sex-mad motorcycle toughies. **1972** R. ADAMS *Watership Down* xix. 111 Few places are far from human noise—cars, buses, motor-cycles, tractors, lorries. **1974** *Times* 18 Mar. 7/1 Five people were killed here in a running battle between motorcycle gangs.

Hence **mo·tor-cycle** *v. intr.*, to ride a motor-cycle; **mo·tor-cycling** *vbl. sb.*; **mo·tor-cyclist,** one who uses a motor-cycle.

1902 *Motor Cycling* 12 Feb. 24/1 Now that motor cycling has come to stay..it may not be out of place to say where improvements may be made that will be beneficial to..all those who motor-cycle. *Ibid.* 19 Feb. 32 Motor cyclists will not require palatial club premises. **1912** G. W. E. RUSSELL *Afterthoughts* xx. 184 Motorists and cyclists, and those strange hybrids the motor-cyclists, seem to disregard weather. **1925** E. F. NORTON *Fight for Everest, 1924* v. 103, I wore a fur-lined leather motor-cycling helmet. **1956** G. N. PATTERSON *God's Fool* ii. 17 Pulling on his motor-cycling gloves savagely, he stalked out. **1972** 'J. & E. BONETT' *No Time to Kill* i. 5 The chef's elder daughter..motor-cycled out for a free lunch in the hotel kitchen. **1973** J. WAINWRIGHT *Pride of Pigs* 92 The motor-cyclist was pinned under his machine.

motordom (mōᵘ·tǒɹdəm). [f. MOTOR *sb.* + -DOM.] The realm or world of motors; motor vehicles, the people who use them, or those who deal in them, considered collectively.

1900 *Captain* III. 225/1 In the world of motordom. **1909** *Westm. Gaz.* 2 Nov. 2/3 There is scarcely a woman in London who has not had to sacrifice the cadences of talk to the Moloch of Motordom. **1910** [see *CRACKER 4 b]. **1916** W. J. LOCKE *Wonderful Year* vi. 84 Fashionable motordom halted at the Hôtel des Grottes. **1961** L. MUMFORD *City in Hist.* xv. 474 The 'progressive' metropolises of motordom, like Los Angeles, exhibit..all the urban evils of the palaeotechnic period.

mo·tored, *a.* [f. MOTOR *sb.* + -ED[2].] Provided with a motor.

1928 *Daily Express* 17 Nov. 9/3 The Wright brothers completed their motored glider—the first real airplane—in their bicycle shop at Dayton on Nov. 17th 1903.

motoric (mǒtǒᵊ·rik), *a.* [f. MOTOR *sb.* and *a.* + -IC.] **a.** Of, pertaining to, or characterized by muscular movement.

1930 *Program 47th Meeting Mod. Lang. Assoc. Amer.* 12 An attempt to illustrate the present status of *Schallanalyse* in its visual, acoustic, and motoric approach **1958** *New Scientist* 14 Aug. 610/2 A simple motoric rhythm in which the animal repeatedly pulled the brush towards himself. **1971** *Nature* 18 June 470/2 The reasons for favouring this method are not quite clear. Motoric convenience, for example, seems an inadequate explanation, in view of normal writing practice.

b. Of a piece of music or its performance: marked by much movement or energy.

1937 *Sat. Rev. Lit.* (U.S.) 23 Jan. 6 Stravinsky's crisp sentences, often naked in their brevity, recall the 'motoric' rhythms of his *Noces.* **1942** *Ann. Reg. 1941* 338 The Symphony..was an interesting..example of what the continental critics used to call 'motoric music'. **1972** *Daily Tel.* 4 May 14/3 Its determined progress was crisply outlined without excessively motoric playing.

motoring, *vbl. sb.* (In Dict. s.v. MOTOR *sb.* and *a.*) Also *attrib.*, as *motoring-cap, chocolate, coat, glove, goggles, map, offence, veil.*

1909 *Chambers's Jrnl.* Sept. 588/2 She raised a little gloved hand and patted the hair under a dainty motoring-cap. **1966** D. HOLBROOK *Flesh Wounds* 130 In handy places here and there the tank men kept their round tins of cigarettes and their bars of motoring chocolate. **1907** G. B. SHAW *John Bull's Other Island* IV. 83 Broadbent enters, soiled and disordered as to his motoring coat. **1931** M. ALLINGHAM *Look to Lady* xx. 204 Mr. Campion in a motoring coat and hatless. **1920** W. J. LOCKE *House of Baltazar* viii. 101 Drawing on his motoring gloves. **1942** *R.A.F. Jrnl.* 3 Oct. 30 There were those first flights..in all the glory of an old flying helmet and motoring gloves. **1903** G. B. SHAW *Man & Superman* III. 78 Tanner and Straker, in their motoring goggles, leather coats, and caps, are led in from the road by the brigands. **1975** 'M. DUKE' *Death of Holy Murderer* ii. 37 She removed a pair of antique motoring goggles. **1926–7** *Army & Navy Stores Catal.* 915/1 Contour Motoring Map of British Isles. **1931** R. H. HEATON *Perfect Hostess* 133 A set of motoring maps of England and Scotland. **1974** *Camping & Caravanning* Sept. 12/1 The R.A.C. have introduced two new series of motoring maps. **1933** M. ALLINGHAM *Sweet Danger* xvii. 213 The young gents who were wanted for a motoring offence. **1972** *Police Rev.* 17 Nov. 1484/1 Although penalties for motoring offences may be low, it is a truism that purely in financial terms it works out cheaper being a petty criminal than being a forgetful motorist. **1973** P. MOYES *Curious Affair of Third Dog* i. 20 He's not a *criminal*... It was only a motoring offence—but unfortunately he killed somebody. **1955** N. MARSH *Scales of Justice* vii. 160 Illustrations of young women in dustcoats and motoring veils. **1971** *Country Life* 14 Oct. 966/3 Intrepid ladies in large hats, goggles, motoring veils and dust-coats. **1974** I. MURDOCH *Sacred & Profane Love Machine* 229 She now donned a floppy green hat and tied it over her head with a sort of motoring veil.

motorism (mōᵘ·tǒriz'm). [f. MOTOR *sb.* + -ISM.] The use or prevalence of motor vehicles; the world of motoring.

1913 *Chambers's Jrnl.* Feb. 132/2 It is but ten or twelve years since the time when the tide of motorism began to flow. **1930** *Time & Tide* 24 Jan. 101 The death-dealing motorism of the highway. **1952** *Birmingham* (Alabama) *News* 20 Sept. 4 If you want to be in the forefront of motorism these days, it seems you have to have headlamps outside the fenders, mudguards that only partially protect, and if possible wire wheels.

motorist. (Later examples.)

1912 *Collier's* 5 Oct. 30/1 In the new Model C-Six the motorist is constantly in a position of rest and free from care or strain. **1960** *Spectator* 30 Sept. 479 Gibberd gave a motorist's-eye view of the town. **1975** *Times* 10 Sept. 3/2 Motorists..would be..invited to discuss their driving with road safety officials.

motorium (motǒᵊ·riɒ̆m). [mod.L., f. *mōtōrius* moving, f. L. *mōt-*, stem of *movēre* to move: cf. -ORY[1].] **1.** *Psychol.* Collectively, the centres in the brain concerned in the function of voluntary muscle; that system of the body capable of initiating and putting into effect muscular movement.

1885 J. ROSS *Handbk. Dis. Nervous Syst.* 73 The central ends of the individual sensory mechanisms are unified by a collective centre—the *sensorium commune*—which is the general centre of nervous connections on the afferent side. It may also be supposed that the individual motor centres are unified by a general centre of nervous connections which may be regarded as a *motorium commune.* **1900** DORLAND *Med. Dict.* 398/1 *Motorium,* (1) a motor center; especially the common center of motor influences; (2) the motor apparatus of the body. **1924** R. M. OGDEN tr. *Koffka's Growth of Mind* 80 The optical sensorium and motorium can not be regarded as two independent pieces of apparatus, since for many types of performance they constitute a unitary organ. **1959** S. KOCH *Psychology* II. 76 For certain purposes, in dealing with transactions with the physical world (walking, performing a motor task, driving a car, etc.), the motorium may be considered to be the muscular apparatus of the organism. Even in such cases, however, it may prove to be useful to consider tools as a part of the motorium.

2. *Zool.* A cytoplasmic structure in some ciliate protozoa forming the centre of the neuromotor apparatus.

1914 R. G. SHARP in *Univ. Calif. Publ. Zool.* XIII. 83 We now come to the description of what is believed to be the most interesting structure in the anatomy of this organism [*sc.* the protozoan *Diplodinium ecaudatum*]... The possibility of this structure functioning..as a neuromotor apparatus is suggested and..the designation neuromotor apparatus will be used, and its constituent parts will be described as a motorium or motor mass. **1926** G. N. CALKINS *Biol. Protozoa* ii. 104 Certain special types of cytoplasmic kinetic elements such as myonemes, motorium, and conductile fibers, are characteristic of the ciliates. **1940** L. H. HYMAN *Invertebrates* I. iii. 65 All these fibrils may center in a small body, the motorium. **1966** *New Scientist* 3 Nov. 242/1 Another interesting feature of *Euplotes* is that, as Taylor first noticed in 1920, some of the cirri are connected by a system of minute fibrils to a structure near the front of the animal. This he called the motorium.

motorization (mōᵘ:tǒrəizēᵻ·ʃən). [f. next + -ATION.] **1.** *Psychol.* The process of making a presentation motorial in character. *rare.*

1901 *Amer. Jrnl. Psychol.* XII. 304 The motorization of an exposed word would suggest another similar in sound. *Ibid.* 309 The single-word motorization does not make so much noise in consciousness.

2. The introduction, use, or possession of motor vehicles; equipment with motor vehicles.

1913 in WEBSTER Add. **1919** *N.Y. Times Mag.* 6 Apr. 11 During the war the motorization of artillery proceeded at an unprecedented rate. **1929** H. ROWAN-ROBINSON *Further Aspects of Mechanization* ii. 9 The motorization of infantry and cavalry divisions furnishes.. additional strategic mobility. **1930** *Time & Tide* 13 Sept. 1134 The world moves largely on rubber, which alone makes motorization possible. **1960** H. HONDERMARD in E. Davies *Roads & their Traffic* vi. 130 The extent of motorization, expressed by the number of vehicles per 1000 inhabitants, has had to be periodically reviewed. *Ibid.* 132 Fig. 6.1..shows a significant correlation between the degree of motorization and national income in different countries. **1960** G. MIKES *How to be Inimitable* 57 This motorisation has developed into a war between the motorists and the authorities. **1969** *Daily Tel.* 26 Aug. 14/3 Full motorisation of Britain's cities..might go as high as £12,000 million.

motorize (mōᵘ·tŏrəiz), *v.* [f. MOTOR *sb.* and *a.* + -IZE.] *trans.* **1.** *Psychol.* To convert (visual or auditory sensations or images) into motorial presentations; to apprehend in a motorial manner. Also *intr.* or *absol. rare.*

1901 *Amer. Jrnl. Psychol.* XII. 308 The word..seems to be motorized as soon as singly presented. *Ibid.* 309 This.. has reference to readers who motorize.

2. To provide or furnish with a motor or with motor vehicles. Hence **mo·torized** *ppl. a.*; **mo·torizing** *vbl. sb.*

1913 WEBSTER Add., *Motorize*, to substitute motor-driven vehicles or automobiles, for the horses and horse-drawn vehicles of (a fire department, city, etc.). **1922** *Daily Mail* 24 Nov. 6 These machines have gone beyond the stage of motorised pedal cycles and are in all respects real motor-cycles. **1924** *Public Opinion* 8 Aug. 130/3 If one should dream of motorising the entire world on the scale of the United States. **1927** *Glasgow Herald* 5 Apr. 8 Serried ranks of tanks advancing against each other.. with motorised artillery bringing up the rear. **1933** ADE *Let.* 13 Nov. (1973) Now there ain't no income from the darn stuff [*sc.* farm lands]. I think it is entirely because of the fact that the world has become motorized but I am not proposing any remedies. **1938** *Times* 16 May 9/1 The extension of the air arm and the motorizing of units. **1938** *Sun* (Baltimore) 31 Aug. 20/3 The regiment is motorized and will come over the Governor Nice Highway to the city. **1958** *Edmonton* (Alberta) *Jrnl.* 24 June IV. 16/6 Motorized toboggans have made their appearance in the Mackenzie River delta. **1972** *Physics Bull.* July 402/2 The construction of a motorized drill table for physically handicapped operators. **1972** 'G. BLACK' *Bitter Tea* (1973) ii. 26 Angels mightn't be watching over them, but a good third of the motorized police in the State were.

motorless (mōᵘ·tǫ̈ɹlės), *a.* [f. MOTOR *sb.* + -LESS.] **1.** Not provided with a motor; performed without the use of a motor; esp. of gliders or flying in gliders.

1897 [see *air-sailer (-or)* s.v. *AIR *sb.*[1] B. III. 5]. **1908** [see *aerodone* s.v. *AERO- b]. **1930** V. W. PAGÉ *Henley's ABC of Gliding & Sailflying* (1931) i. 11 They had proved their aëronautical theories with motorless ships which actually stayed aloft a short-time, supported only by air currents. *Ibid.* iii. 49 (*caption*) Outline Drawings..Showing How Bird Form is Approximated in Creations Intended for Motorless Flight.

2. Of a road, etc.: having little or no traffic.

1970 *Daily Tel.* 19 Sept. 12 Experiments with motorless zones in wild and remote country. **1972** *Listener* 21 Dec. 849 We should drive on motorless roads, praying that conditions would be good.

motor-man. (Further examples.)

1904 F. LYNDE *Grafters* xxiv. 298 The conductor and motorman of an early morning electric car. **1908** [see *dead man's handle* s.v. *DEAD MAN]. **1935** 'J. GUTHRIE' *Little Country* xxv. 367 Ernest..climbed on board a tram... The motorman, instead of moving off immediately, waited a moment. **1956** *Railway Mag.* Nov. 744/1 The back of the motorman's compartment is formed by a glass panel so that passengers can enjoy a good view of the track. **1971** *Railway World* Mar. 127 Someone in High Office..gave orders that motormen should count ten between releasing the air brakes and re-applying power.

motor-minded (stress variable), *a.* [f. MOTOR *sb.* and *a.* + MINDED *ppl. a.*] **1.** *Psychol.* Having a mind in which motor images predominate over visual and auditory ones; thinking largely in terms of movements.

1897 *Psychol. Rev. Monogr. Suppl.* II. 1. 40 This, in itself, does not prove that motor-minded persons are less intelligent readers than auditory- or visual-minded. **1900** *Amer. Jrnl. Psychol.* XI. 297 Consonants were not thought to be generally more important than vowels for word perception. The relative importance of these elements might depend upon the reader's tendency to be motor or auditory minded. **1904** W. JAMES in *Atlantic Monthly* Jan. 98/1 Every one knows that in some of us the material of thought is mainly optical, in others auditory, etc., and the classification of human beings into the eye-minded, the ear-minded, and the motor-minded, is familiar.

2. Interested in motor vehicles.

1927 *Glasgow Herald* 14 Oct. 8 With motor trade exhibitions running..in London (at Olympia) and in Paris.., the motor-minded have got quite a lot to talk about.

So **mo:tor-mi·ndedness**, the state of being motor-minded (sense *1).

1897 *Psychol. Rev. Monogr. Suppl.* II. 1. 41 It is evident that motor-mindedness is far from being an advantage to a reader. **1902** [see *EAR-MINDEDNESS].

† **motorphobe** (mōᵘ·tǫ̈ɹfōᵘb). *Obs.* [f. MOTOR *sb.* + -PHOBE.] One who has a morbid dread or hatred of motor vehicles.

1905 *Automobile Topics* 27 May 448 The time will come when..the motorphobes will wonder what ever possessed them to act so foolishly. **1911** *Chambers's Jrnl.* Aug. 533/1 A motorphobe was quoted as declaring solemnly in 1906, 'In another ten years there will not be half the autocars on the roads that there are now.'

motorway (mōᵘ·tǫ̈ɹwēi). [f. MOTOR *sb.* + WAY[1].] A specially designated class of highway with two or more lanes in each direction, designed and regulated for use by fast motor traffic. Also *attrib.*, as **motorway box**, a rectangular system of motorways; **motorway madness** *colloq.*, reckless driving on a motorway, esp. in fog.

1903 *Car* 4 Nov. 327 (*title*) Concerning motor-ways. *Ibid.* 327/1 The Motor-way is *bound* to come! **1930** TROUBRIDGE & MARSHALL *John Ld. Montagu of Beaulieu* xx. 254 Where the economic conditions guarantee an adequate volume of traffic, as between large cities, direct roads solely for fast traffic, *i.e.* motorways, must be constructed. **1937** [see *AUTOBAHN]. **1955** *Times* 6 July 10/1 Motorways, 345 miles in total length, for motor traffic only, are to be built by the Government. **1959** *Radio Times* 23 Oct. 3/1 A motorway differs from all other types of roads in that it has no crossroads, no traffic lights, no pedestrian crossings. Certain categories of road-users are barred from it altogether; these include pedal cyclists, invalid carriages and 'L' drivers. **1964** *Daily Tel.* 22 Jan. 14 The British are relative newcomers to the motorway age. **1967** *Economist* 4 Nov. 495/1 The more central, shorter, but more expensive 'motorway box' favoured by the GLC. **1971** *Daily Tel.* 14 Sept. 2/6 This supports the 'motorway madness' theory of a false sense of security which makes drivers behave quite differently on motorways than on ordinary roads. **1972** J. MANN *Mrs Knox's Profession* v. 31 She had pulled into the motorway café, hating the look of it. **1973** R. BUSBY *Pattern of Violence* i. 15 He..gave them a name and the time of arrival of a motorway coach. **1973** *Guardian* 15 Oct. 14/1 Fog is the number one motorway menace with irresponsible.. driving coming second. Mix the two, and the headlines next morning scream 'Motorway madness' yet again.

‖ **motoscafo** (mōᵘtoskā·fo). Pl. **motoscafi.** [It.] In Italy: a motor-boat; esp. such a boat used as a public conveyance on the Venetian canals.

1942 *Britannica Bk. of Year* (U.S.) 468 Another type developed considerably in scope and design was the motor torpedo boat... Before the war the Italians were proud of their vessels of this category, officially classed as M.A.S. (*motoscafi anti-sommergibili*) but these had accomplished singularly little. **1950** E. HEMINGWAY *Across River* xxxiv. 210, I will get into the *motoscafo*..and..we will not ever see one another again. **1971** P. LORAINE *Photographs have been Sent* v. i. 143 The father gave up his gondola and bought himself a nice new *motoscafo*. **1975** 'D. RUTHERFORD' *Mystery Tour* iii. 40 There are no motor vehicles in Venice, so..you will be conveyed to the hotel by *motoscafo*.

Motown (mōᵘ·taun). [Shortening of *Motor Town*, nickname for Detroit, Michigan, U.S.A., an important car-manufacturing city.] Music of a type made popular by Negro musicians and singers from Detroit. Also *attrib.* Cf. *TAMLA-MOTOWN.

1970 *Melody Maker* 11 July 19/7 Some of their songs are extremely unusual, for example 'Jesus Buddha Moses Gauranga' which starts with a bit of 2001 string sound and contains one line which is pure Motown. **1971** *New Yorker* 25 Sept. 127 The set included several songs from each of the Band's three albums..and two Motown oldies.

motso, var. *MATZAH.

mott: see *MOT[4], MOTT.

mott, var. MOAT *sb.*[1]

1937 *Times* 16 Nov. 19/6 One pair [of ducks] yearly chose the old moat or 'mott', all among the reeds and the moorhens, [to nest in].

mott, var. MOTE *sb.*[1] 4.

1930 H. WILLIAMSON *Village Bk.* 328 It had looked like a sheaf of reed motts—the unbruised wheaten stalks used for thatching. **1959** *Times* 19 Aug. 9/7 The 'motts' (or stems) are carefully bumped together, butts down, before being tied in bundles for thatching.

motte. Substitute for etym.: [ad. Amer. Sp. *mata* grove, plant, f. Sp. *mata* bush, clump.] (Earlier and later examples of spelling *mott.*)

1848 C. W. WEBBER *Old Hicks* v. 52 Our course bearing west of north, over broken prairie, diversified by clumps or motts of scrubby growth. **1962** E. B. ATWOOD *Regional Vocab. Texas* iii. 42 A small group of trees together, surrounded by open country... *Mott* is rather heavily concentrated in South Central and West Texas.

motte (mǫt), *sb.*[2] [after F. *motte* mound.] Now the usual spelling of MOTE *sb.*[2] 1, esp. in phr. *motte and bailey*, denoting the principal type or design of castle built in Britain by the Normans, consisting of a fort surmounting a mound (*motte*) at the foot of which was an enclosed BAILEY or court.

1884 G. T. CLARK *Mediæval Mil. Archit. Eng.* I. ii. 16 This 'mound', 'motte', or 'burh'..was formed from the contents of a broad and deep circumscribing ditch. **1892** J. H. ROUND *Geoffrey de Mandeville* 336 The *motte*, though its name was occasionally extended to the whole fortress, was essentially the actual keep, the crowned mound. **1900** *Proc. Soc. Antiquaries Scotl.* XXXIV. 269 As these are the proper Norman names, and there are no others, I shall henceforth speak of this type of castle as the motte-and-bailey type. **1912** E. S. ARMITAGE *Early Norman Castles Brit. Isles* vi. 80 The motte-and-bailey type of castle is to be found throughout feudal Europe. **1934** *Proc. Soc. Antiquaries Scotl.* LXVIII. 59 The Peel of Kirkintilloch had been a medieval fortress of the motte-and-bailey type. **1947** T. H. WHITE *Elephant & Kangaroo* (1948) xxi. 169 A Norman castle on a motte. **1962** C. W. HOLLISTER *Anglo-Saxon Mil. Inst.* vii. 142 The motte-and-bailey style was unknown to them, just as it was unknown to their contemporaries on the Continent. **1967** J. B. NELLIST *Brit. Archit.* vi. 145/1 Although the bailey might be captured, the motte as a self-contained unit could still offer resistance. **1971** *Country Life* 27 May 1297/1 At Dunsany the present castle was apparently built in succession to an earlier motte and bailey castle, the mound of which exists to the north-east of the present house. *Ibid.* 11 Nov. 1280/4 The building stands on a raised motte; it had a moat on the south-west side.

2. *Comb.*, as **motte-castle**, a (Norman) fort standing on a motte.

1912 E. S. ARMITAGE *Early Norman Castles Brit. Isles* vi. 83 It is rare indeed to find a motte-castle in a wild, mountainous situation in England. **1926** *Archæologia Cambrensis* LXXXI. 223 The earthen mounds of two of the earlier 'motte' castles—moated mounts which once had wooden towers upon their summits.

motted (mǫ·tėd), *ppl. a. rare.* [f. *MOTT(E *sb.*[2] + -ED[1].] Situated upon a motte or mound.

1947 AUDEN *Nones* (1952) 64 Do they sponsor In us the mornes and motted mammelons?

mottledy (mǫ·t'ldi), *a. rare.* [f. MOTTLED *ppl. a.* + -Y[1].] Having a mottled appearance.

1929 E. BOWEN *Last September* I. vii. 78 Her grey-and-blue 'mottledy' foulard.

motto. Add: **1. c.** (Earlier examples.)

1848 A. H. CLOUGH *Bothie* ii. 12 You ask me to join you in snapping—What but a pink-paper comfit, with motto romantic inside it? **1850** DICKENS *Dav. Copp.* xxxiii. 340 There were crackers..with the tenderest mottos.

4. Freq. *attrib.*, as *motto theme.* (Further examples.)

1934 C. LAMBERT *Music Ho!* v. 316 The ascription of actual individuality to a recurrent or 'motto theme' and the attaching of symbolic significance to its later transformations, devices wholly at variance with the classic principles of symphonic form, are here perfectly justified. **1935** *Downside Rev.* LIII. 30 Against the noble motto-theme of the introduction is set a restless surging subject in the distant tonality of D minor. **1962** *Times* 13 June 13/1 The symphony's motto-theme. **1964** *Listener* 2 Apr. 570/3 The sixth quartet is more difficult to analyse, though the crucial factor is probably the motto-theme which appears in increasingly contrapuntal guise before each movement. **1966** *Ibid.* 17 Nov. 746/3 The first (*Largo*) begins with imitative entries of the 'motto' and quotes the opening of the first symphony, twice.

5. (Further examples.)

1835 *Southern Lit. Messenger* I. 358, I only ate..a few macaronies and mottoes. **1860** *North-West* (Port Townsend, Washington) 5 July 3/3 Candies, Gum drops, Mottoes.

Motu (mōᵘ·tū), *sb.* and *a.* [Native word.] **A.** *sb.* A Melanesian people of New Guinea inhabiting the area of Port Moresby. Also, their language. **B.** *adj.* Of or pertaining to this people. Also, **Motuan.**

1880 O. C. STONE *Few Months New Guinea* iv. 46 The inhabitants of Anuapata and the neighbourhood consist principally of the Motu tribe. **1885** W. B. LAWES *Motu Gram. & Vocab.* p. v, In the grammar of the Motu dialect of New Guinea one peculiarity is in the use of letters so much alike as to be scarcely distinguishable..b and p,.. d and t [etc.]... The Motuan language seems to be a strange mixture of Papuan and Eastern Polynesian. **1894** A. C. HADDON *Decorative Art Brit. New Guinea* 236 Port Moresby..is the centre of the Motu tribe... The Motu make great trading voyages to the Gulf of Papua. **1910** C. G. SELIGMANN *Melanesians Brit. New Guinea* 16 The Koita..have for generations intermarried with the Motu. .. Although the Koita still speak a Papuan language the majority of the males speak Motu, a Melanesian language, and have adopted..certain Motu customs. **1965** *Language* XLI. 169 Motu...is spoken fluently..by a few thousand Koitabuans intermingled among the Motuans themselves. **1967** 'E. LINDALL' *Time Too Soon* xviii. 197 He spoke in Motuan for the valley folk..and then in English for the white man. **1971** *Guardian* 4 Aug. 5/4 Motu, the language of the Port Moresby district.

‖ **motuca** (motū·kă). Also **motuka.** [Native name.] A Brazilian horse-fly, *Hadrus lepidotus*, of the family Tabanidæ.

1836 H. W. BATES *Naturalist on River Amazons* I. vii. 306 In the daytime the Motúca, a much larger and more formidable fly than the mosquito, insisted upon levying his tax of blood. *Ibid.*, The Motúca is of a bronzed-black colour; its proboscis is formed of a bundle of horny lancets. .. Its puncture does not produce much pain, but it makes such a large gash in the flesh that the blood trickles forth in little streams. **1914** *Chambers's Jrnl.* Oct. 630/1 Hornets dispute with motucas and other biting flies over the luckless intruder. **1927** W. M. MCGOVERN *Jungle Paths & Inca Ruins* 224 Unlike the vampire bat, the motuka inflicted a very painful sting. **1933** P. FLEMING *Brazilian*

Adventure I. xvii. 145 There were also *motuca* flies, which looked like a lethal and slightly futuristic form of bluebottle, and whose bites drew blood and oaths but had no worse effects.

|| **motu proprio** (mō͡u·tu prǫ·prio). [L., 'on his, its, etc., own impulse'.] Of one's own volition, on one's own initiative, spontaneously. Also as *sb.*, an edict issued by the Pope personally to the Roman Catholic Church, or to a part of it. Also *attrib.*

1603 C. Heydon *Defence Judicial Astrol.* xxi. 447 But the Moone and other Planets moove also motu proprio. **1613** J. Chamberlain *Let.* 14 Oct. in T. Birch *Court & Times James I* (1848) I. 278 Signor Gabellione, the Duke of Savoy's ambassador, came *motu proprio* about three weeks since to Ware Park. **1620** N. Brent tr. *Soave's Hist. Councel of Trent* iv. 354 Dispatching the dispensations under the name of Motu proprio, or with other clauses, with which the Chancery doth abound. **1848** Godde de Liancourt & Manning *Pius IX* II. xv. 404 The Pope published, on the 2nd of October at Rome, a new *motu proprio* for the organisation of a Senate. **1911** *Catholic Encycl.* X. 602/2 *Motu proprio*, the name given to certain papal rescripts... The words signify that the provisions of the rescript were decided on by the pope personally, that is, not on the advice of the cardinals or others. *Ibid.*, A favour granted *motu proprio* is valid even when counter to ecclesiastical law. **1938** *Oxf. Compan. Mus.* 596/2 *Motu proprio*... The word is often heard in connexion with church music on account of the Motu Proprio of Pius X, issued in the year of his becoming Pope (1903)... Instruments other than the organ were not to be employed without the bishop's special permission. **1964** P. F. Anson *Bishops at Large* x. 455 The Patriarch of the West (in the person of Pope Pius XI) might have been forced to issue a *motu proprio* denouncing the Patriarch of Glastonbury. **1972** *Daily Tel.* 15 Sept. 8/7 Restatement of celibacy rules for deacons and priests came in a separate *motu proprio* decree.

motza, var. *matzah.

|| **mou** (mū). Also **mow, mu.** [Chinese.] A Chinese unit of area, varying according to locality but usu. equivalent to about 670 square metres (800 square yards).

1876 *Encycl. Brit.* V. 39/1 A ground-rent of 15,000 cash (about £3) per *mow* (a third of an acre). **1924** *Other Lands* Jan. 56/2 Having acquired a tract of land on the north bank of thirty to forty thousand mow it has been very successful. **1937** E. Snow *Red Star over China* ii. 71 Here in Shensi a peasant may own as much as 100 *mou* of land and yet be a poor man. **1955** *Ann. Reg.* *1954* 305 'Of the over 80 million mou of the still flooded farmlands, 30 million mou have not yet been drained.'.. A mou was almost exactly one-sixth of an acre. **1957** *Encycl. Brit.* XV. 140/2 Mou... Commonly 806.65 sq. yd. Varies locally. Shanghai = 6,600 sq. ft. (Municipal Council). By Customs Treaty = 920.417 sq. yd., based on ch'ih of 14.1 inches. **1973** *Times* 21 Mar. (China Trade Suppl.) p. xiv/3 Since a *mu* is one sixth of an acre, and a catty is 1.1 lb. these figures come out at 18 cwt and 24 cwt of unhusked rice an acre.

mouche. Restrict † *Obs.* to sense in Dict. and add: **b.** A natural mark on the face similar in appearance to a patch of plaster.

1859 G. A. Sala *Twice round Clock* 143 In a hoop petticoat, a point lace apron, red-heeled *mules*, a *toupet* and a *mouche* on the left cheek. **1959** M. Steen *Woman in Back Seat* I. i. 8 At the angle of the jaw, . . there should be a dark brown *mouche*, about the size of a small pea.

mouchette (mūʃe·t). *Archit.* [Fr.] A motif in curvilinear tracery having the shape of a curved dagger.

1927 *Proc. Soc. Antiquaries Scotl.* LX. 388 The space under the arch bears an heraldic shield supported by a composition of *soufflets* and *mouchettes*. **1949** *Archit. Rev.* CV. 4/1 The mouchettes of the Court School are equally distinctive... They change only within certain fixed limits, . . and yet in a very subtle manner the mouchettes create changes of style. **1955** M. Hastings *St Stephen's Chapel* 179 The fan tracery of Henry VII's chapel is no more than an extremely elaborate combination of mouchettes. **1967** J. B. Nellist *Brit. Archit.* ii. 43/1 The elaborate tracery is almost entirely composed of mouchette shapes.

moue. (Later examples.)

1908 A. Bennett *Old Wives' Tale* iv. i. 429 She gave a *moue* and a flounce in reply, and swished out. **1955** *Times* 18 July 3/1 The hero..seeks the male companionship of sea life only to collapse powerless before the frail charm, the irresistible *moue*, and the wide eyed Frenchness of a passenger on the boat. **1974** 'J. Le Carré' *Tinker, Tailor* xii. 103 'Why, George..it was you who arranged the deal!' With a quaint moue of professional vanity, Smiley conceded..it.

|| **moue** (mū), *v.* [f. the sb.] **1.** *trans.* **a.** To ogle; stare at. **b.** To utter (words) with a moue.

1909 Hardy in *Daily Chron.* 1 Apr. 4/6 Whither have danced those damsels now; Is Death the partner who doth moue Their wormy chaps and bare? **1938** G. Greene *Brighton Rock* v. v. 213 'Work, work, work,' she moued at them.

2. *intr.* To make a moue.

1938 G. Greene *Brighton Rock* vii. ix. 346 They looked up and moued to each other, as much as to say—'Oh well, she wasn't really worth the trouble.' **1968** *Punch* 7 Aug. 202/3 The girls look the same young flappers to me, moueing and mincing and doing the long-lashed come-hither look.

mouf (mauf), repr. a pronunc. of Mouth *sb.*

The examples are taken from Black English sources in the U.S. but the pronunciation is also characteristic of Cockney speech in London.

1909 *Dialect Notes* III. 350 *Mouf*, mouth: a negroism rapidly gaining ground among the whites, especially in the derivatives, as *mouffle* (mouthful). **1935** Z. N. Hurston *Mules & Men* (1970) i. ii. 49 She got plenty hips, plenty mouf and no brains. **1969** R. Fair in A. Chapman *New Black Voices* (1972) 114 Oh, shut yo mouf up man. **1971** *Black World* Oct. 63/2 Like I got hoof and mouf disease and there ain't no hope at all.

moufflon. Add: Further examples of **mouflon**, which is now the usual spelling.

1843 J. Saunders in C. Knight *London* V. cxvii. 261 In the centre..is a curious little open hut, with projecting eaves... A horned sheep, the mouflon, is confined in it. **1932** J. S. Huxley *Probl. Relative Growth* iii. 88 The adult wild Mouflon ewe is in its proportions but little in advance of the improved Suffolk lamb. **1970** *Ashmolean Mus. Rep. Visitors 1969* 14 Omphalos bronze bowl decorated on the inside with mouflon among the trees. **1974** *Environmental Conservation* I. 9/1 Antelope, mouflon, and ostriches, have been exterminated over large areas.

2. The fur of the moufflon; woollen fabric made from the moufflon's coat. Occas. used erron. of the fur of the Mongolian goat. Also *attrib.*

1905 [in Dict.]. **1910** *Encycl. Brit.* XI. 351/2 Many Mongolian goats with the long hairs pulled out are sold as mouflon. **1949** *Amer. Speech* XXIV. 98 There is a species of goat from the mountains of northern China characterized by pelts of downy underhair... These furs are widely used and are called *moufflons* or *pulled goat*. **1952** C. W. Cunnington *Eng. Women's Clothing* 295 *Moufflon serge* ('18), 'a kind of brushed woollen textile'. **1962** *Guardian* 21 July 4/7 A mist of softest peltry—chinchilla, sables, mink, and millinery moufflon. **1973** *Ibid.* 27 Feb. 11/2 Coat in white mouflon wool.

mought (mō͡ut). [See May *v.*[1] 4 c β.] A recurring var. of the pa. t. form *might* in representations of regional English (esp. Black English) in the U.S.

1872, 1885 [see May *v.*[1] 4 c β]. **1927** A. P. Randolph in A. Dundes *Mother Wit* (1973) 203 You can't 'speck des 'nigger' bosses to speak up for our rights when it mought cos dey jobs. **1933** J. M. Brewer in *Ibid.* 248/2 Yuh mought as well die wid de chills. **1938** M. K. Rawlings *Yearling* 144 Mought be, we'll find 'em in a pen some'eres.

moujik, muzhik. Add: Also **mouzhik.**

1949 I. Deutscher *Stalin* iii. 67 Eight or nine soldiers out of ten were mouzhiks. **1961** *Observer* 10 Dec. 7/2 The most fascinating Khrushchev of all is the high-powered *mouzhik*, the super *kulak*.

moulage (mū·lāʒ). [F. *moulage* action of moulding, moulded reproduction, f. *mouler* to mould.] An impression of a (part of a) person or of an object, the material used, or the process of taking an impression. Also *attrib.*

1902 *Encycl. Brit.* XXX. 788/2 In anatomy and physiology, models are specially employed as aids in teaching and study, and the method of *moulage* or chromoplastic yields excellent impressions of living organisms, and enables anatomical and medical preparations to be copied both in form and colour. **1940** R. Morrish *Police and Crime Detection* xii. 120 In these days an attempt is made to create a complete image of the murdered person by casts. This is called the 'Moulage' system. The results are almost as lifelike as the dummies in Madame Tussaud's. **1947** C. Brooks *Well Wrought Urn* iv. 69 A detective making a moulage of a footprint in wet clay. **1947** J. C. Rich *Materials & Methods Sculpture* v. 96 The late Dr. Alphons Poller was among the first to utilize agar as a negative mold material in fashioning molds from flesh. He developed a moulage system and subsequently wrote a book on the subject. Poller's moulage compounds were patented and the trade names of his negative mold compositions.. were registered. **1957** V. J. Kehoe *Technique Film & Television Make-Up* iii. 35 Moulage is a general name for impression materials some of which can be remelted and re-used (regular hydrocolloids)..and others (known as non-reversible hydrocolloids),..which are alginate non-reusable materials. **1969** R. Mayer *Dict. Art Terms & Techniques* 254/1 A specially prepared moulage plaster.. may be used on delicate or valuable materials. **1973** R. C. Dennis *Sweat of Fear* xi. 81 The detection of murder no longer need depend on fingerprints, blood types and moulages.

mould, *sb.*[3] Add: **17.** *mould-cutting, -resisting* adjs. and sbs.; **mould-blowing** *Glass-making*, the blowing of glass inside a mould to give it the required shape; so **mould-blown** *a.*; **mould cavity** (see quots.); **mould-loft**, also *Aeronaut.*; **mould-made** *a.*, of paper, made on a type of machine which produces sheets having characteristics imitating those of hand-made paper, esp. the so-called deckle edge; **mould oil** *Building*, an oil applied to formwork to prevent concrete adhering to it; **mould-runner**, an operative in a pottery responsible for transferring a completed article, still attached to its mould, to the drying-oven; hence **mould-running** *vbl. sb.*

1948 E. B. Haynes *Glass through Ages* 307 Mould-blowing. **1949** P. Davis *Devel. Amer. Glass Industry* iv. 48 Glass for purposes other than glazing..was made by two different processes known technically as 'off-hand blowing' and 'mold-blowing'. **1972** E. Fletcher *Bottle Collecting* iii. 48 Most of the early examples of case bottles to survive have sides which sagged badly after removal from the mould; but the techniques of mould-blowing were soon to improve. **1925** Hodkin & Cousen *Text-bk. Glass Technol.* xxxii. 412 Much of the preliminary work in shaping parisons for mould-blown bottles might be mechanically performed. **1970** *Ashmolean Mus. Rep. Visitors 1969* 15 A clear green glass flask with hexagonal mould blown body decorated with panels of lattice and chevron pattern. **1951** *Gloss. Terms Plastics Industry (B.S.I.)* 37 *Mould cavity* (cavity), the female portion of a mould impression. **1971** W. K. V. Gale *Iron & Steel Industry: Dict. Terms* 136 *Mould cavity*, the impression left in a foundry mould after the pattern has been removed. **1947** J. C. Rich *Materials & Methods Sculpture* v. 114 The author has employed dental floss, which is waxed silk thread, for mold-cutting purposes, with good results. **1947** *Jrnl. R. Aeronaut. Soc.* LI. 307/2 The mold loft consisted of a building with a large floor area, the floor being painted a mat black. **1916** H. A. Maddox *Paper* viii. 120 Mould-made imitations of hand-made paper are produced..by several types of apparatus. **1923** —— *Dict. Stationery* 53 *Mould-made paper*, a class of high-grade paper which closely embodies the characteristic features of handmade. The sheets are made on a special machine which forms them singly and imparts four deckled edges... In selling mould-made note paper the stationer is legally compelled to describe it as such. **1938** *Times Lit. Suppl.* 15 Jan. 40/4 The text of the poem [*sc.* the Nonesuch edition of *Comus*] is printed in Fell types.. on Pannekoek mould-made paper, at the Oxford University Press. **1955** S. C. Gilmour *Paper* vii. 64 Nowadays the relatively few mould-made papers that are produced rank as a close second in character and quality to handmades, though not altogether comparable. **1973** S. Jennett *Making of Bks.* (ed. 5) xi. 182 Mould-made Papers are a paradox. They are in effect hand-made papers made by machine. **1939** W. H. Glanville *Mod. Concrete Construction* I. vi. 166 Mould oils of a variety of types are used in the various fields of concrete products manufacture. **1948** L. J. Murdock *Concrete Materials & Pract.* xvi. 240 The requirements of a good mould oil are that it shall prevent sticking, it shall reduce to a minimum adsorption of water by the formwork, and it shall not harm the concrete either by staining or by softening of the surface. **1962** D. F. Orchard *Concrete Technol.* II. xi. 321 Care must be taken to see that the plywood or hardboard does not buckle through expansion due to atmospheric influences or the absorption of water from the concrete; several coats of mould oil or a brush on plastic are a great help in this respect. **1962** Mould-resisting [see **damp-proofing* vbl. sb.]. **1863** *1st Rep. Children's Employment Comm.* p. ix, in *Parl. Papers* XVIII. 9 As the potter forms the plate or saucer in the mould, the mould runner runs off with it into the 'store'. **1910** A. Bennett *Clayhanger* i. iv. 29 He was 'mould-runner' to a 'muffin-maker', a muffin being..a small plate, fashioned by its maker on a mould. **1961** M. Jones *Potbank* viii. 34 In the older workshops.. the mould-runner really does plenty of running. **1910** A. Bennett *Clayhanger* i. iv. 31 The labour was much lighter than that of mould-running and clay-wedging.

mould, *sb.*[4] Add: **c.** *Comb.* (Earlier and later examples.)

1699 Pepys *Let.* 19 Oct. (1926) I. 200, I have found time ..to looke over all my heads; 'tis only mould-spotts some of them are touched with, by being putt together before they were dry. **1944** J. S. Huxley *On Living in Revolution* v. 64 Some [butterfly wings like dead leaves] even go so far as to be marked with imitation mould-spots and holes.

mould (mō͡uld), *sb.*[6] = Mould-board[1].

1858 *Trans. Illinois Agric. Soc.* III. 367 In fall-plowing we run the share and mould of the plow under the soil and invert it. **1868** *Rep. Iowa Agric. Soc. 1867* 266 There is no clogging, and the mould and lay are so hardened that they scour readily.

mouldability. (Further examples.)

1938 H. I. Lewenz tr. *Brandenburger's Processes & Machinery Plastics Industry* vi. 97 (*heading*) The effect of fillers on the mouldability of compounds. **1956** J. N. Anderson *Appl. Dental Materials* xix. 228 The water also improves mouldability by acting as a plasticizer. **1970** *Cabinet Maker & Retail Furnisher* 23 Oct. 174/3 Melded fabrics..have a sufficient degree of stretch and 'mouldability' to aid the upholstering of curved areas.

mould-board[1]. Add: Also *mould-board plough.*

1808 W. H. Marshall *Rev. Rep. to Board Agric. from N. Eng.* i. 79 The seed is covered in by going once over with a light harrow, or..by a double-mould-board-plough. **1858** *Trans. Illinois Agric. Soc.* III. 366 A bull-tongue or shovel plow put to the same depth, will raise better corn than a mouldboard plow. **1971** *Power Farming* Mar. 31/1 There is a definite place for machines of this type to replace the mouldboard plough under certain circumstances.

moulder, *sb.*[1] Add: **1. b.** (See quot.)

1894 *Gloss. Terms Evidence R. Comm. Labour* 58/1 in *Parl. Papers 1893–4* (C. 7063) XXXVIII. 411 *Moulders*, men in the seed-crushing industry who draw the rolled seed from the fixture wherein it is made hot, and..subject it to a slight pressure.

moulder, *v.* Add: **4.** *intr.* To move *off* in an aimless or lifeless manner. *rare.*

1945 E. Bowen *Demon Lover* 48, I mouldered off by myself..to watch the old clock.

mouldiness. Add: *fig.* A state of boredom or discontent. Cf. *mouldy *a.*[2] 2 b.

1916 'Taffrail' *Stand By!* 23 Our mouldiness in the morning is merely temporary.

moulding, *vbl. sb.*[2] Add: **4.** *moulding machine, -plane* (later example), *powder, -sand* (later examples).

1890 *Cent. Dict.*, Molding-machine. **1921** *Daily Colonist* (Victoria, B.C.) 25 Mar. 8/4 To meet the needs of the small foundry with a varied demand, a British firm has, however, introduced an adaptable molding machine which can be quickly and easily adjusted to take molding boxes and pattern plates of any size within a comparatively wide range. **1964** W. L. Goodman *Hist. Woodworking Tools* 52 The remainder include moulding plane irons,.. rebate- and shoulder-plane irons, and plough irons. **1940** *Chambers's Techn. Dict.* 560/1 *Moulding powder*, the finely ground mixture of binder, accelerator, colouring matter, filler, and lubricant which is converted under pressure into the final moulding. **1957** *Which?* Autumn 9/1 Plastic frames should be made of optical sheet. The reason for this is that frames made from moulding powder are not so practical. **1930** *Engineering* 21 Feb. 247/1 Simple tests have been devised for regular daily foundry control of moulding sands. **1969** Bennison & Wright *Geol. Hist. Brit. Isles* xii. 274 The Pebble Beds are followed by the Upper Mottled Sandstone ≡ Moulding Sand... The term moulding sand refers to their widespread use.

mouldwarp. 1. (Later *poet.* examples.)

1916 Blunden *Harbingers* 59 Mouldwarps working late. **1928** A. D. Mackie *Poems in Two Tongues* 51 Alang his pad the mowdie-worps Like sma' Assyrians lie.

mouldy, *a.*[2] Add: **2. b.** Wretched, boring, depressing, gloomy, sick. *colloq.* or *slang*.

1876 [in Dict., sense 2]. **1896** Farmer & Henley *Slang* IV. 362/1 *Mouldy*,..worthless: *e.g.*, a *mouldy* offer. **1912** F. M. Hueffer *Parnel* I. iii. 93, I slogged like that for Nancy... We could have got along on a major's pay, out there. Just got along! And then the blasted girl goes and gets rotten titles and mouldy houses to her back on the day the bottom drops out of me. **1916** E. V. Lucas *Vermilion Box* 220, I should be mouldy company for you, I fear, because I can't talk. **1916** 'Taffrail' *Pincher Martin* x. 174 Since you're all so mouldy, I suppose I must..turn in. **1924** M. Kennedy *Constant Nymph* iv. xxiii. 322 She looked more wan and frail than ever and he exclaimed: 'You look very mouldy.' **1936** —— *Together & Apart* I. 95 Do please come home soon, for it's mouldy without you. **1956** A. Huxley *Let.* 25 Dec. (1969) 814 One feels a bit low and mouldy after those bouts of flu. **1962** *Guardian* 20 Jan. 3/6 Local support for the event had deteriorated, but it did not deserve to be called 'mouldy'. **1972** *Sat. Rev.* (U.S.) 9 Sept. 92/1 The average cabby is a moldy old fascist.

c. *mouldy fig*: a supporter (occas., a performer) of traditional jazz. Also *attrib.* or as quasi-*adj.*

1945 *Esquire* Mar. 10/2 Why do aforementioned connoisseurs insist upon maintaining that the Chicago and New York (white) styles are the real Jazz, when it's perfectly obvious that New Orleans was—and is—the birthplace of the true 'stuff'?.. Sincerely, Moldy Fig, France. **1945** S. Platt in *Ibid.* June 10/3, I wish to protest against the 'Moldy Fig' genre of music lovers. There seems to be some perverse streak in critics such as Avakian or 'Moldy Fig' which prevents them from liking anything but the very oldest available. **1958** G. Lea *Somewhere there's Music* x. 83 Dixie Cats and the rest of the Moldy Figs, okay for them, they don't need to think. **1959** *Hi Fi Rev.* Apr. 79/2 Lines of seething fury were drawn between the [jazz] traditionalists and the boppers who viewed each other as 'moldy figs', on the one hand, and players of 'all them wrong notes', on the other. **1968** *Listener* 4 Apr. 450/3 Readers over 30 will remember the term 'Mouldy Figge' as contemporaneous with Little Jackie Dennis and Suez. **1968** *Blues Unlimited* Nov. 7 Many collectors are mouldy-fig enough to believe that virtually every worthwhile blues singer was recorded at least once in the '20s and '30s. **1973** *National Observer* (U.S.) 6 Oct. 23/1 Charles Keil satirizes the 'moldy-fig' aspirations of earlier blues scholars.

3. *Comb.*, as *mouldy-minded* adj.

1906 Hardy *Dynasts* II. vi. vii. 320 The rawest Dynast ..Will..Down-topple to the dust like soldier Saul, And Europe's mouldy-minded oligarchs Be propped anew.

mouldy (mōu·ldi), *sb.* *Navy* and *R.A.F. slang.* [Origin unknown.] **1.** A torpedo.

1916 M. T. Hainsselin *In Northern Mists* xvi. 62 A German submarine..kept one of the bug-traps bailed up.. for a week by waiting..ready to squirt a mouldy at her directly she showed her nose outside... To fire a torpedo at her, of course! **1918** *Yachting Monthly* XXIV. 297/1 When H.M.S. Carraco was torpedoed she received the mouldy right forward. **1928** *Observer* 11 Mar. 17/4 The King of Afghanistan will be given a lesson in torpedo firing and himself discharge a 'mouldy' from one of L22's tubes. **1932** *Flight* 19 Aug. 777/1 At the same time, no doubt, the A.A. gunners on board are gleefully telling all and sundry how they simply riddled the 'Horsleys' with shells before ever a mouldy was dropped. **1943** C. H. Ward-Jackson *Piece of Cake* 43 *Mouldy*, a torpedo..was brought into air force use by the Royal Naval Air Service.

2. A confection sold at naval colleges.

1916 G. Franklin *Naval Digression* xii. 105 The various cadets engaged in stuffing themselves with 'pinkmen', 'mouldies'..and suchlike *vinos y comida*. **1962** Granville *Dict. Sailors' Slang* 78/2 *Mouldy*,..confection popular at Dartmouth.

‖ **moule** (mūl). [Fr.] A mussel, *spec.* in **moules (à la) marinière,** mussels served in their shells and cooked in a wine and onion sauce.

1890 E. Lebour-Fawssett *French Cookery for Ladies* 161 *Moules à la Marinière*... After you have taken your mussels out of the saucepan.., put in three onions,..two sliced carrots, [etc.]. **1928** D. L. Sayers *Unpleasantness at Bellona Club* ix. 106, I was just wondering whether to have *moules marinières* or not. **1950** D. Ames *Corpse Diplomatique* iv. 33 She was almost up to her elbows in a dish of *moules à la marinière*. **1959** *Good Food Guide* 36 The cooking is something above 'plain English' and even includes moules marinières quite frequently. *Ibid.* 162 Take moules Mendip (2/6), pâté (2/6), various vol-au-vent (3/-). **1971** Coombes & Wakelin *Good Housek. Advanced Cooking is Fun* 117 *Mussels* (Moules Marinière): These are best eaten from a bowl or soup plate, with a fork to get the mussel from the shell..and a spoon for the liquor.

Mouli (mū·li). Also **mouli.** A proprietary name, shortened from *Moulinette. Also *attrib.*

1937 *Trade Marks Jrnl.* 21 July 862/2 Mouli... All goods included in Class 6. [Machinery of all kinds, and parts of machinery, except agricultural and horticultural machines and their parts.] Mouliware Limited,..London, ..; manufacturers and merchants. **1969** O. John *Dead on Time* I. 11 Homus bathini is made from chick peas.., put..through a mouli. **1972** C. Fremlin *Appointment with Yesterday* vii. 51 The burnt chip-pan. And all that white, sticky stuff in the Mouli-Mixer. **1972** *Times* 12 Aug. 11/1 Pass the soup through a 'mouli' soup mill, this.. keeps back all the stalky bits.

moulin. Add: **2.** A kitchen utensil used for grinding food or reducing it to pulp. (See Mill *sb.*[1] 2 a.)

1959 *Listener* 17 Dec. 1095/1 Put it through a sieve, or a *moulin à legumes*. **1962** *Harper's Bazaar* Aug. 37 Black pepper freshly ground from the *moulin*. **1966** 'K. Nicholson' *Hook, Line & Sinker* viii. 92 In the kitchen Mrs. Chilperic..was urging the apple sauce through the moulin.

Moulin-à-Vent (mulæ̃n a vaṅ). Also **Moulin à Vent.** [Fr. place-name.] The name of a Beaujolais wine produced in the commune of Moulin-à-Vent.

1833 C. Redding *Hist. Mod. Wines* v. 112 The first class of Burgundies in the Saone and Loire, are Moulin à Vent, Torins, and Chenas. **1927** A. E. Housman *Let.* 17 Oct. (1971) 254 We had two bottles of white wine (the first probably Pouilly-Fuissé) and then half a bottle of *Moulin-à-Vent*. **1961** 'J. Welcome' *Beware of Midnight* vi. 79, I ordered..a bottle of Moulin à Vent. **1967** A. Lichine *Encycl. Wines* 121 Such a quintessential Beaujolais as Fleurie will be more characteristic than the bigger wines—the Morgon and Moulin-à-Vent. **1968** 'G. Bagby' *Corpse Candle* vi. 67 There was even a respectable wine, a Moulin-à-Vent.

Moulinette (mūline·t). Also **moulinette.** The proprietary name of a type of food mill.

1936 *Trade Marks Jrnl.* 23 Dec. 1585/2 The Moulinette. .. Food strainers and sieves all of ordinary metal. Mantelet & Boucher.., Bagnolet (Seine), France; manufacturers and merchants. **1951** *Ibid.* 7 Mar. 229/1 Moulinette... Hand operated mincing machines for food. Mouliware Limited,.. London,..; manufacturers and merchants. **1951** E. David *French Country Cooking* 19 A purée-maker or food mill, usually called a *moulinette* in France. For soups, fruit and vegetable purées this is absolutely invaluable. **1961** *Listener* 24 Aug. 295/1 If you enjoy sieved greens, fruits, and other purées, a *moulinette*, or rotary sieve..will pay its way.

moulvi(e. (Examples.)

1862, etc. [see Moolvee]. **1864** J. A. Grant *Walk across Afr.* xi. 239 The Seedees, though knowing nothing of the Mohammedan religion, the majority not being circumcised, were much more particular on those occasions, and offered more opinions than a 'moulvie', or Mussulman priest, would. **1972** *Guardian* 1 Dec. 14/3 The great bulk of [Guyanese] Indians are Hindus or Moslems, and pundits, moulvis and parents always viewed such [Christian] schools with suspicion.

mound, *sb.*[3] Add: **3. c.** In *Baseball*, 'the slightly elevated ground from which the pitcher pitches' (D.A.).

1914 *Collier's* 7 Feb. 7/2 There's a pitcher who never has to be urged to go to the mound. **1957** [see *bull-pen 1 b]. **1974** *Evening Herald* (Rock Hill, S. Carolina) 18 Apr. 6/3 Mussman went the entire nine inning stint on the mound for Rock Hill and was credited with the win.

5. mound ant *Austral.* = *meat-ant* *Meat *sb.* 6); **Mound City** *U.S.*, a name for St. Louis, Missouri; **Mound of Venus** = *Mons Veneris* (s.v. Mons a, b); **mound region,** a region in which there are many mounds.

1907 Mound Ant [see *meat-ant* s.v. *meat *sb.* 6]. **1926** *Austral. Encycl.* I. 68/2 Amongst the objectionable species the Mound Ant (*Iridomyrmex detectus*) is prominent; its huge nests are particularly destructive to garden paths. **1935** K. C. McKeown *Insect Wonders Austral.* 5 The Mound Ants form their great gravel nests in the grassy plains, scouring in search of food..to the dead body of some horse or sheep which has perished in time of drought, the marauders issuing from holes in the carcass in long streams, each ant bearing a fragment of flesh in its jaw. **1855** Mayne Reid *Hunters' Feast* i. 5 On the western bank of the Mississippi..stands the large town of St. Louis, poetically known as the 'Mound City'. **1860** Bartlett *Dict. Amer.* (ed. 3) 282 *Mound-City*, the city of St. Louis, so-called from the number of artificial mounds that occupied the site on which the city is built. **1865** R. Beamish *Psychonomy Hand* 35 The mound of Venus, devoid of lines, is the index of chastity, coldness, tranquility in love. **1963** C. R. Mueller tr. *Büchner's Danton's Death* I. v, in *Compl. Plays & Prose* 20 A woman's thighs will be your guillotine, and her mound of Venus your Tarpeian rock. **1873** J. H. Beadle *Undevel. West* i. 38 This is the centre of the 'Mound Region' of Wisconsin—so called from the many Indian mounds scattered about the valley.

moundy, *a.* Add: (Earlier and later examples.)

1851 W. Kelly *Excursion Calif.* I. vi. 97 Revealing a range of elevated hills stretching north and south, moundy on the surface and where they were broken showing a fine light rabbit sand. **1955** D. D. C. P. Mould *Irish Pilgrimage* iv. 44 Mirage may lift them out of the water, so that they float above the sea, dark moundy masses.

mount, *sb.*[2] Add: **2. c.** An act of copulation.

1896 Farmer & Henley *Slang* IV. 362/1 *Mount*, an act of coition. **1937** Partridge *Dict. Slang* 226/2 *Do a grind, a mount*, to have sexual intercourse (of men). **1970** *Nature* 12 Dec. 1107/1 In mounts from behind, the mounting cat often had its pelvic region well forward on the back of the mounted cat.

4. b. *collect.* A supply of riding- or draft-horses.

1907 S. E. White *Arizona Nights* I. iii. 53 He kept his own mount of horses, took care of them. **1933** *Amer. Speech* VIII. I. 30/1 *Mount*, a string of horses, usually eight or ten, assigned by the boss to one man.

5*. A stuffed and mounted bird-skin.

1935 *Auk* LII. 281 Since the mounts were similarly posed, it seemed that the male Northern Yellow-throat was discriminating between the sexes primarily on a basis of color pattern. **1938** *Brit. Birds* XXXII. 30 The female mount..had a half-spread tail. **1957** J. W. Moyer *Pract. Taxidermy* v. 34 Tie down the feathers with soft, fine thread or string to hold them in place until the mount is dry.

mount, *v.* Add: **8. f.** To rise on to an obstruction, etc.

1930 *Morning Post* 19 July 12/6 He just managed to avoid a crash by cutting out to his right and in doing so he mounted the footpath.

9. (Further examples.)

c **1884** 'Mark Twain' *Speeches* (1923) 109, I renewed my youth, to outward appearance, by mounting a bicycle. **1912** W. Owen *Let.* 1 Feb. (1967) 113, I had arranged to go to the Cyclists...the machine is only £5.19.6!.. It *will* be a *joy-ride* when I am mounted on one of these!

10. (Later examples.) Also of people.

1963 A. Heron *Towards Quaker View of Sex* 54 The young bachelor males of herds where the overlord male jealously protects his harem will mount each other. **1970** *Nature* 12 Dec. 1107/2 A mounting female was frequently immediately mounted by the cat she was mounting, or by another oestrous female. **1970** Masters & Johnson *Human Sexual Inadequacy* 307 The wife once mounted is instructed to hold herself quite still. **1971** 'V. X. Scott' *Surrogate Wife* 19, I was a man, mounting a beautiful and passionate woman. **1973** J. Elsom *Erotic Theatre* ix. 174 Men no longer want to mount women simply because, like Everest, they are there.

11. (Further example.)

1891 'Mark Twain' in *Illustr. Lond. News* 26 Dec. 834/1 Everybody else had..'mounted the train', as they say in those regions [e.g. Geneva].

16. g. *to mount an attack, offensive*, etc. Also *fig.*

1952 *N.Y. Times* 3 May 2/4 Striking at Communist targets in excellent flying weather (Thursday) warplanes of the Far East Air Forces mounted 1,283 sorties. **1957** *Times Lit. Suppl.* 20 Dec. 771/1 A British private-army leader would have mounted, or at least planned, an incessant series of operations. **1965** *Listener* 2 Sept. 334/1 Governments mount big campaigns to secure an 'incomes policy'. **1966** *Ibid.* 20 Oct. 579/2, I am mounting a devastating attack on the seriousness of the book. **1972** *Daily Mirror* 12 Oct. 1 An all-out attack is to be mounted against the porn-pushers in Britain's High Streets.

17. d. (Earlier and later examples.) Also, to put on or produce (a radio or television programme).

1870 *N.Y. Times* 11 Oct. 5/5 'The Two Roses' is.. prettily mounted, and nicely, if not greatly acted. **1962** *Listener* 10 May 808/1 It is the first town that approached us and asked us to mount a festival. *Ibid.* 30 Aug. 328/1 His staff..mounted several brisk little propaganda numbers about social evils in Britain. *Ibid.* 20 Sept. 437/1 The Arts Council has mounted..an exhibition which has certain flaws. **1963** *Times* 8 Feb. 14/2 The production is mounted in the later Brechtian manner. **1971** *Daily Tel.* 2 Dec. 12 The BBC is scrapping normal programme schedules..during Christmas to enable it to mount special productions.

mountain. Add: **2. c.** A stockpile, a surplus.

1969 *Times* 10 Sept. 11/4 In Germany..they are beginning to resent it [*sc.* the price for protection], as the sardonic remarks in the supermarkets about the 'Butter Mountain' reveal. **1974** *Daily Tel.* 5 Feb. 2/4 It is intervention buying that leads to the creation of the Common Market's notorious commodity 'mountains'. **1974** *Times* 1 May 4/7 Measures designed to disperse the Community's growing beef surpluses. The beef mountain now stands at more than 70,000 tons. **1975** *Times* 7 Feb. 4/8 The prospect of a 'cheese mountain' in the EEC.

3. b. *to make a mountain* (*out*) *of a molehill*: see Molehill 2.

6. (Further examples.)

In England also applied to a group of Conservatives at the beginning of the 20th c.

1829 H. Hardinge *Let.* 19 June in C. Arbuthnot *Corr.* (1941) 116 It would, if true, keep the high Whigs disunited from the Mountain, & assist our union with our old Tory party. **1965** E. Fellowes in *Political Q.* XXXVI. 257 Among the Supporters of the Government [in the Parliament of 1918] was the National Party led by Sir Henry Page-Croft, and a group of Conservative backbenchers (the 'Mountain'), not so formally organised, but working in concert... This..group in fact often proved a more successful opposition than the Labour and Liberal parties, who shared the Opposition front bench.

7. a. *mountain-echo, slope, -wreath.*
1805–6 Wordsworth *Prelude* (1959) I. 390 Not without the voice Of mountain-echoes did my Boat move on. **1841** Thoreau *Jrnl.* 4 Mar. in *Writings* (1906) VII. 228 Their way is a mountain slope, a river valley's course. **1930** A. Clarke *Coll. Plays* (1963) 63 To look across Kildare in sun and know The far flocks move along the mountain slope. **1928** Blunden *Retreat* 70 Warm furze-perfume, stern mountain-wreath Of pines.

b. *mountain-climber; mountain-cresting, -walking* adjs.
1880 'Mark Twain' *Tramp Abroad* xxxvi. 375 We were in the..home of the mountain-climbers. **1951** S. Spender *World within World* iii. 179 Then we came to that extraordinary river-encircled, mountain-cresting city of Toledo. **1821** Shelley *Let.* 22 Oct. (1964) II. 361, I.. raised a small turf altar to the mountain-walking Pan.

c. *mountain-clear, -cool* adjs.; *mountain-headed* adj.
1955 P. Larkin *Less Deceived* 36 Their visions mountain-clear. **1919** A. Huxley *Leda* (1920) 1 Brown and bright as an agate, mountain-cool. **1925** Blunden *Eng. Poems* 104 O firmament, O mountain-headed march Of clouds through that blue arch.

e. *mountain-bound, -cradled, -echoed, -guarded, -roofed, -sheltered* adjs.
1860 G. M. Hopkins *Poems* (1967) 3 There is a massy pile above the waste Amongst Castilian barrens mountain-bound. **1954** W. Faulkner *Fable* 158 That thirty-mile-long mountain-cradled saucer. **1860** G. M. Hopkins *Poems* (1967) 6 Then pass'd the wind, and sobb'd with mountain-echo'd woe. **1939** Belloc *Decameron* in *Tablet* 11 Feb. 166/2 Mountain-guarded gardens. **1937** Blunden *Elegy* 90 The rough walls back to Chaucer reach, Near windowless, mountain-roofed, wry-angled. **1924** W. J. Locke *Coming of Amos* xiii. 169 A coast of romantic mountain-sheltered creeks.

8. a. *mountain air* (earlier and later examples), *shelter*.
1807 Southey *Lett. from Eng.* II. xli. 201 The mountain air had made us almost ravenous. **1810** E. Weeton *Let.* 11–15 Nov. (1969) I. 314 The keen mountain air had sharpened our appetites. **1965** *Listener* 30 Dec. 1063/1 The notes of *Colonel Bogey*, played by a military band.., sounding so clearly in the crystalline mountain air. **1922** W. G. Kendrew *Climates of Continents* xxvii. 188 There are almost constant north-west winds, strongest where there is no mountain shelter.

b. *mountain people.*
1881 *Harper's Mag.* Nov. 868/2 They are poor mountain people.

c. *mountain-saddle, wagon.*
1849 F. Parkman *Calif. & Oregon Trail* 145 Though aided by the high-bowed 'mountain-saddle' I could scarcely keep my seat on horseback. **1867** W. H. Dixon *New Amer.* (ed. 6) I. 170, I had the honour of riding in the mountain wagon with an old road-agent.

d. *mountain-mass.* (Cf. quot. 1833 s.v. sense 8 a in Dict.)
1918 A. Huxley *Defeat of Youth* 21 Soon will they lift towards the summer sky Their mountain-mass of clotted greenery.

9. a. mountain-building, the formation of mountains, esp. as a result of folding and thrusting of the earth's crust; **mountain Damara**: see *Damara; **mountain dew,** also used for other, esp. home-made or illicit, whiskies (further examples); **mountain fever** (earlier and later examples); **mountain-folding,** the formation of mountains as a result of folding of the earth's crust; **mountain man,** (*b*) (earlier and later examples); (*c*) *fig.* = Pioneer *sb.* 3; **mountain oyster** = *lamb's fry* (Lamb *sb.* 7); **mountain railway** (earlier example); (*b*) a miniature ascending railway designed for amusement; a scenic railway; a funiculaire; **mountain-schooner,** a wagon used in mountainous country; **mountain-sick** *a.*, suffering from mountain sickness; **mountain slide** (earlier example); **mountain spectre,** a reflection (of persons or things) seen under certain conditions on a mountain (cf. *Brocken); **mountain system,** a group of mountain ranges showing similarity in form, orientation, etc., and assumed to be due to the same general causes; **mountain (standard) time** *N. Amer.*, 'the time of the seventh time zone west of Greenwich based on the 105th meridian and used in west central Canada and the U.S.' (Webster 1961).
1871 J. D. Whitney in *N. Amer. Rev.* CXIII. 238 We cannot separate the phenomena of volcanoes and earthquakes from those of mountain-building and continental growth. **1919** *Jrnl. Geol.* XXVII. 250 Only moderate igneous activity was associated with the mountain building. **1944** J. S. Huxley *On Living in Revolution* p. vii, Periods of mountain-building accompanied by the emergence of more land from the sea. **1971** I. G. Gass et al. *Understanding Earth* i. 26/2 Andesites are typical of the world's greatest volcanoes lying in zones of active mountain building. **1899** R. L. Taylor in B. A. Botkin *Treas. Amer. Folklore* (1944) III. 411 They gathered there on rainy days to talk politics and religion, and to drink 'mountain' dew and fight. **1945** Baker *Austral. Lang.* ix. 168 Illicit whisky, as made in stills in bush areas, is known as *mountain dew*. This is a variation of the Standard English use of the term for genuine Scotch whisky. It is also used in America. **1970** *Times* 15 Oct. 30/3 The distilled spirits industry..wages an expensive propaganda campaign against..mountain dew. **1849** O. W. Lipe *Let.* 15 Aug. in R. P. Bieber *Southern Trails to Calif. in 1849* (1937) 346 There has been much sickness in our company; the disease is mountain fever. *a* **1918** G. Stuart *40 Yrs. on Frontier* (1925) I. 51 A severe attack of mountain fever ..laid me on my back in the wagon. **1970** *Islander* (Victoria, B.C.) 10 May 7/1 An epidemic of mountain fever struck the Kootenays in 1884. **1925** J. Joly *Surface-Hist. Earth* 170 The effects of these conditions on mountain-folding would probably be principally experienced where the geosynclines had forced the continental materials deep into the magma. **1971** *Geogr. Abstr.* A. 445 (*heading*) Fundamental principles of the development of collapses and slips in mountain-folding regions. **1781** *Calendar Virginia State Papers* (1875) I. 494 A late pressing application of General Greene for the aid of the Mountain Men. **1973** R. D. Symons *Where Wagon Led* i. vii. 117 In the United States the 'Mountain Men',—beaver trappers mostly—penetrated the western wilderness at an early date, before and during the middle years of the last century. **1973** *Sci. Amer.* Aug. 113/1 Professor Luria is an authentic pioneer of molecular biology. Even before the first wagon train set out he ventured as a mountain man among bacterial viruses. **1890** *Cent. Dict.* s.v. *Oyster*, *Mountain-oyster*, a lamb's testicle. **1951** E. Paul *Springtime in Paris* xi. 189, I have consumed mountain oysters and prairie dancers that are actually poetic. **1962** *Alberta Hist. Rev.* Autumn 15/2 In the commissariat department [are] 'dope' (butter)... 'Mountain oysters' (calves fries). **1880** 'Mark Twain' *Tramp Abroad* xxviii. 256, I..in the distance detected a long worm of black smoke crawling lazily up the steep mountain. Of course that was the locomotive... we had never seen a mountain railway yet. **1910** *Penny Guide Japan-Brit. Exhib.* 23 Mountain Railway. The visitor enters the cars which travel slowly round and upward until the top of the mountain range is reached. **1925** A. Huxley *Those Barren Leaves* ii. iii. 106 The switchback, the water-shoot and the mountain railway. **1869** C. L. Brace *New West* xiv. 188 It is more than a hundred miles away from the first link with civilization, and yet coaches, wagons, and the stream of 'mountain-schooners' pour into it unceasingly. **1937** *Discovery* June 171/1 People have been very mountain-sick at this hut. **1830** *Mass. Spy* 25 Aug. (Th.), Mountain slides. **1880** *Encycl. Brit.* XI. 399/2 Mountain spectres are caused by reflexion, and often appear accompanied by chromatic halos. **1882** A. Geikie *Text-bk. Geol.* 918 The Alps offer an instructive example of a great mountain system formed by repeated movements during a long succession of geological periods. **1931** C. M. Nevin *Princ. Struct. Geol.* xi. 289 A mountain system is characterized by folding, faulting, and igneous activities that vary in their complexity and relative importance throughout the zone of deformation. **1953** *Q. Jrnl. Geol. Soc.* CVIII. 2 The great mountain systems, or orogens, are zones of extreme compression of the earth's crust weaving a complex pattern of majestic sweeps around the world. **1968** R. A. Lyttleton *Mysteries Solar Syst.* iii. 91 It can be expected that mountain-systems will have formed on Venus comparable with those on Earth. **1935** *World Almanac* (ed. 50) 115/2 Mountain Standard Time is the local time of the 105th meridian. **1968** *Globe & Mail* (Toronto) 5 Feb. 22/8 Sealed tenders..will be received up to 2 o'clock P.M. Mountain Standard Time. **1891** *Cent. Dict.* s.v. *Time*[1] 19, The time of the 105th meridian (called *mountain time*). **1952** B. Malamud *Natural* 12 It looked around half-past five, but he couldn't be sure because somewhere near they left Mountain Time.

c. mountain bluebird *N. Amer.*, a bluebird of western North America, *Sialia currucoides*, distinguished by a blue breast instead of a red one; **mountain boomer**, substitute for def.: *U.S.*, (*a*) the sewellel or mountain beaver, *Aplodontia rufa*; (*b*) the red squirrel, *Sciurus hudsonicus*; also *transf.* (examples); **mountain buffalo** *U.S.*, (*a*) = *mountain sheep 2; (*b*) a mountain variety of the American buffalo, *Bison bison*; **mountain cock,** (*b*) *U.S.* = Prairie-chicken, *cock of the plains* (*cock *sb.*[1] 10); **mountain devil** (later examples); **mountain goat** (earlier and later examples); see also sense 8 b in Dict.; **mountain herring** (earlier example); **mountain jay** *U.S.*, Steller's jay, *Cyanocitta stelleri*; **mountain lion** (earlier and later examples); **mountain plover** *U.S.*, a small plover, *Eupoda montana*; **mountain ringlet,** an alpine butterfly, *Erebia epiphron*, found in limited parts of the Lake District, Scotland, and western Ireland; cf. Ringlet 4; **mountain tortoise,** a large African tortoise, *Geochelone pardalis*, also known as the leopard-tortoise (Leopard 6 b).
1860 S. F. Baird *Birds N. Amer.* I. 224 *Sialia arctica*, Swainson. Rocky Mountain Blue Bird. **1904** I. G. Wheelock *Birds Calif.* 506 The exquisite coloring of the Mountain Bluebird renders him easily the most beautiful of all Californian birds. **1971** *Islander* (Victoria, B.C.) 13 June 13/1 We were fortunate to see such birds as..a sky-blue mountain bluebird. **1858** D. K. Bennett *Chronol. N. Carolina* 94 The only inhabitants we saw on these high points were pheasants, cross bills, ..and mountain boomers, a sort of squirrel. **1859** H. E. Taliaferro *Fisher's River* 33 A mountain 'Boomer' dressed in a linsey hunting-shirt down to his knees. **1922** H. Kephart *Our Southern Highlanders* (new ed.) 87 Out of a tree overhead hopped a mountain 'boomer'. *Ibid.* 280 They call themselves mountain people, or citizens; sometimes humorously 'mountain boomers'. **1940** *Mt. Hood Guide* 21 The sewellel or mountain beaver, sometimes colloquially called 'mountain boomer'..resembles the porcupine and marmot rather than the beaver. **1958** *Amer. Speech* XXXIII. 265 (*table*) Pejorative designations of rural dwellers in the Upper Midwest..mountain boomer. **1868** *Amer. Naturalist* II. 538 'Mountain Buffalo'... The Bighorn is sometimes called so. *Ibid.*, I saw no difference in the skulls, indicating a different species, or 'Mountain Buffalo' of the hunters. **1884** *Encycl. Brit.* Amer. Suppl. I. 540/2 Buffaloes long inhabiting other localities than the open plains, their natural homes, acquire distinguishable varietal characters. They are known as 'wood-buffalo' and 'mountain-buffalo'. **1892** *Scribner's Mag.* Sept. 277/1 There are, besides the ordinary animal of the plains, the 'mountain buffalo',.. the 'wood buffalo',..and the 'beaver buffalo'. **1805** M. Lewis in Lewis & Clark *Orig. Jrnls. Lewis & Clark Expedition* (1905) II. 124 Saw (near the hills) a flock of the mountain cock, or a large species of heath hen with a long pointed tail which the Indians informed us were common to the Rocky Mountains. **1943** H. Drake-Brockman in *Coast to Coast 1942* 158 There were little barking lizards and mountain-devils and eagle-hawks and white owls in the blow-holes. **1966** *Times* 11 Nov. (W. Austral. Suppl.) p. iv/4 The hideous little mountain devil (*Moloch horridus*) ..trades on its frightening aspect while sustaining a perfectly blameless existence on a diet of ants. **1841** G. Catlin *Lett. on N. Amer. Indians* II. 196 His leggings and shirt were of the mountain goat skin. **1936** D. McCowan *Animals Canad. Rockies* xiv. 119 A herd of mountain goats on an immense buttress of rock. **1966** *Globe & Mail* (Toronto) 7 May 41/2 Mountain goat also abound in the mountainous region..in..south-eastern British Columbia. **1877** C. Hallock *Sportsman's Gazetteer* 350 Williamson's Whitefish; Mountain Herring.—*Coregonus williamsoni*. **1872** *Amer. Naturalist* VI. 398 The great-crested, Woodhouse's and the Canada jays were of frequent occurrence in the mountains, the former being familiarly known as the 'mountain jay'. **1917** T. G. Pearson *Birds Amer.* II. 219 Steller's Jay... [also called] Mountain Jay; Pine Jay; Conifer Jay. **1859** G. A. Jackson *Diary* 1 Jan. in *Colorado Mag.* (1935) XII. 204 Killed a mountain lion today. **1936** D. McCowan *Animals Canad. Rockies* ix. 77 The cougar or mountain lion is a large tawny brown cat with a small head, rather slender body and long round tail. **1972** *Radio Times* 1 June 30/1 Wild life to be found in different parts of Canada including a mountain lion and a wapiti. **1858** S. F. Baird in *Rep. Explor. Route to Pacific* (U.S. War Dept.) IX. 693 Mountain Plover..is only known to inhabit the western countries of North America. **1917** T. G. Pearson *Birds Amer.* I. 267 Mountain Plover... Nest: On the open prairies; a depression in the ground, lined with leaves and grass. **1870** F. O. Morris *Hist. Brit. Butterflies* (ed. 5) 53 (*heading*) Small Ringlet. Mountain Ringlet. **1945** E. B. Ford *Butterflies* xiii. 288 The Mountain Ringlet, *Erebia epiphron*, cannot live in England at an altitude of less than 1800 feet, but in Scotland it is able to descend to about 1500 feet. **1975** *Times* 12 Nov. 14/6 The Mountain Ringlet is an extremely rare butterfly that may still exist in the wild, high mountains of Western Ireland. **1958** L. van der Post *Lost World of Kalahari* i. 26 For the equivalent of cello and bass violin he used the shell of our big dark mountain tortoises. **1966** E. Palmer *Plains of Camdeboo* xiii. 228 Mountain tortoises are said to have a great homing instinct. **1971** D. J. Potgieter et al. *Animal Life S. Afr.* 303/2 Mountain or leopard tortoise..is a widely distributed species, extending from the Sudan and Ethiopia in the north to the Cape in the south.

d. mountain beech, (*b*) (earlier and later examples); (*c*) *N.Z.*, the evergreen tree, *Nothofagus cliffortioides*; **mountain-bell,** an alpine species of *Campanula*; **mountain cherry** *U.S.*, substitute for def.: one of several wild cherries (earlier and later examples); **mountain chestnut oak** *U.S.*, an American oak, *Quercus montana*, with leaves resembling those of the chestnut; **mountain daisy** *N.Z.*, a perennial herb of the genus *Celmisia*, belonging to the family Compositæ; **mountain fern,** substitute for def.: *Thelypteris limbosperma* (earlier and later examples); **mountain hemlock,** a large coniferous tree, *Tsuga mertensiana*, of the family Pinaceæ, native to western North America; **mountain mahogany** *U.S.*, (*a*) = *mahogany birch* (*mahogany 7); (*b*) a shrub or small tree of the genus *Cercocarpus*, esp. *C. ledifolius*, belonging to the family Rosaceæ and native to western North America; **mountain maple** *U.S.*, one of several maples found in upland areas, esp. *Acer spicatum*; **mountain pine,** (*b*) *N.Z.*, a small evergreen tree, *Dacrydium bidwillii*, found in boggy or subalpine regions; **mountain pink,** an alpine species of *Dianthus*; **mountain tea** *N. Amer.*, the wintergreen, *Gaultheria procumbens*, or the beverage made from its leaves.
1884 A. Nilson *Timber Trees New South Wales* 92 *L*[*omatia*] *longifolia*.—Mountain Beech.—An erect small tree. **1928** Cockayne & Turner *Trees N.Z.* 154 *Nothofagus cliffortioides* (mountain-beech) is of little value as a timber, for it decays rapidly. **1959** A. McLintock *Descr. Atlas N.Z.* p. xv, The forest is of silver and mountain beech, with traces of red beech and podocarps at low altitude. **1965** *Austral. Encycl.* V. 360/2 *L*[*omatia*] *longifolia* (sometimes called mountain beech), has a hard light-coloured ornamental wood, used for turnery. **1923** D. H. Lawrence *Ladybird* 227 Sometimes the hairy mountain-bell, pale-blue and bristling, stood alone. **1813** H. Muhlenberg *Catal. Plantarum Americæ Septentrionalis* 48 *Prunus montana*,..mountain cherry. **1871** *Harper's Mag.* Oct. 707 We must..gather mountain cherries (*Prunus cerasus*). **1801** A. Michaux *Hist. Chênes de l'Amérique* sig. 6$_1$v Mountain Chesnut Oak. **1821** T. Nuttall *Jrnl. Trav. Arkansa* i. 42 Much of the *Quercus Prima monticola* (or mountain chestnut oak) presents itself on the mountain. **1857** J. T. Thomson in N. M. Taylor *Early Travellers N.Z.* (1959) 335 Half-way up the mountains some pretty flowers were gathered, amongst which the mountain daisy

deserves notice. **1900** A. DENDY in *Canterbury Old & New* 188 Only rivalled in beauty by the marguerite-like flowers of 'cotton plant' or mountain daisy (species of *Celmisia*). **1959** A. MCLINTOCK *Descr. Atlas N.Z.* p. xv, The upper mountain limits were covered with alpine vegetation—mountain daisies (Celmisia), [etc.]. **1840** E. NEWMAN *Hist. Brit. Ferns* 47 (*heading*) Mountain fern. **1879–81** J. BRITTEN *European Ferns* 151 The Mountain Fern, as *L[astrea] Oreopteris* is sometimes called,..is well worthy of cultivation. **1960** P. TAYLOR *Brit. Ferns & Mosses* 155 The Mountain Fern is widely distributed throughout the northern hemisphere. **1884** C. S. SARGENT *Rep. Forests N. Amer.* 572 The timber on these ridges [in Idaho] was often small and scattered..with larch and red fir, balsam, hemlock, and sometimes mountain hemlock. **1969** T. H. EVERETT *Living Trees of World* 64/2 Another western American, the usually bluish-leaved mountain hemlock.., occurs at high altitudes from Alaska to California. **1974** *Daily Colonist* (Victoria, B.C.) 24 Dec. 32/2 The major reason for establishing the reserve..is to allow biologists to study mountain hemlock. **1810** F. A. MICHAUX *Hist. Arbres Forestiers de l'Amérique Septentrionale* I. 26 Sweet birch, [ou] Mountain Mahogany dans Virginia. **1832** D. J. BROWNE *Sylva Amer.* 118 Wherever it grows in the United States, it is known by the name of Black Birch: its secondary denominations are Mountain Mahogany in Virginia, [etc.]. **1875** *Amer. Naturalist* IX. 201 Much more attractive with its glossy foliage and long feathery seeds, is the mountain mahogany *Cercocarpus ledifolius* Nutt. **1951** *Dict. Gardening* (R. Hort. Soc.) I. 440/1 *C[ercocarpus] ledifolius.* Mountain mahogany. Erect slender tree up to 40 ft. **1785** H. MARSHALL *Arbustrum Amer.* 2 *Acer pennsylvanicum*, Pennsylvanian Dwarf Mountain Maple,.. grows naturally upon the mountains in the back parts of Pennsylvania. **1832** D. J. BROWNE *Sylva Amer.* 102 The mountain maple seldom rises above 20 feet in height. **1969** T. H. EVERETT *Living Trees of World* 222/2 Similar in size [to the moosewood] and also favoring shaded locations through much of eastern and central North America is the mountain maple (*A. spicatum*). **1933** L. G. D. ACLAND in *Press* (Christchurch, N.Z.) 4 Nov. 15/7 Mountain... Often used..of a species found in the back country, mostly smaller than their down-country relatives, e.g. mountain pine. **1963** POOLE & ADAMS *Trees & Shrubs N.Z.* 26 *D[acrydium] bidwillii...* Bog pine, mountain pine. Reaching 4 m. Leaves: juvenile linear, sessile, passing abruptly into adult foliage with scale-like, imbricate leaves. **1850** L. SAWYER *Diary* 12 June in *Way Sk.* (1926) 53 We found some grass and some beautiful specimens of what we called mountain pink. It is much smaller than our garden pink, but resembles it somewhat in form, but more in its sweet perfume. **1936** *Discovery* Feb. 46/2 There [*sc.* on a mountain in Yugoslavia] I found tall mountain pinks of deep crimson, single-flowering. [**1765** in D. Campbell *Hist. Prince Edward Island* (1875) 6 The Mountain Shrub and Maiden Hair are also pretty common, of whose leaves and berries the Acadian settlers frequently make a kind of tea.] **1785** H. MARSHALL *Arbustrum Amer.* 53 *Gaultheria procumbens.* Canadian Gaultheria, or Mountain Tea... The leaves have been used as a substitute for Bohea Tea, whence the name of Mountain Tea. **1804** [see **grouse-berry*]. **1830** *Trans. Lit. & Hist. Soc. Quebec* (1837) III. 96 Mountain tea [is] a very small evergreen half-shrubby plant, with strong, shining, leathery leaves. **1832** W. D. WILLIAMSON *Hist. State Maine* I. 121 This 'mountain tea' promotes mammillary secretions. **1858** [see TEA *sb.* 6]. **1886** *Harper's Mag.* June 62/1 Another beverage is 'mountain tea' which is made from the sweet scented golden-rod and from winter-green. **1891** M. E. RYAN *Pagan of Alleghanies* 65 They reached the level above the cliff, the level carpeted with mountain-tea and rabbit-berries. **1941** J. STUART *Men of Mountains* 187, I would love to get out with you and get mountain tea from the knolls. **1964** H. D. WILSON *Tales from Barrett's Landing* 44 To supplement our meals..we ate berries, mountain teas (a leaf that tastes like wintergreen), and seaweed.

mountain ash. 2. b. (Earlier and later examples.)

1884 A. NILSON *Timber Trees New South Wales* 74 *E[ucalyptus] virgata.*—Mountain ash; White-top.—A tree of considerable size. *Ibid.*, *E. micrococca.*—Mountain Ash... Habitat, brush forests, from Illawarra to the Richmond River and New England; also Blue Mountains. **1934** [see *BLACKBUTT]. **1957** *N.Z. Timber Jrnl.* Dec. 59/1 Mountain ash. *Eucalyptus regnans* F. Muell. and *E. delegatensis* R.T.B... Victoria and Tasmania. Also called Tasmanian oak and Australian oak. Moderately hard, heavy, durable, strong, elastic and resilient.

mountain flax. Add: **1. f.** *N.Z. Phormium colensoi*, a smaller and hardier form of the New Zealand flax, *P. tenax*.

1867 E. SAUTER tr. *F. von Hochstetter's New Zealand* vii. 152 We may distinguish about three principal varieties..*Wharariki*, mountain flax, with coarse fibres; little used. **1949** P. BUCK *Coming of Maori* (1950) II. v. 167 Relief in decoration was obtained by spacing tags of the mountain flax (*Phormium colensoi*) which turn a distinct yellow in colour.

mountain laurel. = *KALMIA.

1759 [in Dict. s.v. MOUNTAIN 9 d]. **1810** F. A. MICHAUX *Hist. Arbres Forestiers de l'Amérique Septentrionale* I. 35 Mountain laurel,..dénomination la plus générale. **1832** D. J. BROWNE *Sylva Amer.* 191 The Mountain Laurel is a large shrub, which indifferently bears the name Mountain Laurel, Laurel, Ivy, and Calico Tree. **1845** S. JUDD *Margaret* I. ii. 8 She got running mosses..and mountain laurel blossoms. **1880** *Harper's Mag.* June 80 The mountain laurel, with its deep green foliage and showy clusters peers above that rocky crag. **1887** [in Dict. s.v. MOUNTAIN 9 d]. **1906** J. A. HARRISON *George Washington* 91 The bluish-pink masses of the mountain-laurel. **1955** [see *KALMIA]. **1973** ROBICHAUD & BUELL *Vegetation of New Jersey* 329 Kalmia..latifolia. Mountain laurel.

mountain rescue. Used *attrib.* and *absol.* to designate an organization for rescuing mountaineers (sense 3) in distress.

1956 F. T. K. BULLMORE *Dark Haven* xxiv. 182, I think the best thing I can do is to have all leaders of Mountain Rescue Units up to London for a round-table talk. *Ibid.*, I couldn't help thinking of the many..difficulties that these Mountain Rescue Squads would have to face. *Ibid.* xxvi. 189 Roxborough had been making great progress with the Mountain Rescue Organization. To help him with the technical difficulties of mountaineering he had unearthed..an Austrian mountain guide. **1957** R. G. COLLOMB *Dict. Mountaineering* 108 Mountain districts in Britain and the Alps have their own mountain rescue posts... Mountain rescue teams are local organizations made up of people working in the district. **1959** 'G. CARR' *Swing Away, Climber* iv. 74 Telephone Higgs at the Pen-y-gwryd for the mountain rescue stretcher. **1971** O. NORTON *Corpse-Bird Cries* v. 85 There was a mountain rescue van there. **1973** C. BONINGTON *Next Horizon* i. 26 He..had spent some years with the Royal Air Force in Mountain Rescue, and was a good steady goer.

mountain sheep. 1. [MOUNTAIN 8 b.] Sheep kept in mountainous regions. Cf. SHEEP *sb.* 1 b.

1829 T. L. PEACOCK *Misfortunes Elphin* xi. 141 The mountain sheep are sweeter, But the valley sheep are fatter. **1910** W. DE LA MARE *Three Mulla-Mulgars* 17 The little coat of mountain-sheep's wool. **1961** J. GUNSTON *Profit from Sheep* i. 11 Great experience of local conditions and practice is the only real guide to the proper management of mountain sheep. **1975** *Country Life* 9 Oct. 942/1 The Castlemartin range..is..a custom-built wintering ground for mountain sheep.

2. *U.S.* [MOUNTAIN 9 c.] Either of two species of North American wild sheep, the bighorn, *Ovis canadensis*, or the Dall sheep, *Ovis dalli*.

1802 in *Med. Repository 1803* 240 The mountain ram, or sheep, though not very often seen, is to be met with, in considerable numbers, in some parts of the mountains. **1807** P. GASS *Jrnl.* vii. 82 On the top of the highest [bluff] we saw some Mountain sheep, which the natives say are common about the Rocky mountains. **1837** W. IRVING *Capt. Bonneville* I. iii. 69 This animal is commonly called the mountain sheep, and is often confounded with another animal, the 'woolly sheep' found more to the northward. **1841** G. CATLIN *Lett. on N. Amer. Indians* II. 188 Dressed in a beautiful costume of the mountain-sheep skin. **1846** R. B. SAGE *Scenes Rocky Mts.* xiv. 121 In size the mountain sheep is larger than the domestic animal of that name, and its general appearance is in every respect dissimilar—excepting the head and horns. **1918** T. ROOSEVELT in *Maine my State* (Maine Writers Research Club) (1919) 21 We had a couple of antelope and a yearling mountain sheep. **1947** *Trail & Timberline* Feb. 15/2 We saw moose, bear, caribou, mountain (Dall) sheep, and wolves almost every trip.

mountain side. Add: Also with hyphen or as one word. (Further examples.) Also *fig.*

1910 W. DE LA MARE *Three Mulla-Mulgars* xiii. 175 The bare, snow-flecked mountain-side. **1913** J. HULBERT in *Granta* 7 Mar. 255/1 No man is helped up the mountain side of toil by undue ragging. **1960** *Farmer & Stockbreeder* 23 Feb. Suppl. 2/1, I was late and began to run, panting up the mountainside with my hand under my heart. *a* **1963** L. MACNEICE *Astrol.* (1964) ix. 286 (*caption*) A recent 'end-of-world' forecast was the catastrophe predicted by Indian astrologists in 1962. In Britain, a mountain-side prayer meeting was held to avert this disaster.

mountain snow. 3. (Earlier and later examples.)

1889 'C. E. CRADDOCK' *Despot of Broomsedge Cove* ix. 159 He mechanically noted..how the blooming 'Mountain snow' brushed his mare's fine coat. **1913** BRITTON & BROWN *Illustr. Flora Northern U.S.* (ed. 2) II. 469 *Euphorbia marginata...* In dry soil, Minnesota to Colorado, south to Texas. Introduced into waste places in the Central and Atlantic States. Snow-on-the-mountain... Mountain-snow.

mounted, *a.* Add: **3.** *mounted branch, infantry* (earlier examples), *police*.

1792 *Deb. Congress U.S.* (1849) 18 Sept. 1134 General Harman..detached..the mounted infantry. **1834** R. M. MARTIN *Hist. Brit. Colonies* I. iii. 147 There is a mounted police officered by [Indian] natives. **1858** E. H. D. DOMENECH *Missionary Adventures Texas & Mexico* 177 The Indians were once nearly taking prisoners a whole company of mounted infantry. **1859** J. BLACKWOOD *Let.* 24 July in Geo. Eliot *Lett.* (1954) III. 121 The animal is..under charge of..the veterinary of the Mounted Police. **1878** *Saskatchewan Herald* (Battleford) 25 Aug. 1/2 Shoal Lake has been created the headquarters of the Mounted Police for that district. **1935** N. MITCHISON *We have been Warned* IV. 452 Six mounted police went by at the trot, scattering the crowd. **1963** *Calgary Herald Mag.* 4 Oct. 48/4 An old Mounted Police stable may..be seen. **1970** P. LAURIE *Scotland Yard* ii. 50 A specialist job: the CID.. Mounted Branch.

7. Of a project, exhibition, or radio or television programme: produced, directed, arranged. Cf. *MOUNT *v.* 17 d.

1895 in *Funk's Stand. Dict.* **1966** *Listener* 30 June 945/2 The carefully mounted [broadcast] series for mentally handicapped children. **1971** *Nature* 9 July 74/1 The medical problems of many developing countries,..should be amenable to all kinds of internationally mounted projects.

Mountie (mau·nti). *colloq.* Also **Mounty.** [f. MOUNT(ED *a.* + -IE, -Y[6].] **1.** A member of the Royal Canadian (formerly North West) Mounted Police.

1914 *Eye Opener* (Calgary) 12 Dec. 3/4 Ketchen, the Mountie,..was easily placated. **1924** A. J. SMALL *Frozen Gold* vi. 139 A sentence that is at once the badge and boast of the Mounted—'the Mounties never come in without their man'. **1927** *Sunday at Home* 106/2 The Eskimo borrowed the Mounty's gun and shot him. **1971** D. HEFFRON *Nice Fire & Some Moonpennies* i. 12 We all looked all around us as though there might be a Mountie skulking behind every tree. **1973** *Saturday Night* (Toronto) Feb. 22/1 All I could see was the Mounties' legs.

2. A member of a similar police force outside Canada.

1931 *Skipper* 25 Apr. 112 A detachment of the Camel Corps on the march outside Cairo. These desert 'mounties' keep law and order in Egypt. **1953** R. CAMPBELL *Mamba's Precipice* 125, I wonder why such a smart man with a castle in England has to come out here [*sc.* S. Africa] and work as an ordinary Mountie.

mounting, *vbl. sb.* Add: **1.** (Further examples.)

1828 J. EBERS *Seven Yrs. King's Theatre* xii. 331 The mounting of this, the first performance of the season, afforded me an illustration of the obliging disposition of Madame Biagioli. **1846** *Swell's Night Guide* 43 She undertakes the art of mounting, which she teaches with considerable success. **1959** *Times Lit. Suppl.* 16 Jan. 27/2 Twenty per cent. of the current United States military budget is to be allocated to economic aid and industrial development of the underdeveloped countries, including the mounting of a crash programme for the development of compact and readily transportable atomic power plants. **1962** *Listener* 14 June 1016/2 Ministers of Defence connived at the mounting of an abusive legal action which again jeopardized the journal's financial stability. **1974** H. WAUGH *Parrish for Defence* (1975) xliii. 200 It aroused him, and his second mounting was in the nature of an unbridled emotion.

b. *mounting board, bracket, point, ring, test.*

1854 Mounting board [in Dict., sense 2 a]. **1926** *Paper Terminol.* (Spalding & Hodge) 18 *Mounting boards* are made up of a wood pulp centre lined on one or both sides with paper. **1937** E. J. LABARRE *Dict. Paper* 177/1 *Mounting test*, a method of testing the absorbing power of blotting paper by allowing the ink or water to 'mount' up a strip of blotting, the 'weight test' determining the weight of liquid absorbed. **1944** *R.A.F. Jrnl.* Aug. 292 Strange is the conversation to the uninitiated ear—Mounting rings..—Double engine changes—these are the phrases heard. **1962** *Which? Car Suppl.* Oct. 131/1 The mounting points for the sun visors..were metal and unguarded. *Ibid.* 138/2 The mounting bracket for the accelerator linkage. *Ibid.* 143/1 Safety belt mounting points..are now fitted as standard equipment.

2. a. (Further examples.)

1914 C. F. TWENEY *Dict. Naval & Mil. Terms* 157 *Mountings*, a term applied to the platforms on which heavy naval guns and guns of position for fortresses are mounted. **1962** *Which? Car Suppl.* Oct. 138/2 Flexible gear box rear mounting made gear lever vibrate considerably on rough ground. *Ibid.* 139/2 Fuel pump mounting [was] slightly insecure. *Ibid.*, Central mounting of exhaust system failed.

Mountmellick (mauntme·lik). The name of a town in the Irish Republic used *attrib.* to designate a type of white-work embroidery made there.

1893 E. T. MASTERS *Gentlewoman's Bk. Art Needlework* iii. 77 The material upon which the original Mountmellick embroidery was executed was a stout make of white satin jean, white knitting-cotton of various sizes being used to form the stitches. The designs are usually somewhat naturalistic in style. **1920** A. K. ARTHUR *Embroidery Bk.* viii. 85 Bullion knots are used very frequently in Mountmellick work. **1936** M. THOMAS *Embroidery Bk.* 187 Contrary to most other forms of white work, there are no open or drawn spaces in Mountmellick Embroidery. The stitches are planned to lie on the surface of the material with as little thread as possible beneath, and to provide the sense of 'stitchery in relief'. *Ibid.* 194 The following is a list of stitches, suitable for Mountmellick Embroidery. **1959** *Chambers's Encycl.* V. 156/1 Mountmellick embroidery is an Irish form of white work, using a variety of stitches but no open spaces. **1960** H. HAYWARD *Antique Coll.* 191/2 *Mount Mellick embroidery*, a type of white-work, first introduced about 1830 at Mountmellick in Queen's County, Ireland, and revived as a local industry in the 1880s. **1962** B. MORRIS *Victorian Embroidery* ii. 40 An entirely different type of whitework known as 'Mountmellick embroidery' was popular throughout the Victorian period. **1967** E. SHORT *Embroidery & Fabric Collage* i. 19 *Mountmellick embroidery.* This embroidery relies on padded stitches, knots, etc., giving a raised surface to the embroidery.

Mounty, var. *MOUNTIE.

mourner[1]. 1. d. (Earlier and later examples.)

1834 F. LIEBER *Lett. to Gent. in Germany* xvi. 312 These tents..are divided lengthwise by a bench about a foot high, and called the mourners' bench. **1845** J. J. HOOPER *Some Adventures Simon Suggs* x. 121 Having thus deposited his charge among the mourners, he started out, summarily to convert another soul! *Ibid.* 126 'And then,' continued Simon, 'I had to go yonder—pointing to the mourner's seat. **1857** P. CARTWRIGHT *Autobiogr.* xxvi. 403 You must go to the Methodist's despised mourner's bench. **1888** [see *ANXIOUS *a.* 2]. **1891** *Harper's Mag.* Jan. 214/2 Everybody else war either convicted o' sin, an' at the mourner's bench [etc.]. **1904** *Charlotte* (N. Carolina) *Observer* 27 July 4 In the city police court a motley crowd of prisoners filled the mourners' benches. **1972** *News & Observer* (Raleigh, N. Carolina) 30 Dec. 4/3 The August meeting, the mourner's bench and the amen corner have gone out with stewards who yelled out 'amen' during the sermon.

mournful, *a.* (and *sb.*). Add: **5.** **Mournful Maria** = **Mournful Mary* (*b*); **Mournful**

Mary *Forces' slang*, (*a*) a siren; (*b*) *spec.* the siren used at Dunkirk during the 1914–18 war. ? *Obs.*

1918 K. MacLeish *Let.* 6 May in R. D. Paine *First Yale Unit* (1925) II. 162 The French have installed about six new, loud 'Mournful Marys'. **1918** in J. McG. Grider *War Birds* (1926) 185 Everybody knows when to take shelter and Mournful Mary, the siren, goes off automatically ten minutes before. **1920** G. S. Maxwell *Motor Launch Patrol* ix. 151 Above all the voice of the siren—the famous Mournful Mary—kept up a moaning obbligato. **1925** Fraser & Gibbons *Soldier & Sailor Words* 160 *Mournful Maria*, a nickname given to the Dunkirk syren, employed to give warning of enemy air attacks and long range shelling. **1927** E. W. Springs *Nocturne Militaire* 77 Soon Mournful Mary, the siren in Dunkirk, sounded the All Clear.

mourning, *vbl. sb.*[1] Add: **5.** *mourning armlet, badge, bonnet, card, -dress, handkerchief, hat, hat-band* (later example), *millinery, note-paper, picture, tie, veil*; **mourning-band** (later examples); **mourning envelope**, a mourning-bordered envelope; **mourning iris**, *Iris susiana* (see quots.); **mourning jewellery**, jewellery decorated with miniature funereal ornaments or pictures; **mourning-piece** (further examples); **mourning-vein**, a vein of mourning granite; **mourning warehouse**, a warehouse selling mourning clothes, etc. (cf. Warehouse *sb.* 1 e).

1966 *Olney Amsden & Sons Ltd. Price List* 29 Mourning armlets. **1968** Mrs. L. B. Johnson *White House Diary* 8 Oct. (1970) 718 A mourning badge worn after Lincoln's assassination. *c* **1874** D. Boucicault in M. R. Booth *Eng. Plays of 19th Cent.* (1969) II. 211, I was wrong to come here at all. I feel like a mourning band on a white hat. **1966** J. Potts *Footsteps on Stairs* (1967) ii. 19 Enid kept her loneliness hidden, while Martin's was there for all the world to see; he wore it like a mourning band. **1897** *Sears, Roebuck Catal.* 302/2 Ladies' Mourning Bonnet..a very handsome Bonnet and Mourning Veil. **1804** M. Wilmot *Let.* 2 Jan. in *Russ. Jrnls.* (1934) 72 A Mourning Card was presented to the Princess. **1939–40** *Army & Navy Stores Catal.* 301 Mourning note papers, cards,..and envelopes. **1840** *Knickerbocker* XVI. 70 A conclusive proof that the mourning-dress is an empty ordinance of Fashion. **1843** Dickens *Christmas Carol* ii. 65 A fair young girl in a mourning-dress. *a* **1922** L. Luck in J. Burnett *Useful Toil* (1974) I. 72, I had my new mourning dress torn from my back, through trying to part them when fighting. **1862** Mourning envelope [see Note-paper]. **1907** *Yesterday's Shopping* (1969) 332/1 Mourning envelopes. **1939–40** Mourning envelope [see *mourning card* above]. **1897** *Sears, Roebuck Catal.* 226/3 Mourning Handkerchiefs... with neat fast black hem-stitched borders. **1907** *Yesterday's Shopping* (1969) 819/2 Mourning Handkerchiefs. With black border. **1896** *T. Eaton & Co. Catal.* Spring & Summer 46/3 Telegraph orders for Mourning Hats continue to be received. **1899** in A. Adburgham *Shops & Shopping* (1964) xxii. 261 Mourning hat bands. **1883** W. Robinson *Eng. Flower Garden* 158/1 *I*[*ris*] *susiana* (Mourning I[ris])... The flowers, which are produced in early summer, are very large and densely spotted and striped with dark purple on a grey ground. **1966** M. Price *Iris Bk.* vii. 78 The celebrated silver and black mourning iris.. is easiest. **1895** *Montgomery Ward Catal.* 179 Real onyx and jet mourning jewelry. **1960** H. Hayward *Antique Coll.* 192/1 *Mourning jewellery* became particularly fashionable in the second half of the 18th cent... Earlier mourning jewellery of the 16th and 17th cent..was of a more gloomy kind. **1896** *T. Eaton & Co. Catal.* Spring & Summer 46/3 Mourning Millinery. **1862** Mourning notepaper [see Note-paper]. **1907** *Yesterday's Shopping* (1969) 332/1 Mourning note paper. **1947** T. H. White *Elephant & Kangaroo* (1948) xxi. 170 Two mourning pictures of her father and mother. **1972** *Village Voice* (N.Y.) 1 June 3/4 Crewel work and other kinds of embroidery, mourning pictures, theorems, and stencil work. **1843** *Knickerbocker* XXII. 189 The parlor..was ornamented..among the rest, [with] the indispensable family mourning-piece. **1967** Mrs. L. B. Johnson *White House Diary* 12 Nov. (1970) 588 On the walls are samplers and 'mourning pieces' and quaint American primitive portraits. **1970** *New Yorker* 28 Nov. 158/2 The picture is one of the earliest examples of the mourning piece—a folk genre that originated at the time of Wash.'s death. **1970** B. Knox *Children of Mist* vii. 155 A black mourning tie knotted neatly at his shirt collar. **1897** Mourning veil [see *mourning bonnet* above]. **1872** *Rep. Vermont Board Agric.* I. 662 The other layers most desirable and most valuable are the dark and light mourning veins. *c* **1860** in A. Adburgham *Shops & Shopping* (1964) vi. 65 The London General Mourning Warehouse. **1885** *List of Subscribers, Classified* (United Telephone Co.) (ed. 6) 157 Mourning Warehouses.

mourning, *ppl. a.* **3. mourning dove**, *N. Amer.*, substitute for def.: a blue-grey pigeon, *Zenaidura macroura carolinensis*, distinguished by its plaintive call; (earlier and later examples); **mourning willow**, the weeping willow.

1841 G. Catlin *Lett. on N. Amer. Indians* I. 158 The mourning or turtle-dove..is not to be destroyed or harmed by anyone. **1880** J. M. Farrar *Five Yrs. Minnesota* 166 Mourning-doves fill every wood with their plaintive notes. **1929** M. de la Roche *Whiteoaks* xvi. 203 High in the pines she heard the plaintive notes of a mourning dove. **1968** *Globe & Mail* (Toronto) 13 Jan. 41/2 Once again Ontario gunners are asking for an open season on mourning doves and once again considerations of sentimentality ..will almost certainly defeat them. **1975** A. Dillard *Pilgrim at Tinker Creek* ii. 33, I saw the backyard cedar where the mourning doves roost. **1813** H. Muhlenberg *Catal. Plantarum Americæ Septentrionalis* 91 Mourning Willow.

mouse, *sb.* Add: **2. b.** (Further examples.)

1785 R. Burns *To a Mouse* in *Poems & Songs* (1968) I. 128 The best laid schemes o' Mice an' Men, Gang aft agley. **1937** J. Steinbeck (*title*) Of mice and men. **1938** *Time* 30 May 48/3 Are we mice or men? **1961** *Times* 24 Nov. 15/1 There is a particularly good comic performance by Mr. Denys Graham as the mouse who for one glorious moment believes he is a man. **1975** L. Deighton *Yesterday's Spy* xxii. 169 She gave a mocking laugh. 'What are you?.. A man or a mouse?'

4. e. (See quot.)

1905 *Jrnl. Franklin Inst.* Mar. 185 A fine wire is sometimes drawn through a duct by a conical piece of wood with a thin leather washer filling the duct, and forced ahead by the air pressure at the rear... This piece of wood is termed the 'mouse'.

10. d. *mouse-gnawn* adj.

1921 W. de la Mare *Veil* 1 From crock of bone-dry crusts and mouse-gnawn cheese.

e. *mouse-poor, -quiet* adjs.

1921 R. Graves *Pier-glass* 50 Baffled, aghast with hate, mouse-poor. **1946** —— *Poems 1938–45* 13 And we remain mouse-quiet when they begin Suddenly in their unpredictable way To weave an allegory of their lives.

f. mouse pox = *Ectromelia 2.

1947 F. Fenner in *Austral. Jrnl. Exper. Biol. & Med. Sci.* XXV. 334 Marchal originally proposed the name 'infectious ectromelia' on account of the frequency with which amputation of the extremities occurred. Few subsequent observers have found this at all common... In view of this and of the newly found close relationship of the disease to the mammalian pox diseases, Professor F. M. Burnet has suggested that 'mouse pox' should be used as a synonym for 'infectious ectromelia'. **1948** *Brit. Jrnl. Exper. Path.* XXIX. 77 Mice dying of acute mouse-pox do not shed much virus into the environment. **1955** F. M. Burnet *Princ. Animal Virology* vii. 157 The content of elementary bodies was very clearly shown in ultraviolet micrographs of the..mouse-pox inclusion body. **1970** S. M. Brooks *World of Viruses* v. 47 The so-called variola-like poxviruses cause smallpox,..mousepox,..and turkey-pox.

mouse-deer. Substitute for def.: A chevrotain, a small deer-like mammal of the genus *Tragulus*, found in southern Asia, Sumatra, Borneo, and Java. (Later examples.)

1914 *Oxf. Survey Brit. Empire* II. xii. 383 The Indian pig, the mouse-deer..are found throughout the territories. **1965** R. McKie *Company of Animals* x. 153 Joe's mouse-deer are about nine inches high. **1969** Ld. Medway *Wild Mammals Malaya* 106/1 Mouse-deer are true forest mammals.

mouse-eared, *a.* Add: (*c*) *mouse-eared bat*, a brown bat, *Myotis myotis*, with greyish-white underside, found in Europe, parts of western Asia, and, rarely, in Britain.

1910 G. E. H. Barrett-Hamilton *Hist. Brit. Mammals* I. 191 The Mouse-eared bat, should it occur again in Britain, can hardly be mistaken for any other. **1956** *Proc. Zool. Soc.* CXXVII. 201 The animal was identified as a Mouse-eared Bat *Myotis myotis*..and then photographed *in situ* before being touched. **1975** *Observer* 26 Jan. 1/8 Mr Peter Hardy..said mouse-eared bats survived in Britain in only a single colony.

mouse-hole. Add: Hence **mou·sehole** *v. trans.* and *intr.*, to make a narrow passage or tunnel (through something); **mou·seholed** *ppl. a.*

1950 O. Nash *Family Reunion* (1951) 40 Little mouse Blink strategically mouseholed. **1967** L. Deighton *Expensive Place* xx. 137 It was another half-hour before they had broken into the cellars..and then it took twenty minutes more to mousehole through into Datt's house. *Ibid.* 138 Loiscau's men were moving up from the mouse-holed cellars.

mouse-hunt[2]. Delete *rare*$^{-0}$ and add later example.

1975 *Country Life* 27 Mar. 761/1 Our adopted cat..no longer seems to want to be off on a nocturnal mousehunt.

mouser. 1. (Later examples.)

1921 T. S. Eliot *Let. c* 11 Oct. in *Waste Land Drafts* (1971) p. xxi, Would you be able to house a small cat which we are very fond of?.. It is a very good mouser. **1939** —— *Old Possum's Pract. Cats* 38 No commonplace mousers have such well-cut trousers. **1966** A. Christie *Third Girl* xvii. 178 You're so exactly like a good mouser. A cat sitting over a hole waiting for the mouse to come out.

mousery (mau·səri). [f. Mous(e *sb.* + -ery.] **a.** A place where mice abound; a colony of mice.

1888 F. A. Lucas in *Auk* V. 280 The occasional disturbance of this populous mousery by the visits of Owls. **1925** W. de la Mare *Broomsticks* 109 He never paid the smallest attention to mouse or mouse-hole or mousery.

b. A place where mice are bred or kept.

1935 A. Carrol *Man the Unknown* vi. 207 The mice belonging to one of the strains kept in the mousery of the Rockefeller Institute died of pneumonia in the proportion of fifty-two per cent while subjected to the standard diet. **1946** *All Pets Mag.* Sept. 64/3, I will try and give you a picture of my mousery. I use twelve..breeding units [etc.]. **1949** *Amer. Small Stock Farmer* Sept. 10 Weltytown Mousery. Breeders of white mice for laboratory and research.

mousetrap, *sb.* Add: **1. b.** (Later examples.)

1945 R. Hargreaves *Enemy at Gate* 84 Wounded at the 'mouse-trap' of Dettingen, he was present at Fontenoy. **1966** M. R. D. Foot *SOE in France* viii. 203 All the agents taken in the Villa des Bois mousetrap at Marseilles..were in the noisome Béleyme prison at Périgueux.

d. In various *transf.* and *fig.* uses.

1903 *Dialect Notes* II. 342 *Mouse-trap*, an implement 'for cutting and fishing out rope when matted in the well. It will also take out small pieces of iron or steel, or any small object'. **1929** *Papers Mich. Acad. Sci., Arts & Lett.* X. 309 *Mouse-trap*, a plant at Willoughby, near Cleveland, built for the manufacture of Lewisite. It was so called by the workmen because every one who entered it did so under an agreement not to leave until the end of the war. **1941** *Reader's Digest* Feb. 54 The boys of Britain's R.A.F. have developed a language all their own... 'roller skates' are tanks, and 'mousetraps' submarines. **1953** Rowland & Boyd *U.S. Navy Bureau of Ordnance in World War II* 137 The NDRC project thus became an attempt to combine the respective virtues of the Hedgehog and rockets. By the spring of 1942 the solution was at hand in the Mousetrap, an antisubmarine projector that launched a salvo of sixteen 7″ .2 rockets ahead of the attacking ship. **1957** *Amer. Speech* XXXII. 194 *Mouse trap*, any device of an unorthodox nature attached to a handgun for the purpose of making it more accurate or, less frequently, of making it function more smoothly.

2. Delete † and add: Now used *joc.* to denote inferior or unpalatable cheese. (Later examples.) Also *mousetrap cheese.*

1936 R. Lehmann *Weather in Streets* iii. iii. 299 A portion of mousetrap cheese, extra charge threepence. **1947** F. Smythe *Again Switzerland* iii. 53 The tasty local cheese —what a change from the eternal 'mousetrap'! **1958** *Times Rev. Industry* Sept. 104/3 Statistics are silent as to whether the cheese is 'mousetrap'..a processed type or.. has a character of its own. **1960** *News Chron.* 18 Feb. 3/6, I don't even know what kind of cheese they will be serving. But..mousetrap would be the most suitable. **1972** *Times* 2 Sept. 15/7 Salty butter, red 'mousetrap' cheese. **1975** *Observer* (Colour Suppl.) 27 Apr. 10/1 Although sometimes dismissed as 'mousetrap', Cheddar is much the most popular cheese in Britain.

3. *mousetrap gun, mechanism*; **mousetrap cheese** (see sense *2).

1964 H. L. Peterson *Encycl. Firearms* 325/1 Some collectors called Cochran rifles 'mousetrap guns'. **1969** *Guardian* 25 July 4/4 Watson gave him a smoke grenade which had a 'mousetrap' mechanism.

mousetrap (mau·sˌtræp), *v.* [f. the sb.] *trans.* To entrap, deceive, fool (a person, etc.).

1890 *Cent. Dict.*, *Mouse-trap*, to catch, as a mouse, in a trap; entrap. **1960** Wentworth & Flexner *Dict. Amer. Slang* 346/1 *Mousetrap, v.t.* 1. In sports, to feint an opponent out of position. 2. To fool or mislead by false promises; to entice; to cajole. **1961** *Guardian* 13 Feb. 16/7 The whole system..is close to insane. It is this system which has mouse-trapped Secretary McNamara. **1964** Mrs. L. B. Johnson *White House Diary* 24 July (1970) 183 Bryson Rash used the expression that Lyndon had 'mouse-trapped' Goldwater by leaving him nothing to say about his appointment.

mousquetaire. 2. (Earlier examples.)

1860 M. A. & R. H. M. Wallace-Dunlop *How we spent the Autumn; or, Wanderings in Brittany* 223, I was often struck by the number of fashions we seem to have borrowed from Brittany; for instance, mousquetaire sleeves have their origin there. **1872** *Young Englishwoman* Dec. 651/2 Sleeves with a mousquetaire cuff. **1873** *Ibid.* Oct. 493/2 A mousquetaire hat is of grey felt, turned up with maroon velvet. *Ibid.* 494/1 The redingote tunic of grey poplin, with mousquetaire revers. **1881** C. C. Harrison *Woman's Handiwork* iii. 203 Sachets vary in size..to the ..very long ones, meant to contain sixteen-buttoned or mousquetaire gloves.

‖ **moussaka** (mūsa·kă, mūsākā·). Also **mousaka.** [ult. ad. Egyptian Arab. *musaḳḳ'a* through Turk.: cf. mod. Gr. μουσακᾶς, Rum. *musaca*, Alb., Bulg. *musaka*, etc.] A Balkan and eastern Mediterranean dish of minced beef or lamb, aubergines or potatoes, and onions.

1941 H. D. Harrison *Soul of Yugoslavia* 284 Moussaka is another dish which savours of the east. An earthenware dish is filled with alternative layers of minced mutton and slices of potato or egg plant which have been dipped in batter and lightly fried. Over this is poured a batter of eggs and sour cream and the whole is baked slowly for some hours. **1950** E. David *Bk. Mediterranean Food* 33 (*heading*) Moussaka. Mince 1 lb. of beef or lamb very fine. .. Stir the yolk of an egg into..cream or milk and pour it on top of the Moussaka... The egg and the cream form a kind of custard on the top of the Moussaka. **1957** L. Durrell *Bitter Lemons* 215 We lunched..on a deserted beach to the west of Kyrenia,..eating a *moussaka*. **1960** *Sunday Express* 25 Dec. 8/7 Exotic dishes: stuffed *dolmas, mousaka.* **1962** *Listener* 2 Aug. 191/2 Ask six people for a recipe for the Balkan dish *mousaka* and you will get six different answers, but they are all variations on the theme of minced meat (generally lamb) layered with vegetables. **1966** *Punch* 3 Aug. 189/3 We were suspicious when she started us automatically with ouzo, and brought three bottles of retzina with the moussaka. **1972** J. Aiken *Butterfly Picnic* i. 19 Moussaka..is a sort of super-shepherds-pie with a cheese omelette on top.

mousse. Substitute for def.: A frothy dish made with a savoury or sweet purée or other base, stiffened with cream, gelatine, or egg whites, and freq. served chilled. (Further examples.)

1906 *Mrs. Beeton's Bk. Househ. Managem.* xxxiii. 989 Parfaits, mousses, and soufflés differ from ordinary ices, inasmuch as the cream preparation is at once moulded and placed on ice. **1908** *Daily Chron.* 22 July 7/4 A mousse is nothing more than the addition of whipped

cream instead of plain cream when making ices. **1948** *Good Housek. Cookery Bk.* 490 (*heading*) A mousse or soufflé. A very light frozen mixture, usually containing stiffly beaten egg whites. **1960** E. DAVID *French Provincial Cooking* 445 Nearly everyone knows and appreciates the old and reliable formula for a chocolate mousse—4 yolks beaten into 4 oz. of melted bitter chocolate, and the 4 whipped whites folded in. **1965** L. DEIGHTON *Action Cook Bk.* 119 In France a mousse is part of an ice cream. **1970** SIMON & HOWE *Dict. Gastron.* 269/2 As entrées, main dishes for lunch, or a fine addition to a buffet, savoury mousses of puréed meat or fish, poultry, game or vegetables can be served hot or cold. **1972** K. STEWART *Times Cookery Bk.* ii. 22 (*heading*) Cucumber and cream cheese mousse. *Ibid.*, Allow several hours for mousse to chill. **1975** *Times* 16 Apr. 12 The fruit I can use..for hot crumble or cobbler or cold in a mousse.

‖ **mousseux** (mūsö), *a.* [Fr.] = SPARKLING *ppl. a.*[1] 3 c (often placed after the sb.). Also *fig.* Also as *sb.*, a sparkling wine.

[**1789** A. YOUNG *Jrnl.* 7 July in *Travels* (1792) I. 132, I solaced myself with a bottle of excellent *vin mousseux* for 40*s.*] **1819** H. BUSK *Dessert* 25 The sillery champagne, champagne mousseux, Clear as their taper vase escape the view. **1861** MRS. BEETON *Bk. Househ. Managem.* 889 There are the sparkling wines (*mousseux*), and the still wines (*non-mousseux*). **1906** W. DE MORGAN *Joseph Vance* xl. 400, I feel like the contents of a bottle, and am very curious to know what will happen when the bottle is uncorked. Perhaps I shall be *mousseux*—who knows? **1951** R. POSTGATE *Plain Man's Guide to Wine* v. 92 Not one of the 'mousseux', 'méthode champenoise' or 'gazifiés' possesses the clean, hard flinty taste of champagne. **1968** L. DEIGHTON *Continental Dossier* 29 At St. Péray they make mousseux wine—and say they have made it as long as they have in Champagne. **1973** P. AUDEMARS *Delicate Dust of Death* vii. 95 This is a local *mousseux*... *Mousseux* is drunk after the grapes are gathered—in October and November.

moustache. Add: **6. moustache-lifter,** a device for lifting one's moustache when drinking, sleeping, etc.

1906 *Trans. Asiatic Soc. Japan* XXXIV. II. 122 (*caption*) Ainu moustache lifters. *a* **1930** D. H. LAWRENCE *Phoenix II* (1968) 261 Before the war, in Germany I used to see advertised in the newspapers a moustache-lifter, which you tied on at night and it would make your moustache stay turned up. **1966** J. S. COX *Illustr. Dict. Hairdressing* 100/2 *Moustache lifter*, an implement shaped like a paper knife and used by the male hairy ainu of Japan when drinking, to lift his moustache away from the liquid.

Mousterian, Moustierian (mūstīə·riăn), *a.* and *sb.* [ad. F. *moustiérien* (G. de Mortillet *a* 1873, in *Classification des diverses périodes de l'âge de la Pierre* 4), f. *Moustier* (see below) + -IAN.] **A.** *adj.* Of or pertaining to the people, culture, and tools, esp. the flint industries, typified by remains found in the Moustier cave in the Dordogne region of France, and properly attributed to the Neanderthal peoples living in Europe and round the Mediterranean; of the Middle Palæolithic period (*c* 70,000–30,000 B.C.) during which these tools were made. Also *absol.*, this culture. **B.** *sb.* A Mousterian man or woman.

1890 T. WILSON in *Rep. U.S. Nat. Museum 1888* 614 The Moustierian implements have been found in the river gravels of Europe. **1896** A. H. KEANE *Ethnol.* 86 Moustierian or First Cave Age. *Ibid.* 90 K. Moustierian bed, with typical pointed flint. **1907** *Ann. Rep. Board of Regents Smithsonian Inst. 1906* 374 Glacial period: Mousterian culture. **1912** *Edin. Rev.* Apr. 366 The first discovery of Mousterian man to excite interest was made in 1856 near Düsseldorf. **1912** R. R. MARETT *Anthropol.* ii. 45 Those were the days of the Mousterians who dined off woolly rhinoceros in Jersey. **1927** PEAKE & FLEURE *Hunters & Artists* iv. 39 Breuil thinks that the Neanderthal men of Mousterian culture lived in western Europe from the time of the Riss on through the Würm glaciation. **1927** H. G. WELLS *Short Stories* 679 These Mousterians are also called Neandertalers. **1928**, etc. [see *ATERIAN *a.*]. **1947** J. & C. HAWKES *Prehist. Brit.* (rev. ed.) i. 14 One of the products of the stimulating interaction between the older traditions was a new flake culture, the Mousterian, which enjoyed its heyday during the final glaciation of the Ice Age. **1949** M. E. BOYLE tr. *Breuil's Beyond Bounds of Hist.* 47 A party of courageous hunters is attacking a group of Mammoth with lances and axes of the type known as Mousterian. **1970** J. D. CLARK *Prehist. Afr.* iv. 116 Some forty-five feet of stratified occupation waste and cave earth, showing a long sequence of developing Mousterian overlying an industry made on long blades and blade-like flakes. **1974** *Sci. Amer.* June 101/1 The artifacts ..have been assigned to two successive cultural units. The earlier of the two is known as the Mousterian. *Ibid.* 101/2 The Mousterian stone tools from various Ukrainian sites. *Ibid.* 104/3 Like the Mousterians, Upper Paleolithic peoples often buried their dead.

Hence **Mouste·rioid, Mou·steroid** *adjs.*, resembling the Mousterian culture or tools.

1946 F. E. ZEUNER *Dating Past* ix. 287 Quite probably, many 'mousterioid' industries mentioned in literature are of the same type. **1950** *Proc. Prehist. Soc.* XVI. 176 Among a handful of mousteroid specimens from the cave of Bacho Kiro in Bulgaria a typical specimen of a miniature plano-convex point may be noted. **1969** C. S. CHARD *Man in Prehistory* xi. 114 Since it seems desirable to have a broad term..to designate the flake industries of the neanderthaloid phase in the stretch of contiguous territory from western Europe to Mongolia and south to the Near East and North Africa, which all share certain common features..while retaining their individuality, the label 'Mousteroid' would probably be acceptable.

‖ **Moustiers** (mūstie). The name of a small French town, *Moustiers*-Sainte-Marie, in the Basses Alpes, used *attrib.* or *absol.* to designate a type of faience made there.

1863 W. CHAFFERS *Marks Pott. & Porc.* 96 *Moustiers*... This beautiful ware much resembles porcelain and the early pieces are generally painted in monochrome, in blue, brown, or green; the later specimens are usually in more than one colour. **1870** C. SCHREIBER *Jrnl.* (1911) I. 99 A very fine Moustier Ware dish. **1872** *Ibid.* 162 The specimens were..not equal to fine Moustiers or Marseilles. **1900** F. LITCHFIELD *Pott. & Porc.* vii. 214 Barber's dish of Moustiers faience. **1962** *House & Garden* Dec. 58/2 We've bought..a French Moustiers blue and white dish. **1970** G. SAVAGE *Dict. Antiques* 281/2 (*caption*) *Moustiers.* Dish painted in high-temperature colours with a pastoral scene within rococo scroll borders. Moustiers faience..*c* 1740.

mousy, *a.* Add: **1.** (Earlier and later examples.)

1853 MRS. GASKELL *Cranford* ix. 164, I was..most particularly anxious to prevent her from disfiguring her small gentle mousey face with a great Saracen's-head turban. **1936** K. A. PORTER *Flowering Judas* 107 He could not bear hearing Miriam called a mousy little nit-wit. **1959** W. GOLDING *Free Fall* iv. 82 Fair heads and mousy ones. **1959** 'O. MILLS' *Stairway to Murder* vi. 61 Her skin was sallow, her hair was 'mousey', and her forehead was the lowest Charles had ever seen. **1975** *Times* 15 Feb. 14/2 Hair which is 'light brown' sounds more becoming than hair which is 'mousy'.

4. *mousy-eyed* adj.; *mousy-quiet* (later example).

1909 M. B. SAUNDERS *Litany Lane* I. ii. 13 Only a fold of dark chestnut hair and a hint of red in the lip gave colour—otherwise a little mousy-eyed *gamin* of a thing. **1958** *Observer* 3 Aug. 10/6 Young married business man, cleared by mousey quiet private detective.

moutan (mū·tăn). [Chinese.] The tree peony, *Pæonia suffruticosa*, of the family Ranunculaceæ, a large shrub bearing pale pink flowers, native to China and Tibet, the parent of many garden varieties producing single or double flowers of many colours.

1808 *Curtis's Bot. Mag.* XXIX. 1154 The Moutan, though cultivated in China about fourteen hundred years, is considered in that ancient empire..as rather of modern introduction. **1880** *Encycl. Brit.* XII. 258/1 The Moutans or Tree Pæonies are remarkable for their sub-shrubby habit, forming vigorous plants sometimes attaining a height of 6 to 8 feet. **1963** M. HAWORTH-BOOTH *Moutan* i. 11 In Chinese art each month is represented by a flower, and Moutan is specifically the flower for March.

mouth, *sb.* Add: **3. m.** Also, *to put on* (or *up*) *a poor mouth.*

1892 'MARK TWAIN' *Amer. Claimant* iii. 37 Any selfish tramp..can come and put up a poor mouth. **1949** F. URQUHART *Ferret was Abraham's Daughter* I. vii. 26 'Charity!' Bert shouted. 'Aye puttin' on a poor mouth.'

q. *plum-in-the-mouth* adj. phr.: see *PLUM *sb.*

4. b. *to shoot off one's mouth*: see SHOOT *v.* 23 g in Dict. and Suppl.

20. a. *mouth-aperture, -articulation, -cavity, -gesture, -gymnastics, -heat, -passage, -rim, -sound*; *mouth-honour* (later example); **b.** *mouth-opening* adj.; **d.** *mouth-shrivelled* adj.; **e.** *mouth-blown, -formed* adjs.

1953 K. JACKSON *Lang. & Hist. Early Brit.* 573 The degree of mouth-aperture. **1934** J. J. HOGAN *Outl. Eng. Philol.* 6 The nasal consonants *n* and *m* are stops in their mouth-articulation, opens in their nasality. **1930** R. PAGET *Human Speech* 231 A separate mouth-blown vowel or consonant resonator. **1924** R. M. OGDEN tr. *Koffka's Growth of Mind* iii. 132 The most primitive phenomena are figural; as examples..the too cold or too warm milk in contrast with the temperature level of the mouth-cavity. **1964** C. BARBER *Ling. Change Present-Day Eng.* iii. 38 A vowel is a voiced sound..in which there is a free flow of air out of the mouth, without any audible friction or any obstruction of the mouth-cavity. **1930** R. PAGET *Human Speech* 111 A mouth-formed whistle. **1930** —— *Babel* 60 Making the same mouth-gesture. **1921** H. E. PALMER *Princ. Lang.-Stud.* 89 We must go through a course of mouth-gymnastics. **1942** W. FAULKNER *Go Down, Moses* 103 Not even warmed from mouth-heat. **1907** G. B. SHAW *Major Barbara* Pref. 157 The mouth-honor paid to poverty and obedience by rich and insubordinate do-nothings. **1960** *Guardian* 3 May 7/7 A truly mouth-opening recording of Handel's 'Messiah'. **1964** C. BARBER *Ling. Change Present-Day Eng.* iii. 47 This [l] is a *lateral* consonant: to produce it, you press the tip of the tongue against the teeth-ridge, thus blocking the centre of the mouth-passage. **1933** *Burlington Mag.* June 265/1 It was customary to bind the mouth-rims of bowls and dishes with metal. **1925** BLUNDEN *Eng. Poems* 89 That old man, face like parchment tanned, Wrinkled, mouth-shrivelled. **1929** W. FAULKNER *Sartoris* II. i. 74 All the other mouth-sounds that stood for repose.

21. mouth-board, a wooden instrument to which the mouth is applied, in order to secure a constant position of the head for observation or experiments; **mouth-breather,** a person who breathes through the mouth; **mouth-breeder,** a fish of the families Cichlidæ or Ariidæ which protects its eggs, and sometimes its newly-hatched offspring, by carrying them in its mouth; so **mouth-breeding** *ppl. a.*; **mouth-harp** = MOUTH-ORGAN 1; **mouth music,** (*a*) = **mouth-harp*; (*b*) singing without distinct utterance of words; **mouthparts** *Ent.*, the organs surrounding the mouth of an insect or other arthropod, specially adapted to the particular method of feeding of the animal concerned; **mouth root** (earlier and later examples); **mouth rot,** an oral canker sometimes affecting snakes in captivity; **mouth-to-mouth** *a.*, involving the contact of one individual's mouth with another's; *spec.* applied to a method of artificial respiration in which a person places his mouth tightly over the patient's and blows into him every few seconds so as to inflate his lungs; also *absol.*; (for *fig.* sense see 3 j); similarly **mouth-to-nose** *a.*; **mouth wash,** (*a*) (later examples); also *transf.*; (*b*) nonsense, twaddle; **mouth-watering** *a.* (later examples); **mouth-way,** entrance.

1901 E. B. TITCHENER *Exper. Psychol.* I. II. 245 Materials.—Head-rest, with mouth-board and sighting mark. **1910** *Practitioner* Jan. 69 The child was a mouth-breather and showed signs of adenoids. **1927** *Sunday at Home* June 239/1 The mouth-breeder protects her eggs by carrying them about in her mouth. **1962** K. F. LAGLER et al. *Ichthyol.* x. 298 (*caption*) Mouthbreeding catfish. *Ibid.* 301 Some African fishes, *Tilapia*, are called 'mouth-breeders' because the young when they are hatched escape at time of danger into the oral cavity of the female. **1903** ADE *In Babel* 40 I'd walked from Loueyville over to Terry Hut with a nigger that played the mouth-harp. **1968** *Publ. Amer. Dial. Soc.* XLIX. 15 The lack of familiarity with the musical instrument probably accounts for the decline of *juice harp* and *jew's harp* and the student's use of *mouth harp.* **1972** *Village Voice* (N.Y.) 1 June 76/5 She takes out a mouth harp, fills her cheeks with wind, and blows 'the ballad of the shadows'. **1887** *Lantern* (New Orleans) 3 Sept. 3/2 The music was furnished by a kid with a mouth music. **1936** C. DAY LEWIS *Hope for Poetry* (Postscript) 93 A new language of purely emotive sounds (e.g. the 'mouth-music' of the Hebridean islanders). **1938** L. MACNEICE *I crossed Minch* I. iv. 45 An example of the old 'mouth-music'—Port a Beul—to which the islanders used to dance before they had musical instruments. **1973** BOYD & PARKES *Dark Number* ix. 96 He gave way to a brief rendering of the mouth music of his youth. **1869** A. S. PACKARD *Guide to Study of Insects* 34 We have already treated of the external appendages (mouth-parts) which prepare the food for digestion. **1905** V. L. KELLOGG *Amer. Insects* i. 6 Attached to the thorax are three pairs of legs, which are jointed appendages, homologous in origin and fundamental structure with the mouth-parts and antennæ. **1932** *Times Lit. Suppl.* 17 Mar. 206/2 There are, too, such enigmas as *trophia*, for which we guess mouthparts. **1972** L. E. CHADWICK tr. *Linsenmaier's Insects of World* 24/1 The variations of the insect mouth and mouthparts are nearly limitless. Here we find an assemblage of instruments such as only a surgeon, an artisan, or a burglar might wish for—from a harmless sucking proboscis, through implements for boring, sawing, pinching, and cutting, to such devilish contraptions as poison syringes or stilettos that snap out to pierce the prey. **1974** *Sci. Amer.* Apr. 103/1 When feeding, adult beetles busily squeeze pellets of moist dung between their mouthparts and suck in the expressed juice. **1784** CUTLER in *Mem. Amer. Acad. Arts & Sci.* (1785) I. 457 Goldenthread. Mouth Root... The roots are astringent, and of a bitterish taste. Chewed in the mouth they cure apthas and cankerous sores. **1931** W. N. CLUTE *Common Names of Plants* 123 The canker-root (*Coptis trifolia*) or mouth-root, as it is called,..continues to hold its place among medicines for the cure of sore mouth. **1961** C. H. POPE *Giant Snakes* (1962) 195 Another threat to captive snakes..is mouth rot, which is also called canker mouth and osteomyelitis. **1965** R. & D. MORRIS *Men & Snakes* vii. 145 Snakes are very liable to mouth-rot when their jaws are damaged. **1969** A. BELLAIRS *Life of Reptiles* II. xii. 516 Among the more important bacterial diseases are the oral canker or 'mouth rot' seen in captive snakes and apparently caused by species of *Pseudomonas* and *Pasteurella.* **1909** *Lancet* 13 Mar. 747/2 By 1782 the Royal Humane Society recommended inflation by bellows in preference to the mouth-to-mouth method. **1932** E. STEP *Bees, Wasps, Ants* 32 The first eggs hatch, and the legless little [bee] larvae have to be fed, which is a direct mouth-to-mouth exchange between mother and larva. **1941** *Jrnl. Amer. Med. Assoc.* 6 Dec. 1942/2 Mouth to mouth insufflation has many adherents. It permits an exchange of gases under proper conditions as to temperature, content of moisture and carbon dioxide. **1961** *Sunday Times* 17 Sept. 4/5 Mouth-to-mouth resuscitation, by which a life-saver inflates a victim's lungs with his own breath, was approved officially by the British Red Cross Society last week. **1968** K. WEATHERLEY *Roo Shooter* 113 The bush nurse gave him mouth to mouth and got his heart going again. **1970** S. J. PERELMAN *Baby, it's Cold Inside* 203 Luckily, before Wemyss had to apply mouth-to-mouth breathing, the three of us recovered. **1954** *New Eng. Jrnl. Med.* 6 May 754 Without the mask a mouth-to-nose technic with a handkerchief 'filter' is effective. **1961** *Times* 6 Dec. 9/4 A life-size inflatable doll for demonstrating mouth-to-mouth and mouth-to-nose artificial respiration. **1962** S. MILES *Underwater Med.* xiv. 224 Those who advocate 'mouth to mouth' claim that better inflation is possible, it is more natural and nasal obstruction may be an obstacle if 'mouth to nose' is used. **1920** ADE *Hand-Made Fables* 5 The Cleaners left nothing behind them in Glass Receptacles except Bluing and Mouth-Wash. **1951** M. MCLUHAN *Mech. Bride* (1967) 60/2 Mouth washes, gargles..are backed by long-standing national advertising campaigns. **1957** C. S. LEWIS *Let.* 2 Sept. (1966) 279 Give your imagination a good mouth-wash by a reading..of the *Odyssey.* **1971** *Mod. Law Rev.* XXXIV. 630 Any suggestion that the principle was also

applied can be dismissed as so much mouth-wash. **1960** *Guardian* 7 Oct. 12/5 A mouth-watering bowl of fruit. **1973** *Country Life* 29 Nov. 1796/2 Mouthwatering grills—fish, meat, vegetables. **1920** A. E. W. Mason *Summons* xii. 121 Crossed the road and disappeared into the mouth-way of an alley.

mouth, *v.* Add: **10.** *trans.* To estimate the age of (a sheep) by examining the teeth. *Austral.* and *N.Z.*

1933 *Bulletin* (Sydney) 6 Sept. 24/1 Graziers buy old ewes without troubling to 'mouth' them. *a* **1948** L. G. D. Acland *Early Canterbury Runs* (1951) 404 A competent shepherd should be able to do anything necessary with sheep—draft, shear, mouth, [etc.]. **1972** P. Newton *Sheep Thief* ix. 74, I found the opportunity to mouth several of those double fork sheep—and one was only a four tooth.

mouthful. Add: **b.** Phr. *to say a mouthful*, to make a striking or important statement; to say something noteworthy. *colloq.* (orig. *U.S.*)

[**1790** *Sessions Papers* Sept. 781/1, I never said a *mouth full of ill against her* in my life.] **1922** C. Sandburg *Slabs of Sunburnt West* 7 You said a mouthful. **1924** A. J. Small *Frozen Gold* i. 14 A fight, he says—and he don't know what a mouthful he's said. **1929** A. Conan Doyle *Maracot Deep* vi. 165 He said a mouthful when he asked her to marry him. **1947** L. Hastings *Dragons are Extra* vii. 143 And that says a mouthful. **1973** Wodehouse *Bachelors Anonymous* xii. 153 'Nice nurse?' 'Ah, there you have said a mouthful, Pickering. I have a Grade A nurse.'

mouthing, *vbl. sb.* (Later examples.)

a **1948** L. Acland *Early Canterbury Runs* (1951) 391 s.v. *Race.* Narrow passage in a sheepyard, for drafting, mouthing, branding, etc. **1950** *N.Z. Jrnl. Agric.* Feb. 122 (*caption*) The photograph shows part of the preparation of a breeding flock for the season, which entails mouthing, drafting for wool, age, and other factors.

mouthpiece. Add: **1. b.** The part of a telephone into which one speaks.

1888 *Encycl. Brit.* XXIII. 131/1 The [Reis telephone] receiver consists of an electromagnet made up of a magnetized coil.., with a stout knitting needle for a core. When in use these two instruments are joined in circuit with a battery.., so that under ordinary circumstances a continuous current is flowing through the line. Suppose a sound is then produced in front of the mouthpiece.., the successive variations in the pressure of the air are communicated to the inside of the box, and cause the membrane to vibrate in unison with the sound. **1907** *Sears, Roebuck Catal.* 204/2 Telephone mouthpieces. Male or female thread. **1926** T. E. Lawrence *Seven Pillars* (1935) I. viii. 71 Abdulla went to the telephone..and transferred the mouthpiece to Storrs. **1941** [see *intercom]. **1955** W. Gaddis *Recognitions* II. v. 509 He turned quickly into the other telephone booth, dialed and stood bent rigid before the mouthpiece.

3. b. (Further example.)

1897 J. L. Allen *Choir Invisible* xiii. 197 Her face concealed by a black velvet riding-mask kept in place by a silver mouth-piece held between her teeth.

4. b. (Earlier and later examples.)

1857 'Ducange Anglicus' *Vulgar Tongue* 13 *Mouthpiece*,..counsel. **1914** [see *fixer 1]. **1926** E. Wallace *More Educated Evans* iv. 91 Mouthpiece!.. Why, all these so-and-so lawyers hang together. **1931** [see *bottle *sb.*[2] 1 g (*a*)]. **1960** L. Cooper *Accomplices* III. iii. 164 I'm an Australian citizen and I know my rights and I want to see my mouthpiece before I say any more. **1974** P. B. Yuill *Hazell plays Solomon* xii. 144 The Abreys would get legal aid. The state would fix them up with a good mouthpiece.

mouthy, *a.* Add: **a.** (Later examples.)

1957 M. Spark *Comforters* v. 102 Before they said good night, Eleanor, slurred and mouthy, declared, 'Now, Laurence, take care of Caroline.' **1963** W. H. Boore *Valley & Shadow* ix. 43 Too free you have been..with your talk... Too mouthy all of you. **1968** *Sun Mag.* (Baltimore) 13 Oct. 19/2, I was kind of a big mouth. I wasn't a bully, just mouthy. **1972** *News & Observer* (Raleigh, N. Carolina) 30 Dec. 4/2 Whatever else they are, kids aren't biggity, mouthy [any more].

c. Of a hound: (see quots.).

1946 M. C. Self *Horseman's Encycl.* 457 A hound that is noisy and a babbler is said to be 'mouthy'. **1968** J. Gordon *Beagle Guide* 173 A hound which babbles or is unnecessarily noisy is said to be mouthy.

mouton. Add: **4.** (See quot. 1950.)

1950 Webster Add., *Mouton*, the skin of sheep, usually of Merino Sheep, processed, sheared, and dyed to resemble beaver or a certain type of seal. **1963** *Retail Trading-Standards Assoc. Bull.* Aug./Sept. 3/1 The following names [for furs] may be used notwithstanding the general rule:—*Animal*: Sheep (skin). *Accepted Trade Name*: Lamb or Mouton.

‖ **mouton enragé** (mūtoṅ aṅraʒe). [Fr., lit. angry sheep.] A normally calm person who has become suddenly enraged or violent.

1932 *Times Lit. Suppl.* 27 Oct. 784/4 Her *mouton enragé* of a discarded adorer. **1955** J. Thomas *No Banners* xii. 101 Many of them were peace-loving idealists who, like *moutons enragés*, had been literally goaded into ridding the earth of the Nazi pestilence. **1965** *Economist* 23 Jan. 307/1 The most unenviable reputation as the *moutons enragés* of this Parliament.

Mouton Rothschild (mū·toṅ rǫ·þs,tʃəild). A type of Médoc produced in the Château Mouton-Rothschild, formerly the Château Mouton d'Armailhacq until purchased by the Rothschild family in 1853. Also *ellipt.* as *Mouton.*

[**1860** C. Redding *French Wines & Vineyards* ix. 82 Messrs. Scott,..and d'Armailhac, at Mouton,..are the largest producers... The famous Bran-Mouton is from this district.] **1877** Trollope *Amer. Senator* II. xv. 156, I think you will find that claret what you like... It's a '57 Mouton. **1888** *Encycl. Brit.* XXIV. 605/1 Second Growths. Château Mouton-Rothschild, Pauillac. **1935** M. Morphy *Recipes of all Nations* 102 (*heading*) Growths: Among the best are Château Mouton-Rothschild. **1958** A. L. Simon *Dict. Wines* 115/2 *Mouton-Rothschild, Château*, the first of the second *Crus Classés* of the Médoc (Pauillac). **1974** L. Deighton *Spy Story* xi. 111 What's he going to do..? Put Mouton Rothschild labels on the Algerian? **1974** *Listener* 18 Apr. 487/1 In July 1973 the French Government saw the light and elevated Chateau Mouton Rothschild to one of the top five wines of the Médoc.

‖ **mouvementé** (mūvmaṅte), *a.* [Fr.] Animated, agitated, bustling, full of variety; *spec.* of music: lively.

1918 L. Strachey *Eminent Victorians* 238 The next three years were the most *mouvementés* of his life. **1929** *Theatre Arts Monthly* Mar. 231/2 The chief figure of her time led a life exceedingly *mouvementé*. **1938** *Oxf. Compan. Mus.* 597/1 *Mouvementé*, 'bustling', animated. **1950** A. L. Rowse *England of Elizabeth* vi. 222 We may say that Tudor society was..more flexible and *mouvementé* than is altogether realised. **1961** B. Fergusson *Watery Maze* viii. 201 He had so far had a highly *mouvementé* war, beginning in a Q-ship in Norwegian waters before being appointed navigating officer to the force assembled early in 1941 for the assault on Rhodes. **1963** G. Battiscombe *John Keble* i. 4 Even today..the district round Oxford can hardly be described as *mouvementé.* **1965** *Guardian* 8 Dec. 8/5 Her life has been unusually mouvementé—and erratic.

mouzhik, var. Moujik, muzhik (in Dict. and Suppl.).

movable, moveable, *a.* and *sb.* Add: **A.** *adj.* **7. b.** *Philol.* Designating a consonant or other element affixed to a word, usu. under determined phonetic conditions.

1933 C. D. Buck *Compar. Gram. Greek & Latin* 160 The *ν* movable in forms like λέγουσι(ν), εἶπε(ν), etc., is an added element which, except for a few examples of dat. pl. -σιν in other dialects, is peculiar to Attic-Ionic. **1951** Sturtevant & Hahn *Compar. Gram. Hittite Lang.* (ed. 2) 66, *s* Movable. **1958** Priebsch & Collinson *German Lang.* (rev. ed.) 70 'Movable' *s* is prefixed in Indo-European to many roots. **1973** A. H. Sommerstein *Sound Pattern Anc. Greek* ii. 40 *Moveable Nu.* This is the name given in traditional studies of Greek to a dental nasal which is inserted at the end of certain words that would otherwise end in a vowel, if the following word begins with a vowel or [h] (that is, with a non-consonantal segment), or if a major pause follows.

8. *movable type*: pieces of metal type, individually cast, usu. with reference to early printing.

[**1732** S. Palmer *Gen. Hist. Printing* 5 With the great space so many Pages of Wood must take up, we shall perceive the necessity of inventing moveable Metal Types.] **1770** P. Luckombe *Conc. Hist. Printing* 2 Those who have asserted that Faust was the first inventor of printing, have given for a reason, that they have never seen any book with Guttemberg's name to it; without considering, that their first essays in printing, both by blocks and moveable types,..were anonymous. **1816** W. Y. Ottley *Inquiry Orig. & Early Hist. Engraving* I. 6 The prodigious number of these characters..renders it impracticable for them [*sc.* the Chinese] to print their books with moveable types. **1859** *Abridgements of Specifications relating to Printing* (Patent Office) 15 Where, when, and by whom printing with moveable types was first practised, it seems impossible to determine with any certainty. **1933** T. S. Barber in W. Atkins *Art & Pract. Printing* IV. xx. 239 One of the difficulties encountered in actual printing with movable types was the fact that at times they moved and became displaced when the printer had no desire they should. **1955** S. H. Steinberg *500 Yrs. Printing* i. 22 The available evidence about the invention of printing with movable types cast from matrices is unfortunately less conclusive than might be wished. **1965** J. Moran *Composition of Reading Matter* i. 11 The basis of making pieces of movable type was the punch, matrix and mould. **1974** *Bertram Rota Ltd. Catal.* No. 192. 2 Now the steady advance of film-setting may be heralding the beginning of the end of printing from moveable type.

movant (mū·vănt). *U.S. Law.* [f. Move *v.* + -ant[1]: cf. Movent *a.* b.] One who applies to or petitions a court of law or a judge with the intention of obtaining a ruling in his favour. Also *attrib.* or as *adj.*

1927 *Corpus Juris* XLII. 517/1 A 'renewal' of the motion, so-called, is the remedy usually available to the dissatisfied movant whose motion has been denied. **1949** *Corpus Juris Secundum* LX. 38/1 Relief to Movant... In the absence of a prayer for general relief, the moving party usually is confined to the relief asked for in his motion. **1961** *Words & Phrases State & Federal Courts* XXVII. A. 353/1 Intention was that such statute should be remedial in operation, to permit court to correct errors ..into which it has been led..by the party opposing movant. **1972** *N.Y. Law Jrnl.* 22 Aug. 2/3 Movant is granted and the requested subpoena shall issue. Movant shall furnish a copy of the records produced to the other parties. **1973** *Ibid.* 19 July 11/1 The movant fails to establish either defective service of the notice of petition and petition, upon which the default was granted, or a meritorious defense thereto, since nothing is asserted beyond an expression of dissatisfaction with the award. *Ibid.* 1 Aug. 14/2 It is ordered that this motion by defendant..is denied without prejudice to the right of movant defendant to oppose the application of a general preference made by plaintiffs.

move, *sb.* **6.** For *U.S.* read 'orig. *U.S.*' Now usu. *to get a move on.* (Examples.)

1888 *Troy* (Alabama) *Enquirer* 28 July, Get a move on you. **1893** *Columbus* (Ohio) *Dispatch* 7 July, Now is the time for the mover of dead animals 'to get a move on himself'. **1899** A. H. Quinn *Pennsylvania Stories* 138 Come, get a move on. **1906** E. Dyson *Fact'ry 'Ands* xiv. 183 Get er move on, 'r you'll get ther shoot. **1911** C. E. Mulford *Bar-20 Days* x. 107 Come on! Come on!..Get a move on! Will you hurry up! *Ibid.* xx. 198 But why in Jericho don't you fellers get a move on you? **1914** W. G. Lawrence *Let.* 13 Aug. in T. E. Lawrence *Home Lett.* (1954) 569 In ten days time we should get a move on, but we won't go far. **1920** [see *gas *sb.*[2]]. **1937** D. L. Sayers *Busman's Honeymoon* vii. 149, I only hope they're getting a move on out there. **1973** 'D. Mariner' *Beaufort Dossier* vii. 138 What about getting a move on, then! Get out on the flaming roof an' grab them!

8. *Comb.* **move-man** (see quots.).

1923 J. M. Scott-Maxwell *Costing & Price-fixing* 94 Move-men are the men who move the raw material and manufactured parts from the store to the shop, and move all jobs from one machine to another or one department to another. **1955** *Amer. Speech* XXX. 226 *Move man*, the dispatcher in the [aircraft production] shop who moves parts from one operation to the next.

move, *v.* Add: **1. f.** Also *trans.*, to sell; to cause to be sold.

1938 *Sun* (Baltimore) 20 Sept. 10/1 A drastic tax on chain stores has been defeated in a referendum in California, where the function of the chains in 'moving' citrus-fruit surpluses is now more fully appreciated. **1962** *Guardian* 5 Nov. 3/6 Our displays are moving about 25,000 cans a week. **1971** *Ibid.* 24 Dec. 2/5 The boys..are causing the sales lady a good deal of worry... She simply cannot move Indians this season, even with a wigwam. **1975** *Publishers Weekly* 6 Jan. 54/1 Booksellers should easily be able to move this slender 'autobiography' of Lincoln.

g. *Cricket.* To cause (the ball) to swerve.

1956 N. Cardus *Close of Play* 37 We are supposed to be enlightened by news that Lindwall is 'moving' the ball. **1962** *Times* 24 May 4/2 Platt, however, kept plugging away around the good length mark, moving the ball a little either way and generally looking a thoroughly useful practitioner.

16. g. (Further examples.) So, *to move house.* Also, *to move in on*: to take up residence with (someone), esp. so as to inconvenience or annoy; to attach oneself to, put pressure on, or take control of (a person, project, etc.).

1898 G. B. Shaw *You never can Tell* I. 216, I spent my last sovereign on moving in; and I havnt paid a shilling of rent yet. **1924** R. Macaulay *Orphan Island* ii. 22 Your aunt and Martha and myself have recently moved house. **1941** N. Coward *Australia Visited* vii. 47 God help us when the scenery and properties move in on us, when we have to adapt ourselves to new settings and different furniture. **1945** E. Bowen *Demon Lover* 91 Mona moved out..and moved in on Isobel. **1966** *Listener* 6 Jan. 14/2 The society was formed about four years ago... We still have not moved in. **1967** J. Redgate *Killing Season* (1968) II. xviii. 147 We'll give him a few months to get entrenched in England... Then we'll move in on him. **1968** M. Woodhouse *Rock Baby* xviii. 180 That was the idea, if somebody hadn't moved in on the operation. **1973** 'D. Halliday' *Dolly & Starry Bird* xiv. 205 Sophia deciding to move in on somebody was a sight worth selling tickets for. **1974** R. Rendell *Face of Trespass* 10 If you ever feel like moving house to live among your constituents I'll be happy to oblige.

i. *move on*: also (with hyphen) as *attrib. phr.*

1908 E. J. Banfield *Confessions of Beachcomber* II. i. 246 He was almost knocked down by a move-on sort of shove. **1971** *Ceylon Daily News* 17 Sept. 1/5 The vagrancy laws and the move-on by-law of the Municipality.

k. To go quickly. *colloq.*

1954 *Amer. Speech* XXIX. 100 It can really move. **1959** M. Gilbert *Blood & Judgement* xvi. 164 'What price the law's delays.' 'They can move when they have to.' **1967** 'G. North' *Sgt. Cluff & Day of Reckoning* ii. 23 You'll have to run to catch him:..when he's in that frame of mind, he can move. **1969** J. Fredman *Fourth Agency* vii. 53 The car was rocketing along... We were moving all right. **1973** W. McCarthy *Detail* ii. 77 Immediately the large man..was out of the apartment and through the fire door. It took him little more than two seconds. God, he can move, Ben thought.

l. To dance or play music energetically or with a strong rhythm; to be exciting or dynamic. *colloq.*

1955 *Down Beat* 6 Apr. 15 The only time it does start to move is in the second chorus, with Charlie Shavers. **1958** G. V. Kennard in R. J. Gleason *Jam Session* 176 'It's got to move,' jazzmen say. If it doesn't 'swing', it's not jazz. **1959** [see *drive *v.* 25 c]. **1968** [see *groove *v.* 5]. **1969** N. Cohn *AWopBopaLooBop* (1970) ix. 85 Go to a club one week, go back the next and everyone is moving differently.

19. c. *to move with the times*, to be up to date in one's way of living.

1936 Robinson & Browne *How to live in a Flat* 90 We have no hesitation in offering the following hints to those who—wishing to move with the times..—desire to construct a service-flat for their own use. **1960** L. P. Hartley *Facial Justice* xvii. 144 You must try to move with the times. **1973** *Times* 28 Nov. 22/6 If you change anything, you are accused of eroding history. If you change nothing, you are accused of failing to move with the times.

movement, *sb.* Add: **1. e.** The conveying of cattle from one district to another, often prohibited or restricted during an epidemic of cattle disease.

1869 *Act* 32 & 33 *Vict.* c. 70 § 48 Every local authority and the police of every county..shall..do or cause to be done all things..necessary..for securing, as far as may be, the effectual isolation of infected places in respect of the movement of animals and things. **1878** *Act* 41 & 42 *Vict.* c. 74 § 32 Prohibiting or regulating the movement of animals and persons into, in, or out of an infected place or area. **1954** W. R. Wooldridge *Farm Animals* iv. 74 The Contagious Diseases (Animals) Act..gave adequate powers for the control of all movement of cattle. *Ibid.* vi. 173 Much has been written for and against the policy of suppressing the disease [*sc.* foot-and-mouth] by..rigid control of movement within a wide area.

f. The departure or arrival of an aircraft.

1961 P. W. Brooks *Mod. Airliner* vi. 144, 130 aircraft movements (arrivals and departures) on a peak Summer day. **1969** *Sunday Times* (Colour Suppl.) 17 Aug. 19/1 Many of the major airports are suffering from aerial traffic jams, and the 747 will mean only one movement where there might have been two or more. **1971** *Physics Bull.* Nov. 660/2 Night flying also assumes a significant percentage of the total number of movements.

5. c. *Dancing.* (See quot. 1967.)

1949 Shurr & Yocom *Mod. Dance* v. 135 When the count is finally speeded-up, do *not* omit any of the suspended movements. **1949** *Ballet Ann.* III. 40 Movement after movement was ruined by the broken line. **1967** Chujoy & Manchester *Dance Encycl.* (rev. ed.) 647/2 *Movement*, the fundamental language of dance; a purposeful change of weight or position, as contrasted with motion, which in dance is considered as purely kinetic, i.e. physical, while movement is metakinetic.

6. b. *in the movement* (earlier and later examples).

1894 *World* 5 Sept. 11/2 We have in *The New Woman* a live play, a play which is distinctly in the movement. **1926** C. Sidgwick *Sack & Sugar* xxvi. 299 She..had quite antiquated Victorian ideas of what English people had nowadays if they were in the movement. She had not got beyond shiny chintzes and overmantels.

d. (With capital initial.) A group of English poets in the nineteen-fifties, their characteristics, or their influence. Also *attrib.*

[**1954** *Spectator* 27 Aug. 261/1 Poets of the Fifties... For better or for worse, we are now in the presence of the only considerable movement in English poetry since the Thirties.] *Ibid.* 1 Oct. 399/1 (*heading*) In the Movement. *Ibid.* 399/2 In these columns some weeks ago Mr. Anthony Hartley remarked upon some of the characteristics of this new Movement of the Fifties—its metaphysical wit, its glittering intellectuality, its rich Empsonian ambiguities. *Ibid.* 400/2 Genuflections towards Dr. Leavis and Professor Empson, admiration for people whom the Thirties by-passed, Orwell above all..are indeed signs by which you may recognise the Movement... The Movement, as well as being anti-phoney, is anti-wet. **1958** A. Alvarez in *Internat. Literary Ann.* I. 99, I have been using the past tense because the Movement has now ended and its poets have gone off on their separate ways... The Movement, for all its limitations and negatives, was immensely valuable. **1958** *Times Lit. Suppl.* 17 Jan. 30/4 The poetry-fanciers say that there are two better Movement poets than either Mr Wain or Mr Amis. *Ibid.* 7 Mar. 127/1 The outstanding performer, or even the 'real poet' of the original Movement is Mr. Philip Larkin. **1959** *Ibid.* 27 Feb. 114/2 Around 1953, Mr. Larkin, Mr. Amis, Mr. Wain and the rest of them burst on a startled world—and 'the Movement' restored to English poetry self-control, precision, and clarity. **1961** *Listener* 24 Aug. 268/1 The decade just ended, a decade dominated by a group of university poets usually referred to as the Movement. **1972** *Times Lit. Suppl.* 14 Apr. 411/3 One need only look at the standard Movement and post-Movement poetry of that period. **1972** D. Timms *Philip Larkin* i. 15, I am reminded here of John Wain's description of the Movement as an *avant garde* that was a rear guard.

10. *movement area, -complex, control, -habit, -illusion, -impulse, -melody, order, -response, -sensation, -study, time;* **movement permit**, permission to move cattle from a particular district; **movement restriction**, a ban on the movement of cattle from a district, esp. when cattle disease is present.

1958 *Chambers's Techn. Dict.* 995/2 *Movement area*, that part of an aerodrome reserved for the take-off, landing and movement of aircraft. **1924** R. M. Ogden tr. *Koffka's Growth of Mind* v. 251 Movement-complexes of grasping and touching..are learnt even earlier than walking. **1956** W. A. Heflin *U.S. Air Force Dict.* 334/2 Movement control. **1969** *Times* 6 Jan. 7/7 Secondary effects of movement control and closed markets left a trail of expense and inconvenience. **1972** L. Lamb *Picture Frame* ii. 21 He arranged with movement control to go a different way. **1920** T. P. Nunn *Education* xiii. 169 Recognition-habits of increasing complexity corresponding to the increasingly complex movement-habits of writing. **1894** Creighton & Titchener tr. *Wundt's Human & Animal Psychol.* ix. 137 It has sometimes been thought that the act of will suffices of itself to explain these subjective movement-illusions. **1924** R. M. Ogden tr. *Koffka's Growth of Mind* iv. 156 The sensory impressions and the movement-impulse of the animal under investigation. *Ibid.* v. 259 In this unification a 'movement-melody' composes itself. **1956** W. A. Heflin *U.S. Air Force Dict.* 334/2 Movement order. **1957** P. Kemp *Mine were of Trouble* iii. 51 Your Movement Order will be sent to your Squadron in a few days. **1973** *Radio Times* 8 Nov. 19/2 It's really like the movement order for an operation. You move up to your start line. **1969** *Times* 27 Jan. 10/8 Brucellosis accredited cattle only will be shown at the Surrey county show... Cattle entered there will require only a movement permit. **1954** L. B. Ames et al. *Rorschach Responses in Old Age* xii. 141 Human movement responses become more passive with increasing deterioration of subjects. **1969** *Times* 6 Jan. 7/7 Hogs kept at home, and sometimes in one field because of movement restrictions, fared less well. **1898** G. F. Stout *Man. Psychol.* I. II. vi. 192 The distinction between position-sensations and movement-sensations is important. **1951** J. M. Fraser *Psychol.* xv. 187 It is fatally easy to make movement-study sound difficult. **1952** *New Biol.* XIII. 58 The time between the beginning of his movement and the moment at which he starts to return back again is called 'The Movement Time'. **1968** R. N. Singer *Motor Learning & Human Performance* iii. 67 Movement time may include reflex or reaction time, or, as it is usually viewed in research literature, the time a particular act takes to be completed after it has been initiated.

mover[1]. **5.** Delete ?*Obs.* and add to def.: *spec.* a person migrating westwards; a tenant farmer who moves on after exhausting the fertility of a piece of land. (Earlier and additional examples.)

1810 M. Dwight *Journey to Ohio* (1912) 47 We are.. near a tavern which is fill'd with movers & waggoners. **1878** J. H. Beadle *Western Wilds* xx. 327 Reluctantly the 'movers' consented to his remaining for the night. **1913** J. London *Valley of Moon* 434 The 'movers'..lease, clean out and gut a place in several years, and then move on. **1944** W. Blair *Tall Tale America* 100 Instead of selling the seedlings from these nurseries..he'd..give them to the movers—free. **1945** J. L. Marshall *Santa Fe* 230 'Boomers' and 'movers' tried again and again to take up land, filtering down from Kansas and up from Texas along the Santa Fe track.

6. For ?*U.S.* read *N. Amer.*, and add earlier and later examples.

1838, etc. [see *house-mover* s.v. *house *sb.*[1] 23]. **1894** *Boston Directory* 1944 J. W. Cook & Son,.. movers of pianofortes, furniture, etc. *Ibid.* 1947 T. G. Buckley, piano and furniture mover. **1956** W. H. Whyte *Organization Man* (1957) 286 It's a hell of a day—the kids are crying..and the movers won't be finished till late. **1968** *Globe & Mail* (Toronto) 3 Feb. 3/9 'The honorable gentleman will be glad to know that I will be getting out as soon as I can get a mover,' the Prime Minister replied.

movie (mū·vi). orig. *U.S.* Also † **movy.** [Abbrev. of *moving picture: see -ie, -y[6].] **a.** = *moving picture; also, a moving-picture show; a cinema; *pl.* (freq. *the movies*), motion pictures as an industry, an art-form, or a form of entertainment; a cinema or a cinema-show.

1912 *Survey* (N.Y.) 20 Jan. 1628 (*heading*) 'Movies' and the law. **1912** J. Sandilands *Western Canad. Dict.* 30 *Movie*, a moving picture show. **1913** F. A. Talbot *Pract. Cinematogr.* iii. 22 Taking the 'movies' is quite as simple as snap-shot photography with a Kodak. **1913** *N.Y. Even. Post* 10 July 5/7 Guiding the wheel-chair through the entrance gate of the outdoor 'movie'. **1913** *Home Chat* 27 Sept. 578/1 The comparatively small towns [in America] have installed 'movies'—as they call them over there—in their schools. **1914** M. Carrington *Memories* I. 69 A night at the 'movies'. **1916** 'B. M. Bower' *Phantom Herd* xi. 193 Say, do I get it right that you're in the movies. **1918** C. Sandburg *Cornhusker* 51 There is drama in that point... Griffith would make a movie of it to fetch sobs. **1918** G. B. Shaw *Pen Portraits* (1932) 36 Is an evening with Ibsen as popular as an evening with Mary Pickford at the movies? **1919** —— *Heartbreak House* I. 26 You frequent picture palaces... Talk like a man, not like a movy. **1925** F. Scott Fitzgerald *Great Gatsby* (1926) vii. 150 Those big movies around Fiftieth Street are cool. **1929** H. G. Wells *King who was King* i. 15 It was possible for some of us to forget the crude, shallow trade 'movies' we had seen. **1938** E. Bowen *Death of Heart* II. v. 268 Some of the party wished to go to a movie. *Ibid.* vi. 281 He wanted me to cut off with him somewhere last night, after the movies. **1942** *Short Guide Gt. Brit.* (U.S. War Dept.) 13 The British have theaters and movies (which they call 'cinemas') as we do. **1950** T. S. Eliot *Cocktail Party* III. 148 You must have been living a quiet life! Don't you go to the movies? **1971** *Mod. Law Rev.* XXXIV. 705 There is so much happening in the field of human rights that there is a great temptation to postpone publication until we see how the movie is going to end.

b. *attrib.* and *Comb.*, as *movie actor, actress, ad, advertisement, buff, business, camera, cowboy, fan, film, hero, industry, king, -land, magazine, -maker, -making, -man, medium, picture, play, projector, queen, scenario, script, show, star, studio, test, theatre;* **movie-goer**, one who goes to the cinema; one who frequently attends film-shows; hence **movie-going** *vbl. sb.* and *ppl. a.*; **movie house**, a cinema; **movie palace**, a (palatial) cinema.

1913 *Writer's Mag*, Dec. 264/2 If you want a chance to pay tribute to some 'movie' actor get a copy of the *Ladies World*, and 'full particulars'. **1935** Wodehouse *Luck of Bodkins* xv. 178 The kid points and says: 'Look, mamma. Movie actors!' And the mother says: 'Hush, dear—you don't know what *you* may come to some day.' **1924** 'J. Sutherland' *Circle of Stars* xi. 114 Mountrose is going to marry an American movie-actress. **1949** M. Lowry *Let.* 1 July (1967) 180 My..brother-in-law, who entertains himself..by listening to the chests of movie actresses. **1951** M. McLuhan *Mech. Bride.* (1967) 82/1 In one movie ad the woman says: 'I killed a man for this kiss.' **1918** N. Angell *Political Conditions Allied Success* p. vii, As the movie advertisement of the war play says: 'You can't put up a good fight until your blood boils.' **1973** *Guardian* 30 Mar. 12/6 Imagine the feelings of a movie-buff if he were told he'd have to get along without Bunuel, Bergman, Chabrol, [etc.]. **1916** 'B. M. Bower' *Phantom Herd* v. 71 There's no art for art's sake in the movie business. **1925** H. L. Foster *Trop. Tramp with Tourists* 118 The company's cinema operator had his movie camera set up in one corner. **1934** *Punch* 14 Nov. 536/2 He and another journalist..bought..a couple of small movie-cameras and all the film there was in Australia. **1961** T. Henrot *Belgium* 185 You may bring in..a small movie-camera with fifteen meters of film. **1926** A. Huxley *Let.* 13 May (1969) 269 One mounts a mule and goes off with a movie cowboy down into the gulf. **1941** Auden *New Year Let.* III. 68 Some Texas where real cowboys seem Lost in a movie-cowboy's dream. **1913** *Outlook* 5 Apr. 784/1 The 'movie' fan lays himself open to overtired eye nerves. **1952** S. Kauffmann *Philanderer* (1953) iv. 59 There were seven pulps, ten comic magazines, three movie-fan magazines, three confession magazines. **1922** *Atlantic Monthly* June 775 Half the movie films seem almost to have been made for the flapper. **1959** Halas & Manvell *Technique Film Animation* 11 A movie film exposed at normal speed can..be said to analyse every second of live action in terms of a given number of successive phases of movement. **1923** T. Lane *What's Wrong with Movies* 49 The author's name ..means absolutely nothing to the bulk of movie-goers. **1953** *Time* 27 July 76/1 There is..a danger that some impressionable movie-goers, unable to make up their minds which of the stars they prefer, may go quietly hysterical. **1973** *Sat. Rev. Society* (U.S.) Mar. 80/1 *Deep Throat* has grossed nearly a million dollars from moviegoers. **1938** I. Barry tr. *Burdèche & Brasillach's Hist. Motion Pict.* 68 Further *Nick Carter* series..taught the public the habit of regular moviegoing. **1946** A. Warren in W. S. Knickerbocker *20th Cent. English* III. 312 His conclusions..reassure the parents of movie-going children. **1951** 'J. Wyndham' *Day of Triffids* ii. 43 The great movie-going public. **1958** J. Baldwin in W. King *Black Short Story Anthol.* (1972) 284 A lifetime of moviegoing behind her. **1928** *Manch. Guardian Weekly* 5 Oct. 266/4 The movie hero's knack Of dangling from a trembling wire Across a railway track. **1914** *Automobile Topics* XXXIV. 190/1 Selected bits of the picture..are being shown in the local 'movie houses'. **1932** *Times Lit. Suppl.* 22 Dec. 976/1 Sam, ticket-chopper in a movie-house. **1967** 'La Meri' *Spanish Dancing* (ed. 2) 9 Maria Montero in whose group I danced in vaudeville and the movie houses. **1974** *Times* 19 Jan. 10/1 Local movie houses offering major releases. **1928** H. Crane *Let.* 27 Apr. (1965) 325 'Crashing the gate' ..seems to be exclusively applied to the movie industry. **1917** *Vanity Fair* (N.Y.) Dec. 68 Here we are privileged to behold the interior of a movie king's office. **1914** C. L. Hagen in R. Grau *Theatre of Science* p. xxiv, Is it to be wondered at..that authors, actors, and science await the call to 'movie' land? **1928** *Daily Express* 16 Mar. 4/2 There are few people..better qualified to explain the mysteries of movie-land and of the technical side of films. **1929** E. Wilson *I thought of Daisy* ii. 90 It was a movie magazine called *Photo-Life*. **1955** W. Gaddis *Recognitions* I. v. 180 Movie magazines, simply all sex. **1957** N. Frye *Anat. Crit.* 164 The moviemakers find some difficulty in getting anyone over the age of seventeen into their audiences. **1975** *Listener* 20 Mar. 387 Ingmar Bergman is not everyone's favourite movie maker. **1939** F. Scott Fitzgerald *Lett.* (1964) 415 To be plunged immediately into movie-making. **1973** *Listener* 22 Nov. 716/3 Movie-making depends on movie distributors. **1915** *Pearson's Mag.* Jan. 80 My first action..was to ask a movie-man going home with films, to bring me back a blue serge suit. **1916** 'B. M. Bower' *Phantom Herd* xix. 309 The movie-man that runs this show for the Convention. **1948** *Sun* (Baltimore) 1 Dec. 17/4 Because the most hotly disputed of the series came unexpectedly the movie men did not have their cameras directed at second base. **1951** M. McLuhan *Mech. Bride* (1967) p. vi/1 A film expert, speaking of the value of the movie medium. **1917** *Chicago Defender* 22 Dec., Watch for our new movie palace. **1936** A. Huxley *Olive Tree* 40 When I was last at Margate a gigantic new movie palace had just been opened. **1955** W. Gaddis *Recognitions* I. vi. 220 The woman with me led me down a long street, and we came to a movie palace. **1966** L. Cohen *Beautiful Losers* (1970) I. 22 Let.. no naked flashing breasts lure the dirty laundry of our daily lives into the movie palace. **1916** E. V. Lucas *Vermilion Box* ccxiii. 250 I wish a movie picture could be taken of him. **1917** 'W. Wynning' *Princes St. & Other Otago Rhymes* 11 A girl one sees in 'movie' plays. **1936** Chesterton *As I was Saying* xxxi. 191 The fiction on the film, the partisan version in the movie-play. **1959** *Sears, Roebuck Catal.* Spring & Summer 1396/7 Movie Projectors. **1962** M. McLuhan *Gutenberg Galaxy* 124 The reading of print puts the reader in the role of the movie projector. **1927** U. Sinclair *Oil!* xiii. 314 It's cost me eight million dollars to make a movie queen out of this baby. **1917** H. Crane *Let.* 8 Oct. (1965) 10 Mrs. Walton and I are working out movie scenarios. **1964** M. McLuhan *Understanding Media* (1967) I. v. 65 When the movie scenario or picture story was applied to the *idea* article. **1950** M. Lowry *Lett.* (1967) 2/9 Have written..a detailed movie script. **1973** L. Hellman *Pentimento* (1974) 268 The money I got from the movie script of *The Little Foxes*. **1913** *Technical World* Mar. 17/1 This novel feeling of amused satisfaction over a 'movie' show deepened. **1925** A. P. Herbert *Laughing Ann* 33, I ..wish That life was a little like a movie-show. **1974** M. Z. Lewin *Enemies Within* xxv. 107 I'll..tell Janie about the movie shows at the frat. **1919** H. L. Wilson *Ma Pettengill* ii. 39 [They saw] how much they were paying their president..quoted beside some movie star's salary. **1937** H. G. Wells *Brynhild* vi. 78 Two other of the applicants had 'done publicity' for movie stars. **1973** D. Ramsay *Deadly Discretion* 129 Why do you conceal your beautiful eyes..? You are practising to be a movie star? **1914** *Munsey's Mag.* Jan. 735/2 Then he closed the door and advanced into the 'movie' studio. **1926** A. Huxley *Jesting Pilate* 261 Within the movie studio there shone no sun, only the lamps. **1952** M. McCarthy *Groves of Academe* (1953) x. 197 One of Furness's long-tressed Ritas was promised a movie-test. **1915** *Film Flashes* 13 Nov. 1 It's a long lane that has no movie theatre. **1968** *Michelin Guide N.Y. City* 9 Movie Theaters. —Like the theaters, many first-run movie houses are clustered in the Broadway area.

moviedom (mū·vidəm). orig. *U.S.* Also **Moviedom.** [f. *MOVIE + -DOM.] = *filmdom* (s.v. *FILM *sb.*).

1916 in *Dialect Notes* (1918) V. 7 Methra Morrell, Moviedom's Greatest Actress. **1927** *Daily Express* 28 Nov. 13 Adolphe Zukor, from whose weakening hand the sceptre of Moviedom has been wrested by Joseph M. Schenk. **1947** *N.Y. Times* 27 July II. 4/3 Even in its depiction of moviedom, Hollywood has seen fit to glamourize itself. **1973** *Lebende Sprachen* XVIII. 38/2 US moviedom —BE/US film industry, BE cinema industry—Filmindustrie.

Movieola, var. *MOVIOLA.

Movietone (mū·vitōun). Also **movietone.** [f. *MOVIE + TONE *sb.*] The proprietary name of a system employed in the making of sound films; a film made by this system; also used allusively of the style of presentation of newsreels formerly produced by the Movietone Company. Also *attrib.*

1927 *Daily Express* 27 Aug. 1/3 The 'movietone' is an invention with the same technical basis as the 'phonofilm'. **1927** *Glasgow Herald* 12 Oct. 11/1 The movietone..is a vast improvement on previous talking films. **1927** G. B. SHAW *Platform & Pulpit* (1962) 178, I am an actual real animal; I am not the latest movietone illusion. **1928** *Trade Marks Jrnl* 4 Apr. 534/1 Movietone... Cinematograph transparencies for exhibition. Fox Case Corporation..City..of New York, United States of America; manufacturers. **1928** *Liberty* 11 Aug. 25/2 George Bernard Shaw as he appears in a strip of Movietone film. Note the sound track on the left margin. **1930** *Nature* 19 July 93/1 With such a sound standard at a known distance from the movietone microphone, a record of pitch and intensity of pure notes covering a wide range of frequencies and intensities may be recorded on the film. *Ibid.*, Fig. 1 is a reproduction of a movietone film of an orchestra and the microphotometric record of the music recorded. **1939** *Motion Pict. Herald* 28 Oct. 30/1 Movietone News has devoted two complete issues to the war. **1953** L. J. WHEELER *Princ. Cinematogr.* vii. 213 An invention by Theodore W. Case made possible the Fox-Case Movietone news, photographed by cameras fitted with a device capable of recording sound alongside the picture and on the same negative film. The Movietone camera was made possible by the ability of certain gas-filled lamps to vary in brightness in true relationship to the current which is passing through them. **1969** *Listener* 23 Jan. 123/2 A reading from the Old Testament about the death of Moses delivered in a hushed movietone voice.

moving, *vbl. sb.* Add: **5.** *moving business, -van*; **Moving Day,** (*a*) (earlier and later examples); also (with lower-case initials), any other day on which people move to new premises; **moving-man** *N. Amer.* = MOVER[1] 6.

1973 *Times* 23 Oct. (Pickfords Suppl.) 1 Three hundred years experience in the moving business has helped keep Pickfords the biggest name in household removals. **1832** J. F. WATSON *Hist. Tales N.-Y.* 123 'Moving day' was, as now, the first of May. **1855** *Knickerbocker* XLV. 585 In the southern part of New-Jersey, one who rents or purchases a house or farm usually takes possession of the same on the twenty-fifth day of the present month [*sc.* March], which is therefore denominated 'moving-day'. **1947** *Pasadena* (Calif.) *Star-News* 9 Sept. 16/6 Moving days are ahead for several county departments in the Hall of Records and Hall of Justice, Los Angeles. **1973** Moving day [see *moving-man* below]. **1922** H. L. FOSTER *Adventures Trop. Tramp* xii. 179 While he shipped the furniture from the old place, I was to go down to the new one to see that the moving-men stole none of it en route. **1965** M. MCINTYRE *Place of Quiet Waters* ii. 29 'How right you are, Miss,' said the moving-man. **1973** *National Observer* (U.S.) 3 Feb., When our moving men finally showed up ('removals' in their business, whether you are coming or going, and on moving day we hardly knew which we were) we received another language lesson. **1898** *Kansas City* (Missouri) *Star* 21 Dec. 9/2 The moving vans and pie-wagons of New York are changing their pictures. **1925** T. DREISER *Amer. Trag.* (1926) II. III. xxvii. 334 A venal moving-van company had revealed her address. **1963** *PMLA* Dec. p. vii/2 U.K. removals lorry: U.S. moving van.

moving, *ppl. a.* Add: **3.** Special collocations: **moving average,** an average derived from a series of values in which the interval contributing to it is of constant size but is moved progressively along the series (usually one value at a time) to give a succession of averages; **moving-coil** *attrib.*, denoting electrical instruments and apparatus in which a coil of wire is situated in a magnetic field, so that either the coil moves when a current flows through it or else a current is generated when it is caused to move; similarly **moving-conductor; moving-iron** *attrib.*, denoting electrical instruments and apparatus in which the passage of a current through a fixed coil of wire causes the movement of a piece of iron inside it; **moving map,** a map carried in a ship, aircraft, etc., which is displayed so that as the craft moves its position always corresponds to a fixed point in the middle of the map; **moving pavement,** a section of pavement arranged as a conveyer belt for the carrying of passengers; **moving stair**(**case**), an escalator; also *fig.*; **moving-target** *attrib.*, applied to radar apparatus or techniques which give an indication only of targets moving relative to the transmitter, signals from stationary targets being eliminated.

1912 W. I. KING *Elem. Statistical Method* xv. 168 In determining on the size of groups to be used in calculating a moving average, one should use a period of time approximately equal to the length of the cycle which it is desired to eliminate. **1969** J. ARGENTI *Managem. Techniques* 174 If demand for a product over the past four weeks has been for 20, 23, 19, 19 units respectively, the average demand has been for 20 units. Now suppose another week passes in which the demand is 22 units, the new moving average is 20·5. This is calculated by dropping the earliest figure (20), adding the latest (22) and averaging again. **1896** W. E. AYRTON *Pract. Electr.* (new ed.) I. ii. 144 A very convenient, portable and accurate moving coil ammeter has been perfected by Mr. Weston, of Newark, America. **1903** G. D. A. PARR *Electr. Engin. Measuring Instruments* iii. 106 The ammeters belonging to the class of moving coil instrument measure current indirectly by indicating the fall of potential down a low-resistance 'shunt'. **1930** *Manch. Guardian* 20 Sept. 15/7 Moving-coil loud speakers are, of course, strongly in evidence. **1933** L. E. C. HUGHES *Elem. Engin. Acoustics* v. 77 The three forms of diaphragm action are incorporated respectively in the condenser (Wente) microphone, the moving-coil (Sykes) microphone, and the ribbon (Olson) microphone. **1968** *Radio Communication Handbk.* (ed. 4) ix. 12/2 A miniature moving-coil loudspeaker can sometimes be made to serve as a fairly satisfactory microphone. **1933** K. HENNEY *Radio Engin. Handbk.* xvi. 421 These have practically been superseded by the moving conductor drive (principally electrodynamic) and the larger portion of all loud-speakers in use today are of this type. **1966** *McGraw-Hill Encycl. Sci. & Technol.* VIII. 360/2 A moving conductor microphone consists of a straight-line conductor located in a magnetic field and coupled to a V-shaped diaphragm acted upon by sound waves. **1908** K. EDGCUMBE *Industr. Electr. Measuring Instruments* 27 One of the simplest windings to calculate is that of an ammeter coil such as would be used for a moving-iron instrument. **1940** A. WOOD *Acoustics* xviii. 529 The large diaphragm required in lieu of a horn may also be driven by an arrangement of the 'moving iron' type. **1966** *McGraw-Hill Encycl. Sci. & Technol.* XIV. 372/2 The moving-iron instrument, like the electrodynamic voltmeter, when properly calibrated indicates true rms volts. **1969** *Daily Tel.* 6 Mar. 18 The former Ministry of Aviation applied for Patent No. 926448 in 1960 to cover the moving map developed by that Ministry. **1969** *Sunday Tel.* 30 Mar. 1/4 Throughout the world more than 13,500 ships, 2,000 aircraft and some 1,000 helicopters use Decca navigation equipment including many 'moving map' displays. **1970** *New Scientist* 12 Mar. 508/2 The aircraft's position at any instant is shown by a spot of light at the centre of a six-inch moving-map display, showing the area over which the aircraft is flying. **1960** *Times Rev. Industry* Apr. 28/1 Passenger-carrying conveyor belt..known as moving pavements. **1971** *Guardian* 22 June 6/6 Passenger conveyor systems, popularly known as moving pavements, could become a major form of city transport. **1922** Moving stair [see *ESCALATE *v.* 1]. **1940** L. MACNEICE *Last Ditch* 12 And two people with the one pulse (Somebody stopped the moving stairs): Time was away and somewhere else. **1910** Moving staircase [see *ESCALATOR 1]. **1927** HALDANE & HUXLEY *Animal Biol.* xiii. 309 The gill cilia are so arranged that all food-particles strained off by the gills are driven up to the dorsal groove. Here they become entangled and stuck in the slime, and are passed on by this sort of moving staircase to be digested in the intestine. **1959** *Chambers's Encycl.* V. 389/1 The escalator or moving staircase was originally developed in America; it was exhibited at the Paris Exposition in 1900, and the first to be installed in Britain (in 1911) was at Earl's Court station, London. **1953** PENROSE & BOULDING *Princ. & Pract. Radar* (ed. 4) xxiv. 645 The principles on which moving target indication and permanent echo cancellation work. **1966** E. LARSEN *Radar works like This* (rev. ed.) 39 An important advance in airport radar is the 'moving target indicator'.., a type of radar equipment which shows only moving aircraft on the PPI. **1972** A. SUNDARABABU *Fund. Radar* xviii. 485 (*heading*) Moving target indication.

movingness. Delete † *Obs. rare* and add later examples.

1927 BEERBOHM *Lett. to R. Turner* (1964) 268, I do so agree about the movingness of the Jews at the Süss funeral. **1930** G. GREENE *Two Witnesses* 99 He was touched almost to speechlessness by the movingness of Christ.

moving picture. [f. MOVING *ppl. a.* + PICTURE *sb.*] †**1.** A picture in which objects move, or appear to move, in imitation of their natural motion. *Obs.*

1709 *Daily Courant* 9 May, The most Famous, Artificial and Wonderful Moving Picture that came from Germany. **1709–10** [see MOVING *ppl. a.* 1]. **1713** SWIFT *Jrnl. to Stella* 27 Mar. (1948) II. 647, I went afterwards to see a famous moving Picture, & I never saw any thing so pretty. **1715** *Boston News-Let.* 14 Mar. 2/2 The Italian Matchean, or Moving Picture, wherein are to be seen, Wind-Mills and Water-Mills moving round. **1727** M. W. MONTAGU *Let.* Mar. (1966) II. 73, I now and then peep upon these things with the same coldness I would do on a moving Picture. **1782** *Town & Country Mag.* Apr. 208/2 With moving pictures Loutherburg displays His graphic skill... He derives new pow'rs, To drive fatigue from exhibition hours. **1822** *Hive* I. 66/1 The illustrations consisted of a series of finely painted scenes, which were made to change their effect and constructions, and accompany, in a rapid and beautiful manner, the progress of the story, embodying, as it were, in a moving picture, almost as vivid as the tablet of a camera obscura, every circumstance as it fell from the speaker's lips. **1899** *Science Siftings* XV. 242/1 A second edition has reached us of the 'Motograph Moving Picture Book'... These moving pictures should prove interesting to children.

2. A cinematographic picture or film. Also *attrib.*

1896 QUEEN VICTORIA *Jrnl.* 3 Oct. in *Lett.* (1932) 3rd Ser. III. 87 We were all photographed..by the new cinematograph process, which makes moving pictures by winding off a reel of films. **1897** *Sketch* 13 Oct. 480/2 One guinea and half-a-guinea are being asked for stalls to see the moving pictures of the Corbett-Fitzsimmons fight at the Empress Theatre. **1898** *N.Y. Tribune* 30 Oct. 8/3 The always interesting moving pictures in the biograph..will include..four new scenes. **1906** 'O. HENRY' *Four Million* 3 He cursed the moving pictures. **1907** *Pearson's Mag.* Jan. (Advt.), Moving Picture Machines. **1912** F. A. TALBOT (*title*) Moving pictures: how they are made and worked. **1913** *Punch* 2 Apr. 253/3 It [*sc.* Mexico] contains a town of 10,000 inhabitants where there is no moving picture palace. **1921** G. B. SHAW *Back to Methuselah* III. 103 What earthly interest is there in looking at a moving picture of a lot of people merely because they were drowned? *Ibid.* 105 Weve had moving pictures of all four put on the screen today for this American. **1934** W. SAROYAN *Daring Young Man* 184 This sense of being out of time has driven thousands of people from their homes into moving-picture theatres where new universes appear before them. **1950** T. S. ELIOT *Cocktail Party* I. i. 34 A common interest in the moving pictures Frequently brings young people together. **1959** *Observer* 22 Feb. 19/6 The film is interesting, as a moving-picture record of a movement of our times.

Moviola (mūvi,ōu·lă). *Cinemat.* orig. *U.S.* Also **Movieola,** and with small initial. [f. *MOVIE + *-ola*, after PIANOLA.] The proprietary name of a device whereby the picture and sound of a cinematographic film are reproduced on a small scale so that the film may be edited or checked.

1929 *Photoplay* (Chicago) Apr. 31/2 *Movieola*, miniature projection machine with earphones used in the cutting room of a talking picture studio for rapid viewing of pieces of film. **1931** B. BROWN *Talking Pict.* xi. 276 Lately, a device known as the 'Movieola' has been adopted, ..a miniature peep show projector with a loud speaker. **1933** C. WINCHESTER *World Film Encycl.* 483/1 *Moviola*, a little machine used by the film editors to see and hear the picture. **1944** *Trade Marks Jrnl.* 20 Sept. 455/1 Moviola. .. Projectors, synchronizing apparatus, film measuring machines, sound reading apparatus, sound amplifiers and re-winding apparatus; all for use in editing cinematographic films. Iwan Serrurier, trading as Moviola Company,..Hollywood. **1959** HALAS & MANVELL *Technique Film Animation* xxv. 302 Music track run on a movieola and each note, phrase and sentence marked with grease pencil. **1970** *Daily Tel.* (Colour Suppl.) 6 Feb. 22/3 For ten weeks, three weeks longer than it took to shoot the movie, he works with the editor at the movieola. **1970** *Times* 5 Dec. 19/6 There was no movieola in those days... You just ran the film through your fingers and cut with a pair of scissors.

mow (mōu), *sb.*[6] [f. *MOW *v.*[1] 3 d.] In *Cricket*, a sweeping stroke to leg.

1925 D. J. KNIGHT in *Country Life* 15 Aug. 244/1 Legside shots. They are the glides,..the mow and the pull. **1926** J. B. HOBBS *Test Match Surprise* xvi. 171 What he intended for a leg glance was nothing more than a 'mow' between square leg and mid-on.

mow, *v.*[1] Add: **3. d.** *Cricket.* To make a sweeping stroke to leg as if mowing the grass with a scythe. Also *trans.*

1844 *Bradford Observer* 8 Aug., Holmes cleverly mowed the ball from the off stump to the leg side. **1868** J. LILLYWHITE *Cricketers' Compan.* 81 H. M. Mills..might score well if he did not think it necessary to mow at straight long-hops. **1925** D. J. KNIGHT in *Country Life* 15 Aug. 245/1 Supposing there is a deep square-leg, it is better..to kneel down on your right knee and mow or drag the ball round in the direction of long-leg.

4. Combs. containing the verb stem, as **mow-land** *U.S.*, land where grass is grown for mowing; **mow-lot,** a plot of this land.

1845 S. JUDD *Margaret* II. i. 214 She saw..women.. raking and turning hay among alders and willows that yet flourished in their best mow-lands. **1874** *Rep. Vermont Board Agric.* II. 411 The breeding of wrinkled sheep is like a farmer who ridges up his level mow-land and seeds the ridges with an inferior grass. **1845** S. JUDD *Margaret* II. viii. 325, I kept him here in the mow-lot.

mow, var. *MOU.

mowhay (mōu·hēi, mōu·i). *dial.* [f. MOW *sb.*[1] + HAY *sb.*[2] 2.] A stack-yard, a rick-yard.

Given as Devon and Cornwall in *E.D.D.*

1862 R. S. HAWKER *Let.* 14 Sept. in C. E. Byles *Life & Lett. R. S. Hawker* (1905) xvi. 362 Now I trust to be able to pay my Farm Wages in Wheat as the custom is, while for the last two years I have had to find money instead. To small Farmers and Vicars the Mowhay is the Farm Bank. **1880** M. A. COURTNEY in Courtney & Couch *Gloss. Words Cornwall* 38/2 *Mowhay*, an enclosure of ricks of corn or hay. **1959** *Listener* 22 Jan. 174/2 The granite shafts in the old mowhay.

mowing, *vbl. sb.*[1] Add: **3.** *mowing crook, ground* (later examples), *land, machine* (earlier examples).

1943 *Antiquity* XVII. 203 To use a mowing-crook such as one still sees used in connection with the swap-hook in this country. **1654** *Rec. Early Hist. Boston* (1880) VI. 17 Twenty acres more or lesse of mowing ground upon the marsh. **1722** in *Essex Inst. Hist. Coll.* (1906) XLII. 90 [To

pay damages for] digging in any Corne field, . . mowing ground. **1770** in *Ibid.* (1872) XI. 31 My little mare had provided for herself, by leaping out of a bare pasture into a lot of mowing ground. **1787** G. WASHINGTON *Diaries* (1925) III. 222 The same difference was equally obvious on a piece of mowing grd. not far distant from it. **1640** in *Connecticut Hist. Soc. Coll.* (1912) XIV. 357 One parsell called Swamp, now mowing land. **1704** *Proprietors' Rec. Waterbury, Connecticut* (1911) 60 No man shal stak horses in the moing land in said feild. **1816** *North Amer. Rev.* III. 428 At the distance of five or six miles it begins to wind gently through large tracts of fine rich mowing land. **1858** C. L. FLINT *Milch Cows* 169 The grasses differ widely; and their value as feed for cows will depend . . on the management of pastures and mowing-lands. **1823** *H. R. Doc. 17th U.S. Congress 2 Sess.* No. 36. 6 Improvement in the mowing machine, Feb. 13, [1822], Jeremiah Baily. **1838** H. W. ELLSWORTH *Valley Upper Wabash* v. 47, I have a plan in view . . and that is, to introduce the mowing and grain-cutting machine into this state.

mowra(h), varr. MAHWA (in Dict. & Suppl.).

moxibustion. (Examples.)

1910 E. PLAYFAIR tr. *Neuburger's Hist. Med.* I. 71 Moxibustion . . also serves as a prophylactic. *Ibid.* 78 Moxibustion and acupuncture were also in Japan the favourite methods of treatment. **1958** *Manch. Guardian* 6 Dec. 4/3 This has a history of three thousand years, and works in various ways: by acupuncture . .; by moxibustion . .; and by medicaments prepared from herbs and parts of animals. **1965** *New Scientist* 15 July 129/1 Chinese surgery has clearly advanced at a pretty phenomenal rate. Presumably this is why traditional methods like acupuncture, moxibustion (the burning of a herbal mixture on part of the body to transfer the site of irritation from one place to another) . . are still respected. **1974** *Sci. Amer.* Apr. 25/1 The years since 1949 have seen the general adoption of certain traditional techniques: the use of herbal preparations, of gymnastics and respiratory exercises, and of two related treatments, moxibustion and acupuncture.

moxie (mǫ·ksi). *U.S. slang.* [f. the name of an American soft drink.] Courage, 'guts', 'nerve'; energy, pep.

1930 D. RUNYON in *Collier's* 20 Dec. 32/3 Personally, I always figure Louie a petty-larceny kind of guy, with no more moxie than a canary bird. **1943** M. SHULMAN *Barefoot Boy with Cheek* xv. 158 We knew you had the old moxie, the old get out and get. **1947** S. J. PERELMAN *Westward Ha!* (1949) x. 122 Before I could summon up enough moxie to bolt after them, . . the attendants herded us into Indian file. **1955** *Publ. Amer. Dial. Soc.* xxiv. 94 If he admits his own limitations, he loses his nerve (blows his moxie). **1959** C. WILLIAMS *Man in Motion* iv. 47 She's a real Latin type, dark brown eyes with a lot of moxie in 'em. **1967** *Telegraph* (Brisbane) 6 Mar. 7/2 A girl with all the moxie (outstanding intelligence). **1969** *Maclean's Mag.* Aug. 1/3 The qualities that make business click—qualities such as moxie and timing and stealth. And wealth. **1970** *New Yorker* 29 Aug. 19/1 It takes moxie, skill, and self-reliance. **1975** *Daily Colonist* (Victoria, B.C.) 16 Mar. 17/3, I was very impressed with his all-round moxie. He could snap back at any of them, news reporters, police, and me.

moya (moiā·), *int. Ireland.* Also **maureeyah, mauryah, mor-yah, moyah, moy-yah.** [ad. Ir. *mar dh'eadh*, as if it were so.] Used as an ironic interjection (see quots.).

The spelling in the head-word, which is that of James Joyce, is not otherwise authenticated.

1910 P. W. JOYCE *Eng. as we speak it in Ireland* 296 Mor-yah; a derisive expression of dissent to drive home the untruthfulness of some assertion or supposition or pretence, something like the English 'forsooth', but infinitely stronger. **1911** *Jrnl. Co. Kildare Archæol. Soc.* VI. 535 *Maureeyah*, this expression denotes a strong doubt as to the truthfulness of a statement. 'That notorious poacher, Loughlin Murphy, tould the magistrates he didn't know how to set a snare, Maureeyah.' *Ibid.*, *Moyyah*, this is much the same expression as *Maureeyah*. . . It conveys the same sense as the English saying, 'You may tell that to the Horse Marines'. **1914** JOYCE *Dubliners* 151 And the men used to go in on Sunday morning before the houses were open to buy a waistcoat or a trousers—moya! **1922** —— *Ulysses* 327 Beggar my neighbour is his motto. Love, Moya! **1925** *Blackw. Mag.* Dec. 784/2 'Tis a bad pair to beat we are, moyah! **1939** JOYCE *Finnegans Wake* 375 The wonder of the women of the world together, moya! **1944** *Béaloideas* XIV. 176 Mauryah. A word implying doubt and irony.

Moyen Age (mwayenaʒ). Also **moyen âge**, etc. [Fr.]. The Middle Ages, the medieval period. Also, a representation of medieval life. Also as quasi-*adj.*: of the Middle Ages, medieval.

1849 THACKERAY *Pendennis* I. xxiii. 213 We'll . . furnish the oak room with the Moyen-age cabinet and armour. **1852** E. RUSKIN *Let.* 10 Jan. in M. Lutyens *Effie in Venice* (1965) II. 245 The traditions of their families moved with Moyen-age sentiments of Chivalry. *Ibid.* 26 Jan. A coiffure I have made for myself which John says is decidedly Moyen-age. **1864** G. A. SALA *Quite Alone* I. ii. 37 'If a man wants to get on in life, he can't do better than study the History of the Middle Ages'. To which Moyen Age culture Mr. Blunt owed much of his success. **1870** C. SCHREIBER *Jrnl.* (1911) I. 78, I cannot describe the collection. It was entirely Moyen Age. **1923** R. FRY *Let.* 21 May (1972) II. 535 Spain . . this big rich and on the whole up-to-date civilisation which is yet definitely *moyen age*. **1927** R. H. WILENSKI *Mod. Movement in Art* 66 Moyen-âge elements in their art. **1961** M. LEVY *Studio Dict. Art Terms* 77 *Moyenage*, paintings depicting reconstructed scenes, etc. from the Medieval period. **1962** R. G. HAGGAR *Dict. Art Terms* 219/2 *Moyenage*, pictorial reconstruction of the Middle Ages.

Moygashel (moi·gæʃəl). Also **moygashel.** [Name of a village in Co. Tyrone, N. Ireland.] The proprietary name of a type of Irish linen.

1931 *Trade Marks Jrnl.* 11 Nov. 1506/1 Moygashel . . Linen piece goods. Stevenson & Son, Limited, Moygashel Mills, Dungannon, County Tyrone, Ireland. **1958** *Woman* 1 Mar. 4/2 (Advt.), Unlined suit, trimmed white pique in a moygashel pebble line tweed. **1966** *Punch* 7 Sept. 363/2, I placed the card in the pocket of my moygashel jacket.

moy-yah, var. *MOYA *int.*

Mozambican (mōᵘzæ̆mbī·kăn), *a.* and *sb.* Also † **Mosambican.** [f. MOZAMBIQUE + -AN.]

A. *adj.* Of or pertaining to Mozambique.

1875 *Encycl. Brit.* III. 758/2 The Libyan Subregion . . is then succeeded by the 'Mosambican' Subregion, which continues perhaps to Sofala. **1893** A. NEWTON *Dict. Birds* II. 352 The 'Mosambican' Province next follows. **1970** *Guardian* 1 Aug. 9/1 A Mozambican consciousness, an awareness of African history. **1971** *Standard* (Tanzania) 7 Apr. 4/1 Mozambican freedom fighters. **1974** *Daily News* (Tanzania) 13 Sept. 4/1 This bunch of bandits . . is desperately trying to oppose the Mozambican People's and the Portuguese People's wish for peace.

B. *sb.* A native or inhabitant of Mozambique.

1971 *Standard* (Tanzania) 7 Apr. 4/1 This news was joyfully received by other Mozambicans. **1973** *Times* 17 Feb. (Mozambique Suppl.) p. ii/2 The identity card carried by any Mozambican is exactly the same document as that carried by anyone in Lisbon.

Mozambique. Add: Hence **Mozambi·quer,** a native or inhabitant of Mozambique.

1803 R. SEMPLE *Walks & Sk. Cape Good Hope* iii. 40 Without the inactivity or dulness of the Mozambiquer or the penetrative genius of the Malay, he [*sc.* the Malabar slave] forms an excellent medium between the two. **1876** F. BOYLE *Savage Life* 271 Besides this, we had . . two cooks, a Malay and a Mozambiquer.

Mozartean, *a.* Add: (Further examples.) Also as *sb.*, an admirer or adherent of Mozart; an interpreter of his works.

The usual spelling is now *Mozartian.*

1898 G. B. SHAW *Perfect Wagnerite* 114 The Mozartian method. **1947** [see *CHROMATICISM]. **1947** A. EINSTEIN *Mus. Romantic Era* v. 44 Even in the 19th century there were still many . . who demanded no more than that of music: they were the 'Mozartians', the opponents particularly of Wagner and Liszt. **1955** *Times* 14 May 4/5 It was a curious whim that brought a Mozartian body all the way from Germany in order to play Beethoven's Eighth Symphony. **1958** *Spectator* 10 Jan. 50/2 Despite one or two very lovely movements, this is only for the insatiable Mozartian. **1959** *Listener* 15 Jan. 131/3 The Mozartian aristocracy has long disappeared [in Prague]. **1960** *20th Cent.* Aug. 141 A mood of carnival that one might call Mozartian. **1975** *Daily Tel.* 1 May 13/8 Once again the young Jamaican Nerine Barrett proved last night a natural-born Mozartian.

Also **Mozartia·na** *sb. pl.* (ANA *suff.*), minor works by Mozart; **Moza·rtianly** *adv.*, in the manner or style of Mozart's music; **Mozartism** (later example); **Mozart-lover; Mozart-like, -size** *adjs.*

1925 W. DE LA MARE *Two Tales* 55 The Mozart-like light and sweetness. **1928** *Observer* 24 June 23 The other three . . give the elegant (and in the last movement Mozartianly deep) music an air of special distinction. **1955** H. VAN THAL *Fanfare for E. Newman* x. 147 But he also thought the Finale of Beethoven's *Eroica*, with its 'gentle Mozartisms', unworthy of the rest. **1958** *Spectator* 10 Jan. 50/2 A rarer contribution to recorded Mozartiana is the fifteen one-movement Church Sonatas for chamber orchestra and organ. **1959** D. COOKE *Lang. Mus.* v. 236 True Mozart-lovers of the nineteenth and twentieth centuries. *Ibid.* 245 Only those who have heard the work played in a small hall, by a Mozart-size orchestra with a handful of strings, can be said to have experienced the truly violent impact of the symphony. **1963** *Punch* 3 Apr. 496/3 *Così fan Tutte* is . . brightly and strongly though not always Mozartianly sung.

‖ **mozo** (mōᵘ·þo). *Latin America.* [Sp.] **1.** A male servant or attendant; a groom; a labourer.

1836 C. J. LATROBE *Rambler in Mexico* 49 The remainder were sent in advance under his domestics or mozos. **1847** G. A. F. RUXTON *Adventures Mexico & Rocky Mts.* vii. 48, I at length hired a *mozo* to proceed with me as far as Durango. **1904** CONRAD *Nostromo* I. viii. 107 But Captain Mitchell's right-hand man . . after looking down critically at the ragged mozo, shook his head. **1923** *Blackw. Mag.* July 46/2 The mozo, the ostler lad, . . was a son of the house. **1936** A. HUXLEY *Eyeless in Gaza* xli. 495 The *mozos* had loaded their baggage on to the pack-mules. **1955** W. GADDIS *Recognitions* III. iii. 819 It turned out that the Señorito had asked the same question, and fled directly he got this same answer, leaving this mozo behind, to chat with her.

2. A bull-fighter's attendant.

1926 [see *ESPADA]. **1934** H. BAERLEIN *Belmonte the Matador* iii. 37 Every matador has got a valet, his *mozo de estoques*, whose important days are those on which there is a fight, not only in the dressing of his master but the duties of attendance . . at the ring-side, preparing the muletas and handing to his master the swords as he requires them. *Ibid.* 38 Antonio Conde . . undertook the part of mozo which he kept throughout the years. **1963** *Parade* (Austral.) Dec. 47/1 Meijas had to start at the bottom of the ladder as a 'mozo', the attendant who waits on a matador. **1967** MCCORMICK & MASCAREÑAS *Compl. Aficionado* iv. 146 *Mozo(s)*, the badly paid and often brave ring-attendants who clean up the mess, accompany the picador on foot, [etc.].

mozza, var. *MATZAH.

mozzarella (mǫtsăre·lă). Also **mozarella;** *pl.* **moz(z)arelle.** [It.] In full, *mozzarella cheese.* An Italian cheese originally made in the Naples area from buffalo milk.

1911 C. BESANA in *Bull. Bureau Agric. Intelligence & Plant-Dis.* (Internat. Inst. Agric., Rome) Nos. 8–10. 2231 With Buffalo milk . . 'pasta filata' cheeses are made, which are eaten fresh and much esteemed. These are 'Provature', 'Mozarelle', etc. **1912** *Experiment Station Rec.* (USDA) Oct. 475 Provature, or Provole, and Mozzarelle cheeses are made from buffalo milk. **1935** M. MORPHY *Recipes of all Nations* 160 Slices of Mozzarella cheese. **1962** *Spectator* 16 Feb. 219/2 Was the mozzarella cheese dripping, positively dripping, fresh? **1962** L. DEIGHTON *Ipcress File* ii. 19 The girl in the delicatessen was small, . . and rather delicious. We had been flirting across the mozzarella for years. **1969** *Daily Tel.* (Colour Suppl.) 5 Sept. 33/3 Limpid responsive eyes, and a chin that slopes back from a face as pale and bland as mozzarella. **1974** *Times* 2 Nov. 11/4 Fresh mozarella . . for making pizza.

mozzle (mǫ·z'l). *Austral. slang.* Also **moz, mozz.** [ad. Heb. *mazzāl* luck; cf. *SHEMOZZLE.] Luck; *spec.* in phr. *to put the moz on*, to inconvenience; to jinx. Also as *v. trans.*, to hinder, interrupt.

1898 *Bulletin* (Sydney) 17 Dec. (Red Page), *Mozzle* is luck. . . *Good mozzle* = good luck; *Kronk mozzle* = bad luck. **1903** 'T. COLLINS' *Such is Life* vi. 225 'And how much do you stand to lose, if your mozzle is out?' I asked. **1919** E. DYSON *Hello Soldier!* 32 'Twas rotten mozzle, Neddo. We had blown out every clip. **1941** BAKER *Dict. Austral. Slang* 47 *Moz*, to interrupt, to hinder. 'Put the moz on someone', to inconvenience a person. *Mozzle, to*, as for 'moz'. **1956** A. MARSHALL *How's Andy Going?* 200 'Looking ahead like that never does any bloody good to any man,' observed Pat. 'It puts the moz on him.' **1963** H. PORTER *Watcher on Cast-Iron Balcony* 81 Mother is wishing Miss Brewer some female ill, is putting the mozz on her. **1965** F. HARDY *Yarns Billy Borker* xx. 107 'Don't mozz a man,' I tells him. 'You're well named, I'll say that for you, Calamity.' **1974** J. POWERS *Last of Knucklemen* 49 Don't let him mozz you, Monk. **1974** K. STACKPOLE *Not just for Openers* ii. 32 She felt she put the moz on him . . . She couldn't bear to go in case she was a jinx.

mpalla, var. *IMPALA.

mph ('mh), *int.* Also **mphm.** [Imit.] Used to express an inarticulate sound of disapproval, doubt, or qualified approval. Cf. UMPH *int.*

1876 'MARK TWAIN' *Tom Sawyer* 272 What would people say? 'Mph! Tom Sawyer's gang! pretty low characters in it.' **1949** 'N. BLAKE' *Head of Traveller* vii. 105 To conceal the way he was killed? Mphm. Don't see how it helps us.

Mpret (bret). Also **Mbret, M'pret.** [ad. Alb. *mbret*, f. L. *imperator* emperor.] The title given to William of Wied, elected ruler of Albania after the declaration of Albanian independence in 1913.

1914 *Conc. Oxf. Dict.* Add., *Mpret*, Albanian ruler [L. *imperator*, emperor]. **1915** *Truth* 27 Jan. 133/2 He and not the Prince of Wied ought to be M'pret. **1921** C. TORR *Small Talk at Wreyland* 2nd Ser. 83 When I first went to Greece, they still spelled Byron's name phonetically Mpairon. They pronounce *b* like our *v*, but *mp* like our *b*—a fact unknown to many of the people who talk about the Mpret of Albania. **1954** M. HASLUCK *Unwritten Law in Albania* xv. 154 Esad Pashë Toptani revolted against Prince William of Wied, then *Mbret* (king) of Albania. **1959** *Chambers's Encycl.* I. 221/2 The European ruler selected to be 'mpret' of Albania—the German prince William of Wied.

Mr. Add: **2. d.** One who is entitled to be addressed as 'Mr.'; the word 'Mr.' as a title (in correspondence).

a **1817** JANE AUSTEN *Persuasion* (1818) III. iii. 55 'I have let my house to Admiral Croft,' would sound extremely well; very much better than to any mere *Mr.* ———; a *Mr.* (save, perhaps, some half dozen in the nation,) always needs a note of explanation. **1857** GEO. ELIOT *Let.* 2 June (1954) II. 337 Mr. Eliot . . may be a relation of Mr. Liggins's or some other 'Mr.' who knows Coton stories. **1882** W. PATER *Let.* 4 Nov. (1970) 43 My dear Sharp, (I think we have known each other long enough to drop the 'Mr.'). **1915** R. FRY *Let.* 26 Aug. (1972) II. 389 Dear Waley (May we drop the Mr).

e. Used with following adj. or sb. to denote an exemplar, a type, or a victor in a contest; esp. **Mr. Big,** the head of an organization of criminals; also, any important man; **Mr. Charley, Charlie** (see *CHARLEY, CHARLIE 7); **Mr. Clean,** an honourable or incorruptible politician; **Mr. Fix** (see quot. 1950); **Mr. Fixit,** one who does repairs or odd jobs; one skilled at managing difficult problems or situations; a 'trouble-shooter'; **Mr. Right,** a man who would make the ideal husband; a 'Prince Charming'.

See 1958 *Amer. Speech* XXXIII. II. ii. 84–87.
1814 H. BROUGHAM *Let.* June in T. Creevey *Creevey Papers* (1903) I. ix. 194, I was finally decided in favour of publishing to-day by the apprehension of Alexr., &c., coming in a day or two, and taking off the attention of Mr. and Mrs. Bull. **1913** C. MACKENZIE *Sinister St.* I. I. ii. 28 Because he had been slow in choosing..he had been called Mr. Particular. **1922** JOYCE *Ulysses* 362 Till Mr Right comes along then meet once in a blue moon. **1925** R. LARDNER in *Liberty* 9 May 5 (*title*) Mr. and Mrs. Fix-It. **1937** E. H. SUTHERLAND *Professional Thief* v. 129 Since most of the cases of professional thieves in the stores are taken care of by Mr. Fix, it is evident that the store detectives must get an end. **1940** G. MARX *Let.* 10 Oct. (1967) 26, I may motor east..to see your 'Mr. Big'. **1950** H. E. GOLDIN *Dict. Amer. Underworld Lingo* 139/1 *Mister fix*, a go-between, especially one who shuttles between the underworld and the overworld, handling bribes, ransom payments, etc. **1951** J. CANNAN *And All I Learned* vi. 76 Stevens offered her the last cake on a plate... Mildred laughed and replied, 'What about Mr Manners?' but took the cake. **1952** M. LASKI *Village* i. 24 In the ordinary way you'd expect someone like Miss Margaret to stay at home and go to tennis-parties and things until Mr. Right came along and she could make a home of her own. **1953** R. CHANDLER *Long Good-Bye* xxxii. 200 He was Mr. Big, the winner. **1959** A. W. SHERRING *Tip Off* iii. 28 Hardly the kind of district one would expect to find Mr. Big of London's underworld. **1962** E. CLEAVER in A. Dundes *Mother Wit* (1973) 18/1 To..crown him..Mister..Universe. **1967** P. E. H. DURSTON *Mortissimo* (1968) xii. 100 He's got very little decent for sale. More of what the Americans call a 'Mr. Fixit'. Mends things. **1968** 'J. LE CARRÉ' *Small Town in Germany* v. 71 Do you a girl as well, would he? Mister Fixit, is that it? **1969** C. BOOKER *Neophiliacs* vii. 179 Hints of the existence of a powerful 'Mr. Big'. **1970** G. GREER *Female Eunuch* 88 The whole point of a woman's existence is to be exploited by Mr Right. **1970** *Sunday Times* (Colour Suppl.) 20 Dec. 35/3 Still an entrepreneur and a Mr Fix-it, Levis..died from cirrhosis of the liver. **1972** *Village Voice* (N.Y.) 1 June 15/1 Peter M. Flanigan.. became an assistant to the President and acquired a reputation as 'Richard Nixon's "Mr. Fixit" when it comes to powerful business interests'. **1973** J. MANN *Only Security* x. 132 Sylvester..could have modelled as a Mr Average. **1973** *Times* 21 Nov. 8/4 Mr Elliot Richardson, who resigned as Attorney General..is Mr Clean to many Republicans. **1974** E. MCGIRR *Murderous Journey* 59, I ..asked if I could go through Siskin's papers... He'd been a methodical man... It was more or less the picture of Mr. America. **1974** *Guardian* 28 Jan. 2/5 Mr Shultz himself had never been touched by Watergate... His reputation as a 'Mr Clean'..has led him..to voice a growing sense of unease. **1974** *Observer* 17 Feb. 5/5 Smalls said he had not seen a 'Police 5' TV programme about the Wembley raid, but agreed that Turner's photograph was 'splashed in the papers', accompanied by the title of 'Mr Big'.

mrad: see *M 5 d.

mridangam ('mrida·ŋam). Also **m'ridang(a)**. [a. Sanskrit *mṛdaṃga* a kind of drum.] A double-headed, barrel-shaped drum, once made of clay, now usually of wood, with one head larger than the other, used in southern Indian music. Also *attrib.*

1888 A. J. HIPKINS *Mus. Instruments* 87 The Drum with the striped body and leather braces is a kind of M'ridang. The genuine Drum bearing this name is longer in proportion to its diameter, and has one head larger than the other. *Ibid.*, A good Tabla or M'ridang player will earn from 100 to 150 rupees, per month... The M'ridang is considered to be the most ancient of Indian Drums; its origin is popularly ascribed to the god Mahadeo (S'iva). **1891** C. R. DAY *Mus. & Mus. Instruments S. India* vi. 138 (*caption*) The Mridang is beaten by the hands, finger-tips, and wrists... The smaller head of the Mridang is struck by the right hand, the larger head by the left. **1921** H. A. POPLEY *Mus. India* vii. 120 The *Mṛidaṅga* or *Mardala* is the most common and probably the most ancient of Indian drums... The word *mṛidaṅga* or *mardala* means 'made of clay', and probably therefore its body was originally of mud. **1968** *N.Y. Times* 12 Sept. 56 Palghat Raghu on the mridanga and Alla Rakha on the tabla. **1968** *Daily Tel.* 28 Sept. 13/3 Among them was a drum dialogue between Alla Rakha (tabla) and Palghat Raghu (mridangam), a tour de force of fantastic subtlety and eloquence. **1970** *Ibid.* 6 July 12/6 A musical interlude in which Nagarajan on the mridangam drum had a friendly battle..with the dance director. **1971** *Shankar's Weekly* (Delhi) 4 Apr. 24/1 The infinite variety of the mridangam includes some of the elemental sequences that jazz makes capital out of.

Mrs. Add: **1. b.** A wife (with ellipsis of the name of her husband). *colloq.*

1913 R. BROOKE *Let.* 22 Nov. (1968) 535 He passed through Fiji lately... Mrs, I gather, is not with him. **1938** M. ALLINGHAM *Fashion in Shrouds* vi. 82 Paul Taretan is taking 'three girls from totally different environments', and 'Mrs.' has selected one rather beastly little boy. **1950** J. CANNAN *Murder Included* i. 9 Mr and Mrs Scampnell... Mrs has a daughter by her first husband. **1970** A. MORICE *Death in Grand Manor* iv. 35 Mr Cornford wasn't so bad.. but Mrs was awful. **1974** J. MONTGOMERIE *Implosion* x. 67 Another picture of Mrs., side-view.

c. *the Mrs.*: one's wife. *colloq.*

The examples happen to be U.S. but the use is widespread: cf. MISSIS 1.

1920 [see *monkey suit* s.v. *MONKEY *sb.* 17 a]. **1937** *Amer. Speech* XII. 103 The farmer will often refer to his wife as the Mrs. and he commonly addresses her as Wife. **1944** *Publ. Amer. Dial. Soc.* II. 58 *The Mrs.*, the wife. **1967** E. BULLINS *Theme is Blackness* (1973) 96 I'll have the Mrs. call the doctor as soon as I get home. **1973** *Philadelphia Inquirer* (Today Suppl.) 7 Oct. 42/3 You know, when I go home, the Mrs. says to me: 'Well, what happened tonight, night clerk?'

2. a. Also prefixed to the Christian name of the husband (without a following surname).

a **1817** JANE AUSTEN *Persuasion* (1818) III. vi. 103, I shall tell *you*, Miss Anne..that I have no very good opinion of Mrs. Charles's nursery-maid. **1842** GEO. ELIOT *Let.* 18 Feb. (1954) I. 126, I imagine, from a message my sister Mrs. Isaac told me of, that you had the idea that I was at Griff. **1857** C. M. YONGE *Dynevor Terr.* II. vi. 81 Is it in the nature of things that she should live in such society as Mrs. Walby's and Mrs. Richardson's? People who call her Mrs. James! **1910** E. M. FORSTER *Howard's End* xxxiii. 335 Mrs. Charles is expecting her fourth. **1953** A. CHRISTIE *Pocket Full of Rye* iv. 28 'Who was at breakfast?' 'Mrs. Fortescue, Miss Fortescue, Mrs. Val Fortescue... Mrs. Val and Miss Fortescue always eat a hearty breakfast.' **1971** E. LEMARCHAND *Death on Doomsday* vi. 97 We know Mrs Giles has got a key into the public rooms.

c. Prefixed to the surname of (the husband of) an actual or a fictional married woman, or to a generic sb., indicating esp. a woman of a certain occupation or temperament, as **Mrs. Beeton** (abbr. **Mrs. B.**) [the name of Isabella Mary *Beeton* (1836–65), nominal author of a Book on Household Management], an authority on cooking and domestic subjects; also *transf.*; **Mrs. Dale** [the name of the wife of a doctor in a radio serial], a conventional, middle-class woman; so **Mrs. Dale-ish** *a.*, middle-class; **Mrs. Grundy** (see GRUNDY[3]); **Mrs. Mop(p** [the name of a charwoman in a radio series], (a nickname for) a charwoman; the typical charwoman; also *attrib.*; **Mrs. next-door** (see *NEXT DOOR 1 b); **Mrs. Thing** [THING *sb.*[1] 10 in Dict. and Suppl.], used in place of a married woman's name of which the speaker is uncertain.

1960 *Listener* 7 Jan. 18/2 The modern trick, I am told by Dr. Spock and the other Mrs. Beetons of child care, is not to show anxiety to children. **1970** *Times* 9 Feb. 8/6 Explains Ita Jones, Light's switched-on Mrs B.: 'Though serving up this food may blow some minds, remember that you eat the animal because you love it.' **1954** A. MELVILLE *Simon & Laura* in *Plays of Year* XI. 36 You probably get the idea it's to be a sort of TV 'Mrs Dale'. It's not: we want interesting people who meet other interesting people: people..with a bit of—..glamour, colour, excitement in their lives. **1961** *Times Lit. Suppl.* 24 Nov. 851/1 The setting is suburban, even Mrs. Dale-ish. **1948** J. F. WOLFENDEN *Public Schools To-Day* v. 99 A great deal of the welfare..of a boarding school depends upon the unsung 'warrant officers and N.C.O.s', from the school messenger to Mrs. Mop. **1950** A. CHRISTIE *Murder is Announced* vii. 60 Our Mrs Mopp says he came from one of the big hotels. **1956** 'A. GILBERT' *Riddle of Lady* x. 145 A machine in a Mrs Mopp apron. **1972** *Listener* 27 July 105/1 Today's generation monotonously describe charwomen as Mrs Mops. **1939** N. MARSH *Overture to Death* iii. 41 The other one—Mrs. Thing or whoever she is! **1960** 'R. EAST' *Kingston Black* xiv. 136 Old Mrs. Thing at the exchange may listen in.

Ms[2] (miz). Also **Ms.** (with full stop). [A 'compromise' between MRS. and MISS *sb.*[2]] A title prefixed to the surname of a woman, regardless of her marital status. Hence as *sb.*, a woman so designated. Cf. *MIZ 2.

An increasingly common, but not universally accepted, use.

1952 *The Simplified Letter* (Nat. Office Managem. Assoc., Philadelphia) Jan. 4 Use abbreviation Ms. for *all women* addressees. This modern style solves an age-old problem. **1952** *Ibid.* (rev. ed.) June 4 Use abbreviation Ms. if not sure whether to use Mrs. or Miss. **1970** *Daily Tel.* 28 Aug. 14 The American feminists..object to being addressed as Mrs or Miss but admit that Ms, which the New York Commission on Human Rights has adopted for correspondence, [etc.]. **1970** *New Yorker* 5 Sept. 27 'How come no woman heads a super-agency?' demanded Ms. Komisar. **1971** *Publishers' Weekly* 1 Nov. 22 A crowded New York press conference heard this morning that a new magazine, called *Ms.* (pronounced 'Miz'), will begin publication in January. **1972** *Guardian* 29 Mar. 11 Mrs Chisholm (and it is definitely Mrs not Ms). **1973** *Lancet* 24 Mar. 633/2 We thank Ms Payge Hodapp for technical assistance. **1974** *Daily Tel.* 21 May 1/6 The Passport Office yesterday conceded the right to women to call themselves Ms (pronounced Miz) on their passports instead of Mrs or Miss. This followed a month's campaign by Women's Lib. **1975** *Publishers Weekly* 27 Jan. 232/1 *Sanditon* by Jane Austen and Another Lady..Ms. Austen's seventh and unfinished novel. *Ibid.* 19 May 170/1 Samantha Lay, a comely Ms. who devises gimmicks like a 'flying bullpen'. **1975** *Times* 17 Sept. 16/2 A circular..states grandly: 'Female staff in this department may..use the Ms title (usually pronounced Miz) as an alternative to the Miss or Mrs.' *Ibid.* 16/3 The Civil Service Department..has a fair sprinkling of Mss among its own staff.

msasa ('msa·sa). Also **m'sassa, musaasa.** [Mashona.] A Central African tree, *Brachystegia spiciformis*, of the family Leguminosæ, distinguished by compound leaves, racemes of small, fragrant, white flowers, and a spreading crown of branches. Also *attrib.*

1923 *Kew Bull.* 133 'Musaasa'..is by far the most common of the bark trees and is found all over Southern Rhodesia at an altitude of from 3,000 to 6,000 feet. It grows to 30 or 40 feet in height, has a rough outer bark in the large trees but almost smooth in the young trees... The trunks of the 'Musaasa' vary in diameter from 8 to 24 inches. **1949** K. L. SIMMS *Sun-Drenched Veld* iii. 33 On these islets you can..amuse yourself by trying to pick out the various trees. There is..the crimson-leaved m'sasa.. and the scarlet-flowering kaffirboom. **1951** D. LESSING *This was Old Chief's Country* i. 8 This child could not see a msasa tree, or the thorn, for what they were. **1964** *Listener* 6 Aug. 191/1 The black shadow of the African msasa Squats among the lawn's colonial company. **1973** PALMER & PITMAN *Trees S. Afr.* II. 847 The msasa is one of the few trees, growing beyond the borders of the Republic, that is well-known to South Africans. It is the dominant tree in most of the savannah forest of Rhodesia, reaching northwards to Zambia and Malawi, and is famous for the gorgeous pink, wine red, copper and bronze colours of its spring foliage.

mtepe ('mte·pe). [Swahili.] A sailing craft characterized by a square matting sail, used on the East coast of Africa.

1872 R. F. BURTON *Zanzibar* I. iv. 73 Various native craft..anchor close in shore... The quaintest and freshest local build is to us the Mtepe, which the Arabs call Muntafiyah. **1938** *Jrnl. R. Anthrop. Inst.* LXVIII. 343 It is only when the Swahili coast is reached that the oculus is again encountered. In this region the only sea-going craft that can be classed as indigenous is the *mtepe*. **1942** *E. African Ann.* 1941–2 27/1 His 'M'tepe' squatted, with many others, on the deep waters beyond the jetty. The tapering mast, raking forwards, was now devoid of its lateen sail.

m' tutor: see *M' = my.

mu (miū). [a. Gr. μῦ, name of the letter *M*, μ (see M).] **1.** One micrometre (micron). Usu. denoted by μ.

[**1880:** see *MICRON.] **1888** *Nature* 8 Mar. 438/1 *Micron* is currently used here to express 1/1000 of a millimetre. French botanists call it μ, and seldom use its first decimal because they cannot see such a small space. **1900** DORLAND *Med. Dict.* 398/2 *Mu*, in micrometry, a micron or micromillimeter. **1957** *Jrnl. Anat.* XCI. 2 The mean nuclear volume in six [vole] oocytes was found to be 5200 μ^3. **1958** *Times Rev. Industry* June 53/2 It [*sc.* the Mercast process] yields castings to extremely close dimensional limits, one example quoted being..a surface finish of 60μ an inch or better. **1959** *Listener* 31 Dec. 1161/1 Cell sizes range from a few mu to a few dozens of mu. **1970** AMBROSE & EASTY *Cell Biol.* i. 7 Bacteria..vary greatly in size from a diameter of 5,000 Å for the cocci up to about 20 μ in length for some of the filamentous bacteria.

2. *Electronics.* The amplification factor of a valve.

1918 H. J. VAN DER BIJL in *Physical Rev.* XII. 184 The factor μ_0, which plays a very important part in the theory of operation of the thermionic amplifier, can be more easily and accurately determined with the help of equation (19), which gives the relation between the anode and grid potentials necessary to maintain the current at some convenient constant value. *Ibid.* 192 The voltage amplification μ is given by $\mu = \mu_0 R/(R+R_0)$. **1927** B. F. DASHIELL *Pop. Guide Radio* vi. 98 The amplification constant of a tube, usually designated as mu, is a measure of the relative effect of changing the grid bias compared to changes in the plate voltage. **1931** *Electronics* Apr. 609/1 Mutual conductance meter... The compensator dial is set for the value most nearly corresponding to the 'Mu' of the tube under test. **1962** *Newnes Conc. Encycl. Electr. Engin.* 860/1 A coarse-pitch grid gives a low magnification and requires greater bias to cutoff. In the variable-mu valve the grid is graded, and this gives a valve whose gain can be altered by changing the bias applied to it.

mu, var. *MOU.

‖**Mu'allaqat** (mu,alakā·t), *sb. pl.* Also **Moallakat, Muallakat.** [a. Arab. *mu'allaḳāt*, lit. suspended odes, pl. of *mu'allaqa*.] An anthology of seven pre-Islamic Arabian poems made by the rawi Hammad al Rawija (d. 772). Also in shortened form **Moal.**

1782 (*title*) The Moallakát, or seven Arabian poems.. with a translation..by William Jones. **1834** *Penny Cycl.* II. 219/1 The poems called Moallakat. **1875** *Encycl. Brit.* II. 263/1 Seven of these, known in Arab literature by the title of the *Múallakat* or 'Suspended',..all of them belonging to the 6th century, have become..the..classical standards of Arab poetical composition. **1905** G. BELL *Let.* 12 Feb. (1927) I. 186 At dinner I produced the Muallakat (pre-Muhammadan poems). **1930** R. A. NICHOLSON *Lit. Hist. Arabs* iii. 101, I will now turn directly to those celebrated odes which are well known by the title of *Mu'allaqát*, or 'Suspended Poems', to all who take the slightest interest in Arabic literature. **1959** *N. & Q.* June 216/2 'The Poem of Amriolkais', the *moâl* upon which Tennyson relied for the framework of 'Locksley Hall'. **1964** *Listener* 25 June 1036/1 Behind the *qasidas* of Andalusia lay..the *Mu'allaqat*, the 'hanging odes' of the pre-Islamic oral verse of the Arabian desert.

muccuck, var. *MOCOCK.

much, *a.*, quasi-*sb.*, and *adv.* **A.** *adj.* **2. d.** Delete † *Obs.* and add further examples. Now chiefly *U.S. dial.* and in echoes of quot. 1602 in Dict.

1889 *Kansas City* (Missouri) *Times & Star* 13 Dec., For the latter's fall-down, much thanks. **1890** S. HALE *Lett.* (1919) 253, I have much funny things to tell you. **1928** J. PETERKIN *Scarlet Sister Mary* (1929) xxii. 217 How much chillen you had? **1952** E. O'NEILL *Moon for Misbegotten* I. 17 You didn't get much thanks from Mike, I'll wager, for your help.

B. *absol.* and quasi-*sb.* **2. e.** (Earlier example.)

1847 A. Brontë *Agnes Grey* xvii. 251, I paid more attention to dress than ever I had done before... This is not saying much, for hitherto I had been a little neglectful in that particular.

g. *a bit much*: see *bit *sb.*^{2} 5. Also in similar phrases with the same sense, as *a trifle much*, *rather much*.

1911 O. Onions *Widdershins* 265, I too smiled... 'It *was* rather much, wasn't it?' I said. **1930** R. Lehmann *Note in Music* v. 200 After all, perhaps it would have been a trifle much, applied to mother. **1964** J. Symons *End of Solomon Grundy* I. i. 27 It's enough to break up any party. I must say I thought it was rather much.

C. *adv.* **1. c.** Also still current in *U.S. dial.*

1916 *Dialect Notes* IV. 347, I don't guess she's much old. **1929** W. Faulkner *Sound & Fury* 268, I..went up front. 'Been much busy?' Earl says. 'Not much,' I says.

d. *not much*: certainly not, far from it, 'not likely'; also occas. (ironically), certainly, 'not half'. *colloq.*

1886 *Harper's Mag.* Dec. 148/1 'Go home?—explain?' he began, more calmly. 'Not much.' **1888** 'R. Boldrewood' *Robbery under Arms* I. xviii. 248 Starlight and I wasn't likely to break down—not much—whatever the jury did. **1904** E. Nesbit *Phoenix & Carpet* xi. 212 'He didn't mean stay and be roasted,' said Robert. 'No boys on burning decks for me, thank you.' 'Not much,' said Cyril. **1911** A. Bennett *Card* x. 255 Do you suppose I was going to let you go by that steamer? Not much. **1928** D. L. Sayers *Unpleasantness at Bellona Club* xvi. 188 'They can get it from Robert or George Fentiman,' warned Wimsey. 'Not much, they won't,' said Salcombe Hardy feelingly. **1970** A. Ross *Manchester Thing* 81 'Got a going over, did you?' 'Not much, I got a going over. Want to see the bruises?' **1973** J. Porter *It's Murder with Dover* i. 1 'I am not asking for any preferential treatment,' said Lord Crouch... Not bloody much! thought the Chief Constable..and tried to work out what His Nibs was up to.

e. *not to be* (or *go*) *much on* (or *for*): (*a*) not to be enthusiastic about (something); not to like or care for; (*b*) not to be useful or effective for (a purpose); to be no good at (something). *colloq.*

1896 *Dialect Notes* I. 417 'I don't go much on that', I don't care much for that. **1908** A. Bennett *Buried Alive* v. 111 'I'm not much for these restaurants,' she said, over grilled kidneys. 'No?' he responded tentatively. 'I'm sorry.' **1928** R. Bradford in B. A. Botkin *Treas. S. Folklore* (1949) III. ii. 485 Angels is all right for singin' and playin' and flyin' round, but they ain't much on workin' de crops and buildin' de levees. **1968** A. Munro in R. Weaver *Canad. Short Stories* 2nd Ser. 262 They may not be much on intellectual conversation but their hearts are in the right place.

5. (*a*) *much-abused*, *-admired*, *-branched*, *-criticized*, *-debated*, *-discussed*, *-dreaded*, *-needed*, *-quoted*, *-travelled*, *-used*, *-vaunted*; (*b*) *much talked of* (further example).

1879 W. James *Coll. Ess. & Rev.* (1920) 95 The much-abused subject of mental physiology. **1936** *Discovery* Dec. 382/1 The much abused engine..gave out utterly. **1960** *Farmer & Stockbreeder* 23 Feb. 75/1 The next big price was 3,000gs paid by exporter Mr. James Schofield for Westdrums Winson, Messrs. Boots' much-admired reserve best two-year-old. **1927** Haldane & Huxley *Animal Biol.* i. 35 Most glands..are many-celled tubes or pockets of epithelium, either unbranched or slightly branched..or much-branched like the liver or salivary gland. **1970** T. J. Ross *Film & Liberal Arts* 148 The much-criticized woodenness of her playing is of small matter. **1843** Mill *Logic* I. 9 To this science [*sc.* metaphysics] appertain the great and much debated questions of the existence of matter. **1956** *Nature* 11 Feb. 262/2 The whole of the much-debated line up Borrowdale. **1946** *Ibid.* 23 Nov. 759/2 The much-discussed hypothesis that galactic noise is analogous to the noise associated with solar flares. **1865** G. M. Hopkins *Poems* (1967) 150 You may trust Your footing now to the much-dreaded dust. **1886** E. G. White *Notes of Trav.* in *Hist. Sk. Foreign Missions Seventh Day Adventists* 236/1 We might obtain a little much-needed rest. **1936** *Burlington Mag.* Apr. 202/2 It is a pity not to have given the *Birth of Venus*..a much-needed rest. **1964** *Ann. Reg. 1963* 229 The United States and Canada traditionally supplied much-needed grain. **1927** *Mod. Philology* Nov. 224 The much-quoted example..does not illustrate sound change. **1912** 'Saki' *Chron. Clovis* 196 The County..mustered in full strength to witness the much-talked-of production. **1928** C. Singer *From Magic to Sci.* i. 12 This erudite and much travelled man exhibits great industry. **1890** W. James *Princ. Psychol.* II. xviii. 58 In one it [*sc.* cerebral injury] will throw a much-used brain-tract out of gear; in the other it may affect an unimportant region. **1939** W. S. Churchill *Into Battle* (1941) 150 The magnetic mine..may perhaps be Herr Hitler's much vaunted secret weapon. **1974** *Times* 9 Dec. 12/2 Mr Tanaka rashly published his much vaunted plan for decentralizing industry.

muchacho (mŭtʃā·tʃo). [Sp.] A boy, young man; a male servant. Also *attrib.* So **mucha·cha**, a girl.

1591 Garrard & Hitchcock *Arte of Warre* iii. 212 The followers of the campe, pages and muchachos, who must be chosen able to fight in a day of seruice, for the defence of themselues and their masters baggage. **1852** *San Diego Herald* 10 Apr. 2/2 Gay, dashing muchachos in boots and spurs. **1877** B. Harte *Story of a Mine* 412 Father Pedro had taken a muchacho foundling for adoption. **1888** 'R. Boldrewood' *Robbery under Arms* II. xi. 190 So the muchacha went back on yer. **1904** Conrad *Nostromo* i. viii. 119 Would not the muchachos of Hernandez like to get hold of this insignificant object..? **1963** *Punch* 23 Oct. 589/3 What we're going on with now, muchachos..is how to catch squid.

muchán, mucharn, varr. Machan.

muchi, var. *moocha.

muchocho, var. *mohoohoo.

muchwhat, *sb.* and *adv.* (Later examples.)

1796 'Tim Bobbin the 2nd' *Plebeian Politics* (1801) 29, I think eawer kese is mitchwhot th' same. **1899** B. W. Green *Word-bk. Virginia Folk-Speech* 246 *Much-what*, nearly; almost. For the most part. 'They are all *much-what*.' **1922** Joyce *Ulysses* 388 It was muchwhat indifferent.

mucification (miūsifikēi·ʃən). *Physiol.* [f. Muc(us + -ification.] Transformation (of epithelial cells) into mucus-secreting cells.

1930 *Proc. R. Soc. Edin.* L. 88 Mucification..is typical of the second phase of the genital cycle; it always accompanies true or pseudo-pregnancy. **1957** *Brit. Jrnl. Radiol.* XXX. 243/1 The intermediate cells did not cornify but instead differentiated into mucus-secreting cells, the mucification being most marked on the third and fourth days after the end of treatment. **1973** *Nature* 9 Feb. 398/1 Progesterone administered for 9 weeks..to..3-month-old mice induced a strong intracellular reaction of mucification along the vaginal mucosa.

So **mu·cify** *v. intr.*, to undergo mucification; **mu·cified** *ppl. a.*; **mu·cifying** *ppl. a.*

1930 *Proc. R. Soc. Edin.* L. 95 On sectioning, the wall was found to be thickened and lined with a mucified epithelium. **1941** *Endocrinology* XXVIII. 314, 72 to 96 hours are required for the mucified vagina to become fully cornified after the influence of the corpus luteum hormone has been removed. **1962** *Brit. Jrnl. Cancer* XVI. 648 Castration and progestational hormones have a mucifying effect on the cervico-vaginal epithelium of mice. **1973** *Nature* 9 Feb. 398/1 It is well known that ambivalent cells of the vaginal squamous epithelium..mucify when progesterone acts synergically with oestrogen.

mucilage. 1. c. (Earlier example.)

1859 *La Crosse* (Wisconsin) *Daily Union* 15 Oct. 3/3 Mucilage, sealing wax, playing cards.

mucin. Substitute for def.: **a.** Mucus. **b.** Any of the glycoproteins found in the mucus of various animals. (Add further examples.)

1905 *Chambers's Jrnl.* Jan. 84/2 The mucine which issues from the body of the garden snail. **1938** *Cold Spring Harbor Symp. Quant. Biol.* VI. 91/2 The term 'mucin' is entirely avoided. It should be used only in a physiological sense to denote a viscous fluid of secretory origin. **1966** Schultze & Heremans *Molecular Biol. Human Proteins* I. iv. iv. 769 Salivary mucins are most abundant in sublingual saliva. *Ibid.*, The main sublingual mucin, at least in cattle, differs in composition from submaxillary mucin, as it contains less sialic acid and much more hexose and fucose than the latter product.

muck, *sb.*^{1} **1. d.** Add def.: Soil material consisting of decayed plant remains, similar to peat; in mod. use distinguished from peat by being more thoroughly decomposed (and usu. darker in colour) and having a higher mineral content. (Earlier and later examples.)

1832 H. L. Barnum *Farmer's Own Bk.* 35 On tearing up some handfuls of the ground, this is well blackened of course, and little is thought of looking for the sub-soil, as those invariably do, who have once been deceived by black muck, and these soft beds of leaves. **1839** J. Buel *Farmer's Compan.* ix. 73 Peat earth, or swamp muck, is vegetable food, in an insoluble state, and requires only such a chemical change as shall render it soluable, to convert it into an active manure. **1849** E. Chamberlain *Indiana Gazetteer* (ed. 3) ii. 305 The soil is a black muck, based on clay. **1859** S. W. Johnson *Ess. Peat, Muck, & Commercial Manures* 63 Some intelligent farmers call the surface layers of their swamps, which are loose and light in texture, swamp muck, and to the bottom layers, which are more compact and often serviceable as fuel, they apply the term peat. **1889** *Century Mag.* Dec. 217/2 The soil proved to be a wet muck, overlaying sand with boulders. **1897** G. P. Merrill *Treat. Rocks* ii. ii. 149 An impure variety [of peat] containing a considerable quantity of siliceous sand, and locally known as 'muck', is used as a fertilizer for 'multching' throughout New England. **1928** *Bull. Amer. Soil Survey Assoc.* IX. 44 Peat has been defined as containing over 65% of organic matter and Muck as containing from 25% to 65%. It does not appear desirable to place such definite limits of composition but rather to base the distinction mainly on the degree of decomposition and secondarily on the content of mineral material. **1930** C. E. Thorne *Maintenance Soil Fertility* ii. 15 Beds of muck and peat..are found on the watershed and in some of the river valleys. *Ibid.*, The distinction between peat and muck is that in these bogs the lower strata, being continually covered with water, may still consist of only partially decomposed fibrous matter, brownish in color, while the surface that has been exposed to the air has more completely decayed, losing its fibrous texture and becoming darker in color. Muck and peat, therefore, may be compared to soil and subsoil. **1943** Millar & Turk *Fund. Soil Sci.* ii. 63 When these organic deposits are yet in the crude, fibrous state, they are frequently designated as peat, but when decay has broken down the plant tissues until the material has something of a loamy consistency, it is called muck. **1971** *Gloss. Soil Sci. Terms* (Soil Sci. Soc. Amer.) 11/2 *Muck*, highly decomposed organic material in which the original plant parts are not recognizable.

3. b. (Earlier and later examples.)

1882 'F. Anstey' *Vice Versâ* xvi. 282 'If you think the tea worth racing like that for, I don't,' said Coggs viciously; 'it's muck.' **1928** W. Ponder *Clara Butt* 138 All I can say is..sing 'em muck! It's all they can understand. **1943** K. Tennant *Ride on Stranger* iv. 34 He had a habit of greeting any new dish with a loud: 'What's this muck?' **1959** I. & P. Opie *Lore & Lang. Schoolch.* ix. 162 School dinners are 'muck', 'pig swill', 'poison', 'slops',.. and Y.M.C.A. (Yesterday's Muck Cooked Again). **1967** *Listener* 20 Apr. 524/3 Is this the kind of muck which the National Film Theatre is going to bring to Norwich?

d. Waste material that is removed during mining or civil engineering operations; *spec.* (*U.S.*), surface material that overlies a placer deposit.

1883 W. S. Gresley *Gloss. Terms Coal Mining* 171 *Muck* (Y[orkshire]), see *Dirt* [='clay, bind, or other useless rubbish produced in mining, and which accidentally is sent out of the pit mixed with the coal']. **1897** J. W. Leonard *Gold Fields Klondike* 180 The top 'muck', as it is called by the miners, is, when thawed out, about two-thirds water and one-third sediment. **1908** J. M. MacLaren *Gold* ii. 484 The low-level gravels..lie on decomposed schist bed-rock, and are covered by black frozen 'muck' (silt, vegetable matter, and ice, the last forming 75 per cent. of the mass) of a thickness of 2 to 30 feet. **1914** G. Atherton *Perch of Devil* i. 148 His..hands were white with 'muck', a mixture of rock-dust and water. **1959** *Times* 16 Nov. 8/5 About 400,000 tons of spoil (or muck as the mining engineer calls it) will be brought to the surface. **1960** *Vancouver Sun* 4 June 2/4, 150 vertical feet of muck in the stope above had settled gently down over the mule, the string of cars—and our only way out.

e. Phrases. *as muck*: used emphatically following adj.; *like muck*: used negatively with a statement.

1935 J. C. Masterman *Fate cannot harm Me* viii. 154 He would be out any ball and poor old George would be as sick as muck. **1952** [see *drunk *sb.*^{2} 1].

f. *R.A.F. slang.* (*a*) Hostile anti-aircraft fire; (*b*) (see quot. 1943).

1940 Michie & Graebner *Their Finest Hour* iv. 65, I climbed to 12,000 feet, circling along the outside of the searchlights and all the muck [gunfire] that was coming up. **1943** Hunt & Pringle *Service Slang* 46 *Muck*, dirty weather.

g. *Lord Muck*: see *lord *sb.* 14 c. So *Lady Muck*.

1957 I. Cross *God Boy* (1958) xxii. 190 She sat there, sipping away at her tea like Lady Muck. **1966** 'L. Lane' *ABZ of Scouse* 61 Lady Muck of Muck Hall: A woman who puts on airs, has a condescending manner and is regarded as excessively conceited.

4. b. *to make a muck of*, to do (something) badly; to spoil or bungle.

1906 D. F. T. Coke *Bending of Twig* xiv. 222 There'll be nobody much there, so it doesn't matter if you *do* make a muck of it. **1936** R. Lehmann *Weather in Streets* iii. i. 265, I would like to paint her, but..would make a muck of it. **1947** 'N. Shute' *Chequer Board* iv. 94 He's made a bloody muck o' things, the way I knew he would. **1970** Y. Carter *Mr. Campion's Falcon* xxi. 159 I've made a muck of it. What the hell can I do now?

5. *muck-headed* adj.; (sense 1 d) *muck-bed*, *-land*, *-swamp*; **muck-crome, -crone, -croom** [Crome, cromb *sb.*], a dung-fork; **muck-pot** ?*nonce-wd.* = **muck-spout*; **muck-shifter,** a man who or a machine which removes earth; **muck-shoveller,** (*a*) a farmhand employed in collecting or distributing dung; (*b*) *Austral. slang* (see quot. 1945); so *muck-shovelling* vbl. sb.; **muck soil,** a soil composed of muck (sense 1 d) (see quot. 1928^1); **muck-spout** *dial.* and *slang*, one who uses obscene language or who displays a salacious mentality; **muck-spreader,** a machine for spreading dung; **muck-spreading** *vbl. sb.*, the action of distributing dung over a field; **muck-sweat** (later examples).

1872 A. de Morgan *Budget of Paradoxes* 163, I certainly think the words would never have come together except in this way:—I, quart pyx, who fling muck beds. **1823** E. Moor *Suffolk Words & Phr.* 239 A crooked fork for pulling the article out of carts on to heaps we call muck-crome. **1846** Muck-croom [see Crome, cromb *sb.*]. **1969** G. E. Evans *Farm & Village* x. 111, I got an old *muck-crone* (a fork with curved tines), and I used to put this muck-crone under the door and draw a slab of linseed cake through. **1971** *Country Life* 11 Mar. 533/1, I got out o' me punt and stuck a muck-crome, a muck-rake in it [*sc.* a stranded sturgeon]. **1909** H. G. Wells *Ann Veronica* xiii. 272 'Ass!' he went on, still warming. 'Muck-headed moral ass! I ought to have done anything.' **1847** W. Bacon *Let.* 24 Nov. in *Rep. Comm. Patents 1847* (U.S.) (1848) 358 They have been planted the present year, on deep muck lands. **1936** *Sun* (Baltimore) 17 Jan. 3/4 Shattered remnants of the transcontinental airliner which plunged seventeen persons to death in a nearby muckland. **1950** *Daily Progress* (Charlottesville, Virginia) 24 July 1/2 It plunged into the pine-spotted muckland. **1938** Dylan Thomas *Let.* 6 July (1966) 205 It's a crack at young Georgians,..intellectual muckpots leaning on a theory, post-surrealists and orgasmists. **1880** D. W. Barrett *Life & Work among Navvies* ii. ii. 43 Navvies themselves speak of one another as muck-shifters, or thick-legs. **1961** *Engineering* 9 June 797 Designed to work under rugged off-highway conditions as a muck-shifter. **1967** G. F. Fiennes *I tried to run a Railway* vi. 63 Muck shifting is easy nowadays. **1970** *Daily Tel.* 5 Nov. 13/6 The whole 'muck-shifting' industry changing the shape of the landscape is experimenting all the time with bigger, and sometimes better, machines. **1945** Baker *Austral. Lang.* v. 98

Muck-shoveller, a tin miner. **1960** *Farmer & Stockbreeder* 23 Feb. 105/3 Of these 32 [farmers], 21 simply wanted a muck-shoveller. **1928** *Bull. Amer. Soil Survey Assoc.* IX. 44 *Muck soil*, soil composed of thoroughly decomposed organic material, with a considerable amount of mineral soil material, finely divided and with few fibrous remains. **1928** F. E. BEAR *Theory & Pract. in Use of Fertilizers* xvii. 280 If..more potash can be used to advantage..the ..analysis might well be changed in that direction. This may be the case with muck soils. **1970** *Jrnl. Econ. Entomol.* LXIII. 1283/1 Studies were made to determine the fate of ^{14}C-labeled aldicarb in sand, loam, clay, and muck soils maintained at different moisture levels. *a* **1825** R. FORBY *Vocab. E. Anglia* (1830) II. 223 *Muck-spout*, one who is at once very loquacious and very foul-mouthed. **1916** D. H. LAWRENCE *Let. c* 15 Dec. (1962) 492 And Murry..is a little muck-spout. **1961** *Guardian* 30 May 5/1 In the more developed countries everything from washing machines to muck-spreaders has been mechanised. **1975** *Listener* 29 May 702/2 Gardeners going berserk with mechanical diggers and muck-spreaders. **1903** *Eng. Dial. Dict.* IV. 187/1 [Nottinghamshire] A farmer on being asked in Court when the event occurred, said, 'It wor abaout three weeks afore muck spreading.' **1948** *Brit. Birds* XLI. 358 This is paralleled by the Faeroe farmers' belief that muck-spreading should be completed before the coming of the White Wagtail. **1960** *Farmer & Stockbreeder* 8 Mar. 74/1 An interesting attachment designed for fitting to conventional tipping trailers was this p.t.o.-driven muck-spreading device. **1870** *Rep. Comm. Agric. 1869* (U.S. Dept. Agric.) 270 The soil was..black mud or muck swamp, five feet deep, containing a mixture of sand. **1879** BROWNING *Dramatic Idyls* 115 Publican Black Ned Bratts and Tabby his big wife too: Both in a muck-sweat. **1922** JOYCE *Ulysses* 515 I'm all of a mucksweat. **1953** R. LEHMANN *Echoing Grove* 48 Must have a shower. I've been in a muck sweat all day. **1972** J. PORTER *Meddler & her Murder* i. 10 There's nothing for you to get into a muck sweat about.

muck, *v.* Add: **1.** Also freq. with *out*, and occas. with *off*, and *absol.*

1851 Muck out [in Dict.]. **1914** KIPLING *Divers. Creatures* (1917) 52, I was obligin' Jim that evenin' muckin' out his pig-pen. **1921** [see *CLEANER a]. **1950** *Landfall* XIII. 16 They always want one [*sc.* a cup of tea] after they've finished mucking out. **1958** J. BETJEMAN *Coll. Poems* 252 She can muck out the stables and clean Her snaffle and saddle and bridle. **1952** R. S. SUMMERHAYS *Elem. Riding* (ed. 3) iii. 23 The deep bedding has now been 'mucked out'. **1966** M. TORRIE *Heavy as Lead* xiv. 169 Sir G. had told me special to muck out the pigs. **1967** C. WATSON *Lonelyheart 4122* ix. 91 He would have to be strong, energetic, used to stud work and willing to muck out. **1973** J. BURROWS *Like an Evening Gone* ii. 30 I've mucked out the henhouses.

4. (Later example.) Also, to mix *up*.

1909 H. G. WELLS *Tono-Bungay* III. i. 279 It's a festering mass of earths and heavy metals... There they are, mucked up together in a sort of rotting sand. **1916** 'BOYD CABLE' *Action Front* 109 If it [*sc.* a shell] had fell in the trench, now, and mucked up half a dozen men, there'd have been something to squeal about. **1949** 'J. TEY' *Brat Farrar* xi. 85 You don't want that dazzling outfit of yours to be mucked up.

b. (Earlier and later examples with *up*; later examples with *about.*)

1886 in H. BAUMANN *Londinismen*. **1922** 'R. CROMPTON' *Just—William* viii. 161 You seem to have pretty well mucked it up. **1935** 'N. BLAKE' *Question of Proof* i. 17 Old Simmie will probably muck up the stop-watch like he did last year. **1946** K. TENNANT *Lost Haven* (1947) xi. 180 This is a real good stove... She isn't mucked about and cleaned, and that's what makes her a good stove. **1959** 'M. CRONIN' *Dead & Done With* vi. 99 'Lena could muck it all up.' 'I don't think she will, so long as she's scared about herself.' **1959** ANON. *Streetwalker* iii. 58 Muck me about and you're out. **1966** *Listener* 17 Nov. 719/2, I was delighted to see Mr Bernard Levin..heading a review.. '*Much Ado About Nothing*, by William Shakespeare, the text mucked about by Robert Graves'. **1971** *Nature* 7 May 65/3 Let us not muck up our language, lest we also muddle our minds. **1973** *Nation Rev.* (Melbourne) 31 Aug. 1446/6 But she went and mucked it all up with her television debut.

5. (Earlier and later examples.) Freq. with *with*, and also with *around*.

1856 H. PHILLIPS *Jrnl.* 26 Sept. (typescript) 41 Cutting firewood and mucking about the house. **1918** H. G. WELLS *Joan & Peter* xi. 391 They had long bicycle rides together... They 'mucked about' with Baker's boat. *Ibid.* xiii. 659 He would be climbing trees with Joan, 'mucking about' in the boats with Joan. **1928** D. L. SAYERS *Lord Peter views Body* 276 His art..[is] the one thing a genuine artist won't muck about with. **1935** N. MARSH *Enter Murderer* vii. 90 'E was a-mucking arahnd Trixie. **1946** K. TENNANT *Lost Haven* (1947) x. 152 We been mucking about and mucking about, and got nowhere. **1957** P. MANSFIELD *Final Exposure* ix. 121 Why don't you haul him in instead of mucking around asking me bloody silly questions? **1959** 'M. NEVILLE' *Sweet Night for Murder* xiii. 128 They get fed up with their own wives and have to go mucking about with someone new. **1959** *Engineering* 13 Mar. 343/3 Those Americans are mucking about with their journal titles again. **1963** *Truth* (Wellington, N.Z.) 9 July (*heading*) Don't muck about, Mac. **1973** *Times* 12 Dec. 2/8 The other girls..wanted to muck around with boys.

b. *to muck in with*: to share army rations with; to consort or co-operate with; so *to muck in*, (*a*) to eat; (*b*) to help, to 'pull one's weight', to participate. Also, *to muck in to*.

1919 *Athenæum* 1 Aug. 695/2 'To muck in' with anyone is to share rations with him. **1929** F. MANNING *Middle Parts of Fortune* I. v. 105 'Martlow and I have mucked in together, since you've been in the orderly-room.' 'Well, the three of us can muck in together now,' said Bourne. *a* **1935** T. E. LAWRENCE *Mint* (1955) I. viii. 30 'Muck in', we did, yet still looked lean. **1936** F. RICHARDS *Old-Soldier Sahib* xiii. 223 For nine months he had been mucking-in with a youngster who had only arrived in the country the previous winter. **1942** G. KERSH *Nine Lives Bill Nelson* v. 26 The Army was hell because I couldn't muck in there. **1942** WODEHOUSE *Money in Bank* (1946) iii. 26 When we came to visit here, I understood that that room was reserved for I and my husband. Nobody ever mentioned that we were supposed to muck in with the butler. **1952** M. LASKI *Village* vi. 112 We all muck in together and the jobs get done in no time. **1958** J. CANNAN *And be a Villain* iv. 89 I'm delighted to muck in, but I'm afraid I'm too conscientious for Mrs Langley. **1959** *Encounter* July 27/1 They want men who will muck in as colleagues. **1966** F. SHAW et al. *Lern Yerself Scouse* 42 *Muck in, yer at yer granny's!* Bon Appetit! **1967** *Guardian* 21 Apr. 7/2 Prince Charles..will be able to muck in to all the student activities. **1970** *Times* 13 Feb. 10/8 The company..all muck in, take small or big parts. **1974** J. POPE-HENNESSY *R. L. Stevenson* vi. 128 His readiness to muck in with any of his working-class fellows on boat or train.

c. To search for coal on a coal-tip, a beach, etc.

1935 A. J. CRONIN *Stars look Down* I. ii. 22 'It's my duff,' Softley kept whimpering... 'Aw mucked for it, aw did, for my man to hev a fire.'

6. Euphemistically (chiefly in written work) = *FUCK *v.*

1929 R. ALDINGTON *Death of Hero* x. 376 Spree be mukked—one of you * * fetch his rifle and muckin' near copped me. **1940** E. HEMINGWAY *For whom Bell Tolls* xxii. 273 He may have just mucked off. *Ibid.* xxxv. 369 You're just mucked..you're mucked for good. *Ibid.*, Muck my grandfather and muck this whole treacherous muck-faced mucking country. **1941** *Penguin New Writing* II. 90 'I shall report you to the foreman.' 'Muck the foreman!' I said. **1946** D. HAMSON *We fell among Greeks* vii. 85 Another song I used to perpetrate..was 'I'm a man that's in trouble and sorrow.'..'Muck it,..that's a good song, Denys, let's have it again.' **1949** C. FRY *Lady's not for Burning* 92 Youse only has to say muck off, and I goes, wivout argument. **1950** E. HEMINGWAY *Across River* vii. 58 Now muck off..try and have some fun. **1974** R. ADAMS *Shardik* xxxvi. 300 Come on, now,..you'll get nothing here, so just muck off, there's a good lad.

mu·ck-about. [f. the phrase *to muck about* (MUCK *v.* 5).] **a.** A person who 'mucks about'. **b.** The action of 'mucking about'.

1933 H. G. WELLS *Bulpington of Blup* ix. 353 Rich old women in Paris—middle-aged muck-abouts—art shops. **1968** L. BERG *Risinghill* 122 The boys..were restless, ready for a 'lark' or a 'muck-about' or a 'giggle'.

muck-a-muck (mʊ·kămʊk). [Chinook jargon.] **1.** Used by or with reference to Amerindians of western North America: food.

1847 J. PALMER *Jrnl. Trav. Rocky Mts.* 150 Muck-a-muck, Provisions, eat. **1852** *Oregonian* (Portland) 25 Dec. 2/3 The aborigine..'put' for the settlement with a sort of legs-do-your-duty-for-the-body-is-in-danger resolution for his *muckamuck*. **1863** *Norfolk Reformer* (Simcoe, Ontario) 8 Jan. 3/1 On arriving as far back as Lytton or Lilooet, there was employment..and 'muca muc', as the Indian name implies. **1880** *Forest & Stream* 11 Nov. 285/2 We should have to come ashore and have some 'muck-a-muck'. **1895** H. S. SOMERSET *Land of Muskeg* 167 Yes, all kinds of muck-a-muck at McLeod; jam, cake, biscuits.. plenty plenty muck-a-muck, you see. **1915** R. D. CUMMING *Skookum Chuck Fables* 18 Perhaps he had bought all his luxuries on jaw-bone from one store while he paid cash for his muck-a-muck in another. **1963** R. D. SYMONS *Many Trails* 74 Hi-ya tillicum... You plenty muck-a-muck stop.

2. *fig.* Shortening of *HIGH-MUCK-A-MUCK.

1912 KIPLING *Songs from Bks.* (1913) 159 Shaman, Ju-ju or Angekok, Minister, Mukamuk, Bonze. **1914** *Dialect Notes* IV. 113 *Squeegee*, a person of importance; muckamuck:—used derisively. **1966** H. KANE *Conceal & Disguise* iv. 28 Cape Ulrich was for the muckamucks, the coupon-clippers, the expense account lads, the heavy rich.

mucka-mucka (mʊ·kămʊkă). [Native name.] A name used in Guyana for the large perennial herb, *Caladium arborescens*, native to tropical America and belonging to the family Araceæ. Also *attrib.*

1918 C. W. BEEBE *Jungle Peace* (1919) vi. 123 Mucka-mucka was here and there in the foreground. **1955** *Times* 16 July 7/6 They perched, feeding on the leaves of mucka-mucka, a giant variety of arum. *Ibid.* 23 July 7/6, I sat alone and very still in a primitive dug-out after edging it into the heart of a mucka-mucka plant (*Caladium arborescens*) and tying the boat to one of its thick stems. **1958** J. CAREW *Black Midas* iii. 35 The weeds, the wild cane, the lilies, the mucka-mucka were all still under the burning sun.

mucked, *ppl. a.* Add: **mucked-about,** spoiled, subjected to unnecessary interference; **mucked-up,** bungled, spoiled.

1930 M. ALLINGHAM *Mystery Mile* xxvii. 273, I should be very interested to know how you intend to get away with your reputation all pure and virgie and our Albert's poor little mucked-up corpse lying about. **1930** V. PALMER *Passage* I. iii. 29 It was a mucked-up job. **1966** J. BINGHAM *Double Agent* iv. 52, I don't remember what I ate. Some mucked-about dish of stew.

mucker, *sb.*^{1} Restrict † *Obs.* to senses in Dict. and add: **3.** Euphemistically (chiefly in written work) = *FUCKER. Cf. *MUCK *v.* 6.

1929 R. ALDINGTON *Death of Hero* III. i. 263 Does the old mucker think we're going to run away? **1942** *Penguin New Writing* XV. 19 Suddenly old Bob says: 'I lost my kit, Cockney.' Silly mucker! **1952** M. TRIPP *Faith is Windsock* ii. 38, I thought there was twelve hundred muckers in this raid—where's t' other eleven hundred and ninety-nine?

mucker, *sb.*^{2} Restrict *slang* to sense in Dict. and add later examples.

1914 GALSWORTHY *Mob* I. 8 You're riding for a fall and a godless mucker it'll be. **1916** 'TAFFRAIL' *Pincher Martin* xiv. 270 'Minefield! I thought the one that got you was a floater.' 'Don't you believe it... You can thank your lucky stars you didn't bump one.'.. 'I'm glad we didn't come a mucker—jolly glad!' **1928** GALSWORTHY *Swan Song* I. vi. 41 But for you, old girl, I might have gone a holy mucker myself. **1943** M. AKLOM *Of Social Significance* in *Best One-Act Plays 1942–43* 166 You know what the Guardianship of Infants Act is. They passed it to prevent legal infants coming matrimonial muckers at the age of indiscretion. **1974** G. MITCHELL *Javelin for Jonah* xii. 154, I like old Jimmy boy and I wouldn't want to see him come a mucker.

2. One who, or a machine which, removes muck (*MUCK *sb.*^{1} 3 d).

1899 *Harper's Weekly* 20 May 498/1 [The] Company.. paid $3. for miners and $2.50 for 'muckers', or underground laborers. **1908** [see *JUMBO 1 c]. **1916** C. SANDBURG *Chicago Poems* 21 Twenty men stand watching the muckers. Stabbing the sides of the ditch..for the new gas mains. **1923** 'B. M. BOWER' *Parowan Bonanza* viii. 94 Now you've staked yourself to the luxury of a mucker, you can leave him in charge. **1927** *Dialect Notes* V. 456 *Mucker*, a shovel man. **1931** 'D. STIFF' *Milk & Honey Route* ii. 24 The rawjawed teameos and muckers..who built that railroad got little or no hard cash. **1956** *Fatal Accidents* (Ontario Dept. Mines) Apr. 2 The mucker was hoisted clear of the bottom timber by 10 feet, to where it might normally have been anchored. **1965** S. G. LAWRENCE *40 Yrs. on Yukon Telegraph* iv. 23 A mucker's duties are simply to shovel and wheel out rock, and in those days on a wheelbarrow.

mucker, *sb.*^{3} For *U.S. slang* read orig. *U.S. slang*, and add further examples.

1900 ADE *Fables in Slang* 108 They were not Muckers; they were Nice Boys. **1905** D. G. PHILLIPS *Plum Tree* 35 He used to class himself and me together as 'us gentlemen', in contrast to 'them muckers', meaning my colleagues. **1920** F. SCOTT FITZGERALD *This Side of Paradise* 175 Why is it that the pick of young Englishmen from Oxford and Cambridge go into politics and in the USA we leave it to the muckers? **1936** A. HUXLEY *Olive Tree* 182 There are the refined and aristocratic Muckers in East Prussia, with their ritual of exhibitionism and long-drawn sexual confessions.

† **c.** A youthful townsman, as distinct from a member of a college; a young 'townee'. *Obs. U.S. university slang.*

1893 W. K. POST *Harvard Stories* 75 On the first corner of Harvard Street were stationed three or four boys (the occasionally useful Cambridge muckers) employed as vedettes. **1899** A. H. QUINN *Pennsylvania Stories* 168 Del went through his pockets to the great joy of a limited assortment of muckers who were following. **1948** [see *FÜHRER].

2. [Perh. f. *MUCK *v.* 5 b.] A companion, friend, 'mate'. *slang.*

1947 J. BERTRAM *Shadow of War* VII. v. 239 What's the griff, mucker? **1954** 'S. CARNEGIE' *Noble Purpose* 21 McLeod..was a small dark man of lugubrious appearance. His mucker Reed was fat, fair and cherubic. **1963** 'R. ERSKINE' *Passion Flowers in Italy* v. 56 Well, my father was at Magdalen, but all my muckers seemed to be flocking to the House, so I thought I might as well go there too. **1971** B. W. ALDISS *Soldier Erect* 112 It isn't Taff. It's a mucker of mine down in M/T. Jock McGuffie. He's a real cure. **1972** M. WOODHOUSE *Mama Doll* ix. 120 'Is that my old mucker?' said Bottle. 'None other,' I said.

3. With advbs.: **mucker-in,** one who 'mucks in' (see *MUCK *v.* 5 b); **mucker-upper,** a bungler.

1942 A. P. JEPHCOTT *Girls growing Up* iv. 83 When a girl first goes to a factory she may be a 'mucker in' and have to turn her hand to anything. **1972** *Guardian* 18 Feb. 14/1 A raconteur..good value at a gathering where he knows his audience, a mucker-in, a natural wit. **1942** T. RATTIGAN *Flare Path* I. 9 She's a proper mucker-upper though—she'll go and catch the wrong bus.

mucker, *v.*^{2} Add: **b.** Also with *away*: to squander.

1928 H. G. WELLS *Way World is Going* 15 The Western Powers of Europe..muckered away an enormous amount of war gear and money in supporting crazy 'white hopes' against the nascent new thing in Russia.

muckerdom (mʊ·kərdəm). [f. *MUCKER *sb.*^{3} + -DOM.] The world of muckers or 'townees'; muckers collectively. So **mu·ckerish** *a.*, befitting or characteristic of a mucker; **mu·ckerishly** *adv.*; **mu·ckerism,** the characteristic conduct of muckers; unsportsmanlike behaviour.

1893 W. K. POST *Harvard Stories* 254 In five minutes all the best talent in muckerdom will be there with tin-cans and stones. **1904** *Public Ledger* (Philadelphia) 4 June 6 If a player on the opponent's side happened to make a muff or misplay, cheering by the side benefited was.., in the elegant language of the campus, 'muckerish'. **1906** *Outing* Jan. 494/1 This year there was caterwauling and shouting by cadets individually and muckerishly that was so unusual and unpleasant as to make one discredit one's ears. *Ibid.* 494/2 We hope it does not mean an entrance of muckerism into our Army and Navy games. **1952** C. STEAD *People with Dogs* 330 It's muckerism, saying we all grunt in monosyllables!

muck-heap. Add: (Later examples.) So **mu·ck-heapy** *adj.*

1881 *Punch* 29 Oct. 193/1 We sincerely hope that..His Grace [of Bedford] drove up Wellington Street, made at once for Mud-Salad Market, and..examined the streets 'all round and about that quarter', whose greasy, muck-heapy state is still a disgrace to the Metropolis in general. **1938** 'N. SHUTE' *Ruined City* vi. 112 One didn't finance a muck-heap of a country like Laevatia for fun. **1946** *Coast to Coast 1945* 177 Somebody counted fourteen bottles on old Gormie's muck-heap.

mucking, *vbl. sb.* Add: **2. b.** Also *mucking-about.*

1937 PARTRIDGE *Dict. Slang* 539/2 *Mucking-about*,..an intimate fondling: low (mostly costers'). **1969** *Listener* 27 Feb. 264/3 'Knowledge is conceived in the hot womb of Violence,' said Auden in his poem on Oxford: perhaps he knew what he was doing when he omitted the phrase in his last mucking-about with the piece.

3. Also with *out.* The action of removing muck, esp. dung from a stable or waste material from a mine.

1641 [see MUCK *v.* 1]. **1840** *How to buy a Horse* viii. 160 This Augæan labor is termed 'mucking out'. *Ibid.*, In fact, such an operation as 'mucking out' should, in a well-regulated stable, be an impossibility, for there never should be any 'muck' to take away. **1918** H. L. CARR in R. Peele *Mining Engineers' Handbk.* vii. 260 Mucking, or loading broken rock into hoisting conveyance, occupies 50% of shaft-sinking time. **1932** E. WILSON *Devil take Hindmost* xxi. 218 The men, who had been displaced by new mucking machines (mucking is cleaning out the tunnel after the blast), were to be transferred. **1935** *Mining Mag.* LII. 55/2 Two buckets were used in mucking, one of which was being filled while the other was being hoisted. **1957** *Times* 2 July (Agric. Suppl.) p. vi/3 In a modern fattening house we have also to make provision for minimum labour requirements in feeding, mucking out and weighing. **1960** *New Scientist* 7 Jan. 38/1 'Mucking out', as the removal of the rock fragments is termed, is thus simplified and speeded up. **1961** *Encycl. Brit.* XV. 543/2 The method of mucking is reflected in the choice and design of the haulage system. **1973** K. GILES *File on Death* v. 147 Old Joe keeps the rain channel free on the duck-pond side... Old Joe does a thorough job at mucking-out.

mu·cking, *ppl. a.* [f. MUCK *v.* + -ING^{2}.] Euphemistically (chiefly in written work) = *FUCKING ppl. a. Cf. *MUCK *v.* 6. Also as quasi-*adv.*

1929 R. ALDINGTON *Death of Hero* III. x. 375 What the muckin' hell are you doing, down there? **1933** H. G. WELLS *Bulpington of Blup* vi. 237 Don't be a mucking fool! *Ibid.* 241 Do you think we want to sit round telling ghost stories in this mucking hole? **1935** E. HEMINGWAY *Green Hills Afr.* xiii. 277 And if I ever hit you I'll break your mucking jaw. **1942** *Penguin New Writing* XV. 19 I'll miss the silly mucker... Poor old Bob. Went down with his mucking duffle. **1946** D. HAMSON *We fell among Greeks* v. 61 By Christ, it's that mucking dog. **1974** R. ADAMS *Shardik* xxxvi. 301 You'd better lend him a hand... We'll be 'alf the mucking night else. *Ibid.* xlv. 363 The first man peered in his turn. 'He mucking is, too,' he said. 'Aren't you?'

muckluck (mʌ·klʌk). Also **maclock, mucluc, muklek, mukluk.** [Eskimo.] A high boot made of sealskin, canvas, etc. Also *attrib.*

1868 F. WHYMPER *Trav. Alaska* 136 Their boots vary in length, and in the material used for the sides, but all have soles of 'maclock', or sealskin, with the hair removed. **1901** *Pall Mall Mag.* Jan. 56 We stop on our way..and buy a pair of mucklucks or Esquimaux seal boots. They are water-tight, clumsy, evil-smelling, [etc.]. **1904** E. ROBINS *Magnetic North* I. 51 Nothing like muck-lucks with a wisp of straw inside for this country. *Ibid.* 176 Stretching out his feet, very comfortable in their straw-lined mucklucks. **1913** R. W. SERVICE *Rhymes of Rolling Stone* 118 Then it's down to chewing mucluc, to the water you can *eat*, To fish you bolt with nose held in your hand. **1924** *Chambers's Jrnl.* Jan. 41/1 He was habited..in anorak and skin breeches and mukluks. **1947** *Chicago Tribune* 11 Dec. 20/3 He was presented with..a pair of mukluk boots made to order for Paul Bunyan. **1962** W. NOYCE *To Unknown Mountain* v. 54 Unable to fit his vast feet into any boots but a pair of canvas mucklucks. **1972** *Daily Tel.* (Colour Suppl.) 8 Dec. 10/4 His legs were now swathed almost to the knee in the white sealskin mukluks that are standard issue in the [Canadian National Parks] Service. **1973** *Observer* 29 Apr. 34/8 His mukleks—the Eskimo moccasins with the hard, sealskin soles.

muckna (mʌ·kna). *India* and *Ceylon.* [Hind., f. Skr. *matkuṇa* (among various senses) an elephant without tusks.] A male elephant without tusks, or one having only rudimentary tusks.

c **1780** R. LINDSAY in A. W. C. Lindsay *Lives of Lindsays* (1849) III. 194 The *muckna*, or elephant born without teeth, is thought the best. **1848** tr. *W. Hoffmeister's Trav. Ceylon & India* vi. 207 Of the herd of elephants,..the largest, whose height does not much exceed nine feet, is a '*Muckua*' [sic] *i.e.*, an elephant with short, straight tusks, which never grow. **1878** G. P. SANDERSON *Thirteen Yrs. among Wild Beasts India* vi. 66 Mucknas breed in the herds, and the peculiarity is not hereditary nor transmitted. **1886** G. YULE in Yule & Burnell *Hobson-Jobson* 454/1, I can distinctly call to mind 6 mucknas that I had ..out of 30 or 40 elephants that passed through my hands. **1890** S. W. BAKER *Wild Beasts* I. vi. 226 A tiger sprang from the grass, and seized a large muckna (tuskless male) by the trunk.

mucko (mʌ·ko). *slang.* [? f. MUCK *sb.*^{1} 3 + *-O suffix.] (See quots.)

1937 PARTRIDGE *Dict. Slang* 539/2 *Mucko*, orderly man: military. **1943** BAKER *Dict. Austral. Slang* (ed. 3) 52 *Mucko*, a sailor. (R.A.N. slang.) **1961** PARTRIDGE *Dict. Slang* Suppl. 1191/1 *Mucko*,..esp. a man detailed to serve food to troops aboard ship. **1964** *Punch* 6 May 659/1 No general had..had till then..a mucko–chummo relationship with his men.

muck-rake, *sb.* (Later *attrib.* and *fig.* examples.)

1906 *Sun* (N.Y.) 12 Apr. 8/3 On Saturday the President is to pronounce the formal address at the grave of the Man With the Muck Rake... The Muck Rakers worked merrily for a time in their own bright sunshine, and an unthinking populace applauded their performance. **1906** T. ROOSEVELT in *Cincinnati Enquirer* 15 Apr. 4/4 The men with the muck-rakes are often indispensable to the well-being of society; but only if they know when to stop raking the muck. *c* **1926** 'MIXER' *Transport Workers' Song Bk.* 18 Then you start your muckrake scandel [*sic*] And good men you dare defame. **1968** *Listener* 28 Nov. 726/2 Frank Harris deplored the dismal fate of Sophia in a Paris boarding-house,..regretting that Bennett..preferred to give her a muck rake instead of a soul.

muck-rake, *v. intr.* Delete *nonce-wd.* and add later *fig.* examples.

1954 *Amer. Scholar* XXIII. 421 McCarthy would enjoy himself if he could muckrake in our barnyard. **1970** *Guardian* 6 Mar. 8/3 They need no prompting to register complaints, muckrake among the police, petition for redress against indecencies.

2. *trans.* [Back-formation f. *MUCK-RAKER.] To subject (powerful persons or institutions) to allegations of corruption or other illegal or scandalous behaviour; to discover and publish (such scandals); to examine (political districts) so as to determine the extent of corruption. So **muck-raked** *ppl. a. U.S.*

1910 *N.Y. Even. Post* 10 Dec. 8 Their knowledge of how it feels to be a muck-raked millionaire. **1913** J. LONDON *Let.* 26 June (1966) 388, I..muck-rake the powers that be from one end of the world to the other. **1931** *Time & Tide* 22 Aug. 991/2 Steffens was more successful with his experiments when he was muckraking America's big cities. **1943** M. FLAVIN *Journey in Dark* 193 The country has been muckraked from one end to the other. **1973** G. JENKINS *Cleft of Stars* vii. 86, I couldn't bring myself to muck-rake details of the guard's murder.

mu·ck-raker. [-ER^{1}.] A person who uses a muck-rake. In literary use only *fig.* †**a.** A miser. *Obs.* (Cf. MUCKWORM 2 a.) **b.** One who seeks out and publishes scandals, allegations of corruption, etc., about prominent people, esp. public officials. orig. *U.S.* **c.** A prurient inquirer into private morals; a writer of pornography.

The source of this figurative use in b is T. Roosevelt's speech (itself reminiscent of Bunyan) cited s.v. *MUCK-RAKE *sb.*

1601 A. DENT *Plaine Mans Path-Way to Heaven* 102 We see the world is full of such pinch-pennies, that wil let nothing goe, except it bee wrung from them perforce, as a key out of Hercules hande. These gripple muck-rakers, had as leeue part with their bloud, as with their goods. **1906** S. FORD *Shorty McCabe* xi. 233 That's the style you live in when..you've got to be a top-notch grafter that the muck-rakers ain't jungled yet. **1914** R. BROOKE *Let.* Apr. (1968) 579 Damn it, we're not muck-rakers or German novelists. **1921** G. B. SHAW *Back to Methuselah* IV. I. 159, I leave them to the chumps and noodles, to the blockheads and the muckrakers. **1950** G. BARKER *True Confession* iii. 16 And the muckrakers I have known. **1973** *Guardian* 26 May 1/3 He is a sanctimonious creep..a muck raker. **1974** *Times* 9 May 21/4 In its origins the term 'muckraking' described a tradition of American journalism around the turn of the century which was committed to the exposure of trusts and monopolies and of corruption..; the Muckrakers..were responsible for progressive reforms.

muck-raking, *ppl. a.* (Later examples.)

1951 M. MCLUHAN *Mech. Bride* (1967) 7/1 This exciting suspicion about personal plots and dastard motives everywhere led to the popularity of the muckraking press. **1972** J. PHILIPS *Vanishing Senator* (1973) II. i. 48 A muck-raking journalist who's gotten rich on other people's misfortunes.

mu·ck-raking, *vbl. sb.* [f. MUCK-RAKE *sb.* and *v.* + -ING^{1}.] The employing of a muck-rake, in fig. senses. Also *concr.*, the results of psychological or social inquiries.

1911 *N.Y. Even. Post* 25 Jan. 14 The same articles brought President Roosevelt to the defence of the Senate, and led him to apply the word 'muck-raking' to the literature of higher exposure. **1919** 'W. N. P. BARBELLION' *Jrnl. Disappointed Man* 211 Any eminently 'right-minded' *Times* or *Spectator* reader will ask: 'Who in Faith's name is interested in your introspective muck-rakings?' **1931** L. STEFFENS *Autobiogr.* I. xiii. 105 My first essay into muck-raking cost me nothing. **1959** [see *DEMAGOGUERY]. **1973** 'M. INNES' *Appleby's Answer* xv. 128 Don't imagine I have the slightest wish to be in on your muck-raking.

mu·ck-up. *slang.* [f. phr. *to muck up* (*MUCK *v.* 4).] A mixing or confusing; a confused situation; a blunder, a fiasco, a mess, a muddle; *Austral.* (see quot. 1945).

1930 *Daily Express* 9 Sept. 8/7 The muck-up of society ..is almost complete. **1934** N. MARSH *Man lay Dead* xii. 217 Only Bathgate's prints on the electric switch and a muck-up of everybody's on the bannister. **1939** N. MONSARRAT *This is Schoolroom* I. i. 33 The muck-up the Labour people had left us in, in 1931. **1942** E. WAUGH *Put out More Flags* iii. 209 You seem to have made a pretty good muck-up. **1945** BAKER *Austral. Lang.* xv. 267 Frigg-up or muck-up, a confusion, a row or argument. **1957** W. CAMP *Prospects of Love* III. iii. 159 Mummy..making me do beastly shorthand in case I make a muck-up of the Latin. **1963** B. JAMES *Austral. Short Stories* 46 The 'muck-up' in 4B died down at this announcement. **1967** K. GILES *Death & Mr Prettyman* iii. 72 Old Jabeez made his usual muck-up. **1972** C. DRUMMOND *Death at Bar* ii. 60 The food was probably fry-ups or nasty little continental muck-ups.

mucky, *a.* Add: **1. d.** More widely: grimy, grubby, horrid.

1872 H. T. DUNN *Let.* 10 Sept. in G. Pedrick *Life with Rossetti* (1964) xiii. 121 'The Beatrice' had been got out of the mucky state in which it was, & now looks a very good copy. **1942** *Tee Emm* (Air Ministry) II. 88 Lack of power through mucky plugs..will immediately be seen on the Rev. counter. **1959** I. & P. OPIE *Lore & Lang. Schoolch.* ix. 161 Juvenile repugnance continues to be expressed by the old standbys..mouldy, mucky, nasty, no fair, no good, orrid (usual spelling).

2. (Further U.S. examples.)

1840 C. F. HOFFMAN *Greyslaer* I. I. v. 61 He had laid the logs right down on a piece of deep, mucky soil, made up of old roots, rotten leaves, [etc.]. **1874** *Rep. Vermont Board Agric.* II. 548, I have about five acres of mucky meadow that was mostly covered with alders.

mu·cky-muck. *N. Amer. slang.* [redupl. MUCKY *a.*, after *MUCK-A-MUCK.] = *MUCK-A-MUCK 2. Also *attrib.*

1934 H. MILLER *Tropic of Cancer* 194 One of the big mucky-mucks from the other side of the water had decided to make economies. **1941** E. P. O'DONNELL *Great Big Doorstep* iv. 61 The Governor and the big mucky-mucks from New York with the oil company, was passing close to the levee. **1968** 'E. MCBAIN' *Fuzz* iv. 60 That big mucky-muck got shot. *Ibid.* 61 All them big mucky-muck doctors. **1968** *Globe & Mail* (Toronto) 13 Feb. 27/1 Orpen was always let out at the members' enclosure, but he never sat with the mucky-mucks.

mucluc, var. *MUCKLUCK.

muco-. Add: Also used in *Biochem.* (with broader meaning). **mucoly·tic** *a.*, able to disperse or decompose mucus or mucopolysaccharides; **mucope·ptide** *Biochem.* = *MUREIN; **mucoperio·steum** *Anat.*, a periosteum closely associated with a mucous membrane; **mucopro·tein** *Biochem.*, any of a group of compounds (some of which occur in mucus and other body fluids) whose molecules consist of protein or polypeptides in combination with mucopolysaccharides; **mu:coviscido·sis** *Path.* [VISCID *a.* + -OSIS], a congenital metabolic disorder, usually causing early death, in which exocrine glands (such as the pancreas) secrete very viscid mucus, which accumulates and blocks the passageways of the body; also called *cystic fibrosis* (*of the pancreas*), *fibrocystic disease* (*of the pancreas*).

1939 *Nature* 9 Dec. 977/2 (*heading*) A mucolytic enzyme in testis extracts. **1940** [see *HYALURONIDASE]. **1953** *Jrnl. Soc. Leather Trades' Chemists* XXXVII. 80 It should be possible to produce pelt by removing the mucoids with mucolytic enzymes. **1971** *S. Afr. Med. Jrnl.* XLV. 948/1 In patients with acute obstructive airway disease pancreatic dornase and acetyl-L-cysteine (Airbron) showed excellent mucolytic activity. **1959** MANDELSTAM & ROGERS in *Biochem. Jrnl.* LXXII. 655/1 This class of substances from cell walls, which will be referred to as mucopeptides, constitutes a high proportion of the hot trichloroacetic acid-insoluble material from bacteria. **1962** *Jrnl. Exper. Med.* CXV. 60 A rigid mucopeptide structure, composed of *N*-acetylglucosamine, *N*-acetylmuramic acid, and alanine, lysine, glutamic acid, and glycine, has been identified in the cell wall of each of these three groups of streptococci. **1972** Mucopeptide [see *MUREIN]. **1903** DORLAND *Med. Dict.* (ed. 3) 419/1 Mucoperiosteum. **1906** *Practitioner* Nov. 712 Should the carious tooth be in the upper jaw, the pus may travel down alongside of the fang of the tooth, around the free border of the bone, make its way through the muco-periosteum on the outer side, and then point as a gumboil. **1974** W. J. BANKS *Histol.* xix. 205/3 Because of the intimate relationship of the mucosa to the underlying bone, these structures are referred to collectively as a mucoperiosteum. **1925** *Jrnl. Biol. Chem.* LXV. 700 The carbohydrate radicle isolated from the mucoproteins of the mucus of *Helix aspersa* and *Helix pomatia* belongs to the group of mucoitin sulfuric acid. **1962** D. G. COGAN in A. Pirie *Lens Metabolism Rel. Cataract* 291 The capsule surrounding the lens..stains heavily with periodic acid Schiff (indicating more neutral mucoprotein than most tissues). **1968** Mucoprotein [see *glycoprotein* s.v. *GLYCO-]. **1971** *S. Afr. Med. Jrnl.* XLV. 948/1 Normal human bronchial mucus is a semiviscid substance composed almost entirely of mucoprotein and mucopolysaccharide fibres. **1945** S. FARBER in *Jrnl. Michigan State Med. Soc.* XLIV. 592/2 Until the etiological factors are defined and for the purposes of present convenience only a purely descriptive term suggested by the physical character of the material produced by the mucous glands in this disease may be employed—*muco-viscidosis.* **1949** *New Eng. Jrnl. Med.* 4 Aug. 185 (*heading*) Aureomycin therapy in the pulmonary involvement of pancreatic fibrosis (mucoviscidosis). **1966**

WRIGHT & SYMMERS *Systemic Path.* I. xxiii. 692/1 Farber has suggested that the disease [*sc.* fibrocystic disease of the pancreas] is a manifestation of a generalized abnormality of mucus secretion, for which he proposed the term 'mucoviscidosis'. **1973** L. C. CAREY *Pancreas* ix. 181/2 In mucovisoidosis, steatorrhea is usually present.

mucoid (miū·koid), *sb. Biochem.* [a. G. *mucoid*, f. *mucin* MUCIN + *-oid* -OID.] A mucin-like substance; esp. = *mucoprotein* s.v. *MUCO-.

1900 GIES & CUTTER in *Amer. Jrnl. Physiol.* III. p. vi, We believe that continued investigation will show that the diffirences among the mucins, mucoids, and chondroproteids are not as great as their varying physical proproties and behavior have suggested. **1901** *Ibid.* VI. 155 (*heading*) The composition of tendon mucoid. *Ibid.*, Following Cohnheim's suggestion..we use the term 'mucoid', instead of the previously accepted 'mucin', to designate this substance. We agree with Cohnheim that.. the term 'mucin' may be best applied to the glucoproteids elaborated by true secretory cells, and the term 'mucoid' to similar substances in the tissues. **1945** *Adv. Protein Chem.* II. 250 As mucoids we define substances which contain a mucopolysaccharide in firm chemical union with a peptide, where the hexosamine content is greater than 4 per cent. **1953** [see *mucolytic* adj. s.v. *MUCO-]. **1964** A. WHITE et al. *Princ. Biochem.* (ed. 3) viii. 122 The protein components of mucoids or mucoproteins are combined with large amounts (more than 4 per cent) of carbohydrate, measured as hexosamine. **1967** D. A. L. DAVIES in D. M. Weir *Handbk. Exper. Immunol.* xi. 405 Ovarian cysts are a rich source of mucoids and a classical source of blood-group mucopolysaccharides. **1974** *Nature* 20 Dec. 711/2 Cervical mucus is a heterogeneous secretion, the most important constituent of which is a hydrogel made of glycoproteic mucoids.

mucoitin (miŭkōu·ĭtin). *Biochem.* [f. MUC(IN + *-oitin*, after *CHONDROITIN.] A supposed mucopolysaccharide, now generally considered to be a mixture, occurring in combination with sulphuric acid in the mucin of pigs' stomachs, the cornea, and elsewhere. So *mucoitinsulphuric acid.*

1916 LEVENE & LÓPEZ-SUÁREZ in *Jrnl. Biol. Chem.* XXV. 513 Further work on mucoitin sulfuric acid (as we propose to name this substance) is now in progress. **1925** P. A. LEVENE *Hexosamines* II. iii. 85 A considerable part of the sulphuric acid radicle had been removed in the process of preparation, so that it was possible to determine the properties of mucoitin and of mucoitin sulphuric acid in the same sample. **1925** [see *CHONDROITIN]. **1964** BRIMACOMBE & WEBBER *Mucopolysaccharides* vi. 142 It seems likely that the material originally designated as mucoitin sulphate contained hyaluronic acid admixed with sulphated mucopolysaccharides containing 2-amino-2-deoxy-D-glucose residues. **1967** *Chem. Abstr.* LXVI. 9649/1 The chondroitinsulfuric acid and mucoitinsulfuric acid contents were higher in the umbilical cord and myxoid chondroma.

mucopolysaccharide (miū:kopǫlisæ·kărəid). *Biochem.* [f. MUCO- + *POLYSACCHARIDE.] Any of a group of polysaccharides whose molecules contain amino-sugar residues (*spec.* hexosamine residues) and are often found in complexes with protein molecules, and which include as important examples heparin, hyaluronic acid, keratosulphate, and the blood-group substances.

1938 K. MEYER in *Cold Spring Harbor Symp. Quant. Biol.* VI. 91/1 The mucopolysaccharides of our terminology were formerly included as mucins and as mucoids in the group of conjugated proteins. They occur in nature either as free polysaccharides or as protein salts. **1947** *Physiol. Rev.* XXVII. 335 Hyaluronic acid is a mucopolysaccharide acid which in animal tissues seems to bind water in interstitial spaces. It further holds cells together in a jelly-like matrix and serves as a lubricant and shock-absorber in joints. **1963** R. W. JEANLOZ in Florkin & Stotz *Comprehensive Biochem.* V. vii. 262 Two groups of substances, which in the past had been described under the name of mucopolysaccharide, namely the glycoproteins and the glycolipids, will be discussed in other chapters. **1967** [see *MUCOID *sb.*]. **1971** J. Z. YOUNG *Introd. Study Man* xl. 584 There is polymorphic variation in certain mucopolysaccharide constituents of the red cells of the blood.

mucormycosis (miū:kǫɹməikōu·sis). *Path.* Pl. **-mycoses.** [f. MUCOR + MYCOSIS.] = *PHYCOMYCOSIS.

1918 STEDMAN *Med. Dict.* (ed. 5) 621/2 *Mucormycosis*, a mycosis caused by a fungus or mould of the family *Mucoraceæ*, one of the slime fungi. **1943** *Bull. Johns Hopkins Hosp.* LXXIII. 405 (*heading*) Mucormycosis of the central nervous system. *Ibid.*, These mucormycoses of animals..may be transferred to humans. **1957** *Jrnl. Amer. Med. Assoc.* 9 Mar. 806/2 Rhizopus, rather than Mucor, appears to be the usual cause of human mucormycosis. **1965** WILSON & PLUNKETT *Fungous Dis. Man* xv. 190 Although the term 'mucormycosis' has long been used synonymously with the newer name 'phycomycosis', species of the genus *Mucor* are not often involved. **1974** PASSMORE & ROBSON *Compan. Med. Stud.* III. I. xii. 94/1 Cerebral mucormycosis presents with drowsiness or stupor.

mud, *sb.*[1] Add: **1. e.** *transf.* A 'mud-student' (see Dict., sense 5).

1906 C. G. GREY *Sequel to Story Official Life* 9 Some of the men from across Tweed were very kind to us muds.

f. A liquid (commonly a suspension of clay and other substances in water) that is pumped down the inside of the drill pipe and up the outside during the drilling of an oil or gas well, so as to remove the drill cuttings, cool and lubricate the bit, support the sides of the hole against caving, and prevent the leakage into it of gas or water from the formations encountered; also (with *a* and *pl.*), a kind of mud. Orig. called **mud-laden fluid* and later **mud fluid.*

[**1901** J. G. MCINTOSH tr. *Neuberger & Noalhat's Technol. Petroleum* xxix. 379 It is..by causing a current of water to circulate continually from the surface of the ground to the bottom of the well, and again from the bottom to the surface, that the mud is continually carried away. **1914** *Times Fuel No.* 104/2 Water and heavy mud forced along the column of the pipe..keep the bit clean and bring the detritus up to the surface.] **1922** D. T. DAY *Handbk. Petroleum Industry* I. 249 A column of pure water exerts a pressure of 43 pounds per square inch for each 100 feet in height but with mud-laden fluid this pressure may be increased to 50 or 55 pounds... This lateral pressure forces the mud into sands and porous structures, stabilizes caving formations and effectively shuts off water, gas or oil. **1926** E. R. LILLEY *Oil Industry* vii. 174 In the rotary system mud is introduced continuously and the control of gas seldom becomes a serious problem. **1938** J. G. CROWTHER *About Petroleum* ix. 73 An artificial mud is preferable, as it is more viscous and does not allow the debris to settle. Drilling-mud serves other important functions. **1957** VAN DER HAVE & VERVER *Petroleum & its Products* ii. 59 Three types of drilling fluid are at present in use: water-base muds, emulsion-type muds and oil-base 'muds'. **1970** W. G. ROBERTS *Quest for Oil* iv. 45 A great deal of research continues into the making of suitable muds. **1970** *Daily Colonist* (Victoria, B.C.) 31 Dec. 3/5 Workers cut off a blazing oil well with heavy 'drilling mud'. **1974** *Daily Mail* 3 Apr. 23/2 The mud men ..supervise the texture of the mud in the giant tanks that are reservoirs for the special lubricant which is pumped into the ocean bed.

2. † **c.** A fool. *slang. Obs.*

1708 *Memoirs Right Villanous John Hall* 22 *Mud*, a Fool, or Thick skull Fellow. **1886** in H. BAUMANN *Londinismen.*

d. Opium. *U.S. slang.*

1922 *Dialect Notes* V. 182 *Mud*, obviously so-named from the color and consistency of the drug. **1926** *Flynn's* 16 Jan. 638/2 Some stiffs uses mud but coke don't need any jabbin', cookin' or flops. **1935** *Amer. Speech* X. 17/1 *Hop*, opium. Modern mud, O., pen-yen, tar. **1955** *U.S. Senate Hearings* (1956) VIII. 4161 Opium in the underworld is referred to by various names. For instance, 'mud', 'tar', 'black stuff', 'hop', 'pen yan' and 'yen pocks'. **1974** *Publishers Weekly* 11 Feb. 60/1 Western efforts to open up trade with China in the early to mid-19th century were largely unscrupulous, inspired by the immense profits to be made from 'mud' (opium).

e. Coffee. *slang.*

1925 G. H. MULLIN *Adventures Scholar Tramp* iii. 34, I received punk (bread) and a cup of mud (black coffee) or—to use the familiar hobo expression for the combination—duffer. **1931** 'D. STIFF' *Milk & Honey Route* 210 *Mud*, strong coffee mixed with weak milk. **1945** L. SHELLY *Jive Talk Dict.* 15/1 *Mud*, coffee or a homely person. **1957** 'N. CULOTTA' *They're a Weird Mob* (1958) ix. 135 Got another cuppa mud, Joe?

3. *to fling mud* (earlier U.S. example); (*as*) *sick as mud*: depressed, exasperated, furious; (*here's*) *mud in your eye*: a toast, 'good health!'; *one's name is mud*: one is discredited, held in low esteem, ineffective, unlucky [cf. 2 c, above]; hence, passing into senses suggested by Dict. 2 a, b: one is regarded as a pariah, untrustworthy, with the worst reputation; so in allusive phrases; *up to mud* (Austral.): see quot. 1945.

1823 'J. BEE' *Slang* 122 *Mud*—a stupid twaddling fellow. 'And his name is mud!' ejaculated upon the conclusion of a silly oration, or of a *leader* in the Courier. **1880** 'MARK TWAIN' *Tramp Abroad* 187 These people fling mud at that elegant Englishman..and make fun of him. **1887** *Lantern* (New Orleans) 16 Apr. 2/1 Zeller wants to be Recorder..but his name is mud. **1906** E. DYSON *Fact'ry 'Ands* viii. 92 D'yeh mean to tell me how Hoggy's let you loose agin after you gettin' glorious in his dry-goods, 'n' makin' his name mud all up 'n' down ther town? **1916** C. J. DENNIS *Songs Sentimental Bloke* 13 I'm crook; me name is Mud; I've done me dash. **1927** H. V. MORTON *In Search of England* iii. 60 'Here's mud in your eye!' said one of the modern pilgrims, tossing down his martini. **1929** J. P. MCEVOY *Hollywood Girl* ix. 148 Well, I hope when I'm through I'll have sense enough to know it. Mud in your eye! **1930** K. BRUSH *Young Man of Manhattan* vii. 87 'Well,' somebody said, 'here's mud in your eye.' **1933** *Bulletin* (Sydney) 1 Nov. 42/2 Still, men today are mostly up to mud. **1935** M. DE LA ROCHE *Young Renny* xviii. 152 She hates the thought of his staying on as much as we do. She's as sick as mud about it. **1938** S. V. BENÉT *Thirteen o' Clock* 335 Mud in your eye! **1942** M. DICKENS *One Pair of Feet* vii. 108 Nurse Dickens had no idea of hospital etiquette... Nurse Dickens was too opinionated. Nurse D.'s name, in short, was Mud. **1945** BAKER *Austral. Lang.* vi. 128 *Up to mud, up to tripe,*..describe things that are bad, disliked or out of order. **1949** WODEHOUSE *Mating Season* xxiii. 198 'Skin off your nose, Jeeves.' 'Mud in your eye, sir, if I may use the expression.' **1954** —— *Jeeves & Feudal Spirit* viii. 72 He's as sick as mud about it. He moons broodingly to and fro, looking like Hamlet. **1956** J. SYMONS *Paper Chase* x. 73 Here's mud in your eye, Eileen. **1957** D. ROBINS *Noble One* xviii. 169 If tha' doan't put ring on finger shortly, my lad, tha' name will be mud in Mountaindale. **1973** W. M. DUNCAN *Big Timer* vii. 51 Riordan his name is and so far as I'm concerned from now on it's Mud.

4. a. *mud cabin, floor* (later *fig.* example), *-hut, -land, -puddle, -rush, -scatter, -shoal, -side, -slide, -trap*; **b.** *mud-caked, -chinked, -choked, -greasy, -layered, -moulded, -splashed, -splattered, -stained* adjs.; **c.** *mud-bottomed, -floored, -heaped* adjs.; **d.** *mud-couched, -mattressed, -stuck* adjs.; **e.** objective, as *mud-feeding* adj.; **f.** similative, as *mud-grey* adj.

1908 HARDY *Dynasts* III. VII. iii. 492 Where there is a mud-bottomed stream, the Lasne. **1949** C. LONGFIELD *Dragonflies Brit. Isles* (ed. 2) 132 It inhabits, in England, slow-running, mud-bottomed streams. **1780** A. YOUNG *Tour in Ireland* I. 102 This town appears exceedingly flourishing..yet 40 years ago..there were nothing but mud cabbins in it. **1829** J. MACTAGGART *Three Yrs. Canada* II. 243 It is a singular fact..with the Irish, that if they can get a *mud-cabin*, they will never think of building one of wood. **1922** JOYCE *Ulysses* 324 Their mudcabins and their shielings by the roadside were laid low by the batteringram. **1912** W. DEEPING *Sincerity* xxxix. 281 Grassless fields, mud-caked ponds, and empty wells. **1961** *Times* 11 Jan. 16/4 Their mud-caked forwards battled back into the Eastern Counties' 25. **1946** W. FAULKNER *Portable Faulkner* App. 737 Jefferson Mississippi was one long rambling onestorey mudchinked log building housing the Chickasaw Agent and his tradingpost store. **1922** JOYCE *Ulysses* 98 Past beds of reeds, over slime, mud-choked bottles, carrion dogs. **1936** W. FAULKNER *Absalom, Absalom!* ii. 44 It was that same Akers who had blundered onto the mudcouched negro five years ago. **1926** J. S. HUXLEY *Ess. Pop. Sci.* xvii. 209 The endostyle degenerates together with the rest of the mud-feeding apparatus. **1960** KOESTLER *Lotus & Robot* I. i. 28 It had brought..a mud-floor of starved refugees, increased poverty, land hunger, and the threat of civil war. **1951** —— *Age of Longing* I. vi. 108 All men did that who had.. met in mud-floored rooms before the Great Change. **1921** D. H. LAWRENCE *Sea & Sardinia* ii. 44 Badly paved, mud-greasy..road. **1923** —— *Birds, Beasts & Flowers* 169 You meet a huge and mud-grey elephant. **1935** W. EMPSON *Poems* 26 Empty, mudheaped, through which the alluvial scheme Flows temporary as the modern world. **1803** J. DAVIS *Trav. U.S.* 3, I have entered with equal interest the mud-hut of the negro, and the log-house of the planter. **1858** T. VIELÉ *Following Drum* 125 Half-a-dozen mud-huts neatly thatched with straw..presented a study for an artist. **1941** L. HELLMAN *Watch on Rhine* III. 166 In every town..and every mud hut in the world, there is always a man who..will fight to make a good world. **1971** *Daily Nation* (Nairobi) 10 Apr. 10 The expression traditional housing is a misnomer... The brick homes in the area will have nothing in common with the traditional mud huts. *a* **1865** SMYTH *Sailor's Word-Bk.* (1867) 487 *Mud-lands*, the extensive marshes left dry by the retiring tide in estuaries and river mouths. **1927** *Daily Tel.* 22 Nov. 14/1 This scheme..involves the reclamation of over 400 acres of mudland. **1930** BLUNDEN *Poems* 145 Mud-layered cobble-stones. **1960** S. PLATH *Colossus* (1967) 48 Mud-mattressed under the sign of the hag In a clench of blood, the sleep-talking virgin Gibbets..the moon's man. **1906** HARDY *Dynasts* II. v. viii. 288 We are the only phantoms now abroad On this mud-moulded ball! *a* **1841** W. P. HAWES *Sporting Scenes* (1842) I. 183 The thawing mud-puddles. **1912** KIPLING *Songs from Books* (1913) 76 As a frog shows in a mud-puddle. **1928** KIPLING *Limits & Renewals* (1932) 3 The advance of education and the standard of living would submerge all mind-marks in one mudrush of standardised reading-matter. **1919** J. MASEFIELD *Reynard* 78 Mud-scatters chased him as he scudded. **1842** *Knickerbocker* XX. 309 [He] knew a great deal more about the inconveniences of groping about among mud-shoals in the dark. **1923** G. B. SHAW *Let.* 5 Apr. in *To a Young Actress* (1960) 42, I am here at the mudside (the Bristol channel can hardly be called sea) to recuperate. **1921** *Daily Colonist* (Victoria, B.C.) 29 Oct. 1/7 Mud slides also add to the danger of operating trains until repairs can be effected. **1928** BLUNDEN *Undertones of War* iv. 35 That dugout was a deep one, with a steep mud-slide of an entrance. **1969** *Courier Mail* (Brisbane) 27 Jan. 4/8 Mud-slides buried sleepers alive..as Southern California was deluged by rain. **1908** *Daily Chron.* 28 Sept. 7/4 He sat his mud-splashed saddle, motionless under the moon. **1922** JOYCE *Ulysses* 33 The mudsplashed brakes. **1930** J. DOS PASSOS *42nd Parallel* I. 5 Mudsplattered trouserlegs. *a* **1922** H. LAWSON in *Penguin Bk. Austral. Ballads* (1964) 144 And mud-stained, wet, and weary, He goes by rock and tree. **1908** HARDY *Dynasts* III. VII. iv. 493 His horse got mud-stuck in a new-ploughed plot. **1970** *Motoring Which?* July 93/2 Both cars had areas which may well give trouble in a couple of years' time—mud traps around the headlamp cowls of the 3-litre, [etc.].

5. mud balance, a balance designed for measuring the density of drilling mud; **mud-bar** [BAR *sb.*[1] 15], a bank of mud in a river or off an estuary or a shore; **mud-barge,** a barge transporting dredged mud; **mud-bath,** also *transf.* and *fig.*; **mud box** *Naut.*, a box containing a coarse filter used to trap sediment in bilge-water; **mud-boy** (see quot.); **mud-brick,** brick that is made with mud; also *attrib.*; **mud-chute,** a chute down which mud is discharged (in example, *fig.*); **mud-clerk** *U.S.*, an assistant to the purser on a river steamer; **mud-cone** (earlier example); **mud-crack,** a crack formed in drying mud; **mud engineer,** a person responsible for the quality and supply of drilling mud; **mud fever,** a disease of horses, in which patches of the skin on their feet become inflamed and swollen; **mud flap,** a piece of rubber, metal, etc., hung behind each of the wheels of a vehicle to prevent mud, etc., from splashing; mud-flat, (*b*) a mud-bank in a river

which is not tidal; (*c*) *N.Z.* (see quot. 1947); **mud-flinger**, a person who hurls abuse [from *to fling mud* (MUD *sb.*[1] 3)]; so **mud-flinging** *vbl. sb.*; **mud-flow**, a (fluid or hardened) stream or avalanche of mud, e.g. one consisting of soil made fluid by excessive water, one produced by a mud volcano, or a lahar; also, the flow or motion of such a stream; **mud fluid** = *MUD *sb.*[1] 1 f; **mud flush**, a flush by means of drilling mud; **mudguarded** *a.*, provided with mudguards; **mud hog** = *mud pump* below; † **mud-laden fluid** = *MUD *sb.*[1] 1 f; **mud-lighter** [LIGHTER *sb.*[1]], a barge for transporting mud; **mud-line**, the line on the sea-bed in front of a coast-line which represents the upper limit at which wave action allows mud to settle permanently on the bottom; **mud logging**, examination of the mud (sense *1 f) coming out of a bore-hole for signs of oil or gas or other indications of the strata being drilled; so **mud logger**, a person responsible for this; **mud-lump** (earlier example); **mud-mask, -pack**, a preparation of fuller's earth applied to the face as a beauty treatment; so **mud-mask** *v. trans.*, to treat with a mud-mask; **mud pie**, also *attrib.* and *fig.*; **mud pilot** (earlier, *fig.*, and later examples); so **mud pilotage**; **mud proof** *a.*, impervious to mud; **mud pump**, a pump for circulating mud (sense *1 f) through the drill pipe and up the bore-hole; **mud room** *N.Amer.*, a cloakroom, *spec.* one in which wet or muddy footwear may be left; **mud runner** *U.S.*, a horse which habitually performs well on a wet racecourse; a *MUDDER; **mud-shoe** (see quots.); **mud-show** *arch. slang*, an exhibition or performance held in the open air; so **mud showman**; **mud-sill** (*a*) (earlier Amer. example); (*b*) (later examples); **mud-slinging, -throwing** *vbl. sbs.* (the employment of) abuse, calumny or slander; malevolent gossip; so **mud-sling** *sb.*, **-slinger**; **mud-valve** (U.S. example); **mud volcano**, add further examples and substitute for def.: a mound or cone formed of hardened mud discharged from its centre (usu. of much smaller dimensions than a volcano); also *fig.*; (*b*) *U.S.* = *mud-lump*; **mud wing**, a mudguard, a mud flap.

1960 C. GATLIN *Petroleum Engin.* vi. 70/2 The density of drilling muds is normally measured with a mud balance. **1899** C. J. C. HYNE *Further Adventures Capt. Kettle* i. 10 There was a mud-bar with twenty-four feet, but steamers drawing twenty-seven could scrape over, as the bar was soft. **1906** E. DYSON *Fact'ry 'Ands* xviii. 242 Ther toadstools..was growin'..like mussels on er mudbarge. **1926** W. RUNCIMAN *Collier Brigs* 77 They..took in chalk ballast from the wharves, and occasionally from mud-barges when they could not get a ready turn at the wharves. **1851** J. CHAPMAN *Diary* 26 June in G. S. Haight *Geo. Eliot & J. Chapman* (1940) 184 M[rs] Hennell..thinks ..that..pure monogamy..will only be reached thro' a previous age of general licence! I don't agree with her that such a mud bath is at all necessary. **1856** D. G. ROSSETTI *Let.* 10 Dec. (1965) I. 307 Bath has been a mud-bath ever since I came. **1961** *Times* 12 May 19/2 Mr. Beckett's anti-metaphysical mudbath. **1971** *Sunday Nation* (Nairobi) 11 Apr. 5/1 The remaining cars in the Safari braced themselves for a possible mud bath. **1883** A. E. SEATON *Man. Marine Engin.* xii. 231 Mud boxes. Between the directing box and the pump should be fitted a box with a strainer, which shall intercept such solid matter as would derange the pump valves. **1972** *B.S.I. News* Oct. 28/2 Mudboxes intended for the coarse filtration of bilge water which accumulates in ships' machinery spaces. **1958** *Times* 15 May 14/6 The quality of the mud during drilling operations [for oil] is, therefore, very important, and the mudboy, who is responsible for preparing it, is quite a skilled workman. **1810** Z. M. PIKE *Acct. Expeditions Sources Mississippi* App. II. 7 Houses would be built entirely of mud-brick (like those in New Spain). **1903** *Speaker* 5 Sept. 527/2 The old town being built of mud-brick had vanished. **1934** F. STARK *Valleys of Assassins* I. i. 29 The castle is a mud-brick square with round towers. **1963** M. LAURENCE *Tomorrow-Tamer* 227 Then she was gone, shutting quietly behind her the packing-case door of the mudbrick shanty. **1938** H. G. WELLS *Apropos of Dolores* iv. 211 It is the most awful gabble—but it is nothing more than the inevitable end of this mud-chute called 'history'. **1872** E. EGGLESTON *End of World* xxvi. 171 It was natural enough that the 'mud-clerk' on the old steamboat Iatan should have taken a fancy to the 'striker', as the engineer's apprentice was called. **1912** I. S. COBB *Back Home* 103 Even her two mud clerks, let alone her captain and her pilots, wore uniforms. **1869** 'MARK TWAIN' *Innoc. Abr.* lviii. 632 Groups of mud cones stuck like wasps' nests. **1895** *Funk's Stand. Dict.*, Mud-cracks. **1917** *Jrnl. Geol.* XXV. 135 (*heading*) Some factors affecting the development of mud-cracks. **1968** R. W .FAIRBRIDGE *Encycl. Geomorphol.* 761/1 Mud cracks form largely because of solar radiation. **1970** W. G. ROBERTS *Quest for Oil* iv. 46 The mud engineer and geologist will be examining the mud all the time to find out what sort of rock is being bored. **1975** *Petroleum Rev.* XXIX. 27/3 The toolpusher was ready,..the mud engineers, the experts in every field were ready. **1872** W. WILLIAMS *Princ. & Pract. Vet. Surg.* xxxvii. 623 Mud-fever is occasionally attended with a considerable degree of systemic disturbance. **1901** F. T. BARTON *Vet. Manual* 161 (*heading*) Erythema and Mud-rash. (Mud fever.).. Sometimes there is a slight degree of fever, hence the term 'mud fever'. **1928** *Black's Vet. Dict.* 617/2 Mud fever is the popular name for a variety of erythema that attacks the heels and coronets of horses' feet when these parts are subject to long-continued irritation. **1971** G. W. SERTH *Horse Owner's Guide Common Ailments* vi. 63 Mud fever affects the legs and under the belly. **1963** *Times* 29 Jan. 3/6 Its front wings and front and rear panels are bolted on for easy repair and the car has rubber cushioned over-riders and mud flaps as standard equipment. **1967** *Autocar* 28 Dec. 29/2 Rear mud flaps should be made compulsory in the interest of safety. **1972** *Guardian* 13 Nov. 8/5 The fitting of mud flaps behind the rear wheels should be made compulsory. **1922** H. FOOTNER *Huntress* 134 The only breaks in the endless panorama of cut-banks, mud-flats, willows, and grass were occasional little inlets. **1943** K. TENNANT *Ride on Stranger* ix. 92 The broken grey rocks sloping down to mud flats. **1947** P. NEWTON *Wayleggo* (1949) 154 *Mud-flats*, a high country man's name for down country flats. Heavy land. **1839** THACKERAY *Let.* 1–2 Dec. in A. T. Ritchie *Lett.* (1924) i. 8 Very curious the abuse is of that character. Old Southey is one of the chief mudflingers. **1958** *New Statesman* 22 Feb. 220/2 This latest torrent of mud-flinging was, of course, set off by the letter..from Mr A. H. Milward, Chief Executive of British European Airways. **1964** C. S. LEWIS *Discarded Image* iv. 80 This towering vaunt, this philosophic *panache* which goes beyond mere indifference to mud-flinging and actually courts it, is of Cynic origin. **1901** H. W. MONCKTON in *Q. Jrnl. Geol. Soc.* LVII. 295, I have for several years noted details of landslips in the Drift near Scarborough, and, as in other cases, they may be classed as: (1) Mud-flows. (2) Earth-slips... (3) Falls which, owing to the dryness of the clay, resemble rock-falls. **1902** *Bull. Amer. Mus. Nat. Hist.* XVI. 347 The largest ejected block that we saw was one on the surface of the mud-flow between the rivers Blanche and Sèche and not more than two hundred yards from the sea coast. **1928** *Bull. Geol. Soc. Amer.* XXXIX. 465 (*heading*) Mudflow as a geologic agent in semiarid mountains. **1944** C. A. COTTON *Volcanoes* xiii. 240 The contents of a large crater lake on St Vincent (Antilles) were ejected so as to generate extensive mudflows which rushed down various radial valleys to the sea. *Ibid.* 241 Other destructive mudflows..have been ascribed to the melting of snow and glacier ice by volcanic heat. This has occurred in Iceland. **1963** D. W. & E. E. HUMPHRIES tr. *Termier's Erosion & Sedimentation* x. 206 It is probable that earthquake shocks play an important part in initiating submarine mudflows and it is likely that such processes materially assisted in the filling of oceanic basins. **1970** R. J. SMALL *Study of Landforms* ii. 30 Mud-flows occur in mountain areas after heavy rainfall, in periglacial areas during the thaw season, on the slopes of erupting volcanoes and even in deserts, when a heavily loaded stream-flood is gradually transformed as it loses its water by evaporation and percolation. **1914** HEGGEM & POLLARD *Drilling Wells in Oklahoma by the Mud-Laden Fluid Method* (U.S. Bur. of Mines Techn. Paper No. 68) 23 The mud fluid was then bailed from the inside of the casing and drilling continued. **1921** W. H. JEFFERY *Deep Well Drilling* vii. 240 All this can be prevented by moving the casing as occasion requires, and then the mud fluid will rise uniformly on all sides of the casing and the cuttings will have no chance to pack. **1946** *Mod. Petroleum Technol.* 88 When drilling through porous sands it is often necessary to prepare a mud fluid..which leaves on the walls of the well a thin and impervious sheath which seals the pores. **1949** *Our Industry* (Anglo-Iranian Oil Co. Ltd.) (ed. 2) ii. 32 The next essential operation is to remove by a continuous process the debris formed by the action of drilling; this is accomplished by the use of a mud-flush circulation. **1957** VAN DER HAVE & VERVER *Petroleum & its Products* ii. 59 An accumulation of gas in the mud-flush may lower its density to such an extent that the danger of eruption would increase instead of diminishing. **1923** *Daily Mail* 30 July 6 (Advt.), So well shielded and efficiently mud-guarded that anyone..can ride it in ordinary costume. **1932** *Amer. Speech* VII. 268 Mud-hog. **1939** D. HAGER *Fund. Petroleum Industry* ix. 209 Mud pumps, often called 'mud hogs', are of various sizes. **1914** POLLARD & HEGGEM *Mud-laden Fluid Applied to Well Drilling* (U.S. Bur. of Mines Techn. Paper No. 66) 7 In this paper the term 'mud-laden fluid' is applied to a mixture of water with any clay which will remain suspended in water for a considerable time. **1914** F. A. TALBOT *Oil Conquest of World* iii. 43 In drilling through sand formations mud-laden fluid is used to seal the sides of the borehole temporarily. **1921** W. H. JEFFERY *Deep Well Drilling* vii. 236 Water impregnated with clay, otherwise known as mud laden fluid, is forced by slush pumps down inside the casing,..returning between the casing and the wall of the hole. **1946** *Mod. Petroleum Technol.* 88 The circuit of this mud-laden fluid..begins at the slush-pumps. **1909** *Cent. Dict.* Suppl., Mud-lighter. **1915** W. B. YEATS *Reveries* (1916) 78 He..had nothing to do but work himself into a rage if he saw a mudlighter mismanaged. **1891** *Rep. Sci. Results Voy. H.M.S. Challenger: Deep-Sea Deposits* iii. 185 The greater the extent and depth of the ocean, the greater the depth to which water-movement extends, and consequently the greater is the depth at which the mud-line is formed around the coasts, but the average depth of the mud-line may be taken as approximately about 100 fathoms. *Ibid.* vi. 383 It appears to be most abundant.. in the neighbourhood of what we have termed the mud-ine surrounding continental shores. **1963** D. W. & E. E. HUMPHRIES tr. *Termier's Erosion & Sedimentation* xi. 226 The maximum amounts of organic matter occur in calm waters, either in estuaries (5–15%) or near the edge of the belt of mud which surrounds the land mass, the 'mud line', where the amount is 6%. **1975** *Daily Tel.* 9 Jan. 25 (Advt.), NEC Gas have a limited number of vacancies for experienced Mudloggers and Instrument Technicians with oilfield experience. **1960** C. GATLIN *Petroleum Engin.* xi. 199/1 Continuous mud logging is..an excellent exploratory tool. **1868** *Putnam's Mag.*, May 591/2 *Mud-lumps*, or more properly Mud-volcanoes, have been known to rise to the height of twenty-five feet. **1928** *Daily Express* 16 June 3/4, I suggested that I should like a mud-mask. The assistant appeared to be alarmed. *Ibid.* 22 Dec. 3/5 Faces have been massaged and mud-masked. **1934** M. VERNI *Mod. Beauty Cvlture* iv. 28/2 Fuller's earth is a powdered clay with healing properties. Some forms are called 'clay packs', or 'mud packs', and are used as masks. **1938** L. MACNEICE *Earth Compels* 37 Hot towels for the men, mud packs for the women Will smooth the puckered minutes of your lives. **1971** *New Scientist* 19 Aug. 401/2 The inamorata..wearing a moss-green mud-pack, with hair in rollers. **1927** D. H. LAWRENCE *Mornings in Mexico* 122 The low, square, mud-pie houses. **1958** Mud-pie [see *DRIBBLY *a.*]. **1856** C. NORDHOFF *Merchant Vessel* viii. 94 A Dungeness or *deep-sea* pilot as these are called, in contradistinction to the river men, who are known as mud pilots. **1934** P. H. GODSELL *Arctic Trader* 265 The captains of the whaling vessels always took care to keep between the ice pack and the shore, and for this reason were often contemptuously referred to as 'Mud-Pilots'. **1946** G. MILLAR *Horned Pigeon* xxii. 375 The first guide, a kind of mud-pilot, remained on his bicycle. **1965** R. B. ORAM *Cargo Handling* i. 15 In the port of London, a lesser type of pilot..will take over the ship at the lock from the Trinity House pilot... To indicate his inferior status he is known generally as a mud pilot. **1932** S. G. MCNEIL *In Great Waters* viii. 125, I had to do practically all the mud pilotage myself in the various ports of call. **1897** *Sears, Roebuck Catal.* 255/1 Extra Superfine, strictly rain and mud proof French serge. **1926** E. R. LILLEY *Oil Industry* vi. 137 (*caption*) Duplex slush or mud pumps. **1973** J. W. JENNER in Hobson & Pohl *Mod. Petroleum Technol.* (ed. 4) iv. 115 The heart of the fluid circulating system is the mud pumps. **1950** A. E. BURKE et al. *Archit. & Building Trades Dict.* 212/1 *Mud room*, in building, a small room or entranceway where members of the family remove their muddy overshoes or rubbers before going into any of the other rooms. **1962** F. WILLIAMS *Amer. Invasion* v. 51 The ranch-style houses..with their..sun-rooms, 'bi-level brunch bars', mud rooms [etc.]. **1964** *Calgary Herald* 13 Feb. 16/5 One of the most common places of theft occurrences in the school is in the mud room. **1970** *Globe & Mail* (Toronto) 25 Sept. 36/4 (Advt.), Necessary additions as family room with indoor barbecue,..laundry and mud room..have been architecturally added... **1905** *Evening Sun* (N.Y.) 17 Aug., All the races..were won by the product of stallions that in their day were famous mud runners. **1954** *Mem. Ghost Pine Homesteaders* (Ghost Pine Community Group, Three Hills, Alberta) 119 A chap.. breaking a particularly wet piece of ground, made oval shaped hardwood mud shoes which he fastened to his horses' shoes to keep the horses from miring. **1959** A. HARDY *Fish & Fisheries* xvi. 303 The tractors..will.. have buoyancy tanks so that they are light enough to skim the bottom on their mud-shoes without sinking in. **1969** E. H. PINTO *Treen* 93 Elmwood horse mud shoes, with iron staples,..were used to give a horse better bearing in the cranberry swamps of Wisconsin... Similar devices.. were known as Fen overshoes. **1909** J. R. WARE *Passing Eng.* 178/2 *Mud show*, an agricultural, or other out-door show. **1931** *Amer. Mercury* Nov. 353/2 *Mud show*, the old-time horse-and-wagon circus; now derisive. **1927** K. NICHOLSON *Barker* 150 *Mud showman*, a carnival man. **1685** *Rec. Early Hist. Boston* (1881) VII. 178 The middle of the wall to lie even with northerlie or outward side of the said Simkins Mudsell in the Old Celler. **1935** S. LEWIS *It can't happen Here* xvii. 177 Talking to the dirtiest and tiredest mudsills as warm friend to friend. **1964** *College English* Feb. 333/2 The culturally deprived in our great cities—a more massive social mudsill than the most sanguine dream of Calhoun and other slavocrats ever envisaged, the social converse of Madison Avenue's grey-flanneled dream. **1968** *Times Lit. Suppl.* 4 Apr. 329/3 The mudsill is still Negro, not poor white. **1919** E. POUND *Let.* 1 Feb. (1971) 146 Stings and mud-slings of the ungodly and unco-decorous. **1896** *Advance* (Chicago) 17 Sept. 366 The swarm of caricaturists, libelers and party mud-slingers. **1930** T. S. ELIOT tr. *St.-J. Perse's Anabasis* 27 Instigator of strife and discord! fed on insults and slanders, mudslinger! **1884** *Lisbon* (N. Dakota) *Star* 22 Aug., Campaign lies and mud slinging fail to carry the day. **1914** *National Municipal Rev.* (N.Y.) III. 581 This sweeping provision, if constitutional and enforceable, would have the effect of eliminating 'mud-slinging' in political campaigns, perhaps indeed of revolutionizing campaign methods entirely. **1928** *Sunday Express* 27 May 10/1 The social mud-slinging which gives half society its sole virtuous and intellectual amusement. **1952** R. KNOX *Hidden Stream* xiii. 119 And that something is not affected, really, by all the mud-slinging which starts, among the more embittered kind of Protestants, the moment the sanctity of the Church is mentioned. **1973** J. THOMSON *Death Cap* vii. 98 The accusations..are..not specified, just mud-slinging of a general sort. **1895** W. H. CHAMBLISS *Diary* xxii. 276 They were willing to resort to the most detestable methods of 'mud-throwing'. **1931** *Times Lit. Suppl.* 20 Aug. 633/2 He settles down to protracted mud-throwing with Goodwin Wharton as the target. **1873** 'MARK TWAIN' & WARNER *Gilded Age* 38 The awful thunder of a mud-valve suddenly burst forth. **1868** Mud-volcano [see *mud-lump* above]. **1902** *Ann. Rep. Board of Regents Smithsonian Inst. 1901* 71 Within the region [*sc.* the lower Colorado valley] lie a number of 'mud volcanoes', apparently analogous to the 'mud lumps' of the lower Mississippi. **1914** W. OWEN *Let.* 24 May (1967) 252 My face is certainly satisfactory,..free from whelks and knobs and mud-volcanoes. **1953** *Caribbean Q.* III. II. 80 The mud volcanoes..are caused..by the seepage of natural hydrocarbon gases from underground. They have been given their name because..they erupt intermittently, they extrude flows of 'Mud lava', and they build up cones. **1955** *Bull. Geol. Soc. Amer.* LXVI. 1117/1 One mud volcano on an embankment was particularly instructive. Its cone was 7 or 8 feet in diameter. **1967** K. WILCOXSON *Volcanoes* xv. 158 Mud volcanoes are not true volcanoes at all but have features more in common with hot springs and geysers. **1927** *Daily Express* 9 Sept. 11/3 All the six 1928 models are of improved appearance, with..mudwings which not only look better, but also keep off the mud more efficiently. **1959** *Times* 27 Apr. (Rubber Industry Suppl.) p. vi/1 On many goods and passenger vehicles rubber mud-wings are used.

b. mud cat, substitute for def.: *U.S.* one of several species of catfish found in the Mississippi valley (earlier and later examples); also

fig. and *transf.*, an inhabitant of Mississippi, which was sometimes called the *Mudcat State*; **mud catfish** *U.S.*, the bullhead, *Ameiurus nebulosus* (examples); **mud-dauber,** (*a*) for '*Pelopæus*' substitute '*Sceliphron*' (later examples); (*b*) *U.S.* = **mud swallow*; also *transf.* and *fig.*, a travelling workman; **mud duck** *U.S.*, a domestic duck; **mud dweller,** an animal living in a muddy habitat, esp. a water beetle, *Ilybius fuliginosus*; **mud eel** (earlier example); **mud hopper** = *mud-skipper*; **mud-skipper,** substitute for def.: a small Asian, Australasian, or African fish of the family Periophthalmidæ, which is able to scramble over mud and along tree roots, etc. (later examples); **mud snail,** either of two species of pond snail, *Lymnæa glabra* or *L. truncatula*; **mud swallow** *U.S.*, a North American cliff swallow of the genus *Petrochelidon*, which builds jar-shaped nests of mud; also *attrib.* and *fig.*; **mud trout,** a name used in Newfoundland for the brook trout, *Salvelinus fontinalis*; **mud-turtle** (examples of dial. **mud-turkle**); also *transf.* and *fig.* (examples); so **mud-turtle-shaped** *a.*; **mud wasp** *U.S.*, = *mud dauber* (*a*) in Dict. and Suppl.

1819 D. Thomas *Trav. Western Country* 211 The mud cat is covered with clouded spots, and is a very homely fish. **1872** Schele de Vere *Americanisms* 660 Mississippi is occasionally spoken of humorously as the *Mudcat State*, the inhabitants being quite generally known as Mud-cats. **1883** 'Mark Twain' *Life on Mississippi* liv. 532 He didn't really catch anything but only just one small useless mud-cat. **1935** in Z. N. Hurston *Mules & Men* (1970) I. vii. 159 Not no great big trouts nor mud-cats but li'l perches and brims. **1945** B. A. Botkin *Lay my Burden Down* 27 The next is a mudcat; this kind of a fish likes dark trashy places. **1945** *Chicago Daily News* 16 Aug. 10/7 While we are laying down surrender terms for the Japanese, how about a Declaration on Senator 'Dear Dago' Bilbo, the Mississippi mudcat? **1842** J. E. DeKay *Zool. N.Y.* IV. 187 The Mud Catfish..[is] recognized by the scarified and clouded appearance of its skin. **1964** Mud catfish [see *goujon]. **1866** 'Mark Twain' *Sk. New & Old* (1875) 297 The old mud-dobber tackled the piano, and ran his fingers up and down once or twice. **1899** F. Bergen *Animal & Plant Lore* 34 The building of the mud-daubers, or swallows, on the barn or house is a sign of prosperity to the occupants. **1932** E. Step *Bees, Wasps, Ants* 71 Mud-daubers (*Sceliphron*) of warmer countries..build great clusters of mud cells for their eggs and prey. **1945** H. S. Pearson *Country Flavor* 49 There was often a phoebe's home to explore and dozens of mud daubers' nests. **1963** *Amer. Speech* XXXVIII. 271 Mason: *mud dauber.* **1966** C. Sweeney *Scurrying Bush* v. 76 Mud daubers can be a great nuisance, for they build their nests, stuffed with spiders or caterpillars depending on the species, in any hidden place. **1974** A. Dillard *Pilgrim at Tinker Creek* xii. 214 My life inside the cottage is mostly Tinker Creek and mud dauber wasps. **1857** *Spirit of Times* 26 Sept. 54/2 There is duck of every quality, canvas-back, wood, mud, and various other species. **1903** *Forest & Stream* 27 Feb. 150 They are a cross between the mallard and ordinary mud duck. **1920** E. Pound *Let.* 11 Sept. (1971) 158 If you weren't stupider than a mud-duck you would know that every kick to bad writing is by that much a help for the good. **1952** J. Clegg *Freshwater Life* xiv. 221 The Mud Dweller, *Ilybius fuliginosus*, [is] a bronze-coloured beetle with yellow margins to its wing-cases. **1963** *Times* 19 Jan. 10/6 It [*sc.* the Dublin Bay Prawn] feeds, somewhat indiscriminately like all its kind, on its fellow mud-dwellers. **1823** *Charleston* (S. Carolina) *Courier* 7 Mar. 2/4 The British..fairly chased our militiamen across Broad River, to the huge amazement of the mud eels and cats. **1959** *Listener* 29 Oct. 738/3 The skittering of the mud hoppers, those extraordinary little fish that can climb trees. **1965** *Sunday Mail Mag.* (Brisbane) 21 Nov. 14/1 The mud-hopper belongs to a special group of goby (or small fish) and is notable for its strange eyes and for the stiff fins which it seems to be able to use like limbs. **1957** L. Eiseley *Immense Journey* 58 Of all these fishes the mud-skipper *Periophthalmus* is perhaps the strangest. **1972** *Islander* (Victoria, B.C.) 16 Apr. 4/2 [Queensland] After exploring the mangroves for the amphibious mudskipper fish [etc.]. **1926** A. E. Ellis *Brit. Snails* 111 *L*[*imnæa*] *glabra*..Mud Snail..inhabits ponds and ditches, and frequently lives in places which are left dry in summer. **1972** *Country Life* 2 Mar. 524/3 The damp and muddy slopes where they [*sc.* liver-flukes] can find their next host ..the species of snail called the mud-snail, or..*Lymnaea truncata.* **1873** C. G. Leland *Egyptian Sk.-Bk.* 43 Those curious mud-swallow nests of little villages. **1898** M. Deland *Old Chester Tales* 181 Mud-swallows had built their nests in the corners. **1917** T. G. Pearson *Birds Amer.* III. 84 Cliff Swallow... Barn Swallow; Mud Swallow; Republican Swallow. **1917** *Dialect Notes* IV. 332 *Mud-trout*, the brook-trout. **1969** H. Horwood *Newfoundland* 224 Newfoundland's only native trout..is the speckled brook trout (known locally..as a 'mud trout'). **1884** 'Mark Twain' *Huck. Finn* 69 And so you ain't had no meat nor bread to eat all this time? Why didn't you get mud-turkles? **1909** *Dialect Notes* III. 351 *Mud-turkle*, the mud-turtle: chiefly among the negroes. **1946** *Publ. Amer. Dial. Soc.* vi. 21 *Mud turkle*, a small turtle found in muddy bottoms, in either fresh or salt water. Pamlico. Mainly among Negroes. **1796** *Aurora* (Philadelphia) 17 May (Th.), The crocodile throats of the gentle snappers or mud tortles in the Jersey market. **1873** 'Mark Twain' & Warner *Gilded Age* 48 He's in that pilot-house now, showing those mud-turtles how to hunt for easy water. **1896** *Harper's Mag.* Sept. 527 A mud-turtle of a backsettlement lawyer. **1915** Conrad *Victory* vii. 135 Fancy a mud-turtle like you trying to pass an opinion on a gentleman! **1871** 'Mark Twain' *Screamers* 132 A pickininny, mud-turtle-shaped craft of a schooner. **1824** *Old Colony Memorial* (Plymouth) 6 Mar. (Th.), A sort of would-be dandy; having the bottom of his waist pinched up to the size of a quart pot, and thus resembling in shape what we call a mud wasp. **1861** *Trans. Illinois Agric. Soc.* IV. 338 The common black and yellow mud wasp (*Pelopæus lunatus*) belongs to this group. **1881** *Amer. Naturalist* XV. 443 Baron Osten Sacken..records the breeding of *A*[*rgyramœba*] *cephus*..from the nest of a Texan mud-wasp.

mud, *v.*[1] Add: **2. b.** Also with *off* or *up*. (*a*) *trans.* To seal (porous strata) by causing a layer of mud to be deposited on the sides of a bore-hole. (*b*) *intr.* To become coated in this way. Cf. *mud *sb.*[1] 1 f.

1916 Johnson & Huntley *Princ. Oil & Gas Production* xii. 123 In drilling by the rotary system, usually there is but one size of hole and but one string of casing used, as the sides of the hole are 'mudded up' as drilling proceeds, and caving beds and minor gas and water sands are shut off in this way. **1916** Lewis & McMurray *Use of Mud-Laden Fluid in Oil & Gas Wells* (U.S. Bur. of Mines Bull. 134) 23 When a sand is to be 'mudded off', a comparatively thin mixture is first used. **1921** W. H. Jeffery *Deep Well Drilling* iii. 117 The wire drilling cable now is almost universally used for drilling in deep wet holes and in soft or shale formations that 'mud up'. *Ibid.* xii. 350 The mud fluid under pump pressure has a tendency to 'mud off' an oil or gas producing formation before its paying possibilities may be discovered by the driller. **1924** L. C. Uren *Textbk. Petroleum Production Engin.* ix. 299 It is not always easy to mud an exhausted oil sand, so that it does not continue to absorb fluid. **1926** E. R. Lilley *Oil Industry* vi. 129 Mud fluid is introduced into the hole. This is primarily for the purpose of mudding up the walls of the hole to prevent caving.

‖ **mudalali** (mu·dalali). *India* and *Sri Lanka.* Also **mutalali.** [Marathi, f. *muddal, mudal* capital, principal, stock; cf. Modeliar, and Malayalam *mutalali.*] A proprietor, a businessman, a rich trader.

1855 in H. H. Wilson *Gloss. Judicial & Revenue Terms* 359/1 s.v. *Mutalali.* **1913** J. L. Woolf *Village in Jungle* ii. 31 The fat Sinhalese Mudalali, Kodikarage Allis Appu, had supplied grain and curry stuffs on the same terms. **1971** *Ceylon Daily News* 18 Sept. 4/1 Beggar auctions where.. the beggars themselves have their services bought by bidding beggar mudalalis.

mud-bank. [f. Mud *sb.*[1] + Bank *sb.*[1]] A bank of mud in the bed of a river or on the bottom of the sea. Also *transf.*

1774 *Virginia Gaz.* (Williamsburg) 17 Mar. 2/2 A Sloop ..ran aground on a Mud Bank, a little Way up the Creek. **1832** W. D. Williamson *Hist. State Maine* I. 38 From both [islands] a mud bank extends to the main shore. **1908** *Westm. Gaz.* 30 Dec. 8/2 In spite of the employment of many thousands..on..clearing away the muddy remains of the recent snowstorm, the principal roadways.. presented an extraordinary spectacle of mud-heaps, mud-rivers, and mud-banks. **1963** W. Soyinka *Dance of Forests* ii. 75 From Limpopo to the Nile coils but one snake On mudbanks, and sandy bed. **1974** P. Dickinson *Poison Oracle* i. 18 The heated air rose..above reed-bed and mud-bank.

mudder (mʌ·dəɹ). *slang* (chiefly *U.S.*). [f. Mud *sb.*[1] + -er[1].] A horse which runs well on a wet or muddy racecourse; *transf.*, a sportsman or team similarly proficient.

1903 *Outing* XLIII. 266/2 'He's a mudder,' he growled, 'and the track today will be like lightning.' **1935** *Amer. Speech* X. 315/2 Grand Slam,..winner of the Arlington futurity.., is a good mudder. **1941** *Sun* (Baltimore) 30 Aug. 13/1 Off-Track Seen. Rain today made the prospect for off-going for the first card, thus giving the 'mudders' an opportunity to strut their stuff. **1942** Berrey & Van den Bark *Amer. Thes. Slang* § 683/1 Football player... *mudder, mudlark*, a player for whom a wet field is no great handicap. **1948** *Time* 1 Nov. 44/3 Halfback Jack Swaner, a superior mudder, had a big day scoring all three touchdowns. **1950** *New Yorker* 11 Nov. 121/2 Cornell's last one [*sc.* fumble] gave Columbia, a remarkably good mudder, the chance to tie the score in the fourth quarter. **1952** *Time* 5 May 71/1 Gehrmann and Druetzler proved no mudders and..Purdue's Denis Johansson.. splashed past the leaders on the last lap. **1960** I. Wallach *Absence of Cello* (1961) 29 Will-o'-the-Wisp in the fifth at Hialeah... He's a mudder... It rained all last night in Hialeah. **1969** *Courier-Mail* (Brisbane) 1 Jan. 1/9 Chance for 'mudders'..after last night's flash storm in Brisbane. **1975** *New Yorker* 24 Mar. 64/1 In my book, Stardust Mel is the best mudder in California. Early last month Mrs. Marjorie Lindheimer Everett's rangy gray gelding splattered through the rain and murk to win.

muddied, *ppl. a.* (Later examples with allusion to quot. 1902 in Dict.)

1912 *New Age* 29 Feb. 416/2 The 'flannelled fools' and 'muddied oafs', who come down from Oxford and Cambridge. **1964** C. Mackenzie *My Life & Times* III. iv. 160 No amount of writing about flannelled fools at the wicket and muddied oafs in the goal by Rudyard Kipling could save the British Empire from ultimate collapse.

muddiness. (Later *fig.* examples.)

1915 D. H. Lawrence *Let.* c 7 July (1962) I. 352, I am rid of all my Christian religiosity. It was only a muddiness. **1964** S. Duke-Elder *Parsons' Dis. Eye* (ed. 14) x. 107 'Muddiness of the iris' is the expression used for indistinctness of the pattern, caused by inflammatory exudates.

mudding, *vbl. sb.* Add: **1. b.** The filling of cracks in the walls of a house or log-cabin with mud. *Canad.*

1898 F. Russell *Explor. Far North* 2 The autumnal 'mudding' was poorly done. **1965** E. L. Myles *Emperor of Peace River* ii. iii. 209 On the exterior of the logs treatment was a must if the rooms were to be warm in winter. This treatment consisted of an annual 'mudding', the forcing into the chinks between the logs of a mixture of mud and straw.

muddle, *sb.* Add: **1.** (Earlier example of phr. *in a muddle.*)

1833 J. Constable *Let.* 14 Jan. in *Corr.* (1965) III. 90, I shall be glad when these great pictures are out of doors —but still it's a good thing to be in a muddle.

4. *muddle-thoughted* adj.

1905 E. Phillpotts *Secret Woman* iii. v. 250 What a muddle-thoughted man you be—all in a maze!

muddle, *v.* Add: **5.** Also with *up*.

1944 R. Lehmann *Ballad & Source* 104 Sometimes she doesn't remember our names and muddles us up.

6. Also with *at*.

1895 G. B. Shaw *Let.* 1 Mar. (1965) 491, I should muddle at it until I got it right.

b. *to muddle along* = to muddle through; *to muddle through* (further examples).

1899 J. E. Taylor *Let.* 22 Dec. in D. Ayerst *Guardian* (1971) xviii. 245, I suppose we shall muddle along and suffer the natural results. **1910** Belloc *Verses* 86 A gentleman who cannot jest Remarked that we should muddle through. **1931** *Economist* 21 Mar. 599/1 It reveals us as indolent, complacent, mentally lazy, hide-bound by tradition, content to 'muddle along', neglectful of self-help. **1940** L. MacNeice *Poems 1925–40* 287 Muddling through and glad to have no answer. **1948** D. B. Hawkins in R. O'Sullivan *King's Good Servant* viii. 92 You can muddle through only with the aid of sound instincts; without them you make the muddle but you do not get through. **1972** *Village Voice* (N.Y.) 1 June 9/5 In the absence of a national program, America muddles through to produce its energy.

mu·ddledly, *adv.* [f. Muddled *ppl. a.* + -ly[2].] In a muddled or disorganized manner; with confusion of mind.

1918 E. Marsh in *R. Brooke Coll. Poems* p. cxxv, All these people at the front who are fighting muddledly enough for some idea called England. **1935** F. M. Ford *Let.* 27 Sept. (1965) 243 Though I shall read it..it will probably be rather muddledly.

muddle-head. Add: Also, a disorganized, vague mind.

1938 H. Nicolson *Let.* 11 July (1966) 349 About that I think that your dear muddle-head gets confused.

muddle-hea·dedly, *adv.* [f. Muddle-headed *a.* + -ly[2].] In a muddle-headed manner, confusedly.

1909 G. B. Shaw *Pen Portraits* (1931) 232 Furtively, hypocritically, and muddle-headedly. **1968** *Trans-Action* V. viii. 75 The..letters..are simply too muddle-headedly authoritative to let pass. **1973** *Esquire* May 6 Shortsighted obstructionists, muddleheadedly gumming up the wheels of progress.

muddleheadedness. (Later example.)

1972 *N.Y. Rev. Bks.* 30 Jan. 38/3, I charge them both with muddle-headedness for their own views on this subject.

muddlement. (Later examples.)

1910 *Blackw. Mag.* Sept. 422/1 Nor does any amount of sincerity compensate for muddlement. **1948** W. de la Mare *Chardin* 22 A picture, which, without risk of muddlement between the arts, may be said to be quiet, sonorous, shrill, strident or harsh. **1968** J. R. Ackerley *My Father and Myself* xiii. 146, I had suddenly recollected that my birthday was about to fall and foresaw muddlement.

muddler. Add: **1. b.** *Comb.*, as *muddler-through*, one who conducts affairs without system or foresight (see Muddle *v.* 6 b in Dict. and Suppl.).

1930 *New Statesman* 1 Nov. 110/2 That is my complaint against the peace-lovers, the muddlers-through. **1945** G. Millar *Maquis* iv. 66, I am a muddler-through if ever there was one.

2. (Earlier and later examples.)

1880 W. H. Patterson *Gloss. Words Antrim & Down* 70 *Mudler*, a small metal stamper, used in public houses to crush the lumps of sugar in punch. **1955** M. McCarthy *Charmed Life* (1965) 24 She did them [*sc.* Old-Fashioneds] ..in their best glasses..putting in a silver muddler. **1971** *Scope* (S. Afr.) 19 Mar. 77/4 A 'muddler'—for crushing lump sugar and mixing it with bitters or other flavourings in the bottom of a glass.

muddling, *vbl. sb.* Add: Also *muddling-along*, *-through* (see Muddle *v.* 6 b in Dict. and Suppl.).

1949 Koestler *Promise & Fulfilment* ii. 17 What both Jews and Arabs believed to be a 'diabolic policy' was in fact the traditional muddling-along policy. **1955** *Times* 28 July 3/3 Can it be that..we shall abandon the immemorial practice of muddling through, and discover logic and consistency at last?

mu·ddly, *a.* Also **muddley.** [f. Muddle *sb.* +

-Y^1.] Confused, muddled; passing imperceptibly into: confusing, bewildering.

1909 M. B. SAUNDERS *Litany Lane* II. xvii. 227, I gather it from some of the muddly things he said. **1929** D. H. LAWRENCE *Let.* 24 Aug. (1962) II. 1184, I can't make out if I have to pay this muddley bill for the gramophone or not. **1938** N. MARSH *Artists in Crime* ii. 14, I won't have that sort of thing—it's too muddly. **1959** —— *Singing in Shrouds* viii. 161 A long muddly argument. **1970** 'O. JOHN' *Diamond Dress* i. 8 I'm sorry to be so muddly.

muddy, *a.* Add: **1. c.** As *sb.* The Missouri or Mississippi. Esp. *The Big Muddy,* the Missouri River.

1825 in S. F. COOPER *Rural Hours* (1850) 481 Ye plains where sweet Big-Muddy rolls along, and Teapot, one day to be found in song. **1859** *Trans. Illinois Agric. Soc.* III. 352 In the winter of '55–6, when one wide sweep of destruction laid dead most of the orchard trees north of the Big Muddy. **1884** 'MARK TWAIN' *Huck. Finn* lxvi. 130 When it was daylight, here was the clear Ohio water inshore,..and outside was the old regular Muddy. **1948** *Newsweek* 30 Aug. 21/3 We're going clear to the Missouri River and smash this stuff back across the Big Muddy.

4. d. Of a musical sound: blurred, not clearly differentiated.

1962 A. NISBETT *Technique Sound Studio* iii. 55 The balance to seek is one where you get plenty of reverberation, but not so much that the sound becomes muddy or coloured.

5. (Later examples.)

1876 GEO. ELIOT *Let.* 25 Feb. (1956) VI. 223, I am rather muddy as to the relation of total sales. **1934** A. HUXLEY *Let.* 28 Apr. (1969) 380 Pareto...doesn't, like these 'deep' and muddy Germans, invent gratuitous metaphysical entities.

8. *muddy-grey, -minded* (later examples) adjs.; *muddy oaf* [cf. *MUDDIED *ppl. a.*].

1939 'N. BLAKE' *Smiler with Knife* vi. 96 Her face looked muddy-grey. **1867** TROLLOPE *Last Chron. Barset* II. lxi. 185 Though he knew himself to be muddy-minded and addle-pated, he could see that. **1956** W. H. WHYTE *Organization Man* (1957) iv. 33 People who have been the intellectual founders..have not been as muddy-minded. **1934** R. CAMPBELL *Broken Record* ii. 51 Modern international rugby has been going more and more in the muddy-oaf direction.

muddy, *v.* Add: **1.** *fig.* Also with *up.*

1917 E. POUND *Let.* 10 Nov. (1971) 124 You thank your bloomin gawd you've got enough Spanish blood to muddy up your mind, and prevent the current American ideation from going through it like a blighted collander.

Mudéjar (mūde·hāɹ), *a.* and *sb.* Also **Mudejar,** and with small initial. Pl. **Mudéjares.** [a. Sp. *mudéjar,* f. Arab. *mudajjan* permitted to remain.] **A.** *adj.* Of, pertaining to, or characteristic of the Mudéjares (see below); *spec.* denoting a partly Islamic, partly Gothic style of architecture and decorative art of the 12th to the 15th century. Also *ellipt.* as *sb.,* this style.

1865 H. O'SHEA *Guide to Spain* p. xxix, Moorish architecture may be divided into three periods and styles. 1st. Byzantine–Arabic; 2nd. Mauritane–Almohade; 3rd. Mudejar or Granadine. **1872** M. D. WYATT *Architect's Note-bk. in Spain* p. ix, I have preferred,..in the binding of this volume, to take its ornament in fac-simile from a beautiful little Mudejar casket. **1909** R. TYLER *Spain* ix. 208 The most complete monuments of the Mudejar style are the two synagogues, El Transito and Santa María la Blanca. **1927** G. G. KING *Mudéjar* i. 2 Formerly it was customary to define Mudéjar as a hybrid of oriental and Gothic. **1931** J. B. TREND in Arnold & Guillaume *Legacy of Islam* 15 In later years fine and characteristic work was done by Mudéjar bookbinders. **1938** L. MACNEICE *Earth Compels* 31, I was in Spain... Gobbling..the architecture Moorish mudejar churriguerresque. **1946** E. DIEHL *Bookbinding* I. vi. 91 Their [*sc.* the Spaniards'] mudéjar bindings, showing the Arab influence, were characterized by interlaced strapwork patterns. **1961** *Times* 30 Sept. 11/3 The elaborately joined wood ceilings produced by the Mudejar (Moorish) craftsmen in Spain. **1972** F. M. LÓPEZ-MORILLAS in R. Highfield *Spain in 15th Cent.* 197 Aragon, more bound to the Mudéjar tradition of construction in brick, has nevertheless preserved notable examples of Gothic architecture.

B. *sb.* During the reconquest of the Spanish peninsula from the Moors, a subject Muslim who was allowed to retain his laws and religion in return for his loyalty to a Christian king.

1893 H. E. WATTS *Spain* vi. 167 It was the *mudejar* who drew the design, a *mudejar* who laid the stones, a *mudejar* who painted the walls. **1901** H. C. LEA *Moriscos of Spain* i. 4 When, in 1212, Alfonso IX..won the great victory of Las Navas de Tolosa and advanced to Ubeda, where 70,000 Moors had taken refuge, they offered to become Mudéjares and to pay him a ransom. **1938** B. BEVAN *Hist. Spanish Archit.* xii. 107 In Aragon the Mudéjares were not, as they were elsewhere, a servile minority. **1972** F. M. LÓPEZ-MORILLAS in R. Highfield *Spain in 15th Cent.* 152 In Valladolid on November 9, 1408, both regents signed a law concerning the *Mudéjares* who lived in Castile.

mu·dhead. [MUD *sb.*^{1} 5.] **1.** *U.S. colloq.* A native of Tennessee. *rare.*

1838 [in Dict. s.v. MUD *sb.*^{1} 5]. **1949** *Amer. Speech* XX. 27 Buckshine, Mudhead, or Whelp for a Tennessean.

2. *slang.* A fool.

1882 W. D. HAY *Brighter Britain!* I. ix. 234 Shut up, you Milesian mudhead, and listen to me. **1886** [in Dict. s.v. MUD *sb.*^{1} 5].

3. The name of a ceremonial clown among the Zuñi people who wears a mud-daubed mask.

1959 E. TUNIS *Indians* 129/1 There were other clowns, too, known as *goyemshi,* or Mudheads.

mu·d-hole. Also **mudhole, mud hole.** [f. MUD *sb.*^{1} + HOLE *sb.*] **1. a.** A hole containing mud or in which mud collects, esp. as forming a defect or obstacle in a road or highway.

1760 in *Documentary Hist. Amer. Industr. Society* (1910) I. 310 As soon as one Gets out..he Is In a large due or in a mud hole. **1784** A. ELLICOTT in C. V. Mathews *Andrew Ellicott* (1908) 26 The ground [was] covered with Snow which hid the Mud-Holes. **1857** P. CARTWRIGHT *Autobiogr.* xx. 314, I thought of a desperate mudhole about a quarter of a mile ahead;..many wagons had stuck in it. **1911** E. M. CLOWES *On Wallaby* xi. 291 The water-holding frog found in the central deserts, which can blow its body out with a sufficiency of fluid to support it for a year or more in a dried-up mud-hole. **1937** *Discovery* May 148/1 There are many different kinds of baths available, supplying various mineral waters; boiling mud holes innumerable; waterfalls over which hot water flows side by side with cold; [etc.]. **1948** *Coast to Coast 1947* 71 Those tourist people came and looked at his boiling spring and his bubbling mudhole. **1973** *Sci. Amer.* Apr. 88/3 They find themselves in an alley where they sink into a bottomless mudhole.

b. *transf.* and *fig.*

1784 in *Pennsylvania Mag. Hist. & Biogr.* (1877) I. 51 The general curse of the country, disunion, rages in this little mudhole [*sc.* Uniontown, Pa.]. **1890** *Cent. Dict.,* *Mud-hole,* a salt-water lagoon in which whales are captured. [Whalers' slang, California.] **1938** S. V. BENÉT *Thirteen o'Clock* 317 We've all of us been on your back long enough... I know of twice you pulled Jerry Pye out of the mudhole. **1958** J. CAREW *Black Midas* x. 231 The thought of returning to the mud-hole where I was born made me shy away.

2. A hole at the base of a boiler, condenser, or other apparatus through which sediment can be removed.

1841 W. TEMPLETON *Locomotive Engine* 16 The mud holes..are for the purpose of removing the sediment and scale that constantly accumulate at the bottom of the water spaces. **1893** LANGMAID & GAISFORD *Elem. Less. Steam Machinery* xiii. 123 To allow access to the inside of the boiler, for examining and cleaning, manholes and mudholes are provided.

mud-hook. *slang.* [MUD *sb.*^{1} 5.] **1. a.** An anchor.

1827 J. F. COOPER *Red Rover* I. ii. 44 He would..fasten her to the spot with good hempen cables and iron mudhooks. **1874** W. M. BAINES *Narr. E. Crewe* vii. 138 Cunningly drop your 'mud-hook' so that you exactly swing with the tide over the right spot. **1884** [in Dict. s.v. MUD *sb.*^{1} 5]. **1905** J. C. LINCOLN *Partners of Tide* xii. 230 The partners agreed to undertake the job of recovering the lost 'mud-hook'. **1960** M. SHARCOTT *Place of Many Winds* x. 172 Gusts of wind tore their mud-hooks from the bottom of the anchorage.

b. (See quots.)

1918 'TOMMY' *If I goes West!* 25 Forget old Billy Summers with his board at 'crown and anchor'—'The Mud'ook, boys, and now's the time to bet!' **1919** W. H. DOWNING *Digger Dial.* 34 *Mud-hook*..(2) the anchor in the game of 'Crown and Anchor'. **1943** HUNT & PRINGLE *Service Slang* 46 *Mudhook,* Army name for the Crown and Anchor board used surreptitiously by members of the forces.

2. a. A foot. **b.** A hand.

1850 L. H. GARRARD *Wah-to-Yah* xx. 276 This 'mudhook', holding out his foot, hasn't a moccasin on for nothin'. *a* **1897** F. B. LLOYD *Sk. Country Life* (1898) xl. 239 When a farmer goes to foolin with figgers he is puttin his mudhooks on powerful slippery ground. **1915** *Dialect Notes* IV. 244 *Mud hooks,* n. pl. Feet. **1941** BAKER *Dict. Austral. Slang* 47 *Mudhook,* a foot. (2) A hand. **1952** in Wentworth & Flexner *Dict. Amer. Slang* (1960) 347/2 C'mon, lift them mud hooks!

Mudie (miū·di). The name of Charles Edward *Mudie* (1810–90) used *absol., attrib.,* or in the possessive to designate the lending library opened by him in London in 1842, which continued in business until 1937, or labels, lists, boxes, etc., associated with the library or its contents.

1859 H. C. ROBINSON *Diary* 26 May (1967) 300, I subscribed to Mudie's Library, as I have long intended. *Ibid.* 30 May (1967) 300, I went to Mudie's for the poems of Macdonald. **1864** MRS. GASKELL *French Life* i, in *Fraser's Mag.* Apr. 439/2 They have nothing equivalent to 'Mudie' in Paris. **1879** C. M. YONGE *Magnum Bonum* III. xxxii. 675 'It is the advantage of having no Mudie boxes,' said his mother. 'We are taking up our Southey.' **1885** —— *Nuttie's Father* I. xvi. 191 She could only have recourse to Mudie's box to try to drive dull care away. **1888** *Bks. for Presents & Prizes: Catal. Bks. Best Authors* (Mudie's Select Library) Aug. 1 A few Choice Books in Mudie Calf, Extra Morocco, and other Superior Bindings are also kept in Stock. **1890** S. BUTLER in *Universal Rev.* VIII. 518, I believe I have the smallest library of any literary man in London... I keep my books at the British Museum and at Mudie's. **1908** MRS. H. WARD *Diana Mallory* I. vi. 113 The Book-Club..embraced some ten families who drew up their Mudie lists in common, and sent the books from house to house. **1922** H. S. WALPOLE *Cathedral* I. ii. 28 He looked at them all, with their light yellow Mudie labels, their fresh bindings. **1931** 'G. TREVOR' *Murder at School* ii. 44 He..said you had written a novel... I must get Mudie's to send it down with their next batch. **1966** BERRY & POOLE *Ann. Printing* 230/2 'Mudie's Lending Library'..was to become world famous... As the watch-dog of contemporary literary morals, Mudie soon became a ruthless dictator as to what the people should read... 'What will Mudie say?' became the proverbial question when new fiction was under consideration in publishers' offices. **1970** G. L. GRIEST (*title*) Mudie's Circulating Library and the Victorian novel.

‖ **mudim** (mū·dim). Also 9 **mudin.** [Malay (now *modin*), prob. ad. Arab. *mu'addin* muezzin.] A junior Muslim official in Malaysia, *spec.* one who performs the operation of circumcision.

1817 T. S. RAFFLES *Hist. Java* I. vi. 284 A *Kabáyan*.. with the *Kamitúah* and *Múdin* (priest), formed a court for settling petty village disputes. **1858** *Jrnl. Indian Archipelago* 121 The Mudin or professional circumciser performs the operation in a trice. **1900** W. W. SKEAT *Malay Magic* vi. 360 Among Malays it [*sc.* circumcision] is performed by a functionary called the 'Mudim'. **1966** D. FORBES *Heart of Malaya* xiv. 194 If the traditional *mudim* carries out the operation [*sc.* circumcision] instead of the hospital doctor, he will rub a salve into the wound.

mudir. (Earlier and later examples.)

1844 A. W. KINGLAKE *Eothen* xxvi. 383 The appointment of a special Commissioner—they called him 'the Modeer'. **1902** [see *MAMUR]. **1958** L. DURRELL *Balthazar* v. 99 Local mudirs and sheiks.

Mudjur (mu·dʒuəɹ). Also **Mujur.** The name of a city in central Turkey, used, freq. *attrib.,* to designate rugs made there, usu. with deep borders and prayer arch designs.

1913 W. A. HAWLEY *Oriental Rugs* xvi. 290 Figures of vandykes, which are seen in some Anatolians and Mudjurs, are also a constant feature of Ladiks. **1931** A. U. DILLEY *Oriental Rugs & Carpets* vi. 165 Mujur..prayer rugs [are distinguished] by central panels covered by 'flight-of-stairs roofs'. **1959** *Chambers's Encycl.* III. 137/2 Mujurs, with long pile and glowing reds and greens, can be sumptuous little rugs. **1967** [see *KIR-SHEHR]. **1972** P. L. PHILLIPS tr. *F. Formenton's Oriental Rugs & Carpets* 86 Mudjur carpets are different from Yuruk not only in the fact that they are designed as prayer rugs, but also because of the different colour tones.

mudlark, *sb.* Add: **1.** (Examples.)

1801 T. CAMPBELL *Mobiade* in W. Beattie *Life & Lett. T. Campbell* (1849) I. 380 Or fry the mud-lark's odoriferous wing... The poetical name for a pig, principally used in.. Kilmainham jail. **1833** J. NEAL *Down-Easters* i. 47, I should like to know..what upon irth he means by..mudlarks that's made into Virginny-ham. **1869** *Overland Monthly* III. 129 A hog clandestinely killed outside of camp and smuggled in..was called a 'slow bear'... 'Mudlark' signified the same thing. **1923** *Dialect Notes* V. 240 Boiled potatoes an' mud lark.

2. a. (Later examples.)

1959 *Times* 16 Mar. (Port of London Suppl.) p. xvi/1 'Long apron men' and mudlarks who..waited to pick up goods thrown to them by accomplices on board merchantmen. **1975** *Times* 17 May 8/4 Jack Dash..recalling the Mudlarks, river pirates and knife-belted prostitutes.

3. c. Substitute for def.: A black and white Australian bird, the magpie-lark, *Grallina cyanoleuca,* which builds a nest of mud. Add examples.

1898 MORRIS *Austral Eng.* 278/1 Magpie-Lark..an Australian black-and-white bird..resembling the Magpie in appearance, but smaller; called also Pee-wee, and Mudlark, from its building its nest of mud. **1911** E. M. CLOWES *On Wallaby* xi. 290 The mud larks, rather like our water-wagtails, only much larger, come there with the most wanton flutter of broad black and white tails, to disport themselves upon the patch of green at its verge. **1965** *Austral. Encycl.* V. 460/1 The name 'magpie-lark' was presumably bestowed upon it because it runs on the ground like a lark and has pied plumage;..'mud-lark', owing to its preference for the muddy banks of creeks and waterholes.

4. = *MUDDER. Cf. **mud runner.*

1909 in *Cent. Dict.* Suppl. **1935** A. J. POLLOCK *Underworld Speaks* 78/2 *Mud lark,* a race horse that excels in mud. **1941** BAKER *Dict. Austral. Slang* 47 *Mudlark,* a racehorse that runs well on a muddy course. Also footballers who play on a sodden field. **1975** *Sunday Tel.* (Sydney) 6 Apr. 48 Born Star a Mudlark. Born Star, a two-year-old, yesterday outclassed the field at Sandown in his first start on a rain-affected track.

5. *attrib.,* as *mudlark meet* (see quot.).

1971 *Nat. Geographic* May 719/2 Guernsey invented annual mudlark meets, in which old bangers—near-wrecked automobiles—are raced across the oozing sands at low tide.

mudlarker. (Earlier example.)

1818 'A. BURTON' *Adventures J. Newcome* I. 26 Slopmen, Mud-larkers and Crimps.

mudlarking, *vbl. sb.* (Later example.) Cf. *MUDLARK *sb.* 5.

1960 *Life* (Internat. ed.) 1 Feb. 45/1 The back-bruising sport of mudlarking.., one of England's popular recreations, calls for a special-body car.

‖ **mudra** (mʊdrā·). *Hinduism.* Also **moodra.** [Skr. *mudrā* seal, sign, token.] One of a large number of symbolic hand gestures used in Hindu religious ceremonies and (hence) in Indian dance. Also, a movement or pose in Yoga.

1811 W. WARD *Acct. Hindoos* II. 26 The ceremonies

called moodra; the names of the different moodras.. Certain motions with the hands and fingers. **1832** H. H. WILSON in *Asiatick Researches* XVII. 224 The performance of the *Mudrá*, or gesticulations with the fingers, accompanying the different stages of the ceremony. **1877** M. WILLIAMS *Hinduism* ix. 127 The term *Mudrā* is also used in Tāntrism to denote mystical intertwinings of the fingers so as to form symbolical figures. **1899** MAX MÜLLER *Six Syst. Indian Philos.* vii. 457, I shall abstain from giving descriptions of the Mudrâs (dispositions of upper limbs). **1917** A. COOMARASWAMY in Coomaraswamy & Duggirala tr. *Mirror of Gesture* 8 These poses, chiefly of the hands, are spoken of as *mudrās* (seals), and are more or less familiar to students of Hindū iconography. **1948** G. VENKATACHALAM *Dance in India* xv. 125 There is a regular science of the mudras as there is a science of the mantras. **1952** L. MACNEICE *Ten Burnt Offerings* 84 He was..A dancer..a clown, With his gags, his mudras, his entrechats. **1960** KOESTLER *Lotus & Robot* I. iii. 111 The eight siddhis are promised..in remuneration for the more difficult mudras. **1967** SINGHA & MASSEY *Indian Dances* ix. 93 According to..a text on Kathakali mudras, there are twenty-four basic hand gestures... The significance of a mudra changes according to the position of the hand. **1970** D. BRAHMACHARI *Yogasana Vijñana: Sci. of Yoga* 3 There is..no Mudrā (pose) like Khecarī Mudrā (Khechari pose) and nothing that absorbs one's self completely like Nāda (sound). **1972** R. S. MISHRA *Fund. Yoga* ii. 36 *Mudras*,..movements of limbs and fingers, etc., according to the circulation of *kuṇḍalini* force, magnetic force in the body.

mudwalled, *ppl. a.* (Later examples.)
1892 KIPLING *Barrack-Room Ballads* 171 Put them in mud-walled prisons. **1961** L. MUMFORD *City in Hist.* vi. 159 Did the forms of Phidias rise in this barnyard scattering of workshops..mid these mud-walled huts? **1971** *Inside Kenya Today* Mar. 37/1 The mud-walled and grass-thatched office. **1974** *Nat. Geographic* Aug. 255/1 The traditional mud-walled farmhouse with thatched roof has two bedrooms and a kitchen.

mu·dwalling, *vbl. sb.* [MUD *sb.*[1]] (See quots.)
1905 *Tent Catal.* (John Boyle & Co., N.Y.) No. 8. 15 Both grades are provided with sod cloth (mud walling). **1963** *Which?* Apr. 120/2 The outer tent has a strip of heavier, plastic-coated fabric, called mudwalling, round the bottom to protect the tent's walls. **1970** *Ibid.* May 133 The bottom of the walls [of frame tents] is made from plastic (called mudwalling) so that the canvas does not touch the damp ground, and to keep the wind and rain out. **1974** *Camping & Caravanning* Sept. 39/2 (Advt.), 50″ PVC Groundsheeting or Mudwalling, 66p yd.

muesli (mü·sli, mū·sli). Also **müesli, musli.** [Swiss-Ger.] A dish, originating in Switzerland, consisting of a cereal (usu. oats) and fruit to which milk is added, often eaten as a breakfast dish.
[**1926** BIRCHER-BENNER & BIRCHER *Fruit Dishes & Raw Vegetables* iv. 29 This dish..is popularly known as 'Birchermüesli'.] **1939** *Ibid.* (ed. 2) iv. 29 The fact that it is cold is never harmful as long as the müesli is well chewed and thus sufficiently warmed in the mouth. **1943** M. Y. BRADY *Health for All: Wartime Recipe Bk.* 58 Müesli is a delicious dish, even when modified to suit wartime shortages. **1965** H. RUBINSTEIN *My Life for Beauty* vi. 76, I lived on a diet of Muesli (a mixture of rolled oats, lemon juice, sweetened condensed milk, grated apples and hazel-nuts). **1971** J. AIKEN *Nightly Deadshade* vii. 71, I find them finishing their breakfast of musli. **1971** M. THOMPSON in C. Bonington *Annapurna South Face* App. D. 274 Ideal High Altitude Rations..Readi-Brek *or* Muesli, [etc.]. **1973** [see *INSTANT *a.* 4 c].

muff, *sb.*[2] Add: **3. b.** *slang.* The female pudenda. Also *Comb.*, as **muff-diver,** one who practises cunnilingus.
1699 B. E. *New Dict. Cant. Crew, Muff*, c. a Woman's Secrets. *To the well-wearing of your Muff Mort*, c. to the happy Consummation of your Marriage Madam, a Health. **1935** J. HARGAN *Gloss. Prison Lang.* 5 *Muff-diver*, performer of cunnilingus. **1961** PARTRIDGE *Dict. Slang* Suppl. 1191/2 *Muff-diver*, a cunilingist [*sic*]. **1972** *Screw* 12 June 5/2 Blowjobs are nice, but blowing into her muff can kill her. **1973** H. MILLER *Open City* xiv. 159 The local bookie's got Polaroids of her flashing her muff.

c. A woman or girl, esp. one of low morals; a prostitute. *slang* (orig. *U.S.*).
1914 [see *DRAG *sb.* 3 e]. **1918** *Dialect Notes* V. 26 *Muff*, a girl. South Idaho and University of Idaho. **1965** H. C. RAE *Skinner* I. i. 10 Flappin' about a muff they found up in the woods.

5. muff-box (further examples); **muff pistol,** the smallest size of nineteenth-century pocket pistol believed by some to have been designed to be carried in a muff (but see quot. 1969).
1834 Muff-box [see *bonnet-box* s.v. *BONNET *sb.* 10]. **1868** *Mich. Agric. Rep.* VII. 363 Henry Fowler [exhibited] ..1 dozen muff and collar boxes, combined in one. **1938** J. N. GEORGE *Eng. Pistols & Revolvers* vii. 135 These so-called muff-pistols were not necessarily intended as ladies' weapons. **1956** W. E. BIRD *Off-Trail in Nova Scotia* vi. 181 Another item is a muff pistol that was fired with a percussion cap and ball. **1969** F. WILKINSON *Antique Firearms* 135 Some very small examples..are often described as muff pistols, although it is not at all clear on what basis this term was chosen. Certainly there is little or no evidence to suggest that they were intended primarily for ladies or indeed were ever carried in the muff, for both men and women of the period used muffs.

muff, *v.*[3] **1.** (Earlier and later examples.)
[**1827** W. CLARKE *Every Night Bk.* 84 When one of the fancy dies, the survivors say, that he has..'mizzled'—'morrised'—or 'muffed it'!] **1846** W. DENISON *Cricket: Sk. Players* 24 All the best of our players completely muffed their batting. **1950** *Times Lit. Suppl.* 3 Mar. 131/3 It would be impossible for Sir Max Beerbohm to muff a parody. **1968** J. R. ACKERLEY *My Father & Myself* xiii. 145 A few opportunities occurred. He muffed one of them, I another. **1972** *Jazz & Blues* Oct. 30/1 If Mezz is indeed responsible for this exchange then the author muffs his lines badly. **1973** *Tucson* (Arizona) *Daily Citizen* 22 Aug. 57/3 Third baseman Phil Garner muffed a grounder by Bill Ralston.

muffetee. 2. (Earlier Amer. example.)
1749 in A. M. Earle *Costume Colonial Times* (1894) 165 Men's fine Worsted Gloves and Muffetees.

muffity (mɒ·fiti). [Origin unknown.] A size of Cotswold stone roofing slate.
1914 [see *BACHELOR 4 d]. **1929** N. LLOYD *Building Craftsmanship* 93 The names and sizes of Stonefield [*sic*] Quarry slates..are Muffity or movedays 8 in.

muffle, *sb.*[4] Add: **3.** *muffle furnace* (later examples); **muffle kiln,** a kiln in which the pottery which is being fired is enclosed within a chamber and thus protected from direct contact with the source of heat.
1949 *Electronic Engin.* XXI. 412 An apparatus was constructed for holding a bar-shaped specimen in the muffle furnace. **1974** *Nature* 27 Sept. 305/2 Several single crystals were placed on a glass slide and heated in a muffle furnace at 180° C for 24 h. **1897** SPARKES & GANDY *Potters* i. 43 The pigments..are all mixed in vehicles of an oily nature, and a most necessary step is to fire this oil out... This is done in..a muffle kiln..fired up to red heat only. **1947** W. B. HONEY *German Porcelain* 8 More or less glassy pigments [were] applied over the glaze and fixed by a low-temperature firing in a muffle-kiln. **1971** L. A. BOGER *Dict. World Pott. & Porc.* 260/1 Enamel colors are fired at a comparatively low temperature of 700°C to 900°C in a muffle kiln.

muffledly (mɒ·f'ldli), *adv.* [-LY[2].] In a muffled manner.
1903 CONRAD & HUEFFER *Romance* I. iii. 21 The church clock began muffledly to chime the quarters. **1946** E. O'NEILL *Iceman Cometh* (1947) III. 178 He hides his face on his arms, sobbing muffledly.

muffler. Add: **4.** Also (chiefly *U.S.*) = SILENCER 2.
1895 in *Funk's Stand. Dict.* **1896** [in Dict.]. **1897** [see *BACK-FIRING *vbl. sb.* 2]. **1915** [see *CHUG *v.*]. **1931** *Economist* 28 Feb. 431/2 There is reason to believe that.. mufflers, chassis springs,..and accessories are all being manufactured or obtained in France. **1964** M. BANTON *Policeman in Community* iii. 69 An officer had stopped a driver for a faulty muffler (exhaust silencer) and had given him a ticket. **1973** *Houston* (Texas) *Chron.* 21 Oct. 12/1 Congress is being pressured to ease the auto emission standard that would lead to the installation of catalytic mufflers on new cars sold after Jan. 1, 1975. **1973** J. M. WHITE *Garden Game* 136 There was a horrible grinding and clanking under the car..and I did mental arithmetic about the bill for a new muffler. **1974** *Index-Jrnl.* (Greenwood, S. Carolina) 19 Apr. 5/1 There were also two charges each of muffler violation, disregarding a traffic signal and operating an uninsured vehicle.

mufflered (mɒ·fləɹd), *a.* [f. MUFFLER + -ED[2].] Wearing a muffler; characterized by the wearing of mufflers.
1927 *Daily Express* 13 Mar. 5/1 From the bridge the mufflered figures glanced down at the business men moving across the quayside. **1963** *Times* 3 May 16/7 Raincoated and mufflered, tropical gear a thing of the past, we steamed into cold drizzle and short, steep seas. **1969** *Punch* 26 Mar. 450/2 The hard collar is wilting at last. In a choice between starched indigence and mufflered affluence, proper pride has had it.

mufti[2]. Add: **1.** (Further examples.) Also *transf.* and *fig.*
1930 W. S. MAUGHAM *Cakes & Ale* iv. 52 He looked a little like a dean in mufti on his summer holiday in Switzerland. **1959** *Listener* 16 Apr. 681/3 A time of extravagance already remote from the mufti sobrieties of the Third Republic. **1966** *Ibid.* 13 Oct. 547/1 Students will observe the tears that, Terry-fashion, the actor (in mufti and communing only with the cameras) cannot hold back in the Deposition scene of *Richard II*. **1971** *Illustr. Weekly India* 4 Apr. 23/2 An old man..was nearly killed by a lathi and was carried away by the police in mufti. **1975** A. CHRISTIE *Curtain* xvii. 182 Nurse Craven I saw for the first time in mufti instead of her nurse's uniform.

mug, *sb.*[3] Add: **1. b.** A portrait or photograph of a person, esp. in police records. *slang.*
1887 *Lantern* (New Orleans) 9 July 2/2 He had his mug taken in fireman's clothes. **1889** CLARKSON & RICHARDSON *Police!* xxiii. 323 Circulating thieves' photos... Pushing the mugs round. **1940** R. CHANDLER *Farewell my Lovely* vi. 43 Nulty turned over a photo..and handed it to me. It was a police mug, front and profile.

3. The act of throttling or strangling a person; usu. in phr. *to put the mug on* (someone).
1862 *Sessions Papers Cent. Criminal Court* 26 Nov. 41 Roberts..said, 'You want me for putting the *mug* on, do you? I will put the b—y *mug* on you.' *Ibid.*, *Mug* is slang used by thieves; it means garotting. **1940** *Amer. Speech* XV. 121/1 *To put the mug on* (a mark), to put a strangle-hold on a mark who grows obstreperous after he has been fleeced. **1955** *Publ. Amer. Dial. Soc.* XXIV. 171 A strangle hold is applied... This hold is called..a *mug* on the East Coast.

4. *attrib.* and *Comb.*, as **mug book** *U.S.*, (*a*) (see quot. 1935); (*b*) a book kept by the police containing photographs of criminals; **mug-faker,** a street photographer; **mug shot** *slang* (orig. *U.S.*) = sense 1 b above.
1935 A. J. POLLOCK *Underworld Speaks* 78/2 *Mug book*, a book published for prominent business and professional men who are induced by high pressure solicitors to vividly write about themselves with youthful photographs. They pay well for this blue book privilege. **1958** J. & W. HAWKINS *Death Watch* (1959) i. 19, I couldn't find him in the mug books; his picture isn't there. **1933** 'G. ORWELL' *Down & Out* xxxii. 236 A mugfaker—a street photographer. **1952** M. ALLINGHAM *Tiger in Smoke* i. 16 These old photographers—mugfakers we call 'em—in the street. **1950** in Wentworth & Flexner *Dict. Amer. Slang* (1960) 349/1 Police passed around a mug shot of Willie. **1962** K. ORVIS *Damned & Destroyed* xxvii. 200 The police record plate number..indicates that mug-shot was taken in the Receiving Room. **1970** R. JEFFRIES *Dead Man's Bluff* vii. 66 Check through the mug shots and see if you can find him. **1974** *Daily Tel.* 14 Nov. 2/2 From the mass of information collected, a picture is built up of the personalities in the IRA's command structure, and this is then used in the 'mugshot' booklets carried by soldiers on the streets.

mug, *sb.*[5] Add: **1. b.** mug's game, a thankless task; a useless, foolish, or unprofitable activity. *colloq.*
1910 BELLOC *Pongo* xv. 233 One cannot arrest millionaires with impunity... Even in a wild democracy to arrest them is Mug's game. **1918** *Flying* 12 June 427/2 Flying's a mug's game, mater, A fact I know full well. **1930** G. B. SHAW *Apple Cart* II. 77, I am going out of politics. Politics is a mug's game. **1959** T. S. ELIOT *Elder Statesman* I. 26 Forgery, I can tell you, is a mug's game. I say that——with conviction. **1973** *Times* 9 Nov. 21/2 Running a reserve currency is a mug's game; and the world is running out of mugs.

c. A person, fellow, chap; *spec.* (*a*) a rough or ugly person; a criminal; (*b*) applied by criminals to someone who is not part of the underworld; (*c*) a policeman.
1890 in Barrère & Leland *Dict. Slang* II. 73 'What are *mugs*?' 'Hard characters... Those are thieves from the First Ward, the fellows that rob immigrants, steal cotton from the bales, [etc.]. **1895** E. W. TOWNSEND *Chimmie Fadden Explains* 15 Dat Mr. Paul is de funniest mug you ever see. *Ibid.* 17 De mug what plays de flute has de music all t'himself when de odder mugs in de orchestra don't do nottin. **1903** H. HAPGOOD *Autobiogr. Thief* (1904) xii. 267 I'm only stealin' for certain mugs (policemen) and fer those 'igher up, so they can buy real estate. **1921** [see *GEE *sb.*[4]]. **1930** [see *JITTER *sb.* 1]. **1938** F. D. SHARPE *Sharpe of Flying Squad* i. 13 Underworld men and women speak of all outside their world as 'mugs'. **1960** *Observer* 24 Jan. 5/2 There were recognised prop-men or putters up of jobs, what the mugs called master minds.

2. b. *attrib.*, passing into *adj.*, that is a 'mug' or fool; stupid; easily duped or defeated.
1922 E. WALLACE *Flying Fifty-Five* xxxiii. 197 The mug punter was he who dreamed of long-priced winners and refused to bet on the six to four certainty preferring rather the hopeless proposition that started at twenty to one. **1963** T. TULLETT *Inside Interpol* xvi. 216 There are still thousands of 'mug' criminals..who invariably make mistakes. **1971** *Sunday Australian* 8 Aug. 5/6 Let's just say I'm a good average mug golfer.

mug, *v.*[3] Add: **2.** Also, to fight, beat up, assault; to strangle; (now the prevailing sense) to attack and rob (a person). Also occas. *intr.*, to fight. Cf. *MUGGING *vbl. sb.* 1.
In the more usual current sense not *slang*.
1846 *Swell's Night Guide* 37 Most of them can..mug.. alias fight. *Ibid.* 76 She felt inclined to mug her rival, only she thought it would be no bottle. **1859** HOTTEN *Dict. Slang* 65 *Mug*, to fight, or chastise. **1864** *Ibid.* 183 *Mug*,.. to rob by the garrote. **1866** *London Misc.* 5 May 102 Suppose they had mugged you?..Slogged you, you know. **1904** 'No. 1500' *Life in Sing Sing* 250/2 *Mug*,..to strangle. **1948** *N.Y. Times* 15 Aug. 36 The police said the victims were mugged in the hallways of their homes. **1960** I. WALLACH *Absence of Cello* 23 She's going into Central Park for her constitutional. I hope she gets mugged. **1966** WODEHOUSE *Plum Pie* vii. 166 Somebody mugged Sam last night...Yessir, laid him out cold. **1968** A. DIMENT *Bang Bang Birds* iii. 28 In New York..people conversed about their friends being beaten up and robbed—mugged is the local term. **1971** B. MALAMUD *Tenants* 198 Lesser.. daily fears that..the writer will be mugged on the subway stairs and lie there unable to crawl home. **1972** *Daily Tel.* 7 Oct. 2/6 Judge Hines, Q.C., jailed three youths for three years for 'mugging' a middle-aged man and stealing £7 from his wallet.

3. To take a photograph of (a person), esp. for police records. *U.S.*
1899 'J. FLYNT' *Tramping with Tramps* IV. 395 *Mug*,.. to photograph. **1912** [see *MUGGING *vbl. sb.* 2]. **1929** M. A. GILL *Underworld Slang*, *Mugged*, photographed. **1934** *Sun* (Baltimore) 5 July 13/6 Attempts of Federal authorities to 'mug' him proved futile. When Robert C. Johnson ..prepared to snap a picture of the prisoner, Kent held his hands before his face. **1960** *Wall St. Jrnl.* 3 Nov. 2 More than 15,000 New Jersey securities salesmen are being fingerprinted and 'mugged' at police stations and private detective agencies over the state, under a new state law. **1972** G. V. HIGGINS *Friends of Eddie Coyle* xix. 115 We brought him up to the marshal's office and mugged him and printed him.

4. To kiss, to fondle. Chiefly *Austral.* and *N.Z.*
1916 C. J. DENNIS *Songs Sentimental Bloke* 126 *Mug, to*,

to kiss. **1932** *Amer. Speech* VII. 334 *Mug*, to kiss. **1957** I. Cross *God Boy* (1958) x. 80 You think there is something funny about them mugging up each other like that?

mug, *v.*[4] Add: (Further examples.) Also *trans.*, to supply with beer or liquor; to buy a drink for (someone).

1854 A. E. Baker *Gloss. Northamptonshire Words* II. 38 Come! mug the girls, and they'll get on with their work. **1939** *Daily Mirror* 14 Mar., Are you going to 'mug' us.. Are you going to stand me a drink? **1966** P. Moloney *Plea for Mersey* 23 If ye say to them 'scouse, Mug us dem on de house,' Yerl make Birty and Girty all shirty. **1966** F. Shaw et al. *Lern Yerself Scouse* 42 *Ile mug yer*, allow me to treat you. *Ibid.* 77 Many's the fella dat I use'ter mug.

mug, *v.*[5] Add: Hence **mu·gging** *vbl. sb.*, hard studying, 'swotting'. Usu. with *up*.

1959 I. & P. Opie *Lore & Lang. Schoolch.* x. 179 'Swotting' or 'mugging up' is only considered good form if a person is on the point of taking an exam. **1959** *Daily Tel.* 10 June 10/2 But no one..after yesterday's inauguration of the new electric services from London to the Kent Coast is going to mind mugging up any number of amended arrival and departure times. **1960** *Guardian* 15 July 6/6 Hasty muggings-up and regurgitations of fact.

mug, *v.*[7] For *U.S. slang* read *slang* (chiefly *Canadian* and *Naut.*). (Add further examples.) Also, to have a snack, a meal, or a hot drink.

1917 'Bartimeus' *Long Trick* iv. 78 Coats and mufflers were donned and a bottle of sloe-gin uncorked. 'Mug-up!' cried the Sub. 'Mug-up, and let's get 'appy and chatty.' **1927** G. Bradford *Gloss. Sea Terms* 117/1 *Mug up*, to have a drink of coffee or tea which is always on the galley stove of a fishing schooner. **1929** F. Bowen *Sea Slang* 93 *Mug up, to*, to eat, used principally in the Grand Banks schooners. **1936** A. Stringer *Wife Traders* xv. 214 They fell into the habit of stopping more often to 'mug up' along the trail. **1950** J. Hambleton *Abitibi Adventure* 94 René was just 'mugging up' when the shaggy terrier..sent the blackened tea pail flying. **1972** L. Hancock *There's a Seal in my Sleeping Bag* v. 84 We..mugged up on boiled eggs, toast, jam, and coffee.

Muganda (mugæ·ndă). Also 9 **Mganda.** Pl. *Baganda *sb.* and *a.* [Bantu *ganda* + sing. prefix *mu*.] A native or inhabitant of the former kingdom of Buganda, now a province of Uganda; hence, loosely, any native or inhabitant of Uganda. Also *attrib.* and as *adj.*

1862 J. H. Speke *Jrnl. Discovery Source of Nile* (1863) xi. 299 Turning round with true Mganda impetuosity, he walked away. *Ibid.* 313 Every Mganda will say the first Uganda year dates from the arrival of the first Mzungŭ (white) visitor. **1889** R. P. Ashe *Two Kings Uganda* xxiii. 287 A Muganda mother takes no little pride in her child. *Ibid.* 290 Should any person of position suddenly address a Muganda, he should politely reply, 'Kabaka'. **1905** J. F. Cunningham *Uganda* ix. 185 A Muganda chief looks with loathing on all work in the fields. **1908** *Daily Chron.* 24 Dec. 4/6 Buganda is the country, a Muganda is an individual native, the Baganda are the natives as a whole, and Luganda is the language. **1971** *Sunday Nation* (Nairobi) 11 Apr. 11/7 Possibly he was the greatest Muganda patriot in the four hundred years of the Buganda kingdom's history.

mugearite (mʊ·giˌărəit). *Petrogr.* [f. *Mugeary*, the name of a village in the Isle of Skye, Scotland + -ite[1].] A dark, fine-grained trachyte which has oligoclase as the main feldspar and also contains olivine, orthoclase, and apatite.

1904 A. Harker *Tertiary Igneous Rocks Skye* xv. 257 The other rock..is, when fresh, a black compact-looking rock without phenocrysts... As this rock..belongs to a peculiar type, we..give it a provisional name..'mugearite', a name adopted from that of Mugeary, the crofter village lying at a short distance north. **1928** *Trans. Geol. Soc. Glasgow* XVIII. 348 A characteristic feature which the mugearites share with the Jedburgh basalts is the presence of close-set parallel somewhat irregular platy joints. **1956** *Trans. R. Soc. Edin.* LXIII. 68 The mugearite lava east of Dunsapie Hill, thought to have been the first of the flows, contains a number of phenocrysts of albitised plagioclase. **1971** *Nature* 23 Apr. 510/2 The lavas [of the Baringo District, Kenya] comprise a succession of alkali-olivine basalts, basanites and mugearites.

Hence **mugeari·tic** *a.*, of or containing mugearite.

1927 *Trans. R. Soc. Edin.* LV. 504 We regard the mugearitic and essexitic intrusions of the Dalmahoy syncline as hypabyssal expressions of the magma which gave rise to the accompanying effusive mugearites and allied basalts. **1973** *Nature* 9 Feb. 375/1 There, the volumes of individual hawaiitic and mugearitic lavas are frequently of the order of 0·1 km^3.

mugful (mʊ·gful). Also † **mug-full.** [f. Mug *sb.*[1] + -ful.] The contents of a mug; the amount that a mug will hold (in quot. 1867 = bowlful).

1838 Dickens *Nickleby* (1839) xv. 133 A glass-full of spirits and water for Nicholas, and a cracked mug-full for the joint accommodation of himself and Smike. **1867** J. T. Staton *Rays fro th' Loominary* 110 Aw pusht th' owd woman uv hur bustle in a mugful o dowf [*i.e.* dough]. **1924** J. M. Barrie *Mary Rose* i. 15, I wonder if you would give me a mug of tea. Not a cup, we drink it by the mugful where I hail from. **1973** J. Mann *Only Security* vi. 59 Roger accepted the plastic mugful of tea.

mugger, *sb.*[4] Add: **2.** One who 'mugs' people (see *Mug *v.*[3] 2); *spec.* one who commits robbery with violence. orig. *U.S.*

1865 J. H. Browne *Four Yrs. in Secessia* xlv. 340 The Muggers, like most bullies and ruffians, manifested a fine discrimination respecting the party they attacked, selecting those they thought they could rob with little resistance and entire impunity. **1874** Hotten *Slang Dict.* 220 *Maceman*, or *macer*, a welcher, magsman, or general swindler; a 'street-mugger'. **1942** *N.Y. Times* 3 Oct. 17/1 The police were..tracking down three known..muggers who..had received suspended sentences in a mugging case. **1955** *Sun* (Baltimore) 5 Jan. 2/4 Corporal ——..of Cleveland reported to police early today that he had been attacked by two muggers while walking near the Pennsylvania Station. **1965** Wodehouse *Galahad at Blandings* i. 11 Muggers, stick-up men and hoodlums in general he disliked. **1970** *Daily Mail* 21 Feb. 9/5 Clarendon Road in London's Notting Hill area..is the haunt of the Muggers —men who clobber you and steal whatever you have of value. **1973** *Sun* 18 Jan. 7 (*headline*) Muggers attacked detective.

mugger (mʊ·gəɹ), *sb.*[5] A nail, usually of wrought iron, used for protecting the inner soles of mountaineering boots.

1941 C. F. Kirkus *Let's go Climbing!* v. 68 For the inner part of the sole muggers, rough wrought iron hobnails, are excellent. **1954** C. D. Milner *Wedderburn's Alpine Climbing* (ed. 2) ii. 10 The Alpine mugger is a very good nail, but the alternate freezing and thawing of the sole will soon loosen it. **1970** A. Blackshaw *Mountaineering* (rev. ed.) iii. 99 Soft iron nails which grip as a result of the rock biting into them (muggers and clinkers).

mugger (mʊ·gəɹ), *sb.*[6] and *v.* A slang euphemism for some senses of Bugger *sb.* and *v.* (see quots.).

1945 'N. Shute' *Most Secret* vii. 150 What do you think we stopped to pick the mugger up for? **1948** —— *No Highway* ix. 229 The pilot said, 'I don't give a mugger about that, sir. It's plain bloody nonsense.' **1951** —— *Round the Bend* 69 'Well, I'm muggered,' I said in wonder. **1954** 'G. Carr' *Death under Snowdon* v. 54 Privileges are for the man who works for 'em, not for the mugger who plants his bottom on 'em because his father owned land. **1962** J. P. Carstairs *Pardon my Gun* i. 10 She's muggered off... Hopped it to Italy.

mugginess. (Earlier example.)

1856 Geo. Eliot *Let.* 29 Dec. (1954) II. 284 Don't you enjoy the frost after that long time of mugginess?

mugging (mʊ·giŋ), *vbl. sb.* [f. Mug *v.*[3] + -ing[1].] **1.** orig. *slang.* The action of *mug *v.*[3] 2; *spec.* robbery with violence. Also *attrib.*

1846 *Swell's Night Guide* 75, I knows that 'ere whitehouse warment..would chaff—and you knows I'm soon shirty, and then we should have a mugging match. **1866** J. E. Brogden *Provincial Words Lincolnshire* 131, I gave him a sound mugging, he was so chappy. *a* **1876** E. Leigh *Gloss. Words Dial. Cheshire* (1877) 139 'To receive a muggin' is to be beaten. **1939** *Fortune* July 168/3 The vicious art of 'mugging' by which a Negro thug grabs the wayfarer around the neck, from behind, while two others with knives clean out his pockets. **1942** [see *mugger *sb.*[4] 2]. **1949** *Sat. Even. Post* 8 Oct. 171/2 The only things she reads in our newspapers are the murders and the muggings and the obituaries. **1951** *Manch. Guardian Weekly* 28 June 2/2 The increase in petty thieving, in 'muggings' of night-time strollers, and in prostitution. **1971** B. Malamud *Tenants* 64 Bugsy is shot..in Catshit Alley by two white pigs who had cornered him there after a mugging. **1973** *Guardian* 7 June 9/5 Much of the [crime] increase consists of robberies after sudden attacks in the open, known commonly as mugging.

2. The action of *mug *v.*[3] 3; the taking of photographs of persons. Also *attrib. U.S. slang.*

1899 'J. Flynt' *Tramping with Tramps* iv. 389 In some cities suspicious characters are arrested on general principles and immediately photographed by the police authorities. Such towns are called 'muggin' joints', and the police authorities 'muggin' fiends'. **1912** A. B. Reeve *Poisoned Pen* (1913) ii. 58 An hour later, at headquarters, after the pedigrees had been taken, the 'mugging' done.. O'Connor led the way into his private office. **1912** A. Train *Courts, Criminals & Camorra* 5 'Mugging' was all right, so long as you 'mugged' the right persons.

3. Kissing, love-making, 'necking'. Cf. *mug *v.*[3] 4.

1924 P. Marks *Plastic Age* xxiii. 271, I hate mugging and petting and that sort of thing... Petting is jazzing love; and I hate it. **1926** K. S. Prichard *Working Bullocks* xxvii. 242 But Deb had never kissed her mother, as she had seen children in the township kiss and cuddle up to their mothers... Her mother did not encourage 'mugging', as she called it. **1970** C. Major *Dict. Afro-Amer. Slang* 83 *Mugging*,.. making love.

4. Grimacing; making faces (see also quots.). Also *fig.*

1937 *Amer. Speech* XII. 317/2 *Mugging*, motion picture acting. **1961** *Times* 25 Apr. 20/4 Grimaces and gestures straight out of silent films, properly deserving the name 'mugging'. **1968** *Listener* 25 July 124/2 Paul Daneman made a promising start as Higgins, but dwindled into a kind of verbal mugging.

muggins. Add: **1.** (Earlier and later examples.) Freq. used by a speaker to refer to himself.

1855 *Golden Era* 28 Jan. 2/1 You are a veritable 'Muggins' in [choosing] cigars. **1859** C. E. De Long in *Calif. Hist. Soc. Q.* (1931) X. 167 Spent the evening until late with Jim in having one of our regular old fashioned long talks about women love &c; and both arrived at the conclusion that we were mugginse's. **1973** *Daily Tel.* 29 Aug. 1/3 The letter bomb was not meant for me personally. I was just the muggins who opened it. **1973** E. Lemarchand *Let or Hindrance* 181 'In a nutshell,' Michael said, '..Muggins [*i.e.* himself] has agreed to be in charge.'

2. a. (Earlier examples.)

1855 *Pioneer* (San Francisco) Nov. 358 We returned to the hotel, to engage in the intellectual game of Muggins. Ladies and gentlemen were all decided to be Muggins ere the game had closed. **1865** S. Jex-Blake *Let.* 18 Aug. in M. Todd *Life S. Jex-Blake* (1918) xiii. 165 After the ices we went back to the Hospital, and played a most ridiculous game of cards called 'Muggins', keeping us in roars of laughter half the time.

b. (Earlier U.S. example.)

1868 F. B. Zincke *Last Winter in U.S.* 268 Consoling herself with a kind of dominoes she called 'muggins'.

muggle[3] (mʊ·g'l). *slang* (orig. *U.S.*). [Origin unknown.] *pl.* Marijuana; *sing.* or *pl.*, a marijuana cigarette. Also *Comb.*, as **muggle-head, -smoker,** one who smokes marijuana; so **mu·ggler,** a marijuana addict.

1926 Maines & Grant *Wise-Crack Dict.* 11/1 *Muggle-head*, smoker of Mexican loco weed. **1928** L. Armstrong (*title of gramophone record*) Muggles. **1933** C. de Lenoir *Hundredth Man* i. 10, I found myself on the Mexican border with a bad 'yin', and nothing to relieve me but the native drug marijuana. In New Orleans and other Southern American towns this is known as 'muggles', being sold in the form of cigarettes. **1933** *Fortune* Aug. 90/1 Louis Armstrong, who blew such frenzied tattoos as he has recorded under the titles *Mahogany Hall Stomp*, *Knee Drops*, *Skip the Gutter*, and *Muggles* (named for the Mexican cigarettes drugged with marijuana which have inspired perfectly incredible solos). **1938** *Manch. Guardian Weekly* 2 Sept. 188/3 Many swing players are 'killer-dillers' (first-rate players). Some are 'mugglers' (Marijuana addicts), but very few are 'long-hairs' (people who like classical music). **1946** Mezzrow & Wolfe *Really Blues* (1957) 51 'Ever smoke any muggles?' he asked. **1949** R. Chandler *Little Sister* xxxiv. 248 Desk clerk's a muggle-smoker. **1969** A. Arent *Laying on of Hands* (1971) vi. 50 Offer our guest a muggle. **1972** *Sunday Sun* (Brisbane) 2 July 14 Detectives from the CIB Drug Squad in Brisbane are becoming quite familiar now with words like muggles, griefs, mezz, Mary Jane, jive, tea, rope and locoweed.

Muggur, var. *Magar[2].

mugo (mu·go). Also **mugho(s).** [a. Fr. *mugho*, It. *mugo* mountain pine.] In full, *mugo pine*. The European mountain pine, *Pinus mugo* (or *P. montana*), a large shrub, or one of its many varieties, ranging from dwarf forms to small trees.

c **1756** P. Collinson in L. W. Dillwyn *Hortus Collinsonianus* (1843) 40 Mr. P. Miller received seeds of the Cembro and Mugos Pines from the mountains of Valencia in Spain, Sept. 12, 1753. **1822** J. M. Good *Study of Med.* I. 315 The Hungarian balsam, or distilled oil of that variety of the *pinus sylvestris* which has been called Mughos. **1861** R. Bentley *Man. Bot.* 659 P[*inus*] *Pumilio*, the Mugho or Mountain Pine, yields by spontaneous exudation an oleo-resin called Hungarian balsam. **1951** H. S. Conard tr. *Kerner's Background Plant Ecol.* xxiii. 191 The formation of the Rusty Sedge generally occurs in the calcareous Alps as islands in the dark green mugho pine forest. **1966** H. J. Welch *Dwarf Conifers* v. 266 The Mountain Pine (Mugo is a local name) is a very variable species with a distribution in nature throughout Europe from the Pyrenees to the Balkans. **1967** N. T. Mirou *Genus Pinus* ii. 98 It [sc. *Pinus montana*] grows there [sc. in the Carpathians] in a shrub form and is known as variety *mughus*, or Mugo pine. **1969** T. H. Everett *Living Trees of World* 52/1 The Swiss mountain pine (*P. mugo*) is best known to many Americans in its dwarf variety, the mugho pine (*P. m. mughus*).

‖ **muguet** (müge). [Fr.] Lily of the valley; the smell or scent of lily of the valley. Also *attrib.*

[**1873** *Young Englishwoman* May 234/2 Bodice..edged with muguet fringe of violet silk.] **1919** W. L. Dudley *Askinson's Perfumes* (ed. 4) xvi. 208 *Muguet.* Oil of jasmine... Oil of ylang-ylang... Solution of heliotropin. **1928** H. S. Redgrove *Scent* xi. 66 *Hydroxy-citronellal*.., very useful for making artificial lily of the valley (muguet) perfume. **1957** E. Hyams *Into Dream* ii. iii. 115 She used a little too much scent: Paul identified it as *muguet.* **1970** *Guardian* 12 May 9/2 Coty have recently reformulated their Muguet des Bois fragrance range.

mug-up (mʊ·gʊp, mʊgʊ·p). *slang* (chiefly *Canadian* and *Naut.*). [f. Mug *v.*[7]] A snack, a meal, or a drink.

1933 E. Merrick *True North* 233 Back at the tent we had a mugup, lashed up and said good-bye to the Indians. **1941** *Beaver* Mar. 12 Where the traveller stops long enough to have a 'mug-up', each dog is given about a pound of frozen fish. **1950** R. Moore *Candlemas Bay* 143 They'd warm up the fishhouse and have a mug-up, before Jeb went to work on his traps for the rest of the daylight. **1961** J. W. Anderson *Fur Trader's Story* xxv. 225 The Eskimos too would be entertained, but because of their numbers they would have a picnic 'mug-up' on deck. **1963** J. T. Rowland *North to Adventure* ix. 123 We had a mug-up of hot coffee and turned in. **1970** R. Price *Howling Arctic* iv. 45 Occasionally they stopped for mug-up.

mugwump, *sb.* For *U.S.* read orig. *U.S.* Add: **1.** (Further examples.)

1925 *N.Y. Times* 10 May, The royal red Indian mugwump, the chief, was copiously red-blooded. **1945** [see *BIGWIG].

2. (Further examples.) Also, a person who withdraws his support from any group or organization; one who is aloof, independent, or self-important.

1887 J. D. Billings *Hardtack & Coffee* xv. 286 [The mule's] reputation as a kicker is world-wide. He was the Mugwump of the service. **1894** P. L. Ford *Hon. Peter Stirling* 302 I'd have believed anything but that you [*sc.* a Democrat] would be a dashed Mugwump! **1903** G. B. Shaw *Man & Superman* III. 116, I told him I did not care whether he got into parliament or not; so he called me Mugwump and went his way. **1923** H. E. Buchholz *Of what Use are Common People?* vi. 66 Mugwump may be thought of as a fitting term for the man who because of real or imagined superiority separates himself from the group with which he has been associated. *Ibid.* 73 The proposal of the intelligence mugwumps is that the majority of ordinary minds should step out of the picture of the body politic,..while creatures with better than normal minds should be commissioned to do all the thinking. **1946** *Tuscaloosa* (Alabama) *News* 31 Mar. 4/7 A few moments after Secretary Wallace made his pun, he hastened to add that he himself had been a mugwump. **1975** *Sat. Rev.* 22 Mar. 58/3 Among the delicious names taken by, or given to, minor political parties in the United States (apart from Mugwumps and Bull Moose) are..Quids, Locofocos, [etc.].

3. (Earlier and later examples.)

1887 *Courier-Jrnl.* (Louisville, Kentucky) 8 Jan. 4/5 The Mugwump War Department is a horse-power to the Republican machine. **1923** H. E. Buchholz *Of what Use are Common People?* viii. 108 The various mugwump groups that propose changing the form of the present government. **1931** H. F. Pringle *Theodore Roosevelt* I. ix. 115 Roosevelt's gnawing hatred of the Mugwump independents made it impossible for him to withdraw. **1970** *Times* 9 Dec. 16/2 Even a doubtful and controversial conclusion..would have been more useful than this irritating mugwump approach.

Hence **mu·gwumpish** *a.*, characteristic of a mugwump; professing disinterestedness; pretentiously superior; **mugwumpism** (earlier and later examples).

1886 *Congress. Rec.* 31 Mar. 2968/1 That maudlin political sentiment which we recognize, for want of a better, under the name of 'Mugwumpism'. **1898** G. B. Shaw *Our Theatres in Nineties* (1932) III. 297 It [*sc. Hamlet*] belongs to a detached residence, a select library, an exclusive circle, to no occupation, to fathomless boredom, to impenitent mugwumpism. **1918** F. Hackett *Ireland* ix. 252 This conviction was accompanied..with many mugwumpish strictures such as 'in the main', 'within certain limits', [etc.]. **1923** *Spectator* 22 Sept. 390/1 Racial, intellectual or moral tests..may turn out to be not aristocratic at all, but merely mugwumpish.

Muhammad, Muhammadan. Now the preferred spelling of Mohammed, Mohammedan *a.* and *sb.*

1961 [see *Black Muslim* (*black *a.* 19)]. **1963** *Cambr. Rev.* 20 Apr. 369 (*title*) Oriental Studies at Cambridge: Muhammadan Law and Urdu Literature.

muhimbi (mʊhi·mbi, mʊwi·mbi). Also **muhindi.** [Lunyoro.] An evergreen tree, *Cynometra alexandri*, belonging to the family Leguminosæ and native to East Africa, or the timber obtained from it, which is also called Uganda ironwood.

1906 M. T. Dawe *Rep. Bot. Mission through Forest Districts of Buddu* 43 in *Parl. Papers* (Cd. 2904) LXXX. 41 *Cynometra Alexandri*... Native name, Muhindi: immense and important timber tree. **1939** Eggeling & Harris in L. Chalk et al. *Forest Trees & Timbers Brit. Empire* IV. 27 Two pieces of Muhimbi (Ironwood), buried near a termite hill in 1930, were removed after 16 months, in excellent condition. **1951** *Archit. Rev.* CX. 144/3 Muhimbi, an extremely hard wood from Uganda, is here used for the first time in a floor of any appreciable size in this country. **1956** *Handbk. of Hardwoods* (Forest Prod. Res. Lab.) 158 Muhimbi is a heavy, hard timber of equal weight to East African olive. **1971** F. H. Titmuss *Commercial Timbers of World* (ed. 4) 155 The timber of *Cynometra alexandri*..is now beginning to be much better known under the title of Muhimbi.

muhtar, var. *MUKHTAR.

muid. 1. a. (Later examples.)

1859 R. J. Mann *Colony of Natal* 124 One farmer in the Umvoti country reaped 120 muids (of 2⅔⅔ bushels each) from 30 acres of land which had been sown with 5 muids of seed. **1873** [see *boermeal* (*Boer b)].

muishond (mœ̆ĭ·shɒnt). *S. Afr.* Also 9 **mausehund, mousehund.** [Afrikaans, f. *muis* Mouse *sb.* + *hond* dog; cf. Mouse-hunt[1].] The Cape polecat, *Ictonyx striatus*, which is black with white stripes, or one of several species of mongoose. Also *fig.*

1796 tr. *F. Le Vaillant's New Trav. Afr.* I. 236 It [*sc.* a stranded whale] was attacked..by different species of those small quadrupeds..which, at the Cape, are known under the general name of *muyshond*. *Ibid.* III. 278 My Hottentots of the colony all recognized it as a *muyshond* (mouse-dog), a general name among the inhabitants of the Cape for all the little carnivorous quadrupeds. **1818** C. I. Latrobe *Jrnl. Visit S. Afr.* 36 We observed a tame mongoose or mausehund from Java..which ran about and suffered itself to be handled. **1835** A. Smith *Diary* 5 Jan. (1939) I. 204 A hare and a muishond for sale. **1853** *Edin. New Philos. Jrnl.* LV. 210 Two or three different kinds of Mousehund, or weasel..are commonly seen. **1900** B. Mitford *Aletta* xii. 111 She went round among her fowl-houses, then strolled along the quince hedges to see if any of the hens had been laying out and in irregular places for the benefit of the egg-loving *muishond*, or similar vermin. **1912** F. W. Fitzsimons *Snakes S. Afr.* (new ed.) 30 Within two yards of us was a striped Muishond with his paws firmly planted on an adult Black-necked cobra. **1937** H. Klein *Stage-Coach Dust* xxiv. 208 A muishond (pole-cat) startled the town-bred horse, and away he galloped. **1946** *Cape Argus* 16 Nov. 6/2 Two varieties of muishond now have prices on their heads. **1952** —— 12 Jan. 4/5 His request for tame 'wild' animals has only produced in Cape Town a muishond and a monkey. **1970** *News/Check* (S. Afr.) 12 June 11 An assumption has grown up over the past year or more that South Africa was well and truly isolated, that it remained the *muishond* of the world with whom nobody wanted anything to do. **1974** *Daily Dispatch* (East London, Cape Province) 21 Nov. 10 A rabid muishond has been killed on Arbrook, farm of Mr. George Michau.

muisvoël (mœ̆ĭ·sfōəl). *S. Afr.* Also **muisvoel, muisvogel** (-fōχəl). [Afrikaans, f. as prec. + *voël* bird.] = *mouse-bird* (Mouse *sb.* 10 f).

1822 W. J. Burchell *Trav. S. Afr.* I. xi. 214 Muisvogel (Mouse-bird). *Colius erythropus* of Linnæus. **1849** A. Smith *Illustr. Zool. S. Afr.: Aves* plate ii, *Chizærhis concolor*..As soon as it was observed, the Hottentots declared it to be a *muis vogel*, or *Colius*, Lin...which was not surprising, since it evinces considerable similarity to birds of that genus. **1867** E. L. Layard *Birds S. Afr.* 221 Of the three species of this genus [sc. *Colius*] found in South Africa, and known by the trivial name of Muisvogel or Mouse-bird, this [sc. *C. erythropus*] is the only one that is found in the neighbourhood of Cape Town. **1920** R. Y. Stormberg *Mrs. Pieter de Bruyn* 7 It [*sc.* peachblossom] has been vandalised by swarms of 'finks' and wretched little stiff-tailed 'muisvogels' who snip off the blooms most viciously. **1952** *Cape Times* 27 Nov. 2/3 Muisvoëls are destroying whole orchards of early ripening fruit. **1959** *Ibid.* 20 Jan. 7/3 Sparrows and muisvoels are not a pest in areas where our native birds of prey have not been eliminated. **1973** *Eastern Province Herald* (Port Elizabeth) 19 July 17 How many of us city-dwellers..would know the difference between a mossie and a muisvoël?

mujik, var. Moujik, muzhik. (Examples.)

1833 [see Moujik, muzhik 1]. **1934** *Discovery* Dec. 364/2 The mujiks know that Lenin hath given, but Stalin hath taken away. **1963** V. Nabokov *Gift* iv. 216 He began dabbling in propaganda by conversing with mujiks.

‖ **mujtahid** (mʊdʒtā·hid). Also **mooshtâhed, mujtehid.** Pl. **mujtahids, mujtahidūn.** [Pers. 'one who strives hard to acquire correct and sound views', 'one who has arrived at the highest degree in knowledge of the law'; Arab. 'one who exerts himself'.] In Islamic countries, the title given to a person accepted as an authority on the interpretation of Islamic law. Now only in Iran.

1815 J. Malcolm *Hist. Persia* II. xxiii. 428 That power ..is exercised..by these holy men who are raised, by popular suffrage, to the dignity of Mooshtâhed, or 'high priest'; and who may be deemed at the head of the hierarchy of Persia. **1885** T. P. Hughes *Dict. Islam* 197/2 *Ijtihād* is the deduction made by a single Mujtahid, whilst *Ijma'* is the collective opinion of a council of Mujtahidūn, or enlightened doctors. **1909** *Daily Chron.* 2 Feb. 1/7 The Shah would be well advised to listen to the petition of the Mujtehids and clergy now being presented,..begging for the restoration of the Constitution. **1958** A. Toynbee *East to West* 161 'The veil between us is very thin,' said the old mujtahid. **1961** *Ann. Reg.* 1960 299 The leading *mujtahid* of the day having declared this law to be contrary to the *shari'a* and the Constitution, it seemed likely to remain a dead letter.

Mujur, var. *Mudjur.

mukhtar (mu·ktāɹ). Also **muhtar, muktar.** [ad. Arab. *mukhtār* chosen.] The head of the local government of a town or village in Turkey; a minor provincial official. Hence **mu·khtarship,** the status or office of a mukhtar.

1911 T. E. Lawrence *Let.* 21 May (1938) 104 The Muktar carried off his cousin on his saddle-bow from amid the shrieking women at the spring. **1916** —— *Lett.* (1938) 209 Two Mukhtars and two prominent sheikhs. **1946** [see *dunam]. **1946** Koestler *Thieves in Night* 122 The British rulers had always appointed the most distinguished member of each of the two clans to dual mukhtarship. **1954** F. Stark *Ionia* 65 The mukhtar and the doctor from Pitane..came to give the city's welcome. **1970** *Guardian* 1 Apr. 4/2 The 'muhtar' (local official) of the village of Kakoy. **1974** *Times* 5 Apr. 16/4 The Mukhtar..explained: '..we are Druse and we will never leave our land.'

‖ **mukim** (mū·kim). Pl. **mukim, mukims.** [Malay, ad. Arab. *muḳīm* remaining, resident.] In Malaysia, a Muslim parish, the smallest administrative district.

1839 T. J. Newbold *Pol. & Statistical Acct. Straits of Malacca* I. v. 247 The immediate religious care of the inhabitants of the Mukim (or parish) to which the mosque belongs, devolves upon the Imam, Khatib, and Bilal. **1907** F. A. Swettenham *Brit. Malaya* x. 228 The districts were again sub-divided into *Mukim*. **1911** *Encycl. Brit.* XVII. 482/2 The state is divided into *mukim* or parishes. **1948** *Malayan Pict. Observer* Dec. 1 In Jimah Mukim of Port Dickson District..lies the Chuah Indian Settlement. **1958** J. M. Gullick *Indigenous Political Syst. W. Malaya* ii. 36 A *mukim*, a sub-district which may include several villages ... *Mukim* denotes the area served by a mosque and is sometimes translated 'parish'. **1964** K. G. Tregonning *Hist. Mod. Malaya* vii. 157 By making administration at local *mukim* level the responsibility of people trusted in the kampongs, he created a stable State.

muklek, mukluk, varr. *muckluck.

muktar, var. *mukhtar.

mukti (mɒ·kti, mu·kti). *Hinduism* and *Jainism.* Also 9 **mooktee.** [Skr. *mukti* a setting or becoming free, release, f. *muc* to let loose, free, release.] = *moksha.

1785 C. Wilkins tr. *Bhăgvăt-Gēētā* 140 The Hindoos believe..that an eternal release, which they call *Mŏŏktēē*, is only to be attained by a total neglect of all sublunary things. **1801** *Asiatick Researches* VII. 34 Bhooddha after his death ascended to the Hall of Glory, called Mooktzé, otherwise Nirgoowané. **1807** W. Jones *Works* III. 384 The *Mucti*, or *Elysian* happiness of the *Védánta* school is far more sublime. **1811** W. Ward *Acct. Writings, Relig. & Manners Hindoos* IV. x. 315 The shastrŭs teach that there are four kinds of mooktee, or deliverance. **1832** [see *bhakti]. **1840** [see *moksha]. **1875** M. Williams *Indian Wisdom* iii. 70 The right apprehension of truth..which, if once acquired by the soul, confers upon it final emancipation, whether called Mukti, Moksha,..or Nirvana. **1915** *Encycl. Relig. & Ethics* VIII. 773/2 The evolution of *mukti*, or *mokṣa*, in Jainism cannot be adequately dealt with till its early literature is more fully accessible. **1970** T. W. Organ *Hindu Quest Perfection of Man* ix. 296 *Mukti* is freedom from the individualistic inlook, and the attainment of the divine outlook.

‖ **muktuk** (mɒ·ktɒk). Also **maktuk.** [ad. Eskimo *maktak*.] The skin of any of several species of whales used for food by the Eskimo.

1835 R. Huish *Last Voy. Sir J. Ross Arctic Regions* 701/2 Skin of a whale..Maktuk. **1909** A. D. Cameron *New North* xii. 220 The wedding breakfast consisted of seal-meat, frozen rotten fish, and muktuk (whale meat). **1940** *Beaver* Mar. 25/2 All were chewing *muktuk*—the outer protective skin of the whale—with great enjoyment. **1966** *Star Weekly* (Toronto) 12 Mar. 10/1 The Eskimos love muktuk and eat it raw. It's rather rubbery but doesn't taste bad at all—a bit like hazel nut. **1973** *Nat. Geographic* Mar. 353/1 After the blubber is cut, the Eskimos pare off the tough, rubbery skin and a thin layer of attached blubber—called *muktuk*. A delicacy to the Eskimos, muktuk tastes surprisingly good when boiled and salted. **1974** *N.Y. Times* 30 May 39/2 But the *muktuk*—the skin and outer layer of blubber that is the staple of the Eskimo diet—was fine.

Mukuzani (mukuzā·ni). [Russ.] A red wine from Georgia, U.S.S.R.

1961 *Spectator* 7 Apr. 495 The first Soviet wines to be imported into Britain—Mukuzani, Gurdzhaani and Tsinandali, all from Georgia. **1967** A. Lichine *Encycl. Wines* 470 Some Georgian wines seen abroad are white Myshako Riesling and Ghurdjurni. The Takhetia region is the most successful and the best wines include..the red Mukuzani. **1968** A. H. Gold *Wines & Spirits of World* 467 The wines tend to be full and the red ones dark. *Mukuzani* and *Saperavi* are two dark strong red wines of 14° alcoholic strength from the eastern side of Georgia in the Tiflis region.

Mulana, var. *Maulana.

mulatta. Delete † *Obs.* and add later examples.

1963 *Times* 12 June 16/6 Of the other painters the pioneers were Di Cavalcanti, famous for his sensuous mulatas, and Portinari. **1965** E. Bishop *Questions of Travel* 37 Going out, he met a *mulata* Carrying water on her head.

mulatto, *sb.* and *a.* Add: **A.** *sb.* **4. mulatto-clay** *U.S.*, a dark-coloured clay; **mulatto land** (earlier and later examples); **mulatto loam, mould** = *mulatto land*; **mulatto prairie,** a prairie of mulatto-soil; **mulatto-soil** (later examples).

1741 in *Amer. Speech* (1940) XV. 287/2 A Tract of rich Mulattoe Land, lying in that County. **1788** T. Jefferson *Tour of Amsterdam* in *Writings* (1854) IX. 386 It has a southern aspect, the soil a barren mulatto clay, mixed with a good deal of stone, and some slate. **1883** E. A. Smith *Rep. Geol. Survey Alabama 1881–82* 435 The red or mulatto lands are much the best for cotton. **1837** J. L. Williams *Territory of Florida* 82 The surface is covered with a mulatto or chocolate colored loam. **1838** *Jeffersonian* (Albany) 28 Apr. 88 (Th.), The mulatto mould of the Colorado does not surpass in fatness the alluvial soil of Red River. **1869** *Overland Monthly* III. 130 Then there is the 'chocolate' prairie, and the 'mulatto', and the 'mezquite'. **1819** E. Dana *Geogr. Sk. Western Country* 190 Next to this is very often found a skirt of rich pine land, dark mulatto soil with hickory..characteristic of good land. **1861** *Trans. Illinois Agric. Soc.* IV. 112 He..would not choose the dark prairie mold, but that kind of soil best known in the west as the 'mulatto soil'.

B. *adj.* **1.** (Earlier example.)

1677 *Rec. Court of New Castle on Delaware* (1904) 91 The upholding & detayning of this p[laintiff]'s molatto servant in Maryland.

mulattress. (Earlier and later examples.)

1805 in *Amer. Pioneer* (1843) II. 234 The chief of the

audience is formed of mulatresses and negresses. **1887** *Harper's Mag.* Mar. 609/1 A handsome, strong-limbed, and light-footed mulattress. **1932** *Dict. Amer. Biogr.* VIII. 485/1 He lived openly with a mulattress and was only prevented from marrying her by the law against miscegenation.

mulberry. Add: **3.** (Later examples.)

1951 M. KENNEDY *Lucy Carmichael* I. i. 10, I impressed her with my mulberry house-coat. **1971** *Vogue* 15 Oct. 41 Pullover..in Antwerp Brown, French Navy and Mulberry. **1974** R. HARRIS *Double Snare* xii. 83 Sir Jonathan wore a white doublet, and mulberry trunk hose. *Ibid.* xxviii. 226 The colours; dog-rose pink, green, and mulberry.

3*. In full, *Mulberry harbour*. The code name of the prefabricated harbour used in the invasion of the Continent by British and American forces in 1944; also applied to any artificial harbour. Also *attrib.*

1945 *N. & Q.* 15 Dec. 263/2 The word 'Mulberry' was selected as the secret name for the artificial harbour..from its being that which happened to come next in rotation on the Admiralty's List of Ships' Names then available for use. **1946** J. E. TAYLOR *Last Passage* i. 19 Mulberry is the name given to an artificial harbour erected primarily for the landing of stores off the enemy beaches. **1958** *Listener* 5 June 930/2 Further north—in the island of Schouwen-Duiveland—I saw where it had been necessary to float great mulberry harbour caissons in and sink them in the gaps. *Ibid.* 21 Aug. 258/2 The famous Mulberry Project, the creation of vast artificial seaports on the open coast of Normandy. **1965** R. B. ORAM *Cargo Handling* viii. 152 Movable quays of the war time Mulberry pattern. **1972** *Daily Tel.* 11 May 9/3 Vice-Adml Hughes-Hallett told me he..frankly considered the 'embellishments' of the Mulberries quite superfluous.

4. *mulberry wine*; *mulberry-nosed, -red* adjs.; **mulberry-bird,** (*a*) *Austral.* substitute for def.: the southern figbird, *Sphecotheres vieilloti*; (examples); **mulberry molar** *Med.*, a first molar with a small crown that is nodular and pitted, somewhat like a mulberry, as a result of congenital syphilis.

1891 A. J. NORTH in *Rec. Austral. Museum* I. 113 It [*sc.* the Southern Sphecotheres] is fairly common on the Tweed River, where it is locally known as the 'Mulberry-bird', from the decided preference it evinces for that species of fruit. **1966** N. W. CAYLEY *What Bird is That?* (ed. 4) 21 Southern Figbird... Also called Mulberry-bird and Banana-bird... Flocks may be seen feeding in native fruit- and berry-bearing trees, and sometimes in orchards, where they eat mulberries, figs, and other soft fruits. **1923** *Arch. Dermatol. & Syphilol.* VIII. 794 There is a definite shoulder formation, and the cusps occupy a smaller area ..and..are smaller than normal... The grouping or arrangement of these small cusps have suggested the term 'mulberry' molar. **1941** K. H. THOMA *Oral Path.* v. 242 The mulberry molar is covered on the sides with normal, smooth enamel, but the occlusal surface is pinched together, dwarfed, rough, and hypoplastic, often pigmented. *Ibid.*, Often a supernumerary nodule or pseudo-cusp appears which clinicians emphasize as an important feature of the mulberry molar. **1961** R. D. BAKER *Essent. Path.* ix. 199 Stigmata of congenital syphilis may be found in those who survive. These defects are Hutchinson's teeth, mulberry molars, saddle nose, deafness and keratitis. **1924** R. GRAVES *Mock Beggar Hall* 6 A dissolute Mulberry-nosed philosopher. **1927** Mulberry red [see *ASH *sb.*[2] 1 e]. **1945** W. DE LA MARE *Scarecrow* 35 His large mulberry-red face and eyes like bits of agate. **1723** J. NOTT *Cook's & Confectioner's Dict.* sig. T4 To make mulberry wine. Gather your Mulberries when they are thorough ripe, pick off the Stalks, and press out the Juice. **1971** *Country Life* 23 Dec. 1777/3 There was an abundance of wine, particularly claret, mulberry wine and mead at a peacock feast.

mulctuary, *a.* Delete † *Obs.* and add later example.

1968 *Punch* 25 Sept. 421/2 The taxes used to buy the state industries were collected by savage mulctuary imposts on the rich.

mule[1]. Add: **2. d.** *Naut.* A large triangular sail sometimes used on a ketch. So *mule-rigged* adj.

1932 *Yachting* Sept. 46 'Tidal wave', winner of the race, at the start, with the mule pulling aloft and motor pushing below. **1954** *Ibid.* Apr. 61 The swell rolls the wind out of her spinnaker, but the 'mule' aloft between her masts is pulling like its long-eared namesake. **1954** *Motor Boating* Dec. 29/1 The mule-rigged yawl Flame at the start in Newport. **1964** M. WEEKS *Compl. Boating Encycl.* 366/2 *Mule*, a large triangular staysail sometimes used on a ketch. It sets on the main backstay and is sheeted to the mizzenmasthead.

e. *U.S. slang.* (See quots.)

1935 A. J. POLLOCK *Underworld Speaks* 78/2 *Mule*, person who carries dope for a drug trafficker and passes drug to buyer after a sale has been made. **1951** *Life* 11 June 126/2 He becomes a 'mule' (delivery boy) for a peddler and earns his own heroin by introducing his friends to dope and making customers of them. **1959** 'E. MCBAIN' *Pusher* viii. 78, I bought from him a coupla times. He was a mule, Dad. That means he pushed to other kids.

4. c. (Earlier and later examples.)

1801 C. PYE *Provincial Coins* 3 The endless varieties (not unaptly termed *mules*) produced by a combination of dies not originally intended for the same coin. **1961** G. VAN DER MEER in R. H. M. Dolley *Anglo-Saxon Coins* 183 The variety is an 'Intermediate Small Cross/*Crux*' mule. *Ibid.* 184 The type is a mule of the 'Arm-and-Sceptre' type of 'Cnut' (=Harthacnut) and the '*Pacx*' type of Edward the Confessor.

d. A small tractor or locomotive, usually powered by electricity, used for towing canal-boats, moving trailers, etc. (see quots.).

1903 *Electr. World & Engin.* 14 Nov. 795 The 'mule' has two large hooks for the towropes. **1924** *Chambers's Jrnl.* Nov. 731/2 These wire ropes are stretched from the ship to motor-tractors running on rails the length of the docks. Electric 'mules' the tractors are called... These mules both guide and propel the ship. **1928** *Amer. Speech* III. 366 'Mules' are the little gas and electric tractors used in the studios of Hollywood. **1971** M. TAK *Truck Talk* 109 *Mule*, a small tractor used to relocate dollies in a terminal or warehouse.

5. a. (sense 1) *mule-back* (further examples; also *attrib.* and quasi-*adv.*), *-boy, -bray, -cart, -driver, -hoof, -kick, -load, -man, -meat, -path, -power, -race, -road, -skin, -steak, -team, -track, -trail, -train, -wagon, -way.*

1878 *Harper's Mag.* Jan. 283/2 He put it in his broken English, 'On horse-back or mule-back, and many times on foot-back.' **1897** R. M. STUART *In Simpkinsville* 15 Many's the time..he's rode into town, mule-back, with her settin up in front of him. **1904** 'O. HENRY' *Cabbages & Kings* I. 16 The mule-back system of transport that prevailed between Coralio and the capital. **1968** D. M. SMITH *Medieval Sicily* xviii. 182 All wheat had to be carried to the ports on muleback. **1973** K. BENTON *Craig & Jaguar* iii. 29 An estate..surrounded by high mountain ranges.. and until recently only accessible by mule-back. **1958** J. CAREW *Black Midas* i. 11, I had started work as a mule boy..trotting beside a mounted overseer. **1960** S. PLATH *Colossus* (1967) 20 Mule-bray, pig-grunt. **1847** *Knickerbocker* XXX. 228 Our little mule-cart was but ill-fitted for the passage of so swift a stream. **1929** J. BUCHAN *Courts of Morning* I. 37 Country mule-carts struggled towards the market-place. **1857** P. ST. G. COOKE *Scenes & Adventures* 90 A charge..would have proved disastrous to the mule-drivers. **1909** 'O. HENRY' *Roads of Destiny* 192 He had been mule-driver..and cattleman. **1880** 'MARK TWAIN' *Tramp Abroad* 486 We found the masonry slightly crumbled, and marked by mule-hoofs. **1930** BLUNDEN *De Bello Germanico* 5 That sudden backward mule-kick which gives troop-trains one of their unique charms. **1968** *Globe & Mail* (Toronto) 13 Jan. 24/3 A flying leap known in dancing as a reverse dolphin dive, and in wrestling jargon as a mule kick. **1810** Z. M. PIKE *Acct. Expeditions Sources Mississippi* App. III. 4 There are taken, to be coined, 100 mule-loads of bullion in silver and gold monthly. **1880** 'MARK TWAIN' *Tramp Abroad* 491 We had plenty of company, in the way of wagon-loads and mule-loads of tourists. **1867** in E. CUSTER *Tenting on Plains* (1887) 537 Teams of luggage, dogs, horsemen, mulemen, cross and recross at will. **1952** E. F. DAVIES *Illyrian Venture* iii. 60 Hare gave an order to the mulemen to build the fires. **1970** R. LOWELL *Notebk.* 209 The mule-man lost his footing in the clouds. **1846** R. B. SAGE *Scenes Rocky Mts.* xxix. 251 We ended our fast.. with a feast of mule meat. **1891** *Century Mag.* Mar. 774 We made our Christmas and New Year's dinner on mule meat. **1834** A. PIKE *Prose Sk. & Poems* 25 They would find a mule-path leading from the ford. **1880** 'MARK TWAIN' *Tramp Abroad* 131 Big keel-boats on their way up, using sails, mule power, and profanity. **1914** *Illustr. London News* 12 Dec. 814/3 The mountain gunners can take their gun, by mule-power or man-power, where the Horse and Field cannot follow. **1937** N. N. PUCKETT in A. Dundes *Mother Wit* (1973) 172/1 On plantations with more abundant mule-power, we find appearing..such.. descriptions as Young Beck,..Leader Kit, and even such regular surnames in muledom as Jane Henkel..and Pol Jones. **1883** 'MARK TWAIN' *Life on Mississippi* xlv. 462 The ladies of New Orleans attend so humble an orgy as a mule-race. **1777** P. THICKNESSE *Year's Journey* I. xxiv. 210 The foot-road..is only one thousand three hundred paces;..the mule-road is above four times as far. **1880** 'MARK TWAIN' *Tramp Abroad* 445 We followed the mule-road, a zigzag course. **1970** C. KOPAS *Bella Coola* iii. 55 Applied for a contract to build a mule road from Bella Coola to the mouth of the Quesnel. **1897** *Sears, Roebuck Catal.* 228/2 Men's genuine unlined Mule Skin Gloves. Not very pretty, perhaps, but full of real goodness. **1926** *Daily Colonist* (Victoria, B.C.) 7 Jan. 11/1 Brown Muleskin Gauntlets, warmly lined, cuff has fringe and red star. **1854** J. R. BARTLETT *Pers. Narr. Explor. Texas* I. v. 113 We might reach El Paso by..taking an occasional mule steak. **1846** S. MAGOFFIN *Diary* in *Down Santa Fé Trail* (1926) 25 His mule team (some eighteen or twenty) were.. passing the little wet creek. **1949** L. G. GREEN *In the Land of Afternoon* ix. 131 Every twelve miles along the route a fresh mule team awaited the coach. **1908** A. BENNETT *Old Wives' Tale* I. i. 2 The ineffaceable mule-tracks that had served centuries before..Watling Street. **1975** P. SOMERVILLE-LARGE *Couch of Earth* x. 181 A traditional mule track that crossed the new road. **1859** *Brit. Colonist* (Victoria, B.C.) 29 Jan. 1/4 A good wagon road to Fort Yale, and a mule trail thence equal to the best in California. **1932** *World Today* Feb. 217/2 Twenty miles of mule-trail were built. **1849** H. PAGE *Let.* 8 May in E. Page *Wagons West* (1930) 116 The Indians..will not trouble us, so much as they will the mule trains. **1952** E. F. DAVIES *Illyrian Venture* vii. 129 Chesshire and Kadri went back to find Hare and the mule train at dawn. **1846** P. ST. G. COOKE *Jrnl.* 19 Oct. in P. St. G. Cooke et al. *Exploring Southwestern Trails* (1938) 69 There are three mule wagons to each company. **1863** *Harper's Mag.* June 9/2 With utmost speed, in mule-wagons, they started for the Lower Agency. **1850** J. L. TYSON *Diary of Physician in Calif.* 24 [Down] the only pass..was a narrow mule-way. **1930** T. S. ELIOT tr. *St.-J. Perse's Anabasis* 65 The parties for upkeep of muleways.

c. mule-beater, a stick used for beating mules; **mule chest** (see quot. 1911); **mule-colt** *U.S.*, a young mule; **mule deer,** substitute for def.: *Odocoileus hemionus*, a black-tailed deer native to western North America, and distinguished by its large ears; (further examples); **mule-ear(ed) rabbit** = JACK-RABBIT (in Dict. and Suppl.); **mule-gate,** the space in a spinning-room within which a mule works; **mule-headed** *a.*, stubborn; **mule-killer** *U.S.*, (*a*) (see quot. 1847); (*b*) (see quots. 1890 and 1899); **mule-litter,** a litter borne by mules; **mule rabbit** = **mule-ear(ed) rabbit*; **mule-skinner** (earlier and later examples); also *Canad.*; hence **mule-skinning** *vbl. sb.*; **mule-sweep** = **mule-gate*; **mule-whacker** *U.S.*, a mule-driver.

1909 E. BANKS *Mystery F. Farrington* 123 Pedro took up one of the disused mule-beaters, and laid it on him thick and fast. **1911** BLAKE & REVEIRS-HOPKINS *Little Bks. Old Furnit.: Tudor to Stuart* vi. 96 In some cases during the transition from the simple chest to the chest of drawers, we find a chest with drawer or drawers below and false drawer fronts to match on the upper portion. The old chest lid is still retained. This type, being a hybrid, is known amongst collectors as the 'Mule Chest'. **1923** J. C. ROGERS *Eng. Furnit.* ii. 15 The 'mule chest', or dower chest, with its proverbial bottom drawer. **1972** *Country Life* 21 Dec. 1752/1 A well proportioned 18th century mule chest of well coloured mahogany. **1788** G. WASHINGTON *Diaries* (1925) III. 400 Turned..the two yearling Mule Colts..into the Clover Paddock. **1885** *Rep. Indian Affairs* (U.S.) 11 The increase has been 8 horse and mule colts, 50 calves, and 150 pigs. **1805** M. LEWIS *Jrnl.* 10 May in Lewis & Clark *Orig. Jrnls. Lewis & Clark Expedition* (1904) II. 21 With the mule deer the horns consist of two beams. **1806** W. CLARK *Jrnl.* 11 Mar. in *Ibid.* (1905) IV. 158 The Ears and the tail of this Animale [*sic*] when compared with those of the Common Deer, so well comported with those of the Mule when compared with the Horse, that we have by way of distinction adapted [*sic*] the appellation of the Mule Deer. **1880** *Scribner's Monthly* May 129/1 For meat we have bacon and generally steaks or roasted ribs of elk, mule-deer or mountain sheep. **1936** D. MCCOWAN *Animals Canad. Rockies* xxxi. 265 A full grown Mule deer measures about sixty five inches from nose to tail, stands from forty to forty two inches high at the shoulder and.. weighs from two hundred to two hundred and fifty pounds. **1962** E. LUCIA *Klondike Kate* viii. 170 The big handsome mule deer wandered right into the yard. **1972** *Village Voice* (N.Y.) 1 June 75/2 At dusk mule deer venture out to graze under the apple trees. **1855** *Life Illustrated* 10 Nov. 16/3 She will follow the mountain or 'mule-eared' rabbits. **1885** C. A. SIRINGO *Texas Cowboy* 142, I had just eaten a mule-eared rabbit. **1889** H. H. MCCONNELL *Five Yrs. a Cavalryman* 56 The English hare..is not nearly so large as our jack or 'mule-ear' rabbit. **1892** J. NASMITH *Student's Cotton Spinning* 409 The pillars..are so pitched that they fall into the alleys between the mules and not into the mule-gate. **1884** 'MARK TWAIN' *Huck. Finn* xxix. 278 That mule-headed old fool wouldn't give in then! **1847** *Knickerbocker* XXIX. 161 One might have seen a small French cart, of the sort very appropriately called a 'mule-killer'. **1852** J. EVANS *Let.* 30 Apr. in G. N. Jones *Florida Plantation Rec.* (1927) 67, I would Call the New Waggon a nother Mule killer. **1890** *Cent. Dict.*, *Mule-killer*, the whip-tailed scorpion, *Thelyphonus giganteus*. **1899** *Mem. Amer. Folk-Lore Soc.* VII. 63 Mule-killer, devil's war-horse, praying mantis. *Kansas.* **1887** J. D. BILLINGS *Hardtack & Coffee* xvi. 315 Another invention for the transportation of the wounded from the field was the *Cacolet* or *Mule Litter*. **1904** R. J. FARRER *Garden of Asia* 81 Nor does a mule-litter hurry upon the road. **1857** *Spirit of Times* 28 Feb. 414/3 Some of our expedition.. went farther out, for the purpose of fetching in some of the deer, bar, and mule rabbits aforesaid. **1877** S. W. COZZENS *Crossing Quicksands* 80 More commonly known as the 'mule' rabbit, so called on account of its enormous ears. **1870** J. H. BEADLE *Life in Utah* 224, I took to the plains..in the capacity of a 'mule-skinner'. **1889** J. MCLEAN *Indians* v. 198 The men..are called bull-whackers and mule-skinners, applied to freighters who drive oxen or mules. **1962** A. FRY *Ranch on Cariboo* 160 I'd the repertoire of a mule-skinner, developed behind a wide variety of knotheaded horses. **1881** E. W. NYE *Bill Nye & Boomerang* 34 A practical knowledge of..mule skinning, vocal music, horsemanship. **1945** B. MACDONALD *Egg & I* 50 If only I had studied carpentry or mule skinning instead of ballet. **1971** J. GRAY *Red Lights* vii. 158 Nicholas Sheran gave up mule-skinning for coal mining. **1869** *Overland Monthly* III. 9 Here..is a cotton gin..and ponderous wooden wheels, and the mule-sweep underneath. **1873** J. H. BEADLE *Undevel. West* iv. 88 The streets were thronged with motley crowds of railroad men and mule-whackers. **1889** H. O'REILLY *50 Yrs. on Trail* 357 The town was full of cow-punchers, mule-whackers, [etc.].

mule[2]. **2.** Delete *Obs.* exc. *Hist.* and add later examples.

1922 S. LEWIS *Babbitt* xx. 254 She wore..torn stockings thrust into streaky pink satin mules. **1944** H. CROOME *You've gone Astray* v. 43 Kitty was gone in a light clatter of pink mules. **1973** 'I. DRUMMOND' *Jaws of Watchdog* xii. 160 The girl..padded softly across the room in her fluffy mules.

muled (miū̆ld), *a.*[2] [f. MULE[1] + -ED[2].] Of a coin: that is a mule (sense 4 c).

1914 *Brit. Mus. Return* 115 in *Parl. Papers* LXXI. 193 A muled groat of Henry VIII combining an obverse of the third coinage with a reverse of the second. **1961** DOLLEY & METCALF in R. H. M. Dolley *Anglo-Saxon Coins* 160 *BMC* types III and IV are found muled, though the coins are of the greatest rarity.

Muler, var. *MALER *sb.* and *a.*

Mules (miūlz). The name of J. H. W. *Mules* (d. 1946), Australian sheep-farmer, used *attrib.* or in the possessive to designate an operation developed by him to reduce the incidence of

blowfly strike in sheep by removing folds of skin from the crutch, the area most likely to be affected. So **mulesed** (miū̆lzd) *ppl. a.*, of a sheep, treated in this way; **mu·lesing** *vbl. sb.*, the use of this operation.

1933 *Sci. Bull. Council Sci. & Industr. Res.* (Austral.) No. 40. 9 By the surgical removal of the side folds (e.g., Mules' operation), the breech is opened up, urine soiling reduced, and susceptibility to strike decreased. *Ibid.* 103 By careful surgical procedure on the Mules principle, liability to strike should be reduced considerably, because the folds selected constitute the commonest site of strike. **1946** *Queensland Country Life* 18 Apr. 3 Mulesed sheep are much easier to crutch. *Ibid.*, We don't say that mulesing will stop the fly altogether. **1957** *New Biol.* XXII. 101 This experiment showed clearly that the Mules operation gave good protection against crutch strike in wrinkly breeched sheep. **1965** *Austral. Encycl.* II. 37/1 To effect a permanent improvement in the conformation of the crutch, J. H. W. Mules developed a technique for the surgical removal of the folds of skin occurring in the breech of many ewes. The Mules operation, as it is now called, has been modified and developed to a routine procedure. **1970** *Black's Vet. Dict.* (ed. 9) 558/1 Mules's operation.—This involves the removal of a fold of skin from the crutch of Merino sheep and is carried out by Australian sheepmen for the control of blowfly strike. Mulesing is a synonym.

‖ **muleta** (mūlē·tă). *Bullfighting.* [Sp.] The red cloth fixed to a stick which is used by a matador during the faena.

1838 *Q. Rev.* LXII. 417 The matador must not let the bull run on the muleta above two or three times. **1846** R. Ford *Gatherings from Spain* xxii. 308 The *matador*.. stands before his victim alone... In his left [hand] he waves the *muleta*, the red flag. **1873** J. W. Revere *Keel & Saddle* 111 Taking his stand firmly, he slowly unfolded the scarlet *muleta*. **1931** R. Campbell *Georgiad* i. 10 But leave the banderillos in their place Nor shake the red muleta in its face. **1932** E. Hemingway *Death in Afternoon* 304 The muleta is used to defend the man; to tire the bull and regulate the position of his head and feet. **1971** *Guardian* 20 July 8/6 Rita Hayworth..flaunting her red hair like a muleta.

muley (miū̆·li), *a.*³ Also **muly.** [f. Mule¹ + -y¹.] Mulish, stubborn; sulky.

1871 *Yorks. Mag.* I. 28/2 *Enah* means by and by; *muly*, sulky [etc.]. **1922** J. A. Dunn *Man Trap* v. 68, I got another drink into him, and made a fatal error in doing it, for he turned muley. **1956** *Sat. Even. Post* 21 Apr. 82 With the profits come a steady succession of worries that would discourage any but the most muley.

mulga. 1. Substitute for def.: A small spreading tree, *Acacia aneura*, widespread in dry inland areas of Australia, or one of several related trees found in such regions; also, land covered with vegetation of this kind. Also *attrib.* (Further examples.) Also used *colloq.* in general sense 'uninhabited or inhospitable region'.

1896 H. Lawson *While Billy Boils* 40 Two or three white-washed galvanized-iron roofs start out of the mulga. **1903** 'T. Collins' *Such is Life* 79 When he says 'mulga', he means any tree except pine or currajong. **1909** 'S. Rudd' *From Selection to City* (1910) xiv. 119 We had listened to many lies about the glory of running wild horses and cattle in the mulga. **1911** C. E. W. Bean '*Dreadnought' of Darling* i. 3 Belts of low mulga scrub. *Ibid.* x. 88 The graceful grey mulga trees..came right down to the river. **1928** V. Palmer *Man Hamilton* 26 Manager of this isolated place in the mulga, a hundred miles away from anywhere. **1936** F. Clune *Roaming round Darling* xxii. 223 A mulgawood causeway was built in front for a distance of thirty yards. **1946** F. D. Davison *Dusty* (1947) 1 They live at the bidding of herdsman and drover.., punching stubborn bullocks through the mulga. **1960** *Times* 5 July 11/6 The country was covered with light mulga scrub. **1964** *Punch* 18 Nov. 750/2 To pack a gun around the mulga. **1967** *Sunday Mail Mag.* (Brisbane) 8 Jan. 6/3, I had fancied myself original in conceiving the idea of taking a hot bath at 9 o'clock at night out in the 'mulga' in the middle of winter, and had borrowed a pair of swim trunks for the purpose. **1968** K. Weatherly *Roo Shooter* 5 On the stony hills, the mulga trees gave no shade. *Ibid.* 114 In this mental state he couldn't stay out in the mulga. **1969** *Northern Territory News* (Darwin) *Focus '69* 97/1 Contractors take the fuel off the Track to places out in the sticks and the mulga.

b. *Comb.*, as *mulga-covered, -dotted* adjs.; **mulga madness** *slang* (see quot. 1943); **mulga parrot**, a brightly coloured parrot, *Psephotus varius*, whose plumage includes patches of red, yellow, blue, and green; **mulga scrubber** *slang* (see quot. 1945); **mulga wire** *slang* = *grape-vine 2 a; a rumour, message, or report; a lie or false report.

1936 I. L. Idriess *Cattle King* iv. 27 They rode for thirty miles among the low, mulga-covered ridges that are the foot-hills of the Barrier Range. **1971** *World Archaeol.* III. 170 The mulga-covered flats. **1936** F. Clune *Roaming round Darling* xxii. 226 Steep mulga-dotted headland along Bluff Waterhole. **1943** Baker *Dict. Austral. Slang* (ed. 3) 52 *Mulga madness*, the 'queerness' sometimes developed in lone bushmen or fossickers. **1931** N. W. Cayley *What Bird is That?* 144 Mulga Parrot... Also called Many-coloured Parrot and Varied Parrot. **1941** I. L. Idriess *Great Boomerang* ii. 12 Mulga parrots and blue-bonnets lent a flash of living colour to the light-grey saltbush. **1968** K. Weatherly *Roo Shooter* 115 With the sun would come the parrakeets, mulga parrots, their green wings flashing in the sun. **1945** Baker *Austral. Lang.* iii. 67 The bullock driver and stockman have invented many terms by which to describe their charges. Here are some of the best:..*mulga scrubbers*.., stock that have run wild and deteriorated in condition. **1899** Mulga-wire [see sense 3 below]. **1913** H. Lawson *Triangles of Life* iii, in *Stories* (1964) 3rd Ser. 182 Tom had been out early, or had got what we call a bush telegraphy or mulga wire. **1937** E. Hill *Great Austral. Loneliness* xxiii. 207 Warned by the mulga wires of the approach of a white woman. *Ibid.* 329 *Mulga wires.* Bush telegraph, gossip of the outback. **1940** A. W. Upfield *Bushranger of Skies* ix. 101 This morning I found Itcheroo squatted before a little fire and sending or receiving a mulga wire. **1964** *Evening Post* (Wellington, N.Z.) 3 Mar. 17 The grapevine or 'mulga wire' in opera circles was instrumental in the return to Wellington of [a]..mezzo-soprano.

3. *slang.* Short for *mulga wire.

1899 *Bulletin* (Sydney) 4 Mar. 15/2 A lie or false report is, in N.S.W., a 'Mulga' or 'Mulga-wire'. **1908** E. S. Sorenson *Quinton's Rouseabout* 186 They'll be that delighted to find it was only a mulga that they'd toast you as 'a jolly good fellow'. **1941** Baker *Dict. Austral. Slang* 47 *Mulga*, a falsehood, a rumour. **1950** K. S. Prichard *Winged Seeds* 297 The troops 've had it all by mulga. They've heard too.

muliebrity. (Further examples.)

1888 B. Harte *Phyllis of Sierras* ii. i. 169 This tall.. woman..possessed a refined muliebrity superior to mere liberality of contour. **1911** H. G. Wells *New Machiavelli* ii. ii. 206 She was one of those women who are wanting in —what is the word?—muliebrity.

mull, *sb.*¹ Add: **2.** A suspension of a finely ground solid in a liquid, esp. one used in recording the infra-red spectrum of the solid.

1956 *Mineral. Mag.* XXXI. 193 Spectra were obtained on the Perkin–Elmer model 21 double-beam instrument, using both the 'Nujol' mull technique and pressed KBr pellets. **1964** H. A. Szymanski *IR: Theory & Pract. Infrared Spectroscopy* iii. 78 Hydrocarbon oils as well as halogenated hydrocarbons have been used as the liquid in mulls. **1971** Skoog & West *Princ. Instrumental Analysis* vi. 152 The resulting mull is then examined as a thin film between flat salt plates.

mull, *sb.*⁷ Add: Esp. the fine muslin sometimes stuck to the spine of a book before its cover is put on.

1880 J. W. Zaehnsdorf *Art of Bookbinding* xix. 85 In 'throw up' backs, or in 'flexible not to show', a piece of thin linen or stuff called mull (muslin) is glued on the back first, and one piece of paper on the top. **1951** S. Jennett *Making of Books* xi. 173 A length of mull (the open-weave material that can be seen through the endpapers of most books). **1967** V. Strauss *Printing Industry* x. 673/2 The next preparatory step is lining up. It consists in attaching one or more strips of fabric, known as crash—called mull in Canada—and super, as well as a strip of strong paper to the back of the book.

attrib.

1873 *Young Englishwoman* Dec. 559/1 This edging may be worked on cambric or mull muslin. **1910** *Encycl. Brit.* VII. 277/2 (*Cotton*) The finer kinds, made from Egyptian yarns, are called mull-dhooties. **1960** Cunnington & Beard *Dict. Eng. Costume* 265/1 *Mull muslin*, 19th c., a soft thin muslin, not silky, finer than nainsook.

mull (mɒl), *sb.*¹⁰ *Soil Sci.* [ad. Da. *muld* Mould *sb.*¹ (adopted in this specific sense by P. E. Müller 1879, in *Tidsskrift for Skovbrug* III. 7): etymologically = Mull *sb.*¹] Humus which does not form a distinct layer on top of the soil but is admixed with the underlying mineral soil, which is characteristic of grasslands and hardwood forests and is generally weakly acid to weakly alkaline in reaction. Cf. *mor.

1928 *Ecology* IX. 9 The soil on this..was identified by Dr. Hesselman as a true mull profile. *Ibid.* 10 The mull is deepest under ash and sugar maple. **1931** *Ibid.* XII. 570 Müller distinguished two main types of humus layer called *mull*..and *mor*. **1935** *Forestry* IX. 43 *Mull* or neutral humus..though usually acid in reaction contains sufficient calcium to allow of a crumb or grain structure with a generally 'loose' or 'porous' constitution. **1952** P. W. Richards *Trop. Rain Forest* ix. 218 The humus of rain-forest soils..would appear to resemble the 'mull' rather than the 'mor' of temperate forest soils. **1974** *Encycl. Brit. Macropædia* VII. 537/1 In the temperate regions two major types of organic matter predominate, the mull and the mor.

mull (mɒl), *sb.*¹¹ [f. Mull *v.*³] Mulled wine.

1925 J. Thomas *Bon Vivant's Compan.* 105 (*heading*) Mulls. **1953** D. A. Embury *Fine Art of Mixing Drinks* xiii. 296 A mull, or mulled wine, is simply a spiced and sweetened wine served piping hot. **1959** *Listener* 24 Dec. 1135/3 The mull must be kept hot. **1962** J. Conil *Epicurean Book* xiii. 209 Do not boil the wine, nor allow the mull to reach boiling point. **1972** *House & Garden* Dec. 103/1 The best mulls have as their base an inexpensive, full-bodied red wine.

mull, *v.*¹ Add: **1. b.** *trans.* To convert (solid material) into a mull (*mull *sb.*¹ 2). So **mulled** *ppl. a.*²

1941 *Austral. Jrnl. Dentistry* XLV. 163/2 The writer feels justified in urging all dentists to give up the practice of mulling their amalgams in the bare palm of the hand. *Ibid.* 161/2 It should..be stated that the curves for the mulled specimens are average ones. **1943** *Industr. & Engin. Chem.* (*Analytical Ed.*) XV. 663/2 Samples of insoluble, infusible materials may be prepared for examination by grinding the substance to as fine a powder as possible, then mulling it thoroughly in a straight-chain hydrocarbon, such as Nujol. **1948** *Rev. Sci. Instruments* XIX. 165/1 The present technique is to mull the sample in a mineral oil such as Nujol. **1956** J. N. Anderson *Appl. Dental Materials* xxv. 359 The dentist..may show symptoms of slight mercurial poisoning if he employs the technique of 'mulling' or 'palming' amalgam in the hand over a period of years. **1964** H. A. Szymanski *IR: Theory & Pract. Infrared Spectroscopy* iii. 78 The name given to this technique [*sc.* dispersing a solid in a liquid] is *mulling* the sample.

mull, *v.*⁵ Add: **2.** Delete '*colloq. U.S.*' and add earlier example.

1857 J. G. Holland *Bay-Path* xvii. 200 'What do you do with them [troubles]?' 'Let 'em mull.'

b. *mull over* (an idea, etc.), to turn over in one's mind, cogitate upon.

1880, etc. [in Dict.]. **1910** J. London *Let.* 9 Feb. (1966) 299 If I can get from you a suggestion of a motif.. which, after mulling over, I decide I can do, I could..join you. **1949** B. Woolfe in A. Dundes *Mother Wit* (1973) 529 The Rabbit mulls the problem over. **1958** *Times* 20 Aug. 10/7 Bill and I discovered a mutual hobby in fishing. Rods had to be produced for inspection..and experiences mulled over. **1966** *Listener* 3 Nov. 650/2 Of course one mulls over that.

c. *trans.* To consider, ponder upon. *U.S.*

1923 *Dialect Notes* V. 215 *Mull*, v., to ponder over, to cogitate upon. **1949** *Sun* (Baltimore) 27 Dec. 5/1 At last report, the county was mulling a price. **1958** *Wall St. Jrnl.* 29 Oct. 1/5 The idea of a U.S. pledge to facilitate state and local borrowing is mulled by the joint Federal–state committee on swapping services and revenue sources between the U.S. Government and the states. **1972** *Newsweek* 10 Jan. 39/3 Mr. Nixon is mulling two possible tactics. **1972** *Science* 22 Sept. 1081/1 The Germans.. were mulling a public recommendation from their safety advisory committee.

mull (mɒl), *v.*⁸ [Perh. related to other vbl. uses of Mull.] **a.** *trans.* To moisten (leather) during manufacture so as to make it more supple. **b.** *intr.* Of leather: to become soft by moistening. So **mulled** *ppl. a.*³, **mu·lling** *vbl. sb.*³

1931 F. Plucknett *Boot & Shoe Manuf.* xxvi. 166/2 One of the more recent innovations in the lasting-room is the 'mulling chamber', the idea being that if the upper materials absorb a suitable amount of dampness they will stretch easier. **1953** W. Moore in J. H. Thornton *Textbk. Footwear Manuf.* xx. 277 A criticism of mulling is that the fibre of the leather is adversely affected... The mulled upper after lasting is rather damp. **1962** *New Scientist* 12 Apr. 33/1 Almost any known leather, it is believed, can be mulled in fewer than four minutes. **1963** *Times* 7 Mar. 20/1 In previous shoemaking methods the uppers of the shoes had to remain on 'lasts' for five or six days in order to get their shape. The new process does the job in half an hour by means of pumping moisture into the leather in a special mulling machine. **1969** T. C. Thorstensen *Pract. Leather Technol.* xii. 197 After the oils and greases have been distributed uniformly over the surface, the leather is removed from the drum and allowed to mull, once the initial heat has been removed by air cooling.

mullarkey, var. *malarkey.

Muller (mu·ləɹ), *sb.*⁴ The name of J. P. *Muller* (b. 1866), Danish physical educationalist, used *attrib.* and in the possessive esp. to designate a set of bodily exercises published and promoted by him.

c **1912** J. P. Muller *My Syst. for Ladies* 86 In a pamphlet published by the *Ligue des Mères de Famille* (France), the following letter from Mme. A. de Four appeared:—Two years practice of Muller's exercises has given me muscles sufficiently resistive to enable me to leave off wearing the corset. **1921** A. Huxley *Crome Yellow* xxiv. 260 He would have to try and do his Muller exercises more regularly. **1952** M. Gilbert *Death in Captivity* xii. 182 We must therefore maintain bodily suppleness and agility by means of Muller's exercises before breakfast and a regular physical training class at least once a day.

Müller (mü·ləɹ), *sb.*¹ *Min.* Also **Muller.** [f. the surname (supposedly of its discoverer).] *Müller's glass* (also † *Müller glass*, † *glass of Müller*): = Hyalite.

1794 Müller's Glass [see Hyalite]. **1836** T. Thomson *Outl. Min., Geol.* I. 73 Hyalite or Muller glass. **1852** Glass of Muller [see Hyalite]. **1940** G. F. H. Smith *Gemstones* (ed. 9) xxxii. 302 Hyalite, sometimes called Müller's glass after its discoverer, is a remarkable opal which is as clear as glass. **1962** R. Webster *Gems* I. x. 186 Hyalite is a colourless transparent variety of opal that closely resembles melted glass; it is sometimes called Müller's glass.

Müller (mü·ləɹ), *sb.*² *Anat.* The name of Heinrich *Müller* (1820–64), German anatomist, used *attrib.*, in the possessive, and with *of*-adjunct to designate various anatomical structures of the eye which he described, as: **a.** Neuroglial cells, having the appearance of fibres, which form the supportive ground tissue of the retina.

1856 G. V. Ellis *Demonstrations Anat.* (ed. 4) x. 777 Passing vertically through the retina are other fine threads —fibres of Müller. **1886** C. F. Pollock *Normal & Path. Histol. Human Eye & Eyelids* 127 The fibres of Müller are

the most prominent parts of a supporting matrix, which pervades the retina. **1932** W. PENFIELD *Cytol. & Cellular Path. Nervous Syst.* II. ix. 436 (*heading*) Astrocytes of the retina (Müller's cells). *Ibid.* xvi. 767 In other strata the Müller cells are followed with difficulty. **1961** DUKE-ELDER & WYBAR *Syst. Ophthalm.* II. 256 (*heading*) The fibers of Müller. *Ibid.*, On the vitreal aspect of the retina Müller's fibres terminate in large conical or bulbous expansions. **1971** M. J. HOGAN et al. *Histol. Human Eye* ix. 462 The mature Müller cell is complex in shape.

b. Each of three smooth muscles, of which one is part of the ciliary muscle, one (the orbitalis) is in the orbit, and one (the superior tarsal muscle) is in the upper eyelid.

1875 *Encycl. Brit.* I. 887/2 The inner part of the [ciliary] muscle forms a ring-like arrangement of fasciculi close to the circumference of the iris, and is often called the annular muscle of Müller. **1890** BILLINGS *Med. Dict.* II. 174/1 *Müller's annular muscle*, ciliary muscle. *Ibid.* 174/2 *Müller's muscle*, smooth muscular fibres found in the membrana orbitalis. *Ibid.*, *Müller's palpebral muscle*, a collection of smooth muscle-fibres in the upper eyelid. **1912** A. THOMSON *Anat. Human Eye* i. 13 Corresponding to the bases of the free projecting extremities of the ciliary processes..is a group of fibres..arranged circumferentially; these constitute the circular fibres of Müller. **1921** S. E. WHITNALL *Anat. Human Orbit* 82 This muscle, described by H. Müller in 1858, is known as the 'orbital muscle of Müller', or *musculus orbitalis*. *Ibid.* 296 The palpebral involuntary muscles (of Müller). **1950** *Irish Jrnl. Med. Sci.* 39 (*heading*) Some aspects of Muller's [*sic*] orbital muscle. **1964** [see *ENOPHTHALMUS, -MOS]. **1969** BEARD & QUICKERT *Anat. Orbit* 4 Mueller's [*sic*] sympathetic (superior tarsal) muscle can be seen extending from the junction of the muscular levator and the levator aponeurosis to the superior border of the tarsus.

müller (mü·ləɹ), *v.* Also **muller** (mʊ·ləɹ). [f. the name of Franz *Müller*, a murderer, who was convicted in 1864 on circumstantial evidence in which a hat was of considerable significance.] *trans.* To alter (a hat) in the manner alleged to have been done by Franz Müller. Also as *sb.*, a type of flat-topped felt hat similar to that associated with Müller.

1864 in Farmer & Henley *Slang* (1896) IV. 384/1 In a small shop not far from Sloane-square, Chelsea, may be seen the following tasteful announcement: Hats muller'd here! **1909** *Daily Chron.* 22 Nov. 4/7 Müller's hat..formed the connecting link in a remarkable chain of circumstantial evidence. Henceforth 'mullers', as they were called, were tabooed. **1934** *Trans. Philol. Soc. 1933* 101 A *Müller hat* is a flat-topped, hard felt.

Müllerian (mülɪə·riăn), *a.*² [f. the name of J. F. T. (Fritz) *Müller* (1821–97), German zoologist, who, in 1878, explained this type of mimicry + -IAN.] In *Müllerian mimicry, resemblance*, a form of mimicry (see sense 2 in Dict. & Suppl.) in which insects of different species develop similar patterns of coloration, etc., as a protective device. Also *Müllerian mimic*, an insect exhibiting this type of mimicry.

1899 [see *BATESIAN *a.*]. **1934** *Discovery* July 195/1 Two or more, often many, inedible forms assume a similar aspect and thus enjoy a common advantage by virtue of uniting to share the toll levied on them by experimental tasting. This is the kind of assimilation which was explained by Fritz Müller and often goes by the name of Müllerian mimicry. **1951** *New Biol.* X. 73 'Müllerian' resemblance is when two or more distasteful organisms resemble one another, thereby deriving collective advantage in that a predator has only to 'learn' one pattern which will suffice to protect all the species which have it. *Ibid.*, Müllerian and Batesian mimics may be involved together in nature in a complex mimetic association, all the members of which wear the same livery. **1968** R. D. MARTIN tr. *Wickler's Mimicry in Plants & Animals* vii. 78 Most examples of Müllerian mimicry..involve different species with the same complex patterns. *Ibid.* 79 Müllerian mimicry increases in efficiency the greater the number of species in the system and the better the correspondence in pattern. **1975** *Trans. Roy. Entom. Soc.* CXXVI. 632 *Heliconius* species are frequently highly distasteful, and act as models in many Müllerian systems.

Müller-Lyer (mülər ləi·əɹ). Also erron. **Muller-**. The name of Franz Carl *Müller-Lyer* (1857–1916), German sociologist and philosopher, used *attrib.* (and *absol.*) to designate an optical illusion he described (*Arch. f. Anat. u. Physiol.* (*Physiol. Abth.*) (1889) Suppl. 263–70), by which a line with a V-shaped arrowhead at each end appears shorter than an adjacent line of equal length but with the V-shaped portions reversed and pointing inwards.

1899 *Psychol. Rev.* VI. 241 Brentano's unsuccessful attempt to explain the Müller-Lyer illusion by the general fact that acute angles are overestimated and obtuse angles are underestimated. **1938** R. S. WOODWORTH *Exper. Psychol.* xxv. 646 One of the two Müller-Lyer figures is kept of constant length and used as a Standard, while the other figure is the Variable. **1958** *New Biol.* XXVII. 27 He chose for his experiment the well-known Muller-Lyer illusion. **1969** F. C. SHONTZ *Perceptual & Cognitive Aspects Body Experience* iii. 41 In certain complex stimuli, like the Müller-Lyer illusion, the organization of a perceptual field may lengthen or shorten the apparent length of a line. **1972** *Jrnl. Social Psychol.* LXXXVII. 144 Samples from Western cultures..are more inclined than Eastern ones to see the Muller-Lyer.

mullet¹. Add: **1, 2.** The name, often with an adjective prefixed to it, is used for any fish of the families Mullidæ, or red mullets, and Mugilidæ, or grey mullets. (Further examples.)

1820, etc. [see *KANAE]. **1925** J. T. JENKINS *Fishes Brit. Isles* 123 There are a large number of species of mullets in the genus *Mugil*. **1951** T. C. ROUGHLEY *Fish Austral.* 31 The mullets contained in the family Mugilidae range through the temperate regions of the world. **1962** K. F. LAGLER et al. *Ichthyol.* ix. 277 Neurosecretory cells in the preoptic nucleus of the hypothalamus lose their secretions rapidly in several marine fishes, including.. mullets (Mugilidae) when the fishes are temporarily placed in hypertonic sea water. **1966** *Encycl. N.Z.* II. 600/2 A familiar sight is the gleaming flash as a mullet leaps out of the water and returns to its element. **1969** A. WHEELER *Fishes Brit. Is. & N.-W. Europe* 465/1 Very young mullet are also common in intertidal pools on the Channel coast.

mullet-head. [? f. MULLET¹.] **1.** *U.S.* A freshwater fish with a large flat head.

1866 *Harper's Mag.* Sept. 537/1 Dat fish is a mullet-head; it hain't got any brains. **1873** J. H. BEADLE *Undevel. West* v. 102 There is a fish called the mullethead, that cannot be intoxicated by any amount of liquor. **1893** W. FORBES-MITCHELL *Reminisc. Great Mutiny* vi. 110 That fish, my son, is called a mullet-head: it has got no brains.

2. [Cf. *mull-head* a dull, stupid fellow (*E.D.D.*).] A stupid person. So **mullet-headed** *a.*

1857 *Quindaro* (Kansas) *Chindowan* 6 June 1/3 The men, for the most part sleepy, ignorant, mullet-headed looking wretches. **1884** 'MARK TWAIN' *Huck. Finn* xxxix. 370 They're so confiding and mullet-headed they don't take notice of nothing at all. **1916** *Dialect Notes* IV. 278 Look at that *mullet-head* of a Sam Smith. He don't know beans. **1935** Z. N. HURSTON *Mules & Men* (1970) I. i. 30 Hey, you mullet heads! Get out de way. **1942** BERREY & VAN DEN BARK *Amer. Thes. Slang* § 150/5 *Stupid*,..mullet-headed. *Ibid.* 433/3 *Stupid person*,..mullet-head.

mulligan (mʊ·ligăn). *N. Amer.* [Apparently f. a proper name.] **1.** A stew made from odds and ends of food. Also *attrib.*

1904 *Yukon Midnight Sun* (Dawson, Yukon Territory) 10 Jan. 3/4 All the roadhouses served big Christmas dinners and most of them made a mulligan. **1913** *Collier's* 11 Jan. 16/2, I suppose you never have eaten any 'Mulligan'... The recipe calls for canned Willie, spuds, onions, canned tomatoes, all mixed up together. **1914** *Sat. Even. Post* 4 Apr. 10/1 It was a mulligan. Everything was in that stew—meat, potatoes, onions, bread—an appetizing hodgepodge. **1918** C. SANDBURG *Cornhuskers* 80 Then they go to the bunk cars and eat mulligan and prune sauce. **1926** J. BLACK *You can't Win* vii. 83 There was a grand jungle by a small clean river where they..cooked their mulligans. *Ibid.* xv. 198 He's crazy as a bed bug and the best 'mulligan' maker on the road. **1955** R. P. HOBSON *Nothing too Good for Cowboy* 138 That's what's good for me, a great beeg vegetable mulligan with feesh in it. **1966** H. MARRIOTT *Cariboo Cowboy* ii. 35 Lots of mulligan stew with beef, carrots and onions. **1971** 'R. MACDONALD' *Underground Man* xix. 135 A number of plywood tables had been set up on trestles. A hundred or more men were seated at them, eating mulligan stew.

2. (With capital initial.) *Golf.* An extra stroke awarded after a poor shot, not counted on the score card. *colloq.*

1949 P. CUMMINGS *Dict. Sports* 275 *Mulligan, Golf*, a handicap of a free shot given after a player makes a bad one. **1952** *Golf Digest* May 7 'It's just a friendly match,' he said. 'Wanna take a mulligan?' **1965** H. GRAFFIS *Esquire's World of Golf* xii. 174 Magnanimously, the hustler will allow his prey a Mulligan off the tee now and then. **1971** *Daily Colonist* (Victoria, B.C.) 7 Feb. 1/2 With millions watching on color television, Shepard took another poke—the extra chance golf duffers call a 'Mulligan'—and connected solidly.

mulling, *vbl. sb.*² [f. MULL *v.*¹ + -ING¹.] The process of rubbing or grinding; the conversion of a solid into a mull (*MULL *sb.*¹ 2).

1937 *Austral. Jrnl. Dentistry* XLI. 127 Mixing. This consisted of 1, 1½ or 2 minutes trituration in a standard mortar using about 120 revolutions of the pestle per minute, followed by 1 or 1½ minutes mulling in the hand. **1944** E. R. RIEGEL *Chem. Machinery* xi. 249 Mulling is the second way in which solids may be mixed with solids. The mulling action is comparable to the rubbing, kneading, or smearing action of the mortar and pestle; no grinding is involved. The machine for mulling consists of a circular stationary pan in which is mounted a special combination of mullers and plows which revolves. **1964** H. A. SZYMANSKI *IR: Theory & Pract. Infrared Spectroscopy* iii. 79 One of the disadvantages of mulling is that it cannot be used very conveniently on rubber, plastics, or resinous materials. **1971** ROSENBLATT & DAVIS *Laboratory Course Org. Chem.* iii. 71 Another method for preparing a solid sample is to grind 5 mg of the solid to a fine dispersion in a drop of suitable mulling agent. **1971** *Materials & Technol.* II. iii. 140 Mulling improves the final shape of the grain by knocking off its brittle corners, and this is carried out by impact crushing, pan milling, or air blasting.

mullion. Add: **2.** *Geol.* Each of a series of ribs or columns of rock (*spec.* those composed of the local rock) on a rock face, usu. formed by folding. So *mullion structure*.

1891 E. HULL et al. *Explanatory Mem. Sheets 3–5, 9–11, 15 & 16 Maps Geol. Survey Ireland* iv. 53 To the north of Carnteena, quartzite of the yellowish-white compact variety, forms the bare rocky hills of Crocknaglogh and Croaghnacreggy and in some parts 'mullion structure' was observed—a peculiar fluting due to the shearing of the rocks. **1937** *Q. Jrnl. Geol. Soc.* XCIII. 597 The individual mullions are not always due to the presence of small folds, as is apparently true of the quartz rods of Beinn Thutaig. **1953** *Proc. Geologists' Assoc.* LXIV. 118 Distinction is drawn between mullions which look like 'clustered columns' and are composed of the local country-rock, and rodding. *Ibid.* 124 A remarkable lone mullion resulting from erosion of an abrupt double fold is found at Poll Cròm. **1963** E. S. HILLS *Elem. Struct. Geol.* x. 310 The subdivision of a bed, more particularly a sandstone interbedded with slate, into long parallel slabs with smooth rounded surfaces is known as mullion-structure. **1966** E. H. T. WHITTEN *Struct. Geol. Folded Rocks* ix. 313 Excellent mullions developed in these quartzites, and in the granite close to the northwestern contact zone.

mullite (mʊ·ləit). *Min.* [f. *Mull*, the name of an island off the west coast of Scotland + -ITE¹.] A silicate of aluminium, approximately $Al_9Si_3O_{20}$, that occurs as orthorhombic crystals, is formed naturally or artificially by the action of high temperatures on other aluminium silicates, and is used for making refractory porcelains and bricks.

1924 N. L. BOWEN et al. in *Jrnl. Washington Acad. Sci.* XIV. 184 The occurrence in natural rocks necessitates a mineralogical name and for this [*sc.* the compound $3Al_2O_3.2SiO_2$] we propose the term, *mullite*, after the locality whence came the rocks in which it is here first identified, the Island of Mull. **1930** *Engineering* 26 Dec. 813/3 The successful application of refractories prepared from..synthetic mullite emphasised the effect of 'mullite' content in promoting chemical resistance. **1941** *Proc. Prehist. Soc.* VII. 64 Porcellanite..probably representing a pisolitic bauxitic clay from the inter-basaltic horizon.. is composed of dark spinel and a light fine-grained aggregate of sillimanite and mullite. **1967** M. CHANDLER *Ceramics in Mod. World* i. 19 Some of these later combine with each other to form new crystalline phases, including needle-like particles of crystalline mullite. **1974** *Nature* 2 Aug. 403/1 Quartz samples..were heated in a vacuum in outgassed mullite or alumina tubes.

Hence **mullitiza·tion**, conversion into mullite; **mu·llitized** *ppl. a.*

1939 *Ceramic Abstr.* XVIII. 251/1 Mullite is formed rapidly during the firing of clay... The temperature of firing determines the degree of mullitization. **1948** *Jrnl. Amer. Ceramic Soc.* XXXI. 254 (*heading*) Mullitization of kaolinite. *Ibid.* 258 In more completely mullitized instances, e.g., after firing to 1300°C., groups of mullite needles in associated growth simulate hexagonal aggregations.

mullock, *sb.* Add: **1. b.** *fig.* Worthless information, nonsense. *Austral.* and *N.Z.*

1866 R. BURGESS *Autobiogr.* (typescript) 127 He said, No b....y fear. I should know it was a lot of mullock they were telling for you are not like this Jew. **1911** *Triad* XVIII. 41 We have a lot of trash and maudlin mullock in these days. **1934** *Bulletin* (Sydney) 20 June 47/1 'Cooney,' I said, 'it is madness to present such mullock to an intellectual audience.'

c. *to poke mullock (at)*: to deride, ridicule, make fun of. *Austral.*

1916 C. J. DENNIS *Songs Sentimental Bloke* 126 *Mullock, to poke*—to deride, to tease. **1916** —— *Moods of Ginger Mick* 74, I own me eyes git brighter When I see 'em pokin' mullock at the everlastin' sea. **1931** V. PALMER *Separate Lives* 210 D'you think I'm going to sit in that galley with Curran and the other blokes all poking mullock at me? **1942** G. CASEY *It's Harder for Girls* 153 The chaps poked mullock at me, but it wasn't that that hurt. **1945** BAKER *Austral. Lang.* v. 94 *To poke mullock* (also *muck*) *at*, an extension of *poke borak at*, to make fun of a person. **1957** R. LAWLER *Summer of 17th Doll* 71 Oh, so that's what you got me in for, is it—to poke mullock. **1962** J. MORRISON *Twenty-Three* 86, I heard what you said when you grabbed that rope. Poking mullock at us because we won't go out over an empty hatch.

mullock, *v.* (*Austral.* and *N.Z.* examples.)

1862 *Otago Daily Times* 9 July 5 Whether the flat will pay to reslice at present, from its being so much worked and 'mullocked' and also rather deep, is doubtful. **1893** *Age* (Melbourne) 23 Sept. 14/4 No man could shear 321 sheep in eight hours, although I will admit he might do what we shearers call 'mullock over' that number. **1945** BAKER *Austral. Lang.* 94 *To mullock over*, to work shoddily. **1965** J. S. GUNN *Terminol. Shearing Industry* II. 5 *Mullock over*, to rush the work quickly and carelessly, thus turning out badly shorn sheep.

mully-grub (mʊ·ligrʊb). *Austral.* [Var. of MULLIGRUBS *pl.*] A wichetty grub (cf. WITCHETTY), the larva of various insects, esp. goat-moths of the family Cossidæ and ghost-moths of the family Hepialidæ, which infest the stems and roots of plants, from which they are extracted and used as food by aborigines and as bait by fishermen.

1959 J. WRIGHT *Generations of Men* 28 A gin had gone over to look for mully-grubs in the bush. **1966** *Courier-Mail* (Brisbane) 26 Nov. 8/8 The woman..had told him frequently to 'go and eat his mully grubs', and to 'go back to the bush where you came from'.

multi-. Add: **1.** (From the adjs. are formed advbs. (e.g. *multiserially* in Dict.) and sbs. (e.g. *multicellularity* below).) **a.** *multicelled*,

-molecular, -perforated, -stranded; **multicellular:** hence **mu:lticellula·rity,** the state or condition of being multicellular; **multice·ntric,** pertaining to or having many centres or foci; (of a chromosome or chromatid) having many centromeres; **multicy·clic** *Geol.*, produced by or having undergone many cycles of erosion and deposition; **multidentate,** (*b*) *Chem.* (of a ligand) having more than one point at which it can be attached to a central atom; **multidimensional** (further examples); hence **mu:ltidimensiona·lity,** the property of being multidimensional; **multidime·nsionally** *adv.*, in a manner that involves or requires more than three dimensions; **multifacto·rial,** involving or dependent on a number of factors (*spec.* genes) or causes; hence **multifacto·rially** *adv.*; **multifo·cal,** having or pertaining to several foci, or a range of focal lengths; also as *sb. pl.*, spectacles with multifocal lenses; **multigene·ric,** derived from or involving more than one genus; **multimammate,** having several pairs of mammæ, esp. used to designate the multimammate rat or mouse, *Mastomys natalensis*, a rodent found in tropical Africa; **multipote·ntial** *Med.*, capable of differentiating into any of several kinds of cell or tissue; **multiseriate** (later examples); **multispe·ctral,** operating in or involving several of the regions into which the electromagnetic spectrum is conventionally divided; **multispi·cular** = *multispiculate*; **multista·ble,** (of a system) composed of a number of interconnected subsystems each of which can achieve stability independently of the others; so **multistabi·lity,** the property or state of being multistable.

1968 *Punch* 31 July 157/2 Some urge..has merged it [*sc.* the public] into one worldwide, multicelled acerebral organism. **1972** *Sci. Amer.* Apr. 72/2 The globins were evolving to play several different roles during and after this period, as multicelled organisms arose. **1916** W. TROTTER *Instincts of Herd* 18 Looked at in this way, multicellularity presents itself as an escape from the rigour of natural selection. **1972** *Sci. Amer.* Dec. 95/1 His Mesozoa may yet provide us with valuable evidence on the evolution of multicellularity and on the mechanisms of differentiation and development. **1934** WEBSTER, Multicentric. **1941** *Cold Spring Harbor Symp. Quant. Biol.* IX. 153 Di- and multicentric chromosomes. **1971** *Brit. Med. Bull.* XXVII. 68/2 Multi-centric hypotheses have not proved as popular as multi-stage hypotheses, or theories which assume that a change from a normal to a malignant cell takes place in stages. **1972** *Year Bk. Dermatol.* 185 The present study examined the ultrastructural characteristics of multicentric reticulohistiocytosis. **1952, 1954** Multicyclic [see *MONOCYCLIC *a.* 5]. **1966** G. H. DURY *Ess. Geomorphol.* 128 The degree to which multi-cyclic bevelling is displayed varies widely. **1972** *Science* 3 Nov. 503/1 A large proportion of the grains appears to be multicyclic, having undergone several cycles of erosion and deposition. **1959** *Nomencl. Inorg. Chem.* (I.U.P.A.C.) 64 A group containing more than one *potential* co-ordinating atom is termed a multidentate ligand. **1974** *Chem. Rev.* LXXIV. 351/1 This review deals with the synthesis of multidentate macrocyclic compounds. **1956** E. H. HUTTEN *Lang. Mod. Physics* v. 171 The propagation of the wave must be described as taking place, in most instances, in a multi-dimensional hyper-space, and not in ordinary space. **1963** F. G. LOUNSBURY in J. A. Fishman *Readings Sociol. of Lang.* (1968) 49 Inflection in some languages is carried into several dimensions of variation, resulting in multidimensional paradigms running into hundreds or even thousands of forms. **1970** *Jrnl. Gen. Psychol.* LXXXII. 172 Anxiety is a vague and multidimensional concept. **1967** J. W. JOHNSTON in T. Hayashi *Olfaction & Taste II* 48 This information could be utilized to investigate the relationship between the multidimensionality of odors and the hypothetical sensor units or sites on the receptor membrane. **1968** W. A. SCOTT in Lindzey & Aronson *Handbk. Social Psychol.* (ed. 2) II. 251 The dilemma of multidimensionality stems from the acceptance of a measurement model which equates dimension, in the geometrical sense, with psychological notions of attribute magnitude. **1970** *Computers & Humanities* IV. 210 Meylan has to be selective in what he chooses for encoding, and is unable to represent the entire 'multidimensionality' of the melody (e.g., its complete context). **1957** C. E. OSGOOD et al. in Saporta & Bastian *Psycholinguistics* (1961) 294/2 We may assume at the outset that meanings vary multidimensionally. **1920** W. E. CASTLE *Genetics & Eugenics* (ed. 2) xxxi. 275 It would be a mistake to cover up our present ignorance concerning the inheritance of these characters by classifying them either as unifactorial or as multifactorial. **1937** *Biol. Rev.* XII. 481 The melanism of *Oporinia dilutata* has a multi-factorial basis. **1960** H. J. EYSENCK *Handbk. Abnormal Psychol.* viii. 309/2 Most of the characteristics..are of a quantitatively variable kind, and..regulated by multifactorial and not unifactorial inheritance. **1965** J. POLLITT *Depression & its Treatment* 96 The use of these terms is not in keeping with the view that the ætiology of depression is multifactorial. **1974** *Nature* 10 May 145/2 It can be assumed that the aetiology of cranioschisis is at least complex and multifactorial involving environmental agents as well as genetic factors. **1954** P. M. SHEPPARD in J. S. Huxley et al. *Evolution as Process* 212 (*heading*) The evolution of multifactorially controlled characters. **1973** *Nature* 22 June 433/1 The word genic is extended from its regular use to include multifactorially determined disorders. **1920** T. P. NUNN *Education* 111 The multi-focal view, to which Thorndike has now transferred his allegiance, holds that our abilities fall into a small number of groups. **1928** S. DUKE-ELDER *Pract. Refraction* xxiii. 344 In the multifocal lenses, introduced by Gowland of Montreal, in 1922..the reading portion of the lens has a continuous variable curve, there being a gradual accretion of power from the periphery to the reading centre. **1961** *Brit. Jrnl. Surg.* XLIX. 92/1 Low-grade, primary, multifocal osteosarcoma occurring in middle age appears to be a distinct entity. **1962** L. S. SASIENI *Princ. & Pract. Optical Dispensing* v. 125 The accurate fitting of bifocals and multifocals will be considered later. **1971** *Optometry Today* (Amer. Optometric Assoc.) 12 Special optical devices such as multi-focal lenses, contact lenses and other vision aids are used. **1953** *Internat. Code Nomencl. Cultivated Plants* 25 Such [hybrids] as are trigeneric or multigeneric. **1971** J. Z. YOUNG *Introd. Study Man* xxxii. 445 It may be that ultimately some or all the forms now called *Australopithecus* will be referred to as various species of the genus *Homo*... We prefer to keep a somewhat more conservative (multigeneric) classification. **1902** *Ann. & Mag. Nat. Hist.* IX. 219, I fail to find any point whatever by which *M*[*us*] *Hildegardeæ* can be distinguished externally from the Machakos member of the multimammate group. **1955** *New Biol.* XIX. 108 House rodents such as the native multimammate mouse..and the black rat, which is replacing it, are the reservoirs [of plague in Central Africa] rather than fully rural species. **1959** *Nature* 12 Sept. 794/2 The multimammate rat is a wild rodent which lives in close contact with man in Africa. **1974** *Ibid.* 13 Sept. 101/3 Lassa virus was isolated from a single murine species, the multimammate rat *Mastomys natalensis*, which is a common commensal rodent in West Africa adapted to life both within houses and in the fields. **1944** S. BRUNAUER *Adsorption of Gases* I. 6 When the surface can take up only one layer of the adsorbed gas, the adsorption is called unimolecular; when more than one layer it is called multimolecular. **1969** *Science* 12 Dec. 1365/3 Bacteria, viruses, or cells..often called antigens..really are multimolecular mixtures of polydeterminant antigens. **1928** *Funk's Stand. Dict.*, Multiperforated. **1957** *Jrnl. Brit. Interplanetary Soc.* XVI. 207 It is for such reasons as these that the more complicated multiperforated charge..has been developed, which can have small propellent thickness between the perforations without reducing the loading density, and which has little unused propellent at the end of burning. **1913** O. C. GRUNER *Biol. Blood-Cells* iv. 191 At certain times the wandering cell becomes stationary... In place of migration..it settles down as an essentially multipotential or indifferent cell. **1939** DIBLE & DAVIE *Path.* viii. 152 If the germinal cells for a tumour be split off at this stage, only those tissues can be represented in the growth which are proper to the layer from which these cells have come. Such cells are multipotential but not totipotential. **1966** *Cancer* XIX. 1/1 We have designated these types of tumors as primitive multipotential primary sarcomas of bone:..'multipotential' because each shows differentiation along multiple lines (i.e. bone, cartilage, blood vessels, etc.). **1973** *Nature* 2 Mar. 20/2 The finding of multipotential haemopoietic stem cells (that is, cells capable of becoming any of the mature blood cell types, lymphoid or myeloid) in early mouse embryonic thymus. **1933** *Tropical Woods* XXXVI. 10 Heterogeneous Ray.—A xylem ray composed of cells of different morphological types. (Typically, with the cells of the multiseriate part radially elongated.) **1965** K. ESAU *Plant Anat.* (ed. 2) vi. 138 A ray may be one cell wide and one cell high in the beginning; later, the initial divides or more initials are added to the first. The ray thus increases in height and may increase in width if multiseriate rays are characteristic of the plant. *Ibid.* xvii. 485 A well-known example of a multiseriate epidermis is the velamen of air roots of tropical Orchidaceae. **1966** *Proc. 4th Symposium Remote Sensing Environment* (Univ. Mich., U.S. Govt. AD 638–919) 135 Much additional information is needed before multispectral photography and other remote sensors can be..incorporated into operational urban information centers. **1971** *New Scientist* 27 Apr. 256/2 Placing the Earth under the most detailed observation with multispectral cameras. **1973** L. F. CURTIS in Cruise & Newman *Photogr. Techniques Sci. Res.* ii. 101 Photographic analysis of the data obtained in multispectral studies may include colour enhancement techniques which aim to emphasize the tonal differences between objects. **1902** *Proc. Zool. Soc.* 210 In one of the two specimens [of sponges] in the collection..there are a few multispicular strands in the otherwise very regular unispicular meshwork. **1952** W. R. ASHBY *Design for Brain* xvii. 182 S. 9/4 showed the necessity for ultrastability; is the hypothesis of multistability equally necessary? **1962** A. BATTERSBY *Guide to Stock Control* vii. 65 The effect of this sort of control by interconnected systems is called 'multistability' by cyberneticians. **1952** W. R. ASHBY *Design for Brain* xvi. 171 To study the interactions of these two properties we might start by examining the properties of an ultrastable system whose main variables are all part-functions. But it has been found simpler to start by considering a system defined thus: a multistable system consists of many ultrastable systems joined main variable to main variable, all the main variables being part-functions. *Ibid.* xvii. 179 The concept of the 'multistable' system clearly refers primarily to the nervous system. **1966** J. SINGH *Gt. Ideas Information Theory, Lang. & Cybernetics* (1967) xiv. 221 Every animal is thus built up of a number of ultrastable subsystems organized with the possibility of dispersion of behavior. Such a multistable system can therefore adapt its behavior to settle in a stable resting state in a much shorter time than a single ultrastable system of the kind considered earlier. **1961** *Nature* 11 Mar. 833/1 Multi-stranded deoxyribonucleic acid as determined by X-irradiation. **1970** *New Scientist* 17 Dec. 496/2 The antitumour effects of multistranded RNA which have been reported recently.

b. *multi-authored, -barrelled, -centred, -componential, -consonantal, -cored, -directional, -engined, -ethnic, -faceted* (later examples), *-geminal, -generational, -holed, -hued* (later examples), *-manned, -marbled, -sectional, -sectioned, -secular, -segmental, -syllabic, -tribal, -valued, -volumed*; **mu·ltiplaned,** having or occupying several planes (cf. *MULTIPLANE *sb.* and *a.*); **multi-ta·ped,** recorded from several (magnetic) tapes played simultaneously.

1964 K. WINETROUT in I. L. Horowitz *New Sociol.* 159 *The Lonely Crowd* is multi-authored and *Faces in the Crowd* a research team product. **1974** *Nature* 22 Feb. 581/1 It suffers from the usual disadvantage of a multi-authored book in which no editorial attempt has been made to avoid redundancies and overlap. **1944** *Horizon* Oct. 225 'Moaning Minnies' (multi-barrelled mortars). **1957** K. A. WITTFOGEL *Oriental Despotism* iii. 50 In contrast to the controlled state of multicentered societies, the state of the single-centered hydraulic society was a veritable apparatus state. **1973** *Sci. Amer.* Apr. 90/2 Bruno's belief in a centerless or multicentered universe was derived from..Nicholas of Cusa. **1971** *Archivum Linguisticum* II. 59 Cf. [*make up*] (*sc.* with cosmetics or greasepaint) (verb) and [*make-up*] (noun),..examples whose multicomponential character as idioms is partly revealed by the difference of tonicity or accentuation corresponding to the grammatical distinction indicated. **1974** *Nature* 7 June 571/2 The survival curve of HVS is multicomponential after treatment with heat as well as after treatment with formaldehyde. **1948** D. DIRINGER *Alphabet* ii. 63 They did not employ it [*sc.* the alphabet] when they could use word-signs or multi-consonantal phonograms. **1965** *Language* XLI. 346 Such multiconsonantal clusters as /mb/ and /ngb/ are merely graphic and represent consonants that are phonemically unitary. **1974** D. KYLE *Raft of Swords* ii. 14 Loop after loop of insulated multi cored copper wire. **1942** *Illuminating Engin. Nomencl. & Photometric Stand.* (Illuminating Engin. Soc. U.S.) (ASA Z7.1–1942) 27 Multidirectional illumination on a surface is that produced by several separated light sources of relatively small area. It is characterized by the fact that a small opaque object placed near the illuminated surface casts several shadows. **1964** *Discovery* Oct. 6/2 Control of a vast and complex multi-directional communications network. **1972** *Geo Abstr.* C. 368 (*heading*) Problems of multi-directional development of automobile transport. **1917** *Jrnl. R. Aeronaut. Soc.* XXI. 320 In the case of most single-engined aeroplanes or seaplanes a fuselage of circular cross-section is admirable... This is not so, however, in the case of multi-engined aircraft, in which the power plant units are placed away from the body of the machine. **1931** C. DAY LEWIS *From Feathers to Iron* 14 Bodies we have, fabric and frame designed To take the stress of love, Buoyant on gust, multi-engined. **1967** *Jane's Surface Skimmer Systems 1967–68* 121/2 A drive pad at the rear of the primary box enables the engines of a multi-engined aircraft to be coupled together by spanwise shafting. **1967** 'MALCOLM X' in A. Chapman *New Black Voices* (1972) We Afro-Americans..are not opposed to multi-ethnic associations in any walk of life. **1969** *Alberta Hist. Rev.* Autumn 10/2 Both were born in remote wilderness conditions and embraced multi-ethnic populations. **1965** H. I. ANSOFF *Corporate Strategy* (1968) i. 15 The nature of decisions is multifaceted and continually variable. **1971** *Computers & Humanities* VI. 38 Paralleling this trend toward the multifaceted department articulating with almost all the traditional disciplines is the emergence of the divisional course. **1922** JOYCE *Ulysses* 404 Recorded instances of multigeminal..births. **1965** *New Society* 1 Apr. 25/2 Subjects from multi-generational households have better scores. **1972** P. LASLETT *Household & Family in Past Time* 7 A high proportion of multigenerational extended families among the remaining Dutch peasantry in the 1950s. **1953** *Lancet* 12 Sept. 540/1 A multi-holed catheter had been passed. **1963** A. J. HALL *Textile Sci.* ii. 47 It is pumped at a uniform rate through multi-holed spinnerets into the coagulating bath. **1927** *Daily Express* 13 July 5/2 The hidden wiring of the multi-hued electric lights. **1971** *Sci. Amer.* Oct. 43/1 (Advt.), 'Philippine Birds' contains 569 illustrations..portraying the multi-hued birds. **1973** *Islander* (Victoria, B.C.) 1 July 2/1 Multihued confetti of clouds drifted across the sky. **1961** *Life* 3 Mar. 33/1 The Russians will follow their manned orbiter..with a multimanned moon orbiter..and space station. **1967** *Observer* 5 Nov. 4/5 A multi-manned expedition around the moon and back to earth. **1902** HARDY *Poems of Past & Present* 40 Multimarbled Genova the Proud. **1909** *Westm. Gaz.* 23 Mar. 4/2 The multi-planed helicopter has been abandoned for the biplane. **1959** M. T. WILLIAMS *Art of Jazz* (1960) xii. 110 The nation's misery was mirrored in every facet of its multi-planed existence. **1961** Y. OLSSON *On Syntax Eng. Verb* ii. 33 A classification can be made of the sentences of the language..: I. multi-sectional (consisting of two or more Sections). **1964** *Gloss. Letterpress Rotary Printing Terms* (*B.S.I.*) 22 Multi-sectioned newspapers or magazines. **1922** JOYCE *Ulysses* 655 The multisecular stability of its primeval basin. **1901** C. P. STEINMETZ *Theoret. Elem. Electr. Engin.* 122 A closed coil armature, connected with a multisegmental commutator. **1955** *Trans. Philol. Soc.* 1954 68 We may..classify phonemic features by reference to the *types* of unit, of which they are constituents..; in this way we may establish a broad distinction between (*a*) 'uni-segmental' features, i.e. such as combine within single phonemes, and (*b*) 'multi-segmental' features, i.e. such as can only be extracted from more complex units (syllables, morphemes, words, constructions, or sentences). **1909** *Cent. Dict.* Suppl., Multisyllabic. **1953** N. TINBERGEN *Herring Gull's World* ii. 10 The most elaborate call of the Herring Gull's repertoire is the multisyllabic call. **1972** F. KNEBEL *Dark Horse* (1973) xix. 294 He had long ago passed the point where he sought to impress bewildered laymen by scattering multisyllabic medical terms about. **1955** L. FEATHER *Encycl. Jazz* vii. 245 The unique tonal effects obtained from these multi-taped, multi-speed novelties sold many millions of Capitol records. **1962** *John o' London's* 16 Aug. 162/4 Not all the tracks are multi-taped. **1949** I. DEUTSCHER *Stalin* iii. 69 The multi-tribal cities of the Caucasus. **1934** *Mind* XLIII. 200 Whatever is a proposition of the two-valued logic is recognized as a proposition within the multi-valued 'logic' and *vice versa*. **1965** N. CHOMSKY *Aspects of Theory of Syntax* iv. 171 Regarding each of the dimensions of the

system of paradigms as a multivalued feature, [etc.]. **1963** *Times Lit. Suppl.* 10 May 348/4 Multi-volumed books.

2. mu:ltibillionai·re, one who is worth many billions of money; **mu:lticollinea·rity** *Statistics*, the existence of a perfect linear correlation between a set of variables when the regression of some dependent variable on them is being investigated; **multi-millionaire** (later examples); **multi-ne·gative** *Printing*, an array of many similar images in negative form used in the printing of small items several at a time by photolithography; similarly **multi-po·sitive;** † **multirota·tion** *Chem.* [a. G. *multirotation* (Parcus & Tollens 1890, in *Ann. d. Chem.* CCLVII. 161)] = *MUTAROTATION.

1906 'Mark Twain' in *North Amer. Rev.* Sept. 322 There would not be any multi-billionaire alive, perhaps, who would be able to buy a full set. **1934** R. Frisch *Statistical Confluence Analysis* xi. 75 There exist two or more independent linear relations between the systematic parts of these variates, but..we are not aware of this multicollinearity. **1972** T. H. & R. J. Wonnacott *Introd. Statistics for Business & Econ.* xiii. 296 Suppose demand for a group of goods is being related to prices and income, with the overall price index being the first independent variable. Suppose aggregate income measured in money terms is the second independent variable. If this is real income multiplied by the same price index, the problem of multicollinearity may become a serious one. The solution is to use real income, rather than money income, as the second independent variable. **1921** Multi-millionaire [see *Corona[2]]. **1972** F. Knebel *Dark Horse* (1973) ix. 120 You got multi-millionaires who don't pay more than two or three per cent of their income in taxes. **1933** N. Montague in W. Atkins *Art & Pract. Printing* III. xii. 95 Multi-negatives have become an economic necessity in the case of printing by photo-lithography such things as stamps, coupons, playing cards, and small labels. **1967** E. Chambers *Photolitho-Offset* vi. 70 The automatic operation can be commenced at any part of the layout and an exposure made to any position on the multi-negative. **1933** N. Montague in W. Atkins *Art & Pract. Printing* III. xii. 96 The 'H.L.' step and repeat projecting machine.. is designed for the production of multi-negatives or positives. **1971** D. Potter *Brit. Eliz. Stamps* ii. 23 In the first stages of printing a multipositive is prepared, from which the printing cylinders are made. **1890** *Jrnl. Chem. Soc.* LVIII. 1084 The authors propose to employ the term 'multi-rotation' to denote the change..of rotatory power which takes place in a sugar solution, from immediately after its preparation in the cold until constant rotation is attained. **1904** J. W. Mellor *Chem. Statics & Dynamics* 224 The influence of acids upon the rate of multirotation of sugars. **1935** Tipson & Stiller in Harrow & Sherwin *Textbk. Biochem.* ii. 43 In the course of time other sugars were examined, and it was found that the rotation is not necessarily halved, so the phenomenon was named multirotation.

3. (Compounds of this type are occas. used predicatively, as in quot. 1947 for *multifactor* and quot. 1970 for *multifont.*) *multiaperture, -author, -band, -bed, -billion, -blade, -car, -centre, -class, -component, -cycle* (cf. *multicyclic* in *1 a), *-cylinder* (further examples), *-day, -element, -engine, -family, -floor, -image, -jet, -lane, -lens, -man, -megaton, -microphone, -million, -part, -pin, -plate, -reel, -role, -row, -screen, -seat, -step, -syllable, -track, -tube, -vane, -vitamin, -volume, -way, -word;* **multia·ccess,** pertaining to, involving, or being a computer that may be used simultaneously by independent operators at a number of terminals; **multicha·nnel,** employing or possessing many communication or television channels (*CHANNEL *sb.*[1] 9 d); also = *multitrack* above; **multici·rcuit,** supplying or containing many electric circuits; **mu·lticore,** having many cores; applied *spec.* to an electric cable (cf. Core *sb.*[1] 11); **multi-ele·ctrode,** possessing or involving several electrodes; applied *spec.* to a valve in which there are two or more sets of electrodes, associated with separate electron beams, within a single envelope; **multifa·ctor** = *multifactorial* in *1 a; **multifa·culty,** (of an institution of higher education) possessing several faculties; **multifi·lament,** containing or composed of several filaments; applied *spec.* to a yarn made up of many fine threads; also *absol.*, a multifilament yarn; **mu·ltiflash,** (*a*) *Photogr.* made with two or more flash-bulbs operated simultaneously; (*b*) applied to a process or apparatus for desalinating sea-water in several stages in which water is 'flashed', i.e. converted suddenly into steam, at successively lower pressures; **mu·ltifont,** pertaining to or possessing the ability (of a machine) to read characters of several different 'fonts' (founts) or designs; **mu·ltifuel,** capable of running on more than one kind of fuel; **mu·ltigerm** *Agric.*, (of a sugar-beet variety or seed produced by it) having or consisting of more than one seed in each seed ball (cf. *monogerm* adj. s.v. *MONO- 1); **mu·ltigrade** (see quot. 1972); **mu·ltipath** *Telecommunications*, involving (the receipt of) radio signals that have travelled from a single source by several paths; **mu·ltipoint,** having or serving many points; applied *spec.* to a water-heater serving a number of hot-water taps; **mu·ltistart** *Engin.* (see quot. 1940); **mu·ltiwall,** having many walls; applied *spec.* to a sack or large bag made of several layers of strong paper that are usu. attached to one another along the bottom and the side folds.

1966 *Guardian* 4 May 20/3 By the end of the seventies in Britain there will be more than 300,000 people interested in multi-access computers. **1967** *Economist* 4 Mar. 850/3 This will mean hierarchies of powerful and less powerful multi-access computers linked throughout the country with hundreds of terminals and consoles connected to them from commerce, industry and research establishments. **1968** *Times* 1 Nov. 23/5 Multi-access computing needs data-links between users and computers. **1971** R. A. Wisbey *Computer in Lit. & Ling. Res.* 191 The Atlas multi-access system makes it possible to create and manipulate files of information from remote consoles and to use these files for the initiation of jobs on the Atlas computer. **1966** *Electronics* 14 Nov. 25 Honeywell spokesmen will not disclose details of the new design, beyond saying that it used conventional ferrite cores with one hole, not multiaperture cores. **1968** *New Scientist* 15 Feb. 360/2 The elements, called MADs (multiaperture devices), are specially shaped ferrite discs..which act as very fast switches. **1973** *Nature* 9 Feb. 412/1 As is inevitable in any such multi-author work, the individual chapters vary considerably in scope. **1969** *Sci. Jrnl.* June 64 Vertical aerial view of part of the Carrizo Plains, California, at near right was taken using ordinary Ektachrome film and reveals little trace of the phenomena rendered starkly visible in the enhanced multiband photograph at far right. **1971** *Flying* Apr. 90/1 About our portable multi-band radio. **1964** G. L. Cohen *What's Wrong with Hospitals?* i. 24 To the archetypal American patient of the medical magazines, there is no disgrace in entering a 'multi-bed ward'. **1963** *Observer* 31 Mar. 27/3 A background of multi-billion defence spending. **1971** *New Scientist* 28 Jan. 184 What would be the practical and scientific benefits of a multibillion dollar space station? **1910** *Westm. Gaz.* 24 Mar. 5/2 This is the Pitter multi-blade propellor, which..is claimed to give an enormous thrust at low speeds. **1960** *Farmer & Stockbreeder* 1 Mar. 70 The multi-blade fan located in front of the engine has an output of up to 40,000 cu ft per min. **1962** *Economist* 11 Aug. 526/1 The proportion of multi-car families is continuing to rise. **1965** Phillips & Williams *Inorg. Chem.* I. xi. 403 Metals and metal-like hydrides are similarly electron-deficient... The electrons are thought to be in molecular orbitals embracing all the atoms in the structure, i.e. multi-centre rather than two-centre orbitals. **1930** *Engineering* 31 Oct. 541/2 It is still the only multichannel radio-telephone service in the world. **1955** *Ann. Reg. 1954* 402 There were on exhibition at the radio show ..many television receivers designed for two-band or multi-channel reception. **1962** *Science Survey* III. 315 Indeed one can conceive of such a system in which a multi-channel magnetic tape carries the programme of the plant. **1966** *Punch* 20 July 101/2 The United States, where of course there's multi-channel TV operating more or less round the clock. **1909** *Cent. Dict.* Suppl., *Multicircuit*, having a multiple circuit... *Multicircuit generator*, an electric generator, as for the supplying of arc-lights, which is connected with and feeds several parallel circuits. **1969** *Jane's Freight Containers 1968–69* 536/2 An a.c. drive motor with single and multi-circuit generators built as one unit. **1970** *Sci. Amer.* Feb. 28/2 One obstacle..was that a multicircuit chip would have to incorporate logic gates of several different types and all would have to function perfectly. **1961** *Guardian* 16 June 6/5 The rise of the anonymous, multi-class mass audience. **1934** Webster, Multicomponent. **1966** D. G. Brandon *Mod. Techniques Metallogr.* iii. 125 Identifying the elements in a multicomponent sample. **1971** C. Placek (*title*) Multicomponent fibers. **1908** *Westm. Gaz.* 6 Feb. 4/2 The high-tension wires are moulded in one, forming a multicore cable. **1957** *Railway Mag.* Nov. 760/2 A prototype length of special 'thin'-type multi-core cable was used for certain indication circuits. **1961** *New Left Rev.* Jan.–Feb. 8/1 A multi-core city is gradually taking shape. **1916** C. A. Cotton in *Geogr. Rev.* I. 39 The diagrams..represent stages in the growth of a composite (i.e., two-cycle or multi-cycle) delta. **1918** —— in *Ibid.* VI. 320 In a previously published article the writer called attention to the occurrence of multicycle fault coasts. **1962** *Gloss. Terms Automatic Data Processing* (*B.S.I.*) 91 *Multi-cycle feeding*, a method of processing punched cards in which several fields of a single card are read sequentially on successive machine cycles... The principal use is as a card-saving stratagem when printing names and addresses. **1966** J. C. Pugh in G. H. Dury *Ess. Geomorphol.* 127 Multi-cycle bornhardts can also be found in the form of dome-on-dome residuals. **1904** *Sci. Abstr.* VII. 1080 (*heading*) Multi-cylinder motors. **1909** *Westm. Gaz.* 10 June 4/2 Of the twenty-five pretty little machines which will career round the twenty-three-mile circuit.., no fewer than seventeen are fitted with four-cylinder engines, which shows..the progress that has been made in the multi-cylinder car. **1969** *Jane's Freight Containers 1968–69* 495/3 Insulated flexi-van multi-cylinder high pressure gas holder. **1973** *Nature* 23 Mar. 217/1 By use [in their motor cycles] of multi-cylinder engines, overhead camshafts and such devices as electric starting motors, they have been able to sell products which are in many ways superior to those of British manufacturers. **1971** *Canad. Antiques Collector* May 10/1 These field studies extend up to a week with the multi-day visitors accommodated economically in camps, lodges, schools and private homes. **1973** C. Bonington *Next Horizon* v. 85 He was not interested in the multi-day epic, or the highly technical rock-climb. **1926** *Wireless World* 26 May 722/1 (*heading*) The multi-electrode valve. **1963** Multi-electrode [see *Dekatron]. **1965** *Math. in Biol. & Med.* (Med. Res. Council) iv. 139 Is it possible to recognize automatically particular waveforms in a single channel of a multi-electrode recording [of an electro-encephalogram]? **1961** Y. Olsson *On Syntax Eng. Verb* iv. 85 The 'genitive' is a multi-element term for PRE. **1970** *New Scientist* 24 Dec. 554/2 The Marconi Company..developed a high-gain multi-element vhf aerial. **1934** Webster, Multiengine. **1961** *Economist* 25 Nov. 830/2 Rolls-Royce immediately started hawking its competing multi-engine system round the international market. **1934** R. Frisch *Statistical Confluence Analysis* vii. 49 We get the special hypothesis regarding the correlation coefficients on which Spearman's two factor and Thurstone's multifactor theory are built. **1947** F. A. E. Crew *Genetics Rel. Clin. Med.* v. 84 There is the possibility that certain abnormal characterisations are themselves multifactor in nature. **1966** A. Battersby *Math. in Managem.* iii. 68 The bonus is to be paid at the rate of one shilling for each ton of production in excess of 160... The manager.. undertakes [in addition] to apply a penalty of 10 shillings for a fall of 1 point in the yield, and a corresponding bonus for an increase. Such a scheme is called a 'multi-factor incentive'. **1961** *Technology* Feb. 36/4 The C.A.T.s ..should become multi-faculty institutions with the proportion of science and social studies increased. **1968** *Economist* 13 Apr. 42/1 The schools are to be reduced by amalgamation from twelve to six, and each is to be closely associated with a multi-faculty institution of the University of London. **1965** G. McInnes *Road to Gundagai* xiv. 249 The enormous multi-family picnics that took place. **1972** *Real Estate Rev.* Winter 73/2 The Federal Housing Administration then began requiring its field offices to report on the number of minorities occupying federally assisted multifamily housing. **1937** W. Watson *Textile Design & Colour* (ed. 4) 437 The diameter of each orifice is about 0·1 mm. for ordinary yarns, and may be as small as 0·06 mm. for fine denier multi-filament yarns. **1940** *Chambers's Techn. Dict.* 562/2 *Multi-filament lamp*, an electric filament lamp having more than one filament in the same bulb, so that failure of one filament will not cause the lamp to be extinguished. **1944** *Textile Manufacturer* July 306/1 We made 150/150 yarn of that type but the multifilaments could not compensate for the inherent harsh character of hosiery made from it. **1968** E. Miller *Textiles* 70 Multifilament yarns give more flexibility and cover, the finer and more numerous the filaments are in the yarn the better it is in this respect. **1945** Webster Add., Multiflash. **1956** *Nature* 21 Jan. 109/2 (*caption*) Multiflash photographs..of a typical water-entry trajectory. **1964** *Listener* 21 May 835/1 The new 'multi-flash' distillation process was first realized in this country, and more than two-thirds of all the installations in the world are British. **1971** *Chem. Abstr.* 17 May 195/2 Multiflash evapn. for concg. solns., and producing fresh water. **1938** *Archit. Rev.* LXXXIII. 118/2 A multifloor scheme was devised which, besides allowing high economy of site area, gave other advantages of even greater moment. **1960** *News Chron.* 7 Oct. 8/5 Multi-floor garages. **1961** *Proc. IRE* XLIX. 185/2 Extensions of the notions described will result in improved multifont recognition and in gains toward the isolation of the character separation problem. **1969** *Computers & Humanities* IV. 83 Of all devices for speeding the preparation of text for machines, none has been awaited..with more confidence than some sort of fast, multifont, full page scanner, more appropriately called an optical character recognition (OCR) machine. **1970** *Ibid.* V. 75 The Scan-Data 300 is genuinely multifont. **1959** *Engineering* 9 Jan. 45/1 (*heading*) Multi-fuel engines. **1965** *Economist* 22 May 941/2 The Wankel could come in here, with possibly only marginal disadvantages over available multi-fuel engines. **1950** *Proc. Amer. Soc. Sugar Beet Technologists* VI. 160 (*heading*) Embryology of mono- and multigerm fruits in the genus Beta L. **1962** *Times* 21 May 18/5 The monogerm seed which is still being bred and selected to take the place of the multi-germ seed now used. **1959** *Motor Manual* (ed. 36) x. 237 The 'multi-grade' engine oils now available ..cover a range of ratings. **1972** *Materials & Technol.* IV. ii. 68 Modern motor oils with good viscosity/temperature characteristics may meet the requirements of several SAE [*sc.* Society of Automotive Engineers] grades and are termed multigrade oils (e.g. 10W/30). **1974** *Drive* Autumn 56 Fast-moving engine parts 'snip up' ordinary multigrade oils like scissors. **1962** *Punch* 17 Jan. 133/3 Technicians..explain..what you can and cannot do with a multi-image lens [in television]. **1969** *Focal Encycl. Film & Television Techniques* 472/2 Multi-image films make use of expanding and diminishing pictures. **1963** *Daily Tel.* 21 Nov. 16 The experimental application of multi-jet techniques for lifting transport aircraft vertically. **1966** *McGraw-Hill Yearbk. Sci. & Technol.* 411/2 The multi-jet configuration permits higher speeds..than single-jet turbines. **1974** *Encycl. Brit. Macropædia* XVIII. 637/1 The large transport aircraft, now almost exclusively of multijet design. **1961** *Times* 12 Dec. 14/3 A conservative British driver might envisage a multi-lane nightmare in a wonderland of flyovers and freeways. **1966** *Times* 28 Feb. (Canada Suppl.) p. viii/5 Vancouver's west end, looking northwards over the multi-lane bridge. **1936** *Discovery* Aug. 237/1 This unique camera..is intended for mapping from a higher altitude than has ever before been practical with multi-lens equipment. **1948** E. Raisz *Gen. Cartogr.* (ed. 2) xix. 194/1 The largest multilens camera is the nine-lens camera of the U.S. Coast and Geodetic Survey. **1951** J. M. Fraser *Psychol.* xv. 189 Wherever a number of people are involved in one task at the same time, a multi-man chart can be used to record the task of each individual. **1967** Multi-man [see *EJECTION 1 d]. **1958** J. Blish *Case of Conscience* I. vi. 58 The prettiest multimegaton explosion you ever saw. **1965** H. Kahn *On Escalation* x. 198 Multimegaton weapons appeared to be unusable for any rational, and even for many irrational, purposes. **1941** *B.B.C. Gloss. Broadcasting Terms* 19 *Multi-microphone technique*, method of production in which several microphones, with outputs centralized in a mixer, are used either simultaneously or in succession to reproduce sounds from a single studio or hall. **1957** Manvell & Huntley *Technique Film Music* iv. 194 In England some years ago it was fashionable to use a multi-microphone technique, in which..considerable physical

separation between different sections of the orchestra was necessary to enable each microphone to record only that section which it was intended to cover. **1962** A. NISBETT *Technique Sound Studio* iii. 61 If a close balance is adopted in a multi-microphone mix, artificial 'echo' may be added. **1948** *Amer. Jrnl. Roentgenology* LIX. 771/2 Multimillion volt beta rays and multimillion volt roentgen rays in the treatment of cancer. **1966** *Times* 28 Feb. (Canada Suppl.) p. ix/4 It is a multi-million dollar operation. **1974** *Listener* 23 May 652/2 Multi-million pound shopping precincts. **1928** *Daily Express* 4 May 2/3 The powers given under the Electricity Supply Act of 1926 'to introduce what are known as multi-part tariffs, whereby a consumer, who is willing to use energy for a number of purposes, may pay a fixed charge yearly and then pay a low running charge per unit'. **1936** *Proc. IRE* XXIV. 912 It is..extreme high order harmonic distortion which makes the reception of frequency modulation over a multipath medium far more distorted than the reception of amplitude modulation over the same medium. **1966** *Electronics* 3 Oct. 174 There are three vhf propagation problems that must be considered in designing the Aerocom satellite: fading caused by Faraday rotation, ionospheric fluctuation and sea-water multipath fades. **1970** J. EARL *Tuners & Amplifiers* iii. 75 Multipath interference can severely disturb stereo reception. **1963** *Thorn Electr. Industr. Group Profile* 16 Multi-pin electrical connectors. **1964** R. F. FICCHI *Electr. Interference* v. 72 The package units are less reliable than the individual units. The dependence of [*read* on] multi-pin connectors which have a relatively high failure rate is the cause. **1948** *Motor Manual* (ed. 33) vii. 121 The multi-plate clutch, in which two sets of metal discs were arranged alternately in sandwich fashion. One set was attached to the driving shaft, and the other..to the driven shaft. When a spring was permitted to force them all tightly together, they gripped firmly; but when the spring was restrained by the driver, one set of discs could slip round without turning the others. *Ibid.* 135 For top gear,..there is a separate clutch (sometimes of the multi-plate type) inside the gearbox. **1963** BIRD & HUTTON-STOTT *Veteran Motor Car* 253 Transmission: Multiplate clutch, 4 speeds and reverse, shaft. **1971** *Engineering* Apr. 49 (*caption*) This picture shows the multiplate construction of the differential capacitor probe fitted to the gauging head. **1905** *Trans. Amer. Inst. Electr. Engin.* XXIII. 209 It seems as though the latter class of advantages might be obtained as readily and more simply and cheaply by the use of multipoint control-switches, used in parallel with the ordinary ones. **1931** *Conc. Househ. Encycl.* 531/2 (*caption*) Automatic water heater for multi-point service. **1956** *Bk. Good Housek.* (Good Housek. Inst.) (new ed.) ix. 96/1 Multi-point heaters are now available to fit under a draining-board. **1964** M. LASKI in S. Nowell-Smith *Edwardian England* iv. 160 The bathroom [was] served by..a multi-point pressure heater (the first..came on the market in 1899). **1971** B. SCHARF *Engin. & its Lang.* x. 82 The cutting tools used on machine tools may be conveniently classified as single-point and multi-point tools. **1929** *Encycl. Brit.* XV. 856/2 Multireel pictures began to appear in 1909... A year later screen history was made by releasing multireel pictures in their full length. **1970** *Times* 4 Sept. (Aviation Suppl.) p. iii/1 They include.. the RB 199 turbofan for the Anglo-German MRCA-75 multi-role combat aircraft. **1958** *Chambers's Techn. Dict.* 996/1 *Multi-row radial engine*, a radial aero-engine with two or more rows of cylinders. **1971** *Power Farming* Mar. 11/1 For beans, Herbert had come up with a multi-row harvester which not only reduced the time in the field, but caused less damage. **1967** *Economist* 21 Oct. 267/1 A film in the very latest multiscreen technique extolled the opportunities for everyone in this blossoming province. **1973** *Times* 5 Oct. 25/2 The highlight is the multiscreen show—consisting of what the layman would describe as a cinema screen divided into six parts with different but related films showing on each at the same time. **1958** *Times* 11 Nov. 8/1 The electoral system chosen for Algeria is that of the multi-seat constituency. **1967** *Jane's Surface Skimmer Systems 1967–68* 112/1 Then work began on the Yard's first multi-seat passenger craft. **1940** *Chambers's Techn. Dict.* 564/1 *Multi-start worm*, a worm in which two or more helical threads are used in order to obtain a larger pitch and hence a higher velocity ratio of the drive. **1971** B. SCHARF *Engin. & its Lang.* xii. 158 With single-start worms, lead equals pitch, but on multi-start worms, it amounts to pitch × number of starts (i.e. number of thread sections in a plane at right angles to the axis). **1961** G. R. CHOPPIN *Exper. Nucl. Chem.* xi. 182 If the labeled compound is the end product of a multistep synthesis, in order to obtain a higher final yield, it is best to achieve the labeling at as late a point in the synthesis as possible. **1964** *English Studies* XLV. 383 The difference between a normal one-step process and..the multi-step process..is so great that [etc.]. **1964** *Language* XL. 176 Multisyllable words where a syllabic split in the written word occurs in the sequence vowel–consonant–consonant–vowel. **1958** J. MOIR *High Quality Sound Reproduction* xviii. 545 The film standards used were those previously adopted for multi-track recording in the studios. **1959** W. S. SHARPS *Dict. Cinematogr.* 113/1 *Multitrack recording system*, the system employed for the recording of a multiple sound track. **1969** *Time* 29 Aug. 47 Recording studios also offer new technical means of composing, through such devices as the echo chamber, multi-track recording and tape superimposition. **1935** *Discovery* Feb. 43/2 The multi-tube parachute rocket used for the Harz Mountain experiments. **1959** *Times* 23 Sept. 4 (Advt.), The Oldham Pg battery is unique in possessing a patented double-sleeve multi-tube positive plate. **1909** *Cent. Dict.* Suppl., Multivane. **1963** R. R. A. HIGHAM *Handbk. Papermaking* ii. 25 Situated in the trough [of the hydrapulper] is a multivane rotor, driven by a vertical shaft. **1942** *Endeavour* I. 32/1 On the matter of multivitamin treatment, there are different schools of thought. *Ibid.* 32/2 No multivitamin 'pill'..can at present replace a mixed all-round diet. **1960** *Woman's Own* 19 Mar. 25/3 A course of multi-vitamin tablets are a wise investment. **1968** M. PYKE *Food & Society* ii. 17 But it is different when a manufacturer advertises that..expensive multivitamin tablets protect the well-fed people who can afford them against deficiency diseases they will never experience. **1938** L. M. HARROD *Librarians' Gloss.* 104 *Multi-volume book*, a book in more than one volume. **1962** Y. MALKIEL in Householder & Saporta *Probl. Lexicogr.* 15 Multi-volume encyclopedias shot through..with genuinely lexical entries. **1940** *Dict. Paper* (Amer. Paper & Pulp Assoc.) 234 *Multiwall-bag paper*, normally, a 40- or 50-pound..kraft paper. **1946** *Nature* 6 July 32/1 A review of literature on the acoustics of building, preparatory to carrying out experimental work with particular reference to multiwall units. **1955** *Times* 5 July (Paper Suppl.) p. iii/5 In little more than twenty-five years the development of the multi-wall paper sack..has established new standards of efficiency, convenience and cleanliness in the packaging of powdered and granular products. **1967** *Times Rev. Industry* May 82/1 As cement production grew, so did the use of multiwall sacks. **1974** *Columbia* (S. Carolina) *Record* 25 Apr. 9-D/1 The paper in question is used in multiwall bags, common in grocery stores. **1961** *B.S.I. News* Aug. 16/2 It was agreed that multi-way adapters would not be permitted. **1967** *Gloss. Terms Materials Handling* (*B.S.I.*) III. 10 *Multi-way valve*, a rotatable chamber having a central inlet, and one outlet which can be positioned in line with any one of several radially spaced conveying lines. **1961** R. B. LONG *Sentence & its Parts* i. 15 Many kinds of words and multi-word units function as adjuncts. **1966** G. N. LEECH *Eng. in Advertising* ii. 22 Idioms are treated as multi-word lexical items.

multiar (mɒ·ltiˌɑ̄ɹ). *Electronics.* [f. MULTI- + *ar*, of unknown origin.] A circuit which produces an output signal when a varying voltage applied at one input exceeds an adjustable constant voltage applied at a second input, and which consists of a simple regenerative circuit with a diode and a pulse transformer in the feedback loop.

1946 *Jrnl. Inst. Electr. Engin.* XCIII. IIIA. 321/1 The Multiar..may be made to generate a delayed marker by utilizing the time-base waveform itself. *Ibid.* 1197/2 Two or more complete pick offs of the type described can be operated from a single sawtooth without mutual interaction, and for this reason the circuit is often called the 'Multiar'. **1953** *Electronic Engin.* XXV. 404 The discriminators consist of ten multiars, each with an individual H.T. supply. **1965** MILLMAN & TAUB *Pulse, Digital & Switching Waveforms* xvi. 625 The tube multiar is not useful for positive-going signals because multiple oscillations are obtained. However, a multiar constructed with a *p-n-p* transistor can be used if the input is a positive-going signal.

mu·lti-colouredness. [f. MULTI-COLOURED *a.* + -NESS.] The condition or quality of being multi-coloured.

1953 G. E. M. ANSCOMBE tr. *Wittgenstein's Philos. Investigations* § 47 Multi-colouredness is one kind of complexity.

multicultural (mɒltikɒ·ltiŭrăl), *a.* [MULTI- 1 + CULTURAL *a.* 2.] Of or pertaining to a society consisting of varied cultural groups.

1941 *N.Y. Herald-Tribune Books* 27 July 3 A fervent sermon against nationalism, national prejudice and behavior in favor of a 'multicultural' way of life. **1959** *Times* 18 June (Suppl.) p. iv/4 This multi-cultural, multi-lingual society [of Montreal]..is one of the most cosmopolitan in the world. **1966** *Economist* 22 Jan. 273/2 For the provision of troops and police [to Rhodesia], consideration should be given to states which are multi-cultural (e.g., Canada) or multiracial (e.g., Trinidad, Jamaica, and New Zealand). **1970** P. K. C. MILLINS (*title*) Education in a multicultural society. **1973** *Daily Tel.* 20 July 17 Although Britain has a multi-cultural society, where are the black faces among television announcers, newscasters and sports commentators? **1975** *Globe & Mail* (Toronto) 21 May 5/1 Trustee Daniel Leckie, chairman of the work group, puts it this way: 'Morally, legally and pragmatically we are bound to adopt a thoroughly multicultural approach toward public education in Toronto.'

Hence **multicu·lturalism.**

1965 *Prelim. Rep. R. Comm. Bilingualism & Biculturalism* (Canada) iii. 46 The answer they often gave was 'multiculturalism', or, more elaborately, 'the Canadian mosaic'. **1971** *Daily Colonist* (Victoria, B.C.) 9 Oct. 5/2 A policy of multiculturalism within a bilingual framework commends itself to the government as the most suitable means of assuring the cultural freedom of Canadians. **1972** *Times* 12 Dec. 17/6 The country [*sc.* Canada] faces complex and unresolved problems of..bilingualism and multiculturalism. **1973** *Stornoway Gaz.* 30 June 9/4 A Gaelic Society that has outgrown its original meeting place in just a few short years and enabled the Gaels to meet the new and promising challenge of Multiculturalism.

multidialectal (mɒltidəiăle·ktăl), *a.* [f. MULTI- + DIALECTAL *a.*] Proficient in speaking or comprehending more than two dialects. So **multidiale·ctalism.**

1964 *English Studies* XLV. 27 The individual will acquire either a new dialect, or a new accent, or both. This does not mean..that he thereby loses his former variety of English, but simply that he becomes 'multi-dialectal' in English. **1965** A. H. MARCKWARDT in *Language* XLI. 146 Certainly a fourteenth-century Englishman with Chaucer's range of experience would have been multidialectal. **1971** *Language* XLVII. 194 They show..that command of heterogeneous structure is not a matter of multidialectalism or performance, but a necessary part of unilingual linguistic competence. **1975** *Amer. Speech* 1972 XLVII. 290 Kurath accepts multidialectalism as a linguistic fact.

multidisciplinary (mɒltidisipli·nări), *a.* [f. MULTI- + DISCIPLINARY *a.*] Combining many academic approaches, fields, or methods.

1949 [see **family-oriented* adj.]. **1961** *Times* 13 June 2/4 Senior member of a multi-disciplinary unit. **1965** *Math. in Biol. & Med.* (Med. Res. Council) p. vii, This is no new problem for a multidisciplinary subject like medical research. **1972** *Physics Bull.* Feb. 81/1 Interplay between different branches..follows the wider multidisciplinary trend between branches of science. **1974** *Nature* 10 May 195/1 This is an outstanding, balanced and humane multidisciplinary book which is much more than an introduction to psychology.

Also **multidi·sciplined** *a.*

1950 *Brit. Jrnl. Delinquency* I. 151 For the purposes of this Summer School it was agreed that groups should be 'multi-disciplined'. **1953** A. K. C. OTTAWAY *Educ. & Society* viii. 144 This kind of collaboration has been called the 'multi-disciplined approach'. **1972** *Accountant* 6 Apr. 441/2 The Chartered Institutes should leave the provision of higher qualifications to other multi-disciplined specialist bodies.

multiflora. Substitute for def.: In full, *multiflora rose*. A rose belonging to the species *Rosa multiflora*, which is native to Japan and bears clusters of white or pink flowers, or one of the varieties developed from it; also used *attrib.* to designate a plant bearing several flowers on one stem. (Add earlier and later examples.)

1829 *Western Monthly Rev.* III. 57 It is literally embowered in vines of the multiflora rose. **1839** 'PENCIL' *White Sulphur Papers* 82 A small arbor is covered with the multiflora rose and honey-suckle. **1890** *Harper's Mag.* Jan. 282/1 A multiflora rose, entangled with honeysuckle, clambered up the squat chimney. **1913** H. H. THOMAS *Rose Bk.* iii. 16, I am making a somewhat apologetic introduction of the multiflora roses. **1934** *Times Educ. Suppl.* 24 Nov. p. iv/1 Mermaid, one of the best of modern roses in leaf, flower, and length of flowering season when it is grafted on the *multiflora* stock, deserves to head the analysis of climbing and rambling roses. **1955** C. C. HURST in G. S. Thomas *Old Shrub Roses* ix. 91 Guillot..planted some of these Japanese Multifloras in his nursery. **1971** N. YOUNG *Complete Rosarian* xii. 217 The one unquestionable advantage of the multiflora stock is the fact that it is less prone to throw up suckers than any of the others. **1972** *Daily Tel.* 14 Oct. 8/2 If you are out for a real display in the ground, you might think of using the new multiflora tulips which have only lately turned up from Holland.

multiform, *a.* and *sb.* Add: **A.** *adj.* (Later examples.)

1903 H. JAMES *Ambassadors* xvi. 146 The question of where, among packed accumulations, so multiform a wedge would be able to enter. Were seventy volumes in red-and-gold to be..the fruit of his mission? **1955** *Times* 21 July 7/5 It includes a model, drawings, and photographs of the multiform playhouse which the Questors Theatre at Ealing hopes to build and which could be adapted to five different types of stage.

B. *sb.* (Later example.)

1913 D. H. LAWRENCE *Love Poems* 37 You who are twisted in grief like crumpled beech-leaves,..who fall to earth At last like a bean-pod: what are you, oh multiform?

multifu·nctional, *a.* Also **multi-functional.** [MULTI- 1 b.] Having or fulfilling many functions.

1941 *Industrial & Engin. Chem.* XXXIII. 351/1 The effectiveness of the multifunctional addition agents is improved by the introduction of metal substituents, particularly in respect to antioxidant value. **1946** *Thorpe's Dict. Appl. Chem.* (ed. 4) VII. 391/2 Multifunctional Additives.—Such compounds combine the properties of power-point depressants, viscosity-index improvers and detergency. **1957** *Essays in Crit.* VII. 21 Shakespeare utilizes his multifunctional character, Edgar. **1959** BENN & PETERS *Social Princ. & Democratic State* xii. 255 The family was once a multi-functional organization within which men and women found their work, amusements, and religion under patriarchal government. **1972** *Nature* 28 Jan. 187/2 Dr Walter Marshall, director of the Atomic Energy Research Establishment at Harwell, described his establishment as a 'multi-functional' laboratory.

So **multifu·nction** *attrib.* [MULTI- 3].

1967 *Electronics* 6 Mar. 67/2 The company already has a contract for the beam-forming subsystem of the Nike-X multifunction array radar.

Multigraph (mɒ·ltigrɑf). Also **multigraph.** [f. MULTI- + -GRAPH.] The proprietary name of a small printing machine which uses specially cast type fitted in to grooves on a rotating cylinder. Also *attrib.* So **mu·ltigraphed** *ppl. a.*, printed by a machine of this type.

1905 *Typewriter Trade Jrnl.* Jan. 17/1 Those who were not able to attend the recent show at Madison Square Garden, missed the opportunity of seeing the 'Multigraph', a machine for producing multiple copies of typewritten work. **1908** *Busy Man's Mag.* May 154/1 The multigraph operated by an office boy or girl really typewrites letters individually, but does it at a speed of 2,000 letters per hour. **1921** *Glasgow Herald* 12 Apr. 5 The Gammeter Multigraph, shown by the International Multigraph Co... is an office machine capable of turning out actual printing at over 4000 impressions per hour. **1925** *Daily Tel.* 13 May 20/5 (Advt.), Experienced multigraph operator and stationery buyer required by City firm. **1936** *Brit. Birds* XXX. 32 Explanatory text..is supplied in a multigraphed brochure. **1967** KARCH & BUBER *Offset Processes* 546 Multigraph—A duplicator which prints from specially cast type.

multigravida (mɒltigræ·vidă). *Obstetrics.*

Pl. -idas, -idæ. [f. MULTI- after PRIMIGRAVIDA.] A pregnant woman who has had at least one previous pregnancy (or at least two) (formerly less specific: see quots. 1890, 1900).

1890 BILLINGS *Med. Dict.* II. 175/1 *Multigravida*, a woman who has been pregnant more than once. 1900 DORLAND *Med. Dict.* 399/2 *Multigravida*, a woman who has often been pregnant. 1938 A. L. MUDALIAR *Clin. Obstetr.* II. v. 30 Marked changes take place in the breasts consequent upon pregnancy, and such changes are more obvious in primigravidæ than in multigravidæ. 1943 W. SHAW *Textbk. Midwifery* viii. 146 In normal cases the average duration of the first stage of labour in a primigravida is between twelve and fifteen hours, whereas in a multigravida the duration is usually very much shorter. 1958 *Observer* 3 Aug. 10/5 Nice young upper-middle-class multigravida harassed by children. 1959 *Amer. Jrnl. Obstetr. & Gynecol.* LXXVII. 104 In multigravidas there is practically no distress caused by difficult labor or head pressure in the second stage (although both are seen where the previous pregnancies have been only abortions). 1972 E. C. HUGHES *Obstetr.-Gynecol. Terminol.* 331 A multigravida is a woman who is pregnant and who has been pregnant more than one time.

multihull (mʌ·ltihʌl). [f. MULTI- 2 + HULL *sb.*[2]] A boat with more than one hull; freq. *attrib.* Also **mu·ltihulled** *a.*

1956 *Amat. Yacht Res. Soc. Publ.* No. 10. 4 In spite of the fact that multihulled craft have received such little attention..there is enough interest on the part of amateurs to bring about a high degree of development. 1960 R. B. HARRIS *Mod. Sailing Catamarans* 9 By derivation it [*sc.* catamaran] could include any multihulled craft. With all respect for the many fine existing multihull sailing craft.., this book is concerned only with the twin-hulled sailing craft. 1963 E. F. COTTER *Sailing & Racing Catamarans* ii. 11 Beginning in the late 'Forties, new interest in multi-hulls appeared in widely scattered locations. 1969 C. E. JONES *People in Boats* 129/2 Multihulls are normally sloop or ketch-rigged, but occasionally other types of sail have been tried. 1972 *Observer* 11 June 18/7 If it was multihull weather I would back Tom Follett. *Ibid.*, I don't see another multihull which will outperform her.

multilateral, *a.* Add: **3.** *spec.* Pertaining to or concerning three or more countries, esp. of the trade and financial agreements made by them, or of the control of (part of) their armed forces by a supranational authority.

1946 *Jrnl. R. Aeronaut. Soc.* L. 734/1 These agreements were mostly bilateral, and few were multilateral. 1948 *Hansard Commons* 29 Jan. 1290 The Opposition are asking us to support a conception of multi-lateral trade to which the Government have paid lip-service. 1955 *Times* 29 June 9/3 The west, he [*sc.* J. F. Dulles] said, had worked out the first effective system of multilateral arms control the world had ever known. 1957 *Economist* 30 Nov. 807/1 Commercial and financial relations..can move on to a fully multilateral basis. 1960 *Times Lit. Suppl.* 27 May 334/1 The elaborate build-up of good will by multilateral visits between the heads of government. 1963 [see *MULTINATIONAL *a.* and *sb.*].

4. *Educ.* Of a school providing for two or more types of secondary education; also *ellipt.* as *sb.*, a school of this kind. Cf. *COMPREHENSIVE *a.* 1 d.

1938 *Rep. Consultative Comm. Secondary Educ.* (H.M.S.O.) p. xix, We use the term 'multilateral' to describe a school which by means of separate streams would provide for all types of secondary education with the exception of that provided by Junior Technical Schools. 1947 [see *COMPREHENSIVE *a.* 1 d]. 1956 *Times Educ. Suppl.* 27 Apr. 536/3 The case against big multilateral schools has been so often put that it needs no repetition. 1959 *Punch* 17 June 797/1 He saw it in his mind's eye..as a vast multilateral school bringing instruction in basket-weaving and psychology to all the scattered villages of the hilly north. 1967 *Listener* 13 July 41/2 Soon the multilaterals were being called comprehensive and one or two big authorities were actually building a few.

Hence **multila·teralism**, the quality of being multilateral (sense *3); **multila·teralist** *a.* and *sb.*, (one) advocating multilateral disarmament; **multila·teralize** *v.*, to embrace in an agreement amongst many parties; so **multila:teraliza·tion**, the integration of armed forces under supranational authority; **multilaterally** *adv.*, also, amongst three or more parties.

1928 *Glasgow Herald* 13 June 10/6 M. Briand insisted specifically on the term 'war of aggression' after first talking generically of all war. The reason was the transformation of bilateralism into multilateralism. 1940 *Economist* 20 July 94/1 This element of multilateralism will in future be introduced by appropriate amendments to the Regulations governing each Special Account agreement. 1950 *Sun* (Baltimore) 19 June 10/4 Dr. Dalton says their move to abolish quotas and multilateralize commerce among the nations is really an incitement to class hatred. 1951 *Ann. Reg. 1950* 47 It [*sc.* the European Payments Scheme] was a step towards the complete multilateral system of payments desired by America, and was part of the plan to progress towards world economic multilateralism. 1957 *Essays & Stud.* New Ser. X. 7 No one would willingly admit to our vocabulary so unprepossessing and nebulous a word as *multilateralization*. 1960 *News Chron.* 7 Oct. 6/3 How ought we 'multilateralist' Labour MPs to vote on defence? 1960 *Guardian* 11 Oct. 11/1, I am resolutely opposed to urging any member of the Labour party to resign because he is a unilateralist or a multilateralist. *Ibid.* 22 Oct. 1/1 Mr Harold Wilson..declared that the issue was not multilateralism versus unilateralism, but unity versus civil war. 1964 *Listener* 30 July 169/2 The British Government has recently suggested the mixed manning, the multilateralization, of the so-called tactical nuclear weapons now in western Europe. 1965 *Economist* 17 July 207 The Germans still don't want to non-proliferate until they've been multilateralised. 1972 *Sci. Amer.* Apr. 17/2 Government representatives from East and West met.., bilaterally and multilaterally, to discuss increased trade. 1973 *Current Hist.* May 202/1 Yugoslavia supports the convening of a European Security Conference, which would multilateralize the European territorial status quo.

multilayer (mʌ·ltilēiəɹ), *a.* and *sb.* Also **multi-layer.** [f. MULTI- 3, 2 + LAYER *sb.*] **A.** *adj.* Composed of or taking place in many or several layers.

1923 *Daily Mail* 28 Apr. 5 Modern amateur practice has run violently in the direction of those compact multilayer coils called 'basket', 'pancake', or 'honeycomb' coils. 1932 J. W. McBAIN *Sorption of Gases & Vapours by Solids* x. 325 (*heading*) Monomolecular, multilayer and classical thick films. 1960 *Farmer & Stockbreeder* 29 Mar. 77/1 The front-mounted one..can be used for multi-layer stacking in the barn. 1966 R. J. ROSS *Television Film Engin.* xii. 452 The multilayer Kodachrome film was first developed in a normal negative developer to produce silver images.

B. *sb.* A structure or film composed of many or several layers, *spec.* of more than one monolayer.

1932 J. W. McBAIN *Sorption of Gases & Vapours by Solids* x. 326 No such excitement would be aroused by a demonstration of the actual occurrence of multilayers deriving from the second hypothesis. 1963 R. R. A. HIGHAM *Handbk. Papermaking* viii. 214 Laminating machines are used to apply an adhesive to single or multi-layers of paper which are then bonded together by heat to form one ply. 1966 D. G. BRANDON *Mod. Techniques Metallogr.* i. 34 Films may be prepared from diele[c]tric multilayers (usually alternating zinc sulphide with magnesium fluoride). 1975 *Nature* 24 July 297/1 Its bottom is formed of multilayers of salt deposits separated by films of sand and gypsum.

So **mu·ltilayered** *a.* [MULTI- 1 b].

1935 *Anat. Rec.* LXI. 391 Multilayered follicles were increasing in number and as many as ten or twelve granulosa layers surrounded the ova. 1959 *Biol. Abstr.* XXXIV. 1163/2 (*heading*) The multilayered tube wall as [a] model for the aorta. 1974 *Tetrahedron Lett.* 1573 We have previously described the synthesis of multilayered [2.2] metacyclophanes by way of the Stevens rearrangement.

mu·ltilevel, *a.* Also **multi-level.** [MULTI- 3.] Having, involving, or operating on several levels (in any sense). Also *ellipt.* as *sb.*, a multilevel set of apartments.

1952 *Los Angeles Examiner* 19 Mar. III. 1 (*caption*) Multi-level apartment hotel is planned as the center for the development. 1959 G. TROUP *Masers* iv. 50 One multilevel excitation method is that known as 'optical pumping'. 1959 *Sunday Times* 12 Apr. 21/6 America welcomed the one-storey 'ranch' house and the 'split level'. Today, the development builders, who can find new names for old things, are trumpeting the 'multi level'. 1960 *Guardian* 17 Mar. 9/5 Multi-level traffic to separate vehicles from pedestrians. 1961 L. MUMFORD *City in Hist.* viii. 208 The new marketplaces at Coventry and Harlow, with their upper tiers of shops and offices, are..only a recovery of the admirable Roman multi-level plan. 1964 E. A. NIDA *Toward Sci. Transl.* v. 80 When such vertical divisions are multilevel, that is to say, when the cuts extend through several layers, they mark very important distinctions in the language. 1969 *Jane's Freight Containers 1968–69* 121/3 Unloading automobiles from multi-level cars. 1972 *Village Voice* (N.Y.) 1 June 82/3 (Advt.), Unusual multi-levels. Charming bedroom apts. 1973 *Times* 5 Oct. (Safety Suppl.) p. ii, Junctions are multilevel and local roads..are carried over or under their dual carriageways.

So **multi-le·velled** *a.* [MULTI- 1 b].

1948 *Hudson Rev.* I. 1. 117 But precisely because it is a poem—compact, symbolic, multileveled, all details woven elaborately into the meaning pattern—it cannot be totally accounted for as yet. 1962 M. McLUHAN *Gutenberg Galaxy* 103 When only the eye is engaged, the multi-levelled gestures and resonances of Senecan oral action are quite impertinent. 1964 E. BACH *Introd. Transformational Gram.* iv. 58 A multileveled theory such as is necessary for describing a natural language. 1968 A. LOMAX *Folk Song Style & Culture* iv. 95 The overall impact of the African style is multileveled, multiparted, highly integrated, multi-textured, gregarious, and playful-voiced.

multilineal (mʌltili·niăl), *a.* [f. MULTI- + LINEAL *a.*] Having many lines; *spec.* denoting a kinship system which includes relationships derived from parents, grandparents, etc., of both father and mother. Hence **multilinea·lity**, the fact of multilineal kinship.

a 1800, 1882 [in Dict. s.v. MULTI- 1 a]. 1943 T. PARSONS in *Amer. Anthropologist* XLV. 26 Since the same principle of lack of distinction by sex of intervening relative applies to still higher ascendant generations—the four great- and eight great-great-grandfathers—it is perhaps more accurate to speak of a 'multilineal' than a 'bilateral' system. 1956 R. FIRTH *Two Stud. Kinship in London* 16 The 'multilineal' American family. *Ibid.* 17 It is in this way that the conversion of bilaterality into multilineality occurs. 1965 G. P. MURDOCK *Culture & Society* xiii. 179 The 'multilineal' of Parsons..is inappropriate since..many such systems, including the American, are not in fact 'lineal' in any sense.

multilingual (mʌltili·ŋgwăl), *a.* and *sb.* [f. MULTI- + L. *lingu(a* tongue, language + -AL.] **A.** *adj.* Speaking, characterized by, or written in many languages.

1838, 1880 [in Dict. s.v. MULTI- 1 b]. 1958 *Listener* 2 Jan. 5/2 Indonesia..is multi-racial and multilingual. 1960 E. DELAVENAY *Introd. Machine Transl.* vi. 96 This Cambridge research leads in the direction of a new kind of bilingual or multilingual dictionaries. 1968 *Amer. Speech* XLIII. 127 How is the language variance in multilingual communities best explained?

B. *sb.* One who speaks many languages. Also **multili·nguist.**

1923 W. J. LOCKE *Lengthened Shadow* 187 A white-haired white-moustached multilinguist by the name of Soussouki. 1956 *Essays in Crit.* VI. 67 Fr. Jarret-Kerr is dealing with creative artists who worked in Spanish, Italian, Russian and French—and he confesses himself no multilinguist. 1959 J. C. CATFORD in Quirk & Smith *Teaching of English* vi. 164 Strictly speaking, the alternative use of more than two languages is 'multilingualism' and the persons involved are 'multilingual' (adj.) or 'multilinguals' (n.). 1964 E. PALMER tr. *Martinet's Elem. Gen. Ling.* v. 160 These are the bilingual speakers, or if they possess more than two codes, the multilinguals, whatever degree of perfection they may achieve in handling each of the said languages. 1968 *Amer. Speech* XLIII. 127 What theoretical model most appropriately describes the individual multilingual's speech? 1974 *Daily Tel.* 10 July 18 An Oxford graduate and multilinguist, Saunders worked at the Treasury and the Coal Board.

Hence **multili·ngually** *adv.*; **multili·ngualism**, the ability to speak many languages; the use of many languages.

1940 *Q. Jrnl. Speech* Oct. 394 Problems confronting the speech therapist in the Union are legion, resulting from racial inequalities, multi-lingualism, [etc.]. 1953 U. WEINREICH in *Publ. Ling. Circle N.Y.* I. 1 Unless otherwise specified, all remarks about bilingualism apply as well to multilingualism, the practice of using alternately three or more languages. 1958 *Times Rev. Industry* June 76/1 Working principles are explained multi-lingually through loudspeakers. 1968 J. A. FISHMAN *Readings Sociol. of Lang.* 12 Multilingualism has long been a topic recognized by sociologists, linguists, anthropologists, and others as shedding light on many aspects of language learning. 1972 *Sci. Amer.* Sept. 78/1 Bilingualism or multilingualism ..cannot be rigidly separated from interdialectal fluctuations. 1972 *Physics Bull.* Dec. 136/2 It [*sc.* a European *Physics Bulletin*] would have to be printed multilingually, and would be an extremely expensive exercise. 1973 *Archivum Linguisticum* IV. 55 Another way of putting this is to refer to one of the most common questions faced by those wishing to make sense of multilingualism—how many languages are there here, and how many dialects?

Multilith (mʌ·ltiliþ). Also **multilith.** [f. MULTI- + LITH(OGRAPH *sb.*] The proprietary name of a small, offset-lithographic, printing machine. Also *attrib.* So **mu·ltilithed** *ppl. a.*, printed by a machine of this kind.

1933 *Profit Making Up-to-Date* (Addressograph-Multigraph Corp.) 81 Multilith greatly reduces the necessity of type composition. 1936 *Business Office Training Course* (Addressograph-Multigraph Corp.) xi. 97 The latest addition to the Multigraph line is the 'Multilith'. This term applies to the simplified process of 'offset lithography' developed by the Multigraph Company. 1937 *Geogr. Jrnl.* LXXXIX. 403 Multilith photographer. 1951 *Archivum Linguisticum* III. 106 From 1942 dates the journal *Studies in Linguistics*..published..at first in mimeographed and later in multilithed form. 1965 *Times Lit. Suppl.* 14 Jan. 25/4 A new multilithed newsletter called *Cultural Events in Africa* is appearing monthly. 1968 *Globe & Mail* (Toronto) 13 Jan. 48/2 (Advt.), Pressman..—knowledge of multilith an advantage. 1974 *Oxf. Univ. Gaz.* 19 Dec. 373/1 (Advt.), Academic, literary, and other typing... Multilith duplicating.

multi-me·dia, *a.* [f. MULTI- + *MEDIA.] Designating or pertaining to a form of artistic, educational, or commercial communication in which more than one medium is used. Hence as *sb.*

1962 *Times* 26 Feb. (Canada Suppl.) p. xviii/4 The first prong is a multi-media publicity campaign to encourage school children..to obtain adequate educational qualifications. 1962 *Listener* 5 Apr. 603/3 Both Futurists and Dadaists had a keen interest in multi-media art, in breaking down the technical and formal self-sufficiency of the work of art. 1968 *Sun* (Baltimore) 4 July A. 16/3 The notes of one conference we attended a few weeks ago.. show that speakers were using such terms..as..multimedia and multi-mode curriculum. 1970 *Times* 28 Apr. 7 Late night performances of the Military Tattoo and of the multimedia rock musical *Stomp*. 1970 D. BERGEN in *Americana Ann.* 420 Multimedia information centers with print and audiovisual materials. 1971 *Black Scholar* Jan. 20/2 As originator of the practice of reading poetry to jazz, he not only stitched backwards and forward in his lineage and idiom, but wrought a new force in the now obscenely exaggerated concept of multi-media. 1974 *News & Press* (Darlington, S. Carolina) 25 Apr. 9/7 Hooser creates a multi-media effect that draws the viewer into the picture.

multimer (mʌ·ltiməɹ). *Chem.* [f. MULTI- + *-MER.] An aggregate of molecules held together by relatively weak bonds, such as hydrogen bonds.

1959 M. DAVIES in D. Hadži *Hydrogen Bonding* 560 The use of the term 'polymer' for the associated molecules formed from stable monomers by hydrogen bonding, etc., seems objectionable, and it is suggested that the equivalent, self-explanatory term 'multimer' be used in these

circumstances. **1967** *Arch. Biochem. & Biophysics* CXX. 158 (*heading*) Studies on protein multimers. **1972** H.-G. ELIAS in M. B. Huglin *Light Scattering from Polymer Solutions* ix. 399 A unimer of molecular weight M_I will multimerize to a multimer with a degree of multimerization N̄.

Hence **multime·ric** *a.*; also **mu:ltimeriza·tion**, the formation of multimers; **mu·ltimerize** (or *multi·merize*) *v. intr.*, to associate to form a multimer or multimers; **mu·ltimerized, mu·ltimerizing** *ppl. adjs.*

1971 *Arch. Biochem. & Biophysics* CXLII. 329/1 The experimental basis for supposing that high pressure disaggregates multimeric proteins is already well established. **1972** H.-G. ELIAS in M. B. Huglin *Light Scattering from Polymer Solutions* ix. 451 It is believed that multimerizations occur preferentially in thermodynamically poor solvents as expressed for polyvinyl chloride solutions. *Ibid.* 398 For the multimerized material, we shall use the following nomenclature. *Ibid.* 400 In light scattering studies of multimerizing solutes, many different concentration dependences of the reciprocal apparent weight average molecular weights may be observed. *Ibid.* 441 Cellulose nitrates multimerize in ethanol at temperatures above 20° C. **1973** *Microbios* VII. 53 (*heading*) The multimeric nature of NADPH-nitrate reductase from *Aspergillus nidulans*. **1973** *Nature* 24 Aug. 528/3 Chapter 9 deals with the problems of aggregation or multimerization.

multimeter (mɒ·ltimītəɹ). *Electr.* [f. MULTI- 2 + METER *sb.*³] An instrument designed to measure voltage, current, and usu. resistance, often over several different ranges of value.

The word *Multimeter* is registered as a proprietary name in the U.S.

1910 *Hawkins' Electr. Dict.* 292/1 *Multi-meter*, a 'universal' electronic measuring instrument designed to serve the purpose of a voltmeter, ammeter, ohmmeter, ground detector and Wheatstone bridge. **1926** *Jrnl. Sci. Instruments* III. 346 The vacuum-tube multimeter has three ranges as a voltmeter, and six ranges as an ammeter for each range of the voltmeter. **1929** *Official Gaz.* (U.S. Patent Office) 5 Mar. 23/2 Rawson Electrical Instrument Company, Cambridge, Mass... *Multimeter* for Electric Meters. Claims use since latter part of 1919. **1967** *Electronics* 6 Mar. 117/1 The Instrumentation division of Fairchild Camera & Instrument Corp. has brought the price of a multimeter down to $249. **1971** *Nature* 12 Feb. 482/1 The 1970 resistance measurements were made with a digital multimeter (Fluke '8100A') to the same accuracy as the 1969 measurements. **1975** *Physics Bull.* Jan. 28/2 Sinclair Radionics new DM2 digital multimeter provides the facilities of the conventional multimeter: AC and DC voltage, AC and DC current ranges and resistance measurements, in a portable instrument.

multimodal (mɒltimōu·dăl), *a.* Also (with hyphen) **multi-modal.** [f. MULTI- 1 a + MOD(E *sb.* + -AL.] **a.** Of a frequency curve or distribution: having several modes or maxima (*MODE *sb.* 7 c). Of a property: occurring among different individuals in accordance with such a distribution.

1902 *Biometrika* I. 305 A frequency distribution with more than one true mode is multi-modal. **1932** J. S. HUXLEY *Probl. Relative Growth* VII. i. 210 The body-length for males is irregular, multimodal and skew. **1959** SCHUELL & JENKINS in Saporta & Bastian *Psycholinguistics* (1961) 436/1 The distribution of scores on each test was plotted for the 100-patient sample... Only a few tests yielded irregular multi-modal distributions. **1962** *Lancet* 26 May 1090/1 In both cases distributions in two of the six age-groups are irregular..and of a form which might readily be interpreted as multimodal or bimodal.

b. Characterized by several different modes of occurrence or activity.

1928 D. B. LEARY *Mod. Psychol.* 128 The so-called multi-modal theory..assumes that there are several distinct types of intelligent conduct. **1968** W. A. STEWART in J. A. Fishman *Readings Sociol. of Lang.* (1968) 534 When a language has come to be used in more than one country and has..developed multimodal standardization, the form of standardization prevalent in any one country may [etc.]. **1969** *Jane's Freight Containers 1968–69* 32/3 As shippers adjust to the advantages of an integrated, multimodal transportation system.

Hence **multimo·dalism** (*rare*), **mu:ltimoda·lity**, the property or quality of being multimodal.

1902 *Biometrika* I. 305 Much of the multimodalism interpreted in the case of flowers as polymorphism is due either to misinterpretation.., i.e. is not true multimodalism..or..is due to some heterogeneity..introduced by the gatherer. **1932** J. S. HUXLEY *Probl. Relative Growth* ii. 78 There is a slight tendency to multimodality.. in the male body-length frequency curve. **1972** *Comprehensive Psychiatry* XIII. 391 (*heading*) Impact of a multimodality treatment program for heroin addicts. **1973** D. NELKIN *Methadone Maintenance* i. 24 'Multimodality', an expression coined by Dr. Jaffe, which refers to a concept of rehabilitation that coordinates within a single administrative structure all varieties of approaches to addiction.

multinational (mɒltinæ·ʃənăl), *a.* and *sb.* [f. MULTI- + NATIONAL *a.* and *sb.*] **A.** *adj.* **a.** Comprising or pertaining to many nationalities or ethnic groups. **b.** Possessing branches, factories, offices, etc., in many countries. **B.** *sb.* A multinational company. So **multina·tionally** *adv.*; **multina·tionalism**, the realm of multinational companies.

1926 *Time* 17 May 14 A majority of the multi-national citizens of what is now Hungary. **1940** *Mind* XLIX. 117 Their inequality makes for an intrinsic instability in their relations which causes one to regret the passing of the multi-national Empires, like Austria and Russia, with their stabilising effect. **1957** *Times Lit. Suppl.* 25 Oct. 635/2 The volume contains in fact five separate essays—on the beginnings of the American nation..on the problems of a multi-national nation [etc.]. **1961** *New Scientist* 23 Mar. 733/1 There will be an important multi-national programme of space research, starting in 1962. **1962** *Economist* 15 Dec. 1108/3 Assignments to multinational organisations should be up-graded. **1963** *Guardian* 19 Mar. 11/4 A multinational force would be one composed of Service units already in existence... Multilateral would mean manning.., for example, Polaris surface ships with mixed crews. **1964** *Economist* 17 Oct. 271/2 Very few such companies..seem..to think 'multi-nationally'. **1968** *Listener* 12 Dec. 783/1 The multinational firm transcends national boundaries..through the establishment of subsidiaries in foreign countries. **1971** C. TUGENDHAT (*title*) The multinationals. **1971** *Rand Daily Mail* 4 Dec. 12/2 There are plans for extra senates and supra-parliaments and multinational assemblies. **1972** *Listener* 18 May 652/2 Yours is a multinational group. What are the prospects for multinationalism? **1973** *Daily Tel.* (Colour Suppl.) 22 June 23/2 The five multi-national pilots—as her name implies the Europa is a truly European airship. **1975** *Bookseller* 18 Jan. 155/1 (Advt.), To manipulate the takeover of the Holmes Motor Corporation by an American multi-national and to destroy a rival spying network.

multi-occupa·tion. [MULTI- 2.] Occupation of a house by more than one family, with shared kitchen or sanitary facilities. Hence **multi-o·ccupy** *v. trans.*, to tenant a house with more than one family with such shared facilities; to place tenants in such a house; **multi-o·ccupied** *ppl. a.* Cf. *multiple occupancy, occupation* (s.v. *MULTIPLE *a.* 2 c).

1963 *Guardian* 30 Mar. 2/2 A graduated percentage addition to the rateable value of houses in multi-occupation. **1965** *Ibid.* 3 Sept. 20/8 For every house multi-occupied by Pakistanis..there are many more multi-occupied by Irish. **1967** *Economist* 14 Oct. 177/1 Improvement grants are not available for multi-occupied houses. **1970** *Guardian* 31 July 9/1 The borough council is..planning to multi-occupy its emergency homeless in..a tenement building built in 1878. **1972** *Ibid.* 26 June 7/3 If families are evicted from multi-occupation property, they tend to move to the next street. **1973** C. MULLARD *Black Brit.* xiii. 164 There is still no national code in existence. If there were, multi-occupation and other housing problems would be non-issues.

multip, colloq. abbrev. MULTIPARA (in Dict. and Suppl.).

1948 MENCKEN *Amer. Lang.* Suppl. II. xi. 756 *Primip*, a mother having her first child... At subsequent deliveries she is a *multip*,..or a *para-two, three*, etc. **1967** *Midwives Chron.* Apr. 115/1 The risks to the grande multip cover pregnancy and labour and puerperium.

multipacket (mɒ·ltipækėt). [f. MULTI- + PACKET *sb.*] A cargo boat built in two parts, having the propulsion unit and crew quarters at one end and one or more cargo units at the other. Also *attrib.*

1965 *Daily Express* 11 Nov. 17/2 A design for a cargo ship that splits in half has passed Ministry of Transport tests... The design, called the Multi-packet, has been developed by a Liverpool firm. **1967** *New Scientist* 28 Dec. 743/3 The multipacket vessel can enter harbour, deposit a fully laden cargo unit at the quayside, and depart with a different unit—all within a matter of hours. *Ibid.* 744/1 The greatest technical difficulty to be overcome in the new design is that of connecting and disconnecting the multipacket units quickly and easily.

multipara. Add: Pl. **-paras, -paræ.** Freq. used (in contrast to *primipara*) to include pregnant women with a single previous delivery, the forthcoming birth being anticipated in the enumeration. (Earlier and later examples.)

1860 [see PRIMIPAROUS *a.*]. **1890** tr. *F. Winckel's Text-bk. Obstetr.* III. v. 112 It is by no means easy to distinguish a multipara from a primipara, especially when the previous pregnancy took place many years before. **1938** A. L. MUDALIAR *Clin. Obstetr.* II. vi. 35 In multiparæ the changes in the breasts are not of much diagnostic value, because pregnancy may take place in a lactating woman. **1958** J. R. WILLSON et al. *Obstetr. & Gynecol.* xxviii. 321 In primigravidas the cervix is usually well effaced before the contractions of true labor begin, but preparation of the cervix in multiparas differs slightly. **1967** J. B. LAWSON in Lawson & Stewart *Obstetr. & Gynaecol. in Tropics* i. 5 None of the risks of high parity..are unique to grande multiparae (para 5 and above) but are commoner in this group. **1972** E. C. HUGHES *Obstetr.-Gynecol. Terminol.* vii. 333 A multipara is a woman who has given birth two or more times to an infant or infants, alive or dead, weighing 500 gm or more.

multi-pa·rty, *a. Polit.* [f. MULTI- + PARTY *sb.* 6.] Comprising several parties or members of several parties; of an electoral or political system which results in the formation of three or more influential parties.

1909 *Englishwoman* Apr. 325 The suffrage societies, nominally non-party and really multi-party in their composition. **1935** R. BASSETT *Essent. Parl. Democracy* ii. 43 Under the multi-party conditions prevalent in most continental parliamentary regimes, it is almost certain that no single party will be able to secure a working majority. **1954** B. & R. NORTH tr. *Duverger's Pol. Parties* II. i. 229 The typology of the multi-party system is difficult to establish. **1956** J. KLEIN *Study of Groups* 161 A democratic country with a multi-party system. **1958** A. LEISERSON *Parties & Politics* ix. 358 The multiparty system operates quite differently in a three-party situation..from the way it does when there are five or six fairly identifiable party groupings. **1964** *Ann. Reg. 1963* 204 Dr Raúl Leoni..stated that his party would try to form a multi-party coalition. **1970** B. M. BARRY *Sociologists, Economists & Democracy* v. 125 In a multi-party system, the parties are more precise but it is more difficult to tell what one is doing by voting for one.

Hence **multi-pa·rtism, multi-pa·rtyism,** a political system in which the major interest groups of the electorate are reflected in three or more influential parties. Also *multi-partist* adj.

1946 F. A. OGG *European Govt. & Politics* (rev. ed.) xlv. 901 The error would lie in failure to remember..the total absence of anything approaching Western multi-partyism. **1954** B. & R. NORTH tr. *Duverger's Pol. Parties* II. i. 229 In this sense multi-partism is fairly characteristic of Western Europe, Great Britain excepted but Ireland included. *Ibid.* iii. 393 Great Britain and the Dominions, under a two-party system, are profoundly dissimilar from Continental countries under a multi-partist system. **1962** S. E. FINER *Man on Horseback* xii. 236 In Indonesia, where the sole unifying force in government is the personality of Sukarno, his recent activities provide a grotesque commentary on multi-partyism in a new and divided state. **1967** J. J. LINZ in Lipset & Rokkan *Party Syst. & Voter Alignments* 259 (*heading*) The transition from extreme multipartism to polarized conflict and civil war. **1971** D. W. RAE *Pol. Consequences Electoral Laws* (rev. ed.) iii. 53 An extreme case of 'multi-partism', with, say, ten parties, each polling about one tenth of the total vote.

mu·ltiphase, *a.* [MULTI- 3.] Having or producing two or more phases; in *Electr.* = POLYPHASE *a.*

1890, etc. [in Dict. s.v. MULTI- 3]. **1916** W. H. N. JAMES *Alternating Currents* v. 87 The relative merits of single and multiphase systems depend upon the purpose to which the power is to be applied. **1946** *Nature* 31 Aug. 307/2 The electrolytic polishing of multi-phase metals is usually more difficult than that of single-phase metals owing to differing properties..of the different phases. **1966** D. G. BRANDON *Mod. Techniques Metallogr.* ii. 82 Absorption contrast arises from variations in chemical composition and hence provides information about the composition and distribution of phases in a multiphase alloy.

So **mu·ltiphased** *a.*, occurring in several stages.

1970 *Sci. Amer.* Feb. 103/3 The effect of laser irradiation on the cells varied with the stage of mitosis, the multiphased process of cell division.

multiphasic (mɒltifēi·zik), *a.* [f. MULTI- 1 a + PHAS(E + -IC.] Applied to tests or investigations designed to reveal various phases or aspects of personality, health, etc.

1940 *Psychol. Bull.* XXXVII. 425 The Multiphasic Personality Schedule is a group of 504 items for administration to adults. **1958** M. ARGYLE *Relig. Behaviour* viii. 87 Brown and Lowe (1915) tested a large number of students on the Minnesota Multiphasic Personality Inventory (MMPI) and found that a group of Bible students—who would be extreme Protestants—scored high on hysteria. **1968** *Daily Tel.* 22 Nov. 25/4 Multiphasic screening could disclose much potential sickness and make possible early treatment. **1971** *Brit. Med. Bull.* XXVII. 6/1 In a multiphasic programme the individual will be subjected to a number of tests within a short space of time.

multiplane (mɒ·ltiplēin), *sb.* and *a.* [f. MULTI- 2, 3 + PLANE *sb.*³] **A.** *sb.* An aeroplane or glider having several 'planes' or main supporting surfaces placed one above another. Also *attrib.* or as *adj.*

1909 A. BERGET *Conquest of Air* II. ii. 139 Will the aeroplane be a 'monoplane' or 'multiplane'? *Ibid.* 147 The arrangement employed..is 'partitioning'..and applies to multiplane aeroplanes. **1928** *Jrnl. R. Aeronaut. Soc.* XXXII. 145 The method of obtaining the reduction of drag for a multiplane is described. **1939** C. H. L. NEEDHAM *Aircraft Design* I. vi. 74 When two or more planes are situated one above the other, so as to form biplane, triplane or multiplane arrangements, the low pressure region over the top of the lower wing is closely adjacent to the high pressure area below the upper wing. **1960** C. H. GIBBS-SMITH *Aeroplane* 337 Wenham was the first to build..a multiplane aeroplane, a full-size glider with five wings. **1969** K. MUNSON *Pioneer Aircraft 1903–14* 154/2 In 1904 appeared the first man-carrying multiplane (Phillips I). This had a framework of twenty rigid blade sustainers. **1973** *Country Life* 11 Oct. 1074 In 1903 a multiplane, somewhat similar to the one built in 1893, was constructed and taken to Essex for trials.

B. *adj.* Involving or occupying several distinct planes or layers (not necessarily horizontal); applied *spec.* in *Cinemat.* to a technique employed to give an enhanced impression of perspective.

1909, etc. [see A above]. **1948** E. LINDGREN *Art of Film* vii. 127 Objects in different planes will appear to move at different speeds according to their distance from the camera lens..and the relationship between these

various movements can..suggest almost a three-dimensional effect; this is the principle behind the multiplane technique now employed in the making of cartoon films. **1955** J. Caunter *How to do Tricks in Amat. Films* 65 To give the effect of maximum perspective to a background scene you will have to divide it into more than one layer of scenery... This is the multiplane principle. **1959** Halas & Manvell *Technique Film Animation* ii. 28 Now the animation studios have their own specialized cameras.. capable of photographing multi-plane images with back lighting. **1961** G. Millerson *Technique Television Production* xix. 362 Multiplane captions. Here the caption is comprised of several transparent or cut-out layers, and by revealing or obscuring these layers, we can add or remove detail to order. **1969** *Daily Tel.* 7 Feb. 21/6 A clever white multiplane set is used for the projection of slides and movie-film, either bathing the stage in dazzling colour or else enthroning unexpected VIPs.

multiple, *a.* and *sb.* Add: **A.** *adj.* **2. b.** *multiple shop, store*: one of several shops of the same kind belonging to the same firm, opened in different localities. Cf. *chain store.

1903 J. Hazelip *Multiple-Shop Accounts* 1 There is considerable difference in the class of business carried on by multiple-shop firms. **1909** *Westm. Gaz.* 10 May 9/4 Some of the multiple shops..have been retailing at 9s. 4d. sugar which has cost them 14s. 7½d. to buy. **1927** *Daily Tel.* 14 Mar. 4/7 The multiple shops..have reduced their prices in accord with the drop in wholesale prices. **1929** E. Gill *Art-Nonsense* 315 Politics and social guidance are left to ..novelists, multiple-store keepers, manufacturers of motor-cars. **1959** *Times Lit. Suppl.* 4 Sept. 504/3 *An Introduction to Music* is another of what might be called the multiple-stores books which aim to provide everything for the music-lover. **1963** N. Marsh *Dead Water* (1964) ii. 46 There's a rash of boarding establishments and a multiple store. **1965** *Modern Law Rev.* XXVIII. 553 The new multiple shops and shopping centres in both the United States and England. **1972** N. Marsh *Tied up in Tinsel* vi. 140 There's no joy down your way: big multiple stores robbery.

c. *multiple occupancy, occupation* = *multi-occupation.

1971 *Guardian* 11 June 12/3 There is a certain amount of substandard accommodation largely created through multiple occupation. **1973** *Times* 26 July 4/6 Probably 100 to 120 families are breaking the regulations applicable to multiple occupancy houses. **1975** *Times* 30 Aug. 13/6 Perhaps Mr Cutler..would like to relax controls on houses in multiple occupation so that even more people can share a bath.

3. a. *multiple allele* or *allelomorph*: any allele which is located at a genetic locus known to have three or more alleles; *multiple factor*: any gene which acts in concert with other, non-allelic, genes to control the expression of a character; *multiple fission*: the division of a cell into more than two daughter-cells.

1912 E. A. Minchin *Introd. Study Protozoa* vii. 120 In most cases, probably, of multiple fission the nucleus contains a centriole, and..the centriole multiplies by fission a number of times without the nucleus as a whole becoming divided. **1913** *Amer. Naturalist* XLVII. 234 (*heading*) The Himalayan rabbit case, with some considerations on multiple allelomorphs. **1915** R. Pearl *Modes Res. Genetics* i. 21 In recent developments of Mendelian theory it has been a common practice to assume the existence of multiple factors as the causal agents of a single character. **1938** A. F. Shull *Heredity* (ed. 3) xi. 103 (*heading*) Multiple alleles. **1945** E. Altenburg *Genetics* v. 83 Members of several gene pairs which act in a cumulative way on a trait are known as multiple factors. **1948** *Nature* 30 Oct. 684/1 (*heading*) Multiple allelomorphs in colour vision. **1971** J. Z. Young *Introd. Study Man* xl. 585 Fourteen different systems of blood antigen genes are known... The most familiar of them are three multiple alleles known as G^A, G^B, and G, the first two being both dominant to G. These genes are often called simply *A*, *B*, and *O*. **1972** *Proc. Nat. Acad. Sci.* LXIX. 2346/1 Organisms dividing by multiple fission can be used to study the initiation and control of cytokinesis, because those unique events essential to cytokinesis are separated from events of the cell cycle that pertain to DNA synthesis, mitosis, or cytoplasmic growth.

d. *multiple myeloma* [tr. G. *multiples myelom* (J. von Rustizky 1873, in *Deutsche Zeitschr. f. Chirurgie* III. 163)], = *myelomatosis; *multiple sclerosis*, a chronic, progressive, demyelinating disease in which sclerosis occurs in patches in the brain and spinal cord, which chiefly affects young adults, and is often manifested initially as mild attacks with varying symptoms followed later by successive remissions (often long-lasting) and relapses, but typically leading to weakness and paresis of the lower limbs, intention tremors in the upper limbs, disturbed sight and speech, emotional changes, and mental deterioration; also called *disseminated sclerosis*.

[Multiple sclerosis: cf. quot. 1877 in Dict.] **1885** J. Ross *Handbk. Dis. Nervous Syst.* xx. 674 (*heading*) Multiple sclerosis of the brain and spinal cord (disseminated or insular sclerosis). **1897** *Trans. Path. Soc.* XLVIII. 169 (*heading*) General lymphadenomatosis of bones, one form of 'multiple myeloma'. **1904** Multiple myeloma [see *myelomatosis]. **1917** *Jrnl. Nervous & Mental Dis.* XLV. 454 In multiple sclerosis we had been in the habit of considering the disease incurable and although there might be a remission for a number of months or years, it could not be looked upon as a cure. **1957** S. L. Robbins *Textbk. Path.* xxxii. 1311/2 Studies on animals with injections of nervous tissue and adjuvants may yet prove to be important in multiple sclerosis, but no worker has yet reproduced a convincing replica of the disease. **1961** *Lancet* 5 Aug. 290/1 On paper electrophoresis, macroglobulinæmic sera yield patterns which are indistinguishable from those found in multiple myeloma. **1966** Multiple myeloma [see *myelomatosis]. **1971** *New Scientist* 7 Jan. 6/1 Multiple sclerosis is the commonest disease of the nervous system in northern Europe and the USA. **1972** C. E. Seiverd *Hematol. for Med. Technologists* (ed. 4) xxxvii. 667 Myeloma means marrow tumor; thus, multiple myeloma may be interpreted as simply meaning many tumors of the bone marrow. Multiple myeloma is also referred to by the following terms; myelome, plasmocytoma, plasma cell myeloma, myelomatosis, and Kahler's disease.

j. *Statistics.* Involving the joint effect on the variable under investigation of two or more other variables.

1903 *Phil. Trans. R. Soc.* A. CC. 3 (*heading*) On the fundamental theorem in multiple correlation. **1938** A. E. Waugh *Elem. Statistical Method* xi. 318 Problems that involve the determination of the relationship between one variable and several other variables acting together are called problems of multiple correlation. *Ibid.* 321 The multiple-regression equation must obviously be altered so that we can account for changes in all the independent variables. **1958** M. Argyle *Relig. Behaviour* iii. 18 An alternative procedure for estimating the relative weight of different variables influencing percentages is multiple regression. **1971** *Brit. Med. Bull.* XXVII. 22/1 A multiple regression study showed that..both water calcium and rainfall made significant contributions to the variance of cardiovascular death-rates between the towns studied. **1972** T. H. & R. J. Wonnacott *Introd. Statistics for Business & Econ.* xiv. 350 Whereas the partial correlations measure the significance of regressors one by one, the multiple correlation *R* measures the significance of all the regressors at once.

k. *multiple use*: = *multi-use *a.*

1969 *Gloss. for Landscape Work* (*B.S.I.*) v. 16 *Multiple use*, the use of land for more than one purpose, resulting in a modification in the methods of maintenance, for example, water catchment areas also used for cattle grazing or for forestry. **1969** *Jane's Freight Containers 1968–69* 505 (*caption*) SALwall..incorporates a multiple-use double wall.

4. b. *multiple-beam*; **multiple-access** = *multi-access* (*multi- 3); **multiple-aspect,** applied to a colour-light railway signal capable of displaying at least three aspects; **multiple-choice,** applied to an educational or psychological test in which the subject is asked to select his answer from several items; **multiple-disc,** applied to a kind of friction clutch consisting of a row of co-axial discs, fixed alternately to the driving and the driven parts, which may be brought in contact to transmit the drive from the one to the other; **multiple-unit,** of, pertaining to, or designating a train having a number of coaches provided with engines all of which can be controlled by a single driver; also as *sb.*, a coach of this kind.

1966 *New Scientist* 27 Oct. 160/3 This valuable experience..has..enabled us to take in our stride the 'multiple-access' problem of how to serve a large number of control consoles apparently simultaneously. **1970** O. Dopping *Computers & Data Processing* ix. 130 A control program for a multiple access system must be able to identify a subscriber who requires service, find out which program he needs, and put him in the queue, if any. **1932** *Proc. Inst. Railway Signal Engin.* I. 57 (*heading*) Railway colour light signalling in relation to manual block and multiple aspect signals. **1963** Kichenside & Williams *Brit. Railway Signalling* iii. 24 In colour-light areas, a multiple-aspect signal cannot display a 'green——clear' indication unless the next signal is showing at least a 'caution' if not a 'clear' aspect also. *Ibid.* 25 In colour-light areas..every multiple-aspect signal serves as a distant, home and starting signal at the same time. **1970** *Railway World* Dec. 524 Multiple-aspect colour-light signalling with continuous track circuiting will be installed. **1945** *Proc. R. Soc.* A. CLXXXIV. 41 A multiple beam interferometric procedure..can be used as a powerful method for revealing the details of the surface topography of approximately flat crystal planes. **1966** D. G. Brandon *Mod. Techniques Metallogr.* i. 25 This may be done most simply by placing a half-silvered plate in contact with the specimen, when either two-beam or multiple-beam interference patterns may be obtained. **1928** Orleans & Sealy *Objective Tests* xiii. 220 Facility in framing optional answers for a multiple-choice question comes with practice. **1959** J. Barzun *House of Intellect* 268 A basic defect of multiple choice tests: that they call for choices but not for reasons for choices. **1967** *Observer* 26 Nov. 1/4 In the American 'multiple-choice' examinations the candidate marks one of a number of possible responses to a question, instead of writing an essay on it. **1906, 1909** Multiple disc [see *disc-clutch* (*disc *sb.* 8)]. **1967** *Jane's Surface Skimmer Systems 1967–68* 124/1 Flange-mounted converter automatically changing over from multiple-disc clutch..to converter, operation, then again operation through multiple-disc clutch when moving on foils. **1902** *Encycl. Brit.* XXVIII. 93/1 The train operated by two or more motor cars under a common secondary control. This..is called the 'multiple unit system'. **1955** *Oxf. Jun. Encycl.* VIII. 366/2 In Britain 'in-built' motive-power units have proved more popular than separate locomotives. These have 'multiple-unit' control, that is, one driver can control the current supply and braking throughout the whole train. **1967** *Economist* 21 Jan. 202/1 In October 1965 an agreement was reached between the railway management and the unions on single-manning for passenger and long-distance freight locomotives (and multiple-unit trains that have no loco as such). **1970** *Railway World* Dec. 540 At times of peak traffic, nine-car formations composed of two three-car multiple-units and three additional trailers are often seen.

c. Special collocations: **multiple birth** *Med.*, the birth of more than one child at a single confinement; **multiple exposure** *Photogr.*, the repeated exposure of the same frame of a film so as to produce superimposed images; **multiple image,** a composite image comprising two or more superimposed or adjacent images originally distinct (e.g. resulting from the repeated reflection of light, the reception of television signals that have travelled from the transmitter by different paths, or the simultaneous showing of several scenes on a cinema screen); **multiple personality** *Psychol.*, a dissociative condition in which an individual's personality is apparently split into two or more sub-personalities, each of which may become dominant and then is relatively distinct and complete; **multiple pregnancy** *Med.*, a pregnancy which would normally result in a multiple birth; **multiple resistance** *Med.*, resistance of a micro-organism to the action of more than one antibiotic; so *multiple-resistant* adj.; **multiple shift** *Industry*, a double or treble shift (sense 12); freq. *attrib.*; **multiple switchboard** *Teleph.* (see quot. 1932); **multiple twin,** (*a*) *Telephony*, a cable with a number of cores each of which consists of four wires arranged as two twisted pairs twisted together; usu. *attrib.*; (*b*) *Cryst.*, a twinned crystal composed of alternating lamellæ whose relative orientations are all governed by the same twin law; **multiple valve** *Electronics*, a multi-electrode valve.

1826 *Edin. Jrnl. Med. Sci.* II. 366 (*heading*) Memoir upon multiple or twin births. **1841** *Lancet* 9 Jan. 549/1 (*heading*) Statistics of multiple births. **1966** *Amer. Jrnl. Obstetr. & Gynecol.* XCIV. 490 (*heading*) Pregnancies following treatment with human gonadotropins with special reference to the problem of multiple births. **1968** *Guardian* 3 Oct. 9/2 Multiple births, enormously distressing to the mothers.., are becoming rarer. **1971** Hellman & Pritchard *Williams' Obstetr.* (ed. 14) xxv. 657 Some marriages appear to have an inordinately high frequency of multiple births. Greulich reported the case of a 35-year-old mother who in nine births delivered six pairs of two-egg twins and three single children. **1923** F. A. Talbot *Moving Pict.* xxvii. 382 The perfection of the various devices for accomplishing multiple exposures rendered this manifestation of novelty in photography..easy of ready accomplishment. **1968** *Listener* 18 Jan. 81/2 Multiple-exposure photograph of American mechanical claw used for scrapping up samples of the moon's surface. **1863** Multiple image [see sense A. 3 e]. **1963** A. F. Abbott *Ordinary Level Physics* xxv. 313 (*heading*) Multiple images formed by a thick glass mirror. **1965** Multiple image [see *freeze *v.* 4 f]. **1971** *Gloss. Electrotechnical, Power Terms* (*B.S.I.*) III. iii. 23 *Multiple image; double image; ghost*, a defect apparent in reproduction in which an additional outline (ghost), or succession of outlines (multiple image), of prominent features of a picture may be observed displaced from the correct position of the outline by a noticeable amount. **1972** L. D. Giannetti *Understanding Movies* iii. 100 Multiple images, widely seen at Expo 67, will probably be the next modification of editing... Multiple image filmmaking does not intensify a movie's sense of realism,.. but tends to emphasize the expressionistic aspects of film art. **1901** *Proc. Soc. Psychical Res.* XV. 466 Cases of multiple personality are not very uncommon, but, so far as I know, no attempt has been made to determine the relation which the different personalities bear to each other. **1906** M. Prince *Dissociation of Personality* i. 3 The disintegration resulting in multiple personality is only a functional dissociation of that complex organization which constitutes a normal self. **1942** 'M. Innes' *Daffodil Affair* i. 38 'And did you say dissociation?' 'Yes. What is sometimes called multiple personality.' **1967** M. Argyle *Psychol. Interpersonal Behaviour* iii. 56 Everyone has a number of 'sub-personalities'..—cases of multiple personality are an extreme of what is universal. **1857** Multiple pregnancy [see sense A. 3 d]. **1964** *Obstetr. & Gynecol.* XXIV. 819 (*heading*) Size and number of umbilical vessels, a study of multiple pregnancy in man and the armadillo. **1952** S. K. R. Clarke et al. in *Lancet* 7 June 1132/1 Besides these organisms, called here 'completely resistant', there have appeared staphylococci with what may be called 'multiple resistance'—i.e. resistant to several of these drugs. **1960** *Brit. Med. Jrnl.* 2 Jan. 11/2 It cannot be assumed..that multiple resistance and enhanced virulence are necessarily associated. **1972** *Med. Microbiol. & Immunol.* CLVII. 142 (*heading*) Antimicrobial resistance of the genera *Proteus*, *Providencia* and *Serratia* with special reference to multiple resistance patterns. **1960** *Brit. Med. Jrnl.* 2 Jan. 17/1, 23 of the fatal infections were due to multiple-resistant strains. **1961** *Lancet* 29 July 248/2 It would prevent the selection and breeding of multiple-resistant strains. **1926** *Rep. R. Comm. Coal Industry* I. 175 in *Parl. Papers* (Cmd. 2600) XIV. 1 (*heading*) Advantages of multiple shifts. **1946** M. Dobb *Wages* (rev. ed.) iii. 62 Where it is practicable to introduce a multiple-shift system—two or three working-shifts a day instead of one—the same economy could be obtained together with the employment of additional workers. **1964** T. W. McRae *Impact of Computers on Accounting* vii. 208 Costs arising out of multiple-shift working. **1891** J. Poole *Pract. Telephone Handbk.* viii. 148 (*heading*) Multiple switch-boards. **1932** T. E. Herbert in E. Molloy *Pract. Electr. Engin.* V. 1865/2 A switchboard in which the subscribers' circuits are repeated at several points so as to make each subscriber accessible to every

operator is known as a multiple switchboard. **1969** S. F. SMITH *Telephony & Telegr. A* iv. 98 The need for a series type of multiple connexion which these jacks require on a multiple switchboard has certain disadvantages. **1922** *Encycl. Brit.* XXXII. 709/1 In..the 'multiple twin cable' the centre of yarn is dispensed with, and the cable consists of a number of 4-wire cores. **1932** *Amer. Mineralogist* XVII. 360 The diamond multiple twin..is from South Africa. **1959** J. W. FREEBODY *Telegr.* vi. 173/2 With the multiple-twin type [of cable] the paper insulated conductors are first twisted into pairs and two such pairs are then twisted together to form the two pair core or quad. **1966** *McGraw-Hill Encycl. Sci. & Technol.* V. 208/1 The width of the lamellae in multiple twins of plagioclases is usually about 1 mm and smaller. **1929** *Wireless World* 6 Mar. (*heading*) A Loewe multiple valve for mains operation. **1968** *Radio Communication Handbk.* (ed. 4) ii. 20/1 The trend is to make radio equipment as compact as possible and it is therefore convenient to take advantage of the special multiple valves which have more than one unit contained in a single envelope.

B. *sb.* **4.** *Teleph.* **a.** A section of a multiple switchboard containing one jack for each subscriber.

1905 A. C. BOOTH in M. Maclean *Mod. Electr. Pract.* VI. III. ii. 110 The line shown..is already engaged by the insertion of a plug on the first multiple. **1948** J. ATKINSON *Herbert & Procter's Telephony* (new ed.) I. x. 195/1 In general, a multiple is designed so that the best compromise between vertical and horizontal reach is obtained when the switchboard is equipped with the ultimate number of lines.

b. *in multiple.* Of calling jacks: (connected) between the same pairs of wires, so enabling the same connection to be made at different points.

1943 A. L. ALBERT *Fund. Telephony* viii. 174 The calling jacks of each section must be connected in parallel or multiple with the calling jacks of every other section. **1969** S. F. SMITH *Telephony & Telegr. A* iv. 98 The bush of the jack will be connected to the exchange battery via the plug inserted in one of the other jacks with which it is connected in multiple.

5. A multiple shop or store (see A. 2 b above).

1951 in PARTRIDGE *Dict. Slang* (ed. 4) 1115/1. **1957** *Economist* 5 Oct. 60/1 The multiples have also been ahead in adjusting their range of shoe styles. **1966** *New Statesman* 29 July 156/1 A businessman, stating..that he had sold 'self-owned multiple to avoid capital gains tax'. **1972** *House & Garden* Feb. 100/4 Some of the small merchants ..do a good business with Cape growths. The large multiples..are missing the opportunity.

6. An inexpensive work of art mass-producible by industrial methods.

1968 *Times* 26 Mar. 7 The artist who becomes interested in multiples takes the first step towards involving himself with the demands of technology. **1970** [see *GRAPHIC *sb.* 3]. **1971** P. DICKINSON *Sleep & his Brother* ii. 36 The one touch of art—a bronze and bulbous paperweight, vaguely post-Brancusi—had the look of one of a large issue of multiples. **1973** J. A. WALKER *Gloss. Art, Archit. & Design since 1945* 141 The idea of Multiples was first suggested by Agam and Jean Tinguely. They put their idea to the Parisian gallery dealer Denise René in 1955 but none were produced until 1962.

multiple (mɒ·ltip'l), *v. Teleph.* [f. MULTIPLE *a.* and *sb.*] *trans.* To make (a circuit) accessible to operators at more than one point on a switchboard or switchboards; to provide or employ duplicates of (a device) for this purpose.

1906 BELL & WILSON *Pract. Telephony* (ed. 4) ix. 108 At the outgoing end the lines are multipled three times on every two sections, so that every operator has every line almost directly in front of her. **1932** T. SHERRATT in J. A. Fleming *Electr. Educator* (ed. 2) III. 1194/1 The trunks are multipled to the contacts of a number of line switches, so that several subscribers can gain access to the same trunks. **1942** KNIGHT & PRICKETT *Poole's Telephone Handbk.* (ed. 8) xii. 312 Each answering jack and lamp is multipled every four, six, or twelve panels according to traffic requirements. **1969** S. F. SMITH *Telephony & Telegr. A* iv. 96 It is sufficient..to multiple the jacks without also multipling the calling indicators or lamps.

multiplet (mɒ·ltiplĕt). [f. MULTIPLE *a.* and *sb.* + -ET, after *doublet, triplet.*] **a.** A group of lines in a spectrum that are close together and spaced approximately in accordance with a simple rule; a group of related levels in an atom that differ slightly in energy, esp. a group in which this is due to differing relative orientations of either the electronic spin and orbital angular momenta, giving different values of the quantum number *J* (in the case of fine structure), or the electronic and nuclear angular momenta, giving different values of the quantum number *F* (in the case of hyperfine structure).

1922 M. A. CATALÁN in *Phil. Trans. R. Soc.* A. CCXXIII. 147 As will be seen later there are many 'groups' of lines in the manganese spectrum with similar structure to that of the foregoing 'group', and for this form of regularity the name 'multiplet' is suggested. **1929** *Trans. Faraday Soc.* XXV. 672 Next, the coupling between spin momenta of the electrons gave a 'resultant' spin vector *S*, which determined the multiplicity. The multiplicity was given by $R = 2S + 1$, if *S* was measured in units of $h/2\pi$. Finally, the components of a multiplet were regarded as determined by the coupling between the resultant *L* vector and the resultant *S* vector. **1942** [see *FINE STRUCTURE 1 a]. **1959** *Sci. News* LIII. 87 In order to interpret all the observations, such as the multiplet structure of spectral lines.., it has to be assumed that the electron has, independently of its orbital motion, an intrinsic angular momentum and a magnetic moment. **1967** W. R. HINDMARSH *Atomic Spectra* v. 50 A quantum number *F* can be ascribed to each hyperfine level such that the number increases by one from one level to the next and..the separation between two successive levels is..$A F$ where *A* is a constant for a hyperfine multiplet. **1971** A. G. SHARKEY in R. I. Reed *Recent Topics Mass Spectrometry* 128 High-resolution mass spectrometry is unique in providing a precise mass from which a molecular formula can be derived. The basis of the high-resolution technique is the ability of the instrument to resolve multiplets, having the same nominal mass but differing in precise mass.

b. A group of sub-atomic particles that are alike as regards the values of the various quantum numbers except for the third component of isospin (and hence charge), which is different for each particle and has one of the $2I+1$ values 0, $\pm\frac{1}{2}$, $\pm 1, \ldots, \pm I$ ($I = 0$ or half-integral); also, a larger group (also called a supermultiplet) composed of a number of such charge multiplets, each likewise characterized by a different value of hypercharge (or strangeness) but having the same spin and the same parity.

In quots. 1937 more a *transf.* use of prec. sense.

1937 *Physical Rev.* LI. 106 The structure of the multiplets of nuclear terms is investigated, using as a first approximation a Hamiltonian which does not involve the ordinary spin and corresponds to equal forces between all nuclear constituents, protons and neutrons. The multiplets turn out to have a rather complicated structure, instead of the *S* of atomic spectroscopy, one has three quantum numbers *S, T, Y*. *Ibid.* 117/1 Every one of these six states can be doubly occupied, with a particle $\tau = 1$ and $\tau = -1$ (neutron or proton). The half sum of the τ is denoted by T_ζ and the different T_ζ from $-T$ to T united into a multiplet. **1954** *Proc. Nat. Acad. Sci.* XL. 490 In discussing baryon states we used the intuitive argument of approximate mass degeneracy in a multiplet. **1956** [see *HYPERCHARGE]. **1964** *New Scientist* 20 Feb. 458/3 The particles appear in groups, or 'multiplets', of particles of different charge but very nearly equal mass. **1965** *Ibid.* 18 Mar. 738/3 Just as in the theory of SU(2) the particles are arranged in multiplets, but now they are distinguished within a multiplet by both their charge and hypercharge. The SU(3) symmetry relates not just the proton and neutron one to another, but includes also in one multiplet the six particles known as hyperons. **1970** [see *ISOSPIN]. **1970** D. B. LICHTENBERG *Unitary Symmetry & Elem. Particles* iii. 34 The $2I+1$ different charge states of a particle with isospin *I* constitute a multiplet. However, since isospin is not an exact symmetry, the different states are not exactly degenerate in energy. It is often said under such circumstances that different members of the multiplet are different particles, rather than different states of the same particle. **1973** L. J. TASSIE *Physics Elem. Particles* iv. 39 We now consider the three pions π^-, π^0, π^+ as a charge multiplet or isospin multiplet of multiplicity $2I+1 = 3$ yielding $I = 1$. We identify the $I_3 = +1$ state as the π^+; $I_3 = 0$ as the π^0; $I_3 = -1$ as the π^-. *Ibid.* xi. 134 The arrangement of *N*, Λ, Σ and Ξ into one multiplet, an octet.., is illustrated in Fig. 49.1. The mass splittings between the different isospin multiplets in the octet are about 20 times the mass splitting within isospin multiplets.

multiplex, *a.* and *sb.* Add: **A.** *adj.* **3. b.** More widely in *Telecommunications*, applied to processes and equipment for transmitting two or more independent signals or programmes (to be later separated and recovered) simultaneously over a single wire or channel, and to a composite signal so formed. (Earlier and later examples.)

1873 M. GALLY *Brit. Pat. 1395* 17 Apr. 13 My Invention has particular reference to 'multiplex telegraphy', or the employment of a number of operators sending without conflict a number of different messages upon a single wire. **1883** *Jrnl. Franklin Inst.* CXVI. 479 In the multiplex [system], as I myself have seen, an instantaneous change in the resistance of the line equal to five hundred miles, may be made without practically affecting the synchronous movement of the distributors. **1934** [see *COAXIAL *a.* 2 c]. **1962** A. NISBETT *Technique Sound Studio* 261 Multiplex radio transmissions and the single groove of a stereo disc each contain more than one channel. **1970** J. EARL *Tuners & Amplifiers* ii. 47 Multiplex signal..consists of 19kHz pilot-tone, the A+B mono information and sidebands of the A−B stereo information (the..subcarrier..having been suppressed at the transmitter). **1973** *Mod. Railways* Jan. 12/2 Interlockings within three or four miles of Bristol are operated by individual circuits... Beyond this distance electronic time division multiplex equipment is used.

B. *sb.* **3.** *Electr.* A multiplex system or signal.

1959 J. W. FREEBODY *Telegr.* ii. 50/2 This printer was used in connexion with the Murray multiplex. **1967** *Technology Week* 20 Feb. 4/2 Initial experiments with time-division multiplex have convinced Comsat Corp. that satellite transmission does not produce insuperable synchronization problems. **1970** *Toronto Daily Star* 24 Sept. 26/1 (Advt.), It..tapes for multiplex and even makes 'sound with sound' recordings. **1973** HILLS & EVANS *Telecommunications Syst. Design* I. iv. 92 Modern equipment has group and supergroup limiters applied to the signal prior to their assembly into the higher multiplex.

multiplex (mɒ·ltipleks), *v.* [f. the sb.] *trans.* To incorporate into a multiplex signal or system.

1925 C. A. WRIGHT *Telephone Communication* xiii. 317 The terminal equipment required to multiplex a telephone line is costly and its use is, consequently, justified only with long lines. **1955** *Sci. News Let.* 5 Mar. 158/2 You may soon be able to hear programs from your local FM station —minus commercials—in buses..and on the job. This is just one of the possibilities of a system being considered.. that would allow FM stations to 'multiplex' their broadcasts. In the process, two separate signals would be sent from the same tower using the same radio frequencies. **1966** *McGraw-Hill Encycl. Sci. & Technol.* V. 352/2 When communication channels are multiplexed by time division, a number of messages is propagated over a common transmitting medium by allocating different time intervals in sequence for the transmission of each message. **1969** *Sci. Jrnl.* Dec. 42/3 A colour TV system multiplexes (by frequency division) video, colour and sound information. **1972** *Sci. Amer.* Sept. 120/3 The T1 carrier of the Bell Telephone System, which multiplexes 24 speech signals, is a typical example of a pulse-code-modulation (PCM) system.

Hence **mu·ltiplexed** *ppl. a.*; **mu·ltiplexing** *vbl. sb.* Also **mu·ltiplexer, -or,** a device which multiplexes.

1955 *Sci. News Let.* 5 Mar. 158/3 Multiplexing is only practical on FM broadcasts because at present there are too many technical difficulties in splitting up AM programs. **1957** *Electronic Engin.* XXIX. 159/1 The information received from, say, two channels of the multiplexor are admitted serially to the clamping circuit. **1964** *Ann. N.Y. Acad. Sci.* CXV. 574 Multiplexers can be sequential sampling devices, or electronic commutators, which sample each channel in turn cyclically. **1969** *Sci. Jrnl.* Dec. 42 This spacing of the different signals over adjacent frequency ranges of the communication channel is called frequency-division multiplexing. *Ibid.* (*caption*) Frequency spectrum of a frequency division multiplexed channel shows how..five carriers..are each surrounded by sidebands. **1970** O. DOPPING *Computers & Data Processing* viii. 121 A multiplexor channel has its own facilities for sharing its time between different slow input/output operations. **1973** *Physics Bull.* July 413/3 A multiplexed hologram is produced from the sequence of exposures on the cine film.

multiplication. Add: **6. multiplication constant** or **factor** *Nuclear Physics*, in nuclear fission, the ratio by which the number of neutrons increases during a period equal to the lifetime of a neutron; **multiplication sign**, the sign × placed between two quantities to denote their multiplication; also *fig.*

1956 A. H. COMPTON *Atomic Quest* 137 These 'delayed' neutrons..make the difference between a multiplication constant of less than one and greater than one. **1962** *Newnes Conc. Encycl. Nucl. Energy* 111/1 The actual number of neutrons per fission varies considerably, but has an average value of 2·5. This is a high enough gain per cycle to suggest that a chain-reacting system of uranium could be made with a multiplication constant of at least unity. **1941** E. FERMI *Coll. Papers* (1965) II. 89 The chain reaction may reach a steady state only when the multiplication factor of the neutrons (including neutron losses due to diffusion outside of the reacting mass) is equal to 1. **1974** *Encycl. Brit. Macropædia* XIII. 305/1 If a fission bomb is to be made, the multiplication factor must be as large as possible. **1907** W. D. EGGAR *Elem. Algebra* i. 4 When a number is written in front of a bracket without a sign following it, thus 10(6+5), the multiplication sign is understood, just as when we write 10*a*. **1908** W. OWEN *Let.* 20 July (1967) 46 Best love, and a 'multiplication sign' (×) from your ever loving W. **1973** P. M. AITCHISON et al. *Form Two Maths.* vi. 67 Remember that a multiplication sign connects factors.

multiplicative, *a.* and *sb.* Add: **b.** (Later example of *sb.*)

1928 H. POUTSMA *Gram. Late Mod. Eng.* (ed. 2) iv. 304 The multiplicatives *double, treble, quadruple.*

So **mu·ltiplicatively** *adv.*

1895 in *Funk's Stand. Dict.* **1914** C. D. BROAD *Perception* iii. 180 The strengthening of probability takes place multiplicatively. **1973** *Nature* 23 Feb. 513/1 The latter possibility has an attractive feature, namely that Misner's mechanism, and the one described here would operate simultaneously, the two effects combining multiplicatively.

multiplicator. 1. (Later example.)

1923 *Glasgow Herald* 16 Oct. 7 In Cologne order was restored on Friday night... The price 'Multiplicator', which played a large part in creating the agitation, has been lowered from 1,800,000,000..to 400,000,000.

multiplicity. Add: **1. e.** *Physics.* The number of components (whether one or several) in a multiplet; *spec.* (*a*) the quantity $2S+1$, where *S* is the spin quantum number of a term; (*b*) the quantity $2I+1$, where *I* is the isospin of a charge multiplet.

1923 H. L. BROSE tr. *Sommerfeld's Atomic Struct. & Spectral Lines* vi. 385 Those terms are defined as similar which have the same multiplicity and the same azimuthal quantum number. **1929** [see *MULTIPLET a]. **1934** H. E. WHITE *Introd. Atomic Spectra* xiv. 248 It is found experimentally that the multiplicities of the levels belonging to a given spectrum will either be all even or all odd. *Ibid.* 249 Spectral terms arising from successive elements in the periodic table alternate between even and odd multiplicities. **1948** G. R. HARRISON et al. *Pract. Spectroscopy* x. 241 For two electrons, $S = 0$ or 1, depending on whether

the two spins are antiparallel or parallel. Hence atomic spectra that arise from two electrons (helium and the alkaline-earth metals Be, Mg, Ca, Sr, and Ba) can have multiplicities of 1 (that is, no splitting of levels because of spin) or 3 (splitting of each level into three). **1964** *Sci. Amer.* Feb. 82/2 The number of different charge states in a multiplet, or its 'multiplicity' (*M*), is directly related to the isotopic-spin quantum number *I* by the equation $M = 2I + 1$. **1972** *Physics Bull.* Feb. 92/1 A further interesting feature which these multiplets illustrate is the greater bonding of the states of lower multiplicity. **1973** [see *MULTIPLET b].

f. *Biol.* The ratio of the number of infective particles to the number of susceptible cells; usu. in phr. *multiplicity of infection*.

1947 *Proc. Nat. Acad. Sci.* XXXIII. 259 (*heading*) Dependence of the probability of reactivation on the multiplicity of infection. **1957** *Virology* III. 286 Luria (1947) found that cells of *Escherichia coli* B which had been infected with more than one inactivated particle of phage T2, or other members of the T group of coliphages, yielded active phage. He called this 'multiplicity reactivation'. **1964** W. HAYES *Genetics of Bacteria & their Viruses* xvi. 367 If a suspension of virulent phage is added to a growing culture of sensitive bacteria in broth, so that the number of phage particles exceeds the number of bacteria (multiplicity of infection = > 1),..the culture becomes clear, as a result of the infection and lysis of virtually all the bacteria. **1974** *Nature* 11 Oct. 542/1 Chang cells in suspension were infected at an input multiplicity of 10. *Ibid.* 543/2 Addition of VSV or EMC virus at a multiplicity of infection of 1.

multiplier. Add: **2. b.** *Econ.* (See quot. 1964.)

1936 J. M. KEYNES *Gen. Theory Employment* x. 113 A definite ratio, to be called the *Multiplier*, can be established between income and investment and..between the total employment and the employment directly employed on investment. **1940** G. CROWTHER *Outl. Money* v. 157 In the upward process, the change in the National Income necessary to restore balance and reverse the trend [downwards] may be very many times larger than the original discrepancy... Thus a small original change results in a large ultimate change in the National Income. The ratio between them is usually known as the 'multiplier'. **1963** *Economist* 9 Feb. 481/2 A direct injection of £500 million of new Government spending can sometimes increase total national spending by £1,000 million (i.e. a multiplier of two). **1964** GOULD & KOLB *Dict. Social Sci.* 449/1 *Multiplier*... The term denotes the process (or the index, or coefficient, measuring such a process) whereby initial changes within economic systems (e.g. changes in the levels of investment) have cumulative and, in principle, measurable effects upon the system, its components and its equilibrium.

c. *multiplier effect*, an effect such as could be assessed in terms of the economic multiplier.

1957 R. K. MERTON *Student-Physician* 14 Such an experimental institution for medical education would have multiplier-effects. **1963** *Economist* 16 Feb. 619/1 The multiplier effect..of an injection of purchasing power into personal incomes..is unlikely to exceed unity and may be as low as 0·7. **1964** T. W. MCRAE *Impact of Computers on Accounting* vii. 211 Such improvement will have a 'multiplier effect'. **1965** *Listener* 16 Sept. 405/2 What we can do is to concentrate our help where it will have the highest multiplier effect.

4. (Earlier and later examples.)

1795 T. CAVALLO *Compl. Treat. Electr.* (ed. 3) III. 98 With this machine, which..we shall call the Multiplier of Electricity, the accumulation of the communicated power does not advance..so quick as with the doubler. *Ibid.* 106, I shall now describe a few experiments made with this multiplier. **1938** J. B. HOAG *Electron & Nucl. Physics* vi. 127 In another form of multiplier tube, electrons are oscillated back and forth between two surfaces which are good secondary emitters... At each impact of the electrons with the cathode surfaces, the number of electrons is appreciably multiplied. **1940**, etc. [see *electron multiplier* s.v. *ELECTRON[2] 2 b]. **1950** K. HENNEY *Radio Engin. Handbk.* (ed. 4) xiii. 558 The multiplier phototube has a number of advantages compared with a phototube and separate amplifier. **1973** *McGraw-Hill Yearbk. Sci. & Technol.* 333/1 Because fewer gain stages with higher interstage voltages are needed, the speed of the multipliers has been improved, greatly increasing their usefulness for applications such as laser optical communications.

6. (Examples.)

1969 J. J. SPARKES *Transistor Switching* viii. 200 In the accumulator of this multiplier it is convenient to use flip-flops..which have two separate logic and pulse inputs per flip-flop. *Ibid.* 201 The multiplier circuit operates as follows. **1972** *Daily Tel.* 5 Apr. 10 (Advt.), The world's fastest and smoothest mechanical multiplier. Operates at 360 rpm, lists 10 columns and totals 11.

multiply, *adv.* Restrict *Math.* to terms in Dict. and add: In a multiple manner; many ways or times, or more than once. (Further examples.)

The use of a following hyphen is similar to that described at WELL *adv.* VII.

1892 *Mind* I. 353 The rules for the synthesis of multiply-quantified propositions follow immediately from those for the synthesis of singly-quantified propositions. **1922** F. W. ASTON *Isotopes* 71 These multiply-charged clusters give most reliable values of mass. **1932** LEWIS & LANGFORD *Symbolic Logic* ix. 301 A hierarchy..is involved in multiply-general propositions and functions. **1962** W. & M. KNEALE *Devel. of Logic* ii. 112 Two distinct quantifiers are required, as in the statement '*Some* man does not possess *all* knowledge', and multiply general statements are quite common in science and philosophy, e.g. '*Every* event has *a* cause'. **1963** B. FOZARD *Instrumentation Nucl. Reactors* ii. 12 In many cases only one electron is separated from the parent atom in an ionising process but cases occur where several electrons are emitted and the atom is said to be multiply ionised. **1966** D. G. BRANDON *Mod. Techniques Metallogr.* iv. 204 The ions will be multiply-charged. **1971** *Jrnl. Gen. Psychol.* LXXXV. 165 Almost no studies have been specifically directed to the detection of the relative power of the different kinds of categories into which words seem to be multiply encoded.

multi-ply, *sb.* and *a.* [f. MULTI- + PLY *sb.*, *PLYWOOD.] **A.** *sb.* Plywood comprising more than three layers. **B.** *adj.* Designating textiles, etc., formed by having several threads or webs twisted together; also denoting paper comprising several layers.

1940 *Chambers's Techn. Dict.* 563/2 *Multi-ply*, plywood formed of more than three layers of wood. **1950** *Gloss. Aeronaut. Terms (B.S.I.)* 1. 49 *Multi-ply fabric*, fabric formed of more than one ply. **1951** *Archit. Rev.* CIX. 159 (*caption*) Multi-ply was developed during the war for aircraft propellers. **1962** *Times* 3 Dec. (Agric. Suppl.) p. vii/5 The multi-ply paper sack. **1963** A. J. HALL *Textile Sci.* i. 9 The threads may be single or consist of two, three, or more single threads twisted together to give what are often termed *folded* or *multi-ply* threads. **1966** A. W. LEWIS *Gloss. Woodworking Terms* 52 Laminated boards..include plywood, multi-ply, laminboard, [etc.].

multipolar (mɒltipōu·lăɹ), *a.* [f. MULTI- + POLAR *a.*] Having or pertaining to many poles. **a.** *Anat.* Of a nerve cell: having many processes.

1859 [in Dict. s.v. MULTI- 1 a]. **1885** *Encycl. Brit.* XIX. 27/2 The cells of the spinal ganglia are usually rounded; those of the sympathetic more angular; those of the spinal cord multipolar. **1948** A. BRODAL *Neurol. Anat.* xi. 354 The autonomic ganglion cells in most of the ganglia of the sympathetic trunk and in the peripheral ganglia are usually multipolar and are characterized by possessing numerous and long dendrites. **1964** J. Z. YOUNG *Model of Brain* xix. 307 Multipolar amacrines are numerous in the cell islands of the optic lobes.

b. *Electr.* Of electrical machinery: having more than one pair of magnetic poles in the system of field magnets.

1884 [in Dict. s.v. MULTI- 1 a]. **1903** [see *bar winding* (*BAR *sb.*[1] 30)]. **1964** N. N. HANCOCK *Matrix Analysis of Electr. Machinery* v. 72 To apply the results to multipolar machines it will be necessary to reduce the speed and to increase the torque according to the number of pole-pairs.

c. *Cytology.* Having or involving more than two spindle poles.

1894 *Ann. Bot.* VIII. 313 Nuclear divisions with multipolar spindles. **1896** E. B. WILSON *Cell* ii. 68 The abnormal forms of mitoses are arranged by Hausemann in two general groups, as follows: (1) asymmetrical mitoses,..and (2) multipolar mitoses. **1912** E. A. MINCHIN *Introd. Study Protozoa* vii. 120 In cases where the division of the nucleus is of the karyokinetic type, repeated divisions of the centriole result in the formation of a complicated multipolar mitotic figure, leading to a multiple division of the nucleus. **1937** M. J. D. WHITE *Chromosomes* ii. 19 In many cells such as those of cancerous tissues and in Sea-Urchin eggs which have been fertilized several times as a result of polyspermy, multipolar spindles with a number of equatorial planes intersecting one another are found; there may be as many as 12 poles and 6 equatorial planes. **1950** *Hereditas* XXXVI. 393 (*heading*) Multipolar spindles in human cancer cells.

d. Consisting of, or divided into, more than two (political or other) alliances, ententes, parties, etc.

1968 *Guardian* 4 Dec. 4/6 The most profound challenge to American policy will be..to develop some concept of order in a world which is bipolar militarily but multipolar politically. **1969** S. HENIG in Henig & Pinder *European Pol. Parties* 502 The country-by-country chapters have indicated a threefold classification between bipolar, unipolar and multipolar party systems. In bipolar systems..government will be dominated either by the two parties singly..or by both together in a 'big coalition'. In a unipolar system..the norm is for one party to be easily the largest legislative group... In multipolar systems, neither one nor two parties are dominant even to the extent of always emerging the strongest from succeeding elections. **1975** *Times* 7 Apr. 14/2 Kissinger['s]..concept of a multipolar world, where major powers could compete and co-operate simultaneously.

multipolarity (mɒltipolæ·rĭti). [f. prec. + -ITY.] **a.** Multipolar quality or state.

1947 *Hereditas* XXXIII. 468 The anaphases..all showed serious disturbances, lagging chromosomes, multipolarity..and so on. **1950** *Ibid.* XXXVI. 395 Multipolarity seems..to be fairly independent of the chromosome number in that highly polyploid bipolar as well as multipolar configurations which contain low chromosome numbers are found. **1968** *Guardian* 4 Dec. 2/3 NATO..has yet to adjust to the political multipolarity of the late sixties. **1969** *Punch* 5 Mar. 329/2 Henry Kissinger..has already summed up the Soames affair as an example of 'political multipolarity', spoken of the problems of 'a pluralist world'... All good stuff, if we knew what it meant.

b. *Physics.* The highest order of multipole associated with a state or phenomenon.

1955 *Physical Rev.* XCVIII. 1198/1 (*heading*) Multipolarity of gamma transitions in F^{19} and Na^{23} by Coulomb excitation. **1973** *Nature* 31 Aug. 541/1 There have been speculations that other giant resonances with other multipolarities might exist; for example, quadrupole motions in which the nucleon distributions oscillate between prolate and oblate shapes with quadrupole deformations.

multipole (mɒ·ltipōul), *sb.* and *a.* *Physics.* [f. MULTI- 2 + POLE *sb.*[2]] **A.** *sb.* A system of 2^l monopoles ($l = 1, 2, 3, \ldots$) with no net charge or pole strength and no moment of a lower order than l (cf. *MOMENT *sb.* 8 c); the dipole ($l = 1$) is often treated as a special case and the quadrupole ($l = 2$) regarded as the multipole of lowest order. Freq. *attrib.* or as *adj.*, esp. designating electromagnetic radiation of the kind produced by a multipole with a moment varying sinusoidally in magnitude.

In quot. 1916 this may not be the precise sense.

1916 *Jrnl. Amer. Chem. Soc.* XXXVIII. 764 One or more electrons are held by sufficiently weak constraints so that they may..in the extreme case pass altogether to another atom, thus producing in the molecule a bipole or multipole of high electrical moment. **1929** *Physical Rev.* XXXIV. 1252 Since *m* must change by ± 1,..the transition $j = 0 \rightarrow j = 0$ cannot occur for multipole radiation. **1932** J. H. VAN VLECK *Theory Electr. & Magn. Susceptibilities* i. 12 The omitted terms are sometimes characterized as representing 'multipoles'. The omitted term in ϕ of lowest order, for instance, is..Nq/R^3, where q is the 'quadrupole moment'. **1950** D. HALLIDAY *Introd. Nucl. Physics* ii. 57 If $|\Delta I| = 1$ the multipole order is 2 and we have..a dipole transition; if $|\Delta I| = 2$, the multipole order is 4 and we have a quadrupole transition. **1952** BLATT & WEISSKOPF *Theoret. Nucl. Physics* xii. 586 The electric multipole fields have non-vanishing radial components of **E**, and the magnetic multipole fields have non-vanishing radial components of **H**. The angular momentum carried by one quantum of multipole radiation is $\hbar l$, with *z* component $\hbar m$. Electric and magnetic multipole radiation of order *l*, *m* carry the same angular momentum but differ through their parity. *Ibid.* 587 Any arbitrary field $\mathbf{E(r)}$, $\mathbf{H(r)}$ which obeys the free-space Maxwell equations can be expanded in terms of multipoles. **1962** CORSON & LORRAIN *Introd. Electromagn. Fields* ii. 52 For the general multipole, characterized by the letter *l*, the potential varies as $1/r^{l+1}$. **1970** [see *MOMENT *sb.* 8 c].

B. *adj.* (Freq. written **multi-pole.**) Designed to close or open several circuits simultaneously.

1927 *Wireless World* 22 June 786/3 It is sometimes recommended that a multi-pole switch should be fitted in order to switch off both batteries. **1934** *Pract. Wireless* IV. 667/3 This multi-pole switch converts the usual panel-controlled push-pull action into a lateral movement. **1962** G. A. T. BURDETT *Automatic Control Handbk.* iii. 24 The multi-pole type of control switch is a double break change-over switch especially designed for the switching of squirrel-cage motors.

multi-posi·tion, *a.* [f. MULTI- + POSITION *sb.*] Usable or placeable in more than one position. So **multi-posi·tional** *a.*

1944 *Illustr. Aviation Encycl.* (Aviation Research Associates) 143/2 *Multiposition propeller*: see *controllable pitch propeller*. **1948** F. J. MURRAY *Theory Math. Machines* (ed. 2) i. 3 Another method of indicating the digit which appears in a decimal place in a counter is by means of a multiposition switch. **1961** Y. OLSSON *On Syntax Eng. Verb* iv. 82 A nucleus counts as multi-positional not only if it is identical in all of the Positions in which it occurs, but also if it is combined with a non-nuclear element. **1969** *Jane's Freight Containers 1968–69* 472 (*caption*) Duramin 30 ft ISO Container with side-loading facility and 'Salwall' lining (for multi-position load anchorage). **1971** *Power Farming* Mar. 69/2, 5 ft convertible hay or silage flail mower, straw chopper and haulm pulveriser. Easily adaptable, multi-position wheels.

multipro·cessing, *vbl. sb.* *Computers.* [f. MULTI- 2.] Processing by a number of processors sharing a common memory and common peripherals.

1961 *Communications Assoc. Computing Machinery* Oct. 421/1 Multiprocessing is defined here as the sharing of a common memory and all peripheral equipment by two or more processor units. **1967** C. J. DUNCAN in Cox & Grose *Organiz. Bibliogr. Rec. by Computer* II. 47 The decision as to whether to run the composing machine on-line or off-line will..depend upon the size of the machine, what multiprocessing facilities are available, and the precise machine configuration and loading. **1969** P. B. JORDAIN *Condensed Computer Encycl.* 327 The Honeywell 800 was an early powerful multiprocessing computer. It was equivalent to 8 conventional computers sharing a common memory. A hardware/software executive coordinated the eight processors to ensure efficient operation.

So **multipro·cessor**, a processor capable of performing multiprocessing; usu. *attrib.*

1961 *Communications Assoc. Computing Machinery* Oct. 421 (*heading*) Problems of storage allocation in a multiprocessor multiprogrammed system. **1965** A. G. FAVRET *Introd. Digital Computer Applic.* xvi. 233 In multiprocessor systems the executive routines must be capable of allocating tasks among different processors or deciding which of several inquiries should be given priority. **1970** O. DOPPING *Computers & Data Processing* vi. 97 Two or more computer systems can be interconnected electrically to form a multi-processor system. *Ibid.*, The multi-processor alternative has the advantage that the capacity of the faster machine is always on tap also during input and output operations. **1971** *New Scientist* 25 Feb. 425/2 The 6000 models are well equipped with communications gear, and multi-processor configurations have interconnected memory units and multiplexors as well as processors.

multipro·gramming, *vbl. sb.* *Computers.* [MULTI- 2.] The execution of two or more independent programs concurrently.

1959 *Communications Assoc. Computing Machinery* Nov. 15/1 The normal requirement in multiprogramming is to communicate with a particular program and at the same time allow all other programs to proceed... We now desire to stop a *program* rather than the *machine.* **1965** A. G. Favret *Introd. Digital Computer Applic.* xvi. 234 Multiprogramming techniques will probably also be used in some industrial process control applications where one computer is utilized to control several different processes on a time-shared basis. **1970** A. Cameron et al. *Computers & Old Eng. Concordances* 25 You can do a run on a 360, of course, without tying up the entire 360 through..something called multi-programming. **1973** Murrill & Smith *Introd. Computer Sci.* vii. 260 The objective of multiprogramming is to maintain two or more programs in memory simultaneously so that the processor can be working on one program while it is waiting for an input or output operation to be completed in the other program.

So **multipro·gram, -pro·grammed** *adjs.* [Multi- 3, 1], designed for or pertaining to multiprogramming.

1959 *Proc. Eastern Joint Computer Conf.* Dec. 75 (*heading*) Arithmetic and control in a multiprogram computer. *Ibid.* 80/2 The amount of work which can be accomplished per second..is, of course, increased enormously in a multi-programmed design. **1961** Multiprogrammed [see *multiprocessor]. **1964** T. W. McRae *Impact of Computers on Accounting* vii. 209 By far the most interesting development..has been the introduction of multiprogramme machines, which can process a number of jobs at the same time. **1967** H. Hellerman *Digital Computer System Princ.* ii. 107 In multiprogrammed systems it [*sc.* a control program] also resolves all conflicts among problem programs for calls on common facilities and ensures privacy among the several users that may be sharing these facilities. *Ibid.* viii. 345 The major impetus for storage protection arises in multiprogram sharing of processor storage.

multi-pu·rpose, *a.* [f. Multi- + Purpose *sb.*] Serving, or intended to serve, many purposes; performing many duties.

1935 *Sci. Amer.* Sept. 164 It is capable of handling much larger signal voltages than the diodes incorporated in the multi-purpose type of glass tube. **1937** *New Republic* 6 Jan. 292 The multipurpose TVA dams. **1939** *Electronics* June 48/1 (*title*) Multi-purpose Midget Tubes. **1943** J. S. Huxley *TVA* xviii. 134 A co-operative, unified, multi-purpose undertaking. **1950** *Mind* LIX. 422 An all-round multi-purpose classification. **1959** *Listener* 12 Nov. 810/2 The use of what is now known..as the 'generalist' or 'multi-purpose' worker at village level. **1960** *Farmer & Stockbreeder* 8 Mar. 68 The only multi-purpose oil to be tested by the National Institute of Agricultural Engineering. **1965** *English Studies* XLVI. 30 While it [*sc.* þe] is a multivalent form it is not a multi-purpose form. **1972** *Jrnl. Social Psychol.* LXXXVII. 154 The multipurpose role inner city mothers often assume may explain this [observation] in part. **1972** M. Sheppard *Taman Indera* 65 A long multi-purpose head-cloth of red or blue cotton. **1973** *Country Life* 28 June 1904/1 A new multi-purpose mistblower, suitable for crops of all kinds. **1974** *Daily Tel.* (Colour Suppl.) 29 Nov. 72 Many rooms are multi-purpose, and the use to which they are put by family or friends should be analysed before making any decisions.

multi-ra·cial, multiracial, *a.* Of, pertaining to, or comprising several races, peoples, or ethnic groups; characterized by the co-existence or co-operation of individual members of such groups on amicable and equal terms. Also *fig.* So **multi-ra·cially** *adv.*

1923 *Overseas* Sept. 45 The interests of modern civilisation and, I think, Christian ethics, are better expressed in large, bi-racial or multi-racial States,..where racialism is accounted a public curse rather than a civic virtue. **1933** E. B. Reuter in E. S. Bogardus *Social Probl. & Social Processes* 96 The type of accommodation made is of course an individual matter, but the forms that it takes are.. those familiar in other bi-racial or multi-racial political areas. **1947** *Forum* (Johannesburg) X. 1. 25/1 We, as a multi-racial society, have had our differences, while sharp antagonisms unfortunately exist today. **1957** L. F. R. Williams *State of Israel* 209 The unifying influence which this hostility is exerting upon Israel's multiracial population. **1957** *Economist* 19 Oct. 204/2 He triumphantly created the first multiracial government in Africa at the height of Mau Mau. **1958** *Times Lit. Suppl.* 10 Jan. 21/2 One feels the pleasant relief of a man living a multi-racial life away from the colour bar. **1959** *New Statesman* 28 Feb. 300/1 But it is his attack on the multi-racial clothing industry—involving the dismissal and replacement of 35,000 non-whites—that has frightened the coloured people especially. **1963** *Economist* 30 Nov. 887/3 Such a multi-racially-run world. **1966** *Listener* 6 Oct. 499/3 Closer contact between..the university worker and the industrial scientist, to make a truly 'multi-racial' commonwealth of scholarship. **1972** T. Lilley *K Section* ix. 40 The Dock Labourers' Union was one of the biggest... Multi-racial, it owed allegiance only to itself.

multi-ra·cialism, multiracialism. [f. prec. + -ism.] The condition or quality of being multi-racial; *spec.*, the conception of a state in which members of different races, peoples, or ethnic groups live on amicable and equal terms. So **multi-ra·cialist, multiracialist,** an advocate of multi-racial governments or societies.

1958 *Economist* 3 May 396/2 Its professed multi-racialism was bound to appear an attempt to entrench separate racial streams. **1959** *Manch. Guardian* 25 July 5/3 The concept of partnership or multi-racialism [in Kenya]. **1960** *Guardian* 25 June 5/5 Mr. Blundell is a convinced multi-racialist. **1962** *Times* 4 Jan. 9/2 Britain is pushing the Federation towards a multiracialism that will end in African control. **1962** *Punch* 28 Nov. 758/1 Uncle Tom, a born multi-racialist. **1964** *Ann. Reg. 1963* 326 In September, another Coloured man..escaped to Swaziland..hoping..to represent the case for multi-racialism in South African sport. **1972** *Guardian* 8 Feb. 13/8 Multi-racialism here [*sc.* in Senegal] is not just an experiment. It is a proven fact.

mu·ltisided, *a.* [f. Multi- + Sided *ppl. a.*] = Many-sided *a.* So **multisi·dedness.**

1903 A. W. Patterson *Schumann* xvii. 202 The multi-sidedness of Schumann's genius. **1963** *Times* 30 May 9/6 The first floor elevation has a sawtooth plan with adjoining windows set at an angle to each other so that occupants can look through into each other's rooms, which may disconcert an ambassador seeking privacy; and the resulting multisided rooms may prove awkward in use.

mu·ltistage, *a.* Also **multi-stage.** [f. Multi- 3 + Stage *sb.*] Consisting of, occurring in, or involving several stages (cf. Stage *sb.* IV in Dict. and Suppl.).

1904 *Engineering News* LI. 324/3 The pumps shown and described in the following are multi-stage turbine pumps. **1911** A. M. Greene *Pumping Machinery* xiii. 522 (*heading*) Multi-stage compression. **1920** *Wireless World* Jan. 574/2 (*heading*) The design of multi-stage amplifiers using three-electrode thermionic valves. **1944** [see *intercool* vb. s.v. *intercooling *vbl. sb.*]. **1946** *Nature* 5 Oct. 464/2 It was admitted that these ranges might be attained by the employment of multi-stage rockets. **1962** F. I. Ordway et al. *Basic Astronautics* x. 400 Large boosters..are being designed for use as the initial stage of a multistage space carrier vehicle. **1962** Simpson & Richards *Physical Princ. Junction Transistors* xi. 246 We shall be concerned with typical intermediate stages in a multistage amplifier and not with unusual impedance matching arrangements at the input and output. **1963** R. R. A. Higham *Handbk. Papermaking* vi. 139 Either single- or multi-stage bleaching may be carried out according to the conditions. **1971** *Brit. Med. Bull.* XXVII. 68/2 Multi-centric hypotheses [of the origin of cancer] have not proved as popular as multi-stage hypotheses, or theories which assume that a change from a normal cell to a malignant cell takes place in stages. **1971** B. Scharf *Engin. & its Lang.* xv. 207 Multi-stage turbines may be compound, i.e. they have both impulse and reaction stages.

b. *spec.* in *Statistics.* Applied to sampling carried out in a number of stages, the sample obtained at each stage being divided into smaller units and taken as the population for the next stage of sampling.

1949 F. Yates *Sampling Methods for Censuses & Surveys* iii. 34 Multi-stage sampling introduces a flexibility into sampling which is lacking in the simpler methods. **1966** Kendall & Stuart *Advanced Theory Statistics* III. xxxix. 204 The motive for multi-stage sampling is almost invariably to reduce costs rather than reduce variance directly; the additional resources can, of course, be applied to an increase in sample size. **1973** F. E. Fischer *Fund. Statistical Concepts* ix. 215 The extensive survey work which precedes every national election..is a perfect example of multistage sampling.

So **mu·ltistaged** *ppl. a.* [Multi- 1].

1965 *Times Lit. Suppl.* 25 Nov. 1051/1 It is like a Greek tragedy in which the Furies have been replaced by a multi-staged rocket.

multista·ge, *v.* Also **multi·stage.** [f. prec.] *trans.* To make multistaged. So **multista·ging** *vbl. sb.*, the use of several stages.

1911 A. M. Greene *Pumping Machinery* xiii. 523 Since it is not possible to bring the curve of compression close enough to the isothermal, a method of multi-staging the compression has to be devised. **1944** A. H. Church *Centrifugal Pumps & Blowers* vi. 128 If the total head to be developed by a pump is too large for a single stage to handle, multistaging is resorted to. **1972** *Physics Bull.* Oct. 591/2 In general one would like a higher overall pressure ratio and this can be obtained by multistaging.

multi-sto·ry, -sto·rey, *a.* [f. Multi- + Story *sb.*², storey.] Of many storeys or floors. So **multi-sto·ried, -sto·reyed** *a.*

1918 *N.Y. Times Mag.* 16 June 4 The stenographers.. are here from multi-storied city skyscrapers. **1918** L. Galloway *Office Management* (1919) 50 In a multistory factory building the location of the office within the factory itself vitally affects the efficiency of the clerical force. **1946** *Nature* 3 Aug. 152/2 The framed multi-story construction, to be advocated both on architectural grounds and for blast resistance. *Ibid.* 28 Sept. 439/1 The first remedy was to provide adequate car parks, underground, at ground level, and in multi-storied buildings. **1955** *Times* 31 Aug. 11/6 Rehousing..will create a total overspill of from 35,000 to 54,000, depending on the extent to which multi-storey flats are erected as the old and crumbling tenements come down. **1958** *Manch. Guardian Weekly* 7 Aug. 6/4 The sooner we have more meters the sooner the chaos in our streets will disappear—especially if the profits on metered parking are translated into proper garages and multi-storey parks. **1964** J. Summerson *Classical Lang. Archit.* ii. 15 A building which..is multi-storeyed. **1973** *Times* 28 Feb. (Victoria Centre, Nottingham, Suppl.) p. i/1 The Victoria Centre, Nottingham's new £10m multi-storey shopping centre, is, according to its developers.. the biggest of its type in Europe. **1975** J. Symons *Three Pipe Problem* xviii. 208 The car was in a multi-storey park.

multi-tie·r, *a.* [f. Multi- + Tier *sb.*¹] Having or comprising several tiers or layers. So **multi-tie·red** *a.*; **multi-tie·ring** *vbl. sb.*, arrangement in tiers or layers.

1952 *Flow Q.* Jan. 4 A multi-tier conveyor. **1957** *Textile Terms & Definitions* (Textile Inst.) (ed. 3) 67 *Multi-tier loom*, a loom with a batten having several rows of shuttles. **1958** T. Landau *Encycl. Librarianship* 283/2 The *multi-tier stack*... This system ensures a maximum storage space. Many of these stacks are several tiers high and are connected by book lifts, and occasionally by passenger lifts. **1960** (*title*) The power gain of multi-tiered VHF transmitting aerials (B.B.C. Engin. Monogr. 31). **1965** K. D. Metcalf *Planning Academic & Research Library Buildings* viii. 134/2 Multi-tier book stacks hold themselves up. Each level of stack supports the levels above... A multitier stack provided about as concentrated shelving space as could be found until one or another of the recently developed compact-shelving arrangements began to be used. **1968** *Punch* 27 Nov. 786/2 Dear Public, You've had the Two-Tier System. Now for our fabulous Multi-Tier System, with *Flavorlik*, the new Soft-Centre stamps in *nine exciting flavours.* **1971** *Engineering* Apr. 63/2 If required, the machine will carry out multi-tiering and sleeve-wrapping.

multituberculate (mɒːltitiụbɜ·ɹkiụ̆lĕt), *sb.* and *a. Palæont.* [ad. mod.L. name of order *Multituberculata* (E. D. Cope 1884, in *Amer. Naturalist* XVIII. 687), f. Multi- + Tuberculate *a.*] A small fossil mammal of the order Multituberculata, characterized by teeth bearing many cusps arranged in two or three rows. Also as *adj.*, pertaining to or resembling an animal of this type.

1884 E. D. Cope in *Amer. Naturalist* XVIII. 687 The extinct marsupials belong to three types, as distinguished by the form of their superior molar teeth. These are tri-tuberculate, quadrituberculate, or multituberculate. **1888** [in Dict. s.v. Multi- 1 a]. **1898** A. S. Woodward *Outl. Vertebr. Palæont.* 248 There is also some reason to suspect that other double-rooted multituberculate teeth from the Rhætic of Europe, commonly claimed as mammalian, may be similarly interpreted [as reptilian]. **1926** *Amer. Jrnl. Sci.* CCXI. 228 (*title*) The Multituberculates as living animals. **1933** A. S. Romer *Vertebr. Paleont.* xiii. 257 The multituberculates had the longest history of any known mammalian order, for they appeared in the Triassic as the oldest known forms of mammals and persisted through into the Lower Eocene. **1969** *Sci. Jrnl.* 38/2 Entire skulls, including the basicranial region, of multituberculates have so far been found only in the Palaeocene genus *Ptilodus*, known from North America.

multitudinosity. (Later example.)

1939 R. A. Knox *Let Dons Delight* vi. 161 For all that, sheer multitudinosity has power to oppress the mind.

multi-u·se, *a.* [f. Multi- + Use *sb.*] Having many uses; intended to serve many purposes. Also **multi-u·ser,** having many users.

1952 *Bull. Amer. Inst. Archit.* VI. iv. 11 The multi-use classroom was used to provide for as many as 4 or 5 different functions within a single space. **1960** *Farmer & Stockbreeder* 29 Mar. 125/1 It has been developed from 10 full years of American 'know-how' and British experience into the ideal multi-use machine for any size of farm. **1964** *Daily Tel.* 30 Jan. 14/2 It rejects the transport theory for the 'multi-user' conception. *Ibid.* 19/1 (*heading*) 'Multi-use' policy 'best for Britain's canals'. **1969** *Jane's Freight Containers 1968–69* 183/1 Berth No. 43—Multi-user container berth. **1971** P. Gresswell *Environment* 181 Examples of multi-use park design, and good maintenance, are the great London parks. **1974** *BP Shield Internat.* Oct. 9/1 (*caption*) The multi-user container berth at Tilbury.

multivalent, *a.* Add: **b.** *Med.* Of an antigen or antibody: having several sites at which it can become attached to an antibody or antigen, respectively.

1934 *Harvey Lect.* XXVIII. 198 In this way it has been possible to show that antigen and antibody in this system, too, are multivalent with respect to each other—that is, that the composition of the precipitate varies according to the relative proportions of the reactants. **1948** Kabat & Mayer *Exper. Immunochem.* iii. 67 The immunochemist.. has found it more useful to..consider the visible agglutination as an indication that the antigen particles are linked together by antibody molecules to form aggregates as a result of the combination of multivalent antibody with multivalent antigen on the particle surface. **1963** Humphrey & White *Immunol. for Students of Med.* vi. 185 The combination in multiple proportions depends upon the fact that both antigen and antibody are multivalent. Antibody valencies are restricted to two per molecule but antigen valencies may exceed 200, although they are more usually around 5 to 10 per molecule.

2. *Cytology.* That is (part of) a multivalent.

1929 *Jrnl. Genetics* XXI. 41 The whole process by which multivalent combinations arise has been followed only in the tulips. **1937** C. D Darlington *Recent Adv. Cytol.* (ed. 2) iv. 129 The result seems to depend on..the distribution of the chiasmata in the multivalent chromosome. **1967** *Biol. Abstr.* XLVIII. 983/1 (*heading*) Multivalent associations in oocytes of *Triturus helveticus helveticus.*

3. *gen.* Having many applications, meanings, or values.

1933 *Mind* XLII. 484, I propose to call words which can enter sentences in more than one sense multivalent words. **1952** *Essays in Crit.* II. 99 It is unnecessary to heap up detailed parallels for the reader..; our object is to indicate their multivalent mode of functioning. **1963** *Listener* 31 Jan. 213/2 Spenser's allegory is sometimes naive, often multivalent, and often, indeed, non-existent. **1971** *Archivum Linguisticum* II. 59 Interrogative form con-

sidered in the abstract is as multivalent as the flection *-s* and is variously used..for suggestions.., exclamations.., and so on.

B. *sb. Cytology.* An association of three or more completely or partly homologous chromosomes during the first division of meiosis.

1929 *Jrnl. Genetics* XXI. 12 At post-diplotene stages associations of three, four and five chromosomes are found, clearly the forerunners of the metaphase multivalents. **1937** M. J. D. WHITE *Chromosomes* v. 82 The frequency of formation of multivalents in polyploids varies a great deal and apparently depends in part on the length of the chromosomes and in part on the rapidity of zygotene pairing. **1959** *Biol. Abstr.* XXXIV. 12/1 Multivalent formation and 'secondary association' in the meiotic stages of autotetraploid races of Lycopersicon Mill. **1971** *Nature* 9 Apr. 390/1 Though most of the chromosomes are associated as bivalents, a few multivalents are present.

multivalence, -valency (further examples); also (after *AMBIVALENCE), the property of having many meanings or interpretations.

1933 *Mind* XLII. 49 The solution of these paradoxes lies in the ambiguity... Multivalence would be better. Because it is a multiplicity of use not of meaning. **1937** *Jrnl. Immunol.* XXXII. 119 (*heading*) On the mutual multivalence of toxin and antitoxin. **1940** *Jrnl. Amer. Chem. Soc.* LXII. 2646/1 (*heading*) The bivalence of antibodies and the multivalence of antigens. **1963** HUMPHREY & WHITE *Immunol. for Students of Med.* vi. 218 The so-called 'sandwich' technique for the detection of antibody ..employs a primary layer of a dilute solution of unlabelled antigen. After reacting for 30 minutes or so, this is rinsed off..and then exposed to specific fluorescein-labelled antibody. Such a method depends upon the multivalency of the antigen. **1965** *English Studies* XLVI. 28 This very multivalence..is the crux of a mythological interpretation, by which such a general mother-goddess may be associated with almost anything on earth and sea.

multivallate (mɒltivæ·lēɪt, -ĕt), *a.* [f. MULTI- + VALLATE *a.*] Having encircling ramparts which form multiple lines of defence. Cf. *BIVALLATE *a.* Also **multivalla·tion.**

1948 *Archaeol. Jrnl.* CV. 50 The best developed barbicans are found in multivallate camps. **1954** *Bull. Board Celtic Stud.* XV. 74 Multivallate 'camps' with various types of lateral or oblique entrance. **1963** [see *BIVALLATE *a.*]. **1963** E. S. WOOD *Collins Field Guide Archaeol.* II. ii. 169 The chief areas of multivallation are the south-west.. and Wessex.

multivalve, *a.* Add: **c.** *Electronics.* Having many thermionic valves.

1920 *Wireless World* Jan. 574/2 More than one valve may be connected in cascade to form a multi-valve amplifier. **1957** *Ibid.* July 310 (*heading*) Multi-valve cathode follower circuits.

multiva·riant, *a.* [f. MULTI- + VARIANT *a.* and *sb.*] Influenced by or taking account of several variables; † *spec.* (of a chemical system) having more than two degrees of freedom (*obs.*).

1902 J. E. TREVOR in *Jrnl. Physical Chem.* VI. 136, I would..suggest..that when the variance is successively zero, one, two, three, and more than two, the system be said to be in an Invariant, Univariant, Bivariant, Trivariant, Multivariant, state. **1904** *Ibid.* VIII. 491 The indifferent points of a bivariant or multivariant system form a series analogous to the series of states of equilibrium of a univariant system. **1953** A. K. C. OTTAWAY *Educ. & Society* iii. 47 Enough should have been said to indicate the multiplicity of factors which must be considered in any analysis of social change. That is why the concept of causation is so dangerous in social science; because we are dealing with multi-variant phenomena. **1959** *Biol. Abstr.* XXXIV. 561/2 (*heading*) The application of multivariant analysis to the physical characteristics of Guarao and Caribe Indians.

multiva·riate, *a. Statistics.* [f. MULTI- + *VARIATE *sb.*] Involving or having two or more variates or variables.

1928 *Biometrika* XXA. 32 (*heading*) The generalised product moment distribution in samples from a normal multivariate population. **1939** *Proc. Cambr. Philos. Soc.* XXXV. 180 (*heading*) A note on tests of significance in multivariate analysis. **1958** *Economist* 29 Nov. 782 The multi-variate linear regression technique..is satisfactory only if the explanatory variables vary independently of each other or if the degree of interaction between two or more of them can be measured and allowed for. This is certainly not the case in milk production and it was for this reason that the technique was rejected. **1967** C. BERNERS-LEE in Wills & Yearsley *Handbk. Managem. Technol.* i. 7 Procedures like multivariate regression analysis require a great deal of computation when more than a small number of variables are involved. **1968** R. A. BRADLEY in *Internat. Encycl. Social Sci.* X. 527/1 Multivariate analysis in statistics is devoted to the summarization, representation, and interpretation of data when more than one characteristic of each sample unit is measured. **1972** *Computer Jrnl.* XV. 215/2 Evaluation of the error matrix is therefore reduced to the evaluation of a multivariate polynomial at a number of points. **1973** *Nature* 16 Mar. 210/3 Altogether, the theory of multivariate distributions poses the most difficult problems in mathematical statistics.

mu·ltiverse. [f. UNIVERSE by substituting MULTI- for UNI-.] An alternative suggested for the word UNIVERSE in order to indicate the absence of order or of a single ruling and guiding power.

1895 W. JAMES *Will to Believe* (1897) 43 Visible nature is all plasticity and indifference,—a moral multiverse, as one might call it, and not a moral universe. **1904** *Daily News* 11 Oct. 3 [Reporting Sir O. Lodge], The only possible alternative was to regard the universe as a result of random chance and capricious disorder, not a cosmos or universe at all, but rather a 'multiverse'. **1920** CHESTERTON *New Jerusalem* viii. 163 When I told a distinguished psychologist..that I differed from his view of the universe, he answered, 'Why universe? Why should it not be a multiverse?' **1957** *Times Lit. Suppl.* 11 Oct. 602/1 It is precisely Mr Powys's ever-present contact with the vital, or spiritual, principles within the universe which enables him to explore with so uncanny a penetration the deeper problems of that comparatively small section of the universe—or as he would say multiverse—which constitutes man. **1959** N. N. HOLLAND *First Mod. Comedies* 128 Out of this 'pluralistic multiverse', as Robert Oppenheimer has recently called it. **1975** C. BURT *ESP & Psychol.* ii. 34 Modern physics presents us with a heterogeneous multiverse, in place of the homogeneous universe of Newton and Laplace.

multiversity (mɒltivɜ̄·ɹsɪti). Chiefly *U.S.* [f. MULTI- + UNI)VERSITY *sb.*] A very large university comprising many different departments and activities.

1963 C. KERR *Uses of University* i. 42 The multiversity is in the main stream of events. To the teacher and the researcher have been added the consultant and the administrator. Teaching is less central than it once was for most faculty members; research has become more important. **1966** *Economist* 14 May 713/1 For the second year in succession Dr Clark Kerr, the president of the University of California, has been bitterly attacked for permitting too much freedom by a subcommittee of the State Legislature, which finances this great, sprawling 'multi-versity'. **1968** *Guardian* 30 Nov. 2/3 The inevitable transformation of universities everywhere into 'multiversities' is being achieved with appalling birth pangs in the University of California, which a dozen years ago had two campuses and now has 10. **1969** C. DAVIDSON in Cockburn & Blackburn *Student Power* 337 Transforming the academic landscape into what we now call the 'multiversity'. **1969** *Nature* 13 Dec. 1064/1 By the mid-sixties, the result..was clearly an overloading of the university system as a 'multiversity', to use the word of one of its first victims, Clark Kerr. **1971** *Wall Street Jrnl.* 12 Jan. 1/1 They don't like the way it has grown from a sleepy teachers' college of 3,000 students in 1950 to its present status as a giant, cosmopolitan 'multiversity'.

mu:ltivibra·tor. *Electronics.* [ad. F. *multivibrateur* (Abraham & Bloch 1919, in *Compt. Rend.* CLXVIII. 1107), f. *multi-* MULTI- + *vibrateur* VIBRATOR.] A device that consists of two amplifying valves or transistors, each with its output connected to the input of the other, and produces an oscillatory signal rich in harmonics and capable of being triggered and stabilized by an applied sinusoidal signal of slightly higher frequency (the form of the coupling determining the resonant frequency of the device and whether it is astable, bistable, or monostable).

1919 *Sci. Abstr.* B. XXII. 287 The source of oscillations which has been found very successful in operation has been called a 'multivibrator'. It possesses, besides the fundamental wave-length, all the harmonics from 1 up to two or three hundred. **1940** *Amat. Radio Handbk.* (ed. 2) xiv. 219/1 A multi-vibrator operating on 10 kc can be readily locked by a few volts..of 100 kc frequency, and the harmonics of the multivibrator stage will produce carrier frequencies spaced throughout the radio-frequency spectrum at 10 kc intervals with a precision equal to that of the locking source. **1969** J. J. SPARKES *Transistor Switching* iii. 52 The multivibrator can, of course, produce square waves as well as rectangular waves simply by ensuring symmetry between the two halves of the circuit. **1971** J. H. SMITH *Digital Logic* iv. 75 Digital systems frequently need a multivibrator, or at least a source of continuous signals.

muly, var. *MULEY *a.*[3]

mum, *sb.*[3] For *dial.* read *dial.* and *colloq.*, and add further examples.

1876 C. M. YONGE *Three Brides* I. xvi. 274 You'll never do anything with my Governor..you should hear him and the Mum talking. **1955** M. ALLINGHAM *Beckoning Lady* vi. 88 Charlie Luke has a mum too, hasn't he? **1956** I. BROMIGE *Enchanted Garden* III. iii. 140 This will be our first holiday without the children for a good many years. It'll be good to be with Laurie as a wife and not a mum for a short time. **1960** *News Chron.* 8 Feb. 3/4 The mums from Manchester and Mitcham dressed up in their Sunday best ..had to listen to the principal's report. **1966** AUDEN *About House* 15 The flesh Mum formulated. **1973** A. S. NEILL *Neill! Neill! Orange Peel!* II. 223 Many married men address their wives as Mum.

b. *Sociol.* Used *spec.* to designate the working-class mother who is a dominating influence in the lives of her children, even in their adulthood and marriage.

1957 YOUNG & WILLMOTT *Family & Kinship in East London* iii. 34 Where Mum plays so large a part in the lives of her descendants, she should be honoured for what she does... Since her status as 'Mum' is so high, it is derogatory to call her by any other name. **1958** M. KERR *People of Ship Street* ii. 22 The first characteristic which emerges clearly in this group is the central figure of the Mum. Whatever her personal qualities she is the focus of all the family activities. **1958** *Spectator* 30 May 710/2 The Mum restricts her son-in-law's roles and most of the men in the neighbourhood seem to suffer accordingly. **1958** *Listener* 11 Sept. 395/2 Many families who have been moved out of Bethnal Green..are in most cases perfectly wretched. They crave for their old associations, for Mum, the familiar pub, their pets and the old cosy squalor. **1959** *Ibid.* 4 June 981/2 There is, however, some difference of opinion in the field of 'Mum' sociology.

c. Colloq. phr. *to be mum*, etc. = *to be mother* (see *MOTHER *sb.*[1] 3 e).

1962 N. FREELING *Love in Amsterdam* I. 37 'I'll be Mum,' he said, and poured the coffee. **1965** J. POTTER *Death in Office* xv. 147, I did the chores as mum..the tea-tray ploy was one of the standard fitness tests for prospective employees.

2. *Comb.*, as **mum figure** *colloq.*, one who represents the attributes of a mother; = **mother figure*.

1959 'N. BLAKE' *Widow's Cruise* 23 I'm a Mum figure—everyone coughs it up in my lap. **1960** *Times Lit. Suppl.* 16 Sept. 589/1 His wife is a shadowy mum-figure who collects for good causes.

mum (mɒm), *sb.*[4] Abbrev. of CHRYSANTHEMUM. Also **'mum.**

1924 A. M. MARTINEAU *Gardening in Sunny Lands* ii. 38 The gardeners call chrysanthemums 'mums'. **1949** [see *CUKE]. **1965** J. PHILIPS *Black Glass City* II. ii. 62 A basket of bright-colored fall flowers..mums and asters. **1967** 'E. QUEEN' *Face to Face* lxiii. 197 The enormous basket-spray of shaggy 'mums. **1967** *Times* 4 Apr. 18/1 (Advt.), Captivating Meteor Mums... These chrysanthemums..cascade into bloom in August. **1975** M. H. CLARK *Where are Children?* i. 16 The window boxes.. were filled with yellow and champagne mums.

mum, vulgar var. MA'AM (examples).

1847 A. BRONTË *Agnes Grey* xi. 177 For you know mum he's now't at all to live on, but what he gets fra' th' rector. **1866** TROLLOPE *Belton Estate* (ed. 3) III. vi. 159 The gentleman..was blown up with all the ceremony of which Mrs. Bunce was capable. 'Here he be, mum.' **1973** S. COHEN *Diane Game* (1974) vi. 62 It's me, mum... Are you having dinner in?

mumble-the-peg. Delete restriction of **mumbledepeg** to 7 and **mumblety-peg** to 7, 9 and add **mumbledy-peg** to forms. (Later examples.) Hence **mumblety-pegging** *vbl. sb.*

1931 *Sun* (Baltimore) 18 Feb. 8/7 In my boyhood the spring was ushered in by children rolling hoops, spinning tops, skipping rope, playing mumblety-pegs. **1932** *Ibid.* 17 Sept. 10/7 The Park will attempt next week to match this week's golf tournament with a grand quoit pitchin' and mumblety-peggin' contest. **1938** M. K. RAWLINGS *Yearling* vii. 64 Jody and Fodder-wing lost interest in the talk and went into a corner to play mumbledepeg. Ma Baxter would never have allowed pocket knives to be flipped into her clean smooth floors. **1963** T. PYNCHON *V.* x. 298 They found two more musicians playing mumbledy-peg with clam knives.

mumbo jumbo. Add: **2. b.** Obscure or meaningless talk or writing; nonsense. Also *ellipt.* as **mumbo.**

1896 FARMER & HENLEY *Slang* IV. 386/2 *Mumbo-Jumbo*, 2. (colloquial).—Unmeaning jargon. **1931** E. POUND *Let.* 27 Dec. (1971) 237 The continuation [of a magazine] can be called Poetry, Second Series, or new series, if that hackneyed term is still big heap mumbo on the lake shore. **1938** *Sun* (Baltimore) 16 Nov. 10/1 The Orson Welles mumbo jumbo of a few weeks ago has revived talk of greater public control over this form of communication. **1955** *Times* 2 May 17/3 A mumbo jumbo of meaningless words and phrases. **1969** M. PEI *Words in Sheep's Clothing* (1970) vii. 54 Mumbo jumbo developed by educators to confound the public in general and inquisitive parents in particular. **1973** *Sunday Express* 29 July 12/3 There is a great deal of unnecessary mumbo talked. **1975** *Times* 14 Aug. 14/5 Labour's elected representatives.. mouth the mumbo-jumbo of capitalism: 'The pound must be kept strong', 'We must all buy British'.

mumbudget. Add: **2.** Phr. *to come mumbudgeting* 'to come clandestinely, secretly' (*E.D.D.*). (See also quot. 1909.) *dial.*

1872 HARDY *Under Greenwood Tree* I. II. ii. 115 There was this to be said for him, that you were quite sure he'd never come mumbudgeting to see ye, just as you were in the middle of your work, and put you out with his anxious trouble about you. *Ibid.* II. IV. ii. 110 Now, don't come mumbudgeting so close again. **1909** *Daily Chron.* 30 Apr. 6/5 In Mr. Hardy's 'Under the Greenwood Tree'..mumbudgeting..seems to mean rather 'fussily', a sense in which the word budget is still used in the Midlands. **1939** N. MARSH *Overture to Death* xiii. 139 Whatever be the matter with you, then, mum-budgeting so close to my apron strings?

mumchance, *sb.* and *a.* **B.** *adj.* Delete *arch.* and *dial.*, and add later examples.

1897 *Daily Tel.* 11 Mar. 5/5 The man or woman who can sit 'mumchance'..over a well-acted farce do not deserve to be ranked in the noble army of all-embracing playgoers. **1903** G. B. SHAW *Man & Superman* IV. 167, I couldn't sit mumchance and have everything put on me. **1957** L. DURRELL *Justine* II. 133 For my part I remained always stupefied and mumchance at all the avenues opened up by these thoughts. **1971** F. MEYNELL *My Lives* iv. 42 In a room of awesome vastness with a phalanx of dons at the distant end of it, I was mum-chance.

mu·mchanceness. [f. MUMCHANCE *a.* + -NESS.] Silence, reticence. Also **mumchanciness.**

1910 'A. HOPE' *Second String* xxi. 435 Perhaps his very

mum-chanceness was his saving. Glib protestations would have smacked too strongly of the principal to commend the agent. **1920** J. Joyce *Let.* 29 Aug. (1966) III. 17, I am much inconvenienced by their cursed mumchanciness.

mu-meson (miŭ·mĭ·zǫn, -me·zǫn). *Nuclear Physics.* Also **mu meson.** [f. *MU + *MESON³.] The original name for the *MUON. (Freq. written μ-meson.)

[**1947** Lattes, Occhialini, & Powell in *Nature* 4 Oct. 455/1 There is, therefore, good evidence for the production of a single homogeneous group of secondary mesons. .. It is convenient to refer to this process. .as the μ-decay. We represent the primary mesons by the symbol π, and the secondary by μ. *Ibid.* 455/2 *(heading)* Evidence of a difference in mass of π- and μ-mesons.] **1952** B. Rossi *High-Energy Particles* 566/1 Mu-mesons. **1953** *Jrnl. Brit. Interplanetary Soc.* XII. 203 The final remnants of cosmic-radiation which we observe at sea level are mainly electrons, mu-mesons, gamma rays and a proportionately small component of protons and neutrons. **1969** *Times* 2 Jan. 16/2 The measurements may indicate a means of distinguishing between mu mesons and electrons on grounds other than the difference of mass between the two particles.

Hence **mu-me·sic, -meso·nic** *adjs.* = *MUONIC *a.*

1954 *Physical Rev.* XCIV. 1619/1 Mu-mesonic energy levels. **1957** *Ann. Rev. Nuclear Sci.* VII. 17 *(heading)* Mu mesonic X-rays. *Ibid.* 495 (Index), Mumesic atoms. **1964** W. E. Jones tr. *A. A. Sokolov's Elementary Particles* vi. 52 Since muons are similar to electrons in their properties.., they may form mu-mesic atoms, where the principal role is played by electrical forces, just as in the normal atom. **1969** *New Scientist* 9 Oct. 63/2 The quadrupole moments derived from mu-mesic X-rays can be used to check the reliability of standard calculations in atomic physics.

Mumetal (miŭ·metăl). Also **Mu-metal,** and with small initial. [f. *MU (μ being conventionally used to denote permeability) + METAL *sb.* (and *a.*).] The proprietary name of an alloy of iron that contains approximately 75–78 per cent nickel, 4–6 per cent copper, and 1½–2 per cent chromium by weight and is a useful material for transformer cores and magnetic shields because of its high permeability and low hysteresis loss in weak magnetic fields.

1924 *Trade Marks Jrnl.* 16 Apr. 858 Mumetal... Metallic alloys, unwrought or partly wrought. The Telegraph Construction and Maintenance Company, Limited, . . London, . . manufacturers. **1925** *Jrnl. Iron & Steel Inst.* CXII. 74 The first commercial application of high-frequency melting in Europe was made by a British firm for the preparation of nickel–iron alloys for submarine cables. The research work . . quickly resulted in the perfection of a series of alloys known under the name of 'Mumetal'. **1932** *Discovery* May 142/1 Pure iron, silicon–iron, permalloy, and mumetal are used because they can be magnetized and demagnetized without loss. **1945** *Electronic Engin.* XVII. 384 *(caption)* Recorder unit showing tube enclosed in Mu-metal screen. **1966** *New Scientist* 18 Aug. 351/3 The enclosures were formed of a material (mu-metal) which screens off the Earth's field. **1973** *Physics Bull.* Dec. 719/2 Until now conventional recording heads have had cores of a soft magnetic material, typically ferrite or laminated mumetal.

Mumm (mum). The proprietary name of the champagne produced by the firm of Mumm in Rheims.

[**1851** C. Redding *Hist. Mod. Wines* (ed. 3) vi. 106 The great complaint against Champagne wine has been that it cannot be obtained of a uniform quality... To remedy this evil . . Mumm, Geisler & Co., at Rheims, provided tuns holding twelve thousand litres each.] **1885** *Christie's Auction Catal.* 18 Dec. 17 Three dozens of Champagne, 1868, Mumm. **1907** C. E. Hawker *Chats about Wine* 87 Such names as Cliquot, . . Mumm, Pommery, Roederer, etc., will occur to everyone as carrying with them a guarantee of high-class quality and excellence. **1928** E. Waugh *Decline & Fall* v. 188 The wedding . . was to take place in church with all the barbaric concomitants of bridesmaids, Mendelssohn and Mumm. **1967** 'L. Black' *Two Ladies in Verona* x. 161 A bottle of Mumm Cordon Rouge. I leave the year to you. **1975** J. Symons *Three Pipe Problem* xii. 87 'Glass of Mumm, delicious.' . . 'I shouldn't have thought you could have seen the name.' 'Only the corner of the label. The Mumm label is distinctive.'

mummer (mʌ·məɹ), *v.* [See MUMMER 2.] To take part in a mumming. So **mu·mmering** *vbl. sb.* = MUMMING *vbl. sb.* 2.

1884 F. Madan in *Bodleian Libr. MS. Eng. Poet. c.* 17 39 Christmas mummering at Ducklington, Oxon. **1964** L. Diack *Labrador Nurse* II. xiii. 70 From Christmas Day to Twelfth Night . . was the season for 'Mummering' or 'Janny-ing'. There was much dressing up and disguising, and parties went round from house to house to entertain and have fun. **1969** L. J. Chiaramonte in Halpert & Story *Christmas Mumming in Newfoundland* 91 The single male mummer . . does not always accept a drink at the houses he mummers in. **1969** Widdowson & Halpert in *Ibid.* 147 Disguise is a central element in Christmas mummering throughout Newfoundland.

Mummerset (mʌ·məɹset). Also **Mummersetshire.** [Modelled on *Somerset(shire)*, and perh. influenced by MUMMER.] An imaginary rustic county in the West of England, and its dialect, invented by actors.

1951 J. B. Priestley *Festival at Farbridge* II. ii. 219 'Az tew Papular Antertainment,' he drawled in his best Mummerset. **1952** Granville *Dict. Theatrical Terms* 120 An adviser on regional dialect helps the cast to reach a mean which has earned the jocular nickname *Mummerset-shire*, or actor's dialect. **1957** [see *HONESTLY adv.* 2 b]. **1961** *Punch* 15 Mar. 411/2 Stage yokels from Mummerset. **1961** *Times* 19 June 13/4 How long must we wait for a dialect dictionary in one combined volume with pronunciations in Barsetshire and Mummerset? **1965** *Listener* 25 Oct. 640/3 The characters did speak real dialect, and not Mummerset. **1966** D. Blakelock *Eleanor* x. 77 That exaggerated, bogus country dialect known to actors as 'Mummerset'. **1966** C. Mackenzie *Paper Lives* viii. 114 Nowadays you can't be sure if they *are* eggs, even when somebody on television says they are in B.B.C. Mummerset. **1968** N. Marsh *Clutch of Constables* viii. 203, I sat in the Northumberland Arms . . listening to the dullest brand of Mummerset-type gossip. **1970** *Guardian* 26 Mar. 11/3 The straight English is often sloppy and soft; and throughout there is often a damp sprinkling of mummersetshire such as was never heard or spoken. **1971** *Times* 16 Feb. 10/2 Philip Grout's production selflessly follows the spirit of the piece: it is all Mummerset and wagging bottoms, slack jaws and graceless tussles. **1975** *Times Lit. Suppl.* 28 Feb. 220/2 Ordinary people in British war films became more than lovable Cockneys, Mummerset rustics, or Bunny Doyle Northerners full of blunt common sense.

mummied, *a.* Add: **3.** Of a fruit: brown and dry as a result of brown rot disease, caused by a fungus of the genus *Sclerotinia.*

1909 B. M. Duggar *Fungous Diseases of Plants* xi. 190 These mummied fruits are the chief sources of infection the following season, under ordinary conditions. **1935** *Bull. Min. Agric. & Fish.* LXXXVIII. 1 A fruit so infected [with a fungus of the genus *Sclerotinia*], instead of disintegrating becomes dried up and 'mummied'.

mummified, *a.* Add: **2.** Of a fruit: = *MUMMIED *a.* 3.

1928 F. T. Brooks *Plant Diseases* xi. 143 In New Zealand apothecia [of *Sclerotinia laxa*] are only found where mummified fruits have been buried in hard, compact soil. **1973** H. Martin *Scientific Princ. Crop Protection* (ed. 6) xv. 537 For the control of the brown-rot of stone fruits (*Sclerotinia* spp.) the removal and burning of diseased twigs and mummified fruits is of great importance.

mum-mumble (mʌm,mʌ·mb'l). Onomatopœic variant of MUMBLE *v.*, perhaps under the influence of MUM *v.*

1917 R. Graves *Fairies & Fusiliers* 75 From which the ancient poet was mum-mumbling A song about some Lovers at a Fair. **1956** H. Gold *Man who was not with It* (1965) xxxi. 292 This was our first fret-fingered, mum-mumbling babe.

mummy, *sb.¹* Add: **3. e.** An apple, plum, or other fruit of the family Rosaceæ, made brown and desiccated by the brown rot disease caused by a fungus of the genus *Sclerotinia.*

1909 B. M. Duggar *Fungous Diseases of Plants* xi. 190 The fruit which has decayed may fall to the ground or hang upon the trees, gradually shrinking with evaporation each to a crumpled dried mass, generally known as a mummy. **1952** E. Ramsden tr. *Gram & Weber's Plant Diseases* ii. 153/2 Similar mummies that have fallen and remained on or near the surface of the soil may very rarely produce clusters of small brown-stalked cup-shaped apothecia.

4. a. *mummy-dust;* **b.** *mummy-dead* adj.; **c.** *mummy brown,* a shade of brown akin to that of the pigment mummy; *mummy-case (fig. examples);* *mummy disease,* a disease of mushrooms of uncertain ætiology, indicated by the dying back of young plants, or the distorted shape and hardened gills of older ones.

1886 R. Ridgway *Nomenclature of Colors for Naturalists* II. 92 *Mummy Brown,* a bright brown color, nearly intermediate in tint between burnt umber and raw umber. **1930** Maerz & Paul *Dict. Color* 168/1 *Mummy Brown,* R[idgway] has a color by this name, 15 c 8, which is simply a somewhat reduced tone of the pigment known as 'mummy'. *a* **1936** Kipling *Something of Myself* (1937) i. 13 A tube of 'Mummy Brown'. **1949** *Dict. Colours for Interior Decoration* (Brit. Colour Council) III. 18/2 Mummy Brown, see Clove Brown. **1922** Joyce *Ulysses* 191 Coffined thoughts around me, in mummy cases, embalmed in spice of words. **1922** L. Mumford *City Devel.* (1946) i. 9 What remained of the provincial town in New England was a mummy-case. **1939** W. B. Yeats *Last Poems* 20 Everything else withered and mummy-dead. **1942** Tucker & Routien in *Res. Bull. Missouri Agric. Exper. Station* No. 358. 3 The common name 'mummy disease' was suggested by Dr. [A. M.] Klingman. It is quite appropriate for the symptoms that develop in white strains or varieties, and with Dr. Klingman's permission, will be used here. **1950** R. L. O. Jackson *Mushroom Growing* vii. 66 The Americans have a similar disease called Mummy Disease, which spreads at an alarming rate, and which they think is caused by a virus, but so far this is of doubtful occurrence in this country. **1969** R. Genders *Mushroom Growing for Everyone* xiv. 198 Mummy disease. For long this has been a source of worry to American growers but only since 1950 has it become known to British growers. **1922** E. Sitwell *Façade* 13 When the moon's hurdy-gurdy wheeze Grinds out her slow mummy-dust.

mummy, *sb.²* Add: Also **mummie.** (Earlier and later examples.)

1784 J. Cullum *Hist. Hawsted* iii. 172 *Mummy,* corrupted from mamma. **1903** *Punch* 30 Sept. 231 Mummy dear, of course Uncle Jack is coming to meet us by a Circle Train, isn't he? **1914** 'Bartimeus' *Naval Occasions* ix. 68 Thank you, mummie darling. **1933** E. A. Robertson *Ordinary Families* ii. 39 'Mummy, did you put in my straw hat?' came Marnie's adenoidal whine from upstairs. 'Oh, mummy, you always say yes. Sure you did? Mummee!' **1974** M. Penoyre *Breach of Security* v. 26 Oh, mummy, you're going out. . . I'd hoped you were going to . . read me a story.

2. Phr. mummy's boy = *mother's boy* (*MOTHER *sb.*¹ 15 a).

1927 E. Bowen *Hotel* xv. 177 None of us seem to be making much impression on young Ronald. . . Did you ever see such a Mummy's boy! **1945** E. Taylor *At Mrs Lippincote's* xxi. 180 What a mummy's boy Norman sounds. **1967** 'H. Calvin' *Nice Friendly Town* iv. 49 'Are you a mummy's boy?' 'No,' I said 'but she's a sonny's mum.' **1968** 'P. Hobson' *Titty's Dead* xv. 152 You're not a man at all. Just a mummy's boy. **1975** W. J. Burley *Wycliffe* xi. 173 'What sort of a boy was he?' . . 'Quiet. A bit of a mummy's boy.'

mummy apple, var. *mammee-apple* (MAMMEE 3).

1905 *Daily Graphic* 16 Jan. 4/4 The mummy-apple, a delicate tree-melon, springs up spontaneously wherever land is cleared. **1911** J. London *Adventure* vii. 85 Mummy apples, which he had regarded as weeds, under her guidance appeared as appetizing breakfast fruit.

mump, *sb.* Add: **4.** A block of peat.

1953 A. Jobson *Household & Country Crafts* vii. 84 Each piece of peat was cut to a uniform size. One man cut the blocks or 'mumps', and another carried them away to dry. **1962** *Amateur Gardening* 5 May 1/4 A 'mump' is a block of peat 10 in × 9 in × 9 in.

mumper. (Later examples.)

1882 *Sydney Slang Dict.* 6/1 *Mumper,* beggar. **1967** *Economist* 30 Sept. 1172/1 This is the total number of 'travellers'—Romanies; mixed-blood 'past-rats' and 'didcois'; 'mumpers', who have no Romany blood; and (mostly Irish) tinkers—recorded by a Ministry of Housing census. **1972** *Countryman* Autumn 86 Beside the gypsies there are many other pickers—tramps, mumpers, all sorts.

mums (mʌmz), shortened form of *MUMSY *sb.* and *a.*

1939 L. M. Montgomery *Anne of Ingleside* xxix. 195 It is God who makes everything beautiful, but we can help Him out a bit, can't we, Mums? **1942** J. Cary *To be Pilgrim* cxviii. 254 'How are you really, Johnny?'. . 'Very hungry, Mums darling.' **1942** T. Bailey *Pink Camellia* ii. 18 Say you don't hate me, Mums. **1948** D. Ballantyne *Cunninghams* 8 Dear Mums, I received your ever welcome letter. **1968** 'R. Llewellyn' *End of Rug* (1969) xv. 123 You were always the tough one, Dads. . . I think I've got more of Mums. She'd cry over a hurt dog.

mumsy (mʌ·mzi), *sb.* and *a.* Also **mumsey.** [f. MUM *sb.*³ + -SY.] **A.** *sb.* A playful variant of MUMMY *sb.*² **B.** *adj.* = MATERNAL *a.* (a playful use).

1876 C. M. Yonge *Three Brides* I. xvi. 274 'Well,' says Mumsey, 'it is not what was thought the thing for ladies in my time.' **1916** *Farmer's Wife* Mar. 248/1 'Dear old motherkins!' 'Good old Mumsy!' **1927** M. Ostenso *Mad Carews* (1928) vii. 93 'Hello, Mumsey!' she greeted her mother. **1953** A. Christie *Pocket Full of Rye* xxvii. 184 Poor Mumsy, she was so devoted to Dad, you know. **1961** 'T. Hinde' *For Good of Company* i. 15 They're all three tucked up in one great big mumsy bed. **1970** 'W. Haggard' *Hardliners* vi. 64 The nurse . . was a West Indian woman, large and mumsy. **1972** J. McClure *Caterpillar Cop* ii. 16 To hell with them and all that crap about mumsy-love.

mumu, var. *MUU-MUU.*

mun (mʌn). Colloq. abbrev. of MONEY *sb.* Cf. *MON³.

1896 W. C. Gore *Student Slang* 7 Mun, . . money. **1959** M. Steen *Tower* II. i. 147 You'll adore Kendall—American—tons and tons of lovely *mun*! **1968** J. N. Chance *Rogue Aunt* v. 86 'You should write little tabs, and tie them on,' said Clara. . . 'Tabs corsts mun,' said Barnskin. **1974** *Sunday Times* 22 Dec. 12/7 They were in this gambling club and he won lots and lots of lovely mun.

Munchausen. Add: **b.** Used *attrib.* and in the possessive with reference to a syndrome in which the patient repeatedly feigns a dramatic or severe illness so as to obtain hospital treatment (see quot. 1951).

1951 R. Asher in *Lancet* 10 Feb. 339/1 Munchausen's syndrome. . . Here is described a common syndrome which most doctors have seen, but about which little has been written. Like the famous Baron von Munchausen, the persons affected have always travelled widely; and their stories, like those attributed to him, are both dramatic and untruthful. Accordingly the syndrome is respectfully dedicated to the baron, and named after him. **1959** *Perspect. Biol. & Med.* II. 347 The peripatetic medical vagrant, the itinerant fabricator of a nearly perfect facsimile of serious illness—the victim of Munchausen's syndrome. **1967** *Amer. Jrnl. Med.* XLIII. 579/2 This complex of factors . . distinguishes the Munchausen patient from the malingerer, hypochondriac, hysteric, self-mutilator and drug addict, with all of which the diagnosis of Munchausen's syndrome has been confused in the past. **1967** *Cecil-Loeb Textbk. Med.* (ed. 12) 1453/2 The only ones who can be called malingerers with any confidence are some self-mutilating patients and the remarkable pathological liars, picturesquely called exam-

ples of the Münchhausen syndrome, who travel from hospital to hospital gaining admission by means of dramatic acts of illness.

Munchi (mu·ntʃi), *sb.* and *a.* Also **Midsi, Mitshi, Munshi.** [Native name.] **A.** *sb.* **a.** A Negro people living in Nigeria near the junction of the Niger and Benue rivers; a member of this people. **b.** The language of this people. **B.** *adj.* Of or pertaining to this people.

1854 S. A. CROWTHER *Jrnl. Expedition Niger* (1855) ii. 61 There is a tribe on the south bank called Mitshi. They have been represented all along as a wild people and wicked archers. **1883** R. N. CUST *Sk. Mod. Lang. Afr.* I. xi. 231 Michi, Midsi, Mbidsi is the language spoken by a tribe dwelling on the Left or South Bank of the Binué. **1892** A. F. MOCKLER-FERRYMAN *Up Niger* iv. 76 The Mitshis are a difficult people to deal with, since they acknowledge no one as head of the tribe, and live in independent families, fearing no one, yet feared by all foreign tribes. *Ibid.*, There was a sort of feeling of relief among our crew when..we had left the Mitshi country. **1905** C. PARTRIDGE *Cross River Natives* v. 89 This angle is peopled by the fierce Munchis or Mitshis, a warlike pagan tribe dreaded by their enemies on account of the deadly poison with which they smear their arrows. **1908** *Daily Chron.* 12 Nov. 5/6 At least one-half of the Munchi country is now open to trade. **1913** F. W. H. MIGEOD *Lang. West Afr.* II. xxi. 324 The fact of its being found in Munshi is of special interest... This dual connection, having in view the actual numerals which are similar, brings Munshi into touch with languages far to the west. **1933** J. CARY *American Visitor* viii. 96 When you say pagans, do you mean the Munchis..or the Kukuruku?

munchie (mɒ·nʃi). [f. MUNCH *v.* + -IE.] **a.** A light meal; the name given to any type of food. *slang.* **b.** In *pl.* Hunger induced after ingesting marijuana; also a snack eaten to satisfy this hunger. *U.S. slang.*

In quot. 1917 a family name for a kind of chocolate.

1917 W. OWEN *Let.* 21 Feb. (1967) 437 All I really want is Cigarettes, Munchie, and *plain Cadbury's*. **1959** I. & P. OPIE *Lore & Lang. Schoolch.* ix. 163 Food in general is referred to as 'bait'..'grub', or 'grubber', 'munchie', [etc.]. **1962** *Austral. Women's Weekly* Suppl. 24 Oct. 3/3 *Munchie*, any type of food. **1971** E. E. LANDY *Underground Dict.* 136 *Munchies*, hunger introduced by marijuana—eg. *I have the munchies.* **1971** *Current Slang* (Univ. S. Dakota) VI. 8 *Munchies*, snacks to be eaten after smoking marijuana. **1972** *Dict. Contemp. & Colloquial Usage* (Eng.-Lang. Inst. Amer.) 20 *Munchie*, a snack; food to nibble on. **1973** *Times* 7 Feb. 16/1 There are..munchies (to be hungry usually after ingesting marijuana).

Munda (mŭ·nda), *sb.* and *a.* [Native word.] **A.** *sb.* **a.** A member of an ancient Indian people of pre-Aryan stock which was overrun by invading Caucasians and Mongols and which survives in present times as primitive tribes living in north-eastern India. **b.** The name given to the language group which includes the dialects of the Mundas and is believed to belong to the Austroasiatic family of languages. **B.** *adj.* Of or pertaining to the Mundas or their language. Cf. *KOLARIAN.

1847 B. H. HODGSON *On Aborigines of India* iii. 150 Among the Kóls, I have seen *many* Orauns and Múndas nearly black. **1854** M. MÜLLER in C. C. J. Bunsen *Christianity & Mankind* III. 437 These people, called themselves 'Munda', which as an old ethnic name, I have adopted for the common appellation of the aboriginal Koles... It is said that the Mundas and Uraons lived peaceably together until the Brahmans reached their country. *Ibid.* 438 The dictionaries of the Munda and Tamulian languages differ more than should be the case with cognate dialects. **1866** *Jrnl. Asiatic Soc. Bengal* XXXV. II. (Special Number) 26 There are..'moondahs' and Santals..speaking dialects of a language very different from the Dravidian. **1872** E. T. DALTON *Descr. Ethnol. Bengal* vii. 163 The people I am now about to describe comprise the Múndáris or Múndas of Chútia Nágpúr proper. **1877** A. H. KEANE tr. *Hovelacque's Sci. of Lang.* iv. 138 *Munda.* The language of the Kols, or Kolhs (south-west of Calcutta), would seem, like Sinhalese, to be independent of the Dravidian group. **1888** *Encycl. Brit.* XXIII. 41/2 There are scattered remnants of a still earlier population of India (Mundas, Kolarians), whose race characteristics..do not so essentially differ from those of the Dravidians. **1904** G. A. GRIERSON *Linguistic Survey of India* II. 1 The Mundā order is subject, object, verb, while in Khassi and Mōn it is subject, verb, object. **1912** S. C. ROY *Mundas & their Country* i. 16 The site of the original home of the Mundas will perhaps ever remain hidden from view in the mist of ages. **1933** [see *AUSTRIC *a.*]. **1956** J. WHATMOUGH *Language* ii. 30 Munda is now found chiefly in the eastern Himalayas and in isolated regions in the Central Provinces. **1970** YAMADA RYUJI *Cultural Formation of Mundas* I. i. 13 The Mundas, together with several other Austroasiatic peoples in India, are called an agricultural people. **1975** *Amer. Speech 1972* XLVII. 289 The Indo-Aryan languages have acquired various structural features from the Dravidian and Munda languages spoken by the subjected peoples.

mundanity. Delete 'Now *rare*' and add further examples.

1959 *Listener* 30 July 173/2 The outward mundanity of the master's life. **1963** *Movie* July–Aug. 20/2 The presentation of the torture sequences horrifies by its casual mundanity. **1972** *Daily Tel.* 27 Apr. 8/6 Nothing could be further removed from the mundanities of sausage and haddock than the subject of this book of circumferential recollections. **1974** *Nature* 17 May 199/2 It may mean the moral support that leads to a government grant, permission to work abroad for a spell or even such mundanities as the price of an airline ticket.

mung[2] (mʌŋ). [See MOONG.] In full, *mung bean*. A legume, *Phaseolus aureus*, native to India, where its seeds are an important food.

1866 [see MOONG]. **1868** B. H. POWELL *Handbk. Econ. Products of Punjab* I. 239/1 Másh, múng and channa (gram), are the pulses most in use. **1884** tr. *A. de Candolle's Orig. Cultivated Plants* v. 346 Green Gram or Múng—..A species commonly cultivated in India and in the Nile Valley. **1916** C. J. BAMBER *Plants of Punjab* 600 *Phaseolus mungo*... Mung... Cultivated for its seeds which are eaten as *dal*. **1955** *New Biol.* XIX. 101 Mung bean preparations given succinate consumed oxygen at one-third of the rate shown by the tissue they were derived from. **1960** J. ORGAN *Rare Veg.* iv. 79 There are two kinds of bean used for sprouting, the Soy bean (*Soja max*) and the Mung bean (*Phaseolus aureus*). **1969** *Oxf. Bk. Food Plants* 38/2 Green Gram (*Phaseolus aureus*) is often known by the Indian name of 'mung' and is probably native to India... In China and the United States it is also used to produce bean sprouts..which are popular in certain dishes.

munga[2] (mɒ·ŋgă). *Austral., N.Z.*, and *Forces' slang.* Also **manga, munger, mungey, mungy.** [Said to be f. F. *manger* to eat.] (See quots.) Also *attrib.*

Quot. 1907 may not belong here.

1907 'Q' *Major Vigoureux* xxii. 218 Annet, Linnet, and Matthew Henry sat..and watched their friend Jan eat his mid-morning snack—or 'mungey', as it is called in the Islands. **1919** W. H. DOWNING *Digger Dialects* 34 *Mungy* (Fr., Manger)—Food; a meal. **1925** FRASER & GIBBONS *Soldier & Sailor Words* 161 *Mungy wallah*, a man employed in the Cook House. **1929** *Papers Michigan Acad. Sci. & Arts* X. 309/2 *Mungey*, food in general. **1942** C. BARRETT *On Wallaby* iv. 70 Those munger vendors did a roaring trade. *Ibid.* vii. 152 There were rush-baskets full of mysterious munger; bricks of sugar, bubbly discs of native bread, and piles of vegetables. **1943** *2 N.Z.E.F. Times* 25 Oct. 11 He argued quite a lot until munga time. **1947** D. M. DAVIN *For Rest of Lives* 75 [The Cook] swore he'd give them some good manga to go off with. **1949** 'THE SARGE' *Excuse Feet* ix. 102 Herbert felt quite sure she would have put on a much better act for a bit of army *munga*. *Ibid.* 157 *Munga*, food. **1959** S. H. COURTIER *Death in Dream Time* vi. 69 Come an' get your munga. **1970** *N.Z. Listener* 12 Oct. 12/4 Certainly do feel hungry. How about a plate of steak and eggs now? Or a rich, smoking mutton chop? A man has to eat. White or brown, everyone scoffs the same munga. **1971** *Sunday Mail* (Brisbane) 24 Oct. 42/4 After the munga Ian showed me his cocktail bit.

mungaree (mʌ̆ndʒā·ri). *slang.* Also **mungaree, mungare(er, munjari,** † **numgare.** [ad. It. *mangiare* to eat.] Food.

1861 H. MAYHEW *London Labour* III. 139/2 We [*sc.* strolling actors] call breakfast, dinner, tea, supper, all of them 'numgare'. **1889** *Answers* 11 May 374 Broken meat and scraps of bread ('Bull and Munjari' they are called). **1942** C. BARRETT *On Wallaby* iv. 64 Chameleons..are insectivorous and get their own mungaree (food). **1944** L. GLASSOP *We were Rats* IV. xlvi. 252 Wailed the [Cairene] woman. 'Gibbit *bucksheesh*. Gibbit *mungareer*.'

mungo[4]. Substitute for def.: A fabric made from the short fibres recovered from old hard-woven or felted material. Add further examples.

1961 BLACKSHAW & BRIGHTMAN *Dict. Dyeing & Textile Printing* 116 *Mungo*, the poorest grade of *shoddy*, being that obtained from rags, etc., and from materials which have been felted. **1968** [see *FIBRO, FIBRO 1].

mungofa. (Earlier example.)

1836 J. E. HOLBROOK *N. Amer. Herpetol.* I. 41 *Testudo polyphemus*—Daudin. Synonymes... Gopher and Mungofa, *Vulgo*.

‖ **muni** (mu·ni). *Hinduism & Jainism.* Also **moonee.** [a. Skr. *múni* impulse, eagerness (?), one moved by inward impulse, a seer, saint, etc., f. *man* to think.] An inspired or holy man; a sage; an ascetic or hermit.

1785 C. WILKINS tr. *Bhăgvăt-Gēētā* ii. 41 A man is said to be confirmed in wisdom, when he forsaketh every desire which entereth into his heart, and of himself is happy, and contented in himself... Such a wise man is called a *Mōōnēē*. **1796** [see *DHARMA]. **1811** W. WARD *Acct. of Hindoos* II. 46 How the moonees instruct their disciples in the different kinds of learning. **1828** H. H. WILSON in *Asiatick Res.* XVI. 18 The *Chárvákas* were so named from one of their teachers, the Muni Chárváka. **1854** M. MÜLLER in C. C. J. Bunsen *Christianity & Mankind* III. 285 The Turanian life is no longer a family life, or the life of a troglodyte Muni. **1866** E. T. DALTON in *Jrnl. Asiatic Soc. of Bengal* XXXV. II. (Special Number) 160 There is no tradition even of the 'Munis' having sought retreats amongst its rocks or by its waterfalls for their devotional exercises. **1875** MONIER-WILLIAMS *Indian Wisdom* x. 260 Let him remain without fire, without habitation, feeding on roots and fruits, practising the vow of a Muni. **1949** A. DANIÉLOU *N. Indian Music* I. ii. 39 Mataṅgā Muni considers that the word deśhī (worldly) applies to all earthly music. **1969** W. R. TRASK tr. *Eliade's Yoga* (ed. 2) viii. 327 Let us recall the *muni* of the *Rg-Veda* who, 'in the intoxication of ecstasy', mounted the 'chariot of the winds'. **1971** *Illustr. Weekly India* 11 Apr. 17/1 The Jain Munis believe that the body is a great source of sin and must be subjugated and won over. **1972** P. HOLROYDE *Indian Music* iii. 74 The most famous of all their musical theoreticians: Bharata Muni.

Munich (miū·nik). [G. *München.*] The name of the capital of Bavaria used with reference to a meeting of representatives of Germany, Great Britain, France, and Italy on 29 September 1938, when (by the Munich Agreement) the Sudetenland of N. Czechoslovakia was ceded to Germany; also *transf.* as a typical example of dishonourable appeasement. Hence **Munichee·r, Mu·nichite,** advocates of such an appeasement policy. Also **Mu·nichism,** such a policy. Also *attrib.*

1938 H. NICOLSON *Diary* 8 Oct. (1966) I. 376 Go up to Leicester. Bertie Jarvis says that I have put the women's vote against me by abusing Munich. **1939** *Ann. Reg. 1938* 76 The Prime Minister followed with his defence of the Munich Agreement. **1939** A. HUXLEY *After Many a Summer* I. viii. 106 These last months, since the *Anschluss* and Munich, one had found that political discussion was one of the unpleasant things it was wise to avoid. **1939** L. MACNEICE *Autumn Jrnl.* 36 Glory to God for Munich. **1941** *Amer. Speech* XVI. 66/1–2 *Munichism*..'the spirit of the surrender at Munich; appeasement'. **1942** *R.A.F. Jrnl.* 27 June 13 They do not enter into discussions with dishonourable men..; they have always known the real futility of 'Munichs'. **1942** *Sun* (Baltimore) 5 Aug. 4 (*heading*) Writer finds people hostile to war officialdom, Commons and Municheers. **1944** H. G. WELLS *'42 to '44* 76 The misconduct of the war from Munich onward. **1950** A. WILSON *Such Darling Dodos* 88 Tony was not..unpatriotic, but he had been a great Munichite. **1955** *Ann. Reg. 1954* 24 A further complication..was the absence of normal diplomatic relations between a number of countries... Someone had to provide a channel of communication, even at the risk of being called a 'Municheer'. **1957** R. W. ZANDVOORT in *Wiener Beiträge* LXV. 281 *Munich*.. giving rise to the words *Municheers* and *anti-Municheers*. **1958** *Spectator* 6 June 735/2 The pressure put upon President Benes to accept the Munich agreement. **1960** C. DAY LEWIS *Buried Day* v. 97 The hallucinatory and irresponsible Munich period. **1962** M. FOOT *Aneurin Bevan* I. ix. 285 At Bridgwater, Vernon Bartlett,..won a spectacular victory in the teeth of all the 'peace' propaganda of the Munichites. **1967** *Listener* 5 Oct. 422/3 There are analogies from history—another Munich, another Dunkirk [etc.]—although historians assure us that history never repeats itself. **1973** K. GILES *File on Death* i. 7 Some of the most valuable men in this country were..Men of Munich, vulgarly so called. Now..we have little Munichs every week.

municipal, *a.* Add: *municipal law* (see quot. 1959).

1959 JOWITT *Dict. Eng. Law* II. 1201/1 *Municipal law*, that which pertains solely to the citizens and inhabitants of a State, and is thus distinguished from political law and the law of nations. **1965** *Mod. Law Review* XXVIII. 626 There is a useful review of municipal decisions which points to some areas of prospective conflict between community law and municipal law. **1971** *Ibid.* XXXIV. 602 A miscellany of other changes in United Kingdom law will have to be introduced in order to bring municipal law into closer harmony with Community law.

municipalization. (Later examples.)

1958 *Economist* 13 Dec. 967/2 When Labour's election manifesto two weeks ago turned its back on the party's previous extraordinary scheme for the compulsory municipalisation of virtually all rented houses, Conservative propagandists growled angrily like a dog that was being deprived of a bone. **1970** *Internat. & Compar. Law Quarterly* 4th Ser. XIX. II. 211 The Dutch have..a system of nationalisation of housing with 85 per cent of all housing in municipal ownership. Nor is this a development occasioned by wartime devastation, as municipalisation can be traced back to a statute of 1905. **1972** *Guardian* 2 Nov. 12/4 Anthony Crosland..puts the case for the large-scale municipalisation of low-income rented housing. **1974** *Daily Tel.* 12 Jan. 5/2 The 'municipalisation' of privately rented property—except where the owner-occupier shares a house with a tenant—would be encouraged.

municipalize, *v.* (Later examples.)

1955 *Times* 1 June 7/2 The first action of the revolutionaries was to abolish, without compensation, all private ownership of land; a little later most urban dwellings were 'municipalized'. **1973** *Times* 25 Sept. 17/2 The programme of municipalization includes the building societies. .. It also includes the expensive commitment to municipalize rented housing.

municipalizer (miuni·sipăləizəɹ). [f. MUNICIPALIZE *v.* + -ER[1].] One who favours municipal control of public services, institutions, and the like; = MUNICIPALIST a.

1908 G. B. SHAW *Commonsense of Municipal Trading* p. ix, The most..disinterested of them would..become ardent municipalizers. **1928** *Weekly Dispatch* 24 June 9/3 Within the movement there are (1) prohibitionists,.. (2) municipalisers; (3) advocates of State ownership and control.

municipally, *adv.* Add: **b.** *Comb.*, as *municipally-owned* adj.

1898 E. HOWARD *To-Morrow* vi. 65 It may be found—especially on municipally-owned land—that the field of municipal activity may grow so as to embrace a very large area, and yet the municipality claim no rigid monopoly. **1972** *Guardian* 4 Dec. 6/8 Hull Corporation.. runs the only municipally-owned telephone service in the country.

|| **municipio** (miunisi·pio, -tʃi·pio). [Sp. and It.] A municipality; a corporation, a town council. Also *attrib.*

1896 G. BELL *Let.* 14 Apr. (1927) I. 35 The Municipio appeared in splendid gondolas hung with streamers. **1938** E. HEMINGWAY *Fifth Column* (1939) 275 No one will make any trouble forme in Cortina. I know them at the municipio. **1948** K. DAVIS *Human Society* 317 The *municipios* of Latin America (somewhat similar to our New England townships). **1965** *Language* XLI. 471 All are natives of the large municipio town of Xochistlahuaca, Guerrero. **1972** *Country Life* 2 Mar. 508/1 French is as much in evidence as Italian [in Valle d'Aosta]...it strikes one as odd seeing the word *Mairie* over an Italian Municipio.

munition, *sb.* Add: **2.** Also *colloq.*, the production of munitions; munition-work. *Ministry of Munitions*: a ministry which from 1915 to 1921 controlled the manufacture and supply of munitions. So *Minister of Munitions*.

1915 *Times* 26 May 9/6 The Prime Minister has decided that a new Department shall be created, to be called the Ministry of Munitions. **1915** *Act* 5 & 6 *Geo. V* c. 54 § 4 If the Minister of Munitions considers it expedient..that any establishment in which munitions work is carried on should be subject to the special provisions, [etc.]. **1917** HALL CAINE *Our Girls* i. 11 By permission of Mr. Montague, the Minister of Munitions..we are at the gates of the great Arsenal. **1917** *Dalton* (Lancs.) *Guardian* 28 Apr. 3/5 He had been sent to munitions, and had not been out to the front. **1924** B. GILBERT *Bly Market* 66, I expect..you'll be leaving the schooling and go to the munitions. **1925** D. CARNEGIE *Hist. Munitions Supply in Canada* xxvi. 251 Mr. H. E. Morgan..was sent out to Canada from the Ministry of Munitions. **1935** A. J. CRONIN *Stars look Down* II. vii. 301 There was a future in munitions... They were going to put up a line of sheds..filling sheds. **1957** *Encycl. Brit.* XV. 963/1 On the formation of the first wartime coalition government in 1915, a major change in organization was made by setting up a ministry of munitions, with David Lloyd George as the first minister.

5. *munition factory, girl, -maker, -making, work, worker, works*; also *munitions work, worker*.

1909 *Westm. Gaz.* 9 Oct. 2/2 In 1895 he visited the chief firearm and munition factories of France. **1921** G. A. B. DEWAR *Great Munition Feat* v. 112 The notion that a munition factory was a place full of shirkers and profiteers is grossly ignorant. **1916** M. COSENS (*title*) Lloyd George's munition girls. **1918** *Daily Mirror* 12 Nov. 6/2 Soldiers, sailors, munition girls and mere civilians clung on anywhere. **1916** *Home Companion* 12 Aug. 16/1 This is my last chat to you, little mother munition-makers. **1916** 'B. CABLE' *Doing their Bit* 24 No man or lathe or tool that can be turned to munition-making is possibly doing anything else. *Ibid.* 40 Anything less promising of munition work it would be hard to find. **1918** *Times* 27 Mar. 3/1 These are all chapters in the romance of munitions work in the Midlands. **1915** *Daily Sketch* 18 Aug. 2 (*heading*) Badges for the volunteer munition worker. **1915** W. OWEN *Let.* 16 Oct. (1967) 359 Dr. Rayner says I should become a Munitions Worker at Birmingham. **1925** D. CARNEGIE *Hist. Munitions Supply in Canada* xxvi. 250 One manufacturer said that it cost him approximately $300 to train each munition worker. **1957** *Encycl. Brit.* XV. 964/1 Specialist ladies were set up to deal with the health of munitions workers, especially women. **1917** W. OWEN *Let.* 7 Sept. (1967) 491 The other owner of a large Munition Works. **1932** H. SIMPSON *Boomerang* xvi. 436 The women were haring off to munition-works at five pounds a week. **1940** G. D. H. & M. COLE (*title*) Murder at the munition works.

munition, *v.* Add: **3.** *intr.* To do munition work; to work in a munition factory.

1916 'B. CABLE' *Doing their Bit* 23 A man cast for a commission and refused for the ranks a year ago on account of his eyes has 'gone munitioning'.

munitioneer (miuniʃəniə·ɹ). [f. MUNITION *sb.* + -EER.] A worker in a munition factory.

1916 E. V. LUCAS *Vermilion Box* 254 In the need for copper there is quite a good price for engraved plates, and theirs have been weeded out for the munitioneers. **1919** *Athenæum* 23 May 360/1 'Trinitrotoluene', which the munitioneers shortened to T.N.T. **1927** W. DEEPING *Kitty* xxvii. 342 The men..returned to a land that was not full of heroes... The voice of the yellow dog was heard in it, the snarl of the ex-munitioneer. **1940** *New Statesman* 19 Oct. 376 The munitioneer can see no difference in the management or control of his factory.

munitioner. Add: **c.** = *MUNITIONEER; a maker of ammunition.

1917 *Graphic* 30 June 806 (*caption*) The King with his munitioners.

munitionette (miuniʃəne·t). *colloq.* [f. MUNITION *sb.* + -ETTE.] A female worker in a munition factory.

1915 *Daily Sketch* 9 Nov. 13/1 (*heading*) Munitionettes who receive threepence an hour. **1917** *Daily News* 17 May 3/1 A shell-shop filled with blue-clad mob-capped cheering munitionettes. **1919** *Punch* 7 May 366/2 Work for the ex-munitionette drawing unemployment pay. **1935** A. J. CRONIN *Stars look Down* II. xiii. 381 He had taken a little flutter with a munitionette from the Wirtley Works.

munitionless (miuni·ʃənlės), *a.* [MUNITION *sb.* + -LESS.] Not provided with munitions.

1927 W. S. CHURCHILL *World Crisis 1916–18* I. 224 The mastered agony of the munitionless retreat, the slowly regathered forces;..has he no share in these?

munitionment (miuni·ʃənmĕnt). [f. MUNITION *v.* + -MENT.] Provision with or supply of munitions; munitions collectively.

1915 H. BELLOC in *Land & Water* 29 May 10*/1 If the Austro-German forces under the effect of superior munitionment for the heavy pieces do pierce their opponent's line. **1917** [see *GUNNING *vbl. sb.* 3]. **1929** J. BUCHAN *Courts of Morning* I. 133 Science has now created a norm of weapon and munitionment, which is substantially the same for all armies. **1930** H. JACKSON *Anatomy of Bibliomania* I. VIII. v. 167 Whether they have proved successful as armour or not, they [*sc.* Bibles] are no despicable munitionment of war in other respects.

Munro (mɒnrōu·). *Mountaineering.* Name applied to Scottish mountains of at least 3,000 feet after Sir H. T. *Munro*, who published a list of all such peaks in the Journal of the Scottish Mountaineering Club for 1891.

1903 *Jrnl. Scottish Mountaineering Club* VII. 366 The view from the top was magnificent, all the big Munros in the neighbourhood showing up clear and resplendent. **1972** D. HASTON *In High Places* i. 3 These [*sc.* 'the bigger hills of Scotland'] are relatively small, mostly around 3,000 feet, and called 'Munros'. **1973** SILLAR & MEYLER *Skye* x. 188 Between then [*sc.* 1889] and 1891 H. T. Munro —later Sir Hugh Munro—listed Scottish peaks over 3,000 ft... These are known among Scottish mountaineers as 'Munros'.

Munsell (mɒ·nsĕl). The name of the American Albert H. *Munsell* (1858–1918), used *attrib.* in connection with his classification of colours by means of the three quantities hue, 'value' (lightness or brightness), and chroma, each of which can be assigned, for any particular colour, a numerical value on prescribed scales.

1905 H. E. CLIFFORD in A. H. Munsell *Color Notation* 4 The Munsell photometer..is an instrument of wide range, high precision, and great sensitiveness, and permits the valuations which are necessary in his system to be accurately made. **1913** [see *colour-balance* (*COLOUR *sb.*[1] 17)]. **1937** *Discovery* Oct. 325/2 Other well-known systems besides Ostwald's, such as the American 'Munsell' colour-system. **1950** *Psychol. Abstr.* XXIV. 278/2 The key indicates the Munsell notation for each of the Ridgway color names. **1954** *Archit. Rev.* CXV. 198/2 The following colours from the Munsell range were used: putty-colour on metal panels below windows, [etc.]. **1957**, **1959** [see *CHROMA]. **1964** H. HODGES *Artifacts* xvii. 196 Colour readings using the Munsell Chart are, perhaps, most useful when considering the variation of firing conditions in a large sample of sherds of similar composition. **1971** *Jrnl. Gen. Psychol.* LXXXIV. 24 Ball is beginning to trace saturation changes in monochromatic input, employing Munsell Color Chips as matching targets.

munshi, var. MOONSHEE.

1849 [see MOONSHEE]. **1947** R. O. WINSTEDT *Malays* 152 His father was *munshi* to William Marsden. **1968** D. DUFF *Victoria in Highlands* 360 Abdul Karim advanced to become the Queen's India Secretary and was thereafter known as the Munshi Hafiz Abdul Karim... The Munshi's privileged position led to much opposition. **1975** *Times* 26 July 7/6 The language teacher, or munshi..was larger than I expected.

Munster (mu·nstəɹ). Also **Muenster, Münster.** The name of a town in the Haut-Rhin Department of France used *attrib.* and *absol.* to designate a strongly flavoured, semi-soft cheese made in the Munster valley.

1902 *Encycl. Brit.* XXV. 336/2 Cows are grazed on the S. Vosges in summer and large quantities of cheese (Münster cheese) are made and exported. **1946** G. MILLAR *Horned Pigeon* xvii. 245 A fat chicken, a bottle of Burgundy, and a Münster cheese. **1947** M. GIVEN *Encycl. Cooking* I. 661 Muenster... Ripened 2 or 3 months to develop pronounced flavour. **1954** H. SMITH *Classical Recipes of World* 379 Munster, a French semi-hard, whole-milk fermented cheese. **1960** E. DAVID *French Provincial Cooking* 34 A little bowl of caraway seeds came with the Münster, a strong, rich, creamy textured cheese which, at the right stage of ripeness, is one of the great cheeses of France. *Ibid.* 87 The Münster cheese of Alsace. **1971** *Sunday Times* (Colour Suppl.) 28 Mar. 34/2 The softer a Münster looks the creamier it will be.

munt (munt). *S. Afr.* and *Rhodesian slang.* [ad. Bantu *umuntu*, sing. of *abantu* (see *BANTU *a.* and *sb.*), lit. a person, black person, servant.] A black African: usu. as a term of contempt.

[**1926** G. CALLAWAY *Fellowship of Veld* iii. 25 To the Native the qualities which go to make up *ubuntu*, the qualities which make an *umntu* (person), are largely social. **1937** E. G. MALHERBE *Educational Adaptations in Changing Society* xx. 500 Standard of development will be judged by the extent to which the Native has ceased to be an Umuntu and has become a European.] **1948** O. WALKER *Kaffirs are Lively* 77 It's the towns that muck the *munt* up. **1953** N. GORDIMER *Lying Days* I. iii. 35 Man, there's a whole lota niggers round Ockerts', all over the garden and in the street and everywhere. Just a lot of munts from the Compound. **1962** *New Statesman* 24 Aug. 218/1 The old 'munt', as the African is still widely and insultingly termed. **1964** *Listener* 13 Feb. 257/1 His friends were muttering..about 'cheeky munts', which is the insulting white Rhodesian term for Africans. **1972** P. DRISCOLL *Wilby Conspiracy* (1973) xxiv. 309, I used the whistle too, of course, but those two munts in the truck didn't even hear it.

muntjak. Substitute for def.: A small south-Asian deer of the genus *Muntiacus*, which has been introduced into parts of western Europe. (Later examples.)

1939 *Geogr. Jrnl.* XCIV. 429 The Chinese tufted muntjac, or Mickie's tufted deer. **1963** *Times* 13 Mar. 14/7 A muntjac buck ventured into a well-populated corner of Hertfordshire to lie up beneath a hedge of holly in a secluded garden. **1965** D. MORRIS *Mammals* 384 Muntjacs are usually found singly or in pairs in the thick undergrowth. **1971** *Guardian* 8 Dec. 12/2, I have had the sad task of identifying the corpse of a Muntjac. **1973** *Country Life* 29 Nov. 1763/3 Besides red deer and roe, muntjac have also recently been reported among the Thetford trees.

Muntz (mɒnts). The name of George Frederick *Muntz* (1794–1857), English political reformer and metallurgist, used (now always in *Muntz metal*) to designate a type of brass he patented (*Brit. Pat. 6325* (1832), *11,410* (1846)) that contains about 55–64 per cent of copper (often with 1 per cent or more of lead), can be readily hot-worked, and is used esp. in shipbuilding.

1860 *Chambers's Encycl.* I. 159/1 Muntz sheathing-metal, 16 [parts] copper and 10⅔ zinc. *c* **1865** J. WYLDE *Circle of Sciences* I. 376/1 An alloy of copper,..called Muntz's metal, is..employed for sheathing ships' bottoms. **1866** H. E. ROSCOE *Less. Elem. Chemistry* xxv. 217 The yellow, or muntz metal, used for the sheathing of ships, contains sixty per cent. of copper. **1887** D. A. LOW *Introd. Machine Drawing & Design* xiv. 58 The piston..is attached to a Muntz metal piston rod. **1930** *Engineering* 17 Jan. 68/2 Details of the water cut-offs, consisting of a combination of Muntz metal plates, asphalte and iron sheeting. **1963** *Listener* 17 Jan. 114/2 The Cutty Sark Society is offering an original sheet of Muntz metal [from the hull of the ship] to anyone who pays for a new one. **1969** E. N. SIMONS *Dict. Alloys* 112 Typical Muntz Metal parts are heavy plates, bolting and valve stems, heat-exchanger tubes, hot forgings, and brazing rods for copper alloys and cast iron.

munyeroo (mɒ:nyərū·). *Austral.* Also **munyeru.** [Aboriginal name.] A small, succulent herb, *Claytonia balonnensis*, of the family Portulacaceæ; also, the paste made from its ground seeds mixed with water, formerly used as food by Aborigines in central Australia.

1896 E. C. STIRLING in B. Spencer *Rep. Horn Sci. Exped. Central Austral.* IV. 56 In these districts 'Mŭnyeru' takes the place of the spore cases of 'Nardoo'.., which is so much used in the Barcoo and other districts to the south and east. **1934** A. RUSSELL *Tramp-Royal in Wild Austral.* xx. 127 The munyeroo, a form of pigweed, was also plentiful... The natives collect the seed in large quantities and pound it into flour for bread; they also eat the leaves fresh, both as a food and to relieve thirst. **1935** *Bulletin* (Sydney) 1 May 20/2 The succulent leaves of the munyeroo and parakylia, which the birds feed upon, provide sufficient moisture for their needs. **1941** I. L. IDRIESS *Great Boomerang* xxiii. 174 Some passing shower has fallen here, and the yellow gold is the munyeroo plant in flower. **1956** *Landfall* X. 97 Small black and brown munyeru seeds.

muon (miū·ǫn). *Nuclear Physics.* [f. *MU(-MESON + *-ON[1].] A lepton that appears to be almost identical to the electron, except for being unstable and having a mass about 207 times greater, and is the chief constituent of cosmic radiation at the surface of the earth. (Orig. called a mu-meson, but now no longer classed as a meson.)

1953 *Sci. News Let.* 3 Jan. 14/1 About 20 or so particles exist in or can be knocked out of the atoms. Some of these are well-known oldtimers, like the electron... Others are new and stranger, like the pions, the muons, the V-particles. **1958** *Engineering* 4 Apr. 430/2 The fusion of hydrogen and deuterium (p—D reaction) catalysed by negative muons. The part played by the muon is to bind the two nuclei in a mesic molecular ion, so bringing them close enough together for fusion to occur. **1961** *Guardian* 21 Jan. 2/4 Muons were first discovered in the naturally occurring cosmic rays and identified precisely in 1947.. at Bristol University. **1968** M. S. LIVINGSTON *Particle Physics* iv. 74 Muons are the 'penetrating' component of the ionizing particles in cosmic radiation observed beneath great layers of earth in salt mines. *Ibid.*, Slow μ^- muons can also displace electrons in atomic orbits and form temporarily stable atoms... Eventually, the muon decays into an electron and two neutrinos. **1968** *Times* 28 Nov. 14/1 The muons are created by the collision of cosmic rays with matter in the upper atmosphere of the earth. **1972** *Nature* 14 July 86/1 The mass difference of the electron and muon poses one of the inscrutable problems of particle physics. Except for the mass difference the muon does not appear to be any different from the electron. **1974** *Ibid.* 2 Aug. 377/2 Muons are more penetrating than any other charged particles.

b. Special Comb.: **muon number**, a quantum number assigned to sub-atomic particles that is ± 1 for muons and their neutrinos and 0 for other particles and is conserved in all known interactions.

1961 *Physical Rev.* CXXIII. 1439/2 The possibility of essentially imaginary relative parities can only arise when some quantum number (here, muon number) is multiplicatively conserved. **1970** D. B. LICHTENBERG *Unitary Symmetry* i. 7 Other important symmetries are the invariances under gauge transformations. These sym-

metries are associated with conservation of charge Q, baryon number B, and two lepton numbers, the electron number L_e and the muon number L_μ.

Hence **muo·nic** *a.*, of, pertaining to, or involving a muon, or an atom having a negative muon orbiting the nucleus.

1955 S. S. SCHWEBER et al. *Mesons & Fields* II. 369 The same considerations lead to the conclusion that the two neutrinos ejected in μ decay are like neutrinos, even though a Dirac theory of neutrinos opens the possibility that one is an anti-neutrino... Such conclusions are important in calculating expectations for the muonic processes. **1965** *New Scientist* 1 July 36/1 Studies of the so-called 'muonic' X-ray spectra do not call for high energies. **1969** *Sci. Jrnl.* July 44/1 In a dense material, a muon is slowed down to a velocity corresponding to 1 keV in about 1 nanosecond, after which it is captured into a 'Bohr orbit', forming a hydrogen-like atom known as a muonic atom. **1972** *Physics Bull.* Mar. 149/2 Muonic molecules are systems in which a negative muon binds together two nuclei. Some examples are $(p\mu^-p)^+$, $(p\mu^-d)^+$, and $(d\mu^-d)^+$, and in practice only such ionic states are of interest. **1972** *Sci. Amer.* Nov. 104/3 The behavior of muonic atoms has provided much information about the structure of the nucleus, particularly about the distribution of protons within nuclei.

muonium (miū,ōu·niŏm). *Nuclear Physics.* [f. *MUON + -IUM, after *POSITRONIUM.] A short-lived neutral system, analogous to an atom, consisting of a (usu. positive) muon bound to an electron.

1957 FRIEDMAN & TELEGDI in *Physical Rev.* CV. 1681/2, μ^+ can form 'muonium', i.e. (μ^+e^-). **1960** *Physical Rev. Lett.* V. 63/1 The present Letter reports the formation of muonium in pure argon gas. *Ibid.*, Muonium..can be formed when a positive muon is slowed down in matter and captures an electron from an atom in the stopping material. **1964** S. DEBENEDETTI *Nuclear Interactions* viii. 593 The absence of muonium annihilation, despite the fact that both muons and electrons behave separately as simple Dirac particles, furnishes further evidence for the basic difference between electrons and muons. **1970** G. K. WOODGATE *Elem. Atomic Struct.* ii. 20 The equation therefore applies to all the hydrogenic atoms hydrogen, deuterium, tritium, muonium, positronium, etc.

‖ **muraji** (murā·dʒi). Also, with prefixed ō- 'great'. [Jap.] In early imperial Japan, one of the hereditary titles for a family or clan (cf. *KABANE) who claimed their descent from other gods than the divine ancestors of the emperor. Also, **ō-muraji**, the representative of this family when he was entrusted with affairs of state.

1901 F. BRINKLEY *Japan* I. iii. 53 Such titles as 'great body' (*omi*), 'master of the multitude' (*muraji*), 'honourable intermediary' (*nakatomi*) and so on, were employed as terms of respect, and ultimately passed into use as official titles. *Ibid.*, The head of the clan then came to be distinguished by the prefix *O* (great or senior); as *O-mi* (the senior honourable person), *O-muraji* (the great master of the multitude), and so on. **1931** G. B. SANSOM *Japan* I. ii. 37 The *ō-muraji*, territorial administrative officers of high rank who traced their descent from gods other than the divine ancestors of the emperor. *Ibid.* 39 It became the custom to describe the more important members of a clan or corporation by the name of their hereditary office or by some honorific title granted by the court. Thus we have *muraji*, which means 'leader of a group'. **1964** *Japan* (Unesco) (ed. 2) i. 16/2 The clans..had *kabane* (hereditary family title), to show the status of their families. *Kabane* were divided into *omi, muraji, kimi, atai, obito, miyatsuko* and *fubito*. **1970** J. W. HALL *Japan from Prehist. to Mod. Times* v. 37 Spokesmen chiefs, *Ō-omi* and *Ō-muraji*, were named to serve as chief ministers of state.

mural, *sb.* Restrict † *Obs.* to sense in Dict. and add: **2.** [Short for *mural painting* (MURAL *a.*[1] 2 a).] A painting executed on a wall or ceiling as part of a scheme of decoration. So *mural painter.* orig. *U.S.*

1921 *Quill* Mar. 23 I'm doing big things... 'They satisfy' and such outdoor murals. **1929** *Arts & Decoration* Oct. 63 (*heading*) Arresting murals of classic inspiration in the Long Island home of F. Russell. **1931** H. CRANE *Let.* 4 Nov. (1965) 385 He's fundamentally a mural painter, and even his smaller paintings have a tremendous *scale.* **1936** R. E. SHERWOOD *Idiot's Delight* II. i. 76 He has been out in Australia doing colossal murals for some government building. **1946** H. FEIBUSCH *Mural Painting* 15 H. J. K. Tisdall, the mural painter, helped me with his wide knowledge of technique and materials. **1949** F. MACLEAN *Eastern Approaches* I. ii. 18 The Customs' building [in the frontier station of Negoreloye]..was a fine big, bright room, decorated with murals depicting scenes from Soviet life. **1954** T. GUNN *Fighting Terms* 43 Turn your closed eyes to see upon these walls A mural scratched there by an earlier man. **1964** MRS. L. B. JOHNSON *White House Diary* 17 July (1970) 181 There was a great mural in the Library by Thomas Hare Benton. **1973** F. TAUBES *Painter's Dict. of Materials & Methods* 159 Only a certain portion of a large mural can be completed in one day's work. **1974** *Impressionism* (R. Acad.) 32/2 Saint-Sulpice murals, completed 1861, were a revelation for young artists.

mural, *a.*[1] Add: **2.** (Further example.)

1916 H. F. OSBORN *Men of Old Stone Age* 316 This Art.. is also mural or parietal.., consisting of drawings, engravings, paintings and bas-reliefs on the walls of caverns and grottos.

muralled, *a.* Restrict *rare* to sense in Dict. and add: **2.** Decorated with murals. Cf. *MURAL *sb.* 2.

1962 *UCLA Librarian* (Los Angeles) 25 May 106 The oaken walls and muraled ceiling of the drawing room were pulsing with sweet sound. **1967** A. WEST in *Coast to Coast 1965–6* 218 Stella watched the shadows..as they bobbed on the muralled wall.

muramic (miūᵊræ·mik), *a.* *Biochem.* [f. L. *mūr-us* wall + AM(INE + -IC.] *muramic acid*: an amino-sugar, $C_9H_{17}NO_7$, which is present in combined form in the cell walls of bacteria and in bacterial spores.

1957 *Nature* 27 Apr. 841/2 An acidic hexosamine, first found in a product from bacterial spores, which Strange has provisionally characterized as 3-O-α-carboxyethyl hexosamine and has named 'muramic acid'. **1969** [see *MUREIN]. **1973** *Physiol. Plant Path.* III. 366 Muramic acid and glucosamine are less stable to acid hydrolysis than are amino acids.

‖ **murchana** (mʊ̄·ɹtʃanā). Also **murcchana, murchhana.** [a. Skr. *mūrchanā* modulation.] (See quots.)

1891 C. R. DAY *Music in S. India* ii. 23 The s'rutis are arranged in their different svâras, or intervals of the scale, according to the 'murchanas'. Of what these murchanas consisted is very doubtful. *Ibid.* iv. 41 The following short melodies..show as much as possible the full murchanas of their respective râgas. **1914** [see *JATI, JÂTI]. **1921** H. A. POPLEY *Music of India* vi. 85 We shall notice..the graced notes, these being called in the north Mūrchanā. **1954** *Grove's Dict. Mus.* (ed. 5) IV. 457/1 Now it is clear that the *Sa-grâma* and the *Ma-grâma* are modes of one another. All the same, the Indian theory considers them as separate entities and derives seven octave scales (*mūrchanās*) from each of them. **1968** *Indian Mus. Jrnl.* V. 54 The term '*mūrcchanā*'. In the early sources this refers to an octave-species within a basic tuning-system... One or two 17th-century *śāstra-s*, on the other hand, use the term '*mūrcchanā*'..to refer to that 'pitch-area' within which the phrases of a *rāga* operate. **1972** P. HOLROYDE *Indian Music* 274 *Murchhana...* The word has been variously used: (a) It is the ancient name for the early modes in Indian music before the raga system emerged. (b) According to Popley's book,..murchhana in South India refers to ascending and descending varna or graph-like grace movements. (c) According to Tagore the murchhana is the extending of the note 'to another in the ascending as well as the descending scale (like an *appoggiatura*) without any intermediate break in the disposition of the srutis in the interval'.

murder, *sb.* Add: **1. e.** Phr. *to get away with murder*: see *GET *v.* 54 c.

f. An excellent or marvellous person or thing. *U.S. slang.*

1940 *Music Makers* May 37/3 *Murder*, something excellent or terrific... 'That's solid murder, gate!' **1943** M. SHULMAN *Barefoot Boy* ix. 90 We got on the dance floor just as a Benny Goodman record started to play. 'Oh, B.G.!' cried Noblesse... 'Man, he's murder, Jack.' **1948** H. L. MENCKEN *Amer. Lang.* Suppl. II. 707 The vocabulary of the jazz addict is largely identical with that of the jazz performer...anything excellent is *killer-diller, murder* or *Dracula.* **1970** C. MAJOR *Dict. Afro-Amer. Slang* 83 *Murder*, (1930's–40's) excellent; the best.

3. *to cry blue murder* (earlier and later examples); also *blue murder*, a loud or alarming noise, a great commotion, din, or disturbance; used in intensive phrases as *like blue murder*, at a terrific pace, at top speed. *colloq.*

1859 HOTTEN *Dict. Slang* 8 *Blue-murder*, a desperate or alarming cry. *c* **1874** D. BOUCICAULT in M. R. Booth *Eng. Plays of 19th Cent.* (1969) II. 228 They were standing by and thryving to screech blue murdher. 'Stop their mouths,' said a voice. **1893** G. B. SHAW in *World* 10 May 28/2 What it [*sc.* the slow movement of Stanford's Irish Symphony] does end in is blue murder. **1914** *Evening News* 1 Oct. 2/1 They were off down the road like blue murder. **1921** G. B. SHAW *Back to Methuselah* II. 84 You couldnt produce it. There would be blue murder. It's out of the question. **1959** 'A. GILBERT' *Death takes Wife* xiii. 164 Corpses don't yell blue murder.

4*. In *fig.* and hyperbolic use: (an act of) destruction or spoliation supposed to be tantamount to murder. Also in weakened senses: a situation or condition that is very unpleasant or undesirable.

1857 TROLLOPE *Barchester Towers* II. ii. 37 This cellar is perfectly abominable. It would be murder to put a bottle of wine into it till it has been roofed, walled, and floored... Goodenough never had a glass of wine that any man could drink. **1878** 'R. BOLDREWOOD' *Ups & Downs* ix. 90 What a murder that one should have all these hundredweights of nails,..and forests of posts and wallplates to get all over again! **1924** KIPLING *Debits & Credits* (1926) 316, I was never keen on bombin' myself... But bombin'-instruction's murder! **1951** J. B. PRIESTLEY *Festival at Farbridge* II. ii. 255 Cook's gone, and it's murder trying to do it all myself. **1956** A. J. LERNER *My Fair Lady* (1958) I. i. 8 By right she should be taken out and hung For the cold-blooded murder of the English tongue! **1960** H. PINTER *Room* in *Birthday Party*, etc. 105 *Rose.* You look cold. *Mrs Sands.* It's murder out. Have you been out? **1965** M. BRADBURY *Stepping Westward* i. 64 Private life was simple enough, but the communal centres were murder. **1973** A. ROSS *Dunfermline Affair* 69 An old hip injury... Not so bad when I'm just walking..but murder climbing stairs.

4.** A popular parlour or children's game for a number of participants, which involves a mock murder hunt, led by a 'detective', to find the 'murderer' of one who is playing dead, having been 'murdered' in the dark. Also called **murders, the murder game, murder in the dark.**

1933 PHILLIPS & WESTALL *Bk. Indoor Games* iv. 276 To give as good an idea of 'Murder' as we can, we will describe in narrative form an actual game. **1934** N. MARSH *Man lay Dead* i. 14 Silly games are played... It's going to be Murders this time. *Ibid.* 20 Are we really going to play the Murder Game? **1937** M. HILLIS *Orchids on your Budget* (1938) vi. 103 You can still serve refreshments after bingo played for pennies or the murder game. **1948** C. DAY LEWIS *Otterbury Incident* v. 59 We'd get him interested if we made a detective job of it—sort of Murder Game. **1964** R. JEFFRIES *Embarrassing Death* xii. 147 Did you ever play the game 'Murder'?.. Everybody but the murderer must tell the truth: the murderer may lie. **1972** G. BRANDRETH *Party Games* 24 Murder in the Dark. 6 or more players. A chilling game, definitely not for those with weak hearts.

5. *attrib.* and *Comb.*, as *murder bout, case, charge, film, gun, hunt, story, trial, victim, weapon*; **murder bag** (see quot. 1938); **murder book (file, log)**, a book or file in which are kept details of a police investigation of a murder; **murder game:** see sense 4**; **murder inquiry,** a police investigation into a case of murder; **murder investigation** = **murder inquiry*; **murder-man,** (*b*) a writer of murder stories; cf. *MURDERMONGER; **murder mystery,** a mysterious murder; *spec.* a murder story in which the murderer's identity is concealed by a complicated plot until the dénouement; **murder one** *U.S. colloq.*, (a charge of) first-degree murder; **murder rap** *slang* (orig. *U.S.*), a charge of murder; **murder room,** after the discovery of a murder, a (nearby) room used as a centre for directing a police inquiry into the crime; **murder squad,** a division of the police appointed to investigate crimes of murder.

1938 F. D. SHARPE *S. of Flying Squad* vi. 65 In the Superintendent's office at Scotland Yard repose two plain cowhide bags... They are the Murder Bags which contain all the tools which a detective is likely to need in solving a major crime. **1962** 'J. BELL' *Crime in our Time* v. iii. 156 He takes with him all the necessary apparatus for a detailed examination on the spot, the so-called 'murder bag'. **1972** 'A. GARVE' *Case of Robert Quarry* I. i. 8 Methodically checking the contents of his murder bag. **1972** J. WAINWRIGHT *Requiem for Loser* viii. 162 The final write-up would be bound into a single volume, called 'The Murder Book'. **1973** Murder Book [see *murder log* below]. **1906** HARDY *Dynasts* II. VI. vii. 298 Bonaparte and Alexander ..Are closing to a mutual murder-bout. **1930** A. CHRISTIE *Murder at Vicarage* xv. 118, I should never have suspected that Hawes would take such a keen interest in the details of a murder case. **1974** M. BIRMINGHAM *You can help Me* iii. 52 This is a murder case... To answer a few questions will hardly hurt her. **1937** 'M. INNES' *Hamlet, Revenge!* III. v. 297 There is nobody..who would wish to incriminate me in a murder charge. **1974** *Times* 15 Feb. 1/3 (*heading*) Murder charge after London shooting. **1967** W. KEENAN *Lonely Beat* iv. 39 He picked up the thick murder file... The reports were in chronological order. **1973** Murder File [see *murder log* below]. **1947** M. GILBERT *Close Quarters* xvi. 244 It was a murder film. **1939** E. S. GARDNER *D.A. draws Circle* (1940) v. 57 'What are they, Doug, fingerprints?' 'Yes, on the murder gun.' **1968** *Observer* 28 Apr. 8/2 (*heading*) Murder-hunt police appeal to motorists. **1972** J. WAINWRIGHT *Requiem for Loser* viii. 162 The enquiry was still 'The Murder Enquiry'. **1973** Murder enquiry [see *murder log* below]. **1937** 'M. INNES' *Hamlet, Revenge!* III. i. 220 The scene..suggested..a riot rather than a murder-investigation. **1973** R. LEWIS *Blood Money* iii. 28 This is a murder investigation. Give me your assistance. **1972** J. WAINWRIGHT *Requiem for Loser* viii. 162 The log was still 'The Murder Log'. **1973** —— *High-Class Kill* 123 Bits and pieces which are part of a murder enquiry—the Murder File, the Murder Log..and the Murder Book. **1889** Murder-man [see *blood-curdler* (*BLOOD *sb.* 18)]. **1900** ADE *Fables in Slang* 198 The Book that begins with a Murder Mystery. **1960** AUDEN *Homage to Clio* 26 The sin of Gluttony Is ranked among the Deadly Seven, but in murder mysteries One can be sure the gourmet Didn't do it. **1973** A. MACVICAR *Painted Doll Affair* vi. 68, I bought two of the paperbacks described as 'murder mysteries'. **1975** *Times* 22 Sept. 11/5 They..worked out a scheme about two lexicographers involved in a murder mystery. **1971** 'H. HOWARD' *Murder One* xiv. 177 Murray's going to stand trial charged with murder one. **1972** G. V. HIGGINS *Friends of Eddie Coyle* xxvi. 162 The three of them're up on murder one, they're gonna be having a hearing this afternoon. **1929** D. HAMMETT *Dain Curse* (1930) xv. 169 He hasn't a chance in the world of hanging murder-raps on them. **1972** J. POTTER *Going West* 57 Sergeant O'Leary said how about pulling her in on a murder rap. **1968** P. N. WALKER *Carnaby & Gaolbreakers* xv. 143 I'd like a room set aside as a Murder Room. **1972** G. SERENY *Case of Mary Bell* I. iii. 38 The 'Murder Room' at Newcastle's West End Police..was a hive of activity all night. **1929** M. A. GILL *Underworld Slang, Murder squad*, police who investigate murders. **1958** S. HYLAND *Who goes Hang?* xlv. 220 A straightforward fact..accepted by Macaulay and his murder squad. **1972** C. DRUMMOND *Death at Bar* iii. 84 Sergeant Reed had retired from the pub before the City of London murder squad arrived. **1831** M. EDGEWORTH *Let.* 16 Mar. (1971) 490 Rogers..told me..a capital murder-story. **1929** F. N. HART *Hide in Dark* i. 27 It's despicable to tell a murder story with the lights on. **1888** KIPLING *Let.* 2 May in C. E. Carrington *R. Kipling* (1955) v. 97 He has been concerned in most of the more

distinguished murder trials of the past twenty years. **1973** D. WESTHEIMER *Going Public* iii. 42 Lee went to the *Houston Post* and looked through back issues, studying murders and murder trials. **1971** *Guardian* 11 Dec. 10/5 The weekly number of murder victims [in India] is 283. **1959** M. GILBERT *Blood & Judgment* vii. 71 He had turned up.. the murder weapon, ready furnished with a print of the murderer. **1962** K. ORVIS *Damned & Destroyed* xii. 84 Fay's cap of heroin burned like a murder-weapon in my pocket. **1973** R. LEWIS *Blood Money* iv. 36 Frust..confirmed that..the poker..is the murder weapon.

murder, *v.* Add: **1. g.** (Later examples.)

1857 J. HYDE *Mormonism* vii. 181 These men will fight, lie, rob, murder for Mormonism if commanded. **1910** *New Mag.* Nov. 224/2 Yes. I am the man who murders for the king.

h. *colloq.*, as a jocular threat.

1939 JOYCE *Finnegans Wake* III. 460 So don't keep me now for a good boy for the love of my fragrant saint, you villain,..or I'll first murder you. **1942** T. RATTIGAN *Flare Path* II. ii. 66 *Patricia.* You're ill. I'm going to ring up a doctor. *Teddy.* I'll murder you if you do.

5. *slang.* To defeat (an opponent or rival) totally or conclusively, esp. at a game or sport.

1952 G. TALBOT in Wentworth & Flexner *Dict. Amer. Slang* (1960) 349/2 The National Leaguers..eat up south-paws. They murdered them all season. **1973** 'J. PATRICK' *Glasgow Gang Observed* v. 49 Mick had stepped in and challenged Bertie to a 'square-go'. 'Mick murdered him, man,' Tim recalled. **1974** *Observer* 24 Feb. 23/7 If the passing had got any worse, a team of corporals' grandmothers would have murdered them. They ran like fugitives from a church parade.

murderable (mɒ̄·ɹdərăb'l), *a.* [f. MURDER *v.* + -ABLE.] Giving cause for murder, provoking or inviting murder.

1920 D. H. LAWRENCE *Women in Love* ii. 32 A murderee is a man who is murderable. And a man who is murderable is a man who in a profound, if hidden lust, desires to be murdered. **1927** *Sunday Express* 21 Aug. 10/4 This tendency to associate unpopular opinions with murderable offences seems to be an increasing one on both sides of the Atlantic. **1966** *New Statesman* 18 Mar. 377/1 They had made good, and they *were* good; pre-eminently, they had achieved 'security'. And hence the immediate public terror caused by their murder: the least murderable people in the world, if they could be murdered, then anyone could be murdered.

murderee (mɒ̄ɹdərī·). [f. MURDER *v.* + -EE[1].] A person who is murdered. Also, a person whose character and disposition suggest the passive qualities of an easy victim of murder.

1920 D. H. LAWRENCE *Women in Love* ii. 32 It takes two people to make a murder: a murderer and a murderee. And a murderee is a man who is murderable. **1925** *New Yorker* 28 Mar. 13/2 Some day, somebody is going to write a mystery story in which the murderee will be a swell guy. **1928** F. T. JESSE *Trial of S. H. Dougal* 4 The potential murderer has met the born murderee. **1928** A. HUXLEY *Point Counter Point* xii. 209 He's the real type of murderee ..the obvious victim; he fairly invites maltreatment. **1939** —— *After Many a Summer* 20 You're probably the sort of person that invites persecution. A bit of a murderee ..as well as a scholar and a gentleman. **1958** S. HYLAND *Who goes Hang?* xii. 59, I don't *know* who the murdered man, the 'murderee', was. **1970** *Times Lit. Suppl.* 7 Aug. 883/1 This one hinges on the killing of one of those fiendishly attractive girls who, fictionally at least, are so often murderees. **1973** K. GILES *File on Death* vi. 151 Title wasn't much chop however you look at him, a murderee if ever I investigated one. **1974** *Sunday Times* 31 Mar. 52/3 TV Film...about Elizabeth Montgomery set up as possible next murderee in a storm.

murdermonger (mɒ̄·ɹdəɹmɒ:ŋgəɹ). [f. MURDER *sb.* + MONGER[1].] A dealer in murder, a professional murderer. So *fig.*, a writer of murder stories; fem. (*nonce-wd.*) **murdermongeress.** Also **murder-mongering** *vbl. sb.*, the purveying of news or stories of murder.

a **1889** in Barrère & Leland *Dict. Slang* (1889) I. 139/1 The only one who is annoyed is our own special murder-monger, who has got several blood-curdlers of English extraction up his sleeve. **1900** M. HEWLETT *Richard Yea-and-Nay* II. vi. 299 She knew something of the Marquess, her cousin. Any ally of his must be a murdermonger. **1957** O. NASH *You can't get there from Here* 97, I repeat that one book by this murder-mongeress [*sc.* Agatha Christie] Will last you as long as the Library of Congress. **1967** *Punch* 4 Oct. 524/3 You may think that the enormous sums of money spent on murder-mongering by the newspapers have bred up a lamentable race of scribes.

mureed, var. *MURID.

murein (miū^ə·rīn). *Biochem.* [f. L. *mūr-us* wall + *-ein*, after PROTEIN.] A polymeric substance whose molecules consist of mucopolysaccharide chains interlinked with short peptide chains and which is an important structural component of the cell walls of many bacteria.

1964 WEIDEL & PELZER in *Adv. Enzymol.* XXVI. 195 The new type of polymer from which bacterial sacculi are tailored. We propose the term 'murein',.., in analogy to the trivial name 'protein'. Various other designations presently in use, like 'mucocomplex' or 'mucopolymer', have little to recommend them because they would fit a variety of chemically rather different structures. The term 'mucopeptide' which has also been proposed, appears to be somewhat misleading for a polymer which is..at least as much a polysaccharide as it is a (poly)peptide. **1969** W. G. MURRELL in Gould & Hurst *Bacterial Spore* vii. 236 All spore mureins so far studied..differ from known cell wall polymers in having..a two- to three-fold excess of glucosamine or muramic acid residues over glutamic acid or DAP residues. **1969** *New Scientist* 10 July 64/1 Murein contains an amino sugar, muramic acid, which is not found in higher organisms, and also several amino acids in the unusual D-configuration. **1972** *Nature* 3 Mar. 10/1 The bacterial cell wall is bounded by a fragile cytoplasmic membrane... This is surrounded by, or interwoven with, a more rigid cell wall..built up from a limited number of constituents and known variously as mucopeptide, peptidoglycan or murein.

Muria (miū^ə·riă), *sb.* and *a.* Also **Morea, Moria.** [Native word.] **A.** *sb.* A member of a hill people of Bastar in India, a division of the Gonds. Cf. *GOND *sb.* and *a.* **B.** *adj.* Of or pertaining to this people.

1861 *Selections from Records of Govt. of India* (*Foreign Dept.*) xxx. 8 The Moreas are distributed over the north of the dependency and the vicinity of Jugdulpore, and the Marias to the south and west of it. *a* **1863** S. HISLOP *Aboriginal Tribes of Central Provinces* (1866) i. 22 *Moria Gonds.* These are more civilized than the Márias. *Ibid.* i. 23, I do not possess detailed information regarding the mythology of the Morias. **1877** V. BALL *Jrnl.* 18 Mar. in *Jungle Life in India* (1880) xiii. 620 According to the Dewan, the following are the names of the principal of these races; they are said to possess distinct languages: Bhatra, Muria (=Gond), Purji, Gudwa (or Gudaba), Jhoria, and Mariah or Meriah. **1938** W. V. GRIGSON *Maria Gonds of Bastar* I. iii. 37 In 1931 the tribes enumerated as Gonds in the previous three censuses were separately enumerated under the names Bhattra, Gond, Maria, Muria, Koya and Parja. **1968** P. C. AGARWAL *Human Geogr. Bastar District* xiii. 258 Burha Deo is the principal deity of the Muria tribe. **1971** [see *GOND *sb.* and *a.*].

murid (miū^ə·rī·d). Also **mooreed, mureed** [Arab. *murīd.*] A follower of a Muslim pir; a disciple; a member of the second order of the Sufi 'way', aspiring to join the third order.

1815 J. MALCOLM *Hist. Persia* II. xxii. 396 The person who makes the attempt [for the third class of Sufiism] must be a holy mooreed or disciple, who..has already made a progress that has placed him above the necessity of the common usages and forms of established religion. **1885** T. P. HUGHES *Dict. Islam* 421/2 *Murīd*,..'one who is desirous or willing'. A disciple of some *murshid*, or leader, of a mystic order. Any student of divinity. **1929** E. D. Ross tr. *H. Lammens's Islām* vi. 129 The *murīd* or novice aspiring to be admitted into the congregation. *Ibid.* 135 Admission into a *ṭarīqa* is preceded by a period of trial or noviciate, called *irāda*; whence the name *murīd* given to the *Ṣūfī* aspirant. **1967** F. RAHMAN *Islam* ix. 154 The absolute authority of the Ṣūfī leader, called Shaykh..over his disciples called *faqīr*,..*darwish*, *murīd*..or *ikhwān*.

Muridism (miū^ə·rī·diz'm). [f. *MURID + -ISM.] A revival movement in Islam encouraging the rising of Muslims against their religious and political opponents.

1866 *Chambers's Encycl.* VIII. 656/2 He was one of the zealous disciples of Kasi-Mollah, the great apostle of Muridism. **1875** C. HENEAGE tr. *Von Thielmann's Caucasus, Persia & Turkey* I. iv. 261 This movement, designated Muridism from the name Murid..borne by the initiated, constitutes one of the greatest events in the modern history of Islamism. *Ibid.* 262 The growth of Muridism was to the Russians a matter of fearful import. **1895** *Macmillan's Mag.* July 217/1 It was called Muridism, and was mainly if not avowedly borrowed from Sufism; it was held to be a strictly orthodox form of the Mahommedan religion. **1931** *Times Lit. Suppl.* 12 Feb. 111/2 The doctrine of Muridism united the Mohamedan sects in a common crusade against the Russians. **1973** HOWAT & TAYLOR *Dict. World Hist.* 1034/2 *Muridism*, Muslim mystical..movement originating in Shirvan in the 18th cent... The movement reached its peak under the third imam..and manifested strong egalitarian tendencies.

murillo, var. *MORILLO.

murine, *a.* and *sb.* Add: **A.** *adj.* **b.** Affecting mice or rats; esp. in *murine typhus* [tr. F. *typhus murin* (C. Nicolle et al. 1932, in *Compt. Rend.* CXCIV. 1706)].

1933 *Biol. Abstr.* VII. 395/1 The name 'historic typhus' is proposed for the African (Old-World) form, and 'murine' typhus for the other 2. **1940** *Jrnl. Exper. Med.* LXXII. 417 In marked contrast to the white mouse and cotton rat, the murine virus induces no symptoms whatever..in other rodents. **1947** J. C. SNYDER in F. H. Top et al. *Communicable Diseases* (ed. 2) lix. 879 Unlike the human body louse, which suffers a fatal infection with typhus, the rat flea is unharmed by the multiplication of murine typhus rickettsiae in its tissues. **1955** *Sci. Amer.* Jan. 74/3 Murine typhus, which occurs in many parts of the world including the U.S., is comparatively mild but closely related to epidemic typhus; an attack by one confers immunity after recovery against both. **1970** PASSMORE & ROBSON *Compan. Med. Stud.* II. xviii. 86/1 *Rickettsia prowazekii* is responsible for epidemic typhus, which is transmitted by lice. *R. mooseri* [sic] causes the milder endemic murine typhus, primarily a disease of rats, amongst which it is spread by the rat flea. *Ibid.* xix. 51/2 Murine typhus is not lethal to rats and hence is not accompanied by deviation of rat fleas to man on the scale found in murine bubonic plague.

murky, *a.* Add: **6.** Phr. *the murky past*: confused or 'dubious' happenings at a previous time; an obscure episode or period. Cf. PAST *sb.* 2.

1917 'CONTACT' *Airman's Outings* 141 At times the R.F.C. pilot, like the man with the murky past, is constrained to have clouds for a covering against attack. **1963** J. CLEUGH *Love locked Out* 11 St. Augustine, tormented by the murky past which had preceded his appointment as bishop of Hippo in North Africa. **1966** *Oxf. Univ. Gaz.* 23 Dec. 432/2 If I may go back into the murky past,..these sort of powers..would..have been used at least to influence planning..described..as precipitate and ill-considered.

murmanite (mɒ̄·ɹmănəit). *Min.* [ad. Russ. *murmanit* (A. E. Fersman 1923, in *Doklady̆ Ross. Akad. Nauk* 63), f. *Murman*, name of a shore on the north of the Kola peninsula in Russia + *-it* -ITE[1].] A hydrated silicate of sodium and titanium with lesser and variable amounts of manganese, zirconium, iron, calcium, and niobium, which is found as violet monoclinic crystals.

1924 *Mineral. Abstr.* II. 263 Various new primary occurrences were found for..a new mineral murmanite from Alluaiva, Angvunsiok, and Sengischorr. **1951** *Ibid.* XI. 240 Recalculation of analyses of murmanite..suggests a formula $(Na_2,Ca)TiSiO_5.xH_2O$ analogous to that of sphene. **1968** I. KOSTOV *Mineralogy* II. v. 298 Murmanite and lomonosovite form a complete isomorphous series and are monoclinic like sphene and fersmanite.

murmur, *sb.* Add: **5.** *Comb.* **murmur diphthong,** a diphthong ending with a weak (murmur) vowel; **murmur vowel,** a glide or weak vowel, a *SCHWA.

1892 H. SWEET *New Eng. Gram.* I. 234 There is another class of *murmur diphthongs* ending in (ə), as in *hear, here* (hiə), *fare, faire* (feə). **1933** O. JESPERSEN *Essentials Eng. Gram.* ii. 26 There are three kinds of diphthongs in English: (1) full (long-distance) diphthongs... (2) slow (short-distance) diphthongs... (3) murmur-diphthongs ending in the indistinct central vowel [ə]: [iə] as in *peer*, [eə] as in *pair*, [etc.]. **1965** A. D. CORDTS *Phonics* xii. 228 Today every basic reading system..recognizes the 'short' and 'long' vowel sounds, the diphthongs, the so-called murmur diphthongs and 'digraphs', [etc.]. **1910** Murmur vowel [see *BACK *a.* 1 c]. **1924** W. J. SEDGEFIELD in Mawer & Stenton *Introd. Survey Eng. Place-Names* I. II. i. 8 The vowel that was distinctly pronounced loses under the secondary stress its clear character and becomes either the obscure sound called by phoneticians the 'murmur-vowel' [ə] or an indistinct [i]. **1957** S. POTTER *Mod. Linguistics* i. 27 The inhabitants of Birmingham..call their city [bə:miŋgəm], but Londoners call it [bə:miŋəm]. .. Midlanders raise the velum against the wall of the pharynx and make a plosion with the back of the tongue upon it before passing from agma to the murmur-vowel, whereas the people of London keep the nasal pharynx open at this juncture. **1966** A. WIJK *Rules of Pronunciation for Eng. Lang.* iv. 64 The murmur vowel is..very common in both open and closed syllables when the stress falls on the immediately following syllable.

murmur, *v.* Add: **3.** Also with *out.*

1837 DICKENS *Pickw.* xxviii. 304 Gabriel murmured out something about its being very pretty. **1894** A. CONAN DOYLE *Mem. Sh. Holmes* 41 My lips were parted to murmur out some sleepy words of surprise or remonstrance.

murmuration. Delete † *Obs.* and add later example of sense 1.

1908 *Westm. Gaz.* 5 Aug. 2/1 The plaints and murmurations of these Randlords for the grievances which they clamoured to have redressed.

2. Delete 'An alleged term for' from def., and add later examples.

1932 AUDEN in *New Statesman* 16 July 69/1 Patterns a murmuration of starlings Rising in joy over wolds unwittingly weave. **1938** *Times* 6 Jan. 15/5 Great murmurations of starlings are often represented as a peculiar phenomenon of our own times. **1946** M. PEAKE *Titus Groan* 306 The clearing ended where a derelict stone building..held back a grove of leafless elms, where a murmuration of starlings was gathered. **1966** *Sunday Mail Mag.* (Brisbane) 6 Mar. 6/4 Starlings when they're on the wing have to labor under the collective title of murmuration.

murmured, *ppl. a.* Add: **murmured vowel,** = **murmur vowel*; also, a vowel-sound uttered with slow vibration of free vocal chords.

1933 L. BLOOMFIELD *Language* vi. 102 Some languages ..distinguish different voice-qualities, such as *muffled* vowels, *murmured* vowels, with slow vibration of the vocal chords, or *whispered* vowels. **1952** R. JAKOBSON et al. *Preliminaries to Speech Analysis* ii. 26 It is highly questionable whether there are languages in which..there actually is a..distinctive opposition of voiced and murmured vowels. **1966** M. PEI *Gloss. Linguistic Terminol.* 173 Vowels of weakly stressed syllables are sometimes murmured (reduced vowels), and they tend to lose their identity, contrary to fully voiced and whispered vowels.

murning, var. *MURRNONG.

Murphy[2]. Add: **3.** *Murphy's law*: a name humorously given to various aphoristic expressions of the apparent perverseness and unreasonableness of things (see quots.). orig. *U.S.*

1958 *Nation* (N.Y.) 7 June 506/1 There is an old military maxim known as Murphy's Law which asserts that wherever there is a bolt to be turned, someday there will be someone to turn it the wrong way. **1961** LEEDS & WEINBERG *Computer Programming Fund.* viii. 241 What we desire is the presentation of the information in such an accurate and complete form that the reader will be able to use the sub-routine correctly without hesitation or question. Recalling 'Murphy's law'—'If something can go wrong or be misinterpreted, it will'—should be enough stimulus for the goals we desire. **1962** J. GLENN in *Into Orbit* 85 We blamed human errors like this on what aviation engineers call 'Murphy's Law'. 'Murphy' was a fictitious character who appeared in a series of educational cartoons put out by the U.S. Navy... Murphy was a careless, all-thumbs mechanic who was prone to make such mistakes as installing a propeller backwards. **1970** *Sci. Amer.* June 143 Recently..I learned of a governing principle known as Murphy's first law of biology. It states: 'Under any given set of environmental conditions an experimental animal behaves as it damn well pleases.' **1972** *Oxf. Times* 22 Sept. 12/7 That malign influence which presides over human and typographical enterprises, and which is sometimes described as Murphy's Law ('Things are out to get us'). **1973** G. HART *Right from Start* i. 45 According to Murphy's law, if the worst possible thing can happen, it will. **1974** *N.Y. Times Mag.* 8 Sept. 33/1 'If anything can go wrong, it will,' says Murphy's Law.

4. Name given (in full, *Murphy game*) to a confidence trick in which the victim is duped by unfulfilled promises of money or sex, etc. So *Murphy man*, one who practises confidence tricks of this kind; *Murphy* v. trans., to dupe, to swindle by means of such a trick. *U.S. slang.*

1959 *Washington Post* 2 Oct. B 8/1 The 'Murphy game' is..a confidence game... The victim or 'pigeon' is lured by promises of a woman and then given..paper cut to bill size, in an envelope exchanged for the victim's cash. **1965** *N.Y. Times* 6 Apr. 1/3 Mayor Smitherman..and..a Selma lawyer..were 'murphyed' by the Negro confidence man at 2:30 A.M. today. **1965** *Time* 16 Apr. 16 'The Murphy game' is underworld argot for a slick maneuver in which a victim puts his cash in an envelope and gives it to the con man, who makes a fast sleight-of-hand switch and hands back an identical envelope stuffed with newspaper strips. **1966** *N.Y. Times* 4 Sept. iv. 5 Everybody should have a car... How are you going to get it?.. You know, you can get it playing the Murphy. **1968** W. LABOV et al. in A. Dundes *Mother Wit* (1973) 331 The right of a hand of some murphy man. **1970** C. MAJOR *Dict. Afro-Amer. Slang* 83 *Murphy*, a con game played on innocent (especially white) men who are expecting sex with a prostitute (usually black). **1972** T. KOCHMAN *Rappin' & Stylin' Out* 244 An adept hustler who was playing the 'murphy' game on a white trick. **1972** J. MILLS *Report to Commissioner* 52, I thought he was a complainant...some school kid who'd been Murpheyed. *Ibid.* 55 We stop in a bar..and it's filled with pimps, Murphy men, guys like that.

Murphy³ (mɒ̄·ɹfi). *N. Amer.* The name of William Lawrence *Murphy* (1876–1959), American manufacturer, used *attrib.* in *Murphy bed*, any of various types of folding beds, developed from an original design by Murphy.

1925 *Small Home* Mar. 31 (Advt.), The closet off the living-room has been equipped with a Murphy Bed. **1930** *N.Y. Times* 2 Mar. XIII. 10/2 (Advt.), Apartments Unfurnished... 40s East—Most charming one-room apartment in town; restaurant, telephone service, Murphy beds: $78.50. **1969** L. HELLMAN *Unfinished Woman* vi. 63 They lived in the Murphy-bed, modern apartments that were already the slums off Hollywood Boulevard. **1974** *Apartment Life* May E2/2 The concealed wall bed, best known as a Murphy bed in the 1930s, is coming out of the woodwork again.

murram (mɒ·răm). Also murrum. [Native name.] A hard lateritic material associated with soils with impeded drainage in tropical Africa and locally used as road metal.

1925 *Dollar Mag.* Sept. 120 What first catches the attention..of eyes weary of murrum or black cotton soil.. is the soothing greenness. **1932** G. W. ROBINSON *Soils* iii. 59 In certain types of tropical soils, with impeded drainage, the deposition of iron oxides may result in the development of highly indurated concretionary material, known in Africa as 'murram'. **1935** *Soil Res.* IV. 192 Towards the foot of the slopes are murram soils. **1959** E. HUXLEY *Flame Trees of Thika* i. 7 A plain whose soil was largely murram, a coarse red gravel that baked hard and supported only thin, wiry grass, sad-looking thorn trees and tortured-branched erythrinas. **1961** *Engineering* 2 June 765 A variable thickness of murrum (a tough clay bound gravel). **1963** A. SMITH *Throw out Two Hands* vi. 71 The heavens open in their own African fashion to turn the murram roads into sloshy causeways. **1971** D. CREED *Trial of Lobo Icheka* vii. 78 In the town centre the wide murram road was a bedlam of activity.

Murray¹ (mɒ·ri). Any of the series of guide-books, or of time-tables of all railway trains running in Great Britain, issued by John *Murray* (1808–92) or by his successors. Also in the possessive, and *fig.* So **Mu·rray-less** *a.*

1845 THACKERAY *Leg. Rhine* in *G. Cruikshank's Table-Bk.* Sept. 198 Crowds of English,..armed with Murray's guide-books. **1846** R. FORD *Gatherings from Spain* viii. 86 A solitary wanderer..can read the book of Spain.. dwelling on what he likes, and skipping what he does not, as with a red Murray. **1847** [see *BRADSHAW]. **1862** MRS. GASKELL *Let.* 23 July (1966) 927 We stopped all night in a clean hotel... It is not down in Murray, but ought to be for its cleanliness, civility, and moderate charges. **1864** *Daily Tel.* 26 Sept. 5/1, I hope he found his 'Murray' again, for one would not willingly see him wandering..Murray-less and unguarded. **1885** RUSKIN *Praeterita* I. vi. 183 Murray..did not exist in those days; the courier was a private Murray. **1898** H. G. WELLS *Let.* 22 Jan. in *G. Gissing & H. G. Wells* (1961) 77 The more I see of these Murrays the more I settle to Rome. **1925** A. HUXLEY *Along the Road* I. 42 Old guide-books..make excellent travelling-companions. An early Murray is a treasure. **1961** *Economist* 18 Mar. 1047/2 Murray's ABC Time-table (now a pocketbook..) which sells 75,000 monthly in its two editions for Glasgow and Edinburgh. **1961** E. M. FORSTER *Alexandria* (ed. 3) p. xv, I have always respected guidebooks—particularly the earlier Baedekers and Murrays.

Mu·rray². The name of the main river of a large river-system of south-eastern Australia, used *attrib.* to designate plants or animals native to this region, as **Murray cod**, a large carnivorous food-fish, *Maccullochella macquariensis*, of the family Serranidæ; **Murray lily**, a bulbous plant, *Crinum flaccidum*, belonging to the family Amaryllidaceæ and bearing white, lily-like flowers; also called the Darling lily; **Murray perch** = *CALLOP; **Murray (river) pine**, a cypress pine, *Callitris glauca*.

1875 *Encycl. Brit.* III. 112/2 A very fine fresh-water fish is the Murray cod. **1911** C. E. W. BEAN '*Dreadnought' of Darling* xxxiv. 301 The Murray and the Darling and their tributaries contain a certain large, sluggish fish, which rather reminds one of a big carp, very delicious... They call him the Murray cod. **1952** D. STIVENS in *Coast to Coast 1951–2* The bunyip..was about ten feet long with a body like a Murray cod with gleaming golden-yellow scales. **1966** Murray cod [see *CALLOP]. **1877** F. VON MÜLLER *Introd. Botanic Teachings* xx. 119 This showy genus Crinum furnishes also Victoria with a beautiful species, the *Murray Lily* (Crinum flaccidum), not however to be found away from the Murray-River southward. **1962** J. H. WILLIS *Handbk. to Plants in Victoria* I. 326 Murray Lily (Darling Lily, Macquarie Crinum)..on a few sandy inundated flats along the Murray R. flood-plain. **1880** G. WALCH *Victoria in 1880* 124 (Morris), Our noble old 1400-mile river, the Murray..produces..that finny monster, the Murray cod, together with his less bulky, equally flavourless congener, the Murray perch. **1951** T. C. ROUGHLEY *Fish Austral.* 147 In New South Wales it [*sc.* the callop, *Plectroplites ambiguus*] was until recently referred to as golden perch or yellowbelly,..in Queensland and Western Australia as Murray perch. **1877** F. VON MÜLLER *Introd. Bot. Teachings* 38 Frenela or Callitris verrucosa,..known by the name Murray-Pine. **1933** *Bulletin* (Sydney) 4 Jan. 17 Is nothing to be done in methodical re-afforestation with Murray pine... A beautiful timber white-ant and rot resistant, and its dark rosewood heart and soft cream subcortical layers. **1951** *Dict. Gardening* (R. Hort. Soc.) I. 362/1 C[*allitris*] *glauca*. Murray River Pine. Up to 100 ft... Widely distributed. The wood is in constant use in Australia. **1966** 'J. HACKSTON' *Father clears Out* 100 The solitary Murray Pine in the college paddock was flinging itself about like a windjammer in a gale. **1967** A. M. BLOMBERY *Guide to Native Austral. Plants* 225 Murray Pine. A tree with spreading light-green branches, and cones tending to be longer than broad when ripe.

Murrayism (mɒ·riˌiz'm). [f. *MURRAY¹ + -ISM.] **a.** A mode of expression reminiscent of a guide-book published by Murray. **b.** A tourist's fondness for Murray's guide-books.

1846 in *Downside Rev.* (1945) LXIII. 216 That Rome should be called the Metropolis of Art..'from the miracles of art which it contains' is a Murrayism. **1865** *Daily Tel.* 27 Sept. 7/3, I saw yesterday in the Tribune a British couple who had brought to the races 'Murray's Handbook'. I think Murrayism can scarcely go further.

Murray Valley. The name of the valley of the Murray River (see *MURRAY²), used *attrib.* to designate a severe form of encephalitis and also the mosquito-borne virus that causes it.

1951 *Med. Jrnl. Australia* I. 526/1 A severe human encephalitis of virus origin spread diffusely along the Murray Valley during the early months of 1951. This has been provisionally referred to as Murray Valley encephalitis (MVE). **1955** *Sci. Amer.* Mar. 65/2 The New York laboratory decided to employ the neutralization test to compare each of the 11 new viruses with various other insect-borne viruses, such as the agents of yellow fever, dengue, louping ill, Murray Valley fever, Russian encephalitis, [etc.]. **1966** WRIGHT & SYMMERS *Systemic Path.* II. xxxiv. 1207/1 Epidemics of encephalitis occurred in Australia in 1912, 1918, 1922 and 1926... It is probable that these epidemics were outbreaks of the disease that has become known as Murray Valley fever. **1974** *Sydney Morning Herald* 6 Feb. 7 (*heading*) Mystery of the Murray Valley virus.

murrnong (mɔ̄·ɹnǫŋ). *Austral.* Also **mirr-n'yong, murning.** [Aboriginal name.] A yellow-flowered native herb, *Microseris lanceolata* (also called *M. scapigera*), of the family Compositæ, resembling a dandelion but having clusters of small tuberous roots, formerly used as food by the Aborigines.

1852 J. MORGAN *Life W. Buckley* 85 There was another sort of food very useful to me; this was a particular kind of root the natives call Murning—in shape, and size, and flavour, very much resembling the radish. **1878** R. BROUGH SMYTH *Aborigines Victoria* I. 209 *Murr-nong* or *Mirr-n'yong*, a kind of yam (*Microseris Forsteri*), was usually very plentiful and found in the spring and early summer, and was dug out of the earth by the women and children... The root is small, in taste rather sweet, not unpleasant, and perhaps more like a radish than a potato. **1889** J. H. MAIDEN *Useful Native Plants of Australia* 45 *Microseris Forsteri*... 'Murr-nong' or 'Mirr n'yong', of the aboriginals of New South Wales and Victoria. The tubers were largely used as food by the aboriginals. They are sweet and milky, and in flavour resemble the cocoa-nut. **1965** *Austral. Encycl.* II. 494/1 The most familiar native member of the tribe [*sc.* Compositae] is *Microseris lanceolata* (syn. *M. scapigera*), the 'yam', 'yam daisy', or 'murrnong' of the aborigines, who used its tuberous roots for food.

Murrumbidgee (mɒrɒ̆mbi·dʒī). The name of a river in southern New South Wales used *attrib.* in various Austral. slang collocations, as **Murrumbidgee jam** (see quot. 1943); **Murrumbidgee w(h)aler**, a swagman who camped in the region of the Murrumbidgee or other river, regarded as a classic type of indolent person; so **Murrumbidgee whaling.**

1873 J. C. F. JOHNSON *Christmas on Carringa* 16 Men when on the tramp through the Riverina country often carry a piece of twine and a hook to catch cod or black-fish. This is termed Murrumbidgee Whaling. **1878** 'IRONBARK' *Southerly Busters* 177 Murrumbidgee whalers are a class of loafers who work for about six months in the year —*i.e.*, during shearing and harvest, and camp the rest of the time in bends of rivers, and live by fishing and begging. **1885** *Australasian Printers' Keepsake* 72 [He] eyed Bob very suspiciously, muttering 'spieler' and 'Murrumbidgee whaler'. **1943** BAKER *Dict. Austral. Slang* (ed. 3) 52 *Murrumbidgee jam*, brown sugar moistened with cold tea and spread on damper. **1953** A. RUSSELL *Murray Walkabout* 147 He was a 'Murrumbidgee whaler', the river prototype of the tramping sundowner. **1969** *Sunday Truth* (Brisbane) 2 Nov. 34/1 The so-called Murrumbidgee whalers roamed the inland rivers, particularly for about 50 years from the 1880s, and caught cod which they sold to hotels and farms.

‖ **muru** (mū̆·rū̆). *Obs. N.Z.* [Maori.] (See quot. 1863).

1836 J. A. WILSON *Jrnl.* 24 Aug. in *Missionary Life & Work in N.Z.* (1889) III. 48 We were told the events which led to the burning of the mission station, and the *muru* which followed. **1863** F. E. MANING *Old N.Z.* vii. 96 There were in the old times two great institutions..in Maori land—the *Tapu* and the *Muru*. Pakehas..called the *muru* simply 'robbery'... But I speak of the regular legalized and established system of plundering, as penalty for offences. **1905** W. B. *Where White Man Treads* 32 Hiakai.., forgetting the rules of muru, crashed it [*sc.* the tomahawk] into his enemy's skull. **1921** H. GUTHRIE-SMITH *Tutira* xxvii. 267 Neither..was *muru* an institution likely..to foster foresight. **1949** P. BUCK *Coming of Maori* (1950) III. vi. 421 The custom of *muru* (raiding) was sometimes employed by visitors if a death was due to accident.

‖ **murumuru** (mu·rumu·ru). [Tupi.] A Brazilian palm, *Astrocaryum murumuru*, whose stem is covered with black spines. Also *attrib.*

1853 A. R. WALLACE *Palm Trees of Amazon* 101 On the Upper Amazon cattle eat the fruits of the Murumurú, wandering about for days in the forest to procure it. **1860** MAYNE REID *Odd People* 135 These thorns are the spines of the 'murumuru', or 'pupunha' palm. **1927** R. R. GATES *Botanist in Amazon Valley* vi. 134 We stopped again to take on a canoe load of murumuru nuts. They are sometimes burned in the furnaces and they burn rather like charcoal. **1961** P. B. TOMLINSON *Anat. Monocotyledons* II. 142 *Astrocaryum murumuru* (Murumuru Palm), *A. tucuma* (Tucum Palm), and other spp. are included in a list of Brazilian palms yielding vegetable oils.

‖ **murus gallicus** (miūᵊ·rɒs gæ·likɒs). [L. 'Gaulish wall' (Caesar *De Bello Gallico* VII. xxiii).] A type of late Iron Age Celtic fort having stone walls bound by horizontally placed timber frames. Also called *Gaulish* or *Gallic wall* (*fort*).

1947 J. & C. HAWKES *Prehist. Britain* 265 The specially constructed type known as the Gallic Fort in which stone walls are bound with timber (*murus gallicus*). **1947** *Proc. Prehistoric Soc.* XIII. 16 Moreover the distribution of 'murus gallicus' forts is strictly complementary to, and mutually exclusive with, that of the brochs. **1953** R. J. C. ATKINSON *Field Archaeol.* (ed. 2) ii. 62 Walls of *murus gallicus* type have in addition internal timbering. **1963** *Field Archaeol.* (Ordnance Survey) (ed. 4) 71 This work must not be confused with the special type of timber re-inforcement (*murus gallicus*) which it resembles and which is reported by Caesar as frequent among the Gaulish forts which he assaulted. **1970** BRAY & TRUMP *Dict. Archaeol.* 233/2 One specialized form of timber-laced rampart, the *murus gallicus* or Gaulish wall, was encountered by Caesar during his campaigns against the Celtic tribes.

Murut (mū̆·rŭt). Also **Marut.** [f. Bajau *belud* hill.] A member of a primitive Dyak people originally inhabiting the hill country in the interior of North Borneo, although now more widely scattered; the language of this people. Also *attrib.* or as *adj.*

1846 H. KEPPEL *Expedition to Borneo* II. viii. 171 The Murut inhabits the interior of Borneo Proper. They are

not tattooed,..and have a peculiar dialect. **1846**, etc. [see *KAYAN]. **1848** F. S. MARRYAT *Borneo & Indian Archipelago* 111 The whole space was covered with naked savages. These were the Maruts, a tribe of Dyaks who live in the mountains. **1881** J. HATTON *New Ceylon* iii. 81 The interior of the country is inhabited by the descendants of the aboriginal population, called variously Muruts, Dusuns, or Ida'an. **1896** H. L. ROTH *Natives of Sarawak & Brit. N. Borneo* I. p. xx, British North Borneo has been less fortunate with the Muruts. **1923** *Blackw. Mag.* July 49/2 The Mûruts are not a warlike or courageous people. **1929** O. RUTTER *Pagans of N. Borneo* ii. 31 Speaking generally, the Muruts may be said to inhabit the hilly country of the interior of North Borneo. **1939** A. KEITH *Land below Wind* xi. 197 Here was a Murut headman in only a loincloth. *Ibid.* 198 ·.rusap called to them in Murut. **1968** *Encycl. Brit.* XV. 1012/2 The Muruts..are ..abandoning their communal houses in favour of private dwellings.

Mus' (mɒs), dial. abbrev. of MISTER *sb.*² or MASTER *sb.*¹

1875 W. D. PARISH *Dict. Sussex Dial.* s.v. *Master.* 'Master' is quite a distinct title from 'Mr.', which is always pronounced Mus, thus,—*Mus* Smith is the employer. *Master* Smith is the man he employs. **1906** KIPLING *Puck of Pook's Hill* 224 Oh, Mus' Reynolds, Mus' Reynolds... If I knowed all was inside your head, I'd know something wuth knowin'. **1917** —— *Diversity of Creatures* 68 Whoever pays the taxes old Mus' Hobden owns the land.

musa² (miŭ·ză). *Radio.* Also **MUSA, Musa.** [See quot. 1937.] A radio aerial consisting of a number of rhombic elements in an end-fire array and giving a beam that is varied in direction by varying the phase relations between the elements.

1937 FRIIS & FELDMAN in *Bell System Techn. Jrnl.* XVI. 340 The word MUSA is coined from the initial letters of 'multiple unit steerable antenna'. **1940** *Ibid.* XIX. 309 The principal parts of the two musa receivers occupy three rows of bays each about 25 feet long and 11½ feet high. **1946** *Nature* 10 Aug. 190/1 Vertical angles were measured on transmissions from Rugby received at Holmdel with 'Musa' equipment. **1966** *McGraw-Hill Encycl. Sci. & Technol.* I. 447/2 The multiple unit steerable antenna, abbreviated MUSA,..has a directional pattern 1° wide at 18 Mc.

musaasa, var. *MSASA.

Musak, erron. var. *MUZAK.

1961 *Times Lit. Suppl.* 30 June 396/2 The comfortable times before Musak (relayed music) and large-scale cultural enterprise took over. **1966** AUDEN *About House* 62 The radio in students' cars, Musak at breakfast.

Muscadet (mu·skade). [f. the name of the Muscadet grape from which it is made.] A white wine made in the Loire valley near Nantes.

1920 A. L. SIMON *Blood of Grape* ix. 221 Muscadet white wines are in no way objectionable, and in no way fine. **1951** R. POSTGATE *Plain Man's Guide to Wine* iv. 88 A white wine called Muscadet, from the grape used in it. **1966** H. JOHNSON *Wine* 103 Nobody claims greatness for Muscadet, and yet it is one of the most useful of the lesser wines of France. **1969** R. HUTCHINGS *Lucky in Jeopardy* 21 In lieu of the Hock the Squire usually selects with a curry meal we had a bottle of *Muscadet*, which went down very refreshingly on our scorched palates. **1971** *Guardian* 13 Aug. 9/4 Three magnums, one of Rosé, one of Burgundy, one of Muscadet, from which you could help yourself.

muscarine. Substitute for entry:

muscarine (mɒ·skărin, -īn). *Chem.* Also † **muscarin.** [ad. G. *muscarin* (Schmiedeberg & Koppe *Das Muscarin* (1869) 2, f. L. *muscārius* (see MUSCARIOUS *a.*): see -INE⁵.] A quaternary ammonium base, $C_9H_{21}NO_3$, which is a poisonous alkaloid found in the fungus *Amanita muscaria* and which produces copious secretion by the mucous and sweat glands, nausea, vomiting, contraction of the pupils, and laboured respiration.

1872 *Jrnl. Chem. Soc.* XXV. 830 The physiological action of muscarine is antagonistic to that of atropine. **1878** [in Dict.]. **1910** *Practitioner* June 824 Putrefactive organisms split up proteins into..ptomaines—neurin, cholin, muscarin, cadaverin, [etc.]. **1914** DALE & EWINS in *Jrnl. Physiol.* XLVIII. p. xxv, The choline esters hitherto examined, while showing the peripheral 'muscarine' action in small doses, show in larger doses..a nicotine-like action. **1940** H. A. MCGUIGAN *Appl. Pharmacol.* 576 The action of pilocarpine and muscarine.. seems to be on the parasympathetic nerve endings and not directly on the gland cell. **1951** J. STEINBECK *Log from 'Sea of Cortez'* (1958) 124 Muscarine, the active poisonous principle of *Amanita muscaria* and other fungi. **1951** A. GROLLMAN *Pharmacol. & Therap.* xiii. 246 Muscarine has never been used in medical practice because its powerful parasympathomimetic effects are so generalized as to make it impossible to elicit the desired effects in any given organ. **1961** *Q. Rev.* XV. 154 The story of muscarine revolves round the presentation of three formulae, two erroneous ones $C_8H_{14}O_2N^+$ and $C_8H_{18}O_2N^+$, and the correct one $C_9H_{20}O_2N^+$.

Hence **muscari·nic** *a.*, resembling (that of) muscarine; capable of responding to muscarine; **muscari·nically** *adv.*, in a muscarinic manner.

1941 GOODMAN & GILMAN *Pharmacol. Basis Therapeutics* xix. 339 The nicotinic and muscarinic actions of acetylcholine can be strikingly demonstrated on the intestinal tract of..the tench. **1961** *Nature* 25 Feb. 673/1 Observed differences in the muscarinic activities of the above isomers is [*sic*] therefore explicable in terms of differences in their fit at the muscarinic receptors. **1971** *Ibid.* 16 Apr. 444/1 The muscarinically, weakly active substrates of acetylcholinesterase, acetylthiocholine..and acetylselenocholine..are antiplanar at 72 and 73 both in crystals and in solution. **1974** *Canad. Jrnl. Physiol. & Pharmacol.* LII. 332/2 An alternative explanation..is based on the concepts that there exist separate binding subsites on the muscarinic receptor to accommodate the polar and nonpolar side chains of muscarinic agonists [etc.].

Muscatel. Add: **1.** Also applied to wines made in Australia, California, and England.

1867 *Australasian* 9 Feb. 186/1 Australian Wines in the Indian Market... The Muscatel has plenty of body. **1958** A. L. SIMON *Dict. Wines, Spirits, & Liqueurs* 117 *Muscatel*, the name of a sweet fortified wine made in California. Also, in England, that of a cheap, sweet, white, sparkling wine, usually flavoured with elderberry flowers essence. **1967** A. LICHINE *Encycl. Wines & Spirits* 374/1 In California a regrettable quantity of fortified wine known as 'Muscatel' is sold as a substitute for spirits.

muscicole, *a.* Add: Also as *sb.*

1965 B. E. FREEMAN tr. *Vandel's Biospeleology* ix. 110 These two species are commonplace muscicoles.

muscle, *sb.* Add: **3. b.** Force, violence; an act, or the threat, of violence; fear inspired by force; intimidation; a person employed to use or threaten violence (freq. in *collect.* pl.); strength; influence, the exertion of economic or political influence. Phr. *on the muscle* (see quot. 1950). *slang* (orig. *U.S.*).

1930 *Amer. Mercury* Dec. 457/1 *On the muscle*, angry, quarrelsome. 'He busts up to me strictly on the muscle. So I let him have it.' **1931** *Detective Fiction Weekly* 5 Sept. 436/1 When the police drag his name into every gang killing or big shot feud he makes no denial. This circumstance has given Madden that terrorizing thing known in the underworld as 'muscle'. **1935** C. F. COE *G-Man* ii. 26 Winky and Palmy ain't hot for the muscle. **1942** *Detective Fiction Weekly* May 58/1 You were the best muscle in the whole crowd, Julio. **1950** H. E. GOLDIN *Dict. Amer. Underworld Lingo* 143/2 *On the muscle.* 1. By strong-arm methods; engaged in any criminal activity requiring strong-arm methods. 2. Acquired without paying as the result of a reputation for violence... 3. Belligerent. **1959** *Alfred Hitchcock's Mystery Mag.* Feb. 71/1 Skreen visited ..the organization's punitive department. He gave one of the muscles the name of a pusher who'd taken a junkie's credit. **1962** *Cosmopolitan* Aug. 108/3 A female decoy to set Shanley up and adequate muscle to take care of him. *Ibid.* 122/1 'What kind of people were they?'.. 'They were muscle.' **1968** B. TURNER *Sex Trap* v. 30 Free women, a rent-free pad, and all the muscle you need to keep the things running smoothly. **1968** [see *black power* (*BLACK *a.* 19)]. **1973** H. NIELSEN *Severed Key* xvi. 173 The muscle on the trucks..were free-lancers.

4. a. *muscle power, strain.*

1937 *Jrnl. R. Aeronaut. Soc.* XLI. 1092 The third part deals with the practical side of flying..autogiros, helicopters, muscle power flight, etc. **1959** *Daily Tel.* 2 Nov. 1/2 There has been increasing interest recently in the possibility of achieving sustained flight by the use of muscle power only. **1968** *Brit. Med. Bull.* XXIV. 189/1 Machines through the ages have been principally concerned with deploying muscle power more effectively. **1935** *Mind* XLIV. 353 We know by inference that muscle-strain in our eyes (for instance) is a part-cause of our headache.

b. *muscle(-)relaxant* adj. and sb., *-relaxing* adj., *-training* sb.

1951 *New Biol.* XI. 101 The muscle-relaxant drugs, which are sometimes given in addition to anaesthetics in surgery. **1968** W. C. BOWMAN et al. *Textbk. Pharmacol.* xxii. 613 Mephenesin is useful as a muscle relaxant in the treatment of tetanus. **1947** *Lancet* 18 Jan. 97/1 (*heading*) Muscle-relaxing action of myanesin. **1960** R. W. MARKS *Dymaxion World of Fuller* 94 All the sanitary and muscle-relaxing effects of other types of bathing could be effected without the use of any bathroom. **1969** D. B. TAYLOR in J. A. Bevan *Essent. Pharmacol.* xvii. 162 The neuromuscular junction of voluntary muscle..is..the site of action of a group of valuable muscle-relaxing drugs. **1869** 'MARK TWAIN' *Innoc. Abr.* 622 Who shall say it is not a muscle-training pastime, climbing the pyramids?

d. muscle-bound *a.*, having the muscles stiff and enlarged, esp. as a result of too much exercise or training; also *fig.*; **muscle car** *N. Amer. slang*, = *HOT ROD; **muscle-feeling** (example); **muscle-flexing** *a.*, demonstrating aggression or strength; **muscle sense,** add: also, the sense of position or movement, kinæsthesis (but see quots.); now more commonly used than *muscular sense*; (examples); **muscle spindle** [tr. G. *muskelspindel* (W. Kühne 1863, in *Arch. f. path. Anat. u. Physiol.* XXVIII. 528)], any of numerous small sensory organs within muscle, which consist of a bundle of intrafusal muscle fibres richly supplied with nerves and enclosed in a capsule and which respond to passive stretching and active contraction of the muscle.

1879 W. BLAIKIE *How to get Strong* i. 18 Scarce any man grows earlier muscle-bound [than the coal-heaver], for few backs do so much hard work. **1909** *Westm. Gaz.* 8 June 9/2, I have met many cases where an unintelligent use of such exercises has..so thickened the muscles as to lead to the condition known as being 'muscle-bound'. **1918** *Nation* (N.Y.) 7 Feb. 133/2 There has been a curious sense of leisureliness, of muscle-bound movement. **1946** R. G. COLLINGWOOD *Idea of Hist.* IV. 189 German historians, muscle-bound in their struggle with the facts. **1973** J. WAMBAUGH *Blue Knight* ii. 32, I stopped by the arcade and saw a big muscle-bound fruit hustler standing there. **1969** *Time* (Canad. ed.) 16 May 98/1 It is a hyped-up Mustang—one of Ford's fast-moving contenders in what Detroit calls 'the muscle-car' market, where the best sales pitch is neck-snapping acceleration. **1970** *Wall Street Jrnl.* 16 July 1/6 Two of the insurers' major targets are high-horsepower 'muscle' cars and fragile bumpers that offer little protection in minor accidents. **1974** *Weekend Mag.* (Montreal) 16 Mar. 2/1 But lower drinking ages have crippled the high school dope trade throughout Canada, the big Detroit muscle cars have been displaced by Vivas, MGBs and even Jeeps, and everywhere long hair for boys and short skirts for girls are right out of it. **1975** *Daily Colonist* (Victoria, B.C.) 26 Feb. 17/4 The spokesman said 'muscle cars', today's term for hot rods, had used the stretch up to several times a month. **1890** W. JAMES *Princ. Psychol.* II. xx. 198 Muscle-feeling belongs to that class of general sensations which tell us of our inner states. **1961** *Times* 6 Dec. 17/5 Annoyance at the chest-beating, muscle-flexing, tear-jerking banality of some moments in the second part [of an opera]. **1973** J. ROSSITER *Manipulators* xi. 112 Christou was turned over to you as a sort of muscle-flexing exercise. To prove I could do it. **1895** E. B. TITCHENER in *Amer. Jrnl. Psychol.* VII. 83 *Muskelsinn*, muscle sense. **1933** HEWER & SANDES *Introd. Study Nervous System* (ed. 2) II. i. 71 The sensations produced are those of 'muscle sense', stereognosis, vibratory sense, and a sense of pressure-pain. **1938** R. S. WOODWORTH *Exper. Psychol.* xix. 454 The traditional 'sense of touch' has been broken up by experiment into at least five senses. The first to be split off, early in the nineteenth century, was the muscle sense, kinesthesis. **1968** J. J. GIBSON *Senses considered as Perceptual Systems* vi. 111 The so-called muscle-sense should probably be ascribed no role in detecting the spatial postures and movements of the body, and therefore it had better not be called a sense. **1971** *Jrnl. Gen. Psychol.* Jan. 147 Formerly, kinesthesis was the so-called 'muscle sense'. Now it is known that receptors in joints mediate the appreciation of limb position. **1894** C. S. SHERRINGTON in *Jrnl. Physiol.* XVII. 238 He [*sc.* Kühne] designated the bundles simply in virtue of their shape, muscle-spindles, 'muskelspindeln', the name adopted here as the most suitable of all that have been applied. **1972** P. B. C. MATTHEWS *Mammalian Muscle Receptors* i. 47 With the exception of a few muscles innervated by cranial nerves, muscle spindles have now been found in every striated muscle of every species of mammal in which they have been appropriately sought. **1974** BERGMAN & AFIFI *Atlas Microsc. Anat.* vi. 140 Muscle spindles are found within skeletal muscles. Each spindle is formed of two to ten small muscle fibers, the intrafusal fibers, enclosed within a sheath of connective tissue which is pierced by nerve fibers.

muscle (mɒ·s'l), *v.* [f. the sb.] **1.** *trans.* To move by the exercise of muscular force. *U.S. dial.* and *colloq.*

1913 H. KEPHART *Our Southern Highlanders* xiii. 262 We can muscle this log up. **1969** *New Yorker* 14 June 62/2 Graebner muscles one down the line so fast that Ashe's volley makes a high, awkward parabola. **1974** J. WAINWRIGHT *Hard Hit* 33 The refuse cart is collecting the empties... Three guys..are muscling the bins around.

2. To coerce by violence or by economic or political pressure. *slang* (orig. *U.S. underworld*).

1929 *Chicago Tribune* 18 Jan. 21/4 A certain gentleman in the illicit spirits business was accosted by two sinister characters, who 'muscled' him,..removing from his wallet the sum of $150. **1935** C. F. COE *G-Man* viii. 142 Mebbe it's a new mob. If they're musclin' Rap, it won't be long before they're musclin' us too. **1950** H. E. GOLDIN *Dict. Amer. Underworld Lingo* 143/2 *Muscle out*, to expel by force or threat of force an individual or gang from any racket or area. **1953** in Wentworth & Flexner *Dict. Amer. Slang* (1960) 349/2 If she persists,..she'll be muscled out of the [Free German Youth] movement. **1958** *Time* (Atlantic ed.) 13 Oct. 15/1 The old Union Pacific and Central Pacific railroads had once muscled each other. **1967** *Wall Street Jrnl.* 24 Apr. 32/1 Are aggressive underworld operators beginning to achieve some success in muscling a beachhead among the nation's established securities markets? **1971** *N.Y. Law Jrnl.* 23 Nov. 4/2 Big brewers may be illegally muscling small ones through predatory pricing—that is deliberately using below-cost pricing methods to force competitors out of the market.

3. *intr.* With *in* or *in on* (occas. *into*). To introduce oneself into the business, criminal activities, sphere of influence, etc., of another or others, by force or fraud; to enter forcibly, or uninvited. *slang* (orig. *U.S. underworld*). So **muscling-in** *vbl. sb.*

1929 W. R. BURNETT *Little Caesar* v. iii. 171 If you think you can muscle into this joint you're off your nut. *Ibid.* v. 182 You know, I been watching you ever since you muscled in on Sam Vettori. **1929** E. D. SULLIVAN *Look at Chicago* (1930) iv. 50 When the beer organization, which is trying to muscle in, arrives with its delivery, there is a scene reminiscent of the Fall of Port Arthur. **1931** G. IRWIN *Amer. Tramp & Underworld Slang* 133 *Muscle*, to use force or intimidation so as to secure a share in a 'racket' or graft, or to force one's way into an enterprise or gang by threat of violence. Also 'muscle in'. **1931** F. D. PASLEY (*title*) Muscling in. **1932** WODEHOUSE *Hot Water* vi. 123 You muscle in here, pretending to be the Vicomte de Blissac. **1932** *Observer* 26 June 13/3, I began to feel that he could probably beat Lindrum at billiards and muscle in on Al Capone. **1934** J. O'HARA *Appointment in Samarra* (1935) i. 13 So the feminine members had

muscled in on the smoking-room. **1934** Dylan Thomas *18 Poems* 20, I would not fear the muscling-in of love If I were tickled by the urchin hungers. **1940** Wodehouse *Eggs, Beans & Crumpets* 57 Beetles tried to muscle in between his collar and his neck. *Ibid.* 99 And no more muscling in and trying to dictate the policy of the 'Uncle Joe To His Chickabiddies' page? **1942** E. Waugh *Put out More Flags* iii. 162 You're muscling in on my territory. **1955** *Times Lit. Suppl.* 22 July 415/3 The technical secondary school is failing to challenge the grammar school, which is muscling-in on the occupations to which it primarily looks. **1963** N. Marsh *Dead Water* (1964) vii. 182 Far be me from it—I mean it from me—to muscle in where I'm not wanted. **1973** J. Wainwright *Devil you Don't* 30 'The Ponderosa' was his spread and no cheap, jumped-up, fiddle-foot was gonna muscle in.

4. To make one's way by employing muscular strength.

1961 in Webster. **1972** D. Haston *In High Places* i. 7 He [*sc.* the leader in a rock-climb] doesn't just find something for his hands and muscle up with scrabbling feet. Climbing should be a balanced set of movements.

mu·scle man. *slang* (orig. *U.S.*). Also **muscle-man, muscleman.** [f. Muscle + Man *sb.*[1]] **a.** A person who employs or threatens violence on behalf of a professional criminal, or who commits crimes of violence without instigation. **b.** Used to denote a paragon of powerful physique. **c.** *fig.*

1929 Hostetter & Beesley *It's a Racket!* 232 'Muscle Men' are those who 'muscle' their way. **1931** *Times Lit. Suppl.* 19 Feb. 125/1 O'Banion with the comment 'To hell with the Sicilians!' set his muscle-men moving. *Ibid.* 24 Sept. 728/3 Pinkerton's detectives were the most respectable of numerous bands of hired 'muscle men'. **1932** *Sun* (Baltimore) 23 Nov. 10/2 This country wants a frontal attack on the powerful citadel of muscle-men made rich by illegal beer. **1948** *Daily Mail* 21 Jan. 2/5 Princess MacFarlane..makes presents of boots to all the poor children, touring from slum to slum in a fast black saloon packed with muscle-men. **1952** S. Kaufmann *Philanderer* (1953) xiv. 235 The other kind was the muscle men. You know, right off the farm where they were lifting tractors with one hand. **1953** W. Burroughs *Junkie* (1972) vii. 65 Bert was known as a muscleman. He was a heavy-set, round-faced, deceptively soft-looking young man who specialized in strong-arm routines and 'shakes'. **1960** *Times Lit. Suppl.* 27 May 333/3 *St. Petersburg*..was published..under the comparatively liberal tyranny of the Tsar and proscribed by Zhdanov, Stalin's literary muscle-man. **1962** A. Huxley *Island* xiii. 206 Little muscle-men and muscle-women—children with tendencies towards aggressiveness and love of power. **1966** 'C. Keith' *Elusive Epicure* (1968) v. 76 If there is such a thing as a California type it's the big muscleman with a rather simple mind. **1968** P. Oliver *Screening Blues* iv. 134 With the considerable returns accruing from operating policy wheels the racket came under the control of syndicates with muscle-men and hired gunmen ensuring that their 'rights' were protected. **1975** *Times* 26 Sept. 10/3 Auditions for 'the muscle man with a voice like a bird' [*sc.* Tarzan] will start soon.

Muscovite, *sb.*[1] and *a.* Add: **A.** *sb.* Also, a native or inhabitant of Moscow.

1961 in Webster. **1973** J. Shub *Moscow by Nightmare* x. 113 Are you one of those Muscovites who feel Leningrad is just a provincial town? **1975** *Times* 8 Mar. 13/3 Muscovites expect journalists to strengthen good will between our countries.

muscovite, *sb.*[2] Add: (Earlier example.) Hence **mu:scovitiza·tion**, conversion into muscovite; **mu·scovitized** *ppl. a.*

1850 J. D. Dana *Syst. Min.* (ed. 3) v. v. 356 Muscovite, *D*[*ana*]. **1909** *Cent. Dict.* Suppl., Muscovitization. **1930** *Trans. Geol. Soc. S. Africa* XXXII. 145 Since, however, albitization on an extensive scale generally accompanies the muscovitization, both processes in part merely involve a mutual exchange of alkali-radicles. **1944** *Q. Jrnl. Geol. Soc.* XCIX. 118 In slices they show..scattered plates of partly chloritized or muscovitized biotite. **1956** E. W. Heinrich *Microsc. Petrogr.* ii. 28 Deuteric changes are..muscovitization of biotite [etc.]. **1965** G. J. Williams *Econ. Geol. N.Z.* xiii. 200/1 The granite in the general area of the Tin Range is more or less muscovitized.

Muscovy. Add: **4. Muscovy duck,** also *ellipt.*, as **Muscovy.** (Further examples.) (*b*) = Musk-duck 2.

1822 J. Campbell *Trav. S. Afr. 2nd Journey* I. xiv. 148 We halted at the side of a lake, where one of our people brought down four wild ducks by one shot, and another found eight Muscovy ducks' eggs, as large as those of a turkey. **1911** C. E. W. Bean *'Dreadnought' of Darling* ii. 26 They fairly rushed the cargo into her... Japanese onions, condensed milk, tomato sauce, Worcestershire relish, half a dozen hens, and a dozen Muscovy ducks. **1953** *Amer. Speech* XXVIII. 276 In this type of folk naming, the domesticated varieties of ducks also are not wholly neglected, the large Muscovy, with distinctive head adornment, suggesting the scoters, sizable among wild ducks and with unusually shaped and colored bills. All of our three species are known as bay muscoveys [*sic*] in Maryland. **1956** *Nigerian Field* XXI. 108 The presence of the Muscovy duck in Africa has never been satisfactorily explained. The bird is indigenous to the Americas, hence its presence in Africa as a domesticated fowl must be due to the activity of man. **1972** *Country Life* 2 Mar. 489/1 The China goose can't stand up to the muscovy and retreats before him.

muscular, *a.* Add: **1. b.** (Further examples.) *muscular dystrophy*, any of a group of hereditary disorders (or these disorders collectively) marked by the progressive wasting and weakening of some muscles owing (apparently) to some defect of the muscles themselves.

1886 Muscular dystrophy [see *dystrophy* s.v. Dys-]. **1932** W. Boyd *Text-bk. Path.* xxx. 840 The muscular dystrophies have several clinical divisions, but the basic pathology is the same... The large muscles concerned with fixation (shoulder, girdle, hip) are chiefly affected, the small muscles concerned with active movement (hand, etc.) usually escaping. This is the opposite to what occurs in progressive muscular atrophy. **1939** Dible & Davie *Pathology* lviii. 896 (*heading*) The myopathies or muscular dystrophies. **1961** R. D. Baker *Essent. Path.* xi. 275 In muscular dystrophy the atrophy is due to changes in the muscle fibers themselves... In muscular atrophy the primary change is in the nerves which supply the muscles or in the cord or brain. **1961** *Lancet* 9 Sept. 601/1 We have recently come across a family where five members suffered from muscular dystrophy, inherited apparently as an autosomal or X-linked dominant. **1973** *Nature* 1 June 287/1 The traditional concept that muscular dystrophy is a 'primary degenerative myopathy' has recently been challenged, and the suggestion put forward that the disease may..have a neural basis.

3. b. *muscular Christianity* (earlier example). *muscular Christian* (later examples); so *muscular-Christian* adj.

1857 *Sat. Rev.* 21 Feb. 176/1 We all know by this time what is the task that Mr. Kingsley has made specially his own—it is that of spreading the knowledge and fostering the love of a muscular Christianity. **1966** *Listener* 27 Oct. 613/2 That muscular Christian, Welldon, who was his headmaster and housemaster at Harrow,..always appreciated his [*sc.* Churchill's] merits. **1970** T. Hilton *Pre-Raphaelites* v. 133 The tone of the place [*sc.* the Working Men's College] was heavily muscular-Christian. **1975** J. Blackburn *Mister Brown's Bodies* xviii. 151 Great hulking fellows... Muscular Christians to a man.

muscularis mucosæ (mɒskiulā·ris miukōu·sī). *Anat.* [mod.L., f. mod.L. *musculāris* Muscular + *mūcōsæ*, gen. (?) of Mucosa: the term may be a shortening of *lamina muscularis mucosæ*.] A thin layer of smooth muscle fibres in certain mucous membranes. Also *ellipt.*, as **muscularis.**

[**1854** Busk & Huxley tr. *Kölliker's Man. Human Histol.* II. 89 We find a dense, continuous, reddish layer 0·022–0·044‴ in thickness, (Brücke) the muscular layer of the mucous membrane.] **1867** *Quain's Anat.* (ed. 7) III. p. cxcix, The deepest layer of the alimentary mucous membrane..is formed throughout by non-striated muscular tissue, and is named muscularis mucosæ. **1892** C. S. Minot *Human Embryol.* (1897) i. 2 It is commonly asserted that the muscular coat of the uterus is largely made up of the hypertrophied muscularis mucosæ. **1959** N. Andrew *Textbk. Compar. Histol.* vi. 280 In man the entire length of the intestine shows an inner circular and an outer longitudinal layer of muscularis mucosae. **1974** *Nature* 15 Mar. 238/1 Strips of gastric mucosa (dissected free of the underlying muscularis) were removed from (barbiturate-)anaesthetised adult mongrel dogs.

musculo-. Add: **musculofa·scial** *a.*, of or pertaining to both a muscle and its associated fasciæ; **musculoske·letal** *a.*, of, pertaining to, or involving both muscular and skeletal structures.

1949 *New Gould Med. Dict.* 647/1 *Musculofascial*, consisting of both muscular and fascial elements, as in an amputation flap. **1950** *Jrnl. Amer. Med. Assoc.* 25 Feb. 557/2 (*heading*) Musculofascial pain. *Ibid.* 559/1 A sharp, slender needle may be introduced into musculofascial tissues without harm. **1964** L. Martin *Clin. Endocrinol.* (ed. 4) iii. 115 The musculo-fascial cone behind the eye. **1944** Dorland & Miller *Med. Dict.* (ed. 20) 947/1 Musculoskeletal. **1962** D. Nichols *Echinoderms* iii. 54 Burrowing is apparently effected by musculo-skeletal methods rather than by digging with spines and tube-feet. **1971** *Brit. Med. Bull.* XXVII. 82/2 Rheumatic complaints..are presumed to stem from..the supporting structures of the locomotor or musculoskeletal system. **1972** *Lancet* 2 Sept. 449/1 (*heading*) Musculoskeletal disorders associated with type-IV hyperlipoproteinæmia.

muse, *sb.*[1] Add: **2. d.** In phr. *the tenth Muse*, a muse of inspiration figured as being added to the nine of classical mythology.

1650 A. Bradstreet (*title*) The tenth Muse lately sprung up in America, or Severall poems, compiled with great variety of wit and learning. *c* **1838** C. J. Mathews in M. R. Booth *Eng. Plays of 19th Cent.* (1973) IV. 125 Tell her from me that she's a second Venus, a tenth Muse, a fourth Grace. **1855** A. Trollope *Warden* xiv. 220 It was here that Tom Towers lived, and cultivated with eminent success the tenth Muse who now governs the periodical press. **1957** H. Read (*title*) The tenth Muse: essays in criticism. **1973** *Guardian* 29 June 15/4 Poet confronts poet..they 'talked shop like a tenth muse'.

muse, *v.* Add: **1. d.** To say or murmur meditatively.

1834 A. Marsh *Two Old Men's Tales* II. xviii. 224 'But what can I promise? I who have nothing,' mused she, 'and am now penniless.' **1843** Dickens *Christmas Carol* 32 'You must have been very slow about it, Jacob.'.. 'Slow!' the Ghost repeated. 'Seven years dead,' mused Scrooge 'And travelling all the time?' **1881** Mrs. J. H. Riddell *Senior Partner* I. vii. 150 'That's strange,' mused Mr. McCullagh; 'and you getting on for thirty year of age.' **1922** Joyce *Ulysses* 212 Amused Buck Mulligan mused in pleasant murmur with himself, selfnodding: 'A pleased bottom.'

‖ **museau** (müzo). *colloq.* [Fr., lit. 'muzzle, snout (of animal)'.] A person's face.

1915 D. H. Lawrence *Rainbow* xv. 423 You've got a *museau*, not a face. **1922** —— *England, my England* 228 A young man of twenty-two, with a fresh, jaunty *museau*. **1925** —— *St. Mawr* 7 She, with her odd little *museau*, not exactly pretty, but very attractive. **1955** *Essays in Criticism* V. 79 Lou, with her gipsy wildness, her animal *museau*.

musee. Delete † *Obs. rare*[—1] and add later examples.

Normally in form *musée* as in French.

1861 C. M. Yonge *Young Stepmother* xvii. 233, I shall be most happy to introduce you into my *atelier* and show you my notes on the various *Musées*. **1885** H. James *Little Tour in France* xv. 102 Of course I had time to go to the Musée; the more so that I have a weakness for provincial museums. **1924** R. Fry *Let.* 27 June (1972) II. 553 I've.. seen the much vaunted Musée here [*sc.* in Montpellier]. It's badly lit and worse hung. **1944** *Amer. N. & Q.* Aug. 72/2 In compiling material on the dime museum I could not help being struck with what seems to have been a showman's affectation—the almost universal use of *musee* for *museum*. **1970** B. Whelpton *Painter's Paris* vii. 107 The Musée Cernuschi..houses a superb collection of the art of China.

2. musée imaginaire (‖ *imaʒinɛ̄r*') [Fr., lit. 'imaginary museum']: an imaginary collection of all the works of human artifice.

[**1947** A. Malraux *Musée Imaginaire* 17 Un Musée imaginaire sans précédent s'est ouvert, qui va pousser à l'extrême l'intellectualisation commencée par l'incomplète confrontation des vrais musées; répondant à l'appel de ceux-ci, les arts plastiques ont inventé leur imprimerie.] **1959** *Twentieth Century* Oct. 262 He [*sc.* the culture-vulture]..haunts the limbo of the *musée imaginaire*, where all cultures and styles coexist. **1960** *Ibid.* Sept. 275 In Audenesque abstraction lies the power to keep us from..the object labelled and dismissed in the *musée imaginaire*. **1962** *Listener* 8 Mar. 431/1 We are no longer bewildered by the 'matter' of civilizations now that the *musée imaginaire* has accustomed us to the quick pounce on the artifact that illumines a lost world. **1967** *Ibid.* 7 Sept. 293/2 Dallagret has gone for..a kind of *musée imaginaire* sealed in polythene.

museless. Delete † *Obs.* and substitute *rare*. Also, uninspired. Add later examples.

1882 G. M. Hopkins *Let.* 4 Nov. (1955) 159 My mind is dull and museless. **1958** P. L. Fermor *Mani* i. 6 Nothing in the grace and the enchantment of all this could remind one of museless and unbookish Sparta.

museography. Add: Also = Museology. Also **museogra·phical** *a.*

1935 R. B. Perry *Tht. & Char. of W. James* I. ix. 176 He had no archaeological or museographical interest. **1953** *Times* 4 Mar. 9/6 An exhibition that is certainly a remarkable example of showmanship or, as it is now called, museography. **1973** *Guardian* 20 Jan. 10/2 French museography has improved.

museology. Add: (Later examples.)

1946 *Nature* 9 Nov. 678/2 Another interesting connexion with the University of Chicago is the establishment of university classes in museology in the Department of Anthropology of the Museum. **1957** G. Clark *Archaeology & Society* (ed. 3) i. 36 Prehistoric archaeology was virtually a branch of museology. **1973** *Nature* 21–28 Dec. 541/1 Dr. Carmichael also achieved renown as a science administrator in the worlds of academia, museology and government.

Hence **museolo·gical** *a.*

1949 K. Clark *Landscape into Art* 137 Cézanne's *petite sensation* was transformed into the most cerebral and museological of all styles—cubism. **1960** *Spectator* 4 Nov. 693 Modern methods of reproduction and museological arrangement. **1970** *Times* 18 Mar. 11/7, I..would rather enjoy the image of myself as a kind of museological Hell's Angel or Jesse James.

mu·sery[2]. *rare*[—1]. [Mus(e *sb.*[1] + -ery.] The work of the Muses.

1869 G. Meredith *Let.* 19 Dec. (1970) I. 407 Why, this stuff is not the Muse, it's Musery.

musette. Add: **5.** In full, *musette bag*. A type of canvas haversack. orig. *Mil.*

1923 E. Hemingway *Three Stories* 13 The young gentleman had a musette over his shoulder. **1934** Webster, Musette bag. **1943** [see *flight bag* (*flight *sb.*[1] 14)]. **1949** A. Hayes *Girl on Via Flaminia* iii. 38 He got up from the bed and went to the table where he had placed the musette bag. He began to unbuckle the straps. **1955** J. Thomas *No Banners* xxiii. 229 Alfred had the Sten gun in a canvas *musette* tied with string and slung over his shoulder. **1961** J. Heller *Catch-22* (1962) xiii. 130 Major—de Coverley.. packed his musette bag, commandeered a plane and..had himself flown to that city to rent two apartments. **1965** *Sun* 3 Nov. 11/5 The musette, or featherweight knapsack from the Continent, has largely replaced the saddlebag. **1968** *Amer. Hist. Illustrated* July (rear cover), The diary stayed behind in his musette bag.

museum. Add: **2.** (Further examples.)

1893 M. Howe *Honor* 320, I was expected to give ten thousand to the Art Museum. **1936** *S.P.E. Tract* xlv. 176 There are..a few English words whose meaning in the United States corresponds more closely to that of their French counterparts than to their meaning in England; e.g...*museum*. **1950** [see *gallery *sb.* 6]. **1975** *Times*

27 Sept. 14/6 The first railway museum in Britain was opened..at York in 1928.

b. *attrib.* and *Comb.*, as *museum-goer, interest*; **museum piece**, an object suitable for exhibition in a museum; also *transf.* (usu. with derogatory sense).

1930 *Times Educ. Suppl.* 23 Aug. 362/2 April is the general 'peak' month for museum-goers. **1971** *Daily Tel.* 11 June 16 An admission charge would not of course greatly deter the habitual museum-goer. **1933** P. GODFREY *Back-Stage* xiv. 180 The attempt of recent years to stage a music-hall revival has unearthed a few shaky veterans of variety, who have little more than a museum interest for the post-War generation. **1901** *Brit. Chess Mag.* XXI. 351 The more stately carved pieces (named for the sake of distinction 'museum-pieces'). **1908** R. FRY *Let.* 12 Dec. (1972) I. 306 It would be a great Museum piece, but..the price is high for Ribera. **1920** W. J. LOCKE *House of Baltazar* iii. 31 Quong Ho was admitted to be a museum-piece of discretion. **1923** J. GALSWORTHY *Captures* 228, I felt as if I had a priceless museum piece which a single stumble might shatter to fragments. **1928** —— *Swan Song* I. xi. 82 The girl and her brother had been museum pieces, two Americans without money to speak of. **1936** L. MACNEICE tr. *Aeschylus' Agamemnon* Pref. 8 It is my hope that the play emerges as a play and not as a museum piece. **1949** B. A. BOTKIN *Treas. S. Folklore* I. i. 4 What saves these relics of the past from being mere museum-pieces is their symbolic and often living relation to the culture of the region. **1955** *Amer. Speech* XXX. 94 *Museum piece*,..an old truck. **1960** H. NICOLSON *Let.* 22 Sept. (1968) 385, I had to lunch with such a bore... He is a museum piece; it is like seeing a railway-engine of 1854. **1964** D. VARADAY *Gara-Yaka* v. 48 He..handed over his rifle, an ancient muzzle-loading museum piece. **1974** P. ERDMAN *Silver Bears* xv. 153, I am looked upon as a mildly amusing curiosity—even a museum piece.

muse·umish, *a. colloq.* [f. MUSEUM + -ISH[1].] Resembling a museum or its exhibits.

1926 D. H. LAWRENCE *Let.* (1932) 657, I wouldn't care to live in Assisi..it's too museumish, not enough life in it now. **1937** *Observer* 5 Sept. 13/3, I must confess that I went to 'Ghosts' with some apprehension. Might not these unhappy far-off things seem too far off; might not the echo of battles long ago bring a museumish air to theatre walls?

mush, *sb.*[1] Add: **1.** (Earlier and *attrib.* examples of *mush and milk.*)

1745 E. KIMBER *Itinerant Observations Amer.* (1878) 34 The meaner Sort you find little else but Water amongst, when their Cyder is spent, Mush and Milk, or Molasses, Homine,..and Fish, are their principal Diet. **1817** in *Essex Inst. Hist. Coll.* (1866) VIII. 244 They..gave me a supper of mush and milk. **1866** 'MARK TWAIN' *Lett. fr. Hawaii* (1967) 210 I'm disgusted with these mush-and-milk preacher travels. **1895** *Montgomery Ward Catal.* 534/1 China Oatmeal or Mush and Milk Set..cream pitcher, bowl and plate.

3. d. *slang.* The mouth or face. Freq. pronounced (mʊʃ).

1859 G. W. MATSELL *Vocabulum* 127 *Mush*, the mouth. **1906** E. DYSON *Fact'ry 'Ands* xv. 202 Er stream iv water ..takes Fuzzy fair in the mush, heels him over. **1919** *Dialect Notes* V. 66 *Mush*, the mouth. 'Stop his mush and give us a rest.' **1932** J. T. FARRELL *Young Lonigan* I. i. 20 That time he had pasted Weary in the mush with an icy snowball. **1959** I. JEFFERIES *Thirteen Days* i. 18 He said if anybody opened his mush, he'd kill 'em. **1971** B. W. ALDISS *Soldier Erect* 53 My regret was that I had not given Wally a bunch of fives in the mush while I had the chance. *Ibid.* 194, I hit him smack in the mush. Not very hard but pleasureably hard. My right fist did not hurt a great deal —not as much as his face hurt him. **1974** T. BARLING *Shooter Man* i. 12 A big grin all over his ugly mush.

e. *Surfing slang.* The foam produced when a wave breaks.

1969 *Surfer* IX. 57 Hardy rides and cuts out as the shoulder flattens to mush. **1970** *Surf '70* (N.Z.) 13/2 If there is any flat mush the board tends to stop and lose its turning ability. **1971** *Studies in English* (Univ. Cape Town) Feb. 28 When a surfer is tired, he catches a wave all the way in. For the last part of the distance he will be riding the frommel; the soup; white water; the mush.

4. *Radio.* Interference or noise heard as a hissing or the sound (ʃ); *spec.* (see quot. 1924).

1924 *Harmsworth's Wireless Encycl.* II. 1456 *Mush*, term used for the irregular intermediate frequencies set up by an arc transmitter which interfere with the fundamental wave-lengths. **1927** [see *BACKGROUND *sb.* 3]. **1928** *Observer* 1 July 4/4 In listening to very faint signals from a great distance a limit is put by the 'mush' and statics and other noises brought in from the aerial. **1952** *Electronic Engin.* XXIV. 120 Unwanted low frequency fluctuations of high frequency 'mush'. **1971** *Daily Mail* 17 Nov. 9/3 Were subjected to a continuous 'hissing noise', or 'electronic mush'.

5. *attrib.* and *Comb.*, as (sense 1) *mush pan, pot*; **mush-head**, a person of a yielding disposition; one lacking in firmness; so *mush-headed* adj.; **mush-ice**, water only partly frozen, ice mixed with water; **mush-sugar**, a mixture of syrup and crystals of sugar.

1890 BARRÈRE & LELAND *Dict. Slang* II. 77/2 *Mush-head* (American), a stupid, witless fellow. **1919** H. L. WILSON *Ma Pettengill* ii. 63, I up and told her flat she could never run a boarding-house and make it pay; that no woman could who hadn't learned to say 'No!' and she was too much of a mushhead for that. **1932** *Screenland* Apr. 70/1 She has married the poor little mush-head that had been wished upon her. **1914** R. CULLUM *Way of Strong* III. viii. 294 The game isn't worth it, fighting this mush-headed crowd who have to get other folks to think for 'em. **1815** *Niles' Weekly Reg.* IX. 201/2 You may, by digging down three feet, take a pole sixty feet long and with the strength of your hands run it down the whole length, and find no termination of what is called the mush ice. **1907** J. LONDON *White Fang* 202 The fall of the year, when the first snows were falling and mush-ice was running in the river. **1966** R. M. PATTERSON *Trail* 86 They came..poling and tracking against the slowly drifting mush ice of the fall. **1847** J. S. ROBB *Squatter Life* 59 Betsy Jones' Tumble in the Mush Pan. **1940** H. H. HATCHER *Buckeye Country* 173 When his self-made pasteboard hat fell to pieces..he covered his head with his mush pan. **1847** H. HOWE *Hist. Coll. Ohio* 432 Johnny, who wore on his head a tin utensil which answered both as a cap and a mush pot, filled it with water and quenched the fire. **1868** *Rep. Iowa Agric. Soc. 1867* 178 When sugar is contemplated, White Imphee is..the best, as all I have made went to thick mush sugar immediately.

mush (mʌʃ), *sb.*[3] [f. *MUSH *v.*[3]] A journey made through snow with a dog-sledge.

1910 R. SERVICE *Trail of '98* 341, I was still weak from my illness and my long mush had wearied me. **1926** *Glasgow Herald* 8 Mar. 10/7 From Hudson in northern Ontario it is a twelve-day 'mush' for men and dogs over the frozen sub-arctic prairie to the Red Lake district. **1965** *Kingston* (Ont.) *Whig-Standard* 8 Feb. 8/6 It's 'Mush, Mush' time for Owner-driver Vern Zoschke and his Dogs.

mush (mʊʃ, mʌʃ), *sb.*[4] *Mil. slang.* [? f. MUSH *v.*[2]] A guardroom or cell; a military prison.

1917 W. MUIR *Observations of Orderly* xiv. 228 If one of those 'hooks' [*sc.* pilferers] were caught, he would be first 'rammed in the mush' (put in the guardroom). **1933** E. PARTRIDGE *Words, Words, Words!* III. 204 *Mush*, sometimes spelt and pronounced *moosh*..denotes guard-room or cell(s). **1943** HUNT & PRINGLE *Service Slang* 46 *Mush*, the *glasshouse* or guardroom.

mush (mʊʃ), *sb.*[5] *slang.* [Orig. uncertain.] Man, 'chap'; hence also as a term of address.

1936 J. CURTIS *Gilt Kid* v. 53 I'm a bit of a coring mush, myself. **1961** J. MACLAREN-ROSS *Doomsday Book* vii. 76 Long's you don't go laughing in the wrong place, mush. **1968** A. DIMENT *Bang Bang Birds* v. 57 So this mush is running a string of..houses of ill-repute... So what?

mush (mʌʃ), *sb.*[6] *slang.* Shortened f. MOUSTACHE, MUSTACHE *sb.*

1967 C. DRUMMOND *Death at Furlong Post* xv. 181 Take my oath it's he..with his hair parted..and the mush shaved off his lip. **1969** K. GILES *Death cracks Bottle* xiii. 172 He read one of these Service ads... You know, a young bloke with a mush telling troops to go plunging into the jungle.

mush (mʌʃ), *v.*[3] [Apparently f. Fr. *marchez* or *marchons*, imp. of *marcher* to advance, the command given to sled dogs; cf. *MUSH *sb.*[3]] Also const. *on.* **a.** *intr.* To travel on foot through the snow with a dog-sledge (said also of the dogs); *trans.* to drive dogs through the snow.

[**1862** R. KENNICOTT *Jrnl.* in J. A. James *First Sci. Explor. Russian Amer.* (1942) 130 My dogs are *dogs*! and we will *mouche* very likely, after all.] **1897** *Medicine Hat* (Alberta) *News* 30 Sept. 7/4 It is laughable to hear the driver yell, 'Mush, Mush,' at them. **1900** J. LONDON *Son of Wolf* 5 'Come, mush on there, you poor sore-footed brutes!' he murmured. **1903** *Sun* (N.Y.) 22 Nov., His little boat was cut out, and then he started to 'mush' back over the ice. **1904** S. E. WHITE *Silent Places* xvii. 180 'Mush! Mush on!' shouted Sam. The four dogs leaned into their collars. **1914** R. CULLUM *Way of Strong* I. i. 1 Five great sled dogs crouched in their harness. They were waiting the long familiar command to 'mush'; an order they had not heard since the previous winter. **1927** *Brit. Weekly* 13 Jan. 409/2 They were mushing on to a new strike. **1932** *Sun* (Baltimore) 15 Jan. 1/5 Through a raging blizzard McDowell mushed a dog team the eighty miles to Aklavik. **1934** *Beaver* Sept. 26 Constable Lee and his Indian interpreter, Albert, came mushing up with a jingle of bells from Fort Providence to pay their annual visit to trappers in the bush. **1947** *Mazama* Dec. 6/2 Norris left Mt. McKinley Park station on 11 April and mushed his dog team to Base Camp arriving 15 April. **1963** R. D. SYMONS *Many Trails* 198 And hurry! Hurry! Before it is too late —mush, mush on—the whip cracks hysterically. **1966** *Kingston* (Ont.) *Whig-Standard* 25 Feb. 12/1 There hasn't been so much excitement over sled-dogs in the north since Leonard Sepala mushed through the land of the midnight sun.

b. *transf.* To travel (through snow or ice).

1898 W. N. ROBERTSON *Yukon Memories* 210 You think all the while you are nearing the top, and 'mush on', like viewing a ship at sea. **1906** 'O. HENRY' *Four Million* 106 I never got off the train since I mushed out of Seattle, and I'm hungry. **1958** P. BERTON *Klondike Fever* 19 He thought nothing of making a present of his trousers to a pantless native and mushing home in his red flannels. **1966** *Globe & Mail* (Toronto) 24 Jan. 17/8, I then struck out to mush to the nearest bus stop.

Hence **mu·shing** *vbl. sb.*

1904 *Prof. Papers U.S. Geol. Survey* No. 20. 15 In 'mushing', the best progress is made in relatively cool weather. **1930** W. N. ROBERTSON *Yukon Memories* viii. 114 There is a lingering feeling that the monotonous *mushing* along has not been devoid of its pleasures. **1966** *Kingston* (Ont.) *Whig-Standard* 25 Feb. 12/1 Wilfrid Charles is regarded as a sure-pop betting cinch to retain the mushing title.

mush (mʌʃ), *v.*[4] *colloq.* [f. MUSH *sb.*[1] 3.] Const. *in.* To sink into a soft surface.

1948 N. SHUTE *No Highway* ii. 41 The landing was a hazardous one because of the alternate thaw and freeze: the skis [of the aircraft] mushed in beneath the icy crust. **1962** J. GLENN in *Into Orbit* 13, I..skimmed right over the top of a rice paddy—almost mushing into it.

musha. (Later examples.)

1898 J. D. BRAYSHAW *Slum Silhouettes* 15 Oh, musha! the divil a drown ye'll drown, Murty Hooligan, while there's hemp for the sowing. **1933** DAVIES & THOMSON tr. *O'Sullivan's Twenty Years A-Growing* i. 7 Ah, musha, youth is a queer thing.

musher (mʌ·ʃəɹ). [f. *MUSH *v.*[3] + -ER[1].] A person who mushes; one who travels through snow on foot (with a dog-sledge). Also *fig.*

c **1900** *Western Miner* (1963) Mar. 30/1 Way up north there's a rail road...It followed the tracks of the mushers, Where they grasped the rocks for a hold. **1902** L. MCKEE *Land of Nome* 178, I felt that I had received a very high compliment..when an old-timer in the party..told me that I was a 'musher from hell'. **1925** *Chambers's Jrnl.* July 456/2 Those far northern regions are inaccessible.. except to the most hardy and expert 'mushers'. **1948** *Time* 19 July 34/3 Klondike Mike, the greatest of the mushers, the sourdough who struck it rich and kept his poke, is a living legend. **1973** *Islander* (Victoria, B.C.) 20 May 3/1 Art Fraser, owner and musher of the dog team, was my guide.

mushie (mʌ·ʃi). *Austral. colloq.* shortening of MUSHROOM *sb.* 1.

1935 O. P. MEYER *Four of Us* 52, I don't see many mushies yet. **1972** *Sunday Mail* (Brisbane) 9 Jan. 5/2 Mushies are seldom sold, and are grown so easily from cow manure..that they're usually given away.

mushily (mʌ·ʃili), *adv.* [f. MUSHY *a.* + -LY[2].] In a soft or mushy manner.

1896 'MARK TWAIN' in *Harper's Mag.* Jan. 296/2 The column of inert mortality sank mushily to the ground. **1910** 'O. HENRY' *Strictly Business* xvi. 187 'A cool hundred,' said Fuzzy thoughtfully and mushily. *a* **1935** T. E. LAWRENCE *Mint* (1955) II. xiv. 138 A black east wind froze the sweat mushily over our skins. **1971** 'D. SHANNON' *Ringer* (1972) ix. 147 'That I did,' confirmed Mr. Gebhart mushily. ''Scuse me—get my teeth—.'

mushiness (mʌ·ʃinės). *colloq.* [f. MUSHY *a.* + -NESS.] The condition of being soft or pulpy; also *fig.*, sentimental character, weakness, sloppiness.

1890 [see MUSHY *a.*]. **1893** 'M. RUTHERFORD' *Cath. Furze* II. xiv. 70 Partly this distressing weakness is due to the absence of a clear conviction that we are right;..but frequently it is simple mushiness of character. **1946** A. L. BACHARACH *Brit. Music of our Time* xv. 197 One is perhaps disconcerted by an harmonic mushiness—he was especially fond of the now much-abused chords of the seventh and ninth. **1962** *Yale Rev.* June 540 Pound puts Joyce with Hueffer, diametrically opposite to 'the softness and mushiness of the neo-symbolist movement'.

mu·shrat. = MUSK-RAT 1, 2. *N. Amer.*

1890 *Dialect Notes* I. 74 *Mushrat*, the muskrat or musquash. **1901** R. CONNOR *Man from Glengarry* 19 The Glengarry men..despised the Murphy gang as sawlogmen; 'log-rollers' or 'mushrats' they called them. **1939** W. FAULKNER *Wild Palms* 218 If I took aboard every floating sardine can you sonabitchin mushrats want me to I wouldn't even have room forrard for a leadsman. **1939** T. H. RADDALL *Pied Piper* 45 An' I'm goin' to play hell with you, you game-poachin', fish-spearin', woodstealin' ol' mushrat! **1954** C. BRUCE *Channel Shore* 18 Stan was carrying on..talk of mushrats and rabbitsnaring. **1954** *Encounter* Oct. 3/2 All the lesser beasts—coon and possum and beaver and mink and mushrat (not muskrat: mushrat); they were still there.

mushroom, *sb.* Add: **3. c.** *Archit.* A reinforced concrete pillar that broadens out towards the top, with the reinforcing rods passing upwards and outwards into a reinforced concrete slab forming part of the floor above, which is thereby supported by the pillars without the use of beams. Freq. *attrib.*

1907 *Western Architect* May 51/1 The essential feature of this new construction is the formation of a so-called mushroom at the top of each column, by extending its reinforcing rods, laterally, some four feet or more out into the slab in a radial direction and supporting on these, ring rods, which, in turn, carry the lighter reinforcement for the slab construction. **1927** T. P. BENNETT *Archit. Design in Concrete* 14 A scheme similar in principle has been employed in a number of factory buildings, and has acquired the name of 'Mushroom' construction. **1936** *Archit. Rev.* LXXX. 113/1 (*caption*) These conditions have been met by an adaptation of the 'mushroom' floor slab type of construction. Each floor consists of a reinforced concrete slab, 10 ins. thick, supported on external wall columns, spaced 21 ft. centre to centre, and two internal columns with mushroom caps. **1941** S. GIEDION *Space, Time & Archit.* VI. 374 The American engineer C. A. P. Turner had been experimenting with the mushroom system a year before Maillart, but the Swiss engineer had employed slabs as basic elements in bridges since the beginning of the century. **1963** tr. *Hatje's Encycl. Mod. Archit.* 182/2 His [*sc.* Robert Maillart's] most important invention in the field of high structures was made in 1908 with mushroom slab construction, which he used for the first time on a large scale in 1910. **1969** W. R. DALZELL *Architecture* 41 (*caption*) Reinforced concrete mushrooms support slab constructions.

d. A cloud (of smoke, fire, etc.) that spreads upwards and outwards.

1916 J. BUCHAN *Greenmantle* xxi. 291 There was the dull shock of an explosion and a mushroom of red earth. **1924** A. J. SMALL *Frozen Gold* iv. 110 A sudden, abrupt mushroom of smoke spread out above the building on the uprush of air. **1945** *N.Y. Times* 26 Sept. 16/6 At first it was a giant column that soon took the shape of a supramundane mushroom. **1952** G. WILSON *Julien Ware* xvi. 129 He..pulled energetically at the stem until a mushroom of smoke hung above his head. **1954** *Amer. Speech* xxix. 275 *Mushroom*, a fire which, reaching a ceiling and finding no outlet, starts to spread out and burn downward.

e. A mushroom-shaped implement used in darning.

1931 'R. CROMPTON' *William's Crowded Hours* viii. 172 The cavity through which both her fist and the darning 'mushroom' slipped so unavailingly. **1931** R. H. HEATON *Perfect Hostess* 95 Little comforts for the work-basket... Ribbon threader. Mushroom for darning. **1969** E. H. PINTO *Treen* vii. 134 Cabbage pressers..are larger versions of 'mushroom' darners, usually with the button end about 5 in. in diameter.

6. a. *mushroom lip, minaret, omelette, pickle, sauce* (earlier example), *sculpture*.

1962 D. HARDEN *Phoenicians* xi. 150 In tombs at Carthage jugs with mushroom or trefoil lips abounded. **1930** R. CAMPBELL *Adamastor* 50 Their mushroom minarets and toadstool towers. **1892** *Encycl. Pract. Cookery* I. xiii. 961/2 Mushroom omelet—Either fresh or canned mushrooms may be used for this. **1954** G. M. LAPOLLA *Mushroom Cooking* 78 Mushroom omelette. One way of using mushroom stems. **1972** P. D. JAMES *Unsuitable Job for Woman* iv. 137 She made herself a mushroom omelette. **1747** H. GLASSE *Art of Cookery* ii. 35 Add a Spoonful of Mushroom Pickle, pickled Mushrooms, or fresh, if you have them. **1911** W. OWEN *Let.* 25 Sept. (1967) 85 In the kitchen making mushroom pickle. **1747** H. GLASSE *Art of Cookery* ii. 35 To make Mushroom-Sauce for White Fowls of all Sorts. **1970** *Washington Post* 30 Sept. B 1/5 This holy mushroom sculpture of gray volcanic stone is part of the pre-Columbian art exhibit.

c. mushroom city, = *mushroom town* (below); **mushroom cloud**, the cloud of smoke that forms above the site of a nuclear explosion, with the characteristic shape of a tall pillar with a broad, flattish top; also *fig.*; (cf. sense *3 d); **mushroom-faker** (earlier example); **mushroom-flap** *obs.*, the cap of a common mushroom when fully opened; **mushroom growth**, rapid growth like that of a mushroom; **mushroom hat** (earlier and later examples); **mushroom-headed** *a.* (later example); **mushroom town**, a town that has sprung up rapidly; **mushroom valve**, a lift valve whose moving element somewhat resembles a mushroom in shape.

1860 H. GREELEY *Overland Journey* 140 A rush of three or four hundred, mainly men of broken fortunes from the dead mushroom 'cities' of Nebraska and Kansas. **1948** P. JOHNSTON *Gold Rush* 42/1 By April 1850, Downieville had become a mushroom city of large proportions with a population of about 5000. **1958** *Spectator* 17 Jan. 63/1 If Europe is not to go up in a mushroom cloud we must find an area of agreement with the Soviet Union. **1964** M. GOWING *Britain & Atomic Energy* ix. 267 Dr Penney was one of the scientific observers who saw the mushroom cloud rise from the ruins of Nagasaki. **1965** *Spectator* 5 Feb. 167/1 Hatred grows to mushroom-cloud proportions. **1839** H. BRANDON *Poverty, Mendicity & Crime* 164/1 *Mushroom fakers*, itinerant umbrella makers and repairers. **1747** H. GLASSE *Art of Cookery* xi. 121 Two Quarts of the large Mushroom Flaps rubbed to Pieces. **1861** MRS. BEETON *Bk. Househ. Managem.* 226 Choose full-grown mushroom-flaps, and take care they are perfectly fresh-gathered. **1911** E. WALLACE *Sanders of River* viii. 108 These secret societies he knew well enough... He knew their mushroom growth; how they rose from nothingness with rituals and practices ready-made. **1931** *Economist* 2 May 944/2 Thus has terminated the career of a bank which enjoyed a mushroom growth immediately after the war. **1879** C. M. YONGE *Magnum Bonum* I. xi. 206 She looked up under her brown mushroom hat. **1888** —— *Beechcroft at Rockstone* iv. 73 A..lady in a mushroom hat. **1912** [see *ABLOW *adv.* or *pred. a.*]. **1963** *Guardian* 29 Jan. 7/7 Dots..come on giant mushroom hats. **1875** PITT-RIVERS in *Proc. R. Inst. Gt. Brit.* VII. 514 We see [in the plate] the mushroom-headed waddy, with its projecting ridge flattened, then [in a later stage of development] curved. **1819** R. L. MASON *Diary* 9 Dec. in *Narr. in Pioneer West* (1915) 66 Those mushroom towns in a short time will produce their own death. **1938** H. ASBURY *Sucker's Prog.* 310 The invasion reached its peak with.. the building of the trans-continental railroads which the gamblers followed step by step, carrying on their thieving business in every mushroom town that sprang up along the route. **1957** *Economist* 12 Oct. 105/2 These peasants turned workers..are the most interesting feature of the whole Polish social landscape. The mushroom town.. displays the problem in a nutshell. **1877** *Design & Work* 7 July 114/3 Exhaust valve, consisting of ordinary mushroom valve. **1924** S. G. WHEELER *Marine Engin.* I. vii. 102 Occasionally steam engines are controlled by 'mushroom' valves like internal combustion engines. **1966** J. A. DOLAN *Motor Vehicle Technol.* I. ix. 91 The valves used in motor vehicle engines are called poppet or mushroom valves.

mushroom, *v.* Add: **4.** *intr.* To rise like a mushroom; to expand or increase rapidly; also const. *up, out.* Freq. *fig.*

1903 *Sun* (N.Y.) 2 Nov. 3 The flames had gone up the stairs to the very top of the house, and had then 'mushroomed' out, as the firemen say. **1911** *Ithaca Jrnl.* 10 Aug., The flames mushroomed from the shaft on all floors above. **1937** D. L. SAYERS *Busman's Honeymoon* v. 97 The loosened soot of centuries came plunging in a mad cascade down the chimney; it met the floor with a soft and deadly violence and mushroomed up in a Stygian cloud. **1947** J. C. RICH *Materials & Methods of Sculpture* ix. 249 If the end [of the chisel] receiving the impact of the carving hammer is too soft, it will quickly 'mushroom'. *Ibid.* ix. 261 The untempered ends of working chisels will frequently begin to mushroom..after repeated hammer blows. **1959** *Daily Tel.* 1 Dec. 11/8 A private Bill, promoted by the L.C.C.; it is intended to secure greater control of clubs which have 'mushroomed' into existence in recent years. **1962** *Listener* 9 Aug. 223/2 His characters are huge, they mushroom out one after the other and yet the plays aren't shapeless. **1972** *Language* XLVIII. 429 The number of publishing companies, both in Europe and North America, which have prepared new editions of primary sources [in linguistics] has mushroomed.

mushrooming, *vbl. sb.* Add: **c.** Growth like that of a mushroom, as regards shape (cf. b) or rapidity. Freq. *fig.* Also as *ppl. a.*

1947 J. C. RICH *Materials & Methods of Sculpture* ix. 251 For fashioning chisels... It is advisable to cut the chisel blanks 1 to 2½ extra inches in length, since the occasional fracturing of a point, a mushrooming of the end receiving the hammer blows, and repeated sharpening will slowly shorten the total length. **1954** *Encounter* June 13/1 Over the past decade there has been a fantastic mushrooming of arts and crafts hobbies. **1957** *Listener* 12 Sept. 379/1 Economic changes..have brought..Africans into new jobs and opportunities, and into mushrooming new towns. **1968** A. DIMENT *Great Spy Race* x. 186 The mushrooming fireball of exploding petrol. **1968** *Brit. Med. Bull.* XXIV. 189/1 Recent mushrooming of activity and interest in this subject. **1972** K. S. ROUNDHILL *Prescription for Today's Missionary* 11 Positions for foreign teachers in the mushrooming educational programmes..are often available.

mushy, *a.* Add: (Earlier and later examples.)

1839 *Southern Lit. Messenger* V. 209/2, I soon recognized old *Noth Calinur* in their nasal mushy pronunciation. **1880** 'MARK TWAIN' *Tramp Abr.* xxvi. 267 Mushy, slushy early spring roads. **1952** M. TRIPP *Faith is Windsock* ii. 34 Unfortunately reception was indistinct and towns showed vague and mushy, making identification acutely difficult. **1962** *Which?* (Suppl.) July 86/2 Its handling was described as 'mushy' and our drivers said that it tended to 'wallow' in corners.

2. *fig.* Tender, sentimental, insipid. Also as *adv.*

1870 *Nation* (N.Y.) 3 Feb. 67 The death penalty is disappearing, like some better things, before a kind of mushy and unthinking doubt of its morality and expediency. **1876** [in Dict.]. **1913** G. STRATTON-PORTER *Laddie* vii. 220 They formed a circle around Sally and Peter and as mushy as ever they could they sang, 'As sure as the grass grows around the stump, You are my darling sugar lump,' while they danced. **1928** G. B. SHAW *Intell. Woman's Guide Socialism* 458 You may..be a sharp, cynical sort of person; or you may be a nice, mushy, amiable, goodnatured one. **1951** J. D. SALINGER *Catcher in Rye* xvi. 137 She sings it very Dixieland and whore-house, and it doesn't sound at all mushy. **1971** WODEHOUSE *Much Obliged, Jeeves* i. 7 [Marriage] wouldn't have fitted in with my plans at all, she though physically in the pin-up class, being as mushy a character as ever broke biscuit. **1974** L. LAMB *Man in Mist* i. 12 Some mushy mag. She calls that a book!

3. (See quots. and cf. *MUSH *sb.*[1] 4.)

1924 *Harmsworth's Wireless Encycl.* II. 1456 A mushy note is one which is not absolutely definite or clear cut, and so hard to read. It is a note received by the heterodyne method when damped wires or modulated continuous waves are being received. **1937** *Printers' Ink Monthly* May 39/3 Mushy, poor musical definition of an orchestral pickup.

4. *Surfing.* (See quots.)

1967 J. SEVERSON *Great Surfing* Gloss., *Mushy*, a slow, sloppy wave that has little power. **1969** *Surfer* IX. No. 6, 69 My little board's good for mushy waves, but when it's five foot or over and fast, I use the other. **1972** R. ABBOTT *Science of Surfing* v. 83 It is sometimes possible to 'beat' breaking sections, although this is easiest if the waves are 'mushy'.

music, *sb.* Add: **11.** *to face the music* (earlier U.S. and later examples); *music while you work*: continuous light music played to workers, esp. in factories; *to make* (*beautiful*) *music* (*together*): to have sexual intercourse.

1850 *Congress. Globe* App. 4 Mar. 324/3 There should be no skulking or dodging..every man should 'face the music'. **1920** R. MACAULAY *Potterism* III. viii. 140 If Gideon didn't shove him, he's nothing to be afraid of in our talk, and if he did he'll have to face the music. **1940** *Radio Times* 21 June 3/2 This coming week there will be, twice every day, half-an-hour's music meant specially for factory-workers..under the title 'Music while you work'. **1958** J. BETJEMAN *Coll. Poems* 227 Though 'Music while you work' is now our wont, It's not so nice as 'Music while you don't'. **1958** 'J. BYROM' *Or be he Dead* xv. 186 So the old bitch *did* recognize me! Mrs Kernan and I were pretty sure she had. That's why we did a bunk so hastily, leaving Byron to face the bill and the music. **1960** R. POUND *Selfridge* ii. 40 One of the first applications of the music-while-you-work incentive to modern labour. **1967** F. MULLALLY *Prizewinner* vii. 117 He could say good-bye to any hope of making music later on with the Swede. **1968** S. E. ELLACOTT *Everyday Things in England 1914–68* xi. 162 The factory system of 'music while you work'..was introduced during the Second World War..in munitions factories. In mechanical, repetitive jobs lively music helped production. **1969** H. NIELSEN *Darkest Hour* xxi. 238 You and Buddy can make beautiful music together. **1972** C. SHORT *Naked Skier* xxi. 115, I think we should make music together.

11*. Flexibility or 'give' in the shaft of a golf club. *rare.*

1890 H. G. HUTCHINSON *Golf* iii. 57 A heavy head may bring just the right amount of life—of what Tom Morris calls 'music'—out of a very stiff shaft. **1903** W. J. TRAVIS *Pract. Golf* (rev. ed.) ix. 111 The man with a less rapid swing will get equally as long a ball by using a more supple shaft. The more 'music' there is in the shaft, however, the greater is the liability to slice or pull.

12. a. *music cabinet, critic, -man* (further examples), *-master* (later example), *-rack* (earlier example), *-rest* (further example), *-sheet, -shop* (earlier example), *-stool* (earlier and later examples), *-track*. **b.** *music-lover, -maker, -making, -publisher, -seller; music-hungry, -loving, -sounding, -stunned* adjs.

1883 *Heal & Son Catal.* Sept. 216 Music Cabinet, Walnut or Ebonised. **1911** *Daily Colonist* (Victoria, B.C.) 22 Apr. 4/4 It does not matter to us what style of piano you may have we can give you a music cabinet style to harmonize. **1901** G. B. SHAW *Three Plays for Puritans* p. v, The difference between the leisure of a Persian cat and the labor of a cockney cab horse is not greater than the difference between the official weekly or fortnightly playgoings of the theatre critic and the restless daily rushing to and fro of the music critic. **1956** AUDEN & KALLMAN *Magic Flute* (1957) 58 That is changed Since music-critics learned to feel 'estranged'. **1950** A. LOMAX *Mister Jelly Roll* iv. 181 A gang of music-hungry, life-hungry white kids. **1933** *Maclean's Mag.* 15 July 32/4 Music lovers will thrill at the music of His Majesty's Scots Guards, and thirty other bands. **1963** AUDEN *Dyer's Hand* 507 That great music-lover, Bernard Shaw. **1870** D. J. KIRWAN *Palace & Hovel* xxxiv. 493 Theatre going and music-loving people. **1864** BROWNING *Dramatis Personae* 49 Schumann's our music maker now. **1955** N. CARDUS in H. van Thal *Fanfare for E. Newman* iii. 34 The composer's physiology as music-maker. **1946** Music-making [see sense 12 c below]. **1963** *Times* 12 Feb. 14/4 A recital which had more of the air of a friendly music-making at home than the deadly earnest aspiration usually encountered on this platform. **1937** H. G. WELLS *Brynhild* v. 61 The brightest and best producers, directors,.. cutters, music-men. **1950** L. BENNETT *Anancy Stories & Dial. Verse* 40 Once upon a time Cockroach was a very good music-man an everybody wat have a dance always want Bredda Cockroach fe play fe dem. **1958** *Spectator* 10 Jan. 38/1 Mrs. Legge is what music-men call the flipover. **1845** *Ainsworth's Mag.* VII. 507, I see your ladyship's music-master..in the carriage. **1848** *Knickerbocker* XXXI. 450 Mr. Joseph F. Atwill, one of our most popular music-publishers..is issuing..a musical publication of rare interest. **1885** *List of Subscribers, Classified* (United Telephone Co.) (ed. 6) 157 Music publishers and sellers.. Boosey & Co. **1919** WODEHOUSE *Damsel in Distress* xvi. 199 She was a stenographer in a music-publisher's office when we first met. **1855** *Knickerbocker* XLV. 136 You hide behind the music-rack while Miss Mince passes. **1922** JOYCE *Ulysses* 691 It's musicrest supporting the music.. for voice and piano of *Love's Old Sweet Song*. **1801** T. BUSBY *Dict. Music*, *Music-seller*, one who buys and sells music..likewise all kinds of musical instruments. **1811** JANE AUSTEN *Sense & Sens.* I. xvii. 216 Booksellers, music-sellers, and print-shops. **1914** W. OWEN *Let.* c 3 July (1967) 264 Practically all my Music Sheets..have been stolen! *c* **1760** in Dryden *Alexander's Feast* (title-page), Set to Musick by Mr. Handel. Edinburgh, sold by Robert Bremner, at his Musick-shop, at the Harp and Hautboy. **1925** E., O., & S. SITWELL *Poor Young People* 20 To music-sounding moonlight. **1834** DICKENS *Sk. Boz* (1836). 1st Ser. I. 206 Mr. Wisbottle was describing semi-circles on the music-stool. **1902** CONRAD *Youth* 314 He swung half round on the music-stool, listening with his fingertips at rest on the keyboard. **1975** *Country Life* 2 Oct. 852/1 The wood's great weight also recommended it for pillar furniture: ranging from tea-poy to music stool. *a* **1930** D. H. LAWRENCE *Sex, Literature & Censorship* (1955) 114 The dream of our pathetic, music-stunned young girl of today. **1953** K. REISZ *Technique Film Editing* III. xii. 187 It is most important that the dubbing editor should be able to cross fade from the dialogue to the music track at any time.

c. Delete † and add later examples.

1877 G. B. SHAW *How to become Mus. Critic* (1960) 19 Tristan and Isolde, a music drama which, in order of development, is the latest of Wagner's works. **1885** —— *Ibid.* 91 His allegorical music-play Die Zauberflöte. **1903** R. HUGHES *Musical Guide* I. 207/2 Music-drama. An opera (particularly of the Wagnerian School) in which the text and the action determine the music, and are not interrupted by set arias, duets, etc. **1935** *Discovery* Sept. 250/2 This..building..is now the scene of the Triennial Music Festivals. **1946** MEZZROW & WOLFE *Really Blues* viii. 117 We had a ritual for these music-appreciation classes. **1946** *Penguin Music Mag.* Dec. 10 Since the early eighteenth century the music festival has been one of the most important and sustaining influences in English music-making. **1947** A. EINSTEIN *Music in Romantic Era* xvi. 227 Wagner..considered himself, justifiably, not as a pure musician, but as a music-dramatist. **1966** *Listener* 5 May 663/2 Puccini's *Madama Butterfly*, his only opera that may lay claim to be called a psychological music drama. **1975** *Country Life* 2 Oct. 846/1 Wagner's great works are music-dramas rather than operas in the old sense.

d. music case, (*a*) a container (see CASE *sb.*[2] 9) in which the component parts of a fount of music type are arranged before being set; (*b*) a container for sheet music; **music centre**, a stereophonic system combining record-player, radio, and cassette tape recorder in a single unit, usu. with separate loudspeakers; **music-club**, delete † and add earlier and later examples; **music-hall** (further examples in the *spec.* sense); so **music-hallish, music-hally** *adjs.*,

suggestive of a music-hall; **music line,** a line (LINE *sb.*² 1 e) whose transmission characteristics are good enough for the transmission of music, and along which programme material is usually sent; **music-roll,** (*a*) a receptacle for the carriage of rolled-up sheet music; (*b*) a roll, usually of perforated paper, used in a pianola or player-piano or similar instrument; **music-room** (later examples); **music type,** substitute for def.: a fount of type, including several hundred pieces, used for the typographic printing of music, as distinguished from the use of engraved plates; also *attrib.* (earlier and later examples).

1841 W. SAVAGE *Dict. Art of Printing* 487 All that I shall attempt is to give the plan of a pair of Music Cases, with the characters. **1890** *Cent. Dict.*, Music-case. **1894** *Amer. Dict. Printing & Bookmaking* 383/2 *Music cases*, special cases of a complicated character employed in composing type-music. **1924** *Southward's Mod. Printing* (ed. 5) I. v. 41 Music Cases. This class of case has to be made to suit the founts of different founders, who vary in the number of characters they cast. **1960** K. AMIS *Take Girl like You* ii. 27 Jenny..fetched her music case, with books and not music in, from the classroom. **1974** *Hi Fi for Pleasure* Jan. 15 Model G 2601 KL..is a music centre with everything. **1975** *Gramophone* Nov. 958/2 Decca's Compact 4 music centre now incorporates long wave in its tuner section. **1975** *Which?* Dec. 356/3 Most music centres are designed to be sold with one set of loudspeakers only. **1740** R. VERNEY *Let.* 11 Nov. in M. M. Verney *Verney Lett.* (1930) II. xxix. 185 Mr. Millward on returning..from the inn at East Claydon, where there is a Musicck [*sic*] Club instituted, fell down. **1946** *Penguin Music Mag.* Dec. 7 Gramophone societies and music clubs which flourish all over the country. **1857** J. E. RITCHIE *Night Side London* 145 The new Music Hall, Hungerford Market. **1870** D. J. KIRWAN *Palace & Hovel* xxxiv. 503 A popular street and music-hall song. **1927** J. ADAMS *Errors in School* 112 His music-hall cluster. **1959** *New Statesman* 25 Apr. 574/3 The opening of the prison scene is made the occasion for an interminable drunken charade which destroys the balance of an act that is precarious enough in its original form—all for the sake of a primitive music-hall joke repeated at least a dozen times without variation. **1975** J. WAINWRIGHT *Square Dance* 248 You dress outrageously and you behave like a music-hall comedian. **1893** M. BEERBOHM *Let.* Sept. (1964) 60 A good many common music-hallish people were standing in front of me. **1930** *Observer* 30 Mar. 15 The patriotic song of 1900 should have been sung by someone more robust and music-hallish than the cute and charming Miss Ada-May. **1889** G. B. SHAW *London Music in 1888–89* (1937) 211 The inferior theatre orchestra is music-hally, blatant, thumping, out of tune. **1923** A. CHRISTIE *Murder on Links* xxii. 251 Their voices were..rather thin and music-hally, but attractive. **1941** *B.B.C. Gloss. Broadcasting Terms* 20 Music line. **1962** A. NISBETT *Technique Sound Studio* 246 A control line..is a telephone circuit on which programme details may be discussed, and is so called to distinguish it from the broad band (i.e. high quality) 'music line' along which programme is fed. **1890** *Cent. Dict.*, Music-roll. **1890–1** *T. Eaton & Co. Catal.* Fall & Winter 42/1 Music rolls, in leather... Music rolls, in plush. **1906** *Bazaar, Exch. & Mart* Suppl. 3 Oct. 1322/1 Kastner's upright grand auto-piano for sale,..played by hand or by music rolls. **1907** *Yesterday's Shopping* (1969) 399/3 *Music rolls.* American cloth, lined cloth—1/5. **1913** *Strand Mag.* Jan. 13 (Advt.), For all player-pianos 'Songola' music rolls. **1875** 'MARK TWAIN' *Sketches New & Old* 307 We shall have billard-rooms [*sic*], card-rooms, music-rooms. **1928** 'SAPPER' *Female of Species* x. 173 The music-room appeared to be so-called because there was no trace of any musical instrument in it. **1942** E. BLOM *Music in England* vi. 92 In 1713 a dancing-master named Hickford opened a music room..where the celebrities of the day appeared. **1975** *Listener* 6 Nov. 608/3 My fourth new stopwatch..fell to the tiled floor of our music-room from my nerveless fingers. **1825** T. C. HANSARD *Typographia* Index 11, Music type. **1841** W. SAVAGE *Dict. Art of Printing* 488 (*caption*) C. Hancock's plan of cases for Hughes' music type. **1892** A. POWELL *Southward's Pract. Printing* (ed. 4) xxxi. 292 Most of the letter-founders supply music types. **1923** W. GAMBLE *Music Engraving & Printing* xv. 169 The setting up of music type is a difficult and tedious operation. **1934** C. LAMBERT *Music Ho!* 11 There are few technical terms and no music-type illustrations. **1968** *Listener* 27 June 845/2 To demonstrate this [*sc.* the shapes of this plainchant melody] would need music-type.

‖ **musica** (miū·zikă). [L., = music.] Used in special collocations to designate different kinds of music or musical techniques, as **musica ficta,** in contrapuntal music of the 10th to 16th centuries, the introduction by the singer of conventional chromatically altered tones to avoid unacceptable intervals; **musica figurata,** (*a*) contrapuntal music in which the different melodic strands move more or less independently; (*b*) plainsong with decorated melody; **musica plana** = **cantus firmus*; plainsong; **musica reservata** (see quot. 1972).

1740 J. GRASSINEAU *Musical Dict.* 154 *Musica Figuralis, Figurata,* or *Colorata,* figurate music, wherein the notes are of different values, and the motions various, now slow then quick. **1801** T. BUSBY *Dict. Music, Musica ficta,*..the name given by Franchinus and other musical writers, to the first deviations from the old ecclesiastical modes. **1886** W. S. ROCKSTRO *Hist. Mus.* 482 The Rules of ..Musica ficta..enable us to supply, with certainty, the accidental Sharps and Flats, which the older writers omitted. **1940** G. REESE *Music in Middle Ages* (1941) v. 121 Not until the 13th century did *musica plana* etc. come to connote music in free rhythm as distinguished from measured music, as do the English words 'plainsong' and 'plainchant'. **1944** W. APEL *Harvard Dict. Mus.* 467/2 *Musica reservata* denotes the Renaissance-like clarity, balance, and expressiveness, the full-blooded humanism of the Josquin period, in contrast to the abstract and mysterious transcendentalism of the earlier masters. **1954** A. HUGHES in *New Oxf. Hist. Music* II. xi. 370 The position which called for such a system as *musica ficta* is as simple as the processes of its working out are complex. It is the problem of the tritone. **1954** G. REESE *Music in Renaissance* ix. 512 The expression '*musica reservata*' has become one of the problems of music history. **1963** R. DONINGTON *Interpretation of Early Music* iv. 67 *D* minor, which we notate with a signature of one flat, grew out of the Dorian mode when its leading note, *C*, became habitually sharpened by the workings of *musica ficta*. **1968** *Listener* 23 May 676/2 His [*sc.* Palestrina's] Mass saves music, convinces the Pope that a regression to *musica plana,* plainsong, at the indiscriminate expense of *musica figurata* (the later, florid polyphonic style of the early Flemish composers) would be wrong—wrong metaphysically. **1972** *Composer & Conductor* Aug. 1/1 'Musica reservata'..lends itself to diametrically opposite definitions. Some musicologists describe it as music made suitable for popular use, while others regard 'musica reservata' as literally 'reserved for connoisseurs'.

musical, *a.* (and *sb.*) Add: **A.** *adj.* **1.** (Further examples.)

1790 SHERIDAN *Let.* in T. Moore *Life R. B. Sheridan* (1825) 468 We had a very pleasant musical party last night at Lord Erskine's. **1791** F. BURNEY *Jrnl.* Dec. (1972) I. 95 We have spent a charming Musical Evening at Mr. Burney's. **1814** J. MAYNE *Jrnl.* 7 Nov. (1909) x. 183 Countess Cardelli, who has agreeable musical parties at her house every Sunday evening. **1885** *List of Subscribers, Classified* (United Telephone Co.) (ed. 6) 157 Musical instrument makers..Chappell & Co. **1926** *Punch* 10 Nov. p. iii (Advt.), Recreation for yourself—Dance Parties—Musical Evenings. **1964** W. L. GOODMAN *Hist. Woodworking Tools* 92 These small block planes were very useful to violin and other musical-instrument makers.

10. musical appreciation, informed response to music; **musical arms,** a modification of the game of musical chairs (see quot.); **musical box** (earlier and later examples); also *transf.* and *fig.*; **musical bumps,** a game similar to musical chairs, in which the competitors sit down on the floor or ground when the music stops and the last person to sit is out of the game; also *fig.*; **musical chairs,** a competitive parlour game in which a number of persons walk to music round a smaller number of chairs and each tries to secure a seat when the music stops, or an outdoor game on the same principle played on horseback; also *attrib.* and *fig.*; **musical clock** (later example); **musical comedy,** a light dramatic piece, on stage or in a cinema, consisting of dialogue, songs, and dancing, connected by a slight plot; also *fig.*; **musical director,** the conductor of the orchestra of a theatre, either for opera or for plays; **musical dramatist,** a composer of music-dramas (see *MUSIC *sb.* 12 c); **musical drive,** an exhibition of horsemanship by a military unit in which the horses pull along the military equipment to the accompaniment of music; **musical festival** = FESTIVAL *sb.* 1 b; **musical fright** = **musical chairs*; **musical ride** (later example, here equivalent to *musical drive* above); **musical saw,** a hand-saw held between the knees and 'played' with a violin bow; **musical watch,** a watch which incorporates a comb and cylinder mechanism to produce a tune at specified times.

1929 *Jrnl. Abnormal Psychol.* XXIV. 75 It is possible.. in the teaching of 'musical appreciation' to inculcate dogmas about what is symbolized by certain musical combinations. **1947** C. GRAY *Contingencies & Other Essays* i. 20 The recognition of the truth..has brought about in recent years the development of an activity known as 'musical appreciation', which aims at fostering a love of music among the populace by means of broadcast lectures, evening classes, elementary handbooks and textbooks, educational gramophone records, and so forth; by teaching music, in a word, in very much the same way as one would teach any other subject in the educational curriculum. **1955** P. VINCENT in H. van Thal *Fanfare for Ernest Newman* 174 The courses of musical appreciation that have been taught in schools these last twenty years or so. **1962** M. SARGENT *Outline of Music* p. v, I believe this 'Outline' to be more thorough than many popular books on musical appreciation. **1924** D. C. MINTER *Children's Parties* x. 137 Musical arms. This game is played in the same way as Musical Chairs, without, however, using chairs. [**1821** M. WILMOT *Let.* 16 Apr. (1935) 105 The musical bonbon box, and other trifles to *amuse* the children.] **1829** A. ROYALL *Pennsylvania* I. 10 A small wooden musical box..by mechanical invention produced the name of any capital town you called for. **1925** T. E. LAWRENCE *Let.* 3 Nov. (1938) 486 Our hut now has a little musical box. **1925** E. SITWELL *Poetry & Criticism* 21 No time for darkness there, excepting in the cubes of their musical-box brains. **1932** S. G. HEDGES *Indoor & Community Games* vi. 76 *Musical Bumps*... All march round in single file, while the pianist plays... When the music stops everyone must flop down on the floor—and the one who 'bumps' last falls out of the game. **1967** E. GRIERSON *Crime of One's Own* xi. 92 He..went a few paces and stopped abruptly—the technique one used at the piano to defeat too proficient children at a game of Musical Bumps. **1974** *Listener* 18 July 85/3 England may not be the world champions at soccer, but we are definitely past-masters at musical bumps. **1877** *Cassell's Family Mag.* Dec. 41/1 When there is a piano, 'Musical Chairs' played in the usual way..is quite as interesting. **1916** 'PETER' *Trench Yarns* 25 We had to get the men through the danger zone by a sort of musical-chairs rush. They came slowly up to the entrance, and then dashed in and round the corner into safety behind the bricks. **1933** A. BLEWITT *Ponies & Children* viii. 121 Musical Chairs—the posts are stuck in a small circle, one less than the number of competitors, who have to canter in a wide circle, led by a grown-up on horseback. **1939** R. S. SUMMERHAYS *Riding for All* xiv. 87 The almost inevitable event at all gymkhanas is musical chairs. **1950** G. BRENAN *Face of Spain* x. 202 The Spanish economic system is like a game of musical chairs, in which there are only half as many seats as there are performers. **1973** E. PAGE *Fortnight by Sea* v. 52 How rapidly the years slipped by, with what speed the game of musical chairs was played, how swiftly one was forced out of one role and into another. **1974** *Times* 16 Jan. 12/3 President Bourguiba..was still in the mood of playing musical chairs with his Prime Ministers. **1939** S. SPENDER tr. *E. Toller's Pastor Hall* I. 54 Even the musical clock is afraid of being denounced. **1765** R. CUMBERLAND (*title*) The summer's tale: a musical comedy of three acts. **1791, 1904** Musical comedy [in Dict., sense 6]. **1910** 'SAKI' in *Bystander* 7 Dec. 484/1 Noted lights of the musical-comedy stage. **1923** A. HUXLEY *Antic Hay* iii. 35 He looked..positively soldierly in his black jacket and his musical comedy trousers. **1957** *New Yorker* 12 Jan. 34/1 It was her favorite kind of film, a musical comedy in full color. **1967** *Listener* 3 Aug. 138/1, I thought I'd start in musical comedy,..carry on training as a dancer and singer. **1829** H. FOOTE *Compan. to Theatres* 147 Covent Garden —Season 1828–9... Musical Director and Composer—Mr H. R. Bishop. **1902** W. H. CHANTREY *Theatre Accounts* 73 All reasonable requirements from time to time made by the Manager, and the directors of the Musical Director or Stage Manager. **1885** G. B. SHAW *How to become Mus. Critic* (1960) 73 The most subtle and profound of all musical dramatists. **1963** *Listener* 3 Jan. 45/1 Compared with the microcosm created by the greatest musical dramatists his [*sc.* Puccini's] world is limited in subject-matter. **1930** *Times Educ. Suppl.* 31 May 1/3 The musical drive by 'J' Battery, Royal Horse Artillery, was carried out at the gallop. **1852** DICKENS *Our Bore* in *Househ. Words* 9 Oct. 75/1 He was at the Norwich musical festival. **1879** 'L. HOFFMANN' *Drawing-room Amusements* 24 Musical Fright. **1960** C. DAY LEWIS *Buried Day* v. 93, I seen this regiment..performing their intricate 'musical ride', with guns and limbers, at the Naval and Military Tournament. **1927** *Melody Maker* Aug. 773/2 In the combination are two performers on musical saw, which novelty, says Mr. Haggleton, always goes down well with his audience. **1946** R. BLESH *Shining Trumpets* (1949) v. 104 Exotic instruments may be utilized as well, such as harmonica, kazoo, jug, washboard, wood blocks and musical saw. **1957** W. C. HANDY *Father of Blues* x. 139 The technique..was similar to that used in playing musical saws. **1958** A. JACOBS *New Dict. Mus.* 231 Mayuzumi..has written..music..including..'Tonepleromas 55' for wind and percussion instruments and musical saw. **1973** J. WAINWRIGHT *Devil you Don't* 22 Rawlings will have you warbling *La Traviata*, backwards..with musical saw accompaniment. **1899** F. J. BRITTEN *Old Clocks & Watches* 148 Musical watches of large size with moving figures were a favourite conceit among French makers during the latter part of the eighteenth century. **1952** T. P. C. CUSS *Watches* xi. 145 On earlier musical watches—at the end of the eighteenth century—a pinned cylinder took the place of the disc. **1954** *Grove's Dict. Mus.* (ed. 5) V. 1018/2 Musical watches..were made, usually in Switzerland, at the beginning of the 19th century... There might be one tune.. or, more rarely, an air and variation. **1973** *Watches in Usher Coll.* 12 Musical watch with tiny cylinder playing on 13 teeth.

B. *sb.* **3.** A film or a theatrical piece (not opera or operetta) of which music is an essential element.

1938 *Chatelaine* Jan. 50/2 You can guess what it's about without my telling you—it's a musical. **1940** *Illustr. London News* CXCVI. 464/1 Some of these 'musicals' have proved extremely popular. **1944** [see **cover-girl*]. **1954** T. S. ELIOT *Confidential Clerk* II. 47 *Lucasta*:..But what about taking me to a concert? *Colby*: Only the other day I invited you... *Lucasta*: To go to see that American Musical! **1959** *Listener* 13 Aug. 259/1 A Novello musical. **1973** *Ibid.* 14 June 815/2 Musicals..exist in a far from splendid isolation, endlessly repeating the tricks which once worked.

musicalization (miūzikăləizēi·ʃən). [f. next + -ATION.] The expression or rendering of an art (other than music) in the style or manner of music; the action or process of musicalizing.

1928 A. HUXLEY *Point Counter Point* xxii. 408 The musicalization of fiction. **1930** H. READ *Julien Benda & New Humanism* 14 The cult of vagueness, the musicalisation of all the arts, the general subjectivism and romanticism. **1971** *Listener* 15 Apr. 473/3 The facts behind this 'musicalisation' of our culture..are fairly obvious. But the underlying motives are..complex.

musicalize (miū·zikăləiz), *v.* [f. MUSICAL *a.* + -IZE.] *trans.* To set (a novel, play, or poem) to music; to express or render (an art other than music) in the style or manner of music.

1919 *N.Y. Times* 20 July IV. 2/6 'Kitty Mackaye'.. is another play which is about to be musicalized. **1928** *Sunday Express* 19 Aug. 5/4 He prepared a musicalised version of the..play. **1947** *Penguin Music Mag.* Dec. 72 The art of musicalising films rather than filming music.

1957 MANVELL & HUNTLEY *Technique Film Music* 284 Benjamin Britten had proved particularly adroit at musicalizing the rhythm and intonation of speech beyond their actual use in a vocal line. **1962** *Listener* 3 May 761/2 It was Huxley who showed, in *Point Counter Point*, how fiction could be musicalized. **1966** *New Statesman* 20 May 736/2 Usually with Zukofsky you get..a poem intricately musicalised (he is much affected by Bach's contrapuntal patterns).

musicassette (miū̆zikæse·t). [f. MUSIC *sb.* + CASSETTE.] A tape cassette of prerecorded music.

1966 *Melody Maker* 8 Oct. 13/1 Musicassettes are with us... What exactly is a musicassette? It's the size of a bar of chocolate..and the tape is permanently housed inside the cassette. **1968** *Sat. Rev.* (U.S.) 25 May 50 As yet, of course, musicassettes are more for the uncritical listener to popular music. **1971** *Hi-Fi Sound* Feb. 12 (Advt.), Announcing the new professional musicassette library starting early in 1971. **1975** *Gramophone* Jan. 1293 (Advt.), A stereo musicassette player need not be expensive.

musicianship. (Later examples.)

1903 A. W. PATTERSON *Schumann* iv. 45 Surely a sufficient guarantee of his creative musicianship. **1930** *Times Educ. Suppl.* 2 Aug. 338/3 Miniatures full of dainty musicianship. **1959** *Times* 2 Feb. 1/4 The holder of the post will also be responsible for General Musicianship classes. **1970** P. OLIVER *Savannah Syncopators* 98 But if blues singers appeal because of these talents as well as their musicianship, they are, like the *griots*, frequently considered as lazy, lacking in industry and job application.

musicogenic (miū̆zikodʒe·nik), *a. Path.* [f. MUSICO- + *-GENIC.] Applied to a form of epilepsy in which attacks are precipitated by the hearing of music, and to the attacks themselves.

1937 M. CRITCHLEY in *Brain* LX. 13 The aim of this paper is to describe the occurrence of epileptiform attacks in factual association with the hearing of music... Opportunity has since brought to notice a series of such cases of 'musicogenic epilepsy' (or 'musicolepsia'). **1962** *Jrnl. Amer. Med. Assoc.* 17 Feb. 503/1, 44 patients with musicogenic epilepsy have been reported in the literature. **1972** BOSHES & GIBBS *Epilepsy Handbk.* (ed. 2) xiii. 61 Musicogenic seizures are extremely rare; the patient is usually an adult who is musically orientated.

musicological (miū̆zikŏlǫ·dʒikăl), *a.* [f. *MUSICOLOGY: see -ICAL.] Of or pertaining to musicology. Hence **musicolo·gically** *adv.*

1915 W. S. PRATT in *Musical Quarterly* I. 1 Several handy derivatives, such as 'musicologist'..'musicological', and the like. **1941** G. HAYDON *Introd. Musicology* i. 1 By no means everything written about music qualifies as musicological literature, but only that which exhibits an acceptable quality of scholarship. **1959** D. COOKE *Lang. Music* p. x, We concern ourselves more and more with parochial affairs—technical analyses and musicological *minutiae*—and pride ourselves on our detached, dehumanized approach. **1966** *New Statesman* 23 Sept. 451/2 Musicologically, they are..scrupulous. **1969** *Daily Tel.* 12 Apr. 13 Musicologically sensational and musically highly enjoyable was Alan Hacker's performance on the basset clarinet of Mozart's Concerto, K. 622. **1970** P. OLIVER *Savannah Syncopators* 95 Musicological analyses of the blues have scarcely been undertaken to date. **1973** *Listener* 1 Mar. 286/2 Musicologically-inhibited people catalogue Caruso's liberties as heinous sins.

musicologist (miū̆zikǫ·lŏdʒist). [f. next: see -OLOGIST.] One who studies or practises musicology.

1915 [see *MUSICOLOGICAL *a.*]. **1927** *Observer* 20 Feb. 18/2 The widest co-operation has..been secured from French, Spanish, German, and other foreign musicologists. **1930** *Music & Lett.* Apr. 138 The distinguished list of English musicologists. **1944** W. APEL *Harvard Dict. Mus.* 474/1 The men who undertook to 'discover Bach'..were musicologists in the true sense of the word. **1955** F. TOYE in H. van Thal *Fanfare for E. Newman* xi. 164 Who fifty years ago could have imagined that a musicologist of the calibre of Sir Donald Tovey should sponsor the performance of such an intrinsically popular opera as *Il Trovatore?* **1973** *Oxf. Mag.* 1 June 4/1 The members of the Faculty of Music are for the most part primarily musicologists.

musicology (miū̆zikǫ·lŏdʒi). [ad. F. *musicologie* or f. MUSIC *sb.* + -OLOGY.] The systematic study of music as opposed to the art of composition and performance; *esp.* academic research in music.

1909 M. S. LOGAN (*title*) Musicology. **1915** W. S. PRATT in *Musical Quarterly* I. 3 'Musicology', if it is to rank with other comprehensive sciences, must include every conceivable scientific discussion of musical topics. **1919** *Proc. Mus. Assoc. 1918–19* 106 The foundations of Musicology are the documents, manuscripts or printed music of past times. **1928** *Music & Lett.* Apr. 108 The most valuable piece of musicology is the treatment of the six motets. **1937** R. H. LOWIE *Hist. Ethnological Theory* xiv. 255 Comparative musicology..rose to a new plane with phonographic recordings. **1941** G. HAYDON *Introd. Musicology* i. 7 Musicology, following the lead of philosophy, adopts the epistemological concepts of space and time, and divides its subject matter under the two main headings *systematic* and *historical*. **1958** *Times Lit. Suppl.* 4 July 384/1 Only since the turn of the century has musicology been accepted fully and internationally as an independent branch of scholarship.

musicophile (miū̆·zikofəil). [f. MUSICO- + -PHIL, -PHILE.] One who professes love of music.

1931 J. JOYCE *Let.* 3 Jan. (1957) 298 The wealthy musicophiles in London and New York who control the destinies of opera in those cities.

Musigny (mü·sinʸi). The name of a vineyard in the commune of Chambolle-Musigny in the Côte d'Or department of France used *attrib.* and *absol.* to designate the red Burgundy produced there.

1833 C. REDDING *Mod. Wines* v. 112 To recapitulate the wines of the Côte d'Or: the finest Burgundies are Romanée-Conti [etc.]. Of the second class, Chambolle, Musigny [etc.] among red wines. **1907** *Yesterday's Shopping* (1969) 97/1 Burgundy—Musigny—Vintage 1899—Per doz. bots. 52/0. **1932** A. E. HOUSMAN *Let.* 31 May (1971) 321 The Sommelier insisted on Chambolle-Musigny 1921, which was most excellent. **1966** H. JOHNSON *Wine* 191 Musigny..lingers and spreads in your mouth, making what French tasters call 'the peacocks tail' with its bouquet of flavours and flavours within flavours. **1967** A. LICHINE *Encycl. Wines & Spirits* 374/2 In a good year the wines, in addition to their..feminine delicacy, have an incomparable bouquet... A fine estate-bottled Musigny can be expected..to profit enormously from imprisonment in the bottle.

‖ **musique concrète** (müzik kon̄krę̄t). [Fr. (P. Schaeffer *À la recherche d'une musique concrète* (1952)).] = *concrete music* (*CONCRETE *a.* and *sb.* A. 7). Also semi-anglicized as *musique concrete*, and *fig.*

1952 *Time* 10 Nov. 95/1 Last summer the U.S. got a taste of creative recording in France's *musique concrète*, a compilation of natural sounds..recorded on tape, cut and spliced at patterns to make a composition. **1953** *Musical Quarterly* XXXIX. Oct. 608 A special session was devoted to Pierre Schaeffer's *Musique concrète* and Elektronische Musik developed in the studio laboratories of the Cologne Rundfunk. **1954** *Gramophone Record Rev.* Apr. 297 These experiments come to mind after studying the so-called *Musique Concrète* broadcast recently in the Third Programme. **1957** *Electronic Engin.* XXIX. 350 The recent Musique Concrete in France. To quote a reviewer of records 'This is neither music nor concrete'. **1958** *Oxf. Mag.* 8 May 410/1 The *musique concrète* of dishwasher, duplicator and the pneumatic drills of Restoration Oxford, Thalia shuts her pretty mouth. **1962** A. NISBETT *Technique Sound Studio* xi. 191 *Musique concrète* transformations. **1970** *New Scientist* 30 July 221/2 Modern office workers partial to John Cage and *musique concrète.*

musk, *sb.* Add: **4. a.** *musk-perfumed, -scented* (later examples).

1922 JOYCE *Ulysses* 11 Phantasmal mirth, folded away: muskperfumed. **1891** O. WILDE *Picture of Dorian Gray* (ed. 2) xv. 272 He bathed his hands and forehead with a cool musk-scented vinegar. **1937** *Discovery* Feb. 53/2 A musk-scented lady. **1957** R. CAMPBELL *Coll. Poems* II. 98 Musk-scented lace and fans of ostrich plume.

f. musk lorikeet, an Australian parrot, *Glossopsitta concinna*; = *musk-parrakeet*.

1901 A. J. CAMPBELL *Nests & Eggs Austral. Birds* 596, I have observed many nests of the Musk Lorikeet in Victoria. **1966** EASTMAN & HUNT *Parrots of Australia* 32 Musk lorikeet... Pleasant strong musky odour associated with this Lorikeet.

muskellunge. Now the usual spelling of MASKINONGE, the large North American pike *Esox masquinongy*. (Later examples.)

1946 *Wisconsin State Jrnl.* 18 July 1/4 Gen. Dwight D. 'Ike' Eisenhower and his four brothers all continued their fishing luck Wednesday when they hit the jack pot with a muskellunge each. **1959** E. TUNIS *Indians* 40/2 Not to be despised, however, was the big pike called muskellunge by the Algonquins, the name it still bears. **1963** *Globe & Mail* (Toronto) 13 Apr. 5/6 He is also an officer of the Outdoor Writers of Canada and only in one respect might he come into conflict with his companions on that body—by using the U.S. term muskellunge instead of the accepted, original Canadian name, maskinonge. **1970** R. LOWELL *Notebk.* 251 Each night, a star, gold-on-black, a muskellunge, Dies in the higher sphere that never dies.

musketeer. Add: *musketeer gauntlet, glove*: see MOUSQUETAIRE 2.

1922 JOYCE *Ulysses* 458 Fawn musketeer gauntlets. **1968** *Guardian* 26 July 7/3 There were musketeer gloves and gaiters of sequins.

musketoo·ner. [f. MUSKETOON + -ER[1].] = MUSKETOON 2.

1925 *Chambers's Jrnl.* June 339/2, I felt a tearing blow above my right hip and I knew that the kneeling musketooner had touched me.

muskin[3]. Delete † *Obs. rare*$^{-1}$. and add later allusive example.

1922 JOYCE *Ulysses* 395 The embraces of some unaccountable muskin.

musking-place. A place where weasels or kindred animals deposit musk.

1920 *Chambers's Jrnl.* May 291/2 The wolves have their calling-posts, the beavers have their castor-signs, the weasels have their musking-places.

Muskogean (mɒ:skogī·ăn, mɒskōu·giăn). Also **Muskhogean.** [f. *MUSKOGEE.] An Indian language family in south-eastern N. Amer., consisting of the Creek-Seminole, Hitchiti-Mikasuki, Alabawa-Koasati, Apalachee, and Choctaw-Chickasaw languages. Also *attrib.* or as *adj.*

1891 J. W. POWELL in *7th Ann. Rep. Bureau Ethnol.* 94 (*heading*) Muskhogean family. **1907** F. W. HODGE *Handbk. Amer. Indians* I. 962/2 The Muskhogean population at the time of first contact with Europeans has been estimated at 50,000. **1932** *Times Lit. Suppl.* 8 Sept. 624/3 Forming part of the Muskhogean culture area east of the Mississippi. **1933** [see *CREEK *sb.*[3]]. **1940** *Language* XVI. 142 Curiously enough..certain other Muskogean languages closely related to Muskogee do employ gemination as a grammatical process. **1959** E. TUNIS *Indians* 19/2 Remnants of the temple-mound culture survived into historical times among the Muskhogean Indians of the Southeast. **1972** *Language* XLVIII. 845 Hockett exemplifies 3a with 'Arunta.., Muskogean (except Creek-Seminole).., and Wishram'.

Muskogee (mɒskōu·gī). Also **Muscogee, Muskhogee, Muskhokee, Muskogi, Muskohge.** [f. Creek *maskóki*, perh. of Algonquian origin.] The name of a group of N. American Indians, consisting mainly of Creek Indians; also the language spoken by them; also *attrib.*

1775 J. ADAIR *Hist. Amer. Indians* 161, I had a conversation..with several of the more intelligent Muskohge traders. *Ibid.* 392 A Muskohge warrior..got to a bramble swamp. *Ibid.* 430 The Cherokees and Muscogees still observe that old custom. **1836** *Trans. Amer. Antiq. Soc.* II. 94 The Muskhogees are the prevailing nation... The Hitchittees..speak a dialect of the Muskhogee. **1868** [see *CREEK *sb.*[3]]. **1907** F. W. HODGE *Handbk. Amer. Indians* I. 962/2 The recognized languages of the stock..are as follows:..Muskogee (including almost half the Creek confederacy, and its offshoot, the Seminole). **1948** D. DIRINGER *Alphabet* i. x. 183 The Muskhokee dialect is the principal dialect of the Muskhogean group; politically, the Muskhokee were the dominant tribe of the Creek Confederacy. **1949** E. A. NIDA *Morphology* (ed. 2) vi. 159 Muskogee has some verbs of rather irregular formation which indicate differences of singular, dual, and plural subjects. **1959** E. TUNIS *Indians* 70/2 The principal tribe was the Muskhogee, called Creeks by the English.

musk-rat. Add: **1. b.** (Earlier example.)

1845 in C. Cist *Cincinnati Misc.* 240 The inhabitants of ..Delaware [are called] Muskrats.

3. *musk-rat burrow, cap, skin, study*; **musk-rat house** (later examples).

1870 *Amer. Naturalist* IV. 385 This fish, when the bank was carelessly approached, would withdraw to a deserted muskrat burrow. **1916** C. A. EASTMAN *From Deep Woods to Civilization* 101 We saw that they were colored troopers, wearing buffalo overcoats and muskrat caps. **1962** W. STEGNER *Wolf Willow* III. iii. 230 Crouching in the trench in his muskrat cap, he looked like some digging animal. **1939** *Beaver* June 10 Older men remembered when the muskrat houses had been so thick that the marsh looked like a hayfield in coils. **1962** W. STEGNER *Wolf Willow* III. ii. 150 They had seen muskrat houses built six feet high in the sloughs—and when the rats built high you could depend on a hard winter. **1642** in *Archives of Maryland* (1887) IV. 99, 2. musk-rat skins. **1796** E. P. SIMCOE *Diary* (1911) 315 We..slept well,..but the smell of musk-rat skins..was disagreeable. **1823** in T. L. McKenney *Memoirs* (1846) I. App. 296 Furs and other articles..to wit,..2,500 muskrat skins, [etc.]. **1939** *Amer. Midland Naturalist* XXI. 514 (*title*) Central Wisconsin muskrat study.

musky, *sb.*[2] Add: Also **muskie.** (Later examples.)

1928 *Game Fishes of Canada* 12 The next most definite cult among the anglers are those who devote themselves to muskies. **1936** G. CLARK *Which we Did* i. 20 Jimmie Frise..was successfully commissaried by me to our favorite muskie water for the closing day of the season. **1962** *Times* 12 Apr. 7/3 Waterways full of bass, northern pike and muskies. **1968** *Globe & Mail* (Toronto) 3 Feb. 40/1 They recaptured these previously marked fish: 13 walleyes, three smallmouth bass, 11 largemouth bass, but not one musky. **1975** G. V. HIGGINS *City on Hill* ix. 215, I should spend my days..going after muskies and telling lies when I didn't catch any.

musli, var. *MUESLI.

Muslim. Now the preferred spelling of MOSLEM *sb.* and *a.* Also, = *Black Muslim* (*BLACK *a.* 19).

1961 [see **Black Muslim*]. **1971** *Black Scholar* June 52/1 Submission to democratic centralism instead of the egoism that sent him first against his Muslims.

musquash. Add: **3.** musquash-root (earlier and later examples); **musquash weed**, substitute for def.: (*a*) = *musquash root*; (*b*) = *musk-rat weed* (examples).

1807 *Massachusetts Spy* 22 July (Th.), Five children were lately poisoned in Scipio (New York) by eating Wild Parsnip or Musquash Root. **1857** [see **beaver-poison*]. **1940** E. EARLY *New England Sampler* 309 The Indian had told his grandmother..of a decoction of Cowbane (called Musquash Root) that would make a woman forever sterile. **1767** *Massachusetts Gaz.* 21 May 3/1 Persons (especially Children) would do well to beware of this Weed. It is called wild Hemlock by some, and Musquash Weed by others. **1892** *Jrnl. Amer. Folk Lore* V. 91 *Thalictrum polygamum*, muskrat-weed; musquash weed. **1907** A. B. LYONS *Plant Names* (ed. 2) 457 T[halictrum] polygamum. .. Celandine, Muskrat-weed, Musquash-weed.

Musquito, var. *MISKITO *a.* and *sb.*

muss, *sb.*[4] Add: **1.** (Earlier and later examples.) No longer current.

1830 *Constellation* (N.Y.) 11/3 I've been in many a *scrape* before, but never such a *muss!* **1838** *N.Y. Advertiser & Express* 17 Feb. 4/6 The complainant testified that there was a 'muss' in Chatham Street. **1840** C. F. HOFFMAN *Greyslaer* I. II. iv. 206 That's just what I told Red Wolfert when he showed signs of kicking up a muss. **1864** O. L. JACKSON *Colonel's Diary* (1922) 135 We have just had quite a muss [preceding the battle of Kenesaw Mt.]. **1873** 'MARK TWAIN' & WARNER *Gilded Age* 267 That gentleman delivered the young aspirant for a muss one of his elegant little left-handers. **1903** A. H. LEWIS *Boss* 19 It was nothin' but a cheap muss on the pier.

2. (Earlier and later examples.)

1840 C. F. HOFFMAN *Greyslaer* II. III. iv. 142 All this muss is of Wat Bradshawe's cooking. **1842** *Spirit of Times* (Philad.) 22 Jan. (Th.), I upset my table, spilt my ink, and knocked down my books, making a deuced muss. **1970** *Toronto Daily Star* 24 Sept. 40/1 (Advt.), Here's your cartridge... Instant loading. No muss or fuss. **1972** M. MEAD *Blackberry Winter* ix. 103 The first year Miss Abbott, the head of the dormitory apartments, described us as 'a mental and moral muss', and we accepted this with a kind of wicked glee.

muss, *v.*[2] Add: **1.** (Earlier and later examples.) Hence **mussed** *ppl. a.*; also *mussed-up*.

1837 in *Amer. Speech* (1965) XL. 127 Wish he muss imself [*sic*] up well and arty. **1888** *Detroit Free Press* (Farmer), Neither of us got two winks of sleep during the night on the car... We reached Chicago in a mussed up condition. **1902** C. J. C. HYNE *Mr. Horrocks Purser* 57 If Boy Austen..contrived to get badly mussed up with an undesirable woman [etc.]. **1907** C. E. MULFORD *Bar-20* v. 47, I paid twenty wheels for that [*sc.* a hat] eight years ago, and I don't want it mussed none. **1909** *Philad. Publ. Ledger* 24 June 7/6 (Advt.), Lot 3..Some four hundred soiled or mussed waists, in white lawn & lingerie. **1925** D. H. LAWRENCE *Death of Porcupine* 112 The really quick, Tolstoi loved to kill them off or muss them over. **1930** 'R. CROMPTON' *William's Happy Days* iii. 66 Trampling over his doorstep and 'mussing up' everything. **1955** W. GADDIS *Recognitions* II. ii. 351 The wind hit him,.. mussing his hair from behind. **1973** D. WESTHEIMER *Going Public* ii. 28 Only a little mussed, the kid says! I'm not leaving looking like something the cat dragged in.

mussel, *sb.* Add: **4.** *mussel-gatherer* (earlier example), *-opener*, *-pooled*, *-spawn*; **mussel-cracker** (*b*), **-crusher** = *BISKOP; **mussel mud** (later N. Amer. examples).

1905 *East London* (Cape Province) *Dispatch* 6 Nov. 7/4 Judging by the enormous incisors, and the perfect pavement of rounded molars with which the jaws of these white steenbras are armed, these fish live largely upon shell-fish, hence the local name *mussel cracker* and the Durban name *mussel crusher*. **1930** C. L. BIDEN *Sea-Angling Fishes of Cape* xviii. 256 Mussel-Crusher or Mussel-Cracker. **1951** *Cape Times* 7 Feb. 2/5 Twenty-five mussel-crackers and ten blou stompkop were landed. **1953** J. L. B. SMITH *Sea Fishes S. Afr.* (ed. 2) 502 The name 'Musselcracker' is applied in South Africa mainly to 2 fishes, *Sparodon durbanensis* and *Cymatoceps nasutus*, both of which develop massive jaws and powerful teeth. **1973** *Stand. Encycl. S. Afr.* VIII. 14/1 The musselcracker or musselcrusher (*Cymatoceps nasutus*) is one of the best-known angling fishes in South Africa... The jaws are very powerful, with canine teeth in front and molars behind... Their flesh is coarse, but the head is a delicacy. The young are silvery, yellow and black; the adults are dark, and develop a curious fleshy nose. **1905,** etc. Mussel-crusher [see *mussel-cracker* above]. **1859** A. J. MUNBY *Diary* 18 July (1972) 38, I met the mussel gatherers..fine young women with brown bare limbs. **1825** *Prince Edward Island Register* (Charlottetown) 23 Aug. 1/1 Plenty of manure [is] at hand, either kelp, seaweed, mussle-mud, [etc.]. **1851** J. F. W. JOHNSTON *Notes on N. Amer.* II. 151 Mussel-mud,..or sea-mud full of mussels, abounds in the Bay of St Andrews... This is an excellent fertilising substance... But the most apparently singular way of using it is to put it, with the mussels still living, into the turnip-drills, where it gives alone an excellent crop of turnips. **1973** *Canadian Antiques Collector* Jan.–Feb. 64/1 Of special value [as fertilizer] was the 'deep, black, stinking mud', better known as 'mussel-mud'—which lay thick in the beds of the Island's many tidal estuaries. **1909** *Daily Chron.* 25 Sept. 7/6 (Advt.), Oyster and mussel opener (young) wanted for evenings. **1946** DYLAN THOMAS *Deaths & Entrances* 9 The mussel pooled and the heron Priested shore. **1902** *Chambers's Jrnl.* May 277/2 Some seasons the mussel-spawn is pretty much in evidence here.

Mussolini (mʊsolī·ni). [Name of Benito *Mussolini* (1883–1945), prime minister of Italy and leader of the Fascist Party in Italy.] One who embodies the characteristics of Mussolini; also *attrib.* So **Mussolini-e·sque, Mussoli·nian** *adjs.*, of, pertaining to, characteristic of, or (somewhat) resembling Mussolini; **Mussoli·nism**, the political principles or policy of Mussolini or of the Fascist party in Italy.

1924 *Glasgow Herald* 29 Jan. 9 Signor Mussolini..said that he was unable to accept the antithesis that some people wished to create between Fascism and Mussolinism. *Ibid.* 30 June 11 The working classes needed to be warned against the establishment of 'Mussolinism' in this country. **1928** H. G. WELLS *Way World is Going* ii. 15 The consolidation and reconstruction of China..has not gone on under the direction of some strong-jowled hero of the Diaz or Mussolini type. **1928** *Daily Express* 21 Nov. 19 Mr. [J. W. H. T.] Douglas' stern, unbending look always interests me. So does his Mussolini-esque and frequent call of 'Fight!' **1932** H. NICOLSON *Diary* 15 Mar. (1966) 112 Tom does not wish to end it, being still obsessed by Mussolinian ideas. **1936** [see *HITLER]. **1946** R. CAPELL *Simiomata* II. 86 There are still Mussolinian Italians with the Germans. **1959** *Guardian* 16 Oct. 11/3 He..fails to acknowledge that there were many more sides to 'Mussolinism' than the less creditable later period. **1970** R. A. H. ROBINSON *Origins of Franco's Spain* iii. 134 The policies of Gil Robles meant 'the enslavement, in Mussoliniesque style, of the proletariat'.

Mussulman, *sb.* and *a.* Add: Now falling into disuse. The more usual forms are *Muslim* and *Moslem.*

A. *sb.* **2.** [tr. G. *muselmann.*] pl. Mussulmans, Mussulmen [G. *muselmänner*]. Under the Third Reich, an inhabitant of a concentration camp or extermination camp who had reached a state of physical and emotional exhaustion in which he displayed fatalism and loss of initiative.

[**1950** H. NORDEN tr. *E. Kogon's Theory & Practice of Hell* xviii. 214 Not all the prisoners were what came to be known as 'Moslems', men who were physically and mentally broken, who allowed anything to be done to them.] **1953** G. REITLINGER *Final Solution* xvii. 458 Most of those who died were just *Mussulmen*, the camp slang word for a walking skeleton wrapped up in a bit of blanket. The journey from Auschwitz,..for days on end in open trucks, freezing and without food, was alone sufficient to make a *Mussulman*. **1959** M. LEVIN *Eva* 224 These..were the creatures called mussulmans..in the last stage, when they reacted only as brute animals. **1975** N. FREELING *What are Bugles blowing For?* xxvii. 169 The man..has let himself die. It is a phenomenon similar to what was seen in the camps... The Musselmen they were called.

mussurana (musŭrā·nă). [ad. Pg. *muçurana* f. Tupi, cord.] A Brazilian colubrid snake, *Clelia clelia.*

1914 T. ROOSEVELT *Through Brazilian Wilderness* i. 14 The most formidable enemy of the many dangerous Brazilian snakes is a non-poisonous, entirely harmless, rather uncommon Brazilian snake, the mussurana. **1934** *Discovery* July 207/2 A cannibal snake, known in Brazil as the Mussurana..though harmless to men and animals, lives entirely on other snakes to whose venom it is immune. **1964** G. VEVERS tr. *Vogel's Reptiles & Amphibians* xiii. 162 In Brazil there is a handsome snake, much-loved and protected, which feeds, although not exclusively, on other snakes, particularly poisonous ones. This is the Mussurana, *Clelia clelia*, which is frequently depicted in the act of eating a Jararaca or other poisonous snake. It reaches a length of 7½ ft., is typically a metallic black, although the young are pale, and it lives on the ground. **1970** *East African Standard* 23 Jan. 6/4 The Mussurana, or snake-eater, feeds on deadly snakes, particularly the lethal Fer-de-lance.

mussy, dial. var. MERCY *sb.* Cf. LAWK, LAWKS, *int.*

1823 E. MOOR *Suffolk Words & Phr.* 243 Mussy on us. **1881** J. C. HARRIS *Nights with Uncle Remus* (1883) xii. 67 For mussy sake gin 'im a walkin'-cane. **1903** P. L. DUNBAR *In Old Plantation Days* 63 Lawd a' mussy, 'pon my soul, an' you one of de faifful of de flock! **1909** *Dialect Notes* III. 344 Lawsy mussy (pon my soul). **1935** *Scribner's Mag.* Feb. 120/2 Hab mussy, Jedus!.. When a bull-bat go lak dat he diggin' a grabe.

must, *sb.*[4] Add: **b.** Something that must be done, possessed, considered, etc.; a necessity. orig. *U.S.*

1892 *Dialect Notes* I. 205 An article marked with the word *must* is spoken of as a *must*, or emphatically—if there is absolutely no way of keeping it out of the paper—as a *dead must*. **1941** *Amer. Speech* XVI. 67/1 The *dirndl*, a dress which was a 'must' for every woman in 1937. **1948** 'J. TEY' *Franchise Affair* xxi. 239 The Feathers—one of the 'musts' of American visitors to Britain—was.. famous. **1951** 'J. WYNDHAM' *Day of Triffids* v. 103 It was close on midnight when we had finished adding our own secondary wants to the list of musts. **1957** R. HOGGART *Uses of Literacy* x. 250 These valuable books are *musts* for *you*. **1960** *House & Garden* Mar. 136 Nature in Schweppshire is a top must, is actively encouraged. **1973** *Guardian* 30 Mar. 2/4 A film and a song made the Trevi Fountain a 'must' for tourists.

c. *attrib.* and *Comb.* Essential, mandatory, obligatory. *colloq.* (orig. U.S.).

1912 M. NICHOLSON *Hoosier Chron.* 180 His gratification at being able to write 'must' matter for both sides of a prominent journal. **1937** *Amer. Speech* XII. 8 Roosevelt ..was called..The New Deal Caesar who specialized in must-legislation. **1939** *Canadian Forum* June 94/2 This is a *must* book. **1941** *Britannia & Eve* Sept. 4/1 They had come to accept the fact that mails and government-priority 'must' passengers monopolised the flying boats. **1952** *Manch. Guardian Weekly* 27 Nov. 3/2 A list of suggestions which he [*sc.* Senator Taft] had marked as either 'must' or 'optional' legislation. **1959** *New Statesman* 10 Jan. 32/2 A struggle of some interest..is now taking place among those women's periodicals..which are still 'must-reading' for debutantes with any claim to literacy. **1973** *Black World* May 69/2 His forthcoming paper is a 'must-read'.

must, *a.*[3] and *sb.*[5] Add: **A.** *adj.* Quot. 1886 to read:

1887 KIPLING *Departmental Ditties* (1888) 21 The Commissariat *hathee* had—forgive the rhyme—gone *musth.*

B. *sb.* **1.** (Later and *fig.* examples.)

1959 M. PUGH *Chancer* 35 He suffered from the recurring nightmare that his cameras would go on musth and stampede out of the studios at the second he was due on the air. **1972** *New York* 1 May 10/3 In twenty seconds she can go from emotional neutral to the fury of an elephant in musth. **1973** *Nature* 2 Nov. 17/2 The madness of the animal 'on musth' causes other elephants to avoid him.

must, *v.*[1] Add: **3. c.** *if you must know*: used to introduce information provided against the judgement or inclination of the speaker.

[**1818** SCOTT *Heart Midl.* xxix, in *Tales of My Landlord* 2nd ser. III. iv. 104 He's in Gaffer Gabblewood's wheat-close, an ye maun ken.] **1861** HUGHES *Tom Brown at Oxf.* II. x. 193 Well, if you must know, I never saw her before yesterday. **1885** *Boy's Own Paper* 28 Mar. 403/2 Well, if you must know, it's our boat. **1902** H. JAMES *Wings of Dove* xxxiii. 511 Well, if you must know—and I want you to be clear about it—I didn't even seriously think of a denial to her face. **1927** C. ASQUITH *Black Cap* 250 'If you must know,' she had said, 'well, you've got dirty nails, haven't you? Look.' **1951** J. D. SALINGER *Catcher in Rye* xix. 173 Girl lives in the Village. Sculptress. If you must know. **1972** 'G. HARDING' *Skytrap* ii. 39 If you must know, I wanted to be kissed gently.

musta, must'a' (mʊ·stă), a representation of the colloq. or vulgar pronunciation of *must have* (MUST *v.*[1] 5).

1903 P. L. DUNBAR *In Old Plantation Days* 266 It must 'a' been P'ovidence that directed bofe yo' min's in de same channel. **1927** M. OSTENSO *Mad Carews* (1929) v. 93 You're late... Must'a' stayed at the Phillips' till it was dark. **1938** M. RICHARDSON in B. A. Botkin *Treas. S. Folklore* (1949) III. i. 443 One of the other guards musta told him to bring it in. **1965** J. WAINWRIGHT *Death in Sleeping City* II. 104 They killed—Tommo. They musta—killed Tommo. **1973** *Black World* Jan. 62/2 They laid me out real good... Musta used up most of the insurance money.

mustang. Add: **1.** *attrib.*, as *mustang horse.*

1821 S. AUSTIN *Jrnl.* 5 Sept. in *Texas State Hist. Assoc. Q.* (1904) VII. 300 Mustang horses very plenty saw at least..150. **1941** *Sun* (Baltimore) 30 July 7/6 A Spanish vessel loaded with Mustang horses was shipwrecked years ago.

2. (Earlier and later examples.)

1846 J. GREGG *Diary* 27 Sept. (1941) I. v. 239 There is a large species, called by the Americans, the *Mustang grape* which very much resembles the Muscadine of the western country, except in growing in large bunches or racemes. **1951** *Dict. Gardening* (R. Hort. Soc.) IV. 2250/2 *V*[*itis*] *candicans.* Mustang Grape. Vigorous high climber.

3. An officer in the U.S. services who has been promoted from the ranks; in quots. 1847: a volunteer officer as distinct from a regular-army officer.

1847 G. B. MCCLELLAN *Mexican War Diary* 2 Jan. (1917) 23 'Mind, Mr. Smith,' said the old Mustang [*sc.* General Patterson] the night before, 'mind and appear as early as possible, so that you may not delay us'—all this with that air of dignity and importance so peculiarly characteristic of Mustangs. *Ibid.* 4 Jan. 43, I have repeatedly seen a Second Lieutenant of the regular army exercise more authority over the Volunteers..than a Mustang General. [**1874** L. P. A. D'ORLÉANS *Hist. Guerre Civile en Amérique* I. 35 Le surnom dérisoire de *mustang*.. qu'il appliquait aux volontaires inexpérimentés avant l'épreuve commune.] **1931** *Leatherneck* Feb. 13 We have three..mustangs, two of whom are..completing their probationary periods. **1939** J. B. CONNOLLY *Navy Men* 172 He was a 'mustang'—up from the enlisted ranks. **1950** *Time* 11 Dec. 22 A mustang who had worked his way up from the ranks in 13 years of service. **1953** M. DIBNER *Deep Six* v. 35 A damned 'mustang'. Never went to the Academy or anything. **1962** *Amer. Speech* XXXVII. 288 *Mustang*, a self-made man, i.e., a Marine officer who started as a private instead of as a second lieutenant. **1971** *N.Y. Times Mag.* 5 Sept. 11 The most decorated enlisted man in the Korean War—the mustang everybody thought was the perfect combat commander.

mustard, *sb.* Add: **1. e.** (Earlier and later examples.)

The use of *keen as mustard* is anticipated by the expression *keenest mustard* in quot. 1658 s.v. KEEN *a.* (*adv.*) 4.

1659 [see STRONG *a.* 15 b]. **1672** W. WALKER *Parœmiologia* 25/1 As keen as mustard. **1679** 'T. TICKLEFOOT' *Clod-Pate's Ghost* 4/2 You shall see a man as hot as Mustard against Plot and Plotters. **1916** 'B. CABLE' *Doing their Bit* ii. 36 They get as keen as mustard on it. **1932** R. ALDINGTON *Soft Answers* 185 His famous Uncle Harold.. had unfortunately died insolvent, owing to being as keen as mustard on the form of the Empire's horses and the forms of the Empire's barmaids. **1938** N. MARSH *Artists in Crime* ii. 13 He's as keen as mustard,..and he can talk of nothing but his work.

f. The colour of the condiment, usu. a brownish-yellow. Also *attrib.* or as *adj.* Cf. *mustard-coloured*, *-yellow* adjs.

1848 [see *DANDIE DINMONT]. **1922** JOYCE *Ulysses* 226 She stared at the large poster of Marie Kendall... Mustard hair and dauby cheeks. **1923** *Daily Mail* 17 Apr. 7 (Advt.), In shades of Jade, Mustard, Cherry, Nigger or Grey. **1951** E. PAUL *Springtime in Paris* ii. 33 Most of the young coloured men, yellow, brown, snuff, mustard or ginger in hue, had white girls with them. **1965** J. GALE *Clean Young Englishman* III. 101, I wore my demobilisation suede shoes and a mustard ferreting coat. **1969** G. MACBETH *War Quartets* 60, I rose against a full moon, sharp in mustard light. **1971** *Vogue* 15 Sept. 129/2 Coats..colours: orange, mustard, brick, royal.

g. In fig. phrases: that which enhances the flavour of anything, or adds piquancy or zest;

the best of anything. Phr. *to cut the mustard*: to accomplish, to succeed, to make good; to come up to expectations, to meet requirements. *slang* (chiefly *U.S.*).

1903 A. ADAMS *Log Cowboy* xv. 237 For fear they were not the proper mustard, he had that dog man sue him in court for the balance, so as to make him prove the pedigree. **1904** 'O. HENRY' *Cabbages & Kings* vi. 101 I'm not headlined in the bills, but I'm the mustard in the salad dressing just the same. **1905** 'H. MCHUGH' *You can search Me* 17 Petroskinski is a discovery of mine, and he's all to the mustard. **1907** 'O. HENRY' *Trimmed Lamp* 217 Why don't you invite him if he's so much to the mustard? **1907** —— *Heart of West* x. 163, I looked around and found a proposition that exactly cut the mustard. **1909** —— *Roads of Destiny* 99 'She cut the mustard,' he said, 'all right.' **1922** C. SANDBURG *Slabs of Sunburnt West* 7 Kid each other.. Tell each other you're all to the mustard. **1923** WODEHOUSE *Inimitable Jeeves* iv. 41 Never before had I encountered a curate so genuinely all to the mustard. **1930** —— *Very Good, Jeeves* iii. 70 Life at this juncture seemed pretty well all to the mustard. **1960** J. MITFORD *Hons & Rebels* ix. 56 Perhaps I could get a job as a maid in somebody's house..but Idden convinced me I would never cut the mustard at this occupation. **1966** 'J. HACKSTON' *Father clears Out* 114 Nell was all to the mustard. On her first Sunday afternoon she sat with young Bob Marlow..and, when it was Herby Carter's Sunday, went for a spin with him in his..jinker... For Tom..she sat in the old creek-bed. **1968** *Down Beat* 7 Mar. 18/1 There, in the Apple, his skill was tested in competition with the established ones. If he couldn't cut the mustard, he became part of the anonymous mob. **1974** *Citizen* (Ottawa) 24 Aug. 78 What if it doesn't work out? What if I'm bored with it? What if I'm no good at it? What if I just can't cut the mustard?

h. As quasi-*adj.*: very good, keen, enthusiastic; thorough. Also (*fig.*) hot, pungent.

1925 E. WALLACE *King by Night* ix. 41 That fellow is mustard. **1931** T. LYELL *Slang, Phrase & Idiom* 537 *To be mustard*, to be excellent at anything. It must never be used of the female sex. **1936** WODEHOUSE *Laughing Gas* xvii. 186 Avoid actors. They are mustard. **1959** *Times* 19 June 16/3 He [a batsman] is mustard on anything a trifle short of a length. **1960** L. COOPER *Accomplices* I. vi. 62 He showed me..an extract from a report from..the F.B.I. There wasn't much of it but what there was was mustard. **1966** L. SOUTHWORTH *Felon in Disguise* ix. 131 He could see the couple and what they were doing. 'Blimey, she's mustard,' he thought. **1972** *Daily Express* 4 July 6/8 Britain is particularly hot on calculus. The Russians and the East Germans are mustard on the theory of numbers and on solid geometry. **1973** 'B. MATHER' *Snowline* xix. 231 You can wash out South Africa... They're mustard there. You couldn't smuggle in a grain of wheat. **1973** J. WAINWRIGHT *Touch of Malice* 62 'Careful, Charlie,' warned Sanderson quietly. 'He's mustard.' 'Not mustard,' said Ripley. 'Dynamite—'.

2*. a. = *mustard gas* (see sense *3 c).

1918 *Jrnl. Amer. Med. Assoc.* 7 Dec. 1911/2 (*heading*) Mustard (yellow cross) burns. **1937** A. M. PRENTISS *Chem. in War* ii. 50 If sufficient effort is expended in finding more efficient ways of using it, mustard will undoubtedly yield far greater results. **1966** *Science* 5 Apr. 409/1 Mustard, *bis*(β-chloroethyl)sulfide, shared interest with a series of nitrogenous analogues. **1966** *McGraw-Hill Encycl. Sci. & Technol.* III. 44/2 Wet or perspiring skin absorbs more mustard than does dry skin.

b. *Pharm.* Any of the group of substances that contains mustard gas and the nitrogen mustards (cf. *NITROGEN b).

1946 *Science* 5 Apr. 412/1 The oxidation of pyruvate by brain brei was significantly inhibited by sulfur mustard. **1964** *Brit. Med. Bull.* XX. 91/1 The biological alkylating agents..include the sulphur and nitrogen mustards, epoxides, [etc.]. **1970** *Nature* 6 June 897/1 Quinacrine mustard makes part of the human Y chromosome fluoresce particularly brightly.

3. b. *mustard-keen* (adj.), *-plaster* (earlier and later examples).

1935 G. HEYER *Death in Stocks* iii. 29 I'd had a letter from Arnold, and they were instantly mustard-keen to see it. **1968** 'J. J. MARRIC' *Gideon's River* xviii. 162 Singleton's got the frogmen out already, the Warbler says he's mustard-keen. **1810** E. WEETON *Let.* 25 Feb. (1969) I. 235 Mustard plasters and bottles of warm water were applied to the feet. **1869** 'MARK TWAIN' *Sketches New & Old* (1875) 46 That mustard-plaster of a newspaper. **1909** *Westm. Gaz.* 23 Dec. 4/1 It had lapels that were far too wide,..being what some tailors called 'the mustard-plaster type'. **1975** D. DELMAN *One Man's Murder* v. 95 Let me go home early to a mustard plaster.

c. mustard bush, tree *Austral.* (see quot. 1965); **mustard gas,** dichlorodiethylsulphide, $(ClCH_2CH_2)_2S$, a colourless, oily liquid which is a powerful poison and vesicant, acting directly on the skin, and which was first used in warfare by the Germans in 1917, at Ypres.

1933 *Bulletin* (Sydney) 7 June 25/2 Another hardy northwesterner is the mustard bush. It is of dwarf habit, with a dense growth of leaves relished by sheep. **1965** *Austral. Encycl.* II. 263/1 The mustard-bush or mustard-tree (*Apophyllum anomalum*), an almost leafless tree with small fragrant flowers, is an inland species whose young shoots have a somewhat mustard-like flavour; in spite of its wiry nature it is much relished by stock. **1917** *Nation* (N.Y.) 15 Nov. 524/2 The Germans have just invented a new and particularly powerful weapon in their so-called 'mustard gas'. **1934** *Discovery* Feb. 32/1 As far as can be judged from the sample of casualties officially studied, one in thirty-eight of the British casualties from 'mustard gas' died and about one in four hundred was incapacitated for six months or longer. **1937** J. M. MURRY *Necessity of Pacifism* v. 76 The sword of the Lord is broken in men's hands... The mustard-gas of the Almighty—it cannot be. **1973** G. BEARE *Snake on Grave* xxvi. 160 Less than fifty years ago this place was a sea of blood and mud.. scoured and sterilised by mustard gas.

mustard seed. Add: **1.** *fig.* (Later examples.)

1926 C. VAN VECHTEN *Nigger Heaven* 286 *Mustard-seed*: see high yellow (=mulatto). **1952** DYLAN THOMAS *Coll. Poems* 170 In the mustardseed sun.

3. (Earlier examples.)

1809 T. G. FESSENDEN *Pills Poetical* 8 Her single good gun loaded with mustard seed shot. **1844** *Knickerbocker* XXIII. 440 None of the fine mustard-seed or robin, but the heavy duck-shot.

mustardy, *a.* (Later examples.)

1911 W. J. LOCKE *Glory Clementina Wing* xix. 280 Her ill-fitting mustardy brown stuff skirt. **1936** W. JAMES *Gangways & Corridors* vi. 69 There was a hideous affair of mustardy yellow diagonal serge. **1975** *Times* 5 July 11/3 The plate of crudités, with a mustardy mayonnaise dip.

must-be (mʌ·stˌbī). [f. MUST *v.*[1] + BE *v.*] The inevitable, what is fated to happen.

1907 *Cambr. Hist. Eng. Lit.* I. 4 The must-be often helps an undoomed man when he is brave. **1922** D. H. LAWRENCE *Aaron's Rod* 242 A ghastly atmosphere of must-be. **1970** R. LOWELL *Notebk.* 177 Hope is the must-be, the tomb of a small child.

mustelid (mʌ·stilid). [f. mod.L. family name *Mustelidæ*, f. L. *mustēla* weasel, adopted as the name of a genus by Linnæus (*Systema Naturæ* (ed. 10, 1758) I. 582): see -ID[3].] A small carnivorous mammal of the family Mustelidæ, which includes weasels, stoats, badgers, mink, and others. Cf. MUSTELINE *sb.*[1]

1910 H. F. OSBORN *Age of Mammals* iv. 259 The mustelids were becoming more numerous [in the Miocene]. **1933** A. S. ROMER *Vertebrate Paleontology* xv. 291 Continued emphasis on a flesh-eating diet has..resulted in the retention of well-developed shearing teeth in the greater number of mustelids. **1953** *New Biol.* XIV. 120 Most mustelids and wild dogs and cats do not [have fleas]. **1968** A. S. ROMER *Procession of Life* xv. 247 The mustelids tend to be relatively small in size, short of leg, and primarily forest-dwellers in habitat. **1972** T. A. VAUGHAN *Mammalogy* xii. 201/1 Most mustelids aggressively search for prey in burrows, crevices, or dense cover. **1975** *Nature* 20 Mar. 187/1 Other interesting elements of the fauna include..a new species of gomphothere, a sanid, a mellivorine mustelid.

muster, *sb.*[1] **3. g.** Read: *Austral.* and *N.Z.* A collecting of stock (cattle, sheep, etc.) by riding round the scattered herd and driving it together.

1841 S. REVANS *Lett.* I. 90 (MS.), I am not yet confident of the mode in which flock and stock musters will be dealt with by the natives. **1867** LADY BARKER *Station Life in N.Z.* (1870) xx. 173 It is impossible to estimate our loss until the grand muster at shearing. **1884** [see Dict.]. **1892** W. E. SWANTON *Notes on N.Z.* ii. 97 Previous to the shearing, there is the general muster, which means the rounding up and bringing in of all the sheep, good or bad, on the 'run'. **1946** F. D. DAVISON *Dusty* ix. 90 The paddock..was not the easiest in the world to lift sheep from, but Tom had a feeling..that the count would show a clean muster. **1950** *N.Z. Jrnl. Agric.* Oct. 348/3 After the marking muster musterers proceed to the high country and muster wethers. **1956** *Coast to Coast 1955–6* 35 Whole country's gone dead since muster. **1961** B. CRUMP *Hang on Minute Mate* 75 We're starting the shearing muster in a few days. **1963** *Times* 12 Mar. p. xii/7 (*caption*) A muster of merinos for shearing on Benangaroo, a 40,000 acre sheep and cattle property near Coolac, in the southern tablelands of New South Wales.

9. *muster-field, -ground* (earlier U.S. example).

1838 B. DRAKE *Tales* 179 Our sons..assembling in the 'muster field', divide themselves into armies, and pelt each other with Buckeye balls. **1798** *Deb. Congress U.S.* 15 May (1851) 1707 At the muster ground on the Commons of Portsmouth.

muster, *v.*[1] **6.** Read: *Austral.* and *N.Z.* To collect stock (cattle, sheep, etc.) together for counting, shearing, drafting, branding, etc. Also with *off* and *up*, and with place as obj.

1846 C. J. PHARAZYN *Jrnl.* 23 June 45 (MS.), Assisted in mustering Ewes and Lambs into Stock-Yard. **1852** J. R. CLOUGH *Diary* 4 May in J. Deans *Pioneers of Canterbury* (1937) 292 Port Philip men just arrived..and two of the survey men mustered the cattle this day. **1858** [in Dict.]. **1860** *St. Leonard's Jrnl.* 31 July, To muster stragglers off Isolated Hill. **1867** LADY BARKER *Station Life in N.Z.* (1870) xvi. 122 It is very difficult to 'muster' these ranges. **1875** [in Dict.]. **1878** E. S. ELWELL *Boy Colonists* 208 They all started from the hut to muster off 'Nob' mountain. **1930** L. G. D. ACLAND *Early Canterbury Runs* vii. 164 The country had never been stocked... [They] had once mustered it..and got about 300 wild sheep off it. **1934** A. RUSSELL *Tramp-Royal in Wild Australia* xxiii. 210 Here we loosed the herd and went east to muster up another section of the run. **1946** F. D. DAVISON *Dusty* vi. 65 There were a lot of sheep to be done, to be mustered from the paddock and brought to yard and shears. **1947** P. NEWTON *Wayleggo* (1949) 12 The musterer's job is to muster the sheep off such country into the respective homesteads. **1950** *N.Z. Jrnl. Agric.* Oct. 349/3 While the hill wethers are being shorn the ewes and lambs are being mustered on the various blocks and are brought in.

absol. (Earlier and later examples.)

1874 A. BATHGATE *Colonial Experiences* vii. 80 A shepherd, while out mustering, descried the errant steed on a small plateau. **1878** E. S. ELWELL *Boy Colonists* 173 Walker's men never mustered beyond the 'Saddle'. **1944** F. CLUNE *Red Heart* 18, I found Bob Buck out mustering.

musterer[2] (mʌ·stərəɹ). *Austral.* and *N.Z.* [f. MUSTER *v.*[1] (sense *6) + -ER[1].] One who musters sheep or cattle.

1863 E. C. CHUDLEIGH *Diary* 19 Dec. in Richards *Diary of E. R. Chudleigh* (1950) 114 All the musterers dogs have come home. **1872** LADY BARKER in D. M. Davin *N.Z. Short Stories* (1953) 20 Of course Christmas Day would be a complete holiday, and we had invited shearers and musterers, and all the odd hands which flock to a station at shearing-time, to come up to our house. **1892** W. E. SWANTON *Notes on N.Z.* ii. 97 To accomplish this [muster], ..on large 'runs' additional hands called 'musterers' have to be engaged. **1947** [see *MUSTER *v.*[1] 6]. **1961** B. CRUMP *Hang on Minute Mate* 73 I'm short of a couple of musterers, if you're interested. Done any sheep work before? **1970** *Telegraph* (Brisbane) 4 July 2/1 Lawrence Ryan..worked as a musterer on a South Queensland cattle station 20 years ago.

mustering, *vbl. sb.* Add: (Austral. and N.Z. examples.)

1860 G. DUPPA *Station Diary* Oct. in S. S. Crawford *Sheep & Sheepmen of Canterbury* (1949) v. 47 To collect stragglers for a second mustering. **1874** A. BATHGATE *Colonial Experiences* xv. 206 Life on a sheep-station is rather a dull one. There are periodical 'musterings' and other duties to be attended to. **1878** E. S. ELWELL *Boy Colonists* 172 The mode of mustering adopted by Ernest was this. **1911** C. E. W. BEAN *'Dreadnought' of Darling* xviii. 172 There was the operation of mustering going on as clear and plain as if the hillside were a mile distant. **1968** K. WEATHERLY *Roo Shooter* 95 Tales told in a bush pub; tales of droving, mustering.

b. (Further examples.)

1745 J. HEMPSTEAD *Diary* 6 May (1901) 442 The 1st & 2d Company are viewing Arms &c. Mustering Day through the Colony. **1841** *Southern Lit. Messenger* VII. 768/1 Who should I see..but Mr. Jim Guest himself, in..mustering jacket and trowsers, and tarpaulin hat. **1878** E. S. ELWELL *Boy Colonists* 169 In mustering times Ernest used to set some of the huge boulders on the sides of its cliffs rolling. **1930** L. G. D. ACLAND *Early Canterbury Runs* vi. 138 More stories were told of him in shearers' huts and mustering camps than of any other runholder. **1953** O. E. MIDDLETON in C. K. Stead *N.Z. Short Stories* (1966) 186 See him coming in from the back country at mustering-time.

mut, var. *MUTT.

‖ **muta** (miū·tă). [It. *muta* imp. = change.] In *Music.* a direction to the player (see quots.).

1876 STAINER & BARRETT *Dict. Musical Terms* 298/2 *Muta*, a direction to a player on a horn, trumpet, etc., or on drums, to change the *key* of his instrument. **1880** GROVE *Dict. Mus.* II. 439/1 A word often seen attached to Horn parts—'muta in Es', 'muta in B', etc., meaning simply 'change to E♭ or B♭', etc. **1938** *Oxf. Compan. Music* 602/2 *Muta D in C* means 'change tuning from D to C'. **1959** *Collins' Music Encycl.* 446/1 *Muta*,..a direction to the performer found in parts for wind instruments and timpani, indicating either a change of instrument,.. or a change of crook,..or a change of tuning.

muta, var. *MOOTAH, MOOTER.

mutability. Add: **3.** *Biol.* The tendency to undergo, or capacity for undergoing, mutation.

1908 J. A. THOMSON *Heredity* iii. 92 It is possible that the prolific multiplication in a new environment may have had something to do with the awakening of the impulsive mutability [in *Œnothera lamarckiana*]. **1916** *Genetics* I. 606 (*heading*) Mutability in different species of Drosophila. **1929** *Proc. Nat. Acad. Sci.* XV. 834 That gene..does not influence the mutability of the miniature-gamma gene. **1958** *Nature* 11 Oct. 984/1 The sites in each segment have been plotted in order of decreasing mutability for each mutagen. **1974** *Ibid.* 9 Aug. 493/2 There was no significant difference in mutability between the two strains.

mutable, *a.* and *sb.* Add: **A.** *adj.* **3.** *Biol.* Capable of undergoing mutation; liable to undergo mutation frequently.

1905 F. E. CLEMENTS *Res. Methods in Ecol.* 319 *Mutable*, able to produce mutants. **1908** J. A. THOMSON *Heredity* iii. 91 There he [*sc.* de Vries] found his long-looked-for mutable plant, an evening primrose (*Œnothera lamarckiana*). **1928** *Genetics* XIII. 360 To designate a character showing frequent heritable changes, the terms 'mutable', or 'frequently mutating' will be used. **1941** *Nature* 22 Mar. 356/2 We have carried out an experiment with a mutable gene which produces coloured spots on the petals and stems of *Portulaca grandiflora*. **1972** *Molecular & General Genetics* CXIV. 144 (*heading*) The genetics of a new mutable allele at the *white* locus in *Drosophila melanogaster*.

mutagen (miū·tădʒĕn). *Biol.* [f. MUTA(TION + -GEN.] An agent that causes mutation.

1946 *Proc. R. Soc. Edin.* B. LXII. 220 In unpublished experiments with chemical mutagens, a significant change in the rate of induced lethals was recorded. **1952** *New Biol.* XII. 86 Certain chemical substances, or penetrating radiation such as ultra-violet or X-rays, may increase the mutation rate considerably. Those agents, called 'muta-

gens', are at present being intensively studied. **1971** J. Z. YOUNG *Introd. Study Man* xxviii. 393 Another implication of the randomness of the effects of mutagens is that no amount of them is too small to be biologically irrelevant.

mutagenesis (miūtădʒe·nĕsis). *Biol.* [f. MUTA(TION + -GENESIS.] The production or origination of mutations.

1953 *Nature* 21 Nov. 964/1 (*heading*) Chemical mutagenesis in bacteriophage *T2*. **1961** *Jrnl. Molecular Biol.* III. 121 (*heading*) The theory of mutagenesis. **1972** *Heredity* XXIX. 203 (*heading*) Gamma ray mutagenesis in a strain of *Escherichia coli* deficient in DNA polymerase I.

mutagenic (miūtădʒe·nik). *Biol.* [f. MUTA(TION + *-GENIC.] Causing or capable of causing mutation.

1946 *Proc. R. Soc. Edin.* B. LXII. 211 Muller's classical discovery in 1927 of the mutagenic action of X-rays has provided an extremely useful tool for studying the nature of gene mutation and chromosome breakage. **1952** *New Biol.* XII. 87 All known mutagenic agents also damage the cell. **1959** *New Scientist* 20 Aug. 219/1 Plant geneticists..now combine mutagenic radiations and chemicals with the classic techniques of plant breeding to produce novel plants. **1971** *Nature* 1 Oct. 296/3 Dr Mary Lyon.. argued that the radiation from nuclear fall-out is likely to be less mutagenic than the medical use of X-rays. **1974** *Times* 11 Jan. 16/1 The 'mutagenic' effect of lead compounds.

Hence **mutageni·city**, the property of being mutagenic.

1956 *New Biol.* XX. 30 Different types of radiation were tested for mutagenicity. **1970** *Nature* 30 May 800/1 The concern felt by many scientists about the potential mutagenicity of the ever increasing number of synthetic chemicals in the environment. **1972** *Guardian* 15 Dec. 7/4 Evidence of mutagenicity in a chemical compound is a danger signal.

mutagenize (miū·tădʒĕnəiz), *v.* *Biol.* [f. *MUTAGEN + -IZE.] *trans.* To treat (cells or organisms) with mutagenic agents; also *absol.* So **mu·tagenized** *ppl. a.*

1966 *Virology* XXIX. 339/1 The mutants were produced by mutagenizing with hydroxylamine. *Ibid.* 339/2 A mutagenized phage stock was prepared. **1969** A. M. CAMPBELL *Episomes* ii. 16 From a mutagenized lysogenic culture, some bacteria can be recovered that are no longer lysogenic. **1970** *Nature* 31 Oct. 414/2 Mutagenized stocks of virus. **1972** *Ibid.* 18 Feb. 363/3 Instead of mutagenizing stocks of transforming virus..[they] took mouse 3T3 cells..and..selected for cells which behave at 32° C as typical transformants.

mutalali, var. *MUDALALI.

mutant (miū·tănt), *sb.* and *a.* *Biol.* [ad. L. *mutant-em* pr. pple. of *mūtāre* (see MUTATE *v.*).] **A.** *sb.* An individual (or, formerly, a species or form) which has arisen by or undergone mutation, or which carries a mutant gene (in *Science Fiction*, usu. an individual with freak or grossly abnormal anatomy, abilities, etc.); also, a mutant gene.

1901 *Rep. Brit. Assoc. Adv. Sci.* 848 Two genera of Conifers which are in a period of spontaneous generation, a period in which they do form mutants, to use the terminology of de Vries, which mutants *may* be true to seed. **1919** T. H. MORGAN *Physical Basis Heredity* xx. 249 Of the twelve dominant mutants that have appeared in *Drosophila* each appeared at first in a single individual. **1919** *Jrnl. Exper. Zool.* XXVIII. 363 By aid of these two dominants it is very easy to determine in a single experiment whether a given mutant is in the second or third chromosome. **1929** *Encycl. Brit.* VI. 947/1 There is a mutant or sport of the fruit fly with black coloration of the body. **1930** R. A. FISHER *Genetical Theory Nat. Select.* i. 13 Under the blending theory of inheritance, every individual was regarded as a mutant. **1954** 'J. CHRISTOPHER' *22nd Century* 140 You really can produce a breed of telepathic mutants that will supplant us? **1955** 'J. WYNDHAM' *Chrysalids* ii. 21 The nearest approach to decoration was a number of wooden panels with sayings..burnt into them... Blessed is the norm, and... Watch thou for the mutant! **1962** [see *hypomorph* s.v. *HYPO- II]. **1969** *Nature* 18 Oct. 272/1 (*heading*) Vitamin K-deficient mutants of bacteria. **1974** *Encycl. Brit. Macropædia* XII. 756/1 Better strains of *Penicillium* and other industrial fungi..have been raised from artificially produced mutants.

fig. **1971** *Time* 7 June 7/1 An ominous new mutant of the American tragedy in Viet Nam... The troops who became addicted to heroin while serving in SE Asia.

B. *adj.* Having the attributes of a mutant; produced by mutation.

1903 *Amer. Naturalist* XXXVII. 740 The form, habit and behavior of some of the mutant forms discovered by deVries seventeen years ago. **1928** *Genetics* XIII. 389 In this work two mutant characters have been studied. *Ibid.* 392 The sex-ratio in the mutant stock is normal. **1930** R. A. FISHER *Genetical Theory Nat. Select.* i. 11 In domestication..the rigour of Natural Selection [is] relaxed so that mutant types can survive. **1955** *Bull. Atomic Sci.* June 215/3 There is evidence that a mutant gene frequently does produce some disability of the individual who carries it. **1973** *Nature* 9 Feb. 368/2 Mutant cells resistant to particular drugs..are being routinely used today by somatic cell geneticists.

mutarotation (miūtărŏtēi·ʃən). *Chem.* [f. L. *mūtā-re* to change + ROTATION.] The change of optical activity with time exhibited by the solutions of some compounds (esp. sugars) after being made up. (Orig. called *multirotation* (*MULTI- 2).)

1899 T. M. LOWRY in *Jrnl. Chem. Soc.* LXXV. 213 The essential feature of the phenomenon, however, is the *change* of rotatory power which takes place in the freshly prepared solution, and the term 'mutarotation' may, therefore, be used with advantage to include all those cases in which such a change occurs without reference either to the sign or to the relative magnitude of the initial and final rotations. **1937** *Chem. Rev.* XXI. 65 The brucine salt..was found..to exhibit definite mutarotation. **1971** *Jrnl. Gen. Psychol.* LXXXV. 116 Each quantity of the sugar solution was refrigerated for a day before use at room temperature to allow adequate time for mutarotations.

So **mutarota·tional** *a.*, of, or of the nature of, mutarotation. Also **mutarota·te** *v. intr.*, to exhibit mutarotation; **mutarota·ting** *ppl. a.*

1930 *Jrnl. Chem. Soc.* II. 2618 These two interconvertible, mutarotating forms of mannose are thus assigned different ring structures. **1951** I. L. FINAR *Org. Chem.* I. xviii. 372 These glycosides..do not undergo many of the reactions of the sugars, *e.g.*, they show no reducing properties, they do not mutarotate, etc. **1971** N. L. ALLINGER et al. *Org. Chem.* xxvii. 701 Monosaccharides commonly mutarotate. **1971** M. F. MALLETTE et al. *Introd. Biochem.* v. 145 Because the acetals of carbohydrates are kinetically stable, they do not undergo mutarotational changes. **1973** *Biochemistry* (Easton, Pa.) XII. 2544/1 If the enzyme.. promoted instability by distorting the ring, the mutarotational rate would be enhanced.

mutasarrif, var. *MUTESSARIF.

mutase (miū·tēiz, -s). *Biochem.* [a. G. *mutase* (J. Parnas, at the suggestion of F. Hofmeister, in *Biochem. Zeitschr.* (1910) XXVIII. 284), f. L. *mūt-āre* to change: see *-ASE.] **a.** Any enzyme which brings about a dismutation reaction.

1914 [see *DEHYDRASE a]. **1943** SUMNER & SOMERS *Chem. & Methods Enzymes* xvii. 298 Aldehyde mutase brings about the Cannizzaro reaction. Here, two molecules of an aldehyde undergo an oxido-reduction.

b. Any enzyme which brings about the transfer of a phosphate group from one carbon atom to another in a molecule.

1938 *Jrnl. Biol. Chem.* CXXIV. 552 Mannose-1-phosphate and galactose-1-phosphate, synthetically prepared, were not converted to the respective 6-esters by muscle, liver, or yeast mutase, with or without the addition of accelerating ions. **1964** CORI & BROWN in Florkin & Stotz *Comprehensive Biochem.* XV. vi. 212 In a system consisting of hexokinase, mutase and phosphorylase, glucose could be converted to glycogen, provided that the inorganic phosphate formed in the phosphorylase reaction was removed by barium ions. **1970** R. W. MCGILVERY *Biochemistry* xv. 292 The sequence begins by a freely reversible mutase reaction, in which the phosphate group of glucose-6-phosphate is transferred to form glucose-1-phosphate.

mutassarif, mutasserif, varr. *MUTESSARIF.

mutate, *sb.* Add: **2.** *Chess.* (See quot. 1970.)

1922 HUME & WHITE *Good Companion Two-Mover* 297 We shall see that the term changed mate block (or 'mutate', as Brian Harley has suggested) is often indefinite in that it may include or exclude added mate features according to the individuality of separate problems. **1924** FEAST & WHITE *Simple Two-Move Themes* 62 The changed-mate waiters, or Mutates,..classify more readily. *Ibid.* 66 Every type of mating strategy discussed in Part III may theoretically be treated in Mutate form. **1931** B. HARLEY *Mate in Two Moves* ii. 20 We now come to the last of the big groups into which the two-mover can be divided: the Complete Block both before and after the Key, which changes one or more mates: that is, the Complete Block-Change, or, as I have christened it for short, the Mutate. **1959** B. J. HORTON *Dict. Mod. Chess* 85/1 He [*sc.* Brian Harley] did much to popularize the 'mutate' in his regular chess columns. **1962** K. S. HOWARD *Amer. Two-Move Chess Problem* 11 More than any other type of problem, the attractiveness of a mutate is dependent on the excellence of its construction. *Ibid.* 12 Wurzburg in No. 133 utilizes a mutate setting to show a charming illustration of a Bristol withdrawal key. **1970** J. M. RICE *ABC of Chess Problems* 182 Mutate is the term given to a complete-block problem in which White, with no mere waiting-move at his disposal, is forced to abandon one or more of his set mates and introduce new replies to Black's defences.

mutate, *v.* Add: **2.** *Biol.* **a.** *intr.* To undergo mutation.

1913 *Amer. Naturalist* XLVII. 12 A mutation need not be a loss, and..a recessive may revert in the sense that it may mutate. *Ibid.* 68 There is in *Œnothera lamarckiana* a tendency to mutate in certain definite directions generation after generation. **1926** [see *MUTATING *ppl. a.*]. **1951** E. HAMILTON *Star Kings* xix. 145 They're creatures of this crazy planet... I think they were human once—human colonists who mutated under radioactive influence. **1972** *Sci. Amer.* Apr. 65/2 We have no reason to think the gene for cytochrome *c* mutates more slowly than the gene for hemoglobin. **1974** *Nature* 1 Feb. 261/1 The evolution of enzymes in bacteria is studied by introducing novel substrates and selecting strains that have mutated to be able to use these substrates.

b. *trans.* To cause (genetic material) to undergo mutation.

1961 *Jrnl. Molecular Biol.* III. 142 There are many genetic sites which can be mutated by HA. **1972** *Nature* 14 Apr. 326/1 Clearly, in at least some phage genes certain segments of DNA are more readily mutated than others.

mutated (further examples); **muta·ting** *ppl. a.*, undergoing mutation.

1903 *Amer. Naturalist* XXXVII. 739 This particular factor in distinguishing between fluctuating and mutating variability therefore becomes a safe one, when it is modified to make mutating variability include only newly acquired and transmissible qualities. **1913** *Ibid.* XLVII. 71 Such study should be continued for many years, breeding..from some highly mutating stock. **1919** T. H. MORGAN *Physical Basis Heredity* xx. 248 When these are recessive it is probable..that the actual mutation occurred several generations before the mutated genes came together to produce the mutant character. **1926** *Proc. Nat. Acad. Sci.* XII. 687 The first frequently mutating character observed in *Drosophila virilis* was the body 'reddish', which was found to mutate frequently to wild type. **1945** *Genetics* XXX. 497 From outcrossing flies of the mutating cultures to those of normal cultures (Reedsport) the results..in table 2 were obtained. **1964** *Jrnl. Molecular Biol.* IX. 352 (*heading*) Identification of the altered bases in mutated single-stranded DNA. **1967** *Biol. Abstr.* XLVIII. 3217/1 (*heading*) Notes on mutant forms among Philippine plants. IV. A case of a 'recurrently mutating' banana. **1973** *Guardian* 18 May 18/1 There are reports of mutated fish in the lagoon and radiation sickness from eating the fish.

mutation. **6.** Substitute for def.: **a.** The process whereby detectable and heritable changes in genetic material arise; also, formerly, a process by which de Vries (*Die Mutationstheorie* (1901–3)) supposed a new species to be suddenly produced by a departure from the parent type (in contrast with *variation*). **b.** A change of this kind in the genetic material. **c.** An individual (or, more rarely, an assemblage of like individuals) which has been produced by this process; a mutant. (Further examples.)

1901 *Jrnl. R. Microsc. Soc.* 439 Quite distinct from these are those abrupt.. variations..which sometimes occur, and of which de Vries records a remarkable instance in the genus *Œnothera*. For such variations de Vries proposes the term *mutations*. **1919** *Jrnl. Exper. Zool.* XXVIII. 381 In our opinion, the attempted distinctions between 'saltations', 'mutations', and 'variations of slight degree' have led rather to confusion of thought than to clearer thinking. To us these are all a single class, 'mutations', and the term carries no restrictions of degree, covering the most extreme as well as the slightest detectable inherited variation. **1925** *Genetics* X. 117 If one thinks of mutations as being simply inherited changes, it becomes necessary to distinguish changes that involve whole chromosomes.., changes that involve several adjacent genes.., and what have been called 'point-mutations' or 'gene-mutations'. **1928, 1930** [see *gene mutation* s.v. *GENE 2]. **1955** *Sci. News Let.* 25 June 409 Many mutations are lethal. If man-made irradiation increases the mutation rate, the result is sure to be harmful. **1955** *Sci. Amer.* July 74/2 Reproduction is one of the two essential features of life. Mutation is the other. **1957** I. ASIMOV *Naked Sun* (1958) xi. 145 Even the best gene analysis of parents can't assure that all gene permutations and combinations will be favourable, to say nothing of the possibility of mutations. That's our big concern, the unexpected mutation. **1965** A. H. STURTEVANT *Hist. Genetics* x. 62 It is ironic that few of the original mutations observed by de Vries in Oenothera would now be called mutations. **1971** J. Z. YOUNG *Introd. Study Man* xxviii. 392 The cause of mutation is some faulty copying during replication of the DNA. This..will be inherited only if it occurs in the line of the germ cells. Mutations elsewhere in the body are called somatic mutations... The accumulation of somatic mutations may produce some of the diseases of old age. **1972** [see *MENDELIAN *sb.*]. **1974** *Sci. Amer.* Sept. 82 (*caption*) One-gene mutation is responsible for the difference between the beta chain of a normal hemoglobin molecule..and that of hemoglobin *S*, the variant form responsible for sickle-cell anemia.

7. Special Comb.: **mutation mink,** a mink belonging to a mutant strain with a fur colour different from the normal; fur or a garment made from the skin of such a mink; **mutation pressure,** a tendency for recurring mutation (rather than selection) to alter the frequency of a particular allele within a population; **mutation rate,** the rate at which gene mutations occur (see quot. 1971); **mutation theory,** the theory of de Vries concerning the origin of new species (see *6 a).

1942 H. BOCK in *Amer. Fur Breeder* Oct. 14 (*title*) Mutation mink and their use in coats. **1945** R. G. HODGSON *Mink Book* (ed. 2) 41 Mutation mink got their start in the United States..and the Silverblu..was the important mink to give the industry something to think about. **1956** J. G. LINKS *Book of Fur* 166 The mutation mink names Silverblu, Aleutian, Royal Pastel..each representing a different mutation which had been developed since the original Silverblu. **1958** *Vogue* Jan. 12 Natural pale beige mutation mink. **1966** R. SERJEANT *Mink on my Shoulder* xi. 152 To the fur trade and perhaps also to the general public, the mutation mink means a mink of an abnormal colour or fur pattern that can be repeated at will. **1931** *Genetics* XVI. 100 (*heading*) Mutation pressure. **1962** D. J. MERRELL *Evol. & Genetics* xxiv. 237 Theoretically mutation pressure alone could bring about evolution. **1930** R. A. FISHER *Genetical Theory Nat. Select.* vi. 122 If ..the mutation rates..are high enough to maintain any considerable genetic diversity, it will only be the best adapted genotypes which can become the ancestors of

future generations. **1948** *Proc. R. Soc.* B. CXXXV. 168 It follows that human mutation rates are about twice those of *Drosophila* per nuclear division, and about one two-hundredth of those of *Drosophila* per day. **1971** LEVITAN & MONTAGU *Textbk. Human Genetics* xvii. 649 Mutation rates are usually stated in terms of the number of changed genes per locus per generation. **1904** Mutation theory [in Dict., sense 6]. **1912** *Amer. Naturalist* XLVI. 359 We can distinguish and trace the history of these quantitative variations from generation to generation only when the differences between them are of some size. This has led many to think that only variations of some size are inherited (the mutation theory) and others to deny that such variations can be increased in size by selection. **1962** D. J. MERRELL *Evol. & Genetics* xxi. 213 In the very early days of genetics de Vries (1902) proposed the mutation theory of evolution as an alternative to the theory of natural selection.

mutational (miutēi·ʃənăl), *a. Biol.* [f. MUTATION + -AL.] Of or pertaining to mutation.

1904 *Nature* 25 Feb. 386/2 De Vries's 'mutational' variations. **1931** E. B. FORD *Mendelism & Evolution* iv. 72 This criticism omits all reference to an important condition of the theory: the size of the mutational steps involved. **1955** *Bull. Atomic Sci.* June 210/2 No exposure [to radiation] is so tiny that it does not carry its corresponding mutational risk. **1964** G. H. HAGGIS et al. *Introd. Molecular Biol.* p. xi, Recent refinements in genetic analysis..have made it possible to relate mutational events to modification of nucleic acid structure.

Hence **muta·tionally** *adv.*, as a result of mutation.

1934 in WEBSTER. **1960** *Biochim. & Biophys. Acta* XLIII. 288 (*heading*) The similar properties of tryptophan synthetase and a mutationally altered enzyme in *Neurospora crassa*. **1971** *Nature* 24 Dec. 443/3 Strains of *E. coli* with mutationally altered ribosomal proteins.

mutationist (miutēi·ʃənist). [f. MUTATION + -IST.] One who stresses the importance of mutation as a factor in the evolution of new forms or species.

1904 *Science* 10 June 881/2 It might be inferred that Lamarckians and Darwinians are..regarded as believers in adaptiveness as a factor in evolution, and mutationists are necessarily supposed to hold the opposite view. **1909** *Fabian News* XX. 76/1 The mad mutationist who claims that evolution takes place by mutation only. **1911** A. D. DARBISHIRE *Breeding & Mendelian Discov.* 4 The point at issue between the Selectionist..and the Mutationist.

‖ **mutatis mutandis** (miutā·tis miutæ·ndis), *advb. phr.* [L., f. *mutatis, mutandis*, ablative pl. respectively of pa. pple. and gerundive of *mūtāre* to change.] 'Things being changed that have to be changed', i.e. with the necessary changes; with due alteration of details (in comparing cases).

1498 *Coventry Leet Bk.* (1909) 595 And like billes, mutatis mutandis, were put In ayenst Gloucestre & Worcestre. **1615** T. BONE *Let.* 9 Nov. in J. P. Collier *Egerton Papers* (1840) 472 The very same (*mutatis mutandis* onely) weere put in practize by Foreman. **1666** *Phil. Trans. R. Soc.* I. 289 The like may be fitted to Mars in other positions, *mutatis mutandis*; and so for the other Planets. **1710** SWIFT *Tale Tub* (ed. 5) Author's Apology sig. a1, I know nothing more contemptible in a Writer than the Character of a Plagiary; which he here fixes at a venture, and this, not for a Passage, but a whole Discourse, taken out from another Book only *mutatis mutandis*. **1753** CHESTERFIELD in *World* 14 June 146 The utility of this invention extends, *mutatis mutandis*, to whatever can be the subject of letters. **1817** COLERIDGE *Biogr. Lit.* I. xiii. 288 The actual application of the positions which had so wonderfully enlarged the discoveries of geometry, mutatis mutandis, to philosophical subjects. **1877** *Trans. Connecticut Acad. Arts & Sci.* III. 345 The same may be said, *mutatis mutandis*, of the other symbols of the same type. **1892** [see *HOMOSEXUAL *a.* and *sb.* A.]. **1931** *Times Lit. Suppl.* 23 July 570/2 *Mutatis mutandis*, one might trace a succession from the seventeenth-century divine and Fellow of the Royal Society..to the well-known modern names in philosophy. **1955** *Times* 11 July 13/6 *Mutatis mutandis* these lucid words still apply to the exertions of Russian historians carrying on the same tradition. **1962** S. E. FINER *Man on Horseback* ii. 6 What is said of the army here is to be taken also to apply, *mutatis mutandis*, to the air force and the navy. **1973** *Times* 13 Dec. 18/2 *Mutatis mutandis*, we are going to face a series of enforceable demands by the 'undeveloped' nations, equivalent to the Arabs' demand for higher pay for their oil.

‖ **mutato nomine** (miutā·to nōu·minēi), *advb. phr.* [L., f. *mutato*, ablative sing. of pa. pple. of *mūtāre* to change + *nomine*, ablative sing. of *nōmen* name.] 'The name being changed': applicable in a transferred context if the name of the person, place, etc., is altered accordingly.

The original phrase (cited in quot. 1621) quotes Horace *Sat.* I. i. 69.

1621 BURTON *Anat. Mel.* (Democritus to Reader) 37 Accounting it an excellent thing..to make our selues merry with other mens obliquities, when as he himselfe is more faultie then the rest, *mutato nomine de te fabula narratur*, he may take himselfe by the nose for a foole. *a* **1661** FULLER *Worthies* (1662) Lincs. 153 Which Proverb, *Mutato Nomine*, is used in other Counties. **1828** J. S. MILL in *Westm. Rev.* IX. 146 Nobody would pretend that a man unacquainted with the properties of simple substances would be perfectly capable of performing such an analysis, or that the knowledge of the ultimate elements of bodies was of no service to the chemist. The same observations apply, *mutato nomine*, to the logician, and the syllogism. **1840** J. B. FRASER *Koordistan* II. vi. 152 The words of Burns, *mutato nomine*, describe their country exactly. **1860** THACKERAY in *Cornhill Mag.* May 632 A score of such queer names and titles I have smiled at in America. And, *mutato nomine*?

mutator. Restrict † *Obs. rare*$^{-1}$ to sense in Dict. and add: **2.** *Biol.* Any gene which increases the mutation rate of other genes. Usu. *attrib.*, esp. in *mutator gene*.

1943 *Proc. Nat. Acad. Sci.* XXIX. 138 In determining the abnormal mutation rate we shall consider only those cultures which have given at least one sex-linked recessive, since this is the only indication of the presence of the 'Mutator' gene in the mother. **1945** *Genetics* XXX. 496 Recently, high mutation frequency in a strain of *D. pseudoobscura*, race B, was found to be due to a dominant mutator. **1970** *Jrnl. Molecular Biol.* L. 129 Mutator genes cause a generalized increase in mutation rate. They have been identified in a variety of organisms, including phage and bacteria.

mute, *a.* and *sb.*[1] Add: **B.** *sb.* **3. e.** (Later example.)

1962 WODEHOUSE *Service with Smile* i. 16 That's why she slinks about the place like a funeral mute, is it?

4*. *Cinemat.* A positive or negative film print which has no synchronous sound-track. Also *attrib.* or as *adj.*

1933 A. BRUNEL *Filmcraft* 161 *Mute*, the negative or positive of the pictorial image. **1953** K. REISZ *Technique Film Editing* 281 *Mute negative*, picture negative of a sound film, without the sound-track. *Mute print*, positive print of the picture part of a sound film without the sound track. **1963** E. LINDGREN *Art of Film* (ed. 2) ii. 37 We now have two lengths of negative film, one known as the mute negative (or picture negative or action negative) and the other known as the sound negative. The projection print is made by printing these two negatives on to a single positive film. **1969** W. RUTHERFORD *Gallows Set* ii. 27 We're filming him tomorrow morning... And we're doing a bit of mute, showing him going up to the gate. *Ibid.* iv. 53 There's..a couple of cans on shipbuilding, mostly mute but with a bit of sound.

muted, *a.*[2] Add to def.: Now in extended use; *spec.* of colour = SUBDUED *ppl. a.* 2.

1939 M. B. PICKEN *Language of Fashion* 101/3 Muted, subdued or toned down. Often applied to colours. **1950** *Britannica Bk. of Year* 682/2 *Muted*, of lighting, subdued. **1958** *Oxf. Mail* 9 July 6/2 Sea colours—aquamarine, sapphire blue, muted green. **1964** *Daily Tel.* 7 Feb. 16/2 'It is unlikely that the development of public expenditure on the scale implied will leave much scope for a reduction in taxation.' This muted sentence..must often come to people's minds as they read of new commitments. **1964** MRS. L. B. JOHNSON *White House Diary* 17 July (1970) 181 *My* West is muted brown and green and gray. **1968** *Jazz Monthly* Nov. 23/1 Davis uses that distinctive hard-edged smokey-centred muted tone. **1974** *Impressionism* (R. Acad.) 45/2 He uses a very restricted colour-range to convey an overcast snow-effect—muted blues and greens set off against grey and white.

‖ **mutessarif** (mutəsa·rif). Also **mutasarrif, mutassarif, mutasserif, mutesarrif, mutussarif.** [Turk., ad. Arab. *mutaṣarrif* governor of a sanjak.] In the Ottoman Empire and Iraq, a governor of a province.

1875 *Encycl. Brit.* III. 446/2 Batum..is now the seat of a *mutessarif*, or deputy-governor. **1900** G. BELL *Let.* 2 May (1927) I. 87 There has come a telegram from Damascus to bid me say the Mutussarif fears for the safety of your presence. **1914** T. E. LAWRENCE *Let.* June (1938) 174 All the Consuls & Valis & Kaims & Mutasarrifs & Commandants came out also. **1919** R. WEBB *Let.* 28 June in M. Llewellyn Smith *Ionian Vision* (1973) vi. 106 We were gradually getting the bad Valis, Mutessarifs, &c, removed. **1921** *Blackw. Mag.* June 705/2 A few of the political officers remain in the new capacity of Adviser to an Arab Mutassarif. **1933** *Times Lit. Suppl.* 9 Nov. 760/2 It was in Jerusalem that he was able to watch the simple methods of Rauf Pasha, then Mutessarif of El Kuds. **1969** D. WALDER *Chanak* xi. 199 The Mutessarif of Chanak (a combination of English mayor and French prefect) had taken over the Sanjak. **1972** D. DAKIN *Unification of Greece* viii. 116 The *mutessarifs* (provincial governors) were, if Christian, to have Moslem assessors, and, if Moslems, then Christian assessors.

muthafucka, muthafukka, muthafucking, varr. *mother-fucker, mother-fucking* ppl. adj. (*MOTHER *sb.*[1] 16 a).

1969 H. R. BROWN *Die Nigger, Die* ii. 29 The dirty muthafucka. **1969** R. D. TAYLOR *Drum Song* in A. Chapman *New Black Voices* (1972) 312 Ain't that blackmuthafukka beautiful. **1971** *Black World* Mar. 54/2 The best muthafucking thing that done ever happened to me.

muti (mū·ti). *S. Afr.* Also 9 **booti, mooti.** [ad. Zulu *umuthi* tree, plant, medicine.] Medicine; a medicinal charm (used esp. by a medicine-man or witch-doctor).

1831 W. B. BOYCE *Jrnl.* 23 June in A. Steedman *Wanderings & Adventures in S. Afr.* (1835) II. 282 He mentioned the report of Mr. Shepstone having sent men on horseback to plant booti (bewitching matter) upon his place. **1891** R. MONTEIRO *Delagoa Bay* viii. 172 They [*sc.* the Kaffirs] don't mind saying some are used as 'mooti', physic. **1911** *State* Dec. 659 (Pettman), He produced a few pinches of powder from the *muti* bag suspended round his neck. **1947** *Cape Times* 10 May 1/1 It was thought that the plant had been killed out by witchdoctors, who consider it an important ingredient of a powerful muti. **1957** J. PACKER *Nor Moon by Night* xviii. 176 He may have made *muti* of that boy's eyes and tongue. *Ibid.* xxvi. 234 This *muti* is like the bite of a cobra—it makes a man sleep. **1971** *Sunday Times* (Johannesburg) 28 Mar. 20/3 The club which has often used the rolling of the bones to forecast the results of vital matches need some new 'muti' to revive their form.

mutillid (miuti·lid), *sb.* and *a.* [f. mod.L. family name *Mutillidæ*, f. generic name *Mutilla* (Linnæus *Systema Naturæ* (ed. 10, 1758) I. 582): see -ID[3].] **A.** *sb.* A solitary, parasitic, fossorial wasp of the family Mutillidæ, including insects also known as velvet ants, whose bodies are covered with fine hair. **B.** *adj.* Pertaining to or resembling an insect of this type.

1910 W. M. WHEELER *Ants* xiv. 244 Existing mutillids, however, present two highly specialized characters..: they are, so far as is known, parasitic and their females are wingless. **1913** [see *CLERID *a.* and *sb.*]. **1971** E. O. WILSON *Insect Societies* xviii. 338/1 Several observers.. have witnessed guard bees protecting their nests against mutillid wasps and ants. **1972** L. E. CHADWICK tr. *Linsenmaier's Insects of World* 299/1 The mutillids chirp with a sound like that of boiling water.

muting, *vbl. sb.* (s.v. MUTE *v.*[3]). Add: **b.** *Electronics.* The automatic suppression of the output of an amplifier when the input signal falls below some predetermined level. Freq. *attrib.*

1936 W. T. COCKING *Wireless Servicing Man.* xv. 168 In practically all cases muting is obtained by arranging for a valve to apply a large bias to the last I.F. valve, the detector, or the first L.F. valve in the absence of a carrier, so that the stage is rendered inoperative. **1959** H. N. GANT *Mobile Radio Telephones* ii. 51 Receivers for mobile radio telephony have very large amplification and the transmitter to which they are tuned is only on when a message is to be passed, so there are long periods when the receiver produces only noise, in the form of a loud roaring sound. To prevent this annoyance the more complex receivers often incorporate a muting or squelch circuit to cut off the receiver output in the absence of the signal. **1970** J. EARL *Tuners & Amplifiers* ii. 39 The diodes and four transistors..give a.g.c. for the FET in the f.m. front-end, a potential for the tuning meter and inter-station muting.

mutism[1]. Add: (Further examples.) Also *fig.*

1873 *Nature* 27 Feb. 323/2, I know of two instances where perfect mutism accompanied the deafness in cats. **1882** SALA *America Revisited* I. ix. 138 Behind the counter was a very paragon of mutism in the shape of an hotel clerk. **1894** A. GRIFFITHS *Secrets Prison House* II. IV. viii. 220 There was no other outlet but confession or obstinate mutism. **1969** P. ANDERSON in Cockburn & Blackburn *Student Power* 215 Given the complete mutism of the past, any such initial attempt will inevitably suffer from errors, lapses, [etc.]. **1975** *N.Y. Times Book Rev.* 8 June VII. 21/3 All we can hope is..that the innumerable poems..will not give us nausea, or a new, science-inspired dose of mutism.

b. In *Psychol.* used (in contrast to *aphonia*) to imply the absence of any ascertainable defect of the vocal organs and hence a cause that is primarily psychological rather than physiological.

1892 D. H. TUKE *Dict. Psychol. Med.* II. 827/2 *Mutism*, dumbness from mental defect or disorder. In addition to the cases of Deaf-Dumbness.., mutism occurs in the course of various mental disorders, as Mental Stupor, Delusional Insanity, &c. **1930** *Internat. Jrnl. Psychoanal.* XI. 185 (*title*) On the physiology of hysterical aphonia and mutism. **1940** *Amer. Jrnl. Psychiatry* XCVI. 1445 In psychotic patients mutism is often associated with other manifestations of negativism. **1961** W. R. BRAIN *Speech Disorders* vii. 107 Mutism is the term applied to a complete loss of speech in a conscious patient in the absence of organic disease of the nervous system. **1972** S. CASHDAN *Abnormal Psychol.* ii. 50 In extreme cases, social withdrawal leads to mutism (refusal to speak) and regression (acting in infantile ways).

muto-. Add: **mutoscope** (further examples).

1901 *World's Work* Aug. 1057/2 Prints made from the film are mounted consecutively about a cylinder. As the cylinder is revolved the mounted pictures are held back by a stop, and snap past the eye so that the illusion is of a continuous motion picture. Encased in a box and with the automatic penny-in-the-slot attachment the mutoscope is ready for its common commercial use. **1922** JOYCE *Ulysses* 362 Mutoscope pictures in Capel street: for men only. **1969** *Jabez Elliott* (Ringwood, Hants.) *Miscellany Catal.* No. 6. 7 A little booklet or pad..of 82 photographs of two girls dancing. When the leaves are flicked over the dancers spring to life... These little books, called Mutoscopes, were popular in the early days of the Cinema.

muton (miū·tǫn). *Biol.* [f. MUT(ATION + *-ON[1].] The smallest element of the genetic material (supposedly a single pair of nucleotides) which when altered can give rise to a mutant individual.

1957 S. BENZER in McElroy & Glass *Symp. Chem. Basis Heredity* 71 The unit of mutation, the 'muton', will be defined as the smallest element that, when altered, can give rise to a mutant form of the organism. **1959** [see *CISTRON]. **1970** AMBROSE & EASTY *Cell Biol.* x. 356 It seems probable that the smallest unit of recombination (the recon) has in fact the same dimensions as the smallest unit of mutation (the muton), that is a single nucleotide base pair in the DNA molecule. **1971** J. Z. YOUNG *Introd.*

Study Man iii. 53 Mutation may occur by the change of any single base and these are thus the letters of the genetic language (also known as mutons).

mutsha, mutshi, varr. *MOOCHA.

mutt (mɒt). *slang* (orig. *U.S.*). Also **mut.** [abbrev. *mutton-head* (MUTTON 8 b in Dict. and Suppl.] **a.** One who is stupid, ignorant, awkward, blundering, incompetent, or the like; a blockhead, dullard, or fool; also, non-pejoratively, a person, fellow.

1901 'H. MCHUGH' *Down Line* 79, I knew that Clara Jane would cancel the contract with the mutt that mixed in just as soon as she saw the automobile snap. **1910** O. JOHNSON *Varmint* 377 Engaged to that Ver Planck fellow that was hanging around. I think he's a mutt. **1915** WODEHOUSE *Psmith, Journalist* xvi. 116 This ain't him. This is some other mutt. **1920** *Blackw. Mag.* Feb. 176/2 Dougal, the elder brother, was a quiet, inoffensive kind of a mutt. **1926** *Spectator* 1 May 813/1 Not doubting the poor mutt's love for her. **1929** [see *GOOP]. **1942** 'M. INNES' *Daffodil Affair* iv. 146 Why couldn't you keep to the racket, you poor mut, and leave tinkering alone! **1955** W. GADDIS *Recognitions* II. vii. 597 Got to look up a mutt named Chavenay. **1972** *Police Rev.* 10 Nov. 1444/2 Some male driver—poor mutt!—will be fiddling with the jack. **1973** D. MAY *Laughter in Djakarta* xii. 203 The poor mutt must have driven it along the bank.

b. A term of contempt applied to a dog, *esp.* a mongrel.

Quot. 1904 refers to a horse.

1904 *Outing* XLV. 170/2 Watch that mut curl up out there. **1906** H. GREEN *Actors' Boarding House* 335 A fellow can't leave nothin' on his bed without that mutt chawin' it up! **1911** R. W. CHAMBERS *Common Law* x. 310 Now fat old women..Arrive to exercise their various dogs; And 'round and 'round the little mutts all run. **1927** *Ladies' Home Jrnl.* Dec. 4/1 Be careful the mutt doesn't get into a race with a caterpillar some day, and die of heart collapse. **1932** *Sun* (Baltimore) 15 Oct. 20/5 There are people who especially desire a mutt dog. **1949** *Sat. Even. Post* 16 Apr. 44/2 That cat! That mutt! they fight it out And back and forth they shuttle. **1970** *New Yorker* 29 Aug. 50/3 The cast includes a Sheepdog.., a Mutt Bitch. **1972** C. WESTON *Poor, Poor Ophelia* (1973) vi. 29 Two barefoot hippies were sharing a bag of potato chips with a happy-looking mutt.

c. Phr. *Mutt and Jeff* [from the names of two characters called *Mutt* and *Jeff,* one tall and the other short, in a popular cartoon series by H. C. Fisher (1884–1954), American cartoonist]. (*a*) A stupid pair of men; stupid dialogue; (*b*) (see quot. 1943); (*c*) as *adj.*, deaf.

1917 E. E. CUMMINGS *Let.* 4 June (1969) 26 By failing to get up..I escaped departing with the bums mutts and jeffs (not to say ginks, slobs, and punks) who came over with us. **1937** M. HUXLEY in A. Huxley *Lett.* (1969) 426 A sort of Mutt and Jeff on war and peace and religion. **1937** PARTRIDGE *Dict. Slang* 545/2 *Mutt and Jeff,* the British War Medal and Victory Medal: military: 1918. **1943** C. H. WARD-JACKSON *It's a Piece of Cake* 43 *Mutt and Jeff,* the King George V silver Jubilee and the Edward VIII Coronation medals, or ribbons, worn together; or the 1918 Victory and Overseas medals or ribbons worn together. **1949** *Sun* (Baltimore) 10 Dec. 24/5 Richard ——, identified as the taller man in the recent series of 'Mutt and Jeff' robberies here, yesterday pleaded guilty to armed robbery. **1960** J. FRANKLYN *Dict. Rhyming Slang* 98/2 *Mutt & Jeff,* deaf. 20 C. Current in the theatrical world, and formed on the names of the two famous strip-cartoon characters. **1973** *Washington Post* 21 Nov. C2 The women..call the two cops..'Mutt and Jeff'. Who is Jeff? 'The white one..Mutt is always being kicked around. Jeff makes him do all the work.' **1974** D. SEAMAN *The Bomb* xx. 200 He silently named them Mutt and Jeff. One [man] stood well over six feet..while the other barely reached to his mate's armpits.

muttering, *vbl. sb.* (Later example of sing. use.)

1971 *Guardian* 14 Jan. 1/3 There may be some feminine muttering that in promoting the 'Woman's Guardian' we are perpetuating the idea of the female ghetto.

muttering, *ppl. a.* (Later examples.)

1917 T. S. ELIOT *Prufrock & other Observations* 9 Certain half-deserted streets The muttering retreats Of restless nights in one-night cheap hotels. **1927** JOYCE *She weeps over Rahoon* in *Pomes Penyeach,* The moongrey nettles, the black mould And muttering rain.

mutt-eye (mɒ·tˌəi). *Austral. slang.* [Orig. unknown.] (Cut) corn.

1946 K. TENNANT *Lost Haven* (1947) x. 135 Five sacks of potatoes, three of mutt-eyes, another three of pumpkins. **1966** BAKER *Austral. Lang.* (ed. 2) iv. 84 Bull's eyes, fried eggs; mutt eyes, corn; frog's eyes, boiled sago.

‖ **mutti** (mu·ti). [G., f. *mutter* mother.] A childish or familiar form of 'mother' (used in German-speaking countries).

1906 M. A. VON ARNIM *Princess Priscilla's Fortnight* ii. 32 She's a witch—Mutti, she's a witch! **1939** C. ISHERWOOD *Goodbye to Berlin* 169 'Poor little Mummy, little Mutti, little Mutchen,' he crooned. **1967** A. WILSON *No Laughing Matter* III. 314 And as for Mutti—strange little bent witch-like lady! **1972** *Guardian* 29 July 3/5 An announcement from..the lifeguards. 'Achtung, achtung —morning gymnastics for the ladies..' And off go the Muttis to trim their waistlines, while father relaxes.

mutton. Add: **4.** (Further examples.) So, the genital organs of a woman; copulation. Phr. *to hawk one's mutton,* (of a woman) to seek a lover, to solicit (cf. *hawking* ppl. a. s.v. HAWK *v.*[2]). See also MUTTON-MONGER in Dict. and Suppl.

1864 HOTTEN *Slang Dict.* (ed. 3) 184 *Mutton,* a contemptuous term for a woman of bad character... In that class of English society which does not lay any claim to refinement, a fond lover is often spoken of as being 'fond of his mutton'. **1937** PARTRIDGE *Dict. Slang* 380/2 Hawk one's mutton. **1939** H. HODGE *Cab, Sir?* v. 53 He can't quite believe she hawks her mutton in hexagonal horn-rimmed spectacles. **1964** N. FREELING *Double-Barrel* II. viii. 65 In the army we used to say, of such and such a girl, nurse, waaf, whatever she was, 'That one hawks her mutton.' **1973** 'J. PATRICK' *Glasgow Gang Observed* vii. 73 They're aw cows hawkin' their mutton.

7. *to return to one's muttons* (earlier and later examples); so, *to resume one's muttons;* conversely, *to stick to one's muttons; mutton dressed as lamb*: an elderly or middle-aged woman dressed (coiffured, painted, etc.) as though she were young; *to be one's muttons* (N.Z.): see quot. 1941.

1821 M. EDGEWORTH *Let.* 19 Dec. (1971) 297, I think he is winning..the heart of Lady Caroline—But to return to my muttons. **1895** KIPLING *Brushwood Boy* in *Day's Work* (1898) 348 Look at young Davies makin' an ass of himself over mutton-dressed-as-lamb old enough to be his mother! **1903** A. BENNETT *Leonora* iii. 72, I shall have to return to my muttons directly. **1922** JOYCE *Ulysses* 541 *Passée.* Mutton dressed as lamb. **1930** *Punch* 28 May 606/3 Both houses, having dealt with the Whitsuntide holidays, resumed their muttons. **1933** *Sun* (Baltimore) 3 Mar. 6/7 Let's stick to our muttons, old man radio, and make it music alone. **1937** D. L. SAYERS *Busman's Honeymoon* xv. 307 Aggie Twitterton. Runs arter 'im like an old cat... At *'er* age! Mutton dressed as lamb. **1940** *National Education* (Wellington, N.Z.) Feb. 17 Milk, however, is small Charlie's muttons. **1941** BAKER *N.Z. Slang* vi. 54 The farming community has given us [this century] another useful expression in *our muttons.* When we speak of something *being our muttons* or *a person's muttons* we mean that it is regarded with particular favour, that we like it especially well. **1943** A. HASTINGS *Bright Conversations* 24 Stick to your muttons, and don't talk tripe. **1967** V. S. NAIPAUL *Mimic Men* I. iii. 41 Our middle-aged ladies, mutton dressed as lamb, as our barman says. **1974** N. MARSH *Black as he's Painted* i. 31, I digress... Shall we return to our muttons?

7*. *Printing.* = *mutton quad* (MUTTON 8 b).

1938 *Amer. Speech* XIII. 270 An em quad is a space the square of the type body... In the shop..frequently called muttons or monkeys. **1960** G. A. GLAISTER *Gloss. Book* 122/2 The popular name for an em quad is mutton.

8. b. mutton cloth (see quot. 1957); **mutton-faced** *a.*, having a face suggestive of mutton (as a term of abuse); **mutton fat,** (*b*) in full, *mutton-fat candle*; (*c*) used *attrib.* and *absol.* of jade to designate a creamy white colour valued highly by connoisseurs; **mutton-fisted** *a.*, clumsy, heavy-handed; also *fig.*; **mutton-head** (earlier U.S. and later examples); **mutton-headed** (later examples); **mutton-leg sleeve** = *leg-of-mutton sleeve.*

1923 *Daily Mail* 12 Mar. 2 (Advt.), Stockinette is white mutton cloth in its new form, and everyone knows there is nothing to beat it for any kind of cleaning or polishing. **1957** *Textile Terms & Definitions* (Textile Inst.) (ed. 3) 67 *Mutton cloth,* a plain-knitted fabric of loose texture, usually cotton, made on a multi-feeder circular knitting machine. **1892** STEVENSON & OSBOURNE *Wrecker* xii. 193 'You ——, ——, little, mutton-faced Dutchman,' Nares would bawl. **1864** LE FANU *Uncle Silas* III. xvii. 259 The imperfect light of our mutton-fat candle. **1912** B. LAUFER *Jade* xii. 328 A brown-red tinge passing into light-yellow shades is strewn over a background of a glossy white which the Chinese designate as mutton-fat. **1920** 'K. MANSFIELD' *Let.* 20 May (1928) II. 34 A flamingo in a cage made of mutton-fat jade. **1935** [see *CH'IEN LUNG]. **1936** J. GOETTE *Jade Lore* vi. 104 White jade from Central Asia..shows a greater range than does the Burmese. The native connoisseur has always put great emphasis on what he terms mutton fat. **1969** F. KOVAL tr. *O. Luzzatto-Bilitz's Antique Jade* 46 White jade which is slightly translucent and opalescent is called by the Chinese 'Mutton-Fat Jade'. **1918** Mutton-fisted [see *ham-handed* adj. (*HAM *sb.*[1] 3)]. **1927** *Observer* 27 Nov. 6 A critic of his central sound sense..and mutton-fisted manner of calling a spade a spade. **1934** *Times Lit. Suppl.* 22 Nov. 813/2 But he [*sc.* a hunter] was naturally a little headstrong, and a mutton-fisted stable-boy speedily made of him an incurable puller. **1965** D. FRANCIS *For Kicks* ix. 120, I worked in a slovenly fashion and rode..like a mutton-fisted clod. **1803** T. G. FESSENDEN *Terrible Tractoration* (ed. 2) iv. 159 And couldst thou, pertinacious B—, But maul these mutton heads, most sadly. **1928** D. H. LAWRENCE *Woman who rode Away* 209 That *fool,* Joe, standing there like a mutton-head! **1938** H. NICOLSON *Let.* 11 July (1966) 349, I suppose that some mutton-head might say [etc.]. **1960** I. WALLACH *Absence of Cello* 160 I'm neither an oaf, a boor, or a muttonhead. **1972** 'J. & E. BONETT' *No Time to Kill* xi. 148 Bone-heads, that's what you are. Mutton-heads. Idiots. **1897** G. BARTRAM *People of Clopton* ii. 49 He were sich a mutton-headed fool theer were no valley in oot-wittin' him. **1934** WODEHOUSE *Right Ho, Jeeves* xix. 242 She had caused all the trouble by her mutton-headed behaviour in saying 'Yes' instead of 'No'. **1942** E. PAUL *Narrow St.* xx. 164 A mutton-headed obstinate father. **1830** *Ladies' Mag.* III. 183 Think of such terms as *mutton leg sleeves,* for example. **1845** *Lowell* (Mass.) *Offering* V. 201 Here is a piece of the first dress I ever saw, cut with what were called 'mutton-leg' sleeves. **1922** JOYCE *Ulysses* 431 In..widow Twankey's blouse with muttonleg sleeves buttoned behind.

mutton-bird. Substitute for def.: *Austral.* and *N.Z.* **a.** Either of two species of the genus *Puffinus,* in New Zealand the sooty shearwater *P. griseus,* and in Australia the short-tailed shearwater *P. tenuirostris.* **b.** An Antarctic petrel of the genus *Pterodroma.* Also *attrib.* (Further examples.)

1846 G. H. HAYDON *Five Yrs. Australia Felix* 47 (Morris), The mutton-bird, or sooty petrel..is about the size of the wood-pigeon of England, and is of a dark colour. These birds are migratory, and are to be seen ranging over the surface of the great southern ocean far from land... Many millions of these birds are destroyed annually for the sake of their feathers and the oil of the young. **1905** W. B. *Where White Man Treads* 202 The other day as we opened the mutton-bird burrows, I heard you remonstrate with our lads. **1911** A. E. MACK *Bush Days* 110 On the surface of the water sat a mutton-bird. **1944** A. RUSSELL *Bush Ways* v. 27 The mutton birds make underground nesting burrows. **1954** A. MOOREHEAD *Rum Jungle* ix. 133 It is usually in a gale (known as the 'mutton bird gale')..that the main swarm suddenly appears. **1963** B. PEARSON *Coal Flat* xxii. 375 Mrs Torere brought out..a half-kerosene tin of cooked mutton-birds preserved in fat. **1965** *Courier-Mail* (Brisbane) 24 Mar. 2/7 Mutton bird rookeries can be found on the coasts. **1970** *Southerly* XXX. 226 The children saw countless thousands of mutton birds passing over the farm, returning from ocean wanderings north of the equator to their nesting colonies on the Bass Strait coasts.

2. mutton-bird scrub, tree *N.Z.*, an evergreen shrub or small tree, *Senecio reinoldii,* of the family Compositæ, bearing dark green leaves and clusters of small yellow flowers.

1898 MORRIS *Austral Eng.* 310/1 Mutton-bird Tree.. so called because the mutton-birds, especially in Foveaux Straits, New Zealand, are fond of sitting under it. **1906** LAING & BLACKWELL *Plants N.Z.* 438 *S[enecio] rotundifolius* is the mutton-bird scrub of Stewart Island. Its leaves are much used by tourists for post cards, the white tomentum of the underside affording a suitable surface for writing. **1963** POOLE & ADAMS *Trees & Shrubs N.Z.* 200 *S[enecio] reinoldii* Endl. Mutton-bird scrub. Shrub or small tree reaching 10 m.

d. *slang.* In full, *mutton-bird eater.* (See quot. 1937). Loosely, any Tasmanian.

1937 PARTRIDGE *Dict. Slang* 546/1 *Mutton-Bird* (gen. pl.), a resident in North Tasmania: Southern Tasmanians'. **1941** BAKER *Dict. Austral. Slang* 48 *Mutton-bird,* a resident of Northern Tasmania. Also, 'mutton-bird eater'.

So **mutton-birder,** one who catches mutton-birds in season; one who is engaged in the preparation of mutton-birds for the market. Also **mu·tton-birding** *vbl. sb.*

1881 G. WALCH *Victoria in 1880* 49 Armed with a piece of stout curved wire, fastened at the end of a long stick, the mutton-birder fishes in the holes for his prize. *Ibid.*, One of the sports of the neighbourhood is 'mutton-birding'. **1900** *N.Z. Illustr. Mag.* II. 919 Mutton-birding on Stewart Island. **1965** *Austral. Encycl.* VI. 234B (*caption*) A mutton-birder's hut, with casks of dressed and salted mutton-bird carcasses.

mutton-chop. 2. (Further examples.)

1875 [see *BURNSIDE, BURNSIDE]. **1972** J. WAMBAUGH *Blue Knight* (1973) vi. 83 Some of the boys had mutton-chops and moustaches. **1973** 'D. JORDAN' *Nile Green* xxiv. 97 The mutton-chop whiskered auctioneer. **1975** J. SYMONS *Three Pipe Problem* iii. 24 A square honest face framed by mutton-chop whiskers.

mutton-fish. 2. Substitute for def.: *Austral.* The flesh of a shell-fish of the genus *Haliotis,* esp. *H. iris;* = *PAUA. (Earlier and later examples.)

1840 J. S. POLACK *Manners & Customs of New Zealanders* II. xvi. 176 The *paua,* (mutton-fish) shell. **1843** E. DIEFFENBACH *Travels in N.Z.* II. x. 239 *Haliotis iris*... Inhabits New Zealand... The 'mutton-fish' of the colonists; eaten boiled, but very tough. **1874** A. BATHGATE *Colonial Experiences* xvii. 245 The beautiful iridescent shell of the mutton-fish..is not uncommon in the south. **1944** *Living off Land* ii. 30 In the case of molluscs like mutton fish, cook until most of the natural moisture has boiled out of the shell. **1956** M. WEST *Gallows on Sand* ix. 98 The ecology of *Haliotus asinina*—mutton-fish to you. **1959** W. G. MCCLYMONT *Explor. N.Z.* (ed. 2) 42 They lived on mutton fish.

mutton-monger. Restrict † *Obs.* to sense 2 in Dict. and add later example of sense 1.

1923 J. MANCHON *Le Slang* 201 A mutton-monger, un coureur de filles.

mutual, *a.* Add: **1. a.** spec. *mutual aid, deterrence.*

1539, 1894 [in Dict.]. **1912** J. S. HUXLEY *Individual in Animal Kingdom* v. 135 Mutual aid (though it implies mutual dependence) establishes minimum waste. *Ibid.* vi. 154 The ideals of active harmony and mutual aid as the best means to power and progress. **1927** —— *Religion without Revelation* i. 49 Permanent facts of human existence—..suffering, mutual aid, comradeship, physical and moral growth. **1943** *New Statesman* 20 Nov. 326 Lease lend, now officially named 'Mutual Aid', is giving rise to a great deal of discussion in the United States. **1955** *Ann. Reg. 1954* 149 Canada had previously made 400 Sabres available to the R.A.F. as part of the mutual aid programme. **1955** *Bull. Atomic Sci.* Jan. 16/1 In the non-Communist world a new formula is gaining more and more popularity—'mutual deterrence' by the consideration of the opponent's retaliatory power. **1966** SCHWARZ & HADIK *Strategic Terminology* 61 *Mutual deterrence,* situa-

tion obtaining between nuclear powers when each is deterred from attacking the other (i.e., launching a first strike) because the damage expected to result from the victim's retaliation (second strike) would be unacceptable.

c. (Earlier and later examples.) Also *mutual admiration gang*.

1851 THOREAU *Jrnl.* 27 Feb. in *Early Spring in Massachusetts* (1881) 16 It is the hip-hip-hurrah and mutual admiration society style. **1920** G. B. SHAW *How to become Musical Critic* (1960) 313 A ridiculous little mutual-admiration gang of snobs. **1953** G. HOUGH *Romantic Poets* v. 160 Keats would have been better off at this stage..without so many ladies, or with ladies of a different kind; and some of the familiar sonnets suggest a small and rather silly mutual admiration society. **1969** G. BATTISCOMBE *Queen Alexandra* x. 139 Seldom can there have been a more devoted family: the unkind might even have called them a mutual admiration society.

d. (Further examples.) *Spec.* in phr. **mutual fund** *U.S.*, a unit trust; also *attrib.*; hence **mutual funding.**

1950 J. C. CLENDENIN *Introd. to Investments* 600 (*Index*) Mutual funds (*see* Open-end companies). **1958** *Spectator* 18 July 108/1 In the United States, total investment in Mutual Funds (the American term for unit trusts) stands at over £3,000 million. **1962** S. STRAND *Marketing Dict.* 472 *Mutual Funds Market*, the daily buying and selling transactions of the shares of mutual funds. Companies selling mutual funds are listed on the financial pages of newspapers. **1969** *Times* 30 Apr. 28/3 As a Mutual Society all our profits must go to our policyholders. *Ibid.* 5 May (Suppl.) p. vi/3 The average turnover of mutual fund portfolios rose..to 43 per cent. **1972** *Daily Tel.* 4 Nov. 28/4 By lending those funds on mortgage, the [building] societies, which are mutual and non profit-making, pass on the benefit of the short-term cost of money to long-term borrowers. **1973** *Times* 18 May 29/2 Expanding industries such as insurance or mutual funding.

e. *Electr.* Applied to quantities and properties that depend equally and symmetrically on two circuits or circuit elements and represent an effect on either of a certain kind of change in the other; esp. *mutual inductance* (see *INDUCTANCE), *induction.*

1865 J. C. MAXWELL in *Phil. Trans. R. Soc.* CLV. 507 To find the coefficient (M) of mutual induction between two circular linear conductors in parallel planes. **1886**, etc. [see *INDUCTANCE]. **1896** F. BEDELL *Princ. Transformer* iii. 37 The relation between two circuits is strictly a mutual one, the coefficient of mutual induction having the same value with either circuit as primary or secondary. **1931** MOYER & WOSTREL *Radio Handbk.* vii. 395 In most circuits, the coupling between the input and output circuits is adjusted by changing the mutual reactance. **1959** B. J. LEY et al. *Linear Circuit Anal.* iii. 150 The coefficients Y_{11}, Y_{22},.., Y_{nn} of the principal diagonal terms were called self-admittances and the off-diagonal coefficients Y_{hk} ($h \neq k$) were called the mutual admittances. .. To find the mutual admittance Y_{12} we examine the term $Y_{12}(j\omega)\mathbf{V}_2$ in the first equation of Eqs. (3–69). This term represents the phasor current leaving node 1 when nodes 1, 3,.., *n* are grounded and node 2 has a phasor voltage $\mathbf{V}_2$. **1969** A. M. HOWATSON *Princ. Appl. Electr.* v. 100 The impedance Z_{12} is, physically, the voltage produced in mesh 1 due to unit current flowing in mesh 2. It is called the open-circuit transfer impedance or mutual impedance of mesh 2 to mesh 1, and because $Z_{12} = Z_{21}$ it is also that from mesh 1 to mesh 2.

f. Electronics. *mutual conductance*, the ratio of the change in the anode current of a valve to the change of grid voltage causing it, the anode voltage being held constant; so *mutual characteristic*, a characteristic curve representing the variation of anode current with grid voltage at constant anode voltage.

1918 L. A. HAZELTINE in *Proc. IRE* VI. 64 The effectiveness of the audion as a relay depends primarily on the slope of the characteristic curve. This slope, being the quotient of a current by a voltage associated therewith, is of the dimensions of a conductance and may be called the mutual conductance of the grid towards the plate. **1933** K. HENNEY *Radio Engin. Handbk.* viii. 195 The mutual characteristic, or transfer characteristic of the tube, shows the effect of the grid voltage upon the plate current. **1942** *Electronic Engin.* XIV. 734/1 The alternating potential is applied to control the electron stream at a point where the electron velocity is low, thereby producing a positive feedback which increases the effective mutual conductance of the valve. **1962** D. F. SHAW *Introd. Electronics* xi. 212 The value of g_m is low when I_a is very small but after an initial curvature the mutual characteristics are almost linear and parallel. **1963** B. FOZARD *Instrumentation Nuclear Reactors* x. 116 At middle frequencies where the undesirable effects of the various capacitances are negligible the gain is $g_m R$ where g_m is the mutual conductance of the valve and *R* is the effective anode load resistance.

B. *sb.* **a.** = *mutual friend.* **b.** = *mutual fund* (*MUTUAL *a.* 1 d).

1901 KIPLING *Kim* xii. 314 The wire came in about what our mutual friend said he had hidden... I meet our mutual at Delhi on the way back. **1971** *Financial Mail* (Johannesburg) 26 Feb. 690/1 Some mutual fund men..are once again pressing the Registrar for permission to go ahead with those property mutuals.

mutualism. Add: **1. a.** Esp. in connection with the theory of non-profit credit and voluntary association for the exchange of services advocated by P. J. Proudhon (1809–65).

1849 C. DANA *Proudhon* (1896) 36 But how can they gain possession of this instrument [*sc.* capital]? By the organization of credit, on the principle of reciprocity or mutualism, if we may use a new word. *Ibid.* 40 Mutualism of credit, or credit at cost. **1929** *Amer. Jrnl. Sociol.* XXXIV. 783 By 'mutualism' Proudhon meant a practice of voluntary association for strictly specified and limited purposes. **1968** *Internat. Encycl. Soc. Sci.* XII. 606/1 Federalism, that is, mutualism transferred into the realm of politics, is the solution.

2. (Further examples.) By some writers applied esp. to such a relationship that (*a*) is not necessary for the survival or reproduction of the organisms involved, or else (*b*) is necessary for one or both of the organisms. Also *transf.*

1949 W. C. ALLEE et al. *Princ. Animal Ecol.* xxxv. 711/1 Varying degrees of mutualism exist, from a slight benefit to a remarkable interdependence of both species in the partnership. **1953** *Parasitology* XLII. 261 Symbiosis can be broadly divided into the three well-recognized categories: commensalism (where the host is for all practical purposes unaffected by the presence of the symbiote), parasitism (where the host is injured), and mutualism (where the host is benefited). **1956** T. W. H. CAMERON *Parasites & Parasitism* 231 Commensalism, in turn, grades into mutualism, which implies a certain benefit by the host from the presence of the invader, but the association is not an essential one. **1962** J. D. SMYTH *Introd. Animal Parasitol.* i. 6 An association in which both associates benefit has long been referred to as mutualism by some authors and symbiosis by others... *Symbiosis* could..broadly be used to include all the different kinds of relationship which exist in nature. By usage, however, it has come to be restricted to associations..in which the participating species are dependent on each other for existence... In cases of mutualism, on the other hand, the association is not obligatory to existence. **1962** K. F. LAGLER et al. *Ichthyol.* xiv. 436 [Among fishes] instances of mutualism (symbiosis) are not clearly known; this is the relationship in which neither of two species can reproduce or grow in the absence of the other. **1963** C. J. MCCALL in A. Dundes *Mother Wit* (1973) 420 The relationship is rather one of mutualism, in that it is latently eufunctional for both institutions. **1967** M. E. HALE *Biol. Lichens* v. 70 *Mutualism.* This term describes a mutually beneficial relationship where one or both components may be dependent on the association for survival. **1970** *Nature* 5 Sept. 1001/1 The commonest species, *Remora remora*, is an active cleaner, and the mutualistic relationship between fish and host is strong, but the mutualism is less strong in other species.

mutualist. Add: Also *attrib.*

1909 F. LAWTON *3rd French Republic* xiv. 320 From 1852 onwards, the Mutualist movement extended rapidly. **1929** *Amer. Jrnl. Sociol.* XXXIV. 783 Let exchange take place directly within each 'mutualist' association. **1948** M. NOMAD in F. Gross *European Ideologies* viii. 329 Proudhon's 'mutualist anarchism', with its panacea of a 'People's Bank'. **1969** A. RITTER *Pol. Thought Proudhon* v. 130 The units of a mutualist society are not only to be equal in power; they are also to differ in their occupations, personalities, ideas, inclinations.

mutualistic (miūtiuăli·stik), *a.* [f. MUTUALIST + -IC.] Exhibiting or characteristic of mutualism (esp. sense 2).

1885 *Anarchist* 15 Sept. 2/2 He shews how two principles pervade human society—one mutualistic, which leads to equality, the other, antagonistic, which destroys it. **1911** J. G. MCINTOSH *Manuf. Varnishes* III. 291 Giard does not see that the ants are enemies of the cochineal... Their relations are mutualistic and in no way predatory. **1936** *New Phytologist* XXXV. 129 The presence of the fungus in a mycorrhizal association is to be regarded as an example of controlled parasitic attack and has no mutualistic significance. **1967** V. AHMADJIAN *Lichen Symbiosis* iv. 78 To say that all lichens are mutualistic is as wrong as saying that all are parasitic. **1970** [see *MUTUALISM 2]. **1974** *Nature* 18 Oct. 574/2 Mortimer Starr (University of California, Davis) produced a new classificatory scheme which has the virtue of both clarifying and thinking about the phenomenon and indicating where further experimental work is required—to decide, for example, whether a symbiotic association is mutualistic or obligately parasitic in this respect.

Hence **mutuali·stically** *adv.*

1949 W. C. ALLEE et al. *Princ. Anim. Ecol.* xvii. 251 There does not appear to be any development of a strict taxonomic relation like that in so many examples of mutualistically paired species in which pollination is involved. **1967** V. AHMADJIAN *Lichen Symbiosis* iv. 78 In some *Collema* lichens the fungal hyphae periodically destroy certain parts of the algal colony while living mutualistically with the rest.

mutuality. Add: **1. c.** A system of organizing conditions of work by agreement between the workmen involved and the employer; also **mutuality system.**

1968 *Sunday Tel.* 20 Oct. 19/2 The employers team pressed the unions to surrender the 'mutuality' system. **1970** *Guardian* 4 Dec. 15 'Mutuality'..means that the rates for each job have to be 'mutually agreed' on the shop floor where they are to be carried out and by the people who will perform the tasks. **1972** *Times* 27 Jan. 14/5 The agreement had that degree of mutuality to bring it within the set-off provisions of section 31. *Ibid.* 7 Nov. 19/3 The management has also conceded a large measure of 'mutuality', the arrangement under which shop floor representatives retain bargaining rights on many shop floor working conditions.

mutualization. (Further examples.)

1930 *Economist* 12 Apr. 825/2 It was created four years ago in connection with the 'mutualisation' of the company. **1951** *Ann. Reg. 1950* 5 It [*sc.* the party programme] was followed, two days later, by proposals for 'mutualization', rather than nationalization, of industrial assurance. **1955** *Times* 28 May 9/1 With the return of the Conservative Government measures of re-nationalization, of fresh nationalization, and of mutualization are no longer risks to be discounted, however vaguely, as contingencies just round the corner. **1960** *Times* 15 Jan. 17/2 Yesterday it [*sc.* the Canada Life Assurance Company] asked to be removed from the list because it had completed its 'mutualization' programme by purchasing all its own shares outstanding.

mutually, *adv.* Add: **1.** (Examples of *mutually exclusive.*)

1874 W. WALLACE tr. *Hegel's Logic* ii. 30 Sense..is individual, and as the individual (which, reduced to its simplest terms, is the atom) is also a member of a series, sensible existence presents a number of mutually exclusive units. **1908** A. BENNETT *Jrnl.* 5 Jan. (1932) I. 274 Every day's experience shows the folly of mutually-exclusive generalisations concerning two countries. **1969** D. C. HAGUE *Managerial Economics* vii. 141 To be drawn up correctly, our list of probabilities must be such that if any one event occurs, this automatically rules out the possibility that any other event in the same list could also occur. The events will then be mutually exclusive.

mutuel (mūtŭẹl, miū·tiuĕl). Chiefly *N. Amer.* shortening of PARI MUTUEL in Dict. and Suppl. Freq. *attrib.* and in *pl.* Also *transf.* (see quot. 1949).

1908 *Westm. Gaz.* 12 Dec. 16/2 In France last year 320,000,000 francs passed through the 'mutuel'. **1926** *Daily Colonist* (Victoria, B.C.) 23 July 10/5 Returns from the 'mutuels' show that British Columbians are betting as much as ever, or more so, at the Vancouver races. **1938** D. RUNYON *Furthermore* vi. 113 Then I see Herbie start for the mutuels windows. **1944** *Sun* (Baltimore) 21 Sept. 17/4 The mutuel machines will do close to a $400,000,000 business around New York tracks this season. **1949** *Amer. Speech* XXIV. 193/1 *Race mutuels*, a number game in which the winning number is derived from the racing results of any well-known race track. **1968** *Globe & Mail* (Toronto) 13 Jan. 40/8 The better class horses would attract more patrons who..would accelerate the mutuels play. **1972** *N.Y. Times* 1 June 56/1 The scramble had handled $659,439..meaning the scramble accounted for 8.45 per cent of the mutuel business. **1974** *New Yorker* 25 Feb. 86/2 Serious horseplayers will be sorry to hear..that the take from the mutuels will again be seventeen per cent.

‖ **mutum** (mū·tŭm). [Native name.] = CURASSOW.

1863 [see CURASSOW]. **1933** P. FLEMING *Brazilian Adventure* I. xvi. 137 Sometimes we got a *mutum*, a big black and white turkey with a speckled crest. **1964** A. L. THOMSON *New Dict. Birds* 175/2 The Razorbilled Curassow *Mitu mitu*, which is called 'mutum' by the Brazilians, is black with a bluish sheen in both sexes, with brown on the belly, and with a high narrow frontal comb of the same red colour as the bill; it weighs about 7¾ lb. (3500 grams) and inhabits the Amazon region and northern Brazil.

muu-muu (mū·mū). Also mumu. [Hawaiian *mu'u mu'u* lit. cut off, from the fact that the yoke was originally omitted.] A woman's loose-fitting dress, usually brightly coloured and patterned, which originated in Hawaii as a local adaptation of the 'Mother Hubbard' dress provided by the missionaries.

1923 C. LONDON *New Hawaii* xv. 250 Not far off.. swam a dozen men and women. They wore respectively loincloths and white or red muumuus. **1930** D. BLANDING *Hula Moons* 40 Helen being a woman, put on a yellow *mumu*, a cross between a flour sack and an old-fashioned nightie. *Mumus* were designed by the well-intentioned missionary ladies..as a covering for the Hawaiian women, in the early days when a few flowers sufficed for a garment. **1959** M. JANSMA *Wandering Malihini* ii. 33 A Hawaiian lady, costumed in an attractive *muumuu*,..sang to us songs of welcome and love. **1960** [see *HOLOKU]. **1962** O. RUHEN *Tangaroa's Godchild* xvi. 230 The missionary..invented the Mother Hubbard, from which the muu-muu is derived, to cover the glorious voluptuous bodies of the earth's most beautiful women. **1964** *Daily Mail* 21 Jan. 3/3 Mu-mus or Mother Hubbards describes the beachwear better. **1964** *Sunday Truth* (Brisbane) 19 July 21/7 The new cafe at Brisbane airport is to give a typical Australian welcome..by means of waiters wearing Hawaiian shirts, waitresses with muu-muus and a background aborigine motif. **1964** *Asia Mag.* 16 Aug. 5 (*caption*) A blonde Caucasian girl wears the long muumuu of the islands. **1966** 'O. MILLS' *Enemies of Bride* viii. 76 It was Madeleine, tousle haired, in a short mu-mu with..Ella in a still shorter mu-mu. **1969** C. ARMSTRONG *Seven Seats to Moon* xi. 105 Nanjo with..a blue muumuu concealing her bathing suit..came..and curled herself on the floor.

‖ **muvule** (muviū·li). Also **mvula, mvule, mvuli.** [a. Luganda *muvule*, Kiswahili *mvule.*] The East African name for *IROKO. Also *attrib.*

1911 *Encycl. Brit.* XXVI. 397/1 The largest timber tree [in Tanganyika] is the mvule, which attains vast dimensions, its trunk supplying the natives with the dug-out canoes with which they navigate the lake. **1940** W. J. EGGELING *Indigenous Trees of Uganda Protectorate* 131 Muvule is a tree of great importance to the timber trade of Uganda. **1947** *E. African Ann. 1946–7* 82/1 In the shade of an immense *mvuli* tree, an old man..is sitting. **1962** *Times* 9 Oct. (Uganda Suppl.) p. viii/4 Giant muvule trees (African teak). **1966** B. KIMENYE *Kalasanda Revisited* 77 Hunched over the heavy, old-fashioned mvule desk, they set about answering the numerous personal questions. **1966** C. SWEENEY *Scurrying Bush* ii. 31 Here and there a *Mvule* tree soared upwards.., the smooth, sheer trunks

branchless for the first sixty or seventy feet. **1973** *Daily Colonist* (Victoria, B.C.) 2 May 1/7 Livingstone's heart was buried under a mvula tree in Chipundu.

muvver (mʊ·vəɹ). Representation of a Cockney or childish pronunciation of MOTHER *sb.*[1]
1888 KIPLING *Wee Willie Winkie* 5, I don't fink I'll ever want to kiss big girls, nor no one, 'cept my muvver. **1898** J. D. BRAYSHAW *Slum Silhouettes* 118 A tanner for muvver, an' tuppence for me. **1899** [see *KIP *v.*[2]]. **1924** R. MACAULAY *Orphan Island* viii. 79 Going shopping for my muvver. **1931** S. JAMESON *Richer Dust* xviii. 516, I kep' the letter you wrote poor muvver after you was married. **1958** J. TOWNSEND *Young Devils* x. 83 Andrews has gone to get 'is muvver's washing.

mux (mʊks), *v. dial.* and *U.S. local.* [Of obscure formation; cf. MUSS *v.*[2], MUCK *v.*, and dial. *mucksy* dirty.] = MUCK *v.* 4.
1806 *Balance* (Hudson, N.Y.) 26 Aug. 272 (Th.), To do observance, make obliging mention, Wink lovingly, mux chastity away. **1859** BARTLETT *Dict. Amer.* (ed. 2) 287 To *mux* is much used in New England for *muss*; as, 'Don't *mux* my crinoline.' **1869** BLACKMORE *Lorna Doone* III. x. 157 By vice of mismanagement on the part of my mother, and Nicholas Snowe, who had thoroughly muxed up everything. **1877** J. M. BAILEY *They all do It* 22 Stop muxin' that bread!..you've eaten enough for twenty people. I shan't have you muxing and gauming up the victuals. **1914** *Dialect Notes* IV. 77 *Mux*, to handle, paw over, maul. **1934** *West Virginia Rev.* Dec. 78/1 One may hear *muxed* in certain sections of West Virginia now and then... It is a term synonymous to *messed up*, rather than a form of mixed.

mux (mʊks), *sb. U.S. local.* [f. the vb.] A disordered or muddled state; = MUCK *sb.*[1] 4.
1848 in *Amer. Speech* (1935) X. 41/1 'In a mux.' Confused, disarranged. **1865** E. STODDARD *Two Men* iv. 28, I knew you would come back. Now we are in a mux. **1890** *Cent. Dict.*, *Mux*, work performed in an awkward or improper manner; a botch; a mess; as, he made a mux of it. **1910** *Dialect Notes* III. 454 *Mux*, confusion, 'all in a mux'.

Muzak (miū·zæk). [Cf. MUSIC *sb.*] The proprietary name of a system of piped music for factories, restaurants, supermarkets, etc.; also used loosely, with small initial, to designate recorded light background music generally. Also *attrib.* or as *adj.* Hence (nonce-wds.) **mu·zakal** *a.*, **mu·zakman.** Hence as *v. trans.*, to introduce Muzak to; to equip for the relaying of Muzak; to play in the style of Muzak; so **Mu·zaked** *ppl. a.*
1938 *Trade Marks Jrnl.* 11 May 572/1 Muzak... Instruments and apparatus and parts thereof..for use in the wireless transmission and reception of signals and pictures. Rediffusion Limited,..London,..engineers. **1946** *Ibid.* 27 Mar. 152/1 Muzak... Records of sound, light or electric signals; and instruments and apparatus and parts thereof ..for the production of and reproduction from such records. Rediffusion Limited,..London,..manufacturers. **1954** *Official Gaz.* (U.S. Patent Office) 21 Sept. 497/2 Muzak Corporation..*Muzak.* For transmitting from central locations specially programmed background music to stores, restaurants, homes, hotels, banks, [etc.]. **1959** *Observer* 21 June 10/5 Several firms have already arranged to receive Muzak in the factories. *Ibid.*, Executives in the brave new muzakal world will have a new and special privilege: they alone will be able to switch it off. **1960** *Guardian* 9 May 5/7 Canned music, or Muzak..will to-day ooze into yet another corner of the world. **1965** *Listener* 17 June 898/2 We shall have muzak wherever we go. **1968** *Times* 29 Nov. p. xi/1 If muzak be the food of love, no wonder it is commonly to be found..among the frozen mint-flavoured peas and the crinkle-cut chips. *Ibid.* p. xi/2 In my sort of terms this is what makes it all sound the same, though that is heresy to a professional muzakman. **1969** *Listener* 8 May 661/1 Mifune..walks along a beach to the sound of a Bach chorale, muzak-ed. **1970** M. MOORCOCK *Chinese Agent* xiii. 87 He made the cab stop outside Hennekeys' recently repainted and muzaked pub. **1971** *Daily Tel.* (Colour Suppl.) 11 June 20/3 When subjects were doing a simple manual assembly task, the 'Muzaked' group's output was 17 per cent. up on a 'silent' group. **1971** *New Scientist* 17 June 707/2 The volume has to be kept down to Muzak level so as not to interfere with ..conversation. **1974** *N.Y. Times* 17 Aug. 17/2 'We needed a catchy name and the best known trade name at that time was Kodak,' explained U. V. (Bing) Muscio, current president. 'So we just combined Kodak and music and got Muzak.'

Muzbi, Muz(hu)bee, varr. *MAZHABI.

muzzle, *v.*[1] Add: **3. c.** *transf.* To close (a fishing-net).
1876 F. FRANCIS *Bk. Angling* (ed. 4) xii. 438 The Esk.. is a fine river, and would be finer if the Solway stake nets were only muzzled.
9. (Later example.)
1888 'R. BOLDREWOOD' *Robbery under Arms* II. vi. 106 Jim and I jumped off and muzzled him.

muzzy, *a.* Add: **3.** *Comb.*, as **muzzy-headedness,** a fuddled or intoxicated condition.
1930 R. H. MOTTRAM *Europa's Beast* vii. 169 Cocktails were sheer silliness, a short cut to muzzy-headedness.

mvula, mvule, mvuli, varr. *MUVULE.

Mwami (mwā·mi). [Native title, = chief.] The royal title of the former kings of Ruanda and Urundi in Africa.
On independence in 1962 Rwanda (formerly Ruanda) became a republic; Burundi (formerly Urundi) remained a monarchy until 1966 when the Mwami was deposed by a coup.
1890 H. M. STANLEY *In Darkest Africa* x. 246 The chief was styled Mwani. **1923** *Glasgow Herald* 30 Jan. 12 The Mwami or Sultan of Ruanda..was assisted in his administration of the country by a state religion, and he was in a sense the personification of the deity Imana. **1959** *Times* 9 Nov. 8/6 The Mwami (Paramount Chief) of Ruanda sent a letter..expressing regret that he is unable to come to Brussels, where he was to have been received by the king, with the Mwami of Urundi, in private audience. **1970** A. T. GROVE *Africa South of Sahara* (ed. 2) xi. 201/2 In Burundi the dead Mwami was sewed into the skin of a black bull for burial.

mwchin, var. *MOOCHIN.

Mweru, var. *MERU *sb.* and *a.*

myasthenia gravis (məiˌăsþī·niă græ·vis). *Med.* [mod.L., shortening of *myasthenia gravis pseudoparalytica* (F. Jolly 1895, in *Berliner klin. Wochenschr.* 7 Jan. 7/1), f. MYASTHENIA + L. *gravis* severe, grave.] A rare chronic disease, occurring chiefly in young adults, that is characterized by muscular weakness unaccompanied by atrophy, with temporary paresis following exertion, and is caused by a defect in the mechanism which converts a nervous impulse into a muscular contraction.
1900 CAMPBELL & BRAMWELL in *Brain* XXIII. 278 The disease has received various names. The earlier cases were published as 'cases of bulbar paralysis without discoverable anatomical changes'... Strümpell introduced the term 'Asthenic bulbar palsy'... Other names which have been employed are 'general profound myasthenia', 'Erb's disease', the 'Erb–Goldflam' and the 'Hoppe–Goldflam-symptom-complex'. Jolly has proposed the term 'myasthenia gravis pseudo-paralytica', and this, or for short 'myasthenia gravis', appears to us the most suitable and convenient hitherto suggested. **1939** W. HAYMAKER tr. *R. Bing's Textbk. Nerv. Dis.* v. 182 Myasthenia gravis occasionally appears in more than one member of a family. **1961** *Lancet* 5 Aug. 281/2 The clinical diagnosis of myasthenia gravis is usually easy. **1970** *Toronto Daily Star* 24 Sept. 1/4 The twins have myasthenia gravis, a disease that killed their brother Richard last year when he was 6 months old. Excitement of any kind..can set off the choking, gasping attacks. **1974** PASSMORE & ROBSON *Compan. Med. Stud.* III. xxxiv. 31/2 Myasthenia gravis is also associated with an immunological disturbance.

Mycenæan, *a.* and *sb.* Add: **a.** *adj.* (Later examples.) **b.** *sb.* Also, the language used by the Greeks of the Mycenæan Age.
1930 MAGOFFIN & DAVIS *Romance of Archaeol.* ii. 31 Mycenaean civilization could now be seen to be the mainland exotic of which Minoan island civilization had been the stem and the flower. **1956** VENTRIS & CHADWICK *Documents in Mycenaean Gk.* I. iii. 74 There seems as yet to be little certain indication which dissociates Mycenaean from the Aeolic group. **1958** J. CHADWICK *Decipherment of Linear B* v. 73 The name Mycenaean, originally a label for the culture of the Greek mainland in the Late Helladic period, is now generally extended to the Linear B script and the dialect it contains. **1965** *Language* XLI. 314 Antonio Tovar..comes out..against the Porzig–Risch thesis that Mycenaean represents a form of 'Southern Greek'. **1968** *Encycl. Brit.* XXII. 975/2 The dialect (conventionally known as Mycenaean) is the oldest Greek known and belongs to the Achaean subdivision. **1968** P. MARTIN tr. *Pallottino's Meaning of Archaeol.* 160 The people of the Mycenaean civilization..were neither more nor less than the forebears of the Greeks of history. **1971** L. A. BOGER *Dict. World Pottery & Porcelain* 235/2 The style of painting on the early Mycenaean vases is almost exactly like Minoan Floral and Marine styles. **1972** M. MAGNUSSON *Introducing Archaeol.* iii. 34 Schliemann was convinced he had found the graves of Homer's Mycenean royal family, the graves of murdered Agamemnon and his companions.

myceto-. Add: **myceto·phagous** [-PHAGOUS] *a.* = FUNGIVOROUS *a.*
1906 J. B. SMITH *Explanation of Terms used in Entomology* 86 Mycetophagous: feeding upon fungi. **1920** *Amer. Naturalist* LIV. 314 Many of these mycetophagous insects undoubtedly show a very close association with certain species of fungi. **1946** C. T. BRUES *Insect Dietary* v. 193 Mycetophagous insects..are abundant. **1957** SNELL & DICK *Gloss. Mycology* 101/1 Mycetophagous. Fungivorous; eating fungi. **1974** *Sci. Amer.* Apr. 128/3 Mycetophagous Breeding in the Australian Dung Beetle, *Onthophagus Dunningi*, G. F. Bornemissza.

mycetocyte (məisī·tosəit). *Zool.* [ad. G. *mycetocyt* (K. Šulc 1911, in *Sitzungsber. d. k. böhm. Ges. f. Wissensch.* (*Math.-naturw. Classe*) *Jahrg. 1910* III. 10): see MYCETO- and -CYTE.] Any of the large cells found in some insects, either aggregated into a mycetome or not, which contain symbiotic micro-organisms, esp. yeasts.
1924 *Philippine Jrnl. Sci.* XXIV. 157 In this species there are no specialized 'mycetoms' or 'mycetocytes', as in the aphids. **1946** E. A. STEINHAUS *Insect Microbiol.* iv. 198 The number of mycetocytes present in each individual aphid ranges from about 60 to 70. **1952** *Science* 25 Apr. 459/1 All aphids, except very old ones, contain numerous large cells in the body cavity (mycetocytes) containing many more or less spherical intracellular particles. **1973** W. S. ROMOSER *Sci. Entomol.* iii. 72 In many cases the microbes present are passed from generation to generation. In some insects in which this occurs specialized cells, mycetocytes, and the tissues composed of these cells, mycetomes, can be found associated with the gut, fat body, or, appropriately, the gonads.

mycetome (məi·sītōᵘm). *Zool.* Also **mycetom.** [ad. G. *mycetom* (K. Šulc 1911, in *Sitzungsber. d. k. böhm. Ges. f. Wissensch.* (*Math.-naturw. Classe*) *Jahrg. 1910* III. 10): see MYCETO- and *-OME.] An organ in some insects consisting of an aggregation of mycetocytes.
1924 *Philippine Jrnl. Sci.* XXIV. 143 (*heading*) Studies on the embryogeny and postnatal development of the Aphididæ with special reference to the history of the 'symbiotic organ', or 'mycetom'. **1946** E. A. STEINHAUS *Insect Microbiol.* iv. 190 In 1850 Leydig observed certain organs in aphids which have subsequently been called 'symbiotic organs', 'pseudovitelli', 'green bodies', 'bacteriotomes', and 'mycetoms' or 'mycetomes'. **1946** *Nature* 30 Nov. 795/2 These insects would starve for lack of nitrogenous food were it not for mycetome symbiosis with *Azotobacter*. **1973** [see *MYCETOCYTE].

-mycin (məi·sin), *suffix. Pharmacol.* [f. Gr. μύκ-ης fungus + -IN[1].] Used to form the names of antibiotic compounds derived from fungi, usu. with part of the generic name or specific epithet of the fungus, as *ACTINOMYCIN, *ERYTHROMYCIN, *STREPTOMYCIN, etc.

myco-. Add: **mycomy·sticism,** mystical sensations induced by drugs extracted from mushrooms; so **mycomy·stical** *a.*; **my:cotoxico·sis** [-OSIS], a pathological condition caused by a mycotoxin; **mycoto·xin,** any toxic substance produced by a fungus or bacterium.
1962 A. HUXLEY *Island* ix. 141 Neurotheology, metachemistry, mycomysticism. *Ibid.* 156 The local panel of medical and mycomystical experts. **1948** M. V. GORLENKO in *Amer. Rev. Soviet Med.* V. 164 The moulds..are ubiquitous and not particular as to the substrate upon which they grow. This circumstance, as well as the toxicity, suggests that equine stachybotriotoxicosis is not induced by *Stachybotrys alternans* alone, but may be caused also by other moulds. The disease may be appropriately called mycotoxicosis. **1957** *Rev. Med. & Vet. Mycol.* II. 502 Mycotoxicoses..are stated to be causing great losses among farm animals in the U.S.S.R. **1968** *Prog. Industr. Microbiol.* VII. 156 Alimentary toxic aleukia..appears to be the only mycotoxicosis other than ergotism to have directly affected major segments of human populations. **1962** *Adv. Vet. Sci.* VII. 335 If mycotoxins are indeed present in such grain, sufficient levels of toxin may be added to the mixed feed to be harmful to animals fed thereon. **1974** *Daily Tel.* 26 Mar. 16 The mycotoxins enter the food chain and accumulate in man through his use of milk, eggs, poultry or meat.

mycobacterium (məikobæktīə·riə̆m). [mod. L. (Lehmann & Neumann *Atlas und Grundriss der Bakteriologie* (1896) II. 108), f. MYCO- + BACTERIUM.] A saprophytic or parasitic bacterium of the genus so called, which includes those causing tuberculosis, leprosy, and other diseases in man and other animals; also, a bacterium of the family Mycobacteriaceæ.
1909 E. R. STITT *Pract. Bacteriol.* vii. 66 (*heading*) Study and identification of bacteria. Mycobacteria and corynebacteria. **1949** H. W. FLOREY et al. *Antibiotics* I. iv. 211 The sensitivity to antibiotics of the slow-growing mycobacteria, notably various strains of the tubercle bacillus, has been studied. **1962** *Lancet* 1 Dec. 1153/1 Disease resembling tuberculosis..may be produced by mycobacteria other than tubercle bacilli. **1973** R. G. KRUEGER et al. *Introd. Microbiol.* iii. 62/2 Many types of mycobacteria occur as free-living organisms in soil, water, and dairy products... Some mycobacteria are parasites of animals in which they may cause disease, including tuberculosis.

mycobiont (məikobəi·ǫnt). *Bot.* [f. MYCO- + Gr. βιουντ-, pr. pple. stem of βιοῦν to live, f. βίος life.] The fungal component of a lichen; any fungus which is associated with an alga to form a lichen.
1957 G. D. SCOTT in *Nature* 2 Mar. 486/2 Three new terms are here proposed... They are:..(2) 'mycobiont', applicable to a fungus in association with an alga in the formation of a lichen. **1961** *Science* 10 Mar. 700/2 In our investigation, 11 pure cultures of mycobionts were tested for active compounds. **1969** *Ecology* L. 744/2 In the laboratory the lichen organization breaks down and either the phycobiont..or the mycobiont..overgrows the other partner. **1973** *Phytochemistry* XII. 2249 (*heading*) Sterols of the mycobiont and phycobiont isolated from the lichen *Xanthoria parietina*.

mycologist. (Later examples.)
1903 *Westm. Rev.* 30 Nov. 2/1 The Director..is a botanist; the Assistant-Director..is a mycologist. **1933** *Jrnl. R. Hort. Soc.* LVIII. II. 266 Dr. Dowson..resigned his appointment as mycologist to the Government of Tas-

mania. 1967 M. E. HALE *Biol. Lichens* ii. 33 The definition of the term stroma, however, has not yet been settled even among mycologists.

mycophage (məi·kofēⁱdʒ). [f. MYCO- + *-PHAGE.] One who or that which eats fungi.

1958 *Times Lit. Suppl.* 19 Dec. 742/1 Why do the English and the Celts fear all but the cultivated mushroom, while Slavs and Italians are enthusiastic mycophages? 1965 B. E. FREEMAN tr. *Vandel's Biospeleology* xix. 328 It is generally impossible to classify a cavernicole as a humiphage, xylophage, mycophage, coprophage, or necrophage.

mycophagy. Add: (Later example.) **mycophagist,** also, an animal that eats fungi; **myco·phagous** *a.* = *mycetophagous* adj. (s.v. *MYCETO-).

1919 *Trans. Brit. Mycol. Soc.* VI. 355 (*title*) The red squirrel of North America as a mycophagist. 1922 *Ibid.* VIII. 84 (*title*) Some observations on the mycophagous propensities of slugs. 1939 *Bull. Torrey Bot. Club* LXVI. 1 (*title*) The Snail *Polygyra thyroidus* as a mycophagist. *Ibid.* 5 *P. thyroidus* is decidedly mycophagous in regard to its food preferences. 1950 A. P. KELLEY *Mycotrophy in Plants* xi. 151 As Frank continued to study mycorrhizae, he saw digestion of the mycelium and was led to develop another idea which may be termed 'mycophagy'. According to this concept, the 'fungus-eating plants' are able to draw their victim into the protoplasm,..and finally to digest it.

mycophilic (məikofi·lik), *a.* [f. MYCO- + *-PHILIC.] Fond of mushrooms; feeding upon mushrooms.

1972 *Times Lit. Suppl.* 25 Feb. 211/1 (Advt.), A favourite with mushroom-hunting enthusiasts and mycophilic epicures.

mycophobia (məikofōᵘ·biă). [f. MYCO- + -PHOBIA.] (See quot. 1962.) So **mycopho·bic** *a.*

1958 *Times Lit. Suppl.* 19 Dec. 742/2 The mycophobic hate was back again,..and everything which is not the cultivated mushroom is now banished as 'toadstools'. 1962 *Spectator* 22 June 834/2 Mycophobia, i.e. unreasoning fear of mushrooms.

mycoplasma (məikoplæ·zmă). *Biol.* Pl. **-plasmas, -plasmata.** [mod.L.(J. Nowak 1929 in *Ann. de l'Inst. Pasteur* XLIII. 1349): see MYCO- and PLASMA.] An individual belonging to the genus *Mycoplasma*, comprising a group of pleomorphic, Gram-negative organisms which are much smaller than, and lack the cell wall of, bacteria but, unlike viruses, are capable of growth in artificial media, and which in nature are nearly all animal parasites though only a few are proven pathogens; also called a pleuropneumonia-like organism or PPLO.

[1955 *Internat. Bull. Bacteriol. Nomenclature & Taxonomy* V. 15 (*heading*) Mycoplasma peripneumoniae. Nowak 1929... The generic name *Mycoplasma* was validly published. The older generic names *Asterococcus*, *Coccobacillus*, and *Micromyces* are unavailable. As next in priority sequence *Mycoplasma* apparently is, therefore, the legitimate name of the genus... It should be noted that..the later *Borrelomyces* is more commonly accepted. However, unless some later name is conserved by international action, *Mycoplasma* probably should be recognized as correct.] 1960 *Ann. Rev. Microbiol.* XIV. 140 (*heading*) Nutrition, metabolism, and pathogenicity of mycoplasmas. 1963 *New Scientist* 25 Apr. 200/2 We know, too, of organisms (the mycoplasmata) which multiply inside cells. 1970 AMBROSE & EASTY *Cell Biol.* i. 7 The smallest free-living organisms are the mycoplasmas. These minute cells, the smallest of which are only 1,000 Å in diameter, have been isolated from soil and have been identified as the infective agent in various animal infections. 1971 *Nature* 22 Jan. 231/3 Mycoplasmas also share another important characteristic with bacteria and other cells; they are susceptible to infection by viruses. 1973 *Times* 14 July 1/2 In the United States the term 'viral pneumonia' usually means a lung infection with mycoplasma, an organism intermediate between bacteria and viruses.

So **mycopla·smal** *a.*, of, pertaining to, or caused by mycoplasmas.

1960 *Ann. Rev. Microbiol.* XIV. 154 Mycoplasmal infection of the trachea. 1972 *Science* 5 May 504/2 The structure of the mycoplasmal cell. 1974 *Nature* 31 May 422/1 No viral or mycoplasmal contamination was detected.

mycorrhiza (məikorəi·ză). *Bot.* Pl. **-æ** (-ī) or **-s.** Also **mycorhiza.** [a. mod.L. *mycorhiza* (A. B. Frank 1885, in *Ber. Deutsch. Bot. Ges.* III. 129), f. MYCO- + Gr. ῥίζα root.] A symbiotic or slightly pathogenic fungus growing in association with the roots of a plant. Also *attrib.* Hence **mycorrhi·zal** *a.*

1895 W. R. FISHER in *Schlich's Man. Forestry* IV. III. ii. 376 This altered root with its matted coating of mycelium receives the name mycorhiza, and the fungus has the power of absorbing nutritive matter from the soil and conveying it to the roots of the host. 1898 [in Dict. s.v. MYCO-]. 1900 Mycorhizal [in Dict. s.v. MYCO-]. 1916 *Nature* 2 Nov. 172/1 The abhorrence of lime by the humus-loving rhododendrons appears to be intimately connected with the mycorrhiza, the symbiotic fungus which lives in association with the roots of the rhododendron and heath family. 1924 J. A. THOMSON *Science Old & New* xxvii. 148 In many cases..the partner fungus or mycorhiza confines itself to the outside of the root, forming a dense, absorbing feltwork... The fungus absorbs water and salts and organic materials from the soil and passes these on to the tree; the benefit it gets in return is a supply of carbohydrates from the root. 1926 TANSLEY & CHIPP *Study of Vegetation* ix. 158 Etymologically the word mycorrhiza refers to the fungus–root combination. *Ibid.*, Mycorrhizal fungi may be divided roughly into endotrophic and ectotrophic. 1927 *Forestry* I. 115 Mycorrhiza formation and the mycotrophic habit are of the first importance to trees growing in humus soils. 1934 *Ibid.* VIII. 97 Coralloid clusters of short thick rootlets (mycorrhizas) varying in colour with that of the associated mycelium. 1955 *Jrnl. Ecol.* XLIII. 408 The results of experiments performed with excised mycorrhizal roots may not necessarily be directly applied to mycorrhizas attached to parent trees. 1967 *Punch* 24 May 766/3 The orchid seedling, having no green leaves, depends for its food on the phenomenon of mycorhiza, an association with a resident fungus that is less of a coming together for mutual benefit than an unending war wherein the opposing forces are so perfectly balanced there is no victor, no vanquished. 1967 M. E. HALE *Biol. Lichens* v. 69 Mycorrhizal fungi associated with the roots of trees. 1973 *Nature* 7 Dec. 366/2 The necessity (or not) of raising nursery seedlings under conditions conducive to mycorrhizal infection, are discussed.

mycotrophy (məikǫ·trŏfi). *Bot.* [a. G. *mykotrophie* (R. Falck 1923, in *Mykologische Untersuchungen und Berichte* II. 49), f. MYCO- + Gr. τροφή nourishment: see -Y³.] The state of certain plants which have mycorrhizæ growing in association with their roots, possibly as an aid in the assimilation of nutrients. So **mycotro·phic** *a.*

1927 *Forestry* I. 115 Defining mycotrophy as the capacity to assimilate organic compounds through the agency of specific root fungi, Falck reviews the historical evidence bearing on the significance of mycorrhiza. 1927 [see prec.]. 1930 *Nature* 9 July 80/1 The mycotrophic habit has been shown to be of wide occurrence in many families of plants. 1959 J. L. HARLEY *Biol. Mycorrhiza* i. 6 The mycotrophy of the Ericales is described because it now appears to have something in common with the ectotrophic mycorrhizas of forest trees. *Ibid.* xi. 172 (*heading*) Other mycotrophic plants with septate endophytes.

myctophid (mi·ktŏfid), *sb.* and *a.* *Zool.* [f. mod.L. family name *Myctophidæ*, f. the generic name *Myctophum* (C. S. Rafinesque *Indice d'Ittiologia Siciliana* (1810) 56), f. Gr. μυκτήρ nostril + ὄφις snake: see -ID³.] A small, marine, deep-water fish of the family Myctophidæ, distinguished by luminous organs along its sides; also called lantern-fish. Also as *adj.*, of or pertaining to this family of fishes.

1931 J. R. NORMAN *Hist. Fishes* viii. 151 In the Myctophids or Lantern-fishes (*Myctophidae*) the photophores are fewer in number. 1956 A. HARDY *Open Sea* xii. 233 There are a great many different species of myctophids, but most are very similar in appearance. *Ibid.* 245 (*caption*) A myctophid Lantern-fish *Myctophum punctatum.* 1971 *Nature* 29 Oct. 623/2 The myctophids, or lantern fishes..are among the most common and widely distributed deep-sea fishes known.

myelo-. Add: **myelocœle,** delete entry in Dict. and cf. *MYELOCELE, *MYELOCŒLE; **my:elomonocy·tic** *a.*, designating that form of leukæmia which is characterized by the presence in the circulating blood of myeloid cells of both the monocytic and the myelocytic series; **my:eloproli·ferative** *a.*, characterized by or pertaining to the proliferation of cells of or derived from the bone marrow; esp. in *myeloproliferative syndrome* (see quot. 1974).

1958 DAMESHEK & GUNZ *Leukemia* viii. 161 (*heading*) 'Myelo-monocytic' leukemia. 1960 F. G. J. HAYHOE *Leukaemia* ii. 13 A mixed picture of early monocytic and myelocytic cells is seen, and this variety is called acute myelo-monocytic leukaemia or the Naegeli type of acute leukaemia. 1972 *Nature* 4 Feb. 274/2 High levels of urinary lysozyme activity were observed in acute monocytic and myelomonocytic leukaemia. 1951 W. DAMESHEK in *Blood* VI. 372 (*heading*) Some speculations on the myeloproliferative syndromes. 1962 *Lancet* 19 May 1044/2 The levels were generally normal in various other conditions—kidney disease,..acute or chronic liver disease, and neoplastic or myeloproliferative disease. 1974 R. P. CUSTER *Atlas Blood & Bone Marrow* (ed. 2) xix. 383/1 The term 'myeloproliferative syndrome' was suggested by Dameshek to include a heterogeneous group of disorders characterized by proliferation of any or all cell lines indigenous to the bone marrow at some time during the course of the disease.

myeloblast (məi·ĕloblast). *Anat.* [a. G. *myeloblast* (O. Naegeli 1900, in *Deutsche med. Wochenschr.* 3 May 289/1): see MYELO- and -BLAST.] Any of the immature cells (approximately 15 microns in diameter, with large nuclei and a small amount of densely staining cytoplasm) which are confined to the bone marrow, appearing in the circulating blood only in pathological states, and which, according to the so-called monophyletic (unitary) theory of hæmopoiesis, are the precursors of all other myeloid cells of the blood and bone marrow, or, according to the diphyletic (dualistic) or polyphyletic theories, are the precursors only of the myelocytes and of cells derived from them.

1904 F. P. FOSTER *Appleton's Med. Dict.* 1395/1 Myeloblast. 1909 R. J. M. BUCHANAN *Blood in Health & Dis.* viii. 143 Nägeli termed them 'myeloblasts'. 1911 W. K. HUNTER *Rec. Adv. Hæmatol.* 30 Both the neutrophile and the eosinophile myelocyte are, according to Ehrlich, originally derived from a cell to which the name myeloblast has been given. 1961 *Lancet* 19 Aug. 434/2 The leucoerythroblastosis persisted, although granulocyte precursors, occasionally including myeloblasts, became more numerous than the nucleated red cells in the peripheral blood. 1968 PASSMORE & ROBSON *Compan. Med. Studies* I. xxvi. 11/2 After birth, the production of the granulocytic white cells takes place only in the red marrow... The first stage of development is the myeloblast.

So **myelobla·stic** *a.*, of, pertaining to, or involving myeloblasts; **my:eloblasto·sis** [-OSIS], the condition of having large numbers of myeloblasts in the bone marrow and circulating blood.

1916 L. F. BARKER *Monographic Med.* III. 214 The cells of these myeloblastic proliferations. 1924 *Jrnl. Exper. Med.* XL. 845 (*heading*) Studies on the maturation of myeloblasts into myelocytes and on amitotic cell division in the peripheral blood in subacute myeloblastic leucemia. 1937 KRACKE & GARVER *Dis. Blood* v. 65 A true myeloblastosis, in which the myeloblast is the predominant cell type in both the bone marrow and peripheral blood, occurs only in the terminal, exacerbation stage of chronic myelosis and in acute myeloblastic leukemia. 1938 H. DOWNEY *Handbk. Hematol.* III. xxv. 2014 They [*sc.* the cells] are clearly of the myeloblastic type. 1965 *New Scientist* 17 June 800/2 The three main leukaemias of poultry—lymphomatosis, erythroblastosis and myeloblastosis—are caused by filterable transmissible agents. 1974 PASSMORE & ROBSON *Compan. Med. Studies* III. xxi. 62/1 (*table*) Acute myeloblastic leukaemia.

myelocele (məi·ĕlosīl). *Path.* Also (erron.) **-cœle.** [f. MYELO- + Gr. κήλη tumour, *esp.* rupture, hernia.] **1. a.** = *MYELOMENINGOCELE. **b.** Spina bifida in which tissue of the spinal cord lies exposed over part of its length, without protrusion as a swelling; an area of neural tissue so exposed.

1875 JONES & SIEVEKING *Path. Anat.* (ed. 2) xii. 290 The protruded sac contains some portion of the spinal cord itself, forming the so-called myelocele. 1922 *Brain* XLV. 44 Myelocele... Here..segments of the medullary folds have remained open and the neural ectoderm lies exposed on the surface of the body as a ribbon of delicate tissue down the mid-dorsal line. 1924 J. A. FOOTE *Dis. New-Born* x. 140 Myelocele, or meningo-myelocele, is the name given to the tumor when the spinal cord itself is concerned in the embryonic fissure. 1952 J. E. MORISON *Foetal & Neonatal Path.* xiv. 247 Especially when the tissues are infected a myelocoele may be incorrectly described as a myelomeningocoele. 1963 [see *MYELOMENINGOCELE]. 1974 PASSMORE & ROBSON *Compan. Med. Stud.* III. xxxvi. 9/2 The [spinal] cord may be fully exposed, usually for a length of several segments without any covering from the dura mater, forming a myelocoele.

2. Var. *MYELOCŒLE.

myelocœle (məi·ĕlosīl). *Anat.* Also **-cele, -cœl.** [f. MYELO- + *-cœle* (f. Gr. κοιλία cavity of the body: cf. CŒLO-¹).] **1.** The central canal of the spinal cord.

1885 B. G. WILDER in *N.Y. Med. Jrnl.* 21 Mar. 326/2 (*caption*) Schematic representation of the cavities of the brain and myelon... Encephalocoele. Myelocoele. Neurocoele. 1896 —— in *Jrnl. Compar. Neurol.* VI. 318 (*table*) Myelocele. 1940 *Chambers's Techn. Dict.* 566/1 Myelocoel, the central canal of the spinal cord. 1972 T. W. JENKINS *Funct. Mammalian Neuroanat.* ii. 15/1 The lumen of this division (metacoele) joins the myelocoele without any line of demarcation so that both form the fourth ventricle.

2. Var. *MYELOCELE.

myelocyte. Add: **2.** A cell generally confined to the bone marrow (appearing in the circulating blood only in pathological states) which is smaller than the myeloblast from which it derives, which when mature has neutrophil, eosinophil, and basophil cytoplasmic granules, and which is the precursor of the polymorphonuclear leucocyte of the circulating blood.

1891 *Johns Hopkins Hosp. Bull.* II. 87/1 These elements seem never to acquire the power of amoeboid movement which the polynuclear cells possess. They appear to arise in the marrow and have been called by Ehrlich 'myelocytes'. 1911 [see *MYELOBLAST]. 1962 *Gray's Anat.* (ed. 33) 65 Myeloblasts divide and give rise to smaller cells, the myelocytes. 1968 PASSMORE & ROBSON *Compan. Med. Studies* I. xxvi. 12/1 The myelocyte is a smaller cell with a round nucleus.

So **myelocy·tic** *a.*, of, pertaining to, or involving myelocytes.

1896 *Boston Med. & Surg. Jrnl.* 2 Jan. 6/1 The shape of the myelocytic nucleus..is generally to be contrasted with that of the 'polynuclear' cell. 1972 *Science* 20 Oct. 304/1 Tumor cells derived from patients with both acute lymphocytic and acute myelocytic leukemia.

myelogram (məi·ĕlogræm). *Med.* [f. MYELO- + -GRAM.] **1.** A radiograph obtained by myelography.

1937 *Arch. Neurol. & Psychiatry* (Chicago) XXXVIII. 1126 The method of injection of air and the roentgen technic are discussed and five air myelograms shown. **1942** *Surg., Gynecol. & Obstetr.* LXXV. 735/2 The myelogram..demonstrated a tumor which had invaded the upper thoracic subarachnoid space. **1974** *Daily Colonist* (Victoria, B.C.) 19 Sept. 2/1, I had a whiplash and am being told a myelogram is the only way to determine if I have a ruptured disc.

2. (A list of) the proportions of the various cells in a sample of bone marrow.

1940 *Biol. Abstr.* XIV. 1635/1 Sternal puncture may also aid in diagnosis through modifications of the myelogram. **1949** *Jrnl. Clin. Path.* II. 8/1 Most workers perform differential counts on marrow films, and by presenting the data in the form of a 'myelogram' express the incidence of the various cell types as percentages. **1956** E. PONDER tr. *M. Bessis's Cytol. Blood & Blood-Forming Organs* vii. 172 Some include megakaryocytes in the myelogram, while others do not.

myelography (məiˌĕlǫ·grăfi). *Med.* [f. MYELO- + -GRAPHY.] Radiography of the spinal chord after injection of a contrast medium (often air) into the subarachnoid space.

1937 *Arch. Neurol. & Psychiatry* (Chicago) XXXVIII. 1126 This report is based on 10 cases of lesions of the spinal canal in which the level of the block was found by air myelography. **1943** *Amer. Jrnl. Med. Sci.* CCVI. 691 If..a protruded intervertebral disk in the lumbar region is suspected air myelography should be used. **1969** N. A. LEWTAS in D. Sutton *Textbk. Radiol.* lxiii. 1134/2 Myelography of spinal tumours is best performed as a pre-operative examination.

Hence **myelogra·phic** *a.*, observed using myelography; **myelogra·phically** *adv.*, by myelography.

1940 H. K. PANCOAST et al. *Head & Neck in Roentgen Diagnosis* xii. 892 If there is a difference in the localization of tumors by neurologic and myelographic findings, the possibility of multiple tumors occurring within the spinal chord should be considered. **1950** *Med. Radiogr. & Photogr.* XXVI. 27 To demonstrate myelographically the lesions.., 6 cubic centimeters of *Pantopaque* were injected into the lumbar subarachnoid space. **1957** *Trans. Amer. Neurol. Assoc.* LXXXI. 171 (*heading*) Myelographically demonstrated cervical intervertebral discs, co-existing with tumors. **1969** N. A. LEWTAS in D. Sutton *Textbk. Radiol.* lxiii. 1142/1 There are four principal myelographic signs of disc prolapse.

myeloid, *a.* Add: Also, of, pertaining to, or involving myeloid cells. (Further examples.)

1927, 1961 [see *ERYTHROID *a.* 2]. **1966** WRIGHT & SYMMERS *Systemic Path.* I. iv. 179/2 Leukaemias may arise from any of the stem cells of the leucopoietic series, and the three most frequent types may be classified as myeloid, lymphatic and monocytic. **1971** *Brit. Med. Bull.* XXVII. 66/1 Leukaemia, in the acute and in the chronic myeloid forms, is the type of malignancy which is most frequently induced by whole-body exposures of several hundred rads.

myeloma (məiˌĕlōᵘ·mă). *Path.* Pl. **-omas, -omata.** [f. MYEL(O- + *-OMA.] A tumour composed of bone-marrow cells (see quots.); *spec.* (*a*) (the tumour found in) myelomatosis; (*b*) a giant-cell sarcoma.

1857 MAYNE *Expos. Lex.* 736/1 *Myeloma*, term for a medullary tumour or enlargement. **1894** *Med. News* (Philadelphia) LXV. 239/1 (*heading*) Myeloma: report of a case. **1900** DORLAND *Med. Dict.* 419/2 *Myeloma*, (1) any medullary tumor; (2) giant-cell sarcoma; (3) a slow-growing tumor of a tendinous sheath containing myeloplaxes. **1902** *Encycl. Medica* XII. 449 Myelomata are rare tumours after the age of twenty-five. **1914** *Lancet* 28 Nov. 1236/2 This large class [*sc.* giant-cell sarcoma] is made up of two groups of cases: (1) the myeloid sarcomata, myelomata of some authors; and (2) the malignant giant-cell sarcomata. **1922** J. EWING *Neoplastic Dis.* (ed. 2) xviii. 256 Giant-cell sarcoma of tendon sheaths and aponeuroses.—The specific structure and benign clinical course of a group of giant-cell sarcomas of tendon sheaths of the hand and feet have long been recognized. They have been fully described, especially by French observers, under the terms 'myeloma' or 'xanthosarcoma' (Gross, Paquet, Reverdin, Heurteaux, Spiess, Lit.). **1948** R. A. WILLIS *Path. Tumours* xliii. 680 The changing views regarding the nature of this tumour [*sc.* osteoclastoma or giant-cell tumour of bone] have resulted in a diverse and confusing terminology—'myeloma', 'myeloid sarcoma', 'tumeur à myéloplaxes', 'benign giant-cell tumour', 'osteoclastoma', and 'chronic (non-suppurative) hemorrhagic osteomyelitis', being only some of the names applied to it. 'Myeloma' and 'myeloid' should be discarded, for the tumours are unrelated to the haemopoietic tumours of bone marrow, and in particular are quite distinct from the lesions of myelomatosis. **1966** WRIGHT & SYMMERS *Systemic Path.* I. iv. 185/2 Sometimes myelomas produce extramedullary masses in the viscera. **1967** *New Scientist* 4 May 276/3 The other source of information..about antibody structure has been the discovery of diseases, called myelomas, in which molecules, chemically similar to the immune globulins but without known antibody activity, are produced in the blood of patients suffering from a cancer-like proliferation of cells in the bone marrow and bloodstream. **1970** PASSMORE & ROBSON *Compan. Med. Stud.* II. xxviii. 4/2 An important tumour affecting the bone marrow is the plasma cell myeloma (myelomatosis or multiple myeloma). In this disease the bone marrow becomes packed with plasma cells.

myelomatosis (məi:ĕlomătōᵘ·sis). *Path.* [f. *myelomat-* (taken as stem of *MYELOMA) + -OSIS.] A malignant proliferation of plasma cells causing numerous accumulations of them to form in the bone marrow and abnormal proteins to be present in the blood and urine.

1904 *Jrnl. Path. & Bacteriol.* IX. 173 At the necropsy the bone marrow of all the bones examined was found to be more or less affected by a diffuse sarcoma-like growth of rounded or polyhedral mononuclear cells—a form of 'multiple myeloma' or 'myelomatosis'. **1906** *Jrnl. Amer. Med. Assoc.* 16 June 1893/2 Hoffmann defines myelomatosis as the multiple development of malignant tumors in the bone marrow, originating in hyperplasia of one of the cellular elements of the mother soil [*sic*: ? *read* cell] (lymphocyte, myelocyte, plasma cell). **1961** *Lancet* 16 Sept. 639/2 Neither in myelomatosis in man nor in any of the plasmacytomas of mice..do we ever regularly observe a direct Coombs test or signs of hæmolytic anæmia. **1966** WRIGHT & SYMMERS *Systemic Path.* II. xxxix. 1419/2 Myelomatosis or multiple myeloma is a neoplastic condition originating from the bone marrow.

myelomeningocele (məi:ĕlomīni·ŋgosīl). *Path.* Also (erron.) **-cœle.** [f. MYELO- + *meningocele* s.v. MENINGO-.] Spina bifida in which tissue of the spinal cord and its investing membranes (the meninges) protrudes through the cleft, forming a rounded swelling of the skin usu. slightly above the base of the spine; the tissue so protruding. Also called *meningomyelocele*; cf. *MYELOCELE.

1889 *Buck's Handbk. Med. Sci.* VIII. 471/2 In myelomeningocele the external wall of the sac consists not of dura mater but of pia mater turned inside out. **1924, 1952** [see *MYELOCELE 1]. **1963** *Cecil-Loeb Textbk. Med.* (ed. 11) 1581/1 Myelocele involves a lesser defect of the meninges [than meningocele] with exposure of the spinal cord, but without cystic protrusion. Myelomeningocele is characterized by an incorporation of the spinal nerve roots and cord in the sac of a meningocele. **1974** PASSMORE & ROBSON *Compan. Med. Stud.* III. xxxvi. 9/2 There may be a developmental failure of the spinal cord and then the flat neural plate with its exposed central canal is liable to be involved with the sac and form a myelomeningocoele.

myelosis (məiˌĕlōᵘ·sis). *Path.* Pl. **myeloses.** [f. MYEL(O- + -OSIS.] **1.** The formation of a tumour of the spinal cord.

1891 in *Syd. Soc. Lex.* **1900** in DORLAND *Med. Dict.*

2. The proliferation of blood-cell precursors in the bone marrow.

1916 L. F. BARKER *Monographic Med.* III. 213 (*heading*) Acute myeloid leukemia. (Acute leukemic myelosis.) **1922** V. ELLERMANN *Leucosis Fowls* i. 9 Schnidde's shorter and correcter words, myelosis and lymphadenosis, are now used in several text-books. **1952** *Blood* VII. 767 The term erythremic myelosis is used to indicate the parallelism with the leukemic myeloses. **1974** PASSMORE & ROBSON *Compan. Med. Stud.* III. xxi. 72/2 Pure erythraemic myelosis, di Guglielmo's syndrome, is rare, and is characterized by intense and bizarre proliferation of red cell precursors, which escape into the peripheral blood. *Ibid.* 73/1 Megakaryocytic myelosis is probably a variant of chronic myeloid leukaemia, as the clinical picture, course and prognosis are similar, and it usually terminates with definite evidence of myeloid leukaemia.

Mylar (məi·lāɹ). Also **mylar.** A proprietary name for a polyester which is the condensation product of ethylene glycol and terephthalic acid and is used in the form of films having high strength and heat resistance.

1954 *Trade Marks Jrnl.* 3 Nov. 1110/1 Mylar... Non-mouldable plastics in the form of films for use as a substitute for glass; and electrical insulating materials. E. I. Du Pont de Nemours and Company.., Wilmington, State of Delaware, United States of America; manufacturers. **1962** *New Scientist* 5 Apr. 796/2 A self-inflating balloon made of aluminized mylar was launched in August, 1960. **1966** *McGraw-Hill Encycl. Sci. & Technol.* VIII. 38/1 The tape used in magnetic recording consists of a plastic base with a coating of magnetic oxide. The base material of Mylar or cellulose acetate varies in thickness from 0·0007 to 0·0015 in. **1973** *Daily Colonist* (Victoria, B.C.) 16 May 1/3 Another possibility..is for astronauts to envelop the spaceship with a giant sheet of mylar, an insulating material.

Myleran (məi·ləræn). *Pharm.* A proprietary name for 1,4-di(methanesulphonyloxy)butane, $C_6H_4O_6S_2$, which is a cytotoxic agent with a selective action on bone marrow and is used in the treatment of myeloid leukæmia.

1952 *Trade Marks Jrnl.* 12 Nov. 1049/1 Myleran... The Wellcome Foundation Limited,..London,..manufacturing chemists. **1953** *Lancet* 31 Jan. 207/2 'Myleran'.. showed an intense inhibitory effect on the growth of the Walker rat carcinoma 256. **1959** *Progr. Hematol.* II. 227 With Myleran,.. the margin between the therapeutic dose and the toxic dose, producing irreversible aplastic change in the bone marrow, is relatively narrow. **1968** *Internat. Pharmacol. Abstr.* V. 1509 A 26-year-old woman had to be treated with busulphan (Myleran), 2–8 mg. daily during the first to sixth and 19–30th weeks of pregnancy because of chronic myeloid leukemia.

mylonite. Add: Hence **my:lonitiza·tion, myloniza·tion,** the formation of mylonite; **my·lonitize** *v. trans.*, to convert into mylonite; **my·lonitized** *ppl. a.* = MYLONIZED *ppl. a.*

1910 *Trans. Edin. Geol. Soc.* IX. Spec. Part 'The Thrust-Masses in the Western District of the Dolomites' i. 18 The actual shear-plane is occupied by a finely mylonitized, greenish tuffoid material. *Ibid.* 19 The rock material immediately below the inturned ends is Porphyrite finely mylonitized into a tuff. **1913** B. N. PEACH et al. *Geol. Central Ross-shire* (Mem. Geol. Surv. Scot.) iii. 13 It would appear that the mylonisation of the gneiss is probably due to the passage over it of the great mass of rock brought forward by the Moine thrust-plane. *Ibid.* 112/2 (Index), Mylonitisation. **1926** H. H. READ et al. *Geol. Strath Oykell & Lower Loch Shin* (Mem. Geol. Surv. Scot.) iii. 24 The intrusion is truncated by thrust-planes, and its rocks show evidence of shattering and mylonisation. **1956** E. W. HEINRICH *Microsc. Petrogr.* vii. 187 Such rocks as gabbros and peridotites may also be mylonitized. **1970** *New Scientist* 7 May 275/2 The rocks are crushed, smashed and sheared into an extremely fine grained powder, in a process called mylonization. **1971** *Scott. Jrnl. Geol.* VII. 311 At the western edge of the Moine Nappe mylonitization is the earliest recognizable tectonic event..and involves Cambrian rocks.

myo-. Add: **myoche·mistry,** the chemistry of muscle; **myoepithe·lial** *a.*, (of an animal cell) having characters of both a muscular and an epithelial cell; so **myoepithe·lium,** a tissue composed of such cells; *spec.* the contractile cells outside the epithelium of some mammalian glands, e.g. in the breast; **myofi·lament,** any of the elongated threads, revealed by the electron microscope, which are arranged side by side in bundles to form a myofibril and of which there are two kinds in an ordered arrangement, viz. thick filaments composed of myosin molecules and thin filaments composed of actin molecules; also, one of the related filaments of smooth muscle; **myoge·nesis,** the formation of muscular tissue; **myohæmoglo·bin** *Biochem.* = *MYOGLOBIN; **myo-inositol** (usu. with *myo-* in italics) (see *INOSITOL); **myome·trium** *Anat.* [Gr. μήτρα womb], the muscular coat of the uterus, which forms the bulk of the wall of that organ and surrounds the endometrium; tissue from this muscular coat; so **myome·trial** *a.*; **my·oneme** *Biol.* [Gr. νῆμα thread], any of the minute contractile filaments found in the cytoplasm of many protozoa; **myoneu·ral** *a. Physiol.*, neuromuscular; having characteristics of both muscular and nervous tissue; **my·oplasm** *Anat.* [f. mod.L. *myoplasma* (coined in Ger. by P. Schiefferdecker 1905, in *Sitzungsber. d. niederrhein. Ges. f. Natur- und Heilkunde zu Bonn 1904* B. 90)], the cytoplasm or sarcoplasm of a muscle cell; hence **myopla·smic** *a.*; **myota·tic** *a. Physiol.* [Gr. τατικ-ός exerting tension (f. τείνειν to stretch)], applied to a muscular contraction (usu. a reflex) that occurs as a result of the stretching of the muscle; **myotonic** *a.*, delete entry in Dict. and see *MYOTONIC *a.*; **my·otube** *Biol.* [ad. Sp. *myotubo* (J. F. Tello 1917, in *Trabajos d. Lab. de Investig. biol. de la Univ. de Madrid* XV. 122)], a cylindrical cell that develops from myoblasts during the formation of a muscle fibre (see quots. 1960, 1972).

1962 *Lancet* 1 Dec. 1165/1, I still wonder if two hours' instruction in pathological myochemistry will help the candidate. **1968** *Nature* 2 Nov. 433/2 (*heading*) New myochemistry. **1881** F. M. BALFOUR *Compar. Embryol.* II. 550 In all the Coelenterata, except the Ctenophora, the contractile elements of the body wall consist of filiform processes of ectodermal or entodermal epithelial cells. The elements provided with these processes, which were first discovered by Kleinenberg, are known as myo-epithelial cells. **1904** *Nature* 3 Mar. 431/1 At certain stages complete continuity could be observed between motor nerve trunk and the protoplasmic body of the myoepithelial cell. **1973** R. P. GOULD in G. H. Bourne *Structure & Function Muscle* (ed. 2) II. iv. 192 These are known as myoepithelial, basal, or basket cells, and they are able to act like smooth muscle cells and so aid movement of the secretion into the excretory ducts. **1892** F. P. FOSTER *Med. Dict.* IV. 2367/1 Myo-epithelium. **1943** *Amer. Jrnl. Path.* XIX. 474 Myoepithelium can be demonstrated in the male breast of gynecomastia when the ducts are developed. **1961** L. MARTIN *Clinical Endocrinol.* (ed. 3) i. 16 The act of suckling appears to provoke a reflex secretion of oxytocin whereby the myoepithelium surrounding the alveoli of the breast is stimulated to contract and the milk ducts are simultaneously kept open. **1949** *Jrnl. Clin. Invest.* XXVIII. 770/1 (*heading*) Myofilaments and myofibrils of cardiac muscle. **1970** *Nature* 11 Apr. 180/1 Two to eight cells in each complete transverse section contain what appear to be sparse myofilaments and probably represent degenerate muscle cells. **1973** *Hewer's Textbk. Histol.* (ed. 9) x. 119 Although the fibrous proteins actin and myosin can both be isolated from smooth muscle fibres it is not yet clear what their exact relationship is to the longitudinally orientated myofilaments observed in these cells. **1891** *Syd. Soc. Lex.*, Myogenesis. **1921** *Amer. Jrnl. Physiol.* LVIII. 182 (*heading*) Tension of differential growth as a stimulus to myogenesis. **1956** *Biol. Bull.* CXI. 303 This relationship

prompted a re-examination of the situation in amphibian embryos, where it has been claimed that the notochord is essential to somitic myogenesis. **1974** *Nature* 10 May 106/1 In ways not anticipated, myogenesis has yoked in an uneasy alliance muscle biochemistry, molecular genetics and cell differentiation. **1924** Myohemoglobin [see *COPROPORPHYRIN]. **1934** M. BODANSKY *Introd. Physical Chem.* (ed. 3) xviii. 608 Muscle hemoglobin (myohemoglobin, myoglobin) has been isolated in crystalline form. **1953** J. HUNT *Ascent of Everest* 274 Myohaemoglobin is an oxygen-carrying pigment similar to haemoglobin. **1951** H. G. FLETCHER et al. in *Jrnl. Org. Chem.* XVI. 1241 It is suggested that, since the substance [sc. *meso*-inositol] was first discovered in muscle..and was at one time called 'muscle sugar', it is better called *myo*-inositol. **1965** *Adv. Biochem.* XXXIV. 85 As a degradation product of phytoglycolipid, a complex lipid found in a variety of seed phosphatides, 2-α-D-glucopyranosyl-*myo*-inositol was obtained. **1943** L. R. WHARTON *Gynecology* xxxvii. 542 The prognosis in myometrial sarcoma is poor. **1974** PASSMORE & ROBSON *Compan. Med. Stud.* III. xl. 16/2 Drugs used in labour should not depress myometrial contractility. **1900** DORLAND *Med. Dict.* 421/1 *Myometrium*, the muscular substance of the uterus. **1907** *Practitioner* Dec. 792 The myometrium contained many thick-walled blood-vessels. **1956** *Nature* 10 Mar. 478/2 Progesterone..prevents..œstrogen-induced growth of the myometrium. **1965** *Science* 1 Oct. 67/2 Samples of myometrium were obtained from the uteri of five adult females undergoing hysterectomies. **1901** G. N. CALKINS *Protozoa* ii. 38 The outside is covered by living membranes which may become complicated by the addition of muscular fibrils (myonemes). **1973** E. VIVIER in G. H. Bourne *Structure & Function Muscle* (ed. 2) II. iii. 182 The best characterized myonemes have chiefly been identified in ciliates, in which their structure recalls that of smooth muscle fibers of Metazoa cells. **1905** *Jrnl. Physiol.* XXXII. 436 But when plain muscle developes connection with sympathetic nerves it must at the myoneural junction acquire a mechanism that can receive the nervous impulse. **1960** G. H. BOURNE *Struct. & Function Muscle* I. ii. 48 It has been suggested that the iridial muscles are really myoneural elements rather than true smooth muscle cells. **1963** *Lancet* 19 Jan. 153/1 They also showed that the myoneural junction of a neonatal infant behaves in many respects like that of a patient with myasthenia gravis. **1907** *Alienist & Neurologist* XXVIII. 58 The author [*sc.* Schiefferdecker] suggests a number of new terms. The indifferent protoplasm becomes 'myoplasm' as soon as the cell is plainly recognizable as a muscle cell. **1933** *Physiol. Rev.* XIII. 302 Since the myofibrils represent differentiation products of the original myoplasm, it would seem in accord with a more precise terminology to speak of intra- and interfibrillar sarcoplasm; or, perhaps even better, the protoplasm of the fibrils (sarcostyles) might be designated sarcoplasm, that of the interfibrillar regions myoplasm. **1952** *Jrnl. Physiol.* CXVIII. 348 The aim..was to measure the myoplasm resistance and the membrane resistance and capacity in Purkinje fibres of the mammalian heart. **1975** *Nature* 10 Jan. 97/2 The action potential on the surface membrane depolarises the T-system within the fibre, which in turn triggers the release of Ca^{2+} into the myoplasm from its internal storage site, the sarcoplasmic reticulum. **1970** T. TOMITA in E. Bülbring et al. *Smooth Muscle* vii. 207 The myoplasmic resistance was measured by means of double micro-electrodes in one arm of a bridge circuit. **1975** *Nature* 10 Jan. 100/2 If the ionic current causing this presumed SR potential change was primarily carried by Ca^{2+} moving from one side of the SR to the other, it is interesting to note how much increase in total myoplasmic Ca^{2+} would correspond to a 135 mV potential change. **1881** W. R. GOWERS *Diagn. Dis. Spinal Cord* (ed. 2) ii. 29 It seems..desirable to discard the term 'tendon-reflex' altogether... They may be termed 'tendon-muscular phenomena', but the intervention of tendons is not necessary for their production; the one condition which all have in common is that passive tension is essential for their occurrence, and they may more accurately be termed myotatic contractions. **1924** LIDDELL & SHERRINGTON in *Proc. R. Soc.* B. XCVI. 240 Gowers, in 1881, proposed for the 'tendon-phenomena', then not commonly accepted as reflex, the term 'myotatic contractions'... His suggested adjective would suitably apply to the reflexes brought forward in this paper... Myotatic reflexes could embrace stretch-reflexes in general, including 'jerk' and 'clonus', which we regard as fractional forms of the complete and fully functional myotatic reflex. **1972** J. A. WILSON *Princ. Animal Physiol.* xi. 438/1 The peak of reflex tension in a myotatic reflex occurs at the time of completion of the stretch movement. *Ibid.* 438/2 When the foot of a spinal dog is raised so that the leg is flexed, the leg muscles respond with an extensor thrust—a myotatic reflex. **1933** M. FERNÁN-NÚÑEZ tr. *S. Ramón-Cajal's Histology* xvi. 280 The periphery of the cells exhibits a striated cortex, which goes on successively enlarging. In the axis resides a string of nuclei, as well as an undifferentiated protoplasmic cord (*D*); the ensemble finally represents tubes of contractile material filled with the protoplasm and nuclei (myotubes of Tello). **1960** L. PICKEN *Organization of Cells* vii. 295 By the fourth day of incubation, the multinucleate coenocytic cells (derived from the spindle-shaped, uninucleate myoblasts) have developed a peripheral layer of myofibrils, embedded in sarcoplasm, and a linear series of nuclei occupying the cell axis. These cylindrical cells are conveniently distinguished as a particular stage in the development of the muscle fibres, namely as 'myotubes'. From the seventh day after their appearance, the myotubes begin to multiply by longitudinal fission... The formation of a secondary is prepared by nuclear fission, leading to the formation of a second linear series of nuclei; round which new myofibrils form. **1972** D. A. FISCHMAN in G. H. Bourne *Structure & Function Muscle* (ed. 2) I. iii. 107 The myotube is here defined as the multinucleated syncitium which results from the cytoplasmic fusion of myoblasts. The term is purely descriptive, for it only implies an immature muscle fiber in which the myofibrils are, in general, circumferentially distributed within the cell, and the nuclei occupy the core or central zone of the syncitium. **1973** *Nature* 3 Aug. 253/3 From the fourth to the sixth day of incubation, motor nerve fibres invade the limb-bud muscles [of the chick embryo], and the first myotubes appear.

myocardiac (məiˌokā·ɹdiæ̆k), *a.* [f. MYO- + CARDIAC *a.*] Of or pertaining to the myocardium; myocardial.

1908 *Practitioner* Oct. 610 As the author says, myocardiac deficiency is the chief indication for the Nauheim treatment. **1940** A. HUXLEY *Let.* 7 July (1969) 454, I am still under the weather with..myocardiac weakness.

myoelectric (məiˌoˌĭle·ktrik), *a.* Also (with hyphen) **myo-electric.** [f. MYO- + ELECTRIC *a.*] Applied to (apparatus or techniques using) the currents produced in the body which would normally cause muscular contraction and relaxation.

1955 *Jrnl. Bone & Joint Surg.* XXXVII-B. 506 (*heading*) The use of myo-electric currents in the operation of prostheses. **1963** *Aerospace Med.* XXXIV. 267/1 By attempting to move his arms, the pilot generates muscle action potentials, or myoelectric signals, which may be utilized as a control source. **1964** *New Scientist* 12 Mar. 668/2 A powered prosthetic device with myoelectric control. **1965** D. FRANCIS *Odds Against* xx. 246 The myo-electric arm..worked entirely by harnessing the tiny electric currents generated in one's own remaining muscles. **1972** *Science* 12 May 607/3 The design of myoelectric artificial aids for the physically handicapped.

Hence **myoele·ctrically** *adv.*

1964 *New Scientist* 12 Mar. 671/1 A Russian team..has introduced a myoelectrically controlled hand. **1970** *Ibid.* 5 Mar. 477/1 We constructed in 1966 a myoelectrically controlled hand and arm unit.

myofibril (məiˌofəi·bril). *Anat.* Also in mod. L. form **myofibrilla** (pl. **-fibrillæ**). [f. MYO- + FIBRIL, FIBRILLA.] Any of the elongated cylindrical threads, about one micrometre thick, which arranged side by side in a bundle constitute the contractile components of a striated muscle fibre.

1898 *Jrnl. R. Microsc. Soc.* 64 The muscle-cell produces conducting substance (myofibrils). **1913** DORLAND *Med. Dict.* (ed. 7) 605/1 *Myofibril, myofibrilla*, a muscle-fibril. **1928** *Biol. Abstr.* II. 804/1 The author compares his results on the origin and formation of myofibrillae in striated muscles with those of other investigators. **1933** *Physiol. Rev.* XIII. 318 Thus far it has been assumed that myofibrils are actual morphologic entities. **1960** G. H. BOURNE *Struct. & Function Muscle* I. ii. 34 Hogue (1937) demonstrated cross striated myofibrillae in living cultures of cardiac muscle cells. Microdissection of fresh muscle fibers as a means of demonstrating myofibrils is exceedingly difficult. **1968** *New Scientist* 11 Jan. 70/1 Normal skeletal muscle..is composed of parallel fibres averaging 70 micrometres in diameter. These are in turn made up from hundreds of fine myofibrils, one to two micrometres thick, running the whole length of the fibre. **1970** AMBROSE & EASTY *Cell Biol.* xi. 370 The myofibril is itself composed of fine filaments.

Hence **myofi·brillar** *a.*

1927 *Biol. Abstr.* I. 861/1 Cerebellar ataxia [is due] to loss of 'myofibrillar perceptions'. **1956** *Anatomical Rec.* CXXV. 483 Lacking the regular myofibrillar organization of striated muscles, these filaments appear to span the cell as a loose bundle. **1972** D. A. FISCHMAN in G. H. Bourne *Structure & Function Muscle* (ed. 2) I. iii. 117 Probably no aspect of muscle differentiation has elicited as much interest with biologists as the problem of myofibrillar biosynthesis and assembly.

myogen (məi·ŏdʒĕn). *Biochem.* [a. G. *myogen* (O. von Fürth 1895, in *Arch. f. exper. Path. und Pharm.* XXXVI. 274), f. *myo(sino)gen* MYOSINOGEN.] A mixture of albumins (varying between species) extracted from skeletal muscle plasma; crystalline substances obtained from such mixtures have been designated *myogen A, B, I, II*, etc.

1896 *Jrnl. Chem. Soc.* LXX. II. 48 The proteids in the muscle plasma are three in number, namely paramyosinogen.., myosinogen or myogen 77 to 83 per cent. of the total proteïd, and traces of serum albumin. **1939** *Biochem. Jrnl.* XXXIII. 1342 Baranowski..has recently obtained from rabbit muscle extract a crystalline protein, which he has named myogen A. **1970** R. E. SCOPES in E. J. Briskey et al. *Physiol. & Biochem. of Muscle as Food* II. xxii. 472 It is now clear that..myogen A (when prepared from rabbit muscle) consisted of cocrystallized α-glycerophosphate dehydrogenase (α-GPDH) and aldolase... It has since been shown that pig myogen A is a different enzyme, lactate dehydrogenase. *Ibid.*, Myogens I and II from fish sarcoplasms..have been crystallised; ..neither is related to the myogen A of rabbit.

myoglobin (məiˌŏglōᵘ·bin). *Biochem.* [a. G. *myoglobin* (H. Günther 1921, in *Virchows Arch. f. path. Anat. und Physiol.* CCXXX. 150), f. *myo-* MYO + *globin* *GLOBIN.] A red protein responsible for the transport of oxygen in muscle cells, which differs from hæmoglobin in containing only one hæm group and one peptide chain in its molecule (instead of four of each) and in having a much greater affinity for oxygen.

1925 *Proc. R. Soc.* B. XCVIII. 332 This difference does not justify, however, the introduction of the names 'myochrome' or 'myoglobin' for muscle hæmoglobin proposed respectively by Mörner and Günther. **1956** *New Biol.* XXI. 45 Muscles contain myoglobin, a compound related to haemoglobin which takes up oxygen released by haemoglobin..and stores it for use in time of oxygen shortage. **1958** *Manch. Guardian Weekly* 2 Oct. 12 J. C. Kendrew's molecular model of myoglobin, derived from the first successful X-ray analysis of a protein molecule ever to be made, aroused tremendous interest at the Congress [of Biochemistry at Vienna]. **1968** PASSMORE & ROBSON *Compan. Med. Stud.* I. xv. 11/2 Myoglobin can pick up and store in the cells the oxygen brought by the blood even when the circulation is too inadequate to maintain a high oxygen tension in the tissue fluid interposed between capillaries and muscle cells.

myoid (məi·oid), *a.* and *sb.* [f. MY(O- + -OID.]

A. *adj.* Resembling muscle; composed of muscular tissue.

1857 DUNGLISON *Dict. Med. Sci.* (rev. ed.) 616/1 *Myoid*, an epithet given to tumours composed of fibre cells or muscular fibres of organic life. **1970** *Amer. Jrnl. Anat.* CXXIX. 399 (*heading*) Myoid elements in the mammalian nephron. *Ibid.* 399/1 This procedure revealed myoid features in the nephric tubules. **1973** *Anatomical Rec.* CLXXVII. 525 (*heading*) Myoid cells in the capsule of the adrenal gland and in monolayers derived from cultured adrenal capsules.

B. *sb.* [perh. a different word.] A structural part of the cones and rods of the retina.

1900 *Lancet* 7 July 7/2 The cell-body, traced from the cuticular end, begins as a distinct granular protoplasmic swelling, called the myoid. **1961** S. DUKE-ELDER *Syst. Ophthalmol.* II. iii. 241 In man and other mammals the inner segment of the rod is an elongated slightly barrel-shaped structure, homogeneous in appearance, made up of two elements, an outer ellipsoid and an inner myoid. **1972** *Vision Res.* XII. 1841 (*heading*) Optical function of myoids. *Ibid.*, The myoid is a cylindrical part of the photoreceptor connecting the region of the cell containing its nucleus with the region containing the ellipsoid.

myomectomy (məiˌome·ktŏmi). *Surg.* [f. MYOM(A + *-ECTOMY.] Excision of a myoma, esp. in the uterus.

1886 *Buck's Handbk. Med. Sci.* III. 811/2 The operation of myomectomy..is another product of the fertile mind of Schröder. It has been termed by him myomotomy, but for the sake of greater exactness the other term is to be preferred. **1900** *Lancet* 18 Aug. 501/1 Myomectomy should always be done when it was possible to save the uterus. **1908** *Practitioner* Oct. 608 Vaginal myomectomy. **1974** PASSMORE & ROBSON *Compan. Med. Stud.* III. xxviii. 46/1 Myomectomy is the treatment of choice in cases where it is desirable to preserve the uterus for future pregnancies.

‖ **myon** (myǫ̆n). Also **myen.** [Korean.] A Korean administrative unit approximately equivalent to a rural district or township. Also *attrib.*

1898 I. L. BISHOP *Korea & her Neighbours* II. xxxii. 203 The country is now divided into districts (*Kun*), each *Kun* containing a number of *myen* or cantons, each of which includes a number of *ni* or villages. **1951** C. OSGOOD *Koreans & their Culture* ii. 20 The kun..comprises a series of myŏn, or townships, of which there are said to be currently fourteen in Kanghwa Kun. **1972** P. M. BARTZ *South Korea* 48/2 From provincial governor to rural *myon* chief and city mayor to *dong* head, officials are appointed, not elected. **1972** *Korea Herald* 17 Nov. 1/6 Detailed work on formulation of a plan to construct one factory in each of 770 selected eups and myons throughout the country..began yesterday.

myopic, *a.* (*sb.*) (Later *fig.* examples.)

1955 *Sci. Amer.* Oct. 103/1 Until Maupertuis's death in 1759 Voltaire did not relent in his flood of unmerciful, unscrupulous and myopic ridicule. **1972** G. DURRELL *Catch me a Colobus* v. 82 For some considerable time I had been endeavouring to persuade the BBC to film an animal-collecting trip, but they had been very myopic about the whole thing. **1975** *Times* 3 July 15/2 The Inner London Education Authority..appears to share this myopic vision of the troubles at North London Polytechnic.

myosis. Add: Also **miosis** (now the usual form). (Further examples.)

1890 BILLINGS *Med. Dict.* II. 160/2 *Miosis* (G[erman]), myosis. **1892** A. DUANE tr. *E. Fuchs's Text-bk. Ophthalm.* iv. 257 There is a series of alkaloids which produce either dilatation of the pupil (mydriasis) or its contraction (miosis). [*Note*] From μείωσις, contraction; hence miosis, and not myosis, as it is generally written (Hirschberg). **1910** *Trans. Ophthalm. Soc.* XXX. 163 Miosis on the right side was associated with dilatation of the left pupil. **1947** F. B. WALSH *Clinical Neuro-Ophthalmology* 201 Miosis has already been defined as indicating a pupil 2 mm. or less in diameter. **1964** W. B. SMITH *Allergy & Tissue Metabolism* vii. 78 The pharmacological effects of reserpine administration are: ..miosis (contraction of pupil of the eye), ptosis [etc.].

myotic, *a.* and *sb.* Add: Also **miotic** (now the usual form). (Further examples.)

1892 A. DUANE tr. *E. Fuchs's Text-bk. Ophthalm.* iv. 259 The action of miotics is of shorter duration than that of the mydriatics. **1918** *Jrnl. Amer. Med. Assoc.* 29 June 1992/2 There are contradictory opinions expressed on the effect of miotic drugs in cases of incomplete sphincter. **1946** *Nature* 28 Sept. 432/1 The work ..developed to include other problems, such as the mechanism..of lachrymation, of the action of myotics, etc. **1971** *Lancet* 6 Nov. 1040/2 The use of a miotic..should be regarded as mandatory whatever the mydriatic previously instilled.

myotonia (məiˌŏtōᵘ·niă). *Path.* [mod.L., f. MYO- + Gr. τόν-ος TONE *sb.* + -IA[1].] **1.** The inability to relax voluntary muscle for a period

following its use; any condition characterized by this.

1898 *Jrnl. Nerv. & Mental Dis.* XXV. 509, I think it proper to assign all such cases to the one clinical category of myotonia. *Ibid.* 510 Cases which show symptoms of organic disease..can at once be excluded from the group of myotonias. **1905** *Ibid.* XXIX. 416 Myotonia appears to have been used also in the collective sense. Hochsinger describes as myotonia of infancy the persistent hypertonicity of the flexors, and diagnosticates it from tetany, but if myotonia is used as an inclusive term it is a question if it should not cover tetany itself, while if it is used in the narrow sense it has been preëmpted by Thomsen's disease. **1948** F. B. Carlsen tr. *Thomasen's Myotonia* ii. 15 There is a definite difference in the ages at which the myotonia in Thomsen's disease..on the one hand, and dystrophia myotonica on the other, manifests itself. **1963** Caughey & Myrianthopoulos *Dystrophia Myotonica* p. x, Her father was a London professional man who had myotonia of the grip. **1970** Masters & Johnson *Human Sexual Inadequacy* viii. 220 Specific evidence has been accumulated of the incidence of both myotonia and vasocongestion in the female's pelvis as she responds physiologically to sex-tension elevation.

2. In the (usu. mod.L) names of specific diseases in which myotonia is a prominent feature, as: **a. myotonia congenita** [A. Strümpell 1881, in *Berliner klin. Wochenschr.* 28 Feb. 121/2], **congenital myotonia** (*rare*), a rare hereditary disease manifested soon after birth and characterized by myotonia but without muscular wasting or other symptoms. Also called Thomsen's disease.

1886 *Brain* IX. 113 The eighth article..makes confusion worse confounded by using another term, viz. dysmyotonie congénitale, almost adopting Strumpell's term, congenital myotonia. **1887** *Jrnl. Nerv. & Mental Dis.* XIV. 129 (*heading*) Thomsen's disease (myotonia congenita). **1963** Caughey & Myrianthopoulos *Dystrophia Myotonica* xviii. 216 Myotonia congenita.. was described in detail in 1876 by Dr. Asmus Julius Thomsen who was himself affected and in whose family it had occurred for five generations. **1974** J. T. Hughes *Path. Muscle* iv. 76 In contrast to myotonia congenita and paramyotonia congenita, dystrophia myotonica is frequently diagnosed.

b. myotonia atrophica [tr. F. *myotonie atrophique* (G. Rossolimo 1902, in *Nouvelle Iconographie de la Salpêtrière* XV. 63)], a hereditary condition characterized esp. by myotonia, muscular wasting, cataracts, frontal baldness, and gonadal atrophy. Also called *dystrophia myotonica*.

1908 *Jrnl. Nerv. & Mental Dis.* XXXV. 269 Myotonia atrophica is an extremely rare affection. **1963** Caughey & Myrianthopoulos *Dystrophia Myotonica* p. viii, Dystrophia myotonica has been known as myotonia atrophica, Steinert's disease, dystrophia myotonica or myotonic dystrophy. **1974** J. N. Walton *Disorders Voluntary Muscle* (ed. 3) xv. 595 Dystrophia myotonica (myotonia atrophica) was described by Steinert (1909) and Batten and Gibb (1909).

myotonic, *a.* Substitute for entry s.v. Myo-: **myotonic** (məiˌǒtǫ·nik), *a. Path.* [f. Myo- + Tonic *a.*] Producing, exhibiting, or characteristic of myotonia.

1887 A. de Watteville tr. *H. von Ziemssen's Handbk. Therap.* VI. 213 The Myotonic Electrical Reaction. **1887** *Jrnl. Nerv. & Mental Dis.* XIV. 129 Those [cases] which, although showing the principal symptoms, the 'myotonic disorder of the muscles', still..cannot be considered as true cases of Thomsen's disease. **1887** *Lancet* 14 May 973/2 'Myotonic contractions', which has also been suggested, has the advantage of avoiding prejudice of the question whether the condition is always congenital. **1909** *Brain* XXXII. 190 The muscles did not give the myotonic reaction as described by Erb in Thomsen's disease. **1948** F. B. Carlsen tr. *Thomasen's Myotonia* ii. 18 Myotonic patients may often play the piano without difficulty. **1963** Caughey & Myrianthopoulos *Dystrophia Myotonica* ii. 20 Brown and Harvey (1939) examined myotonic goats electromyographically.

myrcene (mə̄·ɹsīn). *Chem.* [f. mod.L. *Myrc-ia*, name of a genus of tropical trees and shrubs + -ene.] 2-Methyl-6-methylene-2,7-octadiene, $C_{10}H_{16}$, a liquid terpene found in bay, hop, and other essential oils.

1895 Power & Kleber in *Pharmaceut. Rundschau* XIII. 61/1 As this body is not identical with any of the known terpenes, we propose for it the name *myrcene*. **1926** H. Finnemore *Essential Oils* lviii. 528 When 1 part of myrcene was heated..with 3 parts of glacial acetic acid and 1/50 part of 50 per cent sulphuric acid, an oil of lavender-like odour was obtained. **1953** I. A. Preece *Biochem. Brewing* ix. 254 The myrcene content of a hop sample might well prove to be an outstanding factor in determining the storage characteristics of that sample. **1969** *Daily Tel.* 16 Sept. 21/2 The disaster tank..had contained myrcene, an oil closely allied to turpentine, which in certain circumstances can turn into a sticky residue with a low flashpoint.

myriad, *sb.* and *a.* Add: **B.** *adj.* **3.** *Comb.*: parasynthetic, *myriad-accomplished, -islanded -jewelled, -limbed, -minded* (later examples), *-mirrored, -voiced, -wrinkled*; advb., *myriad-flaking, -times, -tinkling, -wise.*

1909 'Mark Twain' *Is Shakes. Dead?* 67 The man who wrote the plays was not merely myriad-minded, but also myriad-accomplished. **1957** R. Campbell *Coll. Poems* II. 106 The Heliades, The myriad-flaking snowstorm of whose boughs Is never still. **1922** Joyce *Ulysses* 48 Tides, myriadislanded, within her. **1909** E. Pound *Personae* 43 Unless it were to make the halo round each one Appear more myriad-jewelled marvellous. **1923** D. H. Lawrence *Birds, Beasts & Flowers* 41 Nude fig-tree... Rather like an octopus, but strange and sweet-myriad-limbed octopus. **1916** Blunden *Harbingers* 12 And wed me with the myriad-minded man. **1968** *Jrnl. Mus. Acad. Madras* XXXIX. 9 Tyagaraja can truly be said to be myriad-minded. **1921** W. de la Mare *Veil* 52 Their myriad-mirrored eyes Great day reflect. **1944** Blunden *Shells by Stream* 26 We may glide Over a myriad-times extended sea And land of life abundant. *a* **1918** W. Owen *Coll. Poems* (1963) 127 The myriad-tinkling flocks. **1883** J. G. Whittier *What Traveller Said* in *Bay of Seven Islands* 48, I dread the myriad-voiced strain. **1917** D. H. Lawrence *Look! We have come Through!* 120 Its oneness veers Out myriad-wise. **1859** Tennyson *Idylls of King: Elaine* 156 Then came an old, dumb, myriad-wrinkled man. **1942** W. Faulkner *Go down, Moses* iii. 75 Then he saw the myriad-wrinkled face.

myriapodal (miriæ·pǒdăl), *a.* [f. Myriapoda + -al.] = Myriapod *a.*

1893 *Rep. U.S. Nat. Mus. 1892* 258 Comparatively little can ever be known concerning the probably great abundance of Insect, Arachnid, and Myriapodal life of former geological time.

myrmeco-. Add: **myrmecologist** (examples); **myrmecophile** (later examples); **myrmecophilism** = *myrmecophily*.

1901 W. M. Wheeler in *Amer. Naturalist* XXXV. 432 It thus becomes necessary to review much that is well known to the myrmecologist. **1972** *Sci. Amer.* Sept. 193/1 Forty-five years ago the American myrmecologist William Morton Wheeler wrote a volume with a very similar title, the fruit of his lifetime study of ants. **1927** H. St. J. K. Donisthorpe *Guests of British Ants* p. xv, A large number of creatures do manage to live in or near ants' nests. Such creatures when associated with, and not merely present with ants, are known as myrmecophiles. **1959** E. F. Linssen *Beetles Brit. Is.* I. 47 Certain beetles are known as myrmecophiles (ant-lovers) from their association with ants. The name myrmecophilism has been given to this curious habit.

myrmekite (mə̄·ɹmĭkəit). *Petrogr.* [ad. G. *myrmekit* (J. J. Sederholm 1897, in *Bull. de la Commission géol. de la Finlande* I. vi. 113) f. Gr. μυρμηκ-ιά anthill, wart + *-it* -ite¹.] An intergrowth of plagioclase with drops or worm-like forms of quartz.

1916 *Bull. de la Commission géol. de la Finlande* IX. xlviii. 1 The intergrowth of plagioclase and 'vermicular' quartz..I have called *myrmekite*. *Ibid.*, I prefer to write *myrmekite*, as analogous to poikilite etc., instead of myrmecite. **1926** H. H. Read et al. *Geol. Strath Oykell & Lower Loch Shin* (Mem. Geol. Surv. Scot.) vi. 154 In slice ..the pinkish medium-grained rock is seen to be composed of quartz, oligoclase, and myrmekite. **1967** *Mineral Mag.* XXXVI. 491 Myrmekite and the other vermicular textures all appear to lack any specific crystallographic or lattice co-relationship between the vermicular and host mineral.

Hence **myrmeki·tic** *a.*, of the nature of or containing myrmekite; **my:rmekitiza·tion**, conversion into myrmekite; a myrmekitic state.

1916 *Bull. de la Commission géol. de la Finlande* IX. xlviii. 120 Myrmekitic intergrowths may occasionally originate like the minerals crystallising in a molten magma, not as crystalloblastic minerals. *Ibid.* 118 The myrmekitization and the formation of the biotite are here obviously independent phenomena. **1944** *Q. Jrnl. Geol. Soc.* XCIX. 118 The plagioclase is sericitized and its larger plates show myrmekitic margins. **1964** *Amer. Mineral.* XLIX. 50 The myrmekite type I..is formed by the myrmekitization of plagioclase already in the rock. **1972** *Mineral. Mag.* XXXVIII. 573 Microprobe and optical measurements have shown the myrmekitic plagioclase of such intergrowths to be very similar compositionally to non-myrmekitic plagioclase.

myrrhy, *a.* Add: Also *Comb.*, as *myrrhy-threaded.*

1865 G. M. Hopkins *Poems* (1967) 21 For sackcloth and frieze And the ever-fretting shirt of punishment Give myrrhy-threaded golden folds of ease.

myrtle, *sb.* Add: **3.** (Earlier example.)

1872 [see *hunter 5 d].

5. myrtle green (later example); **myrtle-of-the-river**, a large evergreen shrub, *Calyptranthes zuzygium*, of the family Myrtaceæ, native to Jamaica and bearing panicles of white flowers; **myrtle warbler** = *myrtle bird.*

1925 E., O., & S. Sitwell *Poor Young People* 2 The colours most in favour are marine Blue Louise, gris bois, grenate, myrtle green. **1919** *Ann. Rep. Board of Regents Smithsonian Inst. 1917* 384 The myrtle-of-the-river..with opposite glossy leaves and clusters of fruit resembling blueberries. **1924** J. A. Thomson *Science Old & New* v. 27 Even the names transport us into a land of pure delight—the paradise tree, the myrtle-of-the-river, the marlberry, and the bois-fidèle. **1892** B. Torrey *Footpath-Way* 95 Not so was it with the myrtle warblers. **1947** *Proc. Iowa Acad. Sci.* LIV. 379 Myrtle Warbler..is often a late migrant, for a warbler. **1963** R. D. Symons *Many Trails* ii. 17 Small birds that at first glance look like myrtle warblers.

myrtly (mə̄·ɹtli), *a.* [f. Myrtle *sb.* + -y¹.] Containing myrtles or redolent of myrtle.

1882 G. F. Armstrong *Garland fr. Greece* 135 Every brake And myrtly jungle seemed to undulate With motions of strange beings.

myself. Add: **5.** Phr. *says I to myself.*

1720, 1825 [see Say *v.*¹ B. 3 b ¶]. **1920** J. Lee *Penitent in Northern Numbers* 81 As I lay in the trenches at Noove Chapelle,..Sez I to mysel', sez I to mysel':—Billy, me boy, here's the end o' you.

Mysian (mi·siăn), *sb.* and *a.* [f. L. *Mysia*, Gr. Μυσία Mysia + -an.] **A.** *sb.* **a.** A native or inhabitant of ancient Mysia in north-west Asia Minor. **b.** The language of Mysia. **B.** *adj.* Of or pertaining to ancient Mysia, its inhabitants or its language.

1555 [see *Bulgarian *a.* and *sb.*]. **1601** Holland tr. *Pliny's Nat. Hist.* v. xxx. 110 Teuthrania, which the Mysians in old time held. **1834** J. S. Mill in *Monthly Repos.* VIII. 837 The most despised of all foreign nations. Witness the phrase *Μυσῶν λεία*, the spoil of the Mysians, applied to any people so poor in spirit, that even the unwarlike Mysians could plunder them with impunity. **1844** A. W. Kinglake *Eothen* iii. 54, I saw, and acknowledged the snowy crown of the Mysian Olympus! **1884** *Encycl. Brit.* XVII. 122/2 Ancient writers all agree in describing the Mysians as a distinct people,..though they never appear in history as an independent nation. *Ibid.* 123/1 The only relic of the Mysian language is a very short inscription,..supposed to be in the Mysian dialect. *a* **1936** A. E. Housman *Coll. Poems* (1939) 216 Up the Mysian entry wending, Lydians, Lydians, what is yon? **1939** L. H. Gray *Foundations of Language* 383 Of *Mysian* we may have a scanty inscription of the fourth or third century B.C., consisting of five lines. **1948** D. Diringer *Alphabet* 466 Some scholars mention a Mysian, a Cilician and a Cappadocian alphabet. **1954** Pei & Gaynor *Dict. Linguistics* 142 *Mysian*, an extinct language, once spoken in Asia Minor... A language of undetermined linguistic affinities, classified as Asianic. **1972** W. B. Lockwood *Panorama Indo-Europ. Languages* 174 In Asia Minor, Mysian is said to have been a living language in the sixth century. **1974** *Encycl. Brit. Micropædia* VII. 151/3 The Mysians..were mentioned by Homer as primitive allies of the Trojans.

mysid (məi·sid). [f. mod.L. family name *Mysidæ*, f. the generic name Mysis (P. A. Latreille in C. S. Sonnini *Buffon's Hist. Nat. Insectes & Crustacés* (1802) III. 36): see -id³.] A small shrimp-like crustacean of the family Mysidæ or the suborder Mysidacea; an opossum-shrimp. Also *attrib.*

1941 Steinbeck & Ricketts *Sea of Cortez* xv. 152 That night we rigged a lamp..and hung it close down to the water... Pelagic isopods and mysids immediately swarmed to the illuminated circle. **1956** A. Hardy *Open Sea* xiii. 254 Many ostracods and copepods, and at least one mysid, are known to flash brightly. **1961** *New Scientist* 15 June 661/1 Small marine crustaceans, called mysids, would orientate themselves preferentially at right angles to the direction of polarization of vertical light. **1965** B. E. Freeman tr. *Vandel's Biospeleology* ix. 117 The mysids are mainly marine Crustacea. **1969** A. Wheeler *Fishes Brit. Is. & N.-W. Europe* 133/2 The 'whitebait herring', i.e. those in their first year,..eat crustacea, the copepod *Calanus*, the larvae of acorn barnacles, mysid shrimps, and the eggs and larvae of decapods and amphipods.

Mysoline (məi·sǒlīn). *Pharm.* Also **mysoline.** A proprietary name for primidone.

1949 *Trade Marks Jrnl.* 12 Oct. 901/2 Mysoline... Pharmaceutical substances for human and veterinary use; sanitary substances and disinfectants;..Imperial Chemical (Pharmaceuticals) Limited,..Slough, Buckinghamshire, England; manufacturers and merchants. **1958** J. H. Burn *Lect. Notes Pharmacol.* (ed. 5) 52 Primidone (Mysoline) is the most effective agent for the form of epilepsy known as 'grand mal'. **1966** *Economist* 30 Apr. 512 Other drugs that ICI hope will attract a large market are..the anti-epileptic Mysoline and the long-established anti-malarial Paludrine. **1973** *Clin. Chim. Acta* XLIV. 383 Both mysoline and phenytoin subjects show a more severely raised GGTP level than those treated with phenobarbitone.

Mysore (məi·sōə·ɹ). The former name of a state in southern India (now Karnataka), used to designate coffee produced there.

1907 *Yesterday's Shopping* (1969) 2 The Mocha and Mysore mixed in equal quantities are recommended for best Coffee. *c* **1938** *Fortnum & Mason Catal.* 7/2 Coffees. ..'Mysore'. **1951** W. H. Brindley in W. G. Copsey *Modern Grocer* (ed. 5) II. viii. 97 The best quality and most widely known coffees from India are Mysores... Mysores are now full-bodied in cup, but often a little rough and dry on the palate. **1965** L. Deighton *Action Cook Bk.* 132/2 Here are some good combinations: Costa Rica with Tanganyika (Chagga); Mocha mixed with Mysore.

Mysorean (məisǒrī·ăn), *sb.* and *a.* **A.** *sb.* A native or inhabitant of Mysore. **B.** *adj.* Of or pertaining to Mysore.

1871 C. M. Yonge *Pioneers & Founders* iii. 61 The Mysoreans complained that the English promises had not been kept. **1932** *Times Lit. Suppl.* 3 Mar. 159/4 A photograph of Mysorean industrial life. **1968** *Jrnl. Mus. Acad. Madras* XXXIX. 74 Kangari Radhakrishnaiya..is believed to have been a Mysorean.

mystagoguery (mi:stægǫ·gəri). [f. MYSTAGOGU(E + -ERY.] = MYSTAGOGY (in trivial or *transf.* sense).

1927 *Observer* 17 July 6 The mystagoguery of weak human beings. **1963** *Times Lit. Suppl.* 4 Jan. 4/5 But mystagoguery like this will not earn for Indian art the friends it so much needs. **1966** *New Statesman* 2 Dec. 838/1 It works out as practically a capitulation..to the literary mystagoguery of France and the United States.

mysterioso (mistiəriōu·so), *a.* [ad. It. *misterioso* adj., mysterious.] Of music: executed in a mysterious manner. Also *transf.* as *sb.*

1953 in H. E. Vizetelly *New Internat. Year Book 1952* 619 *Mysterioso*, a motion-picture, radio or television program which depends upon the element of mystery for its effect. **1957** S. DANCE in S. Traill *Concerning Jazz* 44 In mysterioso numbers suitable for accompanying the more exotic dances in the night-clubs.., there was evoked what was considered a 'jungle' atmosphere. **1957** MANVELL & HUNTLEY *Technique Film Music* ii. 28 The theme is played twice on strings pizzicato, with suitable mysterioso embellishments. **1967** J. SEVERSON *Great Surfing* Gloss., *Mysterioso*, an 'adornment' or surf trick popular in the late fifties... The stance is with the surfer bending over, hiding his head in his hands.

mysterium (mistīə·riŏm). *Astr.* [f. MYSTER(IOUS *a.* + -IUM.] A hypothetical substance to which a galactic radio emission at 1665 megahertz was attributed until it was identified as an exceptionally strong component of a set of four lines emitted by the hydroxyl radical.

1965 H. WEAVER et al. in *Nature* 2 Oct. 30/1 There is no known identification of the strong emission line at 1,665 Mc/s... We shall speak of this unidentified line as arising from 'mysterium'. *Ibid.* 30/2 Our observations indicate that 'mysterium' is found in strong H II regions, but not in all strong H II regions. **1967** *Science* 25 Aug. 885/1 Mysterium has now been identified as OH. **1974** G. L. VERSCHUUR *Invisible Universe* ix. 77 How do we now know that the mysterium signals are in fact OH lines?

‖ **mysterium tremendum** (mistīə·riŏm treme·ndŏm). [L., = tremendous mystery.] A term used to express the overwhelming awe and sense of unknowable mystery felt by those to whom this aspect of God or of being is revealed.

1923 J. W. HARVEY tr. *R. Otto's Idea of Holy* iv. 12 We shall find we are dealing with something for which there is only one appropriate expression, *mysterium tremendum*. *Ibid.* v. 25 We gave to the object to which the numinous consciousness is directed the name 'mysterium tremendum'. **1957** J. S. HUXLEY *Relig. without Revelation* (rev. ed.) ii. 32 The *mysterium tremendum* of religion. **1963** A. HUXLEY *Let.* 17 Feb. (1969) 949 One.. opens oneself up receptively to the *Mysterium tremendum et fascinans* within and without. **1968** *Times* 15 Oct. 11/4 Should we not beware of the mysterium tremendum, the Wrath of God. **1971** *Nature* 13 Aug. 450/2 Their interrelationship [*sc.* that of biology and physical-chemical research] seems to me to represent one of the deepest questions man can ask, a real *mysterium tremendum*.

mystery¹. Add: **12. d.** Shortened form of *bag of mystery* (*BAG *sb.* 17 b). *slang.* **e.** A girl newly arrived in a town or city; a girl with no fixed address; a young or inexperienced prostitute. *slang.* **f.** A mystery story.

d. *a*1890 G. HORNCASTLE in Barrère & Leland *Dict. Slang* (1890) II. 79/2 The peelers I scorn and defy, While strings of these *mysteries* I wave round my head, And then to the people I cry, 'Sassidges, oh, sassidges! Oh, beef and pork and German!'

e. 1937 J. WORBY *Other Half* 278 *Mystery*, a girl who is down and out, come to town to look for a job. **1955** C. H. ROLPH *Women of Streets* x. 120 When you're a new girl they call you a 'mystery'. And you're a mystery until you've been here three or four years. Then you become a 'history'. **1960** *Observer* 28 Feb. 23/4 Many teddys, tearaways and mysteries (drifting girls) are put off by the typical orthodox youth club. **1960** C. MACINNES *Mr Love & Justice* 19 'All those men. Maybe two or three a day...' 'Two or three? Are you kidding? What you take me for—a mystery?' **1962** R. COOK *Crust on its Uppers* (1964) iv. 37 'I Saw a Human Monster in My Bedroom, says Teenager'..means the little mystery's woken up when she wasn't supposed to. **1967** M. M. GLATT et al. *Drug Scene* 117 *Mystery*, girl (young) having left home on arrival in London. **1974** G. F. NEWMAN *Price* v. 169 Instead of calling a couple of mysteries, he called a cab.

f. 1973 *Directory of Dealers in Secondhand & Antiquarian Bks. in Brit. Isles 1973–75* 111 Fantasy, scientific romance, Gothic novel, mystery and detective.

13. *mystery-mongering* adj. and sb.; *mystery-piety*; **mystery-bag** = *bag of mystery* (*BAG *sb.* 17 b); **mystery-man,** (*b*) a man about whom little is known; **mystery-religion** (see quot. 1967); **mystery ship,** an armed and camouflaged merchantman used in the war of 1914–18 as a decoy or to destroy submarines; **mystery story,** a detective or crime story; **mystery tour,** a pleasure trip for which there is no advance announcement of the places to be visited; **mystery train,** a train taking passengers on a mystery tour; **mystery trip** = **mystery tour*; **mystery woman,** a woman about whom little is known; **mystery writer,** a writer of mystery stories.

1889 *Sportsman* 2 Feb. 4/1 But the 'mystery-bags' of Sieur X, if we are to believe the common report, were far from being fragrant. This gentleman has been sentenced to six months' imprisonment for 'making sausages of tainted meat'. **1910** *Encycl. Brit.* III. 570/1 'Adventurer', as applied to Disraeli, was a mere term of abuse. 'Mystery-man' had much of the same intention, but in a blameless though not in a happy sense it was true of him to the end of his days. **1933** H. G. WELLS *Shape of Things to Come* I. 112 That Mystery Man of Mystery Men, Sir Basil Zaharoff, the armaments salesman. **1972** G. LYALL *Blame Dead* ii. 10 You sounded a bit of a mystery man in those stories this morning—they'll want to know more. **1901** W. JAMES *Mem. & Stud.* (1911) vii. 150 With all these things, infected by their previous mystery-mongering discoverers, even our best friends had rather avoid complicity. **1912** MRS. R. DAVIDS *Buddhism* i. 20 There is no evidence..that this late recourse to writing was due to any mystery-mongering or esotericism. **1939** DYLAN THOMAS *Let.* 29 Sept. (1966) 240 Censorship and conscription, mystery-mongering and umbrella-worship. **1939** P. S. WATSON tr. *Nygren's Agape & Eros* II. II. iii. 355 Neoplatonism..to a large extent bears the stamp of Mystery-piety. **1913** H. A. A. KENNEDY *St. Paul & Mystery-Religions* III. 69 There are special strains of religious thought and feeling more or less common to all the Mystery-Religions, such as that of regeneration (in some sense) and union or communion with deity. *Ibid.* 86 This connection with Dionysus leads us into the heart of conceptions typical for mystery-religion, the conception of union with the Divine and attainment of undying life. **1925** S. ANGUS *Mystery-Religions & Christianity* ii. 45 A Mystery-Religion was (1) a religion of symbolism which, through myth and allegory, iconic representations, blazing lights and dense darkness, liturgies and sacramental acts, and suggestion..provoked in the initiate a mystical experience conducing to *palingenesia* (regeneration), the object of every initiation. *Ibid.* 50 II. A Mystery-Religion was a religion of Redemption which professed to remove estrangement between man and God. *Ibid.* 52 III. The Mystery-Religions were systems of *Gnosis* akin, and forming a stage to, those movements to which the name of Gnosticism became attached. **1967** D. T. KAUFFMAN *Dict. Relig. Terms* 322/1 *Mystery religions*, secret cults in pre-Christian Greek and Roman culture, as well as in areas of Egypt and Asia... The mystery religions included the Orphic, Eleusinian, Mithraic. **1914** *Daily Mail* (Greater Manchester ed.) 7/4 The grey, gaunt outline of the mystery ship took definite shape. **1925** Mystery ship [see *DECOY *sb.*² 6]. **1975** B. MEYRICK *Behind Light* xvi. 207 The crew of Mystery Ship 51 listened as the warning boom of their foghorn echoed..through..the Dover Straits. **1908** CHESTERTON *All Things Considered* 115 Mystery stories are very popular, especially when sold at sixpence. **1932** H. CRANE *Let.* 20 Mar. (1965) 404 Even the suspense of the usual mystery story utilizes that device. **1934** Mystery story [see **crime-story*]. **1974** A. PRICE *Other Paths* I. vii. 86 You've been holding on to the book... I can't wait to hear your mystery story. **1947** J. BETJEMAN in *Strand Mag.* Aug. 41 The morning paddle, then the mystery tour By motor-coach inland this afternoon. **1973** C. BONINGTON *Next Horizon* vii. 105 Climbing with Tom Patey was a kind of Magical Mystery Tour, in which no one, except perhaps himself, knew what was coming next. **1933** H. A. PIEHLER *England for Everyman* 35 Recent enterprises include 'mystery' trains for hikers, bound for unknown destinations, and circular tours by special trains through beautiful scenery. **1958** *Listener* 23 Oct. 653/2 An enterprising char-à-banc proprietor advertised 'mystery trips'. **1913** R. C. PRAED (*title*) The mystery woman. **1922** M. ARLEN *Piracy* 321 The *Daily Mail* at once called her a 'mystery woman'. **1974** 'A. GILBERT' *Nice Little Killing* ix. 127 It was something she couldn't afford to be made public... Mrs Brown was the original mystery woman. **1942** *Amer. Speech* XVII. 3 Most of this [*sc.* slang and cant] I have excluded,.. because it is already rather thoroughly recorded in the special dictionaries, out of which, no doubt, the mystery-writers took it in the first place. **1973** *N.Y. Times* 1 Aug. 37/1 Good mystery writers have always known that man himself is the greatest mystery of all.

mystery². **2.** (Later examples.)

1889 'MARK TWAIN' *Conn. Yank.* xxxii. 367 A good blacksmith..[offered]..to..teach him the trade—or 'mystery', as Dowley called it. **1957** *Listener* 25 July 141/1 We usually start with some sort of prejudice against the verse-writer who is better known as a writer of prose: there is a (very proper) feeling that the two are different mysteries.

mystic, *a.* and *sb.* Add: Hence **my·sticness.**

1912 F. LAWRENCE *Let.* in A. Huxley *Lett. D. H. Lawrence* (1932) 75 Her weird mysticness throws a veil over her.

mysticismus: see *-ISMUS.

mystico-. Add: *mystico-humanitarian, -oriental, -religious* (earlier example), adjs.

1932 R. CAMPBELL *Taurine Provence* 53 Our modern mystico-humanitarian scientists who are merely barbarians. **1893** A. BEARDSLEY *Let.* *c*June (1971) 50, I am going to do a full page illustration of the wonderful and gorgeous *Song of Songs*, in mystico-Oriental style. **1834** J. S. MILL tr. *Plato's Phædrus* in *Monthly Repos.* VIII. 636 There are two sorts of madness; one coming from human disease, the other from a divine influence. This last we divided into four kinds: viz., prophetic inspiration ..; mystico-religious, (τελεστικη,) to Bacchus; poetic, to the Muses; and finally, that of which we are speaking, the inspiration or enthusiasm of Love.

mystificatory, *a.* (Later example.)

1927 C. E. MONTAGUE *Right off Map* viii. 68 This mystificatory drug had been working to some effect on the people of Ria's City.

mystify, *v.*² Add: Hence **my·stifyingly** *adv.*

1934 in WEBSTER. **1953** in Botkin & Harlow *Treas. Railroad Folklore* 508 The Delaware and Hudson came tooling up from Pennsylvania with what it mystifyingly called 'Standard gauge; 6 foot and 4 foot, 3 inches'. **1966** *English Studies* XLVII. 19 A conjunction which appears mystifyingly vexing. **1973** *Daily Tel.* 2 Mar. 15/2 *The Wrath of God* (Empire Two, 'X') would seem to parody that novel, mystifyingly, I would say, to most people.

mystique (mistī·k). [F. *mystique*: see MYSTIC *a.* and *sb.*] The atmosphere of mystery and veneration investing some doctrines, arts, professions, or personages; any professional skill or technique which is designed to mystify and impress the layman.

1891 E. DOWSON *Let.* 10 May (1967) 197 Its curious mixture of French technique & the mystique of Rossetti. **1940** *Economist* 14 Sept. 330/1 It is assumed that the only policy which can counter the Hitlerian *mystique* is that of 'European Revolution' which has a *mystique* of its own. **1940** *Time* 21 Oct. 94/2 In the '30s Ernest Hemingway expounded the *mystique* of bullfighting in *Death in the Afternoon.* **1943** H. READ *Politics of Unpolitical* ii. 27 But I do not claim that the principle of equality is a rational doctrine. On the contrary, it is an irrational dogma, a *mystique*. **1949** 'G. ORWELL' *Nineteen Eighty-Four* II. 211 All the beliefs, habits, tastes, emotions, mental attitudes that characterize our time are really designed to sustain the mystique of the Party. **1951** *Observer* 2 Dec. 4/6 The 'mystique' built up around him [*sc.* Stalin] has become a genuine outlet for the Russian religious instinct. **1951** *Sunday Times* 16 Dec. 4 True, the new style [of the Civil Servant] has its own mystique, and the Mr. Alphabet Precis today prides himself on knowing when to write 'Dear' and when 'My dear' [etc.]. **1952** M. MUGGERIDGE in A. Mayor tr. *Ciano's Diaries 1937–8* p. viii, The strange mixture of bombast, lies, cynicism and sincerity which furnished its [*sc.* the Fascist Regime's] mystique. **1952** A. POWELL *Buyer's Market* 141 Money, with its multifarious imagery and restrictive mystique. **1955** H. SPRING *These Lovers fled Away* 316 Talk to me about wine. To me it's something I drink... But to them it's a mystique. **1958** *Times* 25 Apr. 3/1 There is a mystique about violins, especially old violins. **1958** *Spectator* 20 June 813/1 His System has been.. damned by lazy actors as a rarefied mystique. **1959** *Times Lit. Suppl.* 15 May 284/5 The particular virtue of this account is that it shows how the task was done and thereby disposes of its *mystique* without destroying the belief that it was a miracle. **1960** *Times* 7 Jan. 13/2 Flying, both the *mystique* and the technicalities of it, plays its part, too, in the Egyptian stories. **1972** *Guardian* 3 Nov. 12/4 The City, of course, talks its own language and this has helped to add to the mystique.

myth, *sb.* Add: **1. b.** (Further examples.) Also, an untrue or popular tale, a rumour. *colloq.*

1854 GEO. ELIOT *Let.* 23 Oct. (1954) II. 179 Of course many silly myths are already afloat about me, in addition to the truth, which of itself would be thought matter for scandal. **1939** J. S. HUXLEY *'Race' in Europe* 28 Napoleon, Shakespeare, Einstein, Galileo—a dozen great names spring to mind which in themselves should be enough to disperse the Nordic myth. The word *myth* is used advisedly, since this belief frequently plays a semi-religious role, as basis for a creed of passionate racialism. **1940** C. S. LEWIS *Problem of Pain* v. 64, I offer the following picture—a 'myth' in the Socratic sense, a not unlikely tale. **1941** H. G. WELLS *You can't be too Careful* v. i. 240 As the New Deal unfolded, American myth and reality began to take on an increasing parallelism with Europe. **1950** *Scot. Jrnl. Theol.* III. 37 To this inner fellowship of disciples the 'mystery' of the Kingdom of God is disclosed, whereas to outsiders this same Kingdom remains veiled in parables, remains, that is, a figure of speech, a colourful vision, an imaginative dream, or, as we might say, a myth. **1959** *Listener* 31 Dec. 1171/2 The theme of *Sacrilege in Malaya*..is that any institution of this kind needs some myth, that is some nonsense, to make it work. **1961** *Ibid.* 2 Nov. 739/2 Disraeli set himself to recreate a national political party out of the wreckage of Peel's following. A new myth had to be evolved. **1963** *Brit. Jrnl. Sociol.* XIV. 27 We use *myth* in a sense a little different from the popular one. To us it does not mean an untrue or impossible tale, but a tale which is told to justify some aspect of social order or of human experience. **1973** *Times* 13 Nov. 6/6 There is a myth going around that there are an awful lot of empty houses in Windsor Great Park. *Ibid.* 4 Dec. 7/4 Egypt's decision to sit at the table with Israel would 'shatter the myth' surrounding Israel's constant call for 'direct negotiations'.

3. *myth-maker* (later examples), *-making* vbl. sb. (examples), ppl. adj. (later example); *myth-addict, -addiction, -criticism, -monger, -pattern, -play, -removal, -stage, -system, -talk, -transcriber*; *myth-bound, -destroying, -haunted, -producing, -provoking* adjs.

1945 KOESTLER *Yogi & Commissar* II. i. 133 Almost every discussion with myth-addicts, whether public or private, is doomed to failure. **1954** —— *Invisible Writing* ii. 31 It does not matter by what name one calls this mental process—double-think, controlled schizophrenia, myth addiction, or semantic perversion. **1964** *Economist* 8 Aug. 551/2 Trying to educate the myth-bound Americans. **1957** N. FRYE *Anat. Criticism* 72 The most conspicuous today being fantastical learning, or myth criticism. **1949** KOESTLER *Insight & Outlook* x. 153 The only [myth] which his myth-destroying genius embodied into his system. **1940** G. BARKER *Lament & Triumph* 33

The Avalon haven I have in the grave Is now myth-haunted by God like Arthur. **1961** *Guardian* 22 Sept. 10/5 The myth-makers are always quick to produce a propaganda image of the Leader. **1972** *Listener* 10 Aug. 183/1 Why did Buonarroti, who had started life as a court page, become a professional revolutionary and myth-maker, to bore historians for the next 130 years? **1881** J. ROYCE *Let.* 28 Dec. in R. B. Perry *Tht. & Char. of W. James* (1935) I. 791 Ontology, whereby I mean any positive theory of an external reality as such, is of necessity myth-making. **1965** *Times Lit. Suppl.* 25 Nov. 1068/4 The myth-making gestures in her work. **1974** *Listener* 24 Jan. 111/3 There is..no causal connection between art and revolution..to suppose there is one is to take a step towards mythmaking. **1961** *Ibid.* 28 Sept. 479/3 They find their natural allies in the political myth-mongers and the political gangsters. **1951** M. MCLUHAN *Mech. Bride* 5/2 This urgent appetite to have the cake and eat it, too, is widely prevalent in the myth patterns.. of industrial society. **1957** N. FRYE *Anat. Criticism* 282 The scriptural play is a form of a spectacular dramatic genre which we may provisionally call a 'myth-play'. **1954** KOESTLER *Invisible Writing* xxxvi. 390 An indication of the deep, myth-producing forces that were and still are at work. **1966** *Punch* 26 Jan. 139/1 Author explores the myth-provoking north-west coast of Spain. **1951** Myth-removal [see *DEMYTHOLOGIZE *v.*]. **1950** *Scot. Jrnl. Theol.* III. 39 We have seen that..Christians are to..get beyond the myth-stage of spiritual understanding. **1953** A. K. C. OTTAWAY *Education & Society* 42 Every society is held together by a myth-system. **1970** *Jrnl. Ecumen. Studies* VII. 822/1 In this essay, Gilkey is the theologian who establishes guidelines for myth-talk. **1924** D. H. LAWRENCE in *N.Y. Times Mag.* 26 Oct. 3/2 White people always, or nearly always write sentimentally about the Indians—all of them, anthropologists, and myth-transcribers and all.

mythically, *adv.* (Earlier examples.)
1817 COLERIDGE *Biogr. Lit.* (1907) I. ix. 100 The philosopher who cannot utter the whole truth without conveying falsehood..is constrained to express himself either *mythically* or equivocally. **1846** GEO. ELIOT tr. *Strauss's Life of Jesus* II. II. ix. 425 The two narratives in the Old Testament are to be understood mythically.

mythify (mi·þifəi), *v. rare.* [f. MYTHIF(ICATION: see -IFY.] To construct a myth or myths.
1906 *Critic* Feb. 161/1 The truth is that no distinguished actor in modern history has been so recklessly mythified as the great diplomatist [*sc.* Talleyrand]. **1951** AUDEN *Nones* (1952) 50 We have time To misrepresent, excuse, deny, Mythify, use this event While, under a hotel bed, in prison, Down wrong turnings, its meaning Waits for our lives.

mythistory. (Later example.)
1972 *Times* 8 June 16/4 The reason for Eton's interest in Jane [Shore] is that, in the barnacle-encrustation of legend and mythistory that has grown up around her in the past 500 years, she is said to have used her influence with Edward to save Eton from destruction.

mythless (mi·þlės), *a.* [f. MYTH *sb.* + -LESS.] Without a myth.
1924 C. K. OGDEN tr. *Vaihinger's Philos. of 'As If'* 343 The myth..we have lost 'in the abstract character of our mythless existence'. **1936** *Times Lit. Suppl.* 14 Mar. 218/2 In Conrad he finds another writer with an heroic conception of life, but one that is austere, mythless, without veneration for the deep forces of Nature.

mytho-. Add: **my·thomane** = *mythomaniac* in Dict. and Suppl.; also *attrib.*; **mythoma·nia**, the condition or tendencies of a mythomaniac; **mythomaniac,** (*b*) one who has an abnormal or pathological tendency to lie or exaggerate; also as *adj.*; **mytho·nomy** (see quots.); **mythopœ·ia** = MYTHOPŒISM; **my:tho-theo·logy,** theology based on myth.
1954 *Encounter* Dec. 77/2 [Socialism is to be] treated as the way to that abolition of 'injustice' whose necessary existence in any human society these mythomanes find intolerable. **1959** *Ibid.* June 79/1 The mythomanes seized the new means of communication. **1962** *Punch* 26 Sept. 464/3 A mythomane tart with a line in imaginary family grandeur. **1975** *Times* 2 May 11/8 *Paper Tiger*..is a modest..entertainment, with David Niven as a pathological mythomane who..finds himself obliged to live up to his fantasies. **1909** *Cent. Dict.* Suppl., Mythomania. **1955** *Antiquity* XXIX. 197 Deception for the mere fun of deceiving—a sort of mythomania. **1958** *New Statesman* 6 Sept. 311/1 As for the formal principle on which the New Critics plumed themselves, it cannot be said that they ever applied it with any consistency or finesse; and lately it has been giving way to mythomania and symbol-hunting. **1973** *Times Lit. Suppl.* 30 Nov. 1476/1 It proves to have no resemblance to the sculpture, and the assertion is seen as a manifestation of mythomania. **1922** W. S. MAUGHAM *Writer's Notebk.* (1949) 186 She is not only a liar, she is a mythomaniac who will invent malicious stories that have no foundation in fact. **1961** *Times* 15 June 17/3 Mary ends up sadder, if less mythomaniac, than she began. **1973** C. MCCARRY *Miernik Dossier* (1974) 90, I regarded Miernik as a mythomaniac... I did not believe in the existence of the sister. **1882** *Amer. Naturalist* Oct. 829 Mythography... Mythology... Mythonomy. **1890** *Cent. Dict., Mythonomy,* the deductive and predictive stage of mythology. **1939** C. S. LEWIS *Lett.* (1966) 163 We now need a new word for 'the science of the nature of myths'... Would 'mythonomy' do? **1959** H. BLOOM *Shelley's Mythmaking* i. 8, I do not claim that *all* of Shelley's major and mature poems are mythopoeic, especially in the precise and narrow sense of mythopoeia that I insist upon here. **1970** *Listener* 30 July 154/2 Science is not immune to mythopoeia. **1927** J. S. HUXLEY *Relig. without Revelation* vi. 191 They possess a vague and elastic mytho-theology. **1932** R. KNOX *Broadcast Minds* iv. 72 They had ancestors..to whom that mytho-theology was real.

mythogenic (miþodʒe·nik), *a.* [f. MYTHO- + *-GENIC.] Myth-forming; of or pertaining to the creation of myths.
1964 *Economist* 8 Feb. 511/2 The mythogenic dragons of the golden age of steam. **1970** *Time* 5 Oct. 73 Religion has cut itself off from its 'principal sources of nourishment—the soul, the symbolic and mythogenic process, the psychic energy resources'.

mythographic (miþogræ·fik), *a.* [f. MYTHOGRAPHY + -IC.] Of or pertaining to the representation of mythical subjects in art, literature, etc. So **mythogra·phical** *a.*
1939 TILLYARD & LEWIS *Personal Heresy* v. 120 Between Aristotle and the modern mythographical school of Miss Maud Bodkin, Professor Wilson Knight, and Professor D. G. Jame, we find almost nothing. **1955** R. GRAVES *Crowning Privilege* iii. 42 The death of Marvan's pig is a mythographic way of recording the murder of inspired poetry by a new-fangled academicism. **1965** *Listener* 2 Dec. 902/1 A mythographic fantasy *The Complaint of Nature,* diffuse and heady with virtuoso language. **1968** J. A. W. BENNETT *Chaucer's Book of Fame* i. 17 The attraction of this mythographical tradition for Chaucer results in a Venus very different from the divinity he had found described in the *Roman de la Rose.*

mythologem (miþǫlōᵘ·dʒěm). Also **mutholo-gema.** [ad. Gr. μυθολόγημα.] A mythical story; a fundamental theme or motif of myth.
1884 *Jrnl. Hellenic Stud.* V. 236 The apotheosis of Homer and his marriage with Hebè..do not properly belong to the Homeric era, but to the *mutholegema* of later times. **1939** L. BLOOMFIELD in C. F. Hockett *Bloomfield Anthol.* (1970) 424 Any normal human being could analyze this mythologem of 'metrical convenience'. **1961** *Times Lit. Suppl.* 27 Jan. 56/3 Professor Kerényi.. repeatedly inquired of Mann his views on particular images and mythologems. **1973** G. POCOCK *Corneille & Racine* 305 This passion is not merely sexual, but is linked more generally with what, to use a modern mythologem, we would call the unconscious.

mythology. Add: **3.** (Further *transf.* examples.)
1949 'G. ORWELL' *Nineteen Eighty-Four* II. 155 She only questioned the teachings of the Party when they in some way touched upon her own life. Often she was ready to accept the official mythology. **1961** *Listener* 24 Aug. 281/2 This is an antidote to militarism which does not exist in western 'mythology'. **1965** M. SCHOFIELD *Sexual Behaviour of Young People* I. i. 9 The frequent articles in the press and the radio and TV programmes tend to create a teenage mythology. **1975** *Times* 22 Sept. 13/2 Not all private [pension] schemes were in fact as generous as popular mythology suggested.

mythopoetic, *a.* Add: (Further examples.) So **mythopoe·tical** *a.*
1900 R. FRY in *Monthly Rev.* Dec. 152 In such periods the magnifying mythopoetical effect, which for us comes only with time, takes place at once, and swells their contemporaries to heroic proportions. **1959** B. BERNARDI *Mugwe, a Failing Prophet* iii. 52 It constitutes a typical instance of mythopoetical amalgamation. **1965** *Philos. Rev.* LXXIV. 548 Wheelwright is engaged not in metaphysical but in mythopoetic investigation. **1970** J. O. LOVE (*title*) Worlds in consciousness: mythopoetic thought in the novels of Virginia Woolf. **1972** *Times Lit. Suppl.* 7 Apr. 381/2 This mythopoetic quality.

mythos. (Later examples.)
1946 'G. ORWELL' in *Polemic* Jan. 6 The poisonous effect of the Russian *mythos* on English intellectual life. **1957** N. FRYE *Anatomy of Criticism* 52 *Mythoi* or plot-formulas. **1974** *Sat. Rev. World* (U.S.) 2 Nov. 30/2 The same mythos of violence that was indigenous to..the American West.

Mytilenæan, Mytilenean, Mytilenian (mitilī·niăn, mitilenī·ăn), *sb.* and *a.* [f. L. *Mytilenæus,* Gr. Μυτιληναῖος Mytilenæan.] **A.** *sb.* A native or inhabitant of Mytilene, the ancient city and modern capital of the Aegean island of Lesbos. **B.** *adj.* Of or pertaining to Mytilene or its inhabitants.
The form Μιτυληναῖος (L. *Mitylenæus*) also is attested by ancient sources, and is sometimes followed by modern writers in the form *Mitylen(a)ean.* The name of the modern city is frequently transliterated *Mitilini.*
1550 T. NICOLLS tr. *Thucydides' Hystory* III. iii. fol. lxxii, The sayde Mytilenians. **1601** HOLLAND tr. *Pliny's Nat. Hist.* v. xxx. 110 Acheleum..founded first by the Mityleneans. **1790** W. MITFORD *Hist. Greece* II. xv. 227 The principal Mitylenæans had sent offers to the Lacedæmonian administration to renounce the Athenian. *Ibid.* 228 The whole Mitylenæan people would go in procession out of the city. **1900** J. B. BURY *Hist. Greece* x. 413 The Mytilenaeans received secret intelligence and postponed the feast. **1911** *Encycl. Brit.* XIX. 887/1 This base coinage ..ceases about 450 B.C., when the Mytilenaean silver begins. *Ibid.* XXI. 73/2 An assembly was held and under the invective of Cleon it was decided to kill all male Mytileneans of military age. **1945** G. B. GRUNDY *Fifty-Five Years at Oxford* xiv. 221 He could not have supposed that any reader of his history who read the Mytilenian Debate or the Melian Dialogue would regard the Funeral Oration as being a picture of a political..life..at Athens. **1965** T. T. B. RYDER *Koine Eirene* iv. 77 The Athenian people voted a decree of thanks to the Mytileneans for their services in the war against the Spartans. **1968** V. EHRENBERG *From Solon to Socrates* viii. 359 In the Mytilenean debate..Cleon attacks rhetoric. **1972** R. MEIGGS *Athenian Empire* iii. 47 We may prefer the different motivation he attributes to the Mytilenaeans. *Ibid.* xvii. 312 A rich Mytilenaean left two daughters. **1974** *Guardian* 11 Nov. 4/6 Life is rough for the Mytilenians at present.

myxamœba (miksămī·bă). Pl. **-æ.** [f. MYXO- + AMŒBA.] In a slime mould of the division Myxomycota, a cell lacking flagella but capable of amœboid movement; = *myxo-amœba* (s.v. MYXO-). So **myxamœ·boid** *a.*
1887 H. E. F. GARNSEY tr. *A. de Bary's Compar. Morphol. & Biol. Fungi* viii. 423 Swarm-cells with purely amoeboid motion have been unnecessarily distinguished by the name of myxamoebae. **1888** [in Dict. s.v. MYXO-]. **1927** GWYNNE-VAUGHAN & BARNES *Structure & Development of Fungi* 45 In early stages of development they [*sc.* Myxomycetes] appear as small, naked uninucleate amoebae, the myxamoebae. *Ibid.,* Eventually multiplication ceases, the zoospores resume the myxamoeboid form and fuse in pairs. **1947** F. A. & F. T. WOLF *Fungi* I. iv. 40 In moist weather the spore walls open to emit swarm cells (myxamoebae), which ingest bacteria and fungus spores, assimilate them, and grow to become a large, multinucleate, naked mass of protoplasm (plasmodium). **1968** H. HARRIS *Nucleus & Cytoplasm* vi. 118 The experiments..demonstrate the failure of high concentrations of actinomycin D to inhibit decisive events in the differentiation of colonial myxamoebae. **1971** P. H. B. TALBOT *Princ. Fungal Taxonomy* viii. 100 A myxamoeba may put out flagella and become a swarmer, or a swarmer may retract its flagella and become a myxamoeba.

myxo (mi·kso). Abbrev. of *MYXOMATOSIS.
1953 S. J. BAKER *Australia Speaks* 105 Another popular Australian speech habit is to truncate a word and add the suffix *o.* Among words..which fall into this category ..are..*myxo,* the disease myxomatosis, used to kill off rabbits; [etc.]. **1961** PARTRIDGE *Dict. Slang* Suppl. 1193/2 Myxo. Myxomatosis: Australian: since ca. 1945... But, since ca. 1950, also current in Great Britain. **1967** J. MORRISON in *Coast to Coast 1965–6* 135 The myxo'll look after the rabbits. **1970** M. TARMEY *Skinman* i. 22 They reckon myxo'll spread quite a bit this summer.

myxobacterium (miksŏbæktīə·riŏm). Also **myxobacter.** [ad. mod.L. *Myxobacter* (R. Thaxter 1892, in *Bot. Gaz.* XVII. 403), f. MYXO- + BACTERIUM.] A slime bacterium of the order Myxobacterales, which includes predominantly saprophytic bacteria having a vegetative state in which the unicellular rods are embedded in slime to produce thin, flat colonies, and forming spores, often in distinct fruiting bodies. So **myxobacte·rial** *a.,* of or pertaining to an organism of this kind.
1932 D. E. JOHNSON in *Jrnl. Bacteriol.* XXIV. 340 Other cultures had the characteristics of the vegetative stage of Myxobacteria. **1946** *Nature* 23 Nov. 745/1 The lytic effect of certain myxobacteria upon the true bacteria (eubacteria) has been known for some years. **1949** H. W. FLOREY et al. *Antibiotics* I. i. 40 Three other bacteria.. were inhibitory to *Ustilago,* a non-sporing rod, a motile sporing rod, and a myxobacterium. **1957** R. S. BREED et al. *Bergey's Man. Determinative Bacteriol.* (ed. 7) 854 In the vegetative condition, myxobacters consist of unicellular rods which occur in two characteristic shapes. *Ibid.* 855 The myxobacterial colony, also sometimes designated as a swarm or pseudoplasmodium, consists characteristically of a flat, thin mass of vegetative cells which spreads rapidly. **1961** *New Scientist* 16 Mar. 669/1 The predators [in the soil] include also myxo-bacteria, giant rhizopods, acrasieae and others. **1973** R. G. KRUEGER et al. *Introd. Microbiol.* iii. 60/1 Myxobacteria grow as individual cells that are typically embedded in a mass of slime they produce during growth. *Ibid.* 60/2 In soil and in dung, myxobacteria are active in the degradation of complex organic materials.

myxococcus (miksŏkǫ·kǒs). [mod.L., f. MYXO- + COCCUS.] A myxobacterium of the genus so called. Also *attrib.* So **myxoco·ccal** *a.,* of or pertaining to an organism of this kind.
1892 R. THAXTER in *Bot. Gaz.* XVII. 396 In forms like Myxococcus, in which the rods are somewhat scattered, the first preparation for spore production..consists in the appearance of groups of rods moving with a circular tendency. [*Ibid.* 403 Myxococcus n. gen.– Rods slender, curved, swarming together after a vegetative period.] **1932** *Jrnl. Bacteriol.* XXIV. 337 There is some variation in the ability of Myxococcus cultures to fruit on the same types of media. **1946** *Nature* 23 Nov. 745/1 The growth of the myxococcus concerned..results in the production of a true non-enzymic antibiotic substance. *Ibid.,* An inoculum of myxococcal microcysts. **1973** R. G. KRUEGER et al. *Introd. Microbiol.* iii. 61/1 Representatives of the *Myxococcus* group behave in a fashion that requires response of vegetative cells to the presence and behavior of other vegetative cells of the same type.

myxomatosis (mi:ksŏmătōᵘ·sis). [f. *myxomat-* (taken as stem of MYXOMA) + -OSIS, as tr. G. *myxomkrankheit* (G. Sanarelli 1898, in *Centralbl. für Bakteriol.* XXIII. 871). A highly infectious virus disease of rabbits, originally detected in Brazil but now occurring elsewhere, characterized by fever, swelling of the

mucous membranes, and the presence of myxomata; the disease has been artificially introduced into several countries to reduce rabbit populations. Also *attrib.* and *transf.* So **myxo·matized** *ppl. a.*, infected with myxomatosis.

1927 *Proc. Soc. Exper. Biol. & Med.* XXIV. 436 The point of particular interest concerning the myxomatosis of rabbits..is the fact that both epithelial tissue and connective tissue is affected. **1938** *Nature* 16 Apr. 682/2 A field test is now in progress of the virus of myxomatosis, as an agent in reducing rabbit population. **1953** *Times* 20 Oct. 5/4 The Ministry of Agriculture and Fisheries announced yesterday that in the past week myxomatosis, a virus disease of rabbits, was discovered near Edenbridge, Kent. **1953** A. UPFIELD *Murder must Wait* v. 44 'Was the child raised on cow's milk?'..'No, of course not. It wouldn't do, what with cows feeding off the same grass as myxomatised rabbits and things.' **1955** *Sci. News Let.* 5 Feb. 88/3 Myxomatosis..is threatening to wipe out the European rabbit. **1955** *Sci. Amer.* May 32/1 The myxomatosis virus..was recently introduced in France by a doctor who wished to get rid of the rabbits on his estate, and ..the disease soon spread over most of Western Europe. **1958** *Times* 6 Jan. 5/6 Rabbit numbers are increasing in many parts of the country, although isolated outbreaks of myxomatosis have lately occurred in over 30 counties... It seems that myxomatosis is now in a weakened strain. **1966** [see *COLUMNARIS]. **1968** M. PYKE *Food & Society* v. 59 The farmers.., for their own ends, had introduced the disease, myxomatosis, to exterminate the rabbits, which previously kept the brush in check. **1972** R. ADAMS *Watership Down* ii. 8 He had coolly..stood firm during the terrible onslaught of the myxomatosis.

myxophycean (miksofəi·siăn), *a.* [f. mod.L. name of class *Myxophyceæ*, f. MYXO- + Gr. φυκ-ος seaweed + -eæ suffix designating the class (cf. -ACEÆ).] Belonging or pertaining to the Myxophyceæ or Cyanophyceæ, a class of unicellular or filamentous blue-green algae.

1939 G. W. PRESCOTT in F. R. Moulton *Probl. Lake Biol.* 74/1 The greatest pests [in water blooms] are Myxophycean species. **1957** *New Biol.* XXIII. 96 In many respects there is a great similarity between this Myxophycean poison [of *Microcystis aeruginosa*] and that of the Death Cap mushroom, *Amanita phalloides.* **1964** *Oceanogr. & Marine Biol.* II. 214 This internal environment affects the proportion of the Myxophycean endophytes [of *Codium bursa*].

myxovirus (mi·ksovəiərʊ̆s). *Biol.* [mod.L., f. MYXO- (see quot. 1954) + VIRUS.] Any of a group of related viruses that includes the influenza virus (see quot. 1966). (At first the term was used to include the paramyxoviruses, later regarded as a separate group.)

[**1954** *Nature* 3 Apr. 621/1 The group name *Myxovirus* for viruses related to influenza was intended to indicate that the viruses in question have a particular kind of affinity for certain mucins.] **1955** *Virology* I. 180 When tests are made with fowl red cells it has not been shown that the same receptors are involved as with other *Myxoviruses.* **1962** C. H. ANDREWES in *Adv. Virus Res.* IX. 285 The known myxoviruses are: 1. True influenzas. .. 2. Paramyxoviruses... The viruses of the second group differ from the 'true influenzas' in their larger, more variable size, in the absence of filamentous forms (except for NDV) and in normally producing hemolysins as well as hemagglutinins... 3. Viruses possibly related to myxoviruses—measles, distemper, rinderpest. **1966** J. E. PRIER *Basic Med. Virol.* x. 247/1 In effect then, a new definition of the myxovirus group has emerged that is oriented around these biophysical characteristics: (*a*) a size range of 80 to 300 mμ..; (*b*) possession of a coiled ribonucleoprotein inner helix surrounded by an envelope studded with projections; and (*c*) the presence of lipid as an essential constituent of the virus particle. **1968** H. HARRIS *Nucleus & Cytoplasm* v. 90 The virus used in this work was the 'Sendai' virus, a member of the para-influenza group of myxoviruses. **1974** *Sci. Amer.* Feb. 33/2 Myxoviruses (influenza viruses) and paramyxoviruses..have a set of genes that encodes the manufacture of several viral proteins.

myxy (mi·ksi). *Colloq.* shortening of *MYXO-MATOSIS. Also *attrib.* or as *adj.*, suffering from myxomatosis.

1961 R. JEFFRIES *Evidence of Accused* i. 15 Rabbits.. were slowly returning after the second scourge of myxy. **1962** —— *Exhibit No. Thirteen* x. 97 He'd paid a quid for a myxy rabbit which he'd dropped about the warren. **1973** *Daily Tel.* 22 Oct. 18 It is our custom to shoot any 'myxy' rabbits sitting out in the last stages of this horrible disease.

N

N. Add: **I. 1. b.** (See also *EN *sb.*)

c. (Later example.)

1899 J. G. MILLAIS *Breath fr. Veldt* 55 The birds alighting in the background are represented in their usual N-shaped formation.

4. (Further examples.) Also used in place of *bi-*, *di-*, *tri-*, etc., in words (e.g. n-*ary*).

1873 G. SALMON *Treat. Higher Plane Curves* (ed. 2) p. xi, Number of points which determine a *n*-ic. **1903** B. RUSSELL *Princ. Math.* xxxvii. 310 Even an *n*-dimensional series of such terms..is still denumerable. **1924** GALSWORTHY *White Monkey* ix. 193 For the *n*th time it inspired in him a certain liking and confidence. **1940** W. V. QUINE *Math. Logic* 42 The truth table for an *n*-ary mode of composition appears as in Table 3. *Ibid.* 225 A range of *n*-argument functionality..is itself an *n*-adic relation. **1940** W. DE LA MARE *Pleasures & Speculations* 223 Its children's children to the n-th generation. **1954** I. M. COPI *Symbolic Logic* ix. 306 A dyadic or triadic or *n*-adic relation. **1956** F. POHL *Alternating Currents* (1966) 85 Spaceships ran from point to point in n-dimensional hyperspace. **1963** *Dict. U.S. Mil. Terms* (U.S. Dept. Defense) 156 *Nth country*,..the next country of a series to acquire nuclear powers. **1964** E. BACH *Introd. Transformational Gram.* vii. 154 Relations..are accordingly named dyadic, triadic, (or, for *n* terms, *n*-adic) or binary, ternary, and so on. *Ibid.* 155 A relation is the set of ordered pairs (triples, *n*-tuples) for which it holds. **1965** PATTERSON & RUTHERFORD *Elem. Abstract Algebra* v. 156 A vector space, namely the set..of all ordered *n*-tuples $a = [\alpha_1, .., \alpha_n]$ of elements from a field *F*. **1972** H. B. ENDERTON *Mathematical Introd. Logic* i. 50 An *n*-ary connective symbol combines with *n* wffs to produce a new wff. **1974** *Observer* (Colour Suppl.) 1 Sept. 10/1 (Advt.), This is where the standby duty crews wait, in full flying clothing, ready for the off. N-number of aircrew will always be there—24 hours a day, 365 days a year.

b. In *Physics* and *Chem.* *n* represents the principal quantum number of an electronic orbit in an atom, which determines the energy of the orbit (to the first order) and can take the values 1, 2, 3, ... (corresponding to increasing energy). In molecular spectroscopy *n* was introduced to denote the vibrational quantum number of a diatomic molecule (now usu. replaced by *v*), and later (as *N*) the total angular momentum, apart from spin, of diatomic and polyatomic molecules (see also quot. 1962[1]).

1914 N. BOHR in *Phil. Mag.* XXVII. [507 According to Balmer, Rydberg, and Ritz the frequency of the lines in the line-spectrum of an element can be expressed by the formula $\nu = f_r(n_1) - f_s(n_2)$, where n_1 and n_2 are whole numbers and $f_1, f_2, \ldots$ a series of functions of *n*, which can be expressed by $f_r(n) = (K/n^2)\phi_r(n)$, where *K* is a universal constant and ϕ a function which for large values of *n* approaches the value unity.] *Ibid.* 508 We shall assume that this spectrum is emitted by a system possessing a series of stationary states in which, corresponding to the *n*th state, the energy, omitting the arbitrary constant, is given by $A_n = -hK/n^2$. *Ibid.* 509 For $n = 1$, corresponding to the normal state of the atom, we get [etc.]. **1920** *Sci. Abstr.* A. XXIII. 423 If the nuclei are related in a quasi-elastic manner to the equilibrium positions, then the energy values for a diatomic non-rotating molecule are the same as for a Planck oscillator, namely: $E = nh\omega$, where *n* denotes the quantum number for the atomic oscillation. **1922** A. D. UDDEN tr. *Bohr's Theory of Spectra* III. i. 67 This quantum number which will always be denoted by *n* will therefore be called the 'principal quantum number'. **1926** E. C. KEMBLE et al. in *Bull. Nat. Res. Council* No. 57. 5 Some discrepancies in minor details of notation will be found from chapter to chapter in this report. The following major items, however, have been followed consistently: ..Vibrational quantum number for diatomic molecule: *n*. **1951** D. BOHM *Quantum Theory* xv. 348 n = the principal quantum number..defined as one plus the total number of nodal surfaces in the wave function. **1953** *Jrnl. Optical Soc. Amer.* XLIII. 425/1 [Report of Sub-committee of the Joint Commission for Spectroscopy.] Notation for diatomic molecules... *N*. Total angular momentum of the electrons and nuclei, excluding spin... Replaces former *K*. **1962** P. J. & B. DURRANT *Introd. Adv. Inorg. Chem.* vii. 207 The angular momentum due to the rotation of the [diatomic] molecule about an axis at right angles to the internuclear axis is denoted by **N**. **1962** J. POTTER tr. *Messiah's Quantum Mech.* II. xxi. 964 Each quantum number *n* represents the number of vibrational quanta relative to a particular normal mode of vibration. **1966** G. HERZBERG *Molecular Spectra & Molecular Struct.* III. i. 73 For $^3\Sigma$ states each rotational level except the one with $N = 0$ is split into three component levels..corresponding to $J = N+1$, N, $N-1$, respectively. **1973** J. YARWOOD *Atomic & Nuclear Physics* vi. 188 The quantum mechanical treatment [of the one-electron atom] introduces the integral principal quantum number *n* which..decides the total energy of the system, the quantum number *l* which ..has any integral value between 0 and $(n-1)$, and the azimuthal magnetic quantum number m_l which is an integer having $(2l+1)$ values between $+l$ and $-l$.

6. Add: Soon after their alleged discovery it was concluded that such rays do not exist and Blondlot's work was in error. (Further examples.)

1906 *Nature* 1 Mar. 413/1 It would be interesting to know whether anyone has obtained success in repeating the latest experiment designed to show the objective reality of the *n*-rays. **1925** A. HUXLEY *Let.* 25 Jan. (1969) 241 You remember the unanimously favourable verdict in favour of N rays? **1941** W. SEABROOK *Doctor Wood: Mod. Wizard of Laboratory* xvii. 234 According to Blondlot, the rays were given off spontaneously by many metals. A piece of paper, very feebly illuminated, could be used as a detector, for, wonder of wonders, when the N rays fell upon the eye they increased its ability to see objects in a nearly dark room. **1973** *Nature* 12 Oct. 344/2 The protracted error immortalised in scores of publications can be due only to psychological (self-deception), not to chemical causes. The 'anomalous' water belongs to the category exemplified by the N rays of Blondlot.

† **7.** *Radiology.* A unit of neutron dosage (see quot. 1942). *Obs.*

1942 AEBERSOLD & LAWRENCE in *Ann. Rev. Physiol.* IV. 36 In this laboratory, a standard Victoreen *r*-meter with a 100r condenser-chamber is used. The unit of fast neutron exposure is arbitrarily taken as that amount which produces the same reading with this meter as a roentgen of x-ray. Thus an *n* of fast neutrons produces inside this 100r Victoreen thimble chamber the same amount of ionization as produced by an *r* of x-rays. **1948** E. PATERSON in R. Paterson *Treatment of Malignant Dis. by Radium & X-Rays* xxxiii. 593 The *n* unit has fulfilled a useful function, however, in demonstrating differences in effect between X- or gamma-radiation and neutrons when ratios of the dosage required to produce effects are compared.

II. 1. N, naira (formerly, £N = Nigerian pound); N, nuclear; N.A.A.C.P., National Association for the Advancement of Colored People (*U.S.*); N.A.A.S., National Agricultural Advisory Service; N.A.B., National Assistance Board; N.A.C.A., National Advisory Committee for Aeronautics (*U.S.*); NAD(P), nicotinamide-adenine dinucleotide (phosphate); N.B., New Brunswick; N.B.C., National Broadcasting Corporation (*U.S.*); N.B.G., no bloody good (cf. **N.G.*); N.C.B., National Coal Board; N.C.O., non-commissioned officer; N.C.R., no carbon required, the registered trade-name for paper chemically treated so that the pressure of writing or typing alone produces duplicate copies without the use of carbon paper between sheets; *n.d.*, also N.D., (examples); N.D.C., National Defence Contribution; N.D.P., National Democratic Party (*Canad.*); N.E.D., New English Dictionary; N.E.D.(C.), National Economic Development (Council); N.F., New Franc (nouveau franc); N.F.S., National Fire Service; N.F.T., National Film Theatre; N.G., n.g., no go, no good (the latter is the current use, cf. **N.B.G.*); N.H.I., National Health Insurance; N.H.S., National Health Service; NIR [f. the initials of Russ. *Nauchno-Issledovatel'skaya Rabota* scientific research work], a colour television system developed in Russia, similar to SECAM; N.I.R.A., National Industrial Recovery Act (*U.S.*); N.K.V.D. [Russ. *Naródnyĭ Komissariát Vnútrennikh Del*], Soviet Commissariat of Internal Affairs, replacing the *OGPU; N.L.F., National Liberation Front; NNI, noise and number index (see *NOISE *sb.* 3 d); N.O., Naval Officer; N.O.R.A.D., North American Air Defence; N.O.W., National Organization for Women (*U.S.*); n.p. (see quot. 1952); also, not paginated; N.P.D. [G. *Nationaldemokratische Partei Deutschlands*], National Democratic Party of Germany; N.P.L., National Physical Laboratory; N.P.V., Net Present Value; N.R.A., National Recovery Administration (*U.S.*); N.R.D.C., National Research Development Corporation; N.S.P.C.A., National Society for the Prevention of Cruelty to Animals; N.S.P.C.C., National Society for the Prevention of Cruelty to Children; N.S.W., New South Wales (*Austral.*); N.T., Northern Territory (*Austral.*); N.T.S.C., National Television System Committee (*U.S.*); N.U.M., National Union of Mineworkers; N.U.R., National Union of Railwaymen; N.U.S., National Union of Students; N.U.T., National Union of Teachers; N.Y.S.E., New York Stock Exchange. See also *N.A.A.F.I., *N.A.L.G.O., *N.A.S.A., *N.A.T.O., *N.A.T.S.O.P.A., *N.E.P., *NIBMAR, *N.I.C., *N-P-N (as main entries).

1960 *Brit. Exports & Exchange Restrictions* (Swiss Bank Corporation) May 108, 1 Nigerian Pound = 20 Shillings. 1£N = 1£stg. **1973** *Times* 1 Oct. (Nigeria Suppl.) p. xi/3 Each member would be paid N120 a month. **1958** *Oxford Mail* 19 July 1/2 Beirut battle group is part of N-weapon division... U.S. paratroopers..equipped with tactical nuclear weapons. **1958** *Observer* 2 Nov. 6/1 Plenty of Aldermaston badges, with their semaphore symbol of ND—nuclear disarmament. **1910** *Crisis* Nov. 12 (*heading*) The N.A.A.C.P. **1974** *Black Panther* 16 Mar. 4/4 The NAACP filed its first suit attacking segregation and discrimination in education on March 15, 1933, against the University of North Carolina. **1948** *Sci. News* VI. 48 The N.A.A.S., which is the only body giving advice on the whole of agriculture. **1971** *Arable Farmer* Feb. 70/1 A nationwide series recently completed by NAAS, of 77 experiments testing nitrogen, phosphate and potash rates for spring barley. **1953** B. ABEL-SMITH *Reform of Social Security* 27 Malingering is very hard to detect, as the N.A.B. is constantly aware. *Ibid.*, We might keep our whole system on a flat rate basis but take the N.A.B. level as representing the community's present definition of subsistence. **1969** *Listener* 12 June 834/3 In Northborough.. mothers were not allowed to collect the father's weekly contribution..through the NAB. **1922** *Aviation* 13 Nov. 665/1 (*heading*) N.A.C.A. For National Air Policy. **1970** N. ARMSTRONG et al. *First on Moon* i. 17 Vaguely coordinated by something called NACA—the National Advisory Committee for Aeronautics. **1961** *Biochem. Jrnl.* LXXX. 322/1 NAD formation almost certainly involves nucleophilic attack on the α-phosphorus of ATP. **1964** W. G. SMITH *Allergy & Tissue Metabolism* viii. 85 The resulting α-β-unsaturated acid is reduced to its saturated counterpart by an enzyme which requires the reduced form of NADP. **1970** R. W. MCGILVERY *Biochemistry* xvi. 319 In general, NADP is used as an electron carrier for reductive syntheses, such as the formation of fatty acids.., whereas NAD is used more in the processes of energy production. *a* **1912** W. T. ROGERS *Dict. Abbrev.* (1913) 133/1 *N.B.*..New Brunswick. **1929** F. W. WALLACE *Rec. Canad. Shipping* 2 *Abyssinia*, ship, 833 tons. Built 1868, St. John, N.B. **1973** *Fisheries Fact Sheet* (Environment Canada Fisheries & Marine Service) No. 1. 1 (*caption*) Purse seining in Baie des Chaleurs, N.B. **1950** G. MARX *Let.* 7 Nov. in *Groucho Lett.* (1967) 75, I heard you on the NBC radio show. **1969** *Listener* 13 Nov. 667/1 The Duke of Edinburgh 'met the press' recently on America's NBC network. **1903** R. BEDFORD *True Eyes* xxxiv. 195 So see here—this place is N.B.G., Billy, me man. Let's do what I say—sell everythin' an' clear. **1929** C. MACKENZIE *Three Couriers* II. v. 180 Crowder messing about with a typewriter? O.K. Crowder outside an office? N.B.G. **1956** A. WILSON *Anglo-Saxon Attitudes* II. iii. 369 Those Barkers were n.b.g.: I saw quite a lot of their dishonesty at Melpham. **1973** G. MITCHELL *Murder of Busy Lizzie* iii. 42 Bang goes our reason for coming here... She said it was N.B.G. and that seems to be just about right. **1948** *Coal* Dec. 12/2 There are many complaints and criticisms of the N.C.B. It would be surprising if there were not. **1955** *Times* 3 Aug. 11/4 An official of the N.C.B. opencast executive said that the prospecting had shown the site to contain about 750,000 tons of good quality coal. **1963** *Times* 7 Feb. 13/4 It is essential not to impair the work at the N.C.B. which has made it possible to raise productivity four times above the national average. **1803–10** *Orderly Bks. of Manx Fencibles* in *Yn Lioar Manninagh* (1890) I. 152 Any party, consisting of 6 men or upwards, must have a N.C.O...appointed to go with them. **1883** *Army Regulations* II. 102 Report on conviction of N.C.O. by civil power. **1915** *Cornhill Mag.* Mar. 388 Had a chat with my N.C.O.s. **1955** *Times* 11 May 6/7 Corporal J. R. Saunders, who receives the George Medal, was the n.c.o. in charge of fire fighting at the storage unit. **1973** K. GILES *File on Death* i. 5 Old top secrets..guarded by superannuated N.C.O.s. **1954** in *Official Gaz.* (U.S. Patent Off.) (1955) 12 July 104/1 NCR no carbon required paper. **1956** *Brit. Printer* Mar. 42/1 Since its appearance on the US market some 18 months ago, NCR paper..is now being manufactured in this country. The initials NCR represent not only the name of the manufacturers—the National Cash Register Co Ltd—but the particular characteristics of the paper (No Carbon Required). **1967** C. WILSON in Wills & Yearsley *Handbk. Management Technol.* 46 Copies of print-outs are obtained with carbon paper or NCR paper. The latter ('no carbon required') has a chemically coated surface activated by percussion. **1834** *William Pickering's Catal. Manuscripts & Bks.* 19 Angler's Guide... Lond. n.d. **1879** *Blackwell's Catal.* No. 1. 10 Chappell's Old English Ditties..N.D. **1917** T. J. WISE *Bibliogr. Brontë Family* VI. 225 Museum of Brontë Relics..A Descriptive Catalogue. (N.D., but *circa* 1890). **1952** J. CARTER *ABC for Book-Collectors* 124 No date (n.d.). This term, unqualified, means that research has failed (or has not attempted) to establish even an approximate date for the book described. **1959** *N. & Q.* CCIV. 292/1 *A Chronicle History of Portsmouth* by Henry Slight (3d. edit., n.p., n.d.). **1937** *Times* 1 June 17/5 The present N.D.C. scheme..imposes a high rate of tax on excess profits only. **1939** *Times* 4 Jan. 17/2 The figures in each case are struck after provisions for income-tax and N.D.C. **1961** *Edmonton* (Alta.) *Jrnl.* 4 Aug. 17/3 The NDP organizers produced mimeographed songsheets complete with Tommy Douglas lyrics. **1972** *Maclean's Mag.* Mar. 12/2 The NDP..refused to have the issue even raised for discussion. **1904** A. S. PALMER in R. C. Trench *On Study of Words* (rev. ed.) 175 Dr. Murray decides in favour of this explanation, of unknown authorship, and so spurious, uncanonical,—*N.E.D.* **1961** *Essays & Studies* XIV. 35 Of the many accounts of the origin and progress of the dictionary, it may suffice to mention here the following: the *Preface* to Vol. I of *N.E.D.*, [etc.]. **1973** *Jrnl. Soc. Bibliogr. Nat. Hist.* VI. 229 The work is known familiarly as NED, OED, or even 'Murray'. **1975** *N. & Q. for Som. & Dorset* Sept. 127 The single reference cited under lug-fall in the *N.E.D.*..takes the definition a little further. **1962** *Daily Tel.* 9 Feb. 12/2 The NEDC will not be a col-

lection of amateurs or mere theorists. *Ibid.* 7 Mar. 12/2 The collective wisdom of 'NED'. **1964** M. Argyle *Psychol. & Social Probl.* xvi. 199 A new government advisory department, like N.E.D.C. or N.I.C. **1960** *British Exports & Exchange Restrictions* (Swiss Bank Corporation) May 55 Only spare parts from O.E.E.C. countries may be obtained through import certificates when the value is less than NF. 5,000. **1971** A. Diment *Think Inc.* ii. 28, I ..added three $100 bills and two NF 1000 notes to the wad. **1942** *Daily Mirror* 25 Feb. 4/5 It will be necessary to enrol men under 41 for whole-time duties in the National Fire Service... Men over 25 when they registered will still be given an opportunity to express preference for the NFS. **1947** *Science News* IV. 47 Four days after she disappeared a fire broke out in the cellar of the Baptist Church and a passing police officer called the N.F.S. **1965** *New Statesman* 19 Mar. 462/3 Ozu..made some 54 films, of which only nine have ever been seen in London and those only by assiduous patrons of the NFT. **1969** *Listener* 24 July 125/1 Members of the NFT poured into their cinema to hear a discussion between Satyajit Ray and Lindsay Anderson. **1838** *Morning Post* (Boston) 25 June 2/3 They then went together to the plaintiff's to try to settle, but it was n.g. **1840** *Daily Pennant* (St. Louis) 20 June (Th.), The bells, boys, and engines tried to get up a fire last night, but it was N.G. **1922** Joyce *Ulysses* 427 Fish and taters. N.g. **1972** 'L. Egan' *Paper Chase* (1973) x. 160 So that little ride on the merry-go-round was n.g. **1934** Foster & Taylor *National Health Insurance* xiv. 191 Enter on debit side of Cash Book and credit side of N.H.I. Fund Current Account. **1958** *Spectator* 20 June 806/1 A doctor..wrote on what he called unjustified claims by his patients upon the N.H.I. **1948** *Lancet* 20 Nov. 823/3 Other doctors do not discriminate between private and N.H.S. patients. *Ibid.* 4 Dec. 904/1 The pharmacist's principal trouble just now is over delay in payment of his accounts under the N.H.S. **1968** *Listener* 11 July 58/3 One of the hospital committee shown arguing in the NHS film whether or not it should refund the cost of a 7s 11d vest. **1975** *Guardian* 5 Nov. 14/5 There will be the equivalent of 2,500 to 3,000 more beds available for NHS use. **1966** *Economist* 12 Feb. 628 This Russian-designed system offers the best prospect of a single acceptable colour television system for the whole of Europe... The Russians call the Soviet system NIR. **1969** Carnt & Townsend *Colour Television* II. vii. 237 In April, 1963, the Non-linear NIR system had already been anticipated by B. W. B. Pethers of the BBC. This was some two years before the NIR system came to light, but at that time it was felt that NIR did not have any significant advantages over the other systems. **1933** *Sun* (Baltimore) 23 Aug. 1/3 'Threats, intimidation, compulsion, boycotts, blacklists and suppression of opinion,' he declared, 'were never contemplated by the N.I.R.A. and, therefore, have no rightful place in the picture.' *Ibid.* 9 Sept. 1/2 The power of propaganda and the press has had few better illustrations than the way in which the so-called 'Nira' is obscuring the other great Administration activities in Washington and in the country. **1942** V. Conolly *Soviet Asia* (Oxf. Pamphs. on World Affairs) 13 The N.K.V.D. (Commissariat of Internal Affairs, former O.G.P.U.). **1945** Koestler *Yogi & Commissar* iii. iii. 208 The deportees were called for..by the so-called 'Executive Troikas' of the N.K.V.D. **1973** T. Allbeury *Choice of Enemies* vi. 21 He was wearing an NKVD uniform. **1965** *New Society* 22 Apr. 259 Nguyen Huu Tho was made president of the NLF. **1971** *Ink* 12 June 8/3 The delegates ..would have been Thieu/Ky (S. Vietnam), Tho (NLF), Ho Chi Minh (N. Vietnam). **1972** H. Evans *Editing & Design: Newsman's English* vii. 147 When the report says the NLF, the deskman should write in 'the National Liberation Front, political arm of the Vietcong...' This does not offend the reader who knows and it helps the rest, which is most of us. There was at one time, anyway, another NLF—in Aden—and at another an FLN, in Algeria and France. **1963** NNI [see *noise *sb.* 3 d]. **1969** *Guardian* 5 Mar. 9/2 Within such an area noise levels would be 40 NNI. **1970** R. D. Ford *Introd. to Acoustics* vii. 144 An external NNI of 55 has been taken as the recommended limit in the vicinity of London Airport and householders exposed to more noise have been offered a special grant for soundproofing their homes. **1914** 'Bartimeus' *Naval Occasions* xvii. 144 That girl to-night—Molly—I suppose she has refused half a dozen N.O.'s. **1916** G. Franklin *Naval Digression* i. xv. 136 Which brings to light another peculiarity of the average N.O.—how he can adopt a friendly 'hail-fellow-well-met' attitude to all and sundry and lose nothing in respect by it, even should they be ex-service men. **1958** M. Dickens *Man Overboard* i. 14 There'll be a lot of sharks about waiting for the innocent N.O. with his touching faith in human nature. **1959** *Roundel* June 3/1 Creation of the North American Air Defence Command by the governments of Canada and the United States was recognition..that air defence of the continent..is a single, common problem. NORAD is a truly integrated, international Command—responsible to both the U.S. Joint Chiefs of Staff and the Canadian Chiefs of Staff Committee. **1970** *Toronto Daily Star* 24 Sept. 31/3 In NORAD we permitted American nuclear bombers to make provocative flights over Canadian territory. **1966** *N.Y. Times* 22 Nov. 44/1 NOW..was formed three weeks ago in Washington to press for 'true equality for all women in America'. **1970** G. Greer *Female Eunuch* 296 When NOW was formed it was read into the Congressional record. **1973** *Times* 2 June 8/3 Betty Friedan..'founding mother' of NOW in 1966. **1882** Halkett & Laing *Dict. Anon. & Pseudon. Eng. Lit.* I. 122/1 Answer to the Declaration published by the Archbishop of Canterbury... n.p., n.d. Octavo. Pp. 12. *a* **1912** W. T. Rogers *Dict. Abbrev.* (1913) 137/1 *n.p.*, no place (no printer's name). **1952** J. Carter *ABC for Book-Collectors* 124 No place, no printer, no publisher (indiscriminately or collectively shortened to n.p.). **1966** *Dawson's of Pall Mall Catal. No.* 162. 12 Cicero..Laelius de amicitia. (n.p., n.d.) (Cologne..about 1467). **1969** N. B. Eales *Cole Library of Early Med. & Zool.* 330 The Complete Dictionary of Arts and Sciences... 2 vols. Fr., [4], vi, n.p. Pls. 1–11, 14–35, 40–42. **1966** *Guardian* 14 Mar. 21/8 The NPD..won up to 10 per cent in some Bavarian towns. **1969** S. Hyland *Top Bloody Secret* ii. 125 The two people who..organised the first conference of the Neo-Nazi party, NPD. *a* **1912** W. T. Rogers *Dict. Abbrev.* (1913) 137/1 *N.P.L.*, National Physical Laboratory (Bushey, by Teddington). **1920** *Flight* XII. 1131/2 With regard to the staffs at the N.P.L. and at the R.A.E., he said he hoped that provision would be made to maintain these on an adequate scale. **1959** *Ann. Reg. 1958* 388 There was a scientific symposium at the National Physical Laboratory (N.P.L.), Teddington. **1964** *Economist* 26 Sept. 1195/1 Then DCF is no more use than NPV. **1969** D. C. Hague *Managerial Econ.* ii. vi. 128 If we..add together the sums of money in Column C, including the minus £1,000 for Year 0, we are left with a net amount of £10. This is known as the net present value (NPV) of the project. **1933** *N.Y. Times* 3 Aug. 16/4 The most vital issue in the whole National Recovery Program is, of course, the question whether we shall end up speaking of it as the NRA or the N.R.A. People are saying NIRA and NRA but there is no denying the fact that there is a self-conscious air about it. **1933** G. Ade *Let.* 25 Aug. (1973) 170 The country editor..need not ignore the N.R.A. or the Farm Relief Board or any of the agencies intended to bring us back to happier times. **1962** *Amer. Speech* XXXVII. 48 Many such letter groups have entered the American language as items of common exchange: *O.K...N.R.A.* **1954** F. A. Buttress *World List Abbrev.* 186 NRDC, National Research Development Corporation, 1 Tilney Street, London, W.1. **1959** *Engineering* 6 Feb. 182/3 If proof were required that NRDC's activities are useful and beneficial, it is provided by their profitability. **1967** *Jane's Surface Skimmer Systems 1967–68* 30/1 The Company has been granted an NRDC licence. *a* **1912** W. T. Rogers *Dict. Abbrev.* (1913) 137/2 *N.S.P.C.A.*, National Society for the Prevention of Cruelty to Animals. **1895** *Civil Rights for Children* (N.S.P.C.C.) (inside back cover), Mary P. Bolton Asst.-Sec., N.S.P.C.C. **1963** *Social Work* Oct. 20/2 Some will emphasise the word 'neglect' and think in terms of an extended N.S.P.C.C. inspectorate. [**1852** T. Cass *Let.* 1 May in J. Deans *Pioneers of Canterbury* (1937) x. 221, I take the opportunity of sending you a few lines by way of N. S. Wales, a cattle vessel leaving in a day or two.] **1889** H. C. Russell (*title*) The source of the underground water in the western districts... (Read before the Royal Society of N.S.W., August 7, 1889.) **1909** B. Stevens *Golden Treasury of Austral. Verse* 336 *Gidya*, a Queensland and N. S. W. aboriginal word for a tree of the acacia species. **1971** *Sunday Australian* 8 Aug. 3/1 Justice ministers in Victoria and NSW, said yesterday they were considering..changes. *a* **1912** W. T. Rogers *Dict. Abbrev.* (1913) 138/1 *N.T.*,..Northern Territory, -ies (Australia). **1930** A. G. Price *Hist. & Problems of Northern Territory* 64 For labour in the N.T., see reports of Gilruth..and Urquhart. **1969** *Northern Territory News* (Darwin) 11 July 3/3 The NT Police Commissioner..wants breath-analyser tests introduced in the Territory. **1957** *B.B.C. Handbook* 136 The N.T.S.C. system now in use for a public service in the United States of America. **1966** *Economist* 12 Feb. 628/2 The Americans manage to transmit colour from coast to coast by NTSC. **1948** *Ann. Reg. 1947* i. v. 90 The negotiations with the N.U.M. on the method of working overtime ..languished. **1914** *Railway Mag.* Nov. 401/1 It was.. agreed that all existing contracts and conditions of service shall remain in operation,..(signed) for General Managers' Committee:—..for N.U.R.:—..for A.S.L.E.&F.:—. **1955** *Times* 2 May 12/7 The union have won the right to put their case without having representatives of the N.U.R. present. **1975** *Guardian* 17 June 26/8 The NUR executive threw the negotiating ball firmly back into Mr Wilson's court. **1924** *University* I. 21 F. G. Connor..who attended as the representative of the English N.U.S., described the constitution and development of the National Union of Students of England and Wales. **1973** J. H. M. Scott *Dons & Students* xii. 145 The vice-chancellors turned it down, effectively siding with the nus against it. **1889** *Schoolmaster* 4 May 634/1 In place of the familiar initials, N.U.E.T. we have the shorter, and let us hope the improved, form of N.U.T... The objects of the N.U.E.T. remain the objects of the N.U.T. **1973** L. Holcombe *Victorian Ladies at Work* iii. 39 The National Union of Teachers..was organized in 1870... In 1911 the N.U.T. elected its first woman president. **1941** *Exchange* Feb. 3/1 'Secondary distribution!' That's a phrase to make the heart of any floor member of the New York Stock Exchange skip a beat. It means—in most cases, where NYSE stocks are being distributed—that just so much business is not passing through the Exchange. **1964** *Financial Times* 25 Feb. 3/7 A special committee set up by the N.Y.S.E. **1973** *N.Y. Law Jrnl.* 4 Sept. 4/2 It might be possible to include all NYSE-listed securities.

b. N.W., north-west, esp. (usu. followed by a numeral) a London postal district.

1615 T. Roe *Jrnl.* 26 Mar. in *Embassy to Court of Gt. Mogul* (1899) I. 3 Wee..saw land N.W. for the Canarye 8 leauges off. **1857** J. A. Symonds *Let.* 1 Feb. (1967) I. 88 Sunday. Harrow *N.W...* You will wonder what N.W. means on the top of this page. It is in consequence of some Postal arrangements that those letters should be affixed to districts of London. **1899** W. J. Locke *White Dove* (1900) x. 151 Dr. Frodsham..had..[moved] from the house in Weymouth Street into the purer air of the N.W. district. **1965** *Listener* 27 May 792/1 Living with him was his beautiful companion, a Madame de Bargeton of N.W.3, something of a Madame Verdurin also. **1967** *Ibid.* 30 Nov. 733/2 Who could have littered the *Times* with byelines and signed columns and a woman's page so close to NW1's heart? **1971** A. Bennett in D. Nathan *Laughtermakers* iv. 93, I did a series on television with sketches about this area, N.W.1, of which I am a part, and so in a sense it was making fun of myself. But it pinpointed something and since then N.W.1 has been used as a catchphrase to indicate Sunday supplement trendiness which people now find rather suspect.

2. N.B. (later examples).

1861 G. H. Lewes *Jrnl.* 3–6 June in *Geo. Eliot's Lett.* (1954) III. 424 Reposed awhile and chatted (N.B. all the journey we have had fine talk with Trollope). **1965** I. Fleming *Man with Golden Gun* iii. 40 Distinguishing marks: a third nipple about two inches below his left breast. (N.B. in Voodoo and allied local cults this is considered a sign of invulnerability and great sexual prowess.)

3. a. N (also rarely *N*, *n*) (*Chem.*) = *normal *a.* and *sb.* A. 2 b (i).

1863 F. Sutton *Syst. Handbk. Volumetric Anal.* 165 Free iodine is..very readily estimated by solution in iodide of potassium, and titration with N/10 hyposulphite. **1906** *Amer. Chem. Jrnl.* XXXV. 511 A saturated solution of silver chloride..is only about 0·00001N. **1931** J. C. Ware *Analyt. Chem.* iv. 137 Test the solubility of a portion of the precipitate..with 2 cc. 6*n* HNO_3. **1970** M. D. Hawkins *Calculations in Volumetric & Gravimetric Anal.* ii. 35 The solution was titrated against 0·0908N potassium thiocyanate.

b. *n* (also rarely n) (*Chem.*) = *normal *a.* and *sb.* A. 2 b (ii).

1889 G. M'Gowan tr. *A. Bernthsen's Text-bk. Org. Chem.* i. 44 From petroleum have been separated..normal heptane, n-octane, n-nonane, and n-decane. **1938** L. F. Fieser in H. Gilman *Org. Chem.* I. ii. 53 The conversion of *n*-butylcyclopentane into *o*-ethyltoluene on dehydrogenation with palladium charcoal. **1971** N. L. Allinger et al. *Org. Chem.* iii. 28 One isomer, isobutane, has one carbon atom which is bound to three other carbons, and there is no such carbon atom in the other isomer, *n*-butane.

c. In *Physics N* is used to designate the series of X-ray emission lines of longer wavelength than the *M*-series obtained by exciting the atoms of any particular element (cf. *M 4* a); these arise from electron transitions to the atomic orbit of fourth-lowest energy, of principal quantum number 4, which is thus termed the *N-shell*, and electrons in this shell *N-electrons*.

1911 [see *M 4* a]. **1923** H. L. Brose tr. *Sommerfeld's Atomic Structure & Spectral Lines* viii. 505 Our relativistic formula of the fine-structure..furnishes us with a principle of sub-division for the multiplicity of M- and N-lines. *Ibid.* 507 Just as the M-shell belongs to the quantum-number 3, so does the N-shell to the quantum-number 4. **1948** Lapp & Andrews *Nuclear Radiation Physics* v. 74 In the heavier elements such as tungsten ($Z = 74$) the *N* shell is saturated with 32 electrons. **1967** G. L. Clark *Handbk. X-Rays* i. 7 At still longer wavelengths *M-* and *N*-series lines have been measured only for heavier elements. **1968** *Physical Rev.* CLXVI. 944/1 Radiationless transitions are favored in low-*Z* elements and always dominate in the *M*, *N*, and higher shells for the ordinary Auger effect. **1970** E. P. Bertin *Princ. & Pract. X-Ray Spectr. Anal.* i. 27 An electron having just enough energy to expel, say, an *LII* electron can also expel *LIII*, *M*, and *N* electrons, but not *LI* or *K* electrons.

d. N (*Physics*) = newton.

1951 *Symbols, Signs & Abbrev.* (R. Soc. Symbols Comm.) 14/2 Newton... N. **1973** Kleppner & Kolenkow *Introd. Mechanics* ii. 84 Since $g = 9{\cdot}8$ m/s^2, the weight of 1 kg mass is 9·8 N.

'n, 'n' (ən), colloq. shortening of And *conj.*

Esp. common in **rock 'n' roll*.

1858 O. W. Holmes in *Atlantic Monthly* Sept. 497/1 To beat the taown 'n' the keounty. **1906** E. Dyson *Fact'ry 'Ands* xvii. 233 Ther revolvin' arm was bent out, 'n' it got home a left lead 'n' er right cross. **1923** *Radio Times* 28 Sept. 23/2 Dance Programme..One-step, 'By 'n' Bye'. **1925** C. R. Cooper (*title*) Lions 'n' tigers. **1928** F. Hurst *President is Born* v. 67 God bless Mother 'n' Father. **1959** W. Golding *Free Fall* ii. 58 He was helmeted, assured, delicate at the rudder-bar and joystick in the fish-'n-chip smell of the engine oil. **1968** *Listener* 18 July 93/2 Tony Carruthers has turned the whole building into a prison to assist Charles Marowitz's production of a Canadian play about four boys having sex-'n-violence in a reformatory. **1971** *Black World* June 63/1 The President's tryin' his level best to bring more 'n more boys home all the time. **1973** J. Wainwright *Devil you Don't* 30 Dudley was mad.. but good 'n mad.

'n, colloq. reduced form of Than *conj.*

1867 J. T. Trowbridge *Darius Green* in *Oxf. Bk. Children's Verse* (1973) 262 The little chatterin', sassy wren, No bigger 'n my thumb. **1898** J. D. Brayshaw *Slum Silhouettes* 2 That on'y made Bill madder 'n ever. **1903** K. D. Wiggin *Rebecca* i. 8 We've only just started on it,..'it's more 'n two hours'. **1910** C. E. Mulford *Hopalong Cassidy* ix. 63 He hates Greasers worse 'n I do. **1973** 'J. Ashford' *Double Run* viii. 57 The duty would be more 'n Mr. Smith could pay if it's properly declared.

N.A.A.F.I. (næ·fi). Also **NAAFI, Naafi, Naffy.** The Navy, Army, and Air Force Institutes which run canteens, stores, etc., for service personnel; also, a canteen, restaurant, etc., run by this organization. Also *attrib.* Cf. *Naffy.

[**1921** *Times* 7 Jan. 7/3 The joint organization for the administration of canteens for the three Services, hitherto known as the Navy and Army Canteen Board, has been reconstituted with effect from January 1, 1921, under the title 'The Navy, Army, and Air Force Institutes'.] **1927** *Daily Express* 16 Mar. 9/2 Cheering workgirls surrounded the Prince of Wales when he visited the 'Naafi'..headquarters in Kennington yesterday. **1928** J. Fortescue *Canteens in Brit. Army* 73 The general policy of the N.A.A.F.I. is to afford facilities to its members of all three services to purchase commodities of high quality at prices competitive with those of 'multiple' shops. **1940** *War Weekly* 19 Jan. 409/3 N.A.A.F.I., or 'Naffy', as it is affectionately called by the troops. *Ibid.*, The 'Naffy' Institute is a comfortable, red-brick building. **1959** *Times* 17 Jan. 8/4 Common rooms sometimes suggest more the Naafi than the bookman's study. **1959** *Spectator* 23 Jan. 127/3 The NAAFI Is a sort of caafi Where soldiers are rude About the food. **1972** *Oxford Times* 4 Aug. 5 Mr Lewin leaves Oxford for Belfast on Monday to take up an appointment as manager of a NAAFI club in the city. **1973** *Times* 14 May 11/5 Kafka and Brasso make a great

double act with a NAAFI piano. **1974** R. Gentil *Trained to Intrude* ii. 20 At that time Dover.., apart from the pubs and the NAAFI, offered very little comfort to the serviceman.

naan, var. *nan³.

naartj(i)e, varr. *nartjie.

nab, *sb.*³ Restrict '*rare*' to sense 2 and add further examples of sense 1.

1967 *New Yorker* 27 May 32/3, I talk him into splitting the scene and we start hitchhiking back down Sunset, and just like that the Nabs stop us for bumming rides. **1971** J. Wainwright *Dig Grave* 78 All the nabs in the world were in the downstairs front.

nabam (nēⁱ·bæm). *Chem.* [f. *Na*, the chemical symbol for sodium + bisdithiocar*bam*ate (see quot. 1950).] A water-soluble powder used as a fungicide, usu. as a spray with zinc sulphate as a stabilizer; $(NaS{\cdot}CS{\cdot}NH{\cdot}CH_2\text{—})_2$.

1950 *Phytopathology* XL. 118 The Subcommittee on Fungicide Nomenclature of the American Phytopathological Society, cooperating with the Interdepartmental Committee on Pest Control, has selected common names for five commercially-available fungicidal chemicals which are useful in the control of various destructive plant diseases... *Nabam* for the fungicidal chemical, disodium ethylene bisdithiocarbamate. **1960** [see *ferbam]. **1967** L. H. Purdy in D. C. Torgeson *Fungicides* I. vii. 206 Nabam reacted with zinc sulfate was the first commercially used spray fungicide for in-the-row treatment control of cotton seedling diseases.

Nabatæan (næbătī·ăn), *sb.* and *a.* Also **Nabatean, Nabathæan, Nabathean.** [f. L. *Nabat(h)æ-us*, Gr. *Ναβαταῖ-ος*, *Ναβαθαῖ-ος* (cf. *Nebāṭu* the native name of the country) + -an.] **A.** *sb.* One of an ancient Arabian people; their language. **B.** *adj.* Of or pertaining to the Nabatæans.

1601 Holland tr. *Pliny's Nat. Hist.* I. xii. xx. 374 The Troglodyte Nabathæans: who onely of the ancient Nabathæans, there setled and remained. **1875** *Encycl. Brit.* III. 411/2 Two forms of Shemitic writing (the Palmyrenian.., and the Sinaitic or Nabathæan). **1884** *Ibid.* XVII. 160/1 *Nabatæans*, a famous people of ancient Arabia. **1897** F. Hommel in H. von Hilprecht *Recent Res. in Bible Lands* 146 Between the decline of the Nabatean Empire and the appearance of Muhammad. **1898** E. Clodd *Tom Tit Tot* vi. 65 Ibn Khaldun..describes how the Nabathean sorcerers of the Lower Euphrates made an image of the person whom they plotted to destroy. **1911** *Encycl. Brit.* XXIV. 626/1 The language of this country was Nabataean. **1920** *Public Opinion* 9 July 42/3 Little did the ancient..Nabataeans imagine that a people called Americans would one day wander among the ruins of their proud city. **1931** *Times Lit. Suppl.* 29 Oct. 832/2 His new work..is intended to summarize all that is known on the subject of the Nabateans. *Ibid.*, The sources of Nabatean history. **1973** *Times* 9 June 11/7 A fragment of ancient Nabatean pottery. **1974** *Times* 21 Dec. 11/4 The Arava, stretching from the Dead Sea to Eilat, which has been virtually virgin soil since the days of the Nabateans.

nabbie (næ·bi). Also **nabby.** [? f. Nobby *a.*] A type of Scottish boat used esp. in herring-fishing on Loch Fyne and in the Firth of Clyde, and originally having a raking mast, lug-sail and jib. Cf. Nobby *sb.* 2.

1884 R. Hogarth *Herring Fishery* 4 These boats were round-sterned—from fourteen to sixteen feet keel and about seven feet beam. It was not possible to go any distance to look for herrings in boats of this description. They were known by the name of 'nabbies'. **1907** *Yachting Monthly* iv. 366/1 It may interest 'M.I.N.A.' to know that he is quite correct in his use of the word 'nabbie' as applied to the present-day Loch Fyne type of fishing boat. **1955** *Mearns Leader* (Stonehaven) 17 June, 46 ft. 'Nabby' boat, *June Rose*, from Fisherrow. She is very well equipped and powered by a 66 h.p. Kelvin Diesel. **1959** P. Norton *End of Voyage* 85 The Loch Fyne skiff or nabbie is a graceful bird-like craft.

nabe (nēⁱb). *U.S. slang.* [f. the pronunc. of Neighbourhood.] A neighbourhood; *spec.*, a local cinema. Also *attrib.*

1935 *Evening Sun* (Baltimore) 8 Apr. 17 On Sunday two powerful [box office pictures] were released to the nabes. **1937** *Amer. Speech* XII. 317/2 *Nabe*, neighborhood motion picture theatre. **1942** Berrey & Van den Bark *Amer. Thes. Slang* § 50/1 *Nabe, naborhood, neighb*, neighborhood. *Ibid.* § 587/5 Nabe pichouse, a neighborhood motion-picture theater. **1961** A. Berkman *Singers' Gloss. Show Business* 61 Nabes..neighborhood movie houses. **1970** *New Yorker* 20 June 30/1 They picked an aging star, slapped together a moldy script, and sent the result out to the nabes. **1971** *Time* 8 Nov. 73/1 In Portland, where business is also dragging, the nabes (the trade term for the neighborhood houses) are now closed except on weekends.

Nabeshima (næbĕʃī·mă). The name of a baronial family in feudal Japan used *attrib.* and *absol.* to designate the porcelain produced from the kilns established by this family in 1722 at Okawachi on the island of Kyushu in Japan.

1886 W. Chaffers *Marks Pott. & Porc.* (ed. 7) 412 Nabeshimayaki was made at Okawaji, painted principally in blue with plants, fishes, &c., distinct from the Hiradoyaki. **1902** F. Brinkley *Japan* VIII. ii. 95 The *Nabeshima-yaki*, as the Okawachi manufactures were subsequently called, stands first among Japanese porcelains decorated with vitrifiable enamel. **1937** R. L. Hobson *Handbk. Pott. & Porc. Far East* 163 The early Nabeshima porcelain is a good white ware with lustrous glaze of fine texture. **1965** S. Jenyns *Jap. Porcelain* vi. 230 Within their narrow range the saucer dishes of Nabeshima are technically as perfect as any porcelain that the Japanese were able to produce. **1967** H. H. Sanders *World of Jap. Ceramics* 218 The old Nabeshima style is a flat bowl form with a high foot, which has a traditional blue-and-white comb-tooth pattern under the glaze and three underglaze blue patterns on the outside of the bowl. **1971** L. A. Boger *Dict. World Pott. & Porc.* 237/1 Both the underglaze blue and the polychrome enameled Nabeshima are notable for the consummate skill with which the decorations have been applied, particularly the underglaze blue.

‖ **nabi** (nā·bi). Pl. **nebi'im.** [Heb. *nābhi* prophet.] **1.** *Theol.* One inspired to speak the word of God; a prophet, *spec.* a Hebrew prophet of the Old Testament.

[**1765** W. Dodd in *Bible with Commentary* note on Gen. xx. verse 7 The Hebrew נביא *nebia*, signifies a person that speaks something in an eminent and extraordinary manner.] **1877** A. Milroy tr. *Kuenen's Prophets & Prophecy in Israel* iii. 63 The Nabi is, and cannot but be, an improvisatore. **1885** T. P. Hughes *Dict. Islam* 427/1 *Nabi*,..a prophet. One who has received direct inspiration..by means of an angel, or by the inspiration of the heart..; or has seen the things of God in a dream. *Ibid.* 475/2 According to Muhammadan writers a *nabi* is anyone directly inspired by God. **1900** W. W. Skeat *Malay Magic* 99 Of the prophets (Nabi) there are an indefinite number. **1908** R. J. Wilkinson *Life & Customs* (Papers on Malay Subjects 3) i. 14 Other religions had prophets of their own who were nevertheless true prophets like *Nabi Isa*, the prophet of the Christians, and *Nabi Musa*, the prophet of the Siamese. **1918** *Encycl. Relig. & Ethics* X. 384/1 The true religion of Israel..traced its origin to those who bore the title *nabî*. *Ibid.* 384/2 In the Hebrew order of the OT books the *nᵉbî'îm* and the *hăkĕhāmîm* appear in different divisions. **1922** J. Skinner *Prophecy & Religion* i. 4 Amos instances the raising up of *Nĕbî'îm* as a proof of Yahwe's peculiar love for Israel. **1961** B. Vawter *Conscience of Israel* iv. 75 To him Amos was only a *nabi* like the many who grubbed out a living by devising oracles for clients.

2. *Art.* A member of a group of late 19th-century French post-impressionists, including Bonnard, Vuillard, Denis, and Sérusier, who followed the artistic theories of Gauguin.

1931 C'tess de Lauzanne tr. *Basler & Kunstler's Post-Impressionists* xi. 52 All the 'Nabis', all the 'enflammés' who left the Jullian Academy, were attracted by the theories of..Paul Gauguin. **1945** Goldwater & Treves *Artists on Art* (1947) 379 Sérusier gathered about him a group known as the *Nabis* which included..Denis, Bonnard, Vuillard, and later Maillol. **1959** *Listener* 22 Oct. 694/2 Felix Vallotton who worked in Paris and had relations with the Nabis. **1963** L. & E. Hanson *Post-Impressionists* xi. 277 They were..nicknamed the Nabis..because most of them wore beards, some were Jews and all were desperately earnest. **1963** *Times* 2 May 6/5 The 'Nabi' phase of French painting. **1969** M. Bullock tr. *Chassé's Nabis & their Period* i. 14 The Nabis soon became known as devotees of 'beautiful greys' and broken colours. .. When we try to outline Nabism, we always return in the end to the concept of fantasy and dream. **1971** tr. W. Verkade in J. Russell *Vuillard* 85 One day Sérusier said to me: 'Let's go and see the Nabi, Denis, at Saint-Germain.' **1972** L. Lamb *Picture Frame* ii. 24, I should guess that you have got hold of one of the Nabis... If you think it's a Vuillard, it probably *is*. **1973** *Times* 7 May 7/4 Art nouveau, the Nabis, the Pointillistes.

Hence **na·bi'ism, na·bism.**

1922 J. Skinner *Prophecy & Religion* i. 5 *Nabi'ism* had its unprogressive and degenerate representatives. **1969** [see sense 2 above].

nabla (næ·blă). *Math.* [a. Gr. *νάβλα*: see Nable (and cf. quot. 1879 s.v. Nebel).] = *del.

The operator was introduced by Sir William Hamilton, who represented it by the symbol $\lhd$. (In quot. 1837 he uses ∇' as a symbol for any arbitrary function.)

[**1837** W. R. Hamilton in *Trans. R. Irish Acad.* XVII. 236 Considering x as a function ψ of a new variable o' and performing any operation ∇' with reference to the latter variable, $\nabla' f\psi(o') = \nabla' f(1+\Delta)(\psi(o'))^o$. **1846** *Proc. R. Irish Acad.* III. 291 The following.. general characteristic of operation $i\frac{d}{dx} + j\frac{d}{dy} + k\frac{d}{dz} = \lhd$, in which x, y, z are ordinary rectangular coordinates, while i, j, k are his [*sc.* Hamilton's] own coordinate imaginary units, appears to him to be one of great importance in many researches. **1847** W. R. Hamilton in *Phil. Mag.* XXXI. 291 In the paper designed for Southampton..the characteristic was written ∇; but this more common sign has been so often used with other meanings, that it seems desirable to abstain from appropriating it to the new signification here proposed. **1853** —— *Lect. Quaternions* vii. 610 Introducing, for abridgment, as a new characteristic of operation, a symbol defined by the formula $\lhd$ = [etc.].] **1884** W. Thomson *Notes Lect. Molecular Dynamics & Wave Theory of Light at Johns Hopkins Univ.* x. 112 (MS.), I took the liberty of asking Professor Bell..whether he had a name for this symbol ∇^2; and he has mentioned to me *nabla*, a humorous suggestion of Maxwell's. It is the name of an Egyptian harp, which was of that shape. **1892** *Phil. Trans. R. Soc.* CLXXXIII. 431 Physical mathematics is very largely the mathematics of ∇. The name Nabla seems, therefore, ludicrously inefficient. **1939** D. E. Rutherford *Vector Methods* iv. 50 A convenient method of writing grad ϕ is $\nabla\phi$, where ∇ (pronounced 'nabla') is defined as the vector operator $\nabla \equiv \mathbf{i}\frac{\partial}{\partial x} + \mathbf{j}\frac{\partial}{\partial y} + \mathbf{k}\frac{\partial}{\partial z}$. **1964** [see *del]. **1969** L. Young *Systems of Units in Electr. & Magn.* v. 63 The symbol nabla, ∇, is a vector differential operator.

nabob. 4. (Earlier example.)

1803 E. S. Bowne *Girl's Life 80 Yrs. Ago* (1888) 151 Silk nabobs, plaided, colored and white, are much worn, very short waists, hair very plain.

nabocklish (nabǫ·kliʃ), *int. Irish dial.* Also **nabochlish, na bocklish, naboklish.** [Ir. *na* not + *bac*, imp. sing. of *bacaim* 'I meddle' + *leis* with it: lit. 'don't meddle with it'.] Never mind! Leave it alone!

1841 C. J. Lever *Charles O'Malley* I. ii. 10 Arrest him!—na bocklish—catch a weasel asleep. **1843** W. Carleton *Traits & Stories Irish Peasantry* (new ed.) I. 341 But, *naboklish!* what'll ye have? **1867** P. Kennedy *Banks of Boro* xxi. 129 But, *nabochlish*, we will find ourselves in the wrong box, maybe. **1917** J. Morley *Recollections* II. v. iii. 222 When I hear or read some malicious or injurious word in politics, I find real comfort in saying to myself '*Nabochlish!*' **1939** C. Morley *Kitty Foyle* xxix. 285 Like Pop said sometimes, nabocklish! which is Irish for let's not worry too much.

Nabokovian (næbǫ̆kǫ·fiăn, năbǫ·kǫfiăn), *a.* [f. the name *Nabokov* (see below) + -ian.] Of, pertaining to, resembling, or characteristic of the Russian-born novelist and poet Vladimir Nabokov (b. 1899) or his writings.

1959 *Observer* 1 Nov. 21/6 There is a Nabokovian poignancy in leaving such delicate things to be destroyed, as he says with a rueful smile, 'by such booted people'. **1965** *Times Lit. Suppl.* 28 Jan. 68/4 Mr. Nabokov's *Eugene Onegin* will be read not for the learning. It will be read for the brilliant fireworks of his prose and for the beauty of the Nabokovian phrase. **1968** *Punch* 25 Dec. 932/3 Mr. Stegner chooses instead to invest detail with significance, and he overwrites in truly Nabokovian manner. **1972** *Sat. Rev.* (U.S.) 10 June 68/2, I found myself searching for Nabokovian anagrams in the names. **1975** *Times Lit. Suppl.* 31 Oct. 1285/1 The narrative manner similarly alternates between abruptly functional stage or screen-direction and a Nabokovian obliquity in which words take on an energy of their own and skitter away from the matter in hand.

nacelle. Restrict † *Obs. rare*⁻¹ to sense in Dict. and add: **2.** [after the same uses in Fr.] **a.** The basket or gondola of a balloon or airship.

1901 *New Penny Mag.* XII. 440 The 'nacelle', or basket, from which..the aeronaut directs his operations. **1909** *Aero* 13 July 117/2 The dirigible..has a screw at either end of the nacelle or cradle. **1932** *Times* 27 May 13/7 The balloon with which the first ascent was made will be used, but a new *nacelle* will be constructed.

b. The cockpit of an aeroplane; hence, any streamlined structure on an aeroplane for housing something, esp. an engine.

1914 *Scotsman* 8 Sept. 2/7 (Advt.), The Henry Farman seaplane is a biplane of the pusher type... The pilot and passenger have comfortable quarters in a nacelle which is built out from the front of the machine. **1915** *War Illustr.* 10 July 494/2 The machine was apparently a gun-carrying 'pusher' biplane of the type in which the gunman sits right out in the nose of the boat-shaped body—or 'nacelle'. **1918** 'Avion' *Aeroplanes & Aero Engines* v. 59 The engine, tanks, crew, controls, and instruments are accommodated in a body known as the 'nacelle', above which the centre section [of the upper wing] is erected in the usual way. **1920** *Blackw. Mag.* Feb. 195/1 The spirit was not entering the tank, but spilling over the sides on to the floor of the nacelle. **1928** C. F. S. Gamble *Story N. Sea Air Station* i. 56 They could seat two persons in the covered-in *nacelle*, with the pilot in front. **1935** *Jrnl. R. Aeronaut. Soc.* XXXIX. 267 The full anti-drag rings and nacelle cowls merge into the wing. **1943** W. L. Cowley *Aerodynamics of Aeroplane* iii. 53 The engine with a tractor propellor is sometimes placed..in the nose of nacelles or egg-shaped bodies out on the wings. **1973** E. Arnold *Proving Ground* xxix. 309 The planes..upended to show the twin nacelles of P-38s.

c. A similarly shaped structure on or in a motor vehicle.

1959 *Motor* 3 June 603/3 The furnishings belong to the polished walnut school, upon which is superimposed a hooded crackle-finish nacelle in front of the driver containing a full but oddly-framed set of instruments. **1967** E. Rudinger *Consumer's Car Gloss.* (ed. 2) 71 *Nacelle*,.. sometimes used to describe the moulding surrounding a car's lights or dashboard instruments. **1969** *Practical Motorist* Nov. 271/1 Instrumentation is restricted to an oblong speedometer with a small rev-counter perched atop the facia in a separate nacelle. **1970** *Daily Tel.* 7 Apr. 3/1 The Lotus 72's radiator has been moved from the nose and replaced by two smaller radiators mounted in nacelles on the sides of the car.

Nachee, var. *Natchez.

‖ **Nachlass** (na·χlas). [G.] Unpublished writings left by an author after his death.

1842 J. S. Mill *Let.* Apr. in *Wks.* (1963) XIII. 515 She bids me..to ask what you think of Otfried Müller's Nachlass as a subject for translation. **1948** *Mind* LVII. 382 The argument is supported throughout by cogent evidence from Kant's works. The quotations from the *Nachlass* and the *Opus Postumum* are especially valuable. *Ibid.* 524 It has the advantage of making his lectures far better material for publication than that found in the average professor's *Nachlass*. **1961** D. Ross in Aristotle *De Anima* 49 The chapter is apparently a series of jottings which

an early editor found in Aristotle's *Nachlass*, and put together so that nothing of the Master's should be lost.

Nachschlag (na·χ͵ʃlak). *Mus.* [Ger., f. *nach* after + *schlag* blow, note.] A grace note which takes its value from that of the note preceding it.

1879 [see *AGRÉMENT 2]. **1880** GROVE *Dict. Mus.* II. 441/2 In the works of the great masters the Nachschlag, though of very frequent occurrence, is almost invariably written out in notes of ordinary size. **1915** A. DOLMETSCH *Interpretation of Music of 17th & 18th Cents.* iv. 255 C. Ph. E. Bach incidentally mentions the *Nachschlag*, but only to condemn it. **1944** W. APEL *Harvard Dict. Mus.* 476/1 The ornamenting notes constitute a melodic movement away from the preceding note, and are to be performed as a part of this... Thus the Nachschlag is the exact opposite of the appoggiatura. **1960** E. BODKY *Interpretation of Bach's Keyboard Works* v. 180 In bar 20 this version leads to ugly parallel fifths, which Landshoff tries to avoid by changing the short appoggiaturas of bars 19 and 20 into *Nachschläge*.

‖ **Nachtlokal** (na·χtlokal). Pl. **nachtlokale.** [G.] A night-club. Also *attrib.*

1939 E. AMBLER *Mask of Dimitrios* v. 95 'She is the proprietress of a *Nachtlokal* called *La Vierge St. Marie.*' '*Nachtlokal?*' He grinned. 'Well, you could call it a night club.' **1954** P. BOTTOME *Against Whom?* xxiii. 173 Konrad, since it was his free evening, would be at a Nacht-Lokal dancing. **1968** D. HOPKINSON *Incense Tree* viii. 94 We went dancing together in the almost total darkness of a *Nachtlokal*. **1970** S. J. PERELMAN *Baby, it's Cold Inside* 227 Some grisly *Nachtlokal* in the Kurfürstendamm.

Nachtmaal: see *NAGMAAL.

‖ **nacht und nebel** (naχt unt nē·bəl). [G.] The German for 'night and fog', used, freq. *attrib.*, of a situation characterized by mystery or obscurity.

The name of an infamous decree issued by the Nazis in December 1941.

1947 V. H. BERNSTEIN *Final Judgment* xviii. 240 *Nacht und Nebel* was issued over Hitler's signature, but Keitel issued several covering memoranda and interpretations. Indeed, the name of the Chief of the High Command was so closely identified with the order that it was sometimes referred to as the 'Keitel Decree'. **1963** *Times* 21 Feb. 12/5 This was *Tannhäuser* as a would-be music drama, set in a *Nacht und Nebel* thirteenth-century Germany, peopled by symbols and based on the orchestra. **1968** A. MARIN *Clash of Distant Thunder* (1969) i. 5 The transport camp..where captured commandos and *Nacht und Nebel* prisoners were isolated. **1971** D. CORY *Sunburst* vi. 100 Country after country going under, disappearing in the mist of *Nacht und Nebel*. **1973** *Listener* 26 July 123/1 The indescribable verbal miasma, exhalations of *Nacht und Nebel*, that is Scientology's contribution to the encyclopaedia of religious knowledge.

nacker, var. *KNACKER *sb.*[1] 3.

1866 [see *KNACKER *sb.*[1] 3]. **1958** M. PUGH *Wilderness of Monkeys* 79 Oh, smart boy, eh?.. Festival Hall fiddle! Nackers!

‖**nada**[1] (nā·da). *Hinduism.* Also **naad** (nād). [Skr. *nādá* sound.] Inchoate or elemental sound considered as the source of all sounds and as a source of creation; the 'inner' sound of the body.

1913 'A. AVALON' *Tantra of Great Liberation* p. xxiii, It is Nāda..when there is a sound in which there is something like a connected or combined disposition of the letters. **1920** *Encycl. Relig. & Ethics* XI. 93/1 The Sāktas base their doctrines on the assumption that through Śiva and Sakti there is a drop, Bindu, formed which develops into a female element Nāda (sound), containing in itself the names of all things to be created. **1926** *Indian Art & Lett.* II. 79 Nāda as inchoate stressing sound is shown in the form of a crescent-moon on His [*sc.* Siva's] head. **1930** S. N. DASGUPTA *Yoga Philos.* ix. 269 This sound in the stage of pure varṇas is called nāda... But each varṇa vanishes as it is generated, as the sense of hearing has no power to hold them together. **1940** H. E. KENNEDY tr. *Marquès-Rivière's Tantrik Yoga* i. 20 Then there is *Laya Yoga*, based upon the contemplation of the inward parts (nâda), and produced by closing the ears. **1943** D. GASCOYNE *Poems 1937–1942* 50 The incoherent *Nada* of the seer. **1960** SWĀMĪ PRAJÑĀNANANDA *Hist. Dev. Indian Music* ii. 25 The *nāda* or causal sound is the basis or ground of music, and upon this primal ground all the phenomena of Indian music are built. **1960** KOESTLER *Lotus & Robot* I. ii. 99 The last stages before samadhi: the appearance of an 'inner light', and of various 'inner sounds' or nadas. **1968** *Indian Mus. Jrnl.* V. 8 Boundless is the ocean of *Nāda*. **1972** P. HOLROYDE *Indian Music* 274 *Naad* or *Nada*, literally 'resonant sound', but like most Sanskrit words its overtones are more than the literal and precise English. It is much more complex, implying 'vital power'.

‖ **nada**[2] (nā·da, nā·ðа). [Sp., = nothing, f. L. (*res*) *nata* thing born; small, insignificant thing.] Nothing; nothingness, non-existence; a state or condition as of non-existence.

1933 E. HEMINGWAY *Winner take Nothing* 23 It was all a nothing and a man was nothing too... He knew it all was nada y pues nada y nada y pues nada. Our nada who art in nada, nada be thy name. **1939** JOYCE *Finnegans Wake* 521 Vurry nothing, O potators... It amounts to nada in pounds or pence. **1947** *Horizon* XV. 160 The sleepless man—the man obsessed by death, by the meaninglessness of the world, by nothingness, by nada—is one of the recurring symbols in the works of Hemingway. **1962** *Spectator* 25 May 685/1 This sense of the endless *nada* lying beyond the phenomenological world. **1966** E. FIGES *Equinox* 145 A mess, or less than a mess: nothing, nichts, nada, niente, rien. **1974** *Punch* 25 Sept. 493/2 *Hudson*: Will there be anything else, old one? *Mr. Bellamy*: Nada, Hudson. Nada y pues nada y nada y pues nada.

Na-Dene (nā·dəne·). Also **Na-Déné, Nadene.** [f. Athapascan *na* cogn. with Haida *na* to dwell, Tlingit *na* people + Northern Athapascan *Dene* people.] The name given to a North American Indian linguistic family consisting of the Athapascan, Eyak, Haida, and Tlingit languages. Cf. *ATHAPASCAN, *HAIDA.

1915 E. SAPIR in *American Anthropologist* XVII. 534 (*title*) The Na-Dene languages, a preliminary report. *Ibid.* 535 In all Na-dene languages..a large number of stems is found consisting of consonant plus vowel plus consonant. **1932** W. L. GRAFF *Language & Languages* xi. 431 The most important North American branches: Eskimo,..Na-Dene. **1932** D. JENNESS *Indians of Canada* ii. 20 Philologists..have discovered no kinship among any of the eleven Canadian tongues, unless perhaps between Haida, Tlinkit, and Athapaskan, which Sapir would group together under the name of Nadene. **1954** PEI & GAYNOR *Dict. Linguistics* 143 *Na-Dene*, according to Rivet, a family of North American Indian languages, consisting of the Athapascan, Haida and Tlingit. **1957** *Encycl. Brit.* V. 138/1 The *Nadene* languages, probably the most specialized of all, are tone languages, and, while presenting a superficially 'polysynthetic' aspect, are built up, fundamentally, of monosyllabic elements of prevailingly nominal significance. **1965** *Canad. Jrnl. Linguistics* Spring 96 This would be exemplified, hypothetically, by a discovery that Haida does not belong with the other Na-Dene languages. *Ibid.* 97 Na-Dene..also remains essentially as organized by Sapir. **1968** H.-J. PINNOW in *Internat. Jrnl. Amer. Linguistics* XXXIV. 204 (*title*) Genetic relationship vs. borrowing in Na-Dene. **1970** C. LAIRD *Language in America* (1972) iv. 53 Speakers of Na-Dene..are today found in the lush Pacific Northwest. *Ibid.*, One of the Na-Dene languages.

Naderism (nēi·dəriz'm). [f. name of Ralph *Nader* (b. 1934), American lawyer + -ISM.] Public agitation for greater safety and higher quality in consumer goods.

1969 *Britannica Bk. of Year* (U.S.) 800/2 *Naderism*, a protest against defective consumer goods in the manner of the American lawyer Ralph Nader. **1970** *Americana Annual* 725 The phenomenon [*sc.* consumerism] was also called 'Naderism', because of the successful crusades of a young lawyer, Ralph Nader, against unsafe automobiles, industrial hazards, and environmental pollution. **1971** *Guardian* 9 Oct. 10/6 While Medawar is sold on Naderism for his own operation..he has not advised the CA to change their style. **1973** *Listener* 22 Mar. 380/2 It need not be doubted that Naderism, like the Civil Rights campaigns..is..religious in character.

nævus. Add: Also (chiefly *U.S.*) **nevus.** (Further examples.)

1913 *Jrnl. Amer. Med. Assoc.* 1 Feb. 341/1 (*heading*) Melanotic sarcomas resulting from irritation of pigmented nevi. **1961** R. D. BAKER *Essent. Path.* xx. 545 The word nevus has been used to designate skin blemishes of various sorts including 'birthmarks', but in current usage nevus means the ordinary mole of the skin. **1971** *Brit. Med. Bull.* XXVII. 69/1 Trivial congenital defects such as..pigmented or vascular naevi.

Naffy, var. *N.A.A.F.I.

1937 PARTRIDGE *Dict. Slang* 548/2 *Nafy* or *Naffy*; properly *Naafi*; loosely *Narfy* (..pronounced thus by Indian Army officers). The canteen: naval and military: from ca. 1930. **1940** [see *N.A.A.F.I.]. **1943** HUNT & PRINGLE *Service Slang* 47 *Naffy*, the services are supplied on land and sea by the N.A.A.F.I... There are fully equipped shops and grocery stores in addition to the station canteens and mobile canteens which serve outposts. *Naffytime*, the morning break. **1945** J. MACLAREN-Ross in *Penguin New Writing* XXVI. 54 He'd dropped his notebook in a Naffy. **1945** PARTRIDGE *Dict. R.A.F. Slang* 40 *Naffy Romeo*, a ladies' man—addicted to treating W.A.A.F. personnel with Naffy refreshments. *Naffy gong*, 1939–43 star (medal). Since late 1943. **1948** A. M. TAYLOR *Lang. World War II* (rev. ed.) 135 The various NAAFI clubs were almost invariably called Naffies. **1959** 'M. AINSWORTH' *Murder is Catching* 10 Best if I drop you at the Naffy.

nag, *sb.*[3] (Later examples.)

1971 J. GARDNER *Every Night's a Bullfight* ix. 261 They had covered all their separate problems, yet the nag in Douglas's mind left him edgy about the box office situation. *Ibid.* x. 293 The added knowledge served to compound his growing nag of worry.

nag, *v.* Add: **3.** Also *transf.* and *fig.*

1921 *Challenge* 28 Oct. 375/1 He nags his brain into a state of consuming doubt, but dares not arrive at any conclusion. **1958** L. DURRELL *Balthazar* viii. 172 As I examined him a phone started to nag somewhere. **1960** *Times* 20 June 4/2 Laver, a fighter still nagged by his shoulder. **1963** *Times* 4 Mar. 5/1 Barrington was a little out of sorts with himself, and after Yuile..had tied him down by curling the ball into the wind, Reid nagged him out. **1969** *Listener* 6 Mar. 324/1, I am told that R. P. Blackmur used to give a lecture on Jane Austen in which he explored her work in terms of the verb 'to nag' ('she nags out her plots').

naga[1] (nā·ga). *India.* [Skr. *nāgá* serpent, snake.] In Hindu mythology, one of a race of serpent-demons, the offspring of Kadru and the sage Kasyapa, supposed to be the guardians of Patala or the regions under the earth.

1785 C. WILKINS tr. *Bhăgvăt-Gēētā* 151 The *Nāgs* are serpents fabled with many heads. **1810** E. MOOR *Hindu Pantheon* 391 On the other side of Nandi, or the bull, is Naga; his hooded head upreared; his length coiled under him. **1821** J. LEYDEN tr. *Malay Annals* ii. 21 'Make no noise,' said Malin, 'it is some great snake or naga.' **1828** H. H. WILSON in *Asiatick Researches* XVI. 462 Kulika is one of the eight chiefs of the *Nágas*, or serpents of *Pátála*. **1832** C. COLEMAN *Mythol. of Hindus* I. xiii. 254 The fifth lunar day of Sravana is held sacred to the Nagas. **1875** MONIER-WILLIAMS *Indian Wisdom* xiv. 430 All the Nāgas are described as having jewels in their heads. **1909** *Encycl. Relig. & Ethics* II. 809/1 Nāgas are figured on numberless sculptures all over India, and in popular tales they and their beautiful daughters play an important part. **1948** P. J. THOMAS *Epics, Myths & Legends of India* (ed. 3) x. 86 The Nagas are said to be..mortal enemies of their half-brother Garuda. **1967** V. IONS *Indian Mythol.* 117/2 The Nagas called upon Vishnu to save them, and he descended to Patala in the form of Narmada (personification of a river). **1968** B. WALKER *Hindu World* II. 388 The Nāgas possess secrets little dreamt of by creatures living on the surface, and theirs is a realm of magic and magnificence.

Naga[2] (nā·ga). *India.* [a. Hindi *naṅga*, f. Skr. *nagná* cogn. w. NAKED *a.*] A naked mendicant belonging to any Hindu sect, *spec.* such an ascetic belonging to a Dadu Panthi subsect whose members are allowed to carry arms and serve as mercenaries.

1828 H. H. WILSON in *Asiatick Researches* XVI. 80 The *Dádu Pant'his* are of three classes... The *Nágas*, who carry arms, which they are willing to exercise for hire, and, amongst the Hindu princes, they have been considered as good soldiers. *Ibid.* 135 Nagas. All sects include a division under this denomination... They carry their secession from ordinary manners so far as to leave off every kind of covering. **1879** *Rajputana Gazetteer* II. 147 The Nágas of Jaipur are a sect of militant devotees belonging to the Dádu Panthi sect, who are enrolled in regiments to serve the State; they are vowed to celibacy and to arms. **1917** *Encycl. Relig. & Ethics* IX. 123/1 All these Jaipur Nāgās are vowed to celibacy, and their numbers are replenished by children placed by parents under their charge as disciples. **1939** C. VON FÜRER-HAIMENDORF *Naked Nagas* i. 7 A learned Brahmin.., when I told him of my plans to work among the Nagas, thought that I wanted to study people whose nakedness had religious grounds.

Naga[3] (nā·ga). *India.* [Of disputed origin: perh. f. Skr. *nága* mountain or f. Skr. *nagná* naked.] **a.** A member of a group of peoples living mainly in the Naga hills which divide Assam from Burma; a native or inhabitant of Nagaland. Also *attrib.* **b.** The Tibeto-Burman language of these tribes.

1837 J. M'COSH *Topography of Assam* xiv. 156 The next border tribes met with in proceeding westward are the Nagas... The Nagas go literally naked in their hills. **1841** W. ROBINSON *Descr. Acct. Asam* 380 The origin of the word Naga is unknown; but it has been supposed by some to have been derived from the Sanskrit..and applied in derision to the people, from the paucity of their clothing. **1853** *Jrnl. Indian Archipelago* VII. 55 Several of the adjacent languages—Kyen, Heuma, Naga &c., have *v*, *f*, or both. **1872** *Jrnl. Asiatic Soc. Bengal* XLI. I. 84 The Rájah had first intended to fly to the Nágá Hills, but from fear of our army, the Nágás would not afford him an asylum. **1890** KIPLING *Barrack-Room Ballads* (1892) 17 We've chivied the Naga an' Looshai, we've give the Afreedeeman fits. **1903** [see *KACHIN]. **1928** C. DAWSON *Age of Gods* ix. 195 Assam and Manipur, where a degraded form of megalithic culture still survives among the Naga and Kachin tribes. **1939** C. VON FÜRER-HAIMENDORF *Naked Nagas* i. 7, I left Viceregal Lodge enriched..in my knowledge of Naga cuisine. **1964** R. PERRY *World of Tiger* xiv. 207 A man-eater..killed fifty-two Nagas in eight months. **1971** N. RUSTOMJI *Enchanted Frontiers* xvi. 257 At a mammoth meeting held by the Nagas at Mokokchung in October 1959, known as the Third Naga People's Convention, a demand was formulated for the constitution of the Naga hills as a new State within the Indian Union, to be named Nagaland. **1972** PRAKASH SINGH *Nagaland* i. 9 The appellation 'Naga' was quite foreign to the Nagas themselves until very recent times... The appellation 'Naga' was actually given to these hill tribes by the plains people. **1973** *Times* 14 Nov. 18/3 The Nagas are a group of 20 tribes of Sino-Tibetan origin, now numbering about half a million.

‖ **nagaika** (nāgəi·kă). Pl. **-kas, -ki.** [Russ., of Turkic origin.] A thick plaited whip used by Cossacks.

1842 tr. *J. G. Kohl's Russia* 410 The genuine Cossack of the steppe..depends only on his well plaited *nagaika* or whip, with which he rarely fails to cut down a wolf, as with a sabre. **1914** N. JARINTZOFF *Russia: Country of Extremes* vii. 202 The *nagaiki* flashed in the air, heavily lashing people's faces. **1917** *Daily Chron.* 22 June 1/4 The Cossacks..drove off the agitators from the station with their nagaikas. **1928** F. UTLEY tr. *Astrov's Illustr. Hist. Russ. Rev.* I. x. 69 An old, grey-haired police officer..gave the command: 'Charge with the *nagaikas*!' (whips).

nagana (năgā·nă). [ad. Zulu *nakane.*] A disease of domestic animals in southern Africa, characterized by fever, lethargy, and œdematous swellings, and caused by the hæmoflagellate parasite *Trypanosoma brucei* which is transmitted by tsetse flies of the genus *Glossina.* Also *attrib.*

1895 D. BRUCE (*title*) Preliminary report on the tsetse fly-disease, or nagana, in Zululand. **1896** *Nature* 16 Apr. 567/1 Nagana pursues a much slower course in cattle than in horses. **1904** *Q. Rev.* July 120 The 'fly districts' where nagana disease is rife. **1904** *Brit. Med. Jrnl.* 20 Aug. 368 Nuttall of Cambridge..experimented on the conveyance of the nagana trypanosome from sick to healthy animals. **1925** *Times* 29 Dec. 11/3 It was believed that wild game.. formed a permanent reservoir from which tsetses could convey 'nagana' to domestic stock. **1931** J. S. HUXLEY *What dare I Think?* i. 33 Human sleeping sickness and nagana disease of cattle, [are] transmitted by tsetse-flies. **1947** [see *horse-sickness* (*HORSE *sb.* 27 a)]. **1965** *New Scientist* 26 Aug. 504/3 Wild game don't suffer from nagana, the tsetse-borne trypanosome disease that disastrously affects domestic cattle. **1970** JUBB & KENNEDY *Pathol. Domestic Animals* (ed. 2) I. iv. 324/1 *Trypanosoma brucei* is a cause of nagana in most domestic species in Africa, but man is refractory.

nagelfluh (nā·gĕlflū). *Geol.* Also 9 **nagelflue**, and with capital initial. Pl. **-fluhe.** [a. G. *nagelfluh*, f. *nagel* NAIL *sb.* + Swiss Ger. *fluh* (S. Ger, dial. *flüe*) rock face.] A massive conglomerate which accompanies the molasse in the Swiss Alps and contains pebbles supposed to look like nail-heads.

1808 R. JAMESON *Syst. Mineral.* III. ix. 210 Nagelfluh.—This rock is usually composed of fragments of limestone, more or less rounded, and of various magnitudes, cemented together by a basis of calc-sinter. **1849** *Q. Jrnl. Geol. Soc.* V. 229 If the masses of nagelflue which constitute the Rigi mountain near Lucerne, and the still loftier Speer..near Wesen be included in one group, their thickness must be enormous, certainly exceeding 6000 or 8000 feet. **1879** *Encycl. Brit.* X. 321/2 The well-known nagelflue of Switzerland..can be shown from its fossil contents to be essentially a lacustrine formation. **1912** T. G. BONNEY *Building of Alps* i. 25 The gravels, the so-called Nagelfluhe, are occasionally fully a mile in thickness. **1962** L. C. KING *Morphology of Earth* iv. 98 The presence of conglomerates and breccias grading into arkoses shows the rapid erosion of adjacent highlands... Thus arose the coarse *Nagelfluh* outwash of the Alps which passes northward into finer grades of sediment.

nagged (nægd), *ppl. a.* [-ED[1].] That is subject to nagging. Hence, downtrodden, wearied, irritated, annoyed.

1893 K. D. WIGGIN *Polly Oliver's Problem* ix. 107 Existence was wearing a particularly dismal aspect on that afternoon... He felt 'nagged', injured, blue, out of sorts with fate. **1961** M. SPARK *Prime of Miss Jean Brodie* ii. 35 'Mary, don't you *want* to walk tidily?' 'Mary,' said Sandy, 'stop staring at the brown man.' The nagged child looked numbly at Sandy and tried to quicken her pace.

nagging, *ppl. a.* Add: **1.** Also of thirst.

1906 E. DYSON *Fact'ry 'Ands* vi. 67 He sighed frequently; his nagging thirst got at him again.

2. b. (Further examples.)

1946 W. S. MAUGHAM *Then & Now* xxviii. 162 He had not the strength to withstand the nagging arguments of the others. **1953** R. MACAULAY *Let.* 11 Aug. (1961) 106, I think nagging doubts..would always from time to time raise their heads and disturb.

naggingly (næ·giŋli), *adv.* [f. NAGGING *ppl. a.* + -LY[2].] In a nagging or insistent way; in a persistently irritating, annoying, or exhausting manner.

1936 P. FLEMING *News from Tartary* vi. 98 Things had gone quietly, naggingly against us all the way. **1951** M. LEINSTER in D. Knight *100 Yrs. Sci. Fiction* (1969) 209 Haynes wished he could talk with him once more—talk sensibly, quietly, without..this naggingly demanding wonderment.

naggish (næ·giʃ), *a.*[2] [f. NAG *sb.*[1] + -ISH[1].] Of horses: suggestive of a nag; small, inferior.

a **1800** *Spirit Farmer's Museum* (1801) 204, I see some here in gay coats, mounted on naggish horses.

naggy (næ·gi), *a.*[2] [f. NAG *sb.*[1] + -Y[1].] Of horses: inferior in size or quality; naggish.

a **1861** T. WINTHROP *John Brent* (1883) vii. 54 The little villain's mount was a red roan, a Flat-head horse, rather naggy, but perfectly hardy and wiry.

‖ **Nagmaal** (na·χmāl). *S. Afr.* Also **Nagtmaal.** [Afrikaans, f. *nag* night + *maal* meal.] Also **Nachtmaal** [Du., = nightmeal]. The Lord's Supper, or Holy Communion; also the Communion service, or the occasion on which the service is held.

1835 A. STEEDMAN *Wanderings S. Afr.* I. 184 During '*naacht-maal*' (the administration of the Lord's Supper,) the village becomes a scene of great bustle and activity. **1842** R. GODLONTON *Sk. Eastern Districts Cape G.H.* 50 The period for the quarterly administration of the sacrament, (or *nachtmaal*). **1852, 1871** [see *DUTCH *a.* 2 b]. **1916** J. BUCHAN *Greenmantle* iii. 35 It was as slow as a vrouw coming from *nachtmaal*. **1925** *British Weekly* 25 Nov. 182/1 Shy young Dutchmen in 'nachtmaal' clothes. **1930** R. CAMPBELL *Adamastor* 23 The baboons..all their Simian dignity forgot Would hold a sort of Nagmaal on the spot. **1945** *Cape Argus* 7 Aug., The accident occurred while the ..family were on their way to Nagmaal on Sunday. **1948** *Ibid.* 5 June (Mag. Sect.) 2/4 At nagtmaal the farmers drove in from miles around and opened up their little dorp dwellings. **1953** *Cape Times* 15 Apr. 13/4 They would be utter fools to put her there in broad daylight at Nagmaal time. **1974** *Sunday Times* (S. Afr.) 24 Nov. 5 Seldom-worn black suits bought decades before to last a lifetime of weddings, Nagmaals and funerals.

Nago (na·go). [f. Ewe *anagó* a Yoruba Negro.] **a.** A member of an African Negro people, originally Yoruba-speaking, of whom many were taken to the Americas as slaves. **b.** The language of this people, now applied *spec.* to the lingua franca or pidgin form spoken by this people in Brazil. Also *attrib.* or as *adj.*

1775 *Jamaica Gaz.* 25 Mar., [A man] of the Nago country..says his master died when he was a boy and has been run-away ever since. **1793** B. EDWARDS *Hist. Brit. Colonies in W. Indies* II. 73 Many of the Whidah Negroes are found to be circumcised... It is practised universally by the Nagoes. **1825** R. BICKELL *W. Indies* 43 Frank, a Nago, 5 ft 7½ in. no brand-mark, country marks on his face. **1942** D. PIERSON *Negroes in Brazil* iii. 73 It is likely that Nagô was not maintained in a pure form but came to be a patois containing numerous elements from other African dialects as well as from Portuguese. **1949** *Caribbean Quarterly* I. I. 11, 33 were Nagoes..from the Slave Coast. **1968** W. J. SAMARIN in J. A. Fishman *Readings Sociol. of Lang.* 665 As linguistic curios a few others might be cited:..Nago, probably based on Yoruba and ultimately used only in certain Brazilian pseudo-African cults.

nagsman (næ·gzmæ̆n). [f. NAG *sb.*[1] + MAN *sb.*[1] 4 p.] A skilled horseman who is employed to train or show horses.

1891 W. A. KERR *Practical Horsemanship* x. 171 The nagsman who will ride him up and down the yard is pretty certain to be an artist in the saddle, one who, as he gets 'the office', rides either to sell or to buy. **1903** F. M. WARE *First-Hand Bits of Stable Lore* viii. 107 A 'nagsman' handling a green and raw horse may seem..to be rough in his treatment. **1952** R. S. SUMMERHAYS *Encycl. for Horsemen* 191/1 *Nagsman*, a horseman who, by his skill, rides to improve a horse, whether as a ride, or on account of some vice or bad manners. **1955** H. SMITH *Horseman through Six Reigns* xxi. 203 If the rider's body is still..it is generally a sign that the horse is a good ride, though an expert showman or nagsman can cover up a lot. **1959** *Times* 25 Apr. 9/3 What the P.T. instructor and the drill sergeant do for the recruit..the nagsman does for the colt. **1963** E. H. EDWARDS *Saddlery* ix. 78 While it might be of assistance to the experienced nagsman, it could be very dangerous in other hands.

Nagtmaal: see *NAGMAAL.

nah[1] (nā), a representation of a colloq. or vulgar pronunciation of Now *adv.* Also **na.**

1847 E. BRONTË *Wuthering Heights* II. v. 109 He'll hev his lad; und Aw mun tak him—soa nah yah knaw! **1907** SHAW *Major Barbara* II. 245 Wot prawce Selvytion nah? **1954** E. PANGBORN *Mirror for Observers* (1955) II. iv. 135 'Did you think I was sore?' 'You had a right to be.' 'Nah. Hold everything.' **1959** B. KOPS *Hamlet of Stepney Green* I. 108 Na Davey, what can I say to you? **1959** A. WESKER *Chicken Soup with Barley* I. i. 176 Two o'clock they plan to march—nah!

nah[2] (nā), a representation of a colloq. or vulgar pronunciation of No *adv.*[3] Cf. NA *adv.*[2]

1920 C. SANDBURG *Smoke & Steel* 45 Nothin' ever sticks to my fingers, nah, nah, nothin' like that. **1950** *Astounding Sci. Fiction* Nov. 97 'I'll fight you,' offered Borklin. His huge fists closed. 'Nah—why? Wouldn't be a fight, anyway.' **1961** I. JEFFERIES *It wasn't Me!* iii. 46 'I don't need permission..' 'I think you do.' 'Nah,' I said. **1961** J. HELLER *Catch-22* (1962) xxxviii. 393 Havermeyer shook his head thoughtfully. 'Nah, I couldn't do that.' **1966** *New Society* 12 May 9/2 The waiter knows better. 'Nah, you don't want herrings, I'm gonna give you the soup.' **1973** *Time Out* 2–8 Mar. 13/2 Nah, she don't know.

‖ **nahal** (nahā·l). Also with capital initial. [Heb., f. initials of *No'ar Halutzi Loḥem*, Pioneer and Military Youth.] The name of a military youth organization in Israel, used to designate an agricultural settlement manned by members of this organization. Also *attrib.*

1963 D. R. ELSTON *Israel* ii. 79 *Nahal* members are under no compulsion to continue as agricultural settlers once their period of service is over. **1964** L. DEIGHTON *Funeral in Berlin* xlii. 272 Our people in the *nahals* have got to pack a punch. **1969** *Times* 15 Nov. 7/7 The J.N.F. directly promotes the Israeli war effort by helping to establish *nahal* military-agricultural colonies. **1972** I. T. NAAMANI *Israel* ix. 131 in 1950, Pioneer and Military Youth (Noar Halutzi Lohem, or Nahal) was founded. This was an organisation of young people who wished to serve in the army as units and later continue as a group to establish for themselves or help others establish agricultural settlements on the borders. Usually the members of Nahal received several months of intensive military training and then were assigned to a frontier village, where..they underwent rigid agricultural tutoring. **1973** *Guardian* 21 Apr. 3/6 It has always been an axiom of Israeli planning that borders must be peopled... The first 12 villages have already been established. All were started as 'nahal' settlements by young soldiers, combining military and agricultural training.

nahcolite (nā·kǒlait, nākō͞u·lait). *Min.* [f. $NaHCO_3$, its chemical formula + -LITE.] Native sodium bicarbonate, found as colourless, transparent, monoclinic crystals.

1928 F. A. BANNISTER in *Nature* 1 Dec. 866/1 The name nahcolite is proposed for naturally occurring sodium bicarbonate. These incrustations were found lining the walls of a cuniculus near the Stufe di Nerone, Baia, Naples, Italy. **1929** —— in *Min. Mag.* XXII. 60 Dr. L. J. Spencer has very kindly suggested an ingenious name, *Nahcolite*. **1940** *Amer. Mineralogist* XXV. 777 The origin of nahcolite in the Stufe de [*sic*] Nerone and in a lava tunnel at Vesuvius can be easily explained by the action of CO_2 and water vapor upon thermonatrite or trona. **1971** *Prof. Papers U.S. Geol. Survey* No. 750-B. 194 This report describes a new analytical technique for determining the amount of nahcolite in oil shale.

Na'htchi, var. *NATCHEZ.

Nahua, var. *NAHUATL *sb.* and *a.*

1948 D. DIRINGER *Alphabet* 122 The Nahua civilization of Mexico. **1957** E. HYAMS *Speaking Garden* vi. 70 *Tumatl* is a Nahua word. **1962** *Listener* 23 Aug. 270/2 Mexico's own Nahua and Mayan cultures.

Nahuatl (nā·wāt'l), *sb.* and *a.* Also **Nahuat, Nahuatla, Nahuatlac.** [f. Sp., f. Nahuatl.] **A.** *sb.* **a.** A group of peoples of Southern Mexico and Central America which includes the Aztec; a member of these peoples. **b.** The Uto-Aztecan language of this people. **B.** *adj.* Of or pertaining to the Nahuatl people or their language.

1822 J. BLACK tr. *de Humboldt's Essay on Kingdom of New Spain* I. 138 The Toultecs,..the Acolhuas, and the Nahuatlacs, all spoke the same language as the Mexicans. **1873** A. LANG in *Fortnightly Rev.* May 624 The rite itself was actually practised by the Nahuatls in America. **1877** L. H. MORGAN *Ancient Society* II. vi. 181 The question of the organization of these, and the remaining Nahuatlac tribes of Mexico, in gentes will be considered in the next ensuing chapter. **1891** Z. NUTTALL *Atlatl or Spear-thrower of Ancient Mexicans* 6 The Nahuatl text of Sahagun's invaluable Manuscript Historia. **1902** *Encycl. Brit.* XXV. 373/2 The dominant [American] ethnic groups:—Eskimo, on Arctic shores;.. Nahuatla-Maya, Southern Mexico and Central America. **1915** E. SAPIR in *American Anthropologist* XVII. Jan.–Mar. 99 The total number of Southern Paiute consonants that have to be directly accounted for in terms of Nahuatl consonants is considerably less. **1921** —— *Language* iv. 70 The compounded object of a verb precedes the verbal element in.. Nahuatl. **1948** C. L. B. HUBBARD *Dogs in Britain* xix. 215 The Aztecs (tribal name for the last Nahuatl immigrants into the Mexican valleys). **1971** *Language* XLVII. 737 The language as a whole, once called Mexicano, has more recently been referred to as Nahuatl (in some cases Nahuat). **1973** *Guardian* 23 Mar. 12/6, I was going to learn Nahuatl, the Aztec language, which some of the two-dollar whores could speak.

So **Nahuatlan,** the group of Nahuatl dialects; also as *adj.*

1902 *Encycl. Brit.* XXV. 374/1 The [linguistic] families of..Middle America..:—..Nahuatlan, Mex.; Otomitlan [etc.]. **1933** L. BLOOMFIELD *Language* iv. 72 A *Uto-Aztecan* family has been proposed..to include..the great *Nahuatlan* family in Mexico, including *Aztec*... Beside Nahuatlan, we may mention the *Mayan* family in Yucatan. **1953** *Amer. Speech* XXVIII. 62 The ending *-an*..is used after vowels as well as after consonants..*Tibetan*, *Nahuatlan*, [etc.].

naiad. Add: **2.** *Ent.* = NYMPH 3.

1918 J. H. COMSTOCK in *Ann. Ent. Soc. Amer.* XI. 224, I, therefore, propose the restriction of the term nymph to the designating of the early stages of insects with a gradual metamorphosis and the use of the term naiad for designating the immature stages of the Plecoptera, Odonata, and Ephemerida. **1930** W. J. LUCAS *Aquatic (Naiad) Stage Brit. Dragonflies* i. 1 The two stages in a dragonfly's life are no less strikingly unlike... Hence arises the necessity for the student of our dragonfly fauna to study and classify the naiads independently of the imagines. **1942** E. O. ESSIG *College Entomology* i. 11 Naiads of aquatic insects are frequently referred to as nymphs. **1972** SWAN & PAPP *Common Insects N. Amer.* xv. 171 Metamorphosis in the group [*sc.* the Odonata] is incomplete or gradual. The naiads or nymphs are important predators of mosquito larvae.

3. *Bot.* A submerged aquatic plant with linear leaves, belonging to the family Najadaceæ, which includes only one genus, *Najas* (or *Naias*).

1966 *Rhodora* LXVIII. 216 (*title*) Two new naiads from Illinois and distributional records of the Naiadaceae.

naice (nēs), *a.* Representation of an affected pronunc. of NICE *a.*; freq. joc. or derogatory.

1925 A. HUXLEY *Those Barren Leaves* II. iii. 112 'So naice, I always think, these Corner Houses,' says Mrs. Cloudesley. **1941** A. CHRISTIE *Evil under Sun* v. 82 Ay am sure it has always been the quayettest [*sc.* quietest] place imaginable! The people who come here are such naice people. **1950** *Spectator* 29 Sept. 354/2 If you want to read about nice people who are really nice and not in the least 'naice', you will enjoy..*Rain on the Wind*. **1962** J. CANNAN *All is Discovered* iii. 49 Having agreed..that it was a naice morning. **1973** *Observer* (Colour Suppl.) 17 June 46/4 The girls in well-cut tweeds from the 'naice' public schools.

naïf, *a.* Add: **1.** Also as *sb.*

1893 G. B. SHAW in *World* 10 May 28/2 You will sometimes find some naïf doing this, and verdantly assuming that *his* point of view commands the absolute truth. **1932** T. S. ELIOT *Sel. Ess.* 305 He [*sc.* Blake] becomes the apparent naïf, really the mature intelligence. **1968** L.

Durrell *Tunc* ii. 36 Somewhere inside she was a naïf—always a bad sign in a woman connected with politics and public life. **1975** *Times Lit. Suppl.* 20 June 701/1 The Bronowski who concluded this was no mathematical naïf. .. He had spent a whole decade as a senior lecturer in mathematics.

b. *Art.* See *naïve *a.* 1 c.

1947 M. McCarthy in *Partisan Rev.* XIV. 178 As in the case of the *naif* painters, his very faults, the crudity of his conceptions,.. become part of the subject. **1955** —— *Charmed Life* (1956) iii. 58 If Warren had been a carpenter or a plumber, he could have made his marks as a *naif* painter. **1974** *Times* 7 Jan. 8/1 At the age of 39, Haddelsey is one of the world's leading *naif* painters.

nail, *sb.* Add: **13. a.** *nail brush* (earlier example), *enamel, file, lacquer, -pick, polish, scissors* (earlier and later examples, also *transf.*), *varnish*; *nail buffer, clipper(s, polisher.*

1802 M. Edgeworth *Let.* in E. Inglis-Jones *Great Maria* (1959) iv. 65 Enter Miss Linwood who looks not unlike a strolling player... I *wish* she had a nail brush. **1908** *Sears, Roebuck Catal.* 328/1 Solid Silver Nail Buffer, fancy handle, 4½ inches long. **1971** *Petticoat* 24 July 3/4 There are six appliances for the nails—two files, a nail buffer, cuticle stick, nail brush and callous remover. **1945** J. Steinbeck *Cannery Row* xvi. 67 Dora..was there to buy a pair of nail-clippers. **1969** *Sears, Roebuck Catal.* 869/3 Resco Nail Clipper. Helps guard hosiery, furniture, pet's paw-health. **1907** Nail enamel [see *nail polish* below]. **1913** *T. Eaton & Co. Catal.* Spring & Summer 177/3 Lustrite Nail Enamel..will produce a brilliant lustre. **1972** *Vogue* June Special 90 Blueberry Wine Nail Enamel. **1881** *Graphic* 21 May (back cover) (Advt.), Nail file. Cigar cutter. Scissors. **1894** *Country Gentlemen's Catal.* 173/2 Pair nail scissors, button-hook and nail-file. **1922** F. Courtenay *Physical Beauty* 47 When you have shaped the external edge of the nails with a fine pair of scissors, finish with emery or a steel nail file. **1969** *Sears Catal.* Spring/Summer 397 Sapphire-coated Nail File... Two surfaces..one for shaping, one for finishing. **1966** J. S. Cox *Illustr. Dict. Hairdressing* 101/2 *Nail lacquer*, nitro-cellulose dissolved in Butyl Acetate and allied substances forming, when dry, a hard, tough, resistant film on the surface of the nail. **1973** J. Rossiter *Manipulators* viii. 90 A cosmetician's display of nail lacquers and lipstick cases. **1974** *Harpers & Queen* Sept. 50/3 We want to change our nail lacquers as often as our clothes. **1947** J. Steinbeck *Wayward Bus* xvii. 222 He took his gold nail-pick from his pocket and opened it and cleaned his nails. **1907** *Yesterday's Shopping* (1969) 538/3 Diamond Nail Enamel..box 0/10½... Electric Nail Polish..bot. 1/6. **1937** *Discovery* Mar. 86/1 It [*sc.* diatomite] is used in face powders and nail polishes. **1972** 'H. Carmichael' *Naked to Grave* i. 15 A tiny bottle of pink nail polish and another of nail polish remover. **1897** *Sears, Roebuck Catal.* 435/2 Chamois Nail Polisher, fancy Solid Sterling Silver mountings. **1913** E. Wharton *Custom of Country* I. i. 13 Mrs. Heeny, driving her nail-polisher cheeringly. **1854** J. E. Millais *Let.* 5 June in M. Lutyens *Millais & Ruskins* (1967) 222, I have had to operate upon myself with a pair of nail scissors. **1919** W. H. Downing *Digger Dial.* 35 *Nail scissors*, the crossed sword and baton worn as a badge of rank by a General. **1951** *Catal. of Exhibits, South Bank Exhib., Festival of Britain* 60/1 Baby's nail scissors ..Cuticle nail scissors. **1926–7** *Army & Navy Stores Catal.* 495/2 'Elite' Nail Varnish..bot. 1/6. **1936** *Chem. Abstr.* XXX. 7784 Cosmetics in pharmacy... A discussion of face powders, foundation creams,..shampoos and nail varnishes. **1954** *Granta* 6 Nov. 23/2 One uses nail varnish the other not. **1972** *Vogue* Feb. 46/2 Nail Varnish, Revlon's Ultima II. **1974** *She* Jan. 63/4 Nail Varnish Remover pads, 14p for 17.

c. *nail-biting* (further examples).

1941 Koestler *Scum of Earth* 151 But what was the symbolical meaning of all these..nail-biting..figures? **1959** *Ann. Reg. 1958* 190 Sinclair Weeks said..that the outlook was 'far better than the nail-biting pessimists think'. **1973** *Times* 2 Oct. 21/4 The next few weeks will be nail-biting ones for Leonard Grouse.

14. a. *nail boot, factory, machine* (earlier example), *mill*; **nail bomb**, a lethal weapon, used *esp.* by urban guerrillas, made from nails wrapped round a stick of gelignite; **nail-gall**, a nail-shaped gall produced on the leaves of lime and other trees by a mite of the genus *Phytoptus*; **nail-plate** (earlier and later examples); **nail-stubb**, a worn horse-shoe nail; a stub-nail; **nail violin** (see quot. 1959).

1971 *New Scientist* 26 Aug. 483/3 They will assess the effects on the elderly, the sick, children..of the explosives, nail-bomb, indiscriminate rifle and machine gun fire. **1971** *Guardian* 11 Oct. 20/3 A boy of about 10 threw a nail bomb at troops in Belfast yesterday. **1973** R. Clutterbuck *Protest & Urban Guerrilla* x. 111 The same unemployed teenage boys..turned out..almost every evening to throw stones and nail-bombs at army posts and patrols. **1973** 'I. Drummond' *Jaws of Watchdog* x. 135 These revolutionaries were not the ill-shaven back-street throwers of nail-bombs. They were a disciplined corps. **1923** D. H. Lawrence *Ladybird* 242 The other fellows with sticks and nail-boots had now taken heart and were scrambling like crabs past our hero. **1833** H. Barnard in *Maryland Hist. Mag.* (1918) XIII. 374, I found my old friend..who took me to see..a nail factory [etc.]. **1879** *Encycl. Brit.* X. 46/1 The lime-leaf 'nail-galls' of *Phytoptus tiliae* closely resemble the 'trumpet-galls' formed on American vines by a species of Cecidomyia. **1951** *Dict. Gardening* (R. Hort. Soc.) III. 1345/1 Nail-galls. Galls on leaves of Lime and other trees somewhat resembling tin-tacks driven through the leaf tissues. They result from attacks of species of Phytoptus. **1819** E. Dana *Geogr. Sk. Western Country* 77 Zanesville is ..at the falls, whereon various mills are erected..including..an oil mill, nail machine, and woolen factory. **1850** *Rep. Comm. Patents: Agric. 1849* (U.S. Dept. Agric.) 93 Within its present limits are about fifty cotton factories.. seven rolling, slitting, and nail mills. **1797** in *Essex Inst. Hist. Coll.* (1918) LIV. 107 Agreed with Mr. Allen to work at eight shillings pr. ton..cutting every kind of rods and dubble for iron hoops or nail plates. **1945** *Amer. Speech* XX. 115 Since the cut nail is an American invention, the word *nail-plate* must be of American origin. **1851** H. Melville *Moby Dick* III. xxvii. 176 Look ye, blacksmith, these are the gathered nail-stubbs of the steel shoes of racing horses. **1884** E. Heron-Allen *Violin-Making* v. 108 In the year 1740 a German musician, named Johann Wilde,..invented a curious instrument called a Nail-violin. **1944** W. Apel *Harvard Dict. Mus.* 478/1 There exists a quartet by F. W. Rust for nail violin, two violins and cello. **1959** *Collins Mus. Encycl.* 448/2 *Nail Violin*... It consisted of a semicircular resonator of wood into which were driven U-shaped nails of graduated lengths. The sound was produced by a bow.

b. *nail-driver* (transf. examples).

1823 J. F. Cooper *Pilot* I. viii. 106 The cannon, above which were painted the several quaint names of 'boxer',.. 'exterminator', and 'nail-driver'. **1872** *Life of Bill Hickman* 54 (Th.), I had a nail-driver [*sc.* a horse], very swift, and no end to his bottom.

c. nail-tailed wallaby *Austral.*, a wallaby of the genus *Onychogalea*, distinguished by white stripes on the cheeks and at the top of each limb, and a horny nail near the end of the tail.

1896 F. G. Aflalo *Sk. Nat. Hist. Austral.* i. 43 The Nail-tailed (*Onychogalea*) and Hare (*Lagorchestes*) Wallabies are wanting in Tasmania, though three species of each are found on the mainland. **1896** [in Dict., sense 13 c]. **1970** W. D. L. Ride *Guide Native Mammals Austral.* 53 Three species of rather strikingly marked wallabies are called nail-tailed wallabies because they possess a small dark horny nail, rather like a finger nail, hidden in the dark hair at the end of the slender tail.

nail, *v.* Add: **5. b.** Delete *rare*$^{-1}$ and add later example.

1902 'Mark Twain' in *Harper's Mag.* Feb. 431/2 Nailing an alibi where it can't be budged.

8. a. Hence also, to arrest. *slang.*

1889 [in Dict.]. **1918** [see *cut *sb.*^{2} 23 d]. **1931** *Amer. Speech* VII. 111 They nailed me right on the border. **1969** C. F. Burke *God is Beautiful, Man* (1970) 29 The cops..nail Ben for havin' the cup.

nailer. Add: **3. b.** [f. *nail *v.* 8 a.] A policeman or detective. *slang.*

c **1863** T. Taylor in M. R. Booth *Eng. Plays of 19th Cent.* (1969) II. 84 Then there's the Nailer's been after me... What, Hawkshaw, the 'cutest detective in the force? **1935** A. J. Pollock *Underworld Speaks* 79/1 *Nailer*, a uniformed police officer.

nail-head. Add: **1.** Also *fig.*

1855 *Rambler* III. 239 Mr. Forster will have it that the language..scribbled on the rocks of the desert of Sinai, in the Egyptian hieroglyphics, and in the 'nail-head' letters of Assyria and Persia, is all one. **1948** D. Diringer *Alphabet* vi. 358 The vertical strokes ended with wedges or 'nailheads'; this script was therefore termed 'nail-headed'.

2. (Further examples.)

1947 *Sun* (Baltimore) 31 Oct. 3/7 (Advt.), It can look dressed-up or casual with its gold-toned nailheads, oblong gold-toned buckle. **1973** *Philadelphia Inquirer* (Today Suppl.) 14 Oct. 14/1 (Advt.), Zip-front shirt jac with nailhead trim. **1974** *Sumter* (S. Carolina) *Daily Item* 24 Apr. (Belk Stroman Advts. Suppl.) 2 Denim shifts with nailheads, embroidery, polka dot or check trims!

nail-headed, *a.* (Later examples.)

1936 D. Gascoyne *Man's Life is this Meat* 19 In my hand lies the same whispering, nail-headed dude, ever imploring the benefice of a hippograph. **1948** [see *nail-head 1].

nai·l-punch. *Joinery.* [f. Nail *sb.* + Punch *sb.*^{1} 2.] A driving punch for nails.

1899 C. G. Wheeler *Woodworking for Beginners* (1900) xvi. 433 *Nail-Set, or Punch*.., for sinking nail-heads below the surface, is quite important, and it is well to have a large one and a fine one. **1951** *Practical Home Woodworking* ii. 36 A nail-punch has a flat 'point'. **1973** *Practical Woodworking* 34 It is sometimes necessary to drive the head of a nail well below the surface and to fill the resulting cavity with putty... Nail sets, or nail punches, as they are sometimes called are designed for this purpose.

nail-rod. Add: **1. b.** (Earlier example.)

1869 *Rep. Comm. Agric. 1868* (U.S. Dept. Agric.) 433 The most convenient method of destroying the bugs is by using a pair of tongs made of nail-rod.

2. (Further examples.)

Quot. 1896 is U.K.

1890 A. J. Vogan *Black Police* 200 He hands our black friend a piece of 'nailrod' with which to charge his evening pipe. **1896** L. Tracy *Final War* xi. 77 Then joy prevailed, and the fumes of nail-rod mingled in the breeze with the strains of 'Annie Laurie'.

Nailsea (nēi·lsī). The name of a town near Bristol, used to designate a style of glassware first made there in the late 18th century. Freq. *attrib.*

[**1897** A. Hartshorne *Old Eng. Glass* xix. 307 Nailsea, near Bristol, was another [source], with darker coloured glass, sometimes blue. **1907** E. Dillon *Glass* 368/2 (*index*) Nailsea glass-works.] **1910** D. Wilmer *Early Eng. Glass* xi. 205 The manufacture of Nailsea glass continued until about the year 1873, some of the latest productions having gilt decoration. **1926** N. H. Moore *Old Glass* i. 170 The Nailsea glass which is of interest to collectors shows specimens very beautiful in color, like the ornamental flasks which were Nailsea's chief product. **1960** H. Hayward *Antique Coll.* 195/1 *Nailsea glass*, the brownish-green glass speckled with white with which the name of Nailsea, near Bristol, is associated, was used on occasions for the making of wine-bottles, and sealed examples exist. **1961** E. M. Elville *Collector's Dict. Glass* 140/1 Also described as 'Nailsea' are the peculiar love-tokens which were..made at all glassworks near coastal towns. **1966** J. Laver *Victoriana* xiv. 173 (*caption*) Bottles decorated with loops of coloured glass, one of many varieties known as 'Nailsea'. **1971** *Guardian* 23 Mar. 32/8 Nailsea style coloured glass for sale..including walking sticks, bells, bottles, bellows.

nai·l-set. *Joinery.* [f. Nail *sb.* + Set *sb.*^{1} 33.] = *nail-punch.

1899 [see *nail-punch]. **1927** R. A. Freeman *Certain Dr. Thorndyke* ii. xviii, Carpenters don't fix mouldings on with screws. They use nails and punch them in with a 'nail-set' and stop the holes with putty. **1947** J. C. Rich *Materials & Methods Sculpture* vi. 170 The tools required for chasing may be purchased or fashioned by the sculptor either from tool steel,..or from small steel tools called nail sets. If nail-set tools are used it will be first necessary to remove or draw out the temper, prior to shaping the ends by means of filing into the desired forms. **1973** [see *nail-punch].

naio (nai·*o*). Also **naeo, naieo.** [Hawaiian.] An evergreen tree, *Myoporum sandwicense*, of the family Myoporaceæ, native to Hawaii and bearing clusters of pink or white flowers; also called bastard sandalwood, as its wood is fragrant. Cf. *ngaio.

1888 W. Hillebrand *Flora Hawaiian Islands* 339 The wood of the 'Naeo' or 'Naieo', most so that of the roots, becomes fragrant on drying. **1915** W. A. Bryan *Nat. Hist. Hawaii* xvi. 222 The bastard sandalwood or naieo is a tree common on the summit of Kaala, and the higher forest belt generally. **1970** S. Carlquist *Hawaii* xv. 275 The naio, *Myoporum sandwicense*, is a common dry forest tree with relatives in New Zealand and on South Pacific islands.

naira (nəi·rǎ). [See quots. 1972.] A unit of currency in Nigeria, equal to 100 kobo.

1972 *N.Y. Times* 9 Aug. 14 On Jan. 1, 1973, Nigeria will scrap her system of Nigerian pounds,..and begin a decimal currency system with units of money called the naira and the kobo... The name is adapted from the word Nigeria. **1972** *Times* 9 Oct. (Nigeria Suppl.) p. viii/4 The new currency being introduced by the Central Bank of Nigeria consists of naira and kobo. Kobo are coins and naira are notes. The origin of the names has not been fully explained, but naira is said to have been derived from the word Nigeria. *Ibid.*, The various denominations of the naira notes, which are now on display in public places, carry pictures showing various aspects of Nigeria's economic activities. The old Nigerian coins which they replace bear the head of the Queen of England. **1974** *Globe & Mail* (Toronto) 2 Oct. 7/3 A number of firms.. were allowed to stay on, provided they raised their capital to at least 200,000 Naira (roughly $350,000).

naïve, *a.* Add: **1. b.** Philos. *naïve realism.* Also *naïf realism.* [The fem. form, despite being adj. to a sb. which in Fr. is masc., has acquired currency in English.] The belief, attributed to non-philosophers, that the world is directly perceived as it really is, as contrasted with philosophical theories of sense-data, the subjectivity of colour, etc. So *naïve realist.*

1882 W. James *Will to Believe* (1897) 290 Even the most *naïf* realism will hardly pretend that the non-table as such exists *in se* after the same fashion as the table does. **1895** F. Thilly tr. *Paulsen's Introd. Philos.* ii. i. 344 We start out from the popular conception whose standpoint is *naïve Realism.* **1897** B. Russell *Ess. Found. Geometry* ii. 93 Those who have done most to further non-Euclidean Geometry —with the exception of Riemann, who was a disciple of Herbart—have usually inherited from Newton a naïve realism as regards absolute space. **1909** W. James *Meaning of Truth* ii. 50 The reader will observe that the text is written from the point of view of *naïf* realism or common sense. **1914** C. D. Broad *Perception* i. 1 We are going to begin from the position of naïf realism. It is true that our everyday view of the world is not quite naïvely realistic, but that is what it would like to be. **1932** [see *illusion 4 b]. **1932** H. H. Price *Perception* ii. 26 We ask a Naïve Realist what sort of thing it is whose existence he knows of. *Ibid.* iii. 61 The Naïve Realist conception of 'belonging to' would not have been saved. **1954** A. J. Ayer *Philos. Ess.* vi. 142 The naïve realist is not in error. Naïve realism is not a false theory of perception: it is a refusal to play this sort of game. **1971** A. Flew *Introd. Western Philos.* iii. x. 346 The position supported by the uninstructed 'instincts and propensities of nature' is by instructing philosophers labelled contemptuously, 'Naïve Realism'.

c. *naïve painter*: a painter who has not been trained in a formal manner; so *naïve painting.* Cf. *naïf *a.* 1 b.

1957 *Observer* 3 Nov. 14/4 Naive or primitive painting is a discovery of the twentieth century... The innocent eyes of the often untaught naïve painters give an account of the world quite unhampered by preconceptions of what paintings of it should be like. **1961** *Spectator* 28 July 149 A very intense, fat little book on naïve painters, with Henri Rousseau as the grand point of departure. **1970** *Time* 9 Feb. 54 The United States possesses the oldest, the most original, and just about the most authentic naïve painters.

2. *Biol.* and *Psychol.* Not having previously had a particular experience or been the subject of a particular experiment, *esp.* not having taken or received a particular drug; unconditioned. Const. *to.*

1940 *Amer. Jrnl. Psychol.* LIII. 46 (*heading*) Configurational properties considered 'good' by naïve subjects. **1961** *Jrnl. Agric. Sci.* LVII. 401 Assessments of bacon qualities by naïve and experienced judges using photographic reference standards. **1963** *Animal Behaviour* XI. 463 The naive female cat does not exhibit the complete mating pattern on the first opportunity for sexual behaviour. **1969** *Sci. Jrnl.* Sept. 42/1 When research subjects are volunteers who are naive to marihuana, an effective placebo is no problem. **1970** *Nature* 11 Apr. 119/1 Interesting social and psychological similarities and differences were revealed among three groups of subjects: marijuana naïve persons (N), persons not naïve to marijuana (NN) and chronic marijuana users (C). **1974** *Ibid.* 19 Apr. 697/1 Twenty experimentally naïve male albino Wistar rats..were anaesthetised with ether.

naïveness (naˌī·vnės). *rare.* [f. NAÏVE *a.* + -NESS.] = NAÏVETY.

1949 KOESTLER *Insight & Outlook* 387 The reconquest of 'naiveness' is one of the periodic revolutions in painting. **1968** *Classical Q.* XVIII. 208 A weakness of the book ..is a certain naïveness of interpretation.

naked, *a.* and *sb.*[1] **A. 1. b.** Delete †*Obs.* and add further examples.

1654 E. GAYTON *Pleasant Notes Don Quixot* III. iv. 88 As naked and bare as a shorne Sheep, as we say in our English Proverbe. **1860** O. W. HOLMES *Prof. at Breakfast-Table* iii. 39 A friend..had a watch given him ..with a loose silver case... You know them,—the cases that you hang on your thumb, while the..real watch, lies in your hand as naked as a peeled apple. **1879–81** G. F. JACKSON *Shropshire Word-Bk.* 297 W'y yo' bin as naked as a robin. **1890** D. C. MURRAY *John Vale's Guardian* III. xxxviii. 215 Time was I wouldn't ha' married her..without her lands. You can send her now as naked as a robin, if you like. **1939** *N. & Q.* 15 July 42/1 As naked as a needle. **1943** *Amer. Speech* XVIII. 67/2 Naked as a jaybird. **1963** J. T. ROWLAND *North to Adventure* xi. 160 Tell us what you were doing, standing naked as a jaybird. **1974** *State* (Columbia, S. Carolina) 8 Mar. 1-B/1 Just a footnote to ask if there is any truth to the rumor that 'naked as a jaybird' is going to be amended to use 'gamecock'!

e. In printing, *naked forme* (see quots.).

1683–4 J. MOXON *Mech. Exerc. Printing* (1962) 347 *Naked Form*,..is when the Furniture is taken from about all sides of the Form. **1888** C. T. JACOBI *Printers' Vocab.* 86 *Naked forme*, a forme of type waiting for—or stripped of—furniture. **1960** G. A. GLAISTER *Gloss. Bk.* 144/1 A 'naked forme' consists of pages of type secured by page-cord; a 'dressed forme' is one of pages of type with furniture between and around them and the page-cord removed.

6. c. *naked force*, unconcealed, ruthless force.

1963 E. WILSON in *New Statesman* 6 Dec. 847/2 According to the United States State Department, Fidel Castro uses naked force in Cuba.

11. b. (Further examples.) Also *attrib.*

1929 R. GRAVES *Poems* 18 Then it's those naked-light instructions That the muctions plaster up. **1966** *Listener* 18 Aug. 237/1 The naked electric-light bulb had to be left on all day. **1971** *Chambers's Dict. Sci. & Technol.* 787/2 *Naked-light mine*, nonfiery mine, where safety lamps are not required.

15. b. (Further examples.)

1908 *Westm. Gaz.* 11 Aug. 12/1 The other naked-eye planets are too near the sun to be visible. **1930** *Times Educ. Suppl.* 5 Jan. p. iv/3 Within the limit of the naked-eye visibility. **1965** *Listener* 20 May 741/1 Another naked-eye cluster is Præsepe in Cancer, now well placed during the evenings.

17. *naked-footed, -handed* adjs. and advs.; *naked-limbed, -nerved* adjs.; **naked ape,** man, *Homo sapiens*; **naked boys, lady,** see sense A I. 1 c.

1967 D. MORRIS (*title*) The naked ape. **1967** *Spectator* 10 Nov. 577/1 Even before man has destroyed all other animals to make more room for himself, the naked ape may well destroy himself also. **1973** W. BARLOW *Alexander Principle* iii. 33 The 'Naked Ape' has replaced Rousseau's 'Noble Savage'. **1923** D. H. LAWRENCE *Birds, Beasts & Flowers* 16 And yet the soul continuing, naked-footed, ever more vividly embodied. **1848** *Sporting Life* 1 July 210/2 The savage..does not fear to encounter the dangers of his chase naked-handed. **1869** WHITTIER *Hive at Gettysburg* in *Poetical Works* (1898) 380/2 And he who, lone and naked-handed, tore Those jaws of death apart. *a* **1930** D. H. LAWRENCE *Phoenix* (1936) III. 164 There the painted women dance..opposite the naked-limbed men. **1933** DYLAN THOMAS *Let.* Nov. (1966) 48 It is typical of the..naked-nerved..to emphasise its brutality.

nakhlite (nā·kləit). *Geol.* [f. El *Nakhla* el Baharia, the village near Alexandria, Egypt, where the first known examples fell in 1911 + -ITE[1].] Any of a class of achondrites containing about 75 per cent ferroan diopside and 15 per cent olivine.

1916 [see *HOWARDITE 2]. **1962** B. MASON *Meteorites* vii. 116 The diopside-olivine achondrites or nakhlites are represented by two meteorites, Lafayette (Indiana, U.S.A.) and Nakhla (Egypt). **1971** [see *HOWARDITE 2].

Hence **nakhli·tic** *a.*

1963 *Geochim. & Cosmochim. Acta* XXVII. 1077 Abundances of cadmium have been determined by neutron-activation analysis in 31 meteorites:..0·18 and 1·79 p.p.m. in two nakhlitic achondrites. **1971** P. R. BUSECK in B. Mason *Handbk. Elemental Abundances in Meteorites* 365 (*table*) Type... Nakhlitic.

‖ **nakodo** (nǎkōᵘ·do). Also **nakohdo.** [Jap.] In Japan, one who acts as go-between in the arrangement of a marriage.

1890 B. H. CHAMBERLAIN *Things Japanese* 221 The conduct of the affair must be entrusted to a middleman (*nakōdo*)—some discreet married friend, who not only negotiates the marriage, but remains through life a sort of godfather to the young couple. **1895** L. HEARN *Out of East* viii. 258 He was a professional nakōdo, or match-maker, and was..acting in the service of a wealthy rice dealer. **1902** —— *Kottō* x. 123 A majority of Japanese marriages, indeed, are arranged..with the aid of a nakōdo. **1936** K. NOHARA *True Face of Japan* iv. 85 Although he receives monetary compensation for his services, the Nakohdo is not a professional marriage-broker.

nala, var. NULLAH (in Dict. and Suppl.).

N.A.L.G.O., NALGO, Nalgo (næ·lgo). [Acronym f. the initial letters of *N*ational *A*ssociation of *L*ocal *G*overnment *O*fficers.] The name of a trade union of municipal, county, etc., local-government servants.

1909 *Municipal Jrnl.* 29 Oct. 896/2 A change in the Executive Offices of such an organization as the N.A.L.G.O. is always a matter of concern. **1957** *Times* 12 Nov. 8/1 A delegate conference of Nalgo health service branches will be held in London on Sunday. **1962** *Listener* 12 July 74/3 Pompous remarks about Nalgo and the T.U.C. **1975** *Guardian* 5 Nov. 8/8 The social workers, all members of NALGO, say that..the money could be better spent.

nalorphine (næ·lǫ̈ɹfīn). *Pharm.* [f. *N-allylnormorphine*, another name for the compound (see quot. 1953[2]).] A heterocyclic base, $C_{19}H_{21}NO_3$ (or its hydrobromide salt), which is very similar to morphine in chemical structure and is used as an antagonist for that drug and for other narcotics with a similar action.

1953 *Jrnl. Pharmacol. & Exper. Therap.* CIX. 157 N-allylnormorphine (nalorphine) has been shown to have a specific respiratory stimulating effect against the depression caused by morphine,..codeine, methadone. **1953** *Proc. R. Soc. Med.* XLVI. 927 *N*-Allylnormorphine is now officially called nalorphine... A methyl group is removed from the nitrogen [of morphine], hence the term NOR from the German 'Nitrogen ohne radicale'. An allyl group is substituted. **1967** *Martindale's Extra Pharmacopoeia* (ed. 25) 838 Given apart from narcotics, nalorphine may itself cause respiratory depression and disturbing psychotic effects. **1968** J. H. JAFFE in D. H. Efron *Psychopharmacol.* VIII. 854/1 Nalorphine has virtually no abuse potential; its subjective effects are not 'liked' by post-addicts; it does not relieve morphine withdrawal symptoms, but instead precipitates them, and when given over long periods in high doses it produces an atypical physical dependence in which withdrawal symptoms are not associated with craving. **1971** H. W. ELLIOTT in D. H. Clouet *Narcotic Drugs* xxvi. 484 The pharmacological basis for the nalorphine test is an antagonism between nalorphine and the morphine-like drugs, which can be detected by examining the pupil.

naloxone (nælǫ·ksōᵘn). *Pharm.* [f. *N-allylnoroxymorphone*, an alternative name for the compound.] A heterocyclic base, $C_{20}H_{23}NO_4$ (or one of its salts), which resembles nalorphine in its chemical structure and antagonism to narcotics (see quot. 1968).

1964 *Amer. Jrnl. Med. Sci.* CCXLVII. 412 The n-allyl derivative of oxymorphone (Numorphan) has recently been synthesized and found to be a potent narcotic antagonist... It has also been suggested that this preparation (Naloxone), differs from other narcotic antagonists in that its administration simultaneously with a narcotic results in antagonism of the respiratory depression but not of the analgesia induced by the narcotic. **1968** *Clin. Pharmacol. & Therapeutics* IX. 215/1 Unlike nalorphine and cyclazocine, naloxone does not produce miosis, subjective effects, tolerance, or physical dependence. **1973** *Nature* 23 Mar. 228/3 Binding was demonstrated by incubating tissue homogenates with tritium-labelled naloxone, a potent antagonist which precipitates withdrawal in humans addicted to opiates.

Nam (næm, nām). Also **'Nam.** Colloq. abbrev. of *Vietnam.*

1969 *Time* 2 May 33/1 'Nam' or 'The Nam' is widely used by U.S. troops to refer to Vietnam. **1973** R. LUDLUM *Matlock Paper* vii. 66 The early days in 'Nam..those weeks of unreported combat. **1973** J. DI MONA *Last Man at Arlington* (1974) 198 [We] were a unit in 'Nam. **1974** *Publishers Weekly* 30 Dec. 93/3 Four Americans caught in Vietnam... The GIs become buddies in Germany... Now in 'Nam' they hope their camaraderie will be closer still.

Nama (nā·mǎ), *a.* and *sb.* [Hottentot.] **A.** *adj.* Pertaining to or designating one of the four main Hottentot tribes, found in Namaqualand in western South Africa. **B.** *sb.* **a.** A member of this tribe; these people collectively. **b.** Their language, a dialect of Hottentot. Hence **Na·man** *a.* and *sb.*

1864 W. H. I. BLEEK *Reynard the Fox in S. Afr.* p. xxix, To make our available stock of Nama Hottentot literature quite complete. **1881** T. HAHN *Tsuni-‖Goam* i. 3 In the Nama language, one of the Khoikhoi idioms, the Bushmen are called Sā-n (com. plur). *Ibid.* ii. 89, I afterwards made him a present of ammunition, and, as anxious as a Nama is to possess that most precious material, he said: 'No; you want to pay [for] my cow, and I shall not accept it.' **1908** T. G. TUCKER *Introd. Nat. Hist. Lang.* viii. 148 Hottentot dialects: viz. *Nama* (of the Namaqua) to the north-west, [etc.]. **1930** C. G. SELIGMAN *Races Afr.* ii. 34 The customary division of the Hottentots into four main groups—Naman, Korana, Gonaqua, and Old Cape Hottentots. **1944** M. OLDEVIG *Sunny Land* 51 Namas—or Hottentots. *Ibid.* 53 Three different Nama tribes. **1965** [see *HOTTENTOT 2]. **1966** J. H. GREENBERG *Lang. Afr.* (ed. 2) 68 Nama Hottentot indicates the past by an element *go* (in the usual orthography). *Ibid.*, In Nama there is no phonemic distinction between *k* and *g*. **1974** *Times* 14 Jan. 4/6 They have intermarried with Coloured and Nama (Hottentot) people.

Namaqua (nǎmā·kwǎ), *a.* and *sb.* [Hottentot, f. *Nama* (see prec.) + *-qua*, f. *khoi* man.] **1.** = *NAMA *a.* and *sb.*

[**1668** O. DAPPER in I. Schapera *Early Cape Hottentots* (1933) 34 De Hottentots, genaemt *Namaquas*, leggen tegenwoordigh ontrent tachentigh of tuegentigh mÿlen oost-noord-oostwaerts van de kaep van goeder hope, maer zeer verre te landewaerts in.] **1670** J. OGILBY *Africa* 576 The chiefest people hitherto discover'd in this Southerly part of Africa, are the Gorachouqua's, Goringhaiqua's, Goringhaikona's, Kochoqua's,..Namaqua's, Heusaqua's, Brigoudins, and Hankumqua's. **1790** E. HELME tr. *Le Vaillant's Trav. Afr.* I. vii. 133, I had been assured there were some [*sc.* gazelles] in the country of the great *Namaquois*. **1806** J. BARROW *Voy. Cochinchina* 374 Their dwellings..are constructed on the same principle as those of the Namaqua Hottentots. **1822** W. J. BURCHELL *Trav. S. Afr.* I. 582 To the Hottentot Race are referable the tribes denominated Bushmen, the Namaquas, and Koras or Koraquas, as well as the Hottentots proper. **1822** [see *GRIQUA *sb.* and *a.*]. **1849** E. E. NAPIER *Excursions S. Afr.* I. 53 The Dutch became gradually acquainted not only with numerous hordes of Hottentots, similar to those at the Cape; but likewise with a few varieties of the same race, such as the Namaquas. **1851** J. ANDERSON in G. M. Theal *Yellow & Dark-Skinned People Afr.* (1910) iii. 58 The signs of gender were almost identical in the Namaqua and the Egyptian. **1865** [see HOTTENTOT 2]. **1880** *Encycl. Brit.* XI. 731/2, 3000 Bushmen, 1500 Namaqua. **1930** I. SCHAPERA *Khoisan Peoples S. Afr.* I. ii. 48 The Great Namaqua were always the most northerly group of Hottentots, and probably formed the rearguard of their invasion of South Africa. **1932** *Times Lit. Suppl.* 15 Sept. 642/2 There was a little trouble with some Namaqua guides who suddenly refused to go any further. **1959** *Chambers's Encycl.* VII. 248/1 In south-west Africa many of the 15,000 Namaqua retain their Hamitic speech. **1972** *Stand. Encycl. S. Afr.* V. 607/1 The Nama (also called Naman or Namaqua) consisted of two groups: the Little Nama, living in the North-Western Cape south of the Orange River, and the Great Nama, living in South-West Africa.

2. Namaqua dove, a small, long-tailed dove, *Œna capensis*, found in Africa south of the Sudan; **Namaqua grouse, partridge, sand-grouse,** a terrestrial game bird, *Pterocles namaqua.*

1801 J. BARROW *Acct. Trav. S. Afr.* I. iv. 325 Along the road were numbers of that beautiful little pigeon, called here the Namaaqua dove, not larger than a sparrow. **1864** T. BAINES *Explor. S.-W. Afr.* v. 124 A pretty Namaqua dove fluttered about in abortive efforts to sip the water. **1905** J. DU PLESSIS *Thousand Miles in Afr.* 137 Little black-eyed Namaqua doves. **1947** J. STEVENSON-HAMILTON *Wild Life S. Afr.* xxxiv. 291 Doves... The little namaqua (*Oena capensis*) appears to be a winter migrant to the eastern Transvaal low country. **1972** *Shooting Times & Country Mag.* 27 May 24/2 Mourning, laughing and even tiny, wagtail-sized Namaque [*sic*] doves arrive to raid the crops. **1806** J. BARROW *Trav. S. Afr.* (ed. 2) I. iii. 219 Cape partridges and the Namaaqua grouse were equally plentiful. **1867** E. L. LAYARD *Birds S. Afr.* 277 Namaqua Grouse... Namaqua Patrys of Colonists. **1790** E. HELM tr. *Le Vaillant's Trav. Afr.* II. xxi. 434 The Hottentots of the colonies call them perdrix Namaquais, (Namaquai partridges). **1890** A. MARTIN *Home Life Ostrich Farm* xi. 227 The beautiful little 'Namaqua partridges'..are in reality a kind of grouse. **1936** E. L. GILL *First Guide S. Afr. Birds* 113 Namaqua Sandgrouse, Namaqua Partridge... Much the most widespread of the Sandgrouse in South Africa. **1972** Namaqua partridge [see *KORHAAN]. **1893** H. A. BRYDEN *Gun & Camera S. Afr.* xxii. 477 The Namaqua sandgrouse [drinks] between eight and ten in the morning. **1962** MACKWORTH-PRAED & GRANT *Birds S. Third Afr.* 372 Namaqua Sandgrouse... Birds of the desert fringe. A common Sandgrouse of the drier parts of South Africa especially the western side.

‖ **namaskar** (namaskā·ɹ). *India.* Also **namashkar, namaskara.** [Hindi, ad. Skr. *namaskārā*, the greeting '*namas*', obeisance.] = *NAMASTE *sb.*

1930 C. PARSONS *Mysore City* 88 Indian girls..making the silent and beautiful salutation of the 'namaskāra'—folded hands and bent head and bowing figure. **1948** *U.N. World* (N.Y.) Apr. 35 One by one they filed past, some doing *namaskar* (hands placed together in an attitude of prayer), others bowing low. **1966** J. & R. GODDEN *Two under Indian Sun* iv. 102 Instead of a handshake, he uses the namashkar, the graceful movement that means 'to take the other's dust upon you', hands joined together as if in prayer and raised to the forehead or the breast according to the rank or honour of the person saluted. **1967** SINGHA & MASSEY *Indian Dances* iii. 44 Indians always

use joined palms for the namashkar, that is, when they greet anyone, but the position in which they are held indicates the status of the person greeted. **1969** R. Shankar *My Music* i. 12/1 The simplest gesture of the *namaskar*, or greeting (putting the hands palm to palm in front of the forehead and bowing). **1972** 'E. Peters' *Death to Landlords!* viii. 113 Priya offered her *namaskar* shyly.

‖ **namaste** (nā·maste), *sb.* and *int.* *India.* Also **namasthe.** [Hindi, ad. Skr. *nȧmas*, bowing, obeisance + *te* dat. of *tuam*, you (sing.).] **A.** *sb.* A salutatory gesture made by bringing the palms together before the face or chest and bowing. Also *attrib.*

1948 *Time* 16 Aug. 30 In response Nehru closed palms in front of his chest. This traditional Hindu *namasthe* (greeting) is as much a part of his public manner as was the V sign for Churchill. **1951** J. Masters *Nightrunners Bengal* vii. 97 She brought her palms together in front of her face and moved them up to her forehead and down again in the gesture called *namaste*. **1959** M. Brecher *Nehru* 385 A young man stepped forward from the crowd and greeted Gandhi in the traditional *namaste* salutation, joining his hands palm to palm and bowing slightly. **1960** Koestler *Lotus & Robot* i. i. 52 A toothless Brahmin.. walked in and, after a dignified *namaste*, hung a garland round my neck. **1965** E. Linton *World in Grain of Sand* vii. 114, I shall be waiting for a letter from you. Namastes and love from Savitri. *Ibid.*, I join my hands in 'namaste' to you and Chander Kala. **1973** 'B. Mather' *Snow Line* vii. 79 The namaste sign..is with the palms together as in prayer, head bowed reverently and nose touching the fingertips.

B. *int.* Used as a respectful greeting.

1967 D. C. Cooke *c/o American Embassy* (1968) ii. 21 '*Namaste*, Sahib,' the Sikh said. **1969** 'E. Peters' *Mourning Raga* iii. 48 She pressed her hands together in reverence to him, and bowed her head..'Namaste!'

Hence **na·maste** *v. intr.*, to give the *namaste* sign.

1969 J. K. Galbraith *Ambassador's Jrnl.* xxvi. 586 After we had shaken hands, waved, *namasted* and got on board, the crowd lined up by the plane and one of the engines failed to start. **1971** R. Parkes *Line of Fire* xi. 101 He namasted gravely. **1971** *Illustr. Weekly India* 18 Apr. 6 The crowds clustered there drew apart, respectfully '*namasteing*', as the big man at the wheel acknowledged their greetings and drove in.

name, *sb.* Add: **1. c.** *Stockbroking.* The ticket bearing the name of the purchaser of stock, handed over to the selling broker on name-day or ticket-day.

[**1891** G. H. Stutfield *Rules & Usages Stock Exchange* 59 When the issuer of the ticket is a broker,..he has to insert the name of his client as the person into whose name the Stock is to be transferred.] **1907** Poley & Gould *Hist., Law & Pract. Stock Exchange* 178 It is called the ticket or name day because of the passing of tickets or names on that day. **1934** F. E. Armstrong *Bk. Stock Exchange* x. 193 'Names' play an important part in the settlement of Stock Exchange transactions. **1968** J. D. Hamilton *Stockbroking Today* i. iii. 89 Once in the office the names are sorted by the Names Department so that each name or batch of names matches a certain sale..and where there is more than one ticket they are pinned together.

d. (*or*) *my name is not* ——, appended to a statement as an assertion of its truth.

1803 S. Owenson *St. Clair* vi. 29 Sir Patrick will make the walls of the old Abbey ring again, or my name is not Michael M'Carty. **1898** J. D. Brayshaw *Slum Silhouettes* 220, I tell yer straight, if me an' Kitty don't make Soufend sit up, my name ain't Bill Brown. **1962** C. S. Forester *Hornblower & Hotspur* xiii. 174 We'll have a westerly gale, sir, or my name's not William Bush.

e. *to put*, or *write, someone's name down for*: to enter someone's name on a list of those interested in sharing in, acquiring, or taking part in a particular commodity or activity (cf. Put *v.*^{1} 41 i).

1819 M. Edgeworth *Let.* 2 Apr. (1971) 193 Lady Jersey..told me she would put down our names and give me some tickets for Almacks. Of the 5 Patronesses she is supposed to rule. **1821** —— *Let.* 30 Oct. (1971) 248 The Colleges are now so full that a young mans name must be written down 3 or 4 years before he can hope to get in. **1824** [see Put *v.*^{1} 41 i]. **1969** *Guardian* 20 Mar. 20/3 Lord Linley, seven-year-old son of Princess Margaret and Lord Snowdon, had had his name put down for Eton. **1974** *Listener* 25 Apr. 525/3 Frances has her name down for Danesbury [Hospital] just in case something should happen to Ron.

f. *give it a name*: what would you like to drink?

1854 Dickens *Hard T.* i. vi. 43 What thall it be, Thquire... Thall it be Therry? Give it a name, Thquire! ..have a glath of bitterth. *c* **1863** T. Taylor in M. R. Booth *Eng. Plays of 19th Cent.* (1969) II. 88, I hope you'll allow me to stand treat—give it a name, gentlemen... Thank you, I never drink with strangers. **1929** J. B. Priestley *Good Companions* i. vi. 235 The waiter collected orders and told Inigo to give it a name. **1931** T. R. G. Lyell *Slang* 540 'Well, boys, the drinks are on me! Give it a name!' **1951** J. B. Priestley *Festival at Farbridge* i. ii. 59 What are you drinking? Give it a name, chaps—there's everything here.

g. *to have one's name* (*and number*) *on it*: of a bullet, etc.: to be destined to kill a particular person.

1917 A. G. Empey *Over Top* 312 Tommy detests these mortars because..he knows that it is only a matter of minutes before a German shell with his name and number on it will be knocking at his door. **1919** *Athenæum* 18 July 632/2 A soldier refers to the shell that kills him as 'having his name and number on it'. **1925** Fraser & Gibbons *Soldier & Sailor Words* 163 *Name* (*or number*) *on, to have one's*, said of a bullet that hit a man; *i.e.*, that it was destined for him. **1958** R. Storey *Touch it Light* in *Plays of Year* XVIII. 376 *Ted.* That farmer don't like us, sir. Ever since that bomb fell on his cowshed. *Og.* He thought it should have fallen on you? *Syd.* It had our name on it all right. **1973** D. Francis *Slay-Ride* xii. 140 The bomb probably had my name on it in the first place.

h. *no names, no pack-drill*: phr. used to indicate that if nobody is named as being responsible, nobody can be blamed. Cf. *pack-drill* s.v. Pack *sb.*^{1} 14 c.

1923 O. Onions *Peace in our Time* i. ii. 25 Men had a way of omitting the names of those of whom they spoke; no names no pack-drill. **1926** E. Wallace *More Educated Evans* vii. 160 There's a certain party—no names no pack-drill—who's fairly doggin' me to get information. **1931** P. MacDonald *Crime Conductor* i. i. 7 'Meaning?' said Cuthbertson. 'No names,' said Garth Johnson quickly, 'no pack drill!' **1955** M. Allingham *Beckoning Lady* ii. 32 It just means no name, no pack drill, and always speak well of them as has money to sue. **1962** 'B. Graeme' *Undetective* iii. 32 'It's a lie, mister. Who told you?' 'No names, no pack drill.'

i. *to have one's name in lights*: to be a well-known actor and so have one's name displayed in lights outside the theatre.

1929 J. B. Priestley *Good Companions* ii. i. 282 His determination to top the bill and have his name in electric lights. **1972** *Guardian* 15 Jan. 8/4, I couldn't wait to get up there with the best of them and see my name up in lights—topping the bill at the Palladium.

j. *the name of the game* (colloq.): the object or essence of an action, etc.

1966 *Legionary* (Ottawa) Oct. 36/1 Where the knight's concerned, quality is the name of the game. **1967** *Maclean's Mag.* Aug. 27/3 And if this means running up against slum landlords, do-nothing local councils or a hostile white community—well, that's the name of the game. **1970** G. Jackson *Let.* in *Soledad Brother* (1971) 247 We should never make it easy for them—by relaxing—at this stage of the educational process. Examples are crucially important. Well that's the name of the game right now. **1972** *Jazz & Blues* Sept. 7/3 If I can make you feel like you want to holler on your horn then that's the name of the game man. **1972** *Times* 29 Sept. 11/1 The name of the game this week is survival. **1973** *Nature* 6 July 2/1 Call my bluff was the name of the game at last week's meeting of the International Whaling Commission.

5. c. (Later examples of sense 'a celebrity'.) Also *attrib.* or as *adj.* Also in extended use, of a well-known group of people, esp. a jazz band (see *name band* below).

1936 *Variety* 17 June 32/1 The greatest 'names' in the industry, including the cream of its players. **1941** *Sun* (Baltimore) 28 July 11/5 Virtually all of the name horses in the land will be on the scene for the thirty-day meeting. **1943** *Ibid.* 14 Aug. 7/5 At least ten 'name' players, fellows like Gene Sarazen and Craig Wood and Byron Nelson and Walter Hagen, have assured Corcoran that they'd be available. **1945** L. Shelly *Jive Talk Dict.* 15/1 *Name*,.. most popular band at the moment. **1947** *Sat. Rev.* (U.S.) 11 Oct. 53/1 The growing group of record makers who..turn..to the reservoir of fine performing talent that ..lie outside the galaxy of first-rank star names. **1955** J. Betjeman in R. S. Thomas *Song at Year's Turning* 12 His publisher believed that a 'name' was needed to help sell the book. **1960** *20th Cent.* Apr. 342 A big factor in the sale of the more popular 'name' records is the personality cult. **1972** *Times* 12 Dec. 2/6 RIBA circles..had feared that the former Secretary of State, Mr Walker, would appoint a 'name' with glamour to a post where he would have had little real authority or influence. **1973** *Black World* Jan. 28/2 He has concerned himself with the promotional affairs of several 'name' theaters in the Cleveland area. **1973** *Times* 6 Feb. 7/3 There is a narrowing of the opportunities for 'name' designers (couture tailors). **1974** *Times Lit. Suppl.* 18 Jan. 50/3 Professor Eliade is what publishers like to call a 'name', and you cannot ignore him.

d. An underwriter at Lloyd's.

1885 G. van de Linde *Chartered Accountants' Students' Soc. Lect. Biogr. Lloyd's Policy* 10 The respective partners of Blank & Co.,..head the policy by underwriting it to the extent of £10,000 between them, each name being respectively responsible for the amount against the signature. **1928** Wright & Fayle *Hist. Lloyd's* xxiii. 422 Let us consider the career of an underwriting 'Name', that is an Underwriting Member of Lloyd's represented by an Agent. **1937** R. Straus *Lloyd's* xi. 257 Marine underwriters..offered themselves as 'Names' to those Underwriting Agents who specialised in non-marine risks. **1972** G. Lyall *Blame the Dead* iv. 23 He's a Name. *Ibid.* 24 That means a member; they call them Names. **1973** *Daily Tel.* 16 Oct. 3/7 Discussing evidence given earlier by her father, Dr Dugdale said he was a 'name' several times over at Lloyd's, concerned in shipping and aircraft insurance. He made her a 'name' ensuring her a great deal of capital and a very high income.

9. Also *in name only, only in name*: of a marriage without sexual relations.

1894 W. J. Locke *At Gate of Samaria* (1895) xxi. 245 Henceforward Thornton would be her husband only in name. **1972** A. Roudybush *Sybarite Death* (1974) xxi. 173, I married her..but it never even occurred to me that our marriage would be other than a marriage in name only. **1975** R. Player *Let's talk of Graves* ii. 60 She had hated her husband and been his wife only in name.

b. *in all but name*: of a situation or set of circumstances, existing but not officially acknowledged or recognized.

1934 J. E. Neale *Queen Elizabeth* xv. 251 In all but name the Papacy was at war with Elizabeth.

15. *attrib.* and *Comb.*, 'bearing a name', as *name-board* (later examples), *card* (later examples), *-label*, *-ribbon*, *-tab*; 'well-known', of or pertaining to a name (sense 5 or 7), as *name brand*, *-worthy* adj.; 'named after, or giving a name to, one', as *name-daughter* (later example), *name-flower*; in *Logic*, as *name-forming*, *-matrix*, *-relation*, *-variable*; in *Linguistics*: consisting of or pertaining to a proper name, as *name-element*, *-form*, *-giving*, *-group*, *-love*, *-stem*, *-system*; **name-act,** a cabaret act performed by well-known performers; **name band,** a jazz or dance band that has made a name for itself; hence **name band-leader**; **name-calling** *vbl. sb.*, abusive language, mere abuse; hence **name-call** *v.*; **name-dropping** *vbl. sb.*, familiar mention of the names of distinguished people in order to imply one's own importance; also *attrib.*; hence (as a back-formation) **name-drop** *v.*, **name-dropper**; **name-droppingly** *adv.*; **name-part,** also of a book, a ballet, etc.; **name-piece** = **name-poem*, **name-story*; **name-plate,** a metal plate bearing a name; *spec.* one attached to a piece of machinery, or displaying the name of a road or building; also *attrib.* and *fig.*; also as *vb.*; **name-poem,** the poem from which a volume of collected poems is named; **name-story,** the story from which a volume of collected short stories is named; **name-tag,** anything on which a name can be written, to identify the person or object to which it is fixed; **name-tape,** a piece of tape with a person's name woven into it or printed on it, fixed to a person's clothing for identification; hence **name-taped** *ppl. a.*

1942 Berrey & Van den Bark *Amer. Thes. Slang* § 590/15 *Name act*, an act consisting of well-known players. **1949** L. Feather *Inside Be-Bop* iii. 21 The Berry Brothers and several other name acts. **1967** *Stage* 2 Mar. 21/4 (Advt.), Top groups required for one night stands. Name acts for winter season cabaret. **1936** *Amer. Mercury* XXXVIII. p.x/1 *Name band*, a band that has gotten the breaks (whether they're good or not). **1938** *Sat. Even. Post* 2 Apr. 9/1 We are to have an orchestra—'a name-band by all means'. *Ibid.* 9/3 At least $2500 for a name band. **1955** L. Feather *Encycl. Jazz* (1956) 122 His son..is also a drummer, heard w[ith] Erskine Hawkins and other name bands including Count Basie, '55. **1963** *Globe & Mail* (Toronto) 8 Jan. 5/1 Although its popularity declined with the passing of the name bands, Toronto's Palace Pier was still a busy, and apparently profitable operation until yesterday. **1958** P. Gammond *Decca Bk. Jazz* xix. 236 The year 1951 saw the return to Britain of pre-war 'name' bandleader, Roy Fox. **1939** Auden & Isherwood *Journey to War* v. 121 On our left was a little station: we read its name-board, Ling Pao. **1955** J. Cope *Fair House* i. 24 The turn-off to the Boer farm was a gap in the bush at the roadside, no gate or fence or name-board. **1944** *Time* 7 Aug. 38/2 Five times in five minutes the cigaret-counter girl at a Walgreen store in Chicago repeated wearily, 'We have no name brands.' **1973** J. Rossiter *Manipulators* v. 51 Perhaps.. you've been name-calling somebody. And they didn't like it. **1853** Dickens *Nobody's Story* in *Househ. Words* Extra Christmas No. 35/2 Such name-calling and dirt-throwing. **1891** Name-calling [in Dict.]. **1947** *Amer. Speech* XXII. 231/1 *Namecalling*, the attempt to put a person or thing in a bad light by attaching to him or it a word with unpleasant connotations. **1965** G. Jackson *Let.* 16 Mar. in *Soledad Brother* (1971) 69, I have been subjected to the ordeal of hunger, thirst, name-calling, and other uncountable indignities. **1973** R. Ludlum *Matlock Paper* xxvi. 222, I don't want to be responsible for indiscriminate name-calling, any wide-spread panic. **1975** *Verbatim* Feb. 4/1 The argument is a little uneven, for here it delivers a polemic against name-calling, there against grammar. **1907** *Yesterday's Shopping* (1969) 361/2 (Advt.), Menu and name cards. **1925** W. J. Locke *Great Pandolfo* ii. 23 The beautiful lady whose name he had not caught, because, in abstraction, she had turned her name card maddeningly upside down, took little or no interest in him. **1969** A. Cade *Turn up Stone* i. 25 Michael's experience in the Middle East had taught him the importance of the exchange of name cards in many countries. A man without a card was a man without an identity. **1891** R. L. Stevenson *Let.* Nov. (1899) II. 241, I shal begin to despair of everything but my name-daughter. **1955** J. D. Salinger *Franny & Zooey* (1962) 25 There's an unwritten law that people in a certain social or financial bracket can name-drop as much as they like just as long as they say something terribly disparaging about the person as soon as they've dropped his name. **1959** I. Ross *Image Merchants* (1960) v. 94 Newsom does not even have to name-drop. The PR man who can avoid that indulgence has truly arrived. **1969** *Daily Tel.* 22 Aug. 18/3 Mr Walters can name-drop better than most when it comes to generals and film stars. **1947** *San Francisco Examiner* (Pict. Rev.) 7 Sept., Our newest menace. The name dropper. **1959** *Woman's Own* 24 Jan. 31/1 One of my favourite snobs—the name-dropper. **1972** H. Kemelman *Monday the Rabbi took Off* xii. 84 He would be likely to point out important people to his son—the wife of the British consul, the American first secretary. He was no name-dropper, but he wanted so much to have his son think well of him. **1950** M. McCarthy *On Contrary* (1962) 186 The idea that it's smart to be in step, to be liberal or *avant-garde*, is conveyed through the name-

dropping of a Leo Lerman in *Mademoiselle.* **1951** L. Z. HOBSON *Celebrity* (1953) viii. 119 Rex Stout and Oscar Hammerstein... Conversational spice, he had been thinking; nobody could call it name-dropping. **1966** *Philos.* XLI. 359 Plus a wordy, name-dropping Introduction. **1973** *Times* 7 Feb. 4/5 (*heading*) Solicitors appalled by 'name-dropping' in courts. **1966** *Guardian* 30 Dec. 4/8 He becomes absorbed (name droppingly so) into the ranks of the literati. **1922** E. EKWALL *Place-Names Lancs.* 62 It is probably a Scand. name..as *Brand* is hardly with certainty evidenced as an O.E. name-element. **1932** E. WEEKLEY *Words & Names* ix. 134 From the name-element *mun*, thought, etc., were formed a number of names. **1937** *Harvard Univ. Summaries Ph.D. Theses* 272 The deuterotheme..is by far the more stable name-element in the late Germanic period. **1951** *Traditio* VII. 411 The second theme, *-ferth*..is obviously a metathesized form of *frith* (peace) which occurs in many Germanic names both as a first and second name element. **1907** A. QUILLER-COUCH *Major Vigoureux* ii. 20 Glorious trumpet daffodils!..Major [Narcisse] Vigoureux delighted in them. Were they not his name-flower? **1927** *Observer* 24 Apr. 15 Marigold, its heroine, has the unaffected charm of her name-flower. **1946** B. BLOCH in *Language* XXII. 208 The non-past indicative form of a verb, an adjective, or the copula serves as the *name form*, used to refer collectively to all the members of a paradigm. **1951** TRAGER & SMITH *Outl. Eng. Struct.* 60 The uninflected or name-form is the base. **1970** *English Studies* LI. 445 The name-forms are arranged under OE phonemes. Thus under OE *ā* we find head-words like *āc, brād, rāp*. **1955** H. LEBLANC *Introd. Deductive Logic* 2 Semiotic quotes..are a name-forming operator. **1956** J. H. WOODGER tr. *Tarski's Logic, Semantics, Metamath.* 161 Quotation marks provide an example of a name-forming functor with *one* sentence argument. **1957** A. N. PRIOR *Time & Modality* 119 Our *x*'s are given..by means of a name-forming operator on intervals. **1864** Name-giving [in Dict.]. **1898** E. CLODD *Tom Tit Tot* vi. 75 Mungo Park thus describes the name-giving ceremony among the Mandingo people. **1940** A. H. GARDINER *Theory of Proper Names* vi. 20 Certain name-givings..do not give rise to proper names. **1970** G. R. STEWART *Amer. Place-Names* p. xii, European scholars rarely concern themselves with the process of name-giving or its motives. **1950** H. L. LORIMER *Homer & Monuments* iv. 125 Apart from the negative evidence of the Pylos tablets, there is the fact..that certain series of signs in both groups form name-groups which also occur at Knossos in the Palace script. **1963** *English Studies* XLIV. 32 Large name-groups with end-variation, e.g. *Cēolwald, -helm, -bald, -ward*, etc. **1910** *Westm. Gaz.* 14 Mar. 11/2 Affixing red name-labels to their seats in the Council Chamber. **1928** D. H. LAWRENCE *Lady Chatterley* iv. 36 I'd be ashamed to see a woman walking round with my name-label on her. **1924** *Daughter of C. Patmore* iii. 36 At one time she is deep in heraldry and name-lore. **1932** E. WEEKLEY *Words & Names* vii. 82 One of the puzzles of name-lore is the process by which the French name *Jacques* ..was early confused with *Jankin* or *Jenkin.* **1940** W. V. QUINE *Math. Logic* iii. 152 Such expressions might be classed as *name matrices*, for they are related to names as statement matrices are related to statements. **1936** *Times Lit. Suppl.* 25 Jan. 73/2 But Reid, after all, is in the 'name-part'. **1961** *Times* 5 Apr. 13/6 With Dame Margot Fonteyn in a memorable account of the name-part [of *Giselle*]. **1924** *Glasgow Herald* 24 Apr. 4 The name-piece of the volume is a genealogical..account of this branch of the..family. **1882, 1896** Name-plate [in Dict.]. **1904** *Electr. Rev.* 3 Sept. 327 The committee recommends that the ratings of generators and motors, except traction motors, be marked plainly on the name-plate. Two types of service are recommended, continuous working and intermittent working, and the name-plate must state to which service it relates. **1908** [see *FINGER-POST *v.*]. **1967** *Gloss. Terms Builders' Hardware* (*B.S.I.*) IV. 17 *Name plate*, a plate..bearing one or more words fixed to a door, gate or cupboard..to convey information concerning contents, premises, business, profession or individuals. **1971** M. TAK *Truck Talk* 110 *Nameplate finders*, cab-mounted spotlights used to find an address on a building at night. **1972** *Village Voice* (N.Y.) 1 June 20/2 Fiction writers.. start getting asked to do book reviews and being invited to name-plate cocktail parties. **1958** BLUNDEN *War Poets* 29 The name-poem is one of the great achievements. **1956** R. CARNAP *Meaning & Necessity* (ed. 2) iii. 96 The method of the name-relation is an alternative method of semantical analysis, more customary than the method of extension and intension. *Ibid.* 97 Following Russell and Church, I used the word 'denotes' for the name-relation in the first version of this book. However, in view of the ambiguity just described, I now prefer to avoid it. **1905** *Daily Chron.* 23 Feb. 6/5 Name-ribbons may have to be changed. **1924** MAWER & STENTON *Introd. Survey Eng. Place-Names* ix. 166 Recent investigation has shown that many Germanic name-stems which are never recorded in England in historic times were still used by the Angles, Saxons and Jutes of the fifth and sixth centuries. **1953** K. JACKSON *Lang. & Hist. Early Brit.* I. 174 The name-stem *Maglocun* which appears both in Ogam and in Latin. **1927** *Observer* 24 Apr. 8/4 There is an air of strain, as if she were attempting—at any rate in the name-story (the others are nearer her usual vein)—to achieve a high-flown style. **1936** *Times Lit. Suppl.* 25 Jan. 76/4 His 'name-story' is of a poor Australian woman who marries an Afghan trader. **1931** C. L'E. EWEN *Hist. Surnames* iii. 50 Fick concluded that the German name-system exceeded in splendour..others of the Aryan group. **1937** *Harvard Univ. Summaries Ph.D. Theses* 271 The aim of this study is..to study the Old English dithematic name against the background of the general Germanic name-system. **1960** V. JENKINS *Lions Down Under* vi. 95 Mother was almost sewing on name-tabs at the airport. **1973** P. O'DONNELL *Silver Mistress* ii. 25 The clothes..had tailor's name-tabs. **1946** W. S. KNICKERBOCKER *20th Cent. English* 333 Each may usurp the business of the other and lose thereby his special name-tag. **1948** H. LAWRENCE *Death of Doll* x. 230 They did not want name tags pinned to their coat sleeves by Nick. **1953** A. UPFIELD *Murder Must Wait* iv. 36 On some of her clothes is a name tag with the initials P.R. overlaid on others which could be J.O. or J.U. **1958** C. WATSON *Coffin scarcely Used* xvii. 163 Purbright watched Gibbins going through pockets. 'Any name tags?' he asked. **1964** G. L. COHEN *What's Wrong with Hospitals?* i. 16 A parallel substitute for the spoken word is the system of name tags prevalent in America and gaining ground in Europe. 'It saves the staff from having to introduce themselves.' **1899** in A. Adburgham *Shops & Shopping* (1964) xxii. 261 Name tapes. **1932** E. BOWEN *To North* v. 45 She stitched name-tapes on to her new summer-term outfit. **1964** —— *Little Girls* II. vii. 152 Her mackintosh, name-taped as St. Agatha's demanded. **1969** *Guardian* 1 Sept. 7/5 Those new-fangled printed heat-adhesive name tapes. **1971** M. MCCARTHY *Birds of America* 49 Peter would have to have a haircut and name-tapes on his clothes. **1955** A. N. PRIOR *Formal Logic* 182 It would not be possible to lay it down..that in any thesis a description may be substituted for a name-variable. **1957** —— *Time & Modality* 46 Q is enriched by name-variables, predicate variables, and quantifiers. **1963** O. WOJTASIEWICZ tr. *Łukasiewicz's Elem. Math. Logic* 103 We shall be concerned with a certain theory of name variables. **1903** *Chambers's Cycl. Eng. Lit.* (new ed.) III. 695/1 *The Growth of Love*,..*Eros & Psyche*.., are amongst his nameworthy poems.

name, *v.*[1] Add: **1. b.** *to name for*: delete (now only *U.S.*), and add further examples.

1930 ADE *Let.* 20 Aug. (1973) 147 At one time he [*sc.* Peter VanRensselaer] owned thousands of acres in this region and the city of Rensselaer is named for him. **1933** S. HOWARD *Alien Corn* I. 14 We were just saying you must have been named for Wagner's Elsa. **1936** M. DE LA ROCHE *Whiteoak Harvest* vi. 95 You'll have children and perhaps..you'll name a little boy for me. **1957** *Northern Life* June 9/1 Saville Row was named for Col. Sir Geo. Saville, who commanded the garrison of the town [*sc.* Newcastle upon Tyne] in 1776–7 and lived in a house here. **1968** B. FOSTER *Changing Eng. Lang.* v. 226 A very typically American turn of phrase that is showing signs of headway in Britain is the replacing of 'named after' by 'named for'.

5. d. (Later examples.)

1928 [see *LAST *a.* 1 f]. **1972** *Guardian* 11 Feb. 22/4 The Speaker failed to 'name' or suspend Miss Devlin after hitting Mr Maudling. *Ibid.* 15 Mar. 1/4 Mr Charles Loughlin, MP for Gloucestershire West, was named by the Deputy Speaker after telling him that he 'did not give a damn' whether Sir Robert did or did not listen to his point of order. In accordance with the usual custom, the Leader of the House..moved that Mr Loughlin be suspended.

f. To specify officially (someone) by name to whom certain political (usu. Communist) affiliations are imputed, esp. in South Africa under the Suppression of Communism Act, 1950, and in the U.S.A. during the period of McCarthyism. Hence **naming** *vbl. sb.*, **named** *ppl. a.*

1950 *Times* 9 Mar. 5/3 Senator McCarthy has been ordered by Senator Tydings..to name to-morrow the high State Department official who he has alleged in the Senate intervened to protect an employee who was regarded as a bad security risk. **1952** *Economist* 31 May 581/3 He [*sc.* Mr E. S. Sachs] has been 'named' by the Minister of Justice as a Communist under the Suppression of Communism Act. **1956** L. KUPER *Passive Resistance in S. Afr.* II. viii. 188 For most whites, a 'named' person bears a permanent social stigma; he is not acceptable as an employee, or in ordinary intercourse. **1957** S. ADLER *Isolationist Impulse* xv. 460 He [*sc.* McCarthy] said he could name 205, or 57, or 81 Reds (the numbers usually varied with each harangue) in the State Department. *Ibid.* 461 He was unable to substantiate these charges by naming one Communist survivor of the Truman purge. **1958** G. M. CARTER *Politics of Inequality* II. ii. 65 The Minister could then forbid those 'named' to take part in any specified organization. But the 'naming' process is not essential before taking action, for the Minister.. can also prohibit any gathering if it appears to aid the objects of Communism.

g. To cite as co-respondent in a divorce petition.

1971 YELDHAM & CARNE *Rees's Divorce Handbk.* (ed. 4) ii. 27 Unless otherwise directed, where a wife's petition alleges adultery with a woman *named*, the alleged adultress must be made a respondent in this cause. **1971** A. HUNTER *Gently at Gallop* ii. 11 Laing divorced her, naming Berney... Berney was named in another suit, and his first wife petitioned, using that as grounds... He's been named once or twice since then. **1972** *Guardian* 23 Dec. 24/5 The television actress, Linda Thorson..was named yesterday in a divorce suit.

6. e. Phr. *you name it, I* (or *we*) *have* (or *have done*) *it* (also with other verbs), everything that you can think of is available, has been done, etc.; also ellipt., *you name it.*

1962 J. BRAINE *Life at Top* xviii. 213 You name the drink, we have it. **1964** M. S. ALLWOOD *American & British* 137 *American.* You name it! *British*.... or whatever you like. **1967** *Field & Stream* Aug. 63/2 Mallards, gadwall, partridge, quail—you name it—they're up here for the season every year. **1968** *Sun* (Baltimore) 18 Sept. A. 14/4 Bear Creek, Back River, you name it; the story is the same. **1969** N. FREELING *Tsing-Boum* vii. 45 What sort of world are they born into anywhere?—hunger, napalm, you name it and we've got it. **1969** *Rolling Stone* 28 June 17/3 I've written every kind of music there is. You name it, I've written it. All except one thing I couldn't do: rhythm and blues. **1972** D. LEES *Zodiac* 53 He's been a smuggler, a gun runner, a dope peddler—you name it. **1973** *Times* 6 Jan. 9/4 Bits of chicken, port, olive—you name it. *Ibid.* 22 Jan. 9/2 At that time the cops knew me. You name it, I'd done it. **1973** *Black Panther* 8 Sept. 17/1 I've seen police call people slur names such as nigger, mother fuckers, bitches, whores..you name it, they had a name for it.

7. c. *to name no names*: to refrain from mentioning the names of the people involved in an incident, etc., in order to protect them; often with the implication that the hearer or reader could supply these names.

1792 F. BURNEY *Jrnl.* June (1972) I. 212 She desired he would name no names, but merely mention that some ladies had been frightened. **1843** DICKENS *Mart. Chuz.* (1844) iv. 46 Naming no names, and therefore hurting nobody but those whose consciences tell them they are alluded to. **1890** KIPLING *Soldiers Three* 12 Av coorse I will name no names, for there's wan that's an orf'cer's lady now, that was in ut. **1908** K. GRAHAME *Wind in Willows* iv. 89 The Wild Wood is pretty well populated by now; with all the usual lot, good, bad and indifferent—I name no names. **1919** BEERBOHM *Seven Men* 203 But now my sense of duty forces me To a departure from my custom of Naming no names. One name I must and shall Name. **1972** L. LAMB *Picture Frame* xiii. 107 You put that tale around, naming no names, at one o' your police smokers, you'll have 'em all rolling in the aisles.

8. *to name the day* (further examples); also *transf.*

1766 GOLDSMITH *Vicar of Wakefield* I. xvii. 171 'Name, then, your day...' ..She again renewed her..promise of marrying Mr. William ..and..that day month was fixed upon for her nuptials. **1841** DICKENS *Let.* 25 Mar. (1969) II. 243 Chigwell, my dear fellow, is the greatest place in the world. Name your day for going. **1974** *Times* 9 Feb. 16/6 'Health names the day,' shrilled the billboards yesterday. And an elderly couple on a bus said: 'It's about time he got married.'

nameable, *a.* Add: **2.** (Earlier U.S. example.)

1780 J. ADAMS *26 Lett. Revol. Amer.* (1789) 23 The sixth talk is to shew, 'that no person, in America, is of so much influence, power, or credit, that his death, or corruption, by English money, could be of any nameable consequence'.

name-day. Add: **3.** *Stock Exch.* The day on which the seller of registered securities receives from the buyer a ticket with the name and details of the person to whom the securities are to be transferred.

1885 P. CAMPBELL *Stock Exchange* 25 The second [account day] is called 'Name or Ticket Day', devoted by Brokers and Jobbers to concluding Investment operations by completing and delivering transfers. **1895** A. J. WILSON *Gloss. Colloq. Terms Stock Exchange* 170 Each settlement occupies three days—1st, 'contango day'..; 2nd, 'name day', when the names of buyers of registered securities are passed to the sellers; and 3rd, 'pay day'. **1907** [see *NAME *sb.* 1 c]. **1941** DICE & EITEMAN *Stock Market* (ed. 2) x. 155 The second day of settlement is called 'ticket day' or 'name day'. On this day a broker who wishes delivery on stock that he has bought sends a ticket to his jobber, giving the name of the security. **1970** M. GREENER *Penguin Dict. Commerce* 325 Ticket day..is also sometimes called name day.

namesmanship (nēi·mzmănʃip). *colloq.* [f. NAME *sb.* + *-MANSHIP, after *GAMESMANSHIP.] Skill in the use of influential names of people or objects; skill in name-dropping.

1964 *Amer. Speech* XXXIX. 225 Namesmanship at sea. **1967** *Economist* 28 Oct. p. xxii/2 Namesmanship has been in, in Sweden, since the appearance this summer of Mr Ake Ortmark's book on 'The Power Game in Sweden'.

Namibia (nămi·biă). [f. *Namib* (a desert on the western coast of southern Africa) + -IA[1].] A name given to South-West Africa in 1968 by the United Nations in anticipation of its being released from the mandate granted to South Africa by the League of Nations in 1919 (see quots. 1968). Hence **Nami·bian** *sb.*, a native or inhabitant of Namibia; also *adj.*, of or pertaining to the land or people of Namibia.

1968 *Post* (S. Afr.) 4 Feb. 5 We are Namibians and not South Africans. **1968** *United Nations 22nd Session* Suppl. 16A 12 June 1/2 Resolution 2372... Proclaims that, in accordance with the desires of its people, South West Africa shall henceforth be known as 'Namibia'. *Ibid.* 2/1 The Council shall organize a training programme for Namibians. *Ibid.*, Reaffirms the inalienable right of the Namibian people to freedom and independence. **1970** R. HALL *South-West Afr.* (*Namibia*) 3 The Reverend Michael Scott..has won international respect by the tenacity of his fight..to sustain the rights of the Namibian peoples. **1973** *Times* 8 Mar. 6/3 Namibians prefer to be misgoverned or misruled by themselves rather than by others. **1973** *Guardian* 28 June 13/8 The Namibian strikes last year..secured important concessions. **1974** *Stand. Encycl. S. Afr.* X. 145/1 In United Nations circles the territory [*sc.* S.-W. Africa] is called Namibia, a designation derived from the name of the coastal desert, the Namib.

Namierian (nēimiə·riăn), *sb.* and *a.* [f. the name of Sir Lewis B. *Namier* (1888–1960), British historian + -IAN.] **A.** *sb.* An adherent of the methods and theories of Sir L. Namier concerning the structure of, and research into, political history. **B.** *adj.* Of, pertaining to, illustrating, or concerning the historical theories or techniques of Namier.

1958 *Oxf. Mag.* 27 Feb. 330/2 The Namierian revolution in historical method, now a quarter of a century old, destroyed a long accepted view of the nature of political parties in the 18th century. *Ibid.* 332/1 If the party is of

little importance, as the Namierians have proved, then [etc.]. **1961** *Encounter* XVI. 39/2 The general configuration of world history will continue to look much the same, whether one takes the Namierian or pre-Namierian view about the structure of politics in Britain in George III's reign. **1962** *Guardian* 6 July 6/5 The Namierian House of Commons. **1967** *Economist* 6 May 575/3 His expertise with the telescope at one moment and the microscope at another is quite Namierian.

So **Na·mierite** *a.* and *sb.* in same sense. **Namieriza·tion,** the application of Namier's methods and theories to a historical situation; hence **Na·mierize** *v.*; **Na·mierizing** *vbl. sb.*

1948 *Bull. Inst. Hist. Research* XXI. 123, I refer to the process, which I can only call, after its distinguished inventor, the 'Namierizing' of British History: the discovery and exploration of the personal side of parliamentary politics and the parliamentary groups which flourished and manoeuvred, formed, broke and reformed their alliances under cover of debates and constitutional dogmas. **1952** *John o' London's Weekly* 20 June, A really intensely detailed and penetrating piece of analysis is known to historians all over the world as a 'namierisation'. **1957** *Economist* 12 Oct. 120/1 The expression 'to namierise' is a deserved tribute to Sir Lewis's influence. **1958** *Listener* 17 Apr. 661/3 Surely namierite scholarship has.. underlined the great differences..between the political systems of the eighteenth century and our own. **1958** *N.Z. Listener* 5 Sept. 12/4 May one hope that in future volumes he will add a dash of Namierite bitters to the cocktail? **1960** *Observer* 28 Aug. 8/4 Essentially, Namierisation meant a rigorous substitution of accurate detail for the generalisations which had contented older historians. **1961** *Times Lit. Suppl.* 2 June 334/4 This..piece of Namierisation does not offer portraits of any individual members of the group. **1967** *Economist* 22 July 329/3 Are we not, in fact, with the nineteenth century, in danger of much the same kind of difficulties as Namierite zeal landed us in with the eighteenth? **1969** *Listener* 20 Mar. 388/3 A generation ago the Namierites were busy counting heads while the Clapham sect totted up the trade statistics. **1971** *Sunday Times* 30 May 31/4 To 'namierise' is now a well-known historical technique which has been applied—often with far less subtlety—in very different fields. It consists, essentially, of constructing multiple biographies of inarticulate men whose common but unconscious aims may be a force, even a determining force, in history. **1972** *New Society* 13 Apr. 51/2 It [*sc.* the Scarman inquiry into violence in Ulster in 1969] is the Namierisation of a nightmare in which ten people died, [etc.]. **1973** P. A. ALLUM *Politics & Society Post-War Naples* ix. 280 The disappearance of the monarchy left the Vatican as the major institutional support of the *status quo.* In consequence, the Christian Democrats became..a 'Court Party' in the Namierite sense.

naming, *vbl. sb.* Add: **b.** *naming of parts*: the process of becoming acquainted, or of acquainting others, with the essentials of an unfamiliar object or topic.

1946 H. REED *Map of Verona* 22 To-day we have naming of parts. Yesterday We had daily cleaning. And tomorrow morning, We shall have what to do after firing. But to-day, To-day we have naming of parts. **1967** *Listener* 15 June 782/2 The Carnegie Report..begins with a very plain 'naming of parts', which is vital if the different forms of television are to be easily distinguished. **1967** *Punch* 26 July 135/2 We all know the experience, when we take up any new subject..of taking in..an enormous new naming-of-parts, so that we are able to make the distinctions the new subject demands. **1971** *Guardian* 29 Sept. 20/4 Many of the eruptions over topics like sex-education..spring..from a resistance to what may be summed up in the old grammarian's phrase, 'The naming of parts'. **1975** *Nature* 10 Apr. 483/1 (*heading*) Teleost ancestry, or naming of parts. *Ibid.* 483/3 Patterson has been meticulous in naming of parts, that is in tracing homologous structures throughout his series of fishes and naming them accordingly.

namma hole, var. *GNAMMA HOLE. *Austral.*

1893 *Australasian* 5 Aug. 252/4 (Morris), The route all the way from York to Coolgardie is amply watered, either 'namma holes' (native wells) or Government wells being plentiful on the road. **1928** K. S. PRICHARD *Coonardoo* iv. 52 His eyes, namma holes in viscid orbits, glittered at her, as he swung his naked feet.

nam-nam, var. *NUM-NUM.

Namurian (nămiū̆·riăn), *a.* (*sb.*) *Geol.* [f. *Namur,* name of a town and province of southern Belgium + -IAN.] Of, pertaining to, or designating the lowest stage of the Upper Carboniferous in western Europe, lying above the Dinantian; also as *sb.*, the Namurian stage or epoch.

1915 C. SCHUCHERT *Text-bk. Geol.* II. xl. 729 Kayser adds a third series, the Namurian (Namur, Belgium), which is referred to the base of the Middle Carboniferous. **1931** GREGORY & BARRETT *Gen. Stratigr.* vii. 118 Above the Dinantian [in Belgium] is a coarse sandstone, the great Grès d'Ardenne, corresponding to the Millstone Grit; it is called the Namurian. **1938** A. K. WELLS *Outl. Hist. Geol.* 100 The normal facies of the Namurian Stage is deltaic. **1963** D. W. & E. E. HUMPHRIES tr. *Termier's Erosion & Sedimentation* xiii. 292 By the Namurian, subsidence had practically finished and the last reef phase passed into large biostromes. **1967** D. H. RAYNER *Stratigr. Brit. Isles* vii. 200 It is also the type area of the Millstone Grit, where millstones were once fashioned out of the coarser sandstones... The sandstones..probably represent a lesser proportion of Namurian time than their thickness at first sight suggests.

nan[1]**.** (Later example.)

1922 JOYCE *Ulysses* 46 Lambert Simnel, with a tail of nans and sutlers, a scullion crowned.

nan[2] (næn). *colloq.* [Prob. formed on GRANNY, or a shortening of *NANA[1], NANNA.] A grandmother; occas., a children's nurse.

1940 N. MARSH *Surfeit of Lampreys* (1941) iii. 43 Nanny's hands..made a quick involuntary movement. 'You'll be all right, Nan,' added Henry. **1954** —— *Spinsters in Jeopardy* viii. 150 The new Nanny... I didn't think I had to have a Nan over here. **1955** E. BLISHEN *Roaring Boys* iii. 123 'Been to see my nan,' he growled. **1968** L. BERG *Risinghill* 45 Perhaps it is Nan's importance in Islington.. that gives warmth and security to grandchildren. **1969** *Guardian* 15 Sept. 7/3 Her Mum and her Nan aren't a lot of help. **1975** *New Society* 18 Sept. 631/1 Jackie gets £1 a week off her grandmother, who owns a pub: 'My nan's got tons of money.' **1975** *Country Life* 13 Nov. 1277/2 I had a great, great grandmother who was a witch... Old Nan would remove the spell from a churn.

‖ **nan**[3] (nān). Also **naan.** (Hindi.] In Indian and Pakistani cooking, a type of leavened bread.

1967 *Guardian* 8 Dec. 8/4 North Indian or Pakistani [cooking] which depends on the clay oven called a tandoor, into which kebabs..and the special bread called nan are lowered and rapidly cooked. **1971** *Carry Singapore in your Pocket* (Singapore Tourist Promotion Board) (ed. 3) 31 One first-class Kashmiri restaurant..serves..a wide variety of naan and pilau prepared in Kashmiri style. **1972** 'E. PETERS' *Death to Landlords!* iv. 76 The dough-cake type of bread called *nan.* **1973** *Times* 19 June (Bombay Suppl.) p. xv/3 Nan, a leavened bread dotted with poppy seed. **1973** *Sat. Rev. World* (U.S.) 18 Dec. 48/2 *Naan,* bread baked in a special oven by an Indian baker. **1974** R. HOWE in Moraes & Howe *J. K. Galbraith introduces India* 189 It [*sc.* chicken] is eaten with the fingers accompanied by slabs of *nan roti,* a type of bread also made in the *tandur.*

nana[1]**, nanna** (næ·nă). Also **nan-nan.** Forms of address used by a child to a grandmother; occas., a children's nurse.

c **1844** E. PEPYS *Diary* 8 Oct. in *Country Life* (1972) 9 Mar. 577/1, I cut Herbert's hand..he only said 'O, Emy you had better send for Nana.' *Ibid.* 25 Dec. 578/1 Mama rung the bell for Nana. **1869** C. M. YONGE *Release* II. xi. 176 Poor dear Zélie..had been mother's nana. **1899** E. E. CUMMINGS *Let.* 27 Nov. (1969) 3, I am sorry dear Nana but I will be a good boy. **1901** *Punch* 4 Dec. 405/2 Please, Nanna, don't turn on the dark. **1927** W. E. COLLINSON *Contemp. Eng.* 7 Children still use, as in the nineties, and long before, mummy, daddy, nanny or nanna, nursie. [**1928** BARRIE *Peter Pan* I. in *Plays* 18 Nana the nurse.. is a Newfoundland dog.] **1954** *Caribbean Q.* III. I. 5 The role of the *nana* or nurse in preserving folk songs, tales.. herb lore is not to be under-estimated. **1958** M. KERR *People of Ship Street* 48 The granny, or 'nin', or 'nanny', or 'nanna' or 'gran' as she is often called. **1959** D. WALLACE *Richard & Lucy* xv. 210 A mewling toddler, clutching at her grandmother and weeping if Nan-nan were out of sight for more than a minute. **1959** *Woman's Own* 2 May 9/2 Cliffie..lived with his grandparents... Sometimes he would say..'I think I must go home today, thank you. Nana is expecting me.'

nana[2] (nā·nă). *slang* (chiefly *Austral.*). [Perh. f. BANANA.] **a.** A foolish person, a fool. **b.** The head. Also *attrib.*, as in *nana haircut* (see quot. 1941).

[**1894** A. B. PATERSON 'Hughey's Dog' in C. Semmler *The World of 'Banjo' Paterson* (1967) 29 'Off his nanny again,' thought the boss, 'the sooner he goes the better.'] **1941** BAKER *Dict. Austral. Slang* 48 *Nana (hair)cut,* a utilitarian haircut in which the back of the head is closely shaved. **1965** G. MCINNES *Road to Gundagai* ix. 148 Although he was obviously a gent, he was not a 'tonk' or a 'nana'. **1967** *Coast to Coast 1965–66* 35 If you..horror of horrors, had a *nana* haircut. **1967** C. DRUMMOND *Death at Furlong Post* xiii. 165 It seems if you have a bit of cash it snowballs unless you are a proper 'nana. **1968** J. LOCK *Lady Policeman* iv. 41 Do we stand there like a 'nana' holding up our hands to stop invisible traffic? **1971** *TV Times* (Austral.) 18 Dec. 19/4 It's only the famous ones who get fired... They're the ones..making..statements like 'The management is a nana'. **1972** M. FARHI *Pleasure of your Death* iii. 106 The answer, you 'nana. **1974** *Times* 22 Jan. 14/2 A frank admission that he had made a nana of himself. **1974** *Telegraph* (Brisbane) 22 Apr. 2/4 The baby started crying again. I did my nana and I hit him. **1975** *Australian* 8 Feb. 13 'We've all learned to laugh at ourselves and our predicament,' Trevor England said. 'If we hadn't we'd all be off our nanas.'

nanberry, -bury. (Later examples.)

1876 F. K. ROBINSON *Gloss. Words used in Neighbourhood of Whitby* 129/1 *Nanberries,* s. pl. warty spots on the groin of a horse. **1883** A. EASTHER *Gloss. Dial. Almondbury & Huddersfield* 90 *Nanberry* or *Nanbury, sb.* a kind of wart formed on the bag of a cow. **1970** 'J. HERRIOT' *If only they could Talk* xxv. 152 They [*sc.* horses] did get those little dangling growths sometimes—nanberries, the farmers called them. **1973** —— *Let Sleeping Vets Lie* xiii. 113 Oh, and Mr. Ross said would you take some nanberries off a stirk's belly while you're here.

nance (næns). *slang.* = *NANCY[2].

1924 G. C. HENDERSON *Keys to Crookdom* 412 *Nance,* effeminate fellow, sissy man. Nance walk—walk like a woman. **1932** [see *FAG *sb.*[6]]. **1934** *Amer. Speech* IX. 27/1 *Nance,* an effeminate man. **1935** A. J. POLLOCK *Underworld Speaks* 79/1 *Nance,* a fairy; a male sexual pervert. **1941** B. SCHULBERG *What makes Sammy Run?* viii. 158 They were all so different—a titled Englishman and a famous poet and an aesthetic nance and a tough, drunken ex-reporter. **1957** J. G. COZZENS *By Love Possessed* (1958) II. v. 450 Here; I'll sneak out the back. Nances and I don't get on. **1971** F. FORSYTH *Day of Jackal* xx. 336 We're looking for a fellow who screwed the arse off a Baroness.. not a couple of raving nances.

Nancy. (Later example of *Nancy-story.*)

1967 *Times* 24 June 11/5 Here in Guyana, the term 'a nancy story' is common everyday parlance for a far-fetched yarn or even a downright lie... A 'Nancy Story' is ..one of the very few fragments of African culture which survived transplantation with the slaves.

nancy[2] (næ·nsi). *slang.* Also **nancy-boy.** [orig. *Miss Nancy* (MISS *sb.*[2] 2 b), f. pet-form of the female name *Ann.*] An effeminate man or boy; a homosexual. Also as *adj.* Hence **na·ncified** *ppl. a.*; **na·ncifully** *adv.*

1904 'No. 1500' *Life in Sing Sing* 251/1 Nancy, effeminate man. **1918** C. MACKENZIE *Early Life Sylvia Scarlett* I. iv. 123 If you can let that nancified milksop mess you about, you can put up with me. **1930** E. WAUGH *Vile Bodies* 36 Where's my Fairy Prince? Powdering hisself again, I suppose... Come here, Nancy, and put away the beauty cream. **1931** R. CAMPBELL *Georgiad* ii. 36 Sharing out my last desires and fancies With tough old suffragettes and ageing nancies. *Ibid.* 42 Grim guards enough to awe the Nancy race. *Ibid.*, Their flag of truce they raise To bribe his laughter with their public praise, And all their little nancy husbands too. **1933** H. S. WALPOLE *Vanessa* IV. 723 But he isn't one of those, you know, or anything like that. Not a bit nancy. **1936** 'G. ORWELL' *Keep Aspidistra Flying* i. 19 A youth..with gilded hair, tripped Nancifully in. **1937** —— *Road to Wigan Pier* ii. 35 You and I..and the Nancy poets..—all of us *really* owe the comparative decency of our lives to poor drudges underground,..with their lungs full of coal dust. **1937** *Times* 25 Jan. 37/2 That nancyfied nonentity in the Foreign Office. **1937** E. LINKLATER *Juan in China* xxii. 288 You're a fop and a nancified civilian. **1947** L. HASTINGS *Dragons are Extra* x. 224 In the early part of the War I had occasional glimpses of an unfamiliar species known comprehensibly, I believe, as the Nancy Left. **1958** L. DURRELL *Balthazar* ii. 31, I can't stand that Toto fellow. He's an open nancy-boy. **1967** K. GILES *Death & Mr. Prettyman* ii. 58 Beautiful smooth dark rum, not like that nancified white stuff you poms put in your cokes. **1974** L. DEIGHTON *Spy Story* xv. 148 Pop music and nancy-boy actors.

Nancy Dawson (næ·nsi dǭ·sən). ?*Obs.* [See quot. 1890.] A sailor's dance or song; a nancy-boy.

1766 C. ANSTEY *New Bath Guide* ix. 64 With what Grace his Gloves he draws on, Claps, and calls up Nancy Dawson: Me thro' ev'ry Dance conducting. **1771** SMOLLETT *Humph. Cl.* I. 176, I can dance a Welsh jig, and Nancy Dawson. *c* **1810** W. HICKEY *Mem.* (1960) xxv. 418 The dragoons..marched off..the fifes playing 'Nancy Dawson'. **1840** *Family Mag.* (Cincinnati) 332/2 She sailed through the waltz like an elephant dancing 'Nancy Dawson' in the ring of a menagerie. **1890** BARRÈRE & LELAND *Dict. Slang* II. 81/1 *Nancy Dawson,* a name for a molly, an effeminate youth, apathetic, &c... The original Nancy Dawson was a noted prostitute, on whom there is a song still current among sailors.

NAND (nænd). *Computers.* [f. *n(ot) and.*] A Boolean function of two or more variables that has the value zero when all of them are unity, and is otherwise unity; 'not..and..'. Usu. *attrib.*

1958 *IRE Trans. Electronic Computers* VII. 181/3 Using a positive logic (+ is identified with true and ONE) the circuit represents the binary NOR function, $\overline{A_1+A_2}=B$. A negative logic (− is identified with true and ONE) results in the binary NAND function, $\overline{A_1 \cdot A_2}=B$. **1960** N. R. SCOTT *Analog & Digital Computer Technol.* x. 392 Of course, $A\,|\,B=\overline{A \cdot B}$; so this circuit is sometimes called a NOT AND (or NAND) circuit. **1966** *Electronics* 31 Oct. 42 The circuits used..are transistor-transistor NAND logic. **1971** J. H. SMITH *Digital Logic* iv. 48 Due to practical manufacturing reasons the NAND configuration forms the basis of the majority of integrated circuit systems. *Ibid.*, The action of the NAND is that it gives a *0* output when *all* its inputs are *1* signals.

Nandi (næ·ndi), *sb.*[1] [Skr., 'the happy one'.] In Hindu mythology, the name of the bull of Siva which is his vahan or vehicle, and symbolizes fertility; also, a figure or statue of Nandi.

1807 H. T. COLEBROOKE in *Asiatick Researches* IX. 425 Near it stands a bull, intended perhaps for the bull called *Nandi,* a constant attendant of Śiva. **1891** M. MONIER-WILLIAMS *Brāhmanism & Hinduism* (ed. 4) xvii. 440 A shrine for the stone image of Siva's bull (nandi). **1910** *Encycl. Relig. & Ethics* III. 311/2 A representation of his sacred animal, the bull Nandī, is usually placed before him [*sc.* Śiva]. **1953** *Antiquity* XXVII. 169 Worth mentioning also are some clay censers, the handle of one being ornamented with a nandi. **1969** *Hindu Weekly Mag.* (Madras) 3 Aug. p. ii/6 The majestic 'Nandi', the conventional vehicle of Lord Siva in front of the 'sanctum' in the fore-court.

Nandi (næ·ndi), *sb.*[2] and *a.* [Native name.] **A.** *sb.* **a.** An East African people of mixed Nilotic, Hamitic, and Bantu origin which inhabits an area on the Uganda-Kenya border and has given its name to the Nandi plateau;

a member of this people. **b.** The Nilotic language spoken by the Nandi and some neighbouring tribes. **B.** *adj.* Of or pertaining to this people or their language.

1885 J. THOMSON *Through Masai Land* (ed. 3) 469 From this place we could see the high forest region of Nandi... The Wa-nandi are allied in language and customs to the Wa-kamaria and Wa-elgeyo, though much braver and more warlike. **1902** H. H. JOHNSTON *Uganda Protectorate* II. xix. 876 All the Nandi-speaking peoples except the Andorobo make *pottery*. *Ibid.* 882 The Nandi especially believe profoundly in the powers of their medicine men, and follow them implicitly. **1909** C. ELIOT in A. C. Hollis *Nandi* p. xiv, Most of the wild hunting tribes called Dorobo speak a dialect of Nandi. *Ibid.* p. xxi, When a Nandi is ill, it is necessary to discover and propitiate the particular ancestor who has occasioned the disaster. **1909** *Westm. Gaz.* 3 Feb. 4/1 (*heading*) Nandi customs and folklore. **1930** C. G. SELIGMAN *Races Afr.* vii. 163 The Nandi and Suk may be said to live in garden settlements, each man having his own homestead in or near his fields of grain. **1951** in E. E. Evans-Pritchard *Social Anthropol.* i. 12 (*thesis-title*) 'The political organization of the Nandi' (East Africa). **1964** A. N. TUCKER in D. Abercrombie et al. *Daniel Jones* 445 The Nandi Group, comprising Nandi, Kipsigis, [etc.].

b. Nandi bear, a hypothetical animal resembling a bear, said to inhabit parts of East Africa.

1931 C. R. S. PITMAN *Game Warden* xiv. 287 Tales of that elusive monster popularly known in Kenya as the 'Nandi bear' can boast a more substantial basis. **1937** *Discovery* Jan. 2/2 The Wandarobo name 'Keret' or 'Kerit' is applied to the lynx or caracal as well as to the mythical 'Nandi Bear'. **1950** *Sun* (Baltimore) 2 May 13/2 The curious Nandi bear..is often blamed for the killing of humans and domesticated animals in East Africa. Although scientific evaluation is lacking, native and white hunters alike claim to have encountered the beast; and several descriptions of the bearlike creature agree on its shambling gait, shaggy hair, little ears and long snout. **1956** *Nature* 10 Mar. 446/1 This animal may be the dreaded Nandi bear.

Nanga (næ·ŋgă). [Jap., abbrev. *Nanshuga*, f. *nanshu* southern China + *ga* painting, picture.] Used, chiefly *attrib.*, to designate an intellectual style of Japanese painting.

1958 M. L. WOLF *Dict. Painting* 188 *Nanga School*, in Japanese art, a style of painting depicting genre subjects in a manner of Chinese idealism. **1970** J. W. HALL *Japan from Prehist. to Mod. Times* x. 217 The property of the samurai class was the style of 'literati' painting (*bunjinga* or *nanga*). **1970** *Oxf. Compan. Art* 762/1 *Nanga School*, school of painting which arose in Japan at the end of the 17th c.,..and persisted until late in the 19th. *Ibid.* 762/2 The Nanga painters were not all amateurs, but they spurned the professional schools of their day... In general their work represented the art of the intelligentsia as opposed to Ukiyo-e, which was that of the people. **1970** *Ashmolean Mus. Rep. Visitors 1969* 43 A particularly desirable acquisition in connection with the Museum's collection of Nanga painting. **1972** *Times* 18 May 21/6 Ikeno Taiga's *Taigado Gafu*..made £400. This is one of the finest colour-printed Nanga books and extremely rare. It is dated 1803.

Nankeen, Nankin, *sb.* (and *a.*). Add: **6.** (Further examples.)

1784 H. WALPOLE *Descr. Strawberry Hill* 8 A blue and white saucer with a landscape, of fine Nankin china. **1917** D. H. LAWRENCE *Phoenix II* (1968) 113 There were delicate blue Nankin cups. **1921** W. DE LA MARE *Mem. Midget* ii. 12 Dwarf trees..in green Nankin tubs. *Ibid.* xxiv. 157 A little masterpiece: and real old Nankin. **1957** MANKOWITZ & HAGGAR *Conc. Encycl. Eng. Pott. & Porc.* 161/2 Large quantities of porcelain decorated in blue were exported through this town [Nankin], hence the term 'Nankin Blue' or 'Nankin China' or simply 'Nankin'..a synonym for blue-and-white porcelain.

7. A kind of lace.

1865 F. B. PALLISER *Hist. Lace* xv. 199 It was not until 1745 that the blondes..made their appearance. The first silk used for the new production was of its natural colour, 'écrue', hence these laces were called 'nankins' or 'blondes'. **1882** Nankin [see BLOND *sb.* 2 b].

nanna, nan-nan: see *NANA[1].

nannofossil (næ·nofǫsil). *Geol.* [f. as next + FOSSIL *a.* and *sb.*] A fossil of a minute plankton organism.

1963 H. STRADNER in *Proc. 6th World Petroleum Congr.* I. 167/1 Nannofossils (minute calcareous elements of planktonic marine flagellates) were found in sediments younger than Triassic. *Ibid.*, A key for the determination of nannofossil assemblages is given. **1971** *Nature* 3 Sept. 46/1 The ophiolites in those deep-sea troughs were overlain by..radiolarian and nannofossil oozes. **1972** *Sci. Amer.* Dec. 33/2 The white ooze is a typical oceanic sediment, made up almost entirely of the skeletons of microfossils and nannofossils. **1974** *Nature* 13 Sept. 129/2 The chalk contains abundant nannofossils whose preservation is, unfortunately, somewhat marred by calcite overgrowths.

nannoplankton (næ·noplæ:ŋktǫn). *Biol.* Also **nanoplankton.** [a. G. *nannoplankton* (H. Lohmann 1909, in *Verhandl. Deutsch. Zool. Ges.* XIX. 234), f. *nanno-*, used as comb. f. of Gr. νᾶνος, L. *nanus* dwarf + PLANKTON.] Very small forms of plankton.

1912 MURRAY & HJORT *Depths of Ocean* vi. 356 As far as quantity is concerned, the smallest plankton organisms, Lohmann's Nanno-plankton, play a far more important rôle than the whole of the other species caught in our silk nets. **1939** *Nature* 7 Oct. 643/1 There was a nannoplankton consisting entirely of very small flagellates. **1959** *New Biol.* XXIX. 40 Examination of marine nannoplankton, that is the very small plankton organisms which are not retained even by the finest nets, has shown the presence of many colourless forms related to the algae. **1966** R. S. WIMPENNY *Plankton of Sea* iii. 114 The water..is strained through a funnel of fine pipes which filter out the very small organisms of the nannoplankton. **1974** B. H. MCCONNAUGHEY *Introd. Marine Biol.* (ed. 2) i. 7/1 Nanoplankton is, then, simply a size designation that includes parts of both phytoplankton and zooplankton. Strictly speaking, the term nanoplankton is used for organisms ranging from 5 to 60 μm in size.

nanny (næ·ni), *sb.* Also **nannie.** [Appellative use of pet-form of the female name *Ann*(*e*: see -Y[6].] A child's form of address to a nurse; hence, a children's nurse. Also *transf.*, of a person or institution, etc., considered to be unduly protective or apprehensive. Also *attrib.* and *Comb.*

1795 LADY NEWDIGATE *Let.* in A. E. Newdigate-Newdegate *Cheverels* (1898) 154 Nanny Ashcroft got me ye most delightful & perfect Warm Sea Bath last night..after wch I ate my Bason of Milk & went to Bed. **1861** A. HALLIDAY in H. Mayhew *London Labour* (1862) Extra vol. 418/2 An old woman..give me a lodging once for two years. We used to call her Nanny. **1864** *Chambers's Jrnl.* Sept. 506/1 Don't you know I'm a locomotive, and that you should always shunt yourself on to a siding when you hear *me* coming Nanny? **1912** A. N. LYONS *Clara* i. 3 That little boy was..inured to the coming and going of 'nannies'. **1919** [see *CIG]. **1955** T. H. PEAR *Eng. Social Differences* 273 The effect upon the Nannie-cultured Englishman, of two mothers. **1958** A. WILSON *Middle Age of Mrs Eliot* i. 98 He was so clam and soothing and nannylike that she wanted to hit him. **1959** *Listener* 23 Apr. 735/1 Barristers are handled rather like naughty children by their nanny chief clerks. *Ibid.* 2 July 31/2 They can be nursery memories reproducing folk memory: immemorial nanny-lore. *Ibid.* 9 July 49/1 An extraordinarily powerful old bureaucratic nanny..goes stalking up and down the United States, pouncing on people who are telling commercial fibs. **1961** J. WADE *Back to Life* iv. 35 Nan came in... Her nannie days were past. **1965** B. SWEET-ESCOTT *Baker St. Irreg.* v. 147 There was also a good deal of Nanny work we had to do for Professor Pyke... The professor suffered from the traditional absent-mindedness of his kind, and we were expected to keep track of him. **1972** *Times* 2 Aug. 26/1 (Advt.), Country loving nannie. **1973** 'M. INNES' *Appleby's Answer* xvii. 155 Blabbing for your old nanny—that's what you'll be. **1973** *Times* 31 May 10/2 Kicked upstairs by the knighted nannies of his Institute, Hamo is sent on a world tour. **1973** *Listener* 7 June 742/2 The top authorities..who regulate television should [be]..impervious to the huge army of self-appointed nannies. **1974** *Times* 2 Feb. 18/3 Our natural modesty led us to cheer on the rest with encouraging cries..while deprecating our own dazzling accomplishments in the way that Nanny would have wished. *Ibid.* 29 Mar. 19/6 Surely our English cousins, having themselves retired from being 'nanny to the world', must understand how we feel. **1974** J. MANN *Sticking Place* vi. 106 Lorna took Rachel by the arm in a nanny-like way.

Hence **na·nnified** *ppl. a.*; **na·nnify** *v.*; **na·nniness, na·nnyism; na·nnyish** *a.*

1959 *Punch* 8 Apr. 474/1 Of all the nannyisms that have constrained the English middle classes the most inhibiting has been that favourite injunction about not putting ideas into the child's head. **1960** *Guardian* 1 July 8/1 The ponified and nannified Children's Bookland created by middle-class writers. **1962** *Times* 8 Feb. 9/7 Easy for his opponents to smile tolerantly on Wilberforce and make him seem impossibly nannyish. **1962** *Listener* 13 Dec. 1024/1 Is free speech in this country to be nannified out of existence by official vanity? **1972** J. ROSSITER *Rope for General Dietz* iii. 34 The air of nannyish protectiveness she had possessed in her BEA uniform. **1973** *Times Lit. Suppl.* 8 June 647/2 Mr Davidson's gentle male nanniness, initiating charming boys only to lose them.

nanny (næ·ni), *v.* [f. prec.] To act in the manner of a nanny; to be unduly protective. Hence **na·nnying** *vbl. sb.*

1954 J. TRENCH *Dishonoured Bones* ii. 46 Don't nanny me. **1963** *Economist* 6 July 41/3 Labour..would produce a less compulsively nannying piece of legislation. **1969** *Guardian* 11 June 11/7 Professional women get none of this obligatory nannying: their main grudge is inequalities of opportunity rather than of pay. **1971** J. OSBORNE *West of Suez* i. 35 Devoting all his time to Daddy and nannying him like he does. **1972** E. LONGFORD *Wellington: Pillar of State* iii. 31 In the short run, his five-year plan for nannying France—for such it soon seemed to be—could only damage the popularity of Wellington. **1974** E. DEWAR *Dying Business* ix. 110 There was no need for you to come nannying me.

nannygai (næ·nigəi). *Austral.* Also **nannyghai, nennigai.** [Aboriginal name.] A large marine food fish, *Centroberyx affinis*, found off the south-eastern coast of Australia.

1871 A. OLIVER *Fisheries New South Wales* 5 Fish, common to our coast,..when properly smoked or corned, are far superior to any imported codfish or ling... Nothing can surpass a corned 'moorra nennigai'. **1882** J. E. TENISON-WOODS *Fish New South Wales* 52 The Nannygai. .. Colour, a most beautiful pink, with silver stripes on the body. **1896** *Badminton Mag.* III. 206 A great variety of large game fish..the Nannyghai, the snapper, and a dark species of rock cod. **1896** F. G. AFLALO *Sk. Nat. Hist. Austral.* 199 The large-eyed, crimson Nannygai (*Beryx*), taken on the Schnapper grounds. **1947** *Coast to Coast 1946* 237 Morwong, rock-cod, nannygai and the rest, but not a real red fish among the lot. **1965** *Austral. Encycl.* VI. 240/1 Both [fishes] are wrongly called red snapper; the increasing use of this name in the fish trade for different species of nannygai is deprecated because of confusion with the true snapper. **1966** T. C. ROUGHLEY *Fish & Fisheries of Australia* (rev. ed.) 18 In some quarters.. there was a prejudice against the nannygai,..and the New South Wales Fisheries Department therefore condoned the use of the name 'redfish' for it, and the sales were given a helpful impetus.

nanny-goat. Add: **2.** An anecdote. *slang.*

1843 T. C. HALIBURTON *Attaché* 1st Ser. II. vii. 114 The old knight's got an anecdote.., and nanny-goats ain't picked up every day in country. *c* **1895** F. M. FORD *Let.* (1965) 8 That is a subject abt. which I have a nanny goat to commence the next chapter with & it is reserved.

3. *to get* (a person's) *nanny-goat*: to get one's goat (see *GOAT 3 c). Also, *to get* (a person's) *nanny*.

1914 R. LARDNER in *Sat. Even. Post* 15 Aug. 9/3 'Good night, Horseshoes!' he says. That got my nanny up this time. 'Shut up, you lucky stiff!' I says. **1928** E. WALLACE *Double* xi. 122 'She was most kind and gracious—recognised me in an instant. Didn't mention you, by the way,' he dug Dick in the ribs playfully. 'That's got your nanny-goat!' **1972** J. MINIFIE *Homesteader* xvii. 143 Take it easy, old boy... Don't let them get your nanny.

4. A totalisator. *slang.*

1961 PARTRIDGE *Dict. Slang* Suppl. 1194/2 *Nanny-goat*, totalisator... Rhyming on tote. **1970** *Daily Mail* 10 Mar. 8/6 The poor old ailing Tote—the Nanny Goat, as they call it.

nano- (næ·no-, nē̆i·no-, nā·no-), *prefix.* [f. L. *nan-us*, Gr. νᾶν-ος dwarf + -O.] Prefixed to the names of units to form the names of units 10^9 times smaller, i.e. one thousand-millionth part of them (symbol n), as *nanoamp*(*ere*, *-farad*, *-gramme*, *-henry* [*HENRY[3]], *-litre* *-metre*, *-mole* [*MOLE *sb.*[7]] (hence *-molar* adj.), *-volt*, *-watt*; **na·noequivalent**, one thousand-millionth of a gramme-equivalent. Also *NANOSECOND.

1947 *Compt. Rend. de la 14me Conf.* (Union Internat. de Chimie) 115 The following prefixes to abbreviations for the names of units should be used to indicate the specified multiples or sub-multiples of these units:..n nano- 10^{-9} ×. **1952** *Wireless World* May 187/2 The prefixes 'pico' and 'nano' became popular in this country fifteen or twenty years ago, mostly through the technical publications of Philips and others, with 'pico' as favourite. **1973** *Nature* 23 Nov. 190/3 The transient currents generated are small (of the order of a few nanoamps) and flow for a very short time (of the order of 10 nanoseconds). **1962** *Flight Internat.* LXXXII. 634/2 Designers are talking in terms of nanoAmperes. **1967** *McGraw-Hill Yearbk. Sci. & Technol.* 146 Accuracy and precision [of coulometric analysis]..range from a few hundredths of a per cent at the hundred microequivalent level..to approximately 10% at the five nanoequivalent level. **1951** *Wireless World* Nov. 458/1 This is undesirable..if another metric value, the nF (nano-farad) could be accepted for one-milliardth of a farad... Originally introduced—so far as I know—in Germany and also used in other Continental countries before the war, this *nano* abbreviation is now, in the Indonesian PTT, as normal as *km* for length of wire. **1951** *Nature* 8 Dec. 1008/2 Most microanalytical needs are satisfied by the subunits milligram and microgram. This sequence has now been extended by the nanogram (ng = 10^{-9} g) and picogram (pg = 10^{-12} g). **1964** W. G. SMITH *Allergy & Tissue Metabolism* vii. 76 In man, 10^8 platelets contain 60 nanograms (0·06 mg.) of serotonin. **1975** *Nature* 11 Sept. 141/2 Nanogram quantities of DNP-D-GL induced anti-DNP antibody formation, while larger amounts prevented responses to DNP-conjugates, as previously reported. **1975** WILLIAMS & WILSON *Biologist's Guide to Princ. & Techniques Pract. Biochem.* i. 16 Response of isolated organs to nanogramme quantities of active substances has been obtained by this technique. **1968** *New Scientist* 29 Feb. 484/1 The capacitors..are 28 microfarads, 5 nanohenries, 2 milliohms. **1974** *Nature* 26 Apr. 774/2 The use of injection experiments..demands careful quantitative control over the injection of nanolitre volumes of material. **1963** *Calibration & Test Services* (Nat. Bureau of Standards Misc. Publ. 250) 41 Transmittances of these disks at wavelengths from 365 to 390 nm (nanometer, 10^{-9} meter).. will also be determined on request. **1970** *Sci. Jrnl.* Feb. 49/3 Usually points closer than one nanometre (10^{-9}m) can be separated with the electron microscope. **1971** *Sci. Amer.* Sept. 89/2 Blue light at a wavelength of 450 nanometers (a nanometer is a billionth of a meter). **1969** *Nature* 18 Oct. 221/1 They are of such high biological potency that nanomolar concentrations can produce well-marked effects. **1968** *McGraw-Hill Yearbk. Sci. & Technol.* 387/2 Conduction is blocked in isolated, desheathed frog sciatic nerves by a solution [of tetrodotoxin] containing about 3 nanomoles per liter. **1971** *Sci. Amer.* Sept. 98/2 Plants will increase photosynthesis with increasing concentration of carbon dioxide to at least three times the normal concentration of 12·5 nanomoles per cubic centimeter (·03 percent by volume). **1968** *New Scientist* 22 Aug. 391/1 The other problem is how to take just a few microvolts from the national standard of one volt, and to infer its correctness to a few parts of a nanovolt (10^{-9}V). **1968** *Sci. Amer.* Mar. 17 (Advt.), The new COS/MOS units..operate on nanowatts of power in the quiescent state.

nanophanerophyte (næ:nofæ·nəɪofəit). [a. F. *nanophanérophyte* (C. Raunkiær 1905, in *Oversigt K. Danske Videnskabernes Selskabs Forhandl.* 352), f. prec. + *PHANEROPHYTE.] A shrub or sub-shrub between 25 cm and 2 m

in height, bearing its resting buds above the surface of the soil.

1913 W. G. SMITH in *Jrnl. Ecol.* I. 17 Nanophanerophytes less than 2 m. high. **1932** FULLER & CONARD tr. *Braun-Blanquet's Plant Sociol.* xii. 293 The round, woody cushions..are not to be classed with the cushion forms, because of the lignified shoots, but rather among the semishrubs and nanophanerophytes. **1960** N. POLUNIN *Introd. Plant Geogr.* iii. 94 Refinements may be used such as the subdivision of phanerophytes into nanophanerophytes (shrubs) in which the renewal buds lie less than 2 metres above ground, microphanerophytes [etc.].

nanoplankton, var. *NANNOPLANKTON.

na·nosecond (see *NANO-). [f. *NANO- + SECOND *sb.*[1]] A unit of time equal to one thousand-millionth of a second.

1959 W. C. G. ORTEL in *IRE Trans. Electronic Computers* III. 265 (*heading*) Nanasecond logic by amplitude modulation at X band. [*Note*] Although the term *millimicrosecond* has attained some currency, the metric system provides the standard prefix *nano-*, (abbreviated n-), by which the decimal multiplier 10^{-9} may be denoted conveniently without multiple prefixes. **1960** *Times* 17 Feb. 2/6 Pulses of nanosecond duration are being studied by means of fast recording techniques and spectrographic methods. **1964** *Evening Standard* 30 Oct. 19/3 The latest computers are now doing their sums in 'nano-seconds'... According to General Sarnoff, former head of the Radio Corporation of America, 'A nano-second is to a second what a second is to 30 years'. **1966** [see *GIGA-]. **1967** *New Statesman* 14 July 47/3 It takes a nanosecond for an electric signal to travel a foot. **1968** *Dataweek* 24 Jan. 1/3 The 9400 would appear to be slower than the IBM System/360 Model 25 (memory cycle of 600 nanoseconds per two bytes against IBM's 180 nanoseconds per 64 bytes) but faster than the ICT 1902A (3 microseconds per 24-bit word). **1972** *Sci. Amer.* Jan. 121/1 Present atomic clocks keep time to better than 100 nanoseconds per day.

Nansen passport. [f. name of Fridtjof *Nansen* (1861–1930), Norwegian diplomat and explorer, who was responsible for the issue of the papers described below.] A document of identification issued after the war of 1914–18 to a stateless person ineligible for a passport. Also *absol.*

1925 *Measures to help Refugees: Rep. 5th Comm. to 6th Assembly League of Nations* 1 After lengthy negotiations, the Refugee Service has secured recognition for the Nansen Passports from forty Governments in the case of Russians and from twenty-eight in the case of Armenians. **1932** J. B. C. WATKINS tr. *Sörensen's Saga F. Nansen* 285 Nansen called together representatives from the various governments to a meeting at Geneva in July 1922. Thirty-one were represented, and they accepted Nansen's proposal for an identification certificate for each refugee which could be used as a passport. Fifty-two governments have recognized these certificates, which are stamped with Nansen's picture and known as 'Nansen passports'. They may be obtained by Armenian, Chaldean, Turkish, and Syrian refugees. **1944** H. G. WELLS *'42 to '44* 50 The practical organization of the Nansen passports that were for a time a resort for the multitude of people who had lost their national standing through changes of boundaries and similar dislocations. **1958** *Spectator* 14 Feb. 209/2 The 'Nansen passport' was one result. **1975** L. DICKSON *Radclyffe Hall at Well of Loneliness* xvii. 215 Souline had only a 'Nansen', a letter of identity not a passport, allowing her to reside in France. *Ibid.* 220 The long process of obtaining for Souline British naturalization papers, a first step in which was to exchange her French 'Nansen' for an English 'Nansen'.

‖ **nant** (nænt). [W.] A brook; a valley.

1862 G. BORROW *Wild Wales* II. xxxii. 368, I saw a small house close by a nant or dingle. **1883** G. ALLEN *Flowers & their Pedigrees* vi. 184 There was once a time when great glacial sheets spread over the combs and glens of Snowdonia, as they spread to-day over the nants of Chamounix. **1923** *Chambers's Jrnl.* 26 May 409/1 A hill-road scrambles through orchards and vineyards and across dashing *nants* (mountain torrents) to a lofty ledge of pasture-land.

Nantgarw (nænt,gæ·ru). Also **Nantgarrow** (nænt,gæ·ro). The name of a village in Glamorgan, used to designate a translucent soft-paste porcelain produced between 1813 and 1920 at the Nantgarw pottery founded by William Billingsley and Samuel Walker.

1820 W. W. YOUNG *Diary* 28 Oct. in E. M. Nance *Pott. & Porc. Swansea & Nantgarw* (1942) 524 Put Advertisement for the Nantgarw China in *The Cambrian*. **1820** *Cambrian* 28 Oct. in *Ibid.* xiii. 395 (Advt.), For Sale by Auction... At the China Manufactory at Nantgarw on Wednesday the 8th day of November 1820. A Quantity of Nantgarw Porcelain; a considerable portion of this is enamelled and gilded in a superior style. **1849** L. W. DILLWYN *Let.* 5 June in J. Marryat *Coll. Hist. Pott. & Porc.* (1850) ix. 186/2, I believe that all the China with granulated fracture was marked 'Nantgarrow'. **1880** J. RANDALL *Hist. Madeley* 206 Employing agents in Paris to buy up Sevres china in white for the purpose of having it painted in London, as Nantgarw had been. **1948** W. D. JOHN *Nantgarw Porc.* iii. 53 Two glazes were used on the Nantgarw porcelain. **1964** M. KELLY *March to Gallows* i. 10 It wasn't an environment for highflown escape. Nantgarw china and French song, for example. **1973** *Times* 16 Oct. 4/8 The Welsh porcelain brought particularly competitive prices, with one Nantgarw plate painted with fruit and flowers at £714.

Nantucketer (næntʌ·kėtəɹ). [f. *Nantucket*, the name of an American island off the coast of Massachusetts + -ER[1].] A native or inhabitant of Nantucket.

1851 H. MELVILLE *Moby Dick* II. xli. 279 Now some Nantucketers rather distrust this historical story of Jonah and the whale. **1882** E. K. GODFREY *Island of Nantucket* 24 The Nantucketers seem to have a mania for bell-ringing. **1914** R. A. DOUGLAS-LITHGOW *Nantucket* xv. 296 A Nantucketer does not pull, he always 'hauls', he does not tie or fasten anything, he 'splices' it. **1935** *Amer. Speech* X. 38/1 The calm superiority of the Nantucketer is shown in the case of the school boy who began his composition thus: 'Napoleon was a great man..but he was an off-islander.' **1948** *Sat. Even. Post* 26 June 46/3 Russells had also played a part, along with Howlands and Rotches, who had been Nantucketers, in committing New Bedford to the gigantic gamble on whaling. **1974** *Sci. Amer.* Mar. 119/1 The yellowfin-tuna fishery on the Pacific Equator, worked only recently by American and Japanese longliners, is plainly disclosed in the Nantucketers' logbooks.

nap, *sb.*[3] Add: **1. d.** Blankets or other covering used by a person sleeping in the open air. *Austral. slang.*

c **1905** in Stewart & Keesing *Old Bush Songs* (1957) 249 My nap is rather thin, But my rig is pretty good. **1918** C. FETHERSTONHAUGH *After Many Days* 279 That night he could not catch the donkey, and he had to camp without any 'nap' (blankets). **1926** L. C. E. GEE *Bushtracks & Goldfields* 41 The quarts were boiled and an after-dinner supply of coffee made, the 'nap' spread out on soft sandy spots, the two travellers reclined with pipes. **1933** R. B. PLOWMAN *Man from Oodnadatta* 2 The blackboy's nap (blankets, underproof sheet, etc.) filled in the rear compartment. **1934** A. RUSSELL *Tramp-Royal in Wild Austral.* vii. 54 Rolled in our 'nap' with the 'break' at our heads and the camp fire at our feet, we slept snug and comfortable. **1936** —— *Gone Nomad* iii. 15 Here I hobbled out my horse and built a fire, placing beside it my nap and sweat-soaked saddle for pillow. **1945** *Coast to Coast 1944* 157 If you carry enough nap, you goes hungry; if you carry enough tucker you sleeps cold.

nap, *sb.*[5] Add: **2.** *nap hand*, a hand which will probably take all five tricks in the game of nap; a strong hand. Also *fig.*

1862 C. C. ROBINSON *Dial. Leeds* 371 He's a nap hand at his traade! **1899** *Captain* I. 369/2 He showed me the way to deal myself a 'nap' hand, no matter who shuffled the cards. **1955** *Radio Times* 22 Apr. 9/2 Both these races (run over the Rowley Mile) test three-year-olds in the spring and complete the 'nap hand' of classics.

b. (Later *fig.* examples.) In *Austral.* also used neg.

1938 F. S. ANTHONY *Me & Gus* 8 That's why the girls go nap on you the way they do. **1955** P. WHITE *Tree of Man* (1956) vii. 80, I never went nap on the priests meself. **1957** D. NILAND *Call me when Cross turns Over* viii. 184 But he never went nap on the city, he said, and now he had done with it for good. **1959** *Times* 22 Dec. 3/2 That is the sort of thing that poses another problem within the selectors' main one—whether to go nap on the ability that they know a man has in him, or whether to go entirely on the evidence of trials. **1961** A. UPFIELD *Bony & White Savage* vii. 59 The woman who runs the bookshop knows we don't go nap on the sexy stuff. **1967** N. MARSH *Death at Dolphin* x. 256 When you get one of your hunches..I reckon it's safe to go nap on it.

c. A tip that a horse or greyhound is the most likely to win; *spec.* (see quot. 1937). In full, *nap selection*. Also, the horse or greyhound so tipped; a bet on such a horse or greyhound. *colloq.*

1895 *Starting Price* 30 Mar. 1/2 Our 'Outsider's' nap of Docker for the Hainton Stakes. **1926** *Westm. Gaz.* 20 July 1/4 The Whip, which yesterday gave Lightstep, Nap (won 3–1),..continues to hold a strong lead in Naps over the selections of the other racing critics. **1927** W. E. COLLINSON *Contemp. Eng.* 30 He stars this one, and the horse so starred is the nap selection. **1937** E. RICKMAN *On & off Racecourse* ix. 195 Every racing writer gives a single 'nap' or starred selection each day. It is his idea of the most promising bet the programme affords. **1960** *Which?* Mar. 60/1 The figures in the table are based on the correspondent's 'nap' selection—the word comes from a card game —for each day's racing, the horse that he thinks is the best bet. **1971** *Post* (S. Afr., Cape ed.) 9 May 16/5 (Advt.), Information from 'Horseman' includes jackpots, naps, accumulators, duplas, quinellas, doubles.

nap (næp), *v.*[4] [f. *NAP *sb.*[5] 2 c.] *trans.* To recommend (a horse or greyhound) as a likely winner.

1927 *Daily Express* 22 June 17/7 Great Chum napped for White City Cup Final. **1973** *Listener* 28 June 864/3 You start napping odds-on chances, and they get beaten just as easily as the others.

Napa (næ·pă). Also **nappa.** The name of a county, town, and valley in California, U.S.A., used *attrib.* and *ellipt.* to designate (*a*) leather prepared from sheep- or goat-skin by a special tawing process; (*b*) wine grown in the valley.

1883 R. L. STEVENSON *Silverado Squatters* 34 (*heading*) Napa wine. **1895** *Montgomery Ward Catal.* 289/3 Men's Smoke Napa Gauntlet. **1897** C. T. DAVIS *Manuf. Leather* (ed. 2) 275 The staking machine..can be adjusted to any kind of leather, including napa. **1903** L. A. FLEMMING *Pract. Tanning* 51 Coloring black Napa. Black Napa leather is generally colored blue on the flesh side. **1921** B. E. ELLIS *Gloves & Glove Trade* 58 'Nappa' gloves are made from tawed leathers. **1961** *Housewife* Apr. 59/1 Fawn nappa leather handbag. **1971** M. MCCARTHY *Birds of America* 157 Several glasses of Napa Valley wine. **1974** *Country Life* 21 Mar. 688/1 Slip-on mules in coloured nappa leather for £7.

napalm (næ-, nēi·pām), *sb.* orig. *U.S.* [f. *NA(PHTHENATE + PALM(ITATE (see quot. 1946).] **1. a.** A thickening agent consisting essentially of aluminium salts of naphthenic acids and of the fatty acids of coconut oil. **b.** A thixotropic gel consisting of petrol and napalm (or some similar agent), used in flame-throwers and incendiary bombs; jellied petrol.

1942 in L. F. Fieser *Sci. Method* (1964) iv. 47 Novello and Harris will arrive..on Monday morning and deliver 7 small bombs and 7 large ones, each loaded with 100 grams of white phosphorus and with Napalm Polymer Gum prepared in gasoline. **1942** H. C. HOTTEL *Stud. Fuel Projection from Nozzles* (U.S. Govt. Res. Rep. PB 23769, 8 June) Summary, Very striking and extremely promising, however, is the enormous increase in range obtainable by the use of special materials, specifically a starch-water suspension and an incendiary gasoline gel known as Napalm. The latter can be projected three times as far in a one-eighth inch jet as can a conventional hydrocarbon fuel. **1946** L. F. FIESER et al. in *Industr. & Engin. Chem.* Aug. 769/1 It was next found (January 29, 1942) that a combination of aluminium naphthenate with the same 'aluminum palmitate' could be easily incorporated into gasoline to form a promising gel, and we termed this naphthenate-'palmitate' combination a Napalm gel. Subsequently it developed that the supposed 'aluminum palmitate' was actually the aluminum soap of the total fatty acids of coconut oil, and that the specific gelling quality is due to a high content of lauric, not palmitic, acid. **1951** KIRK & OTHMER *Encycl. Chem. Technol.* VI. 580 The U.S. uses a mixture of aluminum soaps, generally referred to as Napalm, as a thickening agent. A fuel of any desired consistency may be prepared by mixing the proper amount of Napalm with gasoline. **1952** R. CUTFORTH *Korean Reporter* xix. 174 He was no longer covered with a skin, but with a crust like crackling which broke easily. 'That's napalm,' said the doctor. **1953** *Armed Forces Chem. Jrnl.* (U.S.) July 8/2 The thickening agent, known popularly as napalm, gelled the gasoline to a honey-like consistency. **1964** L. F. FIESER *Sci. Method* ii. 27 On Feb. 14 [1942], we reported to NDRC development of two lines of gels that could be prepared by stirring with gasoline at room temperature. To one, made from aluminum *na*phthenate and 'aluminum *palm*itate', I gave the name Napalm. *Ibid.* 32 The most interesting sample, Napalm X-104, arrived on April 13, 1942... The material is a brownish, dry, nonsticky powder. When an amount of Napalm powder sufficient to produce a 12% solution is poured into gasoline and given one stir, solvation occurs rapidly and the swollen solvated particles soon fill the container with material of applesauce consistency... After aging for a few hours without attention, the gel reaches its final form, in which it is tough, strong, and sticky. **1966** *Chem. & Engin. News* 14 Mar. 24/3 An Air Force contract to supply 100 million pounds of the new napalm, which contains 50% polystyrene. *Ibid.*, Napalm-B, besides the 50% polystyrene, contains 25% benzene and 25% gasoline. It is replacing the soap-jelled gasoline napalm formulations of World War II and the Korean action. **1966** *Daily Tel.* 16 Aug. 17/3 Mrs. Anne Kerr, Labour M.P. for Rochester and Chatham, said in Tokyo today that the United States should withdraw from South Vietnam 'rather than drop napalm on innocent peasants'. **1967** *Freedomways* VII. 121 We saw a man who was a victim of napalm, and two women who had been tortured in Diem's prisons. **1968** [see *INCENDIJEL]. **1968** V. W. SIDEL in S. Rose *Chem. & Biol. Warfare* iii. 46 The adhesiveness, prolonged burning time and high burning temperature of napalm favour third-degree burns, and such burns are likely to be deep and extensive. **1970** K. LYLE in A. Chapman *New Black Voices* (1972) 293 I-am-wishing for an hour of napalm on ALL Junior Chambers-of-Commerce.

2. *attrib.* and *Comb.*, as *napalm bomb, -bombing, burn, gel, jelly.*

1945 *N.Y. Times* 17 Aug. 2/7 Only a few [new weapons] can be mentioned. Among them were:..the Napalm bomb—jellied gasoline with a detonator in a plane's detachable fuel tank. **1957** S. JAMESON *Cup of Tea for Mr. Thorgill* v. 41 All these years he has done harm—from a position of complete safety and comfort, like a pilot dropping napalm bombs. **1963** *Daily Tel.* 22 Aug. 10/2 The United Arab Republic..admits to using napalm bombs against the Royalist tribes. **1973** *Black Panther* 13 Oct. 14/2 He also charged that the Portuguese had been attacking them with tanks, napalm bombs and highly sophisticated and dangerous weapons supplied mostly by NATO countries. **1955** G. GREENE *Quiet American* 197 What I detest is napalm bombing... The poor devils are burnt alive, the flames go over them like water. **1959** *Times Lit. Suppl.* 23 Oct. 614/3 Fontane sees the war at close quarters—the heat, the dysentery, the napalm-bombing. **1952** *Times* 14 July 7/6 The napalm burns are not necessarily the most painful of wounds. **1968** *Listener* 8 Aug. 170/2 A television shot of a patient suffering from napalm burns in Vietnam. **1946** Napalm gel [see *1]. **1968** V. W. SIDEL in S. Rose *Chem. & Biol. Warfare* iii. 46 The napalm gel proved far superior to the original rubber-based gel. **1966** *Daily Tel.* 2 Nov. 14/8 Pictures showing the full horror of burns in Vietnam caused by the diabolical napalm jelly of phosphorus and petrol.

napalm (næ-, nēi·pām), *v.* [f. prec.] *trans.* To attack or destroy with napalm. Also *fig.* Hence **na·palmed** *ppl. a.*, **na·palming** *vbl. sb.*

1950 *N.Y. Times* 26 Sept. 2/7 Troops were napalmed when they were found hiding in caves at the dead end of a canyon. *Ibid.* 6 Nov. 2/2 Capt. Warren Nichols.. dived down in a napalming attack on a concentration of Red troops. **1952** DYLAN THOMAS *Let.* 8 Oct. (1966) 378, I think it has something to do with what Our Side gives to people after it has napalmed them. **1966** *Punch*

12 Jan. 64/2 The nobility of our democracy obliges us to succour the people..not to napalm them down. **1966** *New Statesman* 26 Aug. 292/2 There is no patience left in Vietnam. It has been napalmed and shot away. **1967** *Observer* 10 Dec. 5/3 The Americans are very busy bombing, rocketing and napalming air fields. **1968** *Economist* 27 Apr. 21/1 The nationalists have no intention of occupying these stockades, since the villages that contain them would then be napalmed or razed. **1968** *Guardian* 1 Oct. 8/4 Napalmed peasants in Vietnam. **1969** R. PETRIE *Despatch of Dove* III. 155 How to get rid of poverty? Blow it up! Napalm it! **1972** *Village Voice* (N.Y.) 1 June 62/2 (Advt.), They said they wanted to napalm draft records instead of people.

nape, *sb.*[1] Add: **1.** (Later *attrib.* example.)

1922 JOYCE *Ulysses* 256 Stooping her fair pinnacles of hair, stooping, her tortoise napecomb showed.

2. b. (Later example.)

1884 G. B. GOODE *Fisheries U.S.: Nat. Hist. Aquatic Anim.* 201 George's fish are very fat fish with white 'napes'.

naphtha. Add: **b.** *naphtha lamp* (earlier example); *naphtha-bearing* adj.; **naphtha engine** (see quot.); **naphtha launch,** a launch powered by a naphtha engine.

1909 *Westm. Gaz.* 2 Dec. 9/2 The leasing of certain areas of naphtha-bearing land contrary to existing regulations. **1892** P. BENJAMIN *Mod. Mechanism* 270 Naphtha-engines, which utilize naphtha both as the fuel under the boiler and as the fluid to be vaporized in the boiler and used in the engine, have recently come into somewhat extensive employment as motors for light launches. **1877** *Scribner's Monthly* Nov. 3/1 It consists of a large reflector behind a common naphtha lamp and mounted upon the bow of the boat. **1887** *Forest & Stream* 8 Dec. 395/3 The success which the naphtha launch has attained in a very short time must be taken as very strong proof of the inherent excellence of the machine itself. **1903** *Mobile* (Alabama) *Advertiser* 2 Jan. 6/3 The big naphtha launch Stella arrived from up the Alabama river yesterday afternoon. **1923** H. E. WILLIAMS *Spinning Wheels & Homespun* xv. 182 There have been times when..skimming away in little naptha [*sic*] launches..has seemed an enviable lot.

naphthalene. (Now the regular spelling.)

naphthaleneacetic (næ:fþălīnăsī·tik), *a.* [f. NAPHTHALENE + ACETIC *a.*] *naphthaleneacetic acid*: either of the two crystalline compounds, $C_{10}H_7CH_2COOH$, obtained by replacing one of the hydrogen atoms of naphthalene by an acetic acid group; *spec.* α-naphthaleneacetic acid, which has the action of an auxin and is used to stimulate the rooting of plant cuttings, to initiate flowering of the pineapple, to prevent premature drop of fruit, and to improve the colour of apples.

1917 *Chem. Abstr.* XI. 3876/2 (Index), Naphthaleneacetic acids. **1936** *Contrib. Boyce Thompson Inst.* VIII. 78 Treating cuttings or shoots of *Ilex, Taxus, Pachysandra, Hibiscus, Acer,* and *Chrysanthemum* with preparations of indoleacetic, indolepropionic, indolebutyric, or naphthaleneacetic acids induced earlier rooting, increased the number of roots, and roots emerged from a greater area of stem tissue as compared with control cuttings. **1942** *Science* 22 May 536/1 Low concentrations of α-naphthaleneacetic acid (the compound used most extensively) applied as foliage sprays induced formation of inflorescences in advance of the normal period, but high concentrations..delayed flowering far beyond that of the controls. **1968** F. C. STEWARD *Growth & Organization in Plants* viii. 394 The application of auxin during the dark period eliminates the photoperiodic induction due to the dark period in a short-day plant like cocklebur. Auxins, whether IAA or a synthetic substitute like naphthalene acetic acid..are all active in this respect.

naphthaquinone, var. *NAPHTHOQUINONE.

naphthene. Add: [ad. F. *naphtène* (Pelletier & Walter 1840, in *Jrnl. de Pharm.* XXVI. 561).] The substance orig. called by this name is now regarded not as a single compound but as a mixture of hydrocarbons, and the term is now *Obs.* in this sense. (Further example.)

1854 THOMSON *Cycl. Chem.* 378 Naphthene. $C_{16}H_{16}$. That portion of mineral naphtha which comes over second in distillation.

b. [ad. F. *naphtène* (coined afresh by Markovnikov & Oglobine 1884, in *Ann. de Chim. et de Physique* II. 447).] Any of a class of saturated cyclic hydrocarbons (including cyclopentane and cyclohexane) that are present in or obtained from petroleum.

1884 *Jrnl. Chem. Soc.* XLVI. 1276 Hydrocarbons of the C_nH_{2n} series, called by the authors naphthenes, constitute the principal part of Caucasian petroleum. **1921** J. S. CHAMBERLAIN *Textbk. Org. Chem.* 38 The saturated cyclic hydrocarbons known as naphthenes are characteristic of Russian (Baku) petroleum and are also found in that from Galicia. **1951** C. R. NOLLER *Chem. Org. Compounds* xxxix. 759 The saturated alicyclic hydrocarbons frequently are called cycloparaffins or cyclanes although petroleum technologists usually call them naphthenes because cyclopentane..and cyclohexane..and their homologs have been isolated from the naphtha fraction of petroleum. **1964** N. G. CLARK *Mod. Org. Chem.* v. 78 The naphthenes (a term used in the petroleum industry for the cyclic paraffins) are mainly cyclopentane and cyclohexane, and their simple derivatives.

naphthenic (næfþī·nik), *a. Chem.* [ad. F. *naphténique* (Markovnikov & Oglobine 1884, in *Ann. de Chim. et de Physique* II. 476), f. *naphtène* NAPHTHENE: see -IC.] **1.** *naphthenic acid*: any of the carboxylic acids obtained in the refining of petroleum, esp. one derived from an alicyclic compound (as cyclohexane or cyclopentane); also, an unspecified mixture of such acids.

1894 *Jrnl. Chem. Soc.* LXVI. I. 532 The methyl salts of the lower natural naphthenic acids were prepared and fractionated with a view to isolate the methyl salt of heptanaphthenic acid (hexahydrobenzoic acid). **1932** *Jrnl. Amer. Chem. Soc.* LIV. 240 We observed that naphthenic acids are formed when linoleic acid is cracked under pressure. **1942** *Chem. Rev.* XXX. 100 The mixture of acids now known as naphthenic acid. **1946** S. B. ELLIOTT *Alkaline-Earth & Heavy-Metal Soaps* ii. 33 Naphthenic acids..are the raw materials from which some of the most important soaps are manufactured. **1957** VAN DER HAVE & VERVER *Petroleum* xiii. 383 The free naphthenic acids also find certain applications, for instance as wetting agents for the pigments used in printing inks and paints. **1966** *McGraw-Hill Encycl. Chem. Technol.* X. 47/2 Naphthenic acid production is about 16,000,000 lb annually.

2. Of, pertaining to, or containing naphthenes.

1931 *Engineering* 2 Jan. 1/2 Cyclohexane, a hydrocarbon of the naphthenic series. **1969** *Sci. Jrnl.* Nov. 32/2 The basic structure of bitumen is that of clusters of naphthenic and aromatic rings... It is called a naphthenic crude oil. **1974** *Sci. Amer.* Dec. 7 (Advt.), Up to this point, the best traction drive lubricants were naphthenic oils.

Hence **na·phthenate,** any of the salts of a naphthenic acid, some of which are used as paint driers, as fungicides, and in lubricants.

1899 *Jrnl. Chem. Soc.* LXXVI. I. 423 (*heading*) Properties of naphthenates and their qualitative distinction from salts of fatty acids. **1924** *Chem. Abstr.* XVIII. 2688 Al naphthenate forms a transparent, colorless, and porous mass which can be powdered; it has a water-proofing action. **1942** *Chem. Rev.* XXX. 103 In the case of castor machine oils, where increased..viscosity..is desired, various naphthenates have been used. **1960** E. L. DELMAR-MORGAN *Cruising Yacht Equipment & Navigation* xiii. 158 It is usually possible to see when power kerosene is deteriorating, by the fact that it becomes bright green in colour, as a result of the formation of copper naphthenate formed by the interaction of the fuel and the metal of a copper or brass tank. **1973** *Biol. Abstr.* LV. 6965/2 Potassium naphthenate significantly increased the ascorbic acid content of green pods of bush bean plants.

naphthoquinone (næfþokwi·nōun). *Chem.* Also **naphtha-.** [f. NAPHTH(ALENE + -O + QUINONE.] Each of the six compounds, $C_{10}H_6O_2$, obtained (theoretically) by replacing two of the ⩾CH groups of naphthalene by carbonyl groups, *spec.* 1,4- (or α-)-naphthoquinone, a volatile yellow solid whose molecule forms part of the structure of vitamin K.

1870 *Jrnl. Chem. Soc.* XXIII. 446/2 (Index), Naphthoquinones. **1914** H. T. CLARKE *Introd. Study Org. Chem.* xxxiv. 417 The *ortho* quinone, β-naphthaquinone,..is a red crystalline solid, which decomposes at 115–120°. **1942** *Ann. Reg. 1941* 344 The four forms of vitamin K proved to be naphthoquinone derivatives. **1951** I. L. FINAR *Org. Chem.* I. xxix. 593 Theoretically, six naphthaquinones are possible... Only three are known, the 1:2-, 1:4- and 2:6-, but it appears that derivatives of 2:3-naphthaquinone have been prepared. **1966** *McGraw-Hill Encycl. Sci. & Technol.* XI. 194/2 The naphthoquinones are prepared by oxidation of the corresponding aminonaphthols.

napkin, *sb.* Add: **1. c.** A rectangular piece of towelling or absorbent material used as a baby's undergarment by folding, drawing up between the legs, and fastening at the waist.

1845 MRS. GASKELL *Let.* (1966) 824 Meta is so neat & so knowing, only, handles wet napkins very gingerly. **1861** MRS. BEETON *Bk. Househ. Managem.* 1021 Soiled baby's napkins should be rolled up and put into a pan, when they should be washed out every morning. **1961** *Brit. Med. Dict.* 1212/1 The skin..is the more easily affected by the free ammonia liberated through the interaction of acid urine and badly washed napkins. **1974** *Janet Frazer Catal.* Spring & Summer 292/2 Fully-bleached terry napkins. Soft and absorbent... Size 24" × 24"..£3·35 (dozen).

4. napkin-ring (earlier and later examples).

1686 in *Narragansett Hist. Reg.* III. (1884–5) 105, 18 Napkins & 9 Napkin Rings. **1972** *Country Life* 21 Dec. 1755 This woven design, using sterling silver ribbons interwoven..is very attractive. There are napkin rings (ideal for a wedding present)... The napkin ring costs £20.

Napoleon. 2. For 'top-boot' read 'long boot'.

3. (Later examples.)

1880 *Harper's Mag.* May 917/1 The artillery is almost entirely the old brass Napoleon. **1897** *Outing* XXX. 80/1 These gun companies were each supplied with one 12-pounder Napoleon gun and one Gatling gun.

4. b. = *NAP *sb.*[5] 2 c.

1895 *Starting Price* 23 Mar. 1/1 With ruinous 'all day wires' and extortionately priced 'Napoleons' we will have nothing to do.

5. One resembling Napoleon I, esp. in having gained supremacy in his own sphere through ruthless ambition. Also *tranf.*

1821 SHELLEY *Let.* 25 Sept. (1964) II. 353 He was a little Napoleon..with a dukedom instead of an empire for his theatre. **1866** J. BLACKWOOD *Let.* 2 Aug. in Geo. Eliot *Lett.* (1956) IV. 293 He is a Napoleon in his Trade is Truefitt. **1879** R. L. STEVENSON *Trav. with Donkey* 144, I had travelled hitherto through a dull district, and in the track of nothing more notable than the child-eating Beast of *Gévaudan*, the *Napoleon Buonaparte* of wolves. **1894** A. CONAN DOYLE *Mem. Sherlock Holmes* 260 He is the Napoleon of crime, Watson. He is the organizer of half that is evil and of nearly all that is undetected in this great city. He is a genius, a philosopher, an abstract thinker. **1907** I. ZANGWILL *Ghetto Comedies* 353 This, then, was the notorious multi-millionaire, 'the Napoleon in dollars'. **1932** Q. D. LEAVIS *Fiction & Reading Public* 312 Northcliffe, being the Napoleon of the Press, naturally disliked having to play second fiddle to the advertiser. **1939** T. S. ELIOT *Old Possum's Pract. Cats* 35 The Cat who all the time Just controls their operations: the Napoleon of Crime! **1969** *N.Y. Rev. Bks.* 18 Dec. 33/2 We had Napoleons of finance, Napoleons of industry, Napoleons of the betting ring. **1973** 'I. DRUMMOND' *Jaws of Watchdog* vi. 79 'Royston,' said Colly. 'What kind of a name is that for a Napoleon of crime?' **1975** *Times* 2 June 10 A Time Prcfile—General Vo Nguyen Giap—Communist Napoleon who conquered South Vietnam.

6. A type of rich cake made from layers of puff pastry filled with cream, custard, or jam. Also *attrib.*

1892 *Encycl. Pract. Cookery* I. 246/1 *Napoleon Cake.* Lay in a Napoleon-cake pan..a layer of puff paste. spread over that a layer of pastry cream, cover with puff paste, glaze the top with sugar, and bake. **1896** E. TURNER *Little Larrikin* xxviii. 342 In the centre were five white-iced Napoleons, ornamented with devices cut from silver tea-paper, this being the nearest the funds would stretch to wedding-cake. **1956** E. STARKIE *Diary* Sept. in J. Richardson *Enid Starkie* (1973) xxviii. 204 There was.. every kind of cake, biscuit and sweet—the most succulent cake was called Napoleon! **1961** J. HELLER *Catch-22* (1962) xxiv. 249 Prune and cheese Danish from Copenhagen, éclairs, cream puffs, Napoleons and *petits fours* from Paris, Reims and Grenoble, [etc.]. **1968** A. BINKLEY *What shall I Cry?* 139 'You got more of those cakes?'.. Lenni handed him a box in which one napoleon remained. **1969** W. S. KUNICZAK *Sempinski Affair* (1970) vii. 69, I..felt my resolve melting like the Napoleon pastries on my plate. **1975** C. NESBITT *Little Love & Good Company* xvi. 201 A plate of luscious Napoleons oozing thick whipped-cream.

7. Used *attrib.* and *absol.* of brandy of supposed great age or special merit.

1930 J. DOS PASSOS *42nd Parallel* II. 207 They were sitting over Napoleon brandy in big bowlshaped glasses and cigars. **1967** C. CHURCHILL *World of Wines* x. 208 'Napoleon Brandy' ranks high among some of the more transparent promotional myths of the industry. **1967** A. LICHINE *Encycl. Wines* 214/2 The worst deception in Cognac brandies is the fraud and fakery connected with alleged 'Napoleon' brandy—but a distinction must be made between brandies pretending to derive from Napoleon's time, and the Napoleon style. **1968** C. FORSYTE *Murder with Minarets* vii. 42 They sat over their Napoleon after dinner. **1968** T. PARKER *People of Streets* 48 Could I have a glass of Napoleon brandy please? **1975** D. BEATY *Electric Train* 147 Liqueurs—two Napoleon brandies. Warm on her stomach.

Napoleonism. Add: (*a*) *spec.* the assumption of absolute control over subject peoples or countries; (*c*) conduct or behaviour resembling that of Napoleon.

1966 *New Statesman* 28 Oct. 828/1 The military life had the advantage of absorbing what could easily have been insidious at this stage: the premature dream of glory, the stupefying effects of youthful Napoleonism. **1969** *Sunday Times* 6 Apr. 27 Personal incompatibility..and the traditional Latin American leader's custom of renouncing ultimate power as soon as he had won it (for fear of accusations of 'Napoleonism'), were less significant than the internal political and social divisions. **1970** *Guardian Weekly* 6 June 2 Without our nation standing up against Russia's modern day mad dog Napoleonism Europe itself would not remain independent through the 1970s.

napoo (nāpū·), *int., a.,* and *v. colloq.* Also **na poo, napooh.** [Corruption of F. (*il n'y e*)*n a plus* there is no more.] **a.** *int.* Finished; gone; done for. **b.** *adj.* Finished; good for nothing; dead. **c.** *v. trans.* To finish, kill, or destroy.

1915 'I. HAY' *First Hundred Thousand* 302 You say 'Na pooh!' when you push your plate away after dinner. .. 'Poor Bill got na-poohed by a rifle-grenade yesterday.' **1917** W. J. LOCKE *Red Planet* xvi. 194 Instinctively I stretched out my hand. He laughed. 'Napoo. You must take it as gripped.' **1919** J. B. MORTON *Barber of Putney* xv. 253 'Can't do nothing,' said Curly, ''e's napoo.' *Ibid.* xviii. 301 Even if they themselves were na-pooed, they'd hate to think of the lousy Boche living in their home. **1925** N. VENNER *Imperfect Impostor* i. 6 If you haven't got a job to do, you're a washout. You might as well be napood right off. **1927** W. DEEPING *Kitty* xvi. 205 A man's phrase—a war-phrase—seemed to trickle into his head. Everything was na poo, a wash-out. His marriage—. **1936** F. CLUNE *Roaming round Darling* vi. 52 All the boys about here..have looked for money in the gullies, and the only thing they ever come across was a rum-keg—empty —'*Napoo*', like the Diggers used to say! **1943** J. B. PRIESTLEY *Daylight on Saturday* xxix. 228 You're as good as dead—just waitin' to stiffen. Fini—napoo! **1973** L. MEYNELL *Thirteen Trumpeters* v. 81 Prudence..fell down dead in the croupier's bag. Fini. Napoo.

nappa, var. *NAPA.

nappe (næp). [a. F. *nappe* table-cloth, NAPE *sb.*[2]] **1.** *Hydraulics.* A sheet of water falling over a weir or similar surface.

1892 Marichal & Trantwine tr. Bazin in *Proc. Engineers' Club Philadelphia* IX. 231 We now proceed to study the form of the sheet of water passing over the weir. [*translator's footnote*] For want of a convenient English equivalent, we shall designate this sheet by its very appropriate French name, the *nappe*, a name applied primarily to a table-cloth, the form of which..is well imitated by the sheet of water passing over the weir. *Ibid.* [*text*], The upper surface of the nappe has already been studied by certain experimenters. **1945** W. P. Creager et al. *Engin. for Dams* II. xi. 357 If the area below the lower nappe is filled with masonry, the shape of the sheet and the discharge will not be changed appreciably. **1966** F. M. Henderson *Open Channel Flow* vi. 177 If the nappe is contained within parallel walls downstream of the weir, it may well enclose the air between itself, walls, and floor.

2. *Geol.* A sheet of rock which has moved sideways over neighbouring strata, usu. as a result of overthrusting.

Earlier used in F. as *nappe de recouvrement* sheet of overlaying (e.g. *Bull. Soc. vaudoise des Sci. nat.* (1893) XXIX. 252).

1922 *Q. Jrnl. Geol. Soc.* LXXVIII. 87 In deciding upon the basal limit to be assigned to any particular nappe, one generally chooses some prominent thrustplane; failing this, one is entitled to select the axial plane of some recumbent anticline or syncline, according to local convenience. **1932** [see *allochthonous *a.*]. **1944** A. Holmes *Princ. Physical Geol.* vi. 81 Tear faults are commonly developed in nappes, where they naturally arise if one part of a nappe has been driven forward further than the adjoining parts. **1970** Linton & Moseley in *Cambr. Anc. Hist.* (ed. 3) I. i. i. 15 The Gulf of Oman, in which a series of 'nappes' or horizontally displaced rock sheets have been successively driven from north-east to south-west.

napper⁴. (Further examples.)

1916 'Taffrail' *Pincher Martin* xii 232 Yer kin be drownded in yer barth, or git a chimney-pot dropped on yer napper in a gale o' wind. **1936** F. Clune *Roaming round Darling* ix. 78 Half a score of Dubboites..waited with suspense and open mouths for a brick to fall back and crack the thrower on the napper. **1936** W. Lawson *When Cobb & Co. was King* v. 81 Fell on his napper on a log. **1947** [see *conk *sb.*¹ c]. **1959** G. M. Wilson *Shadows on Landing* vii. 78 If anyone ever asked for an orangeade bottle on his napper, Fruity did.

nappy, *sb.*² (Later examples.)

1916 *Daily Colonist* (Victoria, B.C.) 1 July 2/1 (Advt.), If it's Cut Glass you want, then we have what you want. Berry Bowls, Bon-Bon Dishes, Nappies, [etc.]. **1969** *Northwest* (*Sunday Oregonian Mag.*) 14 Dec. 24/1 Faceted knife rests, nappies (those flat bottomed, slope-sided little dishes for relish and a myriad of other uses), vases, celery dishes, whatever your budget would support—these offered marriage fitting recognition.

nappy (næ·pi), *sb.*³ *colloq.* = *napkin *sb.* 1 c. Also *fig.*

1927 W. E. Collinson *Contemp. Eng.* 7 Mothers and nurses use pseudo-infantile forms like pinny (pinafore), nappy (napkin). **1938** S. Spender *Trial of Judge* ii. 49 The babe's scream till the nurse brings its nappy. **1955** M. F. Gilbert *Sky High* viii. 118 He's got about as much sense as a baby that kicks its nappy off and then cries because it's sleeping in a puddle. **1959** *Economist* 6 June 921/2 An able minister..will need anything up to six months to get out of his administrative nappies. **1961** *Which?* Apr. 84/1 There are various types of nappy used in this country, including a T-shaped one made of gauze.. and disposable nappies. **1972** Ld. Robens *Ten Year Stint* xvi. 322, I had been a Minister when John Eden was in his political nappies, but had never experienced such peculiar behaviour. **1973** *Guardian* 3 Feb. 24/2 The greatest pollution in this land..was..committed against women 'from the nappy to the coffin'.

b. *attrib.* and *Comb.*, as *nappy-changing, towel*; **nappy pin**, a curved safety pin used for fastening nappies; **nappy rash**, infantile erythema caused by persistent contact with urinary ammonia from a damp nappy; **nappy service**, a commercial laundry service for babies' nappies.

1970 D. Bagley *Running Blind* ii. 17 No nappy-changing for you. **1973** *Guardian* 23 May 9/3, I draw the line at nappy-changing, not because I am a man but because..I don't like surprises of that nature. **1966** *Olney Amsden & Sons Ltd. Price List* 1 *Nappy Pins.* Snaplock curved with enamelled safety cap. **1967** H. W. Sutherland *Magnie* i. 2 He saw Bridie stop and look across at him, a nappy pin in her mouth. **1972** J. Mann *Mrs. Knox's Profession* xv. 110 He wielded the tin of powder and the nappy pins with voluntary attentiveness. **1959** *Which?* Sept. 104/2 Do the synthetic detergents cause dermatitis, or don't they? And does a baby get nappy-rash if its nappies are washed in them? **1966** 'G. North' *Confounding Sgt. Cluff* xvi. 128 An infant red in the face, tormented by nappy-rash, howled in a pram. **1967** *New Scientist* 25 May 449/3 What started out as an effective treatment for nappy rash in infants may now be an essential instrument of modern warfare. **1972** J. Wilson *Hide & Seek* ii. 34 A baby who had teething troubles and nappy rash. **1959** *Manch. Guardian* 8 July 5/5 The nappy service cost 2s 6d a dozen, three times a week. **1970** K. Giles *Death in Church* ii. 47 Auntie..switched me on to Nappy Service, six dozen delivered every morning. **1940** C. Day Lewis tr. *Virgil's Georgics* iv. 89 Her sisters washed his hands Duly with pure water and fetched the nappy towels.

nappy, *a.*¹ Add: **2.** Fuzzy, kinky; used colloquially and freq. derogatorily of Negroes' hair. So **nappy-head**, a Negro; **nappy-haired, -headed** *adjs. U.S.*

1950 A. Lomax *Mister Jelly Roll* (1952) 80 Light-skinned Downtown shared the bandstand with 'real black' and nappy-headed' Uptown. **1956** S. Longstreet *Real Jazz* xviii. 150 To call a man '*nappy*' is to say his hair is kinky—a real insult. **1962** E. Cleaver in A. Dundes *Mother Wit* (1973) 16/1 Good hair, bad hair, nappy hair. **1966** K. L. Morgan in *Ibid.* 606/2 They would come up with black nappy-haired babies. **1967** J. Taylor in A. Chapman *New Black Voices* (1972) 175 One of the new breed of nappy-haired, bangle-wearing nationalists. **1968** J. Pullum in P. Oliver *Screening Blues* iii. 92 Joe Pullum's high-pitched 'black gal, black gal, what makes your nappy head so hard?' **1971** *Black World* June 71/2 Her hair..was in the bushy style that the freedom riders had brought. They called it 'natural'; Bojack called it nappy. **1973** *Ibid.* Apr. 63 All them ol' nappy-heads runnin' up there tryin' to pull his clothes off.

nappy, *a.*² Add: **3.** Of a horse: awkward, disobedient.

1924 G. Brooke *Horse-Sense* v. 36 There are horses that refuse from temper, generally called 'nappy horses'. **1952** R. S. Summerhays *Elem. Riding* (ed. 3) xii. 72 A 'nappy' horse is a horse which can be described as one who will not go forward, will often go sideways and sometimes backwards. **1960** *Times* 23 July 9/2 Do not give the pony more than 20 minutes of this or it will sicken him, and..he may turn nappy and start refusing. **1963** Bloodgood & Santini *Horseman's Dict.* 134 *Nappy* (*to be*), for a horse to be inclined to shy or refuse suddenly and without warning. **1973** J. White *Norfolk Child* 131 My father..was utterly patient with every horse he rode, however nappy.

Nara (nā·ra). [The name of a town in Central Honshu, Japan, capital of Japan A.D. 710–84.] Used *attrib.* to designate the Buddhist sculpture of the period of Japanese history during which Nara was the capital.

1902 F. Brinkley *Oriental Series: Japan* VII. i. 19 As to sculpture, the point of excellence to which it had been carried is attested by several statues which form part of the Nara temple relics. **1903** K. Okakura *Ideals of East* 112 The stone Buddhas of the Tin Tal in Ellora.. are beautiful, with a self-contained grandeur and harmony of proportion. In them we find the sources of inspiration of the Tâng and Nara sculptures. **1955** Paine & Soper *Art & Archit. Japan* iv. 26 The earliest clay images of the Nara period are the groups of figures dating from 711 in the Pagoda of Hōryūji. **1970** *Oxf. Compan. Art* 609/2 During the Heian period..the trend was away from the realism of the Nara period.

narc (nāɹk). *U.S. slang.* Also **nark.** [abbrev. Narcotic *sb.* or *a.*] A federal, state, or local narcotics agent. Cf. *narco.

1967 *N.Y. Times* 17 Oct. 44 Most speed freaks get to a point where they're seeing narks in the trees with cameras. **1968–70** *Current Slang* (Univ. S. Dakota) III–IV. 85 *Narc*, an official of the Narcotics Control Board. *Ibid.*, *Narco, or narc*, narcotics officer. (Drug users' jargon). **1970** E. Tidyman *Shaft* (1971) iv. 50 The police didn't frighten him. The Narcs didn't frighten him. **1972** J. Wambaugh *Blue Knight* (1973) vii. 114 A narco cop nailed him..the narcs busted in the pad. **1973** *Black Panther* 20 Oct. 15/1 Then I made contact for the ring with the narc agent. **1975** *New Yorker* 19 Feb. 96/3 Bo, a rookie detective..is so confused by the Department's manipulations that he doesn't guess that she is an undercover narc.

narcissine, *a.* Add: **2.** Resembling, or of the nature of, Narcissus (see *Narcissus 2); loving or admiring oneself.

1813 E. S. Barrett *Heroine* II. xxii. 77 Flinging off my bonnet, I shook my narcissine locks over my shoulders. **1911** Beerbohm *Zuleika D.* ii. 15 Yet there was nothing Narcissine in her spirit. Her love for her own image was not cold æstheticism.

narcissism (nāɹsi·siz'm). esp. *Psychol.* [f. the name of *Narcissus*, a beautiful youth who fell in love with his own reflection in a fountain (Ovid *Metam.* iii. 370; subsequently referred to by Havelock Ellis in *Alienist & Neurologist* (1898) XIX. ii. 280; the term *Narcissismus* was used by Näcke in *Die sexuellen Perversitäten* (1899)): see -ism.] Self-love and admiration that find emotional satisfaction in self-contemplation; occas. (erron.) **narcism.**

1822 Coleridge *Let.* 15 Jan. (1971) V. 196 Of course, I am glad to be able to correct my fears as far as public Balls, Concerts, and Time-murder in Narcissism. **1905** H. Ellis *Stud. Psychol. Sex* IV. iii. 187, I have referred to the developed forms of this kind of self-contemplation..and in this connection have alluded to the fable of Narcissus, whence Näcke has since devised the term Narcissism for this group of phenomena. **1922** J. Riviere tr. *Freud's Introd. Lect. Psycho-Anal.* xxiv. 347 It is probable that this *narcissism* is the universal original condition, out of which *object-love* develops later without thereby necessarily effecting a disappearance of the narcissism. **1938** H. A. Murray *Explorations in Personality* iii. 180 Narcism (or Egophilia) is technical for self-love. **1946** [see *introjection 3 a]. **1955** H. Marcuse *Eros & Civilization* (1969) viii. 169 The striking paradox that narcissism, normally understood as egotistic withdrawal from reality, here is connected with oneness with the universe, reveals the new depth of the conception. **1969** P. Loewenberg in B. B. Wolman *Psychoanal. Interpretation of Hist.* vi. 182 He [*sc.* Herzl] regressed to the stage of narcissism in which his only sexual object was his own ego and its fantasies. **1970** Hinsie & Campbell *Psychiatric Dict.* (ed. 4) 487/2 *Narcism*, a shortened (and incorrect) form of narcissism.

narcissist (nāɹsi·sist). [f. as prec. + -ist.] A person affected with narcissism. Also *attrib.*

1930 B. Russell *Conquest of Happiness* i. i. 22 A narcissist,..inspired by the homage paid to great painters, may become an art student. **1934** C. Day Lewis *Hope for Poetry* vi. 32 We find, instead of criticism, long narcissist ramblings, the 'reviewer's' views on everything under the sun. **1953** *Essays in Crit.* III. 89 A narcissist indulgence in a 'phantasmal world' of self-reflection. **1958** *Times Lit. Suppl.* 24 Jan. 46/3 The doctrine here is that Shelley is a self-absorbed narcissist, yearning emptily and 'regressively' for death.

narcissistic (nāɹsisi·stik), *a.* [f. as prec. + -istic.] Of or pertaining to narcissism; marked by excessive love of self.

1916 E. Jones tr. *Ferenczi's Contrib. Psycho-Anal.* 174, I was just striving to make clear to a patient her excessive ambition, arising from narcissistic fixation. **1922** J. Riviere tr. *Freud's Introd. Lect. Psycho-Anal.* xxiv. 347 Thus it appeared that auto-erotism was the sexual activity of the narcissistic phase of the direction of the Libido. **1935** S. Spender *Destructive Element* xv. 267 It was not a narcissistic desire to recover lost charms and innocence. **1964** *Economist* 23 May 801/2 Students..would be vastly improved if they were a lot less frowsty and narcissistic. **1973** L. Bellak et al. *Ego Functions* ii. x. 159 Kernberg has discussed 'Barriers to Being in Love' from the standpoint of narcissistic personality features.

narcissistically (nāɹsisi·stikăli), *adv.* [f. prec.: see -ically.] In a narcissistic manner.

1925 T. Dreiser *Amer. Trag.* (1926) I. i. xv. 112 She narcissistically painted her flight. **1962** *Times* 3 May 17/2 Some literary men seem almost narcissistically concerned with themselves and their art. **1968** *Daily Tel.* 13 Nov. 15/5 If you don't go for seeing yourself narcissistically reflected in the shimmering walls, there is the view of lacy trees outside. **1974** D. Meiring *President Plan* x. 84 The father [was] bound narcissistically within the mirrors of his supposed professional importance.

Narcissus. Add: **2.** [See *narcissism.] The name of a youth in classical mythology who died of self-love after seeing his reflection in water and was turned into the flower, used chiefly *attrib.* and *Comb.* allusively for: one who admires himself exclusively, one who resembles Narcissus in handsomeness.

1606 Shakes. *Ant. & Cl.* ii. v. 96 Go get thee hence, Had'st thou Narcissus in thy face to me, Thou would'st appeere most vgly. **1767** W. Kenrick tr. *Misc. Wks. J. J. Rousseau* II. 121 (*title*) Narcissus, or the self-admirer. A comedy. **1860** A. J. Munby *Diary* 10 Feb. in D. Hudson *Munby* (1972) 49 His face..seemed to me weak and self-conscious; a young Narcissus face. **1891** O. Wilde *Pict. Dorian Gray* i. 4 This young Adonis, who looks as if he was made of ivory and rose-leaves. Why, my dear Basil, he is a Narcissus. **1928** R. Campbell *Wayzgoose* ii. 44 Here was a man—I thought it was a mess, A bottle-nosed Narcissus of the Press. **1929** D. H. Lawrence *Pornograhy & Obscenity* 26 The most emancipated bohemians..are still utterly..enclosed within the narcissus–masturbation circle. **1930** —— *A Propos Lady Chatterley* 23 Poor, self-conscious, uneasy, narcissus-monk as he was. **1935** A. Huxley *Let.* 20 Sept (1969) 397 Why is it that when one enters that [*sc.* theatrical] world, one always finds oneself with crooks, imbeciles, narcissus complexes? *a* **1963** C. S. Lewis *Poems* (1964) 89 So should I quickly die Narcissus-like of want. **1964** M. McLuhan *Understanding Media* (1967) v. 66 The frontiers between forms that snap us out of the Narcissus-narcosis.

3. **narcissus fly**, a hover-fly, *Lampetia* (= *Merodon*) *equestris*, whose larva infests the bulbs of narcissus and other plants, causing them to rot.

1903 F. V. Theobald *First Rep. Econ. Entomol.* 107 A correspondent..sent the larvæ of the Narcissus Fly, from Chertsey, with the following note: 'They play havoc with the narcissus bulbs and are evidently the maggot of some fly.' **1926** *Jrnl. Econ. Entomol.* XIX. 249 The observations were made on the larvae of the narcissus fly. **1951** Colyer & Hammond *Flies Brit. Isles* xii. 166 Our last example from the group is *Merodon equestris* F., the 'Large Bulb Fly' or 'Narcissus Fly', which is a serious pest to the horticulturalist. **1966** *Punch* 28 Sept. 485/3 There are in Britain some two hundred and twenty known varieties of hover fly, of which only the Narcissus flies are destructive (to narcissi, naturally).

narco (nā·ɹko). U.S. slang abbrev. of *narcotic* or *narcotics*, used esp. (freq. *attrib.*) = *narc (see also quots.).

1955 *Amer. Speech* XXX. 87 *Narco*, the narcotic hospital in Lexington, Kentucky. **1958** J. & W. Hawkins *Death Watch* 43 This informant is a thief, a narco or a four-bottle bum. **1960** *Sat. Rev.* (U.S.) 6 Feb. 11/3 The Beat Generation has marihuana and the ritual of dodging the 'narcos'—the narcotics squad. **1961** Rigney & Smith *Real Bohemia* p. xvi, *Narco, the*, federal narcotics agents. **1964** *Manhunt* Mar. 67/2, I feel very strongly about helping narco violators. *Ibid.* 68/1 You've gone to bat on forty-three narcos *without a single acquittal*! **1968** *Wall St. Jrnl.* 19 Feb. 1/1 Students also have agitated against university acquiescence in the presence on the campus of 'narcos'—police agents seeking to make arrests for violations of narcotics laws, whose basic premises many of the students question. **1970** K. Platt *Pushbutton Butterfly* (1971) xi. 126 Tina was in the drug racket... The narco squad might have had reason to

suspect her. **1971** 'D. Shannon' *Ringer* (1972) iii. 58 The pedigrees varied from burglary to narco dealing to rape. **1972** [see *narc].

narco- (nā·ɹko). *Psychol.* [f. Gr. *νάρκη* numbness.] Prefixed to a sb. to indicate that use is made, in the treatment specified by the sb., of a drug (usu. a barbiturate such as amylobarbitone or thiopentone sodium) which, while inducing relaxation, facilitates the remembering and verbalizing of repressed emotional experiences. So *narco-analysis*, *-hypnosis* (also *-hypnotic* adj.), *-therapy*; *narco-synthesis*, the acceptance into the conscious self of repressed emotional experiences revealed by the use of drugs.

1936 J. S. Horsley in *Jrnl. Mental Sci.* LXXXII. 416 Narco-analysis is an eclectic technique based on the observation that a combination of narcosis with psychotherapy is quicker and sometimes more effective than the formal methods of analytical psychology. **1943** —— (*title*) Narco-analysis. *Ibid.* i. 3 Clearly any title which suggests that a particular narcotic is essential to the technique is undesirable. Therefore I devised the term 'Narco-Analysis' which is inclusive of all such methods. **1973** E. Rudinger *Treatm. & Care in Mental Illness* (rev. ed.) 161 Narco-analysis or abreaction is a treatment that is also available privately, but the drugs used and the nursing home fee have to be paid in addition to the psychiatrist's fee. **1949** A. Huxley *Let.* 21 Oct. (1969) 605 The world's rulers will discover that infant conditioning and narco-hypnosis are..efficient. **1974** Hawkey & Bingham *Wild Card* v. 51 McElroy was sufficiently promising a subject to be questioned under narco-hypnosis. **1949** A. Huxley *Let.* 9 Dec. (1969) 611 The latest in..narco-hypnotic techniques. **1945** Grinker & Spiegel *Men under Stress* III. v. 102 Here he underwent pentothal narcosynthesis and ventilated his intense anxiety. **1955** A. Huxley *Let.* 10 Jan. (1969) 720 Mescalin..acts in the opposite way to narcosynthesis. **1958** [see *abreaction]. **1963** *Times* 9 Mar. 8/1 It is believed to be the first instance in which narcosynthesis—a technique to help patients release suppressed or forgotten information—has ever been used for this purpose. **1966** P. Polatin *Guide to Treatm. in Psychiatry* v. 50 Narcotherapy is most effective for acute anxiety states, conversion reactions and dissociative phenomena such as amnesias and fugues. **1968** S. Loebl *Exploring the Mind* xv. 184 Hypnotherapy and narcotherapy, as these procedures are called, have by now become part of psychiatry's ever-growing therapeutic arsenal.

narcolepsy. Add: (Earlier and later examples.) [First formed as F. *narcolepsie* (Gélineau 1880, in *Gaz. des Hôpitaux* LIII. 626/2).]

1880 *Jrnl. Nervous & Mental Dis.* VII. 737 Dr. Gelineau [*sic*], *Gaz. des Hopitaux* [sic], Nos. 79 and 80, describes at length, and discusses a case in his practice which.. seems to be one of a new disease, for which he proposes the name 'Narcolepsy'. **1928** *Brain* LI. 78 All narcolepsy is..symptomatic, but at present we do not always know of what pathological or physiological condition it is thus symptomatic. **1969** *Sunday Times* 2 Nov. 10/3 It [*sc.* amphetamine] is the best drug for narcolepsy (uncontrollable attacks of sleeping). **1972** H. L. Williams in Brady & Nauta *Princ., Pract. & Positions Neuropsychiatric Res.* 454 It has been observed that patients with idiopathic narcolepsy frequently move directly from waking to REM sleep.

narcolept (nā·ɹkŏlept). [Back-formation from next.] = *narcoleptic *sb.*

1957 R. A. Heinlein *Door into Summer* (1960) iv. 54 I'm forever deprived, like a narcolept on a honeymoon. **1973** *Times Lit. Suppl.* 19 Oct. 1268/5 Like that later narcolept Edgar Allan Poe.

narcoleptic (nāɹkole·ptik), *a.* and *sb.* [ad. F. *narcoleptique*; cf. Epileptic *a.* and *sb.*] **A.** *adj.* Characteristic of or affected with narcolepsy.

1904 G. S. Hall *Adolescence* I. 264 Sometimes a sense of fatigue, lassitude, and sleepiness, rarely narcoleptic, may supervene. **1912** *Jrnl. Nervous & Mental Dis.* XXXIX. 131 (*heading*) Adipose pituitary syndrome of Lannois with narcoleptic fits. **1949** *Progress Neurol. & Psychiatry* IV. 414 Narcoleptic sleep,..major convulsions, or other 'epileptic' symptoms. **1960** *Arch. Gen. Psychiatry* III. 422/1 This narcoleptic patient is an intelligent 42-year-old married Negro male shipping clerk. **1972** *Ibid.* XXVI. 462/1 The narcoleptic sleep attack is more imperative but of shorter duration than diurnal hypersomniac sleep.

B. *sb.* A narcoleptic person.

1928 *Brain* LI. 84 The sleep of the narcoleptic is to be likened in all respects to normal, healthy sleep. **1957** *Proc. Mayo Clinic* XXXII. 324 A serious problem among the narcoleptics is the tendency to drowse when driving. **1972** *Arch. Gen. Psychiatry* XXVI. 457/2 Hypersomniacs do not fall asleep while eating, speaking, or walking, as narcoleptics do.

narcosis. Add to def.: Also a psychologically therapeutic sleep artificially prolonged by the use of drugs. So *narcosis therapy*.

1936 [see *narco-analysis* s.v. *narco-]. **1943** Curran & Guttmann *Psychological Med.* viii. 97 Probably the most humane method is to give continuous narcosis for the first few days after the drug [*sc.* morphine] has been withdrawn; but relapse is very frequent. **1945** Grinker & Spiegel *Men under Stress* iv. xvii. 394 At the present time, aside from the method of narcosis therapy (continuous sleep), the use of intravenous barbiturates is dignified by three different terms.

narcotic, *sb.* Add: **b.** In extended use: any drug which affects the mind in some way and is prohibited or under strict legal control in many countries owing to the social problems associated with its misuse, but which tends nevertheless to be extensively sold and used illegally. orig. *U.S.*

1926 *Rep. Drug Addiction in Calif.* (Calif. State Narcotic Comm.) 13 When used in this report, the term 'narcotics' or 'drugs' includes all of the following: Cocaine, opium, morphine, codeine, heroin, alpha eucaine, beta eucaine, flowering tops and leaves, extracts, tinctures, and other narcotic preparations of hemp or loco weed, Indian hemp, peyote, or chloral hydrate or any of the salts, derivatives or compounds of the foregoing substances. **1955** *U.S. Senate. Hearings* (1956) VIII. 4160 There are three groups into which the narcotics set forth in division 10 of the Health and Safety Code are divided: 1. Opiate group. 2. Cocaine, marihuana, and lophophora. 3. Synthetic group. **1972** *Daily Tel.* (Colour Suppl.) 11 Aug. 12/1 The Americans prefer the word 'narcotics', which although not entirely accurate—not all banned drugs cause narcosis—is better understood, so it will be used from here on. **1974** A. Goth *Med. Pharmacol.* (ed. 7) xxv. 300 In some state statutes the legal category 'narcotics' embraces the opiates, opiate-like drugs, marihuana, and cocaine. Medically defined, however, the term narcotic refers only to drugs having both a sedative and an analgesic action and is essentially restricted to the opiates and opiate-like drugs. *Ibid.* xxv. 304 Although marihuana is not medically a narcotic, it is classified legally as a narcotic in some states for purposes of control. **1974** *Encycl. Brit. Macropædia* V. 1049/2 Prejudice and ignorance have led to the labelling of all use of nonsanctioned drugs as addiction and of all drugs, when misused, as narcotics.

2. *attrib.* (freq. in *pl.*).

1926 *Proc. 1st World Conf. Narcotic Educ.* 111 How the police catch the crook or the narcotic dealer;..it is only when someone tells the police who the narcotic addict or peddler is that the police get them. *Ibid.* 227 The narcotic squad [in Philadelphia] was under the command of Captain Van Horn. **1929** *Narcotic Educ.* Jan. 46/1 To get sufficient evidence against John Smith it is necessary that a Government agent purchase narcotics from John Smith, but John Smith will only sell..for..$2,500 in advance... Where can a narcotic agent be found who has $2,500 to use? *Ibid.* Apr. 73/1 Out of the gray, neutral shadows cast by the murder of Arnold Rothstein, federal authorities forged a sturdy weapon expected to crush the most gigantic narcotic ring in the history of the illegal drug trade. **1951** *Manch. Guardian Weekly* 28 June 2/2 The State Legislature at Albany ordered an inquiry, which met last week. And this week the American Legion has followed it up with a 'narcotic clinic' of its own. **1953** *Conf. Drug Addiction among Adolescents* (N.Y. Acad. Med., Comm. Public Health Relations) II. 159 He..devised a plan..for the preventive and follow-up care of young narcotics addicts. **1953** W. Burroughs *Junkie* (1972) iii. 37 They found out the narcotics squad had a warrant for him sworn out by the State Inspector. **1963** *Listener* 4 Apr. 585/1 They were the bookies, and money lenders..and the narcotic pedlars. **1972** *Daily Tel.* 4 Sept. 3/1 A national Narcotics Bureau is to be set up in London next month to coordinate the activities of police drug squads in this country. **1973** *N.Y. Law Jrnl.* 19 June 4/5 The defendant argued that the offence itself, sale of dangerous drugs..made it 'appear' that he was a narcotics addict.

‖ **narikin** (na·rikin). [Jap.] In Japan, a wealthy parvenu.

1920 *Glasgow Herald* 2 Sept. 7 'Narikin', or mushroom millionaires, have spent their rapidly amassed fortunes on extravagant living. **1923** in J. Manchon *Le Slang* 203. **1933** *Times Lit. Suppl.* 16 Nov. 784/3 *Narikin*..as commonly used is..a term of reproach, applied to those *nouveaux riches* who made rapid fortunes as profiteers of the War. **1946** R. Benedict *Chrysanthemum & Sword* (1947) iv. 95 Narikin is often translated 'nouveau riche' but that does not do justice to the Japanese feeling... A narikin is a term taken from Japanese chess and means a pawn promoted to queen.

naringin (nări·ndʒin). *Chem.* [ad. G. *naringen* (E. Hoffmann, at the suggestion of Flückiger, 1879 in *Arch. der Pharm.* CCXIV. 140), f. *naringi*, given as Skr. for Orange *sb.*[1], *a.*: see -in[1].] A bitter glucoside, $C_{27}H_{32}O_{14}$, of a tricyclic alcohol which is found in shaddock, grapefruit, and certain types of orange.

1879 *Jrnl. Chem. Soc.* XXXVI. 468 Naringin, the hesperidin of de Vrij, which is found in the fully developed buds of *Citrus decumana* to the amount of 2 per cent., is obtained from the residue left on distillation of the ethereal oil. **1926** *Biochem. Jrnl.* XX. 1305 Naringin, the specific glucoside of the grape-fruit, was found present in the rind and in alcoholic extracts of it. **1957** E. V. Miller *Chem. Plants* viii. 113 Naringin is found in large quantities in the juice of immature grapefruits.. and to a certain extent in the segment walls of mature fruits. **1970** *New Scientist* 1 Jan. 21/1 The most promising [sweetening] compounds are made from naringin isolated from grapefruit, hesperidin from sweet oranges and neohesperidin from Seville oranges.

nark, *sb.* For **1865** *Slang Dict.* (ed. 2) read **1860** in Hotten *Dict. Slang* (ed. 2), 179, and add further examples.

1916 G. B. Shaw *Pygmalion* I. 110 It's a—well, it's a copper's nark, as you might say. What else would you call it? A sort of informer. **1933** Auden *Dance of Death* 37 Quick under the table, it's the 'tecs and their narks, O no, salute—it's Mr. Karl Marx. **1936** J. G. Brandon *Pawnshop Murder* x. 90 Police 'narks', 'noses', and all such kindred brethren. **1954** [see *grass *sb.*[1] 11*]. **1968** *Listener* 19 Dec. 810/3 Don't do it.., he's a copper's nark. **1975** *Times* 9 Jan. 4/4 If it was thought we were coppers' narks it could endanger the lives of our film crews.

b. A policeman.

1891 F. W. Carew *No. 747* vi. 65 If you don't turn up my fair share, I'll put the narks upon you. S'elp me never, I will. **1937** M. Allingham *Dancers in Mourning* xxvii. 327 There's a bunch o' narks at either end of the lane. **1959** A. Sillitoe *Loneliness of Long-Distance Runner* 27 Don't let that gate creak too much or you'll have the narks tuning-in. **1959** I. & P. Opie *Lore & Lang. Schoolch.* xvii. 369 There are, in the London area, at least thirty nicknames current among boys... The Law, Nark or Narker, Nobby, [etc.]. *a* **1966** M. Allingham *Cargo of Eagles* (1968) v. 74 I've 'appened on a little something wot the official narks 'aven't cottoned to yet.

2. *slang* (freq. in *Austral.* and *N.Z.*). **a.** A person who is annoying, unpleasant, obstructive, or quarrelsome. Cf. Knark.

1846 *Swell's Night Guide* 68 They are the rankest narks vot ever God put guts into, or ever farted in a kickses case. **1898** *Bulletin* (Sydney) 17 Dec. (Red Page), An informer or mar-plot is a *nark* or *Jonah*. **1906** E. Dyson *Fact'ry 'Ands* i. 12 'Yeh know, Feathers, she's no bally nark; er bloke kin trust 'er,' he said. **1908** *Austral. Mag.* 1 Nov. 1251 *Nark*, a spoil-sport. **1918** *Aussie* Sept. 2/2 He appealed in vain to Madame... 'Orright, then, Madame, I can be a nark, too! I know where there's..fat, juicy frogs, and you wont get one of 'em!' **1925** Fraser & Gibbons *Soldier & Sailor Words* 164 *Nark*, a bad-tempered man; a spoil-sport... Also, a man eager to curry favour by running about and doing odd jobs for a superior. **1928** V. Palmer *Man Hamilton* 94 'Oh, don't be a nark, Miss Byrne,' he coaxes her. **1933** F. Clune *Try Anything Once* 81 Lieutenant Hennessy fulfilled the most exacting requirements of what a 'nark' should be. **1937** Partridge *Dict. Slang* 551/2 *Nark*... A person on inquiry from head office: London clerks', managers', etc.: from before 1935. **1943** *Penguin New Writing* XVIII. 63 If I said anything..he'd go crook and tell me not to be a nark. **1959** I. & P. Opie *Lore & Lang. Schoolch.* xviii. 391 'It is a way to get your own back on an old nark who has spoilt a game,' declares an Edinburgh 12-year-old. **1965** J. S. Gunn *Terminol. Shearing Industry* II. 6 *Nark*, a troublemaker who interrupts the rhythm of the shed. A nark shearer only hurts himself, but a shedhand or roller who does not keep the board clear can slow up the work of all men handling the fleece.

b. An annoying or unpleasant thing or situation; a source of astonishment or vexation. *slang* (freq. in *Austral.* and *N.Z.*).

1923 J. Manchon *Le Slang* 203 *Nark*.. (rare), rancune, une dent qu'on a contre quelqu'un. **1926** R. R. Terry *Shanty Bk.* II. 25 When they went to church to say 'I will', the drummer got a nark. [*footnote*] *Nark*, a disagreeable surprise. **1937** N. Marsh *Vintage Murder* 114 It's a blooming nark, dinkum it is. **1947** *Book* (Christchurch, N.Z.) IX. 23 'It's a nark, isn't it,' she said. 'I thought you'd get by without the op.' **1948** R. Alley *Gung Ho* 16 Typhoid, malaria, and all the narks. **1966** P. Moloney *Plea for Mersey* 51 Not hardened junkies, when deprived of dope, Ere felt such anger, ere got such a nark As Scouseville driver seeking space to park.

nark, *v.* For **1865** *Slang Dict.* (ed. 2) read **1859** in Hotten *Dict. Slang* 67 and add:

2. *trans.* and *intr.* To annoy, exasperate, infuriate; to complain, grumble. Hence **narked** *ppl. a.*; **na·rking** *vbl. sb.* *slang* (freq. in *Austral.* and *N.Z.*) and *dial.*

1888 J. Dalby *Mayroyd of Mytholm* II. 45 That's just what he's ta'en to him for, just to nark Mayroyd. **1888** S. O. Addy *Gloss. Words Sheffield* 155 *Narked*, vexed, angry... 'He wor narked about it.' **1896** H. Lawson *Shearing of Cook's Dog* in *While Billy Boils* 167 The cook usually forgot all about it in an hour... But this time he didn't; he was 'narked' for three days. **1899** *Bulletin* (Sydney) 25 Feb. (Red Page), Tom was gettin' narked, so I tries to get him to turn in. **1908** E. J. Banfield *Confessions of Beachcomber* I. v. 174 He'll be a bit narked at having wasted a whole bloomin' day. **1916** *Anzac Book* 142 But wot narks us more than any Is to 'ear the sergeant say: 'The sea's too rough to land our stores; There ain't no jam today!' **1916** J. B. Cooper *Coo-oo-ee* xix. 299, I thought you would. That's very like the Tippinses to nark like that. **1930** *Bulletin* (Sydney) 19 Mar. 23/1 It was this that narked me most—'e couldn't see a joke. **1932** L. A. G. Strong *Don Juan & Wheelbarrow* ix. 162 Is it true..that So-and-So is narked as the Cottage 'Ospital be over to 'Arraton, 'stead of here? **1940** F. Sargeson *Man & his Wife* (1944) 49 That got Tom narked. He told George he ought to be ashamed of himself for telling things like that. **1945** *Daily Sketch* 20 Apr. 2/2 Like you, I am all for personal liberty—and so no doubt are the inmates of Wormwood Scrubs—but the fact remains that so long as there is not economic freedom for everybody, what is the point of constantly narking about State-planning? **1947** D. M. Davin *Gorse blooms Pale* 78 It narked her that everyone was eating out of her hand except me. **1958** *Times Lit. Suppl.* 15 Aug. p. xxxii/3 This naturally brings out the worst in their opponents and in the resultant narking and name-calling the 'legitimate contention' is lost sight of. **1962** [see *half *adv.* 3]. **1966** *Crescendo* Apr. 29/2 The narked comments of some respected musicians. **1968** *Daily Progress* (Charlottesville, Virginia) 11 July C.14/1 In Britain, to nark is to nag, scold, annoy or irritate. Mrs. Ewing, a vivacious blonde, narks mostly about home rule for Scotland. She has managed to irritate some members of Parliament and her election victory annoyed Prime Minister Harold Wilson's Labor party. **1970** *New Scientist* 23 July 190/2 The Chinese have naturally been somewhat narked at being left out of the fun. **1973** *Daily Tel.* 2 Nov. 15 If you

feel especially narked about something, you can turn it into a theory of human behaviour.

3. *trans.*, usu. with *it*. To cease, desist, stop, terminate. Freq. in imp. *slang*.

1889 *Sporting Times* 29 June 1/3 And as terseness of expression was an art she'd studied well, She determined that her lady friend should nark it. **1925** in FRASER & GIBBONS *Soldier & Sailor Words* 164. **1933** *Bulletin* (Sydney) 1 Feb. 20 It was 'ard luck when a bloke narked the show. **1936** J. CURTIS *Gilt Kid* xvii. 175 Nark it for God's sake... You'll get us done, yelling around the gaff like that. **1943** M. HARRISON *Reported Safe Arrival* 12 There was a sharp interchange of: 'Nark it!' and 'Oo says so?' I think there had been an interchange of more than words had not the Orderly Officer then appeared. **1943** *R.A.F. Jrnl.* Aug. 30 Nark it, Flight,..you sound like a penny uplift. **1959** I. & P. OPIE *Lore & Lang. Schoolch.* x. 199 Saying by the one being tortured: ''Ere, nark it.' **1973** N. GRAHAM *Murder in Dark Room* xxiii. 162 'Nark it,' I said. 'I want a little bit of information from you.'

narker (nā·ɹkəɹ). *slang*. [f. NARK *v.* + -ER[1].] An informer; a policeman; one who complains or disparages.

1932 NORDHOFF & HALL *Mutiny on Bounty* iii. 39 The captain's 'narker' or spy among the men. **1937** *Sunday Dispatch* 7 Feb. 22/6 The narkers are at it again with their fancy explanation of our Test mistakes. **1959** [see *NARK *sb.* 1 b]. **1959** A. SILLITOE *Loneliness of Long-Distance Runner* 28 I'd..screw my eyes up like I was on my way to the hospital,.. 'Cancer,' I'd manage to say to Narker, which would make his slow punch-drunk brain suspect a thing or two. **1971** *Daily Tel.* 3 May 8/4 His motto will be to celebrate not denigrate, and I commend this to the legion of glib narkers who tend to monopolise the screen.

narks (nāɹks), *sb. pl.* Colloq. abbrev. of nitrogen *narc*osis.

1962 S. MILES *Underwater Med.* vii. 100 Unromantic British divers simply call it 'Narks'. **1967** 'J. PALMER' *Above & Below* i. 9 It's lucky the ship lies in such shallow water. We shan't get the 'narks'.

narky (nā·ɹki), *a. slang.* [f. *NARK *sb.* 2 + -Y[1].] Irascible, vexed, bad-tempered, sarcastic.

1895 *Leeds Mercury Weekly Suppl.* 13 July 3/8 Doan't let's get narky ower it. **1898** B. KIRKBY *Lakeland Words* 105 He were a bit narky ower t' trottin' do. **1943** M. HARRISON *Reported Safe Arrival* 53 Harry was interested. 'Garn!' he said. 'Yer kiddin', Perfess [Professor]!... Shakespeare, eh? Full of swearin', eh? I allus thought 'e wz fer school-kids and blokes like yew, Perfess. I don' mean nothin' narky: on'y 'e ain't the sort of bloke me and de Pen 'ud settle dahn to read a basin of, if yer get me meanin'?' **1958** L. DURRELL *Balthazar* ii. 33 Below the belt... Dirty. Cruel. Narky. **1958** [see *DUCKY *sb.* 2]. **1970** *New Society* 5 Mar. 399/1 Shelter has incurred a lot of narky criticism since it announced its intention of setting up a chain of housing advisory centres. **1973** *Irish Times* 2 Mar. 14/5 My husband is narky in the house. If I was to bring heaven down it would not satisfy him.

‖ **Narodnik** (narǫ·dnik). Also **narodnik.** Pl. **Narodniki, Narodniks.** [Russ., f. *narod* people + *-NIK.] A supporter of the type of populist agrarian socialism originating amongst the Russian intelligentsia in the late 1860s which regarded the peasants and intelligentsia as the only revolutionary forces and denied the revolutionary role of the working class; one who tries to educate politically communities of rural or urban poor while sharing the conditions of their lives. Also *attrib.* and *transf.* Hence **Naro·dnikism,** the theory of making political power a reality for the masses.

1885 E. NOBLE *Russ. Revolt* 204 In the spring of 1877 the members of a revolutionary society called the 'Narodniki' (Party of the People) 'went to the people', establishing a large number of propaganda centres along the line of the Volga. **1904** G. DRAGE *Russ. Affairs* i. 51 A party arose who called themselves *Narodniki* (Nationalists). **1921** M. P. PRICE *My Reminisc. Russ. Revolution* ii. 27 The Narodniks therefore preached 'back to the land'. **1929** L. KRASSIN *Leonid Krassin* vii. 58 The Narodniki, the first organised agrarian party, welcomed..common possession of the soil. **1950** E. H. CARR *Bolshevik Revolution* I. I. i. 4 For the past thirty years [*sc.* 1868–98] the leading Russian revolutionaries had been the *narodniks*—a composite name for a succession of revolutionary groups believing in the theory of peasant revolution and in the practice of terrorism against members of the autocracy. *Ibid.* iii. 52 The peasantry remained for the Mensheviks an essentially anti-revolutionary force; any revolutionary policy which counted on its support was a reversion to the *narodnik* heresy of a peasant revolution. **1965** *New Statesman* 20 Aug. 240/1 Last year's Mississippi Summer Project..was..composed of young Southern Negroes and Northern students on the staff of the Student Non-Violent Co-ordinating Committee... They were the original *narodniks* of the movement. **1966** *Economist* 3 Sept. 887/2 A new *narodnik* movement, a fresh attempt by the intellectuals to 'go to the people'. **1969** J. SAUL in Ionescu & Gallner *Populism* 135 It may seem useful to lump together Russian Narodnikism and North American Populism..because both represent largely rural responses to..'capitalism' or 'modernization' or 'industrialization'. **1970** G. JACKSON *Let.* 25 Mar. in *Soledad Brother* (1971) 197 The dialectic between Narodnik and Nihilist should never break down. **1971** *Graphic* (Durban) 7 May 12/2 Her aunts were active in the populist narodniki movement [in Russia].

narp (nāɹp). *slang.* [Origin unknown.] A shirt.

1839 H. BRANDON *Poverty, Mendicity & Crime* 164/1 *Narp*, a shirt. **1949** in PARTRIDGE *Dict. Underworld* 464/1.

narra[1] (na·rä). *S. Afr.* Also **nara(s).** [ad. Hottentot *'narab*.] A spiny shrub, *Acanthosicyos horrida*, of the family Cucurbitaceæ, found in arid regions of south-western Africa, distinguished by thorns, which replace the leaves of young plants, and yellow flowers; also, the large globular fruit of this plant. Also *attrib.*

1838 J. E. ALEXANDER *Expedition Interior Afr.* II. iii. 68 The 'naras was growing on little knolls of sand; the bushes were about four or five feet high, without leaves, and with apposite thorns on the light and dark green striped branches. **1853** F. GALTON *Narr. Explorer Trop. S. Afr.* i. 21, I have mentioned above the 'Nara, a prickly gourd, which..is the staple food of these Hottentots. **1881** T. HAHN *Tsuni-‖ Goam* 101 !Naras.—This fruit is a *Cucurbitacea*, almost as large as a new-born child's head. The flesh of it is eaten raw, and the seeds are kept for the dry season, when there is no fruit. The seeds taste almost like almonds. **1946** L. G. GREEN *So Few are Free* (1948) xii. 165 The narra, a member of the melon family..sends its roots down through the dunes for fifty feet, if necessary, to find moisture... The ripe narra is full of edible seeds, which are treated in many ways by the Hottentots. Boiled, they make a porridge. Tough pancakes are formed by the narra fluid and stored for months. Narra beer may be brewed from the syrupy juice. **1959** G. JENKINS *Twist of Sand* xiii. 267 The trails of naras creeper would provide some sort of fuel. **1973** *Stand. Encycl. S. Afr.* VIII. 40/2 Naras (properly: narra)... Spiny, much-branched, prostrate shrub of the family *Cucurbitaceae*, found growing on sand-dunes in the dry coastal strip of South-West Africa.

narra[2] (nā·rä). [Tagalog.] The Filipino name for the south-east Asian tree, *Pterocarpus indicus*, of the family Leguminosæ, or its timber; = AMBOYNA. Also *attrib.*

1859 J. BOWRING *Visit to Philippine Islands* xv. 270 (*table*) Narra, or Naga, or Asang... Buildings, furniture, doors and windows. **1890** J. FOREMAN *Philippine Islands* xix. 371 Narra..gives logs up to 35 feet long by 26 inches square. It is the Mahogany of the Philippines. **1911** *Philippine Bureau of Forestry Bull.* No. 10. II. 35 The members of the Narra family mentioned here have simply or doubly compound leaves. *Ibid.*, Narra is found throughout the Philippines. *Ibid.* 36 Narra is the most common commercial name for the wood in the Philippines. **1929** *Amer. Speech* IV. 284 Of the native [Filipino] words, a few have already been accepted... *narra* and *camagon*, hard woods used in fine cabinet work. **1947** J. C. RICH *Materials & Methods Sculpture* x. 292 *Narra* is a Philippine wood related to the Andaman Islands' Padouk. It has a yellow to reddish-brown color and is not always available commercially. **1971** F. H. TITMUSS *Commercial Timbers of World* (ed. 4) 48 This [*sc.* amboyna, *Pterocarpus indicus*] is one of the most important export species of the Philippines (the wood being known as narra on the North American market).

Narragansett (nærăgæ·nsĕt). Also **Nar(r)haganset, Nar(r)ohiganset(t),** etc. [Algonquian *Naiaganset* people of the small point (of land).] **1.** An Algonquian people orig. living in New England; a member of this people. Also *attrib.*

1622 *Relation Eng. Plantation Plimoth, New Eng.* 44 They told us that if they were Narrohigganset men they would not trust them. **1637** T. MORTON *New Eng. Canaan* I. xiv. 45 The cause why these other Salvages of the Narohigansets, came into these parts, was to see what strength we were of. **1682** M. ROWLANDSON *Narr. Captivity among Indians* 5, I was sold to him by another Narrhaganset Indian. **1764** T. HUTCHINSON *Hist. Colony Mass.-Bay* I. 138 At first, the Naragansets gave kind words to the messengers. **1809** 'D. KNICKERBOCKER' *Hist. N.Y.* II. v. iv. 29 He has been secretly endeavoring to instigate the Narrohigansett (or Narraganset).. Indians. **1848** *Trans. Amer. Ethnol. Soc.* II. i. 77 (*table*) *Families... Algonkins. Languages or Dialects...* Narragansets. **1850** R. G. LATHAM *Nat. Hist. Varieties Man* 329 Algonkins... Narraganset.—Extinct. In 1674, in Rhode Island. **1871** C. M. YONGE *Pioneers & Founders* i. 8 The Pequots were..at war..with the Narragansets, or river Indians. **1933** L. BLOOMFIELD *Lang.* 72 The *Algonquian* family..includes the languages..of New England (..*Narraganset, Mohican*, and so on). **1945** C. M. WEBSTER *Town Meeting Country* 11 The Narragansetts on the west shores of Narragansett Bay. **1951** HEPBURN & LOGAN *New England* 84/1 The Old Narragansett Church is worth seeing.

2. In full, **Narragansett pacer** (or **pacing mare**): a breed of pacing horse (now extinct) which originated in Rhode Island.

1777 J. ADAMS in J. & A. Adams *Familiar Lett.* (1876) 272 We are looking about for American curiosities to send across the Atlantic as presents... Narraganset pacing mares, mooses, wood ducks,..have all been thought of. **1809** 'D. KNICKERBOCKER' *Hist. N.Y.* II. VII. iii. 194 A crafty man..bargained him out of his..charger, leaving in place thereof a villainous, spavined, foundered, Narraganset pacer. **1826** J. F. COOPER *Last of Mohicans* I. ii. 18 Giving her Narraganset a smart cut of the whip. **1943** E. FORBES *Johnny Tremain* 92, I never saw a horse his color before... Narragansett breed. **1946** M. C. SELF *Horseman's Encycl.* 286 A noble breed of horses was developed, namely, the Narragansett Pacer. They are said to have had a smooth gliding motion..and were very popular..with the Virginia plantation owners. **1963** BLOODGOOD & SANTINI *Horseman's Dict.* 144 *Pacer.* .. Specifically: a Standardbred pacing horse descended from the Thoroughbred English stallion 'Messenger' and from the native, so-called Naragansett pacing mares.

narratage (næ·rătėdʒ). [f. NARRA(TE *v.* + -AGE.] A technique used in films, plays, and on television in which one of the characters has the role of storyteller.

1948 E. LINDGREN *Art of Film* vi. 112 Other films.. employ a method known as *narratage*, in which one of the characters, usually a minor character in the film, is depicted as telling the story. **1954** *Encounter* Aug. 55/1 Here, still surviving in an age of redundant dialogue and, worse still, explanatory narratage, are stories really told in pictures.

narrate, *v.* Add: **1. b.** To speak the commentary of (a broadcast, film, exhibition, etc.).

1974 *Anderson* (S. Carolina) *Independent* 24 Apr. 1B/2 Rear Adm. Rice narrated a slide show depicting historical portions of Anderson. **1975** *Daily Tel.* 30 Oct. 6/6 The Prince of Wales introduces and narrates 'One Day in November', a £20,000 colour film about the work of the Royal British Legion.

narrative, *a.* Add: **1.** Also in *Painting*. Also *narrative line*, a consecutively developed story.

1902 R. FRY *Let.* 10 Oct. (1972) I. 196 Already he has Giovanni Bellini's *farmito* colours..and he has too the pure narrative style..of the great Venetians. **1962** R. G. HAGGAR *Dict. Art Terms* 221/1 Tissot painted admirable narrative pictures. **1962** *Listener* 22 Feb. 335/2 That rich outpouring of 'narrative' painting which began in England with the Bayeux tapestry, continued through the missals and Books of Hours, to be picked up again by Hogarth, Rowlandson, and Gillray. **1962** *Times* 1 Nov. 8/4 Supporting this narrative line is a cross section of Alf's social background. **1972** *Guardian* 16 Feb. 12/3, I pictured a story with every western cliche in it...Why have a straight narrative line when everybody knows the story?

narrator. Add: **b.** One who speaks a commentary in a broadcast or a film; hence also, a character who relates part of the plot of a play to the audience.

1941 *B.B.C. Gloss. Broadcasting Terms* 20 *Narrator*, person whose role is to deliver, in either his own or an assumed character, narrative passages in a radio-dramatic programme. **1948** E. LINDGREN *Art of Film* vi. 112 There may be.. portions [of film].. in which we see the action of the story, but hear the words of the narrator, which thus become..a form of commentary. **1955** *Radio Times* 22 Apr. 25/1 Bob Hope compères the.. Annual Awards... Narrator, Leslie Mitchell. **1960** *Times* 3 Oct. 16/2 For Ahlsen clearly employs the 'narrator' technique in order to allow his protagonist not only to act out the dramatic scenes..but also to speak his thoughts aloud in monologue form if not actually fire them into the auditorium. **1961** *Times* 23 May 15/1 It is the incidentals of Brecht's method—the narrator-characters half in, half outside the action..which have..proved capable of easy assimilation. **1973** D. GIFFORD *Brit. Film Catal. 1895–1970* 15 *Credits*..Associate Producer.. Director..Narrator [etc.].

‖ **narrischkeit** (nā·riʃkəit). [Yiddish *naarishkeit, narrishkeit*, ad. G. *närrischkeit*, f. *närrisch* foolish.] Foolishness, nonsense; that which is of no consequence.

1892 I. ZANGWILL *Childr. Ghetto* I. 179 What *Narrischkeit*! Why should he die? **1963** *Punch* 4 Dec. 803/1 The piece of *narrischkeit* currently being serialised.

narrow, *a.* and *sb.* Add: **A.** *adj.* **1. c.** *narrow axe* U.S., an axe used primarily for chopping, opp. BROAD-AX; *narrowback* U.S., a citizen of the United States of Irish ancestry (see also quot. 1941); *narrow band* Electr., a band (*BAND *sb.*[2] 14) of frequencies lying within a narrow range; freq. *attrib.* (with hyphen); *narrow boat*, a canal boat, *spec.* one not exceeding 7 feet in width or 72 feet in length; *narrow-cut* adj., applied to filters which transmit only a narrow band of wavelengths; *narrow-range* attrib., restricted in incidence or scope.

1641 *Public Rec. Colony of Connecticut* (1850) I. 444 A broad axe, 2 narrow axes, wimbell & chessells. **1854** THOREAU *Walden* 46, I went on for some days cutting and hewing timber..with my narrow axe. **1941** J. SMILEY *Hash House Lingo* 39 *Narrow back*, dishwasher; cashier. **1957** *N.Y. Times* 29 Sept. X3 William Joseph Patrick (Pat) O'Brien, a Milwaukee-born Irishman or narrowback. **1966** *Publ. Amer. Dial. Soc. 1964* XLII. 39 Irish informants use..*narrowback* for a second generation Irishman who has neither the need, the desire nor the physical equipment to do the work his father had to do. **1975** G. V. HIGGINS *City on Hill* ii. 56 You went out and married the same kind of commoner he always was himself, and a narrowback to boot. **1956** *Nature* 28 Jan. 178/2 A narrow-band tuned amplifier on 16 kc./s. **1962** A. NISBETT *Technique Sound Studio* 261 *Music line*, broad-band circuit for carrying programme (including speech), as distinct from a telephone line which may occupy only a narrow band. **1971** M. S. GHAUSI *Electronic*

Circuits vii. 437 When extremely high *Q* and excellent stability are required in narrow-band bandpass filters, the use of crystal filters is practical. **1951** *Oxf. Jun. Encycl.* IV. 37/2 The narrow boat, or 'monkey boat'.., is possibly the commonest craft on inland waterways in England... because the locks on the group of canals in the Midland counties..can only pass a boat about 7 feet wide and 70 feet long. **1972** *Country Life* 13 Jan. 93/1 Only the deep draught of narrow boats can keep the canals open in the absence of proper dredging. **1975** *Times* 8 Mar. 10/6 Some of the older narrow boats with a three-foot draught are constantly ploughing through mud, for the canals are silted up. **1964** L. A. Mannheim tr. *Clauss & Meusel's Filter Pract.* 63 (*caption*) Absorption curve of a deep red filter (narrow-cut type). **1969** *Focal Encycl. Photogr.* (rev. ed.) 615/1 Special narrow-cut tricolour filter sets are used to make indirect colour separation negatives from colour transparencies. **1932** Faucett & Maki *Study of Eng. Word-Values* 7 It is fair to require of all students of English a mastery of wide-range words but.. it is unfair standardizing of procedure to pass or fail students on their knowledge or lack of knowledge of narrow-range words. **1964** E. Uldall in D. Abercrombie et al. *Daniel Jones* 279 The narrow-range 'smooth' contours..vary most often from one sentence to another.

e. Denoting a type of phonetic transcription in which separate symbols are used to denote all identifiable features (phonemic and non-phonemic) of an utterance; opp. *broad*.

1877 [see *broad *a.* 5 c]. **1908** H. Sweet *Sounds of English* 10 In comparing the sounds of a variety of languages..we require a 'narrow', that is, a minutely accurate notation covering the whole field of possible sounds. **1933** *Amer. Speech* VIII. II. 49/2, I have never been able to understand how there might be any advantage whatever of *broad* over *narrow* transcription for English. **1961** Y. Olsson *On Syntax Eng. Verb* ii. 20 The editing [when linguists transcribe] would not imply a greater crime than a phonetician using a broad, instead of a narrow, notation. **1964** D. Abercrombie *Eng. Phonetic Texts* 35 It is..convenient to use 'broad' as an equivalent of *simple phonemic*, and 'narrow' for any departure from this, either in the direction of comparative or in the direction of *allophonic*, or both together.

3. e. *Econ.* (See quots.)

1935 *Economist* 12 Oct. 712/2 Technically, markets remain 'narrow', and day-to-day price movements are correspondingly exaggerated. **1940** G. Crowther *Outl. Money* vii. 267 The market is at all times 'narrow', that is, quotations are available only for half a dozen of the most important currencies. **1962** S. Strand *Marketing Dict.* 474 *Narrow market*, in the stock market, a dull trading session, generally limited to a few fields. **1965** J. L. Hanson *Dict. Econ.* 288/2 *Narrow market*, a term used more particularly of stock exchange securities of which there is only a small supply available in the market.

7. *narrow-beamed, -billed, -bodied, -gutted, -slitted, -slotted.*

1927 *Observer* 14 Aug. 7/4 Agile, narrow-beamed cars, with plenty of acceleration and 'safety-first' brake-power, are his ideal. **1895** *Funk's Stand. Dict.*, Narrow-billed. **1909** A. E. Mack *Bush Calendar* 9 Birds breeding in August... Chalcococcyx basalis. Narrow-billed bronze cuckoo. **1953** D. A. Bannerman *Birds Brit. Isles* I. 299 There is much to be said in favour of retaining these broad-billed buntings, as distinct from the narrow-billed species, under the specific name *tschusii*. **1949** M. Mead *Male & Female* vi. 133 The slender, narrow-bodied of the Arapesh, Tchambuli, Swede, Eskimo, and Hottentot. **1963** *Times* 1 Feb. 14/5 This narrow-bodied look was extended to coats. **1903** *Dialect Notes* II. 299 (Cape Cod dial.) *Narrow gutted*, mean, ungenerous. **1903** *Eng. Dial. Dict.* IV. 228/2 *Narrow-gutted*, of horses..weak in the loins. *Ibid.*, *Not[tinghamshire]*. A narrow-gutted brute. **1924** D. H. Lawrence *Let.* 29 Oct. (1962) II. 816 A narrow-gutted 'artist' with a stutter. **1965** G. J. Williams *Econ. Geol. N.Z.* xviii. 283/2 Unless the seam is narrow-gutted as at Kawakawa,..it seems certain that coal does not exist above the greywacke. **1905** J. London *Jacket* (1915) xi. 90 His eyes..were cunning and.. narrow-slitted. **1923** Kipling *Irish Guards in Gt. War* I. 234 The narrow-slotted pill-boxes.

narrow, *v.* Add: **1.** Also with *down*.

1906 L. J. Vance *Terence O'Rourke* II. ii. 214 Then it narrowed down to a mere contest of endurance.

2. Also with *down* and *in*.

1885 J. Morris *Kotaka* xi. 106 The entire force and volume of the Fuzikawa being here narrowed down to the width of the gorge. **1885** J. W. Dawson *Egypt & Syria* ii. 39 It is just where the broad expanse of alluvium..is narrowed in by that great promontory. **1889** R. L. Stevenson *Master of Ballantrae* iv. 122 The family was now so narrowed down (indeed, there were..just the father and the two sons) that it was possible to break the entail.

narrow gauge. Add: **2.** *Cinemat.* (See quot. 1959.) Cf. Gauge, gage *sb.* 1.

1951 G. H. Sewell *Amateur Film-Making* (ed. 2) xii. 115 It is not impossible that one day research will place in the hands of the narrow-gauge worker the means of obtaining fully stereoscopic pictures without undue difficulty. **1953** L. J. Wheeler *Princ. Cinematogr.* x. 283 It is interesting to note that the B.K.S. has officially adopted the term 'narrow gauge' [film] in preference to 'sub-standard'. **1959** W. S. Sharps *Dict. Cinematogr.* 100/1 Ciné film is designated according to its width, 35 mm. film..being said to be of 'standard gauge'...the only other professional size of film..is 16 mm. wide and this is termed 'sub-standard', or 'narrow-gauge'.

narrow-mouthed, *a.* **1.** (Later examples.)

1910 W. de la Mare *Three Mulla-Mulgars* xvi. 247 Sipped slowly from their gurgling, narrow-mouthed bags or bottles. **1967** Karch & Buber *Offset Processes* vi. 248 When mixing solution 'A', 'B' or 'C' it is advisable to use a one gallon, narrow-mouthed bottle.

narsarsukite (nāɹsāɹsu·kəit). *Min.* [f. *Narsarssauk, -suk*, name of a plain in SW. Greenland + -ite[1].] A silicate and fluoride of sodium, iron, and titanium, $Na_2(Ti,Fe)Si_4(O,F)_{11}$, which is found as yellow tetragonal crystals.

1900 G. Flink in *Meddelelser om Grønland* XXIV. 154 The new mineral..was the first that attracted my attention on Narsarsuk. None of the other new minerals has been found at so many different localities on the plateau or is so largely distributed there. It may therefore, more than any other mineral, be said to be characteristic of the place. On this ground I propose for it the name narsarsukite. **1935** *Amer. Mineralogist* XX. 598 The narsarsukite was seen only in the quartz veins in the roof rock and upper part on the intrusive. **1968** I. Kostov *Mineral.* II. 300 Baotite is a typical example of silicates with tetragonal rings of silicon tetrahedra $[Si_4O_{12}]$. Narsarsukite has similar rings but they are not isolated as in baotite but linked together along the tetragonal axis in a tube-like manner.

nartjie (nā·ɹtʃi, na·rkʸi). *S. Afr.* Also **naartj(i)e, naatje(e), naretje.** [Afrikaans, f. Tamil *nārattai* citrus.] The tangerine or mandarin orange. Also *attrib.* and *transf.*

1790 E. Helme tr. *Le Vaillant's Trav. Afr.* I. ii. 23 The citrus and oranges (specially the sort called *naretyes* [sic]) are excellent. **1796** tr. *Le Vaillant's New Travels* I. 190 There is a kind of orange..called at the Cape *naretjes*, which, notwithstanding the smallness of its size, is sold at a higher rate. **1870** *Cape Monthly Mag.* Oct. 219 The 'nartjie', a dwarf orange. **1890** A. Martin *Home Life Ostrich Farm* xi. 211 Dutchmen..often bringing with them very good onions, oranges, *naatjes* or mandarines, nuts, dried peaches and figs. **1908** *Westm. Gaz.* 14 Aug. 4/3 The only orange now on the market here is the Cape 'naatjee'. **1909** *Daily Chron.* 15 June 4/3 The little Tangerine..and its bigger relative the Mandarin are called Naartjes in Natal. **1923** *Chambers's Jrnl.* Apr. 269/2 Oranges, nartjes and grape-fruit ripen during June, July and August. **1937** S. Cloete *Turning Wheels* iii. 46 Others handled the seeds they had brought with them—..the pips of nartjes. *Ibid.* xiii. 210 Martha, your heart is like a naartjie. **1947** [see *dennebol]. **1949** A. Wilson *Wrong Set* 41 Oranges of all sizes..from the tiny nartjies, through tangerines and green mandarins to the great navel oranges. **1953** N. Gordimer *Lying Days* III. xxvii. 276 'You've been eating a naartje,' I said. **1966** E. Palmer *Plains of Camdeboo* ii. 33 Fanny's pot-roasted venison and pou, her van der Hum made of brandy, syrup and naartjie peel, her pickled peaches,.. are still remembered. **1967** *Punch* 5 July 17/1 Accept and enjoy a naartje off the tree. **1970** *Rand Daily Mail* 28 Feb. 7/4 Many South African words of Dutch or Afrikaans origin are now part of English usage even in other countries—..naartjie and mealie. **1971** *Sunday Express* (Johannesburg) 28 Mar. 11/4 Couldn't the orange [of air-hostesses' uniforms] be toned down a little and the blue be slightly deeper? No wonder the poor girls are referred to as naartjies. **1972** D. Francis *Smokescreen* vii. 85 The *naartjies* turned out to be like large lumpy tangerines with green patches on the skin. **1974** *Sunday Times* (Johannesburg) 28 July 4/2 The record for the number of naartjies and oranges brought into the ground by spectators is held jointly by Ellis Park, Loftus Versfeld and Kings Park, a total of 200,000 citric fruit units being introduced at each ground. **1975** *Darling* (S. Afr.) 9 Apr. 95 You only feel a naartjie riding in the back of a truck with three drums of pig swill and a stack of moulting lucerne bales for company.

nary, *a.* Add: (Further examples.) Now more widely used, and almost always followed by the indef. article. Also (*U.S.*) *nary (a) red* or *cent*, not a cent.

1746 N. Wright *Jrnl.* 6 Aug. in *New England Hist. & Geneal. Reg.* (1848) II. 209 The Indians..escaped them, and there was no 'spile dunne on nary side'. **1821** *Mass. Spy* 14 Feb. (Th.), He asked her whether she was most fond of writing prose or poetry. 'Nary one,' says she, 'I writes small hand.' **1849** *Picayune* (New Orleans) 6 May 2/6 I'm goin' teu get my breakfuss yere, and not pay 'nary red' till I deu! **1856** *Knickerbocker* XLVII. 99 (Th.), Ain't you gwine to give us three dollars? Nary a red, sung out Hart. **1856** 'J. Phoenix' *Phoenixiana* 125 Playin at billiards and monte Till they've nary red cent to ante. **1872** G. P. Burnham *Mem. U.S. Secret Service* p. vii, *Nary red*, out of pocket; 'broke' of ready funds. **1895** S. Crane *Red Badge of Courage* x. 102 There's too much depending on me fer me t' die yit. No, sir! Nary die; I *can't*! **1906** *Dialect Notes* III. 147 (N.W. Arkansas) Nary a red. **1917** 'H. H. Richardson' *Fortunes R. Mahony* IV. x. 379 She would discover a thousand drawbacks to his scheme, but nary a one of the incorporeal benefits he dreamed of reaping from it. **1920** E. O'Neill *Beyond Horizon* I. ii. 36 They've been thick as thieves all their lives, with nary a quarrel I kin remember. **1932** *New Yorker* 9 Apr. 54/1 We flit hither and thither among the gadgets,..with nary a thought for the morrow. **1941** *Time* 6 Jan. 16/1 From the National Defense Advisory Commission,..there was nary a peep. **1971** M. Torrie *Bismarck Herrings* xi. 156 'Were many turned out during her time?' asked Timothy. 'Nary a one,' replied Mrs Baines. **1973** *New Society* 30 Aug. 522/3 You can wander around the cavernous vaults of the Law Courts in the Strand these days and come across nary a person. **1973** *People's Jrnl.* (Inverness & Northern Counties ed.) 1 Dec. 4/4 And there was nary a stranger on hand to be impressed! **1974** *Verbatim* Dec. 6/2 The computer that did all the dogwork gets nary a mention.

N.A.S.A., NASA, Nasa (næ·sā). [Acronym f. the initial letters of *N*ational *A*eronautics and *S*pace *A*dministration, set up in 1958.] A body responsible for organizing research in extraterrestrial space conducted by the United States.

1958 *Aviation Week* 14 Apr. 25/1 The President's recommendations and proposed legislation to create NASA, using NACA as a nucleus, were sent to Congress before the Easter recess. **1958** D. Eisenhower in *N.Y. Times* 30 July 10/7 The present National Advisory Committee for Aeronautics..will provide the nucleus of the N.A.S.A. **1965** *Economist* 4 Sept. 873/2 The Manned Orbiting Laboratory, a project which President Johnson has decided to entrust not to Nasa but to the Air Force. **1969** *Times* 13 June 7/6 N.A.S.A.'s Apollo applications programme has reached an advanced stage of discussion.

nasalism. (Further examples.)

1887 *Proc. R. Soc. Edin.* XXXII. 349 The Yankee nasalism is another familiar instance of the same kind. **1937** *Evening News* 23 Mar. 4/2 'We just dote on a good English accent,' she said, 'and we've got to get away from nasalism, our teacher says.'

nasalizable (nē·zăləizăb'l), *a.* [f. Nasalize *v.* + -able.] Capable of being pronounced nasally.

1872 S. S. Haldeman *Pennsylvania Dutch* 11 This vowel being nasalisable.

Nasara: see *Nasrani.

Nascapee, Nascapi, varr. *Naskapi *a.* and *sb.*

nascence. (Later example.)

1901 *Science* 21 June 983/1 Formations often disappear through the agency of fires, floods, mankind, etc., in which cases new formations may arise by nascence.

nascent, *a.* **2. c.** Add: (Further examples.) *spec.* applied to hydrogen that has just been released from a compound by electrolysis or chemical action (marked by its great reactivity and reducing power).

1807 H. Davy in *Phil. Trans. R. Soc.* XCVII. 11 It was natural to account for both these appearances, from the combination of nascent oxygene and hydrogene respectively. **1826** —— in *Ibid.* CXVI. 388 Nascent hydrogen was not, as had been generally believed, the cause of the appearance of metals from metallic solutions. **1959** *Proc. Nat. Acad. Sci.* XLV. 1441 Thus there is a protein component which is transiently associated with the ribosomes and has all the characteristics which would be expected in a compulsory precursor of the soluble proteins. It appears that this nascent protein is a polypeptide strand which is formed on the ribosome and is subsequently released as soluble protein. **1965** Phillips & Williams *Inorg. Chem.* I. xi. 412 Nascent hydrogen is an unstable form of hydrogen which has sufficient life or kinetic stability for it to be able to react with Po before it is transformed into normal H_2 molecules. Similarly, the hydrides of phosphorus, arsenic, and antimony can be made by the action of nascent hydrogen on soluble compounds of the element. **1974** *Nature* 1 Nov. 74/2 Experiments..have shown that nascent RNA chains have 5′-triphosphate termini.

nascently (næ·sĕntli), *adv.* [f. Nascent *a.* + -ly[2].] In a nascent manner; incipiently.

1890 W. James *Princ. Psychol.* I. ix. 258 Other processes discharge that ought as yet to be but nascently aroused. **1920** *Times Lit. Suppl.* 29 Apr. 264/2 Notions of the type of mana or orenda are of 'a nascently philosophic order'. **1936** White & Renner *Geogr.* xxiv. 517 The water present in volcanic and geyser eruptions is at least partially of magmatic origin. It is, in that event, nascently formed by the union of hydrogen and oxygen atoms, as these gases are liberated from hot magmatic materials deep in the earth.

nasẖi, nashki, varr. *Naskhi *sb. pl.*

Nashiji (nāʃī·dʒi). Also **Nashidji** and with lower-case initial. [Jap., lit. 'pear ground'.] A Japanese lacquer containing gold or silver flakes. Also, the technique of decorating with this lacquer. Also *attrib.*

1881 J. J. Quin in *Trans. Asiatic Soc. of Japan* IX. 6 The kind of powdered gold lacquer called *nashiji*, from its resemblance to the spotted skin of a pear, was introduced about the beginning of the 10th century. *Ibid.* 7 The groundwork of this box is thick *nashiji*, inlaid with various coloured shells. **1889** J. J. Rein *Industries of Japan* III. iii. 352 Nashi-ji gets its name 'pear ground' from its use in a kind of surface decoration with coarse gold powder or its bronze substitute, which is said to be an imitation in colour of the Japanese pears. *Ibid.* 368 Nashi-ji is one of the most frequent and popular modes of surface decoration. The fine particles of gold dust and foil have at first a brownish yellow colour, but always with age become brighter and more brilliant, because of the greater transparency of the lacquer varnish. **1904** S. Hartmann *Japanese Art* vii. 247 At the beginning of the tenth century, the Nashidji lacquer, of a yellowish orange colour, sprinkled with gold. **1911** J. F. Blacker *ABC of Japanese Art* ix. 176 Now all *Nashiji* on articles intended for exportation is applied by workers in plain lacquer. The best *Nashiji*, the best *Togi-dashi*, the best *Honji*, have the first twenty-two processes alike. **1957** *Encycl. Brit.* XIII. 575/2 In Japanese lacquer, the following are the chief processes used:—*Nashiji* (pear-skin), small flakes of gold or silver sunk to various depths in the lacquer [etc.] **1975** *Country Life* 10 Apr. 907/1 The chests..were..in *Hiramakie* in gold and grey lacquer on a *Nashiji* ground... *Nashiji* (pearskin) is a technique

which can be traced back to AD 905, employing small flakes of gold and silver foil at different levels in the lacquer.

Nasho (næ·ʃo). *Austral. slang.* Abbrev. of 'national serviceman'; also, compulsory military training (discontinued in 1972).

1962 C. Rohan *Delinquents* 52 They..had supper with a couple of national servicemen... 'I'm not keen on Nashos,' she said. **1966** B. Beaver *You can't come Back* (1968) 5 Sam, the new one, was just eighteen and due for his Nasho training. **1966** *Bulletin* (Sydney) 23 Apr. 12/3 The bulk of the Nashos—how the Army loathes that term—have little time for the 'protests'. **1970** *Telegraph* (Brisbane) 8 July 16/3 (*heading*) RSL [*sc.* Returned Services League] wants full Nasho details.

Nashville (næ·ʃvil). The name of the capital city of Tennessee, U.S.A., used *attrib.* and *absol.* to designate a type of country-and-western music originating there.

1963 *Broadcasting* (U.S.) 28 Jan. 74/3 Bill Fuller.. said, 'We play your Nashville numbers in Ireland and they like it because it's our kind of music.' *Ibid.* 78/2 Composer [Harlan] Howard..operates without the benefit of musical education. His 'Pick Me Up on Your Way Down' and scores of others are pure Nashville. **1968** *Sing Out!* Oct./Nov. 57/2 The songs are pleasant, though rarely distinctive (but, of course, that's Nashville). **1969** *Rolling Stone* 28 June 19/1 Along parallel lines a conservative approach to maintaining the Nashville sound could eventually backfire. **1973** *Nation Rev.* (Melbourne) 31 Aug.–6 Sept. 1459/1 The music is pure Nashville. **1975** *Hi-Fi Answers* Feb. 60/2 Musical styling ranges from the almost pure Nashville sound of 'Can't Go Back' to the rocking gospel tune of 'Let It Flow' and the convincing train beat of 'Sunshine Special'.

‖**nasi** (nā·si). [Malay.] Cooked rice. Used usu. in *Comb.* to designate *spec.* dishes, as: **nasi br(i)yani** (briyā·ni) [Malay *beriani, biani*], a type of pilau; **nasi goreng** (gǫre·ŋ), savoury fried rice with a variety of ingredients including meat and/or fish; **nasi Padang**, rice served as in Padang in Sumatra.

1894 N. B. Dennys *Descr. Dict. Brit. Malaya* 331 *Rice* (*padi* and *nasi*). **1900** W. W. Skeat *Malay Magic* v. 226 The rice is..then boiled so that it becomes *nasi* (cooked rice). **1958** *Catal. County Stores, Taunton* June 4 Nasi Goreng (Fried Rice with Pork)—a tin 4/–. **1963** *Times* 16 Feb. 5/5 *Nasi goreng* contains boiled rice, pork, curry powder, soy sauce, sliced omelette and tomatoes. **1971** *Carry Singapore in your Pocket* (Singapore Tourist Promotion Board) (ed. 3) 30 Malay and Indonesian type food is mainly of Sumatran origin and known as Nasi Padang. *Ibid.* 31 One first-class Kashmiri restaurant.. serves nasi bryani. **1972** T. Lilley *K Section* xli. 225 Lunch?..It's only nasi-goreng, but it'll fill a hole. **1972** *New Nation* (Singapore) 25 Nov. 7/5 The nasi briyani was of excellent consistency. **1972** R. McKie *Singapore* 109 Popular Indonesian and Malay food includes nasi Padang, after the town of Padang in Sumatra.

nasion (nē̆i·ziǫn). *Anat.* [a. F. *nasion* (P. Broca *Instruct. gén. pour les Recherches anthropol.* (ed. 2, 1879) iii. 143), f. L. *nās-us* nose: see *-ion².] The centre of the fronto-nasal suture.

1889 *Buck's Handbk. Med. Sci.* VIII. 202/1 (*caption*) *N*, Nasion (junction of the nasal and frontal). **1934** F. Stark *Valleys of Assassins* I. ii. 193 The face is broken off just at the nasion, and only the ends of the molars are present. **1937** Glaister & Brash *Medico-Legal Aspects Ruxton Case* x. 154 The greatest discrepancy..can easily be accounted for by the difficulty of determining the exact position of nasion and prosthion in a portrait. **1971** *Nature* 30 July 311/1 The nasal length [of Olduvai hominid 24] from nasion to the left lateral lip of the nasal aperture is 42·5 mm and nasion to nasospinale 36·0 mm.

Naskapi (næ·skăpi), *a.* and *sb.* Also **Nascapee, -i, Nascopi(e), -upi, Nasquapee, Nescaupick.** [Native name.] **A.** *adj.* Pertaining to or designating an Indian people inhabiting northern Quebec and the interior of Labrador. **B.** *sb.* **a.** This people; a member of this people. **b.** Their language.

1774 G. Cartwright *Jrnl.* 18 June (1792) II. 9 Soon after our arrival there, two canoes of Nescaupick Indians came. **1779** —— *Jrnl.* 7 Mar. (1792) II. 418 My Nescaupick sled..was drawn by the two men, a bloodhound, and a Newfoundland dog. **1849** J. McLean *Notes 25 Years' Service Hudson's Bay* I. 305 The Nascopies, or mountaineers of Labrador, speak a mixture of Cree and Sauteaux, the former predominating. **1863** H. Y. Hind *Explor. Labrador Peninsula* I. iii. 34 On Father Laure's map..the Nasquapees are stated to occupy the country north of this lake under the name of Les Cuneskapi. **1908** *Catholic Encycl.* III. 229/2 To the east are the Micmac, Malecite, Abnaki, Nascapi, and the Montagnais of Labrador. **1934** D. Jenness *Indians of Canada* (ed. 2) xviii. 270 Two tribes (*Montagnais* 'Mountaineers'; *Naskapi* 'rude, uncivilized people') were the first to come into close contact with Europeans. *Ibid.* 271 Much of the Naskapi territory was open plateau covered with grasses and lichens. **1957** *Encycl. Brit.* XV. 741/2 North of the St. Lawrence, the Montagnais and Nascapee resemble the southern Algonkin. **1966** C. F. & F. M. Voegelin *Map N. Amer. Indian Lang.* (*caption*) Algonquian Family. 1. Cree-Montagnais-Naskapi. **1974** *Country Life* 4 Apr. 780/3 A painted deerskin coat of the Naskapi tribe.

‖ **naskhi** (næ·ski), *sb. pl.* Also **nasḫi, nesk(h)i, niskhi**, etc. and with capital initial. [Arab. *naskī*, f. *nasaka* to copy.] The normal cursive Arabic script. Also *attrib.* or as *adj.*

1771 W. Jones *Gram. Pers. Lang.* 15 Our books are printed in the Niskhi hand, and all Arabick manuscripts, as well as most Persian and Turkish histories, are written in it; but the Persians write their poetical works in the Tâlík, which answers to the most elegant of our Italick hands. **1777** J. Richardson *Dict. Pers., Arab., & English* p. iii/1 In this character the Alcoran was originally written: it was afterwards improved under the denomination of Cufik; and continued in use till the appearance of the Niskhi, in the tenth century of our era... The Niskhi, ..with some variation and corruption, is the same which now prevails in Arabia, Persia, India, and other Eastern countries. **1807** in W. Jones *Wks.* XIII. 416 *Zafar Námeh.* A most elegant history of Taimur, written in the Niskh character. **1820** J. G. Jackson *Acct. Timbuctoo & Housa* 350 The Arabs have various modes of writing, the principal of which is that used by the Koreish, the most learned of all the Western tribes, and is denominated the *Nishki*, or upright character: if this is understood, the others may be easily comprehended. **1849** F. Madden tr. *Silvestre's Universal Palæogr.* I. 52 The Arabic Neskhi alphabet, already in use among the Arab tribes, was forced upon Persia with the Coran, and took the place of the ancient cuneiform and other writings. **1854** A. Sprenger *Catal. Arab., Pers. & Hindústány MSS. in Libraries of King of Oudh* I. 8 Copies are not frequent, yet there are five in the Moty Mahall. The best is written in Naskhy. **1879** C. Rieu *Catal. Pers. MSS. in Brit. Mus.* I. 7/2 The Coran in Arabic, with a Persian version written in small Nashki. **1880** *Encycl. Brit.* XIII. 117/2 Arabic epigraphy begins with the rise of Islam. Two systems of writing were used concomitantly, the Cufic or uncial, and the Neski or running hand. **1893** [in Dict. s.v. Cufic *a.*]. **1948** D. Diringer *Alphabet* 271 The two main branches of the Arabic script, Naskhi and Kufic. **1959** *Chambers's Encycl.* XII. 291/1 The earliest form of the North-Arabic script was the Kufic...in this script however many of the signs were inconveniently alike, and the so-called *Nasḫi*-script, in which diacritical points are used to distinguish similar letters, began to take its place as early as the 7th century A.D. **1970** *Oxf. Compan. Art* 634/1 Naskhi inscriptions are common in architecture and the decorative arts.

naskh-ta'lyq: see *nastalik.

Nasmyth (nē̆i·smiþ). The name of James *Nasmyth* (1808–1890), Scottish engineer, used *attrib.* and in the possessive to denote a form of hammer or pile-driver he invented, in which the falling weight is raised by steam pressure on a piston attached to it.

1845 *Jrnl. Franklin Inst.* XL. 283 Nasmyth's steam hammer for pile driving. *a* **1877** Knight *Dict. Mech.* III. 2348/2 Plate LXII shows the new Nasmyth steam-hammer at Woolwich, England. It is at present the largest and most powerful in the world. **1902** L. F. Vernon-Harcourt *Civil Engin.* iv. 56 Nasmyth's pile-driver is the oldest and best-known form of these machines. **1928** R. Bridges in H. Bradley *Coll. Papers* 43 A friend whose mind I used to compare to a Nasmyth's hammer, which can weld a ton of iron or crack a nut without crushing its kernel. **1945** R. Hargreaves *Enemy at Gate* 278 Bringing, in effect, a Nasmyth hammer to the task of cracking a walnut. **1963** A. F. Burstall *Hist. Mech. Engin.* vi. 207 Considerable improvements took place in forging, particularly after the invention of Nasmyth's steam hammer..in 1839.

Nasmyth's membrane (nē̆i·smiþ). *Anat.* [f. the name of Alexander *Nasmyth* (d. 1848), British dentist, who described the membrane in 1839.] A transient membrane covering the crown of young teeth; the primary enamel cuticle.

1853 *Q. Jrnl. Microsc. Sci.* I. 162 The layer is about 1-40th of an inch thick, and consists of an external delicate structureless Nasmyth's membrane. **1906** *Brit. Dental Jrnl.* XXVII. 1017 The interest at the time was centred on the condition of its Nasmyth's membrane. **1973** *Gray's Anat.* (ed. 35) 1235/2 The newly erupted enamel is covered by a two-layered structure (reduced enamel epithelium and primary cuticle). This is called Nasmyth's membrane.

naso-. Add: **nasoci·liary**, applied to a branch of the ophthalmic nerve that supplies the skin and mucous membrane of the nose, the eyelids, and parts of the eyeball, and communicates with the ciliary ganglion; **naso-phary·ngeal** *a.*, of or pertaining to the nasopharynx, or the nose and the pharynx; **na·sopharynx**, the uppermost part of the pharynx, lying above the soft palate and communicating with the posterior nares.

1895 *Quain's Elem. Anat.* (ed. 10) III. ii. 236 The nasal nerve (oculo-nasal or naso-ciliary) enters the orbit between the heads of the external rectus muscle. **1968** Passmore & Robson *Compan. Med. Stud.* I. xxi. 10/2 The ophthalmic nerve..breaks up into its lacrimal, frontal and nasociliary branches while still within the wall of the cavernous sinus. **1872, 1884** Naso-pharyngeal [in Dict.]. **1892** P. McBride *Dis. Throat, Nose & Ear* 281 Naso-pharyngeal Catarrh associated with Crust Formation.—As we have seen, crusts may exist in the nasopharynx in cases of atrophic rhinitis. **1973** *Sci. Amer.* Oct. 32/3 As the term indicates, nasopharyngeal carcinoma originates in the nasal cavity, the pharynx and the rear of the oral cavity. **1877** Nasopharynx [in Dict.]. **1902** D. J. Cunningham *Text-bk. Anat.* 981 This sheet [*sc.* the soft palate]..cuts into the cavity of the pharynx.., and, falling short of the posterior wall, incompletely divides it into two, namely, an upper part or naso-pharynx (pars nasalis), and a lower part or pharynx proper, which is further subdivided..into the oral pharynx..and the laryngeal pharynx. **1935** Imperatori & Burman *Dis. Nose & Throat* xxiv. 283 Most often neoplasms in the nasopharynx really have their origin in the nose but by their growth extend back into the nasopharynx. **1973** *Daily Colonist* (Victoria, B.C.) 3 Nov. 1/3 Snoring results from vibration of the soft tissues of the nasopharynx.

nasogastric (nē̆izogæ·strik), *a. Med.* [f. Naso- + Gastric *a.*] Reaching or supplying the stomach via the nose; effected via such a route.

1958 *Med. Ann. District of Columbia* XXVII. 331 (*heading*) Hypertonic dehydration complicating high protein nasogastric tube feeding. **1961** *Lancet* 2 Sept. 519/2 The uncritical use of naso-gastric suction in all upper abdominal cases should be reconsidered. **1964** *Ibid.* 26 Dec. 1351/1 The indwelling polyvinyl nasogastric tube scarcely disturbs the infant. **1974** Passmore & Robson *Compan. Med. Stud.* III. 10/1 Most nasogastric feeds are based on milk.

nasonite (nē̆i·sǫ̆nəit). *Min.* [f. the name of Frank Lewis *Nason* (1856–1928), U.S. geologist + -ite¹.] A silicate and chloride of calcium and lead, $Ca_4Pb_6(Si_2O_7)_3Cl_2$, which forms hexagonal crystals and is found as white or grey granular masses.

1899 Penfield & Warren in *Amer. Jrnl. Sci.* clviii. 346 Hand specimens usually present a mottled or spotted appearance owing to numerous inclusions of yellow axinite and brown garnet, which are scattered rather uniformly through the massive nasonite. **1935** *Prof. Papers U.S. Geol. Survey* No. 180. 93/2 Nasonite commonly forms the matrix of glaucochroite crystals, and in the few specimens seen is also associated with garnet, axinite, and barite. **1971** *Amer. Mineralogist* LVI. 1177 If one imagines two unit cells of apatite superposed in the *c* direction..and rotates one of them of 60° around the 6_3 axis, one obtains the unit cell of nasonite.

nasospinale (nē̆i:zospinā·li). [app. mod.L., f. Naso- + late L. *spīnāle*, neut. of *spīnālis* Spinal *a.*

So etymologized, e.g., in R. Martin *Lehrb. d. Anthrop.* (1914) 513. But cf. F. *naso-spinal* adj., used and prob. coined (as the fem. *naso-spinale*) by P. Broca (*Mém. de la Soc. d'Anthrop. de Paris* (1875) II. 72) as the epithet of a line 'de la racine du nez à la base de l'épine nasale'.]

‖ The point of intersection of a line joining the lowest points on the anterior nasal apertures with the midsagittal plane.

1920 H. H. Wilder *Lab. Man. Anthropometry* i. 47 (*heading*) Nasospinale... This point is defined as a point (usually within the bone substance), where a line tangent to the two lateral curves of the lower margin of the piriform aperture crosses the median line. **1933** *Jrnl. R. Anthrop. Inst.* LXIII. 44 The definition of the nasospinale we have given above is an elaboration of that which was first given by Broca. **1949** H. Sicher *Oral Anat.* i. 97 The nasal profile angle is the angle formed by the line from nasion to nasospinale with the Frankfort horizontal. **1971** Nasospinale [see *nasion].

Nasquapee, var. *Naskapi *a.* and *sb.*

Nasrani (næzrā·ni). Also **Nasrany**, etc. Pl. **Nasara**, etc. [Arab. *Naṣrānī*, pl. *Naṣārā* cogn. with Nazarene *a.* and *sb.*] A Christian, so called by Muslims; = Nazarene *sb.* 1 b.

1583 J. Newbery *Let.* 15 July in Purchas *Pilgrimes* (1625) II. ix. xviii. 1643 In Aleppo I hired two Nastraynes, and one of them hath the Indian tongue. **1615** G. Sandys *Relation* III. 153 On the twentieth of March with the rising Sunne we departed. A small remainder of that great Caruan; the Nostraines (so name they the Christians of the East) that rid vpon Mules and Asses being gone before. **1792** R. Heron tr. *Niebuhr's Trav. Arabia* II. xxvi. v. 242 In Arabia, the Christians are called *Nassara* or *Nusrani*. **1820** J. G. Jackson *Acct. Timbuctoo & Housa* 510 It is not correct to assert that *Nasari is a general term*, applied to infidels in Muhamed; it is applied to Christians only. **1826** Denham & Clapperton *Narrative* p. xxxi, You were the first man whose hand I ever touched—but they all said it did not signify with you, an *Insara* (a Christian). **1836** E. W. Lane *Account* II. iv. 52 The kelbs before removal from their original places are called *Nasa'ra* (or Christians, in the singular, *Nusra'nee*). **1844** J. H. Drummond Hay *Western Barbary* xi. 76/2 The inhabitants rushed out from their houses to have a sight of the Ensara. **1888** C. M. Doughty *Trav. Arabia Deserta* II. xvii. 514 When I responded,..Sâlem exclaimed, 'Ullah! how truly the Nasrâny speaks!' **1905** *Jewish Encycl.* IX. 195/1 In the Koran also the Christians are called 'Al-Naṣara'. The name may be traced back to Nazareth, Jesus' birthplace. **1912** *Catholic Encycl.* XIV. 681/1 The St. Thomas Christians now prefer to be called *Nasrani* (Nazarenes), the designation given by the Mohammedans to all Christians. **1926** R. Bell *Origin Islam* v. 149 If we could be sure that *Ṣābi'in* denoted the Christians of South Arabia, Naṣārā would then denote specially those of the north. But we shall not..go far wrong in taking it as meant to denote Christians in general. The word Naṣārā is apparently derived from *Nazaraioi*, which is mentioned as the name of a Jewish-Christian sect. **1936** F. Stark *Southern Gates Arabia* iv. 40 About fifty children pursued, calling 'Nasrani' in a monotonous but not insulting way. **1937** R. Bell tr. *Qur'ān* I. xxii. 318/2 Those who have believed, those who have judaised, the Ṣābi'īn, the Naṣārā, the Magians, and the Polytheists—

verily Allah will distinguish between them on the day of resurrection. **1958** L. Durrell *Balthazar* iv. 87 He, a city-bred Alexandrian—almost a despised *Nasrany*—could out-shoot, out-talk and out-gallop..them. **1963** *Times* 14 Feb. 14/7 They drew aside and conferred among themselves since a *Nasrani* or Christian is seldom met in their deserts.

Nass (næs). The name of a river in British Columbia, Canada, used *attrib.* to denote a tribe of the Tsimshian people who inhabit the basin of this river, and whose native name is *Niska. Also as *sb.*, the language of this tribe.

1829 J. S. Green in *Missionary Herald* (Boston, Mass.) (1830) XXVI. 344 The Nass Indians live on the continent. *Ibid.*, The Nass to my ear is harsh and disagreeable. **1911** F. Boas *Handbk. Amer. Indian Lang.* I. 290 The system of vowels of Tsimshian is nearly the same as that of the Nass dialect. *Ibid.* 292 Many *u*-sounds of Tsimshian are *ī* or *ē* in Nass. [**1934** D. Jenness *Indians of Canada* (ed. 2) ii. 18 The Tsimshian of the Nass and Skeena rivers. *Ibid.* xxi. 336 The Tsimshian ('people inside of the Skeena river'), were divided into three groups, the Tsimshian proper around the mouth of Skeena river, the Gitksan ('Skeena River people') farther up the same stream, and the Niska who inhabited the basin of Nass (Niska) river.]

nassa (næ·sǎ). [mod.L. (J. B. P. A. de Monet, Chevalier de Lamarck 1799, in *Mém. Soc. d'Hist. Nat. Paris* I. 71), f. L. *nassa* basket fish-trap.] The shell of a marine gastropod of the genus once so called, now included in the genus *Nassarius*; a basket shell; = Dog-whelk. Also *attrib.*

1853 L. Reeve *Conchologia Iconica* XVI. s.v. *Nassa*, plate 1 The rough Nassa... A very elegantly coronated species, with the spine rising into a sharp turret. **1971** *World Archaeol.* III. 136 String bands to which cowrie or nassa shells are attached. **1974** S. P. Dance *Encycl. Shells* 156/1 *Nassarius fossatus* Gould. Giant Western Nassa. Shell ovate. Conical spire, apex pointed.

Nassauvian (năsǭ·viăn). Also **Nassavian.** [f. *Nassau*, capital city of the Bahama islands + -ian.] A native or inhabitant of Nassau. Also *attrib.* or as *adj.*

1924 F. Holmes *Bahamas during Gt. War* xii. 121 On May 29th [1917], greatly to the satisfaction of all Nassauvians, the Lighting Restrictions were..suspended. **1928** R. A. Curry *Bahamian Lore* vi. 64 Along the side-walks of Bay Street you will meet..the Nassauvian in white clothes. **1961** I. Fleming *Thunderball* xii. 126 A discussion about the merits of Nassavian labour... The Chief of Immigration and Customs was a sleek Nassavian with quick brown eyes. **1973** *Listener* 16 Aug. 202/2 Nassauvians generally have a care for their visitors' feelings.

nassella (næse·lă). [mod.L. (E. Desvaux in C. Gay *Historia Física y Política de Chile, Botánica* (1853) VI. 263), f. L. *nassa* net + *-ella*, fem. of *-ellus*, diminutive suffix.] A coarse grass of the genus so called, native to Chile, but also found in other countries to which it has been introduced, esp. New Zealand, where it has become a troublesome weed. Also *attrib.*

[**1936** H. H. Allan *Introd. Grasses N.Z.* 118 *Nassella trichotoma*, a rather graceful tussocky species, somewhat resembling *Festuca novae-zelandiae* in habit, but with very different spikelets. Recently collected by Professor A. Wall on the Waipara River bed, and in the Omihi Valley, where it appears to be thoroughly established.] **1946** *Nature* 21 Dec. 920/1 Weed problems..such as nassella, constitute a serious threat to good pasture land [in New Zealand]. **1950** *N.Z. Jrnl. Agric.* June 515/1 Nassella tussock... This insidious pest crept almost unawares on to some of our good pastoral country. **1966** G. W. Turner *Eng. Lang. Austral. & N.Z.* viii. 172 In scientific language Latin botanical names often become general. The recently troublesome Nassella tussock has no more popular name. It is controlled in accordance with the Nassella Tussock Act of 1946 by Nassella Tussock Boards.

Nasserite (næ·sərəit). [f. the name of Gamel Abdel *Nasser* (1918–70), President of Egypt from 1956 to 1970 + -ite[1].] A supporter of Nasser. Also *attrib.* or as *adj.* So **Na·sserism,** the political principles or policy of Nasser; **Na·sserist,** a Nasserite; also *attrib.* or as *adj.*

1958 *Times* 18 Mar. 11/3 The argument..between the west-looking policy pursued by President Chamoun and M. Solh and the Nasserite policy espoused by some of the Opposition. **1958** *Observer* 20 July 10/2 We were prepared (as Sir Anthony Eden seemed to be at the time of Suez) to overthrow 'Nasserism' by force. **1958** *Economist* 26 July 300 It is obvious and well understood here that the coup in Iraq means a further link in the encirclement of Israel by Nasserist forces and thus increases Israel's military danger. **1958** *Times* 16 Dec. 9/6 The others are the Nasserists, the Communists, and Brigadier Kassem. **1959** *Daily Tel.* 24 Apr. 12/5 Five visiting Iraqi officers are reported to have recently investigated public feeling here, much to the concern of the Nasserites. **1965** M. Spark *Mandelbaum Gate* iv. 105 Are you a nationalist?.. A Nasserite? **1966** *Economist* 5 Mar. 889/1 If this is not potential 'nasserite material', what is? **1968** *Ibid.* 3 Feb. 23/3 One hears a lot about 'Young Turks', 'Nasserists', and so on these days. **1969** J. Mander *Static Society* viii. 225 We might say that Peron invented 'Nasserism' a decade before Nasser. **1971** *Guardian Weekly* 10 Apr. 7/1 Officially Sadat upholds the Nasserist orthodoxy. He told the Palestinians..that there was no such thing as an Egyptian strategy or a Syrian strategy, but only an Arab strategy. **1973** Howat & Taylor *Dict. World Hist.* 1047/2 *Nasserism*, Western term used to denote first the policies of Egypt..under President Abd Al-Nasir, and second, a generalized movement among Arabs.

‖**nastalik** (næstǎlī·k). Also **nastaliq, nestalik, nestaliq,** etc. [Arab., f. *nasḵī* *naskhi *sb. pl.* + *talik* hanging.] A Persian cursive script, characterized by rounded forms and elongated horizontal strokes. Also called *talik.

1795 W. Ouseley *Pers. Miscellanies* I. i. 7, I must here remark, that in India the Talik hand is generally called Nustaleek... Although used occasionally by the Arabian, and commonly by the Turkish penmen, yet it seems to be more particularly a favourite of the Persians. **1809** C. Stewart *Descr. Catal. Oriental Library of Late Tippoo Sultan of Mysore* 57/1 Octavo, Nastâlik Character, beautifully written. **1854** A. Sprenger *Catal. Arab., Pers., & Hindústány MSS. in Libraries of King of Oudh* I. 89 Myr 'imád of Qazwyn a most exquisite calligraph particularly in Naskh-ta'lyq. **1879** C. Rieu *Catal. Pers. MSS. in Brit. Mus.* I. 5/2 The texts..are given in Arabic, and mostly accompanied with an interlinear Persian version in Nestalik. **1908** Maulavi Abdul Muqtadir *Catal. Arab. & Pers. MSS. in Oriental Public Library at Bankipore: Pers. Poetry* 5 Written in a perfect Nasta'līq, in four columns, with one gold and two ornamental rules. **1913** *Encycl. Islām* I. 391/2 It was probably not until this later period that the *nesta'līḳ* arose (said to be a contraction of *nasḵī* and *ta'līḳ*), a variation of *ta'līḳ*, from which it does not differ in any essential features. **1919** D. C. Phillott *Higher Pers. Gram.* i. 36 The *nasta'līq*.. is a combination of the *nasḵh*..or ordinary hand and the *ta'līq*..: it is a beautiful hand, chiefly used by the Persians for well-written manuscripts; but the modern Arabs call the Persian writing generally *ta'līq*. **1948** D. Diringer *Alphabet* 595/2 (*index*) Nesta'liq script; *see* Ta'liq. **1954** A. F. L. Beeston *Catal. Addit. Pers. MSS. in Bodl. Libr.* 92/1 Main text and index in neat Naksh, the other pieces in Nastaʿlīḳ. **1957** *Encycl. Brit.* XVII. 593/1 In this academy [*sc.* the Academy of Artistic Book-Production at Herat] the Persian texts were no longer written in *naskhi*, but in *nastaliq* an offshoot of the old cursive character, invented by the celebrated Mir Ali of Tabriz. **1966** Hosking & Meredith-Owens *Handbk. Asian Scripts* ii. 20 After 1600 there is a steady deterioration in *Nasta'līk* which becomes larger and coarser, whereas *Naskhī* gradually improves after this date. **1973** 'D. Jordan' *Nile Green* xxiv. 99, I vaguely heard him expounding the difference between *naskhi* and *nasta'liq* script.

nastic (næ·stik), *a. Bot.* [a. G. *nastisch* (E. Strasburger *Lehrbuch der Botanik* (ed. 6, 1904) I. ii. 221), f. Gk. *ναστ-ός* pressed together + -ic.] Of movements of parts of plants: uninfluenced by the direction of an external stimulus.

1908 W. H. Lang tr. *Strasburger's Text-bk. Bot.* (ed. 3) 270 When..the movement results from the internal disposition of the structure it is spoken of as nastic. **1912** *Ibid.* (ed. 4) 300 Nastic movements..are curvatures which bring about a particular position in relation to the plant and not to the direction of the stimulus. **1929** J. C. Bose *Growth & Tropic Movements Plants* xx. 216 If the movement be nastic, then the closure or the opening movement will remain the same, whether the organ be held in normal position or upside down. **1951** M. Abercrombie et al. *Dict. Biol.* 150 Nastic movements are classified according to nature of stimulus, e.g. photonasty, response to alteration in light intensity, thermonasty, response to alteration in heat intensity, seismonasty, response to shock. **1965** Bell & Coombe tr. *Strasburger's Textbk. Bot.* 380 Nastic movements, depending on growth differences on the two sides of the organ concerned, are seen particularly clearly in the perianth segments of the many flowers which open or close according to the temperature.

Nastrayne, obs. var. *Nasrani.

nasturtium. Add: ¶ Used jocularly in place of *aspersion.*

1922 Joyce *Ulysses* 315 Don't cast your nasturtiums on my character. **1933** D. L. Sayers *Murder must Advertise* i. 22 He's been a long time in the firm and doesn't like any nasturtiums cast at it. **1970** *Guardian* 2 Feb. 9/4 No nasturtiums are cast upon anyone's actual hormones.

nasty, *a.* Add: **1. b., 4.** (Further examples.)

1914 G. B. Shaw *Misalliance* 16 Thats what theyre like: theyve nasty minds. With really nice good women a thing is either decent or indecent. **1930** W. S. Maugham *Cakes & Ale* xvii. 162 'Don't bother about it,' she said. 'He's got a nasty mind.' **1933** [see *hot *a.* 6 c]. **1942** Berrey & Van den Bark *Amer. Thes. Slang* § 295/1 *Nasty look*, a reproving look. **1961** [see *equalizer d]. **1969** M. Allingham *Case-Book* 29 One doesn't have to have a nasty mind to wonder.

7. Phrases: *a nasty piece* (or *bit*) *of work* (or *goods*): an unpleasant or contemptible person; *something nasty in the woodshed*, a traumatic experience or a concealed unpleasantness in a person's background.

1923 'Bartimeus' *Seaways* vii. 110 Nasty Bit of Work. I'd go and bash his head for two pins. **1928** 'M. Hoffe' *Many Waters* II. iv. 62 Edith shows in Mr. Rosel. He is really a rather nasty piece of work. **1932** S. Gibbons *Cold Comfort Farm* x. 141 When you were very small.. you had seen something nasty in the woodshed. **1945** G. B. Grundy *55 Yrs. at Oxf.* v. 87 Among the many pupils I had..there was only one I disliked. He was what is called a 'nasty piece of work'. **1949** 'M. Innes' *Journeying Boy* ix. 109 Nasty bit of work, isn't he?.. Specialises in blackmailing adolescents. **1952** A. Christie *Mrs McGinty's Dead* xxvii. 184 She was a nasty bit of goods all right—children know. **1953** 'H. Cecil' *Nat. Causes* xix. 223 He was a nasty piece of work all right. A real blackmailer. **1959** *Sunday Times* 5 July 6/6 He enjoyed a temperate childhood: nothing nasty in his woodshed. **1959** *Listener* 3 Sept. 350/1 Although the idea is no longer entirely respectable (rather akin to 'something nasty in the woodshed'), we [etc.]. **1960** D. Fearon *Murder-on-Thames* xiv. 116 He was a nasty bit of work. I don't know that he actually had a criminal record, but the blighter stank of black market. **1968** B. Bainbridge *Another Part of Wood* ii. 70 They had all, Joseph, brother Trevor, the younger sister,..come across something nasty in the woodshed, mother or father or both, having it off with someone else. **1975** A. Christie *Curtain* v. 46 You do not like him?..What you call the nasty bit of goods.

8. *Comb.*, as *nasty-minded* adj.; *nasty-mindedness.*

1921 D. Canfield *Brimming Cup* xiv. 236 A nasty-minded remark from somebody who didn't know what he was talking about. **1935** *Times Lit. Suppl.* 3 Oct. 613/3 A nasty-minded boy. **1972** 'J. & E. Bonett' *No Time to Kill* vii. 96, I don't want everybody to know about Greg and me. It's not that I'm ashamed... But nasty-minded people make it sound dirty. **1940** M. Marples *Public School Slang* p. x, For some reason food inspires a particular kind of satirical nasty-mindedness. **1960** *Encounter* Mar. 75/1 The nasty-mindedness of the Freudians.

nasty (nɑ·sti), *sb.*[1] [f. the adj.] **1.** (Freq. with capital initial.) Used as a jocular alteration of 'Nazi'.

1935 'R. Crompton' *William—the Detective* vi. 121 I'm jolly well not going to be called Her Hitler... I'll be called Him Hitler... Now I'm Him Hitler an' we four are the nasties. **1939** *Airman's Gaz.* Dec., All aircraft off duty being allowed to..view the stupendous, side-splitting entertainment provided by the Nasty Air Force and our Navy. *Ibid.*, All races won by the Nasties with a three mile start each time. **1940** H. G. Wells *Babes in Darkling Wood* iv. iii. 349 If it helps beat them Nastys,..I'll sit in the 'ole pond all day. **1942** *R.A.F. Jrnl.* 30 May 19 Ole Nasty can hit a hay-stack all right, but it's all he can hit. **1943** J. B. Priestley *Daylight on Saturday* xxi. 163 Cripes, ol' Nasty give us Phoney War all right, didn't 'e?

2. A nasty person; something nasty.

1935 'L. Luard' *Conquering Seas* 39 Fair is foul and foul is fair when Jack nasties step aboard. **1959** *Listener* 2 Apr. 609/2 For a Silver Wedding party there was such a grouping of nasties that one seemed to be involved in a misanthropist's nightmare. **1968** *Saturday Night* (Toronto) Feb. 27 Nasties—they're the newest social force, waiting in the wings to displace the last 1960s social force, the Flower People. They've always been around, the Nasties—disguised as merely unpleasant people. **1970** *Guardian* 8 Aug. 21 Nice nasties are de rigueur these days. **1971** *Ibid.* 22 Feb. 9/1 You come up against all manner of nasties in the woodshed: inadequacy, fear, alcoholism, ignorance, poverty, and hopelessness. **1973** H. Miller *Open City* xiv. 153 Here was a big nasty in a Crombie coat, standing right in the middle of her own living room. She was becoming very frightened. **1974** H. MacInnes *Climb to Lost World* ix. 145, I was convinced that there must be nasties in this territory, but..I found only one spider. **1975** *Country Life* 30 Jan. 257/3 It is the business of museums to present us with nasties as well as with fine things.

nasty (næ·sti), *sb.*[2] *Bot.* [a. G. *nastie* (E. Strasburger *Lehrbuch der Botanik* (ed. 6, 1904) I. ii. 221), f. Gk. *ναστ-ός* pressed together.] A nastic movement.

1936 J. B. Hill et al. *Bot.* ix. 228 Nasties are responses of bilaterally symmetrical organs like leaves and flower petals. **1955** *Sci. Amer.* Feb. 101/2 Nasties (or, more euphoniously, nastic movements) are among a plant's more beautiful motions: a typical example is the opening of a flower. They are the result of differing responses of different parts of the plant structure to the same external stimulus. **1965** Bell & Coombe tr. *Strasburger's Textbk. Bot.* 361 If, however, the direction of the movement is quite independent of that of the stimulus, but is determined solely by the structure of the organ, the movements are designated nasties.

nasute, *a.* Restrict *Obs.* to senses in Dict. and add: **3.** *Zool.* Nose-shaped or having a pronounced proboscis, esp. in reference to a caste of soldier termites of the genus *Nasutitermes.* Also as *sb.*, a termite of this caste.

1884 J. Hall in *Geol. Mag.* Dec. 560 In other forms [of lamellibranchiate molluscs], the anterior extremity becomes nasute or rostrate. **1926** R. J. Tillyard *Insects Austral. & N.Z.* xi. 103 In the family Termitidae the soldiers are sometimes of the nasute type, i.e. they are provided with pear-shaped heads more or less produced anteriorly, above the mandibles, into a narrow, snout-like process. **1934** *Discovery* Nov. 307 (*caption*) Earthen mound built by nasute termites in northern Australia. **1963** A. W. Leftwich *Student's Dict. Zool.* 160 Nasutes. Soldier-termites: specialized forms within the genus *Nasutitermes*, able to defend the colony by discharging an acrid secretion from glands situated at the end of a long snout or rostrum. **1970** F. J. Gay in *Insects of Australia* (Commonwealth Sci. & Industr. Res. Organization) xv. 292/1 *Nasutitermes* is widely distributed throughout Australia, particularly in the northern half of the continent. The soldiers are the typical nasute type.

nasutus (nēⁱsiu·tǝs). Pl. nasuti. [L. *nāsūt-us*, f. *nāsus* nose.] = *NASUTE *sb.*

1869 A. S. PACKARD *Guide to Study of Insects* 587 There also occur among workers [of certain termite species] certain individuals (Nasuti) which have the front of the head prolonged into a horn. **1895** D. SHARP in *Cambr. Nat. Hist.* V. xxi. 371 The prolongation and form of the head of these Nasuti may be fairly described as adaptation to useful ends. **1920** *Bull. U.S. Nat. Mus.* CVIII. 71 Two specimens [of *Nasutitermes costaricensis*] from Texas..; a deälated female and two nasuti.

Nat[1] (næt). *India.* Also **Nut.** [Skr. *naṭa* dancer, actor, tumbler.] A member of an itinerant class of entertainers, fortune-tellers, and the like, found esp. in northern India, but coming from no tribe in particular. Also **Na·ti**, the argot spoken by these people; also *attrib.* or as *adj.*

1801 D. RICHARDSON in *Asiatick Researches* VII. 457 Strictly speaking, these people might be denominated *players* or *actors*, from their Persian name of *Bazee-gur*,.. *juggler* or *tricker*; but the appellation of *Nut* extends to several tribes, and properly belongs to many more. **1855** H. H. WILSON *Gloss. Judicial & Revenue Terms* 369/2 *Naṭa*, *Naṭ*, or *Nuṭ*,..a dancer, an actor, a tumbler, a public performer; applied also to a tribe of vagrants who live by feats of dexterity, sleight of hand, fortune-telling and the like. **1896** W. CROOKE *Tribes & Castes N.-W. Provinces & Oudh* IV. 66 These Nats say that they came originally from Ratanpur and Bilâspur in the Central Provinces. *Ibid.* 70 Their domestic ceremonies are of the usual Nat type. **1908** *Encycl. Relig. & Ethics* I. 451/1 The ritual of the Nats, a tribe of wandering acrobats, is more remarkable. **1917** KIPLING *Eyes of Asia* (1918) 8 The nature of the enemy in this war is like the Nat (juggler) who is compelled to climb a pole for his belly's sake. **1922** G. A. GRIERSON *Ling. Survey India* XI. 121 Any tribe may be represented among the people acting as Naṭs. *Ibid.* 122 The great majority of Naṭī slang words..have been taken from the common Aryan vocabulary of Northern India.

nat[2] (nāt). [Burmese *nat*, f. Skr. *nāthá* lord, protector.] **a.** In the animistic native religion of the Burmese people, a spirit or demon, a supernatural being.

1819 F. HAMILTON *Acct. Kingdom Nepal* I. i. 57 The Bhotiyas..worship all the spirits, that by the Burmas are called Nat. **1826** J. CONDER *Mod. Traveller: Birmah, Siam & Anam* 82 Carved images..are to be seen.., the supposed representatives of different *nats* or demons. **1828** *Asiatick Researches* XVI. 468 In Ava and Siam..in the existence of *Nats*, it is admitted, that other animated creatures than man and animals exist. **1858** C. T. WINTER *Six Months Brit. Burmah* i. 13 The Nats who guard the royal city, palace, and umbrella. **1878** C. J. F. S. FORBES *Brit. Burma* viii. 223 A man going on a journey through a forest, comes to a large and conspicuous tree..and places..an offering to the Nát of the tree. **1923** *Blackw. Mag.* Aug. 149/1 We had been talking..of folk-lore, superstitions, witches, djinns, nats, spookes, ghouls and other inventions of primitive man. **1934** 'G. ORWELL' *Burmese Days* xiv. 209 Sacrificing to the local god. Nats, they call them—a kind of dryad. **1959** C. OGBURN *Marauders* (1960) iv. 115 These were intended to propitiate, entice, or exorcise the nats, or forest spirits. **1968** O. WYND *Sumatra Seven Zero* i. 10 'Rubies..only come out of the ground when their protecting "nats" permit it.'.. 'What is a "nat"?'.. 'A Burmese spirit of the earth and air.' **1974** *Times* 30 Apr. 16/7 A Burmese journalist..asked if I would like to come with him to an evening of 'Nat' Dancing. To the Burmese the Nats are the multitudinous spirits that inhabit all natural phenomena and can exercise at will power over people and objects... The monks are tolerant of Nats: a good many of them are probably Nat-conscious themselves.

b. *Comb.*, as *nat-worship*, *-worshipper*.

1833 A. JUDSON *Let.* 29 Nov. in F. Wayland *Mem. A. Judson* (1853) II. 56 The best outward test is to have refrained from rum, nat-worship, &c. **1910** *Encycl. Relig. & Ethics* III. 21/1 The practical everyday religion of the Burmese peoples is Animism, called generally in Burmese 'Nat-worship'. **1965** M. NASH *Golden Road to Modernity* ix. 320 There is a system of animistic belief (nat worship) which is integrated with Buddhism and gives a villager a belief system reaching from hut to heaven and beyond. **1906** J. G. R. FORLONG *Faiths of Man* I. 257 Its [*sc.* Burma's] population in 1894 was.. Nāt worshipers..420,000. **1923** *Blackw. Mag.* Feb. 183/2 They are all Nat or spirit worshippers.

Nat[3] (næt). [Abbrev. of NATIONAL *a.* and *sb.*, NATIONALIST.] A member of (*a*) the National Party in South Africa; (*b*) the Scottish or Welsh Nationalists.

In S. Afr. also = 'National'.

1934 W. SAINT-MANDÉ *Halcyon Days Afr.* ii. 24 Labour had done right to join forces with the Nats., for the Smuts government would gradually have reduced the white workers to slaves. **1958** *New Statesman* 22 Mar. 367/2 The movement..cannot lose momentum. The Nats must know this, unless the strain of continually having to defend an indefensible position has lost them their sanity. **1967** *Economist* 18 Mar. 1008/2 Both Scotland and Wales could in time do well. But the start of their national lives would be bleak... One cannot take seriously the present Nats who advocate freedom and promise prosperity in one breath. **1968** *Guardian* 20 Sept. 13/2 Jeremy Thorpe's overtures to the Celtic Nationalists... The Liberals would back the Nats on devolution. **1970** B. KNOX *Children of Mist* i. 23 Scot Nats? He'd met all kinds. **1971** *Sunday Times* (Johannesburg) 28 Mar. 2/2 The Transvaler, official organ of the Nat Party in the Transvaal. **1972** M. SINCLAIR *Norslag* ix. 73 'Weren't you with the..' 'Yes, I was an ardent Nat then.'.. MacCaig was already neatly pigeonholed. **1974** *Times* 22 Apr. 7/1 The white people..will be voting overwhelmingly for Mr. Vorster's National Party... The average voter will..continue to vote 'Nat'. **1974** *Sunday Post* (Glasgow) 28 Apr. 5/5 And there are other Labour strongholds where it wouldn't need much of a swing to put in the Nats.

Natal (natā·l), *sb.*[2] The name of a province of the Republic of South Africa used *attrib.* in: **1. Natal sore** *Path.* = *Oriental sore* s.v. ORIENTAL *a.* and *sb.* A. 3 b.

1852 C. BARTER *Dorp & Veld* ii. 13 The Natal sore, a very painful boil. **1855** J. W. COLENSO *Ten Weeks in Natal* 245 The Natal sores or boils..are such as I have known among my parishioners in Norfolk. **1915** O. S. ORMSBY *Pract. Treat. Dis. Skin* 360 As distinguished from the Natal sore, which was chiefly found in the lower part of that country, the veldt sore was most abundant in the high, barren table-lands. **1951** G. PANJA in R. B. H. Gradwohl *Clin. Trop. Med.* xxxiii. 641 Tropical Phagedenic Ulcer... Synonyms... Natal sore.

2. The names of plants and animals found there, as **Natal francolin,** *Francolinus natalensis*; **Natal lily,** a bulbous plant of the family Amaryllidaceæ, *Clivia miniata*, which bears clusters of scarlet flowers, or one of several species of *Crinum*; **Natal mahogany,** either of two evergreen timber trees, *Kiggelaria africana*, of the family Flacourtiaceæ, or *Trichilia emetica*, of the family Meliaceæ; **Natal plum,** one of several shrubs or trees bearing fruit resembling a plum, esp. a spiny evergreen shrub or small tree, *Carissa macrocarpa*, of the family Apocynaceæ, which bears tubular, white, fragrant flowers and an edible purple fruit.

1906 Natal francolin [see *coast-partridge* (*COAST *sb.* 14)]. **1947** J. STEVENSON-HAMILTON *Wild Life S. Afr.* xxxii. 274 The Natal francolin (*Francolinus natalensis*).. may be recognized by its red bill and legs, and white breast with V-shaped black markings. **1855** *Cape of Good Hope Almanac & Ann. Reg. for 1856* 283 The Natal lily is the perfection of beauty and fragrance. **1859** R. J. MANN *Colony of Natal* viii. 152 Most places are commonly covered with another very beautiful amaryllid..which is termed *par excellence* the 'Natal lily'. The flowers of this striking plant are large white pink-ribbed bells, hanging in enormous bunches round the summit of the flower-stalk. **1962** WATT & BREYER-BRANDWIJK *Medicinal & Poisonous Plants S. & E. Afr.* (ed. 2) 1378/1 Crinum sp... Natal lily. **1904** H. STONE *Timbers of Commerce* 3 (*heading*) Natal Mahogany. Kiggelaria Dregeana. **1907** T. R. SIM *Forests & Forest Flora Cape Good Hope* 128 *Kiggelaria africana*, Wild Peach, Natal Mahogany.. does best in open forest. *Ibid.* 161 This tree [*sc. Trichilia emetica*]..is known in the Transkei as Cape Mahogany, Manuti Mahogany, or Natal Mahogany. **1973** PALMER & PITMAN *Trees S. Afr.* II. 1071 *Trichilia emetica* Vahl. Woodland mahogany, Natal mahogany... This is one of the widespread trees of Africa. **1859** R. J. MANN *Colony of Natal* viii. 158 The *Amatungulu* (Natal plum) is the berry of an evergreen periwinkle (*Vinca*) growing as a small shrub on the sea-coast lands. The fruit is about the size of a damson. **1876** H. BROOKS *Natal* v. 168 A plant.. bearing a really valuable fruit which is familiarly known as the Natal plum. **1970** *Country Life* 17 Dec. 1230/3 Scarlet ixoras and the spiny carissa (Natal plum) are used as evergreen hedges. **1973** PALMER & PITMAN *Trees S. Afr.* III. 1901 *Carissa macrocarpa*... Amatungulu, Natal plum..is a common and often conspicuous species in coastal bush, on sand dunes and on the edges of coastal forest... Although it is often a low bush, it can grow into a small tree up to 4 m high, many-branched, spiny, with dense evergreen foliage.

Natalian (natā·liăn), *a.* and *sb.* [f. *NATAL *sb.*[2] + -IAN.] **A.** *adj.* Of or pertaining to the province of Natal in South Africa. **B.** *sb.* A native or inhabitant of Natal.

1867 R. J. MANN in *Intellectual Observer* X. 186 In the year 1842,..the Dutchmen within the Natalian territory became subjects of the British Crown. **1870** A. LINDLEY *After Ophir* ii. 27 The Natalians carry their *penchant* for genteel and sonorous titles nearly as far as the Sicilians. **1878** [see *JIMMY 1]. **1897** J. BRYCE *Impressions S. Afr.* xviii. 359 The Natalians have.. become the less energetic. **1928** R. CAMPBELL *Wayzgoose* i. 10 Seldom do suns such striking talent show As when they set Natalian woods aglow. **1935** S. DESMOND *Afr. Log* xxxix. 191 Throughout the day I see the lovely Natalian landscape roll past. **1960** *Guardian* 14 Oct. 12/5 Natalians are subjects of the Queen. **1973** *Sunday Times* (S. Afr.) 18 Feb. 2 An independent Natal has long been the dream of many White Natalians.

Nataraja (na:tără·dʒă). *India.* [Hindi, lit. 'prince of dancers' f. Skr. *naṭa* dancer, actor + *rājan* prince, king (see RAJA).] A name of Siva, the Hindu god of creation and dissolution, in his role as lord of the dance, when he symbolizes cosmic energy. Also, a figure depicting Siva as lord of the dance.

1911 V. A. SMITH *Hist. Fine Art India & Ceylon* vii. 249 The place of honour may be given to the spirited images of Siva as 'Naṭarāja', 'Lord of the Dance', the first of their kind to be found in Ceylon. *Ibid.* vii. 251 (*caption*) Bronze Siva Nataraja, 3 feet high. **1916** H. KRISHNA SASTRI *S. Indian Images Gods & Goddesses* iv. 77 Naṭarāja ..is the well-known dancing form of god Siva. **1917** COOMARASWAMY & DUGGIRALA tr. *Mirror of Gesture* 15 The image of Śiva as dancer (Naṭarāja, Naṭeśa) and actor is everywhere conspicuous in Śaiva literature. **1918** A. COOMARASWAMY *Dance of Śiva* 66 Explorers of the infinitely great and infinitely small, we are worshippers of Naṭarāja still. **1968** *Indian Mining & Engin. Jrnl.* V. 40 God in his aspect of Naṭarāja, or Lord of the Dance. **1972** P. HOLROYDE *Indian Mus.* i. 42 That first artist who fashioned the Nataraja into a symbolic equation of energy.

natatorium (nēⁱtătōᵊ·riǝm). *N. Amer.* [L. *natātōrium* a place for swimming.] A swimming-pool.

1890 in WEBSTER. **1897** E. BELLAMY *Equality* x. 60, I propose..that we go over to the natatorium and take a plunge. **1900** *Amer. Jrnl. Sociol.* Jan. 473 A considerable number of Wellesley college girls..patronize the Brookline natatorium. **1907** *Amherst College Catal. 1907–08* 104 In the natatorium, swimming is taught by a competent instructor. Every student who on entering college cannot swim, is required to learn the first year. **1911** *Daily Colonist* (Victoria, B.C.) 2 Apr. 2/4 Pearl Moore came to her death by drowning in a pool at the Washington natatorium. **1921** *Ibid.* 6 Oct. 1/5 Plans have been completed for the immediate construction of an up-to-date natatorium in Vancouver. **1966** *Punch* 21 Dec. 921/2 Only in Texas, perhaps, will a man in search of somewhere to swim pick up the Yellow Pages and look under Natatoriums; the directory refers him to Swimming Pools. **1971** *Parks & Recreation* (U.S.) VI. 31 This modern natatorium demonstrated that using a vinyl-coated nylon air-supported structure as the roof in the winter and completely removing it in the summer is a desirable and effective arrangement.

natch (nætʃ), *adv.* Colloq. abbrev. of NATURALLY *adv.* orig. *U.S.*

1945 in L. SHELLY *Jive Talk Dict.* 15/1. **1946** *Sun* (Baltimore) 24 Sept. 3/3 (Advt.), Natch! Mom's gettin' both of us Hen self-starters... Baltimore's most popular 'first shoes for babies'. **1953** *New Yorker* 10 Jan. 21/3 Their disapproving papa..inserted a dime, which, he said, would otherwise have gone to buy them a Coca-Cola... Well, natch, this brought a twenty-dime return. **1957** P. WILDEBLOOD *Main Chance* 132 'You don't mean to say,' she whispered tragically, 'that we're going to eat?' 'Why, natch. We're going to have another drink first, though.' **1962** J. WAIN *Strike Father Dead* 60 We went in: Saloon Bar, natch. Lucille may have been Public Bar in her heart, but she was Saloon Bar on the outside. **1968** *N.Y. Times Bk. Rev.* 23 June VII. 1/3 The banning—in Boston, natch—of 'Fanny Hill' back in 1821. **1970** *Daily Tel.* (Colour Suppl.) 3 July 5/2 A crowd of opulent-looking masochists..were actually savouring this culinary surrealism and, natch, paying through the nose for it. **1971** A. DIMENT *Think Inc.* ii. 20 They blamed you, natch. **1973** *Times* 29 May 8/5, I went down to Bath to celebrate (along with the coronation of King Edgar, natch) the re-opening of the Assembly Rooms.

Natchez (næ·tʃez, nā·tʃī). Also **Nachee, Na'htchi.** [Native name.] A N. Amer. Indian people of Mississippi; a member of this people; also, their language. Also *attrib.* or as *adj.*

1775 J. ADAIR *Hist. Amer. Indians* 86 In the year 1747, a Nachee warrior told me, that while one of their prophets was using his divine invocation for rain..he was killed with thunder on the spot. **1845** *Cherokee Advocate* (Tahlequah, Okla.) 24 Apr. 4/3 The tradition has been widely recorded, that the dominion of the Natchez once extended even to the Wabash. **1848** *Trans. Amer. Ethnol. Soc.* II. i. 77 (*table*) Families... Natchez. **1850** R. G. LATHAM *Nat. Hist. Varieties Man* 340 Disinterred skulls from the Natchez area... Such is a brief notice of the customs of the Natchez. **1890** J. G. FRAZER *Golden Bough* II. 382 The chief solemnity of the Natchez, an Indian tribe on the Lower Mississippi, was the Harvest Festival or the Festival of New Fire. **1891** *7th Ann. Rep. Bureau Amer. Ethnol. 1885–86* 96 The Shetimasha, the language of which is known from a vocabulary to be totally distinct..from the Na'htchi. *Ibid.* 97 The missionary..affirmed the affinity of the Taensa language to that of the Na'htchi... The Taensa language is considered to be a branch of the Na'htchi. **1949** M. MEAD *Male & Female* 396 This was done..by certain women in Natchez Indian society. **1959** E. TUNIS *Indians* 82/2 The Natchez were Muskhogeans who lived on the Mississippi River. **1965** *Canad. Jrnl. Ling.* Spring 99 An 'Eastern Group' comprising Siouan-Yuchi and Natchez-Muskogian. *Ibid.* 145 My Natchez informant..told about the great removal.

nation, *sb.*[1] Add: **4. b.** *two nations*: phr. used of two groups within a given nation divided from each other by marked social inequality; hence *one nation*, a nation which is not divided by social inequalities.

1845 DISRAELI (*title*) Sybil, or The two nations. *Ibid.* I. II. v. 149 Two nations; between whom there is no intercourse and no sympathy; who are..ignorant of each other's habits, thoughts, and feelings..; who are formed by different breeding, are fed by different food,.. and are not governed by the same laws... The Rich and the Poor. **1892** *Youth's Compan.* 8 Sept. 446/1 (*heading*) Salute to the Flag... I pledge allegiance to my Flag and the Republic for which it stands: one Nation indivisible, with Liberty and Justice for all. **1971** *Guardian* 19 Nov. 12/2 There are two nations now within schools... Social inequality is growing. **1973** *Times* 15 Oct. 17/6 The Disraelian doctrine of 'One Nation' has..been in the past little more than an ideal or a pretence. **1974** *Times* 16 Oct. 14/6 God bless the squire and his relations; full speed astern to the Two Nations.

5. d. (Earlier examples.)

1650 *Archives of Maryland* (1883) I. 260 The Ports adjoyning are very much pestered with great Concourse of

Indians of several nations. **1709** J. LAWSON *New Voy. Carolina* 199 Two Nations of Indians here in Carolina were at war together. **1722** D. COXE *Descr. Carolana* iv. 49 Near the Bottom of the Bay..is the fair River of the Miamihas (so call'd because upon it lives Part of a Nation bearing the same Name). **1740** in *South Carolina Hist. Soc. Coll.* (1887) IV. 83, I desire also that you will send me..the Indian presents, with power to distribute them, for much Depends on the Nations.

9. *attrib.* and *Comb.* (see also sense 1 a *ad fin.*), as **nation-building,** the creation of a new nation, *spec.* a newly independent nation; hence **nation-builder; nation-state,** a sovereign state the members of which are also united by those ties such as language, common descent, etc., which constitute a nation; **nation-wide** *a.*, as wide as a nation; extending over, reaching, or affecting the whole nation; also as *adv.*

1907 *Collier's* 12 Jan. 7/2 Next week's issue will be our annual Automobile Number, and, in addition to general news and illustrations concerning the modern vehicle, it will give some lucid arguments for the automobile as a nation-builder. **1920** N. M. BUTLER *Is Amer. Worth Saving?* xvi. 285 (*heading*) Alexander Hamilton, nation-builder. **1933** P. S. CLEARY (*title*) Australia's debt to Irish nation-builders. **1967** *Freedomways* VII. 167 These are the new lessons in old African history that are giving many present-day African nation builders a new consciousness of past achievements. **1913** N. M. BUTLER in *Educational Rev.* (N.Y.) Apr. 405 These six men are.. the moving forces of the constructive nation-building of the American people. *Ibid.* 406 The most prominent in the galaxy of our nation-building heroes. **1928** *Daily Tel.* 4 Sept. 10/4 For such an enterprise of nation-building peace..is the essential condition. **1931** *Economist* 7 Mar. 486/1 One of the urgent needs of India is that the Provinces should have funds available for so-called 'nation building' services. **1971** *Sunday Nation* (Nairobi) 11 Apr. 3/2 The Ambassador advised the students to study hard and return home after graduating to play their part in nation-building. **1973** *Express* (Trinidad & Tobago) 7 Apr. 12/4 Unless we are prepared to..rid ourselves of our petty differences and general smallmindedness, we are not ready for nation building. **1918** J. A. R. MARRIOTT *European Commonwealth* ii. 18 The ultimate genesis of the world conflict of to-day is sought..in..the existing European polity..based upon the recognition of the rights of a large number of Nation-States, entirely independent and nominally coequal. **1935** HUXLEY & HADDON *We Europeans* i. 11 The nation-state is a modern conception and product, the result of certain peculiar social and economic circumstances. *Ibid.* vi. 187 With the sixteenth century, nation-states of the modern type began to appear. **1945** H. KOHN *Idea of Nationalism* i. 19 Nationalism demands the nation-state; the creation of the nation-state strengthens nationalism. **1950** THEIMER & CAMPBELL *Encycl. World Politics* 301/2 Absolutism paved the way for the modern nation-state marked by sovereignty and the repudiation of any superior authority. **1959** *Encounter* July 75/1 Egypt is turning into a modern nation-state. **1971** *Black Scholar* June 29/1 As the cultural revolution and students become more politically sophisticated, the question of an independent black nation-state will become a popular demand. **1973** *Listener* 10 May 616/1 The nation state requires the idea of an entity along with other entities that are equal. **1915** *Munsey's Mag.* May 708/2 The nation-wide primary is coming. **1925** E. S. JONES *Christ of Indian Road* iii. 72 A year ago began a struggle in South India that has had nation-wide consequences. **1928** *Daily Express* 27 Apr. 1 In deciding to publish this most moving..narrative the 'Daily Express' embarks on a venture which will command nation-wide attention. **1958** *Economist* 1 Nov. 413/1 The one real issue of nation-wide importance which this campaign has produced concerns the trade unions. **1960** *Farmer & Stockbreeder* 15 Mar. 72/1 Perhaps F.M.C. could have done more if it hadn't started off on so wide a scale—nation-wide in fact. **1972** *Daily Tel.* 21 Jan. 1/7 Mr. Ian Smith, the Rhodesian Prime Minister, is to make a nationwide broadcast today. **1975** *Lamp* (Exxon Corporation) Winter 3/2 Now being telecast nationwide..each of these television messages pays tribute to an outstanding man or woman.

nation, *adv.*, *a.*, and *sb.*[2] Add: **A.** *adv.* (Earlier and later examples.)

1771 *Trial of Atticus* 26 He is a nation bawdy creature to talk. **1884** 'MARK TWAIN' *Huck. Finn* xix. 186 Looky here, Bilgewater,..I'm nation sorry for you, but you ain't the only person that's had troubles like that.

B. *adj.* (Earlier and later examples.)

1765 in Bartlett *Dict. Amer.* (1877) (ed. 4) 419, I believe, my friend, you're very right, They'll get a nation profit by it. **1962** A. JOBSON *Window in Suffolk* vi. 100 What a nation fule he wur tew be shure.

C. *sb.* (U.S. examples.)

1775 *Yankee Doodle* in O. E. Winslow *Amer. Broadside Verse* (1930) 141/1 A swamping gun..makes a noise like father's gun, Only a nation louder. **1880** *News & Press* (Cimarron, New Mexico) 23 Dec. 1/7 'Well, I've got the g.b.' 'The geebee, Thomas! What in the nation is that?' 'I've got the grand bounce.' **1884** 'MARK TWAIN' *Huck. Finn* xiii. 113 Why, how in the nation did they ever git into such a scrape? **1918** J. C. LINCOLN *Shavings* 213 Now how in the nation did I get it Wood?

national, *a.* and *sb.* Add: **A.** *adj.* **1.** (Further examples.)

1743 BOLINGBROKE *Remarks Hist. Eng.* (1780) ii. 28 A Spirit of Liberty will be always and wholly concern'd about national Interests. **1914** G. B. SHAW *Dark Lady of Sonnets* 132 The very stupid people who cannot see that a National Theatre is worth having for the sake of the National Soul. **1927** 'A. HOPE' *Memories & Notes* xiv. 239, I went to Boston in company with Peter Dunne, whose 'Mr. Dooley' had already made him what the papers in the States call a 'national figure'. **1931** *Hansard Commons* 28 July 2217, I should take no exception to a small sum towards the preservation of such things as Hadrian's Wall and the other national monuments. *c* **1935** E. E. CUMMINGS *Let.* 7 Jan. (1969) 134 Here lies a national hero (Who governed by fits and by starts). **1939** *Hansard Commons* 2 Sept. 232 In the national interest, having in mind the great inroads that war must..make on the youth of our nation, we should see.. that some of our youth are left to carry on in the future. **1966** TACHERON & UDALL *Job of Congressman* vii. 198 And then, you see, some of your friends back home say, 'Why, he is becoming a national figure.' **1966** *Oxf. Compan. Amer. Hist.* 560/1 National monuments include buildings, statues, homesteads, battlefields, cemeteries, and sites of historic, scenic, or political significance. **1969** PLANO & OLTON *Internat. Relations Dict.* vi. 128 When a state bases its foreign policy solely on the bedrock of national interest with little or no concern for universal moral principles, it can be described as pursuing a realistic in contradistinction to an idealistic policy. **1973** *Times* 17 Dec. 15/3 The NUM..cannot be totally indifferent to the national interest. **1973** *N.Y. Times* 22 June 35 One of the most successful codebreaking organizations of those post-war years was the National Security Agency. **1975** *Atlantic Monthly* Jan. 32/2 The Department of Defense could give no adequate definition of 'national security'.

d. Designating a B.B.C. radio service which operated during the 1930s. Also *ellipt.*

1931 *Daily Express* 22 Sept. 13/3 Tonight..on the National begin..the new poetry readings. **1938** W. GOATMAN *By-Ways of B.B.C.* viii. 81 Control-Room engineers are responsible..for controlling three separate programmes—National, Regional, and Empire. **1956** B. PAULU *Brit. Broadcasting* vii. 145 From 1930 to the outbreak of World War II, there was the National Service, uniform throughout the country, consisting mainly of London programs of national appeal. **1965** A. BRIGGS *Golden Age of Wireless* 36 By 1934..there was more light entertainment on the National than on the Regional service. **1971** D. G. BRIDSON *Prospero & Ariel* viii. 177 Back in the thirties, there had been two nation-wide broadcast programmes, the National and the Regional.

e. In the war of 1939–45 used to designate foodstuffs made to official specifications for nation-wide distribution, as *national flour, loaf*, etc.

1940 *Hansard Commons* 25 Jan. 810/2 All butter sold by the Ministry of Food is..described as 'National Butter'. **1941** *New Statesman* 16 Apr. 157 The bakers are equally reluctant to change their habits. They shake their heads with a mournful smile at mention of the national loaf. **1941** *Lancet* 15 Nov. 605/1 When the Medical Research Council drew up its second memorandum on national flour in the spring of 1941 it offered the nation something new. **1943** *Daily Tel.* 20 Dec. 3 National Milk-Cocoa—the new food drink evolved by the Ministry's scientific advisers—is already available to all factories and industrial undertakings in limited quantities. **1945** *ABC of Cookery* (Ministry of Food) vi. 20 National Household Milk is dried skim milk. *Ibid.* xix. 69 The best foods for iron are liver, eggs,..national or wholemeal bread and oatmeal. **1956** W. THOMPSON *Time off my Life* xix. 146, I couldn't stand the stuff they called 'national loaf' in the war.

2. spec. *national football* (Austral.) = **Australian rules*; *national game* (see quots.).

In quots. 1930 and 1963 the game is two-up.

1828 *Oscotian* (ed. 2) I. 35 The day or two previous.. gave employment for our youth, in adjusting the arrangements, necessary for the noble and national game, of Cricket. **1869** W. G. BEERS (*title*) Lacrosse: the national game of Canada. **19..** *Primer Austral. Football* (Austral. National Football Council) 1 Youngsters who are keen to learn and understand the fundamentals of their National Football. **1912** HILTON & SMITH *Royal & Anc. Game of Golf* 34 The Scots themselves have yielded to the softening influences of the South..and the change is reflected in their national game. **1930** L. W. LOWER *Here's Luck* 70 He had a small piece of wood in his hand, on which were balanced two pennies. The national game was in progress. **1958** National football [see **Australian rules*]. **1963** F. HARDY *Legends from Benson's Valley* 108 The demise of the bookmakers increased attendance at the Sunday sessions of Australia's national game.

5. National Assistance, a form of welfare payment combining Unemployment Assistance and Public Assistance, begun in 1948, administered by the **National Assistance Board,** and replaced in 1965 by Supplementary Benefits; **national bank** (earlier example); **national cake** (see *CAKE *sb.* 7 b); **national character,** personality or cultural characteristics which seem to be wide-spread enough in a particular nation or racial group for generalizations to be made concerning either the whole group or individuals belonging to it; so **national characteristic; National Front,** a political group in Britain with extreme reactionary views; **National Government,** a coalition government, esp. one in which party differences are subordinated to the national interest in times of crisis; also in the sense of a government free from external domination (see quot. 1943); **national guard** (further examples); also (with capitals), in the United States, a militia force which may be used by its own state, e.g. for law enforcement, or by the Federal government as part of the U.S. army; **national health,** health as it concerns the nation as a whole; **National Health Service,** the comprehensive health service provided in Great Britain, initiated in 1946 and financed by taxation; freq. *ellipt.* as *National Health*; **National Hunt Committee,** the body which controls steeplechasing and hurdle-racing in Great Britain; freq. *ellipt.* and *attrib.* as *National Hunt*; **national income:** see *INCOME *sb.*[1] 6 a; **National Insurance** = *INSURANCE 4 e; also *attrib.*; **National Mark,** a mark designating grade for use on British agricultural produce; also *attrib.*; **national minority,** a minority group, belonging historically to another nationality, which feels itself or is felt to be culturally or racially separate from the majority in a country; **national park** = PARK *sb.* 2 b; **national product,** the monetary value of all goods and services produced in a country in one year; cf. *gross national product* (s.v. *GROSS *a.* and *sb.*[4] A. 6 c); **National Savings,** a method of saving through investment in British Government securities, started in the war of 1914–18 as National War Savings; also applied to similar schemes in other countries; so *National Savings Certificate*, etc.; **national school,** a school provided for under a system of state-aided education, esp. one of the type set up in Ireland after 1831 under the National System of Education; **national service,** a statutory obligation to serve in the armed forces for a specified period; hence **national serviceman,** one who is performing national service; **National Socialism,** the name adopted by Adolf Hitler for his doctrines of nationalism, racial purity, anti-Communism, and the all-powerful role of the State; so **National Socialist,** a member of the National Socialist Workers' Party led by Adolf Hitler after 1920; = *NAZI *sb.*; also *attrib.*, of or pertaining to this party or to the doctrines of National Socialism; **national theatre** (freq. with capital initials), a theatre endowed by the State; also ellipt., *the National*; **National Trust,** a trust for the preservation of places of historic interest or natural beauty in England, Wales, and N. Ireland, founded in 1893, incorporated in 1907, and supported by endowment and private subscription. Also *NATIONAL GRID.

1948 *Act 11 & 12 Geo. VI* c. 29 §2 (*title*) National Assistance Act, 1948. *Ibid.*, The National Assistance Board (hereafter in this Act referred to as 'the Board') shall exercise their functions in such manner as shall best promote the welfare of persons affected by the exercise thereof. **1958** *New Statesman* 27 Sept. 398/3 Few people are at a worse disadvantage than the man who is fresh from prison and is also homeless. National Assistance methods..must sometimes seem designed to assist such a man back into prison in the shortest possible time. **1959** J. BRAINE *Vodi* viii. 124 There isn't any dole for him. It's bankruptcy first and then National Assistance. **1968** J. LOCK *Lady Policeman* xviii. 152 The National Assistance Board telephoned. **1969** *Listener* 12 June 834/3 The women he has studied are the very poorest, depending almost entirely on National Assistance. **1838** *Democratic Rev.* I. 52 That portion of the plan.. which involved a present non-committalism on the question of a National Bank. **1778** National character [in Dict., sense A. 2]. **1863** *Home & Foreign Rev.* III. 549 Next to those who form the national taste and fix the national character, the greatest geniuses are those who corrupt them. **1908** KIPLING *Lett. of Travel* (1920) 144 'Hustle' does not sit well on the national character. **1967** M. ARGYLE *Psychol. Interpersonal Behaviour* iv. 82 If the people from some cultural group are consistently aggressive, [etc.].., we *can* say that their norms are different; but it may be more useful to say that their level of motivation is different, and to regard this as a feature of their 'national character'. **1960** DUIJKER & FRIJDA *National Character* i. 4 The existence of a stereotype might give rise to a national characteristic. **1967** *Spearhead* Nov.–Dec. 6 (*caption*) On October 7th there took place..an event which may well prove to have historic significance in British politics. This was the first Annual General Meeting of Britain's new party, The National Front. *c* **1970** *Facts: National Front* 2/3 When the National Front comes to power it will know well how to deal with the murderer and the thug. **1973** C. MULLARD *Black Brit.* III. viii. 91 White fascist groups like the National Front are lumped together with progressive, power-demanding groups like the Black People's Alliance. **1931** J. REITH *Diary* 24 Aug. (1975) i. 106 A wire..informed me that the Labour government had resigned, that MacDonald was prime minister of a National government. **1931** *Economist* 17 Oct. 692/1 Sir John Simon..stated that..'if the broad base National Government finds it [*sc.* a tariff] necessary, I am not going on that ground to refuse to support the National Government.' **1936** J. A. SPENDER *Gt. Brit.: Empire & Commonwealth* IV. xliii. 512 National Government [in 1915] was the logical corollary of the party-truce. **1943** *Ann. Reg. 1942* 143 With the security of India threatened, we.. should bring her people into full moral support..by conceding forthwith the demands for a 'National Government', with virtual independence of British authority.

1969 T. A. Neal *Democracy & Responsibility* xviii. 223 Strong arguments may be marshalled to explain MacDonald's formation of the National Government. *Ibid.* xix. 230 In November of the same year [*sc.* 1935], the National Government was re-elected, with a total of 428 supporters in the House of Commons. **1793** *Observer* 27 Jan. in M. Miliband *Observer of 19th Cent.* (1966) i. 4 The train moved on with a slow pace from the Temple to the Boulevards, which were planted with cannon, and beset with National Guards, drums beating, trumpets sounding, and colours flying. **1847** *Santa Fé* (New Mexico) *Republican* 18 Dec. 3/1 Some National Guards that were at San Antonio had a small fight. **1868** *N.Y. Herald* 4 July 6/1 The First division of the National Guard will parade. **1909** *World Today* Oct. 1099 While many of the American states designate their amateur soldiery as 'National Guards', the venerable Bay State still sticks to the thoroughly Yankee caption of 'militia'. **1966** *Oxf. Compan. Amer. Hist.* 530/1 *Militia*, now officially termed the National Guard in the U.S., is the body of armed forces within the states, formed by enlistments. **1973** *Freedomways* XIII. 14 The forces of state power (the police, the army, the National Guard) will be used. **1908** *National Health* I. 1. 18/2 (*heading*) The Women's National Health Association of Great Britain. **1911** Lloyd George *Insurance of the People* 2 A few weeks ago I had the honour of introducing in the House of Commons a measure dealing with proposals for securing the national health. **1935** *Economist* 7 Sept. 456/2 The most important event..in the field of health during the reign was the creation of the scheme of National Health Insurance in 1912. **1946** *Act* 9 & 10 *Geo. VI* c. 81 (*title*) National Health Service Act. **1952** A. Christie *Mrs McGinty's Dead* xii. 96 Nowadays even if you've got a chilblain you run to the doctor with it so as to get your money's worth out of the National Health. **1958** J. Cannan *And be a Villain* i. 23 A doctor w'at was too taken up by 'is posh paying patients to trouble with a National 'Ealth kid. **1958** R. Graves in *Times Lit. Suppl.* 15 Aug. p. x/5 What is even worse, any slight mania or differentiating oddness..they now take along to the National Health psychiatrist, pleading to be de-thinged. **1958** *Listener* 30 Oct. 699/2 The workings of the National Health Service. **1966** J. S. Cox *Illustr. Dict. Hairdressing* 102/1 *National Health wig*, a wig or other similar postiche of necessity supplied by a Wigmaker for a client whose health is said to be affected by lack of hair, to the order of the Ministry of Health. **1967** M. Argyle *Psychol. Interpersonal Behaviour* ix. 174 This [*sc.* counselling] is the most widely practised kind of psychotherapy—it is given by National Health Service psychiatrists in England. **1967** *Melody Maker* 27 May 5 With his bushy sideboards and National Health specs he resembled an animated Victorian watchmaker. **1973** J. Porter *It's Murder with Dover* ii. 13 Gritting his National Health teeth, [he] limped off. **1866** C., J., & E. Weatherby *Racing Calendar for 1866. Races Past* p. vi, Advertisements and reports of Steeple Chases under the Grand National Hunt Rules are included in the Sheet Calendar. **1873** C., J., E., & J. P. Weatherby *Racing Calendar, Steeple Chases Past, for Season 1872–73* p. xiii, Any person running a horse in contravention of this Rule shall (at the discretion of the Grand National Hunt Committee) be disqualified from ever running a horse where these rules are in force. *Ibid.* p. xxv, The following form of certificate is that approved by the National Hunt Committee. **1898** A. E. T. Watson *Turf* ix. 173 Horses are usually put to jumping because for some reason or another their career on the flat has ceased to look promising, it having been so continually proved that failures under Jockey Club Rules were brilliant successes under the Rules of the National Hunt. **1902** *Encycl. Brit.* XXIX. 333/1 None other than thoroughbred horses are nowadays ever found in races run under the rules of the National Hunt Committee, the body which governs the sport of steeplechasing. **1935** *Encycl. Sports* 590/1 National Hunt Rules fix the opening of the steeplechasing season as July 1. **1963** Bloodgood & Santini *Horseman's Dict.* 152 *Point-to-point*, cross-country race for qualified hunters..ridden by amateurs..over a flagged natural hunting country; under the jurisdiction of the National Hunt (England). **1967** *Everyman's Encycl.* VI. 482/2 In 1866, as a result of the efforts of Lord Suffolk, Lord Coventry and the duke of Beaufort, the National Hunt Committee was formed as the authoritative governing body over steeplechasing. **1975** *Oxf. Compan. Sports & Games* 496/1 Over the years, the National Hunt season has gradually become longer, and the 1973–4 season began early in August and will end on 1 June. **1878** Blackley in *19th Cent.* Nov. 834 (*title*) National Insurance: A cheap, practical and popular means of abolishing poor rates. **1911** National insurance [see *insurance 4 e]. **1913** *Q. Rev.* Apr. 510 The labourer has gained something in a pecuniary sense from..national insurance. **1922** *Encycl. Brit.* XXX. 998/2 A few doctors..had started a new organization in opposition to the British Medical Association, called the National Insurance Practitioners Association. **1931** *Times Lit. Suppl.* 20 Aug. 626/3 The indebtedness of the national insurance fund has already risen. **1967** E. Rudinger *Wills & Probate* 60 Matthew's father-in-law had also been receiving the state old age pension, or national insurance retirement pension, as it is properly called. **1968** *Brit. Med. Bull.* XXIV. 207/1 National Insurance records giving the dates on which patients left and returned to work. **1973** *Times* 13 Jan. 19/7 The National Insurance Scheme covers benefits payable by the State (through the Department of Health and Social Security) and covers pensions, widows' benefits, maternity benefits and sickness and unemployment benefits, together with certain minor benefits. **1928** *Times* 8 Aug. 12/3 The Minister of Agriculture and Fisheries has appointed a Committee, to be known as the National Mark Committee,..empowered to authorize the use of grade designation marks. *Ibid.*, An artistic and striking 'National Mark' has been designed,..a silhouette map of South Britain with a circle inset bearing the words around the margin, 'Produce of England and Wales'. **1929** *Daily Express* 7 Nov. 3/4 There has been a greatly increased demand for British beef since the National Mark scheme was introduced. **1931** *Times* 17 Nov. (Suppl.) p. xiv/1 One mark, the National Mark, which is a trade mark registered in the name of the Minister of Agriculture, is being used for all graded produce of England and Wales. **1934** *Daily Tel.* 31 Dec. 14/4 The National Mark Scheme began eight years ago to encourage home producers. **1937** *Food Manufacture* Oct. 340 The National Mark Scheme for Fruit Products..has now been extended to include..fruit juices. **1921** R. W. Seton-Watson in H. W. V. Temperley *Hist. Peace Conf. Paris* IV. 266 National minorities shall enjoy equal rights. **1934** C. A. Macartney (*title*) National states and national minorities. **1945** E. E. Brooke tr. *Azcárate y Florez's League of Nations* p. vii, When those responsible for reconstructing Europe find themselves once again confronted by the difficulties which national minorities have created in the past. **1970** V. Van Dyke *Human Rights, U.S. & World Community* ii. v. 98 A recognition of 'the right of members of national minorities to carry on their own educational activities'. **1868** J. D. Whitney *Yosemite Bk.* i 22 The Yosemite Valley..has been made a National public park and placed under the charge of the State of California. **1871** [see Park *sb.* 2 b]. **1872** *Publ. Colonial Soc. Mass.* VIII. 377 Congress, by an Act approved March 1, 1872, has set apart a tract of land near the head-waters of the Yellowstone River... The reservation so set apart is to be known as the 'Yellowstone National Park'. **1903** [see Park *sb.* 2 b]. **1933** *Discovery* Feb. 68/2 The creation of the great American national parks..has saved the bison from extinction. **1949** *Act* 12 & 13 *Geo. VI* c. 97 An Act to make provision for National Parks and the establishment of a National Parks Commission. **1950** R. N. Hutchins *National Parks & Access to Countryside Act* 1. i. 3 New Zealand..has 10 National Parks and over 200 reserves and public domains. *Ibid.*, In England and Wales, the designation of a National Park will not affect the ownership of the land,..nor will any additional facilities for public access be made available merely by such definition. **1962** *Listener* 1 Mar. 373/1 The Planning Board or committee in charge of a national park has a statutory duty..to 'preserve and enhance' the natural beauty of the landscape. **1974** *Times* 1 Apr. (Yorkshire & Humberside Suppl.) p. ix/1 Within reasonable driving distance of the Humber the choice lies between three national parks, a noble sprinkling of country estates and several attractive cathedral cities. **1945** S. Kuznets *National Product in Wartime* 1. ii. 7 Estimates of peacetime national product assume that economic activity is to produce goods to satisfy ultimate consumers; that production is for man, not man for production. **1962** *Listener* 20 Dec. 1041/1 The French national product rose at a rate of no less than 8 per cent. a year. **1964** Gould & Kolb *Dict. Social Sci.* 454/1 If a series of national product estimates for several years is divided by a price index, each year's national product being divided by the price index for that year, the resulting series is known as *deflated* or *real* national product. [**1917** (*title*) National War Savings Committee... First annual report, in *Parl. Papers 1917–18* (Cd. 8516) XVIII. 703.] **1919** *Saving* 3 Dec. 138/2 The Model Schemes suggested by the National Savings Committee are of various forms. **1922** *Encycl. Brit.* XXXI. 369/2 The system of linking up National Savings certificates with local finance becomes, in effect, a national credit bank spread over the whole country. **1932** *Discovery* Nov. 374/2 The much abused Post Office ..has actually allowed it [*sc.* the Institute of Industrial Psychology] to redesign the National Savings Certificate. **1941** *Picture Post* 3 May 35/3 Buy National Savings Stamps—they cost 6d. and 2/6 each...When you have the right amount you convert them into National Savings Certificates—15/- each. **1964** A. Wykes *Gambling* x. 238 Offering a lottery ticket worth one mark..for every eight marks deposited in national-savings accounts. **1972** *Times* 21 Nov. 19/6 Historically national savings have been treated as a poor relation to other investment media. **1838** *Digest Evidence before Comm. Houses Lords & Commons, 1837, on National Syst. Educ. Ireland* ii. 25 She was highly gratified; indeed she was astonished; she could not have believed that in the national school the Bible was used at all. **1966** *New Statesman* 27 May 774/3 But certain schools, to be called perhaps National Schools, should be placed directly under the Department of Education. **1968** T. Kinsella *Nightwalker* 65 But the authorities Used the National Schools to try to conquer The Irish national spirit. **1972** M. E. Collins *Ireland Three* vi. 49 The National Schools were free, but not compulsory... The National Schools, though in theory of mixed religion, were in practice, separate, and children of each religion went to their own schools. **1916** R. Fry *Let.* 25 Jan. (1972) II. 393, I don't think Ha talked to me of national service. **1916** *Hansard Commons* 19 Dec. 1352 It is proposed to appoint at once a director of National Service, to be in charge of both the military and civil side of universal national service. **1939** *Ibid.* 2 Sept. 240 National Service (armed forces) Bill, 'to make provision for securing and controlling the enlistment of men for services in the armed forces of the Crown; and for purposes connected with the matter aforesaid', presented, accordingly, read the First time; and ordered to be printed. **1940** *Ann. Reg. 1939* 397 The National Service (Armed Forces) Act, which rendered liable for service in the forces all male persons between eighteen and forty-one. **1940** H. G. Wells *Babes in Darkling Wood* 1. i. 21 Romeo and Juliet weren't called on for national service. **1942** G. G. Slack *Liability for National Service* 1. i. 1 The Government powers of control over persons are, in relation to their liability for National Service, exercised by the Minister of Labour. **1944** J. S. Huxley *On Living in Revolution* 21 It is both probable and desirable that some form of National Service will continue after the war is over. **1958** M. Kerr *People of Ship Street* iii. 29 The boys in between 18 and 20 are of course doing National Service. **1970** M. Moorcock *Chinese Agent* xiii. 87 He had avoided being called up for his National Service for two years and, when he had been called up, he'd managed to desert. **1949** *Times* 20 Oct. 5/5 The Secretary of State for War gave an assurance that no national service man would be posted to the Far East with less than 18 weeks' service. **1957** *B.B.C. Handbk.* 170 British National Servicemen. **1957** C. Hunt *Guide to Communist Jargon* vii. 19 Those who have taken up soldiering as a profession as opposed to National Servicemen, who have not. **1973** D. Lees *Rape of Quiet Town* vii. 113 A number of former national service men who had never heard a shot fired in anger. **1931** *Times Lit. Suppl.* 16 Apr. 296/3 Such is the doctrine, not inaptly named National Socialism, which by uniting Moscow and Paris in a common anathema has appealed at once to the quiet steady man and to the boisterous patriot. **1933** J. J. Bronowski in *Granta* 19 Apr. 358/2 National Socialism pictures itself as persecuted, not only by the political world but by art, science and philosophy. **1923** *Times* 23 Aug. 9/6 At the conclusion of a National Socialist meeting last night Herr Hitler's storm troops..attempted to march through Munich. **1931** *Daily Tel.* 21 May 13/1 The National-Socialists (Hitlerites) are now definitely committed to a Hohenzollern restoration. **1933** J. J. Bronowski in *Granta* 19 Apr. 358/1 The National Socialist revolution in Germany is most deeply founded, has its most bigoted and best organised support in the German universities. **1942** E. Barker *Reflections on Govt.* xiii. 369 We have here the ultimate roots of the National Socialist doctrines of the Leader and the Folk which he leads and expresses. **1942** L. B. Namier *Conflicts* 40 The depression..everywhere brought new political forces to the surface, violent and brutal—National Socialists and National Radicals. **1967** D. Eisenberg *Re-emergence Fascism* i. 59 The judge..hit out at Colin Jordan's National Socialist movement. **1973** *Black Panther* 27 Oct. 8/3 On another occasion the National Socialist Party, also known as the 'White People's Party', passed out literature in front of her house pledging to 'get rid of all the niggers'. **1889** G. B. Shaw *London Music 1888–89* (1937) 150 Miss Reimers..upset even my gravity..by asking me..why the splendid, the intellectual, the free English people had no national theatre. **1901** Beerbohm *Around Theatres* (1924) I. 245 The offer made (or *not* made) by Mr. Carnegie to endow with us a national theatre has duly revived that periodic cry to which I have alluded. **1928** G. Hughes *Story of Theatre* xiv. 215 The Burgtheater [in Vienna]..had been founded in 1741 as a Court Theatre..and changed in 1776..into a National Theatre (in imitation of the Comédie Française). **1961** E. Waugh *Unconditional Surrender* 306 The foundation stone was solemnly laid for a National Theatre. **1972** *Listener* 18 May 644/3 The new National Theatre rising on the South Bank. Until the coming of the National, the British theatre had survived..without the alien office of dramaturgs. **1974** *Country Life* 24 Jan. 125 The National has been running successfully for ten years and plays generally to good houses. **1893** *Times* 17 Nov. 9/6 'The National Trust for Places of Historic Interest or Natural Beauty' is an association which held its first meeting yesterday. **1894** *Spectator* 7 July 12/2 Men who love their glens and their hill-tops..would far rather see them go to the National Trust than be put up to auction. **1896** O. Hill *Let.* 26 Oct. in C. E. Maurice *Life O. Hill* (1913) x. 538, I suppose you do not happen to know any gentleman likely to do for, and accept, our National Trust secretaryship? **1907** *Hansard Commons* 21 Aug. 758 The following Bills received the Royal Assent:—..14. National Trust for Places of Historic Interest or Natural Beauty. **1930** J. S. Huxley *Bird-Watching* vi. 115 And he [*sc.* the bird-lover] can help by supporting such bodies as the National Trust and the Royal Society for the Protection of Birds, which are saving wild bits of country from being built over or otherwise developed, or reserving them as actual sanctuaries, inviolate to the birds. **1934** *N. & Q.* 16 June 415/2 East Riddlesden Hall..has just been publicly handed over to the National Trust. **1938** D. Garnett in T. E. Lawrence *Lett.* 873 His cottage at Clouds Hill now belongs to the National Trust. **1958** *Listener* 9 Oct. 556/2 On the preservation of historic buildings many voices must obviously be heard:..art-historians and archivists, the National Trust. **1971** P. Gresswell *Environment* 166 The National Trust..was founded..by Octavia Hill, Sir Robert Hunter and Canon Rawnsley.

B. *sb.* **4. b.** (See quot. 1904.)

1904 J. Westlake *Internat. Law* I. 3 All the members of a state, whether sovereign, subjects or citizens, are denoted by the convenient name of its nationals. **1929** *Times* 31 Jan., The official thanks of the German Government..for the rescue by aeroplane of their nationals in Kabul. **1931** *Times* 22 Sept. 7/4 There is no evidence of any substantial export of capital by British nationals. **1953** *Stroud's Judicial Dict.* (ed. 3) III. 1855 In English courts phrases which refer to the national law of a propositus are prima facie to be construed not as referring to the law which the courts of that country would apply in the case of its own nationals domiciled in its own country with regard..to property in its own country. **1955** *Times* 3 June 6/2 The two Governments have agreed to take measures for the conclusion of a treaty for the purpose of settling questions of citizenship, and with regard to the repatriation of nationals of one contracting party residing in the territory of the other party. **1969** Plano & Olton *Internat. Relations Dict.* xi. 266 *Statelessness*, the condition of an individual who is not recognized by any state as one of its nationals.

5. = *Grand National*: see *grand *a.* 12.

1909 *Westm. Gaz.* 26 Mar. 12/1 A horse that had never run a National. **1931** *Times* 12 Mar. 5/1 Several National horses have been entered at Hurst Park. **1972** L. P. Davies *What did I do Tomorrow?* ii. 26 The only time he backed horses was for the Derby or the National.

6. A national as opposed to a local newspaper; usu. *pl.*

1938 C. Hunt *You want to be a Journalist?* iii. 29 It is when staff increase—on county papers, dailies published from the great cities, London nationals—that specialisation develops. **1960** H. L. Lawrence *Children of Light* v. 68 Some of the nationals had rushed their own men to Keniston, but a flattering number had wired Johnny for coverage. *a***1966** M. Allingham *Cargo of Eagles* (1968) i. 19 She must have sold the idea to the local papers because the nationals picked it up a year or two back. **1966** *Listener* 28 July 129/3 In thirty years' time there could probably be only four nationals left. **1973** J. Porter *It's Murder with Dover* iv. 36 We'll make the front page of the nationals with this!

national grid. [f. National *a.* + Grid.]

1. The grid (sense *8) that interconnects the major power stations and distribution centres in Great Britain; any similar grid in another country. Also *transf.*

1930 *Times* 22 Mar. 19/2 There will be no great rush of new business consequent on the completion of the national 'Grid' system, as was contemplated in some quarters. **1943** [see *GRID 8 b]. **1955** [see *GRID 8 a]. **1967** *Times* 13 Dec. 4/2 Mr. Wilson had said that comparative calculations were not possible for the gas industry, because there was not yet an equivalent of the national grid.

2. The metric co-ordinate system and reference grid used by the Ordnance Survey and printed on its maps, having a false origin west of the Isles of Scilly and a true origin at 2°W., 49°N.

1938 *Final Rep. Dept. Comm. Ordnance Survey* (Ministry of Agric. & Fisheries) 4 We recommend that a National grid should be super-imposed on all large-scale plans, and on smaller scale maps, to provide one reference system for the maps of the whole of the country. **1952** *Proc. Prehist. Soc.* XVIII. 3 The National Grid position on the 6-inch map Sheet XLIV, N.W. is 832642. **1963** *Atlas of Britain* (Clarendon Press) map 1 The National Grid is used in this Atlas with the sanction of the Director General, Ordnance Survey and of H.M. Stationery Office; the Irish Grid is used with the sanction of the Ordnance Survey of Northern Ireland. **1969** C. B. M. LOCK *Mod. Maps & Atlases* i. 32 The Ordnance Survey maps are now prepared on the Transverse Mercator, which enables the National Grid reference system to be easily operated. **1971** *Nature* 5 Feb. 375/1 A combination of these two surveys showed that before 1900 forty-four species..occurred in only one or two 10 km squares of the national grid; by 1930 the number was fifty-nine species.

nationali·stically, *adv.* [f. NATIONALISTIC *a.*: see -ICALLY.] In a nationalistic manner; on nationalistic lines.

1913 H. W. ROBINSON *Relig. Ideas Old Testament* 32 The redemption is differently conceived and nationalistically applied. **1924** *These Eventful Years* (Encycl. Brit.) II. 126 The nationalist problem is renewing itself in the succession states, which are nationalistically as varied as was Old Austria. **1951** *Current Hist.* Sept. 141/2 The nationalistically minded Japanese might be easily made to believe that all the West has done in Japan in the past is nothing but a plot to use the Japanese for its own purposes.

nationality. 3. Add to def.: *spec.* a legal relationship between a state and an individual involving reciprocal rights and duties. Also with reference to the legal device by which ships, aircraft, and companies acquire the protection of the state in which they are registered.

1880 W. E. HALL *Internat. Law* II. v. 188 The more important states recognise..that the child of a foreigner ought to be allowed to be himself a foreigner, unless he manifests a wish to assume or retain the nationality of the state in which he has been born. **1907** L. A. ATHERLEY-JONES *Commerce in War* vi. 345 Every merchant vessel is expected to carry on board some official documents vouching for her nationality. **1928** E. M. BORCHARD *Diplomatic Protection of Citizens Abroad* iii. 555 With the rise of the modern state in Europe..nationality became the test of civil and political status. **1961** N. BAR-YAACOV *Dual Nationality* 3 Having wide discretion to formulate their nationality laws according to their own interests, States adopt different methods for acquisition of nationality, the result being that two States may simultaneously confer their nationality on the same individual. **1964** GOULD & KOLB *Dict. Social Sci.* 456/2 The normal way in which nationality is acquired is through birth... Nationality may also be granted to a person who is originally foreign or stateless. This process is known as naturalization.

5. Also occas., a racial or ethnic group.

1952 S. SELVON *Brighter Sun* v. 88 Whenever he saw a couple of different nationalities he used to hail out to them, and tell Stella that that was the way to live, especially in Trinidad. *Ibid.*, He used to say that all this business about colour and nationality was balls. **1964** GOULD & KOLB *Dict. Social Sci.* 244/1 In the Soviet Union, *nationalities* is more frequently applied to the diverse national-ethnic units who make up the membership of the Union. **1971** *Times* 17 Dec., 'Nationality', in the sense of citizenship of a certain state, must not be confused with 'nationality' as meaning membership of a certain nation in the sense of race.

native, *sb.* Add: **3. b.** (Later examples.)

1818 *London Guide & Stranger's Safeguard* 6 The practices of 'shouldering' passengers, on their own account—doing *the natives* out of articles of life, which they bring to town to dispose of—..bring them [*sc.* coachmen] to 'take care of things', for which there is no immediate owner. **1823** 'J. BEE' *Slang* 124 *Natives*, silly people generally; the untravelled population of any town, wrapt up in incipient simplicity are natives. **1975** D. DELMAN *One Man's Murder* ii. 46 The house, Odum Harborage, corrupted to Odum Garborage by irreverent natives, was a notable mishmash even for Long Island.

c. (Further examples.)

Sense 4 also is current in Australia (of the Aborigines). **1863** R. HENNING *Let.* 21 Sept. (1966) 141 They were natives, and a little colonial, as might be expected. They had just left school in Melbourne. **1886** [see *AUSTRALIAN]. **1895** A. B. PATERSON *Man from Snowy River* (1896) 43 They were long and wiry natives from the rugged mountain side. **1966** G. W. TURNER *Eng. Lang. Austral. & N.Z.* iii. 62 Early writers called them *natives* or *Indians*, but *Indians* fell entirely from use, and the word *natives* was required by Europeans born in Australia, who formed an Australian Natives' Association in 1871.

4. For second part of def. read: now *esp.* one belonging to a non-European race in a country in which Europeans hold political power. (Further examples.)

1896 F. C. SELOUS *Sunshine & Storm Rhodesia* i. 5 No one could have recognised..in the quiet, submissive native..the arrogant savage of old times. **1921** G. PAGE *Jill on Ranch* viii. 184 The native is a strange child, and he needs sympathetic dealing... Make a boy laugh and you can do anything with him. **1924** E. M. FORSTER *Passage to India* II. ii. 33 Whether the native swaggers or cringes, there's always something behind every remark he makes. **1931** E. O'NEILL *Mourning becomes Electra* III. ii. 238 The natives dancing naked and innocent without knowledge of sin. **1934** G. B. SHAW *On Rocks* II. 72 *Sir Bemrose*: If a Conservative Prime Minister of England may not take down a heathen native when he forgets himself there is an end of British supremacy. *Sir Arthur*: For Heaven's sake don't call him a native. You are a native. *Sir Bemrose* (*very solemnly*): Of Kent, Arthur: of Kent. Not of Ceylon. **1944** *Living off Land* ii. 43 The corkwood..blossoms are nourishing. The natives chew these... but..it should be left well alone by the white man. **1948** *Times Lit. Suppl.* 9 Oct. 569/3 'Native' is a good word that may not now be employed without giving deep offence. **1950** M. CHAPPELL *Rhodesian Adventure* xiii. 143 There was nothing here when the pioneers came. Save bushveld and natives and wild animals. **1950** J. C. FURNAS *Anat. Paradise* ii. 24 The meaning of 'Native' can be approximated. It means: Darker. Productive of quaint handicrafts... Greedy for beads..and alcoholic drinks. Suspect of cannibalism. Addicted to drumbeating and lewd dancing. More or less naked. Sporadically treacherous. Probably polygynous and simultaneously promiscuous. Picturesque. Comic when trying to speak English or otherwise ape white ways. **1950** D. LESSING *Grass is Singing* viii. 178 When a white man in Africa by accident looks into the eyes of a native and sees the human being (which it is his chief preoccupation to avoid), his sense of guilt, which he denies, fumes up in resentment and he brings down the whip. **1951** J. MASTERS *Nightrunners Bengal* i. 9 We of the Company's service *live* here all our working lives. We do our work and enjoy ourselves and lord it over the country entirely by the good will of the average native... If you even think of them insultingly, of course they know it and resent it. **1975** C. ALLEN *Plain Tales from Raj* xix. 195 The regimental cook slaughtered a cow... The natives got to know about this and nearly stoned the camp.

c. In U.S. and Canada, a North American Indian.

1636 *Public Rec. Colony of Connecticut* (1850) I. 1 None..shall trade w[i]th the natives or Indians any peece or pistoll or gunn. *a* **1772** J. WOOLMAN *Jrnl.* in *Works* (1774) I. viii. 153 My meditations were on the alterations in the circumstances of the natives..since the coming in of the English. **1846** R. B. SAGE *Scenes Rocky Mts.* xxxiii. 287 Skins furnish to the natives a favorite material for arrow-cases. **1856** R. M. BALLANTYNE *Snowflakes & Sunbeams* vii. 72 This is the trading-store. It is always recognisable, if natives are in the neighbourhood, by the bevy of red men that cluster round it, awaiting the coming of the store-keeper. **1951** R. BULIARD *Inuk* 316 The company nowadays certainly does give help to the natives, in the forms of loans, gifts, and medicine.

d. In phr. *to astonish the natives* (orig. *U.S.*), to shock, or otherwise profoundly impress, public opinion.

1807 *Salmagundi* 27 June 233 He was determined to '*astonish the natives a few*'. *Ibid.* 238 Unfortunate Straddle! may thy fate be a warning to all young gentlemen who come out from Birmingham to *astonish the natives!* **1842** *Ainsworth's Mag.* I. 302 At last, having astonished the natives,..he rolled off to bed. **1852** [in Dict., sense 4]. **1901** M. E. RYAN *That Girl Montana* 96 Much of her afternoon was spent..fashioning a party gown with which to astonish the natives.

e. *to go native*: see *GO *v.* 44 a.

native, *a.* Add: **12. c.** *native son* U.S., a native of a particular state.

1833 *Southern Patriot* (Charleston, S. Carolina) 27 July 2/6 Col. William Drayton..a native son of Carolina..left our shores. **1850** *Ex. Doc. 31st U.S. Congress 1 Sess. Senate* No. 76. 3 The native sons of the United States living in New Mexico knew their right to equality of privilege. **1864** *Weekly New Mexican* (Santa Fé) 25 Nov. 3 Lieut.-Colonel Chaves..is one of New Mexico's favorite native sons. **1913** *Dialect Notes* IV. 27 You can't get a job in California unless you are a native son. **1916** 'B. M. BOWER' *Phantom Herd* 27 [He] backed out of the way of the Native Son, who sprawled himself over the table corner. **1949** *Sun* (Baltimore) 7 Sept. 12/4 A bare victory in Ohio could not be taken as a decisive popular verdict for Mr. Taft's philosophy because the Taft philosophy had been supplemented by loyalty to a native son and that element could not be counted as a safe factor in general calculations. **1974** *News & Reporter* (Chester, S. Carolina) 22 Apr. 2-A/1 The man is a native son, is old enough and has resided in the state long enough.

13. c. *native bear* = *KOALA (later examples); *native cat* = DASYURE (earlier and later examples); *native companion*, the *BROLGA, *Megalornis rubicundus* (later examples).

1863 R. HENNING *Let.* 10 Aug. (1966) 137 It was not rats but a large 'native cat' that had so alarmed John... They are pretty little creatures with soft spotted fur, about the size of a kitten. **1896, 1911** Native companion [see *BROLGA]. **1911** E. M. CLOWES *On Wallaby* xi. 279 You may yet meet with .. a lumbering native bear, like nothing on earth so much as a child's woolly toy, really the most ingratiating creature. Standing about two feet high, and covered with soft, thick fur, it has an odd, blunt, wistful sort of nose. **1916** J. B. COOPER *Coo-oo-ee* xii. 174, I saw for the first time a native bear on the bough of a black butt. **1928** 'BRENT OF BIN BIN' *Up Country* ii. 25 Bert's heelers..were tethered in a number of kennels placed around the fowl-houses as protection against native cats, which could devastate a fowl roost in one attack. **1934** T. WOOD *Cobbers* xvi. 189 Native companions—strange white stalky birds on stilts whose courtship dance is a marvel. **1946** K. TENNANT *Lost Haven* (1968) xiv. 237 The native companions..beating the water with their stumpy wings to frighten the little fish. They seemed to have their legs fastened on backwards at the joints. **1966** G. W. TURNER *Eng. Lang. Austral. & N.Z.* iii. 41 Koalas were more often called native bears in the early years. **1968** *Times* 23 Jan. (Austral. Suppl.) p. xiii/3 He..caught instead a pair of dibblers..believed to be extinct and of importance as a link between the smaller phascogales and the larger native cats.

d. Also, in the names of New Zealand plants; (further examples). Also **native bush** *N.Z.*, woods or forests made up of indigenous trees and shrubs.

1826 Native cherry [see **five corner*(*s*)]. **1884** A. NILSON *Timber Trees New South Wales* 125 *X*[*ylomelum*] *pyriforme.*—Wooden Pear; Native Pear. **1889** J. H. MAIDEN *Useful Native Plants Austral.* 286 *Ricinocarpus pinifolius*, Desf., Native Jasmine. This plant yields abundance of seeds, like small castor-oil seeds. They yield an oil. **1891** R. WALLACE *Rural Econ. Austral. & N.Z.* xxii. 294 *Panicum decompositum*, R. Br.—Barley grass, native millet, umbrella grass. Throughout Colonies, except Tasmania. **1898** MORRIS *Austral Eng.* 5/1 Emu A[pple]—*Owenia acidula*, F. v. M.; called also Native Nectarine. **1905** Native nectarine [see **emu-apple*]. **1908** E. J. BANFIELD *Confessions of Beachcomber* I. i. 20 Strong and spicy are the odours..in the jungle, the so-called native ginger, nutmeg..and many others. **1926** *Trans. N.Z. Inst.* LVI. 662 The word 'native' has been prefixed to almost as many names as the words 'New Zealand'. **1928** 'BRENT OF BIN BIN' *Up Country* iii. 43 Its floor was spread with glowing embers from the bark of the native apple tree, specially suitable for the purpose. **1930** L. G. D. ACLAND *Early Canterbury Runs* vi. 125 The glorious view, native bush and trim gardens make it [*sc.* Peel Forest] one of the most beautiful homesteads in Canterbury. **1933** *Bulletin* (Sydney) 29 Mar. 25/1 Some of the potential plants of these pastures are rib grass, coolah grass..and native wheat grass. *Ibid.* 7 June 25/2 Another ornamental plant is the native jasmine, which grows to about 6 ft. high. This bush is often completely denuded of foliage by stock. **1934** *Ibid.* 15 Aug. 21/4 The thirsty traveller in the western parts of N.S.W. and Queensland welcomes the sight of a native nectarine (*Owenia acidula*) almost as much as a fresh-water spring. **1947** A. VOGT in D. M. Davin *N.Z. Short Stories* (1953) 377 Further back, even here, the hills were thick with native bush. **1959** A. MCLINTOCK *Descr. Atlas N.Z.* 80 Stewart Island..is a popular tourist resort with unspoiled native bush,..and a wealth of birdlife. **1966** W. S. RAMSON *Austral. Eng.* v. 82 In some cases the resemblance to an English species was sufficient for the choice of name, but a qualification was introduced through the use of a particularizer, as, for instance, in..native pear. **1967** A. M. BLOMBERY *Guide Native Austral. Plants* 313 *S*[*antalum*] *acuminatum.* Quandong, Native Peach... A shrub or small tree with light greyish-green, narrow, lanceolate leaves and bright-red fruits.

14. (Further examples.)

1891 R. WALLACE *Rural Econ. Austral. & N.Z.* xiv. 215 Mrs. Donnelly is perhaps one of the most able lawyers in relation to native affairs that New Zealand possesses, and..has earned..the reputation of a Maori Portia. **1914** R. FRY *Let.* (1972) II. 378 Are you going to Tunis? If so..he'll give you Arab dinners in a lovely Arab house in the middle of the native quarter. **1950** M. CHAPPELL *Rhodesian Adventure* ix. 101, I believe the original native name for the place where Salisbury stands was 'Harari'. **1961** G. GREENE *In Search of a Character* I. 14 The 'method' here seems to be to drive around the native town until a likely girl is seen. **1975** C. ALLEN *Plain Tales from Raj* i. 25 The native bazaar was..out of bounds..to all European children.

15. Special Combs., as *Native American*, a North American Indian; also *attrib.* or as *adj.*; *native location* S. Afr., = LOCATION 5 (in Dict. and Suppl.); *native oven* (*N.Z.*) = *COPPER MAORI; a similar oven in Australia; *native question*, the question of relations between colonizers and the indigenous population of a country; *native reserve*, an area of land set aside by a colonial power for the exclusive use of the indigenous population; *native state*, *Native State*, during the period of British dominion of India, the term used to designate a state outside British territory which was governed by a native ruler; also called 'Indian State', 'princely state'.

1956 A. HUXLEY *Let.* 20 Oct. (1969) 809 Thank you for your most interesting letter about the Native American churchmen. **1973** *Black Panther* 7 Apr. 4/1 Appearing at the awards in Brando's behalf was the beautiful, gracious, and now famous Native American woman, Sacheen Littlefeather, who, dressed in the traditional garments of her people, read a prepared statement. **1973** *New Society* 19 July 137/1 Services at a Native American Church, a denomination that combines Indian and Christian beliefs. **1974** *Black Panther* 19 Jan. 3/2 In a vain attempt to cover the highly-political nature of the trial, the government has accused the two Native Americans of crimes such as burglary, larceny, and auto theft rather than accuse them of the real charges: of standing up for the dignity and culture of Indian peoples. [**1855** W. C. HOLDEN *Hist. Natal* viii. 176 The plan of government devised was, to preserve the Natives distinct from the whites; and, for this purpose, large tracts of country were set aside, under

the designation of 'Locations for the Natives'. On these Locations the Natives were to be collected, and governed by their own laws, through the medium of their own chiefs.] **1866** in *Towards Dict. S. Afr. Eng.* (1971) 51 Crime has considerably increased during the year; which is in a great measure to be attributed to the scarcity of food in the native locations. **1881** *Convention of Pretoria* in J. Nixon *Compl. Story Transvaal* (1884) 348 Article 21, Forthwith, after the taking effect of this Convention, a Native Location Commission will be constituted. **1928** R. L. Buell *Native Probl. Afr.* I. I. iii. 50 Each South African city has its native location in which the native population must supposedly live, and in which houses are usually rented from the municipality. **1955** *Problems & Tensions in S. Afr.* 374 In a few Native locations there is adequate provision for good schools, health centres, stores and churches. **1832** A. Earle *Narr. Residence N.Z.* xxviii. 96 On a spot of rising ground, just outside the village, we saw a man preparing a native oven, which is done in the following simple manner:—A hole is made in the ground, and hot stones are put within it, and then all is covered up close. **1834**, **1889** [see *copper Maori]. **1905** W. B. *Where White Man Treads* 101 (*heading*) The haangi—(native oven). **1911** C. E. W. Bean *'Dreadnought' of Darling* xxvi. 227 Menindie..swarms with native ovens and other relics of the blacks. **1917** H. W. Williams *Dict. Maori Lang.* 41/2 *Hāngi*.., native oven, consisting of a circular hole in the ground, in which the food was cooked by heated stones. **1900** (*title*) Native question in South Africa. **1924** E. M. Forster *Passage to India* II. ii. 32 Adela, who meditated spending her life in the country, was a more serious matter; it would be tiresome if she started crooked over the native question. **1927** W. Plomer *I speak of Afr.* 255, I am the only one here who doesn't depend for a living on the native question. **1971** *Oxf. Hist. S. Afr.* II. viii. 403 In 1914 'the Native question' was mentioned only in passing. **1928** R. L. Buell *Native Probl. Afr.* I. v. 71 All land was simply declared public land,..which alienated it to European settlers after establishing in several cases, notable in Natal, native reserves. **1950** M. Chappell *Rhodesian Adventure* ix. 101 The whole area is a native reserve and looks no different today than it has for centuries. **1953** P. Abrahams *Return to Goli* iv. 106 The result is that nowhere else in Africa is land-hunger as acute as it is in the Union's 'Native Reserves'. **1966** M. M. Cole *S. Afr.* (ed. 2) xlv. 687 The Native Reserves in the Republic are incapable of supporting all the Bantu population in agriculture. **1784** *Act* 24 *Geo. III* c. 25 § 15 Treating or negociating with any of the Native Princes or States in India. [*Ibid.* §35 To negociate or conclude any Treaty of Peace..with any Indian Prince or State.] **1823** J. Malcolm *Mem. Cent. India* II. xvi. 280 The present condition of our empire in India requires..in the exercise of political control and superintendence over Native States, a school..distinct from other branches of the service. **1883** J. S. Cotton in Cotton & Payne *Colonies & Dependencies* I. iii. 23 The native states are sometimes called feudatory—a convenient term to express their vague relation to the British crown. **1886** Kipling *Departmental Ditties* (ed. 2) 7 Rustum Beg of Kolazai—slightly backward Native State—Lusted for a C.S.I. **1894** W. Lee-Warner *Protected Princes India* i. 2 The most cursory examination of the Native states brings to light a confusing variety in their size, their origin, and their development. **1931** P. Kendall *India & British* viii. 223 Hyderabad, the largest..of all the Native States, absorbed Golconda centuries ago. **1963** M. A. Rahim *Ld. Dalhousie's Administration* i. 4 As regards the condition of Indian states, there were many so-called independent native principalities or states, but actually..they were firmly controlled by the British Government.

nativism. Add: **1.** (Earlier and later examples.)

1845 *Congress. Globe* 18 Dec. 66 In the City of New York nativism had its origin in the disputes of the Tammany party. **1965** *Guardian* 6 Aug. 5/3 The revived nativism of white, rural, Protestant America. **1968** G. W. Stocking *Race, Culture & Evolution* xi. 297 This reaction was related to the national outburst of nativism which..was to lead finally in 1923 to the passage of legislation which closed the era of mass immigration by non-'Nordics'.

b. *Anthrop.* (See quot. 1972.)

1964 Gould & Kolb *Dict. Social Sci.* 458/1 Examples of nativism would include peyotism and cargo cults. Another example is the Ghost Dance of the American Indians. **1972** D. Davies *Dict. Anthropol.* 132/1 *Nativism*, the movement of societies back toward a reaffirmation of their native tribal cultures as a reaction when acculturation seems to be threatening their tribal identity and culture.

2. b. *Psychol.* and *Linguistics.* The doctrine that certain capacities or abilities, esp. those of sense perception, are innate rather than acquired; the theory that in the development of language an inherent connection exists in the mind between sound and sense.

1924 R. M. Ogden tr. *Koffka's Growth of Mind* i. 1 And even to-day no agreement has been reached between the rival theories of *empiricism* and *nativism*, the first of which emphasizes the influence of environment, and the second the influence of heredity. **1968** D. Price-Williams in J. Clifton *Introd. Cultural Anthropol.* xii. 312/1 Visual illusions have given cross-cultural psychologists a considerable body of data with which to assess the factors of nativism and empiricism in perception. **1970** *Language* XLVI. 139 In the revival of Cartesian philosophical views of language, a number of other moribund doctrines have been brought to spectral life, too: mentalism, nativism (the innate-endowment component in child language studies). **1972** *Encycl. Psychol.* II. 308/1 *Nativism*, the belief that human behavior and particularly human perceptual mechanisms are inborn and determined by genetics, as opposed to the belief that they are the result of learning and experience.

nativist. Add: **2. b.** *Psychol.* and *Linguistics.* One who holds the doctrine of innate capacities, or of an inherent connection between sound and meaning in language.

1924 R. M. Ogden tr. *Koffka's Growth of Mind* iii. § 5. 76 To the empiricist the observed development [of fixation] is regarded as a process of learning; while the nativist regards it as a process of maturation. **1930** W. Leopold in J. T. Hatfield et al. *Curme Vol. Ling. Stud.* 106 It might be possible to find..a tie of union even between views as contrasting as those of Wundt and Marty, of nativists and teleologists, in the philosophy of language. **1971** *Jrnl. Gen. Psychol.* LXXXV. 18 The argument of nativists that the phenomenal experience is not found to be as fluid or flexible as would be expected under an empirical approach.

nativistic, *a.* (Further examples.)

1922 O. Jespersen *Lang.* xxi. 415 A closely related theory is the nativistic, nicknamed the *ding-dong*, theory, according to which there is a mystic harmony between sound and sense. **1943** *Amer. Anthropologist* XLV. 230 The term 'nativistic' has been loosely applied to a rather wide range of phenomena... We may define a nativistic movement as, 'Any conscious, organized attempt on the part of a society's members to revive or perpetuate selected aspects of its culture'. **1946** D. McCarthy in L. Carmichael *Manual of Child Psychol.* x. 501/2 Sapir.. proposes a nativistic theory of phonetic symbolism which has given rise to considerable controversy. **1958** F. M. Keesing *Cultural Anthropol.* xvi. 406 'Nativistic' movements, including the new religious cults spoken of earlier. **1966** M. Pei *Gloss. Ling. Terminol.* 177 *Nativistic theory*, the view that a mystic harmony or connection exists between sound and meaning, and that human speech is the result of an instinct of primitive man. **1968** D. Price-Williams in J. Clifton *Introd. Cultural Anthropol.* xii. 312/1 The results support the Gestalt position and thus the nativistic viewpoint. **1974** *Listener* 7 Mar. 294/1 A nationalist—or as the officials prefer to call it—'nativistic' movement..in the South Pacific.

nativize (nē·tivəiz), *v. Linguistics.* [f. Native *a.* + -ize.] *trans.* To render native; *spec.* **a.** To adapt (a loan word) to the phonetic structure of the native language. **b.** To develop (a pidgin language) into a creole used as a first language. Hence **na·tivized** *ppl. a.*, **na:tiviza·tion.**

1933 L. Bloomfield *Lang.* xxv. 454 From the completely nativized ['šowfr̩] *chauffeur*, we have the back-formation *to chauffe* [šowf]. **1940** *Proc. Amer. Philos. Soc.* LXXXII. 15 'Scandalous examples of Great Russian chauvinism' have often interfered with what is called the nativization of the Soviet apparatus. **1970** *Language* XLVI. 66 A Nupe speaker will consistently 'nativize' [Cɔ] as [Cʷa] and [Cɛ] as [Cʸa]. *Ibid.*, The position supported by this evidence is that the nativization of foreign sounds is a valid indicator of what rules have been internalized. **1971** I. F. Hancock in J. Spencer *Eng. Lang. W. Afr.* 113 When a pidgin supplants a 'full' language, changes must occur... Therefore in becoming *nativised* and thereby *creolised*, it expands its vocabulary, produces more explicit grammatical constructions and becomes more fixed in pronunciation.

N.A.T.O., NATO, Nato (nē·to). [Acronym f. the initials of *N*orth *A*tlantic *T*reaty *O*rganization, set up in 1949.] A military alliance of the United States and Canada with certain European nations. So **Na·to,-ish** *a.*, supporting N.A.T.O.; **Na·toism,** adherence to N.A.T.O.; **Na·toist,** a supporter of N.A.T.O.

1950 *Newsweek* 14 Aug. 40/3 Nato is the newest synthetic word in the international gobbledygook and stands for the North Atlantic treaty organization. **1962** H. O. Beecheno *Introd. Business Stud.* i. 5 Britain had also put her military forces under a unified command in NATO (the North Atlantic Treaty Organization). **1965** *Economist* 28 Aug. 770/3 The Socialist People's party has accused Labour of being too capitalistic and too Nato-ish. **1965** *New Statesman* 24 Dec. 992/2 De Gaulle will not budge on his slightly neutralist type of Natoism. **1966** *Ibid.* 18 Mar. 366/2 The opposition..includes a lot of outright Natoists (Mollet and even Mitterrand also support Nato, with reservations). **1975** *Guardian* 5 Dec. 3/1 Britain is interested in buying several of the aircraft provided that other European NATO countries also join in.

natriuresis (nē:tri-, næ:tri,ⁱurī·sis). *Med.* [f. Natri(um + Gr. οὔρησις urination.] The excretion of abnormally large amounts of sodium in the urine.

1957 H. W. Smith in *Amer. Jrnl. Med.* XXIII. 625/2 An increase or decrease in sodium excretion will be designated as natriuresis and antinatriuresis. **1974** *Nature* 11 Jan. 109/1 The natriuresis produced by the intra-renal release of kallikrein may be effected by vasodilator and permeability effects on the renal vasculature and tubules.

Hence **natriuretic** (-e·tik) *a.*, causing or pertaining to natriuresis.

1957 *Amer. Jrnl. Med.* XXIII. 625/1 The natriuretic effects of the infusion of large volumes of saline solution are in part controlled by the absence of natriuresis after the infusion of iso-oncotic albumin. **1974** *Nature* 11 Jan. 109/1 The data on sodium excretion place substance P amongst the most potent natriuretic substances so far described.

natro- (nē·tro, næ·tro-), comb. form of Natrium, used in *Min.* to form the names of sodium-containing minerals (as Natrolite), and also prefixed to existing mineral names to indicate the (often partial) substitution of sodium for some other metal in that mineral, as **natroa·lunite,** any of the range of basic sulphates of sodium, potassium, and aluminium, $(Na,K)Al_3(SO_4)_2(OH)_6$, which have the proportion of sodium greater than that of potassium and are found as white hexagonal crystals; *spec.* the sodic end-member of this series; **natrocha·lcite** [L. *chalcītes* Chalcites], a basic hydrated sulphate of sodium and copper, $NaCu_2(SO_4)_2(OH).H_2O$, which is found as emerald-green monoclinic crystals at Chuquicamata in Chile; **natroda·vyne** [ad. It. *natrodavyna* (F. Zambonini 1910, in *Atti d. R. Accad. d. Sci. fis. e mat.* XIV. vi. 188)], a silicate and carbonate of aluminium and sodium, found as colourless hexagonal crystals; **natroja·rosite,** a basic sulphate of sodium and iron, $NaFe_3(SO_4)_2(OH)_6$, found as yellow or brown hexagonal crystals; **na:tromontebra·site** [a. F. *natromontebrasite* (F. Gonnard 1913, in *Bull. de la Soc. franç. de Min.* XXXVI. 120)], a basic fluoride and phosphate of sodium, lithium, and aluminium, $(Na,Li)Al(PO_4)(OH,F)$, with more sodium than lithium, which is found as whitish triclinic crystals.

1902 Hillebrand & Penfield in *Amer. Jrnl. Sci.* CLXIV. 220 The name natroalunite might be employed to designate the two varieties of alunite from Colorado.., where the proportion of the soda to the potash molecule is 7:4. **1937** *Amer. Mineralogist* XXII. 944 Small amounts of finely granular natroalunite have attacked the andalusite ores. **1968** I. Kostov *Mineral.* II. 493 Natroalunite is a sodium analogue [of alunite] $NaAl_3(SO_4)_2(OH)_6$. **1969** *Mineral. Abstr.* XX. 146/1 The first occurrence of natroalunite and natrojarosite from Argentina is noted from the area around La Flecha gorge. **1908** Palache & Warren in *Amer. Jrnl. Sci.* CLXXVI. 343 The collection ..was obtained from exhausted copper veins and includes..natrochalcite (a new mineral). **1944** *Econ. Geol.* XXXIX. 274 The SO_3 concentration is so reduced that chalcanthite, natrochalcite, and krohnkite become unstable and antlerite takes their place. **1968** I. Kostov *Mineral.* II. 514 Natrochalcite is monoclinic (*C2/m*), occurring as acute pyramidal green crystals with perfect {001} cleavage. **1913** *Mineral. Mag.* XVI. 367 Natrodavyne... Hexagonal crystals, rich in faces, hitherto referred to nepheline or to davyne. **1963** *Canad. Mineralogist* VII. 632 Dry material of the natrodavyne composition was prepared by mixing α-cristobalite, γ-alumina and Na_2SiO_3 in the correct stoichiometric proportions for the formation of nepheline, and then adding the required weight of anhydrous Na_2CO_3. **1902** Hillebrand & Penfield in *Amer. Jrnl. Sci.* CLXIV. 219 It has seemed to the writers best to designate the new compounds described in this article as natrojarosite and plumbojarosite, the names signifying their relation to a well known species. **1938** *Amer. Mineralogist* XXIII. 757 At Chuquicamata natrojarosite is associated with chalcanthite, kroehnkite and sulphur. **1969** Natrojarosite [see *natroalunite* above]. **1971** *Norsk Geol. Tidsskrift* LI. 195 Natrojarosite is reported as a secondary mineral from Forvik antimony deposit, Helgeland, North Norway. **1915** *Mineral. Mag.* XVII. 355 Natromontebrasite... To replace the name Natramblygonite or Natronamblygonit of W. T. Schaller.., since the mineral is a hydrofluophosphate rather than a fluophosphate. **1955** *Amer. Mineralogist* XL. 1141 Fremontite.., in which Na:Li = 1·7:1 and OH>F, becomes natromontebrasite and possesses the dubious distinction of having been referred to under three different names within 40 years.

N.A.T.S.O.P.A., NATSOPA, Natsopa (næts$\bar{o}^u$·pă). [Acronym f. the initial letters of *Nat*ional *S*ociety of *O*perative *P*rinters and *A*ssistants.] A trade union composed of printing workers; pl., the members of this union.

From 1975 retitled the National Society of Operative Printers, Graphical and Media Personnel.

1917 *Natsopa Jrnl.* May 1/1 Our intentions..will no doubt go to swell the number with which the road to a certain place is paved, but that does not matter,.. because all Natsopas will go the journey to another place, and will require wings to convey them. **1922** *Times* 18 Feb. 4/1 In the January number of *Natsopa*, the official journal of the society, the executive council gave notice that .. the office of general secretary would be declared vacant. **1926** *Glasgow Herald* 3 May 11 The Natsopas.. at Carmelite House took exception to the leading article. **1935** F. D. Klingender *Condition Clerical Labour Brit.* ii. 48 The following remark made by the secretary of the clerical section of Natsopa. **1958** *Oxford Mail* 6 Aug. 1/1 NATSOPA indicate in a statement that..the question of craft and non-craft unions [etc.]. **1963** *Times* 11 Feb. 11/2 Severe disruption of the production of the *Daily Mirror* took place last night as a result of unofficial action by some members of the Natsopa union.

natter, *v.* Add: **1. b.** To chatter, to chat (in an aimless manner). Also with *about, away, of, on.* (Now the usual sense.)

1943 Hunt & Pringle *Service Slang* 47 *Natter*, to chide or chatter in an irritatingly aimless fashion. **1949** M. Allingham *More Work for Undertaker* xxvii. 310 The shares Campion keeps nattering about. **1952** J. Cannan *Body in Beck* i. 9 No human voices..nattering of sodomy and of being bumped by Cat's. **1954** C. P. Snow *New Men* 213 You're saying we ought to find a

bogus reason for putting him in the street—just because some old women might natter. **1958** *Sunday Times* 26 Jan. 17/3 They..nattered away for an hour about nothing. **1959** C. MACINNES *Absolute Beginners* 74 She nattered on. I gave up. 'Well—you win,' I told her. **1972** R. MAUGHAM *Escape from Shadows* iv. 169 Seeing me look like a village idiot when he nattered away at me in Arabic. **1973** *Times* 12 Nov. 10/6 Women who.. natter about discrimination.

2. (Later example.)

1946 J. B. PRIESTLEY *Bright Day* ix. 274 If you've got summat in you that wants to be let out an' goes on natterin' at you day an' night, then you let go of everything else an' get it out.

So **na·tterer**[1]; **nattering** *vbl. sb.* and *ppl. a.* (later examples in various senses); **na·ttery** *a.* = *nattered* ppl. adj.

1825 J. T. BROCKETT *Gloss. North Country Words* 146 *Nattry*, ill natured, petulant. '*Nattry faced*.' **1873** J. STANDING *Echoes Lancs. Vale* 17 One o' thoose nattery owd maids 'at con olez tell so mitch better heaw to bring a family o' childer op nor thoose 'at have 'em. **1900** *Eng. Dial. Dict.* II. 657/2 s.v. *Gnatter*, *Lin[colnshire]*. Eh! Miss, she is such a natterer; she is always nattering about. **1923** *Sunday At Home* Mar. 335/2, I 'ate them skinny owd women—always bad tempered and nattery that kind is. **1937** M. ALLINGHAM *Dancers in Mourning* xvii. 217 Her energy, her constant nattering at one. **1942** *Tee Emm* (Air Ministry) II. 64 Your C.O. tears you off a strip for nattering too much over the R/T. **1949** H. PAKINGTON *Young W. Washbourne* 36 It was no longer a dear old pouch, but a nattering, irritating little pouch that twanged upon the strings of his conscience. **1953** E. SIMON *Past Masters* II. vi. 116 I'm sick and tired of all this lily-livered nattering..behind closed doors. **1956** 'N. SHUTE' *Beyond Black Stump* vii. 207 To kill the nattering of hope that lingered on. **1959** H. HOBSON *Mission House Murder* xviii. 116 'Did this girl talk?' 'Not much... she wasn't one of the natterers.' **1959** G. MITCHELL *Man who grew Tomatoes* i. 23 Do you hold your tongue, now. Like a nattering old mawther, you are! **1966** J. WAINWRIGHT *Crystallised Carbon Pig* x. 47, I was nattery and on edge.

na·tter, *sb.* [f. the vb.] Grumbling, nagging talk; (now esp.) aimless chatter; a chat, a talk.

1866 W. GREGOR *Dial. Banffshire* 119 *Nyatter*, peevish chattering, grumbling. **1943** HUNT & PRINGLE *Service Slang* 47 *Natter party*, a Conference which leads nowhere. **1945** PARTRIDGE *Dict. R.A.F. Slang* 40 *Natter can*, a person—especially a 'Waaf'—prone to talk too much. **1947** *Forum* (Johannesburg) X. I. 23/2 So it is that words like 'interdenominisationalism' and 'polyphiloprogenitive', with which we are wont to sprinkle our normal natter, sound like the mouthings of the village idiot. **1951** *News Chron.* 8 Nov. 6/1 From the swarm he singled out one bird... 'That's Joey,..he usually comes for a natter when there's nothing else doing.' **1955** 'N. SHUTE' *Requiem for Wren* iii. 57 I've got a natter on with the Americans tomorrow evening. **1959** G. FREEMAN *Jack would be Gent.* v. 94 I'd give anythin' to 'ave a natter with some of them blokes. **1966** 'L. LANE' *ABZ of Scouse* 74 *Owd natterbag*, a scolding woman. **1967** N. FREELING *Strike Out* 28 The natter of silly women. **1974** E. LEMARCHAND *Buried in Past* vi. 102 We wanted a natter with you... You can fill us in as nobody else can.

Natterer[2] (næ·tərəɹ). The name of Johann *Natterer* (1787–1843), Austrian naturalist, used in the possessive in **Natterer's bat,** *Myotis nattereri*, a greyish-brown bat with a white underside, found in Europe and Asia. Also *absol.*

1889 J. E. HARTING in *Zoologist* XIII. 245 The present distribution of Natterer's Bat in the British Islands cannot be stated in a few words. **1910** G. E. H. BARRETT-HAMILTON *Hist. Brit. Mammals* I. 178 Natterer's Bat ranges through boreal and temperate Europe and Asia. **1960** *Times* 14 June 14/6 My first encounter with Natterer's bat was a night to remember. *Ibid.*, The most up-to-date bat book today speaks of the Natterer's flight as 'slow and steady'.

Nattier blue (na·tye). [f. the name of the Fr. painter Jean-Marc *Nattier* (1685–1766).] A soft shade of blue much used by Nattier and associated *spec.* with his work.

[**1909** *Westm. Gaz.* 4 May 5/3 We have quoted the painter Nattier for the soft shade of blue he used.] **1912** *Queen* 4 May p. xvii, The bonnet is fashioned of Nattier blue satin. **1918** W. J. LOCKE *Rough Road* xxi. 261 His own bedroom with the satinwood furniture and nattier blue hangings. **1923** [see *BISQUE[2] 3]. **1928** *Times* 9 May 10/3 A train of Nattier-blue satin and silver lace. **1963** *New Yorker* 1 June 34 She wore Nattier-blue with a collar so high it almost reached her ears. **1969** *Queen* 17–30 Sept. 91/1 Nattier blue silk curtains.

Natufian (natū·fiăn). *Archæol.* [f. the name of Wādi an-*Natuf*, seventeen miles north-west of Jerusalem.] Name coined by Prof. D. Garrod for a late Mesolithic culture the type-site of which was discovered by her at Wādi an-Natuf. Also *attrib.*

1932 D. A. E. GARROD in *Jrnl. R. Anthrop. Inst.* LXII. 257 (*heading*) A new mesolithic industry: the Natufian of Palestine. *Ibid.* 261 It was abundantly clear that we were dealing with a microlithic culture that would not fit exactly into any of the pigeon-holes already existing, and I therefore decided to give it a label of its own, adopting the name Natufian from the Wady en-Natuf at Shukba. **1949** [see *food-gatherer* (*FOOD *sb.* 8)]. **1960** K. M. KENYON *Archaeol. in Holy Land* ii. 36 The Natufians of Mount Carmel, and of rock-shelters on the eastern and western slopes of the Judaean hills, lived mainly by hunting. **1960** tr. *S. Moscati's Face of Anc. Orient* i. 13 The Natufian civilization brings two principal innovations: the harvesting of wheat and barley, and the beginnings of the domestication of animals. **1970** BRAY & TRUMP *Dict. Archaeol.* 159/1 The shrine at the base of the Tell at Jericho was built during the early Natufian phase and the descendants of the Natufians built the earliest Neolithic town at the site.

natural, *sb.* Add: **1.** (Later Amer. example.)

1748 in *Maryland Hist. Mag.* (1911) VI. 229, I..am become a Natural of the country or country born as some call themselves.

6. b. (Later example in *sing.*)

1922 JOYCE *Ulysses* 396 Any female..with the desire of fulfilling the functions of her natural.

9. b. Also in other gambling games, any combination or score that immediately wins the stake. Also *fig.*

1762 GOLDSMITH *Citizen of World* I. 165 He had something in his face gave me as much pleasure as a pair-royal of naturals in my own hand. **1929** E. WALLACE *Red Aces* xi. 110 Somebody would draw a six to these, and the banker would have a 'natural'—which means, I understand, that he would win. **1930** J. LAIT *Big House* 15 Dean Ward Kent arrived at the big house with a 'natural' staring him in the face, for that is what the crap-shooting inmates call a seven-year 'stretch'. **1962** K. ORVIS *Damned & Destroyed* xv. 109 The dice bounced to a natural.

13. *colloq.* Short for *natural life* (NATURAL *a.* 9 b).

1893 G. L. GOWER *Gloss. Surrey Words* 27 *In my natural*, phrase for 'in my life', 'at any time'. **1898** J. D. BRAYSHAW *Slum Silhouettes* 220 Yer never see sich a 'owlin' swell as Cocky was in yer born natural. **1911** L. STONE *Jonah* II. ii. 161, I niver 'eard anythin' like that, in my natural. **1913** C. MACKENZIE *Sinister St.* I. I. iv. 46, I never worked so hard in all my natural. **1925** WODEHOUSE *Carry on, Jeeves!* iii. 59, I didn't want to have England barred to me for the rest of my natural. **1967** J. PORTER *Chinks in Curtain* xviii. 185, I couldn't stay like that for the rest of my natural.

14. A person naturally endowed *for* (a role, etc.); one having natural gifts or talents; also, a thing with qualities that make it particularly suitable (*for* some purpose.)

1925 *Hearst's International* June 80/2 The fight was what promoters call a 'natural'. **1929** D. HAMMETT *Red Harvest* xiii. 132 'So you and Noonan are trying to paste his brother's death on me?' 'It doesn't need pasting. It's a natural.' **1930** *Publisher's Weekly* 21 June 2971/2 Mystery fans will devour it; and you can sell it also to anyone who likes a finely written and witty novel. A possible natural. **1933** F. BALDWIN *Innocent Bystander* (1935) xiii. 260 But she's a natural... I watched her walk across the stage..and the audience rose to her. **1939** *Sun* (Baltimore) 2 Jan. 1/8 The Hopkins and Murphy appointments are regarded as 'naturals' for early-session debates. **1946** *Coast to Coast 1945* 125 This is a natural, son. I can pick this one. **1948** F. BROWN *Murder can be Fun* (1951) ix. 132 Hell, it was a *natural* for publicity for a writer. **1955** *Observer* 24 July 13/7 The sort of play which should have been a natural for television. **1958** *Times Lit. Suppl.* 15 Aug. 455/1 But the theme of how the Labour Party was born of the Labour Representation Committee is, as the film-makers say, a 'natural'. Poor Party makes good. **1964** *McCall's Sewing* i. 10/2 You're a natural for high fashion. **1966** *Listener* 24 Nov. 780/1 (Advt.), These five talks..diversified with 64 photos and 8 maps..make up what will be a 'natural' at Christmas, for young and old. **1971** B. MALAMUD *Tenants* 154 I'm not a natural. This present play is my last, I've decided. **1975** *Sunday Times* (Colour Suppl.) 23 Feb. 26/4 He was a natural, and gradually began to pick up something of a reputation. **1975** *Times* 25 Feb. 3/6 Railways are a natural for process control and on-line computer systems.

16. *Bullfighting.* A type of pass made with the cape. Also with Spanish pronunc. (naturāl).

1932 E. HEMINGWAY *Death in Afternoon* xviii. 198 The greatest pass with the muleta, the most dangerous to make.., is the natural. In this the man faces the bull with the muleta held in his left hand, the sword in his right. **1959** V. J. KEHOE *Aficionado!* xiv. 174/1 A natural is always in the direction of the arm that makes it. **1967** MCCORMICK & MASCAREÑAS *Compl. Aficionado* i. 24 A *natural* is a pass; it too may be called a suerte. **1973** *Sat. Rev.* (U.S.) 25 Sept. 29/2 Taking the smaller *muleta*, he ran off several fine *naturales*, bringing the bull tightly round him.

17. *Archæol.* Undisturbed terrain, below the level of cultivation or other working; virgin rock or soil.

1946 R. J. C. ATKINSON *Field Archaeol.* 210 *Natural rock* or '*natural*', the undisturbed material upon which the soil lies. **1950** *Notes on Archaeol. Technique* (ed. 3) 13 Many avoidable mistakes have been made through failure to identify the real 'natural' (undisturbed) layer of a site. Before the excavation proper is started, dig a cutting in undisturbed ground... In one half, stop on the 'natural'; in the other dig well into it. The 'natural' can then be studied in plan and section. **1954** M. B. COOKSON *Photogr. for Archaeologists* i. 14 A sharp right-angle where the last archaeological layer meets 'natural', balks swept at the end of a day's work, will repay the trouble taken a hundredfold.

18. A hair-style among Negroes in which the hair is not straightened or bleached; *spec.*, an Afro haircut. *U.S.*

1969 *Ebony* Feb. 27 There's a lean young cat wearing a natural who knows where it's at and tells it like it is. **1971** B. MALAMUD *Tenants* 42 She wore a natural of small silken ringlets, and a plain white mini with purple tights. **1971** *Black Scholar* Apr.–May 17/1 He has a Black is Beautiful bumper sticker on his car; he has a natural and even wears a dashiki to work. **1973** E. BULLINS *Theme is Blackness* 150, I love you, baby... I sure dig that sexy natural.

natural, *a.* Add: **I. 1.** Add to def.: esp. in phr. *natural law*: in political and legal philosophy and theology, doctrines based on the theory that there are certain unchanging laws which pertain to man's nature, which can be discovered by reason, and to which man-made laws should conform; freq. contrasted with positive laws; also (with hyphen) *attrib.* (Add further examples.)

1899 W. R. INGE *Christian Mysticism* viii. 306 Wordsworth..shows his affinity with the modern spirit in his firm grasp of natural *law*. **1915** tr. *Aquinas's Summa Theologica* II. I. Question 91. Article 2 This participation of the eternal law in the rational creature is called the natural law. **1934** E. BARKER tr. *Gierke's Natural Law Theory of Society* I. III. ii. 111 (*heading*) The natural-law view of the purposes of society and its various groups. **1950** A. VERDROSS-DROSSBERG in *Contemp. Pol. Sci.* (Unesco) 598 They are a residue of the ideas of natural law, since the unanimous agreement among civilized nations on a legal principle shows that the latter satisfies the elementary requirements of the legal conscience of mankind. **1951** A. PASSERIN D'ENTRÈVES (*title*) Natural law: an introduction to legal philosophy. *Ibid.* 15 The belief in natural law, both as a recognition of a law common to humanity and as an assertion of the fundamental rights of man, was..the distinguishing mark of political thought in Western Europe. **1967** *Encycl. Philos.* V. 451/1 The ideal or ethical law, which is contrasted with positive law..is regarded by natural-law theorists..as grounded in something..more enduring than the mere practical needs of men. **1970** W. E. VOLKOMER *Passionate Liberal* iii. 64 The immediate reason for Frank's conversion to natural law would appear to lie in the rise of totalitarianism.

2. c. Also of wind instruments, as *natural trumpet* (see quot. 1959).

1910 K. SCHLESINGER *Instruments Mod. Orchestra* I. xviii. 83 The *natural trumpet* in which the length and pitch are varied by means of crooks. **1959** *Collins' Mus. Encycl.* 450/1 *Natural horn, natural trumpet*, a horn or trumpet which is not provided with any method, such as valves, of altering the length of the tube, and can therefore sound no other notes than those of the harmonic series above its fundamental, except as stopped notes. **1966** P. BATE *Trumpet & Trombone* vi. 99 (*heading*) Natural trumpets: medieval to modern.

e. Also *Zool.*, applied to systems of classification based on the characteristics of the animals concerned, and the groups resulting from a classification of this type.

1841 T. R. JONES *Gen. Outl. Animal Kingdom* i. 2 The apparatus of digestion appears to be among the least efficient for the purpose of a natural division [of the animal kingdom]. *Ibid.* 3 The researches of this profound physiologist [*sc.* John Hunter]..did much to approximate a more natural method of classification. **1945** *Bull. Amer. Mus. Nat. Hist.* LXXXV. 4/1 It is understood that a 'true' or 'natural' classification has, by intention, quite a different basis and expression. **1970** *Nature* 19 Sept. 1272/2 It is always helpful for students to understand thoroughly the natural orders into which insects are divided.

f. *natural order*, the order apparent in the constitution of matter and operation of forces in nature.

1697 M. EARBERY *Answer to Tractatus Theologico Politicus* 18 The one [*sc.* Human Reason] is founded on the Natural Order of things, and therefore subject to those Imperfections, which are common to all the Works of Nature. **1895** F. THILLY tr. *Paulsen's Introd. Philos.* I. ii. 322 The intellectual law of causality is the basis of our belief in the natural order. **1934** *Encycl. Social Sci.* XI. 284/1 The stoics and certain Roman jurists interpreted natural law as that law which conformed to the natural order of the universe. **1941** W. TEMPLE *Citizen & Churchman* v. 83 The 'natural order' by which is meant the consideration of the various departments of life in the light of the essential function of each. **1948** BERGIN & FISCH tr. *Vico's New Sci.* § 2. 3 The philosophers, contemplating divine providence only through the natural order. **1941** C. C. GILLESPIE *Genesis & Geol.* vi. 169 Revealed truth, though indispensable to belief, could be apprehended inductively, by inferring a moral order parallel to natural order. **1953** C. E. RAVEN *Nat. Relig.* i. 2 If grace is radically contrasted with the beauty and truth and goodness of the natural order, then any belief in a real Incarnation is impossible.

g. *natural selection*: see SELECTION 3 b in Dict. and Suppl. Hence *natural selectionist*, a supporter of the theory of natural selection.

1913 G. B. SHAW *Quintessence of Ibsenism Compl.* p. xv, Capitalism, built up by generations of Scotch Rationalists and English Utilitarians, Atheists, Agnostics and Natural-Selectionists..is proclaimed the bulwark of the Christian churches. **1916** —— *Androcles & Lion* p. lxxi, The efforts of Natural Selectionists..to reduce evolution to mere automatism.

h. *natural deduction*, in Logic, the name given to a method devised separately in 1934 by G. Gentzen (1935 *Math. Zeitschrift* XXXIX) and S. Jaśkowski (1934 *Studia Logica* I) whereby formal proofs are obtained solely by the application of rules of inference without appeal to axioms.

1950 W. V. QUINE *Methods of Logic* (1952) § 28. 166 The method set forth in the present pages is of a type known as *natural deduction*, and stems, in its broadest

outlines, from Gentzen and Jaśkowski (1934). **1954** I. M. Copi *Symbolic Logic* iv. 119 The methods of proof so far assembled (techniques for 'Natural Deduction', as they are sometimes called) permit the demonstration of all logically true propositions constructed out of truth-functional connectives and the quantification of individual variables. **1966** *Amer. Philos. Q.* III. 27 (*title*) Natural deduction rules for obligation. **1969** *Aristotelian Soc. Suppl. Vol.* XLIII. 53 The expression 'natural deduction' was introduced, I surmise, under the influence partly of the name bestowed on Herbrand's 'theorem of deduction' and partly of the French expression 'la déduction naturelle'. **1973** B. A. Brody *Logic* iii. 103 Two..methods for showing that inferences are valid. The first, the natural deduction technique, starts from the results of this section.

3. d. (Later examples.) Esp. in phr. *natural causes*.

1889 A. B. Hicks *Hints to Medical Men concerning Certificates of Death* 6 Deaths which may be due to either natural causes, or to neglect or gross carelessness. *c* **1900** H. A. Jones in M. R. Booth *Eng. Plays of 19th Cent.* (1969) II. 382 When I heard this story was being circulated I thought it would be better to take no notice and let it die a natural death. **1921** A. Christie *Mysterious Affair at Styles* xiii. 292 He strenuously, and quite uselessly, upheld the theory of 'Death from natural causes'. **1970** P. Moyes *Who saw her Die?* viii. 105 The death certificate says 'Natural Causes'. That's the doctor's verdict. **1974** 'J. Le Carré' *Tinker, Tailor* xii. 104 Disappeared... May have died of course. One does *tend* to forget the natural causes. **1975** S. Brett *Cast* xi. 104 Assisting her investigations into a perfectly natural death as if it were murder.

e. *natural childbirth*, methods of relaxation and of physical co-operation with the natural process of childbirth, first advocated by G. D. Read in 1933, intended to counteract the muscular tension, resulting from fear, and consequent pain suffered in childbirth esp. by the women of civilized peoples; also *attrib.*

1933 G. D. Read (*title*) Natural childbirth. **1948** H. Heardman (*title*) A way to natural childbirth. **1960** *Guardian* 6 July 5/1 There are still many doctors and hospitals which do little or nothing to teach expectant mothers about the various methods of 'natural childbirth'. **1964** W. Markfield *To Early Grave* (1965) x. 181 Inez, six and a half months gone, was at a natural childbirth class. **1965** W. Lamb *Posture & Gesture* ix. 124 One is the practice of 'natural childbirth', still contentious, but with an organized following. **1971** D. D. Moir *Pain Relief in Labour* ii. 11 The Grantly Dick Read or Natural Childbirth method dates from 1935 and is based on the idea that fear, tension and pain are linked together. **1974** 'E. Lathen' *Sweet & Low* vii. 76 It was not easy.. to become an instant swinger after ten years..of natural childbirth.

6. b. *spec.* in phrs. *natural foundation* (see quots. 1906, 1963); *natural gas* (orig. *N. Amer.*), inflammable gas occurring underground, consisting chiefly of methane and other simple paraffins and often found associated with petroleum; *natural glass*, any of various naturally occurring substances which resemble glass in appearance, having solidified too quickly to crystallize.

1825 *Canad. Courant* (Montreal) 17 Dec. 1/5 This is undoubtedly the first attempt which has ever been made to apply natural Gas to so extensive and useful a purpose. **1846** S. F. Smith *Theatr. Apprenticeship* 102 Many of the stores and shops in the village are lighted with natural gas! **1887** *Encycl. Brit.* XXIII. 813/2 The use of natural gas for illumination, and even for metallurgical purposes, has lately become a matter of importance... The gas obtained from wells or bore-holes was used for illumination in Fredonia, N.Y., as early as 1821. **1906** H. Y. Margary in G. A. T. Middleton *Mod. Buildings* I. iii. i. 71/1 Natural foundation is the name applied to such as are formed on the soil itself, and it is applicable when the soil is practically incompressible. **1917** *Jrnl. Geol.* XXV. 540 Natural glass is, of course, varied in composition in comparison with the various types of igneous rocks, yet the average obsidian is probably not much more varied than some of the amorphous minerals. **1930** *Economist* 22 Mar. 654/2 Interest is being taken in utilities and oils with natural gas possibilities. **1938** E. G. Warland *Building Construction* I. i. 1 Natural foundation beds should be incompressible or equally yielding over the whole area and not subjected to atmospheric or other influences which may alter its nature or powers to resist the loads to be placed upon them. **1942** *Chem. Abstr.* XXXVI. 6452 (*heading*) Transformation of natural glasses into crystalline rocks by subjection to high gas and water-vapor pressures. **1957** *Ann. Reg. 1956* 76 The Government's proposal for financing the natural gas pipeline from Alberta to Ontario. **1963** *Gloss. Gen. Building Terms* (*B.S.I.*) 18 *Natural foundation*, soil requiring no preparation or other foundation to support a building or structure. **1971** W. Vogel *Struct. & Crystallization Glasses* i. 13 In the earliest times of world history, quartz porphyry in particular, and other extrusive rocks, solidified on rapid chilling as natural glasses, e.g. pitchstone, perlite, obsidian or pumice. **1972** *Guardian* 17 Feb. 9 People ran from their homes yesterday because of a gas explosion in Elgin Street, Sheffield... The area had been converted to natural gas about six months ago. **1974** *Sat. Rev. World* (U.S.) 2 Nov. 29/1 Calgary, Canada's oil and natural-gas capital.

d. Esp. in *Forestry*: *natural regeneration*, the growth of young trees from seed of those already established.

1902 B. E. Fernow *Econ. Forestry* vii. 167 There is also a choice of producing the new crop by seeds falling from the trees of the old crop, by 'natural regeneration'. **1928** R. S. Troup *Silvicultural Syst.* ii. 11 Natural regeneration..may be obtained either (1) from seed already on the area, or (2) from seed disseminated from trees outside and usually adjoining it. **1946** *Q. Jrnl. Forestry* XL. 18 A good deal of natural regeneration goes on at Bedgebury and had the seedlings been left..a Scots Pine forest could have been formed on the whole of the Pinetum area without any trouble. **1964** W. E. Hiley *Forestry Venture* iii. 64 The artificial weeding of natural regeneration, in which the young trees are irregularly scattered, is almost an impossible task.

e. Special collocations: *natural area* (see quot. 1964); *natural break*: see *break *sb.*[1] 8 k; *natural cement*: a cement obtained by calcining naturally occurring argillaceous limestone; *natural food* (see quot. 1972); *natural language*: any naturally evolved language, as opposed to artificial languages constructed (*a*) for universal or international communications, or (*b*) for formal logical or mathematical purposes; *natural region*: each of a number of regions of the earth's surface characterized by a certain uniformity and individuality of character (see quots. 1905, 1937); *natural resources* (see quot. 1956); *natural seasoning* = *air-seasoning* vbl. sb. (*air *sb.*[1] B. II).

1932 *Amer. Jrnl. Sociol.* XXXVIII. 339 It is more likely that census tracts near the central business districts of Philadelphia would conform more closely to natural areas than in West Philadelphia. **1964** Gould & Kolb *Dict. Social Sci.* 458/2 A *natural area* is a territorial unit whose distinctive characteristics—physical, economic, and cultural—are the result of the unplanned operation of ecological and social processes. **1970** G. A. & A. G. Theodorson *Mod. Dict. Sociol.* 271 *Natural area*, a territorial area with some common, unifying characteristic. The term has been used primarily in human ecology, and usually refers to an area that emerges without planning from the operation of ecological processes. **1882** *Chem. News* 27 Oct. 187/2 (*heading*) Japanese soils—a natural cement. *Ibid.*, The chemist to the Geological Survey Department of the Japanese Government, was led to look for a natural cement. Such cements are formed by mixing burnt lime with substances of volcanic origin, generally tufas. **1921** W. H. Warren *Engin. Construction* II. iii. 38 In America, Rosendale cement is largely used; it is a natural cement, being first found at Rosendale, Ulster County, N.Y. It is slower setting, weaker, and cheaper than Portland cement. **1966** *McGraw-Hill Encycl. Sci. & Technol.* II. 627/1 Natural cement, a naturally occurring argillaceous limestone, calcined and pulverized, is slower-setting and less uniform in quality than portland cement. **1934** H. C. Sherman *Food & Health* xvii. 160 Natural foods,..nature's wholes of the kinds to which our own bodies have been adjusting themselves throughout our evolutionary history. **1956** I. Orga *Cooking with Yogurt* 8 Yoğurt is a natural food and..only needs the simplest equipment. **1963** B. T. Hunter *Natural Foods Cookbk.* p. xv, Many thoughtful people are..seeking out the good old flavors, textures and nutrients of the natural foods their grandparents enjoyed. **1970** U. M. Cavanagh *Cooking & Catering Wholefood Way* 9 The emphasis is on natural whole foods such as stone-ground wholewheat flour, brown sugar, natural unpolished rice and honey. **1972** *New York* 8 May 49 *Natural food*..refers to food after the growing stage; food that is unprocessed, not treated with preservatives, artificial colorings or flavorings... Ideally the rule is 'nothing added, nothing taken away'. [**1668** J. Wilkins *Ess. Real Character & Philosophical Lang.* i. i. 2 There is scarce any subject that hath been more thoroughly scanned and debated amongst Learned men, than the Original of Languages and Letters. 'Tis evident enough that no one Language is natural to mankind.] **1774** Ld. Monboddo *Orig. & Progress of Lang.* II. iii. xiii. 445 If we understand the sign, we have in effect the definition of the thing, then is the language truly a philosophical language, and such as must be universal among philosophers... It may also be said to be a *natural* language..since it follows the order of the human mind in forming the ideas of which language is the expression. **1864** Max Müller *Lect. Sci. Lang.* 2nd Ser. ii. 58 A grammatical framework, too, is wanted before the problem of an artificial language can be considered as solved. In natural languages the grammatical articulation consists either in separate particles or in modifications in the body of a word. **1871** S. P. Andrews *Primary Synopsis Universology & Alwato* vi. 95 The ideas themselves are the most subtle and embarrassing, and *natural* language then exactly *echoes* this embarrassment. As we descend to more *feasible* domains the words will become correspondingly more *feasible*. **1888** H. A. Strong tr. *Paul's Princ. Hist. Lang.* xxiii. 501 The artificial language of a large area has a tendency to become dialectically differentiated..in much the same degree as the natural language within a particular territory. **1889** *Literary World* 22 June 209/1 The progress of education..will enable each to divest himself of the crudities of his natural language. **1933** L. Bloomfield *Language* xxviii. 506 The political difficulty of getting any considerable number of people all over the world to study, say, Esperanto, will probably prove so great that some natural language will outstrip it. **1956** J. H. Woodger tr. *Tarski's Logic, Semantics, Metamath* viii. 267 Philosophers who are not accustomed to use deductive methods..are inclined to regard all formalized languages with a certain disparagement, because they contrast these 'artificial' constructions with the one natural language—the colloquial language. **1962** U. Weinreich in Householder & Saporta *Probl. Lexicography* 30 Much less can we claim for natural-language lexicography that the definiens should be literally substitutable for the definiendum in normal discourse. **1963** L. Loevinger in H. W. Baade *Jurimetrics* 14 The abstract is recorded in natural language stating the significant index terms. **1970** A. Cameron et al. *Computers & O.E. Concordances* 6 University courses in natural-language programming are now widely available for undergraduates. **1973** M. Dummett *Frege* xiii. 463 A theory of truth which attempts to display the role of the notion of truth..is not a completely separate enterprise from an account of the word 'true' as used within natural language. **1905** J. Herbertson in *Geogr. Jrnl.* XXV. 302 What are the characteristic and distinguishing elements of the areas which we may term natural regions? *Ibid.* 309 We may divide the world up into the following types of natural regions:—1. Polar... 2. The cool temperate regions... 3. The warm temperate regions... 4. (*a*) The west tropical deserts... 5. Lofty tropical or sub-tropical mountains... 6. Equatorial lowlands. *Ibid.*, A natural region should have a certain unity of configuration, climate, and vegetation. **1937** *Geography* XXII. 253 'Natural regions' has been used to cover two distinct types of unit-areas of the earth's surface: (i) those which are marked out as possessing certain common physical characteristics—e.g., a certain kind of structure and surface relief, or a particular kind of climate,—and (ii) those regions which possess a unity based upon any significant geographical characteristics, whether physical, biological or human..as contrasted with areas marked out by boundaries imposed..without reference to any geographical unity of the areas. **1971** *Biol. Conservation* IV. 247 (*heading*) Towards a system for classifying natural regions of the world and their representation by National Parks and Reserves. **1870** Natural resources [see Resource 1 b]. **1921** *Daily Colonist* (Victoria, B.C.) 24 Mar. 13/3 We have toasted our natural resources and talked of the wonderful possibilities of the Province. **1956** J. C. Swayne *Conc. Gloss. Geogr. Terms* 100 *Natural resources*, any materials or conditions existing in nature which may be capable of economic exploitation. **1936** R. R. Rivers *How to buy Timber* iii. 15 Small, specially cut pieces of wood (usually Pine) are inserted crossways between each board in order to let in the air, and so season. That method is called 'air-drying', or 'natural seasoning'. It is a slow process. **1966** A. W. Lewis *Gloss. Woodworking Terms* 87 The two main methods of seasoning are natural or air seasoning, and kiln drying or artificial seasoning.

II. 8. c. *natural right*(*s*), in Western political philosophy, esp. since the 18th century, doctrines derived from concepts of the nature of man and the relationship of the individual to the state whereby certain rights are formulated (see quots.) which the state ought to safeguard.

1689 tr. *B. de Spinoza's Treat. Theol. Pol.* xvi. 343 In Democratical Government, no man so transfers his own Natural Right to another, as for ever after to be excluded from consultation, but only transfers it upon the major part of the Society, of which he still makes one. **1791** T. Paine *Rights of Man* 111 The end of all political associations, is, the preservation of the natural and imprescriptible rights of man; and these rights are liberty, property, security, and resistance of oppression. *Ibid.*, The exercise of the natural rights of every man, has no other limits than those which are necessary to secure to every *other* man the free exercise of the same rights. **1796** *Encycl. Brit.* XVI. 244/1 *Natural* rights are those which a man has to his life, limbs, and liberty; to the produce of his personal labour; to the use, in common with others, of air, light, and water, &c. **1925** A. D. Lindsay *Karl Marx's Capital* iii. 60 The labour theory of value is.., like all theories of natural right, a revolutionary doctrine. *Ibid.* 61 Theories of natural right are always to this extent misleading—that they are statements of ideals which pretend to be statements of fact. **1939** E. Beneš *Democracy* i. 7 The French Revolution became by the declaration of human rights the expression of the whole school of philosophy which for centuries fought for the recognition of the so-called '*natural rights*'—that is, for the innate rights of man, the equality of human beings. **1955** *Philos. Rev.* LXIV. 175, I shall advance the thesis that if there are any moral rights at all, it follows that there is at least one natural right, the equal right of all men to be free. **1971** A. R. Ball *Mod. Pol. & Govt.* vii. 124 The justification for these individual rights was to be found in the theories of natural rights, rights that were beyond the competence of any government interference.

d. *natural frequency*, the frequency at which a mechanical or electrical system oscillates when not subjected to any external forces.

1908 J. A. Fleming *Elem. Man. Radiotelegr.* i. 33 If.. oscillations are maintained which have a frequency different from the natural frequency of [the] circuit, they are called forced oscillations. **1922** Glazebrook *Dict. Appl. Physics* II. 961/1 If the natural frequency is nearly equal to that of the applied force..we have the phenomenon known as resonance. **1962** F. I. Ordway et al. *Basic Astronautics* ix. 370 Very serious problems arise if the lowest natural frequency of the vehicle approaches the control frequency. **1971** L. T. Agger *Introd. Electr.* xxiv. 435 The resonant frequency..in the present simple case is the same as the natural frequency.

12. a. For † *Obs. rare* read 'Now *Hist.*', and substitute for def.: in *Old Med.*, that one of the three spirits (Spirit *sb.* 16) which was held to be produced in the liver and pass thence to the heart (see quots.). (Earlier and later examples.)

1477 Spirit Naturall [see Spirit *sb.* 16]. **1888** *Encycl. Brit.* XXIV. 95/1 The blood-making organ, the liver, separates from the blood subtle vapours, the natural spirits, which, carried to the heart, mix with the air introduced by respiration, and thus form the vital spirits. **1928** C. Singer *Short Hist. Med.* ii. 56 Galen believed that food-substance from the intestines was carried as 'Chyle' by the portal vein to the liver. There it was converted into blood and endowed with a particular pneuma, the Natural Spirit, which bestowed the power of growth and nutrition. *Ibid.* iv. 126 We have already traced the wrecking of the Galenic physiology. With its destruction, the old ideas concerning the three types of spirit, natural,

vital, and animal, went by the board. **1945** D. GUTHRIE *Hist. Med.* v. 77 In the liver the blood, endowed with Natural Spirit, passed to the right ventricle, whence it was distributed to nourish all the tissues and organs, and also to the lungs, in order that impurities might be exhaled.

IV. 18. a. (Examples of *attrib.* and pl. use of *natural science.*) Hence *natural-scientific* adj.

1890 W. JAMES *Princ. Psychol.* I. vii. 184 It is highly important that this natural-science point of view should be understood at the outset. **1924** R. M. OGDEN tr. *Koffka's Growth of Mind* i. § 4. 15 The behaviour of an animal as it takes place is something to be determined as a natural-scientific event. **1944** H. A. HODGES *Wilhelm Dilthey* iii. 49 Natural-science psychology..takes the mind as a thing among things and studies its processes from a causal point of view. **1949** M. FORTES *Social Struct.* p. ix, Their theme was the comparative study of human society by the methods of the natural sciences. *a* **1963** L. MACNEICE *Astrol.* (1964) viii. 262 He began his huge and gallant undertaking while he was still a natural-sciences student at the University of Geneva. **1970** G. E. EVANS *Where Beards wag All* xx. 231 When he [*sc.* the archaeologist] comes..to the question *Why?*, he is forced to look beyond the natural sciences, and his aids are more likely to come from anthropology, history, geography, [etc.].

c. Also *natural scientist.*

1895 F. THILLY tr. *Paulsen's Introd. Philos.* I. i. 59 Natural scientists..are inclined to pursue the former path. **1951** E. E. EVANS-PRITCHARD *Social Anthropol.* iii. 48 This is not the procedure of natural scientists, which most writers of this persuasion—and that means most English social anthropologists—consider themselves to be. **1975** *Notes & Rec. R. Soc.* XXIX. 193 My first intimation of Johnson's views on natural science and on natural scientists came from the *Life of Milton.*

19. Of wool, cotton, silk, etc.: having a colour characteristic of the natural state when unbleached and undyed. Also *natural-coloured* adj. Hence as *sb.* to denote a shade of off-white or creamy beige.

1854 *Morning Post* 7 July 1/5 (Advt.), Aberdeen Linsey Woolseys in granite, heather, and natural wools. *c* **1860** in A. Adburgham *Shops & Shopping* (1964) vii. 74 Vicuna,..woven in its natural colour,..is admirably adapted for Ladies' Cloaks and Gentlemen's Costumes. **1895** *Montgomery Ward Catal.* 9/3 Dress Linen..in the 'natural' flax color only. *Ibid.* 12/3 Plain Habutai Silk in natural (cream) color only. **1927** T. WOODHOUSE *Artificial Silk* 85 Natural-coloured artificial silk yarns. **1930** *Daily Express* 6 Oct. 9/6 (Advt.), Real Italian hand embroidery on pale cream linen, beautifully worked in blue, gold, rose, or natural. **1941** R. STOUT *Red Threads* i. 6 He must have the natural kasha, the one with nubs, by tomorrow afternoon. **1954** [see *ALIZARIN]. **1971** *Vogue* 15 Oct. 144/3 Dress;..colours: cocoa, blue, natural.

20. *natural shoulder* U.S. (see quot. 1973). Freq. *attrib.*

1957 *Men's Wear* (N.Y.) 8 Feb. 69/2 Natural shoulders mark the topcoats as well as the suits. **1958** *Ibid.* 21 Feb. 70/2 What is one man's 'Ivy' is another man's 'natural shoulder garment'. **1962** 'I. T. Ross' *Old Students never Die* i. 13 In a natural-shoulder suit now, instead of a sloppy sweatshirt. **1969** *New Yorker* 11 Oct. 128/1 (Advt.), We don't make outerwear with padding. All our coats are natural shoulder. **1973** *Esquire's Encycl. 20th Cent. Men's Fashions* 670/1 *Natural shoulder.* Term applied to a straight-hanging jacket with medium-width, lightly padded shoulders and a center vent. With this style, favored by university men and others, were worn pleatless, trim-cut trousers.

naturalism. Add: **2.** Also, the view that moral concepts can be analysed in terms of concepts applicable to natural phenomena.

1894 J. SETH *Study of Ethical Princ.* III. ii. 398 We are offered..a new version of the 'Ethics of Naturalism', far superior to the old Utilitarian version, superior because so much more scientific. **1903** G. E. MOORE *Principia Ethica* ii. 40, I have thus appropriated the name Naturalism to a particular method of approaching Ethics. **1945** K. R. POPPER *Open Society* I. v. 60 Ethical naturalism..has recently been used for confusing the whole issue by advertising certain reactionary, and allegedly 'natural' rights as 'natural laws'. **1952** R. M. HARE *Lang. Morals* ii. 30 Professor G. E. Moore's celebrated 'refutation of naturalism'. *Ibid.* v. 92 Naturalism in ethics, like attempts to square the circle..will constantly recur so long as there are people who have not understood the fallacy involved. **1967** *Encycl. Philos.* III. 69/1 According to ethical naturalism, moral judgments just state a special subclass of facts about the natural world.

naturalist. 1. (Further examples.)

1952 R. M. HARE *Lang. Morals* v. 92 It is therefore no answer..to claim that a 'naturalist' might if he pleased define 'good' in terms of some characteristics of his choice. **1964** [see *CONTEXTUALISM 1].

naturalistic, *a.* Add: **1. b.** (Further examples.) Spec. *naturalistic fallacy* (see quot. 1903).

1894 J. SETH *Study of Ethical Princ.* III. ii. 398 In spite of his professed impartiality between matter and mind, Spencer does not hesitate to offer such a materialistic or naturalistic interpretation of the moral life. *Ibid.*, A naturalistic scheme of morality, the correlation of the ethical with the physical process. **1903** G. E. MOORE *Principia Ethica* i. 10 Ethics aims at discovering what are those other properties belonging to all things which are good. But far too many philosophers have thought that when they named those other properties they were actually defining good; that these properties, in fact, were simply not 'other', but absolutely and entirely the same with goodness. This view I propose to call the 'naturalistic fallacy'. *Ibid.* vi. 201 The naturalistic fallacy has been quite as commonly committed with regard to beauty as with regard to good: its use has introduced as many errors into Aesthetics as into Ethics. **1934** C. D. BROAD *Five Types Ethical Theory* vii. 257 Those theories which hold that ethical characteristics *can* be analysed without remainder into non-ethical ones may be called..*Naturalistic Theories.* **1936** A. J. AYER *Lang., Truth & Logic* vi. 157 We have already rejected the 'naturalistic' theories which are commonly supposed to provide the only alternative to 'absolutism' in ethics. **1965** *Philos.* XL. 308 The attack on the naturalistic fallacy..has been welcomed.

‖ **natura naturans** (natiūᵊ·ră næ·tiŭrænz). *Philos.* [L. *nātūra* birth, constitution, etc., f. *nāt-*, pple. stem of *nascī* to be born + med. L. *nātūrans* pres. pple.] Nature creating; the essential creative power or act. Also **natura naturata** (-ā·tă), nature created; the natural phenomena and forces in which creation is manifested. Also *transf.* Cf. NATURE *v.*[1] 2.

1605 [see NATURE *v.*[1] 2]. *c* **1818** COLERIDGE *On Poesy & Art* in *Biog. Lit.* (1907) II. 257 If the artist copies the mere nature, the *natura naturata*, what idle rivalry!.. Believe me, you must master the essence, the *natura naturans*, which presupposes a bond between nature in the higher sense and the soul of man. **1855** BAGEHOT in *National Rev.* I. 57 A school of 'common-sense poets',.. who proceed to describe what they see around them, to describe its *natura naturans*, to delineate its *natura naturata.* **1903** R. A. DUFF *Spinoza's Pol. & Ethical Philos.* i. 3 It might be shown that Spinoza did, and could, make no claim to terms such as substance,..idea, *natura naturans* and *natura naturata*.., nor even to the definitions which he gives of them. **1933** R. TUVE *Seasons and Months* iv. 152 Matfre treats first of the nature and power of God ('natura naturans'), Who has created all 'Natura naturata'. **1950** F. COPLESTON *Hist. Philos.* II. IV. xix. 198 Averroes's..metaphysical scale reaches from pure matter ..to pure Act, God, as the highest limit, between these limits being the objects composed of potency and act, which form *Natura naturata.* (The phrases of the Latin translation, *Natura naturans* and *Natura naturata*, reappear eventually in the system of Spinoza.) **1958** E. F. J. PAYNE tr. *Schopenhauer's World as Will* II. xvii. 175 Such an *absolute system of physics* as described above, which would leave no room for any *metaphysics*, would make *natura naturata* (created nature) into *natura naturans* (creative nature).

nature, *sb.* Add: **2. a.** Also, (one's) *better nature.*

1848 LYTTON *Harold* III. XII. ix. 375 His own better nature which, ere polluted by plotting-craft, and hardened by despotic ire, was magnanimous and heroic, moved and won him. **1919** M. K. BRADBY *Psycho-Anal.* III. x. 129 Any repressed desire which belongs to my undeveloped 'better nature'. **1949** D. SMITH *I capture Castle* xiii. 246 By the time Stephen got home, my better nature had asserted itself and I was terribly worried about his feelings. **1965** M. FRAYN *Tin Men* i. 9 Appeal to their better natures.

4. e. *the nature of the beast.*

1678 J. RAY *Coll. Eng. Proverbs* (ed. 2) 77 It's the nature o' th' beast. *c* **1683** J. VERNEY *Let.* in M. M. Verney *Mem.* (1899) IV. vii. 254 I'me very Sorry John my Coachman Should be soe great a Clowne to you..but t'is the nature of the Beast. **1748** RICHARDSON *Clarissa* III. 218, I might as well have preserv'd the first; for I see it is the *nature of the beast.* **1893** KIPLING *Many Inventions* 254 'Twas the nature av the baste to put the comether on the best av thim. **1969** V. GIELGUD *Necessary End* v. 48 Barry Compayne never made bones about..the number of girls that he had 'laid'... Anthea had chosen deliberately to put down such exploits to 'the nature of the beast'.

f. *nature and nurture, nature–nurture,* heredity and environment as influences on, or the determinants of, personality (see quot. 1874). Also *attrib.*

[**1610** SHAKES. *Tempest* IV. i. 188 A borne-Deuill, on whose nature Nurture can neuer sticke.] **1874** R. GALTON *Eng. Men of Sci.: their Nature & Nurture* i. 12 The phrase 'nature and nurture' is a convenient jingle of words, for it separates under two distinct heads the innumerable elements of which personality is composed. Nature is all that a man brings with himself into the world; nurture is every influence from without that affects him after his birth. **1914** F. W. MOTT *(title)* Nature and nurture in mental development. *Ibid.* 1 The problem of nature and nurture in mental development is one that has recently acquired importance. **1933** L. HOGBEN *(title)* Nature and nurture. **1946** *Brit. Jrnl. Psychol.* May 159 The particular nature-nurture ratio value, or the physiological or anatomical associations which it possesses. **1952** C. P. BLACKER *Eugenics* 267 Unconscious prejudices can throw the nature-nurture controversy into different perspectives. **1965** R. B. CATTELL *Sci. Analysis of Personality* ii. 50 The nature-nurture ratios are not fixed and immutable laws, but statements which may change with culture patterns and the ranges of racial, genetic difference within the given population. **1972** *Times* 2 Sept. 14/3 The argument between the 'nature' and 'nurture' schools of thought. **1974** *Science* 5 July 20/2 The disagreement about the causation of autism... First, there is the usual nature–nurture controversy.

7. Restrict † *Obs.* to sense a and add later example of sense b.

1922 JOYCE *Ulysses* 373 Frightened she was when her nature came on her first.

11. a. *balance of nature*: see *BALANCE *sb.* 13 c.

d. *from nature*: see FROM *prep.* (*adv., conj.*) 13.

12. f. (*one of*) *nature's gentlemen*: a natural gentleman, a person who is a gentleman by nature. Hence in similar phrases, and in extended use: by temperament.

1841 THACKERAY *Second Funeral of Napoleon* iii. 67 In the matter of gentleman democrats, cry pshaw! Give us one of nature's gentlemen, and hang your aristocrats! *a* **1882** TROLLOPE *Autobiogr.* (1883) I. iii. 53 If I say that a judge should be a gentleman..I am met with a scornful allusion to 'Nature's Gentlemen'. **1898** A. J. MUNBY *Diary* 26 Mar. in D. Hudson *Munby* (1972) 423 A splendid woman, full of rustic health & vigour, & one of Nature's ladies. **1901** G. B. SHAW *Admirable Bashville* II. i. 309 You need not be an idle gentleman. I call you one of Nature's gentlemen. **1929** A. HUXLEY *Let.* 9 May (1969) 311 Now..I can write a letter. It will be a poor return for all yours, because I am not one of nature's letter-writers. **1969** L. DURRELL *Spirit of Place* 19 He was one of nature's lobbyers—a tireless and relentless fellow. **1969** *Times* 15 Nov. 10/4 Nature's gentleman one day Bobby [Charlton] will be remembered as the jewel of them all. **1971** P. O'DONNELL *Impossible Virgin* iii. 67 One of nature's innocents. He couldn't dissemble if he tried. **1973** *Guardian* 18 June 9/6 We all know the kind of women who are just nature's doormats and..put up with anything.

13. d. *all nature*, everything, everyone, all creation; *like all nature*, like anything, like blazes. *U.S. colloq.*

1819 *Mass. Spy* 3 Nov. 3/1 Father and I have just returned from the balloon—all nature was there, and more too. **1824** *Woodstock* (Vermont) *Observer* 17 Feb., They said too 'twould shoot like *all nater*, 'Tis singlar what stories they tell. **1825** J. NEAL *Bro. Jonathan* II. 93 Hurra for you—that beats all nater! **1840** C. F. HOFFMAN *Greyslaer* II. III. xiv. 254 The poor critter would have been sucked under, smashed on the rocky bottom, and dragged off like all natur. **1878** MRS. STOWE in *Atlantic Monthly* Oct. 472/2 Cuff would prance round.. and seem to think he..had the charge of *all natur*'. **1892** J. C. DUVAL *Early Times in Texas* vi. 82 'Well, I declar, boys,' said he, 'ef this don't beat all natur.'

14. a. (*d*) (Examples.)

1802 C. WILMOT *Let.* 3 Jan. in *Irish Peer* (1920) 23 My first impression was amazement, at beholding the women from 15 to 70 almost in a state of nature. **1970** *Brewer's Dict. Phr. & Fable* (ed. 12) 747/2 *In a state of nature*, nude or naked.

15. a. *nature-cure* (*attrib.* examples), *-folk, -lover, -loving* (adj.), *-mystic, -mysticism, -myth* (*attrib.* example), *poem, poet, poetry, ramble, -symbol, -symbolism, walk, -worship* (earlier and later examples), *-worshipper, -writer, -writing* (vbl. sb.); **Nature Conservancy**, an organization responsible for the conservation and study of flora and fauna in Britain, which runs nature reserves, research stations, etc.; **nature conservation,** the preservation of wild fauna and flora and the habitat necessary for their continued existence in their native surroundings; **nature-faker** orig. *U.S.*, a person who falsifies reports of natural phenomena, esp. animal behaviour; so **nature-faking** *vbl. sb.* and *ppl. a.*; **nature-name**, a toponym embodying an allusion to a natural occurrence or topographical feature; **nature-notes**, comments on natural history; **nature reserve**, a tract of land managed in order to preserve its fauna, flora, physical features, etc.; **nature sanctuary,** an area in which the fauna and flora are protected from any disturbance; **nature strip** *Austral. local* (see quot. 1966); **nature study**, the study of natural objects and phenomena, esp. as a subject taught in schools; an example of this; so (*rare*) **nature-student; nature trail**, a path linking features of interest, esp. in relation to local natural history, which are described and interpreted by explanatory notices, printed leaflets, or a guide.

1949 *Times* 12 Feb. 3/4 Mr. Herbert Morrison announced in the House of Commons yesterday that arrangements have been completed for forming a Nature Conservancy, and that a separate committee will supervise activities in Scotland... The conservancy—'a more convenient title than conservation board'—would be responsible for the whole of Great Britain. *Ibid.* 5/3 The Nature Conservancy is to have a general charge over all matters relating to the native fauna and flora of Britain. **1959** *News Chron.* 4 Dec. 7/6 The Nature Conservancy has had to abandon plans to establish a warden on Dungeness. **1971** O. NORTON *Corpse-Bird Cries* ii. 25 Nature conservancy, or Snowdonia national park, or something. They've laid out a nature trail at Llyn Coedig. **1974** M. BLACKMORE in Warren & Goldsmith *Conservation in Pract.* xxvii. 427 On March 23rd, 1949, it [*sc.* the Government] created the Nature Conservancy by royal charter as a new research council. **1943** *Nature Conservation & Nature Reserves* (Brit. Ecol. Soc.) 7 The whole problem of nature conservation requires to be viewed against the human or social background. **1948** *Times* 30 Apr. 6/3 Mr. H. Morrison..said that the Government accepted in principle the recommendations..calling for the establishment of a Nature Conservation Board. **1953** *Rep. Nature Conservancy to 1952* 3 Though the Act as a whole does not extend to Scotland, Part III and such other Sections as relate to nature conservation are so extended. **1968** C. BURKE *Elephant across Border* v. 203 You can do more for nature conservation by shocking people..than a

whole heap of discussion groups and bird magazines can do. **1974** M. BLACKMORE in Warren & Goldsmith *Conservation in Pract.* xxvii. 423 Nature conservation illustrates the gradual evolution and development of modern attitudes. **1906** *Chambers's Jrnl.* 24 Nov. 832/1 At Dr. Lahmann's nature-cure sanatorium,..care is taken to cook vegetables so as to retain the nutritive and soluble salts. **1969** C. WATSON *Flaxborough Crab* xvii. 180 What have I to do with this—this nature cure chicanery? **1906** *Everybody's Mag.* June 770 (*heading*) Roosevelt on the nature fakirs. **1909** *Daily Chron.* 8 Dec. 6/4 A President.. who never..'goes for' Congress or nature-fakers or millionaires. **1949** *Natural Hist.* Mar. 131/2 Many nature fakers had obtained free meals..through the gullibility of newspaper reporters. **1921** *Daily Colonist* (Victoria, B.C.) 10 Apr. 17/1, I should be sorry to have Mr. John Burroughs catch me nature-faking. **1923** KIPLING *Land & Sea Tales* 85 To say that William did not sleep a wink that night would be what has been called 'nature-faking'. **1947** *Sports Afield* Dec. 6/3 It was apparent to me that the writer colored his material, particularly in regard to the nature faking episode. **1927** PEAKE & FLEURE *Peasants & Potters* i. 8 They had settled down into a routine, as had many nature-folk the world over before European industrialism touched them in the last century. **1902** *Chambers's Jrnl.* July 426/2 Many an angler and nature-lover is a veritable 'prisoner of Hope'. **1937** *Discovery* Jan. 32/1 The book is a most suitable gift for nature lovers of all ages. **1969** *Islander* (Victoria, B.C.) 31 Aug. 4/1 It is the perfect spot in summertime for lazing on the beach..more than this, it is a nature lover's paradise. **1913** *Eng. Illustr. Mag.* June 254 It is scarcely possible to find a mountain track or woody dell..which has not fascinated and inspired this nature-loving poet. **1927** J. S. HUXLEY *Relig. without Revelation* iv. 123 The nature-mystic. **1958** *Economist* 8 Nov. Suppl. 11/1 Traherne was a visionary possessed of a powerful and discerning mind. To regard him as a lone eccentric or a pre-Romantic Nature-mystic is to under-estimate his stature as a Christian humanist. **1899** W. R. INGE *Christian Mysticism* viii. 302 The true Nature-Mysticism is prominent in St. Francis of Assisi. **1932** C. WILLIAMS *Eng. Poetic Mind* ii. 13 Wordsworth was..not ever writing a child's primer of Nature-mysticism; he left that to his commentators. **1954** E. E. EVANS-PRITCHARD *Inst. Primitive Society* i. 4 Other anthropologists—if we may include Max Müller and the rest of the nature myth school under this heading—were busy explaining religion in terms of personification of such natural phenomena as sun, sky, and rain. **1960** P. H. REANEY *Orig. Eng. Place-Names* ii. 30 Farnborough 'fern-clad hill', Hertford, 'stag-ford'..were originally nature-names from which later settlements near-by took their names. **1906** M. CAWEIN (*title*) Nature-notes and impressions in prose and verse. **1937** *Discovery* Oct. 318 The marvellous journey of Domingo Gonsales..with its ingenious form of aerial transport and its lunar 'nature notes'. **1905** F. H. SHOOSMITH *'Kingsley' Nature Poetry Books* I (*heading*) The 'Kingsley' nature poems. **1946** 'G. ORWELL' *Coll. Ess.* (1968) I. 1, I wrote bad and usually unfinished 'nature poems' in the Georgian style. **1906** A. MACKIE *Nature Knowl. Mod. Poetry* v. 55 (*heading*) Wordsworth as a nature poet. **1925** A. HUXLEY *Along Road* I. 66 A 'nature poet' (the expression is somehow rather horrible, but there is no other). **1938** L. MACNEICE *Mod. Poetry* i. 8 Rooted, as nature-poets should be, in their subject. **1905** F. H. SHOOSMITH (*title*) The 'Kingsley' nature poetry books for schools. **1936** F. R. LEAVIS *Revaluation* v. 186 'Nature poetry', Victorian or Georgian, pays at the best only an equivocal tribute to his [*sc.* Wordsworth's] greatness. **1944** A. THIRKELL *Headmistress* xi. 231 There would be a Nature Ramble at a good brisk pace in Lord Pomfret's grounds. **1965** 'O. MILLS' *Dusty Death* xi. 121 We used to.. go to one of the cookery classes, or go on a nature ramble. **1915** R. LANKESTER *Diversions of Naturalist* ii. 17 A society has been founded for the formation of 'nature-reserves' in the British Islands. **1937** *Handbk. Soc. Promotion of Nature Reserves* 8 Woodwalton Fen, Huntingdonshire. This nature reserve..consists of about 360 acres of primitive fenland, a relic of the once extensive Huntingdonshire fens, and is rich in plant and insect life. **1949** *Act* 12 & 13 *Geo. VI* c. 97 § 15 The expression 'nature reserve' means land managed for the purpose—(*a*) of providing..special opportunities for the study of, and research into, matters relating to the fauna and flora..or (*b*) of preserving flora, fauna or geological or physiographic features of special interest in the area. **1959** *News Chron.* 4 Dec. 7/6 A warden to see that building operations cause as little harm as possible to wild life and plants in what is left of the surrounding nature reserve. **1967** N. FREELING *Strike Out* 39 The sand dunes..have been made into a sort of nature-reserve. **1969** *Times* 3 Mar. 5/8 In a general discussion on establishing nature reserves on farms, the question of unrestricted access and possible vandalism clearly worried some farmers. **1972** *Country Life* 6 Jan. 22/3 Nature-reserve management. **1932** V. E. SHELFORD in *Ecology* XIII. 202 Reports from the Advisory Board and other members of this committee showed them unanimously in favor of nature sanctuaries to which only persons conducting scientific, artistic or literary work of a serious nature are to be admitted. *Ibid.*, Nature sanctuaries should not be given publicity on account of the desire to visit them created thereby. **1972** *Country Life* 6 Apr. 838/3 Where..a marsh has been reclaimed, one cannot expect back-to-the-wilds compensation in the shape of a nature sanctuary. **1966** BAKER *Austral. Lang.* (ed. 2) xvi. 344 *Nature strip*, a strip of lawn beside the footpath outside Melbourne homes in 'garden suburbs'. **1973** *Listener* 25 Jan. 118/1 The ground in front of the house—what the Australians call a 'nature strip'. **1902** *Pall Mall Mag.* Aug. 485 Few of these nature-students are men of leisure. **1896** L. C. MIALL (*title*) Round the year. A series of short nature-studies. **1897** J. H. COMSTOCK (*title*) Insect life: an introduction to nature-study and a guide for teachers, students and others. **1902** *Chambers's Jrnl.* Oct. 683/1 The Nature-study Exhibition which was held at the Botanical Gardens, London, this autumn. **1928** D. PATTON (*title*) Nature study for beginners. **1953** G. BELL *Black Marigolds* i. 19 Bugs got his nature study prize as expected. **1972** J. WILSON *Hide & Seek* ii. 34 Alice taught Mary how to read and how to add up..and they did nature study and learnt about cavemen. **1927** H. CRANE *Let.* 12 Sept. (1965) 305 Pocahontas is the mythological nature-symbol chosen to represent the physical body of the continent. *Ibid.* 307 The mother who died... Her succession to the nature-symbolism of Pocahontas. **1926** F. E. LUTZ (*title*) Nature trails. **1927** *58th Ann. Rep. Amer. Mus. Nat. Hist. 1926* 106 Dr. Frank E. Lutz,..has conducted for some time a Station for the Study of Insects, in Harriman State Park, near Tuxedo, N.Y. In connection with this outdoor station, in 1925 he established and developed a Nature Trail in the vicinity. *Ibid.* 107 This Nature Trail has been a wonderful stimulus to the present-day movement toward the emphasis of the outdoor museum and hundreds of nature trails have been made in various parts of the country, and also in foreign countries. **1950** W. HILLCOURT *Field Bk. Nature Activities* 47 The best location for a nature trail is a park, a camp, a grove adjacent to the school grounds. **1963** *Rep. Nature Conservancy* vii. 103 During the [National Nature] Week the Conservancy set up Nature Trails at Castor Hanglands and Studland Heath National Nature Reserves. **1969** M. PUGH *Last Place Left* iv. 23 All the work of.. laying out nature trails had been undone. **1974** *Country Life* 14 Mar. 583/3 An excellent nature trail has been laid over this land. **1932** R. LEHMANN *Invitation to Waltz* I. vii. 80 She saw two figures..James and Miss Mivart, returning from their nature walk. **1964** O. BLAKESTON *Fingers* i. 9 Drilling the catechism class..and giving the children a yearly 'nature walk' as a treat. **1850** R. W. MACKAY *Progress of Intellect* I. iii. 151 The elements of personification, as well as Pantheism, are in all Nature-worship. **1960** C. DAY LEWIS *Buried Day* vii. 147, I took up nature worship now because it was a poetic thing. **1929** A. HUXLEY *Do what you Will* 158 St. Francis is often hailed as the first nature-worshipper..in Europe since..the Greeks. **1946** BLUNDEN *Shelley* 137 A seer and a nature-worshipper. **1931** —— *Votive Tablets* 259 Some of the..nature-writers mentioned above. **1969** *Times Lit. Suppl.* 16 Jan. 61/1 Thomas's nature writing was good of its kind and time.

b. Restrict *Sc.* to uses in Dict. and add *nature food.*

1847 E. WALKER *Diary* in C. M. Drury *Elkanah & Mary Walker* (1940) viii. 205 The year has been fruitful in nature food. **1971** *Sunday Express* (Johannesburg) 28 Mar. 5/6 He tended the children himself, using nature foods prescribed by Mr. Peter Dowling, a practising naturopath.

nature, *v.*[1] Restrict † *Obs.* to sense 1 and add later example of sense 2 (used as *vbl. sb.*).

1880 G. M. HOPKINS *Note-bks. & Papers* (1937) 312 The whole function, the naturing, the selving of that nature.

naturelle (natürẹl), *a.* [a. Fr. *naturelle* fem. of *naturel* natural. Cf. *NATURAL *a.* 19 above.] Of a pale pink or beige colour; skin-coloured.

1873 *Young Englishwoman* Feb. 78/1 A dark blue marine velvet hat..with black pompom, and long plume naturelle. **1907** *Yesterday's Shopping* (1969) 537/1 Poudre de Riz..in 4 shades (Blanche, Rachel, Naturelle, Rose). **1927–8** *T. Eaton & Co. Catal.* Fall & Winter 367 Pompeian Face Powder..fine and clinging, in White, Rachel, Naturelle or Flesh.

‖ **nature morte** (natür mort). [Fr.] = STILL LIFE. Also *transf.*

1921 R. FRY *Let.* 14 Dec. (1972) II. 518 He's bought.. one superb *nature morte*, and he's two lovely Renoirs. **1923** A. HUXLEY *Antic Hay* xvi. 225 Her face, painted in two tones of red, white, green, blue and black, is the most tasteful of *nature-mortes*. **1938** L. DURRELL *Let.* in *Spirit of Place* (1969) 53 He hasn't painted a stroke..not a bloody *nature-morte* even; and when he admits it he looks rather *nature-morte* himself. **1947** *Horizon* Jan. 17 The fixed elements of cubist nature-morte came to a new life. **1960** *Times* 19 Jan. 13/2 By the religious-minded these *nature morte* passages can be interpreted as a humble hymn to the Creator. **1963** M. MCCARTHY *Group* vi. 123 Pale and lifeless..a veritable *nature morte*. **1970** *Oxf. Compan. Art* 1096/2 Dutch *still-leven*, which..denotes simply a motionless (*still*) aspect of nature (*leven*)... means exactly the same as the French term *nature morte*, which dates from the 18th c.

nature-printing. Add: (Later examples.) **nature-printed** *ppl. a.* (later example); **nature-print** *sb.* (example).

1950 W. BLUNT *Art Botanical Illustr.* xi. 141 Some of these works illustrated by nature printing have considerable charm, especially where the process has been used to record grasses, ferns and delicately formed plants. **1967** CAVE & WAKEMAN *Typographia Naturalis* i. 2 It is appropriate that the earliest description of the original technique of nature printing and the oldest extant nature print should both be by Leonardo da Vinci. *Ibid.* 11 Other nature printed illustrations to books were produced in Germany in the late eighteenth and early nineteenth centuries.

naturism. Add: **4.** A movement for, or the practice of, communal nudity in private grounds.

1933 *Gymnos* Nov. 18/1 This book..is the first serious attempt to link Nudism with..Naturism, and Feminism. **1961** *Daily Tel.* 30 Oct. 11/2 Delegates..at the annual conference of the British Sun Bathing Association... agreed..to substitute 'naturism' for 'nudism'. **1973** *Guardian* 28 June 6/1 The Central Council for British Naturism has launched a publicity campaign..[for] official 'naturist beaches'.

naturist. Add: Also *attrib.*

1950 G. BRENAN *Face of Spain* v. 113 He is a vegetarian and a firm adherent of the Naturist clinic in Malaga, with its theories of opposites and harmonies in foods. **1971** M. MCCARTHY *Birds of America* 184 A naturist diet of fruit and raw vegetables.

2. A practitioner of naturism (sense *4). Also *attrib.*

1929 M. PARMELEE *Nudity in Modern Life* i. 15 We have all heard of so-called 'naturists', who insist that man.. should discard everything artificial such as..clothing, books, cooked food, etc. **1930** *Observer* 27 Apr. 12/5 Advocates of the health cure of complete nudity..spent a holiday in a naturist colony on an island in the Seine. **1958** *New Statesman* 15 Mar. 330/3 Nudist clubs ('actually we prefer the word "naturist"') were in violent competition. **1963** *Daily Tel.* 20 Mar. 22/5 The description 'a nudist camp', according to the naturist terminology, is defunct... Instead club members are asked to use the expression 'sun club' or 'naturist club'. **1973** [see *NATURISM 4].

naturopathy (nēⁱtiŭrọ·păþi). [f. NATUR(E *sb.* + -O + -PATHY (cf. HYDROPATHY).] A theory of the nature of disease and a system of therapeutic practice founded on the supposition that diseases can be cured by natural agencies.

1901 L. STADEN in *Kneipp Water Cure Monthly* Jan. 30/2 There is no doubt that you can get cured without operation by Naturopathy. **1925** [see *KELLGREN]. **1948** [see *CULTISH *a.*]. **1971** *Sunday Express* (Johannesburg) 28 Mar. 5/5 Mr. Fell asked the Supreme Court to reverse the magistrate's findings and to accept that naturopathy is a legitimate form of medicine.

Hence **na·turopath,** one who advocates or practises naturopathy; **naturopa·thic** *a.*

1901 *Kneipp Water Cure Monthly* Jan. 30/2 (*heading*) Naturopathic Adviser. *Ibid.* Nov. 311/2 L. Staden, Naturopath. **1928** S. LIEF *Nat. Cure versus Med. Sci.* v. 14 The crux of the Naturopathic contention is that the suppression of every acute malady—after the Allopathic procedure—lays the foundation for another acute malady. **1937** *Evening News* 20 Jan. 9/1, I suppose that everybody will admit that we owe the present day benefits of fasting to the teaching of naturopaths. **1960** *Spectator* 28 Oct. 647 A number of naturopathic practitioners. **1973** *Times* 8 May 18/8 The conference of the British Naturopathic and Osteopathic Association. **1973** *Nation Rev.* (Melbourne) 31 Aug.–6 Sept. 1434/5, I do take exception to those people who advocate cures for homosexuality as chiropractor and naturopath.

‖ **Naturphilosophie** (natū·rfilǭsŏfi:). Also **natur-philosophie.** [G., f. *natur* nature + *philosophie* philosophy.] The name given to the theory put forward, esp. by Schelling (1775–1854) and other German philosophers, that there is an eternal and unchanging law of nature, proceeding from the Absolute, from which all laws governing natural phenomena and forces derive. Hence **natur·philosoph, -er,** one who adheres to the theory of Naturphilosophie.

1817 COLERIDGE *Biogr. Lit.* I. ix. 148 In Schelling's '*Natur-Philosophie*',..I first found a genial coincidence with much that I had toiled out for myself. *a* **1834** —— in K. Coburn *Inquiring Spirit* (1951) 118 The Natur-Phil[osophen] are apt to mistake the new-naming of a thing..for additional insight. *Ibid.* 251 These..are the passages that annoy me in the *Natur-philosophen*! **1846** J. D. MORELL *Hist. View Philos.* II. v. 109 For the method by which Schelling accounts for the three dimensions in space, we refer the reader to a little work containing the Elements of Schelling's Natur-Philosophie. **1892** W. WALLACE tr. *Hegel's Logic* (ed. 2) 430 The formalism of *Naturphilosophie* may teach *e.g.* that understanding is electricity. **1920** A. N. WHITEHEAD *Concept of Nature* ii. 47 A *Natur-philosoph* raises nature to independence, and makes it construct itself, and he never feels, therefore, the necessity of opposing nature as constructed (*i.e.* as experience) to real nature, or of correcting the one by means of the other. **1946** M. R. COHEN *Pref. to Logic* vi. 102 Since the failure of the romantic *Naturphilosophie* to derive infallible knowledge of nature *a priori*,..it has become generally evident that all our factual knowledge..is only probable. **1957** G. S. CARTER *100 Yrs. Evolution* ii. 16 The German abstract or transcendental zoology, usually called Natur-philosophie..owed its origin to Goethe more than to any other biologist. *Ibid.* vi. 70 The theories of the natur-philosophers might have done this. **1965** *Listener* 3 June 833/1 One of the important influences which shaped the intellectual milieu of early Victorian England was German *Naturphilosophie*. **1974** *Sunday Times* (Colour Suppl.) 9 June 52/4 In Germany *natur-philosophie* often coincided with extreme nationalism.

Naugahyde (nǭᵊ·găhəid). Also (erron.) **naugahide.** [f. *Nauga(tuk*, the name of a town in Connecticut, U.S.A., where rubber is manufactured + *-hyde*, modified form of HIDE *sb.*[1]] The proprietary name of a material consisting of a fabric base coated with a layer of rubber or vinyl resin and finished with a grain like that of leather, which is used in upholstery.

1937 *Official Gaz.* (U.S. Patent Office) 7 Dec. 41/2 United States Rubber Products, Inc... *Naugahyde* for upholstery material, more specifically fabric base which has been treated with rubber and other substances producing artificial leather. **1971** *Flying* Apr. 49/3 He is..a pilot's pilot..for whom 'cockpit' means not a Naugahyde cell with air-conditioning, but a bucket seat and a parachute. **1973** H. NIELSEN *Severed Key* v. 58 The apartment was..finished in contemporary motel naugahide. **1974**

Anderson (S. Carolina) *Independent* 22 Apr. 5B/3 (Advt.), Several Console Stereos. Modern sewing machines. One Duncan Phyfe sofa. covered in Red velvet. One 2 piece den set, covered in naugahyde.

naught, *v.* Add: **b.** To bring to naught; to annihilate. Also **nau·ghting** *vbl. sb.*

1913 E. UNDERHILL *Mystic Way* 137 It is the final disestablishment and 'naughting' of the separate will. **1930** C. WILLIAMS *Poetry at Present* 85 The word death generally suggests a 'naughting' of all that we know. **1958** C. PEPLER *Eng. Relig. Heritage* IV. i. 225 Concentrating only on the outgoing features of simplicity in the naughting of self. **1958** *Times Lit. Suppl.* 10 Oct. 581/3 The Self, the One, in whom a Western mystic..seeks to lose his particular warped and transient self is not Himself naughted, is not naught.

naughty, *a.* Add: **2. b.** Also, *naughty naughty*: a reprimand used to a child; also used jocularly designating disapproval of something, *spec.* concerning sex.

1882 *National Police Gaz.* (U.S.) 4 Nov. 10/1 Those naughty naughty parsons up and at it again. **1938** I. GOLDBERG *Wonder of Words* viii. 150 To a child..we say, 'Nightie-nightie'. Or, if it has been mischievous, 'Naughty-naughty'. **1940** 'G. ORWELL' *Inside Whale* 133 From a mere account of the subject-matter of *Tropic of Cancer* [by Henry Miller] most people would probably assume it to be no more than a bit of naughty-naughty left over from the 'twenties. **1946** —— *Crit. Ess.* 127 The naughty-naughty touches in Dali's autobiography.

3. b. *the naughty nineties* (see quot. 1970).

1925 R. LE GALLIENNE *Romantic '90s* iv. 162 'The '90s' are usually spoken of as if they had only one colour: the 'yellow' '90s, or the 'naughty' '90s, or the 'decadent' '90s. **1930** SELLAR & YEATMAN *1066 & All That* lix. 111 Oscar Wilde..was the leader of a set of disgusting old gentlemen called 'the naughty nineties'. **1937** *Jrnl. R. Aeronaut. Soc.* XLI. 128 He is carrying us back into the nineties of last century..(today I note referred to as the 'naughty nineties'!). **1939** *Burlington Mag.* Apr. 200/2 He was essentially a 'naughty 'nineties' figure. **1970** *Brewer's Dict. Phr. & Fable* (rev. ed.) 748/1 *Naughty Nineties, The*, the 1890s in England, when the puritanical Victorian code of behaviour and conduct gave way in certain wealthy and fashionable circles to growing laxity in sexual morals, a growing cult of hedonism, and a more light-hearted approach to life.

naughty (nǭ·ti), *sb.* [f. the adj.] **1.** *to do the naughty* (slang): to behave in a sexually promiscuous way. Similarly *to go naughty.*

1869 F. HALL in D. Lyndesay *Works* IV. 498 The wealth of the prelates keeps our daughters unwedded. And some of them go naughty. **1902** FARMER & HENLEY *Slang* V. 20/2 Shop and working girls in large towns sometimes say they work for their living, but do the naughty for their clothes. **1937** PARTRIDGE *Dict. Slang* 553/1 *Naughty, do the*, play the whore; to coït (of women only).

2. *Austral.* and *N.Z. colloq.* or *slang.* (An act of) sexual intercourse. Hence as *v. trans.*, to have sexual intercourse with.

1959 D. NILAND *Big Smoke* vii. 169 The woman giggled. .. 'Come on, what about it?' Ocker shook his head, grinning. 'I'd like to oblige, but I can't... It's in me contract, no leaving the job for a naughty.' **1961** PARTRIDGE *Dict. Slang* Suppl. 1195/2 *Naughty, v.* To coït with... 'He naughties her.' **1962** *Times Lit. Suppl.* 12 Oct. 793/4 Would you please whisper in the ear of the young lady who reviewed *The Stuart Case* in your issue of August 10 that 'to have naughty'..is throughout the South Seas the polite and strict analogue of 'to have sexual intercourse'. **1963** F. HARDY *Legends from Benson's Valley* 11, I smiled, remembering his oft-repeated remark: 'I get a lot of knock backs but I get a lot of naughties.' **1967** F. SARGESON *Hangover* vii. 55 He read: 'We'll naughty anyone. No, not on your life, not after Coral.' **1969** *Private Eye* 25 Apr. 12 What bloody fun have I had? Eight kiddies and two more on the way and I haven't even negotiated a naughty!

naughty (nǭ·ti), *adv.* [f. NAUGHTY *a.*] In a naughty or improper manner.

1898 J. D. BRAYSHAW *Slum Silhouettes* 142 He looked a reg'lar dook. He'd a pair o' lavinder-coloured bell-bottom trowsis, cut werry naughty. **1919** MENCKEN *Amer. Lang.* 228 The child behaved naughty. **1922** JOYCE *Ulysses* 441 Naughty cruel I was.

naujakasite (nauyǟkā·zəit). *Min.* [f. *Naujakas-ik*, a point on the southern coast of Tunugdliarfik Fiord, Greenland + -ITE[1].] A hydrated silicate of sodium, iron, and aluminium (with substitution by other metals), $(Na,K)_6(Fe^{II},Mn,Ca)(Al,Fe^{III})_4Si_8O_{26}.H_2O$, which is found as white, platy, monoclinic crystals.

1933 O. B. BØGGILD in *Meddelelser om Grønland* XCII. IX. 7 Among the minerals collected by G. Flink on his mineralogical journey in 1897 there is a specimen labelled 'Chorite?' by Flink. The locality is stated to be Naujakasik... The specimen containing the naujakasite was probably found loose on the ground. **1960** *Mineral. Abstr.* XIV. 370/2 Naujakasite, formerly only known from a loose boulder, has now been found in situ at Tuperssuatsiaq and the northern part of the Ilímaussaq batholith. **1967** *Meddelelser om Grønland* CLXXXI. VI. 14 Naujakasite alters easily through several stages to analcite.

naupliar (nǭ·pliăɹ), *a.* [f. NAUPLI(US + -AR[1].] = NAUPLIAL *a.*

1961 in WEBSTER. **1963** [see *COPEPOID *a.*]. **1975** *Sci. Amer.* Mar. 80/2 In some instances there is enough wax in the egg to carry *E*[*uchaeta*] *japonica* through the entire six naupliar stages. **1975** *Nature* 17 Apr. 591/2 The fresh-water layer of the lake has been colonised by a calanoid copepod, *Pseudoboeckella* sp. (average concentration recorded 0.5 individuals l^{-1}, including naupliar stages).

Nauruan (nau·ruăn), *sb.* and *a.* [f. *Nauru*, an island in the western Pacific + -AN.] **A.** *sb.* A native or inhabitant of Nauru. **B.** *adj.* Of or pertaining to Nauru.

1921 R. D. RHONE in *Nat. Geogr. Mag.* Dec. 563/2 The Nauruans have never been cannibals, but they had the reputation of being savage warriors. *Ibid.* 576/1 In the Nauruan legends the coconut..either owes its eyes and mouth to human ancestry or man owes his eyes and mouth to the coconut. **1925** *Windsor Mag.* Mar. 398/2 A middle-aged Nauruan, clad only in a *ridi*, presents an impressive and ponderous appearance... But..nothing could be more charming than a Nauruan maiden. **1935** A. F. ELLIS *Ocean Islands & Nauru* v. 41 From time immemorial a special kind of fish has been cultivated by the Nauruans in this lagoon. **1951** L. MASON in O. W. Freeman *Geogr. Pacific* x. 296 About a thousand Nauruans were transferred in 1943 to Truk... A postwar sequel in Nauruan history has to do with its new status as a Trust Territory. **1963** *Austral. Encycl.* VI. 257 In the past most of the Nauruans were skilled fishermen. **1969** *Age* (Melbourne) 24 May 2/4 The Acting Chief Secretary (Mr. Manson) warned yesterday that Victorians taking part in the Nauruan pools could face penalties of up to $100.

nausea. Add: Also with pronunc. (nǭ·ziă).

4. Special Comb.: **nausea gas**, a gas used to induce nausea in people.

1966 *Guardian* 10 May 12/4 US Army planes dropped nearly three and a quarter tons of nausea gas on the suspected jungle headquarters of the Vietcong yesterday. **1970** *Globe & Mail* (Toronto) 28 Sept. 17/1 Soldiers fired nausea gas to drive back a stone-throwing mob..in Belfast.

nauseate, *v.* Also with pronunc. (nǭ·zĭ,eit).

nauseous, *a.* Also with pronunc. (nǭ·zĭəs).

Naussie (nǫ·si, nǫ·zi). *colloq.* [f. N(EW *a.* + *AUSSIE *sb.*] = *New Australian* (*AUSTRALIAN *sb.* 2 b).

1959 [see *AUSTRALIAN *sb.* 2 b]. **1959** BAKER *Drum* 129 *Naussie*, a N(ew) Aussie.

nautic, *a.* and *sb.* Add: **B.** *sb.* **b.** A sailor, esp. of the Royal Navy.

1909 *Westm. Gaz.* 3 June 4/2 'Nautics' love the spray of the waves more than they do the dust of the roads. **1943** B. J. HURREN *Eastern Med* vi. 76 A complete reversal of policy was now thrust upon an eager company of flying nautics. **1951** P. BRICKHILL *Dam Busters* xix. 244 A certain..personality at Bomber Command..when he heard the *Tirpitz* was sunk, [said] 'That's one in the eye for the Nautics!' **1973** *Sunday Tel.* 4 Mar. 38/1 The Army did as they had been done by in the first-half. Now it was the Nautics who were under hideous pressure.

navaid (næ·vē͡id). [f. NAV(IGATIONAL *a.* + AID *sb.*] Any navigational device in an aircraft, ship, etc.

1956 S. ROSENBERG *Systems Analysis Approach to Choice of Long Distance Navaid* (Rome Air Devel. Technical Note 56–279, U.S. Govt. Res. Rep. AD 97714, Aug.) 1 Increased interest has been displayed recently on the need for a single, standard long-distance navigational aid (navaid) capable of meeting the latest.. operational objectives. **1960** *Electronics Weekly* 21 Sept. 2 (*heading*) Ocean-based navaid to be tested by US. **1971** *Electronics & Communications Abstr.* XI. 47 An analytical study is presented of a new navaid system designed to assist the navigation of aircraft in remote and low traffic areas by facilitating homing and orbiting on ground beacons. **1971** *Flying* Apr. 53/2 When ranked against the ..expenditures proposed for terminal and en-route traffic control (not counting navaids and landing aids), the FSS money looks like a couple of drops they might spill while pouring.

Navajo (næ·văho), *sb.* and *a.* Also **Nabajo, Nabeho, Navaho, Navajoe.** [f. Sp. *Apaches de Navajó*, f. Tewa *Navahu* large field.] **A.** *sb.* **a.** An Athapascan Indian people of Arizona, Utah, and New Mexico; a member of this people. **b.** The Athapascan language of this people. **B.** *adj.* Of, pertaining to, or characteristic of this people.

[**1629** ZÁRATE-SALMERON in *Papers Archaeol. Inst. Amer.* (1892) Amer. Ser. IV. 294 La nacion de los Indios Apaches de Nabajù.] **1780** in *New Mexico Hist. Soc. Publ.* (1918) No. 21, 36 The war cruelly made upon them [*sc.* pueblos] by the Utes and Navajos. **1822** J. FOWLER *Jrnl.* 8 Mar. (1898) 123 The Spanierds Have Sent 700 men against the nabeho Indeans. **1834** A. PIKE *Prose Sk. & Poems* 99 An Indian girl with her Nabajo blanket, black, with a red border. **1850** [see *JICARILLA]. **1873** J. H. BEADLE *Undevel. West* xxv. 524 John H. Van Order acted as interpreter from English into Spanish, and Jesus Alviso from Spanish into Navajo. Nearly all the employes understood a little Navajo, but not enough to interpret. **1907** [see *APACHE 1]. **1910** G. W. JAMES *Grand Canyon* iii. 18 Gray Navaho rugs cover the brown floor. **1921** [see *APACHE 1]. **1929** D. H. LAWRENCE *Pansies* 39 A Navajo woman, weaving her rug in the pattern of her dream. **1951** see *BEAT-UP *sb.* and *a.*]. **1957** P. WORSLEY *Trumpet shall Sound* 243 The Navaho..were one of the few Indian tribes who remained unaffected by the Ghost Dance of 1890. **1972** A. FOWLES *Double Feature* ix. 173, I stared, instead, at a Navajo rug hanging on the wall. It was worked in small black triangles of black and red, worked in a stark zigzag pattern on a cream background. **1973** T. ALLBEURY *Choice of Enemies* xxviii. 155, I can get by quite happily in Navajo. **1975** *Guardian* 21 Jan. 2/6 The more culturally intact tribes such as the Navajos, the nation's largest.

naval, *a.* Add: **2. d.** *naval brass*, a type of brass containing about 60 per cent copper, 39 per cent zinc, and one per cent tin, used for bolts and other small fittings of ships.

1881 *Calvert's Mechanics' Almanack 1882* 27 In 1874, an alloy, composed of 62 parts of copper, 37 of spelter, and one of tin, was proposed by Mr. Farquharson... The new alloy is specified for all ships built for the Admiralty, and the details now given may be of service to anyone using naval brass. **1928** S. G. WHEELER *Marine Engin.* II. xvii. 510 Naval brass can be rolled or forged, but unless it can be worked in this way has poor strength when cast. **1964** S. H. AVNER *Introd. Physical Metall.* xii. 353 Leaded naval brass with the addition of 1·75 Pb for improved machinability is used for marine hardware. **1969** D. K. ALLEN *Metall.* xiii. 438/2 Naval brass or Tobin bronze.. has increased resistance to salt water spray and is used for condenser plates, welding rod, propeller shafts, and marine hardware.

e. *naval base*, a securely held seaport from which naval operations can be carried out.

1906 F. T. JANE *Heresies of Sea Power* II. ii. 126 These are they who assign the first and second places to the fleet; the shore and the shore forces come but a bad third. The advocates of naval command of naval bases may be found among these. **1941** A. J. MARDER *Brit. Naval Policy 1880–1905* x. 183 England's key position in the Mediterranean, though strongly fortified, could hardly be called a naval base at this time. **1957** P. MACKESY *War in Mediterranean 1803–10* 13 Malta..was the only naval base possessed by England from which the Toulon fleet could be watched and maritime command exercised in the central Mediterranean. **1969** *Islander* (Victoria, B.C.) 9 Nov. 16/2 In the early days Esquimalt was a British naval base, but merchantmen also used the harbor extensively.

f. *naval bank holiday*: (see quot. 1961). *colloq.*

1916 G. FRANKLIN *Naval Digression* vii. 220 We had a typical 'naval bank holiday' on Boxing day—coaling ship. **1948** PARTRIDGE *Dict. Forces' Slang* 124 *Naval bank holiday*, coaling the ship. **1961** —— *Dict. Slang* Suppl. 1195/1 *Naval bank holiday*, a day spent in coaling the ship.

4. d. *naval brigade*, a landing force; a reinforcement force for land troops.

1883 MELTON & OLIPHANT *Cruise of U.S.S. Galena* vii. 80 On several occasions our Naval Brigade was landed upon the breakwater and exercised in marching and counter-marching. **1884** *Naval Encycl.* 510/1 It has been customary in the service to give the name of 'naval brigade' to even a single ship's company, although by rights it refers to a larger organization. **1901** J. BLAKE *How Sailors Fight* xii. 241 Naval brigades took part in the operations with Buller, with Methuen, and with Lord Roberts; but of all it is probable that at the siege of Ladysmith the services rendered were most valuable. **1904** J. S. CORBETT *Eng. in Mediterranean* II. xxiv. 119 The real attack was made from the centre with five battalions of infantry, the naval brigade, and the three troops of British horse. **1937** H. FITCH *My Mis-spent Youth* iii. 14 As a Captain, Beresford had been in charge of the naval brigade during the River War which led up to the battle of Omdurman.

navalist (nē͡i·vălist). [f. NAVAL *a.* + -IST.] One who stresses the importance of having a strong navy. Also *attrib.*

1920 *Glasgow Herald* 30 Dec. 6/3 Mr. Daniels's rather flamboyant allusions to the American naval programme would be utilised by our domestic navalists. **1927** *Observer* 20 Mar. 16/4 'Neon'..is a good old-fashioned navalist and an obsolete politician. **1961** A. J. MARDER *From Dreadnought to Scapa Flow* I. 158 The insistence of navalist opinion..that in an era of international strife it was imperative that the private armament firms be kept in efficient condition. **1963** R. A. HOUGH *Hunting of Force Z* iii. 64 Navalists and airmen and their supporting politicians and suppliers bandied about the old dogmas and statistics. *Ibid.* 72 Bombardment from the air, navalists the world over calculated, was no more than another threat to be added to that of the torpedo-boat and submarine.

‖**navarin** (navarǣn). [Fr.] A mutton stew made with small onions and potatoes. Also **navarin printanier** (prǣntanie), a navarin made with spring vegetables.

1877 E. S. DALLAS *Kettner's Bk. of Table* 309 Navarin is a stupid word which has arisen from a desire to get rid of the unintelligible and misleading name, Haricot de mouton, without falling back on the vulgar phrase, Ragoût de mouton. It was at first selected with a thought of punning upon the *navet* or turnip, which is so prominent in the Haricot de mouton. **1907** A. ESCOFFIER *Guide Mod. Cookery* xv. 448 Navarin Printanier... Transfer the pieces of mutton..to another saucepan with..small, new onions..new trimmed carrots..new turnips..new potatoes..fresh peas, and..French beans. **1951** E. DAVID *French Country Cooking* 111 *Navarin Printanier.* This is a ragoût of lamb or mutton to which spring vegetables give special character... As soon as they [*sc.* peas] are cooked the *Navarin* is ready. **1963** *Economist* 30 Nov. 931/2 A basic recipe like *navarin.* **1966** *Vogue* Nov. 154/3 Dishes of the day may be Navarin Printanier, daube of lamb..or Chicken à la King. **1970** SIMON & HOWE *Dict. Gastron.* 275 *Navarin*, the French culinary

name for a ragoût of mutton..made either with small onions and potatoes or with different vegetables such as carrots, turnips, new potatoes and green peas in which case *à la printanière* is added to its name.

Navarrese (nævărī·z), *sb.* and *a.* Also **Nava·rran.** [f. *Navarr(e* a province of northern Spain, formerly a kingdom which included part of south-west France + -ESE.] **A.** *sb.* The people of Navarre; a native or inhabitant of Navarre. **B.** *adj.* Of or pertaining to Navarre.

[**1699** J. STEVENS tr. *Mariana's Gen. Hist. Spain* VIII. iii. 122 At this time the Count of Toulouse, came in with fresh supplies to assist the Navarrois.] **1846** R. FORD *Gatherings from Spain* xiii. 147 The Navarrese drink their Peralta, the Basques their Chacolet. **1855** C. M. YONGE *Lances of Lynwood* xiv. 219 The swarthy Navarrese mountaineer. **1915** C. C. MARTINDALE *In God's Army* I. 122 His servant, Miguel, was a Navarrese of bad character. **1932** E. HEMINGWAY *Death in Afternoon* xii. 125 Navarrese bulls are almost a different race, smaller and usually of a reddish color. **1943** E. A. PEERS *Spain in Eclipse* I. i. 25 The difficult country north of Reinosa had been negotiated by the Navarrans. *Ibid.* ii. 46 Navarran troops entered Barbastro and a rather slower advance began against Lérida. **1956** P. KEMP *Mine were of Trouble* ii. 26 A young Navarrese officer. *Ibid.* iv. 76 Father Vicente, the Company Chaplain, a stern-faced, lean Navarrese.

nave, *sb.*[1] Add: **1. b. nave plate** = **hub-cap*.

1962 *Which? Car Suppl.* Apr. 67/1 The Austin A60 had a grease gun, nave plate remover and box spanner. **1968** *Radio Times* 13 June 29/3 A rattle from the tail end [of a car],.. sounding .. like a loose wheel nut bouncing about inside the nave plate.

navel, *sb.* Add: **1. a.** *to contemplate* (or *regard*) *one's navel*: to engage in meditation or contemplation; to be complacently parochial or escapist; so *navel-contemplation*. Cf. *navel-contemplator*, **navel-gazer*.

1921 D. H. LAWRENCE *Let.* 2 May (1962) II. 650 *Your* Nirvana is too much a one-man show: leads inevitably to navel-contemplation. **1933** E. O'NEILL *Days without End* (1934) I. 21 His letters..extolled passionless contemplation so passionately that I had a mental view of him regarding his navel frenziedly by the hour and making nothing of it! **1966** *Listener* 24 Nov. 770/1 One sits in a New York traffic jam, contemplating, as it were, the city's navel, and the conclusion is inevitable that death from a combination of congestion and suffocation is not far off. **1974** *Times* 27 June 18/3 To fight off the navel-contemplation mood induced by our move of office. **1975** *Times* 2 June 12/8 Lift our eyes for a moment from the contemplation of our own unlovely navels and look out to where.. our fellow human beings live.

4. navel-cord = NAVEL-STRING; **navel-gazer** = OMPHALOPSYCHITE; also *transf.* (cf. *navel-contemplator*); so **navel-gazing** *vbl. sb.*; **navel-stone,** a stone that marks a navel (sense 2).

1922 JOYCE *Ulysses* 385 Our grandam, which we are linked up with by successive anastomosis of navelcords. **1952** L. MACNEICE *Ten Burnt Offerings* 37 Crystal-gazers, navel-gazers. **1963** *Kenyon Rev.* XXV. 549/1 This piece of navel-gazing also reveals a dangerous and sometimes excessive self-consciousness. **1972** *Publishers' Weekly* 10 July 27/2 David Obst has no monopoly on national navel-gazing. **1917** *Encycl. Relig. & Ethics* IX. 492/2 Zeus, wishing to ascertain the exact centre of the earth, sent forth two eagles to fly simultaneously at equal speed from its eastern and western ends. They met at Delphi, and there in Apollo's temple was set up in commemoration the holy Navel-stone..to mark earth's central point. **1922** A. E. HOUSMAN *Last Poems* 50 Mute's the midland navel-stone beside the singing fountain.

navette (næve·t). [Fr., lit. = little boat, f. med. L. *naveta*, dim. of *navis* ship. Cf. NAVET[2].] A cut of jewel in the shape of a pointed oval; a jewel cut in such a shape. Also *attrib.* Cf. MARQUISE 4.

1908 H. C. SMITH *Jewellery* 246 Many of the best-known collections contain examples of these 'nef' or 'navette' pendants. **1944** *Times* 21 Mar. 2/2 A flower pendant, the six petals formed of diamond navettes with a single ruby centre. **1945** A. SELWYN *Retail Jeweller's Handbk.* xv. 217 Fancy shapes, such as the three-cornered, the marquise or navette.., the pear-shaped..or pendeloque, make unusual jewels, and are generally suggested by the natural form of the diamond itself. **1949** G. F. H. SMITH *Gemstones* (rev. ed.) xii. 153 The commonest distorted shapes are the marquise or navette..and the pendeloque or drop-form. **1963** *Guardian* 15 Nov. 10/5 The leading trend today in diamond cutting is the navette—shuttle-shape an enormous pendant *navette* diamond. **1967** *Times* 21 Feb. 21/7 (Advt.), A navette-shaped diamond single-stone ring. **1973** *Country Life* 18 Oct. (Suppl.) 71 Sunburst brooch..brilliant baguette and navette diamond set.

Nav. House, Nav House, *colloq.* name for the Navigation School in H.M. Dockyard, Portsmouth.

1924 'NAUTICUS' *Sea Ways & Wangles* viii. 48 You will then be sent to the Navigation School or 'Nav. House' as it is more familiarly called. This, as you might expect, is situated ashore, near the main gate of Portsmouth Dockyard. *Ibid.* 52 However you are not likely to become Navigator of a flagship until you have been through another course at the 'Nav. House' to qualify you for first class ships. **1948** PARTRIDGE *Dict. Forces' Slang* 124 *Nav House, the*, the R.N. Navigation School, Portsmouth.

navicert (næ·visəɹt). [f. L. *navis* ship + CERT(IFICATE *sb.*] A consular certificate granted to a neutral ship testifying that her cargo is correctly described in the manifest. Hence as *v. trans.*, to authorize with a navicert.

1923 C. E. FAYLE *Seaborne Trade* II. xx. 304 The 'Navicert System', as it was called, from the code word employed, became, in fact, one of the chief instruments in the prevention of enemy trade. **1939** *Times* 3 Nov. 5/1 Arrangements are approaching completion for introducing the navicert system, which was much used in the last war. **1940** *Times* 21 Mar. 5/5 On Tuesday a vessel came through with no fewer than 200 navicerted items of cargo. **1940** R. W. B. CLARKE *Britain's Blockade* 10 A plan is in operation for issuing compulsory navicerts to all ships coming to Europe and North Africa. **1941** *Ann. Reg. 1940* 7 To make matters easier for neutrals, the 'navicert' system introduced in the last war was being greatly extended. **1941** *Times* 2 Apr. 3/5 After the British Government had agreed to navicert two gift cargoes of flour. **1967** D. L. BUSK *Craft of Diplomacy* ii. 46 During the last war..the British issued what were called 'navicerts'. These guaranteed shippers that 'clean' items of cargo would not be confiscated by the Royal Navy as contraband destined for the enemy.

naviculoid (năvi·kiŭloid), *a.* [f. L. *navicula*, dim. of *nāvis* a ship; (in sense 1) adopted as a generic name by J. B. G. M. Bory de St. Vincent in *Dictionnaire classique d'Histoire naturelle* (1827) XI. 472/2: see -OID.] **1.** Of, pertaining to, or resembling a diatom of the genus *Navicula*.

1894 P. T. CLEVE in *Kongelige Svenska Vetenskaps-akademien Handlingar* XXVI. II. 10 It is by no means an easy task to construct an artificial key of such numerous and variable forms as the naviculoid diatoms. **1916** G. S. WEST *Algæ* I. 90 In some of the larger naviculoid diatoms the cell-wall is destitute of pores. **1946** *Nature* 26 Oct. 588/1 It was found that the form of the protoplasmic bodies was returning to the naviculoid.

2. = NAVICULAR *a.* 3 b.

1961 R. W. BUTCHER *New Illustr. Brit. Flora* II. 172 Seed..naviculoid, rugose, black.

navigable, *a.* Add: **2. b.** (Earlier and later examples.) Also of airships. Now *Obs.* exc. *Hist.*

1783 in S. STUBELIUS *Balloon* (1960) 151 We have received a prodigious number of letters relative to the aerostatic machine of Mess. de Montgolfier. Some of these propose methods for rendering this machine truly navigable. **1835** *Mechanics' Mag.* 15 Aug. 374/2 This has been the case with steam-carriages, steam-boats, and other machines, and why should a navigable balloon be excepted? **1887** *Nature* 13 Jan. 260/1 Captain Renard has recently sent in to the French Academy an account of his experiments with his so-called navigable balloon, *La France*, at Meudon. **1907** *Cornh. Mag.* May 611 We shall not go very far wrong if we say that the limits of speed attainable with navigable balloons are not widely different from those attainable in marine navigation. **1908** H. G. WELLS *War in Air* ii. 41 There were several navigable gas air-ships, not to mention balloons, in the air.

Hence as *sb.*, a navigable balloon. Cf. *DIRIGIBLE *sb. Obs.* exc. *Hist.*

1882 W. N. HUTCHINSON in *United Service Mag.* II. 262 This principle of diminishing buoyancy by diminishing bulk is as applicable to the ordinary balloon..as to the navigable, but..the strain on the material..of the navigable..would be trifling. **1908** H. G. WELLS *War in Air* i. 18 They started ironclads, they started submarines, they started navigables. **1933**—— *Shape of Things to Come* I. §7. 70 That primitive 'navigable' the Zeppelin.

navigate, *v.* Add: **1. c.** *U.S.* To walk steadily; to keep on one's course.

1843 'J. SLICK' *High Life* (1844) I. vii. 109 It warn't no easy matter tu navigate so as not tu git a second ducking, for every nigger in York seemed to be out a washing winders. **1846** *Spirit of Times* 11 July 234/3 Well, by this time I began to think of navigating. **1881** R. T. COOKE *Somebody's Neighbors* 88 What are you navigating round me for? **1904** *Sun* (N.Y.) 9 Aug. 10 She was so drunk that she could barely navigate. **1908** G. H. LORIMER *Jack Spurlock* 117 While he could navigate successfully..he could only just stuttah. **1930** *Randolph Enterprise* (Elkins, W. Virginia) 13 Feb. 1/1 The fellow was..hardly able to navigate as he was carrying a heavy load of Prohibition poison.

3. b. *transf.* and *fig.*

1901 G. B. SHAW *Capt. Brassbound's Conversion* I. 215 Spiritually a little weatherbeaten, as having to navigate his creed in strange waters crowded with other craft. **1934** DYLAN THOMAS *18 Poems* 12 Sleep navigates the tides of time.

c. *absol.* and *transf.* of a motor vehicle.

1965 I. FLEMING *Man with Golden Gun* v. 67 Mary Goodnight had insisted on coming along, 'to navigate and help with the punctures'. **1967** J. CAIRD *Murder Scholastic* viii. 93 Once they were in the car, David said: 'I'll navigate. Turn left at the school gate'. **1967** L. MEYNELL *Mauve Front Door* ix. 117 We all piled into it [*sc.* the car]. Three of us in the front seat, Ray and Zena behind. Tessa navigated. **1971** 'H. HOWARD' *Million Dollar Snapshot* vii. 108 Zombie tossed me the keys. He said, 'You drive, I'll navigate.'

6. *trans.* To manage, direct, sail, or fly (a balloon, airship, aeroplane, or the like) in the air. Hence *spec.* to plot and supervise the course of (an aircraft or spacecraft).

1784 *Universal Mag.* LXXIV. p. ii, By imitating the action of..wings, sails, oars, and a rudder, we may be able to navigate a Globe [*sc.* a balloon] in any direction we please. **1877** *Design & Work* III. 603/1 To build it [*sc.* an airship] in England, and navigate it to Zanzibar. **1910** *Blackw. Mag.* July 5/1 The pilot of an aeroplane is almost wholly occupied with navigating his craft. *Ibid.* 13/2 If we can succeed..in building and in navigating a few score of serviceable dirigibles. **1922** *Encycl. Brit.* XXX. 43/1 Not only had the flying-boats on war service to be navigated but the pilot and observer had also to 'navigate' a bomb to its desired target. **1951** *Oxf. Jun. Encycl.* IV. 289/2 Aeroplanes are navigated first by careful planning before the flight, and then by an attempt to keep the course planned throughout the journey. **1958** C. C. ADAMS et al. *Space Flight* xiii. 326 Seven things must be known to properly navigate a ship [*sc.* a spaceship].

b. To travel or fly through (the air).

1901 *Chambers's Jrnl.* Mar. 207/2 Count Zeppelin's airship, .. with a row of seventeen balloons inside, for navigating the air, has also pointed cigar-like ends. **1902** *Ibid.* July 479/2 In the meantime his efforts to navigate the air have, as a matter of course, resulted in the inauguration of many rival schemes. **1907** *Cornh. Mag.* May 609 Grotesque and fantastic schemes for navigating the air were put forward. **1927** C. L. M. BROWN *Conquest of Air* 8 Stories of wizards and witches who navigated the upper air with the assistance of tubs and broomsticks.

navigating, *vbl. sb.* Add: Also in aeronautical and motoring uses.

1950 M. LASKI in *Contact* May–June 50/2, I must warn you, too, of the danger of letting navigating become an end in itself, of sitting with one's eyes glued to the map until it becomes a substitute for the country outside. **1966** 'E. PETERS' *Piper on Mountain* iii. 51 He enjoyed driving, but to him navigating was a chore. **1971** *Gloss. Electrotechnical, Power Terms* (*B.S.I.*) III. vi. 22 A radar navigating system. **1973** A. ROSS *Dunfermline Affair* 103 Charlie drove, and I did the navigating.

navigation. Add: **1. d.** The action or practice of travelling through the air by means of aircraft; flying. More fully, *aerial navigation*. ? *Obs.*

1804 [see *aerial navigation* s.v. *AERIAL *a.* 5]. **1835** *Mechanics' Mag.* Aug. 290/1 The first experiment of this new system of aërial navigation will be made from London to Paris, and back again. **1870** tr. *F. Marion's Wonderful Balloon Ascents* II. ix. 163 The idea of aerial navigation by means of an apparatus heavier than the atmosphere. **1910** *Blackw. Mag.* July 12/2 The safe navigation of the air. **1920** *Act* 10 & 11 *Geo. V* c.80 §2 Limited to aircraft of any special description, or engaged in any special kind of navigation.

2. b. The art or science of directing the movements of aircraft or spacecraft, esp. in regard to a craft's position and course. More fully, *aerial* (or *air*) or *celestial navigation*.

1922 *Encycl. Brit.* XXX. 14/1 Aerial navigation, as distinct from piloting with the ground in view, developed tardily everywhere, though first in Britain. **1931** *Times* 19 Feb. 17/1 A haze..limited visibility to two miles. Navigation was undoubtedly difficult. **1951** *Oxf. Jun. Encycl.* IV. 291/1 Some methods of navigation employ both radar and radio at the same time... Some of the radar and radio devices..can be used both for the main part of a flight and for the actual landing. **1962** F. I. ORDWAY et al. *Basic Astronautics* ix. 385 (*heading*) Celestial navigation. *Ibid.*, The platform of a celestial navigation system includes an automatic sextant. **1974** *Encycl. Brit. Macropædia* I. 376/2 The flight simulator taught the essentials of air navigation and blind flight to thousands of military pilots during World War II.

c. The action or practice of navigating a car (*NAVIGATE *v.* 3 c) or other vehicle.

1944 *Return to Attack* (Army Board, N. Z.) 9/1 Battalions and regiments entered the wilderness in battle order and exercised in desert navigation. **1950** [see *NAVIGATOR 1 c]. **1973** H. MILLER *Open City* xiii. 148 I'm relying on you for navigation..just keep me on the road.

7. a. (Later example.)

1916 A. BENNETT *Lion's Share* i. 7 Probably the largest yacht that had ever threaded that ticklish navigation.

8. In senses relating mainly to air travel: *navigation beacon, instrument, log*; **navigation light,** one of a set of lights shown by a ship or aircraft at night; **navigation satellite,** a satellite whose orbit is accurately known and made available, so that observations of its position may be used for navigational purposes.

1941 J. MASEFIELD *Nine Days Wonder* 3 In war-time, when the navigation-beacons are extinguished. **1959** F. D. ADAMS *Aeronaut. Dict.* 117/1 *Navigation instrument*, an aircraft instrument that indicates, or that is used to ascertain, information relating to the position of an aircraft in flight, or to the direction in which it is flying. **1922** Navigation light [see **landing light*]. **1939** T. L. STOCKEN *Oncoming Ships* 99/1 Lights..mistaken for navigation lights. **1943** C. D. LANE *Boatman's Manual* x. 355 In addition to the navigation light, the lightship carries a riding light forward. **1951** *Oxf. Jun. Encycl.* IV. 4/1 Small lights attached to the wing tips are navigation lights, similar to those used by ships. **1966** Navigation light [see **collision course*]. **1970** V. CANNING *Great Affair* vii. 117 A helicopter..came low over the villa... It wasn't showing any navigation lights. **1937** Navigation log [see *air speed* (*AIR *sb.*[1] B. III. 1)]. **1961** *Ann. Reg. 1960* 386 Transit IB (U.S.A.)..Navigation satellite. Not transmitting. **1968** *Listener* 27 June 825/1 On 21 April 1964 the U.S. military authorities launched a navigation satellite.

navigational, *a.* (Further examples.)

1920 *Act* 10 & 11 *Geo. V* c.67 §69 Lighthouses, light vessels, buoys, beacons, or other navigational marks.

1903 *Proc. Internat. Illumination Congr. 1931* II. 995 The navigational light on a light-vessel is fitted in a lantern which, in the older types, is made in halves bolted together around the mast. **1951** *Oxf. Jun. Encycl.* IV. 291/1 Another radio navigational aid is the radio compass. **1954** *Communications & Electronics* I. 1. 60 The progress of modern aviation is becoming increasingly bound up with developments in communications and navigational aids. **1962** D. Slayton in *Into Orbit* 21 Carpenter..told us what he was doing about navigational aids, although the word 'navigation' was really a misnomer in our case... When you've been..tossed into either a ballistic trajectory or into an orbit, your course is already set. There is nothing you can do to change it. **1966** *Electronics* 3 Oct. 177 Teldix..supply instrumentation, navigational platforms and sensors. **1971** *Gloss. Electrotechnical, Power Terms* (*B.S.I.*) III. vi. 22 *Navigational radar*, radar equipment installed on a craft as an aid to its navigation. **1973** *Fisheries Fact Sheet* (Environment Canada Fisheries & Marine Service) No. 1. 4/2 Small boats..equipped with..navigational aids and radio.

navigator. Add: **1. b.** One who navigates an aircraft or spacecraft.

1784 *Universal Mag.* LXXIV. 20/1 But they soon lost sight of our aerial navigators. **1825** [in Dict., sense 1 transf.]. **1834**, **1915** [see *air navigator* s.v. *Air *sb.*¹ B. III. 4]. **1929** T. E. Lawrence *Let.* 12 July (1938) 663 The Navigator of the airship will be getting his W/T bearings & time signals all the way, and will plot his course exactly. **1930** *Daily Express* 6 Oct. 3/5 The commander [of the airship] must have known, and the navigator. **1943** [see *air-bomber* (*Air *sb.*¹ B. III. 3)]. **1951** *Oxf. Jun. Encycl.* IV. 290/2 Once in flight, the navigator's task is continually to 'fix' his position by observations. *Ibid.* 291/2 A pilot or navigator..cannot choose any course he pleases, as his is not the only aircraft in the sky. **1960** F. Gaynor *Dict. Aerospace* 161 *Navigator*, a crew member who plots and directs the movement of a space ship from within the ship.

c. One who navigates a motor vehicle.

1950 M. Laski in *Contact* May–June 26/1 It is..possible to take an extended motor-trip abroad without ever coming into contact with the Art of Navigation... Far better to become an Accomplished Navigator, and be free of all roads everywhere. **1964** W. Markfield *To Early Grave* (1965) vii. 120 A groan went round the car. '—we are a little, little bit *fahrblunged*.' 'Our navigator,' fumed Levine. **1968** M. Carroll *Dead Trouble* ii. 25, I sat in the car, content and lazy. Lisa needed no navigator. She seemed to know just where she was going. **1971** 'D. Rutherford' *Clear the Fast Lane* 37 Grant would be responsible for everything to do with the car..whilst Ritchie, who would act as his navigator, would be responsible for maps, routes and the latest road information. **1971** M. Tak *Truck Talk* 110 *Navigator*, the co-driver of a two-man operation who reads the road maps while going through unfamiliar towns.

navy¹. Add: **5. c.** A navy revolver.

1867 *Harper's Mag.* June 131/1 Judge put hand under pillow, drew out 'navy', and fired—*through a looking-glass!* **1875** 'Mark Twain' *Sk. New & Old* 122 She turned on that smirking Spanish fool like a wild cat, and out with a 'navy' and shot him dead in open court. **1931** G. F. Willison *Here they dug Gold* 92 Early boom towns and mining camps generally prefer the Colt 'Navy' (·36). **1968** R. F. Adams *Western Words* (ed. 2) 204 *Navy*, a westerner's term for the Navy Colt revolver.

d. A type of tobacco. Also, cigarette ends, etc., as picked up by tramps.

1872 *Kansas Mag.* 177/1 Another pull at the bottle,..a chaw of navy, and the repast is finished. **1876** G. H. Tripp *Student-Life Harvard* 399 Hawes had smoked 'navy' in it all the year of Sam's probation. **1889** J. W. Riley *Pipes o' Pan* 40, I draw my plug o' navy, and I climb the fence. **1926** *Amer. Speech* I. 652/1 *Navy*, cigar end or 'butts' found on side-walk. **1931** 'D. Stiff' *Milk & Honey Route* 214 *Navy*, butts of cigarettes and cigars. **1934** *Amer. Ballads & Folk Songs* 383 The higher you pitch, the sweeter my navy tastes. **1960** Wentworth & Flexner *Dict. Amer. Slang* 351/2 *Navy*,..a cigar end or butt found on a side walk. Perhaps from 'navy' = a type of chewing tobacco.

e. = navy rum.

1946 J. Irving *Royal Navalese* 121 *Navy*, Service issue; Service ways. Most usually it is a sobriquet for the rum-ration—e.g., 'I'll trade my *Navy* for a turn out of watch!'. **1962** Granville *Dict. Sailors' Slang* 80/1 *Navy, tot of*, measure of Navy rum offered to a guest by one who has saved his ration for some special occasion.

6. Articles as supplied to the navy; *navy biscuit, bread, jacket, -plug, revolver* (earlier example); **navy bean** = Haricot *sb.* 2, **navy bullet**, a bullet used with a navy revolver; **navy catapult** (see quot.); **Navy Cut**, proprietary name of a kind of tobacco; **navy register** (example); **navy stroke**, the style of rowing practised in the navy; **navy-yard** (later U.S. examples).

1897 *Sears, Roebuck Catal.* 15/3 Beans, small Navy, hand picked. **1903** A. Adams *Log of Cowboy* xii. 77 Our supply of flour and navy beans was running rather low. **1951** *Good Housek. Home Encycl.* 349/2 Haricot Beans (called 'navy beans' in U.S.A.). **1955** W. Gaddis *Recognitions* II. iii. 426 She went out..and left Gwyon staring into a plate of white navy beans. **1972** *Arable Farmer* Feb. 55/2 The navy bean crop must remain a matter for research and speculation for at least a year or two. **1973** *Times* 30 Apr. 9/1 The baked beans that pass over the shelves of Britain's supermarkets..originate in the United States. Navy beans grown in the Michigan area are shipped to Britain..for processing and canning. **1975** *New Society* 3 July 6/1 The Scottish Horticultural Institute are developing plants less susceptible to colder northern conditions; and research is going on into the production of a navy bean (baked bean) which can be grown in this country. **1867** 'T. Lackland' *Homespun* II. 216 The people not only want the Word, but they want it as hard and dry as a navy biscuit. **1831** *Constellation* 54/1 Ephraim Treadwell..has for sale..Pilot and Navy Bread. **1848** *Rep. Comm. Patents 1847* (U.S.) 374 The 'navy bread' is usually made out of the coarser particles of the meal. **1873** J. Miller *Life amongst Modocs* 312 Was it possible that this man..could still live with a navy bullet through his body fired at two feet distance. **1914** C. F. Tweney *Dict. Naval & Mil. Terms* 161 *Navy Catapult*, a device for launching hydro-aeroplanes from a ship by means of compressed air. **1907** *Yesterday's Shopping* (1969) 67/3 Cigarettes... Virginia... Navy Cut, mild. **1911** *Trade Marks Jrnl.* 6 Sept. 1309 Player's Navy Cut... Manufactured tobacco. The Imperial Tobacco Company (of Great Britain and Ireland), Limited,..Bristol. **1959** E. Burgess *Divided we Fall* vii. 96 Harry was filling his briar with his favourite navy-cut. **1972** 'G. North' *Sgt. Cluff rings True* i. 15 Harrison inhaled contentedly... 'One third navy-cut, two thirds herb mixture.' **1840** C. Mathews *Politicians* II. i. 30 He..had boasted out of doors he could and would save his life with a word as easily as hem-stitch a navy-jacket! **1864** in *Maryland Hist. Mag.* (1926) XXI. 300 He..had on his navy jacket with bright buttons and pants of the same dark blue. **1870** T. B. Aldrich *Story Bad Boy* 245 Between the beer and the soothing fragrance of the navy-plug, I fell into a pleasanter mood. **1909** 'O. Henry' *Roads of Destiny* xxi. 357 It seems that the only maritime aid I am to receive from the United States is some navy-plug to chew. **1916** 'Taffrail' *Pincher Martin* xiii. 242 'Care for a bit of navy plug?' He..never dreamt of boarding a trawler without a couple of inches of strong navy plug tobacco in his pocket. **1841** *Southern Lit. Messenger* VII. 4/1 Statistics..furnished by the Navy Register will show [etc.]. *a* **1861** T. Winthrop *Canoe & Saddle* (1883) iii. 21 This machine..is called a six-shooter, an eight-inch navy revolver. **1903** Kipling *Traffics & Discov.* (1904) 143 Aren't they rowing Navy-stroke, yonder? **1842** *Knickerbocker* XIX. 107 The General landed at the navy-yard. **1886** *Harper's Mag.* Sept. 619/1 The fact of establishing a navy-yard. **1936** Mencken *Amer. Lang.* (ed. 4) 239 What we call..a navy-yard is a *dock-yard* or *naval-yard*. **1946** E. O'Neill *Iceman Cometh* I. 75 De booze dey dish out around de Brooklyn Navy Yard.

naw, var. of No. Add: Also in *U.S.* use.

1906 *Dialect Notes* III. 147 Naw sir, we didn't do it. **1930** J. P. Burke in *Amer. Mercury* Dec. 455/1 Naw, we don't cut hooch any more; we make the bunk with malt. **1949** C. Himes *Black on Black* (1973) 277 'Naw suh,' Lemuel said. **1959** N. Mailer *Advts. for Myself* (1961) 52 'Does one of you want to go?'.. 'Naw.' **1971** *Black World* June 54/2 Naw, that scene was out. **1973** *New Yorker* 21 Apr. 62/3 'You didn't tear her clothes?' 'Naw, nothing like that.'

Naxalite (næ·ksăləit). [f. *Naxal(bari* (the name of a place in W. Bengal) + -ite¹.] A name given in India to supporters of Chinese-type communism (see quot. 1969¹); also *attrib.* Hence **Na·xalism**, Chinese-type communism as practised in parts of India.

1969 *Times* 9 Jan. 9/1 'Naxalites' are in the headlines and seem to be at work in West Bengal, Andhra, Kerala, and half a dozen other states. The name comes from Naxalbari in West Bengal where Indian communists started arming peasants in the spring of 1967. **1969** *Amrita Bazar Patrika* 5 Aug. 5/5 Classes in Calcutta University..could not be held on Monday following a strike call given by the Naxalite-dominated Students' Action Committee. **1970** *Guardian* 2 July 4/4 Three Naxalites were lynched in the Midnapore district of West Bengal after they had killed a school teacher... The first major sign of popular resistance to Naxalite violence. *Ibid.* 4/6 Nepal..is the place where Naxalites and their Chinese mentors meet. **1970** *Guardian Weekly* 26 Dec. 16 The menace of Naxalism, the Maoist movement in West Bengal, may be less virulent than before. **1971** *Illustr. Weekly India* 11 Apr. 33/2 The authorities saw in it an urgent need to stamp out Naxalism before it became too late to do so. **1972** 'E. Peters' *Death to Landlords!* iii. 58 There are Naxalite bosses who are themselves greedy and tenacious landlords. *Ibid.* v. 88 The Naxalites probably quote the Baghavadgita [*sic*], too. **1974** *Daily Tel.* 18 Mar. 1/6 Four people were killed, one of them a policeman, when Naxalite Communists ambushed a police patrol in a Calcutta suburb yesterday.

Naxian (næ·ksiăn), *sb.* and *a.* [f. Gr. Νάξιος, L. *Naxius* + -ian.] **A.** *sb.* An inhabitant of Naxos, a Greek island in the Cyclades group, or Naxos, a part of Sicily colonized from the island of Naxos. **B.** *adj.* Of, pertaining to, or characteristic of the island or colony of Naxos. So **Naxiote** *sb.* and *a.*

1601 P. Holland tr. *Pliny's Nat. Hist.* II. xxi. xviii. 101 The Naxian Cypirus hath a quicker sent: the Phœnician Cypirus smelleth but a little. **1797** *Encycl. Brit.* XII. 779/2 The Ionians..in time..possessed the whole island; whence the Naxians are, by Herodotus, called Ionians, and ranked among the Athenian colonies. **1835** Mitford & Davenport *Hist. Greece* (new ed.) II. i. 4 The expelled Naxians..consented to guide a Persian army against a Grecian island. **1862** G. Grote *Hist. Greece* (new ed.) II. II. xxii. 522 The oligarchy of Chalkis..sent out..settlers, Chalkidian and Naxian, who founded the Sicilian Naxos. *Ibid.* V. II. lviii. 169 The Naxians cordially received the armament, which then steered southward along the coast of Sicily to Katana. **1885** J. T. Bent *Cyclades* xiv. 334 The Naxiotes were aghast when they heard that they were to be ruled by a Jew. *Ibid.* 348 This fortress..is..the acropolis of the Naxiote valleys. **1911** *Encycl. Brit.* XIX. 318/1 Four Naxian ships took part in the expedition of Xerxes, but deserted and fought on the Greek side at Salamis in 480. **1913** J. B. Bury *Hist. Greece* (ed. 2) xv. 674 The Naxians were the first Sicilians to welcome the deliverer of Sicily to her shores. **1946** R. Capell *Simiomata* I. 33 The Naxian pilot's presence on board was overlooked. *Ibid.* 36 A biggish party of German prisoners has been brought in to join our Naxians. **1968** V. Ehrenberg *From Solon to Socrates* v. 130 The Naxians took to the hills, but a few were taken prisoner. **1972** R. Meiggs *Athenian Empire* vii. 123 The earlier date will..suit the Naxian evidence better.

nay, *adv.*¹ and *sb.* Add: **B.** *sb.* **1.** (Earlier U.S. examples in sense: a negative reply or vote.)

1774 in *Vermont Hist. Soc. Coll.* (1870) I. 8 Passed in the affirmative—all yeas, no nays. **1807** J. Turner *Let.* 23 Jan. in J. Steele *Papers* (1924) II. 492 A Bill has passed the H.R. repealing the duty on salt with only 5 nays. **1871** *Trans. Illinois Agric. Soc.* VIII. 5 Mr. Dalton demanded the yeas and nays.

‖ **naya paisa** (nəi·yă pəi·să). Pl. **naye paise.** [Hindi, = new pice.] A unit of currency in India, equal to 1/100 rupee.

1956 *India: Reference Ann.* (Ministry of Information, Govt. India) xi. 127 The Indian rupee..will be divided into 100 units, each unit being called *naya paisa.* **1957** *Times* 2 Apr. 10/6 India's new decimal coinage was introduced today [*sc.* 1 Apr.]...All business transactions will now be calculated in rupees and *naye paise*, 'new coins', of the value of one hundredth of a rupee. **1957** *Whitaker's Almanack 1958* 974/1 An issue of 600m. coins of one, two, five, and 10 *naye paise* denominations was begun. **1963** *Times* 30 Jan. 12/7 King Edward rupees and everything since even to *naya paisa.* **1969** H. R. F. Keating *Inspector Ghote plays Joker* viii. 114 He plonked down fifteen naye paise, asked if he could use the phone. **1972** 'E. Peters' *Death to Landlords!* xi. 158 At the cost of a few *naye paise* they acquired three satisfied business contacts.

Nayar, var. Nair.

1911 *Encycl. Brit.* XIX. 318/2 *Nayar*.., a caste or tribe on the W. coast of S. India, who form the dominant race in Malabar. Traditionally they are soldiers, but many have taken to professions... Their total number in all India in 1901 was just over one million. **1922** *Edin. Rev.* Jan. 187 Even the Nayar, when he addresses a Brahman, must use the language of deprecation. **1955** M. Gluckman *Custom & Conflict in Afr.* iii. 68 The father's rôle seems to have been reduced to a minimum among the Nayar castes of Malabar in India in the past.

nay-sayer. Delete *rare*⁻¹ and add further examples. Also, one who votes against something.

1939 Joyce *Finnegans Wake* 108 Naysayers we know. **1961** C. MacInnes *England, Half English* 47 In this decade we witness the second Children's Crusade, armed with strength and booty, against all 'squares', all adult nay-sayers. **1962** *Times* 5 Apr. 7/3 Mephistopheles the eternal nay-sayer. **1970** *New Statesman* 12 June 835/2 Food scientists should try to be 'nay-sayers against profit curves'. **1972** *Guardian* 28 Nov. 12/6 The Republican Party began the Nixon years as an unrepresentative minority of nay-sayers. **1974** *Publishers Weekly* 5 Aug. 57/3 Further to refute the nay-sayers, he cites poll after poll in which Americans say they are happy despite their feelings that all is not well with the country.

nay-saying. (Later examples.)

1952 B. Wolfe *Limbo* (1953) iv. 222 His mind brimming with..the necessity for some nay-saying gesture against EMSIAC. **1972** *Jrnl. Social Psychol.* LXXXVI. 220 Subjects who obtained scores of 0, 1, and 11, 12 were dropped from the analysis as representing extremes of yeasaying or naysaying.

‖ **nazar** (næ·zāɹ). *India.* [Hindustani.] = Nuzzer.

1855 H. H. Wilson *Gloss. Judicial & Revenue Terms* 373/2 *Nazr, nazar, najar*,..a present, an offering, especially one from an inferior to a superior, to a holy man, or to a prince [etc.]. **1885** G. C. Whitworth *Anglo-Indian Dict.* 225/2 *Nazar*,..a present, an offering; especially one made by an inferior on his presentation to a superior. **1922** *Glasgow Herald* 11 Feb. 10 Twelve Nobles, each offering 'Nazar', or the symbolic tribute of gold. **1934** E. L. Tottenham *Highnesses of Hindostan* iv. 110 The deputations from the various States were presenting their gifts—the *poshaks* and *nazars*—of valuable cloth and plate. **1956** K. Fitze *Twilight of Maharajas* ii. 41 All Durbaris made their act of homage and obeisance, accompanied by the presentation of coins, known as *nazar*, which..found their way in due course to the Palace treasury. **1973** M. Bence-Jones *Palaces of Raj* x. 169 The civilians offering *nazars* of a few rupees laid on a white handkerchief.

Nazarene, *a.* and *sb.* Add: **A.** *adj.* **2. b.** Of or pertaining to, or characteristic of, the Church of the Nazarene (sense *B. 1 c).

1910 *New Schaff-Herzog Encycl. Relig. Knowl.* VIII. 453/2 As official organs of the church the *Nazarene Messenger*, Los Angeles, Cal.,..and the *Holiness Evangel*, Pilot Point, Tex., are recognized. **1958** M. Argyle *Relig. Behaviour* iv. 33 Many of these sects—the Pentecostal, Holiness, Nazarene churches and others—have increased enormously in proportion to their size during this period [*sc.* 1926–1953]. **1968** [see C.O. (*C III. 3)]. **1968** *War Resistance* II. xxiv. 26 The Nazarene Church is a plain building with simple furniture. *Ibid.* 28 Many do leave for USA, Canada or Australia where there are Nazarene Communities.

4. Of, pertaining to, or characteristic of the school of artists called Nazarenes. Cf. B. 4 below.

1950 *Chambers's Encycl.* XIV. 380/1 In many respects Wackenroder was a forerunner of the Nazarene school of painters. 1952 W. GAUNT *Victorian Olympus* i. 29 The master was found in the Nazarene painter, Jacob Eduard von Steinle. 1959 *Listener* 29 Jan. 217/3 The Bayreuth *Parsifal* has escaped from the old-fashioned 'Nazarene' presentation only to fall into a kind of fashionable 'grimness'. 1965 *Ibid.* 9 Sept. 382/2 For a short time after settling in London in 1846, Brown painted in the Nazarene style. 1970 T. HILTON *Pre-Raphaelites* i. 20 *Wycliffe*, with its light, flat tones and dispersed composition, looks very like a Nazarene painting.

B. *sb.* **1. c.** A member of the Church of the Nazarene, a Protestant sect formed at the beginning of the 20th cent.

1898 P. F. BRESEE in T. L. Smith *Called unto Holiness* (1962) v. 121 It is now somewhat more than two years since..the Nazarenes, putting the old things behind them, went out to follow in the footsteps of Him whose name they bear. 1962 K. S. LATOURETTE *Christianity in Revolutionary Age* V. i. 14 On the Pacific coast denominations of recent American origin loomed larger... the Four-Square Gospel, the Pentecostals, the Churches of God, and the Nazarenes. 1962 T. L. SMITH *Called unto Holiness* iv. 75 Men of the Green Mountain State have been significant leaders among New England Nazarenes. 1968 *War Resistance* II. xxiv. 26 According to a report in the mid-20's there were 12–15,000 Nazarenes in Yugoslavia.

4. A name given to members of a group of German artists called the Brotherhood of St. Luke, founded in 1809, who aimed to restore to art the religious quality found in mediæval painting; cf. PRE-RAPHAELITE *sb.* Also called **Nazarite.** Sometimes in pl. **Nazarener.** Also *transf.*, of a style of musical composition.

1880 J. B. ATKINSON *Schools of Mod. Art in Germany* ii. 11 Enemies in the opposite camp nicknamed the new saints 'Nazarites' and 'Pre-Raphaelites'. 1882 J. B. ATKINSON *Overbeck* iii. 74 The type is ascetic and æsthetic after the pre-Raphaelite pattern affected by the Nazarites. 1889 ARMSTRONG & GRAVES *Bryan's Dict. Painters & Engravers* (rev. ed.) II. 460/1 Schadow..went..to Rome, and joined the 'Nazarenes'. 1911 *Encycl. Brit.* X. 375/1 The group of artists who styled themselves *Nazarener*. 1928 E. WAUGH *Rossetti* ii. 29 Nazarene, Florentine, and Crusader fused into one shadowy figure, glowing and distorted. 1942 *Archit. Rev.* XCI. 29 (*caption*) There is nothing elegant in this interior except for the reredos by William Dyce, the 'Nazarene' amongst English Early-Victorian painters. 1947 A. EINSTEIN *Mus. Romantic Era* xii. 161 The 'Nazarenes' of church music were replaced by the 'Caecilians'. *Ibid.*, Nazarene-like church music. 1965 *Listener* 9 Sept. 382/2 He..had come under various influences, including that of the Nazarenes,..a group of German artists who had founded a 'pre' Pre-Raphaelite movement..in the eighteen-tens. 1973 *Country Life* 20 Sept. 779/2 One of his [*sc.* William Dyce's] Nazarene-type paintings.

Nazarenism (næ·zărīniz'm). [f. NAZARENE *a.* and *sb.*] **1.** The principles, doctrines, or cult, of the Nazarenes (sense *B. 1 c).

1892 T. H. HUXLEY *Let.* in J. S. Huxley *Ess. Pop. Sci.* (1926) 161, I have a great respect for the Nazarenism of Jesus—very little for later 'Christianity'. 1923 *Expository Times* Nov. 73/2 Here..the story of Jesus ends, and the story of Nazarenism begins.

2. The characteristics or artistic principles of the Nazarene school of artists.

1895 E. DOWSON et al. tr. *Muther's Hist. Modern Painting* I. vi. 229 It was of no avail to him [*sc.* Phiip Veit] that he mingled with his Nazarenism a certain air of the world. 1947 A. EINSTEIN *Mus. Romantic Era* iv. 36 The Protestant church turned back to Bach..; the Catholic went back still further, to Palestrina and his time, in whose style it fostered a new musical Nazarenism, comparable to the Pre-Raphaelitism of the English school of painters. 1960 R. H. BOOTHROYD tr. *Novotny's Painting & Sculpture Europe 1780–1880* vi. 69 In the strange mixture of styles pervading his paintings of saints there appear a kind of return to the beginnings of Nazarene and Romantic principles and a breaking down of the narrow confines of academic Nazarenism reminiscent even of Blake.

Nazi (nā·tsi, nā·zi), *sb.* and *a.* [repr. pronunc. of *Nati-* in G. *Nationalsozialist.*] **A.** *sb.* A member of the National Socialist (Workers') Party in Germany, led by Adolf Hitler from 1920 and in power from 1933–45; a member of a similar organization; a person who believes in the aims of Nazism or similar doctrines and in the methods necessary to achieve them. Also *Comb.* So **Na·ziphil(e**, a person sympathetic to the ideology of Nazism.

1930 *Times* 19 Sept. 10/1 Herr Hitler, the leader of the victorious National-Socialists (Nazis), has very carefully refrained from saying anything. 1931 W. LEWIS *Hitler* 57 The Democrats..have not been able to deal with the Nazi because of his Mastery of the Street. 1934 D. TEILHET *Talking Sparrow Murders* xiv. 202 The police are Nazi-controlled even in Heidelberg. 1938 *Sun* (Baltimore) 6 Sept. 1/3 The center of Santiago was kept in turmoil after Chilean Nazis..seized the National University. 1939 *Ann. Reg. 1938* 195 Added a number of minor Naziphile persons to the Cabinet. *Ibid.* 234 The chief change made by the new Premier in the Cabinet was to replace Dr. Homan, a strong Naziphil, with Count Paul Teleki. 1942 W. S. CHURCHILL *End of Beginning* (1943) 222 The horde of divisions provided by Finland, Rumania, Hungary, and others of the Nazi-ridden or Fascist-ridden states. 1946 *R.A.F. Jrnl.* May 169 Lancasters..carried the war from one end of Nazi-controlled Europe to the other. 1956 A. H. COMPTON *Atomic Quest* i. 7 The Nazis saw in the atomic bomb the possibility of a new weapon of decisive importance. 1967 D. EISENBERG *Re-emergence of Fascism* iii. 127 The American Nazi and his uniformed 'storm-troopers' have frequently demonstrated outside the White House against racial integration in the South. 1974 *Times* 21 May 1/3 Mr Begin described Arab terrorists as 'the new Nazis' who made children their targets..adding: 'We must arm the population to fight these Nazis.'

B. *adj.* Of, pertaining to, or connected with the National Socialist Party in Germany or a political organization with similar aims, beliefs, or methods elsewhere. So **Na·zi-ish** *a.*

1930 *Times* 16 Sept. 16 (*caption*) Herr Hitler, the leader of the National Socialists, speaking at the last big Nazi election meeting. 1935 C. ISHERWOOD *Mr. Norris changes Trains* vii. 105 The local Nazi storm-troop. 1939 W. S. CHURCHILL *Into Battle* (1941) 108 There is the Nazi-Fascist ideology, and the Communist ideology. 1939 'N. BLAKE' *Smiler with Knife* x. 154 There's nothing Nazi-ish about it... No talk of labour camps and so on. 1949 KOESTLER *Promise & Fulfilment* I. v. 54 To put the callous policy of the Mandatory Power on a par with the barbarity of Hitlerism, as the Jewish terrorists did in their slogan of the 'Nazi-British', is..unjust and stupid. 1967 W. SOYINKA *Kongi's Harvest* 64 The carpenters end with a march down-stage with stiff mallet-wielding arms pistoning up in the Nazi salute. 1973 *Guardian* 29 Mar. 16/4 'Nazi' has become an indiscriminate political cliché applied to insensitive bureaucrats, Americans in Vietnam, IRA Provos, British paras in Ulster, Black September, Zionists, *et al.* 1974 R. THOMAS *Porkchoppers* xviii. 162 'You mean Peter Majury?' '*Jawohl*,' Gayan said and made a Nazi salute.

Nazidom (nā·tsidəm, nā·zi-). [f. prec. + -DOM.] The concepts and institutions of the Nazis.

1933 *Time* 20 Nov. 19/3 To make sure of a real 'intellectual eruption' last week—an utter blasting of Nazidom's foes—the Chancellor and his chief henchmen have been shouting themselves hoarse. 1935 *Times* 25 June 15/3 Professor Karl Barth..has been finally dismissed by the German Minister of Education. Into the details of his dispute with Nazidom there is no need to enter. 1941 *Ann. Reg. 1940* 387 Do not think that Hitler's Nazidom is going to be easily overthrown. 1947 A. L. ROWSE *End of Epoch* xv. 181 The threat to ourselves and the rest of Europe involved by Nazidom. 1971 D. E. WESTLAKE *I gave at the Office* (1972) 179 The story of his escape from Nazidom took slightly longer than a dental appointment.

Nazify (nā·tsifəi, nā·zi-), *v.* Also **nazify.** [f. as prec. + -FY.] *trans.* To cause or force to adopt Nazism or similar doctrines. Hence **Nazifica·tion; Na·zifying** *vbl. sb.*; **Na·zified** *ppl. a.*

1933 *Times* 7 June 13/3 Dr. Dollfuss..is resisting..the combined efforts of the German and Austrian Nazis to nazify Austria. 1933 *Christian Cent.* 20 Sept. 1164 (*heading*) Nazification of German Protestantism continues. 1934 *Times Lit. Suppl.* 26 July 524/2 It may, of course, be said that the process of 'Nazifying' has not had time to achieve its full results. 1934 *Sun* (Baltimore) 24 Sept. 8/2 Such events do not augur well for the future of the 'unified', *i.e.*, Nazified, Evangelical Church of Germany. 1939 *Ann. Reg. 1938* 199 Preparations for the plebiscite..fully occupied the party and the nazified administration during the preceding weeks. 1941 *Ibid. 1940* 229 Their policy of ..nazifying the population gradually. 1961 R. SETH *How Resistance Worked* vi. 67 Throughout 1941 he issued a number of laws by which he intended to nazify Norway. 1972 C. SHORT *Naked Skier* xvi. 79 This Nazified policeman was on the side of the Countess and against us. 1973 E. OSERS tr. *Waldheim's Austrian Example* iii. 45 At first the new regime made a point of cultivating public opinion, but as the process of Nazification spread to all spheres of public life less and less attention was paid to it.

Nazism (nā·tsiz'm). Also **Naziism, Nazi-ism.** [f. as prec. + -ISM.] The political doctrines evolved and implemented by Adolf Hitler and his followers, esp. those relating to racial superiority, the all-powerful state, and the cult of the leader. So **Na·zist, Nazi·stic** *adjs.*

1934 *Times* 28 Feb. 14/3 Finally it is urged that the disinterested support given by Italy to Nazism should counsel higher respect on her part for Italian foreign policy. *Ibid.* 16 Mar. 20/4 A clever essay on the cultural aims of Nazi-ism. 1938 *Ann. Reg. 1937* 171 Chancellor Schuschnigg rejected the Italian suggestion that he should introduce a representative of Naziism into the Austrian Government. 1938 *Times* 17 Mar. 15/5 In Belgium there is already a semi-Nazist party of Germanic nationality looking for help abroad. 1938 *New Statesman* 25 June 1053/2 Quite recently..a new Nazistic party called the Christian Nationalist Socialist Front has been formed. 1940 A. HUXLEY *Let.* 24 Apr. (1969) 453 The doctrines of Nazism, Communism, nationalism..are manifestly idiotic. 1957 J. S. HUXLEY *Relig. without Revelation* (rev. ed.) iii. 63 Nazism was inherently self-destructive because of its claim to world domination by a small group. 1971 *Nature* 16 July 205/2 Feelings about the scientific community's relationship to Naziism. 1973 *Guardian* 29 Mar. 16/4 Nazism was the ultimate degradation of mankind, singular even in the history of vileness.

N'Dama (n͵dā·mă). Also **N'dama, Ndama.** [Native name.] A West African breed of cattle, usually fawn or light red in colour and bearing lyre-shaped horns; an animal belonging to this breed. Also *attrib*

1938 J. L. STEWART in *Vet. Rec.* 9 Oct. 1291/2 The present day N'Dama is almost identical with the Longhorn of the ancient Egyptian drawings. *Ibid.* 1292/1 The N'Dama cattle until a few years ago were found in the Fouta Djalon mountains of French Guinea but have now spread over a large part of West Africa as this breed is especially good for stock improvement. 1952 *Ann. Trop. Med. & Parasitol.* XLVI. 128 The N'damas were born and bred at the Nigerian Agricultural Department's farm at Ilorin. 1956 *Nature* 21 Jan. 132/2 The West African N'Dama breed of cattle shows a remarkable tolerance to trypanosomiasis. 1973 *Guardian* 20 June 12/3 The Zebu cattle of Senegambia..[are] less resistant than the tougher Ndama breed.

Ndebele (n͵dĕbī·li). [Native name, f. *n-* sing. prefix + *Tebele.*] The name of a Zulu people branches of which are found in Rhodesia and in the Transvaal; also a member of this people; (also **Sin-debele**), the language of this people.

The Rhodesian Ndebele are better known as the Matabele (*ma* = pl. prefix).

1913 J. O'NEIL (*title*) A grammar of the Sindebele dialect of Zulu. 1919 [see *MATABELE]. 1930 C. G. SELIGMAN *Races Afr.* viii. 187 The Zulu-Xosa, chiefly in the coastal region south and east of Drakenberg Mountains,..include ..the Amandebele (Matabele) of Matabeleland. 1937 A. W. HOERNLÉ in I. Schapera *Bantu-Speaking Tribes S. Afr.* iv. 86 Among the Southern Transvaal Ndebele, each ..clan has a special species of animal..which may not be named or eaten or used by the members of that clan... The Rhodesian Ndebele..have introduced a new hierarchy of rank resulting from their conquest of indigenous tribes in their new homes. 1951 P. ABRAHAMS *Wild Conquest* 175 'This one brought the news.' 'An Ndabele?' 'No, a Barolong.' 1971 *Rand Daily Mail* 27 Mar. 6/2 Our Zululand and Ndebele beadwork..has always been regarded as the best in the world. 1973 *Drum* (Johannesburg) 8 Jan. 18/3 My mother language is Shona and I can speak English and Ndebele.

‖ **Ndugu** (n͵dū·gu). [Swahili, = brother.] Used as a general form of address in Tanzania.

1973 *Black World* May 47 San Francisco Afrikans (brothers) Afrikan Afrikans (*ndugu*) West Indian Afrikans (Hey man). 1974 *Sunday Tel.* 16 June 36/3 A [Tanzanian] Government directive says that mister, honourable, excellency and all other honorifics will be replaced by the Swahili word *ndugu*, which means brother. 1974 *Daily News* (Tanzania) 13 Sept. 3/1 One of the passengers Ndugu Mohamed Ismaili had this to say: 'We have a transport problem about buses going to Lindi.' *Ibid.* 3/4 'Ndugu' (to trained nurse) 'you're going to work in the ward for four hours today.'

ne', ne (ne), colloq. shortening of NEVER *adv.*

1934 J. D. CARR *Eight of Swords* ii. 28 His daughter and my son—hurrumph, ne' mind. 1949 C. HIMES *Black on Black* (1973) 277 Ne you mind.

nealie (nī·li). Also **nelia.** *Austral.* [Etym. unknown.] = *needle-bush* (*b*) (*NEEDLE *sb.* 14).

1889 [see *needle-bush* s.v. NEEDLE *sb.* 14]. 1933 *Bulletin* (Sydney) 15 Nov. 21/4 Two miles farther on..was a mile-wide stretch of nelia scrub. 1936 I. L. IDRIESS *Cattle King* xxxviii. 326 Where had all the mulga gone, the white-wood, and acacias, and turpentine bush, the black oak and nelia, and bullocky bush, the thick shrub life that had carpeted this country when he rode through here a boy? 1965 [see *needle-bush* s.v. *NEEDLE *sb.* 14].

Neanderthal (nīæ·ndəɹtāl). Also **Neandertal.** The name of a valley near Düsseldorf in western Germany, used *attrib.* in **Neanderthal man, skull,** etc., to designate the Middle Palæolithic fossil hominid *Homo neanderthalensis*, first identified from a skull found there in 1856, and also known from other remains in Europe, Africa, and Asia. Also *absol.*, *fig.* (with reference to appearance), and as *adj.*

1861 G. BUSK tr. D. Schaaffhausen in *Nat. Hist. Rev.* Apr. 167 The considerations which have led us to compare the Neanderthal cranium with those of the most ancient races are still further confirmed by the discovery ..of skulls exhibiting a yet closer correspondence with it. 1863 T. H. HUXLEY *Evidence Man's Place in Nature* iii. 142 The posterior lobe of the brain of the Neanderthal man must have been as much flattened as I suspected it to be. In truth, the Neanderthal cranium has most extraordinary characters. 1864 *Q. Jrnl. Sci.* I. 88 It is my intention to confine myself to the consideration of the Neanderthal fossil with reference to its place in Nature. *Ibid.* 90 The Neanderthal skull is of an elongated oval form. 1899 A. H. KEANE *Man Past & Present* 9 Certain skulls from South Australia seem cast in almost the same mould as the Neanderthal. 1922 *Encycl. Brit.* XXX. 145/2 Neanderthal man is now revealed as an uncouth race with an enormous flattened head, very prominent eye-brow ridges and a coarse face. 1923 A. L. KROEBER *Anthropol.* ii. 24 Neandertal man was short. *Ibid.* xv. 472 Whenever the origin of a people remains obscure, be they Neandertals, Alpines, Sumerians,..or what not, some one propounds the convenient hypothesis of deriving them from this vast interior land [*sc.* central Asia]. 1928 *Weekly Dispatch* 13 May 12/3 The pictures which show modern influence are even more unpleasant than the streaky bacon sunsets..or the most realistic neanderthal clergymen which otherwise decorate the walls. 1939 'N. BLAKE' *Smiler with Knife* iii. 57 You know what the other side says—..'Woman's place is in the kitchen'—all the rest of that Neanderthal tommyrot. 1966 E. PALMER *Plains of Camdeboo* vii. 117 Neanderthal Man lived here in Southern Africa. 1966 M. WOODHOUSE *Tree Frog* xii. 86 A fourteen-stone Neanderthal with a sub-machine gun appeared. 1970 *Guardian* 9 July 10/4 The Neanderthal men of the military and industrial establishments. 1971 *Observer* 23 May 24/6 Neanderthal grunts over the cornflakes..were the best most husbands could manage. 1973 B. J. WILLIAMS *Evolution & Human*

Origins xi. 176/2 In the material that follows I shall use the term Neandertal *sensu lato*, that is, in the broad sense. The term will designate the early stages of the within-species evolution of *Homo sapiens*. *Ibid.* 185/2 In 1958 part of a Neandertal skull was recovered from a cave at Ma-pa, southern Kwangtung. **1973** A. Price *October Men* xi. 164 He is a creature from the Dark Ages, a man of violence. A Neanderthal. **1973** D. Ramsay *Deadly Discretion* 97 How about your pal Ivan? Does he have sensitive feelings under that Neanderthal exterior?

Hence **Nea·ndertha:ler**, a Neanderthal man; **Neandertha·lian** *a.* and *sb.*; **Neandertha·lic** *adj.* (in quot. *fig.*).

1913 *Science Progress* VIII. 278 The Neandertaler differed from *Homo sapiens* in having an extremely receding forehead, with enormously developed brow-ridges. **1920** H. G. Wells *Outl. Hist.* I. ix. 51/2 The Tasmanians were not racially Neanderthalers. *Ibid.* x. 58/2 The tremendous advance they [*sc.* later Palæolithic men] display upon their Neanderthalian predecessors. **1920** H. Reinheimer *Symbiosis* III. i. 205 Some of them, e.g., the Neanderthalians, reached the stage of the savage beast, marked by chronic acromegaly. **1955** *Sci. News Let.* 19 Feb. 122/2 With succeeding generations Neanderthalers became adapted physically to withstand the cold. **1967** *Boston Sunday Herald* 26 Mar. I. 29/3 Neanderthalic sadists forced near-dead men to run when they scarcely had the strength to put one foot ahead of another. **1971** *Times* 11 Feb. 14/7 He pointed out that Neanderthalers, living as they did in the ice age, might easily have suffered from a deficiency in vitamin D.

Neanderthaloid, *a.* Add: Also as *sb.*

1971 *Nature* 23 Apr. 489/2 Although Swanscombe had long been considered closely affiliated with modern *Homo sapiens* the multivariate analysis indicated a closer resemblance to the neanderthaloids.

neanic (nī,æ·nik), *a. Zool.* [f. Gk. νεανικ-ός youthful.] Designating the early stages of the growth of an animal, esp. the pupal stage of an insect.

1892 Buchman & Bather in *Zool. Anzeiger* XV. 421 Hyatt... Nealogic. Here proposed..Neanic. Literary equivalent..Adolescent. *Ibid.* 430 Neanic. During this stage specific characters and all other morphological features present in the adult, appear and undergo development. **1903** *Amer. Naturalist* XXXVII. 519 At this stage [in the growth of *Sycotypus canaliculatus*], the early neanic, the lines of growth are well marked and of nearly equal strength with the revolving lines, the two together giving the shell surface a reticulated appearance. **1906** J. B. Smith *Explanation Terms Entomol.* 87 Neanic: referring to the pupal stage. **1938** *Nature* 20 Aug. 341/1 It is helpful to distinguish between the very early, or embryonic, stages of development and the later, or neanic stages, during which the young gradually assumes the characteristics of the adult. *Ibid.* 10 Sept. 461/1 In the neanic phase the organism exhibits a combination of less stable characters. **1971** F. E. Eames *Davies's Tertiary Faunas* (ed. 2) I. i. 90 Neanic. Youthful stage in ontogeny.

neanthropic (nī,ænþrǫ·pik), *a.* Also neoanthropic, and with capital initial. [f. Neo- + Anthropic *a.*] Of, pertaining to, or designating the single extant species of man as distinguished from extinct forms known from their fossil remains.

Quot. 1916 may represent an independent coinage.

1894 J. W. Dawson *Meeting-Place Geol. & Hist.* i. 17 The modern, or anthropic [period], is..divisible into two sections—the early modern, or palanthropic, sometimes called quaternary, or post-glacial, and which may coincide with the antediluvian period of human history; and the neanthropic, extending onward to the present time. [*Note*] I have preferred..to call the earlier races of men palaeocosmic and the later neocosmic,..while the periods to which they belong are respectively the Palanthropic and Neanthropic. **1916** G. E. Smith *Primitive Man* 18 Thus the new spirit of man and modern man himself are revealed in the Upper Palaeolithic period. This Neoanthropic phase, as I have called it, thus begins in the Aurignacian period. **1939** McCown & Keith *Stone Age Mt. Carmel* II. xxii. 362 In Neanderthal skulls the great wing and the orbital plate of the malar tend to be wide; in Neanthropic skulls they tend to be narrow. **1959** J. D. Clark *Prehist. S. Afr.* iv. 77 The 'neanthropic' or modern (*Homo sapiens*) form of man. **1973** B. J. Williams *Evolution & Human Origins* xi. 175/1 The neanthropic (new man) line included fossils that were more or less modern throughout time.

neap, *a.* Add: **1.** Also *neap rise* (see quot.).

1888 *Encycl. Brit.* XXIII. 369/2 The height between high-water mark at neap tide and mean low-water mark at spring tide is called the neap rise.

Neapolitan, *a.* and *sb.* Add: **A.** *adj.* **b.** *Neapolitan ice*, a block of ice cream made in layers of different colours and flavours; also *transf.* and *fig.*; *Neapolitan system* (see quots.).

1895 'M. Ronald' *Century Cook Bk.* xxii. 498 *Neapolitan ice-cream.* This cream is molded in brick form in three layers of different flavors and colors. **1911** *Daily Colonist* (Victoria, B.C.) 26 Apr. 7/1 (Advt.), Ice Cream Bricks, Neapolitan, Vanilla, Strawberry, Pineapple, [etc.]. **1933** A. Huxley *Let.* 29 Apr. (1969) 369 Mexico was..very curious. Such a strange Neapolitan ice, with its layers of Indian, mestizo, white. **1954** —— *Let.* 25 Oct. (1969) 714 We have to think of the mind in terms of a stratified Neapolitan ice, with a peculiar flavour of consciousness at each level. **1969** R. & D. De Sola *Dict. Cooking* 158/1 *Neapolitan ice cream*, ice-cream brick containing several flavors arranged in contrasting color layers, usually chocolate, vanilla, and strawberry. **1959** Reese & Dormer *Bridge Player's Dict.* 151 *Neapolitan System*,..one of the principal Italian systems, played by Forquet and Siniscalco and others. It is a one-club system, with a series of artificial responses. **1962** *Listener* 22 Nov. 886/2 West, playing the Neapolitan system, opened Two Diamonds. **1964** *Official Encycl. Bridge* 374/2 *Neapolitan*, a system.. played in many World Championship events by a group of Neapolitan players.

B. *sb.* **d.** A dialect or language of Naples.

1598 Florio *Worlde of Wordes* Epistle Dedicatorie, How shall we, naie how may we ayme at the Venetian, at the Romane, at the Lombard, at the Neapolitane, at so manie, and so much differing Dialects, and Idiomes, as be vsed and spoken in Italie, besides the Florentine? **1901** M. Carmichael *In Tuscany* 99 Had Dante been born not at Florence but in Venice and written in Venetian, had Petrarch been born not at Arezzo but in Naples and written in Neapolitan, there would have been two classical languages in Italy today. **1936** G. F.-H. & J. Berkeley *Italy in Making* II. xviii. 276 As a general rule he spoke French or Neapolitan, not Italian. **1973** A. Price *October Men* xi. 157 The man's Italian was..faultless... There was even..the hint of Neapolitan in it.

near, *adv.*² Add: **1. e.** *so near and yet so far*: describing a person who or thing which is unattainable despite its apparent proximity.

1755 W. Hay tr. *Martial's Sel. Epigrams* I. 15 In the whole town no soul can be So near, and yet so far from me. **1850** Tennyson *In Mem.* xcv. 145 He seems so near and yet so far. **1863** 'Ouida' *Held in Bondage* I. i. 25 The long sunny future that stretched before us in dim golden haze,—so near and yet so far from our young longing eyes. **1863** *Harper's Mag.* Dec. 93/2 Thou art so near, and yet so far! **1920** R. Macaulay *Potterism* I. i. 8 In June and July 1914 the conversation turned largely and tediously on militant suffragists, Irish rebels, and strikers... It was a curious age, so near and yet so far, when the ordered frame of things was still unbroken, and violence a child's dream. **1939** Joyce *Finnegans Wake* 213 I've lost it!.. So near and yet so far! **1962** E. Cleaver in A. Dundes *Mother Wit* (1973) 12/1 The actual conditions to which they aspired were..all around them, as it were 'so near and yet so far'.

8. (Further examples.) Esp. in colloq. phrases: (*as*) *near as dammit* (or *damn-it*), *as near as makes no difference* (or *matter*), extremely near; virtually.

1894 G. F. Northall *Folk-Phrases* 9 As near as two damn it. As near as fourpence to a groat. As near as two ha' pennies for a penny. **1897** Conrad *Nigger of Narcissus* iv. 91 You were as near hanging as damn-it tonight. **1911** A. Bennett *Hilda Lessways* v. i. 338 That first night..I was as near as dammit to letting out the whole thing and chancing it. **1931** [see *dammit]. **1937** D. L. Sayers *Busman's Honeymoon* viii. 171 You left here some time after 6.10 by that clock, which was right as near as makes no difference. **1961** [see *dammit]. **1961** I. Jefferies *It Wasn't Me!* iv. 54 They near as dammit showed interest. **1970** P. Moyes *Who saw her Die?* xiv. 183 Funny, isn't it, Miss Threep ending up in the hospital with Billing? Well, not *with* him, of course, but as near as makes no matter.

21. Delete † *Obs.* and add further examples. Now very commonly prefixed to adjs. in the sense 'almost, nearly, approximately', and to sbs. in the sense 'something that is nearly the same as, or is a substitute for, the thing specified'; 'artificial'; *spec.* **near-beer** orig. *U.S.*, a beverage resembling beer; beer with a very low alcoholic content; also *attrib.*; **near-print** (see quot. 1943); **near-seal** *N. Amer.*, any fur treated and dyed to resemble sealskin; **near-silk**, artificial silk.

1928 *Daily Express* 27 Apr. 12/4 The aspirant painters ..drink near-absinthe instead of beer. **1909** *N.Y. Even. Post* (Semi-Weekly ed.) 23 Aug. 2 The refusal of the Cities Commission to prohibit the sale of imitation beer, commonly known as 'near beer'. **1921** *Daily Colonist* (Victoria, B.C.) 27 Mar. 7/5 The thirty-six near-beer bars in operation here at present pay into the city treasury a total of $5,400 a year in the form of licence fees. **1963** *Times* 14 Feb. 4/7 A hostess in a Soho near-beer club told a jury..that..customers were charged 15s. for two soft drinks made from blackcurrant juice. **1952** *Manch. Guardian Weekly* 4 Sept. 3 Add the near-certainty of Massachusetts. **1822** W. Sewall *Diary* 27 Sept. (1930) 89, I am much troubled with a bowel complaint. This must have been caused by drinking freely of near cider. **1973** L. Snelling *Heresy* I. i. 11 Andover, Yale, fine athlete.., captained the Yale crew, near-effortless Phi Beta key, et cetera. **1926** *Ladies' Home Jrnl.* Apr. 24 The decision was based on..two broken engagements, one near-engagement..and several flirtations. **1949** Koestler *Promise & Fulfilment* II. ii. 218 Each of them means a cherished near-escape story to some member of the commune. **1973** C. Bonington *Next Horizon* xix. 261 Twenty-four hours later the shock of my near-escape really hit me, and manifested itself mainly in a sense of horror at letting down my family. **1942** *Daily Tel.* 22 May 5/3 If the harvest collection should break down through a failure of fuel supplies, then near-famine conditions..may not be far away. **1938** *New Statesman* 3 Dec. 904/2 He must now embrace..not merely those propertied groups which are reliably republican, but near-Fascists of the Flandin type as well. **1926** *Scribner's Mag.* Sept. 34/2 (Advt.), Some more piquant revelations of the great and near-great in English and Continental Society. **1855** W. Whitman *Leaves of Grass* 37 The laughing-gull..laughs her near-human laugh. **1943** *Times* (Weekly ed.) 10 Feb. 5 A British army pitch-forked on to Mars would first smile at and then discover near-human characteristics in any local inhabitants that might appear. **1964** M. Critchley *Developmental Dyslexia* xiv. 81 Many of them..become items within the community of illiterates or near-illiterates. **1955** Koestler *Trail of Dinosaur* 253 The trouble with all near-miracles..is the unpredictability of their timing. **1957** C. S. Lewis *Let.* 6 Mar. (1966) 275, I married..a very sick, save by near-miracle, a dying woman. **1949** Koestler *Promise & Fulfilment* III. i. 391 Transport cooperatives which have..a near-monopoly of cross-country bus services. **1964** *Oceanogr. & Marine Biol.* II. 326 A temperature of 25° C represents near-optimum conditions. **1939** *Ann. Reg. 1938* 261 The condition of the inhabitants was one of near-panic after this merciless destruction. **1956** *Nature* 4 Feb. 239/2 Carbons in which neighbouring ordered regions lie in near-parallel orientation. **1963** C. R. Cowell et al. *Inlays, Crowns & Bridges* ii. 5 The principle of 'near parallelism'—that is, opposing walls must be nearly parallel with only enough divergence to make withdrawal of the pattern or impression possible. **1962** Near-perfect [see *attitude 2 c]. **1934** Dylan Thomas *Let.* 9 May (1966) 124 You've brought 'conventional' poetry..to a point of near-perfection. **1943** E. H. Thompson *A.L.A. Gloss. Library Terms* 106/2 *Processed*, reproduced by duplicating processes other than ordinary printing, as by mimeograph, multigraph, rotoprint, multilith, etc. Also called *Near-print.* **1956** Wilson & Tauber *University Library* 7 Journals, government documents, near-print, newspapers, manuscripts..have to be secured on an unprecedented scale. **1969** *N.Z. National Bibliogr.* II. p. viii, The growing volume of mimeographed and near-print editions has presented particular difficulty. **1949** *Word Study* Apr. 2/2 Cat..gut. Near rhyme..is the most generally accepted name. **1912** J. H. Moore *Ethics & Educ.* 109 That state of near-savagery when any low-browed irresponsible..is allowed to go out and shoot to death everything that has the breath of life in it. **1902** G. H. Lorimer *Lett. Merchant* 184 He leads the nag out..and examines every hair of his hide, as if he expected to find it near-seal. **1906–7** *T. Eaton & Co. Catal.* Fall & Winter 4/1 Near Seal Jacket, made of finest quality skins, closely resembling real seal in appearance. **1919** Mencken *Amer. Lang.* 159 Many characteristic Americanisms of the sort to stagger lexicographers—for example, *near-silk*—have come from the Jews. **1937** D. Canfield *Fables for Parents* (1938) 251 Nude-coloured, near-silk stockings with a run down one leg. **1911** E. Ferber *Dawn O'Hara* iii. 34 Assuming a near-smile, she entered the room. **1950** Koestler et al. *God that Failed* 63 The next five years were for me years of near-starvation. **1962** W. Nowottny *Lang. Poets Use* vii. 169 The treachery of near-synonyms which can slant meaning in a new direction. *Ibid.* 168 Ambiguities (drawn variously from near-synonymity and from rhetorical repetitions involving syntactical similarity). **1910** *Century Mag.* Apr. 891 Clothes and the Man. A near-true story. By Edith Rickert. **1951** S. Spender *World within World* iii. 138 These writers wrote with a near-unanimity, surprising when one considers that most of them were strangers to one another. **1964** *Language* XL. 206 Many of these 'near-universals' involve structural relationships. **1930** *Cambridge Daily News* 25 Sept. 3/2 Never having worn even near-wool within rubbing distance of my skin.

near, *a.* Add: **2. a.** Freq. in phr. *nearest and dearest*; also *absol.* as *sb.*, one's closest and most beloved relatives or friends.

1596 Shakes. *1 Hen. IV* III. ii. 123 Why, Harry, doe I tell thee of my Foes, Which art my neer'st and dearest Enemie? **1610** J. Chamberlain *Let.* 23 Jan. (1939) I. 296 The neerest and deerest frends he hath know not what to guesse of this humor. **1654** [in Dict.]. **1822** T. Creevey *Let.* 23 Dec. in *Creevey Papers* (1963) xi. 186 Brougham arrived here on Saturday, on his way—or rather *out* of his way—to his nearest and dearest. **1839** Dickens *Let.* 21 Jan. (1965) I. 493 For those who are nearest and dearest to me I can realise little more than a genteel subsistence. **1926** F. M. Ford *Man could stand Up* I. ii. 38 Look how you let in your nearest and dearest—those who have to sympathise with you. **1959** J. Burke *Echo of Barbara* ix. 92 One never does know much about one's nearest and dearest. **1975** 'C. Aird' *Slight Mourning* iv. 42 It's always family or friends who do you in... Nearest and dearest, that's who it'll be.

3. c. Of a motor vehicle; usu. in *near side* (freq. *attrib.*).

1926 *Times* 6 May 3/7 The defendant..went to the rear of the car and attempted to rip open the near side wheel with a knife. **1927** [see *dip-stick* s.v. *dip *sb.* 11]. **1959** *Times* 15 Dec. 13/5 The windscreen wipers were so arranged that the nearside blade flicked rain from the off-side blade across the driver's line of vision. **1973** 'H. Howard' *Highway to Murder* i. 12 It felt like they'd got a flat on the nearside front wheel.

4. a. *near space*: space in the immediate vicinity of the earth; inner space.

1962 *New Statesman* 24 Aug. 219/1 The Russians 'have been busily preoccupied with the near-space environment and have ably demonstrated their..de-orbiting accuracies'. **1967** *Economist* 20 May 791/3 The practical uses of 'near-space' in weather observation and in geological surveys of the earth.

c. *near-term*, used *attrib.* = *short-term*; occurring in or pertaining to the near future; opp. *long-term *a.*

1958 *Listener* 18 Sept. 407/1 To turn to Australia. There the near-term position is much more comfortable, unemployment is less than two per cent. **1965** H. I. Ansoff *Corporate Strategy* (1968) iv. 50 If the profitability picture urgently needs a near-term boost, a more modest goal ..will be acceptable. **1971** *Flying* Apr. S1/2 This..certainly does not suggest near-term improvement.

d. *nearest neighbour*, the member of a series or array nearest to that being considered; freq. *attrib.* (usu. with hyphen).

1937 *Jrnl. Appl. Physics* VIII. 654/1 In a liquid the number of nearest neighbors and the interatomic distances are roughly the same as in the crystalline material. **1945** A. F. Wells *Structural Inorg. Chem.* iii. 110 In each of these close-packed arrangements, cubic and hexagonal, each atom has twelve equidistant nearest neighbours, six in its own plane and three in each adjacent layer. **1961**

Jrnl. Biol. Chem. CCXXXVI. 864 (*heading*) Frequencies of nearest neighbor base sequences in deoxyribonucleic acid. **1972** *Computers & Humanities* VII. 40 The statistical analysis of pattern in such horizontal distributions is another area to which some attention is now being given, with nearest-neighbour analysis the most frequently adopted method.

e. *near money*, a deposit, bond, etc., that can easily be converted into ready money.

1948 G. CROWTHER *Outl. Money* (rev. ed.) ii. 65 Bank deposits, in those circumstances, might be something very close to money, but still not quite within the definition. They would be 'near-money'. *Ibid.* 66 We have already come across another example of 'near-money' in the form of the Bill of Exchange. **1968** *Economist* 23 Nov. 83/1 Ottawa itself is relying on a $2 billion 'near-money' savings bond issue at 6¾ per cent to meet its current excessive needs.

6. b. *near miss*, a shot that only just misses a target; also *transf.* and *fig.*; *near thing*, something barely effected; a narrow escape.

1751 FIELDING *Amelia* IV. xi. ii. 123 You certainly know..how hard Colonel Trompington is run at your Town, in the Election of a Mayor; they tell me it will be a very near Thing, unless you join us. **1894** SOMERVILLE & 'ROSS' *Real Charlotte* II. xxiii. 120 'That was a near thing,' remarked Mr. Hawkins complacently, as a slight grating sound told that they had grazed one of these smooth-backed monsters. **1930** W. GIBSON *Hazards* 8 A near thing! But he caught the plane: 'twas well He did not miss it. **1940** *Life* 9 Sept. 120/2 The other was a near miss amidships. **1940** *Illustr. London News* 28 Dec. 829/2 They came back with direct hits on a mine-sweeper and a supply ship, and a near miss on a destroyer to their credit. **1957** F. HOYLE *Black Cloud* i. 17 You mean, Dave, that there's no chance of the cloud missing the solar system, of it being a near-miss, let us say? **1957** *Listener* 21 Nov. 853/2 For those children who are near-misses as well as for those who make the grade. **1964** D. VARADAY *Gara-Yaka* xxi. 190 When one moving coil lashed over the crocodile's head, Mulembe snapped at it with spiky-toothed jaws which almost bit through... It was a near thing for the snake. **1967** G. F. FIENNES *I tried to run a Railway* iv. 38 It had a lot of bomb damage to repair from a near miss whose crater was still unfilled. **1972** 'E. LATHEN' *The Longer the Thread* xiv. 129 The taxi-drive..was..marked by enough near-misses to put from his mind any thoughts but survival. **1973** *Guardian* 7 Mar. 2/1 French and Scandinavian pilots..had reported 11 'near misses' over France to their airlines since Friday.

nearabout (nīə·ɹăbaut), *adv.* Also near about, nearabouts, near 'bout. [f. NEAR *adv.*² + ABOUT *adv.* and *prep.*, ABOUTS *adv.* and *prep.*] † **a.** In this vicinity; nearby. *Obs.* **b.** *dial.* Nearly, almost; approximately.

c **1400, 1634** [see NEAR *adv.*² 1 c]. [**1702** *Rec. Early Hist. Boston* (1882) VIII. 20 The front of the Old house..is neer abt Eleven foot from the street.] **1708** *Ibid.* 81 The mouth of the Said creek bears Neer about North East from ye Knowl of Trees. **1834** W. A. CARUTHERS *Kentuckian in N.Y.* II. 206 Yes, I believe everybody's married, nearabouts, as far as I can learn. *a* **1878** [see NEAR *adv.*² 5 b]. **1907** A. QUILLER-COUCH *Major Vigoureux* xxii. 251 The tide bein' nearabouts on the top of the flood. **1928** 'M. CHAPMAN' *Happy Mountain* iii. 25 All the fields were nearabout flat. **1938** M. K. RAWLINGS *Yearling* i. 9 'I near about give you out, son,' he said. **1941** J. FAULKNER *Men Working* i. 19 We can make twelve bales of cotton, near 'bout, every year.

near by, *adv.*, *prep.*, and *a.* **A.** *adv.* **1.** Delete 'Now chiefly *dial.* and *U.S.*' and add further examples.

1931 *News Chron.* 25 Aug., There had been feverish activity at the Trade Union Congress office nearby. **1965** E. GOWERS *Fowler's Mod. Eng. Usage* (ed. 2) 382/1 *Near by* has been long established as an adverb, and there is no good reason for those who draft police notices to prefer *in the vicinity*.

C. *adj.* Delete 'Chiefly *U.S.*' and add further examples.

1939 JOYCE *Finnegans Wake* 448 Take a good longing gaze into any nearby shopwindow. **1954** *Manch. Guardian Weekly* 26 Aug. 4 He went to the near-by police station. **1973** *Times* 24 May 27/3 There was a slackening interest in nearby metal.

Near East. [NEAR *a.* 4, EAST *sb.*] A region comprising the countries of the eastern Mediterranean, sometimes also including those of the Balkan peninsula, south-west Asia, or north Africa. (Also *Nearer East.*) Also *attrib.* Cf. *FAR EAST, *MIDDLE EAST.

[**1869** *Wesleyan-Methodist Mag.* (Sixpenny ed.) July 312 (*heading*) Peeps at the Near East [*i.e.* Spitalfields in London].] **1891** J. L. KIPLING *Beast & Man in India* iv. 84 There was once a time when in the nearer East..he [*sc.* the ass] was held in high honour. **1898** W. MILLER (*title*) Travels and politics in the Near East. **1902** D. G. HOGARTH (*title*) The Nearer East. **1909** [see *MIDDLE EASTERN *a.*]. **1910** *Chambers's Jrnl.* Dec. 800/1 In the Near East the keynote of cookery is disguise. The Turk brings his oriental love of mystery with him to the dinner-table. **1912** *Review of Reviews* July 70/1 (*heading*) The Near East problem. **1920** *Sat. Rev.* 16 Oct. 320 He took very little notice of Balkan intrigues, because the Near East was not his business. **1923** E. WHARTON *Son at Front* 10 Poor little circumscribed Paul Dastrey, whose utmost adventure had been..an occasional six weeks in the Near East. **1936** *Discovery* Sept. 264/1 The Wellcome Archaeological Expedition to the Near East. **1959** *Listener* 1 Jan. 31/2 Interest in the lands and peoples of the nearer east. **1973** 'D. JORDAN' *Nile Green* xliv. 283 Sue..told the Near East Desk, who..sent a cable to the Cairo Embassy.

Hence Near-Ea·sterly *adv.*, Near-Ea·stern *a.*, Near-Ea·sterner.

1906 *Q. Rev.* Jan. 284 Lord Salisbury and his successor have..skilfully withdrawn England from the Near-Eastern entanglements. **1909** *Ibid.* Apr. 654 (*heading*) The Near Eastern question. **1909** *Daily Chron.* 25 Aug. 3/6 Near-Easterly. Bosnia and Herzegovina have figured recently in European politics. **1925** A. J. TOYNBEE *Survey Internat. Affairs 1920–23* I. 3 They appear..to have refrained from interfering in any way regarding Near Eastern affairs. **1951** E. PAUL *Springtime in Paris* ii. 24 There were a few North Americans, hordes of English, many South Americans, and a few Near-Easterners. *Ibid.* xii. 215 Helen Hatounian put an Armenian record on the gramophone... The afternoon stillness..was rent with the shrill voice of a near-eastern soprano. **1959** *Listener* 15 Jan. 145/2 His predilection for the interval of the augmented second (of the near-Eastern scale).

nearmost, *a.* Delete *dial.* and add further examples.

1913 E. H. BARKER *Wayfaring in France* 468 It is almost a shriek when the wind strikes the nearmost crests [of trees]. **1952** *Times Lit. Suppl.* 7 Mar. 168/4 You are my nearmost, you who have travelled the farthest.

nearshore (nīə·ɹʃōəɹ), *a.* [NEAR *a.* + SHORE *sb.*¹] Situated or occurring (relatively) close to a shore; pertaining to or involving the study of such a zone.

1896 B. WILLIS in *U.S. Geol. Survey Geol. Folio* XXXIII. 2/2 This formation..represents the near-shore, muddier sediment of those times. **1936** *Rep. Comm. Sedimentation* (Nat. Research Council) 3 The main subjects that are contemplated are (1) relation of oceanography to sedimentation, including both physical and biological oceanography, (2) pelagic deposits, (3) inland sea deposits, (4) near-shore deposits, [etc.]. **1957** *Gloss. Geol.* (Amer. Geol. Inst.) 196/1 *Nearshore zone*, in beach terminology an indefinite zone extending seaward from the shore line somewhat beyond the breaker zone. It defines the area of nearshore currents. **1966** R. W. FAIRBRIDGE *Encycl. Oceanogr.* 614/1 Nearshore oceanography may be taken to include the study of all aspects of the area lying between the backshore zone and the outer edge of the continental shelf. **1973** *Nature* 6 Apr. 393/1 The Galana Boi beds..range from coarse-grained fluvial deposits to fine-grained near-shore lacustrine silts. **1974** *Ibid.* 15 Feb. 452/1 Deposition in a shallow, nearshore marine environment.

near-si·ghtedly, *adv.* [f. NEAR-SIGHTED *a.* + -LY².] In a near-sighted manner.

1909 *Daily Chron.* 11 Oct. 7/1 Dr. Shuttleworth blinked near-sightedly throughout the time he was in the witness box. **1971** B. MALAMUD *Tenants* 209 With furrowed brows he reads the marriage contract over and over, then nearsightedly reads it again.

neat, *sb.* Add: **2. b.** *neat beast, -beef, cattle* (earlier examples), *leather* (=NEAT'S LEATHER), *stock*.

1624 in *Essex Inst. Hist. Coll.* (1914) L. 235 All my Cattill nowe upon the farme..as neat bests, horse bests, and swine. **1727** *Rec. Smithtown, N.Y.* (1898) 82 It is agreed on that the pounder shall have for pounding a horse four pence, for a net best four pence. **1755** in S. M. HAMILTON *Lett. to Washington* (1898) I. 135 Not under twelve shillings and sixpence per Hundred Neet Beef. **1619** *Jrnl. House of Burgesses, Gen. Assembly Virginia* (1915) 13 No man without leave from the Governour shall kill any Neat cattle whatsoever. **1648** *Archives of Maryland* (1887) IV. 390 Certaine neate-cattle to the number of 27. **1776** in *New Hampsh. Hist. Soc. Coll.* (1889) IX. 263 Mens Neat Leather Shoes of the best common sort. **1850** *Rep. Comm. Patents: Agric. 1849* (U.S. Dept. Agric.) 94 It is estimated that there are in this country..fifteen thousand two hundred and eighty five neat stock. **1869** *Rep. Comm. Agric. 1868* (U.S. Dept. Agric.) 427 The present winter (1868) he feeds forty-three head of neat stock, equivalent to thirty-four mature animals. **1882** *Rep. Maine Board Agric.* XVI. 265 The way is to fence off such a piece, and allow no neat stock or horses to run in it at any time.

neat, *a.* and *adv.* Add: **A.** *adj.* **3. d.** *neat cement*: a mortar made from cement and water only, without the addition of sand.

1932 T. CORKHILL *Conc. Building Encycl.* 142 *Neat*, a term applied to cement mortar without sand. **1947** J. C. RICH *Materials & Methods Sculpture* xi. 328 Neat cement is a mixture of cement and water. It is not recommended for sculptural use save as a retouching medium. **1964** H. F. W. TAYLOR *Chem. of Cements* I. 2 Mechanical or physical determinations, such as strength tests, are usually made with an aggregate present, as determinations of this type on neat cement pastes can give misleading results.

7. d. Semi-proverbial phr. *neat* (*but*) *not gaudy* and variants. Also *absol.* and *fig.*

[**1602**: see GAUDY *a.*² 3.] **1700** S. WESLEY *Epistle to Friend concerning Poetry* 5 Style is the Dress of Thought; a modest Dress, Neat, but not gaudy, will true Critics please. **1806** C. LAMB *Let.* 26 June (1935) II. 14 A little thin, flowery border round, neat, not gaudy. **1838** RUSKIN in *Archit. Mag.* Nov. 484 That admiration of the 'neat but not gaudy', which is commonly reported to have influenced the devil when he painted his tail pea-green. **1849** THACKERAY *Pendennis* I. xiii. 116 'You seem to like my dressing-gown, sir,' he said to Mr. Tatham. 'A pretty thing, isn't it? Neat, but not in the least gaudy.' **1887** *Lippincott's Mag.* July 116, I have sent, I say, just such manuscript as editors call for, fair, clean, written on one side, not with a pencil, but with a good gold pen, stamps enclosed for return if declined; the whole thing 'neat, but not gaudy, as the monkey said' on the memorable occasion 'when he painted his tail sky-blue'. **1892** *Society* 6 Aug. 757/1 Tennyson when in a rage is neat and not gaudy. **1974** L. DEIGHTON *Spy Story* xxi. 222 If Toliver complains to the Home Secretary you say it was the C.I.A. doing it. Neat, but not gaudy.

11. b. *colloq.* Excellent, desirable, attractive.

1934 J. T. FARRELL *Calico Shoes* 54 A girl in a two-piece bathing suit without brassière walked by them. 'Oh, baby, you can make me so happy!' Don sing-songed. 'Neat!' Jack appraised. **1942** BERREY & VAN DEN BARK *Amer. Thes. Slang* § 29/4 Excellent; first-rate... neat. **1947** *Sat. Rev.* (U.S.) 10 May 26/1 Each of these adjoining rooms has a radio in it, which they find 'neat' and I don't. **1972** D. WESTHEIMER *Over Edge* (1974) i. 10 'I could drive you on into Idyllwild if you want...' 'That would be neat.' **1974** *Washington Post* 24 Feb. H. 13/5 I've passed up some neat dinner invitations.

neaten, *v.* Add: (Later examples.) Often const. *up*.

1942 BERREY & VAN DEN BARK *Amer. Thes. Slang* § 4/4 Arrange; Put in order; Clean up..*neaten up*. **1954** *Daily Progress* (Charlottesville, Virginia) 11 Mar. 10/1 (*heading*) Shrubs and fences neaten up yards. **1970** 'H. PENTECOST' *Plague of Violence* (1972) II. ii. 92 If the killers had tried to neaten up the room after a struggle, they couldn't have put everything back in place just as it had been. **1972** *Daily Tel.* 27 May 9/7 Finally, pulling and weaving neatens the whole nest.

neatnik (nī·tnik). *slang* (chiefly *U.S.*). [Modelled on *BEATNIK.] One who is neat in his personal habits, as opposed to a *BEATNIK.

1959 *N. Y. Times* 30 Aug. 67/1 The beatniks and the neatniks had at each other this week. **1960** *Ibid.* 3 Jan. 48 (Advt.), Seeing how you're a Neatnik, you'll be buying things like soap and ties and stuff from now on. **1961** *Britannica Bk. of Year* 537/1 The reaction of one section of beatniks to the appearance of others produced first *Washed Beatnik* and then *Neatnik*. **1962** *Amer. Speech* XXXVII. 146 *Neatnik*..one who is neat in his personal habits. **1969** *Sears Catal.* Spring/Summer 16 A new look in Rally-back Jeans that can be worn by Neatniks of any age.

neb, *sb.* Add: **3. b.** (Further example.)

1893 R. L. STEVENSON *Catriona* xi. 116, I couldna see the nebs of my ten fingers.

d. 'The pole of an ox-cart' (E.D.D.); *neb ox*, a draught ox.

1710 *New Hampsh. Probate Rec.* (1907) I. 650 All my household goods and four Cows, and a yoak of neb Oxen.. to be for her own proper use. **1865** 'G. HAMILTON' *Skirmishes* II. 7 Men left their oxen standing by the nebs.

‖ **nebbich** (ne·biχ), *sb.* and *a.* Also **nebbish, nebbishe, nebbisher, nebish.** [Yiddish.] A nobody, a nonentity. As *adj.*, innocuous, ineffectual, luckless, hapless, etc. Also as *int.*, an expression of commiseration, dismay, etc.

1892 I. ZANGWILL *Childr. Ghetto* I. 46 '*Achi nebbich*, poor little thing!' cried Mrs. Kosminski, who was in a tender mood. **1907** —— *Ghetto Comedies* 205 '*Nebbich*, the poor little children!' cried Natalya, horrified. **1959** A. WESKER *Chicken Soup with Barley* III. i, in *New Eng. Dramatists* I. 222 It's ach a nebish Harry now. It's not easy for him... Other men get ill but they fight. **1960** *Commentary* June 530/1 The *nebbish*, the cynic, the sophisticate. *Ibid.* 539/1 The sad *nebbishe* Podolsky is the owner of the building. **1960** F. RAPHAEL *Limits of Love* I. i. 11 Your daughter ends up by..marrying a good for nothing, nebbisher nobody. **1962** B. ABRAHAMS tr. *Life Glückel of Hameln* i. 4 All the pleasures and riches he, *nebbich*, was denied here. **1968** *Times* 6 Apr. 21 The central character is so nebbish he has not even a name. **1969** *Atlantic Monthly* Sept. 57 Paranoid psychopaths who, after nebbish lives, suddenly feel themselves invulnerable in the certain wooing of sweet death. **1973** *Jewish Chron.* 9 Feb. 5/1 The kings [in this Jewish chess-set] are dead, long live the nebbishes (the deprived, signifying the decline of royal power). **1975** *New Yorker* 3 Feb. 77/2 Mr. Antonacci is both antic and affecting as the jumpy, craven *nebbish* Honey Boy, and John Bottoms is superb in several roles.

‖ **Nebbiolo** (nebiō͡u·lo), *sb.* and *a.* Also **Nebiolo.** [It.] A black grape of northern Italy; the red table wine made from this grape. Also *attrib.* or as *adj.*

1833 C. REDDING *Hist. Mod. Wines* ix. 246 At Asti, the plants called *Passaretta* and *Malvasia Nebiolo* produce *vins de liqueur*, with the smell of the raspberry. **1875** [see *BAROLO]. **1957** *Encycl. Brit.* XXIII. 664/2 Good honest red drinking wine comes from northern Italy, usually marketed under vine names (Nebiolo, Grignolino, Freisa, Barbera). **1958** A. L. SIMON *Dict. Wines* 117/2 *Nebbiolo*, one of the best black grapes grown in the North of Italy for the making of red table wines. Many of the wines made from Nebbiolo grapes are sold as *Nebbiolo* wines. **1959** W. JAMES *Word-Bk. Wine* 132 *Nebbiolo.* The vine of this name produces some of the best red wines of northern Italy. **1970** SIMON & HOWE *Dict. Gastron.* 275/2 *Nebbiolo*, a black grape grown in Piedmont and Lombardy and used to make red table wines. Among these are Barolo and Barbaresco, two of Italy's best-known wines. **1970** *Sat. Rev.* (U.S.) 12 Sept. 69/1 In Piedmont and Lombardy they have harvested the Nebbiolo grapes (a variety named because it ripens late in the autumnal *nebbia*, or mist). **1970** *House & Garden* May 138/3 Nebbiolo is a red wine named after the most aristocratic of the Piedmont grape varieties.

‖ **nebelwerfer** (nē·bəlvę·rfəɹ, -wǝ̄ɹfəɹ). [G., f. *nebel* mist, fog, haze + *werfer* thrower,

mortar, f. *werfen* to throw.] A German six-barrelled rocket mortar. Also *attrib.*

1943 *Hutchinson's Pict. Hist. War* 4 Aug.–26 Oct. 191 These German gunners have certainly chosen a well-concealed position in which to hide their nebelwerfer (fog-thrower) battery. **1946** C. WILMOT in R. W. Zandvoort et al. *Wartime Eng.* (1957) 163 The nebelwerfers—those many-barrelled mortars that put down the rocket-propelled bombs with the high wailing sobbing note. **1948** A. M. TAYLOR *Lang. World War II* (rev. ed.) 136 *Nebelwerfer*, a German rocket thrower similar to the Russian Katyusha. **1961** W. VAUGHAN-THOMAS *Anzio* vi. 112 The Scots Guards captured a German officer who had driven into their lines while looking for sites for the unpleasant *Nebelwerfers*, or six-barrel mortars.

nebenkern (nē·bĕnkĕᵊɹn). *Cytology.* Pl. **-kerne.** [a. G. *nebenkern* (O. Bütschli 1871, in *Zeitschr. f. wissensch. Zool.* XXI. 527), f. *neben* near + *kern* kernel, nucleus.] Any of various cytoplasmic structures associated with or resembling the nucleus (see quots.).

1898 *Jrnl. R. Microsc. Soc.* 624 (*heading*) 'Nebenkern' in spermatogenesis of Pulmonata. **1901** G. N. CALKINS *Protozoa* i. 14 He [*sc.* Bütschli] held..that in addition to the macronucleus there is a second and a smaller nucleus in Infusoria, and to this he gave the name *Nebenkern* or micronucleus ('76). **1917** *Q. Jrnl. Microsc. Sci.* LXII. 416, I have been unable to find any body in the spermatid formed from 'spindle fibres' or 'yolk granules', and I do not intend to use the term 'nebenkern', which has been, and still is, used without discrimination for almost any granule or body in a cell. For example, Hegner..lately draws attention to the 'granules of Blochmann' in the wasp and two ants, which have also been called 'nebenkerne', quite regardless of whether or no they are of the same nature as the original 'nebenkern' of Bütschli. **1928** E. L. OPIE in E. V. Cowdry *Special Cytol.* I. ix. 246 The name 'nebenkern' or 'paranucleus' has been given to structures situated within the cytoplasm [of the pancreatic acinous cell] and staining like nuclear material... Other chromatin-like bodies designated 'nebenkerne' are spherical and have an even contour. **1958** *Internat. Rev. Cytol.* VII. 223 In other invertebrates..the mitochondrial *nebenkern* is transformed into a spiral wrapping that extends for the greater part of the length of the sperm tail. **1962** D. W. BISHOP *Spermatozoan Motility* 157 In insects, gastropods, and other invertebrates the conspicuous *nebenkern* formed during spermiogenesis arises by fusion of mitochondria. **1965** E. N. WILLMER *Cells & Tissues in Culture* II. xi. 531 The round or oval nucleus of the hair-cell [in the organ of Corti] occupies the third quarter of the cell. The infranuclear part contains a small number of mitochondria and a group of granular cisternae. Occasionally, the granular cisternae might be arranged in a circular fashion forming a 'Nebenkern' which recalls the so-called Retzius Body.

Nebraskan (nėbræ·skăn), *a.* and *sb.* [f. *Nebraska*, name of a state in the central U.S. + -AN.] **A.** *adj.* **1.** Of, pertaining to, or from Nebraska.

1875 E. A. CURLEY *Nebraska* xxii. 289 The Mormon fields, irrigated as they are, are much smaller than those of Nebraskan farmers. **1884** *N.Y. Weekly Tribune* 2 Apr. 10/4 The advantages which the Nebraskan Mennonites secure by co-operative purchasing of their implements, machinery, and supplies of all kinds, are manifestly.. great. **1933** BLUNDEN & NORMAN *We'll shift our Ground* 155 Some thesis writer, Nebraskan or Wisconsinese. **1973** S. DOBYNS *Man of Little Evils* (1974) x. 96 The story concerned a Nebraskan couple who had been..robbed.

2. *Geol.* Of, pertaining to, or designating the first Pleistocene glaciation in North America, now generally identified with the Günz glaciation in the Alps. Also *absol.*, the Nebraskan glaciation or the deposits it produced.

1909 B. SHIMEK in *Bull. Geol. Soc. Amer.* XX. 408 The tough, impervious, bluish-black fill which has been known as the sub-Aftonian or pre-Kansan drift in Iowa, is here so well developed, reaching an exposed thickness of more than 15 feet.., that it can no longer be regarded as merely a remnant, but should rank with other well developed drift sheets... This leaves it without a name, and in view of this fact, and of the wide distribution of this formation, the name *Nebraskan* is proposed for it... The name Nebraskan was suggested to the writer by Professor Calvin. **1930** *Science* 22 Aug. 194/1 The Nebraskan is probably a million years old. **1934**, **1957** [see *ILLINOIAN *sb.* and *a.* B]. **1966** *Science* 11 Nov. 771/3 The Early Pleistocene record in Nebraska is at present interpreted as indicating two stadial advances of the continental glacier during Nebraskan time and three stadial advances during Kansan time. **1970** [see *GÜNZ].

B. *sb.* A native or inhabitant of Nebraska.

1888 [see *MINNESOTAN]. **1900** *Congress. Rec.* 27 Jan. 1241/2 He aided in the nomination of Mr. Bryan for President, and was an enthusiastic supporter of the brilliant Nebraskan. **1948** *Time* 26 Apr. 13/2 Ohioans seemed as friendly to him as Nebraskans. **1969** I. KEMP *Brit. G.I. in Vietnam* iii. 49 The medic, 'Jake' Jacobs..was a pale, thin Nebraskan, recently married.

Nebuchadnezzar (nebiŭkăne·zăɹ). [So called in allusion to *Nebuchadnezzar* King of Babylon, d. 562 B.C.] A very large wine-bottle (see quots.).

1913 A. HUXLEY *Let.* 11 Nov. (1969) 55 Fireworks ensue, then (children dismissed) supper and afterwards, the most magnificent Nebuchadnezzars, and finally a good form of blind man's buff. **1962** [see *BALTHAZAR]. **1967** *Punch* 27 Sept. 484/3 In the thirtieth of fifty-one chapters, Patrick Forbes lists the eleven different sizes of champagne bottle, from the quarter-bottle to the Nebuchadnezzar, eighty times as big. **1967** A. LICHINE *Encycl. Wines* 317/2 Since wine ages more slowly in large bottles, there are many magnums and double magnums in the Lafite cellars, as well as Imperials, which hold eight bottles, and Nebuchadnezzars (ten bottles). **1970** SIMON & HOWE *Dict. Gastron.* 80/2 *Nebuchadnezzar*, 20 bottles.

nebula. **3.** Add to def.: In mod. use the term is applied to (*a*) a cloud of gas or dust situated within the interstellar space of a galaxy (usu. our own) and appearing as either a bright or a dark cloud (according to whether or not there are stars present to make it luminous); (*b*) a galaxy (usu. one other than our own). (Further examples.)

1924 H. DINGLE *Mod. Astrophysics* xvi. 302 A dark nebula is really dark, and not merely too faint for its light to be seen on account of its great distance from us. **1930** R. H. BAKER *Astron.* xi. 465 Frequently a 'nebula' turned out to be a star-cluster, thereby encouraging the opinion, in former times, that all nebulae are really clusters of stars. *Ibid.*, Modern investigations have shown that nebulae, as distinguished from ordinary star-clusters, fall into two classes having entirely different characteristics, namely, the galactic nebulae and the extra-galactic nebulae. **1963** B. & J. LOVELL *Discovering Universe* ix. 114 The Milky Way system is typical of many extra-galactic spiral nebulae, and very much akin to M31 in Andromeda. **1968** P. MOORE *Sky at Night* II. xxxii. 232 With other nebulæ, there are no convenient stars—and so the nebulæ cannot be seen directly, but betray themselves because they blot out the light of the stars beyond... Mention should also be made of the nebulæ which shine by pure reflection. Such is the nebula in the Pleiades. *Ibid.* 235 The old term of 'spiral nebula' has become obsolete, to be replaced by 'spiral galaxy'; a proper nebula is gaseous, and belongs to the Galaxy in which we live. **1971** D. W. SCIAMA *Mod. Cosmol.* iii. 39 In this way he [*sc.* E. P. Hubble] obtained a distance of 800 000 light-years for the Andromeda nebula, and similar values for other spiral nebulae. Now that these nebulae are well established as stellar systems outside our own, we shall henceforth call them galaxies. **1974** F. W. COLE *Fund. Astron.* xiii. 358/1 The Orion nebula is 1600 LY distant and about 30 LY in diameter. In our galaxy, other emission nebulae of the same type are about the same size. Vastly larger emission nebulae are known outside our galaxy; an excellent example is in M33, a spiral galaxy in Triangulum.

nebulium. Add: (Further examples.)

It is now considered that no such element exists, the lines formerly attributed to it having been identified with those produced by known elements.

1937 J. W. T. SPINKS tr. *Herzberg's Atomic Spectra & Atomic Struct.* iv. 157 Bowen..first showed that the nebulium lines, which had been observed in the spectra of many cosmic nebulae but were long a complete mystery, were to be explained as forbidden transitions between the deep terms of O^+ (^4S, ^2D, ^2P), O^{++} (^3P, ^1D, ^1S), and N^+ (^3P, ^1D, ^1S). **1940** *Astrophysical Jrnl.* XCII. 408 The free electrons, liberated from hydrogen by photo-ionization, may excite the 'nebulium' lines by inelastic impact. **1965** PHILLIPS & WILLIAMS *Inorg. Chem.* I. ii. 43 Transitions between these states in atomic spectra are also 'forbidden', but they have been observed for the isoelectronic N^+ and O^{2+} ions in the spectra of cosmic nebulae (so called nebulium lines). **1973** L. OSTER *Mod. Astron.* xiii. 205 For a long time, in fact until 1928, the origin of some of the strongest lines was unclear, and, in desperation, they were ascribed by some astronomers to a hypothetical element called nebulium.

nebulization (nebiŭlaizē¹·ʃən). *Med.* [f. NEBULIZ(E *v.* + -ATION.] **a.** The conversion of a liquid into a mist or spray. **b.** Medical treatment using a nebulizer.

1906 *Index-Catal. Library Surg.-General's Office, U.S. Army* 2nd Ser. XI. 366/1 (*heading*) Nebulizers and nebulization. **1949** *Dis. Chest* XVI. 410 The technique designed ..by us is based on nebulization of the surface anesthetic solution. **1968** *Jrnl. Asthma Res.* V. 253 Each child was subjected to 15 minutes of nebulization, three times daily. **1969** *Daily Tel.* 25 June 15/5 You can have different products incorporated into your nebulisation shower: products to help ease pregnancy scarring, correct dry or greasy skin, [etc.].

nebulize, *v.* Restrict *rare* to sense 2 and add to sense 1: Hence **ne·bulizing** *vbl. sb.* (Further examples.)

1915 WRIGHT & SMITH *Text-bk. Dis. Nose & Throat* i. 58 There are a number of mechanical devices for nebulizing medicated solutions, which have a certain amount of value in tracheal and bronchial affectations. **1944** *Proc. Soc. Exper. Biol. & Med.* LVII. 257/1 The nebulizing unit..consists of a container and a metal atomizer. **1949** *Dis. Chest* XVI. 412 Oxygen or air may be used to nebulize the solution. **1958** *Ann. Allergy* XVI. 628 The liquid is disrupted by the air jet in the nebulizing area and forms an aerosol. *Ibid.* 631 The DeVilbiss No. 40 model nebulizes about twice as much water as the Vaponefrin model. **1973** *Amer. Rev. Respiratory Dis.* CVIII. 511/2 The small deposition of ^{99m}Tc in the lungs in these normal subjects even during slow, deep breathing raises serious doubts that effects claimed for aerosol therapy are related to nebulized fluid.

‖ **nécessaire** (nesesḗr'), *sb.* Also **necessaire.** [Fr. (see NECESSAIRE *a.*).] A small case, sometimes ornamental, for small articles, as pencils, scissors, tweezers, articles of cosmetics, etc.

1800 E. HERVEY *Mourtray Family* III. ix. 177 A chance of his travelling *necessaire*, and all the apparatus of his toilet, being burned. **1854** THACKERAY *Newcomes* I. xxviii. 266 Gousset empty, tiroirs empty, nécessaire parted for Strasbourg! **1876** GEO. ELIOT *Dan. Der.* I. I. ii. 29 Gwendolen..thrust necklace, cambric..and all into her *nécessaire*. **1960** *Times* 16 Feb. 20/7 An old English gold and agate necessaire. **1967** V. NABOKOV *Speak, Memory* (rev. ed.) xiii. 253 The handful of jewels which Natasha, a farsighted old chambermaid,.. had swept off a dresser into a *nécessaire*. **1973** *Times* 11 Dec. 18/5 A George III gold and enamel *nécessaire* attributed to James Cox.

necessary, *a.* and *sb.* Add: **A.** *adj.* **I. 1. a.** *necessary evil* (earlier and later examples).

1547 W. BALDWIN *Treat. Morall Phylosophie* III. xv. sig. O5ᵛ A woman is a necessary euyll. **1765** JOHNSON in Shakes. *Plays* I. Pref. p. lxix, Notes are often necessary, but they are necessary evils. **1776** T. PAINE *Common Sense* 1 Society in every state is a blessing, but Government even in its best state is but a necessary evil; in its worst state an intolerable one. **1815** C'TESS GRANVILLE *Let.* 18 July (1894) I. 54 The humiliation of now having him is great, but he is reasonable about it and thinks it a necessary evil. **1863** *Country Gentleman* 16 Apr. 254/3 The manuring of the vines is regarded as 'a necessary evil'. **1927** E. O'NEILL *Marco Millions* I. iv. 51 Don't waste pity. Her kind are necessary evils.

d. *necessary condition* = CONDITION *sb.* 4; cf. **sufficient condition.*

1817 COLERIDGE *Biog. Lit.* I. ix. 136, I began to ask myself; is a system of philosophy..possible? If possible, what are its necessary conditions? **1859** MILL *On Liberty* i. 9 The consent of the community..was made a necessary condition to some of the more important acts of the governing power. **1949** A. PAP *Elem. Analytical Philos.* x. 212 If a sufficient condition is complex—as it almost invariably is—then it may consist in a conjunction of necessary conditions. **1965** E. J. LEMMON *Beginning Logic* i. 28 Whenever it is the case that only if *P* then *Q*, *P* is a necessary condition for *Q*.

necessitarian, *sb.* and *a.* (Earlier and later examples.)

1796 F. A. NITSCH *Gen. View Kant's Princ. concerning Man* 17 The Necessitarians..make a considerable party in the philosophic world. **1912** KIPLING *Songs from Books* (1913) 154 (*title*) The necessitarian. **1952** C. P. BLACKER *Eugenics* 267 Unconscious prejudices can throw the Nature–Nurture controversy into different perspectives. Those who believe in predestination as an article of religion have a necessitarian bias which might incline them to over-estimate the role of heredity. **1956** E. H. HUTTEN *Lang. Mod. Physics* vi. 212 Ever since Hume the necessitarian interpretation [of determinism] has been rejected. **1966** M. R. D. FOOT *SOE in France* viii. 183 By one of those accidents that baffle the necessitarians, the only sentry awake at the moment of the drop was a newcomer who did not know where the alarm telephone was.

necessitated, *ppl. a.* **2.** (Later example.)

1857 A. & M. WARD *Husband in Utah* xvii. 194 Mrs. Farrow informed me of several sisters, who having inherited money from Eastern quarters, were immediately assailed by the necessitated priest.

nece·ssitator. [f. NECESSITATE *v.* + -OR.] = NECESSITATER.

1904 HARDY *Dynasts* I. vi. iii. 118 O Great Necessitator, heed us now!.. Quicken the issue as Thou knowest how.

necessity. Add: **14.** *attrib.* **necessity-operator** *Logic*, a word or symbol signifying that the proposition to which it attaches is a necessary truth.

1957 A. N. PRIOR *Time & Modality* 57 Church's necessity-operator is not an operator of this sort. **1968** HUGHES & CRESSWELL *Introd. Modal Logic* ii. 24 We shall call *L* the necessity operator. **1973** M. J. CRESSWELL *Logics & Lang.* ii. 32 The simplest is the necessity operator, or as Dana Scott calls it, the universal necessity operator.

neck, *sb.*¹ Add: **1. e.** Phrases. *to get* (*catch, take*) *it in the neck*: to be hard hit (by something); to be severely reprimanded or punished. Conversely, *to give it in the neck*: to assault or reprimand (someone) severely.

1882 *National Police Gaz.* 25 Nov. 3/3 An 'Artless' Young Girl Gives it to Her 'in the Neck', as the Sports Say. **1887** [see *DUB *sb.*⁶]. **1903** A. ADAMS *Log of Cowboy* xi. 175 Old Nat will get it in the neck this time, if that old girl dallies with him as she did with us. **1908** H. G. WELLS *War in Air* ii. 58 They'll get it in the neck in real earnest one of these days, if they ain't precious careful. **1914** D. O. BARNETT *Let.* 31 Dec. (1915) 30 You probably don't know what a village looks like when it has caught it in the neck. **1923** WODEHOUSE *Inimitable Jeeves* iii. 30 Something always comes along to give it you in the neck at the very moment when you're feeling most braced about things in general. **1927** F. NIVEN *Wild Honey* iii. 21 If you sit.. facing ahead, that's called 'punching the breeze'. If you sit..looking back, it's called 'taking it in the neck'. **1928** 'SAPPER' *Female of Species* x. 169 I'd never forgive myself if one of you took it in the neck. *a* **1930** D. H. LAWRENCE *Phoenix II* (1968) 259 Give it the blue-bottles [*sc.* policemen] in the neck! **1955** *Times* 11 July 12/7 Do they belong to an unlucky generation that has got it in the neck before the law can catch up with the swift development of civilian aviation, and insist upon silenced airliners? **1973** *Guardian* 18 June 10/2 It's the poor old vicar who gets it most in the neck... He runs the risk of losing the best-kept-village competition because..the churchyard is looking its shaggiest. **1974** *Times* 12 Dec. 14/4 Giscard..

apparently caught it in the neck from his continental colleagues.

2. d. In Racing, *to win by a neck*, i.e. by the length of the horse's neck. Also *fig.* So *a neck*, such a distance separating two horses at the end of a race. Also of greyhounds.

1823 'J. Bee' *Slang* 94 Won by..indeed 'a neck'. **1865** 'Mark Twain' *Sk. New & Old* (1875) 32 She'd always fetch up at the stand just about a neck ahead. **1873** J. Blackwood *Let.* 7 June in Geo. Eliot *Lett.* (1956) V. 421 There was a grand [golf] match...my man the young champion Tom Morris came in winner by a neck. **1886** [see Head *sb.* 1 c]. **1930** *Daily Express* 6 Oct. 17/6 Three-quarters of a length; neck. Beggarman fourth. **1931** T. R. G. Lyell *Slang* 544 The worst of it is that I only lost by a neck; the other fellow beat me by three marks! **1975** *Times* 21 July 7/4 If Juliette Marny had not cocked her head..a few strides from the post Piggott thought the margin of success would have been half a length rather than a neck.

e. *N.Z.* The wool shorn from the neck of a sheep.

1950 *N.Z. Jrnl. Agric.* Oct. 311 (*caption*) Frames hinged to a wall [in the shearing shed] can be very useful to support a wool pack for bellies, necks, etc.

3. b. Also implying insolent speech or presumptuous behaviour, esp. in phr. *to have a neck.*

1893–4 R. O. Heslop *Northumb. Words* II. 494 *Neck*, forwardness, impudence. 'What a neck ye hev efter aa'!' **1933** *Punch* 25 Jan. 108/3 I'm afraid I was so overcome by his barefaced 'neck' that it never occurred to me to call him back. **1935** G. Heyer *Death in Stocks* iii. 34 He'd had the infernal neck to say I wasn't going to marry the man. **1942** L. A. G. Strong *Unpractised Heart* xii. 77 And then you have the sheer neck, the bloody effrontery to say you think there's more in life than I do. **1960** J. Symons *Progress of a Crime* v. 34 If that doesn't beat anything for hard neck.

e. *to speak* (*talk*) *through* (*the back of*) *one's neck*: to use extravagant or inaccurate words or language; *to stick* (or *put*) *one's neck out*: to expose oneself to danger, reprisal, criticism, etc.; *up to the neck*: fully concerned or deeply implicated in (a transaction, freq. illegal); also *ellipt.*, occupied without intermission; *to breathe down* (*someone's*) *neck*: to be close behind (someone); to keep a close or oppressive watch upon; *dead from the neck up*: see *Dead *a.* 32 h. Also in further miscellaneous uses.

1388 Wyclif *Gen.* xlv. 14 And whanne he hadde biclippid, and hadde feld [*other MSS.* falle] in to the necke of Beniamyn, his brother, he wepte, the while also Benjamin wepte in lijk maner on the necke of Joseph. **1611** Bible *Gen.* xlv. 14 And he fel vpon his brother Beniamins necke, and wept: and Beniamin wept vpon his necke. **1738** Swift *Polite Conv.* i. 47 If ever I hang, it shall be about a fair Lady's Neck. **1896** [see Oafish *a.*]. **1899** E. W. Hornung *Amat. Cracksman* 199 'Don't talk through yer neck,' snarled the convict. 'Talk out straight, curse you!' **1903** A. H. Lewis *Boss* 174 Still I must say you went in up to your neck on sparks and voylets. **1907** *Strand Mag.* June 672/1 We are not slow to tell them they are 'talking through the back of their neck'. **1909** R. Brooke *Let.* 3 Nov. (1968) 192 Your offer is splendid and noble. I fall upon your neck. **1912** Kipling *Songs from Books* (1913) 153 So back I go to my job again, Not.. quite so ready to sob again On any neck that's around. **1923** Conrad *Rover* xii. 203 It's the very spot for hatching treacheries. One feels steeped in them up to the neck. **1923** *Pall Mall Gaz.* 13 Apr. 3/3 Anybody who gets up in this House and talks about universal peace knows he is talking through the back of his neck. **1926** *Univ. Mag.* (Univ. Va.) Oct. 16/2 Absolutely original slang at the University of Virginia includes..*to stick one's neck out.* **1933** *New Republic* 22 Nov. 45/2 Instead, there is a general disposition now to regard him as a fat-headed fellow.. who 'put his neck out' and got what he deserved. **1935** *Planning* III. xlix. 2 Opinion in administration and in industry, among people who are up to the neck in current problems, is far more advanced than opinion among some of those who occupy comfortably detached positions. **1936** R. Chandler in *Black Mask* June 31/2 You sure stick your neck out all the time. **1941** Wodehouse *Berlin Broadcasts* in *Performing Flea* (1961) i. 266 Algy didn't know a thing about it and was almost certainly talking through the back of his neck. **1946** K. Tennant *Lost Haven* (1947) vii. 97 There were big black moths in the wardrobe; not to mention a beastly big mountain breathing down the back of your neck. **1950** H. Hastings *Seagulls Over Sorrento* in *Plays of Year* IV. 64 We've stuck our necks out—we're looking for trouble, see? **1955** R. Frost *Small Hotel* in *Ibid.* XIII. 189 I'll be out of here on my neck as soon as they've got what they want out of me in this court business. **1955** A. L. Rowse *Expansion Eliz. Eng.* ii. 64 Three mayors..were up to their neck in the trade. *Ibid.* viii. 302 The conclusion she [*sc.* Elizabeth] drew from that was not to put out her neck again. **1957** A. Huxley *Let.* 18 Jan. (1969) 816 Selznick is up to his neck in his forthcoming..film and probably won't be able to read the piece for some days. **1959** *Listener* 5 Mar. 414/1 It was likely that he would be thrown out on his neck very quickly. **1959** *Times* 19 May 5/5 Because Kent were always breathing down their necks, Hampshire could never really establish themselves. **1961** *Debates Senate Canada* 5 July 1021/1 So I shall try not to stick my neck out on the legal aspect too much; although, as I say, even from a legal standpoint it does seem rather simple to me. **1961** A. Wilson *Old Men at Zoo* iii. 162 But you shouldn't worry. You can never do the best work that way. Of course with Falcon and Sanderson round your neck, I'm not surprised. **1965** J. Porter *Dover Two* xi. 141 MacGregor rushed..away, delighted to be able to pursue his own line of investigation and..not to have Dover breathing down his neck all the time. **1971** 'F. Clifford' *Blind Side* iv. ii. 157 'I haven't seen him for a couple of days... He's been up to his neck.' 'Who with?' 'Same man.' **1971** A. Price *Alamut Ambush* xiii. 157 You don't have to stick your neck out, David—I'll stick mine out. And it'll be a pleasure! **1973** J. Fleming *You won't let me Finish* ix. 79 You're in it up to the neck whether you like it or not. **1973** *Times* 27 Feb. 14/4 He.. unfortunately began a sentence 'If I disagree with my local party..' whereupon a heckler added loudly 'You'll be out on your neck.' *Ibid.* 24 Apr. 11/7 Shakespeare.. gives the troupe a chance to try something new without the Academie breathing down its neck.

6. c. *neck and crop*: (later examples). Also *attrib.*

1932 Kipling *Limits & Renewals* 398 That does not excuse the neck-and-crop abruptness..of..our expulsion. **1963** A. Ross *Australia 63* v. 110 Titmus,..trying to force an in-swinger away, was bowled neck and crop. **1967** [see *decolonization].

9. a. *neck and neck*: (further examples).

1799 *Sporting Mag.* XIII. 309/1 In this way, neck and neck, whipping and spurring, all the speed of the horses, and all the skill of the jockies exerted, they rode up to the ending post. **1835** Dickens *Let.* 2 May (1965) I. 58 We came in literally neck and neck. **1901** *Chambers's Jrnl.* June 361/2 There a horse fell or staggered, and was instantly recovered. Now we were a few yards ahead, again neck-and-neck with the 'Quicksilver'; and so we raced on until we approached the old bridge at Bow. **1926** P. Guedalla *Palmerston* vii. 320 The republicans, the Orleans princes.., and the President might soon be running neck and neck. **1955** *Times* 23 June 9/4 Production ran neck-and-neck in the studios, but the second version..reached the public screen last.

b. *attrib.* (Earlier and later examples.)

1828 M. R. Mitford *Our Village* III. 204 The strength and luck of the parties were so well balanced, that it produced quite a neck-and-neck race, won only by two notches. **1952** E. F. Davies *Illyrian Venture* v. 84 Nicholls and I had a race across the plain, with a neck-and-neck finish.

9*. *neck-to-knees*: (see quot. 1941). Also *neck-to-knee* attrib. *Austral.*

1941 Baker *Dict. Austral. Slang* 49 *Neck-to-knees*, bathing costumes covering the body from the neck to half-way down the thigh. **1965** G. McInnes *Road to Gundagai* xiv. 261 Refusing to wear the regulation 'neck-to-knee' bathing togs.

11. b. For second part of def. read: *neck of the woods* (orig. *U.S.*), a settlement in wooded country; a small or remotely situated community; a district, neighbourhood, or region. Also *neck of timber*, and *ellipt.* (Earlier and later examples.)

1839 *Spirit of Times* 15 June 175/2 In this neck of the woods. **1874** [see *beatenest *a.*]. **1931** 'Grey Owl' *Men of Last Frontier* 15 A man may be soaking wet, half-frozen, hungry, and tired, landed on some inhospitable neck of the woods, vowing that a man is a fool to so abuse himself. **1955** M. Gilbert *Sky High* vi. 76 They don't come to live in this particular neck of the woods. **1967** *Listener* 19 Oct. 501 Some jerk has applied for a job as the new Cyril Connolly. Perhaps you would look him over, he lives in your neck of the woods. **1973** R. D. Symons *Where Wagon Led* i. vi. 95 Lee said there were springs about two miles up, and any cattle in what he called 'this neck of the woods' would probably be there. **1973** J. Wainwright *Devil you Don't* 21 In this neck, I say what. I also say when.

15. a. *neck-buckle, -gear, -ribbon, -rope, -wear.* **c.** *neck-hold.*

1767 in *Essex Inst. Hist. Coll.* (1917) LIII. 298, 7 pair silver Sleeve Buttons, together with Neck-Buckles, etc. **1888** *Judge* (U.S.) 29 Sept. 401/1 Neck-gear will, as always, cause the torture of dudes and dukes. **1890** Hardy *Melancholy Hussar* ii, in *Three Notable Stories* 167 His head would probably have been bent..but for his stiff neck-gear. **1912** W. Owen *Let.* 3 Apr. (1967) 127 In Church with a neck-gear such as Wordsworth wore. **1905** *Daily Chron.* 23 Feb. 3/5 By means of a peculiar 'neck-hold' he can render his man unconscious. **1852** A. Cary *Clovernook* 97 She selected a white muslin which she thought would do if she only had a new neck-ribbon. **1883** *Century Mag.* Aug. 572/2 Partly to rescue the rest of her raiment from the shower which had ruined her neck-ribbon. **1777** *Horae Subsecivae* (MS.) 302 *Neck-rope*, a wooden bow to come round the neck of a bullock, and fastned above to a small beam, by which bullocks are fastned with a cord or rope in the linney. **1822** J. Fowler *Jrnl.* 18 June (1898) 159 In the evening the Indeans [s]tole all the neck Roaps of our Horses. **1879** Webster Suppl. 1569/1 *Neck-wear*, a collective term for cravats and collars. (*Colloq.*) **1887** *Harper's Mag.* May 947/2 He waited at the corner of the block,..affecting an interest in the neckwear of a furnisher's window. **1910** *Westm. Gaz.* 15 Apr. 4/1 Similar good results have followed upon the use of looser neck-wear. **1924** *Barnsley Brit. Drapery Stores Sale Catal.*, Lace, embroideries and neckwear. **1959** *Sears, Roebuck Catal.* Spring & Summer 145/2 Neckwear... Collar and Cuff Set... Nylon Dickey.

16. neck-canal *Bot.*, in ferns and bryophytes, a central channel in the neck of the archegonium, made up of **neck canal cells**; **neck-cell** (later examples); **neck-lock**, (*a*) in a wig, a sausage-curl (see also quot. 1966); (*b*) in *Judo*, a form of strangle-hold; **neck-oil** *slang*, alcoholic drink, chiefly beer; **neck-rein** *v.* (see quot. 1946); also as *sb.*; so **neck-reining** *vbl. sb.*; **neck-roll**, (*a*) in *Gymnastics*, a swing of the body backwards to rest on the back of the neck: (*b*) (see quot. 1966).

1887 W. Hillhouse tr. *Strasburger's Handbk. Pract. Bot.* xxv. 275 The neck [of the archegonium] is traversed by the neck-canal, which is composed of a series of neck canal-cells, the walls between which are dissolved, and the disorganized contents of the four neck canal-cells are thus fused into a connected string. **1938** G. M. Smith *Cryptogamic Bot.* II. ii. 16 Marchantiales typically have six rows of neck cells. *Ibid.* 17 During the course of development of the neck, the primary canal cell divides to form four neck canal cells. **1957** *New Biol.* XXII. 116 In effecting fertilization the spermatozoid has to traverse a lengthy 'neck-canal', a distance perhaps 200 times its own length. **1965** Bell & Coombe tr. *Strasburger's Textbk. Bot.* 524 The ventral and neck canal cells may be regarded as gametes which have become functionless. **1761** W. Hogarth *Works* (1833) II. facing p. 177 Triglyph membretta or necklock. **1906** Miyake & Tani *Game of Ju-Jitsu* ix. 59 L may make direct opposition to the neck-lock in several ways. **1925** Kelly & Schwabe *Historic Costume* vi. 201 The twisted central neck-lock is a survival of the late seventeenth century dildo. **1962** E. G. Bartlett *Judo & Self-Defence* 56 The Single Wing Necklock... Stranglehold.., pass your left hand under his left armpit and up behind his head, so as to press his head forward. **1966** J. S. Cox *Illustr. Dict. Hairdressing* 169/1 *Neck lock*, the vertical curl at the neck of a barrister's wig. **1860** Hotten *Dict. Slang* (ed. 2) 179 *Neck*, to swallow. *Neck-oil*, drink of any kind. **1880** C. H. Poole *Attempt towards Gloss. Words Stafford* 16/2 *Neck-oil*, ale. A word I once heard at Walsall. **1919** H. Jenkins *John Dene of Toronto* i. 27 They'd be attacked all along the three thousand miles route, and would go down like neck-oil on a permit night. **1936** F. Richards *Old Soldier Sahib* iv. 75 He inquired if we were fond of a drop of 'neck-oil', which like 'purge' was a nickname for beer. **1970** *Private Eye* 2 Jan. 12 A chance encounter..leads Barry to consume a lot of nice neck-oil. **1935** H. D. Chamberlin *Riding & Schooling Horses* iv. 153 'Bearing' or 'Neck Rein'. The right hand is carried just over the crest of the neck, and acts towards the left front. **1940** W. Fawcett *Young Horseman* xii. 151 'Neck reining'... Here the horse is taught with voice, hand and heel to turn away from the side on which he feels the rein against his neck. *Ibid.*, It is very handy to have a horse which is trained to 'neck rein'. **1946** M. C. Self *Horseman's Encycl.* 288 Neck reining a horse is turning him by use of the indirect rein. That is, in turning to the left the reins are carried to the left with no backward pull nor any direct pull on the left rein; the right rein, coming against the neck, gives the signal for the turn. **1953** G. Brooke *Introd. Riding* vii. 76 What in polo language is called 'neck-reining', e.g. when turning or diverging to the right, while applying the left leg, the hand is carried over to the right. **1959** E. Collier *Three against Wilderness* ii. 23, I..neck reined the gelding northward. **1920** *Royal Navy Handbk. Physical & Recreational Training* v. 180 'Tricks of Ground Work'... Neck roll (backwards) to Long-arm Balance. Back Handspring, [etc.]. *a* **1935** T. E. Lawrence *Mint* (1955) ii. xii. 133 Hand-springs and neck-rolls. **1946** G. Millar *Horned Pigeon* xiii. 177 Instead of hitting something very solid,..I found myself doing neck rolls down a granite chip embankment. **1966** J. S. Cox *Illustr. Dict. Hairdressing* 169/1 *Neck roll*, (1) The ends of the natural hair worn in a roll at the nape. (2) A postiche worn at the nape. Also called neck piece.

neck, *v.*[1] **2.** Read: *slang.* To drink, to swallow. (Later examples.)

1860 [see *neck-oil* (*neck *sb.*[1] 16)]. **1889** E. Peacock *Gloss. Words Manley & Corringham, Lincolnshire* (ed. 2) 366 He neck'd a good share o' beer that neet o' th' jewbilee. **1899** C. Rook *Hooligan Nights* i. 13 He wasn't selling 'is meat over-quick, 'cos 'alf the time he was necking four-ale in the pub 'cross the way. **1929** J. Masefield *Hawbucks* 135, I do wish..you'd chuck necking Scotch the way you do.

4. a. *trans.* To clasp (a member of the opposite sex) round the neck; to fondle. **b.** *intr.* To engage in holding and fondling, or to embrace and caress, a member of the opposite sex. Hence **necking** *vbl. sb.*; also *attrib.*, as *necking party.*

1825 A. Crawfurd *Tales my Grandmother* I. 138 Let's see nae mair o' Peter Wallett's neckin' an' touslin' here. **1842** Allnutt *Diary* (MS.) 10 Newcastle... I came rather suddenly upon a man who unceremoniously put his arm round a young lady, and..said..'I was only a-necking on her a little bit, Sir.' **1877** G. Fraser *Wigtown & Whithorn* 272 When sufficiently near him, she necked her supposed partner, greeting him with the following affectionate salute. **1890** J. Service *Thir Notandums* xi. 82 I'm muckle mista'en if I haena seen him neckin' wi' the said Betty. **1922** *Dialect Notes* V. 148 *Necking*, dancing with cheeks together, also known as 'parking'. **1923** *Cosmopolitan* Nov. 72/3 The necking parties in dark nooks about the deck at night. **1924** P. Marks *Plastic Age* xiv. 149 Some of those janes certainly could neck, and they were ready for it any time. **1928** *Daily Tel.* 4 Sept. 7/5 High school children..whose favourite pastime is 'necking' in motor-cars in dark roads with the lights turned off. **1930** *Punch* 26 Mar. 341/3 *Necking-Control.* The Ministry of Transport is now building a chain of illuminated posts... Red means 'stop', amber 'get ready to love' and green 'go'.—*Indian Paper.* **1932** E. Waugh *Black Mischief* v. 179 It's pretty dim for me, floundering about half the day, ..while you neck with the chap who's cut me out. **1935** Wodehouse *Blandings Castle* xii. 296 Do you know who that is that this necker is necking?.. My girl. No less. **1938** E. Bowen *Death of Heart* ii. vi. 278 A spot of necking with Daphne. **1940** J. O'Hara *Pal Joey* 59, I was even surprised I could neck her at all. **1950** G. Barker *True Confession* iv. 24 That this rapscallion Was necking with his legal bride. **1958** *Times Lit. Suppl.* 15 Aug. p. x/3 For the active young non-reader, sport, cars, dancing and necking are the prime immediacies. **1970** G. Greer *Female Eunuch* 181 The best behaved teenager necks. **1971** *Petticoat* 24 July 39/5 In necking and/or petting, a boy may ask his partner to 'make love to him'. **1974** 'J. Le Carré' *Tinker, Tailor* xiii. 115 A loving couple necking in the back of a Rover.

5. To fasten *to* or *together* by means of ropes put around the neck. *U.S.*

1857 D. E. E. Braman *Information Texas* iv. 73 The usual practice of farmers whenever they want work oxen, is to..neck together, with ropes, as many pair of..steers as they desire. **1923** J. H. Cook *50 Yrs. on Old Frontier* 21 Each of them had to be 'necked' to a gentle one, to be led for a time. **1930** J. F. Dobie *Coronado's Children* iii. 102 Every animal in the pen had been roped and led in necked to an old brindle ox. **1933** J. V. Allen *Cowboy Lore* i. 9 *Necking*, in range terminology...On the range an unruly cow or one with roving proclivities will often be necked or tied to a more tractable animal.

6. *intr.* To undergo a local reduction in width when subjected to tension. Usu. with *down*.

1938 J. Newton *Introd. Metall.* iv. 105 The contraction begins to concentrate at some one point on the bar, [and] the piece begins to 'neck down'. **1942** *Industr. & Engin. Chem.* Jan. 56/2 During drawing each filament 'necks down' and takes a smaller diameter. **1964** *Mod. Textiles Mag.* Jan. 67/2 When an undrawn nylon filament is stretched beyond its elastic limit, it suddenly (and irreversibly) 'necks down' to a fraction of its original diameter. **1965** P. I. Vincent in P. D. Ritchie *Physics of Plastics* ii. 84 It may also happen that a specimen does not neck at low speeds because there is not sufficient strain softening.

necked, *a.* Add: **3.** (Further examples.)

1956 R. J. C. Atkinson *Stonehenge* v. 154 Two main groups of population, distinguished by the forms of their pottery as the Bell-Beaker and Necked-Beaker cultures. *Ibid.*, The Necked-Beaker culture..is an indigenous development in England. **1967** *Antiquaries Jrnl.* XLVII. 174 The latter comprised sherds of two pots—part of the body of a probable rusticated beaker and part of the base of a beaker of indeterminate type—probably a necked variety. **1972** *Sci. Amer.* Dec. 54/3 The Taslan process feeds a filament into a rapidly moving airstream at the necked region of a nozzle.

4. [perh. f. *neck *v.*[1] 6.] Reduced in width as a result of having been subjected to tension.

1959 C. E. Birchenall *Physical Metall.* vi. 136 A_f is the cross-sectional area in the necked region. **1964** R. E. Reed-Hill *Physical Metall. Princ.* xviii. 555 Fracture begins at the center of the necked region on a plane that is macroscopically normal to the applied tensile-stress axis.

Necker[1] (ne·kəɹ). [name of Louis Albert *Necker* (1786–1861), Swiss naturalist and mineralogist, who described the phenomenon in 1832 (*Phil. Mag.* I. 329).] *Necker('s) cube*: a line drawing of a transparent cube in which parallel sides are drawn with the same length, so that one seems to look successively down at the top and up at the bottom as the perspective reverses.

1901 E. B. Titchener *Exper. Psychol.* I. ii. ix. 309 The Instructor should have a few prepared as large wall-diagrams:..Schröder's stair-figure, Necker's cube,..the. Müller-Lyer figure. **1938** R. S. Woodworth *Exper. Psychol.* xxv. 628 Many line drawings readily suggest three dimensions and are called figures of ambiguous or reversible perspective. The Necker cube and the Schröder staircase are the best known. **1966** R. L. Gregory *Eye & Brain* xiii. 231 Certain figures..are ambiguously seen in depth, for example the Necker cube. **1975** *Sci. Amer.* Jan. 8/1 Rubin's well-known vase, Schröder's stairs and Necker's cube did almost certainly provide the seed of inspiration for M. C. Escher's work on the regular subdivision of the plane.

necker[2] (ne·kəɹ). [f. *neck *v.*[1] 4 + -er[1].] One who indulges in caresses and fondling.

1923 Mencken *Amer. Lang.* (ed. 3) 373 *Necker*, one given to cheek-to-cheek dancing. **1925** H. L. Foster *Trop. Tramp with Tourists* xvi. 300 Listen, you would-be necker! **1935** [see *neck *v.*[1] 4]. **1947** I. Brown *Say the Word* 81 But they [*sc.* young gentlemen] are not known, I think, as neckers. **1966** 'D. Shannon' *With a Vengeance* (1968) i. 15 Well, it's a body... Found about half an hour ago... By, I gather, a couple of neckers.

neckful (ne·kful). *colloq.* [f. Neck *sb.*[1] + -ful 2.] As much (punishment, vituperation, etc.) as one can endure; cf. phr. *to get* (or *catch, take*) *it in the neck* (*neck *sb.*[1] 1 e). So **ne·ck-full** *a.*, having a full stomach; cf. *neck *v.*[1] 2.

1920 R. Graves *Country Sentiment* 71 On pay-day nights, neck-full with beer, Old soldiers stumbling homeward here. **1950** W. Hammond *Cricketers' School* ii. 30 There was plenty of time..to give them a neckful of their own medicine.

neck-handkerchief. (Earlier Amer. example.)

1642 *Archives of Maryland* (1887) IV. 95, 9 plaine neckcloths and 5 plaine neckhandkercheifes.

necking, *sb.* Add: **3. necking-cord**, in a draw-loom (see quot. 1910).

1910 L. Hooper *Hand-Loom Weaving* 328 *Necking cords*, cords joining pulley cords and leashes in a monture. **1958** A. Hindson *Designer's Drawloom* ii. 26 The doubled part of the cord stretching from top to bottom of the Simple frame is known as the Simple cord and the divided sections from the top of the Simple frame to where they meet the cords from the shafts as the Necking cords.

4. *Archæol.* A circlet around a projection (as the boss of a shield).

1946 *Antiquity* XX. 24 A decorative necking of tinned bronze connects the boss with its wide ornamental border.

necking (ne·kiŋ), *vbl. sb.* [f. Neck *v.*[1] + -ing[1].] (In Dict. s.v. Neck *v.*[1] 4.)

2. (In Suppl. s.v. *neck *v.*[1] 4.)

3. Also **necking down.** A local reduction in width occurring when a sample is subjected to tension.

1957 *Textile Terms & Definitions* (Textile Inst.) (ed. 3) 67 *Necking*, the sudden reduction in diameter occurring on stretching an undrawn filament. **1959** C. E. Birchenall *Physical Metall.* vi. 145 The fcc [*sc.* face-centred cubic] metals, like copper and aluminium, undergo duplex slip and necking without a distinct fracture stage. **1966** *McGraw-Hill Encycl. Sci. & Technol.* VIII. 270/2 Even the tension test, which is in general the most satisfactory, gives some difficulty because of the instability that leads to necking down. **1974** Colangelo & Heiser *Analysis Metall. Failures* ii. 15 When failure occurs, the necking leads to a variety of fracture surfaces, depending on the material's ductility.

necklaced, *a.* (Later example.)

1968 G. Jones *Hist. Vikings* iv. i. 322 Frey was a god of fruitfulness and sexuality. His necklaced sister was his genial counterpart.

ne·ck-line. [Neck *sb.*[1]] †**1.** = Neck *sb.*[1] 10 d. *Obs.*

1672 J. Lacy tr. *Tacquett's Mil. Archit.* 34 Look in the Table for the Neck line, you'l find it to be 169,706. feet. **1810** C. James *New Mil. Dict.* (ed. 3) II, *Neck-line*, an old term in fortification, signifying the gorge.

2. The shape of the neck of a garment; the line of the top of a woman's garment at the front of the neck.

1904 A. K. Smith *Cutting Out* xxviii. 217 Construction lines... The lower line is the 'waist' line and the upper line the 'neck' line. **1923** [see *bateau 2]. **1958** *Times* 5 Dec. 14/4 The bride..wore a gown of ivory-tinted satin with a square neckline. **1964** *McCall's Sewing* viii. 116/2 Neckline fits smoothly without pulling or gaping. **1974** *Country Life* 17 Jan. 106 Sweater with a sweetheart neckline... Spotted pullover..with a fashionable square neckline.

3. (See quot. 1966.)

1931 G. A. Foan *Art & Craft of Hairdressing* iii. 136/1 Note the flat top, ragged crown, high neck line, and straight side-pieces. **1966** J. S. Cox *Illustr. Dict. Hairdressing* 102/2 *Neckline*, (1) That part of the neck where the hair growth begins... (2) The outline at the neck of a cut head of hair. **1972** L. Palladino *Princ. & Pract. Hairdressing* viii. 113 Necklines may be curved, straight, pointed, or graduated high or low.

4. *Archæol.* An ornamental line around the neck of a vessel.

1937 *Antiquity* XI. 394 They show minor differences, additional necklines and bosses on the smaller vessel.

neck-tie. b. Read: *attrib., spec.* in necktie-party, a lynching or hanging. *slang.*

1871 *Harper's Mag.* Nov. 949/2 Mr. Jim Clemenston, equine abductor, was..made the victim of a neck-tie sociable. **1882** in *Nat. Geogr. Mag.* (1929) Aug. 247 If Found within the Limits of this City after Ten O'Clock p.m. this Night, you will be Invited to attend a Grand Neck-tie Party. **1893** [in Dict.]. **1932** 'S. Wood' *Shades Prison House* xxii. 340 An investigation brought to light the remains of the woman and her children, and Mr. Burrows was now booked to play lead at a neck-tie party, shortly to be convened. He walked to and fro with the death guards. **1967** N. Lucas *C.I.D.* x. 157 Oh well—if you have a necktie party, it's a quick way to go. Better than being killed by an atom bomb. **1973** *Listener* 4 Jan. 10/3 A drunk or a loud-mouth could wind up like a rustler—the victim of a neck-tie party.

necro-. Add: **necrobacillo·sis** (pl. **-o·ses**) *Path.* [Bacill(us + -osis], any of several conditions in animals, esp. domestic animals, and occas. in humans, characterized by diffuse or localized necrotic lesions caused by the bacterium *Sphærophorus necrophorus* (also called *Bacteroides funduliformis*, etc.); **necrophi·lia, necro·phily** = *necrophilism*; hence **necrophi·lic, necrophili·stic** *adjs.*; **ne·crophile, necrophi·liac, necro·philist** *sbs.*, one who is morbidly attracted to corpses; also *attrib.* and *fig.*; **necrophilous** *a.*, (*b*) of, pertaining to, or resembling necrophilism; also *fig.*; **ne·crophobe**, one who has a horror of death or of dead bodies; **necrophobia** (examples).

Virginia Woolf preferred to Græcize to *nekro-*.

1907 *Ann. Rep. Bureau Animal Industry, U.S. Dept. Agric. 1905* 18 The presence of only one of the morbid conditions noted may be the starting point of an enzootic outbreak of necrobacillosis. **1933** R. A. Kelser *Man. Vet. Bacteriol.* (ed. 2) xxvii. 284 *Actinomyces necrophorus* is the etiological factor of a variety of 'necrobacilloses' among domestic animals. It is the cause of gangrenous dermatitis of equines, 'foot-rot' and 'lip-and-leg' ulceration of sheep. **1961** M. Hynes *Med. Bacteriol.* (ed. 7) xii. 172 *F*[*usiformis*] *necrophorus* (*Bacteroides funduliformis*) causes calf diphtheria and other animal diseases. In man it is the cause of various infections grouped together as necrobacillosis. **1892** C. G. Chaddock tr. *Krafft-Ebing's Psychopathia Sexualis* iii. 67 Following the preceding horrible group of perversions..come naturally the necrophiles. **1932** V. Woolf *Let. to Young Poet* 20 The large and highly respectable society of nekrophils..who..are even now intoning the sacred and comfortable words, Keats is dead, Shelley is dead, Byron is dead. **1937** M. Hirschfeld *Sexual Anomalies* xxiii. 510 The mentally weak necrophile imagines that it is possible to inflict pain on the corpse. *Ibid.*, The necrophile act is..a frenzied intensification of the aggressive and destructive impulse. **1892** C. G. Chaddock tr. *Krafft-Ebing's Psychopathia Sexualis* iii. 68 The impulse to indulge in acts of necrophilia. **1926** W. McDougall *Outl. Abnormal Psychol.* viii. 164 He [*sc.* Ferenczi] assumes that coprophilia and necrophilia are normal components of the sex instinct. **1946** 'G. Orwell' *Crit. Ess.* 122 [Dali's] most notable characteristic is his necrophilia. **1949** J. Rodker tr. *Bonaparte's Life & Works E. A. Poe* i. xii. 45 The necrophilia of this poet whom death alone inspired, and who was to cast so terrible, though irresistible, a spell on mankind. **1967** D. Pinner *Ritual* x. 105 He keeps corpses in here for amateur necrophilia. **1959** *20th Cent.* Dec. 426 In ghoulism the necrophiliac traffic is one way as it were. **1962** *John o' London's* 14 June 583/3 Lazarus..is trotted out..presumably for the benefit of any necrophiliacs in the audience. **1969** C. Allen *Textbk. Psychosexual Disorders* (ed. 2) xi. 256 Necrophiliacs are very rare, some are insane and inaccessible, and infrequently consult the psychiatrist. **1974** *Country Life* 23 May 1269/1 The sadistic and even necrophiliac horrors of the Symbolists. **1926** J. I. Suttie tr. *Ferenczi's Further Contrib. Theory & Technique Psycho-Anal.* 279 A necrophilic dream was due to anxiety in regard to coitus. **1940** H. Ellis *My Life* ix. 373 She symbolised it [*sc.* this special problem].., making her hero..a fisherman with a kind of necrophilic attraction to corpses. **1955** J. Strachey et al. tr. *Freud's Compl. Psychol. Works* X. 278 A necrophilic phantasy which he once had consciously. **1932** V. Woolf *Let. to Young Poet* 5, I replied after all these years to that elderly nekrophilist—Nonsense. **1949** J. Rodker tr. *Bonaparte's Life & Works E. A. Poe* i. x. 37 The lost and always sought for mother with whom his [*sc.* Poe's] necrophilist soul forever longed to unite. **1950** *John o' London's* 7 July 411/4 There they go, a grubby procession of blasphemers, perverts, lechers, necrophilists and drunkards. **1924** C. Gray *Survey Contemporary Mus.* 185 The general public has taken to its great soft heart the necrophilistic ardours of the *Valse Triste.* **1932** V. Woolf *Let. to Young Poet* 28, I, at any rate, refuse to be nekrophilus. **1956** 'M. Innes' *Old Hall, New Hall* i. v. 51, I don't think he was positively necrophilous. **1967** G. Greene *May we borrow your Husband?* 12, I think she wants something more nubile and less necrophilous. **1971** R. E. Witt *Isis in Graeco-Roman World* iii. 37 Horus, Harsiesis ('Har, Son of Aset'), had been miraculously conceived by Isis in a necrophilous union. **1974** *Time* 7 Jan. 60/2 Chilling psycho-biographies of Sadists Stalin and Himmler, and the necrophilous Adolf Hitler. **1897** tr. *T. Ribot's Psychol. of Emotions* 257, I pass over the extreme cases, those of necrophily, or of sexual erethism. **1905** H. Ellis *Stud. Psychol. Sex* iv. iii. 188 Necrophily, or sexual attraction for corpses,..may perhaps be regarded as a kind of perverted sadism. **1927** *Observer* 8 May 6/4 His circumstances and his griefs, and his disease fostered his necrophily. **1932** V. Woolf *Let. to Young Poet* 20 Nekrophily induces slumber. **1939** T. S. Eliot *Family Reunion* i. ii. 62 Let your necrophily Feed upon that carcase. **1962** *Times* 4 May 20/6 The phœnix rebirth of Toscanini's N.B.C. Orchestra which continued, after the maestro's death, to give Toscanini performances until it became plain to all that photographic reproduction from memory is..a variety of necrophily. **1973** Necrophobe [see *hypochondriac *sb.* 1]. **1833** Dunglison *Dict. Med. Sci.* II. 72 *Necrophobia*... This symptom occurs in patients where the disease is not mortal; as in hypochondriasis. **1936** R. Fleming *News from Tartary* v. i. 189 Since Greys hated anything dead, I gave the goose to her. But necrophobia was rife that morning. **1965** *New Statesman* 30 Apr. 684 (*heading*) Necrophobia.

necromancer. Add: **2.** A silver or pewter dish with closely fitting lid and wide rim (see quots.).

1747 H. Glasse *Art of Cookery* ii. 51 Take a large Pewter or Silver Dish, made like a deep Soop Dish, with an Edge about an Inch deep on the inside, on which the Lid fixes (with a Handle at top) so fast that you may lift it up full, by that Handle without falling; this Dish is called a Necromancer. **1784** S. Maciver *Cookery & Pastry* (ed. 4) iii. 56 A necromancer is a flat white-iron pan with two handles, and a lid that checks in very close. *Ibid.* 57 Send it to the table in the necromancer. **1967** *Canad. Antiques Collector* Apr. 16/2 An interesting if rather odd relative of the chafing dish. It was called a 'necromancer' and was made of silver or pewter and fashioned like a deep soup dish with a well-fitting lid and with a wide rim. When filled with thinly sliced meat, the container was hung by the rim between two chairs. Heat was applied by burning fifteen spills of brown paper.

necromant. (Later example.)

1887 A. Lang *Myth, Ritual & Relig.* I. 105 The power of..Sorcerers and Necromants.

necromantically, *adv.* Delete † *Obs. rare*$^{-1}$ in Dict. and add later examples.

1963 *Times* 1 May 13/6 Voodoo..is seen as a religion of fear in which people become like animals, being possessed by demons and necromantically meddling with the spirits of the dead. **1965** *New Statesman* 12 Nov. 749/1 The most marvellous, necromantically speaking, is probably the title piece, where a boy learns the hazards of magic.

necromantist. For † *Obs. rare*$^{-1}$ read *rare* and add later example.

1910 *Daily Chron.* 8 Apr. 4/4 A sheaf of conjectures.. which have been drawn from the various necromantists.

necropolitan, *a.* (Later examples.)

1914 C. Mackenzie *Sinister St.* II. iv. v. 965 Always in contrast with these necropolitan streets, these masks of human dwellings, were Michael's own thoughts thronged with fancies of himself and Lily. **1916** A. Huxley *Burning Wheel* 48 The necropolitan ground. **1931** A. Gibbs *New Crusade* 78 The long arm of coincidence was in his case the long arm of the law, white sleeved, and it was raised against the further progress of her vehicle to allow a large necropolitan car to come swinging serenely from the Embankment to the left over Westminster Bridge. **1960** *Times Lit. Suppl.* 20 May p. xi/2 The curiously necropolitan conventions of the worst comic strips.

necropsy (ne·krǫpsi, nekrǫ·psi), *v.* [f. the sb.] *trans.* To perform a necropsy on. So **necro·psied** *ppl. a.*

1927 *Arch. Path.* III. 985 It is of interest to compare in some detail the death rates at ages in the necropsied population as a whole, with the life table death rates of a general population, and with that portion of the necropsied population which had some malignant tumor at death. **1958** *Amer. Jrnl. Path.* XXXIV. 863 Kidneys from an unselected series of 200 necropsied patients were sectioned and stained by a modification of the Bowie technique. **1966** *Internat. Encycl. Vet. Med.* II. 964 In 7 per cent. of 52 severely affected pigs necropsied there was inflammation or ulceration of the stomach wall. **1971** *Nature* 16 Apr. 460/2 All surviving animals were killed and necropsied after 60 weeks.

necrosis. 2. *Bot.* (Later examples.)

1901 H. M. Ward *Disease in Plants* xxvi. 240 Necrosis.—This is a general term for cases where the tissues gradually turn brown or black in patches which die and dry up... Necrosis is often due to frost. **1951** L. L. Pyenson *Elem. Plant Protection* xvi. 302 Necrosis. The browning and death of tissues is a characteristic effect of some viruses. *Ibid.* 303 Internal symptoms may show a necrosis of the phloem. **1958** *U.S. Dept. Agric. Yearbk. 1957* 763/1 Necrosis. Death associated with discoloration and dehydration of all or parts of plant ograns, such as leaves.

necrotizing, *ppl. a.* (s.v. Necrotize *v.*). Add defs.: **a.** Undergoing or becoming affected with necrosis.

1899 [see Necrotize *v.*]. **1966** [see *granulomatosis].

b. Causing necrosis.

1901 *Ann. Rep. Bureau Animal Industry, U.S. Dept. Agric. 1900* 276 Dorset and de Schweinitz described the isolation of a necrotizing acid which they obtained from tuberculous cultures. **1957** Smith & Jones *Vet. Path.* xxiv. 831 Each of these latter infections produces a minimum of exudate, but their toxins are no less deadly and the latter two are also necrotizing. Many streptococci also produce necrotizing (lytic) toxins.

nectarious, *a.* (Earlier examples.)

1771 Smollett *Humph. Cl.* III. 4 My dairy flows with nectarious tides of milk and cream. **1791** W. Enfield *Hist. Philos.* II. ii. 53 He [*sc.* Apuleius]..drank freely of.. the nectarious but unfathomable deep of philosophy.

nectarivorous (nektări·vŏrəs), *a.* [f. L. *nectar* (Gk. νέκταρ) nectar + -i- + *vor-us* devouring + -ous, after Carnivorous *a.*, etc.] Of birds or insects: feeding on the nectar of flowers.

1898 *Ann. Rep. Board of Regents Smithsonian Inst. 1896* 421 The nectarivorous insects localize their action upon these nectaries.

necton, var. *nekton.

ned[1] (ned). *Sc. slang.* [? f. *Ned*, a familiar abbrev. of the name *Edward*; cf. *Teddy boy.] Hooligan, thug, petty criminal. Also used as a general term of disapprobation.

1959 *Times* 18 Dec. 5/3 He can..give gloriously funny imitations of Glasgow charwomen, tram drivers, and neds. **1964** B. Gaston *Drifting Death* iv. 57 Lomax..was a tuppeny-ha'penny little ned, not even attached to one of the big mobs. **1968** H. C. Rae *Few Small Bones* ii. i. 71 Even the bloody neds from the newspapers were getting critical with their wisecracks. **1969** B. Knox *Tallyman* ii. 21 Millside had the worst pockets of unemployed and unemployable,..and some of the toughest hooligan 'neds' in the city [*sc.* Glasgow]. **1971** —— *To kill a Witch* i. 10 Most were neds, the city's [*sc.* Glasgow's] verbal shorthand for petty thugs, second-rate criminals and professional layabouts. **1973** P. Malloch *Kickback* xvi. 100 He was a ned. You could always spot them. There was something about them that no trained policeman would ever miss.

Ned[2] (ned). Short for *neddy 3.

1961 *Guardian* 19 Dec. 14/1 His National Economic Development Council (or 'Ned', as it is ominously being called). **1963** *Ann. Reg. 1962* 3 The National Economic Development Council (already familiarly known as Ned or even Neddy). **1964** *New Society* 23 Jan. 23/2 Each little Ned..is going to have a highly individual character, according to the wishes of the industry involved.

neddy. Add: **1. b.** A fool, a simpleton.

1823 'J. Bee' *Slang* 124 *Neddy*—sometimes 'ass-neger', other names for jackass—the living emblem of patience and long suffering. **1853** Thackeray *Newcomes* (1854) I. i. 4 All types of all characters march through all fables:.. victims and bullies; dupes and knaves; long-eared Neddies, giving themselves leonine airs. **1854** A. E. Baker *Gloss. Northamptonshire Words* II. 49 What a neddy you must be, to do that! **1963** L. Deighton *Horse under Water* xlix. 212 'I'm sorry,' he said, 'you must think I'm a terrible neddie.'

c. *Austral. slang.* A horse, esp. a racehorse.

1900 [see *bag *sb.* 17 c(*a*)]. **1918** B. Cronin *Coastlanders* 74 A hot cinder lit on my neddie's rump. **1965** W. Dick *Bunch of Ratbags* 40 My old man was backing the neddies as usual.

3. [Properly a different word.] *colloq.* name for the *N*ational *E*conomic *D*evelopment Council. Also, one of its sub-committees. Also *attrib.*

1962 *Engineering* 1 June 729/2 Since poor Neddy was formed everyone seems to be jumping on to his band wagon. **1963** *Times* 11 June 6/6 The great significance of Neddy is that it is the first time in this country that a concerted effort has been made by the Government, management and the unions to set the country moving on a course which can be steadily sustained. **1964** *Financial Times* 8 Sept., We shall deal with them [*sc.* problems]..most of all through N.E.D.C., which we shall retain, and the regional and industrial Neddies. **1966** *Times* 14 May 17/6 Two little neddies are due to meet, wool on Tuesday and mechanical engineering on Thursday. **1968** W. Davis *Three Years Hard Labour* i. iv. 50 The so-called 'Little Neddies'. These were Councils for individual industries, designed to bridge the gap between Whitehall and industry. **1968** *Times* 18 Apr. 21/7 A Neddy-sponsored questionnaire sent out to 2,000 firms in the wool trade, is the first phase of a £80,000 survey designed to establish the competitiveness of the British wool textile industry. **1969** *Times* 30 Apr. 25/4 New chairman for building Neddy... A new chairman for the building and civil engineering economic development committees has been found.

‖ **Nederlands** (nē·dəɹlants). *S. Afr.* [Afrikaans, ad. Du. *Nederlandsch.*] The Dutch language.

1926 *Spectator* 21 Aug. 278/2 Africaans resembles, in vocabulary, the Dutch of the seventeenth and early eighteenth centuries almost more than modern Nederlands does. **1959** *Cape Times* 8 June 8/5 Nederlands is an old and highly-developed language with a wide literature.

Ned Kelly (ned ke·li). The name of the most famous Australian bush-ranger (1857–1880), used allusively to designate one of reckless courage or unscrupulous business dealings. *Austral. colloq.* See also *game *a.*[1] 2.

1941 Baker *Dict. Austral. Slang* 41 *Kelly, Ned*, any person of buccaneering business habits. **1945** 'R. Rene' *Mo's Memoirs* 24 He was game as Ned Kelly, and he'd ride anything. **1953** D. Cusack *Southern Steel* 41 Is that kid game? Game as Ned Kelly. **1953** R. Braddon in I. Bevan *Sunburnt Country* 129 Such a feat of bluff is known to Australians as a 'Ned Kelly'... It is phrases such as 'do a Ned Kelly' that lend so much verve and colour to the Australian serviceman's vocabulary. **1958** H. D. Williamson *Sunlit Plain* 90 In fact, to pay him his due compliment, he was as game as Ned Kelly. **1965** J. O'Grady *Aussie English* 62 Included in this Ned Kelly category are..characters who overcharge for mediocre work and services, and the bloke who sells you a second-hand, guaranteed, 'every bit as good as new..' vehicle, which falls to pieces in the first hundred miles. *Ibid.*, To say that a man is 'as game as Ned Kelly', on the other hand, is to praise him highly. It means that he..is brave to the point of recklessness in the face of any odds. **1966** D. Crick *Period of Adjustment* 66 'Are you game?' 'As Ned Kelly.' **1973** *Guardian* 19 Mar. 7/7 Sporty boys now..peer out of the windowed skull of the full-face [crash] helmet dubbed Ned Kelly. **1974** *Courier-Mail* (Brisbane) 20 Aug. 12/5 Mr. Bizzell said the council offered him $740 for 74 perches of land, including a 33 perch block he had levelled... 'They are just Ned Kellys,' he said. 'They certainly won't put it back on the market without making a handsome profit.'

2. *Austral.* rhyming slang for 'belly'.

1945 Baker *Austral. Lang.* xv. 271 Here are a few examples of undisguised rhyme that seem to be Australian:..*Port Melbourne Pier*, an ear; *Ned Kelly*, the belly. **1960** J. Franklyn *Dict. Rhyming Slang* 100/1 *Ned Kelly*, belly. **1970** *Private Eye* 27 Mar. 16 If I don't get a drop of hard stuff up me old Ned Kelly there's a good chance I might chunder in the channel.

‖ **née** (ne), *a.* [Fr., fem. of pa. pple. of *naître* to be born.] Born: placed before a married woman's maiden name.

1758 M. W. Montagu *Let.* 27 Nov. (1967) III. 192 The advantage of being casually admitted in the train of Madame de *B.*, *née O.* **1831** M. Edgeworth *Let.* 30 Apr. (1971) 529 This Abroad & at Home is by Mrs. Eaton née Waldy. **1848** Thackeray *Van. Fair* xlviii. 429 The interview between Rebecca Crawley, née Sharp, and her Imperial Master. **1919** T. S. Eliot *Sweeney Among Nightingales* in *Poems*, Rachel née Rabinovitch Tears at the grapes with murderous paws. **1955** *Times* 2 July 8/7 He married, after divorce proceedings, Mary Barrie (*née* Ansell), by whom he was, himself, subsequently divorced. **1973** *Times* 3 Nov. 16/6 Mrs Fanny Harwood, nee Fanny Pain..was born in 1889.

neechee, var. *nitchie.

need, *sb.* Add: **10. c.** *Psychol.* A state of physiological or psychological want that consciously or subconsciously motivates behaviour towards its satisfaction.

1929 J. B. Miner tr. *Piéron's Princ. Exper. Psychol.* iii. 54 These instincts are generally designated by a special name..which expresses in a measure the imperious character of the tendencies; we say that they are needs. **1935** K. Koffka *Princ. Gestalt Psychol.* viii. 329 But needs are..states of tension which persist until they are relieved. **1936** *Jrnl. Psychol.* III. 27 Two commonly used terms for a motivational process are *drive* and *need*, and, since I cannot see that one is to be preferred to the other, I shall..use them interchangeably. Need is a concept to account for certain objective and subjective facts. **1961** F. H. Sanford *Psychol.* viii. 200/2 The need for achievement, referred to in the literature and in the following paragraphs as *n ach.* **1964** L. J. Bischof *Interpreting Personality Theories* ii. iii. 146 In studying the need structure of man, Murray found that he required criteria in order to establish that a need existed.

15. *need-achievement, condition, -disposition, pattern, -push; needs analysis, test.*

1971 F. H. Farley in H. J. Eysenck *Readings in Extraversion–Introversion* III. xlv. 406 The personality variables of anxiety and need-achievement were considered. **1960** N. Maier in Kaplan & Wapner *Perspectives Psychol. Theory* 153 Like all need conditions, social needs select goal-oriented behaviors. **1951** Parsons & Shils *Toward Gen. Theory Action* i. i. 18 The child's development of a 'personality'..is to be viewed as the establishment of a relatively specific, definite, and consistent system of need-dispositions. **1958** D. Emmett *Function, Purpose & Powers* 30 From the point of view of any given actor in the system it is both a mode of the fulfilment of his own need-dispositions and a condition of 'optimizing' the reactions of other significant actors. **1947** G. Murphy *Personality* iii. xvi. 395 It would seem that mood or need patterns can intensify and enrich the world of images. *Ibid.* 992/1 *Need pattern*, total organization of the needs of the organism. **1951** Parsons & Shils *Toward Gen. Theory Action* iii. iii. 308 Identification does involve..locomotion away from some other region of valenced activity because of the stronger need-push to get to the region of love and approval. **1969** J. Argenti *Managem. Techniques* 175 Needs analysis, then, consists of systematically examining the requirements of each job and comparing these with the skills of the incumbent of, or an applicant for, the job. **1932** *Ann. Reg. 1931* i. iv. 102 By the regulations issued by the Ministry of Labour in October, the task of applying the 'needs test' to applicants for transitional benefit had been left to the Public Assistance Committees. **1940** *Economist* 29 June 1106/2 The chief objection is.. that it introduces another needs test. It is now possible that in the same household there will be a means test for an unemployed member..and a means test for pensions of war.

need, *v.*[2] Add: **7. a.** *spec.* In colloq. phrases implying that something is completely unnecessary or unwanted, as *who needs it?* [tr. Yiddish *ver darf es?*], *to need* (*something*) *like a hole in the head*: see *hole *sb.* 11. orig. *U.S.*

1951, etc. [see *hole *sb.* 11]. **1960** *Mademoiselle* Jan. 34/2 Popular idiom deals best with racial prejudice: 'Who needs it?' **1960** *N.Y. Post* 24 Feb. 56/5 Who needs them? **1962** *Sat. Even. Post* 31 Mar. 70 (*heading*) Good news—who needs it? **1963** *TV Times* 11 Jan. 8 It was so easy to say: 'Education? Who needs it?' **1968** *Melody Maker* 23 Nov. 11/3 They envision themselves wearing berets..and crawling about the rubble, throwing Molotov cocktails. 'But who needs Che Guevara? It's not like that.' **1968** M. Woodhouse *Rock Baby* xvii. 164 A twenty-two-year-old bomb disposal expert? I needed a twenty-two-year-old bomb disposal expert like I needed four more thumbs and a teen-age brain surgeon. **1973** R. Hayes *Hungarian Game* xxxi. 185, I needed a cat like I needed a nervous breakdown. **1974** *New Yorker* 17 June 92 True, he's one damn hell of a fine human being. But who needs him?

needful, *a.* Add: **4. a.** (Further examples.) Esp. in phr. *to do the needful.*

1710 J. Lovett *Let.* 1 Apr. in M. M. Verney *Verney Lett.* (1930) I. xii. 210 Waiting on proper persons and doing the needful in all places. **1822** M. Edgeworth *Let.* 27 Jan. (1971) 338, I resolved to write..only 3 or 4 lines just to say the needful. **1831** Scott *Jrnl.* 24 Apr. (1946) 164 Young Clarkson had already done the needful—that is had bled & blisterd severely, and placed me on a very restrictd diet.

needle, *sb.* Add: **1. d.** (Earlier and later examples.)

a **1530** T. Lupset *Compendious Treat. Dyenge Well* (1534) 35 For as harde a thynge it is to plucke through the smale nedels eie a greatte caboull rope, as to brynge a ryche man in at heuens wycket. **1872** Besant & Rice *Ready-Money Mortiboy* III. xiii. 234 A single-hearted.. rich man, for whom the needle's eye is as easy to pass, as for the poorest pauper. **1925** A. Huxley *Those Barren Leaves* i. i. 11 Those roaring lions at Lady Trunion's..had no hope of passing through the needle's eye. **1929** H. W. Nevinson *The English* vi. 43 They are well fitted to carry on the traditions of Victorian vulgarity, and to prove yet again that no camel will ever get through the needle's eye. **1940** V. W. Brooks *New England* xx. 414 People solemnly chewed their food very fine and slowly to be slender enough to pass through the eye of the needle. **1957** F. R. Scott (*title*) Eye of the needle.

2. b. A slender, usu. pointed, indicator on a dial or other measuring instrument, *spec.* on a speedometer.

1928 Kipling *Limits & Renewals* (1932) 60 She preferred cars to her own feet... Her place was at his left elbow, nose touching his sleeve, until the needle reached fifty. **1937** D. L. Sayers *Busman's Honeymoon* xiv. 244 He let the needle drop back to twenty-five and they dawdled on through the lanes. **1958** 'Castle' & 'Hailey' *Flight into Danger* ii. 31 The altimeter needle on the winking instrument panel steadily registered a climb of five hundred feet a minute. **1962** J. Glenn in *Into Orbit* 42 The periscope..gives you an horizon-to-horizon view of the earth below so you can check your actual attitude against the needles. **1973** 'S. Harvester' *Corner of Playground* ii. v. 118 He drove faster, watching the needle flick up to a hundred.

3. b. *spec.* A hypodermic needle used to inject drugs; the use of, or addiction to, injected drugs, esp. in phr. *on the needle*,

engaged in, or addicted to, injecting drugs; also *rarely*, a morphine-addict; a dose of a drug for injection. *slang* (orig. *U.S.*).

1929 M. A. GILL *Underworld Slang* (s.v. *don't*), *Don't break the needle*, don't use all the dope. **1936** L. DUNCAN *Over Wall* i. 21, I saw and became familiar with the hopheads or cokes—the cocaine addicts on the snow; the needles or hypes—morphine users. **1943** *N.Y. Times* 9 May II. 5/6 He's got a band that don't need a five o'clock needle like some other bands. **1953** W. BURROUGHS *Junkie* (1972) x. 94 'You've been hooking that spot so much it's about to get infected,' he said, pointing to a needle welt. **1955** W. GADDIS *Recognitions* I. v. 196 I've heard about her... On the needle. A schiz. **1957** C. MACINNES *City of Spades* II. iv. 102 He's using all his dope allowance now... You know who put him on the needle and supplied him? **1968** R. JEFFRIES *Traitor's Crime* i. 8 'When d'you get your fixes?' asked Elwick. 'In—in the evenings.' 'How much?' 'Fifteen bob a needle.' **1973** *Listener* 6 Sept. 306/1 Middle Britain thinks..one puff on the joint leads to the needle.

d. A thin pointed or tapering rod used to secure fine adjustment in closing apertures, as in valves.

1884 KNIGHT *Dict. Mech.* Suppl. 632/2 In order to regulate the supply of oil [from a needle lubricator], a metallic feed-rod (needle) passes through the tube, and rests upon the shaft to be lubricated. **1909** *Chambers's Jrnl.* Nov. 698/1 The gas-regulator can be adjusted to the fiftieth part of an inch, with dead centralisation of the needle. **1927** G. W. C. KAYE *High Vacua* iv. 52 The needle readily beds itself into its seating, and very little pressure is needed to close the valve completely. **1965** C. M. VAN ATTA *Vacuum Sci. & Engin.* viii. 328 The principal feature of the design [of the needle valve] is the slowly tapering needle fitting snugly into a carefully reamed conical seat.

e. The small pointed jewel or piece of metal, wood, etc., which rests in the groove of a gramophone record when it is being played and communicates the undulations to the pick-up or diaphragm; also, a similar device used to cut the groove; = STYLUS 2.

1902 *Encycl. Brit.* XXXI. 679/2 The marker..instead of being a stiff needle coming from the centre of the membrane or glass plate, is now a lever. **1930** A. B. WOOD *Textbk. Sound* 438 The vibrations of the diaphragm cause a needle to cut grooves on the surface of a prepared cylinder or disc. **1949** FRAYNE & WOLFE *Elem. Sound Recording* xiii. 240 Motion of the needle can be utilized to apply a force to a piezoelectric crystal and thus generate a voltage. **1957** *Records & Recording* Nov. 20/1 These grooves..must be tracked with absolute accuracy by the pickup needle—nowadays it is more usually called a stylus. **1973** D. RAMSAY *Deadly Discretion* 190 The concerto came to an end. The needle began to click against the ungrooved portion of the record.

12. b. (Earlier and additional examples.) Also (sometimes without *the*), anger, bad temper, enmity; esp. *to get the needle*, to become angry or upset, to lose one's temper.

1874 HOTTEN *Slang Dict.* 235 To 'cop the needle' is to become vexed or annoyed. **1884** [see *BIRD *sb.* 5 b]. **1890** BARRÈRE & LELAND *Dict. Slang* II. 84/2 It gives a man the needle when he hasn't got a bob, To see his pals come round and wish him joy. *Ibid.*, To get the needle is to feel very nervous and funky. **1923** *Daily Mail* 1 Aug. 8/2 It may be, of course, that there was too much 'needle' (to employ a boxing term which means bad spirit) about this contest. **1929** H. A. VACHELL *Virgin* viii. 141 The silly ass got the needle, 'cos she asked for the ring. **1959** *Times* 8 June 3/1 Perhaps it was this very lack of needle, this air of unreality in the late evening of Saturday..that failed to see Davies home to a victory. **1967** *Time* 22 Dec. 48 A needle from [Bob] Hope becomes an emblem instead of a scar. **1970** G. F. NEWMAN *Sir, You Bastard* v. 130 He's got the needle with you. You've got to go very careful.

13. b. *needle-painted* (later example).

1910 *Westm. Gaz.* 2 Feb. 5/4 An exhibition of needle-painted wild flowers of South Africa was opened yesterday.

c. *needle-nosed*, *-sharp* adjs.

1955 *Sci. News Let.* 26 Mar. 196/2 An eight-foot-tall, needle-nosed rocket. **1973** *Times* 4 June 1/3 The crash came at the end of the last of three passes the needle-nosed plane made to show off its qualities. **1923** J. GALSWORTHY *Captures* 161 That fellow was needle-sharp, though not always correct in his conclusions. **1973** *Times* 5 Oct. (Safety Suppl.) p. i/3 Everything depends on needle-sharp reflexes.

14. **needle-and-pin**, rhyming slang for GIN *sb.*²; **needle-and-thread**, rhyming slang for 'bread'; **needle bearing**, a bearing using needle rollers; **needle beer** *U.S. slang* (see quot. 1928); **needle board** (see quots.); **needle-bush**, substitute for def.: *Austral.* (*a*) either of two shrubs or small trees of the genus *Hakea*, *H. leucoptera* or *H. vittata*, of the family Proteaceæ; (*b*) the nealie or nelia, *Acacia rigens*, of the family Leguminosæ; (later examples); **needle-cast**, a fungus disease of conifers, causing the leaves to go brown and drop off; **needle contest** = **needle match*; **needlecord**, a finely ribbed cut-pile fabric; **needle-felt**, **needlefelt** = **needle-loom* (b); **needle fight** = **needle match*; **needle game** = **needle match*; **needle gap** *Electr.*, a pair of needle-shaped electrodes placed in line, between which an electric discharge can take place when the potential difference between them exceeds a value dependent on the size of the gap; **needle gate**, a dam or sluice consisting of several thin spars which are placed vertically one after the other into a frame; **needle ice**, ice formed into thin needle-like crystals just beneath the soil surface and often pushing up through it; **needle-loom, needleloom**, (*a*) (see quot. *a* 1877); also *attrib.*; (*b*) carpeting made of felt attached to a base of rubber, hessian, or other material; **needle lubricator, oiler**, a form of lubricator in which the supply of lubricant is controlled by a needle fitted in the supply tube and resting on the shaft to be lubricated; **needle mark**, a mark made by a hypodermic injection; **needle match**, a match or contest that arouses much interest and excitement; a crucial or keenly fought match; a contest in which the contestants have a grudge against each other; a dispute; **needle paper**, a stout black paper orig. used for wrapping up needles; **needle roller**, a roller in the form of a long, thin, sometimes tapered cylinder, used in roller bearings; freq. *attrib.*; **needle scar**, a scar made by a hypodermic injection; **needle shower, spray**, a shower-bath of strong fine jets of water; also *fig.*; **needle-threader**, a device for threading needles; **needle time**, an agreed time during which gramophone records are allowed to be broadcast; **needle track** = **needle mark*; **needle valve**, a valve which works by means of a narrow pointed rod fitting into a conical seating and is operated either automatically or by a screw; **needle-weaving** (see quots.); **needle-wood** = **needle-bush* (*a*); also *attrib.*

1937 PARTRIDGE *Dict. Slang* 555/2 *Needle and pin*, gin. **1973** J. LEASOR *Host of Extras* vi. 118 You owe him some needle and pin—gin. **1859** HOTTEN *Dict. Slang* 144 *Needle and thread*, bread. **1935** A. J. POLLOCK *Underworld Speaks* 80/1 *Needle and thread*, bread. **1930** *Automotive Industries* LXIII. 869/1 The needle bearing offers particular advantages for certain applications in high speed engines, as on crankpins. **1946** L. E. O. CHARLTON *R. Air Force July 1943 to Sept. 1944* 154 (*caption*) Bomber Command launched an attack on a needle-bearing factory..in France. **1972** R. C. GUNTHER *Lubrication* xiii. 408 Needle bearings are suited for slow speeds, or for oscillating and intermittent motion which permits the rollers to return to their required position upon load relief. **1928** *Flynn's* 14 Apr. 29/2 On the same spot you can get your needle beer—near beer shot with alki or ether. **1936** J. DOS PASSOS *Big Money* 81 He..had a session with the helpwanted columns over some glasses of needle beer. **1879** T. R. ASHENHURST *Pract. Treat. Weaving & Designing Textile Fabrics* 63 The pressure thus bestowed upon the crosswires keeps them in position through the needle-board. **1889** *Cent. Dict.*, *Needle-board*, in the Jacquard loom, a perforated board or plate through which the points of the needles presented to the cards pass, and the perforations of which act as guides for the needles when the latter are actuated by the cards. The needle-board holds all the needles in proper relation with the prism or cylinder to which the cards are attached, and with the perforations in the cards. **1961** WEBSTER, *Needle board*, a board covered with very short fine wires that is used for pressing pile fabrics. **1909** A. E. MACK *Bush Calendar* 4 All through the bush the needlebush showed white blossoms amongst its spiky leaves. **1944** *Living off Land* iii. 47 One of the main water supplies of the aborigines came from tree roots, principally those of the mallee, the needle-bush. *Ibid.* 48 The needlebush, a dark green shrub with sharp-pointed needles in place of leaves. **1965** *Austral. Encycl.* VI. 266/2 Needlewood or Needlebush, popular names for *Hakea leucoptera* and *H. vittata*, dry-country shrubs or small trees possessing rigid acicular leaves. *Ibid.*, The so-called 'needle', *Acacia rigens*, is sometimes referred to as needle-bush, because of its long terete phyllodes. **1895** W. R. FISHER *Schlich's Man. Forestry* IV. 408 This sudden shedding of pine needles is the characteristic of the disease so widely spread in Germany, and termed *Schütte*, or needle-cast. **1964** W. E. HILEY *Forestry Venture* iv. 81 We are inclined to associate the trouble with a needle-cast fungus (*Phaeocryptopus gaumannii*). **1922** *Daily Mail* 22 Nov. 11 There is also a 'needle' contest, recently arranged, between two stable-lads. **1963** *Times* 15 Jan. 9/4 And then what about that 'needle' contest, the University match? **1959** *Manch. Guardian* 26 June 5/3 A needlecord in a dove-like grey was excellent for slacks or jackets. **1973** 'D. HALLIDAY' *Dolly & Starry Bird* xvi. 236 Charles had on a needlecord shirt with a flower pattern. **1957** *Textile Terms & Definitions* (Textile Inst.) (ed. 3) 67 *Needle felt*, felt produced by the needleloom process. **1927** *Daily News* 25 May 8/1 England's native champion ..went down in a needle fight with Samuel Robinson, an experienced golfer. **1970** *Globe & Mail* (Toronto) 28 Sept. 21/2 In soccer there is a word for a tense match, it is called a needle game and this one fitted into that category. **1916** C. C. GARRARD *Electr. Switch & Controlling Gear* viii. 563 One source of uncertainty can be removed if needles are used for the measuring gap, in which case the result obtained is termed the 'equivalent needle gap'. **1927** *Ibid.* (ed. 3) viii. 641 Let us assume that this [line] is protected by a needle gap with a breakdown voltage.. of 66,000 volts. **1962** *Newnes Conc. Encycl. Electr. Engin.* 701/2 Needle gaps have been used for measuring voltages of a few kilovolts as they have larger, and therefore more convenient, spacings than sphere gaps at these low voltages. **1909** H. M. WILSON *Irrigation Engin.* (ed. 6) 230 Simple flash-board or needle gates should be used only where the pressure upon them is low. **1918** *Engineering-News Record* 7 Feb. 262/2 The ice columns, or 'needle ice', formed on bare clayey soils are familiar to most people living in regions where the nights are cold enough for heavy frosts. **1939** H. H. BENNETT *Soil Conservation* xii. 284 Where there is sufficient soil moisture, a freeze will produce layers of needle ice, or spew frost, which will lift the overlying soil and vegetation as much as several inches. **1968** R. W. FAIRBRIDGE *Encycl. Geomorphol.* 381 Such 'needle ice' is sometimes called pipkrake. *a* **1877** KNIGHT *Dict. Mech.* II. 1519/1 *Needle-loom*, one in which the weft is carried by a needle instead of a shuttle. The usual form of loom for narrow wares, such as ribbons, tapes, bindings, etc. **1956** *Good Housek. Home Encycl.* (ed. 4) 92/2 Needleloom carpetings have a rubber or plastic back. **1957** *Textile Terms & Definitions* (Textile Inst.) (ed. 3) 68 The needleloom process is essentially a method of attaching a lap or batt..of loose fibrous material to a base, e.g. fabric, paper, rubber and/or plastic materials. **1957** *Observer* 20 Oct. 10/2 Almost all the new *tufted* carpets (which have, to a large extent, superseded the rubber-backed felt called *needleloom*) are made almost entirely of rayon. **1969** A. J. HALL *Stand. Handbk. Textiles* (ed. 7) iii. 161 For the manufacture of needle-loom carpets a machine is used which comprises rows of vertical needles. **1884** KNIGHT *Dict. Mech.* Suppl. 632/2 Needle lubricator. **1887** D. A. LOW *Introd. Machine Drawing & Design* vii. 32 In the block illustrated the journal is lubricated by a needle lubricator. **1949** N. MARSH *Swing, Brother, Swing* ix. 206 He hasn't been long on the injection method... Curtis had a look for needle-marks and didn't find many. **1971** 'D. SHANNON' *Murder with Love* (1972) iv. 69, I doubt very much whether he's really hooked... No needle marks on him. **1923** *Daily Mail* 16 Jan. 9 There will be a 'needle' match in Sheffield if Barnsley beat Swindon and visit the Wednesday. **1952** L. A. G. STRONG *Darling Tom* xvii. 136 (*headline*) Needle match. Family quarrel will be fought out at Olympia. **1962** *Listener* 1 Nov. 732/3 More enjoyable was an off-beat needle match between Hans Keller, who held that Gershwin was a neglected genius, and Deryck Cooke, who didn't. **1965** D. FRANCIS *For Kicks* iii. 41, I..watched Paddy and one of Granger's lads engage in a needle match of dominoes. **1909** *Westm. Gaz.* 3 Apr. 14/2 If needle-paper of the required kind is not available a very excellent substitute can be prepared by placing good stout paper in a solution of gelatine and glycerine to which has been added some good strong black colouring. **1973** *Sci. Amer.* May 118/1 Black needle paper and white typewriter bond differ by about a factor of 15 in reflectance all across the spectrum. **1935** *Jrnl. R. Aeronaut. Soc.* XXXIX. 470 The crankshaft was mounted on roller bearings, and the connecting rod big ends were mounted on needle rollers in split housings. **1951** *Engineering* 26 Oct. 533/1 An open propeller shaft provided with Hardy Spicer needle-roller joints transmits the drive to the rear axle. **1959** R. R. SLAYMAKER *Mech. Design & Analysis* II. xv. 299 Loose needle rollers are now universally used throughout the automotive industry to serve as bearings in planetary gear systems. **1974** 'A. HAIG' *Peruvian Printout* 37 A rubber-wheeled trolley which glided on needle roller bearings. **1962** K. ORVIS *Damned & Destroyed* vii. 52, I made a mental note of the needle-scar item. **1935** A. J. CRONIN *Stars look Down* I. xix. 183 After that a needle shower and a hard rub down. **1973** 'H. HOWARD' *Highway to Murder* iii. 34 Ten minutes under a needle-shower washed the clammy heat out of me. **1974** E. MCGIRR *Murderous Journey* 6, I..shivered under a cold needle shower. **1967** *Freedomways* VII. 153 A scattered needle-spray of unrelated, often ephemeral, facts and events which confuse the readers more than they inform them. **1970** H. MCLEAVE *Question of Negligence* (1973) vii. 54 In the shower room he..focussed the needle spray on his head and body. **1889** *Cent. Dict.*, *Needle-threader*, a device for passing a thread through the eye of a needle. **1964** *McCall's Sewing* v. 66/1 If you have an eye-sight problem, or just find threading needles a chore, use a needle threader. **1962** *Sunday Express* 30 Dec. 1/6 'Needle time'—the number of hours given to records. **1970** *B.B.C. Handbk.* 223 An agreement with *Phonographic Performance Ltd.* provides for the right to broadcast commercial gramophone records 'live', the B.B.C.'s various radio and television services being allocated fixed periods of 'needle time' in return for an annual lump sum payment. **1959** A. K. LANG in H. Q. Masur *Murder Most Foul* (1973) 69 The kid had been a user; they'd know that from the gear in her purse and the needle-tracks in her arm. **1973** J. MARTIN *95 File* 80 He checked her arms but found no needle tracks. **1903** *Sci. Amer. Suppl.* 24 Jan. 59/2 The inventor's idea, in designing the vaporizer, was to do away with the needle-valve usually employed for controlling the flow of gasoline. **1925** N. E. ODELL in E. F. Norton *Fight for Everest 1924* 362 The pressure gauge was connected close to the mouths of the cylinders on the back [of the breathing apparatus], and the rate of flow regulated by a needle-valve close beside it. **1971** *Sci. Amer.* Sept. 222/3 All gases are admitted through needle valves to a manifold that connects to the laser. **1932** D. C. MINTER *Mod. Needlecraft* 16/1 Needleweaving is a form of embroidery worked on the threads of the material when the threads in the opposite direction (i.e. either the warp or the weft) have been withdrawn. **1967** E. SHORT *Embroidery & Fabric Collage* ii. 48 *Needleweaving*. This is a variation of drawn thread work which could be used effectively on accessories such as handbags and belts. **1911** C. E. W. BEAN *'Dreadnought' of Darling* xv. 141 The pretty grey needle-wood. **1936** F. CLUNE *Roaming round Darling* xxv. 286 Plenty of mulga, needlewood, belah, budda, and broad leaf-box. **1941** I. L. IDRIESS *Great Boomerang* i. 1 Upon a needlewood-tree a crow waited. *Ibid.* iii. 22 It [*sc.* the gold] lay by a needlewood bush. **1959** A. UPFIELD *Bony & Black Virgin* xiii. 111 He sat in the shade of the needlewood tree, or rather its trunk, for the narrow leaves give but scant shelter.

needle, *v.* Add: **1. b.** (Further examples.) Also, to goad; to provoke into anger.

1881 G. R. SIMS *Dagonet Ballads* 77 There, he's off! the

young warmint, he's needled; whenever I talks about work He puts on his cap and he hooks it. **1898** G. B. Shaw *Our Theatres in Nineties* (1932) III. 358 Old Indian women get 'fairly needled' at the spectacle of their houses and crops being burnt. **1941** *Time* 7 Apr. 22/3 Some 20 Manhattan reporters gave the Ambassador a going-over for 50 minutes... He did not let it appear that he knew he was being needled. **1958** J. Wain *Contenders* 154 It was that bit about forgetting his business worries that needled Ned. **1959** M. Pugh *Chancer* 177 He was needling me, needling me this night, and I wouldn't provoke. **1972** D. Haston *In High Places* ii. 36 Once again we'd needled each other into a state of open warfare.

3. *U.S. slang.* (See quots.) Also **nee·dled** *ppl. a.* (cf. *needle beer*, *needle *sb.* 14).

1929 *Amer. Speech* IV. 387 Many Kansans..buy the ordinary non-alcoholic near-beer, and add a little alcohol to each bottle. The resulting mixture is called..*needled beer*. **1929** Hostetter & Beesley *It's a Racket!* 233 *Needle*, to inject alcohol or ether into any liquid, such as beer, to make it stimulating. **1930** *Amer. Mercury* Dec. 456/2 *Needle*, to make near-beer intoxicating by injecting ether or alcohol. 'This beer knocks you for a loop. It's needled with ether.' **1931** D. Runyon *Guys & Dolls* (1932) iv. 79 It is sleeping so sound that I am commencing to figure that Butch must give it some of the needled beer he is feeding us.

needleman. Add: **2.** (Spelt as two words, or hyphenated.) A drug-addict, esp. one who is addicted to injecting drugs. *U.S. slang.*

1925 *Flynn's* 11 July 128/1 So surely was Howard a needle man—that is, a hopeless drug addict. **1955** [see *hype *sb.*[1]].

needle-point. Add: **1.** (Examples corresponding to *needle *sb.* 3 e).

1929 *Radio Times* 8 Nov. 444/2 The needle-armature is so light that the needle point actually *feels* its way along the record groove. **1949** B. Semeonoff *Record Collecting* v. 22 The term 'tracking' refers to the path traced by the needle-point as it travels inward towards the centre of a record.

2. (Earlier and additional examples.) Also *attrib.*

1865 F. B. Palliser *Hist. Lace* iii. 28 Lace is divided into point and pillow. The first is made by the needle on a parchment pattern, and termed needle point. **1882** *Encycl. Brit.* XIV. 189/2 A technical peculiarity in making needlepoint lace is that a single thread and needle are alone used to form the pattern. **1902** Jourdain & Dryden *Palliser's Hist. Lace* (rev. ed.) xiii. 195 'Needle point' is the name by which point d'Alençon was alone known in England during the last century. **1967** E. Short *Embroidery & Fabric Collage* ii. 39 Cut work.. later developed into needlepoint lace. *Ibid.*, This delicate embroidery with its contrasts of cut work, eyelets, fine needlepoint fillings, [etc.].

needless, *a.* Add: **2.** Freq. in phr. (*it is*) *needless to say* (or *add*), often used parenthetically.

1770 A. Young *Six Months' Tour North of Eng.* I. 185 It is almost needless to add upon the course of crops in question, that the turnips ought..to be fed off the land by sheep. **1770** Baretti *Journey London to Genoa* I. xx. 148 It is needless to say that thousands and thousands have migrated to other places. **1826** *Kaleidoscope* 31 Jan. 247/3 The Squire was hard hit by this nonchalance, and (as the newspapers say), 'it is needless to add', acted upon Sheridan's suggestion. **1885** Rider Haggard *K. Solomon's Mines* vi. 88 That night we covered nearly five-and-twenty miles, but, needless to say, found no more water. **1902** R. J. Mecredy in A. C. Harmsworth *Motors* vii. 122 Needless to say, the shoulder F is thereby raised. **1930** *Sunday Times* 12 Oct. 5/5 Needless to say, such a visitor is immensely impressed and at once enrols for the Pelman Course in the particular language in which he is interested.

needling, *vbl. sb.* Add: **2. c.** The action of annoying, irritating, or goading (see Needle *v.* 1 b in Dict. and Suppl.). Also as *ppl. adj.*

1941 *Sun* (Baltimore) 10 Jan. 12/7 The word 'needling' ..is being used more and more frequently in the sense of using sharp bits of persuasion to bring a person to adopt a desired course. **1945** *Ibid.* 17 Feb. 7/3 P. K. W...was plainly irked by some sharp needling of his group. **1956** W. H. Whyte *Organization Man* (1957) 246 It was Keefer, with his clever mind, his needling of authority, who led the ordinary people..astray. **1958** *Spectator* 10 Jan. 33/1 Their needling and often impertinent questions. **1959** *Times Lit. Suppl.* 27 Nov. 698/5 She undergoes, still buoyant, the familiar needlings of interrogation. **1962** *Listener* 7 June 999/1 When the next careful, needling letter arrived from Samuel, the black temper broke loose again. **1971** C. Bonington *Annapurna South Face* xi. 128 '..Anyway, if you want to go out in front on this trip, you'd better prove you can keep going.' This kind of needling was the ideal treatment for Mick. **1973** *Islander* (Victoria, B.C.) 28 Oct. 2/1 He was the great complainer of his time, and..Victoria became better place because of his needling.

needs, *adv.* **d.** (Further examples of proverbial use.) Cf. proverbial uses under sense c in Dict.

1835 Southey *Doctor* III. lxxxiii. 77 'Needs must go when the Devil drives', says the proverb: but the Devil shall never drive me. **1853** T. C. Haliburton *Sam Slick's Wise Saws* I. xiii. 267 'Needs must when the devil drives, so here goes,' and off he went for the water. **1886** [see Drive *v.* 1 b]. **1916** E. Wallace *Clue of Twisted Candle* (1918) xi. 133 But needs must when the devil drives, as the saying goes. **1956** G. Durrell *My Family* xiv. 189, I think we had better have a cab. An extravagance, of course, but needs must where the devil drives, eh?

need-to-know (nī:dˌtŭnōu·). [Need *v.*[2] 8.] Used, freq. *attrib.*, to denote a principle or practice, esp. in counter-espionage, whereby people are kept ignorant of things which they do not need to know.

1954 *Amer. Documentation* V. 120 In most security controlled report systems, the dissemination of information is regulated by 'need-to-know' or 'compartmentalization' principles. **1956** W. A. Heflin *U.S. Air Force Dict.* 342/2 *Need-to-know*, n. A criterion used in security procedures that requires a person requesting classified information to establish his need to know such information in terms of his mission. **1966** J. Bingham *Double Agent* ix. 137 Mr. Ryan had then hastily told him to keep that to himself. Nothing further had been said. Mr. List had been naturally dismayed at this gross breach of the need-to-know principle. **1969** A. Marin *Rise with Wind* i. 7 You will notice that there are some gaps in the Clay material. Part of the information is..strictly on a 'need to know' basis. **1970** K. Benton *Sole Agent* xviii. 193 There is the rule about need-to-know. They won't *need* to know the details of your contacts with MI5. **1971** D. Bagley *Freedom Trap* vi. 127 They worked on the 'need to know' principle, and an escapee didn't need to know how he escaped—just that he had done so. **1975** *Observer* 12 Jan. 1/1 The CIA has instructed the companies to limit all knowledge of the exercise to the spymaster's traditional 'need-to-know' criterion. **1975** N. Luard *Robespierre Serial* iv. 27 There was no need for Carswell to be filled in on all the ramifications... On the strict need-to-know basis they simply didn't concern him.

neejee, var. *nitchie.

Néel (nē¹·ĕl). The name of Louis Eugène Félix *Néel* (b. 1904), French physicist, used *attrib.* to designate certain phenomena connected with his work on magnetism, as **Néel point** or **temperature,** the transition temperature for an antiferromagnetic or ferrimagnetic substance, above which it is paramagnetic (analogous to the Curie point for ferromagnetics); **Néel spike,** a sharply pointed triangular domain extending from a small hole or inclusion in a magnetic substance diagonally in relation to the field direction in the surrounding area; **Néel wall,** a type of domain boundary that Néel predicted should occur in thin layers of magnetic material, in which the rotation of the field direction in passing from one side of the wall to the other occurs in the plane of the film.

1949 *Rev. Mod. Physics* XXI. 572/2 Measurement of the ratio of length to width of the Néel domains offers a possible experimental method for determining..the surface energy density of a Bloch wall. **1951** *Jrnl. de Physique et le Radium* XII. 311 (*heading*) Néel 'spikes' around holes in a crystal surface. **1952** *Physica* XVIII. 714 In warming the salt through the region of the Néel temperature a continuous but rapid change occurs from a state in which the spins of the Cu^{++} ions are highly ordered to a state of comparative disorder. **1960** *Jrnl. Appl. Physics* XXXI. 303S/1 The smooth parts of the wall at the thin and thick ends of the film have to be interpreted as pure Néel and Bloch walls, respectively. **1963** J. S. Smart in Rado & Suhl *Magnetism* III. ii. 66 The Néel point..of a ferrimagnet or an antiferromagnet can be determined in a number of different ways, of which magnetic susceptibility is probably the most common and specific heat measurements one of the most accurate. **1966** Carey & Isaac *Magn. Domains* ii. 24 Néel walls become energetically more favourable than Bloch walls for thin films. *Ibid.* 28 In films of thickness less than about 200 Å no cross-tie walls occur but normal Néel walls are observed. *Ibid.* viii. 142 Consideration of the magnetostatic energy associated with large inclusions in iron crystals led Néel to predict the existence of closure domains..now termed Néel spikes. **1973** *Physical Rev.* B. VII. 287 (*heading*) Heat-capacity measurements on manganese dibromide tetrahydrate near its Néel temperature.

neem. (Further examples.)

1876 *Cornh. Mag.* Sept. 320 There was Beena..standing apart under a *nim* tree. **1911** J. Frazer *Golden Bough: Magic Art* (ed. 3) I. v. 293 In order to procure rain people of low caste in the Central Provinces of India will tie a frog to a rod covered with green leaves and branches of the *nīm* tree. **1937** *N. & Q.* 8 May 338/1 The 'nimb' was used by Terence Mulvaney to make 'a thundering big poultice av neem leaves..'. The Indian sais (or groom) still uses the neem leaf as a poultice for galls. **1949** H. W. Florey et al. *Antibiotics* I. xiv. 586 The nim tree (*Melia azadirachta, M. indica*) has been cultivated throughout India on account of its medicinal properties. **1969** T. H. Everett *Living Trees of World* 210/2 The neem or nim tree..common in India and Ceylon, is greatly valued for its bitter, antiseptic resin, which is used in medicines, soaps, lotions and toothpaste. *Ibid.* 211/1 The neem tree is a graceful evergreen, up to 50 feet tall; it thrives in dry climates. Its pinnate leaves have an odd number of curved, pointed, toothed, shiny leaflets. The numerous small, fragrant white flowers occur in loose panicles..followed by small yellow berries. **1971** R. Russell tr. *Ahmad's Shore & Wave* i. 9 There were only tracks on Gipsies' Hill, winding their way through the trees of..bitter-leaved neem among rocks.

neencephalon (niˌense·fălǫn). *Anat.* [a. G. *neencephalon* (L. Edinger *Vorlesungen über den Bau der nervösen Zentralorgane des Menschen und der Tiere* (ed. 7, 1908) II. xvi. 242): see *neo- 1 e and Encephalon.] The phylogenetically younger part of the brain, comprising the cerebral cortex and related structures. So **neencepha·lic** *a.*

1917 *Jrnl. Compar. Neurol.* XXVIII. 216 The emergence of the true cortex (neencephalon, or suprasegmental apparatus of the brain). *Ibid.* 217 Here the picture is uncomplicated by the great neencephalic systems. **1948** *Brit. Jrnl. Psychol.* XXXIX. 71 The infant is born without mental life... Only gradually does the neëncephalon exert its influence. **1972** *Encycl. Psychol.* II. 310/2 *Neencephalon*, the 'new brain' or 'harmonious prolongation' lying above the 'old brain' or paleencephalon. A fairly pure neencephalic area of the brain is the six-layer cerebral cortex (isocortex) in mammals... Under narcosis or the influence of alcohol the neencephalic systems are the first to cease to operate.

ne'er, var. New-year. *Sc.*

nefast, *a.* For *rare*$^{-1}$ read *rare*, and add further example.

1887 R. L. Stevenson *Let.* Oct. (1899) II. 71 In good case and spirits, as I am now, after a most nefast experience of despondency before I left.

nefedyevite (nefedye·vəit). *Min.* Also †**nefediewite, nefedievite.** [ad. Russ. *nefed'evit* (P. Puzyrevsky 1872, in *Zapiski imperat. S.-Peterburgsk. mineral. Obshch.* VII. 15, f. the name of V. V. *Nefed'ev*, 19th-cent. Russian mineralogist: see -ite[1].] A white or pinkish aluminosilicate of magnesium and calcium belonging to the clay family and similar to montmorillonite.

1873 *Jrnl. Chem. Soc.* XXVI. 1210 Nefediewite; a new mineral... This amorphous mineral, very much like lithomarge, occurs, together with fluorspar, in the limestone of Nertschinsk. **1938** *Mineral. Abstr.* VII. 104 Greenish-grey unctuous clay interbedded among Cretaceous limestones, the bulk of which consists of a fibrous crystalline aggregate..and in composition..corresponds to nefedievite. **1961** *Doklady Earth Sci.* CXXXV. 1296/1 In view of the great structural similarity between true montmorillonite and nefedyevite, doubling of the unit cell along the *c* axis can be expected.

neg (neg), colloq. abbrev. of *negative* or *negatively*, esp. = Negative *sb.* 8.

1874 W. H. Jackson *Diaries* (1959) 275 While Bob was saddling and packing up, I made a couple of negs. **1909** *Cent. Dict.* Suppl., *Neg.* An abbreviation (*a*) of *negative*; (*b*) of *negatively*. **1948** M. Allingham *More Work for Undertaker* xv. 185, I told you it was like a neg. Black shadows and everything else a sort of chilly grey. **1959** H. Hamilton *Answer in Negative* i. 8 You don't want to keep negs in the same place as pix..because there's always a risk of fire. **1971** *Hi-Fi Sound* Feb. 71/1 It is not always so difficult to identify 'pos. and neg.' but long practice has made it a habit with me to tie a knot in each negative connection. **1972** *Amat. Photographer* 12 Jan. 29 The resultant negs had a remarkable degree of density.

negate, *v.* Add: **b.** *Gram.* To render negative in sense.

1930 W. Empson *Seven Types of Ambiguity* vii. 269 *Not* may negate *going* or *weeping*. That the ear expects *did go* may mean that all nature wept for Polonius. **1961** R. B. Long *Sentence & its Parts* iv. 105 Even the words that commonly negate clauses do not always do so. **1972** R. Quirk et al. *Gram. Contemp. Eng.* 382 *Not* here functions as a predeterminer in the italicized noun phrase; but it has the effect of negating the whole clause.

negater (nĭgē¹·təɹ). *Computers.* Also **negator.** [f. Negat(e *v.* + -er[1]. Cf. Negator.] = *inverter 2 c.

1962 *Gloss. Terms Automatic Data Processing* (*B.S.I.*) 60 Negater. **1963** *New Scientist* 14 Nov. 387/3 The system employs a 'negator' element—a logical element which reverses, for example, the polarity of the voltage, or the direction of the magnetic flux. **1971** J. H. Smith *Digital Logic* iv. 65 The British standard gives little guidance to the use of a digital buffer amplifier and the reader is recommended to use a single input NOR symbol as an inverting buffer (this is defined as a negater) and the amplifier symbol for the non-inverting buffer.

negation. Add: **1. c.** Also as a logical operation in Computing; = *inversion 2 k. (Further examples.) Also **negation-sign,** the sign or symbol used to indicate negation.

1948 McKinsey & Tarski in *Jrnl. Symbolic Logic* XIII. 1 As regards constants, they are three in number: the negation sign, the conjunction sign, and the possibility sign. **1949** E. C. Berkeley *Giant Brains* iii. 34 The simplest computing operation is negation. **1955** A. N. Prior *Formal Logic* iii. ii. 253 We regard..his negation-sign as meaning impossibility. **1959** E. M. McCormick *Digital Computer Primer* v. 64 The NOT logical operation (negation) results in an output which is opposite to its single input. **1962** T. C. Bartee et al. *Theory & Design Digital Machines* iii. 23 Some authors refer to *x'* as *not x* or as the negation of *x* corresponding to our complement of *x*. **1965** Hughes & Londey *Elem. Formal Logic* x. 67 We used the Law of Double Negation to insert a pair of negation signs. **1969** F. M. Hall *Introd. Abstr. Algebra* II. xi. 313 The negation, or

complement, of *A*, written *A′*, is the statement 'it is false that *A′*', or briefly 'not *A′*'.

negatival (negătəi·văl), *a.* [f. NEGATIVE *sb.* + -AL.] Negative; negativistic; characterized by negation.

1936 J. J. COHEN *Psychotherapy* ii. 7 Psychophonism, or mental logography, is a word which I have coined to distinguish a psychotherapeutic system of negatival auto-suggestion from all rival systems which, all, start from an entirely wrong foundation, this in their being all alike positival in their psychology. **1966** J. E. BUSE in C. E. Bazell *In Memory of J. R. Firth* 56 Phrases are classed as..negatival if they commence with a negative.

negative, *sb.* Add: **1. d.** Used quasi-*advb.*, orig. in radio communication, = No *adv.*³ *colloq.*

Quot. 1946 perhaps illustrates sense 2 a of the adj.

[**1946** J. IRVING *Royal Navalese* 121 Orders for a Church Parade 'Dress for Officers No. 3, negative swords'.] **1955** *Amer. Speech* XXX. 118 *Negative*.., I refuse; I disagree; no (in answer to a question). (For reasons of clarity, any negative expression is expressed over the radio as *negative*...) **1961** E. WAUGH *Unconditional Surrender* I. i. 29 'Any result of my application for the return of my typist?' 'Negative,' said Mr Oates. **1972** C. KEAREY *Last Plane from Uli* vii. 81 'Any snags, Captain?' 'Negative, she's running like a clock.' **1972** P. CLEIFE *Slick & Dead* ix. 69, I shook my head. 'Negative,' I said.

8. b. A mould for, or reverse impression of, a piece of sculpture or the like. Cf. next, sense 11 a.

1911 A. TOFT *Modelling & Sculpture* x. 195 The mould or negative is next coated with a preparation of plumbago or black-lead, and placed in a bath where the metal is deposited into it. **1947** J. C. RICH *Materials & Methods Sculpture* i. 18 The 'negative' is the term applied to the hollow containing form or mold into which the positive, temporarily plastic casting material is poured. *Ibid.* v. 95 If a plaster negative is fashioned over an earth-clay model, the original should not be too dry. **1961** J. CHALLINOR *Dict. Geol.* 134/1 *Negative*, a fossil in the form of an impression. **1973** D. COWLEY *Working with Clay & Plaster* 81 (*caption*) Plaster negative taken from a positive plaster cast.

c. A disc similar to a gramophone record but having ridges in place of grooves.

1918 H. SEYMOUR *Reproduction of Sound* 17 In 1900 he applied the vacuous deposit system in electrolysis to the production of record negatives. **1931** A. NADELL *Projecting Sound Pict.* xiv. 240 This metal plate.. constitutes a 'negative' with which any number of 'positive' records may be stamped. **1974** *Encycl. Brit. Macropædia* XVII. 52/1 Berliner did not, however, contemplate using this etched master as the record to be played; rather, a negative was made from the master by electroforming.

negative, *a.* Add: **2. a.** *negative flag* (see quots.).

1909 *Daily Chron.* 18 Aug. 7/5 If it is hoisted superior to the flag called the Negative flag, it signifies that the man is drowned. **1916** 'TAFFRAIL' *Carry On!* 24 If the 'Negative flag', white with five black crosses, had been displayed, he would have known that the worst had happened, and that a life had been lost. **1948** R. DE KERCHOVE *Internat. Maritime Dict.* 487/1 *Negative flag*, a single-letter signal consisting of letter 'N' of the International Code of signals. Means 'No'.

7. b. (Further examples.) *negative booster*, a booster used to lower the potential of the station end of a negative feeder to below earth potential; *negative feeder*, a wire which connects the rails forming the negative connection for an electric traction vehicle to the bus-bars at a substation.

1890 *Proc. R. Soc.* XLVII. 543 How far the positive charges in the polarising layer and the negative charges projected away from the kathode are *alone* sufficient to account for the whole current, cannot be decided at present. **1902** Negative electron [see *ELECTRON² 1 a]. **1909** P. DAWSON *Electr. Traction on Railways* xv. 475 The negative booster consists simply of a rotating machine driven at a constant speed by an independent motor. *Ibid.* 476 The booster is usually designed so that the E.M.F. produced in the armature is sufficient to cancel out the loss of voltage in the negative feeder. **1932** R. RAWLINSON in E. Molloy *Pract. Electr. Engin.* V. 1598/2 The negative booster is so connected as to reduce the station end of the negative feeder to below earth potential. **1933** *Discovery* Mar. 69/1 The negative electron, the massless unit charge of electricity, was isolated first in the Cavendish Laboratory by Sir J. J. Thomson in 1897. **1956** *Ann. Reg. 1955* 402 The bevatron, at Berkeley, made possible the discovery of a new atomic particle—the negative proton. **1974** *Encycl. Brit. Macropædia* VI. 666/1 The magnitude of the negative charge *e* was obviously of basic importance and a scale parameter for the whole of atomic physics.

d. *negative glow*, the luminous region in a discharge tube between the Crookes dark space and the Faraday dark space.

1890 *Proc. R. Soc.* XLVII. 557 This is the dark interval separating the positive part of the discharge from the negative glow. **1939** H. J. REICH *Theory & Applic. Electron Tubes* xi. 369 The brightness of the negative glow decreases toward the anode, and the glow gradually merges into another relatively dark region, the Faraday dark space. **1971** J. F. WAYMOUTH *Electr. Discharge Lamps* iv. 71 In the negative glow, the rate of ion production required to supply a cathode ion current of 10% of the total may be many times what it is in the positive column.

8. c. Misc. special collocations: *negative capability* (see quot. 1817); now also used (in the light of Keats's other observations on the nature of the creative artist) for *EMPATHY; *negative catalysis* (Chem.) = *INHIBITION 3 b; *negative catalyst* = *INHIBITOR 2 c; *negative eugenics*, an attempt to prevent the birth of children to persons considered unfit to be parents; cf. *DYSGENIC *a.*; *negative feedback*, feedback that tends to diminish or counteract the process giving rise to it; *negative g* or *G*, (a force resulting from) the deceleration of a vehicle, esp. an aircraft or spacecraft; *negative growth*, the cessation or reversal of growth, esp. in lower animals, in response to starvation or other unfavourable conditions; *negative income tax*, a scheme whereby low-paid workers receive a government subsidy to raise their pay to subsistence level; also *negative tax*; *negative* (*phase*) *sequence* (Electr. Engin.), a three-phase system in which the voltages or currents in each phase reach their maxima in the opposite order (i.e. red–blue–yellow) from the positive sequence; *negative resistance*, (the property of) a device in which an increase in the potential difference between its terminals causes a drop in the current flowing through it; *negative transfer*, habits or methods learned for one task which interfere with or transfer negatively to the learning of a subsequent task; cf. *TRANSFER *sb.* 3, *POSITIVE *a.* 8; *negative transference*, the transfer or imputing to a doctor of feelings of hostility, or of resistance and constraint, that may be aroused in the patient through fear of giving expression to his repressed emotions; also, the transferring to a relationship of negative emotions which persist from a previous relationship or experience; cf. *TRANSFERENCE 1, *POSITIVE *a.* 8.

1817 KEATS *Let.* c 21 Dec. (1958) I. 193, I had not a dispute but a disquisition, with Dilke, on various subjects; several things dovetailed in my mind, & at once it struck me, what quality went to form a Man of Achievement especially in Literature & which Shakespeare possessed so enormously—I mean *Negative Capability*, that is when man is capable of being in uncertainties, Mysteries, doubts without any irritable reaching after fact & reason—Coleridge, for instance, would let go by a fine isolated verisimilitude caught from the Penetralium of mystery, from being incapable of remaining content with half knowledge. **1964** S. BARNET et al. *Dict. Literary Terms* 97 Negative capability is sometimes identified with empathy, sometimes with objectivity. **1975** *Studies in Eng. Lit.: Eng. Number* (Tokyo) 167 The poem is representative of the poet [*sc.* Wallace Stevens] in that it is a poem of 'Negative Capability', his basic mental attitude. **1904** *Jrnl. Chem. Soc.* LXXXVI. ii. 113 The simultaneous effect of a positive catalyst (copper sulphate) and a negative catalyst (mannitol or stannic chloride) has been studied, and the experiments support the view that negative catalysis consists in a counteracting of the effect of positive catalysis. **1940** GLASSTONE *Text-bk. Physical Chem.* xiii. 1121 Negative catalysis in gas reactions is probably also to be ascribed to the breaking of reaction chains. **1966** *McGraw-Hill Encycl. Sci. & Technol.* II. 546/2 Such substances, formerly called negative catalysts, are now known to be consumed in the process... Accordingly such materials are not true catalysts. **1968** M. M. JONES *Ligand Reactivity & Catalysis* i. 10 Negative catalysis resulting from the removal of catalytically active metals by a chelating agent, for example, the inhibition of hemoglobin by carbon monoxide. **1908** F. GALTON in *Nature* 22 Oct. 645/2 Little or nothing will be said relating to what has been well termed by Dr. Saleeby 'negative' eugenics, namely,.. hindering the marriages and the production of offspring by the exceptionally unfit. **1914** C. W. SALEEBY *Progress Eugenics* i. 20 It is no less necessary to discourage parenthood among defective individuals, and to this, with Galton's approval, I gave the name of negative eugenics, calling his own scheme positive eugenics. **1931** J. S. HUXLEY *What dare I Think?* iii. 93 Negative eugenics is concerned with preventing degeneration. **1974** J. R. BAKER *Race* iv. 57 He [*sc.* Madison Grant] was harsh in his schemes for negative eugenics... He favoured the forcible sterilization of criminals, diseased and insane persons, and 'worthless race-types', and the enactment of laws against race-mixture. **1934** H. S. BLACK in *Bell Syst. Techn. Jrnl.* XIII. 5, $1/(1-\mu\beta)$ will be used as a quantitative measure of the effect of feedback and the feedback referred to as positive feedback or negative feedback according as the absolute value of $1/(1-\mu\beta)$ is greater or less than unity. Positive feedback increases the gain of the amplifier; negative feedback reduces it. **1956** *Science* 11 May 848/1 (*heading*) Evidence for a negative-feedback mechanism in the biosynthesis of isoleucine. **1966** 'A. HALL' *9th Directive* x. 97, I put in fifty or sixty shots,..gradually allowing the negative feedback data to correct the aim. **1967** M. ARGYLE *Psychol. Interpersonal Behaviour* iii. 62 Such unstable sequences are known as cases of 'positive feedback' (unstable vicious circles) and can be contrasted with self-correcting 'negative feedback', which is also a common feature of social performance. **1952** R. L. CHRISTY in White & Benson *Physics & Med. Upper Atmosphere* 510 Certain unusual attitudes of the aircraft in which irregular accelerations, including negative g, are encountered. **1955** *Aeroplane* 25 Nov. 794/1 The need for a negative-g stressing case for civil aircraft was questioned. **1962** J. GLENN in *Into Orbit* 71 We also made runs to simulate the forces of deceleration, or negative Gs. **1932** J. S. HUXLEY *Probl. Relative Growth* iii. 87 Here [*sc.* in the shore crab Ocypoda] the low point of growth, or 'negative growth-centre', is also in the merus. **1957** G. E. HUTCHINSON *Treat. Limnol.* I. iii. 217 The life of such lower organisms as are capable of negative growth may be greatly prolonged. **1964** A. E. NEEDHAM *Growth Process in Animals* iii. 29 In the lower animals negative growth or degrowth is commonly reversible, sometimes to a remarkable degree. It is a normal response to starvation and to some other conditions. **1967** *Yale Law Jrnl.* Nov. 1 (*title*) Is a negative income tax practical? **1969** *Daily Tel.* 17 Jan. 27/1 The use of 'negative income tax', by which low-wage earners receive a PAYE handout. **1973** *Guardian* 30 Mar. 6/4 The Government's proposed tax credit system—the 'negative income tax' proposed in a Green Paper last year. **1930** M. G. MALTI *Electr. Circuit Analysis* xv. 244 We shall call a negative phase sequence such a sequence of the phases that phase 1 leads phase 3 by 120° and leads phase 2 by 240°. **1896** FRITH & RODGERS in *Phil. Mag.* XLII. 410 [Prof. Ayrton concluded that if an attempt were made to measure the resistance of the arc by altering the P.D. between the carbons and finding the corresponding alteration of current produced, the resistance found by taking this ratio must be *negative.*] *Ibid.*, All these experiments..lead to the conclusion that the arc has a *negative* resistance. **1932** W. L. EVERITT *Communication Engin.* xviii. 479 A negative resistance can be used in a circuit to counteract the effect of positive resistance and so cause a combination of inductance and capacitance to oscillate. **1942** C. L. AMICK *Fluorescent Lighting Manual* ii. 21 The 'negative-resistance' characteristic of fluorescent lamps means that the voltage drop across the lamp decreases as the arc current goes up. **1974** G. J. ANGERBAUER *Electronics for Mod. Communications* xvi. 319 This negative-resistance effect depends upon secondary emission from the plate. **1973** J. R. NEUENSWANDER *Mod. Power Syst.* ix. 175 The revolving field..rotates *with* the rotor while the negative-sequence armature currents..set up a revolving field rotating at the same speed but in opposite direction to the rotor. **1963** M. S. GORDON *Econ. Welfare Policies* vi. 117 A few economists, appalled at the piecemeal character of our approach to welfare policies, have espoused the so-called 'negative tax' proposal. **1921** F. N. FREEMAN *Exper. Educ.* ii. 47 There is strong negative transfer from Set 2 to Set 3. **1933** M. VITELES *Industr. Psychol.* III. xx. 427 The study of transfer effect has indicated that under certain conditions the practice of similar tasks may induce a negative transfer or interference with the acquisition of skill. **1938** R. S. WOODWORTH *Exper. Psychol.* viii. 176 When an act is carried over but impedes the learning of a second act we obviously have positive transfer and a negative transfer effect. **1950** O. MOWRER *Learning Theory & Personality Dynamics* vii. 193 If 'reinforcement' learning were alone operative, the initial 'mis-training' given to the experimental-group subjects should have produced negative transfer. **1966** J. T. & K. W. SPENCE in C. D. Spielberger *Anxiety & Behavior* 303 An investigation..that involved a type of negative transfer design. **1916** C. E. LONG tr. *Jung's Coll. Papers Analytical Psychol.* ix. 270 If it is a 'negative' transference, you can see nothing but violent resistances which sometimes veil themselves in seemingly critical or sceptical dress. **1924** J. RIVIERE et al. tr. *Freud's Coll. Papers* II. xxviii. 319 One is forced to distinguish 'positive' transference from 'negative' transference, the transference of affectionate feeling from that of hostile feeling and to deal separately with the two varieties of the transference to the physician. **1954** R. W. PICKFORD *Analysis of Obsessional* i. 20 A technique for manipulating the positive and negative transferences to the patient's advantage. **1960** L. PINCUS *Marriage* ii. 91 The distress, pain and aggression of a negative transference. **1964** ZALEZNIK & MOMENT *Dynamics Interpersonal Behavior* viii. 268 The negative transference reactions where the individual experiences hatred toward a person in the present because of a past relationship. **1968** A. J. MANDELL in J. Marmor *Mod. Psychoanal.* xi. 283 Side reactions may begin to take the place of verbalized negative transference.

10. b. *negative after-image*, an after-image of complementary colour or brightness to that of the original impression.

1899 L. HILL *Man. Human Physiol.* xxxv. 439 Look steadfastly at a piece of white paper placed on a sheet of black paper, and then look up at a dark wall. You will now see a black spot on a whitish ground. This is a negative after-image... Look steadfastly now at a piece of red paper; a negative after-image appears on looking at the ceiling. This image will not be red, but of the complementary colour greenish blue. **1967** D. A. SCHREUDER in J. B. de Boer *Public Lighting* iv. 167 Complete adaptation [to the luminance of the field of vision] requires a certain length of time. The slowest, and hence in practice the most important process is the disappearance of the negative after-images.

11. a. Of, pertaining to, or designating a mould or reverse impression. Cf. *NEGATIVE *sb.* 8 b.

1911 G. H. WILSON *Man. Dental Prosthetics* ii. 55 An impression is a negative likeness of an object or part taken in a plastic material, from which a cast or positive likeness may be produced. **1939** M. HOFFMAN *Sculpture Inside & Out* xii. 214 While working, it is useful to squeeze the wax often against the negative mold, thereby verifying just what the effect will be. **1940** J. OSBORNE *Dental Mech.* i. 1 The technique necessary for the accurate construction of a model, or positive likeness of the patient's mouth, from an impression or negative likeness. **1947** J. C. RICH *Materials & Methods Sculpture* v. 90 Negative molds are of two varieties: those that are flexible and those that are rigid. *Ibid.* 96 Agar-base negative mixtures are a recent casting development. *Ibid.* 122 Wax is rarely used as a negative material in sculpture. **1966** D. Z. MEILACH *Creating with Plaster* iv. 58/2 Grease the negative mold very well with a

separating medium. **1975** *N.Y. Times* 29 Nov. 19/2 The work, unusual for a cast bronze in that it has a negative impression on the back corresponding to the subject on the front, was apparently designed that way so castings could easily be made from it.

b. Having the character of a negative (*NEGATIVE *sb.* 8 c).

1949 Frayne & Wolfe *Elem. Sound Recording* xiv. 264 A negative matrix or 'stamper' must be made from the original record. **1974** *Encycl. Brit. Macropædia* XVII. 54/1 To make copies of the recording, dies must be made the surface of which is a negative replica of the master-record surface.

12. *Theol.* = *APOPHATIC *a.*

1956, 1961 [see *APOPHATIC *a.*]. **1964** C. S. Lewis *Discarded Image* iv. 70 It is the 'negative Theology' of those who take in a more rigid sense, and emphasise more persistently than others, the incomprehensibility of God.

III. 13. Comb.: **negative-going**, increasing in magnitude in the direction of negative polarity; becoming less positive or more negative; **negative–positive** *a.*, pertaining to or designating a photographic process, device, etc., employing or producing both negative and positive film, or employing negative film to produce a positive image, or vice versa.

1959 J. M. Pettit *Electronic Switching* v. 136 The plate waveforms in Fig. 5–15 are square waves, except for the negative-going spikes and the exponential rise. **1969** J. J. Sparkes *Transistor Switching* v. 121 The logic inputs.. predetermine the direction the circuit will tend to switch next time a negative-going voltage step (from *ECC* to zero) is applied to the pulse inputs. **1936** C. E. K. Mees *Photogr.* 212/1 Negative–positive process, cine film. **1938** G. H. Sewell *Amateur Film-Making* ii. 12 The 'negative–positive' method consists of recording the negative image on one piece of film, and 'printing off' the positive image on to another piece of material in the manner described above. **1958** *Newnes Compl. Amat. Photogr.* 3 The next step [after daguerreotype], technically, was the development by Fox Talbot of a negative–positive process... Light-sensitive paper was the negative, reversed on to a second sheet of sensitised paper for the positive. *Ibid.* v. 85 Negative–positive films are designed to produce colour negatives, from which colour prints can be made. **1967** E. Chambers *Photolitho-Offset* x. 145 The line positive is made on 'lith' film from the negative–positive combination.

negativism. Add: **2.** *Psychol.* Resistance to attempts to impose a change of activity or posture, characteristic of various neuro-psychiatric disorders.

1892 D. H. Tuke *Dict. Psychol. Med.* II. 724/2 As soon as we attempt to produce passive movements of any part of the patient's body, we meet almost always with a powerful resistance; the groups of muscles antagonistic to the attempted movement commence to contract energetically—this has been termed the symptom of negativism. **1902** A. R. Defendorf *Clin. Psychiatry* 63 Negativism consists in the reaction to stimuli which are [*sic*] the reverse of the normal reaction. **1916** A. A. Brill tr. *Freud's Wit & its Relation to Unconscious* iii. vi. 278 This..behavior of antagonistic relationships is probably not without value for the understanding of the symptom of negativism in neurotics and in the insane. **1947** G. Murphy *Personality* ii. ix. 218 Negativism appears..at *any* period in which the external interference is insufficient to redirect behavior but is sufficient to necessitate an extra effort in continuing one's own activities. **1969** *Sci. Jrnl.* June 72/2 The patient continued to maintain his negativism and said 'I don't know'. **1971** *Publishers' Weekly* 30 Aug. 209/3 Solutions to the problems of fear, tension, guilt, loneliness, and negativism.

negativist. Add: Also *attrib.* or as *adj.*

1927 J. S. Huxley *Relig. without Revelation* i. 52 They have..rejected the whole ground of divinity.., and so been forced into a negativist attitude, compelled to satisfy their natural and normal religious needs in other ways and other spheres. **1958** W. Stark *Sociol. of Knowl.* 317 The main representatives of this doctrine which..we wish to label the *negativist* theory, are.. Nietzsche and..Pareto.

negativistic (ne:gătivi·stik), *a.* [f. Negati-v(ism + -istic.] Of, pertaining to, or characterized by negativism.

1902 A. R. Defendorf *Clin. Psychiatry* 64 The negativistic patient shows great equanimity, he seldom defends himself..but merely resists. **1916** C. E. Long tr. *Jung's Coll. Papers Analytical Psychol.* vi. 200 Disposing causes of negativistic phenomena are: the *ambitendency* by which every impulse is accompanied by its opposite. **1930** E. & F. Jensen tr. *Adler's Educ. Children* xii. 213 If an adolescent shows himself very negativistic in regard to the other sex, we will find, if we trace back his life, that he was probably a fighting child. **1957** M. Millar *Soft Talkers* 186, I do hope your negativistic attitude towards me personally won't interfere with your better judgement. **1970** H. McLeave *Question of Negligence* (1973) x. 84 The negativistic attitude of Fairchild, the ministry sneak with the almost psychotic habit of saying no to everything.

negativity. (Earlier and later examples.)

1854 Geo. Eliot tr. *Feuerbach's Essence Christianity* ii. 42 It is true that thus, negativity, as the speculative philosophers express themselves—*nothing* is the cause of the world. **1953** R. Lehmann *Echoing Grove* 41 Had decided to my own satisfaction what it meant, in psychological terms: not tension, not active boredom—simply negativity. **1956** D. Gascoyne *Night Thoughts* 17 The Tyrant Negativity has usurped power. **1975** *Times* 24 Oct. 3/3 Rabies virus was not found in a man who died of the disease after intensive vaccine treatment... 'The negativity of the finding..was perhaps the light at the end of the tunnel.'

negaton (ne·gătǫn). *Physics.* [f. Negat(ive *a.* + *-on[1].] = *NEGATRON 2.

1928 H. D. Hubbard *Explanatory Key to Periodic Chart of Atoms* 20 The positive atom of electricity, the 'proton' is 1845 times heavier than the negative. (Since 'electron' is ambiguous, the term 'positon' is suggested as more explicit, and 'negaton' would avoid ambiguity as the corresponding name for the negative electron.) **1938** *Encycl. Brit. Bk. of Year* 404/1 The prediction of the possibility under certain conditions of the materialization of radiation quanta into a positon and a negaton. **1955** O. Klein in W. Pauli *Niels Bohr* 115 Assuming..that there are no negaton–positon interaction terms. **1955** R. D. Evans *Atomic Nucleus* xviii. 569 The Sixth General Assembly of the International Union of Pure and Applied Physics (Amsterdam, July 8 to 10, 1948) unanimously recommended the use of the terms *positon* and *negaton* as a means of distinguishing between positive and negative electrons. However, common usage, as seen in the periodical literature, still tends to retain the 'r'.

negator. Add: **2.** A word expressing negation; = Negative *sb.* 2.

1961 R. B. Long *Sentence & its Parts* iv. 100 *Not* is by no means the only adjunct with negator force... Negative subjects and negative complements can serve as negators. **1966** G. N. Leech *Eng. in Advertising* xviii. 159 The universal negators *no, never,* etc. **1973** *Archivum Linguisticum* IV. 14 Of these auxiliaries, only one negator /no/ can occur independently. **1974** L. Todd *Pidgins & Creoles* iii. 34 In the 1830 examples the negator occurs in the same position as in the pidgins and creoles we have examined.

3. See *NEGATER.

negatron (ne·gătrǫn). [f. Nega(tive *a.* + *-tron.] **1.** *Electronics.* A kind of valve that exhibits negative resistance, having two anodes (one either side of the cathode) and a control electrode between the cathode and one of the anodes.

1919 J. Scott-Taggart *Brit. Pat. 166,260* 17 Sept., The present invention relates to an electron discharge device, hereinafter to be termed a negatron, which is capable of being used as a negative resistance. **1964** J. Groszkowski *Frequency of Self-Oscillations* iii. 70 The negatron belongs to the voltage-controlled negative resistors.

2. *Physics.* The ordinary, i.e. negatively charged, electron (as distinct from the positron). Cf. *NEGATON.

1934 C. D. Anderson et al. in *Physical Rev.* XLV. 353/1 To remove the ambiguity in the definition of the term 'electron'..the terms 'negatron' and 'positron' are here used. **1955** R. D. Evans *Atomic Nucleus* xviii. 576 Consider the collision of an incident negatron..with an atomic electron. **1961** G. R. Choppin *Exper. Nucl. Chem.* vii. 100 When the gamma energy is greater than 1·02 MeV, a certain probability exists for the creation of a negatron..and a positron. **1971** Stern & Lewis *X-Rays* iii. 47 Triplet production can occur when the photon interacts with an electron and not with a nucleus. Three particles result, the original electron as well as the positron and negatron pair.

negentropy (nege·ntrŏpi). [f. Neg(ative *a.* + Entropy.] Negative entropy, as a measure of order or information.

1950 L. Brillouin in *Amer. Scientist* XXXVIII. 594/1 Every observation in the laboratory..is made at the expense of a certain amount of negative entropy (abbreviation: negentropy), taken away from the surroundings. **1956** —— *Sci. & Information Theory* p. xii, We prove that information must be considered as a negative term in the entropy of a system; in short, information is negentropy. *Ibid.* ix. 117 An isolated system contains negentropy if it reveals a possibility for doing mechanical or electrical work. **1958** *Archivum Linguisticum* X. 137 The calculation of redundancy, by the method taken over from information theory, requires the three terms 'negentropy', 'relative negentropy' and redundancy. **1966** S. Beer *Decision & Control* ix. 188 Hence the energy transferred through the system is exactly balanced by the information flowing the opposite way; to speak of a change in entropy is *ipso facto* to speak of an equivalent change in negentropy. **1970** H. C. Shands *Semiotic Approaches to Psychiatry* xxiii. 386 Knowing systems lose information as physical systems gain entropy. The continuous input of 'negentropy'.. is required to maintain balance in either context. **1971** *Sci. Amer.* Sept. 183/2 Taking commonly accepted average values for the temperatures of the sun and the earth, the $1{\cdot}6 \times 10^{15}$ megawatt-hours of energy radiated to outer space carries with it the capability for an entropy decrease, or 'negentropy flux', of $3{\cdot}2 \times 10^{22}$ joules per degree K. per year, or 10^{38} bits per second.

négligé. Add: Also negligee, negligée. (Further examples.) Cf. Negligee in Dict. and Suppl.

1908 R. W. Chambers *Firing Line* xviii. 313 Cecile, in distractingly pretty negligee, waved him audacious adieu from her window. **1913** E. M. Forster *Let.* 1 Jan. in *Hill of Devi* (1953) 24 Her dress was on the negligee side, but she had not been intending to receive. **1917** 'Taffrail' *Sub* iv. 99 The members of the mess had purchased pictures, most of them of beautiful ladies in rather négligé raiment. **1945** S. Lewis *Cass Timberlane* (1946) xliii. 308 Jinny weaved in, much too pretty in her négligé. **1954** A. Gardiner *Theory of Proper Names* (ed. 2) p. v, The bulk of this book is an exact reprint of a..booklet published..in 1940. Doubtless owing to the circumstances of the times, but possibly also to the original publication's somewhat négligé apparel, this passed almost unnoticed.

negligee. Add: **1.** Also, an informal garment worn by men in the 18th century.

1795 tr. *C. P. Moritz's Trav.* 87 In the morning, it is usual to walk out in a sort of negligèe [*sic*], or morning-dress, your hair not dressed, but merely rolled up in rollers, and in a frock and boots.

b. *negligee shirt* (N. Amer.), a soft-fronted shirt worn by men.

1895 *Montgomery Ward Catal.* 278/3 Men's negligee shirts. **1921** *Daily Colonist* (Victoria, B.C.) 19 Oct. 7/2 (Advt.), Men, if you want the best shirt..buy..these well made Cambric Negligee Shirts, in neat stripes.

c. *transf.* A shroud. *U.S.*

1927 *Amer. Mercury* May 33/1 The corpse is not a corpse nor does it wear a shroud. It is the body, or the remains;..and the garment in which it is wrapped, when there is one aside from ordinary clothing, is a negligée. **1963** J. Mitford *Amer. Way of Death* i. 26 Florence Gowns Inc...exhibited their line of 'streetwear type garments and negligees'..at a recent convention of the National Funeral Directors Association.

3. A woman's dressing-gown, usu. made of flimsy, semi-transparent fabric trimmed with ruffles, lace, etc.

1930 M. Story *Individuality & Clothes* iii. 311 *The negligée*, this garment for intimate occasions may be.. silky, lacy, colorful, and dainty. **1942** H. Pepin *Mod. Pattern Design* x. 219/1 The boudoir negligée is not to be confused with the 'hostess gown'. **1952** S. Kauffmann *Philanderer* (1953) i. 12 She shrugged and walked lazily over to the kitchenette, her filmy negligée heightening the illusion that she floated. **1960** A. Clarke *Later Poems* (1961) 80 Rosalind, in a négligée, Began to sketch me as I lay Naked. **1967** B. Patten *Little Johnny's Confession* 51 A thousand negligées, pyjamas, nightgowns.

negligent, *a.* and *sb.* Add: **B.** *sb.* **2.** A type of wig worn in the 18th century.

1753 in F. W. Fairholt *Costume in England* (1885) II. 320 The pigeon's wing, the comet, the cauliflower,..the rose, the crutch, the negligent, the chancellor, [etc.]. **1762** Goldsmith *Life R. Nash* 74 Nash..had seen flaxen bobs succeeded by majors, which in their turn gave way to negligents. **1971** J. Woodforde *Strange Story False Hair* vii. 46 *Men's—eighteenth century*..Negligent.

‖**négociant** (negosiaṅ). [Fr., = merchant, used *ellipt.* for *négociant des vins.*] A wine merchant.

1910 'Saki' *Reginald in Russia* 104 The little Lemberg *négociant* plucked up heart. **1961** W. E. Massee *Wines & Spirits* 51 A shipper who owns vineyards in one town but ships from another must put the word *négociant* on the label. **1970** *House & Garden* May 38/3 The principal *négociants* of Burgundy are very hospitable to properly introduced visitors who have a serious interest in wine. **1974** *Harpers & Queen* Sept. 73/1 It's a good thing for a young man to have the M[aster of] W[ine]... Continental *négociants* and growers now recognise and respect it.

negotiate, *v.* **4.** (Later examples.)

1909 *Q. Rev.* Oct. 492 Some rival..had 'negotiated'—this we believe to be the sporting phrase—the same 150 miles in forty-seven hours. **1922** H. Titus *Timber* xvi. 151 Pelly negotiated the *cuspidor* safely. **1973** E. Lemarchand *Let or Hindrance* xiii. 157 Toye negotiated the narrow entry, and they arrived in a small enclosed space in which several cars were already parked.

Negress. Add: Now customarily written with a capital initial.

In recent years felt by some to have 'racist' connotations.

1970 J. Updike *Bech: a Book* 113 'In *Travel Light*, for example, you keep calling Roxanne a Negress.' 'But she was one.' He added, 'I loved Roxanne.' 'The fact is, the word has distinctly racist overtones.' **1974** *Times Lit. Suppl.* 21 June 671/1 Blacks all over the world find the term 'Negress' offensive. What is wrong with saying 'a Black woman'?

transf. (Later example.)

1920 E. Sitwell *Wooden Pegasus* 92 The negress Night, within her house of glass Watched the processions pass.

Negri (nēi·gri). *Path.* The name of Adelchi *Negri* (1876–1912), Italian physician, used *attrib.* (and formerly in the possessive) to designate eosinophil cytoplasmic inclusion bodies (first described by him in 1903) found in the neurons of the brains of human beings and animals infected with rabies, the demonstration of which provides the most certain diagnosis of that disease.

1904 *Brit. Med. Jrnl., Epitome of Current Med. Lit.* 30 Apr. 72/2 (*heading*) The minute structure of Negri's bodies. **1905** *Jrnl. Amer. Med. Assoc.* 2 Sept. 744/1 It is just as possible that the Negri bodies are the result of the infection as that they are the cause of rabies. **1906** *Jrnl. R. Microsc. Soc.* 626 (*heading*) Demonstrating Negri's corpuscles. **1952** [see *CHROMATOID *a.*]. **1970** *Sci. Jrnl.* Apr. 38/1 Diagnosis of rabies by the recognition of Negri bodies in the brain of an affected animal.. requires the animal to be dead. **1974** Passmore & Robson *Compan. Med. Stud.* III. xii. 96/2 Smears and

tissue sections should be searched for Negri bodies which stain pink with polychrome stains.

negrification (nɪ:grifikēɪ·ʃən). Also **Negrification.** [f. NEGRO on model of words in *-fication*, as *pacification*. Cf. NIGRIFICATION.] The action or fact of making Negro in character; placing under the control of Blacks. So **ne·grify** *v. trans.*

1929 *Nation* (N.Y.) 9 Jan. 56 At the beginning of 1928 it seemed as if an end would be made to the slave traffic and the 'negrification' of Cuba, when the Government decided to restrict the output of sugar to 4,000,000 tons per year. **1961** *Spectator* 9 June 835 Through the ceremony the negroes 'negrify' themselves. **1962** *Economist* 7 Apr. 28/2 Some young Belgian technicians have complained of the effects of 'negrification'. **1966** P. GREEN tr. *Escarpit's Novel Computer* vi. 76 Suppose..you were asked to join a revolt..to save the Western world from materialism and Arabo-Marxist negrification. **1972** *Daily Tel.* 7 Mar. 11/4 'Black' in Trinidad means black... Hence the need for 'Negrification' of public and private employment.

negritic (nɪ̄gri·tik), *a.* [f. NEGRO + -ITIC. Cf. NIGRITIC *a.*] Of or pertaining to Negroes or Black peoples; nigritic.

1878 C. KEARY *Dawn of Hist.* 220 The reader may consult an interesting paper by Professor Huxley..for some further views concerning the extension of the Negritic family. **1926** *Contemp. Rev.* Apr. 529 The one class that had kept itself pure from negritic intermixture. **1947** E. HOOTON in H. Gladwin *Men out of Asia* p. xi, I am fairly sure that the earliest arrivals here were non-Mongoloids carrying archaic White strains ('Australoids', if you like) probably mixed with Negritic elements. **1950** *Cold Spring Harbor Symposia on Quantitative Biol.* XV. 260/1 Using the living Andamanese as a basis for reference, the negritic migrants may be characterized as of very short stature, dark skin color, woolly hair form, moderate round-headedness, low nasal relief, and a very short and narrow face.

negritize (nɪ̄·gritəiz), *v.* Also **Negritize.** [Irreg. f. NEGRO or *NEGRIT(IC *a.* + -IZE.] *trans.* To make Negro or nigritic in character or appearance.

1901 *Ann. Rep. Board of Regents Smithsonian Inst. 1899* 513 Not one fact is in evidence from which we may conclude that a single neighbouring people known to us has been Negritized. **1930** C. G. SELIGMAN *Races Afr.* v. 112 The less negritized type are of a slight, rather graceful build.

Negrito. (Earlier and later examples.)

1814 J. MAVER tr. *Martinez de Zuñiga's Hist. View Philippine Islands* I. p. xii, It is generally allowed that the language spoken by the Papuans..and Negritos of the Philippines, and adjacent islands, is totally different from the Malayan. **1928** *Times Lit. Suppl.* 9 Feb. 90/4 The Negritoes..live at a primitive level, using wind-breaks and not houses. **1958** J. SLIMMING *Temiar Jungle* ii. 22 Originally much of this part of the Nenggiri was Negrito country. **1965** C. SHUTTLEWORTH *Malayan Safari* i. 16 Negritoes—a small negroid people with crinkly hair. **1969** *Age* (Melbourne) 24 May 12/5 Mr. Robinson..takes it for granted that two 'waves' of Negritos, the Kartans and the Tartangans, preceded the Aborigines to Australia. **1972** *Guardian* 22 Sept. 9/3 At the top of the mud bank was a tiny village of palm shelters, just high enough to sit in and here I met the Negritos, the oldest inhabitants of Malaysia, a short, negroid nomadic group.

Negritude (nɪ̄·gritiud). Also with small initial and in Fr. form *Négritude.* [a. F. *négritude* NIGRITUDE.] The quality or characteristic of being a Negro; affirmation of the value of Black or African culture, identity, etc.

1950 *French Rev.* XXIII. 383 Their [*sc.* pre-1939–45-war young French Colonial Negro authors'] writing would be different, so different that only a new term could describe it; hence they invented the word: *négritude.* **1960** *Guardian* 29 July 4/2 The deeper cultural manifestations of colonialism. The best of this..kind of analysis seems..to be coming from those who have been colonised themselves—in Africa..from 'Présence Africaine's' explorations of *négritude.* **1960** *Observer* 20 Nov. 7/1 A movement for what French Pan-Africanists call 'Negritude'—the recognition of the Negro personality in world civilisation. **1961** *Ibid.* 29 Oct. 13/7 Senghor has been one of the leading prophets of *Négritude*, a literary and philosophical movement which expresses in an almost mystical way the African identity over against Western materialism. **1962** *Times Lit. Suppl.* 10 Aug. 596/4 The recent African Writers Conference..was significant for its hostility to négritude. **1963** *Internat. Year Bk.* 274/1 Aimé Césaire, a Martinique poet, invented the term, 'négritude', to describe the poetry that he and Haitians Jacques Roumain and Léon Laleau, and Léon Damas from Guiana were attempting to write. The word referred to the elevating of Africa as a place toward which all people of Negro blood aspired spiritually, but this Africa was not so much a geographical location as a condition of the mind. **1965** *Time* 27 Aug. 19 The wholehearted attempt by other Negroes to emphasize their Negroid features and hair texture shows their pride in their 'negritude'—a word currently in fashion in Negro communities. **1966** *New Statesman* 18 Nov. 730/1 Negritude is the least characteristic thing about Senator-elect Edward Brooke... On election night..Walter Cronkite told..television listeners that Brooke was 'five-fourths White'. **1969** N. HARE in A. Chapman *New Black Voices* (1972) 435 The debate was kicked off by leading Negritude theoretician, Leopold Senghor. *Ibid.* 436 Negritude.. permitted an escape into excessive glorification of the past and the traditional..so that one found difficulty in incorporating the techniques of the present and the future or in turning them effectively against the oppressor. **1971** *Black Scholar* Apr.–May 8 The laws and order of this nation are contrary to the black man's nature, contrary to our Negritude. **1972** M. RIOFRANCAS in J. Pinkham tr. *Césaire's Discourse on Colonialism* 72 (*tr. interview*) How did you come to develop the concept of Negritude? A[imé] C[ésaire]. I have a feeling that it was something of a collective creation. I used the term first, that's true. .. It was really a resistance to the policy of assimilation. **1975** *Times Lit. Suppl.* 7 Mar. 247/2 (Advt.), Negritude has been defined by Senghor as 'the sum of the cultural values of the black world as they are expressed in the life, the institutions, and the works of black men'.

Negro. Add: In the nineteenth and twentieth centuries also applied (now somewhat less frequently because of the increasing use of the word *Black*) to individuals of African ancestry born in or resident in the United States or in other English-speaking countries. (Now customarily written with a capital initial.) (Further examples.) Cf. *NEW NEGRO, NIGGER *sb.* (in Dict. and Suppl.).

1876 tr. *O. Peschel's Races of Man* 464 Narrow and more or less high skulls are prevalent among the negroes. **1906** *Harper's Weekly* 2 June 763/2 Professor Booker T. Washington, being politely interrogated..as to whether negroes ought to be called 'negroes' or 'members of the colored race' has replied that it has long been his own practice to write and speak of members of his race as negroes, and when using the term 'negro' as a race designation, to employ the capital 'N'. **1911** E. C. SEMPLE *Influences Geogr. Environment* ii. 38 It is generally conceded by scientists that pigment is a protective device of nature. The Negro's skin is comparatively insensitive to a sun heat that blisters a white man. **1930** *N.Y. Times* 7 Mar. 22/5 (*heading*) 'Negro' with a capital 'N'... Major Robert R. Moton..has written..that his people universally wish to see the word 'Negro' capitalized... In our 'style book' 'Negro' is now added to the list of words to be capitalized. It is not merely a typographical change; it is an act in recognition of racial self-respect. **1938** F. BOAS *Gen. Anthropol.* iii. 104 In a strict sense a race must be defined as a group of common origin and of stable type. In this sense extreme forms like the Australians, Negroes, Mongolians, and Europeans may be described as races because each has certain characteristics which set them off from other groups, and which are strictly hereditary. **1965** S. S. SMITH *Ess. Causes of Variety of Complexion & Figure* p. lvii, It remains hazardous..to offer summary findings as to skeletal differences between whites and negroes. **1970** R. D. ABRAHAMS *Positively Black* ii. 33 By espousing the term 'black' for themselves, they are also arguing implicitly that 'Negro' is a status term imposed by whites to underline the white's sense of the place of blacks in the American system. **1970** C. MAJOR *Dict. Afro-Amer. Slang* 84 *Negro*, another way of calling [a] person an *Uncle Tom.* **1971** *Black Scholar* Jan. 53/2 His protagonist, a white-skinned Negro..decides to leave the black race. *Ibid.* Apr.–May 9 The United States of America has..deprived me and my brothers and sisters, the 30 to 60 million so-called Negroes, better known as Asiatic Black people, of life, liberty, and the pursuit of happiness. **1973** *Black World* May 37/2 Upon spotting the Afro-American, the Ghanaians shouted out, 'Hey, Negro!' The other.. retorted angrily, 'I'm a Black Man, not a Negro. Don't call me Negro.'

d. (Earlier example). Also in *Combs.* with a language name, as *Negro-English, -French*, etc.

1704 S. KNIGHT *Jrnl.* (1825) 38 You speak negro to him. I'le ask him. **1808** T. ASHE *Trav. Amer.* 79 The husband..had lived long enough in Virginia to pick up some Negro-English. **1819** R. L. MASON *Narr. in Pioneer West* (1915) 56 Negro-French is the common language of this town. **1862** 'E. KIRKE' *Among Pines* 132 Not to weary the reader with a long repetition of negro-English, I will tell in brief what I gleaned from an hour's conversation with the two blacks. **1932** W. L. GRAFF *Lang.* 436 As a result of European trade a number of creolized trade languages have developed along the Atlantic Coast. They are chiefly Negro-Portuguese, Negro-English, and Negro-French. **1964** *Language* XL. 291 Sravan (also known as..Surinam Negro-English). **1971** J. SPENCER *Eng. Lang. W. Afr.* 9 A pidginised form of Portuguese (often referred to as Negro-Portuguese).

2. *Negro-baiting* vbl. sb. and ppl. a., *-breaker, -breaking, equality, -hate, -holder* (earlier example), *-monger, question, -rank* adj., *slavery, -stale* adj., *-stealer, -stealing, -trader, –white* adj.

1949 *Sat. Rev. Lit.* (U.S.) 24 Sept. 6 Something about Negro-baiting in the South. **1951** KOESTLER *Age of Longing* x. 183 You are a Negro-baiting, half-civilised nation. **1845** F. DOUGLASS *Narr. Life F. Douglass* x. 73 Mr. Covey enjoyed the most unbounded reputation for being a first-rate overseer and negro-breaker. **1855** —— *My Bondage & my Freedom* xv. 216 His proficiency in the art of negro breaking. **1856** *Illinois State Register* (Springfield) 26 June 3/3 The cry for negro equality is on their lips. **1905** N. DAVIS *Northerner* 52 You think I might be nice to Mr. Falls, negro equality and all? **1862** *N.Y. Tribune* 21 Apr., Southern negro-hate, being based on Slavery, is kept within bounds; that of the North, being mainly a hypocrisy or imitation, is affected & exaggerated to caricature. **1780** J. JONES *Lett.* (1889) 47 The negro holders in general already clamour against the project. **1741** T. JONES *Let.* 1 July in *Colonial Rec. Georgia* (1906) IV. 678 This exposes them to the Envy and Hatred of our Negro-Mongers. **1832** *Reg. Deb. Congress U.S.* 2 Apr. 2348 The South must be threatened with the negro question. **1949** *Time* 31 Oct. 84/3 The South gradually transformed 'the Negro question' into a fanatical folk bias, coloring its segregated religion, its sex attitudes, its every moment in life. **1942** Negro-rank [see *Negro-stale* adj. below]. **1831** M. HOLLEY *Texas* (1833) 87 The question of negro slavery..is one of great importance. **1942** W. FAULKNER *Go Down, Moses* 199 It all seemed to stand there about them, intact and complete and visible in the drafty, damp, heatless, negro-stale negro-rank sorry room. **1827** *Western Monthly Rev.* I. 69 It will be the refuge of Negro-stealers and the Elysium of rogues. **1819** *Niles' Reg.* XVI. 160/1 Sentence of death has been pronounced on a fellow in North Carolina, for negro stealing. **1732** in *Rhode Island Hist. Soc. Coll.* (1923) XVI. 108, 4 Negro Traders then on board. **1873** 'MARK TWAIN' & WARNER *Gilded Age* VII. 78 The Hawkins hearts had been torn to see Uncle Dan'l and his wife pass from the auction-block into the hands of a negro trader. **1956** J. C. FURNAS *Goodbye to Uncle Tom* II. 70 Our town then had the largest Negro–white ratio in the North. **1961** *Times* 2 Dec. 11/5 Eight Negroes, mostly of mixed Negro–white descent.

3. *Negro minstrel* (earlier and later examples).

1855 C. E. DE LONG in *Calif. Hist. Soc. Q.* (1929) VIII. 346 A negro minstrel performance at home went to it and took some girls. **1884** *Century Mag.* Mar. 688/1 At that time the negro-minstrel was not a black-faced singer of sentimental songs but a man who sang and jumped Jim Crow..and other genuine plantation songs. **1915** *Scribner's Mag.* June 754 Time was when the Negro-minstrels held possession of three or four theatres in the single city of New York. **1970** *Oxf. Compan. Mus.* (ed. 10) 675/1 Towards the end of the nineteenth century Negro Minstrels were a feature of every considerable British coast resort.

5. *Negro quarters* (later examples).

1813 E. GERRY JR. *Diary* 26 June (1927) 144 Mr. Carrol has 1000 slaves, whose huts, called negro quarters, constitute a small town around the mansion. **1913** W. P. EATON *Barn Doors & Byways* 167 The old foundation stones show that the house was once one hundred and ten feet long, with a gigantic kitchen and outstanding negro quarters.

6. (Further examples.) Spec. of any art form: associated with or characteristic of Negroes. Of clothes, fabrics, etc.: designed to be worn or used by Negroes.

1732 *South Carolina Gaz.* 1 Apr., He had on..blue Negro Boots. *Ibid.* 30 Sept. 4/2 Just imported, white and blue Negro Cloth. **1769**, etc. Negro cloth [in Dict., sense 7]. **1786** *Maryland Jrnl.* 26 Sept., Fine and coarse broadcloths; coatings; Negro cottons. **1818** *Amer. Beacon* (Norfolk, Va.) 19 Dec. 1/4 Negro cotton. 10 Bales just received. **1841** *Picayune* (New Orleans) 3 Mar. 3 Negro Blankets, in store and for sale. **1844** J. COWELL *30 Yrs. among Players* 66 [Blakeley] was the first to introduce negro singing on the American stage. **1847** F. A. KEMBLE *Let.* Dec. in *Rec. Later Life* (1882) III. 279 Do you remember that delightful Negro song, the 'Invitation to Hayti'? **1855** A. M. MURRAY *Lett.* (1856) 395 This morning we have had some negro music. **1912** *Chambers's Jrnl.* Jan. 23/1 Negro songs have always been popular among us, and deservedly so. **1925** W. S. BRAITHWAITE in A. Locke *New Negro* 39 It was the stirring year of 1917 that heard the first real masterful accent in Negro poetry. **1936** A. LOCKE *Negro & his Mus.* i. 1 Negro music is the closest approach America has to a folk music, and so Negro music is almost as important for the musical culture of America as it is for the spiritual life of the Negro. *Ibid.* ii. 15 The Negro dance has the feature, characteristic of Russian, Polish and other Slavic folk-dances, of sudden changes of the pace and daring climaxes of tempo. **1960** A. E. KEEP tr. *Leuzinger's Afr.* (1962) I. i. 13 Negro art attracts and enthrals us by its emotional vigour and clarity of form. *Ibid.* vi. 52 Is negro art primitive? No—if the word 'primitive' is understood to mean something crude, barbaric and contemptible. Yes—if by 'primitive' we mean something honourable, as the term is applied, for instance, to the Fauvists in European painting. **1963** *Times Lit. Suppl.* 18 Jan. 43/2 The rock 'n roll and Negro-jazz rhythms of his American cycle of poems. **1970** R. D. ABRAHAMS *Positively Black* ii. 51 Distrust of even one's closest friends is a constant theme of Negro life and Negro fictions.

7. Negro Renaissance (see quot. 1973); **Negro spiritual,** an American Negro religious song; **Negro State,** any of the Southern States of America in which slavery was legal; **negro yam:** for '*Dioscorea alata*' substitute '*Dioscorea sativa*'; (earlier and later examples).

1925 A. LOCKE *New Negro* p. xi, We speak of the offerings of this book..as culled from the first fruits of the Negro Renaissance. **1952** B. ULANOV *Hist. Jazz in Amer.* (1958) x. 103 The Negro poets who won such a large audience for their work, good, bad, and indifferent, in the intense days of the so-called Negro Renaissance. **1964** J. H. CLARKE *Harlem* 16 The stock market collapse of 1929 marked..the end of the period known as the Negro Renaissance. **1973** BASKIN & RUNES *Dict. Black Culture* 324 *Negro Renaissance*, a creative outpouring in art, music, and literature in the 1920s, giving expression to the discontent of the Negro... Writers of the twenties displayed considerable talent..in developing Negro themes in a highly personal way. **1867** *Atlantic Monthly* June 685/1, I had for many years heard of this class of songs under the name of 'Negro Spirituals'. **1928** *Observer* 22 July 21/1 As important..is their singing of negro spirituals and 'work songs'. **1949** *Oregonian* (Portland) 10 Aug. 8/4 He found time to write books on his hobbies, on alligators and on Negro spirituals. **1970** *Oxf. Compan. Mus.* (ed. 10) 1064/2 The words of Negro spirituals are for the most part adaptations of passages from the Bible. **1780** in *Essex Inst. Hist. Coll.* (1877) XIII. 220 You did not carry home contemptible Ideas enough of the negro States or of this great Braggadocio. **1809** *Deb. Congress U.S.* 20 Jan. (1853) 1152 The Potomac the boundary—the Negro states by themselves! **1696**

H. SLOANE *Catal. Plantarum Jamaica* 219 Negro Country Yam. **1707** —— *Voy. Jamaica* I. 140 Negro Country Yams. This has a great Root a Foot broad... They being cut into pieces and boiled or rosted are eaten by Negros, Slaves, or Europeans, instead of Bread. **1756** P. BROWNE *Civil & Nat. Hist. Jamaica* 359 The Negro Yam... The Yam. Both these plants are cultivated for food, the roots, which grow very large, being mealy and easy of digestion. **1814** J. LUNAN *Hortus Jamaicensis* II. 308 This [sc. *Dioscorea sativa*] is commonly called negro yam. **1864** A. H. R. GRISEBACH *Flora Brit. W. Indian Islands* 789/2 Yams, Negro country: *Dioscorea alata.* **1953** *Caribbean Q.* II. IV. 32 *Dioscorea sativa* the so-called negro-yam, may have been indigenous, for it..sometimes grows wild; but more probably the wild specimens were originally escapes from cultivation. **1971** *Jamaican Weekly Gleaner* 3 Nov. 34/3 (Advt.), Negro yams, yellow yams, sweet potatoes.

Negrodom. (Earlier and later examples.)
1847 *Congress. Globe* 13 Feb. App. 376/1 Our measures have given all that wide region to the empire of negrodom. **1942** Z. N. HURSTON in A. Dundes *Mother Wit* (1973) 31/2 Neither the top nor the bottom of Negrodom. *Ibid.* 32/1 A flight away from Negrodom.

negrofy, *v.* (Earlier example.)
a **1790** B. FRANKLIN *Autobiogr.* in *Writings* (1905) I. 391 Finding he was likely to be negrofied himself, he..grew tir'd of the contest.

negro-head. Add: **2.** (Earlier example.)
1809 'D. KNICKERBOCKER' *Hist. N.Y.* II. vi. ii. 88 He.. thrust a prodigious quid of negro head tobacco into his left cheek.
5. = NIGGERHEAD 2.
1910 F. WOOD-JONES *Coral & Atolls* xxiv. 284 There are many enormous 'negro heads' upon the windward barrier flats of the Southern islands of the Cocos-Keeling atoll. **1943** BAKER *Dict. Austral. Slang* (ed. 3) 54 *Nigger-head*, an anthill-like peak of coral showing above water. Also called 'negro-head'. **1963** D. W. & E. E. HUMPHRIES tr. *Termier's Erosion & Sedimentation* xiii. 280 Reefs are broken into blocks, the large mushroom-shaped fragments are thrown up onto the beaches, where they form 'negro-heads'.

Negroish, *a.* (Earlier example.)
1789 J. MORSE *Amer. Geogr.* 65 The children, by being brought up, and constantly associating with the negroes.. contract a negroish kind of accent and dialect.

Negroism. Add: **1.** (Earlier and later examples.)
1847 *Congress. Globe* 29th Congress 2 Sess. App. 323/2 He..thanked God that he voted against that Wilmot proviso. It smelt rank of negroism. **1935** Z. N. HURSTON *Mules & Men* (1970) 17 When I pitched headforemost into the world I landed in the crib of negroism. **1970** D. CAUTE *Fanon* vi. 80 The vague, cosmic cults of Negroism and Arabism.
2. (Earlier and later examples.)
1859 BARTLETT *Dict. Amer.* (ed. 2) p. viii, The term 'Americanisms'..may then be said to include the following classes of words:..8. Negroisms. **1930** G. B. JOHNSON in B. A. Botkin *Treas. S. Folklore* (1949) IV. iii. 697 *Ax*, ask. Not a Negroism, but a usage which was once good English.

Negroization (nīːgrọ,əizēⁱ·ʃən). [f. NEGRO + -IZATION.] A making or becoming Negro in character.
1898 A. J. BUTLER tr. *Ratzel's Hist. Mankind* III. 258 From them Rohlfs expects an ever-increasing 'negroisation' of the Libyan oasis.

Negroland. Add earlier and later examples and example referring to the Southern States of the U.S.A.
1756 J. WESLEY *Works* (1872) IX. 209 Either in Negroland or round the Cape of Good Hope. **1836** F. A. KEMBLE *Let.* 5 Oct. in *Rec. Later Life* (1882) I. 66 The nearest town to this estate, Brunswick, is..a wretched hole, where I am assured it will be impossible to obtain a decent lodging for me... The owner will go..without us, on his expedition to Negroland. **1931** *Times Lit. Suppl.* 26 Feb. 145/1 Africa south of the Sahara is by no means coterminous with negroland.

Negroness (nī·gronės). [f. NEGRO + -NESS.] Negro qualities and characteristics in the aggregate.
1946 *Sat. Rev. Lit.* (U.S.) 29 June 42 The native suffixes *-hood*, *-ness*, and *-wright* have given us *Hottentothood* and *sahib-hood*; *at-easeness*, *Negroness*, and *tasklessness*; and *filmwright*. **1958** J. KEROUAC *Subterraneans* 31 The old eccentric lady not any more conscious of her *Negroness*. **1965** *Times Lit. Suppl.* 25 Nov. 1047/5 He had to confront being 'Baldwin' without atrophying into an idol, and his method is to transcend enforced initial Negroness, even to avoid being 'a Negro writer', or any 'Negro' trap. **1971** G. S. HOLT in T. Kochman *Rappin' & Stylin' Out* (1972) 155 So identifying someone as 'Jew' or 'Negro' devastates the category of Negroness or Jewishness more so than saying Negro *writer*, Jewish *doctor*. **1973** *Black World* Mar. 19 Bakara asks: 'Where is the Negro-ness of a literature written in imitation of the meanest of social intelligences to be found in American culture, *i.e.*, the white middle class?'

‖ **negroni** (nĭgrō·ni). Also **negrone.** [It.] A drink made from gin, vermouth, and Campari; a glass of this.
1950 E. HEMINGWAY *Across River* vi. 34 They were drinking *negronis*, a combination of two sweet vermouths and seltzer water. **1952** P. BONNER *SPQR* (1953) xx. 174, I called the barman for a *negrone*. **1960** I. FLEMING *For your Eyes Only* v. 146 Bond nodded. 'A Negroni. With Gordon's, please.' **1960** B. MARSHALL *Divided Lady* II. vi. 129 Before I had finished my third *negrone*. **1972** J. D. BUCHANAN *Professional* xvi. 158 Summoning the waiter he ordered a Negroni.

Negrophil. Add further examples of spelling -phile; also example of *attrib.* use.
1934 R. CAMPBELL *Broken Record* iii. 58 Pringle obtained and asserted the freedom of the Press... He had a negrophile bias and misrepresented much. **1936** H. PREECE in A. Dundes *Mother Wit* (1973) 36/2 Our indictments of the professional Negrophiles need not even be so personal. **1958** *Times Lit. Suppl.* 10 Jan. 21/1 Many of the first explorers had an objectivity and sympathy with the indigenous people which would startle a modern negrophile.

Negrophilism. (Earlier and later examples.)
1846 *Congress. Globe* 18 May 838/1 The gentleman from Ohio.., the advocate of *negro-philism.* **1859** *Harper's Mag.* Oct. 694/2 If negrophilism seeks to substitute the Chinaman or the Indiaman for the African, it will neglect all the lessons of experience. **1860** A. B. LONGSTREET in *U.S. Ann. Treas. Rep.* 475 A man..of more negrophilism than brains. **1889** FARMER *Americanisms* 386/2 *Negrophilism*, the anti-slavery movement.

Negrophilistic (nīːgrofili·stik), *a. rare.* [f. NEGROPHIL + -ISTIC.] Having Negrophil characteristics.
1899 *Leisure Hour* Dec. 168/2 The Colonists have always despised the volume [Thomas Pringle's South African poems] because of the Negrophilistic character of some of the pieces therein.

Negrophobe (nī·grofōᵘb). [f. NEGRO + -PHOBE.] One who has a violent aversion to or hatred of Negroes.
1900 *Spectator* 15 Sept. 329/2 Negrophiles may be.. wiser as well as better men than negrophobes. **1962** C. L. BARNHART in Householder & Saporta *Probl. Lexicogr.* 179 A vulgar, offensive term of contempt, as used by Negrophobes. **1974** *Guardian* 23 Jan. 12/2 Edward Long, historian, statistician and so-called absentee sinecurist and negrophobe.

Negrophobia. (Earlier and further examples.)
1819 *Niles' Reg.* XVI. Suppl. 173/2 The gentleman from Kentucky..has charged us..with being under the influence of *negrophobia.* **1859** N. P. WILLIS *Convalescent* 173 His hatred of colored people amounted to a negrophobia. **1945** MENCKEN *Amer. Lang.* Suppl. I. 408 Whenever a new suffix appears in the United States, it is put to use. An example is..*-phobia*, borrowed from the psychiatrists, and made to do heavy duty in a multitude of nouns designating violent aversions *e.g.*,..*negrophobia*..with attendant adjectives in *-phobic.*

Nehru (nēə·ru). [f. the name of Jawaharlal *Nehru* (1889–1964), first Prime Minister of independent India from 1947 to 1964.] A garment of the style often worn by Nehru, consisting of a long narrow jacket with a high, stand-up collar. Usually *attrib.*, as *Nehru coat, collar, jacket, suit*, etc.
1967 *N.Y. Times* 24 May 46 Variations on the narrow 'Nehru' jacket with the stand-up collar continue. **1967** *Time* 25 Aug. 38 There came the groom,..wearing baggy trousers, a white, Nehru-collar tunic with red trim and cowboy boots. **1968** *N.Y. Times* 6 June 50, I wouldn't wear Nehrus or those damn beads either. **1968** *Punch* 24 July 107/2 In, says an informed source, are 'the Nehru coat and the Nehru suit'. Gandhi's turn next? **1969** C. F. BURKE *God is Beautiful, Man* (1970) 47 A new chain to wear with his turtle neck sweater and Nehru jacket. **1971** 'G. BLACK' *Time for Pirates* ii. 33 The man is tall for a Chinese and very thin. He wears a white Nehru jacket over black cotton jeans. **1973** *Caribbean Contact* Feb. 9/4 The Ambassador for the People's Republic of China stands in a corner with the interpreter, wearing a black, Nehru-style shirt.

neighborite (nēⁱ·bŏrəit). *Min.* [f. the name of Frank *Neighbor* (see quot. 1961) + -ITE[1].] A fluoride of sodium and magnesium, $NaMgF_3$, which occurs as colourless orthorhombic crystals, isostructural with perovskite.
1961 E. C. T. CHAO et al. in *Amer. Mineralogist* XLVI. 379 The mineral is named 'neighborite' in grateful acknowledgement of the continued friendly interest and helpfulness of Mr. Frank Neighbor, District Geologist of the Sun Oil Co. at Salt Lake City. *Ibid.* 380 Neighborite was first found as clusters of pink and brown rounded grains in a dark brown to grayish black dolomitic oil shale of the Green River formation of South Ouray, Utah. **1967** *Doklady Earth Sci.* CLXXIV. 140/1 In the USSR neighborite was detected in alkalic metasomatite developed in the Western Urals from porphyry tuff and argillaceous carbonate sediments of Proterozoic age. **1971** *Amer. Mineralogist* LVI. 1520 Neighborite is synthesised from NaF and MgF_2 via a eutectic solidification process in which the product is a two-phase mixture of NaF and $NaMgF_3$.

neighbourhood. Add: **3. c.** *Math.* (i) The set of points whose distance from a given point is less than, or is less than or equal to, some non-zero, usu. small, value (see also quot. 1921).
1891 G. L. CATHCART tr. *Harnack's Introd. Study Elem. Differential & Integral Calculus* I. v. 26 We have attained the conception of the Region or Neighbourhood of a point. By it we mean an arbitrarily small but still always finite interval at both sides of the value *x.* **1921** H. S. CARSLAW *Introd. Theory Fourier's Series & Integrals* (ed. 2) iii. 52 Sometimes the neighbourhood is meant to include the point $x = a$ itself. In this case it is defined by $|x-a| \leq h$. **1939** M. H. A. NEWMAN *Elem. Topology of Plane Sets of Points* ii. 20 If *a* is a point of a space with the metric ρ, and ϵ any positive number, the set of all points, *x*, satisfying $\rho(x, a) < \epsilon$ is called a spherical neighbourhood, and more particularly an ϵ-neighbourhood of *a.* **1956** E. M. PATTERSON *Topology* ii. 22 A convenient way of describing continuity is to introduce the idea of neighbourhood... The set of points whose coordinates *x* satisfy $|x-x_0| < \epsilon$ is called the ϵ-neighbourhood of x_0; it consists of all points whose distance from x_0 is less than ϵ. **1971** M. GEMIGNANI *Introd. Real Analysis* iii. 32 We denote the *p*-neighborhood of *a* by $N(a, p)$. (Thus, $N(a, p)$ consists of all real numbers within distance *p* of *a*.) *Ibid.*, Not only is every *p*-neighborhood an open interval, but every open interval is a *p*-neighborhood.
(ii) Any open set containing a given point or non-empty set; also, any set containing such an open set.
1934 C. C. KRIEGER tr. *Sierpiński's Introd. Gen. Topology* ii. 33 We shall understand by a neighbourhood of an element *a* any open set containing *a.* **1946** E. LEHMER tr. *Pontrjagin's Topological Groups* ii. 28 We shall give a method of defining a topological space by means of neighborhoods rather than by means of the operation of closure. This method is rather important and is often used as the foundation of the axiomatic treatment of the concept of a topological space. **1964** W. J. PERVIN *Found. Gen. Topology* iii. 45 A set is open iff it is a neighborhood of each of its points. **1967** I. ADLER *New Look at Geom.* xii. 372 The sets that belong to this special class of subsets in a topological space are called the open sets of the space or the neighborhoods of the space. **1968** S. MORAN tr. *H. Schubert's Topology* 86 An open set is a neighbourhood of every one of its subsets.
6. c. In urban planning and development, a small sector of a larger inhabited area with an integrated community provided with its own shops and other facilities.
1951 *Social Aspects Town Devel. Plan* (Univ. Liverpool, Social Sci. Dept.) ii. 25 It must be emphasised that the essence of a Neighbourhood from the point of view of the planner and sociologist alike, is the opportunity it provides for people to meet together, to share the burdens of daily life, and to co-operate in an endeavour to overcome their common problems. **1961** *Listener* 2 Nov. 702/2 People are beginning..to insist that their local authorities give proper consideration to all those aspects of life which make a neighbourhood different from an estate. **1961** *Observer* 3 Dec. 23/3 The principle, so depressingly practised in the first batch of British new towns, of grouping low-density housing in so-called neighbourhoods, punctuated by random acres of open space and served by small shopping centres. **1973** *Country Life* 6 Dec. 1952/1 One of London's greatest attractions is..its village-like localities. In planning jargon these are called neighbourhoods or..environmental areas.
7. *neighbourhood bookie, bookstore, centre, council, grocery, market, park, road, school, shop, shopping centre, store, unit*; **neighbourhood friendly** *U.S. colloq.*, a well-known local shop, a neighbourhood shop.
1971 *Black Scholar* June 6/1 A man of some kind is usually around. He may be a boyfriend, an uncle or just the neighborhood bookie. **1973** *N.Y. Law Jrnl.* 17 Apr., Each appellant managed a large neighborhood bookstore. **1961** *Listener* 28 Sept. 470/3 The idea that a neighbourhood centre was a sort of rag-bag where you put all the social functions if you could not find anywhere else to put them. **1973** *Guardian* 24 Dec. 13/6 The idea of neighbourhood councils or 'community councils' or 'urban parish councils' is based on the simple proposition that there is no urban equivalent of the rural parish council and that there should be. **1970** J. HANSEN *Fadeout* (1972) xx. 167 But those envelopes were there. Nine of them. The kind you buy at your neighbourhood friendly. In packs of a dozen. **1966** B. H. DEAL *Fancy's Knell* v. 67 The supermarkets had killed the neighborhood grocery. **1938** *Richmond* (Va.) *News-Leader* 28 Sept. 1/3 The rush of tobacco to market has operated greatly to the advantage of the smaller towns of the belt. Leaf that once was sold in the big centers of North Carolina and Virginia is overflowing into the neighborhood markets. **1961** L. MUMFORD *City in Hist.* xvi. 502 The neighborhood park, conceived either as a Greenbelt around the neighborhood,..or as a ribbon of internal green. **1972** *Village Voice* (N.Y.) 1 June 16/3 Proceeds of the fair will help the association purchase two vacant lots to be developed into a neighborhood park. **1835** W. G. SIMMS *Partisan* II. xxviii. 266 A small track—a common wagon or neighborhood road—wound into the forest. **1843** 'R. CARLTON' *New Purchase* i. 89 Notice here, a neighborhood road does not imply necessarily much proximity of neighbours. **1842** *Southern Lit. Messenger* VIII. 65/1 As this was what is called a 'neighborhood school', the pupils necessarily came from a great distance. **1967** *New Yorker* 31 May 88/2 School integration and the preservation of neighborhood schools have been white-collar movements. **1973** *Times* 19 Apr. 18/1 The tendency for neighbourhood schools to develop on class lines. **1966** B. H. DEAL *Fancy's Knell* v. 67 The shopping centers had killed the neighborhood shops. **1968** *Guardian* 26 Mar. 9/3 Her customers..used to shop in the West End, but are thankful to find a first-rate fashion shop nearer home. The success of such 'neighbourhood shops'..is an interesting trend. **1961** *Listener* 28 Sept. 471/1 Strong neighbourhood shopping centres. **1949** E. S. GARDNER in *Argosy* Apr. 108/3 In that district of small neighbourhood stores, he's in a position to keep irregular hours. **1974** *Amer. Speech 1971* XLVI. 76 *Grocery store*,.. neighbourhood store. **1943** *Archit. Rev.* XCIII. 91/1 Five such residential units make up into one neighbourhood

unit of approximately a thousand families. **1953** P. C. Berg *Dict. New Words* 114/1 *Neighbourhood unit*, one of the residential areas in a planned town, containing about 10,000 inhabitants, complete with schools, shops, and a community centre of its own. **1961** E. A. Powdrill *Vocab. Land Planning* iii. 40 It is by now a fundamental concept of town and country planning that the rehabilitation of existing towns and the building of new towns should be based on the 'neighbourhood unit' principle. **1966** *Listener* 19 May 729/3 It was interesting to discover how much Patrick Abercrombie's neighbourhood-unit concept..had influenced Moscow planners.

b. Attrib. phr. *the, your,* etc., *friendly neighbourhood,* applied to a well-known and popular local person or thing; also *ironical. colloq.*

1955 W. Gaddis *Recognitions* II. ii. 366 Just tell Mummy to ask about *Cuff* next time she visits her friendly neighborhood druggist. **1968** *Peace News* 25 Oct. 7 (*heading*) Your friendly neighbourhood senior detective officer. **1971** *Guardian* 4 June 5/5 Their friendly neighbourhood stockbroker gave his talents free. **1973** 'R. MacLeod' *Nest of Vultures* vii. 154, I feel like I've just made a date with the friendly neighbourhood vampire. **1974** *Times* 22 Mar. 21/4 (*heading*) Your friendly neighbourhood fuel cell.

neighbourize (nē^i·bərəiz), *v. rare.* [f. Neighbour *sb.* + -ize.] *intr.* To associate with others as neighbours; to act in a neighbourly fashion.

1899 G. B. Burgin *Bread of Tears* I. ii. 43 We thought we'd just neighbourise, and happen in to hear what it says.

Neil Robertson stretcher (nī^ə:l rǫ·bəɹtsən). [App. f. a proper name.] (See quots. 1941, 1967.)

1941 N. Hammer *Warwick & Tunstall's First Aid* (ed. 18) xviii. 242 The Neil Robertson stretcher (the hammock stretcher) is made of split bamboo sewn onto stout canvas, on the principle of Gooch splinting. It surrounds and encloses the patient completely and rigidly. **1959** *Times* 16 Mar. (Port of London Suppl.) p. xvi/3 All boats carry a Neil Robertson stretcher designed to remove casualties from such awkward places as the hold or engine room of a ship. **1967** J. Wainwright *Worms must Wait* lxii. 154 The 'Neil-Robertson' stretcher was a contraption of stout canvas, bamboo, leather straps, buckles and rope. Its purpose was (to quote the book of words) 'to lift casualties in any position through small hatches, man-holes, sewer ventilators and for lowering from heights'. **1974** P. McCutchan *Call for S. Shard* xiv. 134 Tuball and his plastered leg safely strapped into a Neil Robertson stretcher with his crutches attached.

‖ **neinei** (nē·nē). *N.Z.* Also **nene.** [Maori.] A New Zealand shrub or small tree of the genus *Dracophyllum*, esp. *D. latifolium*, of the family Epacridaceæ, distinguished by clusters of long, narrow leaves; also called *grass-tree.*

1858 S. P. Smith in N. M. Taylor *Early Travellers N.Z.* (1959) 355 Some of us..found what was to us quite a new kind of tree, called *Nei nei.* **1879** J. von Haast *Geol. Provinces Canterbury & Westland, N.Z.* 78 An undescribed, superb, tree-like *Dracophyllum*..began to appear here... The natives call it Nene. **1882** W. D. Hay *Brighter Britain!* II. 197 The Neinei..is but a small tree. **1949** P. Buck *Coming of Maori* (1950) II. x. 262 The wood [of this flute] is *neinei.* **1966** *Encycl. N.Z.* I. 498/2 Some of the larger-leaved species [of *Dracophyllum*] like nei-nei or *D. latifolium* are true forest plants.

neither. **A.** *adv.* **3. b.** Delete †*Obs.* and add further examples.

1909 L. M. Montgomery *Anne of Avonlea* x. 98 'Davy declares he never saw her since I left.' 'Neither I did,' avowed Davy. **1926** J. Black *You can't Win* xiii. 165 'I wouldn't plead guilty to anything if I were you,' I advised him. 'Me, neither,' said his partner. **1973** R. Busby *Pattern of Violence* iv. 61 'Can you place either of them?' The young detective shook his head. 'Me neither.'

nekoite (ne·ko͵əit). *Min.* [anagram of Okenite.] A triclinic form of the hydrated calcium silicate $Ca_3Si_6O_{15}.6H_2O$ found at Crestmore, California, which differs from the okenite of other localities in its optical and X-ray properties.

1956 Gard & Taylor in *Mineral. Mag.* XXXI. 20 The Crestmore material must be regarded as a new species. Because of the likeness to okenite, the anagram *nekoite* is suggested. **1962** *Ibid.* XXXIII. 70 Nekoite was discovered at Crestmore, California, by Eakle (1917), who identified it as okenite. **1971** *Acta Crystallogr.* B.XXVII. 473/2 When fibre bundles of nekoite are heated to temperatures between 200 and 250°C water is lost reversibly, the apparent limiting water content of the crystal from the 'immediate weight-loss' curve corresponding to the composition $3CaO.6SiO_2.3H_2O$.

nekro-: see *necro-.

nekton (ne·ktǫn). *Zool.* Also **necton.** [ad. G. *necton, nekton* (E. Haeckel 1890, in *Jenaische Zeitschr. Naturw.* XXV. 251, 252), f. Gr. *νεκτόν*, neut. of *νεκτός* swimming, f. *νεῖν* to swim.] A collective name for aquatic animals that are able to swim and move about independently. Cf. *benthos, Plankton. So **nekto·nic** *a.*

1893 G. W. Field tr. *Haeckel's Planktonic Stud.* in *Rep. U.S. Comm. Fisheries 1889–91* 580 We must distinguish the actively swimming nekton from the passively drifting plankton. **1895** *Natural Sci.* July 31 The Plankton, Nekton, and Benthos form three well-marked communities of organisms. **1903** *Amer. Geologist* XXXI. 211 It has been asserted..that slowly creeping organisms preceded the planktonic and nektonic forms. **1909** *Chambers's Jrnl.* Dec. 784/1 The Nekton are those animals which are capable of vigorous swimming movements, and are able to migrate freely from one part of the sea to another. **1923** *Nature* 17 Mar. 374/2 The author concludes that the kerogen has arisen from 'nectons and kelps' which have 'been repeatedly buried by ash and detritus from submarine volcanoes'. **1923** *Glasgow Herald* 17 Nov. 4/2 The animals of the sea are sometimes divided into the Nekton and the Plankton, the swimmers and the drifters. **1956** *Nature* 25 Feb. 375/2 Only one nektonic species apart from *Thyrsites* itself has been found to occur in Bass Strait at the time of year in question. **1969** *Austral. Law Jrnl.* XLIII. 430 The traditional biological classification of fish and fish like creatures into drifters or plankton, swimmers or necton, and the bottom dwellers or benthos. *Ibid.*, The nectonic species of fish are divided into demersal and pelagic. **1974** Lucas & Critch *Life in Oceans* ii. 25 The nekton comprises all those animals, such as squid, cuttlefish, fishes, seals and whales, which are able to swim more or less powerfully and which are therefore independent of water movements for transport. **1975** *Nature* 17 Apr. 591/2 The stomachs of the fish contained the remains of nektonic, planktonic and benthic organisms.

‖ **nekulturny** (nekultu·rni), *sb.* and *a.* Also **nekulturniiy.** [Russ. *nekul'turnyĭ* uncivilized.] **A.** *sb.* One who is by Russian standards considered unenlightened, a boor. **B.** *adj.* Not having cultured manners, boorish. Cf. *kulturny.

1959 I. R. Levine *Real Russia* xxiv. 347 It is *nekulturny* for a man..to put feet up on a desk, to cross legs, or to keep hands in trouser pockets. **1960** W. Miller *Russians as People* vi. 139 To accuse someone of being 'uncultured' (*nekulturny*) is not a light matter... It may signify that you do not clean your teeth, that you never read a book, or that you are pushing rudely or giving way to a coarse expression of opinion. **1962** J. Wade *Running Sand* xiii. 166 To dance so close to a woman was uncultured, *nekulturny*, a sign of western decadence. **1965** *New Statesman* 16 July 71/3 What bothers Washington is that the President is so determinedly *nekulturniiy.* **1967** J. Fores *Desirable Dictator* iv. 97 We are not gangsters, Mr. C.I.A. We leave that kind of *nekulturny* behaviour to the West.

nelia, var. *nealie.

nelly[2] (ne·li). Also **Nelly, Nellie.** [A fem. Christian name.] **1.** Slang phr. *not on your Nelly* [f. rhyming slang *Nelly Duff* = *puff* = breath of life], 'not on your life' (see *life *sb.* 3 d), not likely.

1941 *New Statesman* 30 Aug. 218/3 *Not on your Nelly Duff*,..not likely. **1961** *John o' London's* 14 Dec. 663/1 You might have thought Mr. Samuel Bronston would have rested... Not, as they say, on your nelly. **1961** Partridge *Adventuring among Words* xi. 55 The trouble begins when part, usually the latter part, of the rhyming phrase is omitted, as so often it is, as in..'not on your *Nellie*' for '...Nellie Duff!' = 'not on your *puff*' = 'not on your life' or 'most certainly not' or, less politely, 'like hell, I will!'. **1966** *Times* 15 May 9 That would mean me investing in another man's career. Not on your Nelly! **1968** *Manch. Guardian Weekly* 11 Apr. 15/1 So the Liberals dropped Acton and Dudley and concentrated on Warwick and Leamington? Not on your Nellie! **1972** *Times* 24 June 11/4 Ooh, no, not on your nelly, ah, fearless Francis! **1974** *Globe & Mail* (Toronto) 21 Sept. 35/2, I appear to be giving away most of the plot? Not on your nelly. That's only the beginning.

2. A cheap wine. *Austral. slang.*

1945 Baker *Austral. Lang.* ix. 166 Here is a group of indigenous terms used to describe cheap wines: *Africa speaks*,..*nelly, nelly's death* [etc.]. **1952** A. G. Mitchell in *Chambers's Shorter Eng. Dict.* Suppl., *Nelly*,..(*slang*) cheap wine.—phr. *on the nelly*, given to drinking cheap wine.

3. A weak-spirited or silly person; a homosexual. Also as quasi-adj., of feminine appearance, effeminate. Cf. *nice-nellyism.

1961 *Sunday Times* 17 Sept. 41/4 [Henry] Livings's latest work, 'Sacred Nit'... This same play, now called 'Big Soft Nellie', opens at the Oxford Playhouse. **1962** *Sunday Times* 29 Apr. 12/4 See, what you've got to do is get on the same wavelength as the nellies who write in. **1967** 'T. Wells' *Dead by Light of Moon* (1968) iv. 45 You don't suppose it could have anything to do with that Strangler business, do you? Not that I'm a nervous Nelly type. **1970** K. Platt *Pushbutton Butterfly* (1971) xvi. 182 He..puffed daintily on a long cigarette as he watched the nellies cruising to the 'tearoom'. **1971** *Psychiatry* XXXIV. 187/2 Some guy came up to me and tried to take me for some money, and I knew it, and he said, 'You know, you're very nellie.' **1972** B. Rodgers *Queens' Vernacular* 141 *Nelly*..outrageously effeminate; coy, silly. **1973** C. Wittman in P. Brown *Radical Psychol.* xix. 459 There is a tendency among 'homophile' groups to deplore gays who play visible roles—the queens and the nellies.

4. Slang phr. *sitting next to* (or *by, with*) *Nelly*, learning an occupation on the job by observing how others do it.

1963 J. U. Fraser *Psychol.* (ed. 2) xiv. 173 Observation of a skilled operator (often characterized as 'sitting next to Nellie'). **1966** *Guardian* 30 July 6/5 The generous 'General Trainees Scheme' which allows them to spend up to two years in different departments [of the BBC]—'sitting with Nellie', is the union phrase. **1972** *Listener* 10 Aug. 180/2 Journalists are the casual labourers of the intellectual world... Most training still consists of sitting next to Nellie. **1975** *New Society* 17 July 130/1 It was then made compulsory for doctors from overseas to 'sit by Nellie' for a month. Immigrant doctors had to complete satisfactorily a month's supervision under a consultant supervisor.

Nelson (ne·lsən). [App. f. a proper name.] **1.** *Wrestling.* The name of a class of holds in which one or both arms are passed under the opponent's from behind and the hand(s) applied to his neck; often with words prefixed to indicate the precise form of the hold, as *double nelson, *half nelson, (three-) quarter nelson.* Also *fig.*

1889 W. Armstrong *Wrestling* 233 Probably the most dangerous move in Lancashire and Cornwall and Devon wrestling..is what is called the 'Double Nelson'. **1893** *Lippincott's Mag.* Feb. 211 Among the many holds the Nelson is the most popular one with wrestlers, while the half-Nelson and half-walch-lock are next in order. **1897** [see *hammer-lock* (*hammer *sb.* 7)]. **1900** A. E. T. Watson *Young Sportsman* 644 The principal chips associated with catch as catch can wrestling are the double Nelson, the half Nelson, the heave, the Lancashire lock, the flying mare and the three-quarter Nelson. **1930** P. MacDonald *Link* ix. 168 They lose Dinwater—or lose half the Nelson they've got on him, so immediately they switch on to you.

2. The name of Admiral Lord *Nelson* (1758–1805) used *attrib.* in **Nelson cake** (see quot. 1966); **Nelson eye,** a blind eye: usu. *transf.* and *fig.* (cf. *eye *sb.*[1] 5 e); **Nelson knife,** a combined knife and fork for the use of a one-armed person; **Nelson's blood,** Navy rum; **Nelson touch,** a stroke, action, or manner characteristic of Nelson.

1909 *Daily Chron.* 16 Dec. 4/7 The Nelson cake consists of two thin pieces of reputed pastry, with a dark agglomeration between them of currants and sweet mush. **1966** F. Shaw et al. *Lern Yerself Scouse* 42 *Nelson cake*, a cake made from compressed, broken biscuits, pastry remnants etc. with dried fruit added: the whole soaked in syrup or burnt sugar and stacked in great piles. **1965** *New Society* 7 Jan. 12/3 The police made no attempt to arrest him. The State simply turns a Nelson eye to his presence. **1970** B. Turner *Another Little Death* xxiv. 149 It's often possible for the police to turn a Nelson eye to misdemeanours confessed to them if they can catch a blackmailer by doing so. **1973** J. Leasor *Mandarin Gold* i. 13 He makes most out of opium. Turning a Nelson eye to a trade he should be stamping out. **1902** *Chambers's Jrnl.* 4 Oct. 692/2 The mention of knife *and* fork attached to the one wrist is at first slightly puzzling; but probably the combination was what is called the 'Nelson knife', after its most distinguished user. The handle is like that of an ordinary table-knife; but the end of the blade, instead of being rounded off in the ordinary way, turns up at a right angle in its own plane, and is divided into four fork-prongs. **1974** *Times* 27 Nov. 17/6 A 'Nelson' knife..has a curved blade..and also teeth at the end of the blade... Nelson knives are a Government issue to those..who have lost an arm but they can also be purchased. **1925** Fraser & Gibbons *Soldier & Sailor Words* 166 *Nelson's Blood*, rum. Old Navy, and probably derived from the old story of the sailors on board the *Victory* tapping the cask in which Nelson's body was brought home and drinking the spirits. **1968** *Telegraph* (Brisbane) 26 June 45 To preserve Nelson's body it was placed in the ship's rum ration—that's why rum is now often referred to as 'Nelson's blood'. **1970** A. Draper *Swansong for Rare Bird* ix. 76 After all the Nelson's blood he'd stashed away the night before, I was surprised to see Gorgeous already there. **1805** Ld. Nelson *Let.* 25 Sept. in C. Oman *Nelson* (1947) xix. 607, I am anxious to join the fleet, for it would add to my grief if any other man was to give them the Nelson touch, which *we* say is warranted never to fail. *Ibid.* 1 Oct. 609 When I came to explain to them the '*Nelson touch*', it was like an electric shock. **1898** H. Newbolt *Island Race* 26 But cared greatly to serve God and the king, And keep the Nelson touch. **1963** *Economist* 12 Jan. 90/1 There was a 'Nelson touch' about the bloodless occupation of Jadotville. **1968** B. Turner *Sex Trap* xiii. 116 A little of the old Nelson touch is a big help in getting on with other departments. **1971** D. Cory *Sunburst* i. 20 Only the British, in Intelligence matters, retain the Nelson touch. *What's Fedora doing in Spain?*.. Up goes the old telescope. *Fedora? I see no Fedora.*

Nelsonian (nelsō^u·niăn), *a.* [f. *Nelson 2 + -ian.] Belonging to the time of Nelson; pertaining to, characteristic of, or relating to Nelson. Hence **Nelsonia·na,** a collection of papers, relics, etc., relating to Nelson.

1909 *Daily Chron.* 24 Feb. 3/5 A volume of Nelsoniana, which realised £145. **1913** *Q. Rev.* Apr. 461 We have only to go back to the eighties to find ships..with their..guns still mounted on the Nelsonian trucks worked by handspikes. **1931** *Times Lit. Suppl.* 17 Sept. 699/4 The Nelsonian mannerisms of words, dress and movements. **1958** *Listener* 2 Oct. 519/1 This valuable addition to Nelsoniana is the hundredth volume published by the Navy Records Society. **1969** *Sunday Times* 2 Nov. 8/7 Every editor knows how to turn a Nelsonian eye on a lack of O and A levels if he has a promising journalist before him. **1971** B. Callison *Plague of Sailors* iv. 134 It was conceivable that Their Lords of the Admiralty might have been prepared to turn a Nelsonian blind eye to H.M. Ships shooting up the odd foreign cargo boat.

Nelsonic (nelsǫ·nik), *a.* [f. *Nelson 2 + -ic.]

Pertaining to, relating to, or characteristic of Nelson.

1846 R. Ford *Gatherings from Spain* xvi. 188 They are ill-bred enough, in spite of the Montpensier marriage, and the Nelsonic achievements of Monsieur de Joinville, to consider the words as synonymes. **1909** *Daily Chron.* 13 Sept. 3/3 These Nelsonic qualities in Wolfe do not..come out very clearly in the letters. **1922** *Q. Rev.* Apr. 361 Orders of this nature..are always dangerous in the absence of the Nelsonic spirit. **1972** V. Gielgud *Black Sambo Affair* xxviii. 220 Various persons at the airports were given the hint to turn the Nelsonic blind eye.

nelumbium. In etym. for '(of De Jussieu, 1789)' substitute '(A. L. de Jussieu *Genera Plantarum* (1789) 68)'. Substitute for def.: An aquatic plant of the genus *Nelumbo*, belonging to the family Nymphæaceæ, formerly called *Nelumbium*, and including the East Indian or sacred lotus, *N. nucifera*, which has white or pink flowers, and the American lotus, *N. pentapetala*, which has fragrant yellow flowers. (Earlier and later examples.)

1806 *Curtis's Bot. Mag.* XXIII. 903 The Nelumbium is no longer found in Egypt. **1853** *Harper's Mag.* Nov. 751/2 The broad prairies..are also diversified by lakes, their surfaces shaded from the hot sun by the broad-leafed nelumbium. **1916** L. H. Bailey *Stand. Cycl. Hort.* IV. 2117/1 Nelumbiums are bold plants, suitable for large ponds. **1951** *Dict. Gardening* (R. Hort. Soc.) III. 1359/1 The Nelumbiums need rich soil.

nelumbo (nĭlɒ·mbo). [mod.L. (M. Adanson *Familles des Plantes* (1763) I. 73); see Nelumbium.] = Nelumbium (in Dict. and Suppl.).

1794 E. Darwin *Botanic Garden* (ed. 4) ii. 169 With sweet loquacity Nelumbo sails, Shouts to his shores, and parleys with his gales. *Ibid.*, Linneus [*sic*], who has enlisted all our senses into the service of botany, has observed this rattling of the Nelumbo. **1804** J. E. Smith *Exotic Botany* I. 61 A carved horn of a rhinoceros, sent to Linnæus from China,..is now before me... The whole inverted base of the horn is carved into an elegant leaf of *Nelumbo*, rising from the water. **1818** C. Abel *Narr. Journey in China* v. 103 Fields of *Nelumbo* rearing high its glossy leaves and gorgeous flowers..spread at our feet. **1850** S. F. Cooper *Rural Hours* 275 It is chiefly in our western waters that the Nelumbo is found. **1884** tr. *A. de Candolle's Orig. Cultivated Plants* ii. i. 75 The nelumbo of Indian origin has ceased to grow in Egypt. **1916** L. H. Bailey *Stand. Cycl. Hort.* IV. 2117/1 American Lotus, or Nelumbo... A bold and useful plant for colonizing. **1961** F. Perry *Water Gardening* (ed. 2) vii. 75 Nelumbos are reproduced by means of long creeping rootstocks. *Ibid.* 76 [In India] the stranger is presented with fruit and flowers laid in a simple basket fashioned from Nelumbo leaves.

nemasperm (ne·măspəɹm). *rare*⁻¹. [f. Gr. νῆμα thread + Sperm *sb.*] = Spermatozoon.

1922 Joyce *Ulysses* 411 Must we accept the view of Empedocles of Trinacria that the right ovary..is responsible for the birth of males or are the too long neglected spermatozoa or nemasperms the differentiating factors.

nematic (nemæ·tik), *a. Physical Chem.* [ad. F. *nématique* (G. Friedel 1922, in *Ann. de Physique* XVIII. 277), f. Gr. νῆμα, νηματ- thread: see -ic.] Applied to (the state of) a mesophase in which the molecules all have the same orientation but are not arranged in well-defined planes (as they are in a smectic phase). Also as *sb.*, a nematic substance.

1923 *Chem. Abstr.* XVII. 3267 A complete treatise upon the types and properties of matter existent between the true amorphous and cryst. states. The condition formerly designated as liquid crystals or anisotropic liquids is divided into 2 classifications: smectic.., and nematic. **1940** S. Glasstone *Text-bk. Physical Chem.* vii. 505 Nematic liquids are closer to true anisotropic liquids than are the smectic phases. **1971** *Physics Bull.* June 357/2 One of Marconi's exhibits at this year's Physics Exhibition demonstrated the effective use of organic nematic liquid crystals for visual display purposes. **1972** *Sci. Amer.* Mar. 39/1 (Advt.), We hereby announce the commercial availability of a multicomponent nematic that might suffice to call off some chemists. **1974** *Nature* 25 Jan. 178/3 Nuclear magnetic resonance spectra of molecules oriented in thermotropic and lyotropic nematics.

nematicide (ne·măt-, nemæ·tisəid). [irreg. f. Gr. νῆμα, νηματ- thread + -cide.] = *nematocide* s.v. Nemato-.

1933 [see *nematology]. **1952** *Nature* 8 Mar. 420/2 Work has already been published..on the value of chlorphenol as a nematicide. **1960** *Jrnl. R. Horticultural Soc.* LXXXV. ii. 54 Trial of various nematicides has shown that treatment with methyl bromide gives a yield almost double that of the control plots. **1972** P. Sivapalan in J. M. Webster *Economic Nematology* xiii. 308 In order to improve the trend of the decline in yield in the tea fields infested with *Pratylenchus loosi*, the field is ..treated with suitable nematicides.

Hence **nematici·dal** *a.* = *nematocidal* adj. s.v. *nemato-.

1950 *Helminthol. Abstr.* XVI. 122 Ethylene dibromide is highly nematicidal since 0·1 c.c. will eradicate nematodes from a gallon of soil. **1973** C. A. Anderson in G. Zweig *Analyt. Methods for Pesticides* VII. x. 253 Dasanit® exhibits both insecticidal and nematicidal activity.

nemato-. Add: **nematoci·dal** *a.*, characteristic of a nematocide; **nematogen**, add: [ad. Fr. *nématogène* (E. van Beneden 1876, in *Bull. Acad. R. Belgique* 2 Sér. XLI. 1195)]; (later examples).

1943 *Phytopathology* XXXIII. 1174 The nematocidal effect of chloropicrin was tested in the field against the root-knot nematode, *Heterodera marioni*. **1973** *Biol. Abstr.* LVI. 6884/2 Nematocidal activity, similar to that of trichothecin, was detected in mycelial extracts and volatile substances of *Arthrobotrys*, a predacious fungus. **1899** *Zoologischer Anzeiger* XXII. 171 The mother of vermiform embryos is called a nematogen, the mother of infusoriform embryos a rhombogen. **1972** *Sci. Amer.* Dec. 98/2 Two different wormlike stages of the Mesozoa have been described: 'nematogens' were reported to produce nematogens and 'rhombogens', whereas rhombogens were reported to produce infusoriform dispersal larvae and occasionally to both produce larvae and revert to the nematogen stage. Observations on laboratory populations of Mesozoa make this distinction untenable.

nematodiriasis (ne:mătodirəi·asis). [f. *Nematodir(us + *-iasis.] A disease of young lambs caused by the larvæ of nematodes of the genus *Nematodirus* and characterized by diarrhœa, loss of weight, and dehydration.

1957 Fraser & Stamp *Sheep Husbandry & Diseases* (ed. 3) x. 384 This disease for which the rather ugly word 'nematodiriasis' might be used is characterised by its sudden and dramatic appearance in low-ground flocks during late May and early June. **1967** *New Scientist* 13 July 63/3 Nematodiriasis, a worm-caused disease of young lambs. **1971** *Farmers Weekly* 19 Mar. 66 (Advt.), Frantin Paste halts the scours associated with nematodiriasis and other worm infestations in unweaned lambs.

nematodirus (ne:mătodəi·rɒs). [mod.L. (B. H. Ransom 1907, in *U.S. Dept. Agric. Bur. Anim. Ind.* No. 116. 4), f. Nemato(de *a.* and *sb.* + Gr. δειρή neck.] A parasitic nematode worm of the genus so called, belonging to the family Trichostrongylidæ, which is found in the intestine of many mammals and causes disease in young lambs. Also *attrib.*

1915 *Parasitology* VIII. 146 The *Nematodirus* larvae are able to withstand complete desiccation. **1934** *Jrnl. Agric. Sci.* XXIV. 207 *Nematodirus* larvae can regain the surface after being turned in by the plough. **1956** *Vet. Rec.* 21 July 471 (*title*) Some observations on Nematodirus Disease in Northumberland and Durham. **1957** Fraser & Stamp *Sheep Husbandry & Diseases* (ed. 3) x. 384 Until recently the worm nematodirus was thought to be relatively harmless to sheep. *Ibid.* 385 Nematodirus worms may be present in large numbers. **1960** *Farmer & Stock-breeder* 9 Feb. 64/3 Border farmers..who have never seen nematodirus and who have long ceased to drench for worms. **1963** *Times* 20 May 16/5 Forecasts could now be made of conditions likely to induce..fluke and nematodirus infections.

nematology (nemătǫ·lŏdʒi). [f. Nemat(ode *a.* and *sb.* + -ology.] The study of nematodes. So **nematolo·gical** *a.*, of or pertaining to this study; **nemato·logist**, a person making such a study.

1926 C. W. Stiles in Yorke & Maplestone *Nematode Parasites of Vertebrates* p. v, A few genera..were of some slight interest in human and veterinary medicine, but this fact played a distinctly secondary *rôle* in nematological studies... Zenker..and others, pointed out the far-reaching medical and economic bearings of nematology. **1933** T. Goodey *Plant Parasitic Nematodes* i. 2 In the United States of America these small forms are often called 'nemas'; a word introduced by the late Dr. N. A. Cobb together with several cognate terms such as nematology, nematologist, nematized, and nematicide, &c. **1960** *Times* 7 July 3/6 Research appointments in..plant nematology. **1961** G. Thorne *Princ. Nematology* p. ix, The writer is indebted to the..U.S. Department of Agriculture, for the opportunity to work on nematological problems in many parts of the United States. **1963** *New Scientist* 5 Sept. 490/1 The comparative effectiveness of four nematicides ..has recently been under investigation by the Nematology Department at Rothamsted Experimental Station. **1971** *Nature* 15 Jan. p. xvii (Advt.), A nematologist is required to work in some aspects of the biology of *Trichodorus* species. **1974** *Ibid.* 19 Apr. 715/3, I commend this book to all thoughtful nematologists, plant pathologists and ecologists.

nembie (ne·mbi). Also **nebbie, nemish, nemmie, nimby.** *U.S. colloq.* contractions of *Nembutal.

1950 [see *goof ball]. **1953** W. Burroughs *Junkie* (1972) ii. 23 This night Herman was knocked out on 'nembies' and his head kept falling down onto the bar. *Ibid.* iv. 40 Next day I was worse and could not get out of bed. So I stayed in bed taking nembies at intervals. *Ibid.* 158 *Nembies, Goof Balls, Yellow Jackets*...Nembutal capsules. **1969** R. R. Lingeman *Drugs from A to Z* 182 Nembutal... Slang names: nebbies, nemmies, nemish, yellow jackets. **1971** E. E. Landy *Underground Dict.* 139 Nembutal... Nemish, nemmie, nimby.

Nembutal (ne·mbiutæl). Also **nembutal.** [f. *Na*, chemical symbol for sodium (f. Na(trium) + initial letters of the elements of 5-*e*thyl-5-(1-*m*ethyl*but*yl)barbiturate, chemical name of the compound + *-al* (as in *Veronal, barbital*).] A proprietary name of pentobarbitone sodium, a short-acting barbiturate used as a hypnotic and an anticonvulsant. Also, a capsule of Nembutal.

[**1930** *Anaesthesia & Analgesia* IX. 215/2 Sodium ethyl 1-methyl butyl barbiturate (sodium embutal).] **1930** *Druggists Circular* Dec. 73/2 Nembutal, '844', a new pre-anesthetic sedative and hypnotic,..described as being effective in allaying the apprehension and fear of patients about to undergo an operation. **1931** *Lancet* 10 Jan. 74/1 (*heading*) Nembutal as a basal hypnotic in general anæsthesia. **1931** *Official Gaz.* (U.S. Patent Off.) 21 Apr. 560/1 Nembutal. For hypnotic sedative anesthetic compound. **1936** *Discovery* July 206/2 Another modern method of lessening nervous apprehension is to give the patient a sleeping draught the night before, and then in the morning, sometime before the operation, he is given a capsule of Nembutal or Pronocton. **1937** *Trade Marks Jrnl.* 15 Dec. 1474/1 Nembutal... Medicated preparations for use as hypnotics and sedatives. Abbott Laboratories Limited.., Montreal. **1953** W. Burroughs *Junkie* (1972) xiii. 128, I drank it all with two nembutals and slept several hours. *Ibid.* 158 Nembutal is a barbiturate used by junkies 'to take the edge off' when they can't get junk. **1959** N. Marsh *Singing in Shrouds* ix. 183 I've given her a nembutal. She's asleep in bed. **1962** A. Pirie *Lens Metabolism Rel. Cataract* 429 Rabbit lenses were obtained from the laboratory stock of Dutch rabbits killed by overdose of Nembutal. **1971** J. Wright *Coll. Poems* 274 This was the dream that woke me From nembutal sleep into the pains of grief.

nembutalized (nembiū·tələizd), *ppl. a. Vet.* [f. *Nembutal + -iz(e + -ed¹.] Anæsthetized with Nembutal.

1940 *Amer. Jrnl. Physiol.* CXXIX. 55 Two of the nembutalized dogs included in group II..were adrenalectomized. **1972** *Brain Res.* XXXVI. 350 Presynaptic inhibition in nembutalized cats.

nem. diss. (Further examples.)

1870 *Brewer's Dict. Phr. & Fable* 610/1 *Nem. diss.*, without a dissentient voice. (Latin, *nem'inĕ dissent'ientĕ*.) **1945** R. Hargreaves *Enemy at Gate* 123 The thanks of both Houses were duly agreed *nem. diss.*

Nemedian (nėmī·diăn). [f. *Nemed*, name of a legendary invader of Ireland + -ian.] One of the followers or descendants of Nemed of Scythia, who settled in Ireland, and who were later driven out by the Fomorians.

1876 *Encycl. Brit.* V. 299/2 We find four successive colonies mentioned in the following order:—*Nemedians, Firbolgs, Tuatha Dé Danann*, and *Milesians*. The *Nemedians* are said to have occupied the country during only two hundred years..owing to..their final overthrow, by a people..called Fomorians. **1898** [see *Fomorian]. **1911** *Encycl. Brit.* XIV. 757/2 After undergoing great hardship the Nemedians succeeded in destroying the fortress.. but the Fomorians received reinforcements... Of the Nemedians only thirty warriors escaped. **1950** *Funk's Stand. Dict. Folklore* II. 788/1 *Nemedians*, an early people who invaded Ireland; descendants of Nemed, son of Agnoman of Scythia; the third group to land in Ireland, following next after Partholan and his people. **1971** *It* 2–16 June 24/1 The Partholyans, Nemedians..are all remembered as being of semi-human stock.

nemesia (nĕmī·ʒiă). [mod.L. (E. P. Ventenat *Jardin de la Malmaison* (1803) 41), f. Gr. νεμέσιον a name used by Dioscorides for a similar plant.] An annual or perennial herb of the genus so called, native to southern Africa, belonging to the family Scrophulariaceæ, and usually bearing racemes of flowers of various colours.

1815 F. Pursh *Donn's Hortus Cantabrigiensis* (ed. 8) 196 Nemesia, [English name] Nemesia. Germander-leav. [*sic*]. **1829** J. C. Loudon *Encycl. Plants* 526 Nemesia, Vent[enat. English name] Nemesia...fœtid...horned. **1838** *Edwards's Bot. Reg.* XXIV. 39 (*heading*) Many-flowered Nemesia. **1892** *Gardeners' Chron.* 3 Sept. 269/3 There are many plants that vary to the extent of two or three colours in a wild state, but it is exceedingly rare to find them indulging in such wholesale variation as this Nemesia does. I have seen sixteen varieties of colour. **1927** *Observer* 20 Mar. 24/3 Modern florists and men of science..have made a rainbow out of a single colour (as in the nemesia). **1949** L. G. Green *In Land of Afternoon* v. 72 Hybrid gladioli, nemesias, even the Hottentot fig, were all startling novelties. **1970** C. Lloyd *Well-Tempered Garden* ii. 97 There is a freshness about a display of nemesias.

nemesism (ne·mĭsiz'm). *Psychol.* [f. Nemes(is + -ism.] Feelings of frustration turned inward and expressed by aggression directed against the self. So **nemesi·stic** *a.*, of or connected with nemesism.

1938 S. Rosenzweig in H. A. Murray *Explorations in Personality* vi. 588 The psycho-analyst might appropriately call the turning of aggression upon the individual's own self 'nemesism' from the name of the Greek goddess of vengeance. Nemesism could then be thought of as the counterpart of narcism. **1945** J. C. Flügel *Man, Morals & Society* vii. 78 We propose here to adopt Rosenzweig's suggestion and to use the term 'nemesism' as an alternative and technical term for 'aggression turned against the self'. *Ibid.* 87 The channel for the discharge of the children's aggressiveness towards the natural outer objects being blocked, there may be no alternative for them but to become nemesistic and intropunitive. *Ibid.* xi. 143 This nemesistic urge. **1946** [see *introjection 3 a]. **1968** P. McKellar *Experience & Behav.* ix. 248 Nemesism is a term coined by Flügel.

‖ **nemine contradicente** (ne·mini kǫ:ntrăditʃe·nti). See NEM. CON. Also **nemine con.**

1662 J. DAVIES tr. *A. Olearius's Voyages & Travels of Ambassadors* III. 77 Where, *nemine contradicente*, it was declar'd. **1718** VANBRUGH *Let.* 7 Aug. in *Athenæum* 30 Aug. (1890) 290/2 Amongst many material things in our conversation it was Nemine Contradicente agreed, That your Grace had writ a most Tyrannical letter. **1762** *Monthly Review* XXV. 363 The very vote that should be passed in our favour, would, in all likelihood, be a new grievance; as we should possibly see the honest English resolution, dated, *Die Mercurii, Feb.* 10mo, and concluded with a *Nemine Contradicente.* **1766** H. BROOKE *Fool of Qual.* II. x. 145 They concluded, *nemine con.* to get as speedily as they might from the ministers of darkness. **1962** *Listener* 10 May 798/2 The decision, although not strictly unanimous, can be described as *nemine contradicente.* **1966** *Rep. Comm. Inquiry Univ. Oxf.* I. 316 A special resolution..shall be published..and shall be deemed to have been approved *nemine contradicente.*

nemish, nemmie: see *NEMBIE.

nemmind, nemmine (ne·məin(d), nem-əi·n(d)), representation of a colloq. pronunciation of *never mind.* Chiefly *U.S.*

1914 *Dialect Notes* IV. 77 *Nemmind!*..Contraction of *never mind!* **1935** R. BASS in A. Dundes *Mother Wit* (1973) 389 Nemmine dat. **1960** N. HILLIARD *Maori Girl* III. ix. 241 'You better not do that. They might put you in jail.' 'Nemmine. I get all the baby things, that's all I'm worried about.'

nemo (nī·mo). *U.S.* [Etym. unknown.] (See quots.)

1937 *Printers Ink Monthly* May 39/3 *Nemo,* any program originating outside of the broadcasting studios. A collection of 'remote'. **1942** BERREY & VAN DEN BARK *Amer. Thes. Slang* §619/2 A program originating outside the studio and transmitted to the studio for broadcasting. .. Nemo. **1950** CHESTER & GARRISON *Radio & Television* 527 *Nemo,* a remote, a program originating away from the studio. **1960** O. SKILBECK *ABC of Film & T.V.* 89 *Nemo* (American), a telecast from location: an outside broadcast. **1961** H. B. JACOBSON *Mass Communications Dict.* 222 *Nemo,* a program originating outside of the station's studios.

nenadkevichite (nenæ·dkĕvitʃəit). *Min.* [ad. Russ. *nenadkevichit* (Kuz'menko & Kazakova 1955, in *Dokladȳ Akad. Nauk SSSR* C. 1159), f. the name of K. A. *Nenadkevich* (b. 1880), Russian mineralogist: see -ITE[1].] A hydrated silicate of sodium, calcium, niobium, and titanium, $(Na,Ca)(Nb,Ti)Si_2O_7.2H_2O$, which is found as pale yellow orthorhombic crystals.

1955 *Mineral. Abstr.* XII. 569 (*heading*) Nenadkevichite —a new mineral. **1965** *Doklady Acad. Sci. U.S.S.R. Earth Sci. Sect.* CLX. 118/1 Among the natrolite and feldspar are..large (to 10 cm and more) dull flakes of nenadkevichite of a pale to pinkish yellow color. **1972** *Mineral. Abstr.* XXIII. 225/2 Localities are described representing the alkalic complex of Augusta County [Virginia]... Associated with the alkalic rocks are nenadkevichite, astrophyllite, and bastnäsite.

nenadkevite (nenæ·dkĕvəit). *Min.* [ad. Russ. *nenadkevit,* f. as prec.] Any member of a range of isomorphous, basic, hydrated silicates of uranium(IV), uranium(VI), magnesium, calcium, thorium, and lead.

1955 *1st Internat. Conf. Peaceful Uses Atomic Energy: U.S.S.R. Sci. & Techn. Exhibition* (Eng. ed.) 7 Of interest in the second group of silicates containing tetra- and hexavalent uranium is the new mineral species nenadkevite... This mineral is deposited from hydrothermal solutions in the form of veins. **1960** *Mineral. Abstr.* XIV. 401/1 Rarer uranium deposits include those in which the ore mineral is the silicate nenadkevite.

‖ **nene** (nē[1]·nē[1]). Also **néné.** [Hawaiian.] = *Hawaiian goose* (*HAWAIIAN *a.* and *sb.* II).

1902 H. W. HENSHAW *Birds of Hawaiian Islands* 103 Upon the island of Hawaii the haunts of the nene..are the uplands. **1915** [see **Hawaiian goose*]. **1945** *Condor* XLVII. 34 Direct influences were brought to bear upon the Nene by white men directly and indirectly through altered environment. **1958** [see **Hawaiian goose*]. **1962** *Punch* 1 Aug. 177/3 Various animals whose survival is in question, with the accent on big game rather than..the Hawaiian *ne-ne.* **1972** *Shooting Times & Country Mag.* 1 July 19/2 The Wildfowl Trust established the principle with the Ne-ne or Hawaiian goose. **1975** *Nat. Geographic* Mar. 411/1 A beautiful, unique species of goose called the nene (nay-nay) was being brought back from near extinction here.

nene, var. *NEINEI.

Nenets (ne·nets). Pl. **Nentsi, Nentsy.** [a. Russ. *Nénets,* pl. *Néntsy.*] A Samodian (formerly Samoyedic) people inhabiting the far north-east of Europe and the north of Siberia; a member of this people; their language.

[**1886** *Encycl. Brit.* XXI. 251/1 The names assumed by the Samoyedes themselves are Hazovo and Nyănyăz.] **1944** GREGORY & SHAVE *U.S.S.R.* iv. 162 Occupying territory lying roughly between that of the Palæo-Asiatic groups and the groups of Finnish origin are the peoples commonly known in the past as the Samoyedes, although now more correctly named Nentsi and Ostyak Samoyedes. *Ibid.* viii. 286 The..Nentsi are nomadic tent dwellers. **1954** PEI & GAYNOR *Dict. Ling.* 189 Samoyedic..consists of Samoyed, called *Nenets* by the speakers themselves (with various local dialects), Yurak, Kamassin and Tagvy. **1957** *Encycl. Brit.* XX. 598/1 The earliest known inhabitants of Siberia were the Finno-Ugrian Nentsy. **1962** *Amer. Speech* XXXVII. 68 The phonemic systems of five languages of the Samoyed subgroup (Nenets, Nganasan, Enets, Sel'Kup, Kamas). **1967** D. S. PARLETT *Short Dict. Lang.* 107 The Northern language [of Samoyedic] has three dialects: Yurak (Nenets) with Taiga and Tundra variants, Yenisei (Enets) and Tavgi (Nganasan). **1968** S. P. DUNN tr. *Diószegi's Pop. Beliefs & Folklore Trad. Siberia* 123 An 'Enetsized' Nenets called Yar. **1968** *Encycl. Brit.* XVI. 210/2 The Nenets people, a Finno-Ugrian group formerly known as the Samoyed, make their living chiefly by reindeer herding. **1972** *Language* XLVIII. 206 Soviet scholars usually distinguish three languages: Nenets ('Yurak Samoyed'), Enets..and Nganasan.

neo-. Add: **1. a.** *neo-American* adj., *-Aramaic* adj., *-Aristotelian* adj. and sb., *-Aristotelianism, -Babylonian* adj., *-baroque* adj., *-behaviourism, -behaviourist, -istic* adjs., *-Bloomfieldian* adj., *-Buddhist* adj. and sb., *-Buddhistic* adj., *-capitalism, -capitalist* adj., *-Catholic* (adj.), *-Christian* (adj.), *-Confucian* adj., *-Confucianism, -conservatism, -conservative* adj. and sb., *-critical* adj., *-criticist, -Dada, -Dadaism, -Darwinian* (sb.), *-Darwinism, -Darwinist, -Dixieland* adj., *-Edwardian* adj., *-Elizabethan* adj. and sb., *-expressionism, -expressionist* adj. and sb., *-Fascism, -Fascismo, -Fascist* adj. and sb., *-feminist, -Firthian* adj. and sb., *-Freudian* adj. and sb., *-Freudianism, -Gaullism, -Gaullist* adj. and sb., *-Georgian* adj. and sb., *-Georgianism, -German, -Gothicism, -Hegelian* adj and sb., *-Hegelianism, -Hittite* adj. and sb., *-Humboldtian* adj. and sb., *-imperial* adj., *-imperialism, -imperialist, -isolationism, -isolationist* adj. and sb., *-Kantian* (adj.), *-Kantism, -Keynesian* adj. and sb., *-Keynesianism, -Lamarckian* sb., *-Lamarckism, -liberal* adj., *-Maoist* adj., *-modal* adj., *-modalism, -modality, -nationalism, -Nazi* adj. and sb., *-Nazism, -Nietzschean* adj., *-Norman* adj., *-orthodox* adj., *-orthodoxy, -paganism, -Palladian* adj., *-populism, -positivism, -positivist* adj. and sb., *-primitivism, -Pythagorean* (sb.), *-realism, -realist* adj. and sb., *-realistic* adj., *-revisionist* adj. and sb., *-rococo* adj., *-Romantic* (sb.), *-scholastic* adj. and sb., *-scholasticism, -slave, -slaver, -slavery, -Stalinism, -Stalinist* adj. and sb., *-symbolist* adj. and sb., *-theosophical* adj., *-Thomism, -Thomist* adj. and sb., *-Tory, -Toryism, -traditionalism, -Tudor* adj., *-Victorian* adj. and sb., *-vitalism, -vitalist* adj. and sb., *-vitalistic* adj.

1904 *Amer. Naturalist* XXXVIII. 682 The Neo-American nomenclature is adopted—with synonymic citation where the generic name is unfamiliar to the ordinary reader. **1970** I. REED in A. Chapman *New Black Voices* (1972) 334 So sez d neoamerican hoodoo Church of free spirits. **1948** D. DIRINGER *Alphabet* 289 The east-Syrian or neo-Aramaic dialect. **1931** *Times Lit. Suppl.* 16 July 561/1 The attempt to apply the neo-Aristotlean [*sic*] rules was..doomed to failure. **1947** *College English* VIII. 403 We should not leave the new critics without notice of the neo-Aristotelians who do not accept fellowship with the new critics, nor with the neo-Thomists. **1953** R. S. CRANE *Languages of Criticism* 149 It is not a question of..looking upon ourselves, in any exclusive sense, as forming an 'Aristotelian' or 'Neo-Aristotelian' school. **1962** W. S. SCOTT *Five Approaches of Lit. Criticism* 183 He also arraigns the 'Neo-Aristotelians' for going outside the poem—not to history, psychology, or morality, but to a theory of the genre. **1952** R. S. CRANE *Critics & Criticism* 2 A particular philosophic dogma the nature of which has been defined..as Aristotelianism or neo-Aristotelianism. **1915** L. W. KING *Hist. Babylonia* II. 278 Nebuchadnezzar ..established the Neo-Babylonian empire on a firm basis. **1931** *Times Lit. Suppl.* 31 Dec. 1054/1 Reliefs in glazed brick of the neo-Babylonian revival. **1966** *Daily Tel.* 9 Nov. 17/3 'The Rake's Progress'..is either one of the most enigmatic or the most straight forward, according to the view you take of its neo-rococo or neo-baroque idiom. **1970** *Canadian Antiques Collector* June 10/1 His execution of neo-baroque designs to some degree anticipates the Victorian penchant for period revivals. **1967** *Philos. Rev.* LXXVI. 97 The stimulus-response (S-R) theories of neo-behaviorism. **1964** *Listener* 14 May 785/2 Watsonian Behaviourism is..the foundation on which the..neo-Behaviourist systems of Professor Guthrie, Clark Hull, and Skinner were built. **1952** *Mind* LXI. 349 In *The Concept of Mind* Professor Gilbert Ryle has presented us with a neo-behaviouristic theory. **1964** *Language* XL. 265 Weinreich rejects..the hard-boiled neo-Bloomfieldian behaviorism of such philosophers as Carnap and Quine. **1891** *Literary World* 17 Apr. 357/1 The extracts we have given serve to show the dogmatic assertiveness of the Neo-Buddhist philosophy. **1972** *Times of India* 28 Nov. 11/3 A majority of them come from the Scheduled Castes. Many say they are neo-Buddhists. **1896** A. H. KEANE *Ethnology* xiii. 346 There is something similar in the Neo-Buddhistic teachings. **1968** *Economist* 20 July 25/3 By neocapitalism they mean the new type of industrial economy dominated by the very large industries. *Ibid.,* An educational system which they look upon as the instrument of 'neocapitalist' oppression. **1842** MILL *Let.* 10 Jan. in *Wks.* (1963) XIII. 497 Our neo-Catholic school at [Oxf]ord. **1956** K. CLARK *Nude* viii. 333 The neo-Catholic doctrines of his [*sc.* Rouault's] friend Leon Bloy, by which in the lukewarm, materialistic society of 1900, absolute degradation came closer to redemption than worldly compromise. **1910** WYNDHAM LEWIS *Lett.* (1963) 44 He [*sc.* Masefield] makes Pompey a sort of Tolstoyan or neo-Christian hero. **1948** *Mind* LVII. 535 Dr. Fung..does not, like many Chinese and most Occidental expositors, make Confucius teach medieval Neo-Confucian doctrine. *Ibid.,* Fung continues Chinese traditions by attempting to bring up to date medieval Neo-Confucianism. **1960** *Encounter* Nov. 78/1 If anything can render neo-conservatism intellectually respectable, it is writing of this kind. **1964** K. WINETROUT in I. L. Horowitz *New Sociology* 151 They can turn to Russell Kirk and his fellow neo-conservatives. **1971** *Time* 23 Aug. 31 Judaism and Christianity have always placed primacy in man. Now this primacy is being attacked by what I call the neoconservative ecological approach to life. **1960** *Times Lit. Suppl.* 3 June 357/2 Though it may be short on neo-critical know-how, it will provide valuable ammunition for the literary gamesman. **1925** Neo-criticist [see *EMPIRIO-CRITICAL *a.*]. **1962** *Times* 8 Mar. 16/7 The neo-dada work of which Rauschenberg's 'combine-paintings' (i.e. collages) are the only example here. **1966** *Times* 16 July 7 Perhaps a change in the air encouraged..the recent revival of surrealism and neo-Dadaism. **1895** G. J. ROMANES *Darwin* II. 10 The Neo-Darwinians strain the teachings of Darwin. **1902** J. M. BALDWIN *Development & Evol.* 135 The possible truth of either of the current doctrines of heredity, called Neo-Darwinism and Neo-Lamarckism respectively. **1970** *Observer* (Colour Suppl.) 15 Feb. 18/1 All that neo-Darwinism does at present, the critics say, is to pronounce that 'what survives, survives'. **1895** G. J. ROMANES *Darwin* II. 28, I am not a Neo-Darwinist, and so have no desire to make 'natural selection' synonymous with 'natural causation'. **1972** *Listener* 3 Aug. 138/2 You have said one or two things which would be regarded by neo-Darwinists as treasonable. **1955** L. FEATHER *Encycl. Jazz* vii. 235 The conventional neo-Dixieland jazz of the Eddie Condon variety. **1947** 'N. BLAKE' *Minute for Murder* iv. 84 The hair brushed up from the back in the neo-Edwardian manner. **1909** *Westm. Gaz.* 7 Aug. 7/1 Mr. Figgis is enlightened enough to be a neo-Elizabethan. **1924** R. GRAVES *Mock Beggar Hall* 29 Don't cramp my neo-Elizabethan manner. **1958** *Listener* 3 July 23/3 Conditions would exist that would justify a renewal of the nexus between Church and State; there might be a sort of neo-Elizabethan settlement. **1962** *Guardian* 20 Feb. 5/2 An antiquated system more in keeping with Victoria than with neo-Elizabethan England. **1961** Neo-Expressionism [see *NEO-LIBERTY]. **1955** P. HERON *Changing Forms of Art* 171 The occasional gaunt landscapes by young French neo-expressionists such as Bernard Buffet or Raymond Guerrier. **1968** *N.Y. Times* 20 Jan. 25 Landscape and other subjects are handled by Miss Rosenberger as a series of neoexpressionist clichés. **1946** *Commonweal* (N.Y.) 1 Feb. 398/2 (*title*) Neo-fascism: Italian sample. **1973** *Guardian* 20 June 14 As neofascism under the leadership of Giorgio Almirante makes new gains, suspicions and fears are once again rife in Italy. **1928** *Observer* 29 Jan. 17/1 Herein lies an incident of neo-Fascismo which has no controversial element. **1944** *Birmingham* (Alabama) *News* 28 June 8/5 The Germans had dissolved the Neofascist movement in Northern Italy. **1944** H. MCCLOY *Panic* 143 She—or rather he—is a neo-Fascist and Nazi sympathizer. **1972** *Guardian* 17 Feb. 2/5 Seven people are now in Milan prison in connection with recent neo-Fascist activities. **1969** *Harper's Mag.* Nov. 28 'Are you still against abortion?' Ellen Willis asks, alluding to a position I had once taken which gave me, for a time, some small notoriety among the rest of the neo-feminists. **1964** R. H. ROBINS *Gen. Linguistics* p. xix, Several of the principles taught by [J. R.] Firth..are continued in the work of those who are coming to be known as 'neo-Firthians'. **1964** *Language* XL. 305 The term 'neo-Firthian linguistics' may be suggested to characterize the recent work of M. A. K. Halliday, R. M. Dixon, and others. **1948** L. SCHNEIDER *Freudian Psychol. & Veblen's Social Theory* v. 166 Some of the work of the neo-Freudians..suggests that the strain in Freud above referred to has not quite been eliminated. *Ibid.* 173 This lacuna in neo-Freudian literature is..quite evident in Fromm's *Escape From Freedom.* **1959** Neo-Freudian [see *BIOLOGISTIC *a.*]. **1958** W. J. H. SPROTT *Human Groups* iv. 64 The 'neo-Freudianism' of Karen Horney. **1958** *Spectator* 6 June 720/2 A neo-Gaullism that has little to do with anything he [*sc.* General de Gaulle] has sought to represent. **1958** *Ibid.* 30 May 677/1 All the neo-Gaullists who have been utilised by M. Soustelle to create the situation in which the General [*sc.* de Gaulle] is invited to act as supreme arbitrator. **1958** *Times* 19 Dec. 8/1 The innovation was proposed by the leader of the neo-Gaullist Union for the New Republic. **1915** *Truth* 24 Mar. 459/2 Essentially early nineteenth century in character, he was hopelessly out of his element in this neo-Georgian era. **1923** HARDY *Coll. Poems* (ed. 2) 525 The launching of a volume of this kind in neo-Georgian days by one who began writing in mid-Victorian, and has published nothing to speak of for some years, may seem to call for a few words of excuse or explanation. **1923** W. DEEPING *Secret Sanctuary* xix. 195 The Jinkses with their drink-philosophy, their blatant motor-bike, their stout insensitiveness, were Neo-Georgians. **1933** *Archit. Rev.* LXXIV. 130/2 The Kirkgate and the Briggate..cast off their Georgian glory and assumed the Jacobean,..the Perpendicular and the neo-Georgian, in Leeds phorpres brick and stone and terra-cotta. **1955** J. BETJEMAN in R. S. Thomas *Song at Year's Turning* 12 The 'wain and stook' pastoral poetry of the neo-Georgians. **1970** *English Studies* LI. 270 The insipidly 'pleasant' strain which.. became a conditioned reflex in the 'neo-Georgian' ripplings of the Squire–Turner–Freeman school. **1940** *Scrutiny* IX. 289 The 'simplicity' of Auden's later manner merges into neo-Georgianism. **1940** *Tablet* 4 May 421/1 This is the feat attempted only by the neo-Germans of the two Great Wars. **1964** *Daily Tel.* 3 Feb. 12 It savours of all the neo-Gothicism of Sir Walter Scott. **1885** W. JAMES *Let.* 13 Aug. (1920) I. 254 Why don't you have a special 'Neo-Hegelian Department' in 'Mind',..

which educated readers skip? **1928** *London Aphrodite* Aug. 6 This analysis is carried on so as to involve anyone at all who admits Time as a philosophic symbol, whether he be an academic neo-Hegelian like Bosanquet, or an intelligent one like Croce. **1917** *Encycl. Relig. & Ethics* IX. 300/2 Neo-Hegelianism is a title which has been given to that current of thought inspired by Hegel and the idealists of Germany which began to make itself felt in British and American philosophy in the third quarter of the 19th century. **1971** *Jrnl. Gen. Psychol.* Apr. 253 Philosophical tendencies have also influenced the practice of psychology in the course of the nineteenth century: in particular neo-Kantianism, neo-Hegelianism, [etc.]. **1925** J. B. BURY et al. *Cambr. Anc. Hist.* III. p. vii, Dr Hogarth ..discusses the successors of the Hittites, and the history and art of the Neo-Hittite states of North Syria. **1952** O. R. GURNEY *Hittites* i. 40 The language and the religion of these 'Neo-Hittite' inscriptions are not those of the Hittites of Hattusas. **1964** L. ROUX *Anc. Iraq* xvii. 223 We reach, in the extreme north of Syria, the realm of the people called 'Hieroglyphic Hittites' or, more simply, 'Neo-Hittites'. *Ibid.* 224 It is important to emphasize that there was no break in the transmission of Hittite culture in those regions, and that the term 'Neo-Hittite' is no more than a convenient appellation. *Ibid.* xviii. 245 The Neo-Hittite and Aramaean princes whom Ashurnaṣirpal had caught by surprise had had time to strengthen themselves. **1952** H. BASILIUS in J. A. Fishman *Readings Sociol. of Lang.* (1968) 447 (*title*) Neo-Humboldtian ethnolinguistics. *Ibid.* 458 The basic point of departure for the Neo-Humboldtians is always Wilhelm von Humboldt's idea that language is simply 'the human being approaching the objective idea'. **1962** *Language* XXXVIII. 319 Karl-Otto Apel provides an excellent illustration of the interconvertibility of Neo-Humboldtian and Existentialist terminology. **1968** *N.Y. Times* 17 Mar. IV. 12 This analysis could embrace not just neoimperial China and neoimperial Russia. **1962** *Listener* 5 Apr. 583/2 It does..make sense to regard this neo-imperialism of the left as an extension of its traditional Little Englanderism. **1971** *Yearbk. World Affairs* XXV. 136 Neo-imperialism is more broadly defined to include the creation and maintenance of an economic sphere of influence by one or more developed countries embracing one or more countries at a very much lower stage of economic development. **1967** *Atlantic Monthly* Jan. 55, I believe that, in fact, we are in danger of seeing the isolationists of the 1920s and 1930s replaced by the neoimperialists, who somehow imagine that the United States has a mandate to impose an American solution the world around. **1952** *Britannica Bk. of Year* 666/2 *Neo-isolationism*, an isolationism in which military preparedness plays a part. **1971** *Atlantic Monthly* Jan. 4 Disillusionment about the Indochina War and preoccupation with domestic ills will bring on neoisolationism in the United States. **1950** *N.Y. Times* 30 Dec. 12/1 The neo-isolationists..propose to retreat to the Western hemisphere, with some outlying bases. **1967** *Listener* 21 Dec. 813/1 People who think we ought not to be in Asia are neo-isolationists. **1971** *Atlantic Monthly* Jan. 4 This month's magazine offers a considerable dose of anti-neoisolationist nourishment: two articles on Egypt and the Middle East situation, reports on Berlin, Canada, and China policy; as well as a lighthearted exercise in the ways of England. **1886** S. H. HODGSON *Let.* 23 Nov. in R. B. Perry *Tht. & Char. W. James* (1935) I. 640 Bradley's *Logic*..belongs to that Neo-Kantian line of thought from which, except as mental gymnastic, I hope nothing. **1958** W. STARK *Sociology of Knowledge* p. x, Heinrich Rickert was a member of the neo-Kantian school. **1904** W. JAMES *Ess. Rad. Emp.* (1912) i. 5 If neo-Kantism has expelled earlier forms of dualism, we shall have expelled all forms if we are able to expel neo-Kantism in its turn. **1959** *Encounter* Jan. 52/1 Neo-Keynesian models. **1968** *Time* 25 Oct. 31 [Senator Hubert H.] Humphrey pledges to continue neo-Keynesian policies that have helped stimulate the nation to 7½ years of unprecedented growth in jobs, wages and production. **1970** *Times* 7 Sept. 19 It was also recognized that monetary policy could be effectively exploited for purposes of stabilization policy, and this position is accepted by Neo-Keynesians and monetarists alike. **1965** *Times Lit. Suppl.* 25 Nov. 1039/3 It was only towards the end of his life that the neo-Keynesianism of his professional advisers prevailed. **1899** J. A. THOMSON *Sci. of Life* xvi. 228 The Neo-Lamarckians have added breadth and subtlety to Lamarckism. **1910** *Contemp. Rev.* Jan. 107 This important factor of direct action, which has been brought so much into prominence by the Neo-Lamarckians. **1902** Neo-Lamarckism [see *neo-Darwinism* above]. **1966** *Economist* 14 May p. xii/3 The restrictive view of the common market as a strictly neo-liberal free trade affair would win the day. **1970** *Times* 21 Feb. 7 If a neo-Maoist China is to take shape after the cultural revolution and the ninth congress one can say that it is still very murky and that its institutional life is not in sight yet. **1959** D. COOKE *Lang. Mus.* ii. 76 The austere nature of modal and neo-modal music. **1930** *Music & Lett.* XI. I. 62 Polytonality or atonality on the one hand, and neo-modalism on the other, must set the bounds of our next enquiry. **1958** *Times* 6 June 4/4 The neo-modalism of Vaughan Williams nor the neo-primitivism of Carl Orff. **1947** *Penguin Music Mag.* Sept. 11 They needed a stronger purgative, needed a new instrument—neo-modality, atonality, polytonality, quarter-tonality. **1968** *N.Y. Times* 11 May 13 Signs that 'middle-class radicalism and neo-nationalism' were growing in West Germany. **1950** Neo-Nazi [see *neo-Nazism* below]. **1952** *Time* 9 June 30 Threateningly resurgent neo-Nazis. **1952** *Harper's Mag.* Dec. 33/1 Fissures are appearing in Communist and neo-Nazi parties. **1973** D. BAGLEY *Tightrope Men* xxv. 172 Who the hell cares what happens to a lot of neo-Nazis? **1974** *Washington Post* 18 Jan. A29/5 The facade of the Euram Building looks almost neo-Nazi. **1950** *Britannica Bk. of Year* 739/2 *Neo-Nazism*, a rightist movement designed to revive former nazi principles and beliefs (1947; neo-Nazi, 1938). **1966** *Daily Tel.* 15 Aug. 17/8 Deep concern about an increase in neo-Nazism and other forms of bigotry was expressed at the end of the International Conference on Jewish–Christian Co-operation. **1974** *Times* 22 Oct. 5/1 National Front members.. have been embarrassed..by Mr Tyndall's vulnerability to the charge of neo-Nazism. **1920** E. POUND *H. S. Mauberley* 25 Mildness, amid the neo-Nietzschean clatter. **1958** *Listener* 19 June 1025/3 The neo-Nietzschean oracles of Colin Wilson. **1960** J. BETJEMAN *Summoned by Bells* v. 46 St. Andrew's first, with neo-Norman apse. **1958** *New Statesman* 6 Sept. 296/2 Serious neo-orthodox theologians regard the Billy Grahams and Norman Vincent Peales with revulsion. **1952** *Britannica Bk. of Year* 666/2 *Neo-orthodoxy*, certain new interpretations, especially on original sin, the righteousness of God, and the Bible as a source of revealed religious truth to which man must respond in every situation by a decision involving obedience or disobedience. **1880** J. MCCARTHY *Hist. Own Times* IV. 542 Pre-Raphaelitism..has got mixed up with æstheticism, neo-paganism, and other such fantasies. **1940** *Burlington Mag.* Sept. 79/2 The Neo-palladian architecture in England from the twenties of the eighteenth century onwards. **1972** *Newsweek* 27 Mar. 3 Once dismissed as a racist demagogue, Alabama Gov. George Wallace brings a quirky but potent neopopulism to 1972 Presidential politics—as witnessed by his triumph in the Florida Democratic primary. **1975** *Times Lit. Suppl.* 31 Jan. 116/5 In small, localized communities, the tyranny of social control and of majority pressures can be all the more dangerous, as the neopopulism of Mid-Western small towns and the American South amply illustrates. **1935** *Mind* XLIV. 540 (*title*) Some metaphysical assumptions and problems of neo-positivism. **1963** R. CARNAP in P. A. Schilpp *Philos. of R. Carnap* 866 Since Lenin's book against Mach's philosophy, no author in the Soviet Union has dared to discuss neo-positivism with sympathy. **1935** *Mind* XLIV. 540 Neo-positivists who define the class of possible operations by reference to *future* acts of verification can do so only by assigning some metaphysical status to time. **1964** *English Studies* XLV. Suppl. 109 Present-day British philosophers of the analytical or neo-positivist schools have therefore one criterion, namely the contribution to positive knowledge. **1927** *Observer* 24 Apr. 14/4 Post-impressionism, Expressionism, Neo-primitivism. **1971** *Times Lit. Suppl.* 31 Dec. 1622/1 He would have denounced their neo-primitivism, the Rousseauian belief that poverty and roughness are closer to nature than austerity and civilized habits, and therefore more authentic and morally pure. **1891** *Chambers's Encycl.* VII. 436/2 Neopythagoreans may be divided into two groups. **1916** *Mind* XXV. 314 The theory of neo-realism that colours, shapes and sounds must be accepted at their face value whatever the difficulties. **1955** *Times* 4 July 12/3 The earnest talker on films, the *cinéaste*, finds his brother in the balletomane and his cousin in the first-nighter..and his conversation is full of words like montage, neo-realism, and audio-visual correspondence. **1917** A. S. PRINGLE-PATTISON *Idea of God* x. 191 The opening years of the twentieth century have been marked..by a strong attack on the fundamental tenet of Mentalism on the part of thinkers who call themselves Realists or Neo-Realists. **1931** G. F. STOUT *Mind & Matter* 171 The Neo-Realist holds that when we see a star the star itself becomes in one aspect of its being an immediate content of our actual sense-experience. **1940** *Mind* XLIX. 122 The 'neo-realist' positions of Russell, Alexander, and Whitehead. **1974** *Times* 11 Dec. 14/4 *Downpour*, a gentle neo-realist study of the difficulties of a young teacher. **1955** *Times* 26 May 13/3 The neo-realistic Italian cinema has made English audiences familiar with the poverty and crime that flourish in the back streets of Italian cities. **1970** *Times* 26 Feb. 6 One of the Maoists' main targets is the Marxist Communist Party, branded by Peking as neo-revisionist to distinguish it from the pro-Moscow Communist Party. **1970** *Guardian Weekly* 18 July 5 The Indian Marxists have often been denounced by Radio Peking as 'neo-revisionists'. **1926** A. HUXLEY *Two or Three Graces* 76 That sham *dix-huitième* language, those neo-rococo sentiments. **1899** BEERBOHM *More* 95 The Neo-Romantics, the dalliers with pretty sentiment, would paint admirable sign-boards. **1947** A. EINSTEIN *Music in Romantic Era* xv. 221 That crude, scribbling materialism with which the French neo-Romantics amuse themselves. **1915** *London Q. Rev.* Jan. 49 The 'Neo-scholastic' movement would have attracted no attention outside Catholic circles, had it not been for the literary activity of the Louvain professors. **1930** *Times Lit. Suppl.* 26 June 524/4 It is true that there are certain neo-Scholastics and certain naturalists who divide into neo-Realists and critical Realists influenced both by William James and Mr. Bertrand Russell. **1915** *London Q. Rev.* Jan. 46 It is strange that a movement with so much verve as 'Neo-scholasticism' has attracted so little attention in Britain. **1934** C. S. LEWIS *Let.* 7 June (1966) 157 Beware of people who are at present running what they call 'neo-scholasticism' as a fad. **1970** G. JACKSON *Let.* 4 Apr. in *Soledad Brother* (1971) 211 Part of the credo of the neoslave, the latter-day slave,..is to shuffle away from any situation that becomes too difficult. *Ibid.* 214 The neoslaver destroyed the uneconomic plantation, and built upon its ruins a factory. **1965** —— *Let.* 30 Mar. in *Soledad Brother* (1971) 70 Our people react in different ways to this neoslavery. **1969** *Guardian* 30 Sept. 12/2 Those who are allowed to speak to the [Czech] nation speak with the accents of neo-Stalinism. **1974** *Times* 27 May 4/2 The [Yugoslav] climate changed and the attacks began to centre on neo-Stalinism. **1960** *Guardian* 28 July 9/6 The neo-Stalinists..are now prepared to make their stand known in public. *Ibid.* 9/7 This is also the neo-Stalinist view in China. **1973** A. MANN *Tiara* i. 3 Things are beginning to simmer again in Moscow, and the neo-Stalinists or hard-liners..have recovered a good deal of influence. **1930** *Times Educ. Suppl.* 3 May 197/2 The schools or coteries of the last few decades—the symbolists, neo-classicists, neo-symbolists, synthetists..and so forth. **1960** *Guardian* 19 Aug. 4/5 How to combine the neo-symbolist image..with the language of rational discourse. **1907** W. DE MORGAN *Alice-For-Short* viii. 75 A neo-theosophical reincarnationism without so much as a single Himalayan Brother to back you up! **1964** P. F. ANSON *Bishops at Large* ix. 367 He [*sc.* Steiner] founded his own neo-theosophical body. **1915** *London Q. Rev.* Jan. 51 Neo-scholasticism is essentially 'Neo-Thomism'. **1968** P. B. AUSTIN *On being Swedish* xxiii. 168 Neo-Thomism is also making its voice heard. **1928** H. CRANE *Let.* 17 Apr. (1965) 323 This method is reversed—as with the neo-Thomists. *c* **1928** R. FRY *Lett.* (1972) II. 632 He [*sc.* Herbert Read]'s one of this neo-Thomist lot with a whole bag of metaphysical nostrums on his back. **1947** Neo-Thomist [see *neo-Aristotelian* adj. and sb. above]. **1945** 'G. ORWELL' *England Your England* (1953) 56 All Neo-Tories are anti-Russian, but sometimes the main emphasis is anti-American. *Ibid.*, The real motive force of Neo-Toryism..is the desire not to recognise that British power and influence have declined. **1962** *Economist* 19 May 674/1 Neo-traditionalism was now so strong that Buganda became its own political 'party'. **1932** AUDEN *Orators* III. 103 In the neo-Tudor club-house the captains frown. **1960** J. BETJEMAN *Summoned by Bells* vi. 57 And not far off the neo-Tudor shops. **1929** GALSWORTHY *Modern Comedy* p. x, Such subsidiary neo-Victorians as the self-righteous Mr. Danby. **1959** Neo-Victorian [see *BETJEMAN]. **1902** *Encycl. Brit.* XXXI. 712/2 These efforts..by their unfortunate designations of Vitalism and Neo-vitalism give rise to entirely false conceptions. **1899** J. A. THOMSON *Sci. of Life* 9 The rise of a school of 'neovitalists', who have helped to save the science from self-conceit by their emphasis on the partial nature of all physiological analysis. **1920** A. S. PRINGLE-PATTISON *Idea of God* (ed. 2) p. vi, I have added some detailed criticism of recent neo-vitalist statements from which I wish to dissociate myself. **1966** C. G. HEMPEL *Philos. of Nat. Sci.* vi. 72 All that the neovitalist doctrine enables us to do is to make the *post factum* pronouncement. **1902** *Encycl. Brit.* XXXI. 712/2 All the so-called neo-vitalistic efforts..have nothing to do with the older vitalism.

b. neoarsphe·namine, a bicyclic arsenic compound, $H_2NC_6H_3(OH)As{:}As(OH)C_6H_3\text{-}NHCH_2SO_2Na$, which is a derivative of arsphenamine and is a toxic yellow powder formerly much used in the treatment of syphilis; **neohespe·ridin** [a. G. *neohesperidin* (Kolle & Gloppe 1936, in *Pharmazeut. Zentralhalle* LXXVII. 425)], a bitter compound, $C_{28}H_{34}O_{15}$, which is a glycoside of a flavone and is found in Seville oranges; **neosa·lvarsan** [a. G. *neosalvarsan* (E. Schreiber 1912, in *München. med. Wochenschr.* 23 Apr. 905/1)] = *neoarsphenamine* above; **neosti·gmine** [*PHYSO)STIGMINE], the aromatic quaternary ammonium ion $(CH_3)_2N{\cdot}CO{\cdot}O{\cdot}C_6H_4N^+(CH_3)_3$ or its bromide or methylsulphate salts, which are white crystalline compounds used in treating myasthenia gravis and other muscular complaints.

1918 *Public Health Rep.* (U.S.) XXXIII. 1003 Previous to the year 1914, all of the arsphenamine (salvarsan) and neo-arsphenamine (neosalvarsan) on the market was manufactured by a single German firm. **1951** A. GROLLMAN *Pharmacol. & Therap.* xxx. 698 Neoarsphenamine is easier to prepare and administer than arsphenamine; causes fewer reactions; and is less irritant to the tissues. **1969** *Radiation Res.* XXXIX. 579 Neoarsphenamine, a sulfhydryl-binding agent, sensitizes hypoxic suspensions of *E. coli*..to irradiation. **1936** *Chem. Abstr.* XXX. 6509 The new glucoside '244', for which the name *neohesperidin* is suggested, is split on hydrolysis in 2 phases in accordance with the following scheme. **1962** *Anal. Biochem.* IV. 110 The isolation and identification of neohesperidin, a 7-rhamnoglucoside of hesperetin..from a commercially produced grapefruit flavonoid preparation containing mostly naringin. **1970** Neohesperidin [see *NARINGIN]. **1912** *Chem. Abstr.* VI. 2111 Neo-salvarsan is more easily sol. than salvarsan, thus simplifying this part of the salvarsan therapy and preventing the effects produced by NaOH. It is more easily tolerated than salvarsan; intestinal disturbances and collapse are nearly entirely absent. **1932** SCHAMBERG & WRIGHT *Treatment of Syphilis* x. 159 The product known as '914' or 'neo-salvarsan' (neoarsphenamine) possessed the very desirable property of being more freely soluble in water and being neutral in reaction. **1970** PASSMORE & ROBSON *Compan. Med. Stud.* II. xx. 2/1 Salvarsan tended to be toxic and was soon replaced by a less toxic compound called neosalvarsan, which was universally employed until it was superseded by penicillin in 1945. **1943** *Proc. Soc. Exper. Biol. & Med.* LIV. 254/1 Oral administration of 0·2 mg/kg of neostigmine bromide to mice reduces mortality in severe anoxia but larger doses are not prophylactic. **1951** A. GROLLMAN *Pharmacol. & Therap.* xiii. 253 Neostigmine, like physostigmine, exerts its action by inactivating cholinesterase. **1973** *Exper. Eye Res.* XV. 35 The increase in blood flow in the ciliary processes may be due to a direct effect on the muscarinic receptor of neostigmine, which is a quaternary compound, but it may also be due to an ability of neostigmine to release acetylcholine from the nerve terminals besides protecting it.

Spec. (after *neoparaffin*: see Dict.), denoting compounds and radicals in which one carbon atom is linked to four others, as *neohexane*, *neohexyl*; **neope·ntane**, an isomer, $C(CH_3)_4$, of pentane which is an easily condensable gas and which is found in small amounts in petroleum; **neope·ntyl**, the radical $(CH_3)_3\text{-}C{\cdot}CH_2$— derived from neopentane.

1876 *Phil. Mag.* I. 207 (*caption*) Neohexane. **1942** V. J. CLANCEY *Chem. & Aeroplane* iv. 64 Neo-hexane, with an octane value of 94, has been produced for use in blending with normal aviation fuels. **1957** G. I. BROWN *Introd. Org. Chem.* vi. 83 Ethylene and iso-butane react.. at 500°C and 250 atmospheres to form neo-hexane. **1968** R. O. C. NORMAN *Princ. Org. Synth.* viii. 263 The simplest example of an efficient alkylation is the preparation of neohexyl chloride..from t-butyl chloride and ethylene. **1938** *Encycl. Brit. Bk. of Year* 145/1 The highly symmetrical neopentane molecule. **1966** *McGraw-Hill Encycl. Sci. & Tech* nol.I. 249/1 Two alkanes, neopentane (dimethylpropane) and neohexane (2,2-dimethylbutane) are named unambiguously by using the prefix 'neo'. **1876** *Phil. Mag.* I. 209 The paraffin- or alcohol-monad radicals propyl, butyl, isobutyl, pentyl, isopentyl or amyl, and neopentyl, &c. **1933** *Jrnl. Amer. Chem. Soc.* LV. 3803 Because of the

importance of the neopentyl system in rearrangements the preparation and properties of the parent hydrocarbons have been studied. **1969** A. NICA *Theory & Pract. Lubrication Syst.* vi. 168 The neopentyl polyol esters were used in gas turbine engines when the temperatures..prohibited the utilisation of diesters.

c. In anatomical terms designating parts of the brain which are considered to be of relatively recent development phylogenetically, as *NEENCEPHALON, *NEOCEREBELLUM, *NEOCORTEX, *NEOPALLIUM, *NEOSTRIATUM, *NEOTHALAMUS. Cf. *PALÆO-, PALEO- b.

2. ne·oblast *Zool.* [-BLAST], any of the specialized cells in annelid worms by the division of which a lost portion of the body can be regenerated; **neoge·nesis,** chiefly in scientific use: the formation of something new; the renewed formation of something formed previously; **Neo-Gre·c** [F. *grec* Greek], a modern style of architecture based on classical Greek architecture; **neomorpho·sis** *Biol.*, a type of regeneration (see quot.); **neona·tally** *adv.*, soon after birth; **neopho·bic** *a.*, fearing or disliking what is new; **neota·ntalite** *Min.* [ad. F. *néotantalite* (P. Termier 1902, in *Bull. de la Soc. franç. de Minéral.* XXV. 37)], a mineral found as yellow octahedra in Allier, France, that was formerly thought to be a tantalate and niobate of iron, manganese, and sodium but is now thought to be an impure microlite; **neote·nin** *Ent.* [*neoten(ia* s.v. NEO- 2] = *juvenile hormone* s.v. *JUVENILE *a.* 4.

1891 H. RANDOLPH in *Zoologischer Anzeiger* XIV. 154 The new mesoderm is formed in great part from specialized cells in the region of the peritonaeal epithelium of the ventral longitudinal muscles, on each side of the ventral nerve cord between it and the ventral row of setae. These cells, which I propose to call neoblasts, are distinguishable from the cells of the peritonaeum by their great size and by the presence of a cell body. **1930** *Jrnl. Linn. Soc.* XXXVII. 186 The cells concerned in the phagocytosis and replacement of tissues are derived from neoblasts in the ventral body-wall. **1972** *Jrnl. Morphol.* CXXXVII. 217/2 The confusion between peritoneal cells, so-called neoblasts, and oocytes in polychaetes has a considerable historical basis. **1903** *Ibis* III. 15 But the opposite hypothesis, that we have in this singular small Owl a case of neogenesis—i.e. the *ex-abrupto* formation of a new type with sufficient differential characters to constitute, if maintained, a new species,—can, I believe, be upheld. The term neogenesis was first used to explain this sudden origin of new forms from old-established species, if I am not mistaken, by my friend and colleague Prof. Paolo Mantegazza, many years ago; it has been since used, more or less in the same sense, by the late Prof. Cope and by others. **1946** *Nature* 10 Aug. 202/1 The situation is essentially different in coma, in the sense that although neogenesis of sugar occurs (high blood sugar during fast) storage of glycogen in the liver is no longer possible. **1959** *Ann. N.Y. Acad. Sci.* LXXXIII. 507 (*heading*) Neogenesis of human hair follicles. **1972** *Gloss. Geol.* (Amer. Geol. Inst.) 477/1 *Neogenesis*, the formation of new minerals, as by diagenesis or metamorphism. **1931** C. H. REILLY in W. Rose *Outl. Mod. Knowl.* 989 The next stage, generally called the Neo Grec, was probably due to the indirect influence of the Gothic revivalists. **1939** *Archit. Rev.* LXXXV. 52/3 No better background could be imagined for the parade ground manoeuvrings of red-coated guards than these stern, unadorned neo-grec façades. **1901** T. H. MORGAN *Regeneration* i. 24 In one case [of heteromorphosis] the new part is not only different from the part removed, but is also an organ that belongs to a different part of the body (or it may be unlike any organ of the body). This we may call 'neomorphosis'. **1945** *Ann. Amer. Acad. Political & Social Sci.* CCXXXVII. 140 Puerperal fatality increases sharply when the infant is either stillborn or dies neonatally. **1974** *Nature* 7 June 564/2 No significant increase in tumour incidence has been observed in either neonatally thymectomised..mice or congenitally athymic..mice. **1925** *Glasgow Herald* 20 June 4 The greeting extended to the steamship was quite as neophobic. **1971** W. HANLEY *Blue Dreams* iii. 22 Her unfailingly neophobic response to those attempts. **1903** *Mineral. Mag.* XIII. 374 Neotantalite... Minute, regular octahedra resembling pyrochlore, in kaolin from dép. Allier, France. **1932** *Mineral. Abstr.* V. 185 The several minerals (..microlite, neotantalite, atopite, [etc.]..) of this group [*sc.* pyrochlore-romeite]..crystallize as small octahedra and have the same type of crystal-structure. **1973** *Ibid.* XXIV. 282/1 'Neotantalite' is a microlite $A_2B_2O_6$(OH,F) with large deficiences in the *A* ions which may be Ba, Pb, U, or Ca. Microprobe analyses show that the Fe and Mn included in the first description..are impurities. **1954** V. B. WIGGLESWORTH *Physiol. Insect Metamorphosis* iv. 56 The 'inhibitory hormone'..has..been called for preference the 'juvenile hormone'. If a Greek term is preferred it might be called 'neotenin'. **1966** tr. *V. J. A. Novák's Insect Hormones* 79 (*heading*) The juvenile hormone (neotenin), JH (=inhibitory hormone, Wigglesworth, 1935; = status quo hormone, Williams, 1952; = das Larvalhormon, Weber, 1954). **1968** *New Scientist* 16 May 354/1 In larval insects, moulting and metamorphosis are controlled by two hormones produced by epithelial endocrine glands:..neotenin from the corpora allata controls the change towards the adult form.

neoanthropic, var. *NEANTHROPIC *a.*

neocerebellum (nīˌoserĭbe·lǝ̆m). *Anat.* [mod.L., f. *NEO- 1 e + CEREBELLUM.] The phylogenetically youngest portion of the cerebellum, comprising mainly its lateral lobes ('hemispheres').

1925 W. H. F. ADDISON tr. *Villiger's Brain & Spinal Cord* (ed. 3) 80 The hemispheres constitute the neocerebellum, and the vermis and flocculus constitute the palaeocerebellum. **1954** JANSEN & BRODAL *Aspects Cerebellar Anat.* vi. 384 We may appropriately close this discussion by commenting briefly on the much debated concepts paleocerebellum, comprising the vermis and the flocculus, and neocerebellum, comprising the cerebellar hemispheres... From the point of view of gross morphology these concepts may appear well founded. On the basis of fiber connections, however, a paleocerebellum and a neocerebellum *sensu strictiori* are not distinguishable. **1974** *Encycl. Brit. Macropædia* XII. 990/2 This new part of the cerebellum, or neocerebellum, coordinates skilled movements initiated at cortical levels.

So **neocerebe·llar** *a.*, of or pertaining to the neocerebellum.

1914 *Jrnl. Nerv. & Mental Dis.* XLI. 540 (*heading*) Neocerebellar hemiatrophy. **1948** A. BRODAL *Neurol. Anat.* v. 126 The neo-cerebellar syndrome. Here homolateral hypotonia and atactic movements, asynergic and clumsy, appear, and when the dentate nucleus is involved tremor also develops. **1958** *Jrnl. Neurophysiol.* XXI. 3 Stimulation of some neocerebellar areas, however, resulted in equilibratory changes.

neo-cla·ssic, -cla·ssical, *a.* [NEO-.] Of, pertaining to, or characteristic of a style of art, architecture, music, literature, etc., that is based on or influenced by classical style or by a style that has become established as 'classical'; *spec.* of such a style in 18th-century literature, late-18th-century art and architecture, or 20th-century music.

1877 *Contemp. Rev.* Feb. 360 The imagination of the men of Spenser's time was affected by his use of the neo-classical mythology of the Renaissance. **1881, 1882** [see NEO- 1 a]. **1923** C. GRAY *Contingencies* (1947) ii. 65 We find throughout almost all the work of Brahms..the perpetual striving after the ideal of a grandiose, neo-classic art. **1927** *P.M.L.A.* Mar. 237 This linguistic attitude, expressing itself in grammars of arbitrary rules, seems to be but another manifestation and *survival* of that tendency called the neo-classic creed of literary criticism. **1933** *Archit. Rev.* LXXIV. 79/2 Many is the ill-built block of London flats whose internal planning has been sacrificed for some ponderous neo-classical façade. **1934** C. LAMBERT *Music Ho!* II. 101 Stravinsky's neo-classical period,..apart from the adoption of eighteenth-century forms and titles, is chiefly noticeable for its attempt to create melody by synthetic means. **1944** *Burlington Mag.* Apr. 97/1 A fully developed neo-classic sculptor. **1964** J. SUMMERSON *Classical Lang. Archit.* v. 37/1 The Panthéon is the first major building which can be called neo-classical—'neo-classical' being the expression which has come to be used for architecture which..tends towards the rational simplification advocated by Cordemoy and Laugier and..seeks to present the orders with the utmost antiquarian fidelity. **1966** *English Studies* XLVII. 150 In the period up to the Civil War the neo-classic Happy Husbandman becomes the neo-Stoic Contemplator of the world. **1974** *Times Lit. Suppl.* 15 Mar. 259/4 Throughout the book—as for example in the emphasis on jobs rather than on the ownership of capital as a key determinant in occupational mobility—the authors assume the validity of neo-classical economics as taught in the United States.

Hence **neo-cla·ssicism,** neo-classic style or principles; **neo-cla·ssicist,** a follower or exponent of neo-classic style or principles.

1893 Neo-classicism [see NEO- 1 a]. **1930** *Times Educ. Suppl.* 3 May 197/2 The schools or coteries of the last few decades—the symbolists, neo-classicists, neo-symbolists, [etc.]. **1934** C. LAMBERT *Music Ho!* II. 73 *Pulcinella*..marks the beginning of the movement sometimes dignified with the name of neo-classicism. *Ibid.* IV. 245 It may seem contradictory to condemn composers like Honegger for basing their work on the contemporary scene after complaining that the neo-classicists are so out of touch with contemporary life. **1943** *Philological Q.* XXII. 143 The fairy tales about 'neo-classicism' and 'romanticism' in the eighteenth century which have so long been allowed to come between us and the direct appreciation of eighteenth-century texts. **1944** *Burlington Mag.* Apr. 97/2 He..gives no hint of any sympathy with the principles of the Neo-Classicists. **1947** *Penguin Music Mag.* Sept. 24 Both men [*sc.* Schumann and Mendelssohn] turned to a sort of neo-classicism before they had done. **1965** *Times Lit. Suppl.* 25 Nov. 1063/2 The 'lower order' was one which allowed Gay his particularly delicate critical assimilation of the vulgar writers and the 'trivial' moderns, while himself remaining, in theory at least, in the camp of the neo-classicists. **1972** *Listener* 21 Sept. 361/3 What was then called the 'True Style' which we now tend to call Neo-Classicism.

ne:o-colo·nialism. [f. NEO- + COLONIALISM.] The acquisition or retention of influence over other countries, esp. one's former colonies, often by economic or political measures. So **ne:o-colo·nial** *a.* and *sb.*; **ne:o-colo·nialist** *a.* and *sb.*; **ne:o-colo:nializa·tion; ne:o-colo·nial-ized, ne:o-co·lonized** *adjs.*

1961 *New Statesman* 20 Jan. 82/1 The most dangerous type of colonialism is neo-colonialism. **1961** *New Left Rev.* July–Aug. 12/1 One of the effects of EEC is therefore to deepen the split between independent and neo-colonial Africa. **1961** *Economist* 16 Dec. 1113/2 Casuistry worthy of the most devious neo-colonialist. **1963** *Ann. Reg. 1962* 98 Accepting the Indonesian Communist Party's definition of 'Malaysia' as a 'neo-colonialist' device. **1964** K. NKRUMAH *Consciencism* v. 111 Just as a liberated territory can be produced by the application of D (na > pa), so a neo-colonized territory can be produced by the application of D (pa > na). **1965** —— *Neo-colonialism: the Last Stage of Imperialism* p. ix, In place of colonialism as the main instrument of imperialism we have today neo-colonialism. The essence of neo-colonialism is that the State which is subject to it is, in theory, independent and has all the outward trappings of international sovereignty. In reality its economic system and thus its political policy is directed from outside. **1966** *Economist* 26 Mar. 1226/1 Libya is not nearly so neo-colonialised as a country like Algeria with its government-to-government oil and development agreements with France. **1967** *N.Y. Times* 5 July 12 The 'neocolonials' (the Belgians) and the 'imperialists' (the Americans). **1969** *Listener* 3 July 12/2 You'll always have people moving from a stage of neo-colonialisation back to capitalism. **1971** *Black Scholar* Apr.–May 9 The black people in the United States..are de facto neocolonial subjects. **1972** *Sci. Amer.* Apr. 19/3 Strong elements of neocolonialism persist in the economic relations of the rich and poor countries. **1973** J. REX *Discovering Sociology* ix. 109 The inhabitants of the former British and French empires..addressed themselves to the twin tasks of dealing with their own poverty and fighting neo-colonialism. **1973** *Times* 1 Jan. 14/4 One of the black speakers..mentioned Europe in passing as a 'massive neo-colonialist conspiracy to castrate black men everywhere'.

neocortex (nīˌokǫ·ɹteks). *Anat.* Also (with hyphen) **neo-cortex.** [mod.L., f. *NEO- 1 e + CORTEX.] The phylogenetically youngest portion of the cerebral cortex, which is co-extensive with the neopallium.

1909 C. U. A. KAPPERS in *Arch. Neurol. & Psychiatry* IV. 162 Just as in the pallium there can be distinguished three territories according to the connections which they exhibit, so the cortical structures occurring in them should be distinguished, according to the same principle, into a palæo-cortex, archi-cortex and neo-cortex. **1947** H. C. ELLIOTT *Textbk. Nerv. Syst.* vii. 87/1 This first, or paleo-cortex..is soon overshadowed by the development of a general, or neocortex. **1948** [see *NEOPALLIUM]. **1964** J. Z. YOUNG *Model of Brain* xiv. 234 Although it is notoriously dangerous to try to speak of the locality of 'engrams' in a mammal, there can be little doubt that they reside largely in the neocortex. **1972** T. W. JENKINS *Functional Mammalian Neuroanat.* xvi. 250/2 The area of the canine neocortex is 84·2 per cent of the entire hemispheric area. **1972** *Science* 19 May 804/1 We have used the development of the neocortex..as an index of generation length in extinct taxa.

Hence **neoco·rtical** *a.*, of or pertaining to the neocortex.

1909 *Arch. Neurol. & Psychiatry* IV. 163 The upper part of the lateral cortex layer has certainly already a neo-cortical character. **1971** *Nature* 11 June 397/1 All rats were killed 4 h later and the RNA was extracted from hippocarpal, thalamic and medial neocortical tissue. **1971** *Daily Colonist* (Victoria, B.C.) 7 Oct. 5/1 There are other species like ourselves who through evolutionary quirk if not neocortical ascendancy lack biological commands to insure reasonable populations.

neodymium (nīˌodi·mĭǝ̆m). *Chem.* [mod.L., f. G. *neodym* (C. A. von Welsbach 1885, in *Monatshefte f. Chem.* VI. 490), f. *neo-* NEO- + *di)dym* DIDYMIUM: see -IUM.] A metallic element that is a typical member of the lanthanide series, forms red compounds in which it has a valency of three (some of the salts being used for colouring glass and for glazes), and can also have a valency of two or four. Atomic number 60; symbol Nd.

1885 *Jrnl. Chem. Soc.* XLVIII. II. 1113 By repeated crystallisation of a mixture of the double nitrates of lanthanum and didymium with ammonium, the lanthanum salt was obtained pure, whilst the didymium salt separated into the salts of two new elements, neodymium and praseodymium. **1923** *Glasgow Herald* 16 Feb. 11 Number 61 is a rare-earth metal in the midst of that troop of strange elements with stranger names found chiefly in Scandinavian minerals; its neighbours are neodymium and samarium. **1971** *Sci. Amer.* June 20/3 At present solid-state ruby and neodymium-glass laser materials are used to obtain the highest peak-power output in pulsed operation. **1974** *Encycl. Brit. Micropædia* VII. 253/2 Of the rare earths, only cerium and yttrium are more plentiful than neodymium.

neoglacial (nīˌoglē̆i·siăl, -glē̆i·ʃăl), *a.* Also **Neo-.** [f. NEO- + GLACIAL *a.*] Of or pertaining to a neoglaciation; also *absol.*, a neoglacial period.

1960 *Amer. Jrnl. Sci.* CCLVIII. 325 Some Neoglacial ice bodies are judged to have attained a length of nearly two miles. **1970** *Sci. Amer.* June 103/3 In 1794, George Vancouver observed the position of ice in Glacier Bay. At that time glaciers in southern Alaska had begun to retreat from a maximum neoglacial position attained earlier in the 18th century. **1974** *Nature* 20/27 Dec. 680/1 During the Neoglacial, the three major advance phases of alpine and polar glaciers around 4,590–5,260, 2,100–2,940 and 40–460 yr b.p. were exactly contemporaneous with the three major post-Wisconsin volcanic phases..in New Zealand, Japan and southern South America.

neoglaciation (nī:oglē̆isiē̆i·ʃǝn). Also **Neo-.** [f. NEO- + GLACIATION.] A minor, short-lived increase in glaciation following the major glacial retreat at the end of the Ice Age.

Though freq. attributed to F. E. Matthes, the term appears not to have been used by him in print.

1951 J. H. MOSS *Early Man in Eden Valley* v. 62 In the Sierra Nevada, Matthes (1939) has described a similar set

of small, very fresh moraines fronting the existing glaciers... They contrast sharply with the older moraines slightly farther down the valley. Matthes suggested the name Neo-glaciation for the minor glacial pulsation represented by these moraines, and pointed out that it probably postdates the so-called Climatic Optimum. **1954** *Jrnl. Geol.* LIV. 340/1 Most of the moraines described in the literature which have been correlated with the Neoglaciation are close to, or in contact with, existing ice masses and are devoid of all vegetation. **1970** *Sci. Amer.* June 102 Historical records of the latest glacier fluctuations during neoglaciation are available from many alpine regions.

ne:o-gramma·rian, ne:ogramma·rian. [f. NEO- + GRAMMARIAN.] A member of the *JUNGGRAMMATIKER. Also as *adj.*

1885 *Encycl. Brit.* XVIII. 782/2 This younger school (often branded with the name of Neo-Grammarians, 'Junggrammatiker', by its opponents real and imaginary) is marked by certain distinct tendencies. **1933** L. BLOOMFIELD *Lang.* xx. 354 The neo-grammarian insists..that his hypothesis..sorts out the resemblances that are due to factors other than phonetic change. *Ibid.* 355 The opponents of the neo-grammarian hypothesis claim that resemblances which do not fit into recognized types of phonetic correspondence may be due merely to sporadic occurrence or deviation or non-occurrence of sound-change. **1947** E. STURTEVANT *Introd. Linguistic Sci.* vii. 70 In the 1870's a number of scholars announced..that phonetic laws have no exceptions. The earliest declaration..seems to have been made by August Leskien in 1876, but the discovery really belonged to a group, who, from that time to this, have been called the neo-grammarians (*Junggrammatiker*). **1965** *Language* XLI. 188 Mention of the neogrammarians..can elicit so much emotional noise that no one can hear what you are saying. **1972** *Ibid.* XLVIII. 437 The subsequent section illustrates ..the Neogrammarian position. *Ibid.*, Arens refers to Saussure's association with the Neogrammarians.

ne:o-impre·ssionism. Freq. with capital initials. [ad. F. *néo-impressionnisme*, f. NEO- + IMPRESSIONISM.] A movement or style in art, originated by the French painter Georges Seurat (1859–91), and characterized by a systematic use of divisionism. Cf. *POINTILLISM. So **ne:o-impre·ssionist** *a.* and *sb.*

[**1886** F. FÉNÉON in *L'Art Moderne* 19 Sept. 302/1 La vérité est que la méthode néo-impressionniste exige une exceptionnelle délicatesse d'œil.] **1892** *Mag. of Art* p. xxxv/1 Though neo-impressionism has, indeed, asserted itself in the exhibitions of the Twenty, symbolism and realism also hold their own. *Ibid.*, M. Camille Pissaro, a neo-impressionist in his pictures, betrays Japanese influence in his woodcuts. **1901** *Sat. Rev.* 23 Feb. 240/1 Impressionism in France had..passed through the phases of luminism, vibration, pointillisme, independence and neo-impressionism, all comparatively short-lived extreme phases. **1903** *Studio* XXIX. 112/1 Coteries of artists.. have..tried to 'go one better', the most formidable and temporarily successful being that of the 'Néo-Impressionists'. **1908** R. FRY *Let.* Mar. (1972) I. 299 These neo-Impressionists follow straight upon the heels of the true Impressionists. **1914** A. J. EDDY *Cubists & Post-Impressionism* (1915) 27 Neo-Impressionism was the logical outcome of Impressionism. It was simply the attempt to paint light in still more scientific fashion, by the use of the primary colors laid on in fine points in such a manner that at the proper distance the points fuse and produce the tone desired. **1938** *Burlington Mag.* June 289/2 A confirmed disciple of the neo-impressionists. **1944** *Ibid.* Apr. 104/1 A history of the whole Neo-Impressionist movement. **1968** *Michelin Guide N.Y. City* 37 Adepts of Neo-Impressionism, like Seurat. **1972** *Country Life* 23 Nov. 1369/2 These artists' [*sc.* Futurists'] neo-Impressionist brushwork and Expressionist colour is invariably awful. **1975** *Physics Bull.* Feb. 59/2 Our start is the beginning of the 20th century, taking for granted the legacy of Leonardo Da Vinci, photography and the effects of the theories of colour on the neoimpressionists.

ne:o-La·tin. Also **Neo-Latin.** [f. NEO- + LATIN *sb.*] **a.** = ROMANCE *sb.* 1. **b.** Latin in use since the end of the Renaissance. Also *attrib.* or as *adj.* Hence **ne:o-La·tinist**, a writer of neo-Latin.

1850, 1880–1 [see NEO- 1 a]. **1946** H. JACOB *On Choice of Common Lang.* 16 Idiom Neutral is considered a neo-Latin rather than an autonomic system. **1951** [see *COPULATIVE *a.* 1]. **1964** *Archivum Linguisticum* XVI. 4 The author's uniquely panoramic view of the neo-Latin languages. **1965** J. LAWLOR in J. Gibb *Light on C. S. Lewis* 79 Lewis consistently turned his neo-Latin authors into sixteenth-century English. **1966** *English Studies* XLVII. 150 Miss Røstvig stresses the importance of the hitherto neglected neo-Latinist Casimir Sarbiewski. **1970** B. M. H. STRANG *Hist. English* 130 These learned written sources, usually referred to as *Neo-Latin*, are not confined to the donation of whole words. *Ibid.*, The following suffixes come from Neo-Latin.

Neo-Li·berty. Also **Neoliberty.** [f. NEO- + LIBERTY *sb.*] A movement or style in architecture originating in Italy, a revival of *art nouveau.*

1959 *Archit. Rev.* CXXV. 232/2 Paolo Portoghesi seems to have been the first to call the style of the Retreat by the apt term 'Neoliberty' as late as the end of 1958. **1961** *Listener* 16 Feb. 300/1 There is Neo-Liberty in Italy, there is quite a lot of Neo-Gaudí, and there is Neo-Expressionism.

neo-li·nguist. Also **neolinguist.** [f. NEO- + LINGUIST.] A member of a school of linguistics which arose in opposition to the neo-grammarians, rejecting the claim that phonetic laws have no exception, and maintaining that linguistic change results from individual innovation. So **neo-lingui·stic** *a.*; **neo-lingui·stics** *sb. pl.*

[**1925** M. BARTOLI (*title*) Introduzione alla neolinguistica.] **1937** J. ORR tr. *Iordan's Introd. Romance Linguistics* i. 29 Here..is..the source of the misunderstanding between the neo-linguists..and the Italian neo-grammarians of to-day, with regard to their attitude towards Ascoli. *Ibid.* iii. 273 The so-called Neo-linguistic School, whose tenets..are little more than a somewhat hard-and-fast formulation of certain of Gilliéron's ideas. **1944** *Jrnl. Amer. Oriental Soc.* LXIV. 177 The *areal* theory of linguistics..has been developed and brought into a system by the Italian neolinguistic school. **1946** *Language* XXII. 273 Bartoli's 'Neo-Linguistics' has both a negative and a positive side. **1953** J. H. GREENBERG in A. L. Kroeber *Anthropology Today* 265/1 The reconstructions of the neo-linguistic school are not generally accepted by other scholars. **1972** *Language* XLVIII. 439 The Neo-Humboldtians in Germany and the Neolinguists in Italy.

neolocal (nī,olōᵘ·kăl), *a.* *Anthrop.* [f. NEO- + LOCAL *a.*] Denoting a place of residence chosen by a newly-married couple which is independent of parental or family ties. Hence **neolo·cally** *adv.*

1949 G. P. MURDOCK *Soc. Structure* i. 16 When a newly wedded couple, as in our own society, establishes a domicile independent of the location of the parental home of either partner..residence may be called neolocal. **1958** F. M. KEESING *Cultural Anthrop.* x. 264 The married couple may.., as in the modern urban society, set up a home apart from the parents of both: neolocal (new-place). **1967** J. DEETZ *Invitation to Archaeology* 95 We Americans reside *neolocally*, apart from both parents. **1973** *Times Lit. Suppl.* 6 July 774/5 Many young married couples must live 'neolocally': that is, away from the extended family households characteristic of other kinds of area.

neologism. Add: **1. c.** *Psychol.* An invented or concocted word or word-sound without recognizable meaning, freq. interpolated in otherwise correct sentences, and used by persons in a variety of neuropsychiatric disorders.

1905 A. J. ROSANOFF tr. *Rogues de Fursac's Man. Psychiatry* ii. 46 Neologisms the meaning of which may remain absolutely enigmatical to the patient himself. *Ibid.* viii. 200 Neologisms are frequent in the period of dementia. **1906** J. H. MACDONALD tr. *Bianchi's Textbk. Psychiatry* III. xiii. 680 In the typical form [of mania].. neologisms and symbols are found in great number. **1932** CANNON & HAYES *Princ. & Pract. of Psychiatry* 378 The verbal repetition of these 'new' words—neologisms or senseless words invented by himself. **1960** R. F. C. HULL tr. *Jung's Coll. Wks.* III. I. 25 Word-formations, which are so bizarre that they immediately bring to mind the neologisms of dementia praecox. **1969** W. MAYER-GROSS et al. *Clin. Psychiatry* (ed. 3) v. 286 Other patients refer the origin of neologisms to hallucinatory experiences.

neologistic, *a.* (Further examples.)

1935 *Mind* XLIV. 524 Philosophers who have absorbed a glut of new systems of logistic during the last decade.. must face the invention of yet another neologistic language with something like dismay. **1936** *Theology* XXXII. 73 The Catholic is quite sure that there is a God, and that in no neologistic sense.

ne:o-Malthu·sian, *a.* and *sb.* Also **Neo-Malthusian.** [f. NEO- + MALTHUSIAN *a.* and *sb.*] **A.** *adj.* Of or pertaining to the belief that the size of population should be controlled, *spec.* by the use of contraceptives. **B.** *sb.* An advocate of birth control or the limitation of population. So **ne:o-Malthu·sianism.**

1885 Neo-Malthusianism [see NEO- 1 a]. **1901** J. A. GODFREY *Sci. Sex* II. vi. 253 The main points to be proved by the Neo-malthusian are, therefore, that it is advisable for society to have some means of checking the increase of population in advance, and that the means now at hand are both harmless and effective. **1910** G. B. SHAW *Brieux: a Preface* 31 Just about forty years ago the propaganda of Neo-Malthusianism changed the bearing of children from an involuntary condition of marriage to a voluntary one. *Ibid.*, The expectation of the Neo-Malthusians that the regulation of births in our families would give the fewer children born a better chance of survival..has no doubt been fulfilled in some cases. **1911** HAVELOCK ELLIS *Stud. Psychol. Sex* VI. xii. 594 James Mill was the pioneer in advocating Neo-Malthusian methods. **1934** A. HUXLEY *Beyond Mexique Bay* 255 You cannot teach primitive Indians to practise the Neo-Malthusian techniques and expect them to remain primitive Indians. **1934** H. G. WELLS *Experiment in Autobiogr.* II. vii. 436 The spreading knowledge of birth-control,—Neo-Malthusianism was our name for it in those days—seemed to justify my contention that love was now to be taken more lightly than it had been in the past. **1962** *Punch* 3 Jan. 52/1 Some neo-Malthusians have been heard to suggest that the bomb is Nature's Way..of checking..the..over-spawning of our species. **1967** *Listener* 20 July 94/2 Mr Eversley..dispelled any doubt in the minds of those listeners who felt guilty about having '*two* children and a motor-car'—apparently anti-social luxuries in the neo-Malthusian wave.

Ne:o-Melane·sian. [f. NEO- + MELANESIAN *sb.*] (See quots.)

1961 WEBSTER, *Neo-melanesian*, an English-based pidgin language used in New Guinea and the Solomon islands. **1962** *Listener* 20 Sept. 418/2 This word 'neo-Melanesian' is an indication of the changed status that pidgin English has in south-east Asia. The name is given to the pidgin that is spoken particularly in places like New Guinea, and a translation of the Bible has appeared in neo-Melanesian; grammars of neo-Melanesian and a dictionary of neo-Melanesian have appeared. **1972** W. B. LOCKWOOD *Panorama Indo-European Lang.* 120 An important language used in the South Seas, technically known as Neo-Melanesian, but more popularly as Beach-la-Mar... Beach-la-Mar came to denote the Pidgin English spoken between East Australian and Melanesian tripang fishermen... Neo-Melanesian is..of obvious political importance. **1973** *Sunday Times* (Colour Suppl.) 10 June 42/2 Pidgin is taught as a subject at Brisbane University and is referred to by some American scholars as 'Neo-Melanesian'.

neomorph (nī·omǭɹf). [f. NEO- + *-MORPH.] **1.** *Biol.* An anatomical structure or feature that is of recent origin phylogenetically.

1886 W. N. PARKER tr. *Wiedersheim's Elem. Compar. Anat. Vertebrates* 33 It is uncertain whether the dermal skeleton present in Armadillos..is to be derived directly from that of Reptiles, or whether it is to be considered as formed independently, that is, as a new acquisition or 'neomorph' (Gadow).

2. *Genetics.* A mutant allele which effects a different character from that effected by the wild-type allele.

1932 H. J. MULLER in *Proc. Sixth Internat. Congress Genetics* I. 245 Somewhat different from the negatively acting, competing mutant genes, or antimorphs, is the class which I am provisionally terming 'neomorphs'. A good example is the dominant mutant, Hairy wing, near the left end of the X chromosome. **1946** *Nature* 12 Oct. 520/1 Among spontaneous mutations which are known to occur at this locus some would be expected to be neomorphs. **1967** *Evolution* XXI. 850 (*heading*) Latent neomorphs and the evolution of dominance.

Hence **neomo·rphic** *a.*, of, pertaining to, or being a neomorph (in either sense).

1903 *Rep. Brit. Assoc. Advancement of Sci. 1902* 631 Madagascar has yielded a Physa (*P. lamellata*) with a neomorphic gill, a character shared by species of Planorbis (*P. corneus* and *P. marginatus*). **1922** W. GARSTANG in *Jrnl. Linnean Soc.: Zool.* XXXV. 99, I propose in future to use *palæogenetic* and *neogenetic* when referring to ontogenetic processes, and *palæomorphic* and *neomorphic* when contrasting primitive and modified types of structure. **1932** H. J. MULLER in *Proc. Sixth Internat. Congress Genetics* I. 245 (*heading*) Neomorphic mutations. **1940** G. R. DE BEER *Embryos & Ancestors* xiv. 89 A palaeomorphic character may of course..have made its first appearance in early stages of ontogeny. Conversely, characters of more recent origin, to which Garstang applies the term neomorphic, may have originated in terminal ontogenetic or adult stages. **1966** E. A. CARLSON *Gene* xiii. 113 In this neomorphic class, Muller placed Bar eyes.

neomycin (nī,omɔi·sin). *Pharm.* [f. NEO- + *-MYCIN.] An antibiotic that is a mixture of two stereoisomers produced by a selected strain of *Streptomyces fradiæ*, is active against many strains of Gram-positive and Gram-negative bacteria, and is used (as the sulphate) in lotions and injections for treating a wide variety of infections and orally as an intestinal antiseptic; also, either of the two constituent isomers (*neomycin B* and *C*) or an inactive degradation product of them (*neomycin A*).

1949 WAKSMAN & LECHEVALIER in *Science* 25 Mar. 305/2 In search for new compounds, particular attention was paid to those that would be effective against streptomycin-resistant bacteria, notably against the streptomycin-resistant strains of *M*[*ycobacterium*] *tuberculosis.* The discovery of such an agent, designated as neomycin, is reported here. **1949** R. L. PECK et al. in *Jrnl. Amer. Chem. Soc.* LXXI. 2590/2 Evidence has been obtained that the neomycin activity is due to more than one chemical entity; hence one may define it as a 'neomycin-complex'. The substance isolated as described herein, has been designated neomycin A. **1960** M. E. FLOREY *Clinical Applications of Antibiotics* IV. v. 140 Neomycin.. was expected to replace streptomycin since it was much less liable to induce resistance in pathogenic organisms. **1963** *Lancet* 19 Jan. 161/2 The infant [*sc.* a *Salmonella heidelberg* excretor] was treated with neomycin, and thereafter all specimens were negative. **1970** PASSMORE & ROBSON *Compan. Med. Stud.* II. xx. 30/1 Neomycin and kanamycin reduce ventilation during general anaesthesia by a neuromuscular blocking action. **1974** M. C. GERALD *Pharmacol.* iii. 45 The antibiotic neomycin is used to sterilize the gastrointestinal tract prior to abdominal surgery.

neon. Substitute for def.: **1.** One of the inert or noble gases, which is present in low concentration in the earth's atmosphere and is used at low pressure in discharge tubes, where it emits an orange-red glow. Atomic number 10; symbol Ne. (Add further examples.)

1905 *Chem. News* 5 May 204/1 A fair quantity of the mixture of neon and helium was prepared by liquefying air. **1935** *Industr. & Engin. Chem.* Jan. 116/1 Neon is characterized by its high electrical conductivity and light-emissive powers when an electrical current is discharged through it. **1966** *McGraw-Hill Encycl. Sci. & Technol.* IX. 36/1 Neon is used as the current-carrying agent in lightning arrestors; virtually no current is carried at voltages below the breakdown potential of the neon, but

when lightning strikes, the neon is ionized and allows the current to flow to ground. **1966** COTTON & WILKINSON *Adv. Inorg. Chem.* (ed. 2) xxiii. 598 Helium, neon and argon have so far not been brought into chemical combination..and it seems unlikely that they are capable of reaction.

2. A neon lamp or tube; neon lighting. Also *fig.*

1934 S. GOLD *Neon* 18 Whilst the customer may want his name expressed in neon and surrounded by a border, it is up to the sign-man to supply it with 'finish'. **1957** J. BRAINE *Room at Top* vi. 54 Too clean and well-lighted. They'll be installing neons soon. **1958** *Spectator* 30 May 687/3 The dialogue [of a play] is stuffed as full of metaphors as a copywriter's prose and Tony Richardson's production sets up each phrase in neon. **1969** A. GLYN *Dragon Variation* v. 162 To the left it was the glare of the rest of the Strip, the great river of neon, the jazziest in the world. **1974** R. BUTLER *Buffalo Hook* iii. 26 The neons were flashing over the plushy restaurants.

3. a. *attrib.* and *Comb.*, as *neon advertisement, glow, lighting, strip, wilderness, world; neon-blazing, -bright, -coupled, -filled, -lighted, -lit* adjs.

1972 D. HASTON *In High Places* iv. 57 There was a neon advertisement by the entrance. **1962** K. ORVIS *Damned & Destroyed* xxvii. 206 The city's wide, neon-blazing Sunset Strip. **1958** *Spectator* 25 July 133/3 A neon-bright café. **1946** *Nature* 21 Sept. 414/1 The rectified signal from the second detector was amplified by a neon-coupled two-stage D.C. amplifier. **1935** MILLER & FINK *Neon Signs* iii. 37 (*caption*) Relative light energy from a neon-filled tube. **1966** *McGraw-Hill Encycl. Sci. & Technol.* IX. 36/1 A very small wattage produces visible light in neon-filled glow lamps. **1935** MILLER & FINK *Neon Signs* iii. 37 Why is it, then, that the neon glow has such a powerful effect? **1945** A. HUXLEY *Time must have Stop* xxx. 276 The neon glow from those technological New Jerusalems beyond the horizons of the next revolution. **1936** C. ROUSE *Old Towns* i. 21 Inside, a neon-lighted glass sign directs you to 'Ye olde Beamed Tudor Cocktail Bar'. **1954** *Encounter* Feb. 37/2 It begins, in the West, with the neon-lighted brilliance of the Kurfürstendamm. **1913** *Trans. Illum. Engin. Soc.* (U.S.) 371 (*heading*) Neon lighting. **1933** *Times* 5 Dec. (Electricity Supply Number) p. xxiii/7 Neon lighting can be seen in almost every town of any size in the country. **1958** *Times Lit. Suppl.* 31 Jan. 63/2 His wrath is only excited by the Subtopia, the neon lighting, the petrol fumes, the 'soulless concrete' of our time. **1954** Neon-lit [see *ASPIRIN]. **1958** *Spectator* 14 Feb. 197/1 The actress, the best-selling author, or the famous film star who..remain tragically single, trapped in their own accursed, neon-lit achievement. **1972** R. BUSBY *Reasonable Man* iii. 24 They left the car outside the store and went..into the brash, neon-lit interior. **1939** 'J. STRUTHER' *Mrs. Miniver* 243 This part of the town was almost unrecognizable—a street of angular lettering and neon strips. **1973** 'H. HOWARD' *Highway to Murder* xiii. 149 Over the dressing chest a neon strip shone down on jars and bottles. **1953** *Encounter* Nov. 8/1 The neon wilderness of noise and music, fun and sin, boredom and high, desperate spirits. **1959** *Listener* 10 Dec. 1048/3 The American neon-wilderness. **1959** *New Statesman* 28 Feb. 302/3 Living in a neon-world of semi-legality, its leadership organises conferences and 'stay-at-homes' as if keeping the government informed about its intentions was a rule in the revolutionary game.

b. Special Comb.: **neon fish** = **neon tetra*; **neon lamp, light,** a lamp in which an electric discharge is passed through neon (giving an orange-red coloured light) or a mixture of neon with other gases (giving other colours); **neon sign,** a sign incorporating a neon light (usu. a neon tube), and often serving as an advertisement on a building; **neon tetra,** a small characin, *Hyphessobrycon innesi*, native to the Amazon, and remarkable for its colouring, which is dark green and white with a shining blue-green stripe; **neon tube,** a neon light in the form of a tube.

1938 L. MACNEICE *Zoo* 182 The tiniest fish here are the neon fish. **1911** *Chem. Abstr.* V. 1024 In contradistinction to the Hg vapor lamp the neon lamp's light is rich in red rays. **1931** *B.B.C. Year-bk.* 447/1 A special type of neon lamp is now used in television receivers to convert the electrical impulses back into light impulses, dependent for its action on a linear relation between light response and applied electrical potential and on an absence of time-lag. **1940** L. MACNEICE *Last Ditch* 15 And the neon-lamps of London Stain the canals of night. **1966** AINSWORTH & ROBINSON in Hewitt & Vause *Lamps & Lighting* xix. 309 Neon lamps using the positive column as the light source do exist however, the conventional 'neon lamps' used in advertising displays being of this type. **1913** *Trans. Illum. Engin. Soc.* (U.S.) 376 The neon light is physiologically excellent on account of its dull luminescence. **1931** H. G. WELLS *Work, Wealth & Happiness of Mankind* (1932) v. 211 This Neon light has great penetrating power in a fog. **1958** J. BETJEMAN *Coll. Poems* 231 So up I rose and went along To that old village alehouse where In neon lights is written 'Bear'. **1972** J. POTTER *Going West* 38 'Aloha', the airport tower announced in neon lights... Aloha meant welcome. **1927** *Advertising & Selling* 28 Dec. 34/3 Neon signs overcome the handicap of high first cost by lowered current consumption. **1934** *Times* 19 Feb. 13/5 In two of our quiet residential streets flaring neon signs have been put up to announce that the houses on which they are placed are hotels. **1958** J. BETJEMAN *Coll. Poems* 232 The neon sign's a work of art and visible for miles. **1973** *Black World* Mar. 62 Pulsating rock music seemed to control the flashing neon signs. **1936** W. T. INNES in *Aquarium* V. 82/2 The recent feat of bringing some wonderful new Characins, Neon Tetras (*Hyphessobrycon innesi* Myers), from Germany to the Shedd Aquarium in Chicago..in less than 60 hours. *Ibid.* 135/2 Regarding the Neon fishes... Four of these fishes were dead when the airship arrived... The red coloring from the fishes had made bright red blotches on the paper. *Ibid.* 136/2 The very good descriptive popular name for the fish, 'Neon Tetra' or 'Neontet' was originated by M. Lepaut, of Paris... The name is so fitting that Mr. Lew Willumsen, on seeing the new importation, independently hit upon the same name for them. **1952** D. GOHM *Tropical Fish* 100 The Neon Tetra is generally regarded as the most beautiful of all aquarium fish. **1962** *Listener* 22 Nov. 852/2 One [*sc.* tropical fish] which seemed to be lit up by a greenish blue light running from his head to his tail—this was a neon tetra. **1971** *Ceylon Observer Mag. Ed.* (Colombo) 19 Sept. 2/6 (Advt.), Goldfish, Angelfish, Neontetras. **1904** *Electr. World & Engin.* XLII. 583/2 The wavelength of the oscillator's vibration can..be measured by isolating a complete wave on the helix by means of a sliding earthed saddle using a neon tube as indicator. **1936** *Discovery* Nov. 364/2 The manufacture, erection, and maintenance of all neon tubes for advertising and display purposes. **1945** R. C. WALKER *Electronic Equipment & Accessories* xi. 211 Fig. 187 shows an application of the neon tube as a voltage stabiliser in a valve-rectifier circuit. **1962** A. NISBETT *Technique Sound Studio* 272 Stroboscopes work best with neon tubes.

neonate (nī·onēⁱt). *Med.* [f. NEO- + L. *nāt-us* born.] A recently born individual; *spec.* an infant less than four weeks old. Also *attrib.* or as *adj.*

1932 M. B. MCGRAW in *Child Development* III. 292/1 Most 'partunates'[1] display a decidedly helpless response to the force of gravity. [*Note*] [1] A term indicating infants who are just born... It covers about the first fifteen or thirty minutes of life since it includes the time during and immediately following parturition. When the umbilical cord is dressed and the baby is taken to the maternity nursery, then he becomes a 'neonate'. **1936** *Q. Rev. Biol.* XI. 70 (*heading*) Problems in the classification of neonate activities. **1951** L. CARMICHAEL in S. S. Stevens *Handbk. Exper. Psychol.* viii. 289/1 The fetus shows most of the specific patterns of response that can be elicited in the neonate. **1962** *Lancet* 12 May 1026/2 Neonates are capable of withstanding quite profound hypothermia for a short period of time. **1967** *Nature* 10 June 1099/2 The dentate gyrus is considerably more mature in the neonate guinea-pig than in the rat. **1973** *Jrnl. Genetic Psychol.* CXXII. 320 The overall body proportions of the typical neonate, 2-year-old, 6-year-old, [etc.].

neonatology (nīˌonēⁱtǫ·lŏdʒi). *Med.* [f. prec. + -OLOGY.] The branch of medicine concerned with the disorders and problems of recently born infants. Hence **neonato·logist,** an expert or specialist in neonatology.

1960 A. J. SCHAFFER *Diseases of Newborn* 1/1 We trust we shall be forgiven for coining the words 'neonatology' and 'neonatologist'. We do not recall ever having seen them in print. The one designates the art and science of diagnosis and treatment of disorders of the newborn infant, and the other the physician whose primary concern lies in this specialty. *Ibid.* p. vi/1 The situation of the pediatrician practising neonatology differs but little qualitatively from his everyday posture with respect to older infants and children. **1967** *Obstetrics & Gynecol.* XXX. 890 The obstetric trainee would assume the role of a pediatric resident in the field of neonatology. **1972** *Daily Colonist* (Victoria, B.C.) 3 Aug. 26/5 The intensive care unit..combines the disciplines of both fetology and neonatology. **1975** *Sci. Amer.* Jan. 51 (Advt.), Most neonatologists contend that many of these tragedies can be prevented by specially-trained perinatal medical teams using intensive care techniques.

neoned (nī·ǫnd), *a.* [f. NEON + -ED[2].] Illuminated by neon lighting.

1945 *Tomorrow* Mar. 46 The shadow went, he hardly noticed that he was already moving again toward the neoned glare. **1968** *Punch* 29 May 778/3 We..came upon an imperfectly neoned structure which might have passed for a church hall. **1973** J. WAINWRIGHT *Devil you Don't* 34 The neoned entrance to the *Roll-a-Ball Arcade.*

neopallium (nīˌopæ·liɒm). *Anat.* Also (with hyphen) **neo-pallium.** Pl. **-pallia.** [mod.L., f. *NEO- 1 e + PALLIUM.] The phylogenetically youngest portion of the pallium of the brain, which appears first among the more advanced reptiles and which among the mammals has become the largest part of the brain. Cf. *NEOCORTEX.

1901 G. E. SMITH in *Jrnl. Anat. & Physiol.* XXXV. 431 It is only one of the three histological formations which constitute the true pallium; and, as it is the latest of these to reach the height of its development, we may call it the 'new pallium' or..'neopallium', in contradistinction to the 'old pallium' of the Sauropsida and earlier Vertebrata, which is *chiefly* formed of the other two pallial areas. **1907** *Arch. Neurol.* III. 51 Maps have been obtained of these neopallia which are fairly full. *Ibid.* 52 The term neopallium is employed throughout in the sense suggested by Elliot Smith to indicate the variable area intercalated between the 'basal pallium' or pyriform lobe and the marginal pallium, or hippocampus. **1922** *Glasgow Herald* 23 Dec. 4/2 When our ancestors, with their free hands, their enlarged cerebral cortex or neopallium, and their capacity for co-operative action, had resources sufficient to enable them to stand up to Carnivores.., they left the trees and became once more terrestrial. **1948** A. BRODAL *Neurol. Anat.* x. 323 With the development of the neopallium or neo-cortex, the two more primitive areas are finally pushed medially, and in man are found entirely on the medial aspect of the hemisphere. **1973** *Gray's Anat.* (ed. 35) vii. 921/1 In the course of evolution visual, auditory and other conduction paths have been transferred, through the thalamus, to the pallium of the cerebral hemispheres... Consequently, each cerebral hemisphere enlarges as a result of the formation of an additional region, the neopallium.

Hence **neopa·llial** *a.*, of or pertaining to the neopallium.

1907 *Arch. Neurol.* III. 112 This appears to be the lowest grade of conscious neopallial association—*i.e.*, of psychic function. **1921** TILNEY & RILEY *Form & Functions Central Nervous Syst.* xlii. 772 (*heading*) Neopallial projection system. **1953** G. A. G. MITCHELL *Anat. Autonomic Nerv. Syst.* v. 66 This neopallial responsibility for autonomic activities is shared by subcortical centres in the hypothalamus. **1962** E. C. CROSBY et al. *Correl. Anat. Nerv. Syst.* vii. 411/1 Neopallial cortex makes up the major portion of the cerebral cortex in man.

neophilia (nīˌŏfi·liă). [f. NEO- + *-PHILIA.] Love for, or great interest in, what is new; a love of novelty. So **neophi·liac,** a person characterized by neophilia; also **neophi·li(a)c** *a.*; **neo·phily.**

1932 B. MALINOWSKI in R. F. Fortune *Sorcerers of Dobu* p. xxvii, Terminological neophily..is a habit to which I have always been hostile. **1966** R. & D. MORRIS *Men & Apes* vii. 217 There is a perpetual struggle going on inside the brain, between the fear of the new (neophobia) and the love of the new (neophilia). The neophobic urges keep the animal out of danger, while the neophilic urges prevent him from becoming too set in his ways. **1969** C. BOOKER (*title*) The neophiliacs. **1971** R. PETRIE *Thorne in Flesh* xi. 142 From where Thorne had sat, without neophiliac needs, he had seen..not spangles but sweating flesh. **1972** *Daily Tel.* 2 Aug. 2/2 The exaltation of novelty (neophilia) had been turned into a cult. *Ibid.*, Neophiliacs suffer from a collective fantasy which leads them to describe every change as inevitable and an improvement on what preceded it.

neophyte. Add: **3.** *Bot.* A plant found in an area in which it has not been recorded before.

1916 B. D. JACKSON *Gloss. Bot. Terms* (ed. 3) 248/1 Neophyte..a newly introduced plant (Rikli). **1970** *Watsonia* VIII. 157 Besides these three widespread neophytes, some other exotic taxa occur as ornamentals in gardens and parks.

neopilina (nīˌopilǝi·nă). [mod.L. (H. Lemche 1957, in *Nature* 23 Feb. 414/1), f. NEO- + *Pilina*, name of a similar fossil genus of molluscs.] A primitive, deep-sea mollusc of the monotypic genus so called, belonging to the order Monoplacophora.

1957 H. LEMCHE in *Nature* 23 Feb. 416/1 It would seem probable..that one of the main food-sources of *Neopilina* is radiolarians. **1959** *Listener* 12 Feb. 300/2 The recent discovery of *Neopilina*..is scientifically quite as important as that of the coelacanth. **1968** A. S. ROMER *Procession of Life* v. 101 Belief as to the primitive nature of these little ancient molluscs was abundantly confirmed by the discovery by a Danish oceanographic vessel a few years ago of specimens of a modern descendant of *Pilina*, living in deep oceanic waters off the west coast of South America; American exploration has resulted in further finds of this small mollusc, appropriately named *Neopilina*... Little *Neopilina* has aroused little public interest, but scientifically it is far more important than *Latimeria*... *Neopilina* sheds much light on the origin of a whole animal phylum. **1973** P. TASCH *Paleobiol. Invertebrates* viii. 325/2 *Neopilina* is segmented (that is, has internal metamerism) in a way similar to that of annelid worms and arthropods.

neoplasia (nīˌoplēⁱ·ziă). *Biol.* and *Med.* [f. NEO- + Gr. πλάσις formation: see -IA[1].] The formation of neoplasms; the state or condition of having neoplastic growth.

1890 C. P. MITCHELL *Philosophy Tumour-Dis.* i. 7 (*heading*) Explanation of the self-dependence of tumours: neoplasia identified with genesis in the Protozoa. **1926** *Glasgow Herald* 22 May 7/2 No one who had made a broad study of neoplasia of all varieties could support either of those theses. **1947** *Radiology* XLIX. 358/2 The late effects resulting from exposure to penetrating radiations..consisted of generalized atrophy and neoplasia of hemopoietic organs. **1962** *New Scientist* 12 Apr. 48/2 These processes do resemble in certain respects neoplasia. **1970** *Nature* 18 Apr. 290/1 The general belief in clinical circles is that bladder tumours are..produced as the result of chemical constituents in the urine which act on the urinary epithelium and produce neoplasia.

ne:o-pla·sticism. Freq. with capital initials. [ad. F. *néoplasticisme*, f. NEO- + PLASTICISM.] A movement or style in art originated by the Dutch painter Piet Mondrian (1872–1944), characterized by the use of primary colours and abstract forms. So **neopla·stic** *a.*[2]; **neoplasti·cian; neopla·sticist** *a.*

[**1920** P. MONDRIAN (*title*) Le Néo-plasticisme.] **1933** *Gallery of Living Art Catal.: A. E. Gallatin Coll.* (N.Y.), Mondrian, the neo-plastician. **1934** J. J. SWEENEY *Plastic Redirections in 20th Cent. Painting* 40 Piet Mondrian, member of the Dutch 'de Stijl' group and founder of the Neoplastic school, can..be taken as a producer of.. 'abstractions'... Yet, Mondrian has said, 'It is a great error to envisage a Neoplastic work as a total abstraction from life.' *Ibid.* 69 Such groups as the Purists, the Neoplasticians, and the Constructivists. **1935** *Art Digest* 15 Jan. 9/1 The Gallery of Living Art at New York University..has reopened after redecoration... In the rearrangement, emphasis has been placed on the work of the Cubists and on Constructivism and Neo-plasticism. **1936** A. H. BARR in *Cubism & Abstract Art* (N.Y. Mus. Mod.

Art) 140 (*heading*) Abstract art in Holland: *de Stijl* and Neo-Plasticism. *Ibid.* 144 This project is clearly a three-dimensional projection of a Neo-Plasticist painting. **1970** *Oxf. Compan. Art* 770/2 Neo-plasticism..was distinguished from Cubism in that it did not make use of figurative elements even as a starting-point for abstraction.

Neoplatonic, *a.* Add: Hence as *sb.* = NEOPLATONIST.

1840 E. Cox tr. *Döllinger's Hist. Church* i. 71 The Neoplatonics endeavoured, therefore, to unite the different systems of philosophy, especially the Pythagorean, Platonic, and Aristotelean, in one body with the principles of oriental learning. **1879** *Dublin Rev.* Apr. 524 On the Catholic side no theologian has followed Scotus Erigena: his system may be called an offspring of the Neoplatonics.

neoprene (nī·oprīn). [f. NEO- + *-prene*, after *ISOPRENE, *CHLOROPRENE.] Any of various synthetic rubbers made by polymerizing chloroprene (2-chloro-1,3-butadiene, CH_2:-CCl·CH:CH_2) and useful for their resistance to oil, heat, and weathering and their higher strength than natural rubber.

1937 *Du Pont Mag.* Feb. 16/3 As of December 15th the name *Neoprene* has been adopted to describe our chloroprene rubber formerly sold under the trade-mark 'DuPrene'. **1939** *Jrnl. R. Aeronaut. Soc.* XLIII. 150 In the matter of fuel tank construction, there are just about as many welded tanks as riveted tanks, the latter using duprene or neoprene as a leak preventative. **1950** *Archit. Rev.* CVIII. 411 Exterior butt joints are sealed with a flexible neoprene tube which is compressed when the panels are bolted together. **1957** H. L. FISHER *Chem. Natural & Synthetic Rubbers* ix. 101 The neoprenes are available in several types of latexes. **1959** *Observer* 27 Sept. 4/3 Diving-suits, made out of 'expanded neoprene' (a kind of foamed rubber), are now coming on the market. **1959** J. P. MUNN in M. Morton *Introd. Rubber Technol.* xiii. 339 Neoprene Type KNR is a soft, chemically plasticizable type, suitable for the production of cement, paints, and in spreading compounds. **1969** *New Scientist* 28 Aug. 430/3 The pyrotechnical compound is ignited by applying a soldering iron or propane gas flame to a small ignition hole. The heat makes the neoprene gasket expand to form a continuous seal. **1974** 'J. GRAHAM' *Bloody Passage* i. 24, I took down a neoprene wetsuit in black and pulled it on.

neostriatum (nīˌostraiˌēi·tǝ̆m). *Anat.* [mod. L., f. *NEO- 1 e + *STRIATUM.] The phylogenetically younger portion of the corpus striatum, consisting essentially of the caudate nucleus and the putamen.

1909 *Arch. Neurol. & Psychiatry* IV. 163 As the nucl. med. thal. (and also the nucl. rotund.) receive trigeminal fillet-fibres, it results that the first neocortical tactile region is one of oral sensibility (just as the first neostriatum). **1929** *Physiol. Abstr.* XIV. 398 (*heading*) Morphogenesis of neo- and palæostriatum in man. **1972** T. W. JENKINS *Functional Mammalian Neuroanat.* xvi. 237/1 Functionally the neostriatum (caudate nucleus and putamen) differs from the paleostriatum (globus pallidus). **1974** *Nature* 1 Feb. 284/1 Brains from other animals prepared similarly were dissected into neostriatum, nucleus accumbens, [etc.].

Hence **neostria·tal** *a.*, of or pertaining to the neostriatum.

1936 C. U. A. KAPPERS et al. *Compar. Anat. Nervous Syst. Vertebr.* II. ix. 1475 It..forms a hypopallial (or neostriatal) area. **1958** L. HAUSMAN *Clin. Neuroanat.* xxxiii. 287 (*heading*) The efferent neostriatal connections.

Neo-Synephrine (nīˌosine·frin, -īn). *Pharm.* Also **neo-synephrin(e, neosynephrine.** [f. NEO- + *synephrine* (f. SYN- + *EPIN)EPHRINE.] A proprietary name for phenylephrine.

1934 *Jrnl. Amer. Med. Assoc.* 16 June 2024/1 Neo-synephrin hydrochloride is a vasoconstrictor which is active when administered orally. **1937** *Amer. Jrnl. Ophthalmol.* XX. 176/2 In ophthalmoscopy neo-synephrine has the properties of other epinephrines. It produces mydriasis as quickly, as fully, and as safely as any mydriatic. **1950** *Trade Marks Jrnl.* 2 Aug. 711/1 Neo-Synephrine... Vasoconstrictors and antispasmodics being pharmaceutical preparations. Winthrop-Stearns, Inc... City and State of New York, United States of America; manufacturing chemists. **1972** *Obstetr. & Gynecol.* XL. 23/1 The nonsuture technic using a neosynephrine injection procedure for hemostasis..is recommended. **1974** M. C. GERALD *Pharmacol.* vi. 109 Drugs such as..phenylephrine (Neo-Synephrine) activate the adrenergic receptor directly.

neotechnic (nīˌote·knik), *a.* [f. NEO- + Gr. τεχνικ-ός (see TECHNIC *a.* and *sb.*).] Denoting, or belonging to, the most recent stage of industrial development. Hence **neote·chnics**, neotechnic technology.

1915 P. GEDDES *Cities in Evolution* iv. 64 Simply substituting *-technic* for *-lithic*, we may distinguish the earlier and ruder elements of the Industrial Age as Paleotechnic, the newer and still often incipient elements disengaging themselves from these as Neotechnic. **1927** Neotechnics [see *geotechnics* (*GEO-)]. **1934** [see *EOTECHNIC *a.*]. **1963** *Punch* 21 Aug. 284/1 The forms, symbolism and idiom of neotechnics. **1967** *Punch* 27 Sept. 451/1 The country would be rejigged to meet the challenge of the neotechnic revolution.

neotene (nī·otīn). *rare*$^{-1}$. [Cf. next.] A species (or member of a species) in which the period of immaturity is indefinitely prolonged.

1959 AUDEN *Homage to Clio* (1960) 25 The neotene who marches Upright and can subtract.

neoteny (niˌǫ·tǝni). *Zool.* [ad. G. *neotenie* (J. C. E. Kollman 1884, in *Verh. Naturf. Ges. Basel* VII. 391), f. Gr. νέος young + τείνειν to extend.] **a.** The retention of juvenile characteristics in adult life. **b.** The possession of sexual maturity by an animal still in its larval stage. Cf. *neoteinia, -tenia* (NEO- 2).

1901 H. GADOW in *Cambr. Nat. Hist.* VIII. iii. 65 These cases of neoteny are therefore instances of more or less complete retardation, or of the retention of partially larval conditions. **1920** *Conquest* Apr. 278/2 Neoteny.. here means the abnormal time-extension of youthful characters. **1932** J. S. HUXLEY *Probl. Relative Growth* vii. 237 It is clear that changes in rate-genes could as easily lead to the opposite of recapitulation as to recapitulation. Many examples of neoteny would fall under this head. **1962** D. NICHOLS *Echinoderms* xiv. 178 An interesting embryological phenomenon known as neoteny, in which, by the acceleration of development of the gonads, an animal becomes sexually mature while still retaining the larval body form. **1965** *New Scientist* 14 Jan. 86/1 The retention of the puppy characteristic (neoteny) of floppy ears. **1971** J. Z. YOUNG *Introd. Study Man* xxxiv. 479 Such a change, technically called neoteny (or paedomorphosis), has in fact occurred often in the course of the evolution of diverse animals.

Hence **neote·nic, neo·tenous** *adjs.*, **neo·tenously** *adv.*

1901 H. GADOW in *Cambr. Nat. Hist.* VIII. iii. 64 Not unfrequently typical neotenic and overgrown specimens occur side by side with others which have completed their metamorphosis. **1930** G. R. DE BEER *Embryol. & Evol.* 27 Some animals have become permanently committed to this neotenous state. **1932** J. S. HUXLEY *Probl. Relative Growth* ii. 67 Workers [*sc.* termites] have been derived from soldiers by a suppression of their final development into the normal big-jawed type—..in fact, they are neotenic. **1957** *New Biol.* XXIII. 103 Animals which breed as juveniles or larvae are described as 'neotenous'. **1963** R. P. DALES *Annelids* iii. 72 The fusiform typhloscolecids...were possibly derived neotenously from phyllodocid stock. **1965** B. E. FREEMAN tr. *Vandel's Biospeleology* xiv. 233 All the troglobious urodeles are neotenous. They do not undergo metamorphosis and thus retain their larval characters throughout life.

neoterical, *a.* Delete ? *Obs.* and add later *arch.* example.

1941 E. R. EDDISON *Fish Dinner* (1972) xvi. 266 For the more mockery, let it arise from the sea: a very neoterical Anadyomene.

neothalamus (nīˌoþæ·lǎmǝ̆s). *Anat.* [mod. L. (L. Edinger *Vorlesungen über den Bau der nervösen Zentralorgane des Menschen und der Tiere* (ed. 7, 1908) II. xv. 234), f. *NEO- 1 e + THALAMUS.] The phylogenetically younger portion of the thalamus, which includes its lateral part.

1917 *Jrnl. Compar. Neurol.* XXVIII. 217 These parts of the thalamus..are termed by Edinger the neothalamus by reason of their functional relationship with the neopallium. **1921** TILNEY & RILEY *Form & Functions Central Nerv. Syst.* xxxi. 567 The neothalamus is an addition to the pars thalamica appearing in mammals only. **1973** *Gray's Anat.* (ed. 35) 893/1 The anterior and medial part of the thalamus, together with some of the smaller groups of nuclei, are often regarded as phylogenetically the older regions, and designated paleothalamus in contrast with the lateral part or neothalamus, which reaches its greatest development in anthropoid apes and man.

So **neotha·lamic** *a.*, of or pertaining to the neothalamus.

1909 *Arch. Neurol. & Psychiatry* IV. 163 The upper part of the lateral cortex layer has certainly already a neo-cortical character, as is proved by the fact that a certain amount of fibres, originating in a neo-thalamic nucleus of the fillet.., end in it. **1936** C. U. A. KAPPERS et al. *Compar. Anat. Nervous Syst. Vertebr.* II. ix. 1481 Here for the first time there are projection fibers from neothalamic centers.

neotocite. Read: (nīˌotōᵘ·kǝit). *Min.* Also † **neotokite.** [ad. G. *neotokit* (N. Nordenskiöld *Verzeichn. d. in Finland gefund. Min.* (1852) (Dana)), f. Gr. νεότοκ-ος new-born, recent (f. νέος new + τόκος offspring, childbirth) + G. *-it* -ITE¹.] A hydrated silicate of manganese and iron, approximately $Mn_2Fe_2Si_4O_{12}.6H_2O$, which is found as black amorphous masses.

1854, etc. [in Dict.]. **1921** *Jrnl. Washington Acad. Sci.* XI. 27 Some specimens of the bementite rock are cut by thin veinlets of dark brown to black amorphous neotocite. **1932** *Amer. Mineralogist* XVII. 18 Areas of neotocite, several centimeters across are characterized by glistening black color and conchoidal fracture. **1968** I. KOSTOV *Mineralogy* 351 The amorphous silicate of manganese known as neotocite, occurring as black, opal- or coal-like masses is found as a weathering product of rhodonite and as a volcanogenic-sedimentary mineral.

neotype (nī·otəip). [f. NEO- + TYPE.] **1.** (In Dict. s.v. NEO- 2.)

2. *Taxonomy.* [a. F. *néotype* (A. E. M. Cossman *Essais de Paléoécologie Comparée* (1896) II. 2 and (1904) VI. 9), f. NEO- + *TYPE *sb.*¹ 8.] A specimen designated as a type, in the absence of any other type material.

1905 C. SCHUCHERT in *Bull. U.S. Nat. Mus.* No. 53. 13 The term is here used as redefined by Cossman in 1904.. as follows: Neotype for the specimen afterwards taken as the type of a species when the original type has been destroyed. **1961** G. G. SIMPSON *Princ. Animal Taxonomy* i. 32 Neotype: a substitute for a type that has been lost or (in some usages) is otherwise inadequate for the type role. (Neotypes have not hitherto been recognized in the Rules, but there are proposals to incorporate them therein.) **1966** *Internat. Code Bot. Nomenclature* ii. 19 A neotype is a specimen or other element selected to serve as nomenclatural type as long as all of the material on which the name of the taxon was based is missing.

N.E.P., NEP, Nep⁴ (nep). [f. the initial letters of *New Economic Policy.*] A programme initiated in the Soviet Union in 1921 for the revival of the wage system and private ownership in industry. Hence **ne·pman, NEP-man,** one engaged in this programme.

[**1922** *Communist Rev.* June 107/2 The basic task of 'Nepa' (New Economic Policy),..is to establish a close connection between the socialist economy..and the economy of the peasant masses.] **1924** *Glasgow Herald* 2 Jan. 7 The wholesale arrest of thousands of persons, including many 'Nepmen' supporters of the new economic policy. **1927** *19th Cent.* Nov. 655 In 1921 the economic catastrophe threatened to bury under its ruins even the Soviet Government. It was then that Lenin proclaimed the New Economic Policy or 'N.E.P.' This 'Nep' was nothing else than a whole series of concessions to life—it was the victory of life over the deadly system inaugurated by the Soviet Government. **1929** *Daily Tel.* 22 Jan. 10/7 The Nep..is continually reasserting itself, in spite of the persecution and restrictions under which the Nepmen suffer. **1949** E. POUND *Pisan Cantos* lxxiv. 25 But in Russia they bungled and did not apparently Grasp the idea of work-certificate And started the N.E.P. with disaster And the immolation of men to machinery. **1951** KOESTLER *Age of Longing* vi. 98 There were rich and poor again; though the rich were now called NEP-men. **1961** C. COCKBURN *View from West* ix. 127 The British upper middle classes..richer and happier than ever—the great NEP-men of the 1950s. **1971** W. H. MCNEILL in A. Bullock *20th Cent.* 48/1 Extreme economic disruption even compelled Lenin to abandon Communist principles to the extent of allowing limited private trading (NEP or New Economic Policy, 1921). **1973** *Times Lit. Suppl.* 3 Aug. 910/3 The wickedness, real or alleged, of Nepmen became a favourite theme of official propaganda.

Nepalese (nepǭlī·z), *a.* and *sb.* Also **Nepaulese.** [f. *Nepal*, name of a country on the north-eastern frontier of India + -ESE.] **A.** *adj.* Of, pertaining to, or connected with Nepal. **B.** *sb.* A native or inhabitant of Nepal; these people collectively. Also, the language of this people.

The form *Nepali* (*a.* and *sb.*) also occurs, esp. as the name of the language of the Nepalese.

[**1811** W. KIRKPATRICK *Acct. Nepaul* vii. 207 The Nepaulians most commonly barter it for the rock salt and borax of Tibet.] **1819** F. HAMILTON *Acct. Nepal* I. i. 39 The following account of the Nepalese, or rather Newar, architecture, I have taken from papers communicated by Colonel Crawford. The Nepalese possess a great advantage in having an excellent clay for making bricks and tiles. **1848** J. D. HOOKER in L. Huxley *Life J. D. Hooker* (1918) I. xiii. 251 The Sikkim Rajah, whose territories were once the prey of the Nepalese. *Ibid.* 263 Accepting the invitation of Major Thoresby, the Nepaulese Resident. **1884** *Encycl. Brit.* XVII. 343/1 In all matters of domestic policy the Nepalese brook no interference. **1885** G. C. WHITWORTH *Anglo-Indian Dict.* 226/2 *Nepáli*, an inhabitant of Nepal or an emigrant from that country. The principal Nepáli tribes are the Gurkhás, the Gurungs, the Newárs and Limbus, the Kirátis, the Bhutiás, the Lepchás. Also the name of the language of the country, which is a dialect of Hindi. **1908** T. G. TUCKER *Introd. Nat. Hist. Lang.* 187 *Gujarāti, Sindhi, Punjābi, Kashmiri*, and *Nepāli* in the regions which their names imply. **1911** *Encycl. Brit.* XX. 453/1 Khas-kurā,.. passes under various names. The English generally call it Nēpālī or Naipālī (i.e. the language of Nepal), which is a misnomer, for it is not the principal form of speech of that country. **1920** *Mission News* June 45/2 He has translated..the whole of the Bible into his own Nepali language. **1927** *Chambers's Jrnl.* June 370/1 The bungalow.. remained in charge of a Nepali. **1931** *Times* 16 Mar. 22/5 Nepalese bronzes and brass work. **1961** *Listener* 10 Aug. 211/1, I had once known Nepali almost as well as I know English. **1964** R. PERRY *World of Tiger* iv. 52 The Nepalese stockmen were only too well aware of this habit. **1969** *Sunday Tel.* 12 Jan. 7/3 Many of the hippies..left Nepal..in 1968. The Nepalese didn't like them. **1971** C. BONINGTON *Annapurna South Face* i. 13 He spoke fluent Nepali. *Ibid.* iii. 40 The Internal Departures office, an open shed crammed with Nepalis and hippies. **1973** *Times* 14 Apr. (Nepal Suppl.) p. ii/2 It was only after the unification of the country under the royal house of Gorkha that Nepali became the *lingua franca* of the whole of Nepal. *Ibid.* p. ii/3 Traditionally Nepali Hindus are extremely conservative.

neper (nī-, nēi·pǝɹ). Also †**napier.** [f. *Neperus*, Latinized form of the name of John *Napier* (or *Neper*) (see NAPIER'S BONES).] A unit used in comparing the power levels in

two communication circuits or the intensities of two sounds: their difference in nepers is equal to half the natural logarithm of their ratio.

1924 K. S. JOHNSON *Transmission Circuits for Telephonic Communication* vii. 46 The transformer loss (expressed in napiers). **1929** [see *BEL]. **1931** [see *decineper* (*DECI- 1)]. **1954** *Electronic Engin.* XXVI. 91 The short line with which we are concerned in this article is defined as one for which the overall attenuation coefficient is small, say not greater than 0·2 neper, although the line may be several wavelengths long. **1972** J. M. TAYLOR tr. *Meyer & Neumann's Physical & Appl. Acoustics* i. 11 One neper corresponds to 8·69 dB.

nepeta (nĕpī·tă). [L. *nepeta* catmint, perh. f. *Nepeta* ancient name of Nepi, a town in central Italy, adopted as the name of a genus by Linnæus (*Genera Plantarum* (1737) 170) and earlier botanists.] An annual or perennial herbaceous plant of the genus so called, belonging to the family Labiatæ; = CATMINT.

1915 H. H. THOMAS *Bk. Hardy Flowers* 304 Some of the Nepetas are little more than weeds, though a few kinds are attractive. **1939** R. E. CLARKSON *Magic Gardens* ii. 21 If you like, the gray santolina (but only for wide edgings), the nepetas, French thyme. **1961** *Times* 28 Jan. 9/3 Interplanted with the nepeta were daffodils. **1975** *Country Life* 6 Mar. 561/2 Blue anchusas..rising from misty blue nepeta.

nephanalysis (nefănæ·lĭsis). *Meteorol.* Pl. **-ses.** [f. Gr. νέφ-ος cloud + ANALYSIS.] An analysis of the amounts and kinds of cloud present over an area; *esp.* a chart showing this in symbolic form.

1945 F. A. BERRY et al. *Handbk. Meteorol.* xi. 882 Synoptic studies of clouds (nephanalysis) indicate the possibility of a visual weather analysis based on cloud observations. *Ibid.* 905 Observations plotted on maps for nephanalysis include clouds, weather, [etc.]. **1961** *N.Y. Times* 21 Sept. 31/5 Meanwhile the meteorologists were translating the cloud pictures into diagrammatic meteorological charts, known as 'nephanalyses'. **1965** *Q. Jrnl. R. Meteorol. Soc.* XCI. 526 The latest Tiros 9 weather satellite is on a polar orbit and facsimile nephanalyses are received twice daily at Bracknell for an area close to or covering the British Isles. **1973** BARRY & PERRY *Synoptic Climatology* ii. 52 With the NIMBUS and ESSA satellites, global coverage is now available on a daily basis and nephanalyses are prepared from the photography.

nephelauxetic (nefĕlǭkse·tik), *a.* *Physical Chem.* [f. Gr. νεφέλ-η cloud + αὐξητικ-ός AUXETIC *a.*] Causing an expansion of the *d*-electron cloud of a central atom, i.e. a decrease in the inter-electron repulsion parameter; *nephelauxetic series*, a series of ligands arranged in order of their nephelauxetic effects.

1958 SCHÄFFER & JØRGENSEN in *Jrnl. Inorg. & Nuclear Chem.* VIII. 147 We shall propose to call this series the nephelauxetic (cloud expanding) series, as it corresponds to a development of the *d* shell in the region of the ligands. The neo-greek word was constructed by Professor Kaj Barr from the University of Copenhagen. **1965** *Molecular Physics* X. 7 The red shift of the ligand field bands in metal complexes with respect to the free ions has been explained..as being due to the nephelauxetic effect. **1966** PHILLIPS & WILLIAMS *Inorg. Chem.* II. xxviii. 402 The nephelauxetic (cloud-expanding) series.., it is suggested, represents the spread of the electron away from its parent nucleus on increase of covalent character in the binding of a given cation. **1973** *Chem. Soc. Rev.* II. 177 The *cis*-influence of ligands increases in accordance with their position in the nephelauxetic series.

nepheline. Add: **nepheline-syenite** [ad. G. *nephelin-syenit* (H. Rosenbusch *Mikrosk. Petrogr.* (1877) II. 203)], a rare plutonic rock which resembles syenite in containing alkali feldspars such as orthoclase as essential minerals and usu. dark ferromagnesian minerals also (commonly amphibole or pyroxene), but differs in containing nepheline as an additional essential mineral, in being rich in soda but always lacking quartz, and in the frequent occurrence of rare minerals as accessories.

1892 F. H. HATCH *Text-bk. Petrol.* (ed. 2) vi. 143 The syenites and diorites are plutonic granitoid rocks, less acid than granite, and consequently containing little or no free silica. They may be divided into—Syenites. Nepheline-syenites. Diorites. **1938** A. JOHANNSEN *Descr. Petrogr. Ign. Rocks* IV. 78 The nepheline-syenites are generally gray rocks with a greasy luster, usually moderately dark... Yellows, reds, and blues are not unknown. **1967** M. J. COE *Ecol. Alpine Zone Mt. Kenya* 11 The lava cooled slowly and produced a material that is highly crystalline. These rocks are called nepheline-syenite and contain large Felspar crystals up to 3 cm long as well as smaller nepheline crystals.

nephelinite. Add: Hence **nephelini·tic** *a.*, containing or characteristic of nephelinite.

1909 J. P. IDDINGS *Igneous Rocks* I. ii. ii. 386 Rocks rich in feldspar have a trachytic texture; those rich in nephelite have a nephelinitic texture. **1944** C. PALACHE et al. *Dana's Syst. Min.* (ed. 7) I. 733 Pegmatites of the contact zone of the nephelinitic intrusive of the Chibina tundra, Kola. **1974** *Nature* 8 Feb. 354/1 An older series of basaltic-trachytic shield volcanoes, together with smaller nephelinitic centres.

nephelinization (nefĕlinəizē̆·ʃən). *Petrol.* [f. NEPHELIN(E + -IZATION.] The alteration of a rock to one in which nepheline is an essential constituent.

1943 *Science* 26 Mar. 286/2 It is believed that the nephelinization is post-folding, since the flow marble contains fragments of all rocks except those containing nepheline. **1969** *Bull. Brit. Mus. (Nat. Hist.) Mineral.* II. 214 The nepheline syenites and ijolites are capable of desilicating the enclosing rock envelope—nephelinization. *Ibid.*, The nephelinization at Tundulu has been shown.. to be related to the main ring-dyke of foyaite.., while at Dorowa the nephelinized fenite..surrounds a body of foyaite and ijolite.

So **ne·phelinized, ne·phelinizing** *ppl. adjs.*

1943 *Science* 26 Mar. 286/2 (*heading*) The nephelinized paragneisses of the Bancroft region, Ontario. **1946** *Jrnl. Geol.* LIV. 167/2 The nephelinizing solutions.. carried..soda and alumina, with quantities of volatiles, including H_2O, Cl, P, and others. **1959** W. W. MOORHOUSE *Study Rocks in Thin Section* xv. 311 The nephelinized gneisses include a wide variety of melanocratic to leucocratic rocks. **1969** Nephelinized [see above].

nephelo-. Add: **nephelometer,** (*b*) any of various instruments by which the turbidity of a suspension, culture, etc., can be measured or compared with a standard by means of the light scattered (at right angles) by it; **nephelometric,** *a.*, add: or to nephelometry (examples); **nephelome·trically** *adv.*, by nephelometry; **nephelo·metry** *Chem.*, the technique of quantitative analysis using a nephelometer.

1895 T. W. RICHARDS in *Proc. Amer. Acad. Arts & Sci.* XXX. 385 Since the opalescence was so faint that one could only with difficulty see it at all under ordinary conditions, a piece of apparatus, which may be named a 'nephelometer' (νεφελη, a cloud), was devised for detecting it. **1906** MCFARLAND & L'ENGLE in *Medicine* (Detroit) XII. 249/1 It occurred to us that uniformity in the number of bacteria..could be secured with reasonable accuracy by some means of measuring and standardizing the turbidity of the fluid containing them. We therefore devised a simple instrument, for which we suggest the name *nephelometer*.., by which it became easy to secure any desired degree of turbidity. **1936** F. D. & C. T. SNELL *Colorimetric Methods of Anal.* viii. 91 In the usual nephelometer the opaque tubes with clear glass bottoms used in colorimetry have been replaced with clear glass tubes with opaque bottoms. **1969** *Atmospheric Environment* III. 561 The multi-wavelength adaptation of the integrating nephelometer makes possible the local measurement of the wavelength dependence of the extinction coefficient due to scatter of atmospheric air. **1974** *Times-Herald-Record* (Middletown, N.Y.) 12 May, (*caption*) Researchers set up a light scattering instrument called an integrating nephelometer atop Mount Beacon. The tests were part of an air-pollution study. **1905** *Jrnl. Amer. Chem. Soc.* XXVII. 485 The application of these observations to the nephelometric analysis of a very dilute silver chloride solution is obvious. **1929** P. A. KOBER in J. H. Yoe *Photometric Chem. Anal.* II. vi. 71 Precipitants for the production of nephelometric suspensions are as varied as the substances precipitated. **1971** P. R. HESSE *Textbk. Soil Chem. Anal.* xii. 314 The only difference between turbidimetric and nephelometric measurement of sulphate is in the measurement of the final turbidity. **1905** *Jrnl. Amer. Chem. Soc.* XXVII. 507 When in a day or two the precipitate had settled and the mother-liquor had become clear the latter was examined nephelometrically. **1971** P. R. HESSE *Textbk. Soil Chem. Anal.* xvi. 423 Silver is extracted from soil by acid digestion and is classically determined nephelometrically as the chloride. **1876** T. P. BLUNT in *Chem. News* 7 Jan. 7/2 It would appear that the usefulness of colorimetry, and also of judgment by turbidity, which may provisionally be termed 'nephelometry', might be widely extended. **1906** *Amer. Chem. Jrnl.* XXXV. 113 In order to save the time of those attempting nephelometry, the precautions for several typical cases are here collected. **1929** J. H. YOE *Photometric Chem. Anal.* II. iii. 18 When colorimetry or nephelometry is used at all, in routine analytical work or in research problems, it is apt to be used almost continuously. **1966** *McGraw-Hill Encycl. Sci. & Technol.* IX. 40/1 The advantage of nephelometry [over turbidimetry] is its greater sensitivity, accuracy, and precision in the determination of small amounts of turbidity.

nepheloid, *a.* Delete *rare*—⁰ and add examples referring to the ocean; chiefly in *nepheloid layer*, a layer about a kilometre thick in the deep water of the western North Atlantic and elsewhere that is turbid owing to suspended mineral matter.

1965 EWING & THORNDIKE in *Science* 12 Mar. 1291/1 Strong background haze in some of our ocean bottom photographs has been difficult to explain by any cause other than clouded (nepheloid) water. *Ibid.* 1291/2 The degree to which the water is nepheloid. *Ibid.* 1291/3 A sample of 200 liters obtained from the nepheloid layer was found..to contain some organisms and about 0·50 g of suspended lutite. **1972** ETTREIM & EWING in A. L. Gordon *Stud. Physical Oceanogr.* II. 123 The turbulence associated with the vigorous bottom currents of the western North Atlantic maintains a nepheloid layer with an average thickness of one kilometer. **1974** *Nature* 6 Sept. 43/2 The thickness of this nepheloid layer is several orders of magnitude greater than the characteristic thickness of the turbulent Ekman layer at the ocean floor.

nephometer (nefǫ·mĭtəɹ). [ad. F. *néphomètre* (L. Besson 1906, in *Annuaire de la Soc. météorol. de France* LIV. 241), Gr. νέφ-ος cloud + -OMETER.] = *nephelometer* s.v. NEPHELO-.

1910 J. MOORE *Meteorol.* (ed. 2) xvii. 218 Spherical Mirror Nephometer.—This instrument..permits the cloud-percentage (nebulosity) to be measured without any fear of an error in the number of the tenths. The description of, and the method of using, this new nephometer have been given by the inventor, M. L. Besson. **1959** R. E. HUSCHKE *Gloss. Meteorol.* 388 *Nephometer* (also called *nephelometer*), a general term for instruments designed to measure the amount of cloudiness.

nephrectomize, *v.* Add: (Further example.) So **nephre·ctomized** *ppl. a.*, deprived of a kidney by surgery.

1949 FLOREY & JENNINGS in H. W. Florey et al. *Antibiotics* II. xl. 1286 The slopes of the curves showing the disappearance of the two penicillins from the plasma were roughly parallel for both normal and nephrectomized dogs. **1953** Nephrectomized [see *hypokalæmic* adj. s.v. *HYPO- II]. **1972** *Science* 9 June 1146/3 Rats..either had their ureters ligated or were bilaterally nephrectomized.

nephridiopore (nefri·diopōᵊɹ). [f. NEPHRIDIUM + PORE *sb.*¹] The excretory opening of a nephridium.

1888 F. E. BEDDARD in *Q. Jrnl. Microsc. Sci.* XXVIII. 397 There are more than one pair of nephridiopores in each segment of the body. **1946** *Nature* 9 Nov. 665/2 Overton observed an initial loss of weight on handling the worm, and attributed this to the expulsion of fluid through the nephridiopores. **1963** R. P. DALES *Annelids* v. 98 The fluid which issues from the nephridiopores of an earthworm does not have the same composition as the coelomic fluid.

nephridiostome (nefri·diostōᵘm). [f. NEPHRIDIUM + STOMA.] = *nephrostome* s.v. NEPHRO-.

1902 *Encycl. Brit.* XXXIII. 882/2 The Hesionidæ have compound organs, serving both as excretory and as genital ducts, formed by the grafting of the coelomostome on to the nephridiostome. **1963** R. P. DALES *Annelids* i. 29 In many other polychaetes..and in oligochaetes and leeches, an open funnel or nephridiostome is formed.

nephro-. Add: **ne:phrocalcino·sis,** deposition of concretions of calcium compounds in the kidneys; **nephrocyte** *Zool.* [ad. G. *nephrocyt* (A. Korotneff 1894, in *Mitt. Zool. Stat. Neapel* XI. 344)], a cell in insects which stores or excretes waste products; **nephromi·xium** (pl. **-mixia**) *Zool.* [Gr. μῖξις mingling], in certain polychaetes, an organ formed by the fusion of the coelomoduct and the nephridium; **nephropathy,** for 'diseases' read 'disease' and add examples; hence **nephropa·thic** *a.*; **ne·phropexy** *Surg.* [Gr. πῆξις fixing], the operation of securing an abnormally movable kidney; **nephrosclero·sis,** thickening and hardening of the walls of the blood vessels of the kidney, which is often associated with hypertension and can lead to renal failure; **nephro·-stomy** *Surg.* [ad. F. *néphrostomie* (Guyon & Albarran 1898, in *Rev. de Chir.* XVIII. 1052), f. Gr. στόμα mouth], the operation of making an opening from the surface of the body directly into the pelvis of the kidney; **ne·-phrotome** *Zool.* [ad. G. *nephrotom* (J. W. van Wijhe 1889, in *Arch. f. mikrosk. Anat.* XXXIII. 465): see *-TOME], a block of tissue at the edge of a somite, giving rise to the excretory organs; **nephroto·xic** *a.*, having a toxic effect on the kidneys; so **ne:phrotoxi·city,** the property or effect of being nephrotoxic; **ne·phrotoxin,** (*a*) a nephrotoxic antibody produced by injecting kidney tissue into an animal; (*b*) any nephrotoxic substance.

1934 F. ALBRIGHT et al. in *Amer. Jrnl. Med. Sci.* CLXXVII. 60 The initial disturbance, however, is not an inflammation, but presumably a deposition of calcium. Therefore, the term chronic nephro-calcinosis would seem preferable. **1951** A. C. ALLEN *Kidney* xi. 366/2 Parenchymal nephrocalcinosis rarely interferes with renal function to any significant degree. **1974** PASSMORE & ROBSON *Compan. Med. Stud.* III. xxiii. 51/1 In nephrocalcinosis calcium is deposited in the basement of renal tubules in cortex and medulla, in tubular lumina and in small foci in the interstitial tissue. **1895** *Jrnl. R. Microsc. Soc.* 165 He [*sc.* Korotneff] finds colossal cells, whose possible function is suggested in the title 'nephrocytes'. **1932** BORRADAILE & POTTS *Invertebrata* xiv. 390 Nitrogenous end products are found in the nephrocytes (cells found commonly associated with the fat body and the pericardium [of insects]). **1969** R. F. CHAPMAN *Insects* xxv. 494 Nephrocytes, or pericardial cells, are cells occurring singly or in groups in various parts of the body. They may be very large, as in dipterous larvae, or small and numerous and usually they contain more than one nucleus. **1900** E. S. GOODRICH in *Q. Jrnl. Microsc. Sci.* XLIII. 742 The ordinary wide-mouthed segmental

organs of the Polychæta, formed by the fusion of the nephridium with the genital funnel, may be called Nephromixia... Kindly suggested to me by Professor E. Ray Lankester. **1900** E. R. LANKESTER *Treat. Zool.* II. ii. 37 The composite organ thus formed may be termed a 'nephromixium' or 'nephromix', in reference to its hybrid composition. **1932** BORRADAILE & POTTS *Invertebrata* ix. 229 Nephromixia may take on the functions of coelomoducts where these do not exist independently. **1963** R. P. DALES *Annelids* i. 30 In other polychaetes the coelomoducts may be grafted on to the stem of the nephridium to form a nephromixium, which may be used both as a genital and as an excretory duct. **1917** DORLAND *Med. Dict.* (ed. 9) 655/1 Nephropathic. **1973** *Nature* 3 Aug. 289/2 In the nephropathic form of cystinosis, patients appear normal at birth. **1916** Nephropathy [see *NEPHROSIS b]. **1956** ROOT & WHITE *Diabetes Mellitus* xv. 189 Diabetic nephropathy is commonly first indicated by recurring edema, persistent albuminuria and in many cases an increase in the plasma lipids. **1968** A. WALSH tr. *J. Hamburger's Nephrology* I. xvi. 529/1 Even in the group of nephropathies of toxic origin, mercury poisoning takes second place..after carbon tetrachloride. **1897** *Jrnl. Amer. Med. Assoc.* 11 Dec. 1190/1 Nephropexy is a legitimate and established procedure in all cases in which it can be established that the kidney is not only displaced, but is at the same time the direct cause of the manifold symptoms which such a condition may and often will produce. **1932** BALL & EVANS *Dis. of Kidney* xiii. 394 Nephropexy has proved a sufficient method of treatment of mild degrees of hydronephrosis associated with excessive mobility of the kidney. **1968** Nephropexy [see *FIXATION 3 c]. **1890** BILLINGS *Med. Dict.* II. 199/2 Nephrosclerosis. **1926** H. ELWYN *Nephritis* xvi. 280 Arteriosclerosis of the kidney with its end stage of primary contracted kidney was classified under the term nephrosclerosis. **1951** A. C. ALLEN *Kidney* xiii. 397/1 The color of the kidneys with malignant nephrosclerosis is brownish or greyish red. **1966** *McGraw-Hill Encycl. Sci. & Technol.* VII. 343/2 Nephrosclerosis is only part of a generalized disorder of arteries. **1900** KEEN & DACOSTA *Amer. Yr.-bk. Med. & Surg.* II. 184 MM. Guyon and T. Albarran discussed the subject of nephrotomy at the French Surgical Congress of 1898. They restrict the term nephrotomy to the making of an incision into the kidney; but when the pelvis of the kidney is opened through the kidney-substance, and the wound is kept open and a fistula is formed, they call the operation nephrostomy. *Ibid.*, Nephrostomy is employed, in the first place, to relieve renal retention, septic or aseptic. **1932** *Jrnl. Amer. Med. Assoc.* 8 Oct. 1229/2 Nephrostomy on only one side makes the care of the urinary drainage apparatus much easier. **1967** S. TAYLOR et al. *Short Textbk. Surg.* xxv. 357 If the patient is too ill for a major operation nephrostomy or drainage of the kidney only may be possible, with secondary nephrectomy later, a very difficult operation. **1895** GADOW & ABBOTT in *Phil. Trans. R. Soc.* B. CLXXXVI. 166 Concerning the segmentally arranged mesodermal products (omitting nephrotomes and gonotomes) the following subdivision is adhered to. **1949** A. S. ROMER *Vertebrate Body* xii. 378 In our embryological story we noted that in every trunk segment the mesoderm includes, on either side, a nephric region, often segmentally distinct as a nephrotome, a small discrete block of tissue interposed between somite and lateral plate. **1974** M. HILDEBRAND *Analysis of Vertebrate Structure* xiii. 308 Relatively few nephrotomes are incorporated [in the pronephros]. **1902** VAUGHAN & NOVY *Cellular Toxins* (ed. 4) vii. 144 The blood of animals in which one ureter has remained tied for some time becomes laden with a nephrotoxic substance. **1937** Nephrotoxic [see *nephrotoxin* below]. **1973** *Jrnl. Pharmacol. & Exper. Ther.* CLXXXVI. 593/1 Administration of the nephrotoxic agent uranyl nitrate to rats specifically stimulated organic base accumulation by renal cortical slices. **1961** *Lancet* 22 July 179/1 The new preparation.. appeared..to be devoid of..nephrotoxicity. **1970** PASSMORE & ROBSON *Compan. Med. Stud.* II. xxxii. 4/2 Mercury poisoning is the oldest and best understood type of nephrotoxicity. **1902** *Jrnl. Chem. Soc.* LXXXIV. ii. 443 Repeated injections into the rabbit..of kidney cells from the dog..provoke the appearance in the rabbit's blood of a substance, nephrotoxin, which is most harmful to the kidney cells of the dog. **1937** *Jrnl. Exper. Med.* LXV. 564 The nephrotoxic effect induced by anti-kidney serum is dependent upon a relatively organ specific antibody, nephrotoxin. **1961** A. G. WHITE *Clin. Disturbances of Renal Function* v. 153 Among the nephrotoxins encountered most frequently in clinical practice is carbon tetrachloride. **1970** R. C. MUEHRCKE in F. W. Sunderman *Lab. Diagnosis Kidney Dis.* xxxvii. 444/1 Other nephrotoxins such as sulfonamides produce their adverse pathopharmacological effects through a hypersensitivity reaction.

nephron (ne·frǫn). *Anat.* [a. G. *nephron* (H. Braus *Anat. d. Menschen* (1924) II. 351), f. Gr. νεφρός kidney.] Each of the numerous filtration units in the kidney, which consist of a tube divided (in higher forms) into a glomerulus, a proximal convoluted tubule, a loop of Henle, a distal convoluted tubule and a collecting tubule, and through which the glomerular filtrate passes, undergoing selective reabsorption and emerging as urine.

1932 *Anat. Record* CIV. 185 The nephron of the sculpin was nevertheless compared with that of the toadfish. **1937** *Amer. Jrnl. Anat.* LXI. 21 (*heading*) Observations upon the structure of the nephron in the common eel. **1965** *New Scientist* 24 June 868/2 A human kidney contains approximately one million units called nephrons, each consisting of a thin tube about 20 to 50 micrometres wide and 50 millimetres long. **1974** PASSMORE & ROBSON *Compan. Med. Stud.* III. xxii. 11/1 Such surviving nephrons would be in a state of continuous osmotic diuresis. **1975** A. DILLARD *Pilgrim at Tinker Creek* viii. 133 The nephron..is a filtering structure which produces urine and reabsorbs nutrients.

nephrops (ne·frǫps). [mod.L. (W. E. Leach 1816, in *Trans. Linn. Soc.* XI. 344), f. NEPHR(O- + Gr. ὤψ eye.] = *Dublin (Bay) prawn* (*DUBLIN); = *Norway lobster* (s.v. NORWAY[1] in Dict. and Suppl.).

[**1830** *Edin. Encycl.* VII. 398/2 This last [sc. *Astacus Norvegicus*] is considered as a distinct genus by Mr. Leach, under the name of Nephrops, from the kidney shaped eye.] **1961** *New Statesman* 23 June 1000/3 She is fishing off Barra, both seine-netting and after nephrops (scampi), a new and at present a paying type of fishery. **1971** *Nature* 29 Jan. 299/1 *Nephrops* tends to stay hidden away during the day, coming out during the night.

nephrosis (nefrōᵘ·sis). *Path.* Pl. **-oses.** [f. NEPHR(O- + -OSIS.] †**a.** (See quot.) *Obs.* exc. as in *b.

1900 DORLAND *Med. Dict.* 428/1 *Nephrosis*, any disease of the kidney.

b. [a. G. *nephrose* (F. Müller 1905, in *Verhandl. d. Deut. Path. Ges.* IX. 65).] A syndrome characterized by œdema, albuminuria, a fall in the plasma albumin, and usu. an increase in the blood cholesterol, formerly attributed to degeneration of the renal tubules but now known to arise from increased permeability to protein of the glomerular capillary basement membranes.

1916 L. F. BARKER *Monogr. Med.* III. 954 (*heading*) Toxic degenerative tubular nephropathies without marked glomerular involvement (the so-called nephroses). **1926** H. ELWYN *Nephritis* v. 74 Tubular degenerations occurring in the course of other diseases, when presenting definite renal symptoms, may be similarly designated by the term nephrosis of the particular disease in which they occur. **1929** *Amer. Jrnl. Path.* V. 619 Lipoid nephrosis is to be regarded as a form of glomerulonephritis in which the glomeruli are damaged but their capillaries are only partially obstructed. **1946** E. T. BELL *Renal Dis.* vi. 217 The tubular atrophy in lipoid nephrosis is due to disuse and anemia. **1973** J. BROD *Kidney* xix. 405/1 Unlike glomerulonephritis pure nephrosis is encountered mostly in children under 5 years of age.

nephrotic (nefrǫ·tik), *a.* *Path.* [f. prec.: see -OTIC.] Of, associated with, or suffering from nephrosis.

1928 *Amer. Jrnl. Path.* IV. 633 Every case of glomerulonephritis has a certain nephrotic element. **1940** *Jrnl. Clin. Invest.* XIX. 317/1 The albumin was much reduced in plasma, but unlike a nephrotic serum with a similar diminution of albumin, the globulin increase was most striking in the γ-fraction. **1954** *Amer. Jrnl. Physiol.* CLXXVIII. 329/2 The results demonstrated either an unchanged or a diminished hepatic synthesis of cholesterol by the nephrotic rat. **1966** *McGraw-Hill Encycl. Sci. & Technol.* III. 141/2 An example of edema formation secondary to a decrease in the colloid osmotic pressure of the plasma proteins is nephrotic edema.

b. *nephrotic syndrome* = *NEPHROSIS b.

1939 *Arch. Internal Med.* LXIII. 646 Throughout the last fifteen months of the patient's illness all the cardinal signs of the nephrotic syndrome were repeatedly found. **1961** *Lancet* 5 Aug. 290/2 Specimens were obtained from.. 2 [patients] with the nephrotic syndrome. **1974** PASSMORE & ROBSON *Compan. Med. Stud.* III. xxii. 30/2 In the case of toxic or allergic nephrotic syndrome the offending agent should be removed.

nephsystem (ne·fsistĕm). *Meteorol.* [f. Gr. νέφ-ος cloud + SYSTEM.] (See quot. 1959.)

1945 F. A. BERRY et al. *Handbk. Meteorol.* xi. 903 Cloud forms and cloud species over large areas form synoptic entities (called nephsystems) usually surrounded by fair-weather areas of clear sky, cumulus humilis, or cirriform clouds. **1959** R. E. HUSCHKE *Gloss. Meteorol.* 113 *Cloud system* (or *nephsystem*), an array of clouds and precipitation associated with a cyclonic-scale feature of atmospheric circulation. **1974** E. C. BARRETT *Climatol. from Satellites* iv. 116 Especially heavy and prolonged rain may be expected from major nephsystems within the meteorological tropics.

nepionic (nīpi,ǫ·nik), *a.* *Zool.* [f. Gr. νήπιος child + *-onic* as in *embryonic.*] Larval; in an early stage of development.

1889 A. HYATT in *Smithsonian Contrib. Knowledge* XXVI. ii. 9 The first larval or næpionic stage of a Nautiloid was, therefore, represented by the apex of the conch in that order. **1893** —— in *Proc. Boston Soc. Nat. Hist.* XXVI. 94 Larval or young: nepionic. Here first used as a substitute for 'næpionic'. **1898** A. S. PACKARD *Text-bk. Ent.* 706 As regards the organization of larval (nepionic) as compared with imaginal forms, the nymphs and larvæ of insects are, with the exception of many Diptera, nearly as perfectly developed as the adult. **1903** *Amer. Naturalist* XXXVII. 517 The nepionic stage of shell growth begins with the second whorl.

‖ **nepitella** (nepite·lă). [It.] = CALAMINT.

1926 D. H. LAWRENCE *Sun* iv. 13 The paths were all grown high with grass and flowers and nepitella.

nepman, NEP-man: see *N.E.P. (as main entry).

nepotistic (nepǒti·stik), *a.* [f. NEPOTIST + -IC.] Characterized by, or given to, nepotism.

1936 *Fortune* Jan. 133 Mr. Aldrich's sudden elevation, whereas it may have been dramatic, was certainly not nepotistic. **1949** KOESTLER *Promise & Fulfilment* II. v. 296 The one-time pioneers have, as so often happens, developed into a somewhat nepotistic coterie of the ancients. **1955** W. GADDIS *Recognitions* II. i. 305 The Viareggio, a small Italian bar of nepotistic honesty before it was discovered by exotics.

Neptune. 3. Add to def.: and lying beyond Uranus. (A more distant planet, *PLUTO[1], was discovered in 1930.)

Neptunism (ne·ptiŭniz'm). *Geol.* [f. NEPTUN(E + -ISM.] = NEPTUNIANISM.

1905 A. GEIKIE *Founders of Geol.* (ed. 2) viii. 257 Powerful as an advocate for the Vulcanist doctrines in opposition to the prevailing Neptunism of his time, he wrote some excellent monographs on the geology of different parts of Italy. **1951** C. C. GILLISPIE *Genesis & Geol.* ii. 46 The appeal of Neptunism is easier to understand than its acceptability. **1953** S. F. MASON *Hist. Sci.* xxxiii. 321 In the period 1790–1830..the Vulcanist view became associated with the theory that rock strata had gradually evolved, and Neptunism with the theory that the strata were formed suddenly and catastrophically. **1966** *Mercian Geol.* I. 291 The geological concepts Plutonism and Neptunism have, until recently, been thought to belong more properly to the igneous and sedimentary environments respectively.

Neptunist. 2. For '*attrib.*' read '*attrib.* or as *adj.*', and add further examples.

1905 A. GEIKIE *Founders of Geol.* (ed. 2) viii. 262 He would have run some risk of being regarded as having gone over to the Neptunist camp. **1951** C. C. GILLISPIE *Genesis & Geol.* ii. 44 The Neptunist synthesis explained stratification by postulating that all rock formations had been precipitated from an aqueous solution and suspension. **1965** M. SMITH *Essent. Mod. Geol.* vi. 101 Considerable controversy existed in the eighteenth century until the Vulcanists, led by Nicholas Desmarest, finally overcame the opposition of the Neptunists.

neptunite (ne·ptiunəit). *Min.* [ad. Sw. *neptunit* (G. Flink (at the suggestion of N. O. Holst) 1893, in *Geol. Förening i Stockholm Förhandl.* XV. 196): see NEPTUNE and -ITE[1]. (So called because of its occurrence with ÆGIRITE, Ægir being the Scandinavian god of the sea.)] A silicate of sodium, potassium, iron, manganese, and titanium, $(Na,K)_2(Fe^{II},Mn)TiSi_4O_{12}$, which is found as black monoclinic crystals.

1895 *Mineral. Mag.* XI. 100 Owing to the close similarity of the crystal angles to those of sphene, neptunite is placed in the titanite group. **1926** *Mineral. Abstr.* III. 102 Neptunite has been found at eight spots in the Kola peninsula. **1950** *Mineral. Mag.* XXIX. 27 The main point of interest in the new material is the presence here and there of the rare mineral neptunite in the syenite, a mineral previously unknown in the British Isles. **1966** *Doklady Acad. Sci. U.S.S.R.* (*Earth Sci. Sect.*) CLXVI. 121/2 The pyroxenic structure of neptunite is typically apparent from the endless zigzag baroque columns, in which Ti and Mn octahedra connected by common edges alternate in pairs.

neptunium (neptiū·niǒm). *Chem.* [mod.L., f. NEPTUN(E + -IUM.] † **1.** [coined in G. (R. Hermann 1877, in *Jrnl. f. prakt. Chem.* XV. 105).] A supposed element similar to tantalum found in a sample of tantalite from Haddam, Connecticut, U.S.A. *Obs.*

1877 *Jrnl. Chem. Soc.* XXXII. 167 Neptunium is distinguished from tantalum by the fact that its fluoride forms an easily soluble double salt with potassium fluoride. **1877** *Potter's Amer. Monthly* Sept. 238/2 Hermann calls it neptunium.

2. An artificially produced transuranic element (traces of which have subsequently been found in nature) which is a silvery metal and whose longest-lived isotope has a half-life of about $2\frac{1}{4}$ million years. Atomic number 93; symbol Np.

The word does not occur in the article by McMillan and Abelson (*Physical Rev.* (1940) LVII. 1185) in which they announced the discovery of the element, though McMillan is often said to be the coiner (e.g. quot. 1945; cf. also *Jrnl. Amer. Chem. Soc.* (1948) LXX. 1128 (an abridgement of a secret report of 1942)).

1941 *Sci. News Let.* 30 Aug. 135/1 The uranium outpost was passed some years ago by Prof. Enrico Fermi..with his discovery of the radioactive element No. 93, now called neptunium. **1945** *Chem. & Engin. News* 10 Dec. 2190/3 Element 93 was given the name neptunium by McMillan after Neptune, the planet immediately beyond Uranus, which gives its name to uranium. **1946** *Electronic Engin.* XVIII. 88 On bombarding the 238 isotope of uranium with a neutron of resonant energy value, a new isotope of uranium..is formed. This isotope is unstable.. and emits one electron to become a new element..called neptunium. **1950** M. LOWRY *Let.* 6 Mar. (1967) 200 Oddly enough I put neptunium in but abandoned it for niobium... I just took the elements out of the dictionary. **1968** *New Scientist* 23 May 410/2 Neptunium-237 is an important isotope because it is the precursor of plutonium-238. **1974** *Encycl. Brit. Micropædia* VII. 261/3 Neptunium is chemically reactive and similar to uranium with oxidation states from +3 to +6.

neral (nīə·ræl). *Chem.* [f. *NER(OL + AL(DEHYDE.] A colourless oily aldehyde, $C_{10}H_{16}O$, which is the *cis* form of citral (*CITRAL[2] b) and gives nerol on reduction.

1939 [see *CITRAL[2]]. **1953** [see *GERANIAL]. **1973**

Zoon Suppl. I. 56 The main components of the secretion [of four species of *Prosopis*] have been identified as the two isomers of citral, geranial..and neral.

neram (nera·m). [Malay.] A large evergreen tree, *Dipterocarpus oblongifolius*, of the family Dipterocarpaceæ. Also *attrib.*

1927 F. W. Foxworthy *Commercial Timber Trees of Malay Peninsula* 41 *D*[*ipterocarpus*] *oblongifolius*..is known as Neram and is not used commercially. **1940** E. J. H. Corner *Wayside Trees of Malaya* I. 211 The *Neram* is the big tree that arches over the rocky rivers in the eastern and northern states of Malaya. **1965** R. McKie *Company of Animals* i. 24 Neram trees, with trunks that weigh many tons and sprawling root systems ..reached thirty degrees from the jungle banks to meet above the centre of the stream.

nerf (nɔ̄ɹf), *v. slang* (orig. *U.S.*). [Origin unknown.] *intr.* In drag-racing, to bump another car. Hence **ne·rf-bar, ne·rfing-bar,** a bumper fitted to a car used in drag-racing.

1953 Berrey & Van den Bark *Amer. Thes. Slang* (1954) § 728/1 *Nerfing*, bumping another car out of the way. **1955** *Hot Rod Mag.* May 28 The nerf bar itself is mounted in a 'slip tube' that is welded permanently to the reworked bumper irons. **1960** Wentworth & Flexner *Dict. Amer. Slang* 352/2 The nerfing bar that supports the bumper on most cars. **1962** *Punch* 17 Oct. 561/1 A custom-built nerfing bar (bumper). **1969** R. E. Jennings *Automotive Dict.* 158/1 *Nerf bar:* see 'Nerfing Bar'. *Nerfing bar*, small, lightweight, vertical bumpers normally used on race cars, hot rods, and custom cars. *Ibid.*, *Nerf*, to bump, shove, or push a car during a racing event with another racer. Nerfing is very popular on short tracks.

nerine (nĭrəi·nĭ). *Bot.* Also **nerina.** [mod.L. (W. Herbert 1820, in *Curtis's Bot. Mag.* XLVII. 2124), f. L. *Nērīnē* (Virg. *Ecl.* vii. 37), Gr. νηρηίς a water nymph; see Nereid.] A South African bulbous plant of the genus so called, belonging to the family Amaryllidaceæ and including *Nerine bowdenii*, widely cultivated for its autumn-blooming pink flowers, and the Guernsey lily, *Nerine sarniensis*. Also *attrib.*

1820 *Curtis's Bot. Mag.* XLVII. 2124 Rose-coloured Nerine... Nerine is probably confined to South Africa. **1837** W. Herbert *Amaryllidaceæ* 285, I have no hesitation in saying that it is a Nerine. **1886** G. Nicholson *Dict. Gardening* II. 446/2 When in flower, Nerines are amongst the most beautiful of greenhouse bulbous plants. **1923** *Chambers's Jrnl.* Dec. 786/2 The scarlet or rose-red nerine (the Japanese spider lily) appeared next. **1929** *Amateur Gardening* 3 Aug. 292/3 Nerines, or Guernsey lilies, are attractive flowering bulbs. **1949** L. G. Green *In Land of Afternoon* v. 69 They [*sc.* lilies growing on the Guernsey coast] were identified as the nerinas of the Table Mountain ledges. **1955** K. A. Thompson *Great House* iv. 116 A Nerine lily glistening like rose-crystal. **1961** *Amateur Gardening* 14 Oct. 19/3 Nerines are often looked upon as bulbs to grow in favoured gardens. **1974** R. L. Fox *Variations on Garden* 165, I prefer its [*sc.* the amaryllis's] cousin, the Nerine or Guernsey lily.

neritic (nĭri·tik), *a.* [a. G. *neritisch* (E. Haeckel 1890, in *Jenaische Zeitschr. Naturw.* XXV. 253), perh. f. Nerit(a + -ic.] Of, pertaining to, or inhabiting the region of water bordering coasts, down to a depth of a hundred fathoms.

1891 Murray & Renard *Rep. Deep-Sea Deposits* iv. 251 The organisms living in mid-ocean in the great oceanic currents are quite different from those in the surface waters near land, and Haeckel proposes to designate the former oceanic Plankton, and the latter neritic Plankton. **1909** [see *holoplankton* (*holo-)]. **1913** J. Murray *Ocean* vii. 136 The neritic area surrounds all continents and islands. **1926** [see *bathyal adj.]. **1957** *Sci. News* XLIII. 71 Certain environments, such as the neritic zone of the ocean, are much more commonly represented in the fossil record than others. **1967** *New Scientist* 16 Mar. 546/2 Marine fish from the 'neritic' zone between the low-water mark and the edge of the continental shelf. **1974** Lucas & Critch *Life in Oceans* i. 24 The pelagic division is divided into the region inshore of the continental edge, known as the 'neritic province', and the remainder, called the 'oceanic province'.

Nernst (nĕ̄ɹnst, nɔ̄ɹnst). [Name of Walther Hermann *Nernst* (1864–1941), German physical chemist.] **a.** Used *attrib.* to designate an electric incandescent lamp invented by Nernst in which an unenclosed rod or wire consisting of a mixture of rare earths and other metallic oxides (as magnesia or zirconia) is made hot and luminous by the passage of an electric current (after being first brought to a conducting state by heating), and which is used esp. as a source of infra-red radiation.

1899 *Chambers's Jrnl.* 25 Mar. 269/2 For some time there have been rumours of an electric lamp on an entirely new principle, and..the contrivance was recently exhibited at the Society of Arts, London. It is known as the Nernst incandescent electric lamp, and its chief peculiarity is that it employs a rod of refractory earth in place of the usual carbon filament, and that this material is not enclosed in a glass exhausted of air. **1912** W. S. Franklin *Electric Lighting* v. 134 There are five important kinds of glow lamps as follows:... (*e*) The Nernst lamp in which the glower is a small rod of porcelain-like material. **1950** L. J. Brady in M. G. Mellon *Analytical Absorption Spectrosc.* viii. 444 One serious objection to the Nernst glower is the frequent mechanical failure of the source due to the poor bonding of the platinum leads to the element itself. **1962** R. E. Dodd *Chem. Spectrosc.* i. 16 For use in the infra-red region, mainly beyond 2μ, the hot body takes the form of a rod of semi-conducting lanthanon oxides, a Nernst glower. *Ibid.* 17 The Nernst filament is only suitable for the near infra-red and visible.

b. Used *attrib.* with reference to a thermomagnetic effect investigated by Nernst, in which a temperature gradient in a metal subject to a magnetic field at right angles to the gradient gives rise to an e.m.f. in a direction at right angles to both.

1901 M. G. Lloyd in *Amer. Jrnl. Sci.* CLXII. 57 It has already been proposed† to call the galvano-magnetic temperature-difference, the thermo-magnetic temperature-difference, and the thermo-magnetic potential-difference by the respective names, Ettingshausen effect, Leduc effect and Nernst effect. [*Note*] † Thesis: The Transversal Thermo-magnetic Effect in Bismuth, M. G. Lloyd, Philadelphia, 1900; Beiblätter, 24, p. 1014. **1911** *Physical Rev.* XXXIII. 300 Both the Hall electromotive force and the Nernst electromotive force seem to be proportional to the intensity of magnetization in the plate rather than to the magnetic field. **1960** E. H. Putley *Hall Effect & Related Phenomena* ii. 27 In the Nernst effect, electrons attempting to diffuse down a temperature gradient are deflected by a magnetic field but a transverse electric field is set up to balance out the Lorentz force. *Ibid.* 28 The units for the Nernst coefficient are cm² sec⁻¹ (°K)⁻¹ or m² sec⁻¹ (°K)⁻¹.

c. Used *attrib.* and in the possessive to designate a theorem in thermodynamics enunciated by Nernst: the change in entropy accompanying a chemical reaction between pure crystalline solids tends to zero as the temperature at which it occurs tends to absolute zero. (Also called the third law of thermodynamics, esp. in more generalized formulations.)

1913 J. R. Partington *Text-bk. Thermodynamics* xvii. 484 The required information is furnished by a hypothesis put forward in 1906 by W. Nernst, and usually called by German writers 'das Nernstsche Wärmetheorem'. We can refer to it without ambiguity as Nernst's Theorem. **1928** J. K. Roberts *Heat & Thermodynamics* xviii. 354 Such a wide range of reactions is considered that we are certainly justified in regarding the Nernst Heat Theorem as being established as a first approximation. *Ibid.* 355 If the Nernst Theorem as originally stated should prove to be only a first approximation, the theorem does not on that account become less important. **1971** G. Socrates *Thermodynamics & Statistical Mech.* vii. 139 An alternative statement of Nernst's heat theorem is: It is impossible to reduce the temperature of any system to absolute zero in a finite number of operations.

nerol (nĭə·rǫl). *Chem.* [a. G. *nerol* (Hesse & Zeitschel 1902, in *Jrnl. f. prakt. Chem.* LXVI. 498): see Neroli and -ol.] An oily unsaturated primary alcohol, $C_{10}H_{18}O$, which is present in neroli and some other essential oils and is used in perfumery, having a fragrance similar to but finer than that of geraniol, with which it is stereoisomeric.

1903 *Jrnl. Chem. Soc.* LXXXIV. I. 189 Nerol, $C_{10}H_{18}O$, is an oil which boils at 225–227° under 765 mm. pressure.. and is distinguished from geraniol by its odour of roses. **1949** E. Guenther *Essent. Oils* II. 174 Nerol and its acetic ester have been found in several volatile oils, for instance, in oil of helichrysum (30–50 per cent), neroli, bigarade, petitgrain, rose, linaloe, lavender, bergamot, Ceylon citronella, etc. **1949** T. F. West et al. *Synthetic Perfumes* iii. 19 Nerol is a superior odorant [to geraniol] in exquisite rose compositions as it provides them with that velvety blossom top-note of freshly cut dark-red roses. **1974** *Jrnl. Chem. Soc.: Perkin Trans. I* 1637 Treatment of geraniol or nerol with fluorosulphonic acid at low temperatures gave good..yields of a novel iridoid ether.

nerts (nɔ̄ɹts), repr. a colloq. or euphemistic pronunc. of *nuts* (*nut *sb.*[1] 7 e).

1932 *Amer. Speech* VII. 334 (Johns Hopkins jargon) Nerts—exclamation of incredulity or disgust. (Nuts?) **1932** *Sun* (Baltimore) 28 Sept. 10/6 The first couple of months are devoted to getting the right title, suggestions running all the way from 'Alors, Mes Enfants' to 'Nerts'. **1933** M. Allingham *Sweet Danger* xviii. 222 'Life's very beautiful, isn't it?' 'Speaking as a soul not yet mated, nerts,' said Amanda. **1937** Hemingway *To have & have Not* iii. 128 Oh, nerts to you. **1937** B. Howard in *New Statesman* 9 Jan. 52/1 Heaven knows that no little word of mine can possibly be heard above the deepening hosannas, but all the same, I shall say it, and it is Nerts. Nerts to everybody, all round, except the authoress. **1948** D. Ballantyne *Cunninghams* ii. xiii. 222 Nerts, you did your part bringing them into the world.

nerve, *sb.* Add: **8. b.** Phr. *to live on one's nerves:* to lead an emotionally exhausting life.

1927 *Daily Tel.* 1 Nov. 7 The correspondence about the dramatic version of 'The Secret Agent'..is almost interminable. One sees that Conrad lived on his nerves, as the French say, and that he took a secret delight in parading his petty cares. **1932** Auden *Orators* i. 16 Dare-devils of the soul, living dangerously upon their nerves.

d. (Earlier and later examples.)

Quots. ?1792 and 1839 perhaps belong in sense 8 b.

? **1792** I. Pigot *Let.* in A. Leslie *Mrs Fitzherbert* (1960) ix. 87 She says her spirits are so damped and her nerves so bad, she must go out to..soothe her mind by change of scene and country. **1839** Dickens *Let.* 5 Mar. (1965) I. 519 Recovering from an attack 'on the Nerves'. **1914** G. W. Young *From Trenches* vii. 143 The control of the population is admirable in its restraint. We have no 'nerves' here yet. **1920** H. Crane *Let.* 23 Nov. (1965) 46 I'm sorry to know you are having such an ordeal of 'nerves'. **1948** A. Christie *Taken at Flood* i. i. 20 The poor girl was blitzed and had shock from blast... She's a mass of nerves.

e. Phr. *to get on one's nerves:* to (begin to) affect one with irritation, impatience, fear, or the like.

1903 'C. E. Merriman' *Lett. from Son to his Self-Made Father* vi. 75 I've worried a lot since you went away. The business seems to have got on my nerves. **1908** H. G. Wells *War in Air* iv. 125 This flying gets on one's nerves. *Ibid.* v. 174 All this looking down and floating over things and smashing up people, it's getting on my nerves. **1910** *Chambers's Jrnl.* Mar. 155/2 Sometimes I hate this accursed country... It gets on one's nerves at times. **1920** B. C. Cronin *Timber Wolves* ii. 34 Hotel hogs, I call 'em. Come in and jolly a chap as if they owned the whole joke. Gets on your nerves when you've been out of your bed all night. **1941** A. L. Rowse *Tudor Cornwall* xi. 276 The siege..got on people's nerves. **1959** T. S. Eliot *Elder Statesman* iii. 99, I remember, when I came home for the holidays How it used to get on my nerves, when I saw you Always sitting there with your nose in a book. **1972** J. Wilson *Hide & Seek* vii. 118 Alice and I are really close, even if we do get on each other's nerves sometimes.

f. *war of nerves:* the use of hostile or subversive propaganda to undermine morale and cause confusion and uncertainty; psychological warfare.

1940 *Ann. Reg. 1939* 81 The British public..did not allow the 'war of nerves' organised by the Nazi Government to interfere in the least with its August holiday. **1953** E. Simon *Past Masters* iv. ii. 223 War of nerves... Best thing to do is take no notice. **1974** P. Wright *Lang. Brit. Industry* ii. 26 Recent threats of conflicts have produced, e.g., *cold war* and *war of nerves.*

10. b. *colloq.* Audacity, impudence, cheek. Esp. in phr. *to have a nerve* or *to have the nerve to.*

1887 *Lantern* (New Orleans) 6 Aug. 3/3 Oh, this is a nerve, sure. **1890** Barrère & Leland *Dict. Slang* II. 84/2 *Nerve* (Eton), impudence. *a* **1911** D. G. Phillips *Susan Lenox* (1917) I. xx. 352 More money!.. You *have* got a nerve!—when factories are shutting down everywhere. **1921** *Daily Colonist* (Victoria, B.C.) 5 Apr. 4/2 No one had the nerve to claim this should be done, because it would have been laughed out of court immediately. **1925** Wodehouse *Sam the Sudden* xxv. 219 'You mean to tell me that you had the—the nerve—the insolence—.' He gulped. **1929** [see *honestly *adv.* 2 b]. **1930** V. Sackville-West *Edwardians* vi. 220 The cabby exclaimed that the young toff had a nerve and no mistake. **1942** *Q. Jrnl. Speech* Feb. 6/2 In low brow programs..we note..'you've got a nerve'. **1975** S. Brett *Cast* xiii. 136 Joanne Menzies looked at him coolly. 'You've got a nerve.'

11. a. *nerve-channel, -end* (*fig.* examples), *-network, -pill, -test, -tester, -tip, -world.*

1902 *Chambers's Jrnl.* 15 Feb. 166/1 Muscular repose means that the muscles are relaxed and the nerve-channels free. **1951** J. M. Fraser *Psychol.* ii. 13 A message.. will be sent along a nerve-channel to the brain. **1953** R. Lehmann *Echoing Grove* 159 In the silence Dinah's nerve ends crept, contracted, listening for the guns, the sirens. **1969** *Listener* 22 May 733/3 In Debussy's case this led to Impressionism, which lived at the nerve ends. **1947** *Mind* LVI. 57 In the nervous system the 'variables' are mostly impulse-frequencies at various points in the nerve-network. **1972** *Sci. Amer.* Feb. 88/2 The major part of the sympathetic nerve network stimulates the secretion of norepinephrine. **1907** *Yesterday's Shopping* (1969) 505/1 Carter's little liver pills... Nerve pills. **1975** M. Crichton *Great Train Robbery* xiii. 78 He was forced to down two Carter's Little Nerve Pills and some tincture of opium for his pain. **1909** *Westm. Gaz.* 29 May 8/3 (*heading*) A zoological nerve-test. **1894** *Strand* Feb. 119/1 A visit to this place is the finest and most complete nerve-tester in the world! **1890** W. James *Princ. Psychol.* I. vi. 150 This must be because the number of sensations from the elementary nerve-tips affected was too small. **1936** F. R. Leavis *Revaluation* v. 184 The sentiments and attitudes of the patriotic and Anglican Wordsworth..are external, general and conventional; their quality is that of the medium they are proffered in, which is..not felt into from within as something at the nerve-tips, but handled from outside. **1890** Nerve-world [see *mind-world].

b. Objective, as *nerve-lacerating, -racking, -shaking* (earlier and later examples), *-shattering, -testing, -wracking; nerve-wrackingly* adv.; instrumental, as *nerve-drawn, -racked, -ridden* (further examples), *-shattered, -worn, -wracked.*

1937 V. Woolf *Years* 388 A queer face; knit up; nerve-drawn; fixed. **1911** W. Owen *Let.* 17 Sept. (1967) 83 The nerve-lacerating speech of the pompous vigilator. **1933** A. N. Whitehead *Adventures of Ideas* xvi. 245 A red-irritation is prevalent among nerve-racked people and among bulls. **1812** Shelley *Let.* 27 Dec. (1964) I. 347 My removal from your nerve racking & spirit quelling metropolis. **1908** *Westm. Gaz.* 22 Feb. 2/3 The nerve-racking work of the telephone-girls. **1909** *Chambers's Jrnl.* Mar. 205/2 In all the large towns in Britain there is also far too much nerve-racking, unnecessary noise. **1973** *Times* 30 June 13/5 My own King Charles's head is the use of 'nerve-wracking' for 'nerve-racking'. **1930** R. Macaulay *Staying with Relations* xxi. 313 Adrian..had already shown himself a husband too impatient and too nerve-ridden to endure for long so much irrational excitement at his side. **1939** D. Cecil *Young Melbourne* vi. 150 He [*sc.* Byron] was a raw, nerve-ridden boy of genius. **1820** Keats *Let.* ?Feb. (1958) II. 262 The medicine I am at present taking..is of a nerve-shaking nature. **1933** J. Cary *Amer. Visitor* vii. 88 Uli shrank away from the white men and uttered another nerve-shaking yell. **1929** *Observer* 17 Nov. 11/3 Jean Jacques Bernard's interesting

play..about a nerve-shattered and unreasonably jealous husband. **1975** C. DENNIS *Somebody just grabbed Annie!* 195 Close-up of a nerve-shattered Ilima. **1909** *Westm. Gaz.* 28 Sept. 4/2 The work of the engine-driver and fireman is ..by no means of the nerve-shattering description that some would have us believe. **1973** *Nation Rev.* (Melbourne) 31 Aug. 1464/3 Marasco's nerve-shattering novel *Burnt offerings*. **1973** D. FRANCIS *Slay-Ride* vii. 80 A nerve-testing isolation. **1792** J. BYNG *Torrington Diaries* (1936) III. 5, I will not accord to the unnatural hours. Nerve-worn, and with reason, I must..take the field. **1922** D. H. LAWRENCE *Let.* 15 May (1932) 547 In many ways it [*sc.* Australia] is older: more nerve-worn. **1911** E. POUND *Canzoni* 46 How our modernity, Nerve-wracked and broken, turns Against time's way. **1925** Nerve-wracked [see *GONE *ppl. a.* 3 b]. **1909** *Daily Chron.* 9 Feb. 5/1 Despite his nerve-wracking experience, he had the courage to endeavour to return to search for him. **1973** *Guardian* 28 June 11/1 The worst thing is getting a call in the middle of the night saying that the windows of my husband's business have been blown in again...It's nerve wracking sitting here. **1963** A. ROSS *Australia 63* i. 42 The handsome and the hazardous were jostling nerve-wrackingly together.

12. nerve block, blocking, inactivation of the nerve supplying a particular area of the body, esp. by use of a local anæsthetic; **nerve cell** (earlier example); **nerve-centre** (later *fig.* examples); **nerve current,** a signal propagated along a nerve; a series of nerve impulses; **nerve-doctor,** a specialist in the treatment of nervous diseases; **nerve gas,** any poisonous gas or vapour that has a weakening or paralysing effect on the nervous system, esp. for use in warfare; also *fig.*; **nerve impulse,** a wave of excitation in a nerve fibre accompanied by a brief, temporary change in electrical potential, motion of which constitutes transmission of a stimulus along the fibre; **nerve net,** a diffuse network of neurones found in cœlenterates, echinoderms, and other organisms which conducts excitations in all directions from the area stimulated; **nerve-path,** a route (assumed to be inborn or developed through use) by which a specific sensory stimulus or motor response is propagated through the nervous system; **nerve-patient,** a patient suffering from a nervous disorder; **nerve physiology** = *neurophysiology* s.v. NEURO-; so *nerve-physiologist*; **nerve-route** = *nerve-path* above; **nerve-sick** *a.*, suffering from nervous illness; **nerve-specialist** = *nerve-doctor* above; **nerve war** = *war of nerves* (*NERVE *sb.* 8 f); also *joc.*

1923 *Jrnl. Amer. Med. Assoc.* 29 Sept. 1079/1 (*heading*) The value of sacral nerve block anesthesia in obstetrics. **1941** *Brit. Jrnl. Psychol.* July 69 The simplest explanation of the blindness [due to pressure] is that the stoppage of circulation produces retinal anoxia and nerve-block, probably in the ganglionic layers. **1970** W. H. PARKER *Health & Dis. in Farm Animals* viii. 94 Dehorning is the removal of horns already in existence on older cattle, essentially a veterinarian's job involving nerve block anaesthesia. **1906** J. M. PATTON *Anaesthesia & Anaesthetics* (ed. 2) xvii. 208 Bodine sees no reason why all major surgery should not be done by Corning's nerve-blocking method of injecting directly into the nerves supplying the limb. **1972** *Jrnl. Pharmacol. & Exper. Ther.* CLXXXII. 442/1 The nerve blocking action of the insecticide, allethrin, is unique in the sense that it is highly dependent on temperature. **1858** G. H. LEWES *Let.* 19 July in G. S. Haight *Geo. Eliot Lett.* (1954) II. 469 It was so very amusing to find myself thinking of 'nerve cells' amid the grand mountains, and of physiological processes on the shores of a lake. **1910** *Blackw. Mag.* July 9/2 The nerve centres of London, such as the General Post Office, the Telephone Exchanges, the Bank of England,..the Railway Termini, and so on. **1930** Nerve-centre [see **control room*]. **1939** *War Illustr.* 29 Dec. 526 The superstructure is the nerve centre of the ship from which she is navigated and her gunfire controlled. **1942** D. JENKINS *Nature of Catholicity* ii. 48 This brings us to the doctrine of Reformation according to the Word of God which is the nerve-centre of the Reformed doctrine of the Church. **1959** *Daily Tel.* 30 Nov. 19/3 A 'nerve centre' opens to-day opposite Victoria Station for cross-Channel steamer car traffic. **1971** 'D. HALLIDAY' *Dolly & Doctor Bird* v. 71, I was being dragged..through the nerve-centre [*sc.* Miami] of the Sunshine State. **1879** *Mind* IV. 317 All feeling whatever.. seems to depend for its physical condition not on simple discharge of nerve-currents, but on their discharge under arrest, impediment or resistance. **1951** J. M. FRASER *Psychol.* ii. 13 These cells..send a nerve-current along the olfactory nerve to the brain. **1892** W. JAMES *Coll. Ess. & Rev.* (1920) 327 The men who care little or nothing for ultimate rationality, the biologists, nerve-doctors, and psychical researchers. **1940** *Sun* (Baltimore) 13 May 1/5 A specialist in nervous diseases and a chemist..said tonight that a 'nerve gas', reported possibly used by the Nazis..was 'entirely within the range of possibility'. **1960** KOESTLER *Lotus & Robot* II. xii. 274 Once a balm for self-inflicted bruises, it [*sc.* Zen Buddhism] has become a kind of moral nerve-gas. **1962** L. DEIGHTON *Ipcress File* xxi. 141 They won't be using kids' stuff like this bomb. It will be area saturation with suitable nerve gases. **1968** *Observer* 16 June 9/1 The nerve gases are liquids which are most lethal when inhaled as fine droplets, but can also be absorbed through the skin. **1975** *Times* 6 Jan. 1/2 MPs are to question ministers about a report that the formula for a lethal nerve gas has been taken off the secret list. **1900** *Nature* 26 July 291/1 The futility of those hypotheses which would explain the passage of the nerve-impulse as a mere propagated polarisation. **1927** HALDANE & HUXLEY *Animal Biol.* v. 123 (*caption*) Diagram to illustrate the course of nerve-impulses concerned in a spinal reflex. **1966** *McGraw-Hill Encycl. Sci. & Technol.* IX. 52/2 The rate of conduction of nerve impulses varies in proportion to the diameter of the nerve fiber. **1971** J. Z. YOUNG *Introd. Study Man* ii. 28 This is best known for nerve cells, whose signals the nerve impulses (action potentials) are propagated by serial breakdown of the charged surface membrane, allowing sodium to enter and potassium to leave. **1904** C. S. SHERRINGTON in *Nature* 8 Sept. 460/1 We can distinguish two main types of [nervous] system according to the mode of union of the conductors.—(i.) the nerve-net system, such as met in Medusa and in the walls of viscera, and (ii.) the synaptic system, such as the cerebro-spinal system of Arthropods and Vertebrates. **1942** O. LARSELL *Anat. Nervous System* i. 3 The older view of the nerve net as a conduction apparatus for diffusing nerve impulses by protoplasmic continuity of the nerve cell processes has largely yielded to the conception of a synaptic system, even in coelenterates. **1968** D. W. WOOD *Princ. Animal Physiol.* x. 214 The nerve nets found in phyla other than the Coelenterata are mostly peripheral to a more organized central nervous system. **1890** W. JAMES *Princ. Psychol.* I. xi. 458 A downward nerve-path is thus kept constantly open during concentrated thought. **1926** J. S. HUXLEY *Essays in Popular Science* vi. 65 The secretions of ovaries pick out and bring into action the nerve-paths appropriate to females, those of testes the paths appropriate to males. **1968** *Biol. Abstr.* XLIX. 2670/1 (*heading*) Age changes of the optic nerve path. **1909** *Chambers's Jrnl.* Dec. 818/1 Every medical practitioner..obtains an increasing number of nerve-patients year after year. **1890** W. JAMES *Princ. Psychol.* I. i. 5 In still another way the psychologist is forced to be something of a nerve-physiologist. **1860** *Rep. Brit. Assoc. Adv. Sci. 1859* II. 166 (*heading*) Necessity of a reform in nerve-physiology. **1890** W. JAMES *Princ. Psychol.* I. ii. 23 The conception of *all* action as conforming to this type [*sc.* reflex] is the fundamental conception of modern nerve-physiology. **1927** J. S. HUXLEY *Relig. without Revelation* iv. 135 How, precisely, these experiences are generated, psychology and nerve-physiology must learn and tell us. **1890** A. HILL tr. *H. Obersteiner's Anat. Central Nerv. Organs* 162 One must be very careful in assigning an object to nerve-routes, especially when they exceed an internode..in length. **1933** A. N. WHITEHEAD *Adventures of Ideas* xiv. 276 Also incipient sense-percepta may be forming themselves in the nerve-routes. **1929** W. FAULKNER *Sartoris* III. 173 His thin, nerve-sick face clouded over with a fine cold distaste. **1930** R. MACAULAY *Staying with Relations* xv. 219 Poor child, to be born of quarrelling, nerve-sick parents into a home of strife. **1889** Nerve-specialist [see SPECIALIST 1]. **1920** A. J. CUMMINGS in 'W. N. P. Barbellion' *Last Diary* p. xxx, I persuaded him..to see a first-class nerve specialist. **1941** *Argus* (Melbourne) *Week-End Mag.* 15 Nov. 1/4 *Nerve war*, grousing or complaining to get things done. **1942** *Ann. Reg. 1941* 212 The firm stand..against Japanese blackmail, cajolery, threats, and 'nerve-war'. **1943** *Daily Tel.* 26 Aug. 6 Berliners are really panicky... The nerve war has reached a climax which I never thought possible. **1946** F. WILLIAMS *Press, Parliament & People* iii. 61 They [*sc.* the Germans]..convinced themselves that the message had been put out deliberately as part of a clever piece of nerve war to mislead them and try to make their defence forces jumpy.

nerver (nɜ̄·ɹvəɹ). [f. NERVE *sb.* or *v.* + -ER[1].] Something, esp. a drink, that gives one 'nerve' or courage.

1886 BAUMANN *Londinismen* 117/2 *Nerver*, eins für den Durst, Magenlikör. **1889** *St. James's Gaz.* 10 Aug. 3/2 His dose..possibly contains cardamums, hydrocyanic acid, and tincture of capsicum; a capital 'nerver' in its way. **1895** 'G. MORTIMER' *Like Stars that Fall* iii. 33 You'll pull through all right. I'll give you a nerver of pale sherry and a drop of brandy before you go on.

nervily (nɜ̄·ɹvĭli), *adv.* [f. NERVY *a.*: see -LY[2].] In a nervy manner; boldly; agitatedly.

1911 [see *CLASSISM]. **1928** *Daily Express* 15 June 9/4 The blue eyes were not as serene as he would like to have seen them. The professor's grey ones roved nervily from side to side. **1957** M. SPARK *Comforters* iii. 63 Caroline jogged round nervily as the door opened.

nerviness. Delete *rare*—⁰ and add: **2.** The state or character of being nervous (sense 9) or nervy (sense *5).

1921 *Glasgow Herald* 15 June 8 The home men had only to shake off their 'nerviness' to reduce the Australian bowling to trundling of good class. **1924** J. SUTHERLAND *Circle of Stars* xxiii. 232 At every footstep he started... Indeed he was so unlike himself that even Barbara commented upon his nerviness. **1975** J. RATHBONE *Kill Cure* I. i. 16 Bury, she supposed, was all right, but there was a nerviness about him that she did not quite like.

nervo-. Add: † **nervo-electric** *a.* = *neuro-electric* adj. s.v. *NEURO-; so **nervo-electricity.**

[**1792** A. GALVANI *De Viribus Electricitatis in Motu Musculari* IV. 48 Nerveo-electrici fluidi excursum per musculum ad nervum illum esse.] **1860** A. C. GARRATT *Electro-Physiol. & Electro-Therapeutics* iv. 216 (*heading*) Effects of heat and cold on the nervo-electric batteries. *Ibid.* vi. 349 May not the brain be thus incessantly charged, says Dr. Watson, if indeed it be..'an electric pile constantly in action', discharging itself by the nerves at brief intervals, 'when the tension of the nervo-electricity, developed, reaches a certain point'?

nervous, *a.* Add: **2. c.** (Examples of *nervous energy*.) Also, *nervous tension*.

1849 THOREAU *Week Concord Riv.* 338 They..handled their paddles unskilfully, but with nervous energy and determination. **1933** *Burlington Mag.* Feb. 54/1 Everywhere the nervous tension is relaxed, the rhythms are less vital and less consistent. **1936** *Discovery* Nov. 357/2 His nervous tension is surely not lessened if precautions are taken against his actually watching the operation [on himself]. **1951** M. MCLUHAN *Mech. Bride* (1967) 33/1 Books on how to relax would seem just about to cancel out books on how to build up nervous tension for success drive. **1953** J. S. HUXLEY *Evolution in Action* iv. 91 Behaviour is always the result of a flow of something—what many psychologists and most laymen call nervous energy. Unfortunately, the physiologists are driven to say 'excitation', because *energy* is another word the physicists have taken over from ordinary speech and given a restricted scientific meaning. Perhaps the term 'neurergy' would serve.

7. b. *nervous breakdown*: see *BREAK-DOWN 1 c; *nervous fever* (earlier and later U.S. examples). Also *nervous exhaustion, nervous headache.*

1787 H. MORE *Let.* June (1925) 120 A very tedious nervous headache has made me less than ever qualified to traffic with you. **1807** A. PUTNAM in *Danvers Hist. Soc. Coll.* (1917) V. 57 Mr. David Tapley is very sick with the nervous fever. **1857** J. A. SYMONDS *Let.* 16 Nov. (1967) I. 125, I must..not work much these trials since yesterday I had the same sort of nervous headache. **1924** H. CRANE *Let.* 23 Sept. (1965) 190 The sneezing and nervous fever.. begin to subside. **1927** 'R. CROMPTON' *William—in Trouble* viii. 207 He's suffering from *nervous exhaustion.* **1973** E. BERCKMAN *Victorian Album* 142 The thought of any considerable threat to her happiness..is always enough to give me a nervous headache.

9. Also, *nervous wreck. colloq.*

1899 [see WRECK *sb.*[1] 7 b]. **1906** W. JAMES *Let.* 9 May (1920) II. 251, I did n't hear one pathetic word uttered at the scene of disaster, though of course the crop of 'nervous wrecks' is very likely to come in a month or so. **1932** H. CRANE *Let.* 22 Apr. (1965) 412 It certainly has about made a nervous wreck of me. **1936** J. BUCHAN *Island of Sheep* I. vi. 110 He started at every noise. He was the very model of a nervous wreck.

nervuration (nɜ̄ɹviurēɪ·ʃən). [f. NERVURE + -ATION.] = NEURATION.

1899 D. SHARP in *Cambr. Nat. Hist.* VI. v. 319 In the aberrant moths of the genus Costina the nervuration is unusually complex.

nervy, *a.* Add: **2. b.** (Earlier and later examples.) *U.S. colloq.*

1896 ADE *Artie* viii. 75, I just received your nervy letter. **1904** E. ROBINS *Magnetic North* II. 118 Feeling that it is a little 'nervy'..to walk into another man's house uninvited. **1948** *Pauls Valley* (Okla.) *Daily Democrat* 2 May 4 Wouldn't it be rather nervy to ask her help?

5. Having one's nerves disordered; easily excitable, 'jumpy'; = NERVOUS *a.* 9.

1891 R. T. COOKE *Huckleberries gathered f. New England Hills* 319, I expect I be sort o' nervy, what with takin' a journey and the thought o' seein' Melindy. **1906** *Sat. Rev.* 3 Mar. 254 They are very 'nervy' in Russia. **1916** *Daily Mail* 21 Sept. 7 (Advt.), When you are weak, anæmic, 'nervy', run-down, [etc.]. **1923** W. DEEPING *Secret Sanctuary* viii. 77 You can explain that your brother was shell-shocked, and that he is still a bit nervy. **1932** A. CHRISTIE *Peril at End House* iii. 40, I have been worried to death. Everybody's been telling me I'm nervy. **1973** J. BURROWS *Like Evening Gone* v. 63 Greta was grey as paper and peevish and nervy.

Nescafé (ne·skæfe). The proprietary name of a brand of instant coffee; a drink made of Nescafé. Also *colloq.* abbrev. **Nes**; [cf. *CAFF] **Nescaff.**

1946 *Trade Marks Jrnl.* 4 Sept. 475/2 Nescafé... Preparations of coffee in powder form. Nestlé's Milk Products Limited,..London,.. Manufacturers. **1959** [see *ABLUTE *v.*]. **1962** A. LEJEUNE *Duel in Shadows* xi. 156 'Only Nescaff, I'm afraid,' said Fiona Stewart-Long. **1966** *Observer* 19 June 29/5 Silk shantung dress in Nescafé brown. **1966** *New Statesman* 24 June 939/3 Maurice Ronet as a devil-may-care sadist, and George Segal in Nescafé as an old Algerian buddy. **1968** H. READE *Comeback for Stark* xii. 175 Sure you won't have a cup of nes? I prefer it to anything except the real bottled yellow. Take it cold in the summer. **1968** *Listener* 18 Apr. 515/1 How many spoonfuls of Nescafé did the Chancellor of the Exchequer have in his elevenses that vital morning? **1970** J. FLEMING *Young Man, I think you're Dying* ii. 33, I could make you a cuppa hot Nescaff, eh? How about it? **1971** 'P. HOBSON' *Three Graces* viii. 54 Downstairs for a cup of Nes. **1975** N. FREELING *What are Bugles blowing For?* iv. 17 We'll have some coffee—or to be accurate, Nes. *Ibid.* v. 21 La Touche seemed to be waking up... Shock wearing off, or the stimulus of Nescafé.

Nescaupick, var. *NASKAPI *a.* and *sb.*

nesh, *a.* **1. a.** (Further example.)

1915 R. C. THOMPSON *Pilgr. Scrip* 71 The road from the bridge is like an English lane with blackberry hedgerows.. and a nesh track for a morning gallop.

Nesite (ne·səit). Also **Nesian, Nesitic.** [f. Hittite *našili, nešumnili*, f. *Nešaš* name of an ancient Hittite city in Asia Minor (identified by B. Hrozný 1929, in *Archiv orientální* (Prague) I. 273–99) + -ITE[1].] **a.** A name given to the official language used in Hittite documents, suggested as an alternative to *KANE-

SIAN. **b.** A member of the Hittite people who used this language.

The meaning of *našili* and *nešumnili* in Hittite texts has been disputed, but the view of Hrozný (above, and 1931, in *Journal Asiatique* CCXVIII. 318–19) is now generally accepted, that the words relate to the former Hittite capital Nešaš (or Nesa) and designate the Indo-European Hittite aristocracy and its language (see also quot. 1954).

[**1920** A. H. SAYCE in *Jrnl. Royal Asiatic Soc.* 605 Literary Hittite is once called 'Luvian', *Lûi-li*, 'in Luvian', taking the place of the more usual *nâsi-li*. **1921** M. BLOOMFIELD in *Jrnl. Amer. Oriental Soc.* XLI. 197 The supposedly I. E. Hittite [in the Boghazköi inscriptions] seems, according to both authors [*sc.* Forrer and Hrozný], to be well entitled to the name Kanesian, named after the city of Kaneš. But this latter designation is never indicated by an ethnical adjective... Instead there occurs, more frequently than the mention of Kaneš, the ethnical designation Nâšili, which Forrer takes to be the same as Kanesian. **1929** B. HROZNÝ in *Archiv orientální* (Prague) I. 296 Les Nêsites sont donc en effet les fondateurs du grand empire hittite... La langue hittite doit donc être nommée..la langue nésite.] **1933** E. H. STURTEVANT *Compar. Gram. Hittite Lang.* i. 28 Hrozný.. may be correct in thinking that the word *Nesumnili*..refers to official Hittite and therefore in calling the latter Nesite. **1949** F. O. STEIN tr. *L. Matouš's Bedřich Hrozný* 26 Later, in a paper published in Volume I of '*Archiv orientální*' (Oriental Archives).., Hrozný shewed that the Indo-European Hittites originally called themselves *Nesites*, from their ancient city *Neshash*, and that therefore their language should more correctly be called *Nesitic*, and not Hittite, as had always been taken for granted. **1954** O. R. GURNEY *Hittites* (ed. 2) 122 While Hrozný adopted the name 'Nésite' (i.e., the language of the city Nesa), Forrer preferred 'Kanisisch' (i.e., the language of Kanesh). It is now generally agreed that 'Nésite' or 'Nesian' (derived from the Hittite adverb *našili* or *nešumnili*) is indeed the true name of the language. **1959** *Chambers's Encycl.* VII. 155/1 The language..was seen to be mainly Indo-European in structure and vocabulary. In the Hittite texts it is sometimes called the speech of Nesas, and has therefore been termed Nesite. **1964** G. ROUX *Ancient Iraq* xiv. 191 The Luwians..settled to the west of Cilicia, along the coast,..and the so-called Nesites in Cappadocia... Centuries later, those Nesite-speaking invaders conquered the centre of the Anatolian plateau.. **1972** W. B. LOCKWOOD *Panorama Indo-Europ. Lang.* xiv. 262 The terms used are *nasili* (or *nisili*) and *nesumnili* meaning respectively 'in the language of Nesa' and 'in the language of those of Nesa', and Hittite has since occasionally been called Nesite.

nesk(h)i, varr. *NASKHI *sb. pl.*

‖ **nespola** (ne·spŏlă). [It.] = MEDLAR.

1883 LADY MONKSWELL *Jrnl.* 29 Apr. in *Victorian Diarist* (1944) 104 On the entrance terrace were lemon trees in pots, trees of magnolia (not in flower) & nespola. **1920** D. H. LAWRENCE *Let.* 7 May (1932) 504 Nespoli look like apricots, and taste a bit like them—but they're pear-shaped. They're a sort of medlar. **1922** *Blackw. Mag.* Feb. 157/2 Florindo threw a number of nespole with deadly accuracy.

nesquehonite (neskwihōᵘ·nəit). *Min.* [f. *Nesquehon-ing* (see quot. 1890) + -ITE¹.] Magnesium carbonate trihydrate, $MgCO_3.3H_2O$, found as colourless monoclinic crystals.

1890 GENTH & PENFIELD in *Amer. Jrnl. Sci.* CXXXIX. 122 The clear crystals..proved on examination to be a new mineral, having the composition $MgCO_3.3H_2O$, to which we have given the name Nesquehonite, after the locality where the mineral was found, the Nesquehoning Mine being one of the best known in Pennsylvania. **1934** *Mineral. Abstr.* V. 431 Galleries in the Cogne magnetite mine in serpentine rocks, at an elevation of 2500 metres in the Piedmontese Alps, have a constant temperature of 4°C., and this has favoured the formation of lansfordite.. and nesquehonite. **1957** G. E. HUTCHINSON *Treat. Limnol.* I. x. 665 At ordinary temperatures the carbonate that precipitates when saturation is reached at from 10^{-3} to 10^{-1} atm. of CO_2 is $MgCO_3.3H_2O$, or nesquehonite. **1971** *Contrib. Mineral. & Petrol.* XXXIII. 88 The 'cauliflower' crusts mainly consist of hydromagnesite and/or nesquehonite with traces of monohydrocalcite and calcite.

nessberry (ne·sberi). [f. the name of Helge *Ness* (d. 1928), American horticulturist + BERRY *sb.*¹] A variety of *Rubus*, produced by crossing a dewberry and a raspberry, introduced by Helge Ness in 1921.

1925 H. NESS in *Bull. Texas Agric. Exper. Stat.* No. 326. 19 This new fruit has been named the Nessberry by the authorities of the College. *Ibid.*, The Nessberry is of an excessively strong growth, some of its branches attaining a length of 10 to 15 feet in a single season. **1948** J. S. SHOEMAKER *Small Fruit Culture* (ed. 2) iii. 232 Nessberry..has a delightful flavor and thrives well in East Texas, but it proved unpopular because of poor picking quality and difficulty in propagation. **1952** *New Biol.* XIII. 46 Among the newer crops which have arisen by allopolyploidy..the most notable are the various berries related to blackberry and raspberry... Two typical examples are the nessberry and loganberry. **1972** BROOKS & OLMO *Register of New Fruit & Nut Varieties* 164 Nessberry... Fruit: larger than Logan; size variable; hemispherical; skin deep to blood red.

Nesselrode (ne·səlrōᵘd). The name of Karl R. *Nesselrode* (1780–1862), Russian statesman, used *attrib.* in *Nesselrode pie, pudding*, etc., an iced dessert made with chestnuts, cream, preserved fruits, etc., and freq. flavoured with rum. Also ellipt. *Nesselrode*.

1845 E. ACTON *Mod. Cookery* xx. 441 *Nesselrode Cream*, .. Chestnuts .. sugar .. isinglass .. cream .. vanilla [etc]. *Ibid.* 461 Nesselrode pudding. We give Monsieur Carème's own receipt..as it originated with him. **1877** E. S. DALLAS *Kettner's Bk. of Table* 311 (*heading*) Nesselrode pudding was invented..by Mony, cook to the famous Count Nesselrode. **1894** E. SKUSE *Compl. Confectioner* 155 Nesselrode or Ice Pudding. Prepare a custard of one pint of cream, [etc.]. **1952** S. J. PERELMAN *Ill-Tempered Clavichord* (1953) 12, I wouldn't bolt that Nesselrode if I were you. **1965** *Harper's Bazaar* Nov. 136/2 Make a Nesselrode pudding such as Françoise made for Monsieur de Norpois the first time he went to dine with the Prousts. **1972** *New Yorker* 15 Apr. 35/2 Toward the back of the shop are two refrigerated cases—one for birthday cakes, the other for ice-cream cakes and for desserts composed of perishable whipped cream, such as Nesselrode pie.

Nessie (ne·si). *colloq.* Also **Nessy.** [f. *Ness* (see below) + -IE or -Y⁶.] A name for a monster or monsters supposedly inhabiting Loch Ness in northern Scotland. Cf. *LOCH NESS.

1945 *Sun* (Baltimore) 25 June 2 'Nessie', the unidentified Loch Ness monster which used to disport itself in those Scottish waters before the war..has reappeared, according to several women residents. **1960** in T. Dinsdale *Loch Ness Monster* (1961) v. 76 According to substantiated reports, Nessie was seen a number of times last spring..and a few times in the autumn. **1968** *New Scientist* 26 Dec. 729/1 The trouble with Nessie was that she became an immediate newspaper sensation. **1971** *Ibid.* 10 June 641/2 Nessy has lost her mythical charm and has become the target of serious-minded technocrats. **1974** *People's Jrnl.* (Inverness & Northern Counties ed.) 29 June 2/6 They sighted Nessie as they returned from a delivery at Inverfarigaig. **1975** *Nature* 11 Dec. 467/3 Should the Nessies wish to breathe quite frequently, they would not be detected easily if the nostrils were at the topmost point to break surface.

Nessler (ne·slər). *Chem.* The name of Julius *Nessler* (1827–1905), German agricultural chemist, used *attrib.* and in the possessive with reference to a delicate test for ammonia he devised; as **Nessler('s) reagent** or **solution**, an alkaline solution of potassium mercuric iodide, which gives a yellow or brown colour or precipitate when added to an aqueous solution containing ammonia; **Nessler('s) tube**, a glass cylinder marked with a line indicating a certain volume and depth, used in nesslerization and other colorimetric procedures.

1865 *Jrnl. Chem. Soc.* XVIII. 125 The distillate is divided into two equal portions; one of these is submitted to Nessler's test for ammonia. **1868** *Ibid.* XXI. 87 Mr. Chapman..recommends that the ammonia determination should be made by the application of Nessler's solution directly to the water. *Ibid.*, Waters containing chalk in solution become turbid on the addition of the Nessler test. **1873** *Chem. News* 11 July 13/2 The time required for the development of the Nessler colour. *Ibid.*, One sample of Nessler reagent gives its maximum of colour almost immediately, and another takes a quarter of an hour or an hour. **1913** CUMMING & KAY *Text-bk. Quantit. Chem. Anal.* IV. 156 Measure into a 100 c.c. Nessler tube a portion of the solution containing from 0·1 to 3 mgrm. of iron. **1946** *Thorpe's Dict. Appl. Chem.* (ed. 4) VII. 579/1 The action of ammonia on an alkaline solution of potassium mercuri-iodide..is the basis of the Nessler test for ammonia. **1963** SKOOG & WEST *Fund. Analytical Chem.* xxviii. 656 In its simplest form, colorimetry consists of visual matching of the color of the solutions of the substance with a set of standards. For such a procedure flat-bottomed tubes called Nessler tubes are frequently employed. **1970** Nessler's reagent [see *NESSLERIZATION].

nesslerize, *v.* Add: Also **Nesslerize.** Substitute for def.: *trans.* To treat with Nessler's reagent in order to test for the presence of ammonia; also, to test for (ammonia) by this means. Also *absol.* (Earlier and later examples.) So **ne·sslerized** *ppl. a.*, **ne·sslerizing** *vbl. sb.*

1873 *Chem. News* 11 July 13/2 Whether the Nesslerising takes a couple of minutes, or whether it takes an hour, is a matter of vital importance to those persons who are working the ammonia process of water analysis. **1884** *Jrnl. Amer. Chem. Soc.* VI. 122 Such a tube was found.. to be unsuitable for comparison with the color of Nesslerized liquids. **1890** *Amer. Chem. Jrnl.* XII. 426 Standards and distillates are made ready for nesslerisation during the day, and all stand on the same table overnight. In the morning they are nesslerised and compared. **1916** *Jrnl. Biol. Chem.* XXVI. 473 It was hoped that it would be possible to Nesslerize directly the ammonia produced by the destructive digestion of the urine. *Ibid.* 481 It is better when working in urine to dilute the final Nesslerized solution to 200 cc. instead of to 100 cc. **1956** *Jrnl. Lab. & Clin. Med.* XLVII. 645 In one the clot is dried and weighed to the nearest microgram; in the other it is nesslerized and assayed colorimetrically. *Ibid.* 646 If a microbalance is not available, the fibrin may be estimated by digesting it in sulfuric acid and hydrogen peroxide, nesslerizing, and determining the color density.

nesslerization (examples).

1890 [see above]. **1916** *Jrnl. Biol. Chem.* XXVI. 475 This sediment does not interfere with the Nesslerization of the ammonia, but it must be removed before the color comparison is made. **1964** *Oceanogr. & Marine Biol.* II. 148 They determine ammonia in the digest by Nesslerization. **1970** *Nature* 12 Sept. 1136/2 L-Glutaminase and L-asparaginase assays were performed..as previously described except that the colour formed by nesslerization of ammonia was measured 1–3 min after addition of Nessler's reagent.

Nessus (ne·sŏs). Name of the centaur slain by Hercules and in whose blood was soaked the tunic which consumed Hercules with fire, used allusively in *Nessus robe, Nessus shirt, shirt of Nessus* of any destructive or expurgatory force or influence.

1606 SHAKES. *Ant. & Cl.* IV. xii. 43 The shirt of Nessus is vpon me. **1835** CARLYLE *Lett. to his Wife* (1953) 108 It is now almost my sole rule of life: to clear myself of Cants and formulas, as of poisonous Nessus' shirts. **1905** S. J. WEYMAN *Starvecrow Farm* xxxii. 297 Remorse is the very shirt of Nessus. It is of all mental pains the worst. **1924** R. GRAVES *Mock Beggar Hall* 10 The Nessus-robe that beauties wear, Burning away their beauty. **1931** *Times Lit. Suppl.* 5 Mar. 162/2 The Nessus-robe of vice clings festering about him. **1957** E. SITWELL *Coll. Poems* 414 Then the heart that was the Burning-Bush May change to a Nessus-robe of flame. **1961** M. WEST *Daughter of Silence* iv. 116 Accept the guilt, know yourself for what you are, wear the knowledge like a Nessus shirt on your own back and bear the pricks and the poison with as much dignity as you can muster.

Nessy, var. *NESSIE.

nest, *sb.* Add: **2. d.** *Mil.* An emplaced group of machine-guns.

1914 E. A. POWELL *Fighting in Flanders* v. 120 Other wagons..contained 'nests' of nine machine-guns. **1949** 'G. ORWELL' *Nineteen Eighty-Four* I. 8 A maze of barbed-wire entanglements, steel doors and hidden machine-gun nests. **1959** R. POSTGATE *Every Man is God* xviii. 157 The Germans come out of the machine-gun nest holding up their hands.

6. (Further examples.)

1807 R. SOUTHEY *Lett. from England* I. 155 Here is also a nest of tables for the ladies, consisting of four, one less than another, and each fitting into the one above it. **1924** R. KEABLE *Recompence* iv. 76 A delightful nest of occasional tables. **1973** J. LEASOR *Host of Extras* i. 17 A nest of spanners and some lengths of wire that might come in useful in starting an engine. **1975** *Country Life* 20 Feb. Suppl. 32d/2 A rare nest of five rosewood 'quartetto' tables..English, circa 1820.

8. *nest-burrow, -factory, -mate, -material, -relief, -scrape, -site; nest-raiding.*

1948 *British Birds* XLI. 341 During our short stay we saw no trace of nest burrows of the Great Shearwater. **1961** G. DURRELL *Whispering Land* ii. 55 Once the parent bird [*sc.* a penguin] reached the edge of the colony it had run the gauntlet of several thousand youngsters before it reached its own nest-burrow and babies. **1908** *Westm. Gaz.* 19 Aug. 5/3 The Hungarian Government go so far as to pay large sums of money in subsidies to artificial nest factories, these nests being fixed in the forests by the thousand and regularly looked after. **1913** G. STRATTON-PORTER *Laddie* v. 146 If a young bird failed to get the bite it wanted, it sometimes grabbed one of its nestmates by the bill..and tried to swallow it whole. **1941** J. S. HUXLEY *Uniqueness of Man* x. 214 The nestling cuckoo.. does not know why he is murdering his fellow nest-mates. **1923** —— *Essays of Biologist* iii. 121 We invariably find the seizing of nest-material in the beak as a part of courtship. **1953** N. TINBERGEN *Herring Gull's World* vii. 68 We often wondered how another gull knew whether a grass-pulling gull was in an aggressive mood or merely collecting nest-material. **1937** *British Birds* XXXI. 205 The evidence for nest raiding is so scanty as to lead to the conclusion that it is not a usual habit. **1953** D. A. BANNERMAN *Birds Brit. Isles* I. 15 It is in the early morning ..that the crow carries out most of its nest-raiding. **1923** J. S. HUXLEY *Essays of Biologist* iii. 112 After the eggs [of the Louisiana Heron] are laid both sexes brood, and there is a nest-relief four times in every twenty-four hours. **1953** N. TINBERGEN *Herring Gull's World* xvi. 136 The variation in the behaviour of the birds at nest-relief is primarily due to variations in the intensity of the incubation urge. *Ibid.* ii. 11 When the birds of a pair make a nest-scrape together..they make a queer rhythmical sound. **1964** *Oxf. Bk. Birds* 48/1 The nest scrape [of the kestrel] may be in a hollow tree. **1930** J. S. HUXLEY *Bird-Watching* iii. 53 Each breeding pair occupies and defends against intrusion a considerable area around its nest-site. **1964** A. L. THOMSON *New Dict. Birds* 531/1 Summer migrants may select a nest site and begin building on the same day.

nest, *v.* Add: **2. c.** *U.S. colloq.* To squat. (Cf. *NESTER 2.)

1918 C. E. MULFORD *Man from Bar-20* xi. 114 Not satisfied with nestin' on a man's range, you had to start a little herd.

4. b. (Later example, not in pa. pple. Also, examples referring to abstract entities; cf. *NESTED *ppl. a.* 2.)

1925 N. E. ODELL in E. F. Norton *Fight for Everest 1924* 362 Two saucepans that nest into one another. **1961** D. V. HUNTSBERGER *Elem. Statist. Inference* ix. 230 Situations of this sort, where every classification is nested within the next larger one, are called nested or hierarch[ic]al classifications. **1967** KLERER & KORN *Digital Computer User's Handbk.* I. i. 16 Groups of loops need not be strictly nested and may have parts which are done in parallel or parts which are done in series. **1968** J. LYONS *Introd. Theoret. Linguistics* vi. 233 In subordinative constructions one modifier may be recursively 'nested' within another. **1970** P. M. SHERMAN *Techn. Computer Programming* iii. 43 In many problems one loop is nested within another one. This occurs when a loop contains a box with a repetitious process that itself can be drawn as a loop.

nestalik, nestaliq, varr. *NASTALIK.

nest-box. *2.* (Later examples.)

1893 *Burpee's Farm Ann.* 64 These gourds are useful for many household purposes, such as..nest-boxes, soap

and salt dishes. **1946** *Q. Jrnl. Forestry* XL. 83 The habit of maintaining a territory also leads to birds being well scattered over the area, and as a consequence nest boxes should not be too close together. **1963** *Times* 8 June 12/7 Your Correspondent recalls a horrid stench from a nest-box after seven or eight young great tits had flown. **1971** *Country Life* 2 Sept. 541/1 Many bird-lovers put up two or three nest-boxes in their gardens.

nested, *ppl. a.* Add: **2.** Such that each item or constituent contains or is contained within another similar item in a hierarchical arrangement. **a.** Of concrete objects (cf. Nest *v.* 4 b).

1921 *Glasgow Herald* 1 June 7 Two or three 'nested' dishes, the biggest one large enough to take two plates side by side. **1969** 'S. Troy' *Swift to its Close* vi. 81 A little man carrying three nested chairs brushed past. **1972** *Sci. Amer.* Apr. 32/1 The magnetic field in the compressor is supplied by a nested set of copper coils.

b. Of abstract entities.

1959 E. L. Lehmann *Testing Statistical Hypotheses* vii. 290 (*heading*) Nested classifications. **1963** Ervin & Miller in J. A. Fishman *Readings Sociol. of Lang.* (1968) 80 Preliminary evidence suggests that nesting is learned early... It is difficult to assess the evidence, however, because nested constructions are usually delineated by markers which are largely lacking in the early grammatical systems. **1965** N. Chomsky *Aspects of Theory of Syntax* i. 12 The phrases *A* and *B* form a nested construction if *A* falls totally within *B*, with some nonnull element to its left within *B* and some nonnull element to its right within *B*. **1967** [see *nesting *vbl. sb.* 2]. **1968** J. F. Hart et al. *Computer Approximations* iv. 68 Consider a polynomial given in the conventional power form $P_n(x) = \sum_{i=0}^{n} a_i x^i$. It can be written in nested form $P_n(x) = [\ldots(a_n x + a_{n-1})x + \ldots + a_1]x + a_0$. **1970** P. M. Sherman *Techn. Computer Programming* iii. 43 Some flowcharts contain three or more nested loops. **1973** A. M. Cohen et al. *Numerical Anal.* ii. 21 The computation of a polynomial function is usually done by means of 'nested multiplication'. **1973** *Computers & Humanities* VII. 226 Procedures for handling nested loops and subscripted variables.

nest-egg, *sb.* Add: **1.** (Later examples.)

1939–40 *Army & Navy Stores Catal.* 989/2 Poultry nest eggs. **1973** *Country Life* 18 Oct. 1129/3 What happened to the old-fashioned nest-egg, the white pot egg one could once..buy to ensure that hens would lay where they were supposed to lay?

4. (Later examples.)

1968 J. R. Ackerley *My Father & Myself* 41 This nest-egg towards the cost of the farm. **1975** *Radio Times* 24 Apr. 12 (Advt.), Williams & Glyn's Nest Egg is a regular savings plan.

nester. Delete *rare* and add: **1.** (Earlier example.)

1887 *Ibis* 95 It [sc. *Cisticola cursitans*] is both an early and late nester.

2. *N. Amer.* An opprobrious term for a person who settles permanently in a cattle-grazing region as a farmer, homesteader, etc. (Cf. *Nest *v.* 2 c.)

1880 *Ft. Griffin* (Tex.) *Echo* 3 Jan., [A sheep man is] a tramp, an ingrate, a 'Nester', and a liar. **1907** C. E. Mulford *Bar-20* xix. 192 Ain't th' Panhandle full of nesters (farmers)? **1918** —— *Man from Bar-20* iii. 27 He had found the ruins of a burned homestead..and he guessed that it had been used by 'nesters'. **1970** *Alberta Hist. Rev.* Summer 9/2 The one small cloud on this otherwise sunny horizon was the would-be farmer, or as he was more inhospitably known to the cattlemen—the 'sod-buster' or 'nester'. **1973** R. D. Symons *Where Wagon Led* p. xx, You plant a garden and someone'll see it an' we'll have nesters.

nesting, *vbl. sb.* Add: **b.** *nesting-burrow, -call, -cover, -ground, -habit, -hole, -territory, -tree*; **nesting-box** = Nest-box 2 (in Dict. and Suppl.); also *fig.*

1873 *Young Englishwoman* May 225/1 The space beneath the nesting-boxes should be partitioned from the rest of the cage. **1895** W. Schlich *Man. Forestry* IV. ii. 148 The wooden nesting-boxes..are made out of half-inch boards, and tarred. **1933** H. Nicolson *Diary* 5 Jan. (1966) 131 Up Broadway and Madison to the hotel. Nesting-boxes. **1938** *Brit. Birds* XXXI. 331 Noticing..a Blue Tit..entering about dusk a nesting box..I began watching. **1970** *New Yorker* 8 Aug. 56/3 We're building nesting boxes and doing everything else we can think of to encourage the kestrels. **1937** *Brit. Birds* XXX. 237 On Rona the thrift-grown banks..are riddled with nesting burrows of Leach's Petrels. **1959** Van Tyne & Berger *Fundamentals of Ornithology* x. 277 The Turquoise-browed Motmot..may dig nesting burrows over 5 feet long. **1924** J. A. Thomson *Sci. Old & New* xxi. 116 The selection is marked by the bird's remaining near the chosen spot and giving the nesting-call to the mate. **1936** *Brit. Birds* XXIX. 28 Elstree reservoir..is about 80 acres in extent with relatively little suitable nesting-cover for the Great Crested Grebe. **1921** *Daily Colonist* (Victoria, B.C.) 27 Oct. 10/3 The purchasing of suitable marsh and swamp lands to furnish nesting grounds for the birds in the North. **1961** O. L. Austin *Birds of World* (1962) 38/2 They [*sc.* diving petrels]..are nocturnal on the nesting grounds. **1936** *Brit. Birds* XXX. 98 The average size of the broods of the Swallow..and other questions connected with their nesting-habits..bring the enquiry to a close. **1964** *Oxf. Bk. Birds* 102/2 They [*sc.* rock doves] build on ledges in caves and crevices and have..nesting habits like other doves. **1936** *Brit. Birds* XXIX. 379 The height above ground of the nesting-hole varies according to the choice there is of decayed wood. **1961** O. L. Austin *Birds of World* (1962) 173/2 Guatemalans have always claimed that the Quetzal selects a nesting hole with two entrances ...Recent studies have shown this to be pure legend. **1923** J. S. Huxley *Ess. Biologist* vii. 291 The sense of being a trespasser so often shown by a bird that has ventured upon the nesting-territory of another. **1959** Van Tyne & Berger *Fundamentals of Ornithology* x. 268 Small nesting territories of colonial and some non-colonial birds—a small area round the actual nest. **1974** *Country Life* 14 Feb. 285/3 Fulmars..lay claim to sites, even when there is frost... Ravens, too, patrol a nesting territory. **1935** *Brit. Birds* XXVIII. 347 Return to nesting-trees.—First seen on February 18th.

2. (The making of) a nested arrangement (see *nested *ppl. a.* 2).

1957 D. D. McCracken *Digital Computer Programming* xvii. 207 The truncated series is factored: $e^x = 1 + x/1! + x^2/2! + x^3/3! + x^4/4! + x^5/5! + x^6/6! = 1 + x[1 + \frac{1}{2}x[1 + \frac{1}{3}x[1 + \frac{1}{4}x[1 + \frac{1}{5}x[1 + \frac{1}{6}x]]]]]$. The factored series is then evaluated 'from the inside out', which is also called nesting. **1958** C. F. Hockett *Course in Mod. Linguistics* xxi. 189 The presence of certain attributive constructions in the nesting precludes the occurrence of certain others at a more inclusive level: we can say *this fresh milk*, but not *fresh this milk*. **1963** [see *nested *ppl. a.* 2 b]. **1965** *Language* XLI. 71 Internal layering and multiple nesting characterize many syntagmemes. **1966** Y. Bar-Hillel in *Automatic Transl. of Lang.* (NATO Summer School, Venice 1962) 11 The same degree of nesting is also assigned to the terminal expression as analysed by this tree. **1967** Klerer & Korn *Digital Computer User's Handbk.* i. iii. 75 Another technique to reduce operations is by nesting when increasing powers of a variable are to be calculated. For example, the expression $AX^3 + BX^2 + CX + D$ may be written in nested form as $((B + Ax)x + C)x + D$ which requires less arithmetic. **1972** Hartmann & Stork *Dict. of Lang. & Linguistics* 150/2 *Nesting*, the embedding of a phrase or clause within an endocentric phrase to modify its head word.

nesting, *ppl. a.* Add: **2.** Of a table, chair, etc.: that forms part of a set of similar articles which can be fitted into one another (cf. Nest *sb.* 6).

Passing into the *vbl. sb.*

1934 H. Read *Art & Industry* ii. 89 Another chair designed by Alvar Aalto. The plywood process combined with tubular steel to make nesting-chairs. **1934** A. Woollcott *While Rome Burns* 29 He [*sc.* Harpo, a French poodle] was gracious, for instance, toward Erich Maria Remarque, a dachshund who fitted under him like a nesting table. **1958** J. Cannan *And be a Villain* iii. 57 In the meagre lounge, half-heartedly modernized with nesting chairs and formica-topped tables. **1959** N. Mailer *Advts. for Myself* (1961) 436 Hand-worked nesting tables. **1961** G. Millerson *Technique Telev. Production* viii. 150 (*caption*) Nesting sets may be placed one within the other, the inner one being struck to reveal the outer. **1969** *Guardian* 26 Sept. 11/7 Nesting tables..5 gns. each or £15. 10s. per set of three. **1970** *Washington Post* 30 Sept. B8/5 (Advt.), Front-zipped cotton luggage... Six nesting sizes. **1975** *Harpers & Queen* May 145/2 Gladstone bags in woven rush; 3 nesting sizes.

nestle-chick = Nestle-cock.

1932 R. Macaulay *They were Defeated* i. 32, I couldn't spare her—my last nestle-chick, and the best. **1937** —— *I would be Private* 36 It was to have been her..nestle-chick.

net, *sb.*[1] Add: **2. a.** *spec.* In Games and Sports: a piece of netting used as part of the equipment for the game; esp. *Cricket*, the netting used to divide off practice wickets; hence in *pl.*, a name for such a wicket. Also, the safety net used by acrobats.

1845 'N. Felix' *Felix on Bat* i. i. 7 The way to secure much practice..is to procure a large net, about twenty yards long and six feet in height, [etc.]. **1856** [in Dict.]. **1884** E. M. Butler in F. Gale *Life R. Grimston* (1885) xii. 191 In the evenings he would stand behind the nets when the eleven were practising, and coach them very thoroughly. **1889** [in Dict.]. **1899** *Captain* II. 127/1 The most difficult shot for a goal-keeper to stop is a low one that crosses him into the corner of the net... Beware lest..you shoot outside the net. **1903** G. B. Shaw *Man & Superman* iv. 144 There is no tennis net nor set of croquet hoops. **1905** A. Bennett *Tales of Five Towns* ii. 250 We should..flash past each other in mid-flight.. and soar to opposite platforms again, amid frenzied applause. There were no nets. **1915** W. S. Maugham *Of Human Bondage* xvii. 67 They practised at nets in the summer. **1937** [see *hoop *sb.*[1] 8 c]. **1947** *Sun* (Baltimore) 8 Nov. 12/2 Although Friends took the ball on several long runs down the field, the Bryn Mawr defense was too effective to be penetrated and Goalie Jo Nelson found little to do in the nets. **1955** *Times* 6 July 3/6 With his left side heavily plastered he batted in the nets before the Yorkshire game resumed. **1958** [see *graft *v.*[3]]. **1958** J. Betjeman *Coll. Poems* 50, I adore you, Pam, you great big mountainous sports girl, Whizzing them over the net. **1960** N. Streatfeild *Look at Circus* iv. 80 In any properly run circus under the trapezes or high tight-rope act a net is stretched. **1961** J. S. Salak *Dict. Amer. Sports* 295 *Net* (ice hockey), the goal. **1965** *Men's Hockey* ('Know the Game' Series) 6 Nets are attached to the goal-posts, cross bar and ground behind the goal. Goal-boards..are placed at the foot of the goal-nets. **1967** C. B. Mills *B. Mills Circus* viii. 109 Fritzi Bartoni..did one very difficult trick in which she fell forward from a trapeze and caught herself by her heels on the cross bar and she had been doing this without a net. **1975** *Times* 4 Dec. 10/1 Their goalkeeper..rolled out a ball that rebounded..to Summerill who sent Hart away to run the ball into an empty net.

c. *Lawn Tennis.* = Let *sb.*[1] 2. *colloq.*

1904 J. P. Paret et al. *Lawn Tennis* 344 *Net*,..also (same as 'let'), a ball that touches the net and goes into the proper court. **1929** D. Mackail *How Amusing!* 450 Clampson served a let. They actually—yes, in the twentieth century and the Centre Court—they distinctly called it a 'net'.

4. c. A network; *spec.* (*a*) a network of spies; (*b*) a broadcasting network.

1919 J. Buchan *Mr. Standfast* iii. 63 By the middle of 1915 most [enemy spies]..had been gathered in. But there remained loose ends, and..somebody was very busy combining these ends into a net. **1952** *Brewer's Dict. Phr. & Fable* (rev. ed.) 644/2 *On the Old Boy net*, to arrange something through a friend (originally, someone known at school) instead of through the usual channels. **1959** *Listener* 22 Oct. 668/2 Television programmes are to be exchanged among the East European countries and the Soviet Union... A coaxial cable is already being laid on the Soviet-Polish section of the net. **1961** H. B. Jacobson *Mass Communications Dict.* 222 *Net*, abbreviation for radio network, which is merely a group of stations joined by wires to release a given program simultaneously. **1966** 'H. Talbot' *Catch me Traitor* i. 14, D. I. 6 was probably short of yet another carefully built up net in the East German People's Republic. **1966** *Electronics* 17 Oct. 129 Capt. D. A. Jones..cautioned that 'our national security could be affected by the dissemination of data by these geodetic nets'. **1967** M. Childs *Taint of Innocence* (1968) ii. 97 She's got her own net going in that nest of vipers and I'd stake a lot on it. **1969** J. Elliot *Duel* i. i. 25, I had a regular weekly spot on a national net—thirty-six in a year. **1969** A. Marin *Rise with Wind* xiv. 168 Whenever a net was surfaced..the word went around the *intelligence community*. **1971** C. Bonington *Annapurna South Face* iii. 33 He eventually got an agreement that the set in Katmandu should be kept in the Nepalese Army headquarters so that they would have control of the wireless net. **1972** 'W. Haggard' *Protectors* iv. 42 Shay was after the gold, on information received through the usual net.

5. a. *net-fishing* (later examples), *game, -man* (earlier and later examples), *-owner, -pocket, shot*; **d. net-bag** (earlier and later examples); **net-cord**, the cord passing along and supporting the top of a net, esp. a tennis net; so **net-cord (stroke)**, in lawn tennis, a stroke which hits the net cord but still crosses the net; **net curtain**, a curtain made of net, usu. now fixed permanently across windows to ensure privacy; hence **net-curtained** *a.*; **net-drifter**, earlier term for **net-layer*; also *attrib.*; **net-fish** *v. intr.*, to fish with a net; **net-layer**, a vessel which lays anti-submarine nets; hence **net-laying** *vbl. sb.*; **netminder** = *goal-tender* (*goal *sb.* 6); **net-player** *Lawn Tennis* and *Badminton*, a player who advances close to the net; hence **net play**; **net-practice**, cricket practice at the nets.

1598 J. Florio *Worlde of Wordes* 61/1 *Carnero, Carniéro*, a net-bag to carie meat in, a hawking bag. **1934** *Discovery* Sept. 261/1 In those days the wild fowler had not learnt the trick of curving the pipes, and so had to trust to frightening the duck into the net bag, or some such contraption. **1951** Colyer & Hammond *Flies Brit. Isles* 324 This instrument can often be used under conditions where a net-bag is liable to be torn, e.g. on thorn or bramble. **1970** *New Yorker* 28 Nov. 51/1 On the third bed lay a bulging net bag. **1844** Net-cord [in Dict.]. **1887** *Boy's Own Paper* 3 Sept. 778/1 If you are tall enough, take it before it descends to the level of the net-cord. **1904** J. P. Paret et al. *Lawn Tennis* 345 Net-cord stroke. **1959** *Times* 1 Sept. 3/3 It was the third game when twice MacKay got away with net cords. **1961** F. C. Avis *Sportsman's Gloss.* 258 *Net cord stroke*, one that causes the ball to contact the net, the ball afterwards going into the proper court. **1931** M. Allingham *Look to Lady* xxii. 224 There was a thin net curtain over the windows, but the light inside rendered it transparent. **1935** A. Fremantle tr. *Wynne Diaries* I. i. 2 The Curé of Berkheim's house is very pretty. There is in it a sofa and net curtains which he himself has made. **1967** E. Short *Embroidery & Fabric Collage* iii. 83 On net curtains, permanently in place across a window, designs of a more pictorial type would be quite suitable. **1972** J. Mann *Mrs Knox's Profession* x. 78 The local style was for picture windows, sometimes net curtained. **1973** C. Egleton *Seven Days to Killing* xviii. 188 The net-curtained window. **1919** R. Bacon *Dover Patrol 1915–17* I. vi. 157 The procedure of the mine-net drifters was simple. As each division arrived at its mark-buoy, the rear boats proceeded to shoot their nets, and, after steaming a definite time interval, each succeeding pair stopped and shot their nets to complete the line. *Ibid.*, In addition to the above, the 10th, 11th, and 12th Divisions of net-drifters anchored parallel to the West Hinder and shot their nets. **1923** E. K. Chatterton *Auxiliary Patrol* iii. 41 Net-drifter bases were quickly established also at Peterhead..and Larne. **1925** *Home Waters* (Naval Staff Monogr., Historical, XIII.) iv. vii. 126 By the beginning of March [1915] the term 'Net Drifter Flotillas' was in use to designate units of drifters working indicator nets, or other anti-submarine devices. **1891** *Chambers's Encycl.* VIII. 256/1 He may be arrested if he is net-fishing, but not if he is fishing in another way. **1968** J. Arnold *Shell Book of Country Crafts* 228 As no new licences are being granted, net fishing on the upper stretch of the river will die out. **1961** F. C. Avis *Sportsman's Gloss.* 259 *Net game*, that kind of play taking place in the vicinity of the net, and thus the opposite of base line game. **1930** *Economist* 8 Mar. 513/1 Five submarines, one submarine depôt ship, two sloops and one netlayer. **1957** *Observer* 1 Dec. 1/1 H.M.S. Protector, a converted net-layer. **1923** E. K. Chatterton *Auxiliary Patrol* xv. 229 One hundred and two ships were secretly assembled, and the actual operation of net-laying was carried out in an hour and a half. **1847** C. Lanman *Summer in Wilderness* xxvi. 160 A false movement of the net-man will cause the canoe to be swamped. **1915** [see *cross-court* adj. s.v. *cross- B]. **1934** R. Graves *Claudius the God* xxx. 518 He was disarmed and a net-man was standing over him with his trident raised. **1942** Berrey &

Van den Bark *Amer. Thes. Slang* §662/2 *Net minder*,..a goalkeeper. **1961** J. S. Salak *Dict. Amer. Sports* 296 *Net minder* (ice hockey), the goaltender. **1968** *Globe & Mail* (Toronto) 15 Jan. 19/1 Eddie Shack spoiled Montreal net-minder Rogatien Vachon's chance for a shutout when he scored. **1973** *Cleveland* (Ohio) *Plain Dealer* 6 Apr. 10-C/1 Cheevers has come on strong to maintain his reputation as one of the best netminders in hockey. **1901** *Chambers's Jrnl.* Sept. 585/1 The estuary limits..have been fixed more in the interests of net-owners than in those of the salmon. **1961** J. S. Salak *Dict. Amer. Sports* 296 *Net play* (badminton), the player returning the bird from a position close to the net. **1919** S. Lenglen *Lawn Tennis for Girls* 53 The net player..has a free hand at the net. **1930** *Amer. Speech* VI. 118 California's net players. **1902** *Chambers's Jrnl.* Jan. 48/2 The younger man..swung the captive ashore in the net-pocket. **1899** *Captain* I. 378/2 Net practice is good in moderation, but nothing is so good as practice games. **1975** *Country Life* 19 June 1625/3, I waited to greet the Australians for their first net practice. **1961** J. S. Salak *Dict. Amer. Sports* 296 In mixed doubles the lady is usually responsible for the net shots.

net, *a.* Add: **3. a.** Also as *sb.*

1910 *Gt. Central Railway Rep.* 11 Feb. 7 Deducting from our receipts..our expenses of £1,488,474, we have a net of £796,956. **1961** H. B. Jacobson *Mass Communications Dict.* 222 *Net*, the amount paid to the advertising medium by the advertising agency after deducting the agency commission. **1969** *N.Y. Rev. Books* 2 Jan. 6/4 Its net after taxes..after allowing for sales of assets,..was only $9 million.

b. *spec.* in phr. *net book*, a book sold at the net price; *Net Book Agreement*, the formal arrangement between publishers and booksellers, binding the latter not to sell below the net price; also, an agreement between publishers and public libraries to adhere to a set discount; *net (and) net*, used to indicate that the price of a book so marked cannot be subject to any discount whatever; *net system*, the system laid down in the Net Book Agreement for the sale of net books.

1890 *Bookseller* 6 Mar. 244/2 With the hearty co-operation of the retail trade, the *net* system could easily be introduced. **1893, 1894** [in Dict.]. **1911** *Encycl. Brit.* XXII. 630/1 The Booksellers' Association signed an agreement to charge the full published price for every net book. *Ibid.* 630/2 The net system was gradually introduced, net books and discount books being issued side by side. *Ibid.* 631/2 In 1901 the net system, as adopted in Great Britain, was partially introduced into America. **1938** L. M. Harrod *Librarians' Gloss.* 105 *Net book agreement*, an agreement drawn up in 1929..between the Publishers' Association, the Booksellers' Association, and the Library Association, enabling rate-supported libraries and other libraries..to receive a discount of 10 per cent on all new books purchased. **1939** M. Plant *Eng. Bk. Trade* xx. 441 Net books were to come, but not in that way. It was Frederick Macmillan who was to take the lead. He wrote to the *Bookseller* in 1890 suggesting the publication of net books. **1952** *Bookseller* 5 Jan. 27 This list is..published..at quarterly intervals..with Classified List, May 6/- net net. **1959** L. M. Harrod *Librarians' Gloss.* (ed. 2) 187 *Net book*, one which..may be sold to a signatory to the agreement at a recognized discount. **1960** G. A. Glaister *Glossary of Book* 274/2 The 1901 Net Book Agreement, now replaced, was based on the right of the Publishers Association to act on behalf of its publisher members in ensuring that the conditions of supply of net books were observed. *Ibid.* 275/2 *Net net*, an indication that a book so marked or described must be sold at the full published price, and that the publisher will not allow any discount to the book trade... Confined almost exclusively to reference works published at the lowest possible sum for the benefit of the trade. **1961** M. C. Turner *Bookman's Gloss.* (ed. 4) 113 When an English book carries no trade discount, it is sometimes called a 'net net' book. **1963** Kenneison & Spilman *Dict. Printing* 133 *Net net*, term indicating that a book will not be sold to the book trade at any discount. **1972** C. Bingley *Business Bk. Publishing* iv. 135 The validity of the British Net Book Agreement does not extend beyond the U.K.

c. *net reproduction rate*: a reproduction rate representing the average number of girls born to each woman of a population who can be expected to reach their mothers' age at the time of birth, calculated from the average fertility rates and death rates of each age-group during the period considered.

1928 R. R. Kuczynski *Balance Births & Deaths* I. iii. 46 The net reproduction rate, as we may call it, was 1·435. **1952** C. P. Blacker *Eugenics* viii. 170 Gross and net reproduction rates have been published for France since 1806. **1972** *Nature* 7 Apr. 270/1 In a population which is just barely reproducing itself, the Net Reproduction Rate should, of course, be 1·0. **1973** *Sci. Amer.* Apr. 19/1 Under conditions of high mortality the difference between the net reproduction rate and the gross reproduction rate is large.

d. *net worth* (see quot. 1930).

1930 *Economist* 17 May 1108/2 'Net worth' (that is, the stockholders' equity, made up of preferred and common stock outstanding, surplus account and undivided profits, taken at the beginning of the fiscal year). **1955** *Times* 13 July 13/1 Some estimates..have now been made..of the net worth of consumers. **1964** Gould & Kolb *Dict. Social Sci.* 465/2 The expression *net worth* is becoming obsolete. The British now frequently use the expression *total equity*.

e. *net national product* (see quot. 1964 and *national product*, *national *a.* 5).

1945 S. Kuznets *National Product in Wartime* I. ii. 13 Net national product consists of (a) flow of goods to consumers, (b) net nonwar Capital formation, (c) net war output, i.e., net additions to the inventory of war goods. **1945** S. E. Harris *Inflation & American Economy* i. 31 (*table*) Output rises. The percentage rise of 1939–43:..Net national product. **1962** *Listener* 25 Oct. 679/1 The proportion of the net national product going to property and enterprise..has fallen relative to that going to wages and salaries. **1964** Gould & Kolb *Dict. Social Sci.* 453/2 In defining national product,..one has a choice about whether or not to subtract from the total an allowance for the depreciation of capital goods that occurs during the period... If one does make such a subtraction, the results are called *net* national product... Net national product measures the value of goods and services produced, *after setting aside* whatever is required to maintain the stock of capital goods as it was at the beginning of the period.

4. *Comb.*, as *net-priced* adj.

1909 *Daily Chron.* 16 July 3/2 In his new net-priced series. **1973** *Writers' & Artists' Year Bk.* 218 They agree to sell their net-priced books to booksellers.

net, *v.*[1] Add: **1. a.** To fasten *down* with a net.

1909 H. G. Wells *Tono-Bungay* iii. iii. 363 Practically I contracted my sausage gas-bag by netting it down.

2. a. (Later example.) Hence in *colloq.* or *slang* use, to acquire (cf. Land *v.* 3 b).

1900 Ade *Fables in Slang* 178 The Management of the Bazaar was pleased to learn that the Sixty-cent Vase had Netted over Seven Hundred Dollars. **1912** Galsworthy *Inn of Tranquility* 126 The dusk is falling... Some stars are already netted in the branches of the pines. **1936** H. L. Mencken *Amer. Lang.* (ed. 4) v. 199 The favorite verbs of the newspaper copy-desk are those of three letters, *e.g.*, *to air*,..*to net*. **1975** *Publishers Weekly* 10 Feb. 52/3 Miss Read begins her summer holiday with a mishap, a fall that nets her a broken arm and an injured ankle.

4. *trans.* and *absol.* In ball games in which a net is employed: to send (a ball) into the net.

1906 *Peel City Guardian* 10 Mar. 8/3 It seemed as if they meant to force the custodian into the net, not net the ball. **1907** *Ibid.* 26 Oct. 5/2 A rush in the goal resulted in Cain netting. **1927** *Daily Express* 20 Apr. 13/2 Scriven netted for Birmingham in the first five minutes. *Ibid.* 22 June 2/2 Raymond, striving for extra speed, netted and outed a succession of returns. **1942** Berrey & Van den Bark *Amer. Thes. Slang* §648/5 *Score*,..net, net a goal. **1970** *Times* 1 Oct. 10/4 Reading gained ground at the expense of Bradford City, Williams netting the only goal. **1972** D. Delman *Sudden Death* (1973) vi. 169 A shocking bounce on a shoddy return, and I net what I should have put away. **1975** *Football Echo* (Liverpool) 12 Apr. 14/3 Winsford knocked up their 100th Cheshire League goal of the season when Haughton netted their second goal.

Ne·therla:ndic, *a.* [f. *Netherland* + -ic.] = Netherlandish *a.*

1902 *Encycl. Brit.* XXXI. 294/1 Wienecke is interesting for the sake of his early Netherlandic manner. **1972** E. Krispyn in A. Dixon tr. *Boon's Chapel Road* p. i, Louis Paul Boon, born in 1912, is one of the most interesting and controversial contemporary prose writers in the Netherlandic area. *Ibid.* p. ii, The medieval Netherlandic story of Reynard the Fox. **1973** *Mod. Lang. Assoc. Newsletter* Mar. 1 There are Provencal and Netherlandic groups, but with the exception of 'Chinese Language and Literature', which presently has provisional status, there are no groups in Oriental or African languages or literatures. **1975** *Times Lit. Suppl.* 28 Nov. 1429/1 There is also one [series of books] of international studies and translations, including a Dutch (or, as the publishers call it, Netherlandic) section.

Netherlandish, *a.* Add: **b.** *sb.* The language of the Netherlands; Dutch.

1890 *Chambers's Encycl.* V. 744/2 The origin of new Netherlandish or Dutch is to be found with the *Rederijkers*. **1944** *Britannica Bk. of Year* (U.S.) 759/1 Languages: Spanish, English, French and Netherlandish. **1954** *Word* X. Apr. 91 He [*sc.* Geschiere] admits that lg. *amo* ('orge hâtive,' barley) may come from German; or may come from Netherlandish. What he does not add explicitly is that lg. *amo* may have a fourfold source: German plus Netherlandish plus limbourgeois plus eupenois. **1974** *N.Y. Times* 3 Feb. 14 The great majority, especially the educated and young, do not call the language they speak 'Vlaams', or Flemish; they call it 'Nederlands', meaning Dutch, or Netherlandish.

netherward(s, *adv.* Add: Also (in form *netherward*) as *adj.*

1865-6 W. Whitman *When Lilacs last in Door-Yard Bloom'd* 6, I watch'd where you pass'd and was lost in the netherward black of the night. **1878** Hardy *Ret. Native* I. vii. 149 But celestial imperiousness, love, wrath, and fervour had proved to be somewhat tnrown away on netherward Egdon.

netherworld (ne·ðəɹwɔ̄ɹld). [f. Nether *a.* 6 + World *sb.*] = Underworld 4.

1930 *Sat. Evening Post* 26 July 145/1 Who could possibly deny his skill in the affairs of the netherworld? **1955** P. Heron *Changing Forms of Art* 106 It seems in itself a symbol of the artist, and particularly of his work in recent years: for it is a sort of ambassador of the Dark, of the vast netherworld which psychologists call the Unconscious. **1973** *Daily Tel.* 5 Apr. 15/2 When to admit a new word is always a problem, but President Nixon has made it with 'netherworld' ('the netherworld of deceit, subversion and espionage'). **1975** *Times Lit. Suppl.* 13 June 679/1 Occasionally he even descended from Baltimore into this netherworld of benighted yokels and hillbillies.

netsman. (Further examples.)

1937 H. Pope *St. Augustine of Hippo* vi. 245 One of the netsmen has just been bitten by a crab. **1962** *Punch* 21 Feb. 328/2 Who but a lunatic or a salmon netsman would be astir? **1973** *Nature* 27 July 232/1 Many were caught by netsmen off other neighbouring salmon rivers. **1975** *Times Lit. Suppl.* 7 Mar. 258/5 The salmon netsmen of the east coast of Scotland were the first to complain of the damage done by seals.

netter. Add: **3.** *U.S. colloq.* A lawn-tennis player.

1932 *Sun* (Baltimore) 6 Sept. 14/1 (*heading*) Coast netter stops invader. Stoefen injects drama into Forest Hills meet defeating Japanese. **1974** *Anderson* (S. Carolina) *Independent* 23 Apr. 6A/3 The Anderson College netters took an 8–1 win over Gainesville here Monday but the AC No. 1 doubles team of Rajiv Kapur and Elango Ranganathan dropped its first match after 18 straight wins.

netting, *vbl. sb.* Add: **1.** (Earlier example.)

1785 E. Sheridan *Jrnl.* 20 June (1960) ii. 58, I called at the toyshop and desired my purchases to be properly pack'd..—there is a box for you to put your netting in while you work it and to keep it in when you are idle, with lock and key.

b. *netting-case, -cotton, -needle* (earlier and later examples).

1790 F. Burney *Diary* Jan. (1905) IV. xlii. 348 The air of common employment was such, that..everything of that sort was spread about..—workboxes, netting-cases, etc. etc.! *a* **1817** Jane Austen *Northanger Abbey* (1818) II. x. 194 Assured of Isabella's having matched some fine netting-cotton. **1865** Mrs. Gaskell *Wives & Daughters* (1866) II. xviii. 185 The netting-cotton she was using kept continually snapping..from the jerks of her nervous hands. *a* **1817** Jane Austen *Persuasion* (1818) III. xi. 234 He fashioned new netting-needles and pins with improvements. **1832** in A. Adburgham *Shops & Shopping* (1964) iv. 38 Knitting, netting and mending needles. **1847** C. Brontë *Jane Eyre* II. ii. 44, I try to concentrate my attention on these netting-needles, on the meshes of the purse I am forming. **1918** N. Duncan *Battles Royal* 6 It is said of our people that they are born with a netting needle in their hand and an ax by the side of their cradle. **1942** [see *battle-twig]. **1973** W. Elmer *Terminol. Fishing* iv. 256 Two instruments are used for braiding or mending nets, the *netting-needle*, on which a certain amount of twine is wound, and the *spool*.

nettle, *sb.*[1] Add: **2. d.** *to cast (throw) one's frock* (or *cassock*) *to the nettles* [=Fr. *jeter le froc aux orties*], to renounce the clerical life; also *transf. rare.*

1916 W. J. Locke *Wonderful Year* xviii. 255 Now, indeed, he had burned his boats, thrown his cap over the windmills, cast his frock to the nettles. **1918** —— *Rough Road* vi. 58 Young parsons..threw their cassocks to the nettles and put on the full..panoply of war.

4. a. *nettle beer* (further examples), *-field.*

1910 A. Bennett *Clayhanger* I. xii. 103, I won't have them apprentices drinking!.. Mrs. Nixon'll give 'em some nettle-beer if they fancy it. **1953** *Word for Word* (Whitbread & Co.) 12/2 *Nettle beer*, brewed from nettles as opposed to barley. **1919** *Chambers's Jrnl.* May 298/2 In the boggy regions..people have begun to cultivate nettle-fields. **1965** G. B. Schaller *Year of Gorilla* vii. 171 The guard and I cut a narrow trail through the stands of lobelias and nettle fields.

b. nettle-weed *U.S.*, a plant of the nettle family.

1843 'R. Carlton' *New Purchase* I. xix. 159 They gathered a peculiar species of nettle, (called there nettle-weed,) which they succeeded in dressing like flax. **1867** 'T. Lackland' *Homespun* I. 18 Their blackened skeletons ..overgrown with nettleweeds and long grasses.

network. Add: **2. c.** (Further examples.) Also without *of.*

1869 *Bradshaw's Railway Manual* XXI. 346 The Antwerp and Rotterdam, in conjunction with the East Belgian and the Sambre and Meuse, is now worked under the title of the Great Central Belgian. The network thus constituted comprises 310 miles. *Ibid.* 348 The concessions accorded by a new convention..may be said to constitute a seventh great French network. *Ibid.* 366 The guarantee of interest given by the State on the new network capital. **1890** A. Hill tr. *Obersteiner's Anat. Cent. Nervous Organs* 161 The richer the network of rails the more numerous are the connections, the 'tracts' between the two chief termini. **1937** *Discovery* May 163/2 Few people realise how vast is the network of airlines which now links up the United States with Central and South America. **1950** *Britannica Bk. of Year* 682/2 *Network*, any system of related but not necessarily interconnected units; *e.g.*, a network of naval bases. **1966** G. F. Allen *British Rail after Beeching* viii. 243 Each Region drafted a scheme to..thin out its depots to a network sited so that they could be economically served by feeder services direct from a yard handling long-distance trains.

d. (Further examples.) Also *attrib.* Also, a representation of interconnected events, processes, etc., used in the study of work efficiency. Hence **networking** *sb.*

1959 S. Beer *Cybernetics & Management* xi. 95 Each of the dots in the network represents some binary situation. **1964** K. G. Lockyer *Introd. Critical Path Analysis* i. 4 This could then be simplified to the diagram (now known as a network). **1964** A. Battersby *Network Analysis* ii. 13 It is not the purpose of this book to discuss such methods of charting in detail..but rather to point out why their inadequacies have made necessary a new method of charting: arrow diagrams, otherwise known as networks. **1966** S. Beer *Decision & Control* ix. 191 Naturally, the critical path through a converging network can be discovered under any criterion or balance of criteria. **1966** *Economist* 3 Dec. 1042/2 If one wanted to

work out what was involved in doing something, an engineer would use a bar chart. (The 'hard way' in our charts showing the networking of a cup of tea.) **1967** S. WOODGATE in Wills & Yearsley *Handbk. Management Technol.* v. 73 Network planning techniques first came into general use in 1957. *Ibid.* 74 Since 1957 hundreds of variations of network planning systems have proliferated and many of these variations have perished while undergoing the supreme test of operational effectiveness. *Ibid.* 98 *Network*, a schematic representation of events and activities which shows their inter-relationships. **1968** *Listener* 4 July 13/2 They propose..a 'network' system which would allow variety and versatility to be developed. **1970** O. DOPPING *Computers & Data Processing* xxii. 345 Network planning helps to reveal all the possibilities for parallel operations, identify critical activities, and follow up the job... A network is built up of the different *activities* which constitute the project. **1970** *Canadian Jrnl. Linguistics* XV. 103 Once we express a grammar in terms of a relational network, intermediate symbols become completely superfluous. *Ibid.* 108 One can organize types of grammar in a two-by-two table. There are re-write grammars and network grammars.

e. A system of cables for the distribution of electricity to consumers; *spec.* one in which interconnections are such that each consumer is supplied by more than one route; hence, any system of interconnected electrical conductors or components, sometimes including a source of e.m.f., that provides more than one path for the current between any two points.

1883 *Jrnl. Soc. Telegr.-Engineers & Electricians* XII. 551 (*heading*) On a method of calculating the total horse-power expended in a network of conductors (such, for instance, as a system of street mains). **1914** J. W. MEARES *Electr. Engin. in India* iii. 47 The terms 'network' and 'distributor' are also applied to any system of distributing mains. **1930** DANNATT & DALGLEISH *Electr. Power Transmission & Interconnection* v. 110 Any network can be divided into conducting polygons or meshes. **1940** *Proc. IRE* XXVIII. 415/1 Figs. 3 and 4 represent mathematically identical networks, even though they refer to physically different systems. **1962** *Newnes Conc. Encycl. Electr. Engin.* 201/1 Distribution systems can be classified into the following basic categories: (*a*) Radial system. (*b*) Ring system: (i) h.v. feeders ring. (ii) l.v. distribution ring. (*c*) Network system. **1966** *McGraw-Hill Encycl. Sci. & Technol.* IX. 72/1 A network may be solved when it is possible to set up a number of independent equations equal to the number of unknown quantities.

f. A broadcasting system, consisting of a series of transmitters capable of being linked together to carry the same programme; also, in a more general sense: a nation-wide broadcasting company; the broadcasting companies as a whole. Also *attrib.*

1914 W. A. DU PUY *Uncle Sam's Modern Miracles* 170 This great network of stations may not merely hurl forth its messages. **1933** *B.B.C. Year Bk.* 37 In step with the gradual nationalisation of the network, local autonomy has declined. **1941** *B.B.C. Gloss. of Broadcasting Terms* 20 *Network cue*, cue consisting of a standardized phrase which constitutes a signal for the performance of technical operations at switching centres and transmitting stations forming part of a network. **1956** *Newsweek* 7 May 59 On its three wholly owned TV stations, exclusive of network operations, CBS reported a total net investment as of Dec. 31, 1953, of $3.322.023. **1957** *Listener* 21 Nov. 853/3 His hour-by-hour account of what the networks were saying. **1961** *Washington Post* 17 Feb. A14 The Columbia Broadcasting System's handling of its excellent TV show 'The Spy Next Door' on Wednesday night at 10 is a good illustration of what is amiss with network television. **1966** *Publ. Amer. Dial. Soc.* XLII. 46 A Southern rustic's imitation of 'network' pronunciation. **1969** *New Statesman* 11 Apr. 506/1 If there were 100 commercial stations..on the air all day they would either have to negotiate..or have back-up programmes from some central concern—virtually a network outfit. **1970** *New Yorker* 28 Feb. 29/2 The more general avoidance of controversial issues which has been noticeable among politicians and on the networks and in the press. **1972** *Daily Tel.* 14 Aug. 7/6 The plans for Radios 1 and 2 are designed to put the networks into an impregnable position when the commercial companies start. **1972** *Sci. Amer.* Sept. 117/1 The radio and television broadcasting networks provide the people of the world with on-the-spot news reports, entertainment and educational programs through a billion radio and television receivers. **1972** J. L. DILLARD *Black English* vi. 261 Many a preacher of this type [*sc.* 'storefront'] presents a better performance on Sunday than is ever to be seen on network television.

g. A structure proposed for glass in which the non-oxygen atoms (usu. silicon) are joined together in a three-dimensional array by oxygen atoms.

1932 W. H. ZACHARIASEN in *Jrnl. Amer. Chem. Soc.* LIV. 3842 As in crystals, the atoms in glasses must form extended three dimensional networks. **1947** *Jrnl. Soc. Glass Technol.* XXXI. 117 A quantitative factor may be deduced which is..an indication of the extent to which these atoms may be expected to take part in the glass network. **1971** *Oxidation of Metals & Alloys* (Amer. Soc. for Metals) 42 Oxides of the form..M_2O_3 can form a network if the oxygens form triangles around each metal atom.

h. An interconnected group of people; an organization. Also *attrib.*

1947 *Science News* IV. 37 He [*sc.* the habitual criminal].. is matching his brain and slender resources against all the might of a vast police network with infinite resource. **1954** [see *GIRL *sb.* 2 a]. **1957** E. BOTT *Family & Social Network* iii. 62 Intermediate degrees of conjugal role-segregation and network-connectedness. *Ibid.* 92 Although the networks of husband and wife are distinct, it is very likely, even at the time of marriage, that there will be overlapping between them. **1960** *Analog Science Fact/Fiction* Dec. 68/1 As long as they're allowed to think they haven't been spotted, they may lead the way to other spies or spy net-works. **1960** L. PINCUS *Marriage* I. 15 Supports and satisfactions..normally provided by participation in.. social and kinship networks are sought, and often not found, within the resources of marriage. **1972** *Daily Tel.* 19 June 2/1, I was paid..about £500 for infiltrating the IRA network in London. **1973** *Times* 15 Aug. 21/7 'Multinational organizations are becoming increasingly integrated..', especially in the case of 'network' companies having subsidiaries in many countries. **1974** 'J. LE CARRÉ' *Tinker, Tailor* xxii. 196 Moscow..was busy denouncing him for blowing the San Francisco network.

5. *attrib.* and *Comb.*, as **network analyser**, an assembly of inductors, capacitors, and resistors used to model an electrical network and facilitate its analysis; **network analysis**, (*a*) *Electr.*, calculation of the currents flowing in the various meshes of a network; (*b*) *Work Study* (see quot. 1968; cf. sense 2 d above); **network former**, (a substance containing) an atom which can become part of the network of a glass; so **network-forming** *a.*; **network modifier**, (a substance containing) a metal ion which can occupy an interstice in the network of a glass; so **network-modifying** *a.*; **network structure** *Metallurgy*, the structure of an alloy in which one component forms a continuous network around the grains of the other component; **network theorem**, any of various theorems about the currents and voltages in an electrical network that can be used to determine their values in any particular case.

1930 H. L. HAZEN et al. in *Trans. Amer. Inst. Electr. Engin.* XLIX. 1102/1 The following paper deals with an improved form of network-computing device... The Network Analyzer, as this device is called, is installed in the Electrical Engineering Research Laboratory. **1945** *Physical Rev.* LXVII. 48/1 The tests reported here.. indicate that it is practical to use for this purpose [*sc.* determining eigenvalues and eigenfunctions of the Schrödinger equation] existing a.c. network analyzers. **1974** *Encycl. Brit. Macropædia* VI. 625/2 Since World War II, digital computers have largely replaced network analyzers. **1930** *Trans. Amer. Inst. Electr. Engin.* XLIX. 1102/1 Several types of experimental computing devices or miniature systems for network analysis have been developed. **1945** H. W. BODE *Network Analysis & Feedback Amplifier Design* xvi. 360 Expressions having the mathematical form of a reflection coefficient appear frequently in network analysis. **1962** *Operations Res.* X. 728 Network analysis—also known as PERT (program evaluation and review technique), PEP (program evaluation procedure), CPM (critical-path method), CPS (critical path scheduling), and arrow diagramming—for the planning and control of research and industrial projects and programs has been the subject of many published articles. **1966** *Economist* 3 Dec. 1043/1 The Post Office Savings Bank has made massive use of network analysis to control its move to Glasgow. **1968** *Gloss. Terms Project Network Analysis* (*B.S.I.*) 5 *Project network analysis*, a group of techniques for presenting information to assist the planning and controlling of projects. The information, usually represented by a network, includes the sequence and logical interrelationships of all project activities. **1969** *Power System Protection* (Electr. Council) I. iii. 201 Network analysis by manual computation may involve a very considerable amount of labour. **1973** A. PARRISH *Mech. Engineers' Ref. Bk.* xx. 73 Network analysis is a general term which is used to embrace a whole series of similar planning methods dealing with project control. **1947** *Jrnl. Soc. Glass Technol.* XXXI. 114 For some years it has been customary to classify the various constituents of glass into network formers, such as SiO_2 and B_2O_3; intermediates..; and modifiers. **1966** C. R. TOTTLE *Sci. Engin. Materials* iii. 83 Aluminium occurs in the natural glass obsidian, as a network former, in the proportion of one aluminium to five silicon ions, with sodium and potassium to modify the network. **1950** KIRK & OTHMER *Encycl. Chem. Technol.* V. 723 Oxygen ratio is defined as the total number of oxygen ions to the total number of network-forming ions. **1971** FEHLNER & MOTT in *Oxidation of Metals & Alloys* (Amer. Soc. for Metals) 43 Ionic transport by anions is expected in network-forming oxides. **1961** *Progress Ceramic Sci.* I. 7 Systematic measurement of elastic properties of glasses, containing various proportions of the single network former SiO_2, and a single univalent network modifier, would be of great value in assessing the role of the network former in determining theoretical strength. **1971** *Materials & Technol.* II. vi. 335 Aluminium, when in tetrahedral coordination..is undoubtedly a network former, and when in octahedral configuration it is a network modifier. **1950** KIRK & OTHMER *Encycl. Chem. Technol.* V. 732 The 'holes' between these tetrahedral groups are considered to be occupied by the network-modifying ions. **1966** C. R. TOTTLE *Sci. Engin. Materials* iii. 83 Healing glass containing metallic ions that are network-modifying tends to move them into positions that are network-forming and so varies the colour. **1939** E. C. ROLLASON *Metall. for Engin.* vii. 101 If sufficient time is allowed for the diffusion phenomena all the ferrite is precipitated, whilst the pearlite occupies the centre forming a network structure. **1940** E. J. TEICHERT *Ferrous Metallurgy* III. xiv. 317 Slow cooling will induce the Widmanstatten and rapid cooling will promote the network structure. **1965** A. D. MERRIMAN *Concise Encycl. Metall.* 594 When the structure of an alloy is such that one constituent occurs partly or completely surrounding the crystals of another constituent, then the appearance of an etched section taken across the grains shows as a network structure. **1930** DANNATT & DALGLEISH *Electr. Power Transmission & Interconnection* vii. 220 (*heading*) Network theorems. **1966** *McGraw-Hill Encycl. Sci. & Technol.* IX. 75/2 In the solution of specific problems, much time can often be saved by making use of special methods or relations, known as network theorems.

network (ne·twɜːk), *v.* [f. the sb.] **a.** To cover with a network.

1887 *Courier-Jrnl.* (Louisville, Kentucky) 24 Jan. 8/1 It is only a question of time when railroads will net-work the Pan-handle. **1914** *Cycl. Amer. Govt.* III. 139/1 Whole regions are networked, and one can go by trolley car from the Atlantic to the Middle West. **1928** E. WRIGHT *Great Horn Spoon* xviii. 217 Gourds and several varieties of squashes networked the compound with their vines.

b. To broadcast simultaneously over a network of radio or television stations.

1940 [implied in *networking* vbl. sb. below]. **1952** *Sun* (Baltimore) 12 Feb. 14/3 Matthews beat Murphy in a bout networked out of Madison Square Garden. **1957** *Times* 28 Aug. (Radio & Television Suppl.) p. iii/3 This practice of networking the major items will continue. **1958** *Observer* 21 Sept. 16/6 The first sample of *This Wonderful World* to be networked in England came up to high expectation. **1968** *Times* 13 Nov. 1 (Advt.), Early in 1969 Thames Television are networking twelve one hour documentaries about one man. **1973** *Times* 8 Jan. 3/2 His series on the castles of Wales is being networked.

Hence **ne·tworked** *ppl. a.*; **ne·tworking** *vbl. sb.* and *ppl. a.*

1940 PORTERFIELD & REYNOLDS *We present Television* iv. 149 Television, now that a practicable means of networking has been developed, has been supplied with the final implement necessary for the creation of what will eventually be a nation-wide service. **1956** *Newsweek* 7 May 59 The television networking business is a complicated and delicate business. **1962** *Rep. Comm. Broadcasting 1960* 159 in *Parl. Papers 1961–2* (Cmnd. 1753) IX. 259 They must..use an old recorded networked programme. **1968** *Listener* 8 Aug. 187/1 The new companies..operate within a networking system still dominated by Granada, ATV and Thames. **1970** *New Statesman* 4 Sept. 281/3 A small [television] company can rely on getting full networking for just about four programmes a year... This figure of about four hours' worth of fully networked television time ought to be placed beside..the fact that STV is obliged..to do nine hours' output of its own every week. **1971** *Writing for B.B.C.* 65 Scotland contributes to all the networked series described under the 'Drama' heading... Plays intended for networking..should not be so Scottish that they cannot be readily understood by listeners in the other parts of the British Isles.

Neuchâtel (nøʃatel). The name of a town and a canton in western Switzerland, used *attrib.* or *absol.* to designate the white wine, or the less common red one, made there.

1903 S. WEYMAN *Long Night* i. 8 The landlord.. vanished, to return..with four tall glasses and a flask of Neuchatel. **1967** A. LICHINE *Encycl. Wines & Spirits* 516/1 The Neuchâtel white wines, grown in a chalky soil, are light and sprightly. *Ibid.* 516/2 Neuchâtel is the most widely exported wine of Switzerland. **1969** N. DENNY tr. *Veraldi's Spies of Good Intent* viii. 114 My brother's a wine-grower and he keeps the best of his Neutchatel [*sic*] for me.

‖ **Neue Sachlichkeit** (noi·ə za·χliχʸkəit). [G., 'new objectivity'.] A movement in the fine arts, music, and literature, which developed in Germany during the 1920s and was characterized by realism and a deliberate rejection of romantic attitudes.

1929 G. F. HARTLAUB *Let.* 8 July in *Arts* (1931) XVII. 237 The expression *Neue Sachlichkeit* was in fact coined by me in the year 1924. A year later came the Mannheim exhibition which bore the same name. The expression ought really to apply as a label to the new realism bearing a socialistic flavor. **1938** C. FULLMAN tr. *Thoene's Modern German Art* 87 The new group..wanted super-concrete precision; after the elimination of objects, journalistic reporting of time and place. This was the starting-point for German *vérisme*, the 'Neue Sachlichkeit', and the art of such men as Max Beckmann, Otto Dix, George Grosz and their like. **1950** B. S. MYERS *Modern Art in Making* xix. 351 There appeared a movement since classified as *Neue Sachlichkeit*, or New Objectivity, begun in 1920 by Otto Dix and George Grosz. **1954** *Grove's Dict. Mus.* VI. 53/1 *Neue Sachlichkeit*.., a term that came into fashion in Germany between the two world wars. It describes a tendency in some composers of that time to write music entirely detached from sentiment and free from any pictorial suggestion. **1959** J. WILLETT *Theatre of Bertolt Brecht* vii. 194 A deliberately impersonal quality marks much of the art of that time [*sc.* the late 1920s], as the words 'Neue Sachlichkeit' themselves imply. **1964** *Listener* 17 Sept. 445/1 After its first performance in 1923..[Hindemith's] *Marienleben* was hailed as a shining example of *Neue Sachlichkeit*, a new matter-of-fact contrapuntal style then emerging, which represented a conscious reaction against the hyper-romantic attitude prevalent earlier this century. **1970** *Oxf. Compan. Art* 772/2 *Neue Sachlichkeit*, a movement in German art and literature that arose in the mid 1920s. It represented a sharp reaction against experimental and idealistic art of any sort... Artists strove for an 'honest objectivity' (Sachlichkeit), depicting with matter-of-fact literalness their everyday experience.

Neufchâtel (nøʃatel). The name of a small town in Normandy, NE. of Rouen, used *attrib.* or *absol.* to designate the soft, white cheese originally made there.

c **1865** E. C. GASKELL *Let.* 6 Oct. (1966) 778 Lunch.. chocolate, cold meat, bread & butter Neufchatel Cheese & grapes. **1902** [see *BONDON]. **1951** *Good Housek. Home Encycl.* 568/2 *Neufchâtel Cheese*, a soft whole-milk cheese prepared in Normandy and other parts of France. **1966** P. V. PRICE *France: Food & Wine Guide* 283 *Neufchâtel*, the name of the best cheese produced in the Pays de Bray.

It may be eaten when it has only been kept for a few days, in which case it is creamy, soft and mild..; if allowed to ferment and ripen it..is fairly strong.

Neumann (noi·man). The name of Johann G. *Neumann*, 19th-cent. Austrian geologist(?), used *attrib.* to designate narrow bands, lines, or lamellæ parallel to crystallographic planes which are seen in α-iron (ferrite) subjected to a sudden shock, and are usu. attributed to twinning (investigated by Neumann *c* 1848).

1886 *Proc. Amer. Acad. Arts & Sci.* XXI. 498 On different sections of meteorites Widmanstättian figures and Neumann lines can be exhibited in every gradation, from the broadest bands to the finest markings. **1914** *Jrnl. Soc. Chem. Industry* 15 Aug. 791/2 The Neumann lamellæ occurring in any given grain are parallel to not more than 6 planes corresponding to the crystalline orientation of the grain itself. **1922** *Chem. Abstr.* XVI. 3845 (*heading*) Neumann bands as evidence of action of explosives upon metal. **1946** *Jrnl. Iron & Steel Inst.* CLIV. 129P/1 The Neumann band is primarily a shearing or faulting movement operating along the pre-existent planar disjunctions of the mosaic structure, and..as a secondary operation twinning may be completed, as is known to be possible in ferrite. **1966** C. R. Tottle *Sci. Engin. Materials* iii. 64 In alpha iron (b.c.c.) impact loading at room temperature can produce shear twins, called Neumann bands (which are found, incidentally, in metallic meteorites).

neurally (niūᵊ·răli), *adv.* [f. Neural *a.* + -ly².] **a.** By a nerve or nerves.

1902 W. James *Var. Relig. Exper.* p. vii, All states of mind are neurally conditioned. **1974** *Nature* 13 Dec. 591/2 Neurally-evoked responses.

b. As regards one's 'nerves'.

1936 L. C. Douglas *White Banners* vi. 141 He was too far spent, neurally, to offer any resistance.

neuraminic (niūᵊrămi·nik), *a. Chem.* [tr. G. *neuraminsäure* neuraminic acid (E. Klenk 1941, in *Zeitschr. f. physiol. Chem.* CCLXVIII. 51): see Neur-, Amine and -ic.] *neuraminic acid*: a crystalline carboxylic acid, $HOOC \cdot CO \cdot CH_2 \cdot CHOH \cdot CHNH_2 \cdot (CHOH)_3 \cdot CH_2OH$ (or a cyclic form of this), acyl derivatives of which are the sialic acids.

1942 *Chem. Abstr.* XXXVI. 3204 (*heading*) Neuraminic acid, the cleavage product of a new brain lipoid. **1956** *Nature* 17 Mar. 524/2 Klenk *et al.* have also investigated the amount of ganglioside in human brain by determining the content of neuraminic acid. **1966** *McGraw-Hill Encycl. Sci. & Technol.* II. 12/1 Neuraminic acid, an important constituent of carbohydrate-protein complexes of animal cells and tissues, has been reported in polymeric form in cultures of *Escherichia coli.*

Hence **neura·minate**, a salt or ester of neuraminic acid.

1970 R. W. McGilvery *Biochemistry* xxiv. 585 Part of the neuraminates contain an additional 4–O–acetyl group.

neuraminidase (niūᵊrămi·nidēⁱz, -s). *Biochem.* [f. *neuramin(ic *a.* + -id⁴ + *-ase.] (See quot. 1957.)

1957 A. Gottschalk in *Biochim. & Biophys. Acta* XXIII. 646 We propose the name 'neuraminidase' for the enzyme and define its action as the hydrolytic cleavage of the glycosidic bond joining the keto group of neuraminic acid to D-galactose or D-galactosamine and possibly to other sugars. **1960** —— in P. D. Boyer et al. *Enzymes* (ed. 2) IV. xxvii. 472 The wide distribution of neuraminidase among microorganisms inhabiting the respiratory and intestinal tracts would suggest that the enzyme has been evolved as a vital mechanism to guard the microbe against solitary confinement in a coating of host mucin. *Ibid.* 473 Neuraminidase has not been met in animal tissues. It is not a metabolic enzyme but a tool to facilitate accommodation of a parasite or symbiont within its host. **1970** *New Scientist* 8 Jan. 51/1 Influenza viruses possess another surface protein, the enzyme neuraminidase. *Ibid.* 31 Dec. 608/3 The enzyme neuraminidase, injected into mice as a post-coital contraceptive, seemed to be the most effective base for a 'morning-after pill' of any yet tried.

neurasthenia. (Further examples.)

1922 J. Riviere tr. *Freud's Introd. Lectures on Psycho-Anal.* xxiv. 325 We distinguish three pure forms of actual neurosis: neurasthenia, anxiety-neurosis and hypochondria. Even this classification has been disputed. The terms are certainly all in use, but their connotation is vague and unsettled. **1926** J. I. Suttie tr. *Ferenczi's Further Contrib. Theory & Technique Psycho-Anal.* ii. 35 The obsessional neuroses are nowadays mostly ranked among the 'neurasthenias'. **1965** Rosen & Gregory *Abnormal Psychol.* xii. 250/1 Neurasthenia is observed with such frequency in housewives who are bored and feel neglected by their husbands that it has often been called 'housewives' neurosis'. **1968** C. Rycroft *Crit. Dict. Psychoanal.* 96 *Neurasthenia*, obsolescent medical and psychiatric term for a state of excessive fatiguability and lack of vigour. **1974** M. Sainsbury *Key to Psychiatry* xiv. 234 Much disagreement is in evidence through the years regarding the status of neurasthenia as a nosological entity.

neurastheniac (niūᵊræspī·niæk). *rare.* [f. Neurasthenia: see -ac.] = Neurasthenic *sb.*

1904 *Lancet* 18 June 1737/2 The 'neurastheniacs' that present themselves at the clinic for diseases of the nervous system.

neurilema, neurilemma. Add: Also neuro-. **c.** The thin outer sheath that is seen with the light microscope surrounding the axon (and the myelin sheath, if present) of an individual peripheral nerve fibre; also called *sheath of Schwann.* (The usual sense: senses a, b are now *rare* or *Obs.*) (Further examples.)

1852 Neurolemma [in Dict. s.v. Neuro-]. **1874** A. E. J. Barker tr. *Frey's Histol. & Histochem. of Man* 307 The existence of an envelope on the nervous tube [*sc.* fibre] is easily inferred... This neurilemma may be seen not infrequently as [etc.]. *Ibid.* 317 The nerves of the brain and spinal cord..become clothed with a delicate envelope at their exit from the nervous centres. This covering receives another addition from the *dura mater* of connective-tissue bundles in its passage through the latter, and.. constitutes what was formerly known as 'neurilemma', but which we will designate from henceforth 'perineurium'. **1890** *Gray's Anat.* (ed. 12) 42 The tubular sheath of the funiculi, called the neurilemma or perineurium. **1892** E. A. Schäfer *Essent. Histol.* (ed. 3) xviii. 83 Outside the medullary sheath is a delicate but tough homogeneous membrane, the primitive sheath or nucleated sheath of Schwann... The primitive sheath is also known as the neurolemma. **1930** Maximow & Bloom *Text-bk. Histol.* xii. 251 Some European writers, like Cajal, apply the term 'neurilemma' to the epineurium and not to the sheath of Schwann of the individual fibers. **1966** Wright & Symmers *Systemic Path.* II. xxxiv. 1252/1 Neurolemmomas arise from the cells of the neurolemma, or nerve sheath. It is believed that the cell of origin is the Schwann cell. **1968** Bloom & Fawcett *Textbk. Histol.* (ed. 9) xii. 321/1 The myelin is actually part of the Schwann cell, consisting of spirally wrapped layers of its surface membrane... The outer membrane..and the protein-polysaccharide boundary layer on its outer aspect were resolved with the light microscope as a single layer, which has traditionally been called the neurilemma.

Hence also **neurile·mmal** *a.* (now the usual adj.).

1903 *Rep. Brit. Assoc. Adv. Sci. 1902* 782 From the microscopic study of the distal portions of divided nerve-trunks we arrived at the conclusion that the activity of the neurilemmal cells has some relation to the development of the new nerve-fibres. **1937** E. E. Hewer *Text-bk. Histol.* 96 Within the central nervous system there is no neurilemmal sheath. **1954** T. L. Peele *Neuroanat. Basis Clin. Neurol.* i. 13/2 The neurilemmal sheath of the spinal nerves, and of those cranial nerves possessing it, terminates (or begins) a short distance from spinal cord or brain stem. **1973** H. M. Ráliš et al. *Techniques Neurohistol.* i. 19 The neurilemmal sheath plays an important role in the nutrition and protection of nerve fibres.

neurilemoma, neurilemmoma (niūᵊrilemōᵘ·mă). *Path.* Also neuro-. [f. Neurilem(a, neurilemm(a + *-oma.] A tumour formed by proliferation of the neurilemma.

1935 A. P. Stout in *Amer. Jrnl. Cancer* XXIV. 752 Therefore it seemed advisable to take this phrase 'nerve sheath tumor'..and to construct from it a new name for the neoplasm. After consultation with Dr. G. F. Laidlaw and Dr. F. H. Vizetelly, editor of the *New Standard Dictionary*, the word 'neurilemoma' has been constructed and it is proposed to use this term for the tumor under discussion. *Ibid.* 753 Neurilemomas can be found sometimes in cases of von Recklinghausen's disease. **1948** J. M. Beattie et al. *Text-bk. Path.* (ed. 5) II. xxix. 1310 On the supposition that this word is derived from the Greek words νεῦρον, *neuron*, a nerve-fibre.., λέμμα, lemma, a skin or sheath..we ventured to alter the spelling of Dr. Purdy Stout's term 'neurilemoma' to 'neurilemmoma'... Dr. Purdy Stout..has persuaded us of the error of our ways. .. It is a pleasure..to take this opportunity of altering our spelling of the word back to..'neurilemoma'—though we are still in some doubt as to whether..it might not with propriety take the form 'Neurolemoma'. **1948** R. A. Willis *Path. Tumours* liv. 828 Masson's and Stout's names 'Schwannoma' and 'neurilemmoma', and Mallory and Penfield's name 'perineural fibroblastoma', express the two opposing views regarding the histogenesis of this distinctive nerve-sheath tumour. **1954** Ackerman & Del Regato *Cancer* (ed. 2) vii. 202 Neurilemomas [*ed.* 1 (1947): neurilemmomas] have also been reported to arise in the nasal fossa. **1962** *Lancet* 29 Dec. 1354/2 The preoperative diagnosis rested between a neurilemmoma of the posterior tibial nerve and compression of the nerve by the retinaculum. **1966** Neurolemmoma [see *neurilema].

neurinoma (niūᵊrinōᵘ·mă). *Path.* Pl. -omas, -omata. [mod.L. (J. Verocay 1910, in *Beitr. z. path. Anat. u. z. allgem. Path.* XLVIII. 65), f. Neur- + Ino- + *-oma.] = *neurilemoma, neurilemmoma.

1913 in Stedman *Med. Dict.* (ed. 2) 600/1. **1917** H. Cushing *Tumors of Nervus Acusticus* vii. 195 Though the term 'fibrosarcoma' predominates, other terms, which have been met with in cases which appear to be unquestionably acoustic tumors, are as follows: steatoma of the older writers,..neurinoma (Verocay), fibroblastoma (Borst). **1928** W. G. MacCallum *Text-Bk. Path.* (ed. 4) liv. 966 Such neurinomata occur only in peripheral nerves in which there are the sheath cells of Schwann. Of this character is the so-called acusticus tumor which is a neurinoma (formerly called neurofibroma). **1932** W. Penfield *Cytol. & Cellular Path. Nervous Syst.* III. xix. 968 These tumors contain long slender fibers of even caliber which tend to be arranged in parallel sheaves. Verocay (1910) considered these fibers to be nerve fibers and the type cell to be the sheath of Schwann cell... He therefore suggested the term neurinoma, meaning nerve fiber tumor. **1935** *Amer. Jrnl. Cancer* XXIV. 751 It is proposed..to limit the discussion to that specific encapsulated tumor composed of highly differentiated tissues which is so characteristic of the nerve sheath within which it develops. ..Neurinoma is the term most widely used,..but there is the insuperable objection to it that it means 'nerve fiber tumor'. Whatever else..all authorities are convinced that this is not a nerve fiber tumor but a nerve sheath tumor. **1948** A. Brodal *Neurological Anat.* vii. 240 Likewise it may happen that patients affected with a neurinoma of the VIIIth nerve tell a story of their sufferings starting with a pain situated deep in the ear. **1961** R. D. Baker *Essent. Path.* xx. 554 Neurinomas (neurilemmomas) of the skin are rare.

neuristor (niuri·stəɹ). *Electronics.* [f. Neur- + -*istor*, as in *resistor, transistor.*] Any device that is effectively a transmission line along which a signal will travel without attenuation (generally with a supply of energy along its length).

1960 H. C. Crane in *IRE Trans. Electronic Computers* IX. 370/1 A novel device and its properties have been hypothesized and possible digital systems employing it are briefly outlined in this note. The device, termed Neuristor, may be used to synthesize all digital logic functions... A neuristor may be visualized as a one-dimensional channel along which signals may flow. A signal propagates along the channel in the form of a discharge... A discharge signal has the following properties: 1) attenuationless propagation, 2) uniform velocity of propagation, 3) a refractory period. These characteristics are somewhat similar to the gross properties of transmission of discharge pulses by neurons in the nervous system —hence the name neuristor. **1963** *New Scientist* 7 Feb. 285/1 The concept of devices called 'neuristors', which behave like the axon or connection process of the neuron in the brain, is exciting to medical workers. **1965** *Electronics Lett.* I. 134/1 In most cases, neuristors which can propagate pulses have been considered, but one which can only propagate a discharge has also been studied. **1972** *Nuclear Instruments & Methods* CIV. 593 (*heading*) On the possibility of using superconducting neuristor line as particle detector.

neurite (niūᵊ·rəit). *Anat.* [f. Neur- + -*ite*, after *dendrite 3.] An axon or dendrite (formerly, an axon only).

1894 P. A. Fish in *Jrnl. Compar. Neurol.* IV. 173 For the axis-cylinder process the term neurite is proposed and for the other processes of the cells, retain the word dendrites. **1898** *Jrnl. R. Microsc. Soc.* 64 Nerve-cells with a long neurite (Purkinje's cells). **1924** R. M. Ogden tr. *Koffka's Growth of Mind* ii. 53 At its end this neurite divides into a fine net-work. **1956** *Nature* 28 Jan. 185/2 Individual nerve cell bodies and a part of their neurites 100–200μ long were dissected out by micromanipulation. **1973** *Gray's Anat.* (ed. 35) vii. 750/1 The neurites..may be divided into those which conduct broadly towards the cell body..and another one which may branch more or less profusely, and conducts away from the cell body.

neuro-. Add: **neuroana·tomy,** the anatomy of the nervous system; hence **neu:roanato·mical** *a.*, **neuroana·tomist; neurobio·logy,** the branch of biology which deals with nervous tissue; hence **neu:robiolo·gical** *a.*, **neurobio·logist; neu:robiota·xis** *Biol.* [Bio- + Taxis], a tendency of nerve cells, in the course both of development and of evolution, to remain close to their source of stimulation by migrating; so **neu:robiota·ctic** *a.*; **neuroblasto·ma** (pl. **-omas, -omata**) *Med.* [*-oma], a tumour composed of neuroblasts; *spec.* a malignant tumour composed of small cells with darkly staining nuclei and little cytoplasm, which is common in infants and usually appears in the adrenal gland; **neuroche·mistry,** (the study of) the chemical composition and processes of nervous tissue; hence **neuroche·mical** *a.*, **-che·mist; neu:rocircula·tory** *a. Med.*, of or pertaining to the nervous system and the circulatory system jointly; chiefly in *neurocirculatory asthenia* = *irritable heart* s.v. *irritable *a.* 2 b; **neurocra·nium** *Anat.* = Cranium 1 a; **neu·rocrine** (-krəin) *a. Physiol.* [a. F. *neurocrine* (Masson & Berger 1923, in *Compt. Rend.* CLXXVI. 1750), after *olocrine* holocrine, *endocrine* endocrine, etc.], secreting or secreted directly into nervous tissue; **neu·rocyte** [-cyte], a neurone, a nerve cell; hence **neurocyto·ma** (pl. **-omas, -omata**) *Med.* [*-oma], a tumour composed of nerve cells; **neu:rodermati·tis** (pl. **-dermatitides**) *Path.* [ad. F. *névrodermite* (Brocq & Jacquet 1891, in *Ann. de Dermatol. et de Syphiligraphie* II. 98)], lichen simplex chronicus or atopic dermatitis, esp. when aggravated by a nervous disorder; also more widely, = next; **neu:rodermato·sis** (pl. **-oses**) *Path.*, any skin disorder that is nervous or psychosomatic in nature; **neuro-effe·ctor** *a. Physiol.*, pertaining to or composed of both a nerve and an effector; also as *sb.*, a neuro-effector system; **neuroele·ctric** *a.*, of or pertaining to the electrical phenomena and properties of the nervous system; cf. *nervo-electric* adj. s.v. *nervo-; also **neuroele·ctrical**

a. (*rare*), **-electri·city; neuroembryo·logy,** the science which deals with the development of the nervous system in embryos; hence **neu:roembryolo·gic** (chiefly *U.S.*), **-lo·gical** *adjs.*; **neuroembryo·logist,** a specialist or expert in neuroembryology; **neuroe·ndocrine** *a.*, involving both nervous and endocrine participation; **neu:roendocrino·logy,** the study of the interactions between the nervous system and the endocrine system; hence **neu:roendocrinolo·gical** *a.*, **-endocrino·logist; neuro-fi·bril, -fi·brilla,** any of the fibrils visible within the body of a nerve cell using light microscopy; hence **neurofi·brillar, -fi·brillary** *adjs.*; **neurofi·lament,** a long filamentary structure, typically about 100 ångströms in diameter, visible in the cytoplasm of neurones under electron microscopy; **neurogla·ndular** *a.*, involving or possessing both glandular and nervous tissue or functions; **neuro-hæ·mal** (*U.S.* **-hemal**) *a.*, designating any of the organs, esp. among insects, which are composed of a group of nerve endings closely associated with the vascular system and are believed to have a neurosecretory function; **neurohisto·logy,** the histology of the nervous system or of nervous tissue; so **neu:rohistolo·gic** (chiefly *U.S.*), **-lo·gical** *adjs.*; **neuro-histo·logist,** an expert or specialist in neurohistology; **neu:ro-interme·diate** *a. Anat.*, used to designate the posterior lobe (pars nervosa) of the neurohypophysis together with the adjacent pars intermedia (which is usu. regarded as part of the adenohypophysis); **neuroki·nin** *Med.*, a kinin reported to have been obtained from subcutaneous fluid in the scalp during attacks of migraine; **neu·rokyme** *Psychol.* [ad. G. *neurokym* (O. Vogt 1895, in *Zeitschr. f. Hypnotismus* III. 300), f. Gr. κῦμ-α wave] (see quot. 1908); **neurolingui·stic** *a.*, of or connected with the application of neurology to linguistic research; so **neuroli·nguist,** an expert or specialist in neurolinguistics; **neurolingui·stics** *sb. pl.* (const. as *sing.*), neurological linguistics; **neuromuscular** *a.*, add to def.: having characteristics of both nervous and muscular tissue; being or pertaining to a junction between a nerve fibre and a muscle fibre (earlier and later examples); **neuromy·al** *a.* [MYO-] = prec.; **neu:ropharmaco·logy,** the study of the action of drugs on the nervous system; hence **neu:ropharmacolo·gic** (chiefly *U.S.*), **-lo·gical** *adjs.*, **neu:ropharmacolo·gically** *adv.*, **neu:ropharmaco·logist; neuro-physin** (-fəi·sin) *Biochem.* [ad F. *neurophysine* (J. Chauvet et al. 1960, in *Biochim. & Biophys. Acta* XXXVIII. 266), f. *neuro(hypo)physe* *NEUROHYPOPHYSIS], any of a group of proteins which are found in the neurohypophysis in complexes with oxytocin and vasopressin and are believed to act as carriers for these hormones during their passage from the hypothalamus; **neurophysiolo·gic** *a.* (chiefly *U.S.*), neurophysiological; **neurophysiolo·gically** *adv.*, with respect to neurophysiology; **neuro-physio·logist,** an expert or specialist in neurophysiology; **neu·roplasm,** the cytoplasm of a neurone; occas. applied to that of the cell body, as distinguished from *AXOPLASM; hence **neuropla·smic** *a.*; **neuropsycho·sis** *Psychol.*, a neurotic condition in which certain features characteristic of a psychosis can be recognized; **neuroradio·logy** *Med.*, radiology of the central nervous system; hence **neu:roradiolo·gic** (chiefly *U.S.*), **-lo·gical** *adjs.*; **neuroradio·logist,** a specialist or expert in neuroradiology; **neu·roscience,** any of the sciences (as neurochemistry or psychology) which deal with the nervous system or mental phenomena; such sciences collectively; hence **neurosci·entist,** a specialist in a neuroscience; **neurosecre·tion,** (*a*) the process of secretion by a (specially adapted) nerve cell; (*b*) the substance secreted in this process; so **neurosecre·tory** *a.*, performing, produced by, or pertaining to neurosecretion; **neurosema·ntic** *a.*, of or connected with a neurological approach to semantics; **neurose·nsory,** pertaining to or involving both nervous and sensory properties; *spec.* applied to a sensory nerve cell, esp. one in which the cell boby (usu. situated in epithelium) is the receptor and has a single process by which impulses are transmitted to a ganglionic neurone or an effector organ; **neu·rosurgeon,** one who practises neurosurgery; **neurosu·rgery,** surgery of the nervous system; hence **neuro-su·rgical** *a.*; **neurosy·philis** *Path.*, syphilis involving the central nervous system; hence **neu:rosyphili·tic** *a.* (also as *sb.*, a neurosyphilitic person); **neurote·ndinous** *a.*, of or pertaining to a nerve fibre and a tendon, esp. the termination of a nerve in a tendon; **neuro-toxi·city,** (*a*) toxicity towards the nerves; (*b*) poisoning by a neurotoxin; **neurotu·bule,** a microtubule of a neurone; **neurovi·rulence,** virulence towards the nervous system.

1904 *Biol. Bull.* VI. 90 These facts point toward either a specialization or a modification in function which is of interest because of its bearing upon certain neuro-anatomical facts. **1971** H. A. WHITAKER in W. O. Dingwall *Survey of Linguistic Science* 148 It is plausible ..that there is a universal neuroanatomical substrate for the language system. **1931** H. L. HOLLINGWORTH *Abnormal Psychol.* iv. 68 This condition would be difficult to understand if it were not that the neuroanatomist had mapped out the course of the various sensory pathways in the spinal cord. **1963** *Zeitschr. für Zellforschung* LX. 815 The basis of the neuron doctrine was established by the work of a few eminent neuroanatomists. **1974** *Nature* 6 Sept. 83/1 For the neuroanatomists of the nineteenth century, the cerebellum was a source of fascination. **1900** DORLAND *Med. Dict.* 441/1 Neuro-anatomy. **1913** *Official Publ. Cornell Univ.* IV. xvi, Strauss, Israel. A.B., M.D., Instructor in Neuro-Anatomy, 1911. **1931** H. L. HOLLINGWORTH *Abnormal Psychol.* iv. 77 We may illustrate the 'fictional' or hypothetical notion of explanation also in the field of neuro-anatomy. **1971** *Sci. Amer.* May 89/3 In view of the basic neuroanatomy of the visual system, this means that the visual effects must have been the result of neuronal activity in the brain rather than in the eye itself. **1959** *Internat. Rev. Neurobiol.* I. p. vii, Progress in neurobiological research must maintain a delicate balance between the fascination of basic explanation of clinical and physiological phenomena by means of chemical and physical concepts on the one hand and the pressing needs for the development of new and effective treatments of disease on the other. **1971** *Nature* 5 Mar. 25/1 The neurobiological approach to mental health. **1957** H. READ *Tenth Muse* xiii. 110 If one reads a neurobiologist such as J. R. Smithies one has the feeling, perhaps deceptive, that the problems discussed by Professor Ayer are being discussed more realistically. **1971** J. Z. YOUNG *Introd. Study Man* p. vii, What the neurobiologist finds out about the brain must surely be relevant to fundamental views of the nature of all this knowledge. **1906** *Index-Catal. Library Surg.-General's Office, U.S. Army* 2nd Ser. XI. 622/1 (*heading*) Neurobiology. **1960** *Times* 22 Sept. 4/2 Researches cover neurobiology—such as 'eye movements and optogyral illusion'. **1972** *Sci. Amer.* Sept. 51/1 Thus neurobiology has now shown why it is human—and all too human—to hold Euclidean geometry and its non-intersecting co-planar parallel lines to be a self-evident truth. Non-Euclidean geometries of convex or concave surfaces, although our brain is evidently capable of conceiving them, are more alien to our built-in spatial-perception processes. **1908** C. U. A. KAPPERS in *Jrnl. Physiol.* XXXVII. 143 Another feature of the autonomic system might find its explanation in the neurobiotactic influence of the axon stimulation. **1948** A. BRODAL *Neurological Anat.* vii. 192 The neurobiotactic influences (Kappers) of which the above-mentioned fact is an example, are also revealed in other morphological features. **1908** C. U. A. KAPPERS in *Jrnl. Physiol.* XXXVII. 140 Referring for further details concerning these phenomena of neurobiotaxis to my former papers on this subject, I only wish to state here that..it is obvious that the motor cells migrate in the direction whence they get the greatest quantity of stimuli. **1961** P. GLEES *Exper. Neurol.* vi. 168 In accordance with his hypothesis of neurobiotaxis.. Kappers (1920) believes that the dendrites grow from the cell towards the source of their afferent stimuli. **1910** J. H. WRIGHT in *Jrnl. Exper. Med.* XII. 556 The essential cells of the tumor are considered to be more or less undifferentiated nerve cells or neurocytes or neuroblasts, and hence the names neurocytoma and neuroblastoma. **1925** *Arch. Neurol. & Psychiatry* (Chicago) XIV. 193 In our Brigham Hospital records..many of them have in the past been designated neurocytomas or neuroblastomas. **1948** R. GREENE *Pract. Endocrinol.* iv. 128 The neuroblastomata are highly malignant tumours. **1974** *Nature* 17 May 224/1 The C1300 mouse neuroblastoma has been useful for studies of the differentiation and trophic interactions of nerve cells. **1949** KOESTLER *Insight & Outlook* v. 68 Their neurochemical substratum [*sc.* that of our emotional impulses] cannot be worked off in overt activities. **1963** *Lancet* 12 Jan. 79/1 If their effect on the brain could be evaluated, understanding of the neurochemical changes in depression might follow. **1972** *Sci. Amer.* Nov. 28/3 The hypothesis proposed that hypothalamic control of the secretory activity of the anterior pituitary could be neurochemical. **1958** *Neurology* VIII. (Suppl. 1) 27/2 Many investigators using such methods would not consider themselves neurochemists, but they certainly contribute to the growing body of neurochemical data. **1971** *Nature* 22 Mar. 130/3 Undoubtedly, it [*sc.* myelin] now has the added attraction to neurochemists that it can be obtained in bulk from the mammalian nervous system. **1955** *Neuropharmacology* I. 11 There are enough problems and enough possibilities for an entire science in the field of 'neuro-chemistry' or/and 'neuro-pharmacology'. **1969** *Nature* 11 Oct. 118/2 A significant development in neurochemistry has been the finding that thiol groups and disulphides are involved in the functioning and activity of neurones. **1918** 'T. LEWIS' [*i.e.* B. S. Oppenheimer et al.: see *Jrnl. Amer. Med. Assoc.* (1918) 21 Sept. 994] in *Military Surgeon* XLII. 410 An appreciable number of soldiers present a well-defined symptom-complex, in which certain nervous and circulatory symptoms are associated with an increased susceptibility to fatigue. The descriptive name of Neuro-Circulatory Asthenia ('N.C.A.') is suggested for this syndrome in preference to Disordered Action of the Heart ('D.A.H.'). **1953** R. A. MCFARLAND *Human Factors in Air Transportation* vi. 305 The effect of smoking on neurocirculatory efficiency..may be of particular importance to the airman since this test is often used to appraise fitness. **1971** Neurocirculatory [see *irritable heart* (*IRRITABLE *a.* 2 b)]. **1907** W. N. PARKER tr. *Wiedersheim's Compar. Anat. Vertebrates* (ed. 3) 75 The portion of the skull which is situated along the main axis in continuation of the vertebral column and which encloses the brain, is known as the brain-case or cranium (neurocranium). **1942** GROVE & NEWELL *Animal Biol.* xv. 257 Other cartilage is laid down at the sides and above the brain until it becomes enclosed in a cartilaginous box, the brain box or neurocranium. **1972** *Nature* 24 Mar. 143/2 A sulcus on the outer face of the neurocranium in front of the supposed foramen for the vagus nerve is interpreted as the lateral occipital fissure. **1925** *Physiol. Abstr.* IX. 544 The secretion of these 'neurocrine' glands acts directly on the nerves. **1947** *Phil. Trans. R. Soc.* B. CCXXXII. 394 The relationship of the pars distalis of the pituitary and the possible neurocrine secretion by the hypothalamic nuclei to the water balance of the body are still debatable points. **1962** *Science Survey* III. 264 There exist equally interesting relationships between odours and animal behaviour on a different and perhaps more profound level..which are very likely mediated by the vegetative nervous system and the neurocrine and other endocrine glands. **1890** BILLINGS *Med. Dict.* II. 209/1 *Neurocyte*, nerve-cell. **1894** P. A. FISH in *Jrnl. Compar. Neurol.* IV. 174 For the equivalent of a nerve unit including the nerve cell with all its processes to the uttermost filament, the term neurocyte is suggested. It has not been possible to trace the word to its originator. It is in use in the French language and is included in the dictionary of the New Sydenham Society and Gould's New Medical Dictionary with the simple definition; a nerve cell. **1932** W. PENFIELD *Cytol. & Cellular Path. Nervous Syst.* III. xviii. 941 Between the neurocytes are numerous smaller cells. **1910, 1925** Neurocytoma [see *neuroblastoma* above]. **1948** R. GREENE *Pract. Endocrinol.* iv. 127 The most malignant tumours are the neuroblastomata or neurocytomata. **1966** WRIGHT & SYMMERS *Systemic Path.* II. xxxiv. 1246/1 A ganglioneuroma (neurocytoma) of the brain is a slowly growing tumour composed of neurons. **1896** *Amer. Year-bk. Med. & Surg.* 715 (*heading*) Vitiligo, lichen ruber planus, and chronic circumscribed neurodermatitis. **1935** Neurodermatitis [see *neurodermatosis* below]. **1947** *N.Y. State Jrnl. Med.* XLVII. 1889/2 MacKenna and others have suggested that the neurodermatitides may have a corresponding symbolic meaning. **1954** *Bull. Muscogee County Med. Soc.* Aug. 9 A large list of diseases has been included under the term 'psychosomatic',..it includes..certain skin diseases—notably the so-called neurodermatitides. **1974** PASSMORE & ROBSON *Compan. Med. Stud.* III. xxxi. 13/1 The condition [*sc.* lichen simplex chronicus] is sometimes referred to as neurodermatitis because it is most frequently encountered in obsessional and anxious individuals. **1909** *Cent. Dict.* Suppl., Neurodermatosis. **1911** M. MORRIS *Dis. Skin* (ed. 5) iv. 54 (*heading*) Neuroses of the skin. Classification of neuro-dermatoses. **1935** *Jrnl. Amer. Med. Assoc.* 5 Oct. 1099/1 A group of eighty patients presenting typical clinical examples of the neurodermatoses..was selected.., with diagnoses as follows: neurodermatitis (dry type), nineteen; pruritus ani or vulvae, five; neurodermatitis (exudative type), twenty-eight; dyshidrosis, four; [etc.]. **1941** S. H. KRAINES *Therapy of Neuroses & Psychoses* xiv. 313 Clearing up of these neurodermatoses is more difficult than removal of many other emotionally conditioned physical symptoms. **1961** *Lancet* 12 Aug. 369/1 MacKenna very artistically described neurodermatosis when he stated that 'in some cases the skin is an organ of stress which bears the brunt of nervous agitation, acting as the canvas on which the perturbation of the mind is painted.' **1935** *Q. Rev. Biol.* X. 335/2 According to the data available, the following is the sequence of functionally related events which probably occur in the electrical excitation of a neuro-effector system. **1937** CANNON & ROSENBLUETH *Autonomic Neuro-Effector Systems* p. viii, Previous researches on autonomic neuro-effectors and the occurrences at their synapses. **1973** *European Jrnl. Clin. Pharmacol.* VI. 92/1 Further investigations are possible..of the possible role of these [neuronal] pools in the control of NA exchanges at the level of the sympathetic neuro-effector junction. **1973** *Science* 16 Feb. 693/2 (*heading*) Neuroeffectors controlling mucus release by the leech. **1849** G. BIRD *Lect. Electr. & Galvanism* i. 24 The neuro-electric theory of Galvani. *Ibid.* 25 Valli..believed the neuro-electric fluid to be secreted by the capillary arteries supplying the nerves. **1956** L. S. FRISHKOPF in *Technical Rep. Res. Lab. Electronics Mass. Inst. Technol.* No. 307 (*title*) A probability approach to certain neuroelectric phenomena. **1965** *Math. in Biol. & Med.* (Med. Res. Council) IV. 131 Modern electrophysiological techniques permit the recording of several types of neuroelectric potentials, and the patterns of voltage-versus-time traces provide the electrophysiologist's basic data. **1974** *Nature* 15 Feb. 481/1 An exactly similar method is widely used in studying EEG visual evoked responses and other neuroelectric phenomena. **1914** *Practitioner* June 838 The immediate cause of an epileptic attack is a neuro-electrical brain storm. *Ibid.* 831 The chemical generation of nerve force (neuro-electricity) in the human body. *Ibid.* 832 The grey matter of the brain must be the site of generation of this neuro-electricity. **1933** *Science* 18 Aug. 132/1 A notable beginning was made in neuro-embryologic study of behavior. **1950** HAMBURGER & LEVI-MONTALCINI in P. Weiss *Genetic Neurol.* 129 The *in vitro* culture of nerve cells made important contributions to the solution of neuro-embryological problems. **1970** D. BODIAN in F. O. Schmitt *Neurosciences: 2nd Study Program* xiii. 139/2 The considerable insight gained in recent times through analysis of neuroembryological processes. **1950** HAMBURGER & LEVI-MONTALCINI in P. Weiss *Genetic Neurol.* 141 The neuroembryologist is largely concerned with the further elaboration of these elementary patterns of the early

neural tube. **1970** M. V. Edds in F. O. Schmitt *Neurosciences: 2nd Study Program* v. 51/2 The roster of experimental neuroembryologists active since Harrison opened the field early in the century includes some of the most able developmental biologists. **1933** *Science* 18 Aug. 137/1 The whole subject of neuro-embryology of higher vertebrates should be reexamined. **1950** Hamburger & Levi-Montalcini in P. Weiss *Genetic Neurol.* 131 The material used in experimental neuroembryology has been confined largely to teleosts, amphibians, and the chick embryo. **1974** *Nature* 22 Mar. p. xi/1 (Advt.), By combining the facts of neurophysiology, neuroembryology, and behaviour, a new theory is built up. **1922** P. Fridenberg in L. F. Barker et al. *Endocrinol. & Metabolism* II. 769 (*heading*) Neuro-endocrin control of intra-ocular tension. **1944** Neuro-endocrine [see *hypothalamico-hypophysial *a.*]. **1959** T. Lidz in S. Arieti *Amer. Handbk. Psychiatry* I. xxxii. 650/1 The hypothalamus..is now understood to form a critical juncture in a circular feedback system that mediates and regulates neural impulses concerned with emotions and neuro-endocrine activity. **1973** *Folia Biol.* (Cracow) XXI. 329 It has been suggested that alterations in the..secretory pattern of the neuroendocrine components are due to the action of stress. **1963** *Annales d'Endocrinol.* XXIV. 198 (*heading*) Introduction to the neuro-endocrinological study of the pineal gland. **1974** *Nature* 17 May 213/1 Recent neuroendocrinological findings of most of the leading laboratories in Europe were discussed informally. **1969** *Britannica Yearbk. of Sci. & Future 1968* 389 These organic compounds, which were thought to act as chemical mediators (neurohumors) at synaptic junctions..were of interest to neuroendocrinologists. **1922** P. Fridenberg in L. F. Barker et al. *Endocrinol. & Metabolism* II. 757 (*heading*) Ophthalmic neuro-endocrinology. **1961** *Lancet* 19 Aug. 442/2 In 1952 he was appointed senior lecturer in experimental neuroendocrinology at the Institute of Psychiatry. **1967** E. Bajusz (*title*) An introduction to clinical neuroendocrinology. **1898** *Jrnl. R. Microsc. Soc.* 64 The general conception [of Prof. Apáthy] may be briefly stated. The nerve-cell is analogous to the muscle-cell, producing conducting substance (primitive fibrils, neurofibrils), as the muscle-cell produces contractile substance (myofibrils). **1970** A. Peters et al. *Fine Struct. Nervous Syst.* iv. 62/2 The precise correlation between the classical neurofibrils of silver preparations and the structures seen in electron micrographs remains uncertain. **1973** Neurofibril [see *neurofibrillary* adj. below]. **1902** *Jrnl. Nerv. & Mental Dis.* XXIX. 435 (*heading*) The neuro-fibrillae in nerve cells and nerve fibers of the retina. **1963** R. P. Dales *Annelids* vii. 138 Hess suggested that the irregularly shaped refractory body directed the light on to a dense reticulum of neurofibrillae which joined to form the basal nerve fibre. **1902** *Jrnl. R. Microsc. Soc.* 542 (*heading*) Neurofibrillar theory. **1949** Neurofibrillar [see *neurofibrillary* adj. below]. **1971** *Jrnl. Compar. Neurol.* CXLIII. 395/2 Neurofibrillar boutons appear following section of the axons. **1902** *Jrnl. Nerv. & Mental Dis.* XXIX. 435 The author concludes..that a neuro-fibrillary structure of nerve cells and their processes..is abundantly proven. **1949** B. W. Lichtenstein *Textbk. Neuropath.* iv. 46 Neurofibrillary abnormalities occur in a variety of disease states. The normal configuration of the neurofibrillar apparatus is well seen in preparations impregnated with silver according to Bielschowsky's method. **1973** H. M. Ráliš et al. *Techniques Neurohistol.* iv. 89 Methods for neurofibrils may also be used to demonstrate..the neurofibrillary tangles which are found in certain pathological conditions. **1955** Palay & Palade in *Jrnl. Biophysical & Biochem. Cytol.* I. 78 Neurofilaments.—Fine, long threads, 60 to 100A in diameter and of indefinite length, traverse the cytoplasmic matrix [of the neuron] between masses of Nissl substance and other organelles. **1965** *Progress Brain Res.* XIV. 57 Electron microscopical studies have shown that the neurofibrils of light microscopists are made up of fine, long, apparently non-branching structures approximately 100 Å in diameter. These are the neurofilaments. **1968** G. A. Horridge *Interneurons* i. 11 Throughout the animal kingdom..many axons and dendrites of nerve cells have tubules in the axoplasm; others, such as the squid giant axon, have neurofilaments that are thinner and less obviously tubular. **1969, 1970** Neurofilament [see *neurotubule* below]. **1909** *Cent. Dict.* Suppl., *Neuroglandular*, having the characteristics of sensory and glandular organs: as, the neuroglandular pit of some *Nemertini*. **1941** *Jrnl. Compar. Neurol.* LXXIV. 106 Neuroglandular cells are described in three species of cockroaches... The main center of neurosecretory activity is found to be the suboesophageal ganglion. **1943** H. Read *Education through Art* 26 Temperament..is closely connected with the neuro-glandular system and the relations of the cortex to the sub-cortex. **1964** J. Z. Young *Model of Brain* xviii. 296 There must be some common principle involved to produce these similar neuroglandular arrangements in completely independent phyla. **1953** Carlisle & Knowles in *Nature* 29 Aug. 405/1 It seems preferable to call these organs by some purely topographical name which does not denote any function, actual or supposed. The adjective 'neurohæmal' seems to us to be the most appropriate topographical name denoting the common feature of these organs. The organs may thus be referred to collectively as neurohæmal organs, while the adjective may be combined with any of the pre-existing names for these various organs, as, for example, 'the post-commissural neurohæmal organ' and 'dorsal neurohæmal lamella'. **1967** C. A. G. Wiersma *Invertebr. Nervous Systems* x. 125 (*heading*) Correlation of propagated action potentials and release of neurosecretory material in a neurohemal organ. **1973** *Nature* 12 Oct. 288/2 Thus another useful criterion for the definition of a neurosecretory neurone—that it ends in a neurohaemal organ—loses its generality. **1957** *A.M.A. Arch. Path.* LXIII. 3/2 Histologic analysis of these alterations does not require special neurohistologic methods. **1940** *Jrnl. Anat.* LXXIV. 413 (*heading*) Observations on the neurohistological basis of cutaneous pain. **1973** H. M. Ráliš et al. *Techniques Neurohistol.* iv. 82 (*heading*) Neurohistological staining methods. **1901** *Buck's Handbk. Med. Sci.* (ed. 2) II. 336/1 Until further knowledge has been gained it is safer for the neurohistologist to work with the various methods [etc.]. **1968** Clarke & O'Malley *Human Brain & Spinal Cord* ii. 87 Two opposing groups of neurohistologists arose. On the one hand were those who believed that the nerve cells and their processes..constituted independent units in contiguity with other units but not in continuity... Their opponents..considered the cells and fibres to be in direct continuity with one another by way of a network to which the fibres contributed. **1897** *N.Y. Med. Jrnl.* 15 May 652/2 The most important contributions of Golgi in the domain of neuro-histology consisted in (1) the invention of the silver method of staining; (2) the recognition within the central regions of cells of different types..; and (3) the discovery of lateral branches from the axis-cylinder process. **1940** *Jrnl. Anat.* LXXIV. 426 The neuro-histology of this area establishes that in the human skin pain is subserved by fine nerve fibres bearing free nerve endings. **1973** H. M. Ráliš et al. *Techniques Neurohistol.* v. 146 This final chapter..mentions histochemical methods used in neurohistology as well as some applications of autoradiography in the study of nerve tissue. **1926** G. R. de Beer *Compar. Anat. Pituitary Body* ii. 28 The anterior lobe consists only of the pars anterior, but the posterior lobe, which always contains the partes intermedia and nervosa, may or may not also be associated with the pars tuberalis, since many authors fail to distinguish between the latter and the pars intermedia. In order to avoid ambiguity the term *neuro-intermediate lobe* may be used to include the pars nervosa and the pars intermedia, since they are always in the closest morphological association. **1965** Lee & Knowles *Animal Hormones* ii. 28 In fishes the pituitary gland is conveniently divided into three portions... Closely associated with the posterior portion of the adenohypophysis (pars intermedia), and extending into it, is the pars nervosa; the term neuro-intermediate lobe is often applied to this region. **1973** *Nature* 28 Sept. 207/2 Pituitary control of sebaceous gland activity has generally been assumed to be a function of the anterior lobe. The possibility that the neurointermediate (NI) lobe is involved was first suggested when we found that its removal led to a decrease in sebum secretion. **1960** L. F. Chapman et al. in *Trans. Assoc. Amer. Physicians* LXXIII. 263 Specimens collected from the head during the headache attacks contained a substance that could be distinguished from serotonin,..acetylcholine and histamine... The heat stabilized substance had many of the properties of bradykinin, Kallidin, or 'plasma kinin'... This polypeptide has been labeled 'neurokinin' and has been found..to be released during neuronal excitation. **1969** J. Pearce *Migraine* vii. 39 More recently the polypeptides and kinins have been examined more critically, because of the claims of isolation of neurokinin from the scalp tissue fluid in migraine attacks. **1908** W. McDougall in *Brain* XXXI. 247 This distinction between chemically stored or potential nervous energy and the liberated active nervous energy is, I feel sure, one of the first importance for neurological speculation... Oscar Vogt..has proposed to mark it by calling the freed nervous energy 'neurokyme'... I adopt Vogt's term. **1926** —— *Outl. Abnormal Psychol.* v. 104 All mental activity involves the discharge of neurokyme from the sensory to the motor side of the brain. **1944** W. Brown *Psychol. & Psychotherapy* (ed. 5) v. 57 McDougall regards the passage of nervous energy (neurokyme) across the synapses of the cerebral cortex as the physical correlate of the psychical process. **1961** *Studies in Linguistics* XV. 70 Ideally, the neurolinguist would have thorough training in scientific linguistics and in neuroanatomy and neurophysiology. **1936** Neuro-linguistic [see *neuro-semantic* adj. below]. **1961** *Studies in Linguistics* XV. 70 Neurolinguistic work has certainly been carried out under other names, by people who work with aphasia, by neurosurgeons and neurologists, [etc.]. **1970** J. Laver in J. Lyons *New Horizons in Linguistics* iii. 61 The healthy adult brain is not itself accessible to neurolinguistic experiment. There is thus no possibility of directly observing the neural mechanisms involved in constructing a neurolinguistic program. **1961** E. C. Trager in *Studies in Linguistics* XV. 70 Neurolinguistics is the term proposed here for a field of interdisciplinary scientific study which does not as yet have a formal existence. Its subject matter is the relationship between the human nervous system and language. **1970** J. Laver in J. Lyons *New Horizons in Linguistics* iii. 61 In neurolinguistics the subdisciplinary boundary between phonetics and linguistics, which has always been of doubtful validity, is largely disappearing. **1973** *Tuscaloosa* (Ala.) *News* 10 Apr. 5/4 She is interested in neurolinguistics and studies of aphasia. **1975** *Canad. Jrnl. Linguistics* XX. 94 *A Study in Neurolinguistics* is perhaps the first publication in the form of a monograph in the field of 'language and the brain' with the term 'neurolinguistics' in its title. **1864** *Jrnl. Mental Sci.* X. 37 There appears to be a neuro-muscular, as well as a purely mental retentiveness. **1892** J. A. Thomson *Outl. Zool.* iii. 36 In some Cœlenterates it is possible that some of the external cells combine contractile, nervous, and even other functions. Under this impression many call them 'neuro-muscular'. **1904** *Jrnl. Physiol.* XXX. 494 If our conception of this neuro-muscular junctional tissue is correct the name nerve-ending is obviously a misnomer. **1937** *Physiol. Rev.* XVII. 538 It may be concluded that synapses and neuro-muscular junctions are essentially similar, there being close contact but not protoplasmic continuity. **1948** *Federation Proc.* VII. 452/1 The fundamental change which accounts for the neuromuscular block produced by curare itself is a decrease in the end-plate potential. **1950** J. H. Burn *Lect. Notes Pharmacol.* (ed. 2) 14 Neostigmine restores neuromuscular transmission. **1963** R. P. Dales *Annelids* vi. 119 The failure to respond is not due to failure of the giant fibre itself, but to the relay or to the neuromuscular junction. **1926** *Physiol. Rev.* VI. 564 Comparable data on muscle and the neuromyal junction. **1965** *Jrnl. Pharmacol. & Exper. Therap.* CXLVII. 350 (*heading*) Pharmacological actions of oxamides and hydroxyanalinium compounds at frog neuromyal junction. **1913** *Ibid.* V. 107 We now approach the subject of the susceptibility of the central heat-regulating mechanism to more specific neuro-pharmacologic influences. **1973** *Folia Biol.* (Cracow) XXI. 331 The CAH-positive cells of the brain in the cockroach undergo most of the alterations..after the administration of various types of neuropharmacologic agents. **1959** *Jrnl. Pharmacol. & Exper. Therap.* CXXVI. 312/1 Thioridazine hydrochloride..and chlorpromazine hydrochloride..have been examined for neuropharmacological properties in mice and rats. **1971** *New Scientist* 9 Dec. 119 These various poisons have proved novel tools in neuropharmacological research, especially in elucidating the mechanism of nervous conduction. **1971** *Nature* 24 Sept. 285/2 Other neuropharmacologically-active or serotonin-related drugs were also tested. **1966** *Sci. News Let.* 1 Jan. 6 Rats..given the compound..retained what they had learned longer, Dr. N. P. Plotnikoff, an Abbott neuropharmacologist, reported. **1973** *Nature* 14 Dec. p. xvi/1 (Advt.), We seek a Technician to join a team of neuropharmacologists. **1955** Neuro-pharmacology [see *neurochemistry* above]. **1973** *Nature* 28 Sept. p. xx/3 (Advt.), General experience of either neurochemistry, neurophysiology, or neuropharmacology is essential. **1960** *Biochim. & Biophys. Acta* XXXVIII. 266 From sheep posterior hypophysis a complex was obtained containing 90% of the oxytocic and vasopressic activity of the gland. The complex is an association of oxytocine and vasopressine with a protein, neurophysine [*sic: Eng. summary of article in Fr.*]. **1970** *Biochem. Jrnl.* CXVI. 908/2 The neurophysins of the pig form a group of proteins of different electrophoretic mobilities but all possessing the capacity to bind oxytocin and [8-lysine]-vasopressin. **1973** *Nature* 2 Mar. 63/1 This system is characterized immunochemically by the neurophysins, the specific carrier-proteins for vasopressin and oxytocin. **1937** *Surgery* I. 132 The vast literature on recent neurophysiologic research. **1972** *Science* 12 May 607/1 Any changes in the action potentials of trained motor units..must reflect neurophysiologic changes of the single neuron supplying the motor unit. **1962** C. L. Buxton *Study of Psychophysical Methods for Relief Childbirth Pain* vii. 60 Attempts were made also to explain neurophysiologically how it might be possible for fear and tension to increase the pain and length of labor. **1971** *Jrnl. Gen. Psychol.* LXXXIV. 141 In the early experimentation, there was no way to isolate a channel neurophysiologically. **1949** Koestler *Insight & Outlook* iv. 44 The demonstration or refutation by the neuro-physiologist of the existence of corresponding mechanisms in the central nervous system. **1966** I. Asimov *Fantastic Voyage* i. 17 The extension of the technique could be of great importance to the neurophysiologist. **1973** *Sci. Amer.* July 96/3 Between 1900 and 1920 Charles S. Sherrington, the foremost neurophysiologist of the time, applied the technique of electrical stimulation to study how the cerebrum controlled movement. [**1892** *Syd. Soc. Lex.*, *Neuroplasma*, Kupffer's term for a fluid which he supposed to lie between the fibrils of the cylinder-axis of a nerve.] **1894** Gould *Dict. Med.* 869/1 Neuroplasm. **1896** E. L. Billstein tr. *Stöhr's Text-bk. Histol.* II. i. 81 Each fibrilla [of the axon] represents a special conducting path and is cemented to neighboring fibrillae by a small amount of finely-granular interstitial substance—neuroplasm. **1960** L. Picken *Organization of Cells* vii. 291 In the light of electron microscope studies..it is likely that the axoplasm differs from the neuroplasm rather in the relative abundance and orientation of the various components..than in absolute composition. **1970** *Nature* 5 Sept. 1006/2 It is generally believed that neuroplasm is constantly synthesized in the cell body and moves as a gel down the axon (and probably also along the dendrites). **1909** *Cent. Dict.* Suppl., Neuroplasmic. **1965** *Acta Neuropath.* IV. 33 Neuroplasmic swellings were found within dendrites. **1970** P. A. Weiss in F. O. Schmitt *Neurosciences: 2nd Study Program* lxxiii. 840 (*heading*) Neuronal dynamics and neuroplasmic flow. **1900** Dorland *Med. Dict.* 442/2 *Neuropsychosis*, nervous disease complicated with mental disorder. **1918** A. A. Brill tr. *Freud's Totem & Taboo* iii. 158 The system formation is most ingenious in delusional states (paranoia) and dominates the clinical picture, but it also must not be overlooked in other forms of neuropsychoses. **1924** J. Riviere et al. tr. *Freud's Coll. Papers* I. 59 (*heading*) The defence of neuropsychoses. **1936** A. Myerson in *Amer. Jrnl. Psychiatry* XCIII. 281, I formally introduce the concept of the neuropsychosis. The neuropsychosis comes into being by an intensification of the symptomatology of the neuroses. **1964** Taveras & Wood *Diagnostic Neuroradiol.* 2 The use of gamma rays from radioactive isotopes for scanning, and the use of heat waves in thermography, ..are being incorporated in neuroradiological clinical practice. **1962** *Brit. Jrnl. Radiol.* XXXV. 501/1 Problems of neuroradiological nomenclature and the radiographic projections were discussed. **1955** *Brit. Jrnl. Surg.* XLIII 8/1 A very high proportion of successful angiograms justifies a wider trial. Even if it may not be equally successful in other hands I believe that it will become an important part of the armamentarium of neuroradiologist and neurosurgeon. **1961** *Lancet* 30 Sept. 746/1 Dr. J. L. G. Thomson, the neuroradiologist in Bristol, and all of the neurosurgical team are now performing about 700 angiographies a year. **1938** Wakeley & Orley (*title*) A textbook of neuro-radiology. **1964** Taveras & Wood *Diagnostic Neuroradiol.* 1 During the last fifteen years, angiography has arrived at its appropriate place of importance in diagnostic neuroradiology. **1963** (*title of periodical*) Neurosciences research program bulletin. **1964** *New Scientist* 10 Sept. 643/1 Man's search for the physical basis of mental processes has evolved a number of disparate neurosciences. Some of these, such as neurology, neuroanatomy, neurophysiology, neurochemistry, neuropathology, and psychology, have advanced to the status of mature sciences. **1970** *Nature* 5 Sept. 1006/1 During the past few years neuroscience, comprising the sciences of brain and behaviour, has been differentiating, integrating, regrouping. **1974** *Times Lit. Suppl.* 18 Oct. 1151/3 It will transform the established neuro-sciences until they become increasingly able to comprehend the problems of behaviour, possibly even of mind. **1967** R. B. Livingston in G. C. Quarton et al. *Neurosciences: Study Program* 500/1 Neuroscientists are drawn to this field..by a desire to learn more about ourselves as human beings. **1974** *Nature* 1 Mar. p. v/1 (Advt.), This new book by the well-known neuroscientist Elliot S. Valenstein. **1941** *Jrnl. Compar. Neurol.* LXXIV. 93 Neurosecretion is present in both vertebrates and invertebrates. **1961** *Biol. Abstr.* XXXVI. 1201/1 (*heading*) Neurosecretions in the insect. **1963** R. P. Dales *Annelids* viii. 166 Neurosecretion may be of major importance in the co-ordination of the annelid

body. **1968** *New Scientist* 16 May 355/1 It is quite possible that neurosecretions are the 'oldest' hormones in the animal kingdom. **1973** *Proc. Indian Acad. Sci.* B. LXXVII. 148 Involvement of neurosecretion in some of the physiological activities of this scorpion will be reported here. **1940** *Nature* 17 Feb. 264/1 (*heading*) Neurosecretory cells in the ganglia of Lepidoptera. **1956** *Ibid.* 17 Mar. 532/1 In the cockroach, activity rhythms may have a neurosecretory basis. **1963** R. P. DALES *Annelids* viii. 166 In *Nephthys* the cells in the blood greatly increase and take up neurosecretory material from the back of the brain during posterior regeneration following amputation. **1968** H. O. HOFER in G. H. Bourne *Struct. & Function of Nervous Tissue* I. xi. 471 The neurosecretory substances act as hormones, long-range and long-acting; and they are not directly transmitted, but are released in a circulating body fluid as acting agents. **1936** A. KORZYBSKI in *Amer. Jrnl. Psychiatry* XCIII. 29 By using the term *evaluation* as a fundamental term, we bridge methodologically and linguistically the exact sciences with other sciences, psychiatry included. We gain thereby powerful neuro-linguistic and neuro-semantic direct methods for education and psychotherapy. **1946** S. A. HAYAKAWA in W. S. Knickerbocker *Twentieth Century English* 47 In accounting for human behavior it postulates the 'neuro-semantic environment'—the environment, that is, of dogmas, beliefs, creeds, knowledge, and superstitions to which we react as the result of our training—as a fundamental and inescapable part of our total environment. **1929** C. U. A. KAPPERS *Evolution Nervous Syst. Invertebr., Vertebr. & Man* 3 The different forms of nervous conductors are three: the neurosensory cell, which generally retains its place in an epithelial layer, the primitive or asynaptic ganglion cell and the polarized or synaptic neurone, both of which are nearly always located under the epithelium. **1940** O. LOWENSTEIN *Parker & Haswell's Text-bk. Zool.* (ed. 6) I. I. 36 The photosensitive cells in the retina of the vertebrate eye and the olfactory receptor cells situated in the epithelium coating of the vertebrate nose have the structure of neurosensory cells. **1946** L. A. WHITE in W. S. Knickerbocker *Twentieth Century Eng.* 93 The animal hearing them understands them..by virtue of his own inborn neurosensory equipment. **1962** D. NICHOLS *Echinoderms* iii. 43 Besides the general scattering of neurosensory cells over the asteroid body, there are five light-sensitive optic cushions, one at the base of each terminal tentacle. **1974** *Sci. Amer.* Nov. 14/3 Reader in neurosensory physiology. **1925** *Arch. Neurol. & Psychiatry* (Chicago) XIV. 192 It.. is important, more especially for the neurosurgeon..that his clinical experiences should be correlated with a more detailed classification of the gliomas than is customary. **1972** *Oxford Times* 26 May 6/7 Mr R. Gye, consultant neurosurgeon, explained the many uses to which the blanket could be put. **1904** *Alienist & Neurologist* XXV. 404 (*heading*) Neurosurgery. Trigeminal neuralgia treated by intraneural injections of osmic acid. **1937** *Surgery* I. 132 With the later days of Victor Horsley in England and the early days of Harvey Cushing in America, neurosurgery may truly be said to have been born. **1966** *Lancet* 24 Dec. 1400/1 A speciality like neuro-surgery requires an extra year's training. **1932** *Glasgow Med. Jrnl.* CXVIII. 137 (*heading*) The work of a neuro-surgical clinic. **1955** A. HUXLEY *Let.* 25 Sept. (1969) 767 Penfield says, absence of evidence, in the present state of neurosurgical knowledge, proves nothing. **1974** *Nature* 13 Dec. 582/2 Recordings of unit activity during neurosurgical operations have demonstrated neuronal activity in cortex and subcortical structures. [**1877** *Med. Times & Gaz.* 10 Nov. 511/1 Nerve-syphilis appears to affect with preference those persons in whom there is the neuropathic constitution.] **1878** *Boston Med. & Surgical Jrnl.* XCVIII. 278 Neuro-Syphilis.—As nervous diseases of syphilitic origin are more amenable to treatment than the corresponding idiopathic ones, a correct diagnosis may at times be sufficient to save a life otherwise lost. **1915** *Ibid.* CLXXIII. 996/1 (*heading*) The significance of changes in cellular content of cerebrospinal fluid in neurosyphilis. **1946** *Nature* 17 Aug. 243/2 Penicillin sodium in saline solution is effective to a greater or lesser degree in all aspects of neurosyphilis studied. **1974** PASSMORE & ROBSON *Compan. Med. Stud.* III. xiii. 6/1 In all forms of neurosyphilis the results of treatment depend on the number of neurones already destroyed. **1877** *Med. Times & Gaz.* 10 Nov. 511/1 Neuro-syphilitic affections belong generally to the later portions of the secondary stage, or to the tertiary period of the complaint. **1918** *Jrnl. Amer. Med. Assoc.* 28 Sept. 1023/2 We can..control the majority of the early infections of the [cerebrospinal] fluid and greatly limit the number of neurosyphilitics in the future. **1921** *Ibid.* 2 July 3/2 In eight of the twenty-one neurosyphilitic partners the type of neurosyphilis was the same as in the original patient. **1954** D. NABARRO *Congenital Syphilis* viii. 282 Unless neurosyphilis is actively sought by routine C.S.F. investigations upon patients, many neurosyphilitics will be overlooked. **1972** *Afr. Jrnl. Med. Sci.* III. 195 Cases..diagnosed as neurosyphilitic on clinical grounds should be given the benefit of adequate penicillin therapy. **1901** *Gray's Anat.* (ed. 15) [52] (*heading*) Organ of Golgi (neuro-tendinous spindle) from the human tendo Achillis. **1920** S. W. RANSON *Anat. Nervous Syst.* v. 72 Somewhat analogous structures [to the neuromuscular end organs] are the neurotendinous end organs or tendon spindles where myelinated nerve-fibers end in relation to specialized tendon fasciculi. **1962** E. C. CROSBY et al. *Correlative Anat. Nervous Syst.* ii. 87/2 The dendritic endings may be of neuromuscular or neurotendinous type (that is, muscle spindles or tendon spindles). **1949** *Jrnl. Compar. Neurol.* XCI. 339 Only such procedures as bear specifically on the comparative neurotoxicity of this drug for various animals will be set forth here. **1959** *Arch. Internat. de Pharmacodynamie et de Thérapie* CXXII. 98 Rats on a diet deficient in pyridoxine developed signs of neurotoxicity when administered IDPN. **1968** W. C. BOWMAN et al. *Textbk. Pharmacol.* xxviii. 722 All of the potent compounds which cause neurotoxicity are inhibitors of butyryl cholinesterase. **1971** *Nature* 20 Aug. 525/2 Between them the two proteins manifest ferocious neurotoxicity. **1948** DE ROBERTIS & SCHMITT in *Jrnl. Cellular & Compar. Physiol.* XXXI. 3 Although unequivocal proof of the structure of the fibers cannot yet be given, the available evidence is consistent with the view that they are tubular, possessing a thin wall of relatively high electron density and a core of low density. To facilitate description they will be called 'neurotubules'. **1969** *Nature* 15 Nov. 710/1 The chief axoplasmic components, extending beyond the neurone cell body, are neurofilaments and neurotubules. **1970** P. A. WEISS in F. O. Schmitt *Neurosciences: 2nd Study Program* lxxiii. 845/2 In contrast to the straight neurotubules, the neurofilaments, 70–100 Ångström units in diameter, show a more wavy course. **1961** *Lancet* 23 Sept. 717/2 The Cox strains..exhibit a much higher level of monkey neurovirulence. **1973** *Nature* 26 Jan. 248/2 The vaccine was used on a limited scale but was withdrawn after Dick had claimed that he had detected a reversion to neurovirulence.

neuroepithelial (niūə:ro,epiþī·liăl), *a. Histology.* Also **neuro-epithelial.** [f. *NEUROEPITHELI(UM + -AL.] **a.** Of or pertaining to neuroepithelium (sense *a); applied *spec.* to an epithelial nerve cell that is a sensory receptor.

1889 MCKENDRICK & STOEHR *Text-bk. Physiol.* II. XI. i. 448 In certain medusæ, the transition between a neuro-epithelial cell and a ganglionic or nerve cell may be traced. **1907** G. A. PIERSOL *Human Anat.* 1463 The inner lamella [of the retina] may be subdivided..into the neuro-epithelial and the cerebral layers. **1952** HABEL & BIBERSTEIN tr. *Trautmann & Fiebiger's Fund. Histology Domestic Animals* iii. 32 The neuroepithelial cells occur in taste buds, the olfactory epithelium, the cristae and maculae staticae, the organ of Corti, and the retina. **1966** T. S. & C. R. LEESON *Histology* xiv. 267/2 The neuroepithelial taste cells are distributed between the supporting cells and number only 4 to 16 in each taste bud. **1974** P. CONSTANTINIDES *Functional Electronic Histology* vi. 81/2 (*heading*) Neuro-epithelial synapses.

b. Composed of or derived from neuro-epithelium (sense *b).

1948 R. A. WILLIS *Path. Tumours* lii. 818 While it is possible that the tumours containing undoubted embryonic neuro-epithelial tissue..were indeed pure embryonic neuro-epithelial growths, this remains uncertain. **1949** B. W. LICHTENSTEIN *Textbk. Neuropath.* iv. 47 One generally recognizes two varieties of interstitial tissue in the fully developed nervous system—the neuroglia of neuro-epithelial origin and the microglia of mesenchymal origin. **1971** J. MINCKLER *Path. Nervous Syst.* II. clvii. 2111/1 Very primitive tumors occasionally occur in peripheral nerves which are regarded as neuroepithelial.

neuroepithelium (niūə:ro,epiþī·liŭm). *Histology.* Also **neuro-epithelium.** [mod.L., f. NEURO- + EPITHELIUM, as tr. G. *neuroepithel* (G. Schwalbe in Graefe & Saemisch *Handb. d. ges. Augenheilkunde* (1874) I. 358).] **a.** The sensory epithelium in organs of special sense, such as the eye or the nose.

1885 W. STIRLING tr. *Landois's Text-bk. Human Physiol.* II. 960 The layer of rods and cones or neuro-epithelium of Schwalbe. **1899** F. H. GERRISH *Text-bk. Anat.* 43 Sensory epithelium, or neuro-epithelium cells, are found in close relation with the filamentous terminals of the nerves devoted to taste, smell, hearing, and sight. **1929** S. DUKE-ELDER *Recent Adv. Ophthalm.* (ed. 2) iii. 104 As the primary optic vesicle invaginates, two layers are formed... The inner layer shows two well-differentiated regions: a marginal layer.., and deep to this the cells proper of the primitive neuro-epithelium. **1943** FISCHER & WOLFSON *Inner Ear* x. 319 There was a circular fold of neuro-epithelium segmenting the utricle. **1952** HABEL & BIBERSTEIN tr. *Trautmann & Fiebiger's Fund. Histol. Domestic Animals* ii. 32 (*heading*) Sensory epithelium (neuro-epithelium).

b. Embryonic ectoderm that develops into nervous tissue.

1889 *Nature* 10 Jan. 260/2 The epithelium of this ciliated groove..is the only part of the primary central cylinder which is ciliated, and which does not form ganglion elements, and hence it is the only part which is not neuro-epithelium. **1940** S. A. K. WILSON *Neurol.* II. lxxii. 1176 In the epiblast of the embryo there appears a medullary tube lined by primitive neuroepithelium. **1958** R. A. WILLIS *Borderland Embryol. & Path.* iii. 115 This undifferentiated prospective nervous tissue, from which neurones, neuroglia and epenchyma will all arise, is neuro-epithelium. **1971** —— in J. Minckler *Path. Nervous Syst.* II. cxlvi. 1938/2 Malignant teratomas in adults.. may contain nervous tissue at all stages of development, from early neuroepithelium to its fully differentiated derivatives.

neurofibromatosis (niūə:rofəibrōumătōu·sis). *Path.* [f. *neurofibromat-* (taken as stem of *neurofibroma*, s.v. NEURO-) + -OSIS.] Any condition characterized by multiple neurofibromas; *spec.* a condition in which multiple (often very numerous) palpable neurofibromas occur on the peripheral nerves (also called *von Recklinghausen's disease*).

1899 *Lancet* 29 July 271/2 The nature of Recklinghausen's disease or, as it has sometimes been called, generalised neuro-fibromatosis. **1900** A. THOMSON (*title*) On neuroma and neuro-fibromatosis. **1966** WRIGHT & SYMMERS *Systemic Path.* II. xxxiv. 1236/1 The rare condition that is sometimes referred to as central neurofibromatosis, or Wishart's disease, may occur in association with neurofibromatosis of the peripheral nerves (von Recklinghausen's disease), or it may exist without the latter. **1973** *Daily Colonist* (Victoria, B.C.) 4 Oct. 2/3 A rare condition called neurofibromatosis is featured by multiple bumps.

neurogenesis (niūərodʒe·nĭsis). *Biol.* [f. NEURO- + -GENESIS.] The development of nervous tissue.

1900 in DORLAND *Med. Dict.* **1908** *Jrnl. R. Microsc. Soc.* 27 Arguments based on embryonic neurogenesis. **1928** R. M. MAY tr. *Ramón y Cajal's Degeneration & Regeneration Nervous Syst.* I. xvi. 381 The ideas of Harrison..are perfectly applicable to normal neurogenesis as well as to nervous regeneration. **1967** M. V. EDDS in G. C. Quarton et al. *Neurosciences: a Study Program* 232/1 Faced with the limitations imposed by working with the embryo, investigators of neurogenesis have often turned to older organisms with the fortunate capacity of regenerating amputated nerve fibers.

neurogenetic (niūərodʒĕne·tik), *a.* [f. NEURO- + -GENETIC.] = *NEUROGENIC *a.* 2.

1889 *Jrnl. R. Microsc. Soc.* 494 The primordial cells of the embryonic brain are therefore neurogenetic, giving rise to the special nerve-cells. **1928** R. M. MAY tr. *Ramón y Cajal's Degeneration & Regeneration Nervous Syst.* I. xvi. 383 In the neurogenetic process the following factors come into play.

neurogenic (niūərŏdʒe·nik), *a.* [f. NEURO- + *-GENIC.] **1. a.** Of a theory: implying or assuming control (esp. of the heart-beat) by the nervous system.

1901 *Buck's Handbk. Med. Sci.* (ed. 2) III. 111/1 The neurogenic theory is based on the following considerations: Muscular tissue..depends upon its motor-nerve impulses to set it into action. **1922** C. P. HOWARD in L. F. Barker *Endocrinol. & Metabolism* I. 313 Biedl has come to the conclusion that the neurogenic theory was based upon inconclusive experiments.

b. Caused or controlled by (a disorder of) the nervous system.

1904 [see *myogenic* adj. s.v. MYO-]. **1949** KOESTLER *Insight & Outlook* v. 69 They [*sc.* digestive disorders] could be called neurogenic rather than psychogenic. **1961** *Lancet* 19 Aug. 409/1 The book..ends with a detailed account of the surgical treatment of neurogenic disorders of the entire urogenital tract. **1974** *Nature* 8 Mar. 106/3 In the singing katydids..relatively high rates of sound pulses..are controlled by synchronous, or neurogenic, muscles in which each contraction is initiated by a nerve impulse.

c. *neurogenic bladder*, abnormal functioning of the bladder owing to disturbances of nervous control.

1930 *Urologic & Cutaneous Rev.* XXXIV. 541/2 (*heading*) Treatment of the neurogenic bladder with the slow sinusoidal current. **1952** P. A. HERBUT *Urological Path.* I. iii. 323 In neurogenic bladder the sphincteric mechanism ceases to exist as an efficient functioning structure and the detrusor mechanism dictates the behavior of the bladder. **1966** WRIGHT & SYMMERS *Systemic Path.* I. xxv. 782/1 The neurogenic bladder is in effect a functional obstruction of the urinary tract.

2. Of or pertaining to neurogenesis; giving rise to nervous tissue.

1915 J. A. NELSON *Embryol. of Honey Bee* viii. 127 The neurogenic area..comprises two longitudinal thickenings, the primitive swellings..which are separated by a median furrow. **1928** R. M. MAY tr. *Ramón y Cajal's Degeneration & Regeneration Nervous Syst.* I. xvi. 381 Some of the neurogenic factors mentioned by Harrison seem to us highly doubtful. **1941** JOHANNSEN & BUTT *Embryol. of Insects & Myriapods* xv. 242 A thin layer of elongated cells, the neurilemma, probably arising from the outlying ganglion cells, covers the neurogenic tissue dorsally.

Hence **neuroge·nically** *adv.*, by the nervous system or by nerves.

1960 *Arch. Neurol.* III. 229/1 The result is a sterile inflammatory reaction, neurogenically induced. **1967** *Jrnl. Pharmacol. & Exper. Therap.* CLV. 37/2 Phentolamine blocked with equal facility..the norepinephrine- and neurogenically evoked constriction. **1971** *Nature* 28 May 264/2 Increased sensitivity at the receptor level could play a role in enhancement of neurogenically mediated responses.

neurogram (niūə·rogræm). [f. NEURO- + -GRAM.] An enduring structural change postulated as being produced in the nervous system by experience and as being the physiological basis of memory.

1914 M. PRINCE *Unconscious* v. 131, I have been in the habit of using the term *neurograms* to characterize these brain records... Richard Semon..has adopted the term Engramm with much the same signification that I have given to Neurogram. **1921** M. GARNETT *Educ. & World Citizenship* v. 42 Examples of neural dispositions, or neurograms, are furnished by the functional systems of nervous arcs. **1939** —— *Knowledge & Character* iv. 54 The same neurones and systems of neurones may form part of several different neurograms.

neurography. Add: **3.** A name proposed for: all the neurograms of an individual, considered collectively.

1921 M. GARNETT *Educ. & World Citizenship* v. 63 In the course of life's experience, then, an individual's neurography—if we may so describe all his neurograms, however distributed and arranged—tends to become organised into interest-systems. **1939** —— *Knowl. & Character* xi. 215 That our neurographies do tend to correspond to the realm of facts..is so important that we must insist further upon it.

neurohormone (niūərohǭ·ɹmōun). *Physiol.* [f. NEURO- + *HORMONE.] Any hormone or neurotransmitter released by the nervous system.

1941 A. GROLLMAN *Essent. Endocrinol.* i. 2 This definition [of true hormones] excludes the..neurohormones,..for these are..local in their effects or are transported by diffusion. **1955** J. H. WELSH in Pincus & Thimann *Hormones* III. iii. 99 In this chapter an attempt will be made to see what all neurons have in common with respect to production, transport, storage, and release of regulator substances. It is proposed that the term 'neurohormone' be used to designate these substances. We may well continue to speak of 'neurohumors' and of 'neurosecretory materials', but it appears highly desirable to have an exclusive term, and 'neurohormone', previously used in this sense without precise definition,..seems highly appropriate. *Ibid.*, The term neurohormone.. may be defined as an organic compound produced by neurons and released at their endings to act as a chemical messenger or hormone, either locally or at a distance. **1965** J. POLLITT *Depression & its Treatment* iv. 53 Monoamines are neurohormones regarded as essential for normal activity of the brain, and the two substances of this group playing particularly important roles in mood regulation, are serotonin..and noradrenalin. **1972** *Sci. Amer.* Nov. 28/3 The hypothesis that pituitary function is controlled by neurohormones originating in the hypothalamus was soon well established. **1974** *Nature* 15 Mar. 238/1 Many hormones, including noradrenaline, the neurohormone of the sympathetic nervous system.

So **neurohormo·nal** *a.*, involving both the nervous system and the endocrine system; of or pertaining to a neurohormone.

1949 KOESTLER *Insight & Outlook* v. 69 Digestive disorders..may be explained in direct neurohormonal terms. *Ibid.* viii. 127 The neurohormonal excitation may persist for a while like the duffed-down pain. **1962** *Science Survey* III. 266 The neuro-hormonal chain of events leading to the olfactory pregnancy block has to some extent been explored. **1965** LEE & KNOWLES *Animal Hormones* ii. 32 The ejection of milk at suckling.. is a neurohormonal reflex. **1974** *Sci. Amer.* Sept. 8/3 What magic gives Grinspoon and Singer the power to know that a behavioral condition..is not due to, say, a neurohormonal deficiency?

neurohumoral (niūᵊrohiū·mŏrăl), *a. Physiol.* [a. F. *neuro-humoral* (H. Fredericq 1927, in *Compt. Rend. des Séances de la Soc. de Biol.* XCVII. (Réunion plénière) 3), f. *neuro-* NEURO- + *humoral* HUMORAL *a.*] Of, involving, or being a neurohumour. Cf. *HUMORAL *a.* 1 a.

1929 P. BARD in C. Murchison *Foundations Exper. Psychol.* xii. 449 (*heading*) The neuro-humoral basis of emotional reactions. **1947** *Jrnl. Endocrinol.* V. 136 The possibility of a neurohumoral transmission of stimuli has been tentatively suggested on many occasions. **1966** G. B. KOELLE in Rodahl & Issekutz *Nerve as Tissue* 291 The neurohumoral theory is most consistent with the known facts concerning transmission at the vast majority of synaptic and neuro-effector junctions. **1971** *Nature* 31 Dec. 570/1 Neurohumoral agents from the hypothalamus were discharged into the portal vessels for transmission to the anterior lobe of the pituitary to affect the secretion of hormones.

neurohumour (niūᵊ·rohiūməɹ). *Physiol.* Also (*U.S.*) **-humor.** [f. NEURO- + HUMOUR, HUMOR *sb.* Cf. next.] A neurohormone, esp. a transmitter.

1933 *Proc. Soc. Exper. Biol. & Med.* XXX. 556 That this stripe should be dark is due to the fact that the severance of the nerve fibers excites the discharge of an expanding neurohumor whereby the melanophores are made to enlarge and thus to darken the skin. **1948** *Special Publ. N.Y. Acad. Sci.* IV. 292 Fries..has obtained considerable evidence pointing to the conclusion that xanthophores are also doubly innervated and believes that neurohumors are involved. **1959** J. H. WELSH in A. Gorbman *Compar. Endocrinol.* 123 Although it is convenient to refer to the products of ordinary neurons as neurohumors and to those of neurosecretory cells as neurosecretory substances, their common role as regulatory agents must be recognized. **1971** *Compar. Biochem. & Physiol.* XXXVIII. A.239 The neurohumor, serotonin, has been shown to be functionally involved in hibernation in the ground squirrel.

neurohypophysial (niūᵊ:rohəipofi·ziăl), *a. Med.* Also **-physeal** (-fi·ziăl, -fisī·ăl). [f. next after *HYPOPHYSIAL *a.*

In sense a, f. NEURO- + HYPOPHYS(IS + -AL.]

a. Pertaining to the neural tube and the hypophysis (in the embryo). ?*Obs.*

1893 *Q. Jrnl. Microsc. Sci.* XXXV. 301 The process of constriction by which the tube, or, as it may at once be called, the neuro-hypophysial canal, comes to be entirely separated from the cerebral vesicle has therefore now commenced. *Ibid.* 306 The hypophysis and the ganglion ..have been gradually differentiating themselves from the common neuro-hypophysial tube. **1929** *Ibid.* LXXII. 79 The whole of the adult nervous system [in Ascidians] is a new development proliferated from a minute remnant of the embryonic neural canal. The region in which this proliferation takes place is usually included in the neurohypophysial canal.

b. Of or pertaining to the neurohypophysis.

1934 *Physiol. Abstr.* XIX. 481 (*heading*) The central effect on blood pressure of the neurohypophyseal circulation hormone. **1939** *Res. Publ. Assoc. Res. Nerv. & Mental Dis.* XX. 444 There is some question..that the antidiuretic substance in the urine is of neurohypophysial origin. **1963** MONTGOMERY & WELBOURN *Clin. Endocrinol.* viii. 336 Any condition which damages the integrity of the neurohypophyseal system causes diabetes insipidus. **1973** C. EZRIN et al. *Systematic Endocrinol.* iii. 21/2 Recovery follows because damage to the supraoptic neurohypophyseal tract is mild enough to be reversible. **1973** *Nature* 12 Oct. 287/2 This also means that the rat now has two neurohypophysial hormones and two neurophysins.

neurohypophysis (niūᵊrohəipǫ·fisis). *Med.* [f. NEURO- + HYPOPHYSIS.] The portion of the hypophysis that develops from the embryonic brain, comprising the posterior lobe and usually the infundibulum and median eminence, and differing from the adenohypophysis in having little glandular activity and in being richly supplied with nerve fibres, which originate in the hypothalamus (being the means by which the latter exercises its control of the hormonal activity of the anterior lobe) and release the hormones oxytocin and vasopressin following their production in the hypothalamus.

1912 H. CUSHING *Pituitary Body & its Disorders* I. 2 The tip becomes thickened into the infundibular body (neurohypophysis, or pars nervosa). *Ibid.* 3 The neurohypophysis itself is connected with the tuber cinereum by a stalk which varies in length in different species. **1939** *Res. Publ. Assoc. Res. Nerv. & Mental Dis.* XX. 24 It is convenient to regard the neurohypophysis as being divisible into two major divisions, namely, the neural lobe and the neural stalk. **1954** L. C. MARTIN *Clin. Endocrinol.* (ed. 2) i. 2 The neural division or neuro-hypophysis consists of the pars nervosa or infundibular process, the pituitary stalk or infundibular stem, and the median eminence of the tuber cinereum. **1968** A. VAN TIENHOVEN *Reproductive Physiol. Vertebr.* viii. 249/1 Some of the hypothalamic hormones, e.g. oxytocin and vasopressin, are stored in the neurohypophysis. **1968** PASSMORE & ROBSON *Compan. Med. Stud.* I. xxv. 15/2 The neurohypophysis is a point of contact between neurological and hormonal control mechanisms. **1972** *Sci. Amer.* Nov. 24/3 This double organ..is the pituitary gland, or hypophysis. The part that migrated from the brain is the posterior lobe, or neurohypophysis; the part that migrated from the pharynx is the anterior lobe, or adenohypophysis.

neuroleptic (niūᵊrole·ptik), *a.* (*sb.*) *Pharm.* [ad. F. *neuroleptique* (Delay & Deniker 1955, in *Bull. de l'Acad. Nat. de Méd.* CXXXIX. 145), after *psycholeptique* *PSYCHOLEPTIC *a.*] Able to reduce nervous tension; tranquillizing; also as *sb.*, a neuroleptic drug; a tranquillizer.

1958 *Science* 10 Jan. 59/1 Others [*sc.* terms for psychopharmacologic drugs] are *ataraxic*.., and *neuroleptic* and *neuroplegic*, indicating diminutions in the intensity of nerve functions. **1959** *Jrnl. Clin. & Exper. Psychopath.* XIX. 286 We believe..the higher dosage of neuroleptics, combination of neuroleptics with other medications, or combinations of neuroleptics is frequently responsible for the unfavorable reactions. **1965** J. POLLITT *Depression & its Treatment* v. 67 This drug [*sc.* chlorpromazine] is neuroleptic, producing Parkinsonism. **1968** *New Scientist* 21 Nov. 417/1 Schizophrenics treated over long periods with neuroleptics have sometimes shown symptoms typical of endogenous depression. **1971** *Nature* 26 Nov. 224/2 All patients remained on their previous neuroleptic medication throughout the study. **1972** *Encycl. Psychol.* II. 310/2 After acute application in healthy subjects, even in low doses, neuroleptics only seldom induce motor relaxation and emotional stabilization.

neurologically (niūᵊrolǫ·dʒikăli), *adv.* [f. NEUROLOGICAL *a.* + -LY^{2}.] From a neurological point of view; as regards neurology.

1936 *Acta Med. Scand.* LXXXVIII. 479 Nothing neurologically abnormal was found. **1971** *New Scientist* 5 Aug. 335/1 Psychiatric disorders in neurologically handicapped children. **1974** *Sci. Amer.* July 106/1 Neurologically speaking, brains whose organization was essentially human were already in existence some three million years ago.

neuromast (niūᵊ·romæst). *Zool.* [f. NEURO- + Gr. μαστ-ός breast.] An organ of sensory perception forming part of the lateral line system of fishes and larval or aquatic amphibians.

1912 J. S. KINGSLEY *Compar. Anat. Vertebrates* 167 Distally the fibres terminate in peculiar collections of sense cells known as sense hillocks or neuromasts occurring in the inner ear and in the lateral line organs of the ichthyopsida. **1937** *Proc. R. Soc.* B. CXXIII. 474 The distinction between pit organs and canal neuromasts is purely conjectural. **1957** O. LOWENSTEIN in M. E. Brown *Physiol. Fishes* II. ii. 156 Fundamentally the end-organs of the lateral line system consist of groups of secondary sensory cells called neuromasts. **1962** K. F. LAGLER et al. *Ichthyology* iii. 105 Each ampulla contains sensory nerve endings (neuromast cells) in a gelatinous terminal cup. **1974** M. HILDEBRAND *Analysis Vertebr. Struct.* xvi. 395 The lateral line system..is present in fishes and in both larval and aquatic adult amphibians. It consists of thousands of microscopic organs called neuromasts.

neuromotor (niūᵊ·romōᵘtəɹ), *a.* [f. NEURO- + MOTOR *sb.* and *a.*] Pertaining to or involving both the nervous system and motor activities; applied *spec.* to a system of minute ectoplasmic fibrils connecting some of the cirri to the motorium in some ciliate protozoa.

1914 [see *MOTORIUM 2]. **1940** L. H. HYMAN *Invertebrates* I. iii. 169 It is probable that at least some of the fibrils of the neuromotor system are conductile and serve to coordinate ciliary activities..; but others are presumably of a supporting nature. **1959** W. ANDREW *Textbk. Compar. Histology* xiv. 539 The neuromotor system of Stylonichia appears to be very similar to that of Oxytricha... Some authors have ascribed a neuromotor function to certain fibrils connected to the basal granules of flagellates. **1966** *New Scientist* 3 Nov. 242/1 These neuromotor fibres have since been generally accepted as indicating the presence of an elementary intracellular 'nervous system'. **1966** *Amer. Speech* XLI. 226 Speech production by control of vocal tract configuration changes treats..phonemic distinction in terms of neuromotor commands. **1971** *Language* XLVII. 51 We have now reached the stage where automatic phonetic and phonological rules take over, converting the sequences of segments into actual neuro-motor commands to the muscles in the articulation of the utterance.

neuron. Add: **2.** (Earlier and later examples.) *Obs.*

1893 [see *DENDRON]. **1897** *Med. Chron.* VII. 234 We notice that Mr. Schäfer uses the word 'neuron' in a somewhat different sense from that applied to it by Waldeyer, who used it—and we believe that in his sense it is extensively, if not universally, used—to denote a nerve cell with all its processes. Mr. Schäfer uses it to designate the axis-cylinder process of a nerve cell. **1930** HARTRIDGE & HAYNES *Histol.* 114 Nerve processes are of two kinds, long and short. The long are called axons, axis cylinders,..and neurons.

3. [a. G. *neuron* (W. Waldeyer 1891, in *Berliner klin. Wochenschr.* 13 July 691/1).] (Earlier and later examples.)

The spellings *neuron* (niūᵊ·rǫn) and *neurone* (niūᵊ·rōᵘn) are both still widely current.

1891 *Brain* XIV. 569 [*Abstr. of Waldeyer*, 1891] Thus a nerve element, a nerve entity, or 'neuron', as I propose to call it, consists..of the following pieces:—(*a*) a nerve cell, (*b*) the nerve process, (*c*) its collaterals, and (*d*) the end-branching. **1896** L. F. BARKER in *Johns Hopkins Hosp. Bull.* VII. 201/1 Van Gehuchten has adopted Waldeyer's word, spelling it in French 'le neurone', and French writers generally employ it. The leading investigators in Spain and Italy have also adopted the same term... The question arises, how is Waldeyer's form to be anglicized? Would it be justifiable to bring it into English through the French and to spell it *neurone*, pronounced neurōne, or could it be brought into English directly from the Greek and be so spelled and pronounced? **1904** E. B. TITCHENER tr. *Wundt's Physiol. Psychol.* I. vi. 326 This spatial connexion may..consist either in the immediate proximity of neurones lying upon the same side of the brain, or in the union of distant areas by association fibres. **1939** W. E. LE GROS CLARK *Tissues of Body* xii. 294 Within the central nervous system impulses are conducted from one part to another along a chain of neurones. **1950** A. HUXLEY *Themes & Variations* i. 94 The gulf between thought..and..neurones and electric charges is just as wide as that which in Biran's day divided thought from fluids and fibres. **1964** *New Scientist* 10 Sept. 643/1 The brain is estimated to contain ten thousand million nerve cells (neurons) and ten times as many glial cells. **1971** J. Z. YOUNG *Introd. Study Man* xxii. 296 Neurons are probably lost steadily in the later decades of life. **1973** H. M. RÁLIŠ et al. *Techniques Neurohistol.* i. 16 The nerve cell can make contact with a large number of other neurones through the multiple branches of dendrites.

4. Special Comb: **neuron(e theory,** the theory (now generally accepted) that the nervous system is composed of individual cells which, though effectively in contact with one another, are structurally distinct units all derived from a single neuroblast in the embryo.

1897 *Cincinnati Lancet-Clinic* LXXVIII. 565/1 (*heading*) The histological basis of the neuron theory. **1939** W. E. LE GROS CLARK *Tissues of Body* xii. 320 At one time the neurone theory excited considerable controversy, and even to-day some anatomists question its validity. **1972** M. L. BARR *Human Nervous Syst.* ii. 9/1 The Neuron Theory, as opposed to the view that nerve cells form a continuous reticulum, was advanced by His on the basis of embryological studies, by Forel on the basis of the response of nerve cells to injury, and by Ramón y Cajal from his observations with silver staining methods... Wholly convincing evidence in support of the Neuron Theory had to await the introduction of electron microscopy.

neuronal (niurōᵘ·năl), *a.* [f. NEURON + -AL.] Of or pertaining to a neurone or neurones.

1901 *Brit. Med. Jrnl.* 29 June 1610/2 (*heading*) Changes in the neuronal centres in beri-beric neuritis. **1946** *Nature* 9 Nov. 647/2 Nachmansohn deals with the theory (his own) that acetylcholine is released at the neuronal surface during the passage of an impulse. **1953** *Brit. Jrnl. Psychol.* XLIV. 304 The final verification of an explanatory hypothesis in psychology will not come from its direct identification in terms of neuronal systems. **1971** CHIN-WU KIM in W. O. Dingwall *Survey of Linguistic Sci.* 32 Lenneberg..is of the opinion that the orders of neuronal firings are adjusted so as to achieve a temporal coincidence at the neuro-muscular juncture. **1974** [see *NEURONOPHAGIA].

Hence **neuro·nally** *adv.*, by a neurone or neurones.

1960 *Exper. Neurol.* II. 364 (*heading*) Effects of various drugs on activity of the neuronally isolated cerebral cortex. **1975** *Nature* 6 Feb. 448/1 The contractile responses are neuronally mediated.

neurone: see NEURON 3 in Dict. and Suppl.

neuronic, *a.* (s.v. NEURON). Add: (Further examples.) Now a less common word than *NEURONAL *a.*

1906 *Athenæum* 1 Sept. 246/2 The controversy on the neuronic theory still continues. **1931** *Brit. Jrnl. Psychol.* XXII. 141 If there be some such automatic regulating device in the neuronic mechanism, we must assume that it is in operation in the intact animal. **1964** S. DUKE-ELDER *Parsons' Dis. Eye* (ed. 14) xxii. 334 The disease is a primary lipid neuronic degeneration of the whole of the central nervous system.

neuronophagia (niūᵊ:rǫnǒfē̆ⁱ·dʒiă). *Med.* Also anglicized as **-phagy.** [f. NEURON + -O + Gr. -φαγία eating (*sb.*).] The destruction of neurones by phagocytes.

1911 STEDMAN *Med. Dict.* 584/1 Neuronophagia, neuronophagy. **1932** M. BIELSCHOWSKY in W. Penfield *Cytol. & Cellular Path. Nervous Syst.* I. iv. 153 The neuroglia cells not only multiply, but some of them invade the marginal hollows and vacuoles. This process is included under the rather ill-chosen name of neuronophagia. **1958** J. G. GREENFIELD et al. *Neuropath.* ii. 62 Neuronophagy is specially common in all forms of encephalomyelitis which affect the grey matter. **1974** PASSMORE & ROBSON *Compan. Med. Stud.* III. xxxiv. 128/2 The occurrence of perivascular lymphocytic cuffing may distract attention from the more subtle isolated neuronal necrosis, each dead cell being surrounded by a ring of satellite phagocytes (neuronophagia).

neuropathologic (niūᵊ:rǫpæþǫlǫ·dʒik), *a.* Chiefly *U.S.* [f. NEUROPATHOLOG(Y + -IC.] = NEUROPATHOLOGICAL *a.*

1950 *Veterinary Bull.* XX. 278 The neuropathologic diagnosis of hog cholera. **1973** *Neurology* XXIII. 561/1 Neuropathologic studies of 10 cases of Huntington's disease are known to us.

neuropathologist (niūᵊrǫpăþǫ·lǒdʒist). Also **neuro-pathologist.** [f. NEUROPATHOLOG(Y + -IST] = NEUROPATHIST.

1876 VAN DUYN & SEGUIN tr. *Wagner's Man. Gen. Path.* I. 5 Physicians have distinguished themselves as humoralists or solidists. Among solidists the neuropathologists and cellular pathologists must be separately designated. **1903** *Proc. Soc. Psychical Res.* XVIII. 23 Conservatives in anthropologic science will immediately say that Myers used the concept of the 'subliminal' far too broadly, and that the only safe demarcation of the term is that of the neuro-pathologists. **1932** M. BIELSCHOWSKY in W. Penfield *Cytol. & Cellular Path. Nervous Syst.* I. iv. 147 In his method of study the neuropathologist must amalgamate investigation of localization together with investigation of the pathological process. **1973** *Neurology* XXIII. 561/1 The striking clinical disparity between the manifestations of Huntington's chorea in children and those in adults is a challenge to the physiologist and neuropathologist.

neuropil (niūᵊ·rǫpil). *Neurology.* Also **neuropile** (-pəil). [prob. a shortening of next: cf. PILE *sb.*[5]] **a.** A network of interwoven unmyelinated nerve fibres and their branches and synapses; hence, esp. in organisms with simple nervous systems, a structure composed of, or a region in which is concentrated, such a network. **b.** *rare.* An ultimate branch of a nerve fibre.

1899 L. F. BARKER *Nervous System* xxiii. 271 This investigator..isolated the neuropil of the second antenna of Carcinus—in other words, he removed the ganglion cells of the neurones supplying the antenna, but left their processes and side branches. **1900** tr. A. Bethe in J. Loeb *Compar. Physiol. Brain* iii. 45 It was easy to decide this question by separating the ganglion-cells with their axis-cylinder process from the motor neurons without injuring the neuropiles. **1934** *Jrnl. Compar. Neurol.* LIX. 95 In some parts of the [amphibian] brain much branched and contorted unmyelinated axons form a dense entanglement which is termed neuropil. **1941** JOHANNSEN & BUTT *Embryol. Insects & Myriapods* ii. 21 The neuropile (Punctsubstanz, fibrillar substance, nerve fibers) develops in the ganglia in the older stages. **1953** *Nature* 29 Aug. 405/1 The neurohæmal organs of the heart ligaments [in higher Crustacea] are..neuropiles. **1964** R. M. & J. W. FOX *Introd. Compar. Entomol.* vi. 179 A ganglion..has a central mass of medullary tissue (neuropile) consisting of the intermixed axons and dendrons of motor and internuncial neurons and the terminal arborizations of sensory dendrons. **1974** *Sci. Amer.* Jan. 41/1 In addition to the major branches running through roots and connectives there are many such processes within the neuropil, the region in the center of the ganglion where synaptic connections are made. **1974** *Nature* 4 Oct. 428/1 The ganglia..have a central fibrous neuropile containing most of the synapses.

†neuropilema (niūᵊrǫpəilī·mă). *Obs.* Also **neuropilem.** [ad. G. *neuropilem* (W. His 1890, in *Arch. f. Entwickelungsges.* (*Anat. Abth.*) Suppl. 113), f. Gr. νεῦρο-ν nerve + πῖλημα felt.] = *NEUROPIL a.

1891 *Brain* XIV. 568 Nerve-felt, neuro-pilema, *His.* **1900** A. HILL tr. *Obersteiner's Anat. Cent. Nervous Organs* (ed. 2) iii. 156 The last and finest ramifications of the cell-processes, collaterals and arborescent systems alike, are closely interwoven in the grey substance, forming not so much a network as a felt-work, the neuropilema or neurospongium. **1900** *Jrnl. Nerv. & Mental Dis.* XXVII. 476 He [*sc.* Waldeyer] acknowledges that his ideas of the mode of conduction are based on the view that no anastomosing nerve networks occur, but only a nerve feltwork (neuropilema, His). **1902** BALDWIN *Dict. Philos. & Psychol.* II. 175/2 *Neuropilem,* a meshwork of nervous arborizations forming a system of intercommunication between various neurocytes. **1929** C. U. A. KAPPERS *Evolution Nervous Syst. Invertebr., Vertebr. & Man* 43 In the higher Molluscs..they are arranged peripherally to the neuropilema as in Annelids.

neuropsychiatry (niūᵊrosəikəi·ătri). *Med.* [f. NEURO- + PSYCHIATRY.] Psychiatry which relates mental or emotional disturbance to disordered brain function; neurology and psychiatry as a single discipline.

1918 M. W. BROWN (*title*) Neuropsychiatry and the war. **1945** *Times* 11 Jan. 2/4 Smith was examined by Major Thomas March, chief of the section of neuropsychiatry at a United States service hospital. **1955** *Psychiatric Q.* XXIX. 392 The brain has been enthroned once again as the organ of thought, and a new era of neuropsychiatry is about to unfold. **1971** *New Scientist* 5 Aug. 335/1 This careful and scholarly investigation is of great help to the understanding of this difficult aspect of neuropsychiatry; it also..stresses the necessity of close cooperation between paediatricians, neurologists, and psychologists.

So **neu:ropsychia·tric** *a.*; **neuropsychi·atrist,** an expert or specialist in neuropsychiatry.

1918 M. W. BROWN *Neuropsychiatry & the War* 113 A plea..for the establishment also of medico-legal centers to collaborate with the medical and neuro-psychiatric centers. **1922** *N.Y. State Jrnl. Med.* XXII. 512/2 The neuropsychiatrist..has to deal with the structure and functions in health and in disease of the most highly organized part of man, namely the multi-neuronic integrate known as the nervous system. **1952** *Sun* (Baltimore) 28 Feb. 11/3 The neuropsychiatrist conducts his interviews in an office apart from the hospital buildings. **1953** *A.M.A. Arch. Neurol. & Psychiatry* LXX. 428 (*heading*) Neuropsychiatric aspects of infantile eczema. **1971** *New Scientist* 5 Aug. 335/1 For anyone who has struggled with the diagnosis of mild conditions in psychologically affected children *A Neuropsychiatric Study in Childhood* comes as very welcome help.

neuropsychology (niūᵊrosəikǫ·lǒdʒi). *Med.* [f. NEURO- + PSYCHOLOGY.] The field of study concerned with the relationship between behaviour and the mind on the one hand, and the nervous system, esp. the brain, on the other; neurological psychology.

1893 DUNGLISON *Dict. Med. Sci.* (ed. 21) 751/1 *Neuropsychology,* neurology including psychology. **1955** *Sci. Amer.* 72/2 Neuropsychology is Lashley's specialty, and.. its studies of cerebral function and neurological structure have been conducted under his personal direction. **1963** *Neuropsychologia* I. 1 Under the term 'neuropsychology', we have in mind a particular area of neurology of common interest to neurologists, psychiatrists, psychologists, and neurophysiologists. This interest is focused mainly..on the cerebral cortex. Among topics of particular concern to us are disorders of language, perception and action. **1964** R. L. ISAACSON *Basic Readings Neuropsychol.* p. vii, Since the work of Lashley, neuropsychology has become a major branch of physiological psychology. **1973** *Daily Tel.* 23 Aug. 7/1 A high degree of specialisation by each of man's 'two brains'—the cerebral hemispheres—have [*sic*] been shown by recent work in neuro-psychology.

So **neu:ropsycholo·gical** *a.*; **neuropsycho·logist,** an expert or specialist in neuropsychology.

The mod. use appears to be independent of quots. 1851, where the meaning is rather less specific.

1851 T. LAYCOCK tr. *Unzer's Princ. Physiol.* p. ii, The neuro-psychological essays he inserted in it are frequently referred to in the present work. *Ibid.* p. vi, Sylvius.. followed Descartes, while Willis was influenced..by the doctrines of Paracelsus. There was, however, yet another neuro-psychologist. **1949** D. O. HEBB (*title*) Organization of behavior: a neuropsychological theory. **1970** *Sci. Amer.* Mar. 67/3 Of the various lesions in the second block of the brain those in the tertiary zones are particularly interesting to us as neuropsychologists. *Ibid.* 72/3 The neuropsychological approach provides a valuable means of dissecting mental processes as well as diagnosing illness. **1973** B. HAIGH tr. *Luria's Working Brain* 12 The author.. attempts to fit the facts obtained by neuropsychological studies of individual brain systems into their appropriate place in the grand design of psychological science. **1974** *Nature* 31 May 495/1 Thus was born the 'frontal lobe syndrome', the study of which in modern times owes much to the Russian neuro-psychologist Alexander Luria.

neurotic, *a.* Add: **3. b.** Characteristic of a neurosis or a neurotic. Also *fig.*

1918 A. A. BRILL tr. *Freud's Totem & Taboo* iii. 143 Neurotics live in a special world in which..only the 'neurotic standard of currency' counts. **1948** L. MACNEICE *Holes in Sky* 31 The taut-necked donkey's neurotic-asthmatic-erotic lamenting. **1972** *Newsweek* 10 Jan. 3/1 The Nixon Administration has blundered again—having become enslaved by its neurotic emphasis on seeking re-election in '72 at all costs. **1975** M. BABSON *There must be Some Mistake* xix. 161 My husband simply disappears.. and I was foolish enough to get upset about it. Neurotic of me, wasn't it?

neurotically (niurǫ·tikăli), *adv.* [f. NEUROTIC *a.* + -AL + -LY[2].] In a neurotic manner; as the result of a nervous disorder. Also *fig.*

1890 W. JAMES *Princ. Psychol.* II. xxviii. 685 In many cases..the parental alcoholics are themselves degenerates neurotically. **1919** M. K. BRADBY *Psycho-Anal.* 78 Many..thrust their qualms into the unconscious and become neurotically deaf, blind or what not. **1924** R. GRAVES *Mock Beggar Hall* 21 A row of post-war villas, neurotically built, Standing each at different curious angles to the road. **1961** C. WILLOCK *Death in Covert* iii. 69 He had a dark, keen, neurotically intelligent face. **1972** *Daily Tel.* 20 Apr. 10/6 Christopher Dowson, who slides into a house-party uninvited.., yearns neurotically after an unchanging situation.

neuroticism (niurǫ·tisiz'm). [f. NEUROTIC *a.* + -ISM.] The condition or state of being neurotic; a tendency towards neurosis; esp. as a factor showing liability to neurosis included in certain types of personality assessment.

1900 *Daily Chron.* 5 June 4/5 The holiday season has been darkened by the reports of suicides which suggest.. the neuroticism of Paris. **1902** W. JAMES *Var. Relig. Exper.* i. 25, I think that I may let the matter of religion and neuroticism drop. **1922** *Glasgow Herald* 5 Oct. 5 The brilliant neuroticism of recent novels. **1952** H. J. EYSENCK *Sci. Study of Personality* ii. 58 We have extracted a general factor of 'neuroticism' from the intercorrelations of fifteen tests for normal and neurotic groups separately. **1957** P. LAFITTE *Person in Psychol.* iii. 34 Neuroticism and psychoticism are defined with scrupulous statistical care in terms of factorial scores..: but neither is directly related to ordinary behaviour. **1959** *Times Lit. Suppl.* 31 July 445/1 Mr. Johnston is subtle and satisfying when he shows them needling one another into neuroticism. **1973** *Jrnl. Genetic Psychol.* CXXII. 197 Iranian female subjects had scored higher than their male counterparts on neuroticism but lower on both extraversion and psychoticism.

neu·rotransmi:tter. *Physiol.* [f. NEURO- + TRANSMITTER.] A substance which is released at the end of a nerve fibre by the arrival of a nerve impulse and, by diffusing across the synapse or junction, effects the transfer of the impulse to another nerve fibre, a muscle fibre, or some other receptor.

1961 *Lancet* 2 Sept. 530/1 In these sections appears much of the most recent work on the metabolic as well as the neurotransmitter actions of these amines. **1965** LEE & KNOWLES *Animal Hormones* ix. 123 Acetylcholine is also released in the ganglia of the autonomic nerves and at the endings of the parasympathetic nerves, acting as a neurotransmitter substance. **1971** *New Scientist* 17 June 669/1 The neurotransmitter serotonin stimuiates salivation in the salivary gland of the housefly. **1974** *Sci. Amer.* June 59/1 Neurotransmitters make the heart beat faster or slower and make muscles contract or relax. They cause glands to synthesize hormone-producing enzymes or to secrete hormones.

So **neurotransmi·ssion,** the transmission of nerve impulses.

1961 *Harvey Lect.* LV. 43 (*heading*) Neurotransmission in the adrenergic nervous system. **1973** *Nature* 15 June 426/1 Reviews on biochemical aspects of neurotransmission.

neurotrophic (niūᵉrotrōᵘ·fik, -trǫ·fik), *a.* [f. NEURO- + *-TROPHIC.] Of or pertaining to the control of cells exerted by nervous tissue, esp. in relation to cellular nutrition.

1887 T. W. MILLS in *Med. Record* 22 Oct. 529/2, I propose..to substitute for mechanical explanations as applied to cardiac pathology, neuro-trophic ones. **1899** [in Dict. s.v. NEURO-]. **1935** *Amer. Jrnl. Cancer* XXIV. 416 Every epithelial cell is normally under constant neurotrophic control. **1970** *Nature* 28 Feb. 824 (*heading*) Neurotrophic control of protein synthesis in the regenerating limb of the newt, *Triturus. Ibid.,* We have examined the chemical nature of the neurotrophic action in a system which is clearly nerve-dependent, the regenerating salamander limb.

neurotropic (niūᵊrotrōᵘ·pik, -trǫ·pik), *a.* [f. NEURO- + *-TROPIC.] **1.** *Path.* Tending to attack or affect the nervous system preferentially.

1903 *Buck's Handbk. Med. Sci.* (ed. 2) VI. 270/2 Thus the poisons which have at the same time neurotropic and lipotropic effects..will have a much more marked influence upon the nervous system in an emaciated animal than in one which is very fat. **1922** *Med. Jrnl. Australia* II. 261/2 Vaccinia is the least neurotropic, while poliomyelitis is the most exclusively neurotropic. **1933** *Amer. Jrnl. Cancer* XIX. 648 Thus the tumor employed is not neurotropic. **1939** *Lancet* 4 Mar. 497/1 (*heading*) A neurotropic strain of human influenza virus. **1961** R. D. BAKER *Essent. Path.* viii. 136 Venoms of snakes are hemolytic or neurotropic. **1973** *Nature* 26 Jan. 247/1 The MV strain of [poliomyelitis] virus..was then shown to be so adapted to monkey brain passage and so neurotropic that it would no longer grow in cells from other organs.

2. *Anat.* Of or pertaining to the control or regulation of nerves, esp. in relation to their growth and regeneration.

1912 *Jrnl. Nerv. & Mental Dis.* XXXIX. 774 Is the comparative incapacity of the nervous system to regenerate due to some incapacity of the mechanical obstacles, absence of preestablished routes, or to some peculiar defect in the Schwann cells, the chief if not the only elaborators of neurotrophic [*sic*] material? **1928** R. M. MAY tr. *Ramón y Cajal's Degeneration & Regeneration Nervous Syst.* I. 374 Several neurotropic currents may act simultaneously on the same cone of growth. *Ibid.,* This fact bears out the view that the neurotropic material is an enzyme segregated by the living cells, instead of a product of the decomposition or

disintegration of the nervous tissue. **1968** A. F. W. Hughes *Aspects Neural Ontogeny* i. 33 For Ramon y Cajal the association of a regenerating fibre with the bands of Büngner was an instance of neurotropic attraction. **1968** S. Sunderland *Nerves & Nerve Injuries* xxxii. 405 Whether or not the tissues of the distal stump exert a neurotropic influence on the regenerating process..is still unsettled.

neurotropism (niūᵊrotrōᵘ·piz'm, niūᵊrǫ·trǭpiz'm). [ad. G. *neurotropismus* (J. Forssman 1900, in *Beiträge z. path. Anat. u. z. allgem. Path.* XXVII. 408): see *NEUROTROPIC *a.* and -ISM.] **1.** *Anat.* The supposed attraction (or repulsion) exerted by one mass of nervous (or other) tissue upon another mass of nervous tissue which is in the process of growing or regenerating.

1905 Gould *Dict. New Med. Terms* 380/1 *Neurotropism*, the attraction or repulsion exercised upon regenerating nerve-fibers. A substance is said to have positive neurotropism when these regenerating nerve fibers have a tendency to grow toward and into it. **1912** *Jrnl. Nerv. & Mental Dis.* XXXIX. 774 (*heading*) Influence of neurotropism on regeneration. **1955** B. H. Willier et al. *Analysis of Devel.* VII. i. 356/2 Such 'distance action', commonly referred to as 'neurotropism' and assumed to be a form of either galvanotropism or chemotropism, has been invoked to explain oriented nerve growth in the embryo.., as well as during later nerve regeneration. **1968** A. F. W. Hughes *Aspects Neural Ontogeny* i. 34 The two principles which have been proposed as forces which direct the growing nerve fibre, the 'contact-guidance' of Weiss.., and the neurotropism of Ramon y Cajal, both rest on inference from the behaviour of growing fibres under various circumstances, and at present on nothing more.

2. *Path.* The tendency of a virus or other pathological agent to attack the nervous system preferentially.

1911 Stedman *Med. Dict.* 585/2 *Neurotropism*, the attraction of certain pathogenic microorganisms, poisons, and nutritive substances, toward the nerve-centers. **1925** *Jrnl. Exper. Med.* XLII. 523 His theories of dermotropism and neurotropism of viruses. **1933** *Amer. Jrnl. Cancer* XIX. 647 (*heading*) Neurotropism of neoplasms in the mouse. **1940** *Nature* 2 Nov. 596/1 A curious characteristic of the yellow fever virus..is its manifestation of two types of virulence, namely, 'viscerotropism', meaning that it attacks such viscera as the liver, kidneys and heart, and 'neurotropism', meaning that it damages the nervous system. **1959** *New Scientist* 19 Mar. 620/1 Sabin himself admits that there is some return of virulence—neurotropism he calls it, the power to cause paralysis.

neurula (niū̆ᵊ·rŭlă). *Embryol.* Pl. **neurulæ**. [mod.L., f. Neur- + *-ula*, as in *BLASTULA, GASTRULA.] An embryo at the time when it is developing a neural tube from the neural plate. So **neurula·tion**, the formation of a neurula.

1888 *Amer. Naturalist* XXII. 470 The neurulation is normal. **1909** *Cent. Dict.* Suppl., Neurula. **1926** J. S. Huxley *Essays Popular Sci.* xviii. 259 The late gastrula or neurula is bisected as a whole. **1973** *Nature* 2 Mar. 55/2 In amphibian neurulae following initial removal of much of the totipotent blastula, abnormally few cells create a whole pattern. *Ibid.* 56/2 Gastrulation and neurulation movements are unaffected by mitomycin C.

neuston (niū·stǫn). [a. G. *neuston* (E. Naumann 1917, in *Biol. Zentralbl.* XXXVII. 99), f. Gr. νευστόν neuter of νευστός swimming, f. νεῖν to swim, after *plankton*.] A collective term for minute organisms inhabiting the surface layer of fresh water. Also *attrib.*

1928 K. E. Carpenter *Life in Inland Waters* ii. 35 Neuston.—This term, applied..especially to minute forms, such as bacteria and Protista, which float against the surface-film, may be extended to include all types especially associated with the film. **1939** *Nature* 28 Jan. 139/1 It [*sc.* the book under review] divides the plankton into plankton proper and the so-called 'neuston'—a term new to us—which means the organisms the peculiar province of which is the surface-film. **1957** G. E. Hutchinson *Treat. Limnol.* I. vi. 418 The organisms may be associated with the surface film and the resultant coloration should then be termed *neuston color* rather than section color. **1968** *New Scientist* 26 Sept. 669/2 Neuston are the organisms which live in the surface layer of [*sic*] film of water. **1974** A. Mayr-Harting tr. *Rheinheimer's Aquatic Microbiology* iii. 31 In the neuston—that is, the living community which develops during calm weather on the surface of lakes at the water-air interface—a characteristic microflora develops. **1974** *Nature* 4 Jan. 30/2 Thirty-seven surface tows were made with a neuston net to collect particulate pollutants quantitatively.

Neustrian (niū̆·striăn), *sb.* and *a.* [f. med.L. *Neustria* + -AN.] **A.** *sb.* A native or inhabitant of Neustria, the western part of the Frankish empire in the Merovingian period. **B.** *adj.* Of or pertaining to Neustria or its inhabitants.

1794 W. Beckford *Hist. France* I. vi. 104 The Austrasians..assisted by the Neustrians..drove him from the throne, and raised Childeric..to the sovereignty. **1874** [see *AUSTRASIAN *a.* and *sb.*]. **1918** A. Hassall *France Mediaeval & Modern* i. 6 In spite of the efforts of Ebroin, the Neustrian Mayor,..the tendency of Austrasia and Burgundy towards independence was too strong to be resisted. **1924** *Public Opinion* 27 June 618/2 The descendants of the Neustrian Franks now garrison the conquered Rhineland. **1927** O. M. Dalton *Gregory of Tours's Hist. of Franks* I. II. ii. 165 We are told that Charles addressed his Neustrians in 'Roman'. *Ibid.* 168 The Neustrian army of Charles was harangued in the Latin vulgar tongue. **1951** B. & R. North tr. *Martin's Making of France* iv. 37 Aquitanians fought with Neustrians, and Austrasians with Burgundians in battles in which the unity of Roman Gaul was undone. **1968** *Encycl. Brit.* XVI. 302/1 In the later Merovingian period the names Neustria and Francia were used interchangeably by Neustrian writers to designate the kingdom of which they were subjects, thus betraying their conviction that Neustria formed the heart and core of the Frankish lands. **1975** F. Heer *Charlemagne & his World* i. 16 After Ebroin was murdered..Pepin defeated the Neustrians in battle. He crushed Neustria as an independent state by confiscating the lands of the great Neustrian magnates and rewarding his own followers with them.

neutral, *a.* and *sb.* Add: **A.** *adj.* **2. c.** *neutral corner*: (see quot. 1954).

1952 *Amateur Boxing* ('Know the Game' Series) 29 When a boxer is 'down', his opponent must immediately retire to the farther neutral corner where he shall remain until ordered to resume boxing by the Referee. **1954** F. C. Avis *Boxing Reference Dict.* 89 *Neutral Corners*, the two corners of the ring not occupied, between the rounds, by the boxers and their seconds.

3. c. *neutral tint* (see also quot. 1911). Also *neutral orange* (see quots. 1934 and 1969).

1835 G. Field *Chromatography* xx. 170 Several mixed pigments of the class of gray colours are sold under the name of Payne's gray, neutral tint, &c. **1869** T. W. Salter *Field's Chromatogr.* (new ed.) xi. 253 Neutral orange or Penley's Neutral Orange, is a permanent compound pigment composed of yellow ochre and the russet-marrone known as brown madder. **1911** M. Toch *Materials for Permanent Painting* xiv. 145 Neutral tint..is a complex mixture of ultramarine, sienna, lamp black or ochre and lamp black, and..is an excellent color which is perfectly permanent. *Ibid.*, Neutral orange..has many of the characteristics of mars orange, but sometimes is made by mixing a brilliant yellow, free from lead, with a bright oxide of iron. **1924** F. W. Weber *Artists' Pigments* 98 Payne's Gray, like Neutral Tint, is prepared by various color manufacturers. **1934** H. Hiler *Notes on Technique Painting* ii. 113 Neutral orange, Penley's orange, a mixture of cadmium yellow with Venetian red. It is only used in water colour. **1969** R. Mayer *Dict. Art Terms & Techniques* 262/1 *Neutral orange*, a prepared artists' color made of mixed pigments. The best grades would contain cadmium orange or deep cadmium yellow and light red.

e. *Phonetics.* Of the central, usu. unstressed, vowel sounds [ə] and [ɨ], produced with the tongue in a rest position and having indefinite quality.

1891 L. Soames *Introd. Phonetics* I. iii. 50 The obscure vowel 'a' in attend.., sometimes called the *natural* or the *neutral vowel*. **1948** J. R. Firth *Papers in Ling. 1934–51* (1957) ix. 131 The weak, neutral, or 'minimal' vowel... The term neutral suits it in English, since it is in fact neutral to the phonematic system of vowels in southern English. **1956** D. Abercrombie *Problems & Principles* iii. 33 The ubiquitous English 'neutral' vowel ə. **1965** W. S. Allen *Vox Latina* 4 The so-called 'neutral' vowel of standard southern British English, as at the end of *sofa*. **1972** R. A. Palmatier *Gloss. Eng. Transformational Gram.* 103 *Neutral vowel*, .. the mid central vowel 'schwa' [ə]—or the high central vowel 'barred i' [ɨ]—to which insufficiently stressed vowels are reduced.

f. *Philos.* Belonging neither to the mental nor to the physical; esp. as *neutral monism*, the theory that there is but one substance of existence of which mind and matter are varying arrangements. So *neutral monist*.

1904 W. James in *Jrnl. Philos., Psychol. & Sci. Methods* 1 Sept. 487 Matter we know, and thought we know, and conscious content we know, but neutral and simple 'pure experience' is something we know not at all. **1912** R. B. Perry *Present Philos. Tendencies* II. iv. 79 It is evident that Mach's view can only mean a reduction of both the physical and the mental order to a manifold of neutral elements. **1914** B. Russell in *Monist* XXIV. Apr. 161 'Neutral monism'—as opposed to idealistic monism and materialistic monism. *Ibid.* 171 Neutral monists..infer that the mental and the physical are composed of the same 'stuff'. **1920** S. Alexander *Space, Time & Deity* II III. viii. 216 Nor are we free to suppose that there is a neutral non-mental world containing illusions amongst other neutral objects, neither mental nor physical. **1925** C. D. Broad *Mind & its Place in Nature* iii. 133 It might be so on a Double-Aspect theory, or on a theory of Neutral Monism. **1944** J. E. Boodin in P. A. Schilpp *Philos. B. Russell* xv. 495 It seems to me that Russell's neutral monism is an illusion. Our sensory awareness—'sensation' as Russell calls it—is real. But it is not identical with a mathematical equation. **1973** A. Quinton *Nature of Things* III. 237 There is the kind of phenomenalistic or neutral monist theory intimated by Hume and Mill. *Ibid.* xi. 318 Minds, for the neutral monist, are literally composed of impressions.

4. f. Electr. Engin. *neutral point*, the point in an electrical system which has the same potential that the junction of equal resistances would have if they were connected at their other ends to the lines making up the system; (see also sense 4 c in Dict.); *neutral wire*, a wire connected to a neutral point (and usu. also to earth).

1896 R. Robb *Electr. Wiring* iii. 44 The taps are taken off from the neutral wire and either of the other two in such a way that the loads on the two sides of the system will balance as nearly as possible. **1907** J. F. C. Snell *Distribution Electr. Energy* 19 A usual practice is to require the middle of the star, or neutral point, to be earthed. **1930** *Engineering* 7 Mar. 321/3 The necessary apparatus for earthing the neutral point of a three-phase system. **1962** *Newnes Conc. Encycl. Electr. Engin.* 543/1 If no neutral point on a system is earthed and one of the line conductors becomes accidentally earthed, the other two line conductors will immediately assume line voltage to earth and the neutral will assume the line-to-neutral voltage. **1972** Smith & Hosie *Basic Electr. Engin. Sci.* ix. 238 The current in the neutral wire of a balanced 3-ph[ase], 4-wire star-connected system is zero and the conductor may be omitted.

g. *neutral-density* (Photogr.): applied to a filter that absorbs light of all wavelengths to the same extent and so causes no change in its colour.

1938 K. Henney *Color Photogr.* iii. 58 By the use of a neutral-density filter of the proper transmission, in addition to the colored separation filters, it is possible to lengthen the exposure of the green and the red filters. **1962** M. L. Haselgrove *Photographers' Dict.* 151 Mainly used in sensitometry and color work, a neutral density filter is sometimes resorted to in black and white photography when the camera is loaded with a film of very high speed. **1965** M. J. Langford *Basic Photogr.* xi. 195 Other, colourless, filters include neutral density (grey) filters for reducing image brightness without affecting colour reproduction.

6. Denoting various classes of dyes. **a.** Applied to various basic azine dyes: *neutral blue*, a brown crystalline compound, $C_{24}H_{20}N_3Cl$, which dyes cotton a dull blue but has poor fastness; *neutral red*, a dark green crystalline compound, $C_{15}H_{16}N_4.HCl$, which forms a red solution in water or alcohol and is used as an acid–base indicator and for staining granules and vacuoles in living cells; *neutral violet*, a dark green crystalline compound, $C_{22}H_{24}N_6.HCl$, which is occasionally used as a biological stain or an indicator.

1889 *Cent. Dict.* s.v. *blue*, Neutral blue. **1890** Thorpe *Dict. Appl. Chem.* I. 229/2 The commercial product [*sc.* toluene red], which contains a certain amount of impurities, is sold under the name of 'neutral red'... A similar product is..sold under the name of 'neutral violet'. **1905** Cain & Thorpe *Synthetic Dyestuffs* xviii. 133 The only other Eurhodine of importance is Neutral violet.., prepared by the oxidation of a mixture of *p*-amidodimethylaniline and *m*-phenylenediamine. *Ibid.* 140 Neutral blue..and its derivatives, Basle blue B..and Azine green GB..are important tannin cotton dyes. **1914** *Chem. Abstr.* VIII. 723 (*heading*) Neutral red as indicator in determination of the alkalinity of the serum. **1930** *Stain Technol.* V. 133 Dyes employed in the vital staining are:.. neutral red, neutral violet, fuchsin, [etc.]. **1950** *Proc. Linn. Soc.* CLXII. 69 He [*sc.* the French cytologist Paiat] saw there no net: on the contrary, he saw separate spheres, and these he called neutral red vacuoles, because he was accustomed to colour them in the living cell with neutral red. **1952** K. Venkataraman *Chem. Synthetic Dyes* II. xxv. 768 A further distinction has been made between Rosindulines..and *iso*Rosindulines, such as Neutral Blue,..in which the auxochrome is in the benzene part of the naphthophenazine nucleus. **1967** *Oceanogr. & Marine Biol.* V. 364 She ascertained the region of epithelial elongation using Neutral Red marks. **1971** E. Gurr *Synthetic Dyes* 110 Neutral violet is only occasionally used as a biological stain.

b. Applied to textile dyes which can be used directly in an approximately neutral dye-bath. So *neutral-dyeing* ppl. adj.

1892 Collin & Richardson tr. *Nietzki's Chem. Org. Dyestuffs* 14 The salts of certain azosulphonic acids may be termed neutral dyestuffs. They may be directly fixed on vegetable fibres. **1920** J. M. Matthews *Application of Dyestuffs* v. 156 A separate group of dyestuffs is frequently made of the eosin or phthalein dyes. This group includes certain of both the acid and basic dyes, which.. might be termed 'neutral' dyes... They are applied in neutral or slightly acid bath, and are largely used for the dyeing of silk. **1955** A. J. Hall *Handbk. Textile Dyeing & Printing* iii. 49 Acid wool dyes are sometimes divided into two groups, *viz.* acid dyeing and neutral dyeing. **1955** H. E. Woodward in H. A. Lubs *Chem. of Synthetic Dyes & Pigments* iii. 151 Many neutral-dyeing dyes are aggregated more than level-dyeing acid dyes. **1962** [see sense A. 6 c below].

c. *Histology.* [Introduced in this sense by P. Ehrlich 1880, in *Zeitschr. f. klin. Med.* I. 557.] Applied to biological stains or dyes precipitated on mixing an acid dye and a basic dye.

1893 *N.Y. Med. Jrnl.* LVII. 2/2 Other granules react only to basic, or still others only to neutral colors. **1925** H. J. Conn *Biol. Stains* viii. 86 Compound dyes of this sort are sometimes referred to as neutral dyes or neutral stains. This terminology, of course, does not indicate that they are neutral in reaction any more than do the corresponding terms acid and basic dyes. A dye chemist, in fact, uses the term neutral dye in an entirely different sense. **1958** J. R. Baker *Princ. Biol. Microtechnique* xiv. 263 The granules of polymorphonuclear leucocytes are coloured by both the components of the neutral dye, and that is why Ehrlich called them 'neutrophil'. He regarded the specific dyeing of these granules as an important property of the neutral dyes, not to be obtained without their use. **1962** E. Gurr *Staining Animal Tissues* 31 Neutral 'dyes' should not be confused with 'neutral' or compound stains. The latter are formed by chemical union between a basic and an acid dye.

B. *sb.* **4.** *Electr.* A neutral point or conductor (cf. *A. 4 f above).

1900 *Jrnl. Inst. Electr. Engin.* XXIX. 538 Each of these boards receives from the main generator board five cables, a pair of 'outers' for lighting, a similar pair for power, and a common neutral. **1930** H. P. SEELYE *Electr. Distribution Engin.* vi. 98 On many systems, the neutral of the primary circuit, whether or not it is brought out as a four-wire circuit, is grounded at the substation. **1973** [see *LIVE *a.* 4].

5. = *Idiom Neutral* (s.v. *IDIOM 5). Also *attrib.*

1907 W. J. CLARK *Internat. Lang.* II. v. 99 Members of the academy..carry on their business by means of circulars, drawn up, of course, in Neutral. **1922** A. L. GUÉRARD *Short Hist. Internat. Lang. Movement* II. vi. 137 International words were selected..and were altered only in order to conform to Neutral spelling. **1928** O. JESPERSEN *Internat. Lang.* I. 49 Occidental... It forms in that respect a continuation of Neutral and especially of Rosenberger's Reform–Neutral. **1947** H. JACOB *Planned Auxiliary Language* ii. 45 The most favoured systems [based on ethnic languages] were Esperanto, Neutral, Novlatin, and Universal.

6. A position of the driving and driven parts in a gear mechanism in which no power is transmitted. Also *fig.*

1912 G. HARRIS et al. *Audel's Answers on Automobiles* 442 With clutch still disengaged, the transmission lever is moved from neutral to first speed position. **1925** *Morris Owner* Jan. 1154/1 Don't lose your head and start the car in gear. Take things quietly, put the lever in neutral, [etc.]. **1926** 'J. J. CONNINGTON' *Death at Swaythling Court* xiii. 250 The Colonel slipped his gear into neutral. **1958** *Spectator* 22 Aug. 251/2 A time-waster filling the hours when the brain is in neutral. **1962** J. BRAINE *Life at Top* xix. 222 She turned the ignition key; the car jerked forward convulsively, then stopped. 'Put it in neutral, first.' **1971** R. DENTRY *Encounter at Kharmel* iii. 42 Pepper threw the gear stick into neutral, applied the handbrake firmly, switched off. **1973** 'D. JORDAN' *Nile Green* xxxv. 174 Sue's face went into neutral. **1975** T. ALLBEURY *Special Collection* xix. 132 The Special Collection [Operation] has been put into neutral by the Presidium.

neutralism. Add to def: *spec.* a policy of maintaining neutrality and attempting conciliation in conflicts between major world powers. (Further examples.)

1951 *Here & Now* (N.Z.) May 5/1 The second feature of French opinion which seems important today is..the anxiety to keep out of future wars and is summed up in the term 'neutralism'. **1955** *Times* 6 July 11/3 Russia might take a favourable view of some at least of Japan's requests in order to stimulate Japanese 'neutralism' and the adoption of a foreign policy less friendly to the western Powers. **1958** *Listener* 27 Nov. 864/2 The interests of the Arabs require the political neutralization of their countries. This should mean genuine neutrality, and not neutralism; that is, exacerbating and exploiting the rivalries of the great powers, for immediate political advantage. **1959** *Times* 26 Oct. 11/2 Neutralism differs from neutrality in that it is an attitude of mind in time of peace rather than a legal status in time of war. **1963** M. BRECHER *New States of Asia* iv. 112 *Neutralism* has in common with non-alignment an expressed desire to remain aloof from bloc conflict. But neutralism goes much further, for it involves a positive attitude towards bloc conflicts. A neutralist state assumes an obligation to help reduce tensions between blocs with a view to maintaining peace or bringing about peace, and more particularly to prevent the outbreak of war.

neutralist. (Further examples.)

1915 *Morning Post* 1 Feb. 8/6 A meeting of neutralists, held here to-day, was broken up by Republicans, who shouted 'Long live the war!' **1920** *Glasgow Herald* 26 May 9/2 The Neutralist elements..hate the very idea of celebrating Italy's entrance into the war. **1957** *Economist* 28 Dec. 1114/2 They have been supported by perhaps an equal number of pacifists, near-pacifists and neutralists. **1963** *Ann. Reg. 1962* 351 The congress called for the withdrawal of American influence from South Vietnam and the formation of a neutralist Government there. **1975** *Nature* 6 Feb. 482/2 Neutralists, however, are delighted to find that this molecule of a living fossil underwent changes at least as rapidly as the homologous molecules in highly-evolved species.

neutralistic (niū·trăli·stik), *a.* [f. NEUTRAL *a.* + -ISTIC.] Characterized by a neutral attitude.

1949 *Mind* LVIII. 57 The element in, for example, a sensation of blue..will be susceptible to Mr. Gallie's neutralistic analysis.

neutrality. Add: **4. a.** (Later example.)

1883 J. S. STALLYBRASS tr. *Grimm's Teutonic Mythol.* II. 883 Out of the Goth. fairguni's neutrality unfolded themselves both a male *Fiörgynn* and a female *Fiörgyn.*

neutralization. Add: **1. b.** (Earlier example.)

1817 COLERIDGE *Biog. Lit.* I. ii. 45 This is one instance among many of deception, by the telling the half of a fact, and omitting the other half, when it is from their mutual counteraction and neutralization, that the *whole* truth arises.

c. *Ophthalm.* Combination of a lens with one or more of known power, as a means of finding its power.

1897 J. THORINGTON *Retinoscopy* iv. 34 This movement, at such a point in neutralization, may give a hint as to the presence of astigmatism. **1946** DICKINSON & HALL *Contact Lenses* vii. 82 The lenses should be checked for accuracy of focus and curve. In the absence of a refractionometer, neutralization may be employed. **1974** JALIE & WRAY *Pract. Ophthalmic Lenses* 5 The measurement of the focal power of lenses can be done in many ways. Two main methods are used for ophthalmic lenses: (1) Neutralization. (2) Vertex power measuring instruments.

d. *Electronics.* The cancellation of internal feedback in an amplifier, etc. (see *NEUTRALIZE *v.* 3 c).

1923 *Wireless World* 21 Apr. 69/2 Neutralisation is secured provided coils L and L_1 are correctly coupled. **1943** F. E. TERMAN *Radio Engineers' Handbk.* v. 469 Cross neutralization is used with push-pull amplifiers... It can be thought of as a form of neutrodyne that takes advantage of the fact that the voltages on the two sides of a push-pull amplifier are of opposite polarity, thus giving the phase relations required for neutralizing. **1961** GRAY & GRAHAM *Radio Transmitters* iii. 64 Many systems of neutralization are based on forming a balanced bridge with the tube grid-to-plate capacity forming one of the arms of the bridge. **1962** SIMPSON & RICHARDS *Physical Princ. Junction Transistors* vii. 132 It is possible to determine the elements of an external feedback circuit which will accomplish the required neutralization. Since the transistor is thereby made into a one-way device, in which an input signal can influence the output but the reverse is not true, the compensation process is often called 'unilateralization'. **1968** [see *NEUTRALIZE *v.* 3 c].

3. *Linguistics.* The levelling out of certain phonemic or morphemic distinctions in particular contexts.

1942 C. F. HOCKETT in *Language* XVIII. 10 Any talk of neutralization or cancellation or archiphonemes confuses the facts without adding anything. **1947** K. L. PIKE *Phonemics* 243/2 *Neutralization of oppositions*, the occurrence in some environment of a segment phonetically similar to and mutually exclusive with two other contrasting segments. **1949** A. MARTINET *Phonology as Functional Phonetics* 7 Care should be taken not to mistake the non-appearance of a phoneme in a given position with a neutralization. **1962** *Amer. Speech* XXXVII. 69 Review of extant phonemic analyses of Modern Icelandic..and proposal of a third solution hinging on the Prague concept of neutralization. **1964** E. PALMER tr. *Martinet's Elem. General Linguistics* iii. 69 Where an archiphoneme is manifested there is said to be neutralization. **1968** *Language* XLIV. 475, I understand neutralization to mean the lack of consonance between form contrasts and function contrasts in all parts of a single linguistic sub-system. **1972** HARTMANN & STORK *Dict. Lang. & Ling.* 151 *Neutralisation*, the cancelling of a phonemic opposition in certain positions. **1973** *Word 1970* XXVI. 102 Morphological neutralization occurs in such examples as *alemães* and *alemãs* (both pronounced [the same]).

neutralize, *v.* Add: **3. b.** *Ophthalm.* To annul the refractive power of (a lens) by combination with one or more other lenses (of known power).

1902 TAYLOR & BAXTER *Key to Sight Testing* xxxvi. 243 A deep convex, if it could be made infinitely thin, would practically neutralize a concave of the same power. **1962** L. S. SASIENI *Optical Dispensing* (ed. 2) xv. 354 When plastic lenses have to be neutralized, the trial lenses should on no account be allowed to touch the outer surface. **1974** JALIE & WRAY *Pract. Ophthalmic Lenses* 8 It may be necessary for unknown lenses of high focal power to be neutralized by a combination of two neutralizing lenses.

c. *Electronics.* To cancel internal feedback in (an amplifier stage, valve, or transistor), esp. that due to interelectrode capacitance, by providing an additional external feedback voltage of equal magnitude but opposite phase.

1924 MOYER & WOSTREL *Pract. Radio* viii. 123 The adjustment of each neutralizing capacity is made by tuning to the radio current of some transmitting station, turning out the filament of the vacuum tube to be neutralized..and adjusting the capacity until all the sounds in the telephone receiver disappear. **1948** A. L. ALBERT *Radio Fund.* ix. 367 Triodes used in radio-frequency amplifiers must be neutralized, otherwise feedback from the plate to the grid through the interelectrode capacitance may cause oscillations. **1962** SIMPSON & RICHARDS *Physical Princ. Junction Transistors* vii. 132 We now consider a general determination of the circuit constants required to neutralize a *CB* or *CE* amplifying stage. **1968** ROMANOWITZ & PUCKETT *Introd. Electronics* x. 410 Push-pull circuits operating at high frequencies also require neutralization. They may be neutralized by a criss-cross connection of two capacitors, one from each tube plate, to the end of the input parallel circuit that is connected to the grid of the other tube.

5. In motor rallying, to exempt (a section of the course) from having to be covered at a set average speed, so that that section has no effect on the result of a race.

1902 *Encycl. Brit.* XXXI. 13/2 Deducting the Swiss portion of the route (which was neutralized), the distance was 615 miles. **1903** *Sci. Amer. Suppl.* 20 June 22958 A number of different villages were neutralized, and the chauffeurs were given from 5 to 25 minutes to make the passage. **1971** P. BROWNING *Rally Manual* vi. 54 My immediate reaction was to neutralize the frontier crossing—that is to say..disregard the time taken to pass between the two officials. **1972** H. S. VILLARD *Great Road Races 1894–1914* vi. 115 The Taunus Circuit took in eight neutralized control areas..and was eighty-seven miles in length.

neutralizing, *vbl. sb.* (Later examples, in sense *3 b of the vb.)

1902 TAYLOR & BAXTER *Key to Sight Testing* xxiii. 148 The lenses used for testing should not be used for neutralizing. **1962** L. S. SASIENI *Optical Dispensing* (ed. 2) xv. 355 The usual practice in neutralising is to hold the neutralising lens against the front surface of the spectacle lens and with the front surface towards the observer.

neutretto (niū̆tre·to). *Nuclear Physics.* [f. *NEUTR(INO + It. *-etto*, dim. suffix (see -ET).] † **a.** A neutral pion. *Obs.* **b.** A neutral particle having low rest-mass. *rare.*

1938 ARLEY & HEITLER in *Nature* 23 July 159/1 Neutrons would have a much smaller penetrating power and there is no process known by which neutrinos could produce heavy electrons in sufficiently large numbers. We therefore think that we have to deal in these experiments with the neutral counterpart of the heavy electron, for which we propose the name neutretto. *Ibid.*, A neutretto (denoted by Y°) can be transformed into a heavy electron, $Y^{\pm}$, during a collision with a proton (P) or neutron (N) and vice versa: $Y^{\circ} + N \rightleftarrows P + Y^{-}$ or $Y^{\circ} + P \rightleftarrows N + Y^{+}$. **1939** *Physical Rev.* LV. 24 These non-ionizing particles must be much more penetrating than photons. This high penetrating power suggests their identification with the neutrettos (neutral particles having mass and other properties similar to the barytron) postulated by Heitler. **1947** *Sci. News* IV. 123 A neutral meson is also expected to appear; the romantic name Neutretto is ready waiting for it. **1948** *Rev. Mod. Physics* XX. 550/1 If the neutral particle is a neutrino, the electron energy should be almost exactly one-half the rest energy of the meson, i.e., 50 Mev. If the neutral particle is considerably heavier than an electron (neutretto) the energy of the decay electron should be correspondingly smaller. **1952** R. E. MARSHAK *Meson Physics* vi. 208 If one is willing to consider the possibility of a new neutral decay particle of small rest mass (we shall call it a neutretto and denote it by μ°), then an alternative decay scheme would be $\mu^{\pm} \rightarrow e^{\pm} + \nu + \mu^{\circ}$. **1963** *New Scientist* 1 Aug. 255 The terms 'electron neutrino' and 'muon neutrino' respectively for 'neutrino' and 'neutretto' are probably more common at present in distinguishing these two particles.

neutrino (niutrī·no). *Nuclear Physics.* [a. It. *neutrino* (E. Fermi 1933, in *La Ricerca sci.* II. 491), f. *neutro* NEUTER *a.* and *sb.*, neutral + *-ino*, dim. suffix.] Either of two stable, uncharged leptons (associated respectively with the electron and the muon) which have zero or negligible mass and an extremely low probability of interaction with matter; also, the antiparticle of either of these, one of which is produced (along with an electron and a proton) in the beta decay of a neutron.

1934 *Sci. Abstr.* A. XXXVII. 383 A quantitative theory of the emission of β-rays is explained. This admits the existence of the 'neutrino', a new particle proposed by Pauli having no electric charge and mass of the order of magnitude of that of the electron or less. **1938** *Ann. Reg. 1937* 354 The neutrino was generally accepted as a useful working hypothesis, but at least one attempt was made to show that the beta-ray spectrum could be explained without assuming its existence. **1948** *Sci. News* VI. 79 Beta decay is very slow compared to the times taken by other nuclear reactions, and one must, therefore, expect the reverse process, i.e., the capture of a neutrino, also to be very rare. On the Fermi theory, a neutrino could indeed go very many times across the interior of the earth and still have practically no chance of hitting anything. **1956** *Time* 2 July 46/3 For 20 years nuclear physicists have used neutrinos (small, uncharged particles) in their calculations... But no known apparatus has ever detected neutrinos... Last week from the Atomic Energy Commission came big news. Neutrinos do exist. **1958** *New Scientist* 25 Dec. 1567/1 Pauli produced the sorely needed explanation for the variability of the energy of beta-particles thrown out by radioactive materials. He postulated the simultaneous emission of a ghost particle which carried away part of the energy but which had no charge and virtually no mass and so was not observable directly. The neutrino..has been fully vindicated and now occupies a position of great importance in contemporary theory. **1962** *Physical Rev. Lett.* IX. 36/1 The neutrinos we have used produce μ mesons but do not produce electrons, and hence are very likely different from the neutrinos involved in β decay. *Ibid.* 42/2 The most plausible explanation for the absence of electron showers..is then that $\nu_{\mu} \neq \nu_{e}$; i.e., that there are at least two types of neutrinos. This also resolves the problem raised by the forbiddenness of the $\mu^{+} \rightarrow e^{+} + \gamma$ decay. **1968** M. S. LIVINGSTONE *Particle Physics* iv. 74 The muon decays into an electron and two neutrinos: $\mu^{-} \rightarrow e^{-} + \bar{\nu}_{e} + \nu_{\mu}$. **1969** *Times* 20 Feb. 17/5 Neutrinos are emitted as by-products in a great many nuclear reactions. **1974** *McGraw-Hill Yearbk. Sci. & Technol.* 306/1 The neutrino is the only known particle that has only weak interactions. Thus, the neutrino is a unique tool in the study of the weak forces, since the interactions are free of the effects of the strong and the electromagnetic interactions, which are many orders of magnitude stronger. **1974** *Sci. Amer.* Dec. 115/1 At proton accelerators muon neutrinos are produced about 100 times more copiously than electron neutrinos.

neutro-. Add: **neutrope·nia** *Med.* [Gr. πενία poverty, need], the presence of an abnormally low concentration of neutrophils in the blood; hence **neutrope·nic** *a.*, suffering from neutropenia; **neutrophil**(**e** *a.*, add: [a. G. *neutrophil* (P. Ehrlich 1880, in *Zeitschr. f. klin. Med.* I. 558)], and substitute for def.: that can be stained with neutral dyes (*NEUTRAL *a.* and *sb.* A. 6 c); not strongly stained by acid or basic dyes; also as *sb.*, a neutrophil cell;

(further examples); so **neutrophi·lic** *a.*, neutrophil; of or pertaining to neutrophil cells.

1931 *Arch. Otolaryngol.* XIII. 864 The term agranulocytosis has come into the literature because of its brevity. The name is not strictly correct... At present, the name applied by Tuerk, 'malignant neutropenia', seems to be more appropriate. **1973** *Acta Haematol.* L. 223 Neutropenia early in haemodialysis is probably due to the return into the circulation of leucocytes damaged by the first contact with the dialyzing surface. **1961** WEBSTER, Neutropenic. **1963** *Federation Proc.* XXII. 671/1 (*heading*) Potentiation of arthus reactivity in neutropenic rabbits. **1973** *Jrnl. Infectious Dis.* CXXVIII. 248 Both normal and neutropenic mice were treated with gentamicin. **1893** *N.Y. Med. Jrnl.* LVII. 3/2 The neutrophile granules of the polynuclear cells are not stained by this solution. **1954** Neutrophil [see *DRUMSTICK 2 e]. **1973** *Daily Tel.* 2 Oct. 19/2 Neutrophil cells in a healthy person are usually six per cent. of the total number of white blood cells. *Ibid.*, A medical expert said last night: 'An increase of neutrophils to 12 per cent. in a two-year-old is a thoroughly satisfactory reaction to an ear infection.' **1893** *N.Y. Med. Jrnl.* LVII. 4/2 The uninuclear leucocyte does not show neutrophilic granulations. **1962** LUNTZ & WRIGHT in A. Pirie *Lens Metabolism Rel. Cataract* 321 Group A... These show mainly neutrophilic infiltration.

neutrodyne (niū·trodəin). *Radio.* [f. NEUTRO- (taken as repr. *neutralize*, *-ization*) + *-DYNE.] A type of high-frequency valve amplifier in which neutralization was first employed to prevent oscillation throughout a range of frequencies. Freq. *attrib.*

1923 *Wireless World* 21 Apr. 68/2 Professor L. A. Hazeltine has designed receivers in which the valve capacity coupling is neutralised. The capacity coupling is neutralised with the aid of fixed condensers, and the receivers are called by him 'Neutrodyne' receivers. **1924** *Mod. Wireless* II. 590/2 In the receivers to be described here, a fixed coupling is used between the anode coil and the neutrodyne coil. **1924** MOYER & WOSTREL *Pract. Radio* viii. 124 The neutrodyne works best on an antenna but may be used on a loop. **1936** R. S. GLASGOW *Princ. Radio Engin.* ix. 256 The neutrodyne circuit was used quite extensively in broadcast receiving sets prior to the general introduction of screen-grid tubes in 1929. **1943** [see *NEUTRALIZATION 1 d]. **1964** GHIRARDI & DINES *Radio & Television Receiver Circuitry* (rev. ed.) iii. 79 A modification of the famous Hazeltine 'neutrodyne' circuit is perhaps the most widely used in commercial receivers that employ triodes.

Hence **neu·trodyning** *vbl. sb.* and *ppl. a.*, neutralizing (see *NEUTRALIZE *v.* 3 c).

1924 *Mod. Wireless* II. 590/3 The reaction is controlled entirely by this neutrodyning condenser. **1926** R. W. HUTCHINSON *Wireless* 217 Several methods have been devised for the control of this oscillation; neutrodyning, as it is termed, is one of the best. **1943** C. L. BOLTZ *Basic Radio* xiv. 226 This [instability] was decreased by using condensers to provide negative feed-back to nullify the positive feed-back. These were called neutralizing condensers, and the process was one of neutralization or neutrodyning.

neutron (niū·trǫn). *Physics.* [f. NEUTRAL *a.* and *sb.* + *-ON[1].] An electrically uncharged sub-atomic particle whose mass (939·6 MeV) is very slightly greater than that of the proton, which can decay into a proton, an electron, and an antineutrino (as in beta decay), and which is a constituent (with the proton) of all atomic nuclei except that of the common isotope of hydrogen; it is now usu. regarded as a particular state of a nucleon.

Before its discovery in 1932 it was conceived as a close association of a proton and an electron. Rutherford (who communicated Glasson's 1921 paper to the Royal Society) discusses this concept in a paper of 1920 cited by Glasson, but without using the word *neutron*. Harkins (of Chicago) seems to have coined the term independently. (The use in quot. 1899 is unrelated to the current use.)

[**1899** W. SUTHERLAND in *Phil. Mag.* 5th Ser. XLVII. 273 If the electrons are distributed through the æther, we must suppose that in æther showing no electric charge each negative electron is united with a positive electron to form the analogue of a material molecule, which might conveniently be called a neutron.] **1921** W. D. HARKINS in *Ibid.* 6th Ser. XLII. 309 Any complex atom has a mass and weight 0·76 per cent. less than the hydrogen atoms (neutrons) from which it may be assumed to be built. *Ibid.* 315 The term neutron represents one proton plus one electron. **1921** J. L. GLASSON in *Ibid.* 597 In the ordinary atom of hydrogen we have a single electron separated from the nucleus by a distance of the order of 10^{-8} cm. It is here contemplated that a more intimate union of the two is possible... Such a particle, to which the name neutron has been given by Prof. Rutherford, would have novel and important properties. It would, for instance, greatly simplify our ideas as to how the nuclei of the heavy elements are built up. **1930** E. RUTHERFORD et al. *Radiations from Radio-Active Substances* xvii. 523 The existence of a neutron, i.e. a close combination of a proton and electron, has been suggested. **1932** J. CHADWICK in *Nature* 27 Feb. 312/1 (*heading*) Possible existence of a neutron. *Ibid.*, These results..are very difficult to explain on the assumption that the radiation from beryllium is a quantum radiation, if energy and momentum are to be conserved in the collisions. The difficulties disappear, however, if it be assumed that the radiation consists of particles of mass 1 and charge 0, or neutrons. The capture of the α-particle by the Be^9 nucleus may be supposed to result in the formation of a C^{12} nucleus and the emission of the neutron. **1938** R. W. LAWSON tr. *Hevesy & Paneth's Man. Radioactivity* (ed. 2) ix. 94 We must regard these protons and neutrons as the ultimate constituents of the nuclei, and consider the α-particle as a kind of 'molecule' of the 'nuclear atoms' possessing especial stability, and arising from the union of 2 protons and 2 neutrons. **1950** GLASSTONE *Sourcebk. Atomic Energy* xi. 287 One of the most striking arguments for the wave-particle duality of matter..has been provided by the diffraction of neutrons. **1951** S. DUSHMAN *Fund. Atomic Physics* xiii. 227 The U-235 nucleus, in splitting, emits high-speed neutrons which may produce fission in other U-235 nuclei, thus initiating a chain reaction. **1968** M. S. LIVINGSTONE *Particle Physics* ii. 25 The nucleus could now be conceived as a closely packed assemblage of protons and neutrons, with the atomic charge number *Z* given by the number of protons and the atomic weight number *A* by the total of protons and neutrons. **1972** *Physics Bull.* June 349/1 Although it is comforting and often convenient to consider the proton and neutron as elementary particles with no internal substructure, they are in fact particles in a state of continual change... The neutron divides its time between being a neutron and a composite proton-negative pion system, while remaining electrically neutral. **1973** A. J. MACLEOD *Instrumental Methods Food Analysis* vii. 684 Isotopes of an element possess different numbers of neutrons in their nuclei, but are otherwise identical.

2. *attrib.* and *Comb.*, as *neutron absorption, bombardment, flux; neutron-absorbing* adj.; **neutron activation,** the process of making a substance radioactive by irradiating it with neutrons; freq. *attrib.*, esp. in *neutron activation analysis*, activation analysis in which this is employed; **neutron bomb,** a bomb that would produce large numbers of neutrons but little blast, and would consequently be harmful to life but not destructive of property; **neutron capture,** the absorption of a neutron by an atomic nucleus; **neutron chopper,** a device for converting a continuous beam of neutrons into a pulsed beam by passing it through a rotating slotted disc or cylinder; **neutron diffraction,** diffraction of a beam of neutrons; **neutron excess,** the excess of the number of neutrons in an atomic nucleus over the number of protons; **neutron number,** the mass number of a nucleus minus its atomic number, taken as being the number of neutrons it contains; **neutron radiography,** radiography in which the radiation employed is a beam of neutrons; **neutron star** *Astr.*, a hypothetical extremely dense kind of star composed predominantly of closely packed neutrons, which is believed to have a mass similar to that of the sun but a diameter of only a few kilometres; cf. *PULSAR; **neutron therapy,** radio-therapy in which the radiation employed is a beam of neutrons.

1947 *Physical Rev.* LXXII. 16 Introduction of a neutron-absorbing substance into a pile decreases the re-activity. **1964** M. GOWING *Britain & Atomic Energy* 29 The Paris group also worked out the idea of controlling the reaction by introducing neutron-absorbing material to limit the multiplication of neutrons. **1947** *Physical Rev.* LXXII. 16 (*heading*) Method for measuring neutron-absorption cross sections by the effect on the reactivity of a chain-reacting pile. **1951** *Analyst* LXXVI. 644 (*heading*) The estimation of tantalum in mixtures by neutron activation analysis. **1960** *Nature* 16 Jan. 196/2 (*heading*) Neutron activation analysis of ancient Roman potsherds. **1965** D. GIBBONS in Lenihan & Thomson *Activation Analysis* x. 68 Phosphorus and barium can be determined, rapidly and non-destructively, in lubricating oil in the range 0·01–1% and 0·05–2% using 14 MeV neutron activation and γ-ray spectrometry. **1966** *Encycl. Industr. Chem. Analysis* I. 52 With the high neutron flux of a nuclear reactor, neutron activation analysis (NAA) provides the most sensitive means of detection of low concentrations known today for most of the elements of the periodic system. A typical limit of detection is about one part per billion (ppb) in a 1-g sample. **1973** A. J. MACLEOD *Instrumental Methods Food Analysis* vii. 695 Of the three methods described for separation and analysis of the products of neutron activation, gamma ray spectrometry is by far the most common. **1960** *Congress. Rec.* 12 May 10138/3 Although there have been a few fragmentary references to the neutron bomb in the press, I was told.. that the matter was classified. **1962** L. DEIGHTON *Ipcress File* xxiv. 155, I guessed that it was a neutron bomb that they were about to explode. **1967** *New Scientist* 14 Sept. 534/1 Whenever the possibility of a neutron bomb was discussed in the late 'fifties and early 'sixties it was with particular reference to the military interest in the application of tactical nuclear firepower in a controlled and highly selective fashion. **1937** G. GAMOW *Struct. Atomic Nuclei* x. 193 These phenomena (of induced activity by neutron bombardment) were observed by Fermi for many very heavy elements also. **1964** M. GOWING *Britain & Atomic Energy* ii. 55 It was known that in some nuclei fission occurred spontaneously, without neutron bombardment. **1945** H. D. SMYTH *Gen. Acct. Devel. Atomic Energy Mil. Purposes* i. 17 [By 1940] neutron-capture cross-sections had been measured. **1959** *Listener* 19 Nov. 872/1 At slow or 'thermal' speeds neutron capture by nuclei of Uranium 238 is less important. **1966** PHILLIPS & WILLIAMS *Inorg. Chem.* II. xxxv. 635 Neutron-capture efficiencies are usually measured in terms of nuclear cross-sections, for which the whimsical unit the 'barn' has been devised. **1950** GLASSTONE *Sourcebk. Atomic Energy* xi. 306/2 Three main techniques have been developed for making measurements with neutrons of specific energies; these are the time-of-flight velocity selector..; the mechanical selector, sometimes referred to colloquially as a 'neutron chopper'..; and the crystal spectrometer. **1971** *New Scientist* 8 July 72/1 Another rotating component developed at Harwell has been the so-called 'neutron chopper'... When it rotates, the beam is chopped into pulses of neutrons of the same energy level. **1949** *Physical Rev.* LXXVI. 1256/2 (*heading*) Detection of antiferromagnetism by neutron diffraction. **1973** J. YARWOOD *Atomic & Nuclear Physics* xiii. 381 Whereas X-ray diffraction cannot readily lead to a knowledge of the positions of hydrogen atoms in a crystal because the scattering is dependent on the number of orbital electrons.., neutrons are strongly scattered by hydrogen nuclei. The technique of neutron diffraction therefore supplements that of X-ray diffraction. **1955** R. D. EVANS *Atomic Nucleus* iii. 99 (*N–Z*) is called..the 'neutron excess'. **1947** *Science* 9 May 491/1 Facilities will include..another pile with 100 times the neutron flux of the first. **1971** *Engineering* Apr. 34/2 The neutron flux reaching the sample is in excess of 10^7 neutrons cm^{-2} sec^{-1}. **1955** R. D. EVANS *Atomic Nucleus* iii. 99 Nuclei having the same neutron number are isotones. **1973** *McGraw-Hill Yearbk. Sci. & Technol.* 181/1 Theoretical calculations..have shown that the same r-process which synthesizes the actinides.. may also synthesize the predicted superheavy elements with atomic number $Z \sim 114$ and neutron number $N \sim 184$. **1948** H. KALLMANN in *Research* I. 254/1 The first successful experiments in neutron radiography are due to the author and his collaborator E. Kuhn, who in the years 1935–39 developed and partly tried out the fundamental methods of neutron radiography. **1962** *Sci. Amer.* Nov. 107/2 Neutron radiography has become practical with the advent of nuclear reactors and particle accelerators, which can provide a source of neutrons of the required intensity. **1971** *Engineering* Apr. 37/1 An advantage of using neutron radiography is the possibility of detecting small amounts of low density materials, within sections of high density materials such as lead or steel. **1934** BAADE & ZWICKY in *Physical Rev.* XLV. 138/2 We advance the view that supernovae represent the transitions from ordinary stars into neutron stars, which in their final stages consist of extremely closely packed neutrons. **1968** *New Scientist* 16 May 331/1 Neutron stars, if they exist, could have densities as much as ten million times higher even than a white dwarf. **1970** B. LOVELL in *Times* 19 Aug. 9/7 It is now generally accepted that the pulsars are the remnants of stars which have collapsed to form neutron stars. **1974** *Nature* 13 Sept 99/3 The neutron star represents the most extreme density of matter in the observable Universe (greater densities lead to unobservable black hole matter). **1947** *Radiology* XLVIII. 431/1 (*heading*) Possible progress in the radiotherapy of cancer (neutron therapy, Joliot therapy, alpha therapy, beta therapy..). **1974** *Nature* 25 Jan. 173/1 Because of Hammersmith Hospital's success in the use of neutron therapy for the treatment of cancer a second British hospital is to be supplied with a compact cyclotron. *Ibid.*, The effectiveness of neutron therapy depends on the ability of the neutrons to destroy cancer cells even in the absence of oxygen.

neutronic (niutrǫ·nik), *a. Physics.* [f. prec. + -IC.] Of, pertaining to, or employing neutrons.

1934 [see *ISOMER 2]. **1952** *Proc. Nat. Acad. Sci.* XXXVIII. 450 Particles which are heavy in the sense used here may be said to have unit neutronic charge. The neutronic charge should play the same role for the conservation law of heavy particles as the electric charge plays in the conservation law of electric charges. **1955** *Sci. News Let.* 28 May 349/1 Drs. Fermi and Szilard originally filed application for a patent on the 'neutronic reactor', on Dec. 19, 1944. **1958** *Times* 2 Jan. 2/4 Neutronic calculations on the steady state performance of thermal reactors. **1971** *Nature* 26 Nov. 217/2 If the reflecting box is expanding, all enclosed quantal systems will be decaying and emitting quanta of [*printed* on] all sorts of electromagnetic, electronic, neutronic and so on, waves.

névé. 1. (Earlier example.)

1843 J. D. FORBES *Travels through Alps of Savoy* 31 The part of a glacier covered with perpetual snow is what I understand to be meant by the term *névé* in the writings of the modern glacialists, although that term is vaguely defined.

never, *adv.* Add: **1. d.** (Further examples.)

1896 A. MORRISON *Child of Jago* xii. 120 'I never,' protested Dicky stoutly. **1926** A. BENNETT *Lord Raingo* II. lxxi. 322 She faintly annoyed him by her ingenuous exclamations: Oh my! Well, I never! Well I never did! *a* **1930** D. H. LAWRENCE *Phoenix II* (1968) 21 'I never, I never!!' he declared, more emphatically. **1939** L. M. MONTGOMERY *Anne of Ingleside* xxv. 171 'I've an idea Bruno has gone back there.' 'Six miles? He'd never!' said Jem. **1950** [see *INJUN b]. **1972** N. MARSH *Tied up in Tinsel* ii. 49 'A booby-trap.' 'I never!' Mervyn burst out. 'My God..I swear I never.' **1974** N. BENTLEY *Inside Information* xv. 151 'There's a fellow..got a gun—a pistol.' 'Never!'

e. With suppression of the personal pronoun as subject.

1874 HARDY *Far from Madding Crowd* I. vi. 76 Never heard the man's name in my life. **1968** *Listener* 7 Nov. 610/2 He said: 'Never heard of it.'

2. *never fear, never mind* (further examples); *to make* (or *pay*) *no nevermind* (U.S.), to make no difference; to pay no attention.

1795 tr. *C. P. Moritz's Trav.* 261, I do not recollect to have heard any expression repeated oftener than this *never mind it!* A porter..fell down, and cut his head.. 'O, never mind it!' said an Englishman who happened to be passing by. **1849** G. E. JEWSBURY *Sel. Lett. to Jane Welsh Carlyle* (1892) 344 Dear child, the solution will come to you, never fear. **1935** H. DAVIS *Honey in Horn* xvi. 264 That ain't no neverminds to me, though. **1946** MEZZROW & WOLFE *Really the Blues* (1957) xii. 225 He pays it no nevermind. **1968** *Guardian* 27 Dec. 8/1 We still have to adapt to Prime Ministers and Presidents, never mind astronauts, who have the essential quality of ordinariness. **1971** B. MALAMUD *Tenants* 177 Those are old books of his he wrote long ago, says Willie. Both been published. Then it makes no nevermind if we burn them.

3. c. *Never say die* (see quot. *a* 1865); also *attrib.*

***a* 1865** SMYTH *Sailor's Word-Bk.* (1867) 497 *Never say die*, an expressive phrase, meaning do not despair, there is hope yet. **1971** *Scope* (S. Afr.) 19 Mar. 10/2 Israel is a land that lives by the maxim: 'Never say die.' **1974** *Country Life* 5 Dec. 1717/2 The mental stamina, and the never-say-die spirit.

6. c. (Further examples.)

1917 E. WALLACE *Just Men of Cordova* ii. 32 One never-to-be-forgotten occasion. **1925** R. GRAVES *Welchman's Hose* 59 In the compilation Of their Grand Dictionnaire de la Langue Française, The full, the final, never-to-be-gainsaid. **1935** L. MACNEICE *Poems* 56 That never-to-be-touched Vision is your mistress.

7. a. *never-broken, -come, -conquered* (later example), *-contented, -dreamt, -ended* (earlier example), *-erased, -glutted, -lost, -quelled, -rebuked, -satisfied* (later example), *-tarnished, -tracked.*

1817 COLERIDGE *Biog. Lit.* II. xv. 16 A series and never broken chain of imagery. **1873** J. R. LOWELL *Cathedral* in *Poetical Wks.* 452/1 Never-broken secrecies of sky. **1892** W. B. YEATS *Let.* Nov. (1954) 218 The ever-coming never-come light of that ideal peace and freedom. **1951** L. MACNEICE tr. *Goethe's Faust* 235 Now even my army, I fear, must needs Obey the conquering, never-conquered woman. **1845** POE *Fairy-land* in *Raven & Other Poems* 86 Those butterflies, Of Earth, who seek the skies, And so come down again (Never-contented things!). **1951** L. MACNEICE tr. *Goethe's Faust* 302 Make to *this* good soul concession—Only once misled by pleasure To a never-dreamt transgression. **1855** D. G. ROSSETTI *Let.* 25 Nov. (1965) I. 282 One of his neverended stories was about an anonymous letter. **1855** W. WHITMAN *Leaves of Grass* 83, I see your rounded never-erased flow, I see neath the rims of your haggard and mean disguises. **1843** J. R. LOWELL *Prometheus* in *U.S. Mag. & Democratic Rev.* Aug. 149 This bitter peak, This never-glutted vulture, and these chains. **1957** A. MILLER *Coll. Plays* (1958) iv. 27 His terror springs from his never-lost awareness of time and place. **1860** W. WHITMAN *Leaves of Grass* 368 Those with a never-quell'd audacity. **1950** D. GASCOYNE *Vagrant* 12 The serene, robust air as of never-rebuked gaiety. **1940** C. DAY LEWIS tr. *Virgil's Georgics* I. 16 That crop..Will answer at last the prayers of the never-satisfied Farmer. **1944** AUDEN *For Time Being* iii. 29 Present to the speculative eye an ever-shining, never-tarnished proof of her amazing unheard-of power to combine and happily contrast. **1848** J. R. LOWELL *Growth of Legend* in *Poems* 2nd Ser. 71 The lake's frore Sahara of never-tracked white.

b. *never-diminishing, -ebbing, -eldering, -hastening, -intermitting, -lifting, -moving, -pardoning, -rejecting, -sinking, -stopping.*

1898 'MARK TWAIN' *Man that Corrupted Hadleyburg* (1900) 326 The war of epithets crashes along with never-diminishing energy for a couple of hours. **1866** J. G. WHITTIER *Our Master* in *Tent on Beach* (1867) 143 Immortal Love, forever full, Forever flowing free, Forever shared, forever whole, A never-ebbing sea! **1876** G. M. HOPKINS *Wreck of Deutschland* xviii, in *Poems* (1967) 57 Tears; such a melting, a madrigal start! Never-eldering revel and river of youth, What can it be, this glee? **1950** W. DE LA MARE *Inward Companion* 13 With never-hastening feet Time pursues the Infinite. **1849** J. S. MILL in *Westm. Rev.* LI. 34 The immense majority are condemned..to a life of never-ending, never-intermitting toil. **1885** W. B. YEATS *Island of Statues* I. iii, in *Dublin Univ. Rev.* May 84/1 Where their sinewy might is strung In the never-lifting dark. **1913** J. MASEFIELD *Daffodil Fields* 24 The stars did house Their lights like lamps upon those never-moving boughs. **1923** R. GRAVES *Whipperginny* 54 This never-pardoning life we live May earn God's blackest punishment. **1849** J. R. LOWELL *Day in June* in *National Anti-Slavery Standard* 8 Mar. 162/1 O never-rejecting roof of blue. **1849** THOREAU *Week Concord Riv.* 244 The unwearied, never sinking shore. **1931** R. GRAVES *To Whom Else?* 9 What drew the legs along Was the never-stopping, And the senseless frightening Fate of being legs.

c. *never-anxious, -quiet.*

1889 W. B. YEATS *Wanderings of Oisin* I. 5 And always never-anxious sleep. **1913** J. MASEFIELD *Daffodil Fields* 2 The never-quiet joy of dancing daffodils.

8. never-fail, (*a*) a person who never fails (one); (*b*) an Australian grass, *Eragrostis setifolia*, used as pasture in areas of low rainfall; **never-was,** a person who has never been great, distinguished, useful, or the like; also **never-waser, -wozzer.**

1850 H. C. WATSON *Camp-Fires of Revolution* 188 Morgan's one of the never-fails. **1936** F. CLUNE *Roaming round Darling* xiii. 114 He has a marvellous collection of native grasses, nardoo, Mitchell, neverfail, and a dozen others. **1964** *Austral. Encycl.* IV. 367/1 *E[ragrostis] setifolia* ('never-fail') is a drought resistant species of the inland. **1967** *Coast to Coast 1965–66* 191, I had been riding through..the high grained heads of the grasses, the spinifex and the neverfail. **1911** J. C. LINCOLN *Cap'n Warren's Wards* xv. 238 One of 'em's a used-to-be, and the other's a never-was. **1923** 'B. M. BOWER' *Parowan Bonanza* i. 14 'Nope, I'm a never-was,' Bill retorted shamelessly. **1938** L. MACNEICE *I crossed Minch* I. iii. 36 You ninny, you, you automaton, You Never-Was, you As-Good-As-Gone! **1891** *Sportsman* 1 Apr. 2/6 He is one of the 'has beens' or else one of the 'never wasers', as Dan Rice, the circus man, always called ambitious counterfeits. **1915** A. S. NEILL *Dominie's Log* xiv. 155 The average married woman is a 'has been' in thought, while not a few are 'never wasers'. **1931** WODEHOUSE *Big Money* viii. 176 It's always been half-way between a may-be and a never-waser. **1974** *Economist* 9 Nov. 6/1 With respect, it is silly, on the strength of a typical remark of some anonymous Brussels diplomat, no doubt a strong advocate of the absurd procedure rules of the council of ministers, to describe them as 'has beens' or 'never wasers'. **1929** Neverwozzer [see *HAS-BEEN *sb.*].

9. (Further examples.)

1882 A. J. BOYD *Old Colonials* 202 My soliloquy ends with the inquiry, 'What on earth is to be done in this wretched Never-never country?' **1890** 'R. BOLDREWOOD' *Colonial Reformer* 174 But here it seems to be the Never-Never country, and no mistake. **1916** J. B. COOPER *Coo-oo-ee* iii. 39 He had not forgotten the palship that is often made between men tramping along the bush distances that cover the sunburnt tracks to the Never-Never. **1942** C. BARRETT *On Wallaby* iii. 43 Tim..owned a copper show in the Never Never country near the West Australian border. **1963** V. B. CRANLEY *27,000 Miles through Australia* v. 34 It was far beyond Yuendumu along the great desert traverse..back in the Never-Never, as they call those wastes. **1969** 'A. GARVE' *Boomerang* ii. 71 His intention was to enjoy this trip..not to 'do a perish' in the Never-Never.

b. *Never(-Never) Land*, an imaginary, illusory, or Utopian place; freq. with allusion to the ideal country in J. M. Barrie's *Peter Pan* (see quots. 1904 and 1908).

1900 *N.Y. Dramatic Mirror* 3 Nov. 16/1 At Wallack's on Tuesday evening Sarah Cowell Le Moyne supplemented The Greatest Thing in the World with the initial performance of The Moment of Death; or, The Never, Never Land, a drama in one act and three scenes, by Israel Zangwill. **1904** J. M. BARRIE *Peter Pan* (1928) I. 34 *Wendy.* Where do you live now? *Peter.* With the lost boys... They are the children who fall out of their prams when the nurse is looking the other way. If they are not claimed in seven days they are sent far away to the Never Land. **1907** *Canadian Mag.* XXIX. 135/1 But instead of the unreal *never-never-land*..the scene is dear old England. **1908** J. M. BARRIE *When Wendy grew Up* (1957) 17 Do they ever wish they were back in the Never Never Land? *Ibid.* 28 The dear Never Never Land. **1938** AUDEN & ISHERWOOD *On Frontier* I. i. 24 Dream of your never-never land, where the parks are covered with naked cow-like women, quite free. **1938** L. MACNEICE *Mod. Poetry* v. 80 William Morris..looking wanly..back to a medieval Never-Never Land. **1958** *Spectator* 8 Aug. 203/1 It was no longer the real India they wanted to escape to; it was the Never-Never Land of the East. **1961** *Times* 1 Nov. 13/1 This commercial never-never land. **1968** MRS. L. B. JOHNSON *White House Diary* 4 Apr. (1970) 647, I was back at the White House by 3 o'clock from my brief visit to that beautiful never-never land—Mrs. Merriweather Post's home. **1971** *Nature* 30 July 287/1 The result is that the report of the committee under Sir Frederick Dainton on the reorganization of civil research,..has disappeared into never-never land. **1975** *Times* 16 Oct. 13/8 Sending the hero and heroine at the end into an azure never-land that is clearly some distance from both Dorset and London.

c. *never-never* adj., *colloq.* (or *joc.*), denoting a system of paying for articles by periodic instalments over an extended period; = *hire-purchase*; also *ellipt.* as *sb.*, and as *never.*

1926 E. WALLACE *More Educated Evans* ii. 39 Her uncle ..drove a taxi which he..had purchased on the 'never never' system. You pay £80 down and more than you can afford for the rest of your life. **1939** 'N. SHUTE' *What Happened to Corbetts* viii. 261 We could have the radiogram... Even if we had to put it on the Never-Never. **1957** F. KING *Man on Rock* i. 7, I can't even afford to pay the never-never on a wireless. **1960** *News Chron.* 29 Apr. 6 Twenty per cent is a small deposit for hire purchase, and the most reputable 'never-never' firms have been asking that. **1967** M. PROCTER *Exercise Hoodwink* iii. 21 'I'm getting it on the never. Anybody can do that.' 'Not a new Rover.' **1973** J. WILSON *Truth or Dare* ii. 24 They've still not paid off their mortgage, you know, and I wouldn't mind betting that Rover of theirs is on the never-never.

d. *never-never* adj., unrealistic, unrealizable, imaginary. Also applied to a person who says 'never, never'.

1928 D. H. LAWRENCE *Lady Chatterley* xiv. 243 'So when you did get a woman who wanted you..you got a bit too much of a good thing.' 'Ay! Seems so! Yet even then I'd rather have her than the never-never ones.' **1950** [see *CLOUD-CUCKOO-LAND]. **1952** DYLAN THOMAS *Let.* 21 Nov. (1966) 384 A day's life in a small town in a never-never Wales. **1955** *Bull. Atomic Sci.* Jan. 36/2 Norman Thomas, who had the courage to deplore our never-never attitude to the recognition of Red China, did so with an acute sense of his own isolation. **1956** H. GOLD *Man who was not with It* (1965) xiii. 113 She predicted the never-never happiness of others. **1958** *Sunday Times* 16 Nov. 21/7 The atmosphere of some never-never hotel is certainly caught.

10. Colloq. phrases: *never a dull moment!*: see *MOMENT *sb.* 1 c; *never again!*, a phrase expressing emphatic refusal to repeat an experience, etc.

1873 HARDY *Pair of Blue Eyes* II. iv. 51 Thank you. But never again. **1901** ADE *Forty Modern Fables* 161 And everybody said, 'Never Again.' **1915** T. F. A. SMITH *Soul of Germany* 298 The oft-quoted phrase is applicable to the case: Never again!

never (ne·vəɹ), *sb. Naut. slang.* [f. the adv.] In phr. *to do a never*: to shirk; to loaf.

1946 J. IRVING *Royal Navalese* 121 *Never, to do a*, to dodge work. **1948** PARTRIDGE *Dict. Forces' Slang* 124 *Doing a never* means—in the Navy—shirking work. **1961** F. H. BURGESS *Dict. Sailing* 74 *Doing a Never*, loafing on a job.

never-fading, *a.* (Later example.)

1916 BLUNDEN *Pastorals* 32 Nor where the never-fading rainbow plays.

nevermore, *adv.* Add: **B.** as *sb.*

1951 KOESTLER *Age of Longing* II. v. 257 The evermore of desire and the nevermore of satiety. **1952** R. CAMPBELL tr. *Baudelaire's Poems* 50 It's by such charms the Nevermore Intoxicates us in the Now.

‖**Nevers** (nevę̄r). The name of a city in central France, used freq. *attrib.* to describe a type of deep blue-ground faience in the style of Italian majolica, made there from the latter part of the 16th century to the 18th.

1863 W. CHAFFERS *Marks Pott. & Porc.* 93 *Nevers*, fine Faïence, in the Italian style, decorated in colours, sometimes like Faenza ware; also in blue *en grisaille*, as well as in a deep blue ground of enamel with splashes or spots of white. **1900** F. LITCHFIELD *Pott. & Porc.* vii. 219 Specimens of Nevers are difficult to identify, owing to the similarity of their characteristics to those of the Rouen and other similar faiences. **1960** H. HAYWARD *Antique Coll.* 198/1 *Nevers faience*, the chief Nevers pottery was founded early in the 17th cent. by Italian potters... Nevers glass. **1960** R. G. HAGGAR *Conc. Encycl. Cont. Pott. & Porc.* 68/1 Nevers faience decorated with pseudo-oriental or oriental motifs in white, or white, yellow and orange. **1971** L. A. BOGER *Dict. World Pott. & Porc.* 241/2 The so-called Bleu Persan or Décor Persan was introduced during the second half of the 17th century and is probably the most important Nevers creation. **1972** *Times* 21 June 16/4 A charming seventeenth-century Nevers glass picture depicting Diana surprised by Actaeon.

neves (ne·vės). *Back-slang.* Also **nevis.** [Reversed form of 'seven'.] Seven years' hard labour.

1901 FARMER & HENLEY *Slang* V. 31/2 *Nevis*,..Seven. .. Nevis-stretch = seven year's hard. **1958** F. NORMAN *Bang to Rights* 22 Your f——ing lucky, I'm doing a bleeding neves.

nevus, var. NÆVUS (in Dict. and Suppl.).

nevvy, nevy, colloq. abbrevs. of NEPHEW.

1847 DICKENS *Dombey* (1848) xv. 149 'He might die a little sooner for the loss of—' 'Of his Nevy,' interposed the Captain. **1903** WODEHOUSE *Tales of St. Austin's* 138 Yes, prarper good runner, his nevvy. **1940** M. MARPLES *Public School Slang* 133 Nunky and nevvy, uncle and nephew, are quoted by Wrench's WB as current before 1901 at Winchester; they are certainly now obsolete. **1959** E. POUND *Thrones* civ. 91 Sammy's nevvy got the gold out of the palace bed-room.

nevyanskite (nevyæ·nskəit). *Min.* Also † **newjanskite.** [ad. G. *newjanskit* (W. Haidinger *Handbuch der bestimm. Min.* (1845) 558), f. *Newjansk* Nevyansk, a city in Russia: see -ITE[1].] A variety of iridosmine containing about 35 to 50 per cent of osmium.

1854 J. D. DANA *Syst. Min.* (ed. 4) II. vi. 20 At a high temperature..Newjanskite is not decomposed and does not give an osmium odor. **1938** *Mineral. Abstr.* VII. 162 Ruthenium-bearing nevyanskite was found in alluvial deposits associated with serpentine of the Great Laba river, northern Caucasus. **1963** *Mineral. Mag.* XXXIII. 714 Iridosmine for the hexagonal phase (with Nevyanskite and Sysertskite as varieties) and Osmiridium for the cubic phase.

new, *a.* and *sb.*[2] Add: **A.** *adj.* **2. a.** *a new one* (*spec.* an anecdote or a joke; also, a circumstance not previously encountered). Usu. const. *on* (a person). orig. *U.S.*

1887 *Lantern* (New Orleans) 17 Dec. 2/3 Isn't this a new one on you, Messrs. Police? **1900** ADE *Fables in Slang* 74 The Pew-Holders didn't even admit among themselves that the Preacher had rung in some New Ones. **1930** D. L. SAYERS *Strong Poison* xx. 256 'I warn you..that you still have to establish evidence as to means and opportunity.' 'I know that. Tell us a new one.' **1931** T. H. DEY *Leaves from Bookmaker's Bk.* iii. 72 Charles Austin, Wilkie Bard and Ernie Lotinga too, are excellent private raconteurs and George Robey has always got a 'new one'. **1939** C. ISHERWOOD *Goodbye to Berlin* 72 That's a new one on me... I never suspected the boy of having a mind at all. **1940** J. CARY *Charley is My Darling* xv. 77 Ginger reflects a moment and says then: 'It's a new one on me', meaning that he has not yet broken the law. **1952** 'M. INNES' *Private View* iii. 45 He said there was blood pouring through his ceiling. That was a new one on the station sergeant. **1971** 'A. GILBERT' *Tenant for Tomb* vi. 93 Her brother?.. That's a new one on me.

4. (Further examples.) *new breed*: see BREED *sb.* 2 c in Dict. and Suppl.; *new order*, a new regime or government; *spec.* (cf. G. *die neue Ordnung*), Hitler's plan for the reconstitution of the States of Europe on the basis of a National-Socialist regime. Of a coinage: replacing a former monetary unit, e.g. *new franc, new penny.*

1842 New order [see ORDER *sb.* 16]. **1917** KIPLING *Divers. Creatures* (1917) 333 He and his friends had helped the World a step nearer the Truth, the Dawn, and the New Order. **1936** *Discovery* Sept. 295/1 The higher motives of a new order. **1940** *Times* (Weekly ed.) 27 Nov. 16 Every effort of the Quisling Government to induce the Norwegian people to believe that the 'new order' in Norway means the real liberation of the people and the erection of a new and happier Norway, freed from party strife and class distinctions, seems to have fallen on very deaf ears. **1941, 1944** New order [see *CO-PROSPERITY SPHERE]. **1944** G. B. SHAW *Everybody's Political What's What?* viii. 67 There is much talk at present of a New Order to follow the war. **1960** *Whitaker's Almanack 1961* 864/2 The *New Franc*, worth 100 old francs, came into use on Jan. 1, 1960, in metropolitan France and Algeria. **1966** H. YOXALL *Fashion of Life* xxiv. 221 A *menu gastronomique* at twenty-five new francs. **1966** *New Statesman* 16 Dec. 896/3 The government has opted for a pound divided into

100 'new pennies'. **1969** *Times* 21 July p. i/3 In 1971 our coins will be $\frac{1}{2}$p, 1p, 2p, 5p, 10p, and 50p, each new penny equalling 2·4 of our present pennies. **1971** 'J. FRASER' *Death in Pheasant's Eye* xxvi. 163 Game bird soup at twenty new pence a helping. **1972** D. LEES *Zodiac* 47 I've won twenty-five thousand new francs—it's a fortune. **1973** *Listener* 22 Feb. 258/3 If the Nazis considered it worth their while to be so subtle in their propaganda, surely we should be at least as discerning in our exposure of the New Order.

b. *new bug* (slang), a new boy. Cf. *BUG *sb.*^{2} 4 c. Also (rare) *new tick*. Cf. *NEW BOY, *NEW GIRL.

1900 FARMER *Public School Word-Bk.* 139 *New-bug*, a new boy. **1934** 'G. ORWELL' *Burmese Days* v. 79 New-tick Flory does look rum. **1936, 1960** New bug [see *BUG *sb.*^{2} 4 c]. **1971** 'M. INNES' *Awkward Lie* v. 90 It mayn't be too bad an idea for the new bugs.

f. *new thing* (freq. with capital initials): something avant-garde or innovative; *spec.* a type of experimental jazz music of the 1960s dispensing with the normal harmonic and rhythmic framework. Also *attrib.* Hence *new thinger*. *slang* (orig. *U.S.*).

1928 [see *MUCKER *v.*^{2} b]. **1962** *Down Beat* 12 Apr. 20 Coltrane's cohort Eric Dolphy, a member of that group of musicians who play what has been dubbed the 'new thing'. **1966** *New Statesman* 25 Mar. 438/3 'Pure feeling, pure expression, pure movement' (I quote from *Change/1*, an extended manifesto of the New Thingers). **1966** *New Yorker* 1 Oct. 214 The newest rock 'n' roll groups are tuning in on the new thing. *Ibid.* 217 Charles Lloyd..wears new-thing clothes (an Army officer's jacket, tinted glasses, and bell-bottom trousers). **1967** *Melody Maker* 28 Jan. 15 Near the end, Dolphy had adopted a determinedly 'new thing' attitude, becoming more and more anarchistic in his playing, especially on alto. **1970** C. MAJOR *Dict. Afro-Amer. Slang* 84 *New thing*, in jazz, an aggressive and original attitude and feeling..; in black writing, the 'new thing' trend is best indicated through..*The New Black Poetry*.

5. a. *the New Humanism*, in the U.S., a school of cultural thought based on the pragmatic philosophy of Dewey and others and emphasizing man's superiority to the natural order through the use of his reason; so *New Humanist*, a proponent of the New Humanism; *the New Kingdom*, a name given collectively to the Eighteenth, Nineteenth, and Twentieth Dynasties, which ruled Egypt from the sixteenth to the eleventh centuries B.C.; *the new mathematics*, a system of teaching mathematics to younger children in which an emphasis is laid on investigation and discovery on their part and topics are included that are not in the traditional school curriculum (as set theory, symbolic logic, and number systems); usu. abbreviated to *the new maths* (U.S. *math*); also without *the*; *the new psychology*, a term denoting new and major fields of psychological investigation, such as experimental psychology in the 19th century and esp. those theories in the 20th century that recognize the irrational and unconscious motivations of human behaviour.

1899 W. JAMES *Talks to Teachers* ii. 20 In the light of some of the expectations that are abroad concerning the 'new psychology', it is instructive to read the unusually candid confession of its founder Wundt. **1920** A. G. TANSLEY (*title*) The new psychology. *Ibid.* i. 9 Before we consider the developments of the New Psychology we must first glance at the causes of this failure of the older psychology... Not very many years ago the subject-matter of psychology was almost entirely limited to what is called the 'content of consciousness'. **1928** N. FOERSTER *Amer. Criticism* v. 236 A better way to consider the reconstruction proposed by the new humanism would be to examine its fundamental assumption. **1928** C. DAWSON *Age of Gods* viii. 173 The Late Minoan [corresponds] to the New Kingdom [in Egypt]. **1930** *Proc. Brit. Acad.* XVI. 414 The 'new psychology' with its perhaps exaggerated stress on the hidden roots of our conscious convictions and purposes in the depths of our unconscious mind, had not yet brought all reasoning into suspicion of being merely the 'rationalization' of irrational impulses. **1930** C. H. GRATTAN *Critique of Humanism* 6 In attacking the New Humanism, then, I am not casting aspersions upon the attitude which more than any other will lead to the good life. **1930** K. BURKE in *Ibid.* 169 The men whom the New Humanists in America recognize as their colleagues in France are advocates of Catholicism. **1942** S. R. K. GLANVILLE *Legacy of Egypt* 105 His tomb..bore witness to a period when the art of the New Kingdom had..reached its highest point. **1957** *Antiquity & Survival* II. 122/1 One of the raids carried out by one of the New Kingdom Pharaohs along the Palestinian coast. **1958** *Time* 3 Feb. 48/2 (*heading*) The new mathematics. **1958** I. ADLER (*title*) The new mathematics. [*In the text referred to as* modern mathematics.] **1960** *Math. Teaching* July 21 The self-styled Public Relations Officer for the New Mathematics..declared himself the herald of New Mathematics. **1961** A. H. GARDINER *Egypt of the Pharaohs* iii. 40 It is a matter of some surprise that the much less pleasing sandstone should have supplanted it [*sc.* limestone] from the New Kingdom (*c.* 1500 B.C.) onwards. **1963** J. S. BRUNER in Z. P. Dienes *Exper. Study of Math.-Learning* p. xii, In recent years there has been much misguided debate about the introduction of 'the new mathematics' into the schools. **1965** R. WELLEK *Hist. Mod. Criticism* IV. 59 His theory of commonplaces..is practically the same as that of the American new humanists. **1966** MEYER & HANLON (*title*) Fun with the new math. **1967** *Punch* 8 Mar. 332/1 If we realised..how much the New Maths derived from a foreign professor attending to the babbling of infants.. our suspicions would be even deeper and darker. **1971** R. A. PARKER in J. R. Harris *Legacy of Egypt* (ed. 2) i. 22 A papyrus known as the Turin Canon..listed the kings of Egypt from the earliest dynasties down to the end of the Hyksos period, that is just prior to the New Kingdom. **1973** *Sci. Amer.* Apr. 101/1 The triumph of the 'new math' in the elementary schools of America during the past decade. **1973** H. WHITNEY in E. Choat *Preschool & Primary Math.* 9 After centuries with little change in the mathematics curriculum in schools, we find ourselves in an era of 'new maths', typified by the acquisition of concepts.

b. *new entry*: a recruit; *collect.*, persons who have recently qualified or become eligible to do something. Also *transf.* and *attrib.*

1919 W. LANG *Sea Lawyer's Log* 5 Approaching him with diffidence our spokesman modestly announced us as 'new entries'—the Navy does not deal in 'recruits'. **1958** *Listener* 20 Nov. 812/1 If the electoral behaviour of the new entry [of voters] differs from that of those who have joined the great majority, there will be a swing one way or the other in consequence. **1962** *Economist* 18 Aug. 623/3 Competition seems to have prevented prices from ever going near their new-entry ceiling.

d. In names of inhabitants of countries, provinces, etc. whose names include the word *New*. Cf. NEW ENGLANDER, NEWFOUNDLANDER, *NEW MEXICAN, NEW ZEALANDER.

1874 C. M. YONGE *Life J. C. Patteson* I. viii. 214 The little New Caledonian remained at Taurarua. **1890** W. A. FOSTER in R. Reid *Canadian Style* (1973) ii. 40 All we need is a sentiment which shall make us feel not as Ontarions or Quebeckers, Nova Scotians or New Brunswickers, but as Canadians proud of our country as a whole. **1911** *Encycl. Brit.* XIX. 469/1 Many New Caledonians having black skins and woolly hair with Polynesian superiority of limb. **1957** *Ibid.* XVI. 696/2 The newcomers spoke languages of the Austronesian..family, which were in time adopted by most of the coastal New Guineans. **1973** *Country Life* 13 Sept. 745/1 Shell jewellery still valued for its magical powers by the New Guineans.

6. Used of colour names.

1897 *Sears, Roebuck Catal.* 360/3 Colors for Artists... Neutral Tint, New Blue, Olive Lake. *Ibid.* 361/1 Water Colors... Dark Green, New Rose, Flesh, New Violet. **1927** [see *DAWN *sb.* 1 b]. **1948** F. A. STAPLES *Watercolor Painting* iv. 49 *New Blue*, bright blue transparent.

f. Recently formed; *spec.* (see quot. 1958): said of deposits of ice or snow, esp. in polar regions.

1860 *Jrnl. R. Dublin Soc.* Jan. 374, I have before stated that we were frozen in on the 7th of September, 1857; the new ice then forming around us was of specific gravity 1·0235 (30°). **1918** FINCH & HAWKS *Water in Nature* vi. 126 Nansen has given us particulars of thickness attained by the ice of the Polar seas... 'This formation of new ice on the underside was owing to the layer of fresh water which, by reason of the surface thaw on the ice, now floated above the cold, salt water.' **1935** *Handbk. Weather, Currents & Ice, for Seamen* (Meteorol. Office) vii. 102 Between the Arctic Pack and the fast ice is a moving belt consisting partly of new ice and partly of broken ice from the pack and from the fast ice. **1958** ARMSTRONG & ROBERTS *Illustr. Ice Gloss.* 94 *New snow*, a recent snow deposit in which the original form of the ice crystals can be recognized; usually the daily new snowfall, measured in the morning. **1966** T. ARMSTRONG et al. *Illustr. Gloss. Snow & Ice* 28 *New ice*, a general term for floating ice recently formed. It includes frazil ice, grease ice, slush, shuga, ice rind, milas and pancake ice.

8. (Later examples.) Cf. *New Australian* (*AUSTRALIAN *sb.* 2 b).

1807 SOUTHEY *Lett. from England* II. xxix. 27 The heretical sects in this country... form a curious list! Arminians, Socinians, Baxterians, Presbyterians, New Americans, Sabellians, [etc.]. **1907** H. A. KENNEDY (*title*) New Canada and the New Canadians. **1919** *Ladies' Home Jrnl.* Sept. 35 The New Americans. **1939** J. M. GIBBON *Canadian Mosaic* ix. 231 Anthology of verse written by New Canadians. **1940** *Chatelaine* Jan. 40/1 Native-born and new Canadians work together for the nation's good. **1965** *Listener* 10 June 860/2 The idealist who saw his vision of the New Man shattered by harsh reality. **1970** *Guardian* 14 Apr. 11/5 The machines..are obviously the New Men, the ultimate revolutionaries. **1970** *Toronto Daily Star* 24 Sept. 7/6 If New Canadians prefer to learn English from Eaton's or Simpson's catalogue, there must be something wrong?

d. spec. *new rich*: in recent use, common as a translation of the French *nouveaux riches*, persons who have recently acquired wealth. Also as *adj.* Hence *new poor*, recently impoverished persons; *new money*, a fortune recently acquired, funds recently raised; so by metonymy, the new rich.

1886 *Harper's Mag.* Oct. 795/2 There are..the sons of the 'new rich' who are like men drunk with new wine. **1920** *Punch* 6 Oct. 279 *Exhausted War Profiteer.* 'Deer forests for the 'idle rich' be blowed! The 'new poor' can 'ave 'em for me.' **1923** 'B. M. BOWER' *Parowan Bonanza* xiii. 157 You've never seen *me* look New-rich, have you, Bill? **1926** A. BENNETT *Lord Raingo* I. xxxv. 165 He had demonstrated publicly..that he belonged to the type of the new rich. **1942** H. C. BAILEY *Dead Man's Shoes* x. 46 Not a drop of fizz for you. I am the new poor and proud of the title. **1958** *New Statesman* 23 Aug. 222/2 How typical is his new-rich business man, seen leaving an elaborate Tudoresque house..who seemed genuinely to feel no animosity either towards the class to which his father, a jobbing gardener, had belonged or towards the class in which, economically at least, he now finds himself. **1961** 'W. HAGGARD' *Arena* iii. 25 They had most of the new money: all the new men used them, the takeover boys, the property men. **1967** M. PROCTER *Exercise Hoodwink* xvii. 119 He moves with a pricey crowd, though I wouldn't call 'em classy. Small business people. New money. **1969** *Triumph* (U.S.) Mar. 25/1 The new poor, the misplaced workers, who are a by-product of our technology. **1970** *Daily Tel.* 2 June 20/3 'New money' raised in the United Kingdom during May by the issue of marketable securities was £32 million. **1973** R. LUDLUM *Matlock Paper* xvi. 139 The blooded first families..migrated just a little west to avoid the new rich. **1975** *Daily Tel.* 30 Aug. 13/4 The amount of new money raised in August at £120·1 million was the lowest since last January.

9. (Later examples.)

1903 MRS. H. WARD *Lady Rose's Daughter* xiv. 230 He was a good deal of a politician, himself a 'new man', and on the side of 'new men'. **1936** M. MITCHELL *Gone with Wind* iii. 52 Gerald was a 'new man', despite his nearly ten years' residence. **1943** D. W. BROGAN *English People* iii. 81 Lord Reading was the first Marquess of Reading, a 'new man'. **1962** *Spectator* 30 Mar. 392 It strikes fear, not into the manual worker so much as into the hearts of the new men.

10. a. *new-old* (later examples).

1926 D. H. LAWRENCE *Plumed Serpent* xvii. 279 They seized upon the new-old thrill, with a certain fear, and joy, and relief. **1932** H. CRANE *Let.* 31 Mar. (1965) 405 An environment not half so strange and distractingly new-old curious as this. **1961** *Guardian* 14 June 10/6 These new-old problems that face our daughters.

b. *new-face* = *modern-face(d)* adjs. (*MODERN *a.* 2 g); *new time*: in the Stock Exchange: of dealings, having the settlement postponed to the next settling-day; of prices, quoted for the next settling-day before the previous settlement is completed; also in more general contexts; *new wheat disease*: a pyelonephritis affecting young poultry, possibly caused by a virus; also called *blue comb* (*disease*) (*BLUE *a.* 13) or *pullet disease* (*PULLET 3).

Some of these expressions also occur in non-*attrib.* contexts.

1900 H. HART *Cent. Typogr.* 120 These are the first examples of what are called nowadays 'new-face' types. *a* **1910** 'MARK TWAIN' *Autobiogr.* (1924) I. 198 Any other old-time or new-time palace on the continent of Europe. **1912** *Century Mag.* Jan. 476 Open Letters... On the New-time Negro. **1922** New-time [see *CARRY-OVER]. **1927** *Daily Express* 27 Sept. 10/1 The price for 'new time' was about 15s. 6d., compared with a making up price of 14s. *Ibid.* 10/3 The 'new time' price at one time touched the new record of $4\frac{1}{2}$. **1950** New wheat disease [see *blue comb* (*disease*) s.v. *BLUE *a.* 13]. **1957** L. ROBINSON *Mod. Poultry Husbandry* (ed. 4) xx. 677 Since outbreaks usually occur in late summer and autumn, the disease has been called 'New Wheat disease'. There is no evidence, however, that new wheat is responsible. **1964** *Financial Times* 25 Feb. 17/1 First Dealings... 'New time' dealings may take place two business days earlier.

d. *new style*: in Chronology, see STYLE *sb.* 27; gen., forming attributive compounds.

1914 'I. HAY' *Lighter Side School Life* vii. 193 The new-style parent breaks right away from tradition—kicks over the traces, in fact. **1937** B. H. L. HART *Europe in Arms* iii. 26 These new-style formations were not shown to the foreign officers and military publicists. **1961** *Times* 18 May 19/4 The new-style Arab. **1965** *New Statesman* 7 May 707/2 Such a department, like the rest of a new-style Transport House, would have to have a long-term career structure.

B. *absol.* or as *sb.* **5.** A naval cadet during his first term in a training-ship.

1909 J. R. WARE *Passing Eng.* 181/2 *New* (*Britannia training ship*), fresh arrival, last addition. Used in the plural. **1914** 'BARTIMEUS' *Naval Occasions* ix. 63 The path of the 'New' in those days was by no means strewn with roses. **1953** J. MASEFIELD *Conway* (rev. ed.) IV. 224 The 'News' very rarely ventured into the upper room. **1962** GRANVILLE *Dict. Sailors' Slang* 81/1 *New!*, HMS *Britannia's* equivalent of the public school's 'Fag!'

new, *adv.* Add: **3. a.** *new-baked, -bought, -crowned, -cut, -dated, -fulfilled, -gnarled, -nurtured, -scored, -skeined, -washed.*

1793 W. BLAKE *Visions Daughters Albion* in *Compl. Writings* (1972) 191 The new wash'd lamb ting'd with the village smoke, & the bright swan. **1821** BYRON *Don Juan* v. clvi. 289 The new-bought virgin, made her blush and shake. **1865** G. M. HOPKINS *Poems* (1967) 21 New-dated from the terms that reappear, More sweet-familiar grows my love to thee. **1877** —— *Ibid.* 68, I hear the lark ascend, His rash-fresh re-winded new-skeinèd score In crisps of curl off wild winch whirl. **1889** W. B. YEATS *Wanderings of Oisin* III. 35 Whiter than new-washed fleece. **1909** KIPLING *Actions & Reactions* 51 Over their heads in the branches Of their new-bought ancient trees. **1913** —— *Songs from Books* 43 My new-cut ashlar takes the light. **1918** E. SITWELL *Clown's Houses* 14 In new-washed air. **1922** JOYCE *Ulysses* 155 Steam of newbaked jampuffs. **1934** E. BLUNDEN *Choice or Chance* 37 Yet one I knew who most of all seemed sent Among earth's flowers for new-fulfilled content. **1935** W. EMPSON *Poems* 27 With plump or splash on the new-nurtured field To Reason's arm they proper homage yield. **1942** *R.A.F. Jrnl.* 3 Oct. 7 The wheels kicking up a frenzied cloud of new-cut grass. **1943** L. B. LYON *Evening in Stepney* 20 A script of blackening girders, New-scored by old despair. **1948** E. POUND *Pisan Cantos* (1949) lxxx. 107 Nor is the white bud Time's inquisitor Probing to know if its new-gnarled root Twists from York's head or belly of Lancaster. *a* **1963** C. S. LEWIS *Poems* (1964) 69 A seminal breeze from the far side Calls to their new-crowned race.

b. *new-awakened, -kerned, -landed.*

1851 H. MELVILLE *Moby Dick* I. xxiii. 169 One Bulkington was spoken of, a new-landed mariner, encountered in

New Bedford. **1908** HARDY *Dynasts* III. VII. ii. 486 The peaceful produce of the grange,..new-kerned apples, hairy gooseberries green. **1918** E. SITWELL *Clown's Houses* 7 The new-awakened flower-strange hair.

4. *new-awakened, -crushed, -desired.*

1878 O. WILDE *Ravenna* 13 Thou hast not drunk this wine From grapes new-crushed. **1917** D. H. LAWRENCE *Look! We have come Through!* 131 Now here was I, new-awakened. **1959** BLUNDEN *Hong Kong House*, Except when they, of one tree tired Into another new-desired Over the lawn and scattered playthings chose to glide.

6. b. With active forms of intransitive verbs, as *new-dapple, new-nestle.*

a **1885** G. M. HOPKINS *Poems* (1967) 193 As sure as what is most sure, sure as that spring primroses Shall new-dapple next year. *a* **1889** —— *Ibid.* 185 Say it is áshboughs: whether on a December day and furled Fast ór they in clammyish lashtender combs creep Apart wide and new-nestle at heaven most high.

7. *new-dawning.*

1820 J. TRUMBULL *Poetical Wks.* II. 108 Prove to the world in these new-dawning skies, What genius kindles and what arts arise.

b. With pres. pples. of intransitive verbs that are const. with predicative adverbs, as *new-looking, -seeming.*

1905 J. JOYCE *Let.* c 12 Oct. (1966) II. 121 A good new-looking..suit. **1928** D. H. LAWRENCE *Lady Chatterley* xv. 276 The man's face, that was smooth and new-looking with love. **1951** S. SPENDER *World within World* 87 Raindrops..through which the sun..would gleam with a new-seeming whiteness. **1969** *Sears Catal.* Spring/Summer 15 Enamel colors oven-baked to stay new-looking longer.

New Aca·demy. Also **new Academy.** [ACADEMY 2.] A name given to schools of philosophy founded in Athens by the successors of Plato as Heads of the Academy and developing some of its principles, *spec.* (*a*) that founded by Arcesilaus (316/15–242/1 B.C.) in the third century B.C. (now more usually called **Middle Academy*); (*b*) (more usually) that founded in the second century B.C. by Carneades of Cyrene (214/13–129/8 B.C.) and developing the mainly sceptical philosophy of Arcesilaus. Also *attrib.* So **New Acade·mic** *sb.* and *a.*

1659 T. STANLEY tr. *Sextus Empiricus's Pyrr. Hyp.* in *Hist. Philos.* III. IV. 33 Those of the new Academy, though they say all things are incomprehensible, differ from the Scepticks... Now the new Academicks, before Phantasie which is simply credible, preferre that which is credible and circumcurrent. **1702** S. PARKER tr. *Cicero's De Finibus* v. 280 For all that, I'll venture to dissuade you from following the new Academicks, and bespeak you in behalf of the Old ones. **1744** W. GUTHRIE tr. *Cicero's Morals* p. v, It was by Sincerity alone that the New Academy could hope to recommend that Moderation which was their peculiar Distinction. *Ibid.*, Thus, The New Academic, by admitting a Degree of Comprehension, preserv'd a Principle of Agency. *Ibid.* 321 This they call'd the new Academy, tho' it appears to me to be the old one, at least we may look upon Plato to have been of the old. **1853** C. D. YONGE tr. *Cicero's Academic Questions* p. xxix, *Arcesilaus*, or *Arcesilas*, flourished about B.C. 280... On the death of Crantor he succeeded to the chair of the Academy, in the doctrines of which he made so many innovations that he is called the founder of the New Academy. **1856** W. A. BUTLER *Lect. on Hist. of Ancient Philosophy* II. IV. i. 318 The sceptical side of Platonism represented by the New Academy, the doctrinal by the Neo-platonists. **1874** J. S. REID *Cicero's Academica* p. lvi, Cicero..merely attaches Philo's name to those general New Academic doctrines which had been so brilliantly supported by the pupil of Clitomachus in his earlier days. **1902** BALDWIN *Dict. Philos. & Psychol.* II. 496/2 The New Academy, under Philo of Larissa (about 100 B.C.) and Antiochus, turned to dogmatism and eclecticism. **1946** F. C. COPLESTON *Hist. Philos.* I. xxxviii. 414 The founder of the Third or New Academy was Carneades of Cyrene. **1967** P. MERLAN in *Cambr. Hist. Later Greek & Early Medieval Philos.* 61 Plutarch even has kind words for the scepticism of the New Academy.

Newar (nɪwā·ɹ). A member of one of the castes of Nepal, of Mongol or partly Mongol origin. Also *attrib.* So **Newa·ri,** a language of partly Tibetan origin spoken by the Newars.

1811 [see *MAGAR[2]]. **1819** F. HAMILTON *Acct. Kingdom Nepal* I. i. 49 They afterwards settled in the valley of Nepal, and are the people now called Newars. **1877** [see *BAEL, BEL]. **1877** D. WRIGHT *Hist. Nepal* App. vii. 306 (*heading*) Newārī songs. **1893** A. L. WADDELL in *Indian Antiquary* XXII. 292 The Nêwârs are the aborigines of Nêpâl Proper, that is, of the valley in which the present capital Khâṭmâṇḍû stands. *Ibid.* 293 The original name of this section of the Pâl country, which contained the home of the Nêwârs, seems to have been *Nê*, while the people were hence called by the Hindus *Nêwâr*, or '*Inhabitants of Nê*'. **1911** FRAZER *Golden Bough: Magic Art* (ed. 3) I. v. 294 The Newars..worship the frog. **1928** P. LANDON *Nepal* II. App. xvi. 236 He was buried in the little Christian cemetery with an inscription in two languages, Latin and Newari. **1971** J. PEMBLE *Invasion of Nepal* i. 6 Jaya Yaksha Malla..patronized native letters and raised Newari to the status of an official language. **1972** W. B. LOCKWOOD *Panorama Indo-European Lang.* 208 Spoken in 1952–4 by close on 400,000 persons in Nepal, Newari is the only Himalayan language of the Tibeto-Burman group to have developed a considerable literature. The Newars have evolved a high degree of material culture. **1973** *Times* 14 Apr. (Nepal Suppl.) p. ii/5 The three towns of Katmandu, Patan and Bhadgaon are the creation of Newars. **1974** M. PEISSEL *Great Himalayan Passage* xiv. 206 The Newars do not like anyone to die in their houses, so they turn the dying outside on mats. *Ibid.*, All the windows of traditional Newar houses have to be entirely closed by wooden lattices, as these are believed to stop evil spirits entering.

Newark (niū·ăɹk, nū·ăɹk). The name of a city in New Jersey, U.S.A., used *attrib.* or in *Comb.* in various special collocations (see quots.).

1787 in T. F. De Voe *Market Book* (1862) I. 181 (New) *Jersey*, a Burlington ham and Newark cyder. **1804** A. F. M. WILLICH *Domestic Encycl.* III. 111/1 *Newark Pippin*... It is said to have been imported from France. **1858** S. P. AVERY *Harp of Thousand Strings* 289 A well-known sporting character of the city had made a bet that he would drive his 'Newark waggon' (a light carriage with two horses) the whole length of Broadway. **1870** R. TOMES *Bazaar Bk. Decorum* 136 He will be sure to detect the Newark cider in your Champagne bottle. **1910** A. E. BOSTWICK *Amer. Public Library* 45 In the type of two-card system known as the 'Newark' system.., an additional record of the date is made on a flap attached to the inside of the book. **1961** T. LANDAU *Encycl. Librarianship* (ed. 2) 261/1 *Newark charging system*, the method of recording book loans which is most widely used in America.

New Art, new art. = *art nouveau* (*ART *sb.* VI. e).

1903 W. B. YEATS *Let.* 14 May in *Florence Farr, Shaw, Yeats* (1946) 38, I have had a letter from the editor of the 'Daily News' asking permission to interview me on the Theatre and the New Art. **1906** M. H. BAILLIE-SCOTT *Houses & Gardens* i. 13 A bizarre striving after originality and eccentricity of design,..posing as the 'new art'. **1909** *Cottage Furniture* (Heal & Son) 1 The 'new art' overmantel smothered in rococo photograph frames. **1909** H.G. WELLS *Tono-Bungay* III. i. 266 Beautiful jam-pots! Get one of those new art chaps to design all the things they make ugly now. **1912** L. WEAVER *House & its Equipment* 35 The superficial clevernesses of the New Art movement. **1914** C. MACKENZIE *Sinister Street* II. III. vi. 617 New Art flower vases. **1938** G. GREENE *Brighton Rock* I. iii. 46 He touched a little buzzer, the New Art doors opened. **1969** J. GLOAG *Short Dict. Furniture* (ed. 2) 469 New Art was characterized by the free use of naturalistic motifs: chairs, tables, cabinets and bedsteads were contorted by writhing plants, exuberant blossoms, and intricate arabesques, while surfaces were punctuated by inserted patches of hammered copper and coloured enamel, and pierced by heart-shaped apertures.

new ball. *Cricket.* A previously unused ball, such as is brought into use at the beginning of an innings or after a prescribed number of overs; freq. used *attrib.* (with hyphen) of an opening bowler or of the type of bowling (usu. fast) in which the new ball is employed. Also *fig.*

1956 R. ALSTON *Test Commentary* 12 The most devastating pair of new-ball bowlers in the world. **1960** J. FINGLETON *Four Chukkas to Australia* vi. 65 We saw a magnificent piece of new-ball bowling. **1963** *Times Lit. Suppl.* 18 Jan. 27/3 One has the impression [in reading a novel] of waiting for the new ball to become available. **1971** *Times* 15 Feb. 8/1 Edrich and Luckhurst..batted with the greatest of ease against some modest new-ball bowling. **1975** *Cricketer* May 23/2 It was the finest display of new-ball bowling I ever saw.

newberyite (niū·bĕrɪ,əit). *Min.* [ad. G. *newberyit* (G. vom Rath (at the suggestion of G. Ulrich) 1879, in *Sitzungsber. der niederrhein. Ges. in Bonn* XXXVI. 8), f. the name of J. Cosmo *Newbery* (19th-cent. Australian mineralogist) + *-it* -ITE[1].] A hydrated magnesium acid phosphate, $MgH(PO_4).3H_2O$, which is found as colourless orthorhombic crystals.

1879 *Mineral. Mag.* III. 108 Newberyite... Found at Skipton Caves, Victoria, with Hannayite. **1928** *Amer. Mineralogist* XIII. 397 (*heading*) Newberyite and other phosphates from Ascension Island. **1957** *Mineral. Mag.* XIII. 190 Newberyite, together with pyrrhotine and vivianite, was found in cracks of mammoth tusk buried in clay. **1966** *Amer. Mineralogist* LI. 1764 Subsequent submergence and removal of the source of ammonia permitted the replacement of struvite by newberyite in a subaqueous environment.

new-born, *ppl. a.* Add: Also **newborn, new born. 3.** *absol.* as *sb.* A new-born individual; chiefly in *the new-born* (usu. with pl. or collective sense).

1879 A. JACOBI in A. H. Buck *Treat. Hygiene & Public Health* I. I. 75 Landau's essay on 'The Melæna of the New-Born, with Notices on the Obliteration of the Fœtal Blood-Vessels', proves that..but little attention has been paid to the subject. **1907** *Jrnl. Amer. Med. Assoc.* 31 Aug. 775/1 Occurrences of vaginal hemorrhage of the new-born are..rare. **1929** R. HURWITZ tr. *Bernfeld's Psychol. of Infant* 2 The new-born is not capable of maintaining life for itself. **1937** *Amer. Jrnl. Dis. Child.* LIV. 1215 Tetany of the new-born..may occur at any time during the neonatal period. **1968** PASSMORE & ROBSON *Compan. Med. Stud.* I. xxxix. 6/2 The distribution and amount of brown fat in the newborn varies among different species. **1974** *Nature* 6 Dec. 514/3 A doubtful study..indicating that newborns can orient visually to a voice source in space.

new boy. Also **new-boy, newboy.** [NEW *a.* 8.] A schoolboy during his first term(s) at a school, esp. one at a preparatory school or English public school. Also *transf.*, a (young) man newly come into a given set of circumstances. Cf. *NEW *a.* 4 b, *NEW GIRL.

1847 DICKENS *Dombey* (1848) xli. 410 Here is the table upon which he sat forlorn and strange, the 'new boy' of the school. **1847** *Punch* 25 Dec. 255 (*caption*) Here's a New Boy, Johnny Russell. Now you see that nobody bullies him. **1905** R. BROOKE *Let.* 12 Mar. (1968) 18 Such brave souls can be content with the admiration of one another, and of the new boys. **1935** H. NICOLSON *Diary* 21 Nov. (1966) 229 He says the rather dramatic circumstances of my election may arouse some jealousy in that old hen the H. of C. I must do the new-boy for six months at least. **1948** PARTRIDGE *Dict. Forces' Slang* 124 *New boy*, a new member of a ship's ward-room. **1953** A. HUXLEY *Let.* 5 Apr. (1969) 667 He had been part of my Order of Things for almost fifty years, ever since we first met as newboys at our preparatory school in the autumn of 1903. **1970** E. PACE *Saberlegs* (1971) x. 87 He was a new boy here, a novice 'philanthropoid', as people in the foundation business called themselves. **1973** *Washington Post* 13 Jan. A. 22/2 Neither the anxious war critic Mr. Hughes nor the cautious new boy Mr. Clements was familiar with the unequivocal policy statement..made.. just two years ago. **1974** 'J. LE CARRÉ' *Tinker, Tailor* i. 10 Roach was a new boy... Thursgood's was his second prep school.

new broom. [In allusion to the prov. *new brooms sweep clean* (SWEEP *v.* 13 b).] One newly appointed to a position who vigorously makes changes in personnel or procedures; one who effects fundamental or numerous alterations. Also (with hyphen) *attrib.* and as *v. trans.* and *intr.*

[**1776** G. COLMAN (*title*) New brooms! An occasional prelude. *Ibid.* 15, I am glad he is gone. *Catcall.* Glad! *Phelim.* To be sure I am glad. *New Brooms*, you know.] **1855** [see BROOM *sb.* 3 b]. **1925** [see *CLEAN *v.* 6 c]. *a* **1930** D. H. LAWRENCE *Phoenix II* (1968) 114 The Reverend Mr. Flewitt is newly arrived on the circuit, and wants to sweep the chapel very clean of sin, being a new broom. **1938** *Ann. Reg. 1937* 93 The War Ministry, where Mr. Hore-Belisha was proving himself a veritable 'new broom'. **1951** N. MARSH *Opening Night* v. 114 Our little stranger.. seems to be new-brooming away. **1963** *Economist* 10 Aug. 496/3 Lord Hill of Luton, new-brooming his way through the Independent Television Authority. *Ibid.* 7 Sept. 809/1 The new government's new-broom mentality. **1969** *Listener* 14 Aug. 205/1 This seems to me exactly what is happening at the BBC, new brooms bustling about tidying up, rationalising and sorting out on very ill-thought-out principles.

ne·wbuilding. [tr. Da. *nybygning* new building, new ship: NEW *adv.* 8.] A newly constructed ship; the construction of ships.

1948 *N.Y. Maritime Register* 12 May 3/2 The new-buildings include a number of large fast cargo liners. **1957** *Times* 19 Dec. 16/6 It is the intention of that company to arrange a time charter on its newbuilding. **1968** *Marine West* Mar.–Apr. 2 The extra thick plates and oversize scantlings once used in tanker new buildings. **1968** *Marine Digest* 13 July 23 There is a steady trickle these days of newbuilding contracts for sale.

Newcastle[1] (niū·kɑs'l; also with main stress on second syllable). [Name of a city (in full *Newcastle upon Tyne*) in the north of England.] **1.** Phr. *to carry coals to Newcastle*: see COAL *sb.* 13.

2. Used *attrib.* in various special collocations: **Newcastle brown,** a strong brown ale; **Newcastle disease,** an infectious, often fatal, virus disease of poultry, first recorded in Britain near Newcastle in 1927 and characterized by lethargy followed by paralysis and difficulty in breathing; also called **fowl pest*; **Newcastle glass,** a type of colour-free glass manufactured in Newcastle; also *ellipt.*; **Newcastle pottery,** a type of coarse pottery manufactured around Newcastle.

1972 J. WAINWRIGHT *Requiem for Loser* ii. 43 A beer?.. There's a can o' Newcastle Brown in the fridge. **1973** 'J. PATRICK' *Glasgow Gang Observed* iii. 29 Pints of lager, heavy beer and bottles of Newcastle Brown were ordered. **1927** T. M. DOYLE in *Jrnl. Compar. Path. & Therapeutics* XL. 144 In order to facilitate description we propose to refer to it [*sc.* a virus disease of fowls] as 'Newcastle disease'. **1938** *Poultry Keepers' Year Book* v. 178 Newcastle Disease is notifiable to the Ministry of Agriculture... Recognisable by dribbling from beak and sudden death of many birds at the same time. **1955** *Sci. News Let.* 21 May 326/3 Newcastle disease virus, cause of a frequently fatal epidemic in poultry..can also cause eye inflammation in humans. **1968** *New Scientist* 5 Dec. 561/1 The infection—the dreaded Newcastle disease—is normally so lethal to chickens that a strict quarantine is imposed on imported poultry. **1972** *Daily Colonist* (Victoria, B.C.) 9 Jan. 35/5 Vaccination of hens against Newcastle disease is being urged by the B.C. Poultry Commissioner. **1767** in *Sc. Nat. Dict.* (1968) VII. 17/1 All the windows to be glazed with Newcastle crown glass, bedded and backpottied, and all hung with paces. **1779** COWPER *Let.* 26 May in *Corr.* (1904) I. 153, I shall be obliged..if you will inquire at a glass-manufacturer's how he sells his Newcastle glass, such as is used for frames and hothouses. **1883** J. W. MOLLETT *Illustr. Dict. Art & Archæol.* 225/1 *Newcastle glass*, a crown glass, held the best for windows from 1728 to 1830... It was of an ash colour,..and frequently

warped. **1923** H. J. Powell *Glass-Making in Pottery* vii. 93 In later years John Tyzack's warehouse for Newcastle glass near the Old Swan Stairs was well known. In 1691 Newcastle cut window-glass was sold at 13s. per 100 feet. **1965** P. M. Hubbard *Hive of Glass* i. 9 It was..[a] quite faultless Newcastle light baluster..ten inches high, the rounded perfect bowl perched on a breathless series of knobs. **1972** *Country Life* 28 Dec. 1783/2 The great rarities in this sale were two Dutch engraved Newcastle glasses of the mid-18th century. **1874** L. W. *Eng. Pott. & Porc.* 40 The principal marks on Sunderland and Newcastle pottery are (stamped in the clay or printed in transfer). **1971** R. C. Bell *Tyneside Pottery* ii. 95/2 The Willett Collection in the Brighton Museum contains two rare earthenware mugs marked 'Newcastle Pottery'.

Newcastle². The title of Henry Pelham-Clinton, fifth Duke of *Newcastle*-under-Lyme (1811–64), used as the name of a classical scholarship at Eton College, established by him in 1829. Also *attrib.*

1832 *Eton College Mag.* 25 June 7 It was on the second of April..that we went up for the last Newcastle scholarship. **1845** J. Patteson *Let.* in C. M. Yonge *Life J. C. Patteson* (1874) I. ii. 46 Do not distress yourself about this unfortunate failure as to the Newcastle. **1875** H. C. Maxwell-Lyte *Hist. Eton College* xix. 369 One Newcastle Scholar is elected annually after a competitive examination open to Oppidans and Collegers alike. **1879** C. M. Yonge *Magnum Bonum* ii. xxiv. 484 But you did like Eton so, and you were going to get the Newcastle and the Prince Consort's Prize. **1884** E. W. Hamilton *Diary* 5 Nov. (1972) II. 725 Dined at Dilke's—Chamberlain, Sir L. Playfair, Lord Advocate, L. Lawson, Romer, and Kennedy (the Newcastle Scholar of my day). **1922** S. Leslie *Oppidan* vii. 83, I would rather get the Newcastle than make a century at Lord's. **1953** H. Nicolson *Diary* 3 Jan. (1968) 236, I feel as if I had got a fourth prize in scripture when I should have liked the Newcastle. **1959** *Chambers's Encycl.* V. 422/1 The classical tradition in Eton education, strengthened by the institution of the Newcastle scholarship in 1829, remains strong to-day. **1975** *Times* 18 Oct. 7/5 My [*sc.* Harold Macmillan's] brother Daniel had won the Newcastle at Eton.

new-comer. (Further examples: used of things.)

1886 W. B. Yeats *Mosada* iii. 8 Yonder a leaf Of apple blossom circles in the gloom, Floating from yon barred window. New-comer, Thou'rt welcome. **1930** *New Statesman* 27 Dec. 357/2 The Gum-trees or Eucalypts are newcomers to California. **1966** *B.B.C. Handbk.* 23 A newcomer to many schools is 'radio-vision'.

New Commonwealth. [*commonwealth 4 c.] *collect.* Those countries which have achieved self-government within the British Commonwealth since 1945, opp. the old Dominions; also used *attrib.* of persons from (or whose parents came from) such countries; a genteelism for persons considered 'non-white'.

1960 *New Commonwealth* Oct. 626/3 The Rt. Hon. Ian Macleod, M.P., Secretary of State for the Colonies, will be the guest-of-honour at the next New Commonwealth luncheon, to be held at Claridges. **1964** *Listener* 6 Feb. 219/1 A respected voice from the new Commonwealth, that of Professor Rajan of the Indian School of International Studies, declared that [etc.]. **1964** S. A. de Smith *New Commonwealth & its Constitutions* iv. 137 In a new Commonwealth country there is a presumption against leaving the power of appointment exclusively in the hands of the executive. **1970** *Guardian* 10 Mar. 7/3 The number of 'new' Commonwealth immigrants admitted during the whole year fell by very nearly one-third. **1973** *Times* 4 Oct. 4/7 About 547,000 people whose parents were born in the New Commonwealth live in Greater London. **1975** *Times* 28 Feb. 3/2 The total New Commonwealth population in Britain. **1976** *Times* 27 Jan. 4/3 The total number of births [in Britain] to New Commonwealth and Pakistan mothers fell.

new-create, *v.* (Later examples.)

a **1930** D. H. Lawrence *Last Poems* (1932) 77 Then I have been dipped again in God, and new-created. **1952** R. Campbell tr. *St. John of the Cross's Poems* 25 And have been new-created There where your mother first was violated.

New Criticism, new criticism. [New *a.* 5.] An approach to the analysis of literary texts, associated spec. with American critics who subscribed to the procedures outlined by John Crowe Ransom (see quots. 1941), which concentrates on the linguistic organization of a text with particular emphasis on irony, ambiguity, paradox, etc. So **New Critic; New Critical** *a.*

1941 J. C. Ransom (*title*) The new criticism. *Ibid.* p. vii, He [*sc.* R. P. Blackmur] is nevertheless a 'new' critic in the sense of this book. *Ibid.* i. 3 Discussion of the new criticism must start with Mr. Richards. **1948** *Poetry* LXXIII. 153 The Father of the New Criticism is probably I. A. Richards. **1948** [see *concrete *a.* and *sb.* A. 4 b]. **1951** R. P. Blackmur in *Hudson Rev.* III. iv. 501 The one thing the 'new critics' shared was skill in analysis. **1952** M. McCarthy *Groves of Academe* (1953) x. 212 The true attitude of Eliot, he suspected, was manifest in his disciples, who in all their voluminous New Criticism had given Joyce scarcely a word of exegesis. **1955** J. Wain *Interpretations* 215 Poetic difficulty..is not identical with grammatical difficulty..nor is the 'New Critic'..simply the old note-maker writ large. **1956** A. Wilson *Anglo-Saxon Att.* i. iii. 59 Hardy was back from New York with some frightfully funny stories about the New Criticism boys. **1960–1** M. Spilka in *Modern Fiction Studies* VI. iv. 285 The concept of the author is conspicuous, in New Critical thought, by its absence. **1963** P. West *Mod. Novel* iii. ii. 291 Robert Penn Warren..one of the old New Critics. **1969** *Encycl. Brit.* VI. 781/2 In 1941 John Crowe Ransom coined the term 'new criticism' for what is in certain essential respects a return to the Renaissance rhetoricians' principle that a poem is an arrangement of words, to be apprehended in their interaction. **1973** *Observer* 8 Apr. 37/5 The so-called New Critics in America made a great deal of their capacity to submit poems or prose-passages to detailed, word-by-word analysis. **1973** *College English* XXXIV. 573 The pattern is the same as he moves from one caricature of a 'New Critical' assumption to the next.

new deal, new dealer: see *deal *sb.*² 4 d. So **New Dealing, New Dealish** *a.*, **New Dealism.**

1934 *Sun* (Baltimore) 23 Oct. 1/2 In many sections Republican candidates have gone New Dealish. **1936** *Rocky Mt. News* (Denver, Colorado) 7 May 10/3 Two towers of progressive strength, more 'New Dealish' than most Democrats, will be lost to the administration in the next Congress. **1939** in *Amer. Speech* (1941) XVI. 309/1 New Dealism..is nothing but the American form of Communism. **1962** R. B. Fuller *Epic Poem on Industrialization* 21 Lugubrious New Dealing Of a mixed pack Of bright new cards And dirty old ones. **1965** *Punch* 27 Oct. 593/1 Somehow President Johnson has managed to inject his countrymen with a new, and better, shot of New Dealism. **1965** *New Statesman* 29 Oct. 634/3 By that time Mr Johnson may have done all the New Dealing he thinks necessary. **1973** *New Yorker* 13 Jan. 56/2 Melvin Laird.. saved everyone's dignity by declaring that the name—Family Security System—sounded 'too New Dealish'.

Newdigate (niū·digĕt). The name of Sir Roger *Newdigate* (1719–1806), M.P. for Oxford University, used *attrib.* and *absol.* to designate an English verse prize founded by him at Oxford University in 1805, or the poetry associated with this prize.

1852 *Prospective Rev.* VIII. 523 These [*sc.* the mechanical parts of rhythm and metre] any industrious person will find in any collection of the Newdegate forms [ed. 1965 Newdigate poems]. **1856** C. M. Yonge *Daisy Chain* ii. v. 383 You should try for the Newdigate Prize. *Ibid.* viii. 414, I am not going to have the Newdigate prizeman shown as brother to a scare-crow. **1860** J. A. Symonds *Let.* 15 June (1967) I. 245, I am so glad you are pleased about the Newdigate. **1929** Ld. Birkenhead *Hundred Best Eng. Ess.* 386 He subsequently entered Christ Church, Oxford, and won the Newdigate Prize. **1931** 'G. Trevor' *Murder at School* i. 12 So far he seemed to have done nothing in life except win the Newdigate. **1969** G. Smith in A. Huxley *Lett.* 11, 1915... His Byronic poem on Glastonbury fails to gain the Newdigate Prize. **1975** *Times* 25 Aug. 5/7 John Buchan..won the Newdigate and was President of the Union.

New England. [See New Englander.] **a.** Used to denote a form of U.S. speech characteristic of New England, and *attrib.* of persons, produce, etc., native to New England; of mentality, idiom, etc., marked by the characteristics of New England.

1638 J. Underhill in *Mass. Hist. Soc. Coll.* (1837) 3rd Ser. VI. 5 Let the clamor be quenched.., that New England men usurp over their wives. **1655** *Deeds Suffolk County, Mass.* (1883) II. 166 Thirty quintalls he reciued.. was New England fish. **1709** W. Byrd *Secret Diary* (1941) 13 Parson Ware sent to me for a pint of canary, he being sick of the gripes with the New England rum. **1715** S. Sewall *Diary* (1882) III. 56 Gave Mr. Short's daughter a New-England shilling. **1787** M. Cutler in Parker & Cutler *Life M. Cutler* (1888) I. 195 [You are] acquainted with the institution of a Company in the New England States by the name of the Ohio Company. **1839** *Southern Lit. Messenger* V. 112/2 Noah Webster..will ere long succeed in giving us a New England tongue which shall not be intelligible in Britain. **1842** Dickens *Let.* 29 Apr. (1974) III. 217 A New England Poet buzzed about me on the Ohio, like a gigantic Bee. **1845** J. F. Cooper *Chainbearer* II. xiv. 466 The supercilious feeling of the New Englandman can very easily be traced to his origin in the mother country. **1850** W. C. Fowler *Eng. Gram.* ii. iii. 92 To pass over the local peculiarities of smaller districts, there are certain generic dialectal differences which characterize, 1. New England. 2. The Southern States. 3. The Western States. **1905** R. Fry *Let.* Jan. (1972) I. 228 The Philadelphia Quakeress..said 'You know I can't bear it because I've got a New England conscience.' **1917** T. S. Eliot *Prufrock* 34 The barren New England hills. **1934** Webster p. xlviii/1, Another variety of short *o* is the 'New England short *o*'. This is acoustically intermediate between ŏ (*nŏte*) and ŭ (*nŭt*), being practically an ŭ sounded with rounded lips. **1935** A. C. Baugh *Hist. Eng. Lang.* 446 In the English language spoken in America three major dialects can be distinguished: New England, Southern, and General American. **1951** *Language* XXVII. 425 The division into Northern, Midland, and Southern (instead of the older New England, General American, and Southern) does not come as a shock. **1952** S. Kauffmann *Philanderer* (1953) iii. 33 They had just been graduated from a small New England college. **1975** *Daily Colonist* (Victoria, B.C.) 26 Oct. 30/8 New England peachblow [glass] is made in one layer shading from red to white. **1975** P. Organ *House on Cheyne Walk* v. 31 We could stand a little New England uprightness here. One tires of the bohemian life.

b. In special collocations, as **New England aster,** a large Michaelmas daisy, *Aster novæ-angliæ*; **New England boiled dinner,** a *boiled *dinner*, esp. one including corned beef; **New England mayflower,** a prostrate, evergreen shrub, *Epigæa repens*, belonging to the family Ericaceæ, native to the eastern half of North America, and better known as trailing arbutus; **New England theology,** a movement in American Congregationalism, also affecting other American Protestant bodies, which repudiated much Calvinist doctrine.

1814 J. Bigelow *Florula Bostoniensis* 199 *Aster Novæ Angliæ.* New England aster... A tall, and very beautiful plant. Stem three feet high, brown, very hairy. **1931** W. N. Clute *Common Names of Plants* 140 The New England aster (*Aster Nova* [sic] *Angliæ*), which lingers long in the fields and fence corners, is further distinguished as last-rose-of-summer. **1968** Peterson & McKenny *Field Guide to Wildflowers Northeastern & Northcentral N. Amer.* 356 New England Aster. *Aster novæ-angliæ.* Our most showy wild aster, deeper violet than the others; rarely rose-colored. **1936** F. M. Farmer *Boston Cooking-School Cook Bk.* (new ed.) 277 New England boiled dinner. Served warm, unpressed corned beef with cabbage, beets, turnips, carrots, and potatoes. **1975** *Times Lit. Suppl.* 20 June 703/2 We have a New England boiled dinner as well as pot-au-feu. **1855** *Harvard Mag.* I. 232 Most admired of our spring flowers is the Ground Laurel, *Epigæa repens*, commonly called Trailing Arbutus, or New England Mayflower. **1952** A. G. L. Hellyer *Sanders' Encycl. Gardening* (ed. 22) 178 *Epigæa... repens*, 'American Ground Laurel', 'New England Mayflower', 'Trailing Arbutus', white, fragrant. **1899** G. N. Boardman (*title*) A history of New England theology. **1967** D. T. Kauffman *Dict. Religious Terms* 329/1 *New England theology*, term for the movement in New England in the latter part of the eighteenth century and the first half of the nineteenth century to tie Calvinism to human reason and experience.

New-Englandism. (Earlier and later examples in sense: An idiom or mode of expression characteristic of New Englanders.)

1831 *Boston Transcript* 7 Sept. 2/3 Mr Pickering, however, thinks *hub* a New-Englandism only. **1948** Mencken *Amer. Lang.* Suppl. II. 198 Dr. R-M. S. Heffner, who was born in 1892 at Bellefontaine, in the west central part of the State [*sc.* Ohio], testifies that New Englandisms were common there in his boyhood.

new-fallen, *a.* **1.** (Later example.)

1926 J. Fergusson in *Oxford Poetry* 23 Like a shield New-fallen on a stricken field.

Newfie (niū·fi, nū·fi). *colloq.* [Hypocoristic, f. Newfoundland, Newfoundlander: see -ie.] Newfoundland; a Newfoundlander. Also *attrib.* or as *adj.*

1942 Berrey & Van den Bark *Amer. Thes. Slang* § 49/4 Newfie, New Foundland [*sic*]. *Ibid.* § 385/5 Newfie, Newfier, a Newfoundlander. **1945** W. H. Pugsley *Saints, Sinners & Ordinary Seamen* 81 This certainly is a change after those winters off Sydney and Newfie. **1958** *In Flight* (Montreal) Summer 8/1 Cod fishing has..long been synonymous with Newfoundland, but today the canny 'Newfies' are no longer putting all their economic eggs in one basket. **1963** R. I. McDavid *Mencken's Amer. Lang.* 166 Colonial days, when rum was actually the chief tipple of American dipsomaniacs... It still is in Newfoundland, where screech or Newfie screech designates the cheapest grade. **1965** *Globe & Mail* (Toronto) 29 Jan. 7/6 Nobody in Newfie..underestimates Joey Smallwood's abilities as a propagandist. *Ibid.* 7 Dec. 6/4, I described a rail trip (on the famous Newfie Bullet) through the great dead heart of the island-province. **1971** S. E. Morison *European Discovery Amer.: Northern Voy.* vi. 180 The rocky surface of eastern Newfoundland is full of small depressions..; swarms of mosquitoes breed therein and make life miserable for all but most hardened 'Newfies'. **1972** *Evening Telegram* (St. John's, Newfoundland) 24 June 10/4 It was Newfie entertainment at its best.

Newfoundland. Add: (Earlier examples of *Newfoundland dog.*)

1773 M. Rishton *Let.* 25 Apr. in F. Burney *Early Diary* (1889) I. 204 We intend getting a very large Newfoundland dog before we leave this place. **1779** W. Coxe *Sketches of Swisserland* v. 49 How we contrived to arrange ourselves, our servants, a large Newfoundland dog, and the baggage, in so narrow a compass.

b. (Earlier example.)

1827 Disraeli *Vivian Grey* V. vii. v. 29 They were instantly saluted by an immense Newfoundland.

New Frontier. [cf. Frontier *sb.* 4 b.] A new approach to reform and social betterment; *spec.* the name given to a programme of social improvement advocated by J. F. Kennedy, President of the U.S. from 1961 to 1963. Hence **New Frontiersman, new frontiersman,** a proponent of this programme.

1934 H. A. Wallace (*title*) The new frontier. **1960** J. F. Kennedy in *N.Y. Times* 16 July 1/8 The New Frontier of which I speak is not a set of promises—it is a set of challenges. **1962** *Listener* 21 June 1057/2 Even the most ardent new frontiersman..would agree that Mr McCormack was probably not exaggerating. **1963** *Guardian* 22 Feb. 11/4 The energy and sophistication of the New Frontiersmen. **1964** *New Statesman* 10 Apr. 574/1 Baulked of any hope of keeping up with the new frontiersmen of science, it is determined to keep tabs on the new backwoodsmen of architecture. **1969** C. Booker *Neophiliacs* vii. 162 Kennedy's New Frontier America. **1973** R. Thomas *If you can't be Good* (1974) ii. 14 The doctoral thesis I had been researching when summoned to the New Frontier.

Newgate. Add: **Newgate hornpipe,** a hanging; **Newgate novel,** a picaresque novel of the

second quarter of the nineteenth century; so *Newgate novelist, Newgate school.*

1829 W. MAGINN in Partridge *Dict. Slang* (1937) 558/1 Toeing a Newgate hornpipe. **1854** C. KNIGHT *Old Printer & Modern Press* vi. 281 The host of penny Newgate novels ..may continue to be sold; but, as far as we can trace, there are no novelties in this once popular literature of the gallows. **1959** *Brno Studies in English* I. 104 The 'Newgate novelists' of the 'thirties (Edward Bulwer, W. H. Ainsworth, and Charles Whitehead) represent a literary school, which is generally called 'the Newgate School' or 'Bulwer's school'. **1963** K. HOLLINGSWORTH *Newgate Novel 1830–47* i. 14 A series of novels having criminals as prominent characters aroused widespread attention. Contemptuous critics at the time called them Newgate fiction, and later writers have grouped them under the label of the Newgate novel. **1965** S. MARCUS *Dickens: from Pickwick to Dombey* ii. 67 In *Catherine*..Thackeray..identified Dickens with the Newgate novelists. **1970** G. M. FRASER *Royal Flash* 188 And then it would be the Newgate hornpipe for Flashy, with the whole damned crew of Sons of the Volsungs hauling on the rope. **1971** R. L. WOLFF *Strange Stories* I. 24 The vogue of the 'Newgate' novel—as the new genre was called after the famous prison, where some of the most affecting scenes usually took place, and after the Newgate Calendar of crime—ran fast and furious.

new girl. [NEW *a.* 8.] A schoolgirl during her first term(s) at a school, esp. one at an English boarding-school; also *transf.*, a (young) woman newly come into a given set of circumstances. Also (with hyphen) *attrib.* or as *adj.* Cf. *NEW BOY.

1853 MRS. GASKELL *Ruth* I. i. 16 Most new girls get impatient at first; but it goes off. **1924** D. MOORE *Fen's First Term* v. 59 A dozen people charged hospitably at the new girl with biscuits and milk. **1936** M. KENNEDY *Together & Apart* I. 130 New girls are always sort of freaks. **1951** N. MITFORD *Blessing* I. viii. 93 She was a new girl, she must watch her step. **1968** 'R. LLEWELLYN' *End of Rug* (1969) xix. 151, I went from school to school... I was rather new-girl at times, of course. A little lonely.

new ground. [GROUND *sb.* 16.] **a.** Ground which has been cleared and cultivated only recently. *U.S. local.* **b.** A part of a goldfield unexploited until recently. *Austral.* (Cf. *to break (new) ground* s.v. *GROUND *sb.* 11 b.)

1624 J. SMITH *Gen. Hist. Virginia* IV. 126 We haue ordinarily foure or fiue [barrels of produce an acre], but of new ground six, seuen, and eight. **1771** in *Maryland Hist. Mag.* (1919) XIV. 134 Our new ground tob[acc]o here has been housed 3 or 4 days past. **1862** *Burrangong* (New South Wales) *Courier* 13 Aug. 2/3 The rush to the Three Mile Diggings..is..going ahead in a most satisfactory manner, and a large extent of new ground has lately been taken up. **1868** *Mining Surveyors & Registrars' Rep.* (Victoria, Dept. Mines) Sept. 36 At Barkly some new ground has been opened south of the main lead. **1915** *Dialect Notes* IV. 186 *New-ground*, virgin land prepared for cultivation. **1937** *Shenandoah* (Va.) *Nature Jrnl.* I. III. 11/1 Each year the acre and half of rough rocky mountain and perhaps a little 'new ground' patch were tilled by hand. **1949** H. HORNSBY *Lonesome Valley* 44 The next time he looked back Chester's place was like a newground that had been burned over. **1953** *Amer. Speech* XXVIII. 251 [Bedford Co., Pa.] *New ground*... Pronounced with a heavily accented *new* and as if it were a single word, *newground*. 'There are lots of teaberries this year out on John Bussard's new ground.' In general use.

New Hall. The name of a site at Shelton, Staffordshire, used to designate china and porcelain produced there.

1829 S. SHAW *Hist. Staffordshire Pott.* viii. 201 The partners..settled the manufactory at the New Hall, Shelton..; on which account the Porcelain had the appellation of *New Hall China*. **1896** E. A. DOWNMAN *Eng. Pott. & Porc.* (new ed.) 132 As no distinguishing mark was used before 1820, New Hall porcelain is difficult to identify. **1969** [see *BRISTOL 2 b].

newie (niū·i). *colloq.* Also **newy.** [f. NEW *a.* + -IE.] **a.** Something new, as a new joke, story, or suggestion. **b.** A person without previous experience in professional entertainment. **c.** A song recently issued on a gramophone record. **d.** = *NEW BALL.

1947 *Amer. Speech* XXII. 157 On the 'Can You Top This?' radio show of November 16, 1946, one of the principal characters said, 'Here's a *new-y*.' His reference was to a joke. **1951** CUSACK & JAMES *Come in Spinner* 495 'Yeah! I seem to have heard your propositions before.' Kim leaned over and took the bottle from her. 'Put that down and listen to me. You haven't heard this one, this is a newy.' **1961** A. BERKMAN *Singers' Gloss. Show Business* 61 *Newies* (Var.), novices; neophytes. **1966** *Melody Maker* 26 Nov. 2 Dave Dee's newie 'Save Me' has an 'African sound with cowbells'. **1971** *West Indian Weekly* 12 Nov. 14/4 The Staples Singers are turning out some incredible soul discs of which their newie, 'Respect Yourself', is a classic in the message song genre. **1972** *Shout* Mar., When this newie turned up..I snatched up a copy. **1975** *Saturday Night* (Toronto) July/Aug. 29/1 Mostly, synectics involves sticking big pieces of paper up around the walls, writing down every bright remark that anyone comes up with, and then winnowing these down to a few golden newies. **1975** *Daily Tel.* 6 Sept. 14/5 But did I say 'ball?' How old-fashioned can one get? 'Ah, the new cherry,' mutters Trevor Bailey with nostalgia in his voice. 'It's the newie,' exclaims Brian Johnston.

New Jersey. The name of one of the eastern states of the United States, used *attrib.* in the names of plants native to the region, as **New Jersey pine** = *Jersey pine* (*JERSEY²); **New Jersey tea** = *Jersey tea* (*JERSEY²).

1759 [see *Jersey tea* (*JERSEY²)]. **1785** H. MARSHALL *Arbustrum Americanum* 27 American Ceanothus, or New-Jersey Tea-tree,..is a low shrub, growing common in most parts of North America. **1818** W. P. C. BARTON *Compendium Floræ Philadelphicæ* II. 183 *P[inus] inops*... New Jersey Pine. Scrub Pine. Pitch Pine. A low straggly, and very common species particularly in Jersey. **1832** D. J. BROWNE *Sylva Amer.* 234 New Jersey Pine. **1877** *Rep. Vermont Board Agric.* IV. 159 Riley recommends persons..to plant a small patch of New Jersey Tea (*Ceanothus*)..as a decoy near the strawberry bed. **1941** R. S. WALKER *Lookout* 59 The New Jersey tea or redroot ..grows profusely on the summit as well as on both sides of the mountain. **1958** G. A. PETRIDES *Field Guide to Trees & Shrubs* 139 New Jersey Tea, *Ceanothus americanus* L... A low shrub. Leaves egg-shaped to triangular... Flowers white in dense heads.

New Left, new left. [Phr. coined by C. Wright Mills (1916–62), American political sociologist.] The name of a movement originated by young radicals opposed to the philosophy of the 'old' liberal society; now applied to many movements of protest. Also *attrib.* Hence **New Lefter, New Lefty,** a supporter of radical policies; **New Leftish** *a.*, **New Leftist** *a.* and *sb.*

1960 *New Left Rev.* Jan.–Feb. 1 Our hope is that people in the New Left will feel, with a special urgency, the poverty of ideas in the Labour Movement. *Ibid.* Mar.–Apr. 70/2 The 'anarchism' of young New Lefters. *Ibid.* Sept.–Oct. 15/2 Stop the new-leftist dogs from yapping. **1960** New Lefty [see *HOBOHEMIA]. **1961** *New Left Rev.* Jan.–Feb. 51/1 What can..be called 'new left' student opinion. **1966** *Economist* 3 Sept. 887/1 The phrase 'new left' is applied to all sorts of protesters in the United States, to Provos in Amsterdam, to dissatisfied intellectuals in eastern Europe. **1967** *Philosophy* XLII. 287 The emphasis is rather New-Leftish and Gramscian. **1967** *Time* 28 Apr. 15 The New Leftists have a mystical faith in the purity and wisdom of the poor, 'uncorrupted' by the Establishment. **1968** *Listener* 3 Oct. 442/1 The would-be Monday Clubber and the New Lefter will both shut up when they hear of the accident in the Headrow. **1971** *Daily Tel.* 18 Nov. 15/3 Berkeley City Council—first and only city government in America to represent the 'New Left'—has passed an astonishing resolution..to offer asylum to military deserters. **1973** *Times Lit. Suppl.* 23 Nov. 1422/5 Whose sympathies are clearly more towards the New Left than towards bureaucratic communism. **1975** *Listener* 13 Feb. 209/1 All over Europe in the Sixties you could see a proliferation of political sects—Marxists, Trotskyists, Maoists, Castroists... This New Left..was, above all, a manifestation of youth.

new light. [LIGHT *sb.* 6 d.] **1. a.** Novel religious views or doctrines (see LIGHT *sb.* 6 d).

1650–1785 [see LIGHT *sb.* 6 d]. **1806** T. G. FESSENDEN *Democracy Unveiled* II. 181 Altho' not bless'd with second sight, Divine inflation, or new light.

b. Any of the religious sects or doctrines of the 'New Lights'.

1750 J. BIRKET *Voy. N. Amer.* (1916) 4 There is two Presbyterian meeting houses here, one of the Newlight, and one of the old. **1819** J. G. LOCKHART *Peter's Lett. to his Kinsfolk* III. lxii. 100 The Old Light Antiburghers enjoy the ministrations of..Dr. McCrie... The New Light.. are ruled *in spiritualibus* by Dr. Jamieson. **1850** W. H. FOOTE *Sk. Virginia* 373 In his discourse he..read a hue and cry, for the arrest of 'the new light'. **1874** [see LIGHT *sb.* 6 d]. **1943** J. MACLEOD *Scottish Theology* 229 As a term, New Light came especially to be used in connection with the change that took place in the thinking of the Seceders towards the end of the 18th century.

2. A person holding 'new lights' or novel (religious) doctrines; a revivalist; a member of any of various schisms from several Protestant churches in Scotland and N. Amer. during the eighteenth and nineteenth centuries.

a **1734** R. WODROW *Analecta* (1842) II. 169 You have brought in a stranger, one of the neu-lights, among us. **1743** J. HEMPSTEAD *Diary* 30 Mar. (1901) 407 All come to settle the disorders that are subsisting among those called New Lights which follow Mr Davenport. **1750** J. BIRKET *Voy. N. Amer.* (1916) 22 There is Nineteen different places of Worship in the Town (to wit) thirteen of the Independents Presbyterians & newlights &Ca. **1796** GROSE *Dict. Vulgar T.* (ed. 3) *New Light*, one of the new light; a methodist. **1807** R. MCNEMAR *Kentucky Revival* 29 These ..taught as an important truth, that the will of God, was made manifest to each individual..by an inward light... Hence they received the name of 'New-Lights'. **1828** J. MCGREGOR *Sk. Maritime Colonies Brit. Amer.* II. 465 Let us leave abstract points of Christian doctrine to theological disputants, and the raving of *new lights*. **1847** R. DAVIDSON *Hist. Presbyterian Church in Kentucky* 219 In the Great Revival, Mr. Stone was conspicuous..[in] the subsequent formation of societies, known under the various names of New Lights, Christians, Arians, Marshallites, and Stoneites. **1872** [see *HICKORY 4 a]. **1888** J. M. BARRIE *Auld Licht Idylls* iii. 60 The congregation..had split, and as the New Lights (now the U.P.'s) were in the majority, the Old Lights..had to retire to the community. **1949** *William & Mary Q.* Jan. 43 The New Brunswick group, the 'new lights', wished to give eloquence in preaching precedence over formal knowledge. **1959** *Chambers's Encycl.* XII. 309/1 The original seceders..formed themselves into a body independent of the state church in 1733. The new group of separatists were divided in 1747 by the anti-Jacobite burgess oath into burghers and anti-burghers. Subsequently each of these bodies split into Old and New Lights (1799 and 1806 respectively).

b. *transf.* = *CAMPBELLITE 2.

1877 *Bull. U.S. Nat. Museum* No. 9. 21 *Pomoxys annularis*... Throughout Kentucky it is known as the 'New Light', and sometimes as 'Campbellite'. **1884** [see *CAMPBELLITE 2].

3. *attrib.* or as *adj.* **a.** Belonging to or holding the views of the 'New Lights'.

1732 SWIFT *Advantages repealing Sacramental Test* 10 The Quarrel between Old and New Light-Men, is managed with more Rage and Rancour, than any other Dispute. **1742** J. HEMPSTEAD *Diary* 20 Dec. (1901) 402, 2 of them Newlight Exhorters begun their meeting. **1744** [see LIGHT *sb.* 6 d]. **1793** 'T. THRUM' *Look before ye Loup* 3, I took the advice of a *newlight* neighbour upo' this knotty point. **1807** R. MCNEMAR *Kentucky Revival* 46 Taking what is called the *New-light* doctrine, as the rudiments of divine truth, they proceeded to consider the nature of justification, reconciliation to God, etc. **1837** W. JENKINS *Ohio Gazetteer* 373 There are in this county..eight christian (or newlight)..and five dunkard churches. **1874** [see LIGHT *sb.* 6 d]. **1883** P. SCHAFF *Relig. Encycl.* II. 1634/2 [New England divines] announced a few principles, which were called 'New-Light Divinity', or 'New Divinity'. **1949** *Canad. Hist. Rev.* Mar. 75 Henry Alline, the New Light evangelist, was shattering the less sedate Dissenting congregations of the Nova Scotian out-ports.

b. *transf.* Novel, newfangled.

1831 J. N. CATRON *Let.* 1 May in N. N. Scott *Mem. H. L. White* (1856) xii. 249 A union of N. Light Federalists with Kentucky republicans..cannot last. **1833** J. B. WYETH *Oregon* 4 What the *new-light* doctrine of Phrenology calls the disposition bump of *Inhabitiveness*. **1839** *Spirit of Times* 26 Oct. 399/3 *Abbreviations*... We heard of this 'new light system' being carried so far as to be adopted by a lady.

Hence **New Lightism**, new-light doctrines.

1755 in *Essex Inst. Hist. Coll.* (1916) LII. 78 He seems a grave, close heavy Man, not given to talk & deeply immerged in New Lightism. **1857** P. CARTWRIGHT *Autobiogr.* 32 B. W. Stone stuck to his New Lightism.

new look. [*LOOK *sb.* 2 f.] **1.** (Freq. with capital initials.) A style of women's clothes introduced in Paris by Christian Dior in 1947, characterized esp. by skirts longer and fuller than those previously worn. Also applied to more recent new styles.

1947 *Time* 15 Sept. 87 What was going on [in fashion]? The search for the 'New Look'. What was the New Look? No one knew precisely. **1948** *Economist* 14 Feb. 285/2 Clothing in styles which the New Look has superseded. **1949** *Ann. Reg. 1948* 59 The 'new look' had swept the great cities. **1957** *Daily Mail* 25 Oct. 10/2 When Christian Dior launched the New Look in 1947 it met with an enthusiasm which amounted to hysteria. **1958** *Spectator* 8 Aug. 187/1 The [fashion] trade now bitterly resents St. Laurent's new look.

2. In wider use: a change in policy or procedure; a renovated or up-to-date presentation or appearance. Also (with hyphen) *attrib.*

1948 *Melody Maker* 3 Apr. 3/3 (*heading*) The 'New Look' in jazz has come to stay. **1952** *Economist* 27 Sept. 765/2 (*heading*) Czech trade unions reorganized... The 'new look' given to, and by, the trade union officials at once brought them into conflict with the rank and file of the movement. **1952** *Science News Let.* 25 Oct. 258/1 A 'New Look' for veterans with smashed noses due to wartime injuries is being developed. **1955** *Ann. Reg. 1954* 169 On January 12 the Secretary of State, Mr. Dulles, announced what came to be called the 'New Look' policy. **1956** E. J. RUPPELT *Report on Unidentified Flying Objects* 85 In early 1949 the term 'new look' was well known. The new look in women's fashions was the lower hemlines, in automobiles it was longer lines. In UFO circles the new look was cuss 'em. **1958** J. CANNAN *And be a Villain* iii. 61 How different life looked now, and how strange that the begetter of this New Look was..the depraved and disgraced Jonathan. **1959** *News Chron.* 2 Nov. 5/1 The new-look colours and markings which are to be on all B.E.A. airliners. **1960** *Guardian* 28 Apr. 6/6 The 'new look' which..the Glasgow business man who now runs the Tourist Board, is giving to tourist centres. **1966** *Melody Maker* 15 Oct. 19 A slightly new-look Johnny Parker band restored to full vigour. **1974** S. GULLIVER *Vulcan Bulletins* 107 It's the new-look Libyan justice. Or rather, it's medieval but recently revived.

Hence **new-loo·kish** *a.*

1950 *Christian Sci. Monitor* 20 Feb. 10/1 Visitors recently returned from Moscow report that it is the most New Lookish of any Russian city.

newly, *adv.* Add: **1. c.** (Further examples.)

1690 LOCKE *Ess. Hum. Understanding* III. x. § 32 He that, in a newly-discovered country, shall see several sorts of animals and vegetables, unknown to him before, may have as true ideas of them, as of a horse or stag. **1831** MILL *Let.* 22 Oct. (1910) I. 19 They have formed a plan for a new colony,.. on the coast of Southern Australia, near the place where the newly discovered navigable river discharges itself into the sea. **1834** —— in *Monthly Repos.* VIII. 163 The many are..likely to make a most dangerous use of their newly-acquired power. **1848** S. M. GRAY *Let.* 11 Apr. in M. Lutyens *Ruskins & Grays* (1972) xi. 107 Many compliments [were] paid to the newly married couple. **1937** *Burlington Mag.* Apr. 173/2 Prince of a newly-constituted State. **1968** R. A. LYTTLETON *Myst. Solar Syst.* v. 166 It endows the newly-formed comets with orbits that are almost parabolic. **1974** J. WAINWRIGHT *Evidence I shall Give* viii. 35 Lennox was bringing the newly-arrived Sugden up to date on the murder.

d. newly-wed, newlywed, a person newly married.

1918 *Cosmopolitan* Feb. 90/2 It seemed that a Newly-wed can live on Marmalade for about three months. **1932** AUDEN *Orators* III. 103 To-day may mean division for the newly-weds. **1935** *Discovery* Mar. 91/1 Generation upon generation of newly-weds are tempted to 'come and live in leafy ——'. **1938** J. I. RODALE *King's English on Horse-back* 146/1 Newlyweds. First-nighters. **1959** G. FREEMAN *Jack would be Gentleman* viii. 163 'Quite the blissful newly-weds, aren't we?'..'Well, we are newly-weds.' **1973** *Guardian* 12 Mar. 9/6 The advertisement..was one of a series which featured a newly-wed, an insurance man and a saleslady.

Newmania (niū̆mēⁱ·niă). [f. the name of J. H. *Newman* (see NEWMANISM) + -IA¹, punning on MANIA.] Enthusiastic support for Newmanism. Also *attrib.* Also **Newmanic** (niū̆mæ·nik) *a.*, pertaining to or characteristic of J. H. Newman or his views.

1838 J. ROMILLY *Diary* 9 Dec. (1967) 158 A very objectionable sermon..as faulty as the 'Newmania' sect at Oxford. **1849** F. D. MAURICE *Let.* 9 Mar. in J. F. Maurice *F. D. Maurice* (1884) I. xxv. 518 Froude's hero.. adopted the Newmanic theory. He gave God credit for being a tyrant. **1900** W. TUCKWELL *Reminisc. of Oxford* ii. 17 Men who formed in Oxford what was known as the Noetic school.., provoking by their political and ecclesiastical liberalism the great revolt of the Newmania. **1958** *Spectator* 7 Feb. 167/3 The Newmania [in Oxford] was succeeded by the Railway Mania.

Newman–Keuls (niū̆:măn,köls). *Statistics.* The names of D. *Newman* (of the Dept. of Statistics, University College, London) and M. *Keuls* (of the Institute of Horticultural Plant Breeding, Wageningen, Holland), used *attrib.* to designate a test they devised for assessing the significance of differences between the means of different sets of observations, using the ranges of the sets contributing to the means.

1955 D. B. DUNCAN in *Biometrics* XI. 26 The Newman–Keuls Test. A test proposed by Newman..in 1939 and again by Keuls..in 1952 succeeds very simply in raising all of the low protection levels of the multiple *t* test. This test is equivalent to a multiple *t* test preceded by several preliminary range tests. **1962** B. J. WINER *Statistical Princ. Exper. Design* iii. 85 The level of significance for the Newman–Keuls procedure is considered individually with respect to each test. **1970** *Jrnl. General Psychol.* LXXXII. 159 The Newman Keuls test..was run on the means for the different diagnostic classes.., with results indicating significantly more cartoon enjoyment for normals than for the neurotic and sociopathic Ss. No other differences reached significance.

Newmarket. Add: **1.** *Newmarket boot*; **Newmarket coat** (earlier example).

1837 B. WEBSTER *My Young Wife & my Old Umbrella* in *Acting National Drama* I. 7 Green Newmarket cut coat. **1933** J. BUCHAN *Prince of Captivity* II. iv. 248 She had been gardening..and wore Newmarket boots. **1958** *Times* 6 Oct. 13/1 The foot which would be warm and practical with sheepskin or Newmarket boots.

New Mexican, *a.* and *sb.* [f. *New Mexico*, one of the United States.] **a.** *adj.* Of or belonging to New Mexico. **b.** *sb.* A native or inhabitant of New Mexico.

1834 A. PIKE *Sketches* 137 To an American, the first sight of these New Mexican villages is novel and singular. *Ibid.* 170 Even the New Mexicans call him a great rascal. **1893** C. F. LUMMIS *Land of Poco Tiempo* 294 Twenty miles south of the New Mexican hamlet of Manzano..is.. the pueblo of Abó. **1940** E. FERGUSSON *Our Southwest* 228 Few families are so completely urbanized as not to have a little ranch somewhere, and New Mexicans care for their own as long as they can.

new-mown, *ppl. a.* Add: *new-mown hay*, as the name of a scent.

1890–1 *T. Eaton & Co. Catal.* Fall & Winter 42/2 Jockey club, new-mown hay, lily of the valley, 25 c. per bottle. **1926–7** *Army & Navy Stores Catal.* 490/2 Perfumes ..Lilas Blanc, New Mown Hay, Oeillet Blanc. **1971** *Guardian* 17 Aug. 7/2 Their new Meadowsong fragrance range..based on..newmown hay, honeysuckle, clover.

New Negro, new negro. *U.S.* **a.** During the period of slavery, a Negro brought from Africa to the New World. **b.** An artist belonging to the *New Negro Movement*, the efflorescence of Negro writing, etc., during the 1920s. **c.** A Negro claiming equal status with a white American.

1701 C. WOLLEY *Two Years' Jrnl. N.-Y.* 32 In Barbados new Negro's (*i.e.* such as cannot speak English) are bought for twelve or fourteen pound a head. **1732** *Calendar State Papers Amer. & W. Indies* (1939) 55 Except proof were made that they were all new negroes and not been above 6 months in America. **1860** S. MORDECAI *Virginia* 350, I do not speak of the New Negros, as the imported Africans were called, but of their descendants. **1922** A. P. RANDOLPH in A. Dundes *Mother Wit* (1973) 400/1 It does not occur to the Old South that there is a 'New Negro'; that the 'Uncle Toms' are passing. **1925** A. LOCKE in *Survey* (N.Y.) Graphic No., 1 Mar. 632/1 The Negro is being carefully studied, not just talked about and discussed. In arts and letters, instead of being wholly caricatured, he is being seriously portrayed and painted. To all of this the New Negro is keenly responsive as an augury of a new democracy in American culture. **1953** S. A. BROWN in A. Dundes *Mother Wit* (1973) 40/1 We go then to what is called the New Negro Movement. *Ibid.* 43/2 She wouldn't let anybody kick her around (something like the New Negro). **1963** in J. H. Clarke *Harlem* (1964) 40 For a racial dilemma in Negro art, a racial solution was necessary. This came in the mid-twenties from the inspiration of the New Negro Movement with its crusade of folk expression in all of the arts. *Ibid.* 49 Many of the New Negroes were unwilling victims of an inverted racialistic nationalism,..priding themselves that they could sing, paint and write as well as their white-skinned patrons.

Newnhamite (niū̆·nămait). [f. *Newnham* (see below) + -ITE¹.] One who is, or has been, a student at Newnham College, one of the Cambridge colleges for women.

1896 [see GIRTONIAN]. **1907** R. BROOKE *Let.* 28 Nov. (1968) 115 Most of the committee are Newnhamites, strange wild people. **1913** J. VAIZEY *College Girl* xx. 282, I am proud to be a Newnhamite. **1936** M. V. HUGHES *London Girl of Eighties* vi. 119 Miss Rogers, a large and genial Newnhamite.

New Orleans (niū̆ ǭlī·ănz, -lī·nz). The name of a city in SE. Louisiana, giving its name to various commercial and natural products; used *spec.* to designate a style of jazz which originated there.

1807 C. SCHULTZ *Travels* (1810) I. 132 Kentucky and New-Orleans boats from one dollar to one and a half a foot. **1849** G. G. FOSTER *N.Y. in Slices* 82 The grocery-keeper..buys a barrel of common New Orleans molasses at twenty-five cents per gallon. [**1905** (*title of tune composed by Jelly Roll Morton*) New Orleans Blues. **1922** (*name of jazz band*) New Orleans Rhythm Kings.] **1935** *Swing Music* July 120/1 The expressions 'Chicago Style', 'New Orleans Style' were certainly invented by the American musicians, and not at all by European hot fans. **1938** D. BAKER *Young Man with Horn* I. v. 42 Jeff's band..had two styles of playing, known to the present trade as Memphis style and New Orleans style. *Ibid.* 43 Memphis style is sometimes called 'take your turn', and New Orleans has everybody in at the same time. **1952** B. WOLFE *Limbo* (1953) II. ix. 102 Program of jazz recordings... Maybe New Orleans had come back..to a world it..belonged to. **1955** R. BLESH *Shining Trumpets* (ed. 3) iii. 58 They prophesy New Orleans jazz as clearly as they recall Africa. **1958** OSBORNE & CREIGHTON *Epitaph G. Dillon* I. 14 Do you mind if we do without New Orleans just for the moment? **1965** G. MELLY *Owning-Up* xi. 128 What the revivalists thought of as 'New Orleans Jazz' was the music of Armstrong, Morton and Oliver—New Orleans musicians but based on, and recorded in, Chicago, during the Prohibition era. What the traditionalists meant by New Orleans Jazz..was the music played by musicians who had never left the city. **1973** J. DRUMMOND *Bang! Bang! You're Dead!* xiii. 34 One of the early New Orleans rags.

New Realism, new realism. *Philos.* Chiefly *U.S.* Doctrines of Realism as revived at the beginning of the twentieth century to refute certain tenets of Idealism, emphasizing the existence of objects in the external world independently of the way they are subjectively experienced. (For the contemporary movement in Britain, cf. *REALISM 1 c.) So **New Realist** *sb.* and *a.*, an adherent or advocate of, pertaining to, New Realism.

1906 J. S. MACKENZIE in *Mind* XV. 308 (*heading*) The New Realism and the Old Idealism. *Ibid.*, Some of the leading supporters of the new Realism (especially Mr. Moore and Mr. Russell) connect it with an extremely nominalistic type of Logic. **1920** W. R. SORLEY *Hist. Eng. Philos.* xii. 297 Forms of what is called the new realism seem to have been started independently in the United States and in this country. **1929** C. I. LEWIS *Mind & World-Order* ii. 39 Immediacy is thus emphasized ..by the American new-realists. **1947** *Mind* LVI. 290 As everyone knows, the revolt against Idealism, initiated chiefly by Moore and Russell in this country and by the New Realist group in the United States, proved quite prodigiously successful. **1966** F. COPLESTON *Hist. Philos.* VIII. v. xvii. 387 The new realists were at any rate agreed on the truth of a basic tenet.., 'things known are not products of the knowing relation nor essentially dependent for their existence or behaviour upon that relation'.

news, *sb.* (*pl.*) Add: **2. c.** *no news is good news* (further examples).

1616 JAMES I *Let.* 13 May in A. J. Kempe *Loseley Manuscripts* (1835) 403 No newis is better then evill newis. **1850** F. E. SMEDLEY *Frank Fairleigh* x. 101 Arguing.. (on the 'no-news being good-news' system) that I should have heard again if anything had gone wrong, I dismissed the subject from my mind. **1916** 'TAFFRAIL' *Pincher Martin* xviii. 336 They could not bring themselves to believe that 'no news was good news'. **1941** A. HUXLEY *Let.* 27 Nov. (1969) 473 Matthew never writes; but we interpret no news as good news.

e. *that* (or *it*) *is news to me*: I did not know that. *colloq.*

1898 S. WEYMAN *Castle Inn* xvi. 159 For the rest, which this gentleman says, about who she is and her claim.. it is news to me. **1919** D. ASHFORD *Young Visiters* viii. 69 Ethel he said blushing a deep red I always wished to marry you some fine day. This is news to me cried Ethel still peevish. **1943** J. B. PRIESTLEY *Daylight on Saturday* xii. 76 If you've had any trouble with your husband, I'm sorry, but it's news to me. **1968** S. B. HOUGH *Sweet Sister Seduced* xv. 79, I had thought we were in tune with one another...that my reactions were her reactions. It was news to me, as she told me in round phrases, that in fact they weren't. **1974** M. Z. LEWIN *Enemies Within* xxxiv. 154 'I'm going to Chicago shortly.' News to me. But not a bad idea.

f. *bad news*, used to designate something or someone unpleasant, unlucky, or undesirable (see quots.). *colloq.*

For the literal use cf. quot. 1821 in Dict.

1926 MAINES & GRANT *Wise-Crack Dict.* 5/2 *Bad news*, piece of pasteboard handed by the waiter after a meal. **1929** M. A. GILL *Underworld Slang*, *Bad news*, shot gun. **1930** *Amer. Mercury* Dec. 454/1 *Bad news*, trouble. 'Sucker, stay out of me district! It's bad news if you don't.' **1935** A. J. POLLOCK *Underworld Speaks* 120/1 *The bad news*, the bill (check) in a restaurant, speakeasy or night club. **1942** BERREY & VAN DEN BARK *Amer. Thes. Slang* § 256/1 *Difficulty, trouble..*, bad news. **1963** I. FLEMING *On H.M. Secret Service* i. 13 Their waiter.. had simply put them in the category of 'bad news' and hoped they would soon be on their way. **1964** *Amer. Speech* XXXIX. 189 *Bad news*, 'a poor social evening, a wasted night'. **1968** 'J. WELCOME' *Hell is where you find It* iv. 67 'Where is she?' I said... 'Listen, I don't know. She's bad news, that one.' **1973** 'E. MCBAIN' *Let's hear It* v. 69 Bikies had begun drifting into the area, sporting their leather jackets and their swastikas... The bikies were bad news. **1973** H. MILLER *Open City* xviii. 197 Any kind of witness would be bad news on a job with such a tight specification. **1974** D. GRAY *Dead Give Away* iii. 31 Milly these days was plain bad news. Her fascination had evaporated.

g. A person, place, etc., regarded as a topic of discussion or note.

1912 KIPLING *Diversity of Creatures* (1917) 192 The great Baron Reuter himself..flashed that letter in full to the front, back, and both wings of this scene of our labours. For Huckley was News. **1946** E. WAUGH *When Going was Good* v. 260 Abyssinia was News. Everyone with any claims to African experience was cashing in. **1965** *Listener* 23 Sept. 452/2 The reading boom..has made poets news, and it has made them think about being news. **1974** V. GIELGUD *In Such a Night* vii. 58, I am not what is commonly called 'news'. But..my wife is 'news' in the biggest possible way.

5. c. A television or radio programme in which the news is announced and sometimes discussed; a newsreel. Also *attrib.*

1923 *Radio Times* 28 Sept. 9/1 10.0. — Time signal, general news bulletin. Broadcast to all stations, followed by London News and Weather Report. **1925** *Daily Herald* 23 June 4/3 To hear the news from your favourite announcer is like buying your favourite newspaper. **1932** G. GREENE *Stamboul Train* II. i. 66 Janet Pardoe said that she wanted to see the news and they both stayed [in the cinema]. **1939** T. S. ELIOT *Family Reunion* II. i. 97 And now it is nearly time for the news We must listen to the weather report And the international catastrophes. **1940** 'G. ORWELL' in *World Rev.* (1950) June 21, I went to the pub to hear the 9 o'clock news. **1947** AUDEN *Age of Anxiety* (1948) I. 17 Now the news. Night raids on Five cities. **1953** M. LASKI *Victorian Chaise Longue* 64 It was that programme just before the news. **1968** 'D. RUTHERFORD' *Skin for Skin* iv. 95 Crisp...glanced at his watch. 'Five minutes till news time... Can you look after her while I listen to the news?' **1972** D. DELMAN *Sudden Death* (1973) iv. 121 It was news time so..I turned on the TV. **1973** J. DRUMMOND *Bang! Bang! You're Dead!* xxxvi. 126 The ginger-headed Crabbe was watching the nine o'clock news.

6. a. *news-dealer* (earlier and later examples), *-gatherer* (later examples).

1861 *Chicago Tribune* 15 Apr., We..are now prepared to furnish News Dealers and Booksellers with Every Paper, Periodical and Book. **1966** R. ELLISON in A. Chapman *New Black Voices* (1972) 407 One newsdealer in Harlem. **1963** *Punch* 20 Feb. 273/1 He is a seer rather than an exclusive news-gatherer. **1971** *Guardian* 20 Dec. 11/1 The Guardian's specialist correspondents are not only newsgatherers but also distinguished commentators.

b. *news-gathering*; *news black-out, -board, bulletin, conference, editor, feature, film, item, magazine, -matter, media, -print* (earlier example), *story, summary, value.*

1944 *Sun* (Baltimore) 17 Aug. 1/6 The whole sector east of the Falaise bottleneck was under an Allied news blackout. **1945** [see *BLACK-OUT 2]. **1974** HAWKEY & BINGHAM *Wild Card* xxiii. 192 To reduce the risk of panic..a news blackout was requested. **1922** JOYCE *Ulysses* 116 A stately figure entered between the newsboards. *Ibid.* 218 He passed Grogan's the tobacconist against which newsboards leaned. **1915** (*title*) News Bulletin (Aero Club Amer.). **1923** [see sense 5 c above]. **1925** News bulletin [see *BULLETIN 2 b]. **1973** C. EGLETON *Seven Days to Killing* xx. 211 Julyan sat..listening to the transistor radio... The music faded to give way to the news bulletin. **1966** 'G. BLACK' *You want to die, Johnny?* i. 11 At a news conference in Los Angeles..Lil had said to television cameras..: 'Boots and I think God is a drag.' **1972** *N.Y. Times* 3 Nov. 1/1 The Prime Minister's announcement at a televised news conference was a rejection of demands..that the Liberal Prime Minister resign. *a* **1883** G. W. BAGBY *Old Virginia Gentleman* (1910) 190 Pollard he declared was 'the best news editor in the whole South'. **1931** *Daily Express* 16 Oct. 11/3 Before I die, I wish to see the countenance of my own news editor when I stand before him admitting a similar circumstance. **1951** *Oxf. Jun. Encycl.* IV. 300/2 The news editor also receives a great deal of information from Government departments. **1974** *Times* 16 Nov. 15/5 The issue at the *Kentish Times* is..whether six journalists styled 'district editors'..are in fact the editors of newspapers... Each..works under the direction of the news editor of the *Kentish Times*. **1912** *International* (N.Y.) Apr. 79/1 It is wonderful what a variety of cultured subjects are concentrated in the Gould article—economics

..and heart interest 'news feature' as the daily papers would say. **1973** 'S. Harvester' *Corner of Playground* II. i. 81 She loved news-features about herself. **1940** J. Reith *Diary* 16 Jan. (1975) v. 238 Very bothered about a news film..in which Hore-Belisha was cheered and Gort received in silence. **1941** E. Niggeman *Let.* 2 Jan. in H. Nicolson *Diaries & Lett.* (1967) 136, I also went to a News film and saw the film of London's fire. **1965** *B.B.C. Handbk.* 65 The BBC's own newsfilm cameramen. **1974** *Times* 9 Dec. 13/2 Producers of television.. want..access to Parliament for the making of news film on the big occasions. **1918** W. G. Bleyer *Profession of Journalism* 27 The Allied governments abroad and our courts at home have struck a hard blow at the Hearst news-gathering concern. *Ibid.* 114 The Associated Press is the child of the first effort at cooperative news-gathering ever made. **1966** *B.B.C. Handbk.* 52 General news-gathering facilities have been enlarged. **1972** H. Evans *Newsman's English* i. 1 This news-gathering is a prodigious if familiar achievement. **1844** *Knickerbocker* XXIV. 179 News-items, matters of information, actual discoveries. **1930–1** G. Ade *Let.* Dec.–Jan. (1973) 149 Here are some news items which have not been printed but which come from pretty reliable sources. **1938** News-item [see *cover design* s.v. *cover *sb.*[1] 8]. **1958** *New Statesman* 20 Dec. 871/1 The second intrusive news-item concerns the budget. **1923** (*title*) Time, the weekly news-magazine. **1953** *Encounter* Nov. 5/1 He shifted to the weekly news-magazine, *Der Spiegel*. **1968** *Listener* 4 Apr. 442/3 His job was to compile the early morning news magazine which I shall present at ten past seven. **1923** O. G. Villard *Some Newspapers & Newspapermen* 88 His rivals and critics accuse him..of going to the very edge of the salacious in some of his news-matter and fiction. **1959** *Times* 14 Jan. 12/5 The setting and make-up of newsmatter. **1962** *Amer. Speech* XXXVII. 44 The news media in Moscow relayed to the American press the sensational story of Gagarin's space flight. **1972** J. Mann *Mrs. Knox's Profession* xiv. 105 The news media had got on to the story very quickly. **1973** *Sat. Rev. Soc.* (U.S.) May 69/3 Survey results can be disseminated through the news media. **1843** *Knickerbocker* XXII. 283 The news-prints kept their works and worth before the public eye. **1932** News story [see *money *sb.* 6 b]. **1974** M. G. Eberhart *Danger Money* (1975) xiii. 136 She can't stop the news stories but perhaps she can soften them. **1941** *B.B.C. Gloss. Broadcasting Terms* 20 News summary: (1) Brief statement of salient news items, broadcast at a fixed time. (2) Brief statement of principal news items, broadcast as a preface in a news bulletin. **1973** A. MacVicar *Painted Doll Affair* ii. 33, I turned on the dashboard radio... The pop music was interrupted by a news summary. **1906** J. London *Let.* 8 Apr. (1966) 198 But what I did propose to you was 'events of large news-value'. **1926** T. Beer *Mauve Decade* 172 He had no 'news value'—Julian Ralph invented the phrase in 1892 although it would be long before it became sacred. **1941** [see *ephemeral *a.*]. **1960** G. Butler *Death lives Next Door* vii. 149 Ezra could see at once that he had news value. **1972** P. Black *Biggest Aspidistra* III. viii. 229 Lord Hill..justified the occasional trivialisation as better than some academic selection of news values.

c. news agency, (*a*) a business that sells newspapers and periodicals; (*b*) a business organization that collects and supplies news to subscribing newspapers, broadcasters, etc.; **news-boat** (earlier example); **news break,** a newsworthy item (see also quot. 1969); **news butch(er)** *U.S. colloq.* [*butcher *sb.* 3 b], a seller of newspapers, sweets, etc., on a train; **news cinema,** a cinema which shows a succession of short films, cartoons, and newsreels; **news desk,** the department of a newspaper office responsible for collecting and reporting the news; **news-dick** *literary nonce-wd.*, a newshawk, a news-hound; **news flash** (see *flash *sb.*[2] 1 d); **news-girl,** a girl who sells newspapers; **news-hawk, -hound** *colloq.* (orig. *U.S.*), a newspaper reporter; **news peg,** a news story that forms the basis of an editorial, interview, cartoon, etc.; **newsprint,** cheap paper made from mechanical and chemical wood-pulp, and used chiefly for newspapers (see also 6 b); also **news-printing** *vbl. sb.*; **news-reader,** a person who reads the news on radio or television (see also 6 a); hence **news-reading** *vbl. sb.*; **news-reel, news reel,** a short cinema film dealing with news and current affairs; also *attrib.*; **news room,** (*b*) the office in a newspaper, radio, or television station, etc., where the news is processed; **news-stand** (earlier and later examples); **news theatre** = **news cinema*; **news ticker,** a telegraphic recording instrument which automatically prints the news on to a tape; **news-work** (earlier and later examples).

1873 F. Hudson *Journalism* 521 News agencies.. branched out and extended into colossal news companies as a..necessity of the age. **1883** *Encycl. Brit.* XX. 405/2 The demand for such reporting had led, on the passing of the telegraphs into the hands of the state, to the formation of news agencies which undertook to supply the provincial newspapers. **1887** *Postal Laws* (U.S.) 147 In admitting second-class publications sent from a news agency, postmasters will observe the following [rules]. **1890** [see *burglar *v.*]. **1933** J. Buchan *Prince of Captivity* III. ii. 291 A statement to an international news agency. **1959** *New Statesman* 25 Apr. 564/3 Chancellor is a brilliant journalistic administrator who deserves a very large part of the credit for the wartime and post-war recovery of that famous world news-agency, but he has had no previous experience in actual magazine or newspaper publication. **1974** J. Banning *How I fooled the World* iv. 23 One difference..between working for a newspaper and working for a news agency was that a news agency correspondent is much more vulnerable. **1830** *Boston Transcript* 1 Sept. 2/2 The news-boat, T. H. Smith, belonging to the Associated Morning Papers, boarded the packet ship Caledonia,..25 miles outside Sandy Hook, and before she was boarded by any other news-boat. **1954** D. Dodge *Lights of Skaro* vi. 218 Filing coverage on one of the news breaks of our time. **1959** J. Thurber *Years with Ross* v. 80 Newsbreaks, those garbled..items from American journals..which conveniently fill out..*New Yorker* columns. **1969** *New Yorker* 11 Oct. 43/1 We've just received a letter..enclosing three newsbreaks (those little items we print at the bottom of the page) for our consideration. **1930** A. Henderson *Contemporary Immortals* 54 In connection with his profession as 'news butch' or seller of newspapers, candy and the like, he established a printing press and a small laboratory upon the train. **1894** *Daily Ardmoreite* (Ardmore, Okla.) 1 Jan. 3/1 Ben R. Wheeler, an old time and popular news butcher on the Santa Fe..is in the city. **1930** J. Dos Passos *42nd Parallel* 294 He got a concession as newsbutcher on the daily train. **1947** L. M. Beebe *Mixed Train Daily* 85 The news butcher..still carries as stock in trade the immortal volume of senescent anecdotes, Thomas W. Jackson's *On a Slow Train Through Arkansas*. **1935** *Punch* 14 Aug. 192/1 Trousers go wrong the moment you move in them. The news-cinemas and photographs in the papers tell you that. **1965** M. Stewart *Airs above Ground* i. 16 There was an hour to Angy's train and we wanted somewhere to sit, so we went to the news cinema. **1950** *Kemsley Man. Journalism* 1. 67 Touch must constantly be kept with the picture news desk which controls the photographers. **1962** A. Lejeune *Duel in Shadows* i. 11 The staff of the Night News Desk could be seen in their usual state of harassment. **1973** *Times* 21 Sept. 5/3 He asked to be put through to the news desk. **1974** *New Society* 7 Feb. 308/1 Wrote for British newspapers through more than three decades of lack of interest on London foreign newsdesks. *a* **1953** Dylan Thomas *Quite Early One Morning* (1954) 80 Two typewriter Thomas the ace news-dick. **1904, 1938** News flash [see *flash *sb.*[2] 1 d]. **1972** J. Wilson *Hide & Seek* vi. 111 He was in control now. News-flashes couldn't scare him. **1974** E. Ambler *Dr. Frigo* 1. 56 There was a television news flash. The announcer didn't get your father's name quite right. **1868** *Putnam's Mag.* Apr. 518/1 A few years ago, a news-girl was as rare a sight as a Dodo. **1870** *Scribner's Monthly* I. 115 Old and young are enlisted in the street-vending service from the grey-haired grandsire..to the tiny news-girl. **1937** B. Board (*title*) Newsgirl in Palestine. **1931** *Amer. Speech* VI. 283 *Newshawk*.., used for 'reporter'. **1935** [see *big time* (*big *a.* B 2)]. **1940** *Illustr. London News* CXCVI. 544/1 News-hawks reading the tape-machines in New York and California. **1970** E. K. Walker in W. King *Black Short Story Anthol.* (1972) 54 Bull, flanked by his sergeant, the newshawk, and his cameramen, walked to the ambulance. **1974** N. Freeling *Dressing of Diamond* 17 Just ringing the police..is equivalent to inviting the newshawks. They'll be here in half an hour. **1918** *Hatchet* 7 Apr. 48/2 'Got what all figured out,' queried the news hound eagerly. **1926** *Time* 12 July 22/3 In a jazzed age no news hound delved through the reference 'morgue' of his paper to turn up the great story. **1936** E. Ambler *Dark Frontier* x. 163 'What have you been doing with yourself?' 'Trying to be a good newshound.' **1973** 'S. Harvester' *Corner of Playground* 1. iv. 41 You newshounds never spare yourselves once you've gotten latched onto a story. **1974** H. MacInnes *Climb to Lost World* ii. 35 Our trip was getting more like Conan Doyle's Lost World expedition every day, and I was obviously being cast as Ed Malone of the *Daily Gazette*. 'That stalwart news-hound of the cleft sticks', as Neil put it. **1960** *20th Cent.* Apr. 357 These jousts don't seem to need a news peg. **1960** *New Statesman* 15 Oct. 556/2 The BBC's interview programme *Face to Face*..subjects selected public figures to sustained personal questioning before the cameras—without necessarily any particular topical news-peg. **1909** *Westm. Gaz.* 3 June 2/2 The duty of 5 dollars a ton on news-print. **1935** *Geogr. Jrnl.* LXXXVI. 354 A large mill on the Wirral which manufactures newsprint. **1967** Karch & Buber *Offset Processes* xi. 485 Newsprint.., (Use) Newspaper, hand-bills, posters. **1974** *Publishers Weekly* 18 Feb. 44/2 Newsprint remains a headache for most paperback publishers [in Britain] and one was shocked recently to find himself quoted a price almost twice what he usually pays. **1937** *Tablet* 2 Oct. 436/2 The growth of large newspaper combines makes competition increasingly difficult, because the large proprietors are in fact deeply interested in the allied industries like the manufacture of news printing. **1925** *Daily Herald* 23 June 4/3 Instead of receiving a shock at a national calamity, the news reader breaks it to you in a calm and quiet voice. **1959** P. McCutchan *Storm South* i. 6, I hadn't realized it was News-time... I heard the news-reader's voice coming over. **1973** *Times* 15 Jan. 14/8 Mr William Alexander Moyes, the former BBC news reader and announcer, has been found dead at his flat. **1975** J. Wood *North Kill* xii. 181 A BBC news-reader was announcing the details. **1951** in M. McLuhan *Mech. Bride* (1967) 8/3 The Editors of *Time* hope to give..a clearer picture of the world of news-gathering, news-writing, and news-reading. **1971** T. F. Mitchell in *Archivum Linguisticum* II. 38 Although the implication of spoken utterance is less assured for some written functions than others, nevertheless rehearsals.., newsreading, lecturing and public address, though not 'colloquial' language, illustrate speech with the implication of writing and vice versa. **1916** *Wells Fargo Messenger* V. 39/3 Some companies issue their news reels twice a week. **1928** *Manch. Guardian Weekly* 26 Oct. 335/1 There are four motion picture newsreel cameramen, and four 'still' photographers. **1934** *B.B.C. Year-Bk.* 60 There has been another development of this new service by 'special correspondent' in the five-minute topical talk which in turn has now been extended to the 'News Reel'. **1944** L. MacNeice *Christopher Columbus* 15 The radio play..is competing with the Soviet art-cinema rather than with Hollywood or the standardised news-reel. **1949** *Radio Times* 15 July 15/2 Radio Newsreel, a summary of events of the past week. **1973** 'D. Jordan' *Nile Green* xliii. 218 We were safe.. bowling across the desert like old newsreels of the Eighth Army chasing Rommel into the sea. **1929** C. N. Warren *News Reporting* i. 2 Ed Markham, reporter, entered the *Times* local news room, ready to start his work for the day. **1959** *Times* 5 May 13/5 The news-room scoop is almost a thing of the past—an exciting aspect of newspaper life remembered only by the journalist whose career began in the heady Fleet Street days before the war. **1973** *Scotsman* 13 Feb. 15/6 (Advt.), The Scotsman Publications Limited require a newsroom typist... You will be typing our news stories as phoned in live by 'The Scotsman' reporters. **1872** E. Eggleston *Hoosier Schoolm.* viii. 77 You can buy trap-doors..dirt-cheap at the next news-stand. **1926** G. Ade *Let.* 29 Nov. (1973) 116 You.. finally met out west the news-stand girl who had been your friend. **1932** E. Wilson *Devil take Hindmost* iii. 19 Communist publications, sold openly on news-stands. **1973** 'J. Ashford' *Double Run* vi. 42 Ryan crossed the main hall of Charing Cross station to the Smith news-stand in the centre. **1973** *Philadelphia Inquirer* (Today Suppl.) 14 Oct. 7/2 The Digest..has lowered its newsstand price a dime. **1933** J. B. Priestley *Wonder Hero* iii. 95 He paid his shilling and entered one of the little News Theatres. **1961** S. Chaplin *Day of Sardine* ii. 54 We nipped into the News Theatre one night and saw one of these Barbecue affairs, in colour. **1974** E. Lemarchand *Buried in Past* ix. 152 Enquiries at steak houses and news theatres in the Tottenham Court Road area. **1902** News ticker [see Ticker[3] b]. **1933** Balmer & Wylie *When Worlds Collide* v. 46 The news-ticker carried, as additional information, only the effect of the announcement on the markets in Europe. **1967** Mrs. L. B. Johnson *White House Diary* 1 Aug. (1970) 550 It was 11 when we got back..and Lyndon wanted me to go into his office with him to take that last look at the news ticker. **1820** *Rep. Comm. Working on Newspapers* in E. Howe *London Compositor* (1947) xv. 378 The Committee commenced their labours by tracing the Regulations for News Work back to a certain period. **1971** *Library* XXVI. 302 If we can trust the 'oral testimony' reported in 1820, long galleys were in use in newswork as early as 1770.

news-boy. (Earlier and later examples.)

1764 in O. E. Winslow *Amer. Broadside Verse* (1930) 205 The news-boy's christmas and new-year's verses. **1939** T. S. Eliot *Family Reunion* 1. i. 43 The hidden shall be exposed and the newsboy shall shout in the street.

new·scast, *sb.* [Modelled on *broadcast *sb.* 2.] A broadcast of the news on radio or television. Also as *vb.* So **new·scaster,** (*a*) a person who reads out the news on radio or television; (*b*) (see quot. 1966); **new·scasting** *vbl. sb.*

1930 *Observer* 28 Sept. 21 Graham MacNamee, the news-caster of our American newspaper newsreel, takes the part of an unseen dramatist. **1934** M. Weseen *Dict. Amer. Slang* xii. 169 *Newscast*, to broadcast news by radio; a radio report of news. **1943** *Amer. Speech* XVIII. 147 The *-cast* of *broadcast* long since cast loose to attach itself in *newscast*. **1956** *Ann. Reg. 1955* 358 I.T.A. news was planned, intentionally, as something different from the traditional, wholly dignified, and impartial B.B.C. news, and was given instead from a personal angle, from less orthodox sources, by a skilful team of 'newscasters'. **1958** *New Statesman* 26 July 106/2 ITN one evening played martial music..during the newscasting between shots. **1966** *Times* 8 Mar. 4/5 An electric newscaster is to be erected in Piccadilly Circus. A newscaster was one of three illuminated signs for the Circus approved by the Minister..last month... Headline news bulletins, containing up-to-the-minute news from all over the world, will be flashed direct from the Press Association. Interspersed with the news bulletins will be advertising 'commercials' in four colours. **1970** *Toronto Daily Star* 24 Sept. 30/4 When the CBC hits it lucky, nobody can beat its newscasts. **1972** J. Wainwright *Requiem for Loser* viii. 171 He, too, momentarily disbelieved the B.B.C. newscaster... The wireless set continued to broadcast the news item. A lot of people listened to the newscast. **1972** 'G. Black' *Bitter Tea* (1973) xi. 180 The American style of newscasting, a breathless outpouring of words. **1973** *Daily Tel.* (Colour Suppl.) 9 Mar. 21/4 We've always had great success using newscasters for our appeals, and we prefer to use them, to make it a current affairs thing. The BBC don't see it our way, quite. **1973** *Daily Tel.* 3 Dec. 14/2 The first business to become a victim, presumably unintentionally, of the Government's ban on outdoor illuminated display advertising is Newscaster Publicity, which runs the newscaster on the outside of the Swiss Centre in Leicester Square.

new school. a. An advanced or liberal faction of a party or organization, *spec.* applied to the section of the Presbyterian Church of the United States which was separated from the rest of that Church between 1838 and 1869. Chiefly *attrib.*

1806 T. Fessenden *Democracy Unveiled* 1. 113 That were not justice in arrears, These New School folks would lack their ears. **1816** *Emigrant's Guide* 17 Local politicians assume various appellations, such as New School and Old School Democrats, Snyderites, Clintonians, and many others, mostly derived from the name or principles of some popular demagogue. **1837** W. Jenkins *Ohio Gaz.* 317 The public buildings consist of..two presbyterian churches, one of the old, and one of the new school. **1837** J. M. Peck *Gaz. Illinois* (ed. 2) 1. 72 McDonough College ..is identified with the interests of the 'old school' Presbyterians, as the Illinois College at Jacksonville is with the 'New School' Presbyterians. **1872** R. G. McClellan *Golden State* 406 The Old and New School Presbyterians have..2,600 members and 3,500 Sunday-scholars. **1884** P. Schaff *Relig. Encycl.* III. 2306/1 The 'New-Haven Theology'..was one of the most influential

of the types of so-called 'New School Divinity'. **1959** *Chambers's Encycl.* XI. 184/1 The controversies of the old country were reflected in the colony, for instance, in the divisions of the Philadelphian presbyterians into the Old and New sides or schools. **1961** K. S. LATOURETTE *Christianity in Revolutionary Age* III. 87 The congregations which had sprung up from the Plan of Union, the 'New School' Presbyterians, were made up mainly of New Englanders and their descendants. **1967** D. T. KAUFFMAN *Dict. Relig. Terms* 329/2 *New School*, term for that part of American Presbyterianism in mid-nineteenth century which favored liberal positions in theology, church government, and social issues such as slavery.

b. *transf.*

1837 *Southern Lit. Messenger* III. 107 As I once read medicine..under a disciple of the 'new school' (vulgarly called steam doctors). **1838** J. F. COOPER *Eve Effingham* II. iii. 84 But they evidently inclined to the opinion that the new school of pews was far better than the old. **1974** *Times* 18 Apr. 19/6 We conclude that the New School are mistaken in relying on some 'black box' stability in the relationships between the various sectoral balances.

newsie (niū·zi). Chiefly *U.S.* and *Austral. colloq.* Also **newsy.** [f. NEWS *sb.* (*pl.*) + -IE, -Y^6.] = NEWS-BOY.

1875 *North Alabamian* (Tuscaloosa, Ala.) 1 July 3/2 A newsboy on the M. and C. road was cruelly beating a dog which had jumped on the train, when its owner suddenly appeared at the car door, knocked 'newsy' off and commenced to pay him in his own coin. **1889** *Kansas City Times & Star* 12 Jan., Nearly 900 'newsies' applied for licenses and badges. **1904** *N.Y. Times* 16 July 7 He approached the 'newsy' and offered to buy a paper. **1916** C. SANDBURG *Chicago Poems* 42 The newsies are pitching pennies. **1953** BAKER *Australia Speaks* iv. 105 *Newsie*, a paper seller. **1962** *John o' London's* 4 Jan. 7/2 To be polite the newsie took a couple of swigs of it. **1962** J. ONSLOW *Bowler-Hatted Cowboy* i. 10 One early morning as the 'newsy' passed my berth, I leant out to ask him quietly for some fruit. **1969** 'E. LATHEN' *Murder to Go* (1970) xvi. 161 The newsie in the lobby.

newsily (niū·zili), *adv.* [f. NEWSY *a.* + -LY^2.] In a newsy manner or style.

1949 'N. R. NASH' *Young & Fair* 17 Have a nice summer? *Patty* (Newsily): Oh, fine. We got here in August. **1967** *Listener* 3 Aug. 136/3 Twenty years ago it [*sc.* a newspaper] was laid out rather newsily too.

news-letter. Delete 'Now only *Hist.*' and add further examples. Also, a periodical sent or handed out to subscribers, members of an organization, etc.

1880 'GEO. ELIOT' *Let.* 19 Sept. (1956) VII. 325 Your 'news-letter' was very welcome, and I was especially glad to know that Gertrude tries to keep up her health by little devices of change. **1914** *Writer's Mag.* Jan. 313/2 Some of the journals take daily news letters. **1936** *Time* 29 June 26/2 He runs a publishing house with offices in Chicago and Philadelphia, keeps his friends informed in periodic news-letters which he calls 'Rainbow-Graphs'. **1961** 'E. LATHEN' *Banking on Death* (1962) xi. 91 Martin seems to be a persistent reader of stock market newsletters. **1972** *Physics Bull.* Sept. 562/2 The purpose of the new Group will be..to circulate newsletters to Group members and to promote the general advancement and dissemination of knowledge in the field of neutron scattering.

news-man. Also **newsman.** Add: **1.** Also, a newspaper reporter, a journalist.

1953 *Manch. Guardian Weekly* 7 May 2. **1958** *Church Times* 24 Jan. 4/3 None the less, the theatre critic or the theatre newsman, each with his seat in the stalls on most nights in the year, must sit through many weary hours. **1968** *Globe & Mail* (Toronto) 17 Feb. 7/5 Some newsmen were concerned about Mr. Trudeau's talk of a government information service. **1970** N. ARMSTRONG et al. *First on Moon* iii. 64 Deke Slayton went outside to tell newsmen, standing in the glare of television camera lights, that the crew would soon be out. **1973** *Nature* 2 Feb. 300/1 A high-ranking newsman from the BBC. **1974** *Anderson* (S. Carolina) *Independent* 23 Apr. 3B/3 The Envoy Towers was evacuated and among its dazed occupants a newsman counted three dozen persons, children included, bleeding from head and body cuts sustained when windows blew in.

newspaper, *sb.* Add: **b.** *newspaper account, advertisement, advertising, agent, article, boy* (further examples), *carrier, clipping, column, correspondence, corresponding, critic, cutting, directory, editor, hack, kiosk, letter, man* (further examples), *office, owner, paragraph* (earlier example), *postage, press* (earlier and later examples), *printing, proprietor, reader, reporter, round, seller, selling, stand, syndicate, woman* (further examples), *wrapper.*

1851 D. B. WOODS *Sixteen Months at Gold Diggings* 199 Divesting the newspaper accounts from California of certain expressions bordering rather too much upon the hyperbolic order, they amount to the fact that the outcrops of certain veins [of goldbearing quartz] have been removed. **1936** *Discovery* Dec. 384/2 It was not until February, 1626, that the first newspaper advertisement appeared. *Ibid.*, The next step was newspaper advertising. **1874** 'G. HAMILTON' *Twelve Miles* ii. 30 The religious newspaper-agents bore into your house like worms of the dust. **1832** J. S. MILL in *Tait's Edin. Mag.* II. 343 Books are run through with no less rapidity, and scarcely leave a more durable impression than a newspaper article. **1858** *Missouri Democrat* 23 Oct. 2/2, I have not seen the letter, and but very few of the newspaper articles on the subject. **1972** D. WAINWRIGHT *Journalism made Simple* iv. 109 A magazine article needs an attractive and if possible startling opening sentence, like a good newspaper article. **1920** M. BEER *Hist. Brit. Socialism* II. IV. xiii. 249 He played the part of a newspaper-boy. **1974** P. LOVESEY *Invitation to Dynamite Party* iii. 32 Newspaper-boys..bawled their wares. **1851** C. CIST *Sk. Cincinnati in 1851* 50 Occupations. .. Newspaper publishers, 9; Newspaper carriers, 23. **1926** *Daily Colonist* (Victoria, B.C.) 9 Jan. 14/3 With the neck broken and a deep gash in the head, the body of William Merchant, fourteen-year-old newspaper carrier, was found last night. **1906** W. CHURCHILL *Coniston* II. xi. 374 She had brought a note from her father... Two newspaper clippings fell out of it. **1958** C. WATSON *Coffin scarcely Used* iv. 33, I am here now instead of concocting a mysterious message from newspaper clippings. **1974** J. BANNING *How I fooled World* iv. 23 Rosemary was putting teleprinter and newspaper clippings into the filing cabinet. **1843** M. FULLER *Summer on Lakes* (1844) vi. 185 Has ever Art found..a richer theme..sketched carelessly in the newspaper column of to-day? **1868** 'MARK TWAIN' *Lett. to Publishers* (1967) 14, I have cut my newspaper correspondence down a good deal. *Ibid.* 15 If you can stand an advance, I wish you would, and relieve me of this newspaper corresponding until July. **1859** B. BODICHON *Let.* 28 June in Geo. Eliot *Lett.* (1954) III. 103 The book could not have succeeded if it had been known as hers; *every newspaper critic would have written against it* (!!!). **1907** *Yesterday's Shopping* (1969) 436D Albums for Newspaper Cuttings. **1886** 'MARK TWAIN' *Lett. to Publishers* (1967) 206 Please take a glance..at your Newspaper Directory and tell me the aggregate number of dailies in the U.S., big cities and all. **1785** *Daily Universal Register* 1 Jan. 4/1 A Newspaper Editor..should rest himself on truth and facts. **1837** H. MARTINEAU *Society in America* I. I. iii. 151 The majority of newspaper editors made themselves parties to the act, by refusing, from fear, to reprobate it. **1972** C. WINTOUR *Pressures on Press* i. 6 It is essential for newspaper editors to be concerned with accuracy. **1885** Newspaper-hack [see *CIPHERER 2]. **1894** E. L. SHUMAN *Steps into Journalism* 65 One of the most prolific newspaper hacks in Chicago once remarked that he did not consider a man..a reporter unless he could make good reading out of anything. **1975** N. LUARD *Robespierre Serial* xvii. 151 Carswell..stopped at a newspaper kiosk. **1868** 'MARK TWAIN' *Lett. to Publishers* (1967) 15 In order to give to the book the amount of attention it really requires I shall have to cut loose from everything but one, and sometimes two, newspaper letters a week. **1954** G. KERSH in D. Knight *100 Yrs. Sci. Fiction* (1969) IV. 217 I'm a war correspondent, and newspaperman, and so I have the right to ask impertinent questions. **1966** *Listener* 21 July 79/1 For newspapermen throughout the world Washington has always been the Mecca of journalism. **1972** J. MOSEDALE *Football* v. 71 Newspapermen..confessed they could not look on him objectively. **1834** J. S. MILL in *Monthly Repos.* VIII. 173 The priest of the nineteenth century..sets up his pulpit in a newspaper office. **1915** R. FRY *Let.* 27 Aug. (1972) II. 390 Those who encounter the enemy in the newspaper offices are the most bloodthirsty. **1966** HARRIS & SPARK *Pract. Newspaper Reporting* iii. 34 Different newspaper offices mean different things when they refer to 'district reporting'. **1975** A. FRASER *Whistler's Lane* x. 159 I'll take the bus into Clitheroe...that's where the nearest newspaper office is. I want to look up the files. **1959** *Chambers's Encycl.* IX. 845/2 The fears of journalists in Britain that similar systems of chain newspapers, all propagating the views of one newspaper owner, might have ill effects both on the journalistic profession and on the newspapers. **1961** A. CLARKE *Later Poems* 92 The leader of the Dublin capitalists was William Martin Murphy, a newspaper owner and ruthless clericalist. **1798** *Deb. Congress U.S.* 5 July (1851) 2107 The gentleman from Connecticut.. had communicated to the House..a number of newspaper paragraphs. **1812** *Niles' Reg.* I. 361/1, I..admit your publication to be a newspaper and to be rated at Newspaper Postage. **1829** J. S. MILL *Let.* 7 Nov. in *Wks.* (1963) XII. 38 You know in how low a state the newspaper press of this country is. **1837** H. MARTINEAU *Society in America* I. I. iii. 75 Of all newspaper presses, I never heard any one deny that the American is the worst. **1959** *Chambers's Encycl.* IX. 843/1 In America only the periodical press is national and therefore has priority for advertising purposes over the newspaper press. **1824** J. JOHNSON *Typographia* II. 651 (*heading*) Newspaper printing offices. **1847** H. HOWE *Hist. Coll. Ohio* 241 Kenton..now contains..1 newspaper printing office. **1974** *Encycl. Brit. Macropædia* XV. 243/1 The practice resulted in considerable overmanning in newspaper printing departments. **1885** *List of Subscribers, Brighton* (S. of Eng. Telephone Co.) 14 Printers and Newspaper Proprietors. **1933** J. BUCHAN *Prince of Captivity* I. iv. 114 Falconet was..a newspaper proprietor on a large scale. **1974** *Encycl. Brit. Macropædia* XV. 243/2 Many of Scripps' methods were adopted by his rivals and by newspaper proprietors in other countries. **1935** *Discovery* Aug. 244/1 To the average newspaper-reader, Mongol is but a generic term. **1959** *Chambers's Encycl.* IX. 842/2 The steadily growing body of potential newspaper readers which increased educational facilities had brought into being. **1813** *Theatrical Inquisitor* II. 213 Newspaper critics and reporters..have had a prodigious addition to their necessary employments. **1910** 'O. HENRY' *Strictly Business* 87 The newspaper reporters dug out of their trunks the old broad-brimmed hats and leather belts. **1963** L. E. & B. RYAN *So you want to go into Journalism* i. 27 Newspaper reporters make modest salaries. **1948** C. DAY LEWIS *Otterbury Incident* iv. 48, I was a bit late, the newspaper-round taking longer than I expected. **1973** J. WAYNE *Brown Bread & Butter* x. 183 Was she eating breakfast, wasn't the newspaper round too much? **1927** C. PARSONS in *Oxford Poetry* 24 Beneath me in the windy stir Newspaper-sellers advertise The death of a philosopher By unintelligible cries. **1974** *Country Life* 28 Nov. 1656/3, I had a word..with a newspaper seller outside the building. **1957** J. KEROUAC *On Road* (1958) 58 The little midget newspaper-selling woman. **1893** W. K. POST *Harvard Stories* 31 At a news-paper stand he bought all the picture papers. **1889** W. D. HOWELLS *Hazard of New Fortunes* II. 120, I told 'em I hadn't much practice with Go-devils in the newspaper syndicate business. **1891** 'MARK TWAIN' *Lett. to Publishers* (1967) 275 McCluny..the manager of the newspaper syndicate. **1925** F. SCOTT FITZGERALD *Great Gatsby* vi. 120 Ella Kaye, the newspaper woman. **1954** D. DODGE *Lights of Skaro* ii. 55 She was a very good newspaperwoman, and not too scrupulous. **1971** B. GRAHAM *Spy Trap* i. 13 Christ! A bloody newspaper woman! He told her everything! **1873** *Brit. Postal Guide* 1 Jan. 21 Every Head Postmaster is required to keep, for sale to the public..newspaper wrappers bearing an impressed halfpenny stamp, and Post Cards. **1926–7** *Army & Navy Stores Catal.* 363/2 *Newspaper wrappers.* Size $12\frac{1}{8} \times 4\frac{5}{8}$ in., plain, gummed.

c. newspaper English, the style of English used in newspapers; journalese; **newspaper stamp,** a stamp tax imposed on newspapers between 1711 and 1855.

1888 *Harper's Mag.* May 962/2 The phrase 'newspaper English' has come to have a significance which is not flattering to newspapers. **1942** P. G. PERRIN *Writer's Guide & Index* 606 Good newspaper English is simply informal English applied to the daily recording of affairs. It is a style written to be read rapidly and by the eye—tricks of sound outside the headlines are out of place. **1947** PARTRIDGE *Usage & Abusage* 38/2 *Betrothal* [for 'engagement'] and *betrothed* are current in American newspaper-English. **1835** J. S. MILL in *London Rev.* I. 513 It was understood..that the ministry intended to take off the newspaper stamps. **1956** J. E. GERALD *British Press under Govt. Econ. Controls* i. 5 The newspaper stamp duty..was allowed to lapse in 1855.

2. *Underworld slang.* (See quots.)

1926 MAINES & GRANT *Wise-Crack Dict.* 11/2 *Newspaper*, crook's term for thirty days in jail. **1931** G. IRWIN *Amer. Tramp & Underworld Slang* 134 *Newspaper*, a thirty days' gaol sentence. **1949** PARTRIDGE *Dict. Underworld* 467/2 *Newspaper*, a thirty-days jail sentence. ..The time it takes an illiterate to read one.

newspaper (niū·zpeⁱpəɹ), *v. U.S. rare.* [f. the sb.] To work on a newspaper, to do newspaper work. Cf. NEWSPAPERING *vbl. sb.* in Dict. and Suppl.

1943 *Time* 8 Mar. 64 He had newspapered in Hawaii. **1959** *Time* (Atlantic ed.) 6 July 11 Who newspapered in Chicago.

newspaperdom. (Further examples.)

1933 *Times Lit. Suppl.* 30 Mar. 223/4 *Shooting the Bull*..is a tongue-in-the-cheek march through newspaperdom. **1946** *Sun* (Baltimore) 9 May 12/3 [A] new era of independent journalism in country newspaperdom.

newspapered, *ppl. a.* (Further examples.)

1855 DICKENS in *Household Words* 29 Sept. 193/1 Every house was shut up and newspapered. **1926** W. W. BISHOP *Backs of Books* 229 We are the most newspapered and magazined nation on earth, I suppose. **1973** E. WILLIAMS *Emlyn* i. 7, I saw my two brothers sitting at the table neatly newspapered to save the cloth.

newspapering, *vbl. sb.* (Later examples.)

1911 E. FERBER *Dawn O'Hara* iii. 29, I would fall to thinking of those years of newspapering—of the thrills of them, and the ills of them. **1968** L. J. BRAUN *Cat who turned on & Off* (1969) i. 11 Interviewing artists, interior decorators and Japanese flower arrangers was not Qwilleran's idea of newspapering. **1971** *Daily Colonist* (Victoria, B.C.) 26 Sept. 2/1, I care because newspapering is my business—make that my life, not business.

newspaperish, *a.* (Earlier and later examples.)

1825 M. WILMOT *Let.* 26 Sept. (1935) 225 And so ends my story, which is a stupid newspaperish sort of thing, tho' it was exceedingly interesting and amusing and pretty to look at at the time. **1929** A. NOYES *Return of Scare-Crow* iv. 54, I know that it's all very noble and distinguished and broad-minded and generally newspaperish.

new·spaperland. [f. NEWSPAPER + LAND *sb.*] = NEWSPAPERDOM.

1910 *Daily Chron.* 22 Mar. 8/2 As he is one of those who sit in the high places of newspaperland his voice is an authority that must not be overlooked. **1931** G. B. SHAW in *Ellen Terry & Bernard Shaw* 338 In newspaperland a slander is interesting news, always welcomed by news-editors. **1931** T. H. PEAR *Voice & Personality* ii. 20 In newspaper-land, too, persons in danger when sleeping, escape in 'night attire'.

new·spaperless, *a.* [f. NEWSPAPER + -LESS.] Without a newspaper.

c **1889** 'MARK TWAIN' *Speeches* (1923) 152 This was a newspaperless globe. **1909** *Westm. Gaz.* 10 Aug. 7/2 Newspaperless Sweden... No newspapers..are published here this morning. **1920** *Glasgow Herald* 1 Sept. 6 The demand for a distantly printed issue imported into Liverpool was a revelation of the eagerness with which a newspaperless public will snatch at anything conveying a semblance of the news of the day.

Newspeak (niū·spīk). Also **newspeak.** [f. NEW *a.* + SPEAK *v.*] The name of the artificial language used for official communications in G. Orwell's novel *Nineteen Eighty-Four*, freq. applied to any corrupt form of English, *spec.* the propagandist and ambiguous language of some politicians, broadcasters, etc. Also *attrib.*

1949 'G. ORWELL' *Nineteen Eighty-Four* I. 51 Syme was a philologist, a specialist in Newspeak. Indeed, he was one of the enormous team of experts now engaged in

compiling the Eleventh Edition of the Newspeak Dictionary. *Ibid.* II. 133 Do you know the Newspeak word *goodthinkful*? *Ibid.* App. 299 Newspeak was the official language of Oceania and had been devised to meet the ideological needs of Ingsoc, or English Socialism. In the year 1984 there was not as yet anyone who used Newspeak as his sole means of communication, either in speech or writing. **1950** A. A. ROBACK *Personality in Theory & Practice* i. 27, I do not think it necessary to resort to 'Newspeak' in order to write scientifically. **1959** *New Statesman* 2 May 602/2 This cynical 'newspeak' naming of Nationalist legislation has, in recent months, been matched by a remarkable change in the language used by their press and politicians. **1961** Y. OLSSON *On Syntax Eng. Verb* vi. 148 Even George Orwell's progressive Newspeak still preserves a few 'clumsy remnants of a bygone past'. **1963** *Guardian* 8 Mar. 10/6 Mr John Snagge, Head of Presentation at the BBC, is asking applicants for jobs as announcers to read aloud the 'Guardian's' leading article about 'newspeak', a method of speech, said by the writer to have become common among broadcasters, in which fullstops are put in the middle of sentences. **1966** *Punch* 27 July 140/1 Accusing the Prime Minister of 'the same old excuses', it [*sc.* the *Daily Telegraph*] labelled 'redeployment' as 'new-speak', which would be 'victimisation of the workers' in any but a Labour Government. **1972** *Guardian* 17 Feb. 14/5 The Orwellian Newspeak style. **1972** *Times Lit. Suppl.* 11 Aug. 935/2 The new party line, directed this time against 'rootless cosmopolitans'—newspeak for Jews. **1975** *Ibid.* 31 Jan. 115/4 A Khrushchevian panache which still makes a refreshing contrast with the computerized newspeak that passes for political discourse among many of his successors.

newst, var. *NOUST.

newsworthy (niū·zwɒ̄ɪðɪ), *a.* [f. NEWS *sb.* (*pl.*) + WORTHY *a.*] Of sufficient interest to the general public to warrant mention in the news. Also **new·sworthily** *adv.*; **new·sworthiness.**

1932 *Time* 15 Feb. 4/2 *Time* is grateful for support and criticism of its policy, and repeats its promise to cause the minimum of offense in respect to newsworthy oaths. **1936** L. C. DOUGLAS *White Banners* v. 88 The manner of the taciturn chemist's departure had doubled the insurance his widow would have received in the event of his having died less newsworthily. **1940** *Harper's Mag.* Nov. 588a The Nazi offensive..is, judging from our newspapers, apparently the only newsworthy topic on Latin America. **1951** L. Z. HOBSON *Celebrity* (1953) x. 145 They were finding his speech a shade less newsworthy than they were supposed to. **1957** *Observer* 29 Sept. 10/7 His lot is harder than Mr. Colvin's, if not so newsworthy. **1960** 'M. CRONIN' *Begin with Gun* vii. 82 A celebrated French *modiste* who had become eminently newsworthy..had consented to be interviewed. **1961** *Guardian* 22 Mar. 10/4 Publicity-conscious people..make 'newsworthiness' a determinant of their actions. **1967** G. PLAYFAIR *Prodigy* vii. 167 His newsworthiness had dwindled. **1969** *Listener* 24 July 113/2 Not that by living life more newsworthily one could hope to provide more than the raw material. **1970** G. F. NEWMAN *Sir, You Bastard* iii. 89 They might get a lot of newsworthy items, but no exclusives. **1972** M. WILLIAMS *Inside Number 10* xiv. 345 While the general public will know the names of the political heads of the more newsworthy ministries, there is rarely any knowledge of the names of the permanent features of the departments, the Civil Service heads. **1973** *Guardian* 13 Apr. 11/2 The newsworthiness of the [Black Panther] movement.

newsy, *a.* Add: **2.** Likely to create news.

1959 *Vogue* Nov. 83 A newsy new car, the red sleek Daimler. **1971** *Daily Tel.* 28 July 11 Tweed sprouts all over the collection, best in separates such as..the ponchos worn over slim skirts or (far more newsy) skin-tight tweed trousers.

newsy, var. *NEWSIE.

New Thought, new thought. [THOUGHT[1] I.] A theory of the nature of disease, a system of therapeutic practice, and a religious sect believing in these, founded on principles formulated by Phineas P. Quimby of Portland, Maine, U.S.A. Hence **New Thoughter**, one who holds and practises 'new thought'; a member of the sect following the principles of Quimby. Also *transf.*

1887 W. H. HOLCOMBE *Condensed Thoughts Christian Sci.* (ed. 6) 45 New thought always excites combat in the mind with the old thought, which refuses to retire. **1899** H. W. DRESSER *Voices of Freedom* ii. 22 The term 'New Thought', now the accepted appellation of a doctrine which has differentiated itself from..mental science.. and become the representative teaching of those who..are not worshippers of personality, are not bound to certain books, but remain independent. *Ibid.* 23 The New Thought..is both a philosophy of life and conduct and a mode of healing. **1902** W. JAMES *Var. Relig. Exper.* iv. 94 A current..has recently poured over America..to which..I will give the title of the 'Mind-cure movement'. There are various sects of this 'New Thought', to use another of the names by which it calls itself. **1907** —— in *American Mag.* Nov. 58/2 To relax, to say to ourselves (with the 'new thoughters') 'Peace! be still!' is sometimes a great achievement of inner work. *a* **1910** —— *Some Probl. Philos.* (1911) i. 18 Compare Prentice Mulford and others of the 'new thought' type. **1937** D. CANFIELD *Fables for Parents* 128 Being a Congregationalist and not a Christian Scientist or a New Thoughter. **1942** A. HUXLEY *Let.* 30 Dec. (1969) 485 The strengthening and extension of such religions as Christian Science, Theosophy, New Thought, 'I Am', in which the stress is wholly on powers, personal advantages and future time. **1949** *Sun* (Baltimore) 7 Sept. 12/4 Loss of that strength would weaken the old-line men as against the groping 'new-thoughters' in the party. **1967** D. T. KAUFFMAN *Dict. Relig. Terms* 330/1 *New Thought*, American religious movement,..emphasizing 'the divinity of man and his infinite possibilities..'. Groups are now found in many parts of the world.

Newton (niū·tən). [Name of Sir Isaac *Newton*: see NEWTONIAN *a.* and *sb.*] **1.** *Newton's rings*: a set of concentric circular fringes seen surrounding the point of contact when a convex lens is placed on a plane surface (or on another lens), which join points where the intervening thin layer of air has the same thickness and are caused by interference between light reflected from its upper and lower surfaces. When used *attrib.* also *sing.*

[**1807** *Phil. Trans. R. Soc.* XCVII. 180 (*heading*) Experiments for investigating the cause of the coloured concentric rings, discovered by Sir Isaac Newton, between two object-glasses laid upon one another. **1809** *Ibid.* XCIX. 299 In order completely to account for the Newtonian rings.] **1835** *Phil. Mag.* VII. 363 In examining Newton's rings I was induced to place a convex lens.. between two surfaces of plate-glass, in order to effect the superposition of the rings. **1904** A. SCHUSTER *Introd. Theory of Optics* iv. 72 The colours observed in Newton's rings are the colours of thin films, the film being the layer of air included between the lens and the plate. **1969** S. G. & H. LIPSON *Optical Physics* xii. 382 Lens surfaces can be tested to a high degree of accuracy by forming Newton's rings with a known surface. *Ibid.* 383 Coefficients of thermal expansion of quite small crystals can be measured by counting the fringes that pass through the centre of a Newton's ring system as the crystal is heated.

2. (Written **newton.**) The unit of force in the metre-kilogramme-second system (now incorporated in the S.I.): the force that would give a mass of one kilogramme an acceleration of one metre per second per second; 100,000 dynes (approximately the weight of 102 grammes or 3·6 oz.). Abbrev. N.

1904 D. ROBERTSON in *Electrician* 22 Apr. 25/1 The writer suggests that the name 'Newton' be given to the unit of force (10^8 dynes). **1919** *Nature* 4 Sept. 13/2 A fourth matter..which was discussed was the proposal to adopt in future legislation for metric countries the M.K.S. system of units... On this system the unit of force is the 'Newton'. **1935** HARTSHORN & VIGOUREUX in *Ibid.* 7 Sept. 397/2 In the M.K.S. system..no name has yet been assigned to the unit of force... G. Giorgi has provisionally used the word 'vis'... We venture to suggest that 'newton' would be more appropriate. **1942** H. HOWE *Introd. Physics* iv. 57 The awkwardly large numbers in Ex. 2 would have been avoided had mks units been used; the answer would have been F = 300 newtons. **1962** CORSON & LORRAIN *Introd. Electromagnetic Fields* ii. 29 In these units Coulomb's law is written as $\mathbf{F}_{ab} = (1/4\pi\epsilon_0)\,(Q_aQ_b/r^2)/\mathbf{r}_1$, where the force $\mathbf{F}$ is measured in newtons; the charges Q_a and Q_b, in coulombs..; and the distance r, in meters. **1970** *Daily Tel.* 14 May 18 In the S I the force is measured not in kilogrammes, but in newtons—spelt with a small 'n' but abbreviated with a large one, 'N'. One newton (reinforcing the legend) is roughly the pull of gravity on one apple.

Newtonically (niūtǫ·nikăli), *adv. rare.* [f. the name of Sir Isaac *Newton* (see NEWTONIAN *a.* and *sb.*) + -ICALLY.] In the manner of Sir Isaac Newton.

1869 J. S. MILL *Let.* 30 Jan. (1910) II. xii. 181 In regard to the Darwinian hypothesis,..Darwin has found (to speak Newtonically) a *vera causa.* **1953** K. BRITTON *John Stuart Mill* v. 182 His [*sc.* Mill's] preference for a mechanical view of forces..arises in part from his insistence upon 'speaking Newtonically' in opposition to the Baconian language of Macaulay and the empiricists.

New Town, new town. A planned urban area designed to ease the congestion of a nearby large city, usu. one with special provision for housing, employment, and amenities for a delimited population. Also *transf.* Also *attrib.*, as *New Town blues*, despondency or anxiety suffered by a person resident in a New Town. Hence **New Towner**; **New-Townish**, *a.*

1918 (*title*) New towns after the war. **1946** *Hansard Commons* 17 Apr. 2710 *New Towns Bill* 'to provide for the creation of new towns by means of development corporations, and for purposes connected therewith' presented by Mr. Silkin. **1948** 'J. TEY' *Franchise Affair* xxiii. 266 The little house on the outer rim of the 'new' town. **1958** *Engineering* 21 Feb. 227/1 Suburban railway peak problems could be eased by more New Towns. **1958** *Spectator* 8 Aug. 191/1 An immense new-town bicycle shed. **1958** *Listener* 23 Oct. 655/2 His analysis of the Hellenistic 'new town', Priene. **1959** *Manch. Guardian* 6 Aug. 4/2 The new-town voters. **1960** *News Chron.* 2 July 3/5 He was born in St. Pancras, London, and is now a Hemel Hempstead new towner. **1962** *Britannica Bk. of Year* 546/1 In Great Britain a topical term was New Town Blues, used to describe the dissatisfied, discontented condition of people from large cities who found the recreational amenities of the new towns inadequate. **1962** *Harper's Bazaar* Aug. 58/1 Castries, the capital..is entirely modern and rather New-Townish. **1964** *Daily Tel.* 4 Feb. 14/2 The new environment, though brighter, cleaner and more commodious, is said to lack the social attraction of the old. Hence the so-called complaint of the 'new town blues'. **1965** *Economist* 6 Nov. p. x/2 New towners also pay rates at the level set by the local authorities in whose territory they lie. **1970** *Americana Ann.* 176 The high hopes that 'new towns'.. could provide a solution to congestion, high population densities, and the erosion of public services have collapsed. **1971** P. GRESSWELL *Environment* 174 A visit to one or more of the new towns is essential to anyone interested in architecture and environment. **1973** *Guardian* 30 May 7/1 The fears of the old-towners are certainly understandable. The population has declined... Runcorn new town has been growing. **1975** *Ibid.* 20 Jan. 15 Milton Keynes..is the latest (possibly the final?) refinement of new town theory.

Newtown (niū·taun). Also **Newton.** The name of a town on Long Island in New York state, used *attrib.* or *absol.* to designate two varieties of dessert apple first introduced there, the **Newtown Pippin** and the **Newtown Spitzenburg.** So **New·towner**, a Newtown apple.

1760 G. WASHINGTON *Diary* 30 Mar. (1925) I. 147 Grafted 10 of the New Town Pippin from Collo. **1770** in *Maryland Historical Mag.* (1918) XIII. 69 Things sent by the wagon 4 Barrills of Apples Russetins, Golden Pippins, Newtown Pippins & Pairmains. **1785** G. WASHINGTON *Diary* 12 Nov. (1925) II. 435 Received two New Town and 2 Golden Pippin trees. **1803** A. F. M. WILLICH *Domestic Encycl.* (Amer. ed.) III. 110 Newton Pippin. *Ibid.* IV. 182/2 The New-town Pippin, or New-York Rennet, a noble American apple. **1817** W. COXE *View of Cultivation of Fruit Trees* 126 Newton Spitzemberg [*sic*]. This apple is in some parts of this State [*sc.* Pennsylvania] called the English, or Burlington Spitzemberg: it was brought from Newton on Long-Island. **1840** *N.Y. Mirror* 4 Apr. 327/2 Dealers in Newton pippins and maple candy tell you.. they can't afford their accommodations so low as they can be afforded in Chatham and Church streets. **1846** J. F. COOPER *Ravensnest* I. i. 27 Their *poire beurrée*, here at Paris..will not compare with the Newtowners we grow at Satanstoe. **1860** R. HOGG *Fruit Manual* 18 Newtown Pippin, D. — Medium sized, roundish, rather irregular, and obscurely ribbed... Requires a wall in this country. December to April. **1863** *Rep. Comm. Agric. 1862* (U.S. Dept. Agric.) 168 Newtown Spitzenberg... A very hardy tree; good bearer; fruit of superior quality; keeps and bears transportation well. **1877** E. S. DALLAS *Kettner's Bk. of Table* 34 Newtown Pippin... Named after Newtown, Long Island. This apple is imported from America. *Ibid.* 36 Kitchen Apples... Newtown Spitzemberg [*sic*]... Named by William Cobbett 'the matchless'. **1913** J. LONDON *Valley of Moon* 364 Every year he goes to England, and he takes a hundred carloads of yellow Newton pippins with him. **1925** B. D. DRAIN *Essent. Systematic Pomology* v. 78 Newtown Spitzenburg Group. Medium size, round–oblate, red-striped, high quality. **1953** BROOKS & HESSE *Western Fruit Gardening* 97 Yellow Newtown is most widely grown in the coastal districts... The fruit is medium to large, roundish to flattened, green to yellow.

new wave. Also New Wave. = *NOUVELLE VAGUE. Also (with hyphen) *attrib.* Hence **new wavish** *a.*

1960 *News Chron.* 19 July 6/8 A 'new wave' is emerging here [in Spain], too, with an up-to-date philosophy. *Ibid.* 6 Aug. 6/7 Cy Grant will sing 'Carnival' from the French new-wave movie. **1960** *Guardian* 15 Oct. 5/2 The Italian neo-realists..and..the Frenchmen of the 'New Wave' have all been pursuing the same course. **1961** *Sunday Times* 12 Feb. 11/8 Blanchflower is the very crest of the New Wave among professional footballers. **1962** *Spectator* 23 Feb. 242/1 Her central situation concerns a new-wave actress. **1963** *Punch* 20 Feb. 285/1 Perhaps she's New Wavish enough to scorn love. **1967** *Economist* 18 Mar. 1008/2 The new-wave nationalists have not bothered to think out what sort of nationalism they want. **1972** *Newsweek* 10 Jan. 22/1 As New York's new-wave mayor in 1966, he had portrayed himself as a reform insurgent battling the city's 'power brokers'. **1974** *Publishers Weekly* 25 Nov. 47/1 Malzberg is rather on the New Wavish side, writing 'speculative' rather than straight science fiction. **1975** *Times Lit. Suppl.* 21 Nov. 1374/2 The defining characteristic of the New Wave, and its ambiguous legacy to all films made since 1958–61, was selfconsciousness... The New Wave brought the film director to the public's immediate attention as a potential cultural hero.

new-wed, *a.* and *sb. arch.* [NEW *adv.* 3.] **A.** *adj.* Recently married. **B.** *sb.* = *newly-wed* (*NEWLY *adv.* 1 d).

1886 KIPLING *Departmental Ditties* (ed. 2) 21 Jones had left his new-wed bride to keep his house in order. **1893** W. B. YEATS *Celtic Twilight* 94 The new-born or the new-wed moves henceforth in the bloodless land of Faery.

new woman, etc.: see WOMAN *sb.* 1 i.

New World, new world. [WORLD *sb.* 11.] Used *attrib.* to designate phenomena characteristic of, or territories pertaining to, the western hemisphere. Hence **New-Worlder, New-Worldling**, a native or inhabitant of the western hemisphere; **newworldward** *adv.*, towards the western hemisphere.

[**1823** BYRON *Don Juan* IX. xxxix. 24 How the new worldlings of the then new east.] *a* **1855** C. BRONTË *Professor* (1857) II. xviii. 7 Some natural and graphic touches disclosed to the reader the scene of virgin forest and great, New-World river—barren of sail and flag. **1863** H. W. BATES *Naturalist on Amazons* II. v. 324 All the New World genera of apes..are represented in the Amazon regions. **1867** O. W. HOLMES *Guardian Angel* 216 There is a double proportion of oxygen in the New-World air. **1876** H. MELVILLE *Clarel* I. II. xxvi. 256 Oh, that a New-Worlder should talk so! **1901** *Munsey's Mag.* XXIV. 530/1 These and other causes have acted and reacted to

bring about, in this new world metropolis,..a crowding together of the poor. **1930** *Tablet* 24 May 686/1 Old Worldlings in Europe..the New-Worldlings of the U.S.A. **1935** E. E. CUMMINGS *Let.* 29 Jan. (1969) 134 Delighted to learn that you're casting your anchor and blowing newworldward!!!!! **1944** *Amer. Fern Jrnl.* XXXIV. 69 (*heading*) The New World species of *Azolla.* **1951** in M. McLuhan *Mech. Bride* (1967) 77/2 A new-world man towering free and confident in an untroubled generation. **1957** P. J. DARLINGTON *Zoogeography* vi. 346 Whether one of them [*sc.* a primitive primate] reached South America and evolved the New World monkeys..is unknown. *Ibid.* 390 Erethizontidae, New World porcupines. **1965** *New Statesman* 24 Sept. 435/1 Great Victorian relics, long since peeled of their paint, electric-light bulbs and courteous service—especially toward dollar-bearing New Worlders. These are some recent experiences of myself and a pair of Montreal acquaintances. **1968** *Times* 15 Nov. 8/7 The New World monkeys, or Ceboidea, include such species as the marmosets and the howler monkeys. **1970** *Nature* 24 Oct. 382/1 In Jamaica the fifth instar larvae of the New World hawkmoth, *Erinnyis ello,* exhibit four basic colours.

newy, var. *NEWIE.

new-year. Add: **1. a.** *to see the new-year in*: see *YEAR 7.

2. *New-year('s) honours list*: see *honour(s) list* (*HONOUR *sb.* 10).

3. Also with ellipsis of *day. N. Amer.*

1845 *Knickerbocker* XXV. 128 Stay away on New-Year's and you stay away all the year. **1909** *Springfield* (Mass.) *Weekly Republ.* 4 Nov. 1 The general elections are not now expected until after New Year's. **1952** J. REANEY in R. Weaver *Canad. Short Stories* (1960) 383 The Christmas holidays were haunted for me by my fear of what would happen when I went back there after New Year's. **1975** F. DECKER in S. Terkel *Working* IV. 190 She's just lucky he's home Christmas and New Year's.

New York (niū yǭ·ɹk, nū yǭ·ɹk). The name of a city and state in the United States used *attrib.* in various special collocations (see quots.).

1714 S. SEWALL *Diary* 14 Apr. in *Mass. Hist. Soc. Coll.* (1879) 5th Ser. VI. 440, I had my New York Biscuit to eat. **1771** T. PENNANT *Synopsis Quadrupeds* 367 New York Bat with a head shaped like that of a mouse. **1842** J. E. DEKAY *Zool. N.Y.* I. 140 Index, New York Weasel. **1843** J. TORREY *Flora State of New-York* II. 497 *Aspidium Noveboracense*... New-York Shield-fern. Moist woods and thickets. **1862** *Amer. Ann. Cycl. 1861* 307/2 The highest, lowest, and average quotations..at the New York Stock Exchange for the stocks most largely dealt in. **1892** *Scribner's Mag.* Sept. 386/1 A fellow-pupil dictated to him Latin and Greek, and he printed the text in New York point. **1901** C. MOHR *Plant Life Alabama* 316 *Dryopteris noveboracensis*... New York Shield Fern... Alleghenian and Carolinian areas. **1943** H. W. SHIMER *Origin & Significance Plant Names* 47 New York fern, Dryopteris noveboracensis. **1955** R. BLESH *Shining Trumpets* (ed. 3) xii. 275 New York jazz, even at its best, was inept. **1956** B. COBB *Field Guide to Ferns* 50 The Marsh Ferns, the Massachusetts Ferns, and the New York Fern have upright, narrow, oblong leaves... These five species of the genus *Thelypteris* have been moved from one genus to another... Elsewhere they are classified in the genus *Dryopteris.* **1974** *Guardian* 23 Jan. 4/7 The poultry industry..called in a slim blonde to wheel to the platform a 30-lb New York dressed turkey—New York dressed being a dying species.

New Yorker. Add: (Further examples.) Also *attrib.*, pertaining to or characteristic of the magazine *The New Yorker* (founded 1925).

1859 G. H. LEWES *Let.* 6 Sept. in *Geo. Eliot's Lett.* (1954) III. 146 To-day a letter has come from the editor of a 'Parish Magazine'—and really G. E. was almost more likely to be tempted by that audience than by the New Yorkers. **1884** MATTHEWS & BUNNER *In Partnership* 127 'Are you a New Yorker, sir?' 'From the north of the State.' **1902** *Chambers's Jrnl.* July 450/1 The New Yorker defends this wretched state of affairs by a peculiar argument. **1916** H. L. WILSON *Somewhere in Red Gap* 398 The New Yorker was now sunk deep in a trance. **1934** *Fortune* Aug. 75/1 No advertising man is believed, by the editors, ever to have understood a *New Yorker* joke. **1948** *Hearst's International* May 175/1 Literary critics and editors of other magazines are always referring to 'The New Yorker style of writing'. **1948** *N.Y. Star* 30 June 14/3 The Board of Transportation is appealing to New Yorkers to put up patiently with the confusion. **1951** R. HOGGART *Auden* iii. 68 We consign much of this to the part of the mind which is tickled but put on its guard by the 'New Yorker' profiles. **1959** *Times Lit. Suppl.* 2 Jan. 4/2 He surveys the established Old Guard.., the new 'realists'.., the *New Yorker* School. **1974** *Times* 4 Mar. 14/8 Brenda Bedansky, a New Yorker, dressed to resemble a man trying to look like Marlene Dietrich.

Hence **New Yo·rkerish** *a.*, characteristic or reminiscent of the magazine *The New Yorker*; **New Yo·rkerism**, an idiom, expression, or word peculiar to *The New Yorker.*

1948 H. F. PRINGLE in *'48: Magazine of Yr.* Apr. 87/2 His [*sc.* H. W. Ross's] sense of comedy is properly *New Yorker*ish and fantastic. **1951** *Time* 22 Oct. 102/2 Many a New Yorkerism (e.g., Cartoonist Carl Rose's 'I say it's spinach, and I say the hell with it') has become a part of the language. **1961** *Punch* 4 Jan. 81/3 The drawings.. [are] well suited to the captions, many of which have a *New Yorker*ish elliptical quality. **1967** *Guardian* 20 Oct. 7/4 Just another New Yorkerish monologue. **1970** D. L. EMBLEN *Peter Mark Roget* xv. 276 Punch in its *New Yorkerish* way, picking up a slip in some Scottish paper.

New Yo·rkese. [-ESE.] The regional form of English used in New York City. Cf. *MANHATTANESE *sb.*

1894 *Harper's Mag.* Oct. 695/1 'Cafe'..is New Yorkese for dram-shop. **1935** F. M. FORD *Let.* 11 Sept. (1965) 242 Perhaps it is the latest New Yorkese which, I know, is always welcome in Hampstead. **1951** TRAGER & SMITH *Outl. Eng. Structure* I. 23 The sequence /əy/ has always been known to him as 'New Yorkese' or 'Brooklynese'. **1973** E.-J. BAHR *Nice Neighbourhood* vii. 71 'So continue,' said Don... He sometimes lapses into New Yorkese.

New-Yo·rkish, *a.* [-ISH[1].] = next.

1913 F. H. BURNETT *T. Tembarom* xxiv. 305 How thoroughly New Yorkish it was that he should march into a fashionable shop and see that he got..the worth of his money! **1962** *John o' London's* 19 Apr. 385/3 That most New Yorkish of all musical comedies, *Guys and Dolls.*

New-Yo·rky, *a.* [-Y[1].] Suggestive or characteristic of New York.

1908 E. WHARTON *Hermit* 150 To be compared to her! to be accused of being 'New-Yorky'! **1963** *Guardian* 25 Jan. 6/6 The 'Partisan', New York-y too, but out of a cosmopolitan liberal intelligentsia. **1973** R. L. SIMON *Big Fix* (1974) ix. 66 The accent was nasal and New Yorky, the voice scratchy.

New Zealand. 1. The name of an Australasian country, used *attrib.* to designate plants native there, as **New Zealand flax,** an evergreen plant, *Phormium tenax,* of the family Agavaceæ, cultivated for the fibre it produces or the ornamental value of its tufts of long, stiff, pointed leaves; **New Zealand passion flower,** a climbing plant, *Tetrapathæa tetrandra,* of the family Passifloraceæ; **New Zealand spinach,** an annual herb, *Tetragonia tetragonioides* (*T. expansa*), of the family Aizoaceæ, cultivated for its thick leaves which are used as a substitute for spinach.

1811 W. AITON *Hortus Kewensis* (ed. 2) II. 284 New Zealand Flax. Nat[ive] of New Zealand. Introd[uced] about 1789, by the Right Hon. Sir Joseph Banks. **1832** *Curtis's Bot. Mag.* LIX. 3199 The seeds brought home by Sir Joseph Banks in 1771 did not succeed, but the New Zealand Flax was introduced through the medium of the same enlightened individual in 1789, and thence has been liberally distributed. **1883** W. ROBINSON *Eng. Flower Garden* 195/1 New Zealand Flax (*Phormium tenax*). **1910** [see *INANGA 2]. **1973** *Islander* (Victoria, B.C.) 4 Feb. 2/4 The harakeke or New Zealand flax..doesn't resemble its European cousin. **1853** J. D. HOOKER *Bot. Antarctic Voy.: Flora Novæ-Zelandiæ* I. 72. The New Zealand Passion-flower is a perfectly smooth climbing plant, with alternate, simple, petiolate leaves, axillary tendrils, and small axillary panicles of green flowers. **1951** LAING & BLACKWELL *Plants N.Z.* (ed. 5) 281 *Tetrapathaea tetrandra* (The New Zealand Passion-flower). A slender climber, with glossy leaves. **1822** J. ANDERSON in *Trans. Hort. Soc.* IV. 488 (*heading*) Account of a new Esculent Vegetable called *Tetragonia*, or New Zealand Spinach. **1867** E. SAUTER tr. *F. von Hochstetter's New Zealand* vii. 157 New Zealand Spinach..was first brought into notice by Captain Cook, who found it useful as an anti-scorbutic. **1898, 1944** [see *ICE-PLANT]. **1951** *Dict. Gardening* (R. Hort. Soc.) III. 1369/2 New Zealand Spinach is an excellent substitute for the common Spinach for use during the hot dry months. **1973** *Parade* (Melbourne) Sept. 35/1, I have seen New Zealand spinach..growing on the sandhills along the beach..north of Perth.

2. New Zealand rabbit, also **New Zealand black, New Zealand red, New Zealand white,** various American breeds of domestic rabbit. Also *absol.*

1914 ROTH & COLEMAN *Rabbit Culture* 95 Standard of the New Zealand Rabbit... Larger than the Belgian Hare and of a beautiful reddish buff color... Everybody's friend wherever known. **1917** C. P. GILMORE *N.Z. Red Rabbit* 8/1 The New Zealand Reds are..business rabbits for general or utility purposes. *Ibid.*, The New Zealand is practically a new rabbit in the American fancy. **1920** F. L. WASHBURN *Rabbit Bk.* ii. 43 The New Zealand Red. This rabbit is a close second to the Belgian and Flemish in the race for popularity. **1921** C. A. RICHEY *Rabbit & Cavy Bk.* (ed. 4) 21 A new breed..called the White New Zealand..having the type of the New Zealand, but a pure white coat with pink eyes. **1953** C. GOODCHILD *Keeping Rabbits* ii. 80 The New Zealand Red was first imported into this country around 1920. It was originated in the U.S.A., and was a breed much favoured by the Californian breeders for the frying trade. *Ibid.* 82 Although the New Zealand White has only recently been adopted in this country, they have been one of the most popular breeds in the U.S.A. for over a quarter of a century. **1965** *Amer. Rabbit Breeders' Assoc. Official Guide Bk.* 32 The New Zealand Rabbit had its origin in the United States in the early 1900's. *Ibid.* 33 The standard of perfection for all New Zealands is identical with the exception of the color of the fur, eyes and nails... The Black New Zealand is the newest variety of the New Zealand breed. Blacks were started in California in 1949. **1971** *Guardian* 28 Dec. 1/6 Half the consignment [of rabbits] will be New Zealand Whites which have red eyes. **1973** M. I. FAIVRE *How to raise Rabbits* i. 11 The New Zealand breed may be divided into three distinct categories: New Zealand Red, New Zealand Black, and New Zealand White... Although all three types are excellent meat rabbits, the New Zealand White fur is in greatest demand by garment makers because it takes a variety of dyes successfully.

New Zealander. Add: **a.** (Earlier example.) Also (occas.) *attrib.* **b.** (Earlier and later examples.)

1773 CAPT. J. COOK *Jrnl.* (1961) II. 268 The New Zealanders cut and scar themselves on the same account. **1837** *Sydney Gaz.* 11 Dec., in R. McNab *Old Whaling Days* (1913) ix. 167 They saw the chief officer, James George Bailey, a New Zealander. **1841** M. EDGEWORTH *Let.* 14 Mar. (1971) 586 A New Zealander boy with large head and frizzled black hair and face as yellow as dirty gold. **1886** J. A. FROUDE *Oceana* xx. 323 The Australian, the New Zealander, the Californian will have as much in them..of the ancient 'Merry England' as the severely earnest Northern American. **1966** MRS. L. B. JOHNSON *White House Diary* 20 Oct. (1970) 430 We departed in a New Zealand airplane with the Prime Minister and Mrs. Holyoake to the tune of a thousand New Zealanders singing.

New Zea·landism. [-ISM.] An idiom or word peculiar to the English spoken in New Zealand.

1957 *N.Z. Listener* 22 Nov. 4/3 'Creek' and 'paddock' are New Zealandisms, because they mean something quite different in the English of England. **1964** A. S. C. Ross in Ross & Moverley *Pitcairnese Lang.* 13 The two letters which I published in New Zealand about possible new zealandisms in Pitcairnese.

nexal, *a.* Add: **2.** *Linguistics.* Of or pertaining to a nexus (sense *1 c).

1933 *English Studies* XV. 148, I don't wish to speak to you ever again..is a more polite formula for: I wish never to speak to you again. We have here a very curious case of 'cleaving of *never*' and 'nexal attraction'. **1937** V. MATHESIUS in *Mélanges de Linguistique et de Philologie offerts à J. van Ginneken* 82 Professor Jespersen has repeatedly called attention to the difference between what he calls *special negation* and what he calls *nexal negation.*

next, *a., sb.,* and *adv.* Add: **A.** *adj.* **2. c.** *the next man* (*one, person,* etc.): the average man; a typical man; the next comer. orig. *U.S.*

1857 *Lawrence* (Kan.) *Republican* 18 June 2 The Judge ..will probably talk as long to a crowd without tiring them as the next man. **1897** KIPLING *Captains Courageous* i. 5 Guess I've as good right here as the next man. **1900** ADE *More Fables in Slang* 175 Lutie was just about as Nifty as the Next One. **1902** S. G. FISHER *True Hist. Amer. Revol.* 146 We do not surrender our property to the next man who is an abler business manager. **1925** S. O'CASEY *Juno & Paycock* II, in *Two Plays* 105 We have to live as well as th' nex' man. **1933** E. CALDWELL *God's Little Acre* iii. 37 Will can dig as good as the next one, if he wants to. **1938** G. GREENE *Brighton Rock* III. iv. 135 He'd been a loyal old geezer, he hadn't done as much harm as the next man. **1941** L. BROMFIELD in *Hearst's International* May 131/2 She thought: I'll show them that I'm as good as the next woman. I'll take care of myself. **1961** *Sunday Times* 5 Mar. 15/2 Cecil Beaton..can appreciate the 'excruciatingly bad taste' of a Lancashire living-room as well as the next designer. **1962** L. PETERS *Snatch of Music* ix. 155, I can read a paperback translation with the next man. **1966** A. E. LINDOP *I start Counting* xviii. 222, I can take a hint as well as the next person—and I know when I'm not wanted. **1973** *Sunday Bulletin* (Philadelphia) (Discover Suppl.) 14 Oct. 8/2, I feel you owe me a smidgin more than the next person.

10. (Further example.)

1835 DICKENS *Let.* ?June (1965) I. 64 It will give me pleasure;..and I am sure will be excellent practice for you against Christmas next.

13. c. *to get* (or *be*) *next* (*to* or *on*): to become acquainted or intimate with, to come to know; to find out about, to understand, to become worldly-wise, to acquire self-knowledge. Also *to put next* (*to*): to acquaint (one) (with). *U.S. slang.*

1896 [see *BRASH *a.*[2] b]. **1896** ADE *Artie* xvi. 146 I've been next, I'll tell you those. **1900** —— *More Fables in Slang* 109 She knew that the Treasurer of the Shoe Factory was Next to all these Boarding School Tactics. **1902** 'D. DIX' *Fables of Elite* 85 'Do you get Next to my Meaning?' 'I am on..and I apprehend that a wink to the Wise is sufficient.' **1906** B. L. TAYLOR *Extra Dry* 24 Then along comes Paul Potter, and puts me next on how to write a play. **1908** K. MCGAFFEY *Show-Girl* 72 You had better drop in your penny and get next to yourselves. **1910** W. M. RAINE *B. O'Connor* 225 Mrs. Mackenzie will put you next to the etiquette wrinkles where you are shy. **1910** WODEHOUSE *Gentleman of Leisure* vii. 66 Sure, he will... He'll be good. He's next to de game, sure. *Ibid.* x. 98 Boss, what's doin' here? Put me next to de game. **1913** E. C. BENTLEY *Trent's Last Case* vi. 59 'Has he any friends?' interjected Trent. Mr. Bunner [an American] glanced at him sharply. 'Somebody has been putting you next, I see that.' **1936** J. TULLY *Bruiser* iv. 41 She took me for a hundred before I got next. **1950** A. LOMAX *Mr. Jelly Roll* 19 If you could shoot a good agate.., I'm telling you were liable to get next to that broad. **1957** R. STOUT *If Death ever Slept* (1958) vi. 73 Maybe you can get a lead to it through Brigham. Get next to him. **1969** 'H. PENTECOST' *Girl Watcher's Funeral* (1970) II. iii. 114 He found out I was an actor... He told me he could put me next to some guy who was making underground films. **1973** *Black World* Sept. 4/2 If he can't get next to what we're about, we'll just have to school him.

next door. Add: **1. b.** By extension, the occupant of the adjoining house; so *Mrs. next-door.* Also, *next-door-but-one,* the occupant of the house two doors away.

1855 DICKENS *Prince Bull* in *Household Words* 17 Feb.

51/1 One answered, 'I will if next door will;' and another, 'I won't, if over the way does.' **1933** D. C. PEEL *Life's Enchanted Cup* xi. 127 It..occurred to him that our extra pair of guests might belong to one of the 'next doors'. **1935** *Punch* 27 Nov. 590/1 Next-door-but-one was rather a strain. Have you ever imagined canvassing through a speaking-tube? **1951** W. MORUM *Gabriel* I. i. 20, I showed it to Mrs. Next-door. *Ibid.* vii 95 Aunt Amy came in carrying a roast chicken... 'One of next-door's,' she said. **1960** WILLMOTT & YOUNG *Family & Class in London Suburb* ix. 107 Next door but one has pussy when we go on holiday. Last year she broke her arm and I used to go in and help her. **1962** *Guardian* 30 July 4/3 Most of us have had to pick up Mrs Next-Door's torn-up letters.

2. b. *boy next door*: see *BOY *sb.*¹ 8; (*the*) *girl next door*: see *GIRL *sb.* 2 h.

nexus. Add: **1. c.** In Jespersen's terminology, a group of words containing a verb, or a predicative (with ellipsis of verb); a predicative relation or a construction treated as such. Freq. *attrib.*

1924 O. JESPERSEN *Philos. Gram.* vii. 97 If now we compare the combination *a furiously barking dog*..with *the dog barks furiously*, it is evident that the same subordination obtains in the latter as in the former combination... We shall call the former kind *junction*, and the latter *nexus*. *Ibid.* ix. 122 A nexus-object is often found: 'I found *the cage empty*', which is easily distinguished from 'I found *the empty cage*' where *empty* is an adjunct. *Ibid.* 126 The subject-part (primary) of a Latin nexus-subjunct may be an accusative-with-infinitive or a clause. *Ibid.* x. 138 Nexus-substantives are also often convenient in cases where idiomatic usage does not allow a dependent clause, as after *upon* in 'Close upon his resignation followed his last illness and death'. *Ibid.* xxii. 303 We may therefore call questions of this kind [i.e. yes-or-no] *nexus-questions*. **1928** —— *Internat. Lang.* II. 130 To form so-called 'abstracts' (i.e. in my terminology predicative nexus-words) from adjectives we use the suffix *-eso*. **1933** [see *ADNEX]. **1936** J. R. AIKEN *Commonsense Gram.* xvii. 212 The clause is basically a nexus performing a single function within a communication. **1937** O. JESPERSEN *Analytic Syntax* 16 Nexus-substantive, e.g. work, kindness. **1946** —— *Mod. Eng. Gram.* VI. v. 47 Something looking like a nexus-tertiary is continued with its S[ubject] as the real subject of the sentence. **1951** A. GARDINER *Speech & Lang.* 261 Jespersen has given to this subject-predicate relation..the name of 'nexus'. **1957** S. POTTER *Mod. Linguistics* iii. 71 General or nexus-questions which may be answered by 'yes' or 'no'. **1966** *English Studies* XLVII. 55 Those with nexus-objects (e.g. I believe Williams the murderer = Williams to be the murderer).

Nez Percé, Nez Perce (nez pɔ̄ɪs). [Fr., lit. 'pierced nose'.] A member of a group of North American Indians; also, the language of this people. Also *attrib.*

1812 in *S. Dakota Hist. Coll.* (1908) IV. 157 The..Nez Perce nation have a tradition that the human race spring from this dog [*sc.* the prairie dog] and the beaver. **1832** in *Overland to Pacific* (1934) IV. 120 Here we found about 120 Lodges of the Nez Perces and about 80 of the Flatheads. **1841** G. CATLIN *Lett. on N. Amer. Indians* II. 108 The *Nez Percés* who inhabit the upper waters..of the Columbia,..are seldom known to flatten the head. **1910** F. W. HODGE *Handbk. Amer. Indians* II. 67/1 Practically the only rupture in these relations was the Nez Percé war of 1877. **1926** L. A. CLARE tr. *Lévy-Bruhl's How Natives Think* iv. 157 With the Nez-percés, verbs assume different forms according to whether the subject or object is advancing or retreating. **1937** R. H. LOWIE *Hist. Ethnol. Theory* ix. 133 The Nez Percé myths dictated by an old native woman to her college-bred son form another notable instance. **1949** *Pacific Discovery* May–June 16/1 According to some it is derived from the Nez Percé word meaning 'muddy water'. **1959** E. TUNIS *Indians* 112/1 The northern Shoshone, the Nez Percé, and some other tribes obtained horses and were transformed into reasonable facsimiles of Plains Indians. **1965** *Canad. Jrnl. Linguistics* X. 78 Languages of sure affiliation... Nez Perce (Penutian). **1968** [see *IBO *a.* and *sb.* B. 1 b]. **1969** *Language* XLV. 45 Sahaptian..has two members: Nez Perce and Sahaptin. Nez Perce was spoken in parts of present-day Oregon, Washington, and Idaho. **1973** *Times Lit. Suppl.* 23 Nov. 1425/1 Joseph, last of the Nez Percé, non-treaty chiefs, was restricted to a Washington reservation.

ngaio (nai·o). Also 9 ngaiho. [Maori.] An evergreen shrub or small tree, *Myoporum laetum*, of the family Myoporaceæ, native to New Zealand and bearing clusters of white flowers. Also *attrib.*

1853 J. D. HOOKER *Bot. Antarctic Voy.: Flora Novæ-Zelandiæ* I. 205 *Myoporum lætum*... Nat[ive] name 'Ngaio', Col[enso]. (Cultivated in England.) **1861** A. S. ATKINSON *Jrnl.* 6 Mar. in *Richmond–Atkinson Papers* (1960) I. 693 Sat down in the shade of the ngaiho's which bordered the beach. **1873** *Descr. Catal. Exhibits from N.Z. Vienna Exhib.* 24/1 *Myoporum lætum.* (Ngaio). A small ornamental tree. Wood light, white, and tough. Used for gun stocks. **1876** *Trans. N.Z. Inst.* IX. 206 A common New Zealand shrub, or tree, which may be made useful for shelter, viz. the Ngaio. **1921** H. GUTHRIE-SMITH *Tutira* xii. 102 In this light bush, tawa..mahoe or hinahina (*Melicytus ramiflorus*), ngaio (*Myoporum laetum*)..were the most common trees and shrubs. **1946** *Jrnl. Polynesian Soc.* LV. 161 Fancy ngaio not being in the Dictionary; ngaio, so reminiscent of the story of Ngaio and her translation to the moon with her calabash and the ngaio tree she clung to for support and stay. **1959** *Listener* 30 Apr. 769/2 The New Zealand 'properties'—ngaio, bluegum, etc.—enter naturally into what he [*sc.* J. K. Baxter] has to say. **1966** *Encycl. N.Z.* II. 681/2 Ngaio grows to a height of about 30 ft and is a much-branched, rounded tree. The leaves are bright green and somewhat fleshy... They are thickly studded with oil glands in which bacteria live. Flowers are small and appear as little clusters in the axils of leaves.

Ngala, var. *LINGALA.

nganga, var. *MGANGA.

‖ **ngarara** (narā·rā). [Maori.] A name used for various extinct, unidentified, New Zealand lizards; also, in Maori mythology, a lizard-like monster. Also *attrib.*

1874 J. W. STACK in *Trans. N.Z. Inst.* VII. 296 Ngarara burrows were frequently met with on the plains. *Ibid.*, A ngarara known as Te iha was kept a long time at Kaiapoi. **1882** W. D. HAY *Brighter Britain!* II. 115 There is a little emerald-green lizard in the bush, called by the Maori ngarara. It is dreadfully tapu. **1901** A. A. GRACE *Tales of Dying Race* 190 'The Ngarara—you never heard of him?' said the old woman. 'He is *the* Ngarara—the real one. Big body, eight feet long; big webbed feet; big wings like a bat's, with which he flies and catches fish; long tail like a *tuatara* lizard's, but bigger; skin like the bark of the red pine.' **1905** W. B. *Where White Man Treads* 38 His [*sc.* the Maori's] existence was burdened with the knowledge of huge reptilian monsters, ngarara on land,and taniwha in the water. **1949** P. BUCK *Coming of Maori* (1950) I. iv. 61 The crew and passengers of the [canoe] Mangarara consisted of reptiles and insects. The reptiles (*ngarara*) were lizards. **1966** *Encycl. N.Z.* I. 48/2 Less improbable were Maori tales of the *ngarara*, lizards which were larger than the tuatara... Certain prominent Maoris ..claimed not only to have seen but also to have handled and eaten them. It seems that the *ngarara*, which frequented manuka scrub, varied in size from 2 to 3 ft in length and from 10 to 20 in. in girth. There was also a smaller *ngarara*, about 18 in. long, found in streams. The Maoris attributed the disappearance of the large *ngarara* to scrub-fires and the attacks of cats and..perhaps the Norwegian rat.

Ngbaka (ŋ,bā·kă). [Native name.] A Bantu language of the northern parts of Zaire.

1949 E. A. NIDA *Morphol.* (ed. 2) 63 Ngbaka, a language of the Belgian Congo. **1965** *Language* XLI. 347 A few short Ngbaka texts.

Ngbandi (ŋ,ba·ndi). [Native name.] A Bantu language of the Central African Republic and northern Zaire.

1955 J. H. GREENBERG *Studies in African Linguistic Classification* 12 An enumeration of the membership of the Niger-Congo family by tentative genetic subfamilies follows:..14. Eastern Branch: Gbaya-Manjia,..Sango-Yakoma-Ngbandi. **1964** E. A. NIDA *Toward Sci. Transl.* ix. 199 In Ngbandi, a language of northern Congo, tense distinctions are generally indicated by tonal differences on the subject pronouns, while aspectual differences are signaled by differences of tone on the verbs. **1967** W. J. SAMARIN *Grammar of Sango* 17 Vernacular Sango, one of the dialects of the Ngbandi complex (which itself is a language of the Adamawa-Eastern group of Greenberg's Niger-Kordofanian), at one time came to be used as a lingua-franca. **1969** *Language* XLV. 659 Sango is a pidginized variant of a Ngbandi language of the Central African Republic.

‖ **ngege** (ŋ,ge·ge). [Native name.] A cichlid food fish, *Tilapia esculenta*, found in Lake Victoria in E. Africa. Cf. *TILAPIA.

1928 *Times* (Weekly ed.) 12 Jan. 54/2 His nets were full of the prime fish of the lake, the carplike ngege. **1932** *Discovery* Jan. 16/1 The fish of economic importance is called the ngege, a carp-like species which is found in Lake Victoria.

Ngoko (ŋ,ōᵘ·ko). [Native name.] The popular written or spoken form of modern Javanese.

1893, 1925 [see *KROMO]. **1948** D. DIRINGER *Alphabet* vii. 424 Ngoko, the language of the commoner. **1963** R. T. MCVEY *Indonesia* x. 443 Semar..speaks to the god in Ngoko (low Javanese) and is answered in high Javanese.

‖ **ngoma** (ŋ,gōᵘ·mă). [Swahili *ngoma, goma,* drum, dance, music.] In East Africa, a dance, a social gathering where dancing is general, a night of dancing.

1926 *Glasgow Herald* 27 Jan. 10 They..console them for the temporary absence of their dancing partners at ngomas. **1935** E. HEMINGWAY *Green Hills of Africa* I. i. 16 That is what you should see. The big *ngomas*. The big native dance festivals. **1947** *E. African Ann.* 1946–7 57/1 Most include in their headdresses a 'halo' of giraffe or zebra hair, and one I saw at a Victory ngoma (dance) had his horned headdress crowned by a..teapot. **1960** *Spectator* 29 July 179 They would keep it up far into the night, drinking and drumming; a jolly social party not like the ngomas I used to see which always had a hint of magic and, it seemed, of menace. **1966** C. SWEENEY *Scurrying Bush* v. 65 It was not until I went to a *ngoma*, or beer-dance,..that I appreciated the tremendous volume of noise that human beings could produce. **1971** *Standard* (Dar es Salaam) 7 Apr. 1/8 There will be dances in all dancing halls,..competitions in ngomas and singing, [etc.].

Ngoni (ŋ,gōᵘ·ni), *sb.* and *a.* [Native name.] **A.** *sb.* An African people belonging to the Nguni branch of the Bantu. (Groups of Ngoni migrated from their original home in Zululand in about 1830 and are now found in Malawi, Tanzania, Zambia, etc.) **B.** *adj.* Of or pertaining to this people.

1883 R. N. CUST *Mod. Lang. Africa* II. xii. 300 Bands of marauders, or Nomads, are met with as far North as the neighbourhood of the Victoria Nyanza under the names of..Ba-Ngoni, Wa-Ngoni, and Ma-Ngoni. The uniform testimony of travellers is that they speak Zulu. **1891** W. A. ELMSLIE (*title*) Introductory grammar of the Ngoni (Zulu) language, as spoken in Mombera's kingdom. **1911** *Encycl. Brit.* XXVIII. 1050/2 In the 19th century various Zulu hordes successively invaded and overran a great part of east-central Africa... Throughout these regions they are variously known as Ma-Zitu, Ma-Ravi, Wa-Ngoni (Angoni), [etc.]. **1948** J. A. BARNES *Material Culture of Ft. Jameson Ngoni* i. 4 The principal difference between the Ngoni and their surrounding neighbours is in their form of centralised chieftainship, inherited from father to son. **1950** —— *Marriage in Changing Society* iv. 71 The Ngoni regard uxorilocal residence as part of the obligation a man has towards his wife's parents. **1966** C. G. SELIGMAN *Races of Africa* (ed. 4) ix. 141 Reflex movements northwards had produced disorder long before Arab raids and Ngoni incursions spread ruin and desolation.

Nguni (ŋ,gu·ni), *sb.* and *a.* [Zulu.] **A.** *sb.* A subdivision of the Bantu people which includes the Zulu-Xhosa tribes; also the languages spoken by this group, i.e. the Zulu-Xhosa-Swazi languages. **B.** *adj.* Of or pertaining to this group of peoples or languages.

1929 A. T. BRYANT *Olden Times in Zululand & Natal* i. 3 The natives of South-Eastern Africa we distinguish as of three separate families, which we call respectively Ngûni, in Zululand, the Transvaal, Natal and the Cape; Sutû..; and Tònga. *Ibid.* 5 Captured Bushwomen became common in their homes... And the children..adopted..in a Bantuized form, much of the slave-girl's speech... Hence the clicks in Ngûni speech. **1940** M. GLUCKMAN in Fortes & Evans-Pritchard *African Political Systems* i. 29 In the earlier period of Nguni history, political allegiance tended to coincide with kinship affiliation. **1950** RADCLIFFE-BROWN & FORDE *African Systems of Kinship & Marriage* 58 In the Nguni tribes the personal name that a woman has in her own family, as a daughter, may not be used by her husband's family. **1957** C. G. SELIGMAN *Races of Africa* (ed. 3) viii. 168 This group [*sc.* Eastern Southern Bantu] consists of two main subdivisions Nguni and Tsonga. The former include the Cape Nguni of the Ciskei and Transkei.. together with the 'Fingo', fugitive remnants of tribes broken up in Natal..; the Natal Nguni, or 'Zulu' of Natal and Zululand, with their offshoot the Ndebele (Tebele) of Southern Rhodesia; the Swazi of Swaziland and the Eastern Transvaal; and the 'Transvaal Ndebele' of Central and Northern Transvaal. **1970** W. SMITH *Gold Mine* xxxiv. 88 Basuto is also one of the fighting tribes of the N'guni group.

ngwee (ŋ,gwī·). Pl. **ngwee.** [Chibemba, lit. 'bright'.] A small coin of Zambia.

1966 *Guardian* 10 Mar. 12/4 Zambia..is to go over, by January 1968, to a decimal currency based on the kwacha (worth 10s of the present pound), divided into 100 ngwee. **1969** *Reporter* (Nairobi) 16 May 12/4 Zambia's white farmers..appear fairly satisfied with the 38 ngwee per pound average. **1975** *Stand. Encycl. S. Afr.* XI. 573/1 The kwacha was equivalent to half of the pound and itself was made up of 100 ngwee.

niacin (nəi·ăsin). *Biochem.* [f. *NI(COTINIC *a.* + AC(ID *a.* and *sb.* + -IN¹.] **a.** = **nicotinic acid*. **b.** The pellagra-preventing vitamin, which can be either nicotinic acid or nicotinamide.

1942 *Cooperative Consumer* 28 Feb. 5/3 'Niacin' is the new name for 'nicotinic acid', the ingredient of enriched bread which was first discovered as a potent preventive and cure for pellagra. The new name was found to be necessary because some anti-tobacco groups warned against using enriched bread because it would foster the cigaret habit... Federal Security Administrator Paul McNutt..approved the name. **1956** A. HUXLEY *Let.* 25 Dec. (1969) 814 Are there any published papers on the use of niacin in the treatment of high cholesterol conditions? **1968** PFEIFFER & MURPHREE in D. H. Efron *Psychopharmacology* 696/2 The majority of schizophrenic patients given niacin or niacinamide had fewer hospital readmissions..when compared to non-vitamin treated control groups. **1970** *Nature* 16 May 665/2 Niacin is now acceptably defined as a blanket word for the acid and amide. **1972** *Materials & Technology* V. xix. 676 The best dietary sources of niacin are yeast, liver, lean meat, poultry, and legumes.

niacinamide (nəi,ăsi·năməid). *Biochem.* [f. prec. + AMIDE.] = *NICOTINAMIDE.

1951 *Addendum to Brit. Pharmacop.* 23 Injection of Nicotinamide. *Synonym.* Niacinamide Injection. **1955** W. W. DENLINGER *Compl. Boston* II. 34 The need for niacinamide, calcium pantothenate and pyr[i]doxine..has not yet been established as pertains to the nutrition of dogs. **1968** [see prec.]. **1972** *Arch. Dermatol.* CV. 574/2 In our patient, oral and parenteral administration of niacinamide..led to rapid clearing of the pellagrous dermatitis.

Niagara. 1. (Earlier and later examples.)

1841 F. A. KEMBLE *Let.* 28 Dec. in *Rec. Later Life* (1882) II. 153 Such a Niagara of information did surely never pour from the lips of mortal man! **1909** *Chambers's Jrnl.* June 383/1 In the savage blizzards of a frozen Sahara this [ice-]drift becomes a roaring, hissing, blinding Niagara of snow, rising hundreds of feet into the air. **1912** I. S. COBB *Back Home* 321 Rivers of red pop had

already flowed, Niagaras of lager beer and stick gin had been swallowed up. **1931** A. Huxley *Let.* 24 Aug. (1969) 352 We are reading *Monte Cristo* aloud. What a book! I had never read it before: it is a kind of Niagara! **1970** P. Laurie *Scotland Yard* iii. 86 A Niagara of tinted hair. **1974** *Times* 9 Jan. 6/5 Mr Nixon was swept towards what the White House once called a 'Niagara' of accusations last spring.

nialamide (nəiˌæ·læməid). *Pharm.* [f. the proprietary name *Niamid* by insertion of *-al.*] A crystalline hydrazide, $C_{16}H_{18}N_4O_2$, which is a monoamine oxidase inhibitor used as an antidepressant.

1959 *Proc. Soc. Exper. Biol. & Med.* CI. 832 (*heading*) Pharmacological studies with nialamide, a new antidepressant agent. **1960** A. Carlsson et al. in J. R. Vane et al. *Adrenergic Mechanisms* 434 Fig. 1 shows the action of nialamide, which is a very potent and long-acting monoamine oxidase inhibitor though its action sets in fairly slowly. **1971** *Brit. Med. Bull.* XXVII. 28/2 First nialamide..and then tranylcypromine..began to be used for the treatment of depression.

Niam-Niam (nī·ămˌnī·ăm). [Dinka, lit. 'great eaters'.] = *Zande.

1861 J. Petherick *Egypt, Soudan, & Central Africa* xxvi. 469 Attached to the girdle, a strong leather sheath containing a knife, hilt downwards, is worn by every Neam Nam. *Ibid.* 473 The Neam Nam recognise no superior chief; but, like the Dôr, the tribe is divided into numerous chieftainships. **1873** E. E. Frewer tr. *Schweinfurth's Heart of Africa* II. xiii. 3 The name Niam-niam is.. so universally incorporated into the Arabic of the Soudan, that it seems unadvisable to substitute for it the word 'Zandey', the name by which the people are known among themselves. **1891** A. W. Buckland *Anthrop. Studies* v. 59 In Africa, the typical home of the stalwart Negro.. we find the Bushman and Hottentot in the South, and the Akkas and Niam-Niams in the centre, very small in stature and yellow in colour. **1902** *Encycl. Brit.* XXXI. 230/1 The Niam-Niam, or Zandeh people, as they call themselves..are now found to stretch, with interruptions, from the White Nile above the Sobat confluence to the Shari affluent of Lake Chad. **1931** J. G. Leyburn *Handbk. Ethnography* 176/2 Niam-Niam. Between the Welle, a tributary of the Ubangi, and the Nile. **1966** R. & D. Morris *Men & Apes* viii. 238 The Niams-Niams, apparently, still adorn themselves with colobus monkey skins wound round the waist.

‖ **niaouli** (nī̆ˌăˌuli). [Native name.] An evergreen tree, *Melaleuca quinquenervia*, of the family Myrtaceæ, native to New Caledonia. Also *attrib.* and *transf.*, a personification of New Caledonia.

1921 *Public Opinion* 29 July 109/2 A mat of pandanus leaves served for his sail and a paddle of niaouli wood for its helm. **1943** *Amer. Speech* XVIII. 14 It would be.. impossible to root them [*sc.* English words] out of the Niaouli's everyday language. *Ibid.* 15 Our expression 'to go bush' has its counterpart in Niaouli pidgin... Niaouli is the name of a tree which..has come to be regarded as a national symbol [of New Caledonia]. **1965** *Univ. Iowa Stud. Nat. Hist.* XX. vii. 52 (*caption*) This frequent burning maintains the enormous area of fire-resistant niaouli.

nib, *sb.*[1] Add: **3.** (Further examples.)

1901 J. Black *Carp. & Builder Series: Slating & Tiling* 13 The ordinary pantile..is provided on the underside with a small projection known as a nib. **1940** *Chambers's Techn. Dict.* 578/1 *Nib*, a small projection, sometimes continuous, formed on the under-side at the top of each tile, enabling the tile to be hung on battens. **1955** *Railway Mag.* May 307/2 The main feature of the detachable nibs in the relay baseboards is that disconnection points are available without the necessity of providing independent terminal boards for each relay. **1962** *Gloss. Terms Glass Industry* (*B.S.I.*) 43 *Nib*, a small protrusion at the corner of a piece of flat glass due to faulty cutting. **1968** *Gloss. Formwork Terms* (*B.S.I.*) 17 *Kicker* (nib), a small concrete upstand cast above floor level to position wall or column forms for the next lift and to assist the prevention of grout loss.

7. A speck of solid matter in a coat of paint or varnish.

1940 in *Chambers's Techn. Dict.* **1958** *Listener* 11 Sept. 399/1 You can now tidy it [*sc.* the undercoat of paint] up with fine sandpaper—just enough to remove any dust nibs or brush marks. **1965** W. N. Lapper in *Applic. Surface Coatings* (Oil & Colour Chemists' Assoc.) iii. 37 A coagulation of pigment can cause 'nibs' or bittiness in the film. **1968** *Pract. Motorist* Feb. 611/3 Once the first coat is fully dry rub it down very gently with wet-or-dry (grade 320) to remove any 'nibs' and runs.

nib, *sb.*[3] (Later example.)

1936 Wodehouse *Laughing Gas* viii. 81 You don't run to an English butler in Hollywood unless you are a pretty prominent nib.

nibble, *v.* Add: **1. e.** To produce by nibbling.

1867 A. J. Evans *St. Elmo* xxi. 296 Just see what a hole the pretty little wretch has nibbled in my new Swiss muslin dress!

2. b. (Later *fig.* examples.) Also *absol.*

1921 W. J. Locke *Mountebank* xvi. 208 Moignon was in touch, on his behalf, with powerful American agencies... Moignon had said: 'They are nibbling for the winter.' **1973** *Times* 20 Mar. 21/3 Since the Broadspeed Turbo Bullit..was announced in January, motor manufacturers have been nibbling at the idea.

d. *Cricket.* To play (indecisively) at a ball bowled outside the off stump.

1926 P. F. Warner *Fight for Ashes* 16 Bardsley.. showed a distinct weakness in nibbling at good-length balls outside the off-stump. **1932** E. Blunden *Face of England* 71 'Tom's out.' 'He shouldn't have nibbled at that.'

nibbled (ni·b'ld), *ppl. a.* [f. Nibble *v.* + -ed[1].] That has been nibbled or cropped.

1865 R. D. Blackmore *Cradock Nowell* (1866) I. viii. 68 Over the nibbled sward..came wandering the lightest foot that ever passed. **1905** J. B. Firth *Highways Derbyshire* viii. 119 The Dove flows between closely nibbled hill slopes. **1949** *U.S. Employment Service, Dict. Occup. Titles* 891 May file and grind excess metal and rough edges of nibbled parts to specified dimensions.

nibble-nip, *v.* [f. Nibble *sb.* or *v.* + Nip *v.*[1]] *intr.* To give a nibble, a trifling nip (only *fig.*). So **nibble-nipped** *ppl. a.*

1883 G. Meredith *Poems & Lyrics of Joy of Earth* 26 Haggard Wisdom, stately once, Leers fantastical and trips: Allegory drums the sconce, Impiousness nibblenips. **1937** *Sunday Times* 10 Jan. 8/3 The conversation distinguished, sedate, and rather wintry (even Newman had at first felt nibble-nipped) of the Oriel Common Room.

nibbler. Add: **1. b.** *Engin.* A type of metal-cutting tool in which a rapidly reciprocating punch knocks out a line of overlapping small holes from sheet or plate.

1939 *Jrnl. R. Aeronaut. Soc.* XLIII. 144 Practically all of the standard means of cutting are used in all factories. These are the oxy-acetylene torch,..the nibbler; the saw; and the uni-shears. **1958** *Engineering* 28 Mar. 409/2 A nibbler for sheet up to 16 s.w.g. **1961** *Aeroplane & Astronautics* CI. 272/3 On display is a complete range of tools, including drills, screwdrivers, nutrunners, grinders, rivet and bolt millers, nibblers and shears.

nibcocked (ni·bˌkǫk't), *a. rare*—[1]. [f. Nib *sb.*[1] + Cock *sb.*[1] 20 + -ed[2].] ? Having a penis like the point of a pen.

1939 Dylan Thomas *Let.* Mar. (1966) 226 The English poets now are such a pinlegged, nibcocked, paperhearted crowd you could blow them down with one bellow out of a done lung.

nibful (ni·bful). *rare.* [f. Nib *sb.*[1] + -ful.] As much as a nib can hold.

1930 V. Woolf *Writer's Diary* 29 Apr. (1953) 158, I have just finished, with this very nib-ful of ink, the last sentence of *The Waves.*

niblick. (Earlier, *attrib.*, and later examples.)

1857 H. B. Farnie *Golfer's Manual* (1947) iii. 18 It is called a *Niblick.* **1886** H. G. Hutchinson *Hints on Golf* xiii. 33 In the typical niblick shot the ball lies in a heel-mark or other cup in the sand, with the face of the bunker in front. **1909** *Bystander* 13 Oct. 90/2 Herd..saved an apparently lost hole by a most masterly niblick pitch. **1955** R. Browning *Hist. Golf* 145 Even the niblicks were originally wooden clubs: the first iron-headed niblicks were excessively short in the blade. **1961** M. Spark *Prime of Miss Jean Brodie* v. 141 Sandy gave a hack with her niblick.

ni·blick, *v. Golf.* [f. the sb.] *trans.* To hit (a ball) with a niblick.

1909 *Westm. Gaz.* 15 Jan. 4/2 If bunkered..he would have to niblick the ball out sideways.

Nibmar, NIBMAR (ni·bmāɹ). [f. the initials of '*n*o *i*ndependence *b*efore *m*ajority *A*frican *r*ule'.] The policy of opposing recognition of the minority government which proclaimed the independence of Rhodesia in 1965.

1966 *Time* 23 Sept. 31 They demanded that he agree to something called NIBMAR. **1966** *Economist* 17 Dec. 1222/1 They suspect Britain is on the point of making a settlement with Mr Smith which would snatch from them the apple of Nibmar. **1970** *Times* 12 Nov. 6 Britain, he said, had never accepted a commitment to Nibmar from the United Nations.

nibong, var. Nibung (in Dict. and Suppl.).

nibs. Add: Esp. *his nibs*, *His Nibs*, an employer, a superior; a self-important person. (Further examples, including occas. uses with other possessive pronouns.)

1846 *Swell's Night Guide* 57 She flokessed his nibs, and hooked it off to his crib. **1877** *Brooklyn Monthly* Oct. 21/2 Salute the hostess by saying: 'Cully, how's his nibs?' **1882** G. W. Peck *Sunshine* 131 A respectable merchant was going to the opera with a friend from the country, when a couple of sirens met them and one said to the other, 'Look at his nibs.' **1906** E. Dyson *Fact'ry 'Ands* ii. 18 They're settin' her nibs t'-day. **1906** [see *dilly *a.*[1]]. **1919** G. S. Gordon *Let.* 30 June (1943) 115 We get on to the *Caesar*, and find their nibs strolling the quarterdeck after dinner. **1928** 'Brent of Bin Bin' *Up Country* ii. 33 Gifts..including a splendid meerschaum pipe for his Nibs. **1933** M. Allingham *Sweet Danger* xxi. 218 What if 'Is Nib's boy friends spot us before? **1944** [see *Hampshire b]. **1957** H. Croome *Forgotten Place* 175, I wish I could just lie on a bed and smoke, like His Nibs. **1967** A. Wilson *No Laughing Matter* i. 21 His father smiled. 'Trust His Nibs to have noticed that deficiency.' **1973** A. Hunter *Gently French* i. 9 Since when were you on first-name terms with His Nibs? **1974** O. Manning *Rain Forest* ii. i. 141 Her nibs don't like me calling him 'old bugger'. There's a snobby bitch, if you like!

nibung. Substitute for def.: A Malaysian palm, *Oncosperma filamentosa.* (Earlier and later examples.)

The usual sp. is now *nibong.*

1779 T. Forrest *Voyage to New Guinea* ix. 121 We made very good curry; stewing it with the heart of the aneebong, or cabbage tree. **1783** W. Marsden *Hist. Sumatra* 77 The *neebong* or cabbage tree, a species of palm, grows wild in too great abundance to require being cultivated. **1820** J. Crawfurd *Hist. Indian Archipelago* I. iv. 417 The *nibung* is the true mountain cabbage. **1839** T. J. Newbold *Straits of Malacca* I. iv. 139 Thatch of Atap, and floors of split nibong, called lantei. **1898** Conrad *Tales of Unrest* 275 Two tall nibong palms.. leaned slightly over the ragged roof. **1907** F. Swettenham *Brit. Malaya* vii. 151 The floor..is of planks, *nibong*, or split bamboos. **1954** R. H. Holttum *Plant Life in Malaya* ii. 22 Other kinds of palm have many trunks; for example, the Sago palm and the Nibong. **1966** *Listener* 6 Oct. 502/3 Nearly 14,000 people live in wooden houses built on stilts of tough nibong palms.

N.I.C., NIC, Nic (nik). [Acronym f. the initial letters of '*N*ational *I*ncomes *C*ommission'.] The name of a body giving advice to the government on economic policy. Cf. *Nicky *sb.*[2]

1962 *Daily Tel.* 27 July 24/5 He saw the N.I.C. primarily as a means of 'educating public opinion'. **1962** *Times* 27 July 13/2 (*heading*) To Neddy add Nic.

Nicaraguan (nikăræ·giuăn), *a.* and *sb.* [f. Nicaragua: see -an.] **A.** *adj.* Of, pertaining to, or characteristic of Nicaragua. **B.** *sb.* A native or inhabitant of Nicaragua.

1847 R. G. Dunlop *Trav. Central America* iii. 105 The Caroline, a schooner chartered by the Nicaraguan government. **1852** E. G. Squier *Nicaragua* I. ii. ii. 77 The average rate of duty exacted under the Nicaraguan tariff, is about 21 per cent. ad valorem. *Ibid.* 78 All its inhabitants were, and with the exception of a few.., still are Nicaraguans. **1868** F. Boyle *Ride across Continent* I. p. xxi, The universal legend of the surrounding peoples—Indians, Caribs, Nicaraguans, and Costa Ricans,—declares the Guatuso race to be distinguished by fair hair and blue eyes. *Ibid.* iii. 120 He stayed with us through all our Nicaraguan experiences. **1884** *Encycl. Brit.* XVII. 478/2 The Nicaraguan fauna differs in few respects from that of the other Central-American states. **1923** Ld. Charnwood *Theodore Roosevelt* vii. 151 The Nicaraguan route would be cheaper for a canal. **1934** [see *Honduran, Hondurean *a.* and *sb.*]. **1946** E. A. Peers *Fool of Love* vii. 121 The Nicaraguan, Rubén Dario, took up the picturesque phrase. **1973** *Time* 25 June 17/1 Nicaraguan Ambassador Guillermo Sevilla-Sacasa said sympathetically [to Julie Nixon Eisenhower]: 'Your father still has one friend.'

nice, *a.* Add: **14.** *spec.* Of a cup of tea.

1899 R. Whiteing *No. 5 John St.* iv. 38 Her sex's universal restorative... 'You shall have a nice cup of tea.' **1928** R. Knox *Footsteps at Lock* v. 41 You'd have got a nice cup of tea down at the Gudgeon. **1937** A. P. Herbert *Nice Cup of Tea* (song), I like a nice cup of tea in the morning, For to start the day you see. **1937** 'G. Orwell' *Road to Wigan Pier* v. 88 There is generally a cup of tea going—a 'nice cup of tea'. **1961** I. Fleming *Thunderball* iv. 38 The dimity world of the Nice-Cup-of-Tea. **1974** L. Deighton *Spy Story* xxi. 221 'I'll pour him some tea,' said Dawlish. 'There's nothing so reviving as a nice cup of tea.'

15. a. *nice girl* (of an adult). Freq. somewhat derisive.

1876 C. M. Yonge *Womankind* xvi. 126 Though a well managed, innocent and select rink is quite possible, 'nice' girls would do well to abstain from those where a chance public shares the sport. **1901** W. D. Howells *Heroines of Fiction* I. 12 They imagined the heroine who was after all a Nice Girl; who still remains the ideal of our fiction. **1905** E. Wharton *House of Mirth* i. xv. 239 He had never wanted to marry a 'nice' girl: the adjective connoting..certain utilitarian qualities..apt to preclude the luxury of charm. **1910** *National Police Gaz.* 16 July 3/1 That's what tells and it pulls the nice girls down with a sudden rush that takes their breath away. **1933** E. O'Neill *Ah, Wilderness!* (1934) iii. i. 89 You're a darned nice girl. **1938** N. Marsh *Artists in Crime* viii. 108 She tries to talk 'Slade'..but the original nice-girl gush oozes out. **1968–70** *Current Slang* (Univ. S. Dakota) III–IV. 86 *Nice Girl*, a sexually permissive girl. **1975** I. S. Black *Man on Bridge* ii. 26 'She's pretty.'.. 'More than that, she looked what used to be called a nice girl.'

Phr. (Further examples.)

1839 Dickens *Let.* 5 Mar. (1965) I. 521 A capital bed, and all as nice as nice could be. **1937** G. & I. Gershwin *Nice Work if you can get It* (*song*), Holding hands at mid-night 'Neath a starry sky, Nice work if you can get it, And you can get it if you try. **1938** *Sun* (Baltimore) 20 June 8/2 Ruth said, 'Nice going, kid,' and that simple compliment pleased the young Cincinnati pitcher more than all of the other praises he received. **1954** R. Bissell *High Water* xxiii. 279 'Nice going, George,' I said. **1958** *Listener* 2 Oct. 492/1 The Frenchman..may well reply with impatience: 'Nice work if you can get it.'

d. (Earlier and later examples.)

1836 Dickens *Let.* 29 Dec. (1965) I. 217, I have been clearing off all the rejected articles to-day, and nice work I have had. **1892** I. Zangwill *Childr. Ghetto* I. i. xi. 248 Well, you're a nice friend of his, I must say. **1896** E. Turner *Little Larrikin* xviii. 209 Aren't you going to stop and see Clem off?..you *are* a nice one. **1939**

L. M. MONTGOMERY *Anne of Ingleside* v, S'posin' he et a lot of the little green apples..and got nice and sick?

nicely, *adv.* Add: **3. c.** (Later examples.)

In quots. 1935 and 1938 = 'merry from the effects of drinking'.

1935 G. HEYER *Death in Stocks* xvi. 178 It was quite obvious he'd been at a pub all the time, because he was quite nicely. **1938** N. MARSH *Death in White Tie* v. 55 I'm not inebriated..but I am..a little exalted. What I believe is nowadays called nicely thank you. **1949** —— *Swing, Brother, Swing* ix. 207 'How are you, Mr. Fox?' 'Nicely, thank you, sir. And you?' **1954** A. S. C. Ross in *Neuphilologische Mitteilungen* LV. 43 Possible negative non-U answers are *I'm doing nicely, thank you* and *(Quite) sufficient, thank you.* **1943** *Times* 31 May 10/8 Aurelia Weatherbournes generally do quite nicely, thank you, on council estates.

Nicene, *a.* (and *sb.*) Add: Cf. *ISNIK.

nice-nellyism (nəisˌne·liˌiz'm). *N. Amer. slang.* Also **nice-nellieism.** [f. *nice Nelly,* a conventional name for a respectable woman, a prude + -ISM.] Prudery; genteelism; excessive prudishness of speech or behaviour: usually applied adversely. Cf. *NELLY² 3.

1936 *New Republic* 28 Oct. 337/1 Perhaps, it is true, as charged that the British press is displaying a brand of Nice Nellyism in refusing to mention the subject [*sc.* the divorce of Mrs Simpson, later Duchess of Windsor]. **1942** *Sun* (Baltimore) 17 June 10/7 Mr. Adams accused the editor [of a new book of soldier songs] of Nice Nellieism in dealing with the songs. **1947** *Sat. Rev.* (U.S.) 15 Feb. 9/2 It takes more than..nice-Nellyism in the name of patriotism to obliterate that spirit. **1952** *New Yorker* 18 Oct. 159/1 Mr. Pyles attributes much of the nice-nellyism that blighted polite speech and writing during the nineteenth century to Webster's Puritan prudishness. **1956** *N.Y. Times Book Rev.* 30 Sept. 2/2 None of the words which Ned Sheldon..found so obnoxious seems to me acutely distasteful, with the exception of 'funeral parlor', which carries nice-nellieism to the nth degree. **1960** I. WALLACH *Absence of Cello* (1961) 174 'Experience', as absurd a nice-Nellyism for copulation as she could conceive. **1973** *Saturday Night* (Toronto) Oct. 15/1 The public had been made comatose by the greyness of Mackenzie King and the nice nellyism of Middle Powermanship.

nicey, nicy (nəi·si), *a. colloq.* [f. NICE *a.* + -Y¹.] Nice. Also as *sb.*, a nice person or thing.

1859 TROLLOPE *Bertrams* I. vi. 120 The musty fusty people, and the nicy spicy people, and the witty pretty people do severally assemble and get together as they ought to do. Bertram's next-door neighbour was certainly of the nicy spicy order. **1879** C. M. YONGE *Burnt Out* viii. 132 Oh, you're a tell-tale-tit! Catch me giving you nicies again! **1914** *Conc. Oxf. Dict.* Add., *Nicy*..(nursery), sweet, lollipop. **1922** JOYCE *Ulysses* 363 Go home to nicey bread and milky and say night prayers with the kiddies. **1959** *Listener* 3 Dec. 1008/1 Young nasties after lots of lolly, and young nicies to foil them at last.

niche, *sb.* Add: Also with pronunc. (nīʃ). **2. c.** = *MIHRAB 2. In full, *prayer niche.*

1911, etc. [see *MIHRAB 2]. **1962** C. W. JACOBSEN *Oriental Rugs* 251 The prayer niche is typical and each is in this shape unless, by chance, it is one that has three prayer niches.

3. c. *Ecol.* The position of a plant or animal within its community.

1927 C. ELTON *Anim. Ecology* v. 63 It is therefore convenient to have some term to describe the status of an animal in its community, to indicate what it is doing and not merely what it looks like, and the term used is 'niche'. *Ibid.* 64 The 'niche' of an animal means its place in the biotic environment, its relations to food and enemies. **1937** [see *BIOTOPE]. **1960** N. POLUNIN *Introd. Plant Geogr.* xiv. 431 The large lianes comprise..by far the more numerous synusiae (groups of plants of similar life-form, each filling much the same ecological niche and playing a similar role). **1962** *Listener* 13 Sept. 388/2 Divergence is related to the existence of ecological niches. *Ibid.*, On the existence of niches, he [*sc.* Darwin] was already clear in 1837... Even more apposite is his question on how a niche is entered. **1965** B. E. FREEMAN tr. *Vandel's Biospeleology* i. 6 A number of terrestrial planarians are endogeans, occupying a similar niche to the earthworms. **1974** BENNETT & HUMPHRIES *Introd. Field Biol.* (ed. 2) ii. 8 Each animal species has its own typical food relationships with other species, so in a given community at a given time each is said to have its characteristic food niche. *Ibid.* 12 Its habitat niche can be thought of as the sum total of its many effective environments throughout life. *Ibid.* 13 The term 'niche' on its own is much misused in ecological writing to mean food-niche, habitat-niche, habitat or microhabitat.

Nichrome (nəi·krōᵘm). Also **nichrome.** A proprietary name of various alloys of nickel with chromium (10–20 per cent) and sometimes iron (up to 25 per cent).

1911 *Jrnl. Amer. Chem. Soc.* XXXIII. 190 The nichrome triangles..when used with city gas..lost, at most, one milligram an hour. **1933** *Official Gaz.* (U.S. Patent Off.) 4 July 18/1 Driver-Harris Company, Harrison, N.J. ..Nichrome. For alloys of nickel, chromium, and iron in the form of wire, ribbon, strip, [etc.]. **1937** *Jrnl. Brit. Interplanetary Soc.* IV. 7 The nozzles were machined from nichrome steel rod, threaded at the lower end so that they could be screwed into the exhaust end of the combustion chamber. **1947** J. C. RICH *Materials & Methods of Sculpture* ii. 46 For low-temperature firing, electric kilns equipped with nichrome wire heating elements are very efficient. **1950** *Jrnl. R. Aeronaut. Soc.* LIV. 20/1 For general purposes, the wire used in strain gauges is a straightforward cupro-nickel, or nickel-chrome alloy, such as Eureka, Brightray, Nichrome. **1951** *Trade Marks Jrnl.* 7 Mar. 228/1 'Nichrome'... Unwrought and partly wrought alloys composed mainly of nickel-chromium; and rods, tubes, bars, wire, sheets and pellets, all being goods..made from alloys composed mainly of nickel-chromium. British Driver-Harris Company Limited,.. Manchester,..manufacturers. **1964** S. H. AVNER *Introd. Physical Metallurgy* xii. 387 Some nominal compositions are 80Ni-20Cr (Chromel A, Nichrome V, and others) used as electric heating elements for household appliances and industrial furnaces; 60Ni-16Cr-24Fe (Chromel C, Nichrome, and others) used as electrical heating elements for toasters..and hot-water heaters. **1968** E. R. PETTY *Physical Metall. Engin. Materials* xiii. 276 There are two main groups of heater wire, one based on 80% nickel–20% chromium (Nichrome) with or without amounts of iron, and the other based on ferritic chromium steels... The former alloy is well known as the basis of the Nimonic high temperature alloys.

‖ **nicht wahr** (niχt vāɪ). [G., lit. 'not true'.] Is it not true?

1924 M. KENNEDY *Constant Nymph* xii. 167 We shall do very well without one [*sc.* a maid] for a little, *nicht war?* **1941** M. TREADGOLD *We couldn't leave Dinah* vi. 106 They are nice liddle horses, *nicht wahr,* Karl? **1948** W. STEVENS *Let.* 25 Oct. (1967) 621 One has a sense that the world was never less new than now... Nicht wahr? **1967** 'G. CARR' *Lewker in Tirol* v. 69 Today it is so hot that tempers are not good—*nicht wahr?* **1971** J. HENDERSON *Copperhead* (1972) xiii. 162 He was going over to the other side. Such is truly a form of suicide, *nicht wahr?*

nick, *sb.*¹ Add: **1. d.** *Squash* and *Real Tennis.* (See quot. 1961.)

1890 J. M. HEATHCOTE et al. *Tennis, Lawn Tennis, Rackets, Fives* I. iv. 69 When the odds of touch-no-walls.. are given, a ball returned by the giver of odds, which makes a nick, is counted for the striker. **1926** C. ARNOLD *Handbk. on Squash Rackets* iii. 34 Winners can also be made by what is known as a dead service nick, the ball being made to meet the back or side wall and the floor at the same time. **1961** J. S. SALAK *Dict. Amer. Sports* 296 *Nick* (court tennis)—the junction of the wall and the floor, or a return when the ball, as it drops or falls, touches the wall and the floor simultaneously. **1963** *Times* 8 Jan. 3/5 This Binns did with his usual touch strokes, boasting with precision and, on his forehand drops, turning his racket over like a butterfly net to impart top spin and make the ball die in the nick. **1973** R. HAWKEY *Beginner's Guide Squash* iv. 41 One must avoid..allowing a service to drop into the 'nick' between the back wall and the floor.

13. (Earlier and later examples.)

1824 D. BLAINE *Canine Pathol.* (ed. 2) 109 Some rearers of game fowls..are favourable to breeding from the third remove, which they call a nick. **1927** J. E. PLATT *Thoroughbred Race-Horse* iv. 31 All the well-known nicks and blending of bloods must be observed, and the leading lines of sires and dams carefully considered. **1973** *Country Life* 15 Nov. 1545/1 The nick owed little to studies of genetics and line breeding [of harriers].

14. Phrases. *in good nick* (slang, orig. dial.), in good condition; *(in the) nick* (slang), (in) prison, (at a) police station.

1882 *Sydney Slang Dict.* 6/2 *Nick (The),* gaol. **1905** WRIGHT *Eng. Dial. Dict.* Suppl. 151/1 *In good nick,* in good condition. **1949** F. SARGESON *I saw in my Dream* 61 They [*sc.* tennis courts] seemed to be in good nick. **1952** 'N. SHUTE' *Far Country* 5 She's in good nick. **1957** *Railway Mag.* June 431/1 It does not mean..that an 'A4' in good 'nick'..is not capable of performances well up to the pre-war standard. **1957** P. WILDEBLOOD *Main Chance* 122 'Arrest me,' said Ron. 'Go on, take me to the nick.' **1959** *Listener* 9 Apr. 645/3 Sundry knaves have been routed and put in 'the nick'. **1962** R. COOK *Crust on its Uppers* i. 20 The boys down at Chelsea nick. **1968** *Listener* 8 Aug. 178/2 A second-'and British slave in good nick. **1968** J. LOCK *Lady Policeman* i. 7 An address much nearer than the 'nick'. *Ibid.* 8 Back at the nick the station officer was very cross. **1969** [see *BUST *sb.*³ f]. **1970** P. LAURIE *Scotland Yard* iii. 66 The Inspector calls the nick. **1971** 'F. CLIFFORD' *Blind Side* II. ii. 81 Reports are that he's in fair enough nick.

nick, *v.*² Add: **4.** (Later examples of *intr.* use.)

1876 *Rep. Vermont Board Agric.* III. 132 There is another strain or peculiarity among these Canadians, that seems to nick well with the Morgans. **1974** *Country Life* 3–10 Jan. 43/3 The colour-marking Hereford 'nicks' well with virtually all beef and dairy breeds.

7. d. Of a ball in squash, real tennis, etc.: to strike the floor and wall simultaneously.

1898 W. MORGAN *'House' on Sport* 251 By volleying the service you prevent the ball 'nicking', i.e., so pitching in the angle formed by floor and wall as to be unplayable. **1926** C. ARNOLD *Handbk. on Squash Rackets* iii. 34 It [*sc.* the ball] should be made just to nick on to the side wall and floor and there lie dead. **1960** *Times* 29 Nov. 17/3 Oddy was nicking the side wall more often. **1973** *Times* 31 Jan. 8/7 The pace was ferocious, the 22-year-old Jehan hitting a stream of nicked winners.

8. a. Add to def.: to arrest, to put in gaol. Hence **ni·cking** *vbl. sb.*

1836, etc. [in Dict.]. **1958** *Encounter* May 11/2 He'd got nicked for ponceing off his old woman. **1959** 'M. CRONIN' *Dead & Done With* x. 152 They nicked your chum for killing his wife. **1962** *John o' London's* 25 Jan. 82/2 'Arrest' has many Cant synonyms including..*nick.* **1968** J. LOCK *Lady Policeman* iii. 30, I don't sleep rough any more. I've learnt a thing or two since you nicked me. **1970** G. F. NEWMAN *Sir, You Bastard* i. 28 Even on leave he looked for possible nickings. **1973** J. WAINWRIGHT *Devil you Don't* 32, I am talking to you, copper..either nick me..or close that bloody door.

c. (Later examples.) Also, to rob.

1901 'J. FLYNT' *World of Graft* 220/1 *Nick,* to make a 'touch'. **1903** J. LONDON *People of Abyss* xxiii. 280 'At ten we 'ops the wag; at thirteen we nicks things; an' at sixteen we bashes the copper.' Which is to say, at ten they play truant, at thirteen steal, and at sixteen are sufficiently developed hooligans to smash the policemen. **1914** JACKSON & HELLYER *Vocab. Criminal Slang* 62 *Nick*... To surreptitiously extract something from the person. **1916** H. L. WILSON *Somewhere in Red Gap* vi. 236 'I did hear that you'd had your pocket picked.'.. 'That's right. .. Some lad nicked me for my roll and return ticket.' **1954** WODEHOUSE *Jeeves & Feudal Spirit* ix. 81 Despite this, you succeeded in nicking him for what must have been a small fortune. **1966** J. PORTER *Sour Cream* xiii. 169, I had Azatov's own pass which I had nicked from him at the airport. **1973** *Courier Mail* (Brisbane) 21 June 7/4 Nicking toys from chain stores. **1974** S. GULLIVER *Vulcan Bulletins* 29 The Libyans will try to nick Javits' shipment.

13. b. *Austral.* To slip away, depart hurriedly.

1896 E. TURNER *Little Larrikin* xxiii. 274 Trying to induce the driver of the motor, for whom he had a friendship, to promise at the end of the journey to 'nick away and come too'. **1928** 'BRENT OF BIN BIN' *Up Country* viii. 120 Bert and I could just nick down to Mungee. **1959** BAKER *Drum* II. 129 *Nick, do a,* to decamp, slip away unnoticed. Also, *nick off.*

14. Substitute for def.: Of animals, to mate with excellent results. (Later examples.)

1942 R. B. KELLEY *Sheep Dogs* 51 When the progeny of a bitch by a particular dog are outstanding the parents are said to have 'nicked'. **1959** *New Scientist* 22 Oct. 737/2 Where the offspring's performance is conspicuously superior to that of its parents the mating [of poultry] is said to 'nick'. **1971** *Daily Tel.* 4 Jan. 7/6 Breeders..know from bitter experience that matings do not always 'nick' and that..they are sure to suffer many a disappointment.

nickel, *sb.* Add: **2. c.** Five dollars' worth of marijuana. *U.S. slang.*

1967 *Boston Sunday Herald* 26 Mar. 1/2 Nickel bags of marijuana (in hippie lingo a 'nickel' is $5 worth). **1968–70** *Current Slang* (Univ. S. Dakota) III–IV. 86 *Nickel*.., one-eighth to one-fourth of an ounce of marijuana costing about five dollars. Five dollars. (Drug users' jargon).

3. a. *nickel-candy, -cigar, -faced* (also *-face* vb.), *-facing, -plated* adj. (also *fig.*); **nickel-and-dime,** (*a*) rhyming slang for 'time'; (*b*) *adj.*, designating a store in which articles are cheaply priced; also *transf.* and *fig.*; **nickel bag** *U.S. slang,* a bag containing, or a measure of, five dollars' worth of a drug, esp. heroin or marijuana; **nickel-in-the-slot** *a.*, of a machine, etc.: operated by the insertion of a nickel; **nickel note** *U.S. slang* (see quots.); **nickel nurser** *U.S. slang,* a miser.

1935 A. J. POLLOCK *Underworld Speaks* 80/1 *Nickel and dime,* time. **1960** J. FRANKLYN *Dict. Rhyming Slang* 100/2 *Nickel and dime,* time. **1970** *New York* 16 Nov. 42/2 Pinned to its banks are proud, homely nickel-and-dime towns..with sides made of asphalt shingles. **1972** *Times* 16 May 1/3 The first Mrs Wallace had worked in a nickel-and-dime store. **1974** 'E. LATHEN' *Sweet & Low* viii. 84 You've got a lot of members who do nickel-and-dime business. **1967** WENTWORTH & FLEXNER *Dict. Amer. Slang* 672/1 The usual quantities or sizes of 'bags' are: 'trey' = $3 worth (esp. cocaine and heroin); 'nickel bag' = $5 worth (esp. marijuana, cocaine, or heroin). **1971** *Black World* Apr. 38/2 Black men and women and their children exchange expensive gifts of death—in small nickel bags. **1973** *Ibid.* June 79/2 If..he gets high and blurts it out to a stranger in some bar that he got his nickel bag from Joe, the pusher, then Joe's livelihood is endangered. **1972** *Village Voice* (N.Y.) 1 June 13/4 Nickel candy is 12 cents. **1894** R. KIPLING *Let.* 28 July in C. Carrington *Rudyard Kipling* (1955) ix. 217 There's a smell of horse-piss, Italian fruit-vendor, nickel cigars. **1894** *Amer. Dict. Printing & Bookmaking* 402/1 Electrotypes are often nickel-faced when they are to be used with colored inks, as copper injures the color. **1964** E. A. D. HUTCHINGS *Printing by Letterpress* I. xii. 207 The usual copper shell can be nickel-faced after the plate has been finished. This type of plate is termed a nickel-faced electrotype. **1892** A. POWELL *Southward's Pract. Printing* (ed. 4) lxxii. 696 (*heading*) Electrotyping.. finishing the plate..nickel facing. **1946** W. H. CHURCH in H. Whetton *Pract. Printing & Binding* xiii. 169/1 No further finishing of the surface of the plate can be undertaken after the nickel facing is applied, without risk of the nickel peeling off when the plate is in use. **1889** *Tacoma* (Washington) *News* 13 Dec. 3/5 The latest nickel-in-the-slot scheme is really a stroke of genius and is destined to revolutionize cheap literature in this country. **1893** *Harper's Mag.* Mar. 494 [In Jacksonville] there were the same..nickel-in-the-slot machines [as in Asbury Park]. **1901** *Daily Colonist* (Victoria, B.C.) 20 Oct. 10/3 So long as..there is no means of obtaining..official reports,..so long will mining stock investment remain on the level of 'nickel-in-the-slot' gambling. **1926** *Amer. Speech* I. 652/1 *Nickel note,* five dollar paper bill. **1970** C. MAJOR *Dict. Afro-Amer. Slang* 85 *Nickel note,* five-dollar bill. **1926** MAINES & GRANT *Wise-Crack Dict.* 11/2 *Nickle nurser,* one who has a passion for seeing that his nickles don't stray. **1945** L. SHELLY *Jive Talk Dict.* 29 *Nickel nurser,* tightwad. **1884** *Encycl. Brit.* XVII. 488/2 The manufacture of cooking utensils and other useful articles out of..nickel-plated iron. **1885** 'MARK TWAIN' in *Century Mag.* Dec. 194 He had some pathetic little nickel-plated aristocratic instincts. **1910** *Daily Chron.* 10 Dec. 9/5 This five-shilling watch..is made in cases of nickel or of gunmetal nickel-plated, with a crown bow. **1970** T. HUGHES *Crow* 39 The tears are nickel-plated. **1974** R. C. DENNIS *Conversations with Corpse* iii. 19 A revolver..

or a pistol? Nickel-plated or blue steel? Regulation or snub-nosed?

b. nickel-antigorite [ad. G. *nickel-antigorit* (H. Strunz *Mineral. Tabellen* (ed. 3, 1957) 323)], a nickelian variety, $(Mg,Ni)_3Si_2O_5(OH)_4$, of antigorite; **nickel-chlorite** [ad. G. *nickelchlorit* (H. Strunz *Mineral. Tabellen* (ed. 3, 1957) 317)], a basic silicate and aluminate of magnesium, iron, nickel, and aluminium, $(Mg,Fe,Ni,Al)_6(Si,Al)_4O_{10}(OH)_8$, which has been synthesized but whose natural occurrence is uncertain; **nickel-iron**, any alloy of nickel and iron; freq. *attrib.*; **nickel-skutterudite**, an arsenide of nickel and cobalt, $(Ni,Co)As_3$, with nickel predominating, found as white or grey isometric crystals; also, the cobalt-free compound $NiAs_3$; **nickel spinel** [ad. G. *nickelspinell* (H. Strunz *Mineral. Tabellen* (ed. 3, 1957) 137): see SPINEL], an artificially produced oxide of nickel and aluminium, $NiAl_2O_4$.

1961 *Mineral. Mag.* XXXII. 972 Nickel-antigorite... An unnecessary name for nickelian antigorite. **1968** *Proc. Indian Acad. Sci.* B. LXVII. 178 The '*d*' spacings of this mineral can also stand a fair comparison with nickel-antigorite. Therefore, this sample could be either nepouite or nickel antigorite. **1961** *Mineral. Mag.* XXXII. 972 Nickelchlorite... Some of the natural nickel silicates may be members of the chlorite group. **1969** *Clays & Clay Minerals* XVII. 233 Nickel-chlorite has been obtained by the co-precipitation of nickelous hydrous oxide and montmorillonite at an OH/Ni ratio of 2·0. **1875** *Geol. Mag.* Decade II. II. 21 Nickel-iron, containing 15·3 per cent. of nickel, constitutes 3·5 per cent. of the stone, a less quantity than is found in the Pultusk meteorites. **1946** *Thorpe's Dict. Appl. Chem.* (ed. 4) VII. 458/1 Silicon-irons and nickel-irons with alloy additions are noteworthy. *Ibid.*, The nickel-iron alloys ('Permalloys') are used in compressed powder form at telephonic and radio frequencies. **1971** I. G. GASS et al. *Understanding Earth* viii. 116/1 Nickel-iron is practically absent from terrestrial rocks. **1971** *Gloss. Electrotechnical, Power Terms (B.S.I.)* I. iii. 14 *Nickel-iron sleeve*, longitudinally split sleeve of nickel-iron alloy, the use of which enables a winding to have a higher impedance at speech frequencies. **1892** WALLER & MOSES in *School of Mines Q.* XIV. 51 This would be a mineral of the type of skutterudite $CoAs_3$... If further analysis confirms these results, the name *Nickel-Skutterudite* is suggested. **1935** *Amer. Mineralogist* XX. 723 Microscopic study of material from the Bullard's Peak district, New Mexico, shows native silver associated with nickel-skutterudite. **1968** I. KOSTOV *Mineralogy* II. 134 The analogous $NiAs_3$ (nickel-skutterudite) contains Ni 20·71%, As 79·29%. **1961** *Mineral. Mag.* XXXIII. 973 Nickelspinel. **1963** *Jrnl. Amer. Ceramic Soc.* XLVI. 581/2 The other ternary phase assemblage, liquid, NiO, and nickel spinel, exists over wide ranges of temperature (1450° to ~1775° C) and composition (~20 to 100 mole % $NiAl_2O_4$).

nickel, *v.* Add: **b.** To foul (the bore of a gun) with nickel off the bullet-casing; *intr.*, to become fouled. **nickeling,** (*b*) the fouling of the bore of a gun with nickel; metallic fouling.

1918 E. S. FARROW *Dict. Mil. Terms* 407 Nickeling, in gunnery, metallic fouling caused by a portion of the cupro-nickel of the envelope of the bullet being left on the surface of the bore. **1920** G. BURRARD *Notes on Sporting Rifles* 31 When a barrel has once been nickelled it is always liable to nickel again very quickly. *Ibid.* 30 Nickelling at first is impossible to detect with the eye. **1958** J. A. BARLOW *Elements of Rifle Shooting* (ed. 5) i. 6 It may be as well here to touch on the problem presented by metallic fouling, generally known as nickelling... Nickelling is mainly due to small particles of the bullet envelope being cut off by roughness or excrescence in the bore.

nickelian (nikī·liăn), *a. Min.* [f. NICKEL *sb.* + *-IAN 2.] Of a mineral: having a (small) proportion of a constituent element replaced by nickel.

1930 W. T. SCHALLER in *Amer. Mineralogist* XV. 571 Nickel—nickelian. **1951** C. PALACHE et al. *Dana's Syst. Min.* (ed. 7) II. 503 A nickelian variety [of kirovite] (2·5 per cent NiO) occurs in the Mt. Diablo district. **1974** *Encycl. Brit. Macropædia* XII. 41/1 There is simply a gradually thickening crust of iron oxides—a mixture of goethite, hematite, and nickelian magnetite.

nickeline, *sb.* (in Dict. after NICKEL *sb.*). Add: (See quot. 1971.) (Further example.)

1971 *Mineral. Mag.* XXXVIII. 104 Recommendations of the Commission [on New Minerals and Mineral Names, of the International Mineralogical Association] on minerals for which more than one name is in common use: ..Nickeline, not niccolite or nickelite.

nickelodeon (nikəlōᵘ·diən). *U.S.* [f. NICKEL *sb.* 2; app. after MELODEON.] **1.** A theatre or motion-picture show for which the admission fee is a nickel; a place containing automatic machines to provide amusement, which can be used for a nickel. Also *attrib.*

1921 *Ladies' Home Jrnl.* June 79/1 It is this class which first patronized the old nickelodeon, and undoubtedly it imposed its tastes and its traditions on the picture makers. **1927** F. HURST *Song of Life* 292 The nickelodeons and the gewgaw shops of the most terrific city in the world. **1930** *Time & Tide* 27 Sept. 1206 The film was.. handed over by the scientists to the 'nickelodeons' of America. **1938** *Encycl. Brit. Bk. of Year* 422/2 The old nickelodeon programmes. **1939** C. MORLEY *Kitty Foyle* 68 A dance floor and a nickelodeon piano. **1955** G. GREENE *Quiet American* 188 It must have belonged to the same era as the nickelodeon. **1973** *Publishers Weekly* 10 Sept. 45/2 The development of American movies from nickelodeon days to the 1970s.

2. A 'jukebox'; a machine that automatically plays selected gramophone records on the insertion of a coin. Also *attrib.*

1938 *Florida Review* Spring 25/1 The requisites of a place entitling it to the name *jook* are..presence of the nickelodeon, and..of the dance-floor. **1949** *Sat. Even. Post* 15 Jan. 88/3 A nickelodeon at the end of the street emits a tinny piano tinkle. **1957** J. FRAME *Owls do Cry* 76 Putting money in the nickelodeon. **1971** *Daily Colonist* (Victoria, B.C.) 18 Aug. 8/2 The former shepherd boy who used a $4,000 nickelodeon as a springboard to the top.

nicker (ni·kəɹ), *sb.*[6] *slang.* [Origin unknown.] One pound sterling.

1910 *Sessions Papers* 1 June 128, I suppose this has cost you a couple of 'nickers'. **1939** [see *CASER[2]]. **1960** D. LESSING *In Pursuit of English* ii. 66 It's a little matter. A hundred nicker. And it'd double itself in a year. **1966** F. SHAW et al. *Lern Yerself Scouse* 34 *Five nicker*, five pounds; five pound note. **1975** J. SYMONS *Three Pipe Problem* xv. 138 Who said there'd be trouble? Anyway, it's a hundred nicker.

nickie tam, nickie tom, varr. *NICKY TAM.

nicking, *vbl. sb.*[1] Add: **1. d.** A method of pruning in which an incision is made below the base of a bud in order to curb its growth.

1949 C. R. THOMPSON *Pruning of Apples & Pears* ii. 53 The top bud should be prevented from growing vigorously by making a knife incision at its base, a treatment referred to as 'nicking'. **1972** G. E. BROWN *Pruning of Trees* ii. 24 Nicking is carried out below selected buds in order to reduce their vigour.

nickpoint, var. *KNICKPOINT.

nick-tailed (ni·kˌtēᵢld), *a.* Having the tail nicked.

1841 *Southern Lit. Messenger* VII. 219/1 Brenda, mounted on Paul Clifford, nick-tailed sorrel pacer. **1853** J. G. BALDWIN *Flush Times Alabama* 97 The horse, a nick-tailed trotter, Tom had raffled off. **1867** G. W. HARRIS *Sut Lovingood* 19 A nick tailed, bow necked, long, poor, pale sorrel horse.

Nicky (ni·ki), *sb.*[2] [f. *N.I.C. (main entry), infl. by *Nicky*, dim. of *Nicholas*, a male name.] Colloq. name for the National Incomes Commission. Also *attrib.*

1962 *Daily Tel.* 27 July 1/1 The Commission, likely to be known as 'Nicky', will consider pay questions in both private and public sectors. **1962** *Ibid.* 10 Aug. 20/5 (*heading*) 'Nicky' report for TUC. **1963** *Ann. Reg. 1962* iii. 30 Nicky was expected to run the rule over wages claims.

nicky tam (ni·ki tæm). *Sc.* Also **knicky tom, nickie tam, nickie tom,** and with hyphen. [f. K)NICK(ER[2] + -Y[6] + *tam* (see TAUM).] (See quot. 1965.)

1911 *Aberdeen Jrnl. N. & Q.* IV. 17/2 *Knicky-toms*, garters worn over trousers. **1917** E. S. RAE *Private John Macpherson* 54 An' Geordie, ma foreman, a dacenter lad Ne'er wore nickietoms, nor plooed up a fleed. *a* **1931** in E. MACCOLL *Scotland Sings* (1953) 96, I..buskit roond my nappin' knees a pair o' Nicky Tams. **1965** *Sc. Nat. Dict.* VI. 422/3 *Nickie-tam*... One of a pair of straps, or a piece of string in lieu, tied by farmworkers over the trousers-legs immediately below the knee to keep the legs clear of the soil and dust, etc. **1967** *Listener* 12 Oct. 472/3 The Scots word for 'a tying worn below the knee to keep the bottom of the trouser-leg lifted clear in dirty work or to exclude dust'. It is a nicky-tam. **1972** *Daily Mail* 29 July 6/3 We are about to lose the English word 'yorkers' or what the Scots called 'Nicky Tams'.

Nicobarese (nikŏbărī·z), *sb.* and *a.* [f. *Nicobar* (see below) + -ESE.] **A.** *sb.* **a.** The people of the Nicobar Islands in the Bay of Bengal. **b.** The Mon-Khmer language of this people. **B.** *adj.* Of or pertaining to this people. Also **Nicoba·rian** *sb.* and *a.*

1790 G. HAMILTON in *Asiatick Res.* II. 344 The people of Carnicobar have a tradition among them, that several canoes came from Andaman..and that the crews.. killed several of the Nicobarians. **1846** *Jrnl. Asiatic Soc. Bengal* XV. 368 The Nicobarian Pigs appear to have been derived from the Chinese domestic species. **1859** *Sel. Rec. Govt. India Home Dept.* No. 25. 61 Their language bears no affinity to that of the Nicobarians. **1875** F. A. DE ROEPSTORFF *Vocab. Dial. Nicobar & Andaman Is.* (ed. 2) 14 The Nicobarese have all they want, yet they like very much to barter with foreigners. **1884** ——*Dict. Nancowry Dial. of Nicobarese Lang.* p. xiii, Nicobarese is a wholly uninflective tongue. **1889** E. H. MAN (*title*) Dictionary of the central Nicobarese language. **1924** G. WHITEHEAD *In Nicobar Is.* ii. 47 The Nicobarese keep a great number of domestic pigs, which they feed on coco-nut. **1972** W. B. LOCKWOOD *Panorama of Indo-European Lang.* 229 Nicobarese..is spoken by 15,000 islanders. *Ibid.*, The population of the Nicobars has been swollen in the last two decades by settlers from all parts of India, forming a polyglot element..about as numerous as the native Nicobarese.

Nicodemite. (Later example.)

1921 *Outward Bound* Apr. 29/2 This is no time to play the Nicodemite.

Nicol[2]**.** Add: Also **nicol.** (*Nicol* (or *nicol*) *prism* is now more usual than *Nicol's prism*.) (Earlier and additional examples.)

1863 E. ATKINSON tr. *Ganot's Elem. Treat. Physics* VII. viii. 485 The Nicol's prism is one of the most valuable means of polarising light. **1906** *Jrnl. Chem. Soc.* LXXXIX. II. 1150 The nicols were rotated. **1937** *Discovery* Aug. 242/2 A Nicol prism (which is two portions of a rhomb of Iceland spar cemented together with Canada balsam). **1955** W. GADDIS *Recognitions* III. v. 874 If we can fix a microscope up with polarized light and put a particle of the pigment under it, we can see whether it's isotropic or anisotropic, for that we use nicol prisms.

Niconian, var. *NIKONIAN *sb.* and *a.*

nicotinamide (nikoti·nămaid). *Biochem.* [f. *NICOTIN(IC *a.* + AMIDE.] **a.** The amide, $(C_5H_4N)CONH_2$, of nicotinic acid, which can be converted into the acid *in vivo* and so can replace it in the diet.

1895 *Jrnl. Chem. Soc.* LXVIII. I. 391 On heating ethylic nicotinate with alcoholic ammonia..it is converted into nicotinamide, which melts at 121°. **1951** in M. McLuhan *Mech. Bride* (1967) 91/1 (Advt.), It is nicotinamide, an important component in the familiar Vitamin B Complex pill. **1957** A. HUXLEY *Let.* 12 Dec. (1969) 837 The Italians have been using massive doses of Nicotinamide (a variant on nicotinic acid) in psychological cases for some time. **1968** PASSMORE & ROBSON *Compan. Med. Stud.* I. v. 14/2 In Great Britain, the U.S.A. and many other countries, nicotinamide must by law be added to white flour used for bread making.

b. *Comb.* **nicotinamide-adenine dinucleotide,** a compound of adenosine monophosphate and nicotinamide mononucleotide which is a co-enzyme for the oxidation of a wide variety of substrates *in vivo*; NAD; co-enzyme I; diphosphopyridine nucleotide.

1961 *Biochem. Jrnl.* LXXX. 323/1 The rate of formation of nicotinamide–adenine dinucleotide from adenosine triphosphate..and nicotinamide mononucleotide..was measured. **1969** J. R. HOLUM *Introd. Org. & Biol. Chem.* xi. 381 Nicotinamide (niacinamide) is a vitamin used by the body in making the coenzyme nicotinamide adenine dinucleotide.

nicotinate (ni·kotineᵢt). [f. *NICOTIN(IC *a.* + -ATE[4].] The anion, or a salt or ester, of nicotinic acid.

1879 *Jrnl. Chem. Soc.* XXXVI. 809 If..potassium nicotinate is treated with phosphorus pentachloride, energetic action ensues. **1934** *Jrnl. Amer. Chem. Soc.* LVI. 2426/1 Folkers prepared ethyl nipecotate..by the hydrogenation of ethyl nicotinate. **1970** R. W. MCGILVERY *Biochemistry* x. 185 Nicotinate and its enzyme occur in all organisms.

nicotine. Add to def.: in small doses it has a stimulating action, but in larger amounts it blocks the actions of autonomic ganglion cells and skeletal muscle fibres. (Further examples.)

1915 W. S. MAUGHAM *Of Human Bondage* xlvii. 231 She had long, beautiful hands, with fingers deeply stained by nicotine. **1940** H. A. MCGUIGAN *Appl. Pharmacol.* 589 When nicotine is injected intravenously, an enormous rise in blood pressure occurs. **1951** A. GROLLMAN *Pharmacol. & Therapeutics* xv. 285 Nicotine produces extreme nausea and vomiting when taken even in comparatively small quantities. **1966** *McGraw-Hill Encycl. Sci. & Technol.* IX. 100/2 Poisoning has occurred from accidental ingestion of insecticide sprays containing nicotine.

b. *attrib.* and *Comb.*, as *nicotine-brown*, *-free*, *-like*, *-stained* adjs.; *nicotine poisoning* (further example).

1945 DYLAN THOMAS *Let.* 30 July (1966) 278, I can hear..my uncle Bob drinking tea and methylated spirits through eighty years of nicotine-brown fern. **1967** *Daily Tel.* 20 Jan. 17/7 The pleasure of nicotine-free smoking. **1914** Nicotine-like [see *MUSCARINE]. **1948** J. H. BURN *Lect. Notes Pharmacol.* 15 Nicotine is a substance which possesses the nicotine-like actions of acetylcholine. **1951** A. GROLLMAN *Pharmacol. & Therapeutics* xv. 282 In the treatment of nicotine poisoning, artificial respiration should be instituted. **1936** C. DAY LEWIS *Friendly Tree* 12 A plump man with a nicotine-stained moustache. **1967** A. MARSHALL in *Coast to Coast 1965–66* 121 He rubbed his chin with a nicotine-stained finger.

Hence **ni:cotiniza·tion**, subjection to the action of nicotine; **ni·cotinized** *ppl. a.*, containing or drugged with nicotine. (Delete entry for **nicotinic** *a.* and see next.)

1873 Nicotinized [in Dict.]. **1911** *Jrnl. Physiol.* XLIII. 181 The partial contraction suggests an anodic inhibition in the nerve cell like that which occurs in certain nicotinized striated muscles. **1940** *Ibid.* XCIX. 73 Acetylcholine injections have been observed to produce vasoconstriction in the nicotinized as well as in the normal perfused guinea-pig lungs. **1945** *Amer. Jrnl. Physiol.* CXLIV. 192 The nicotinization was maintained by adding nicotine (2 mgm./liter) to the perfusion fluid of the heart. **1966** *Punch* 9 Feb. 215/1 Today nicotinisation is complete with our own men taking the first breath of the day through a tube, lighting up automatically at the appearance of food, and thickening the bedroom air well into the early hours of the morning.

nicotinic (nikoti·nik), *a. Chem.* and *Biochem.* [f. NICOTIN(E + -IC.] **1.** *nicotinic acid* [tr. G. *nicotinsäure* (H. Weidel 1873, in *Ann. d. Chem. und Pharm.* CLXV. 330)]: a white crystalline heterocyclic acid, $(C_5H_4N)COOH$, which is widely distributed (usu. in the form of a complex of its amide) in foods such as yeasts, wheat germ, and meat, is formed when nicotine is oxidized, and can be synthesized in the body from tryptophan; it is a B vitamin, deficiency of which causes pellagra in man; 3-pyridinecarboxylic acid. (Cf. *NIACIN.)

1873 *Jrnl. Chem. Soc.* XXVI. 509 Acetyl chloride has no action on nicotinic acid. **1913** J. WALKER *Org. Chem.* 279 The *β* acid, or nicotinic acid, may also be produced by the oxidation of the alkaloid nicotine. **1942** *Industr. & Engin. Chem. (Analytical Ed.)* XIV. 663/1 The dietary position of cereals and cereal products in relation to their pellegra [*sic*]-preventive attributes has recently been given considerable prominence by the inclusion of nicotinic acid or niacin in the list of required components of enriched flour. **1968** PASSMORE & ROBSON *Compan. Med. Stud.* I. v. 14/2 Like thiamine, nicotinic acid is present in the whole-wheat grain in good quantities, but most is removed by the millers in preparing fine flours or polished rice.

2. Resembling (that of) nicotine; capable of responding to nicotine.

1941 [see *MUSCARINIC *a.*]. **1961** A. GOTH *Med. Pharmacol.* iii. 44 The nicotinic receptors may be divided into the ganglionic receptors, which are hexamethonium sensitive, and the skeletal muscle receptors, which are sensitive to *d*-tubocurarine. **1970** *Nature* 5 Dec. 917/1 The pharmacological actions of acetylcholine..outside the central nervous system could be divided into two categories, nicotinic and muscarinic. **1973** *Jrnl. Pharmacol. & Exper. Therap.* CLXXXV. 649 The data..suggest that both stimulant drugs and competitive antagonists interact on a one-to-one basis with the nicotinic receptor of the guinea-pig lumbrical muscle.

nictate, *v.* Delete 'Only in *nictating membrane*' and add further example.

1960 V. NABOKOV *Invitation to Beheading* iv. 40 Emmie was still squatting,..her long, pale, almost white lashes nictating as she looked across the table-top at the door.

nictitation. Add: Also *transf.*

1962 V. NABOKOV *Pale Fire* 160 A couple..whose blundering Cadillac half entered my driveway before retreating in a flurry of luminous nictitation.

nicy: see *NICEY *a.*

nidation (nəidēi·ʃən). *Physiol.* [f. NID(US + -ATION.] † **a.** (See quots.) *Obs.*

1874 J. H. AVELING in *Obstetr. Jrnl.* II. 210 The act of nidation consists of the periodical development of the mucous membrane lining the interior of the body of the uterus. **1892** *Syd. Soc. Lex., Nidation*,..Aveling's term for the monthly renewal of the epithelium of the mucous lining of the womb during the intermenstrual period.

b. = *IMPLANTATION 6.

1892 *Syd. Soc. Lex., Nidation*,..also, a term for the reception of the fertilised ovum in the uterine mucous membrane. **1921** B. M. ANSPACH *Gynecol.* iv. 72 These [changes] have for their purpose suitable nidation and nourishment of the ovum. **1966** *New Statesman* 17 June 880/1 Surely an abortifacient is something which interferes with an established pregnancy and not something which prevents the nidation of a fertilised ovum. **1970** *Sci. Jrnl.* June 63/2 It is apparently by this thickened trophoblastic plate that the penetration of the maternal tissues—called nidation or implantation—is accomplished.

niddy-noddy (ni·diˌnǫ·di), *sb. Hist.* [Prob. f. NIDDY-NODDY *adv.* and *v.*] A frame on which to skein and measure wool yarn.

1890 G. S. HALL in *Proc. Amer. Antiquarian Soc.* VII. 111 It was taken from the spindle sometimes on a niddy-noddy held in the hand, at two rounds per yard, but more commonly on a reel, in rounds of two yards each. **1927** M. N. RAWSON *Candle Days* ii. 28 The graceful 'swifts', the 'niddy noddy', or hand reels, was also of home construction in wood. **1968** *Beaver* Winter 43/1 A cross between the hand looms..has been found practical, as has been..the English niddy-noddy and butterfly yarn winders. **1969** E. H. PINTO *Treen* 318 The earlier device, which was in general use..was the cross reel, in English speaking countries almost universally known as a niddy-noddy. *Ibid.*, The niddy-noddy, which was held in one hand by the central stem, was wound with a waving motion, to the rhythm of a song, the opening line of which ran, 'Niddy-noddy, niddy-noddy, two heads and one body.'

Niderviller (nidęrvilę̄r). The name of a town in Lorraine, east France, used, freq. *attrib.*, to designate the porcelain and faience made there from 1754.

1857 H. G. BOHN *Guide Knowl. Pottery, Porcelain* 480 *Niderviller.* Hard paste. Manufacture of François Lanfray,..about 1790. Stencilled in blue. **1863** W. CHAFFERS *Marks Pott. & Porc.* 208 *Niderviller*, the letter N., for Niderviller, occurs on a set of plates, on one of which is the double C, and on another the letter N. **1903** M. L. SOLON *Hist. Old French Faïence* 112 The Niderviller faïence is amply represented in the Nancy Museum. **1948** A. LANE *French Faïence* ix. 39 The Niderviller figures belong to a class peculiar to the Lorraine region. **1960** R. G. HAGGAR *Concise Encycl. Cont. Pott. & Porc.* 329 The flower painting on Niderviller faience was of high quality and exploited the range of tints which 'purple of Cassius' crimson could be made to yield. **1963** *Times* 16 Feb. 4/4 A Niderviller part dinner-service of 37 pieces, painted with landscapes, the borders with butterflies, ladybirds and other insects, made £170. **1971** H. WYNTER *Introd. European Porc.* iii. 105 Niderviller characteristics..Hard-paste... Shapes and decoration..similar to rococo Strasbourg.

nidicolous (nidi·kŏləs), *a. Ornith.* [f. mod.L. group name *Nidicolæ* (H. F. Gadow in A. Newton *Dict. Birds* (1894) 629) (f. L. *nīdus* nest + *col-ere* to inhabit) + -OUS.] Of a bird: bearing young which are helpless at birth and remain in the nest until they are sufficiently developed to live without parental care. So **ni·dicole** *sb.*, a bird of this type.

1902 H. F. GADOW in *Encycl. Brit.* XXVI. 257/1 Order Sphenisciformes.—Nidicolous, marine. Flightless, wings transformed into rowing paddles. **1927** A. L. THOMSON *Birds* ix. 155 Birds may..be divided into two main types, those having nidifugous or 'nest-quitting' young, and those having nidicolous or 'nest-dwelling' young. **1945** S. SMITH *How to study Birds* iv. 74 Birds whose young are born naked, helpless and blind (the so-called nidicolous birds). **1962** J. C. WELTY *Life of Birds* xvii. 319/1 The altricial bird, is born naked, or nearly so, is usually blind, and is too weak to support itself on its legs... Such birds remain confined to the nest for some days or weeks. They are therefore called nidicoles or nest-dwellers. **1974** I. C. J. GALBRAITH tr. *Dorst's Life of Birds* I. xiii. 247 The parents are entirely responsible for feeding nidicolous young.

nidifugous (nidi·fiŭgəs), *a. Ornith.* [f. mod. L. group name *Nidifugæ* (H. F. Gadow in A. Newton *Dict. Birds* (1894) 629) (f. L. *nīdus* nest + *fug-ere* to flee) + -OUS.] Of a bird: bearing young which are well developed at birth and leave the nest almost immediately. So **ni·difuge** *sb.*, a bird of this type.

1902 H. F. GADOW in *Encycl. Brit.* XXVI. 257/1 Order Colymbiformes.—Plantigrade, nidifugous, aquatic. **1927** [see *NIDICOLOUS *a.*]. **1945** S. SMITH *How to study Birds* iv. 74 Birds whose young are born strong, with plenty of down, and able to run within a few hours of the hatch (the nidifugous birds). **1962** J. C. WELTY *Life of Birds* xvii. 318/2 Nidifuges are often ground-nesting species that, as adults, are good runners or good swimmers and feed either on the ground or in the water. These precocial birds include such forms as the ostrich and its relatives, loons, grebes, ducks, [etc.]. *Ibid.* 319/2 (*caption*) The one-day-old, precocial, or nidifugous chick of the Ruffed Grouse. **1974** I. C. J. GALBRAITH tr. *Dorst's Life of Birds* I. xiii. 245 Nidifugous birds also have visual means of communication.

nid-nod, *a. poet.* [f. NID-NOD *v.*] That nid-nods.

1921 W. DE LA MARE *Veil* 88 Of whispering boughs, and feathery, nid-nod grass. **1937** —— *This Year, Next Year*, Poppy, cornflower, nid-nod wheat, The sheaves are ripe for rick. **1941** —— *Bells & Grass* 50 The nid-nod daffodil.

nidor. (Later example.)

1923 *Blackw. Mag.* Feb. 159/2 A nidor was to him an agony impossible to endure.

nielsbohrium (nīlzbōə·riŏm). *Chem.* [f. *Niels Bohr* (see *BOHR) + -IUM, as ad. Russ. *nil'sborii*, a name used by G. N. Flerov and co-workers (e.g. in Flerov & Zvara *Report D7-6013* (Joint Inst. Nuclear Res., Dubna, U.S.S.R., 1971) 56), though no explicit coinage of the word has been traced in the literature available.] (A name proposed for) an artificially produced transuranic element, of atomic number 105. (The name *HAHNIUM has also been proposed for it.)

1973 *Nuclear Sci. Abstr.* XXVIII. 1209/2 Proposed names for Nos. 103–105 are Lawrencium (Lr), Kurchatovium (Ku), and Nielsbohrium (Bo). **1975** *Nature* 27 Mar. 288/2 As a sign of the rival claims elements 104 and 105 have been christened Rutherfordium and Hahnium in the USA and Kurchatovium and Nielsbohrium in the USSR.

Niemann–Pick disease (nīmănˌpi·k). *Path.* Also **Niemann–Pick's disease.** [f. the names of Albert *Niemann* (1880–1921) and Ludwig *Pick* (1868–?1944), German physicians, who described the disease in 1914 and 1926 respectively.] A rare, inherited metabolic disorder, usu. fatal in childhood, which is characterized by the accumulation within the body cells of a lipid (sphingomyelin).

1928 *Jrnl. Amer. Med. Assoc.* 7 Apr. 1166/1 (*heading*) Niemann–Pick disease. *Ibid.* 30 June 2077/2 The stored material in Niemann–Pick's disease is phosphatide. **1942** M. M. WINTROBE *Clin. Hematol.* xii. 521 The cells of Niemann–Pick's disease are round, oval, or polyhedral and are filled with small round hyaline droplets in clusters which give the appearance of foam or a honeycomb. **1966** WRIGHT & SYMMERS *Systemic Path.* I. v. 246/1 Niemann–Pick disease is considerably rarer than Gaucher's disease. **1973** *Sci. Amer.* Aug. 90/3 Another disorder involving enlargement of the liver and the spleen and mental retardation, Niemann–Pick disease, was shown..to involve the accumulation of the phospholipid sphingomyelin.

Niersteiner (nīə·ɹʃtəinəɹ). [f. *Nierstein* a town in west central Germany near Mainz + *-er*, G. adj. suffix.] A much esteemed white Rhine wine produced at Nierstein.

[**1825** SCOTT *Talisman* in *Tales of Crusaders* IV. xi. 200 He invited them to a goblet of nierenstein.] **1833** C. REDDING *Hist. Mod. Wines* vii. 207 The wines of Bischeim ..are very pleasant wines; those of the most strength are ..Rüdesheimer, and Niersteiner. **1852** T. MCMULLEN *Handbk. Wines* xi. 112 Some are of opinion that the Marcobrunner, Rüdesheimer, and Niersteiner, possess more fulness and body. **1907** *Yesterday's Shopping* (1969) 99/3 Still Hock..Niersteiner Pettenthal—Per doz. bots. 30/0. **1939** [see *HEURIGE 2]. **1961** *Guardian* 3 Mar. 12/3 She was eating alone, with a bottle of Niersteiner. **1967** A. LICHINE *Encycl. Wines & Spirits* 447/2 Of some 550 parcels, about two dozen produce the soft, elegant, full-bodied, peak wines known around the world as Niersteiners. Look for Riesling on the label: the best Niersteiners are from the Riesling grape.

Nietzschean (nī·tʃĭăn), *sb.* and *a.* Also **Nietzschian.** [f. the name of the German philosopher, Friedrich *Nietzsche* (1844–1900) + -AN.] **A.** *sb.* A follower, admirer, or imitator of Nietzsche; one who holds or supports Nietzsche's principles or views, esp. his theories of the superman, and the division of humanity into masters and slaves. **B.** *adj.* Of, pertaining to, or characteristic of Nietzsche or his views.

1904 *To-Day* XLIV. 49/2 This moustache..was Nietzschean at the root, to end in the twirl of the sub-officer. **1908** G. B. SHAW *Sanity of Art* 6 The Nietzscheans were only too glad to see Tolstoy catching it. **1908** M. A. MÜGGE *Friedrich Nietzsche* III. ii. 331 There is no doubt that Goethe was a Nietzschean aristocrat. **1910** *Daily Chron.* 9 Feb. 6/3 The volumes of this edition are beginning to make me believe that Nietzsche's greatest enemies are the Nietzscheans. **1915** *London Q. Rev.* Jan. 92 One need only take up any of Nietzsche's books at random to see how alien this is to the 'Nietzschian' spirit. **1921** *Glasgow Herald* 24 Nov. 6 It is only fitting that the standpoint of that eminent Nietzschean, Mr A. M. Ludovici, should have an individuality of its own. **1932** WYNDHAM LEWIS *Emperor of West* i. 22 The ironic pen of Machiavelli drew.. the portrait of the ideal Prince:..the original Nietzschean Non-Moral Overman. **1959** [see *BOUNDERISH *a.*]. **1968** *Times Lit. Suppl.* 25 Apr. 436/3 In his earlier years he [*sc.* Orage] was a Theosophist, a Nietzschean, and a Fabian Socialist. **1973** *Listener* 9 Aug. 170/1 The Nietzschean idea that since God is dead, everything is permitted.

Hence **Nie·tzscheanism; Nie·tzscheanite; Nie·tzscheism; Nie·tzscheite.**

1908 H. L. MENCKEN *Philos. Nietzsche* III. ii. 278 We have a hero who calls himself a dionysian and offers Nietzscheism as a substitute for Christianity. **1908** M. A. MÜGGE *Friedrich Nietzsche* I. ii. 82 It was the Dawn of Nietzscheanism. *Ibid.* III. ii. 352 Nietzscheanites hope their master's influence will create in England a sense for the true higher culture. **1909** CHESTERTON *Orthodoxy* iii. 73 If Nietzsche had not ended in imbecility, Nietzscheism would end in imbecility. **1910** —— *G. B. Shaw* 180 You must make sure of the presence of some Nietzscheite professor, who will explain to him that such a course might possibly serve to eliminate the unfit. **1914** *Times* 31 Oct. 7/1 Mistaken Nietzscheanism always tempts to the development of the devil in man. **1916** GALSWORTHY in *Scribner's Mag.* Jan. 21/2 The Neo-German conception of the State..may be inverted Nietzscheism. **1968** *Times Lit. Suppl.* 25 Apr. 437/1 This untidy mixture of socialism, Nietzscheanism, and mysticism is a fair expression of Orage's untidy thought.

Nife (nəif). Also **nife.** [f. *Ni* + *Fe*, chem. symbols for *ni*ckel and iron (L. *fe*rrum) respectively.] Nickel-iron; *spec.* [a. G. *Nife* (E. Suess *Das Antlitz der Erde* (1909) III. II. xxiv. 626)], the earth's core or the material composing it.

1909 H. B. C. & W. J. SOLLAS tr. *Suess's Face of Earth* IV. xv. 544 We assume the existence of three zones..as determining the structure of the earth, namely, the barysphere or the Nife (Ni-fe), Sima (Si-Mg), and Sal (Si-Al). *Ibid.* 547 A nucleus of Nife and heavy metals extends from the centre outwards for three quarters of the radius. *Ibid.* xvii. 606 We may suppose that..these gases and with them our volcanic eruptions do not proceed from the depth of the Nife but from Sima. **1924** J. G. A. SKERL tr. *Wegener's Orig. Continents & Oceans* x. 146 The core of the earth, probably composed chiefly of nickel and iron, has been termed the 'nife' by E. Suess. **1932** J. A. STEERS *Unstable Earth* iv. 159 Following Suess, Wegener assumed that the outer 'skin' of the earth was sial..; under this is the sima, and the interior core of the globe is the nife. **1927** *Wireless World* 19 Jan. 87/1 Batteries, Limited,.. have recently drawn attention to the need of floating a layer of paraffin on the electrolyte of their Nife cells. [**1966** *McGraw-Hill Encycl. Sci. & Technol.* XIII. 158/1 In the original types of Ni-Cd (Jungner) cells the materials and structural features are quite similar to those described for the Ni-Fe cell.]

niff (nif), *sb.*[1] *colloq.* and *dial.* Also **nif.** [Origin unknown.] Resentment, offence. Freq. in phr. *to take a niff*, to take offence.

1777 *Horae Subsecivae* 303 Let her alone, her've o'ny a-got a bit of a niff her'll zoon come o' that again. **1865** R. HUNT *Pop. Romances W. of Eng.* 2nd Ser. 78 The woman took a nif, and for a long time never spoke to our John. **1903** in *Eng. Dial. Dict.* IV. 267/2 You're taking the niff. **1914** *Dialect Notes* IV. 77 *Niff*, a quarrel, grudge, or spite. **1946** *Amer. Speech* XXI. 308 To 'take a niff' at a person was to conceive a violent dislike for him.

niff (nif), *sb.*[2] *slang.* [Perh. f. S)NIFF *sb.*] A disagreeable smell; a whiff.

1903 in *Eng. Dial. Dict.* **1921** *Chambers's Jrnl.* Mar. 202/1 They found themselves within an outer circle of bee hive huts, fires that had died to red glimmers, and—a 'niff', if I may thus gently put it. **1960** D. FEARON *Murder-on-Thames* ii. 27 It wouldn't be nice for Rachel if some niff of ancient scandal caught up with her poor papa. **1975** *Draconian* Christmas 16922/1 The customary Oxford autumn niff, usually readily recognisable, redolent as it is of bonfires and long grass.

niff (nif), *v.*[1] *colloq.* and *dial.* [Origin unknown.] To quarrel, to be offended. So **niffed** (nift) *ppl. a.*

1875 W. D. PARISH *Dict. Sussex Dial.* 79 *Niff*, to quarrel; to be offended. **1880** COURTNEY & COUCH *Gloss. Words in Use in Cornwall* 40/1 She's gone away niffed. **1893** D. JORDAN *Forest Tithes* 99 Ye wunt feel niffed like when we meets ye, if we gives ye plenty o' elber-room, mister. **1906** E. PHILLPOTTS *Portreeve* III. xii. 310 Then—just because you'm niffed about something—you lift your hand to her to let out your bile. **1924** LAWRENCE & SKINNER *Boy in Bush* viii. 119 At last Monica..was niffed. She thought him a muff. **1927** W. E. COLLINSON *Contemp. Eng.* 116 Anger is expressed by such phrases as these in ascending order of intensity: he was niffed or peeved, he got shirty or hairy, he got his rag out, [etc.].

niff (nif), *v.*[2] *slang.* Also **nif.** [See *NIFF *sb.*[2]] *intr.* To have a disagreeable smell.

1927 [see *HUM *v.*[3]]. **1934** WODEHOUSE *Thank you, Jeeves* iii. 34 I've started breeding mice and puppies. And, of course, they nif a bit. **1938** —— *Code of Woosters* viii. 177 Scotties are smellie... You will recall how my Aunt Agatha's McIntosh niffed to heaven while enjoying my hospitality. **1950** A. BARON *There's no Home* v. 57 This ol' street may niff a bit, but it don't smell as bad as the water out of polluted wells. **1967** K. GILES *Death in Diamonds* iv. 66 It smelled... 'Niffs, don't it?' said one of the youths. **1974** WODEHOUSE *Aunts aren't Gentlemen* xvii. 145 'Nasty slinking-looking bleeder.'.. 'He don't half niff.'

niffy (ni·fi), *a. slang.* [f. *NIFF *sb.*[2] + -Y[1].] Having a disagreeable or strong smell. Also as *sb.* Hence **ni·ffiness.**

1903 *Eng. Dial. Dict.* IV. 267/2 *Niffy*, adj. odorous. **1925** FRASER & GIBBONS *Soldier & Sailor Words* 209 *Niffy, a*, a strong nasty smell. **1934** 'BARON CORVO' *Desire & Pursuit of Whole* ix. 81 The niffy silted-up little Rio della Croxe. **1934** WODEHOUSE *Right Ho, Jeeves* x. 113 The garden was full of the aroma of those niffy white flowers. **1946** —— *Money in Bank* iv. 31 Well anyway, Stinker, putting aside for the moment the question of your niffiness, wasn't it notorious that you couldn't tell the truth without straining a ligament?

nifontovite (nifǫ·ntǒvəit). *Min.* [ad. Russ. *nifontovit* (Malinko & Lisitsyn 1961, in *Doklady̆ Akad. Nauk SSSR* CXXXIX. 188), f. the name of P. V. *Nifontov*, 20th-cent. Russian geologist: see -ITE[1].] A hydrated borate of calcium, $CaB_2O_4{\cdot}2{\cdot}3H_2O$, found as colourless monoclinic crystals.

1961 *Mineral. Mag.* XXXII. 990 Nifontovite... Small anhedral grains in skarn deposits in the Urals. **1971** *Soviet Physics—Crystallogr.* XVI. 186/1 The description and investigation of a group of endogenic calcium metaborates: calciborite, korzhinskite, uralborite, nifontovite, frolovite, and pentahydroborite.

niftily (ni·ftili), *adv.* [f. NIFTY *a.* + -LY[2].] In a nifty manner.

1919 *Amer. Mag.* LXXXVII. 93/1 That was a clever girl you had against you tonight. I don't believe in pacifism much, myself, but she used it very niftily for her argument. **1960** P. MORTIMER *Saturday Lunch with Brownings* 202 She lay down on her stomach, lifting up the chest with one hand while niftily tucking the carpet down under its foot with the other. **1971** *New Yorker* 13 Nov. 126/3 (Advt.), Our famous Whale Tie..in a niftily contemporary 4½ inch width. **1974** D. SMITH *Look Back with Love* xi. 106, I..particularly liked one story..in which the hero fought his way through an army by niftily manipulating a chair.

niftiness (ni·ftinės). *colloq.* [f. NIFTY *a.* + -NESS.] The quality of being nifty; smartness, cleverness.

1923 M. WATTS *Luther Nichols* 27 His fixed purpose was to keep it so or to increase its niftiness. **1974** *Punch* 13 Feb. 268 Some have even been moved to congratulate him on the niftiness of his own footwork—particularly when it comes to the waltz.

nifty, *a.* Add: (Later examples.) Also, clever, nimble, adroit.

1907 C. E. MULFORD *Bar-20* ix. 107 I've heard of Smith of Topeka, an' he's mighty nifty with his hands. **1916** H. L. WILSON *Somewhere in Red Gap* v. 213 Hetty.. looking so fresh and nifty and feminine. **1921** WODEHOUSE *Indiscretions of Archie* xiii. 141 Don't you think it's a nifty scheme? **1923** —— *Inimitable Jeeves* iii. 32 Roville ..is a fairly nifty spot where a chappie without encumbrances in the shape of aunts might spend a somewhat genial week or so. **1930** CHESTERTON *Four Faultless Felons* iii. 196 He's awfully nifty with his fingers. **1933** G. ADE *Let.* 6 Apr. (1973) 166 You..tell a nifty little story at the finish. **1938** D. SMITH *Dear Octopus* II. i. 52 I'm very nifty on a step-ladder. **1949** N. MARSH *Swing, Brother, Swing* iv. 57 Now that's quite a nifty little idea. **1958** J. CANNAN *And be a Villain* i. 19, I..got the niftiest white overalls. **1968** *Globe & Mail* (Toronto) 3 Feb. 35/4 Bruce Kelly scored a tying goal..on a nifty pass from John DeDiana. **1973** R. HAYES *Hungarian Game* xxxi. 184 'Try that coffee now. Tell me if you like it.'.. It was good. 'It's nifty,' I said. **1975** *Observer* 19 Jan. 22/4 Duncan was nifty on occasions, indeed scored an immaculate goal, but was at other times rather daintily ineffective.

nifty (ni·fti), *sb. slang.* [f. the adj.] A joke, a witty remark or story.

1925 WODEHOUSE *Carry on, Jeeves* vi. 145 Every time I started to pull a nifty, Sir Roderick swung round on me with such a piercing stare that it stopped me in my tracks. **1929** D. MACKAIL *How Amusing!* 237 He..released no less than six of the wisecracks or nifties which he had been carefully hoarding for his next story. **1957** O. NASH *You can't get there from Here* 65 Had he sought his answers just below where Broadway bisects the lower Fifties, He would have come up with some nifties.

nig, Nig, *sb.*[3] Add: (Earlier and later examples.) Now only in derogatory use.

1828 T. D. RICE *Jim Crow* x, De Nigs in ole Virginny Be so black dey shine. **1840** *Picayune* (New Orleans) 20 Sept. 2/2 Two little nigs..had a most scientific set-to at the corner. **1905** E. W. PRINGLE *Woman Rice Planter* 160 Her manner is what the 'nigs' call 'stiff'. **1916** J. B. COOPER *Coo-oo-ee* xvi. 245 He never wipes the glass slobbered over by dozens of dirty nigs! Gosh, it's a good place to get out of! **1939** J. CARY *Mister Johnson* 162 You don't know wot it costs us, you nigs, to tidy up things for you. **1961** C. WILLOCK *Death in Covert* i. 11 Like many of these nigs, he could shoot. Dammit, back home in steaming wogland he probably did nothing else. **1974** R. GADNEY *Something worth fighting For* xii. 85 Judd read National Front puts Britain First. Someone had scribbled Nigs Out.

Niger[2] (nəi·dʒəɪ). Also written **niger. 1.** The name of a West African river, used *absol.* or *attrib.* to designate a type of morocco produced in regions near the river and used for bookbinding.

1898 C. EYRE in *Bookbinding by Women* 4 From Chiswick there are a number of examples of the very beautiful Niger-morocco bindings. **1901** D. COCKERELL *Bookbinding* xix. 278 The leather that I have found most useful is the Niger goatskin, brought from Africa by the Royal Niger Company. *Ibid.* 279 It is to be hoped that before long some of the manufacturers interested will produce skins as good in quality and colour as the best Niger morocco. **1930** *Times Lit. Suppl.* 18 Dec. 1081/3 (Advt.), Bound in whole natural niger goat-skin. **1952** J. CARTER *ABC for Book Collectors* 124 True niger, which comes from West Africa, is a soft skin with an unemphatic, variable grain. It is locally tanned and dyed... The slight variations of grain and colour which give niger its character are seldom achieved in the imitations of it. **1963** B. C. MIDDLETON *Hist. Eng. Craft Bookbinding Technique* xi. 122 Niger goatskin..was popularized by Douglas Cockerell more than sixty years ago.

2. Niger seed, the seeds of *Guizotia abyssinica*, of the family Compositæ, native to West Africa and cultivated elsewhere for the oil obtained from its seeds; also, the plant itself (cf. RAMTIL); **niger (seed) oil,** the oil produced from niger seeds.

1884 *Encycl. Brit.* XVII. 746/1 Niger oil is the produce of the seeds (properly achenes) of *Guizotia oleifera*, a plant native of the east coast of Africa, but cultivated throughout India and to some extent in Germany. The fruits, which are small, tooth-like in form, and shining black in colour, contain from 40 to 45 per cent. of oil... In Western countries niger oil is principally employed in soap-making and as a lubricant. **1889** G. S. BOULGER *Uses of Plants* 138 *Guizotia abyssinica*, Cass., Niger or Ramtil seeds, came into the English market about 1851. It is a native of Tropical Africa, but is cultivated in India and Germany. It is used in Europe for soap and lubricating oil. **1917** *Chambers's Jrnl.* May 293/2 Niger-seed oil is used as a substitute for linseed-oil when the latter is scarce. **1944** *Living off Land* ii. 40 Niger-seed..looks like a sunflower. **1974** F. N. HOWES *Dict. Useful & Everyday Plants* 175 Niger seed. *Guizotia abyssinica*, an oil seed and much favoured for cage birds. **1974** G. USHER *Dict. Plants used by Man* 288/2 The plant [sc. *Guizotia abyssinica*] is cultivated for the seeds which yield an oil (Niger Seed Oil, Ramtilla Oil, Werinnua Oil). The plant is cultivated mainly in India, but also in E. Africa, W. Indies and Germany... It is used for soap-making and cooking fats.

Niger–Congo (nəi·dʒəɪ,kǫ·ŋgo). [f. the names of the rivers *Niger* and *Congo*.] A group of languages which includes those spoken by most of the indigenous peoples of western, central, and southern Africa.

1955 J. H. GREENBERG *Studies in African Linguistic Classification* 8 To the entire family consisting of the West Sudanic nucleus inclusive of Bantu, plus this eastward extension, I have preferred to adopt a new name of a non-committal geographic nature, Niger–Congo, from the two great rivers in whose basins these languages predominate. **1961** F. G. CASSIDY *Jamaica Talk* iii. 31 The Niger–Congo languages are characterised by differences of meaning which depend upon pitch—or 'tone'—and stress. **1970** R. FINNEGAN *Oral Lit. in Africa* iii. 55 In the opinion of some recent scholars, even this large Bantu group is only one subdivision within a much larger family, the 'Niger–Congo' group, which also includes most of the languages of West Africa. **1972** *Language* XLVIII. 273 Accounting for the various kinds of syntactic evidence in the Bantu languages, such as the consistent use of prefixes which often correspond to suffixes of the Niger–Congo languages, will require considerable historical study.

Nigerian (nəidʒīə·riăn), *sb.* and *a.* [f. *Nigeria* (see below): see -AN.] **A.** *sb.* A native or inhabitant of Nigeria, a republic in West Africa occupying the basin of the lower Niger. **B.** *adj.* Of or pertaining to Nigeria or its inhabitants.

1860 W. COLE *Jrnl.* 6 May in *Life in Niger* (1862) 170 This is the general mode in which the Nigerians make known their losses. **1905** F. L. SHAW *Tropical Dependency* xlv. 425 The names, alas, of more than one of the first small Nigerian group are engraved now upon tombstones on that border of the Empire which they helped to make. *Ibid.* li. 481 There are now in all..about 400 white men in the Northern Nigerian service. **1908** *Daily Chron.* 31 Jan. 3/3 When she came back from her first journey still hale and happy, she was accepted as a full-fledged Nigerian. **1923** *Blackw. Mag.* Apr. 514/2 His early days have gone down in Nigerian history. **1954** R. ST. B. BAKER *Sahara Challenge* vii. 73 This is the secret of the successful growing of groundnuts, which has been known to the Nigerians for many generations. *Ibid.*, We slept just outside a Nigerian resthouse. **1973** *Listener* 14 June 782/1 There is a confidence and exuberance about Nigerians which lifts the spirits. **1973** *Guardian* 19 June 18/4 The Niger herdsmen are paid in Nigerian pounds. They buy Nigerian goods, recross the border and sell the goods.

Nigerianization (nəidʒīə:riănəizēi·ʃən). [f. *NIGERIAN *sb.* and *a.* + -IZATION.] The process of making Nigerian, *spec.* the transfer of posts in government and industry from foreigners to native Nigerians.

1954 *Rep. Lagos Conf.* 80 in *Parl. Papers 1953–4* (Cmd. 9059) XI. 122 We are determined to press forward with the Nigerianization of the Civil Service. **1955** *Times* 23 Aug. 7/4 The 'Nigerianization' of the public service had not kept pace with the speed of the advance of self-government. **1959** *Times* 4 Dec. 9/3 He..pursued a vigorous policy of Nigerianization, particularly in the Post and Telegraphs Department. **1960** *Economist* 8 Oct. 132/1 Nigerianisation will go on, as it ought to do. **1961** *Aeroplane* CI. 450/2 A programme of development has recently been agreed by the board of Nigeria Airways... Steps will be taken leading eventually to the complete 'Nigerianization' of all activities. **1973** *Times* 1 Oct. (Nigeria Suppl.) p. viii/3 Within Nigeria British business continues to play a highly significant role, despite the effects of Nigerianization.

Nigerianize (nəidʒīə·riănəiz), *v.* [f. *NIGERIAN *sb.* and *a.* + -IZE.] To make Nigerian in character. Hence **Nige·rianized** *ppl. a.*

1960 *Guardian* 4 Nov. 10/3 The politicians..are themselves fully 'Nigerianised'. **1966** J. P. MACKINTOSH *Nigerian Govt. & Politics* iv. 175 The Eastern and Western Government were composed of men determined to Nigerianize their Public Services with the utmost speed. **1969** I. F. NICOLSON *Administration of Nigeria* ix. 251 There are several justifications for the somewhat arbitrary choice of the year 1948 as the starting point of the process of transforming alien 'administocracy' into the apparatus of modern, federal, parliamentary government, complete with Nigerian Ministers and 'Nigerianized' career public services. **1971** J. S. COLEMAN *Nigeria: Background to Nationalism* iv. 103 The first major effort to Nigerianize the clergy..was made by the Church Missionary Society.

nigerite (nəi·dʒĕrəit). *Min.* [f. *Niger-ia*, the name of the country in which it was discovered + -ITE[1].] A basic oxide of zinc, iron, magnesium, tin, and aluminium, $(Zn,Fe^{II},Mg)(Sn,Zn)_2(Al,Fe^{III})_{12}O_{22}(OH)_2$, found as brown or red hexagonal platelets.

1946 JACOBSON & WEBB in *Bull. Geol. Surv. Nigeria* No. 17. 11 The dykes to the south-east of Oke Oloke are of special interest on account of the discovery of a new tin-zinc mineral, nigerite, which occurs in quartz–andalusite–sillimanite veins associated with the albitized pegmatites. **1947** *Times* 2 Dec. 6/3 Specimens of nigerite, a new tin mineral, recently analysed and described by the Museum's Department of Mineralogy, have been given. **1974** *Mineral. Mag.* XXXIX. 837 (*heading*) Nigerite in the tin-tantalum pegmatites of Amapá, Brazil.

nigga (ni·gă). Also **niggah.** Repr. a Southern U.S. pronunciation of NIGGER *sb.* Cf. *NIGGUH, NIGGUR.

Now virtually restricted to publications in which Black English vernacular is set down.

1925 L. R. HARRIS in A. Dundes *Mother Wit* (1973) 563/2 Howdy niggahs,..how's you all dis mawnin'. **1937** C. HIMES in *Black on Black* (1973) 139 Niggah, ef'n yo is talkin' tuh me, Ah ain' liss'nin'. **1969** in A. Dundes *Mother Wit* (1973) 655/1 They end up losing all of their money to that big nigga who is supposed to be the epitome of 'nigga-ness'. **1973** *Black World* Apr. 58 My wandering niggah done slipped up on me. **1974** *Ibid.* Dec. 23 In the grammaticality of the mid nighttime sky when them sweet blue nigga dialects of the flesh rise.

nigger, *sb.* Add: **1.** Except in Black English vernacular, where it remains common, now virtually restricted to contexts of deliberate and contemptuous ethnic abuse. (Further examples.)

1931 D. L. SAYERS *Five Red Herrings* i. 11 Waters.., like all Englishmen, was ready enough to admire and praise all foreigners except dagoes and niggers. **1934** G. B. SHAW *On Rocks* II. 70 Pandranath: you are only a silly nigger pretending to be an English gentleman. *Ibid.*

71, I am called nigger by this dirty faced barbarian whose forefathers were naked savages worshipping acorns and mistletoe..whilst my people were spreading the highest enlightenment yet reached by the human race from the temples of Brahma... You call me nigger, sneering at my colour because you have none. The jackdaw has lost his tail and would persuade the world that his defect is a quality. **1936** M. Mitchell *Gone with Wind* 401 'You're a fool nigger, and the worst day's work Pa ever did was to buy you,' said Scarlett slowly... There, she thought, I've said 'nigger' and Mother wouldn't like that at all. **1937** C. Himes in *Black on Black* 132 Uncle Tomism, acceptance, toadying—all there in its most rugged form. One way to be a nigger. Other Negroes did it other ways—he did it the hard way. The same result—*a nigger.* **1948** [see *coon *sb.* 2 c]. **1948** G. Greene *Heart of Matter* I. i. 3, I hate the place. I hate the people. I hate the bloody niggers. Mustn't call 'em that you know. *Ibid.* II. i. 179 A clerk knocked and said, 'There's a nigger for you, Wilson, with a note.' **1949** B. A. Botkin *Treas. S. Folklore* p. xxiii, In turning his laughter on himself as well as the whites, the Negro has taken over the objectionable word 'nigger' (though not 'darky') and made it a term of praise or blame. **1964** L. Hughes in J. H. Clarke *Harlem* iv. 251 A klansman said, 'Nigger, Look me in the face—And tell me you believe in The great white race.' **1966** *Stage & Television Today* 6 Oct., When 'Ten Little Niggers' opened for a week's run at Birmingham Theatre on Monday members of the co-ordinating committee against racial discrimination (CARD) staged a protest demonstration outside. **1968** C. Brown in A. Dundes *Mother Wit* (1973) 232/1 Perhaps the most soulful word in the world is 'nigger'. **1969** D. L. Lee in A. Chapman *New Black Voices* (1972) II. 286 Change, stop being an instant yes machine. Change. Niggers don't change they just grow. That's a change; Bigger and better niggers. **1971** *Black World* Apr. 56 Who the hell you think, nigger? **1972** D. Onyeama *Nigger at Eton* iii. 83, I remember that in conversation, some boys occasionally used 'nigger' in reference to black people. I never dreamt that it was a racial name and generally used with contempt; I just reckoned it was a harmless slang word for a black man. **1973** *Black World* Aug. 61/1 Even credit-card niggers didn' really trust banks. **1973** *Times Lit. Suppl.* 14 Dec. 1536/1 You do not reduce to only a ticket-collector, only an asthmatic, only a voter, only a politician, only a pools-winner, only a nigger.

b. (Further Austral. examples.)

1941 I. L. Idriess *Great Boomerang* xxii. 169 The cranky nigger who was on the job broke the only shovel. **1946** K. Tennant *Lost Haven* (1968) 6 No grandson of mine,..is going to be brought up by them thieving, godless, nigger Detwinters. *Ibid.* xviii. 312 When that old nigger went past she turned up her nose.

c. *to work like a nigger*, to work exceptionally hard. orig. *U.S.*

1836 C. Gilman *Recoll. Southern Matron* in *Southern Rose* 23 July 186/1, I have toiled night and day, I've worked like a nigger, and more than any nigger. **1861** Geo. Eliot *Let.* 13 Apr. (1954) III. 404 Charles..will..work like a nigger at his music. **1880** 'Mark Twain' *Tramp Abroad* 40 He laid into his work like a nigger. **1889** E. Dowson *Let.* 19 May (1967) 80, I have simply worked like a nigger this week. **1920** R. Fry *Let.* 20 June (1972) II. 481, I have worked like a nigger to arrange it [*sc.* an exhibition] well. **1931** D. L. Sayers *Five Red Herrings* ix. 99 Dalziel has been working like a nigger all day, getting him identified by his family and by the station-master at Pinwherry and by the people at Larne.

d. *a nigger in the woodpile* (or *fence*): a concealed motive or unknown factor affecting a situation in an adverse way. orig. *U.S.*

1852 in *Kans. Hist. Quarterly* (1942) XI. 235 No 'nigger in the wood pile' here..; white men are at the bottom of this speculation. **1862** *Congress. Globe* 3 June 2527/1 [These gentlemen] spoke two whole hours..in showing—to borrow an elegant phrase, the paternity of which belongs, I think, to their side of the House,—that there was 'a nigger in the wood-pile'. **1897** *Congress. Rec.* 18 Feb. App. 61/1 Like a great many others ignorant of facts, he finds 'a nigger in the wood pile' when there is neither wood pile nor nigger. **1911** Woodrow Wilson in *Outlook* 11 Aug. 944 If you go through the schedules you will find some nigger in every wood pile. **1930** *Cambridge Daily News* 24 Sept. 7/6 Unless..there is a nigger in the wood pile,..the shares ought to be worth a mild flutter at round 8s. 6d. **1952** A. Christie *They do it with Mirrors* xii. 109 Well now, let's have your point of view. Who's the nigger in the woodpile? The G.I. husband? **1958** *Listener* 13 Feb. 285/1 'The starry heaven that we know.. is inside us'.. The nigger in the woodpile is to be found in the word 'know'. **1958** 'A. Gilbert' *Death against Clock* 72 The nigger in the woodpile on this occasion being an elderly spinster of decided views. **1960** *Daily Tel.* 16 Jan. 8 This seems to be the nigger in the woodpile—the woodpile being an industrial recovery and activity remarkable by any standard. **1974** M. Gilbert *Flash Point* ii. 19 It wouldn't have been easy to spot... It's taken Jonas himself all this time to spot the nigger in the woodpile.

1850 *California Courier* (San Francisco) 4 Sept. 2/6 The majority of the papers, however, think that there 'is a nigger in the fence' somewhere. **1888** B. Harte *Phyllis of Sierras* I. iii. 90 Ef he aint scooped up by Jenny Bradley he'll guess there's a nigger in the fence somewhere. **1911** H. Quick *Yellowstone Nights* xi. 286 He's always looking for a nigger in the fence.

2. d. Used in Comb. to denote a dark shade of colour, as *nigger-brown* (also *ellipt.*), *-grey*, *-pink*.

1914 *Lady's Pictorial* 4 July p. v (Advt.), Soft Taffeta Hat..In Black,..Nigger, Mole, and White. **1915** *Home Chat* 2 Jan. 11/1 Nigger-brown cloth. **1917** *Ibid.* 3 Nov. 139/2 Nigger or, as it is now called, 'Zulu', is also to be seen. **1922** D. H. Lawrence *England, my England* 116 She was wearing a wide hat of grey straw, and a loose, swinging dress of nigger-grey velvet. **1923** [see *desert-brown adj.]. **1930** J. Dos Passos *42nd Parallel* I. 124 On each table there were niggerpink and vermilion paper flowers. **1960** V. Williams *Walk Egypt* 89 A dry-goods store showed a dress of 'nigger-pink'. **1973** *Times* 12 Nov. 4/4 Decorations in autumnal colours, that is, coral pink and what used to be nigger brown.

3. a, b. (Examples.)

1867 J. A. Hosmer *Trip to States by Yellowstone & Missouri* 58 The boat..struck the bar; they then began to work with the spars and nigger, and at two o'clock we got off. **1878** J. H. Beadle *Western Wilds* 378 Then oaths, spars, 'nigger-engine' and all the other available machinery were set in operation. **1882** *Harper's Mag.* Jan. 175/2 One of the 'nigger' engines is suddenly called into service to tighten a two-inch rope, or wind up a discarded cable. **1900** *Atlantic Monthly* LXXXV. 103/2 'Carriages', bright with red and green lanterns..rush to and fro, seizing the logs as they come from the 'kickers' and 'niggers'. **1910** S. E. White *Rules of Game* I. v. 32 When the car had flown back to its starting-point, the 'nigger' rose from obscurity to turn the log half-way round. **1929** *Encycl. Brit.* XIV. 482/1 A steam or air 'nigger' (mechanically operated steel arms) helps to place the log in the proper position.

4. c. *slang.* (See quot. 1960.)

1934 *Tit-Bits* 31 Mar. 12/1 The film world has a colourful compilation of expressions unlike those in other walks of life. 'Niggers' are not men of colour, but blackboards used to 'kill' unwanted reflections from the powerful lights. **1937** A. Buchanan *Film Making* iii. 52 'Niggers' are wooden oblong screens used to 'nigger-off' or shield light from faces, or shadows on walls, and so 'Her face needs a nigger' is not such an alarming statement as it sounds to the uninitiated. **1957** Manvell & Huntley *Technique Film Music* ii. 32 In silent film days we had all the apparatus we needed in the studios, with miles of cables, banks of arcs, and great screens (known in the industry as 'niggers') to reflect light and help shadow effects. **1960** O. Skilbeck *ABC of Film & TV* 89 *Nigger*, an adjustable Mask on a stand, used on the Floor to shield the camera from, or to achieve effects with, lights.

5. *nigger-breaker*, *-chaser*, *-dealer*, *-driver*, (earlier example), *-lover*, *-stealer*, *-trader*; also *nigger-loving* adj.

1845 F. Douglass *Narr. Life F. Douglass* 57 All of this added weight to his reputation as a 'nigger-breaker'. **1921** C. E. Mulford *Bar-20 Three* xvi. 217 Most likely they'll be nigger-chasers, th' way some folks'll be steppin' lively to get out of th' way. **1853** F. W. Thomas *John Randolph* 285 You know Robinson the nigger-dealer, who has the pen down town. **1833** J. Neal *Down Easters* I. 70 When the nigger-drivers falls out among themselves. **1909** R. E. Knowles *Attic Guest* xiii. 178 'Then you can take what you deserve, curse you for a nigger-lover,' I heard the Colonel retort madly. **1924** *American Mercury* Feb. 135/2 Shorty—Nigger-lover! *He throws the money in her face.* **1930** J. Dos Passos *42nd Parallel* II. 140 'Niggerlover,' yelled Joe in her ear... Janey began to cry. **1958** *Church Times* 21 Nov. 6/4 You can call a man a *Kaffir-Boetie* in Johannesburg and a nigger-lover in the Southern States; but both mean precisely the same thing and have the same accent. **1959** *Encounter* Dec. 45/2 They nick our boys and let the Spades go!..Nigger-lovers! **1972** *Guardian* 3 July 8/2 Black Mountain College..was a seat of free love, communism, and nigger-lovers. **1914** S. Lewis *Our Mr. Wrenn* 3 Mrs Zapp was too conscientiously dolorous to be much cheered by the sympathy of a nigger-lovin' Yankee. **1962** *Guardian* 3 Oct. 1/6 It is still wise not to..admit you represent such a Nigger-loving Red publication as the 'Guardian'. **1975** J. Rathbone *Kill Cure* III. iv. 106 You nigger-loving bitch. **1839** R. M. Bird *Adventures R. Day* I. xxv. 181, I was 'a kidnapper, a Georgeye nigger-stealer'. **1884** 'Mark Twain' *Huck. Finn* xxxiii. 314 Only I couldn't believe it. Tom Sawyer a nigger-stealer. **1853** F. W. Thomas *John Randolph* 285 He's not in favor of these regular nigger-traders is he? **1884** 'Mark Twain' *Huck. Finn* viii. 60 But I noticed dey wuz a nigger trader roun' de place considerable lately en I begin to get oneasy.

6. a. *nigger-blood*, *boy*, *-lips*, *mouth*; also *nigger-blooded*, *-skinned* adjs.; *nigger-dead* adj.; *nigger minstrel*, one of a group of entertainers performing songs and dances typical of or based on plantation life in the Southern U.S., freq. by white men with blackened faces; also ellipt., *nigger*.

1833 J. Neal *Down-Easters* I. 66 If there's a drop of nigger-blood in 'em, they'll always show it in their temper. **1932** W. Faulkner *Light in August* v. 96 'Take your black hand off of me, you damn niggerblooded —' The hand shut down again. **1825** J. Neal *Bro. Jonathan* III. 207 Nobody there, I guess, but a nigger boy. **1970** R. D. Abrahams *Positively Black* ii. 26 'Nigger boy,' he said to me, 'how'd you like to meet your maker right now?' **1970** W. Ford in O. Coombs *We speak as Liberators* 43, I would tell of being Black and Proud and Black and Loud and Black and Bowed and Black and niggerdead. **1922** Joyce *Ulysses* 219 From the hoardings Mr. Eugene Stratton grinned with thick niggerlips at Father Conmee. **1860** A. J. Munby *Diary* 17 Mar. in D. Hudson *Munby* (1972) 56 My 'comic' friend suggested that I should apply to certain 'niggers', who had just bowed themselves off the stage... In this den were two or three men with blackened faces, taking off their shabby nigger costume. **1860** E. Cowell *Diary* 13 Sept. in *Cowells in America* (1934) 155 A Company of 'nigger minstrels' are to be here tomorrow night. **1917** A. Waugh *Loom of Youth* II. i. 93 And do you think he really imagines he is doing any good to his form by giving that nigger minstrel entertainment up there? **1959** I. & P. Opie *Lore & Lang. Schoolch.* i. 13 Nellie Bligh..was the heroine of a mid-nineteenth-century nigger minstrel song by Stephen Foster. **1922** Joyce *Ulysses* 365 The dark one [*sc.* girl] with the mop head and the nigger mouth. **1938** Nigger-skinned [see *fawn-eyed adj.].

b. *nigger culture*, *dialect*, *melody* (earlier and later examples), *music*, *show*, *song*.

1970 J. B. Cole in A. Chapman *New Black Voices* (1972) III. 493 When blacks refer to 'Nigger culture', they often very explicitly speak of soul and style. **1834** *Knickerbocker* III. 445 And I would say too, that although *mighty smart*, and a *mighty smart chance*, *mighty big*, and *mighty little* was excellent 'nigger' dialect, yet it was not so refined, as an orator might use. **1846** *Ibid.* XXVIII. 244 Captain Marin would give a touch from a sea-song, or a specimen of a 'nigger-melody'. **1857** J. D. Borthwick *Three Yrs. in Calif.* xii. 212 My entertainers, producing two violins, favoured me with a selection of Nigger melodies. **1894** G. du Maurier *Trilby* I. III. 219 He..can even scream with laughter at..a nigger melody. **1948** A. Lomax in A. Dundes *Mother Wit* (1973) 472/1 If you like this nigger music. **1856** C. E. De Long in *Calif. Hist. Soc. Q.* (1930) IX. 60 Went to a nigger show. **1884** 'Mark Twain' *Huck. Finn* xxvi. 261 They never go to the circus, nor theatre, nor nigger shows, nor nowheres. **1909** R. E. Knowles *Attic Guest* xiii. 156 They'll be flaunting that Uncle Tom's Cabin nigger show under their noses. **1844** *United Service Jrnl.* XLIV. 21 He was never at rest,—now singing a nigger song on the deck. **1851** H. Mayhew *London Labour* I. 273/1, I sell ballads and manuscript music.., which is 'transposed'..from the nigger songs.

c. nigger cloth = *negro cloth* (Negro 7); **nigger corner** *U.S.*, a part of a public building to which Negroes were confined; **nigger fish**, a small grouper, *Cephalopholis fulvus*, found in the West Indies and off the coast of Florida; = Cony, coney *sb.* 7 b; (earlier example); **nigger goose** *N. Amer. local* (see quots.); **nigger heaven** *U.S. slang*, the top gallery in a theatre; **nigger heel** *Naut.* (see quot.); also **nigger-heeled** *a.* (see quot. 1961); **nigger hunt**, the organized pursuit of Negroes for the purpose of attacking them; so **nigger-hunter, -hunting**; **nigger lice** *U.S.*, informal name of the prickly awns of various species of plants, esp. of the genus *Desmodium*; **nigger luck**, exceptionally good luck; **nigger shooter** *U.S. slang*, a catapult; **nigger-stick** *U.S. slang* (see quot. 1974); **nigger toe** *U.S.*, a Brazil nut.

1857 *Chambers's Jrnl.* 3 Jan. 3/2 The garments of.. copper-coloured nigger cloth. **1860** J. G. Holland *Miss Gilbert's Career* iv. 61 You see he sells some of his nigger cloth for goods. **1955** W. Foster-Harris *Look of Old West* i. 38 Typically the cloth was linsey-woolsey... 'Nigger cloth' it was called. It had been much used for slaves' garments, [etc.]. **1894** 'Mark Twain' in *Century Mag.* June 233/1 In the 'nigger corner' sat Chambers. **1876** G. B. Goode *Catal. Fishes Bermudas* 60 The red form corresponds to *Terranus ouatalibe*, and is known as the Nigger-fish. **1917** T. G. Pearson *Birds of Amer.* I. 97/2 The Cormorants have many local names, such as 'Shag', 'Lawyer', and 'Nigger Goose'. **1941** R. Faherty *Big Old Sun* 313 You can eat curlew, or kill duck or coot or niggergoose if they come flying out yonder. **1947** *National Geographic Mag.* Sept. 339/1 A large flight of cormorants, called there [*sc.* in North Carolina] 'nigger geese', passed close aboard. **1957** W. L. McAtee *Folk-Names Canad. Birds* 5 Double-crested Cormorant.. nigger goose (in allusion to its colour and its goose-like appearance, especially when in flight in the V-formation so closely associated with the common Canada goose). **1878** A. Daly in J. F. Daly *Life A. Daly* (1917) 249 There is a 'Nigger Heaven' (as the third tier is called in Troy) here, & as 'tis very capacious I have been liberal with my pencilled passes. **1931** 'D. Stiff' *Milk & Honey Route* xiv. 151 These..entertainments..have raised their prices beyond the reach of the hobo, unless he wants to go to 'nigger heaven'. **1973** A. Dundes *Mother Wit* 222 This extension or transformation of the 'Nigger Heaven' stereotype has no doubt contributed to the continued currency of Harlem folk speech. **1901** *Rudder* XII. 302/2 The after leech would take an incurve or 'nigger heel', as sailmakers call it. **1922** C. G. Davis *How Sails are Made* (ed. 2) 63 A double-bighted sail would, if not carefully handled and hauled out too hard on peak and clew, become 'nigger-heeled', as a hollow leech was called. **1934** *Yachting Monthly* LVII. 11/1 We were watching a hawse-fallen sloop beating in under a badly nigger-heeled mainsail. **1961** F. H. Burgess *Dict. Sailing* 150 *Niggerheeled*, said of the leech of a sail that curves inward of a line from peak to clew, and is therefore not roached. **1834** *Chambers's Edin. Jrnl.* III. 135/3 When a slave runs away..a party is made up for a nigger hunt. **1940** E. Caldwell *Trouble in July* x. 165 This ain't no nigger-hunt—this here's a jawing match! **1959** *Encounter* Mar. 87 The young 'nigger-hunters' of Notting Hill. **1834** *Chambers's Edin. Jrnl.* III. 135/3 In Kentucky..nigger-hunting is a favourite sport. **1958** *Encounter* Dec. 4/2 They had then armed themselves,..and had gone on what they described..as a 'nigger-hunting expedition'. **1971** in C. Mullard *Black Britain* (1973) IV. xi. 142 The racists, who were no doubt nigger-hunting, as they call it, felt that this was easy meat. **1933** *Sun* (Baltimore) 11 Sept. 6/7 The iron weed with its deep color, and..great clumps of 'nigger lice'. **1940** H. L. Mencken *Happy Days* 43 Sometimes a black-hearted boy would sneak into the adjacent brickyard, which was covered in large part with Jimpson weeds, plantains and other such vegetable outlaws, and return with a large ball of nigger-lice. **1946** *Sun* (Baltimore) 2 Oct. 12/3 When I spoke the other day of 'nigger lice', I was referring to the tick trefoil, its scientific name. **1851** R. Glisan *Jrnl. Army Life* (1874) 90, I occasionally made him a little envious by my nigger-luck, as he is pleased to term it. **1900** R. H. Savage *Midnight Passenger* (1901) 135 It has been a great stroke of nigger luck. **1909** *Dialect Notes* III. 352 You can't beat me playing dominoes. It's jest your nigger-luck that gets away with me. **1876** E. W. Heap *Diary* 26 Feb. in *Publ. Amer. Dial. Soc.* (1969) LII. 53, I had a job on hand making Nigger shooters for Dr's children. **1883** Sweet & Knox *On Mexican Mustang through Texas* 339 Just about the time people have got used to tops buzzing about their ears, the 'nigger-shooter' mania breaks out. **1901** Ade *Forty Mod. Fables* 172 All you wanted to do was to tear out with those Toughs and kill Birds with Nigger-Shooters. **1963** R. I. McDavid *Mencken's Amer. Lang.* vi. 284 In the South it [*sc.* a slingshot] is still sometimes called a *nigger-shooter.* **1971**

Guardian 18 Sept. 11/7 Conditions inside American prisons... Prisoners live their lives at the end of gun barrels and what are often known as 'nigger-sticks'. **1973** *Black Panther* 15 Sept. 17/3 They were attacked and brutally beaten by 50 to 60 guards armed with tear gas, plexiglass shields and four-foot long 'nigger sticks'. **1974** *Guidelines to Volunteer Services* (N.Y. State, Dept. Correctional Services) 42 *Niggerstick*, officer's baton. **1896** *Dialect Notes* I. 421 *Nigger toes*: for *Brazil nuts*. **1958** J. M. LACY in A. Dundes *Mother Wit* (1973) 597/2 He buys..nuts called 'nigger toes'. **1973** *Times* 27 Aug. 5/8 In Virginia brazil nuts are called *nigger-toes* and chewed with great relish.

nigger, *v.* Add: **1. b.** (Earlier and later examples.)

1833 S. SMITH *Life & Writings J. Downing* 22 He laid sticks across the large logs.., and *niggered* them off with fire, and then roolled them up in piles. **1843** 'R. CARLTON' *New Purchase* I. xx. 188 In addition to the 'niggering off', it became necessary, as the cold increased, to chop off logs. **1905** M. G. SHERK *Pen Pictures of Early Pioneer Life in Upper Canada* 49 To save the time and labor of cutting the fallen trees into lengths for being drawn together by the oxen, they were often 'niggered'.

2. To work 'like a nigger'; to work very hard; quasi-*trans.* with *it*.

1857 J. HYDE *Mormonism* v. 120 Many of the people express satisfaction in seeing these 'better-dressed fellers' obliged to 'nigger it' as well as themselves. **1878** J. H. BEADLE *Western Wilds* 349 Was it not more of an honor to be the 'bishop's fourth'..than the 'slavey' of a poor mechanic, to 'nigger it on love and starvation'?

3. *refl.* To make (oneself) resemble a Negro, by blackening the face.

1881 M. CROMMELIN *Miss Daisy Dimity* I. ii. 21 Jemmy the third, was 'niggering' himself, by adorning his rosy cheeks with black.

niggerdom. (Earlier examples.)

1862 *Congress. Globe* 28 Mar. 1414/2 New England, where they hate niggerdom worse than the devil. **1868** *Good Words* 1 Oct. 603/2 The conquering nigger..caught many of the Aborigines, blacked them over, and sent them off to proclaim the glories of Niggerdom.

niggerhead. Add: **1.** For *U.S.* read *N. Amer.* (Later examples.) Also, *N.Z.*, the tussocks formed in swampy ground by species of *Carex*, esp. *C. secta*.

1882 T. H. POTTS *Out in Open* 76 Penetrating the dead massy root of an old plant of nigger-head (*carex virgata*). **1904** J. LYNCH *Three Yrs. Klondike* 41 We plunged into a mire of muddy water and 'nigger-heads'. 'Nigger-heads' are detachments of dark moss about a foot in diameter, lifting their heads just above the water or marshy subsoil. **1910** R. W. SERVICE *Ballads of Cheechako* 19 And there was the little lone moose trail... By muskeg hollow and niggerhead it wandered endlessly. **1921** H. GUTHRIE-SMITH *Tutira* xii. 103 The outer edges of these marshes were rough with nigger's-head (*Carex secta*). **1947** J. H. BROWN *Outdoors Unlimited* 314 The ptarmigan cackled in the manner of a Bronx cheer as it flew to a nearby nigger-head. **1950** *N.Z. Jrnl. Agric.* Apr. 356/3 Excellent crops and pastures..where before only nigger-heads, rushes, and swamp plants were flourishing. **1958** P. BERTON *Klondike* 44 The great clumps of grass 'nigger-heads' that marked the mouth of Rabbit. **1961** C. VYVYAN *Arctic Adventure* xxi. 126 We had to negotiate about a mile of open country across nigger-heads.

b. *U.S.* A spherical prickly cactus belonging to the genera *Ferocactus* or *Echinocactus*.

1877 H. C. HODGE *Arizona* 244 The kind [of cactus] commonly called the nigger head is round, of the size of a cabbage, and covered with large, crooked, catlike thorns. **1881** [see **barrel cactus*]. **1940** E. C. JAEGER *Calif. Deserts* (rev. ed.) 181 Closely allied to this is the Mohavean niggerhead. **1966** E. Y. DAWSON *Cacti of Calif.* 51 (*heading*) Nigger Heads (*Echinocactus polycephalus*).

c. *U.S.* The black-eyed Susan, *Rudbeckia hirta*, a yellow composite flower with a dark centre.

1893 S. F. PRICE *Flora of Warren County, Kentucky* 15 *Rudbeckia..fulgida*... Cone Flower. 'Nigger-head'. **1931** W. N. CLUTE *Common Names of Plants* 45 A number of composites with yellow rays and dark centers are commonly known as niggerheads, though the more polite term is black-eyed Susan. **1966** *Publ. Amer. Dial. Soc. 1964* XLII. 21 Niggerhead... The black-eyed Susan (*Rudbeckia hirta*).

2. A rock, stone, lump of coral, etc. (Earlier and further examples.)

1847 H. HOWE *Hist. Coll. of Ohio* 569 It was a saw mill, with a small pair of stones attached, made of boulders, or 'nigger heads', as they are commonly called. **1885** in *Amer. Speech* (1961) XXXVI. 295 The term 'Nigger head' is used by the Kanawha miners to designate a hard, heavy, impure coal often resembling cannel. **1901** *Chambers's Jrnl.* Sept. 634/1 He tightened his grip on the reins as he caught the dim outline of a treacherous nigger-head stone. **1908** E. J. BANFIELD *Confessions of Beachcomber* I. ii. 57 Nothing was left of the big ship save some distorted fragments of iron jammed in among the nigger-heads of coral. **1916** C. SANDBURG *Chicago Poems* 41 A boy passes and throws a niggerhead that chips off the end of the nose [of a statue]. **1948** E. N. DICK *Dixie Frontier* 4 Bears rolled 'nigger head' stones over and ate the grubs and field mice. **1956** M. L. WEST *Gallows on Sand* viii. 89 We moored the skiff to a niggerhead, one of those jutting stumps of dead coral which are found all over the reefs, and which have the lock of a frizzled skull on top of a stumpy neck.

3. (Earlier and later examples.)

1843 J. LUMSDEN *Amer. Memoranda* (1844) 14 My next communication will probably contain full details of the methods adopted by the Virginian planters in the manufacturing of the nigger-head, ladies'-twist, [etc.]. **1860** *Nor'Wester* (Red River Settlement) 28 June 4/5 After that I would smoke half a plug of 'nigger-head tobacco'. **1884** 'MARK TWAIN' *Huck. Finn* xxi. 194 You borry'd store tobacco and paid back nigger-head. **1936** *Beaver* Mar. 7/2 It is probably the lineal descendant of the nigger-head tobacco used in the Indian trade years ago, and as it came in ropes it was sold by the inch. **1956** CRATE & WILLIAMS *We speak for Silent* 3 Groceries—particularly tea and 'nigger-head' (a trade-tobacco for smoking and chewing)—are his more necessary 'luxuries'.

5. (Later example.)

1946 W. S. KNICKERBOCKER *20th Cent. English* 149 Niggerhead... After the Civil War it was used for a person in favor of full political equality for Negroes.

6. A type of fabric (see quot. 1950).

1892–3 *T. Eaton & Co. Catal.* Fall & Winter 10/2 In the plain cloth jackets the materials are beavers, niggerheads, serges and worsted. **1950** '*Mercury*' *Dict. Textile Terms* 366/1 *Niggerhead Curl*, a fancy dress cloth made from spiral yarn warp and mixture weft (cotton and wool).

7. (See quot.)

1927 G. BRADFORD *Gloss. Sea Terms* 119/1 *Niggerheads*, a name for bollards, and sometimes applied to winch heads.

ni·ggering, *vbl. sb.* [f. NIGGER *v.* + -ING[1].] The action of the verb in various senses.

1843 'R. CARLTON' *New Purchase* I. xx. 188 Niggering belongs mainly to very large timber, and pertains rather to the science of log-rolling than of preparing fuel. **1894** 'R. ANDOM' *We Three & Troddles* xix. 174 'Busking' be it known is the technical term for amateur niggering. **1948** E. N. DICK *Dixie Frontier* 126 Morning and evening dry limbs were laid in the widening gap until the log was burnt into length. After about a week the fires had done their work. This was called 'niggering off'.

niggerish, *a.* (Earlier example.)

1825 J. NEAL *Bro. Jonathan* II. 67 Ye great niggerish lookin', wap-sided haw.

niggerism. (Further examples.)

1844 *St. Louis* (Missouri) *Reveille* 24 Nov. 2/4 Scrub and whitewash your spiritual niggerism, or you will forever rest in the valley of *Sheol*! **1856** *Illinois State Register* (Springfield) 19 June 2/1 For every democrat who deserts to niggerism, one hundred old line whigs join the democracy against it. **1873** *Porcupine* 19 Apr. 38/3 For the occasional dash or suspicion of niggerism in the mangling of the words, common custom and coincidence will quite account. **1970** G. JACKSON *Let.* 10 June in *Soledad Brother* (1971) 33 He and my mother went to great pains to impress on me that it was the worst form of niggerism to hook and jab..at other blacks.

niggerize (ni·gərəiz), *v.* [f. NIGGER *sb.* + -IZE.] *trans.* To make Negro in character; to treat (a Negro) with contempt. Also *intr.*, to act or dress up as a Negro.

1969 V. FERDINAND in A. Chapman *New Black Voices* (1972) 379 Blk people have done it to the english language, they have niggerized it. **1973** *Times* 13 Feb. 16/4 As people, we are tired of being niggerized, ostracized..and ossified. **1974** J. MARKS' *Mick Jagger* 92 Mick niggerising with a fake, greasy dialect and a very heavy debt to Bo on 'I'm a King Bee'.

nigger's head. *Naut.* An ornamental knot; = TURK'S HEAD 2.

1925 *Glasgow Herald* 3 Oct. 4 The glittering ship's bell with its pendant of brightly painted niggershead knotting.

niggery, *a.* (Earlier and later examples.)

1855 'Q. K. P. DOESTICKS' *Doesticks, What he Says* xxiii 204 Coffee, which I sweeten with niggery brown sugar. **1935** E. HEMINGWAY *Green Hills Afr.* (1936) IV. ii. 241 The long, clean niggery legs. **1936** M. MITCHELL *Gone with Wind* 427 The faint niggery smell which crept from the cabin increased her nausea. **1940** C. MCCULLERS *Heart is Lonely Hunter* (1943) I. iii. 43 Portia had a certain kind of niggery craziness, but she was O.K.

nigget (ni·dʒėt). *dial.* Also **nidget.** [Origin unknown.] A small insect; *spec.* one used by a witch or sorcerer as a familiar.

1875 W. D. PARISH *Dict. Sussex Dial.* 79 *Nidget*, a little bug. **1915** *Times* 3 Sept. 5/2 'Oh, what are niggets?' 'Why those creepy-crawly things that witches keep all over them. She was sitting down with her niggets all round her, feeding them with little bits of grass all chopped up.' **1925** R. O. WINSTEDT *Shaman, Saiva, & Sufi* ii. 21 But the best known of these familiars..is of the nigget type and takes the shape of a house-cricket.

niggle, *sb.* Add: **2.** A complaint or criticism, esp. one that is petty or trifling; a worry, annoyance; nagging or irritation.

1886 F. T. ELWORTHY *West Somerset Word-Bk.* 512 Her's always 'pon the niggle way un. **1956** I. BROMIGE *Enchanted Garden* III. iii. 144, I even feel a few little niggles of uneasiness myself. **1960** *Guardian* 11 June 1/5 The poor quality of contemporary furniture..can be the only niggle. **1966** *New Statesman* 8 July 51/3 How much of us will be recognisable in the pages of the history books of 2066? This egoist's niggle spiralled up into my mind. **1972** M. GILBERT *Body of Girl* xii. 106 If the boys in blue can get in a niggle at you, they will. **1974** *Times Lit. Suppl.* 15 Feb. 158/3 In view..of the fact that his book should..go into a second edition.., one or two minor niggles may conveniently be ventilated.

niggle, *v.*[2] Add: **1. d.** (Earlier and later examples.)

1844 W. BARNES *Poems Rural Life* 1st Coll. 330 *Niggle*, to complain of trifles from ill temper or bad humor. **1929** W. DEEPING *Roper's Row* xxviii. 312 He would niggle at his food. **1966** 'L. LANE' *ABZ of Scouse* 75 *Niggle*, to question; to raise objections. **1974** *Sunday Post* (Glasgow) 21 Apr. 16 (Advt.), Your accounts director won't niggle at the bill at the Ormonde Restaurant (just a high-speed lift away from your room).

3. d. To annoy, irritate; to criticize, nag.

1886 F. T. ELWORTHY *West Somerset Word-Bk.* 512 *Niggle*, same as to nag. To aggravate. Her'd niggle anybody's live out o' them, nif they'd let her to. **1959** I. & P. OPIE *Lore & Lang. Schoolch.* x. 178 A short-tempered person is spoken of as being..niggled or niggly. **1968** A. DIMENT *Great Spy Race* iv. 47 He is liable to start demanding mass executions when niggled. **1971** A. PRICE *Alamut Ambush* 6 He was mildly niggled that Maitland had found himself some other pressing engagement.

niggliite (ni·gli,əit). *Min.* [f. the name of Paul *Niggli* (1888–1953), Swiss mineralogist + -ITE[1].] A mineral containing platinum and tin (or perhaps tellurium), found at Insizwa in Cape Province, Republic of South Africa.

1936 D. L. SCHOLTZ in *Publ. Univ. Pretoria* 2nd Ser. I. 184 (*heading*) Mineral F (niggliite). **1955** *Amer. Mineralogist* XL. 693 Niggliite..was found in a concentrate which was obtained by panning large amounts of oxidized sulphide ore from Waterfall Gorge, Insizwa, South Africa. **1968** I. KOSTOV *Mineralogy* 115 Various other formulae have been given to niggliite, PtTe, PtSn, and Pt_2Sn_3; its structure appears to be that of niccolite. **1972** *Mineral. Mag.* XXXVIII. 796 The close similarity of niggliite to synthetic PtTe..led Groeneveld Meijer (1955) to suggest that they were identical. Ramdohr (1960) suggests that the formula is Pt_2Sn_3 but in Ramdohr (1969) the composition is given as 'PtTe, perhaps a mixed crystal with isostructural PtSn'. Scholtz..reports that re-examination showed niggliite is essentially PtSn. *Ibid.* 798 Niggliite from the type locality has been shown to be an antimonian-bismuthian variety of PtSn.

niggly (ni·gli), *a.* [f. NIGGLE *v.*[2] + -Y[1].] = NIGGLING *ppl. a.*; also, irritable, short-tempered.

1840 W. HARCOURT *Let.* in A. G. Gardiner *Life W. Harcourt* (1923) I. ii. 24, I think his trees *niggly* as you would say, and he teaches an odd doctrine about trees. **1862** C. C. ROBINSON *Dial. Leeds* 40 Ah doant want to live soa as fowks could cawal us niggly. **1898** B. KIRKBY *Lakeland Words* 107 He was as niggly ower a penny as many a yan is ower a pund. **1952** M. TRIPP *Faith is Windsock* iii. 43 Well, aren't you a niggly old bastard? **1959** [see *NIGGLE *v.*[2] 3 d]. **1967** E. SHORT *Embroidery & Fabric Collage* iv. 106 Care must be taken to avoid niggly detail and a temptation to imitate a pencil line or brush stroke exactly. **1973** A. ROSS *Dunfermline Affair* 65 'What about ..going to get the bloody stuff?' Thomson said. He was niggly, and showed it.

niggra (ni·gră). *U.S.* (See quot. 1960.) Cf. *NIGRA.

1960 WENTWORTH & FLEXNER *Dict. Amer. Slang* 354/2 *Niggra* = nigger. A pronunciation used by Southerners of Southern breeding and ancestry. Conjuring up the period of Negro slavery, the pronunciation is even more derog. than 'nigger'. **1968** *Guardian* 25 Oct. 2/3 We know our niggras and we love them. **1969** P. CROSS in A. Dundes *Mother Wit* (1973) 654/2 They had the niggras on their plantation.

nigguh, niggur (ni·gə), varr. NIGGER *sb.* *U.S. slang.* Cf. *NIGGA.

1968 *Amer. Speech* XLIII. 217 The mountain trapper.. was *this Injun*, ..*this niggur*, or *this hoss*. **1969** G. BROOKS in A. Chapman *New Black Voices* (1972) 202 Lord! Forgive these nigguhs that know not what they do. **1970** J. CORTEZ in O. Coombs *We speak as Liberators* 17 Love Lives And I wanta taste myself inside Mmmmmmmm that pure nigguh pain. **1973** *Black World* Sept. 70 His sound now turns to nigguh notes.

night, *sb.* Add: **4. f.** An evening or night devoted to the performance of a play, or of music by a specified composer or artist, or celebrations in honour of a particular person, etc.; freq. with defining word prefixed, as in *first night* (see FIRST *a.* (*sb.*) and *adv.* C 2). Cf. quot. 1711 under sense 4 b in Dict.

1707 *Muses Mercury* Jan. 4 This Prologue was forbidden to be spoken the second Night of the Representation of the *Prophetess*. **1784** in C. B. Hogan *London Stage 1660–1800* (1968) v. 760 *Il Curioso Indiscreto*... This Night, the last of performing before the Holidays, will not be counted a Subscription Night, but the Tickets admitted as usual. **1793** in *Ibid.* v. 1584 *Othello*... Paid Music 4 Nights £35 19*s*. 4*d*. **1842** DICKENS *Let.* 12 Nov. (1974) III. 368 Mrs. Dickens begs me..to say that if you can oblige her with your box at Covent Garden on any of Miss Kemble's nights, she will be very thankful. **1847** *Punch* XIII. 60 (*caption*) Melancholy scene at the opera on a Jenny Lind night. **1859** G. A. SALA *Twice round Clock* 260, I have brought you to her Majesty's Theatre, and this is unfortunately a Verdi night. **1861** GEO. ELIOT *Let.* 6 Oct. (1954) III. 456 We are enjoying a great, great pleasure—a new grand piano; and last evening we had a Beethoven night. **1959** *Observer* 18 Jan. 14/4 The Burns Night circles the globe like a sputnik. **1969** M. R. BOOTH *Eng. Plays of 19th Cent.* II. 346 *Mrs. Dane's Defence* ran for 209 nights on its first appearance. **1970** *Listener* 10 Sept. 326/3 The years of the romantic biographers and the Beethoven pianists, of Beethoven nights at the old Queen's Hall.

g. *the night*, the first occasion on which a play, entertainment, etc., is publicly per-

formed; freq. in phr. (*it will be*) *all right on the night*, an expression of optimism that a performance will go well when it is given publicly, even if rehearsals are unpromising; also *transf.*

1911 O. ONIONS *Widdershins* 26 I've not got on very well with it. But it will be all right on the night, as you used to say. **1938** R. G. COLLINGWOOD *Principles of Art* xiv. 322 In the rehearsal of any given passage..the actors may move and speak exactly as they will 'on the night'. **1939** S. BOX in J. W. Marriott *Best One-Act Plays of 1939* (1940) 296 *Juliet.* God-a-mercy! PROMPT!.. *Nurse.* Ah, well! 'Twill be all right on the night! **1949** *Economist* 23 July 172 The hope that the Atlantic Pact would 'turn out all right on the night'. **1967** J. GARDNER *Madrigal* ii. 22 Boysie..began to build up a mental block. It would be all right on the night, he thought with a nervous laugh. **1973** E. LEMARCHAND *Let or Hindrance* xiii. 165 Penny may fly off the handle, but she's always all right on the night.

h. (Also *'night.*) Ellipt. for GOOD NIGHT I. *colloq.*

1912 MULFORD & CLAY *Buck Peters, Ranchman* viii. 92 'Good-night. I'm goin' to roost.' 'Night, Dave.' **1922** JOYCE *Ulysses* 589 *Corny Kelleher.* Good night, men. *The Watch.* (*Saluting together.*) Night, gentlemen. **1933** A. THIRKELL *High Rising* vii. 151 'Good night. We're going to bed now.' 'Night,' said Stoker. **1967** K. GILES *Death & Mr. Prettyman* i. 21 'Seven ack emma tomorrow if you can manage.' 'Night, sir,' Honeybody lumbered off. **1972** 'H. HOWARD' *Nice Day for Funeral* v. 80 'I could sleep standing up.' 'Then let's call it a day...' ''Night...'

5. a. *night out* (examples); also, an evening or night spent in enjoyment or revelling away from one's home; a spree (cf. OUT *adv.* 15 b); so *night off*, a night free from work or one's usual duties.

1885 A. DALY in A. Nicoll *Hist. Eng. Drama 1660–1900* (1959) V. 333 (*play-title*) A night off; or, a page from Balzac. **1890** W. BOOTH *In Darkest Eng.* II. v. 190 The weekly Church service or 'night out' with nowhere to go. **1908** G. SANGER *Seventy Yrs. a Showman* ix. 30 For these people Lansdown Fair was, as they put it, their 'night out'. **1910** *Blackw. Mag.* Jan. 149/1 Mr. Lloyd-George declined to deliver a speech on the ground that it was 'the Prime Minister's night out'! **1916** E. V. LUCAS *Vermilion Box* 129 We have the pictures here, of course, and I go there regularly on my night out. **1943** J. B. PRIESTLEY *Daylight on Saturday* xix. 152 'I'm staying late tonight.' 'Then we can't have our night out,' she cried. **1947** N. CARDUS *Autobiogr.* 277 Whenever his 'night off' occurred he bought a ticket. **1961** H. PINTER (*title*) A night out.

13. a. *night-air* (earlier example), *-ascent, -attack* (earlier and later examples), *-calm, -city, -class, -damp, -duty* (further examples; freq. *attrib.*), *-fancy* (further examples), *-fear, -fight, -flight* (further examples), *-haunt, -hospital, -lunch, -music, -noise, -nursery, -perfume, -raid, -rate, -rehearsal, -road, -school* (further examples), *-self, -smell, -sound, -speech, -talk, -town, -train* (earlier and later examples), *-web, -wonder, -world.*

1788 LD. AUCKLAND *Jrnl.* 25 June (1861) II. 55 He is afraid of the night air. **1866** *Chambers's Jrnl.* Oct. 644/2 One night-ascent has been made in this way. **1844** *Knickerbocker* XXIII. 117, I knew that Indians in a night attack make signals by imitating the cry of some animal. **1952** R. CAMPBELL tr. *Baudelaire's Poems* 127 Like enemies preparing night-attacks. **1817–19** WORDSWORTH *MS.* in E. de Selincourt *Prelude* (1959) 136 The night-calm over sea and land. **1970** T. HUGHES *Crow* 55 Seeing the night-city..He bellows laughter. **1891** A. BEARDSLEY *Let.* July (1971) 24 Two hours' daily work is quite sufficient for me, so, as you suggest, I mean to attend night classes. **1936** N. COWARD *Fumed Oak* i, in *Tonight at 8.30* II. i. 47 Your father was a gentleman, which is more than your husband ever will be, with all his night-classes and his book reading—night-classes indeed! **1851** H. MELVILLE *Moby Dick* III. xliv. 250 The unheeded night-damp gathered in beads of dew upon that stone-carved coat and hat. **1921** A. CHRISTIE *Mysterious Affair at Styles* viii. 170 She had kindly offered to remain on night duty. **1959** [see *BEIGEL]. **1966** J. BINGHAM *Double Agent* vi. 93 The phone rang. It was the Night Duty Officer with a deciphered message from Vienna. **1973** 'B. MATHER' *Snowline* vii. 83 Mukherjee wasn't at the [police] station, and the night duty havildar couldn't tell me where he was. **1823** C. LAMB *Elia* 156 My night-fancies have long ceased to be afflictive. **1904** W. H. HUDSON *Green Mansions* xxii. 292 Half-delirious night-fancies. **1823** C. LAMB *Elia* 148 (*heading*) Witches, and other night-fears. **1923** KIPLING *Irish Guards in Great War* I. 7 The 3rd Coldstream Guards ..beat off that attack in a night-fight. **1918** *War Illustr.* 13 July 372/2 My first night-flight was during one of the earlier Zeppelin raids on London and the Eastern Counties. **1973** L. COOPER *Tea on Sunday* xxxi. 228, I must get a plane to Milan tonight..a night flight. **1859** A. J. MUNBY *Diary* 20 Mar. in D. Hudson *Munby* (1972) 28 A large & still flourishing crop of secret dens & night haunts. **1950** G. GREENE *Third Man* xi. 96 He might have been in any third-rate night haunt in any other shabby capital. **1963** 'Night' hospital [see *day-hospital* s.v. *DAY *sb.* 23]. **1964** G. L. COHEN *What's Wrong with Hospitals?* viii. 174 He started a night hospital... Executives and professional men who would not otherwise contemplate treatment come by night to bare their unconscious. **1933** M. PELL *S.S. Utah* 12 Anybody know where the night lunch hangs out? **1945** *Seafarers' Log* 17 Aug. 6/5 Men coming back from shore leave are not able to get into night lunch. **1910** W. DE LA MARE *Three Mulla-Mulgars* ix. 128 It pleased Battle mightily, this night-music—music of all the kinds they knew, white man's, Jaqquamusic, Nugga-music, and Mulla-mulgars'. **1952** M. J. WARD (*title*) A little night Music. **1954** J. R. R. TOLKIEN *Fellowship of Ring* I. xii. 214 He lay tossing and turning and listening fearfully to the stealthy night-noises. **1844** T. WEBSTER *Encycl. Domestic Econ.* XXVI. i. 1189 Night nurseries require little furniture beyond bedding, and utensils for washing and bathing. **1937** Night nursery [see *BUDDY *sb.*]. **1974** J. POPE-HENNESSY *R. L. Stevenson* i. 34 Louis's night-nursery..was a small room to the east of the day-nursery. **1918** E. SITWELL *Clown's Houses* 7 Tulip-trees Spilling night-perfumes on the terraces. **1932** AUDEN *Orators* 110 The shamming dead, the night-raid, the feinted retreat. **1939** R. A. KNOX *Let Dons Delight* ix. 247 My host returned, voluble..in his anathemas over the cheap night-rate for telephoning. **1975** J. R. L. ANDERSON *Death in North Sea* iv. 73 'Can you get a helicopter out tonight?' 'I can, but..night-rates for the crews make it rather expensive.' **1812** *Dramatic Censor for 1811* 312 The Public are respectfully informed, that it being found absolutely necessary to have a general night rehearsal of the new Burlesque Tragic Drama, there will be no performance in the Theatre this evening. **1866** M. MACKINTOSH *Stage Reminiscences* 98 We rehearsed the piece, without music, after which a night rehearsal, including the orchestra, was called. **1933** W. DE LA MARE *Fleeting* 42 The empty night-road to the sea. **1780** *New Jersey Jrnl.* 22 Nov. 4/2 Wanted, to be bound, a Boy;..he shall be..sent to night school if required. **1858** Night-school [see *cottage lecture* s.v. *COTTAGE 6]. **1973** E.-J. BAHR *Nice Neighbourhood* i. 14, I met Don at night school. He was learning to be an accountant. **1922** D. H. LAWRENCE *Fantasia of Unconscious* xv. 271 The night-self is the very basis of the dynamic self. **1965** *Punch* 3 Nov. 665/1 The struggle in man between the day-self and the night-self. **1936** C. MORGAN *Sparkenbroke* IV. iv. 344 From the darkness of the garden came the soft patter of invisible rain and the earthy night-smell of plants. **1904** W. H. HUDSON *Green Mansions* xx. 272 Nor had I any choice then but to listen to the night-sounds of the forest. **1953** S. BECKETT *Watt* 33 Listening to the little nightsounds in the hedge behind him. **1954** J. R. R. TOLKIEN *Fellowship of Ring* II. vi. 352, I hear nothing but the night-speech of plant and stone. **1910** W. DE LA MARE *Three Mulla-Mulgars* iv. 51 Soon the long-billed river-birds began their night-talk across the water. **1922** JOYCE *Ulysses* 422 The Mabbot street entrance of nighttown. *Ibid.* 598 A word of caution *re* the dangers of nighttown, women of ill fame and swell mobsmen. **1971** *Guardian Weekly* 5 June 18 Where all seeing readers join is in delight at the architecture of his [*sc.* Maurice Sendak's] Manhattan nighttown of towering pots and packets and jars. **1848** C. BRONTË *Let.* 4 Sept. in *Studies in Bibliogr.* (1971) XXIV. 103 Anne & I..walked through a thunderstorm to the station, got to Leeds and whirled up by the Night train to London. **1954** T. S. ELIOT *Confid. Clerk* I. 30 We took the night train, and did the Channel crossing. **1906** HARDY *Dynasts* II. VI. v. 276 Is it where sky-fires flame and flit, Or solar craters spew and spit, Or ultra-stellar night-webs knit? **1909** E. POUND *Personae* 22 The strange night-wonder of your eyes Dies not. **1939** DYLAN THOMAS *Map of Love* 75 The clean winter sounds of the nightworld.

b. *night-express, -ferry, -latch, -refuge, -shelter, -sock, -stand, -suit, -wrapper.*

1877 J. BLACKWOOD *Let.* 25 June in *Geo. Eliot's Lett.* (1956) VI. 390 We propose to come down by the night express. **1975** N. LUARD *Travelling Horseman* iii. 63 He was on the road to Edinburgh..to catch the night express back to London. **1954** I. MURDOCH *Under Net* xiii. 188, I set off to Victoria to catch the night ferry. **1967** E. WYMARK *As Good as Gold* xiv. 200, I gave them Camilla's address on the Avenue Foch. I omitted to mention that she was already on the Night Ferry. **1854** O. S. FOWLER *Home for All* 113 The front door..secured..with a night-latch and two keys. **1967** KARCH & BUBER *Offset Processes* viii. 321 Turn night latch lever to 'night latch' position. **1872** B. JERROLD *London* xxi. 185 We are in the receiving home of a night refuge—the home of the ragged scholars whom Lord Shaftesbury has befriended—of the wild young clients of the devoted city missionaries. **1911** *Rep. Labour & Social Conditions in Germany* (Tariff Reform League) III. 223 We also had a visit to the Berlin night refuge. **1910** W. DE LA MARE *Three Mulla-Mulgars* xiii. 177 They would sneak off and hide in their night-shelter. **1941** *Times* (Weekly ed.) 5 Feb. 4 Hours spent in night-shelters and tours of devastated areas. **1899** in A. Adburgham *Shops & Shopping* (1964) xxii. 261 Night socks and hose. **1906** GALSWORTHY *Man of Property* III. iii. 305 To ask June whether she had worn night-socks up in those high hotels where it must be so cold of a night. **1961** *John o' London's* 28 Sept. 345/1 This won't be a show-off collection [of books]. Rather, a cross-section of what's on my night-stand. **1939** C. DAY LEWIS *Child of Misfortune* 195 Oliver watched her fastening two children's night-suits. **1863** A. D. WHITNEY *Faith Gartney's Girlhood* ix. 78 Miss Sampson entered..to put on her night-wrapper and make ready for her watch.

c. *night-editor, guard* (later example), *nurse, -patrol, people, police, porter* (later examples), *sister, tourist.*

1868 M. H. SMITH *Sunshine & Shadow in New York* lxxviii. 639 Henry Winson is city editor, and Governier Carr is night editor. **1873** Night editor [see *day editor* s.v. *DAY *sb.* 24]. **1949** *Time* 30 May 69/1 Stewart..had been night editor, sports editor and state editor of the Scripps-Howard *Press.* **1973** R. L. SIMON *Big Fix* (1974) xx. 174 Ask for the night editor. **1914** 'BARTIMEUS' *Naval Occasions* xvi. 128 'Night Guard,' said the Lieutenant curtly. **1844** Night-nurse [see *day-nurse* s.v. *DAY *sb.* 23 c]. **1944** A. THIRKELL *Headmistress* ii. 36 The day nurse went off duty and the night nurse came on. **1971** 'F. CLIFFORD' *Blind Side* v. i. 190 Doctor O'Sullivan reckons Mrs. Lawrence needs a regular night nurse. **1864** J. T. TROWBRIDGE *Cudjo's Cave* xxiii. 201 They discovered some horsemen drawn up before them beside the road. It was the night-patrol. **1971** B. PATTEN *Irrelevant Song* 64 Leave it out among the night-patrols and the lovers. **1957** *N.Y. Post* 20 Sept. M4 Night people, the professor and his wife used to retire at about 2.30 or 3 A.M. **1963** *Times* 8 Jan. 10/4 The 'night people', cleaners, maintenance men, and so on, who occupy the London Underground after the last train has gone. **1877** E. S. PHELPS *Story of Avis* 153 To recommend to the Faculty a stricter régime of night police for those boys. **1887** in C. E. Pascoe *Joyous Neighbourhood Covent Garden* 126 (Advt.), Rougemont hotel, Exeter... Night porter on patrol. **1963** N. MARSH *Dead Water* (1964) ix. 231 The night porter was reading behind his desk. **1969** H. MACINNES *Salzburg Connection* viii. 118 A little late, perhaps, to telephone but he knew the night porter there. **1886** E. C. E. LÜCKES *Hospital Sisters & their Duties* vi. 138 The Night Sister's object is to help the Day sister by giving the supervision to her patients and Nurses which the latter cannot exercise both night and day. **1920** F. NORTON *Duties of Sisters in Small Hospitals* v. 54 The routine duties of the Night Sister consist in taking the day report, making periodical visits to the wards, supervising the admission of accidents and of emergency operation cases. **1934** P. BOTTOME *Private Worlds* 3 The door of the night-sister's room was open. **1958** Night-sister [see *GARBO[1]]. **1973** 'E. PETERS' *City of Gold & Shadows* xii. 191 The night sister on duty was an old friend. **1963** L. DEIGHTON *Horse under Water* v. 28 They send me on a Night Tourist aeroplane. **1971** P. PURSER *Holy Father's Navy* xviii. 88 The last plane will have gone, anyway Unless there are night tourist flights.

d. night snake, a name used for several nocturnal African snakes.

1931 R. L. DITMARS *Snakes of World* ix. 93 The so-called Bush Snakes or Night Snakes are rear-fanged species. **1954** J. A. PRINGLE *Common Snakes* 12 Olive Night-Snake..non-venomous..is a quiet, docile snake.. mainly confined to the coastal belt from Cape Town to north of Durban. **1962** V. F. M. FITZSIMONS *Snakes S. Afr.* 112/1 *Lamprophis aurora...* Aurora- or Night-snake.

e. *night-primrose* = *evening-primrose* (EVENING *sb.*[1] 5 b, in Dict. and Suppl.) (earlier and later examples); *night stock* = *night-scented stock* (sense *14).

1759 P. MILLER *Gardeners Dict.* (ed. 7) s.v. *Œnothera.* Tree Primrose... From the Flower opening in the Evening, many Persons call it the Night Primrose. **1931** A. HUXLEY *Cicadas* 12 Your pallid beauty Like a pale night-primrose. **1918** D. H. LAWRENCE *New Poems* 33 The night-stock oozes scent.

14. night-adapted *a.* = *dark-adapted* ppl. adj. s.v. *DARK *sb.* 6; **night adder,** a nocturnal, venomous, African viper of the genus *Causus*, esp. *C. rhombeatus*, a grey snake with darker patches, common in southern Africa; **night-blooming cereus,** one of several tropical plants belonging to the genera *Hylocereus* and *Selenicereus* of the family Cactaceæ, esp. *H. undulatus*, having very large, fragrant, white flowers that open only at night; **night-blue** (further examples); also *attrib.* or as *adj.*; **night bomber,** an aircraft that drops bombs at night; also, the pilot of such an aircraft; hence *night-bombing*; **night-bound** *a.*, bound, confined, or impeded by night or darkness; **night-box** = **boîte de nuit*; **night chain,** a chain for securing a door at night; **night-climber,** one who climbs on buildings at night, esp. at the Universities of Oxford and Cambridge; so *night-climbing*; **night clock,** a clock which is illuminated so that it can be seen in the dark; **night-club,** † (*a*) *U.S.* = **night-stick*; (*b*) a club or similar establishment that opens at night, usu. providing food, drink, and entertainment; also *attrib.*; hence **night-club** *v. trans.* and *intr.*, to take or go to a night-club; **night-clubber,** one who frequents night-clubs; **night-clubbing,** the frequenting of night-clubs; **night-clubby** *a.*, characteristic or fond of night-clubs; **night-coach,** (*a*) a coach that travels at night; (*b*) *U.S.*, a commercial aircraft providing a night service; **night crawler** *N. Amer.*, a large earthworm, esp. one caught at night to be used as bait in fishing; **night cream,** cosmetic cream that is applied to the face at night; **night-driving,** the driving of a motor vehicle at night; also *attrib.*; so **night-drive** *v. intr.*, to drive a motor vehicle at night; **night effect,** irregularity of the strength and apparent direction of received radio waves of certain frequencies that is especially marked at night, owing to the reception of polarized waves reflected by the ionosphere; so **night error**; **night eye,** (*a*) *U.S.* = CHESTNUT 6; (*b*) an eye adapted for seeing in the dark (usu. *pl.*); **night-fighter,** a fighter (*FIGHTER 3) used, or designed for use, at night; also, the pilot of such an aircraft; also *attrib.*; so *night-fighting*; **night-flowering cereus** = **night-blooming cereus*; **night-fossicker** *Austral. Hist.*, a nocturnal thief of gold dust or quartz; so *night-fossicking*; **night-herd** *N. Amer.*, the herding or guarding of cattle at night; hence as *v. intr.* and *trans.*, to herd or guard (cattle) at night; **night-herder,** one who night-herds; **night-herding,** the work of a night-herder; **night-horse,** (*a*) a horse used for work at night; (*b*) a punning alteration of NIGHTMARE *sb.*; **night-lark,** a person who goes about at

night; **night-life,** manifestations of life at night; *spec.* the activities of, or urban entertainments open to, pleasure-seekers at night; **night-lifer,** one who enjoys night-life; **night-office** *R.C.Ch.*, (until 1971) the part of the canonical office performed during the night hours; **night op** or **operation,** a military operation at night; **night paddock** *Austral.* and *N.Z.*, a field where stock, esp. dairy cows, are kept overnight; **night parrot** *Austral.*, a nocturnal green and yellow ground parrot, *Geopsittacus occidentalis*; **night rider,** one who rides by night, esp. on horse-back; *spec.* in *U.S.*, one of various gangs of mounted men who commit acts of violence in order to intimidate or punish (see also quots.); so *night-riding* vbl. sb. and ppl. adj.; **night-safe** (see quot. 1930); **night-scented stock,** a small annual herb, *Matthiola tristis* or *M. bicornis*, of the family Cruciferæ, whose fragrant lilac flowers open at night; **night-side,** (*a*) the dark or bad aspect of a person or thing; (*b*) *Shetland dial.*, in phr. *in the night-side*, in the evening; (*c*) (see quot. 1927); (*d*) the side of a planet that is facing away from the sun and is therefore in darkness; **night-sight,** (*b*) a rifle-sight designed for shooting at night; (*c*) = Night-vision 2 a; **night spot,** a night-club or similar place open to pleasure-seekers at night; **night starvation,** hunger at night; also *transf.*, lack of sexual gratification; **night-stick** orig. *U.S.*, a stick or truncheon carried by a policeman or the like, esp. at night; also *attrib.*; **night-stop,** a place where one stops for the night; the action of stopping at such a place; hence as *v. intr.*, to stop for the night; **night storage heater** or **radiator,** an electric heater in which heat can be accumulated at night and released during the day; so *night-stored* ppl. adj.; **night-watchman,** (*a*) a person employed to keep watch at night; (*b*) in *Cricket*, a batsman who goes in to bat just before the end of a day's play.

1961 I. Jefferies *It wasn't Me!* x. 132 When the moon was up I let an hour pass to make sure my eyes were night-adapted. 1972 J. Poyer *Chinese Agenda* (1973) xi. 144 Just enough light for Gillon's night-adapted vision. 1834 Night adder [in Dict., sense 13 d]. 1915 *Chambers's Jrnl.* July 437/2 The night-adder, as its name implies, is most in evidence after sundown. 1947 J. Stevenson-Hamilton *Wild Life S. Afr.* xxxvi. 329 The Night Adder (*Causus rhombeatus*). *Ibid.*, I have often seen my cats eating night adders which they have caught and killed. 1966 C. Sweeney *Scurrying Bush* vii. 98 The night adder was writhing in some discomfort. 1832 J. Lindley *Introd. Bot.* IV. 402 Of a night (*nocturnus*); which appears during the night, and perishes before morning; as the flowers of the night-blooming cereus. 1890 *Harper's Mag.* Mar. 613/1 My wife has a sweet face of her own, but one bearing the same relation to Miss Jasmine's as that existing between a sprig of mignonette and a night-blooming cereus. 1936 *Times Lit. Suppl.* 20 June 521/2 The flowering of the night-blooming cereus..is very lovingly described. 1971 E. L. Wardman *Bermuda Jubilee Garden* 199/2 Night-blooming cereus. A vine-like plant with triangular stems... Useful for clambering over a wall or rock face and even growing up a tree... Its very beautiful flowers open only after sunset and shrivel and die before morning. 1908 *Paris Fashions* 18 Jan. 23/2 Costume of night-blue cloth. 1938 L. MacNeice *I crossed Minch* II. viii. 106 The sky part of the landscape was night-blue. 1956 D. Gascoyne *Night Thoughts* 45 That profound night-blue abyss of starry vacancy. 1970 R. P. Warren *Incarnations* 17 On night-blue the tetter of cloud-scud. 1918 *Flying* 4 Sept. 221 (*caption*) A British night-bomber photographed by searchlight. 1919 R. H. Reece *Night Bombing with Bedouins* 57 These calculations are all important to the long-distance night bomber. 1936 *Economist* 11 Jan. 85/2 The Fairey Company is an air-frame concern which is chiefly interested in the 'Hendon' night bomber. 1975 *Listener* 13 Mar. 335/1 Scheduled air services began on 25 August 1919..using ten- and 12-seated converted night bombers. 1942 W. S. Churchill *End of Beginning* (1943) 118 These two great night-bombing raids mark the introduction of a new phase in the British air offensive against Germany. 1925 A. S. M. Hutchinson *One Increasing Purpose* I. xxvi. 161 As if the phrase were a path on which, nightbound and groping, he suddenly had stumbled. *Ibid.* II. ii. 203 A finger-post whose word the nightbound traveller hates to obey yet may not disbelieve. 1954 L. MacNeice *Autumn Sequel* 123 From my seat I see my night-bound double, slumped apart On a conveyor belt. 1938 *New Statesman* 23 July 154/1, I have very rarely been overcharged in France (except in the grotesque night-boxes of Montmartre). 1973 E. McGirr *Bardel's Murder* iv. 108 Night boxes.. came and they went, and the more crowded the more successful. 1904 E. Glasgow *Deliverance* 45 He had fastened the night-chain and shot the heavy bolt. 1973 'E. McBain' *Let's hear It* xiv. 205 Kling heard the night chain being slipped off, the lock turning. 1968 J. M. White *Nightclimber* iv. 28, I had repeated the whole series of safaris among the tiles and chimneypots pioneered by the Night-climbers. *Ibid.* 27, I didn't realise you were interested in night-climbing. 1911 F. J. Britten *Old Clocks & Watches* (ed. 3) v. 266 A night clock..is of ebony on oak, and the top lifts off to allow the insertion of a lamp. Showing through a curved slit in the upper part of the dial is a disc with perforated hour numerals so that the time can be seen at night. The light would also shine through a keyhole-shaped aperture above which serves as a pointer. 1972 *Times* 7 Nov. 25/4 (Advt.), A rare 17th century night clock, by Edward East, London. 1882 J. D. McCabe *New York* 383 The entire force on duty at the station dashed into the street, armed with their long night clubs. 1894 W. J. Locke *At Gate of Samaria* (1903) xxvii. 319 They went together to East End music-halls,.. night clubs in the West End, where ladies are admitted free on a member's introduction. 1906 R. Machray *Night Side of London* i. 21 Finishing up, perhaps, at some night-club, or in some other den. 1915 Night club [see *cabaret[1] 2 b]. 1928 F. B. Young *My Brother Jonathan* II. viii. 355 A life of night-clubs and jazz-bands. 1938 *Amer. Speech* XIII. 194 Pleasure seekers at first went to night clubs; now, at least in the columns of the Broadway gossips, they simply *night-club*. 1965 *New Statesman* 9 Apr. 557/2 The sharp limitation in the circumstances in which business-men can wine and dine and nightclub other businessmen. 1972 P. Driscoll *Wilby Conspiracy* (1973) xi. 138 That bitch of a nightclub singer. 1974 *Listener* 31 Jan. 131/1 The foreboding, the mounting menace, that we can trace through, say, the night-club songs of the Weimar republic. 1952 B. Ulanov *Hist. Jazz in Amer.* (1958) xv. 177 From the general hubbub of night clubs and the particular cries and grunts of night-clubbers..Bubber made his music. 1953 'S. Ransome' *Hear No Evil* (1954) xv. 138 Bendley, a confirmed night-clubber. 1936 R. Lehmann *Weather in Streets* I. v. 90 No, she never married. .. Does some little odd jobs and goes lunching and dining and night-clubbing. 1941 Hermer & May *Havana Mañana* p. xii, There have been no books about Havana that show tourists how to get more than their money's worth out of stopping, eating, sightseeing and nightclubbing. 1947 *Sun* (Baltimore) 4 Aug. 1/2 Senator Pepper (D. Fla.) today tabbed as possibly 'base judgment' the 1943 night clubbing activities which Elliott Roosevelt will be asked to explain tomorrow to senators investigating Howard Hughes's wartime plane contracts. 1971 D. Bagley *Freedom Trap* viii. 181 Too much damned night-clubbing. 1933 G. B. Shaw *Political Madhouse in Amer.* 48 You have become a wonderful night clubby sort of nation. 1958 *New Statesman* 6 Sept. 314/2 A nightclubby girl 'with a spurious American accent' is a minor character in the recent *Sober as a Judge* by Henry Cecil. 1844 Night-coach [in Dict., sense 13]. 1959 *Wall St. Jrnl.* (Eastern ed.) 7 Oct. 8/4 Standard first class Miami–New York fare one-way is $80.80, regular daycoach is $54.55 and regular nightcoach is $46.80. 1960 *Daily Progress* (Charlottesville, Va.) 6 Jan., A National Airlines night coach flying non-stop from New York to Miami crashed with 34 persons aboard. 1924 *Collier's* 2 Feb. 3/1 He could stay up till 10 and hunt night crawlers in the garden with a lantern. 1948 *Esquire* Mar. 88 Members of the Huck Finn school of fishing..have been looking for some way to enliven the almost impossibly sluggish night crawler. 1951 T. Capote *Grass Harp* (1952) ii. 64 Night-crawlers slithered away from its lurching light. 1971 B. Malamud *Tenants* 12 Lesser tried to scare off the nightcrawlers on his floor.. by playing loud his hi-fi at night. 1973 *Islander* (Victoria, B.C.) 5 Aug. 13/2 Sympathy and practical help poured in from every direction. Small donations of native worms—night crawlers—were the most practical help. 1926–7 *Army & Navy Stores Catal.* 496/2 Day Cream... Massage Cream... Night Cream. 1963 D. Gray *Murder in Mind* iii. 23 Except for a thick night cream, she took so little [care] of her face. 1956 *This Week* 29 July 11/2 If you must night-drive, keep the dash-lights as dim as possible—this particular glare is hypnotic. 1929 *Times* 31 Oct. 21/3 Those who have used this latest device under actual night-driving conditions are unanimous in their praise. 1936 *Discovery* Oct. 302/1 The application of a sheet of.. Polaroid..should remove one of the greatest inconveniences of night driving. 1962 L. S. Sasieni *Optical Dispensing* xiii. 327 There have been introduced from time to time certain glasses said to increase vision in low illumination—and so-called night-driving glasses. There are many arguments as to the merits and demerits of tinted glasses for night driving. 1914 R. Stanley *Text-bk. Wireless Telegr.* x. 114 The difference between day and night effects on the transmitted ether energy might possibly be caused by a change in the position of the upper conducting layer of atmosphere. 1932 F. E. Terman *Radio Engineering* xvi. 591 Since the sky wave is always strongest at night the errors that result from downcoming horizontally polarized waves are frequently referred to as 'night effects' although they are always present to some extent in daytime. 1962 J. H. & P. J. Reyner *Radio Communication* viii. 333 A phenomenon which considerably affects D.F. work is what is known as 'night effect'. 1921 *Flight* XIII. 664/1 Aircraft when within an area northward of the parallel of latitude 51° 10′ 00″ N., and westward of the meridian of longitude 8° 30′ 00″ W., should not ask for bearings from Carnsore, as such bearings..will probably be unreliable on account of the effect of the coastline, the night error in particular being of considerable magnitude. 1936 *Jrnl. R. Aeronaut. Soc.* XL. 161 These wave-lengths are subject to night error which affects the accuracy of bearings taken on medium wave direction finders. 1948 *Sat. Even. Post* 29 May 116/1 Six photographs are taken—a front view, side view and close-ups of the horse's four 'chestnuts', or 'night eyes', which are the rough protrusions of scaly, hardened skin that are on the inner side of each leg. 1954 J. R. R. Tolkien *Fellowship of Ring* II. ix. 402 It was dark, but not too dark for the night-eyes of Orcs. 1956 I. Fleming *Diamonds are Forever* viii. 80 'The Jockey Club are going to change to photos of the night eyes [to help identify race horses].' 'What are night eyes?' 'They're those callouses on the inside of a horse's knees. The English call them 'chestnuts'. Seems they're different on every horse. Like a man's fingerprints.' 1957 'J. Wyndham' *Midwich Cuckoos* ii. 21 The last customers to be persuaded out of The Scythe and Stone had lingered for a few minutes to get their night-eyes and gone their ways. 1963 M. A. Stoneridge *Horse of your Own* ii. 75 Inside each of the horse's legs you will notice a sort of horny excrescence called Chestnuts or Night Eyes, which are vestigial toes (remember, prehistoric horses had four or five of them). Night Eyes vary in form with no two alike; they are as individual as human fingerprints and recorded as part of the identification system for thoroughbred race horses and registered trotters. 1941 *Aeronautics* Jan. 41/3 The effective range of fire of night fighter aircraft will have to be increased. 1941 *Times* (Weekly ed.) 5 Feb. 15 The defence by night-fighter aeroplanes was the most difficult task of anti-aircraft defences. 1942 *Tee Emm* (Air Ministry) II. 62 That..is the gist, or guts, of the night-fighter pilot's training. *Ibid.* 85 Particularly important this for night-fighters. 1947 J. Mulgan *Report on Experience* vi. 80 Meeting sometimes night-fighters or flak coming back over the coast defences. 1933 *Meccano Mag.* Feb. 109/1 Night fighting consists chiefly of individual attacks at close range. 1947 Crowther & Whiddington *Science at War* 60 The radar air interception equipments, used in the early night-fighting battles. 1789 W. Aiton *Hortus Kewensis* II. 152 Great Night-flowering Cereus. Nat[ive] of Jamaica and Vera Cruz. 1853 C. R. Read *What I heard, saw, & did at Austral. Gold Fields* 150 (Morris), The man was what they called a night fossicker, who slept, or did nothing during the day, and then went round at night to where he knew the claims to be rich, and stole the stuff by candle-light. 1889 *Cent. Dict.*, Night-fossicking. 1884 R. Aldridge *Life on Ranch* 62 When on night-herd the men usually keep singing all the time as they ride round. 1903 A. Adams *Log of Cowboy* ii. 11 Forrest night herded them using five guards. *Ibid.* vii. 97 We night herded as usual. 1955 R. P. Hobson *Nothing too Good for Cowboy* viii. 71 Simrose and Rob came in from their night-herd shift. 1962 W. Stegner *Wolf Willow* III. ii. 163 Everything he said or played or sang during his hours on the night herd was meant seriously. 1963 R. D. Symons *Many Trails* 37 We certainly did not propose to night herd. 1873 J. H. Beadle *Undevel. West* v. 98 The 'night-herder' Billy Keyes, and two other drivers..were Gentiles. 1891 Night herder [in Dict., sense 13 c]. 1888 *Chambers's Jrnl.* Apr. 221/1 This is called night-herding. 1890 Night-herding [in Dict., sense 12 b]. 1908 *Sat. Even. Post* 24 Oct. 10/1 A long-eared, reddish, sleepy-eyed..mule frequently used in night-herding. 1933 J. V. Allen *Cowboy Lore* IV. 71 David went from night-herding to using a sling. 1908 *Sat. Even. Post* 4 July 22/3 They made Blackie a night horse, for his sure-footedness was remarkable. 1925 J. Farnol *Loring Mystery* xlii. 283 'Talking o' bed,' quoth Mr. Shrig .., 'do you ever dream —— d'ye ever have the night-'orse?' 1929 *Amer. Speech* V. 67 Usually the 'kept horses' or 'herding horses' are also 'night horses', those used for 'night herding'. 1937 *Dialect Notes* VI. 618 The night horse is one staked near the cowpuncher's bed for immediate use in some such emergency as a stampede. 1959 C. MacInnes *Absolute Beginners* 81 The capital was a night-horse dream. 1967 *Coast to Coast 1965–66* 195 The smell of the night-horse nearby and the cattle a little beyond will tie you to reality. 1895 G. Meredith *Amaz. Marriage* I. xxiii. 258 Night-larks of different classes, both sexes. 1852 H. Melville *Pierre* XVI. i. 322 All the garish night-life of a vast thoroughfare, crowded and wedged by day, and even now, at this late hour, brilliant with occasional illuminations. 1913 H. L. Mencken *Let.* 17 Aug. (1961) 32 The title 'Night Life in Vienna'..has the air of a lure held out to the Puritanical and dirty-minded. 1927 G. Ade et al. *Let.* 4 Mar. (1973) 119 Our fellow-passengers ..were ashore last night, dancing and hunting up a second-rate African imitation of night life in Paris. 1929 D. L. Moore *Pandora's Letter Box* iii. 53 'Night life'—to use the popular expression for habitual nocturnal dancing and drinking. 1972 *Sat. Rev.* (U.S.) 25 Mar. 68/3 The Kabarett, with its sharp political satire, was part of Berlin night life. 1967 W. Soyinka *Kongi's Harvest* 13 A few night-lifers pick up their drinks and go in. 1767 A. B. *Short Acct. Life Mary of Holy Cross* 84 In the Time of St. Peter Damian, only the Clergy rose to the Night Office. 1909 M. B. Saunders *Litany Lane* I. iii. 34 A small chapel in which the brothers held their short night-office. 1957 *Oxf. Dict. Chr. Church* 960/1 *Night office*, another name for Mattins, the liturgical office prescribed for the night. 1916 W. Owen *Let.* 6 Apr. (1967) 388 We had 'Night Ops.' yesterday till 9.30! *Ibid.* 10 Apr. 390 We had Night Operations again. 1930 *Bulletin* (Sydney) 29 Jan. 62/4 He strode up to the big, heavily-capped yards in the corner of the night-paddock. 1950 *N.Z. Jrnl. Agric.* Jan. 71/2 Night paddocks on dairy farms showed least response [to potash topdressing]. 1966 *Te Reo* IX. 54 The apparently Australian innovation lies..in the adoption of the refined terminology of the *home paddock* and the *night paddock*. 1917 *Chambers's Jrnl.* Feb. 89/1 Even on moonlight nights I could never catch a glimpse of the flying night-parrots. 1934 *Bulletin* (Sydney) 9 May 21/1 The night parrot..continues to hide itself from human ken, and is always referred to either as the elusive parrot or mystery bird. 1965 *Austral. Encycl.* VII. 27/2 A second remarkable parrot of the ground is one known as the night parrot, sole member of the genus *Geopsittacus*, which is, or used to be, distributed widely throughout the drier parts of the inland region. It is closely associated with the spiny spinifex or porcupine-grass, hiding in the thick clusters by day, feeding on their seeds at night. 1877 J. M Wells *Chisolm Massacre* x. 118 They said that night-riders had shot into the houses of the colored people. 1879 *Congress. Rec.* 20 May 1480/1 There was much said..of kuklux, white leagues, and night-riders... There are..no night-riders in the State of Louisiana. 1882 F. W. P. Jago *Anc. Lang. & Dial. Cornwall* 226 *Night-riders*, Piskey (Fairy) people who have been riding Tom (the name of a horse) again. 1906 Kipling *Puck of Pook's Hill* 10 Leprechauns, night-riders, pixies, nixies. 1907 *Lit. Digest* 28 Dec. 976 The first appearance of the night riders was in November, 1906, when they destroyed some tobacco-barns and small factories in Todd County. 1911 J. Masefield *Jim Davis* ii. 12 They were the night-riders or smugglers. 1936 J. G. Miller *Black Patch War* 18 The Night Rider burnt his warehouse and his purchase with it. 1948 E. N. Dick *Dixie Frontier* 94 Patrols, called patterols by the slaves, were organized by the whites, and these night riders endeavored to enforce the regulations. 1970 *New Yorker* 12 Dec. 166/3 Night riders who fire shotgun blasts at the home of an anti-war leader..are routine. 1973 J. Cleary *Ransom* viii. 184 As a plainclothesman he had travelled on late trains out of Sydney to the suburbs, riding shotgun as it were against hooligans... Night riders, he guessed, were the same everywhere. 1875 *Chicago Tribune* 6 Nov. 3/6 To-night..there is to be a 'night riding' and shooting..to arouse a degree of uneasiness in the darky's mind and cause him..not to go to the election. 1909

Chambers's Jrnl. Feb. 104/1 Night riding began as soon as the farmers' associations were organised. **1952** C. Day Lewis tr. *Virgil's Aeneid* x. 215 The gentle Moon's Night-riding horses were pacing halfway across the heavens. **1930** W. Thomson *Dict. Banking* (ed. 7) 501/2 *Night safes.* In order that customers may deposit cash or cheques after a bank has closed for the day or for the week-end, night safes were introduced in 1928. The entrance to these safes is in the outside wall of the bank, the opening being fitted with a locked cover to which customers who wish to avail themselves of the safe are supplied with a key. **1959** *Times* 18 Feb. 11/5 Night safes don't cash cheques. **1975** 'M. Yorke' *Small Hours* iii. 31 Ray had tracked down one of the night-safe depositors. [**1824** H. Phillips *Flora Historica* I. 336 We have no plant that exhales so delightful a fragrance in the night as the..Night-smelling Rocket, or Night Odorous Stock.] **1849** Night-scented stock [see *night-scented*, sense 12 c]. **1870** W. Robinson *Wild Garden* II. 54 Night-scented Stock... May be established on the sunny sides of old ruins and walls. **1914** E. A. Bowles *My Garden in Summer* xiv. 259 The old Night-scented Stock of one's great-grandmother, is another half-hardy indispensable. **1972** *Country Life* 23 Mar. 690/1 Seeds of small annuals such as night-scented stock..I broadcast by scattering them over the ground. **1848, 1855** Night side [in Dict., sense 13]. **1898** *Shetland News* 10 Dec., If Willie id been some boys, diel wird he'd sung i' da night side. **1900** *Ibid.* 26 May, Dis kirn is no laek ta brak i' da night side. **1927** *Amer. Speech* II. 242/2 On papers having both morning and afternoon editions one also hears references to the two divisions of the staff as the 'day side' and the 'night side'. **1951** A. C. Clarke *Sands of Mars* viii. 94 It was a live programme, beamed to Mars from somewhere on the night-side of Earth. **1970** *Nature* 7 Mar. 925/1 On the nightside of Venus at altitudes between 750 km and 1,450 km the presence of a light ion was inferred. **1973** G. Greene *Honorary Consul* v. iii. 285 Suppose the night-side of God swallows up the day-side altogether? Suppose it is the good side which withers away? **1974** *Nature* 4 Jan. 24/1 The orbit is near-polar with the north-going passes on the nightside at about 2230 LT, and the south-going passes on the dayside at about 1030 LT. **1915** *Chambers's Jrnl.* Apr. 269/2 The night-sight does not interfere with the ordinary front-sight for daylight shooting. **1971** *Guardian Weekly* 6 Nov. 12 Our marksman..saw him clearly through his night-sight. **1972** B. Everitt *Cold Front* xv. 143 My night-sight is good and I drove on side-lights only. **1973** 'D. Halliday' *Dolly & Starry Bird* ii. 29 At night the full lights in the cupola never go on. They would spoil the plate and ruin your night sight. **1936** *Swing Music* Mar. 9/1 The management at the Friar's Inn, well-known Chicago night spot, was very anxious to feature this new type of music. **1947** *Sun* (Baltimore) 4 Aug. 1/2 He was the guest of John Meyer, publicity man, in a costly round of New York night spots. **1959** F. Usher *Death in Error* i. 18 They went to a night spot.. where they drank champagne. **1973** *Express* (Trinidad & Tobago) 26 June 4/6 A flash fire..swept through a New Orleans night spot. **1936** 'G. Orwell' *Keep Aspidistra Flying* xii. 311 What they asked for was a really telling slogan; something in the class of 'Night-starvation'..that would rankle in the public consciousness. **1949** Partridge *Dict. Slang* (ed. 3) Add. 1119/1 *Night starvation,* sexual deprivation, lack of sexual intimacy. **1970** *Southerly* XXX. 286 David's head is in the right place—night starvation—Horlicks—Venus de Milo. **1971** D. Lees *Rainbow Conspiracy* viii. 117 It wasn't as if I was suffering from night starvation. Val was easily one of the best screws in the business. **1974** *Harpers & Queen* Sept. 135/1 My bread rolls she secretes..against night starvation. **1887** W. E. S. Fales *Brooklyn's Guardians* ii. 30 In the wealthier thoroughfares the brawls were of so frequent occurrence that the sight of two watchmen..pounding each other with their night-sticks, occasioned no comment. **1893** S. Crane *Maggie* xi. 102 The officer made a terrific advance, club in hand. One comprehensive sweep of the long night stick threw the ally to the floor. **1904** 'No. 1500' *Life in Sing Sing* i. 10 Big clubs, heavier and more formidable than a policeman's night stick. **1905** *N.Y. Times* 15 July, San Juan Hill and the Gut were under nightstick law until early this morning. **1932** *New Yorker* 4 June 23 There's a lot of law at the end of a nightstick. **1963** T. & P. Morris *Pentonville* x. 209 Hospital officers do not carry night sticks. **1973** J. Wambaugh *Blue Knight* i. 18 A beat cop has to be big..or..somebody'd take the nightstick off him and shove it up his ass. **1975** *Daily Tel.* 30 June 1/5 Police chased the demonstrators down the streets [of Delhi], stopping occasionally to swing at anyone in their way with heavy wooden nightsticks. **1791** J. Byng *Diary* 3 July in *Torrington Diaries* (1935) II. 360 Dunnington, a small market-town, where I dined..in a quiet house, but not a night-stop. **1951** 'N. Shute' *Round the Bend* 232 Next day took us to Karachi, where we night-stopped before going on to Bahrein. **1959** *New Statesman* 8 Aug. 151/1 When coming back from India took five days, with agreeable night-stops along the way, it was quite pleasant. **1972** C. Kearey *Last Plane from Uli* ii. 34 'Are you night-stopping, sir?' the Immigration Chief asked curiously. 'No, I'm taking off for Lagos as soon as the refuelling's finished.' **1975** *Daily Tel.* (Colour Suppl.) 4 Apr. 16/1 Had the supervisors declared the plane unserviceable, another 747..due to night-stop in London would have been allocated to take her place. **1963** *Good Housek. Setting up Home* iii. 30 Electric night storage heaters. These are electric heaters which..absorb and store heat during the night when off-peak rates for electricity are available, releasing it during the day. **1970** *House & Garden* Mar. 94/3 The eight-hour-charge night-storage radiators..are able to store enough heat to give an even heat output for the rest of the day. **1973** *Guardian* 23 May 9/6 Night storage heaters are metal boxes filled with bricks wired for electric heating. **1962** *Daily Tel.* 20 Aug. 16/2 (*heading*) Night-stored heat from electricity. **1863** A. D. Whitney *Faith Gartney's Girlhood* xxviii. 261 Michael Garvin, the night-watchman,..had left. **1874** Night-watchman [in Dict., sense 13 c]. **1926** J. Masefield *Odtaa* xiii. 214 There must be at least a caretaker or night-watchman. **1949** Partridge *Dict. Slang* (ed. 3) Add. 1119/1 *Night-watchman,* a (usually a second-rate) batsman sent in to 'hold up an end' until the close of play. **1971** *Sunday Times* 2 May 24 The fifth [ball] was caught by Turner off the nightwatchman Wasim Bari's glove and shoulder.

night-bird. **2.** (Later examples.)

1870 D. J. Kirwan *Palace & Hovel* xxxii. 481 When the dancing places..close, this door remains open to catch all stray night birds who can find no other resting place. **1871** G. Easton *Trav. Amer.* 41 In Boston the cars run till midnight, and after that time one car runs every hour through the principal thoroughfare for the accommodation of 'Night Birds'. **1900** [see *brunch]. **1939** Joyce *Finnegans Wake* 438, I have every reason to know that rogues' gallery of nightbirds and bitchfanciers. **1974** 'J. Le Carré' *Tinker, Tailor* xxxv. 313 It was nearly midnight... He was a night bird.

night-cap. Add: **3.** Also, a non-alcoholic drink taken at bedtime.

1930 *Daily Tel.* 9 Apr. 11/7 (Advt.), 'Ovaltine'... The world's best 'night-cap' to ensure sound, natural sleep. **1959** *New Statesman* 1 Aug. 141/3 A greater number of housewives than ever before realised the goodness of Bovril..for use as a beverage during the day, a night-cap, and for adding to savoury dishes. **1975** 'C. Aird' *Slight Mourning* ii. 18 Sloan's own nightcap was usually milky coffee.

4. The final event in one day's series of sporting contests; *spec.* the second of two baseball games played by the same two teams on a single day. *N. Amer. colloq.*

1939 Webster Add., *Nightcap,* the final race or contest of a day's sports. **1941** *Sun* (Baltimore) 22 Sept. 1/1 The Cardinals pulled the opening game out of the fire with a daring bit of base running..to win 6–5, and took the nightcap, 7–0. **1942** Berrey & Van den Bark *Amer. Thes. Slang* § 675/6 Second game of a 'double-header',.. *nightcap.* **1969** *Internat. Herald Tribune* (Paris) 6 Nov. 13/1 In the nightcap, Baltimore's Wes Unseld..sat out much of the game because of foul trouble. **1970** *Toronto Daily Star* 24 Sept. 17/1 In the nightcap, Jerry Reuss permitted seven hits. **1974** *Union* (S. Carolina) *Daily Times* 22 Apr. 6/2 The Orioles edged New York 6–5 in 13 innings in the opener of a doubleheader and then protested the nightcap, which they lost 3–0.

night-dress. Add: **2.** *attrib.,* as **night-dress bag, case,** a bag or other container in which a night-dress can be placed when it is not being worn.

1975 *Times* 25 Nov. 2/6 He tried to punch her and hit a toy dog nightdress bag instead. **1907** *Yesterday's Shopping* (1969) p. xlvi/4 Night Dress Cases. **1932** D. C. Minter *Mod. Needlecraft* 218/2 A triangular embroidered night-dress case. **1969** 'G. North' *Procrastination of Sergeant Cluff* xv. 151 The night-dress case in the shape of a toy Koala-bear that growled when she lifted it.

ni·ght-flying, *vbl. sb.* [f. Night *sb.* + Flying *vbl. sb.*] Flying in an aircraft by night. Also *attrib.* Hence **ni·ght-fly** *v. intr.*

1907 A. C. Johnson *How to find Time at Sea* (ed. 6) 9 Steering by the stars, for night flying, night marching and night boat-work. **1918** *War Illustr.* 13 July 372/2 The petrol or electric flares, which are placed on all night-flying aerodromes for landing purposes. **1927** *Daily Tel.* 31 May 13/2 We night-fly regularly in America. It's the ideal time for flying in the States. **1935** [see *directional *a.* 5]. **1945** *Tee Emm* (Air Ministry) V. 42 He thought the obstructions were left over from the previous night's night-flying taxi path. **1973** 'A. Hall' *Tango Briefing* xviii. 222 'Is there any chance of a flarepath on that strip?' 'No. They don't night-fly.'

nightglow (nəi·tglōᵘ). *Meteorol.* [f. Night *sb.* + Glow *sb.*] The faint light emitted by the upper atmosphere at night.

1951 Roach & Pettit in *Jrnl. Geophysical Res.* LVI. 325 Many investigators..have reported that the intensity of the green nightglow line at 5577 Å has a maximum near the observer's local midnight. *Ibid.,* The general term 'airglow' is used for radiations originating in the upper atmosphere. We use the term 'nightglow' to connote airglow at night to distinguish it from similar radiations which may be present (though not observable) in the daytime. **1955** *Sci. Amer.* Sept. 150/2 These studies show that the nightglow is faintest at the zenith overhead and grows in intensity down the sky until it reaches a maximum about 10 degrees above the horizon. **1967** R. W. Fairbridge *Encycl. Atmospheric Sci. & Astrogeol.* 9/1 It has become usual to distinguish these differing kinds of airglow by the names 'twilight glow' and 'dayglow', in distinction to the 'nightglow'. **1972** *Sci. Amer.* Jan. 78/2 The nightglow can be observed with a photometer or a spectrometer.

night-hawk. **1. b.** Substitute for def.: A predominantly nocturnal bird of the genus *Chordeiles,* esp. *C. minor,* belonging to the nightjar family, Caprimulgidæ. (Earlier and later examples.)

1793 W. Bentley *Diary* 22 Aug. (1909) II. 48 We observed a great number of the birds, called here [*sc.* at Charlestown, N.H.] night hawks, playing in the air. **1913** W. P. Pritchard *Barn Doors & Byways* 119 The naturalists tell us that the night-hawks nest on top of the Manhattan skyscrapers. **1962** O. L. Austin *Birds of World* 163/2 The plaintive buzzing calls of Nighthawks are now commonly heard above the traffic noises of many American cities as the birds course high over the rooftops in their buoyant, dancing search for flying insects. **1968** R. M. Patterson *Finlay's River* 123 The dew was starting to fall..and the thrum of the night-hawk was sounding from the upper air. **1974** D. Sears *Lark in Clear Air* vi. 73 A night-hawk beeped high and out of sight.

2. (Further examples.) Also, one who stays up late at night; a person who goes out or works at night; *spec.* = **night-herder* (see also quots.).

1868 'Mark Twain' *Let.* 8 Jan. (1920) 80 Jack Van Nostrand, Dan and I, (all Quaker City night-hawks,) had a blow-out at Dan's house. **1903** W. D. Coburn *Rhymes from Round-up Camp* (rev. ed.) 18 Cotton-Eye, the night-hawk, Was then a top cow-hand. **1915** *Dialect Notes* IV. 209 *Night-hawk,* a thief or harlot. 'Those night-hawks ought to be taken up and sent home if they don't know enough to go.' **1929** F. Bowen *Sea Slang* 95 *Night hawks,* night watchmen stewards. **1934** A. Woollcott *While Rome Burns* 180 Your correspondent, a nighthawk of parts in those days, was within ear-shot. **1948** *Sierra Club Bull.* (San Francisco) Mar. 22 Ed Thistlethwaite..was our night hawk. It was to be his job..to get up and watch the dawn in the high and relatively high pasture lands to which the stock had been pushed, then to round them up and bring them down to work. **1972** J. Metcalf *Going Down Slow* vi. 108 As the hour wore on to eleven p.m. she excused herself and retired, always calling them 'night-hawks'.

nightie, nightie-night(ie): see *nighty *sb.,* *nighty-night *int.*

nightingale[1]**.** Add: **1. c.** Also *Cambridgeshire nightingale.* The edible frog, *Rana esculenta,* which was introduced into East Anglia early in the nineteenth century.

1881 *Brewer's Dict. Phr. & Fable* (ed. 12) 615/2 Cambridgeshire nightingales, edible frogs. **1975** *Country Life* 20 Feb. 455/2 The lakes, canals and meres of East Anglia became well stocked with [edible] frogs... Locals called these invaders Cambridgeshire nightingales.

4. nightingale floor, in Japan, a floor that emits a high-pitched sound when it is trodden on.

1959 S. Sitwell *Bridge of Brocade Sash* v. 113 As for the squeaking,..the Japanese..will not allow it to be a 'nightingale floor', and leave it at that, but have to remark it is so constructed that 'at every step the boards emit a sound resembling that of *uguishu,* Japanese bush warbler'. **1964** I. Fleming *You only live Twice* v. 62 This..is what the Japanese call a 'nightingale floor'... Imagine trying to get across here without being heard.

nightingale[2]**.** Add: **2.** *attrib.,* as **Nightingale ward,** a type of hospital ward designed to accommodate several patients in one room.

1964 G. L. Cohen *What's Wrong with Hospitals?* ii. 37 Long after the austere open dormitory had been abandoned abroad, Britain doggedly went on building 'Nightingale wards'. **1970** *Guardian* 10 Sept. 13/1 Cubicles instead of Nightingale wards mean that nurses escape being constantly overseen.

night letter. [f. Night *sb.* + Letter *sb.*[1]] **a.** In full **night telegraph letter,** a cheap-rate inland telegram delivered overnight. (Said in the 1945 P.O. Guide 'to be suspended'. The similar *overnight telegram* service was introduced in 1955.) Cf. *lettergram.

1912 *Post Office Guide* Apr. 94 A service of night telegraph letters is in operation between London and Aberdeen and between London and Belfast. The rate is 6*d.* for 36 words or less and ½*d.* for every 3 words beyond 36. Night Telegraph letters are delivered (except on Sunday) by the first post next morning. **1912** *Times* 29 May 3/4 Night telegraph letters may be posted prepaid at the rates given above. **1938** E. T. Crutchley *G.P.O.* vii. 146 There are various by-products of the telegraph system about which the ordinary man-in-the-street remains strangely ignorant. For instance there is the Night Telegraph Letter which provides a means of communication after the usual posting hour, and at a cheaper rate than by the ordinary telegraph service. **1940** *Post Office Guide* Aug. 413 Night telegraph letters, which are accepted at any time and delivered by first postal delivery the next week-day or by special messenger shortly afterwards. Minimum charge 1*s.* 3*d.* for 36 words. **1953** H. Robinson *Britain's Post Office* xix. 258 A successful effort was made [*sc.* in the 1930s] to give the public a knowledge of the advantages of night-telegraph letters.

b. In full **night letter telegram,** a cheap-rate overseas telegram (see quots.). (Discontinued after 1949.)

[**1913** *Post Office Guide* Jan. 883 The Night and Week-end Cable Letter Services are not available viâ the Commercial or French Telegraph Cable Companies' routes... Night Cable Letters are accepted on the condition that they will not be delivered before the day after they are received at the Cable Companies' Stations.] **1914** *Ibid.* Apr. 896 (*heading*) Night and week-end letter telegrams for Canada, Newfoundland and the United States. *Ibid.,* Night Letter Telegrams are accepted on the condition that they will not be delivered before the day following that on which they are received at the Telegraph Companies' Stations. **1934** 'E. M. Delafield' *Provincial Lady in America* 234 She gets such quantities of night letters and cables from abroad. **1949** *Post Office Guide* July 229 Night Letter Telegrams (NLT) may be sent to North and South America, British territories in Africa, Egypt, West Indies, certain British territories in the Far East, India, Pakistan and many other places outside Europe at one-third the rates for ordinary telegrams. They are normally delivered on the morning following the day of handing in. The minimum charge is as for 25 words. **1966** N. Freeling *King of Rainy Country* 33 The War Office in London ..promised to get him off a night letter. **1973** T. Tobin in Ade *Lett.* 1 George Ade sent the above night letter to Ashton Stevens in reply to the drama critic's request for an autobiographical sketch to insert in his *Chicago Herald*

and Examiner column, April 30, 1930. The night letter to Stevens illustrates the image Ade manifested throughout his career.

nightman. Add: **2.** (Earlier and later examples.) Also, one who works illegally at night; a burglar.

1851 H. MELVILLE *Moby Dick* III. xlix. 293 The solitary night-man at the fore-mast-head. **1928** *Amer. Mercury* May 78/1 *Rowdy-dowdy*..was borrowed from the more aristocratic *night-men*, who use it in this manner: 'Charge on a town, make as many clouts on the *kiester* (safe) as necessary, and then battle the irate citizens in a *rowdy-dowdy* get-a-way.' **1957** M. BANTON *W. Afr. City* v. 87 The people hated any type of investigator because so many of them were 'night men' (i.e. made an illegal living after dark). **1960** *Times* 29 Sept. 7/1 A company taxi is usually driven by both a day-man and a night-man.

nightmare, *sb.* Add: **2. b.** (Further examples.)

1909 *Chambers's Jrnl.* Feb. 75/2 From tip to tip of its outstretched arms this nightmare of the deep measured 56 feet. **1956** A. L. ROWSE *Early Churchills* 32 A great deal of genuine learning is displayed, a nightmare of authorities cited in the Elizabethan fashion. **1975** M. BABSON *There must be some Mistake* xiii. 100 'It's a nightmare,' Karen agreed. '..I wake up and it's still there.'

3. *nightmare-dreamer, -land; nightmare-like* adj. and adv.; *nightmare-ridden* adj.

1954 KOESTLER *Invisible Writing* vii. 76, I am a chronic nightmare-dreamer. **1957** E. HYAMS *Into Dream* 246 For twenty-four hours he had been living in wonderland, nightmareland. **1847** J. R. LOWELL *Let. from Boston* in *Pennsylvania Freeman* 1 Jan. 3/3 His words burn as with iron-searers, And nightmare-like he mounts his hearers. **1919** WODEHOUSE *Damsel in Distress* xv. 176 This blister had become the one great Fact in an unreal nightmare-like universe. **1926** C. PLUMB in *Oxford Poetry* 36 Plagued, nightmare-ridden by a million lusts. **1961** *Times* 10 Nov. 18/7 Schoenberg's nightmare-ridden territory.

nightmarey, var. NIGHTMARY *a.*

1851 [see NIGHTMARY *a.*]. **1934** H. NICOLSON *Diary* 24 Mar. (1966) 172, I am..very apprehensive and nightmarey.

nightmarishly, *adv.* (Further examples.)

1915 A. BENNETT *These Twain* (1916) II. xv. 297 The longer Hilda regarded, the more nightmarishly numerous seemed the doors. **1934** A. HUXLEY *Beyond Mexique Bay* 249 Then, nightmarishly proliferating, appear the Pittsburgs and Birminghams, the Osakas and Calcuttas of this unhappy world. **1973** *Nation Rev.* (Melbourne) 31 Aug. 1453/5 Backdrops as nightmarishly accurate as the best of Goya.

night-night (nəi·tˌnəi:t), *int.* Also **night, night.** [Cf. *NIGHT *sb.* 4 h.] = GOOD NIGHT I.

1896 G. F. NORTHALL *Warwickshire Word-Bk.* 158 *Night-night*, good-night: spoken to children. **1905** R. FRY *Let.* 9 Jan. (1972) I. 229 Night, night, dear heart. Thanks for your cheering letter. **1945** W. DE LA MARE *Burning-Glass* 24 Night-night, my Precious!

night-owl. Add: **2.** A person who is up or out-of-doors late at night. orig. *U.S.*

1847 W. T. PORTER *Quarter Race Kentucky* 163 You no-souled, shad-bellied, squash-headed, old night-owl you! **1880** 'MARK TWAIN' *Tramp Abroad* 270 He calculated to be off before night-owls like me turned out of bed. **1963** M. MCCARTHY *Group* xii. 286 Her father, who was a night owl, was still awake. **1975** *Listener* 11 Sept. 343/3 Jazz lovers have to be night owls..for only two programmes feature early evening jazz.

nights, *adv.* Add: (Further examples.) Also *colloq.*

1786 *Exchange Advertiser* (Boston) 19 Oct. (Th.), Not a flute that has a hole in it, but that is employed very successfully nights. **1861** O. W. NORTON *Army Lett.* (1903) 29 To-morrow we do guard duty. It is tiresome work. No sleep nights. **1938** T. WILDER *Our Town* 34 From my window up there I can just see your head nights when you're doing your homework over in your room. **1964** *Panorama* (Brisbane) Sept. 7/1, I don't know who writes the lyrics for their songs, but professionals can still sleep nights. **1970** *Globe & Mail* (Toronto) 25 Sept. 12/1 (Advt.), She wanted a place that would stay up nights to serve her.

night-scape, nightscape (nəi·tskēɪp). [f. NIGHT *sb.* + SCAPE *sb.*[3]] = NIGHT-PIECE.

1915 T. BURKE *Nights in Town* 14 There is a short street in Walworth Road..which is as perfect as any nightscape ever conceived by any artist. *Ibid.* 272 Even as a child I was conscious of the call of these wicked nightscapes. **1949** *Archit. Rev.* CV. 248 (*caption*) Nightscape, suspended animation. **1958** L. DURRELL *Mountolive* xiii. 250 The youthful figures of himself and Leila moved..to the punctuation of a single soft finger-drum across a violet night-scape.

night-shift. 1. (Later examples.)

1863 QUEEN VICTORIA *Let.* 8 Apr. in R. Fulford *Dearest Mama* (1968) 192 Poor, dear Alice had the same night shift on which I had when you were all born! **1923** CONRAD *Rover* v. 76 If she had a petticoat over her night-shift, that was all. **1958** *New Yorker* 13 Dec. 69/2 (Advt.), The beautiful night shift..by Barbizon in..nylon satin.

night-soil. Add: **2.** *attrib.* and *Comb.*, as *night-soil cart, collector, man.*

1967 O. WYND *Walk Softly, Men Praying* ix. 145, I had to steer past a chain of night-soil carts. **1960** *Spectator* 19 Feb. 244 The nightsoil collectors of Lagos's slums were so thoughtless as to go on strike. **1957** M. BANTON *W. Afr. City* viii. 158 Loko men are ridiculed by other tribes for working as night-soil men. **1960** C. ACHEBE *No Longer at Ease* ii. 16 As soon as the night-soil-man passed swinging his broom..and trailing clouds of putrefaction the boy quickly sprang to his feet and began calling him names. **1965** J. R. HETHERINGTON *Selina's Aunt* 42/2, I then learned that he *worked* for the council—in the capacity of night-soilman.

night telegraph letter: see *NIGHT LETTER a.

night-time. Add: Also *attrib.*

1935 T. S. ELIOT *Murder in Cathedral* ii. 76 The night-time heaping of the ashes. **1955** *Sci. News Let.* 26 Feb. 138/1 Sirius, the dog-star, brightest of all the stars in the nighttime sky.

night-times (nəi·tˌtəi:mz), *adv.* Chiefly *dial.* [f. NIGHT-TIME + -S.] At night; during the night.

1884 'MARK TWAIN' *Huck. Finn* 41 Just tramp right across the country, mostly night-times. **1886** F. T. ELWORTHY *West Somerset Word-Bk.* 513, I goes to work, but I goes to school night-times. **1902** 'L. HOPE' *Garden of Kama* 18 We rested, night-times, on the sand By the rare waters of this weary land. **1940** *Sat. Even. Post* 20 Jan. 36/3 Cut the rest of his fence, nighttimes.

night-vision. Add: Also as two words. **2. a.** (Later examples.)

1946 V. TEMPEST *Near the Sun* vii. 53 The medical people were..confined to assisting the overcoming of.. the effects of height and lack of oxygen,..the difficulties of night vision and the psychological approach to flying. **1961** *Housewife* (Ceylon) Dec. 19 Vitamin A..assists our eyesight, especially 'night vision'. **1969** P. KAVANAGH *Such Men are Dangerous* (1971) iii. 49 He might even wait until dark. Fine. My night vision was always good. **1973** J. ROSSITER *Manipulators* xxvi. 249 Ferris would have been watching his progress through his night-vision glasses.

ni·ght-walk, *v.* [f. NIGHT *sb.* + WALK *v.*[1]] *trans.* To walk or travel across (a place) by night. Also *transf.*

1845 THOREAU *Jrnl.* 6 Aug. in *Writings* (1906) VII. 377 Fallen spirits who once in human shape night-walked the earth. **1899** KIPLING *Five Nations* (1903) 8 Consider what toils we [*sc.* cruisers] endure, Night-walking wet sea-lanes, a guard and a lure.

night-walking, *vbl. sb.* Add to def.: Also, sleep-walking.

1621 [in Dict.]. **1943** A. M. MAYNARD in D. Ibberson *Our Towns* 135 Look for signs of bitten finger-nails, night walking or excitability.

nighty, *sb.* Add: Also **nightie.** (Earlier and later examples.) Also *attrib.* and *Comb.*

1871 'S. MAY' *Prudy keeping House* 98 After a nice bath ..the little one was dressed in her nightie. **1894** S. HALE *Lett.* (1919) 286 A blind I opened (thereby drenching me and my nighty) banged and smashed a big pane. **1908** *Daily Chron.* 14 Sept. 5/5 So I folded up my nightie and went into the street. **1913** R. BROOKE *Let.* in *Coll. Poems* (1918) p. lxxx, We may only find each other in a whiter world, nighty-clad, harped, winged, celibate. **1934** R. NICHOLS *Fisbo* 36 Frivolous and frolicsome and flighty As the naughtiest flapper in her newest nightie. **1968** 'O. MILLS' *Sundry Fell Designs* iii. 29 Vicky's got a mangy old nightie-case she won't go to bed without. **1972** 'G. BLACK' *Bitter Tea* (1973) x. 157 The hospital nighty..felt slightly scratchy.

ni·ghty-night, *int.* Also **nightie-night(ie), nighty-nighty.** [See -Y[6].] = GOOD-NIGHT I.

1876 A. F. PARKER *Gloss. Words Oxfordshire* 118 *Nighty-nighty*, good-night, a phrase used by *very old* people. **1888** *Texas Siftings* 7 Jan. 4/1 His nibs wants yer ter fire in yer stuff ter-morrow by eleven sharp. Nighty-night, dovey. **1929** E. BOWEN *Joining Charles* 193 Mrs. Moysey would say, 'Well nightie-night I suppose,' and get finally up. **1957** L. STERN *Midas Touch* II. xviii. 136 Nighty-night, Barbara. Sleep tight. **1959** I. & P. OPIE *Lore & Lang. Schoolch.* iii. 52 To one colloquially saying good-night 'Nightie, nightie', their good-humoured riposte is 'Pyjama, pyjama'. **1971** *Southerly* XXXI. 103 They kissed each other 'nightie night'.

nig-nog[1] (ni·gˌnɒg). *slang.* [Perh. f. NIGMENOG fool.] A foolish person; hence, a raw and unskilled recruit. Cf. *NING-NONG.

1953 *Punch* 9 Dec. 692/3 All must be represented on a strict basis of proportion of the number of citizens for whom they cater: Football-pool promoters (six representatives), barrow-boys (two representatives), sharepushers, erks, nig-nogs, [etc.]. **1962** A. WESKER *Chips with Everything* I. iii. 17 A straight line, you heaving nig-nogs, a straight line. **1967** *Times* 30 Nov. 10/8 'Nig-nog' was used on the railways and elsewhere long before coloured immigrants appeared... It is usually taken as a mildly contemptuous but good-humoured name for an unskilled man or novice.

nig-nog[2] (ni·gˌnɒg). [Redupl. shortened form of NIGGER *sb.*] A coarsely abusive term for a Negro.

1959 M. PUGH *Chancer* 85 First lot, and look lively. Lot of nig-nogs off the trees. **1971** J. GARDNER *Every Night's a Bullfight* xiii. 405 I'm talking about you and your precious Juliet, your beloved Carol bloody Evans that nig-nog tart. **1972** D. ONYEAMA *Nigger at Eton* x. 199 The word 'wog'..was one racial name which I always seemed to fear at Eton. Together with 'nig-nog', it was the term of abuse which..I did not, to start with, understand the meaning of. **1974** *Times* 14 Feb. 16/8 I'm not going to vote until they get me a house and get rid of the nignogs. **1975** J. SYMONS *Three Pipe Problem* v. 36 He wanted to send the nig nogs and the Pakis back where they belong, in the jungle.

nigra (ni·gră). *U.S.* Also **nigrah** (ni·grā). [f. NEGRO.] Variant form of 'Negro', used principally in the Southern States. Cf. *NIGGRA.

1944 *Amer. Speech* XIX. 166 In the South it is commonly heard as *nigrah*, and not only from white lips. Indeed *nigrah* is also used by Northern Negroes, including some of the most eminent. **1959** *New Statesman* 6 June 800/1 In the autumn of 1956 I asked a young plantation owner in Mississippi if he had noticed any change in his relations with Negro employees since the Supreme Court rulings against segregation. 'Well,' he said slowly, 'I guess you can say the nigra ain't loyal any more.' **1965** L. WHITTEN *Progeny of Adder* (1966) 69 The guy has some kind of funny accent, it ain't Jewish or Italian and it ain't Nigra or Southern. **1969** F. RICHARDS *Risky Way to Kill* (1970) xi. 140 'Pretty little thing, as nigras go, Mrs. Prender said.' "Nigras"? Like that, Henderson?' 'Way it sounded to me.' 'It's a Southern variant,' Heimrich said. 'Between "nigger", which they're beginning—some of them are beginning—not to use so much and "Negro", which a lot of them can't get used to.' **1973** L. HEREN *Growing up Poor in London* v. 109, I was with Martin Luther King Jr. on his 1961 freedom ride, and the church in which he preached in Montgomery, Alabama, was attacked. This led to a stopover of three or four days, during which several well-meaning whites, in spite of all the evidence, sought to persuade me that their niggers—or rather, nigras—were happy, well loved, and free to do whatever they wanted.

Nigritian, *a.* (Earlier examples.)

1757 J. DYER *Fleece* IV. 128 Sailing the western coast of Afric's realms, Of Mauritania and Nigritian tracts. **1856** J. L. WILSON *Western Africa* I. ii. 30 The inhabitants of Northern Guinea are known as the Nigritian family, from their supposed descent from the great Negro families living in the valley of the Niger.

Nigritic, *a.* (Examples.)

1883 R. N. CUST *Sk. Mod. Lang. Afr.* I. iv. 54 Krapf.. became aware of the existence of two distinct Groups of Languages on the East Coast, about the line of the Equator, and called them Nilo-Hamitic, or Nilotic, and Nigro-Hamitic or Nigritic respectively. **1938** M. HAILEY *African Survey* iii. 76 Dr. Westermann..proposes a four-fold division: (*a*) Nigritic, or Old Sudanic. **1963** C. J. MCCALL in A. Dundes *Mother Wit* (1973) 420 'Hoodoo represents the syncretistic blend of Christian and Nigritic religious traditions.

nigromancer, -mancy. Delete *obs.* and add examples (quot. 1970 involves a pun on 'Negro').

1922 E. R. EDDISON *Worm Ouroboros* xxxi. 388 Yet was it apparent to one so deeply learned in nigromancy and secrets astronomical that this thing was fatal. **1970** I. REED in A. Chapman *New Black Voices* (1972) 329 He who meddles w/ nigro-mancers courts his demise.

nihilism. Add: **2.** (Further examples.)

1909 A. M. LUDOVICI tr. *Nietzsche's Will to Power* I. 5 Nihilism, i.e., the absolute repudiation of worth, purpose desirability. *Ibid.* 16 The extremest form of Nihilism would mean that *all* belief—all assumption of truth—is false: because no real world is at hand. **1964** P. ROUBICZEK *Existentialism* vii. 125 Thus it is no cause for surprise that Sartre lands himself in complete nihilism. **1972** M. NATANSON in L. Embree *Life-World & Consciousness* 302 Value-free science as it has been interpreted by many contemporary social scientists does endorse a kind of *cultural nihilism.*

c. *Psychol.* In some forms of severe mental illness, the belief that the outside world, the patient's self, or parts of either, have ceased to function or to exist.

1889 *Jrnl. Mental Sci.* XXXIV. 137 Though not a mental affection in the strict sense of the word, nihilism is a psychical factor very liable to devolve into insanity. **1927** HENDERSON & GILLESPIE *Text.-bk. Psychiatry* viii. 160 The most characteristic involutional qualities lie in the content of the psychosis, especially in the apprehension, hypochondriasis and nihilism. **1957** E. MAYER in P. A. Schilpp *Philos. K. Jaspers* xi. 451 Jaspers vividly describes nihilism as a symptom of mental illness or..as a manifestation of ultimate situations in which a human being can find himself in depressions and schizophrenias. **1965** J. POLLITT *Depression & its Treatment* iii. 33 The most extreme form of hypochondriacal delusion, referred to as 'nihilism'.

nihilistic, *a.* Add: **c.** *Psychol.* Of or characterized by delusions of nihilism (first described by J. Cotard *Du délire des négations* in *Archives Neurologiques* (1882) IV. XI. 152). See *NIHILISM 2 c.

1925 STRECKER & EBAUGH *Pract. Clin. Psychiatry* iii. 45 Nihilistic ideas deny the existence of things. As an aspect of a depressive trend there may be self-depreciation. **1927** HENDERSON & GILLESPIE *Text-bk. Psychiatry* xi. 294 The feature of the depression is the frequency with which absurd nihilistic ideas are expressed. Patients claim that they are dead, that their blood has ceased to circulate,.. that their bodies are utterly destroyed. **1944** LICHTENSTEIN & SMALL *Handbk. Psychiatry* ii. 34 Nihilistic delusions, in which there is a more or less complete denial of

reality and existence. **1967** A. T. Beck *Depression* i. ii. 38 A typical nihilistic delusion is reflected in the following statement: 'It's no use... The world is empty. Everybody died last night.' **1974** M. Rohde tr. *Cotard's Nihilistic Delusions* in Hirsch & Shepherd *Themes & Variations European Psychiatry* xiv. 354, I would tentatively suggest the name 'nihilistic delusions' (*délire de négations*) to describe the condition of the patients to whom Griesinger was referring.

‖ **nihil obstat** (ni·hil ǫ·bstæt). [Lat., 'nothing stands in the way'.] Words appearing on the title-page or elsewhere in the preliminary pages of a Roman Catholic work indicating that it has been approved as free of doctrinal or moral error. Also *fig.*

1886 in P. Soulier *Life St. Philip Benizi* p. iv, Nihil obstat: Guglielmus T. Gordon, *Congr. Orat. Presbyter.* **1932** J. L. Stocks in *Hibbert Jrnl.* XXX. 622 He loves beauty, he admires character, he feels the thrill of poetry and art. He believes in God. For all this the utmost that he can get out of science is a *nihil obstat.* **1933** *Times Lit. Suppl.* 21 Dec. 904/2 The selection [of anthems] carries with it the *nihil obstat* of two such eminent Church musicians as Sir Walford Davies and Dr. Henry Ley. **1938** *Mind* XLVII. 93 The parallel to the *Nihil Obstat* of Roman Catholic censorship is obvious. **1955** *Times* 6 July 11/4 Authoritarians wish that one dictionary enjoyed dictatorial rights. Reference to it then would finally close any argument; its *nihil obstat* would give the green light to *imprimatur.* **1958** *Spectator* 22 Aug. 260/1 This is a lucid, judicious book, with a '*Nihil obstat*' discreetly tucked away in the title pages. **1973** *Times* 11 Aug. 2/8 Mgr. Guazzelli said: 'The *nihil obstat* and the imprimatur were duly signed, and the censor and myself, as the responsible bishop, acknowledge this fact.'

-nik (nik), *suff.* from Russian (cf. *kolkhoznik, *Narodnik, *sputnik) and Yiddish, appended to sbs. and adjs. to denote a person or thing involved in or associated with the thing or quality specified, as **beatnik*, **folknik*, **no-goodnik*, *nudnik, **peacenik.* Often with humorous or pejorative connotations.

1945 A. Kober *Parm Me* 17 That stuck-upnick fomm the lodge, Sister Leshinsky..she's a regella Yenkee. **1958** *Amer. Speech* XXXIII. 154 On learning that a dog was in the Soviet Moon, the Detroit *News* (and almost every other paper)..referred to the satellite as *Muttnik*... From then on there was no end of -niks. **1959** *Observer* 14 June 22/7 It happened that Mr. Werth arrived in Columbus, Ohio, just as the Russian Sputnik soared into the cosmos; before he left the American flopnik had burnt out on its launching pad. **1965** *Newsweek* 1 Nov. 31/3 The crowded headquarters of the young draftniks and Vietniks pulse with an almost religious fervor. **1965** *Time* 12 Nov. 4 Those guitar-plunking protestniks whose St. Joan is Baez. **1966** *Economist* 5 Mar. 883/1 These protestants represent only a small faction, no more important politically than the nuclear disarmers were in Britain or the Vietniks are in America. **1966** *Sat. Rev.* (U.S.) 22 Oct. 59 Despite the alarums of the computerniks..the book would appear to be here to stay. **1968** B. Foster *Changing Eng. Lang.* ii. 110 This borrowing [*sc.* sputnik]..has given a new lease of life to the suffix *-nik* which had already made its appearance, at any rate in the U.S.A., as a loan from Yiddish... New creations..have usually been..humorous..; thus a device which failed to go into orbit was derided in..1957 as a Kaputnik (*Daily Express*), a Flopnik (*Daily Herald*), a Puffnik (*Daily Mail*), and a Stayputnik (*News Chronicle*). **1968** L. Rosten *Joys of Yiddish* 265 *-Nik* lends itself to delightful *ad hoc* inventions. A *sicknik* would be one who fancies 'sick' or 'black' humor. A *Freudnik* would be an uncritical acolyte of the father of psychoanalysis. And recently homosexuals began to refer to heterosexuals, with some amusement, as 'straightniks'. **1973** *Indexer* VIII. 227/2 Publishers and computerniks can create decadent search systems.

nikau (nī·kau). [Maori.] A New Zealand palm tree, *Rhopalostylis sapida*, or its leaves, once used as a sort of thatch. Also *attrib.*

1831 H. Williams *Jrnl.* 15 Nov. in H. Carleton *Life of Henry Williams* (1874) I. 100 We..erected a tent, with a shed of nikau for the boys. **1844** C. Chapman *Let.* 30 Nov. in A. Drummond *Married & gone to N.Z.* (1960) 70 Another tree called the Nikau is said to be very good; I have tasted a little bit and found it very nice. **1847** *N.Z. Jrnl.* No. 191. 105/1 From Teapu southward the country is ..wooded with rata and nikau, or cabbage palm, down to the high water mark. **1853** J. M. Richmond *Let.* 11 Nov. in *Richmond–Atkinson Papers* (1960) I. iii. 133 It [*sc.* their dwelling] is in fact a roof on the ground, thatched with nikau, a palm, the only one in N.Z. **1891** R. Wallace *Rural Econ. Austral. & N.Z.* xvi. 242 The tree fern and the common Nikau Palm of the country dotted the hillsides and gave..a semi-tropical appearance to the landscape. **1905** W. B. *Where White Man Treads* 16 He could supplement his dry fare with..the tender leaves of the nikau. **1920** J. Mander *Story N.Z. River* 315 He built a nikau whare. **1935** J. Guthrie *Little Country* iv. 98 Nikaus, rata vine, and lycopodium..brought to the hall the charms of the New Zealand bush. **1949** P. Buck *Coming of Maori* (1950) ii. i. 87 The middle part of the top of the trunk of the *nikau* palm, just under the leaf spread, was eaten raw. **1959** M. Shadbolt *New Zealanders* 66 He explained how easy it was to live off the bush if you wanted, eating..the juicy white insides of nikau palms. **1966** *Encycl. N.Z.* II. 690/1 The Maoris used the nikau leaves in their whares.

Nike (nəi·ki). [Gr. νίκη victory.] **1.** In Greek art: a winged statue representing Nike, the goddess of victory.

1867 H. M. Westropp *Handbk. Archæol.* 195 *Nike.—Victory.* Victory is represented in a short tunic, with wings, and usually carries a palm. She is also represented writing on a shield, and frequently sacrificing a bull. **1924** A. D. Sedgwick *Little French Girl* iv. iii. 327 She's a Nike..on the prow of a Greek ship. **1960** R. Carpenter *Greek Sculpture* v. 147 The running Nike is an interesting study in formal drapery. **1968** V. Ehrenberg *From Solon to Socrates* vii. 315 There are the figures of a number of winged *Nikai.*

2. Any of a range of surface-to-air guided missiles developed by the U.S., initially as defensive weapons.

1952 *Britannica Bk. of Year* 431/2 Limited production for operational trials of the U.S. army's Nike missile for the anti-aircraft artillery was begun in 1951. **1955** *Times* 4 July 9/7 Short-range guided weapons such as the American Nike are useless for the air defence of Britain. **1961** E. Burgess *Long-Range Ballistic Missiles* vii. 194 On a recent tour of a Nike-Zeus installation the writer saw ..the tremendous complexity of the anti-missile missile system. **1970** J. W. R. Taylor *Rockets & Missiles* ii. 56 Typical of first-generation anti-aircraft missiles was America's two-stage Nike-Ajax, made up of a liquid-propellent second stage and a solid-propellent first-stage booster. **1974** *Encycl. Brit. Micropædia* VII. 344/1 Nike Zeus, first antimissile missile, was about 50 feet long... A further development was Nike X, which had a fixed radar antenna that could be electronically scanned. Nike Cajun, a sounding rocket, was capable of lifting a 50-pound payload of scientific instruments to a height of 90 miles.

nikethamide (nike·þǎməid). *Pharm.* [f. *nic*otinic acid di*eth*yl*amide*, its chemical name, by alteration.] A colourless or yellowish oily liquid or crystalline solid, $(C_5H_4N)CON(CH_2CH_3)_2$, which is used as a respiratory stimulant and analeptic.

1940 *Jrnl. Amer. Med. Assoc.* 20 Jan. 249/2 The Council consulted Ciba Pharmaceutical Products, Inc., and agreement was reached on the name 'Nikethamide'..as the nonproprietary name for the substance introduced in medicine under the proprietary name of Coramine. **1951** A. Grollman *Pharmacol. & Therapeutics* viii. 168 Because of its analeptic action, nikethamide is used in acute respiratory depression of anesthesia, alcoholic intoxication, and overdosage with hypnotics. **1969** [see *Coramine].

Nikonian (nikōu·niǎn), *sb.* and *a.* Also **Niconian.** [f. *Nikon*, the name adopted by Nikita Minin (1605–81), 6th Patriarch of Moscow + -ian.] **A.** *sb.* An orthodox member of the Russian Church who accepted the reforms introduced by Nikon. **B.** *adj.* Of or pertaining to Nikon or his reforms. Hence **Niko·nianism.**

1874 J. H. Blunt *Dict. Sects, Heresies* 373/1 *Niconians*, a name applied by Russian dissenters to the orthodox members of the Established Church who accepted the reforms introduced by the Patriarch Nicon in the year 1654. **1877** D. M. Wallace *Russia* xx. 308 Believing these 'Nikonian novelties' to be heretical. **1888** S. M. Kravchinskii *Russ. Peasantry* II. 454 They [*sc.* the Stranniky] look upon their co-religionists..with the same disgust and abhorrence as they lavish on the Niconians. **1957** *Encycl. Brit.* XIX. 695/2 A long struggle began between the faith of the Old Believers and the Nikonianism, as the official church was now generally called.

nil[2]. Add: **1. a.** (Later examples.)

1936 A. W. Clapham *Romanesque Archit.* i. 5 Of all the various structures referred to or described by Isidore of Seville..the surviving remains are almost nil. **1952** C. Day Lewis tr. *Virgil's Aeneid* viii. 172 Visibility was reduced to nil. **1955** *Times* 6 July 4/4 The British Isles Rugby Union tourists beat South West Africa by nine points to nil in their match here to-day.

2. *Comb.*, as **nil-grade** *Philol.*, the most reduced form of weak ablaut grade, in which the vowel disappears; **nil norm** *Econ.*, during a wage-freeze a standard under which no wage increases are normally allowed.

1922–3 *Modern Philology* XX. 197 The nil-grade of the root vowel is represented by OE *-tyllan* (in *fortyllan* 'to seduce'). **1928** *Language* IV. 163 It follows that *šd* is the nil-grade of ***sed-* 'sit'. **1935** *Mod. Lang. Notes* L. 523 Pre-English uncontracted *Lāamkō* (with nil-grade of the *k*-suffix). **1972** *Language* XLVIII. 9 The difficulty disappears if we start from a root *kʷerp*, whose nil-grade developed into Aryan *kṛp-* and Goidelic *kri.* **1966** *Sunday Times* 14 Aug. 8 For all the traditional wage demands some principle does need to be hammered out to establish who will be permitted to breach the nil norm. **1967** *Economist* 23 Dec. 1204/1 Britain is still supposed to be operating in conditions of a 'nil norm' for wage increases. **1968** *Manch. Guardian Weekly* 1 Feb. 8 The £1 a week rise would not qualify as an exception to the nil norm laid down in the summer.

b. Passing into *adj.*, containing, reporting, or consisting of nothing.

1959 *Punch* 27 May 704/3 The thoughtless might suppose that hail-watching was dull work, with long blank intervals offering nothing better than a nil return. **1972** *Guardian* 14 Mar. 2/8 They..returned because of nil visibility. **1974** L. Lamb *Man in Mist* ix. 55 In view of my constable's nil report, *could* it be that nothing ever happened?

‖ **nil admirari** (nil ædmirā·ri). [L.] An attitude of indifference to the distractions of the outside world, advocated by Horace (*Epistles* i. vi. 1): *nil admirari prope res est una..quae possit facere et servare beatum*, 'to wonder at nothing is just about the only way a man can become contented and remain so.' Hence, a person adopting this attitude. Also *attrib.* or as *adj.*

Also used erron. with the meaning 'to admire nothing'.

1748 Chesterfield *Let.* 27 Sept. (1774) I. 345 This book..will both divert and astonish you; and at the same time, teach you *nil admirari.* **1749** Fielding *Tom Jones* III. vii. i. 8 The famous *Nil admirari* of Horace, or in the English Phrase, *To stare at nothing.* **1785** Boswell *Jrnl. Tour Hebr.* 118 But Dr. Johnson has much of the *nil admirari* in smaller concerns. **1821** Byron *Don Juan* v. c. 185, I ne'er could see the very Great happiness of the 'Nil Admirari'. **1822** Shelley *Let.* 18 June (1964) II. 715 The *nil admirari*..seems to me a bad sign in a young person. **1857** Trollope *Barchester T.* III. xvi. 277 Very many men now-a-days..adopt or affect to adopt the *nil admirari* doctrine. **1866** Mrs. Gaskell *Wives & Daughters* I. xxii. 287 Every inflexion of the voice breathed out.. admiration! And this from the *nil admirari* brother. **1935** J. Buchan *House of Four Winds* vi. 139 Mr Glynde's *nil admirari* countenance..registered surprise. **1951** N. Annan *Leslie Stephen* x. 278 *Nil admirari* was his precept, the salute to genius his practice. **1961** M. Kelly *Spoilt Kill* iii. 193 Why was I always preaching *nil admirari*?

‖ **nil desperandum** (nil despəræ·ndǒm), *int.* Also **ni:hil despera·ndum.** [L.] An exhortation to have hope in difficult circumstances and not to despair, deriving from Horace *Odes* i. vii. 27 *nil desperandum Teucro duce et auspice Teucro*, 'no need to despair with Teucer as your leader and Teucer to protect you'.

[**1617** T. Adams *Souldiers Honour* sig. A3v, Nil desperandū Christo Duce, & Auspice Christo.] **1628** R. Burton *Anat. Melancholy* (ed. 3) iii. ii. 527 *Nihil desperandum*, there s hope enough yet. **1749** Fielding *Tom Jones* III. viii. vi. 189 All I have is at your Service, and at your Disposal... Nil desperandum est Teucro duce et auspice Teucro. **1774** J. Adams *Wks.* (1851) IV. 12 *Nil desperandum* is a good motto. **1872** E. Braddon *Life in India* iii. 75 But *nil desperandum* was the cry of the Vauxhall partisans. **1921** W. de la Mare *Memoirs of Midget* xx. 142 *Nil desperandum*, Mr. Crimble. And you know what they say about fish in the sea. **1955** *Times* 5 May 15/4 There is..a key-note running through the essays and magazine articles here reprinted—'a note of *nil desperandum*'. **1974** J. Mann *Sticking Place* iii. 46 Edward had thought the job his for the asking... Well, *nil desperandum*..he might yet be moving in.

Nile (nəil). The name of a river in North Africa, used *attrib.* to designate animals native to the region, as **Nile crocodile,** the African crocodile, *Crocodylus niloticus*; cf. Crocodile 1; **Nile monitor** = *iguana 2; **Nile perch,** a large food fish, *Lates niloticus*, found in the rivers and lakes of north and central Africa.

1860 T. H. Huxley in *Jrnl. Linn. Soc.* (*Zool.*) IV. 8, I could find neither in the British Museum, nor in the Museum of the Royal College of Surgeons, any authentic skeleton of this, the so-called Nilotic Crocodile.] **1898** J. Anderson *Zool. Egypt* I. 1 The Nile crocodile was described, so long ago as 1699, by Oligeus Jacobæus. **1915** A. M. Reese *Alligator & its Allies* i. 39 The African or Nile Crocodile..is found throughout the continent of Africa. **1974** *BP Shield Internat.* Oct. 28/4 Nile crocodiles are a prominent feature of the lake fauna. **1900** H. A. Bryden *Animals of Africa* xv. 173 The Nile Monitor, a big lizard, attaining a length of six feet,..is often miscalled an 'iguana'. **1964** C. Willock *Enormous Zoo* vii. 125 The Nile monitor, an immense and really powerful lizard which sometimes reaches four feet in length, has a banquet when crocodile hatching time comes around. [**1905** A. Sedgwick *Student's Text-bk. Zool.* II. 235 *Lates* C. and V., *L. niloticus*, the perch of the Nile.] **1931** J. R. Norman *Hist. Fishes* ix. 162 (*caption*) Skeleton of the Nile Perch. **1949** L. J. McCormick in Vesey-Fitzgerald & Lamonte *Gamefish of World* 367 In colour and form the Nile perch looks like an overgrown cod. **1965** A. J. McClane *Standard Fishing Encycl.* 616/2 Various species of the Nile perch are distributed in the big rivers and lakes of tropical Africa. **1974** *Encycl. Brit. Macropædia* XIV. 46/2 The nile perches (Latidae) have been found as mummies in ancient tombs in Egypt.

Nile-blue, *sb.* and *a.* Add: (Earlier and later examples.) Also *ellipt.* **Nile.**

The ellipt. examples may represent *Nile-green.*

1873 *Young Englishwoman* Feb. 77/2 Dark maroon velvet and Nile blue silk rep. **1895** *Montgomery Ward Catal.* 7/3 Plain Crepe Picardie... Colors: Lilac,..nile, black [etc.]. **1926** *Daily Colonist* (Victoria, B.C.) 21 July 16/6 (Advt.), A 4-ply worsted wool in shades of pink.. nile, [etc.]. **1950** Maerz & Paul *Dict. Color* (ed. 2) 199/1 Nile Blue.

2. Also **Nile blue.** A tetracyclic quaternary ammonium ion which is an azine dye and is used as a biological stain to colour fatty acids blue; also, a salt (usu. the sulphate) of this ion.

1888 *Jrnl. Soc. Dyers & Colourists* IV. 96/1 On wool and silk, Nile blue is applied in a neutral bath, and yields red shades of blue. **1920** *Physiol. Abstr.* VI. 617 The affinity of Nile blue sulphate for fat is small. Oleic acid and its esters are the most stainable. **1942** V. Hamburger *Man. Exper. Biol.* 46 A small particle of agar stained with Nile blue sulphate or neutral red is pressed against the surface of the blastula for a short period. **1971** Ayyangar & Tilak in K. Venkataraman *Chem. Synthetic Dyes* IV. iii. 107 It has been shown that Rhodanile Blue is nothing but a mixture of Rhodamine B and Nile Blue.

Nile-green (earlier and later examples).

1871 *Scribner's Monthly* June 209/1 'Nile green' will turn some people into oranges, though twenty empresses ordain its adoption. **1944** R. CHANDLER *Lady in Lake* xvi. 93 The nile green tiles of the bathroom floor. **1969** 'I. DRUMMOND' *Man with Tiny Head* xv. 176 He used his palms against the nile-green hull. **1973** 'D. JORDAN' (*title*) Nile green.

Nili (ni·li). [Acronym f. Heb. *Netzach Israel lo Ishakare*, the strength of Israel will not lie (1 Sam. xv. 29).] A Jewish espionage group in Turkish-ruled Palestine during the 1914–18 war.

1930 H. B. SAMUEL *Unholy Memories of Holy Land* viii. 119 Aronson..leapt to prominence in the war by organizing the celebrated Nili Society..whose 'intelligence' was largely instrumental in the success of Lord Allenby's campaign. **1938** W. B. ZIFF *Rape of Palestine* vi. 66 Of.. great importance was the voluntary intelligence service rendered by the celebrated Nili Society all over the Holy Land. **1959** A. ENGLE *Nili Spies* ix. 99 Nili became the name of the espionage group, adding a new word to the Hebrew language. *Ibid.* xi. 113 The actual details of Nili's work were never known... But the existence of a group of people carrying on espionage and plotting rebellion could not be concealed. **1973** *Jewish Chron.* 2 Feb. 12/4 The Nili Group..sprang up during the First World War, when Turkish treatment of the Palestine Jewish community raised questions of its survival.

Nilo-. Used as combining form of *Nile* in names of language groups common to inhabitants of the Nile area and of some other specified area. Cf. next.

1932 W. L. GRAFF *Lang.* 434 *Kanuri*, of the Nilo-Chadian group. **1938** [see *NILO-HAMITIC *a.*]. **1939** L. H. GRAY *Foundations of Language* 401 The Nobades (the supposed ancestors of the modern Nilo-Chadian Nuba). *Ibid.* 402 The divisions of *Sudano-Guinean*, according to Delafosse, may now be enumerated:..(2) *Nilo-Abyssinian* (fifteen languages) with evident traces of classes and class-pronouns and tones, and including Shiluk, Dinka, etc. *Ibid.*, (5) *Nilo-Congolese* (nineteen languages) with traces of classes, and including Mangbetu, Mbuda, etc. **1966** J. H. GREENBERG *Languages of Africa* (ed. 2) 130 To the new grouping which consists of Songhai, Saharan, Maban, Fur and Coman in addition to Chari-Nile, the name Nilo-Saharan is given. **1969** *Language* XLV. 665 Of the 33 languages and language groups surveyed in *Hdbk 66*, 21 fall into Greenberg's Nilo-Saharan family.

Nilo-Hamite (nəi:lo,hæ·məit). [f. *NILO-HAMITIC *a.*: see -ITE[1].] A member of the Nilo-Hamitic group of peoples.

1932 C. G. & B. Z. SELIGMAN *Pagan Tribes Nilotic Sudan* i. 5 There can be no doubt as to the persistent influence, physical and cultural, of the Hamites on the Nilotes and Nilo-Hamites. **1953** G. W. B. HUNTINGFORD *Southern Nilo-Hamites* 9 The majority of the Southern Nilo-Hamites are pastoralists practising..a little agriculture. **1955** P. H. GULLIVER *Family Herds* iii. 55 Another tribe of the northern Nilo-Hamites, the Lotuko, makes the same distinction [of kinship terms]. **1966** C. G. SELIGMAN *Races of Africa* (ed. 4) vii. 102 The Nilo-Hamites..speak Nilotic languages with Hamitic elements, and are predominantly pastoral Negroids. **1974** J. R. BAKER *Race* xiii. 226 The Aethiopids have hybridized secondarily with Nilotid Negrids to give rise to tribes referred to under the general title of Niloto or Nilo-Hamites (or sometimes Half-Hamites).

Nilo-Hamitic (nəi:lo,hæmi·tik), *a.* Also **Niloto-Hamitic, Nilohamitic.** [f. *NILO- + HAMITIC *a.*] **a.** Used (originally by German philologists) to designate the groups of languages spoken by East African peoples of mixed Negro and Hamitic descent. **b.** Of, pertaining to, or designating any one or all of the peoples who speak a language belonging to this group.

1883 R. N. CUST *Sk. Mod. Lang. Afr.* I. iv. 54 Krapf.. became aware of the existence of two distinct Groups of Languages on the East Coast, about the line of the Equator, and called them Nilo-Hamitic, or Nilotic and Nigro-Hamitic or Nigritic respectively. **1920** G. W. MURRAY in *Jrnl. R. Anthrop. Inst.* L. 328 The Hamito-Semitic influence on these first three languages is so strong that we may certainly call them Niloto-Hamitic with Westermann. **1938** W. M. HAILEY *Afr. Survey* iii. 77 The Nilotic..comprises tongues spoken in the Upper Nile region as far south as Lake Victoria. Two main branches are distinguished, Nilo-Sudanic..and Nilo-Hamitic. **1955** J. H. GREENBERG *Studies in African Linguistic Classification* 66 The term Nilo-Hamitic has been used by different writers with widely varying meanings. **1955** P. H. GULLIVER *Family Herds* i. 1 In East Africa..it so happens that many of the pastoral peoples are of the Nilo-Hamitic strain, which tends to give them a more striking physique than their Bantu neighbours. **1957** C. G. SELIGMAN *Races of Africa* (ed. 3) vii. 161 Their kinship is rather with the Nilo-Hamitic tribes of East Africa. **1967** M. J. COE *Ecol. Alpine Zone Mt. Kenya* 1 For centuries the peak of Mount Kenya has held a magical and religious significance for the Bantu and Nilohamitic peoples.

Nilome·tric, *a.* [f. NILOMETER + -IC.] Of or pertaining to a nilometer, or the measurement of the height of the Nile.

1921 G. A. F. KNIGHT *Nile & Jordan* ix. 96 The Second Cataract where Nilometric markings with his cartouche are recorded.

Nilot. Add: Also **Nilote.**

1932 C. G. & B. Z. SELIGMAN *Pagan Tribes Nilotic Sudan* i. 13 The Nilotes..are essentially proud, aloof, tenacious of their old beliefs and ideas, intensely religious, and by far the most introvert of the peoples of the Sudan. **1934** D. WESTERMANN *African Today* ii. 24 The Masai and tribes related to them..show strong Hamitic influence but are on the other hand relatives of the Nilotes. **1966** C. G. SELIGMAN *Races of Africa* (ed. 4) vii. 110 The second great group of hamiticized Negroes are the Nilotes..geographically limited to the Nile Valley or its immediate neighbourhood.

Nilotic, *a.* Add: **2.** Of, pertaining to, or designating the group of East African Negro tribes including the Dinka, Luo, Nuer, and Shilluk, or the sub-group of Sudanic languages spoken by them.

1915 A. WERNER *Lang. Families of Africa* iii. 41 These ..may perhaps be grouped together as a 'Nilotic' subdivision of the Sudan family. **1930** C. G. SELIGMAN *Races of Africa* vii. 173 The Acholi and Belanda no doubt are of Nilotic origin. **1932** C. G. & B. Z. SELIGMAN *Pagan Tribes Nilotic Sudan* p. xxiii, In the Nilotic languages the *p* and *f* approach each other and seem to be interchangeable. **1949** tr. *L. Homburger's Negro-Afr. Lang.* ii. 42 Central Nilotic languages have no *s*, *z*; in them Arab *suk* becomes *šuk*. **1966** J. H. GREENBERG *Lang. of Africa* (ed. 2) 85 The closest relatives of these languages [*sc.* the Nilo-Hamitic languages] are the group of languages traditionally called Nilotic... The term Nilotic may be extended to include both the Nilotic and Nilo-Hamitic languages. **1973** *Sci. Amer.* July 74/2 The Sebei, a Southern Nilotic people who live on the northern slopes of Mount Elgon in Uganda. **1973** A. MANN *Tiara* xvii. 158 The indefinite tyranny of the Northern Arabs over the Nilotic and Nilo-Hamitic Southerners.

Nilotic (nəilǫ·tik), *sb.* **a.** = NILOT. **b.** A subdivision of the Sudanic group of languages.

1924 *Chambers's Jrnl.* Jan. 11/2 The Nilotics are in nearly every case the aggressors. **1938** W. M. HAILEY *Afr. Survey* iii. 77 The third family included in the Negro division—namely Nilotic—comprises tongues spoken in the Upper Nile region as far south as Lake Victoria. **1963** *Times* 4 June 14/6 Hieroglyphics, and Demotics, and Nilotics, and Cryptics, and Cufics.

nilpotent (nilpōᵘ·tĕnt), *a. Math.* [f. NIL[2] + L. *potent-*, *potens* powerful, POTENT *a.*[1]] Becoming zero when raised to some positive integral power (see also quot. 1949).

1870 B. PEIRCE in *Amer. Jrnl. Math.* (1881) IV. 104 When an expression raised to the square or any higher power vanishes, it may be called nilpotent. **1937** A. A. ALBERT *Mod. Higher Algebra* (1938) iv. 87 Two nilpotent matrices of index two are similar in **F** if and only if they have the same rank. **1949** S. KRAVETZ tr. *Zassenhaus's Theory of Groups* iv. 111 A group **G** is said to be nilpotent if the ascending central series contains the whole group as a member. **1971** I. T. ADAMSON *Rings, Modules & Algebras* xxiii. 194 We say that *I* is a nilpotent ideal if there exists a positive integer *n* such that I^n is the zero ideal. **1974** T. W. HUNGERFORD *Algebra* vii. 100 We obtain a sequence of normal subgroups of *G*, called the ascending central series of *G*: $\langle e \rangle < C_1(G) < C_2(G) < \ldots$ A group *G* is nilpotent if $C_n(G) = G$ for some *n*. *Ibid.* 102 A group *G* is said to be solvable if $G^{(n)} = \langle e \rangle$ for some *n*.. Every nilpotent group is solvable.

nim (nim), *sb.*[2] Also **Nim.** [Orig. uncertain: perh. suggested by NIM *v.* or G. *nimm* (imp. of *nehmen* to take).] A game in which two players alternately take one or more objects from any one of several heaps, the aim being to compel one's opponent to take the last remaining object (or, sometimes, to take it oneself).

1901 C. L. BOUTON in *Ann. Math.* III. 35 Nim. A game with a complete mathematical theory... The writer has not been able to discover much concerning its history, although certain forms of it seem to be played at a number of American colleges, and at some of the American fairs. It has been called Fan-Tan, but as it is not the Chinese game of that name, the name in the title is proposed for it. **1939** USPENSKY & HEASLET *Elem. Number Theory* i. 16 It should be interesting to present an application of the binary system..to the theory of the game of Nim. **1955** *Sci. News Let.* 26 Feb. 134/2 A 17-year-old senior at Newton High School..can boast of having an electronic player that almost never loses in the ancient game of wits, known as 'nim'. **1968** CORLETT & TINSLEY *Pract. Programming* iv. 66 In a game of Nim..two players move alternately and take any number of matches from one pile, the winner taking the last match. If a player can set up a winning position, he cannot lose unless he makes a mistake in a subsequent move.

nim, var. NEEM (in Dict. and Suppl.).

nimble, *a.* (and *adv.*). Add: **7. nimble-pimble** *v. intr.* (*nonce?*), to behave in a sentimental or trifling manner (toward); **nimble Will,** substitute for def.: a slender grass, *Muhlenbergia schreberi*, found in the central United States and sometimes used for pasture.

1927 D. H. LAWRENCE *Let.* 6 Feb. in E. & A. Brewster *D. H. Lawrence: Reminisc. & Corr.* (1934) 115, I feel an infinite disgust at the idea of having to be there while the fools nimble-pimble at the dialogue. **1816** D. THOMAS *Jrnl.* 10 July in *Travels through Western Country* (1819) 168 He pointed out to me a grass, of which I had heard much, known through all the western country by the name of nimble Will. **1817** S. R. BROWN *Western Gazetteer* 109 This is the short, nutritious grass called 'nimble will', which has completely overspred with astonishing celerity, almost every spot of waste or uncultivated ground. **1865** *Trans. Illinois Agric. Soc.* V. 863 The *Muhlenbergia diffusa*, or Nimble Will, is a common grass, which is rather known as a troublesome weed. **1894** J. M. COULTER *Bot. W. Texas* III. 523 Nimble Will... Dry hills and woods, northern Texas and northward.

8. *nimble-throated* adj.; *nimble-tongued*, *-winged* (later examples).

1930 BLUNDEN *Poems* 310 The girls are quicker, more nimble-throated. **1951** *Essays in Criticism* I. II. 165 She [*sc.* Mrs. Behn]..is nimble-tongued indeed at the expense of a military fop who was ready to damn her play. **1960** S. PLATH *Colossus* (1967) 37 Each thumb-size bird Flits nimble-winged in thickets.

nimble, *v.* **3.** (Later example.)

1938 E. BOWEN *Death of Heart* II. ii. 191 She nimbled in with the tray.

nimble-witted, *a.* (Later example.)

1922 V. WOOLF *Jacob's Room* iv. 86 The talkative, nimble-witted people have taken themselves to towns.

nimbostratus (nimbostrā·tŏs, -strēⁱ·tŏs). *Meteorol.* [mod.L., f. NIMB(US + -O + STRATUS.] A form of cloud, which usually occurs as a thick, low, extensive layer, which is grey and often dark, and from which rain, sleet, or snow falls (not necessarily reaching the ground) unaccompanied by lightning, hail, or thunder.

Quot. 1887 represents a different sense. The present use appears to have originated independently in 1932, and quot. 1909 is difficult to account for.

1887 R. ABERCROMBY *Weather* iii. 112 Weilbach..gives three varieties [of nimbus]—..and nimbo-stratus, the rain-cloud, in rear of cyclones, which we have designated cumulo-nimbus [i.e. a 'rocky cumulus cloud from which rain falls in squalls or showers']. **1909** *Cent. Dict.* Suppl., *Nimbo-stratus*, same as *nimbo-pallium* [*sc.* 'a broad sheet of cloud from which rain is falling']. **1932** *Internat. Atlas Clouds* (Internat. Meteorol. Comm.) (abridged ed.) I. 14 In the present Atlas it was intended to give the cloud (*a*) the new name of Nimbostratus, which is a better name than nimbus for a continuous layer which is formed by evolution from altostratus. **1940** W. J. HUMPHREYS *Physics of Air* (ed. 3) 295 The nimbostratus, formerly called nimbus, is any thick, extensive layer of formless cloud from which rain or snow is falling or seemingly on the point of falling. **1957** J. I. M. STEWART *Use of Riches* I. ii. 23 Charles pointed to the horizon. 'Nimbostratus. There's going to be rain.' **1967** R. W. FAIRBRIDGE *Encycl. Atmospheric Sci. & Astrogeol.* 687/1 Nimbostratus generally grows out of altostratus, thickening downward.

‖ **nimbu-pani** (ni·mbu,pā·ni). Also **nimboo-pani, nimbo-pani.** [Hindi; cf. Punjabi *nimbū* lemon, lime, Pali *pāna-* drink.] An Indian non-alcoholic drink comprising lemon-juice or lime-juice with sugar and ice or water.

1961 MRS. B. SINGH *Indian Cookery* 184 Nimboo pani or fresh lime juice and a little sugar dissolved in water is a very popular drink in India during the hot weather. **1968** P. LAL *Indian Recipes* 259 Rose-flavoured nimbu pani... Squeeze the juice out of the lemons and add the sugar... Add..iced water and the rosewater. Pour into serving glasses and serve with crushed ice. **1971** *Illustr. Weekly India* 4 Apr. 6/1 Portugal does not believe in *nimbu-pani*. *Ibid.* 25 Apr. 8/3 Nuzzling into a glass of nimboo-pani placed by his side. **1973** 'B. MATHER' *Snowline* xvi. 197 Nimbo-pani..is the juice of fresh limes squeezed on to cracked ice and sugar.

nimby: see *NEMBIE.

niminy-piminy, *a.* (Earlier examples.)

1786 J. BURGOYNE *Heiress* III. ii. 55 *Lady Emily*...You have only, when before your glass, to keep pronouncing to yourself nimini-primini. *Miss Alscrip.* Nimini-pimini-imini, mimini—oh, it's delightfully enfantine. **1786** G. WHITE *Let.* 25 Mar. in R. Holt-White *Life & Lett. G. White* (1901) II. 154, I hope you practice every day at your Glass; and that you are by this time perfect mistress of '*Nimini pimini*'.

nimite (ni·məit). *Min.* [f. *N*ational *I*nstitute for *M*etallurgy + -ITE[1].] A basic silicate, aluminate, and oxide of nickel, magnesium, iron, and aluminium (with nickel as the dominant cation), $(Ni,Mg,Fe,Al)_3(Si,Al)_2O_5(OH)_4$, which belongs to the chlorite group and is found as yellowish-green monoclinic crystals near the Scotia talc mine in Transvaal.

1968 HIEMSTRA & DE WAAL in *S. Afr. Nat. Inst. Metall. Res. Rep.* No. 344 (*title*) Nickel minerals from Barberton. II. Nimite, a nickelian chlorite. **1970** *Amer. Mineralogist* LV. 21 The exothermic reaction..at 921°C most probably is due to recrystallization of the nimite to a substance that by X-ray diffraction analysis proved to be mainly spinel.

nim-nosed (ni·m,nōᵘzd), *a. rare*[−1]. [f. *nim* (*dial.* shortening of NIMBLE *a.*) + NOSED *a.*] Quick-nosed, swift to pick up the scent.

1936 J. MASEFIELD *Let. from Pontus* 68 The keeper with his nim-nosed dog.

Nimonic (nimǫ·nik). Also **nimonic**. A proprietary name of various nickel-based alloys similar to those known by the name *INCONEL.

1941 *Trade Marks Jrnl.* 9 Apr. 136/2 *Nimonic*... Cast and wrought alloys of nickel sold in the form of bars, sheets, rods,..and other shaped pieces. Henry Wiggin & Company Limited,..London,..manufacturers. **1947** *Official Gazette* (U.S. Patent Office) 22 July 529/2 Henry Wiggin & Company Limited, London, England..*Nimonic*. **1947** A. W. JUDGE *Mod. Gas Turbines* iv. 79, 1270°C (abs.)..is about the limiting value for the turbine blades when made in Nimonic 80 alloy. **1957** *Technology* Aug. 213/1 Ordinary high-temperature alloys, like the nimonics, have reached the limits of development. **1966** [see *INCONEL]. **1968** [see *NICHROME]. **1968** D. R. CLIFFE *Technical Metall.* xvii. 357 Nimonic 75 contains approximately 80:20 Ni:Cr, with 0·2 to 0·6% Ti and up to 0·15% C. Nimonic 80 and 80A have, in addition, 0·5–1·8% Al, and Nimonic 90 and 95 have 15–21% Co replacing nickel. **1971** *New Scientist* 25 Mar. 667/1 Scientists within the UKAEA had been studying a selection of nickel-based alloys, and in particular a nimonic alloy called PE16.

‖ **n'importe** (nænport'), *phr.* [Fr.] It does not matter, it is immaterial.

1775 H. WALPOLE *Let.* 16 Sept. (1904) IX. 257 *N'importe*; we know many sages that take great pains to pass their time with less satisfaction. **1779** [see SOMETHING *sb.* 1 b]. **1837** DICKENS *Let. c* 14 June (1965) I. 271 This is a bad look-out, but n'importe—we will mend it. **1856** S. O. BEETON *Let.* in N. Spain *Mrs Beeton* (1948) I. vi. 97 N'importe, a little more than a month, and I hope and think you will be a happy little wife. **1909** *Manch. Guardian* 24 Nov. 10/1 Dresses by the 'Maison N'Importe' and all the rest of it. **1929** R. HUGHES *High Wind in Jamaica* vii. 149 He imagined..rescuing Rachel—or Laura, *n'importe*—from new and complicated dangers. **1952** 'M. COST' *Hour Awaits* 113 'I'm so sorry, Fanchon.' '*N'importe!* You and Albert Augustus were cut out for tight-rope walking from birth.'

Nimzo-Indian (ni:mzo,i·ndiăn), *a. Chess.* [f. *Nimzowitsch* (see next) + INDIAN *a.*] Designating a form of Indian defence popularized by A. Nimzowitsch, in which Black plays his king's bishop to Kt5 instead of fianchettoing it.

1935 *Chess* I. 103/1 Nimzo-Indian Defence... White simply sought to *combat* and not to *refute* the Nimzo-Indian Variation. **1957** *Griffith & White's Mod. Chess Openings* (ed. 9) 261 The Nimzowitsch-Indian Defence, 'Nimzo-Indian' for short, was first worked out in detail by Aron Nimzowitsch, the Latvian-Danish Grandmaster. **1958** *Listener* 13 Nov. 803/3 If you prefer positional play.. you will probably do best to specialize in some form of the Ruy Lopez or English with White, and with the French and Nimzo-Indian Defences with Black.

Nimzowitsch (ni·mzovitʃ). *Chess.* Also **Nimzovitch**, etc. The name of A. *Nimzowitsch* (1886–1935), Latvian-born chess-player, used *attrib.* and in the possessive to designate various methods of opening play introduced or popularized by him.

1925 *Griffith & White's Mod. Chess Openings* (ed. 4) 57 Nimzovitch's Defence. **1932** *Ibid.* (ed. 5) 105 Nimzovitch's Attack. **1957** Nimzowitsch-Indian [see *NIMZO-INDIAN *a.*]. **1961** *Times* 25 Mar. 7/2 The game started with exactly the same variation of the Nimzovitch defence that was played in the first and third games. **1972** *Times* 2 Sept. 4/3 This had started with 1.P–Q4 and had been defended by Fischer, satisfactorily enough with a Nimzowitsch defence.

nin[2] (nin). [ad. W. *nain* grandmother.] In Liverpool working-class use: grandmother.

1958 M. KERR *People of Ship Street* 48 The granny, or 'nin', or 'nanny', or 'nanna' or 'gran' as she is often called. **1966** P. MOLONEY *Plea for Mersey* 22 Every true wacker has three relations, viz. 'Me Mar, Me Nin, an me Anti-Mury'.

nincompoopiana (ni:nkǫmpūpi,ā·na). [f. NINCOMPOOP + *-IANA.] (See quots.)

1895 BEERBOHM in *Yellow Bk.* Jan. 279 Long before this time there had been in the heart of Chelsea a kind of cult of Beauty... 'Nincompoopiana' the craze was called at first, and later 'Æstheticism'. **1970** *Sunday Times* 18 Oct. 49/3 'Nincompoopiana' began in the 1880s and was triggered off by the aesthetic movement which rebelled against the pretty and the respectable, and by the 'new woman'.

nine, *a.* and *sb.* Add: **A.** *adj.* **2. b.** *attrib. nine o'clock news*: see *NEWS *sb.* (*pl.*) 5 c. Also *ellipt.*

1942 T. RATTIGAN *Flare Path* II. i. 117 Anyone hear the nine o'clock? I clean forgot the time. **1952** M. LASKI *Village* i. 11 Since the King had spoken on the nine o'clock.

c. (Further examples.)

1635 F. QUARLES *Emblemes* v. iii. 254 'Tis not the sacred wealth of all the Nine Can buy my heart from Him. **1757** J. DYER *Fleece* IV. 145 My Muse..Be thou the first of the harmonious Nine From high Parnassus. **1803** [see MUSE *sb.*[1] 1]. **1852** M. ARNOLD *Empedocles on Etna* 69 'Tis Apollo comes leading His choir, The Nine. **1933** KIPLING in *Times* 23 Feb. 16/1 He called the obedient Nine to aid The varied chase. And Clio kissed.

d. *nine-to-five, nine-till-five*, used *attrib.* (*a*) of a person working between 9 a.m. and 5 p.m.; so *nine-to-fiver, nine-till-fiver*; (*b*) of an occupation pursued between these hours, or of the mentality concerned with such an occupation, or with work only between such hours. So *nine-to-five* (*it*) v., to work between such hours.

1959 *Manch. Guardian* 16 June 5/1 These people are just workers like everybody else..they're all nine-to-fivers. **1960** *News Chron.* 13 Sept. 4/5 An electronic computer, working the nine-to-five shift. **1960** F. RAPHAEL *Limits of Love* I. vi. 80 What do you want him to be? A nine till fiver? **1961** *Oxf. Mag.* 4 May 318/2 The so called '9 to 5' atmosphere and routine. **1962** R. COOK *Crust on its Uppers* i. 25 The game we play, it's got its risks, but it's.. better than nine-to-fiving it. **1965** *Listener* 10 June 856/2 Some 60 per cent. of the students are home-based—a statistic to which the president of the students' union attributes nine-till-five attitudes. **1966** O. NORTON *School of Liars* i. 19 'I hate having my corn measured by someone else's bushel. Especially when it's a tinpot suburban bushel. The nine-to-five world.' That amused him. 'But you're a nine-to-fiver's wife.' **1969** *Times* 13 Mar. 20/3 (Advt.), 9 to 5 men come cheaper by the dozen. **1972** *Nature* 25 Feb. 412/3 The contract people tend to be exclusively '9 to 5' scientists whereas the scientists on grants have the traditional university attitude of ignoring the clock. **1972** F. WARNER *Lying Figures* II. 9, I couldn't stand a nine-to-fiver. **1975** P. G. WINSLOW *Death of Angel* i. 41 Wants a nine to five... That's her type, not a policeman coming in at all hours.

4. c. *nine-hours' day*: a working day of nine hours. So *nine-hours' movement*. Cf. *nine-hour* in Dict., sense 4 a.

1859 *Times* 5 Aug. 3/3 It appears that the 'Conference of the United Building Trades'..is established for the special purpose of carrying the nine hours' movement. **1862** *Leisure Hour* 28 June 413/2 They agreed upon an effort to shorten working time, and fixed upon a nine-hours' day. The phrase includes nine hours' *actual* work.

5. *nine-banded, -spotted* adj.

1909 *Biol. Bull.* XVII. 181 (*title*) A case of normal identical quadruplets in the nine-banded armadillo [sc. *Dasypus novemcinctus*]. **1964** G. DURRELL *Menagerie Manor* i. 34 The nine-banded armadillo..trots about his cage. **1861** *Trans. Illinois Agric. Soc.* IV. 347, I found numerous specimens of a nine-spotted lady-bird (*Coccinella novemnotata*, Herbst,) under dry cow-dung. **1972** SWAN & PAPP *Common Insects N. Amer.* xx. 410 Nine-spotted lady beetle... In California..they are heavy feeders on aphids in alfalfa.

B. *sb.* **4. b.** (See also *LONG NINE.)

6. b. *up to the nines* (earlier and later examples).

1859 HOTTEN *Dict. Slang* 68 *Nines*, 'dressed up to the *nines*', in a showy or recherché manner. **1928** GALSWORTHY *Swan Song* I. viii. 63 Women then were defended up to the nines. **1963** N. C. E. KENRICK *Story Wiltshire Regiment* ix. 86 The 99th's sartorial perfection at this time [*c* 1850] is said to have given rise to the expression 'Dressed up to the nines' as the other Regiments in Aldershot were constantly trying to achieve the same standard. **1965** *Listener* 20 May 742/2 So there they are, whenever a concert is given by their own orchestra, dressed up to the nines and bursting with pride.

c. *nine-nine-nine*, a telephone number dialled in an emergency in order to obtain a connection to the ambulance service, fire brigade, police, etc.; also written *999*.

1937 *Rep. Proc. 14th Conf. ASLIB* 76 The first burglar caught by dialling 999—the new telephone alarm signal. **1939** G. GREENE *19 Stories* (1947) 159 He chose..a telephone box and dialled..999. **1954** I. MURDOCH *Under Net* x. 136 'Better call the police if you see me.'.. 'You go and dial nine nine nine.' **1954** M. PROCTER *Hell is City* I. i. 16, I stopped..and dialled nine-nine-nine. *a* **1956** W. DE LE MARE *Compl. Poems* (1969) 713 Dial 999, and gain at once, Safety from fire, police and ambulance. **1966** 'W. HAGGARD' *Power House* viii. 89 She staggered to the telephone..dialled Nine Nine Nine. **1966** 'A. YORK' *Eliminator* v. 85 Should something happen to him I don't see Lucinda dialling Nine-Nine-Nine. **1973** *Express* (Trinidad & Tobago) 17 Mar. 10/4 We have introduced the 999 system with four cars to cover Morvant, San Juan and Santa Cruz areas. **1974** 'M. INNES' *Appleby's Other Story* vii. 55 He put through a 999 call to the police.

nine-holes. Add: **1. c.** *in the nine-hole*(*s*: in a difficulty. *U.S.*

1863 'E. KIRKE' *My Southern Friends* 76 He owned har [*sc.* a slave] till he got in the nineholes one day, and sold har to the Gin'ral. **1877** *Congress. Rec.* 3 Nov. 230/1 We have put the gentleman in the 'nine-holes'; and there we intend to keep him. **1890** *Ibid.* 12 June 6002/1 The bill.. has passed the Senate, and, to use a Western expression, it will put me 'in the nine-hole' if I do not get it through. **1906** B. L. RIDLEY *Battles & Sk. Army Tennessee* 295 The only time he ever got Johnston apparently in 'a nine hole' was at Resaca, on May 15, 1864.

ninepence. Add: **1.** (Earlier and further examples.)

1546 [see SHILLING 5]. **1607** R. C. tr. *Estienne's World of Wonders* xv. 81 Hauing brought their twelue-pence to nine-pence, and their nine-pence to nothing. **1659** J. HOWELL *Eng. Proverbs* 11/1 As fine as fippence, as neat as nine pence. **1670** J. RAY *Coll. Eng. Proverbs* 206 As like as nine pence to nothing. **1850** F. E. SMEDLEY *Frank Fairlegh* l. 444 Well, let her say 'no' as if she meant it,..and then it will all be as right as ninepence. **1884** *Temple Bar* Aug. 525 The trick of alliteration is often useful to give point to old proverbs. In such familiar sayings as 'fine as fivepence', 'nice as ninepence', 'to lie by the legend', its importance is most curious. **1968** 'C. AIRD' *Henrietta Who?* iv. 37 A rare old state it was in..but your mother.. had it right as ninepence in next to no time.

b. (*nobbut, no more than*) *ninepence in the shilling*: of imperfect intelligence, mentally retarded. *dial.* and *colloq.*

1889 E. PEACOCK *Gloss. Words Manley & Corringham, Lincolnshire* (ed. 2) 370 *Nine-pence-to-the-shilling*, below the average in common sense. 'How's Mr..? Thaay do saay as he's nobut nine-pence-to-th'-shilling.'—M. F., *Scotton*, 1876. **1951** J. B. PRIESTLEY *Festival at Farbridge* III. ii. 521 She's got a husband who's..ninepence in the shilling, a bit barmy. **1957** M. KENNEDY *Heroes of Clone* II. iii. 97 She's ninepence in the shilling. **1964** 'A. GILBERT' *Fingerprint* v. 77 While they might be sympathetic, it was more likely they thought her child no more than ninepence in the shilling.

ninepenny, *sb.* and *a.* Add: **A.** *sb.* **2.** Ale that costs ninepence a gallon.

1886 HARDY *Mayor of Casterbridge* I. xiii. 160 I'm in such a low key with drinking nothing but small table ninepenny this last week or two.

niner. Add: **2.** Formerly, a senior naval cadet in the training-ship *Britannia*.

1914 'BARTIMEUS' *Naval Occasions* ix. 63 Jerry had to submit to strange indignities and stranger torments at the hands of Olympian 'Niners' (Fourth-term Cadets).

nineteen, *a.* (and *sb.*). **2. b.** (Earlier and later examples.)

1785 E. SHERIDAN *Jrnl.* 7 Aug. (1960) ii. 63 The Mother good humour'd and Civil but talks nineteen to the dozen. **1916** 'BOYD CABLE' *Action Front* 187 They must be charging, I think, or our front line's fallen back, because the rifles is going nineteen to the dozen. **1936** A. CHRISTIE *Murder in Mesopotamia* v. 39 Presently Mr Coleman bustled in and took the place beyond Miss Johnson... He talked away nineteen to the dozen. **1956** V. H. COLLINS *Bk. Eng. Idioms* 228 *Talk nineteen to the dozen*... Why 'nineteen'? The obvious numeral would be the round number 'twenty'. Possibly 'nineteen' was chosen just because, not being what might have been expected, it seemed to give a more striking effect.

nineteen eighty-four. The year-date (freq. written in form *1984*): the title of an apocalyptic novel (1949) by 'George Orwell' portraying a society in which government propaganda and terrorizing destroy consciousness of reality; freq. used allusively. Also *1984-ish*. Cf. *DOUBLETHINK, DOUBLE-THINK, *NEWSPEAK.

1959 BENN & PETERS *Social Principles* x. 225 Our antipathy to nineteen eighty-four methods may be due in part to the evil ends with which we associate them, or with the physical and mental cruelty involved in particular techniques. **1959** *Times* 6 May 15/7 We had a constant 1984-ish feeling as we worked in these vast abandoned castles. **1961** L. MUMFORD *City in History* xvii. 527 Whether they extrapolate 1960 or anticipate 2060 their goal is actually '1984'. **1968** *Listener* 29 Feb. 261/1 David Brinkley..pointed to the spokesman who claimed, 'We had to destroy that village to save it,' and commented that 1984 Newspeak had come to 1968. **1970** *Time* 16 Nov. 14 The political uses of television advertising and packaging of candidates were heralded by..doom-sayers as the ominous forerunner of 1984.

nineteenth, *a.* and *sb.* Add: **A.** *adj.* (Earlier and later *Comb.* examples.)

In quot. 1951 used in a quasi-*adj.* phr.

1872 W. F. BUTLER *Gt. Lone Land* (ed. 2) xvi. 241 Terrible deeds..never perhaps more sickening than now in the full blaze of nineteenth-century civilization. **1923** J. W. HARVEY tr. *Otto's Idea of Holy* p. vii, A fair expression of the limitations and bias of the nineteenth-century mind. **1951** C. P. SNOW *Masters* xxxiv. 272 His views were eccentric for an old man, but his manners had stayed gentle and nineteenth century. **1956** R. C. ZAEHNER in A. Pryce-Jones *New Outl. Mod. Knowledge* 65 Nineteenth-century optimism, then, is comparable to Buddhism in the emphasis it lays on individual effort in the battle for salvation.

2. *the nineteenth hole*: the bar-room in a golf club-house. Also *ellipt.* and in extended use. *slang* (orig. *U.S.*).

1901 W. G. VAN T. SUTPHEN (*title*) The nineteenth hole, being tales of the fair green. **1926** *Daily Colonist* (Victoria, B.C.) 11 July 4/3 The immeasurable distance of the nineteenth hole on standard courses is altogether beyond our physical capacity on these hot and golden Summer days. **1928** *Daily Express* 3 Jan. 9/2 Most courses have been completely unplayable, except at the nineteenth hole. **1948** 'J. TEY' *Franchise Affair* i. 7 A good chap who played a very steady game and occasionally, when it came to the nineteenth, expanded into mild indiscretions. **1956** [see *EAR-BASH *v.*]. **1971** *Good Food Guide* 317 The Golf Tavern Nineteenth Hole.

nineteenth-ce·nturyism. The distinctive spirit, outlook, or character of the nineteenth century; a feature or trait suggestive of the nineteenth century.

1846 TENNYSON in H. Tennyson *Alfred Ld. Tennyson* (1897) I. 238 They seem to be very clever and full of a noble 19th century-ism (if you will admit such a word). **1891** 'L. MALET' *Wages of Sin* II. v. iii. 214 There is another of your perverted nineteenth-centuryisms!

ninety. Add: **1. b.** **ninety-day wonder** *U.S. Services' slang*, a graduate of a ninety-day officers' training course; an inexperienced, newly-commissioned officer; also *attrib.* or as *adj.*

1917 R. Lord in *Captain Boyd's Battery, A.E.F.* (1919) ii. 23 Two tents of Shavetails (i.e... Ninety-Day Wonders ..) have been attached to us for instruction purposes. **1919** K. M. Cortelyou et al. *From Arizona to Huns* 106 'A ninty [*sic*] day wonder' fresh from O.T.S. **1921** F. L. Field *Battery Book* 15 The inexperience of officers was a circumstance of tremendous significance. The fact that we used to call them 'ninety-day wonders' indicates our attitude..at the time. **1926** L. H. Nason *Chevrons* 136 You ninety-day wonder!.. Haven't you got brains enough to know this brook runs east and west? **1928** A. C. Havlin *Hist. Company A, 102nd Machine Gun Battalion* 1 As usual, they were dubbed 'ninety-day wonders'. **1956** E. N. Rogers *Queenie's Brood* 307 The draft law and the ninety-day-wonder officers came in for much discussion also. **1970** W. C. Woods *Killing Zone* 5 A pale punk kid to run my company, another ninety day wonder.

2. b. *spec.*, the years between 1890 and 1899. Also *attrib.*

1911 W. G. Blaikie Murdoch *Renaissance of Nineties* 34 Subtlety and delicacy are not more prominent in the painting of the nineties than in the period's literature. *Ibid.* 45 If Life was the watchword of the men of the nineties, Freedom was the motto on their banner. **1913** H. Jackson *Eighteen Nineties* i. 27 Max Beerbohm, in a delightful essay which could only have been written in the Nineties. *Ibid.* ii. 40 *The Yellow Book* and *The Savoy*.. were the favourite lamps around which the most bizarre moths of the Nineties clustered. There were few essential writers of the Nineties who did not contribute to one or the other. **1920** B. Muddiman (*title*) The men of the nineties. **1938** L. MacNeice *Modern Poetry* i. 7 The nineties poets did to some extent criticize life. **1954** A. S. C. Ross in *Neuphilologische Mitteilungen* LV. 32 It was apparently U and was certainly thriving in the nineties. **1971** P. Muir *Victorian Illustrated Books* viii. 194 (*heading*) Other Nineties people. **1972** *Country Life* 23 Nov. 1414/3 The Nineties in Paris were not all decadence, can-can and absinthe. **1975** *Times* 5 Dec. 13/4 A mock-innocent return to the 'nineties.

ninetyish (nəi·nti,iʃ), *a.* [f. Ninety *a.* and *sb.* + -ish[1].] Of, belonging to, or characteristic of 'the nineties' of the nineteenth century; resembling, or suggestive of, what was then current. So **ni·netyism**, the spirit of 'the nineties'; **ni·netyishness**, ninetyish characteristics.

1909 *Westm. Gaz.* 2 Mar. 2/2 What the *Standard* had hoped was that 'there might be a return to the rule of the 'nineties, when the seat was won or lost by a margin between two and five hundred votes'. Certainly there is nothing ninety-ish about Saturday's figures. **1918** E. Marsh *Rupert Brooke* 13 He entertained a *culte*..for the literature that is now called 'ninetyish'—Pater, Wilde and Dowson. **1931** *Times Lit. Suppl.* 23 Apr. 327/4 Thus 'Proteus' in the *New Statesman* describes me as 'engagingly ninety-ish'. **1941** L. MacNeice *Poetry of Yeats* iv. 66 He ceased to be 'ninetyish' with the Nineties. How saturated with 'Ninetyism' he had been can be seen [etc.]. **1959** *Times* 13 Feb. 13/4 Consider the subjects, or titles, of *Verklärte Nacht, Pierrot Lunaire, Wozzeck, Lulu*, all in varying measure products of a decadent romanticism, ranging from 'ninetyishness' to post-Freudian psychopathology. **1973** *Guardian* 28 Mar. 10/1 Firbank seemed negligible..his fictions artificial, *naughty* and Ninetyish.

ning-nong (ni·ŋ,nɒŋ). *dial.* and *Austral. slang.* Also **ning-nang.** [Origin unknown.] A fool, a stupid person. Cf. *nig-nog[1].

1832 *Whitehaven Poll Bk.* 34 He looks parlish like a ning-nang. **1864** Hotten *Slang Dict.* 188 *Ning-nang*, horse-coupers' term for a worthless thorough-bred. **1881** J. Sargisson *Joe Scoap's Jurneh through three Wardles* ii. 189 Wad teh believe't noo, t'Ning-nang can nowder read ner write. **1957** 'N. Culotta' *They're a Weird Mob* (1958) i. 15, I 'ave ter get landed with a bloody ning nong who doesn't know where he's bloody goin'. **1973** *Telegraph* (Brisbane) 14 Mar. 71/1 Even ning-nongs can win prizes on Channel 0's daily quiz show.

Ningre Tongo (niŋgre tɒŋgo). [prob. Taki-Taki, ad. Eng. Nigger *sb.* + Tongue *sb.*] An English-based creole language of Surinam, less divergent from English than **Jew Tongo*.

1933 L. Bloomfield *Lang.* xxvi. 474 Ningre Tongo or taki-taki is spoken by descendants of slaves along the coast. **1939** L. H. Gray *Foundations of Language* 37 The languages are termed *creolised*, examples being the *Taki-Taki* (or *Ningre Tongo*). **1968** [see *Jew Tongo* (*Jew *sb.* 3 c)].

ningyoite (ni·ŋgyo,əit). *Min.* [f. *Ningyo*, the name of a pass in Tottori Prefecture, Japan + -ite[1].] A hydrated phosphate of calcium and uranium, $CaU^{IV}(PO_4)_2.1\frac{1}{2}H_2O$, in which there is some replacement of uranium by lanthanons and which is found as brown or brownish-green orthorhombic crystals.

1959 T. Muto et al. in *Amer. Mineralogist* XLIV. 634 The new mineral, ningyoite, is named for the locality, Ningyo Pass. *Ibid.* 649 The synthetic ningyoite ignited at 600°C. in air for 5–10 minutes still retained the original orthorhombic structure. **1962** *Mineral. Jrnl.* III. 306 Ningyoite contains almost all the rare earths and their abundance ratio resembles that of apatite. **1970** *Econ. Geol.* LXV. 470 For the formation of ningyoite, fixation of much sulfur in comparison with carbonaceous matter should occur before the penetration of uranium-carrying solutions.

ninhydrin (ninhəi·drin). *Chem.* [prob. partially f. the chemical name, *triketohydrindene*, and app. first formed (as a trade name) in Ger.] A brown crystalline compound, $C_9H_6O_4$, which forms coloured products with amines and is particularly used for detecting and estimating amino-acids; triketohydrindene hydrate; 1,2,3-indantrione hydrate. Freq. *attrib.*

[**1912** *Warenzeichenblatt* Nov. 2500/2 Ninhydrin... Farbwerke vorm. Meister Lucius & Brüning, Aktiengesellschaft, Höchst a/M... Geschäftsbetrieb: Chemische Fabrik. Waren: Pharmazeutische und therapeutische Präparate.] **1913** *Chem. Abstr.* VII. 3765 Ninhydrin is a valuable reagent for the detection of non-biuret dialyzable amino acids. **1915** *Jrnl. Biol. Chem.* XX. 218 This discovery [of Ruhemann's] was confirmed and extended by Abderhalden, who applied it to the detection of pregnancy and cancer, triketohydrindene hydrate now being a commercial product under the name of 'ninhydrin'. *Ibid.* XXIII. 382 Free from soluble nitrogen capable of giving the ninhydrin test for amino-acids. **1949** Abraham & Heatley in H. W. Florey et al. *Antibiotics* I. ii. 107 The positions of the separated amino acids on the paper were made visible by the coloration they gave with ninhydrin. **1962** Dardenne & Kirsten in A. Pirie *Lens Metabolism Rel. Cataract* 416 In these hydrolysed lens extracts we detected some 30 non-protein-bound substances which could be determined by the ninhydrin reaction. **1974** W. J. Burley *Death in Stanley St.* x. 161 [We] decided to try a new test for latents. It's supposed to be better than the old ninhydrin test for some surfaces.

ninon (nīnoṅ). [Fr.] A light-weight fabric, used esp. in dresses, made in a plain weave from silk, rayon, or nylon.

1911 *Daily Colonist* (Victoria, B.C.) 15 Apr. 24/1 (Advt.), Three large shipments just to hand making our stock replete with every desired line of silks..Bengaline,..Tamaline..Ninon. **1913** W. J. Locke *Stella Maris* xiii. 160 Dressed in a soft grey ninon gown. **1923** *Daily Mail* 24 Feb. 11 Novel ninons are patterned with designs resembling finely worked embroideries. **1929** D. L. Moore *Pandora's Letter Box* xiv. 254 Everything must be of silk, georgette, triple ninon and so forth. **1948** G. L. Fraser *Textiles by Britain* 165 *Ninon*, fine and closely woven plain-weave semi-transparent dress cloth made either in silk or rayon. **1968** Hollen & Saddler *Textiles* (ed. 3) xvi. 140/1 *Ninon* is a filament sheer widely used for curtains.

ninth, *a.* and *sb.* Add: **B.** *sb.* **2.** Also, a note eight diatonic degrees above or below another note. **b.** In full, *ninth chord.* The chord of such notes; a ninth added to a triad. (Later examples.)

1845 *Encycl. Metrop.* IV. 799 As to pentachords, such as what have been called the major and minor ninth, and compound sharp sixth,..they are..only chords of the seventh..with a fifth note violently forced in. **1876** Stainer & Barrett *Dict. Mus. Terms* 303/1 *Chord of the major ninth*, a chord formed by a combination of thirds starting with the dominant or fifth of the scale, called by some writers the 'added ninth', because it consists of a chord of the dominant seventh, with the addition of the ninth; by others the 'dominant ninth', because it occurs on a dominant bass. *Ibid.* 303/2 *Chord of the minor ninth*.. consists of a dominant, its major third, major (perfect) fifth, minor seventh, and minor ninth. **1926** A. Niles in W. C. Handy *Blues* iii. 16 The device..of ending up the tune on the diminished seventh chord..lately sometimes on the chord of the ninth. **1934** [see *eleventh *sb.* 2]. **1949** L. Feather *Inside Be-Bop* ii. 50 By the 1920's it had become fashionable to end on a seventh or ninth chord. **1952** R. Eldridge in B. Ulanov *Hist. Jazz in Amer.* (1958) xix. 238, I was full of ideas. Augmented chords. Ninths. **1969** *Rolling Stone* 28 June 17/3 In those days country music was very loose in both meter and lyrics... No one had ever heard of a ninth chord.

niobian (nəi,ōᵘ·biăn), *a.* *Min.* [f. Niob(ium + *-ian 2.] Of a mineral: having a (small) proportion of a constituent element replaced by niobium.

1962 [see *ilmenorutile]. **1972** *Nature* 31 Mar. 215/1 Terrestrial dysanalyte is a niobian perovskite which contains about 26% CaO and no detectable ZrO_2.

niocalite (nəi,okæ·ləit). *Min.* [f. Nio(bium + Cal(cium + -ite[1].] A basic silicate and fluoride of niobium and calcium, $Ca_4NbSi_2O_{10}(OH,F)$, found as yellow orthorhombic crystals.

1956 E. H. Nickel in *Amer. Mineralogist* XLI. 785 A new mineral species, for which the name 'niocalite' is here proposed, has been identified in rock from the Oka district, 20 miles west of Montreal, Quebec. **1958** *Canad. Mineralogist* VI. 264 The niocalite occurs as randomly oriented, coarse, prismatic crystals up to one centimetre in length, and occasionally even longer, embedded in the calcite. **1966** *Soviet Physics—Doklady* XI. 197/2 The Patterson projections show that niocalite does not have a screw axis.

niopo (ni,ōᵘ·po). [Native name.] A narcotic snuff used by certain South American Indian tribes, prepared from the seeds of the tropical American trees, *Piptadenia peregrina* and related species. Also *attrib.*

1860 Mayne Reid *Odd People* 134 Snuffing the niopo is not exclusively confined to the Mundrucu. *Ibid.*, The niopo-taker who has one [*sc.* a device for taking snuff, made from the forked bone of a bird], esteems it as the most valuable item of his apparatus. **1900** Dorland *Med. Dict.* 444/1 Niopo-snuff... An intoxicating snuff made from the seeds of *Piptadenia peregrina*, a tree of tropical America. **1966** *New Scientist* 21 Apr. 156/1 Some natives of tropical America use a snuff made from seeds of the tree *Piptadenia peregrina*... This is called cohoba, niopo or parica. **1969** R. R. Lingeman *Drugs from A to Z* 204 A hallucinogenic snuff is made by South American Indians by pulverizing the seeds of the legumes *Piptadenia peregrina*, *P. colubrina*, and *P. macrocarpa*... Among different tribes it is known variously as yopo, niopo, cohoba, and huilca. These tribes are centered in the Orinoco basin of Colombia and Venezuela and in the Peruvian Andes.

nip, *sb.*[1] Add: **I. 1.** *fig.* phr. *to put in the nips*, to cadge, to ask for a loan. Cf. *nip *v.*[1] 2 c. *Austral.* and *N.Z. colloq.*

1919 [see *nip *v.*[1] 2 c]. **1937** Partridge *Dict. Slang* 564/1 *Put the nips in(to*, to ask a loan (from a person): Australian and New Zealand: from ca. 1908. **1949** L. Glassop *Lucky Palmer* 230 You can't put the nips into old Alf. He's got death adders in his pockets. **1955** D. Niland *Shiralee* 41 He was here yesterday, too. Put the nips into me for tea and sugar and tobacco in his usual style. **1963** B. Pearson *Coal Flat* x. 190 'The woman's getting too serious,' he thought; 'she's putting the nips in.' **1973** F. Huelin *Keep Moving* 48 Parsons, priests, doctors, lawyers and professional people generally were legitimate prey, and we had no scruples about 'putting the nips' into them.

4. *Cricket.* Restrict † *Obs.* to sense in Dict. and add: **b.** The quality in bowling which causes the ball to rise sharply from the pitch.

1963 A. Ross *Australia 63* iii. 75 Coldwell had been varying pace and direction skilfully and only that lack of final nip which Bedser possessed prevented him from being even more troublesome.

6. For (U.S.) read (chiefly U.S.). (Earlier and later examples.) *nip and tuck folder*: see quot. 1964.

1832 J. K. Paulding *Westward Ho!* I. 172 There we were at rip *and* tuck [*sic*], up one tree and down another. **1847** W. T. Porter *Quarter Race in Kentucky* 16 (Th.), It will be like the old bitch and the rabbit, nick and tack every jump. *Ibid.* 123 (Th.), Then we'd have it again, nip and chuck. **1857** *Knickerbocker* L. 498 (Th.), [I got the trout off the fire] by the head, and the dog got him by the tail, and it was nip and tuck, pull Dick, pull devil. **1890** Barrère & Leland *Dict. Slang* II. 87/1 *Nip and tuck* (Cornwall), a close contest. An old term in wrestling. **1906** J. London *Let.* 1 Dec. (1966) 226 This means..loss of money in the first months of the voyage, during which time things will be just nip and tuck with me. **1948** *Economist* 8 May 764/2 It is nip and tuck whether such a last great achievement of the bipartisan foreign policy can be ratified before..the Presidential race. **1964** *Gloss. Letterpress Rotary Print. Terms* (*B.S.I.*) 25 *Nip and tuck folder*, a type of folder in which the fold at right angles to the run of the web is formed by a blade thrusting the web between folding jaws. **1968** *Economist* 9 Nov. 28/3 The Vice President said that there were still several important states nip-and-tuck. **1974** *State* (Columbia, S. Carolina) 5 Mar. 6–A/1 It was nip and tuck the rest of the way with two straight Cunningham baskets to open the fourth quarter knotting the count, 40–40, with 7:28 left to play.

8. c. The narrow gap or area of contact between two rollers; the rollers themselves.

1884 W. S. B. McLaren *Spinning* 250 Nip of rollers, the point where a pair of rollers touch each other, and where, consequently, they hold or nip the wool. *Ibid.* iii. 35 The lowest rollers..have their nip below the level of the suds. **1946** A. J. Hall *Stand. Handbk. Textiles* iv. 171 The fabric receives a light squeeze as it passes between the nip of the mangle rollers. **1969** W. R. R. Park *Plastics Film Technol.* ii. 12 Aluminium foil is made by passing hot sheet through a series of hot, highly polished, precision finished metal roll nips. **1972** *Materials & Technol.* V. 515 The opening between the two rolls—the nip—is adjusted in such a way that when pieces of rubber are fed into the nip they are gripped and squeezed through the opening.

III. 10. *Geol.* A low cliff cut along a gently sloping coastline by wave action; also, a notch cut along the base of a pre-existing coastal cliff by wave action.

1897 *Geogr. Jrnl.* IX. 542 Where the aggradation begins at the shoreline at the foot of the earlier formed 'nip'. **1919** D. W. Johnson *Shore Processes & Shoreline Development* v. 259 If the lagoon waves are too feeble, the nip may be entirely lacking. **1939** A. K. Lobeck *Geomorphology* x. 347 The smaller waves advance landward and cut low cliffs in the weak material of which the land is usually composed. Thus a nip is produced. **1942** C. A. Cotton *Geomorphology* (ed. 3) xxix. 409 Erosion may be so rapid that in cliffs of tough, unjointed rock a nip is cut—that is, a notch along the base, above which the cliff overhangs. **1958** Sparks & Kneese tr. *Guilcher's Coastal & Submarine Morphology* iii. 64 That notches or nips at the base of cliffs are due to mechanical erosion is often much more improbable.

nip, *sb.*[2] Add: **2.** *Comb.* **nip bottle,** a miniature bottle of spirits (literally, one containing enough for one drink); **nip joint** *U.S.*, an establishment illegally selling (small quantities of) spirits.

1915 A. D. Gillespie *Lett. from Flanders* (1916) 150 The etcetera now includes goggles, respirators, and 'nip bottles' of chemicals. **1939** *Sun* (Baltimore) 18 Aug. 24/7 A hearing by the Liquor Board on the advisability of banning the sale of miniature, or 'nip' bottles of alcoholic drink. **1936** *Ibid.* 28 Jan. 9/1 The bills were opposed by.. Raye O. Lawson,..who said the legislation would increase bootlegging and 'nip joints'. **1938** *Ibid.* 10 Sept. 4/1 The court ordered restored to the owners a house which had been padlocked on conviction of a tenant for operating a 'nip joint'.

Nip, *sb.*^{6} and *a.* [Abbrev. of *NIPPONESE.] (A) Japanese. *slang.*

Usually abusive.

1942 *Time* 9 Feb. 23/3, I visited a command post in one sector where they had just rounded up a bunch of Nips. **1942** *R.A.F. Jrnl.* 31 Oct. 13 The Nip pilots. **1947** J. BERTRAM *Shadow of War* I. ii. 12 The Nips keep bombing the airfields. **1965** R. T. BICKERS *Scent of Mayhem* iii. 30 La belle Pauline was a secretary at the Nip Embassy in Paris. **1971** J. OSBORNE *West of Suez* I. 27 Few little Nips popping away with cameras. **1973** *Islander* (Victoria, B.C.) 19 Aug. 12/2 Who hadn't quite made up their minds about what should be done with Hitler and Mussolini and the Nips.

nip, *v.*^{1} Add: **1. d.** (Earlier and later examples.)

1850 S. OSBORN *Stray Leaves Arctic Jrnl.* (1852) 72 Penny had passed a long way inside of the spot the steamers had been beset and nipped in. **1937** *Beaver* June 13/2 The 'Fort James', a Company schooner, was 'nipped' in the ice at Tuktuk. **1966** T. ARMSTRONG et al. *Gloss. Snow & Ice* 29 *Nip*, ice is said to nip when it forcibly presses against a ship which is *beset*. A vessel so caught, though undamaged, is said to have been nipped.

2. c. To borrow, to obtain by wheedling. Cf. *NIP *sb.*^{1} 1 *slang* (chiefly *Austral.*).

1919 W. H. DOWNING *Digger Dial.* 35 *Nip*, to cadge (or 'Put in the Nips'). **1925** FRASER & GIBBONS *Soldier & Sailor Words* 209 *To nip*, to cadge.

4. Restrict † to senses in Dict. and add: **c.** To defeat narrowly (in a sporting contest). *U.S.*

1942 BERREY & VAN DEN BARK *Amer. Thes. Slang* §649/3 Defeat..nick, nip, outbeat, outwin. **1942** *Sun* (Baltimore) 29 Apr. 19/1 Miss Goshen, under Eddie DeCamillis, came along in the stretch to take the second by two lengths. Sobriquet got up to nip Spare the Rod for second honors. **1951** *Amer. Speech* XXVI. 230/2 Oregon nips St. Mary's. **1966** *N.Y. Times* (Internat. ed.) 22 Apr. 12/1 The Pirates nipped the Reds, 3–2. **1969** *Eugene* (Oregon) *Register-Guard* 3 Dec. 1D/5 The Ducks.. will continue their three-game..against highly rated Florida State, which nipped touring Oregon State 69–68 Tuesday night. **1974** *Anderson* (S. Carolina) *Independent* 19 Apr. 4B/2 Danny Ford banged out four hits and knocked in two runs as Augusta College nipped Erskine, 6–5, here Thursday.

5. Also with *off*.

1902 *Chambers's Jrnl.* Nov. 742/2 Small establishments for the treatment of manufacturing refuse..are nipped off by a rise in the price of fuel.

12. (Later examples. In quot. 1919 *trans.*) Freq. *fig.*, as to cut *in*, and in extended use, to move informally or unobtrusively, often quickly, *away*, *out*, etc. Occas. without adv.

1908 H. G. WELLS *War in Air* v. 155 She [*sc.* a ship] had..nipped in between the *Susquehanna* and the *Kansas City*. **1909** A. QUILLER-COUCH *True Tilda* xiii. 169 'If they catch up with us we must nip into a gateway,' panted Tilda. **1919** *Times Lit. Suppl.* 27 Feb. 107/3 'The light-hearted snottie' who nipped in his piquet boat across the knife-edged ram of a fast-travelling cruiser. **1920** *Blackw. Mag.* Jan. 111/2 Your friend..nips in and takes up the running, and you are out of the hunt. **1920** D. H. LAWRENCE *Let.* 9 Apr. in C. Mackenzie *My Life & Times* (1966) V. 177 Nip over here for a short while! **1926** T. E. LAWRENCE *Seven Pillars* lviii. 355 So, watching the time, one or two of the quicker youths nipped across to drag back the saddle-bags. **1930** M. ALLINGHAM *Mystery Mile* xxi. 199 'Shall we nip off?' said Knapp nervously. **1930** W. S. MAUGHAM *Bread-Winner* 115 If Uncle Alfred wants us to get out we'd better nip before Daddy comes back. **1930** J. B. PRIESTLEY *Angel Pavement* vi. 299 Now then,.. just nip back for the plates. **1947** *People* 22 June 7/5 Meantime, Club No. 2..nipped in, handed the 'very famous footballer' the thousand smackers.., and clinched the transfer. **1955** M. GILBERT *Sky High* viii. 115 If you nip along now..you could catch her before the practice starts. **1962** C. OMAN *Mary of Modena* v. 187 All the visiting English who could manage it quietly nipped off to see the Prince of Wales. **1969** *Listener* 14 Aug. 205/2 Nipping out for a smoke during the odd bit of Schoenberg. **1973** A. MANN *Tiara* xiii. 118 Piccoli's will still be open. Shall I nip down and get pictures of all these types?

b. Of a cricket ball: to come sharply *off* the pitch; also *absol.*

1899 *Captain* I. 516/1 Another..makes the ball nip off the pitch like a marble off a granite wall. **1903** P. F. WARNER in H. G. Hutchinson *Cricket* xiv. 399 Matting on the bare grassless ground favours the batsman, though I am inclined to think that a really good bowler ought always to be able to make the ball 'nip' a bit.

nipa. 2. In def. substitute 'native to coastal regions in tropical Asia and Australia' for 'native to the coasts and islands of the Indian seas'. (Earlier and later examples.)

1779 T. FORREST *Voy. New Guinea* i. 16 She was covered almost entirely with the leaves of a certain Palm tree, called Nipa, such as the natives cover houses with on the south-west coast of Sumatra, and in almost all Malay countries. **1783** W. MARSDEN *Hist. Sumatra* 46 Those [people] of the lowest class have their fillet of the leaf of the *neepah* tree. **1817** [see *ATTAP]. **1926** E. BLATTER *Palms Brit. India* 553 Nipa is the vernacular name of the palm in the Philippines. **1954** R. H. HOLTTUM *Plant Life in Malaya* ii. 23 One of the most peculiar of all palms is Nipah, which grows on muddy river banks near the sea. **1962** B. HARRISSON *Orang-Utan* iv. 139, I had boarded ship at the mouth of the Rejang River where it had anchored alongside mud, mangrove and nipah-palms. **1966** D. FORBES *Heart of Malaya* xiii. 161 The wooden beach bungalows. thatched with the nipa palm,..were all empty. **1969** J. M. GULLICK *Malaysia* iv. 160 *Nipah* is a type of palm whose fronds are plaited for use as thatch. **1973** *Telegraph* (Brisbane) 2 Apr. 12/1 They tied the two women up in a nipa (thatched grass) hut.

Nipkow disc (ni·pkǫf). *Television.* [f. the name of Paul *Nipkow* (1860–1940), Polish electrical engineer, who invented it in 1884.] A scanning disc used in some early television transmitters and receivers having a line of small apertures near the circumference arranged in a spiral of one complete turn, so that on each revolution of the disc an area is scanned equal in height to the radial distance between the first and last apertures.

1934 J. H. REYNER *Television* xiv. 161 Until recent times most of the Continental systems..have been of the Nipkow disc type, and in that main respect similar to the Baird system. **1962** G. A. T. BURDETT *Automatic Control Handbk.* xxi. 6 There are three types of scanning device in existence,..the Nipkow disc,..the flying-spot scanner and the pick-up tube. *Ibid.*, A development of the Nipkow disc has recently been produced in the U.S.A. for use as a slow-scan device for the transmission of documents. **1974** *Encycl. Brit. Macropædia* XVIII. 105/2 Until the advent of electronic scanning, all workable television systems depended on some form or variation (*e.g.*, mirror drums, lensed disks, etc.) of the mechanical sequential scanning method exemplified by the Nipkow disk.

nipper, *sb.*^{1} Add: **3.** (Later examples.)

1968 *Courier-Mail* (Brisbane) 21 Nov. 3/5 The men, employed by the Public Works Department, claimed the job foreman would not let their 'nipper' patronise the sandwich shop of his choice. A nipper is a boy or man who boils the billies, runs messages, buys lunches, and does similar jobs. **1971** R. ROBERTS *Classic Slum* viii. 125 The nippers, carters' helps. The nipper looked after the horse and sat guard over goods at the tail end of the vehicle.

b. (Earlier, *attrib.*, and later examples.) Also, a girl; a child of either sex; the smallest or youngest of a family.

[**1847** DICKENS *Dombey* (1848) xxiii. 240 Florence endeavoured to believe that the Captain was right; but the Nipper..shook her head in resolute denial.] **1859** HOTTEN *Dict. Slang* 68 *Nipper*, a small boy. **1875** W. D. PARISH *Dict. Sussex Dial.*, *Nipper*, a common nickname for the youngest member of the family, or for one who is unusually small for his age. **1901** M. FRANKLIN *My Brilliant Career* x. 81 By George, you're a wonderful-looking girl!.. You are such a little nipper. **1928** J. MASON *Before Mast in Sailing Ships* 128 Next to Clarke was a Scottish lad by the name of Nisbet, from Inverness-shire. He was the smallest, and was called the 'Nipper'. **1941** *Lilliput* Mar. 371/1 A family party..arrived on the scene: Mother, aunty, two nippers—a girl and a boy. **1959** I. & P. OPIE *Lore & Lang. Schoolch.* ix. 170 Little 'uns..midge, nipper, penguin, pint-size. **1967** *Courier-Mail* (Brisbane) 3 Feb. 6/8 The establishment of 'nipper clubs' for boys aged from eight to 13 would guarantee the future of the surf club movement. **1969** VISCT. BUCKMASTER *Roundabout* ii. 35 He [*sc.* a butler] was..always in domestic trouble from the arrival of what he would call 'another little nipper'. **1972** *Times* 3 June 19/1 When I was a nipper at school in Glasgow [etc.].

4. c. (Earlier and later examples.)

1821 D. HAGGART *Life* 94 That's one of the bulkies from Dumfries, wanting to clap the nippers on me. **1876** J. S. INGRAM *Centenn. Exposition* viii. 235 The curious part of this [hardware] exhibit consisted in the police nippers. **1910** *Encycl. Brit.* X. 296/1 Several recently invented appliances are used as handcuffs, *e.g.* snaps, nippers, twisters. They differ from handcuffs in being intended for one wrist only... The nippers can be instantly fastened on the wrist. **1918** *Outlook* (N.Y.) 25 Sept. 126/1 A newly appointed policeman..has to buy ..a pair of nippers. **1939** *Fortune* July 104/1 At 2145 one of the detectives put nippers on the prisoner's wrist. **1950** H. E. GOLDIN *Dict. Amer. Underworld Lingo* 145/2 We hit a scorf joint (went into an eating place), and the dick (detective) took the nippers off.

nippet, nippit, Sc. varr. NIPPED *ppl. a.* (chiefly in senses: miserly; scanty; starved; of restricted mental attitude; bitter, sarcastic).

1535 [see NIPPED *ppl. a.*]. **1808** JAMIESON, *Nippit*, adj. 1. Niggardly, parsimonious... 2. Too small, scanty. **1814** C. I. JOHNSTONE *Saxon & Gaël* I. ix. 121 Na, na, I ne'er liket to be nippit or pinging, gie me routhrie o' a'thing. **1857** H. S. RIDDELL *St. Matthew* xxv. 24, I kennet thee that thou art ane nippet man, sheerin' whare thou hestna sawn, an' getherin' whare thou hestna strinklet. *c* **1860** in *Scotsman* (1912) 13 Sept., 'She is a puir nippet creater' —A poorly-fed child. **1875** N. ELLIOTT *Nellie Macpherson* 165 As regards the langidge, ye maunna be ower nippet on that point. **1924** A. DODD *Poppies in Corn* 33 Ye're naewise mean or nippit. **1925** *Glasgow Herald* 23 May 4/4 Nannie..rejected nothing—but oatcakes. The misguided and 'nippet' woman at the Sluices once offered these, conspicuously ill-baked. **1935** D. KIRKWOOD *My Life of Revolt* 222 Philip Snowden's views were precise, narrow, and moulded by the immediate circumstances. The Scotsmen used to call him 'nippet'. **1962** *Buchan Observer* 24 July 2 Nippet words an' soor ill-naiter Gart her man an' bairns behave!

nippily, *adv.* Delete *rare*$^{-1}$ and add later examples.

1972 *Guardian* 10 Nov. 11/1 The new 3-Door Renault 5 ..[will] take you nippily through town traffic snarl-ups. **1974** *Times* 3 Jan. 23/3 The 128 [Fiat] handles nippily, with good roadholding.

nippiness (ni·pinės). [f. NIPPY *a.* + -NESS.] Nimbleness, agility.

1923 U. L. SILBERRAD *Lett. J. Armiter* ii. 50 Jethro is smitten with admiration of her agility; 'nippiness' he calls it. **1932** *Daily Express* 2 July 11/2 Perry's volleys, Hughes' return of service and overhead smashing, and the perpetual nippiness of our two men, gave us the victory.

nipping, *ppl. a.* (and *adv.*). Add: **5.** ***nipping-roller.***

1920 *Discovery* Mar. 88/1 The padded goods are well squeezed through nipping-rollers, and then dried and 'backed'. **1964** *Gloss. Letterpress Rotary Printing Terms* (*B.S.I.*) 25 *Nipping rollers*, a pair of rollers adjustable to exert pressure to set a fold. **1967** V. STRAUSS *Printing Industry* vi. 382/2 The cutting cylinder cuts the web after it passes the nipping rollers.

nipple, *sb.* **4. c.** **nipple cactus**, for '*Mamillaria*' substitute the correct spelling '*Mammillaria*'. (Examples.)

1876 *Encycl. Brit.* IV. 625/2 Mammillaria.—This group..is called Nipple Cactus. **1971** D. WENIGER *Cacti of Southwest* 122/1 *Mammillaria similis*... 'Nipple Cactus'.

Nippon (ni·pǫn). [Jap., f. *ni*(*chi* the sun + *pon*, *hon* source.] **1.** The Japanese name for Japan.

1727 J. G. SCHEUCHZER tr. *Kæmpfer's Hist. Japan* I. I. iv. 58 This Empire is by the Europeans call'd *Japan*. The Natives give it several names and characters. The most common, and most frequently us'd in their writings and conversation, is *Nipon*, which is sometimes in a more elegant manner, and particular to this Nation, pronounc'd Nifon... It signifies, *the foundation of the Sun*. **1859** K. CORNWALLIS *Two Journeys to Japan* I. vii. 187 It was against the laws of Nipon—in speaking of their own country this was the invariable term and pronunciation. **1890** B. H. CHAMBERLAIN *Things Japanese* 174 Our word 'Japan', and the Japanese *Nihon* or *Nippon* are alike corruptions of *Jih-pên*,..literally 'sun-origin' a name given to Japan by the Chinese. **1914** M. KLEIN *By Nippon's Lotus Ponds* v. 62 Nippon's old custom wills that the..wife or..servant girl closely seal up the house with..big rain-doors. **1940** E. POUND *Cantos* lviii. 74 Sinbu put order in Sun land, Nippon, in the beginning of all things. **1942** *R.A.F. Jrnl.* 13 June 5 The sons of Nippon had become aware that their destiny was to establish a New Order in the East. **1975** O. SELA *Bengali Inheritance* xviii. 160 The Indians in Nippon dominated territory.

2. Nippon vellum = *Japanese vellum* (*JAPANESE *a.* b).

1926 *Brit. Weekly* 3 June 185/3 They will simultaneously issue special editions on nippon vellum. **1958** J. R. BIGGS *Woodcuts* 91 *Nippon Vellum* and *Jappon Vellum*.. are imitation vellum papers whose smooth, creamy kindly surface is just right for some prints.

Nipponese (nipǫ̆nī·z). [f. *NIPPON + -ESE.] **a.** The Japanese people; an individual Japanese. **b.** The Japanese language. Also *attrib.* or as *adj.*

1859 K. CORNWALLIS *Two Journeys to Japan* I. 205 Beyond..was to be seen the houses of the town of Napa.. wherein were moored several large junks, native and Niponese. **1860** R. H. DANA *Jrnl.* 24 Apr. (1968) III. 1027 This island, Yeso, is a conquest of the Japanese (Niponese). **1927** E. POUND *Let.* 9 Nov. (1971) 214 At present it is the scattered fragments left by a dead man, edited by a man ignorant of Japanese. Naturally any sonvbitch who knows a little Nipponese can jump on it or say his flatfooted renderings are a safer guide to the style of that country. **1931** *Lit. Digest* 16 May 45/1 Your Nipponese..looks as tho nothing short of an earthquake would startle him. **1935** J. JOYCE *Let.* c 18 Feb. (1966) III. 343 He wore a kimono and scarlet vest. I suppose the Nipponese evening dress. **1942** [see *crash-dive vb.]. **1944** *Sun* (Baltimore) 25 Nov. 2/4 Nipponese planes were shot down. **1948** A. KEITH *Three came Home* i. 33 The war was coming to the East, and..the Nipponese were coming to Borneo. **1973** 'S. HARVESTER' *Corner of Playground* I. viii. 66 The apparent end of traditional Nipponese spiritual values under the steam-roller of post-war materialism.

Nipponian (nipōᵘ·niăn), *a.* [f. *NIPPON + -IAN.] Of or pertaining to Japan, Japanese. So **Ni·pponism**, the furtherance of Japanese nationalistic interests.

1909 *Daily Chron.* 19 Aug. 4/6 The best English account of the conflict from the Nipponian point of view. **1914** *Encycl. Relig. & Ethics* VII. 489/1 The cry of 'Nipponism' ..was raised in a somewhat extravagant fashion.

Nippy (ni·pi), *sb.* [f. the adj.] Formerly, a waitress in one of the restaurants of J. Lyons & Co. Ltd., London; hence, any waitress.

1925 *Punch* 11 Feb. 167/2, I can't mike up me mind weyver to be a lidy's 'elp or a 'nippy'. **1941** J. SMILEY *Hash House Lingo* 39 *Nippy*, waitress. **1948** G. V. GALWEY *Lift & Drop* vi. 161 His hands stuck out in front of him like a Nippy carrying a tray. **1973** *Country Life* 22 Nov. 1736/1 Biba's shiny black tea boxes have three Nippies in gold decorating the label. **1974** W. FOLEY *Child in Forest* II. 251 The big brightly lit clean teashop in Oxford Street where I worked as a Nippy.

Nirvana. Add: **b. Nirvana principle** *Psychol.*, in psychoanalytic theory, the attraction felt by the psyche for a state of non-existence,

which Freud connected with the death-instinct, countering the tensions set up by the pleasure principle.

1920 B. Low *Psycho-Analysis* (ed. 2) iii. 73 It is possible that deeper than the Pleasure-principle lies the Nirvana-principle, as one may call it—the desire of the newborn creature to return to that stage of omnipotence, where there are no non-fulfilled desires, in which it existed within the mother's womb. **1924** J. Riviere tr. *Freud's Econ. Problem in Masochism* in *Coll. Papers* II. xxii. 256 For this tendency that has been presumed by us Barbara Low has suggested the name Nirvana-principle, which we accept. But we have unquestioningly identified the pleasure-pain-principle with this Nirvana-principle. *Ibid.* 257 The *Nirvana*-principle expresses the tendency of the death-instincts. **1936** *Brit. Jrnl. Psychol.* Jan. 286 In the biological-physical conception of a tendency to death (for which they would reserve the name 'Nirvana principle') there is no room for Eros. **1973** L. Bellak et al. *Ego Functions* II. xiv. 212 Do these data invalidate the Nirvana principle, or can that tenet be modified to include the seemingly contradictory clinical observations?

Hence **Nirva·na-ing** *vbl. sb.*, experiencing the state of nirvana; **Nirva·nist,** one who experiences this state.

1898 G. B. Shaw *Perfect Wagnerite* 106 He rested himself as a Pessimist and Nirvanist. **1921** D. H. Lawrence in *Reminisc. & Corr.* (1934) 23 Nirvana-ing is surely a state of continuing as you are. **1922** —— *Aaron's Rod* xxi. 309 And you've never got to think you'll dodge the responsibility of your own soul's self, by loving or sacrificing or Nirvanaing. *a* **1930** —— *Sex, Lit. & Censorship* (1955) 101 Even the Nirvanists consider man as a fixed entity.

‖**Nisan** (ni·săn, nɪ·sān). Also † **Nysan.** [Heb. *Nīsān.*] The first month of the Jewish ecclesiastical year and the seventh of the civil year, formerly called Abib.

1382 Wyclif *Neh.* (2nd text) ii. 1 Forsothe it was doon in the monethe Nysan, in the twentithe ȝeer of Artaxerses, kyng. **1535** Coverdale *Neh.* ii. 1 In the moneth Nisan of the twentieth yeare of kynge Artaxerses. **1611** Bible *Neh.* ii. 1 And it came to passe, in the moneth Nisan,..that wine was before him. **1737** W. Whiston tr. *Josephus' Works* 9 Moses appointed that Nisan, which is the same with Xanthicus, should be the first month, for their festivals; because he brought them out of Egypt in that month. **1846** Geo. Eliot *Let. c* Apr. (1954) I. 213 The evening of the 13th Nisan..would be what Strauss calls the *Vorabend* des Pascha. **1934** T. S. Eliot *Rock* i. 35 In Shushan the palace, in the month Nisan, He served the wine to the King Artaxerxes. **1972** C. Raphael *Feast of History* i. 32/1 A hand-written Hebrew-Russian calendar..open at Nisan, the month of Passover.

nisei (ni·sē[1]). Also **nissei,** and with capital initial. Pl. **nisei.** [Jap., f. *ni-* second + *sei* generation.] An American born of Japanese parents. Also *attrib.*

1943 S. Menefee *Assignment: U.S.A.* 191 The War Relocation Authority, after a delay of many months, finally began to release those Nisei, or American-born Japanese. **1945** Mencken *Amer. Lang.* Suppl. I. 608 The designation *nisei*..for Japanese of American birth was seldom heard, before Pearl Harbor, save on the Pacific Coast... *Nisei* is sometimes spelled *nissei.* **1948** *Newsweek* 30 Aug. 20/1 The 29-year-old Nisei claimed that she had taken a job with the Tokyo radio merely 'for the experience'. **1957** *New Yorker* 16 Nov. 125/1 It would be difficult for a Japanese born student to..date a nisei girl. **1972** J. Ball *Five Pieces of Jade* v. 51 The bespectacled, crew-cut, Babbitt-looking Nisei detective. **1973** *Publishers Weekly* 3 Sept. 48/3 This diary, kept for eight months in 1942 by a 26-year-old Nisei.

nish, var. Nesh *a.*

1925 *Dialect Notes* V. 237 *Nish*.., delicate. **1963** *Amer. Speech* XXXVIII. 299 [Newfoundland] *Nish, adj.* (1) Tender. (2) Easily injured. **1964** L. E. F. English *Historic Newfoundland* 31 Nish, tender, easily injured.

nisin (nəi·sin). *Pharm.* [See quot. 1947 and -in[1].] A mixture of closely related polypeptides produced by the bacterium *Streptococcus lactis* which is active against Gram-positive bacteria and is used in some countries as a food preservative.

1947 Mattick & Hirsch in *Lancet* 5 July 5/1 We have already given some account..of the action in vivo of an inhibitory substance*, isolated from lactic streptococci, against streptococcal infections of the mouse. [*Note*] *Group N Inhibitory Substance: (G) Nisin. **1959** *Times* 9 Mar. (Britain's Food Suppl.) p. viii/2 Nisin is an easily digested protein. **1963** *B.S.I. News* Feb. 13/2 The bacteriological examination of butter, milk, cheese and ice-cream, and for the detection and assay of nisin. **1972** *Sci. Amer.* Mar. 18/3 A number of countries have permitted such antibiotics as tetracyclines, nystatin, nisin..as direct or indirect additives to chilled or raw fish.

Niska: see *Nass.

1895 F. Boas in *Rep. Brit. Assoc. Adv. Sci.* 569 The customs of the Nîsk·a and those of the Tsimshian..are practically identical. *Ibid.* 583 The Nîsk·a does not differ very much from the Tsimshian. **1973** *Times* 27 Dec. 6/4 There is also a portrait mask of an old woman (c 1825–1850) from the Niska of British Columbia, of wood inlaid with abalone shell.

niskh(i), varr. *naskhi *sb. pl.*

Nissen (ni·sən). [Name of the inventor, Lt.-Col. Peter Norman *Nissen* (1871–1930).] Used *attrib.* and *absol.* of a tunnel-shaped hut made of corrugated iron with a cement floor.

1917 E. F. Wood *Note-Book of Intelligence Officer* 224 Recently I met the inventor of the now famous Nissen hut. **1932** Auden *Orators* iii. 114 These nissen huts if hiding could Your eye inseeing from Firm fenders were. **1942** *R.A.F. Jrnl.* 16 May 3 In Nissen huts, with orders coming through from Flight Commander all day and night. **1948** G. Greene *Heart of Matter* iii. i. 191, I would never go back there, to the Nissen hut, if it meant that she were happy. *Ibid.* 192 The rain hammered on the Nissen roofs. *Ibid.* 222 He's living in one of the Nissens now. **1954** W. Faulkner *Fable* (1955) 86 It was not the Nissen walls which trembled. **1973** J. Wainwright *Pride of Pigs* 72 There's a glorified Nissen hut—a bit of a youth club—on the site.

Nissl (ni·s'l). *Med.* The name of Franz *Nissl* (1860–1919), German neurologist, used *attrib.* and in the possessive to designate esp. a methylene blue stain (*Nissl('s) stain*) used for the cell bodies of neurones; the application of this stain (*Nissl('s) method*); and hence the small cytoplasmic structures (*Nissl('s) bodies, granules*) revealed in the cell bodies of neurones by this method. Also **Nissl degeneration,** degeneration of the cell bodies of neurones, accompanied by disappearance of their Nissl bodies; **Nissl('s) substance,** the Nissl bodies collectively.

1898 *Jrnl. Mental Sci.* XLIV. 730 The Nissl bodies.., which stain deeply with basic dyes. **1899** *Jrnl. R. Microsc. Soc.* 448 (*heading*) New Nissl method. **1899** L. F. Barker *Nervous System* 110 He thinks it very wrong that these should be thrown all together and designated either 'Nissl's substance' or 'tigroid substance'. **1901** *Jrnl. Exper. Med.* V. 551 The principles of Nissl's method are extremely simple. *Ibid.* 553 A definite reaction to the Nissl stain. *Ibid.* 554 He finds the Nissl granules embedded in a homogeneous coagulum-like mass. **1905** Gould *Dict. New Med. Terms* 129/1 Staining with Nissl's stain (methylene-blue). **1911** Stedman *Med. Dict.* 586/2 Nissl degeneration. **1933** *Amer. Jrnl. Anat.* LIII. 153 The cells are indeed very light; the Nissl substance is scanty. **1943** Strong & Elwyn *Human Neuroanat.* iii. 28/1 The significance of the Nissl stain.. lies in the fact that..each type of nerve cell always presents the same appearance or 'equivalent picture' in normal conditions. **1966** Wright & Symmers *Systemic Path.* II. xxxiv. 1147/1 In the cytoplasm of the neuron, certain polygonal, basiphile structures, known collectively as Nissl substance, are present. **1968** Passmore & Robson *Compan. Med. Studies* I. xiv. 2/2 Nissl granules are present in the perikaryons of all neurones. **1971** *Sci. Amer.* July 48/2 The Nissl method made it possible to outline and identify well-defined regions in the brain. **1971** J. Z. Young *Introd. Study Man* xi. 147 Nerve cells are characterized by a large amount of ribonucleic acid in the cytoplasm—the basophilic Nissl bodies. **1974** Passmore & Robson *Compan. Med. Studies* III. ii. xxxiv. 33/2 The parent cell bodies undergo central chromatolysis (Nissl degeneration).

nit, *sb.*[1] **2.** Delete †*Obs.* and add further examples. Now esp., a stupid or incompetent person. *colloq.*

Influenced by *nitwit.

1941 Baker *Dict. Austral. Slang* 49 *Nit*, a simpleton or fool. **1961** *Sunday Times* 17 Sept. 41/4 Livings's latest work, 'Sacred Nit'. **1962** *Melody Maker* 11 Aug 6/1 I could see he wasn't very impressed with this nit sitting across the table. **1963** [see *coot *sb.*[1] 4]. **1967** S. Knight *Window on Shanghai* xxiii. 97 You ask a crazy question —Xmas ???!!! The Chinese certainly enjoy celebrating, but for goodness sake! You nit, Mum—can you imagine them trooping to church on December 25? **1972** P. Cleife *Slick & Dead* ii. ix. 70 If you think..I would be willing to allow you..to board my aircraft..then you must be a nit.

4. *Comb.*, as *nit-comb.*

1943 D. Ibberson *Our Towns* iii. 72 A square-toothed steel nit-comb..is too expensive for the poorest. **1959** F. Donaldson *Child of Twenties* iii. 39 My mother washed her head again and again, and combed her hair with a nit-comb.

nit (nit), *sb.*[2] *Austral.* [Origin unknown; but cf. Nix[1] 3, a parallel use.] **1.** A word used as a signal that someone is approaching.

1899 H. Lawson *If I could Paint* in *Stories* (1964) 3rd. Ser. 416 I'd call it 'Nit! There's Mother.' **1911** L. Stone *Jonah* 8 Suddenly there was a cry of 'Nit! 'Ere's a cop!' and the push bolted like rabbits.

2. Usu. in phr. *to keep nit,* to keep watch, to act as guard. Hence **ni·tkeeper,** one who acts as sentinel, usu. while some illegal activity is being carried on.

1935 *Bulletin* (Sydney) 22 May 21/1 That outlaw the sulphur-crested cockatoo is not the only bird to post a 'nit-keeper' when transgressing against society. **1940** I. L. Idriess *Lightning Ridge* 20 Bill kept nit for his elder brother who was courting a girl, and earned a shilling. **1943** D. Stewart *Ned Kelly* ii. i. 97 We keep nit and keep quiet. Ned's good watch-dogs! **1947** N. Lindsay in B. James *Austral. Short Stories* (1963) 6 On condition of you kids scooting up the flat to keep nit, case the old man comes down this way. **1952** T. A. G. Hungerford *Ridge & River* 10 Send two men a couple of hundred yards up and down the track to keep nit. **1963** F. Hardy *Legends from Benson's Valley* 108 An elaborate network of nitkeepers on all sides frustrated the new policeman for three weeks. **1971** D. Ireland *Unknown Industrial Prisoner* 77 They had transgressed the unwritten law that you didn't let yourself go to sleep while you were keeping nit for your mates.

nit (nit), *sb.*[3] *U.S. colloq.* [Of obscure origin; perh. a corruption of Naught *sb.*, Nought *sb.*: cf. *nit *adv.*] None; nothing.

1910 'O. Henry' *Strictly Business* v. 66 'You fool... Why did you do it? 'The Stuff,' explained Thomas briefly. 'You know. But subsequently nit. Not a drop.'

nit (nit), *sb.*[4] *Physics.* [a. F. *nit* (formally adopted in 1948 at the 11th meeting of the Commission internationale de l'Éclairage, and published in its *Recueil des travaux* (1950) 145), f. L. *nit-ēre* to shine.] A unit of luminance equal to one candela per square metre.

1953 J. W. T. Walsh *Photometry* (ed. 2) v. 136 On the c.g.s. system the unit [of luminance] is the stilb, equal to one candela per sq. cm. or the nit, equal to one candela per sq. metre. There is no name for the corresponding unit on the British system; the candela per sq. inch or per sq. ft. is generally employed. **1965** G. A. Fry in R. Kingslake *Appl. Optics* II. i. 18 One nit of luminance is equal to one lux of illuminance per steradian of solid angle. **1965** R. Kingslake in *Ibid.* v. 198, 1 ft-L is equal to 3·43 nits. **1969** *Amateur Photographer* 19 Mar. 80/3 A brightness (or luminous intensity) of 1 Candela per square metre is termed a Nit. Therefore, for example, 60 Candelas per square centimetre equals 600,000 Nits.

nit (nit), *adv.* [? f. Yiddish.] = Not *adv.* Cf. *nit *sb.*[3]

1895 W. C. Gore in *Inlander* Nov. 63 *Nit*.., not; sometimes an emphatic not. **1896** *Dialect Notes* I. 421 *Nit*, a decided negative, much stronger than *no.*

nit (nit), *v.*[2] *Austral.* [Cf. *nit *sb.*[2]] To escape, decamp; to hurry away.

1882 *Sydney Slang Dict.* 10/2 *Nit*, get away (usually from a foe), make tracks. **1897** W. T. Goodge *Hits! Skits! & Jingles!* (1899) 150 And to 'nark it' means to stop it, And to 'nit it' means to fly! **1941** Baker *Dict. Austral. Slang* 49 *To nit*, to decamp, get away (from a foe).

nital (nəi·tæl). *Metallurgy.* Also **Nital.** [f. Nit(ric *a.* + Al(cohol.] An etchant consisting of a few per cent of concentrated nitric acid in ethyl or methyl alcohol.

1925 M. A. Grossmann tr. *Heyn's Physical Metallogr.* iv. 144 Alcoholic Nitric Acid (Martens)... Abbreviation HNO_3/Alc., or nital. **1936** *Metals Handbk.* (Amer. Soc. for Metals) 557 Nital brings out ferrite junction lines clearly while both Nital and Picral etch pearlite clearly. **1950** *Engineering* 24 Mar. 339/1 The barrel is etched with 7 per cent. nital solution. **1963** B. Harocopos *Princ. Structural Metall.* v. 55 Occasionally nital will produce pits in the vicinity of non-metallic inclusions, and in such cases amyl alcohol may be used as a solvent instead. **1975** *Nature* 21 Aug. 635/1 The Nital etch did not reveal recrystallisation in the taenite.

nitchie (ni·tʃi). *Canad.* Also **neche, neechee, neejee, nichi, nichiwa, nidge, nitchee, nitchy.** [Algonquian.] Originally (among North American Indians), a friend; hence as a (usu. derogatory) term for a North American Indian.

1791 J. Long *Voy. & Trav. Indian Trader* 268 Neejee, or neecarnis, friend, or companion. **1838** A. Jameson *Winter Stud. & Summer Rambles Canada* III. 83 Thus, one man addressing another says 'nichi' or 'neejee', my friend. **1850** J. J. Bigsby *Shoe & Canoe* II. 161, I sallied forth, and found the Nidges loading the canoes, drest in their best. **1852** C. P. Traill *Canad. Crusoes* vi. 180 While she called Louis, 'Nee-chee', or friend. **1857** J. Palliser *Jrnls.* (1863) 52 Our Indian friend..to whom we had given the name Nichiwa, or friend. **1878** C. Hallock *Amer. Club List & Sportsman's Gloss.* p. viii, *Nitchee*, a common word among Indian tribes signifying brother. **1903** R. Cullum *Devil's Keg* xxii. 242 A neche was leisurely cleaning up round Lablache's store. **1910** R. W. Service *Ballads of Cheechako* 118 Then came I to a land I knew no man had ever seen, a haggard land, forlornly spanned by mountains lank and lean; The nitchies said 'twas full of dread, of smoke and fiery breath. **1930** J. Beames *Army without Banners* 131 Have to see if I can dig up a Nitchie an' trade whitefish for tobacco or something. **1947** *Beaver* Mar. 4 'These confounded nitchies,' he was wont to exclaim, 'are lazy, good-for-nothings.' **1956** *Saturday Night* 8 Dec. 16/2 And since when have Americans or British freely discussed Clear Grits, Digby chickens, Socreds, the Land of Little Sticks, separate schools, nitchies, longlinermen? **1960** in E. Fowke et al. *Canada's Story in Song* 127 They leave their homes on starving pay to take the nitchies' lives. **1973** R. D. Symons *Where Wagon Led* i. viii. 132 'Quick, you fellows,' he said, 'them Nitchies are crawling up all around.'

nite (nəit), *sb.*[2] An arbitrary respelling of Night *sb.* Also *attrib.* and *Comb.* Hence **ni·tely** *a.* and *adv.*

A widespread vulgarism.

1931 *Amer. Speech* VI. 379 Write *rite* (for right) and *nite* (for night). **1934** B. J. Thompson in *Catholic World* Aug. 523 *Nite* connotes speakeasies, gin, cheapness and vulgarity. **1960** *Punch* 27 Apr. 584/1 Didn't you know? It's Rock Nite at the Darby and Joan. **1961** A. Berkman *Singers' Gloss. Show Business* 62 Nite Club, Nite Spot. **1968** *Blues Unlimited* Nov. 6 Both he

and Myers were discovered by Johnny in Jackson 'nitespots'. **1970** *Toronto Daily Star* 24 Sept. 32/2 (Advt.), Nitely dancing to an excellent European trio. **1970** *Globe & Mail* (Toronto) 25 Sept. 9/1 (Advt.), Train for Court Reporting..Special nite classes. **1971** *Times* 25 Aug. 11/7 (Advt.), Where it's at in Yorkshire... Mood with good food, nitely til 2... And for a romping, Bavarian-style nite out, visit the Intercon Bier Keller in Wakefield. **1971** *Leader* (Durban) 7 May 4/3 (*caption*) Elaine Meyers needs no introduction to nitelifers. *Ibid.*, Around the nitespots. **1973** *Black World* June 61 Sister Habiba knew how to give parties alright: three flights up—Saturday nite. **1974** *Marlboro Herald-Advocate* (Bennettsville, S. Carolina) 18 Apr. 7/8 (Advt.), Free parking in paved lot in rear of store. Open all day Wednesday. Open Fri. nite 'til 6:30.

nitery (nəi·təri). *U.S. slang.* Also **niterie.** [f. *NITE *sb.*[2] + -ERY.] A night club.

1934 M. H. WESEEN *Dict. Amer. Slang* x. 147 *Nitery*, a night club. **1935** *Vanity Fair* (N.Y.) Nov. 38/1 We'll never catch a wire in a decent nitery. **1938** *Amer. Speech* XIII. 239/1 The most recent market nose dive played hob with what Abel Green calls 'the niteries'. **1946** *Sat. Rev.* (U.S.) 19 Oct. 20/3 His reportage is accurate in capturing the contemporary nitery scene. **1955** PRIESTLEY & HAWKES *Journey down Rainbow* 129 All darkened niteries and dimmed hot spots. **1958** [see *DREAM *sb.*[2] 4 h]. **1962** *New Statesman* 19 Jan. 95/3 This negro comedian, who refuses to be winkled out of the grimy little niterie in which he made his reputation. **1967** *Boston Sunday Herald* 30 Apr. (Show Guide) 14/3 Our story begins in a narrow strip of niteries on 52nd Street. **1972** *Daily Tel.* (Colour Suppl.) 1 Dec 62/3 The Body Shop..is a nitery of the topless/bottomless variety, and reminds one that this is..LA's own porno-strip. **1972** *Guardian* 13 Dec. 9/1 El Cubano (the New Niterie with the Olde Worlde Flavor).

Nitinol (ni·tinǫl). [f. *Ni*, chem. symbol for nickel + *Ti*, chem. symbol for titanium + the initial letters of *N*aval *O*rdnance *L*aboratory, Silver Spring, Maryland, U.S.A., the place of work of the metallurgists who discovered the alloy and invented its name.] An alloy of nickel and titanium; *esp.* one composed of equimolecular proportions of these elements, which has the property that after deformation it will return to its former shape when heated to a certain transition temperature.

1968 BUEHLER & WANG in *Ocean Engin.* I. 105 (*heading*) A summary of recent research on the Nitinol* alloys and their potential application in ocean engineering. [*Note*] *Name derived from Ni-Ti-NOL. Prefix numeral value (e.g., 55-Nitinol) indicates the nominal nickel content in weight per cent, balance titanium. *Ibid.*, The 55-Nitinol was found to be a single phase alloy containing only TiNi phase.., while nickel-rich TiNi alloys showed a $TiNi_3$ phase that co-existed in varying quantity with the TiNi phase. Nominal 55-Nitinol..exhibits a very unusual 'mechanical memory'. *Ibid.* 106, 55-Nitinol and 60-Nitinol must be considered as separate and distinct alloy types. **1969** *Nature* 29 Nov. 844/2 An object made of 'Nitinol' can be deformed to an arbitrary shape, briefly heated to 'fix' that shape, and then possesses a 'memory'. **1971** *Sci. Amer.* Mar. 48/1 At present the only commercial use of Nitinol is in a heat-shrinkable tube coupling.

nitkeeper: see *NIT *sb.*[2] 2.

† **niton** (nəi·tǫn). *Chem. Obs.* [f. L. *nit-ēre* to shine + *-ON[2].] = *RADON.

1911 GRAY & RAMSAY in *Proc. R. Soc.* A. LXXXIV. 550 To show its relation to gases of the argon series, it should receive a similar name...The name 'niton', Nt, which has been used in this paper is suggested as sufficiently distinctive. **1912** *Bath & Wilts. Chron.* 12 Mar. 4/2 Solid niton causes the glass or silica tube in which it is necessary to confine it to glow with a brilliant light. **1926** G. BIRTWISTLE *Quantum Theory of Atom* xv. 154 The conclusions..agree with Bohr's general scheme, which gives niton orbits up to quantum number 6. **1947** *Science News* V. 157 In the six years 1894–1900 there were added to the periodic table five new elements, constituting a group soon to be completed by niton (the radioactive emanation).

nitpicker (ni·tpikəɹ). Also **nit-picker.** [f. NIT *sb.* + PICKER[1].] A pedantic critic; one who searches for and over-emphasizes trivial errors. Hence **ni·tpicking, nit-picking** *vbl. sb.* and *ppl. a.* Hence (as back formations) **ni·t-pick** *v.* and *sb.*

1951 *Collier's* 24 Nov. 67/1 Two long-time Pentagon stand-bys are *fly-speckers* and *nit-pickers*. The first of these nouns refers to people whose sole occupation seems to be studying papers in the hope of finding flaws in the writing, rather than making any effort to improve the thought or meaning; nit-pickers are those who quarrel with trivialities of expression *and* meaning, but who usually end up without making concrete or justified suggestions for improvement. **1956** *Time* 16 Jan. 17 The members of the Cabinet commented on the draft of the message, then commented upon one another's comments. 'No nit-picking,' Vice President Nixon adjured his colleagues, but the Cabinet eventually sent out to the President a file of verbatim reaction that piled 1½ inches high. **1959** *Washington Post* 3 July A 12/2 When the nit-pickers and the parliamentary horse-traders had finished with it, the program had shrunk to much smaller proportions. **1961** *Flight* LXXX. 525 Contributions have not sought to attract the jackdaws nor the 'nitpickers'. **1962** W. SCHIRRA in *Into Orbit* 34 We all tried to avoid nit-picking with each other on these things. **1964** *New Statesman* 14 Feb. 261/3 Some of the..modern buildings..which provide a real feast for art-historical nit-pickers. **1968** *Listener* 4 July 22/1 Knox's essay was a stylistic send-up of German *apparatus criticus* nit-picking in the Bible and the classics. **1970** P. ST. PIERRE *Chilcotin Holiday* 93 Let us bring it down to the point where no nitpicking critic can disagree. **1970** *New Scientist* 10 Sept. 542/1 If I am giving an impression of nit-picking, I can only apologise. **1971** 'D. SHANNON' *Ringer* (1972) vi. 108 Don't nitpick. **1972** *Times Lit. Suppl.* 18 Feb. 179/1 A savage, malicious, and nitpicking attack on Malone's great Variorum edition of 1790. **1972** *Guardian* 10 June 10/2 A nit-picking approach would be dangerous and impractical. **1972** *N.Y. Times* 19 Dec. 65/7 Every niggling detail is carefully nitpicked. **1973** *Times* 28 Nov. 4 Nit-picking is an occupational activity of MPs. **1974** *Sat. Even. Post* Jan.-Feb. 32/3 Protect yourself and your leaders from preoccupation with the trivial and the picayune: let people control their own time; don't nitpick procedures. **1975** *Time Out* 1 Aug. 3/3, I don't argue about the inaccuracies (though they're so nit-picking as to infer that everything about the film must be defended at all costs). **1975** *Times Lit. Suppl.* 15 Aug. 922/4 Professor Laqueur's nitpicks force me to comment.

Nitralloy (nəi·trăloi). Also **nitralloy.** [f. *nitr*(*iding* vbl. sb. (s.v. *NITRIDE *v.*) + ALLOY *sb.*] A proprietary name for any of a range of alloy steels specially manufactured for nitriding and usu. containing (among other elements) about one per cent of aluminium and 0·2 to 0·5 per cent of carbon.

1928 *Machinery* XXXI. 478/2 Nitralloys are suitable for crankshafts, camshafts, timing gears, wrist pins, worms,..etc. **1930** *Flight* XXII. 170g/1 The Hispano-Suiza patents do not cover the actual hardening process, but its application to cylinder liners of an alloy steel known as Nitralloy, which is especially suitable for this form of heat treatment. **1952** J. WULFF et al. *Metall. for Engineers* x. 182 Steels (especially Nitralloy, which contains aluminium) may be case-hardened by heating in ammonia at 450–540°C. **1966** *McGraw-Hill Encycl. Sci. & Technol.* XIII. 314/1 The special alloy steels used for nitriding are known as nitralloy. **1972** *Trade Marks Jrnl.* 1 June 1059/1 Nitralloy...Unwrought and partly wrought nitriding steel. Firth Brown Limited,..Sheffield,..manufacturers and merchants.

nitrate, *sb.* Add: **2. b.** Cellulose nitrate (i.e. nitrocellulose), used as a base for cinematographic films. Usu. *attrib.* (see *3).

1949 W. H. OFFENHAUSER *16-mm Sound Motion Pictures* iii. 20 The weight of nitrate, however, is but a fraction of one per cent of the total weight of the film. **1971** L. B. HAPPÉ *Basic Motion Picture Technol.* 348 *Nitrate*, cellulose nitrate, a highly inflammable material once used as film base.

3. *nitrate base, film, reduction*; *nitrate-reducing* adj.; **nitrate reductase,** an enzyme or group of enzymes which brings about (the second step in) the reduction of nitrate to nitrite.

1936 A. B. KLEIN *Colour Cinematography* I. iii. 172 Standard nitrate base for motion picture film is coated with three layers of emulsion containing dyes. **1925** *Chem. Abstr.* XIX. 728 Addn. of 16·6% camphor to one to [*sic*] the strongest nitrate films increased the tensile strength from 3·43 to 8·56 kg. per sq. mm. **1975** *Oxford Jrnl.* 6 June 8 The old one [*sc.* projector room] was fire-proof..because of the highly inflammable nitrate film that was used. **1927** S. A. WAKSMAN *Princ. Soil Microbiol.* vii. 180 The bacteria, which reduce nitrates only to nitrites or to ammonia, but not to nitrogen gas (elementary form and oxides), may be best spoken of as nitrate reducing bacteria, reserving the term denitrifying bacteria for the other organisms. **1967** *Oceanogr. & Marine Biol.* V. 194 Inactivation of the nitrate-reducing system occurred on prolonged incubation at elevated pressures. **1939** *Chem. Abstr.* XXXIII. 2176 Reduction of $—NO_3$ to $—NO_2$ by this bacterium [sc. *E. coli*] involves 2 enzymes, an ordinary reductase and a special nitrate reductase... The special reductase transfers the H [from an intermediate acceptor] to the $—NO_3$. **1964** *Oceanogr. & Marine Biol.* II. 216 Nitrate reductase is found in various green seaweeds. **1974** *Arch. Biochem. & Biophysics* CLX. 269 The enzymatic complex nitrate reductase from *Chlorella fusca* is inactivated by simple thiols. **1919** *Jrnl. Bacteriol.* IV. 267 (*heading*) The use of the nitrate-reduction test in characterizing bacteria. **1973** *Jrnl. Gen. Microbiol.* LXXV. 419 The function of cytochromes in the metabolism of bifidobacteria seems to be associated with nitrate reduction.

nitrazepam (nəitrē̆i·zĭpæm). *Pharm.* [f. NITR(O- + AZ(O- + *-ep*(*ine* (suffix designating an unsaturated seven-membered ring containing nitrogen) + AM(IDE.] A tricyclic, yellow, crystalline compound, $C_{15}H_{11}N_3O_3$, which is a rapidly acting non-barbiturate hypnotic. Cf. *MOGADON.

1965 [see *MOGADON]. **1970** PASSMORE & ROBSON *Compan. Med. Stud.* II. v. 35/1 Nitrazepam is also used as a night sedative and induces sleep without the hang-over effects attributed to the barbiturates.

nitre, *sb.* Add: **1. d.** A sediment produced during the refining of maple syrup.

1872 *Rep. Vermont Board Agric.* I. 219 The gritty sediment from maple syrup, commonly termed 'nitre'. **1882** *Ibid.* VII. 65 The higher the tree is tapped the more of nitre or malate of lime is found. **1949** *Highway Traveler* Feb. 39/1 Strainers..through which the hot syrup is passed to remove the 'nitre', or 'sugar sand', a fine gritty substance, before it is canned.

5. *nitre works.*

1775 *South Carolina Hist. Soc. Coll.* (1858) II. 66 If he was assisted with a sufficient sum..he says he could bring the nitre works to a great degree of perfection.

Nitrian (ni·triăn), *a.* [f. the name *Nitria*: see -AN.] Of, pertaining to, or designating the desert region of Nitria in Egypt, *spec.* the Christian hermit monks, renowned for asceticism, who lived there in the fourth century.

1867 C. M. YONGE *Pupils of St. John* ix. 149 Christians ..are said to have preferred the Nitrian valley because of the words of Jeremiah—'though thou wash thee with nitre'. **1892** I. G. SMITH *Christian Monasticism* vii. 186 In the famous monastery of St. Gall, in Switzerland, as in the Nitrian monasteries of the fifth century, the whip.. was suspended from a pillar in the chapter-house. **1904** J. O. HANNAY *Wisdom of Desert* 6 Journeying still southwards over about forty miles of utterly desolate land, he would come to a long valley extending east and west between two ranges of mountains..covered with.. dangerous rocks. This is the famous Nitrian desert... At the end of the fourth century the Nitrian mountains were dotted over with hermits' cells. **1923** T. E. LAWRENCE *Let.* 14 May (1938) 416 This sort of thing must be madness... It's terrible to hold myself voluntarily here, and yet I want to stay here till it no longer hurts me... It's a lurid flash into the Nitrian desert: seems almost to strip the sainthood from Anthony. **1958** L. DURRELL *Balthazar* iv. 80 His mind winged away like a swallow across the dunes into the Nitrian desert itself.

nitridation (nəitrəidē̆ⁱ·ʃən). *Chem.* [f. NITRID(E + -ATION, after *oxidation*.] A reaction analogous to oxidation but involving nitrogen or its compounds rather than oxygen, water, etc.; *spec.* = *NITRIDING *vbl. sb.*

1911 BROWNE & WALSH in *Jrnl. Amer. Chem. Soc.* XXXIII. 1728 One..purpose of this research has..been to study the phenomena of ammono-oxidation, or nitridation. **1929** *Chem. Abstr.* XXIII. 3888 (*heading*) Study of surface-hardening of steel by nitridation. **1931** *Jrnl. Amer. Chem. Soc.* LIII. 1478 Browne.. applied the term 'nitridation' to all those reactions which for the ammonia system of compounds are essentially similar to oxidation reactions for the familiar water compounds... Nitridation reactions are today classed under the broader conception of oxidation reactions. **1974** *Jrnl. Materials Sci.* IX. 1362/2 Nitridations under identical conditions in tubes of two types of commercial sintered alumina resulted in the formation of greatly increased proportions of the beta phase.

nitride (nəi·trəid), *v.* [f. the sb.] *trans.* To convert into a nitride or nitrides; *spec.* to heat in the presence of ammonia or other nitrogen-containing gas so as to form nitrides near the surface and improve the hardness and corrosion resistance.

1928 *Machinery* XXXI. 479/1 The parts to be nitrided are placed in a gas-tight box. **1958** AITCHISON & PUMPHREY *Using Steel Wisely* 1. ix. 155 A number of high-alloy steels—such as those employed for aero-engine exhaust valves—are nitrided with very beneficial results. **1966** *McGraw-Hill Encycl. Sci. & Technol.* XIII. 314/1 It is possible to nitride some of the common alloy steels which do not contain appreciable amounts of aluminium, although the hardness in this case is much lower than with nitralloy. **1972** *Nature* 28 Jan. 219/2 The alloys were nitrided in pure, dry nitrogen at 7 atmosphere pressure at 1,050°C.

Hence **ni·trided** *ppl. a.*, **ni·triding** *vbl. sb.*; *nitriding steel*, steel made with a composition to fit it for nitriding.

1928 *Machinery* XXXI. 478/2 Standard electric furnaces can easily be adapted to the nitriding process. **1928** *Jrnl. Iron & Steel Inst.* CXVII. 855 Photo-micrographs show the nitrided case after nitriding for 90 hrs. at 900°F. **1931** *Ibid.* CXXIV. 615 With the exception of aluminium, all metals present in nitriding steels are transition elements, the nitrides of which have a metallic character. **1952** KIRK & OTHMER *Encycl. Chem. Technol.* IX. 26 Nitriding improves the fatigue endurance limit of the heat-treated nitriding steels. **1967** *Trans. Inst. Engin. & Shipbuilders Scotl.* CX. 32 A photograph of a frigate's fine-tooth coupling with barrelled, crowned and nitrided teeth. **1967** M. CHANDLER *Ceramics in Mod. World* vi. 171 Silicon nitride..is formed in the nitriding process, which consists of taking the element silicon, pressing it into the required form, and then heating to a temperature of about 1400°C in an atmosphere of nitrogen.

nitridizing (nəi·tridəiziŋ), *ppl. a. Chem.* [f. NITRID(E + -IZ(E + -ING[2].] Bringing about nitridation.

1911 BROWNE & WALSH in *Jrnl. Amer. Chem. Soc.* XXXIII. 1728 In case the hydrogen pernitrides in liquid ammonia possess properties similar to those of hydrogen peroxide in aqueous solution it is to be expected that under proper conditions they should act in a sense as oxidizing agents, or more strictly as nitridizing agents. **1930** *Ibid.* LII. 2430 Mercuric nitride and bismuth nitride have been shown to have the properties of nitridizing agents.

nitrifiable, *a.* Add: (Earlier example.) Hence **ni:trifiabi·lity,** the property of being nitrifiable.

1827 *Phil. Mag.* I. 177 Tufa, chalk and nitrifiable materials act in nitrification both as absorbents of water

and air, and as presenting a base which solicits the formation of nitric acid. **1884** *Jrnl. Chem. Soc.* XLV. 651 Evidence of the nitrifiability of rape-cake.

nitrification. 1. (Earlier and later examples.)
1827 [see *NITRIFIABLE *a.*]. **1897** *Bull. Minnesota Agric. Exper. Station* No. 53. 7 Although a corn crop takes more nitrogen from the soil than a wheat crop, the cultivation of the corn crop favors nitrification (production of nitrates from humus) and results in leaving more available nitrogen in the soil. **1926** TANSLEY & CHIPP *Study of Vegetation* vii. 122 This process of nitrification..carried out by special bacteria, is of the first importance in humous soils. **1966** *McGraw-Hill Encycl. Sci. & Technol.* IX. 111/1 A well-aerated, fertile, neutral to slightly alkaline soil will provide optimum conditions for nitrification.

nitrifier (nəi·trifəiˌəɹ). *Biol.* [f. NITRIFY *v.* + -IER[1].] An organism or soil which nitrifies.
1903 *Lancet* 6 June 1590/1 The bacterial organisms themselves are..the real nitrogen bringers or nitrifiers. **1931** E. ASHBY tr. *Lundegårdh's Environment & Plant Devel.* viii. 241 Mycorhiza occur more commonly in soils which are poor nitrifiers, than in soils in which the nitrification is good. **1973** *Communications Soil Sci. & Plant Analysis* IV. 280 Greater populations of nitrifiers were found by the NPN method than by silica gel plating for most soils.

nitrify, *v.* Add: **1.** (Earlier and later examples.) *spec.* To convert (ammonia) into nitrite or nitrate. Also *absol.*
1827 *Phil. Mag.* I. 174 The putrescent blood was at the distance of two feet from the carbonate of lime, which it is pretended that it nitrified. **1932** FULLER & CONARD tr. *Braun-Blanquet's Plant Sociol.* viii. 239 Probably all communities of the Molinion nitrify abundantly. **1957** G. E. HUTCHINSON *Treat. Limnol.* I. xvi. 837 A considerable part of the ammonia so formed is nitrified. **1962** H. S. MCKEE *Nitrogen Metabolism in Plants* iv. 112 These heterotrophs nitrify more completely than the autotrophic species.
2. (Earlier examples.)
1827 *Phil. Mag.* I. 176 Chevraud met with compact chalks which did not nitrify. **1878** *Jrnl. Chem. Soc.* XXXIII. 46, 10 grams of a vegetable soil, known to nitrify with ease, were washed with water.
nitrifying *ppl. a.* (earlier and later examples). Quot. 1827 is *vbl. sb.*
1827 *Phil. Mag.* I. 175 Why..does it exhibit no nitrifying power without the cooperation of carbonate of lime? **1900** *Jrnl. Chem. Soc.* LXXVIII. II. 97 Experiments with amides, proteids, wine, &c., showed that the nitrifying organisms are not able to attack organic nitrogen; the nitrogen must first be converted into ammonia. **1932** FULLER & CONARD tr. *Braun-Blanquet's Plant Sociol.* viii. 236 The nitrogen compounds in the soil must generally be converted into nitric acid... But this transformation can only take place with the cooperation of nitrifying bacteria. **1969** F. E. ROUND *Introd. Lower Plants* i. 4 The nitrifying bacteria operate in the nitrogen cycle by utilizing ammonia ions which they convert into nitrite (nitrile bacteria), which is then excreted to be absorbed by nitrate bacteria which convert the nitrite into nitrate.

nitrile. Add: **2.** Special Comb.: **nitrile rubber,** any of the copolymers of acrylonitrile with butadiene in various proportions, which have properties resembling those of natural rubber and are used esp. when oil resistance is necessary, as for fuel hoses, containers, and adhesives.
1947 *Mod. Plastics* Oct. 91/2 The particular difference between nitrile rubber and the more commonly used Buna-S or GR-S synthetic rubber is the use of acrylonitrile instead of styrene. **1954** W. L. SEMON in G. S. Whitby *Synthetic Rubber* xxiii. 818 One of the largest uses for nitrile rubber is in the form of latex, in which form it finds application as an adhesive, as a modifier for other water-dispersed resins, and as an impregnant for paper, textiles, and leather. **1972** *Materials & Technol.* V. xiv. 481 The first nitrile rubbers were hot polymerized; later on cold rubbers also became available, which are easier to process.

nitritoid (nəi·trəitoid), *a. Med.* [f. NITRIT(E + -OID.] Resembling the effect of nitrite; said of the crisis which may follow the administration of arsphenamine, which mimics the effect of nitrite poisoning.
1921 in STEDMAN *Med. Dict.* (ed. 6) 677/2. **1943** *Ann. Allergy* I. 144 Urbach was able to prevent nitritoid crisis from arsphenamine, for example, by a similar technique.

nitro-. Add: In sense d also used without hyphen as quasi-adj.
b. nitrofu·ran, any of the furans having a nitro group attached to one of the carbon atoms of the furan ring, some of which (with the nitro group attached to a carbon atom next to the oxygen atom) are used as bacteriostatics; **nitrome·thane,** an oily liquid, CH_3NO_2, which is used as a solvent, as a rocket fuel, and in the production of nitro-compounds; **nitrophe·nol,** any compound containing a nitro and a phenolic hydroxyl group; esp. any of the three possible compounds, $C_6H_4(NO_2)OH$, obtained by substituting a nitro group for one of the nuclear hydrogen atoms of phenol, *spec.* 2- (or *ortho-*)*nitrophenol,* a yellow crystalline compound used as a dyestuff intermediate, and 4- (or *para-*)-*nitrophenol,* a colourless or yellow crystalline compound used in the manufacture of phosphorus-containing pesticides and azo-dyes; **nitroto·luene,** any of the four possible compounds, $C_7H_7NO_2$, obtained by substituting a nitro group for one of the hydrogen atoms of toluene, two of which (the *ortho* and *para* isomers) are used as intermediates for dyestuffs.
1930 *Jrnl. Amer. Chem. Soc.* LII. 2550 In connection with the preparation of aminofurans and their diazo-compounds, it was necessary to have a series of readily accessible nitrofurans and their derivatives. **1950** *Jrnl. Pharmacol. & Exper. Therap.* XCVIII. 163 Of the nitrofurans fed in this study, the ones which result in appreciable antibacterial activity in the urine are characterized by a side-chain of the semicarbazone, semioxamazone, or closely related type in the 2-position of the furan ring. **1959** *Times* 7 Dec. (Agriculture Suppl.) p. vii/4 To prevent coccidiosis in chickens, nitrophenid, a sulfonamide, or a nitrofuran is added to the feed. **1970** W. H. PARKER *Health & Dis. in Farm Animals* xiii. 180 When the vaccine is used antibiotics and nitrofurans must only be used..for calves showing actual symptoms. **1872** *Jrnl. Chem. Soc.* XXV. 804 Nitromethane is a heavy oil, of a peculiar odour; it boils at 99°. **1950** *Sci. News* XV. 78 A third group..is the monergols, which contain the oxygen needed for their own combustion. Members of this group, such as nitromethane (CH_3NO_2), tend to be unstable, and research is now being intensively carried out with the object of making them safe to handle. **1972** *Materials & Technol.* IV. xv. 548 Nitromethane is used as a solvent for cellulose esters and vinyl resins. **1852** Nitrophenol [in Dict.]. **1905** CAIN & THORPE *Synthetic Dyestuffs* xviii. 149 The formation of these compounds [*sc.* the Nigrosines] is brought about by heating crude nitrophenol..with aniline and aniline hydrochloride. **1949** P. W. VITTUM tr. *Fierz-David & Blangey's Fund. Proc. Dye Chem.* I. 148, *o-* and *p*-nitrophenols are the starting materials for *o-* and *p*-phenetidine and anisidine. **1972** *Materials & Technol.* IV. xv. 554 The nitrophenols are extremely hazardous materials; not only as a fire risk but also because the polynitrophenols are explosive. **1871** *Jrnl. Chem. Soc.* XXIV. 871 (*table*) Nitrotoluene. **1915** *Dyestuffs & Coal-Tar Products* i. 24 2-Nitrotoluene may be..reduced to *o*-azoxytoluene, which is then acidified..and reduced to tolidine sulphate. **1964** N. G. CLARK *Mod. Org. Chem.* xix. 377 A substituent in the side-chain of toluene may be designated 'α-'; for example, α-nitrotoluene, $C_6H_5.CH_2.NO_2$. **1972** *Materials & Technol.* IV. xv. 551 *para*-Nitrotoluene, a brownish-yellow solid.., is employed in the manufacture of *para*-toluidine.
d. nitrobacte·rium [ad. F. *nitrobactérie* (S. Winogradsky 1891, in *Ann. de l'Inst. Pasteur* V. 92)], any nitrifying bacterium; *esp.* one of the genus *Nitrobacter,* which oxidizes nitrites to nitrates; **nitro-cellulose** (further examples); now usu. without hyphen; **Ni·trochalk, ni·tro-chalk,** the proprietary name of a fertilizer consisting of a mixture of ammonium nitrate and calcium carbonate; **nitro-compound,** change stress to *ni·tro-co:mpound* and add to def.: any compound containing a nitro group; (further examples); **nitro group,** the radical $—NO_2$, present in nitric acid; **ni·trolim(e** [LIME *sb.*[1]], calcium cyanamide, or a mixture of it with carbon, obtained by treating calcium carbide with nitrogen and used as a fertilizer.
1891 *Jrnl. R. Microsc. Soc.* 680 M. Winogradsky, who at one time ascribed the nitrifying faculty to a single species of bacteria.., has..satisfied himself that morphological differences exist in these organisms, and they are now classed together in a group of 'Nitrobacteria', the common characteristic of which is the oxidation of the ammoniacal nitrogen. **1906** E. W. HILGARD *Soils* ix. 146 The oxidation of the nitrites into nitrates by..rod-shaped bacilli, named nitrobacteria. **1965** B. E. FREEMAN tr. *Vandel's Biospeleology* xix. 335 The nitrobacteria have the effect of mineralising proteins. **1911** E. C. WORDEN *Nitrocellulose Industry* I. xiii. 459 The nitrocellulose silks dissolve in concentrated sulphuric acid. **1931** *Economist* 28 Feb. 431/2 There is reason to believe that nitro-cellulose, lacquers, oils..are all being manufactured or obtained in France. **1955** F. D. MILES *Cellulose Nitrate* vi. 221 On account of its capacity to swell in nitroglycerine and to absorb it, nitrocellulose is an almost indispensable component of both the two principal classes of explosive—blasting explosives..and propellant explosives. **1962** F. T. DAY *Introd. to Paper* v. 53 Nitrocellulose finishing is now an established process for printing work, the smooth and polished surface being obtained by coating on the machine. **1972** *Materials & Technol.* V. xi. 336 Nitrocellulose paints and varnishes dry very fast to give hard, flexible, and reasonably durable films. **1927** *Daily Express* 7 Dec. 12/4 To replace Chilean nitrate we shall make..nitrochalk, a rich mixture of nitrogen and calcium. **1936** *Trade Marks Jrnl.* 4 Nov. 1355/1 Nitro-Chalk... Artificial fertilisers for soils... I.C.I. (Fertilizer & Synthetic Products) Limited,.. London,..manufacturers. **1954** *Jrnl. Brit. Grassland Soc.* IX. 323 (*heading*) The influence of 'Nitro-Chalk' on established lucerne leys. **1966** WEBSTER & WILSON *Agric. in Tropics* viii. 197 It would seem wise to consider other types of nitrogenous fertilizer, such as nitro-chalk (15·5 per cent N) or ammonium nitrate.., as alternatives to the long-continued use of sulphate of ammonia. **1928** ADKINS & MCELVAIN *Elem. Org. Chem.* x. 101 Many of these nitro compounds are of considerable importance. **1962** P. J. & B. DURRANT *Introd. Adv. Inorg. Chem.* xix. 679 The nitro compounds are made by the action of silver nitrite on the alkyl iodide. **1886** E. F. SMITH tr. *V. von Richter's Chem. Carbon Compounds* 79 The nitro-group always exerts such an acidic influence upon hydrogen linked to carbon. **1938** C. D. HURD in H. Gilman *Org. Chem.* I. vii. 628 The peculiar activity of the fourth nitro group in $C(NO_2)_4$ should be mentioned. **1964** J. W. LINNETT *Electronic Struct. Molecules* iv. 65 There is much evidence which suggests that the nitro-group (NO_2) is a very stable group in many different molecules. **1908** *Trans. Faraday Soc.* IV. 104 A great outcry was, and still is, made warning farmers against the use of calcium cyanamide, popularly known as nitrolim, or at least advising that it should be employed with the utmost caution. **1909** *Jrnl. Chem. Soc.* XCVI. 893 (*heading*) Formation of 'Nitrolime'. **1923** J. HENDRICK *Farmer's Raw Materials* x. 156 When nitrolim is applied to the soil its nitrogen quickly turns to ammonia, and the ammonia in turn changes to nitrate. **1962** J. H. WHITE *Inorg. Chem.* xxi. 331 Nitrolime is a soluble fertilizer, rich in nitrogen.

nitro. Add pronunc. (nəi·tro). **2.** Abbrev. of NITROGLYCERINE. *slang.*
1935 N. ERSINE *Underworld & Prison Slang* 54 *Nitro,* nitroglycerine. **1950** R. CHANDLER *Let.* 18 May in *R. Chandler Speaking* (1966) 80 Opening a good safe (without a time lock) requires expensive and heavy tools, the finest drills either to drill out the lock or to get in the nitro if he is a peterman. **1972** J. GODEY *Three Worlds* (1973) iii. 30 They had an old-time safe... I hit it with a fat charge of nitro.

nitrofurantoin (nəitrofiŭræ·ntoˌin). *Pharm.* [f. NITRO- + *fur-furyl* (f. FURFUR-OL + -YL) + HYD)ANTOÏN in the chemical name of the compound, 1-(5-*nitrofur*furylideneamino)-hyd*antoïn.*] A yellow crystalline bicyclic compound, $C_8H_6N_4O_5$, which is an antibacterial agent used in treating infections of the urinary tract.
1953 *Antibiotics & Chemotherapy* III. 151 A new antibacterial nitrofuran, Furadantin, Eaton, brand of nitrofurantoin. **1963** *Amer. Rev. Respiratory Dis.* LXXXVIII. 712/2 Most tubercle bacilli with increased resistance to isoniazid also manifest increased susceptibility to nitrofurantoin. **1972** M. ROWLAND in Melmon & Morrelli *Clin. Pharmacol.* ii. 30/2 The most common side effect associated with nitrofurantoin is gastrointestinal irritation and occasional emesis due to a central action of the drug, probably dependent on high concentrations of nitrofurantoin in blood.

nitrofurazone (nəitrofŭ·răzōun). *Pharm.* [f. NITRO- + *FUR(FURALDEHYDE + *SEMICARB)AZONE in the chemical name of the compound, 5-*nitrofur*furaldehyde semicarb*azone.*] A yellow crystalline cyclic compound, $C_6H_6N_4O_4$, which is an antibacterial agent used locally on burns, wounds, and skin infections, and in veterinary medicine.
1947 F. K. OLDHAM et al. *Essent. Pharmacol.* xxiv. 323 5-nitro 2-furaldehyde semicarbazone (nitrofurazone) has been recently introduced under the name of furacin as a dressing for wounds and chronic ulcers. **1957** *Veterinary Rec.* LXIX. 1415/2 In Great Britain the drug nitrofurazone has been widely used and flocks of domestic poultry very commonly are given this drug continuously as a preventative measure against Eimeria infections. **1972** *Cancer Research* XXXII. 2623/1 Nitrofurazone chemotherapy was usually initiated after both surgery and radiotherapy had failed to arrest the metastatic invasion of testicular cancer to the lungs and its subsequent growth.

nitrogen. Add: **b.** *nitrogen-containing* adj.; **nitrogen cycle** *Biol.,* the cycle of changes whereby nitrogen is interconverted between its free state in the air and combined states in organisms and the soil; **nitrogen fixation,** the conversion of free, gaseous nitrogen into a combined form; cf. *FIXATION 2 d; so **nitrogen fixer,** a nitrogen-fixing organism; **nitrogen-fixing** *ppl. a.,* bringing about nitrogen fixation; **nitrogen mustard,** any of the group of substances containing the group $—N(CH_2CH_2Cl)_2$, which are cytotoxic as a result of their alkylating property and some of which are used in treating neoplastic diseases, such as Hodgkin's disease and lymphosarcoma; **nitrogen narcosis,** a narcotic state, common among divers, induced by breathing air under pressure.
1956 *Nature* 4 Feb. 234/1 A nitrogen-containing acid. **1967** *Oceanogr. & Marine Biol.* V. 168 If some of the nitrogen-containing gases (evolved during the digestion procedure) escape..the values obtained may be too low. **1908** HALL & DEFREN tr. *Abderhalden's Text-bk. Physiol. Chem.* x. 198 The discovery that ordinary nitrogen can be directly assimilated closes the chain of the nitrogen cycle, which had apparently been broken open by the discovery of the denitrifying organisms. **1931** E. ASHBY tr. *Lundegårdh's Environment & Plant Devel.* viii. 242 The nitrogen cycle..lies to a great degree, though not exclusively, in the soil. **1966** *McGraw-Hill Encycl. Sci. &*

Technol. IX. 111/2 The nitrogen cycle comprises the processes of ammonification, nitrification, denitrification, and nitrogen fixation. **1895** LAWES & GILBERT *Rothamsted Exper.* 164 Recently acquired knowledge in regard to nitrogen fixation. **1938** *Nature* 12 Nov. 878/1 Diverse workers..have previously affirmed nitrogen fixation by Blue-green Algæ. **1970** *Sunday Times* (Colour Suppl.) 16 Aug. 13/1 It is likely that Germany would have collapsed before 1918 but for the nitrogen fixation plants built in 1914–16. **1912** E. J. RUSSELL *Soil Conditions & Plant Growth* iv. 83 In all these cases leguminous plants are present in greatest extent where the gains in nitrogen are greatest, but they are not necessarily the only nitrogen fixers. **1932** FULLER & CONARD tr. *Braun-Blanquet's Plant Sociol.* viii. 235 Anaerobic and aerobic nitrogen fixers often occur associated together in the same soil. **1968** *Jrnl. Gen. Microbiol.* L. 487 As these small colonies grew abundantly on nitrogen-poor agar, it was thought possible that some of them might be nitrogen-fixers. **1899** F. H. KING *Irrigation & Drainage* 233 The nitrogen-fixing tubercles were already developed. **1929** WEAVER & CLEMENTS *Plant Ecol.* x. 249 Both nitrifying and nitrogen-fixing bacteria thrive in the humus. **1966** *New Statesman* 2 Dec. 826/1 The first new component isolated from the Du Pont nitrogen-fixing system. **1970** *Nature* 25 July 378/1 The nitrogen-fixing enzyme complex, nitrogenase, catalyses various reductions as well as the formation of ammonia from dinitrogen. **1946** *Jrnl. Amer. Med. Assoc.* 21 Sept. 132/1 Although indications and contraindications for the use of the nitrogen mustards remain to be established definitively, it is felt that these agents are deserving of further clinical trial. **1951** *New Biol.* XI. 97 In the treatment of leukaemia..several different classes of chemicals show some value. There are some compounds, such as the nitrogen mustards, which imitate the action of radiation on the cell, and dislocate nuclear division. **1970** PASSMORE & ROBSON *Compan. Med. Stud.* II. xxix. 5/1 Chlorambucil..can be given by mouth and is the slowest acting and least toxic of all the nitrogen mustards in clinical use. **1937** *U.S. Naval Med. Bull.* XXXV. 379 It is well known that if pressure is applied too quickly the diver becomes dizzy and often is so dazed as to require several minutes to orient himself. Consequently, if the cause were nitrogen narcosis, the difficulty would increase with exposure rather than decrease. **1962** *Listener* 29 Mar. 562/1 Free deep-sea divers—that is to say, divers wearing cylinders filled with compressed air—may suffer at varying depths from a mild intoxicating effect, or 'rapture of the deep', known as nitrogen narcosis. **1972** *Aerospace Med.* XLIII. 1079 (*heading*) Diver performance: nitrogen narcosis and anxiety.

nitrogenize *v.*, add to def.: *spec.* = *NITRIDE *v.*; also **nitrogeniza·tion**, the action or result of nitrogenizing.

1896 *Jrnl. Iron & Steel Inst.* L. 161 Iron specially nitrogenised by the action of ammonia is materially altered in character. **1903** *Lancet* 6 June 1590/1 The increased nitrogenisation of the soil by the widened use of phosphatic manures. **1916** *Engineering* 3 Mar. 218/2 A sample of iron was taken, nitrogenised at 600 deg.,..and then thrown out from the Heraeus furnace into very cold water. **1922** *Ibid.* 29 Sept. 413/1 To obtain positive evidence of nitrogenisation both unannealed and annealed specimens of armco iron were analysed for nitrogen. **1926** *Chem. Abstr.* XX. 2138 In Ni and Mn steels nitrogenization produced hardly any increase in hardness.

nitrogenase (nəitrǫ·dʒěnēiz, -s). *Biochem.* [f. NITROGEN + *-ASE.] The enzyme which combines with molecular nitrogen as the first step in biological nitrogen fixation.

1934 D. BURK in *Ergebnisse der Enzymforschung* III. 24 Nitrogenase is the specific enzyme within the azotase system that combines directly with N_2 with characteristic affinity. **1950** *Federation Proc.* IX. 548/1 The remarkable effect of molecular nitrogen appears to require activation of nitrogenase which in some way results in simultaneous activation of the dehydrogenases which are thereby enabled to compete successfully with the hydrogenase systems. **1975** *Nature* 3 Jan. 7/3 It is now a tacit assumption of all model studies that a metal ion, most probably molybdenum, is responsible for binding dinitrogen in nitrogenase.

nitrogenate (nəitrǫ·dʒěnēit), *v.* [f. NITROGEN + -ATE[3].] *trans.* To combine with nitrogen; *spec.* = *NITRIDE *v.* So **nitro·genated** *ppl. a.* Also **nitrogena·tion**, the action or process of nitrogenating.

1926 *Jrnl. Iron & Steel Inst.* CXIII. 600 Parts to be case-hardened by nitrogenation must be completely machined and finished off before case-hardening. **1927** *Ibid.* CXV. 893 Brinell tests were made on a chrome-aluminium steel nitrogenated by heating in ammonia. **1938** *Chem. Abstr. Third Decennial Index* 6205/3 *Nitrogenation*, see *nitridation*. **1967** *Biol. Abstr.* XLVIII. 1394/2 Ways of controlling nitrogenation [of soil] are.. treated. **1969** KUNII & LEVENSPIEL *Fluidization Engineering* xv. 517 (*heading*) Conversion of a particle in the nitrogenation of calcium carbide. **1971** *Biol. Abstr.* LII. 8948/2 (*heading*) Tests of the 'Pro-Milk Automatic Apparatus' for use in the serial determination of nitrogenated matter in milk.

nitron (nəi·trǫn). *Chem.* [ad. G. *nitron* (Busch & Mehrtens 1905, in *Ber. d. Deut. Chem. Ges.* XXXVIII. 4049), f. *nitro-* NITRO- + *-on*.] A heterocyclic compound, $(C_6H_5)_3$-C_2HN_4, which is used in gravimetric analysis as a precipitant for nitrate, perrhenate, and some other ions.

1906 *Jrnl. Chem. Soc.* XC. I. 118 As a test for nitrates nitron is even more delicate than was stated previously. **1939** A. I. VOGEL *Text-bk. Quantitative Inorg. Analysis* i. 165 The following acids form slightly soluble salts with nitron..perchloric, thiocyanic,..and nitrous acids. **1971** *Mikrochim. Acta* 478 Small amounts of gold can be extracted into dichloroethane as nitron tetrachloroaurate.

nitronium (nəitrōu·niǝ̆m). *Chem.* [mod.L. (coined in Ger. by A. Hantzsch 1925, in *Ber. d. Deut. Chem. Ges.* LVIII. 943): see NITRO- and *-ONIUM.] † **a.** The cation which was supposed to be formed by ionization in pure nitric acid and formulated as $[NO(OH)_2]^+$ or $[N(OH)_3]^{2+}$. *Obs.*

1925 *Chem. Abstr.* XIX. 2312 The fairly high cond[uctivity] of pure HNO_3 is probably due not to ionization of H^+ and NO_3^-, but to formation of 'nitronium nitrate' $[NO(OH)_2][NO_3]$ or $[N(OH)_3][NO_3]_2$.

b. The cation NO_2^+, which is the nitrating agent in mixtures of concentrated nitric acid with another strong acid and is formed by the dissociation of nitric acid itself.

1946 R. J. GILLESPIE et al. in *Nature* 5 Oct. 480/1 The freezing point evidence..provides an unambiguous proof that the cation into which nitric acid is actually converted in sulphuric acid is..the nitronium ion, NO_2^+. **1961** *Aeroplane* CI. 549/2 New oxidizers such as nitronium perchlorate are being applied experimentally in propellents containing well established binder systems. **1972** S. J. WEININGER *Contemp. Org. Chem.* xv. 371 Salts of the nitronium cation containing nonnucleophilic anions may be prepared and..used as nitrating agents.

nitrophilous (nəitrǫ·filəs), *a. Bot.* [f. NITRO(GEN + -PHILOUS.] Of a plant: growing best in a habitat rich in nitrogen. So **ni·trophile** *sb.*, a plant of this type.

1909 GROOM & BALFOUR tr. *Warming's Oecol. Plants* xvii. 68 Nitrophilous plants..thrive best in soil where compounds of ammonium and nitric acid are abundant. **1932** FULLER & CONARD tr. *Braun-Blanquet's Plant Sociol.* iv. 63 Here [*sc.* among ecologically specialized forms] belong many mycotrophic species, saprophytes, nitrophiles. *Ibid.* viii. 240 Nitrophilous communities are very widely distributed in dry, subtropical regions. **1964** V. J. CHAPMAN *Coastal Vegetation* iv. 97 These [*sc.* marsh plants] are probably nitrophiles. **1967** M. E. HALE *Biol. Lichens* iv. 58 This phenomenon [*sc.* lichens growing on guano] has given rise to a large literature on nitrophilous or ornithocoprophilous lichens. **1972** A. MITCHELL in Leigh & Noble *Plants for Sheep in Australia* v. 42 In eastern Victoria..the native perennial grasses could be maintained in the sward with the introduced clovers without the same tendency to invasion by nitrophilous weeds.

nitrosamine (nəitrōu·sămīn). [ad. G. *nitrosamin* (O. N. Witt 1875, in *Ber. d. deut. Chem. Ges.* VIII. 857): see NITROSO- and AMINE.] Any of the class of compounds containing the group >N—NO, which can be prepared by the action of sodium nitrite and a strong acid on secondary amines.

1878 O. N. WITT in *Jrnl. Chem. Soc.* XXXIII. 202 The term 'nitrosamine' I apply to any substituted ammonia which contains, instead of at least one atom of hydrogen, the univalent nitrosyl group,—NO, in immediate connection with the ammoniacal nitrogen. **1912** *Chem. Abstr.* VI. 2319 (*heading*) The nitrosamine of *p*-nitro-*o*-anisidine as a red resist under aniline black. **1942** FUSON & SNYDER *Org. Chem.* x. 118 The nitrosamines are really amides of nitrous acid and as such would be expected to be neutral compounds. **1954** *Chem. Abstr.* XLVIII. 7305 (*heading*) Printing of cotton with nitrosamine dyes using a neutral developer. **1975** *Daily Colonist* (Victoria, B.C.) 15 May 3/2 Animal research studies have shown that nitrate and nitrite preservatives may produce cancer-causing chemicals, called nitrosamines, in the stomach.

nitrosate (nəi·trosēit), *v. Chem.* [f. NITROS(O- + -ATE[3].] *trans.* To introduce a nitroso group into (a compound).

1920 F. A. MASON tr. *G. von Georgievics's Text-bk. Dye Chem.* 66 The monoazo dyes derived from resorcinol can be nitrosated, but the mordant dyes obtained possess too slight tinctorial powers to be of much technical value. **1952** K. VENKATARAMAN *Chem. Synthetic Dyes* II. xxv. 783 Rhoduline Pure Blue 3G is prepared by nitrosating diethyl-*m*-phenetidine, and condensing with *m*-diethylaminophenol. **1973** *Nature* 12 Oct. 326/1 The mutagenicity of MG nitrosated in human gastric juice was studied by the spot test.

Hence **ni·trosated, ni·trosating** *ppl. adjs.* Also **nitrosa·table** *a.*, capable of being converted into a nitroso compound; **nitrosa·tion**, the process of converting into a nitroso compound.

1920 F. A. MASON tr. *G. von Georgievics's Text-bk. Dye Chem.* 66 On nitrosation, *p*-nitroso derivatives are obtained where the *para* position is free. **1968** R. O. C. NORMAN *Princ. Org. Synthesis* xi. 385 Nitrosation is limited to the very reactive nuclei of phenols and tertiary aromatic amines. **1970** R. PRICE in K. Venkataraman *Chem. Synthetic Dyes* III. vii. 371 Certain of the complexes which are disclosed are derived from nitrosated *o*-hydroxyarylazoresorcinol dyestuffs. **1972** *Science* 7 July 66/3 These are also the nitrosating species for secondary amines and alkylureas. *Ibid.* 67/3 Addition of ascorbate to certain foods containing nitrate or nitrosatable compounds might be worth considering. **1973** *Nature* 12 Oct. 326/1 Nitrosated MG was found to be mutagenic at up to six-teen-fold dilution of the original reaction mixture. **1974** *Ibid.* 8 Nov. 179/1 Ascorbate might be used to block *in vivo* formation of N-nitroso compounds from nitrosatable chemicals.

nitroso-. Add: Also used without hyphen as quasi-*adj.* **nitroso group**, the nitrosyl radical, —N:O.

1885 *Jrnl. Soc. Dyers & Colourists* I. 177/2 Tetramethyltolylenediamine seems to give a similar nitroso compound. **1906** J. M. MATTHEWS tr. *Alexeyeff's Gen. Princ. Org. Syntheses* ii. 58 (*heading*) Substitution of the nitroso group. **1911** I. W. FAY *Chem. Coal-Tar Dyes* v. 71 Naphthol green B. is a nitroso dye which, unlike the other members of this class, does not require a mordant upon the fabric to be dyed. **1938** C. D. HURD in H. Gilman *Org. Chem.* I. vii. 635 This tendency for nitroso compounds to change to oximes..is apparent even in the nitroso alcohols or acids. **1971** N. L. ALLINGER et al. *Org. Chem.* xxii. 604 Aliphatic nitroso compounds which bear at least one hydrogen on the carbon *α* to the nitroso group are isomerized rapidly and irreversibly by acid or base to oximes.

nitrous, *a.* Add: **2. g.** *nitrous vitriol*, a solution of oxides of nitrogen in sulphuric acid produced in the Gay-Lussac tower in the lead-chamber process.

1879 *Chem. News* 30 May 237/2 In a paper about to be published, I [*sc.* G. Lunge] have proved that denitration by hot water or steam is insufficient when the nitrous vitriol, by faulty work, contains nitric acid. **1933** W. T. READ *Industr. Chem.* xi. 165 A portion of the acid from the coolers is sent to the top of the cold tower. As it passes down the cold tower it picks up the oxides of nitrogen in the form of nitrosyl sulfuric acid and becomes..'nitrous vitriol'. **1954** KIRK & OTHMER *Encycl. Chem. Technol.* XIII. 472 The Glover tower receives the hot burner gas, and is fed at the top with the nitrous vitriol from the Gay-Lussac tower, and with 52° Bé. (65%) acid from the chambers.

nitto (ni·to), *v. Criminals' slang.* [Cf. *NIT *sb.*[2]] (See quot. 1959.)

1959 J. GOSLING *Ghost Squad* ii. 25 'Nitto' means 'stop' or 'Be quiet'. **1962** D. WARNER *Death of Bogey* iv. vi. 169 You guys better nitto. The Sparrow's got a line to your run-in.

nitty-gritty (ni:ti,gri·ti). *slang* (orig. *U.S.*). [Etym. unknown.] The realities or basic facts of a problem, situation, subject, etc.; the heart of the matter. Also *attrib.* or as *adj.*

1963 *Time* 2 Aug. 14/2 The Negroes present would know perfectly well that the nitty-gritty of a situation is the essentials of it. **1963** *Wall St. Jrnl.* 12 Sept. 14/1 Says W. C. Patton, field secretary for..the National Association for the Advancement of Colored People. 'Now we' re down to the nitty-gritty, the hard core who' ve never been interested in politics.' **1967** *Freedomways* VII. 186 All those 'nitty gritty' actions and styles which set Negroes off from the rest of American society. **1967** *N.Y. Times* 27 June 20 He's not afraid to get down to the nitty-gritty of unpleasant problems. **1968** *Times* 15 Nov. 17/2 To get down to what the American will call the 'nitty-gritty' of the matter—the heart, sir, the heart. **1969** *Listener* 25 Sept. 420/2 The Animals were already into the nitty-gritty of blues history. **1973** *Computers & Humanities* VII. 163 Most of the Harris work covers the nitty-gritty problems of subject analysis. **1974** *Financial Times* 6 Mar. 36/2 Mr Wilson is expected to appoint a trade union MP or two as junior Ministers at the Department of Employment to make up for Mr Foot's lack of experience in the 'nitty-gritty' of trade union negotiations. **1975** *Publishers Weekly* 13 Jan. 56/3 He still can startle the reader with his abrupt shifts from nitty-gritty reality to far-out fantasy.

nit-weed (ni·twīd). [f. NIT *sb.* + WEED *sb.*[1]] A North American herb, *Hypericum gentianoides*, of the family Guttiferæ, having wiry stems, scale-like leaves, and yellow flowers; also called orange grass and pine-weed.

1818 A. EATON *Man. Bot.* (ed. 2) 422 Nit-weed, false john's wort... On the sandy plain west of Ball's spring, New Haven. **1843** J. TORREY *Flora N.Y.* I. 89 Ground Pine. Nitweed. Pine-weed. **1907** A. B. LYONS *Plant Names* (ed. 2) 414 Sarothra... Orange-grass, Pine-weed, Bastard Gentian, Ground Pine, Nit-weed, False Johnswort.

nitwit (ni·twit). *colloq.* [Perh. f. NIT *sb.* 2 (in Dict. and Suppl.) + WIT *sb.*] A stupid person, a person of little intelligence. Also *attrib.* and *transf.*

1922 *Dialect Notes* V. 142 Nit-wit. **1926** L. NASON *Chevrons* v. 170 Listen, nit-wit. The rocket you want is a yellow smoke. **1928** *Daily Express* 1 June 9 The Vice-President announced loudly that he wanted a large cup of coffee with his dinner, and none of these 'nit-wit, pee-wee, demi-tasses'. **1930** *Musical Times* Nov. 987 Music..of the type that the nitwits who write..to the *Radio Times* call dry and highbrow. **1933** *Punch* 8 Feb. 157/2 *Barbara.* It's awful explaining to a nitwit. When you're out you put down. *Me.* Put what down? *Barbara.* Your cards, idiot! **1958** *Times Lit. Suppl.* 11 Apr. 193/3 Like some nitwit from a slapstick comedy, Turvey may be outwitted, but he is never really worsted. **1975** J. DRUMMOND *Slowly the Poison* II. 168 For God's sake, Beryl, don't be such a nitwit.

ni·twitted, *a.* [f. prec. + -ED[2].] Lacking in intelligence. Hence **nitwi·ttedness**, stupidity.

1931 *Observer* 6 Dec. 11 Many of the American films are

just as shoddy, just as nitwitted. **1942** A. CHRISTIE *Body in Library* ix. 85 That half-baked nitwitted little slypuss. **1952** *Canad. Forum* XXXII. 13 These gems of phony surprise, of noxious nitwittedness.

nitwittery (nitwi·təri). [f. *NITWIT + -ERY.] Imbecility, stupidity, lack of intelligence; foolish behaviour.

1936 *Punch* 29 Apr. 504/1 Eight of the stories are adventures which befell members of that singular focus of nitwittery, the Drones Club. **1949** C. FRY *Lady's not for Burning* 96 Last, vulgarity, cruelty, trickery, sham And all possible nitwittery. **1965** *New Statesman* 6 Aug. 194/1 It does not advance dramatic art to..tolerate nitwittery for the sake of a Cause.

Niuean (niˌū̆·ăn, niū̆·iăn), *sb.* and *a.* [f. *Niue*, native name (= 'world') of an island in the S. Pacific + -AN.] **A.** *sb.* **a.** A native or inhabitant of Niue. **b.** The language of the Niuean people. **B.** *adj.* Of or pertaining to Niue, the Niueans, or their language.

[**1893** *Jrnl. Polynesian Soc.* II. 11 The words were obtained from the New Testament translated into Niue by the Rev. Frank Lawes. *Ibid.* 13 The missionaries..'induced' two of the Niue youths to accompany them.] **1901** *Jrnl. R. Anthrop. Inst.* XXXI. 138 The Tongan mode of warfare was frontal attack by desperate charges; the Niuéan, a series of feints intended to frighten the enemy, and entice him into ambush. **1902** B. THOMSON *Savage Island* p. v, I went to the Niuéans in the name of the Queen and Empress whom the world is still lamenting. **1924** R. W. WILLIAMSON *Social & Pol. Syst. Cent. Polynesia* II. xiv. 53, I have..referred to Tregear's dictionary and to a Niuean vocabulary provided by Williams. **1954** K. B. CUMBERLAND *Southwest Pacific* vi. 270 It was native missionaries, Samoans mainly, who converted the Niueans. **1962** H. LUKE *Islands S. Pacific* xii. 222 In the latter half of the [19th] century..Niuean men would voluntarily leave the island..to work phosphate for good wages on Malden Island. **1968** *Encycl. Brit.* XVIII. 205/2 The best known of the dialects [of the Polynesian language] include Hawaiian,..Tongan, Tahitian, Niuean,..and Tuamotuan. **1973** *Guardian* 21 May 13/4 The Cook Islanders and Niueans are New Zealand citizens, have free right of entry... The Fijians and Tongans need individual permits.

nivation (nəivēⁱ·ʃən). *Geol.* [f. L. *niv-*, *nix* snow + -ATION.] Erosion of the ground beneath and at the sides of a snowbank, mainly as a result of alternate freezing and thawing.

1900 F. E. MATTHES in *21st Ann. Rep. U.S. Geol. Survey* II. 183 These névé effects..I shall, for the sake of brevity, speak of as effects of nivation. **1918** *Proc. Nat. Acad. Sci.* IV. 288 (*heading*) The importance of nivation as an erosive factor, and of soil flow as a transporting agency, in northern Greenland. **1957** G. E. HUTCHINSON *Treat. Limnol.* I. i. 59 A few cases may be found where nivation, or the freezing and thawing of water round patches of snow, has produced small closed depressions in jointed or fractured rocks. **1968** R. W. FAIRBRIDGE *Encycl. Geomorphol.* 123/2 When a deep snowdrift fails to melt away during summer, periodic freezing and thawing of the constantly moistened ground around and beneath it leads to the breakup of the rock particles which are then removed by meltwaters. This process is known as nivation.

ni:velliza·tion. *rare.* [f. F. *nivel-er* to level + -IZATION.] A making level or equal.

1879 VIGFUSSON & POWELL *Icelandic Reader* 469 There is a nivellization of all vowels as to their quantities. **1947** R. WELLEK in H. Smith *Columbia Dict. Mod. Europ. Lit.* 186/1 There was after the war a most impressive expansion —with the concomitant dangers in a break with tradition, in commercialization and nivellization.

Nivernois (nivẽ̄rnwa). [f. the title of Louis Jules Mancini Mazarini, Duc de Nivernais or *Nivernois* (1716–98), f. Nivernais, *Nivernois*, a former province of central France.] A tricorn hat with a wide brim, fashionable in the late eighteenth century. Also *attrib.*

1765 in Cunnington & Beard *Dict. Eng. Costume* (1960) 147/1 He wears this large umbrella-like hat. This is the Nivernois. **1766** C. ANSTEY *New Bath Guide* x. 68 What with my *Nivernois*' Hat can compare? **1770** E. P. *Art of Dressing Hair* 8 For they to shining Balls the Camp prefer'd, Nor e'er of Powder and Pomatum heard, Of silken Suits, or Nivernois genteel. **1960** CUNNINGTON & BEARD *Dict. Eng. Costume* 147/1 *Nivernois hat*, a tricorne hat with broad spreading brim rolled over a flat crown; known as the 'Nivernois cock'. **1969** R. T. WILCOX *Dict. Costume* (1970) 248/1 *Nivernois*, a diminutive tricorne worn by the English Macaronies with the cadogan wig in in 1770's.

‖**Nivose** (nivō̆ᵘ·z). [F. *Nivôse*, ad. L. *nivōsus* snowy: see NIVOSITY.] The fourth month of the French revolutionary calendar, extending (in 1793–94) from 21 Dec. to 19 Jan.

1802 C. WILMOT *Let.* 3 Jan. in *Irish Peer* (1920) 21 Sunday—3rd Jany. 1802. 13 Nivose, An 10. **1838** H. NICOLAS *Chronol. Hist.* (ed. 2) 184 The French Republicans ..used the number of the day of each month of their Calendar. For example: 1,2,..30 Nivose. **1884** *Encycl. Brit.* XVII. 266/2 He arrested and transported one hundred and thirty persons, whom he knew to be innocent of the plot... This is Nivose, an act as enormous as Fructidor, and with a perfidy of its own. **1957** *Ibid.* IX. 804/1 The winter months were *Nivôse*, the snowy, *Pluviôse*, the rainy, and *Ventôse*, the windy month. **1972** R. COBB *Reactions to French Revol.* iv. 134 On 7 Nivôse year VI (27 Dec. 1798), the *Ministre*..reported to his colleague.

nix^1. Add: **1.** (Further examples.) Also, = No *adv.*^{3}; not possibly.

1909 *Dialect Notes* III. 352 *Nit, nix(y*, adv. Variants of *no*. Slang. **1926** J. BLACK *You can't Win* vi. 67 'I'll go to the farmhouse..and buy something.' 'Nix, nix,' said one; 'buy nothin'.' **1929** A. CONAN DOYLE *Maracot Deep* 14 If I pull down fifty bucks a week it's not for nix. **1932** D. L. SAYERS *Have his Carcase* xxiii. 309 As for getting an experienced actor and giving him a show in the part—nix! **1951** GREEN & LAURIE *Show Biz* 570/1 *Nix*, no, veto, thumbs-down. **1959** 'J. R. MACDONALD' *Galton Case* (1960) xvi. 132 'He..wanted his old job back. Nix.' A gesture of his spread hand swept Lemberg into the dust-bin.

c. Phr. *nix on*, enough of, have done with, no more of. *colloq.*

1902 'H. MCHUGH' *It's up to You* iii. 55 We decided before we stepped on the Pullman that it would be nix on the sweetheart talk. **1923** R. D. PAINE *Comrades of Rolling Ocean* iv. 62 Camp Stuart at ten o'clock. Nix on that kid stuff. **1941** BAKER *Dict. Austral. Slang* 49 *Nix on it!*: Stop it! Lay off!

d. = No *a.*; none, negligible. (Also directly from G. *nix* (or *nichts*), in bilingual conversation.)

1906 E. DYSON *Fact'ry 'Ands* vii. 84 No man can reasonably expect t' live ther life iv er hindependent gent on er nix income. **1928** H. CRANE *Let.* 31 Jan. (1965) 315 One can generally 'place' people to some extent; but out here it's mostly nix. **1945** G. MORGAN *Only Ghosts can Live* xii. 144 'Nix Fish-Tins.' *Gefangener*—German for '*Nicht verstehen*': I don't get you. **1971** *Daily Tel.* (Colour Suppl.) 12 Nov. 21/2 Oh, I just said battery kaput, nix lights, nix motor... And we fix. But all European trucks stop for each other here.

3. (Earlier example.) Also, as a children's 'truce-word'.

1860 in HOTTEN *Dict. Slang* (ed. 2). **1959** I. & P. OPIE *Lore & Lang. Schoolch.* viii. 152 *Nicks* or *nix*. Prevailing term [as a truce-word] in Warwick.

nix, *v.* [f. NIX^1.] **1.** *trans.* To cancel, forbid, refuse. Freq. as imp., beware, cease (doing something).

1903 H. HUTCHINS *Autobiogr. Thief* viii. 180, I started in to talk about old times in the stir and..he answered me by saying 'Nix', which meant 'Drop it'. **1914** [see *EYEFUL *sb.* c]. **1934** M. H. WESEEN *Dict. Amer. Slang* xxi. 371 *Nix*, to refuse an offer; a refusal; to deny a request; a denial. *Nixy* is a variant. **1945** in Wentworth & Flexner *Dict. Amer. Slang* (1960) 356/1 The blue-penciler nixed the story. **1961** *New Left Rev.* July/Aug. 53/1 Every time somebody nixes..paid work to fulfil an unpaid commitment..my faith..is..restored. **1969** R. V. BESTE *Next Time I'll Pay* ii. 22 He could have been more explicit... If he had been his holiday would have been nixed, that was for sure. **1973** *Tucson* (Arizona) *Daily Citizen* 22 Aug. 11/1 (*heading*) Nude bathing nixed. **1974** *Maclean's Mag.* Dec. 19/1 It was the inner voice that nixed the deal—the savings contract that the salesman was pushing ensured that I wouldn't break even until after the first eight years.

2. *nix out* (*on*): *U.S. slang* in various senses (see quots.).

1940 *Music Makers* May 37/3 *Nix out*, to eliminate, get rid of. Ex. 'I nixed that chick out last week'. 'I nixed my garments' (undressed). **1945** L. SHELLY *Jive Talk Dict.* 29/2 *Nix out*, to erase. **1946** MEZZROW & WOLFE *Really Blues* (1957) 84 The owner nixed big crowds out. **1969** Nix out on [see *FADE *sb.*^{1}]. **1970** C. MAJOR *Dict. Afro-Amer. Slang* 85 *Nix out*, to throw away.

nixie^1. (Later poet. examples.)

1918 D. H. LAWRENCE *New Poems* 62 It seems to me The woman you are should be nixie, there is a pool Where we ought to be. **1952** R. CAMPBELL tr. *Baudelaire's Poems* 214 If your gaze the gaze transfixes Of satyresses or of nixies.

nixie^2 (ni·ksi). Also **nixy.** [f. NIX^1 + -Y^6, -IE.] **1.** = NIX^1 1 b. Also *attrib. U.S.*

1890 *Cent. Dict.*, Nixy^2. **1901** *Congress. Rec.* 17 Jan. 1145/6 These poor 'nixie' clerks in the postoffices of this country. **1904** *Springfield* (Mass.) *Republ.* 29 Oct. 4 He was made what is known in the office as a 'nixy' clerk.. one who looks up misdirected letters. **1905** *N.Y. Even. Post* 8 Feb. 5 What the railway postal clerks most dread is the class of mail they know as 'nixies'. **1929** *Lit. Digest* 5 Oct. 67/1 The similarity in appearance of the letters N.Y. and N.J...is responsible for many letters reaching the 'Nixie' division. **1949** *Amer. Speech* XXVI. 136/1 *Nixie*, a piece of mail so damaged or illegible that it can go no farther in the mails. The *Nixie* section rewraps and tries to discern the scribbled addresses on mail. **1956** *Daily Progress* (Charlottesville, Va.) 19 Sept. 28/1 '*Nixie*' is mail that can't be delivered because the address is incorrect, illegible, or insufficient.

b. = NIX^1 1 a (in Dict. and Suppl.).

1906 E. DYSON *Fact'ry 'Ands* xviii. 249 Er storm centre ..redooced..land values t' nex' t' nixie.

2. *adv.* No, certainly not. Freq. as expletive.

1886 H. BAUMANN *Londinismen* 120/1 *Nixey*..nein, nicht. **1903** *Pedagogical Seminary* X. 373 Nixy... Don't you believe it. Not much. **1914** G. ATHERTON *Perch of Devil* I. 108 They're all right to marry,..but to sacrifice your life for, nixie.

Nixonian (niksō̆ᵘ·niăn), *a.* [f. the name of Richard M. *Nixon* (b. 1913), Vice-President of the United States 1953–61 and President 1969–74 + -IAN.] Of, pertaining to, or resembling Richard M. Nixon.

1959 *Listener* 10 Sept. 376/1 Thomas Edmund Dewey was a Nixonian sort of man. **1970** *Harper's Mag.* July 30/3 It was not, after all, critics of the Administration who defined Nixonian language for us—Don't watch what we say, watch what we do—it was the Administration spokesmen themselves. **1971** *Between Lines* (Newtown, Pa.) 1 Nov. 1/1 Voluntarism, the theme of the new Nixonian-economics, puts capitalism to its most severe test. **1972** *N.Y. Times Book Rev.* 29 Oct. 46/3 Herblock analyzes Nixonian techniques such as the Happening or Non-Event in which the Vice President is photographed standing at a podium addressing the President and full Cabinet and telling them what a great job they are doing. **1973** *Nation Rev.* (Melbourne) 31 Aug. 1445/1 Change indeed in nixonian Washington!

Hence **Nixonite** (ni·ksŏ̆nəit), a supporter of Nixon or his policies; **Nixonization** (ni:ksŏ̆nəizēⁱ·ʃən), development of a Nixonian character; subjection to the influence of or domination by supporters of Nixon; **Nixonomics** (niksŏ̆nǫ·miks) *sb. pl.* [f. *econ*)*omics* (ECONOMIC *sb.* 2 c)], the economic policies of Nixon.

1958 *Time* 17 Nov. 22 A staunch Nixonite. **1960** *Guardian* 10 Nov. 10/7 There were some Nixonites present. **1969** *Demo Memo* (Washington, D.C.) 29 Oct. 1 Walter Heller..challenges the soundness of 'Nixonomics'. **1971** *New Statesman* 16 Apr. 516/3 Alternatives to the Hobson's choice of possibly counterproductive street protest or mute acquiescence in the Nixonisation of the war. **1971** *N.Y. Times* 19 Sept. 2E/2 The President dredged up a term he had always treated with derision as a symbol of economic blundering by his Democratic predecessors and converted it to the dynamics of the new Nixonomics. **1972** *Newsweek* 16 Oct. 89/1 Phase two of the new Nixonomics has changed nearly all the rules— and as one result, quite a few companies these days..are going out of their way..to cut profits down. **1973** *Black World* Mar. 68 There is certain to be greater Nixonization of government at every level. **1975** *Maclean's Mag.* Jan. 6/1 Richard Nixon was able to take dramatic economic action over a single weekend in August, 1971 (remember the new Nixonomics?) without a word of sass or backtalk from Congress.

nkonze, var. *KONZE.

Nkrumahism (nˌkrū̆·măˌiz'm). Also **Nkrumaism.** [f. the name of 'Kwame *Nkrumah*' (Francis Nwia Kofi) (1909–72), Ghanaian political leader: see -ISM.] The principles and policies associated with Kwame Nkrumah; adherence to or support of these principles. So **Nkru·ma(h)ist** *a.* and *sb.*, (supporting, one who supports) the policies and principles of Nkrumah; of or pertaining to these policies and principles. Also **Nkru:mahiza·tion,** the making of changes in accordance with his policies and principles.

1960 *Sunday Times* 28 Aug. 5/1 Orgy of phrases... These phrases..have cropped up constantly..'Nkrumahism' (off-stage among Ghanaians). **1962** *Listener* 23 Aug. 272/2 Bishop Roseveare had 'tried to subvert the Nkrumahist revolution'. **1964** *Economist* 1 Feb. 396/2 The forming of regional groups is not inimical to pan-African unity (as Nkrumahism says it is). **1968** *Listener* 11 July 53/1 In 1964, 'local conditions'—that is to say, Kwame Nkrumah—demanded that the University appoint certain known 'Nkrumahists' to key positions. The sole specific intellectual content of 'Nkrumahism' was the implied infallibility of Kwame Nkrumah. *Ibid.*, At the University we had the choice of accepting 'Nkrumahisation' or 'sheltering behind political freedom.' **1973** *Ann. Reg. 1972* 247 There were those who saw the new military regime in Accra as returning to a form of 'Nkrumaism without Nkrumah'. *Ibid.*, General Nathan Aferi..was reported as saying..'There are Busiaites and Nkrumaists and uncommitted.'

No., N^o. Add: (Further examples.)

No longer restricted to the designation of individual things and persons.

1840 DICKENS *Let.* 4 Feb. (1969) II. 18, I am curious to see how the idea of the first No. of my projected work strikes you. **1905** *Strand Mag.* Apr. 376/1 George II.. made a present of No. 10 [Downing Street] to his Prime Minister, Sir Robert Walpole, and his successors. **1924** J. BUCHAN *Three Hostages* xvii. 242 It was eventually arranged that the district-visitor should call at No. 4 the following afternoon. **1937** N. MARSH *Vintage Murder* v. 47 He was advancing a No. 4 company in St. Helens. I was selling tickets for the worst show in England. **1972** *Oxford Times* 15 Sept. 18/1 Conversion of house into 2 No. self contained flats. **1974** M. GILBERT *Flash Point* ii. 14 It's No. 276 Coalporter Street.

b. *No. 9* (mil.): see quot. 1917.

1911 *Pharmaceutical Formulas* (ed. 8) 922/2 (*heading*) Army Pill No. 9. **1917** A. G. EMPEY *Over Top* 301 'No. 9.' A pill the doctor gives you if you are suffering with corns or barber's itch or any disease at all.

no, *a.* Add: **I. 1. a.** (Later examples.) Still *dial.* or illiterate.

1896 [see *CON *v.*]. **1897** [see *CLASS *sb.* 5 b]. **1968** *Listener* 20 June 796/3 He's not going to be put in no poorhouse.

3. b. (Earlier U.S. examples.)

1832 J. P. KENNEDY *Swallow Barn* II. xvii. 220 Which ..would produce a cure 'in almost no time'. **1868** G. G. CHANNING *Early Recoll. Newport R.I.* 143 The money was

..arranged as to facilitate the payments in 'no time', understood in my day, to mean the shortest period.

II. 5. b. (Further examples.)

In quot. 1948 the sense is 'without the use of the hands'. **1940** *Ann. Reg. 1939* 253 A vote of no-confidence was carried in the Lower Chamber. **1948** D. Ballantyne *Cunninghams* I. xviii. 92 Ralph showed off, riding no-hands and skidding in the loose metal. **1954** F. C. Avis *Boxing Reference Dict.* 75 *No contest*, a declaration of the referee that the fight is null and void, usually because both contestants are making no serious efforts at boxing. *Ibid.*, *No-count*, a slipping to the floor of the ring but getting up again before the count begins. **1956** J. G. Porter in A. Pryce-Jones *New Outl. Mod. Knowledge* 142 Adaptable as he [*sc.* man] is, can he exist for any length of time under conditions of no-gravity? **1957** L. F. R. Williams *State of Israel* 158 The four years of the legislature's statutory life (which is, of course, always liable to be shortened by a vote of no-confidence). **1960** *Times* 5 July 18/2 Edwards has had 10 contests and won nine of them, featuring rather unluckily in a no-contest (or double disqualification). **1973** *Houston* (Texas) *Chron. Mag. People, Places, Pleasures* 14 Oct. 8/4 Agnew..pleaded no contest—in effect, guilty—to cheating on his income tax.

d. Used in various colloq. phrases, as *no strings*, no conditions or obligations; also *attrib.* (cf. *STRING *sb.*); *no stuff*, no joking; *no sweat*, no bother, no trouble.

1909 'O. Henry' *Options* (1916) 50 I've told you..my oral sentiments, and there's no strings to 'em. **1946** Mezzrow & Wolfe *Really Blues* (1957) 376 *No stuff*, no kidding. **1952** A. Huxley *Let.* 12 Oct. (1969) 658 The thing should start in a small way, but with adequate equipment, no strings and no red tape. **1955** *Amer. Speech* XXX. 118 *No sweat, no strain* n. phr. used adjectivally, easy, no trouble, no difficulty. **1960** *Ibid.* XXXV. 122 *No sweat*, the GI's reaction to an unpleasant, but necessary task. **1963** *Daily Mail* 11 Nov. 8/8 Mumblemouth especially knows how to blow flicks that cop bread, no-sweat style (knows how to succeed in movies without really trying). **1965** *Economist* 6 Mar. 980/3 In effect, the family doctors will get a no-strings pay rise averaging 9 per cent. **1970** *Times* 18 Aug. 15 Following the February £13m no-strings pay deal..union officials have been conducting a wages and conditions survey of motor plants in Britain. **1970** C. Major *Dict. Afro-Amer. Slang* 85 *No stuff*, expression that implies sincerity. **1972** 'H. Howard' *Nice Day for Funeral* iii. 45 He respects me as a person. No strings. **1972** *Publishers Weekly* 16 Oct. 17/1 Mrs Wallach complains that she cannot use plastic book jackets on books with maps on the inside covers. No sweat! We paste the book pocket..on the next inside page, [etc.]. **1973** K. Giles *File on Death* vi. 153 No sweat, mate...We're not looking for trouble.

e. Denoting the complete emptying of the mind described in Buddhist, and esp. Zen, philosophy as *no-mind, no-thought*, etc.

1934 D. T. Suzuki *Essays in Zen Buddhism* III. ii. 84 'Mind is still subject to measurement. Who is the Buddha?' 'No-mind is he.' **1949** —— *Zen Doctrine of No-Mind* 29 When..the seeing of self-nature has no reference to a specific state of consciousness, which can be logically or relatively defined as a something, the Zen Masters designate it in negative terms and call it 'no-thought' or 'no mind', *wu-nien* or *wu-hsin*. **1956** A. Huxley *Adonis & Alphabet* 34 No-thought not-thinks about the world in terms of no-things. *Ibid.*, In Zen the virgin consciousness was called *Wu-nien* or *Wu-hsin*—no-mind or no-thought. **1959** C. C. Chang *Practice of Zen* ii. 59 The so-called No-mind (Chinese: *Wu hsin*) is not like day, wood, or stone, that is, utterly devoid of consciousness; nor does the term imply that the mind stands still without any reaction when it contacts objects or circumstances in the world. It..is natural and spontaneous at all times... There is nothing impure within it; neither does it remain in a state of impurity. When one observes his body and mind, he sees them as magic shadows or as a dream... When he reaches this point, then he can be considered as having arrived at the true state of No-mind. **1959** D. T. Suzuki *Zen & Jap. Culture* iv. 74 All things are accomplished when one attains a mind of 'no-mind-ness' according to the great Zen master. **1960** A. Koestler *Lotus & Robot* II. x. 240 It [*sc.* Zen] proclaims to be the philosophy of no-mind (Wu-hsin), of no-thought (Wu-mien)..and of 'going ahead without hesitation'. **1966** P. Kapleau *Three Pillars of Zen* II. v. 201 Mindlessness, on the other hand, or 'no-mindness' as it has been called, is a condition of such complete absorption that there is no vestige of self-awareness.

6. b. (Further examples.) Also, denoting absence of necessity for. See also *NO-FINES *a.* (*sb.*).

1902 R. Machray *Night Side of London* ii. 23 The clubs, both high-class and no-class, are not all closed. **1930** E. Pound *XXX Cantos* vii. 27 Brown-yellow wood, and the no colour plaster. **1936** 'J. Beynon' *Planet Plane* 58, I didn't think we were going to hit the no-gravity zone so soon. **1939** No class [see *billiard-hall* (*BILLIARDS 2)]. **1955** *N.Y. Times* 13 Feb. III. 8/1 The favorite fabric is the no-iron type. **1958** *Economist* 1 Nov. 435/2 Nobody really doubts that 'no deposit' business will also be done. **1961** P. White *Riders in Chariot* viii. 233 For Chrisake! Who am I to know what is up to every no-hope Jew that comes to the country? **1963** B. Fozard *Instrumentation Nuclear Reactors* xi. 132 The reading of the voltmeter may be corrected to zero under no-signal conditions. **1969** *New Statesman* 18 July 80/1 'It's a gas, man, it's a rave,' says a no-bra girl. **1970** *Globe & Mail* (Toronto) 26 Sept. 1/5 (*caption*) Empty cans and no-deposit bottles lie around a tree. **1971** *Flying* (N.Y.) Apr. 18/2 The evidence seemed clear that the no-accident day had been moved from Thursday to Tuesday. **1972** *Guardian* 2 Nov. 10/3 A no-hope telephonist with an invalid mother, an illegitimate child and a bad communication problem. **1973** *Times* 19 Mar. 21/1 The United States Justice Department filed both civil and criminal suits. Ford entered a 'no contest' plea and last month was fined a total of $7m. **1973** Gagnon & Simon *Sexual Conduct* (1974) x. 291 The no-bra look is serving both males' fantasies and a return to naturalness.

7. b. (Later example.)

1916 Joyce *Portrait of Artist* (1969) i. 50 His nocoloured eyes looking through the glasses.

no, *adv.*[1] **1.** (Later *Sc.* examples.)

a **1894** R. L. Stevenson *Weir of Hermiston* (1896) viii. 245 Oh, my dear, that'll no dae! **1931** A. J. Cronin *Hatter's Castle* II. xiii. 435 What was't he said, 'a loyal wife and a devoted mother,' wasn't no? **1973** *People's Jrnl.* (Inverness & Northern Counties ed.) 28 July 4/5 Who says the Scots are a dour lot? No' us anyway! **1975** M. Russell *Murder by Mile* iii. 22 What's holding ye up?..Was the tyre no' checked?

no, *adv.*[2] *no better than* (one) *should* (or *ought to*) *be*: see *BETTER *a.* 5.

no, *adv.*[3] and *sb.* Add: **A.** *adv.* **1.** (Further examples.)

1853 *Harper's Mag.* Feb. 402/1 This is the gentleman who can't say no. **1853** T. C. Haliburton *Sam Slick's Wise Saws* I. v. 119 You first of all force yourself into my cabin, won't take no for an answer, and then complain of oncivility. **1861** G. H. Lewes *Let.* 20 Aug. in Geo. Eliot *Lett.* (1954) III. 446 She allows herself to be preyed upon dreadfully by the boys—she can't say No. **1930** W. S. Churchill *My Early Life* iv. 74 Come on now, all you young men... Don't take no for an answer, never submit to failure. **1961** *Family Jrnl.* Dec. 15/3 'But he would not take "No" for an answer,' she went on. **1961** *Listener* 21 Dec. 1065/2 He was made Minister of Labour in a season when the Government's economic policy meant saying 'no' to wage demands. **1974** M. Butterworth *Man in Sopwith Camel* viii. 89 I'm warning you that I'm not taking no for an answer. **1975** C. Storr *Chinese Egg* vii. 41 'I can manage. You keep sitting down.' 'I shan't say, No. It's a long drag up to St. Monica's.'

3. c. *no, you don't*: see *DO *v.* 29 b.

No,[2] **Nō**: see *NOH.

noa (nō͞u·ă). [a. Hawaiian (Maori, Tahitian) *noa* (something) free from taboo, ordinary.] An expression substituted for a taboo word or phrase. Freq. in *Comb.*

1925 O. Jespersen *Mankind, Nation & Individual* ix. 169 This harmless word that has been substituted, the Polynesians call *noa*. *Ibid.* 179 Both the above Danish names for devil are originally noa-names. *Ibid.* 184 Certain words and expressions are taboo for certain persons and must therefore be replaced by other words, by noa-words. **1951** S. Ullmann *Words & their Use* III. iii. 75 If a word is struck by a taboo ban, it must be replaced by a harmless alternative, a so-called *noa* term. **1956** *Trans. Philol. Soc. 1955* 1 The special terms used by the [Faroese] fishermen to replace ordinary words when these became tabooed are designated as noa words or noa names, etc. Noa denotes the opposite of taboo, in the present context it stands for what is allowed in contrast to that which is forbidden. **1975** W. B. Lockwood *Lang. Brit. Isles* 55 [Cornish] *pajerpaw* 'newt', lit. 'four foot'..clearly a noa name.

no-account, *a.* orig. *U.S.* Of no account, importance, value, or use; insignificant, worthless. (See also *NO-'COUNT *a.*)

1845 *Spirit of Times* 1 Feb. 583/2 I'll just tell you that the land I'm after is a d–d, little, no-account quarter section, that nobody would have but me. **1886** *Pall Mall Gaz.* 29 Sept. 4/1 We submit to be..treated as no-account people in all affairs of State. **1898** H. S. Canfield *Maid of Frontier* 109 It seems to me..that Charlie is gettin mighty no account. **1900** Conrad *Lord Jim* v. 47 The other two no-account chaps spotted their captain, and began to move towards us. **1902** G. H. Lorimer *Lett. Merchant* vi. 69 A mailing-clerk so no-account as to be writing personal letters in office hours. **1936** 'J. Tey' *Shilling for Candles* v. 51 'You mean she thinks he's a wrong 'un?' 'No. Just no account.' *Ibid.* vii. 71 We both felt no-account and were afraid people'd find it out. **1952** C. Day Lewis tr. *Virgil's Aeneid* XI. 246 Are we, we no-account souls, to litter the plains? **1973** M. Mackintosh *King & Two Queens* xii. 180 I'm only a no-account Irisher, but I like to pay my debts.

B. *sb.* A 'no-account' person.

1896 'Mark Twain' in *Harper's Mag.* Sept. 523 Who ever had anything agin that poor trifling no-account? **1936** J. Dos Passos *Big Money* 169 The child of a no-account like Fred. **1970** W. Garner *Puppet-Masters* XXX. 222 Why is a no-account like Lindsay collected from a police court by a Special Branch cop? **1973** *Philadelphia Inquirer* (Today Suppl.) 14 Oct. 43/2 Others—those Gypsies most respected and strongest in the community—will not challenge him because they believe he is a 'no-account'.

Noah's Ark. Add: **5.** *U.S.* An orchid of the genus *Cypripedium*, esp. the pink *C. acaule* and the yellow *C. calceolus* var. *pubescens*.

1826 W. Darlington *Florula Cestrica* 95 C[*ypripedium*] *pubescens*... Noah's Ark. Yellow Mocasin [*sic*] flower. **1898** C. A. Creevey *Flowers of Field* 296 Stemless Lady's Slipper. Noah's Ark. Moccasin-flower. *Cypripedium acaule*. **1949** E. L. Palmer *Fieldbk. Nat. Hist.* 148/2 It bears a number of common names such as Noah's ark, squirrel's shoes, camel's foot, nerveroot, old goose, Indian moccasin, and two lips.

6. *Rhyming slang.* **a.** A police informer. **b.** *Austral.* A shark. (See also quots. 1941, 1960.)

1898 *Bulletin* (Sydney) 17 Dec. (Red Page), An informer or mar-plot is a nark or a Jonah or a Noah's Ark. **1941** Baker *Dict. Austral. Slang* 49 *A Noah's ark*, a dull, witless fellow. A rhyme on 'nark'. **1941** 'V. Davis' *Phenomena in Crime* xix. 254 A stoolie, Noah's Ark, a grasshopper, a nark or informer. **1952** *Chambers's Shorter Eng. Dict.* 800/1 *Noah's ark* (*slang*), a shark. **1960** J. Franklyn *Dict. Rhyming Slang* 101/1 *Noah's ark*, (1) nark (an informer), (2) park. (1) has been in use in England since the first decade of the 20 C. It is also used in the form of a Spoonerism '*oah's Nark*, the first word having the inference, '*whore's*' and when thus inverted it is the supreme expression of contempt.

7. (See quot. 1968.)

1945 *Archit. Rev.* XCVII. 59/3 In the 1920's an import from Germany, simpler in erection, faster and thus more thrilling, threatened the supremacy of the switch-back... This new machine—the Noah's Ark..had decorative features which continued the tradition of coarse splendour. **1965** *Observer* (Colour Suppl.) 29 Aug. 10/2 The showmen are setting up their stalls and heavy riding machines: Dodgems, Noah's Arks, Waltzers, Shows, and Hurricane Jets. **1968** D. Braithwaite *Fairground Archit.* 153/2 The term 'Noah's Ark' referred to a circular ride having an undulating track..and a variety of fixed animals carried on segmental platforms, all contained within a static enclosure.

nob, *sb.*[2] Add: **1.** *bob a nob*: see *BOB *sb.*[8] 2.

no ball, no-ball, *sb.* Add: **2.** (Earlier and later examples.)

1876 *Haygarth's Cricket Scores* V. 176 Mr. Hankey was bowled by a no ball..; he afterwards carried out his bat. **1955** *Times* 6 Aug. 4/3 The loping run, all arms and legs, and the no-ball were not forgotten. **1974** *Sunday Tel.* 3 Mar. 33/7 Hayes, his middle stump removed by a Holder no-ball.., remained to fight another day. **1975** *Cricketer* May 19/2 There were at least three occasions when he bowled batsmen with no-balls.

3. *fig.* (also *attrib.*).

1922 [see *BEAVER[4]]. **1939** *John o' London's* 9 June 361/2 Mr. Chance's solution is much too complicated, and he does not play the game quite fairly, because he has two men who are related and can pass for each other, which..has been considered a 'no-ball' in detective fiction for a long time. **1966** *Sunday Times* (Colour Suppl.) 4 Dec. 73/2 GI Jargon. *No-ball Target*, Air Corps nickname for a German rocket launching site.

no-ball, *v.* (Earlier examples of both senses.)

1862 *Baily's Mag.* Oct. 201 John Lillywhite..also 'No balled' the third, fourth, fifth, sixth, and seventh delivered by Willsher, who thereupon walked off the ground. **1867** G. H. Selkirk *Guide to Cricket-Ground* iv. 60 Dean, as umpire, no balled Mr. C. D. Marsham three times in one over.

nobbily, *adv.* (Examples.)

1859 Hotten *Dict. Slang* 69 *Nobby*, fine or showy; *nobbily*, showily. **1877** 'Mark Twain' in *Atlantic Monthly* Nov. 591 Two hundred Bermudians..all of them nobbily dressed, as the poet says. **1880** *Punch* 25 Dec. 299/1 There wasn't a chap in the room so good-looking or nobbily drest.

no·bbiness. [f. Nobby *a.* + -ness.] Smartness; affected elegance.

1909 *N.Y. Even. Post* 7 Aug. 2 He unwittingly errs.. on the side either of a certain scrubbiness or of an even more unfortunate 'nobbiness'. **1935** *Amer. Speech* X. 10/1 Around 1900 when the present-day elderly good-people were criminal Dapper Dans, their lingo was the last word in linguistic nobbiness.

nobble, *v.* Add: **1.** (Later examples.)

1933 Wodehouse *Heavy Weather* iii. 34 At any moment ..the bounder was liable to come sneaking in, with mask on face and poison-needle in hand, intent on nobbling the favourite. **1951** *News Chron.* 18 Dec. 1 Lord Rosebery confirms today that his horse which was nobbled was Snap.

b. (Earlier and later examples.) Also in somewhat weakened sense: to reduce the efficiency of (a person, etc.) by some means.

1856 Ld. Clarendon *Let.* in H. R. C. Wellesley *Paris Embassy* (1928) 103 Morny..seems to have talked with enthusiasm about the Empress-mother, and to have been quite nobbled by her. **1912** F. M. Hueffer *Panel* I. ii. 31 'I want to point out to Miss Delamere that you can't reform the theatre without reforming the conventional idea about marriage.'.. 'Oh, I see,' the major said amiably, 'you want to nobble her before she makes any business arrangements with my uncle.' **1939** H. Nicolson *Diary* 20 Sept. (1967) 36 Margesson insisted that..he [*sc.* Churchill] must be 'nobbled' by having a department which would occupy all his time. **1960** J. Fingleton *Four Chukkas to Australia* xvii. 142 He was left bereft when this particular style of 'nobbling' the opposition was outwitted in the first Test. **1963** *Times* 13 May 6/6 Unions felt that if they were to take part in the work of the National Incomes Commission they would be 'nobbled at the start.' **1973** 'M. Underwood' *Reward for Defector* v. 39 What about the rest of the delegation?.. No chance of nobbling one of them?

3. Also, to strike; to kidnap; to 'steal'.

1841 C. H. Hartshorne *Salopia Antiqua* 517 *Nobler*, a man whose duty it is to remind inattentive youths in church, of their misbehaviour, by '*nobling*' them, or hitting them on the head with a wand. **1865** Milton & Cheadle *N.-W. Passage by Land* xv. 306 His son had succeeded in 'nobbling' a brace of partridges, knocking the young birds out of the trees with short sticks, missiles they used with great dexterity. **1922** Joyce *Ulysses* 497 You once nobble that, congregation, and a buck joy ride to heaven becomes a back number. **1928** E. Waugh *Decline & Fall* vii. 66 'What sort of job?' I says. 'Nobbling,' he says, meaning kidnapping. **1932** H. J. Massingham *World without End* 296 Off he goes to 'bibble' a

mug of scrumpy and 'nobble' a hunk of cheese. **1968** M. WOODHOUSE *Rock Baby* viii. 64 We've got this Shackleton we've nobbled off Coastal Command.

nobbler[2]. Add: (Further Austral. and N.Z. examples.) Also, a small glass or container for liquor.

1852 'G.F.P.' *Gold Pen & Pencil Sk.* XIV. (Morris), The summit gained, he pulls up at the Valley, To drain a farewell nobbler to his Sally. **1853** J. SHERER *Gold-Finder of Australia* 177, I have only had two nobblers (as they are called) since I came to the place, and paid 1s. 6d. per nobler. **1859** F. FOWLER *Southern Lights & Shadows* 52 (Morris), To pay for liquor for another is to 'stand' or to 'shout'... The measure is called a 'nobbler' or a 'breakdown'. **1873** TROLLOPE *Austral. & N.Z.* II. xi. 201 A nobbler is the proper colonial phrase for a drink at a public-house. **1885** R. C. PRAED *Austral. Life* 103 Having accepted at my hands the customary 'nobbler', he would sit down for half-an-hour, talking. **1908** D. FERGUSON *Bush Life in Austral. & N.Z.* (ed. 4) xxxv. 274 Nor did their thirst for ardent spirits appear to be in the least moderated by the price of the beverages..the good old colonial charge of one shilling per 'nobbler'. **1936** M. FRANKLIN *All that Swagger* xix. 181, I took a nobbler of your poisoned grog. **1949** D. M. DAVIN *Roads from Home* 216 He..was pouring it into two nobblers he had fished out of the pocket. **1957** D. NILAND *Call me when Cross turns Over* ii. 30 He poured himself nobbler after nobbler and drank them straight. **1971** *Walkabout* (Austral.) Nov. 73/1 Whisky costs around 300 rupiahs, or some 75 cents, for a generous nobbler.

nobbut, *adv.* **1.** (Later *dial.* examples.)

1929 J. B. PRIESTLEY *Good Companions* I. v. 196 It's nobbut Thursday, isn't it? Well, it seems like months. **1957** 'B. BUCKINGHAM' *Boiled Alive* xi. 61 There was nobbut a bunch of dirty foreigners here. **1963** *Times* 25 May 9/7 Mr. Vernon Horsfall still makes clogs. 'But it's a mak a finished is t'trade, you know. It's nobbut farmers and folk in weaving sheds.'

nobby, *sb.* Add: **2.** Also used more widely around the Irish Sea, and by the Royal Navy.

1936 E. VALE *Seas & Shores England* ii. 19 The Morecambe Bay fishermen with their specially evolved cutter-rigged smack called a *nobby* have been for generations famous throughout the three western seas of Britain. **1948** R. DE KERCHOVE *Internat. Maritime Dict.* 491/1 *Nobbie, nobby.* 1. A round-sterned, two-masted, lug-rigged fishing boat found on the south coast of Ireland... 2. A pointed-stern fishing boat of the Mersey estuary rigged with a jib, a dipping lug foresail, and a standing lug mizzen. **1953** J. MASEFIELD *Conway* (rev. ed.) IV. 209 We had three sailing dinghies—and the nobby—a heavier boat of about eighteen feet. **1970** E. J. MARCH *Inshore Craft Gt. Britain* II. viii. 280 The early smacks, 'nobbies' to use the local name, were about 36 ft long, and drew 4 ft of water. **1973** W. ELMER *Terminol. Fishing* i. 26 In the west, an impressive pattern is formed by the distribution of the *prawners* and *shrimpers* of the Cumberland and Lancashire coast, and the Lancashire *nobby*.

3. *Austral.* Black opal found as a silica drop (the characteristic form at Lightning Ridge, N.S.W.).

1924 T. C. WOLLASTON *Opal* I. ii. 10 Characteristic forms of the Black Opal are locally known as 'Nobbies'... pseudomorphs after sponges and corals. **1948** E. F. MURPHY *They struck Opal* 140 Nobbies are..scattered here and there like shells on the beach. **1963** A. LUBBOCK *Austral. Roundabout* 79 These petrified..bubbles are called 'nobbies'; and they are prised out..by the opal digger. **1967** S. LLOYD *Lightning Ridge Bk.* Introd., Dug out a cleanskin nobby. It was a bonza stone and a whopper too.

Nobel (nōᵘbe·l). [The name of Alfred *Nobel* (1833–96), Swedish chemist and engineer, inventor of dynamite and other high explosives.] **Nobel prize,** one of five prizes, established by the will of Alfred Nobel, which are awarded annually to the person or persons adjudged by Swedish learned societies to have done the most significant recent work in physics, chemistry, medicine, and literature, and to the person or persons adjudged by the Norwegian parliament to have rendered the greatest service to the cause of peace. So *Nobel award, bequest, laureate* (see *LAUREATE *sb.* 1 d), *prize-man, prize-winner, prize-winning* adj. Also *ellipt.*

A sixth prize, for economics, was first awarded in 1969.

1900 *Sci. Gossip* Nov. 164/2 Just before going to press we have been furnished..with copies of the official statutes and regulations of the Nobel Bequest. *Ibid.* Dec. 195/1 Each candidate for a Nobel prize must be proposed in writing by some one qualified to make such proposal. **1904** *To-Day* 28 Dec. 252/2 (*heading*) The Nobel Prizemen. **1932** *Discovery* Oct. 327/2 Ross..was..awarded the Nobel Prize for Medicine. **1956** Nobel award [see *GUGGENHEIM]. **1958** *Listener* 6 Nov. 749/1 His great discovery, a Nobel-prizewinning matter. **1962** *Ibid.* 8 Nov. 775/1 Deservedly a Nobel Prize winner, O'Neill..was perhaps the greatest twentieth-century dramatist writing in English. **1968** J. D. WATSON *Double Helix* xxii. 163 Though the odds still appeared against us, Linus had not yet won his Nobel. **1969** *Times* 29 Sept. 10/8 An award for economics is, I hear, to be added to the list of Nobel prizes for peace, literature, physics, chemistry, and medicine. It has been endowed after a bequest from the Royal Bank of Sweden, which has celebrated its 300th anniversary this year. **1973** D. ROBINSON *Rotten with Honour* 66 Our own people rate this man's work at Nobel standard. **1973** *Times* 19 Oct. 21/2 Professor Wassily Leontief, of Harvard University, yesterday won the Nobel Prize for Economics. He will receive an award of £41,000. **1975** J. AIKEN *Voices in Empty House* ii. 73 August's lab assistants gave him this set when he won his Nobel.

Nobelist (nōᵘbe·list). [f. *NOBEL + -IST.] A winner of a Nobel prize.

1941 *Sci. News Let.* 30 Aug. 135/1 Prof. Enrico Fermi, Nobelist now working at Columbia University. **1965** *Amer. N. & Q.* Sept. 9/2 *Joseph Breuer as Nobelist*—Is there any evidence that Joseph Breuer (1842–1925), physiologist, was ever seriously considered as a candidate for a Nobel Prize? **1972** *Impact of Science on Society* (Unesco) XXII. IV. 282 Nobelists everywhere have emerged from the laboratory corner, the literary alcove or the private study to become involved with the plight of the race.

nobelium (nōᵘbī·-, nōᵘbe·liŏm). *Chem.* [f. *NOBEL + -IUM.] An artificially produced transuranic element, the longest-lived isotope of which has a half-life of about three minutes. Atomic number 102; symbol No.

1957 P. R. FIELDS et al. in *Physical Rev.* CVII. 1461/2 We suggest the name nobelium, symbol No, for the new element in recognition of Alfred Nobel's support of scientific research and after the institute where the work was done. **1957** *Times* 10 Sept. 11/1 He compared the building up of new elements beyond uranium to the ascent of Everest... In the making of nobelium, the advanced camp had been curium 244, made in the materials testing reactor in Idaho, United States. **1963** *Sci. Amer.* Apr. 70/2 The investigators proposed the name 'nobelium' for element 102, and the name was accepted by the Commission on Atomic Weights of the International Union of Pure and Applied Chemistry. The acceptance turned out to be premature. All attempts..to duplicate the Stockholm experiment have failed. **1974** *Encycl. Brit. Micropædia* VII. 368/2 Radiochemists have shown nobelium to exist in aqueous solution in both the +2 and +3 oxidation states.

nobility. Add: **1. c.** *pl.* Instances of nobleness of nature.

1921 R. HICHENS *Spirit of Time* iv. 71 He pointed to the nobilities, the self-sacrifice,..the marvellous examples of courage.

d. The property (of an element) of being noble or relatively unreactive. Cf. NOBLE *a.* 7 b in Dict. and Suppl.

1907 [see *NOBLE *a.* 7 b]. **1974** *Sci. Amer.* Aug. 48/2 The supposed 'nobility' of the elements that make up Group Zero in the periodic table was first compromised in 1962, when Neil Bartlett..synthesized xenon hexafluoroplatinate.

4. b. (Later example.)

1927 [see *DIVINELY *adv.* 2].

noble, *a.* and *sb.*[1] Add: **A.** *adj.* **4.** *noble savage,* primitive man, conceived of in the manner of Rousseau as morally superior to civilized man.

1672 [see SAVAGE *sb.* 2]. **1914** C. MACKENZIE *Sinister Street* II. III. vi. 628 Every new writer who commands any attention drags out the old idol of the Noble Savage and invites us to worship him. Only now the Noble Savage has been put into corduroy trousers. **1933** J. CARY *Amer. Visitor* vii. 72 Her publisher..belonged to the most modern school of anthropologists and believed in the Golden Age, the noble savage, and all the other resuscitated fancies of Rousseau. **1947** *English Studies* XXVIII. 1 He is prevented from depicting the enemies.. in..sinister colours by his interest in the romantic dream of the noble savage. **1954** W. S. MAUGHAM *Ten Novels* I. viii. 201 Let us not forget that *Typee* is a glorification of the noble savage, uncorrupted by the vices of civilization, and that Melville looked upon the natural man as good. **1971** G. STEINER *In Bluebeard's Castle* iii. 52 The myth of the noble savage had interiorized a powerful hierarchic dogma. **1972** *Daily Tel.* 11 Dec. 11/1 They believe in the moral superiority of primitive over civilised man. As a potent idea, the Noble Savage died 100 years ago. But it lives for the Ardens in..the Indian peasants, the exploited Irish.

7. b. *spec.* of a metal: resisting oxidation; relatively unreactive. Hence of any element: low in the electrochemical series. (Further examples.)

1907 E. S. MERRIAM tr. *Danneel's Electrochem.* v. 134 Metals whose solution pressure is less than that of hydrogen..have a negative potential. The same thing is meant when we speak of the 'nobility' of the metals; silver is more noble than zinc, and zinc is less noble than hydrogen, etc. **1938** R. W. LAWSON tr. *Hevesy & Paneth's Man. Radioactivity* (ed. 2) xxii. 218 They can only be contemplated for those radio-elements which are to some extent electrochemically noble, and hence especially for the isotopes of lead, bismuth, and polonium. **1956** E. C. POTTER *Electrochem.* x. 234 We may summarize this mode of corrosion..by saying 'it is unwise to permit a metal to contact an aqueous solution of a salt of a metal more noble than itself'. **1973** *Nature* 20 July 137/1 After a beta transformation the daughter element is electrochemically more noble than the mother element. **1974** *Sci. Amer.* Jan. 33/3 If..one puts the corroding metal in contact with a 'nobler' (less active) metal on which the cathodic reaction can proceed more easily, the corrosion current and hence the rate of dissolution of metal can be increased significantly.

(ii) *noble gas*: = *inert gas* (*b*) s.v. *INERT *a.* 1 c. So *noble liquid,* one of the noble gases in the liquid state.

noble gas is now the term officially preferred by the International Union of Pure & Applied Chemistry.

1902 J. I. D. HINDS *Inorg. Chem.* xviii. 151 The name *Noble Gases* has been given by Erdmann to the several rare and inactive elements which have recently been discovered. **1927** [see *INERT *a.* 1 c (*b*)]. **1950** *Electronic Engin.* XXII. 108 Electron tubes filled with a noble gas such as argon, neon or helium are now widely employed. **1971** *Nomencl. Inorg. Chem.* (I.U.P.A.C.) (ed. 2) 11 The use of the collective names..alkaline-earth metals (Ca to Ra), and noble gases [ed. 1 (1959): inert gases] may be continued. **1971** *Nature* 29 Oct. 617/1 We are working towards the development of a thin multiconductor chamber filled with a noble liquid. **1974** *Sci. Amer.* Aug. 48/3 Soon after Bartlett's announcement several other noble-gas compounds were made, chief among them the xenon fluorides (XeF_2, XeF_4 and XeF_6) and xenon trioxide (XeO_3).

f. *noble rot* = **pourriture noble.*

[**1924** H. W. ALLEN *Wines of France* ii. 114 The Botrytis produces a grey mould, which gives to other wines a most unpleasant taste, but in Sauternes that mould is the *pourriture noble,* the 'noble rottenness', which bestows on the grapes and the wines made from them their extraordinary richness of sweetness and perfume.] **1935** SCHOONMAKER & MARVEL *Compl. Wine Bk.* i. 12 It is necessary to leave the grapes on the vine until they are.. over-ripe, sugary and shrunken, until that so-called 'noble rot' (*la pourriture noble*) has set in. **1959** W. JAMES *Word-Bk. Wine* 133 The noble rot also produces glycerine, which gives the wine a fine liqueur-like oiliness. **1965** A. SICHEL *Penguin Bk. Wines* 194 To every hectolitre (22 gallons) off the fermenting must of the Furmint and Harslevelii grape they [*sc.* Hungarians producing Tokay] add 3, 4, 5 or 6 *puttony* of the grapes concentrated by the 'noble rot'. **1973** *Country Life* 15 Nov. 1535/3 The German vintage..lacking the 'noble rot' which produces the more luscious *auslese* and *beerenauslese* wines. **1975** P. VANDYKE PRICE *Taste of Wine* 53/1 The primarily sweet wines may have some grapes affected by noble rot, but there is a profundity and a distinctive after-taste to those that are chiefly made with nobly rotten grapes.

B. *sb.* **1. c.** A leader or protector of men hired to replace striking workers. *U.S. slang.*

1930 *Amer. Mercury* Dec. 456/2 *Noble,* a guard for strike breakers. 'Me work? Don't be foolish. I'm a noble, I am.' **1937** *N.Y. Times* 22 Dec. 22 *Noble,* a lieutenant of strike operations usually in charge of a detachment of guards, sluggers and finks. **1950** H. E. GOLDIN *Dict. Amer. Underworld Lingo* 145/2 *Noble* (rare), a guard hired to protect strike-breakers. **1960** WENTWORTH & FLEXNER *Dict. Amer. Slang* 356/2 *Noble.* 1. A strike-breaker's guard. 2. The boss of a gang of strike-breakers; a chief fink.

nobleite (nōᵘ·b'ləit). *Min.* [f. the name of Levi F. *Noble,* 20th-cent. U.S. geologist + -ITE[1].] A hydrated calcium borate, $CaB_6O_{10}.4H_2O$, found as colourless, monoclinic crystals at Furnace Creek, Death Valley, California.

1961 R. C. ERD et al. in *Amer. Mineralogist* XLVI. 560 The naturally occurring hydrous calcium borate, CaO.-$3B_2O_3.4H_2O$..is named nobleite in honor of Dr. Levi F. Noble, geologist in the U.S. Geological Survey since 1909, in further recognition of his fundamental contributions to geologic knowledge of the Death Valley region. **1964** *Ibid.* XLIX. 1549 Tunellite..is isostructural with the Ca analogue, nobleite. **1968** I. KOSTOV *Mineralogy* 435 Colemanite Group. The following minerals belong to this group:.. nifontovite..tunellite..nobleite.

‖ **noblesse oblige** (noble·s oblī·ʒ), *phr.* [Fr.] Phrase suggesting that noble ancestry constrains (to honourable behaviour); privilege entails responsibility. Also in extended use. Also as *sb.* and *attrib.*

1837 F. A. KEMBLE *Let.* 1 Aug. in *Rec. Later Life* (1882) I. 86 To be sure, if 'noblesse oblige', royalty must do so still more. **1864** J. H. NEWMAN *Apol.* I. 10 Do you think I can let you go scot free instead of myself? No; *noblesse oblige.* Go to the shades, old man. **1873** C. M. YONGE *Pillars of House* IV. xxxix. 150, I always regarded you as a sacred personage, condemned to *noblesse oblige,* and all that! **1896** BEERBOHM *Happy Hypocrite* in *Yellow Bk.* Oct. 12 *Noblesse oblige*.. an aristocrat should be very careful of his good name. **1903** CHESTERTON *Robert Browning* v. 114 When someone excused coarseness..on the ground of genius, he said, 'That is an error: Noblesse oblige.' **1923** D. H. LAWRENCE *Birds, Beasts & Flowers* 65 Blessed are the pure in heart and the fathomless in bright pride; The loveliness that knows *noblesse oblige.* **1932** J. M. S. TOMPKINS *Popular Novel in England 1770–1800* iv. 153 The Magdalens of gentle blood.. descend..to the family vault. It is a clear case of *noblesse oblige.* **1968** *Listener* 6 June 713/2 *Noblesse oblige* Toryism ..is giving way to..managerial Conservatism. **1973** J. SHUB *Moscow by Nightmare* xiii. 150 He was pleased to inform the servants of his whereabouts; it simplified their reporting for the KGB. *Noblesse oblige.*

Nobodaddy (nōᵘ·bodædi). [Blend of NOBODY + DADDY.] Used by William Blake, and others after him: a disrespectful name for God, esp. when regarded anthropomorphically. Also *transf.,* someone no longer held in esteem. Also *attrib.*

c **1793** W. BLAKE in *Compl. Writings* (1972) 171 (*title*) To Nobodaddy. *Ibid.* 187 Then again old Nobodaddy swore He ne'er had seen such a thing before, Since Noah was shut in the ark. **1921** G. B. SHAW *Back to Methuselah* p. lxiii, It did not occur to us that Old Nobodaddy, instead of being a ridiculous fiction, might be only an impostor. *Ibid.* p. lxvi, The moment Nobodaddy was slain by Darwin, Public Opinion, as divine deputy, lost its sanctity. **1922** JOYCE *Ulysses* 203 Whether these be sins or virtues

old Nobodaddy will tell us at doomsday leet. *Ibid.* 388 But the braggart boaster cried that an old Nobodaddy was in his cups it was muchwhat indifferent and he would not lag behind his lead. **1926** A. MacLeish *(title)* Nobodaddy. **1962** *Listener* 29 Nov. 932/1 Goethe is in danger of turning into a Nobodaddy—a booming, boring member of that depressed class, the Illustrious Dead. **1976** *Guardian* 8 Jan. 12/7, I believe we see here [*sc.* in the poetry of Tristan Tzara] the great Nobodaddy Dadaist losing out to the truthful inclusiveness of our women's contemporaries.

nobody. 1. Delete † and add earlier and further examples of proverbial use.

1611 Cotgrave *Dict.* s.v. *Ouvrage,* Euerie bodies worke is no bodies worke. **1725** Defoe *(title)* Every-body's business is no-body's business. **1828** Macaulay in *Edin. Rev.* Sept. 103 The business of every body is the business of nobody. **1829** Cobbett *Advice to Young Men* vi. 345 Public property is never so well taken care of as private property; and this, too, on the maxim, that 'that which is every body's business is no [*sic*] nobody's business'.

2. Phr. *nobody's business* (see *business 16 f); *nobody's fool,* a person who cannot be taken advantage of.

Further examples s.v. *business 16 f.

1839 *Spirit of Times* 8 June 163/1 As to eating, jist go to Snowden's, and the way you can git good things is nobody's business. **1923** H. C. Witwer *Fighting Blood* xi. 323 He's a little too big..for us... And, another thing, Ryan is nobody's fool. **1940** N. Marsh *Surfeit of Lampreys* (1941) xv. 232 They've displayed a surprising virtuosity. They're nobody's fools. **1942** [see *death *sb.* 17 c]. **1956** *Times* 12 Sept. 1 What she could do with a pencil, notebook, and typewriter was simply nobody's business. **1959** 'A. Fraser' *High Tension* x. 103 He smiled slightly, and I made a note that he was nobody's fool. **1962** 'E. Peters' *Funeral of Figaro* i. 32 'He can sing like nobody's business,' said Stoker positively. **1975** *Times* 20 Sept. 9/7 Poirot..adds..'Never do I pull the leg.' That, alas, is not true. He teased poor Hastings like nobody's business.

b. (Examples with the indef. article.)

1886 G. Meredith *Let.* 15 Nov. (1970) II. 838 In origin I am what is called here a nobody. **1922** Joyce *Ulysses* 316 And who was he, tell us? A nobody. **1950** G. B. Shaw *Farfetched Fables* 67, I replied that if he did not realize that without them he would be a nobody he was no gentleman. **1961** New Eng. Bible 2 Cor. xii. 11 In no respect did I fall short of these superlative apostles, even if I am a nobody. **1975** *Listener* 4 Dec. 752/2 Out there, he could become a 'somebody'; in London, he felt he was a 'nobody'.

3. nobody-crab, a marine arachnid of the order Pantopoda (or Pycnogonida), having a small body and four pairs of very long, thin legs; = *pycnogonid* (s.v. Pycno-), Sea spider 1 b.

1881 [see *pycnogonid* (s.v. Pycno-)]. **1935** *Discovery* Sept. 282/1 Those queer creatures the Pycnogonida, the so-called No-body Crabs, real Tom Noddies, with only enough body to hold together the legs, in which are situated the vital organs. **1945** T. H. Savory *Spiders Brit. Isles* (ed. 2) 20 Sea-spiders or nobody-crabs are found only in the sea, where they range from the littoral regions to the depths of the ocean.

no bon (nō^u boṅ), *adj. phr. slang.* [No *adv.*¹ + Bon *a.*] No good.

1918 W. Owen *Let.* 29 May (1967) 554 Music—no bon! Painting—nah pooh! **1929** *Papers Mich. Acad. Sci., Arts, & Lett.* X. 310/2 *No bon,* no good.

no-ca·lorie, *a.* [f. No *a.* + Calorie.] Of a food substance or diet: free from, or very low in, calories. Abbrev. **no-cal.**

1961 S. Price *Just for Record* x. 101 Morosely munching their no-calory diet. **1969** *Guardian* 6 Oct. 11/4 Young mothers..whose entire diet consists of cottage cheese, yogurt, and gallons of 'no-cal' pop. **1971** *Petticoat* 17 July 5 They are no-cyclamate, no-calorie, no-aftertaste sweeteners.

no can do, *colloq. phr.* [f. No *adv.*¹ + Can *v.*¹ + Do *v.*] It is not possible; it is not within the power of (the speaker).

1914 'Saki' *Beasts & Super-Beasts* 289 'Sorry, my dear, no can do,' said Suzanne. **1915** A. D. Gillespie *Lett. from Flanders* (1916) 69 'Nap poo'..was once 'il n'y a plus', but now it's used like the Chinese 'no can do' for everything. **1923, 1958** [see *can *v.*¹ 8 c]. **1962** 'E. Ferrars' *Busy Body* v. 53 Sorry, no can do—not tonight.

nocardiosis (nō^ukāɹdiō^u·sis). *Path.* [f. mod.L. *Nocardi-a,* the name of a genus of actinomycetes (f. the name of E. I. E. *Nocard* (1850–1903), French veterinary pathologist + -ia¹) + -osis.] Infection with, or a disease caused by, an actinomycete of the genus *Nocardia,* esp. *N. asteroides,* which is occas. pathogenic in humans, producing local lesions or more often generalized disease beginning in the lungs but tending to spread to other organs, esp. the brain, and often proving fatal.

1907 J. H. Wright in Osler & McGrae *Mod. Med.* I. xvi. 341 It has been pointed out that if the name Actinomyces be not used for these microörganisms then the only permissible generic term to apply to them..is Nocardia, and disease processes produced by them should be called nocardiosis. **1920** *Arch. Dermatol. & Syphilol.* II. 137 *(heading)* Nocardiosis cutis resembling sporotrichosis. **1949** *Amer. Jrnl. Path.* XXV. 1 *(heading)* Pure granulomatous nocardiosis: a new fungus disease distinguished by intracellular parasitism. **1963** C. W. Emmons et al. *Med. Mycol.* ix. 75 Nocardiosis is recognized in the dog oftener than in other domesticated animals. **1974** Passmore & Robson *Compan. Med. Stud.* III. i. xii. 90/2 Nocardiosis and mucormycosis are infections usually acquired by inhaling dusts.

‖ **noceur** (nosö̆r). [Fr.] A reveller, rake, libertine; one who stays up late at night.

1908 Nevill & Jerningham *Piccadilly to Pall Mall* iv. 157 The French *noceur* is only too pleased to show himself in the company of some well-known 'horizontale'. **1918** J. Agate *Buzz, Buzz!* i. 11 In Ibsen the characters who bother themselves about the arts are invariably humbugs or hypocrites or *noceurs.* **1931** W. Rothenstein *Men & Memories* I. ix. 94 Though I could, on occasion, sit up most of the night, I was not a *noceur.*

noci- (nō^usi), comb. form of L. *noc-ēre* to do harm, used in a few terms, esp. in neurology, as **nocice·ptive** *a. Physiol.* [(Re)ceptive *a.*], (of a stimulus) painful; responding to or caused by such a stimulus; hence **nocice·ptor** [(Re)ceptor], any sensory receptor for painful stimuli; **nocife·nsor** *a.* [L. *dē-fens-,* ppl. stem (in Defensive *a.,* etc.): cf. L. *dēfensor* defender] (of a nerve) concerned in the transmission of the sensation of pain.

1904 C. S. Sherrington in *Nature* 8 Sept. 463/1 In this reaction the reflex arc is (i) the receptive neurone.. (nociceptive) from the foot to the spinal segment, (ii) perhaps a short intraspinal neurone, and (iii) the motor neurone..to the flexor muscle. *Ibid.,* Stimulation (nociceptive) of the foot causes flexion of its own leg and extension of the opposite. **1956** *Nature* 18 Feb. 340/1 In the lightly anæsthetised preparations, nociceptive stimuli, twisting the pinna and electrical stimulation of the reticular activating system produced transient changes in the cortical blood-flow. **1961** *Lancet* 2 Sept. 546/2 Dr. W. Koll..described his work on the action of various pharmacological substances on nociceptive spinal reflexes. **1974** *Sci. Amer.* Jan. 43/1 The nociceptive (*N*) cells require still stronger mechanical stimuli. **1906** C. S. Sherrington *Integrative Action Nervous Syst.* ix. 330 The reaction initiated by a noci-ceptor..is to be regarded as consummatory. **1967** *Jrnl. Physiol.* CXC. 541 Seventy-four fibres conducting between 6 and 37 m/sec were classified as nociceptors because they responded only to damaging mechanical stimulation of the skin. **1936** T. Lewis in *Clin. Sci.* II. 402 It will be evident that any system of nerve fibres, which in the exercise of its function gives rise to no obvious and distinctive external manifestations, will tend to escape recognition... The need to postulate a new system of nerves has arisen to explain hitherto unrecognised phenomena. The nerves of this system are at present unnamed. Because they are associated with local defence against injury I propose to call them the 'nocifensor nerves'. **1964** J. Z. Young *Model of Brain* xiii. 209 They are presumed to be nocifensor (pain) fibres, coming either direct from the periphery or after synapse in the sub-vertical lobe.

no-city, *a.* Also **no-cities.** [No *a.*] Of a strategy in a nuclear war: (see quot. 1966).

1962 *Economist* 8 Dec. 1014/1 Many Americans are sceptical of this 'no cities' doctrine. **1965** H. Kahn *On Escalation* vi. 124 If the war were conducted as a no-city war. **1966** Schwarz & Hadik *Strategic Terminol.* 102 *No-cities strategy,* strategy based on the principle that only the enemy's forces are to be targets of nuclear strikes, and that enemy population centers are to be avoided completely or as much as possible.

‖ **nockerl** (nǫ·kərl). Pl. **nockerln.** [Austrian G., little dumpling.] A small, light dumpling, made with a batter including eggs, and usually fried; **Salzburger nockerl,** a sweet version of this dumpling, using extra eggs which make the mixture puff up when it is cooked.

1855 E. Acton *Mod. Cookery* (rev. ed.) xxxii. 620 *(heading)* A Viennese soufflé-pudding, called Salzburger Nockerl. **1954** G. Beer *Austrian Cooking* 89 A *Nockerl* is tiny to medium-sized, oval in shape and not really a dumpling at all. The only reason why I continuously refer to them as such is for want of a better name. *Ibid.* 90 The *Nockerln* must not brown. *Ibid.* 106 Salzburger Nockerl. .. Remove *Nockerln* carefully with a palette knife... Dust liberally with icing sugar... The centre should be light and creamy, the outside golden brown and puffed. **1958** J. Grossinger *Art Jewish Cooking* (1960) 31 Soup Nockerl... Beat the eggs, water and salt together. Mix in the flour and baking powder. Drop by the teaspoon into boiling salted water. Cook until they rise to the surface.

no claim(s, *attrib. phr.* [No *a.*] Designating a discount allowed on a motor-vehicle insurance premium if no claim has been submitted during the preceding year(s).

1933 G. W. Gilbert *Motor Insurance* iii. 66 *(heading)* No claim bonus. This is allowed..only at a flat rate of 10 per cent of the renewal premium. If more than one cycle is insured the bonus is payable 'per cycle'. *Ibid.* iv. 75 No Claim Bonus is paid..if the policy as a whole runs free of claim for one or two or three succeeding years. **1955** *Times* 24 Aug. 7/3 The 'tariff' companies are credited with the intention of still further increasing the 'no-claims' bonus. **1968** D. Devine *Sleeping Tiger* i. 15 'Take it up with the insurance company, would you?..' 'It's not worth losing your no-claim bonus. I'll pay for it to be re-sprayed myself.' **1970** *Motoring Which?* July 91/1 Before no-claims bonus and other discounts, fully comprehensive insurance will probably cost you around £45 to £90 for the 3-litre. **1975** *Times* 24 Sept. 3/2 The no-claim bonus is no longer, because of inflation, a sufficient incentive.

no comment: see *comment *sb.* 2 c. Also (with hyphen) as attrib. phr.

1966 S. B. Jackman *Davidson Affair* iii. 22, I thought he was strictly a no-comment man. **1971** 'L. Black' *Death has Green Fingers* iii. 32 The police simply didn't know any more yet. When they did, the 'no comment' answers would begin. **1971** E. Fenwick *Impeccable People* xix. 103 Ben wore his no-comment expression.

no-'count, *a.* Aphetic form of *no-account *a.* Cf. *'count. Also as *sb.*

1853 'P. Paxton' *Stray Yankee in Texas* 282 (Th.), Yes, Massa, dem no 'count calves done fool me again. **1885** H. Jackson *Zeph* iii. 82 Ye miserable, mean-spirited, no-'count critter! **1902** A. D. McFaul *Ike Glidden* xviii. 145 It wasn't enough for your sickly, no-'count mother to waste my grub and money in idleness. **1920** C. E. Mulford *Johnny Nelson* xiii. 135 Judgin' from th' way those no-'count hosses was pullin' when they come over th' hill..I reckoned you got th' hides. **1936** M. Mitchell *Gone with Wind* iv. 65 Dey is de shiflesses, mos' ungrateful passel of no-counts livin'.

noct-. Add: Also used in place of Nocti- in words in which the following element begins with a vowel; **nocta·mbulate** *v. intr.,* to walk at night; **nocta·mbulator,** one who walks at night; **noctambula·tory** *a.* = *noctambulous* adj.; **noctu·ria** [-uria], the condition of being aroused from one's sleep abnormally often by the need to urinate.

1955 H. Spring *These Lovers fled Away* 206 Now and then I would noctambulate through the city. **1962** V. Nabokov *Pale Fire* 221 If you..pull up the window, and..roll out..there is always the chance of knocking clean through into your own hell a pacific noctambulator walking his dog. **1913** C. Mackenzie *Sinister Street* I. ii. vii. 259 Conversations with Brother Aloysius were sufficiently thrilling journeys, and Michael was always ready to follow his footsteps as one might follow a noctambulatory cat. **1911** Dorland *Med. Dict.* (ed. 6) 558/2 *Nocturia,* excessive urination at night. **1928** Eisendrath & Rolnick *Text-bk. Urology* xlvi. 707 The patient has noticed that..there has been an increase in the number of times, he or she, experienced the desire to void urine. This may have occurred only at night i.e. nocturia, or during the day. **1961** *Lancet* 12 Aug. 335/2, 1 patient was troubled by nocturia. **1971** Golden & Maher *Kidney* ii. 36 Nocturia may thus be an early symptom of renal failure.

nocti-. Add: **noctilucent** *a.* (examples); *spec.* in *noctilucent cloud,* a cloud of a kind occas. seen at night in summer in high latitudes, which occurs at a height of about 80 kilometres (at the mesopause) and which some authorities believe is composed purely of cosmic dust and others of ice condensed round cosmic dust particles; cf. **mother-of-pearl cloud.*

1890 *Cent. Dict., Noctilucent,* shining by night or in the dark; noctilucid; as, the noctilucent eyes of a cat. **1910** W. L. Moore *Descriptive Meteorol.* xi. 198 Certain clouds that are seen about midnight in summer have for twenty years received considerable attention from Abbe and others..; sometimes they are called nacreous..at other times noctilucent, because they shine at night. **1936** N. Shaw *Man. Meteorol.* (ed. 2) ii. iii. 44 The lower type, known as Perlmutter or iridescent clouds, show brilliant prismatic colours and occur at heights between 20 and 30 kilometres. They differ from noctilucent clouds by appearing almost exclusively in winter. **1940** *Chambers's Techn. Dict.* 581/1 *Noctilucent (Zool.),* phosphorescent, light-producing. **1956** *Nature* 18 Feb. 308/1 The technique of observing noctilucent clouds has been improved recently. **1963** *New Scientist* 25 July 169/2 There has been considerable dispute in the past about whether the noctilucent clouds are composed of ice particles or dust particles.

noctuary. (Later example.)

1910 *Chambers's Jrnl.* Sept. 594/2 My sceptical friends.. say I kept myself awake on purpose to write this noctuary

nocturnal, *a.* Add: **1.** *nocturnal emission:* involuntary ejaculation of sperm during sleep.

1928 H. B. English *Student's Dict. Psychol. Terms, Nocturnal emissions,* loss of semen during sleep. **1948** A. C. Kinsey et al. *Sexual Behavior Human Male* xv. 516 In the male, nocturnal emissions or wet dreams are generally accepted as a usual part of the sexual picture. **1951** M. McLuhan *Mech. Bride* (1967) 47/1 The [sexual] 'outlets' are..'nocturnal emission', etc.]. **1958** M. Argyle *Relig. Behaviour* x. 123 *Nocturnal emissions* for Kinsey's devout males were insignificantly more frequent, for his devout females sex dreams to the point of orgasm were less frequent.

nod, *sb.*¹ Add: **1.** In phrases which imply approval, as *to get* or *give the nod.* Chiefly *U.S.*

1948 W. O'Sullivan in *Thrilling Sports* July 55/1 Rebel felt sure of his surmise on the hidden-crew game when his bunch got the nod to start against the highly regarded Tiger crew. **1953** *Wall St. Jrnl.* 23 Apr. 1/3 Paul L. Troast got the G.O.P. nod, beating his nearest rival, State Sen.

Malcolm Forbes, by more than 53,000 votes. **1962** *New Yorker* 17 Nov. 43/2 Industry has at last given literature the nod. **1967** *Boston Globe* 20 May 2/2 (*heading*) Desalting funds get U.S. nod. **1970** *New Yorker* 28 Nov. 151/1 We will not be surprised if the museum gives this piece the nod. **1973** *Bulletin* (Sydney) 25 Aug. 30/2 Perhaps he sees himself—if he gets the nod—as a natural successor to Sir Kevin Ellis in the Speaker's chair of the Assembly. **1975** *Cleveland* (Ohio) *Plain Dealer* 31 Mar. 2-D/2 The five outfielders certainly will include regulars Charlie Spikes, George Hendrick, and Oscar Gamble, meaning the two other jobs will be fought for among Ken Berry, Leron Lee and Rick Manning, with Berry and Lee probably getting the nod.

Prov. (Earlier and later examples.) (See also WINK *sb.*¹ 2.)

1794 GODWIN *Caleb Williams* I. viii. 171 A nod is as good as a wink to a blind horse. **1935** T. S. ELIOT *Murder in Cathedral* i. 24 My Lord, a nod is as good as a wink. A man will often love what he spurns. **1974** N. FREELING *Dressing of Diamond* 200 All right; a nod's as good as a wink... You've got these people in mind.

d. *on the nod* (later examples).

1907 'IAN HAY' *Pip* ix. 286 He looked all round the room, and I *knew* he knew everything in it had been got on the nod. **1934** *Bulletin* (Sydney) 25 July 46/4 Drunks with determined minds to get bacon, bread, cheese, on the nod. **1945** B. NAUGHTON in C. Madge *Pilot Papers* I. 106 Edith ..got them a house,..and Edith filled it with furniture on the 'nod'.

e. *on the nod*, with a merely formal assent; by abstention from voting.

1959 *Times* 14 Mar. 4/2 The Bill..was given a second reading 'on the nod' by the House. **1969** *Sunday Times* 12 Jan. 4 The agenda, usually the cause of great friction, was accepted 'on the nod'. **1973** C. MULLARD *Black Britain* III. vii. 85 The late Lord (Learie) Constantine, then a member of the Board, opposed the appointment of John Lyttle on the nod, and urged that the job should be advertised in the press.

2. c. A state of drowsiness brought on by narcotic drugs. *Esp.* in phr. *on the nod.*

1942 BERREY & VAN DEN BARK *Amer. Thes. Slang* § 509/22 *Play the nod*, to be drowsy as a result of overindulgence in narcotics. **1946** B. TREADWELL *Big Bk. of Swing* xvi. 125/1 *Nod*, tired feeling, sleepy, fatigued. **1951** *Life* 11 June 126/2 Instead of a warming, bright 'charge', he merely becomes comatose and lethargic (goes on the nod in junkie parlance). **1953** W. BURROUGHS *Junkie* (1972) iv. 43 Don't ever invite him to your home... He'll go on the nod in front of your family. He's got no class to him. *Ibid.* xiv. 147 When he arrived in Mexico, I gave him half a grain of M and he went on the nod. **1962** K. ORVIS *Damned & Destroyed* v. 37 While I was on the nod. **1965** *New Statesman* 20 Aug. 248/3 In addict's language—'going on the nod' (becoming senseless). **1969** H. WAUGH *Young Prey* (1970) xxiii. 180 Once you went into the nod, the surroundings no longer mattered.

nod, *v.* Add: **2. d.** (See quot.)

1968–70 *Current Slang* (Univ. S. Dakota) III–IV. 86 *Nod*, to drift in and out of consciousness while under the influence of a drug.

nodal, *a.* Add: **1.** Similarly *nodal surface.*

1937 J. W. T. SPINKS tr. *Herzberg's Atomic Spectra & Atomic Struct.* i. 41 For $n > 1$, ψ goes once, or more than once, through the value zero before the exponential decrease sets in; that is, on certain spherical surfaces about the nucleus, the ψ function is always zero. These are the nodal surfaces of the ψ function corresponding to the nodes of a vibrating string.

nodality (nodæ·lĭti). [f. NODAL *a.* + -ITY.] **a.** The degree to which a place is a point of convergence for routes, roads, or the like.

1897 *Geogr. Jrnl.* IX. 78 A higher degree of 'nodality', to use Mr. Mackinder's term, is found where several such furrows [*sc.* shallow valleys in the chalk] meet to form a well-marked though by no means deep hollow. **1902** H. J. MACKINDER *Britain & British Seas* xix. 330 A spot upon which more numerous land and water roads converge, as in a defile past some natural obstacle, may be said to have a higher degree of nodality. **1953** J. M. HOUSTON *Social Geogr. Europe* ix. 205 In cities of long history, such as Paris, it is easy to point out the geographical advantages of the site and the elements of nodality, whether at a bridge-head, a crossing of routes or at a transfer point.

b. The number of nodes of an oscillation.

1905 *Trans. R. Soc. Edin.* XLI. 602 In any given lake, seiches of all degrees of nodality, i.e. uninodal, binodal, trinodal, etc., are possible. **1957** G. E. HUTCHINSON *Treat. Limnol.* I. v. 299 In the case of Loch Earn, periods have been identified which may belong to a nodality as high as the sixteenth.

nodalize (nōᵘ·dăləiz), *v. rare.* [f. NODAL *a.* + -IZE.] *trans.* To make nodal in form or arrangement; to concentrate in a node.

1915 D. H. LAWRENCE *Rainbow* xv. 412 For what purpose were the incalculable physical and chemical activities nodalised in this..speck under her microscope?

nodding, *vbl. sb.* Add: **a.** Also = *NOD *sb.*¹ 2 c.

1970 H. E. ROBERTS *Third Ear* 10/2 Nodding out, a drug stupor. **1972** C. WESTON *Poor, Poor Ophelia* (1973) xxiv. 149 He's high on something. Nodding, I think they call it.

b. (Further examples.)

1825 H. WILSON *Mem.* (ed. 2) II. 108 Having only a sort of bowing, nodding acquaintance with him. **1959** I. & P. OPIE *Lore & Lang. Schoolch.* viii. 122 Childhood is on nodding terms with the supernatural. **1969** *Times* 22 July p. ii/6 Nobody volunteers that they are not at least on nodding terms with their hero. **1972** H. C. RAE *Shooting Gallery* ii. 74 Three thousand students in this establishment. I know, on nodding terms, about forty of them. **1972** *Times* 7 Aug. (Jamaica Suppl.) p. ii/5 A health care plan..should give many Jamaicans at least a nodding acquaintance with health services.

node, *sb.* Add: **3. c.** *Anat.* Any small mass of differentiated tissue; also applied to the interruptions (called *nodes of Ranvier*: see *RANVIER) of the myelin sheath of myelinated nerve fibres.

1885 *Encycl. Brit.* XIX. 23/2 The medullary sheath shows at certain intervals interruptions called the 'nodes of Ranvier'. **1892**, etc. [see *lymph node* (*LYMPH 5)]. **1902** *Trans. Chicago Path. Soc.* V. 151 (*heading*) Are the hemolymph nodes organs *sui generis?* **1917** *Amer. Jrnl. Anat.* XXI. 375 The frequent close association of lymph and hemal nodes makes differentiation of the early stages in development naturally very difficult. **1962** *Gray's Anat.* (ed. 33) 89 At its [*sc.* the primitive streak's] headward end a further area of exceptionally active growth forms a knob-like thickening which is termed the primitive node. **1968** PASSMORE & ROBSON *Compan. Med. Stud.* I. xxviii. 9/1 The part of the heart with the highest spontaneous rate..provides the source of excitation of the whole heart, and this pacemaker is normally the sinuatrial (SA) node. *Ibid.* 10/1 Situated low in the right atrium, near the opening of coronary sinus and tricuspid valve, is another group of cells with a specialized conducting function, the atrioventricular (AV) node.

6. a. (Further examples.) Hence also, a point at which a spherical harmonic or similar function has the value zero.

1905 *Trans. R. Soc. Edin.* XLI. 601 At these points, which are called nodes, the level of the surface [of the lake] is unaltered by the seiche. **1927** T. M. MACROBERT *Spherical Harmonics* iii. 59 The middle point..is always at rest, and this point is called a node, the end-points also being nodes. For the *n*th mode there are $n-1$ nodes, as well as the two end nodes. **1957** G. E. HUTCHINSON *Treat. Limnol.* I. v. 299 While the periods and positions of the nodes depend on the form of the lake basin, the amplitude of the seiche depends only on the source of energy that generates it. **1964** J. W. LINNETT *Electronic Struct. Molecules* i. 6 For $n = 3$, the $l = 0$ function would be multiplied by a radial function varying with r, the distance from the nucleus, which had two nodes (i.e. it may be considered, rather approximately, as made up of 3 half-waves).

b. Delete the def. in Dict. and transfer the quots. to 6 a.

c. *Electr.* A point on an aerial or in a circuit where the current or voltage is zero.

1915 A. E. SEELIG tr. *Zenneck's Wireless Telegr.* ii. 25 In a lineal oscillator..the current amplitude is greatest at the middle and zero at the ends of the oscillator. In other words, there are 'current nodes' at each end and a 'current anti-node' at the middle... The 'potential' or 'voltage anti-nodes' occur at each end of the oscillator, the 'potential node' being at the middle. **1947** E. K. SANDEMAN *Radio Engin.* I. xvi. 645 At the voltage antinodes (current nodes) the incident and reflected voltages are in phase and therefore add, while the incident and reflected currents are 180° out of phase and therefore subtract. **1968** *Radio Communication Handbk.* (ed. 4) xiii. 3/1 The positions of maxima are usually known as current (or voltage) anti-nodes or loops and the intermediate positions as nodes or zeros.

7. b. A point or vertex of a network or graph (sense 1). Also *node point.*

1864 H. J. S. SMITH in *Rep. Brit. Assoc. Adv. Sci. 1863* I. 768 Let an infinite plane area be divided by two systems of parallel lines into similar and equal parallelograms. The vertices of these parallelograms we shall call nodes. **1892** G. B. MATHEWS *Theory of Numbers* I. iv. 124 Let the plane of reference be divided up into a system of equal and similar parallelograms..; such a system will be called a net,..and each joint, where two lines cross, a node. **1941** *Proc. Cambr. Philos. Soc.* XXXVII. 194 Let N be a network (or linear graph) such that at each node not more than n lines meet (where $n > 2$), and no line has both ends at the same node. **1957** N. CHOMSKY *Syntactic Structures* vii. 68 The phrase structure of a terminal string is determined from its derivation, by tracing segments back to node points. **1964** J. J. KATZ in Fodor & Katz *Struct. of Lang.* 526 The amalgam is assigned to the set of paths associated with the node (i.e., the point at which an *n*-ary branching occurs) that immediately dominates the sets of paths from which the paths amalgamated were drawn. The amalgam provides one of the meanings for the sequence of lexical items that the node dominates. **1964** A. BATTERSBY *Network Analysis* ii. 14 The beginning and end of a job are events; they are represented as numbered circles called nodes. *Ibid.* 19 The nodes which represent the events are numbered successively from the beginning to the end of the network. **1966** S. BEER *Decision & Control* ix. 194 In the first place, the nodes in the network which now represent individuals are not very tidily placed in ranks of equivalent importance. **1967** *Electronics* 6 Mar. 132/1 The feedback loop is formed by connecting the amplifier's inverting input..to potentiometer R_3. When power is first applied..the voltage at the common node rises quickly to 6·6 volts. **1971** [see *GRAPH *sb.*¹ 1]. **1972** *Sci. Amer.* June 52/3 By last month the network..included 24 computer centers ('nodes' in the terminology of the system), ranging from Massachusetts to California. **1975** *Language* LI. 388 The use of the empty node in the derivation of truncated passives is not motivated empirically, but rather is a way of retaining a transformational analysis of passives.

nodular, *a.* Add: **4.** *Metallurgy.* Of cast iron: containing all the graphite in the form of small spheroids rather than flakes, which results in increased strength and ductility and can be brought about by adding a suitable inoculant. Cf. *SPHEROIDAL *a.*

1947 *Machinery* LXX. 420/1 (*heading*) Nodular cast iron. **1950** [see *INOCULATION 2*]. **1967** A. H. COTTRELL *Introd. Metallurgy* xxv. 520 In nodular cast irons the structure is developed directly, in an as-cast grey iron, by adding a small amount of magnesium or cerium alloy to the metal in the ladle.

nodularity (nǫdiŭlæ·rĭti). [f. NODULAR *a.* + -ITY.] The state or condition of being nodular.

1948 L. MARTIN *Clin. Endocrinol.* x. 200 Nodularity so extreme as to be obviously pathological. **1953** *Brit. Jrnl. Urology* XXV. 27 Radial striation on the fractured surface of a calculus is often associated with nodularity of the external surface. **1971** *Amer. Jrnl. Public Health* LXI. 241 (*heading*) Thyroid nodularity in southwestern Utah school children exposed to fallout radiation.

nodulate (nǫ·diŭlēⁱt), *v. Bot.* [f. NODUL(E + -ATE³, or back-formation from NODULATED *a.*] **a.** *trans.* To produce root nodules on.

1939 *Soil Sci.* XLVII. 67 A velvet bean culture..produced nodules on six plant species included within the cowpea group yet did not nodulate three other plant members. **1973** *Nature* 17 Aug. 460/1 The *Trema* root nodule bacterium is the first of the rhizobia known to effectively nodulate a non-legume.

b. *intr.* Of a plant: to undergo nodulation.

1956 *Biol. Rev.* XXXI. 111 The degree to which an individual plant can be induced to nodulate earlier by root exudates depends wholly upon its normal nodulating habit in their absence. **1968** GIBBS & SHAPTON *Identification Methods for Microbiologists* 61 Only about 1200 species have been examined for the presence of nodules and not all of these nodulate.

Hence **no·dulating** *vbl. sb.* and *ppl. a.*

1944 *Proc. Soil Sci. Soc. Amer.* IX. 95 (*heading*) The nodulating performance of three species of legumes. **1960** *Dissertation Abstr.* XX. 3003/1 Experiments using.. nodulating and non-nodulating soybeans were established. **1971** M. ALEXANDER *Microbial Ecol.* xi. 259 The nodulating habit is particularly prominent among genera of Podocarpaceae, a family that includes trees important as timber.

nodulated, *ppl. a.* (Further examples: cf. prec.)

1932 E. B. FRED et al. *Root Nodule Bacteria & Leguminous Plants* ii. 17 In 1905 Norton & Walls... suggested that the wild Leguminosae, nearly all of which are nodulated in Maryland, are important agents for adding nitrogen and humus to the soils. **1957** *Canadian Jrnl. Microbiol.* III. 120 In the nodulated plants the nitrogen content was fully twice the seed nitrogen. **1971** M. ALEXANDER *Microbial Ecol.* xi. 259 In addition to the plants cited, several gymnosperms are nodulated, and they may be capable of assimilating N_2.

nodulation. (Further examples: cf. *NODULATE *v.*)

1924 *Soil Sci.* XVII. 439 Fellers found that under many conditions nodulation was increased by an application of phosphorus, calcium, or potassium. **1973** *Nature* 17 Aug. 459/1 Roots of *Trema aspera* Decaisne plants growing between rows of tea in..New Guinea showed abundant nodulation, similar to the nodules found on many tropical legumes.

nodule. Add: **3.** Esp., one formed on the root of a leguminous plant by symbiotic bacteria. Also *attrib.* (Later examples.)

1890 *Proc. R. Soc.* XLVII. 104 The limited growth in pot I..is coincident with the entire absence of nodule-formation. **1922** *Encycl. Brit.* XXX. 72/1 The so-called 'nodule' organisms (*Pseudomonas radicicola*)..live in symbiosis with the leguminous plants. **1965** BELL & COOMBE tr. *Strasburger's Textbk. Bot.* 303 In the development of the nitrogen-fixing nodules on the roots of the Leguminosae the first process is a normal infection of the rootlets by various races of the aerobic *Rhizobium leguminosarum*..living saprophytically in the soil.

nodulize (nǫ·diŭləiz), *v. Metallurgy.* [f. NODUL(E + -IZE.] *trans.* To convert (esp. finely-divided iron ore) into nodules. So **no·dulized** *ppl. a.*, **no·dulizing** *vbl. sb.*

1905 *U.S. Patent 794,673* 1/1 A new and useful Improvement in Methods or Processes of Purifying and Nodulizing Metalliferous Materials. **1905** *Iron Age* LXXVI. 590/1 The National Metallurgic Company has erected what it terms an ore purifying and nodulizing plant. **1906** *Jrnl. Iron & Steel Inst.* LXXI. 359 One rotary kiln..has produced an average of 75 to 90 tons of nodulised desulphurised pyrites cinder per day of twenty-four hours. **1921** W. GOWLAND *Metallurgy of Non-Ferrous Metals* (ed. 3) 139, 62 per cent. of the concentrate is nodulized, 14 per cent. sintered, and 24 per cent. reduced direct. **1968** E. N. SIMONS *Outl. Metallurgy* i. 3 Nodulizing..passes the ore too fine for use through a rotary kiln, in which it is heated with a relative movement between an internal rotary drum and an outer shell. Nodulizing has some advantages over sintering. *Ibid.* iii. 34 The graphite is present as tiny round balls, i.e. it is nodulized.

Hence **noduliza·tion,** the process of nodulizing.

1915 *Chem. Abstr.* IX. 590 Nodulizing iron ores..by subjection first to a reducing flame at a temp. only slightly below that required for nodulization and then to an oxidizing flame which suddenly raises the temp. of the material above the nodulizing point. **1921** W. GOWLAND *Metallurgy of Non-Ferrous Metals* (ed. 3) 138 In the pro-

cess of nodulization the proportion of sulphur has been reduced from 28 to 18 per cent. **1968** E. N. SIMONS *Outl. Metallurgy* iii. 34 Nodulization or spheroidization renders the iron stronger and more ductile.

nodum (nōᵘ·dɒ̆m). *Ecology.* Pl. **noda.** [mod. L., perh. f. L. *nōdus* knot] (See quot. 1955.)

1955 M. E. D. POORE in *Jrnl. Ecol.* XLIII. 243 The additional term Nodum has been introduced to apply to an abstract unit [of vegetation]..of uncertain status. *Ibid.* 259 The term nodum is being adopted to apply to abstract vegetation units of any category. It corresponds to the term taxon in systematics. *Ibid.*, Both the *Rhacomitrium-Carex bigelowii* and the *Nardus* noda..are clearly defined communities. **1961** *Watsonia* V. 76 The nodum is only developed on south- to west-facing slopes of 10 to 15°, fully exposed to wind and salt spray. **1971** *New Phytologist* LXX. 1155 The noda are related to environmental factors. *Ibid.*, A strongly marked relationship between the percentage of maritime species in a nodum and the sodium-organic ratio is noted. **1973** H. J. B. BIRKS *Past & Present Vegetation of Skye* iv. 24/2 A community is any aggregation of plants constituting a certain spatial whole... It is regarded as synonymous with Poore's general term 'nodum'. *Ibid.* 25/2 Where the vegetational unit is rather heterogeneous, it is termed a *nodum*. The word is italicised when it is used to refer to a specific vegetational unit that does not merit the rank of association.

noegenesis (no,idʒe·nėsis). [f. Gr. *νόη-σις* NOE(SIS + -GENESIS.] The generating of new knowledge from experience through the apprehension of experience, the eduction of relations and the eduction of correlates; the obtaining of knowledge thus. So **noegene·tic** *a.*, of, pertaining to, or concerned with, noegenesis.

1923 C. SPEARMAN *Nature of 'Intelligence'* iv. 61 'Noegenesis'. Another basal property of the manifestations of all the principles is that they, and they alone, are generative of new items in the field of cognition. If then, it be desired to depict these three principles summarily, taking into account both their noetic and their generative properties, we must compound some such name as 'noegenetic'. **1931** F. AVELING in W. Rose *Outl. Mod. Knowl.* viii. 336 The noegenetic principles, though accounting for the origin of knowledge, do not cover the entire cognitive field. **1936** F. BANKS *Conduct & Ability* xii. 232 Clearly some word like *eduction* was needed to distinguish this noegenetic process from the 'merely associative'. *Ibid.* xv. 308 The third principle of noegenesis will also be found adequate to explain the inventions of science. **1938** *Mind* XLVII. 378 Very proper complaint is registered to the effect that Psychologists have always neglected the problem of the perception of relations. Here again Prof. Spearman may reflect with pride on his own contribution in the shape of the 'noegenetic laws'. **1972** L. S. HEARNSHAW in Cox & Dyson *20th-Cent. Mind* I. vii. 235 Spearman contributed a powerful and erudite analysis, and though once again his theory of noegenesis, or creative intelligence, has not altogether stood up to subsequent scrutiny, it proved practically useful. **1973** H. J. EYSENCK *Inequality of Man* ii. 45 Spearman (1927) tried to lay down in his 'noegenetic laws' the essence of this cognitive ability.

noem (nōᵘ·em), **noeme** (nōᵘ·īm). *Philos.* and *Linguistics.* [f. Gr. *νόημα* thought.] A term used to denote that aspect of a unit of speech which is concerned with meaning as distinguished from sound.

a **1866** J. GROTE in *Jrnl. Philol.* (1872) IV. 55 It will be necessary for me to make use of one or two new-coined words, which I will begin by defining as accurately as I can... When I mean words as thought I shall use the term *noem*. *Ibid.* 56 Logically, a noem may be called a concept, a notion, or what we will; but I would have the term bear simply a relation to language, and mean the thought-word, that, whatever it is, which the sound stands for. **1926** L. BLOOMFIELD in *Language* II. 161 The meaning of a glosseme is a noeme. **1940** *Mod. Lang. Q.* June 178, I have recently encountered the *enthymeme*,..the *noeme*, the *philosopheme*, [etc.]. **1966** M. PEI *Gloss. Ling. Terminol.* 180 *Noeme*, the meaning of a glosseme.

noema (nōᵘ,ē·mă, nōᵘ,ī·mă). *Philos.* Pl. **noemata** (no,ī·mătă). [ad. Gr. *νόημα* thought.] A term first used by Husserl for that which is perceived or thought as the self experiences it. (See quot. 1966.)

1931 W. R. B. GIBSON tr. *Husserl's Ideas* III. iii. § 88. 258 Corresponding at all points to the manifold data of the real (*reellen*) noetic content, there is a variety of data displayable in really pure (*wirklich reiner*) intuition, and in a correlative '*noematic content*', or briefly '*noema*'—terms which we shall henceforth be continually using. **1957** B. LONERGAN *Insight* p. xxv, The *noēma* or *intentio intenta* or *pensée pensée*, illustrated by the lower contexts, *P, Q, R*,... and by the upper context that is Gödel's theorem. **1966** A. GURWITSCH *Stud. Phenomenology & Psychol.* vii. 132 What has just been described by these allusions is the *noema* of perception—namely the object just (exactly so and only so) as the perceiving subject is aware of it. *Ibid.* 133 Noemata are not to be found in perceptual life alone. There is a noema corresponding to every act of memory, expectation, representation, [etc.]. **1972** H. DREYFUS in L. Embree *Life-World & Consciousness* 138 If the noema were an abstract entity, we could indeed reflect on the higher order noemata involved in reflecting on the first-order noema.

noematic (no,imæ·tik), *a.* [f. Gr. type *νοηματικός*, f. *νόημα* thought.] **a.** Of or pertaining to a noem. **b.** Of, pertaining to, or connected with a noema.

a **1866** J. GROTE in *Jrnl. Philol.* (1872) IV. 55, I shall use the adjectives *phonal* and *noematic*; and I shall give the name of phonal or noematic *schematisms* to modifications of the primary noems and phones. **1931** [see *NOEMA]. **1934** *Mind* XLIII. 310 Kant obviously contemplated the possibility of a noematic 'given'. **1943** M. FARBER *Found. Phenomenology* xvi. 526 The *noematic* side (referring to what is correlatively involved, as 'that which is experienced, thought, etc.'). **1957** B. LONERGAN *Insight* II. xiv. 415 The pure forms of noetic experience terminating in noematic contents. **1973** J. N. MOHANTY in Carr & Casey *Explor. Phenomenology* 212 An awareness of the truth of its own noematic content.

noem-noem, var. *NUM-NUM.

no end. (See END *sb.* 21.) (Further examples.)

1871 F. C. BURNAND *More Happy Thoughts* (ed. 2) xix. 143 He 'makes no end of stuff', or 'loses no end of stuff'..on the Derby. **1903** R. E. KNOWLES *Attic Guest* (1909) 54 You'll have no end of fun with him. **1912** *Chambers's Jrnl.* Dec. 769/1 'I really must show this to Champneys,' thought Michael; 'it will please him no end.' **1955** *Essays & Studies* VIII. 5 A few clean strokes of Occam's razor would have helped Mr. Jackson no end. **1958** H. BABCOCK *I don't want to shoot an Elephant* 8, I often walk fifteen miles a day while hunting... This puzzles my wife no end. **1970** *New Yorker* 3 Oct. 90/2 Thomas had been impressed no end by the sight of Klüver ..fixing an art-and-technology malfunction with a pair of pliers.

no entry. [ENTRY 1.] Used *attrib.* to designate an area to which entrance is forbidden; also, to designate a sign marking this instruction.

1967 *Guardian* 15 Dec. 3/5 Bollards and no-entry signs to deflect vehicles. **1968** *Ibid.* 13 Aug. 5/3 Potential suicides swerve into 'No entry' streets. **1969** S. COULTER *Embassy* xviii. 195 They had reversed the traffic along the Avenue Gabriel. No Entry signs—white-barred red discs —were now planted in concrete bases on either sidewalk. **1971** *Guardian* 30 Oct. 20/1 Mrs. Joy Johnson..demolished a 'No Entry' sign while driving a double-deck bus.

noesis. Add: Pl. noeses. **c.** *Philos.* In phenomenology, that which is involved in the act of thinking or perceiving. Cf. *NOEMA.

1931 W. R. B. GIBSON tr. *Husserl's Ideas* III. iii. § 92. 268 Our glance, instead of passing through the noeses of perception..goes through a noesis of remembrance into a world of memory. **1957** B. LONERGAN *Insight* p. xxv, There is also the *noēsis* or *intentio intendens*, or *pensée pensante* that is constituted by the very activity of inquiring and reflecting, understanding and affirming, asking further questions and reaching further answers. **1967** B. JAGER tr. *Kockelmans's Edmund Husserl's Phenomenological Psychol.* v. 244 A consideration and analysis of the related *noeses*, of the different acts in and through which the ego is conscious of something. **1970** E. PIVČEVIĆ *Husserl & Phenomenology* vi. 67 'Noesis'.. must of course be strictly distinguished from the sensory content of an experience.

noetic, *a.*² and *sb.* Add: **A.** *adj.* **1.** (Further examples.)

1907 W. JAMES *Pragmatism* v. 166 This is the hypothesis of *noetic pluralism*, which monists consider so absurd. **1925** *Brit. Jrnl. Psychol.* Oct. 106 In the following pages the word 'noetic' is used for brevity's sake instead of the more elaborate though more correct 'noegenetic'. *Ibid.* 115 The tests..measure the 'Noetic' and the 'Generative' powers of the subject. **1957** J. S. HUXLEY *Relig. without Revelation* (rev. ed.) ix. 204 Some new term..in which communicable mental activities play a predominant rôle. If so, I suggest the term *noetic*. *Ibid.*, Religions are thus noetic organs of evolving man. **1972** *Encycl. Psychol.* II. 327/2 *Noetic superstructure*, a term applied by strata theorists..to individual thought processes (power of abstraction, judgment, logical reasoning, etc.) that take place, together with voluntary activities, above the endothymic basis.

b. In phenomenology, that which is concerned with or pertains to the act of thinking or perceiving (see *NOESIS c). Cf. *NOEMATIC *a.* b.

1931 [see *NOEMA]. **1943** M. FARBER *Found. Phenomenology* xvi. 526 This applies to the *noetic* side ('I think', 'I experience', etc.) as well as to the *noematic* side. **1969** R. MCKEON in R. Klibansky *Contemp. Philos.* III. 105 The difference of knower and known disappear in the description of the experiencing (or the 'noetic') and experienced (or the 'noematic').

B. *sb.* **1.** (Later example.)

1931 W. R. B. GIBSON tr. *Husserl's Ideas* II. iv. § 59. 176 So too..we cannot suspend general Noetics, which expresses our essential insight into the rationality or irrationality of the judging activity generally.

noetical, *a.* Delete †*Obs.* and add later example.

1931 W. R. B. GIBSON tr. *Husserl's Ideas* III. iii. § 87. 256 It is a long..way that leads from meaning, from ontological and noetical insights.

no-fault. *U.S.* Used *attrib.* to designate a form of motor vehicle insurance (see quot. 1973¹).

1967 *Wall St. Jrnl.* 7 Nov. 1 Support for no-fault auto insurance in the U.S. **1968** *Economist* 13 July p. xviii/2 American motor insurance is now to be put under the microscope. And a no-fault compensation system is being discussed. **1973** C. L. BARNHART et al. *Dict. New Eng.* 318/7 *No-fault*, of or relating to a form of automobile insurance by which an accident victim is compensated for damages or expenses by his own insurance company, whether the accident was his fault or not. **1973** *Washington Post* 13 Jan. A.22/2 Governor Holton's call for a strong no-fault insurance bill. **1974** *Aiken* (S. Carolina) *Standard* 22 Apr. 1-A/2 The bill, to come up today, would assure that victims are paid for their losses regardless of who is at fault. It would require every car owner to buy insurance to protect himself and his family against losses arising from traffic accidents. The no-fault bill heads the Senate agenda for the week as Congress returns from a 10-day recess.

no-fines (nōᵘfəi·nz), *a.* (*sb.*) [f. No *a.* + pl. of *fine* sb. (FINE *a.* B).] Applied to concrete made from an aggregate composed of lumps larger than about 9 mm. (and smaller than about 18 mm.), which results in increased porosity and better thermal insulation. Also as *sb.*

1946 A. F. BOYD *Rep. Tests No-Fines Concrete* (Commonwealth Exper. Building Station, Sydney) 1 Little technical information was available on the strength of no-fines concrete as applied to building construction. **1954** *Archit. Rev.* CXVI. 410/3 Hills themselves also made no-fines walling blocks about 7 in. thick..for facing their steel-framed houses. **1955** *Times* 5 July 17/3 (Advt.), We handed over during the year some 19,500 permanent dwellings, most of them built by the Wimpey 'No-Fines' technique, which continues to make a wide appeal to those wanting speed combined with a high standard of construction. **1960** M. BOWLEY *Innovations in Building Materials* ix. 209 Dense concrete properly made is impervious to moisture..but provides poor heat insulation... 'No fines', on the other hand, is more pervious..but provides better heat insulation. **1969** E. C. ADAMS *Sci. in Building* III. viii. 139 No-fines is made by mixing a coarse aggregate with cement and water. *Ibid.*, No-fines concrete is not subject to capillarity, and can..provide a weatherproof wall in one thickness..if rendered externally.

no-frill(s. [*FRILL *sb.*¹ 1 e.] Used *attrib.* to designate a lack of ornamentation or embellishment.

The more usual form is *no-frills*.

1960 *Farmer & Stockbreeder* 16 Feb. 3/2 A no-frill piggery. **1967** 'E. LATHEN' *Murder against Grain* iv. 48 The no-frills exterior of Halloran's garage. **1969** *Listener* 27 Mar. 436/2 *World in Action* has an aggressive investigatory policy combined with tight editing and a no-frills presentation. **1969** *Daily Tel.* (Colour Suppl.) 3 Oct. 20/4 The 61st is a no-frills working regiment that spends most of its time in khaki field uniforms.

nog, *sb.*² **2.** (Earlier examples.)

1851 A. O. HALL *Manhattaner* 10, I tremble to think of the juleps, and punches, and nogs, and soups. **1881** A. W. TOURGÉE *Zouri's Christmas* in *Royal Gentleman* viii. 527 Then he tried to drain the glass, but a part of the foamy nogg remained in it despite his efforts.

Nogai, var. *NOGAY.

‖**nogaku** (nō·gaku). [Jap. *nōgaku*, f. *nō* talent, accomplishment, *NOH, No² + *gaku* music.] The Japanese dramatic form called Noh; the genre of the Noh drama.

1916 JOLY & TOMITA *Jap. Art & Handicraft* 7 The *Nô Gaku* originated in the Oyei era close upon the beginning of the XVth century. **1932** B. L. SUZUKI (*title*) Nōgaku: Japanese Nō Plays. **1938** D. T. SUZUKI *Zen Buddhism & its Influence on Jap. Culture* I. v. 101 The beginning of *haiku*, nōgaku theatre,..is to be sought in them. **1948** *Introd. Classic Jap. Lit.* (Kokusai Bunka Shinkokai) p. xvi, The earliest theatrical performances were those of the *nôgaku* (Noh drama), and the *nô-kyôgen* (Noh farces). **1959** W. P. MALM *Jap. Music* iv. 105 (*heading*) Nohgaku, the music of the noh drama.

Nogay (nǫ̆gai·). Also † **Na-, Nogai. a.** A Turkic-speaking people inhabiting the north-western Caucasus region of the U.S.S.R. **b.** The language of this people, a member of the Kipchak branch of Turkic languages. Also *attrib.* or as *adj.* So **Nogai·an** *a.*

1652 Nagaian [see *KIRGHIZ *sb.* and *a.*]. **1840** *Penny Cycl.* XVI. 248/1 The Nogays are a Tartar or Turkish nation, dispersed over the steppes which extend between the lower course of the river Dnieper and Mount Caucasus. **1886** [see *KAZAKH]. **1888** [see *KIRGHIZ *sb.* and *a.*]. **1948** D. DIRINGER *Alphabet* 568 The Arabic character has also been adopted for..Nogai Turkish, spoken by nearly 200,000 people to the north-west of the Caucasus and in the Crimea. **1958** *Everyman's Encycl.* IX. 268/1 *Nogay*, Turkic-speaking people of N. Caucasus, who live in the Groznyy oblast and Circassian Autonomous Oblast. **1974** *Encycl. Brit. Micropædia* VII. 376/1 Nogay belongs to the northwestern, or Kipchak, division of the Turkic languages, along with such languages as Kazakh and Tatar.

noggin. Add: **1. b.** The head. orig. and chiefly *U.S.*

1866 J. FINLEY *Hoosier's Nest* 90 But Matty's topknot..Wasn't there, for his noggin was bald. **1885** 'PHUDGE PHUMBLE' *Adventures Greenhorn in Gotham* 25 The full force of it against his noggin. **1931** D. RUNYON *Guys & Dolls* (1932) 286 She smacks Rusty Charley on the side of the noggin with the bat. **1951** *Landfall* V. 202 'Thanks, chum,' said Vic, 'You used your noggin.' **1957** *New Yorker* 2 Nov. 34/3 The Right Honourable Our Man Stanley, his Lock hat set firmly on his noggin, dropped by

the office the other day and deposited the following dispatch. **1972** J. E. Franklin in W. King *Black Short Story Anthol.* 354 Her hair was short,..and a dozen of those little twig-plaits tucked under and pinned looked like knots rising on her noggin. **1975** P. G. Winslow *Death of Angel* iv. 86 A rap on the back of the noggin that knocked her out.

c. A pail or bucket. *local U.S.*

1885 'C. E. Craddock' *Prophet Gt. Smoky Mts.* x. 175 Mirandy Jane, seated on an inverted noggin, listened tamely to the conversation. **1889** —— *Despot of Broomsedge Cove* xviii. 324 Isabel sat idle on an inverted noggin.

no-go. Add: (Further examples.) Freq. *attrib.*

1946 *Ann. Computation Lab. Harvard Univ.* I. 26 If.. the calculator finds that all multiples of the divisor are greater than the dividend or the remainder under consideration, a zero or 'no-go' is entered in the quotient counter and a new comparison made one column to the right. **1961** *Flight* LXXX. 542/1 A self-checking capability was therefore built into the machine so that, whenever a 'No Go' condition occurred, this part..carried out a self-checking routine to ensure that the fault was in the aircraft and not in the tester. **1962** A. Shepard in *Into Orbit* 170 When a particular station is on a 'No Go' status, the appropriate symbol lights up to indicate which of the several systems there is non-operative. **1966** *Electronics* 17 Oct. 93 Usually one test was sufficient to provide a go or no-go indication. **1969** *Guardian* 14 June 7/3 The astronauts would have had to end the mission there for, in space jargon, this was potentially a 'no-go' situation.

b. Used *attrib.* of an area: impossible to enter (because of barricades, etc.); to which entry is forbidden for specified persons, groups, etc.

1971 *Guardian* 13 Nov. 1/6 For journalists and others, the Bogside and Creggan estates are 'no-go' areas, with the IRA in total effective control. **1972** *Times* 24 May 16/1 The UDA organized the Protestant 'no go' areas in Belfast last weekend. **1972** *Guardian* 29 May 8/1 The Duke of Norfolk has decreed the Royal Enclosure at Ascot a 'no-go' area for the miniskirted or hotpanted lass. **1972** *Times* 3 June 2/7 Gypsy Council Names Four 'No-Go' Districts. The first four English boroughs likely to be designated as 'no go' areas for gypsies were named yesterday. **1972** *Daily Tel.* 11 Nov. 2/5 As a result, soldiers have been injured in rioting in the former 'no go' areas. **1974** *Times* 12 Feb. 2/8 Since the dispersal of the IRA leadership from inside the city to Donegal, after the British Army moved into the 'no-go areas' in 1972.

no-God. Used *attrib.* of a set of beliefs, etc., based on atheism. Also (*nonce-wd.*), a personified non-deity. So **no-Goddism, no-Goddite.**

1931 Belloc *Essays of Catholic* viii. 174, I have seen one very monstrous Myth reach maturity..and..explode. That was the Myth of Natural Selection. The enthusiasm which supported it and gave it the atmosphere in which to grow was no-Goddism. **1933** Chesterton *St. Thomas Aquinas* iv. 126 The Bolshevist No-God movement in the twentieth century. **1940** L. MacNeice *Last Ditch* 15 The horses ride..To a place where God and No-God Play at pitch and toss. **1952** R. A. Knox *Hidden Stream* vii. 60 If your atheist friend was a really reasoned no-Goddite, he would hoot with laughter.

no-good. orig. *U.S.* [A sb. use of the phr. *no good*: see Good C. 5 g.] **1.** A useless or valueless person or thing. Also *attrib.* Hence **no-goo·der,** (*U.S. slang*) **no-goodnik** [*-nik], a no-good person.

1908 E. J. Banfield *Confessions of Beachcomber* II. i. 250 A no-good-boy wantonly brought about a big wind. **1924** A. J. Small *Frozen Gold* i. 14 I'll learn you half-suckled no-goods what it means. **1931** M. Allingham *Look to Lady* v. 59 A pack of crazy no-goods—strutting about in funny clothes. **1936** S. P. Spivey in P. Oliver *Screening Blues* (1968) vi. 246 Oh you dirty no-gooder, you don't mean me no good. **1944** *This Week Mag.* 22 Oct. 21/2 Any newspaper reader of the late '20's would remember this no-gooder. **1944** S. J. Perelman *Crazy like Fox* (1945) 9 A parasite, a leech, a bloodsucker—altogether a five-star nogoodnick! **1947** D. M. Davin *Gorse blooms Pale* 28 Taking that no-good Calaghan girl to every dance. **1948** J. Steinbeck *Russ. Jrnl.* (1949) 100 The slovenly, no-good girl. **1958** 'A. Gilbert' *Death against Clock* 67 He recognized her almost at once for what she was, a gold-digger, a no-good. **1958** R. Graves in *Times Lit. Suppl.* 15 Aug. p. x/2 And the committee would, I am sure, be a snuggery of all the no-goods and do-goods whom I have spent half my life successfully avoiding. **1958** *Listener* 9 Oct. 569/2 A splendid comic performance by Alberto Sordi as a no-gooder from the city. **1959** *News Chron.* 19 June 8/2 Holly..gets herself involved with a no-good hoofer in a low night club. **1960** *Sunday Express* 10 July 15/6 He is a lazy no-good. **1960** *Guardian* 23 Sept. 11/7, I know their type... Bums and nogoodniks, the lot of them. **1968** *N.Y. Times* 3 Mar. 37 Lew Archer's job is to find a 17-year-old girl who has run off with a 19-year-old no-goodnik. **1971** *Black Scholar* Sept. 38/2 It was snowin' when your no good daddy left me for that hussy. **1973** W. M. Duncan *Big Timer* x. 67 This no-good whom I do not even see for weeks on end.

2. Phr. *no good to Gundy*: (see quots.) *Austral.*

The explanation in quot. 1945 seems improbable.

1919 W. H. Downing *Digger Dial.* 35 *No good to gundy*, of no advantage. **1945** Baker *Austral. Lang.* iv. 90 *No good to Gundy*, an elaboration of the simple 'no good', has been current since 1907 or before, and probably had its origin in America... The origin is more likely to be found..in the old U.S. phrase, *according to Gunter*. Gunter was a noted mathematician who gave his name to works of precision and accuracy. **1966** G. W. Turner *Eng. Lang. Austral. & N.Z.* vi. 118 The unexplained phrase *no good to Gundy*, meaning simply 'no good' perhaps appeals because of its alliteration.

Noh, No² (nōu). Also Nō. [Jap.] The traditional Japanese masked drama evolved from the rites of Shinto worship and substantially unchanged since the 15th c.; the oldest form of drama in Japan. Freq. *attrib.*

1871 A. B. Mitford *Tales of Old Japan* I. 156 A kind of classical opera, called Nô, which is performed on stages specially built for the purpose. **1899** [see *kyogen]. **1911** *Encycl. Brit.* XV. 169 Briefly speaking, the Nō was a dance of the most stately character, adapted to the incidents of dramas. **1917** W. B. Yeats *Lett.* (1954) IV. 631 The music to my Noh play *The Dreaming of the Bones*. **1927** E. Pound *Let.* 9 Nov. (1971) 214, I wonder if Iwasaki is trained in No or if you and he want to undertake revision of my redaction of Fenollosa's paper on the Noh (or No; better I think spelled with the 'h'). **1938** D. T. Suzuki *Zen Buddhism & its Influence on Jap. Culture* I. iv. 70 The Noh-play 'Kokaji' gives us some idea about the moral and religious significance of the sword among the Japanese. **1958** [see *kyogen]. **1960** B. Leach *Potter in Japan* vii. 155 A grey, wooden, thatched, open-air Nō stage where the monks still perform under an August moon. **1964** I. Fleming *You only live Twice* i. 15 'Grey Pearl'..was so thickly made up that she looked like a character out of a No play. **1973** *Times* 20 Mar. 9/5 The bare events of the tragedy are retained and acted out in trance-like, Noh-play fashion. **1974** S. Marcus *Minding the Store* (1975) xiv. 281 Billie gave me..a Noh mask from Japan.

no hit. 1. *Cricket.* (See quot. 1835.)

This rule no longer applies.

1827 *Sussex Weekly Advertiser* 9 July, The umpire called no hit. **1835** *Hoyle's Games* 426 When the striker shall hit the ball, one of his feet must be on the ground, and behind the popping crease, otherwise the umpire shall call *no hit*.

2. *Baseball.* (See quots. 1961.) So **no-hitter.**

1948 *Richmond* (Va.) *Times-Dispatch* 15 Mar. 17/4 Even without this new delivery Blackwell..came within two outs of pitching two successive no-hitters. **1949** [see *left field* (*left *a.* 3 c)]. **1955** A. Budrys in D. Knight *100 Yrs. Sci. Fiction* (1969) 255 Walker's a good pitcher, all right—but he didn't pitch any no-hitters. And he only won eighteen games. **1961** J. S. Salak *Dict. Amer. Sports* 298 *No-hit no-run game*, a game in which the pitcher permits the opposing team no base hits and no runs for the entire game or for at least the first nine innings of the game. **1961** Webster, *No-hitter*, a no-hit game in baseball. **1973** *Tucson* (Arizona) *Daily Citizen* 22 Aug. 60/2 Bahnsen said he was aware he had a no-hitter going and started bearing down in the seventh inning. **1974** *News & Reporter* (Chester, S. Carolina) 22 Apr. 10-A/8 Blackwell struck out 13 batters in the contest and pitched five innings of no-hit ball before Burton ended his hopes for a no-hitter.

no-ho·per. *Austral. slang.* [f. No *a.* + Hoper.] **a.** A horse with no prospect of winning, an outsider. **b.** A useless or incompetent person, one from whom no good can be expected.

1943 Baker *Dict. Austral. Slang* (ed. 3) 54 *No-hoper*, an outsider. (Racing slang.) **1945** T. Ronan *Strangers on Ophir* (1966) 79 There were actually eight runners in it: the three favourites, three no-hopers hardly up to hack-race standard, [etc.]. **1953** [see *drongo 3]. **1957** D. Niland *Call me when Cross turns Over* i. 27 This son was not a no-hoper. **1959** Baker *Drum* (1960) iii. 33 The suggestion that a heart of gold beats in the breast of every no-hoper. **1959** *Times Lit. Suppl.* 25 Dec. 753/2 Shanty towns where the 'no-hopers' drink their big cheques away. **1967** J. Morrison in *Coast to Coast 1965–66* 137 He's a bit of a no-hoper. **1971** *Sunday Australian* 8 Aug. 5/1 He prefers that they go north to the mining towns to..staying in the cities where they are dragged down to the level of no-hopers they pick up with.

nohow, *adv.* Add: **1. b.** (Earlier and later U.S. examples.) Esp. in phr. *no how you* (*they*) *can fix it*. Cf. Fix *v.* 14 c.

1833 J. Hall *Harpe's Head* 91 (Th.), They don't raise such humans in the Old Dominion, no how. **1835** W. G. Simms *Partisan* 506 It won't be an easy journey, ma'am, no how, I tell you. **1836** [see *fix *v.* 14 c]. **1840** *Knickerbocker* XVI. 19, I mean my name ain't G. Washington Mortimer, no how. **1843** 'R. Carlton' *New Purchase* I. xviii. 141, I..couldn't read a chapter in the Bible no how you could fix it. **1929** H. W. Odum in A. Dundes *Mother Wit* (1973) 187 Boys jes' natchelly tired an' don't want to work no-how. **1970** R. P. Warren *Incarnations* 48 Did he merely blow, and never Was rightly your husband, no how. **1973** C. Williams *Man on Leash* (1974) x. 146 You won't be thinkin' about yore hairdo nohow.

nohowish, *a.* (Earlier and later examples.)

1826 Disraeli *Vivian Grey* II. xii. 171, I was altogether *no-howish* by the time I got home. *a* **1897** [see *all A. 10 a]. **1935** J. M. Murry *Between Two Worlds* viii. 110 Within a fortnight I was feeling nohowish.

‖ **noia** (noi·ă). [It.] Boredom, weariness, ennui.

1944 'Palinurus' *Unquiet Grave* I. 22 The secret of happiness lies in the avoidance of Angst (anxiety, spleen, noia, guilt, fear, remorse, cafard). **1962** *Encounter* XIX. 69 Let us hear what Moravia has to say about *noia*, the fundamental..situation of all his books. **1967** *Listener* 2 Nov. 583/2 The revenge play is the pretext for all that Renaissance introspection and *noia* and *Angst*.

Noilly Prat (nwaʸi pra). [Name of the manufacturers.] The proprietary name of a French vermouth; a drink of this.

1906 *Hatch, Mansfield Price List* May 32 Liqueurs... Vermouth (Noilly, Prat)..2/7-litre. **1907** *Yesterday's Shopping* (1969) 100/3 Vermouth... French, Noilly Prat —Per bot. 2/7. **1950** D. Ames *Corpse Diplomatique* i. 10, I found Dagobert..sipping a *Noilly Prat*. **1964** E. Bowen *Little Girls* I. iv. 53 We are also right at the end of the Noilly Prat. **1965** *Harper's Bazaar* Jan. 80/3 Haut Savoie, historically the cradle of French vermouth, though Noilly-Prat has always been made well to the west of it. **1966** J. Pearl *Crucifixion of Pete McCabe* (1967) v. 65 He uncorked the Noilly Prat vermouth. **1974** D. Winsor *Death Convention* v. 40, I want a very dry martini. With Noilly Prat.

noir. Add: **2. a.** The black numbers in the game of roulette.

1850 *Bohn's Hand-bk. Games* 348 The other chances are also designated on the green cloth.., 'le pair, le passe, et le noir'. **1928** M. Carol *How to play Roulette* ii. 21 Among other divisions, or spaces for the stakes, you will find *Passe, Pair, Manque, Impair, Noir, Rouge*. **1939** T. King *Twenty-one Games to play for Money* 31 Even chances are given when a stake is placed on:..*Noir*, meaning any black number that turns up. **1964** A. Wykes *Gambling* ix. 215 The European betting table is divided into six areas labelled *pair, impair, passe, manque, rouge*, and *noir* (even, odd, high, low, red, black). **1971** P. O'Neil-Dunne *Roulette for Millions* iv. 36 You may be regarded as socially inferior in French casinos, if you do not understand the following French expressions: *Rouge:* Red *Noir:* Black *Impair:* Odds [etc.].

b. The black colour in the game of *rouge et noir* (cf. *Rouge et Noir* s.v. Rouge *sb.*¹ 4).

1850 *Bohn's Hand-bk. Games* 343 The first parcel of cards played, is usually for noir, the second for rouge. **1850** [see *inverse *sb.* 3]. **1928** M. Carol *How to play Roulette* iv. 56 The even money chances are Rouge or Red, Noir or Black, Coleur [*sic*] and Inverse. **1964** A. Wykes *Gambling* vii. 171 (*caption*) The dealer lays out two rows of cards (*le noir* and *le rouge*) until each totals 31 or more. Players bet that one or the other row will be nearer to 31 by placing chips on *rouge* or on *noir*.

noise, *sb.* Add: **2. d.** An utterance, usu. in phr. *to make noises*: to express (something) vocally; freq. with defining adj. prefixed.

1951 N. Marsh *Opening Night* vii. 152 Dr. Curtis said: 'I'd better go and make professional noises at him.' **1955** *Times* 21 July 8/6 If this is so, 'why then the noise about the 12 German divisions in W.E.U. and N.A.T.O.?' **1956** N. Marsh *Off with his Head* (1957) v. 91, I suppose I ought to make a polite noise. **1965** *N.Y. Times* 15 Sept. 42 Left-wing Liberals have made neutralist noises in the past. **1967** *New Scientist* 22 June 718 General Electric and Alcoa, for example, are making noises about getting into city building. **1969** S. Hyland *Top Bloody Secret* iii. 232, I made the right kind of encouraging noises. **1971** *Guardian* 14 May 24/2 There is a temptation to see the hand of Tate and Lyle and Mr Cube in any political noises from the sugar trade. **1971** P. Worsthorne *Socialist Myth* iii. 32 The Labour Party cannot make the classical patriotic noises as convincingly as the Tories. **1973** *Times* 8 Jan. 3/3 Although the city council is, as they see it, making more friendly noises, its policies on development and road building..set it on a collision course.

3. c. *noises off*: sound effects, usu. loud or confused, produced off the stage but to be heard by the audience at the performance of a play. Also *transf.*

1924 H. A. Vachell *Quinney's Adventures* 46 As he did so, he heard what is called in stageland a 'noise off'. 'Put them in your pocket,' commanded madame, in a hurried whisper. **1932** Wodehouse *Hot Water* ii. 66 He's got a job with the British Broadcasting Company... He does the noises off. **1934** *B.B.C. Year-bk.* 44 Plays, for example, need their effects, which in their turn call for the studio and staff allocated specially for producing 'noises off'. **1937** N. Marsh *Vintage Murder* xi. 122 'And what..is Scotland Yard's part in the proceedings?' 'Noises off, Mr Ackroyd,' replied Alleyn good-humouredly. **1940** 'G. Orwell' *Inside Whale* 38 The aristocracy and the big bourgeoisie exist in his books chiefly as a kind of 'noises off', a haw-hawing chorus somewhere in the wings. **1949** F. Maclean *Eastern Approaches* iii. v. 359 After some time had elapsed, there were 'noises off' from which those of us who remained concluded that the attention of the enemy was fully engaged elsewhere. **1958** *Times* 7 July 9/4 There are 'noises-off', however, that add to the harmony. **1972** *Daily Tel.* 31 May 10/4 In fact the rustlings of the wind-blown trees were perfect noises-off for Shakespeare's uninhabited island.

d. *noise and number index*: a quantity used in evaluating aircraft noise in terms of its intensity and duration.

1963 *Final Rep. Comm. Probl. Noise* 218 in *Parl. Papers 1962–3* (Cmnd. 2056) XXII. 657 During the Social Survey made in 1961 in the vicinity of London (Heathrow) Airport, measurement of noise levels and studies of the numbers of aircraft likely to be heard were made... The results have been combined..to form a Noise and Number Index (NNI). **1971** *Physics Bull.* Nov. 660/3 An exposure index for aircraft noise has been developed from this survey, called the noise and number index. This index is a combination of the average noise level measured at a point on the ground and the number of times a person is exposed to aircraft noise during a given period of time.

6. b. Also (without preceding *make* or *keep*) used of a person, esp. in phr. *the* (or *a*) *big noise*: a person of great importance. orig. *U.S.*

1908 G. H. Lorimer *Jack Spurlock* vii. 153 A lot of people are beginning to think that Teddy's a mere noise. **1911** R. W. Chambers *Common Law* vi. 169 Well, sister,

take it from muh, she thinks she's the big noise in the Great White Alley. **1927** T. E. LAWRENCE *Let.* 8 Feb. (1938) 506 Drill Parades bi-weekly when a big noise draws near—Sir Sam. **1931** GALSWORTHY *Maid in Waiting* vi. 42 Saxenden is a big noise behind the scenes in military matters. **1939** C. DAY LEWIS *Child of Misfortune* III. iii. 296 Elderton was the big noise in the Home Office. **1942** J. B. PRIESTLEY *Black-out in Gretley* iii. 32 He's rather a big noise here. Landed man really, but has a seat on our Board, and a local J.P. **1957** M. KENNEDY *Heroes of Clone* I. v. 50 Say you don't want him. You're the big noise here.

d. Joc. phr. *to make a noise like*, to pretend to be.

1920 'SAPPER' *Bull-Dog Drummond* v. 126 Make a noise like a sturgeon, and he'll think it's caviare. **1928** D. L. SAYERS *Lord Peter views Body* 87, I s'pose I'd better make a noise like a hoop and roll away. Night, night, everybody. **1961** PARTRIDGE *Dict. Slang.* Suppl. 1199/1 *Noise like a—, make a..* dates from ca. 1908. Baden Powell, in his *Scouting for Boys*, instructed scouts in danger of detection to take cover and make a noise like a (say) thrush.

6*. In scientific use, a collective term (used without the indef. article) for: fluctuations or disturbances (usu. irregular) which are not part of a wanted signal or which interfere with its intelligibility or usefulness.

1923 *Telegraph & Telephone Jrnl.* IX. 119/2 The variations in noise were plotted, and their effect at times was to reduce the intelligibility to 20 or 30 per cent. **1930** *Proc. IRE* XVIII. 253 Circuit for measuring noise on the plate side of a vacuum tube. *Ibid.* 259 The ratio of signal to noise in the input circuit. **1932** F. E. TERMAN *Radio Engin.* vi. 207 The output currents obtained..in the absence of a signal voltage produce what is commonly referred to as 'noise' when flowing through a..loud-speaker, and it is also common practice to apply the term 'noise' to the corresponding radio-frequency currents obtained in the output of a radio-frequency amplifier, although these lie above the range of audible frequencies. **1940** ZWORYKIN & MORTON *Television* vi. 194 If the noise is appreciable compared with the picture signal, it appears in the reproduction as a myriad of constantly changing bright specks. **1953** J. B. CARROLL *Study of Language* vii. 201 It is..necessary to study the effect of the signal-to-noise ratio on the efficiency of communication, noise being defined as that part of a received transmission which is extraneous to the original message. **1962** A. NISBETT *Technique Sound Studio* 262 In all electronic components and recording or transmission media the signal must compete with some degree of background noise. **1966** *New Scientist* 16 June 714/3 In this way a radar echo which may otherwise be hidden by 'noise' is rendered visible. **1968** J. LYONS *Introd. Theoretical Linguistics* ii. 88 The distortions produced in one's handwriting in a moving train can be attributed to 'noise'. **1970** O. DOPPING *Computers & Data Processing* i. 21 Information theory deals largely with what happens when a random interference ('noise') is superimposed on the desired signal. **1973** *Computers & Humanities* VII. 160 Knisbacher uses a generalized (context-free) grammar in his algorithm [for machine translation] but avoids the 'noise' of too many resultant analyses for each sentence by simulating context sensitivity within that context-free framework. **1974** *Nature* 10 May 192/1 As normally viewed, displays of video noise ('snow') have the appearance of fields of small speckles which seem to dart about at random.

7. *noise abatement, control, level, measurement, meter, pollution, reduction, suppression*; *noise-free, -measuring* adjs.; **noise check** *Motor Rallying*, the use of a decibel metre to ensure that cars do not make too much noise; **noise contour**, an imaginary line or surface joining points where the noise level is the same; **noise factor** or **figure** *Electronics*, a quantity representing the additional noise introduced by a signal-processing device such as an amplifier (see quots.); **noise filter** *Electronics*, a filter for selectively reducing noise; **noise limiter** *Electronics*, a circuit or device for selectively reducing certain types of noise, esp. by momentarily reducing the output or the gain during peaks of greater amplitude than the desired signal; **noise storm** *Astr.*, a radio emission from the sun consisting of a succession of short bursts or pips in the megahertz range that lasts for a period of hours or days and is associated with sunspots.

1923 *Health* II. 438 A real want, a very great want, and a very immediate want is a Noise-Abatement Society. **1973** *Scotsman* 13 Feb. 8/3 It would be very hard to sustain a reasonable argument against them on noise abatement grounds. **1960** S. TURNER *Rallying* vi. 68 One other sort of check which you must treat with respect is a noise check. **1963** [see *dust-raising* adj. (*DUST *sb.*[1] 8 b)]. **1963** P. DRACKETT *Motor Rallying* iii. 37, I was remarkably unimpressed by the secrecy displayed by noise-check marshals on one big rally. **1971** *Physics Bull.* Nov. 656/1 During design studies of rotorcraft the noise of various designs is assessed by predicting an appropriate noise contour (usually 90 PN dB) and comparing it with the design noise target. **1973** *Times* 25 Apr. 19/6 If there were a prospect of drastically curtailing operations from Heathrow and Gatwick..before the time when the noise contours will start contracting through the increasing use of quieter aircraft, then there would be some point..in building Maplin. **1960** *McGraw-Hill Encycl. Sci. & Technol.* IX. 120/1 The first step in noise control is an analysis of the nature and extent of the problem. **1937** A. G. TYNAN in *Radio Engin.* July 21/2 Such a factor is very easily arrived at by multiplying the noise-signal ratio..by the sensitivity of the receiver in microvolts. This may be conveniently christened the noise factor. **1952** *Wireless World* June 224/1 There are various slightly different definitions of noise factor (in America, 'noise figure'). *Ibid.*, The noise factor is 3. It means that the result of amplifier noise is to make the noise 3 times as bad as in the ideal case where the signal source is the sole noise generator. *Ibid.*, In an ideal amplifier or receiver the noise factor..would be 1. **1962** *Rep. Comm. Broadcasting 1960* 333 in *Parl. Papers 1961–2* (Cmnd. 1753) IX. 259 The Band V tests have also shown that the noise factor of receivers in this Band is at present relatively high. **1944** *Proc. IRE* XXXII. 420/2 The noise figure *F* of the network is defined as the ratio of the available signal-to-noise ratio at the signal-to-generator terminals to the available signal-to-noise ratio at its output terminals. **1952** Noise figure [see *noise factor* above]. **1968** *Wireless World* Dec. 455/2 Noise figure = Total noise output power/ Noise output power due to sources only. *Ibid.* 457/2 Negative feedback..has no effect whatever on the noise figure of an amplifier at any given frequency. *Ibid.* 458/2 A noise figure at 1,000 Hz of 0·02 dB. **1960** *McGraw-Hill Encycl. Sci. & Technol.* IX. 130/1 The tone control of a radio or record player can act as a noise filter, as when high-frequencies are cut down to reduce record noise. **1967** E. L. GRUENBERG *Handbk. Telemetry & Remote Control* ix. 15 The characteristics of the noise filter are determined by the sampling rate, the overall system accuracy, and the allowable crosstalk between successive samples. **1934** *Discovery* Dec. 348/1 Standard practice in noise-free construction is now available for architects. **1966** D. G. BRANDON *Mod. Techniques Metallogr.* 162 Careful design of the collection system for backscattered electrons yields practically noise-free images. **1925** *Sci. Amer.* June 422/3 The limit of radio..is the static—what the radio engineers call the 'noise level' of the disturbances in the ether. **1932** V. O. KNUDSEN *Archit. Acoustics* ix. 257 The average street noise level in New York varies from about 47 to 80 db. **1959** *Daily Tel.* 24 Apr. 20/7 It must be shown that helicopter operations can be carried out at a noise level tolerable to the public. **1972** R. ADAMS *Watership Down* xix. 111 Nowadays, among fields and woods, the noise level by day is..too high for some kinds of animal to tolerate. **1939** *Wireless World* 5 Jan. 15 (*heading*) Noise limiters suppressing interference in the receiver. **1954** E. MOLLOY *Radio & Television Engineers' Ref. Bk.* xxxiii. 8 Noise limiters tend to be less efficient when used in receivers possessing extremely high selectivity. **1934** *Discovery* Dec. 345 Efforts..are being made to provide standards of noise-measurement. *Ibid.* 347/1 The expert with his noise-measuring gear. **1964** R. F. FICCHI *Electr. Interference* vii. 120 About twenty years ago, a new approach to the problem of measurement was taken when it was stated that the most practical type of noise-measuring instrument is, essentially, a radio receiver with an indicating means. **1931** *Proc. IRE* XIX. 1953 This instrument, which has been called a 'circuit noise meter', consists of an amplifier, a frequency weighting network, a rectifier, and an indicating meter. **1950** *Jrnl. R. Aeronaut. Soc.* LIV. 699/1 The microphone..has been calibrated by the makers in conjunction with the noise meter. **1970** *Britannica Bk. of Year 1969* 798/3 *Noise pollution*, pollution consisting of annoying noise (*noise pollution* caused by automobile traffic, a jet airplane, or a vacuum cleaner); called also *sound pollution*. **1970** *Sci. Jrnl.* Mar. 5 The greatly improved noise pollution characteristics of VTOL compared not only with conventional aircraft (CTOL) but with short take off and landing craft (STOL). **1972** J. MADDOX *Doomsday Syndrome* iv. 98 'Noise pollution' is a phrase in everyday use. **1931** *Proc. IRE* XIX. 1763 The noise reduction advantage of the arrays..is some 15 decibels over that of a nondirectional antenna. **1959** W. S. SHARPS *Dict. Cinematogr.* 114/2 In photographic recording and reproducing, noise reduction is a process whereby the average transmission of the sound track of the print..is decreased for signals of low level and increased for signals of high level. **1947** C. W. ALLEN in *Monthly Notices R. Astron. Soc.* CVII. 391 All solar noise storms..in Figs. 2 and 3 coincide with near meridian passage of spots. **1974** G. L. VERSCHUUR *Invisible Universe* iii. 36 Sunspots also produce characteristic radio bursts, called storm bursts or bursts of type I. These are very short-lived intense pips of radio emission, each lasting only a fraction of a second, although thousands of these might be emitted every hour and the noise storm (a string of bursts) may last for days. **1933** *Practical Wireless* II. 37/2 (*heading*) Noise suppression on the short waves. **1968** *IEEE Jrnl. Quantum Electronics* IV. 644 (*heading*) Noise suppression in the Argon FM Laser.

noiseless, *a.* Add: **b.** Characterized by a virtual absence of noise (sense 6*).

1931 A. NADELL *Projecting Sound Pictures* xiv. 244 The recently developed 'noiseless recording' is achieved by passing a 'bias' current through the value ribbons, in addition to the usual speech current. The effect of the bias is to eliminate the former spacing of 2, or 1½ mils, and to keep the ribbons always closed when no speech current is passing. **1944** *Phil. Mag.* XXXV. 394, *r̂* must be regarded as a noiseless shunting resistance. **1957** *Sci. Amer.* Feb. 82/2 The maser would..be useful in astronomy and cosmology. As a noiseless amplifier it would eliminate the noise generated in the circuits of radio telescopes. **1972** J. M. TAYLOR tr. *Meyer & Neumann's Physical & Applied Acoustics* ix. 351 In variable-area recording..the bright side of the sound track is darkened for small amplitudes in the region that does not contribute to sound generation (noiseless recording).

noisy, *a.* Add: **1. b. noisy scrub bird** *Austral.*, a ground-dwelling bird, *Altrichornis clamosus*, found in parts of Western Australia.

[**1848** J. GOULD *Birds Austral.* III. tab. 34 (*heading*) *Altrichia clamosa*, Gould. Noisy Brush-bird.] **1901** A. J. CAMPBELL *Nests & Eggs Austral. Birds* I. 504 The Noisy Scrub Bird..lives in the thickets of undergrowth. **1933** *Bulletin* (Sydney) 1 Feb. 21 One of the rarest and most curious of Australian birds is the 'noisy scrub-bird'.. whose home, if perchance the secretive creature survives, is in the dense forest of the Leeuwin Peninsula. **1966** *Evening Standard* 14 July 18/2 One of Australia's rarest birds, the noisy scrub bird, has forced the Western Australian State Government to abandon plans to establish a new town. The town..was to have been in the heart of the noisy scrub bird country near Albany, 300 miles south of Perth. *Ibid.* 18/3 Between 1889 and 1961 the bird was neither seen nor heard. But then it reappeared... The noisy scrub bird is extremely elusive. The male has a call like the crack of a whip. **1972** G. DURRELL *Catch me a Colobus* x. 218 In Australia they rediscovered the Noisy Scrub Bird which had been thought to be extinct.

2. b. (In the sense of *NOISE *sb.* 6*.)

1944 *Phil. Mag.* XXXV. 394 If [the resistance] *r̂* were thermally 'noisy'. **1949** *Proc. R. Soc.* A. CXCVII. 480 (*facing caption*) Noisy background chiefly due to imperfections of illuminating objective. **1951** *Sci. Amer.* Aug. 14/3 Transistors..were 'noisy'. **1973** *Nature* 5 Oct. 258/1 In the galactic plane, the 1,420 MHz line is noisy, which decreases its attractiveness.

‖ **noix** (nwa). [F., lit. 'nut'.] (See quot. 1961.)

1845 E. ACTON *Mod. Cookery* ix. 210 That part of the fillet [of veal] to which the cat or udder is attached;.. Called by them [*sc.* French cooks] the *noix*. **1893** *Encycl. Pract. Cookery* II. 699/2 Beat the noix well, trim it to a nice shape, and lard with thin fillets of fat bacon. **1906** A. FILIPPINI *Internat. Cook Bk.* 162 (*heading*) Noix of veal, braisée, fermière. **1923** C. H. SENN *Cent. Cookery Bk.* (new ed.) 565 Noix de veau à la Viart..1 small cushion or kernel part of veal [etc.]. **1960** E. DAVID *French Provincial Cooking* 371 A *noix* of veal, the cut approximating to the topside of the leg in beef. **1961** N. FROUD et al. tr. *Montagné's Larousse Gastronomique* 993/1 The *noix* of veal is the topside (rump), the fleshy upper part of the leg, cut lengthwise. **1967** A. WILSON *No Laughing Matter* III. 193 They hungrily devoured the noix de veau and carrots at lunch. **1974** *Times* 2 Nov. 11/5 Everything from stewing steak to dainty noix de veau.

no-knock. Used *attrib.* (occas. *absol.*) of a search or raid by the police made without permission or warning. *U.S.*

1970 *Atlantic Monthly* Oct. 57 John Mitchell puts on a happy face and suggests that the name of the 'no-knock' law be changed to something more felicitous, like 'quick-entry'. **1971** *New Yorker* 10 Apr. 30 The 'no-knock' and 'preventive-detention' provisions of the District of Columbia Crime Control Act have violated, respectively, the public's right to be secure against unreasonable searches and seizures and the traditional presumption of innocence. **1973** *Black Panther* 8 Sept. 8/3 The California State Supreme Court last week refused to decide in favor of a no-knock rule. In a four to three decision the court held that a search warrant specifically providing that a police officer can enter a home without announcing himself cannot be issued. **1973** *Houston* (Texas) *Chron. Mag. People, Places, Pleasures* 14 Oct. 4/6 Can't the people see the implications of a thing like 'no knock'? It's a Gestapo tactic.

no-licence. A stipulation that no licence is granted, e.g. for the sale of liquor. Freq. *attrib.*

1908 *Daily Chron.* 24 Apr. 4/3, I have been a police officer for thirty-seven years, and am consequently quite familiar with the conditions prevailing before the no-license law..came into effect. **1909** *Ibid.* 27 Feb. 5/7 A no-license resolution, which means that no certificate for the sale of excisable liquors shall be granted. **1921** E. O'FERRALL in Murdoch & Drake-Brockman *Austral. Short Stories* (1951) 163 I've decided to reform and join the No-licence crowd. *Ibid.*, I'm goin' t' vote No-licence! **1969** *Austral. Encycl.* V. 312/1 There was to be no compensation for licensees in the event of a vote for no-licence.

no-limit. Used *attrib.* of a game, betting, etc., in which no limits are laid down.

1915 *Munsey's Mag.* LIV. Apr. 485/1 Poker game to-night... We'll have a real game this time—a no-limit game. **1954** F. C. AVIS *Boxing Ref. Dict.* 75 *No-Limit Boxer*, a heavyweight, from the fact that there is no restriction of weight among the 'heavies'. **1962** K. ORVIS *Damned & Destroyed* xv. 110 Play on the no-limit table was completed. **1973** *Times* 12 Apr. 12/6 Ladbroke.. aside from the £50m spending spree planned on hotels, is quite happy to welcome no-limit betting.

nolition. (Later example.)

1857 in *Appleton's Illustr. Handbk. Amer. Trav.* 237 Do not allow..the nolition of your womankind..to prevent you.

nolle, *v.* (Later example.)

1910 *Springfield* (Mass.) *Weekly Republ.* 24 Nov. 10 (*headline*) Case against Haskell Nolled.

‖ **nolle** (nǫ·li), *sb.* *U.S.* Abbrev. of NOLLE PROSEQUI.

1871 E. EGGLESTON in *Hearth & Home* 23 Dec. 1010/3, I now enter a *nolle* in his case..and I ask that this court adjourn. **1878** J. H. BEADLE *Western Wilds* xxxi. 507 He had been indicted along with the others, and a *nolle* entered.

‖ **nolle pros.** = *NOLLE *sb.*

1895 *Denver Times* 5 Mar. 1/3 John Doyle was dismissed on a nolle pros in both cases against him.

nolle prosequi. Add: (Later examples.) Also (quot. 1971) *joc.*

1964 *Mod. Law Rev.* XXVII. 268 The jury failed to agree whether there was a trade dispute. The Attorney-General entered a *nolle prosequi*, but wished it to be 'clearly understood' that strikes not in pursuit of trade disputes had no statutory protection. **1971** WODEHOUSE *Much Obliged, Jeeves* x. 104 When an aunt has set her mind on a thing, it's no use trying to put in a nolle prosequi.

nolle-pros(s, *v.* Add: Also **nolle prosse, nol-pros.** (Earlier and later examples.)

1880 G. A. Pierce *Zachariah* 436 Judge Spalding informed Zach..that the case could be 'nolle prossed' when it came up. **1905** *Springfield* (Mass.) *Weekly Republ.* 15 Dec. 2 The court heard petitions for a new trial, and upon these being granted the cases were nol prossed and the brothers set free. **1926** D. L. Colvin *Prohibition in U.S.* 505 In the two years 14,567 cases were nolle-prossed or dismissed. **1974** D. Tidyman *Dummy* ix. 127 The State would move to *nolle prosse* the case against Donald Lang.

no-load (nō͞ᵘ:lō͞ᵘ·d), *attrib. phr.* [No *a.* 6 b.] **1.** *Electr.* Corresponding to or involving an absence of any load.

1907 G. W. O. Howe tr. *Thomälen's Text-bk. Electr. Engin.* viii. 180 The no-load loss for a given excitation can generally be looked upon as a constant loss. **1951** W. Sluckin *Princ. Alternating Currents* vii. 175 Calculation of the..iron losses is based on the results of the so-called open-circuit or no-load test. **1966** N. Jones *Basic Electrotechnology* xi. 150 The motor exhibits a practically constant speed characteristic, the full-load speed being about 5% less than the no-load speed.

2. Of shares: sold at net asset value. Also as *sb.*

1964 P. Wyckoff *Dict. Stock Market Terms* 174 *No load fund*, a mutual fund which charges little or no commission (*load charge*) to the buyer of its shares. No sales organization is involved. **1968** *Maclean's Mag.* Oct. 22 A handful or so Canadian funds are 'no-loads'—are offered without any sales charge and are generally available through investment dealers. **1969** *Times* 5 May (Suppl.) p. vi/3 No-loads are more likely to be performance funds because they have no salesmen to sell them. **1972** *National Observer* (U.S.) 27 May 8/6 (Advt.), The Scudder Special Fund is a no-load mutual fund seeking above-average growth of capital and may invest in securities with above-average risk. You pay no sales commission when you invest in this Fund.

‖**nolo contendere** (nō͞ᵘ·lo kǫnte·ndĕre). [L., 'I do not wish to contend'.] 'A plea by the defendant in a criminal prosecution that without admitting guilt subjects him to a judgment of conviction as in case of a plea of guilty but does not preclude him from denying the truth of the charges in a collateral proceeding' (Webster, 1961).

1872 G. P. Burnham *Memo. U.S. Secret Service* p. vii, *Nolo contendere*, don't wish further to contend. **1960** *Times* 9 Dec. 11/2 Counsel for these companies told the court that their pleas of Guilty and *nolo contendere* were not an admission of all allegations on the indictment, but were made with a desire to terminate what would otherwise be protracted and expensive litigation. **1972** *N.Y. Law Jrnl.* 24 Nov. 3/1 [He] entered a plea of nolo-contendere to ten counts of securities fraud of an indictment charging him with sixteen counts of securities law violations.

‖**nom.** Add: **c.** *nom de Dieu* (noṅ də dyö), a mild oath.

1867 'Ouida' *Under Two Flags* III. ix. 228 'Nom de Dieu, Miladi!' she swore in her teeth. **1922** E. E. Cummings *Enormous Room* viii. 176 *Nom de dieu*, I thought vaguely. Am I or am I not completely asleep? **1961** *Amer. Speech* XXXVI. 35 Another basic oath is *nom de Dieu.*

d. *nom de théâtre* (noṅ də teˌatr'), a stage name.

1874 W. P. Lennox *My Recollections* I. viii. 189 After leaving the army, he appeared on the regular boards under the *nom de théâtre* of Calcraft. **1935** Wodehouse *Blandings Castle* xi. 278 A short list of names, one of which she proposed as a *nom de théâtre* as soon as her screen career should begin. **1952** Granville *Dict. Theatrical Terms* 122 *Nom de théâtre*, a stage name. These were adopted at the time when connection with the stage was not considered respectable. **1974** *Times* 6 Apr. 14/2 Erik Weisz..in 1890..set himself up as a stage musician under the *nom de théâtre* of Harry Houdini.

e. *nom de vente* (noṅ də vāṅt), a name assumed by a buyer at an auction who wishes to remain anonymous.

1955 *Times* 21 May 5/4 This, it is understood, is the *nom-de-vente* for a member of the nobleman's family. **1959** *Times* 26 Feb. 12/5 All three bought by Felham, a *nom de vente.*

nomadism. (Later examples.)

1963 *Punch* 13 Nov. 721/1 Centuries of fierce nomadism. **1964** Gould & Kolb *Dict. Social Sci.* 724/2 Usages of transhumance..agree in contrasting the term with *pastoral nomadism.* **1974** *Environmental Conservation* I. 12/1 If traditional nomadism finally disappears..it will be impossible to recreate it.

nomadization. Add: **b.** A making or becoming nomadic in character or nature.

1920 H. G. Wells *Outl. Hist.* 606/2 What we now call democracy, the boldness of modern scientific inquiry and a universal restlessness, are due to this 'nomadization' of civilization.

nomadize, *v.* Add: **b.** *trans.* To make nomadic in character.

1902 D. G. Hogarth *Nearer East* 156 The incomers 'nomadised' the south-east. *Ibid.* 272 The southern oases are the most 'nomadised'.

nomady (nō͞ᵘ·mădi). [f. Nomad *sb.* and *a.* + -y³.] The state, condition, or life of a nomad.

1909 Beerbohm *Yet Again* 126 Had nomady been my business, had I been a commercial traveller or a King's Messenger. **1920** —— *And Even Now* 263 The Bohemian, as tending always to nomady, feels that [etc.].

no man. Add: **1. b.** [see No *adv.*³ and *sb.*] A man who says 'no'; one who is accustomed to disagree or to refuse requests in a resolute manner. *colloq.*

1953 Berrey & Van den Bark *Amer. Thes. Slang* (1954) § 400/3 Obstinate person..'no' man. *Ibid.* § 421/1 Critic; opposer..'no' man (*vs.* 'yes man'). **1959** *Listener* 30 July 168/1 He [*sc.* Metternich] was the great 'No-man'. One can make a long list of the changes he did not like. **1961** *Sunday Express* 19 Feb. 8/4 Prince Philip..attacked what he called the 'no-men' who stood in the way of those with energy and imagination. **1967** *Listener* 26 Jan. 143/1 The only role of the abominable no-men of Whitehall was to frustrate him at every turn.

2. a. *no man's land.* (Earlier and additional examples.) See also quots. 1966 and 1972.

1598 Stow *Survey of London* 356 Ralph Stratforde Bishop of London, in the yeare 1348. bought a peece of ground called no mans land, which he inclosed with a wall of Bricke. **1876** H. Brooks *Natal* 234 In 1866..the Government of the colony took possession of 'No-man's-land'. **1902** *Chambers's Jrnl.* Jan. 34/1 The independent warlike tribes formerly sandwiched in a No Man's Land between Afghanistan and India. **1909** *Westm. Gaz.* 21 Aug. 14/1 This place has a higher attraction..for it is no-man's-land, eligible for building on, threatened, but as yet unoccupied. **1910** *Chambers's Jrnl.* Aug. 495/1 These cottages had been built..on ground between two roads, which was a kind of 'no man's land' and rent free. **1921** C. A. W. Monckton *Some Experiences New Guinea Resident Magistrate* xxvi. 306 The country we were camped in was a sort of 'no man's land' or border land lying between the Baruga tribe and their mountain enemies. **1966** G. E. Evans *Pattern under Plough* xiii. 136 The belief that a piece of land in the parish should be left untilled. In English villages this is sometimes called *Jack's Land* or *No-Man's Land.* **1972** P. Newton *Sheep Thief* 187 *No Man's Land*, those areas of wild rough country, bounding the Southern Alps, which are not stocked. **1975** *Country Life* 19 June 1637/1 Until the Dutchman Vermuyden came on the scene..to control ..the river Great Ouse..much of the region was a marshy no-man's-land through which..the only means of transport was by boat.

c. *fig.*

1870 H. A. Nicholson *Man. Zool.* I. 6 Some observers have established an intermediate kingdom, a sort of no-man's-land, for the reception of those debatable organisms. **1888** H. A. Strong tr. *Paul's Princ. Hist. Lang.* ii. 28 This 'no man's land' forms a boundary wall through which the influences cannot pass from one side to the other. **1892** [in Dict., sense 2 a]. **1954** M. Beresford *Lost Villages* v. 166 The crucial years lie half in a no-man's-land of English historical research. **1959** *Wall St. Jrnl.* 9 Nov. 16/4 One aim of the new law was to abolish the so-called 'no-man's-land' between Federal and state authority in labor cases. **1973** *Archivum Linguisticum* IV. 51 This is indeed a No Man's Land, virgin territory one might say. **1974** 'H. Carmichael' *Motive* iv. 53 One question chased another..questions that got lost in a no-man's-land of conjecture. **1974** *Kingston* (Ontario) *Whig-Standard* 11 Jan. 7/1 Dossers are..men and women squeezed into a no-man's-land by an increasingly affluent society.

d. *Mil.* The terrain between the front lines of armies entrenched opposite one another.

1908 *Blackw. Mag.* Dec. 761 Here and there in that wilderness of dead bodies—the dreadful 'No-Man's-Land' between the opposing lines—deserted guns showed up singly or in groups. **1915** G. Adam *Behind Scenes at Front* 101 Perilous work it is repairing wire in the No Man's Land between trenches. **1936** M. Plowman *Faith called Pacifism* 97 The order I received..to go out across No-man's-land, and cut the throat of the nearest German lad on sentry. **1973** R. Hill *Ruling Passion* III. ii. 173 They were keeping steadily on neutral ground and she was finding it a pleasant experience. Like football in no-man's-land during a Great War Christmas.

e. *Lawn Tennis.* (See quot. 1931.)

1931 Doeg & Danzig *Elem. Lawn Tennis* 65 If you hesitate you are caught in what is known as 'No Man's Land', the territory between the service line and the baseline. **1969** *New Yorker* 14 June 68/3 Graebner, in no man's land, drives the ball far into Ashe's backhand corner.

no-mar (nō͞ᵘˌmāɹ), *attrib. phr.* [f. No *a.* + Mar *v.*] That is designed not to mar, spoil, etc.

1970 *Globe & Mail* (Toronto) 26 Sept. 52/4 (Advt.), Trays..of stain-resistant woodgrain, with raised frame and no-mar, plastic tipped feet. **1973** *Washington Post* 13 Jan. A. 19/1 (Advt.), Round extension table with..walnut bronze no-mar top table.

nomen (nō͞ᵘ·mĕn). [L.] **1.** *Taxonomy.* **nomen nudum** (niū̆·dŏ̆m) [L., naked name], a Latin name which has no standing because it was introduced without publication of the full description demanded by the rules governing botanical and zoological nomenclature. Also occasionally used for a popular name that cannot be attached to a definite species (see quot. 1957).

1906 *Verhandl. Int. Bot. Kongr. Wien 1905* VIII. 205 A genus or any other group of higher rank than a species, named or announced without being characterised conformably to article 37 cannot be regarded as effectively published (*nomen nudum*). **1925** A. S. Hitchcock *Methods of Descriptive Systematic Bot.* xii. 114 A new name appearing without description is called a *nomen nudum.* **1957** *N. & Q.* Feb. 83/2 Since, however, no such variety has been described or bred, Chub-eel (× *Aminguilla*) remains a *nomen nudum.* **1963** Davies & Heywood *Princ. Angiosperm Taxonomy* viii. 290 It is permissible..to use a name for a new species that already exists as a *nomen nudum*—i.e. has never been validated by a description and therefore has no standing under the Rules [of botanical nomenclature]. **1969** E. Mayr *Princ. Systematic Zool.* xiii. 347 A name published without satisfying the conditions of availability is generally called a *nomen nudum*... A *nomen nudum* has no standing in zoological nomenclature and is best never recorded, not even in synonymy.

2. *Philol.* In phrases: **nomen actionis** (æktiō͞ᵘ·nis), a noun of action; **nomen agentis** (age·ntis), an agent noun.

1928 C. Bergener *Contrib. to Study of Conversion of Adjs. into Nouns* ii. 18 When a nomen agentis is contrasted with an absolute past participle of the corresponding verb (as in Galsw., Flower I, ch. vi: *the tortured does not salute her torturers*). **1930** T. Sasaki *On Lang. Bridges' Poetry* III. ii. 80 The use of the gerund and the noun of action (nomen actionis)..have in common certain grammatical functions. **1932** A. Gardiner *Theory of Speech & Lang.* iii. 107 In all these languages..the equivalent of 'speech' is a *nomen actionis* for the activity of which the most evident symptoms are articulation and audibility. **1963** F. T. Visser *Hist. Syntax Eng. Lang.* I. iv. 357 With a plural subject the ending *-end* of the nomina agentis appeared as *-ende.* **1966** *English Studies* XLVII. 53 This is an old trait in Germanic where the pres. participles had the character and regimen of nomina agentis. **1970** *Archivum Linguisticum* I. 9 One other class of words seems to have had fluctuating secondary stress: these are the nomina agentium in *-ari, eri, -iri.*

nomenclatorial, *a.* Delete *rare*⁻¹ and add further examples.

1897 *Nature* 19 Aug. 364/1 To distinguish those [references] that relate to habits and biology from those that are systematic and nomenclatorial. **1935** *Jrnl. Heredity* XXVI. 461/1 It has been..a continuing nomenclatorial tragedy that parents..label helpless infants..with the cognomen of the political (or other) hero popular at the moment of birth. **1946** F. E. Zeuner *Dating the Past* viii. 271 This [*sc.* a difference in dating Chinese geological formations] appears to be due to nomenclatorial rather than factual differences. **1953** *Parasitology* XLII. 260/2, I wish also to make reference to another nomenclatorial problem. **1970** *Nature* 5 Sept. 1065/2 Fortunately, the informational content of volume eight of *Primates* is in no way affected by these nomenclatorial niceties.

nomenclatural, *a.* (Later examples.)

1937 N. N. Puckett in A. Dundes *Mother Wit* (1973) 167/1 The enticement may have been the ceremony [of baptism] rather than a delusion of nomenclatural grandeur. **1939** [see *homotype 1]. **1951** G. H. M. Lawrence *Taxon. Vascular Plants* ix. 196 In many countries the nomenclatural patterns and practices were set by botanists of considerable prestige. **1961** G. G. Simpson *Princ. Animal Taxon.* i. 29 Personal preferences and emphases also frequently affect rearrangements of supraspecific taxa..although this is not an important cause of nomenclatural change. **1972** *Nature* 24 Nov. 239/1 The difference between them is more apparent than real and stems from nomenclatural rather than biological considerations. **1974** *Ibid.* 1 Nov. 85/3 He has kindly and lucidly drawn attention to the intricacies of the correct nomenclatural procedures to be used.

Hence **nomenclatu·rally** *adv.*

1944 S. A. Cain *Found. Plant Geogr.* xxx. 473 The first described form in a group is the species and the later forms are varieties, nomenclaturally. **1967** R. E. Blackwelder *Taxonomy* xx. 423 Nomenclaturally it [*sc.* the type specimen] serves as an anchor for the name.

nomic, *a.*² Add: **2.** *Philos.* and *Math.* That pertains to or is concerned with a discoverable scientific or logical law. Hence **no·mically** *adv.*

1892 K. Pearson *Gram. of Sci.* iii. 114, I shall, for convenience, however, speak of natural law in the old sense, or, as a mere routine of perceptions, as law in the *nomic* sense. Law in the nomic sense is thus no product of the reason, but a pure *order* of perceptions. **1905** *Nature* 30 Mar. 517/2 The correlation..is..of nomic heteroscedasticity. **1921** W. E. Johnson *Logic* I. iv. 61, I should propose that *nomic* (from νόμος, a law) should be substituted for necessary as contrasted with contingent. Thus a nomic proposition is one that expresses a pure law of nature. *Ibid.*, The nomically possible. **1959** K. R. Popper *Logic of Sci. Discovery* 434 A 'necessary conditional' or a 'nomic conditional'. **1961** E. Nagel *Structure of Sci.* iv. 51 The distinction between accidental and nomic universality can be brought out in another way. **1973** N. Rescher *Conceptual Idealism* iv. 59 This nomological necessity of laws is generally called 'nomic necessity'.

nominal, *a.* and *sb.* Add: **A.** *adj.* **1. a.** (Further examples.) (See also quots.)

1924 O. Jespersen *Philos. of Gram.* ix. 120 Here we first encounter the so-called nominal sentences, containing a subject and a predicative, which may be either a substantive or an adjective. **1928** H. Poutsma *Gram. Late Mod. English* (ed. 2) I. i. 2 Predicates are of two kinds, viz.: (*a*) verbal predicates..; (*b*) nominal predicates, i.e. such as are made up of a copula or link-verb and a nominal. **1929** *Ibid.* x. 557 *And* is used to..bring about a junction of a sentence with an undeveloped nominal- or infinitive-clause. **1939** L. H. Gray *Foundations of Lang.* 230 There is only one case in which the sentence does not require a verb, i.e., the nominal sentence of the type of the Latin *omnia praeclara rara* 'all splendid things (are) rare'... Contrary to popular opinion, the nominal sentence does not omit the copula, and none is to be supplied. **1949** *Archivum Linguisticum* I. 183 The hybrid nature—nominal–verbal—of the participle. **1954** Pei &

GAYNOR *Dict. Ling.* 147 *Nominal sentence,* a sentence in which the principal part..is a noun or nominal form. **1973** *Archivum Linguisticum* IV. 3 Some verbal forms occur as nominal modifiers, others not.

5. d. (Earlier and later examples.)

1869 *Bradshaw's Railway Manual* XXI. 369 The nominal capital now consists of 92,000 original shares of 5*l* each; 38,000 preference shares of 4*l* each: and 32,000 obligations of 4*l* each. **1964** *Lebende Sprachen* IX. 98/2 The amount of capital stated in the memorandum of association which a joint-stock company may issue is called *nominal* or *authorized capital.*

6. (See quot. 1970^{2}.)

1966 *Aviation Week & Space Technology* 5 Dec. 30/1 The mission is to launch the 800-lb. Prime vehicle to effect a nominal re-entry at 400,000 ft. following injection at 26,000 fps. **1970** N. ARMSTRONG et al. *First on Moon* vi. 124 An example of misuse is our use of the word 'nominal', which most of the English-speaking world interprets as meaning small, minimal—and we usually use it in the sense of being average or normal. **1970** R. TURNILL *Lang. Space* 94 *Nominal,* a favourite word, meaning within prescribed limits; anything from 'perfect' to acceptable. **1972** *Daily Colonist* (Victoria, B.C.) 26 July 3/1 As one engineer said, 'She is phenomenally nominal'—nominal being space jargon for operating-as-planned.

B. *sb.* **5.** *Gram.* (See quot. 1972.)

1928 H. POUTSMA *Gram. Late Mod. Eng.* (ed. 2) I. i. 2 A nominal (a noun or adjective) or a nominal equivalent (i.e. a word or word-group doing duty as a nominal). **1935** H. STRAUMANN *Newspaper Headlines* 49 Words of these formal characteristics will be called nominals. **1961** *Amer. Speech* XXXVI. 159 It is customary to describe the English nominal as consisting of a sequence of constituents: predeterminers, determiners, adjectives, the noun head, and finally certain postnominal modifiers, such as relative clauses. **1968** J. LYONS *Introd. Theoretical Linguistics* 347 Let us..draw a distinction between what we will call *first-order* and *second-order* nominals in English, and say that only second-order nominals may occur in sentences whose underlying structure is Nominal + Time. **1972** HARTMANN & STORK *Dict. Lang. & Ling.* 151/2 *Nominal,* a name given..to a word which functions as a..noun, but does not have all the formal characteristics of a noun (i.e. in English the distinction between singular and plural and between common and possessive cases). **1974** *Nature* 25 Oct. 705/1 One could defend the thesis that sentences are remembered by forming an associative structure linking representations of their nouns and verbs by arguing that the associative machinery deals with nominals derived from verbs in a very similar way to verbs themselves.

nominalist. Add: Also as *adj.*

1965 *Listener* 9 Dec. 942/1 How much more nominalist, in a way, the whole society is.

nominalistic, *a.* Add: (Later example.) Hence **nominali·stically** *adv.*

1932 C. C. J. WEBB *John of Salisbury* 154 In philosophy he favoured the views of the Nominalistic school. **1939** *Mind* XLVIII. 246 To save himself he would have to read 'satisfaction' nominalistically.

nominalize, *v.* Delete † $Obs.\ rare^{-1}$ and add later examples. Hence **nominali·zable** *a.*; **nominaliza·tion**; **no·minalized** *ppl. a.*; **no·minalizer**; **no·minalizing** *ppl. a.*

1951 Z. S. HARRIS *Methods in Structural Linguistics* xvi. 277 There is no noun class in Hidatsa, only a stem class (neither noun nor verb), a class of nominalizing suffixes, and a class of verbalizing suffixes. **1955** T. BURROW *Sanskrit Lang.* iv. 125 Such transference is common in nominalised adjectives throughout the system. **1960** R. B. LEES in *Internat. Jrnl. Amer. Linguistics* XXVI. (*title*) The grammar of English nominalizations. **1965** N. CHOMSKY *Aspects of Theory of Syntax* ii. 87 Nominalizable adjectives. **1965** *Canad. Jrnl. Linguistics* X. 117 The nominalizer *-ma* is attached directly to the future durative suffixes. *Ibid.* 160 These articles are obligatory with every noun or nominalization appearing as subject or object of a verb. **1967** Z. VENDLER *Linguistics in Philos.* v. 124 In technical terms, we will end up with a list of nominalized sentences. **1968** J. LYONS *Introd. Theoretical Linguistics* 265 The constituent-string is transformed ('nominalized') into an N[oun] P[hrase] of the form A[djective] + N[oun]. **1972** A. MAKKAI *Idiom Structure* 140 *The king stepped down,* nominalizable as **the downstepping of the king.* **1972** *Science* 23 June 1306/2 When a surgeon uses a phrase such as the [*sic*] 'the bleeding of the vessels', the only admissible origin for the nominalization 'bleeding' would be 'the vessels bled' and not 'someone (that is, the surgeon) bled the vessels'. **1972** J. W. BRESNAN in *Language* XLVIII. 334 It must be noted that *-ation* is not an isolated case...Many other nominalizing affixes affect internal stress: contínue, continúity; oppóse, opposítion; [etc.]. **1974** H. ESAU (*title*) Nominalization and complementation in modern German.

nominate, *ppl. a.* Add: **1. d.** *Taxonomy.* (See quot. 1967.)

1948 A. L. RAND *Mammals Eastern Rockies* 100 The Alberta form is the nominate subspecies [of badger]: *Taxidea taxus taxus* Schreber. **1967** R. E. BLACKWELDER *Taxonomy* xix. 398 A nominate taxon is the subordinate taxon which contains the type of the subdivided 'higher' taxon. **1968** PERRING & SELL *Critical Suppl. Atlas Brit. Flora* 146 The question of the use of the nominate subspecies in this case [sc. *Eleocharis palustris*] is complex and disputed. **1971** *Nature* 10 Dec. 360/1 The European stock [of the Atlantic salmon], binomially named by Linnaeus, must become the nominate subspecies and, therefore, should bear the name *Salmo salar salar* Linnaeus. **1974** *New Phytologist* LXXIII. 802 The presence of the nominate subspecies in some cases..and not in others..is not explained.

nominate, *v.* Add: **5.** In horse breeding, to choose (a mare) as suitable for mating *to* a particular stallion.

1950 H. WYNMALEN *Horse Breeding* vi. 109 The considerations set out in the preceding chapter will be found helpful in selecting a suitable stallion to which to nominate our mare. **1972** *Harper's Bazaar* Apr. 63/1 [The mare] gave the stallion she was nominated to such a hell of a time he wouldn't touch her with a barge-pole.

nomination. Add: **6.** In horse breeding, the planned mating of a particular mare and a particular stallion.

1912 *Bloodstock Breeders' Rev.* I. 169/2 (*heading*) Free nominations for mares. *Ibid.*, The Board, in 1911, allotted for award by County Committees 777 nominations for the free service of mares by the King's Premium stallions. **1927** J. E. PLATT *Thoroughbred Race-Horse* iv. 29 It is necessary to book nominations for two, three, or even four years ahead. **1950** H. WYNMALEN *Horse Breeding* vi. 110 If the horse is of a type and character that pleases you.. you are not likely to go wrong in fixing upon your nomination. **1969** G. E. EVANS *Farm & Village* x. 118 They gave them assisted nominations to encourage horse-breeding. **1974** *Country Life* 14 Mar. 584/1 The highest price was given for a nomination to the American horse, Never Bend.

nominative. Add: **B.** *sb.* **3.** *nominative absolute.*

1858 C. P. MASON *Eng. Gram.* 97 This adverbial relation may be sustained... By a substantive (accompanied by some attributive adjunct) in the nominative absolute; as '*The sun having risen,* we commenced our journey'. **1916** E. A. SONNENSCHEIN *New Eng. Gram.* III. 44 The nominative absolute construction is an equivalent of an adverb-clause: *We sitting,* as I said, the cock crew loud. **1949** BAILEY & HORN *Eng. Handbk.* vii. 266 Begin some sentences with a nominative absolute... Dr. Carver having proved his point, sweet potatoes and peanuts were planted in abundance. **1963** PENCE & EMERY *Gram. Present-Day Eng.* ii. 62 The nominative absolute is a perfectly proper construction as far as grammar is concerned... Although a nominative absolute has no *grammatical* function in the statement in which it appears, it should have a logical function. **1972** HARTMANN & STORK *Dict. Lang. & Linguistics* 152/2 *Nominative absolute,* absolute construction.

‖ **nominativus pendens** (nǫ:minătəi·vɒ̆s pe·ndenz). [L.] (See quot. 1926.)

1867 WHARTON *Law-Lexicon* (ed. 4) 647/2 *Nominativus pendens,* a nominative case grammatically unconnected with the rest of the sentence in which it stands. **1926** FOWLER *Mod. Eng. Usage* 611/2 *Nominativus pendens..*, 'hanging nominative'. A form of anacoluthon in which a sentence is begun with what appears to be the subject, but before the verb is reached something else is substituted in word or in thought, & the supposed subject is left in the air. **1929** C. MACKENZIE *Gallipoli Memories* viii. 124 And I would have turned a gerund into a participle here and there..and probably there would be a vile *nominativus pendens.* **1929** BLUNDEN *Near & Far* 12 While the pallid herd Of Grecians limit their pedantic gaze To some prodigious *nominativus pendens.* **1963** F. T. VISSER *Hist. Syntax Eng. Lang.* I. I. i. 61 This subject is sometimes called 'nominativus pendens' or 'dangling subject'.

‖ **nominatum** (nǫmineⁱ·tɒ̆m). [L., neut. of *nōminātus*, pa. pple. of *nōmināre* NOMINATE *v.*] 'The thing that is named by a sign, word, or linguistic expression' (Webster, 1961).

1947 R. CARNAP *Meaning & Necessity* iii. 96 The customary method of meaning analysis regards an expression as a *name* for a (concrete or abstract) entity, which we call its *nominatum.* **1949** H. FEIGL tr. G. Frege in Feigl & Sellars *Readings in Philos. Analysis* 89 A proper name (word, sign, sign-compound, expression) expresses its sense, and designates or signifies its nominatum. We let a *sign express* its sense and *designate* its nominatum. **1962** W. & M. KNEALE *Devel. of Logic* viii. 496 'Nominatum' is too obviously artificial. **1966** S. CECCATO in *Automatic Transl. of Lang.* (NATO Summer School, Venice 1962) 77 However, since thought is always constituted by correlations made up of correlata in a given order, it is clear that the second example requires a repetition of the nominatum of 'water' which is not required in the first example.

no-mind: see *NO *a.* 5 e.

nominee. Add: **4.** One in whose name, though he is not the owner, a stock or registered bond certificate is registered. Also *attrib.*

1869 *Bradshaw's Railway Manual* XXI. 157 The directors..be authorised to offer such new shares to the holders of ordinary stock..or to the nominees of such holders. **1930** *Economist* 22 Mar. 634/2 Again, many securities registered in the names of British banks or even individuals, as nominees, are really the property of foreigners. *Ibid.* 15 Nov. 896/1 Our own figures for 1929 are on the low side owing to the growth of nominee holdings in recent years. **1960** *Times* 24 Oct. (Financial Review) p. xvii/4 The nominee companies endeavour to facilitate the handling and supervision of portfolio investment. **1964** *Financial Times* 12 Mar. 19/5 Nominee..is a holder who, as respects the exercise of any rights in respect of a security, is not entitled to exercise those rights except in accordance with instructions given by the owner. **1975** *Guardian* 24 Feb. 20/7 Mr Marcus Lipton, the Labour MP for Lambeth Central will, however, ask the Government this week to outlaw nominee shareholding.

‖ **nominis umbra** (nǫ·minis ɒ·mbră), *phr.* [L. (Lucan I. 135)] The shadow or appearance of a name; a name without substance.

1856 BAGEHOT in *National Rev.* Apr. 363 Taylor's theorem will go down to posterity,..but what does posterity know of the deceased Taylor? *Nominis umbra* is rather a compliment; for it is not substantial enough to have a shadow. *c* **1874** W. JAMES in R. B. Perry *Tht. & Char. W. James* (1935) I. xxxi. 525 The British school say that the laws are nil—*nominis umbra.* **1896** [see *BOOKFUL *a.* 2]. **1959** JOWITT *Dict. English Law* II. 1230/2 *Nominis umbra,* the shadow of a name, *e.g.*, a one-man company.

nomism (nōᵘ·miz'm). [f. Gr. νόμ-ος law + -ISM.] (See quots.)

1905 *Jewish Encycl.* IX. 326/1 *Nomism,* that religious tendency which aims at the control of both social and individual life by legalism, making the law the supreme norm. **1917** *Encycl. Relig. & Ethics* IX. 380/1 'Nomism' or 'legalism' is the name given to the view that moral conduct consists in the observance of a law or body of laws.

nomisma (nōᵘmi·zmă). Pl. **nomismata.** [ad. Gr. νόμισμα money, f. νομίζ-ειν to use customarily, f. νόμος usage, custom.] = BEZANT I.

1908 W. WROTH *Catal. Imperial Byzantine Coins Brit. Mus.* p. lxxiv, Under Alexius I, the nomisma..was issued in several different metals simultaneously. **1957** *Encycl. Brit.* XV. 699/1 The principal coin, the *nomisma,* popularly called bezant, was derived from the Roman gold solidus. **1959** E. POUND *Thrones* xcvii. 24 Vasa Klipped for the people, Lycurgus, nomisma, And 'limitation is the essence of good nomisma'. **1960** H. HAYWARD *Antique Coll.* 200/1 *Nomisma,* the gold coin of the later Byzantine Empire. Usually scyphate in form with types of the Emperor, Christ, the Virgin and saints.

nomogram (nǫ·mŏgræm). [ad. F. *nomogramme,* f. Gr. νομο- NOMO- + F. *-gramme* -GRAM.] A diagram representing a relationship between three or more variables in the form of a number of (straight or curved) scales, so arranged that the value of one variable corresponding to given values of the others can be read off by means of one or more straight lines drawn to intersect the scales at the appropriate values.

1909 in *Cent. Dict.* Suppl. [with Fr. reference]. **1910** R. K. HEZLET in *Jrnl. R. Artillery* XXXVI. 460 Fig. 5 shows..the 'nomogram' constructed for the formula on this plan. [*Note*] Coining an equivalent to the French 'nomogramme'. **1918** *Inst. Automobile Engin. Proc.* XII. 191 When..this 'intersection' diagram is changed to a 'nomogram' or 'alinement' diagram, all these difficulties disappear and the reading is rendered much more accurate. **1920** *Chem. Abstr.* XIV. 2440 (*heading*) Nomograms for the functions $\log p = -(Q_0/4{\cdot}57T) + 1{\cdot}75 \log T + C$ and $\log P = -(Q_0/4{\cdot}57T) + 1{\cdot}75 \log T - aT + 3{\cdot}3$. **1938** *Jrnl. R. Aeronaut. Soc.* XLII. 8 Nomograms for picking the best airscrew diameter. **1947** *Electronic Engin.* XIX. 100 Line drawings, tables, charts and nomograms are liberally used. **1957** G. E. HUTCHINSON *Treat. Limnol.* I. ix. 582 (*caption*) Nomogram for determining O_2 saturation at different temperatures and altitudes. **1965** A. S. LEVENS *Graphical Methods Res.* II. 39 There are two general types of nomograms: one recognized as a Cartesian coordinate chart (or concurrency chart) and the other as an alignment chart.

nomograph (nǫ·mŏgrɑf). [f. NOMO- + -GRAPH.] = prec.

1909 in *Cent. Dict.* Suppl. **1921** *Chem. Abstr.* XV. 3233 The methods of calcg. and plotting nomographs are explained. **1939** *Nature* 4 Mar. 371/2 In the third chart a third series of horizontal and vertical lines leading to a final nomograph either confirms the horizontal shear strength as adequate or shows the correction required. **1965** A. S. LEVENS *Graphical Methods Res.* II. 81 The nomographs provide a means for the rapid evaluation of the relative merit of various materials for the design of ablating shields on re-entering vehicles. **1975** G. J. KING *Audio Handbk.* ii. 30 The intrinsic noise of the power amplifier is always fed to the loudspeaker, and the attenuated preamplifier noise adds in vector sum (see the nomograph in Fig. 1.5).

nomography (nŏmǫ·grăfi). [ad. F. *nomographie* (M. d'Ocagne *Nomographie. Les calculs usuels effectués au moyen des abaques,* etc. (1891)), f. Gr. νομο- NOMO- + F. *-graphie* -GRAPHY.] The technique of using or devising nomograms.

1909 in *Cent. Dict.* Suppl. [with Fr. reference]. **1913** R. K. HEZLET (*title*) Nomography. **1918** *Inst. Automobile Engin. Proc.* XII. 187 Nomography can be an aid to efficiency in the drawing office and factory. **1951** *Engineering* 3 Aug. 160/1 Although nomography is by no means a new branch of mathematics, the use of nomograms seems never to have become widespread. **1965** [see NOMOGRAPHIC *a.* below].

Hence **nomo·grapher,** one who employs nomography; **nomogra·phic** *a.*, involving or being a nomogram; **nomogra·phically** *adv.*, by means of a nomogram.

1915, 1918 Nomographic [see *ALIGNMENT 6]. **1947** DOUGLASS & ADAMS *Elem. Nomography* p. v, This book

uses the term 'nomographic chart' in the popular sense to refer to alignment diagrams. *Ibid.* p. vii, However, the successful rule-of-thumb or short-cut nomographer is not to be criticized for his approach. **1965** W. H. BURROWS *Graphical Techniques for Engin. Computations* p. ix, A modification of existing theory..pointed the way towards the development of a new theory of nomographic representation, the hyperbolic coordinate method from which have grown generalizations and extensions covering the entire field of nomography. **1965** A. S. LEVENS *Graphical Methods Res.* II. 81 The amount of material given up during ablation..can be determined nomographically for heat input rates from 100 to 5,000 Btu/ft.²-sec.

‖ **nomoli** (nǫ·moli). Also **nomori, numori.** [Mende.] (See quots.)

1910 T. J. ALLDRIDGE *Transformed Colony* xxix. facing p. 286 (*caption*) Numori... Steatite figures found in caves and supposed to be of very great antiquity. **1925** T. N. GODDARD *Handbk. Sierra Leone* III. iii. 56 Another superstition of much interest is that associated with the steatite stone figures known locally as 'Nomori'... A Nomori is venerated for its supernatural powers and the good luck it is supposed to bring. **1926** F. W. H. MIGEOD *View Sierra Leone* xiv. 180 Owing to the demand of Europeans for steatite images which, of unknown origin, have frequently been dug up in various parts of Mende country, the manufacture of them has begun again... Their name in Mende is Nomoli. **1951** K. L. LITTLE *Mende of Sierra Leone* xi. 223 The steatite *nomoli* which the farmer turns up when he is hoeing in old bush are looked upon as the genii's handiwork and can be used to make the rice prosper. **1954** R. LEWIS *Sierra Leone* xvii. 161 Small soapstone figures of men and animals called Nomoli, which are found only in Sierra Leone, are not the artistic productions of any existing tribe, though they are greatly valued as bringers of good luck and fertility; at the time of planting rice they are whipped to make them 'work'. They are, apparently, the handiwork of an earlier bush culture and are found in the gravel of rivers or in the bush. They have, however, been convincingly counterfeited by Mende craftsmen for European collectors. **1961** *Times* 12 Aug. 10/5 Called 'Nomoli' by the Mende, these [figures] are credited with a supernatural origin.

nomological, *a.* (in Dict. s.v. NOMO-). Add: (Later examples.) Also as *sb.* Hence **nomolo·gically** *adv.*

1947 H. REICHENBACH *Elements of Symbolic Logic* viii. § 61. 360 We shall call these formulas *nomological formulas*. The term 'nomological'..is chosen to express the idea that the formulas are either laws of nature or logical laws... The term 'nomological' is therefore a generalization of the term 'tautological'. **1961** E. NAGEL *Structure of Sci.* iv. 51 Such use is characteristic of all nomological universals. *Ibid.* 53 They contend only that genuine nomologicals are logically necessary. **1967** *Philosophy* XLII. 134 My theory permits me nomologically to derive the statement. **1970** J. N. FINDLAY tr. *Husserl's Logical Investigations* I. xi. 230 One could say..that these sciences are *nomological*, in so far as their unifying principle, as well as their essential aim of research, is a law. **1973** *Jrnl. Genetic Psychol.* CXXIII. 11 The beginnings of a nomological network may have been laid in this experiment. **1973** [see *NOMIC *a.*²].

nomori, var. *NOMOLI.

nomos (nǫ·mǫs). *Theol.* [ad. Gr. νόμος usage, custom, law.] The law; a law of life.

1938 P. S. WATSON tr. *Nygren's Agape & Eros: Part 2* I. 35 The *Commandment* of love was easier to grasp, and it led back to the Old Testament level, so that Agape was again brought under the scheme of Nomos. **1948** J. L. ADAMS tr. *Tillich's Protestant Era* iv. 56 The words 'autonomy', 'heteronomy', and 'theonomy' answer the question of the *nomos* or the law of life in three different ways. **1954** *Scottish Jrnl. Theol.* VII. 260 The Church follows Christ as justified, reconciled, and risen with Him, and is therefore differently related to the *nomos*-form of this age.

nomothetic, *a.* Delete *rare* and add: That pertains to or is concerned with the study or discovery of general (scientific) laws, esp. as contrasted with idiographic study.

[**1894:** see *idiographic* adj. s.v. *IDIO-.] **1904** *Jrnl. Philos., Psychol. & Sci. Methods* 21 Jan. 42 This is the same distinction as that made by Windelband under the names nomothetic and idiographic sciences. *a* **1943** R. G. COLLINGWOOD *Idea of Hist.* (1946) 166 Windelband..laid it down that history and science were two different things. ..There were two kinds of science..: nomothetic science, which is science in the common sense of the word, and idiographic science, which is history. **1948** *Brit. Jrnl. Psychol.* XXXVIII. 160 (*heading*) Nomothetic and idiographic [perspectives in psychology]... Two aims: the discovery of general laws of mind, or the description..of the unique undivided personality... Well-balanced psychologists ought to keep in mind both the nomothetic and idiographic aims. **1955** F. H. ALLPORT *Theories of Perception* xi. 263 Conditions that are truer to life than those in which the exact or 'nomothetic' laws of nature are sought. **1964** *Listener* 16 Apr. 617/2, I [*sc.* G. Freeland] have coined..the term 'nomothetic corrections'. This group of corrections is intimately tied up with scientific laws. **1970** *Daily Tel.* 19 Sept. 9/7 Is musicology—or rather *musikwissenschaft*, which means science of music—a nomothetic or an idiographic discipline? Ought it to emulate physics and concern itself with establishing generally applicable laws or must it, like history, describe what is unrepeatable?

non-, *prefix*. Add: The prefix has continued to be one of the great formative elements in English. The sections that follow contain a selection of the more frequently occurring formations during the last hundred years or so.

1. Prefixed to nouns of action, condition, or quality, as *non-achievement, -activity, -ambiguity, -aspiration, -candidacy, -class, -commitment, -communication, -commutativeness, -commutativity, -comparability, -comprehension, -conservation, -contemporaneity, -creativity, -deposition, -derivability, -disclosure, -discrimination, -employment, -equilibrium* (later examples; see also *4), *-equivalence, -finality, -happening, -implication, -inclusion, -independence, -influence, -invitation, -involvement, -occurrence, -pathogenicity, -planarity, -possession, -reality, -reception, -recognition* (earlier and later examples), *-recurrence, -simultaneity, -stationarity, -stoich(e)iometry, -support, -transitivity, -uniformity, -uniqueness, -universality, -validity* (later examples).

1934 WEBSTER, Nonachievement. **1946** *Nature* 17 Aug. 236/2 The residual carbon dioxide in the inhibited oxidation gases..is shown in the graph by the non-achievement of 100 per cent inhibition. **1847** W. SMITH tr. *Fichte's Characteristics Present Age* 6 Every one would accept the proof of *non-existence* at a particular time, as equivalent to the proof of *non-activity* at the same time. **1949** A. PAP *Elem. Analytical Philos.* iii. 74 How could we..insure non-ambiguity of a proper name? **1958** E. FISCHER-JØRGENSEN in Saporta & Bastian *Psycholinguistics* (1961) 140/1 The non-aspiration of final /t/ and the non-closure of final /d/ should be considered as part of the syllable boundary. **1968** *Gainesville* (Florida) *Sun* 16 Jan., All this randomly built superstructure of his non-candidacy could..come tumbling down. **1971** *New Yorker* 4 Dec. 47 In addition to repeatedly asserting his non-candidacy, [Senator Edward] Kennedy had made some forceful speeches in recent months. **1940** W. V. QUINE *Math. Logic* 123 The distinguishing feature of a non-class *y* is this: '$x \in y$' amounts, for every object *x*, to '$x = y$'. **1973** 'TREVANIAN' *Loo Sanction* (1974) 11 A dour young man.. flaunting his non-class by drinking beer. **1959** *Brno Studies in English* I. 133 This is not so much non-commitment..as withdrawal. **1962** W. NOWOTTNY *Lang. Poets Use* iv. 94 A tone of non-commitment is established. **1960** *News Chron.* 28 July 6/6 Critics talk a lot about the problem of non-communication amongst my characters. **1973** *N.Y. Times* 11 Aug., One is struck by the talent of the lawyers for non-communication. **1940** *Mind* XLIX. 459 It is not always the case that *ab* = *ba*. This non-commutativeness is quite essential to its use in physics. **1964** E. A. POWER *Introd. Quantum Electrodynamics* vi. 83 The order of the factors **p** and **A(q)** in the first term of (56) is immaterial despite the non-commutativity of $\mathbf{p}_\alpha$ and $\mathbf{q}_\alpha$ in the quantum theory. **1909** W. JAMES *Pluralistic Universe* 335 The only real relations in comparison are absolute identity and absolute non-comparability. **1973** *Computers & Humanities* VII. 158 A. A. Lyne..spoke on 'The Problem of Non-Comparability of Word-Frequency Counts'. **1910** *Daily Chron.* 3 Mar. 4/4 To non-comprehension of the true meaning of that golden rule..can be traced practically every defect of our system. **1962** *Times* 15 Feb. 15/2 Across a vast abyss of non-comprehension. **1941** *Physical Rev.* LIX. 441 A natural consequence of this nonconservation of spin angular momentum is a dependence of the scattering cross section upon the spin magnetic quantum number of the incident beam. **1968** M. S. LIVINGSTON *Particle Physics* vii. 146 As another example of nonconservation of parity in a weak interaction, it shows a correlation between spin and direction for the product photon. **1950** F. E. ZEUNER *Dating Past* (ed. 2) iv. 78 This evidence bears out what has been said on p. 54, that the land rose faster than the sea-level in the northern Baltic region, and that the non-contemporaneity of the maximum in different parts of the Baltic may be due to this fact. **1969** BENNISON & WRIGHT *Geol. Hist. Brit. Isles* i. 5 The noncontemporaneity of geological events..makes some scale of reference imperative. **1957** P. SUPPES *Introd. Logic* 154 Criterion of Non-creativity. **1965** B. MATES *Elem. Logic* xi. 190, ϕ will satisfy the criterion of non-creativity. **1843** MILL *Logic* I. III. ix. 499 The presence or absence of an uninterrupted communication with the sky causes the deposition or non-deposition of dew. **1969** BENNISON & WRIGHT *Geol. Hist. Brit. Isles* i. 8 The older strata may be tilted..during the period of non-deposition. **1957** A. N. PRIOR *Time & Modality* ii. 14 If we wish to express the non-derivability of *CMpp*. **1964** G. KREISEL in Benacerraf & Putnam *Philos. of Math.* 157 Hilbert emphasized the consistency problem which is so to speak the weakest non-derivability result. **1908** *Westm. Gaz.* 24 July 8/4 Defendants resisted the plaintiff's claim under the policy upon the grounds of the misstatement and non-disclosure. **1950** *Mind* LIX. 248 There is always a possibility..of non-disclosure or lies. **1923** *19th Cent.* Jan. 135 Shinto favours racial nondiscrimination. **1958** *Listener* 16 Jan. 88/1 To say that the Communists, who claim world brotherhood,..practise non-discrimination in the fullest sense on the racial side, [etc.]. **1843** MILL *Logic* II. v. iv. 398 It is not the nature of the faculties..but the non-employment of them. **1966** A. BATTERSBY *Math. in Management* iii. 74 The quick answer 'use machinery wherever possible because it is cheaper' is not necessarily the best when the non-employment of labour is unjustified on social or moral grounds. **1938** J. NEWTON *Introd. Metallurgy* vi. 162 The iron–carbon equilibrium diagram.. is the best diagram to illustrate the meaning of equilibrium and non-equilibrium. **1971** *Contrib. Mineral. & Petrol.* XXXII. 165 Some magnetites..that show a wide variation of Cr content also give very erratic oxygen isotopic results, suggesting non-equilibrium. **1894** J. N. KEYNES *Stud. & Exerc. Formal Logic* (ed. 3) II. iii. 111 To establish their non-equivalence we may proceed as follows. **1955** A. N. PRIOR *Formal Logic* 212 The connected non-equivalence of $\Pi xM\phi x$ and $M\Pi x\phi x$. **1896** W. CALDWELL *Schopenhauer's System* viii. 370 Religion alone pretends to answer the question, why it is that non-finality and non-attainment and illusoriness seem to characterise all human experience and all human life. **1971** D. CRYSTAL *Linguistics* 133 The..sentence ends with a rising movement.., giving the impression of non-finality. **1892** W. JAMES *Coll. Ess. & Rev.* (1920) 319 Our conscious states are temporal *events*,..the conditions of whose happening or non-happening from one moment to another, lie certainly in large part in the physical world. **1968** *Gainesville* (Florida) *Sun* 13 Feb., The [TV] medium's extraordinary ability to suggest that a true happening resides in a non-happening. **1878** H. MACCOLL in *Proc. London Math. Soc.* IX. 180 Thus in a non-implication, as in an implication, the rule is *Transpose and change signs.* **1887** J. N. KEYNES *Stud. & Exerc. Formal Logic* (ed. 2) II. ii. 77 The implication or non-implication of existence in propositions. **1932** LEWIS & LANGFORD *Symbolic Logic* ix. 281 Facts like these about non-implication and independence. **1972** M. A. BODEN *Purposive Explanation in Psychol.* viii. 318 The logical characteristics of indeterminacy,..and non-implication of embedded clauses. **1885** J. VEITCH *Institutes of Logic* § 383 *All* are thus excluded, through the non-inclusion of *any*. **1952** *Mind* LXI. 526 We interpret the non-inclusion of a conjunction as the exclusion of one *or* the other of the conjuncts. **1874** W. WALLACE tr. *Hegel's Logic* 293 A mean which combines in itself the centrality with the non-independence of the objects. **1965** HUGHES & LONDEY *Elem. Formal Logic* xviii. 131 (*heading*) PM (IV)—independence and non-independence. **1838** W. HOWITT *Rural Life of Eng.* I. I. v. 79 Those who ..believe in the nonsense of the economists on the non-influence of absenteeism. **1907** W. JAMES *Pragmatism* iv. 138 All these systems of influence or non-influence may be listed under the general problem of the world's *causal unity*. **1908** *Daily Chron.* 24 July 4/3 Invitations would be robbed of their grace, and non-invitations be invested quite unnecessarily with the air of a slight. **1940** *Economist* 11 May 853/1 Japan's policy, for all her declarations of 'non-involvement' (a new type of non-belligerency?) is bound to be that of fishing in troubled waters. **1970** *Guardian* 31 Dec. 7/8 A devastating..argument for non-involvement as a starting-point for social research. **1807** R. KIRWAN *Logick* I. 178 Their occurrence or non-occurrence being consonant to common observation. **1963** J. LYONS *Structural Semantics* i. 8 The non-occurrence of the large set of grammatical, but nonsensical, sentences. **1971** *Nature* 12 Mar. 97/8 It should..be possible to improve greatly the efficacy of live cholera vaccines by preparing them from bacteria in which non-pathogenicity has been induced by a very specific genetic mutation. **1967** A. BATTERSBY *Network Analysis* (ed. 2) xi. 177 There are, however, some minor ones [*sc.* obstacles], including integer restrictions and non-planarity. **1843** MILL *Logic* I. I. ii. 52 The non-possession of any given attribute is also an attribute, and may receive a name as such. **1959** D. COOKE *Lang. Mus.* ii. 69 The feeling is..of non-possession, non-acceptance, need. *a* **1866** J. GROTE *Treat. Moral Ideals* (1876) 360 We may assume four degrees of reality or non-reality in the moral ideals. **1909** W. JAMES *Pluralistic Universe* iv. 234 Zeno..has no alternative but to say that our intellect repudiates motion as a non-reality. **1924** W. E. JOHNSON *Logic* III. i. 7 A verbal formula that..gives the true test of non-reality. **1878** TROLLOPE *Is he Popenjoy?* II. ii. 20 Mr. Holdenough had made no attempt after the reception—or rather non-reception—awarded to his wife. **1963** *Times Lit. Suppl.* 1 Mar. 152/4 His [*sc.* Chopin's] reception—or non-reception—by the English. **1838** J. S. MILL in *London & Westm. Rev.* Aug. 484 His non-recognition of them does not put them out of existence. **1862** BAGEHOT *Coll. Works* (1965) II. 257 Its non-recognition by what is called the public. **1946** *Nature* 9 Nov. 679/1 A further factor which stems progressive action is the non-recognition of the educational potentialities of museums. **1965** A. J. P. TAYLOR *Eng. Hist. 1914–45* x. 373 In February 1932 Stimson, the American secretary of state, announced that the United States would not recognize territorial changes brought about by force... 'Non-recognition' became a League [of Nations] principle. **1847** A. DE MORGAN *Formal Logic* xiii. 278 The demand for non-recurrence of words arises from the public (I beg its pardon) not knowing how to read. **1911** J. WARD *Realm of Ends* xv. 335 In place of the existing certainty of evil, there will be an even chance of its non-recurrence. **1855** H. SPENCER *Princ. Psychol.* II. v. 121 The simultaneity or non-simultaneity of certain events. **1904** *Mind* XIII. 214 The non-simultaneity of perception and object, where internal perception is concerned, need cause no difficulty. **1953** C. E. BAZELL *Linguistic Form* 44 Non-simultaneity has different degrees of validity. **1965** *Math. in Biol. & Med.* (Med. Res. Council) IV. 158 Non-stationarity of the EEG signals during each of the 10-second epochs does not pose the same limitations. **1974** *Jrnl. of Business* (Chicago) XLVII. 518 (*heading*) Investigations of nonstationarity in prices. **1962** SIMPSON & RICHARDS *Physical Princ. Junction Transistors* iii. 35 In the latter materials any unbalance (non-stoichiometry) between constituents degrades physical properties such as mobility and lifetime to a marked extent. **1909** *Daily Chron.* 20 Jan. 6/2 The Englishwoman makes a charge of non-support against her husband. **1939** *Mind* XLVIII. 532 Obviously true of non-transitivity since that is 'ambiguous' with respect to transitivity or intransitivity. **1974** *Sci. Amer.* Oct. 120/2 If the nontransitivity is so counter-intuitive as to boggle the mind, we have what is called a nontransitive paradox. **1902** *Encycl. Brit.* XXVIII. 456/2 Non-uniformity of convergence of the series does not necessarily imply discontinuity in the sum. **1962** SIMPSON & RICHARDS *Physical Princ. Junction Transistors* vi. 116 For high-power transistors, other factors such as the non-uniformity of current distribution across the base region may become important. **1957** J. D. O'CONNOR in Saporta & Bastian *Psycholinguistics* (1961) 102/1 The acceptance of the nonuniqueness of phonemic solutions. **1974** *Physics Bull.* Dec. 587/3 Questions of nonuniqueness and stability in nonlinear continuum mechanics. **1846** J. D. MORELL *Hist. View Philos.* I. ii. 102 He attempts to prove their non-universality. **1893** W. MINTO *Logic* 70 The expression of Quantity, that is, of Universality or non-universality, is all-important. **1952** W. V. QUINE *Methods of Logic* § 9. 50 Interchange of equivalents.. preserves consistency, nonvalidity, nonimplication, and

nonequivalence. **1964** P. F. ANSON *Bishops at Large* viii. 271 The validity or non-validity of Anglican orders.

2. Prefixed to agent-nouns and designations of persons and objects, as *non-actor, -addict, -body, -breeder, -candidate, -Christian, -clitic, -cognitivist, -dancer, -drinker, -driver, -electrolyte, -fact, -friend, -Jew, -joiner, -linguist, -motorist, -musician, -owner, -participant, -people, -philosopher, -reader, -scientist, -self, -sentence, -slaveholder, -socialist, -speaker, -structuralist, -swimmer, -theist, -theorem, -visualizer, -writer*; **non-secre·tor**, a person whose saliva and other secretions do not contain his blood-group antigens.

1937 *Times* 17 Aug. 8/3 The air of reality, the judicious use of non-actors, the social consciousness of the Russian film. **1955** *Publ. Amer. Dial. Soc.* XXIV. 34 The natural revulsion which nonaddicts feel toward addicts. **1933** DYLAN THOMAS *Lett.* (1966) 72 The life of the non-body.. is capable..of creating an artistic progeny. **1949** G. RYLE *Concept of Mind* vi. 189 Perhaps it is because of the absurdity of such collocations that so many people have felt driven to describe a person as an association between a body and a non-body. **1944** J. S. HUXLEY *On Living in Revolution* ix. 99 About 17,000 breeding pairs: with the non-breeders, about 40,000. **1950** *Chem. Engin. Progress* XLVI. 112/1 The nonbreeders are pointed essentially toward power production. **1967** *Time* 22 Sept. 22 (*heading*) The non-candidates. **1972** *Daily Colonist* (Victoria, B.C.) 12 Jan. 16/5 Miami—Sen. Edward Kennedy, a steadfast noncandidate, was one of a dozen Democrats whose names have been entered in the..primary. **1671** A. WOODHEAD *Consid. Council of Trent* xv. 240 Nor may such separation be understood from Infidels, Heathens, or non-Christians only. **1941** W. TEMPLE *Citizen & Churchman* iv. 68 Children grow up in it who are schoolfellows of non-Christians. **1949** Nonclitic [see *ADDITIVE *sb.*]. **1952** *Mind* LXI. 546 The non-cognitivists are usually regarded as a relatively homogeneous group. **1963** R. CARNAP in P. A. Schilpp *Philos. R. Carnap* 1008 Both cognitivists and non-cognitivists agree that beliefs play a very important role in the origin of attitudes and decisions. **1965** Noncognitivist [see *IMPERATIVISM]. **1863** TROLLOPE *Rachel Ray* I. vii. 136 Now the room was partially cleared, the non-dancers being pressed back. **1929** L. BETTANY in W. J. Temple *Diaries* p. lxxiv, Bored as a Whig, as a non-drinker, as a scholar, and as an opponent of blood sports, by the only society he could generally enter. **1975** E. MOSBACHER tr. *Herlin's Commemorations* 4 A tall, thin, fair man.., a non-smoker and non-drinker. **1953** *Essays in Criticism* III. 422 The customary impression of the non-driver, that handling a car by night involves merely the switching on of headlights, and the turning of a wheel. **1891** *Jrnl. Chem. Soc.* LX. II. 971 (*heading*) Freezing points of dilute aqueous solutions of non-electrolytes. **1964** N. G. CLARK *Mod. Org. Chem.* i. 4 With salts very much in mind, he probably associates inorganic chemistry with electrolytes... However,..this branch of chemistry embraces..many compounds which neither dissolve in water nor produce ions, i.e. typical non-electrolytes. **1926** FOWLER *Mod. Eng. Usage* 576/1 Utopia, the realm of non-fact or the imaginary. **1964** *Listener* 9 Jan. 48/2 Our opinions..should not be based on non-facts, or dubious facts. **1971** *Harper's Mag.* Sept. 57 'There are people here who are not our friends.' The nonfriends were expelled. **1973** *Jrnl. Genetic Psychol.* CXXIII. 70 Cliques of friends and nonfriends. **1967** W. Q. DE FUNIAK *American-British Dict.* 115 *Non-Jew*, Gentile. **1973** R. PERRY *Nowhere Man* 6 For a non-Jew to have risen so high [in Israel] was testimony enough to his ability. **1964** R. MILIBAND in I. L. Horowitz *New Sociology* 78 Mills was a determined non-joiner, with an intense dislike of togetherness. **1974** *Listener* 14 Feb. 210/2 It was an efficient way of getting people into a group, turning non-joiners into joiners. **1936** *Language* XII. 93 Non-linguists..constantly forget that a speaker is making noise, and credit him, instead, with the possession of impalpable 'ideas'. **1965** *English Studies* Feb. 58 A terminology as simple and as familiar to the non-linguist as possible. **1908** *Westm. Gaz.* 31 Dec. 4/1 Non-motorists can join on equal terms. **1936** *Discovery* Apr. 108/2 Even the non-motorist may enjoy the adventure, as a comfortable bus service has been established. **1949** *Penguin Music Mag.* Feb. 40 This is utterly meaningless to a non-musician, and obvious and therefore unnecessary to a musician. **1912** BELLOC *Servile State* 3 This principle of compulsion applied against the non-owners. **1948** *Mind* LVII. 228 The political opinions of automobile-owners are not very symptomatic of the political opinions of non-owners. **1883** 'MARK TWAIN' *Life on Mississippi* 379 Could you come nearer to reproducing it [*sc.* the siege of Vicksburg] to the imagination of a non-participant? **1971** *Jrnl. Gen. Psychol.* LXXXV. 266 All three categories (doublers, singlers, nonparticipants) are compared. **1967** B. KAUFMAN in S. Henderson *Understanding New Black Poetry* (1973) III. 206, I am writing these lines to the responsible non-people. **1969** *Guardian* 26 Sept. 11/2 His shiny, plastic world of nonpeople attending nonevents. **1897** W. JAMES *Will to Believe* 210 In all this the philosopher is just like the rest of us non-philosophers. **1956** F. C. COPLESTON in H. D. Lewis *Contemp. Brit. Philos.* 122 By the term 'ordinary man'..I mean simply the non-philosopher. **1938** S. BECKETT *Murphy* 162 Murphy, a strict non-reader. **1964** M. CRITCHLEY *Developmental Dyslexia* iv. 16 Monroe, too, preferred the old-fashioned phonic approach, saying darkly that it was better to be a slow reader than a non-reader. **1897** W. JAMES *Will to Believe* 320 We all, scientists and non-scientists, live on some inclined plane of credulity. **1959** C. P. SNOW *Two Cultures* i. 5 The non-scientists have a rooted impression that the scientists are shallowly optimistic. **1950** *Sci. News* XV. 111 Most people secrete the appropriate blood group substances (antigens) in bodily secretions such as saliva and tears. About one-seventh of the population, however, do not do this, and are called 'non-secretors'. **1971** J. Z. YOUNG *Introd. Study Man* xl. 586 Those who get duodenal ulcers include more group O than would be expected. Non-secretors are more liable to the disease than secretors. **1874** J. CUNNINGHAM *New Theory of Knowing* 98 The bodily organism is the 'debateable land' between self and non-self. **1949** KOESTLER *Insight & Outlook* viii. 120 Our understanding of other personalities, of the nonself by the self. **1970** *New Scientist* 19 Feb. 345/1 When a foreign protein enters the body the immune system recognizes the invader as non-self and produces antibodies which destroy it. **1940** BRYANT & AIKEN *Psychology of Eng.* 21 The phrase is any other group of words with a unitary idea, within a sentence or a nonsentence. **1966** M. GROSS in *Automatic Transl. of Lang.* (NATO Summer School, Venice 1962) 124 Certain strings on *V* are clearly understood by speakers of *L* as sentences of *L*, others are clearly recognized as nonsentences. **1832** T. J. RANDOLPH *Speech on Abolition of Slavery* 16 The burden of this defence..is to fall upon the less wealthy class of our citizens; chiefly upon the non-slaveholder. **1895** G. B. SHAW *Let.* 15 Dec. (1965) 578 The third division falling to Horobin, a non socialist. **1964** M. A. K. HALLIDAY et al. *Linguistic Sciences* 63 A non-speaker of the language. **1971** J. Z. YOUNG *Introd. Study Man* xxxvi. 518 The selection of those individuals who were competent in such skills became unusually severe at the expense of the non-speakers. **1952** *Archivum Linguisticum* IV. 89 To the non-structuralist at least, the book appears to throw less light on the essential nature of the French language than on the present state of structural linguistics. **1932** BLUNDEN *Face of England* 159 Our young men are non-swimmers. **1962** J. F. POWERS *Morte d'Urban* xiii. 285 Paul, the non-swimmer, had probably been thinking of the return voyage when he pinched the life preserver. **1908** *Lit. Guide* 1 Sept. 141/2 This false charge—viz., that non-theists are morally inferior persons. **1944** W. TEMPLE *Let.* 6 Mar. (1963) 148 But there is a Christian way of living and it is possible for non-theists to appreciate it and try to follow it. **1954** I. M. COPI *Symbolic Logic* vi. 185 A purely formal criterion for distinguishing between theorems and non-theorems of the system. **1972** A. CHURCH in Rudner & Scheffler *Logic & Art* x. 198 The expected consequences of any assertion, even of a non-theorem. **1924** G. B. SHAW *St. Joan* p. xxi, Some other people see imaginary diagrams and landscapes ..and are thereby able to perform feats of memory and arithmetic impossible to non-visualisers. **1953** A. HUXLEY *Let.* 21 June (1969) 676, I am a non-visualizer, and got very little in the way of imagery. **1940** V. WOOLF *Writer's Diary* 29 Mar. (1953) 330 All the detail that seems to the non-writer so easy..to me is torture. **1958** *New Statesman* 15 Nov. 664/2 It might even lure some of the great non-writers in the historical profession into putting pen to paper.

b. *spec.* Prefixed to a sb. with an implication of pretence, to denote a person who, or thing which, is not wholly, adequately, or genuinely what is specified by the sb.; used esp. of forms of art or literature, freq. with the implication that they are new or unconventional forms of the things specified (cf. *ANTI-[1] 2 c); as *non-answer, -architecture, -book, -budget, -conversation, -country, -debate, -drama, -film, -information, -issue, -lecture, -music, -news, -newspaper, -novel, -play, -policy, -problem, -sherry, -story*. See also *NON-ART, *NON-EVENT, *NON-HERO.

1966 *Listener* 21 July 84/1 Public men have learned to apply the technique of the non-answer, a technique in many cases mastered and perfected at the Commons dispatch-box. **1968** *Gainesville* (Florida) *Sun* 11 Mar. 8 They were non-answers—words calculated solely as a physical response to solve the immediate need for some kind of a response generated in a news conference. **1960** *20th-Cent.* Oct. 357 Manchester..is a city with no architecture, only an inert mass of *building*. I believe that the adherents of the Betjemanesque cult of Victorian bad taste find things to admire in examples of Manchester non-architecture. *Ibid.* May 441 Technical language and presentation are necessary; they do not excuse so many non-books. **1972** *Scholarly Publishing* III. 101 Non-books are of several kinds; but their differences notwithstanding, they all share two common features: they tend to be written for market rather than for intellectual reasons, and they are all means rather than ends. **1967** *Observer* 16 Apr. 10/2 The crescendo of the roll call of defeat..came just two days after the Chancellor of the Exchequer's non-Budget. **1960** *News Chron.* 28 July 6/8 Pinter is..a writer over-occupied with the externals of behaviour. The non-conversations..can stale into nothingness. **1970** *Gainesville* (Florida) *Sun* 24 Sept. A6 Jordan was and remains a non-country, created out of sandscape by Britain to pay off a dynastic debt. **1971** *Britannica Bk. of Year* (U.S.) 779/3 *Noncountry*, a country whose size, location, and economic resources are inadequate for economic self-sufficiency and development. **1970** *Times* 21 May 8 The debate on the amendments to end the Indo-China war was the usual non-debate. **1968** *Sat. Rev.* (U.S.) 20 Jan. 33 Most of the noise is made by Mailer, who, as principal player in a turgid nondrama.. barks sometimes like a dog and sometimes like a seal. **1963** *Listener* 31 Jan. 201/1 Their [*sc.* the Situationists'] violent and derisory manifestations—such as the non-film *Hurlements en faveur de Sade*—are all intended to create situations..such as will produce certain kinds of human behaviour, usually disgust or disorientation. **1970** *Times* 16 Apr. 5 The ritual exchange of non-information. **1965** *New Society* 9 Sept. 5/3 The brain drain is a non-issue. **1972** *Time* 20 Nov. 28 Unfortunately for the country, there were a lot of non-issues in this campaign. **1953** E. E. CUMMINGS (*title*) I: six nonlectures. **1958** *Publ. Amer. Dial. Soc.* XXX. 41 There has always been a tendency in some circles to regard jazz as non-music. **1969** *Listener* 3 July 26/1 Easily the most interesting and successful work in the programme was the one which kept consistently and coherently to the realms of non-music, and could thus be listened to without difficulty on its own terms. **1963** Non-news [see *NON-EVENT]. **1972** *Wall St. Jrnl. Index* 681/1 President Nixon clears desk with sweep of proclamations and orders, other (yawn) nonnews items. **1973** *Nation Rev.* (Melbourne) 31 Aug. 1443/4 There's a new type of newspaper occurring in the world: the *non newspaper*. **1961** *Guardian* 27 Oct. 6/5 Henry Miller's two remarkable non-novels. **1963** *New Yorker* 8 June 120 A non-novel, 'Why Not Try God?' **1968** *Ibid.* 28 Dec. 2 Dustin Hoffman does his brave best to make us believe that this non-play by Murray Schisgal is a touching comedy about the ignominy of young manhood. **1962** E. CLEAVER in A. Dundes *Mother Wit* (1973) 20/1 The fallacious stupidity of the non-policy of segregation. **1969** *Guardian* 7 Nov. 12/2 The apostles of relevance..bring massive expertise to bear on non-problems. **1967** *Economist* 5 Aug. 477 The non-sherries have carved themselves out healthy chunks of the fortified wine market on the basis of what they really are, more than by pretending to be the real Spanish thing. **1967** *Gainesville* (Florida) *Sun* 19 Mar., The latest non-story out of New Orleans on the Kennedy assassination 'plot'. **1968** *Listener* 11 July 49/2 The House of Lords vote on Rhodesia..was the great 'non-story' of recent weeks. **1971** M. RUSSELL *Deadline* xiii. 157 This promises to be the non-story of the month. **1973** L. HEREN *Growing up Poor in London* vii. 179 The coming and going of ships were regularly reported by local stringers, but tarantula spiders among the bananas and other non-stories were always available.

3. Prefixed to adjectives, as *non-academic, -actinic, -adaptive, -addictive, -æsthetic, -alcoholic, -alphabetic, -alphabetical, -ambiguous, -analytic, -antigenic, -aquatic, -aqueous, -articular, -assertive, -assimilable, -atomic, -auditory, -automatic, -axiomatic, -basic, -behavioural, -binary, -biodegradable, -British, -calcareous, -causal, -causative, -cellulosic* (also as *sb.* (*sc.* fibre)), *-chemical, -Christian, -chromosomal, -circular, -classical, -cognitive, -coherent, -coital, -collinear, -combustible, -commercial, -communicative, -Communist, -communistic, -commutative, -compact, -competitive, -complementary, -complex, -compound, -conceptual, -concrete, -conscious, -conservative, -consonantal, -constructive, -contiguous, -continuous, -contrastive, -controversial, -corrosive, -critical, -crystalline, -cumulative, -cyclic, -deductive, -degenerate, -delinquent, -demonstrative, -denominational, -denumerable, -derivative, -descriptive, -designative, -deterministic, -diffusible* (also *-able*), *-directive, -discriminatory, -dispersive, -dispositional, -disruptive, -dissipative, -dominant, -dramatic, -economic, -electrolytic, -electronic, -elementary, -emotional, -emphatic, -English, -enumerative, -enzymatic, -enzymic, -equivalent, -ethical, -exclusive, -existential, -explanatory, -explosive, -extensional, -factual, -fatty* (cf. *non-fat* in *4), *-final, -finite, -finitist, -fissile, -fissionable, -formal, -functional, -generic, -genetic, -geometrical, -German, -Germanic, -grammatical, -gravid, -habitual, -hæmolytic, -Hermitian, -historical, -homogeneous, -identical, -ideological, -illusory, -imitative, -independent, -indigenous, -individual, -Indo-European, -inductive, -industrial, -infectious, -infective, -inferential, -inflammable* (later examples), *-inflected, -inflexional, -initial, -insightful, -integral, -intellectual, -intuitive, -involved, -irritant, -Jewish, -judg(e)mental, -kosher, -lethal, -lexical, -linguistic, -literary, -local, -magnetic, -manual, -marine, -material, -mathematical, -measurable, -mechanical, -medical, -Mendelian, -mental* (also as *sb.*), *-mentalistic, -metabolizable, -metaphorical, -metaphysical, -metrical, -migratory, -military, -mimetic, -minimal, -modal, -molecular, -monetary, -motile, -musical, -mystical, -national, -native, -Nazi, -negative, -negligible, -negotiable, -null, -numerical, -nutritious, -observational, -official, -operational, -organic, -pathogenic, -perceptual, -perfective, -perishable* (also as *sb.*), *-permissive, -phallic, -phenomenal, -philosophical, -phonemic, -phonetic, -physical, -planar, -poetic, -poisonous, -polarizable, -porous, -predicative, -predictable, -pregnant, -prepositional, -prescriptive, -productive, -professorial, -progressive, -propositional, -psychological, -public, -purposeful, -purposive, -quantitative, -racial, -radioactive, -reactive, -realistic, -reciprocal, -recurrent, -redundant, -relational, -relative, -relativistic, -religious, -renewable, -representational, -representative, -reproducible, -revolutionary, -Roman, -roman, -routine, -saponifiable, -sceptical, -sectarian, -selective, -sensational, -sensory, -sensuous, -sentential, -sharp, -shrinkable, -simultaneous, -social, -socialist, -spatial, -spherical, -stationary, -statistical, -statutory, -steady, -structural, -subjective, -suppurative, -syllogistic, -symbolic, -symmetric(al, -synchronous, -synonymous, -syntactic, -systematic, -tautologous, -technical* (later examples),

-teleological, -temporal, -terminal, -theatric(al, -theistic, -theological, -theoretical, -tonal, -totalitarian, -toxic, -traditional, -transitive, -turbulent, -typical, -ultimate, -uniform, -urban, -utilitarian, -vacuous, -valid, -veridical, -visual, -vital, -vocal, -vocalic, -vocational; **non-cli·nical,** not clinical; *esp.* not accompanied by directly observable symptoms; **non-dime·nsional,** (of a quantity) = *DIMENSIONLESS *a.* 1 d; (of an equation) composed of dimensionless terms; **non-homo·logous,** not homologous; *spec.* in *Genetics* (cf. *HOMOLOGOUS *a.* 4 b); **non-Oh·mic** *Electr.*, not obeying or in accordance with Ohm's law; **no:n-stoich(e)iome·tric** *a. Chem.*, containing or representing atoms of the different elements in numbers that do not bear a simple ratio to one another.

1918 *Nation* (N.Y.) 28 Mar. 335 The real trouble with American universities has been their inability to 'get it across' to the 'man in the street', the 'roughnecks', and all those other fearsome beasts that inhabit the non-academic jungles. **1937** *Mind* XLVI. 124 That ease, forcefulness, and felicity of expression which made him so welcome a speaker, alike to academic and to non-academic audiences. **1957** C. S. LEWIS *Let.* 16 Mar. (1966) 275 In *writing* I do regard all non-academic works..as being leisure occupations. **1975** *Times* 6 Dec. 3/2 To chop £500,000 off the budget of a college means fewer jobs for staff, academic and non-academic. **1909** *Westm. Gaz.* 16 Oct. 14 The real essential in comfort..is the use of one of the scientifically prepared light screens which gives us all the possible non-actinic light. **1935** *Discovery* Apr. 97/1 The non-actinic paper in which photographic plates were wrapped. **1926** J. S. HUXLEY *Ess. Pop. Sci.* xviii. 276 An artificial and non-adaptive tendon. **1955** *Sci. Amer.* Apr. 93/1 The modification of T2 is 'nonadaptive'; that is, the modified virus cannot grow in the host that changed it. **1967** *Economist* 7 Oct. 20/1 The 'non-medical', non-addictive drugs such as marijuana and LSD. **1934** C. LAMBERT *Music Ho!* iv. 251 Music for organized and non-aesthetic action such as military marches and fox-trots. **1957** T. VEBLEN *Theory of Leisure Class* 164 The limits..are fixed by requirements of a non-aesthetic kind. **1907** *Yesterday's Shopping* (1969) 59/2 Hop Bitter Beer, non-alcoholic. **1909** [see *BEERLESS *a.*]. **1966** B. KIMENYE *Kalasanda Revisited* 58 There he was..nursing a glass of non-alcoholic, fizzy liquid. **1960** E. DELAVENAY *Introd. Machine Translation* vi. 90 A meaningful group of signs, alphabetic and non-alphabetic (spaces, hyphens, etc.). **1973** *Computers & Humanities* VII. 151 A provision must be made for the concurrent appearance of any number of non-alphabetic characters in any position. **1948** D. DIRINGER *Alphabet* 21 The crudest forms of writing.. are non-alphabetical. **1964** E. PALMER tr. *Martinet's Elem. General Linguistics* iv. 114 A non-ambiguous form. **1971** J. ANDERSON in A. J. Aitken et al. *Edin. Stud. Eng. & Scots* 76, I want now to turn to the (non-ambiguous) distinction hinted at above. **1890** W. JAMES *Princ. Psychol.* II. xxii. 351 In certain stages of the hypnotic trance the subject seems to lapse into the non-analytic state. **1939** *Mind* XLVIII. 202 The class *k* of non-analytic declarative sentences formulable in a given language. **1949** A. PAP *Elem. Analytical Philos.* viii. 152 A synthetic statement would simply be defined as a non-analytic statement. **1934** WEBSTER, Nonantigenic. **1948** J. H. BURN *Lect. Notes Pharmacol.* 75 The protein must, of course, be non-antigenic. **1951** WHITBY & HYNES *Med. Bacteriol.* (ed. 5) vi. 69 Enzymic digestion of antitoxic sera is also used, and by this means even the antibodies themselves may be split into non-antigenic fractions without loss of activity. **1963** D. W. & E. E. HUMPHRIES tr. *Termier's Erosion & Sedimentation* xvii. 338 Sediments of nonaquatic origin, such as those of deserts, can receive rain water. **1904** R. A. LEHFELDT *Electro-Chem.* I. i. 84 These laws..are only very partially applicable to non-aqueous solutions. **1957** G. E. HUTCHINSON *Treat. Limnol.* I. iii. 202 The only other non-aqueous natural liquids are the complex mixtures of hydrocarbons and other organic compounds known as petroleums. **1967** G. M. WYBURN et al. *Conc. Anat.* iv. 111/1 The [parotid] gland occupies the nonarticular part of the mandibular fossa of the temporal bone. **1901** A. SIDGWICK *Use of Words* viii. 224 Some statement of theirs is ambiguous, and therefore..non-assertive. **1940** *Kenyon Review* II. 282 The poetic statement..falls between the two poles of full assertion..and pure non-assertive tension between plurisigns. **1920** H. G. WELLS *Outl. Hist.* 563/1 There has hitherto existed in the States no organization for and no tradition of what one may call non-assimilable possessions. **1972** P. GREEN *Shadow of Parthenon* 70 Everything that conventional historiography finds non-assimilable, from science to tragedy. **1943** *Mind* LII. 26 It is supposed that..all complex or non-atomic assertions are just aggregates of atomic propositions linked by 'and', 'on', or 'if—then'. **1955** KOESTLER *Trail of Dinosaur* 239 The value of an atomic stockpile against non-atomic, local aggression. **1890** W. JAMES *Princ. Psychol.* I. ii. 50 The momentary loss..of our *non*-auditory images.. makes us mentally deaf. **1938** *Times Lit. Suppl.* 8 Oct. 649/3 Calvin was not hostile to art as such, but merely to the use of any non-auditory art in connexion with worship. **1953** C. E. BAZELL *Linguistic Form* i. 1 Non-automatic alternations between phonemes differing in respect of one minimal feature alone are seldom more frequent than similar alternations between phonemes differing in respect of several features. **1964** E. BACH *Introd. Transformational Gram.* iii. 44 The number suffixes show different forms for these two classes (nonautomatic). **1896** L. T. HOBHOUSE *Theory of Knowl.* 480 We shall have to discard any other principle..as non-axiomatic in character. **1966** *Jrnl. Philos.* LXIII. 435 We are not inclined to admit intuition or nonaxiomatic knowledge about sets. **1939** *Mind* XLVIII. 489 The discrimination of basic from non-basic predicates. **1964** R. H. ROBINS *Gen. Linguistics* 235 Non-basic endocentric constructions. **1946** C. MORRIS *Signs, Language & Behavior* 201 The explanation has the merit of not invoking non-behavioral factors. **1953** *Mind* LXII. 231 We have not yet enquired whether a machine is essentially distinct from a man in non-behavioural respects. **1947** *Math. Tables & Other Aids to Computation* Oct. 361 It is convenient to use as many selections as there are basic binary places in the computer, or in nonbinary machines as many as on-off signal channels. **1962** F. I. ORDWAY et al. *Basic Astronautics* vi. 287 By taking an inventory of nonbinary, solar-type stars with low angular momenta, we may at the same time be taking an inventory of stars with planetary systems. **1967** *New Scientist* 31 Aug. 440/1 Organic substances which are largely or totally nonbiodegradable are currently being used in both domestic and industrial applications. **1971** *Ibid.* 27 Apr. 260/1 Pollution created by non-biodegradable products has created immense environmental problems. **1955** *Times* 2 May 18/4 The pressing need of giving non-British immigrants to the Dominions some idea of British standards and culture. **1934** WEBSTER, Noncalcareous. **1946** *Nature* 21 Sept. 421/2 The non-calcareous type of surface waters, chiefly found in mountainous areas of the north and west, requires little or no treatment in the best cases. **1964** V. J. CHAPMAN *Coastal Vegetation* vi. 139 Two main types of dune, i.e. calcareous and non-calcareous. **1911** W. JAMES *Some Probl. Philos.* xii. 201 Non-causal sequences can be reversed; causal ones follow in conformity to rule. **1939** *Mind* XLVIII. 422 But very often in determining the dates of events we use non-causal Law-propositions. **1959** *Archivum Linguisticum* XI. 15 *Feed* can also have the non-causative sense: 'we feed at eight'. **1931** *Jrnl. Physical Chem.* XXXV. 469 The walls [of Corallines] are non-cellulosic. **1959** *Times Rev. Industry* Sept. 4/1 Man made fibres..have seen the development of non-cellulosic fibres. **1964** *Financial Times* 25 Feb. 2/2 Output of all man-made fibres, including non-cellulosics, in the U.K. was 15 per cent. higher in 1963. **1964** N. G. CLARK *Mod. Org. Chem.* vii. 119 This and other non-chemical uses of acetylene today account for only about 20 per cent of the amount consumed. **1974** *Verbatim* Dec. 1/1 The elements for which there is likely to be a nonchemical ..name. **1936** T. S. ELIOT *Ess. Anc. & Mod.* 132 There may always be schemes, initiated by non-Christian and non-Catholic minds with purely temporal motives and aims, to which we can give unqualified support. **1965** *English Studies* Feb. 3 Such scenes in earlier non-dramatic narrative, where the roots are probably non-Christian. **1975** *Times* 18 Dec. 10/8 The beauty of ancient non-Christian mystical texts. **1960** *New Biol.* XXXI. 109 The special value of *Paramecium* for genetics depends not on its use in the analysis of heredity by Mendelian methods but on its revelation of other hereditary or quasi-hereditary systems, based on non-chromosomal or cytoplasmic elements. **1922** A. D. UDDEN tr. *Bohr's Theory of Spectra* III. iii. 100 The non-circular orbits will correspond to a firmer binding than the circular orbits having the same value for the principal quantum number. **1935** *Mind* XLIV. 373 This interpretation..shows the appeal to the divine veracity to be both non-circular and epistemologically necessary. **1926** S. R. JAMES *Seventy Years* ix. 72 In those days the non-classical masters [at Eton College] who held houses were known as 'Dames'. **1955** A. N. PRIOR *Formal Logic* 258 A non-classical calculus developed by the Russian logician A. Kolmogorov in 1925. **1934** WEBSTER, Nonclinical. **1960** *Farmer & Stockbreeder* 9 Feb. 77/1 The prohibition has been made since the discovery that a form of non-clinical rhinitis exists in pigs in Ireland. **1971** *Brit. Med. Bull.* XXVII. 33/1 The range of conditions is gradually progressive, from normal veins to veins that are elongated, tortuous and dilated but which give rise to no symptoms or to one symptom referrable to the legs; these have been termed 'non-clinical' varicose veins. **1890** W. JAMES *Princ. Psychol.* II. xvii. 9 Plato's earlier pupils used to admit Sensation's existence, grudgingly, but they trampled it in the dust as something corporeal, non-cognitive, and vile. **1963** R. CARNAP in P. A. Schilpp *Philos. R. Carnap* 45 The view that these sentences and questions are non-cognitive was based on Wittgenstein's principle of verifiability. **1962** F. I. ORDWAY et al. *Basic Astronautics* v. 207 (*caption*) Coherent and non-coherent converters. **1967** M. CHANDLER *Ceramics in Mod. World* iii. 98 The glaze at this stage is a feeble layer of noncoherent particles. **1971** G. H. BOURNE *Ape People* x. 255 Among humans the amount of sexual play..and..noncoital sex in general seem to be related to the social level..and intelligence in the individual concerned. **1973** I. SINGER *Goals Human Sexuality* i. 35 Claiming that all coital orgasms are physiologically indistinguishable from noncoital ones. **1914** S. E. RASOR tr. *Burkhardt's Theory of Functions* i. 24 Three points *A, B, C* in the plane such that *oA, oB, oC* are non-collinear. **1918** VEBLEN & YOUNG *Projective Geom.* II. iii. 96 The triads of points..are all triads of noncollinear points. *Ibid.* 97 A, B, C are any three noncollinear points. **1966** OGILVY & ANDERSON *Excursions in Number Theory* vi. 69 How many non-collinear points in a plane can be spaced at integral distances each from each? **1969** *Gloss. Terms Fire* (*B.S.I.*) 1. 7 *Non-combustible*, not capable of undergoing combustion. **1975** *B.S.I. News* May 10 The term 'incombustible' as a synonym for 'non-combustible' is deprecated in BS 4422: Part 1: 1969 and should not be used in standards. **1901** *Edin. Rev.* Apr. 492 The 'dumping' abroad at non-commercial prices of goods manufactured in excess of the requirements of the protected home market. **1933** DYLAN THOMAS *Let.* Jan. (1966) 14 It is prose..but an utterly non-commercial prose. **1973** *Listener* 30 Aug. 295/3 This concern to tailor the news to the listener has even spread..to National Public Radio, the non-commercial radio network. **1953** C. F. HOCKETT in Saporta & Bastian *Psycholinguistics* (1961) 63/2 Information theory does not deal with the way in which a source maps a noncommunicative stimulus into communicative output. **1920** B. RUSSELL *Pract. & Theory Bolshevism* v. 76 If they elected a non-Communist representative he could not obtain a pass on the railway. **1972** 'G. BLACK' *Bitter Tea* (1973) vi. 82 Singapore is now the real focal point for the whole of non-Communist Chinese life. **1852** MILL *Pol. Econ.* (ed. 3) I. II. i. 258 The two elaborate forms of non-communistic Socialism known as St. Simonism and Fourierism. **1863** *Rep. Brit. Assoc. Adv. Sci. 1862* II. 7 An algebra of non-commutative symbols. **1964** E. BACH *Introd. Transformational Gram.* vii. 159 Ordinary arithmetical multiplication and addition form groups of a special character called commutative (or Abelian) groups, since they obey the commutative law: $x+y=y+x$; semi-groups are in general noncommutative. **1954** *Proc. Nat. Acad. Sci.* XL. 1150 The quotient *G/K* of a simple noncompact group with center reduced to {*e*} by a maximal compact subgroup carries a Hermitian symmetric structure invariant under *G* if and only if *K* has a nondiscrete center. **1959** E. M. PATTERSON *Topology* iii. 63 The transformation operates on a non-compact space. **1964** E. BACH *Introd. Transformational Gram.* v. 114 It is only at the lowest levels that the noncompact nature of the morphemes appears. **1906** *Daily Chron.* 10 Aug. 8/7 This club is extending the idea of holding a long-distance non-competitive run to Bath and back. **1935** *Discovery* Mar. 64/1 We have never ceased advocating this non-competitive use of available idle labour. **1953** C. E. BAZELL *Linguistic Form* 40 Non redundancy (non-complementary distribution). **1961** R. B. LONG *Sentence & its Parts* i. 22 But the distinction between complementary and noncomplementary contained modifiers can generally be disregarded. **1936** *Mind* XLV. 316 The third class.. actually includes non-complex ideas revived by imagination. **1972** *Jrnl. Social Psychol.* LXXXVI. 36 Complex groups perform better than noncomplex groups. **1887** J. N. KEYNES *Formal Logic* (ed. 2) vi. 381 The proposition..is supposed to be non-compound. **1954** I. M. COPI *Symbolic Logic* iv. 66 We must develop methods for analyzing non-compound statements. **1897** W. M. URBAN *Hist. Princ. Sufficient Reason* iv. 41 The postulate of ground..is not..unlogical, and non-conceptual, as Schopenhauer later maintained. **1929** A. N. WHITEHEAD *Process & Reality* 344 Physical feelings form the non-conceptual element in our awareness of nature. **1964** F. BOWERS *Bibliogr. & Textual Criticism* I. v. 27 Not as words that have meaningful values—but, instead, as impersonal and non-conceptual inked prints. **1928** E. & C. PAUL tr. *Marx's Capital* II. iii. 117 The money serves as an ideal, as a non-concrete, means of purchase. **1912** J. S. HUXLEY *Individual in Animal Kingdom* iii. 84 To discriminate between conscious and non-conscious brains. **1972** *Computers & Humanities* VII. 111 We propose to do a feasibility study to see if the role of language in the formation of nonconscious belief systems can be ascertained. **1867** THOMSON & TAIT *Treat. Nat. Philos.* ii. 280 It is easy to arrange a system artificially, in connexion with a source of energy, so that its forces of position shall be non-conservative. **1962** CORSON & LORRAIN *Introd. Electromagn. Fields* vi. 219 We shall now extend the discussion to include time-dependent magnetic fields and the nonconservative electric fields which accompany them. **1965** H. KAHN *On Escalation* xii. 241 Almost everybody looks for ways to improve a situation, and 'non-conservative' behavior..becomes very possible. **1964** R. H. ROBINS *Gen. Linguistics* 157 Opposed acoustic features:..consonantal, non-consonantal. **1908** *Westm. Gaz.* 8 Aug. 14/1 Non-resistance is for the non-constructive man. **1964** G. KREISEL in Benacerraf & Putnam *Philos. of Math.* 158 Brouwer ignores non-constructive mathematics altogether. **1964** *Language* XL. 24 Noncontiguous dialect areas. **1865** G. M. HOPKINS *Jrnls. & Papers* (1959) 103 All figures must be composed of continuous or of non-continuous lines or of both. **1973** *Archivum Linguisticum* IV. 4 A past time auxiliary which refers to recent non-continuous actions. **1964** R. H. ROBINS *Gen. Linguistics* 130 The equally non-contrastive [t] and [t^h]. **1928** J. REITH *Diary* 13 Apr. (1975) i. 100 Winston Churchill..said he would like to.. speak for 15 minutes the next night, factual and non-controversial. **1943** *Mind* LII. 274 This covers only the elementary, non-controversial portions of the system. **1960** E. L. DELMAR-MORGAN *Cruising Yacht Equipment* v. 66 A modern sextant is..made of non-corrosive light metal alloy. **1969** *Jane's Freight Containers 1968–69* 472/2 Floor screws, flat head, self-tapping with non-corrosive finish. **1893** G. B. SHAW *Let.* 3 Mar. (1965) 386 Assuring you, in our personal, non-artistic and non-critical relations, of my unmitigated defiance. **1967** A. BATTERSBY *Network Analysis* (ed. 2) iii. 26 The systematic analysis of a network sorts out the individual jobs into two main classes, critical and non-critical. **1851** *Phil. Mag.* I. 178 It is..desirable that a complete theory of magnetic induction in crystalline or non-crystalline matter should be established independently of any hypothesis of magnetic fluids. **1966** D. G. BRANDON *Mod. Techniques Metallogr.* ii. 64 In electron microscopy the contrast is most commonly caused by elastic scattering only, that from non-crystalline replica materials being due to non-coherent scattering, that from thin crystalline films being diffraction contrast. **1908** *Westm. Gaz.* 15 Aug. 15/1 Home Railway Preference stocks are non-cumulative, **1954** G. I. M. SWYER *Reproduction & Sex* xiv. 173 An efficient spermicide..should be non-toxic, non-irritating, and non-cumulative;..it should preferably be non-absorbable. **1946** F. E. ZEUNER *Dating the Past* xi. 341 There are superimposed cycles, or non-cyclic changes of a considerably longer duration. **1962** CORSON & LORRAIN *Introd. Electromagn. Fields* v. 203 If the vectors are permuted in noncyclic order, the sign is changed. **1914** B. RUSSELL *Our Knowl. External World* ii. 34 The ultimate result of the introduction of the inductive method seems not the creation of a new kind of non-deductive reasoning. **1968** R. A. LYTTLETON *Mysteries Solar Syst.* vii. 250 An intricate subjective psychological process must be concerned, of a non-deductive character. **1900** *Trans. Amer. Math. Soc.* I. 462 This represents the most general non-degenerate quadric. **1929** Non-degenerate [see *DEGENERATE *a.* B. 3 a]. **1968** C. G. KUPER *Introd. Theory Superconductivity* xi. 183 The *n*-fold degenerate pair state has been split into an $(n-1)$-fold level and a non-degenerate lower state. **1941** *Manch. Guardian Weekly* 14 Mar. 214/4 Now is my chance..to synthesize the ideology and emotional attitudes of juveniles and adolescents (cross-sectional and non-delinquent) during their vacational activities. **1970** *Jrnl. General Psychol.* LXXXII. 265 Delinquent and nondelinquent subjects. **1944** *Mind* LIII. 344 We must admit non-demonstrative principles of inference which are not derivable from experience. **1965** P. CAWS *Philos. of Sci.* xxvi. 193 The most common name for such non-demonstrative inference is induction. **1908** *Daily Chron.* 19 Nov. 4/4 The Churches..together with all the ethical and non-denominational societies

should be summoned to co-operate. **1953** E. Smith *Guide to Eng. Traditions & Public Life* 17 A non-denominational chapel was commonly provided for religious services. **1905** *Ann. Math.* VI. 175 An example of a non-denumerable class is the class of all non-terminating decimal fractions. **1937** *Mind* XLVI. 59 The properties of integers are non-denumerable. **1968** J. J. C. Smart *Between Sci. & Philos.* vii. 245 A non-denumerable infinity of points. **1902** W. James *Let.* 29 July in R. B. Perry *Tht. & Char. W. James* (1935) II. 650, I may maximize unduly the non-derivative character of these forces, which you minimize. **1956** J. Whatmough *Language* 39 The derivative *manly* as compared with the simple 'non-derivative' word *man*. **1892** A. Sidgwick *Distinction* 182 Normally all proper (or non-descriptive) names have once been general (or descriptive). **1925** L. P. Smith *Words & Idioms* iii. 83 The non-descriptive, non-explanatory, and purely identifying term of the French Précieuses, *je ne sais quoi*. **1944** *Mind* LIII. 241 A formal distinction can be made..between *descriptive* symbols on the one hand and *nondescriptive* or logical symbols on the other. **1946** C. Morris *Signs, Language & Behavior* 116 Knowledge about the adequacy of non-designative signs is a powerful factor in their control. **1952** *Mind* LXI. 459 These theories proposed that ethical terms function like 'hurrah' and 'blast', as non-designative expressions. **1960** *Encounter* XV. v. 42 A markedly non-deterministic interpretation of psycho-analysis. **1965** A. Shimony in M. Black *Philos. in America* 260 As a result of the measurement there is a non-deterministic transition from the initial state to a final state. **1885** Non-diffusible [see Particulate *a.*]. **1951** Whitby & Hynes *Med. Bacteriol.* (ed. 5) iv. 57 The toxins of bacteria which do not produce exotoxins are termed endotoxins and are thought to be firmly bound to the bacterial proteins in a non-diffusible form. **1962** H. Heath in A. Pirie *Lens Metabolism Rel. Cataract* 362 Nondiffusable high polymers. **1967** *Oceanogr. & Marine Biol.* V. 380 Part of the calcium content of the blood is in the form of non-diffusible compounds of calcium with protein. **1956** A. A. Townsend *Struct. Turbulent Shear Flow* v. 91 By substituting in the equation of mean motion.., the non-dimensional equation is obtained. **1956** *Nature* 24 Mar. 548/2 The rather bewildering array of non-dimensional numbers that confronts the student in this subject [*sc.* combustion]. **1971** *Ibid.* 13 Aug. 447/3 The system is then arranged so that the equations of motion have the same form whether they are dimensional or non-dimensional. **1951** *Mind* LX. 398 The Rogerian non-directive technique is of no avail. **1954** J. A. C. Brown *Social Psychol. of Industry* 78 'Non-directive' interviewing in which the interviewer listens rather than talks. **1961** *Ann. Reg. 1960* 467 The expansion of world trade on a multilateral non-discriminatory basis. **1962** W. B. Thompson *Introd. Plasma Physics* ii. 11 These oscillations have the unusual character of being non-dispersive. **1966** D. G. Brandon *Mod. Techniques Metallogr.* 155 Such needle counters hold great promise in the field of 'non-dispersive' analysis. **1941** *Mind* L. 339 So it does not seem as if ϕ can be a non-dispositional, non-relational characteristic. **1949** A. Pap *Elem. Analytical Philos.* xii. 289 The dispositional predicate is said to be reducible, by means of the reduction-sentence, to non-dispositional predicates. **1970** *Manch. Guardian Weekly* 24 Oct. 9 The colleges on their side would agree to permit non-disruptive occupations and boycotts of classes. **1940** *Chambers's Techn. Dict.* 582/1 *Non-dissipative network*, a network designed as if the inductances and condensers are free from dissipation, and with components of minimum loss. **1964** R. F. Ficchi *Electr. Interference* iv. 38 A cavity resonator is described as a cylindrical box with perfect conductivity and containing within itself a nondissipative medium. An oscillation, once started within the box, should continue indefinitely. **1961** *Amer. Speech* XXXVI. 204 The reasons for the persistence of non-dominant languages. **1972** *Jrnl. Social Psychol.* LXXXVII. 92 Ring electrodes were slipped onto two fingers of the subject's nondominant hand. **1947** C. Gray *Contingencies* v. 120 Avoiding..the pitfall of non-dramatic music-making into which so many of his contemporaries and predecessors had fallen. **1965** *English Studies* Feb. 3 It is possible to find such scenes in earlier non-dramatic narrative. **1920** B. Russell *Pract. & Theory Bolshevism* ii. 123, I do not think that non-economic factors can be neglected. **1965** J. D. Chambers in Glass & Eversley *Population in Hist.* xiii. 344 There is more reason to relate the change to non-economic causes. **1853** *Phil. Mag.* V. 398 Nothing is known with certainty regarding the non-electrolytic resistance of liquid conductors. **1964** R. F. Ficchi *Electr. Interference* v. 55 Capacitors, both electrolytic and nonelectrolytic. **1964** *Times Rev. Industry & Techn.* Jan. 22/2 The operation was put straight on to a computer without an intervening non-electronic stage. **1964** *Language* XL. 191 The simple words which by our definitions are nonelementary. **1965** Hughes & Londey *Elem. of Formal Logic* xxiii. 177 Even the full Lower Predicate Calculus..raises problems of a non-elementary nature. **1941** *Mind* L. 168 Expressed in non-metaphoric and non-emotional words. **1961** R. B. Long *Sentence & its Parts* vi. 147 This occurs in subordinate-declarative clauses following ideas of appraisal, emotional or non-emotional. **1901** W. James *Let.* (1920) II. 153 The optimism and healthy-mindedness are yours... But the moderate and non-emphatic way of putting things is not. **1966** *English Studies* XLVII. 257 The normal non-emphatic character of the subject. **1955** *Publ. Amer. Dial. Soc.* xxiv. 20, I have on tape some argots which might at first appear to be non-English. **1941** *Mind* L. 129 We know the truth of a universal non-enumerative proposition, *All A is B*, only by apprehending, in a particular instance, that the universal A-ness necessitates the universal B-ness. **1956** J. O. Urmson *Philosophical Analysis* v. 63 The case becomes still more favourable to general facts if we take the non-enumerative universal proposition of traditional logic—'All As are B'. **1960** *New Biol.* XXXI. 26 A mutation (change) of a single chromosomal gene can lead to a corresponding chemical change in a non-enzymatic protein. **1964** *Oceanogr. & Marine Biol.* II. 347 Luciferin..is a non-enzymatic protein which luminesces in the presence of calcium ions. **1934** Webster, Nonenzymic. **1946** *Nature* 28 Sept. 433/2 Mackworth finds the other —SH enzymes..much less sensitive, requiring concentrations of the order of $M/1{,}000$, and this was also found by Morgan and Dixon for —SH groups in non-enzymic proteins. **1965** Peacocke & Drysdale *Molecular Basis Heredity* x. 115 Work on non-enzymic proteins. **1885** J. Veitch *Institutes of Logic* §560 What are equivalent, or non-equivalent, to a common third term, are equivalent or non-equivalent to each other. **1973** J. J. Zeman *Modal Logic* v. 80 The systems which have an infinite number of non-equivalent irreducible modalities will generally be called 'absolutely strict' systems, while systems containing only a finite number of non-equivalent modalities will, in general, be called 'systems of complete modalization'. **1925** C. D. Broad *Mind & its Place* xi. 487 Purely ethical characteristics..cannot be identified with or defined in terms of non-ethical or 'natural' characteristics. **1964** E. A. Nida *Toward Sci. Transl.* v. 93 It might seem strange at first glance that in the above treatment of *jwok* in Anuak we have not indicated such traditional componential contrasts as ethical vs. non-ethical and secular vs. sacred. **1847** A. De Morgan *Formal Logic* iv. 75 We may say that each is *participant*, or *non-exclusive*, of the other. **1963** Auden *Dyer's Hand* 402 Friendship is a nonexclusive, nonpossessive relationship. **1903** B. Russell *Princ. Math.* I. li. 450 The consideration of existence itself leads to non-existential propositions, and so contradicts the theory. **1949** A. Pap *Elem. Analytical Philos.* iv. 85 Such discourse about connections of properties without any regard to particulars exemplifying them, is often called 'non-existential'. **1901** A. Sidgwick *Use of Words* iv. 119 Some kind of non-explanatory verbiage. **1966** *Jrnl. Philos.* LXIII. 446 The author's typical non-explanatory explanations. **1946** F. E. Zeuner *Dating the Past* xii. 381 The *quality* of the species-steps during the period of explosive evolution differs from those of the period of ordinary, non-explosive evolution. **1971** I. G. Gass et al. *Understanding Earth* xxi. 301/2 Non-explosive fissure eruptions. **1949** *Mind* LVIII. 63 We need a modal or non-extensional language which contains such words as 'necessarily' or 'accidentally'. **1955** A. N. Prior *Formal Logic* 269 Modal operators (and non-extensional operators generally). **1934** Webster, Nonfactual. **1936** *Mind* XLV. 359 According to Mr. Ayer every significant, non-factual proposition is analytic; every factual proposition is synthetic. **1934** Webster, Nonfatty. **1935** *Discovery* June 170/1 For analytical purposes, milk is divided into three parts: fat or cream; non-fatty solids..; and water. **1953** C. E. Bazell *Linguistic Form* iv. 47 The opposition in French between 'close e' and 'open e' in non-final syllables is similarly marginal. **1973** *Word 1970* XXVI. 103 In such compounds, nonfinal primary stress is supposed to become secondary. **1923** J. S. Huxley *Ess. Biologist* vii. 264 Man's ideals are in themselves unlimited, non-finite. **1971** *Computers & Humanities* V. 307 Stylistic uses of the non-finite verb clause in Shakespeare's plays. **1940** *Mind* XLIX. 248 The theory that the non-finitist symbols used in pure mathematics are to be interpreted as 'ideal elements'..would provide a fruitful starting-point for a consideration of certain aspects of scientific method. **1956** J. H. Woodger tr. *Tarski's Logic, Semantics, Metamath.* 260 On account of its non-finitist nature the rule of infinite induction differs fundamentally. **1909** Webster, Non-fissile. **1953** Non-fissile [see *fissile *a.* 2]. **1961** J. E. Radford *Nuclear Energy Simplified* ii. 29 The non-fissile isotope U^{238}..has now become exceedingly valuable because plutonium can be transmuted from it. **1950** *Chem. Engin. Progress* XLVI. 110/1 An immediate concern should be to make use of the relatively large amount of nonfissionable U-238. **1974** *Sci. Amer.* June 36/1 The fusion neutrons can also be used to convert nonfissionable isotopes of uranium or thorium to fissionable isotopes. **1903** B. Russell *Princ. Math.* I. iii. 41 This is simply an instance of the non-formal principle of dropping a true premiss. **1964** R. H. Robins *Gen. Linguistics* v. 194 Those [definitions of the word unit] relying on non-formal, extra-grammatical criteria.. are of little value. **1926** J. S. Huxley *Ess. Pop. Sci.* xviii. 301 The embryonic or non-functional period. **1965** *English Studies* XLVI. 420 The attempt to save the *Gesetz* by saying that in all these cases the alliteration of the verb is non-functional can hardly be taken seriously. **1959** *Brno Studies in English* I. 42 The non-generic indefinite article. **1932** J. S. Huxley *Probl. Relative Growth* vii. 207 The bulk of the observable differences in size and proportions between the existing Scottish strain of Red deer and (a) the existing Carpathian strain and (b) the sub-fossil Scottish type are non-genetic and of no taxonomic significance. **1964** *Oceanogr. & Marine Biol.* II. 314 Others imply a nongenetic character of the changes involved or a combination of both genetic and nongenetic components. **1926** A. Huxley *Essays New & Old* 131 The grandest sight I saw in non-geometrical Holland was Zaandam. **1936** *Mind* XLV. 466 Some non-geometrical kind of analysis. **1861** Mill *Repr. Govt.* xvi. 292 East Prussia.. must..be either under a non-German government, or the intervening Polish territory must be under a German one. **1964** *English Studies* XLV. 395 The use of *Textbuch* in the non-German sense may be due to carelessness of translation. **1937** *Jrnl. Eng. & Gmc. Philol.* 4 Oct. 463 Rules are given..and a comparison made between the vocabulary of German and English and the non-Germanic languages. **1965** *English Studies* XLVI. 419 This [*sc.* Gregorian chant] is of non-Germanic origin. **1955** J. L. Austin *How to do Things with Words* (1962) i. 3 The mistake of taking as straightforward statements of fact utterances which are *either* (in interesting non-grammatical ways) nonsensical *or else* intended as something quite different. **1965** *Canad. Jrnl. Linguistics* XI. 47 The moment a 'non-grammatical' sentence is uttered or written, it ceases to be 'non-grammatical'. **1961** L. C. Martin *Clinical Endocrinol.* (ed. 3) i. 15 Oxytocin has little or no effect either upon the non-gravid human uterus or upon the gravid uterus until the time of parturition. **1967** *Oceanogr. & Marine Biol.* V. 161 The perivisceral fluid..constitutes only 25% of the mass of a small (non-gravid) sea urchin. **1964** C. Barber *Present-Day Eng.* vi. 142 This habitual/non-habitual criterion is not typical. **1946** *Nature* 31 Aug. 294/1 It is non-hæmolytic and does not produce any pyrogenic effect on intramuscular injection in man. **1964** W. G. Smith *Allergy & Tissue Metabolism* v. 61 They also caused the formation of hæmolytic lysolecithin-like substances and non-hæmolytic SRS. **1955** W. Pauli *Niels Bohr* 37 This group distinguishes two kinds of complex (non-Hermitian) fields..which are multiplied by gauge-transformations with opposite phase factors. **1970** G. K. Woodgate *Elem. Atomic Struct.* 207 We find it convenient to use two non-Hermitian operators. **1896** W. Caldwell *Schopenhauer's System* ix. 508 A metaphysical analysis of the world must naturally always be taken in a timeless or ideal (non-historical) sense. **1935** *Mind* XLIV. 235 The historical essays..are mostly concerned with Greek philosophy..; and two of the essays are ostensibly non-historical. **1957** L. Fox *Two-Point Boundary Probl.* vii. 190 A change..in the non-homogeneous part of the equation. **1927** *Jrnl. Heredity* XVIII. 269/1 One might suppose that a portion of one chromosome has become attached to a member of a non-homologous pair. **1956** *Nature* 25 Feb. 386/1 'Centric fusion' of non-homologous autosomes. **1971** *Perceptual & Motor Skills* XXXII. 639 Synchrony of bimanual wrist movements by 12 normal *Ss* was compared when homologous muscles (e.g., left and right wrist flexors) and when non-homologous muscles (e.g., left flexors and right extensors) were simultaneously active. **1971** *Chromosoma* XXXV. 247 Rieger (1957) reported a high level of pairing between non-homologous chromosomes in haploid forms of *Antirrhinum majus*. **1890** R. Adamson in W. S. Jevons *Pure Logic* p. xi, Non-identical contents presented to it. **1965** *Language* XLI. 280 The nonidentical subject constituents. **1964** Rousseas & Farganis in I. L. Horowitz *New Sociology* 270 The non-ideological liberal is uncommitted. **1975** *Times* 25 Nov. 8/8 The [Chinese] authors..have been writing cultural books, largely non-ideological, since the 1930s. **1932** H. H. Price *Perception* v. 110 Some few and as it were privileged expanses (normal or non-illusory ones). **1928** L. P. Smith *Words & Idioms* 114 The non-imitative arts, architecture and music. **1973** *Jrnl. Genetic Psychol.* CXXIII. 145 The reinforced group emitted significant more physical, verbal, and nonimitative aggression than the nonreinforced group. **1874** W. Wallace tr. *Hegel's Logic* 208 The non-independent and changeable. **1965** Hughes & Londey *Elem. of Formal Logic* xviii. 131 A4..can be proved from the other axioms... We express this fact by saying that A4 is a non-independent axiom. **1894** C. Dixon (*title*) The nests and eggs of non-indigenous British birds. **1964** *Language* XL. 93 Regional and nonindigenous influence. **1926** D. H. Lawrence *Plumed Serpent* vii. 128 Men, dark, collective men, non-individual. **1949** A. Pap *Elem. Analytical Philos.* iv. 88 The use of non-individual variables commits the logician to the use of names of abstract entities, like properties, classes or propositions. **1934** Priebsch & Collinson *German Lang.* ii. v. 251 A residue of untraced words which have led some scholars..to postulate a non-Indo-European strain in the early vocabulary. **1965** W. S. Allen *Vox Latina* i. 13 Many of the words..are probably non-Indo-European. **1899** *Jrnl. Inst. Electr. Engin.* XXVIII. 17 A practically non-inductive wire resistance. **1957** G. Ryle in C. A. Mace *Brit. Philos. in Mid-Cent.* 259 Pure mathematics is a non-inductive..science. **1938** *Mind* XLVII. 247 It is this aspect of Dr. Myers' essay that is of interest to the non-industrial reader, though there is much of value in it about the prevention of accidents in industrial occupations. **1909** Webster, Noninfectious. **1956** *Nature* 21 Jan. 131/1 The purified protein alone was found to be non-infectious. **1965** McKeown & Brown in Glass & Eversley *Population in Hist.* xii. 291 Infectious and non-infectious cases. **1956** *Nature* 18 Feb. 304/1 Extracts from infected plants contain a range of specific proteins that resemble the virus..but are not infective... Beans appear to contain an unusually large proportion of non-infective protein. **1971** *Brit. Med. Bull.* XXVII. 9/1 It may have a predominantly non-infective allergic origin. **1897** B. Russell *Essay on Foundations of Geometry* ii. 61 This element must be non-inferential. **1935** *Mind* XLIV. 48 The last phrase suggests a less positive stand in regard to the non-inferential apprehension of the objective. **1936** *Discovery* Apr. 106/2 Helium gas is used as a non-inflammable substitute for hydrogen in balloons and airships. **1969** *Jane's Freight Containers 1968–69* 476/2 Both achieved by in-situ foamed non-inflammable urethane. **1837** J. S. Mill *Let.* Sept. in *Wks.* (1963) XII. 350 Our non-inflected language. **1928** *Mod. Lang. Rev.* Apr. 136 Then we shall have two genitives in English, one inflected and one non-inflected. **1924** H. E. Palmer *Gram. Spoken Eng.* 81 All other classes of qualificatives..form the comparative..and superlative by the non-inflexional method. **1940** *Mind* XLIX. 436 The syntax of the Aryan languages differs fundamentally from that of non-inflectional languages, in particular Chinese. **1953** K. Jackson *Lang. & Hist. in Early Britain* ii. 286 He gives substitution by AS. *i, y*, or *e* in all cases, apparently not considering Pr.W. stressed *ï* in non-initial syllables. **1965** *Language* XLI. 453 Medial (i.e. noninitial and nonfinal) dissyllabic sequences. **1962** *Listener* 20 Sept. 436/2 The differences between insightful and non-insightful problem-solving behaviour. **1968** M. S. Livingston *Particle Physics* ii. 18 The non-integral atomic weights were explained as isotopes. **1897** W. James *Will to Believe* 11 Evidently..our non-intellectual nature does influence our convictions. **1946** *Mind* LV. 51 This, so far as it depends on denying the possibility of other sorts of non-intellectual intuition than the sensible, is certainly dogmatic. **1957** N. Chomsky in Saporta & Bastian *Psycholinguistics* (1961) 41/2 Our ultimate aim is to provide an objective, non-intuitive way to evaluate a grammar. **1960** *Suppl. Oxf. Med. Treatment of Disease* VIII. 804 Non-involved. **1973** S. Fisher *Female Orgasm* xv. 434 A signal for potential future sexual difficulties is..a distant, non-involved relationship with the father. **1946** *Nature* 14 Dec. 876/2 Physiological effect on man: non-irritant. **1963** J. Osborne *Dental Mechanics* (ed. 5) i. 9 It [*sc.* the impression material] should be non-irritant to the mouth tissues. **1935** Huxley & Haddon *We Europeans* iii. 96 In each country the Jewish population overlaps with the non-Jewish. **1973** *Guardian* 17 Apr. 15/8 The Passover meal, to which non-Jewish passengers like me were invited. **1965** M. Morse *Unattached* i. 44 His impartial and non-judgemental attitude. **1972** *Jrnl. Social Psychol.* LXXXVI. 224 Low authoritarian subjects are..flexible and nonjudgmental. **1949** Koestler *Promise & Fulfilment* iii. iii. 317 The Cabinet has capitulated to the

rabbis and no non-kosher meat will be imported into Israel. **1968** D. Hopkinson *Incense-Tree* iv. 38, I was considered by Jews to be a Jewess. Accordingly I ought not to..eat non-kosher food. **1930** R. A. Fisher *Genetical Theory of Natural Selection* iii. 64 With non-lethal mutants..a process of modification of the homozygote may be expected to commence. **1965** H. Kahn *On Escalation* xii. 234 The 'nonlethal central confrontations'..were not repeated. **1955** P. Strevens *Papers in Lang. & Lang. Teaching* (1965) ix. 118 The non-lexical effects arise chiefly from the absence of a system of interdependent stress and intonation. **1971** *Archivum Linguisticum* II. 131 The terms Pre-article and Post-article can be used when talking about arrangements of non-lexical formatives in surface structure. **1927** *Mod. Philology* Nov. 217 An ear trained to other languages will hear differences between the [t]'s of [tik, stik, botr, bit] which are not distinctive, that is, in English non-linguistic. **1956** J. Whatmough *Language* 7, May 'thought' be not merely sub-linguistic, but also non-linguistic, or both? **1960** W. V. Quine *Word & Object* 270 Discourse about non linguistic objects would have been an excellent medium. **1971** D. Crystal *Linguistics* 72 Modern linguists..do not want to gear their descriptions to non-linguistic standards of correctness. **1889** *Granta* 17 May 9/1 To a non-literary man, like myself, the post of Editor offered temptations well-nigh irresistible. *a* **1943** R. G. Collingwood *Idea of Hist.* (1946) 258 Non-literary sources, such as coins and inscriptions. **1965** *English Studies* XLVI. 256 These three themes are all copiously illustrated with quotations, the vast majority being drawn from non-literary sources. **1908** *Westm. Gaz.* 3 Feb. 2/2 He has in three weeks done all that any non-local candidate could do. **1965** *English Studies* Apr. 140 Non-local forms of their names can hardly..affect the outcome of an investigation. **1829** *Phil. Mag.* VI. 146 This ore is remarkable on account of its being entirely non-magnetic. **1903** Non-magnetic [see *oersted b]. **1968** C. G. Kuper *Introd. Theory Superconductivity* ii. 22 Since the normal phase has been assumed to be nonmagnetic g_n is independent of the field. **1956** J. E. Floud *Social Class & Educational Opportunity* i. i. 7 In South West Hertfordshire the non-manual occupations are much better represented. **1946** *Nature* 31 Aug. 299/1 The non-marine Lamellibranchs have become of extreme economic importance in the correlation of seams in British and Continental coalfields. **1965** G. J. Williams *Econ. Geol. N.Z.* xviii. 324/2 The non-marine Orauea mudstone consists in the lower part of grey to brown sandy mudstone. **1937** R. H. Lowie *Hist. Ethnol. Theory* vii. 83 Tylor's mistake sprang from the difficulty of applying the evolutionary scale to elements of non-material culture. **1967** Cox & Grose *Organiz. Bibliogr. Rec. by Computer* ii. 41 E.D.P. offers both the low data input error rate and the non-material manipulation required. **1847** A. De Morgan *Formal Logic* xii. 232 The terms by which the non-mathematical logician indicates his degrees of belief. **1937** *Mind* XLVI. 38 The rejection from the interpretation of nature of everything *non*-mathematical. **1973** *Sci. Amer.* Apr. 103/3 Nonmathematical scholars tend to view with profound indifference the tortures that mathematicians suffer over such basic issues as the nature of number. **1920** A. S. Eddington *Space, Time & Gravitation* 4 What you are comparing it with is not some non-measurable ideal of length, but some attainable, or at least approachable, ideal of material constitution. **1949** A. Pap *Elem. Analytical Philos.* vii. 128 The only legitimate distinction between 'primary' and 'secondary' qualities is that between measurable qualities..and non-measurable qualities. **1855** H. Spencer *Princ. Psychol.* iii. ix. 416 The non-mechanical sequences occurring in them [*sc.* organisms]. **1939** L. H. Gray *Found. Language* 144 Language..has two aspects: physiological or mechanical, and psychological or non-mechanical. **1834** Mill in *Monthly Repos.* VIII. 818 The most important facts of the human organization, explained in a manner peculiarly well suited..even to non-medical readers. **1967** Non-medical [see *non-addictive* above]. **1902** W. Bateson *Mendel's Princ. Heredity* p. xiii, Non-Mendelian phenomena. **1968** H. Harris *Nucleus & Cytoplasm* i. 7 Where there is good evidence that the specifications for a particular characteristic are encoded in cytoplasmic DNA, as, for example, in the case of the chloroplast, genetic analysis reveals a non-mendelian or cytoplasmic form of inheritance. **1878** W. James *Coll. Ess. & Rev.* (1920) 62 It is perfectly possible to express the existence of interests in non-mental terms. **1936** *Mind* XLV. 182 From these three assertions, it would immediately follow that a mental act, in being experienced, is an *-ed* as well as an *-ing*, that is to say, is non-mental as well as mental. **1959** *Encounter* Jan. 3 It prepares the philosophical student for the belief that mind has some kind of supremacy over the non-mental universe. **1973** *N.Y. Times* 22 Aug. 1/6 The Secret Service continued today to press its investigation of what was described as a 'very serious, very large' conspiracy by 'nonmentals' to assassinate President Nixon during his visit to New Orleans yesterday. **1936** L. Bloomfield in *Language* XII. 95 Now let us re-word the statement in non-mentalistic terms. **1968** P. M. Postal *Aspects Phonol. Theory* p. xv, The recent attempt of C. F. Hockett to formulate an antimentalistic theory of sound change within the general framework of a nonmentalistic interpretation of autonomous phonemics. **1962** R. van Heyningen in A. Pirie *Lens Metabolism Rel. Cataract* 400 The interconversion of sugars..can, in certain micro-organisms, enable the incorporation into a major metabolic pathway of an otherwise non-metabolizable sugar. **1973** *Nature* 9 Mar. 122/2, 3-MG is a non-metabolizable sugar which is transported into brain but does not react with hexokinase. **1962** W. Nowottny *Lang. Poets Use* iv. 85 Non-metaphorical poetry. **1865** Mill *Exam. Hamilton's Philos.* xiii. 249, I ask..whether to the natural, or non-metaphysical man, it is not as great a paradox [etc.]. **1892** W. Wallace tr. *Hegel's Logic* (ed. 2) 66 In these material, non-metaphysical surroundings, thought is free. **1937** *Mind* XLVI. 120 He lays stress on the resolution made by the Congress to produce an International Encyclopaedia which is to represent in a unified, physicalistic, non-metaphysical terminology the Unity of Science. **1933** A. N. Whitehead *Adventures of Ideas* viii. 142 Geometry, developed in this fashion, has been termed 'Non-metrical Projective Geometry'. **1963** *Times* 22 Feb. 16/5 The original non-metrical notation. **1909** Webster, Non-migratory. **1926** J. S. Huxley *Ess. Pop. Sci.* 171 This occupation of territory [by birds] takes place in..the same way in migratory and non-migratory forms. **1964** *Oceanogr. & Marine Biol.* II. 186 That it is independent of species is apparent from comparison of examples such as the brown trout and sea trout, non-migratory and migratory forms respectively of the species, *Salmo trutta*. **1869** Mill *Subj. Women* iv. 158 Gentleness, generosity, and self-abnegation, towards the non-military and defenceless classes generally. **1956** A. H. Compton *Atomic Quest* 239 A nonmilitary atomic demonstration. **1965** G. McInnes *Road to Gundagai* i. 20 His decision to pursue what the A.I.F. called Non-Military Employment. **1957** N. Frye *Anatomy of Criticism* 290 Farce, being a non-mimetic form of comedy, has a natural place in the masque. **1959** J. L. Austin *Sense & Sensibilia* (1962) xi. 137 Consider, he says, the statement, 'I hear a car'. This is non-minimal, he says. **1966** G. N. Leech *Eng. in Advertising* viii. 84 A complete measure of grammatical complexity would require a similar calculation for all non-minimal units. **1928** H. Poutsma *Gram. Late Mod. Eng.* (ed. 2) i. i. i. 37 Also non-modal *may* is frequently attended by emotional *perhaps*. **1953** *Mind* LXII. 398 The philosophical character of a modal system turns in the first place on which non-modal expressions are flagged as necessary. **1957** A. N. Prior *Time & Modality* 60 The non-modal part of the theory of reference..could be ..formalized. **1961** *Lancet* 19 Aug. 435/1 No constant abnormality was observed in the non-modal cells. **1971** J. Anderson in A. J. Aitken et al. *Edin. Stud. Eng. & Scots* 102 Note, however, that the complex modals can have only the future interpretation, as is also the case with their non-modal equivalents. **1890** W. James *Princ. Psychol.* I. viii. 215 Fichte calls it [*sc.* the soul] the inner body, Ulrici likens it to a fluid of non-molecular composition. **1965** Phillips & Williams *Inorg. Chem.* I. vi. 193 Most non-molecular solids give this type of spectrum, but salts do not. **1951** R. Firth *Elements of Social Organization* iv. 133 A non-monetary economy does provide for a great deal of direct matching of goods and services. **1909** *Cent. Dict.* Suppl., Non-motile. **1956** *Nature* 11 Feb. 257/2 One of the strains—*Proteus X* 1—..was under some conditions motile and under others non-motile. **1902** W. James *Var. Relig. Exper.* xvi. 421 Music gives us ontological messages which non-musical criticism is unable to contradict. **1965** *B.B.C. Handbk.* 200 Suggestions for non-musical light entertainment programmes. **1902** W. James *Var. Relig. Exper.* iv. 90 More ordinary non-mystical conditions of rapture suffice for my immediate contention. **1941** *Mind* L. 128 One would like there to be a uniformity of knowing-power in such straightforward non-mystical matters. **1937** S. Spender *Forward from Liberalism* 272 The U.S.S.R. offers the world the example of the non-national state. **1942** L. B. Namier *Conflicts* 11 A line of independent States arose between Austria and Turkey which, with the backing of Russia, were to become a menace to both these non-national Empires. **1909** *Westm. Gaz.* 2 Sept. 2/1 The country which is..dependent upon intelligent work for non-native wealth. **1968** P. M. Postal *Aspects Phonol. Theory* vi. 126 When languages borrow large bodies of vocabulary they very often borrow nonnative phonological matrices. **1975** *Verbatim* May 5/2 Nonnative speakers seem to lack the security of being able to admit they are ignorant of a word. **1934** *Political Q.* V. 135 For expressions of non-Nazi opinion we have to go outside Germany. **1939** *War Illustr.* 9 Dec. 394 Written by a non-Nazi German who was interned in England. **1885** J. Veitch *Institutes of Logic* xxxiv. 464 Our expectation of recurrence in the future is determined by the condition that we do not know that any negative or destructive cause has been at work. The theory of the Inductive Principle is at once positive and negative, or rather is positive and non-negative. **1937** *Mind* XLVI. 58 Gödel's procedure of arithmetization consists essentially of the establishment of a one–one correlation between all possible series of symbols belonging to the 'object language' (*i.e.*, a certain system of mathematics) and certain non-negative integers. **1966** *Mathematical Rev.* XXXI. 22/1 Representations of natural numbers as sums of nonnegative *k*th powers. **1957** L. Fox *Numerical Solution Two-Point Boundary Probl.* vii. 180 This involves..a non-negligible difference correction in the finite-difference equations. **1972** *Science* 27 Oct. 407/1 Account had to be taken of the very small, but nonnegligible, declination motion of the satellite. **1927** Haldane & Huxley *Animal Biol.* ix. 177 In the higher animals, the living capital is locked up in non-negotiable forms to a much greater extent. **1969** *Listener* 8 May 632/1 These demands are almost always called 'non-negotiable', so that the university's offer to negotiate is..meaningless. **1973** M. & G. Gordon *Informant* xxv. 101 About the securities, even the theft of the non-negotiable ones could hurt us badly. **1959** E. M. Patterson *Topology* (ed. 2) ii. 49 The only non-null open set is the whole space, and so no separation condition is possible. **1974** *Canad. Jrnl. Linguistics* XIX. 198 Substitution rules are defined as including both deletion rules and rules substituting a non-null element for a term in the Structural Index. **1903** B. Russell *Princ. Math.* xxxii. 264 Other instances of non-numerical functions are afforded by dictionaries. **1940** W. V. Quine *Math. Logic* 68 The analogous use of letters in non-numerical fields. **1973** *Computers & Humanities* VII. 173 It conveys an erroneous impression to science students concerning the present state of so-called non-numerical data processing. **1964** *Oceanogr. & Marine Biol.* II. 260 Reeve (1963) working with *Artemia salina*..showed that it does not discriminate between nutritious and non-nutritious particles when filter-feeding. **1973** *Sci. Amer.* Dec. 66/1 It is then given over to savannas of coarse, non-nutritious grasses, bamboo thickets and stands of bracken and other ferns. **1945** *Mind* LIV. 4 The theory [of matter] itself contains a large number of highly abstract, non-observational terms such as 'atom', 'electron', 'nucleus', 'dissociation', 'valence'. **1960** W. V. Quine *Word & Object* 47 He can translate the non-observational occasion sentences. **1850** *Punch* Aug. 57/2 We subjoin a specimen of the two styles of reports, the one official, and the other non-official. **1970** *Jrnl. General Psychol.* LXXXII. 215 Analyses of a variety of official and non-official documents. **1946** *Nature* 23 Nov. 742/1 (*heading*) Silicon carbide non-ohmic resistors. **1973** *Physics Bull.* Dec. 741/1 The final chapter..describes the nonohmic behaviour observed in several semiconductors. **1942** *Tee Emm* (Air Ministry) II. 63 The C.M.E. has passed me 'fit for non-operational flying at home'. And the Blitz has started! **1949** A. Pap *Elem. Analytical Philos.* v. 97 A non-operational definition. **1946** C. Morris *Signs, Language & Behavior* 18 The non-organic world. **1968** C. A. Doxiadis *Between Dystopia & Utopia* 34 Cities continued to spread in what seems to be a non-organic pattern. **1884** E. Klein *Micro-Organisms & Disease* xviii. 169 (*heading*) Vital phenomena of non-pathogenic organisms. **1964** M. Hynes *Med. Bacteriol.* (ed. 8) ii. 10 Fæcal streptococci resist 60° C. for 30 minutes and non-pathogenic thermophilic bacteria may actually grow at 75° C. **1904** W. James *Ess. Radical Empiricism* (1912) i. 16 These non-perceptual experiences have objectivity as well as subjectivity. **1963** P. Gardiner *Schopenhauer* ii. 52 Attempts to describe or explain the physical world in non-perceptual terms. **1962** B. M. Strang *Mod. Eng. Structure* viii. 142 Thus, *he is eating* is non-interrogative, non-negative, non-passive, non-perfective, but is durative. **1973** *Archivum Linguisticum* IV. 34 The behaviour of transitive verbs in non-perfective sentences is exactly parallel to that of intransitive verbs in both perfective and non-perfective sentences. **1922** Joyce *Ulysses* 287 Nonperishable goods. **1962** R. B. Fuller *Epic Poem on Industrialization* 212 The 'non-perishables', chiefly the industrial metals. **1974** *Times* 21 Dec. 9/4 Shop for all non-perishable foods this weekend. **1975** *Times* 9 Dec. 16/6 Non-perishables, such as grain and butter. **1967** *Punch* 27 Dec. 976/1 We can't simply go back one square, trying to apply to Them what our non-permissive parents practised on Us. **1973** S. Fisher *Female Orgasm* iv. 102 Femininity seemed to be maximized by a parental orientation that was nonpermissive and punitive. **1928** D. H. Lawrence *Let.* 13 Mar. (1932) 711, I feel one still has to fight for the phallic reality, as against the non-phallic cerebration unrealities. **1973** S. Fisher *Female Orgasm* iii. 69 The female experiences her body as nonphallic, in contrast to the male whose body feelings are saturated with phallic qualities. **1879** W. James *Coll. Ess. & Rev.* (1920) 94 Such relations, represented as non-phenomenal entities, become thus the *bête noire* and pet aversion of many thinkers. **1954** R. Wells in Saporta & Bastian *Psycholinguistics* (1961) 276/1 In that case we invent or postulate some non-phenomenal circumstance. *a*1866 J. Grote *Exam. Utilitarian Philos.* (1870) xvi. 243 Only the older utilitarianism..has any sympathy with this non-philosophical spirit. **1965** *Language* XLI. 511 A nonphilosophical writer like Euripides? **1933** L. Bloomfield *Language* ix. 147 Non-phonemic, gesture-like features may become fairly fixed. **1953** C. E. Bazell *Linguistic Form* 22 This is most strikingly illustrated in Zoque, where the impermissibility of many sequences of consonants leads to a non-phonemic transposition of phoneme-order in the event of suffixation. **1965** *Canad. Jrnl. Linguistics* X. 147 The illusion of objective non-phonemic recording. **1964** *Archivum Linguisticum* XVI. 43 The main non-phonetic or non-French features of the *graphie occitane*. **1973** *Sci. Amer.* Feb. 60/2 Given the nonphonetic nature of the Chinese writing system, it may seem an impossible task to reconstruct how the language was spoken many centuries ago. **1920** A. S. Eddington *Space, Time & Gravitation* xii. 194 The matter..can only differ in a mysterious non-physical quality—that of identity. **1957** G. Ryle in M. Black *Importance of Lang.* (1962) 166 All three maintained the doctrine of a third realm of non-physical, nonpsychological entities. **1934** Webster, Nonplanar. **1945** *Jrnl. Inst. Electr. Engin.* XCII. i. 163/2 This procedure breaks down if the old circuit cannot be drawn without crossings between some of its branches ('non-planar' networks). **1964** N. G. Clark *Mod. Org. Chem.* xviii. 366 This work suggests that the basic units of vitrinite consist of small benzenoid groups joined together... These elongated, non-planar, rather rigid units have a molecular weight of 1000 to 3000. **1925** I. A. Richards *Princ. Literary Criticism* 250 In ordinary, non-poetic, non-imaginative experience. **1964** W. S. Allen in D. Abercrombie et al. *Daniel Jones* 7 Sequences of words in the course of non-poetic utterance. **1935** *Discovery* Nov. 316/1 White non-poisonous pigments. **1968** *Times* 2 Oct. 12/6 Butterflies reared on non-poisonous plants. **1878** Non-polarizable [see Polarizable *a.*] **1966** Phillips & Williams *Inorg. Chem.* II. xxv. 243 (*caption*) Upper plot (type A) corresponds to a non-polarizable ligand, lower plot (type B) to a polarizable ligand. **1946** *Nature* 5 Oct. 475/1 Compact, non-porous sorbing media such as wool. **1966** A. W. Lewis *Gloss. Woodworking Terms* 62 *Non-porous woods*, woods from conifers, i.e. softwoods, which do not contain vessels or pores. **1950** *Mind* LIX. 262 This book..claims to show how the predicative activities of judgment arise out of earlier, non-predicative forms of awareness. **1964** E. Palmer tr. *Martinet's Elem. General Linguistics* iv. 133 Units which are all capable of assuming predicative and non-predicative functions. *Ibid.* iii. 88 An accent with a non-predictable position. **1946** *Nature* 26 Oct. 590/1 The sera studied were taken from umbilical blood, infants up to the age of eighteen months, and adults in the pregnant and non-pregnant state, as controls. **1954** G. I. M Swyer *Reproduction & Sex* vi. 83 The normal non-pregnant uterus is approximately 7·5 cm. (3 in.) long. **1904** H. Poutsma *Gram. Late Mod. Eng.* i. i. iii. 130 Both the objects are non-prepositional. **1933** M. Callaway *Consecutive Subjunctive in O.E.* i. 11 In the *Lindisfarne Gospels* we find few Consecutive Subjunctives Introduced by Non-prepositional Correlative Particles. **1964** E. Palmer tr. *Martinet's Elem. General Linguistics* i. 15 In the case of linguistics it is particularly important to insist on the scientific and non-prescriptive character of our approach. **1922** Non-productive [see *direct *a.* 6 f]. **1961** *Brno Studies in English* III. 18 The type to which they belong is a traditional, non-productive one. **1974** P. H. Matthews *Morphology* xii. 221 The formation of *breadth* is wholly non-productive. **1946** *Nature* 26 Oct. 578/1 Several departments in the College have non-professorial heads. **1969** H. Perkin *Key Profession* i. 15 Non-professorial tutors and lecturers. **1909** Webster, Non-progressive. **1950** B. Russell *Unpopular Essays* ix. 166 Learning in Babylonia seems..to have become

stereotyped and non-progressive. 1973 Archivum Linguisticum IV. 7 The action involved is of a continuous nature as is clear..from a comparison with a non-progressive future. 1937 Mind XLVI. 103 Of course, she could not discuss in detail the question of non-propositional truth in so short a volume. 1903 B. Russell Princ. Math. iii. 35 If I may be allowed to use the word assertion in a non-psychological sense. 1965 B. Mates Elem. Logic i. 7 Leibniz..wishes to use the..word [sc. 'inconceivable'] in what may be termed a 'non-psychological' sense. 1946 Nature 14 Sept. 381/2 Within the scope of non-public management lie such special fields as industrial administration, commercial or business administration, [etc.]. 1938 Mind XLVII. 251 In any case I cannot see any other way of defining a 'higher' centre than by saying that it is a class of happenings which facilitate 'purposeful' series and inhibit 'non-purposeful' ones. 1926 J. S. Huxley Essays of Biologist (ed. 3) i. 41 Apparently purposive structures could arise by means of a non-purposive mechanism. 1965 P. Caws Philos. of Sci. xl. 312 The goal itself may emerge from an originally nonpurposive activity. 1940 W. V. Quine Math. Logic 7 To the scientist longing for non-quantitative techniques, ..mathematical logic brings hope. 1971 Computers & Humanities V. 317 Quantitative data covering this aspect of the story are supplemented by a narrative based on traditional (non-quantitative) sources. 1909 Westm. Gaz. 7 Apr. 3/1 It is to be conducted on 'absolutely non-racial and non-party lines'. 1971 Rand Daily Mail 3 Apr. 1/3 We stand for nonracial not multiracial cricket and..believe in selection on merit, irrespective of colour. 1972 Jrnl. Social Psychol. LXXXVII. 150 It may be that these nonsignificant results were due to the nonracial nature of the communications. 1904 E. Rutherford Radio-Activity 397/2 Preparation of non-radio-active thorium. 1937 Discovery Apr. 127/1 An isotope of a non-radioactive element. 1909 Webster, Nonreactive, without inductance or capacity. 1962 Simpson & Richards Physical Princ. Junction Transistors vi. 107 Another non-reactive extrinsic effect is sometimes added to the low-frequency equivalent circuit. 1969 Jane's Freight Containers 1968–69 550/1 The braking safety and non-reactive road holding characteristics required by today's operators. 1941 Mind L. 163 A difficulty which Price doubts whether any non-Realistic theory can completely remove is that quite specific statements may be made purporting to be about unperceived objects for the existence of which there is no evidence. 1965 J. Lawlor in J. Gibb Light on C. S. Lewis 75 The non-realistic nature of a large part of Shakespearian characterization. 1949 Mind LVIII. 3 A 'determining' element which qualifies it in some non-reciprocal way. 1935 B. Russell Relig. & Sci. ii. 45 What was unusual or non-recurrent was assigned directly to the will of God. 1973 Univ. Oxf. Ann. Rep. 1970–71 6 The Institute received £150 as a non-recurrent supplement to the departmental grant. 1939 Mind XLVIII. 399 Russell long ago emphasised that Peano's axioms, for instance, could be satisfied in infinitely many ways by objects other than the integers. The same is true of all non-redundant sets of axioms. 1972 J. L. Dillard Black English iii. 93 Non-redundant tense marking... This system of tense marking persists into Black English today. 1903 B. Russell Princ. Math. iv. 49 Subject-predicate propositions are distinguished by just this non-relational character. 1954 I. M. Copi Symbolic Logic v. 145 The non-relational premiss that all greyhounds are dogs. 1843 Mill Logic I. ii. § 7. 1. 53 The fifth leading division of names is into relative and absolute, or let us rather say, relative and non-relative; for the word absolute is put upon much too hard duty in metaphysics, not to be willingly spared when its services can be dispensed with. 1934 Mind XLIII. 202 Such an independence of non-relative properties is what the operationalist theories, with the exception of Mead's, come to. 1930 Nature 20 Dec. 954/1 Non-relativistic wave mechanics. 1970 G. K. Woodgate Elem. Atomic Struct. ii. 12 Schrödinger's equation is equivalent to the non-relativistic form of the classical equation of conservation of energy. 1902 W. James Var. Relig. Exper. viii. 176 In these non-religious cases the new man may also be born either gradually or suddenly. 1929 D. H. Lawrence Pansies 66 The mind is non-religious. 1964 E. A. Nida Toward Sci. Transl. v. 109 It would have been possible to use the label 'religious vs. nonreligious'. 1956 Ld. Boyd-Orr in A. Pryce-Jones New Outl. Mod. Knowledge 539 This great accelerating rate of increasing consumption of non-renewable sources of energy. 1974 Guardian 27 Aug. 14/6 Human time..is the ultimate non-renewable resource. 1923 Gramophone June 25/2 Music to assert itself has become representational; painting to assert itself has become non-representational. 1958 Times 20 Aug. 11/1 The non-representational third symphony. 1855 S. Bailey Lett. on Philos. Human Mind 212 Ideas of a non-representative character. 1925 I. A. Richards Princ. Literary Criticism 159 From Raphael..to Rembrandt..all degrees of participation between non-representative form and represented subject ..can be found. 1942 W. Churchill End of Beginning (1943) 180 The outstanding fact which has so far emerged from the violent action of the Congress Party has been their non-representative character. a1910 W. James Some Probl. Philos. (1911) v. 82 What I am contending for is that the non-reproducible part of reality is an essential part of the content of philosophy. 1908 Daily Chron. 4 May 3/3 If Socialism was to come in England,..it must needs have come in a slow, quiet, non-revolutionary, almost invisible way. 1959 Brno Studies in English I. 121 The non-revolutionary Fabian standpoint. 1905 Tablet 14 Oct. 608/2 Some mission or other that called itself Catholic but confessed itself non-Roman. 1964 R. H. Robins Gen. Linguistics v. 193 The use of orthographic spaces, or other marks as in some non-roman scripts. 1956 Nature 31 Mar. 610/2 Professional advisory service of a non-routine nature. 1964 F. Bowers Bibliogr. & Textual Criticism III. i. 69 The occurrence of error through non-routine copying. 1934 Webster, Nonsaponifiable. 1946 Nature 28 Dec. 950/1 Prelog, Ruzicka and Stein isolated a compound..from the non-saponifiable portion of extracts of pig spleen. 1967 Oceanogr. & Marine Biol. V. 173 Using alcoholic KOH, lipids may be separated into a saponifiable fraction..and a non-saponifiable fraction including the sterols, carotenoids, wax-alcohols, and hydrocarbons. 1875 W. James Coll. Ess. & Rev .(1920) 4 (As is almost always the case with non-skeptical systems) it simply ends by 'indorsing' common-sense. 1941 N. K. Smith Philos. of D. Hume p. v, This doctrine is the key to the non-sceptical, realist teaching which Hume has expounded. 1831 J. S. Mill Lett. (1910) I. 4 The clergy of a non-sectarian church. 1937 J. M. Murry Necessity of Pacifism v. 81 The Adelphi Centre is a centre of non-sectarian Socialism. 1948 E. Waugh Loved One 138 All non-sectarian services expeditiously conducted at competitive prices. 1975 G. Seymour Harry's Game xiii. 180 Most of the farmers round were Prods but..the market was 'non-sectarian', as they'd say these days. 1927 R. H. Wilenski Mod. Movement in Art 95 It was the artist's duty to rival the camera in purely mechanical non-selective vision. 1958 Observer 20 July 21/5 The danger lies in the enforcement of the non-selective principle in the vast majority of schools which will continue as separate units in existing buildings. 1909 W. M. Urban Valuation iv. 98 The non-sensational aspects of any experience are..describable in functional terms. 1921 B. Russell Analysis of Mind iv. 81 (heading) Non-sensational elements in perception. 1937 Mind XLVI. 307 Kant holds that we are never acquainted with existence in a wholly non-sensory way. 1855 J. M. D. Meiklejohn tr. Kant's Critique Pure Reason II. i. 56 The understanding was defined above only negatively, as a non-sensuous faculty of cognition. 1934 Mind XLIII. 364 Locke taught that we can have a non-sensuous intuition of agreement and disagreement of ideas. 1939 Mind XLVIII. 483 It is full sentences that serve for communication, not isolated or non-sentential signs. 1966 Jrnl. Philos. LXIII. 665 Propositions in a nonsentential sense were unavailable,..so facts seemed all the more needed. 1960 Amer. Speech XXXV. 232 Correlates of Central Romance palatals..are best interpreted as members of a three-way set: plain (nonsharp).., sharp.., and palatal. 1967 E. Chambers Photolitho-Offset vii. 80 An anastigmatic lens gives a flat field and corrects any spherical shape of the image area which otherwise is non-sharp towards the edges of the image. 1897 Sears, Roebuck Catal. 239/2 Men's heavy winter weight..wool shirts... Non-shrinkable. 1963 A. J. Hall Textile Sci. v. 242 This shrunk non-shrinkable finish is then set by passing it (with drying) around the hot cylinder of a Palmer machine P. 1890 W. James Princ. Psychol. I. xi. 411 The 'difficulty', in the cases of which Wundt speaks, is that of forcing two non-simultaneous events into apparent combination with the same instant of time. 1953 C. E. Bazell Linguistic Form 44 The fact that the units concerned may occur as units in a functionally discrete sequence is one criterion for treating the units as non-simultaneous. 1944 J. S. Huxley On Living in Rev. ii. 18 Powerful monopolies develop, which, from being merely non-social, may become definitely anti-social. 1964 M. Argyle Psychol. & Social Probl. xiv. 176 Social structures often change as the result of non-social factors in the situation—technical, economic and so on. 1949 Koestler Promise & Fulfilment III. i. 305 The political record of the only strong non-Socialist opposition Party in Israel is one of frustration and sterility. 1959 New Statesman 13 June 833/2 The idea of a planned hospital service had been developed by non-socialist doctors by 1920 (Dawson Report). 1888 W. James Let. 22 Aug. in R. B. Perry Tht. & Char. of W.J. (1935) II. 86 By the Kantian view..I mean the doctrine of a supersensational construction. For Kant there is a non-spatial sensational chaos before there is space in the mind. 1897 B. Russell Essay on Foundations of Geometry iv. 181 The argument rests on a petitio principii, for only if sensations are necessarily non-spatial does their projection demand a subjective space-form. 1851 Phil. Mag. I. 177 Poisson.. does not overlook the possibility of these magnetic elements being non-spherical and symmetrically arranged in crystalline matter. 1971 I. G. Gass et al. Understanding Earth vii. 98/1 The uneven attraction of the non-spherical Earth. 1940 S. Glasstone Text-bk. Physical Chem. xiii. 1063 One of the results of non-stationary chains is the phenomenon of explosion limits. 1968 P. A. P. Moran Introd. Probability Theory iii. 173 This is a non-stationary pure birth process. 1922 A. D. Udden tr. Bohr's Theory of Spectra II. i. 22 This is of great importance, since it represents the first instance in which the quantum theory was applied to a phenomenon of non-statistical character. 1949 A. Pap Elem. Analytical Philos. ix. 179 We use the word 'probable' in a non-statistical sense. 1963 Higher Educ. (Cmnd. 2154) 315 The form of government, including financial and other relations with central and local government, with non-statutory bodies and with industry. 1946 Nature 5 Oct. 475/2 He laid the foundation for a fundamental study of the kinetics of dyeing by deriving four differential equations to describe the non-steady state of flow. 1960 Times 1 Sept. 2 Application of non-steady flow theory. 1975 Sci. Amer. Nov. 81 The muscle-powered flight of birds, bats and insects depends on the flapping of the wings, which introduces a degree of nonsteady airflow. Nonsteady aerodynamics is thus inherent in natural flapping flight. 1946 Nature 24 Aug. 275/2 Some years ago, LeBlanc and Eberius reported that in the decomposition of lead dioxide, PbO_2, a range of homogeneous oxides of non-stoichiometric formulae was formed. 1965 Phillips & Williams Inorg. Chem. I. viii. 267 There are compounds of the type $Fe_{0.95}O$, $GeTe_{1.025}$, $Ti_{1.103}S_2$. Such non-stoicheiometric compounds are found largely amongst minerals, alloys, and those compounds which contain one or more elements giving rise to at least two valence states. 1954 U. Weinreich in Saporta & Bastian Psycholinguistics (1961) 379/2 The interplay of structural and non-structural factors. 1965 Hughes & Londey Elem. of Formal Logic iii. 16 In doing this we have by-passed the non-structural features, i.e. the particular content of the propositions. 1902 W. James Var. Relig. Exper. xviii. 433 Logical reason drawing rigorous inference from non-subjective facts. 1965 F. Sargeson Memoirs of Peon vii. 192 Unless there had been some non-subjective displacement in the timing of events. 1907 J. H. Parsons Diseases of Eye xi. 258 (heading) Non-suppurative keratitis. 1951 Whitby & Hynes Med. Bacteriol. (ed. 5) xv. 273 Prostration is extreme, with..a characteristic non-suppurative arthritis floating from joint to joint. 1849 H. L. Mansel Aldrich's Artis Logicæ App. 38 Aquinas..admits the ἔκθεσις as a non-syllogistic process, being an appeal to the senses, not to the reason. 1971 Jrnl. Gen. Psychol. Apr. 239 This was an effort to present deductive reasoning demands in a nonsyllogistic form. 1903 B. Russell Princ. Math. I. ii. 18 There are much greater difficulties in the way of non-symbolic exposition of the ideas embedded in our symbolism. 1933 Chapman & Henle Fundamentals of Logic 226 There has been a complete separation between the 'informal' non-symbolic postulates and the 'formal' symbolic ones. 1961 L. F. Brosnahan Sounds of Language viii. 182 Features of sound complements (which are, of course, non-symbolic). 1964 E. Bach Introd. Transformational Gram. vii. 155 It [sc. a relation] is nonsymmetric if there is at least one pair such that $R(x, y)$ and not $R(y, x)$... Loving is nonsymmetric, as numerous poems testify. 1948 H. Reichenbach Elem. Symb. Logic iii. 119 We include both mesosymmetrical and asymmetrical functions in the group of nonsymmetrical functions. 1955 H. Leblanc Introd. to Deductive Logic 188 A relation R is said to be non-symmetrical in a class A if it is neither symmetrical nor asymmetrical in A. 1912, 1940 Non-synchronous [see *asynchronous a.]. 1971 Engineering Apr. 6/1 With synchronous or non-synchronous controls. 1953 in M. Macdonald Philos. & Analysis (1954) 63 Some clearly non-synonymous names or predicates apply to exactly the same objects. 1965 B. Mates Elem. Logic v. 79 The indicated procedure can lead to different, and plainly non-synonymous, translations for the same formal sentence. 1957 R. W. Zandvoort Handbk. Eng. Gram. IX. i. 283 Such a non-syntactic group as happy-go-lucky. 1965 N. Chomsky Aspects of Theory of Syntax iv. 158 One can cite cases of perfectly grammatical strings that are incongruous on nonsyntactic grounds. 1960 Non-systematic [see *impressionistic a. 2]. 1964 E. A. Nida Towards Sci. Transl. v. 87 It must be recognized, however, that semantic space may be orthogonal, i.e. regular and systematic, or it may be nonorthogonal, i.e. irregular and nonsystematic. 1949 Mind LVIII. 69 This simply begs the central question at issue, viz. whether there can be any necessary non-tautologous propositions. 1955 A. N. Prior Formal Logic 139 'Analytic' and 'synthetic' are now often used as synonyms for 'tautologous' and 'non-tautologous' respectively. 1920 A. S. Eddington Space, Time & Gravit. xii. 180 But this mode of development of the theory cannot be described in a non-technical book. 1944 W. Temple Let. 5 Jan. (1963) 132 The non-technical mind of the ordinary Churchman. 1971 Engineering Apr. 26/1 He spends his time on non-technical activities. 1949 Koestler Insight & Outlook x. 153 Like all means towards an end (or subfunctions in nonteleological language). 1972 M. A. Boden Purposive Explan. in Psychol. v. 180 The nonteleological factors involved may include learnt motor habits. 1924 R. M. Ogden tr. Koffka's Growth of Mind v. § 1. 244 The images that occur can scarcely be called non-temporal. 1933 A. N. Whitehead Adventures of Ideas xiii. 209 The everlasting nature of God, which in a sense is non-temporal and in another sense temporal. 1954 I. M. Copi Symbolic Logic v. 132 The words 'always', 'never', and 'sometimes' frequently have a strictly non-temporal significance. 1962 H. C. Conklin in Householder & Saporta Problems in Lexicography 129 The same segregates may be classed..as terminal or nonterminal categories in another taxonomy. 1965 Language XLI. 292 Certain nonterminal constituents. 1959 New Statesman 14 Nov. 661/1 The film was made by the BBC Television Service, and is scheduled for non-theatric distribution; which means that it will only be seen by film societies and non-paying audiences. 1966 BBC Handbk. 39 The distribution of programmes for non-theatric use in schools. 1927 T. S. Eliot in Newton's Seneca (Tudor Translations) I. p. xi, This curious freak of non-theatrical drama. 1964 F. Bowers Bibliogr. & Textual Criticism VI. i. 160 A non-theatrical manuscript such as an author's 'foul papers'. 1879 Dublin Rev. Apr. 263 It seems to be the wish of the prominent non-theistic writers of our own day to be called Agnostics. 1964 E. Fromm in I. L. Horowitz New Sociology 191 Marx's theory..is close to Pelagius' heresy; it is a doctrine of salvation in non-theistic terms. 1962 H. R. Loyn Anglo-Saxon England (1963) vi. 285 Interest was also shown in non-theological matters. 1943 Mind LII. 130 Clearly the outcome of a maze learning experiment is completely devoid of any significance in the latter, non-theoretical sense. 1963 P. Gardiner Schopenhauer v. 216 At a non-theoretical level, Schopenhauer suggests, such features of aesthetic awareness are..recognized by sensitive and perceptive persons. 1959 D. Cooke Lang. of Music p. xiii, The new non-tonal language..must be restricted to expressing what chromaticism always was restricted to expressing. 1963 Listener 21 Feb. 345/3 Schoenberg went on from there to write first non-tonal and later twelve-note music. 1964 R. H. Robins Gen. Linguistics iii. 111 English, a non-tonal language. 1941 J. S. Huxley Uniqueness of Man xi. 235 The T.V.A. in America is perhaps the largest social experiment ever undertaken, at any rate in a non-totalitarian country. 1967 H. Arendt Orig. Totalitarianism (new ed.) ix. 279 Non-totalitarian countries..generally have shied away from mass repatriations. 1946 Nature 31 Aug. 294/1 Animal experiments with guinea pigs and rabbits have shown polyporin to be completely non-toxic. 1971 Engineering Apr. 30/1 Since the introduction of plastics enabled the use of non-tainting, non-toxic, and non-staining materials. 1938 Wyndham Lewis Let. 1 May (1963) 253 A non-traditional (and so a 'fashionable') policy. 1957 Manvell & Huntley Technique Film Music iii. 169 The term 'synthetic sound' is generally used to cover a wide variety of new, non-traditional methods of making noise, sound effects, music, and speech, by electronic, magnetic, mechanical, optical, and other means. 1914 B. Russell Our Knowl. External World ii. 48 A relation is said to be non-transitive whenever it is not transitive. Thus 'brother' is non-transitive, because a brother of one's brother may be oneself. All kinds of dissimilarity are non-transitive. 1964 E. Bach Introd. Transformational Gram. vii. 155 Friend is nontransitive if you are my friend and have friends who are not my friends. 1974 Sci. Amer. Oct. 120/1 Familiar games abound in transitive rules (if poker hand A beats B and B beats C, then A beats C), but some games have nontransitive (or intransitive) rules. 1946 Nature 14 Sept. 361/2 Another means of attaining greater efficiency in flight..is to design the wing section

so that the flow in the very thin 'boundary-layer' of air near the wing surface remains non-turbulent over as much of the surface as possible. **1964** J. C. CATFORD in D. Abercrombie et al. *Daniel Jones* 30 Airflow through the glottis is non-turbulent and consequently silent. **1890** W. JAMES *Princ. Psychol.* I. iii. 93 When we begin to react in the 'extreme sensorial' way, Lange says that we get times so very long that they must be rejected from the count as non-typical. **1959** *Brno Studies* I. 106 The non-typical nature of his [*sc.* Bulwer's] figures. **1874** W. WALLACE tr. *Hegel's Logic* 299 Finite things as finite ought in justice to be viewed as non-ultimate. **1935** *Mind* XLIV. 351 He ought to say that such facts as 'orange is between red and yellow' are incomplete or non-ultimate. **1886** G. S. CARR *Synopsis Elem. Results Pure & Appl. Math.* I. II. 905/1 (Index), Non-uniform functions. **1920** A. S. EDDINGTON *Space, Time & Gravit.* ii. 40 An absolute non-uniform motion through space is just as impossible to imagine as an absolute uniform motion. **1968** *Economist* 23 Mar. 48/2 The 40-month contract..reportedly gives workers giant but nonuniform wage increases. **1909** *Daily Chron.* 12 Apr. 4/4, I revisit America and wander off into the non-urban—there are no really rural—parts. **1953** K. JACKSON *Lang. & Hist. in Early Britain* 230 A state of affairs that was essentially non-urban. *a* **1866** J. GROTE *Exam. Utilit. Philos.* (1870) p. xvii, Mr. Mill gives up points objected to in the old utilitarianism, and approximates to non-utilitarian schools. **1965** F. SARGESON *Memoirs of Peon* i. 10 My grandmother was entirely non-utilitarian, a dreamer. **1939** *Mind* XLVIII. 202 And if *s* does express a proposition, thereby being subject to non-vacuous application of this [verification] principle, it could be the case [etc.]. **1965** N. CHOMSKY *Aspects of Theory of Syntax* i. 39 At least one rule $A \rightarrow x$ being obligatory for each category *A*, so as to guarantee that each cycle is nonvacuous. **1881** MAX MÜLLER tr. *Kant's Critique Pure Reason* (1896) 323 All those predicates are with regard to intuition non-valid, entailing no consequences with regard to objects of experience. **1935** *Mind* XLIV. 504 The content of a sentence is said to be the class of its non-valid consequences. **1919** A. C. DOYLE *Vital Message* iii. 102 Thus though 'non-veridical', to use the modern jargon, they do conform to all our canons of evidence. **1942** *Mind* LI. 43 But if there need be no 'intrinsic difference'..between veridical and non-veridical experiences, then how can you tell, at any given time, whether your perceptual experience is veridical or non-veridical? **1890** W. JAMES *Princ. Psychol.* II. xx. 212 Berkeley..concluded that distance could not possibly be a visual sensation, but must be an intellectual 'suggestion' from 'custom' of some non-visual experience. **1971** J. Z. YOUNG *Introd. Study Man* xxx. 421 Some lemurs have scent-glands on the fore-limbs; these are common among non-visual mammals. **1933** *Discovery* Sept. 278/1 It is, in fact, not an *aposeme* to frighten an enemy away..but an *episeme*, to distract attack from a vulnerable to a fortified or non-vital region. **1936** J. R. KANTOR *Objective Psychol. Gram.* xiii. 184 There is still left the question of interjectional acts or even non-vocal behavior. **1946** C. MORRIS *Signs, Language & Behavior* 192 That there are non-vocal languages is not generally disputed. **1964** R. H. ROBINS *Gen. Linguistics* iv. 157 Opposed acoustic features: vocalic, non-vocalic. **1930** *Times Educ. Suppl.* 15 Feb. 70/2 What was known as non-vocational education. **1963** *Higher Educ.* (Cmnd. 2154) 317 Courses of a mainly non-vocational character.

4. Prefixed to a sb. (or vbl. sb.) forming a phrase used attributively, as *non-citizen, -class, -combat, -copyright, -corridor, -county, -craft, -dollar, -equilibrium* (see also sense 1 in Dict. and Suppl.), *-fat* (cf. *non-fatty* in *3), *-food, -image, -jazz, -kernel, -language, -league, -narrative, -pedigree, -print, -profit, -protein, -speech, -structuralist, -teaching, -title, -vintage*; **non-association** (see quot. 1940).

Occas. such phrases are used predicatively (as in quot. 1956 for *non-protein*).

1909 *Installation News* II. 180 The standard qualities listed are:— (1) A class equivalent to what is generally designated throughout the trade as Non-Association Cable. (2) A grade equivalent to that manufactured by members of the Cable Makers' Association, and sold by the latter under the Association's label as Association-made Cable. **1940** *Chambers's Techn. Dict.* 582/1 *Non-association cable*, cable which is not manufactured or designed in accordance with the standards of the Cable Makers' Association. **1970** *East African Standard* 2 Jan. 15/2 In the Market Square in Kampala, which is one of the areas proscribed for non-citizen businessmen, there are several empty shops. **1957** R. N. CAREW HUNT *Guide to Communist Jargon* xxxii. 111 The ideologists of the imperialist bourgeoisie, hypocritically screening themselves behind a non-class approach. **1971** *Jrnl. Gen. Psychol.* Apr. 313 Centred on each of these cards was a column of 12 words, one of which was the correct response, the other 11 words being nonclass, low associate, masking words. **1944** D. WECTER *When Johnny comes marching Home* 547 He must also be persuaded that an important job waits for him, either in non-combat duty or in civil life. **1971** *Fremdsprachen* XV. 209 In the last three months of 1970, aircraft accidents were the chief cause of noncombat deaths. **1947** *Penguin Music Mag.* Dec. 37 British non-copyright masterpieces such as *David Copperfield*. **1908** *Daily Chron.* 31 July 1/7 The door on the non-corridor side of the train was found open. **1966** M. CATTO *Bird on Wing* vi. 93 It was one of those old-fashioned non-corridor trains. **1909** *Westm. Gaz.* 1 May 9/2 Property owned and leased by county and non-county boroughs. **1963** *Times* 7 June 3/7 It contains a detailed breakdown of the rates levied by the 83 county boroughs and 28 metropolitan boroughs, and there is also a representative selection of 226 non-county boroughs, 219 urban districts and 144 rural districts. **1961** *Spectator* 7 Apr. 474/2 These craft divisions, particularly those between what is considered 'craft' and 'non-craft' work, are apparently carried much further in Britain than elsewhere. **1958** *Ann. Reg.* 1957 88 Japan was placed on the same footing as other..non-dollar countries. **1951** S. R. DE GROOT *Thermodynamics of Irreversible Processes* xi. 220 (*heading*) Non-equilibrium thermodynamical functions. **1962** SIMPSON & RICHARDS *Physical Princ. Junction Transistors* i. 2 The higher energy states will be empty except in a non-equilibrium condition when an electron is excited to a higher state by some external influence. **1971** *Nature* 17 Dec. 393/1 Nonequilibrium thermodynamics, as developed by Onsager and others, has been successful in correlating many physical, chemical and biological phenomena. **1969** *Listener* 30 Jan. 159/3 The bonus payments scheme takes into account not merely the important nutrients in milk (protein, vitamins and minerals, commonly known as the 'non-fat solids') but also fat content, which doesn't matter a hoot to anyone who doesn't want to make butter or cheese. **1946** *Nature* 7 Sept. 324/1 Possible non-food industrial utilizations of the wheat protein. **1974** *Index-Jrnl.* (Greenwood, S. Carolina) 19 Apr. 1/5 Sharply higher food prices and a record jump in nonfood commodities pushed the cost of living up 1.1 per cent in March. **1953** KIRK & OTHMER *Encycl. Chem. Technol.* XI. 139 The moisture film produced on the plate is continuous on the nonimage areas of the plate. **1964** *Gloss. Letterpress Rotary Printing Terms* (*B.S.I.*) 9 *Blacking up*, printing of the non-image areas. **1926** WHITEMAN & MCBRIDE *Jazz* viii. 168 The orchestrations for bands, jazz and non-jazz are almost as important as the song plugger himself. **1958** P. GAMMOND *Decca Bk. Jazz* xv. 189 His fault at the moment..is his quick switching from jazz to non-jazz phrasing. **1963** *Amer. Speech* XXXVIII. 295 Nonkernel, derived sentences such as 'The man is on the corner'. **1936** J. R. KANTOR *Objective Psychol. Gram.* vi. 74 B's action may be connected with a non-language response—namely, handing over the book. **1946** C. MORRIS *Signs, Language & Behavior* 6 The differences between non-language and language signs. **1938** C. E. SUTCLIFFE et al. *Story of Football League* 12 The boycott of non-League clubs..was withdrawn. **1963** *Times* 28 Jan. 3/3 Nairn county, another non-league club still in the competition, came down from the Highlands on Saturday to cause a surprise by holding Hamilton Academicals, leaders of the second division, to a draw. **1975** *Liverpool Echo* (Football ed.) 11 Jan. 8/3, I cannot recall..so many non League clubs doing so well [in the F.A. Cup]. **1964** M. A. K. HALLIDAY et al. *Linguistic Sci.* 237 It shows the written language in use in non-narrative registers. **1931** *Times Lit. Suppl.* 13 Aug. 620/4 Others in favour are the Border, the Lakeland, the Fox, the Sealyham (but with these two it is generally specified that they must be 'non-pedigree' or 'old type'). **1960** *Farmer & Stockbreeder* 9 Feb. 85/3 The few non-pedigree cattle on offer were of moderate class and sold to 130gs. **1971** *Computers & Humanities* VI. 96 Such classes of material as technical reports, government documents, and microforms and other non-print media. **1972** *Guardian* 5 Dec. 9/7 The shift to non-print means of communication —television, the telephone. **1974** *Spartanburg* (S. Carolina) *Herald* 25 Apr. C. 2/5 Kawamura's laboratories are in the Mitsubishi Chemical Co.'s nonprofit Institute of Life Sciences which it set up in 1971 at a cost of $6·6 million. **1942** *Agenda* Oct. 305 The T.V.A...is required by statute to give preference to States, counties, municipalities, and non-profit co-operative associations. **1972** *Accountant* 28 Sept. 389/2 The interest rates are high, being 11 per cent for a with-profit policy and 10 per cent for a non-profit policy. [**1934** WEBSTER, Nonprotein, *n.*] **1946** *Nature* 2 Nov. 610/1 The now demonstrated ability of ruminants to utilize non-protein nitrogen in the form of urea. **1956** *Ibid.* 28 Jan. 190/2 Binkley..obtained a soluble fraction..which was apparently non-protein in nature. **1967** *Oceanogr. & Marine Biol.* V. 159 The biochemical analysis of marine invertebrates, especially their content of macromolecules..and reserves (lipids, carbohydrates, non-protein nitrogenous compounds (NPN)). **1954** F. G. CASSIDY *Robertson's Devel. Mod. Eng.* iv. 54 The phonetician..must include the entire range of speech sounds... Pike would have him investigate non-speech sounds too. **1953** C. E. BAZELL *Linguistic Form* 5 The earlier distinction of morpheme and semanteme is obsolete except in non-structuralist circles. **1959** *New Statesman* 21 Feb. 259/3 Hours are wasted each week in administrative, non-teaching duties such as special staff meetings, frequent house meetings, tutorial group meetings. **1973** *N.Y. Times* 28 Jan. 21/2 This is a nontitle fight and there is no weight restriction on heavyweights. **1953** D. PARRY *Going Up——Going Down* vi. 318 At dinner Clive ordered up four bottles of non-vintage champagne. **1959** *Listener* 5 Mar. 422/1 Bratby is here, of course, a non-vintage work half way between the 'larder' period and what is happening at his current exhibition. **1975** *Country Life* 2 Oct. 838/3 No non-vintage champagne may be sold until it has been a year in bottle.

5. b. Prefixed to an infinitive forming a phrase used attributively in the sense 'that does not ——', 'that is designed not to ——', as *non-crease, -crush, -dazzle, -shrink.* Cf. *NON-SKID *a.*, *NON-SLIP *a.*, *NON-STICK *a.*

1944 A. THIRKELL *Headmistress* ix. 200 Utility non-crease (though they were neither) ready-made dresses. **1969** *Punch* 5 Feb. 195/1 You *should* wear non-crease clothes. **1924** *Times Trade & Eng. Suppl.* 29 Nov. 247/2 It must be remembered that the heavy weight non-crush costume linens absorb an enormous quantity of flax in spinning. **1961** *Times* 4 Dec. (Agric. Suppl.) p. iii/5 An optional extra to be combined with a non-crush cab. **1962** *Times* 5 May 9/4 A non-dazzle protective covering for our remaining pictures. **1965** *Economist* 27 Feb. 929/2 An alternative pair of non-dazzle lamps.. [for] meeting other traffic. **1962** J. T. MARSH *Self-Smoothing Fabrics* xv. 256 The anti-shrink effect so often ignored by later publications on non-shrink processes. *a* **1963** L. MACNEICE *Astrology* (1964) vii. 237 The Zodiac..signs are featured..in advertisements for..non-shrink cottons.

6. a. Prefixed to ppl. adjs., as *non-aspirated, -associated, -centralized, -ciliated, -classified, -clogging, -coloured, -committed, -corroding, -defining, -dividing, -fabricated, -fattening, -flying, -glottalized, -graphitizing, -growing, -increasing, -interacting, -introduced, -ionized, -ionizing, -living, -medullated, -nasalized, -overlapping, -palatalized, -playing, -polarized, -polluting, -proliferating, -recurring, -referring, -reflecting, -scripted, -slaveholding, -specialized, -teaching, -terminating.*

1934 PRIEBSCH & COLLINSON *German Lang.* I. iii. 42 The non-aspirated mediae are treated differently from the aspirated mediae. **1964** E. A. NIDA *Toward Sci. Transl.* vi. 132 In one language in Central Africa there is a contrast between aspirated and nonaspirated consonants. **1934** C. LAMBERT *Music Ho!* ii. 78 Surrealism may conveniently be defined as the free grouping together of incongruous and non-associated images. **1974** *Information Handbk.* 1974–5 (Shell Internat. Petroleum Co.) 85 Non-associated gas – either from structures capable of producing only gas economically or from condensate reservoirs which yield relatively large amounts of gas per barrel of light liquid hydrocarbons. **1893** G. B. SHAW *Let.* 11 Jan. (1965) 377 My present intention is to go uncompromisingly for..non-centralized local organization of the Labor Party. **1956** *Nature* 3 Mar. 432/1 A well-defined zone of non-ciliated epithelium which lies along the medial sides of the lips of the endostylar groove [in *Ciona intestinalis*]. **1958** *New Statesman* 19 Apr. 494/1 The Columbia Inspection Project, a private, non-classified study of disarmament techniques. **1973** A. PRICE *October Men* x. 136 He is in charge of the non-classified printed material—newspapers, periodicals and journals. **1910** *Daily Chron.* 12 Mar. 8/5 A truly efficient non-clogging lubricant has been used. **1960** *Farmer & Stockbreeder* 16 Feb. 106/2 Automatic recoil-starter eliminating the use of loose starting rope; special non-clogging, fast-cutting blades, 18 in. cutting width. **1962** E. CLEAVER in A. Dundes *Mother Wit* (1973) 15/1 Blue eyes, long straight blonde hair, and non-colored skin. **1964** S. M. MILLER in I. L. Horowitz *New Sociology* 306 That can be done most effectively by outsiders—non-colored, non-poor—coming into the impoverished areas. **1901** R. FRY *Let.* 14 Mar. (1972) I. 180 Shannon, coming to such design from the Impressionist side,.. goes off into vague non-committed tastefulness. **1970** Non-committed [see *NON-ALIGNMENT]. **1908** *Daily Chron.* 21 Nov. 9/3 As evidence of their non-corroding quality specimens are shown in glass bottles immersed in water uninjured. **1967** E. CHAMBERS *Photolitho-Offset* xii. 189 The turntable consists of a non-corroding alloy. **1926** FOWLER *Mod. Eng. Usage* 635/2 The closer connexion between a defining, (or *that-*) clause & the antecedent than between a non-defining (or *which-*) clause & the antecedent. **1970** *Dict. Sci. Biogr.* I. 250/2 His [*sc.* Aristotle's] distinction..between defining and non-defining characteristics. **1945** KOESTLER *Yogi & Commissar* III. iv. 242 Non-dividing organic constituents (proteins, enzymes, hormones, etc.). **1939** *Mind* XLVIII. 170 The first objection asserts that all universals are fabricated, and no non-fabricated universals exist. **1971** *Woman's Own* 27 Mar. 30/2 It's expensive to eat non-fattening foods. **1941** N. MACMILLAN *Air Strategy* 53 Safeguarding the health and efficiency of the non-flying personnel. **1949** E. A. NIDA *Morphology* (ed. 2) 287 The contrasts in such changes are..glottalized, non-glottalized. **1973** *Word* 1970 XXVI. 6 A regular interchange..between nonglottalized and glottalized stops. **1951** Non-graphitizing [see *GRAPHITIZABLE *a.*]. **1971** *Nature* 30 July 306/2 The graphitizable carbon fibres probably have superior tensile properties..than the equivalently heated non-graphitizing carbon fibres. **1937** *Discovery* June 173/1 The non-growing tip must have some control over the growing region below it. **1968** H. HARRIS *Nucleus & Cytoplasm* iii. 54 In cells growing exponentially, ribosomal RNA appears to be essentially stable, and in non-growing cells, it turns over at a very much slower rate than the rapidly labelled RNA. **1962** D. R. COX *Renewal Theory* i. 3 Clearly $\mathscr{F}(0) = 1, \mathscr{F}(\infty) = 0$ and $\mathscr{F}(x)$ is a non-increasing function of *x*. **1951** A. C. EWING *Fundamental Questions Philos.* vi. 125 The same substance appearing under parallel non-interacting aspects. **1962** W. B. THOMPSON *Introd. Plasma Physics* viii. 170 For the case of non-interacting particles..eq. (8.1.1) may be integrated to yield the collisionless Boltzmann equation. **1957** R. W. ZANDVOORT *Handbk. Eng. Gram.* v. ii. 217 Note the following example of a non-introduced clause (with *so*): *I paid him double, I was so pleased.* **1966** *English Studies* XLVII. 262 The non-introduced type is normal in adjunct clauses to verbs, and in adjunct clauses to adjectives. **1902** *Encycl. Brit.* XXVIII. 15/1 In the case of non-electrolytes and of all non-ionized molecules this analogy completely represents the facts, and the phenomena of diffusion can be deduced from it alone. **1963** B. FOZARD *Instrumentation Nuclear Reactors* viii. 78 Thus glow transfer can be caused by applying a negative pulse to the cathode of the non-ionized gap. **1974** M. C. GERALD *Pharmacol.* iii. 39 At the physiological pH of body fluids, drug molecules exist as a mixture of the nonionized or uncharged molecular form and the ionized or charged form. **1903** *Nature* 3 Dec. 103/2 If non-ionising solvents like the hydrocarbons be substituted for water, the absence of effects attributable to ionisation might be discernible. **1968** M. S. LIVINGSTON *Particle Physics* iv. 83 Nonionizing neutral particles..were assumed also to be produced. **1926** J. S. HUXLEY *Ess. Pop. Sci.* 261 For Haldane, regulation places organisms in a different category from any non-living systems. **1971** J. Z. YOUNG *Introd. Study Man* ii. 14 It is not enough to base our biology only on familiar concepts with which we describe the non-living world. **1881** J. ROSS *Treat. Dis. Nervous Syst.* I. I. i. 22 (*heading*) Non-medullated nerve-fibres. *Ibid.* 23 A fatty material of a very special character accumulates in the interior of the protoplasm..in order to account for the development of the medullated from the non-medullated fibres (Ranvier). **1949** J. B. SPEAKMAN in J. M. Preston *Fibre Science* xvi. 277 Turning..to non-medullated fibres, Chamberlain found that the sulphur content of human hair, which had been descaled.. was identical with that of the original untreated hair. **1962** *Gray's Anat.* (ed. 33) 50 Fibres with a myelin sheath

are described as myelinated, medullated or white. Those devoid of it are termed unmyelinated, amyelinated, non-medullated or grey fibres. **1953** K. JACKSON *Lang. & Hist. in Early Britain* 642 (Apparently) non-nasalised spellings are found in MW. beside nasalised (non-nasal-ised even occurring in later MSS. when the earlier MS. copied has nasalised). **1950** *Mind* LIX. 202 The division is exhaustive and non-overlapping. **1968** P. A. P. MORAN *Introd. Probability Theory* iv. 185 A set function, ϕ (A), is said to be σ-additive on a σ-field, if ϕ (ΣA$_i$) = Σ ϕ(A$_i$) for every finite or enumerable set of non-over-lapping sets A$_i$ such that ϕ (ΣA$_i$) is bounded. **1956** JAKOBSON & HALLE in Saporta & Bastian *Psycho-linguistics* (1961) 348/2 Consonants: palatalized vs. non-palatalized. **1898** H. E. BYERS in W. A. Morgan '*House*' *on Sport* 206 The non-playing men alternately shout their approbation and make heavy bets. **1958** *Atlantic Monthly* Nov. 184/2 One solution is to..subsidize a trip to the movies for the nonplaying members of the family. **1959** *Times* 11 Sept. 9/3 The British team's non-playing captain. **1876** PREECE & SIVEWRIGHT *Telegraphy* iii. 60 A non-polarized relay..is not much used in England. The forms of relay more largely used are called polarized, because their armatures are either permanent magnets or are maintained in a magnetized condition. **1946** *Nature* 30 Nov. 794/2 The erythrocytes become dipoles.. and form chain-like aggregates... Sedimentation-rates of such red-cell aggregates will be greater than those of single non-polarized blood cells. **1967** *Economist* 8 July 107/3 Tenants in some rural areas had to prostrate them-selves at a safe, non-polluting distance on the one day they saw their Brahmin landlord, rest day. **1974** *Listener* 14 Feb. 212/2 What is needed is..cycleways and en-couragement for people to use this non-polluting form of transport. **1946** *Nature* 21 Dec. 900/1 The processes listed are mainly brought about by non-proliferating suspensions of bacteria or yeasts. **1910** *Daily Chron.* 7 Mar. 1/7 They did not mix up recurring and non-recurring expenditure. **1973** *Ann. Rep. Curators Bodl. Libr. 1971-2* 49 A total balance of £1,614 from special non-recurring grants for stock-piling. **1957** A. N. PRIOR *Time & Modality* 61 Genuinely non-referring names..are excluded. **1963** F. T. VISSER *Hist. Syntax* I. iii. 236 Another [construction] of very recent introduction, in which *it* is non-referring. **1946** *Nature* 21 Sept. 422/1 The anti-reflexion or non-reflecting thin transparent film deposited on the surface of the lens. **1962** L. S. SASIENI *Optical Dispensing* x. 271 Coating the lens surfaces with a non-reflecting coating. **1974** *Country Life* 21 Mar. 659/2 The black non-reflecting surface. **1972** P. BLACK *Biggest Aspidistra* III. iv. 179 The non-scripted shows made an important contribution to the art of radio. **1955** *Nation Rev.* (Melbourne) 31 Aug. 1453/1 *Lonesome cowboys* is a collection of heads playing themselves in non scripted situations. **1819** *Deb. Congress U.S.* 17 Feb. (1855) 1235 A line..shall divide the slaveholding from the non-slave-holding States. **1909** S. & B. WEBB *Break-up of Poor Law* I. i. 11 Here and there we meet exceptionally gifted natures, whose faith and love..enable them..to with-stand the deadening influence of the non-specialised institution. **1964** M. A. K. HALLIDAY et al. *Linguistic Sci.* 37 'Context'..thus corresponds roughly to 'meaning' in the general, non-specialized sense of the term. **1963** *Times* 5 Feb. 6/3 Other factors are £880,000 for aid to pupils and £621,000 for non-teaching staff. **1975** *Listener* 4 Dec. 757/2 Non-teaching Fellows and professors. **1936** *Mind* XLV. 105 Popper, indeed, recognises that falsifica-tion, too, is a non-terminating process. **1966** OGILVY & ANDERSON *Excurs. Number Theory* x. 121 Therefore if the irrationals have continued fraction expansions (and indeed they do), these must be nonterminating.

b. Prefixed to combs. formed with ppl. adjs., as *non-English-speaking, -habit-forming, -information-carrying, -interest-bearing, -profit-making.*

1949 M. MEAD *Male & Female* xvi. 330 The division of labour among non-English-speaking immigrants. **1975** *Nature* 20 Feb. p. xiv/1 (Advt.), The work..involves.. language correction of contributions written by non-English-speaking authors. **1933** *Radio Times* 14 Apr. 112/2 This pleasant, gentle laxative..is non-habit-forming. **1949** M. LOWRY *Let.* 16 Feb. (1967) 169 One or other of the non-habit-forming barbiturates should be often used in preference to strychnine or chloral. **1974** M. C. GERALD *Pharmacol.* xi. 198 Virtually all of these nonbarbiturate compounds have been initially promoted as being nonhabit-forming. **1967** Cox & GROSE *Organiz. Bibliogr. Rec. by Computer* iv. 85 These are a set of words which the user defines as non-information carrying words. **1937** E. SNOW *Red Star over China* vi. 233 Some $70,000 in non-interest-bearing loans had been invested by the Government in the co-operatives. **1959** E. POUND *Thrones* ciii. 85 Trying (T.C.P.) 50 years later to keep some of the non-interest-bearing etc. in circulation as currency. **1933** *Planning* I. VIII. 11 A non-profit-making organisation for this purpose could probably obtain a large interest in British farming. **1971** *Guardian* 16 Dec. 1/8 A railway porter..has been told to stop his non-profit making early-morning hot drink service to passengers.

8. Prefixed to adverbs, as *non-adaptively, -denumerably, -enzymatically, -enzymically, -inferentially, -relativistically, -spatially, -uni-formly.*

1931 *Brit. Jrnl. Psychol.* XXII. 126 The reaction is not adaptive. It is one in which the past..does not function; or if it does function at all, it does so inefficiently, non-adaptively. **1945** E. T. BELL *Devel. of Math.* (ed. 2) viii. 171 Non-denumerably infinite classes of rational numbers. **1965** B. MATES *Elem. Logic* viii. 141 The question thus arises whether one could find a consistent set of sentences that is satisfiable only by interpretations having non-denumerably infinite domains. In view of the Löwen-heim-Skolem theorem, the answer is negative. **1953** *Adv. in Protein Chem.* VIII. 169 labeled amino acids may combine nonenzymatically with certain proteins in other ways than through sulfur linkage. **1974** *Nature* 4 Jan. 4/1 The inhibitory alcohol also reacts, non-enzymically with the antennal protein. **1962** H. HEATH in A. Pirie *Lens Metabolism Rel. Cataract* 366 Glutathione readily and

non-enzymically reduces dehydroascorbic acid to as-corbic acid. **1860** A. DE MORGAN *On Syllogism* 214 Non-inferentially and immediately seen. **1956** J. O. URMSON *Philosophical Analysis* iii. 42 Now some of these philoso-phers..inferred the existence of such things as God, substance, universals, the ego, which they did not claim to be non-inferentially discoverable. **1957** BETHE & SALPETER *Quantum Mechanics of One- & Two-Electron Atoms* I. xix. 97 We treat the electron nonrelativistically throughout. **1934** *Mind* XLIII. 299 What confronts the mind, in this sense..is (perhaps non-spatially) *there* to be found, or haply to be found out, by searching. **1893** HARKNESS & MORLEY *Treat. Theory of Functions* iii. 72 A non-uniformly convergent series may be continuous. **1969** *Listener* 2 Jan. 11/1 Stars generally spin non-uniformly, rotating faster near the equator than at the pole.

non-, form of *NONA- used before a vowel.

nona- (before a vowel **non-**), comb. form of L. *nōnus* ninth. **a.** In scientific words, as NONAGON, *NONAPEPTIDE, *NONIC *sb.* and *a.* **b.** *spec.* in *Chem.*, used in naming the alkane with nine carbon atoms in its molecule, NONANE, and compounds and radicals which contain a similar carbon chain, as NONOIC *acid*, NONYL.

non-aggre·ssion. [NON- 1.] Absence of the will, desire, or intention to show aggression on the part of nations, governments, or politicians; freq. *attrib.*, esp. in phr. *non-aggression pact.*

1903 J. MORLEY *Life of Gladstone* III. x. viii. 508 Then he would go on—'..—My name stands in Europe as a symbol of the policy of peace, moderation, and non-aggression.' **1925** A. TOYNBEE *Survey Internat. Affairs* 26 The proposed pledge of non-aggression would not have power to deprive the Allies of the right conferred on them by the Treaty of Versailles. *Ibid.* 31 Mr. Lloyd George broached to the French delegation his project for a Pact of Non-aggression. **1935** *Ann. Reg. 1934* [217] The Polish Ambassador in Moscow signed a Protocol extending the Non-Aggression Pact between the two countries till December 31, 1945. **1941** KOESTLER *Scum of Earth* 19 The classical form for non-aggression treaties had been so far to promise neutrality. **1955** *Ann. Reg. 1954* 106 The two countries [*sc.* India and China] based their relationship on..mutual non-aggression.

non-ali·gned, *a.* [NON- 6.] Of a country, government, etc.: pursuing a policy of non-alignment. Also *absol.* as *sb.* Hence **non-ali·gnedness, non-ali·gner.**

1960 *New Left Rev.* Nov.–Dec. 10/2 The non-aligned powers have grown in strength. **1962** *Guardian* 7 Nov. 18/7 The concept of political non-alignedness. **1963** *Economist* 28 Dec. 1325/1 India's professional non-aligners. **1965** *Times Lit. Suppl.* 25 Nov. 1056/4 The attitudes of allies and of the non-aligned. **1966** *Guardian* 14 Oct. 12/2 The Canadians..believe that there is a real strategic danger of a nonaligned block composed of Austria, Switzerland, and France cutting Europe into two. **1970** *Guardian Weekly* 30 May 6 The two groups in Indonesia opposing each other are the 'nonaligneds' and the 'interventionists'. **1973** *Caribbean Contact* Feb. 9/3 The need..for the Non-Aligned world to probe beyond the detente between the big powers.

non-ali·gnment. [NON- 1.] Lack or absence of alignment; *spec.* in *Politics*, absence of political or ideological affiliations with other nations, esp. with the most powerful nations. Also *transf.*

1934 in WEBSTER. **1955** *Times* 6 May 11/4 He extolled 'non-alignment' and co-existence. **1963** M. BRECHER *New States of Asia* iv. 111 *Non-alignment*..is a political status. It refers to a state that declares itself aloof from bloc conflicts; nothing more. It proclaims itself free from *a priori* alliances, notably military entanglements with any bloc or Great Power anywhere in the world. **1970** E. BULLINS *Theme is Blackness* (1973) 153 My non-alignment with reality is quite evident and explainable.. my being Black and non-committed to any political truths. **1973** 'D. JORDAN' *Nile Green* xx. 81 The Egyptians ..prefer to hang on to what's left of their non-alignment status and not rely on the Russians.

non-alle·rgic, *a.* [NON- 3.] Not allergic; *spec.* not causing allergy.

1936 H. GOODMAN *Cosmetic Dermatol.* xxv. 368 In the field of cosmetics and beauty-application preparations, the words *allergy* and *nonallergic* are mentioned more and more often. **1938** *Words* Jan. 11/2 'Cosmetics are non-allergic.' Donna Ray broadcast Oct. 24 [19]37. **1954** L. MARTIN *Clin. Endocrinol.* (ed. 2) vii. 150 The eosinophil count will..be lowered by..50 per cent or more in non-allergic subjects. **1964** W. G. SMITH *Allergy & Tissue Metabolism* iii. 42 Inflammation of non-allergic origin. **1972** *Islander* (Victoria, B.C.) 18 June 7/3 Dacron fibrefill II is non-allergic and moth, vermin and mildew resistant.

non-American, *a.* (*sb.*). [NON- 3.] Not American. Occas. as *sb.*, one who is not an American.

1904 G. SAINTSBURY *Hist. Criticism* III. 640 The poet who seems to some possibly rash non-American persons to divide with Poe the prize due to the worthiest in American poetry, was also a critic—less of the professional kind, much more *borné*, but more concentrated. **1924** S. P. SHERMAN *Genius of America* 213 He laughed at all the non-American world. **1936** *Mind* XLV. 15 Insuffi-

ciently known and appreciated, not only among non-American philosophers, but even among his own colleagues in the United States. **1962** H. A. GLEASON in House-holder & Saporta *Problems in Lexicography* 88 Diction-aries with good..citations..have been mostly produced by people outside the fraternity—non-American linguists, or people laying no claim at all to the title of linguist. **1965** J. POTTER in Glass & Eversley *Population in Hist.* xxvii. 631 For non-Americans,..it can have an important bearing on their own attempts to interpret the European ..data.

nonane. Add: Hence **nonano·ic** *a.* = NO-NOIC *a.*; **nonano·ate,** the anion, or an ester or salt, of nonanoic acid.

1947 K. S. MARKLEY *Fatty Acids* xv. 407 Armstrong and Hilditch described a method for the disruptive oxida-tion of methyl oleate in acetone solution which they claim yields 80% to 90% of the theoretical amount of nonanoic acid. **1967** I. L. FINAR *Org. Chem.* (ed. 5) ix. 211 Nonanoic acid is obtained by the oxidation of oleic acid. **1974** *Ber. der Bunsen-Gesell. für physikal. Chem.* LXXVIII. 874 (*heading*) X-ray-studies of cholesteric-smectic-pretransitions in mixtures of cholesteryl chloride and cholesteryl nonanoate.

nonapeptide (nǫnăpe·ptəid). *Biochem.* [f. *NONA- + *PEPTIDE.] Any peptide composed of nine amino-acid residues.

1960 *Helv. Chim. Acta* XLIII. 1358 The synthesis of a nonapeptide exhibiting bradykinin-like properties is described. **1972** *Science* 22 Sept. 1108/3 Animals were given the nonapeptide Pyr-Trp-Pro-Arg-Pro-Gln-Ile-Pro-Pro, a potent inhibitor of the angiotensin-converting enzyme.

non-art. [NON- 2 and *2 b.] Something that is not art; *spec.* a form of art which avoids artifice or which rejects conventional modes and methods.

1936 L. DURRELL *Spirit of Place* (1969) 49 It [*sc. Tropic of Cancer*] bore out a few theories about writing that I had been trying to formulate. The art of non-art... Real art being absolutely devoid of 'artifice', in the literary sense. **1949** *Horizon* XIX. 379 The great artists of the past..are not replaced by others because we are moving into a world of non-art. **1958** *New Statesman* 20 Sept. 377/1 The great illusion of current non-art lies in the belief that numerous meanings can be expressed without searching. **1965** ZIGROSSER & GAEHDE *Guide Coll. Orig. Prints* iii. 35 The distinction..between art (as we know it now) and non-art might lose its force. **1971** R. A. CARTER *Manhattan Primitive* (1972) xxii. 215 You haven't transformed it into art—you've just set it down. It's non-art, Bess. Anti-art.

non-A·ryan, *a.* and *sb.* [NON- 3, 2.] **A.** *adj.* Of a language or a person: not Aryan or of Aryan descent; used *spec.* of Jews in Nazi Germany.

1878 [see ARYAN *a.*]. **1878** [in Dict. s.v. NON- 3]. **1898** R. BROWN *Semitic Influence in Hellenic Mythol.* III. iii. 86 The mixed peoples of Asia Minor, Aryan, and non-Aryan. **1931** *Times Lit. Suppl.* 11 June 461/2 It is interesting..to encounter variants of familiar ballads in a non-Aryan language. **1933** *New Statesman* 15 Apr. 465/2 A slight relief has been given by a Reich decree which allows an increase in the number of 'non-Aryan' lawyers who may practise. **1942** L. B. NAMIER *Conflicts* 133 More logical were those who attempted amalgama-tion: but even this, as a mass movement, could only pro-duce Marranos or 'non-Aryan Christians'. **1964** *Archi-vum Linguisticum* XVI. 76 Nicula-, probably non-Aryan.

B. *sb.* One who is not an Aryan; used *spec.* of Jews in Nazi Germany.

1933 [see *ARYAN *sb.* 2). **1935** AUDEN & ISHERWOOD *Dog beneath Skin* II. i. 75 Rumour-monger!.. Non-Aryan! **1944** J. S. HUXLEY *On Living in Rev.* 174 It is thus absurd to distinguish between 'non-Aryans' and 'Europeans'.

no-na·tion, *a.* *dial.* [f. No *a.* 6 b + NATION *sb.*[1]] (See quots.)

1825 J. JENNINGS *Observ. Dial. W. Eng.* 57 *Nonation*, difficult to be understood; not intelligent; incoherent; wild. **1856** P. THOMPSON *Hist. Boston* XVI. 716 *No-nation place*, an out-of-the-way locality, or lawless neighbourhood. **1868** J. C. ATKINSON *Gloss. Cleveland Dial.* 357 *No-nation*, strange, remote, out-of-the-way; scarcely known, geographically; and, hence, uncivilised and rough. **1914** *Dialect Notes* IV. 77 *No-nation*,.. worthless. 'You *no-nation* cuss!' **1932** *Times Lit. Suppl.* 27 Oct. 792/1 He was a 'no-nation' boy and he had no name other than Duke.

non-atta·ched, *ppl. a.* [NON- 6.] Not attached; *spec.* unconcerned or uninvolved with material things. So **non-atta·chment.**

1856 [in Dict. s.v. NON- 6]. **1937** A. HUXLEY *Ends & Means* i. 3 The ideal man is the non-attached man. Non-attached to his bodily sensations and lusts. Non-attached to his craving for power and possessions... Non-attached to his anger and hatred. *Ibid.* 4 The practice of non-attachment entails the practice of all the virtues. **1940** AUDEN *Another Time* 23 Over the talkative city like any other Weep the non-attached angels. **1950** 'G. ORWELL' *Shooting an Elephant* 108 In this yogi-ridden age, it is too readily assumed that 'non-attachment' is..better than a full acceptance of earthly life.

non-bank, *a.* [NON- 4.] Not connected with, or transacted by, a banking house; of an institution: not being a bank.

1946 C. C. ABBOTT *Managem. Federal Debt* v. 87 Should a boom or a price inflation develop and conditions

call for a restriction of deposits, this policy of relying upon increases of bank credit to take up obligations not wanted by nonbank holders would aggravate the situation. **1961** *Ann. Reg. 1960* 485 The Bank of England commented..that..in the light of the need to attract purchases of stock by 'non-bank' investors, 'a somewhat higher level of gilt-edged yields would now be appropriate'. **1961** *Economist* 25 Nov. 822/3 The gilt-edged market (which provides the Exchequer with non-bank finance). **1964** GOULD & KOLB *Dict. Soc. Sci.* 438/2 Like every other nonbank institution, savings and loan associations..must keep accounts with commercial banks. **1973** *N.Y. Law Jrnl.* 4 Sept. 3/5 (Advt.), We are..the largest non-bank firm—providing complete corporation securities services.

non-belli·gerent, *a.* and *sb.* [NON- 3, 2.] **A.** *adj.* Not actively engaged in hostilities; not aggressive. **B.** *sb.* A country which abstains from active involvement in a war but which more or less openly favours one side. Hence **non-belli·gerence, -belli·gerency,** the status or attitude of a non-belligerent country.

1909 *Westm. Gaz.* 14 June 5/3 When the defence has been on anything like a great scale, the non-belligerent defenders have very largely exceeded in number the armed defenders. **1940** *War Illustr.* 5 Jan. 556 'The position assumed by Italy on September 1,' he [*sc.* Count Ciano, the Italian Foreign Minister] said, 'was a position of non-belligerency strictly in conformity with the German intention of localizing the conflict.' **1940** *Manch. Guardian Weekly* 1 Mar. 162 Today all the Balkan states are neutral, Italy is a 'non-belligerent', Turkey is a firm friend, Russia is uncertain. **1946** *Ann. Reg. 1945* 76 The Spanish Government had publicly followed a policy not of neutrality but of non-belligerence. **1953** P. C. BERG *Dict. New Words* (ed. 2) 115/1 A non-belligerent attitude between contending parties or powers. **1975** *Times* 19 Aug. 13/2 A formal pledge of non-belligerency is something which President Sadat cannot or will not give.

non-biolo·gical, *a.* [NON- 3.] Not belonging to biology or forming part of its subject matter; not occurring in, involving, or pertaining to living organisms.

1931 J. S. HUXLEY *What dare I Think?* i. 32 There have been Boards of Pest Control which were not too anxious to find their occupation gone with the going of their particular pest. Leaving such non-biological or hyper-biological considerations on one side, there have been many pests which have so far baffled research. **1956** *Nature* 21 Jan. 110/2 Photochemistry in higher plants and in non-biological systems. **1957** G. E. HUTCHINSON *Treat. Limnol.* I. xvi. 866 The existence of non-biological mechanisms of oxidation of ammonia. **1962** F. I. ORDWAY et al. *Basic Astronautics* vi. 247 An understanding of much corollary evidence and supposition from nonbiological fields. **1971** I. G. GASS et al. *Understanding Earth* ix. 125/1 All known extra-terrestrial environments and many geological environments are still non-biological.

Hence **non-biolo·gically** *adv.*

1974 *Nature* 6 Sept. 43/1 A rapid, routine, new tool for the differentiation of biologically and nonbiologically produced dicarboxylic acids.

non-black, *a.* and *sb.* [NON- 3, 2.] **A.** *adj.* Not black; *spec.* (also *non-Black*), of, pertaining to, or being a person or persons who are not black. **B.** *sb.* A non-black person.

1926 D. M. LIDDELL *Handbk. Non-Ferrous Metallurgy* I. ix. 283 No radiation pyrometer has been found to be very useful for measuring temperatures of non-black bodies. **1930** *Social Sci. Abstr.* June 1011 In the non-black land the rush toward individual appropriation was naturally less than in the black soil belt. **1970** *Guardian Weekly* 22 Aug. 7 At the University of Natal, non-white students..refer to whites as 'non-blacks'. **1971** *Black Scholar* Jan. 27/2 The argument goes that black artists..must move beyond race in their work to some mythical human (non-black) understanding. **1973** *Black World* Apr. 20/2 Expertly directed by a non-Black, the musical played to standing-room audiences. **1973** S. HENDERSON *Understanding New Black Poetry* 9 Is it possible that, given a Black Poetic Structure, a non-Black can create in this form—as whites play jazz, for example?

non-ca·pital, *a.* [NON- 3]. Of a murder or other offence: for which a convicted person is not punishable by the death penalty.

1898 C. ILBERT *Government of India* i. 15 The Company were in the habit of procuring for each voyage a commission to the 'general' in command, empowering him to inflict punishments for non-capital offences, such as murder or mutiny. **1956** *Hansard Commons* 15 Nov. 1237/1 The distinction between non-capital murders and capital murders which is made in this part of the Bill must lead to many inconsistencies and anomalies. **1964** MORRIS & BLOM-COOPER *Calendar of Murder* viii. 328 The legislature..sought..to mitigate considerably the incidence of the death penalty..by declaring certain categories of murder non-capital. **1968** *Globe & Mail* (Toronto) 13 Feb. 3/8 Two men were jointly charged yesterday with the non-capital murder of..a taxi driver.

non-Ca·tholic, *sb.* and *a.* [NON- 2, 3.] **A.** *sb.* One who is not a Roman Catholic.

1793 [in Dict. s.v. NON- 2]. **1859** MILL *Liberty* iv. 154 What do Protestants think of these perfectly sincere feelings, and of the attempt to enforce them against non-Catholics? **1971** J. C. HEENAN *Not Whole Truth* i. 12 His church was half-filled every Monday evening with enquirers who came to hear his talks to non-Catholics.

B. *adj.* That is not Roman Catholic.

In a somewhat wider sense in quot. 1936.

1823 C. BUTLER *Continuation of A. Butler's Lives of Saints* p. lxii, Their anti-christian and non-catholic adversaries. **1867** F. OAKELEY in H. E. Manning *Ess. Relig. & Lit.* 2nd Ser. 130 The world persists in thinking that the Catholic and non-Catholic ideas are in diametrical opposition. **1936** T. S. ELIOT *Essays Ancient & Modern* 132 There may always be schemes, initiated by non-Christian and non-Catholic minds..to which we can give unqualified support. **1966** *Publ. Amer. Dial. Soc.* XLII. 35 To recall many abusive terms for non-Catholic Christians.

nonce. Add: **4. nonce-word** (examples); similarly *nonce-borrowing, -combination, -form, -formation, -meaning.*

1954 U. WEINREICH in Saporta & Bastian *Psycholinguistics* (1961) 385/1 At the time of his utterance, it is a 'nonce-borrowing'. **1943** *Amer. Speech* XVIII. 301 A number of them..also meet the condition of not being independent words used in some nonce-combination. **1962** H. A. GLEASON in Householder & Saporta *Problems in Lexicography* 88 A dictionary-maker need not include a non-idiomatic nonce-form. **1957** *Archivum Linguisticum* IX. 122 It clearly functions morphemically as everyday nonce-formations testify. **1943** C. L. WRENN *Word & Symbol* (1967) 97 The most surprisingly beautiful result of Spenser's experimenting in poetic language is in the use..of the word *Cheuisaunce,* which may be described as having acquired for special purpose what I would call a nonce-meaning. **1884** Nonce-wd. [see ANOTHERNESS]. **1927** *Englische Studien* Nov. 99 If an alternative explanation presents itself, topographical nonce-words ought to be avoided. **1957** R. W. ZANDVOORT *Handbk. Eng. Gram.* I. ii. 43 Some of them are nonce-words, i.e. spontaneous creations by a speaker or writer, coined for the occasion.

non-ce·ntral, *a.* [NON- 3.] **1.** *Statistics.* Having or corresponding to a non-zero mean.

1928 *Proc. R. Soc.* A. CXXI. 670 This interpretation of the distribution..is seen to replace the χ^2 distribution of the analysis of variance for cases in which the sum of squares corresponding to n_1 degrees of freedom is derived theoretically for non-central deviations with fixed central displacements. **1949** *Biometrika* XXXVI. 202 In the case of the well-known tests using χ^2, *t* and *F,* the evaluation of their power functions involves the use of what have been called non-central distributions. **1968** P. A. P. MORAN *Introd. Probability Theory* vii. 323 The quantity χ^2 in (7.121) is then said to have a non-central χ^2-distribution.

2. *Physics.* Of a force: not central, i.e. not in general directed along the line joining the bodies it acts between.

1948 *Physical Rev.* LXXIII. 1403/1 (*heading*) The effect of non-central forces on the collisions of high energy neutrons with protons. **1962** *Encycl. Dict. Physics* V. 610/1 The magnetic forces due to electric currents also have this non-central character. **1966** D. L. LIVESEY *Atomic & Nuclear Physics* ix. 414 There are noncentral forces between neutron and proton. **1970** G. K. WOODGATE *Elem. Atomic Struct.* vii. 107 In the central-field approximation we neglected the residual electrostatic term in the Hamiltonian which represents a non-central force.

Hence **non-centra·lity,** the property of being non-central.

1959 H. SCHEFFÉ *Anal. of Variance* 412 The ordinary or central chi-square distribution is the special case of the noncentral distribution when the noncentrality parameter $\delta = 0$. **1969** H. O. LANCASTER *Chi-Squared Distribution* xi. 231 It is required to determine the parameters of non-centrality of the test of independence in two dimensions.

non-committal, *sb.* (*a.*). **b.** (Earlier and later examples.)

1829 H. ORNE *Lett. of Columbus* 18 The non-committal system prevailed. **1973** *Archivum Linguisticum* IV. 18 The same applies in..(5), which may be interpreted as a 'non-committal' statement.

non-communicating, *vbl. sb.* and *ppl. a.* Add examples in the sense: 'not communicating or conversing'.

1917 A. S. PRINGLE-PATTISON *Idea of God* iii. 57 It is impossible to treat the world of religious belief and the world of fact..as if they were two non-communicating spheres. **1960** K. AMIS *New Maps of Hell* (1961) i. 20 Some excellent stories have been written about non-communicating aliens, from *The War of the Worlds* onwards. **1972** *Where* May–June 158/2 The parent who protested that her LEA was sending her non-communicating child 200 miles away from home and so she would not be able to visit, when the child could not write or use a phone, had a real case.

non-concur, *v.* Add: (Later example.)

1823 W. TUDOR *Life of James Otis* 239 The Council non-concurred this resolve.

b. *intr.* To fail or refuse to concur; to disagree. Usu. const. *in* or *with.*

1855 *Chicago Times* 3 Mar. 3/5 The House non-concurred with the Senate amendment. **1862** *Congress. Globe* 9 July 3214/1, I hope the house will non-concur in that amendment of the Senate. **1907** *Springfield* (Mass.) *Weekly Republican* 20 June 1 The Senate has non-concurred with the House amendments. **1911** PARTON & MANNING in C. E. Persons et al. *Labor Laws* 53 The House went on record as favorable to the resolution. The State nonconcurred. **1974** *Spartanburg* (S. Carolina) *Herald* 18 Apr. A. 2/4 Arthur was one of several House members to take the floor Tuesday to urge the legislators to non-concur in the Senate amendments.

nonconforming, *ppl. a.* Add to def.: Also in non-religious contexts; *spec.* (see quot. 1961).

1899 'MARK TWAIN' *Man that corrupted Hadleyburg* (1900) 273 Worn officially, our nonconforming swallow-tail is a declaration of ungracious independence in the matter of manners. **1961** E. A. POWDRILL *Vocab. Land Planning* iv. 67 When industry of this nature [*sc.* general industry] is located in an area the primary use of which is residential, shopping, or other non-industrial uses, it is said to be 'non-conforming', in that it does not conform, in usage, to the primary use. **1972** *Jrnl. Social Psychol.* LXXXVI. 16 When a non-conforming response was made by an *S* in the low or high reward condition..he automatically received a coin. **1973** *N.Y. Law Jrnl.* 26 July 2/2 The effect of such a zoning law change is to make the property a non-conforming use.

nonconformist. 2. Delete † *Obs.* and add later example.

1952 [see *FEATHER-BEDDING *vbl. sb.*].

3. Esp. in phr. *nonconformist conscience.*

1890 *Times* 28 Nov. 8/6 The *minimum* demand of the great Nonconformist party is the unconditional abdication of Mr. Parnell, and his immediate retirement from Parliamentary life... Nothing less will satisfy the Nonconformist conscience. **1893** O. WILDE *Lady Windermere's Fan* III. 90 There is nothing in the whole world so unbecoming to a woman as a Nonconformist conscience. **1894** BEERBOHM in *Yellow Bk.* III. Oct. 250 The Nonconformist Conscience makes cowards of us all. **1931** *Times Lit. Suppl.* 10 Sept. 670/1 The difficulties of governing Ireland and keeping the Nonconformist conscience quiet.

4. A moth, *Lithophane lamda,* found in northern Europe, Russia, and North America.

1869 E. NEWMAN *Illustr. Nat. Hist. Brit. Moths* 428/2 The Nonconformist... Their colour is bluish-gray in some specimens, prettily varied with darker and lighter gray in others. **1961** EDELSTEN & FLETCHER *South's Moths Brit. Is.* (ed. 4) 228 The Nonconformist (*Lithophane lamda,* Fab.).

non-conju·nction. [NON- 1.] **1.** *Cytology.* The failure of homologous chromosomes to pair at meiosis. *rare.*

1925 J. BELLING in *Jrnl. Genetics* XV. 256 Non-conjunction. This term is used instead of non-conjugation, because in most cases it cannot be told whether conjugation, that is, parasynapsis, has taken place or not, with regard to the chromosome pair in question... Non-conjunction cannot be distinguished from true non-disjunction, in the later stages.

2. *Logic.* The relation of the terms in a proposition asserting the negative of a conjunctive proposition ('not both..and..').

1926 H. M. SHEFFER in *Isis* VIII. 229 The authors consider one of the cardinal improvements in the new edition to consist in their substitution, for the two operations of propositional *negation* and *disjunction,* of the single operation of *non-conjunction.* **1956** A. CHURCH *Introd. Math. Logic* (rev. ed.) I. ii. 134 Sheffer uses the sign of disjunction, ∨, inverted as a sign of non-disjunction; he introduces non-conjunction only in a footnote and uses no special sign for it. *Ibid.* 135 Taking non-conjunction as the only primitive connective, give definitions of the singulary and remaining binary connectives. **1957** *Encycl. Brit.* XIV. 306/1 We shall use..the sign | to denote non-conjunction ('$p|q$' to mean 'not both *p* and *q*'). *Ibid.,* If the sign of non-conjunction (Sheffer's stroke) is taken as primitive, all the other connectives can be defined from this one. **1965** HUGHES & LONDEY *Elem. Formal Logic* viii. 54 The following are valid: (i) $(p \uparrow q) \equiv \sim (p.q)$, (ii) $(p \downarrow q) \equiv \sim (p \vee q)$, which suggests the names 'non-conjunction' and 'non-disjunction' for '↑' and '↓' respectively.

non-consumption. (Later example.)

1961 L. E. DAVIS et al. *Amer. Econ. Hist.* iii. 54 The net..addition to a nation's capital stock..must be the result of nonconsumption of national product.

non-conti·ngent, *a.* [f. NON- 3 + CONTINGENT *a.* 4.] That does not happen by chance or depend on a variable.

1890 J. RANKINE *Erskine's Princ. Law Scotl.* (ed. 18) III. vii. 405 The running of prescription is suspended during the minority of the person who is *verus dominus,* being lawfully vested with a non-contingent title to compete for possession, or of him who is the true creditor. **1939** KURTZ & EDGERTON *Statistical Dict. Terms & Symbols* 99 *Mathematically independent,* unaffected by the happening of another event or by the size of another variable. Also called independent, non-contingent, and uncontingent. **1971** *Jrnl. General Psychol.* Apr. 326 Ss were given either 30%, 50%, or 70% noncontingent positive *E*-administered reinforcement. **1973** *Jrnl. Genetic Psychol.* Sept. 16 The final design contained two levels of noncontingent preference value within subjects.

non-contri·butory, *a.* [NON- 3.] Of a pension, a pension-scheme, or the like: not involving contributions from the pensioner or beneficiary.

1911 *Q. Rev.* July 198 The provision for old age in our system is non-contributory and wholly paid by the State. **1935** *Planning* II. XLII. 5 The first of these is the non-contributory State pension of 10s a week available at 70 subject to a declaration of means. **1975** *Times* 1 Dec. 12/8 The question of moving from a non-contributory to a contributory [pensions] scheme has been reopened in Whitehall.

non-co-opera·tion. [NON- 1.] Failure or refusal to co-operate; *spec.* used as a means of resistance or protest, esp. against the British in India before 1947. Also *attrib.*

1795 [in Dict. s.v. NON- 1]. **1860** RUSKIN *Unto this Last* (1862) IV. 141 The most accurately nugatory labour is.. that of which not enough is given to answer a purpose effectually... Also, labour which fails of effect through non-co-operation. **1920** A. BESANT (*title*) Gandhian non-co-operation; or, shall India commit suicide? **1922** *Telegraphic Corr. India* 3 in *Parl. Papers* (Cmd. 1586) XVI. 578 The origins of the non-co-operation movement. **1937** J. M. MURRY *Necessity of Pacifism* vi. 91 The only possible creative issue for the German Socialist movement was by way of non-violent non-co-operation. **1946** J. S. HUXLEY *Unesco* i. 7 The non-cooperation or even withdrawal of a number of nations. **1973** C. MULLARD *Black Britain* IV. xiii. 156 This resistance has been passive in the tradition of civil disobedience and of Martin Luther King's philosophy of nonco-operation.

Hence **non-co-o·perate** *v. intr.*, to refuse to co-operate; **non-co-o·perating** *ppl. a.*, **non-co-o·perative** *a.*, that refuses or fails to co-operate; **non-co-o·perator**, one who practises or advocates non-co-operation.

1921 *Daily Tel.* 28 Sept. 9/1 The leaflet..asks the Moplahs actively to non-co-operate with the Government. **1922** J. T. GWYNN *Let.* 17 May in *Indian Politics* (1924) iii. 17 A Non-Co-operating politician. *Ibid.*, Non-Co-operative propaganda. *Ibid.* 18 The first-raters may be looked for either among the Co-operators or among the practising Non-Co-operators. **1928** *Observer* 19 Feb. 17/3 The non-co-operators expected to win in the division. **1958** *Punch* 29 Jan. 187/2 The water-fowl are non-co-operative, bobbing about indistinguishably on the far side of the water.

non-cro·ssover. *Biol.* [NON- 2, 4.] A gamete or individual which does not exhibit the results of crossing-over between any two genetic loci. Also *attrib.*

1916, 1919 [see *CROSS-OVER 4]. **1962** *Lancet* 12 May 1026/1 In the three families there were six children who could be considered non-cross-overs. **1971** LEVITAN & MONTAGU *Textbk. Human Genetics* x. 379 To whom the *AB/ab* parent contributed non-crossover gametes. *Ibid.*, The former could identify a noncrossover gamete of the *AB/ab* parent.

noncurantist, *a.* Add: (Further example.) Also **noncurance**, indifference; **noncurant** *a.*, indifferent.

1904 F. ROLFE *Hadrian the Seventh* iii. 84 He began to undress..with the noncurance of one accustomed to swim in Sandford Lasher. *a***1913** —— *Desire & Pursuit of Whole* (1934) viii. 78 The most elegant young stranger.., exquisitely noncurant in carriage. *a***1913** —— *Nicholas Crabbe* (1958) iii. 28 In the matter of money, he was extravagant, chimerical, quixotic, noncurant, to a degree. *Ibid.* xxiii. 158 Some unknown boy, noncurant, saucy, shrilly whistling. **1928** *Times Lit. Suppl.* 12 July 510/4 He contrasts the Italian measures against manifestations in favour of Enosis (union with Greece) with the completely noncurantist tolerance of them by the British authorities in Cyprus. **1931** *Ibid.* 5 Nov. 870/3 Some of the [Masonic] symbols and ceremonies discarded in the days of uninquiring ignorance and self-satisfied noncurance.

non-destru·ctive, *a.* [NON- 3.] That does not involve destruction, esp. of an object or material that is tested.

1929 *Trans. Amer. Soc. Steel Testing* XVI. 771 (*heading*) Nondestructive testing. *Ibid.*, A number of independent investigators have been working on various methods of nondestructive inspection. **1930** *Mining & Metallurgy* XI. 308 (*heading*) Destructive and non-destructive tests of welds. **1946** *Nature* 19 Oct. 539/2 It was pointed out that the X-ray method is the only non-destructive way of determining surface residual stresses. **1959** *Jrnl. Iron & Steel Inst.* CXCI. 299/2 The economic importance of non-destructive testing is emphasized. **1962** *Gloss. Terms Automatic Data Processing* (*B.S.I.*) 63 *Non-destructive reading*, a reading process which does not change the record of the data which has been read. **1962** *B.S.I. News* June 12/1 Points covered in the section on welding are the quality of welds, tests on welds..and non-destructive examination. **1971** *Engineering* Apr. 37/1 Facilities at Harwell have become available to industry through the Nondestructive Testing Centre. **1975** G. BRAM *Manufacturing Technol.* ii. 66 Research and development of methods of non-destructive testing has increased considerably over the past thirty years.

Hence **non-destru·ctively** *adv.*

1930 STOUGHTON & BUTTS *Engin. Metallurgy* (ed. 2) iii. 54 (*heading*) Tests sometimes made non-destructively. **1945** A. N. SACHANEN *Chem. Constituents of Petroleum* iii. 130 Petroleum fractions are completely and non-destructively hydrogenated so that the ring structure of the naphthenes formed corresponds to the original ring structure. **1969** P. B. JORDAIN *Condensed Computer Encycl.* 336 Magnetic tapes, disks, drums, and cards are usually read nondestructively. **1971** *Engineering* Apr. 33/1 To be able to examine critically the insides of welds or castings non-destructively has improved fabrication technology.

non-dire·ctional, *a.* (*sb.*) [NON- 3.] Lacking directional properties; *esp.* equally sensitive, intense, or the like, in all directions. † Also as *sb.*

1903 *Nature* 22 Oct. 610/1 In Prof. Henrici's algebra the products of two vectors *α*, *β* are:— (*αβ*) a non-directional or 'scalar',..and [*αβ*] a vector perpendicular to the plane drawn through *α* and *β*. **1931** *Proc. IRE* XIX. 1754 When the noise comes from more than one direction the effects produced by sunrise or sunset upon the noise intensity as received on a nondirectional antenna become somewhat involved. **1946** H. JACOB *On Choice of Common Language* iii. 107 In addition to the primarily spatial directives, *for*, *of*, and *till* are used on the same analogy, as non-directional prepositions. **1964** *Oceanogr. & Marine Biol.* II. 448 The usual response of untrained fish in aquaria to non-directional sounds is one of non-orientated quickened swimming, often momentary. **1967** E. SHORT *Embroidery & Fabric Collage* iii. 59 This non-directional type of design is important in an article which may be carelessly thrown down.

non-disju·nction. [NON- 1.] **1.** *Cytology.* The failure of one or more pairs of homologous chromosomes (at meiosis) or sister chromatids (at mitosis) to separate and move away normally from the equatorial plate during nuclear division, usu. with the result that one of the daughter nuclei has too few chromosomes and the other too many.

1913 *Jrnl. Exper. Zoöl.* XV. 587 (*heading*) Non-disjunction of the sex chromosomes of Drosophila. **1925** *Jrnl. Genetics* XV. 251 Non-disjunction was long ago observed in the diploid *Oenothera*. **1961** *Lancet* 5 Aug. 319/2 The mosaicism reported here could have originated in several ways. Mitotic nondisjunction in a normal diploid embryo could result in 1 cell with forty-eight chromosomes (trisomy for chromosome 21 and chromosome 19 or 20) and 1 non-viable cell with forty-four chromosomes. **1962** *Ibid.* 15 Dec. 1270/1 Three types of meiotic non-disjunction have been recognised. **1971** LEVITAN & MONTAGU *Textbk. Human Genetics* iii. 63 Changes in the total number of chromosomes most frequently result from the occasional failure of chromosomes to move to opposite poles or disjoin during anaphase of cell division. Such a failure is called nondisjunction.

Hence **non-disju·nctional** *a.*

1913 *Jrnl. Exper. Zoöl.* XV. 589, 10 per cent of the eggs of such a female matured in a non-disjunctional manner. *Ibid.* 590, I counted the offspring of the non-disjunctional male only with respect to white and pink. **1930** *Genetics* XV. 11 These seven non-disjunctional males were red. **1971** LEVITAN & MONTAGU *Textbk. Human Genetics* iii. 66 Nondisjunctional error in meiosis could involve *all* 23 pairs of chromosomes.

2. *Logic.* The relation of the terms in a proposition asserting the negative of a disjunctive proposition ('neither..nor..').

1956, 1965 [see *NON-CONJUNCTION 2].

non-disti·nctive, *a. Linguistics.* [NON- 3.] Not distinctive (see *DISTINCTIVE *a.* 1 b).

1916 JONES & PLAATJE *Sechuana Reader* p. xiv, The consonant sounds c, ɪ̄, ɥ, and the vowel sound ʉ are probably 'non-distinctive'... By this we mean that the substitution of the sounds t, l, w, u respectively..would probably never change the meaning of any word. **1933, 1942** [see *DISTINCTIVE *a.* 1 b]. **1964** L. S. HULTZÉN in D. Abercrombie et al. *Daniel Jones* 92 There is of course a great deal of grammatically non-distinctive variation in utterance.

none, *pron.*, *a.*, and *adv.* Add: **C.** *adv.* **3. a.** Freq. with *too* and an adjective forming combs. used *attrib.*

1928 H. CRANE *Let.* 31 Jan. (1965) 315 Crowds of ambitious but none-too-successful strumpets of movie-dom. **1941** *Amer. Speech* XVI. 57/2 This none-too-accurate article on the DAE. **1963** D. BALLANTYNE in C. K. Stead *N.Z. Short Stories* (1966) 151 His none-too-searching questions had already disclosed that the psychologist..was sophisticated enough to take an irreverent view of Freud. **1970** 'M. HEBDEN' *Mask of Violence* (1971) i. 3 He was dressed in shabby jeans and a none-too-clean shirt. **1974** *Country Life* 26 Dec. 2016/2 Its class of none-too-hardy evergreens.

b. (Later examples.)

1852 J. B. JONES *Col. Vanderbomb* xv. 198 Our adventurers slept none that night. **1890** J. SERVICE *Thir Notandums* i. 3, I would weary nane. **1906** *Advocate of Peace* Mar. 52 Has civilization advanced none from the barbaric days of the 5th century? **1956** B. HOLIDAY *Lady sings Blues* (1973) xviii. 151, I had never cared what the hell people thought, and jail hadn't changed that none. **1973** E. BULLINS *Theme is Blackness* 65 Now, now, don't you worry none about that, Mother. We'll find a way.

non-ele·ctive, *a.* [NON- 3.] Not appointed by election.

1909 W. S. CHURCHILL in *Westm. Gaz.* 9 Oct. 9/4 The claim of the House of Lords—that is, the claim of a non-elective and unrepresentative Chamber—to make and to unmake Governments. **1910** *Blackw. Mag.* Aug. 283/1 The independent opinion of men formed in the comparatively 'dry light' of the non-elective chamber has a value of its own.

non-e·mpty, *a. Math.* and *Logic.* [NON- 3.] Not empty; having at least one member or element.

1937 *Mind* XLVI. 375 There is another non-empty sub-set..of sentences of C_2 which are nonsensical but not *α*-nonsensical. **1956** E. M. PATTERSON *Topology* vi. 113 A complex *K* is said to be connected if it is not the union of two non-empty subcomplexes which have no simplexes in common. **1957** P. SUPPES *Introd. Logic* 198 At least one of the three small regions is non-empty. **1965** P. CAWS *Philos. of Sci.* xvii. 130 The restriction must be added that the domain be non-empty. **1971** G. GLAUBERMAN in Powell & Higman *Finite Simple Groups* i. 54 Let $\mathscr{A}$ be a non-empty set of subgroups of *S*.

Hence **non-e·mptiness**, the property of being non-empty.

1937 A. SMEATON tr. *Carnap's Logical Syntax of Lang.* 261 We introduce conditions which require for symmetrical, reflexive, and transitive relations the property of non-emptiness. **1950** W. V. QUINE *Methods of Logic* (1952) 80 The bar..can be made to lie across a boundary and thus indicate non-emptiness of a compound region. **1957** P. SUPPES *Introd. Logic* ix. 198 Another kind of symbol is needed for non-emptiness. **1965** HUGHES & LONDEY *Elem. Formal Logic* xlvi. 339 Each schema..is valid under the hypothesis of the non-emptiness of some one term.

none·ntitize, *v.* [f. NONENTITY + -IZE.] *trans.* To make into a nonentity.

1903 G. B. SHAW *Man & Superman* I. 21 We're beaten——smashed—nonentitized, like her mother. **1913** R. W. SERVICE *Rhymes of Rolling Stone* 176 Sober am I nonentitized; drunk am I more than half a god.

non-entitous, *a.* (Further example.) Also **non-entitious.**

1951 W. SANSOM *Face of Innocence* (1954) 77 The girls nubile and the men nonentitous. **1954** C. E. M. JOAD *Folly Farm* vi. 143 Henry, the husband, a decent civil servant, utterly non-entitious—another character without a face..without a body of any kind. **1968** *Listener* 15 Aug. 212/3 Much of the rebuilding is elephantine and nonentitious.

non-entry. 2. (Later example.)

1962 H. R. LOYN *Anglo-Saxon Eng.* ix. 359 A factor that determined entry or non-entry in Domesday Book.

none-so-pretty. Add: **1.** (Later examples.) Also as *adj.*

1771 in A. M. Earle *Costume Col. Times* (1894) 173 None-so-Pretty Tapes. **1804** W. CLARK in *Orig. Jrnls. of Lewis & Clark Exped.* (1905) VI. 271 For Indians Presents..10 pieces Nonsoprettys. **1969** R. T. WILCOX *Dict. Costume* 248/1 *None-so-pretties*, fancy, decorative tapes used for trimming garments in the eighteenth century in the American Colonies.

non est. (Further examples.)

1945 MRS. BELLOC LOWNDES *Let.* 21 July (1971) 261 *Eggs* are practically *non est*, unless one has hens. **1959** R. FULLER *Ruined Boys* I. v. 34 The weights you put on it at the end of the arm thing were *non est.*

nonesuch, *sb.* and *a.* Add: **1. c.** *Nonesuch* (or *Nonsuch*) *chest*: a type of wooden chest made in the 16th and 17th centuries, inlaid with stylized designs supposedly representing views of Nonsuch Palace (see 1 b in Dict.); also *Nonesuch ornament.*

1905 F. S. ROBINSON *Eng. Furnit.* v. 71 A somewhat rare type of chest..called a 'Nonesuch' chest. **1920** *Connoisseur* Dec. 205 The 'Nonsuch chest'..possesses the flat surface unrelieved by mouldings, which is characteristic of many of the earlier inlaid pieces. **1960** H. HAYWARD *Antique Coll.* 200/1 *Nonesuch chest*, chest, dating from the second half of the 16th cent., decorated with an inlaid design representing an ideal building resembling the Palace of Nonesuch. **1970** D. ASH *Dict. Eng. Antique Furnit.* 107/2 Ornament of this kind probably originated in Italy, but quite possibly reached England from Germany without any connection with the palace from which its name is derived. Some pieces of furniture bearing Nonsuch ornament and long regarded as English may well have been imported. **1973** *Country Life* 7 June 1690 English oak chest, with..bands of stylised zig-zag ornament reminiscent of so-called Nonesuch chests... Circa 1630.

2. b. (Later U.S. examples.)

1821 A. ROYALL *Lett. from Alabama* (1830) li. 123, I went to hear this none such. **1927** 'S. ROHMER' *Moon of Madness* 18 He was a poisonously handsome none-such. *Ibid.* 26 Da Cunha danced perfectly, with all the sensuous grace of a none-such.

nonet. Add: **2.** *Nuclear Physics.* A multiplet (sense *b) of nine sub-atomic particles.

1963 S. OKUBO in *Physics Lett.* V. 166/2 We have to take into account of [*sic*] the ninth boson *ϕ* together with the octet. This means that we are dealing with a nonet rather than an octet, and a singlet. **1970** *New Scientist* 29 Oct. 211/3 To reconcile the A2 meson with current theory, it is necessary to show that the other members of its SU(3) nonet display similar double structure.

nonetheless (nʊnðəle·s, nʊ·nðəles), *adv.* Also **none the less, none-the-less.** [See NONE *adv.* 1 b, LESS *adv.* 1 a.] Nevertheless.

1847 DICKENS *Dombey* (1848) xlii. 419, I thank you none the less. **1875** [see NONE *adv.* 1 b]. **1924** G. B. SHAW *St. Joan* v. 66 But you will be none the less alone: they cannot save you. **1930** *Principal's Rep., Armstrong College* (*Newcastle*) *1929–30* 4 The elevation of Sir William Noble..to the peerage..has been a matter of pride and pleasure..which nonetheless has been qualified subsequently. **1955** *Times* 13 July 7/5 Later than *Nabucco*.., it is, nonetheless, not such a good opera. **1972** *Nature* 8 Dec. 327/1 Although some research fields seem to grow from a single, germinal experiment, others take root in accidents set off by workers stumbling from one preserve to another—and are none-the-less interesting for that.

non-Europe·an, *a.* and *sb.* [NON- 3, 2.] **A.** *adj.* Not European.

1907 W. JAMES *Pragmatism* v. 182 At this stage of philosophy all non-European men without exception have remained. **1923** D. H. LAWRENCE *Birds, Beasts & Flowers* 31 A set, stoic endurance, non-European. **1967** *Guardian* 15 May 6/6 Another such Russian idea..is that all 'non-European' nuclear weapons should be banned from European soil and seas.

B. *sb.* A person who is not European; esp. in South Africa: a non-white.

1926 M. NATHAN *South Africa from Within* viii. 166 According to this [*sc.* a 1921 census in British S. Africa], there were 1,519,488 Europeans.., and 5,409,092 non-Europeans. **1935** A. M. CARR-SAUNDERS in Huxley & Haddon *We Europeans* viii. 242 In the Union of South Africa there are under 2 million Europeans and about 6 million non-Europeans. **1939** J. S. MARAIS *Cape Coloured People* p. vii, This book is..a study..of the relations between the Europeans and that group of non-Europeans with whom the former have been longest..in contact. **1958** *Ann. Reg. 1957* 95 The so-called 'open' universities, Cape Town and the Witwatersrand, had a long tradition of admitting non-Europeans. **1970** *Cape Times* 28 Oct. 18/2 (Advt.), Personal loans, for Europeans and non-Europeans.

non-eva·luative, *a.* [NON- 3.] Of or pertaining to that which does not evaluate but is concerned only with fact.

1937 *Jrnl. Philos.* XXXIV. 237 It is a basic rule of valuational logic that an evaluative conclusion can not be deduced from non-evaluative, that is to say factual, premises. **1958** W. STARK *Sociol. of Knowl.* I. iv. 152 'Knowledge' in the context of gnosio-sociology is a non-evaluative term. **1973** 'J. PATRICK' *Glasgow Gang Observed* xxi. 219 Adolescents..did not know how to react to the non-evaluative, non-judgmental approach of the street worker.

non-eve·nt. [*NON- 2 b.] An unimportant or unexciting event, *spec.* one which was expected or intended to be important; occas., something that did not happen.

1962 *Spectator* 30 Nov. 853/1 The chief non-event of Gilmour's campaign was also, he says, the product of the 'serious' press. **1963** I. GILMOUR in *Hansard Commons* 7 May 272 Drugged by their normal diet of non-news stories and non-events, the newspapers tend to lose their heads when..faced with..a news story. **1965** *Listener* 30 Sept. 480/2 For all its admirable achievements in science and technology and the arts, the Soviet Union is still a great place for the non-event and the non-person, a category in which Mr. Khrushchev is at present languishing. **1966** K. AMIS *Anti-Death League* 186 To find this view supported by events, or as now by non-events, was depressing. **1967** *Listener* 23 Nov. 679/2 Here was a non-event to compare with those other annual and totally insignificant English non-events—Ascot, the Boat Race and the Queen's Speech. **1972** *Guardian* 22 Jan. 15/3 The exchange of signatures is a non-event.. it is neither truly historic nor of much practical significance.

non-existence. 1. (Later examples.)

1854 K. H. DIGBY *Compitum* VII. iii. 255 Books of dogmatic scepticism, and expositions of the non-existence of virtue and honour. **1968** P. A. P. MORAN *Introd. Probability Theory* vi. 269 The fact that this is not analytic at t = 0 corresponds to the non-existence of the moments in this case.

non-fe·rrous, *a.* [NON- 3.] Containing no iron; of or pertaining to metals other than iron.

1887 [see *FERROUS *a.* 2]. **1909** *Westm. Gaz.* 4 Sept. 4/3 The non-ferrous metal trades. **1936** *Times Educ. Suppl.* 13 June p. iv/1 A non-ferrous survey ship..is being fitted out and will probably start work in the Southern Indian Ocean. **1940** LAING & ROLFE (*title*) Non-ferrous foundry practice. **1963** H. R. CLAUSER *Encycl. Engin. Materials & Processes* 120/1 Nonferrous centrifugal castings are produced from copper alloys, nickel alloys, and tin and ead-base bearing metals. **1971** *Nature* 23 July 215/1 Britain's imports of non-ferrous metals cost £600 million annually.

non-fi·ction. [NON- 2.] Prose writings other than fiction (see FICTION 4). Also *attrib.* or as *adj.*, esp. in **non-fiction novel,** a novel written about real situations or characters.

1909 *Westm. Gaz.* 2 June 5/2 In Capetown the percentage of non-fiction to the total number of volumes is 58. **1922** HOLLIDAY & VAN RENSSELAER *Business of Writing* 174 Successful works of non-fiction not infrequently are later issued in cheaper forms by the original publisher. **1930** *Times Educ. Suppl.* 31 May 248/3 One of the most pleasing features was an increase of 344 issues of non-fiction literature. **1951** L. Z. HOBSON *Celebrity* (1953) xvi. 255 In this bad slump, nonfiction's the only thing selling—apart from one or two novels a year. **1965** *Vogue* 15 Oct. 94 [Truman] Capote is an experimenter, an adventurer. His newest experiment is *In Cold Blood*, a unique book, for it is the first non-fiction novel, a precise documentary, in many ways brilliantly composed. **1967** *New Mexico Q.* Autumn 243 (*heading*) The 'non-fiction' novel. **1969** *Times* 30 Oct. 10/7 Non-fiction paperbacks.

Hence **non-fi·ctional** *a.*, of, pertaining to, or characteristic of non-fiction.

1903 *Library World* Mar. 227 Mr. Doubleday's allusions to the expedients that have been adopted to advertise the non-fictional wares remind me of another point. **1911** A. BENNETT *Let.* 28 July (1966) I. 159 This clause would prevent me from publishing anything whatever non-fictional until they issued the book. **1938** D. BAKER *Young Man with Horn* II. i. 92 The author's right, as author, to furnish himself, as hero, with everything he lacked in his non-fictional life. **1966** G. N. LEECH *Eng. in Advertising* v. 54 Credibility is a dominant consideration in both fictional and non-fictional indirect address. **1967** *Britannica Bk. of Year 1966* 803/3 *Nonfictional novel*, a completely factual narrative characterized by the use of fictional techniques; *nonfictional novelist*.

non-fi·gurative, *a.* [NON- 3.] Not figurative; *spec.* in art = *ABSTRACT A. 4 d. So **non-figura·tion.**

1927 O. JESPERSEN *Mod. Eng. Gram.* III. xiv. 294 *Play* in the non-figurative sense has often *to*: he played Beethoven to us. **1934** *Burlington Mag.* Aug. 94/1 Cubism or non-figurative art is dismissed as an ephemeral movement. **1955** P. HERON *Changing Forms of Art* iii. 40 Until painting became non-figurative, the spatial configuration which the painter registered upon his canvas consisted of forms that could be read as illusionistic references to real objects; objects, that is, that were external to the picture. *Ibid.* 41 In 1945 pure non-figuration began to predominate in Paris. **1961** *Guardian* 16 Nov. 7/4 Abstract pattern deriving from Islamic ornament..to transcend..Western non-figuration. **1962** *Listener* 19 July 94/1 The non-figurative painter avoids stereotypes by means of marks and shapes, the interpretation of which is arbitrary, since the truly non-figurative is infinitely ambiguous.

non-flam, *a.* [NON- 3.] That is not inflammable. Hence as *sb.*, something that is not inflammable. So **non-fla·mmable** *a.*

1906 *Chambers's Jrnl.* 24 Nov. 831/2 A British firm, the patentees of 'Non-Flam' goods, of Aytoun Street, Manchester, points out that however efficacious Professor Doremus's prescription may be, it will need to be applied to the curtains every time they are washed. **1908** *Daily Chron.* 20 Oct. 3/6 It would be a good thing if the Government would..prohibit the use of any but 'non-flam' or other permanently incombustible flannelette for infants' garments. **1909** *Ibid.* 27 Feb. 4/7 'Non-Flam'..will not flare when brought into contact with fire. **1927** *Daily Tel.* 25 Oct. 14 In France from Jan. 1 next no celluloid film may be used unless made from this so-called 'non-flam' film. **1961** *Daily Mail* 20 July 9/4 A resolution urging the association to do more to promote the use of non-flammable clothing was accepted. **1968** *Punch* 17 Jan. 77/2 (*caption*) You've sure got a point there, Senator—non-flam draft cards. **1970** N. ARMSTRONG et al. *First on Moon* iii. 65 It was made of foam and covered with nonflammable tape. **1975** L. DEIGHTON *Yesterday's Spy* xxx. 221 Non-flam helium would not have burned.

non-fraterniza·tion. [NON- 1.] An absence of fraternization (see *FRATERNIZATION b). Also abbrev. (*slang*) **non-frat.** Also *attrib.*

1945 F. GILLARD in Hawkins & Boyd *War Report* (1946) xx. 383 The Germans don't like our non-fraternization rule, and they don't like the way in which our troops are obeying these rules. *Ibid.* 384 The attitude of these people makes our non-fraternization policy more necessary than ever. **1945** Non-fraternisation [see *FRATERNIZATION b]. **1945** Non-frat [see *FRATTING *vbl. sb.*]. **1957** *Wiener Beiträge* LXV. 280 Soldiers abbreviated the long words *fraternisation* and *non-fraternisation* to *frat* and *non-frat*.

nong (nǫŋ). *Austral. slang.* Also **nong-nong.** [Origin unknown.] A fool; a stupid person. Cf. *NING-NONG.

1953 BAKER *Australia Speaks* vii. 171 *Nong*, a simpleton or fool. **1959** —— *Drum* viii. 61 'Nong' (or the duplicated form 'nong-nong') was equivalent not only to dill, but also to drube, dope, and drongo. **1961** *Sunday Mail Mag.* (Brisbane) 5 Feb. 5/1 Nicholson and Fenton were not complete nongnongs. **1970** M. KELLY *Spinifex* vii. 113 Todd whirled, rifle at hip, 'You nong!' 'That's what they call me,' Reid commented affably. **1972** *Telegraph* (Brisbane) 5 Dec. 3/4 Mrs. Margaret Whitlam today emphatically denied that she had referred on Saturday night to journalists as 'nongs'.

nongenary (nǫndʒī·nări). [f. L. *nongēnārius* containing nine hundred, after CENTENARY *sb.* 3.] A nine hundredth anniversary, or the celebrations connected with it.

1926 FOWLER *Mod. Eng. Usage* 72/2 A list of not intolerable forms is here offered... Centē'nary,..octingē'nary, nongē'nary, millē'nary. **1965** E. GOWERS *Fowler's Mod. Eng. Usage* (ed. 2) 83/1 Nor is anyone, however passionate a supporter of etymological correctness, likely to try to introduce *sescenary, septingenary, octingenary*, or *nongenary*. **1966** *New Statesman* 8 Apr. 511/2 The painters are in no way concerned with the nongenary of the Battle of Hastings.

non-grea·sy, *a.* [NON- 3.] Not greasy.

1907 *Yesterday's Shopping* (1969) 537/1 Violet Oatmeal Skin Cream... Non-greasy and without stickiness. **1937** *Discovery* Oct. 297 An offset—a print made in a non-greasy powdered chalk. **1967** E. CHAMBERS *Photo-litho-Offset* xvi. 242 Gravure inks are difficult in make-up, being very fluid, finely ground, non-greasy and drying mainly by evaporation. **1974** *Harpers & Queen* Sept. 112 Some foundations are non-greasy, ideal for oily skins.

no·n-hero. [*NON- 2 b.] One who is the opposite or the reverse of a hero; one who is not genuinely a hero. Cf. *ANTI-HERO.

1940 *Sun* (Baltimore) 7 Sept. 10/7 In my list of non-heroes, Carol of Rumania stands close to the top. **1948** E. E. CUMMINGS *Let.* 27 Jan. (1969) 181 Since our (as he's doubtless already boasted to you) non-hero was once a candidate for honours. **1959** *Times Lit. Suppl.* 13 Nov. 657/1 These two novels..take lovable, weak, defeated men as non-heroes. **1972** *Sat. Rev.* 17 June 52/3 Our existential nonhero wanders through the story.

nonic (nōᵘ·nik), *sb.* and *a. Math.* [f. *NON(A- + -IC.] **A.** *sb.* A nonic curve or equation. **B.** *adj.* Of the ninth order or degree.

1879 *Amer. Jrnl. Math.* II. 233 (*heading*) Nonic. **1894** *Phil. Trans. R. Soc.* A. CLXXXV. 103 The nonic was proved..to have only three real roots. **1958** *New Biol.* XXV. 16 By an elementary transformation I have thrown his rather formidable nonic equation into a form which allows numerical tabulation.

nonillion. (Earlier example.)

1690 [see BILLION 1].

non-intervention. Add: (Further examples.) Hence **non-interve·ne** *v. intr.*, not to intervene; **non-interve·ner,** one who does not intervene or who advocates non-intervention; **non-interve·ning** *ppl. a.*

1849 S. P. CHASE *Let.* 30 July in J. Schuckers *Life of Chase* (1874) xii. 102 For what will be the cost to the Democracy of the alliance with the slaveholders in a presidential campaign?.. It is non-intervention upon the subject of slavery. **1901** K. D. BEST *Victories of Rome* (ed. 4) p. xii, The State..is exhibiting to a non-intervening circle of Catholic kingdoms the newest and latest development of Liberté, Egalité, Fraternité. **1937** H. NICOLSON *Diary* 27 July (1966) 309 Anthony Eden.. says that the French really did take the initiative in non-intervention [in Spain] and were not put up to it by us. **1937** A. P. HERBERT in *Punch* 8 Sept. 275/1 The Non-Intervention Committee are meeting, The Non-Interveners are meeting again. *Ibid.* 275/2 So let every soldier go non-intervening—Oh, fly with me Southward and non-intervene! **1939** S. SPENDER *Poems for Spain* 10 Satire, like Edgell Rickword's on Non-Intervention, in which the fundamental ideas are turned against the politicians. **1942** 'A. BRIDGE' *Frontier Passage* iv. 53 Mr. Crumpaun..was playing bridge with the elderly clergyman and two Non-Interveners. **1959** *Ann. Reg. 1958* 51 A discreet non-intervention in the debate was observed by the Leader of the Party. **1969** *Guardian* 29 Aug. 8/4 Mr Chamberlain..threatened to..'non-intervene' on Hitler's side against Czechoslovakia, as they were doing in favour of General Franco in Spain. **1975** *Times* 16 Oct. 15/2 The Soviet Union feels free to propagate its ideas in the west, so the west should not be shy about propagating its ideas in the east... The passages on non-intervention are aimed..at..physical intervention.

non-io·nic, *a.* and *sb.* [NON- 3.] **A.** *adj.* Not ionic; *spec.* (esp. of a detergent) not dissociating into ions in aqueous solution.

1943 *Chemical Industries* LII. 327/1 Non-ionic surface active agents, as their name implies, are not ionizable and owe their effectiveness to a proper balance between certain hydrophilic (polar) and lyophilic (non-polar) groups in their molecules. **1959** *Spectator* 4 Sept. 294/1 Together with the nonionic 'Nonidet' products, they have scores of applications throughout industry both for cleaning and maintenance. **1963** A. J. HALL *Textile Sci.* vi. 296 Surface active agents or surfactants can be usefully classified into three main groups—anion-active, non-ionic, and cation-active. **1964** M. HYNES *Med. Bacteriol.* (ed. 8) vii. 90 It depends on such forces as attraction between polar non-ionic groups..and van der Waal[s] attraction. **1965** PHILLIPS & WILLIAMS *Inorg. Chem.* I. v. 171 The difference between the equilibrium lattice energies U and U_i is seen to be approximately equal to the additional non-ionic binding energies.

B. *sb.* A non-ionic substance or detergent.

1952 *Mod. Sanit. & Build. Maint.* IV. 63/1 Considerable interest has been shown as to just what happens when iodine is dissolved in nonionics... It has been observed that nonionics render iodine soluble in aqueous solutions providing the amount of iodine does not exceed 25% based on the nonionic. **1972** *Materials & Technol.* V. x. 308 In several of the different classes of these non-ionics, it is possible to obtain products ranging from completely oil-soluble to completely water-soluble.

non-iron, *a.* [Cf. *NON- 5 b.] Of clothes, fabrics, etc.: that does not require ironing after being washed.

1957 *Woman* 16 Nov. 25/4 Cottons and rayons with a special finish—that is ones that have been made crease-resistant, drip-dry or non-iron cannot be dyed at home. **1971** *Vogue* 15 Sept. 43/1 Thick soft American towels, non-iron sheets. **1975** *Times* 27 Sept. 16/1 Easily washable and non-iron fabrics.

nonlea·ded, *ppl. a.* [f. NON- 6 + *LEADED *ppl. a.* e.] Of petrol: containing no added tetraethyl lead to counteract 'knocking'.

1955 *Sci. News Let.* 22 Jan. 54/1 The best way to remove carbon monoxide from auto fumes appears to be the use of nonleaded gasoline and a catalytic converter, Dr. W. L. Faith, chief engineer of the Southern California Air Pollution Foundation, said. **1971** *McGraw-Hill Yearbk. Sci. & Technol.* 212 The two most desired types of gasoline components for nonleaded gasolines are highly branched paraffins and the common aromatic components such as benzene, toluene, and xylene. **1971** J. D. ROBERTS et al. *Org. Chem.* iii. 58 The manufacture of engines capable of running on nonleaded gasoline is also being undertaken.

non-li·near, *a.* [NON- 3.] Not linear, in sense 3 of the adj.; involving terms of an equation that are not of the first degree; involving or possessing the property that the magnitude of an effect or output is not linearly related to that of the cause or input.

1844 *Phil. Trans. R. Soc.* CXXXIV. 282 The integration of non-linear differential equations. **1905** *Drapers' Company Res. Mem. Biometric Ser.* II. 21 In the cases of non-linear regression..I have..had to deal with, I find that parabolæ of the 2nd or 3rd order will suffice as

a rule to describe the deviation from linearity. **1925** F. C. MILLS *Statistical Methods* xii. 432 (*heading*) Non-linear correlation. **1930** T. E. SHEA *Transmission Networks & Wave Filters* ii. 43 Waves would tend to lose character in propagation, because of what is called non-linear distortion. **1949** O. G. SUTTON *Sci. of Flight* ii. 43 The inertia terms in these equations contain both squares and products of the velocities and the equations are thus non-linear. **1968** FOX & MAYERS *Computing Methods for Scientists & Engineers* i. 7 The Runge–Kutta method, or one of its variants, is a useful general-purpose routine for non-linear first-order equations. **1969** *Sci. Jrnl.* Apr. 53/3 Non-linear optics..is the study of the behaviour of materials subjected to light of such intensity as to change some of the parameters of the material. **1973** [see *LINEARIZE *v.*].

b. *Linguistics.* = **suprasegmental* adj.

1947 C. F. HOCKETT in *Internat. Jrnl. Amer. Ling.* XIII. 258/2 Features of stress or tone, for example, which normally stretch over more than a single vowel or consonant, have been called non-linear or suprasegmental, in contrast to the linear or segmental vowels and consonants. **1947** —— in *Jrnl. Amer. Oriental Soc.* LXVII. 258/1 Since it is inconvenient to transcribe other than linearly, we derive the symbols for inclosure between solidi from the symbols defined above in such a way as to eliminate the need for non-linear notation.

Hence **non-li·nearly** *adv.*

1943 *Jrnl. Amer. Chem. Soc.* LXV. 381/2 The ratio π/c of osmotic pressure to concentration has been found..to vary non-linearly with concentration. **1964** R. F. FICCHI *Electrical Interference* iii. 24 Components should not be permitted to operate nonlinearly since this causes harmonics to generate. **1973** *Jrnl. Genetic Psychol.* CXXII. 325 Body proportions..vary nonlinearly with figure age.

non-linea·rity. [NON- 1.] The property of not being linear; *esp.* lack of proportionality between two related quantities (as input and output).

1929 *Physical Rev.* XXXIII. 633 (*heading*) Non-linearity of photoelectric response near long wave-length limit. **1937** J. ORR tr. *Iordan's Introd. Romance Linguistics* iv. 379 Non-linearity of structure is shown to be present when a sign 'cumulates' more than one function. **1948** *Proc. IRE* XXXVI. 37/1 Any transmission system containing vacuum tubes is more or less nonlinear, with the degree of nonlinearity increasing with increasing signal level. **1965** *Math. in Biol. & Med.* (Med. Res. Council) VI. 266 In some cases, such as an excessively branching syncytial network, the gross non-linearities may be completely smoothed out and virtually linear polarizing current–voltage relations could then be obtained. **1967** *Oceanogr. & Marine Biol.* V. 30 Part of the non-linearity in the latter equations arises from the assumption that the bottom friction is proportional to the square of the bottom current. **1973** *Sci. Amer.* July 29/3 The presence of such nonlinearity in the control characteristics gives rise to additional frequencies at double, triple and quadruple the frequency of the basic oscillation.

non liquet. (Later example.)

1952 *Archivum Linguisticum* IV. II. 99 Hofmann..has also returned a verdict of *non liquet* on the question of etymology.

non-li·terate, *a. Anthropol.* [NON- 3.] Denoting a person or culture that has no written language. Hence as *sb.*, a non-literate person.

1948 M. J. HERSKOVITS *Man & his Works* II. v. 75 The..form, *nonliterate*, simply describes the fact that these people do not have written languages... Nonliterate, because it is colorless, conveys its meaning unambiguously, and is readily applicable to the data it seeks to delimit, is thus to be preferred to all the other terms we have considered. **1956** R. REDFIELD *Peasant Society & Culture* i. 6 Among these non-literates there was no history to learn. **1958** A. R. RADCLIFFE-BROWN *Method in Soc. Anthropol.* II. iii. 155 The customs of ancient times might be better understood in the light of the resemblances they show to customs of non-literate peoples of later times. **1970** G. A. & A. G. THEODORSON *Mod. Dict. Sociol.* 276 Sometimes the term *preliterate* is used as synonymous with nonliterate; however, preliterate is associated with certain theoretical assumptions..that are no longer accepted.

non-natural, *a.* and *sb.* **A.** *adj.* **1.** (Earlier example.)

1621 BURTON *Anat. Mel.* I. ii. 86 Necessary..are those six non-naturall things, so much spoken of amongst Physitians.

non-naturalism. Add: **2.** *Philos.* A theory of ethics which opposes naturalism; intuitionalism in ethics.

1939 *Mind* XLVIII. 464 The practitioners of a certain kind of ethical theory, which is dominant in England and capably represented in America, and which is variously called objectivism, non-naturalism, or intuitionism, have frequently charged their opponents with committing the naturalistic fallacy.

non-naturalist. Add: **b.** *Philos.* Of or pertaining to non-naturalism.

1966 *Amer. Philos. Q.* III. 299/2 Such a derivation, if valid, might be..a counter-example to the non-naturalist thesis.

B. *sb.* [NON- 2.] *Philos.* An adherent of non-naturalism.

1939 *Mind* XLVIII. 5 It is not indeed the only sense of good which the non-naturalist will hold incapable of reduction to naturalistic terms. **1966** *Amer. Philos. Q.* III. 305/2 Both non-naturalists and their critics seem to be seriously mistaken.

Hence **non-naturali·stic** *a.*; **non-naturali·stically** *adv.*

1902 W. JAMES *Var. Relig. Exper.* vi. 143 Brahmans, Buddhists, Christians, Mohammedans, twice-born people whose religion is non-naturalistic. **1939** W. D. ROSS *Foundations of Ethics* i. 6 If you define 'good' as meaning 'such that it *ought* to be desired', you are putting forward a non-naturalistic definition. Consequence theories also may be either naturalistic or non-naturalistic. **1940** *Mind* XLIX. 228 In the Introduction Ross divides attempted definitions of ethical terms into 'attitude-theories' and 'consequence-theories', and then sub-divides each of these into a naturalistic and a non-naturalistic sub-class. **1952** *Mind* LXI. 544 Any moral system is taken to be grounded non-naturalistically which is deduced from principles held to be certain and inviolable.

non-net, *a.* [NON- 3.] Of a book: not subject to the normal conditions of sale of net books.

1939 in F. D. Sanders *Brit. Bk. Trade Organisation* 79 The sale of books published at non-net prices is not covered by the terms of the Net Book Agreement. **1951** B. N. LANGDON-DAVIES *Practice of Bookselling* ii. 21 In respect of non-net books the only condition is that the bookseller may not sell them at less than the price he gave for them. **1963** 'R. FINDLATER' *What are Writers Worth?* 11 'Non-net' books are mainly educational ones, sold in bulk for use in schools by contractors rather than through the bookshops. **1972** *Bookseller* 2 Dec. 2545/2 Many of them [*sc.* textbooks] will be non-net, and not have prices printed on them.

non-Newto·nian, *a.* [NON- 3.] Not Newtonian, in sense 1 of the adj.; used esp. in connection with the flow of fluids (see quot. 1937).

1913 *Phil. Mag.* XXV. 157 The Einstein transformation equations, and the other principles of non-Newtonian mechanics. **1937** *Rep. Progress Physics* III. 22 It is rather with impure liquids, semi-liquids and semi-solids, that we have to deal in every-day life. Of these a large proportion may be described as 'non-Newtonian', i.e. the rate of shear is not proportional to the shearing stress, and they do not obey Poiseuille's or Stokes's law. **1943** *Amer. Speech* XVIII. 220 We are..on the threshold, he says, of a third stage: the 'non-aristotelian', non-Euclidean, non-Newtonian stage. The complete revolution Einstein has produced in physics is only part of a general revolution that must eventually affect all human knowledge. **1946** *Nature* 17 Aug. 245/1 The measurement of viscosity of non-Newtonian liquids. **1971** *Biorheology* VIII. 79 The 'overall viscosity'..exhibited non-Newtonian behavior.

non-no·rmal, *a.* [NON- 3.] Not normal; *spec.* in *Statistics* (cf. *NORMAL *a.* and *sb.* A. 2 e).

1929 *Biometrika* XXI. 124 (*heading*) On the distribution of the ratio of mean to standard deviation in small samples from non-normal universes. **1966** *English Studies* XLVII. 194 In this last phrase [*sc.* 'Mallice domestique'] the contrasting adjective 'domestique', given emphasis by its non-normal position, brings into full prominence the 'hatred' which the noun contains. **1968** P. A. P. MORAN *Introd. Probability Theory* vii. 300 The distributions..converge to a proper distribution, $F(x)$, which can be chosen to be non-normal if the theorem is false. **1973** J. J. ZEMAN *Modal Logic* ix. 146 The PC connectives behave in non-normal worlds precisely as they do in normal ones.

So **no:n-norma·lity**, the property or state of being non-normal.

1935 *Proc. Cambr. Philos. Soc.* XXXI. 230 The test of significance of a correlation coefficient has been shown..to be little vitiated by non-normality. **1962** E. S. KEEPING *Introd. Statistical Inference* viii. 208 If there is reason to suspect non-normality, from the nature of the data, it is advisable to try a transformation. The logarithm of the variate, or the square root,..may be more nearly normal. **1968** *Brit. Med. Bull.* XXIV. 212/1 The emphasis placed so far on non-Normality is somewhat misleading, in that other kinds of departure from the usual statistical model are often more important.

non-nu·clear, *a.* [NON- 3.] That is not nuclear (in various senses); *spec.* not possessing nuclear weapons; esp. in *non-nuclear club*, a group of nations that agrees not to possess nuclear weapons. Hence as *sb.*, something non-nuclear; *spec.* a nation that has no nuclear weapons.

1920 W. W. STRONG *New Philos. of Mod. Sci.* 103 Present day theories of the atom assume that the positive charge on the nucleus is equal in magnitude to the charge of the non-nuclear or planetary electrons. **1932** H. H. PRICE *Perception* viii. 258 If the sense-datum is a non-nuclear one, we cannot possibly move *towards* it. **1950** *New Biol.* VIII. 20 The unequal distribution of some non-nuclear hereditary substance. **1956** *Bull. Atomic Sci.* June 204/1 The nonnuclear nations may have the feeling that they alone constitute the stakes in the great struggle for world hegemony that the East is waging with the West. **1957** *Ibid.* Sept. 260/2 The U.S. on June 26 also proposed a reduction of nonnuclear weapons. **1959** *Daily Tel.* 6 July 6/2 His [*sc.* Mr. Gaitskell's] promise to try to form a non-nuclear club under British leadership. **1961** Y. OLSSON *Syntax Eng. Verb* vi. 95 The most restricted collocability gives the nucleus and the most general collocability gives the non-nuclear elements. *Ibid.* 127 The Nᵛ-expansion contains no non-nuclears. **1966** *Economist* 13 Aug. 634/1 Keeping the devices out of non-nuclear hands (and sight), but providing the service at a much lower cost than the non-nuclears would face. **1967** *Observer* 26 Feb. 10/6 The current leader of the non-nuclear club is Germany. **1968** MRS. L. B. JOHNSON *White House Diary* 1 July (1970) 692 The United States, Great Britain, and the Soviet Union, as well as fifty-eight non-nuclear nations, signed the Treaty.

nonny bag, var. *NUNNY BAG.

no-no (nō͡ᵘ-nō͡ᵘ). *colloq.* (orig. *U.S.*). [Redupl. No *sb.*] Something that must not be done, used, etc.; something that is forbidden, impossible, or not acceptable; a failure.

1942 BERREY & VAN DEN BARK *Amer. Thes. Slang* §310/1 *No-no*,..something that should not be done. **1968** *Washington Post* 30 Sept. A.20/2 What she was doing was a no-no, the protectors of our health announced... She must stop baking things for sale. **1970** *Islander* (Victoria, B.C.) 25 Oct. 16/3 Colonial Secretary Young at Victoria had to remind them that the Admiralty timber reserve was a 'no no'. **1972** *New Yorker* 17 June 29/1 Our people in Accounting tell me that cash payments are a no-no. **1972** *Observer* 17 Sept. 34/8 *Nationwide*..has my strict instructions never to touch the subject of rock music again: its piece on Bob Dylan was a total no-no. **1975** *Sunday Advocate-News* (Barbados) 15 June 3/1 Plants that require a great deal of moisture are no-noes unless you have your own well.

non-object. 1. [NON- 2.] **a.** Something which is not a material body.

1914 C. D. BROAD *Perception* i. 8 We must accept the possibility of real non-objects, though there cannot be apparent non-objects.

b. The condition of not being a grammatical object.

1964 E. A. NIDA *Toward Sci. Transl.* v. 109 Semantic markers are primarily of two types: (1) those which mark positive–negative dichotomies, e.g. nonobject vs. object and verbal vs. nonverbal.

2. *attrib.* [NON- 4.] **a.** Not corporeal. **b.** Not functioning as grammatical object.

1963 F. T. VISSER *Hist. Syntax of Eng. Lang.* I. iv. 429 For its [*sc.* 'the self's'] use in non-object relations see 1959 Carstensen p. 226. **1971** *Gloss. Electrotechnical, Power Terms* (*B.S.I.*) IV. ii. 9 *Non-object* (*perceived*) *colour*, colour perceived as non-located in depth, such as that perceived as filling a hole in a screen.

non-obje·ctive, *a.* [NON- 3.] Not objective; *spec.* in art = *ABSTRACT A. 4 d. Hence **non-obje·ctivism, non-obje·ctivist, non-objec·ti·vity.**

1905 W. JAMES in *Jrnl. Philos., Psychol. & Sci. Methods* II. 286 That..is enough to save them from being classed as absolutely non-objective. **1936** *Amer. Mag. of Art* Mar. 154 (*heading*) Non-objectivity at Charleston. **1936** *Design* June 13 (*heading*) Definition of non-objective painting. **1937** H. READ *Art & Society* vii. 260 A heightened sensibility to the purity of form..can best be induced and refined by the creation and appreciation of non-objective works of art. **1946** D. D. RUNES *Encycl. Arts* 680/1 The non-objectivist uses his medium, line and color..to create freely following his intuition. **1952** *Time* 16 June 61 He enjoys swimming against the current of non-objectivism. **1958** *Times* 24 Nov. (Canada Suppl.) p. xvi/6 In our contracting world few countries can escape the impact of the international artistic trend towards non-objectivity. **1959** *Listener* 3 Dec. 980/2 The non-objectivist Alexander Rodchenko painted three canvases, one red, one blue, one yellow, and announced 'the death of art'. **1960** E. H. GOMBRICH *Art & Illusion* viii. 286 Even nonobjective art derives some of its meaning and effects from the habits and mental sets we acquired in learning to read representations. **1962** J. SÖDERLIND in F. Behre *Contrib. Eng. Syntax* 110 Non-objective *of*-groups offer some difficulties.

no-no·nsense, *a.* [The phr. *no nonsense* (NONSENSE *sb.* 1 c) used as an adj.] That does not tolerate foolish or extravagant conduct; sensible, business-like, realistic, practical.

1928 *Sat. Even. Post* 12 May 25/1 From a no-nonsense business man he has become a romantic. **1943** J. B. PRIESTLEY *Daylight on Saturday* xiii. 92 Her own breezy, no-nonsense line. **1957** *Observer* 27 Oct. 16/3 The tunes are vigorous no-nonsense affairs. **1959** W. MCGIVERN *Savage Streets* (1960) i. 7 A blunt, no-nonsense sort of person. **1963** [see *go-anywhere* adj. s.v. *GO *v.* VIII]. **1973** J. WAINWRIGHT *Pride of Pigs* 113 Its bare-brick walls were painted white. Its floor was no-nonsense concrete.

non-o·rientable, *a. Math.* [NON- 3.] Of a surface: such that a figure in the surface can be continuously transformed into its mirror image by taking it round a closed path in the surface; not orientable.

1949 S. LEFSCHETZ *Introd. Topology* ii. 76 The combination of the first type is called nonorientable. **1952** P. NEMENYI tr. *Hilbert & Cohn-Vossen's Geom. & Imagination* vi. 306 The classification of surfaces into two-sided and one-sided surfaces is identical with the classification into orientable and non-orientable. *Ibid.*, A surface is non-orientable if and only if there exists on the surface some closed curve *s* which is such that a small oriented circle whose center traverses the curve continuously will arrive at its starting point with its orientation reversed. **1965** S. BARR *Exper. Topology* ii. 22 The Moebius strip is what is called non-orientable—which is less open to misinterpretation than saying it is 1-sided.

Hence **no:n-orientabi·lity**, the property of being non-orientable.

1949 S. LEFSCHETZ *Introd. Topology* ii. 83 A closed surface..is completely characterized by the value of its Betti number..and by its orientability or nonorientability. **1964** H. LEVY *Projective & Related Geometries* v. 388 We shall derive two properties of L_2 that are strongly suggestive of its nonorientability.

nonose (nōu·nōus, -z). *Chem.* [a. G. *nonose* (E. Fischer 1890, in *Ber. d. Deut. Chem. Ges.* XXIII. 934): see *NONA- and -OSE².] Any monosaccharide having nine carbon atoms in the molecule, esp. when these are all in an unbranched chain.

1890 *Jrnl. Chem. Soc.* LVIII. 1234 (*table*) Nonose. **1915** *Jrnl. Biol. Chem.* XXIII. 327 When it was found later that the glucononose was not fermentable, the configurations of the two nonoses became of great interest. **1945** *Adv. Carbohydrate Chem.* I. 7 Distinctly different nonoses were obtained in the two researches by the reduction of the respective lactones. **1972** BRIMACOMBE & WEBBER in Pigman & Horton *Carbohydrates* (ed. 2) IA. xiv. 497 Extension of the cyanohydrin synthesis to this nonose gave a decitol.

non-parame·tric, *a.* *Statistics.* [NON- 3.] Not involving any assumptions as to the form or parameters of a frequency distribution.

1942 J. WOLFOWITZ in *Ann. Math. Statistics* XIII. 264 Most of these developments have this feature in common, that the distribution functions of the various stochastic variables which enter into their problems are assumed to be of known functional form, and the theories of estimation of and of testing hypotheses about, one or more parameters..the knowledge of which would completely determine the various distribution functions involved. We shall refer to this situation..as the parametric case, and denote the opposite case, where the functional forms of the distributions are unknown, as the non-parametric case. **1956** S. SIEGEL (*title*) Nonparametric statistics for the behavioral sciences. **1957** KENDALL & BUCKLAND *Dict. Statistical Terms* 87 Distribution-free inference or distribution-free tests are sometimes known as non-parametric but this usage is confusing and should be avoided. It is better to confine the word 'non-parametric' to the description of hypotheses which do not explicitly make an assertion about a parameter. **1962** E. S. KEEPING *Introd. Statistical Inference* x. 251 Non-parametric tests are generally simple to apply... In those cases where a parametric test would also be applicable a non-parametric test will naturally be less powerful than the parametric one. **1966** *Lancet* 31 Dec. 1434/1 To avoid making assumptions concerning normality and homogeneity, the nonparametric one-way analysis [of] variance by ranks..was carried out. **1972** *Jrnl. Social Psychol.* LXXXVIII. 204, I have typically used a nonparametric correlation to illustrate the association between awareness and experimental performance.

non-partisa·n, *a.* [NON- 3.] Not partisan. Also as *sb.*, one who is not a partisan. Hence **non-partisa·nship.**

1885 *Century Mag.* Apr. 823 A citizens' ticket, largely non-partisan in character, was run for certain local offices. **1888** *Voice* 9 Feb., The non-partisans have for some time been making Mr. Johnson's position very uncomfortable for him. **1888** G. H. CARROW (*title*) Non-partisanship; or, do not take temperance into politics. **1932** *Times Lit. Suppl.* 11 Feb. 95/4 Critical, non-partisan, and bright in style, this book is a veritable compendium of the theories, claims, and actual achievements of psychology. **1952** G. SARTON *Hist. Sci.* I. xii. 319 His nonpartisanship, objectivity, and honesty. **1957** *Economist* 7 Sept. 850/2 For most of the time, he has put on a determined show of nonpartisanship. **1964** *Ann. Reg. 1963* 215 The latter.. dealt in a relatively non-partisan spirit with contemporary Western culture. **1974** *Nature* 25 Jan. 169/1 The inferior quality of the recent Commons debate on the fuel shortage does not bode well for informed non-partisan discussions.

non-passive, *a.* and *sb.* *Gram.* [NON- 3, 2.] **A.** *adj.* Not in the passive voice.

1962 C. L. BARBER in F. Behre *Contrib. Eng. Syntax* 26 Of these [finite verbs], 28% are passive, and 72% non-passive. **1963** F. T. VISSER *Hist. Syntax of Eng. Lang.* I. iv. 562 In the non-passive construction the predicative adjunct is usually preceded by *for*: 'Hig hæfdon hyne for ænne witegan'. **1965** *Language* XLI. 107 The non-passive aorist in Greek. **B.** *sb.* A construction not in the passive voice.

1962 C. L. BARBER in F. Behre *Contrib. Eng. Syntax* 27 A much smaller number of passives—only 3%, against 97% non-passives.

non-past. *Gram.* [NON- 2.] A tense that is not the past tense; usually, the present tense, or the present and future tenses. Also *attrib.* or as *adj.*

1946 *Language* XXII. 213 The non-past indicative of the copula, *dá*, is replaced by a zero alternant (i.e. drops out). **1951** TRAGER & SMITH *Outl. Eng. Structure* II. 60 Verbs are inflected for 3D Person SG. Non-past, Past, Past Participle, Present Participle. **1962** S. E. MARTIN in Householder & Saporta *Problems in Lexicography* 157 In many parts of the world, verbs are usually entered under the plain present (or non-past) form. **1966** *Amer. Speech* XLI. 201 The present, which many structuralists have preferred to call the 'nonpast'. **1971** *Archivum Linguisticum* II. 25 It is important to notice that [in Classical Latin] both potential and unreal conditions could refer to past and to non-past time. *Ibid.* 27 It is possible to visualize, in Old Spanish, the maintenance of the category of 'non-past, unreal', a category which..existed in Latin. **1972** *Language* XLVIII. 473 One feature of emphatic transformations from verbal bases is the replacement of the verb form of the base clause by an emphatic form; this is a special form in the non-past or past corresponding to the simple forms in the same tenses.

non-pa·trial, *sb.* and *a.* [NON- 2, 4 + *PATRIAL *a.* (*sb.*) 3.] **A.** *sb.* One who is not a patrial. **B.** *adj.* Applied to a person who is not a patrial.

The 1971 Immigration Act does not use the term 'non-patrial'. **1971** *Telegraph* (Brisbane) 25 Jan. 5/3 Under the Government's new Immigration Act, everyone who regards himself as a UK citizen is to be defined as a 'patrial' or 'non-patrial'. **1971** *Daily Tel.* 11 Oct. 1/5 The Police Federation asked the Government four months ago to drop the proposal in the Bill for 'non-patrial' Commonwealth citizens to register with and report to the police, as aliens do. **1972** *Guardian* 25 Nov. 10/2 A non-patrial Commonwealth citizen who wants to work here. **1973** C. MULLARD *Black Britain* II. v. 63 Others—'non-patrials' —do not have an automatic 'right of abode'.

non-perio·dic, *a.* [NON- 3.] Characterized by or exhibiting a lack of periodicity; without regular recurrence; = *APERIODIC *a.*

1843 *Scientific Mem.* III. 221 (*heading*) On the non-periodic variations in the distribution of temperature on the surface of the earth. **1902** *Encycl. Brit.* XXVII. 161/2 The non-periodic comets appearing since 1700 are nearly all in the hands of computers. **1932** W. L. GRAFF *Language & Languages* 17 Many so-called musical tones are nonperiodic. **1965** *Math. in Biol. & Med.* (Med. Res. Council) IV. 141 If the time occupied by one complex cycle is assumed to increase to infinity, then a Fourier Integral ..may be developed which describes, again in terms of sines and cosines, the waveform of a transient or non-periodic function.

no·n-person. [NON- 2.] A person who is regarded as nonexistent or unimportant; someone who is ignored, humiliated, or forgotten.

1959 *Times Lit. Suppl.* 2 Oct. 555/3 The belief that all Africans, students and dockers alike, are the same; the notion that they are 'non-persons', with a kind of animal anonymity which relieves whites of their inhibitions. **1965** [see *NON-EVENT]. **1968** *Daily Tel.* 7 Nov. 22/4 Pets are in highest demand in the wealthy Protestant West, with all its rejects and 'non-persons'. **1973** R. HAYES *Hungarian Game* xxiii. 145 Neither AVH nor KGB had a watch on Mityas' house. He'd become such a non-person that not even they worried about whom he saw.

non-pe·rsonal, *a.* and *sb.* [NON- 3, 2.] **A.** *adj.* Not personal. **B.** *sb.* Something that is not personal, or not a person; *spec.* a pronoun representing a non-personal noun.

1902 W. JAMES *Var. Relig. Exper.* xx. 500 The contention of the survival-theory that we ought to stick to non-personal elements exclusively. **1925** GRATTAN & GURREY *Our Living Lang.* 189 With Non-Personals the idea of possession is commonly not present—for example —I have recovered this book and mended *the* (not *its*) back. **1928** O. JESPERSEN *Internat. Lang.* II. 128 If there is an apparatus called in this way, the word belongs to the non-personal class: *telegrafe* (the apparatus), *telegrafa* vb, *telegrafo* telegraphing. **1933** L. BLOOMFIELD *Lang.* ix. 146 It has the class-meanings of substantives, singulars, nonpersonals. *Ibid.* xv. 253 The English definite or third-person pronouns..differ.., in the singular, for *personal* and *non-personal* antecedents: *personal he, she,* versus non-personal *it*. **1957** R. W. ZANDVOORT *Handbk. Eng. Gram.* IX. ii. 315 The addition of *-ish* to other personal nouns: *boyish, girlish* (= proper to the nature of), and to a few non-personal nouns (*feverish*). **1965** *English Studies* XLVI. 228 It perfectly focusses the gap between a personal standard and the non-personal sonorities of Roman 'honor'.

non-plu·ral, *sb.* and *a.* [NON- 2, 3.] **A.** *sb.* The fact or condition of being only one in number.

1941 N. K. SMITH *Philos. of D. Hume* xxiii. 500 Tending to equate 'unity' with 'the simple', in the sense of the non-plural.

B. *adj.* *Linguistics.* Not in the plural form.

1958 L. KRASNER in Saporta & Bastian *Psycholinguistics* (1961) 81/1 When used to reinforce nonplural responses, both stimuli tended to increase the frequency of such responses. **1961** R. B. LONG *Sentence & its Parts* viii. 184 The 'singular' forms are really nonplural rather than singular in the strict sense. **1970** *Jrnl. Gen. Psychol.* July 7 Greenspoon noted that both of these reinforcing stimuli effected an increase in the emission of nonplural responses.

non-po·lar, *a.* [NON- 3.] Not polar; *spec.* in *Chem.* and *Physics*, (composed of molecules) having no electric dipole moment.

1892 *Electrician* 29 Jan. 329/1 He [*sc.* G. Forbes] had carried out some encouraging experiments with a dynamo..built on his 'non-polar' principle. **1896** FISHER & SCHWATT tr. H. Durège's *Elem. Theory Functions* vii. 126 A non-polar discontinuity. **1913** *Jrnl. Amer. Chem. Soc.* XXXV. 1443 Polar and non-polar bonds may..appear in the same formula. *Ibid.*, There are two distinct types of union between atoms: polar, in which an electron has passed from one atom to the other, and non-polar, in which there is no motion of an electron. *Ibid.*, Characteristics of the non-polar type [of substance] are the ability to form chain compounds, and the existence of separable isomers. **1951** *New Biol.* X. 124 Water molecules, being polar, that is, with electric charges not distributed uniformly, are attracted by other polar molecules or parts of molecules that have no affinity for non-polar groups. **1965** PHILLIPS & WILLIAMS *Inorg. Chem.* I. iv. 135 Polar molecules will have higher.. boiling points than otherwise similar non-polar molecules.

1967 E. CHAMBERS *Photolitho-Offset* i. 8 Lithographic etches produce non-polar deposits not capable of absorbing an acid.

non-poli·tical, *a.* and *sb.* [NON- 3, 2.] **A.** *adj.* Not involved in politics. **B.** *sb.* One who is not involved in politics.

1860 DICKENS *Uncommercial Traveller* (1958) xvii. 172 If the prisoner..had committed every non-political crime in the Newgate Calendar..nothing would have been easier than..to obtain his release. **1882** E. W. HAMILTON *Diary* 27 July (1972) I. 312 It appears that H.M., regarding the matter as 'non-political', has also taken the advice of Lord Cranbrook and Northcote about it. **1920** B. RUSSELL *Practice & Theory Bolshevism* I. ii. 25, I was able..to find out how the whole system appears to the ordinary non-political man and woman. **1926** R. MACAULAY *Crewe Train* (1967) II. iii. 67 She enjoyed her mother's party, though she found at it too many non-politicals. **1958** *New Statesman* 1 Feb. 131/1 Even in South Africa (I would argue) it was all right for us to live our non-political lives. **1962** *Guardian* 22 Dec. 3/1 The other non-politicals contented themselves with brief speeches.

non-prolifera·tion. [NON- 1.] The prevention of an increase in the number of countries possessing nuclear weapons. Freq. *attrib.*

1965 *Times* 13 July 12/3 It would, however, only be prepared to subscribe to an east-west agreement on non-proliferation when the problem of nuclear security within the Atlantic Alliance had been satisfactorily settled. **1965** *Newsweek* 26 July 36/2 The price for a Russian agreement on a non-proliferation pact. **1974** *Friend* 1 Feb. 114/2 The premier..is committed under the Non-Proliferation Treaty to negotiate an end to the nuclear arms race. **1974** *Times* 20 May 15/2 Some Afro-Asian countries.. maintained that the non-proliferation treaty was..a plot to maintain the hegemony of those who already had the bomb.

non-provi·ded, *a.* [NON- 6.] Of schools or education: that is not provided (see PROVIDED *ppl. a.* 4 b).

1918 A. QUILLER-COUCH *Foe-Farrell* 44 He..zigzagged off into Education 'Provided' and 'Non-Provided', lunging and floundering with the Church Catechism and the Rate-book. **1921** *Act* 11 & 12 *Geo. V* c. 51 §29 *marg.*, Conditions to be observed in conduct of non-provided schools. **1960** R. WILLIAMS *Border Country* 162 The entrance to the school, Glynmawr Non-Provided.

non-ra·ndom, *a.* [NON- 3.] Not random. Hence **non-ra·ndomly** *adv.*; **non-ra·ndomness.**

1942 *Genetics* XXVII. 531 (*heading*) The non-random distribution of mutants in the progeny of certain flies. **1943** J. S. HUXLEY *Evolutionary Ethics* 73 A non-random sample of the population. **1958** *Oxf. Univ. Gaz.* 27 Jan. 524/2 A model of non-randomness in threshold experiments. **1961** L. F. BROSNAHAN *Sounds of Language* v. 90 Sounds..occur in apparently non-random distributions which unite languages of different language groups. **1966** D. G. BRANDON *Mod. Techniques Metallogr.* 251 Spatial non-randomness may be either orientation-dependent or orientation-independent. **1972** *Science* 5 May 545/1 Alleles of polymorphic loci, in the absence of direct selection, will tend to become nonrandomly associated with closely linked overdominant loci. **1972** *Jrnl. Soc. Psychol.* Aug. 223 A nonrandom sample of collective behaviour. **1973** *Nature* 16 Mar. 166/1 Human chromosomes are segregated non-randomly into hybrid clones.

non-ra·tional, *a.* [NON- 3.] Not rational. Also *absol.* as *sb.* Hence **non-rationa·lity.**

a **1871** G. GROTE *Eth. Fragm.* (1876) v. 183 Aristotle classifies the phenomena of..the non-rational soul into three. **1896** W. CALDWELL *Schopenhauer's System* i. 16 His experience of life was such as to bring the *non-rational* side of things prominently before his mind. **1902** W. JAMES *Var. Relig. Exper.* iii. 74, I do not yet say that it is *better* that the subconscious and non-rational should thus hold primacy in the religious realm. *a* **1910** —— *Some Probl. Philos.* (1911) viii. 136 The only alternative allowed by monistic writers is to confess the world's non-rationality—and no philosopher can permit himself to do that. **1951** R. FIRTH *Elements of Social Organization* vii. 245 The possibilities of intellectual and emotional satisfaction to be derived from religious belief are increased by the resort of that belief to non-rationality. **1957** J. S. HUXLEY *Relig. without Revelation* iii. 52 Mythical thought, which is basically non-rational. **1972** *Listener* 21 Dec. 854/2 Reliance on the non-rational means that courses of action are followed without regard for their long-term consequences.

non-refere·ntial, *a.* [NON- 3.] Of hypothesized mental events, such as the awareness of thought or of an image: having no reference to anything beyond themselves.

1925 C. D. BROAD *Mind & its Place* vi. 305 Purely inspective situations would belong to the latter class. So would pure sensation, the mere awareness of an image, etc... I am inclined to think that pure sensations, etc., are ideal limits rather than actual facts... Let us call situations of the..second kind 'non-referential'. **1943** *Mind* LII. 176, I..shall say something more about the non-referential interpretation of 'copy'. **1971** J. Z. YOUNG *Introd. Study Man* x. 125 All the words of the mental language are said to be 'non-referential'.

non-refle·xive, *a.* [NON- 3.] **1.** *Gram.* Not reflexive (REFLEXIVE *a.* 5).

1949 O. JESPERSEN *Mod. Eng. Gram.* VII. 170 As a reflexive use of the *self*-forms we must also reckon the predicative in 'he is quite himself again' = 'in a normal

condition', though NED takes it to be the emphatic, i.e. non-reflexive use. **1965** D. WARD *Russ. Lang. Today* v. 139 As a general rule, such nouns are formed from imperfective non-reflexive verbs. **1968** J. LYONS *Introd. Theoretical Linguistics* 361 Many languages..have a set of reflexive pronouns distinguished for person and number..; others..draw a distinction between reflexive and non-reflexive objects only in the third person.

2. *Philos.* Of a relation which may, but need not, hold between a thing and itself. Cf. *IRREFLEXIVE *a.*, *REFLEXIVE *a.* 3.

1947 H. REICHENBACH *Elem. Symbolic Logic* iii. 120 The nonreflexive functions comprise the irreflexive and the mesoreflexive functions. **1954** I. M. COPI *Symbolic Logic* v. 143 Relations which are neither reflexive nor irreflexive are said to be non-reflexive. The phrases: 'loves', 'hates', and 'criticizes' designate non-reflexive relations. **1955** A. N. PRIOR *Formal Logic* III. iii. 274 Not everybody is a shaver of himself, but some are. These [relations] are sometimes called 'non-reflexive'. **1964** E. BACH *Introd. Transformational Gram.* vii. 155 If there is at least one term in its domain that does not bear the relation to itself, then it is classed as *nonreflexive*... *Admiring* is presumably non-reflexive; i.e., there are people who admire someone and do not admire themselves. **1965** HUGHES & LONDEY *Elem. of Formal Logic* xxxix. 274 Every dyadic relation must be either reflexive or irreflexive or non-reflexive.

non-resident, *sb.* Add: **3.** A person who uses some of the facilities of a hotel without residing there.

1910 *Bradshaw's Railway Guide* Apr. 1081 Sea and fresh water baths in the hotel..are open to non-residents. **1960** *Harper's Bazaar* Oct. 101/1 Even at the Dorchester.. the bar is closed at 11 p.m. to non-residents. **1971** 'A. GILBERT' *Tenant for Tomb* vii. 132 A printed invitation to non-residents to use the bar and the dining-room.

non-resident, *a.* Add: **3.** *U.S.* Of land: owned by a person who does not reside on it.

1849 E. CHAMBERLAIN *Indiana Gaz.* (ed. 3) 313 The large amount of non-resident lands has hitherto retarded improvements. **1881** *Mich. Gen. Statutes* (1882) I. 385 Such notice to owners of such non-resident lands, shall be served by posting up the same in three public places.

non-resistance. Delete 'Now only *Hist.*' and add further examples.

1838 W. L. GARRISON in *Liberator* (Boston) 28 Sept. 154/5 We shall adhere to the doctrine of non-resistance and passive submission to enemies. **1861** W. ROWNTREE *War & Christianity* 6 The great principle of non-resistance. **1898** [see INTERNATIONALISM]. **1934** G. B. SHAW *On Rocks* 155 It is easy to suggest that they [*sc.* evildoers] should be reformed by gentleness and shamed by nonresistance. **1973** R. V. SAMPSON *Tolstoy: the Discovery of Peace* vi. 109 It is very rare for a writer to allow Tolstoy's arguments in support of the doctrine of non-resistance to evil—the essence of Tolstoy—to be heard.

non-resistant, *a.* and *sb.* **B.** *sb.* (Earlier example.)

1755 in S. M. Hamilton *Lett. to Washington* (1898) I. 91 The fighting Faction..threaten to put to Death all the Non-resistents—Dunkers, Moravians, Dutch and Quakers.

non-resi·ster. [NON- 2.] = NON-RESISTANT *sb.*

1851 J. A. QUITMAN in J. F. H. Clairborne *Life & Corr. J. A. Quitman* (1860) II. 147 By the election of Nonresisters to the Convention, a majority of the people have declared against the course of policy on the slavery questions.

non-restri·ctive, *a.* [NON- 3.] Not restrictive; *spec.* in *Gram.*, denoting a word, phrase, or clause that does not restrict or limit the meaning of the word or words to which it is added.

1924 O. JESPERSEN *Philos. of Gram.* viii. 111 Next we come to *non-restrictive adjuncts* as in *my dear little Ann!* **1927** —— *Mod. Eng. Gram.* III. iv. 82 Restrictive or defining clauses,..give a necessary determination to the antecedent, and thereby make it more precise... Nonrestrictive or loose clauses..might be discarded without serious injury to the precise understanding of the sentence as a whole. **1953** J. S. HUXLEY *Evolution in Action* vi. 142 What is difficult is to discover just how any one step is effected, still more to distinguish desirable from undesirable change, and restrictive from non-restrictive improvement. **1966** G. N. LEECH *Eng. in Advertising* xiv. 132 Proper nouns do occasionally combine with modifiers of non-restrictive force: 'fair Helen'..; 'beautiful Britain'. **1971** *Archivum Linguisticum* II. 14 To separate nonrestrictive progressive relative clauses from the preceding clause.

non-retu·rnable, *a.* [NON- 3.] That may not be returned; *spec.* of containers, bottles, etc.: that may not be returned empty to the suppliers. Also *absol.* as *sb.*

1903 T. E. YOUNG *Insurance* x. 265 The premiums in the event of death happening prior to the adult age agreed upon may be either non-returnable..or returnable in full. **1907** *Yesterday's Shopping* (1969) p. x/1 All empties, except 'non-returnable cases'..must be returned within a reasonable period. **1926–27** *Army & Navy Stores Catal.* p. ix/1 Goods sent by Rail or by Carter Paterson are packed in non-returnable cases for which no charge is made. **1961** *New Scientist* 16 Mar. 700/2 The milk bottle.. is about five times cheaper than the non-returnable carton. **1968** *Economist* 27 Jan. 59/3 Now that the nonreturnable bottle—and breathalysers—are here to stay, grocery stores are the growth point in drink sales. **1971** *Wall St. Jrnl.* 5 Mar. 26/4 About 70 such laws were debated last year by various local, state and federal bodies. Bowle, Md., actually banned nonreturnables. **1971** *Nature* 6 Aug. 359/2 Potential customers should..make appropriate non-returnable deposits as marks of their good faith. **1973** *Times* 11 Dec. 6/4 It is absurd for continuance of non-returnable bottle production still to be allowed.

nonrewa·rd. *Psychol.* [NON- 1.] In learning experiments: deliberate withholding of an expected reward. Hence **nonrew·arded** *ppl. a.*

1951 N. E. MILLER in S. S. Stevens *Handbk. Exper. Psychol.* 458/1 The cues produced by nonreward. *Ibid.*, The interspersing of a number of nonrewarded trials during training with primary drive and reward (i.e. partial reinforcement) may increase the resistance of a learned reward to experimental extinction. **1970** *Jrnl. General Psychol.* Oct. 185 The role of frustrative nonreward in instrumental escape conditioning. **1973** *Jrnl. Genetic Psychol.* Mar. 89 Association with frustrative nonreward alters the affective value of the stimulus.

non-ri·gid, *a.* [NON- 3.] Not rigid; *spec.* denoting an airship which has no framework to support the envelope, and whose shape is maintained solely by the pressure of the gas inside. Also occas. as *sb.*, an airship of this kind.

1909 A. BERGET *Conquest of Air* I. v. 108 These airships are non-rigid. **1909** *Daily Chron.* 3 Aug. 1/7 The two non-rigids that are to come from France. **1930** *Daily Express* 6 Oct. 2/4 He..was captain of non-rigid airships in home waters and the East Mediterranean. **1961** *B.S.I. News* Dec. 20/2 Rigid plastics; semi-rigid plastics; nonrigid plastics.

non-sche·duled, *a.* orig. *U.S.* [NON- 6.] Not scheduled; *spec.* of an airline: operating without fixed or published flying schedules; of or pertaining to such an airline. So **non-sched, -sked** (nǫnske·d), a non-scheduled airline; also *attrib.* or as *adj.*

1946 *Harper's Mag.* Oct. 324/1 The non-scheds naturally look with envy at the mail subsidies now granted to the big airlines. **1949** *Aviation Week* 30 May 7/1 The nonsked may barely break even as a result. **1949** *Industrial Arts Index* June 7/2 Air carriers: non-scheduled operations. **1960** *Wall St. Jrnl.* 12 Jan. 30/2 The ultimate outcome of the case apparently will affect several other suits brought by 'non-skeds' which seek an additional $154.6 million in damages. **1961** *Flight* LXXX. 645/1 The Flying Tiger Line has leased an L.1049H Super Constellation to Trans-International Airlines Inc, a Florida-based 'non-sked'. **1971** *Flying* Apr. 113/2 Cargo and non-scheduled carriers described. **1975** *Publishers Weekly* 3 Mar. 73/2 This is like being stuck on a nonsched junket to the most obvious European spots.

nonsense, *sb.* Add: **1. a.** *to knock the nonsense out of*: see *KNOCK *v.* 6 e.

b. Delete † and add later examples; also *concr.*; also, a muddle, fiasco, esp. in phr. *to make a nonsense (of)*.

1803 SCOTT *Let.* 14 Sept. (1932) I. 204, I daresay I shall go on scribbling one nonsense or another to the end of the chapter. **1942** E. WAUGH *Put Out More Flags* iii. 212 Everyone said, 'Lyne made a nonsense of the embarkation.' *Ibid.* 242 'It was all rather a nonsense' said the subaltern, in the classic phraseology of his trade which comprehends all human tragedy. **1957** *Listener* 30 May 873 Size is essential for efficiency. A small steel works.. is an economic nonsense. **1960** L. COOPER *Accomplices* II. i. 71 He's made a complete nonsense of the whole thing and got the sack. *Ibid.* vi. 135, I knew you'd make a nonsense of it so I told Wallis to be ready to take over. **1962** *Movie* June 6/2 Ambitious nonsenses like *The Entertainer* and *Flame in the Streets*. **1966** A. PRIOR *Operators* xv. 225 An occasion that could make a nonsense of any Op. Bad intelligence, weather, flak. **1970** *New Statesman* 16 Jan. 88/3 'Structure' is one of those useful nonsenses in the vocabulary of the fiction critic, the mystery ingredient with the secret formula.

d. Used, usu. in the spelling *non-sense*, without connotations of absurdity: something that is not sense or that differs from sense.

Not clearly separable from sense 1 a in Dict.

1942 T. S. ELIOT *Music of Poetry* 14 His [*sc.* Lear's] nonsense is not vacuity of sense: it is a parody of sense, and that is the sense of it. **1943** *Amer. Speech* XVIII. 221 Men struggle over non-sense questions. **1965** *English Studies* XLVI. 322 A 'steep ford' is quite obvious nonsense.

6. a. *nonsense song* (later examples); **nonsense syllable**, a syllable formed by putting a vowel between any two consonants, used in memory experiments and tests; **nonsense verses** (earlier and later examples); also **nonsense verse**, comically nonsensical or whimsical verse; *spec.* a limerick; **nonsense word**, a word which has no accepted meaning; also = **nonsense syllable*.

1968 *Radio Times* 28 Nov. 65/2 A nonsense song from Virginia, 'Poor Howard'. **1975** *Listener* 6 Mar. 305/2 When Charlie finally opened his mouth in *Modern Times*, out came a nonsense song no one needed to understand. **1890** W. JAMES *Princ. Psychol.* I. xvi. 667 Mr. Burnham.. suggested..one ought to test one's self *à la* Ebbinghaus on series of nonsense-syllables. **1924** R. M. OGDEN tr. *Koffka's Growth of Mind* i. 29 Impressing certain material (preferably nonsense-syllables in an ordered series)..upon the observer. **1971** *Jrnl. General Psychol.* LXXXV. 139 Ss were allowed to work 10 nonsense-syllable examples. **1799** *Public Characters* II. 423 Although few *men* in England could equal him in writing *sense* prose, yet many *boys* might surpass him in writing *nonsense* verses. **1819** KEATS *Let.* 17 Sept. (1931) II. 438, I cannot get on without writing as boys do at school a few nonsense verses. **1851** [see AMPHIGOURI, -GORY]. **1898** [see LIMERICK]. **1938** A. DAVIDSON *Edward Lear* ii. 18 It is possible that these extemporized nonsense-verses were in the limerick form. **1940** *Essays & Studies* XXV. 7 The nonsense verse also was well worth having—who had believed, else, that Housman had it in him either to be happy or to write nonsense. **1919** J. B. WATSON *Psychology* ix. 336 Nonsense words or syllables are made by separating two consonants with a vowel as *ver, gax* and *moc*. **1935** B. MALINOWSKI in M. Black *Importance of Lang.* (1962) 72 Have we to imagine that magical speech starts from sheer nonsense words..? **1954** J. R. R. TOLKIEN *Fellowship of Ring* I. vi. 130 Out of a long string of nonsense-words (or so they seemed) the voice rose up loud and clear and burst into this song.

c. *Biol.* Denoting a codon that does not specify any amino-acid, or a mutation which gives rise to such a codon (and may thus prematurely bring about a blocking of polypeptide synthesis).

[**1957** F. H. C. CRICK et al. in *Proc. Nat. Acad. Sci.* XLIII. 418 We shall assume that there are certain sequences of three nucleotides with which an amino acid can be associated and certain others for which this is not possible. Using the metaphors of coding, we say that some of the 64 triplets make sense and some make nonsense.] **1961** [see *MISSENSE *a.*]. **1964** G. H. HAGGIS et al. *Introd. Molecular Biol.* xii. 318 They then calculated that the sixty-four triplets could be divided..into two classes, with twenty meaningful triplets in one class and forty-four nonsense triplets in the other. **1969** A. M. CAMPBELL *Episomes* ix. 122 Nonsense mutations of *lacZ*..produce reduced levels of the permease coded by *lacY*. **1974** *Encycl. Brit. Micropædia* IV. 464/2 It is now known that there may be several codes for one amino acid and that there are nonsense codes that do not code anything.

nonsense (nǫ·nsěns), *v. rare.* [f. the sb.] *intr.* To talk nonsense.

1822 M. EDGEWORTH *Let.* 30 May (1971) 404 We have given most elegant repasts as I shall have the honor of describing to you soon when we are all together nonsenseing round Lucys sofa. **1909** R. A. WASON *Happy Hawkins* 67, I nonsensed a while, tryin' to get her to laugh an' cut up, but not her.

non-se·quence. *Geol.* [NON- 1.] An interruption in the deposition of adjacent conformable strata that was too short (in geological terms) for significant erosion to take place and consequently has to be inferred from a gap in the fossil record.

[**1895** S. S. BUCKMAN in *Q. Jrnl. Geol. Soc.* LI. 391 Nonsequential strata, when the sequence is incomplete, but the planes of the deposits are practically parallel.] **1904** *Ibid.* LX. 349 (*heading*) Evidence for a non-sequence between the Keuper and Rhætic series in North-West Gloucestershire and Worcestershire. **1933** *Ibid.* LXXXIX. 163 If..the oolitic and nodular beds are at this horizon.. their position immediately overlying slates with *Didymograptus bifidus* would indicate that they mark a considerable non-sequence. **1969** BENNISON & WRIGHT *Geol. Hist. Brit. Isles* i. 7 Naturally non-sequences are unprovable in barren unfossiliferous rocks..or in rocks so altered that fossils have failed to be preserved.

non-signi·ficant, *a.* [NON- 3.] Not significant. Also *absol.*

1902 S. H. BUTCHER *Aristotle's Theory of Poetry & Fine Art* (ed. 3) x. 377 In Plautus the number of names etymologically significant and appropriate largely preponderates over the non-significant. **1903** C. G. D. ROBERTS *Barbara Ladd* 219 His wife was a non-significant, abundant, gently acquiescent pudding of a woman. **1923** J. S. HUXLEY *Ess. Biologist* iv. 139 These differences may be biologically speaking non-significant, mere accidents of the primary difference. **1973** *Jrnl. Genetic Psychol.* CXXIII. 10 A nonsignificant correlation of −.10 was obtained. **1974** *Nature* 22 Nov. 272/2 Unobserved objects (black holes, dead white dwarfs and so on) must only make up a non-significant percentage of the galactic mass.

non-sked: see *NON-SCHEDULED *a.*

non-skid, *a.* and *sb.* [NON- 4 or *5 b.] **A.** *adj.* That does not skid, or is designed to prevent skidding. **B.** *sb.* A tyre, substance, etc., designed to prevent skidding. So **non-ski·dding** *ppl. a.*

1908 *Sears, Roebuck Catal.* 169/1 We have added to this tire a link chain non-skid tread, the most practical and scientific tread ever made. **1908** *Daily Report* 12 Sept. 8/4 It is absolutely incumbent upon all owners of such cars to only use this sort of non-skid in the winter. **1909** *Chambers's Jrnl.* June 404/1 A perfect non-skidding wheel. **1911** *Daily Colonist* (Victoria, B.C.) 2 Apr. 10/1 (Advt.), Michelin 'Semelle' Non-Skids, unlike so-called non-skids made wholly of rubber, do not wear down into ordinary smooth treads. **1920** *Motor Cycle* 29 July 129/2 Non-skid chains. **1925** *Public Opinion* 11 Dec. 588/3 We want light-coloured, waterproof, nonskid surfaces. **1937** [see *AUTOSTRADA]. **1944–45** *Jane's Fighting Ships* (1946) 459 Armoured flight deck is..covered with non-skid surface material. **1972** *Country Life* 15 June 1577/2 A useful top oddments shelf with non-skid surface. **1972** *Islander* (Victoria, B.C.) 25 June 2/2 Many busy weeks and months were spent painting and putting non-skid on the decks.

non-slip, *a.* [Non- 4 or *5 b.] That does not slip, or is designed to prevent slipping. So **non-sli·pping** *ppl. a.* and *vbl. sb.*

1904 G. B. Shaw *Common Sense of Municipal Trading* vii. 56 To ride bicycles through greasy mud..on tires advertized as 'non-slipping'. **1909** Webster, Nonslip. **1912** *Chambers's Jrnl.* Jan. 78/2 The gyroscope non-slipping device has been subjected to many exacting tests, but has established its capabilities to overcome skidding. **1933** *Archit. Rev.* LXXIII. 219 The staircase is in concrete, and the steps are rendered non-slip on the nosings. **1956** [see *granolithic *a.*]. **1959** *Times* 27 Apr. (Suppl. Rubber Industry) p.vi/7 Special non-slipping mineral grain-filled flooring is used for safety walks and service corridors. **1973** *Times* 19 Oct. 14/3 (*caption*) Non-slip. They are unlikely to get pushed across the kitchen floor.

non-smo·ker. [Non- 2.] A person who does not smoke.

1846 in H. C. Webster *Railways for All* (1950) xv. 114 Smokers and non-smokers should be apart, but why should smokers exclusively be indulged with the use of the best carriages on the line? **1860** *Pharmaceutical Jrnl.* II. iii. 190 Dividing the pupils..into..the smokers and the non-smokers, it is shown that the smokers have proved themselves in the various competitive examinations far inferior to the others. **1891** W. Morris *News from Nowhere* vi. 37 Bob is always telling me that we non-smokers are a selfish lot. **1898** K. Baedeker *Spain & Portugal* p. xv, Every train is bound to have a first-class compartment..and another for non-smokers. **1921** G. B. Shaw *Back to Methuselah* ii. 84 They believe the tee-totallers and non-smokers live longer. **1973** K. Giles *File on Death* i. 10 No car, two suits a year, non-smoker, allows more than he should afford on drink.

b. A compartment in a railway carriage, or other conveyance, where smoking is not permitted. *colloq.*

1962 J. Braine *Life at Top* v. 74 All the first-class compartments seemed to be full; finally I got a seat in a non-smoker. **1971** 'L. Black' *Death has Green Fingers* iii. 29 When the woman angrily lit a cigarette, he pointed out to her..that she was in a non-smoker.

non-smo·king, *a.* [Non- 4, 6.] Denoting a railway compartment, carriage, etc., in which smoking is not permitted.

1891 H. Spencer *Let.* 27 Mar. in G. S. Layard *Mrs. Lynn Linton* (1901) xx. 278 One may persist in putting down smoking in a non-smoking compartment of a railway carriage. **1909** *Daily Chron.* 17 Sept. 4/7 A well-known clergyman was travelling in a non-smoking compartment of a train. **1922** C. E. Montague *Disenchantment* (1924) vi. 86 Trains are divided into 'non-smoking' and 'smoking'. **1936** *Punch* 5 Feb. 141/3 Discovering as we finish lighting our pipes that we are in a Ladies Only Non-Smoking carriage. **1963** *Mod. Railways* May 359/1 The sliding door to the non-smoking compartment is often left open by passengers.

b. Denoting a person who does not smoke.

1946 *R.A.F. Jrnl.* May 178 Les, non-smoking but not teetotal,..will never fail to stand by for a duty. **1972** J. Mosedale *Football* v. 65 The non-smoking, non-drinking Graham, of whom it was said, 'His idea of a big night is eating chocolate ice cream.' **1975** V. Canning *Kingsford Mark* v. 74 Are you still non-smoking and non-drinking?

non-spe·cialist, *a.* and *sb.* [Non- 3, 2.] **A.** *adj.* That is not specialist. **B.** *sb.* One who is not a specialist.

1919 W. Lewis *Caliph's Design* iii. 53, I am..only giving so much general matter..as is necessary to remind a non-specialist public of the rough points of the position. **1933** *Discovery* Sept. 286/2 He has just written a remarkable book, where the non-specialist will find much of interest. **1958** *Times Lit. Suppl.* 24 Jan. 46/2 An editor whose speciality is to be non-specialist. **1971** J. Spencer *Eng. Lang. W. Afr.* p. viii, If our explorations prove to be of interest to the non-specialist, while at the same time stimulating the specialist to embark upon further research, we shall be very well satisfied. **1975** *Listener* 28 Aug. 280/3 The performance criteria were clear to non-specialists.

non-speci·fic, *a.* [Non- 3.] Not specific; esp. in *Med.*, not specific as regards cause or effects. Hence **no:n-specifi·city.**

1938 R. W. Lawson tr. *Hevesy & Paneth's Man. Radioactivity* (ed. 2) xv. 147 Non-specific adsorption forces do not play a part in this process. **1939** H. Kogan et al. in Saporta & Bastian *Psycholinguistics* (1961) 534/2 Gestalt psychology..left unaltered the postulate of its non-specificity. **1942** Darlington & Mather *Genes, Plants & People* (1950) iv. 37 The difference between activity and inertness would then be the difference between specificity and non-specificity. **1964** W. G. Smith *Allergy & Tissue Metabolism* ii. 29 Promethazine produces considerable antagonism, but the effect is probably a non-specific one. **1971** *Brit. Med. Bull.* XXVII. 61/1 This group of diseases might be referred to as 'chronic non-specific lung disease'. **1971** J. Z. Young *Introd. Study Man* xxvi. 372 The first organism included only one enzyme, a non-specific phosphokinase. **1975** I. K. Martin *Regan & Manhattan File* 88 He made some non-specific enquiries to the FBI.

non-sta·ndard, *a.* [Non- 3.] Not standard; esp. of language that is not standard (see *standard *a.* 3).

1924 *Simplified Practice Recommendation* (U.S. Nat. Bureau Standards) XVI. 61 These tables include certain illustrative combinations of standard, and nonstandard, widths and thicknesses. **1927** *Reliable Poultry Jrnl.* Feb. 33 Whatever may be said of the policy of showing the non-Standard colors, there can be no doubt..that a class of all Standard colored birds makes a much better impression on the lay visitor than a class of mixed shades of color. **1933** L. Bloomfield *Language* iii. 48 'Bad' or 'vulgar' or, as the linguist prefers to call it, *non-standard* English. **1962** A. Battersby *Guide to Stock Control* viii. 77 Another multiplier of stock items is the non-standard product. **1971** *Engineering* Apr. 117 Diameters can be altered slightly to produce non-standard sizes. **1973** *Archivum Linguisticum* IV. 107 It might well only give evidence of a socially determined Nonstandard English.

b. *Math.* Involving infinitesimals and infinities, as quantities which are not defined in the real number system but can be rigorously accommodated in a model which includes that system.

1961 A. Robinson in *Proc. K. Nederlandse Akad. v. Wetensch.* A. LXIV. 432 (*heading*) Non-standard analysis. *Ibid.* 437 Let $f(x, t)$ be a standard function defined in a standard set S_1, and let $g(x) = f(x, \omega)$, where ω is non-standard, e.g. infinite or infinitesimal. **1966** —— *Non-Standard Analysis* p. vii, In the fall of 1960 it occurred to me that the concepts and methods of contemporary Mathematical Logic are capable of providing a suitable framework for the development of the Differential and Integral Calculus by means of infinitely small and infinitely large numbers. I first reported my ideas in a seminar talk at Princeton University (November 1960) and, later, in an address at the annual meeting of the Association for Symbolic Logic (January 1961) and in a paper published in the Proceedings of the Royal Academy of Sciences of Amsterdam... The resulting subject was called by me Non-standard Analysis since it involves and was, in part, inspired by the so-called Non-standard models of Arithmetic whose existence was first pointed out by T. Skolem. **1972** *Sci. Amer.* June 86/2 We define the instantaneous velocity not as the ratio of infinitesimal increments, as L'Hôpital did, but rather as the standard part of that ratio; then *ds*, *dt* and their ratio *ds/dt* are nonstandard real numbers. We have as before $ds/dt = 32 + 16dt$, but now we immediately conclude, rigorously and without any limiting argument, that *v*, the standard part of *ds/dt*, equals 32.

non-sta·rter. [Non- 2.] One who does not start something; esp. one who fails to start in a race or other contest; hence, a useless or ineffective person or thing; an impracticable idea.

1909 in Webster. **1932** *Brit. Jrnl. Psychol.* July 31 Besides the 33 non-starters, only two made no attempt at this test. **1934** Wodehouse *Right Ho, Jeeves* ii. 27, I reminded myself that this non-starter and I had been at school together. **1942** 'A. Bridge' *Frontier Passage* iii. 49 That's one reason why non-intervention is such a non-starter. **1952** A. J. Ayer *Philosophical Essays* (1954) iii. 42 A statement..might be a non-starter, in the sense that the question of its truth or falsehood did not arise. **1973** C. Mullard *Black Britain* iii. ix. 109 People began to dub the council a nonstarter.

non-stick, *a.* [*non- 5 b.] That does not stick or allow sticking; *spec.* of a cooking utensil: to which food does not adhere.

1958 *Listener* 4 Dec. 967/1 Silicones are used..for..coating cooking pans to make them 'non-stick'. **1960** *Farmer & Stockbreeder* 1 Mar. 152/3 (Advt.), Men's non-stick P.V.C. plastic oilskin coats. **1968** *Guardian* 9 July 7/3 The cost of the non-stick oven lining adds £6 10s to the price of a cooker. **1973** 'D. Jordan' *Nile Green* ii. 14 Sticky non-stick frying pans in the sink.

non-stop, *a.*, *sb.*, and *adv.* [Non- 4 or *5 b.] **A.** *adj.* That does not stop; *spec.* of a railway train or other conveyance: that travels between two (usually distant) places without stopping at intermediate ones; of a journey, etc.: made or done without a stop; of a variety show or the like: in which there is no interval between the various acts.

1903 *Work* 11 July 364/1 The L. & N.W. Railway long non-stop run..presents no difficulty. **1904** *Windsor Mag.* Dec. p. ix (Advt.), Awards gained for Glasgow to London non-stop trials. **1910** *Punch* 15 June 441/2 *Platelayer* (to passenger who has jumped from the London-Plymouth Non-stop Express). Jumped aht? did yer.—Wof for? **1914** *Whitaker's Almanack 1915* 822/1 Britannia trophy awarded to Capt. Longcroft, R.F.C., for non-stop flight Montrose to Farnborough. **1923** Wodehouse *Inimitable Jeeves* xv. 192, I was fairly tired, having swung a practically non-stop shoe from shortly after dinner till two a.m. **1932** *Sunday Express* 3 July 17/6 Of all the people in non-stop variety, the one I should most hate to annoy is Veronica, the dancer. She can do fifty high kicks in twenty-five seconds. **1938** *Times Lit. Suppl.* 15 Jan. 44/1 A job as chorus girl in a very undressed non-stop revue. **1957** *Economist* 28 Dec. 1120/2 The sum total of his economics is that a non-stop increase in money wages is..a Good Thing. **1967** G. F. Fiennes *I tried to run a Railway* vii. 86 Averages of 75 m.p.h. for the non-stop business expresses. **1973** 'I. Drummond' *Jaws of Watchdog* i. 9 The party will be out to sea. A seventy-two hour trip, way the hell out, a non-stop party. **1973** *Country Life* 23 Aug. 476/2 The Windmill Theatre..became famous as the home of live, non-stop revue.

B. *sb.* A non-stop train; a non-stop journey or run; (see also quot. 1925; *Obs. slang*).

1909 *Westm. Gaz.* 8 Sept. 2/1 The innovation and growth of 'non-stops' upon the Metropolitan and District electric lines. **1911** *Motor Cycle* 27 Apr. 428/1 He..has now made six successive non-stops. **1922** V. Woolf *Jacob's Room* ix. 183 The hordes crossing Waterloo Bridge to catch the non-stop to Surbiton. **1925** Fraser & Gibbons *Soldier & Sailor Words* 210 *Nonstop, a*, a trench expression used of a long range shell passing high overhead. **1957** *Railway Mag.* Jan. 22/2 Thus the non-stops to and from Sheffield were suspended. **1958** J. Betjeman *Coll. Poems* 202 They ..caught the first non-stop to Willesden Green.

C. *adv.* Without stopping.

1920 'Ixion' *Motor Cycle Remin.* 15 The beastie [*sc.* a motor cycle] did the outward journey non-stop. **1927** *Daily Tel.* 14 June 11/3 The second attempt to fly non-stop to India. **1942** *R.A.F. Jrnl.* 16 May 9 The test pilot..flew the aircraft non-stop from Moscow to Baku and back. **1953** A. Upfield *Murder must Wait* xvii. 147 We were talking non-stop. **1963** *Ann. Reg. 1962* 447 One station in New York (WBAI) gave the whole *Der Ring des Nibelungen* in 17 hours non-stop. **1965** W. Soyinka *Road* 21 Have you known any other driver take an oil-tanker from Port Harcourt to Kaduna non-stop since Muftan died? **1968** M. Bragg *Without City Wall* x. 112 Both he and Richard went on non-stop about London, their friends, politics, anything that came up.

non-subscriber. 2. (Further examples.)

1816 T. J. Howell *Stranger in Shrewsbury* 65 The public libraries in Shrewsbury are wretchedly furnished except one, and to *that* entrance is almost denied to strangers and non-subscribers. **1884** *List of Subscribers* (London & Globe Telephone Co.) [3] Subscribers..must not allow non-subscribers to use their instruments for the transmission of messages.

non-sylla·bic, *a.* and *sb.* *Linguistics.* [Non- 3, 2.] **A.** *adj.* **a.** = *asyllabic *a.*; *spec.* denoting a speech-sound that does not constitute the predominant sonority of the syllable in which it occurs. **b.** Not syllable-timed. **B.** *sb.* A non-syllabic speech-sound.

1909 Webster, Nonsyllabic, *a.* **1933** L. Bloomfield *Language* vii. 120 Some of the phonemes are more sonorous than the phonemes (or the silence) which immediately precede or follow... Any such phoneme is a *crest of sonority* or a *syllabic*; the other phonemes are *non-syllabic*. Thus the [e] in *red* and the [r] in *bird* are syllabics, but the [r] in *red* and the [d] in *red* and *bird* are non-syllabics. **1947** K. L. Pike *Phonemics* 30/1 The acoustic quality is quite similar to that which is found when they are acting as nonsyllabics. **1957** H. Whitehall in N. Frye *Sound & Poetry* 143 The first distinction would be drawn between syllabic and non-syllabic rhythms. **1961** R. B. Long *Sentence & its Parts* xvii. 382 Such monosyllabic complexes employing nonsyllabic suffixes as *truth* and *fourth.* **1965** *Language* XLI. 32 Since the first element of these clusters always represents the syllable peak.., I have not separately indicated the nonsyllabic nature of the second element. *Ibid.* 476 According to their function in the syllable, the consonants are non-syllabics or syllabics.

non-thema·tic, *a.* [Non- 3.] **1.** *Linguistics.* = *athematic *a.* 1.

1933 E. H. Sturtevant *Compar. Gram. Hittite Lang.* vi. 217 There is also, as in I[ndo-] E[uropean], a distinction between thematic and non-thematic conjugation. **1955** T. Burrow *Sanskrit Lang.* vii. 318 The verbs are divided into two major types, (a) non-thematic..and (b) thematic.

b. Not conveying new information; constituting part of the rheme; = *rhematic *a.*

1959 *Brno Studies in English* I. 43 The indefinite article and its zero plural variant..play an important part in that co-operation of means which may render non-thematic even such a subject as occurs at the very beginning, or very near the beginning, of the sentence.

2. *Mus.* = *athematic *a.* 2.

1946 G. Abraham in A. L. Bacharach *Brit. Mus.* 55 *Neptune, the Mystic*, which shares with *Saturn* the distinction of being one of the most remarkable purely impressionistic, practically non-thematic pieces of music ever written.

non-trea·ty. *N. Amer.* [Non- 4.] Used *attrib.* or *absol.* to designate an American Indian who is not subject to a treaty made with the Government.

1878 *Saskatchewan Herald* (Battleford) 18 Nov. 2/2 The non-treaty Indians invade them. **1885** J. L. Onderdonk *Idaho* 15 Councils were held at Lapwai to apportion lands to the various chiefs of the Non-treaties. **1945** *Beaver* Mar. 12/1 Some four hundred Chipewyans and one hundred Crees, the latter being mixed treaties and non-treaties. **1956** C. Relander *Drummers & Dreamers* 121 The intruders occupied the scurfy land along the Columbia where the non-treaty people lived. **1964** W. Duff *Indian Hist. Brit. Columbia* I. 70 The generalization, often heard, that the Indians of British Columbia are 'non-treaty' Indians is not wholly true.

non-tri·vial, *a.* [Non- 3.] Not trivial; significant; *spec.* in *Math.*, such that not all variables or terms are zero.

1915 R. D. Carmichael *Diophantine Analysis* ii. 52 Prove that a non-trivial solution does not exist when *b* is a square number. **1940** *Mind* XLIX. 366 This view has non-trivial consequences. **1948** F. D. Murnaghan *Introd. Applied Math.* i. 12, *n* plane vectors are linearly dependent when, and only when, there exists a nontrivial linear combination of the *n* vectors which is the zero vector. **1953** C. E. Bazell *Linguistic Form* 19 It is only when there are relations of conversion between constructions that complementary distribution is non-trivial. **1971** *Amer. Jrnl. Physics* XXXIX. 486/1 Our aim..is to derive a list of all values of $\Omega > 0$ for which there exist nontrivial *q* satisfying (11) and (12). **1973** *Sci. Amer.* Feb. 81/2 The ratio of those who received nontrivial injuries was 70 percent higher among the unbelted than among the belted.

So **non-tri·vially** *adv.*

1940 W. V. QUINE *Math. Logic* 222 We can speak non-trivially of *the x* of *y*. **1971** POWELL & HIGMAN *Finite Simple Groups* i. 2 A conjugate class of *G* that interests *S* non-trivially.

nontronite. Add: *Nontronite* rather than *chloropal* is now the usual name for the mineral. (Further examples.)

1928 *Amer. Jrnl. Sci.* CCXV. 10 A large number of names have been proposed for the hydrous silicates of ferric iron; and of these nontronite, chloropal, pinguite, fettbol, and graminite are recognized by most mineralogists as belonging to the species nontronite. **1935**, etc. [see *MONTMORILLONITE]. **1945** *Prof. Papers U.S. Geol. Survey Paper* No. 205-B. 28/1 The name chloropal has a slight priority over nontronite. However, the material has been shown to be definitely crystalline by both optical and X-ray methods, and the name chloropal, suggesting a deeply colored opaline mineral, is unsuitable. Dana (1892, p. xliii) has laid down the rule that a name having priority may properly be set aside when its signification is glaringly false. Mineralogists for some time have used the name nontronite as the most suitable for this mineral. **1963** M. H. HEY *Index Min. Species* (ed. 2) App. 117 *Nontronite*.. The older name Chloropal has passed out of common use.

non-U (nǫnˌyū·, nǫ·nˌyū), *a.* and *sb.* [f. NON- 3 + *U 4.] **A.** *adj.* Not upper-class; not characteristic of upper-class people; esp. with reference to linguistic usage. **B.** *sb.* Non-U persons or characteristics collectively; non-U language. Hence **non-U-ness.**

1954 A. S. C. ROSS in *Neuphilologische Mitteilungen* LV. 21 (*title*) U and non-U. *Ibid.*, In this article I use the terms *upper class* (abbreviated: U), *correct, proper*,..to designate usages of the upper class; their antonyms (*non-U, incorrect, not proper*,..) to designate usages which are not upper class. *Ibid.* 22 As a boy I heard *not quite a gent* ..used by non-U speakers. *Ibid.* 23 The non-U slang phrase *He's left his visiting card*. *Ibid.* 27 The U-rules for ending letters are very strict; failure to observe them usually implies non-U-ness. *Ibid.* 45 *Pardon!* is used by the non-U in three main ways. **1956** *Times* 13 Jan. 9/4 The cosh is, of course, definitely non-U, whereas the old-fashioned blunt instrument was perfectly *comme il faut*. **1957** O. NASH *You can't get there from Here* 16 The Wicked Queen said 'Mirror, mirror on the wall' instead of 'Looking glass, looking glass on the wall'... So the Wicked Queen exposed herself as not only wicked but definitely non-U. **1958** *Times Lit. Suppl.* 18 July 411/2 They phrase their advice just seriously enough to encourage the uninitiated, or non-U, yet just facetiously enough to reassure the *cognoscenti*. **1960** R. LISTER *Decorative Cast Ironwork* iv. 141 Letter racks, tobacco jars, spittoons ('salivaria' in non-U). **1964** H. KÖKERITZ in D. Abercrombie et al. *Daniel Jones* 140 These pronunciations..might..be classified as U rather than non-U. **1967** M. ARGYLE *Psychol. Interpersonal Behaviour* iii. 47 Others may be divided simply into the 'saved' and the 'not-saved', U and non-U, or into finer sub-groups. **1973** *Listener* 29 Nov. 755/2 Empty-headed chat, mixed with non-U euphemisms.

non-ultra. (Earlier examples.)

1611 CORYAT *Crudities* sig. b 3ᵛ, To give the *Non vltra* of him in a word, he is so Substantive an Author as will stand by himselfe. *a* **1666** EVELYN *Diary* 8 Feb. an. 1645 (1955) II. 354, I left this Ode..as the Non ultra of my Travells.

non-union. Add: **1.** (Further examples.)

1909 *Daily Chron.* 17 Feb. 1/6 Dr. Jameson..warned his hearers of the dangers of non-union, which might possibly lead to internecine war. **1963** *Lancet* 12 Jan. 86/2 There are only two causes of delayed union or non-union of fractures.

2. (Further examples.)

c **1926** 'MIXER' *Transport Workers' Song Bk.* 28 Your ranks are broken through By the carping critic 'ring-necks'. And non-union alienage. **1964** S. M. MILLER in I. L. Horowitz *New Sociol.* 309 The importance of organizing the non-union and rapidly growing white-collar workers. **1973** L. SNELLING *Heresy* II. i. 61 Even if they stayed away I'm sure you could shoot the thing [*sc.* a film] with non-union people. **1974** *Times* 10 May 11/6 The *Daily News*..has continued to be printed..by non-union staff.

Hence **non-u·nionize** *v. trans.*, to make non-union in character; to supply with non-union employees in place of union members; also **non-u·nionized** *ppl. a.*

1926 *Glasgow Herald* 26 July 7 A motion was carried condemning the action of those Scottish newspaper proprietors who had non-unionised their offices since the strike. **1961** W. SHEED *Middle Class Education* xviii. 334, I resent every last butler of yours. And when I think of those non-unionized chambermaids—cheezt! **1968** *Economist* 20 July 19/2 If no union can attain 50 per cent of the votes, the plant remains non-unionised. **1974** *Black Panther* 16 Mar. 15/4 Many non-unionized enterprises were forced to close down as well.

non-uti·lity, *a.* [NON- 3.] Not utility or not for utility; used chiefly of clothes that are of better quality than *UTILITY garments.

1948 *News Chron.* 7 Apr. 1 Children's non-utility garments. *Ibid.*, Non-utility tables, desks, chairs. **1950** *Engineering* 6 Jan. 11/3 'Nonutility generation' is defined as 'generation by producers..for the purpose of supplying electric power required in the conduct of their industrial or commercial operations'. **1957** R. CAMPBELL *Portugal* 82 In Portugal there are still the regional dresses of the people (strictly non-utility). **1960** I. JEFFERIES *Dignity & Purity* iv. 55 My suits happened to be new and very non-utility.

non-va·lent, *a. Chem.* [f. NON- + *-VALENT.] **a.** Not capable of entering into chemical combination; inert.

1908 *Athenæum* 28 Mar. 390/1 All the 'non-valent' elements—I should prefer to describe them as the elements which are inert at atmospheric pressure and temperature—should sublime.

b. Having a formal oxidation state of zero.

1950 N. V. SIDGWICK *Chem. Elements & their Compounds* II. 1429 Nickel is of course non-valent in the carbonyl $Ni(CO)_4$. **1962** P. J. & B. DURRANT *Introd. Adv. Inorg. Chem.* xxiv. 981 None of the elements [of sub-Group VI T] forms any compounds in which it is non-valent.

non-va·nishing, *ppl. a. Math.* and *Physics.* [NON- 6.] Not becoming zero, or not zero.

1907 M. BÔCHER *Introd. Higher Algebra* v. 54 The non-vanishing *r*-rowed determinant stands in the upper left-hand corner of the matrix. **1922** G. N. WATSON *Theory Bessel Functions* xix. 636 Schlömilch series with non-vanishing coefficients. **1956** *Physical Rev.* CIV. 257/1 The particle has a nonvanishing spin. **1962** CORSON & LORRAIN *Introd. Electromagn. Fields* ii. 76 In Eq. 2–197 it must include all regions of space in which the field intensity **E** is nonvanishing.

non-ve·rbal, *a.* [NON- 3.] **a.** Not employing or including words; unskilful in the use of words.

1927 B. RUSSELL *Outl. Philos.* xxiv. 271 This keeps us in the verbal realm, and does not get us outside it to some realm of non-verbal fact. **1934** H. C. WARREN *Dict. Psychol.* 181/2 *Non-verbal test*, a type of mental (generally intelligence) test, in which no words are used in the test content, but the directions for giving the tests may be either verbal or by pantomime. **1953** W. BURROUGHS *Junkie* (1972) xv. 152 What I look for in any relationship is contact on the non-verbal level of intuition and feeling, that is, telepathic contact. **1972** J. L. DILLARD *Black English* i. 33 There may be many reasons, most of them cultural, why a child may appear 'non-verbal' in certain contexts.

b. Not employing or including a verb; not a form of a verb.

1932 A. H. GARDINER *Theory of Speech & Lang.* iv. 219 Old Egyptian dispensed with the copula in more than one common sub-class of nominal or, as I prefer to call them, non-verbal sentences. **1965** D. WARD *Russ. Lang. Today* iv. 102 Non-verbal predicators include **не** and **нет**, as in **Он не там** *He is not there*. *Ibid.* v. 123 **Пред-** is productive, however, in non-verbal derivatives. **1973** *Archivum Linguisticum* IV. 49 In respect of their association with a verbal or non-verbal form in the sentence, the suffixes often alternate more or less freely.

So **non-ve·rbalized** *ppl. a.*, not verbalized; **non-ve·rbally** *adv.*, not verbally.

1949 KOESTLER *Insight & Outlook* xxiv. 342 It is in the very nature of this type of nonverbalized experience that ordinary language..is insufficient to convey it. **1955** J. L. AUSTIN *How to do Things with Words* (1962) ix. 118 The means for achieving its ends non-verbally must be conventional. **1958** B. BERNSTEIN in J. A. Fishman *Readings Sociol. Lang.* (1968) 233 The child is born into a world in which personal qualifications are established non-verbally in the sense that the personal qualifications are left out of the structure of the sentences. **1961** *Countryman* LVIII. III. 462 Most of his waking life the berger is communicating with animals in grunts, cries and other non-verbalized sounds.

non-vi·able, *a.* [NON- 3.] Not viable; *spec.* (*a*) of living beings or living matter: = *INVIABLE *a.*; (*b*) not economically viable.

1879 [in Dict. s.v. NON- 3]. **1946** *Nature* 9 Nov. 678/1 The cells become non-viable. **1956** A. HUXLEY *Adonis & Alphabet* 204 The wall, which now divides the ancient city from the new, the non-viable state of Jordan from the non-viable state of Israel. **1959** *Times* 6 Mar. 11/5 Her Majesty's Government..is struggling..to build up a primitive people in a non-viable country to a point where they may one day hope to achieve a genuine form of democracy. **1959** *Economist* 18 Apr. 218/1 Agricultural policy is belatedly growing more rational, which means tougher towards the 'non-viable' farm. **1971** J. Z. YOUNG *Introd. Study Man* xxvii. 385 Producing a new version that is not a non-viable freak. **1974** *Nature* 1 Nov. 64/2 The consideration that cells defective for such processes should be non-viable.

non-vi·olence. [NON- 1.] The principle or practice of abstaining from the use of violence.

1920 M. K. GANDHI in J. Nehru *Autobiogr.* (1936) xii. 83, I believe that non-violence is infinitely superior to violence, forgiveness is more manly than punishment. **1936** [see *CONSCIENTIOUS *a.* 2]. **1942** KOESTLER in *Horizon* June 384 His [*sc.* Gandhi's] slope..gradually made him slide down to his present position of non-violence towards the Japanese aggression. **1968** M. LUTHER KING *Trumpet of Conscience* iv. 77 Nonviolence is no longer an option for intellectual analysis, it is an imperative for action. **1974** *Peace News* 1 Feb. 3/1, I knew myself pretty well and knew a little about nonviolence.

So **non-vi·olent** *a.*, characterized by, believing in, or practising non-violence; **non-vi·olently** *adv.*, in a non-violent manner.

1920 M. K. GANDHI *Non-Violence* 9 Mar. (1922) in *Young India 1919–22* 288 We must not intend harm to the English or to our co-operating countrymen, if and whilst we claim to be non-violent. **1923** C. M. CASE (*title*) Non-violent coercion. **1937** J. M. MURRY *Necessity of Pacifism* i. 22 A Socialism of voluntary community and absolute but non-violent resistance to war. **1948** A. HUXLEY *Ape & Essence* (1949) 2 Gandhi..just couldn't do anything but resist oppression non-violently. **1971** M. MCCARTHY *Birds of America* 82 Peter replied non-violently. 'It's for my mother.' **1973** J. FERGUSON (*title*) The politics of love: the New Testament and non-violent revolution.

non-vo·coid. *Linguistics.* [NON- 2.] A speech sound that is not a vocoid; = *CONTOID *sb.*

1943 K. L. PIKE *Phonetics* vii. 143 All nonvocoids are contoids. **1952** A. COHEN *Phonemes of English* 37 Pike suggests using the terms vocoids and non-vocoids in phonetic, and vowels and consonants in phonemic analysis.

non-vo·latile, *a.* [NON- 3.] Not volatile. **a.** Of substances (cf. VOLATILE *sb.* and *a.* B. 3).

1866 WATTS *Dict. Chem.* IV. 230 They possess a bitter taste, are non-volatile, and do not suffer any change when exposed to air. **1903** *Phil. Mag.* V. 577 In other cases.. the new matter is itself non-volatile. **1957** G. E. HUTCHINSON *Treat. Limnol.* I. viii. 553 Evaporating the water to dryness, so obtaining the total solids per unit mass or volume, and then igniting the residue to obtain the non-volatile solids per unit mass or volume. **1971** I. G. GASS et al. *Understanding Earth* 114 It is widely believed that the average composition of meteoric matter provides the best information on the relative abundances of the non-volatile elements.

b. *Computers.* Of a store or storage (cf. *VOLATILE *a.*).

1950 W. W. STIFLER et al. *High-Speed Computing Devices* xiv. 313 The storage unit is said to be nonvolatile because it can sustain loss of power without losing all the information stored. **1962** *Gloss. Terms Automatic Data Processing* (*B.S.I.*) 65 A non-volatile store..retains its content when the power supplies are switched off normally, but the content may be lost if power failure occurs. **1969** P. B. JORDAIN *Condensed Computer Encycl.* 563 Non-volatile storage (almost all magnetic; some optical and some punched-hole media) will hold onto its data through any mishaps.

Hence **non-volati·lity**, the property of not being volatile.

1964 N. G. CLARK *Mod. Organic Chem.* v. 67 The highest members [of the paraffin series], e.g. the waxes, because of their non-volatility, possess no smell.

non-white, *a.* and *sb.* Also **non-White.** [NON- 3, 2.] **A.** *adj.* Not having a white skin; of or pertaining to people who are not white. **B.** *sb.* A non-white person. Also *collect.*

1921 *Sci. Amer.* 20 Aug. 125 The States that have the greatest proportion of non-white residents. **1952** B. DAVIDSON *Rep. S. Afr.* I. i. 27 No serious South African will argue any longer (at least in private) that *apartheid*, the complete and geographical segregation of the white from the non-white at all levels, can work. **1953** P. ABRAHAMS *Return to Goli* II. iii. 57 They are the most prejudiced and colour conscious of all the non-White groups. **1956** *Time* 9 Jan. 61/2 The rarity of skin cancer among non-whites..is thought to be caused by a 'true racial difference in susceptibility'. **1959** V. PACKARD *Status Seekers* (1960) vi. 86 If white residents of an area are in no hurry to leave, but non-whites are eager to come in, the pressure of non-white demand may bid up the price of houses. **1973** E. BULLINS *Theme is Blackness* 3 America's educational institutions are predicated upon keeping Black men ignorant of themselves and the other nonwhite four-fifths of the world. **1973** *Black Panther* 5 May 5/2 Eleven non-whites and five civil rights organizations last week charged the San Francisco Police Department with discriminatory employment practices against non-whites and women.

no·n-word. [NON- 2.] A word that is not recorded or not established.

1961 *Life* 27 Oct. 4 (*heading*) A non-word deluge. **1963** *Punch* 16 Jan. 95/1 The aesthetically displeasing non-word 'annoyment'. **1967** D. G. HAYS *Introd. Computational Linguistics* v. 87 But for that to be practical, the memory would have to be large enough so that every string of letters shorter than the longest word in the language could serve as a cell index, and almost all the cells in the memory would be empty—since almost every letter string is a nonword. **1970** *Sun* (Gainesville, Florida) 8 Jan., The School Board's petition to the Supreme Court contained an error, the non-word 'predominately'.

non-woven, *a.* and *sb.* [NON- 3, 2.] **A.** *adj.* Not woven (see quot. 1968). **B.** *sb.* A non-woven fabric or material.

1945 *Forbes* (N.Y.) 15 Oct. 16/2 The new non-spun and non-woven cloth will be cheaper, not only because it eliminates so many operations but also because it requires much less of the basic fiber to cover a given area. **1959** A. J. HALL *Standard Handbk. Textiles* iii. 156 It is obvious that non-woven fabrics can never entirely take the place of woven or knitted fabrics. **1963** —— *Textile Sci.* i. 11 The characteristics of non-woven fabrics are capable of wide variation. **1968** J. IRONSIDE *Fashion Alphabet* 242 *Non-woven fabrics*. A 'non-woven' ought..to refer to any fabric not made on a loom, but the generally accepted meaning..is that it is any fabric which is not woven, knitted or spun but built up by interlocking fibres by means of chemical bonding agents, and (for fusible fibres) by mechanical means, chemical action, moisture and heat. .. Paper is also ilncuded in this definition. **1970** *Cabinet Maker & Retail Furnisher* 23 Oct. 173/2 The chemically or adhesively bonded non-wovens use bonding elements that behave as glueing binders. **1973** *Times* 28 Aug. 17/7 That other branch of the disposable paper industry, nonwovens, is being addressed in the same optimistic tones.

non-ze·ro, *a.* [NON- 4.] Not equal to zero.

1905 *Proc. London Math. Soc.* III. 273 This assumption is valid in the case of functions of finite (non-zero) order.

1925 C. E. Cullis *Matrices & Determinoids* III. i. xxvii. 440 Two sets of non-zero positive integers whose sums are respectively *m* and *n*. **1951** *Physical Rev.* LXXXIII. 1235/1 Small but nonzero errors in the results. **1970** G. K. Woodgate *Elem. Atomic Struct.* vii. 132 The admixture of the $^1P_1$ level accounts for the non-zero intensity of the line 2,537 Å.

noodle, *sb.*[1] Add: **b.** *slang.* The head. cf. Noddle *sb.*[1] 2 b, 3.

1914 Jackson & Hellyer *Vocab. Criminal Slang* 62 *Noodle*.., the human head; brains; savoir faire; mentality. **1923** T. Fane *What's wrong with Movies* vi. 101 To the masses the cinema is only an entertainment, and using their noodles has long been classed..as one of life's hard labors. **1945** M. Trist in *Coast to Coast 1944* 207 Take no notice... She's off her noodle.

noodle (nū·d'l), *sb.*[3] *Jazz.* [Origin unknown.] A trill or improvisation on an instrument. Cf. *noodle *v.*[3] below.

1926 Whiteman & McBride *Jazz* x. 220 'Noodles', that is, fancy figures in saxophone such as triple trills, often crowd out the melody. **1958** *Jazz Review* Nov. 25 My one complaint is that Monk here allows too many of his favourite piano 'noodles' (all pianists seem to have them).

noodle (nū·d'l), *v.*[2] *Austral.* [Origin unknown.] **a.** *intr.* and *trans.* To search for opals (in opal dumps or 'mullock'). **b.** *trans.* To obtain (an opal) in this way. So **noo·dling** *vbl. sb.*[1]

1902 *Geol. Survey* No. 177 (Queensland Dept. Mines) 20 Some splendid opal is found..by turning over and searching the old heaps and mullock—'noodling'. **1931** M. S. Buchanan *Prospecting for Opal in Austral.* 10 Produced ten thousand pounds, with what was 'noodled' or picked up from the dumps. **1940** I. L. Idriess *Lightning Ridge* (1948) xiii. 79 Send the dirt up in the bucket where his mate..would carefully 'noodle' it, seeking tell-tale potch and colour. **1962** R. Webster *Gems* I. x. 191 The practice of picking over old mine dumps for overlooked opal is another form of 'mining'. Such procedure is termed 'noodling'. **1963** A. Lubbock *Austral. Roundabout* 79 Anyone can poke about..and 'puddle' or 'noodle' in the gravelly tailings of the mines. **1967** *Sunday Mail Mag.* (Brisbane) 8 Jan. 6/7 If you do the work by hand, sitting on the mullock heap like a shag on a rock, and patiently sift through the dirt, you are 'noodling'.

noodle (nū·d'l), *v.*[3] orig. *U.S.* [f. the sb.; cf. *noodle *sb.*[3]] *intr.* To improvise or play casually on a musical instrument, esp. in jazz; to play an elaborate or decorative series of notes; also occas. *trans.* Freq. as **noo·dling** *vbl. sb.*[2] Also *fig.*

1937 *Printers' Ink Monthly* May 39/3 *Noodling*, the tuning up of musical instruments with practice runs, trills, scales, etc. **1941** *Sun* (Baltimore) 19 July 8/3 There is something rather exciting about the notion of 'Old Man River', already a folk song, being poured out by the whole choir of woodwinds, with the strings noodling away in the background like rolling waters. **1946** R. Blesh *Shining Trumpets* (1949) ix. 212 Shield's clarinet part..revolves in little runs around lead notes (this is called 'noodling'). **1957** *Nugget* Dec. 5 Every time a jazz musician noodles a passable break these days he is followed by a show of bravura on an open Underwood fingered by a jazz writer. **1960** H. O. Brunn *Story of Orig. Dixieland Jazz Band* 164 Larry Shields will go down in history as the father of the 'noodling' style and possessor of one of the most powerful clarinet tones on record. **1966** Auden *About House* 44 In the half-dark, members of an avian orchestra Are already softly noodling, limbering up for An overture at sunrise. **1970** *Globe & Mail* (Toronto) 26 Sept. 27/2 Each piece [of writing] has the feel of jazz, the sense of building, of noodling around here, improvising there and finally resolving.

noodler (nū·dləɹ). *Austral.* [f. *noodle *v.*[2]] One who 'noodles' (see *noodle *v.*[2]).

1940 I. L. Idriess *Lightning Ridge* (1948) xvi. 96 All stones thus missed were regarded as the legitimate prey of the noodlers. **1945** *Walkabout* (Austral.) 1 Mar. 15 Other noodlers use a wire-screen and a shovel. **1967** S. Lloyd *Lightning Ridge Bk.* 38 A champion noodler. First to use shear blade to cut opal dirt on dumps.

noodly (nū·dli), *a. rare*$^{-1}$. [Presumably f. Noodle *sb.*[1] + -y[1].] Stupid, silly.

1922 Joyce *Ulysses* 646 A big foolish nervous noodly kind of a horse.

noogenesis (nōuˌodʒe·nėsis). [ad. F. *noögenèse*, f. Gr. νόο-ς mind + Genesis.] The coming into being of the stage or sphere of the mind, according to Pierre Teilhard de Chardin's theory of evolution (see quot. 1959).

1959 B. Wall tr. *Teilhard de Chardin's Phenomenon of Man* iii. i. 181 Psychogenesis has led to man. Now it effaces itself, relieved or absorbed by another and a higher function—the engendering and subsequent development of all the stages of the mind, in one word *noogenesis.* **1966** C. F. Mooney *Teilhard de Chardin* ii. 43 'Noogenesis' will therefore be spiritual and social, that is to say, it will concern itself with the development of individuals as persons and with society on the level of interpersonal relationships.

noogenic (nōuˌodʒe·nik), *a.* [ad. F. *noögénique*, f. Gr. νόο-ς mind + *-genic.] Pertaining to or connected with noogenesis, or to that which exists in the sphere of the mind.

1959 B. Wall tr. *Teilhard de Chardin's Phenomenon of Man* 307 Without doubt, the 'noogenic' forces of compression, organisation and interiorisation, under which the biological synthesis of reflection operates, do not at any moment relax their pressure on the stuff of mankind. **1964** I. Lasch tr. *V. E. Frankl's Man's Search for Meaning* (rev. ed.) ii. 102 Existential frustration can also result in neuroses. For this type of neuroses, logotherapy has coined the term 'noögenic neuroses' in contrast to.. psychogenic neuroses. Noögenic neuroses have their origin ..in the noölogical (from the Greek 'noos' meaning mind) dimension of the human existence. **1968** *Time* 2 Feb. 38 Dr Frankl makes great play with words beginning with noö—, from the Greek *noös* (mind), as in noödynamics and noögenic neuroses.

Noogoora (nūgū·rā). The name of a Queensland sheep station, used attrib. in **Noogoora burr** to designate a composite plant, *Xanthium chinense*, treated as a noxious weed in Australia because of its hooked burrs which become entangled in wool.

1883 F. M. Bailey *Synopsis Queensland Flora* 259 *X[anthium] strumarium*,..known as 'Noogoora Burr', and supposed injurious to stock. **1900** —— *Queensland Flora* III. 857 Noogoora Burr. A tall wide-spreading annual... A widespread weed of warm countries. **1934** *Bulletin* (Sydney) 12 Sept. 22/1 Through not obeying a Lands Department order to clear his holding of Noogoora burr, a N[orth] Q[ueensland] grazier has been served with a notice of forfeiture. **1961** *Times* 7 June 3/1 A cerambycid beetle..[is] to be liberated in Queensland in 1962 against the important weed Noogoora burr. **1961** *Coast to Coast 1959–60* 41 When we saw how he looked at our note-book, we knew he was a dairy farmer, because his eyes classified us—with drought, fire, the pear, flood and Noogoora burr. **1965** *Austral. Encycl.* IX. 227/2 One of the worst offenders [*sc.* plants whose burrs cling to wool] is noogoora burr (*Xanthium chinense*) which causes annual wool losses of at least £50,000. Since the 1860s it has occupied sheep country from the Gulf of Carpentaria to Sydney... Noogoora burr, indigenous to South America. is supposed to have been introduced with cotton seed.

nook (nŭk), *sb.*[2] *U.S.* representation of an abbreviated form of 'nuclear (weapon)'. Cf. *nuke *sb.*[2]

1964 *Daily Mirror* 24 Aug. 4/5 The generals should be allowed to decide whether to use tactical nuclear weapons, or as the current ugly phrase has it: 'Where and when to put in the nooks.' **1967** *Word Study* Oct. 8/1, I heard a grim, affectionate diminutive: 'nook' (nŭk). 'If the bird is carrying nooks.'

nooky, *a.* (Earlier example.)

1813 M. Edgeworth *Let.* 19 Apr. (1971) 19 Railed-in nice gardens, little *nooky* green spots.

nooky (nu·ki), *sb. slang.* Also **nookie.** [Orig. uncertain; perh. f. Nook *sb.* 3.] Sexual intercourse; hence also, a woman or girl considered as a sex object.

1928 Hecht & MacArthur *Front Page* i. 46 *Mollie Malloy enters. She is a North Clark Street tart...* Well, well! Nookie! **1930** J. Dos Passos *42nd Parallel* v. 400 Hendriks said he'd picked up with a skirt that was a warm baby and he was getting his nookie every night. **1932** J. T. Farrell *Young Lonigan* vi. 242 Schreiber was a good guy, but you know he liked his nooky, and he was always mixed up with some woman or other. **1948** N. Mailer *Naked & Dead* (1949) ii. v. 161 A woman that likes her nookie ain't gonna be satisfied with one man after she gits used to him. **1953** *Landfall* VII. 250 But I've had my bit of nookie on toast... A sheila of thirty, hot and spry. **1960** A. West *Trend is Up* (1961) iii. 95 Still nooky was nooky he told himself, and who cared what the woman was like if the lay was good. **1964** W. Markfield *To Early Grave* (1965) vi. 108 He starts telling me how tough it is for him to break in another nookie, how he's tired of having to make up reading lists for them. **1972** M. Woodhouse *Mama Doll* vii. 83 All the money he'll make as well as the nooky.

noon, *sb.* Add: **6.** *noon-dew, -height, -reek, rest* (later example), *-scape, -top*; *noon-clear, -fierce, -hot, -maned, -slight, -wide, -wild* adjs.; *noon-aglow* adv.

1919 W. De La Mare *Flora* 33 Her billowing summits heaving noon-aglow. **1874** Hardy *Far from Madding Crowd* II. i. 5 In her noon-clear sense that she had never loved him she forgot for a moment, [etc.]. **1953** E. Sitwell *Gardeners & Astronomers* 9 Holding small stars for seeds And planets of noon-dew. **1954** W. Faulkner *Fable* (1955) 42 He would whisper the one word against the noon-fierce stone under his face. **1869** D. G. Rossetti *Let.* 26 Aug. (1965) II. 720 Every sense..Now labours o'er the stark noon-height To reach the sunset's desolate disarray. **1940** Auden *Another Time* 37 Every crevice of the noon-hot landscape. **1946** Dylan Thomas *Deaths & Entrances* 17, I see the togron in tears In the androgynous dark, His striped and noon maned tribe striding to holocaust. **1922** Joyce *Ulysses* 155 The heavy noonreek tickled the top of Mr Bloom's gullet. **1873** J. H. Beadle *Undevel. West* xxviii. 615 We found water enough for our noon rest in the hollowed surface of a rock. **1926** V. Sackville-West *Land* 71 Then, with the noonscape, underneath the hedge ..the random reaper drains his pint of ale. **1936** L. B. Lyon *Bright Feather Fading* 16 He loved to shoulder A far cloud or brush the noon-Slight sickle moon. **1933** C. Day Lewis *Magnetic Mountain* 9 Spirit mating afresh shall discern him On the world's noon-top purely poised. **1935** —— *Time to Dance* 25 Buoyed, embayed in heaven's noon-wide reaches. **1936** L. B. Lyon *Bright Feather Fading* 41 Battlement that once glowed Noon-wild is warier lit.

b. noon-basket *U.S.*, a lunch-basket; **noon-halt,** a halt made in the middle of the day; **noon-house** *U.S.*, a house used for rest and meals at midday; now *Hist.*; **noon-mark,** a mark which indicates when it is noon; midday; now *Hist.*; **noonshine,** joc. form of Nuncheon; **noon-spell** *U.S.*, a rest taken in the middle of the day.

1865 A. D. Whitney *Gayworthys* vi. 71 Don't you remember what we used to say at school, when we opened our noon-baskets? **1843** J. C. Frémont *Rep. Exploring Expedition* 15 At our noon halt, the men were exercised at a target. **1854** J. R. Bartlett *Pers. Narr. Explor. Texas* II. xxxvii. 395 On our return we made a noon halt on the banks of the river. *a* **1918** G. Stewart *On Frontier* I. 115 John Dickery rode ahead from our noon halt to try to kill a sage hen. **1845** S. Judd *Margaret* i. 110 Several elderly men and women retired to what was called a 'Noon House', a small building..where they ate dinner and had a prayer. **1891** A. Earle *Sabbath* 102 There might have been seen a hundred years ago, by the side of many an old meeting-house in New England, a long, low, mean, stable-like building... This was the 'noon-house', or 'Sabba-day house'... It was a place of refuge in the winter time, at the noon interval between two services. **1854** B. F. Taylor *Jan. & June* i. 131 The sun..has reached the noon-mark on the threshold. **1889** R. T. Cooke *Steadfast* xxv. 275 Goodness! tis most noon-mark and I haven't took a step towardst dinner. **1948** *Amer. N. & Q.* Nov. 121/2, I should like to know whether..the term 'noon mark' was once common. **1808** Jane Austen *Let.* 20 June (1952) 195 The Moores came..between one & two o'clock, &..after the noonshine which succeeded their arrival, a party set off for Buckwell. *Ibid.* 24 Oct. 228 The tide is just right for our going immediately after noon-shine. **1839** C. M. Kirkland *New Home* xlv. 300 Even the 'noon-spell' shines no holiday for the luckless subjects of her domination. **1887** J. Kirkland *Zury* 18 Wait till noon-spell, then we'll see! **1889** R. T. Cooke *Steadfast* ii. 30 Its nigh about noonspell now.

noon-time. Add: (Later (*fig.*) example.) Also as *adv.*, **noontimes** *U.S.*, at mid-day.

1938 T. Wilder *Our Town* 11 Quarter of nine mornings, noontimes, and three o'clock afternoon's, the hull town can hear the yelling and screaming from those schoolyards. **1951** E. Paul *Springtime in Paris* i. 3, I concluded that he was posting the Dove bills noontimes, on a volunteer basis. **1965** *Times Lit. Suppl.* 25 Nov. 1036/3 The noon-time of the genre [*sc.* the musical] was over.

noosphere (nōu·osfīəɹ). [a. F. *noösphere*, f. Gr. νόο-ς mind + Sphere *sb.* 7.] The name given by Pierre Teilhard de Chardin in his theory of evolution to the stage or sphere characterized by the emergence of consciousness and mind which follows the stage of the establishment of human life (see quot. 1959). Also *fig.* Hence **noosphe·ric** *a.*

1953 J. S. Huxley *Evolution in Action* iv. 110 It provides a new kind of environment for life to inhabit. It needs a name of its own: following Père Teilhard de Chardin, the French paleontologist and philosopher, I shall call it the *noösphere*, the world of mind. **1959** B. Wall tr. *Teilhard de Chardin's Phenomenon of Man* iii. i. 182 Much more coherent and just as extensive as any preceding layer, it is really a new layer, the 'thinking layer', which.. has spread over and above the world of plants and animals. In other words, outside and above the biosphere there is the noosphere. **1962** M. McLuhan *Gutenberg Galaxy* 32 This externalization of our senses creates what de Chardin calls the 'noosphere' or a technological brain for the world. **1965** *Times Lit. Suppl.* 6 May 350/5 Linguistic anthropologists are at least asking questions about language which pull that phenomenon down from its cold noosphere back into the warm current of social living. **1966** *New Statesman* 6 May 659/2 Stock fictional characters in some kind of noöspheric organisation run by Conchis for his own enlightenment. **1967** *New Scientist* 26 Jan. 227/2 In practice we all act as if the mental aspect of Chardin's noösphere really is a guiding and determining factor in human existence. **1970** *Sci. Amer.* Sept. 53/3 Just before his death on January 6, 1945, he wrote..'I think that we undergo not only a historical, but a planetary change as well. We live in a transition to the noosphere.' By noosphere Vernadsky meant the envelope of mind that was to supersede the biosphere.

noost, var. *noust.

Nootka (nū·tkă, nu·tkă), *sb.* and *a.* [f. *Nootka* Sound, an inlet on the coast of Vancouver Island, British Columbia.] **A.** *sb.* **a.** A North American Indian people of north-western Washington state and Vancouver Island; a member of this people. **b.** The Wakashan language of the Nootka people.

[**1841** *Jrnl. R. Geogr. Soc.* XI. 221 The second or Southern Family of the insular tribes may be also denominated *Nootka–Columbian*, from the two places in which they have had most intercourse with Europeans.] **1846** H. Hale *Rep. U.S. Exploring Exped.* VI. 198 (*heading*) The North-Oregon division. All the tribes north of the Columbia..belong to this division... The *Nootkas*.. also belong to it. **1868** G. M. Sproat *Scenes Stud. Savage Life* iv. 22 The men (the Nootkahs) are below the middle height, with thick-set limbs, broad faces..and rough, coppery, and tanned skins. **1875** H. H. Bancroft *Native Races of Pacific States* I. iii. 176 The Nootkas are of less than medium height..but rather strongly built. **1910** F. W. Hodge *Handbk. Amer. Indians* II. 82/1 The Nootka form one branch of the great Wakashan family. **1915** E.

SAPIR *Abnormal Types of Speech in Nootka* 1 In Nootka there are special words used in speaking of obscene matters to or in the presence of women. **1934** *Language* X. 122 In Nootka a monosyllabic word may end in a consonant or a long vowel, but never in a short vowel. **1959** *Chambers's Encycl.* I. 339/2 The tribes of the coast and islands of north-west Canada comprise..southward, coast Salish, Nootka, Chinook, [etc.]. **1972** *Language* XLVIII. 274 Languages like Nootka, in which it seems difficult to distinguish between nominal and verbal roots.

B. *adj.* **1.** Pertaining to or designating the Nootkas or their language.

1846 H. HALE *Rep. U.S. Exploring Exped.* VI. 220 We might..add to the synopsis and map the *Nootka Family*, comprising the tribes of Vancouver Island. **1875** H. H. BANCROFT *Native Races of Pacific States* I. iii. 177 The Nootka complexion..is decidedly light. **1890** J. G. FRAZER *Golden Bough* II. iii. 113 Amongst the Nootka Indians of British Columbia, when a bear had been killed, it was brought in and seated before the head chief. **1915** E. SAPIR *Abnormal Types of Speech in Nootka* 3 More specialized Nootka examples to be given presently. **1955** P. DRUCKER *Indians of Northwest Coast* 12 They [*sc.* the Chinook Indians] traded slaves from the Californian hinterland up the coast for Nootka canoes.

2. Designating trees native to the Pacific coast of North America, as **Nootka (false-) cypress, Nootka Sound cypress,** a coniferous tree, *Chamæcyparis nootkatensis*, of the family Cupressaceæ, also known as the yellow cedar; **Nootka fir** = *Douglas fir* (*DOUGLAS[1]).

1892 A. C. APGAR *Trees Northern U.S.* 195 Nootka Sound Cypress... Tree 100 ft. high in Alaska. **1897** G. B. SUDWORTH *Nomencl. Arborescent Flora U.S.* 79 Yellow Cedar... [Also called] Nootka Cypress... Nootka Sound Cypress. **1957** M. HADFIELD *Brit. Trees* 116 The Nootka cypress grows on the Pacific coast of North America, from southern Alaska to southern Oregon. **1969** T. H. EVERETT *Living Trees of World* 33/2 The Nootka false-cypress.. has quadrangular, drooping branchlets and leaves without white markings on their undersides. A native from Oregon to Alaska, this slender tree is often 120 feet tall. **1974** *Country Life* 12 Dec. 1855/1 Two big Nootka cypresses (*Chamaecyparis nootkatensis*). **1803** A. B. LAMBERT *Descr. Genus Pinus* I. 51 Nootka Fir... A specimen in the Banksian herbarium, brought home by Mr. Menzies, by whom it was discovered on the North-west coast of America. **1889** G. S. BOULGER *Uses of Plants* vii. 186 *Pseudotsuga Douglasii*, Carrière, the Oregon Pine, or Douglas or Nootka Fir, abundant in North-west America, furnishes fine, straight, and durable timber. **1957** *N.Z. Timber Jrnl.* Dec. 59/2 *Nootka fir*, Douglas fir.

So **Noo·tkan** *a.* and *sb.*

1841 *Jrnl. R. Geogr. Soc.* XI. 224 Whoever will compare the list of Nootkan words..with the Tlaoquatch vocabulary..will find that there is very little difference between them. *Ibid.* 225 The Kawitchen tribe..appears..to be a mixed race, compounded of Shahaptans and Nootkans. **1848** *Jrnl. Ethnol. Soc. London* I. 234 Nootkans. **1973** *Amer. Speech 1969* XLIV. 232 Chinook jargon [has].. Nootkan and Algonkian lexical elements.

no parking. [*PARKING *vbl. sb.*] Used *attrib.* and *absol.* to designate an area, place, etc., where vehicles may not be parked; also, to designate a sign bearing this instruction.

1946 *Rep. Departmental Comm. Traffic Signs 1944* (Ministry of Transport) 51 We do not consider it desirable that the words 'Halt' or 'No Parking' should be marked on the carriageway. **1956** F. CASTLE *Violent Hours* (1966) x. 97 The car was in a no-parking zone. **1964** I. FLEMING *You only live Twice* iv. 51 A smart Toyopet saloon waiting in a no-parking area. **1964** J. MASTERS *Trial at Monomoy* ii. 49 That's a *No Parking* zone. **1968** S. B. HOUGH *Sweet Sister Seduced* iv. 15 He reached the grass, the No Parking signs. **1971** A. PRICE *Alamut Ambush* i. 12 A parked car is just a parked car if it's not in a 'no parking' zone. **1972** M. SINCLAIR *Norslag* x. 85 A 'No Parking' sign by the kerb.

nope (nōᵘp), *adv. slang* (orig. *U.S.*) Extended form of No *adv.*[3] Cf. YEP.

1888 *N.Y. Life* 12 May, Cover 3/2 'I suppose you will be a literary man, like your father, when you grow up.' 'Nope,' said the little boy..'Literary nuthin'! I'm goin' to be a ten-thousand-dollar cook.' **1891** *Harper's Mag.* Nov. 970/1 The professor, wishing to express negation, made use of the objectionable form 'nope'. **1908** C. E. MULFORD *Orphan* ii. 24 Nope, I reckon not—seven husky Apaches are too much for one man to go out of his way to fight. **1918** E. WALLACE *Down Under Donovan* x. 129 'Have you been in Europe before?' 'Nope,' she replied shortly. **1941** R. STOUT *Red Threads* iii. 30 'You don't paint in oils, do you?' 'Nope.' **1956** E. POUND tr. *Sophocles' Women of Trachis* 27 Nope, no proof without data. **1964** MRS. L. B. JOHNSON *White House Diary* 8 Apr. (1970) 103 And General George Marshall said, 'I'll be damned if I will have people calling me "Marshal Marshall". Nope, we'll just have five-star Generals.' **1971** H. C. RAE *Marksman* I. viii. 72 'Anybody asking for me?' 'Nope.'

no-place, *sb.* and *adv.* [f. No *a.* + PLACE *sb.*]

A. *sb.* A place which does not exist.

1929 E. BOWEN *Last September* xi. 131 To be enclosed in nonentity, in some ideal no-place. **1934** L. B. LYON *White Hare* 12 Now is the new page turned and the new light falling From the no-place of the spirit. **1958** *Listener* 28 Aug. 304/2 Neither to accept nor to rebel Is that no-place which I call hell. **1963** *Colorado Portfolio* No. 1 31/3 And in some noplace in some notime he would take out a tiny book..and write.

B. *adv.* (usu. *colloq.*) Nowhere; (in double negative) anywhere. Chiefly *U.S.*

1934 in WEBSTER. **1942** PARTRIDGE *Usage & Abusage* 211/1 *No place* is illiterate for *nowhere*, as in 'The jewel was no place to be found'. **1956** H. GOLD *Man who was not with It* (1965) ix. 74 'Where are you going?' I..cried out: 'Noplace!' **1969** M. PUGH *Last Place Left* xxv. 187 You're going no place until Herb gets here. **1971** D. E. WESTLAKE *I gave at the Office* (1972) 192 We was in two trucks, packed in tight so you couldn't hardly sit down noplace.

nor, *conj.*[1] Add: **II. 6.** As *sb.* or *adj. Computers.* (Written in capitals.) A Boolean function of two or more variables that has the value unity if all the variables are zero and is otherwise zero; 'neither..nor..'. Usu. *attrib.*

1957 *Trans. Amer. Inst. Electr. Engin.* LXXVI. I. 263/1 The transistor NOR circuit was introduced because of the desire to have a single logic element which would combine well in logic configurations with a minimum concern for matching and element loading. A NOR element has a signal output only if there are no input signals. *Ibid.*, P-n-p and n-p-n transistor NOR circuits..cannot be readily intermixed. **1958** [see *NAND]. **1969** J. J. SPARKES *Transistor Switching* iv. 96 For NOR gates the Boolean expression is first reduced to its simplest form containing the product of sums. **1971** J. H. SMITH *Digital Logic* iv. 42 The NOR function is used extensively, especially in resistor–transistor logic systems. **1972** *IEEE Trans. Computers* XXI. 153/1 Optimal networks consisting of NOR–OR gates (each gate produces the NOR and/or the OR of its inputs) are tabulated for all Boolean functions of three variables.

nor- (nǭɹ), *prefix. Organic Chem.* [f. NOR(MAL *a.* and *sb.*] **1. a.** Prefixed to the names of organic compounds to denote the replacement of one or (esp. in terpenes) all the (methyl) side-chains by hydrogen atoms.

The use arose from the designation of a compound $C_8H_6O_5$ as 'normal opianic acid', of which opianic acid was supposed to be a dimethyl derivative: **1868** MATTHIESON & FOSTER in *Jrnl. Chem. Soc.* XXI. 358 We therefore propose to call the compound $C_9H_8O_5$ monomethyl-normal opianic acid, or if the contraction is admissible, methylnoropianic acid.

norbo·rnane [*bornane* f. BORN(EOL + -ANE], the crystalline bicyclic hydrocarbon, C_7H_{12}, which is obtained by replacing the three methyl groups of bornane (camphane) by hydrogen atoms and is the parent compound of a number of terpenes; bicyclo[2.2.1]heptane; **nordihy:droguaiare·tic acid** [f. *guaiaretic acid*, f. GUAIA(C + Gr. ῥητ-ίνη resin of the pine], a crystalline phenol, $C_{18}H_{18}(OH)_4$, which is used as an antoxidant for oils and fats; **nore·phedrine,** the crystalline, optically active compound, $C_9H_{13}NO$, which is obtained by replacing the methylamino group of ephedrine by an amino group and has actions and uses resembling those of ephedrine; **norethi·sterone,** a crystalline compound, $C_{20}H_{26}O_2$, which has actions similar to those of progesterone and is used as a contraceptive and in the treatment of amenorrhœa and functional uterine bleeding; **(β-)norni·cotine** [a. F. *nornicotine* (M. & M. Polonovski 1927, in *Compt. Rend.* CLXXXIV. 1333)], an optically active liquid alkaloid, $C_9H_{12}N_2$, found with and resembling nicotine; **norsyne·phrin(e** = *OCTOPAMINE; **nortesto·sterone,** the 19-norsteroid derived from testosterone.

1952 *Chem. & Engin. News* 3 Mar. 930/3 Corresponding to these six types [of bicyclic compounds] are the four-parent ring systems northujane.., norcarane.., norpinane..and norbornane. **1962** E. L. ELIEL *Stereochem. Carbon Compounds* x. 302 Norbornane, despite its easy accessibility, is an appreciably strained system. **1974** *Jrnl. Chem. Soc.: Perkin Trans. II* 322 (*heading*) Inhibition of ring expansion reactions in the norbornane system by neighbouring methyl groups. [**1919** *Chem. Abstr.* XIII. 991 Schiff's norguaiaretic acid is shown to be norhydroguaiaretic acid.] **1944** *Oil & Soap* XXI. 33/1 An investigation was made of the antioxydant properties of nordihydroguaiaretic acid. **1945** *Jrnl. Amer. Pharm. Assoc.* (*Sci. Ed.*) XXXIV. 81/1 One, if not the most active, of the bactericidal agents present in [the shrub] *Larrea divaricata* Cav. has been characterized as nordihydroguaiaretic acid. **1956** M. K. SCHWITZER *Margarine & Other Food Fats* viii. 323 Nordihydroguaiaretic acid..was permitted to be used in the United States in December, 1943 at the rate of 0·01 per cent. The antioxidant effect is very marked in animal fats... It is less effective in vegetable fats. **1971** P. TOOLEY *Fats, Oils & Waxes* iv. 125 Oxidation can cause serious deterioration in a lipstick producing unpleasant rancid odours and taste... This can be largely prevented by the use of antioxidants such as..nordihydroguaiaretic acid. **1929** *Chem. Abstr.* XXIII. 2431 Reduction of $PhCH(OH)CH(NO_2)Me$ with Zn dust and dil. H_2SO_4 gave norephedrine..and nor-ψ-ephedrine. **1943** *Jrnl. Lab. & Clin. Med.* XXVIII. 704 Norephedrine and pseudonorephedrine together constitute propadrine, of which the commercial preparation contains also a small amount of ammonium chloride. **1973** *Biochem. Jrnl.* CXXXVI. 769/1 Norephedrine is extensively metabolized in the rabbit but not in man. **1956** *Proc. Soc. Exper. Biol. & Med.* XCI. 419/2, 10 mg nor-ethisterone given twice daily represents a reproducibly effective dose in women for the production of marked progestational changes. **1964** Norethisterone [see *ETHINYLŒSTRADIOL]. **1973** *Nature* 10 Aug. 351/1 If inferences can be drawn from this preliminary study using mouse foetal hearts, it would seem that the concentration of norethisterone acetate in the pill should be kept to a minimum. **1927** *Chem. Abstr.* XXI 3905 (*heading*) β-Pyridyl-α-pyrrolidine (nornicotine). **1936** *Jrnl. Econ. Entomol.* XXIX. 854 Macht & Davis..observed that β-nornicotine was more toxic for certain vertebrates..than natural nicotine. **1951** A. GROLLMAN *Pharmacol. & Therapeutics* xv. 281 Nornicotine, which has similar actions to nicotine, lacks only the CH_3 group in the pyrrolidine nucleus. **1968** LARSON & SILVETTE *Tobacco* Suppl. I. 682/1 Nornicotine inhibited development of the chick-embryo, and was even more potent than nicotine in causing hydrops. **1952** Norsynephrine [see *OCTOPAMINE]. **1952** *Ricerca Sci.* XXII. 1576 Sympathomimetic amines (tyramine, norsynephrine, adrenaline, noradrenaline). **1960** *Biochim. & Biophys. Acta* XLIII. 568 The enzyme responsible for norsynephrin formation is dopamine β-oxidase. **1950** *Jrnl. Chem. Soc.* 367 This βγ-unsaturated ketone has now been isomerised..to the αβ-unsaturated ketone.., which is a 10-nortestosterone. **1955** H. HIRSCHMANN *Hormones* III. xi. 544 19-Nortestosterone on the other hand, is inferior to testosterone as an androgen but equal to it in its myotrophic..effect. **1973** *Jrnl. Appl. Physiol.* XXXV. 378/2 Nortestosterone esters are more potent than testosterone in their capacity to stimulate erythropoietic activity in mice.

b. Denoting the contraction of a chain or ring of carbon atoms by one methylene group, as **norchola·nic acid** [*cholanic* f. CHOL- + -AN + -IC], a crystalline, optically active compound, $C_{23}H_{38}O_2$, obtained by shortening the side-chain of cholanic acid by one methylene group; **norpi·nic acid,** a crystalline dicarboxylic acid, $C_8H_{12}O_4$, existing in *cis* and *trans* isomers and differing from pinic acid in having a carboxyl group attached to the cyclobutane ring in place of a carboxymethyl group.

1927 *Chem. Abstr.* XXI. 590 Oxidation of I [*sc.* cholanic acid] by CrO_3 in AcOH yielded the next lower homolog, norcholanic acid. **1958** C. W. SHOPPEE *Chem. Steroids* iv. 192 Similar reactions have been carried out in the norcholanic acid..series. **1909** *Jrnl. Chem. Soc.* XCV. 1170 Our experiments have, however, shown that this ring, in norpinic acid, exhibits quite unusual stability. **1932** J. L. SIMONSEN *Terpenes* II. iii. 129 By the action of dilute hydrochloric acid at 180° [on the *cis*-isomer], an equilibrium mixture of *cis*- and *trans*-norpinic acids is obtained. **1960** A. R. PINDER *Chem. of Terpenes* v. 91 The molecular formula and properties of norpinic acid suggested it was derived from *cyclo*butane.

2. Denoting the normal (unbranched chain) isomer of the compound to whose name it is prefixed, as **norleu·cine** [ad. G. *norleucin* (E. Abderhalden et al. 1913, in *Zeitschr. f. physiol. Chem.* LXXXVI. 455)], an optically active, crystalline, non-essential amino-acid, $CH_3(CH_2)_3CH(NH_2)COOH$; **norva·line** [ad. G. *norvalin* (Abderhalden & Kürten 1921, in *Fermentforschung* IV. 328)], an optically active crystalline amino-acid, $CH_3(CH_2)_2$-$CH(NH_2)COOH$.

1913 *Jrnl. Chem. Soc.* CIV. I. 1049 The acid, for which the name norleucine is proposed, has been combined with glycine and leucylglycine to form polypeptides. **1932** *Jrnl. Biol. Chem.* XCVII. 342 Norleucine has been isolated from spinal cord protein. **1961** D. M. GREENBERG *Metabolic Pathways* II. xiv. 111 Norleucine is readily oxidized to CO_2 in the intact animal. **1971** *Nomencl. Org. Chem.* (I.U.P.A.C.) (ed. 2) C.42 193 (*table*) Norleucine..Norvaline. [*Note*] Use of 'nor' in these names to denote a 'normal' (unbranched) chain conflicts with more recent usage. **1921** *Jrnl. Chem. Soc.* CXX. I. 547 *dl*-α-Amino-*n*-valeric acid,..to which the name *norvaline* is given, is prepared by the usual methods from *n*-valeric acid. **1933** *Ann. Rev. Biochem.* II. 73 Further evidence of the occurrence of norvaline in proteins has been furnished by Abderhalden & Heyns..who report its occurrence in steer horn. **1969** *Biochem. Jrnl.* CXV. 621 Kinetic studies of glutamate dehydrogenase were made with wide concentration ranges of the coenzymes NAD^+ and $NADP^+$ and the substrates glutamate and norvaline.

nor (nǭɹ), *a. Organic Chem.* [f. prec.] Applied to compounds or groups of compounds conventionally named by adding the prefix *NOR- to the name of a parent compound, esp. with a prefixed numeral indicating the methyl group lacking or a prefixed capital letter indicating the ring which is contracted as compared with the parent compound.

1940 *Chem. Abstr.* XXXIV. 5455 Diminution from a 6-ring to a 5-ring by loss of C atoms..in rings A, B and C gives rise to the corresponding A-nor, B-nor and C-nor compds. **1946** *Jrnl. Biol. Chem.* CLXII. 589 The nor, bisnor, and etio homologues of 3,11-dihydroxy-12-ketocholanic acid have been prepared. **1954** *Jrnl. Amer. Chem. Soc.* LXXVI. 4092/2 The efficacy of this 19-nor analog..in human females has been established. **1972** *Adv. Steroid Biochem. & Pharmacol.* III. 93 Two of the 19-nor steroids, norgestrel and allylestrenol, appear to show differences from norethisterone and lynestrenol.

noradrenaline (nǭræ̆dre·nălin, -ǣdrī̆nălin). *Med.* Also **-in.** [f. *NOR- 1 a + *ADRENALINE.] An amine, $(HO)_2C_6H_3{\cdot}CHOH{\cdot}CH_2$-$NH_2$, related to adrenaline, having a hydrogen atom in place of the methyl group; 1-(3,

4-dihydroxyphenyl)-2-aminoethanol; *spec.* the lævorotatory isomer, which is the transmitter substance of sympathetic nerves and at some synapses in the central nervous system, is also synthesized in the adrenal medulla, and whose acid tartrate is used, usu. by intravenal infusion, as a vasoconstrictor for raising blood pressure.

1932 *Arch. Internat. de Pharmacodynamie et de Thérapie* XLI. 366 This compound..is referred to occasionally as nor-adrenaline. **1948** *Science* 6 Aug. 135/2 The facts..point to the existence of two highly active sympathomimetic substances: nor-adrenaline and adrenaline. **1962** A. HUXLEY *Island* xiii. 206 The power generated by fear or envy or too much noradrenalin. **1965** J. POLLITT *Depression & its Treatment* iv. 53 Monoamines are neurohormones.., and two substances of this group playing particularly important roles in mood regulation are serotonin and noradrenalin. **1968** [see *DRIP *sb.* 2 b]. **1971** J. Z. YOUNG *Introd. Study Man* xliii. 629 Carnivorous animals are said to secrete large amounts of noradrenalin, which makes them aggressive. **1973** *Daily Colonist* (Victoria, B.C.) 30 June 12/1 Both humans and rats secrete a large amount of noradrenaline when they shiver.

Hence **noradrene·rgic** *a.* [after *ADRENERGIC, *CHOLINERGIC *adjs.*], (of a nerve-cell) stimulated by or liberating noradrenaline; **noradrene·rgically** *adv.*

1963 *Arch. Internat. de Pharmacodynamie et de Thérapie* CXLII. 257 The hindleg vasoconstriction, spleen contraction and cardioacceleration, which occur in response to a threshold stimulation of the corresponding postganglionic noradrenergic nerve supply, are not sensitized by intravenous infusion of noradrenaline. **1973** *Naunyn-Schmiedebergs Arch. Pharmakol.* CCLXXIX. 53 An α-receptor-mediated feed-back control of noradrenaline release, previously demonstrated in postganglionic sympathetic nerves, also operates in central noradrenergic neurones. **1975** *Nature* 21 Aug. 659/2 Peripheral, noradrenergically innervated tissue.

norate (nǭrēi·t), *v.* *U.S. dial.* Also **norrate.** [? Corruption of NARRATE *v.*] **a.** To announce; to spread (information) by word of mouth. **b.** To denigrate. So **nora·tion, norration.**

1853 J. W. PAGE *Uncle Robin* 231 Der's some folks who tells de people, dar, dat massers in dis country [*sc.* in the South], when der niggers runs away, puts out a noration, dat dey will give four hundred dollar' to anybody who will bring one o' der runaway niggers to um, dead or live. **1895** *Dialect Notes* I. 373 'We will *norate* the preaching' (i.e. announce the services to be held). **1905** *Ibid.* III. 89 [Arkansas] A French specialist has given out the '*noration*' that kissing is not a hurtful process. **1914** *Ibid.* IV. 110 Norate... Also, norration, noration, *n.* **1921** J. C. CAMPBELL *Southern Highlander & his Homeland* 145 [In the Southern Appalachians] a man wishing to hold a public meeting has it *norated*, that is, the announcement of it spread by report. **1938** *Amer. Speech* XIII. 6/2 [S.E. Arkansas] It is norated about that he is a crook. **1941** H. SKIDMORE *Hawk's Nest* 22 Norratin' it round bout them wanten men to work. **1949** H. HORNSBY *Lonesome Valley* 10 'You're planning to norate the word,' he said... 'More than apt they'll expect me to do the preaching.' **1954** *Publ. Amer. Dial. Soc.* XXI. 33 [South Carolina] *Norate*: *v.t.*, to depreciate. Usually of persons.

norbergite (nǭ·ɹbəɹgəit). *Min.* [f. *Norberg*, the name of the village in Sweden near which it was discovered + -ITE[1].] A basic silicate and fluoride of magnesium, $Mg_3SiO_4(F,OH)_2$, which is found as pink or whitish orthorhombic crystals.

1926 P. GEIJER in *Geol. Förening. Stockholm Förhand.* XLVIII. 84 Norbergite. Only in massive aggregates, crystal system unknown... The proposed name is derived from the name of the district, since that of the mine is unsuitable for an international nomenclature. **1928** *Amer. Mineralogist* XIII. 349 The norbergite occurs in a coarsely crystalline limestone from the Nicoll Quarry, and grains or crystals are commonly several millimeters across. **1968** *Mineral. Mag.* XXXVI. 966 The polyhedral distortions in norbergite are smaller than in forsterite in accord with the decreased number of shared edges.

nordenskiöldine (nǭɹdenʃö·ldīn, -ski,ö·ldīn). *Min.* [ad. Sw. *nordenskiöldin* (W. C. Brögger 1887, in *Geol. Förening. Stockholm Förhand.* IX. 255), f. the name of Baron Nils Adolf Erik *Nordenskiöld* (1832–1901), Swedish geologist and explorer: see -INE[5].] A borate of calcium and tin, $CaSnB_2O_6$, found as colourless or yellow rhombohedral crystals.

1890 *Jrnl. Chem. Soc.* LVIII. 1078 Nordenskiöldine, named after the celebrated traveller, is of great rarity in the Norwegian veins. **1935** *Mineral. Abstr.* VI. 46 An ore pipe in marble near a granite contact at Arandis, South-West Africa.., contains near its margin cassiterite, tourmaline, and small colourless plates of the rare mineral nordenskiöldine. **1966** *Doklady Earth Sci.* CLXIV. 131/1 Macroscopically, the nordenskiöldine synthesized is a dense white mass in which hexagonal, heavily tabular crystals up to 0·005 mm in size are discernible under the microscope.

Nordic (nǭ·ɹdik), *a.* and *sb.* [ad. F. *nordique* (J. Deniker 1898, in *L'Anthropologie* IX. 127) f. *nord* NORTH: see -IC.] **A.** *adj.* Of or pertaining to the Scandinavian people or their languages; *spec.* of or pertaining to a physical type of northern Germanic peoples characterized by tall stature, bony frame, light colouring, and dolichocephalic head.

In Nazi doctrine the 'Nordic race' was regarded as essentially 'superior' to other races.

1898 W. Z. RIPLEY in *Pop. Sci. Monthly* Oct. 744 A direct physical relationship between the three [peoples], referring them all to a so-called nordic race, is confirmed by the very latest and most competent authority [*sc.* J. Deniker]. **1921** *Contemp. Rev.* Jan. 56 All the talk about Nordic supremacy is vanity when we look at the facts in Europe. **1929** CHESTERTON *Thing* xiv. 113 Englishmen who now call themselves Nordic used to call themselves Teutonic. **1937** [see sense B. 1 below]. **1938** G. HEYER *Blunt Instrument* ii. 37 You ought to have seen me giving my impression of a Nordic public-school man with a reverence for good form and the done-thing. **1939** H. G. WELLS *Holy Terror* IV. ii. 419 The new generation of Germans were ashamed of the Hitler period and the Nordic legend. **1940** —— *All Aboard for Ararat* i. 24 The third, Japhet, was what the Germans would consider a Nordic type, all milk and roses. **1957** M. BELOFF *Europe & Europeans* iv. 86 The Nordic languages, especially Old Norse, borrowed important words from Anglo-Saxon. **1959** *Chambers's Encycl.* XIV. 319/1 The term viking is Nordic in origin. **1966** W. P. LEHMANN in Birnbaum & Puhvel *Anc. Indo-Europ. Dialects* 16 The most striking innovation common to Gothic and the Nordic languages is the development of a stop in geminate *j* and *w* clusters. **1968** G. JONES *Hist. Vikings* 69 As Wessén says, at the beginning of his history of the Swedish language:..We have then come to the *Primitive Nordic language*, the parent tongue of the present Nordic vernaculars, common to the Scandinavian countries down to the beginnings of the Viking Age. **1970** FOOTE & WILSON *Viking Achievement* 3 Some of the Nordic provinces had sent out tribes in the Migration Age to join the more southerly Germanic peoples as they cut their way through the old domains of the Roman Empire. **1973** G. BEARE *Snake on Grave* vii. 36 A crowd of Nordic drunks at a table near him was singing. **1974** *Encycl. Brit. Micropædia* VII. 386/3 *Nordic Council*, organization of the Nordic states of Denmark, Finland, Iceland, Norway, and Sweden for the purpose of consultation and cooperation on matters of common interest.

b. Of a skiing competition involving cross-country or jumping events.

1954 *Brit. Ski Yr. Bk.* XVI. 70 The greatest of all of the Nordic competitions—Holmenkollen. **1960** *Ski-ing* ('Know the Game' series) 24/2 The Nordic events include cross-country races and jumping competitions. **1966** S. ERIKSEN *Come ski with Me* 44 Norwegian had won the Nordic Combination and the 18 km. cross-country in Holmenkollen. **1969** M. HELLER *Ski* xiii. 170 Nordic skiing is the original and basic form of ski-ing... The fundamental techniques are self-evident—the diagonal stride, double poling with and without a stride and uphill strides —in other words, walking on skis. **1972** *Evening Telegram* (St. John's, Newfoundland) 24 June 23/1 Rolf Kjaernsli of Norway has been named nordic skiing program director to develop nordic and cross-country skiing in Canada.

B. *sb.* **1.** A person of the Nordic type.

1901 *Cassell's Mag.* June 110/2 The tall blonde race of northern Europe, sometimes called 'Teutons', but more scientifically 'Nordics'. **1928** WODEHOUSE *Money for Nothing* ii. 32 Well, all I can say is,..it's no life for a refined Nordic. **1936** H. G. WELLS *Anat. Frustration* xv. 176 It is for the treatment of the Jews that we are most frequently urged to condemn Hitlerism... Their [*sc.* the Jews'] racial purity is as much a falsehood as the racial purity of the 'Nordics'. **1937** A. HUXLEY *Ends & Means* xiii. 242 Hitlerian theology affirms that there is a Nordic race, inherently superior to all other. Hence it is right that Nordics should organize themselves for conquest.

2. The northern branch of the Germanic languages.

1955 T. BURROW *Sanskrit Lang.* 8 Germanic..may be divided into East Germanic or Gothic (extinct), Nordic or Scandinavian, and West Germanic. **1967** *Scandinavian Studies* XXXIX. 16 (*title*) Proto-Scandinavian and Common Nordic. **1972** in Van Coetsem & Kufner *Toward Gram. of Proto-Germanic* 78 The close relationship of 'Nordic' and 'Gothic'.

Nordicism (nǭ·ɹdisiz'm). [f. *NORDIC *a.* and *sb.* + -ISM.] **a.** The state or condition of being Nordic; the characteristics of the Nordics. **b.** The belief in or doctrine of the cultural and racial supremacy of the Nordic people. Hence **No·rdicist**, one who believes in the supremacy of the Nordic people.

1923 J. H. ECKENRODE *Jefferson Davis* (1924) ii. 24 The modernism of the North and the Nordicism of the South came more and more into conflict. **1924** *Glasgow Herald* 7 Apr. 8 Doubtless he was not as strong on Nordicism as his biographer. **1925** *Nation* (N.Y.) CXX. 516/1 The transition from Aryanism to Nordicism in Germany. **1929** R. HUGHES *High Wind in Jamaica* vii. 151 The Nordicism of captain and mate kept the rest looking clean enough. **1934** A. TOYNBEE *Study of Hist.* I. II. 221 The Nordicists claim it [*sc.* the monopoly of the unique magical quality in Mankind] for all White Men with fair hair and blue eyes. **1957** G. CLARK *Archaeol. & Society* (ed. 3) viii. 259 Much..was corrupted by doctrines which stemmed directly from Gustaf Kossinna (1858–1931), an ardent exponent of Pan-Germanism and Nordicism.

nordite (nǭ·ɹdəit). *Min.* [ad. Russ. *nordit* (V.I. Gerasimovsky 1941, in *Doklady Akad. Nauk SSSR* XXXII. 496): see quot. 1941 and -ITE[1].] A silicate of sodium, strontium, manganese, calcium, and lanthanides, found as light brown orthorhombic crystals.

1941 V. I. GERASIMOVSKY in *Compt. Rend.* (*Doklady*) *de l'Acad. des Sci. de l'URSS* XXXII. 496 A more detailed study of the mineral has shown that it cannot be identified with any of the minerals already known, and therefore it was given a new name—nordite (because of its northern origin). **1958** *Chem. Abstr.* LII. 12701 The predominance of La over Ce in nordite is an exception to the Oddo-Harkins rule. **1970** *Amer. Mineralogist* LV. 1167 The structure of nordite is closely related to the structures of melilite and datolite-gadolinite, and can be considered as an unusual combination of both.

nordmarkite (nǭ·ɹdmāɹkəit). [f. *Nordmark*, name of an area in Sweden + -ITE[1].] **1.** *Min.* A brown manganesian variety of staurolite.

1868 J. D. DANA *Syst. Min.* (ed. 5) v. 389 *Manganese-Staurolite, Nordmarkite* (anal. 28); from dolomite in Nordmark, Sweden, of chocolate-brown color, with H. = 6·5, G. = 3·54, and presenting the usual crystalline form. Its easy fusibility is reason for here giving this variety the distinctive name *Nordmarkite.* **1968** I. KOSTOV *Mineralogy* 289 Staurolites rich in manganese are termed nordmarkite.

2. *Petrogr.* [a. G. *nordmarkit* (W. C. Brøgger 1890, in *Zeitschr. f. Kryst. und Mineral.* XVI. I. 55).] A syenite composed mainly of microperthite, with lesser amounts of quartz and usu. oligoclase and biotite, which has a trachytoid or granitic texture.

1895 *Mineral. Mag.* XI. 115 The corresponding abyssal or plutonic rock is nordmarkite. **1928** *Mineral. Abstr.* III. 498 The differentiation of the Lung Wang Miao åkerite has given rise to a whole series of granitic derivatives: nordmarkite, alkali-granite-aplite, and quartz-porphyry. **1942** *Amer. Jrnl. Sci.* CCXL. 362 Nordmarkite porphyry from a dyke at Blindern, by Oslo, Norway. **1970** *Meddelelser om Grønland* CXC. II. 15 The nordmarkites are grey or fawn in colour and are fairly coarse-grained rocks. *Ibid.* 16 In most of the nordmarkites the ferromagnesian minerals occur in small clusters.

Hence **nordmarki·tic** *a.*, composed of, or having the nature of, (the rock) nordmarkite.

1947 *Mineral. Mag.* X. 90 At Dorowa [S. Rhodesia] nordmarkitic granite occurs with syenite in the outer ring. **1953** *Q. Jrnl. Geol. Soc.* CIX. 161 Keratophyres, kersantites and nordmarkitic rocks occur on both sides of the outcrop of the Moine thrust-plane.

nordstrandite (nǭ·ɹdstrăndəit). *Min.* [a. F. *nordstrandite* (D. Papée et al. 1958, in *Bull. Soc. chim. de France* 1306/2), f. the name of Robert A. van *Nordstrand*, 20th-cent. U.S. chemist: see -ITE[1].] One of the phases of aluminium hydroxide, $Al(OH)_3$.

1962 *Nature* 20 Oct. 265/1 The nordstrandite varies from almost colourless to coral pink and reddish-brown, the coloration being largely due to inclusions of finely divided goethite. **1968** *Mineral. Abstr.* XIX. 176/2 Nordstrandite occurs in all (6) Hungarian brickclays examined and is the only phase in the Debrecen clay.

norepinephrine (nǭ:repine·frin). *Biochem.* [f. *NOR- + *EPINEPHRINE.] = *NORADRENALINE.

1948 *Jrnl. Pharmacol. & Exper. Therap.* XCII. 369 Norepinephrine ('Arterenol'), a racemic compound,..is 1·5 times more pressor than racemic epinephrine. **1951** A. GROLLMAN *Pharmacol. & Therapeutics* xi. 205 Norepinephrine is a vasoconstrictor and unlike epinephrine does not decrease the peripheral resistance or increase the cardiac output. **1962** J. GLENN et al. *Into Orbit* 115 The flow of norephinephrine [*sic*] from his adrenal glands during the flight had been more than 2½ times what it had normally been. **1971** *Nature* 2 Apr. 330/1 Some, if not all, states of mental depression may be associated with a deficiency in norepinephrine..at functionally important receptor sites in the brain.

norethynodrel (nǭreþi·nǭdrĕl). *Pharm.* [f. *NOR- + ETH(ANE + *-YN(E + *-odrel*, of unknown origin.] A synthetic hormone, $C_{20}H_{26}O_2$, with actions and uses similar to those of norethisterone, with which it is isomeric.

1957 *Endocrinology* LX. 804 Norethynodrel has been examined for its ability to produce endometrial gland development in the estrogen-primed spayed or immature rabbit. **1962** *New Scientist* 7 June 506/3 Most contraceptive pills consist of a mixture of two steroids obtained from yams. One is norethynodrel..which is believed to inhibit ovulation. The other is an oestrogen. **1970** PASSMORE & ROBSON *Compan. Med. Stud.* II. xii. 6/1 Shift of the double bond in the A ring of norethisterone from the 4–5 to the 5–10 position produces the isomer, norethynodrel.

Norfolk. Add: **b. Norfolk dumpling,** (*b*) a plain dumpling made from bread dough; **Norfolk jacket** (earlier and later examples); **Norfolk reed,** the common reed, *Phragmites australis*, grown in East Anglia for use as thatching material; **Norfolk spaniel,** a name formerly used for the English springer spaniel, a breed once associated with the estates of the Duke of Norfolk; **Norfolk suit,** a suit with a Norfolk jacket and knee breeches; **Norfolk terrier,** the drop-eared variety of the Norwich terrier (see *NORWICH).

c **1600**, etc. [see DUMPLING 1 a]. **1747** H. GLASSE *Art of Cookery* ix. 112 *Norfolk Dumplings.* Make a good thick

batter... Eat them hot. **1877** *Cassell's Dict. Cookery* 458/1 Norfolk Dumplings... When bread is made at home, take a little of the dough.., make it up into small balls.., drop them into fast-boiling water... Send melted butter, sweetened and flavoured with lemon juice, to table with them. **1933** C. H. SENN *Century Cookery Bk.* (ed. 10) 1013 *Norfolk Dumplings*,—Make an ordinary bread dough... Serve with a boat of rich gravy or other suitable sauce. **1972** *Mrs. Beeton's Family Cookery* 449 Norfolk Dumplings..Boiling water, Salt, Bread, Dough... Make the dough... Cream the yeast with the sugar and add the warm water and the melted fat... Serve with..jam, treacle, golden syrup, *or* butter and sugar. **1866** J. MACGREGOR *Thousand Miles in Rob Roy Canoe* i. 9 The 'Norfolk jacket' is a loose frock-coat, like a blouse, with shoulder-straps, and belted at the waist, and garnished by six pockets. **1969** *Queen* 17–30 Sept. 76 Norfolk jacket in cream leather; long side vents; belt..45 gns. [**1925** E. G. BLAKE *Roof Coverings* ii. 18 The reeds are grown principally in the eastern counties, especially on the Norfolk Broads.] **1952** *Oxf. Jun. Encycl.* VI. 440 A well-bedded thatch of Norfolk reed..has been known to last as long as 50 years. *Ibid.*, Although Norfolk reed is by far the most durable, it is also the most expensive. **1965** P. WAYRE *Wind in Reeds* ix. 111 Norfolk reed is in much demand for thatch, being most durable and of good length—often exceeding eight feet. **1971** *Country Life* 18 Nov. 1403/1 The great tithe barn at Tisbury, in Wiltshire, has just been re-thatched with Norfolk reed. **1859** *Field* 5 Mar. 180/3 Will any of the readers of *The Field* kindly inform me what spaniels are considered the best for woodcock-shooting—the Sussex, Clumber, Norfolk, &c.? **1867** 'STONEHENGE' *Dogs Brit. Is.* I. iii. 40 The Norfolk is one of the four descriptions of spaniels known as 'springers'. *Ibid.*, The Norfolk spaniel is now seldom to be obtained mute. **1945** C. L. B. HUBBARD *Observer's Bk. Dogs* 65 The old name of Norfolk Spaniel..is obsolete. **1896** *Junior Army & Navy Stores Catal.* p. xxxvi/2 Norfolk Jackets.. Suits. **1913** C. MACKENZIE *Sinister St.* I. I. vii. 112 An exciting Monday spent in buying a Norfolk suit and Eton collars. **1938** J. CARY *Castle Corner* iii. 116 He was seen every day walking about Knockeen with his solemn, fierce air and his smartest norfolk suits. **1964** *Kennel Gaz.* 419/2 On September 22, 1964, the General Committee of the Kennel Club agreed to register drop-eared Norwich Terriers as Norfolk Terriers, a separate breed and not a variety. **1968** C. G. E. WIMHURST *Bk. Terriers* xxi. 154 The Norfolk Terrier is one of the smallest of the terriers. **1971** F. HAMILTON *World Encycl. Dogs* 463 The Norfolk Terrier was, until September 1964, the drop-eared Norwich Terrier. *Ibid.* 467 There is little or no difference in character between the Norwich and the Norfolk.

d. *ellipt.* A Norfolk jacket. In pl., a Norfolk suit.

1902 E. NESBIT *Five Children & It* ii. 47 Nine pockets in my Norfolks. *Ibid.* viii. 215 A giant little boy—in Norfolks like my brother's. **1904** *T. Eaton & Co. Catal.* Spring & Summer 87/1 Brownie Norfolks, made of dark green Tweed. **1969** R. T. WILCOX *Dict. Costume* 248/1 The coat of the Duke of Norfolk's hunting suit, the first 'Norfolk', appeared in the 1880's with knickerbockers, a revival of knee breeches for day wear. **1970** S. J. PERELMAN *Baby, it's Cold Inside* 28 Where'd you get that Norfolk?.. Brooks hasn't carried that model in years.

Norfolk Island (nǭ·ɹfǒk əi·lænd). The name of a South Pacific island about five hundred miles north-west of New Zealand, used *attrib.* in **Norfolk (Island) pine** to designate a large conifer, *Araucaria heterophylla* (formerly *excelsa*), of the family Araucariaceæ, native to this island.

[**1778** J. R. FORSTER *Observations made during Voyage round World* v. 174 In the opposite, or Westernmost part of the South-Sea, lies a small isle, which has obtained the name of Norfolk-Island... Peculiar to this isle, and to the Eastern end of Caledonia, we found a species of coniferous tree, from the cones probably seeming to be a cypress: it grows here to a great size, and is very heavy but useful timber.] **1803** A. B. LAMBERT *Descr. Genus Pinus* I. 87 Norfolk Island Pine... This tree..is the tallest at present known. **1836** *Agriculturist's Manual* (P. Lawson & Son) 354 The Norfolk Island Pine..was first discovered by the celebrated circumnavigator Captain Cook, in his second voyage, on Norfolk Island and New Caledonia. **1854** J. C. PATTESON *Let.* 24 Aug. in C. M. Yonge *Life J. C. Patteson* (1874) I. v. 175, I shall write to you very often, and send you ferns and seeds, and tell you about the Norfolk Island pines. **1920** C. COLTMAN-ROGERS *Conifers* vi. 227 The Norfolk Island Pine..is fast becoming quite a common corner-window side-show in many English homes. **1933** *Bulletin* (Sydney) 27 Dec. 20/4 Almost as well known overseas as the eucalypts is the Norfolk Island pine. **1940** F. SARGESON *Man & his Wife* (1944) 91 A very old settled place with a row of Norfolk pines planted along the beach. **1966** *Times* 28 Mar. (Austral. Suppl.) p. xv/2 The home unit blocks are growing taller than the two Norfolk pines. **1968** *Southerly* XXVIII. 172 Halfway up the west face of the valley was a double row of Norfolk Island pines. **1974** A. MITCHELL *Field Guide Trees Britain* 57 One tender species, the Norfolk Island Pine, *A[raucaria] heterophylla* (*excelsa*), frequent as a pot plant and growing to 30 m at Tresco, Isles of Scilly.

norgestrel (nǭɹdʒe·strěl). *Pharm.* [f. *NOR- + *PRO)GEST(OGEN + *-rel*, prob. after *NORETHYNODREL.] An artificial steroid hormone, $C_{21}H_{28}O_2$, which has actions similar to those of progesterone and is used in some contraceptive pills.

1966 R. A. EDGREN et al. in *Internat. Jrnl. Fertility* XI. 389 Norgestrel..is a highly potent, totally synthetic progestogen chemically related to norethisterone and norethynodrel. **1974** *Nature* 8 Mar. 98/3 Ovranette contains a progestogen called norgestrel which is not converted to oestrogen in the body. In fact it is actively anti-oestrogenic, reversing some of the changes brought about by oestrogen.

‖**nori** (nǭə·ri). [Jap.] A Japanese food prepared from fronds of a seaweed of the genus *Porphyra*, eaten either fresh or dried, when they stick together to form small sheets. Cf. *LAVER *sb.*[1] 2.

1892 E. ARNOLD *Japonica* II. 86 Large slices of broiled *tai*, and *tsubo* or *nori*, sea-weed,..of which the Japanese are fonder than the foreigner is likely to prove. **1966** P. S. BUCK *People of Japan* (1968) xiv. 167 Rice covered with shredded egg and *nori*. **1973** A. BROINOWSKI *Take One Ambassador* xi. 174 We all collected *nori*, the seaweed along the beach.

no-right (nōᵘ,rəit). [f. NO *a.* + RIGHT *sb.*[1] 7.] In Jurisprudence, an obligation not to prevent the exercise of a privilege.

1913 W. N. HOHFELD in *Yale Law Jrnl.* XXIII. 32 As indicated in the above scheme of jural relations, a privilege is the opposite of a duty, and the correlative of a 'no-right'. **1923** —— *Fundamental Legal Conceptions* i. 39 The correlative of X's right that Y shall not enter on the land is Y's duty not to enter; but the correlative of X's privilege of entering himself is manifestly Y's 'no-right' that X shall not enter. **1938** M. RADIN in *Harvard Law Rev.* LI. 1150 The phrase 'no right' was subjected to a great deal of critical and destructive comment. 'A "no-right" ', one critic once declared, 'might be an elephant.' **1972** W. A. WILSON in *Juridical Rev.* Aug. 162 The correlative of a liberty is a no-right. The jural opposite of a right is a no-right.

nork (nǭɹk). *Austral. slang.* [See quot. 1966.] A woman's breast. Usu. *pl.*

1962 C. ROHAN *Delinquents* 157 Hello, honey, that sweater—one deep breath and your norks will be in my soup. **1966** BAKER *Austral. Lang.* (ed. 2) x. 215 *Nork*, a female breast, usually in plural. (Ex Norco Co-operative Ltd., a butter manufacturer in N.S.W.) The form *norg* is reported from Melbourne. **1969** *Private Eye* 21 Nov. 14 She's a top model with norks out to here. **1972** I. HAMILTON *Thrill Machine* iii. 17 She's only a body, all she's got is big norks. **1973** P. WHITE *Eye of Storm* 593 Hits herself in the eye with an independent nork it isn't any laughing matter.

Norland[2] (nǭ·ɹlănd). The name of the *Norland* Institute (see below), now the Norland Nursery Training College, used *attrib.* to designate the methods of child care taught there, a nurse trained in these methods, or a nursery following them. Also *ellipt.*, a Norland nurse.

[**1892** *St. James's Gaz.* 28 Sept. 12/2 It will be interesting to watch the experiment being made by Mrs. Walter Ward, who has just opened the Norland Institute for the training of kindergarten nurses. **1893** *Farm, Field & Fireside* 10 Feb. 460/1 The Norland Institute is situated at 9, Norland Place, Holland Park Gardens, London, W. It was started by Mrs. Walter Ward (Miss Emily Ford) for the training of ladies as children's nurses on Froebelian principles.] **1894** *Nursing Record & Hospital World* 7 Apr. 234/2 As a Norland Nurse, I have now had opportunity of seeing the value of the work to both employer and employée. **1899** *West-End* 23 Aug. 14/1 [The nurse] must receive a certificate, and do a further three months as probationer in a family.., or at some special Institution, before she dons her pretty neat brown uniform, and sallies forth as a fully-fledged Norland nurse. **1945** N. STREATFEILD *Saplings* ii. 19 Lena would have liked..a young Norland or the equivalent, looking smart in her uniform. **1959** *Times* 29 Sept. 2/7 Norland/Trained Nurse required. **1972** J. GATHORNE-HARDY *Rise & Fall of Brit. Nanny* vi. 178 From the first a Norland Nurse was forbidden to hit a child... This enlightened view..has remained a key feature of the Norland training. **1975** *Harpers & Queen* May 139/2 When they were eighteen months old they went to a Norland nursery. **1975** *Times* 4 Aug. 5/6 Each weekend they go to Barnwell with [the baby] Alexander and his Norland nanny.

norm. Add: **a.** (Further examples.)

1911 R. BROOKE *Coll. Poems* (1918) 154 All of the accents upon all the norms!—And ah! the stress on the penultimate! We never knew blank verse could have such feet. **1941** J. P. MARQUAND *H.M. Pulham, Esquire* iv. 44 Beatrice considered that I was utterly characteristic, completely true to type; once she called me a norm. **1961** S. R. HERMAN in J. A. Fishman *Readings Sociol. of Lang.* (1968) 505 Frequently the newcomer arrives with the belief that the prevailing norm about using Hebrew to the exclusion of other languages is more rigidly observed than is actually the case... Soon, however, the newcomer becomes aware of the wide range of deviations from the norm. **1964** M. ARGYLE *Psychol. & Social Probl.* iii. 38 One particular respect in which a group equilibrium develops is in the formation of norms—shared patterns of behaving, feeling and thinking. All social groups develop norms, particularly about matters connected with the group's main purposes and activities. ..When group members deviate from the norms, various kinds of persuasion, pressure and sanctions are exerted in order to make them conform. **1965** *Economist* 13 Feb. 645/2 The other vital point will be the 'norms' or 'guiding lights' [for incomes] recommended for each year.

b. (Earlier and later examples.) Also defined analogously for other quantities. [Introduced as L. *norma* by Gauss 1832, in *Commentationes Recentiores Soc. R. Scient. Gottingensis* VII. Class. math. 98.]

1856 W. R. HAMILTON *Notebook* in Halberstam & Ingram *Math. Papers Sir W. R. Hamilton* (1967) III. 657, $a + ib$ is said to be a complex number, when a and b are integers, and $i = \sqrt{-1}$; its norm is $a^2 + b^2$; and therefore the norm of a product is equal to the product of the norms of its factors. **1932** TURNBULL & AITKEN *Introd. Theory Canonical Matrices* iv. 38 This fundamental Hermitian inner product of $\bar{x}$ and x is often called the norm of the complex vector x... The square root of the norm, taken with positive sign, $(\bar{x}x)^{\frac{1}{2}}$, is sometimes denoted by $|x|$. **1949** A. ALBERT *Solid Analytic Geom.* i. 3 The norm of a vector P is defined to be the inner product $P \cdot P = x_1^2 + \ldots + x_n^2$. **1952** C. MØLLER *Theory of Relativity* iv. 99 It then follows ..that the 'square of the magnitude of the four-vector', or the norm of the vector, $\sum_i a_i^2 = \sum_i a'_i{}^2$, is an invariant. **1967** MACLANE & BIRKHOFF *Algebra* v. 187 Each quadratic field $Q(\sqrt{d})$, with the elements $\sigma = r + s\sqrt{d}$, has as automorphisms the identity and $\sigma \mapsto \bar{\sigma} = r - s\sqrt{d}$. The product $\sigma\bar{\sigma} = r^2 + s^2 d$ is called the norm $N(\sigma)$ of σ.

(ii) The positive square root of the quantity defined in sense b; more generally, a quantity defined on a vector space over the real or complex field which represents a generalization of the concept of length or magnitude and has the properties that $\|u\| > 0$ if $u \neq 0$ ($\|u\|$ being the norm of the vector u), $\|u\| = 0$ if $u = 0$, $\|au\| = |a|\,\|u\|$ (a being a real number), and $\|u+v\| \leqslant \|u\|+\|v\|$ (v being another vector).

1921 *Proc. Nat. Acad. Sci.* VII. 84 The notion of norm or numerical value of a complex quantity, $c = a + b\sqrt{-1}$, namely, $|c| = \sqrt{(a^2 + b^2)}$, as it arises in algebra, has a more or less immediate generalization to more extensive matric systems. **1951** P. R. HALMOS *Introd. Hilbert Space* i. 13 The norm of a vector α in the inner product space..coincides with the absolute value of the complex number α. **1955** L. F. BORON tr. *I. P. Natanson's Theory of Functions of Real Variable* I. vii. 199 Let $f(x) \in L_p$. The number $\|f\| = \sqrt[p]{\left(\int_a^b |f(x)|^p dx\right)}$ is called the norm of the function $f(x)$ (considered as an element of L_p). **1962** KACINSKAS & COUNTS tr. *L. S. Pontryagin's Ordinary Differential Equations* iv. 152 The maximum modulus of this function..will be called its norm. **1965** PATTERSON & RUTHERFORD *Elem. Abstract Algebra* v. 184 A norm can be defined in a vector space having an inner product by writing $\|x\| = \sqrt{(x \cdot x)}$... There exist norms which cannot be expressed in this way in terms of an inner product. In the case where an inner product exists, it is clear that the length of a vector satisfies the requirements for a norm. *Ibid.* 185 Let $M_{2,2}(\mathbf{C})$ be the vector space of 2×2 matrices over the complex field. Then the mapping $\left[\begin{smallmatrix} a & b \\ c & d \end{smallmatrix}\right] \to \max(|a|, |b|, |c|, |d|)$ defines a norm in $M_{2,2}(\mathbf{C})$. The mapping $\left[\begin{smallmatrix} a & b \\ c & d \end{smallmatrix}\right] \to \sqrt{(|a|^2+|b|^2+|c|^2+|d|^2)}$ defines another norm. **1970** F. A. MATSEN *Vector Spaces & Algebras* i. 11 The norm N_c of c is defined by $N_c = (cc^*)^{1/2} = \sqrt{(a^2 + b^2)}$.

c. In Communist countries, a standard unit of work prescribed.

1935 S. & B. WEBB *Soviet Communism* II. ix. 706 They [*sc.* piece-work rates] are, in some cases, even progressive, the rate rising by stages for output beyond the norm. **1952** *Manch. Guardian* 6 June, Stakhanovite women miners in the Donetz basin are performing four, nine, and eleven norms each. **1959** *Times* 12 Mar. 13/6 This moulding process may vary from the crudest regimentation and subordination..to factory-like specification and 'norms' to mere pilotage..towards the Marxist haven.

2. *Petrol.* A hypothetical mineral composition of a rock calculated by assigning the compounds present to certain relatively simple minerals in accordance with prescribed rules.

1902 [see *MODE *sb.* 5 b]. **1932** A. JOHANNSEN *Descr. Petrogr. Ign. Rocks* II. 272 (*heading*) Table 135. Norms of rhyolites. **1973** *Jrnl. Petrol.* XIV. 35 The norms used are not based on stoichiometric formulae..but approach the compositions of the constituents as actually found in natural rocks. *Ibid.* 250 The C.I.P.W. norms which accompany the analyses were calculated using an Fe_2O_3/FeO ratio estimated to be appropriate for the quartz-fayalite-magnetite-buffered charges.

3. *attrib.* and *Comb.*

1934 *Archit. Rev.* LXXVI. 42/1 It represents a return to the machine, regarded realistically and as mechanism to produce mechanical norm-types. **1958** M. ARGYLE *Relig. Behaviour* v. 57 All these findings can be regarded as instances of social learning, mediated by the usual processes of persuasion, imitation and norm-formation. **1961** J. N. FINDLAY *Values & Intentions* ix. 399 The religious object..must tend more and more towards the pattern of a detached, suprapersonal, norm-setting *mind*. **1964** I. L. HOROWITZ *New Sociology* 32 Why do people choose rapid industrialization with its attendant psychological turmoil over social stability and norm adherence? **1966** *Mathematical Rev.* XXXI. 8/2 Since norm-sentences are neither true nor false, logical connectives undergo reinterpretation. **1969** J. F. SZWED in Halpert & Story *Christmas Mumming in Newfoundland* 116 During socialization, each person acquires an awareness of social sanctions and at the same time becomes 'norm-oriented'.

norm (nǭɹm), *v. Math.* [f. the sb.] **1.** *trans.* = *NORMALIZE *v.* 3 a. ?*Obs.*

1931 P. DIENES *Taylor Series* viii. 274 We 'norm' the mapping with respect to $u = a$ by requiring that $a_1 k = 1$. **1941** R. V. CHURCHILL *Fourier Series* iii. 38 The functions of the set are normed by dividing each function $g_n(x)$ by $[N(g_n)]^{1/2}$.

2. *trans.* [back-formation from *NORMED *a.*] To define a norm on (a space).

1959 L. F. BORON tr. *Naimark's Normed Rings* i. 73 The space $X/\mathfrak{M}$, normed by formula (1), will be called a normed factor-space. **1964** D. E. BROWN tr. *Kantorovich & Akilov's Functional Analysis in Normed Spaces* ii. 51 The metric spaces. . are also linear sets and can be normed. **1972** A. G. HOWSON *Handbk. Terms used in Algebra & Analysis* xxii. 111 The vector space $\mathscr{L}(E,F)$ can be normed in the following way.

Hence **no·rming** *vbl. sb.*

1967 L. RÉDEI *Algebra* I. iv. 307 In different rings norming is carried out in different ways.

normal, *a.* and *sb.* **A.** *adj.* **2. b.** Substitute for def.: (i) Of a salt: containing no acidic hydrogen.

1860 W. A. MILLER *Elements Chem.* (ed. 2) II. x. 338 The most usual form of salt, in which 1 atom of a protoxide is united with 1 atom of an acid to form the normal salt. **1869** [in Dict.]. **1915** P. W. OSCROFT *Adv. Inorg. Chem.* iv. 38 It must not be understood that normal salts are always neutral bodies with regard to their action with litmus; this is far from being the case. **1965** B. J. MOODY *Comp. Inorg. Chem.* xiii. 188/2 Both sodium sulphate and trisodium orthophosphate are normal salts.

(ii) Of (the concentration of) a solution: having one gramme-equivalent of solute per litre.

1863 F. SUTTON *Syst. Handbk. Volumetric Anal.* 19 The normal solutions prepared on the gramme system are equally applicable for that of the grain, and *vice versâ*. **1892** [in Dict.]. **1915** P. W. OSCROFT *Adv. Inorg. Chem.* v. 48, 25 c.c. of a caustic potash solution required 15 c.c. of a normal sulphuric acid solution for neutralization. **1955** C. R. N. STROUTS et al. *Analyt. Chem.* I. xii. 258 A solution of one-tenth normal strength is designated as N/10. **1967** R. FULTON *Course in Titrimetric Anal.* ii. 7 Normal solutions are more widely used [than molar solutions].

(iii) (Composed of molecules) containing an unbranched chain of carbon atoms in an alkane molecule or alkyl radical.

1869 C. SCHORLEMMER in *Proc. R. Soc.* XVII. 373, I had obtained the normal propyl alcohol by this method. **1871** —— *Ibid.* XIX. 487 The first group, which I called normal paraffins, contain the carbon atoms linked together in a single chain. **1876** [in Dict.]. **1932** I. D. GARARD *Introd. Org. Chem.* ii. 20 At average room temperature, those normal paraffin hydrocarbons containing four carbon atoms or less are gaseous, and those from five to seventeen, liquids. **1968** J. A. MONICK *Alcohols* iii. 86 If the [parent] hydrocarbon consists of an unbranched carbon chain, the equivalent primary alcohol is called normal.

c. *Physics.* Of, pertaining to, or being a mode of vibration in which every particle executes simple harmonic motion at the same frequency and in phase (or 180° out of phase).

1867 THOMSON & TAIT *Treat. Nat. Philos.* ii. 274 There are in general. . *i* distinct determinate displacements, which we shall call the normal displacements, fulfilling the condition, that if any one of them be produced alone, and the system then left to itself for an instant at rest, this displacement will diminish and increase periodically according to a simple harmonic function of the time, and consequently every particle of the system will execute a simple harmonic movement in the same period. **1877** [see *MODE *sb.* 4 c]. **1927** TOFT & KERSEY *Theory of Machines* xiv. 362 Any type of oscillation other than a normal mode may be considered as being the sum of a number of motions each of which is a normal mode. **1942** SYNGE & GRIFFITH *Princ. Mech.* vii. 209 The periods and frequencies of normal modes are called normal periods and normal frequencies. **1962** P. J. & B. DURRANT *Introd. Adv. Inorg. Chem.* viii. 229 There may be several normal vibrations of different frequencies characteristic of a given molecule. **1971** *Amer. Jrnl. Physics* XXXIX. 484/2 The major purpose of this paper is to determine. . the normal-mode longitudinal-vibration frequencies of the chain.

d. *Geol.* Applied to a fault and to faulting in which the relative downward movement occurred in the strata situated on the upper side of the fault plane. So *normal-faulted* adj.

1876 A. H. GREEN *Geol.* xi. 382 The direction of the hade in a normal fault. **1878** J. LECONTE in *Amer. Jrnl. Sci. & Arts* XVI. 99 Thus arise two distinct slips: In the one, the more common or normal, the strata drop on the hanging-wall side of the fissure, in the other or reverse fault, the strata on the hanging-wall side is slidden up and over the other side by the sheer force of the horizontal pressure. **1902** *Jrnl. Geol.* X. 873 Orographic blocks may. . display an arrangement in zigzags or *en échelon*, which it is difficult to explain upon any other basis than that of normal faulting. **1944** A. HOLMES *Princ. Physical Geol.* vi. 79 Normal faults involve an extension of the faulted beds. **1974** FLINT & SKINNER *Physical Geol.* iv. 293/2 Normal faults are caused by tensional forces that tend to pull the crust apart, and also by forces tending to expand the crust by pushing it upward from below. *Ibid.* 294/1 In the Earth's crust are many zones that have been deformed repeatedly by normal faulting. **1975** *Nature* 1 May 22/2 This part represents a tensional arm. . bifurcating into normal-faulted shear zones south of Sinai.

e. *Statistics.* = *GAUSSIAN *a.* b.

1893 K. PEARSON in *Nature* 26 Oct. 615/2 As verification note that for the normal probability curve $3\mu_2^2 = \mu_4$ and $\mu_3 = 0$. **1894** —— in *Phil. Trans. R. Soc.* A. CLXXXV. 72 A frequency-curve, which, for practical purposes, can be represented by the error curve, will for the remainder of this paper be termed a normal curve. **1897** *Proc. R. Soc.* LXII. 176 A random selection from a normal distribution. **1920** [see *GAUSSIAN *a.* b]. **1928** T. C. FRY *Probability & its Engin. Uses* viii. 244 Both the Binomial and the Poisson Laws, under suitable conditions, approach the Normal Law as a limit. **1938** A. E. WAUGH *Elem. Statistical Method* vi. 94 Many phenomena of biology, economics, psychology, education, etc., even though not exactly normal in distribution, can be described roughly by the normal curve. **1951** DIXON & MASSEY *Introd. Statistical Anal.* v. 63 Many practical problems have statistical answers based on the 'assumption' that the distribution of the population is normal. . . The truth of this assumption may be checked by plotting the sample cumulative-percentage points on normal-probability paper. **1968** *Brit. Med. Bull.* XXIV. 211/1 One of these [alternatives for small samples] consists simply in plotting the individual sample values. . on 'Normal-probability' graph paper—this is a special graph paper whose vertical scale has been 'stretched' in such a way that the S-shaped cumulative Normal curve is transformed graphically into a straight line.

f. *Med.* Of a saline solution: containing the same concentration of sodium chloride as the blood.

1895 *Jrnl. Physiol.* XVIII. 50 Neither can the injection of normal saline be of much benefit. **1924** L. CLENDENING *Mod. Methods Treatment* ii. 153 Normal salt solution given in subcutaneous areolar tissue (beneath the breasts or in the thighs) or intravenously is very frequently used in surgical shock. *Ibid.*, In normal salt solution with glucose any concentration could be used, without hemolysis. **1970** F. N. DOUGLAS *Essentials Pharmacology in Clinical Nursing* iii. 22 Physiologic normal saline (0·9 per cent) is used for treating dehydration in the absence of acidosis.

g. Physics. *normal state* = *ground state* (*GROUND *sb.* 18).

See also sense *2 i.

1914 [see *N I. 4 b]. **1922** A. D. UDDEN tr. *Bohr's Theory of Spectra* II. ii. 32 All the atoms exist in that stationary state in which the value of the energy is a minimum. This state I shall call the normal state. **1952** R. W. DITCHBURN *Light* xvii. 550 The atom very quickly makes a transition back to the normal state re-emitting the radiation. **1963** G. F. LOTHIAN *Electrons in Atoms* iii, Mercury atoms have quantized energy levels . . above the normal or 'ground' state.

h. *spec.* = heterosexual.

1914 E. M. FORSTER *Maurice* (1971) xxii. 106 Against my will I have become normal. I cannot help it.

i. *Physics.* Pertaining to or characteristic of a substance that is not in the superconducting state.

1927 *Nature* 3 Dec. 818/2 The resistance became normal at a certain critical value of the magnetic field. **1938** D. SHOENBERG *Superconductivity* i. 4 Apart from the loss of resistance the metal appeared to have identical properties both in the superconducting and normal states. **1955** H. B. G. CASIMIR in W. Pauli *Niels Bohr* 119 The theory describing the normal state when the absolute temperature tends towards zero is extremely simple. **1968** C. G. KUPER *Introd. Theory Superconductivity* i. 6 An upper bound for the resistance in the superconducting state can be established. If R_n is the resistance of the specimen when normal, then $R/R_n < 10^{-15}$.

j. *normal forest*, a collection of trees at various stages of development, organized to provide a regular yield of timber.

1928 R. S. TROUP *Silvicultural Systems* i. 1 With the object of ensuring future sustained yields the ideal of the normal forest has been created. Such a forest contains a regular and complete succession of age-classes. . in correct proportion, density, and distribution. . . The normal forest can hardly be said to exist in reality; rather it should be regarded as an ideal to be aimed at. **1962** C. E. HART *Practical Forestry* vi. 109 The term normal forest is used for a forest or woodland or group of woodlands containing a regular and complete succession of age classes, from the youngest to the oldest.

k. *Physics.* Applied to a component of a superfluid that is regarded as not having the properties of a superfluid and as co-existing at the atomic level with a component that does have them, in a proportion that decreases with decreasing temperature.

1947 L. TIZAS in *Physical Rev.* LXXII. 842/2 The density [of the Bose-Einstein liquid]. . will be subdivided into two parts: $\rho = \rho_n + \rho_s$ where ρ_n is the density connected with the 'molecules' of the gas and ρ_s refers to the 'background' in which the molecules are moving. The subscripts refer to 'normal' and 'superfluid', a terminology which will be explained below. *Ibid.* 853/2 In this 'anomalous' region [*sc.* between about 1°K and 2·19°K] the liquid is a mixture of a normal component (like helium I) and a superfluid component. **1967** J. WILKS *Properties of Liquid & Solid Helium* iii. 39 Two baths of liquid helium II. . at slightly different temperatures. . are connected by a fine capillary. The capillary almost completely inhibits the flow of the normal fluid, on the other hand the superfluid having zero viscosity, may pass freely. **1975** *Nature* 10 Apr. 480/3 At a finite temperature the superfluid phase [of ⁴He] behaves like a mixture of two fluids: a 'normal' component, behaving like an ordinary viscous liquid. .; and a 'superfluid' component,. . closely associated with the atoms in the Bose condensate.

3. (Later examples.) Also *ellipt.* = *normal school.*

1888 *Nat. Educ. Assoc. U.S. Addresses & Proc. 1887* 478 We say that normal-school training is as essential to good teaching as the work of a medical school to the physician. *Ibid.* 502 A course of normal instruction. **1925** in P. W. Slosson *Great Crusade* (1931) xv. 431 Unlawful for any teacher in any of the universities, normals, and all other public schools. . to teach. . that man has descended from a lower order of animals. **1939** H. G. WELLS *Holy Terror* IV. i. 359 An increasing number of women are taking up professions now; at architecture, catering, various industries, normal teaching. . they are practically as good as men or better. **1960** P. E. BURRUP *Teacher & Public School Syst.* IV. vii. 275 'Normal Schools' for the preparation of teachers. . have been replaced by teachers' colleges, liberal-arts colleges, and universities, each with a college of education. **1960** CURTIS & BOULTWOOD *Introd. Hist. Eng. Educ.* xii. 277 In that year [*sc.* 1836] a normal school of design was established. *Ibid.* 278 The Normal School of Design became the Royal College of Art in 1896.

4. Philos. *normal form* (see quot. 1950).

1948 *Mind* LVII. 173 He [*sc.* Boole] introduced two notions which are of the greatest importance, namely, that of a *truth-function* and that of a *normal form.* **1950** L. M. HAMMOND et al. tr. *Hilbert & Ackermann's Math. Logic* i. §3. 11 (*heading*) Normal form for logical expressions. *Ibid.* 12 Any combination of sentences can be brought into a certain normal form by means of equivalence transformations;. . this normal form consists of a conjunction of disjunctions in which each component of the disjunction is either an elementary sentence or the negation of one. **1952** *Mind* LXI. 564 The procedure is to be applied to normal forms, reduction to which is a matter of propositional logic. **1965** E. J. LEMMON *Beginning Logic* 189 Normal forms have a certain interest in connection with the truth-table method, since they provide an independent test as to whether a wff is tautologous, contingent, or inconsistent; and they are also used in certain proofs of the completeness of the propositional calculus. **1973** J. J. ZEMAN *Modal Logic* viii. 117 The normal-form theorem holds for systems LS1° and LS1.

B. *sb.* **4.** (Later example.)

1957 M. SPARK *Comforters* v. 114 She snapped back at him. And so, in his need for their relations to return to a nice normal, he said peaceably, [etc.].

5. A normal variety of anything; that which, or a person who, is healthy and is not impaired in any way.

1894 W. BATESON *Study of Variation* 17 For the belief that such races are descended from the putative normal scarcely ever rests on proof. **1901** *Amer. Jrnl. Psychol.* XII. 235 The blind rats learned the original task as well as the normals. **1908** *Daily Chron.* 14 Oct. 4/4 We might divide them [*sc.* criminals] into three groups:— Normals, Juveniles and children; and The degenerate. **1916** J. S. HALDANE *Organism & Environment* (1917) iv. 102 The normals of anatomy are not mere physical structures, nor are the normals of physiology mere averages: they are manifestations of the life of an organism regarded as a whole. **1940** *Psychol. Bull.* XXXVII. 425 Scales may be successively discovered and standardized on a reservoir sample of normals. **1964** M. CRITCHLEY *Developmental Dyslexia* vii. 40 Measuring the reaction time. . in normals and in dyslexics. **1973** *Nature* 12 Jan. 99/1 The response of lymphocytes from normals or leukaemics to low (7μg ml.$^{-1}$) doses of PHA.

b. A heterosexual person.

1966 *New Statesman* 29 Apr. 623/3 He [*sc.* Coward]'s working for the same kind of audience—Knightsbridge normals—and still going as near the knuckle as he thinks they can abide. **1971** M. MCCARTHY *Birds of America* 304 A female *clocharde* had reason to shrink from 'normals'.

normalcy. Add: Now freq. (esp. in U.S.) used in the senses of NORMALITY.

1920 W. G. HARDING in F. L. Allen *Only Yesterday* (1931) ii. 41 America's present need is not heroics but healing; not nostrums but normalcy; not revolution but restoration. **1929** G. N. CLARK in *S.P.E. Tract* XXXIII. 417 If. . 'normalcy' is ever to become an accepted word it will presumably be because the late President Harding did not know any better. **1932** G. K. CHESTERTON *Sidelights* II. xiv. 182 Life in a modern town, whatever else it is, is not Normalcy. **1939** *John o' London's* 9 June 369/1 That insistent normalcy of men who cannot afford to permit themselves to be thrown off balance. **1951** M. MCLUHAN *Mech. Bride* 47/1 Professor Kinsey's surveys, with their economist-like normalcy charts. **1957** V. J. KEHOE *Technique Film & T.V. Make-up* i. 17 On stage, where strong lights and distance of the actors from the audience wash out and flatten the features, make-up restores to the face the look of normalcy in both color and contour. **1965** *New Statesman* 7 May 733/1 A kind of spectral normalcy.

normalism (nǭ·ɹmăliz'm). *rare.* [f. NORMAL *a.* and *sb.* + -ISM.] The quality or state of being normal.

1891 F. W. BAIN *Antichrist* ii. 113 The planing away of all gnarled and knotty characteristics, the reducing each individual to precisely the same external appearance. This is the essence and the consequence of the impulse to normalism.

normality. Add: **1. b.** *spec.* in *Statistics* (cf. *NORMAL *a.* and *sb.* A. 2 e).

1928 *Amer. Jrnl. Psychol.* XL. 348 We can change 0·93 into a P.E. [*sc.* probable error] by multiplying by 0·845 (assuming normality of distribution). **1938** A. E. WAUGH *Elem. Statistical Method* vi. 95 In most statistical problems there is no a priori reason for expecting normality of distribution—no reason for believing in advance that the data will be distributed as are the coefficients of the expansion $(\frac{1}{2}+\frac{1}{2})^n$. **1968** *Brit. Med. Bull.* XXIV. 211/1 The assumption of Normality is central to the most powerful statistical techniques. **1974** *Nature* 22 Mar. 288/1 A weighted least squares analysis of the two sets of correlations. . provides (given normality) a test of goodness of fit of the model.

2. *Chem.* The concentration of a solution as a proportion of the normal concentration.

1903 *Sci. Abstr.* VI. 315 Boric acid was agitated. . with an excess of aqueous hydrochloric acids of different normalities. **1928** A. W. WELLINGS *Volumetric Analysis* ii. 41 The normality of the acid solution will be 0·1N. × 18·6/50. **1966** *McGraw-Hill Encycl. Sci. & Technol.* III. 361/2 In double-decomposition reactions normality may be an ambiguous concept unless referred to a specific reaction. **1972** *Nature* 8 Sept. 69/3 At higher concentra-

tions of the salt. .the viscosity was considerably smaller (1·60 at a normality of 0·50).

normalizable (nǭ·ɹmăləizăb'l), *a.* [f. NORMALIZ(E *v.* + -ABLE.] Capable of being normalized.

1939 V. ROJANSKY *Introd. Quantum Mech.* i. 37 If *u* and all of its derivatives approach zero when $|x| \to \infty$, and if $\int_{-\infty}^{\infty} \bar{u}u\,dx$ is finite, we call *u* a normalizable function (this use of the term is not standard in the literature). **1955** O. KLEIN in W. Pauli *Niels Bohr* 116 There may be some reason to expect that the most obvious formulation of the interaction problem on these lines should already give rise to a normalizable theory, the effect of the 'wrong' states being limited to further infinite contributions to the mass and charge of the electron. **1968** *Physics Bull.* Nov. 373/2 A normalizable state ϕ_0.

normalization. Add to def.: More widely, the process of normalizing (in any sense). (Further examples.)

1916 *Jrnl. Iron & Steel Inst.* XCIV. 10 It is not suggested to abandon the term 'normalise', but to define normalisation as a treatment which will give equalisation and not metal of abnormal variations. **1929** [see *NORMALIZE *v.* 3 a]. **1944** GREGORY & SIMONS *Heat-Treatment Steel* xx. 273 The steels not requiring normalization after forging should be cooled off in lime, then annealed. **1959** E. M. MCCORMICK *Digital Computer Primer* xi. 155 To facilitate normalization, many computers have a special instruction. .that counts the positions the number must be shifted left to be normalized. This count is then used to modify the exponent. **1967** C. L. WRENN *Word & Symbol* p. xii, The problem of normalisation for Old English still requires scholarly attention. **1972** BERGMAN & BRUCKNER *Introd. Computers & Computer Programming* vi. 169 The only exception to the normalization rule is zero; there are many ways in which we can represent zero. **1972** P. W. WILLIAMS *Numerical Computation* ix. 162 One method of normalization is to divide all the elements of a vector by the largest element so that vectors have unity as the largest element. Alternatively, each element could be divided by the sum of the squares of the elements of the vector in which case vectors have unit length. **1973** *Amer. Speech 1969* XLIV. 220 Two sociolinguistic problems: immigrant bilingualism and language normalization.

b. *Psychol.* The subconscious process whereby the mental image of a shape, pattern, etc., is changed to resemble something more familiar; also *attrib.* So **normali·zing** *vbl. sb.*

1929 J. J. GIBSON in *Jrnl. Experimental Psychol.* XII. 3 The first kind [of change] he [*sc.* Wulf] calls *normalizing* (Normalizierung), *i.e.* a change (presumably in the reproductions) in the direction of a familiar object. **1935** K. KOFFKA *Princ. Gestalt Psychol.* xi. 499 Normalizing occurs when the reproductions approach successively a familiar form. *Ibid.*, Autonomous changes occur against the forces of normalization and pointing. **1970** L. ZUSNE *Visual Perception of Form* vii. 312 Making the reproduced figure resemble some well-known shape (normalizing). **1971** J. HOCHBERG in Woodworth & Schlosberg *Experimental Psychol.* (1972) xii. 469 The normalization effects might thus simply be instances of the figural after effects produced by satiation.

c. *Politics.* The achieving of 'normal' or stable political relationships between two countries, freq. between a major power and a weaker or dependent country.

1938 *Times Review of 1937* p. vii/1 The 'normalization' of Polish-German relations. **1955** *Times* 22 Aug. 5/3 The Yugoslav Press has been complaining for some time that the process of 'normalization' with Albania was lagging behind other east European countries. **1956** *Ann. Reg. 1955* 260 'Normalization' of relations with the satellites. **1962** *Daily Tel.* 18 Sept. 12/2 President Tito can be well pleased. 'Normalisation' has been attained without compromise of Jugoslavia's freedom of action, in defence of which he broke with Stalin. **1968** *Economist* 7 Sept. 33/1 It will permit Mr. Dubcek, his party leadership and government to resume the road towards what is laughingly called 'normalisation' just so long as they stick to Moscow's interpretation of normality.

normalize, *v.* Add: **1. b.** *intr.* To become normal.

1923 *Contemp. Rev.* Mar. 366 If a rise in the price of tin should follow on the already normalising price of materials.

2. *Metallurgy.* To heat (steel) to above the transformation range (about 700°C or more) and allow to cool in still air at room temperature, so as to remove any effects of strain-hardening, produce a finer grain structure, and improve the mechanical properties and machinability.

1902 *Jrnl. Iron & Steel Inst.* LXI. plate XIV (*caption*) Mr. Stead's Austenite normalized. **1916** *Ibid.* XCIV. 26 (*heading*) Effect of heating to 850°C., quenching in oil and tempering at 550°C., compared with the same steels simply normalized by heating to 1000°C. and cooling in air. **1937** R. T. ROLFE *Steels for User* vi. 114 Since quenching in a liquid medium was for a long time prohibited, these castings were either annealed or normalised, followed by a tempering process. **1970** E. N. SIMONS *Dict. Ferrous Metals* 155 The rate of cooling differs according to the mass of the piece, a thin cross-section cooling more rapidly than a thick, so that in the large masses the core is annealed rather than normalized. **1971** B. SCHARF *Engin. & its Lang.* ii. 13 Steel is often normalised before hardening or machining.

3. a. Chiefly *Math.* and *Physics.* To multiply (a series, function, or variable) by a factor that makes the norm or some associated quantity (as an integral) equal to a particular value, usu. unity.

1921 *Proc. Lond. Math. Soc.* XX. 125 The sequence $\{\psi_n(x)\}$ being normalised and orthogonal. **1929** CONDON & MORSE *Quantum Mech.* i. 30 Of course, when $\Psi\bar{\Psi}$ is to be used as probability it has to be so normalized, by choice of a constant multiplier for Ψ, that $\int \Psi\bar{\Psi}\,dv = 1$. . . The same normalization is required from the distributed charge standpoint to express the fact that the total charge is *e*. **1934** W. V. HOUSTON *Princ. Math. Physics* ix. 134 A function can be normalized by multiplying it by a constant. When it is normalized, $\int_a^b R_i^2\,dx = 1$. **1956** *Math. Tables & Other Aids to Computation* X. 2 The fundamental sequence was normalized so that $-1 \leqslant u_j \leqslant 1$. **1961** POWELL & CRASEMANN *Quantum Mech.* ix. 286 A vector of unit norm is said to be normalized. . . Every nonzero vector can be normalized. **1975** *Nature* 13 Feb. 563/1 To normalise variations among tissues, responses are reported as percentage of the maximum increase, calculated for each preparation.

b. *Computers.* To express (a number in floating-point representation) in the standard form as regards the position of the radix point, which is usually immediately preceding the first non-zero digit.

1946 *Ann. Computation Lab. Harvard Univ.* I. 495 The quantity to be normalized lies in storage counter A. **1957** D. D. MCCRACKEN *Digital Computer Programming* xvii. 205 The first two steps convert the code number into an unnormalized floating point form. The third does nothing but normalize it, i.e., it brings the first nonzero digit into position three of the accumulator. **1962** HUSKEY & KORN *Computer Handbk.* xv. 23 It is desirable to obtain as many significant figures in the answers as possible. In floating-point systems this can be accomplished by normalizing the nonzero numbers at each step. **1973** H. DINTER *Introd. Computing* v. 167 The decimal exponent will be a value that is adjusted for normalizing the number. For example, if the number 26·5 is to be expressed in normalized form, it will be presented as $\cdot265 \times 10^2$.

normalizer (nǭ·ɹmăləizəɹ). [f. NORMALIZE *v.* + -ER[1].] Someone or something that normalizes.

1926 *Heating & Ventilating Mag.* (U.S.) Oct. 110/1 (*caption*) The Sjostrom Atmospheric Normalizer. *Ibid.* 110/2 When the Normalizer is operating it moves about 800 cu. ft. of air per minute. **1946** *House Beautiful* Nov. 290 If you live in a hard-water area, it helps to use a good water normalizer. .in the water. **1960** P. DORF tr. M. M. Guxman in J. A. Fishman *Readings Sociol. of Lang.* (1968) 773 The puristic strivings of the German normalizers of the 17th and 18th centuries were ridiculed, the striving of many normalizers both in Western as well as Eastern countries to counteract the appearance of the new vital tendencies of the colloquial variety of the language was underscored. *Ibid.* 777 It is a known fact that the French normalizers of the 15th and 16th centuries oriented themselves towards the language of Paris, but towards the form in which it was spoken at court.

normalizing (nǭ·ɹmăləiziŋ), *vbl. sb.* [f. NORMALIZ(E *v.* + -ING[1].] The action of the vb. NORMALIZE (in Dict. and Suppl.).

1909 *Jrnl. Iron & Steel Inst.* LXXIX. 350 (*heading*) Normalising. **1935** A. B. KINZEL in *Symp. Welding Iron & Steel* (Iron & Steel Inst.) II. iii. 424 Complete normalising or stress-relieving of the entire structure should be considered essential if high internal stress exists. **1970** O. DOPPING *Computers & Data Processing* vii. 112 In computers with built-in operations for floating-point arithmetic. .normalizing usually occurs as a special operation.

normally, *adv.* Add: **5.** *Statistics.* In accordance with the normal distribution.

1928 T. C. FRY *Probability & its Engin. Uses* viii. 243 It is absurd to speak of a man of negative height:. .it simply cannot occur. Yet if height were distributed normally, the second property of the Law would assign a finite probability to this absurdity. **1951** DIXON & MASSEY *Introd. Statistical Anal.* v. 63 Often a research worker has sufficient data and enough experience. .to be able to specify the type of transformation of measurement which will give a normally distributed variable. **1971** *Nature* 3 Sept. 19/1, I take as my datum the fact that Englishmen are normally distributed in height with a mean of 5 feet 8 inches.

normalness (nǭ·ɹmălnės). *rare.* [f. NORMAL *a.* and *sb.* + -NESS.] = NORMALITY.

1854 GEO. ELIOT tr. *Feuerbach's Essence Christianity* xvi. 159 The agreement of others is therefore my criterion of the normalness, the universality, the truth of my thoughts. **1972** *Language* XLVIII. 314 We suspect that for some speakers, some of the sentences that we have claimed to be 'odd' will sound quite normal. This is to be expected if the oddness or normalness of a given stress contour depends partly on the speaker's ability to provide a satisfactory context.

Normandy (nǭ·ɹmăndi). [Name of a region of northern France.] *Normandy butter*: butter made in Normandy. Also *ellipt.*

1902 J. T. LAW *Grocer's Man.* (ed. 2) 632/2 Normandy butter. **1962** L. DEIGHTON *Ipcress File* ii. 19, I. .bought. . some Normandy butter and garlic sausage. **1973** *Guardian* 26 Jan. 9/1 'Butter is half the price here, even French butter,' she said, packing pounds of best cream Normandy into her shopping trolley. **1975** R. BUTLER *Where all Girls are Sweeter* i. 5 There was still a slab of Sainsbury's Normandy butter.

b. *Normandy vellum*, a strong, hand-made paper designed to imitate the qualities of parchment.

1935 S. BECKETT *Echo's Bones*, This edition is limited to 327 copies of which 25 on Normandy vellum signed by the author are numbered 1 to xxv. **1968** *Amer. N. & Q.* VI. 158/1 There were only 212 copies [of the magazine *Pages*] of which 12. .are on Normandy vellum.

Normanist. Add: **b.** (See quot. 1970.) Also as *adj.*

1943 G. VERNADSKY *Anc. Russia* VII. iv. 276 Let us then turn to an appraisal of the results of the tournement of the *Norsephiles* ('Normanists') and *Mysosnorses* ('Anti-Normanists'), so famous in the annals of the Russian historiography. *Ibid.* 277 The whole argument of the first Normanists was based on the premise that the very name of Rus spread from north to south and not otherwise. **1968** G. JONES *Hist. Vikings* III. iv. 247 The most readable 'Normanist' statement is still V. Thomsen's *Relations.* G. Vernadsky presents a summary of evidence for the 'anti-Normanist' view. *Ibid.* 264 To the disengaged it may well seem that the Normanist case has been as over-presented by a majority of Scandinavian historians as it has been played down by a majority of the historians of Russia. **1970** FOOTE & WILSON *Viking Achievement* vi. 220 Scholars have tended to side with one of two factions; the first firmly believing in the importance of the Scandinavian element in the founding of Russian towns and of the Russian state itself, the second discounting this influence almost completely (these two schools of thought are labelled in technical literature by the unfortunate terms 'Normanist' and 'anti-Normanist'). *Ibid.*, Discussion of the validity of this evidence is at the basis of the Normanist controversy. *Ibid.* 222 Both Normanists and anti-Normanists are more or less agreed that Ladoga was at one time dominated by Scandinavian traders.

normative, *a.* Add: **a.** (Later examples.) Deriving from, expressing, or implying a general standard, norm, or ideal. Also *absol.*

1897 J. H. GULLIVER et al. tr. *Wundt's Ethics* I. 1 The normative point of view considers objects with reference to *definite rules*, which find expression in them, and to which they are at the same time required to conform. *Ibid.*, From the normative point of view, it is the purpose of the inquirer to estimate the relative values of facts. **1912** L. BLOOMFIELD in *Jrnl. Eng. & Germ. Philol.* XI. 622 The scientific study of language has nothing to do with the normative (i.e. purely pedagogic) purpose of teaching people of ('fixing') the use or the better use of a literary language. **1931** M. R. COHEN *Reason & Nature* III. iv. 403 Instead of refuting the normative standpoint of the old natural law, these writers substitute an unconscious natural law of their own. **1932** E. C. TOLMAN *Purposive Behav.* v. xxiii. 389 Relations to pre-individual or 'normative psychology'. *Ibid.* 397 Normative psychologies. .tend to take an average (normal) individual or. .sample of individuals. .and then to apply all sorts of different stimuli. **1941** [see *GENETIC *a.* 1 f]. **1954** *Mind* LXIII. 264 As examples of 'normatives' he gives 'I ought to go' [etc.]. **1963** H.-N. CASTAÑEDA in Castañeda & Nakhnikian *Morality & Lang. of Conduct* vii. 279 A complete elucidation of the nature and structure of normatives requires an understanding of the logic of imperatives. **1968** A. ETZIONI in Lindzey & Aronson *Handbk. Social Psychol.* (ed. 2) V. xliii. 547 The world situation warrants an approach that would emphasize common interests—above all, peace—as the key normative principle. **1970** R. C. ZAEHNER *Concordant Discord* iii. 46 It is the custom of nature mystics to assume that their own experience, even though it last only for a few moments, must be normative of all such experiences. **1973** *Archivum Linguisticum* IV. 107 It is hazardous to state correlations between social status and speech behaviour, especially if it is done in this normative fashion.

b. In special collocations: *normative grammar*: grammatical rules set up as a fixed standard to which language in use must conform; also, a treatise setting out such rules; so *normative grammarian*; *normative science*: a discipline such as ethics or æsthetics which aims at evaluation as well as description; *normative system*: a system based on what is established as the norm.

1901 H. OERTEL *Lect. on Study of Lang.* ii. 87 Normative or didactic grammar sets up a certain standard as correct. **1933** L. BLOOMFIELD *Language* i. 7 This gave the authoritarians their chance: they wrote *normative grammars*, in which they often ignored actual usage in favor of speculative notions. **1966** L. J. COHEN *Diversity of Meaning* (ed. 2) i. 9 The late eighteenth century was the first period to treat words' meanings as raw material for historians as well as normative grammarians. *Ibid.*, Some bold spirit had to cry down the pretensions of normative grammar and lexicography. **1968** *Word* XXIV. 387 Normative grammarians come into being when a society begins to concern itself with its language. **1895** F. THILLY tr. *Paulsen's Introd. Philos.* 26 Three normative sciences are added: Logic, practical philosophy based on psychology, and technology based on physics. **1921** W. E. JOHNSON *Logic* I. xiv. 224 Any study of which imperatives constitute the subject-matter has been called a normative science. **1934** COHEN & NAGEL *Introd. Logic* vi. 110 Logic has. .been defined as the normative science which studies the norms distinguishing sound. .from unsound thinking. **1953** G. E. M. ANSCOMBE tr. *Wittgenstein's Philos. Investigations* I. 38[e] F. P. Ramsey once emphasized in conversation with me that logic was a 'normative science'. **1966** *Mathematical Rev.* XXXI. 8/2 (*title*) The principles of a logic of normative systems. **1967** C. MARGERISON in Wills & Yearsley *Handbk. Management Technol.* 31 The normative system is a central factor in

securing group participation. *Ibid.* 32 Various studies have indicated how the group's activity can be structured and led to bring about a normative system consonant with the organizational goals. **1973** *Jrnl. Genetic Psychol.* Mar. 56 Internalization was defined as correspondence between the child's normative system (i.e., his generalized expectations) and the parent's behavior or own normative system.

2. *Petrol.* Of or pertaining to the norm of a rock.

1902 W. CROSS et al. in *Jrnl. Geol.* X. 604 The standard minerals which make up the norm are to be called the normative minerals, not the normal ones, since the latter adjective has the meaning of usual or common. **1909** J. P. IDDINGS *Ign. Rocks* I. II. iii. 420 Normative minerals are frequently not the normal ones in certain rocks, though they may be the normal minerals in many others. **1962** *Jrnl. Petrology* III. 353 The normative components in basalts closely approximate the mode in most cases. **1973** *Ibid.* XIV. 35 (*heading*) Normative composition.

Hence **no·rmatively** *adv.*; **no·rmativeness**; **no·rmativist**; **normati·vity**.

1945 Normativity [see *FACTICITY]. **1948** J. TOWSTER *Pol. Power in U.S.S.R.* 16 The normativists (Kelsen etc.), too, say that every law is state (public) law. **1953** J. G. PERISTIANY in *Durkheim's Sociol. & Philos.* p. xv, The generality of a fact.. is significant in this context only in relation to its generality, in the sense of its normativeness. **1957** *Archivum Linguisticum* IX. I. 75 Among the normativists both Gaertner/Passendorfer and Slonski admit of both genders. **1958** W. J. H. SPROTT *Human Groups* ix. 144 Normativeness as such is a prerequisite for continuous interaction. **1964** GOULD & KOLB *Dict. Soc. Sci.* 495/2 This rules out..any items of conduct which are not founded on past experience (in their words 'normatively regulated'). **1970** J. N. FINDLAY tr. *Husserl's Logical Investigations* I. ii. 78 Has not the concept of normativity got an inherent relation to a guiding aim. **1973** *Nature* 23 Nov. 228/2 The intent of these very simple models is neither to forecast, even implicitly, the levels reached in either population or food, or to forecast 'normatively', to set a target and then to deduce what is needed to achieve it.

normed (nǭɹmd), *a.* *Math.* [f. NORM + -ED[2].] Having a norm.

1935 *Trans. Amer. Math. Soc.* XXXVIII. 360 We now add the permanent assumption that 𝔅 is 'normed', that is, that there is associated with 𝔅 a rule assigning to every $\xi \in \mathfrak{B}$ a number $\|\xi\|$ called the 'norm' of ξ, and satisfying [etc.]. **1947** *Ibid.* LXII. 193 A normed linear vector space is a Banach space..if it is furthermore complete. **1959** L. F. BORON tr. Naimark (*title*) Normed rings. **1962** C. WEXLER *Analytic Geom.* ii. 29 The most important normed linear spaces are those that have one additional property, that of completeness. **1972** A. G. HOWSON *Handbk. Terms used in Algebra & Analysis* xxii. 111 A space with a norm is known as a normed space; it is..a metric space with metric $d(x, y) = \|x - y\|$.

no·rmlessness. [f. NORM + -LESS + -NESS.] Without any relevant standard or norm.

1944 H. P. FAIRCHILD *Dict. Sociol.* 206/1 *Normlessness*, the absence of any appreciable norm. **1951** R. K. MERTON *Soc. Theory & Soc. Structure* II. iv. 128 There develops what Durkheim called 'anomie' (or normlessness). **1961** B. R. WILSON *Sects & Society* IV. v. 350 The individual is sheltered from the wider social anomie..the normlessness of the modern world. **1964** I. L. HOROWITZ *New Sociology* 20 All agree that anomie is defined by a 'condition of normlessness'. **1969** R. BLACKBURN in Cockburn & Blackburn *Student Power* 198 Seeman suggests reducing the concept [*sc.* alienation] to five psychological dimensions (feelings of normlessness, meaninglessness, powerlessness, isolation and self-estrangement).

normo- (nǭɹmo), comb. form of L. *norma* (see NORMA) used in several biological and medical words, esp. in physiology, to express the condition of being close to the average in respect of any particular character which varies (often contrasted with HYPER- and HYPO-). **normochro·mic** [Gr. χρῶμ-α colour] *a.*, having the normal amount of hæmoglobin; (of anæmia) characterized by the presence of red blood cells with the normal content of hæmoglobin; **no·rmocyte** [-CYTE], an erythrocyte which is normal (esp. in size); so **normocy·tic** *a.*, of or pertaining to a normocyte; (of anæmia) characterized by the presence of erythrocytes which are normal in size, etc., but reduced in numbers; **normoglycæ·mia** (*U.S.* **-e·mia**), a normal concentration of sugar in the blood; so **normoglycæ·mic** *a.*, characterized by normoglycæmia; **normote·nsive** [*HYPER-, *HYPO)TENSIVE *adjs.*] *a.*, having, or being, a normal blood pressure; hence as *sb.*, one who has such a blood pressure; **normothe·rmic** *a.* [Gr. θέρμ-η heat], characterized by or occurring at a normal body temperature; **normovolæ·mia** (*U.S.* **-e·mia**) [VOL(UME *sb.* + Gr. αἷμα blood], the condition of having a normal volume of circulating blood in the body; so **normovolæ·mic** *a.*, characterized by or pertaining to normovolæmia.

1935 WHITBY & BRITTON *Disorders of Blood* iii. 48 The technical terms used are, firstly, 'hypochromic', 'normochromic' and 'hyperchromic', which indicate whether the cells contain an amount of hemoglobin which is less than, equal to, or more than normal. **1958** Normochromic [see *HYPOCHROMIC *a.* 1]. **1974** *Nature* 7 June 551/1 Clinically the disease is characterised by proteinuria, corneal opacities and normochromic anaemia with decreased erythrocyte life span. **1900** *Buck's Handbk. Med. Sci.* (rev. ed.) I. 273/1 The red cells..are spoken of as microcytes, normocytes, and megalocytes, according to their size. **1935** WHITBY & BRITTON *Disorders Blood* iii. 49 Hypochromia may be found with microcytes and normocytes. **1969** W. R. PLATT *Color Atlas & Textbk. Hematol.* ii. 28/1 The erythrocyte (normocyte or red blood cell) measures 6–8 μ in diameter. **1911** DORLAND *Med. Dict.* (ed. 6) 559/2 Normocytic. **1935** WHITBY & BRITTON *Disorders of Blood* iii. 48 The technical terms used are.. 'microcytic', 'normocytic' and 'macrocytic', which indicate whether the [red] cells are smaller than, equal to, or larger than normal. **1971** *Indian Jrnl. Med. Res.* LIX. 427 In 60% of the cases the anemia was of the normocytic normochromic type. **1932** DORLAND & MILLER *Med. Dict.* (ed. 16) 871/2 Normoglycemia. **1961** *Lancet* 16 Sept. 637/2 To maintain normoglycæmia a [diabetic] woman of 81 needed 45 units P.Z.I. before the course but only 15 units after it. **1973** *Nature* 17 Aug. 447/2 Direct injection of pancreatic islets into the portal vein resulted in normoglycaemia and normal urine volumes in the five rats studied. **1933** *Stedman's Med. Dict.* (ed. 12) 733/2 Normoglycemic. **1961** *Diabetes* X. 322/1 The ketonuria may..represent the relatively benign normoglycemic ketosis of hunger or starvation which usually responds to increase in the amount of carbohydrate in the diet. **1969** *Hormone & Metabol. Res.* I. 266 (*heading*) Insulin levels during pregnancy or obesity in normoglycemic women with a positive history of diabetes mellitus. **1941** DORLAND & MILLER *Med. Dict.* (ed. 19) 982/1 *Normotensive*, marked by normal blood pressure. **1948** *Federation Proc.* VII. 41/2 (*heading*) The immediate pressor effect of desoxycorticosterone acetate in hypertensive and normotensive subjects. **1953** *Lancet* 12 Sept. 541/2 None of the other normotensives exceeded 0·9 ml. per minute. *Ibid.* 543/2 Ten normotensive women. **1962** *Ibid.* 26 May 1092/1 Possible sources of irregularity in the distribution of blood-pressure include..the observer's subconscious distinction between normotensive and hypertensive levels of pressure. **1972** *Aerospace Med.* XLIII. 1225 (*heading*) Effect of hydrochlorothiazide on $+G_z$ tolerance in normotensives. **1959** *Surg., Gynecol. & Obstetr.* CIX. 721 (*heading*) Normothermic perfusion and replantation of the excised dog kidney. **1960** *Amer. Jrnl. Physiol.* CXCIX. 163/1 The heart was cooled while maintaining the rest of the body normothermic. **1974** *Nature* 22 Feb. 568/2 Obviously the destruction of cells by growth of virus may also be different in hypothermic and normothermic conditions. **1925** Normovolemia [see *hypervolæmia* s.v. *HYPER- IV]. **1966** *Ann. Surg.* CLXIV. 51 (*heading*) Effects of adrenergic blocking agents on renal blood flow in normovolemia and experimental hypovolemia. **1947** *Acta Cardiologica* II. 134 This method.. permitted comparisons of sequential cardiovascular changes which occurred in the same animal during oligemic shock and normovolemic shock (i.e., shock with essentially normal blood volume). **1966** *Amer. Jrnl. Physiol.* CCXI. 878/1 Normovolemic anemia was produced by removing from a femoral artery 40 ml/kg blood while infusing an equal volume of 6% dextran in saline into a femoral vein.

Norn, *sb.*[1] Add: Also pl. **Nornir.**

1859 G. W. DASENT *Pop. Tales from Norse* p. xli, The worshippers of Odin and the Nornir were gradually converted into votaries of the Virgin Mary. **1875** *Encycl. Brit.* I. 211/1 The three principal Norns or Nornir are Urd, past time; Verdandi, present time; and Skulld, future time. **1959** R. W. V. ELLIOTT *Runes* vii. 105 Other possibilities occur to one: such as that the figures represent the Nornir, the 'three fatal sisters' of Northern mythology.

Norn, *a.* and *sb.*[2] Delete *dial.* and add to def.: **a.** *adj.* Also, of or pertaining to Norn. **b.** *sb.* Also formerly spoken on parts of the northern mainland of Scotland. Also *the Orkney* (or *Shetland*) *Norn.* (Further examples.)

1932 *Times Lit. Suppl.* 6 Oct. 712/3 Jakobsen's great dictionary of the Norn language in Shetland. **1956** 'H. MACDIARMID' *Stony Limits & Scots Unbound* 48 The old Norn words. **1966** E. W. MARWICK in J. Shearer et al. *New Orkney Book* iv. 25 At the beginning of the eighteenth century some of them were still speaking the old Norn language. **1966–69** *Saga-Book* XVII. 11 In Appendix II he printed specimens of the Orkney Norn of the fourteenth and fifteenth centuries. **1972** W. B. LOCKWOOD *Panorama Indo-Europ. Lang.* vii. 122 Norse obliterated the Pictish of Orkney and Shetland and hastened its demise on the mainland. Known locally as Norn, the language lived on there and across the Pentland Firth in Caithness until modern times. *Ibid.* 127 On the Scottish mainland generally, Norn was ousted by Gaelic during the Middle Ages, except in the North-East of Caithness where it appears to have lingered on until the sixteenth century. **1970–73** *Saga-Book* XVIII. 382 The section on the Orkney and Shetland Norn..is most noteworthy in this respect.

Norse, *sb.* and *a.* **A.** *sb.* **2.** Also, any native or inhabitant of ancient Scandinavia. (Further example.)

1972 W. B. LOCKWOOD *Panorama Indo-Europe. Lang.* vii. 126 As many as 5,000 Norse are believed to have lived in Greenland.

3. For '(sometimes loosely used to include early Swedish and Danish)' read 'Also, the North Germanic language which was the immediate ancestor of the Scandinavian languages'. (Further example.)

1927 E. V. GORDON *Introd. Old Norse* p. xvi, The structure of Gothic..reveals its affinity with Norse, but the differences between the oldest surviving Gothic ..and Norse of the same period are too great for Gothic to be included in the Norse group of tongues.

B. *adj.* Also, of or pertaining to ancient Scandinavia or the Norse peoples as a whole. (Further examples.)

1885 *Encycl. Dict.* V. I. 216/1 *Norse*,..of or pertaining to ancient Scandinavia or its inhabitants; Norwegian. **1927** E. V. GORDON *Introd. Old Norse* p. xv, The home of the oldest Norse culture and the oldest Norse traditions was Sweden. *Ibid.* p. xxxv, The oldest Norse poetry preserved traditions which belonged not merely to the Norse peoples but to the Germanic race as a whole. **1970–73** *Saga-Book* XVIII. 208, I may insert a word of warning on Dr Marwick's old-fashioned and narrowly correct use of the term 'Norse'—to him it translates *norsk*, Norwegian and then especially *landsmål*.

Hence **No·rseness**, the state or quality of being Norwegian or Scandinavian.

1961 *Listener* 7 Sept. 363/3 Ibsen's characters are always about to take flight into fantasy but their manner, their stubborn Norseness, holds them fast in a two-dimensional theatre. **1968** G. JONES *Hist. Vikings* III. iv. 264 The adoption of Slavonic customs had quietly eroded the Norseness of the Rus.

norseller (nǭ·ɹs'ləɹ). Also **orseller.** [f. NORSEL *sb.* and *v.* + -ER[1].] A person who fits nets with norsels.

1921 *Dict. Occup. Terms* (1927) §398 *Net orseller, norseller*, attaches orsells or norsells (short lines about ten inches long) to top and bottom of fishing net at regular intervals.

Norseman. Add: Also, any native or inhabitant of viking-age Scandinavia.

1864 *Chambers's Encycl.* VI. 792/2 The first Danish Norsemen made their appearance on the eastern and southern coasts of England in 787. *Ibid.* 793/2 The Swedish Norsemen directed their expeditions chiefly against the eastern coasts of the Baltic. **1935** *Ibid.* VII. 527/2 *Northmen*, or Norsemen, were the sea-rovers who came from the north—Denmark, Norway, Sweden. **1943** G. VERNADSKY *Anc. Russia* VII. iii. 273 It seems highly probable that..a band of Norsemen—more exactly, of Swedes—established their control over the lower Don and Azov area. **1948** *Oxf. Jun. Encycl.* I. 137/1 *Danes.* These are a Scandinavian people, as are their neighbours the Swedes..and Norwegians... The ancestors of all three were the Norsemen or Vikings. **1968** G. JONES *Hist. Vikings* IV. iii. 395 Ireland was different. The Norsemen (part Danes, part Norwegians) had established a number of important trading towns in the southern half of the island. **1970** FOOTE & WILSON *Viking Achievement* i. 14 Saxon political influence went hand in hand with Saxon efforts to convert the Danes to Christianity. The archbishopric of Hamburg-Bremen..was intended as a missionary outpost with prime responsibility for bringing the heathen Norsemen to the true faith.

norsethite (nǭ·ɹsĕþəit). *Min.* [See quot. 1959[2] and -ITE[1].] A carbonate of barium and magnesium, $BaMg(CO_3)_2$, that is found as whitish crystals with a vitreous or pearly lustre, similar to calcite and dolomite.

1959 C. MILTON et al. in *Bull. Geol. Soc. Amer.* LXX. 1646 Norsethite, $BaMg(CO_3)_2$, was found in dolomitic, black oil shale below the main trona bed in the Westvaco trona mine. *Ibid.*, Norsethite is named in honor of Mr. Keith Norseth, engineering geologist of the trona mine at Westvaco, Sweetwater County, Wyoming. **1967** *Amer. Mineralogist* LII. 1770 The occurrence of norsethite, $BaMg(CO_3)_2$, in large quantities in a newly discovered zinc-lead-copper deposit in South West Africa, is reported. It is one of the major gangue minerals of the deposit, is closely associated with calcite and is apparently of hydrothermal origin. **1968** I. KOSTOV *Mineralogy* II. xi. 540 Norsethite is probably trigonal-trapezohedral with distinct rhombohedral {10$\bar{1}$1} cleavage.

norsteroid (nǭɹstiᵊ·roid, -ste·roid). *Biochem.* [f. *NOR- + *STEROID.] A steroid lacking a methyl side chain (esp. the one containing the carbon atom numbered 19), or having one of its rings contracted by one methylene group.

1950 *Jrnl. Chem. Soc.* 367 The synthetic approach to nor-steroid hormones has now been greatly simplified by Birch and Mukherji's method of reduction. **1954** *Ibid.* 1984 Values for 2-substituted A-norsteroids..may be considered. **1970** *Indian Jrnl. Biochem.* VII. 116/1 Since the introduction of 19-norsteroids as the synthetic progestational agents, it has become necessary to know their role as regulators of metabolic processes.

nortes, *sb. pl.* Add: Also in *sing.*

1926 *British Weekly* 21 Jan. 398/5 We hear of the *norte*, the wind from the Equatorial belt... When the *norte* blows, many temperamental folk are apt to become unbalanced.

north. Add: **A.** *adv.* **1. b.** (Later example.)

1955 J. R. R. TOLKIEN *Return of King* 197 Going swiftly to lesser posts and strongholds north-away.

B. *sb.* **1. b.** *Bridge.* A person occupying a position opposite 'South'.

1926 [see *EAST *sb.* 4]. **1958** *Listener* 2 Oct. 541/2 North bid Three Clubs. **1965** *Ibid.* 20 May 758/2 The bidding should have made it clear to him that North was hoping to play in Two Hearts doubled. **1973** *Country Life* 21 June 1842/3 Study this deal... Dealer, North. North-South vulnerable.

2. c. (Earlier examples.)

1796 WASHINGTON *Messages & Papers* (1898) I. 217 The North, in an unrestricted intercourse with the South. **1831** J. M. PECK *Guide for Emigrants* II. 81 The

result would be more disastrous to the south and west, than the influx of foreign goods was to..the north..in 1816.

3. b. *North-of-England*, used *attrib.*, of, pertaining to, or characteristic of, the north of England.

1816 SCOTT *Antiq.* III. ii. 34 His father was a north-of-England gentleman. **1847** C. BRONTË *Jane Eyre* I. xii. 212 A North-of-England spirit, called a 'Gytrash'; which,.. haunted solitary ways. **1907** F. E. E. BELL *At Works* vi. 127 Watching football matches, a comfortless thing enough to do in a North of England winter. **1973** J. WAINWRIGHT *High-Class Kill* 221 North-of-England conformity — best-clothes-on-Sunday-speak-when-you're spoken-to.

5. north and south *Rhyming slang*, mouth; **north canoe,** a birchbark canoe once used north and west of Lake Superior, North America; **northpaw** *U.S. slang* (see quot. 1960).

1858 A. MAYHEW *Paved with Gold* II. x. 169 'I'll smash your "glass case", and damage your "north and south",' roared Bill, referring to the *face* and *mouth* of his opponent. **1928** M. C. SHARPE *Chicago May* 287/2 North and South, mouth. **1958** F. NORMAN *Bang to Rights* 36 Dust floating about in the air, which gets in your north and south. **1972** *Lebende Sprachen* XVII. 8/2 *North and south*, mouth. **1819** W. F. WENTZEL *Let.* in L. F. R. Masson *Bourgeois de la Compagnie du Nord-Ouest* (1889) I. 134 Sir Alexander Mackenzie has suggested that one north canoe with Canadian voyageurs, and six small Indian canoes, would be a fitter outfit. **1879** H. M. ROBINSON *Great Fur Land* 31 The North canoe..is a light graceful vessel about thirty-six long, by four or five broad, and capable of containing eight men and three passengers. **1956** V. FISHER *Pemmican* 250 A north canoe; twenty-five foot long and from four to five feet wide, it could carry a crew of eight or nine men and their supplies, as well as three passengers. **1969** *Islander* (Victoria, B.C.) 23 Nov. 12/3 Ahead roared the Rapids of the Drowned. They gained their name after one of the Hudson's Bay Company's large north canoes capsized there with the loss of several men. **1960** WENTWORTH & FLEXNER *Dict. Amer. Slang* 358/1 *Northpaw*.., a right-handed baseball pitcher; any right-handed person. **1968** *Listener* 19 Sept. 357/1 A skilful person is 'dextrous': in its way as insulting to left-handers (they call us southpaws, though I have never heard anyone described as a northpaw) as 'white man', for someone of worthy character, is offensive to Negroes. **1972** *Daily Mail* 1 Aug. 2/6, 20 per cent of Americans are tired of grappling with things designed for northpaws.

C. *adj.* **1. d.** *North Oxford*, of, pertaining to, or characteristic of the suburban part of Oxford north of the university area, where many dons and their families live. Also as *sb.*

1935 N. MITCHISON *We have been Warned* IV. 462 She had..a Sybil Dunlop moonstone on a long silver chain. A bit North Oxfordy? Well, she was North Oxford! **1950** A. WILSON *Such Darling Dodos* 79 The whimsical humour of North Oxford. *Ibid.* 97 Why you should have to drag Coleridge in, only your staunch North Oxford spirit can explain. **1973** *Country Life* 13 Sept. 720/1 The houses behind (Carolean or North Oxford Gothic?) ..seem oddly familiar. **1974** F. EMERY *Oxfordsh. Landscape* vii. 214 Between the rustic variety of Summertown and the old suburbs of St Giles lies the Victorian perfection of North Oxford proper.

2. d. North Circular (**Road**), a road passing through the northern outskirts of London.

1944 M. LASKI *Love on Supertax* xi. 102 After a prolonged..journey by 'bus, Clarissa alighted way out on the North Circular Road. **1968** J. LLOYD *Death at Roman Farm* xviii. 171 You go straight through town and send the other car round the North Circular. **1974** 'A. GARVE' *File on Lester* xxxi. 118 He became silent, concentrating on his driving on the busy North Circular.

4. *Comb.*, **north-facing,** facing the north; *spec.* of a window.

1952 A. G. L. HELLYER *Sanders' Encycl. Gardening* (ed. 22) 205 Position, semi-shaded or north-facing. **1973** 'I. DRUMMOND' *Jaws of Watchdog* xii. 156 A large window. North-facing so I guess a studio.

North African, *a.* and *sb.* [f. *North Africa* the countries of northern Africa, *spec.* the region including Morocco, Algeria, Tunisia, Libya, and Egypt.] **A.** *adj.* Of or pertaining to North Africa or its inhabitants. **B.** *sb.* A native or inhabitant of North Africa.

1867 'OUIDA' *Under Two Flags* II. iii. 56 The blaze and heat of the North African day. **1932** KIPLING *Limits & Renewals* 321 His speech—to suit his hearers—ran From pure Parisian to gross peasant, With interludes North African If any Legionnaire were present. **1961** E. WAUGH *Unconditional Surrender* II. v. 140 Stirred by the heavy North African wine de Souza's imagination rolled into action. **1962** P. BRICKHILL *Deadline* vi. 88 The noise made by four North Africans on a dais. *Ibid.* 89 Belly dancing seemed to be the forte of the North African smart spots in Paris. **1972** D. LEES *Zodiac* 107 The couscous was being ladled out by a grinning North African.

North American, *sb.* and *a.* [f. *North America* the name of the northern part of the continent of America including Central America, Mexico, U.S., and Canada.] **A.** *sb.* A native or inhabitant of North America, esp. of the United States or Canada.

1766 [see NORTH *a.* 1 c]. **1783** A. STOKES *Brit. Colonies* 144 The North Americans will refuse them their assistance. **1825** J. NEAL *Bro. Jonathan* II. 1 The man of America—the Original North American..the 'Indian' as he is called. *Ibid.* III. 413 The brave North American was dead. **1974** 'E. ANTHONY' *Malaspiga Exit* ii. 25 You could disguise every feature except the magnificent dentistry of the North Americans.

B. *adj.* Of or pertaining to North America or its inhabitants; belonging to or characteristic of North America, living in North America, etc.

1770 J. OTIS in W. Tudor *Life J. Otis* (1823) 476 My humble North American word of honour for it, my lord, these volumes will hurt neither thee, nor thy master. **1771** FRANKLIN *Autobiogr.* (1909) 171 This was the mother of all the North American subscription libraries, now so numerous. **1775** BURKE *Speech on Conciliation with America* 22 Mar. in *Wks.* II (1792) 31 The export trade to the colonies consists of three great branches. The African..the West Indian; and the North-American. **1776** (*title*) The North-American and the West-Indian Gazetteer. **1783** (*title*) The North-American Calendar. **1837** *Southern Lit. Messenger* III. 695 A declaration of the independence of the North American States. **1880** G. W. CABLE *Grandissimes* iv. 23 She had..the nerve of the true North American Indian. **1916** G. B. SHAW *Androcles & Lion* p. li, Jesus himself had referred to that psalm (LXXXII) in which men who have judged unjustly and accepted the persons of the wicked (including by anticipation practically all the white inhabitants of the British Isles and the North American continent, to mention no other places) are condemned. **1923** A. L. KROEBER *Anthropol.* xiii. 356 It would be extravagant to maintain that throughout the North American continent every matrilineal tribe was culturally more advanced than every patrilineal one. **1949** *Chicago Tribune* 8 Nov. 1. 12/2 The very rich head of a business is vanishing as rapidly as the North American Indian. **1952** *Oxf. Jun. Encycl.* X. 105/1 The example of the North American colonists roused other oppressed colonists to bid for freedom. **1959** M. SCHLAUCH *Eng. Lang.* iii. 78 Words connected with the life of North American Indians also appeared after 1600. **1974** E. AMBLER *Dr. Frigo* II. 96 He was still speaking Spanish but adulterating it now with ..North American business jargon. **1975** *Country Life* 6 Nov. 1250/3 *Q*[*uercus*] *coccinea* is the North American scarlet oak.

north-bound, *a.* Also **northbound.** [NORTH *adv.*] Bound for the north; travelling northwards; also, intended for such travellers, serving as a point of departure for the north. Also as *sb.*, a north-bound train.

1903 KIPLING *Five Nations* 115 We gather and wait her coming—The wonderful north-bound train. **1904** W. N. HARBEN *Georgians* 217 The young man was at the seven-o'clock north-bound train when it stopped in the antiquated brick car-shed. **1939** G. HOUSEHOLD *Rogue Male* 78 At the bottom of the Piccadilly escalator you turn left for the north-bound trains... I ran on to the north-bound platform. **1973** *Sci. Amer.* June 26/2 A slowing of the northbound Coastal Current. **1975** D. BEATY *Electric Train* 232 'When's the next train?' 'No more northbounds tonight.'

north country. Add: **2.** (Later examples.) Also a native of the north country of England.

1823 J. G. LOCKHART *R. Dalton* II. v. v. 289 You're north-country, I believe. **1966** *Listener* 7 Apr. 501/1, I can play cockney, I can play north country. **1972** C. DRUMMOND *Death at Bar* ii. 60 'If you borrow you make bad friends'—a flash of honest north-country peeped through the trained accent. **1974** *Times* 30 Dec. 4/7 Gracie Fields..reverts to the characteristic mixture of North Country, standard English and American overtones.

2. (Later example.)

1975 J. MITCHELL *Smear Job* x. 69 Her accent was harshly Sicilian, but lurking in it was a hint of the North Country she had picked up from the soldiers.

3. (Further examples.)

1896 D. C. MURRAY (*title*) A capful o'nails: a North-Country story. **1933** M. ALLINGHAM *Sweet Danger* x. 129 A comfortable, homely voice with an unexpected North Country accent. **1959** R. LONGRIGG *Wrong Number* ii. 30 They..left in a gruff welter of north-country gratitude. **1964** V. S. NAIPAUL *Area of Darkness* ix. 243 The newcomer was a commercial Englishman, middle-aged, fat and red-faced. He spoke with a North Country accent.

northen, *a.* (Later U.S. examples.)

1772 D. TAITT in N. D. Mereness *Trav. Amer. Col.* (1916) 541 The Inhabitants of the Tuskigees are a remnant of Northen Indians and speak a different Language from the Creek. **1773** C. CAROLL *Let.* 26 Mar. in *Maryland Hist. Mag.* (1920) XV. 58 Keep the Boy if the Northen Post be not Come in untill Monday.

norther, *sb.* Add: **1.** (Earlier and later examples.)

1827 *Western Monthly Rev.* I. 320 We were struck by a gale, that they call a norther. **1831** M. HOLLEY *Texas* (1833) i. 19 Our voyage..is..not without hazard, on account of the Northers; as they are called. **1946** *Sun* (Baltimore) 30 Dec. 11/1 St. Mary's football squad arrived in Houston early this morning to be greeted by a Texas 'norther'. **1969** 'J. MORRIS' *Fever Grass* xiii. 121 A fresh 'norther' was blowing from the Gulf. **1973** *Houston* (Texas) *Chron.* 21 Oct. 1/3 (*caption*) A delightfully persistent Indian Summer lingered over Houston, luring people to parks for langorous hours of contentment before looking ahead to winter and the prospect of rain and blue northers.

2. A strong north wind blowing in other parts, esp. on the Pacific seaboard of North America.

1835 J. F. COOPER *Monikins* II. iii. 71 It may be even now questioned whether the ship would claw off..with a sending sea, and this heavy norther. **1850** in *Harper's Mag.* (1878) Jan. 279 We met a norther in coming out of the Gulf of California. **1891** *Scribner's Mag.* X. 283 The weather along the Pacific highway has been uniformly pleasant, for northers are infrequent. **1893** KIPLING *Seven Seas* (1896) 28 We've slipped from Valparaiso With the Norther at our heels. **1903** —— *Five Nations* 53 That night the Norther found me—Froze and killed the plains-bred ponies.

northern, *a.* and *sb.* Add: **A.** *adj.* **1. c. northern canoe** = ***north canoe.**

1820 R. HOOD *To Arctic* (1974) 110 Late on the 21st Mr. Robertson, of the Hudson's Bay Company arrived, and furnished us with a guide, but desired that he might be exchanged when we met the northern canoes. **1860** S. HANCOCK *Narr.* (1927) 163 What is termed a northern canoe is much larger and differently shaped from those made and used by the Indians south of the Straits of Fuca. **1867** J. T. ROTHROCK *Flora Alaska* 434 From it the celebrated 'northern canoes' are made. These canoes, 'dug' from a single trunk and afterwards steamed into shape, will often carry four tons. **1938** *Beaver* Dec. 13/1 The northern canoe carried a crew of five or six men, apart from passengers. **1954** M. W. CAMPBELL *Nor' Westers* 44 Each northern canoe held twenty-five ninety-pound packs instead of the sixty loaded into the Montreal canoes.

3. b. *Northern Spy*, an American variety of red-skinned, late-ripening, dessert apple. (Earlier and later examples.)

1847 J. M. IVES *New England Bk. Fruit* 46 Northern Spy.—This new native fruit, originated near Rochester, N. York. It is a fine winter apple, and is one of the most popular fruits in New York. **1850** *New England Farmer* II. 404 Northern Spy Apple. We had hoped to be able to test the qualities of this apple ourselves. **1917** D. CANFIELD *Understood Betsy* iii. 61 Those Northern Spies are just getting to be good about now. When they first come off the tree in October you could shoot them through an oak plank. *Ibid.* xi. 241 A basket..half full of striped red Northern Spies. **1944** *Poetry Chap Bk.* Fall 14 And fragrant windrows of crisp Northern Spies Are scattered in the tumbled twisted sheaves. **1965** MRS. L. B. JOHNSON *White House Diary* 15 Jan. (1970) 221 'What are your best brands [of apple]?' asked Gromyko. Without hesitation and with honesty General McNaughton replied, 'Our best brands are Northern *Spies* and McIntosh *Reds*.'

northerner. 1. (Earlier and later examples.)

1831 J. M. PECK *Guide for Emigrants* II. 60 Such for beauty and splendor and fragrance, the *Northerners* have never seen. **1928** I. C. WARD *Phonetics of English* i. 3 A Northerner's pronunciation of *but*..is called 'broad'. **1945** *Chicago Daily News* 1 Feb. 8/7 It's about time we long-suffering Northerners got it off our chest.

northernism (nǭ·ɹðəɹniz'm). [f. NORTHERN *a.* and *sb.* + -ISM.] Northern quality; a Northern characteristic, esp. a Northern form of expression.

1930 *Times Lit. Suppl.* 9 Jan. 28/4 Anything tainted with northernism or 'Lutheranism' is poison for Italy. **1964** *English Studies* XLV. 249 Identified..as a northernism. **1965** H. KÖKERITZ in Bessinger & Creed *Medieval & Linguistic Stud.* 294 Notwithstanding a few seeming northernisms..there is no vestige of his father's dialect.

northernness. Add: **2.** The quality of being from the north.

1939 C. S. LEWIS *Rehabilitations* ii. 37, I knew one who could come no nearer to an explanation of Morris's charm than to repeat 'It's the Northernness—the Northerness'. **1955** E. BLISHEN *Roaring Boys* ii. 74 To our grey northern-ness they brought a southern gleam. **1968** G. JONES *Hist. Vikings* 2 Though they had many ties..to remind them of a shared northernness, they had but little sense of a separate Danish, Swedish, or Norwegian nationality. **1975** C. N. MANLOVE *Mod. Fantasy* iv. 100 Despite lifelong fascination for 'Northernness', and interests in the medieval School of Chartres and in the Renaissance, he never felt the urge to visit their sources in Scandinavia, France or Italy.

north-light. Add: Also **north light. 3.** A window, esp. in a roof, that faces north. So *north-light roof.*

1904 F. E. KIDDER *Architects' & Builders' Pocket-Bk.* (ed. 14) 1304 With the 'Maze' glass, the artist may have, in all weather and in all directions, what is in effect a much-desired 'north-light'. **1919** R. FRY *Let.* 29 Nov. (1972) II. 473, I went to his tiny studio..he'd simply put a high north light in the roof of a small bedroom. **1931** *Engineering* 9 Jan. 33/2 The older bays had roofs of the saw-tooth pattern, with north lights. **1940** *Chambers's Techn. Dict.* 583/1 *North light roof*, a pitched roof of unequal slopes, of which the steeper is glazed and arranged to receive light from the north. **1958** *Times* 20 Aug. 13/6 Where only day shifts are worked the cost of installing fittings to produce the whole of the necessary illumination, instead of only those required to supplement daylight from windows or north-light roof must also be reckoned. **1961** E. E. CUMMINGS *Let.* 22 July (1969) 272, I asked a firstrate carpenter..to make me a real—with a North Light—studio in the barn. **1972** E. LEMARCHAND *Cyanide with Compliments* ix. 117 Could be a studio... I can't make out if it's got a north light, though.

northman. Add: **2.** *U.S.* = NORTHERNER 1.

1836 *Southern Lit. Messenger* II. 434 From my very heart, northman as I am, I admire and affect this good remnant of olden time. **1837** *Ibid.* III. 337 Between the Virginians and the North-men there was a wide variance.

northmost, *a.* (Later examples.)

1888 SWINBURNE *Armada* III. i, Darker far than the tempests are that sweep the skies of her northmost clime. **1921** R. L. JACK (*title*) Northmost Australia.

North Sea. Add: **1. b.** *attrib. North Sea gas, oil*: raw materials discovered beneath the North Sea.

1965 *Times* 22 Sept. 10/6 The BP gas find radically alters the North Sea oil and gas search. **1967** *Guardian* 4 Jan. 3/1 Bringing North Sea gas ashore in Norfolk. **1972** *Ibid.* 8 June 9/1 The tests were carried out in households supplied by North Sea gas and those supplied by town gas. **1973** *Ibid.* 2 Mar. 15/7 North Sea oil will go a long way to reducing Britain's dependence on the volatile Middle East. **1974** *Sunday Times* (Colour Suppl.) 28 Apr. 20 It is a feature of the story of North Sea oil that men encountering its immensities can find themselves in conflict with their previous positions. **1975** *Sat. Rev.* 25 Jan. 16/3 Britain retiring into a new insularity fueled by North Sea oil.

North Star State. *U.S.* The state of Minnesota.

1862 *American Odd Fellow* I. 196/2 In the North Star State here, we rejoice in having a Grand Master, who knows no such word as fail. **1909** *World To-Day* Oct. 1108 The North Star State has been the scene of her greatest usefulness. Mrs. Potter commenced her educational work in Minneapolis. **1946** C. McWilliams *Southern Calif. Country* 173 Floats move through the streets of Long beach with captions as 'Corn is King',..'Minnesota: The North Star State'.

Norway[1]. Add: *Norway lobster* = *Dublin* (*Bay*) *prawn* (*Dublin) (earlier and later examples); *Norway pine* (see Pine *sb.*[2] 2) (earlier and later examples).

1777 T. Pennant *Brit. Zool.* (ed. 4) IV. 17 Cancer Novegicus... Norway. L[obster] with a long spiny snout. **1911, 1963** [see *Dublin* (*Bay*) *prawn* (*Dublin)]. **1720** R. Palmer *Let.* 4 Oct. in M. M. Verney *Verney Lett.* (1930) II. xxiv. 81, 36 Norway Pines and Yews for a Hedge of 38 yards long. **1784** M. Cutler *Jrnl.* 22 July in Parker & Cutler *Life & Corr. M. Cutler* (1888) I. iii. 99 We rode five miles over pitch and Norway-pine plains, with very low shrubs. **1829** J. C. Loudon *Encycl. Plants* 804 The pitch pine, *P*[*inus*] *resinosa* is generally known in its native country by the name of Norway pine; sometimes, particularly among the Canadian French, red pine. **1838** J. F. Cooper *Homeward Bound* I. xvi. 252 [He] applied his knife to try the quality of the wood, and pronounced the Norway pine of the spars to be almost equal to anything that could be found in our own southern woods. **1896** M. E. Wilkins *Madelon* 1 There were evergreens—Norway pines, spruces and hemlocks—bordering the road. **1969** T. H. Everett *Living Trees of World* 51/1 Eastern American species with paired leaves include the red pine or Norway pine (*P. resinosa*). It may at first seem to be misnamed, but its popular designation refers to the Maine village of Norway and not to the land of the Vikings. **1973** *Saint Croix Courier* (St. Stephen, New Brunswick) 26 July 1 Dories are planked with Norway (Red) Pine and clench-fastened with galvanized boat nails.

Norwegian, *a.* and *sb.* Add: **A.** *adj.* **b.** *Norwegian steam* (see quot. 1960).

1944 *Amer. Speech* XIX. 106 Norwegian steam is brute manpower,..from the tradition of the fine sailing ships. **1947** R. O. Boyer *Dark Ship* vii. 53, I heard another sailor say 'We got there by Norwegian steam' and asked him what he meant. 'By rowing,' he said. **1958** E. S. Land *Winning War with Ships* iv. 66 The power on deck for such work as weighing anchor was 'Norwegian steam'. **1960** Wentworth & Flexner *Dict. Amer. Slang* 358/1 *Norwegian steam,* manpower; muscle power. A little jocular use, esp. maritime use. **1970** *Sea Breezes* Nov. 717/2 All the hoisting and hauling is done by hand—'Norwegian steam' as we used to say years ago.

nor'-wester. Add: **1.** Esp. in the South Island of New Zealand. In full, *Canterbury nor'-wester.*

1871 Lady Barker *Christmas Cake in Four Quarters* iv. ii. 267 How many of us would be in that valley on a Christmas Day in the far future, when these trees would have struggled up against their enemy the Nor'-wester. **1933** L. G. D. Acland in *Press* (Christchurch) 2 Dec. 15/7 The ordinary man in the paddock in Canterbury recognises only three winds: east (from N.E.), sou'-wester (from S.E., S., etc., S.W., etc.), and nor'-wester. **1959** A. McLintock *Descr. Atlas N.Z.* 22 In summer the hot, dry 'Canterbury Nor'wester' is generally a most unpleasant wind. **1966** G. W. Turner *Eng. Lang. Austral. & N.Z.* viii. 163 The Canterbury *nor' wester* resembling the European *Föhn* wind..and the *three-day sou'wester* in New Zealand.

3. Also, a strong oilskin or waterproof coat worn in rough weather. In full *norwester coat.*

1689–90 J. Greenvill in W. S. Pelletreau *Early Long Island Wills* (1897) 46 My will is that my norwester Coat.. may be given to Christopher Leaming.

Norwich (nǫ·ritʃ, -idʒ). [The name of the city and county town of Norfolk.] Used *attrib.* in various collocations, as *Norwich crape* (see Crape *sb.* 1); *Norwich damask, poplin, shawl*; also *Norwich school*, an English school of painting of the early nineteenth century associated with Norwich; *Norwich stuff*, a textile fabric manufactured, or as manufactured, in Norwich; *Norwich terrier*, a small, thick-set, red or black-and-tan, rough-coated terrier with pricked ears, belonging to a breed developed in East Anglia; in North America and formerly in Britain also used for the drop-eared variety of the breed, now called the Norfolk terrier; also ellipt. *Norwich.*

1618 T. Roe *Advise for Goodes* in *Embassy* (1899) II. 487 Some light coullored Norwich stuffes wrought in flowers for triall, the lighter the better. **1685, 1709** [see Crape *sb.* 1]. **1741** Richardson *Pamela* IV. xiii. 75 So many Yards of Norwich Stuffs for Gowns and Coats for Girls. **1774** H. Walpole *Descr. Strawberry-Hill* 65 The room is hung with crimson Norwich damask. **1790** M. Dunsford *Hist. Mem. Tiverton* iv. 235 This year [*sc.* 1752] was introduced to Tiverton the manufacture of Norwich stuffs, camblets, tarborates, [etc.]. **1816** J. Crome *Let.* Jan. in W. F. Dickes *Norwich Sch. Painting* (1906) v. 111 You wish me to give you my opinion of your picture... How pleased I was to see so much improvement in the figures, so unlike our Norwich School; I may say they were good. **1821** *Times* 15 Aug., The ladies to wear..dark Norwich crape. *c* **1860** in A. Adburgham *Shops & Shopping* (1964) ix. 100 Paisley, Norwich and French shawls. *Ibid.*, Irish and Norwich poplins. **1877** *Encycl. Brit.* VII. 596/2 *John Crome* (1769–1821), English landscape painter, founder and chief representative of the 'Norwich School'. **1906** W. F. Dickes *Norwich Sch. Painting* 11 The Norwich School has had a powerful influence upon the Art of Great Britain. **1929** *Official Guide to City of Norwich* 25 The.. Jacquard loom for the weaving of the beautiful Norwich shawls of coloured silks. **1931** J. Lucas *Hunt & Working Terriers* xxiii. 189 In 1880 a Mr. Nichols of Wymondham, Norfolk, was breeding a small red dog which he called the Norwich terrier. **1950** *'Mercury' Dict. Textile Terms* 368/1 *Norwich crepe*, a cloth very similar to georgettes, and made from fine silk warp and cotton weft, the crepe being produced by the weave. **1950** A. C. Smith *Dogs since 1900* xi. 179 Some of their admirers..asked permission to have them registered at the Kennel Club as Norwich Terriers. In 1932 they were admitted to registration. **1951** *Short Guide Norwich School Pictures* 3 The old masters of Holland..influenced so profoundly the Norwich School. **1958** *Times* 12 Dec. 1/7 (Advt.), Norwich Terrier for sale. **1967** R. M. R. Young *Guide to Bridewell Museum* 11 The traditional Oriental design now often called 'the Paisley pattern' was also used by the Norwich shawl makers. **1971** F. Hamilton *World Encycl. Dogs* 466 From these red East Anglian terriers..sprang the breed which was recognized..as the Norwich terrier. *Ibid.* 467 The Norwich is very hardy and adaptable. **1972** *Times* 21 June 16/5 Two large, fine views by Henry Bright, the late Norwich school landscapist. **1974** *Country Life* 28 Nov. 1652/1 The Castle Museum at Norwich has long specialized in the..Norwich School.

nose, *sb.* Add: **1. e.** In Horse-racing: the nose of a horse used as an indication of the distance between two finishing horses. Phr. *to bet* (etc.) *on the nose*: to back a horse to win (as opposed to betting for a place, or betting each way).

1908 L. Mitchell *New York Idea* I. 11 Flying Cloud slipped by the pair and won on the post by a nose in one forty nine! **1951** *Publ. Amer. Dial. Soc.* xvi. 13 Bet on the nose. **1955** *Amer. Speech* XXX. 26 Laymen.. will say that a horse won by a neck, head, or nose to describe any race which was extremely close. In this country a bet on a horse to win..is said to be on the nose. **1963** 'J. Prescot' *Case for Hearing* iv. 71 Every afternoon that lad of mine is in the betting shop slapping as much as fifty quid a time on the nose. **1973** *Times* 12 Apr. 12/6 Ladbroke..assured me that I could lay £30,000 on the nose if I wished.

2. b. *fig.* (Further examples.)

1875 W. Hyde in C. F. Wingate *Views & Interviews on Journalism* 196 The 'nose for news', by which is meant unwearying alertness and insatiable hunger for something 'ahead of the other papers'. **1934** C. Lambert *Music Ho!* ii. 86 He had an astounding 'nose' for the growth of any particular movement of taste or snobbism. **1942** E. Waugh *Put out More Flags* ii. 118 One does not work in the East without acquiring a nose for a deal. **1960** *Times* 20 June 4/1 The crowds who always have a nose for personality. **1972** 'J. Cassells' *Profit for Picaroon* v. 36 He was a damned good reporter..and he had a nose for a story.

c. Also, of wines.

1936 F. C. Lloyd *Art & Technique Wine* xv. 146 The bouquet, or 'nose' to use a more technical word, is very important and serves to reveal the characteristics of wines to a connoisseur. **1952** A. Lichine *Wines of France* x. 107 Its tremendous nose—*bouquet* is too delicate a word—makes it [*sc.* Chambertin] a veritable Cyrano. **1971** *Guardian* 12 Nov. 9/2 The dry white of Beaucaire.. has an aromatic 'nose' and plenty of body.

d. *on the nose* (Austral.): offensive, annoying; smelly.

1941 Baker *Dict. Austral. Slang* 49 *Nose, on the*: (said of things) disliked, offensive. **1945** T. Inglis Moore *We're going Through* 18 Withdraw! That's on the nose! **1946** K. Tennant *Lost Haven* (1947) vi. 86 'Christ! Alec,' he complained. 'This bait's a bit on the nose, ain't it?' He spat over the side as the reek of fish-heads a week old.. caught his stomach. **1953** D. Cusack *Southern Steel* 138 The beer's on the nose and the plonk'd make a willy-wagtail fight an emu. **1974** *Australian* 12 Dec. 13 She renounced her Australian citizenship and swore everlasting loyalty to the Stars and Stripes. A bit on the nose, we think.

5. (Earlier and later examples.)

1789 G. Parker *Life's Painter* xv. 151 Nose.—Snitch. **1928** E. Wallace *Gunner* xviii. 145 He was just a little thief and a nose. **1954** [see *grass *sb.*[1] 11*]. **1961** *John o' London's* 30 Nov. 610/3 Other words used for him [*sc.* an informer] include *grass, nose,* [etc.]. **1974** R. Edwards *Dixon of Dock Green* 7 He knew that CID men are allowed to drink on duty because much of their time is spent with 'noses' or informants.

6. (Later examples.)

1917 R. Fry *Let.* 23 Nov. (1972) II. 420 Millions of people..catch me on the telephone the moment I just put my nose inside the Omega. **1922** Joyce *Ulysses* 322 In Shanagolden where he daren't show his nose. **1935** J. Buchan *House of Four Winds* i. 42, I should like to put my nose inside Evallonia just to say I'd been there. **1947** M. Lowry *Under Volcano* i. 25 Geoffrey's 'nose was always in a book'. **1963** Nose wide open [see *fox *sb.* 2 c]. **1968** M. Jones *Survivor* ii. 33 It was considered anti-social to 'have your nose stuck in a book'. **1970** C. Major *Dict. Afro-Amer. Slang* 85 *'Nose wide open'* is to be in love.

7. c. *on the nose* (U.S.): accurately, precisely, to the heart of the situation; accurate, precise (esp. of time).

1937 *Printers' Ink Monthly* May 40/1 *On the button,* a program ending exactly on time... *On the nose,* see 'On the button'. **1943** *New Yorker* 30 Oct. 21/1 I'll meet you there happest twelve, but on the nose. **1944** W. C. Greet *World Words* p. v, This book has been prepared in great haste. To be readily understood, and, in radio parlance, to be on the nose, were its prime requirements. **1958** B. Holiday *Lady sings Blues* (1973) ii. 27 'You were supposed to be out weeks ago,' they told one girl. But I got out right on the nose at the end of four months. **1959** N. Mailer *Advts. for Myself* (1961) 240 Malcolm Cowley was right on the nose when he wrote that *The Deer Park* was a far more difficult book to write than *The Naked and the Dead.* **1962** P. Gregory *Like Tigress at Bay* i. 14 'That's it.' he said. 'You've hit it right on the nose.' **1972** R. H. Copperud *Dict. Contemp. & Colloq. Usage* (Eng.-Lang Inst. Amer.) 21/1 *On the nose*, right on target; exactly; accurately; on the button. **1974** Hawkey & Bingham *Wild Card* xxii. 176 The cerebroid was properly docked in the flight couch. 'Right on the nose,' Stillman said.

8. b. (Earlier example of usage with *poke.*) Conversely *to keep one's nose clean,* to behave properly, keep out of trouble (see also quot. 1909).

1850 Thackeray *Pendennis* II. xxxvi. 347 Beck! leave the room. What do *you* want poking your nose in here? **1887** *Lantern* (New Orleans) 13 Oct. 5/3 There's worse fellows than you looking for it, and if you only keep your nose clean, we'll let you have it. **1909** J. R. Ware *Passing Eng.* 162/1 *Keep your nose clean* (Army), avoid drink. **1934** J. O'Hara *Appointment in Samarra* ii. 54, I give you the sawbuck because you've just got out of the can. Keep your nose clean **1945** P. Cheyney *I'll say she Does!* i. 12 You're a guy who has gotta reputation for keepin' his nose clean, but..you're in bad with the big boy. **1959** N. Mailer *Advts. for Myself* (1961) 350 You boys on Channel Five want to keep your nose clean, now don't you? **1960** C. MacInnes *Mr. Love & Justice* 15 What we're offering you is—well, influence... How you manage there, provided you keep your nose clean, is really up to you. **1970** N. Armstrong et al. *First on Moon* i. 23 Do what people tell you, keep your nose clean and work out your academic progress. **1974** A. Ross *Bradford Business* 64 Denis Fitzgerald..a known associate of villains, but managed to keep his own nose clean.

c. Also, *to look down one's nose.*

1921 Galsworthy *To Let* iii. xi. 306 That chap Jolyon's water-colours were on view there. He went in to look down his nose at them—it might give him some faint satisfaction. **1932** *Sun* (Baltimore) 24 Oct. 8/1 It is getting more difficult for a lawyer to look down his nose at the courtroom, with consequent impairment of the prestige of the courts. **1956** A. Wilson *Anglo-Saxon Att.* i. iv. 102 When you were all little babies, I used to sing and dance all day. The English neighbours would say 'That young Mrs Middleton's quite mad', and look down their noses—so! **1973** *Times* 24 Apr. 5/4 The portrait of the famous widow, who invented the topsy-turvy logic of *remuage* and *dégorgement*..looks down her nose down the stairs at her successors in the craft.

e. *to hold one's nose*: to compress the nostrils between the fingers in order to avoid perceiving a (bad) smell. Also *fig.*

a **1592** Greene *Jas. IV* (1905) II. i. ii. 102 A stiffe docket,—hold your nose, master. **1830** Coleridge *Table-T.* 8 July (1884) 102 Son of Jacob! Thou stinkest foully. See the man in the moon! he is holding his nose at thee at that distance. **1900** *Fortn. Rev.* Jan. 74 Surely there are times when he is forced to hold his nose and shut his eyes to shut out the abominable visions he conjures up for us. **1973** *Times* 18 Sept. 18/2 Then abolish all alternatives to this public system of education, at which they hold their noses.

f. *to thumb one's nose*: to put one's thumb to one's nose and extend the fingers as a gesture of derision: to 'cock a snook'. Also *fig.* orig. *U.S.*

1903 R. Dunn *Diary* 25 July (1907) ix. 109 He thumbed his nose at us. **1929** A. C. & C. Edington *Studio Murder Myst.* iv. 37 Underlings in the studio thumbed their noses at his back. **1947** W. Motley *Knock on any Door* 119 Behind Ma's back Ang thumbed her nose at him and stuck out her tongue. **1973** J. Wainwright *High-Class Kill* 163 They are already thumbing their snotty, aristocratic noses at us.

g. *to get it up one's nose*: in P. G. Wodehouse (*a*) to become angry; (*b*) to become infatuated.

1925 Wodehouse *Carry on, Jeeves!* iii. 67 This lad seems to have chucked all the principles of a well-spent boyhood. He has got it up his nose! **1934** —— *Right ho, Jeeves* xvii. 220 So thoroughly had Gussie got it up his nose by now that it seemed to me that had he sighted me he might have become personal about even an old school friend. **1961** —— *Service with Smile* (1962) ix. 135, I have seldom seen a man who has got it so thoroughly up his nose. **1971** —— *Much Obliged, Jeeves* iii. 20 He had spoken of her..with devotion in every syllable. Plainly he had got it up his nose and didn't object to being bossed. **1973** —— *Bachelors Anonymous* viii. 92 'See what I mean?.. Got it right up his nose,' said Mr. Llewellyn. 'I have seldom seen a case where the symptoms were more clearly marked,' said Mr. Trout. 'He is taking her to dinner.'

h. *to get up someone's nose*: (see quot. 1951).

1951 Partridge *Dict. Slang* 1120/2 *Nose, get up one's*, to upset, annoy, irritate, render 'touchy'. **1975** *Daily Mail* 6 Aug. 7/1 The implication that granny was a little winning knockout with a system that couldn't be bettered ..does, I'm afraid, get rather up my nose. **1975** *Times Lit. Suppl.* 26 Sept. 1102/2 The police pulled them [*sc.* homeless alcoholics] in whenever they got up the public's nose too much.

i. *to get one's nose down* (*to*): to work arduously and concentratedly (at). Cf. Grindstone 2 b.

1962 *Times* 31 May 4/1 Getting their noses really down to business. **1966** Wodehouse *Plum Pie* i. 11 One would certainly have expected him by this time to have raised the price of a marriage licence and had the Bishop and assistant clergy getting their noses down to it.

9. e. Also, *to rub* (occas. *push*) *one's nose in it*: to remind (someone) humiliatingly of his error; to make (someone) acutely aware of (a fault, etc.).

1963 P. M. Hubbard *Flush as May* xiii. 121 I'm sorry. I've said I'm sorry... Don't rub my nose in it. **1967** 'M. Hunter' *Cambridgeshire Disaster* vii. 47 It makes a change, I suppose,.. having your nose rubbed in it. **1971** D. Lees *Rainbow Conspiracy* i. 18 Using me on a hard news story would be pushing their noses in it—treating them like a branch office with printing facilities. **1972** *Times Lit. Suppl.* 3 Mar. 234/1 Discontinuity will not do on its own for a resolute dualist and Bataille wants to rub our noses in the idea of the continuous.

13. Also, the corresponding part of an aeroplane, motor vehicle, torpedo, surfboard, etc.

1899 *Royal Mag.* Jan. 251/1 In the 'nose' of the torpedo. **1899** H. G. Wells *When Sleeper Wakes* xxiv. 320 The nose of the machine jerked upward steeply. **1903** *Science Siftings* 7 Nov. 68/1 When the operator wishes to descend he pulls on a line which lowers the nose of the kite. **1906** *Strand Mag.* May 516/2 In such cases they put the nose of the machine to the opposite side. **1914** *War Illustr.* I. 406 A British Army biplane that collapsed and fell with its nose in the earth. **1942** *R.A.F. Jrnl.* 13 June 33 Always face the nose of the bomb. When I say 'nose' I mean the end which is away from the explosive charge. **1962** S. Carpenter in *Into Orbit* 57 The engineers designed the capsule so that the blunt-nose would come down first. **1962** T. Masters *Surfing made Easy* 64 *Nose*, the front of the surfboard. **1968** W. Warwick *Surfriding in N.Z.* 3/2 The nose was rounded with a slight uplift or rocker. **1971** M. Tak *Truck Talk* 110 *Nose*, the foremost part of a trailer.

14. e. A projecting part of an electric traction motor by which it is suspended from the framework of the bogie or vehicle.

1907 Parshall & Hobart *Electric Railway Engin.* x. 451 In the case of a heavy motor there is usually a nose in the frame casting which rests on a bar carried by springs on the transom. **1927** R. E. Dickinson *Electric Trains* vi. 110 On the other side of the motor case a projecting 'nose' is cast and this nose is fixed on the bogie transom with a stiff spring above and below it. **1955** E. A. Binney *Electric Traction Engin.* vii. 126 The nose end of the motor is resiliently supported on the bogie transom.

17. a. *nose-bone, -jam, -net, -peg, -pin, -tip* (later example), *weight*.

1890 W. F. Butler *Sir Charles Napier* xiii. 188 Others..have not had the nerves torn by a jagged ball passing through, breaking nose-bones and jaw-bones, and lacerating nerves. **1956** H. Gold *Man who was not with It* (1965) i. 7 Even if the sharpest nosebones worked *their* way into my cheeks. **1922** Joyce *Ulysses* 168 Sheepsnouts bloodypapered snivelling nosejam on sawdust. **1883** *Illustr. Sporting & Dramatic News* 6 Jan. 407/2 He calls it a 'nose net'. It consists of an ordinary bag net, just large enough to encircle the muzzle of a horse... The effect..is to make a horse keep his mouth shut and..to prevent him pulling. **1963** E. H. Edwards *Saddlery* xii. 88 A very simple device is the nose-net. ..It is put over the nose and fastened fairly tightly to the noseband and will stop the majority of tearaways. **1909** *Cent. Dict.* Suppl. II. 875/1 *Nose-peg*, a pin or stud attached to the quadrant-arm in a spinning-mule to effect an acceleration of the spindle in forming the cop. **1935** H. H. Finlayson *Red Centre* xii. 118 The nose-peg..is a hardwood cylinder expanding to a disk at one end and a smaller pointed cone at the other... The young camel is thrown, the cartilage of the left nostril pierced.., and the peg pushed through the wound. **1966** G. W. Turner *Eng. Lang. Austral. & N.Z.* iii. 39 Cook noticed the nose-pins worn by native men. **1971** *World Archaeology* III. 140 There might be an occasional stone nose-pin. **1927** W. de la Mare *Told Again* 246 The Fox then brushed himself nose-tip to stern with his brush. **1959** '*Motor*' *Man.* (ed. 36) xiii. 270 A caravan with a heavy nose weight tows more steadily than one without.

b. *nose-blowing*.

1864 J. S. Le Fanu *Uncle Silas* I. xxiv. 292 The boisterous nose-blowing that suddenly resounded from the passage. **1967** E. A. Gollschewsky in *Coast to Coast 1965–6* 87 The vehement nose-blowing..that marked her progress from room to room.

c. *nose-dropping*.

1905 J. Joyce *Let.* 19 Jan. (1966) II. 78 O, blind, snivelling, nose-dropping, calumniated Christ.

18. nose-bridge, (*a*) = Nose *sb.* 1 d; (*b*) *Archæol.* denoting a type of handle found on pottery of the Copper Age in southern Europe; **nose-candy** *U.S. slang*, a drug that is inhaled (illegally), *spec.* cocaine; **nose-clip,** a clip excluding water from the nose of a swimmer or diver; **nose door** *Aeronaut.*, a forward-facing door in the nose of an aeroplane, **nose drive,** the positioning of the engines at the front of a space rocket; so **nose-driven** *a.*; **nose drops,** a medicament intended to be administered as drops into the nose; **nose-glasses** *U.S.* (examples); **nose hangar** *Aeronaut.* (see quot. 1960); **nose-heavy** *a. Aeronaut.*, having a tendency for the nose to drop relative to the tail; hence **nose-heaviness**; **nose-nippers** *pl.* = Pince-nez; **nose-paint** *slang*, intoxicating liquor; also, a reddening of the nose ascribed to habitual drinking (cf. *nose-painter, -painting* s.v. Nose *sb.* 17 b); **nose paste** = *nose putty* below; **nose print,** a drawing of the facial characteristics of an animal, used as a means of identification; so **nose-printing** *vbl. sb.*; **nose putty,** a putty-like substance used in the theatre for altering the shape of the nose, etc.; **nose-ride** *v. intr.*, to stand on the nose (cf. *Nose *sb.* 13) of a surfboard (usu. as *vbl. sb.*); **nose-riders** *pl.*, spectacles; **nose suspension,** a method of supporting a traction motor from the framework of the bogie or vehicle at one end and on an axle at the other (cf. sense *14 e); so **nose-suspended** *a.*; **nose-thumbing** *vbl. sb.*, the action of thumbing one's nose (*Nose *sb.* 8 f); an instance of such behaviour; so (as a back-formation) **nose-thumb** *sb.*; **nose-to-tail** *adv.* and *a.*, (of motor vehicles) travelling, or placed, behind one another and very close together; **nose-trick,** the inadvertent inhalation or expulsion of liquid through the nose when drinking; **nose wheel** *Aeronaut.*, a wheel under the nose of an aircraft; **nose wipe** *sb.* = *nose-wiper*.

1923 A. Huxley *Antic Hay* x. 156 Shell rims with gold ear-pieces and gold nose-bridge. **1939** V. G. Childe *Dawn Europ. Civilization* (ed. 3) xiv. 245 In the pottery [of Sardinia before the nuragic age] we might distinguish: ..carinated cups and other vessels with nose-bridge handles, which persist into the nuragic age. **1935** A. J. Pollock *Underworld Speaks* 81/1 *Nose candy*, cocaine. **1935** C. F. Coe *G-Man* ii. 25 I'll lay off the booze an' you lay off the organizin', the nose-candy and the stick-ups. **1960** *Time* 25 Jan. 88/2 Cocaine..is put into crystalline form. This enables users to sniff it ('nose candy'). **1974** *Globe & Mail* (Toronto) 28 Sept. 33/4 The movie omitted the morphine and left the cocaine because nose candy is the trendy drug. **1959** *Elizabethan* Apr. 9/2 Following the orders of the sergeant I had..fitted the nose clip in place [on an under-water breathing apparatus]. **1971** A. Diment *Think Inc.* vii. 123, I bit on the rubber mouth-piece, put on the nose-clip and flipped down my face mask. **1960** Nose door [see *beaver-tail* s.v. *Beaver[1] 6]. **1969** *Jane's Freight Containers 1968–69* 454/1 Loading is via a vizor-type, straight-in, nose-door with full-width integral ramps. **1937** *Discovery* Sept. 270/2 First he [*sc.* Goddard] directed his attention to the so-called 'nose-drive' construction. **1947** W. Ley *Rockets & Space Travel* (1948) v. 134 The gases were to be ejected through a system of nozzles at the top of the rocket; the nozzles were to pull the rocket upward, instead of pushing it upward as planned in the original Oberth Rocket... This system, known as 'nose drive'.., offered a great number of advantages. The rocket did not have to be constructed as sturdily nor did it require an elaborate steering mechanism. **1952** E. Burgess *Rocket Propulsion* v. 131 It has been stated that nose-driven rockets..are inherently more stable than those in which the motor is situated at the extreme rear. This is another common fallacy, for providing the thrust line of the motor passes through the centre of gravity of the rocket, the actual position of the motor cannot affect stability. **1942** T. Sollmann *Man. Pharmacol.* (ed. 6) 165 'Nose drops', *i.e.*, solutions in liquid petrolatum for instillation into the nares, should not contain more than 1 per cent of eucalyptol or camphor. **1970** *Women's Household* July 12/1 When he needed nose drops badly he would come over to one of us and stick up his nose. **1890** *Cent. Dict.* V. 4020/2 Nose glasses. **1901** Ade *Forty Mod. Fables* 22 He said 'Whom,' and wore Nose Glasses. **1929** D. Runyon in *Hearst's International* Oct. 64/1 To look at Judge Henry G. Blake, with his..nose glasses. **1971** *Lebende Sprachen* XVI. 11/2 US nose glasses —BE/US pince-nez. **1948** *Jrnl. R. Aeronaut. Soc.* LII. 573 In the civil field the 'nose hangar', such as that used successfully by KLM for the Constellation last winter, is a realistic effort to provide shelter where it is needed, instead of enclosing space at random. **1960** G. Blanchet *Search in North* v. 66 Nose hangars were built—sheds in which the front of a plane could be sheltered and work done on its engines. **1970** R. & J. Paterson *Cranberry Portage* xiv. 87 A great deal of time was spent warming aircraft engines with roaring fire-pots inside the canvas nose-hangars. **1919** A. Klemin *Text-bk. Aeronaut. Engin.* xv. 178 The down stream from the propellers..is said to increase the safety from the point of view of longitudinal balance, giving tail heaviness with power, and nose heaviness without power. **1930** R. Duncan *Stunt Flying* iii. 26 Nose-heaviness, or tail-heaviness, can be corrected by adjusting the horizontal stabilizer. **1959** *Times* 8 Sept. 13/6 There is no feeling of nose-heaviness, and the steering does not have any tricks on corners. **1914** S. L. Walkden *How to understand Aeroplanes* ii. 5 This 'front-heavy,' or 'nose-heavy' machine..is devoid of a self-righting effect. **1917** *Flying* I. 217/1 A stable aeroplane has its centre of gravity well forward, and normally the centre of pressure is behind the centre of gravity. Without a fixed tail plane it would therefore be nose heavy. **1945** R. von Mises *Theory of Flight* xvii. 501 If the state of motion changes or the loads are shifted, the airplane will become slightly nose- or tail-heavy so that the pilot has to operate the elevator. **1895** J. Davidson *Old Aberdeenshire Ministers* 26 The *Aberdeen Journal*, which he read aloud..in a loud monotone, nasalised by the light grip of a large pair of nose-nippers worn low. **1900** Conrad *Lord Jim* v. 40 He saw the old man lift his head from some writing so sharp that his nose-nippers fell off. *a* **1913** F. Rolfe *Desire & Pursuit of Whole* (1934) vii. 61 Smirking female with the thinnest of pinched lips and nose-nippers. **1880** A. A. Hayes *New Colorado* (1881) xi. 158 We saw..a sign, in which a name which I have never encountered elsewhere was given to stimulating beverages. This sign was '*Nose-paint* and *Lunch*'. **1901** F. E. Taylor *Folk-Speech S. Lancs.*, *Nose-paint*, a jocular term for alcoholic drink. **1922** Joyce *Ulysses* 615 A strong suspicion of nosepaint about the nasal appendage. **1968** *Amer. Speech* XLIII. 303 He [*sc.* the cowman] drinks..*nose paint* instead of 'whiskey'. **1951** N. Marsh *Opening Night* vii. 156 One cardboard box containing false hair, rouge, substance labelled 'nose paste'. **1961** Bowman & Ball *Theatre Lang.* 233 *Nose paste*, a plastic substance used to alter the appearance of an actor's nose, chin, etc. **1934** *Sun* (Baltimore) 15 Sept. 15/2 The 'nose print' of a dog is as distinctive as the finger print of a human being. **1952** *Ibid.* 8 Dec. 10/4 Three dairy scientists of the South Dakota Agricultural Experiment Station at Brookings, S.D., have worked out a system of nose prints by means of which it is possible to identify one individual cow from a million others. **1970** B. Knox *Children of Mist* iii. 56 Sometimes breeders..try to work a switch of animal. So we keep one nose-print on file in special cases..ready for comparison **1973** *Times* 26 Nov. 17/5 Four investigators followed the trail of the animals, to establish 'contact' with them and where possible, to draw 'noseprints'—simple drawings of nostril shape and facial wrinkles—to identify the particular animals and their approximate stages of development. **1934** *Sun* (Baltimore) 15 Sept. 15/2 A plan for nation-wide identification of dogs by 'nose printing' to eliminate 'dognapping'. **1960** A. Christie *Adventure of Xmas Pudding* 223 Why did I feel..I was talking to..an actor playing a part!.. What did I see..the beaked nose (faked with that useful substance, nose putty), [etc.]. **1969** K. Vonnegut *Slaughterhouse-Five* v. 88 Rosewater was a big man, but not very powerful. He looked as though he might be made out of nose putty. **1965** Farrelly & McGregor *This Surfing Life* 138 *Nose-ride*, to ride on the nose of the surfboard. **1875** E. H. Dering *Sherborne* II. xviii. 53 Sir Thomas..put on a pair of those glasses which are popularly known as nose-riders. **1962** *Austral. Women's Weekly* Suppl. 24 Oct. 3/3 *Nose-riding*, standing right at front of the board while riding a wave. **1971** *Studies in English* (Univ. Cape Town) Feb. 25 Until the end of the nose-riding era, the run of Cape Town surfers identified with the Californian scene as portrayed in *Surfer*. **1927** R. E. Dickinson *Electric Trains* vi. 111 Fig. 48 shows a bogie with two nose-suspended motors in place. **1948** D. W. & M. Hinde *Electric & Diesel-Electric Locomotives* ii. 25 During the past past few years, however, nose-suspended motors mounted on bogies have become standard practice on all American diesel-electric locomotives. **1894** K. Hedges *Amer. Electr. Street Railways* vii. 75 In the case of the G.E. 800 type when the side suspension is used, the whole of the weight is taken off the axle, whereas by the older method half the weight only was on the cross bar, resting on springs, and the remainder on the axle. One method is known as the End or Nose Suspension, the other as the Side Bar Suspension. **1927** R. E. Dickinson *Electric Trains* vi. 111 For multiple unit trains the nose suspension is practically universal. **1948** D. W. & M. Hinde *Electric & Diesel-Electric Locomotives* ii. 24 Where hammer-blow on the track and axle-loading are not limiting factors and provided that there is one motor per driven axle, nose-suspension is the simplest form of drive obtainable. **1963** *Guardian* 11 Feb. 2/6 Their medical officer of health ..is leaving his post because of the council's continued nose-thumb at the Clean Air Act. **1959** I. & P. Opie *Lore & Lang. Schoolch.* xiv. 317 That peculiar form of recognition variously known as 'the five-finger salute', 'nose thumbing',.. 'cocking a snook', or 'taking a sight' used, thirty years ago, to be demonstrated by every child in the country. **1970** *Globe & Mail* (Toronto) 26 Sept. 23/5 A nose-thumbing gesture comes as a blessed relief in a movie so painfully earnest. **1959** *Manch. Guardian* 20 July 2/5 Four L-drivers nose to tail on a busy road. **1960** *Guardian* 7 June 6/1 The accustomed queues of nose-to-tail traffic on main roads. **1963** *Times* 11 June 5/4 Yet above the garage cars sit nose-to-tail on free space within the park, and scour Mayfair for vacant meters. **1974** C. Fremlin *By Horror Haunted* 48 The nose-to-tail crawl along the motorway. **1954** P Frankau *Wreath for Enemy* II. i. 58 It was the 'Prendergast' that made me do what is vulgarly called the nose-trick with my lemonade. **1972** P. Dickinson *Lizard in Cup* ix. 132 Pibble almost did the nose-trick with the dung-smelling local brandy. **1934** *Flight* 6 Dec. 1301 A castor nose wheel allows the fullest use to be made of the wheel brakes of the Hammond Model Y. **1940** *Illustr London News* CXCVII. 315 (*caption*) The 'Boston' has.. an undercarriage of the tricycle type—two rear wheels retracting into the rear of the engine nacelles and the nosewheel retracting rearwards and upwards into the fuselage. **1974** *Daily Tel.* 5 Oct. 1 A Belgian airliner.. pitched on to its nose on the main runway at Southend airport when the nosewheel collapsed shortly before takeoff. **1919** W. Deeping *Second Youth* ii. 13 Yer dirty little wretch yer; ain't yer got a nose-wipe?

nose, *v.* Add: **6. c.** (Later examples.)

1926 E. F. Spanner *Naviators* i. 9 The car nosed its way ahead on bottom gear, and at a snail's pace. **1937** *Discovery* Feb. 38/2 We nosed our way through the reeds. **1973** P. Moyes *Curious Affair* i. 14 The station wagon nosed its way along the narrow road.

d. To direct the nose of (a motor vehicle, etc.) in a certain direction.

1954 'N. Shute' *Slide Rule* iv. 89 The elevator coxswain nosed her [*sc.* an airship] upwards to about a thousand feet. **1972** D. Delman *Week to Kill* 139, I nosed the car out of town and on to 118, where I zapped it into high.

8. b. (Earlier and later *fig.* examples.)

1879 'Mark Twain' *Let.* 21 Jan. (1920) I. 187 The detectives were nosing around after Stewart's loud remains. **1887** *Lantern* (New Orleans) 3 Dec. 2/3 We

nosed around to try and find out why. **1917** WODEHOUSE *Uneasy Money* iv. 43 There's no harm in my nosing round, is there? Be a good chap and give me the address. **1925** —— *Carry On, Jeeves!* i. 28 He began to nose about. He pulled out drawer after drawer. **1955** A. HUXLEY *Let.* 25 Sept. (1969) 766 While in Guildford I read, or rather nosed about in, Penfield's book on Epilepsy. **1958** P. KEMP *No Colours or Crest* iii. 36 We nosed around the Islands, sometimes less than a mile off shore, searching for indications of our quarry.

c. (Later example.) Also with *among*.

1936 R. LEHMANN *Weather in Streets* II. 189, I thought of her nosing in my room for signs. **1941** A. CURNOW in Chapman & Bennett *N.Z. Verse* (1956) 148, I am the nor'west air nosing among the pines.

d. To inform; † to turn king's evidence. *Criminals' slang.*

1811 [see TWIST *v.* 9 c]. **1822** *J. Mackcoull Mem. Life* 112 *Nosed*,..watched and informed against. **1846** tr. *E. Sue's Myst. of Paris* cli. 743/1 Gros Boiteux..has already wanted to *escarper* him, (make him a stiff 'un—kill him,) because he has *mangé* (nosed, informed upon some one). **1923** E. WALLACE *Missing Million* xix. 156 When a copper comes to one of the 'boys' for expert advice, it means he wants him to 'nose'. **1930** —— *White Face* x. 147 You come down 'ere an' expect us to 'nose' for you, and everybody in the court knows we're 'nosing'.

9. Also *transf.* with *ahead*, to go into the lead by a small margin.

1960 *Times* 1 July 18/1 So Miss Truman had nosed ahead at last. **1971** WODEHOUSE *Much Obliged, Jeeves* xiii. 134 If the McCorkadale nosed ahead of him in the voting, Florence would in all probability hand him the pink slip.

11. nose down *Aeronaut.*: to direct the nose of an aircraft downwards, to produce or undergo a (downward) steepening of the flight path.

1916 H. BARBER *Aeroplane Speaks* 85 If a sharp turn necessitates banking beyond that angle, he must 'nose-down'. *Ibid.* 88 The C.G. being forward of the C.P... causes the aeroplane to nose-down. **1938** V. W. PAGÉ *Airplane Servicing Man.* xxiv. 818 It is considered advisable, if the engine should stop, that the plane will nose down automatically, instead of tending to stall. **1958** R. D. BLACKER *Basic Aeronaut. Sci.* xi. 195/1 The vertical portion of the lift was not as great as the weight of the airplane and it nosed down, losing altitude. **1974** J. MONTGOMERIE *Implosion* xii. 86 We crossed the coast, nosing down over pewter sea... Runway rose towards us.

12. Of an aircraft: to fall *over* on its 'nose'. Of a surfboard: to plunge downward nose first.

1928 V. W. PAGÉ *Mod. Aircraft* xii. 523 Always pick as smooth and level a piece of ground as possible when making a landing, as, if the ground is very soft or if there are hummocks or ditches, the machine is very likely to 'nose over'. **1953** BERG *Dict. New Words* 115/2 *Nose over*. .. *Flying*. To fall nose forward. **1963** *Surfing Yearbk.* 42/2 *Nosing*, when the nose of the surfboard goes under water while riding a wave. **1965** J. POLLARD *Surfrider* ii. 20 Don't let your board 'nose'. This is what happens when the front of the surf board digs in.

nosing *vbl. sb.*: also *Comb.*, as **nosing motion** (see quot. 1940).

1883 H. E. WALMSLEY *Cotton Spinning* 30 The terminal velocity of the spindles may be increased in the same ratio, as their diameter decreases. This object is attained by Platt's automatic nosing motion. **1884** R. MARSDEN *Cotton Spinning* ix. 264 The last invention.., which seems to answer all needs, is the automatic nosing motion brought out by Messrs. Platts, and which consists of a scroll placed upon the end of the winding-on drum. **1932** W. SCOTT-TAGGART *Cotton Machinery Sketches* (ed. 4) p. xviii, Diagram of Cop, etc., illustrating Principle of Nosing Motion. **1940** *Chambers's Techn. Dict.* 583/2 *Nosing motion* (Cotton Spinning), a motion on the mule spinning frame which, as the diameter lessens, increases the speed of the tapering spindle on which a cop is being wound.

nose-bag. Add: **1. b.** Also, the practice among holiday-makers of taking their own food or refreshments with them. Also *attrib.*, as *nose-bag crowd*.

1908 *Daily Chron.* 4 Aug. 3/4 Neither was it, as one of Messrs. Lyons's managers observed with appreciation, a 'nose-bag' crowd. **1909** *Ibid.* 7 June 5/2 The 'nose-bag' grows and flourishes.

3. Food, a meal. Also allusively. Phr. *to put* (occas. *get*) *on the nose-bag*, to eat. *slang.*

1874 HOTTEN *Slang Dict.* 239 To 'put on the nose-bag' is to eat hurriedly, or to eat while continuing at work. **1886** F. T. ELWORTHY *West Somerset Word-Bk.* 521 Well! hon I zeed zo many o' they there whit-neckangkecher fullers comin', I thinks to mysul, there's a bit of a nose-bag a-gwain on in there. **1898** J. D. BRAYSHAW *Slum Silhouettes* 155 Come in, we'll jist 'ave five minutes wiv the nose-bag. **1921** R. LARDNER *Big Town* v. 201 We couldn't stop to put on the nose bag at the Graham. **1925** WODEHOUSE *Carry On, Jeeves!* vi. 145 Biffy's man came in with the nose-bags and we sat down to lunch. **1926** *Amer. Speech* I. 652/1 *Nose-bag*, lunch handed out in paper bag. **1930** D. L. SAYERS *Strong Poison* xi. 137 Thanks awfully, I've had my morning nosebag. **1962** *New Statesman* 21 Dec. 897/3 The precise time the family get the nose-bag on. **1973** WODEHOUSE *Bachelors Anonymous* xiv. 185, I must rush. I'm putting on the nosebag with a popsy.

4. A gas-mask. *colloq.*

1915 D. O. BARNETT *Let.* 11 May 135 Every one was ready and had their nose-bags on, and the gas had no effect whatever. **1940** *Everybody's Weekly* 2 Mar. 4/1 Londoners call their masks 'Dicky-birds', 'Canaries' and 'Nose-bags'.

nose-bagger. [f. NOSE-BAG + -ER[1].] = NOSE-BAG 1 b.

1931 *Morning Post* 17 Oct. 12/5 The friendly little South Coast town, where only the 'nose-baggers'..are frowned upon.

nose-bleed. 2. (Earlier, later, and *fig.* examples.)

1848 *Asmodeus* (N.Y.) 73 (Th.), What's the best cure for nose-bleed, doctor? **1914** G. S. GORDON *Let.* 11 Aug. (1943) 59 Germany will get the nose-bleed of her life. **1953** 'J. R. MACDONALD' *Imaginary Blonde* in *Manhunt* (1964) XII. 138/1 It was a little scuffle. One of the guests suffered a nosebleed. **1960** WODEHOUSE *Jeeves in Offing* xv. 161 Half way through the second act..Catsmeat Potter-Pirbright, who was playing Lord Fancourt Babberley, left the stage abruptly to attend to an unforeseen nose bleed. **1972** 'L. EGAN' *Paper Chase* (1973) x. 160 Just a nosebleed... Somebody banged me on the nose.

no·se-cap. [f. NOSE *sb.* + CAP *sb.*[1]] **1.** (See NOSE *sb.* 18.)

2. *Aeronaut.* **a.** (See quot. 1950.)

1909 KIPLING *Actions & Reactions* 112 From her North Atlantic Winter nose-cap (worn bright as diamond with boring through uncounted leagues of hail, snow, and ice) to the inset of her three built-out propeller-shafts is some two hundred and forty feet. **1950** *Gloss. Aeronaut. Terms* (*B.S.I.*) I. 49 *Bow cap* (*nose cap*), a structure forming the extreme forward end of the envelope or hull.

b. (See quots.)

1919 BLACKBURN & NEWBY *All about Aircraft* 106 *Nose cap*, a conical cap placed over the propeller boss to reduce head resistance. **1949** *Gloss. Aeronaut. Terms* (*B.S.I.*) II. 19 *Nose cap*, a boss or hub fairing filled coaxially and rotating with the propeller. It does not extend aft of the front of the blade roots.

3. The metal cap on the nose of a shell or bomb which contains the device for setting the time fuse.

1917 A. G. EMPEY *Over Top* 301 *Nosecap*, that part of a shell which unscrews and contains the device and scale for setting the time fuse. **1919** W. DEEPING *Second Youth* xxix. 244 St. Roman was not a nice place that night, with 'dud Archies' and nose-caps falling into it, as well as bombs. **1942** 'R. CROMPTON' *William carries On* iii. 65 Rich in nose-caps and time-fuses and casings.

4. A cover protecting the nose.

1973 *Times Lit. Suppl.* 18 May 544/2 The middle-aged on the beaches clearly felt no self-consciousness in wearing little paper nose-caps as protection from the sun.

nose cone. Also **nose-cone, nosecone.** [f. NOSE *sb.*] A conical nose-cap; *spec.* the cone-shaped front part of a rocket, which is designed to withstand the severe heating caused by atmospheric friction and generally contains any instruments that may be carried.

1949 *Jrnl. Brit. Interplanetary Soc.* VIII. 233 A diagram of the rocket is shown in Fig. 1. The equipment space is within a thin ogival-shaped aluminium nose-cone. **1956** *Spaceflight* I. 26/1 At this stage..the ballistic nose-cone (which protects the satellite package from aerodynamic heating) can be thrown off. **1963** *Guardian* 30 Mar. 1/5 The plane was struck by lightning .. A hole was made in the fibre nosecone. **1964** J. L. NAYLER *Dict. Astronautics* 177 The nose cone may become the satellite itself..or, after shielding the satellite.., be separated by an explosive cartridge. **1974** A. PRICE *Other Paths* II. ii. 128 They were trying to take the brass nose-cone off one of our howitzer shells.

no·se count. [f. the phr. *to count noses* (NOSE *sb.* 6 d).] An enumeration, esp. of votes; a decision by majority vote. Hence **no·se-counting** *vbl. sb.*, assessment by numbers.

1938 *Life* 6 June 22/3 Meantime in London peace-yearning Prime Minister Chamberlain again tried to quarantine the Spanish war by proposing a nose-count and withdrawal of foreign troops. **1951** *True Police Cases* (U.S.) Nov. 42 At nose-counting time in the..hoosegow. **1958** *Listener* 30 Oct. 708/1 Was that nose-counting success due only to some adventitious notion..that *Salome* is salacious? **1960** *Times* 14 Sept. 12/6 There was much talk just then of the coming 'Nose Count' over the U.S.A. which was one way of making their census sound more personal and pointed. **1966** *Economist* 29 Oct. 450/1 The prospects of an effective tightening of Rhodesian sanctions must depend far more on the major powers' real readiness to apply a tighter squeeze than on the nominal nose-count in the Security Council. **1967** M. MCLUHAN *Medium is Massage* 22 Nose-counting, a cherished part of the eighteenth-century fragmentation process, has rapidly become a cumbersome and ineffectual form of social assessment.

no·se-dive, *sb.* Also **nose dive, nosedive.** [f. NOSE *sb.* + DIVE *sb.*] **1.** *Aeronaut.* A sudden or rapid descent by an aircraft nose first. Also *transf.*

1912 *Flight* 31 Aug. 787/1 The machine at once started a spiral nose-dive. **1914** HAMEL & TURNER *Flying* iii. 57 M. Adolphe Pégoud introduced side-slips, tail-dives, and nose-dives into his exhibition repertory of flying. **1917** 'I. HAY' *Carrying On* i. 17 Next moment she [*sc.* the aeroplane] lurched again, and then took a 'nose-dive' straight into the British trenches. **1922** *Encycl. Brit.* XXX. 21/2 The aeroplane may..drop one wing and pass into a steep spiral glide known as a 'spinning nose-dive'. *a* **1930** D. H. LAWRENCE *Last Poems* (1932) 15 The dolphins leap ..and flip! they go! with the nose-dive of sheer delight. **1932** AUDEN *Orators* II. 52 *Nose-dive*—Nightmare to nerves And needed by no one And dash toward death. **1952** R. S. PORTEOUS in *Coast to Coast 1951–1952* 146 If this tub rolls over or takes a sudden nose-dive to the bottom. **1955** H. KLEIN *Winged Courier* viii. 52 It looked as if the 'Pioneer' was crashing to its doom in an uncontrolled nose-dive. **1975** *Aeroplane Monthly* Nov. 572 When a down-draught was encountered or the control column was pushed forward..this resulted in a nose-dive to earth.

2. *fig.*

1920 R. MACAULAY *Potterism* VI. iv. 241 If you chuck the *Fact* you take away its last chance. It'll do a nose-dive now! **1946** *Sun* (Baltimore) 8 Nov. 21 An unexplained nose dive in surplus sales occurred in the July-August-September quarter. **1973** *Guardian* 28 May 6/6 After a really splendid first week, the Festival took a nosedive from which it never recovered.

no·se-dive, *v.* Also **nosedive.** [f. prec. sb., or DIVE *v.*] **1. a.** *intr.* To perform a nose-dive.

1915 *Sphere* 24 July 94/2 Its engines stopped, and it nose-dived to a level of 2,000 ft. **1920** *Chambers's Jrnl.* Mar. 208/1 Checking any tendency [of a motor-boat] to nosedive. **1923** *Daily Mail* 27 Mar. 9 His aeroplane nose-dived from a height of about 150 feet and crashed on to the aerodrome. **1930** E. BLUNDEN *Poems* 42 A hundred feet he nose-dives. **1930** *Daily Express* 6 Oct. 3/3 Then with all the lights on the airship nose dived. **1930** J. S. HUXLEY *Bird-Watching & Bird Behaviour* (1949) ii. 35 They [*sc.* birds] must be protected against side-slipping and nose-diving. **1968** W. WARWICK *Surfriding in N.Z.* 2 He then ran to the front of the board so that it nosedived.

b. *trans.* To put into a nose-dive.

1919 PIPPARD & PRITCHARD *Aeroplane Structures* vi. 55 There is a moment upon the wings tending to nose dive the aeroplane still further. **1928** *Daily Tel.* 16 Oct. 17/5, I have nose-dived this machine at 250 miles an hour.

2. *fig.* Esp. to drop or decrease abruptly.

1920 R. MACAULAY *Potterism* VI. iv. 241, I can't stop it [*sc.* a newspaper's collapsing]. But I'm jolly well not going to nose-dive with it. I'm clearing out. **1926** *Spectator* 13 Mar. 492/1 We will nose-dive straight into the middle of Mr Cobham's book. **1954** *Sun* (Baltimore) 16 Dec. 24/1 Business..has nosedived since the expressway was opened to intercity traffic. **1958** S. HYLAND *Who goes Hang?* xviii. 78 'Is that all you wanted to ask me?' He said it falsetto. 'Well, as a matter of fact, no.' 'Good.' His voice nose-dived. **1969** *Daily Tel.* 23 Jan. 4/1 Allied Investments nosedived again yesterday. The market pushed the shares down another 2s to 3s 6d.

Hence **no·se-diving** *vbl. sb.* and *ppl. a.*

1917 E. W. WALTERS *Heroic Airmen* xii. 102 He was compelled to resort to nose-diving. **1931** *Handbk. Aeronautics* (R. Aeronaut. Soc.) iv. 288 The fuselage must have a load factor the same as for the main planes in nose diving. **1958** *Engineering* 7 Mar. 295/1 Nose diving under hard braking is no more than on more conventional vehicles. **1970** T. HUGHES *Crow* 39 The nosediving aircraft concludes with a boom.

nose-do·wn, *a.* and *sb. Aeronaut.* [f. NOSE *sb.* + DOWN *adv.* or the phr. *to nose down* (*NOSE *v.* 11).] **A.** *adj.* With the nose directed downwards. Also as quasi-*adv.*

1916 H. BARBER *Aeroplane Speaks* 87 [An inclinometer] will indicate a nose-down position by increase in airspeed. *Ibid.* 113 The aeroplane may have a tendency to fly 'nose-down'. **1933** *Jrnl. R. Aeronaut. Soc.* XXXVII. 67 She..goes into a second dive, being 1,160 ft. below her starting height at $t = 80$, and 1,440 ft. below at $t = 100$, when she is 13·5° nose down. **1965** C. N. VAN DEVENTER *Introd. Gen. Aeronaut.* v. 88 If the engine fails the airplane will automatically assume a slightly nose-down position ready for a glide.

B. *sb.* A descent.

1942 *Tee Emm* (Air Ministry) II. 94 That steep nose-down which is often so dangerous if the sea is met sooner than expected. **1944** J. R. HOYT *Safety after Solo* xii. 217 It is time to start the nose down toward point 3.

no-see-em (nōusī·ĕm). *N. Amer.* Also **no-see-um.** [Corruption of *no see them.*] A name used for several small, blood-sucking insects, esp. biting midges of the family Ceratopogonidæ.

1848 THOREAU *Maine Woods* 2 In the summer myriads of black flies, mosquitoes, and midges, or, as the Indians call them, 'no-see-ems', make travelling in the woods almost impossible. **1902** W. D. HULBERT *Forest Neighbors* (1903) 129 The mosquitoes and black-flies and no-see-'ems had bitten him until his skin was covered with blotches. **1903** S. E. WHITE *Forest* 154 The midge, again, or punkie, or 'no-see-'um', just as you please, swarms down upon you suddenly. **1934** A. CHRISTIE *Parker Pyne Investigates* 198 The no-see-ums are biting good and hard. **1939** K. PINKERTON *Wilderness Wife* xvi. 166 No-see-ums are after dark prowlers. **1964** *Atlantic Advocate* July 67/1 Near the bottom we struck swamp ground, a paradise for no-see-'ems, those minute flies whose burning bites are inversely related to their size. **1970** *Observer* (Colour Suppl.) 19 Apr. 59/1 Down on the banks [of a Canadian river] there were awful blood-sucking insects called 'no-see-um', giant mosquitoes. **1975** *New Yorker* 24 Feb. 82/3 No-see-ums are so small they go right through the screening of the tent. They home on flesh.

nose-end. [NOSE *sb.* 17 a.] **a.** The tip of the human nose. **b.** The end of a nose in any of the transferred senses.

1611, etc. [see NOSE *sb.* 17 a]. **1960** S. PLATH *Colossus* (1967) 65 The nose-end that twitches. **1961** *Times* 16 Dec. 11/5 Make sure..that mud does not enter the nose-ends [of a gun].

Hence **nose-ender.** **a.** (See NOSE *sb.* 18.) **b.** (See quots.)

1854 [in Dict. s.v. NOSE *sb.* 18]. **1929** F. C. BOWEN *Sea Slang* 96 *Nose ender*, a strong head wind. **1946** J. IRVING *Royal Navalese* 123 *Nose-ender*, a head wind and sea; regular Destroyer Weather. **1962** W. GRANVILLE *Dict. Sailors' Slang* 82/1 *Nose-ender*, wind blowing from dead ahead, literally into one's nose.

nose-flute. Add to def.: Later used also in North America and Europe. (Later examples.)

1962 *New Yorker* 21 July 68/2 They are the manzello and the stritch, early forbears of the saxophone; a pocket-sized nose flute; the..melodica, a kind of accordion that is blown, not pumped. **1963** *Economist* 23 Nov. 775/2 Invented [jazz] instruments like the stritch and a nose-flute. **1969** *Listener* 3 Apr. 470/3 He has a large gong, a kind of..battery-run accordion, various whistles, and a nose flute.

nose-hole. **1.** (Later examples.)

1922 JOYCE *Ulysses* 51 His leprous nosehole snoring to the sun. **1950** R. MOORE *Candlemas Bay* 242 You know how Candy looks when she's mad, like death, them black eyes and her noseholes thin.

nosema (nosī·mă). [mod.L. (C. W. von Nägeli 1857, in *Amtlicher Bericht über die Versammlung Deutscher Naturforscher* XXXIII. 133), f. Gr. νόσημα disease.] A microsporidian protozoan parasite of the genus so called, esp. *Nosema apis*, identified in 1909 as the cause of an infectious dysentery affecting bees; also, the disease itself. Also *attrib.*

1911 FANTHAM & PORTER in *Proc. Zool. Soc.* 625 That *Nosema apis* was fatal to bees and allied Hymenoptera had been shown..by feeding healthy hive-bees, mason-bees, and wasps with honey infected with *Nosema* spores. **1912** *Ann. Trop. Med. & Parasitol.* VI. 149 Bees infected with *Nosema* seem unable to preserve their spotless cleanliness. *Ibid.* 159 Wasps have been observed carrying away bees dead of *Nosema* and then feeding their larvae on the corpses. **1914** *Bull. U.S. Dept. Agric.* no. 92, 6 The name 'Nosema disease', which the writer [*sc.* G. F. White] suggests as the common name for this disease, is, it will be observed, only a translation of the German name used by Zander. *Ibid.* One is justified in at least drawing the conclusion that Nosema infection in a colony tends to weaken the colony. **1937** W. HERROD-HEMPSALL *Bee-Keeping* II. xxx. 1427 Nosema Disease is caused by a microscopical animal parasite (*Nosema apis*) infesting the food canal of the bee. *Ibid.* 1429 Nosema infected bees do not, as a rule, lose the power of flight. **1955** *Sci. News Let.* 1 Oct. 214/3 Antibiotics..will give successful control over the destructive diseases, American and European foulbroods, that attack larval bees, and nosema, a killer of adults. **1973** *Times* 19 Apr. 27/5 It is against these very diseases [of bees], notably the two 'foul brood' types, but not forgetting acarine and nosema, that the Ministry is acting.

no·se-pick. [PICK *sb.*[1] 5.] An instrument for clearing the nose of mucus, etc. **no·se-picker** [PICKER[1]], a person who picks his nose (with his fingers); **no·se-picking** *vbl. sb.* and *ppl. a.*

1825 *Kaleidoscope* 11 Oct. 114/3 Appended to it, by a silver chain, was..an ivory nose-pick. **1959** I. & P. OPIE *Lore & Lang. Schoolch.* iii. 47 To a nose-picker they chant: Friday, pie-day, Keep your nose tidy. **1960** KOESTLER *Lotus & Robot* I. i. 62 Only the nose-picking disciple kept up his activities. **1975** J. AIKEN *Voices in Empty House* iv. 116 The nose-picking in itself made me feel sick... *Nobody* in polite society *ever* picked their nose.

nose-piece. Add: Also nose piece. **3. a.** *Aeronaut.* (See quot.)

1918 W. E. DOMMETT *Dict. Aircraft* 32 *Nose piece*, conical metal piece attached to the propeller boss, its contour being continuous with the engine cowling.

† **b.** *Astronautics.* = *NOSE CONE. *Obs.*

1946 H. HARPER *Dawn of Space Age* III. viii. 113 During the initial thrusting period, while the space-vessel is ascending from the earth, the heat resisting carapace—or nose-piece..will obscure any view forward.

nose-ring. Add: **2.** (Earlier and later examples.)

1819 KEATS *Cap & Bells* (1848) II. 227 His turban wreath'd of gold,.. Mustachios, ear-ring, nose-ring, and his sabre keen. **1964** S. M. SHDEEK *Windswept & Other Stories* (1969) 14 Earrings and nose-rings twinkled.

Hence **no·se-ringed** *ppl. a.*

1925 E., O., & S. SITWELL *Poor Young People* 7 Like my black Nose-ringed lumbering bear.

no·se-up, *a.* *Aeronaut.* [f. NOSE *sb.* + UP *adv.*[2]] With the nose directed upwards.

1933 *Jrnl. R. Aeronaut. Soc.* XXXVII. 60 The lighter air[ship]..takes 20 seconds longer than the neutral ship to return to the horizontal, beyond which it only proceeds to 1° nose up. **1971** *Flying* Apr. 35/3 All you have to do s open the throttles, accelerate to that speed, rotate to a 10- or 12-degree nose-up attitude, and blast on out of the aerodrome. **1975** *Flight Internat.* 2 Oct. 506/2, I.. adjusted the attitude..because it was more markedly nose-up than expected.

nosey, *a.* Add: Also **nosy.** **3.** *slang.* Inquisitive, esp. objectionably so; curious.

1882 F. W. P. JAGO *Anc. Lang. & Dial. Cornwall* 226 *Nosey*, impertinent, intrusive. **1910** H. G. WELLS *Hist. Mr. Polly* vi. 163 I'm not such a blooming Geezer..as not to be able to sell goods a bit. One has to be nosy over one's buying, of course. **1928** *Daily Express* 11 Sept. 7 Marylebone man: Being nosey, I goes to 'ave a look. Magistrate: Being what? Clerk: Nosey; meaning curious. **1957** M. SPARK *Comforters* iv. 91 She saw Laurence examining Eleanor's cigarette case in his nosey way. **1973** P. EVANS *Bodyguard Man* xv. 104 'A nosey man...' 'Very nosey, very smart, very perceptive.'

b. *Nosey Parker, nosey parker*: an inquisitive person. Hence *Nosey-Parkering, nosey-parkering* ppl. a. and vbl. sb. and (as a back-formation) *nosey-park* v. intr.; *nosey-parkerdom, Nosey-Parkerism, nosey-parkery*, the display of inquisitive behaviour, the exercise of oppressive questioning; *nosey-parkerishness*, inquisitive tendencies.

1907 *Picture post card* (London View Co. Ltd.) (*caption*) The adventures of Nosey Parker. **1912** C. MACKENZIE *Carnival* xxi. 217 'I saw you go off with a fellah.' 'What of it, Mr. Nosy Parker?' **1915** WODEHOUSE *Something Fresh* v. 163 'But Nosey Parker is what *I* call him,' she said. 'He minds everybody's business as well as his own.' **1925** W. DEEPING *Sorrell & Son* xxx. 302 A rodent, a nasty, acute little man of the Nosey Parker genus. **1929** H. A. VACHELL *Virgin* xviii. 280 I'm a pestering nosey-parkering, shilly-shallying sort of an idiot, eh? **1930** J. B. PRIESTLEY *Angel Pavement* iv. 156 That's what takes your time, my boy—doing your bit of nosy-parkering. **1932** H. WILLIAMS in *Hansard Commons* CCLXII. 1359/2 What I call the modern spirit of 'nosey-parkerism' in legislation and administration. **1937** N. MARSH *Vintage Murder* viii. 86 Shut up, Gordon... Don't nosy-park. **1939** —— *Overture to Death* xi. 118 Asking questions..out of.. nosey-parkerishness. **1947** T. H. WHITE *Mistress Masham's Repose* xx. 150 'Good-bye.' 'And none of your Nosey-Parkering.' **1958** E. HYAMS *Taking it Easy* II. iii. 195 Is Bachelor still connected with military intelligence, or security, or whatever fancy name they have for official nosey-parkering? **1961** *Economist* 4 Nov. 426/3 This kind of officious nosey-parkery gives the British immigration authorities a bad name. **1966** C. MACKENZIE *My Life & Times* V. 157 The original 'nosy parker'..was one who played Peeping Tom to love-making couples in Hyde Park. **1969** *Daily Tel.* 25 Apr. 18 Goodness knows what all this massive exercise in nosey parkerdom is costing in terms of printing, manpower, administration, etc. **1971** L. LAMB *Worse than Death* iii. 29 Mrs Marshman nosey-parked..in Mrs Marble's cupboard. **1973** *Times* 17 Feb. 14/8 As ducks are 'parkers', it is easier to understand why exploratory and curious ducklings became 'nosy parkers'. **1974** 'D. CRAIG' *Whose Little Girl are You?* i. 19 All nosey parkers in this street. **1974** J. COOPER *Women & Super Women* 23 The social security ladies come nosy-parkering round.

B. *sb.* An inquisitive person, a 'Nosey Parker'.

1937 N. MARSH *Vintage Murder* xiv. 155 He may be a bit of a nosy, but he doesn't look like a murderer. **1942** BERREY & VAN DEN BARK *Amer. Thes. Slang* § 399/1 *Meddler or inquisitive person*,..nosy. **1975** H. R. F. KEATING *Remarkable Case* ii. 25 Tomorrow she would be out there in time, before all the noseys come out.

noseyness (nōu·zinės). Also **nosiness.** [f. NOSEY *a.* + -NESS.] Impertinent curiosity.

1919 F. HURST *Humoresque* 14 Haven't I learned it to you often enough a slummer must pay for her nosiness? **1941** *Penguin New Writing* X. 10, I do not think the men read these letters out of pure noseyness. **1952** J. STEINBECK *East of Eden* xviii 179 This isn't nosiness. This is the law. **1973** *Daily Tel.* 5 Oct. 17/3 Noseyness was the main motive; we always spent a lot of time speculating about other people's marriages. **1975** L. DEIGHTON *Yesterday's Spy* viii. 60 Curiosity—even nosiness—is not yet against the law.

nosh (nǫʃ), *sb. colloq.* [Yiddish; cf. next word.] **a.** A restaurant, a snack-bar. More usually *nosh bar, -house.*

1917 R. FRY *Let.* 11 May (1972) II. 411 Come with me to Kettners' nosh at 8.0. **1959** C. MACINNES *Absolute Beginners* 154 After a quick bite at a Nosh, and two strong black coffees, I felt up to the ordeal. **1969** I. DRUMMOND *Man with Tiny Head* i. 21 We're going to your nosh-house. **1970** *New Scientist* 2 Apr. 5/2 What dishes will they have at the epicurean nosh-houses up west? **1973** *Jewish Chron.* 2 Feb. 22/4 The quasi-kosher-culture of the nosh bar. **1974** J. GARDNER *Corner Men* viii. 67 Wanted to set up a couple of class nosh houses in the Smoke, here.

b. Food, a meal. Also *nosh-up*, a (good) meal.

The more usual sense in the U.K.

1963 *Daily Mail* 15 May 4/1 Why is it that whenever I read anything about freedom from hunger it's accompanied by pictures of people having a nosh-up? **1964** *Cherwell* 4 Nov. 12 At the unofficial opening..two old ladies were dragged in off the street and given free nosh and free coats. **1968** *Punch* 14 Feb. 220 I've always found Chinese nosh both cheap and filling. **1968** A. DIMENT *Great Spy Race* ii. 19, I like him enough to buy him some alcohol and the occasional cheap nosh. **1970** A. DRAPER *Swansong for Rare Bird* ix. 79 Like most birds she didn't want to lose out on a nosh-up. **1972** C. DRUMMOND *Death at Bar* vi. 159 Burglars go for plain, healthy English nosh.

c. A snack eaten between meals; a titbit. Chiefly *U.S.*

1965 *N.Y. Times* 9 Apr. 40 Advertising copy will stress that the company makes everything from 'soup to nosh'. (A nosh is a snack.) **1968** L. ROSTEN *Joys o fYiddish* 267 Many delicatessen counters display plates with small slices of salami, or pieces of halvah, with a legend affixed to a toothpick: 'Have a nosh.'

nosh (nǫʃ), *v. colloq.* [Yiddish; cf. G. *naschen* to nibble, eat on the sly.] **1. a.** To nibble, to eat a snack between meals. Chiefly *U.S.*

1957 *Observer* 3 Nov. 8/5 One eats breakfast or lunch, but one noshes in between. *Ibid.*, 'Women don't know how to nosh,' he continued, 'except chocolate and sweets.' **1958** I. BROWN *Words in Our Time* 76 Women, the salesman complained, only nosh chocolates and the true nosher is a connoisseur of cheeses at once sharp and ripe. **1968** L. ROSTEN *Joys of Yiddish* 267 To *nosh* is to 'have a little bite to eat before dinner is ready', or to 'have a little something between meals'. **1970** *Time* 12 Oct. 42 The politician, equipped with a trowel and the Fixed Smile, gobs mortar on a cornerstone, or noshes his way along the campaign trail. **1973** *Impetus* (Toronto) June 44/2 By nightfall, when mosquitoes as large as vampire bats were noshing on my exposed flesh, I had hoed a row and a half.

b. More generally, to eat; occas., to drink.

The more usual sense in the U.K.

1962 R. COOK *Crust on its Uppers* ii. 34, I finally bought a quart of grappa... Mrs. Marengo had noshed her half down. **1965** G. MELLY *Owning Up* xiv. 170 After our huge meal, we were forced to refuse although, as Mick said, 'I'd have noshed the lot if I could have done.' **1972** *Annabel* Jan. 8/3 There I sat in my steaming bath, noshing my favourite food. **1972** C. DRUMMOND *Death at Bar* v. 122 The Sergeant..morosely noshed the veal-and-ham pie.

2. To practise fellatio (with). *coarse slang.*

1965 *Listener* 18 Nov. 803/1 Such typical modernisms as *snog, nosh, dildo*, [etc.]. **1968** [see *GAMAHUCHE *v.*]. **1972** B. RODGERS *Queens' Vernac.* 142 *Nosh*.., to suck cock.

Hence **no·shable** *a.*; **no·shing** *vbl. sb.*

1957 *Observer* 3 Nov. 8/5 Noshing—derived from the German verb *naschen*—is to sample desirable food voluptuously, surreptitiously. **1965** J. P. CARSTAIRS *Concrete Kimono* i. 12 Too much noshin' and drinkin' the night before. **1965** W. YOUNG *Eros Denied* xiv. 137 *Gamming*, from the French *gamahucher*, or *blowing*, or *plating*, or *noshing*, from the Yiddish *nosh*, to nibble, or eat between meals. **1966** M. WADDELL *Otley* xi. 114 A particularly noshable repast—chop and peas and potatoes. **1966** *Crescendo* Nov. 10/1 This saga of happy noshing.

nosher (nǫ·ʃəɪ). *colloq.* [f. *NOSH *v.* + -ER[1].] A person who samples food before buying it; one given to eating snacks; a customer at a restaurant.

1957 *Observer* 3 Nov. 8/5 He jerked his head towards a round-bellied, cheerful man..who was biting large segments of Gruyère held lovingly in his hand. 'A nosher,' said the shopkeeper sentimentally. **1958** I. BROWN *Words in Our Time* 76 The salesman's much-liked noshers paid up properly as they nosed and nuzzled and chewed their way from one of his cates to another. **1969** *Sunday Times* 23 Mar. 28 Hot meal vending machines in the lobby for late night noshers. **1974** *Ibid.* 20 Jan. 24/7 Gourmet foods to salivate the palates of jaded British noshers.

noshery (nǫ·ʃĕri). *colloq.* [f. *NOSH *v.* + *-ERY 2 b.] A restaurant; a snack-bar.

1963 R. I. MCDAVID *Mencken's Amer. Lang.* v. 261 Miami Beach and similar outposts of civilization are full of *nosheries*... A *Chinese Noshery* was opened in the posh Georgetown section of the District of Columbia, *c.* 1955. **1970** A. DRAPER *Swansong for Rare Bird* ix. 78 Let's skip your noshery and I'll take you out for some grub. **1972** K. O'HARA *Company of St George* xiii. 118 The place I'm thinking of for lunch..has the reputation of a very superior noshery. **1975** *Spectator* 11 Jan. 36/1 A chain of nosheries have just sent out a drinks guide that shows sherry in that abominable receptacle known as an 'Elgin' or 'schooner'.

noshi (nǫ·ʃi). Also **nosi.** [Jap.] A Japanese token of esteem, originally a piece of dried awabi or more recently a specially folded piece of paper, forming part of the wrapping of a Japanese gift.

1855 R. HILDRETH *Japan* xli. 434 *Nosi*, a species of edible sea-weed, of which small pieces are attached to every congratulatory present. **1891** A. M. BACON *Japanese Girls & Women* i. 2 Tied with a peculiar red and white string, in which is inserted the *noshi*, or bit of dried fish daintily folded in a piece of coloured paper, which is an indispensable accompaniment of every present. **1954** J. M. MORRIS *Wise Bamboo* iv. 61 It was wrapped as a Japanese wedding gift, tied with gold and white cords in the traditional knot and with a paper *noshi*, the Japanese sign of a gift, on the wrapping. **1971** R. HARBIN *More Origami* 39 A simple Noshi which is a good luck item given with anything.

no show, *sb.* orig. *U.S.* Also **noshow,** (with hyphen) **no-show.** [f. NO *a.* + SHOW *v.*] A person who reserves a place on a train, boat, or esp. an aircraft, and fails to claim or cancel it. Also *transf.* and *attrib.*

1941 *Collier's* 27 Sept. 67 He's what the Airlines call a 'no show'. **1946** *Sun* (Baltimore) 3 Sept. 6 (Advt.), The traveling public has long been aware of the so-called 'no show'. He is the person who reserves airline space, buys a ticket and then neglects to cancel his reservation when he decides not to go. **1948** *Time* 10 May 89/3 Last week ship lines were still accepting tentative bookings—but only to replace last-minute no-shows. **1949** *Birmingham* (Alabama) *News* 17 Feb. 40/3 Many passengers who were denied seats could have occupied those left empty by

'noshows'. The airlines are in the red largely because of 'noshow' passengers. **1959** *Economist* 17 Jan. 248/1 To be sure of a seat or a sleeping berth, the 'no show' traveller books on several different services and sits back to decide at leisure which booking to take up. **1961** *Flight* LXXX. 489/1 IATA announce that transatlantic operators, in order to alleviate the no-show problem, are to introduce a reconfirmation rule. **1963** *Times* 8 Feb. 19/6 Booking and cancellation charges and 'no-show' charges. **1972** R. K. SMITH *Ransom* i. 25 The phone rang... Another 'no show', the Cable boy. Wasn't that on Ben Carter's route? **1973** *Daily Colonist* (Victoria, B.C.) 7 July 9/2 No-shows, passengers who simply fail to turn up for flights they've booked, have long been a major headache for airlines. **1974** *Index-Jrnl.* (Greenwood, S. Carolina) 19 Apr. 6/5 The regulatory agency said there was an increase in the number of no-shows, fans who purchase tickets but don't attend the game.

no side. *Rugby.* The (announcement of the) conclusion of a game.

1857 T. HUGHES *Tom Brown's School Days* I. v. 125 Five o'clock strikes. 'No side' is called, and the first day of the School-house match is over. **1874** *Rugby Union Football Ann. 1874–75* 39 Glasgow were again compelled to touch the ball down before the call of 'No-side', when the match was declared drawn in favour of Edinburgh. **1882** [see SIDE *sb.*[1] 20 b]. **1904** WODEHOUSE *Gold Bat* xi. 126 The whistle blew for no-side. **1931** *Times* 16 Feb. 5/1 They had looked a beaten team when, a quarter of an hour from 'no side', England at last managed to score a try. **1957** *Times* 14 Nov. 17/1 When no-side arrived the Australians had had all that they wanted. **1968** *Listener* 8 Aug. 189/1 The Lions took the lead ten minutes from no side, at which point the referee began awarding penalty kicks at goal to the Transvaal side.

nosiness, var. *NOSEYNESS.

no sir: see *NOSSIR.

no siree (nōu sərī·). *U.S. colloq.* Also **no sirree.** [f. NO *adv.*[3] + SIRREE.] No indeed; certainly not. Cf. SIRREE.

1848 [see SIRREE]. **1851** *Knickerbocker* XXXVIII. 496 'Can you take two to Whitlockville by five o'clock?'.. No, Siree!' **1861** [see SIRREE]. **1883** *Wheelman* Apr. 2/2 No, sir-e-e, you can't have any of my boats. **1936** J. DOS PASSOS *Big Money* (1937) 83 No more of that stuff, nosiree. **1973** J. DI MONA *Last Man at Arlington* (1974) 49 The senator wouldn't protect him. No siree.

no-sky (nōu̦skai·), *adj. phr.* [f. NO *a.* 6 b + SKY *sb.*[1]] *no-sky line*: a line in a room behind which no sky is visible from table height.

1927 *Illumination Res. Techn. Paper* (Dept. Sci. & Industr. Res.) No. 7. 12 This experience of adequacy and inadequacy in front of and behind the 'no-sky' line appears to be more or less independent of weather, so long as no sun is shining into the room. **1961** J. W. T. WALSH *Sci. Daylight* xi. 255 The first step in preparing a daylight plan is, usually, to plot the no-sky line.

no smoking, *vbl. sb.* [NO *a.* 4.] Usu. *attrib.*, = *NON-SMOKING *a.*; also a formula used on a notice, sign, etc., indicating that smoking is not permitted.

1944 J. GUNTHER *D Day* i. 13, I wanted to smoke, but fell asleep before the No SMOKING sign was switched off. **1952** T. J. MULVEY *These are your Sons* v. 108 The light over the cabin door flashed red. NO SMOKING. FASTEN YOUR SEAT BELTS—the glass panel warned. **1955** G. WILLANS *Fasten Your Lapstraps!* i. 17 Inside the airport there are more notices. 'No Entry', 'No Smoking', 'Staff Only'. **1961** *John o' London's* 1 June 608/3 One doesn't always notice the no-smoking sign. **1970** *New Yorker* 16 May 46/3 The no-smoking lights go out and the loudspeaker confirms that the passengers may now unfasten their seatbelts and smoke. **1971** P. AUDEMARS *Stolen like Magic Away* i. 15 The No Smoking notice was prominently displayed. **1973** J. ASHFORD *Double Run* vi. 44 He reached..for a pack of cigarettes. 'This is a no-smoking compartment,' said the woman.

noso-. Add: **no·sophile** *rare* [-PHIL, -PHILE], a person who is morbidly attracted by sickness or disease.

1895 tr. *M. Nordau's Degeneration* v. i. 539 Sadists, 'bestials', nosophiles, and necrophiles, etc., find legal opportunities to gratify their inclinations. **1905** *Smart Set* Sept. 113/2 Names of Satanic painters from Hell-Fire Breughel to Arnold Böcklin..passed through the halls of this nosophile's memory.

nossir (nōusə·ɪ). Chiefly *U.S. colloq.* Also **no sir.** [Corruption of *no sir.*] A formula of emphatic denial or refusal: certainly not. Cf. *NO SIREE.

1856 *Knickerbocker* XLVII. 544 *Examiner*: Has it effected that object? *Student*: No, Sir-r-r! I don't think it has. **1930** I. Low *His Master's Voice* ii. 15 Most of his replies to questions were in the nature of 'Yessir!' 'Nossir!' or their present-day Russian equivalent. **1932** MRS. P. CAMPBELL *Let.* 29 Mar. in *B. Shaw & Mrs. Campbell* (1952) 298 Please don't think..that I am such a foolish creature as to look upon these letters as bouquets to *me* 'No, Sir' —as the Americans say, with the accent on the 'sir'. **1939** A. HUXLEY *After Many a Summer* I. iv. 43 She really cared for her old Uncle Jo, and cared for him, what was more, not merely as an old uncle—no, *sir.* **1955** POHL & KORNBLUTH *Space Merchants* xv. 156 'I want to look at your books.' He shook his head emphatically. 'Nossir. Only the old man himself gets to see the books.' **1968** E. MCGIRR *Lead-lined Coffin* ii. 51 Joe Silverman don't like his neck being breathed down. Nossir. **1970** R. CRAWFORD *Kiss Boss Goodbye* II. ii. 64 '*Nobody* gave you an answer?' 'Nossir,' Dell said. **1973** *Listener* 19 Apr. 501/3 In Texas, do you think they're going to inquire about the hanging of the venison..? No, sir. They wonder if there's any shepherd's pie.

nostalgia. Add: (Earlier example.)

1770 J. BANKS *Jrnl.* in J. Cook *Jrnls.* (1955) I. 409 The greatest part of them [*sc.* the ship's company] were now pretty far gone with the longing for home which the Physicians have gone so far as to esteem a disease under the name of Nostalgia.

2. *transf.* Regret or sorrowful longing *for* the conditions of a past age; regretful or wistful memory or recall of an earlier time.

1920 D. H. LAWRENCE *Lost Girl* xv. 344 The terror, the agony, the nostalgia of the heathen past was a constant torture to her mediumistic soul. **1928** A. WAUGH *Nor Many Waters* vi. 231 He pictures with a sense of nostalgia, too acute almost to be endured, all that marriage to Marian would have meant. **1933** D. GARNETT *Pocahontas* xx. 234 Seeing all these things again filled her heart with that violent sentimental nostalgia..felt by the very young about the very recent past. **1943** KOESTLER in *Tribune* 26 Nov. 13/1 Even the names of Paris underground stations..become the nostalgia-imbued stimuli of conditioned reflexes. **1945** AUDEN *For Time Being* 37 We and They are united in the candid glare of the same commercial hope by day, and the soft refulgence of the same erotic nostalgia by night. **1951** L. P. HARTLEY *My Fellow Devils* xxxiii. 339 The faults for which she had been obliged to sack him no longer counted:..she was free to dwell with some nostalgia on his virtues. **1957** *Listener* 3 Oct. 512/1 When grown-ups become passionately interested in them [*sc.* children's books] some kind of nostalgia is involved. **1957** B. & C. EVANS *Dict. Contemp. Amer. Usage* 322/2 Now a vogue word, *nostalgia* has come to mean any vague yearning, especially for the past and especially..when tinged with tenderness and sadness. **1959** *Observer* 8 Feb. 7/5 Nostalgia for one's childhood does not necessarily mean that the childhood was a happy one. **1971** *Sunday Times* 30 May 32/2 Nostalgia's all right, But it's not what it was.

nostalgic, *a.* Add: **3. a.** That evokes a wistful and sentimental yearning for the past. **b.** Feeling or indulging in nostalgia.

1944 *Evening News* 11 Dec. 1/3 Britain, that nostalgic lover of vanished thrones. **1950** A. L. ROWSE *England of Elizabeth* v. 184 That nostalgic figure, the Town Crier, was becoming familiar. **1952** *N.Y. Herald Tribune* 28 Aug. 16/7 The Empire Theater, fifty nine years old and 'one of the fine old nostalgic houses' will be torn down next spring. **1958** B. NICHOLS *Sweet & Twenties* viii. 112 The charming thing snapped open, releasing a cloud of dust and a host of memories. The very sound of it was nostalgic. **1959** *Observer* 18 Jan. 19/1 It had a sudden sharp nostalgic appeal for me because I immediately recognised in one of the chief testifiers a former assistant master at my preparatory school. **1965** *Church Times* 18 June 6/4 The departure on Friday afternoon of the last train to be drawn out of Paddington Station..by a steam locomotive was..a nostalgic occasion.

nostalgically (nǫstæ·ldʒikăli), *adv.* [f. NOSTALGIC *a.*: see -ICALLY.] In a nostalgic way; in evocation of the past.

1928 GALSWORTHY *Swan Song* III. xi. 298 A long time he sat there, nostalgically bemused, strangely unwilling to move. **1937** A. HUXLEY *Ends & Means* i. 2 The poor and downtrodden have always dreamed nostalgically of a man ideally well-fed, free, happy and unoppressed. **1945** *John o' London's Weekly* 24 Aug. 216 Its style of binding is nostalgically akin to that of those A.A. handbooks which one used to find (sometimes) in seaside hotels. **1957** A. E. COPPARD *It's Me, O Lord!* iii. 37 There is something nostalgically primitive about the woodwind instruments. **1958** *Listener* 20 Nov. 842/2 Mesens..uses these elements lyrically and nostalgically. **1975** J. MELDRUM *Semonov Impulse* iii. 57 You're going nostalgically north?.. See the boys?

‖ **nostalgie de la boue** (nǫstalʒi də la bū). [Fr., lit. = yearning for mud (Émile Augier *Le Mariage d'Olympe* (1855) I. i).] A desire for degradation and depravity.

1897 G. B. SHAW *Our Theatres in Nineties* (1932) III. 168 To him those habits were 'morality'; and what was counter to them was 'nostalgie de la boue'. **1905** H. A. VACHELL *Hill* vi. 121 She..said that I suffered from what the French call *la nostalgie de la boue*; that means, you know, the homesickness for the gutter. **1920** G. DICKINS *Hellenistic Sculpture* ii. 27 The Hellenistic sculptors.. suffered as much as any modern decadent from 'la nostalgie de la boue'. **1928** D. H. LAWRENCE *Lady Chatterley* xix. 358 You're one of those half-insane, perverted women who must run after depravity, the *nostalgie de la boue.* **1957** C. MACINNES *City of Spades* II. xii. 181 It's the crude animal type that attracts you... It's simply another form of *nostalgie de la boue.* **1965** *Listener* 9 Sept. 391/2 A cultural *nostalgie de la boue* for the nonsense of the 'thirties is surely perverse. **1969** R. LOWELL *Notebook 1967–68* 105 The Muse shouts vacation in my ear: *Nostalgie de la boue* that shelters ape And protozoa from the rights of man. **1971** *Southerly* XXXI. 11 There may be a suggestion of *nostalgie de la boue* in his choice of sexual partners.

Similarly *nostalgie de la banlieue* [Fr., = suburbs], *des adieux* [Fr., = farewells], *du divin* [Fr., = divine], *du pavé, trottoir* [Fr., = pavement], etc.

1933 D. L. SAYERS *Murder must Advertise* iii. 41 There is a *nostalgie de la banilieu* [*sic*] as well as *de la boue*. **1941** Nostalgie des adieux [see *FAUTE DE MIEUX]. **1944** *Horizon* IX. 13 My reaction to everything not urban has been either one of acute melancholy or an urgent *nostalgie du pavé.* **1944** M. LASKI *Love on Supertax* ix. 88 'Every man has an urge to go Mayfairing once in his life.'..'*Nostalgie du trottoir,*' agreed Tatiana. **1948** W. STEVENS *Let.* 6 May (1967) 596 He speaks of the nostalgie du divin, (which is obviously epidemic in Dublin). **1972** *Times* 27 Sept. 5/3 The archetypal early twentieth-century laboratory scented evocatively with *Nostalgie de la Bunsen Burner.*

nostoma·niac. *rare.* [f. NOSTOMANIA: see -AC.] A person affected with nostomania.

1913 R. W. SERVICE *Rhymes of Rolling Stone* 50 The Nostomaniac.

nostos (nǫ·stǫs). Also **Nostos.** Pl. **nostoi.** [Gr. νόστος a return home.] A homecoming, applied *spec.* to the homeward journeys of Odysseus and the other heroes of Troy. Also, the story of such a homecoming or return, esp. as the conclusion of a literary work.

In quots. 1883, 1901, and 1962[1] *Nost(o)i* is the title of a lost poem of the Epic Cycle dealing with the return of the Greek heroes from the Trojan War.

1883 D. B. MUNRO in *Jrnl. Hellenic Studies* IV. 319 A passage of Pausanias (x. 28, 7), mentions, as the poems which contain descriptions of the infernal regions, the *Odyssey*, the *Minyas*, and the *Nostoi*. **1901** —— *Homer's Odyssey Bks XIII–XXIV* 380 We may regard the *Nosti* as a tragic *Odyssey*. **1920** J. JOYCE *Let.* 12 July (1957) I. 143 A great part of the Nostos or close was written several years ago and the style is quite plain. **1924** T. W. ALLEN *Homer: Origins & Transmission* 333, I have found a reference to their Nostos in Plutarch. **1957** N. FRYE *Anat. of Criticism* iii. 159 It is rare, in literature as in life, to find even a domesticated animal peacefully living through its full span of life... The exceptions, such as Odysseus' dog, are appropriate to the theme of *nostos* or full close of a cyclical movement. **1962** M. BOWRA in Wace & Stubbings *Compan. to Homer* iii. 40 The tradition that he composed the *Iliad* and the *Odyssey* becomes less impressive when he is credited by different authorities with the *Thebais, Epigonoi, Cypria*, and *Nostoi*. **1962** THOMAS & STUBBINGS in *Ibid.* ix. 292 Agamemnon, on his *nostos*, was carried away as he approached Malea. **1968** C. R. BEYE *Iliad, Odyssey & Epic Tradition* v. 161 The story of homecoming had a name: *nostos*. The several *nostoi* are a leitmotiv throughout the *Odyssey* which is over-all a *nostos*, being the return of Odysseus. There is a hint in the *Odyssey* that epics of *nostoi* were currently fashionable.

Nostraine, obs. var. *NASRANI.

Nostratic (nǫstræ·tik), *a.* Also **Nostratian.** [ad. G. *nostratisch*, f. L. *nostrās, -ātis* of our country: see -IC.] (See quots.)

1931 J. W. SPARGO tr. *Pedersen's Linguistic Science in Nineteenth Century* viii. 338 As a comprehensive designation for the families of languages which are related to Indo-European, we may employ the expression *Nostratian Languages* (from Latin *nostrās* 'our countryman'). **1966** B. COLLINDER in Birnbaum & Puhvel *Anc. Indo-Europ. Dial.* 199 Holger Pedersen used to speak about a 'nostratic' family of languages, comprising Indo-European, Semitic-Egyptian-Hamitic, Uralic, Altaic, Yukagir, and Eskimo. **1966** M. PEI *Gloss. Linguistic Terminol.* 136 *Japhetic*, a hypothetical language family claimed to include North Caucasian, South Caucasian, Sumerian, Elamite, Asianic, Basque, Etruscan, etc... *Synonyms*: Alarodian, Nostratic. **1973** *Jrnl. R. Asiatic Soc.* 46 The term Nostratic is defined by the words in brackets following the title of the book, 'Semito-Hamitic, Kartvelian, Indo-European, Uralian, Dravidian, Altaic'.

nostril (nǫ·stril), *v.* [f. the sb.] To look like or function as a nostril; to inhale or exhale through one's nose. So **no·strilled** *ppl. a.*, having nostrils, freq. of a particular kind.

The *transf.* use in quot. 1942 is unusual.

1909 *Athenæum* 31 July 125/1 The characteristically Irish 'nostrilled' portraits of the four Evangelists. **1939** E. HEMINGWAY *Fifth Column* 131 His outstretched, wide-nostrilled muzzle. **1942** A. L. ROWSE *Cornish Childhood* (1943) 36 The blue summer sea curling round the ships of those emigrant miners, the water nostrilling the stem. **1971** A. HUNTER *Gently at Gallop* v. 49 He was smoking a small, sooty briar... He nostrilled a couple of wisps of smoke.

nosy, var. NOSEY *a.* (in Dict. and Suppl.).

not, *adv.* and *sb.* Add: **I.** *adv.* **1. c.** With ellipsis of dependent clause after certain verbs, as *do, have, know, say not.* colloq.

1906 KIPLING *Puck of Pook's Hill* 147 'Did *you* have a governess, then?' 'Did we not? A Greek too.' **1918** C. MACKENZIE *Early Life Sylvia Scarlett* II. vii. 450 '..Do you remember a man called Leopold Hansberg?' 'Do I not?' Sylvia exclaimed. **1936** M. ALLINGHAM *Flowers for Judge* iv. 74 'I suppose they've been questioning you..?' 'Have they not!' Mike spoke explosively. **1973** C. AIRD *His Burial Too* ii. 28 Your father always puts it in the book... I've never known him not.

2. b. Freq. with *that.*

1939 'N. BLAKE' *Smiler with Knife* i. 13 You never knew when..Nigel [would] be dragged into some queer criminal tangle. Not that they really needed the substantial fees he charged. **1967** *Listener* 7 Dec. 762/3 We should recall our initial experience of a creative personality as strong as Mahler's... Not that Koechlin is a Mahler, but at best he is an original.

4. Esp. with imperative force; freq. in colloq. phr. *not to worry*, do not worry.

1872 GEO. ELIOT *Middlem.* II. xxxvii. 258 And he objects to a secretary: please not to mention that again. **1958** *Daily Mail* 24 July 6/5 Not to worry. By the time he ..had finished with me..I'd be doing long division. **1965** L. MEYNELL *Double Fault* I. iii. 31 'We'll send it for you.' 'Not to bother. I'm going down to the country this evening.' **1967** *Spectator* 11 Aug. 160/1 In short, to borrow one of Mr. William's own favoured colloquialisms, not to worry. **1970** V. CANNING *Great Affair* xiv. 269 He gave me a big grin and said, 'Not to be overcome, son.'

7. c. *not half* (see HALF *adv.* 3 in Dict. and Suppl.).

d. *not all that*, not exceptionally (so).

1964 T. WHITE tr. *Simenon's Maigret & Saturday Caller* iv. 70 'Were they heavy?'.. 'Quite heavy, but not all that.' **1970** *Guardian* 24 Jan. 1/5 Asked how he assessed the capacity of the present relief system of the Federal authorities to cope with widespread starvation, Lord Hunt said: 'Now I don't feel all that confidence in the Nigerian Government's ability to do this.' *Ibid.* 28 Jan. 8/3 Without her voice, Callas is not all that impressive an actress. **1974** *Sat. Rev. World* (U.S.) 19 Oct. 56/2 Several years ago..I asked him, 'How was the picture?' He..said, 'Not all that good.' The expression 'not all that good', as far as I know, was fairly new at the time.

10. c. (Further example.) (See also *BAD *a.* I c.) Also as *sb.*, **not-bad.**

1843 THOREAU *Let.* 24 Jan. in *Corr.* (1958) 77 He is, at any rate, one of the not-bad. **1871** GEO ELIOT *Middlem.* I. I. ix. 128 She had got nothing from him more graphic about the Lowick cottages than that they were 'not bad'. **1973** A. ROSS *Dunfermline Affair* 41 A not-bad job, Farrow. Not bad at all. **1975** *Times* 20 Sept. 8/5 Brian Armstrong's *Bags of Swank* consisted of three not-bad scripts about his National Service.

II. 13*. As *sb.* or *adj.* *Computers.* (Usu. written in capitals.) A Boolean function of one variable that has the value unity if the variable is zero, and *vice versa.* Usu. *attrib.*

1950 W. W. STIFLER *High-Speed Computing Devices* xiii. 270 This device, called a half adder, will consist of *and*, *or*, and *not* circuits..arranged so as to carry out the operations exemplified in Table 13-1. **1955** R. K. RICHARDS *Arithmetic Operations in Digital Computers* ii. 29 A fundamental concept which is found in Boolean algebra and which has no counterpart in ordinary algebra is the 'not' function, as indicated by a line over a symbol. **1957** GOODE & MACHOL *System. Engin.* xxv. 394 There is.. evidence that certain synapses are inhibitory, i.e. NOT gates. **1969** P. B. JORDAIN *Condensed Computer Encycl.* 341 NOT is a unary operation since it has only one argument, and it is one of the most fundamental logic operators. **1970** O. DOPPING *Computers & Data Processing* i. 26 All logical connections between two-valued variables can be expressed by means of the three functions NOT, AND, and OR. **1972** *IEEE Trans. Computers* XXI. 153/2 When digital computers are synthesized with gates other than AND, OR, and NOT gates, it is difficult to design optimal ..networks directly from the Boolean expressions.

III. 14. d. (Further example.)

1867 MILL *Exam. Hamilton's Philos.* (ed. 3) xiii. 289 A complete idea of a closed figure, and of the boundary which incloses it—the outline separating object from not-object.

15. d. Freq. with *so* or *too* and an adj. forming combs. used as *sb.*, *adv.*, or *adj.*

1748 RICHARDSON *Clarissa* II. xiii. 72, I [say]..she is too wise; that is to say..Not so young as she has been. **1851** LYTTON (*title*) Not so bad as we seem. **1866** MRS. GASKELL *Wives & Daughters* I. xxi. 235 It was also evident to her that Osborne was not too happy at home. **1870** GEO. ELIOT *Let.* 15 Nov. (1956) V. 120 We..cannot yet decide whether we should..have a modest little refuge in the not-too-distant country. **1931** J. S. HUXLEY *What dare I Think?* vi. 190 Man believing himself the inhabitant of the Universe's central globe,..looking forward to a not-too-distant end of this terrestrial home, cannot well have the same religion as man knowing himself descended by slow evolution from the brutes. **1935** *Discovery* Sept. 262/1 The not-so-distant days of the pirates. **1941** M. ALLINGHAM *Traitor's Purse* xx. 229 'I say, it's pretty serious, isn't it?' He nodded. 'Not so hot. Time's short.' **1943** G. ADE *Let.* 5 Feb. (1973) 238 The not-so-good-news in regard to the soy bean crop does not come as a surprise. **1945** [see *ATOMIC *a.* 2 f]. **1945** *Sun* (Baltimore) 29 Oct. 4 A British rubber inspection committee sent out to the plantations of Malaya..reported today that conditions were 'not too bad'. **1951** S. SPENDER *World within World* iii. 143 One of their not-too-distant neighbours was Lytton Strachey. **1952** A. G. L. HELLYER *Sanders' Encycl. Gardening* (ed. 22) 270 Soil, cool, slightly moist, and a not-too-hot position in the rock garden. **1955** *Radio Times* 22 Apr. 5/1 Where the making of home entertainment is not just a pleasant memory of the not-so-young. **1957** *Times Lit. Suppl.* 13 Dec. 762/5 The not-so-rich lady in the subway solemnly knitting a double-necked jersey. **1960** *Guardian* 20 May 4/5 Access is limited for the not-so-young, the not-so-robust, and those who like to amble. **1962** R. H. SMYTHE *Anatomy of Dog Breeding* iv. 77 Bred from ancestors of not-so-long-ago. **1965** *Listener* 27 May 766/2 They accepted all the good things..and the not-so-good things, with fatalistic acquiescence. **1971** *Good Motoring* Sept. 3 This incredible phenomenon is the Giant's Causeway, known to most people by pictorial sight but, oddly, not too many know its location. **1972** E. LEMARCHAND *Cyanide with Compliments* i. 3 Olivia watched the launch filling up. The not-so-young predominated. **1974** *Sat. Rev. World* (U.S.) 19 Oct. 41/1 All of this is seen through the eyes of a not-too-bright country boy.

notability. 1. c. (Earlier example.)

1832 J. S. MILL *Lett.* (1910) I. 33 There is need that the march of mind should raise up new spiritual notabilities; for it seems as though all the old ones with one accord were departing out of the world together. In a few days or weeks the world has lost the three greatest men in it in their several departments—Goethe, Bentham, and Cuvier.

notal (nōu·tăl), *a.*[2] [f. NOTE *sb.*[2] + -AL.] Of, pertaining to, or employing notes.

1884 *Encycl. Brit.* XVII. 85/1 The treachery of tradition is exemplified in the loss of the rules for this once generally understood practice of notal inflexion. **1924** LUCAS & BONAR tr. *Knapp's State Theory of Money* ii. 113 There are metalloplatic and papyroplatic notal money systems, with or without hylodromy.

notam (nōu·tăm). [f. initial letters of *no*tice *to* *airm*en.] A (warning) notice to pilots of aircraft.

1946 F. HAMANN *Air Words* 38/1 *Notam*, notice to airmen. **1955** R. J. SCHWARTZ *Compl. Dict. Abbrev.* 128/2 *Notam*, International Notices to Airmen. **1963** *Times* 25 Jan. 4/4 He added that until two months ago 'notams'—notices warning aviators and mariners to keep out of the way of Nato exercises—were also issued and had nearly a worldwide circulation. **1967** *Times* 16 May 10/3 All went well until the second Spanish 'notam' (notice to airmen), a week ago.

NOT AND (nǫt ænd). *Computers.* [f. NOT *adv.* + AND *conj.*] = *NAND.

1960 [see *NAND]. **1962** SIMPSON & RICHARDS *Physical Princ. Junction Transistors* xvi. 402 Parallel *p-n-p* inverters form a 'NOT AND' gate, for which all must be one to maintain a zero output.

notaphily (nōutæ·fili). [f. NOTE *sb.*[2] 18 + -PHILY.] The collecting of bank-notes as a hobby. Hence **nota·philic** *a.*; **nota·philism**; **nota·philist.**

1970 *Daily Tel.* 7 Nov. 15/2 Stanley Gibbons has created a new word, 'Notaphilly' [*sic*], which derives from Latin and Greek meaning 'lover of notes'... A banknote is a notaphilic item and the collector is a notaphilist. (Say it like 'philatelist'.) **1970** *Guardian* 2 Dec. 11/2 The charm of bank notes..is their history... Notaphily is the name of the hobby. **1972** *Daily Tel.* 28 Oct. 29/4 Colin Narbeth compares the position of today's notaphilist with that of Edward Stanley Gibbons..when he bought a kit bag containing thousands of Cape Triangulars for £5. **1973** *Times* 13 Dec. 17/8 Collectors have coined the ugly name notaphilists to describe themselves. About twenty of the highest-denomination notaphilists came to the auction. **1976** *Times* 27 Jan. 17/4 Biafran £1 notes..found their way on to the notaphilic market.

notarikon (notæ·rikǫn). *Jewish Lit.* Also **notaricon.** [late Gr. νοταρικόν, f. L. *notārius* shorthand-writer, NOTARY *sb.*] In cabalistic phraseology, the art of making a new word from letters taken from the beginning, middle, or end of the words in a sentence.

1911 'SEPHARIAL' *Kabala of Numbers* I. iii. 31 *Notaricon.* —Selection was made of certain letters according to the rules of the art, these letters being taken from the beginning, middle, or end of the words in a sentence, so as to produce a single word from their combination. **1941** G. G. SCHOLEM *Major Trends Jewish Mysticism* iii. 90 Techniques..popularly supposed to represent the heart and core of Kabbalism, such as *Gematria*.., *Notarikon*, or interpretation of the letters of a word as abbreviations of whole sentences. **1951** *John o' London's Weekly* LX. 716/2 Hempe..is a Tudor notarikon... Hempe is formed of the initial letters of the Tudor sovereigns Henry, Edward, Mary, Philip and Elizabeth.

notarize (nōu·tăraiz), *v.* [f. NOTAR(Y *sb.* + -IZE.] *trans.* To have (a document) legalized by a notary. Usu. in **no·tarized** *ppl. a.*

1935 *Sun* (Baltimore) 22 Nov. 10/1 In a series of notarized cases a prominent journal recently stated that in the installation of industrial machinery totaling $8,000,000 the savings effected by these installations were approximately $55,000 per plant per year. **1939** W. FAULKNER *Wild Palms* 19 There was no sworn notarised statement attached. **1960** *Times* 2 Aug. 7/4 Boys under 21 and girls under 18 must be accompanied by their parents to obtain a marriage licence, or else present a notarized letter of consent. **1972** *Scholarly Publishing* III. 182 Sometimes.. he has practically to sign his life away to get his meagre five dollars or so. In extreme cases the publisher once even had to get the form notarized.

not at all. = *don't mention it* (see MENTION *v.* I c).

1936 WODEHOUSE *Laughing Gas* ii. 19, I was not-at-alling and shoving the handkerchief up my sleeve again. **1963** 'E. MCBAIN' *Ten plus One* vii. 88 'Well, thank you,' Carella said. 'Not all. My pleasure,' Richardson answered. **1973** J. BURROWS *Like an Evening Gone* i. 13 She ..pretty well knocked him flying... 'So sorry.' 'Not at all.'

notate (notēi·t), *v.* [f. as NOTATE *a.*] **a.** To set down in musical notation. **b.** To record, note. So **nota·ted** *ppl. a.*; **nota·ting** *vbl. sb.*

1922 W. J. LOCKE *Tale of Triona* xii. 128 He could play, ..by ear—knowledge of notated music he disclaimed. **1965** *Listener* 16 Dec. 990/2, I would say it would help any composer to conduct if he had the gift, because, in the first place, you learn how to notate your music more precisely, so that a performing musician will know exactly what you mean. **1971** S. CAVELL *World Viewed* ii. 17 Such troubles in notating so obvious a fact. **1974** *Times Lit. Suppl.* 13 Dec. 1411/2 To sing through the variants of even a single song—for example, of the beautiful 'Seeds of Love', the first which [Cecil] Sharp notated—is an enlargement of the spirit... Once notated versions of the songs exist, are the rhythmic quirks ironed out?

not at home, *adv. phr.* Not prepared to receive visitors or accessible to callers. Also as *sb.*

1829 [see AT HOME I b]. **1874** HARDY *Far from Madding Crowd* I. ix. 123 'I can't see him in this state. Whatever shall I do?' Not-at-homes were hardly naturalized in Weatherbury farm-houses, so Liddy suggested—'Say you're a fright with dust, and can't come down.' **1923** *Mrs. Beeton's Bk. Househ. Managem.* i. 35 When visitors present themselves the servant charged with the duty of opening the door will..answer without hesitation if the family are 'not at home', or 'engaged'.

notatin (notēi·tin). *Biochem.* [f. L. *notāt-us*, pa. pple. of *notāre* to mark, NOTE *v.*[2] + -IN[1].] A flavoprotein produced by the mould *Penicillium notatum* which is an enzyme that catalyses the direct oxidation of glucose to gluconic acid and hydrogen peroxide and is used in the detection and estimation of glucose; = *PENATIN, *PENICILLIN A, B.

1942 C. E. COULTHARD et al. in *Nature* 28 Nov. 634/2 When a selected strain of *Penicillium notatum* Westling is grown on a Czapek-Dox medium an anti-bacterial substance is produced which differs in the majority of its properties from penicillin. This anti-bacterial substance was originally named 'Penicillin A', but in order to avoid confusion with penicillin we now prefer the name 'notatin'. **1949** N. G. HEATLEY in H. W. Florey et al. *Antibiotics* I. iii. 136 For the assay of 'notatin' (known also as 'penicillin B' or 'penatin') the medium must contain glucose, for this so-called antibiotic is an enzyme..and exerts its effect purely through the hydrogen peroxide which is formed. **1954** A. WHITE et al. *Princ. Biochem.* xii. 264 A curious example of an antibiotic isolated from the mold *Penicillium notatum* is the substance notatin, which was later found to be the enzyme glucose oxidase containing flavin adenine dinucleotide. **1963** R. BENTLEY in P. D. Boyer et al. *Enzymes* (ed. 2) VII. xxiv. 568 The following materials, originally described as antibiotics, are actually enzymes similar to, or identical with, the glucose oxidase of Müller: notatin (originally penicillin A).., penatin.., and penicillin B. *Ibid.* 569 Much of the work described in this chapter has been carried out with purified preparations of notatin, and an unqualified reference to glucose oxidase in the rest of this chapter will indicate notatin.

notation. 2. (Later examples.)

1929 J. GALLISHAW *Twenty Probl. Fiction Writer* 228 The wise writer depends upon recorded observations, and makes notations. **1932** L. C. DOUGLAS *Forgive our Trespasses* (1937) vii. 128 The papers submitted on Tuesday were, in the main, satisfactory. They would be returned, with notations, to their makers, at the close of the hour.

notational, *a.* Add: (Further examples.)

1955 A. N. PRIOR *Formal Logic* 293 Introducing 'classes' as merely a notational device. **1964** P. K. BOCK in J. A. Fishman *Readings Sociol. of Lang.* (1968) 217 The structural description of any one situation occurring in a human community must, necessarily, refer to other situations; therefore, a notational system was devised to facilitate cross-referencing. **1964** E. BACH *Introd. Transformational Gram.* vii. 145 A certain amount of facility in handling symbols and practice in manipulating the notational conventions is all that is needed. **1965** HUGHES & LONDEY *Elem. of Formal Logic* xxxvi. 249 We can..reduce the welter of bracketing..by the following notational convention. **1965** *Language* XLI. 485 Using the same notational devices as before. **1970** J. D. MCCAWLEY in P. L. Garvin *Cognition* x. 231 A system of semantic representation that is along the lines of the notational systems used in symbolic logic. **1973** J. HINTIKKA *Logic, Language-Games & Information* xi. 252 A formula which is like one of the constituents or a-constituents we have defined..will be called its *notational variant.* We shall call two constituents or a-constituents *different* only if they are not notational variants of each other.

b. *spec.* Of or pertaining to musical notation.

1925 P. A. SCHOLES *Second Bk. Gramophone Record* 162 Under the notational description of 6/8 we get sometimes *two groups* in a bar, sometimes *three groups*.

Hence **nota·tionally** *adv.*

1896 *Musical Herald* 1 Feb. 43/1 With regard to *ba*, Mr. McNaught admitted that, notationally, there was something to be said in favour of abolishing the name, but, educationally, it was better to keep it. **1940** W. V. QUINE *Math. Logic* 33 A mode which consists notationally of compounding the statements by means of 'implies' and the two pairs of quotation marks.

nota·tionist. [f. NOTATION + -IST.] One who uses or advocates a particular style of musical notation.

1896 *Musical Herald* 1 Feb. 41/2 Every singer should be a two-notationist. **1897** *Ibid.* 1 June 188/2 There is no reason why..Sol-faists and staff notationists should not come to a common understanding and agreement. **1928** *Musical Times* July 619 All those brought up on the Staff would benefit by a grounding in Tonic Sol-fa... The dual notationist is, in fact, the best-equipped musician.

not-being, *sb.* **1.** (Later examples.)

1907 J. R. ILLINGWORTH *Doctrine of Trinity* i. 8 We cannot possibly conceive a passage from not-being to being, as the Greeks phrased it,..except through the operation of some energy which is already actual,..and adequate. **1917** D. H. LAWRENCE *Look! We have come Through!* 147 It wounds me to death with my own not-being. **1933** C. DAWSON *Enquiries Relig. & Culture* III. ii. 194 The element of nothingness or not-being which is inherent in the world of sensible experience.

notch, *sb.* Add: **1. b.** (Later examples.)

Quot. 1970 perh. belongs to I a.

1929 W. FAULKNER *Sound & Fury* 399 Luster took still another notch in himself and gave the impervious Queenie a cut with the switch. **1947** *Sun* (Baltimore) 15 May 2/8 The notch, instead of $67, is $38.50, and it stops at $265.52. **1958** *Sunday Times* (Johannesburg) 21 Sept. 4/9 Each of the Transvaal's 13,000 teachers will have their pay raised by at least one notch on October 1. **1958** *Cape Times* 29 Oct. 15/5 Applicants must have auctioneering experience... The notch for appointment will depend on previous experience. **1970** E. MCGIRR *Death pays Wages* vii. 146 He turned up the central heating a notch.

d. A slit in the ground made to take the roots of a seedling tree.

1891 W. SCHLICH *Man. Forestry* II. ii. 126 An enlarged notch may be produced by swaying it [*sc.* the notching spade] to and fro. **1934** *Forestry* VIII. 21 A deep vertical notch..with adequate firming, is the best method of planting. **1970** H. L. EDLIN *Collins Guide to Tree Planting & Cultivation* vii. 107 In its simplest form, the notch is just a slit cut into the ground, into which the tree's roots are inserted.

e. An incision made in a twig to stimulate the growth of a bud lower down the twig.

1916 tr. K. Koopmann in L. H. Bailey *Pruning-Manual* v. 127 Notches are made on twigs of one year's growth or more, to influence a particular bud in various ways. **1974** R. GROUNDS *Practical Pruning* iii. 28 Cut a notch just above the buds that you wish to form branches during April.

4. b. *spec.* An opening extending above the water level in a surface placed across a stream like a weir; also, the surface itself.

1789 [in Dict.]. **1845** *Encycl. Metrop.* III. 238/1 Theoretically the quantity discharged through a rectangular notch, which reaches to the surface, is two-thirds of what would issue through an equal orifice placed at the whole depth below the level of the fluid. **1907** W. C. UNWIN *Treat. Hydraulics* v. 96 Notches for measuring purposes are weirs fitted with a plate in which an open notch is formed through which the water passes. **1908** A. H. GIBSON *Hydraulics* v. 137 (*heading*) Flow over notches and weirs. **1914** W. M. WALLACE *Hydraulics* xii. 188 Where it is possible to provide an artificial section for the stream the gauge notch is used, of which there are three standard forms, viz., (1) rectangular, (2) circular, (3) triangular. **1959** [see *FLUME *sb.* 3 a]. **1974** J. A. FOX *Introd. Engin. Fluid Mech.* iii. 99 In the case of orifices and rectangular notches the coefficient of discharge varies with both the Reynolds number and the value of *l/h*.

6. notch-back, a back on a motor car that extends approximately horizontally from the bottom of the rear window so as to make a distinct angle with it; a car having such a back; also *transf.*; opp. *fast back* (*b*) s.v. *FAST *a.* 11; **notch-bar test** *Engin.* = *notched-bar test* (*NOTCHED *ppl. a.* 1); **notch-brittleness** *Engin.*, susceptibility to fracture at a notch when a sudden load is applied; hence (as a back-formation) **notch-brittle** *a.*; **notch effect** *Engin.*, the increase in the susceptibility of a specimen to fracture caused by the presence of a notch; **notch factor** *Engin.* (see quot. 1968); **notch filter** *Electronics*, a filter that attenuates signals within a very narrow band of frequencies; **notch-house** *slang*, a brothel (cf. NAUTCH *sb.* 2); **notch-ladder** (see quot.); **notch-planting** = *NOTCHING *vbl. sb.* 3; **notch-sensitive** *a. Engin.*, characterized by a high notch sensitivity; **notch-sensitiveness** or **-sensitivity** *Engin.* (see quot. 1970); **notch-toughness** *Engin.*, the opposite of **notch-brittleness*; *spec.* the result (in units of energy) of a notched-bar test on a specimen.

[**1959** *Motor* 28 Oct. 447/2 The Special Continental saloon..was notable for the abandonment of the sloping tail in favour of a notched back treatment.] **1965** J. LAWLOR *How to talk Car* 76 *Notch-back*, body design with a separate distinct rear deck. The term is used to distinguish conventional styling from fast-back design. **1967** *Wall St. Jrnl.* 24 Apr. 6/3 The Charger will drop its fast-back roofline in 1968 in favor of a 'notchback' in which the roofline slopes more abruptly to the rear fender. **1971** *Flying* (N.Y.) Apr. 40/1 In 1962, the Cessna 182 got the Omni-Vision treatment, with a notchback after fuselage and auto-style rear window. **1972** *Practical Motorist* Oct. 69/2 In 1961..a Capri based on the notch-back Ford Classic was introduced. **1957** *Financial Times Ann. Rev. Brit. Industry* 61/4 To predict the service behaviour of the steel..the information derived from small notch bar tests is being amplified. **1966** *McGraw-Hill Encycl. Sci. & Technol.* VIII. 272/2 Notch-bar tests are usually made in either of two convenient arrangements, in both of which the specimen is broken by a freely swinging pendulum. **1958** A. D. MERRIMAN *Dict. Metallurgy* 212/1 In notch brittle materials the notch or crack is propagated with great rapidity under sudden loading conditions. **1963** ALEXANDER & BREWER *Manuf. Prop. of Materials* i. 16 There is a fairly well-defined threshold value of temperature below which the steel is notch-brittle and above which it exhibits relatively ductile behaviour. **1929** *Jrnl. Iron & Steel Inst.* CXX. 514 The authors first discuss two diagrams representing the ratios of the notch-brittleness obtained by means of Mesnager test-pieces and large Charpy test-pieces for a large number of steels. **1965** MATSUO & INOUE tr. *T. Yokobori's Strength, Fracture & Fatigue of Materials* vii. 162 The classical theory of Griffith explains notch brittleness as the increase of the plastic constraint factor *qe* arising from fibrous cracks induced in the early stages of the process. **1925** M. A. GROSSMANN tr. *Heyn's Physical Metallogr.* v. 299 With decreasing *b*, hence with increasing notch effect, the values for *q* and ϵ_e decrease. **1970** C. C. OSGOOD *Fatigue Design* iii. 104 The scale of notch sensitivity for a material then varies between no notch effect, $q = 0$, and full theoretical notch effect at $q = 1$. **1939** *Jrnl. R. Aeronaut. Soc.* XLIII. 728 The notch-factor was plotted against the notch-depth, and the resulting curve indicated that, as the notch-depth increases, the notch-factor increases up to a critical value of the notch-depth, and thereafter decreases. **1968** F. A. D'ISA *Mechanics of Metals* vii. 326 The actual effectiveness of stress concentration on fatigue strength is measured by the fatigue notch factor, K_f, which is defined as the ratio of the fatigue strength of a specimen with no stress concentration to the fatigue strength at the same number of cycles with stress concentration for the same conditions. [**1950** *Electronics* July 75/3 (*heading*) Notching filters.] **1962** *Electronic Technol.* XXXIX. 332/1 At v.h.f. it is desirable to construct notch filters from coaxial elements. **1974** *Physics Bull.* Mar. 107/3 A fully tunable notch filter for removing line frequency pick-up. **1931** *Amer. Mercury* Nov. 353/2 *Notch house*, a house of prostitution. **1956** H. GOLD *Man who was not with It* (1965) xxx. 277 Nancy ran a notch-house for travelers who loved to see things. **1902** *Chambers's Jrnl.* Oct. 657/2 A notable feature of these smaller mines is the notch-ladder system of conveying the ore from the interior to the pit-head. Two masts, notched like bear-poles, form the means of ascent and descent for a more or less continuous chain of *peons*. **1953** H. L. EDLIN *Forester's Handbk.* ix. 145 Notch planting..is the simplest and cheapest method, by which the majority of forest trees are planted today. **1970** —— *Collins Guide to Tree Planting & Cultivation* vii. 107 (*heading*) Notch planting. **1946** *Metallurgia* XXXIII. 250/1 A forthright statement of which material is the more notch sensitive seems impossible. **1956** M. C. SMITH *Princ. Physical Metallurgy* x. 377 Because a notch creates locally a condition of triaxial tension, all metals are notch-sensitive. **1967** LEE & NEVILLE *Handbk. Epoxy Resins* iv. 9 Cyclization, together with randomly occurring areas of low bond density for other reasons.., will lead to internal flaws within the polymer network to create notch-sensitive defects. **1934** *Jrnl. Iron & Steel Inst.* CXXX. 653 The investigation of notch sensitiveness, the use of the index of notch sensitiveness..and the connection between the index and the chemical composition..are discussed. **1934** *Jrnl. Res. Nat. Bureau of Standards* (U.S.) XIII. 535 Even for annealed copper, notch sensitivity evidently is equal to that of steels with tensile strength five times as great. **1970** C. C. OSGOOD *Fatigue Design* iii. 104 The ratio between the apparent increase in local stress [due to the presence of a notch or other stress concentrator] in fatigue and the increase predicted by the elastic theory of stress concentration has been defined..as notch sensitivity. **1926** *Jrnl. Iron & Steel Inst.* CXIII. 624 This method of testing enables it to be judged whether a material has been brought to its best condition in regard to notch-toughness. **1972** E. N. SIMONS *Testing of Metals* v. 85 A component designed for a hot climate may not give the same degree of notch toughness in a cold one if the temperature of the latter lies below the transition temperature.

notch, *v.* **3.** (Later *fig.* examples.)

1911 *Chambers's Jrnl.* Oct. 702/1 A speed of one hundred miles an hour has been notched on more than one occasion. **1963** *Sunday Express* 6 Jan. 23/5 Her earnings now are well above the £10,000 she was notching up a few years ago. **1969** 'D. RUTHERFORD' *Gilt-Edged Cockpit* i. 17 In about three minutes Mascot would have notched up the victory they so desperately needed. **1973** *Daily Tel.* 23 Apr. 5/4 When..'Andre Previn's Music Night' notched up audiences of six million last year, he was understandably delighted and encouraged. **1974** *Nature* 29 Mar. 373/3 Albright and Wilson managed to notch up an increase in profits.

notched, *ppl. a.* Add: **1.** *notched-bar test*: any of several impact tests (as the Izod or the Charpy test) in which the energy absorbed in breaking a notched specimen in a single blow is measured.

1918 *Proc. Inst. Automobile Engin.* XII. 250 Untreated bright drawn mild steel bar..usually gives a low result on the notched bar test. **1966** *McGraw-Hill Encycl. Sci. & Technol.* VIII. 272/2 Notched-bar tests are made to estimate the ductility that may be expected in the presence of defects in structures.

notcher. Add: Also, an instrument for making notches.

1879 *Organ Voicing & Tuning* 8 Tools for voicing and tuning... 1. The *notchers* of various sizes.

notching, *vbl. sb.* Add: **3.** A method of planting seedling trees in which a slit is made in the earth to take the roots of the plant. Also *attrib.*

1847 J. BROWN *Forester* iii. 85 He [*sc.* the superintendent] must examine almost each tree as it is put into the ground, whether it may be done by the pitting or notching system. **1851** *Ibid.* (ed. 2) iii. 237 The method of planting termed notching, or slitting, is done with the common spade or planting mattock. **1891** W. SCHLICH *Man. Forestry* II. ii. 126 Notching..differs from planting with a peg in the shape of the planting hole, which is that of a notch. *Ibid.*, The notching spade is wedge-shaped. **1930** *Forestry* IV. 18 Notching. The idea behind this type of planting is to..make an opening quickly which is of sufficient size to take in the roots of small plants. **1953** H. L. EDLIN *Forester's Handbk.* ix. 145 A proper straight notching spade..has no 'crank' between handle and blade. **1967** C. E. HART *Practical Forestry* (ed. 2) iv. 63 The most usual method [of planting] is notching with a spade or a mattock.

4. A type of pruning in which twigs are partially cut to stimulate the growth of a bud lower down the twig.

1913 J. C. NEWSHAM *Propagation & Pruning* 23 Notching is used to force the development of particular buds, the notch being made in the bark and young wood immediately above the selected bud. **1916** L. H. BAILEY *Pruning-Manual* v. 127 Notching into the wood above a bud tends to produce strong growth from that bud. **1972** G. E. BROWN *Pruning of Trees* ii. 24 'Notching'..is carried out during the dormant season, when a notch is cut about 10 to 15 mm. above the bud, completely removing a wedge-shaped piece. **1974** R. GROUNDS *Practical Pruning* iii. 29 The lowest branches resulting from the first year's notching are pulled down and tied at the horizontal.

notchy, *a.* Add: **2.** Of a manual gear-changing mechanism: difficult to use because the lever has to be moved accurately (as if into a narrow notch).

1967 *Autocar* 28 Dec. 20/2 The gear change is rather notchy, which is somewhat typical. **1972** *Drive* Spring 150/2 Short, precise movements..are features of the four-speed gearbox, though the lever has a slightly notchy feeling. **1975** *Daily Tel.* 16 Apr. 12/6 The short gear lever is a trifle notchy in operation although I always find this preferable to vague sloppiness.

note, *sb.*² Add: **5. c.** In perfumery, one of the basic components of the fragrance of a perfume which give it its character.

1905 F. W. BURBIDGE *Bk. of Scented Garden* 34 Dr Piesse goes so far as to say that one false note amongst odours will destroy the whole harmony of the chord, just as in music or in colour. **1945** E. SAGARIN *Science & Art of Perfumery* xii. 145 The odors were like sounds..and a scale could be created going from the first or lowest note, the heavy smell, to the last or highest note, the sharp smell. **1954** A. J. KRAJKEMAN tr. *Jellinek's Pract. Mod. Perfumery* IV. 180 Honey-like odours, combining a sweet-floral with an animal note. **1960** A. ELLIS *Essence of Beauty* xii. 142 The characteristic a discerning and discriminating user looks for in a perfume..is what the perfumer calls '*the soft odour note*'. **1970** *Daily Tel.* 16 Dec. 11/6 The top notes are the lightest and most volatile. **1973** E. MAPLE *Magic of Perfume* vi. 51 There has long existed in perfumers' language a system of 'musical notation' in which the constituents of perfume are accorded 'top notes', 'middle notes' and 'bass notes'.

10. *note of interrogation*: see INTERROGATION 2 b in Dict. and Suppl.

21. (sense 1) *note-head, -value*; (sense 2) *note-singing; -spinning* vbl. sb. and ppl. adj.; (sense 13) *note-block, -pad, -taker* (later examples), *-taking*; (sense 16) *note-writing* (earlier example); also as *adj.*; **note-broker** *U.S.* a broker who deals in promissory notes and bills of exchange; **note-cluster,** several neighbouring notes played simultaneously; **notehead paper,** business notepaper having a printed heading; **note-holder,** a holder of notes (sense 17) issued by a business company or the like for temporary financing; **note-layer** (sense 18), a petty thief who operates a short-change swindle; **note-row, -series** = *tone-row* (*TONE *sb.* 11).

1927 R. A. FREEMAN *Certain Dr. Thorndyke* II. xiv. 207 Jotting down on a note-block a few brief memoranda. **1870** W. W. FOWLER *10 Yrs. Wall St.* 226 This man..is an English Jew, who has gone into the business of a note broker. **1929** *Encycl. Brit.* IV. 233/1 Bill-brokers are practically unknown in the United States; their general analogue is the note-broker. **1934** C. LAMBERT *Music Ho!* v. 330 Van Dieren's attitude towards harmony is more indicative of future developments than the 'note clusters' of Henry Cowell. **1965** *New Statesman* 24 Sept. 458/3 A younger composer like Peter Sculthorpe attempts to enter the heart of the Australian experience by way of a static technique of cumulative ostinati and note-clusters that is more Asiatic than occidental. **1946** H. Foss in A. L. Bacharach *Brit. Mus. of our Time* iv. 78 Warlock wrote with exquisite precision:..the shape of the note-heads, the uprights, the binds and ties, were of enormous interest to him. **1974** G. READ *Music Notation* v. 63 The note-head..is somewhat oval in shape, and is either open (or 'white'..) or closed ('black'..). **1909** *Westm. Gaz.* 20 May 7/2 The..notehead paper of a London firm of stock, share, and bond dealers. **1927** *Daily Tel.* 21 June 2/3 Shareholders were prepared for unfavourable figures by the necessity for an arrangement regarding..the rights of the note-holders. **1968** *Globe & Mail* (Toronto) 13 Jan. B. 1/2 Fraudulent financial statements and a false prospectus were means used..to defraud 8,500 noteholders of Prudential Finance Corp. Ltd. of $20-million. **1928** Note-layer [see *CREEP *sb.* 1 d]. **1938** D. CASTLE *Do Your Own Time* viii. 83 They boast of having been knock-off gees, gow peddlers,..note layers, and torpedo men. **1950** H. E. GOLDIN *Dict. Amer. Underworld Lingo* 146/1 The note-layer usually works with an accomplice. **1922** A. BENNETT *Lilian* I. iv. 41 She repeated the number, even writing it on her note pad. **1961** *Encounter* Apr. 29/2 He asked me for one of my notepads. **1975** D. BAGLEY *Snow Tiger* xi. 95 Smithers consulted his note-pad. **1955** *Oxf. Compan. Mus.* (ed. 9) 698/1 Note-row... This is a rigid method of composition introduced by Schönberg... All the twelve notes of the octave are employed in every composition, and all the notes are treated in such a way as to enjoy an equal footing. **1961** *Listener* 12 Oct. 578/3 He spoke of his contrapuntal technique, of note rows, their combinations and inversions. **1947** *Penguin Music Mag.* Dec. 20 'Twelve-tone technique', in which the twelve notes of the chromatic scale are used in an order known as a 'note-series', which remains the same throughout the work. **1962** *Times* 19 Oct. 18/6 The American group admit to working from a note-series. **1896** *Musical Herald* 1 Feb. 41/1 Thousands of teachers waste time in note-singing practice. **1908** E. M. SNEYD-KYNNERSLEY *H.M.I.* xxiv. 288 The clergy encouraged note-singing for the sake of their choirs. **1946** H. FOSS in A. L. Bacharach *Brit.*

Music of our Time iv. 67 He [*sc.* 'Peter Warlock'] was no devotee of note-spinning, of blowing up frog-ideas into bull-like proportions. **1961** *Listener* 20 Apr. 717/3 The ideas in the other two movements are of an altogether lower standard and there is some tiresome note-spinning. **1970** *Times* (Sat. Suppl.) 18 Apr. p. iii/5, I confess to finding it rather like late, not very strongly motivated, note-spinning Schumann. **1935** *Essays & Studies* XX. 123 All these matters can be conscientiously taught to the plodding note-taker and be redelivered at examinations. **1961** *Sunday Express* 29 Jan. 9/6 Police note-takers filled four foolscap pages. **1954** J. MASTERS *Bhowani Junction* II. xii. 107 They didn't want me for any more note-taking. **1955** H. ROTH *Sleeper* xi. 92 The stilted feeling that note-taking causes in some interviewees. **1975** *Times* 5 July 2/5 Jurors..were often required to perform fantastic feats of attention and memory..without the aid of note-taking. **1915** *Musical Quarterly* I. 191 An Indian [*sc.* North American Indian] can give short note-values corresponding to eighth or sixteenth notes with perfect distinctness. **1917** H. JAMES *Middle Years* iv. 46 Whereas the smartness and newness beyond the sea supposedly disavowed the low, they did so but thinly and vainly, falling markedly short of the high; which the little boxed and boiled Albany attained to some effect of,..just by having its so thoroughly appreciable note-value in a scheme of manners. **1944** W. APEL *Harvard Dict. Mus.* 497/2 The illustration shows the note values with their American terminology. **1955** G. ABRAHAM in H. van Thal *Fanfare for E. Newman* ii. 10 The first two bars were originally written as four, in double note-values. **1963** *Listener* 17 Jan. 141/2 It [*sc.* the basic five-note figure] is repeated eight times in succession, with progressively lengthening note-values. **1814** JANE AUSTEN *Mansfield Park* II. xiii. 291 Quite unpractised in such sort of note-writing. **1967** G. KELLY in *Coast to Coast 1965–66* 101 He became the victim of their gum-chewing, note-writing, hair-combing inattention.

note, *v.*[2] **6. a.** (Later example.)

1897 *Musical Herald* 1 June 189/1 They organise vocal music competitions, but they have no sight-singing, and no noting music by ear.

notelet. Add: **3.** A folded card or sheet of paper on which a note may be written, having a picture or design on the face of the first leaf.

1955 *Stationery Trade Ref. Bk.* 71/1 Macniven & Cameron Ltd...manufacturers of social and gift stationery. 189/1 Notelets Products. Macniven & Cameron Ltd. **1971** *Countryman* Autumn 205/2 (Advt.), S.A.E. brings our list of Christmas gifts, cards, notelets, calendars for country lovers. **1972** *Stationery Trade Rev.* Aug. 39/2 Many of the Waverley gift stationery boxes also includes [*sic*] Notelets.

note-shaver. (Earlier and later examples.)

1816 *Massachusetts Spy* 4 Sept. (Th.), We have too many note-shavers; too many gentlemen. **1905** D. G. PHILLIPS *Plum Tree* 11 But my clients were poor, and poor pay, and slow pay. Nobody was doing well but the note-shavers. **1911** R. D. SAUNDERS *Col. Todhunter* viii. 113 Old Eph Tucker was a note-shaver long before he was a politician, and he's got note-shavin' in his blood bigger'n a mule. **1942** BERREY & VAN DEN BARK *Amer. Thes. Slang* ix. 520 *Shaver, note shaver,* a discounter of notes at an exorbitant rate.

no·te-shaving. *U.S. slang.* [f. prec.] The profession of a note-shaver; the making of an excessive profit on the discounting of notes.

1828 *Yankee* (Portland, Maine) I. 52/1 [By] the system of note-shaving that prevails here..the industrious and active are held in a state of bondage to the more wealthy and more lazy. **1855** P. T. BARNUM *Life* 138 Had I termed the deed an extortion or note-shaving..the verdict might have been different—but I had called the act 'usury'. **1902** W. N. HARBEN *Abner Daniel* 38 He began to utilize this capital in 'note shaving', and other methods of turning over money for a handsome profit. **1911** [see *NOTE-SHAVER].

‖ **notes inégales** (nǫtsinegal), *pl. Mus.* [Fr., lit. 'unequal notes'.] In Baroque music, notes performed by convention in a rhythm different from that shown in the score.

1927 *Grove's Dict. Mus.* (ed. 3) II. 708/2 To avoid all uncertainty, authors frequently make use of the expression *notes égales* or *notes inégales*. **1954** *Ibid.* (ed. 5) IV. 479/2 In common 4-4 time semi-quavers or quavers but not crotchets or minims are eligible as 'notes inégales'. **1965** *Times* 9 July 16 Chief among these 'errors' is the convention of *notes inégales*, which decreed that with certain specified or understood exceptions, pairs of stepwise quavers (or, in some time-signatures, semiquavers) were to be played unevenly, the first note rather longer than the second. **1970** *Sat. Rev.* 31 Oct. 55 Mr. Weaver shows a commendable awareness of performance practice, even though scholars are not unanimous—namely the *notes inégales* in the finale of No. 3 where he adjusts the left hand to the triplet meter in the right. **1972** *Times* 22 Nov. 11/5 A sound knowledge of the more ticklish stylistic points to be observed, *notes inégales*, for instance in music from Couperin's Ninth Suite. **1975** *Times Lit. Suppl.* 9 May 503/4 (Advt.), Notes on ornamentation, bowing, *notes inégales*, and other performance problems.

‖ **note verbale** (nǫt vẹ̄rbal). [Fr., lit. 'verbal note'.] An unsigned diplomatic note, of the nature of a memorandum, which is written in the third person.

1855 E. GRENVILLE MURRAY *Embassies & Foreign Courts* xvii. 264 Certain diplomatic worthies invented a double-faced document called a *note verbale*, or summary of conversation. These notes are unsigned. Their object is merely to refresh the diplomatic memory... They are supposed..to combine all the advantages of writing and conversation. **1911** *Encycl. Brit.* XIX. 823/2 The so-called *notes verbales* are unsigned, and are merely of the nature of memoranda (of conversations, &c.). **1917** E. SATOW *Guide to Diplomatic Practice* vii. 75 As not many *Notes Verbales* are to be met with in print, it seems worth while to reproduce it here. **1939** H. NICOLSON *Diplomacy* x. 246 *Note verbale.* This is a type of communication which is less formal than a signed Note and more formal than a memorandum. It is unsigned, but it is customary that it should contain at the end some conventional expression of courtesy. It is, in fact, merely the addition of this polite tag which differentiates it from the mémoire. **1955** *Times* 20 May 8/1 Among the papers now issued by the secretariat is a *note verbale* from the permanent delegation of the United Kingdom to the United Nations. **1970** R. G. FELTHAM *Diplomatic Handbk.* iv. 42 The Note Verbale is not common, but it is used to clarify or confirm points raised in a previous conversation or to list items which one could not expect to be recalled precisely. **1973** I. M. SINCLAIR *Vienna Convention on Law of Treaties* ii. 36 The conference decided otherwise, no doubt influenced by the growing practice of constituting treaties by an exchange of unsigned *notes verbales*.

not-go (nǫ·tgō), *a. Engin.* [f. NOT *adv.* + GO *v.*] Designating (part of) a gauge so made that it will not enter, or will not admit, an object whose dimensions are within a designated limit.

1917 *Proc. Inst. Mech. Engin.* Jan. 58 Those gauges that were considered right might be put into one lot.. the tests being made solely by 'go' and 'not go' check gauges. **1951** [see *GO *a.* 1]. **1964** S. CRAWFORD *Basic Engin. Processes* xiv. 296 The 'Not-Go' end is of such a size that it will not enter the hole when the hole is up to the highest limit.

'nother, colloq. var. ANOTHER *a., pron.*

1934 D. MACKAIL *Summer Leaves* x. 341 'How long have you got here?'..''Nother month, I expect.' **1935** in Z. N. Hurston *Mules & Men* (1970) 20 People told one 'nother that God was talking in de mountains. **1972** 'L. EGAN' *Paper Chase* (1973) xii. 195 'Nother little bit of the thing just occurred to me. **1973** H. MCCLOY *Change of Heart* iv. 39 'Nother cup of coffee, gramps?

nothing, *sb.* and *adv.* Add: **A.** *sb.* **I. 1. f.** As *adj.* or *interj.* Not at all; in no respect. *colloq.* (orig. *U.S.*).

1883 G. W. PECK *Mirth for Million* 325 'You are pretty rough on the old man..after he has..given you nice presents.' 'Nice presents nothin. All I got was a "Come to Jesus" Christmas card.' **1888** [see *NOPE *adv.*]. **1899** A. NICHOLAS *Idyl of Wabash* 175 'My account—nothing!' was her scornful ejaculation. **1899** B. TARKINGTON *Gentleman from Indiana* i. 10 'But you only wait—' The editor smiled sadly. 'Wait nothing. Don't threaten, man.' **1911** H. QUICK *Yellowstone Nights* xi. 288 Stop nothing! Federal injunction won't do it. **1922** M. B. HOUSTON *Witch-man* xviii. 238 'He could have found it, of course.'.. 'Found it, nothing. I saw other things he'd taken.' **1925** WODEHOUSE *Sam the Sudden* xiii. 93 'Two million smackers it's going to get him,' retorted Dolly. 'Two million smackers nothing! The stuff's hidden in a place where he'd never think of looking in two million years.' **1946** K. TENNANT *Lost Haven* (1968) ii. 43 'How about the spooks?'.. 'Spooks nothing.' **1966** A. E. LINDOP *I start Counting* xxii. 275 Grandad said, poor little mite nothing. The man that gave her a lift told the police she'd done her best to seduce him. **1969** R. RENDELL *Best Man to Die* xii. 117 'Did you wait for him?' 'Wait, nothing!' said Cullam hotly. 'Why would I?' **1972** D. LEES *Zodiac* 46 'Francs?' 'Francs nothing—pounds.' **1974** T. BARLING *Shooter Man* iii. 23 'It just slipped out.' 'Slipped nothing. You couldn't resist.'

g. *as slick as nothing at all*: very promptly or quickly, 'in the twinkling of an eye'. *rare.*

1884 'MARK TWAIN' *Huck. Finn* xl. 410 Done it just as slick as nothing at all.

h. *with* (or *having*) *nothing on,* wearing no clothes, undressed, naked.

1719 DEFOE *Robinson Crusoe* 62, I stripp'd..having nothing on but a Chequer'd Shirt, and a Pair of Linnen Drawers. **1908** KIPLING *Let.* in C. E. Carrington *Rudyard Kipling* (1955) xvi. 399, I cannot help blushing when I am rung-up by women—with nothing on but spectacles and a bath-towel. **1971** E. PAUL *Reluctant Cloak & Dagger Man* xi. 137 We always swam here with nothing on.

i. *nothing doing*: see *DO *v.* 34 c.

j. *like nothing on earth*: strange, ugly, wretched, etc., in a superlative degree.

1923 A. CHRISTIE *Murder on Links* xxvi. 286 She looked like nothing on God's earth. **1927** W. E. COLLINSON *Contemp. Eng.* 117 To look or feel like nothing on earth (*very bad*). **1974** M. G. EBERHART *Danger Money* (1975) iv. 39 'What's he like?' 'Nothing on earth... I wouldn't trust him with a nickel.'

k. *there is nothing* (*much*) *in it*: there is no important feature of interest or value in something; there is no significant difference between two things, etc.

1927 *Observer* 18 Dec. 19/3 The first round there was nothing much in it. In the second round Angus..punched Mansfield round the ring. **1950** PARTRIDGE *Dict. Clichés* (ed. 4) 156 *Nothing in it,* esp., *there's nothing...* (there is no appreciable—or important—difference): c. 20.

l. *to have nothing on* (someone): to be no match for (someone). See *HAVE *v.* 14 h.

3. c. As *adj.* in trivial use: of no account, insignificant, meaningless, insipid, dull; (of a dress, etc.) discreet, elegantly unobtrusive.

1961 *Time* (Atlantic ed.) 18 Aug. 60 All these beautiful people with nothing faces. **1964** 'E. MCBAIN' *Axe* vi. 118 This is a *nothing* game, you dig? A buck, two bucks a time, that's all. **1965** *Vogue* Aug. 43/2 Little 'nothing' sweaters and shirts for wearing with suits. **1967** W. MURRAY *Sweet Ride* iv. 46 It was a nothing place, just a few booths and a counter. **1969** P. KAVANAGH *Such Men are Dangerous* (1971) ii. 30 The characters..were all hung up on trivia, little nothing problems in their careers and marriages. **1971** *Sunday Times* (Colour Suppl.) 23 May 53/1 A girl in one of those 'nothing' dresses with the Quant signature written all over it. **1972** P. DICKINSON *Lizard in Cup* vi. 97 It's a nothing thing, like I said... But drugs aren't a nothing thing, no.

6. e. (Earlier and later examples.)

1835 J. F. COOPER *Monikins* III. iv. 93 In this happy land, there was no registration, no passports, 'no nothin' —as Mr. Poke pointedly expressed it. **1905** KIPLING *Actions & Reactions* (1909) 8 'No roads, no nothing!' said Sophie. **1948** H. L. MENCKEN *Amer. Lang.* Suppl. II. ix. 392 There may not be no nothing. **1968** *Washington Post* 21 Sept. A.12/1 His [*sc.* Wallace's] appeal is to racial animosity, no-nothing policies.

II. 8. b. (Further examples.) Also used to typify theorizing which attempts to reduce, simplify, or explain concepts in such a way that they seem to accord with the theory propounded; so *the nothing-but*; also *nothing-but-ism, nothing-buttery.*

c **1838** W. H. MURRAY in M. R. Booth *Eng. Plays of 19th Cent.* (1973) IV. 160 Mark me: no amendments, no conferences—I'll have '*the* bill, the *whole* bill, and *nothing* but the bill'. **1884** *Encycl. Brit.* XVII. 701/2 Witnesses are sworn: 'The evidence you shall give..shall be the truth, the whole truth, and nothing but the truth. So', &c. **1923** R. H. THOULESS *Introd. Psychol. Relig.* x. 129 The essential requirement of this theory is that it should be shown that religion contains nothing but elements of this kind, and this is exactly what Mr Schroeder makes no attempt at all to prove. **1934** J. G. BRANDON *One-Minute Murder* iv. 32 As far as that poor devil's concerned..it's accident and nothing but. **1935** *Mind* XLIV. 91 Jung's formulation..is the antithesis of '*nothing-but*'-ism. **1937** A. HUXLEY *Ends & Means* xiv. 257 All who advance theories of mind containing the word 'nothing but', tend to involve themselves in this kind of contradiction. The very fact that they formulate theories which they believe to have general validity..constitutes in itself a sufficient denial of the validity of 'nothing-but' judgments concerning the nature of the mind. **1951** M. LOWRY *Let.* 25 Aug. (1967) 252 You might call it pseudo-Freud and the philosophy of the 'nothingbut'. **1961** *Mind* LXX. 100 There is much else in the literary idiom of nature-philosophy: *nothing-buttery*, for example, always part of the minor symptomatology of the bogus. 'Love is.. nothing more, and nothing less, than [etc.]'. **1973** *Black World* June 30 A poet ain't nothin' but a bird.

10. a. (Later examples.)

1885 'M. RUTHERFORD' *M. Rutherford's Deliverance* iv. 65 She had learned that she was nothing specially to him. **1947** E. O'NEILL *Iceman Cometh* I. 79 He's nothing to you —or to me, either. *Ibid.* II. 105 The good old Cause means nothing to you any more.

c. *there's nothing to it*: it is very easy to do; there is no difficulty involved.

1934 E. O'NEILL *Ah, Wilderness!* I. 21 There (*with a grin*). I know there's nothing to it, anyway. **1951** H. WOUK *Caine Mutiny* viii. 77 There's nothing to it, really, except making damn sure none of your watch-standers sit down or fall asleep standing up. **1953** F. STARK *Coast of Incense* iv. 232, I am puzzled when asked what makes my style, for there is nothing to it except a natural ear for cadence and the wish to get the meaning right. **1963** 'S. WOODS' *Taste of Fears* i. 13 'There's nothing to it if you're quick, or so I'm told,' he added. **1971** D. EDEN *Afternoon Walk* vii. 83 'You used to automatic drive?' 'Yes.' 'Then there's nothing to it.' **1974** *Country Life* 14 Feb. 322/1, I mentioned that I was spending the following night at a Japanese inn. He assured me that there was nothing to it.

15*. *nothing to write* (or *cable, wire*) *home about,* denoting something that is unworthy of comment, unremarkable or mediocre. *slang* (orig. *Forces*').

1917 W. MUIR *Observations of Orderly* 227 Miserable conditions.., bad accommodation, doubtful food.. these, in the lingo of our now much-travelled and stoical troops, are 'nothing to write home about'. **1937** AUDEN & MACNEICE *Lett. from Iceland* iv. 38 Fare from Hull to anywhere in Iceland, £4 10s. plus 5 kr. a day for food. The latter is nothing to write home about but eatable. **1942** BERREY & VAN DEN BARK *Amer. Thes. Slang* i. 33 Fair to middling,..nothing to..shout about, nothing to wire *or* write home about.

16. b. *nothing-saying.*

a **1817** JANE AUSTEN *Persuasion* (1818) IV. viii. 160 After a period of nothing-saying amongst the party.

c. (Further examples.)

1906 *All-Story Mag.* (U.S.) Aug. 593/1 The nothing-doingness of things in general outside the office. **1924** R. GRAVES *Mock Beggar Hall* 16 A formless lumpish, nothing-in-particular. **1924** D. H. LAWRENCE *England, My England* 98 They passed an agreeable, casual, nothing-in-particular evening.

nothofagus (nǫþofē̆·gǒs). [mod.L. (K. L. Blume *Museum Botanicum Lugduno-Batavum* (1850) I. 307). f. Gr. νόθος false + φηγός beech tree.] An evergreen or deciduous tree of the genus so called, belonging to the family Fagaceæ and native to Australasia and South America; also called southern beech.

1914 W. J. BEAN *Trees & Shrubs Hardy in Brit. Isles* II. 100 Of the Nothofagus group of beeches, this [*sc. N. Moorei*] has the largest leaves of any cultivated out-of-doors in this country. **1956** *Handbk. Hardwoods* (Forest Prod. Res. Lab.) 76 *Nothofagus* is the beech of the south-

ern hemisphere. **1961** *Times* 18 July 11/7 The dark and light greens of the nothofagus forest. **1974** R. L. Fox *Variations on Garden* 138 Foresters are beginning to realize the merits of a cousin of the beech tree called nothofagus... These southern beeches grow wild in New Zealand and South America... Their leaves are small, like a small beech or hornbeam, and their autumn colouring is most remarkable: each leaf changes individually to its own shade of orange, red, brown or plain green.

nothomorph (nǫ·þomǭɹf). *Bot.* [f. Gr. *νόθος* cross-bred + *μορφή* form.] A plant produced by hybridization.

1939 R. Melville in *Proc. Linn. Soc.* CLI. 158, I therefore propose the term nothomorph (nothomorphus = hybrid form) for all hybrid forms of sexual origin, whether F_1 segregates or back-crosses. **1949** *Jrnl. R. Hort. Soc.* LXXIV. 43 This original seedling and its vegetatively produced offspring may..be the product of hybridization, i.e. a nothomorph. **1953** *Rep. Proc. 7th Internat. Bot. Congr. 1950* XII. 544/2 These forms are recognized as nothomorphs; when desirable they may be designated by an epithet preceded by the binary name of the group and the term nothomorph. **1963** Davis & Heywood *Princ. Angiosperm Taxonomy* xiv. 482 The term nothomorph can be used to distinguish different derivatives of hybridisation between the same species.

nothosaur (nǫ·posǭɹ). *Palæont.* [f. mod.L. name of suborder *Nothosauria*, f. generic name Nothosaurus (Georg, Graf von Münster 1834, in *Neues Jahrb. f. Min.* 525).] An extinct marine reptile belonging to the suborder Nothosauria, known from Triassic fossil remains in Europe.

1933 A. S. Romer *Vertebr. Paleont.* vii. 153 A nothosaur in which this pterygoid union had not been quite completed would make an ideal plesiosaur ancestor. **1962** *New Scientist* 5 July 34/2 Some of the nothosaurs seem to have been very lightly built, others larger and more sturdy. They all had fairly long, flexible necks and long jaws with many pointed teeth. They must have caught their food in the shallow waters..paddling along with their stubby webbed feet. **1971** *Nature* 15 Jan. 172/1 In a great many aquatic and marine reptiles, past and present, ichthyosaurs, placodonts, nothosaurs,..the external nares are just in front of the eyes.

no-thought: see *no *a.* 5 e.

no-throw. [f. No *a.* + Throw *sb.*[2]] In various games or sports, a throw disallowed because it does not comply with the rules.

1959 *Times* 14 Sept. 3/2 Ellis..won the hammer.. with his second throw.., thereafter having four no-throws. **1964** A. Wykes *Gambling* iii. 62 The bettors place their money on whether the coins will land as two heads or two tails; a head and a tail is a 'no-throw'. **1967** Ward & Watts *Athletics* xii. 115 *Major fault 9*: point [of javelin] not coming down—no mark is made, and hence there is a 'No throw'.

not-I, not-me. [f. Not *adv.* 14 d + I, Me *pers. prons.*] That from which the subjective or personal is excluded.

1846 J. D. Morell *Hist. View Philos.* I. 59 In the same manner as *the me* implies the notion of a *not-me* from which it is distinguished..so the notion of the limited and the finite implies the correlative one of the unlimited and the infinite. **1854** A. G. Henderson tr. *Cousin's Philos. of Kant* vii. 179 The me..could only become cognizant of the not-me by means of the faculties it possesses. **1895** tr. *M. Nordau's Degeneration* III. i. 245 It has.. jumped to the conclusion that the 'I' has actually no knowledge of a 'not-I', of an external world. *Ibid.*, These wise men repeated, in a tone of conviction, the doctrine of the non-existence of the 'not-I'. **1917** D. H. Lawrence *Look! We have come Through!* 147, I suppose ultimately, she is all beyond me, She is all not-me, ultimately. **1950** A. Huxley *Themes & Variations* i. 114 Not the hyper-organic 'I', still less the divine not-I, which transcends the ego and is its ground. **1953** S. Spender *Creative Element* ii. 54 He [*sc.* Rimbaud] was attempting to remove the barrier which divides subject from object, the 'I' from the 'not I'. **1953** H. L. Sullivan *Interpersonal Theory of Psychiatry* x. 162 The personification of not-me is..very emphatically encountered by people who are having a severe schizophrenic episode. **1965** *Listener* 4 Nov. 691/2 We are accustomed to distinguish so sharply between 'I' and 'not-I' and between 'now' and 'not-now' that any blurring of the dichotomy may seem unnatural to us. **1974** A. Plant in M. Fordham et al. *Technique in Jungian Analysis* II. 215 The analyst can be of use by letting the patient experience him as a 'not-me' possession.

notice, *sb.* Add: **1. c.** (Earlier example of *at —— minutes' notice.*)

1839 Dickens *Let.* 25 July (1965) I. 569 There is *always* a bed for you at five minutes' notice.

2. b. (Earlier examples.)

1765 Earl of Malmesbury *Let.* 16 Sept. (1870) I. 129 It is 150 florins, or fourteen guineas, a-year; but I am to try it first, and may, at any time after, quit it by giving six weeks' notice. **1836** Dickens *Let.* 5 Nov. (1965) I. 191, I have deemed it right to beg you to accept my notice from to-day.

c. An announcement read to a church congregation (freq. *pl.*).

1855 F. Procter *Hist. Bk. Com. Prayer* II. iii. 322 The correct interpretation concerning notices to be given in church. *a* **1870** 'Mark Twain' *Let.* in C. Clemens *My Father* (1931) i. 11 The local minister had read sixteen 'notices' of Sunday-school and Bible-class and church and sewing-society and other meetings. **1967** *Alternative Services (Second Series): An Order for Holy Communion* 4 Banns of Marriage and other notices may then be published, if they have not been published before the service.

8. a. Also, a review of a play or any public entertainment. (Earlier and later examples.)

1835 Dickens *Let.* 23 Nov. (1965) I. 97 If I take a cab and put off writing my notice 'till we return, I can easily manage it. I shall come straight from the Theatre. **1952** Granville *Dict. Theatrical Terms* 123 *Notice*, the newspaper critique following a first-night performance. **1959** N. Marsh *False Scent* (1960) ii. 76 'She's playing Eliza Doolittle,' Gantry remarked. 'Of course. Nice notices,' Marchant murmured.

9. b. notice paper, a parliamentary paper giving the current day's proceedings.

1844 T. E. May *Law, Privileges Parliament* viii. 166 Any member [of the House of Commons] may propose a question... But in order to give the House due notice of his intention, he is required to state the form of his motion on a previous day, and to have it entered in the Order Book or Notice Paper. **1884** E. W. Hamilton *Diary* 3 Apr. (1972) II. 588 After the unprecedent[ed] number of questions had been disposed of (no less than 73 being on the Notice paper).. Sir S. Northcote moved the adjournment of the House. **1956** P. & G. Ford *Guide to Parliamentary Papers* I. i. 3 The White Paper (Notice Paper)..contains certain portions of the Blue Paper and relates to the current day's sittings.

notice, *v.* Add: **3. b.** colloq. phr. *not so as you'd notice*: not to a noticeable degree.

1937 A. Christie *Murder in Mews* iii. 172 '*He* was fond of *you?*' 'Not so that you'd notice it..he rather resented my existence.' **1938** N. Marsh *Artists in Crime* (1954) xvi. 216 Garcia's not innocent, dear, not so's you'd notice it. **1966** 'N. Blake' *Morning after Death* xiii. 198 'Was Chester interested?' 'Not so as you'd notice.' **1970** W. J. Burley *To kill a Cat* xi. 189 'Any luck?' 'Not so's you'd notice.'

c. *intr.* To be seen, to show, to be noticeable.

1961 Y. Olsson *On Syntax Eng. Verb* vii. 177, I have mended the hole now. I don't think it notices.

7. To write a review or 'notice' of a book, play, etc.

1854 *Punch* 15 July 20/1 The reporter who 'noticed' the diplomatists. **1859** G. H. Lewes *Let.* 5 Feb. in *Geo. Eliot Lett.* (1954) III. 10 Perhaps also you will send the 'Times' should that 'publication' notice the carpenter [sc. *Adam Bede*].

noticeability. Add: **b.** The quality, state, or fact of being noticeable.

1926 Fowler *Mod. Eng. Usage* 639 The reader will perhaps conclude that its noticeability is not a grace.

noticeable, *a.* **2.** (Earlier example.)

1809 *Mem. Amer. Acad. Arts & Sci.* III. 248 The moon's limb exhibited very little of that rough or serrated appearance, which was so noticeable in 1806.

noticing, *ppl. a.* (Later examples.)

1903 E. Wharton *Sanctuary* II. i. 79 You know she's an uncommonly noticing person, and little things tell with her. **1905** J. C. Lincoln *Partners of Tide* ii. 20 Bradley, being what his late 'Uncle Solon' had called a 'noticin' boy', remembered Captain Titcomb's hint. **1940** R. Postgate *Verdict of Twelve* i. 12 Father was not 'noticing'; Mother was, and what's more would twist your arm till you screamed if you sulked and wouldn't answer. **1959** A. Christie *Cat among Pigeons* xx. 205 She's not what I'd call a noticing kind of child.

no-time. [f. No *a.* + Time *sb.*] A time which does not exist (*poet.*); a very short time (*U.S. local*).

a **1918** W. Owen *Poems* (1931) 69 And in the happy no-time of his sleeping Death took him by the heart. **1942** W. Faulkner *Go Down, Moses* 224 After a no-time he returned. **1943** D. Gascoyne *Poems 1937–1942* 22 Black was the No-time at the heart Of Time (the frameless mirror's back). **1963** [see *no-place *sb.*].

notion. Add: **7.** (Earlier example of *to take a notion.*)

1776 J. Verrieul *Let.* 17 Apr. in F. Chase *Hist. Dartmouth Coll.* (1891) I. vi. 347 Ther was Ten Regt ordert to march for Newyoark, and I toock a notion to go with them.

9. b. (Earlier and later examples.) Now *spec.* in haberdashery.

1803 F. Asbury *Jrnl.* (1821) III. 106 How would it tell to the South, that priests were among the notions of Yankee traffick? **1913** F. H. Burnett *T. Tembaron* xx. 264 The young lady from the notion counter (those wonderful shops!). **1964** *McCall's Sewing* ii. 22 While making a list of the fabrics and trims needed, check the 'Notions' section to see what notions are needed. *Ibid.* 30/2 *Notions*, all dressmaking supplies that are used in the construction of a garment: thread, zippers, tape, buttons, etc. **1965** 'L. Egan' *Detective's Due* (1966) iv. 39 Varallo and Katz were led past Notions, Gift Cards and Cameras, to a counter in the center of the store.

c. *notion-peddler* (or *-pedlar*), *-peddling*, *-seller*.

1932 L. C. Douglas *Forgive our Trespasses* (1937) i. 1 The steel-bowed spectacles that had been her mother's, had of a notion peddler for two dozen eggs & a pound of butter. **1809** 'D. Knickerbocker' *Hist. N.Y.* I. iv. iii. 214 He swore that he would have nothing more to do with such a squatting, bundling, guessing,..notion-peddling crew. **1839** *Chemung* (N.Y.) *Democrat* 17 Apr. (Th.), A 'notion seller' was offering Yankee clocks, &c.

notional, *a.* Add: **1. c.** *Economics.* Of a figure, profit, etc.: speculative, hypothetical; for the purposes of a particular interpretation or theory.

1958 *Spectator* 8 Aug. 204/3 The profit attributable to Iraq is the notional one which the oil companies regard as economic. **1960** *Economist* 15 Oct. 278/1 Costs per ton of storage, mainly notional interest charges, were put at roughly £5 for lead and zinc. **1964** *Financial Times* 3 Mar. 15/6 The formula for calculating this standard price has been drawn up so that it would leave the Corporation with a notional profit of £1·8 m. before tax. **1972** *Accountant* 17 Aug. 197/1 A company..will be able to obtain relief..on a notional figure.

4. b. (Earlier example.)

1791 *Gazette of U.S.* (N.Y.) 9 Feb. (Th.), If a man is a little odd in his ways, his friends say he is a notional creature, or full of notions... Love is the most notional passion.

6. *Gram.* Used (orig. by Jespersen) in relation to the semantic content, real or apparent, of grammatical forms and categories; of a word: carrying full meaning, not merely grammatical; of a verb: principal, main, not auxiliary.

1924 O. Jespersen *Philos. Gram.* iii. 56 Our examples of gender and sex will make it clear that the relations between the syntactic and notional categories will often present a similar kind of network to that noticed between formal and syntactic categories. **1933** —— *Syst. Gram.* 20 In 'he happened to fall' the notional subject is a nexus 'he..to fall'. **1942** Partridge *Usage & Abusage* 148/2 Jespersen's *The Philosophy of Grammar*..urges us to consider all words..in their three aspects, form, syntactic function, and 'natural or logical meaning'; this third aspect he calls 'notional'. **1957** R. W. Zandvoort *Handbk. Eng. Gram.* I. v. 64 The opposite of 'auxiliary' is 'notional verb', 'principal verb', or 'verb of full meaning'. **1966** M. Pei *Gloss. Linguistic Terminol.* 182 *Notional word*, a word that carries a full meaning ('he *has* luck' vs. 'he *has* gone'). **1971** P. J. Lucas in *Archivum Linguisticum* II. 19 There is a considerable degree of overlap (in Capgrave's *Chronicle*) between the notional signs on the one hand, and, between the grammatical signs on the other, but there is no overlap between primarily notional and primarily grammatical signs.

not-life. [Not *adv.* 14 d.] Inanimate matter, esp. as contrasted with that which contains life. So **not-living** *a.* and *sb.*

1869 T. H. Huxley in *Fortn. Rev.* 1 Feb. 140 The assumption of the existence in the living matter of a something which has no representative or correlative in the not living matter which gave rise to it. **1895** [see Not *adv.* 14 d]. **1943** J. S. Huxley *Evolutionary Ethics* i. 7 The scientific study of change, of becoming, of the production of novelty, whether of life from not-life, of a baby from an ovum. **1953** Massingham & Hyams *Prophecy of Famine* iii. 57 The harmony..between the living creature..and the not-living habitat itself. *Ibid.* viii. 169 A short-circuiting of the life-cycle in terms of not-life. **1964** Gould & Kolb *Dict. Social Sci.* 607/1 Birth rituals.. signifying the separation of the infant from the world of the dead (or not-living) and his aggregation to that of the living.

not-me: see *not-I.

not-ness. *rare.* [f. Not *adv.* + -ness.] The quality or state of not accepting something; something negative.

1933 Dylan Thomas *Let.* Sept. (1966) 21 Your 'not-ness' alone is worth all the superlatives at my command. **1945** H. Miller *Air-Conditioned Nightmare* 12 It was something negative, some not-ness of some kind or other.

notornis. Insert in etym. [mod.L. (R. Owen 1848, in *Proc. Zool. Soc.* 2).] Substitute for def.: A flightless New Zealand bird of the genus so called, which includes the single species *Notornis mantelli*, belonging to the family Rallidæ, and distinguished by blue-green plumage and pink bill and legs; = Moho[1], *takahe. (Later examples.)

The bird was believed to be extinct until Dr. G. B. Orbell rediscovered it in a mountain valley near Lake Te Anau in November 1948.

1882 *Trans. N.Z. Inst.* XIV. 253 It has always been acknowledged that Notornis is a degenerate rail. **1930** W. R. B. Oliver *N.Z. Birds* 350 Suspecting that it was a Notornis, Connor took it to the station where he carefully skinned it, preserving both the skin and the bones. **1950** *Discovery* July 217/2 The news of the discovery of *Notornis* was announced on the following day—November 21 [1948]. **1962** J. Frame *Edge of Alphabet* xii. 74 There's a valley of the notornis, the flightless bird. **1970** *Notornis* XVII. 67 This encounter [with a Takahe] was approximately 12 km from the closed Notornis area.

no-touch (nōutʊ·tʃ), *a.* *Med.* [f. No *a.* + Touch *sb.*] Applied to a method of dressing wounds in an environment that is not aseptic in which no one is allowed to touch either the wound or its dressings.

1944 *Med. Res. Council Special Rep. Ser.* No. 249. 24 'No-touch' technique, and dry instruments are used throughout. **1950** *Lancet* 18 Feb. 294/1 A no-touch technique was used for all wounds; this was not a theatre technique, but comprised the exclusive use of sterile instruments and dressing swabs. **1961** R. Hare *Bacteriol. & Immunity* v. 74 For most wounds, a method of dressing

known as the 'no touch' (or 'non-touch') technique is the method of choice.

not-out, *a.* Add: (Earlier and later examples.) Also as *sb.*: (*a*) A batsman who is 'not out'; (*b*) a 'not out' innings. Also *transf.*

1860 *Baily's Monthly Mag.* Sept. 426 We were most pleased with the two 'not-out' innings of 15 and 12 played by Mr. C. D. Marsham. **1869** *Ibid.* July 22 On the Tuesday the two not outs resumed their innings. **1898** *Field* 11 June 873/1 At the outset Troup and Townsend, the not-outs, were very slow. **1900** W. J. Ford *Cricketer on Cricket* 140 Last year..in 56 innings he had an average of over 30, with only one not-out to help him. **1960** *Times* 14 June 16/2 With the aid of a number of not-outs Statham's batting average for England..is more than 30. **1974** *Daily Tel.* 12 June 34/4 Graves added a not-out 55 at a run a minute.

not-quite, *a.* and *adv.* [f. Not *adv.* 10 + Quite *adv.*] **A.** *adj.* Almost, not wholly; *spec.* (*a*) not wholly committed or involved; (*b*) not wholly acceptable or respectable. Also as *sb.*

1920 D. H. Lawrence *Let.* 28 May (1962) I. 632 There is always a kind of half-measure, half-length, 'not quite' feeling about. **1948** L. MacNeice *Holes in Sky* 39 He spelled out True and Good, With their interleaving of half-truths and not-quites. **1955** N. Marsh *Scales of Justice* xii. 236 Kitty, over-painted, knowledgeable, fantastically 'Not-quite'. **1961** M. Beadle *These Ruins are Inhabited* (1963) vii. 96 We awoke on Sunday to not-quite-fog. **1962** *Punch* 15 Aug. 241/3 Marriage by special licence will be Not Quite. **1968** 'Han Suyin' *Birdless Summer* 281 The 'half-caste'. The Anglo-Indian, the chi-chi, the not-quite.

B. *adv.* Nearly, almost.

1940 W. Faulkner *Hamlet* I. i. 20 The other [face] pumping up and down with metronome-like regularity to the wheel's not-quite-musical complaint. **1944** Auden *Sea & Mirror* in *For Time Being* iii. 33 The notable absence of the slightest shiver or not-quite-inhibited sneeze. **1975** M. Babson *There must be Some Mistake* xiii. 93 Karen and Jill exchanged glances of not-quite-mock despair.

no trump(s), *phr. Bridge.* Also **no-trump, notrump.** [f. No *a.* 1, 6 + Trump *sb.*²] **1.** *ellipt.* A call which provides for the playing of a hand without a trump suit; the play at bridge without trumps; also with preceding number (as *three no trumps*), referring to the number of tricks (above six). Also *fig.*

1899 A. Dunn *Bridge* 19 The dealer should declare 'no trumps' when he holds four aces. **1902** *Encycl. Brit.* XXVI. 370/2 With an established black suit of 5 or 6 cards the dealer should declare no-trump if he has another suit protected. **1904** J. B. Elwell *Adv. Bridge* 236 It is the rule at 'no-trump' to return partner's suit with your highest card. **1910** *Blackw. Mag.* Dec. 809/2 Nine times out of ten it is No Trumps, but sometimes the class element creeps in. **1929** M. C. Work *Compl. Contract Bridge* ii. 9 He may overcall a No Trump with a suit-bid, or overcall a suit-bid with another suit or No Trump. **1933** [see *bid *v.* 3 c]. **1952** Phillips & Reese *Bridge with Mr. Playbetter* iv. 20 Mrs. Rougenoir responded One No Trump. This was a good bid on her part. **1965** *Listener* 20 May 758/2 West has a minimum strong No Trump in terms of high cards. **1969** A. Truscott *Gt. Bridge Scandal* xx. 237 Schapiro opened this hand with a non-vulnerable weak notrump. **1974** *Country Life* 16 May 1239/3 You have to find a way to make Three No Trumps.

2. *attrib.* Made or played without a trump suit; of or pertaining to such a call.

1902 *Encycl. Brit.* XXVI. 369/2 If in a no-trump hand the partners conjointly hold 3 aces, they score 30 for honours. *Ibid.*, Each trick above 6 counts..12 in a no-trump declaration. **1906** W. Dalton *'Saturday' Bridge* 41 This is an undoubted No Trump call for the dealer. **1931** G. F. Hervey *Headlights on Contract Bridge* viii. 69 When the dealer has made an initial No-Trump bid and second hand has passed, the third hand has three courses open to him. **1973** Reese & Dormer *Compl. Bk. Bridge* v. 71 The partner of the notrump bidder..is able to judge the combined assets at once and can often select the final contract with his first call. **1975** *Way to Play* 90 In 'no trump' games, the four aces are honors. *Ibid.*, A no trump call ranks above all suits.

no-tru·mper. [f. prec. + -er¹.] A no-trump call, or a hand on which a no-trump bid is or can be made; a person who makes a no-trump call.

1899 A. Dunn *Bridge* 29 As the dealer's hand is not worth a single trick, a light 'no-trumper' means absolute ruin. **1906** W. Dalton *'Saturday' Bridge* 42 Both of the hands quoted above are sound No Trumpers. **1929** M. C. Work *Compl. Contract Bridge* ii. 12 In deciding whether to advance the No Trump..the no trumper's partner uses the same count.

not-seeing, *vbl. sb. Literary.* [f. Not *adv.* and *sb.* 14 a + Seeing *vbl. sb.*] The state of not seeing.

a **1930** D. H. Lawrence *Last Poems* (1932) 250 In not-looking, and in not-seeing Comes a new strength. **1932** W. Faulkner *Light in August* (1933) viii. 177 In the notseeing and the hardknowing as though in a cave he seemed to see a diminishing row of suavely shaped urns. **1963** *Listener* 10 Jan. 71/2 To the not-seeing of the flat surface of Renaissance painting Abstract Art opposes the not-seeing of figures or patterns.

not-self. Add: (Further examples.) So **not-se·lfness.**

1872 *Dublin Rev.* July 145 A philosophy that shall confirm the existence of an independent Not-Self. **1901** J. McTaggart *Stud. Hegelian Cosmol.* ix. 277 But I mean that the characteristic which experience possesses of being not-self—its 'not-selfness', if the barbarism is permissible,—will always remain as an external and alien element. **1927** J. S. Huxley *Relig. without Revelation* viii. 285 The objective outer world and the subjective un-self-organised parts of the mind are usually interwoven in what is felt as 'not-self'. **1949** D. L. Sayers tr. *Dante's Divine Comedy* I. 68 That experience of the Not-self—which, by arousing his adoring love, has become for him the God-bearing image. **1958** *Times Lit. Suppl.* 10 Oct. 581/1 Reality for him belongs exclusively to the Atman, the one impersonal Self or not-Self with which we can, and should, identify ourselves by shedding all that is personal, desirous and therefore fatally separatist in ourselves. **1960** C. Day Lewis *Buried Day* i. 25 His proper concern is with the object to be created—an object which, however much of himself goes into it, must end up as not-self.

not-the·reness. [f. Not *adv.* + There *adv.* + -ness.] The state of being absent or pre-occupied.

1934 A. Huxley *Beyond Mexique Bay* 261 There is something profoundly horrifying in this immense, indefinite not-thereness of the Mexican scene. **1950** —— *Themes & Variations* 86 Rushing from one soirée to another in a strange state of alienation and not-thereness.

Nottingham (nǫ·tiŋəm; also *locally* nǫ·tiŋgəm). The name of a city in the Midlands of England, used *attrib.* to denote: **a.** Any of a variety of articles made or found there; something originating there.

1708 in *Bagford Ballads* (1877) I. ii. 389 With Nottingham Ale At every Meal. **1748** M. W. Montagu *Let.* 18 Aug. (1966) II. 410 If you would order me six dozen of Nottingham ale..it would be very acceptable. **1851** J. Pycroft *Cricket Field* vii. 151 Practise each kind of cut..and the Nottingham forward cut, with left leg over. **1866** 'Capt. Crawley' *Cricket* 29 If the ball is far-pitched, carry the left foot across the front of the wicket.. and hit the ball on to the ground in a direction between point and mid-wicket. This is the 'Forward Cut', or 'Nottingham Drive'. **1869** J. C. Patteson *Let.* 24 Nov. in C. M. Yonge *Life J. C. Patteson* (1874) II. xi. 392 Nottingham drill, good towelling, huckaback, &c., ought to be worthwhile to send out. **1931** *Star* 8 May 8/3 She [*sc.* the housewife] would be even more annoyed if we were to prove to her that she had been burning Nottingham Top Hard for years to her satisfaction. **1963** *Homes & Gardens* May 81/3 The pink Nottingham brickwork for the outside walls. **1973** *Country Life* 29 Nov. 1798/2 The pale creamy-grey of the Nottingham stone of which the house is built.

b. Nottingham catchfly, a white-flowered, perennial herb, *Silene nutans*, of the family Caryophyllaceæ, distinguished by the soft hair on its leaves and stems and the stickiness of the upper part of the plant.

[**1690** J. Ray *Synopsis Methodica Stirpium Britannicarum* 140 *Lychnis sylvestris alba*... Wild white Catchfly. On the walls of Nottingham-Castle, and thereabout; shewn us first by Tho. Willsel.] **1762** W. Hudson *Flora Anglica* 165 Nottingham catchfly. Habitat in pratis montosis. On the walls of Nottingham-castle, and thereabout. **1852** A. Pratt *Wild Flowers* I. 158 No less fragrant are the flowers of one variety of the Nottingham Catchfly. **1960** *Oxf. Bk. Wild Flowers* 72/2 Nottingham Catchfly is a rare plant of dry, stony places and sea cliffs in England and Wales. **1963** W. Blunt *Of Flowers & Village* 106 Fresh seed of the Nottingham catchfly (*Silene nutans*) germinates better in the dark.

c. A type of stoneware produced at Nottingham until the end of the eighteenth century.

1855 E. Acton *Mod. Cookery* (rev. ed.) xii. 243 Fill a brown upright Nottingham jar with alternate layers of mutton..potatoes, and..onions. **1957** Mankowitz & Haggar *Conc. Encycl. Eng. Pott. & Porc.* 167/1 Examples of Nottingham stoneware may be seen in the Victoria and Albert Museum. **1960** H. Hayward *Antique Collecting* 200/2 *Nottingham earthenware*, pottery made in Nottingham from the 13th cent. and its production continued along characteristic lines until about 1800. The manufactories making Nottingham wares are unidentified. **1973** *Times* 25 Aug. 12/4 The Nottingham bear jugs and owl jugs, weirdly modelled, are particularly sought after.

d. A type of machine-made flat lace originally produced at Nottingham (also *N. net*).

1859 Geo. Eliot *Adam Bede* I. ix. 182 Hetty's dreams were all of luxuries: to sit in a carpeted parlour..to have Nottingham lace round the top of her gown. **1881** C. C. Harrison *Woman's Handiwork* iii. 187 Nottingham lace is now sold in excellent block patterns. *Ibid.* 188 Edgings of the common Nottingham antique lace at eight to ten cents a yard. **1919** T. Wright *Romance of Lace Pillow* xv. 213 The low prices at which machine lace could be sold caused great consternation among the Bucks workers. 'Nottingham Net' was followed by 'Urling's Figured Imitations'. **1921** *Daily Colonist* (Victoria, B.C.) 5 Oct. 7/7, 50 Pairs of Nottingham Lace Curtains at $1.95 a Pair. **1939** O. Lancaster *Homes Sweet Homes* 60 Small tight-shut windows, the light from which is further dimmed by a barrage of Nottingham lace. **1963** *Times* 5 June 17/2 The future of Byard Manufacturing, the Nottingham lace and textile manufacturers, was plunged into even greater obscurity yesterday by the announcement of yet another offer for the company. **1967** *Guardian* 3 July 4 Some of us still think of machine-made lace as 'Nottingham' and equate it with soot-soiled curtains in back streets. **1969** *New Yorker* 29 Nov. 55/1 Her denigratory glance travelled from the plush tablecloth to the Nottingham-lace curtains.

e. *Nottingham white* (see quot. 1969).

1883 J. W. Mollett *Illustr. Dict. Art & Archeol.* 227/2 *Nottingham white*, white lead. **1897** *Sears, Roebuck Catal.* 360/3 Colors for Artists... New Blue, Nottingham White, Olive Lake [etc.]. **1934** H. Hiler *Notes on Technique of Painting* ii. 91 White lead..also called flake-white,..Nottingham white, [etc.]. **1969** R. Mayer *Dict. Art Terms & Techniques* 263/2 *Nottingham white*, an obsolete name for white lead, used in England during the 19th century.

f. A style of fishing; also, a type of reel (see quots.).

1900 A. E. T. Watson *Young Sportsman* 22 The principle of the Nottingham men was the travelling tackle, or 'long corking'... The special tackle for this is a long and supple rod, upright rings, a Nottingham reel without check or complications..and quill or cork float. **1939** 'G. Orwell' *Coming up for Air* ii. iv. 87, I could give you all the details about gut-substitute and gimp and Limerick hooks..and Nottingham reels. **1963** *Newnes Encycl. Angling* 156/1 Nottingham reel, a reel made in wood instead of the usual brass. *Ibid.* 156/2 The tackle used in Nottingham-style fishing is heavier than that generally adopted in the Sheffield style.

g. Nottingham (one club) system *Bridge*, a system originating at Nottingham.

1954 M. Burns (*title*) The Nottingham club system of contract bridge. **1959** *Listener* 8 Jan. 84/2 In this town our convention is the Nottingham One Club. **1959** Reese & Dormer *Bridge Player's Dict.* 154 Of the many one-club systems that were popular in the early days of contract, one of the few that have survived in Britain and America is the Nottingham system. **1959** *Listener* 31 Dec. 1178/2 The Skegness pair were convincing, using the Nottingham One Club system. **1964** *Official Encycl. Bridge* 385/1 *Nottingham Club*, a system popular in the English Midlands.

Nouba, var. *Nuba.

nougatine (nūgatī·n). [f. Nougat + -ine¹.] A form of nougat freq. covered with chocolate.

1894 E. Skuse *Compl. Confectioner* 58 Nougatines. 4 lbs. Ground Almonds. 7 lbs. Castor Sugar. **1897** *Sears, Roebuck Catal.* 7/2 Almond Nougatines. **1916** *Daily Colonist* (Victoria, B.C.) 21 July 14/5 (Advt.), Chocolate Fig Nougatines. *c* **1938** *Fortnum & Mason Price List* 8/1 Chocolate Nougatine Batons—per lb. 5/-.

'nough (nʌf). An aphetic form of Enough; phr. *'nough said*: used to emphasize and conclude a statement. Cf. *nuff.

1839 *Philadelphia Gaz.* 12 Nov. 2/1 N.S.M.J., 'nough said 'mong gentlemen. **1903** K. D. Wiggin *Rebecca* ii. 24 L.D.M. was talented 'nough to *get* Reely's money, but M.D.L. would 'a' ben practical 'nough to have *kep*' it. **1934** *Amer. Speech* IX. 319/2 *'Nough said.* Implies the ending of all discussion by acceptance of proposition or challenge. **1944** C. Himes *Cotton gonna kill me Yet* in *Black on Black* (1973) 197 Ain't got sense 'nough to be mad. **1973** *Amer. Speech 1970* XLV. 76 Sure 'nough is.

nought, *sb.*, *a.*, and *adv.* Add: **A.** *sb.* **2. d.** A score of no points in a game.

1862 *Lillywhite's Cricket Scores* I. 354 It is certainly curious that Beldham should have made two noughts in this contest. **1876** *Haygarth's Cricket Scores* V. 165 Thirty-three noughts were obtained in the match.

B. *adj.* **4.** *at nought feet*: in *Aeronaut.*, very close to the ground, just above the ground.

1945 *Aeroplane Spotter* 20 Sept. 218/1 Other noteworthy flying displays were given by the Messenger I, showing off its manœuvrability at nought feet. **1949** F. Maclean *Eastern Approaches* iii. vi. 372 A large three-engined German flying boat..scared the life out of our cook by skimming past our house at what is known by the R.A.F. as 'nought feet'. **1960** *Observer* 17 Jan. 9/6 If there were an emergency at 'nought feet' the airmen could not afford the precious seconds needed to jettison the cockpit canopy normally.

noughting, *vbl. sb.* (Later example.)

1926 A. E. Taylor *Plato* ix. 225 The 'noughting' and remaking of the soul is the greatest business of life.

‖ **nouille** (nūiyə). [Fr.] = Noodle *sb.*² Usu. in *pl.* Also (in *sing.*) *attrib.*, as *nouille paste.*

1845 E. Acton *Mod. Cookery* i. 6 (*heading*) To make nouilles;..Wet, with the yolks of four eggs, as much fine, dry, and sifted flour as will make them into a firm but very smooth paste. *Ibid.* 13 Make into nouille paste the yolks of four fresh eggs. **1938** *Times Lit. Suppl.* 9 July p. iii/1 Excursions to Soho to buy the authentic *nouilles* and the right kind of cheeses. **1960** *Good Housek. Cookery Bk.* (rev. ed.) 266/1 (*heading*) Noodles (Nouilles).

noumenal, *a.*, etc. Add: Now also with pronunc. (nū-).

noumenalism (nū·mĕnăliz'm, nau-). [f. Noumenal *a.* + -ism.] = Noumenism.

1902 *Encycl. Brit.* XXX. 679/2 Fechner regarded every composite body as the appearance of a spirit;..This noumenalism would not do for Lewes. **1925** J. E. Turner *Theory Direct Realism* 22 Noumenalism, meaning by this term that the character and existence of the real physical world are essentially different from and independent of the existence and attributes of sensed content.

noumenalist (nū·mĕnălist, nau-). [f. as prec. + -ist.] A believer in noumenalism. Also *attrib.* or as *adj.*

1904 G. S. Fullerton *Syst. Metaphysics* v. 88 The hypostatized abstractions of the noumenalist and the neo-Kantian. **1925** J. E. Turner *Theory Direct Realism* 8

The term 'Direct' is intended to imply further the complete absence of any representative or noumenalist factors in the process and object of perception.

noumenon. Add: Now also with pronunc. (nū·mĕnǫn). (Earlier and later examples.)

1796 F. A. Nitsch *Gen. View Kant's Princ. concerning Man* 118 The conception we have of the world of Noumena, contains no knowledge of that world, but is a mere conception of demarkation [i.e. *Grenzbegriff*, or limiting concept]. **1967** *Listener* 27 July 123/3 It was a revelation, a vision of the noumenon..and I fear that—for quite a long time—we will glory in the sensuous bliss of it all and become uncritical of the human content.

noun. Add: **1. c.** *noun-adjunct, -complement, -compound, -equivalent, -modifier, phrase, -stem*; *noun-like* adj.; **noun–adjective** *a.*, of or pertaining to the relationship between a noun and an adjective.

1963 *Times Lit. Suppl.* 22 Mar. 193/4 The English noun–adjective relationship..as in 'church'—'ecclesiastical'. **1962** H. A. Gleason in Householder & Saporta *Probl. Lexicogr.* 93 Among the nouns is a considerable subclass including, *United States,..Hague,...* These are..always preceded by *the* except in noun-adjunct position. **1964** C. Barber *Ling. Change Present-Day Eng.* v. 121 The tendency of *economy* used as noun-adjunct to develop the meaning of 'large'... The largest packet is frequently called 'economy size'. **1963** F. T. Visser *Hist. Syntax Eng. Lang.* I. iv. 624 The adoption of numerous French verbs which were construed with *à* before a noun-complement. **1966** *English Studies* XLVII. 51 Concerning the noun-complement the author discusses two points. **1914** L. Bloomfield in C. F. Hockett *Leonard Bloomfield Anthol.* (1970) 67 Any one who reads Brugmann's section on noun-compounds..will be impressed by the endless deviations..of composition-stems from independent words. **1965** J. E. Cross in *English Studies* XLVI. 108 Such noun-compounds having *wulf* as the second element are used simply of warriors to express the idea that they are anxious to fight and kill. **1935** *Jrnl. Eng. & Gmc. Philol.* XXXIV. 416 All that the primaries..have in common is their noun character; it would be simpler and clearer to call them nouns and noun-equivalents. **1954** Pei & Gaynor *Dict. Ling.* 149 *Noun-equivalent*, a word (pronoun, participle, adjective) or group of words used in the sense and function of a noun. **1963** F. T. Visser *Hist. Syntax Eng. Lang.* I. iv. 410 The direct object might be defined as the (pro)noun or noun-equivalent not preceded by a preposition. **1935** G. K. Zipf *Psycho-Biol. of Lang.* (1936) v. 31 Not all languages make, say, noun-like and verb-like distinctions. **1958** C. F. Hockett *Course Mod. Ling.* xxvi. 222 A few stems which show no inflection show syntactical behavior so nounlike that we class them as nouns. **1971** D. Crystal *Ling.* 92 We may have isolated a few noun-like words. **1955** Quirk & Wrenn *Old Eng. Gram.* iii. 68 (*heading*) Noun modifiers and pronouns. *Ibid.* iv. 109 An example of a common noun-modifier is *and* —, which has the force of 'opposite' or 'corresponding to'. **1958** W. N. Francis *Struct. Amer. Eng.* vi. 298 Nouns appear very frequently as heads of structures of modification. The modifiers in such structures may belong to any of the four parts of speech... The most common noun-modifier is the adjective. **1964** C. Barber *Ling. Change Present-Day Eng.* vii. 147 In the phrase *an old grey stone wall*,..we have the headword *wall* and as noun-modifiers the adjectives *old* and *grey*. **1951** *Mind* LX. 425 A noun-phrase used predicatively. **1965** N. Chomsky *Aspects of Theory of Syntax* ii. 63 *Frighten the boy* is a Verb Phrase.. consisting of the Verb..*frighten* and the Noun Phrase..*the boy*. **1973** *Amer. Speech* 1970 XLV. 133 The grammatical transformation..operates so as to convert the noun phrase that follows the verb into the derived subject. **1935** G. K. Zipf *Psycho-Biol. of Lang.* (1936) iv. 166 The number of different *verb-stems* and *noun-stems* which enter into compounds far surpasses the number of available prefixes which may be used in compounds. **1957** R. W. Zandvoort *Handbk. Eng. Gram.* ix. i. 278 Sometimes combinations of genitive + noun and of noun-stem + noun exist side by side: *a large schoolboy hand*. **1973** *Archivum Linguisticum* IV. 37 The premiss that a noun-stem has an inherent gender.

3. (Later example.)

1930 W. Empson *Seven Types Ambiguity* viii. 300 Here we have the English language..given particular meaning by noun–adjectives in apposition.

nounal, *a.* Add: (Later examples.) Also, of an author's style: containing many nouns.

1952 *Scrutiny* XVIII. iv. 306 That same test on Milton generally bears out her observation that Milton is predominantly nounal and adjectival in the sense of described scenery rather than re-enacted experience. **1961** R. B. Long *Sentence & its Parts* xiii. 292 The demonstratives have very considerable nounal use. *This* is fun... Who's *that*?

nounally *adv.* (Later example.)

1961 R. B. Long *Sentence & its Parts* xiii. 292 But demonstratives used nounally of people can be emotional also. *That's* a good fellow.

nou·nism. *rare.* [f. Noun + -ism.] In an author's style: a marked preference for nouns.

1904 G. S. Hall *Adolescence* II. xvi. 467 Adjectivism, adverbism, and nounism, or marked disposition to multiply one or more of the above classes of words.

nou·nize, *v. rare.* [f. Noun + -ize.] *trans.* To make into a noun.

1871 J. Earle *Philol. Eng. Tongue* 190, 2 Henry IV, iv. i. 71 *there* (nounized).

nou·nness. [f. Noun + -ness.] The quality or nature of a noun.

1971 D. Crystal *Linguistics* 124 We might arrive at an explicit notion of nounness. **1971** R. Fowler in *Archivum Linguisticum* II. 143 A Pronoun..represents features proper to *N* (gender, noun-ness, [etc.]).

‖ **nounou** (nū·nū). [Fr.] A child's name for a nurse; a wet nurse.

1894 G. du Maurier *Trilby* II. vi. 208 In the formal dusty gardens were the same pioupious and zouzous still walking with the same nounous. *Ibid.*, Nounou——a wet-nurse with a pretty ribboned cap and long streamers. **1900** *Glasgow Herald* 17 July 4 He was in the charge of a nou-nou (wet nurse). **1930** *Observer* 23 Feb. 12/1 The 'nounous' which it was naturally the chief object of the 'pioupious' of that period to dazzle. **1951** M. Sharp *Lise Lillywhite* i. 9 A sea-sick *nounou*.

nou·ny, *a. rare.* [f. Noun + -y[1].] Having or using many nouns; having the nature of a noun.

1926 Fowler *Mod. Eng. Usage* 654 It is as an unfailing sign of a nouny abstract style that a cluster of *-ion* words is chiefly to be dreaded.

So **nou·niness,** the state or quality of a noun.

1973 *Ann. N.Y. Acad. Sci.* CCXI. 170 Degrees of adjectiveness, degrees of nouniness.

nourishable, *a.* Restrict † *Obs.* to sense 1 and add: **2.** (Later example.)

1876 G. Meredith *Lett.* (1912) I. 269 The dear heart of him so frankly nourishable by flattery that [etc.].

nourishment. Add: **4.** *spec.* The treatment of leather with some substance to keep it soft or pliant.

1897 C. T. Davis *Manuf. Leather* (ed. 2) xlii. 596 For the nourishment of fine glacé leather, yolk of eggs is..used.

nous. 2. (Later examples.)

1927 F. B. Young *Portrait of Clare* 509 'Upon my soul, Clare,' Aunt Cathie declared, 'I thought you had more nous.' **1928** Galsworthy *Swan Song* i. ii. 12 They've got no more *nous* than a tom-cat. **1930** R. Campbell *Adamastor* 26 Had Creswell, Smuts or Hertzog half his nous, There would be far more goats on the Karroo And far less in the Senate and the House. **1945** R. Hargreaves *Enemy at Gate* 291 Nothing compensated for ignorance or lack of *nous* in a leader. **1946** [see *common *sb.*[1] 16]. **1956** [see *backwoods b]. **1959** [see *can *sb.*[1] 1 f]. **1972** *Daily Tel.* 8 Dec. 14/6, I do know how easy it would be for anyone with a camera and a little nous to film 'The Breakdown of Life' in Britain. **1973** *Times* 22 Feb. 25/1 If we had had a bit of *nous* we'd have probably discovered this earlier. **1975** *Daily Tel.* 29 Jan. 17 The City, extraordinary as it may sound, has very limited political nous.

‖ **nous autres** (nuzōtr'). [Fr., lit. 'we others'.] The personal pronoun *we*, somewhat stressed or emphasized.

1860 C. Lever *Day's Ride* in *All Year Round* III. 470/1 We were, in fact, henceforth 'nous autres'. **1870** J. C. Patteson *Let.* 9 Dec. in C. M. Yonge *Life J. C. Patteson* (1874) II. xii. 472 We fail to understand him, *nous autres* I mean, outside the sanctuary. **1911** E. M. Clowes *On Wallaby* v. 140 It gave us a nasty lumpy feeling in our throats—*nous autres* who had nobody to come and see us.

noust (naust, nūst). *Sc. dial.* Also † **newst, noost,** † **nowst.** [ad. Norw. dial. *naust(r)*, *nøst*, f. ON. *naust* boat-shed, dock.] 'The place in which a boat is hauled up, gen. a scooped-out trench at the edge of a beach surrounded by a shallow wall of stones, a boat-stance in gen.' (Sc. Nat. Dict.) Also *fig.*

The pronunc. (naust) is used in Orkney, (nūst) in Shetland.

1613 *Court Bk. Orkney & Shetland* (1967) 76 William Ewinsone..found her lying..beneath the boat nowst in Wytfoord. *a* **1693** T. Brown *Diary* (1898) 63 Ther wes a great boat blowen owt of the Newst at the Air. **1869** J. T. Reid *Art Rambles* 41 Down to the boat-noust the trio hirpled. **1894** L. J. Nicolson *Songs of Thule* 79 My fecht is owre wi' wind an' wave Da Noost is noo da quiet grave. **1922** *Glasgow Herald* 22 July 86 Her bow could be seen in the 'noust'. *Ibid.*, In the afternoon at ebb tide they went down to take the boats out of the 'nousts'. **1931** J. Nicolson *Tales* 55 When a boat was taken from its 'noost', and put into the water, the bow had to be turned 'sun-gaets'. **1956** C. M. Costie *Benjie's Bodle* 7 Jamie Peace sitting at the noust sorting his creels. **1971** G. M. Brown *Fishermen with Ploughs* 69 He coughed his way to the noust And launched the *Belle*.

‖ **nous verrons** (nū verọn). [Fr.] We shall see; it remains to be seen.

1764 H. Walpole *Lett.* (1857) IV. 262 *Nous verrons*—the temptation [to go to Paris] is strong, but [etc.]. **1840** Dickens *Let.* ?9 Sept. (1969) II. 125, I have opened the second volume with Kit; and I saw..on looking out at sea an affecting thing that I can do with him bye and bye. Nous verrons. **1861** G. Meredith *Let.* 17 May (1970) I. 81, I think it will be my best book as yet... *Nous verrons.* **1889** E. C. Dowson *Let.* 21 Feb. (1967) 39, I don't feel much like matinizing at the moment mais *nous verrons.* **1951** A. Huxley *Let.* 23 Dec. (1969) 639, I may collaborate on a film about Gandhi..but feel a little hesitant, in view of the precarious condition of my eyes... *Nous verrons.*

nouveau art (nūvo ār) = *art nouveau.

1911 G. B. Shaw *Lett. to Granville Barker* 11 Jan. (1956) 170 Olivier's new poet-earthquake [*sic*] palace of reinforced concrete is a masterpiece of *nouveau* art. *a* **1946** J. M. Keynes 'Dr Melchior' in *Two Memoirs* (1949) 35 The raised pattern of the *nouveau art* wall-paper. **1947** E. Taylor *View of Harbour* (1954) xi. 159 A picture of Our Lord carrying a *nouveau*-art lantern.

‖ **nouveau pauvre** (nūvo pōvr'). Pl. **nouveaux pauvres.** Also fem. **nouvelle pauvre** (*rare*). [Fr., after next word.] A person who has recently become poor. Also (with hyphen) *attrib.* or as *adj.*, newly impoverished.

1965 *Punch* 27 Oct. 619/1 Maigret, holidaying with his wife in a small Normandy fishing port, is summoned to the home of a morally rotten, nouveau-pauvre family where a maid has died of arsenic poisoning after swallowing her mistress's sleeping draught. **1970** *Time* 3 Aug. 49 One of every four Americans 65 or over lives at or below 'the poverty line'. Some of these 5,000,000 old people were poor to begin with, but most are bewildered and bitter *nouveaux pauvres*, their savings and fixed incomes devoured by spiraling property taxes and other forms of inflation. **1975** *Country Life* 13 Feb. 413/1 Nouveau-pauvre? Could you do with an extra bedroom? **1975** *Harpers & Queen* May 101 Crisis for coiffeurs... Some of the *nouvelles pauvres* are clamouring for Brillo-pad mouse, the new colour and the new texture.

‖ **nouveau riche** (nūvo rīʃ). Pl. **nouveaux riches.** Also fem. **nouvelle riche** (*rare*). [Fr.] One who has recently attained to wealth; usu. with connotation of ostentation or vulgar show. Also *attrib.* or as *adj.*

1813 M. Edgeworth *Let.* 6 Apr. (1971) 15 Larry the footboy and Mrs. Rafferty's dinner are nothing to what has been seen at the dinners of les nouveaux riches at Liverpool and Manchester. **1828** Lytton *Pelham* I. xxiii. 193 You never pass by the white and modern mansion of a *nouveau riche*. **1838** W. H. Prescott *Hist. Reign Ferdinand & Isabella* III. ii. xxvi. 560 This same *nouveau riche* used to serve gold dust, says Herrera, instead of salt, at his entertainments. **1853** C. M. Yonge *Heir of Redclyffe* II. xvii. 278 His manner became so dry and repellent that visitors went away moralizing on the absurdity of *nouveaux riches* taking so much state on them. **1863** 'Ouida' *Strathmore* (1865) I. vi. 96 She was a *nouvelle riche*, and brought him money. **1899** E. Wharton *Greater Inclination* 187 She had none of the *nouveau riche* prudery which classes poverty with the nude in art. **1936** F. Clune *Roaming round Darling* vi. 58 The hovels they occupy are made of mud, except a few palaces of their *nouveaux riches*. **1957** A. E. Coppard *It's Me, O Lord!* iii. 37 Modern upstarts such as the piano are as inelegant as *nouveaux riches* in a cathedral. **1957** *New Yorker* 2 Nov. 76/1 The elder members of the two families..are..rather crudely drawn caricatures of the *nouveau riche*. **1959** G. Savage *Antique Collector's Handbk.* 238 The industrializing process which started in the 1750s had gained considerable ground by the end of the century, and the Napoleonic Wars, by creating a *nouveau riche* class, succeeded in debasing taste to an extremely low level. **1966** R. Ellison in A. Chapman *New Black Voices* (1972) 404 Some of the *nouveau riche* oilmen who were members of the club. **1972** T. Aronson *Queen Victoria & Bonapartes* ix. 111 The society of the Second Empire—the courtesans, the financiers, the foreign adventurers, the *nouveaux riches*.

‖ **nouveau roman** (nūvo romaṅ). [Fr., lit. new novel.] 'A type of novel developed chiefly in France in the 1960's by such writers as Alain Robbe-Grillet, Michel Butor, Marguerite Duras, and Claude Mauriac, characterized by lack of moral, social, or psychological comment and by precise descriptions that suggest the mental state of the person experiencing or seeing them.' (C. L. Barnhart et al. *Dict. New Eng.* (1973).)

1961 *Listener* 24 Aug. 289/1 *The Key*..reads very like something young and French: it has the soberness of the *nouveau roman*. **1962** *Times* 13 Dec. 14/3 The *nouveau roman* is already a bit *vieux jeu* in France. **1965** *Harper's Mag.* July 112 The characters are many and the story jumps from one to another, often (in the manner of the *nouveau roman*) with no names other than 'he' or 'the boy' to tell you whose episode it is. **1965** *New Society* 12 Aug. 26/3 The author obviously owes a big debt both to Beckett and to the French exponents of the *nouveau roman*, with their insistent emphasis on the depiction of physical detail and visual objectivity. **1967** *Listener* 23 Mar. 391/3 One of the most successful recent attempts, for instance, is to be found in a novel by one of Robbe-Grillet's fellow-practitioners of the *nouveau roman*, Michel Butor's *Passing Time*, which combines a narrative giving us the hero's present experience and a diary containing his experiences of several months before. **1974** *Times Lit. Suppl.* 25 Jan. 69/2 The sources of Mr Gordon's off-the-peg technique are fairly clear: some Kafka; the Burroughs scissors; but mostly the *nouveau roman*. The novel, so this modish dogma asserts, is a 'vision of things', and the universe no more than the sum of the author's sensations.

‖ **nouvelle** (nūvel). [Fr.] A short piece of fictitious narrative, freq. one dealing with a single situation or a single aspect of a character or characters.

1680 H. Savile *Let.* 24 Feb. in W. D. Cooper *Savile Corr.* (1858) 140 Disposed to those kind of books you mention of *nouvell's* and other *entretiens* of folly and levity. [**1717** M. W. Montagu *Let.* 1 Jan. (1965) I. 293 Would you have me write novelles like the Countess of D'Aunois?] **1887** *Athenæum* 1 Jan. 10/2 M. de Maupassant's 'Petite Roque', a collection of *nouvelles* written with his usual cleverness. **1917** G. Saintsbury *Hist. Fr. Novel* I. iv. 88 The faults of long-windedness, of otiose padding, of un-

necessary episodes, etc., are almost mechanically or mathematically impossible in the *nouvelle*. **1935** S. SPENDER *Destructive Element* 48 Many other of the stories of this period, especially what he [*sc.* Henry James] called the 'nouvelles', as distinct from the short stories which are more in the nature of the anecdote. **1959** *Times Lit. Suppl.* 27 Mar. 182/1 *Mademoiselle B*— is a *nouvelle* in a recognizable style (it reads as if it had been intelligently translated from the French) and a familiar convention. **1975** *Times* 5 Apr. 5/7 What we learnt from Henry James to call a *nouvelle*, which I take to be a fictional narrative longer than a long short-story and shorter than a short novel.

nouvelles. (Later example.)
1894 E. DOWSON *Let.* 30 July (1967) 307 Write and give me your nouvelles.

‖ **nouvelle vague** (nūvɛl vag). [Fr., f. *nouvelle* (fem.) new + *vague* wave.] A new movement or trend; *spec.* one in film-making originating in France in the late 1950s; also applied to other arts; also *attrib.*
1959 *Times* 4 Sept. 5/4 It is a film made by one of the old guard rather than by a member of the *nouvelle vague.* **1960** *Times* 1 Nov. 16/4 The film is in no important sense *nouvelle vague.* **1962** *John o' London's* 19 Apr. 371/2 If no clique, trend, *avant garde* or *nouvelle vague* has yet arisen to claim the creative heritage of social change, perhaps it is because the upheaval is still with us. **1962** *Movie* Sept. 34/1 *Paris Nous Appartient* is arguably the most important Nouvelle Vague film to date. **1965** *Philos. Rev.* LXXIV. 53 The *nouvelle vague* of mathematics teachers. **1973** 'E. MCBAIN' *Let's hear It* xiv. 209 Teddy normally enjoyed films, except when she was submitted to the excesses of a sadistic *nouvelle vague* camera. **1974** *Times* 26 Apr. 16/3 In terms of chronology the celebrated *nouvelle vague* of the late Fifties must by now be reckoned the old guard.

nova. 2. Add: In mod. use, a star that suddenly increases in brightness by several magnitudes and then, after a period of maximum brightness lasting from a few days to several years, decreases to its former brightness over a much longer period. (Further examples.)
Now distinguished from a *SUPERNOVA.
1927 H. N. RUSSELL et al. *Astronomy* II. xxii. 777 The brightest stars ever recorded have been novæ. Nova B Cassiopeiæ, known as 'Tycho's star', which appeared in November, 1572, was for some days as bright as Venus at her best (visible in the daytime), and then gradually waned. **1939** *Nature* 15 July 122/2 Some of these extra-galactic novæ have a brightness equal to nearly 100 million suns... In 1934 Baade and Zwicky suggested that these extremely bright objects were not ordinary novæ, but presented a class by themselves—the class of super-novæ. **1955** *Sci. News Let.* 9 July 31/1 Because of a sudden break-down of the normally stable energy conditions in its interior, a nova abruptly flares up to thousands of times its normal brightness, so that a star never before visible from the earth bursts into brilliance. **1956** R. A. LYTTLETON *Mod. Universe* v. 167 Every year on the average about a score of stars within our own galaxy undergo this catastrophic development and become what are termed novae. **1968** *Times* 2 Dec. 17/2 Most of the X-ray sources are located in the Milky Way and some of them have been identified with old novae—stars that flared brightly a long time ago and are now fading.

nováčekite (nɒvā·tʃĕkəit). *Min.* Also **novacekite.** [f. the name of Radim *Nováček* (see quot. 1951) + -ITE[1].] A hydrated oxide and arsenate of magnesium and uranium, $Mg(UO_2)_2(AsO_4)_2.12H_2O$, which is a member of the autunite group and is found as yellow, tetragonal crystals.
1951 C. FRONDEL in *Amer. Mineralogist* XXXVI. 682 In the course of examination of a small suite of secondary uranium minerals from Schneeberg, Saxony,..two specimens were found of a mineral that has proved to be a new hydrated magnesium uranyl arsenate member of the autunite group. The name novacekite is proposed for this species after the Czech mineralogist Radim Nováček (1905–1942), who made important contributions to the knowledge of the mineralogy of uranium. **1956** *Ibid.* XLI. 152 (*heading*) Novacekite from the Wichita Mountains, Oklahoma. **1965** G. J. WILLIAMS *Econ. Geol. N.Z.* xiii. 206/2 The novacekite-like secondary uranium mineral is consistent with the presence of arsenopyrite. **1971** *Mineral. Abstr.* XXII. 226/2 Localities are mentioned for ..nováčekite, especially in NE Brazil.

Novachord (nōᵘ·văkɒ̄ɹd). Also **novachord.** [f. L. *nova* new + CHORD *sb.*[2]] Name of an electronic musical instrument of the organ family.
1940 *Chambers's Techn. Dict.* 584/1 *Novachord*, an electronic musical instrument using a single keyboard, sustaining and swell pedals. **1944** W. APEL *Harvard Dict. Mus.* 237/1 The *Novachord*, a six-octave, single-manual instrument which..resembles the spinet in form, employs a purely electronic tone-generating system. **1952** B. ULANOV *Hist. Jazz in Amer.* (1958) xxiii. 324 He made Shearing-like records with rhythm section and Novachord. **1955** L. FEATHER *Encycl. Jazz* (1956) 111 LPs: Bruns. 58048 (trio & Terry Gibbs);..Dec. 5297 (novachord, w. Hampton). **1970** *Oxf. Compan. Mus.* (ed. 10) 325/1 Akin to oscillating valve organs is the *Novachord*, a domestic six-octave keyboard instrument giving fourteen different tonal qualities.

novákite (nɒvā·kəit). *Min.* Also **novakite.** [ad. G. *novákit* (Johan & Hak 1959, in *Chem. der Erde* XX. 49), f. the name of *Jiří Novák*, 20th-cent. Czechoslovakian mineralogist: see -ITE[1].] A tetragonal arsenide of copper, Cu_4As_3, found at Černy Důl, Czechoslovakia, which is steel-grey on fresh fracture but becomes almost black on exposure to air.
1959 *Amer. Mineralogist* XLIV. 1321 From the powder pattern, novakite is tetragonal..and..pseudocubic. **1961** *Mineral. Abstr.* XV. 292/2 Novakite occurs (with chalcocite and löllingite) as impregnations in carbonate rocks in Cu–Co–As ores. **1970** *Amer. Mineralogist* LV. 1084 (*caption*) Polished surface of kutinaite..intergrown with novákite..and calcite.

Nova Scotian (nōᵘvă skōᵘ·ʃiăn), *sb.* and *a.* **A.** *sb.* A native or inhabitant of the province of Nova Scotia in Eastern Canada.
1867 B. MURDOCH *Hist. Nova Scotia* III. xxxix. 536 Captain Stewart..assured them he was a Nova Scotian in temperament. **1879** *Rep. of Nova Scotia Hist. Soc.* I. 28 As Nova Scotians, the duty of the moment..is to garner up the materials of Provincial History before they perish. **1913** B. WILSON *Nova Scotia* (ed. 2) iii. 29 Cherishing of the memory of their worthy forerunners is perhaps the most marked characteristic of Nova Scotians today. **1968** *Globe & Mail* (Toronto) 13 Feb. 3/2 A Nova Scotian, he is the only declared candidate from the Atlantic provinces. **1971** E. JONES in J. Spencer *Eng. Lang. W. Afr.* 67 The Sierra Leone settlement consisted of the following groups of people: The Black Poor, the Maroons and Nova Scotians, and the West African recaptives.
B. *adj.* Of or pertaining to Nova Scotia.
1866 B. MURDOCH *Hist. Nova Scotia* II. p. iii, By almost imperceptible degrees the people acquire habits, sentiments and pursuits suited to the land in which they live.. and thus the Nova Scotian character is gradually developed. **1869** *Bradshaw's Railway Manual* XXI. 390 The Nova Scotian Government secured the passage of an Act to authorize the extension of the trunk line. **1902** W. JAMES *Var. Relig. Exper.* viii. 173 The autobiography of Henry Alline, the Nova Scotian evangelist. **1969** in Halpert & Story *Christmas Mumming in Newfoundland* 24 South coast Newfoundlanders..manned a substantial part of the Nova Scotian..deep-sea fishing fleets.

novel, *sb.* Add: **3. b.** (Earlier example.)
1639 J. S. *Clidamas* pref. sign. A2 *recto*, Here I present you with this little Novel..which though in it selfe it be nothing, yet..may prove something.
5, 5. b. *novel-form, -hero, -length, -reader* (later example), *-reading* (earlier example), *-review, -reviewer, -reviewing.*
1903 A. BENNETT *Truth about Author* xii. 150, I was almost bound to pander to the vulgar taste..in my short stories, but I had sworn solemnly that I would keep the novel-form unsullied. **1967** A. BURGESS *Novel Now* ii. 27 In *The Waves*, whose poetic prose now reads very awkwardly, we seem to get as far away from the novel-form as possible. **1838** J. S. MILL in *Westm. Rev.* XXVIII. 439 He ..fulfils with propriety the essential functions of a novel-hero. **1948** F. R. LEAVIS *Great Tradition* iii. 138 He wrote ..other 'American' classics. Not to speak of short-stories and things of less than novel-length. **1972** E. ROUTLEY *Puritan Pleasures of Detective Story* vi. 72 [Austin] Freeman..was not stylist enough to sustain the technique through a story of full novel-length. **1921** P. LUBBOCK *Craft of Fiction* (1926) iii. 41 There is nothing more familiar to a novel-reader of today than the difficulty of discovering what the novel in his hand is about. **1789** A. SEWARD *Let.* 17 Aug. (1811) II. 319 The contemptible rage for novel-reading, is a pernicious and deplorably prevalent taste. **1947** 'G. ORWELL' in *Tribune* 31 Jan. 8/1 Raymond Postgate, who was then editor, had asked me to do the novel reviews from time to time. **1951** *Observer* 8 Apr. 7/4 Novel-reviewers receive letters from readers asking why the books we choose to notice are all..'sad, bad and mad'. **1893** E. DOWSON *Let. c* 20 Sept. (1967) 292 The opinion of the average novel-reviewing Le Gallienish animal.

novelette. Add: (Earlier and later examples.) Now freq. applied to a short romantic or sentimental novel of inferior quality.
1814 J. C. DUNLOP *Hist. Fiction* II. vii. 127 The endless variety of tales, or *Novelettes*,..which form so popular and so extensive a branch of Italian literature. **1914** G. B. SHAW *Misalliance* 66 'You want to be the hero of a romance and to get into the papers... A son revenges his mother's shame. Villain weltering in his gore...' *The Man* 'Oh, rot! do you think I read novelettes?' **1919** W. S. MAUGHAM *Moon & Sixpence* xix. 161 If I am rhetorical it is because Stroeve was rhetorical. (Do we not know that man in moments of emotion expresses himself naturally in the terms of a novelette?) **1962** *Woman's Own* 3 Nov. 14/3 A ghost-lover..is a mixture of novelettes, and film stars, and pop singers, and a girl's inner yearnings as to what she thinks she wants in a man. **1965** R. PAULSON *Novelette before 1900* p. v, Novelette..designates a distinctive, yet certainly vague, genre; a narrative in prose that is longer than a short story and shorter than a novel. .. It lacks the diffuseness as well as the length of a novel, and it covers more ground as well as more space than its modern offspring, the short story. **1967** A. BURGESS *Novel Now* i. 16 We're unwilling to dignify books of, say, fifty thousand words and under with the title of novel, preferring to use the Italian term *novella* ('novelette' disparages not only length but content).

novele·ttish, *a.* Also **noveletteish.** [f. NOVELETTE + -ISH[1].] Pertaining to or characteristic of a novelette.
1904 J. C. SNAITH *Broke of Covenden* xv. 222 Our dear stiff-backed..simple-minded, penny-noveletteish feudal baron. **1921** *Sat. Westm. Gaz.* 10 Sept. 15/2 The blue-eyed make-up of the novelettish débutante. **1940** *Illustr. London News* CXCVII. 98 What an incredible creature is Maxim de Winter himself, with his novelettish name and his novelettish riches and mansion. **1963** *Listener* 31 Jan. 217/1 The abortive seduction scene, with the couple's novelettish dialogue..was unfortunate enough. **1972** *Daily Tel.* 16 Nov. 10/4 The writing is uneven, often degenerating into the novelettish.

novelettist. (Later examples.)
1898 G. B. SHAW *Our Theatres in Nineties* (1932) III. 327 Mr Ogilvie is no mere twaddling novelettist. **1904** BEERBOHM *Around Theatres* (1953) 313 The plot of it was just that which even our worst novelettists have outgrown. **1955** *Times* 28 July 3/5 She was the novelettist of the repressions of a vanished social world.

novelize, *v.* Add: **2. b.** *intr.* To write novels. *rare.*
1889 G. B. SHAW *Let.* 31 Aug. (1965) 221 Some time ago I tried novelizing again. **1961** *Times Lit. Suppl.* 27 Jan. 62/2 Dr. Johnson would certainly not have wanted to bring women novelizing into his analogy about dogs standing on their hind legs—even women novelizing at sixteen.

‖ **novella** (nove·lă). [It.] A short narrative (as the stories of Boccaccio's *Decameron*), = NOVEL *sb.* 3; a short novel or long short-story.
1902 W. D. HOWELLS *Literature & Life* 116 Few modern fictions of the novel's dimensions..have the beauty of form many a novella embodies. **1911** *Encycl. Brit.* XIX. 834/2 After Bandello the decline of the Italian *novella* is evident. **1934** *Times Lit. Suppl.* 6 Dec. 868/1 A brilliant *novella* of life in a remote Welsh valley. **1957** *Ibid.* 30 Aug. 517/3 Why is any story of more than fifty pages now called 'a short novel' or 'novella'—have publishers invented a new literary category? **1958** *Ibid.* 15 Aug. 458/2 The novella is a simpler medieval form brought to perfection in the *Decameron*. Essentially the novella is an anecdote about people you know, or know of. **1959** *John o' London's* 17 Dec. 350/1 H. E. Bates has made the *novella*, which is more generally referred to as the 'long-short story' a form of fiction which is very much his own. **1974** *Times* 23 May 10/8 There are two novellas here, both written entirely in dialogue.

novelty. Add: **1. d.** An often useless, but decorative or amusing, object which relies for its appeal on the newness of its design. Hence **novelty shop.**
1901 *Daily Colonist* (Victoria, B.C.) 19 Oct. 4/6 (Advt.), Sterling Silver Novelties. An English manufacturer's range of samples: no two pieces alike. Puff Boxes, Tooth Brush Boxes, Vases, Cigarette Cases, Match Boxes, Napkin Rings. **1911** *Woman's Home Companion* Apr. 28/3 This idea can be carried out to any extent by having quantities of things which are more or less novelties to sell. **1933** *Planning* I. XVI. 14 The climax to this orgy of designs is reached at Christmas-time when the shops are filled with 'novelties' that no customer would think of wanting for himself. **1972** *Guardian* 23 Dec. 1/1 A cracker-making contract..has been withdrawn because blue jokes were found with the paper hats and novelties. **1973** 'I. DRUMMOND' *Jaws of Watchdog* xi. 145 The only retailer who handled the macabre Belgian masks had a novelty shop in High Holborn.
4. *novelty-hunter* (so *-hunting*), *-value*; **novelty number, song** (see quot. 1952).
1926 FOWLER *Mod. Eng. Usage* 387/2 If each novelty-hunter struck out a line for himself, we could be content to register novelty-hunting as a useful outward sign of inward dullness, and leave such writers carefully alone. **1938** I. GOLDBERG *Wonder of Words* xviii. 372 We all know the novelty-hunter who uses his neologisms because he wishes to stun his reader. **1940** *Scrutiny* VIII. 397, I am thinking mostly of course of the hack of Tin Pan Alley and the ubiquitous and cynically named 'novelty' number. **1952** B. ULANOV *Hist. Jazz in Amer.* (1958) 352 *Novelty song*: a song that depends on some obvious contrivance for its appeal, such as a reorganized nursery rhyme..or an infectious sort of gibberish. **1955** L. FEATHER *Encycl. Jazz* (1956) 79 Novelty songs such as *Ol' Man Mose* and *Brother Bill* began to edge out the jazz material in his repertoire. **1959** *Times* (Suppl. Britain's Food) 9 Mar. p. vii/6 Novelty-value has its own appeal. **1968** 'J. CHRISTOPHER' *Pendulum* v. 42 The novelty value won't last.
b. Of fabrics, etc.: see quot. 1968.
1945 M. D. POTTER *Fiber to Fabric* iii. 51 Novelty yarns produce the attractive nubby effects seen in tweeds. **1950** *'Mercury' Dict. Textile Terms* 368/2 *Novelty suitings*, a name applied originally to plain homespun weaves with rough, irregular fillings of different colours, but now referring to all weaves, especially brocaded or jacquard effects. **1968** J. IRONSIDE *Fashion Alphabet* 94 *Novelty*, when used of fabrics this indicates that the material is made from more than one basic fibre and may be in an unusual weave. **1974** *Guardian* 26 Mar. 16/1, 12 leading French cloth manufacturers will be showing..jerseys, shirtings, novelty silks.

Novemberish, *a.* (Later examples.)
1939 *War Illustr.* 9 Dec. p. ii/2 We are approaching the shortest day, and the weather has been thoroughly Novemberish, in London especially. *a* **1945** E. R. EDDISON *Mezentian Gate* (1958) xxxvii. 193 Even in that Novemberish raw weather of her years, some strength of lost youth, some glory,..lived on.

Novial (nōᵘ·viăl). [See quot. 1928[1].] Name of an artificial language created by Otto Jespersen in 1928 for use as an international auxiliary language. Hence **No·vialist,** a speaker of Novial; an advocate of Novial.

1928 O. JESPERSEN *International Language* I. 52 As such a scheme must have a name, I have called it NOVIAL = Nov(new) I.A.L., where I.A.L. stands for International Auxiliary Language. *Ibid.* II. 67 In Novial..we simplify the spelling in all words containing double letters in the national languages, from which the words are taken. *Ibid.* 137 N[ovial] therefore adopts botn suffixes, but Novialists need not commit to memory which words take one and which the other ending. **1930** *S.P.E. Tract* XXXIV. 462 Novial will be suspiciously easy; keen Novialists will rattle it off together in the family circle. **1943** F. BODMER *Loom of Language* xi. 471 Novial departs from English usage in one particular. The dictionary form does the work of our past participle in compound past tenses. **1947** H. JACOB *Planned Auxiliary Lang.* iv. 83 Jespersen's Novial has many features which are advocated by the naturalistic school of interlinguists, the use of auxiliary verbs, the revised system of spelling, a certain number of flexional elements in indirect derivation, the abolition of so-called pleonastic endings, the plural form in *-s*. **1973** *Trans. Philol. Soc. 1972* 16 This work extended over many years and led eventually to the invention of his own auxiliary language, Novial... He came to think, later on, that he could have put that time to better use.

novice. Add: **3. d.** Applied to animals entered in a competitive event which have not previously (or before a specified date) won other than very minor prizes; also a competition restricted to such animals.

1903 *Forest & Stream* 21 Feb. 151 (Cent. Suppl.), Novice dogs was a large class, 28 in all. **1909** *Daily Chron.* 19 June 7/6 'Canterbury Belle' headed the list in a fine show of novice hacks. **1962** D. FRANCIS *Dead Cert* iii. 26, I was riding him in novice hurdle races. **1969** [see *CHASE *sb.*[1] 1 f]. **1975** *Country Life* 13 Nov. 1281/2 Brown Lad was a novice chaser last year... He is an absolutely top-class horse, and he stays three miles readily.

‖ **novillada** (novi·lʸā·da). [Sp.] A bullfight in which three-year-old bulls are fought by novice matadors.

1897 *Encycl. Sport* I. 152/2 Bulls for a *novillada* or second-rate bull-fight cost far less. **1932** E. HEMINGWAY *Death in Afternoon* ii. 23 At a novillada the spectator may see the mistakes of the bullfighters, and the penalties that these mistakes carry. **1955** K. TYNAN *Bull Fever* ii. 14 A matador's career..nowadays rarely exceeds ten years. Manolo González, who fought his first novillada in 1946 and retired rich in 1952, is a fair example. **1964** G. ERIK *Corrida* v. 21 He can become a novice matador..fighting three year old bulls with *picadors*. Such fights are known as '*corridas de novillos-toros*' or '*novilladas*'. **1967** MCCORMICK & MASCAREÑAS *Compl. Aficionado* iii. 78 They are walking back from a novillada.

‖ **novillero** (novilʸē·ro). [Sp.] An apprentice matador who has fought only in *novilladas*.

1921 L. FITZ-BARNARD *Fighting Sports* III. 166 They enter the troupe of some matador and serve an apprenticeship..; and as they improve become *novilleros*. **1932** E. HEMINGWAY *Death in Afternoon* xiii. 152 The novilleros you see killed are all victims of economics. **1955** K. TYNAN *Bull Fever* ii. 27 He took his doctorate at Seville in the spring of 1948, after a riotously successful career as novillero. **1969** *Telegraph* (Brisbane) 13 Jan. 8/1 This year could see him leaving the ranks of the novillero..and moving into the arenas of big bulls and big money. **1970** *Times* 4 May 8/7 He was the leading novillero in Spain in mid-season last year, but three bad gorings put him out of action.

‖ **novillo** (novi·lʸo). [Sp.] A young bull; *spec.* a fighting bull not more than three years old.

1838 *Quarterly Rev.* LXII. 398 A calf, a 'novillo'—which true bull-fighters place on a par with a cow. **1846** R. FORD *Gatherings from Spain* xxi. 292 The villagers..amuse themselves with baiting *novillos*, or bull-youngsters—calves of one year old. **1925** E. HEMINGWAY *The Undefeated* in *This Quarter* II. 205 You can..kill two novillos... Whatever stuff they've got in the corrals. **1967** MCCORMICK & MASCAREÑAS *Compl. Aficionado* ii. 32 The neophyte.. while gaining experience, faces not toros (four-year-olds and up) but novillos (three-year-olds).

‖ **novio** (nō·vio). [Sp.] A boy friend, lover.

1920 *Chambers's Jrnl.* June 359/1 She has a novio, a sweetheart. **1929** J. LANGDON-DAVIES *Dancing Catalans* iii. 63 She had a 'novio', a bad young fisherman. **1950** G. BRENAN *Face of Spain* xii. 249 They trip gaily along with their *novio* by their side.

novobiocin (novobəi·ōsin). *Pharm.* [prob. f. as next + BIO- + *-MY)CIN.] A weakly acidic tetracyclic phenol, $C_{31}H_{35}N_2O_{11}$, that is produced by certain actinomycetes of the genus *Streptomyces* and is used in treating infections with bacteria resistant to less toxic antibiotics; also, the sodium or calcium salt of this phenol, in which forms it is usually administered.

1956 *Antibiotics & Chemotherapy* VI. 195 It has been announced that by mutual agreement of The Upjohn Co. and of Merck & Co., Inc., the generic name of novobiocin would be used for the antibiotic previously called streptonivicin and cathomycin. **1961** *Lancet* 23 Sept. 688/2 Kanamycin..was changed to a combination of erythromycin..with novobiocin 500 mg. six-hourly. **1967** *Martindale's Extra Pharmacopoeia* (ed. 25) 990/1 The usefulness of novobiocin is limited by the frequent occurrence of side-effects. *Ibid.*, Novobiocin sodium is usually administered by mouth. **1972** *Jrnl. Pharmacy & Pharmacol.* XXIV. 972 Novobiocin..is used infrequently because micro-organisms rapidly develop resistance to it.

novocain (nōᵘ·vŏkēin). *Pharm.* Also **novocaine**, and with capital initial. [f. *novo-*, comb. form of L. *novus* new + Co)CAIN(E.] A proprietary name for procaine.

1905 *Trade Marks Jrnl.* 22 Nov. 1450 Novocain... Chemical substances prepared for use in medicine and pharmacy. Farbwerke vorm. Meister Lucius & Brüning, Hoechst a/Main, Germany; manufacturers. **1910** *Practitioner* Feb. 255 For regional anaesthesia novocain has given good results. **1926** *Glasgow Herald* 25 Aug. 10 Mrs Mary Agnes Brown..died..following injections of cocaine hydrochlorate, which had been mistakenly administered instead of novocaine solution. **1952** MORIN & SMITH tr. *Herzog's Annapurna* xvi. 232 It meant injecting novocaine into the nerve ganglion. **1961** C. MCCULLERS *Clock without Hands* iii. 55 Poke, Doc's brother, just drew the tooth for me—with novocain and antibiotics. **1972** 'G. BLACK' *Bitter Tea* (1973) ix. 139, I sat like a man coming from dental extractions under Novocaine, given a time of numb reprieve before the pain flared.

Novocastrian (nōᵘvokæ·striăn), *sb.* and *a.* Also with lower-case initial. [f. L. *novo-* reduced form of *novum* new + *castr(um* castle + -IAN.] **A.** *sb.* A native or inhabitant of Newcastle upon Tyne. **B.** *adj.* Of or pertaining to Newcastle or its inhabitants.

1888 L. A. SMITH *Music of Waters* 123 They must have been scarcely as sensitive and refined as one would like to imagine the ancestors of the..Novocastrians. **1915** E. CORRI *30 Yrs. Boxing Ref.* 228, I had no friends in Newcastle when I arrived, but made many during that short visit, coming away with a tremendously high opinion of Novocastrian hospitality. **1949** H. L. HONEYMAN *Northumberland* I. vi. 104 Ralph Gardiner, a renegade Novocastrian and pupil of its Grammar School, settled at Chirton near Shields in 1650. **1959** E. L. MASCALL *Pi in High* 26 What coals to Novocastrians are, To Generals what caviare, To Hecubas what divers he's, Were mushrooms to Ozonides. **1969** C. GEESON *Northumberland & Durham Word Bk.* 4 Wilfred Whitten, the distinguished original editor of *John O' London's Weekly*, spoke of his native Novocastrian tongue as 'that abominable dialect'. **1973** I. CARR in B. S. Johnson *All Bull* 107 He quizzed me about distinguished novocastrian citizens. **1974** *Times* 29 Apr. 5/4 Mr T. Dan Smith will be remembered as the man who changed the face of Newcastle upon Tyne... The pace and scale of the change have..frightened Novocastrians.

novolak (nōᵘ·volæk). Also **novolac.** [f. as prec. + (alteration of) LAC(QUER, LACKER *sb.*] Any of a range of soluble, fusible resins formed by condensing formaldehyde with phenol using an acid catalyst, which are used extensively in varnishes.

1909 L. H. BAEKELAND in *Jrnl. Industr. & Engin. Chem.* Aug. 547/2 In order to simplify matters, I propose to call this substance *Novolak.* **1944** H. R. FLECK *Plastics: Sci. & Technol.* ix. 203 Such properties as the durability and hardness of the Novolac type of resin were obviously very desirable properties to have in a varnish. **1970** E. PARKES et al. in K. Strauss *Appl. Sci. in Casting of Metals* ix. 359 The novolac produced in this way, when cooled down, is a hard glass-like solid and may be ground for use in the manufacture of precoated sand by the hot-coating technique. **1973** *Materials & Technol.* VI. viii. 590 The prime use of moulding powders based on novolak resins is for the production of articles and components in the electrical engineering field.

‖ **novus homo** (nōᵘ·vŏs hǫ·mo). Pl. **novi homines.** [L., lit. 'new man'.] Orig. used in ancient Rome of the first man in a family to rise to a curule office; hence, a man who has recently risen to a position of importance from insignificance; an upstart.

1589 T. SMITH *Commonw. of Eng.* I. xx. 36 Those which were *noui homines*, were more allowed, for their vertues new and newly shewen, than the old smell of auncient race. **1764** SMOLLETT *Let.* 2 July in *Trav.* (1766) I. xvii. 280 Of these, three or four families are really respectable: the rest are *novi homines*, sprung from Bourgeois, who have saved a little money by their different occupations and raised themselves to the rank of noblesse by purchase. **1824** J. S. MILL in *Westm. Rev.* II. 391 The military leaders, being *novi homines*, were the great opponents of the aristocracy. **1956** A. TOYNBEE *Historian's Approach to Relig.* xvi. 211 All of which had to draw their diplomats from among *novi homines*. **1960** *Times* 17 Sept. 7/2 The competition of radical politicians—the *novi homines* of Africa—has weakened it [*sc.* the tribal system].

novy (nōᵘ·vi). Also **Novy.** Shortened colloq. form of Nova Scotia, used ellipt.: (*a*) a type of local boat; (*b*) a person from Nova Scotia.

1885 *Bull. U.S. Fish Comm.* V. 8 The boats used in the ordinary fishing [along the Labrador coast] are of two kinds; those called 'novies' or Nova Scotia boats, being long and narrow. **1897** KIPLING *Captains Courageous* vi. 138 'Git aout, you Novy!' To call a Gloucester man a Nova Scotian is not well received. **1942** BERREY & VAN DEN BARK *Amer. Thes. Slang* § 385/5 *Novy*, a Nova Scotian. **1970** J. F. LEAVITT *Wake of Coasters* xvii. 165 In deep water parlance, Nova Scotia and New Brunswick vessels were usually spoken of as 'Bluenoses', but along the coast they were more frequently called 'Novies'.

now, *adv., conj., sb.*[1], and *a.* Add: **I.** *adv.* **1. c.** Phr. *now-it-can-be-told*, used *attrib.* to designate a book, story, etc., which reveals previously classified or unknown facts.

1932 *N.Y. Times Book Rev.* 7 Feb. 15/3 Colonel Reeve's book belongs in the now-it-can-be-told class—and he has a lot to tell. **1948** Q. WRIGHT in J. Towster *Political Power in the U.S.S.R.* p. ix, Correspondents..have produced books of the 'now-it-can-be-told' variety.

d. In colloq. expression of the type —— *now and* —— *later.*

1965 N. FREELING *Criminal Conversation* I. vii. 44 Van der Valk the tally-boy; live now and pay later. **1970** *Guardian* 18 Mar. 19/2 Profit now and pay later. **1973** *P.O. Telephone Directory* (§ 101 London area A–D) 4/1 Telephone credit cards. Talk now—pay later.

IV. 16. Revived in adjectival use: modern, fashionable, up-to-date, 'with it'.

1963 *New Yorker* 8 June 72 A black crepe dress..a now-and-future shaping of pebbly acetate-and-rayon crepe. **1967** *Time* 7 Apr. 20 The more mature of the unmarried in the Now Generation say that, far from promoting promiscuity, the pills impose a sense of responsibility. **1967** *Listener* 2 Nov. 564/2 'Drag', of course, is very now (as the copy-writers are saying). **1968** *Sat. Rev.* (U.S.) 28 Dec. 18 *Bullitt*, I find, is completely typical of the 'now' look in American movies—a swift-moving, constantly shifting surface that suggests rather than reveals depths. **1970** G. GREER *Female Eunuch* 255 Even a poet as *now* as Dylan has two kinds of female character in his imagery. **1972** *Sat. Rev.* (U.S.) 27 May 18/2 Dig the now scene. **1973** E. BULLINS *Theme is Blackness* 167 Everybody in our integrated circle of mod people is with it, man. We're the Now Crowd.

17. a. *now-forgotten.*

1785 A. SEWARD *Let.* 30 Mar. (1811) I. 53 Mr. Warton demonstrates, that the general plan of L'Allegro, Il Penseroso, was suggested to Milton by a now-forgotten work of one Burton. **1951** M. MCLUHAN *Mech. Bride* (1967) 132/2 Mere attacks on salesmanship are confusing..when these now-forgotten assumptions are missed.

nowackiite (novā·ki,əit). *Min.* [f. the name of Werner *Nowacki* (b. 1909), Swiss crystallographer + -ITE[1].] A sulphide of copper, zinc, and arsenic, $Cu_6Zn_3As_4S_{12}$, found as grey or black rhombohedral crystals at Lengenbach, Switzerland.

1965 MARUMO & BURRI in *Chimia* XIX. 501/2 Our mineral, for which we—together with Mr. J. Imhof—suggest the name *nowackiite*, in honour of Professor Werner Nowacki (Bern). **1967** *Zeitschr. für Kristallogr.* CXXIV. 354 The structure determination of nowackiite was undertaken to determine the coordination around the As atoms in the mineral, and to clarify the structural relationship to the zincblende type.

no waiting. Used (with hyphen) *attrib.* and *absol.* to designate an area, place, etc., where vehicles may not be parked.

1959 *Times* 8 Dec. 5/1 In streets where there is unilateral no-waiting, the signs only indicate the side of the road on which waiting is not allowed. **1963** M. LEVINSON *Taxi!* v. 66 A taxi-driver..must wait for..a passenger if he is asked to do so..although this law..is cancelled out by the no-waiting restrictions. **1969** *Morning Star* 18 Nov. 3 Mr Callaghan said the inquiries were about a car causing obstruction in a no-waiting area of Brixton. **1969** *Highway Code* 43 Along the edge of the Carriageway. No waiting.. at times shown on nearby plates or on entry signs to controlled parking zones. **1970** O. NORTON *Dead on Prediction* ii. 22 They had painted yellow no-waiting lines all the way.

now-a-nights. Delete *rare*[−1] and add earlier and later examples.

1841 THOREAU *Let.* 21 July in *Corr.* (1958) 45 Now-a-nights I go on to the hill. **1920** M. BEERBOHM *And Even Now* 120 The Golden Drugget is not outspread nowanights across the high dark coast-road between Rapallo and Zoagli. **1939** JOYCE *Finnegans Wake* 15 And still nowanights and by nights of yore do all bold floras..say only: Cull me ere I wilt to thee!

noway, *adv.* Add: In colloq. use (usu. written as two words): it is impossible, it can't be done.

1968–70 *Current Slang* (Univ. S. Dakota) III–IV. 86 Can we get out of the test? No Way! **1970** J. G. VERMANDEL *Dine with Devil* vii. 36 'No way I can do it any faster than that'... But Peter Angel was shaking his head. 'No way, sorry.' **1973** *Observer* 16 Dec. 40/1 A letter was dispatched to the Foreign Office asking HMG to foot the bill for any damage done—no way. **1973** *Chicago Sun-Times* 29 Dec. 25/1, I say Fred Astaire played a drunk in the made-for-TV movie 'The Over-the-Hill Gang Rides Again'. My brother says, 'No way.' Who is right? **1974** *Nature* 15 Feb. 420/2 Suppose then that an ingenious scribe..decided to use the very compound which wasn't used again for that purpose until about 1920? No way, says McCrone. **1975** *New Yorker* 20 Jan. 29/1 He said he wouldn't start up a gang today—no way.

nowhere, *adv.* Add: **4. a.** (Earlier and later examples of *transf.* use.)

1831 MACAULAY *Essay on Boswell's Life Johnson* in *Edin. Rev.* Sept. 16 Boswell is the first of biographers.. and the rest nowhere. **1928** C. A. NICHOLSON *Hell & Duchess* vi. 108 Don't imagine you have a fortune there. A hundred francs goes nowhere these days.

5. *sb.* **b.** A remote or inaccessible place; freq. in colloq. phr. *the middle of nowhere.*

1908 *Dialect Notes* III. 312 *Forty miles from nowhere*, far from any civilized or settled section. **1951** E. COXHEAD *One Green Bottle* vii. 182 My uncle's farm is on the road to nowhere... They often don't see a new face for months on end. **1960** *Times* 21 Nov. (Canada Suppl.) p. xi/2 Hydro-Quebec is starting to move far up the Manicouagan, in the middle of nowhere. **1963** A. LUBBOCK *Austral. Round-*

about 30, I got going again pretty quickly as I didn't want to be caught by the storm in the middle of nowhere. **1967** MRS. L. B. JOHNSON *White House Diary* 7 July (1970) 544 The country was sparsely populated and it was surprising to come upon such an enormous church, out in nowhere. **1967** E. COUSINS *Death in Quiet Place* i. 10 'I never heard of Boling Green.' 'You wouldn't, old boy. Fag-end of nowhere, down a two-mile lane from the second-class road.'

c. A dull person, place, or thing. Passing into *adj.*: insignificant, unsatisfactory, dull; non-existent. In most contexts *slang.*

1940 L. MACNEICE *Last Ditch* 14 The here and there and nowhere birds. **1948** L. SPITZER *Linguistics & Literary History* i. 18 The priestess Bacbuc (whose ambiguous response: '*Trinc!*' is just a nowhere word). **1953** W. BURROUGHS *Junkie* x. 110 The others [*sc.* patients] were a beat, nowhere bunch of people. The type psychiatrists like. **1956** B. HOLIDAY *Lady sings Blues* (1958) viii. 82 A Rolls is built for pleasure... But it's nowhere for highballing a hundred and fifty miles to make a gig. **1959** 'F. NEWTON' *Jazz Scene* xii. 220 The hipster classifies..an undesirable state as *nowhere*. **1959** *Esquire* Nov. 70J *Nowhere*, the absolute of nothing. Example: That guy is nowhere. **1966** *Melody Maker* 7 May 5/2 We all thought it was the most nowhere record we'd made. **1970** *Globe & Mail* (Toronto) 26 Sept. 12/2 He wants to spread this physical act as a sign..and then..see work expanding in the nowhere parish to merge with the national scene. **1974** *Ibid.* 14 Sept. 27/4 What you'll remember is the casual dreariness of the nowhere towns and the faded dreams of the guys who never managed to get out of them.

nowhereness. Delete *nonce-word* and add later examples.

1928 D. H. LAWRENCE *Let.* 15 Dec. (1932) 766 A ghastly slummy nowhereness—but France seems all like that. **1929** —— *Pansies* 105 We can but howl the lugubrious howl of idiots, The howl of the utterly lost Howling their nowhereness.

nowheres (nōᵘ·hwēəɹz), *adv.* *U.S. dial.* = NOWHERE *adv.*

1884 'MARK TWAIN' *Huck. Finn* xli. 415, I hain't been nowheres. **1909** *Dialect Notes* III. 353 *Nowheres*, nowhere.

no-win, *a.* [f. NO *a.* + WIN *sb.*[1]] Of a contest or struggle: that cannot be won.

1962 *Economist* 30 June 1310/1 He recommended an agreement with the Russians—a 'no-win' approach, in fact, 'an accommodation with tyranny'. **1966** *Ibid.* 5 Nov. 565/1 Both attack Washington for a 'no-win war policy' in Vietnam. **1973** *Daily Colonist* (Victoria, B.C.) 24 July 5/3 So the trail of broken fixes has put Nixon in a no-win position.

nowness. Delete *rare* and add: (Later examples.) Also, the quality of taking place in the present time.

1891 [see -NESS *suff.* 2 a]. **1926** *Spectator* 22 May 871/1 We enter upon a consideration of 'thenness' and nowness. **1928** A. S. EDDINGTON *Nature of Physical World* iii. 49 From this point of view the 'nowness' of an event is like a shadow cast by it into space. **1962** *Punch* 1 Aug. 153/2 Once the viewer has tasted..This-is-actually-happening, or what we might..describe as Nowness, he's going to waste no time in demanding it. **1973** *Sci. Amer.* Apr. 8/2 Nowness and Permanence. Thanks to the former, it is possible for an art historian to give at least an approximate date for its making.

nowst, var. *NOUST.

nowt (s.v. NOUGHT *sb.*, *a.*, and *adv.* In Dict.). Add later examples.

1913 [see *BLEEDER 3]. **1963** *Times* 11 Mar. 3/6 The verdict was just, anyway, for Yorkshire took their chances like men who seldom get 'owt for nowt', and were better disciplined on a day that demanded it. **1975** *Daily Tel.* 13 Dec. 9/1 There's nowt else possible in this weather.

noxa (nǫ·ksă). *Med.* Pl. **noxæ.** [L., = 'hurt, damage'.] Anything harmful to the body.

1894 GOULD *Dict. Med.* 877/2 *Noxa*, an injurious principle; especially a pathogenetic microörganism, or other *materies morbi.* **1960** BLOOD & HENDERSON *Vet. Med.* I. iii. 44 The embryo..does not react to noxa in the same way as the fœtus since no inflammation or leucocytosis develops. **1966** *Ann. N.Y. Acad. Sci.* CXXV. 884 What became obviously and inevitably clear..was the extreme 'communicability' of a purely symbolic 'noxa' in working with patients in the valley of the shadow of death. **1971** *Nature* 2 July 18/2 Aspirin does not lessen pain in skin, elicited by noxious substances, but it does lessen pain in other sites, when elicited by similar noxae.

noxious, *a.* Add: **3. noxious weed,** a weed growing on neglected land, esp., in Australia and New Zealand, one considered harmful to animals, which may be the subject of regulations governing attempts to control it.

1913 F. M. BAILEY *Comprehensive Catal. Queensland Plants* 259 Many of the species [of *Calotis*] are noxious weeds, but it would be impossible to get rid of them by Act of Parliament. **1923** R. MACAULAY *Told by an Idiot* III. 256 As to Ireland, a bill was passed to reduce her docks, thistles, and noxious weeds: no other bill. **1966** G. W. TURNER *Eng. Lang. Austral. & N.Z.* vii. 142 Inspectors call [on New Zealand farmers] to make sure.. that noxious weeds, weeds officially proscribed, are controlled. **1971** *Guardian* 12 Aug. 1/5 She is not opposed to the killing..of clumps of noxious weeds like docks or thistles. **1973** *Stand. Encycl. S. Afr.* VIII. 103/2 A 'wild flower' is defined as a plant indigenous to the Republic of South Africa, except noxious weeds.

noy (noi), *sb.*[2] *Physics.* [repr. the pronunc. of the first part of *noise.*] A unit of perceived noisiness, defined so that the number of noys is proportional to the noisiness of a sound, and one noy is equal to the noisiness of a sound of specified bandwidth and intensity (see quot. 1959).

1959 K. D. KRYTER in *Jrnl. Acoustical Soc. Amer.* XXXI. 1424/1 The following..steps were taken in arriving at the procedure suggested for the calculation of the perceived noise kind of a sound: Step 1. First, the word 'noy' was coined for the units on the scale of perceived noisiness. The numerical value of 1 was assigned to the perceived noisiness of the band from 910–1090 cps of random noise at a sound pressure level of 40 db *re* 0·0002 μ bar. **1963** JERRARD & MCNEILL *Dict. Sci. Units* 96 The noisiness of a jet aircraft taking off is about 110 noys. **1970** R. D. FORD *Introd. Acoustics* vii. 138 The relationship between PN dB and noys is exactly the same as that between phons and sones. **1971** B. J. SMITH *Acoustics* ii. 29 Find the total noisiness N from $N = N_{max} + 0{\cdot}3(\Sigma N - N_{max})$ where N_{max} = highest noy value and ΣN = sum of the noy values in all octave bands.

noyade. Add: (Further examples.) Also *fig.*

1899 E. WHARTON *Greater Inclination* iv. 126 He and she..were bound together in a *noyade* of passion that left them resisting yet clinging as they went down. **1955** AUDEN *Shield of Achilles* iii. 76 Some autumn night of delations and noyades.

noyau. Add: (Earlier example.)

1787 W. DYOTT *Diary* (1907) I. 38 We dined at half-past three and drank pretty freely till eight, when we had coffee, and after noyau, etc.

b. A type of sweetmeat related to nougat.

1913 C. MACKENZIE *Sinister St.* I. I. vii. 103 Richer boys emerged from the tuckshop, sucking gelatines and satin pralines and chocolate creams and raspberry noyau. **1963** —— *My Life & Times* II. 135 A small boy tried to make up his mind whether he would invest a penny in a bar of raspberry, or greengage, or apricot noyau... Noyau was a second-best to nougat.

2. *transf.* A nucleus (of people).

1965 *Listener* 27 May 792/1 They picked out, from the far from 'little' *noyau* of young, hopeful writers who had gathered around them, any Lucien de Rubempré..who came their way. **1966** R. ARDREY *Territorial Imperative* (1967) v. 167, I have taken from the French ethologist Jean-Jacques Petter the term '*noyau*' as a label for the society of inward antagonism... It has seemed wise..to get..away..from all those English words like 'community' or 'society' which inevitably bear connotations of co-operation. *Noyau*—meaning, roughly, a nucleus—is correct in that it implies a primitive evolutionary step towards societies characterized by mutual aid.

nozzer (nǫ·zəɹ). *Naut. slang.* [Orig. uncertain: ? f. colloq. repr. of *No, sir*; but see quot. 1962.] A new recruit, a novice sailor.

1943 'TAFFRAIL' *White Ensigns* ii. 32 To make matters worse the 'nozzers', or novices, usually had their soap and water purloined by those who had been longer on board and knew the ropes. **1962** GRANVILLE *Dict. Sailors' Slang* 82/2 *Nozzer*, new entry boy at the training establishment, HMS *Ganges*... These boys have been called *nozzers*..since the establishment opened, because the petty officer in charge was nicknamed 'Nosey'.

nozzle, *sb.* **2. b.** Add to def.: Also to those in other engines, e.g. turbines (for directing the fluid on to the rotor), internal-combustion engines (for injecting fuel into the carburettor or the combustion chamber), and jet engines (for increasing the speed of the ejected fluid). (Further examples.)

1906 W. H. S. GARNETT *Turbines* I. v. 56 When it is required to reduce the power more rapidly..it is usual to deflect the nozzle so that the jet misses the buckets. **1912** *Motor Manual* (ed. 14) i. 10 When the suction of the engine occurs petrol issues through the nozzle, and an in-rush of air..passes upwards, carrying the sprayed petrol with it, and thus forming the explosive mixture. **1946** [see *AFTER-BURNING *vbl. sb.* 2]. **1949** G. P. SUTTON *Rocket Propulsion Elem.* i. 3 When a rocket unit operates, a chemical reaction occurs which generates high temperature, high pressure gases; these..are ejected through a nozzle. **1950** SKROTZKI & VOPAT *Steam & Gas Turbines* ix. 371 Mechanical spray nozzles for injecting fuel oil into combustion chambers. **1962** D. SLAYTON in *Into Orbit* 22 The job of keeping the capsule in its correct attitude during flight is taken care of by small jet nozzles fastened on the outside of the spacecraft. **1966** *Aviation Week & Space Technol.* 6 Dec. 24/1 A rocket engine with a conventional bell nozzle. **1971** B. SCHARF *Engin. & its Lang.* xiv. 207 In impulse turbines, the high pressure steam ..expands through nozzles or guide blades shaped to form nozzles.

n-p-n (e:n,pī:e·n). *Electronics.* Also **npn,** and in capitals. Designating a semiconductor device in which a *p*-type region is sandwiched between two *n*-type regions.

1951 W. SHOCKLEY et al. in *Physical Rev.* LXXXIII. 151/1 The *p-n-p* transistor has been discussed previously. .. In this article we shall consider..the *n-p-n* transistor. **1962** SIMPSON & RICHARDS *Physical Princ. Junction Transistors* iii. 46 In the manufacture of *n-p-n* grown-junction transistors, the *p*-type section is grown for a very short time to give a thin base layer. **1967** *Electronics* 6 Mar. 4/2 Transistors Types: PNP and NPN. **1969** J. J. SPARKES *Transistor Switching* v. 126 Using *npn* transistors, pulsed *R–S* flip-flops using three basic types of pulse steering are available.

‖ **nritta** (n,ri·tă). Also **nrtta.** [Skr. *nṛitta* dance.] A type of 'pure', abstract Indian dance (see quots. 1967).

1917 COOMARASWAMY & DUGGIRALA tr. *Mirror of Gesture* 14 Nṛtta is here dismissed with a merely negative definition, as the object of the Abhinaya Darpaṇa is to explain how to express by gesture definite themes. **1953** F. BOWERS *Dance in India* 24 Sanskrit has no single word for dance in our sense... *Nritta*..refers to dance pure and simple, unadulterated by meaning, interpretation, gesture, or language. **1967** SINGHA & MASSEY *Indian Dances* 24 Nritta is the rhythmic movement of the body in dance... It visualizes and reproduces music and rhythm by means of abstract gestures of the body and hands... Nritta..is concerned solely with rhythmic movement in dancing and is therefore loosely termed 'pure dance'. **1967** CHUJOY & MANCHESTER *Dance Encycl.* 457/2 The repertoire of the Bharata Natya dancer includes nrtta, nrtya, and nautch. Nrtta is an abstract dance of pure lyricism; nrtya is an expressive dance, pantomimic in content; nautch is a combination of song and dance. **1971** *Femina* (Bombay) 30 Apr. 49/1 Kuchipudi is the regional variation of Bharata Natyam. Both share classical Carnatic music and the Nritta (pure dance) and Nritya (expressional dance) aspects.

‖ **nritya** (n,ri·tyă). Also **nrtya.** [Skr. *nṛitya* dance, play.] A type of Indian dance through which ideas or emotions are expressed.

1875 MONIER WILLIAMS *Indian Wisdom* xv. 463 The root *naṭ* and the nouns *nāṭya* and *nāṭaka*, which are now applied to dramatic acting, are probably mere corruptions of *nṛit*, 'to dance', *nṛitya*, 'dancing'. **1917** COOMARASWAMY & DUGGIRALA tr. *Mirror of Gesture* 14 Nṛtya should be seen by a royal audience in the court of kings. **1953** F. BOWERS *Dance in India* 25 *Nritya*..refers to expression, interpretation, and gesticulation with meaning. In other words, dance when it conveys sense and ideas. **1967** SINGHA & MASSEY *Indian Dances* 24 Nritya is that element of the dance which 'suggests *ras* (sentiment) and *bhava* (mood)'. Both..are conveyed through facial expressions and appropriate gestures... The object of both natya and nritya..is to depict ideas, themes, moods and sentiments. **1967, 1971** [see *NRITTA].

Nsima, var. *NZIMA.

nth: see N I. 4 (in Dict. and Suppl.).

n-tuple: see *-TUPLE.

n-type (e·ntəip), *a.* *Physics.* [f. *N* (repr. *negative*) + TYPE *sb.*[1]] Applied to (a region in) a semiconductor in which electrical conduction is due chiefly to the movement of holes. Opp. *P-TYPE *a.*

1946 J. A. BECKER et al. in *Trans. Amer. Inst. Electr. Engin.* LXV. 714/1 The theoretical and experimental physicists have established that there are two types of electronic semiconductors which can be called *N* and *P* type, depending on whether the carriers are negative electrons or are equivalent to positive 'holes' in the filled energy band. *Ibid.* 715/1 *N*-type oxides, such as ZnO... *P*-type oxides, such as NiO. **1948** TORREY & WHITMAN *Crystal Rectifiers* iii. 49 A semiconductor that conducts principally by electrons in the nearly empty band is said to be an '*n*-type' semiconductor. **1962** SIMPSON & RICHARDS *Physical Princ. Junction Transistors* i. 8 If this type of impurity semiconduction is predominant the material is said to be an *n*-type extrinsic semiconductor, or simply of *n*-type. **1967** *Electronics* 6 Mar. 60/2 Light-sensitive diodes are produced by diffusing islands of boron into a substrate of n-type silicon.

‖ **nu** (nŭ), *int.* [Yiddish, f. Russ. *nu* well, well now.] An exclamation variously used to express interrogation, surprise, emphasis, doubt, etc.

1892 I. ZANGWILL *Childr. Ghetto* I. I. ii. 52 '*Nu*, Pesach, another glass of rum,' said Mr. Beleovitch genially. **1945** A. KOBER *Parm Me* 134 '*Nu*,' she said, 'is lust by you the tunk, you can't give a person a hello when you coming home?' **1967** C. POTOK *Chosen* vii. 139 'Nu,' Reb Saunders said, smiling, 'how should you not know that?' **1968** L. ROSTEN *Joys of Yiddish* 268 *Nu* is so very Yiddish an interjection that it has become the one word which can identify a Jew. **1970** L. M. FEINSILVER *Taste of Yiddish* ii. 155 Growing impatience makes for Nu-nu? and nu-nu-nu? **1971** D. MEIRING *Wall of Glass* xvii. 147 *Nu?* thought Geyra, So what?

nuance (nŭ,āns), *v.* [f. the sb.] *trans.* To give nuances to. Hence **nu·ancing** *vbl. sb.*

1897 W. ARCHER *Theatr. World 1896* 94 Nor the elocutionary skill to give variety to a long speech, *nuancing* it, if I may say so, by means of his voice alone. **1959** M. SCHLAUCH *Eng. Lang. in Mod. Times* II. iii. 53 Some tendencies toward such nuancing may be detected in the late medieval distribution of *thou* and *ye* for the singular. **1973** P. A. ALLUM *Politics & Society in Post-War Naples* vi. 191 We can nuance this conclusion and reveal that in some communes the relation of the first to the fourth candidate was 2:1..; in other communes the difference between first and fourth was less than 1,000 votes out of 5,000. **1975** *Gramophone* Oct. 652/1 Take the Wagner piece.., and note the impassioned recitative, nuanced as by the human voice.

‖ **nuancé** (nŭ,ãnse). [Fr.] = *NUANCED *ppl. a.*

1963 *Times Lit. Suppl.* 1 Feb. 71/1 Life..was extremely *nuancé*. *Ibid.* 3 May 318/5 His answer is extremely *nuancé*. **1973** P. A. ALLUM *Politics & Society in Post-War Naples* vi. 181 Macciocchi's judgement of Amendola is more *nuancé*.

nuanced (nǖ,ãnst), *ppl. a.* [f. *NUANCE *v.* + -ED¹.] Possessing or exhibiting delicate gradations in tone, expression, etc.

1920 [see *BOSTONIAN *a.*]. **1965** *Listener* 21 Oct. 613/1 Marxists often distinguish between 'Marxism' and 'vulgar Marxism'... The former is subtle, profound, nuanced,.. and dialectical. **1969** N. FREELING *Tsing-Boum* xi. 71 An immensely nuanced and confused double-think. **1971** *Daily Tel.* 23 Mar. 16/5 He brought a wealth of finely nuanced expression to the eloquently fashioned vocal line. **1972** *Language* XLVIII. 457 In a study devoted to discriminations among adverbs, one would expect a nuanced feeling for them, and to a large extent this is borne out.

nub, *sb.*¹ **3.** Delete *U.S.* and add earlier and later examples.

1834 S. SMITH *Sel. Lett. J. Downing* 205 That's pretty much the *nub* of the business. **1933** WODEHOUSE *Heavy Weather* viii. 166 'The problem..is, How the hell is one to get it away from the blighter?' 'Quite.' 'That is, as you might say, the nub?' **1963** *Guardian* 11 Mar. 13/6 Speaking on the election of vice-presidents, he came to the nub of the unrest among active athletes. **1974** *Times* 22 Oct. 14/6 The nub of the judges' difficulty lay in Lord Widgery's reference to the claim..that the judge had no authority in law to give a direction binding on the press.

Nuba (nū·bă). Also **Nouba.** [See NUBIAN *a.* and *sb.*] The name of a group of peoples of southern Kordofan in the Sudan; a member of these peoples. Also *attrib.* or as *adj.*

1827 J. CONDER *Mod. Traveller: Egypt, Nubia, & Abyssinia* II. 242 The male Noubas, in Egypt as well as in Arabia, are preferred to all others for labour. **1884** *Encycl. Brit.* XVII. 316/2 Certainly none of the chief native races in Soudan..Maba in Wadai, Nuba in the Nile valley..can be considered as of pure Negro descent. **1910** *Ibid.* II. 51/2 The Nuba and Nuer [of the Upper Nile] worship the bull. **1911** *Ibid.* XV. 907/2 The Nubas have their own language, though the inhabitants of each hill have usually a different dialect... In the northern hills [of Kordofan] are communities of black people... They speak Arabic and are called Nuba Arabs. **1911** J. G. FRAZER *Golden Bough: Magic Art* (ed. 3) I. iii. 122 When a Nuba of north-eastern Africa goes to El Obeid for the first time, he tells his wife not to wash or oil herself. **1936** *Discovery* June 170/1 The Nubians (not to be confused with the Nuba of Kordofan). **1949** J. S. TRIMINGHAM *Islam in Sudan* i. 3 Here live the settled 'Arab' population of Kordofān, the Baqqāra cattle-breeding Arabs, the pastoral negroid Shilluk, and the pagan Nūba in the hills. **1962** OLIVER & FAGE *Short Hist. Afr.* iv. 47 The kingdom of the Nuba who are above upper Egypt. **1966** C. SWEENEY *Scurrying Bush* iii. 46 The Nuba of Kordofan..say that it was the baboon that stole the *Kako's* (hyrax's) tail. **1970** *Man, Myth & Magic* v. 138/3 Victorious Nuba wrestlers are awarded branches which are burnt; the wrestler covers himself with the ashes before the next fight. **1972** J. C. FARIS in Cunnison & James *Ess. Sudan Ethnogr.* i. 3 The Southeastern Nuba have suffered locally at the hands of a series of raiders and slavers for a long time.

nubbin. Add: (Earlier and later examples.) Also *transf.* and *fig.*, esp. something small or something that remains when the main part is worn away.

1692 in *Maryland Hist. Mag.* (1918) XIII. 209 Jones saw him buy one beaver skin..for thirty ears and nubbins of corn. **1838** B. DRAKE *Tales & Sketches* 150 A handfull of salt and a few nubbins of corn. **1857** *Harper's Mag.* Feb. 399/2 They served me, at the 'American', with a little hard *nubbin* of steak. **1904** H. F. DAY *Kin O'Ktaadn* 93 She'd squizzle all to nubbins a speech an hour long. **1910** 'O. HENRY' *Strictly Business* vi. 76 A red nubbin of corn. **1915** A. C. LAWSON in *Bull. Dept. Geol. Univ. Calif.* IX. III. 38 Broad alluvial embankments..rise by a gentle slope to the summits of the ranges, where there are residual rock crests, or 'nubbins'. **1931** *Times Educ. Suppl.* 11 July 275/4 One may find 'nubbins'—hard, undeveloped, useless things—the result of non-fertilization. **1945** B. MACDONALD *Egg & I* (1946) I. iii. 45 Many of the trees bore nothing or merely two or three wizened nubbins. **1954** G. I. M. SWYER *Reprod. & Sex* App. I. 249 Shortly before puberty..a small nubbin of tissue appears beneath the areola, converting it to a cone. **1954** DYLAN THOMAS *Quite Early One Morning* I. 56 The Telecinema..blobs and nubbins and rubbery squirls receding. **1969** D. BAGLEY *Spoilers* i. 10 The lipstick was worn right down... Another lipstick worn to a nubbin.

nubbly, *a.* Add: Also *fig.*

1958 *Economist* 8 Nov. 487/1 Labour had seemed in danger of becoming obsessed with the nubbly problems of publicity. **1963** *Times Lit. Suppl.* 8 Feb. 96/5 A nubbly and idiosyncratic style.

3. Of cloth or fabric: rough-textured. Also as *sb.*

1935 *Amer. Speech* X. 192/1 A dress of *nubby* crepe may have *nubbly* knots. **1958** J. D. MACDONALD *Executioners* (1959) v. 72 She wore a green nubbly suit. **1964** *McCall's Sewing* i. 8/1 A pebbly crêpe will not noticeably add pounds, but a very rough, nubbly wool tweed may have a decided effect. **1972** *Daily Tel.* 20 Nov. 15 Janice is shopping..for new fabrics..and her mood is for nubblies, for lots of texture. **1973** J. BURROWS *Like an Evening Gone* iii. 39 A jacket of the same nubbly tweed material as the victim's skirt.

nubby, *a.* Add: Also, = *NUBBLY *a.* 3.

1935 [see *NUBBLY *a.* 3]. **1938** *Times* 19 Jan. 17/2 The nubby type jacket to the waistline is worn with vivid coloured woollen frocks. **1967** *Boston Sunday Globe* 23 Apr. 24 (Advt.), An elegant new drapery in a nubby solid and open weave design. **1974** *Union* (S. Carolina) *Daily Times* 19 Apr. 5/3 Also, when washing acrylic sweaters, socks and other wash-and-wear things turn them inside out before washing and they do not get nubby and I think they wear longer.

nubile. Add: **3.** Of women: sexually attractive.

1973 *Times* 8 Mar. 3/1 Some of the slimmest and most nubile girls in London, animadverted on by the Chancellor in his Budget statement, were on parade in London yesterday beneath the chandelier and haze of perfume of Christian Dior's thrice-repeated display of spring fashion. **1973** N. MAILER in *Atlantic Monthly* Aug. 52/2 A woman so sensitive and alive, so nubile as flesh and so evanescent as a wisp of vapour. **1975** *New Society* 17 July 154/2 Most women of my acquaintance..prefer the nubile bodies and erotic accessories of the female nudes. **1975** T. HEALD *Deadline* ii. 22 Waiting by the lift doors was a nubile blonde.

nubk. Substitute for def.: A spiny, evergreen shrub or tree of the genus *Zizyphus*, esp. *Z. spina-Christi*, belonging to the family Rhamnaceæ, native to north Africa and south-western Asia and bearing edible fruit. Cf. *ILB. (Further examples.)

1958 L. DURRELL *Mountolive* xvi. 304 He made his way ..to the great *nubk* tree standing up starkly in its clearing. **1960** —— *Clea* I. iii. 57 The 'nubk' forms the great circular palisade of trees which encircles the Moslem Paradise.

nucellar (niuse·lăɹ), *a. Bot.* [f. NUCELL(US + -AR¹.] Of, pertaining to, or involving the nucellus; derived from or produced in the nucellus.

1904 *Jrnl. R. Microsc. Soc.* 665 Two series of vascular bundles run in the ovule, and it is proved that the inner series, frequently described as 'nucellar', belong to the soft inner layer of the integument. **1949** DARLINGTON & MATHER *Elem. Genetics* 406 *Nucellar embryony*, a form of apomixis where the embryo arises directly from the nucellus. **1953** K. ESAU *Plant Anat.* xviii. 555 The nucellar epidermis is sometimes highly resistant and may proliferate into a nucellar cap with relatively thick walls. **1972** *Theoret. & Appl. Genetics* XLII. 314 (*heading*) Differentiation between nucellar and zygotic citrus seedlings by leaf shape.

nuck, var. *KNUCK.

nucleant (niū·kliănt), *a.* and *sb.* [f. NUCLE(US *sb.* + -ANT¹.] **A.** *adj.* Forming a nucleus. *rare*⁻¹.

1953 S. BECKETT *Watt* 142 In his own vitals, nucleant, he knew them clasped.

B. *sb.* A particle that initiates nucleation; = *NUCLEUS *sb.* 9.

1968 *Jrnl. Appl. Meteorol.* VII. 858/1 The relatively high base temperatures of the convective clouds makes [*sic*] it rather unlikely that their precipitation can be increased by the injection of ice nucleants. **1969** G. F. BOLLING in *Solidification* (Amer. Soc. Metals) (1971) xi. 364 The effective nucleants seem to be those active in the melt, in the sense of having been freshly formed in the melt.

nuclear, *a.* (and *sb.*). Add: **1. c.** Central, cardinal; *spec.* in *Linguistics* and *Phonetics*, being or constituting a linguistic or phonetic nucleus. Hence as *sb.*, a nuclear word, sound, etc. Cf. *NUCLEUS *sb.* 12.

1912 *Housemaster's Lett.* 91 You will forgive me if I tell you what I consider the nuclear fault underlying all this writing. **1940** H. G. WELLS *All Aboard for Ararat* ii. 82, I must look round to find those nuclear men who are needed to carry through the next revolution.

1941 *Language* XVII. 224 In the structure of the syllable vowels are nuclear, consonants marginal. **1949** E. A. NIDA *Morphol.* (ed. 2) 84 A nuclear structure consists of or contains the nucleus... In the word *formal* the nuclear element is *form-* and the peripheral element *-al*. *Ibid.* 118 There are a number of morphological classes represented by the nuclear immediate constituent. For example, there are single-morpheme nuclears, e.g. count, poet.., and multiple-morpheme nuclears, e.g. waiter, hunter. **1952** A. COHEN *Phonemes of English* 39 In general, independent nuclear words are first examined, i.e. words which do not carry morphological characteristics in the shape of phonemes and which do not show 'outer sandhi' (= external open juncture). **1962** A. C. GIMSON *Introd. Pronunc. Eng.* x. 245 In the sense that the nuclear syllable stands out from amongst its neighbours (both accented and unaccented syllables), the nucleus and its situation may be said to have a special contrastive function. **1966** G. N. LEECH *Eng. in Advertising* v. 48 The italicised portion represents a nuclear syllable. **1971** *Language* XLVII. 586 Linguists have long also recognized the existence of stress originating from phrasal structure: Chomsky and Halle call this the Nuclear Stress Rule. **1973** *Archivum Linguisticum* IV. 25 The different varieties of the same nuclear tone.

d. *Psychoanalysis.* Central to the development of the sexual components of the ego; pertaining to or being the emotional nucleus of a neurosis, esp. the Oedipus complex.

[**1913** C. G. JUNG in *17th Internat. Congr. Med.* XII. 67 The unconscious existence of manifold phantasies, which have their final root in the infantile past and turn around the so-called 'Kern-complex', or nucleus-complex, which may be qualified in male individuals as the Œdipus-complex and in females as the Electra-complex.] **1916** B. M. HINKLE tr. *Jung's Psychol. of Unconscious* II. iv. 195 Taken at the roots in the case of our patients, the 'nuclear complex' (Freud) reveals itself as the incest problem. **1925** A. & J. STRACHEY tr. *Freud's Case of Obsessional Neurosis* in *Coll. Papers* III. 345 The formation of that complex which deserves to be called the nuclear complex of the neuroses. It is the complex which comprises the child's earliest impulses, alike tender and hostile, towards its parents and brothers and sisters, after its curiosity has been awakened. **1939** E. GLOVER *Psycho-analysis* x. 74 Findings of this order give rise to the tenet that the Oedipus complex is the nuclear complex of the neurosis. **1968** —— *Birth of Ego* i. 11 My views on the theoretical concept of the ego, and in particular on the 'nuclear theory' of its development. *Ibid.* 17 If one were prepared not to stick too slavishly to the idea of a *fixed* nuclear system one could put the psychic situation of the Oedipus complex in clearer perspective.

e. *nuclear family* (Sociology): a term for the basic family unit or group, consisting normally of father, mother, and offspring.

1949 G. P. MURDOCK *Social Structure* i. 1 The first and most basic, called herewith the nuclear family, consists typically of a married man and woman with their offspring. **1963** A. HERON *Towards Quaker View of Sex* 56 This taboo is of social origin, designed to protect the basic unit of society—the 'nuclear' family—from disintegration. **1966** D. JENKINS *Educated Society* iii. 98 The extended, as distinct from the nuclear, family. **1971** *Guardian* 24 Mar. 11/6 If they get rid of the nuclear family there won't be grannies any more than there will be widows. **1973** *Times Lit. Suppl.* 29 June 736/1 This is a loose network of ordinary nuclear families.

2. For 'a nucleus' read: a nucleus or nuclei, esp. atomic nuclei; also, with or by (atomic) nuclei. (Further examples.)

1914 *Engineering* 20 Nov. 607/2 A point raised by Professor Rutherford concerning the effective nuclear charge. **1920** L. DONCASTER *Introd. Study Cytol.* ii. 17 It is from the chromatin that the bodies called chromosomes, which play a great part in nuclear division, are formed. **1929** *Physical Rev.* XXXIV. 1501 The new quantum number is associated with the nucleus intrinsically in the same way that *s* is associated with the electron, and because of its similar properties might be interpreted as a nuclear spin moment. **1933** *Discovery* Apr. 106/2 With this generator, it is hoped to produce currents of the order of 1 milliampere at 5 to 10 million volts, and to insert a large vacuum tube between the sphere and ground for nuclear bombardment. **1934** *Proc. Nat. Acad. Sci.* XX. 470 When certain substances are bombarded with deutons, many and varied nuclear reactions take place. **1935** *Discovery* May 150/1 The interpretation of atomic, molecular, and nuclear radiation. **1936** [see *CYCLOTRON]. **1945** H. D. SMYTH *Gen. Acct. Devel. Atomic Energy Mil. Purposes* vi. 59 The pile was first operated..on December 2, 1942... This was the first time that human beings ever initiated a self-maintaining nuclear chain reaction. **1958** *Times Rev. Industry* Aug. 7/1 An article..on the nuclear bombardment of reactor metals..is evidence of the valuable work now being done. **1961** G. R. CHOPPIN *Exper. Nuclear Chem.* i. 4 Nuclear transformations are on the order of 10^5 to 10^6 more energetic than chemical reactions on an individual molecular or atomic basis. *Ibid.* iii. 27 Nuclear scattering is a more important factor for electrons than it is for heavy particles. **1963** *Oxf. Univ. Gaz.* 9 May 1183/2 The University has established a Professorship of Nuclear Structure in the Department of Nuclear Physics. **1966** C. R. TOTTLE *Sci. Engin. Materials* x. 235 The term nuclear cross-section is used to define the effective area that the target nucleus presents to the neutron as it moves through the lattice, on a statistical or probability basis. **1969** *Times* 20 Feb. 17/5 A single type of nuclear reaction in the sun is thought to bathe each square centimetre of the earth's surface with a flux of 10 million neutrinos every second. **1970** AMBROSE & EASTY *Cell Biol.* v. 161 During cell division in both plant and animal cells the nuclear membrane disappears.

b. *nuclear energy* or *power*: = *atomic energy* (*ATOMIC *a.* and *sb.* A. 2 d). So *nuclear-powered* adj.

In quot. 1930, merely 'energy possessed by a nucleus'.

[**1926** D. H. LAWRENCE *Plumed Serpent* vii. 130 She was attracted, almost fascinated by the strange *nuclear* power of the men in the circle.] **1930** *Nature* 20 Dec. 953/2 When a nucleus passes from an excited state into a state of lower energy, two different processes may occur: either a γ-quantum is emitted or one of the extra-nuclear electrons [is] thrown out of the atom..; in this case we speak of internal conversion of nuclear energy. **1941** in M. Gowing *Britain & Atomic Energy* (1964) 431 The results..indicate that it should be possible to develop a nuclear energy machine on these lines. **1945** H. D. SMYTH *Gen. Acct. Devel. Atomic Energy Mil. Purposes* xiii. 135 The possible uses of nuclear energy are not all destructive. *Ibid.*, There is no immediate prospect of running cars with nuclear power. **1945** [see sense *3 b]. **1948** *Time* 5 July 44/1 Since atomic fuel would have over two million times as much energy as gasoline, a 'nuclear-powered' plane could fly on and on. **1951** *Jane's Fighting Ships 1951–52* 6 The contract for the first nuclear-powered submarine has been awarded to the Electric Boat Co. **1958** *Daily Express* 11 Mar. 7/1 He was speaking on the hazards which arrive from the peaceful use of nuclear energy. **1962** H. D. BUSH *Atomic & Nucl. Physics* vii. 137 For an isotope to be considered as a source of nuclear power, not only must fission be induced by neutrons of moderate energies but also the cross section must be reasonably high. **1970** *Daily Tel.* 30 June 4/8 A nuclear-powered cardiac pacemaker has been placed in an unidentified female patient in the second such operation in France.

c. Applied to research and fields of study concerned with the atomic nucleus (as *nuclear chemistry, physics*) and to specialists in those fields (as *nuclear physicist*).

1933 *Discovery* Jan. 31/2 Lord Rutherford of Nelson, to whom so much of what is best in modern nuclear physics is due. **1934** *Times* 12 Dec. 19/3 The new field of nuclear chemistry was opening up with great rapidity. **1935** *Discovery* Oct. 291/1 The nuclear chemist, Professor Aston prophesied, 'will transmute and synthesise atoms as his elder brother had done molecules'. **1936** N. FEATHER *Introd. Nucl. Physics* i. 2 The astronomer and modern physicist..discard inconvenient powers of ten for ease in forming mental pictures... But they invite danger

whenever they forget what they have discarded. To such danger the nuclear physicist is particularly liable. **1945** H. D. SMYTH *Gen. Acct. Devel. Atomic Energy Mil. Purposes* 247 The first man-made atomic explosion, the outstanding achievement of nuclear science, was achieved at 5:30 a.m. of that day. **1947** *Sci. News* V. 158 The most recent development of all is the production of new elements and isotopes by bombardment of elements with neutrons or other particles, but this so-called nuclear chemistry..is really a branch of physics. **1948** *Nucleonics* June 2 Nuclear engineering, concerned with the design, construction, and operation of nuclear fission reactors. **1956** A. H. COMPTON *Atomic Quest* 5 The use of the cyclotron was of epochal importance in nuclear physics. *Ibid.* 7 Nuclear research as a subject for wartime study. **1956** *N.Y. Times* 23 July 6/5 The coming years will bring to mankind limitless ways in which this new nuclear science can advance human welfare. **1964** M. GOWING *Britain & Atomic Energy* i. 33 The sobriety of the notes and articles concealed an intense excitement amongst the nuclear scientists. *Ibid.* x. 282 Ideas whose problems were to preoccupy the nuclear engineers for many years to come. **1969** *Times* 25 Jan. 17/5 Gamma rays are a familiar form of radiation to nuclear physicists. **1970** *New Scientist* 29 Oct. 230/1 About five years ago, the University of London decided to set up the first and still the only department in the United Kingdom awarding a first degree in nuclear engineering. **1973** 'D. HALLIDAY' *Dolly & Starry Bird* xviii. 278 He had offered to help track down some rather worrying leaks from our brave nuclear physicist boys.

3. Pertaining to or employing nuclear energy. (In senses a and b opp. *CONVENTIONAL *a.* 4 c.) **a.** Employing nuclear energy as a source of propulsive power or electricity.

1945 *Engineering Jrnl.* XXVIII. 757/1 A large stationary power installation might be used for heat and motive power in the Arctic or Antarctic regions..where the difficulty of transporting other fuels..outweigh[s] the disadvantages and difficulties of operating and maintaining a nuclear power plant. **1955** *Tribune* 22 Apr. 4/2 Nuclear power stations are designed to be safe. **1956** *Jrnl. Brit. Interplanetary Soc.* XV. 235 The range between the energy concentrations of the typical chemical combustion rockets with moderate exhaust velocities and those of not yet realized true nuclear rockets. **1957** *Newsweek* 12 Aug. 65/2 Nuclear-power plants capable of driving jets, rockets, or even space ships tremendous distances are being developed. **1957** *Jane's Fighting Ships 1957–58* 7 Advances in nuclear propulsion enable submarines to remain submerged indefinitely. *Ibid.* 50 It was officially stated in the 1957–58 Navy estimates that progress is being made with the design of the nuclear submarine 'Dreadnought'. **1959** *Daily Tel.* 24 Feb. 11/8 The day has not yet arrived when nuclear ships can prove commercially much more attractive to ship owners than ships using conventional fuel. **1960** *Aeroplane* XCVIII. 772/2 During its development the first nuclear aircraft will inevitably have alternative chemical propulsion. **1961** *Daily Tel.* 4 Oct. 21/5 The United States plans to start flight tests of nuclear rocket engines by 1967. **1968** *New Scientist* 18 Jan. 147/2 There are still no plans for a British nuclear ship, and now the Japanese are coming into the field. **1968** *Brit. Med. Bull.* XXIV. 260/2 It offers the possibility of biological monitoring of workers such as nuclear-power-station employees who are exposed to unusual environmental hazards. **1974** L. DEIGHTON *Spy Story* xii. 118 He pointed down at the War Table... Ferdy had wiped out nuclear subs.

b. Of a weapon: deriving its destructive power from the rapid, uncontrolled release of nuclear energy.

1945 *Engineering Jrnl.* XXVIII. 752/1 In view of the source of the energy, the current terms 'atomic bomb' and 'atomic power' might well be replaced by the more exact terms 'nuclear bomb' and 'nuclear power'. **1948** *Nuclear Science Abstracts* 30 Sept. 265 Fourth, nuclear weapons have not reached their maximum size in the present type bomb. **1954** *Commonweal* 1 Oct. 621/2 It has been suggested that the nuclear warhead may be small enough to be fitted to an air-to-ground rocket. *Ibid.* 10 Dec. 279/2 The vocabulary of the nuclear age began to grow:.. 'nuclear device' vs. a deliverable weapon; [etc.]. **1955** [see *DETERRENT *sb.*]. **1956** *Time* 25 June 34/3 Hopping off on his inspection of nuclear-weapons testing grounds at Eniwetok and Bikini. **1956** *Newsweek* 3 Sept. 17/2 A nuclear device can mean either hydrogen or atomic. **1957** *Observer* 28 July 6/4 To keep the British nuclear deterrent up to date on its present scale in relation to the Soviet defence will cost more and more each year. **1958** *Times Lit. Suppl.* 15 Aug. p. xxxviii/3 After all, scientists put their skill in making nuclear bombs at the service of those who believe in things; so why cannot artists act correspondingly? **1958** in *Ann. Reg. 1958* (1959) 519 The United States Government shall provide nuclear warheads for the missiles transferred to the United Kingdom Government. **1965** H. KAHN *On Escalation* vi. 101 The U.S. should be willing to adopt the concept that the only purpose of nuclear weapons is to negate nuclear weapons... It should not try to get any 'positive' benefits from its nuclear weaponry. **1973** C. BONINGTON *Next Horizon* xxi. 283 The argument seemed settled, but then Don came on the air with the effect of a small nuclear weapon.

c. Of, pertaining to, possessing, or employing nuclear weapons; *nuclear club*, the nations that possess nuclear weapons; *to go nuclear*, to acquire nuclear weapons.

1954 *Commonweal* 30 Apr. 83 (*heading*) Nuclear war: a false dilemma. **1954** *Newsweek* 8 Nov. 30/1 Talk and thought in government circles about nuclear weapons still seems to be geared largely to the period during which we alone had the capacity to wage nuclear warfare. **1956** *Foreign Policy Bull.* 1 Jan. 59 (*heading*) Nuclear tests: psychological defeat for West. **1957** *Observer* 28 July 6/3 It does not take a very elaborate calculation to realise that our contribution to the strategic Anglo-American nuclear striking force must be very small. **1957** *Christian Science Monitor* 15 Aug. 1 *Nuclear club*, those nations which possess nuclear weapons. The only current members are the United States, Britain, and the Soviet Union. **1958** *Ann. Reg. 1957* 166 The risk of leaving no alternative save nuclear retaliation in the event of war. *Ibid.* 347 The resolution urged that the United Nations and the 'nuclear' Powers should immediately suspend all such tests. **1958** *New Statesman* 22 Feb. 218/1 The response to last Monday's inaugural meetings of the Campaign for Nuclear Disarmament suggests that it is becoming a focus for a real movement of opinion on this issue. **1958** *Economist* 22 Mar. 1006/1 The starting point of most current speeches made by the nuclear disarmers is that a hydrogen-bomb war would be an unspeakably terrible thing. **1958** *Spectator* 15 Aug. 211/2 It seems impossible to convince them that a nuclear war, should it come, will not be like that. **1959** *Daily Tel.* 27 Feb. 10 There was real anxiety lest what we should need for non-nuclear wars had been excessively cut down in favour of what is needed to deal with nuclear threats. *Ibid.* 23 Mar. 18 The rate of descent from the stratosphere of radio-active debris, including strontium 90, from nuclear explosions. **1960** *Spectator* 26 Aug. 303 The American nuclear umbrella is a myth. **1963** *Daily Tel.* 1 Feb. 22/2 The Soviet Union might threaten us with nuclear attack. *Ibid.*, A sort of last-ditch argument now being used by Conservatives under the heading of 'nuclear blackmail'. **1964** *Ann. Reg. 1963* 133 The nuclear test ban treaty..symbolized their mutual determination to secure an abatement of the arms race. *Ibid.* 138 The treaty..did at least symbolize a new and welcome flexibility of outlook on the part of the leading nuclear Powers. **1964** M. GOWING *Britain & Atomic Energy* xiii. 346 Sir John Anderson's forebodings about a nuclear arms race between competing power blocs were not the result of his concern over the specific problem of the French. **1964** J. H. ROTHSCHILD *Tomorrow's Weapons* iii. 24 Nuclear warfare would include atomic (fission) bombs, shells, and mines, and hydrogen (fusion) bombs and missile warheads. **1965** H. KAHN *On Escalation* vi. 94 Alain Enthoven has described the nuclear threshold as follows: 'In efforts to limit violence, there is..a recognizable, qualitative distinction that both combatants can recognize and agree upon if they want to.' *Ibid.* 98 As Soviet nuclear capability has grown, the Soviets have..become less aggressive. *Ibid.* 297 A nuclear stalemate..exists when the balance of central war forces is such that neither side is capable of making a disarming first strike. **1967** *Listener* 11 May 607/2 The decision of certain powers to go nuclear would have the effect of making endemic regional conflicts totally insoluble. **1970** [see *GO *v.* B. 44 a]. **1973** *Times* 22 Feb. 16/4 He was attacking the nuclear disarmers or some such, who had for a time been predicting that we would all be blown up or poisoned by the Bomb. *Ibid.* 9 Nov. 20/1 The nuclear umbrella is now demonstrably in shreds. **1974** *Sci. Amer.* July 46/1 India became the sixth member of the nuclear club on May 18 by carrying out what it called a 'peaceful nuclear explosion experiment using an implosion device'.

d. = *ATOMIC *a.* 2 f.

1954 *Commonweal* 10 Dec. 279/2 With that tragic event the facts of the nuclear age were spread out for all to see. **1960** KOESTLER *Lotus & Robot* 11 The first generation of the Nuclear Age seems to have found a like solace in Zen.

4. Special collocations: **nuclear atom,** (*a*) the concept of the atom as having the charges of one sign surrounding those of the opposite sign, which are regarded as concentrated in a much smaller central volume; (*b*) an elementary constituent of an atomic nucleus (*nonce-use*); **nuclear battery,** an electric battery that utilizes the separation of positive and negative charges accompanying radioactivity; **nuclear emulsion,** a fine-grained photographic emulsion specially designed for recording the tracks of sub-atomic particles in it; **nuclear force,** a force that acts between nucleons; now *spec.* the strong interaction; **nuclear fuel** = *FUEL *sb.* 2* d; so *nuclear-fuelled* adj.; **nuclear isomer** (see *ISOMER 2); **nuclear magnetic resonance,** magnetic resonance (see *RESONANCE) exhibited by atomic nuclei; **nuclear magneton** (see *MAGNETON); **nuclear medicine,** the branch of medicine concerned with the use of radioactive substances in research, diagnosis, and treatment; **nuclear pile** = **nuclear reactor* (see also *PILE *sb.*[3]); **nuclear reactor,** an apparatus or structure in which fissile material can be made to undergo a controlled, self-sustaining nuclear reaction with the consequent release of energy; **nuclear sap** *Biol.* (see *SAP *sb.*[1]). Also *NUCLEAR FISSION, *NUCLEAR FUSION.

1922 A. D. UDDEN tr. *Bohr's Theory of Spectra* III. i. 61 The conception of atomic structure which will form the basis of all the following remarks is the so-called nuclear atom according to which an atom is assumed to consist of a nucleus surrounded by a number of electrons whose distances from one another and from the nucleus are very large compared to the dimensions of the particles themselves. **1936** *Discovery* Jan. 31/1 The quantum mechanical theory of the nuclear atom. **1938** Nuclear atom [see *ALPHA 3 e]. **1961** POWELL & CRASEMANN *Quantum Mech.* i. 14 A nuclear atom had already been considered mathematically by Nagaoka in 1904, but it was Rutherford's analysis that established this concept as an experimental fact. **1970** G. K. WOODGATE *Elem. Atomic Struct.* i. 1 Bohr's theory of hydrogen, based on Rutherford's nuclear atom and incorporating the ideas of Planck, was the famous starting point for atomic structure. **1955** *Jrnl. Brit. Interplanetary Soc.* XIV. 85 The nuclear battery, thermo-couples, photo-electric effects, etc., present further possibilities. **1962** SIMPSON & RICHARDS *Physical Princ. Junction Transistors* iv. 74 'Nuclear batteries' in which the radiation consists of fast electrons from a β-emitter have also been built. **1949** H. YAGODA *Radioactive Measurements with Nucl. Emulsions* i. 6 These emulsions, intended for the registration of alpha-particle, proton, and fission-fragment tracks, are conveniently referred to as Nuclear Emulsions. **1958** K. M. HORNSBY tr. *Glafkides' Photogr. Chem.* I. xxiii. 409 Nuclear emulsions..have a very high concentration of silver bromide (80%), fine grain (0·1 to 0·5 μ), and are coated in very thick layers. **1966** *McGraw-Hill Encycl. Sci. & Technol.* IX. 584/2 Nuclear emulsion plates are important particle detectors for research in high-energy nuclear physics. **1935** *Sci. Abstr.* A. XXXIII. 2 (*heading*) Constitution of elementary particles and nuclear forces. **1955** FRIEDMAN & WEISSKOPF in W. Pauli *Niels Bohr* 144 Our present difficulties in understanding the saturation of nuclear forces on the basis of the free nucleon–nucleon interaction speak in favour of some change in the internucleon potential when the nucleons are closely packed. **1972** *Sci. Amer.* Oct. 100/2 Although the nuclear force acts between all nucleons, whether they are protons or neutrons, it must overcome the disruptive influence of the electrical repulsion between the positive charges of the protons in the nucleus. **1946** *Scientific & Techn. Aspects of Control of Atomic Energy* (U.N. Dept. Public Information) i. 8 The nuclear fuel provided by nature is uranium-235. **1948** Nuclear fuel [see *FUEL *sb.* 2* d]. **1970** *Daily Tel.* 4 Nov. 5 Russia is prepared to supply West Germany with enriched uranium as nuclear fuel for peaceful purposes. **1968** *Times* 18 Oct. 16/7 The element [*sc.* gadolinium] can be used in the design of nuclear-fuelled batteries. **1942** *Physica* IX. 591 (*heading*) Negative result of an attempt to observe nuclear magnetic resonance in solids. **1970** G. K. WOODGATE *Elem. Atomic Struct.* ix. 174 Some of the most accurate values of nuclear moments have been obtained directly by nuclear magnetic resonance. **1952** (*periodical title*) The American journal of roentgenology, radium therapy and nuclear medicine. **1975** *Univ. of London Bull.* Feb. 5/2 This University stands alone in the United Kingdom in having supported since 1961, in one of its medical schools, an academic department devoted solely to nuclear medicine. **1955** *Gloss. Terms Radiology* (*B.S.I.*) 17 Nuclear pile. **1962** F. I. ORDWAY et al. *Basic Astronautics* xii. 497 The effects in general would be the same as those experienced by victims of an atomic bomb blast or an accident in a nuclear pile. **1964** M. GOWING *Britain & Atomic Energy* x. 284 Now the doctors..also appreciated the great usefulness of nuclear piles for medical and biological purposes. **1945** *Sci. Amer.* Nov. 285/3 The radiation emitted by present nuclear reactors requires..heavy shielding. **1948** *Electronic Engin.* XX. 148 An atomic pile, or nuclear reactor, consists usually of an assembly of uranium metal in a pile of graphite. **1955** *Times* 16 July 6/4 The first atomic stations of the Central Electricity Authority will have two nuclear reactors each, together providing a net output of electricity of 100 to 200 megawatts. **1966** J. BETJEMAN *High & Low* 31 No nuclear reactors Bulge hideous on the downs.

B. *ellipt.* as *sb.* **a.** A nuclear weapon. Also *Comb.*, as *nuclear-armed*, *-free*, *-tipped* adjs.

1957 *Time* 15 Apr. 29/1 The British decision to convert almost completely to nuclear-armed missiles had deep meaning for all of the world. **1958** *New Statesman* 5 Apr. 423/1 The SPD are demanding in effect no nuclear weapons for the Bundeswehr, none for foreign troops stationed on German territory, and a nuclear-free zone in central Europe. **1959** *Economist* 14 Feb. 615/2 A nuclear-tipped anti-aircraft missile. **1962** *Listener* 29 Mar. 541/2 What difference does the presence of nuclear weapons make to the strategy and tactics of conventional war?.. What is it that prevents either side from going to nuclears on the battlefield? **1964** *Ann. Reg. 1963* 73 The A.L.P. supported moves to establish a 'nuclear-free zone'. **1964** *Economist* 7 Mar. 892/1 Armed with nuclear-tipped missiles. **1972** *Daily Tel.* 2 May 16 The current Nato strategy is one of flexible response, implying that both sides will seek to put off firing nuclears until the last possible moment. **1975** *Nature* 27 Mar. 281/2 It is widely believed that the CIA failed to retrieve the two chief items it wanted—the nuclear-tipped missiles and code machines.

b. A nuclear-powered submarine.

1969 *New Scientist* 28 Aug. 420/2 One can imagine an enemy submarine lying in wait..to pick up the trail of one of our patrolling 'nuclears'. **1974** 'M. HEBDEN' *Pride of Dolphins* I. v. 50 'Would you say Nanjizel was a good submariner?' 'He'd done his stint in nuclears.'

nuclear fission. [f. NUCLEAR *a.* + FISSION.] **1.** *Biol.* The division of a cell nucleus (cf. FISSION 2).

1889 *Jrnl. R. Microsc. Soc.* 728 (*heading*) Phenomena of indirect nuclear fission in inverting epithelia. **1960** L. PICKEN *Organization of Cells* vii. 295 The formation of a secondary [myotube] is prepared by nuclear fission, leading to the formation of a second linear series of nuclei.

2. *Nuclear Sci.* = *FISSION 4.

1939 *Physical Rev.* LV. 418/2 As pointed out by Meitner and Frisch, the recent discovery..of the appearance of a radioactive barium isotope as the product of such transmutations offers evidence of a new type of nuclear reaction in which the nucleus divides into two nuclei of smaller charges and masses with release of an energy of more than a hundred million electron volts. The direct proof of the occurrence of this so-called nuclear fission was given by Frisch. **1945** H. D. SMYTH *Gen. Acct. Devel. Atomic Energy Mil. Purposes* i. 1 Such a conversion is observed in the phenomenon of nuclear fission of uranium. **1958** J. BETJEMAN *Coll. Poems* 230 Where Hodge sits down beside his wife And talks of Marx and nuclear fission With all a rustic's intuition. **1958** *Listener* 19 June 1005/1 Reactors operating by nuclear fission. **1971** *Sci. Amer.* June 24/3 Nuclear-fusion fuels such as deuterium and tritium liberate more energy per nucleon (neutron or proton) than nuclear-fission fuels. Unfortunately these hydrogen isotopes only burn efficiently at high temperature.

nuclear fusion. [f. NUCLEAR *a.* + FUSION.] **1.** *Biol.* The fusion of cell nuclei.

1900 *Jrnl. R. Microsc. Soc.* 73 The generation in which the nuclear fusion occurs is probably in all cases degenerate. **1970** *Protoplasma* LXX. 292 Once the outer cell surfaces have joined and two nuclei are in a common cytoplasm, nuclear fusion nearly always seems to follow.

2. *Nuclear Sci.* = *FUSION 3 d.

1952 [see *FUSION 3 d]. **1959** *Ann. Reg. 1958* 137 The Secretary-General expressed the hope that progress would be made on..the potentiality of nuclear fusion to solve the world's energy problems. **1969** *New Scientist* 25 Sept. 640/1 The Tokamak machines..have formed the basis of the main Soviet research effort into achieving controlled nuclear fusion during the past few years. **1971** [see *NUCLEAR FISSION 2].

nuclearist (niū·klĭărist). [f. *NUCLEAR *a.* 3 + -IST.] One who advocates the possession or use of nuclear weapons; a nation that possesses nuclear weapons. (See also quot. 1952.) So **nu·clearism** (see quot. 1970[1]).

1952 *Time* 26 May 73 In Venice last week, 13 Italian painters who call themselves 'spatialists' and 'nuclearists' gave their answer with an exhibit 'inspired by the atomic bomb'. The canvases were almost as explosive as the bomb itself: furious fireballs of bright colors and bold contrasts. **1962** *Times Lit. Suppl.* 7 Dec. 948/3 In the great debate on nuclear disarmament..the advantages of sober logic and clear thought have usually lain with the anti-unilateralists, sometimes called the nuclearists. **1964** *Listener* 6 Feb. 220/2 The inclusion of a number of uncommitted countries..has..made of the Commonwealth a useful bridge,..a witness that even neutralists and a nuclearist can work closely together. **1969** *Bull. Atomic Sci.* June 39/2 The weapons..become grotesque technological deities for a debased religion of nuclearism. **1970** *Atlantic Monthly* Oct. 106 The most extreme state of contemporary deformation is..'nuclearism'. By this term I mean to suggest the passionate embrace of nuclear weapons as a solution to our anxieties..and as a means of restoring a lost sense of immortality. *Ibid.*, This deity is seen as an all-powerful force,..and the nuclear believer, or nuclearist, allies himself to that force.

nuclearize (niū·klĭărəiz), *v.* [f. *NUCLEAR *a.* 3 + -IZE.] **1.** *trans.* To supply or equip (a nation) with nuclear weapons. So **nu·cleariza·tion.**

1960 *New Left Rev.* Nov.–Dec. 4/1 A generalised discontent with the prospects of a nuclearised Germany. *Ibid.* 8/1 The NEC is against the nuclearisation of West Germany. **1967** *Times* 20 Jan. 11/7 The difficulty of predicting the resolution of crises in advance, from the blockade of Berlin to the nuclearization of Cuba.

2. To render (a family, etc.) nuclear in character (see *NUCLEAR *a.* 1 e). *rare.*

1972 P. LASLETT *Household & Family in Past Time* 55 The extent to which the domestic group has been 'nuclearised', that is, has lost extension and multiplicity.

nuclearly (niū·klĭărli), *adv.* [f. NUCLEAR *a.* + -LY[2].] In a nuclear manner (in quot. 1959, with nuclear weapons).

1959 *Listener* 17 Dec. 1062/1 The conventional forces, whether or not nuclearly armed, should be..reduced in the Soviet Union. **1966** J. E. BUSE in C. E. Bazell *In Memory of J. R. Firth* 56 Statives..also occur nuclearly in the verbal phrase.

nuclease (niū·klĭĕiz, -s). *Biochem.* [a. G. *nuclease*, f. *nucl-* (in *nucleoproteïd* nucleoprotein): see *-ASE.]

The Ger. word was coined by Emmerich and Löw 1899, in *Zeitschr. für Hygiene* XXXI. 10, but in a different sense (see quot. 1902); the present meaning originated with L. Iwanoff 1903, in *Zeitschr. für physiol. Chem.* XXXIX. 43.]

Any enzyme that catalyses the hydrolysis of polynucleotides or oligonucleotides into smaller units.

1902 VAUGHAN & NOVY *Cellular Toxins* (ed. 4) ix. 175 It is proposed that bacteriolytic enzymes be given the general name of nucleases, because they digest the nucleoproteids of the bacterial cells. *Ibid.*, In their second paper Emmerich and Löw detail the methods which they have employed in the preparation of their nucleases and immuneproteids. **1903** *Jrnl. Chem. Soc.* LXXXIV. II. 679 Various fungi..decompose nucleic acid with the liberation of phosphoric acid and purine bases; this appears to be a ferment action... The name *nuclease* is suggested for the enzyme responsible for the action. **1911** *Jrnl. Biol. Chem.* IX. 129 The term nuclease is usually understood to designate a ferment..through whose agency nucleic acid is decomposed with the liberation of purine bases. **1949** H. W. FLOREY et al. *Antibiotics* I. i. 20 The active material was supposed to be an enzyme—it was even stated to be a nuclease. **1954** A. WHITE et al. *Princ. Biochem.* xx. 582 The intestinal mucosa is also believed to form nucleases which aid in the digestion of the high unilateral weight nucleic acids and polynucleotides. **1970** R. W. McGILVERY *Biochem.* xx. 481 The effect of the lysosomal nucleases is to cleave the molecule [of nucleic acid] into smaller polynucleotide fragments, with the liberation of only a few free nucleotides.

nucleate, *a.* Add: (Examples.)

1962 R. P. LEVINE *Genetics* ix. 115 Gene recombination among the sexually reproducing nucleate organisms can occur as a result of both independent assortment and crossing over. **1972** *Nature* 28 Jan. 211/2 Cultures..of nucleate and enucleate sea urchin egg halves.

b. Applied to a kind of boiling process in which streams of bubbles rise from specific sites on a hot surface in the liquid and are recondensed in the surrounding liquid.

1938 *Trans. Amer. Inst. Chem. Engin.* XXXIII. 449 'Nucleate boiling' is what is ordinarily seen when a pan of water boils upon a stove. **1948** *Trans. Amer. Soc. Mech. Engin.* LXX. 372/1 The boiling was nucleate in the sense that the bubbles originated at favored spots on the metal surface. **1975** *Nature* 27 Mar. 322/2 This [*sc.* pulsation boiling] then progressively changes to nucleate boiling from the front of the sphere to the back.

nucleate, *v.* Add: **1. b.** To form nuclei in; to act as or provide a nucleus for.

1952 *Industr. & Engin. Chem.* June 1273/2 Such fluctuations [in local density] are occurring continuously but it is only under very special, almost critical, conditions that they become of sufficient magnitude to nucleate the phase for a transition to a more stable state. **1961** J. W. MULLIN *Crystallization* v. 109 Ethyl acetanilide can nucleate methyl acetanilide. **1969** D. K. ALLEN *Metall.* vii. 179 (*caption*) Bainite is nucleated by a ferrite crystal. **1972** *Physics Bull.* Nov. 656/1 They do predict static fatigue (since for example the probability of nucleating a crack of critical size increases with time). **1973** *Nature* 23 Nov. 212/2 Freezing nuclei are defined as particles capable of nucleating ice in supercooled water.

2. Add after 'nucleus' in both parts of def.: or nuclei. (Further examples.)

1959 *Engineering* 30 Jan. 152/2 Many of the domains appeared to 'nucleate' at crystalline imperfections. **1961** J. W. MULLIN *Crystallization* v. 104 A saturated solution cannot nucleate spontaneously. **1969** P. G. SHEWMON *Transform. in Metals* vi. 210 If ferrite containing virtually no carbon..is to nucleate in a given region of austenite containing much more carbon, several changes must occur. **1974** *Sci. Amer.* Dec. 94/2 Inclusions can nucleate, multiply and grow dendritically just as the primary metallic phase does.

nucleating *ppl. a.* (further examples); also as *vbl. sb.*

1948 *Jrnl. Colloid Sci.* III. 569 The rate of nucleation in the water drops on the metal plate is much larger than that in the water drops in a cloud, probably because of the nucleating effect of the surface of the plate and chance impurities. **1961** *New Scientist* 28 Sept. 813/1 Nucleation is associated with the similarity in spacing between the lattices of the ice crystal and of the nucleating substance. **1969** G. F. BOLLING in *Solidification* (Amer. Soc. Metals) (1971) xi. 364 (*heading*) Inoculating, nucleating and alloying. **1974** F. D. RICHARDSON *Physical Chem. of Melts in Metallurgy* II. xii. 459 Small unfilled crevices in containers can act as nucleating sites for the evolution of gases from metals at very small supersaturation pressures.

nucleate (niū·klĭĕit), *sb. Biochem.* [f. NUCLE(IC *a.* + -ATE[4].] Any salt of a nucleic acid.

1907 *Jrnl. Chem. Soc.* XCII. I. 266 In the estimation of purine bases, much smaller yields of guanine are obtained when the copper nucleate is hydrolysed instead of the free acid. **1952** *Jrnl. Biol. Chem.* CXCVIII. 85 They attributed this discrepancy to the formation of ion pairs between sodium ions and the phosphate residues of the nucleate.

nucleated, *a.* **2.** Add to def.: esp. of buildings in villages. (Further examples.)

1942 *Rep. Comm. Land Utilisation in Rural Areas* II in *Parl. Papers 1941–2* (Cmd. 6378) IV. 421 In other parts, especially where the community was organised under the feudal or manorial systems, nucleated settlements or villages are the rule. **1954** M. BERESFORD *Lost Villages* vii. 233 One such district is the plain of Lancashire. Here, at first blush, we might seem to have nothing but a countryside of compact, nucleated villages. **1970** N. CHADWICK *Celts* v. 125 Houses..were grouped together in small nucleated settlements. *Ibid.*, Most settlement sites, whether nucleated or individual, were enclosed.

nucleation. Delete *rare*[-1] and add to def.: esp. by the aggregation of molecules into a new phase within a medium. **b.** The formation of something, esp. a crystal, droplet, or bubble, on or into a nucleus.

1902 *Science* 31 Jan. 177/1 After nucleation the first dense fogs were vaguely annular during the first.. exhaustions. **1906** S. S. LAURIE *Synthetica* I. iii. 39 A nucleation or involution or articulation or specific determination of Universal Being whereby an independent centre of actuality is constituted *in rerum natura.* **1906** H. T. BARNES *Ice Formation* iv. 106 An appropriate term, nucleation, might be applied to the formation of ice-crystals throughout the volume of the water, on nuclei supplied by fine particles of sand. **1933** H. G. WELLS *Shape of Things to Come* II. §3. 147 What we now call social nucleation was failing; the grouping of human beings in families and working communities was not going on. *Ibid.* 158 This chaotic nucleation of human beings about gangs and organizations for frankly criminal purposes. **1947** DOAN & MAHLA *Princ. Physical Metallurgy* (ed. 2) vi. 224 In the transformation of a solid solution, such as austenite, the rate of nucleation is limited further by the rates of diffusion of the atoms forming the precipitate. **1950** *Engineering* 13 Jan. 36/2 If the gas concentration is fairly low and the nucleation of bubbles difficult. **1966** C. R. TOTTLE *Sci. Engin. Materials* vii. 167 In b.c.c. metals, some of which do show ductile failure, the nucleation of cavities occurs at piled-up dislocation sites. **1967** A. H. COTTRELL *Introd. Metallurgy* xii. 153 Many metallurgical processes occur by nucleation and growth, e.g. the formation of CO bubbles in a steelmaking bath. *Ibid.* 154 When the probability of forming a nucleus is the same everywhere, the system is in a state suitable for homogeneous nucleation.

nucleator (niū·klĭ̆ĕitəɹ). [f. NUCLEAT(E *v.* + -OR.] A substance which provides nuclei.

1903 *Nature* 3 Dec. 103/1 Phosphorus as a nucleator suddenly bursts forth into maximum activity at about 13°. **1961** *New Scientist* 28 Sept. 813/1 Steroids can act as effective ice nucleators. **1965** *Ibid.* 4 Nov. 341/1 Glass-crystalline materials that are made from special glassy compositions containing crystal nucleators.

nucleic, *a.* Add pronuncs. (niuk lĭ̆·ik, -ĕi·ik, niū·klĭ̯ik) and substitute for def. of *nucleic acid:* Any of the naturally occurring polynucleotides present in most cells (chiefly in the chromosomes and ribosomes), which either store genetic information or translate this into the structure of proteins; they fall into two distinct classes, deoxyribonucleic acid (DNA) and ribonucleic acid (RNA), each of which consists of long unbranched molecules of very high molecular weight and usu. occurs in combination with protein (nucleoprotein). [prob. tr. G. *nucleïnsäure* (R. Altmann 1889, in *Arch. für Anat. u. Physiol.* (*Physiol. Abth.*) 524).]

1892 *Jrnl. Chem. Soc.* LXII. 224 The preparation of nucleic acid from nucleïn by Altmann..gives a further means of distinguishing between the two groups. **1908** [see *glycoprotein* s.v. *GLYCO-]. **1942** *Endeavour* I. 104/1 Nucleic acid renders a further invaluable service—it makes the chromosomes visible. **1958** *Listener* 31 July 165/1 The advances of organic chemistry in the last 100 years, advances culminating in the nucleic acid story, lately so much discussed. **1960** L. PICKEN *Organization of Cells* iv. 126 The Watson and Crick helical model of nucleic acid suggests that accurate replication of a unique serial order of nucleotides might readily occur if the two helical chains could be partially uncoiled, so that each might serve as a mould for a new chain. **1972** *Sci. Amer.* June 41/3 The only other compounds that are as important in living systems are the nucleic acids, which are the repository of genetic information and direct the synthesis of proteins.

nucleo-. Add: **nu:cleo-cytopla·smic** *a.*, existing or taking place between the nucleus and the cytoplasm; relating the nucleus to the cytoplasm (with respect to some property); **nucleoge·nesis,** the formation of nuclei; *spec.* = *nucleosynthesis* below; **nucleohi·stone** (also formerly -hi·ston) *Biochem.*, a nucleoprotein in which the protein component is a histone; **nucleopro·tamine** *Biochem.*, any nucleoprotein in which the protein component is a protamine; † **nucleoproteid** *Biochem.* = *NUCLEOPROTEIN; **nucleosy·nthesis** *Astr.*, the cosmic formation of atoms more complicated than the hydrogen atom; hence **nucleosynthe·tic** *a.*

1905 *Publ. Carnegie Inst. Washington* No. 37. 66 In order that the nucleo-cytoplasmic equilibrium may be maintained, it [*sc.* the ascus] must be provided with an excess of nuclear material as compared with the other cells of the ascogenous hyphæ and the ascogonium. **1956** *Nature* 4 Feb. 236/2 The mean nucleo-cytoplasmic ratio was then measured by the method of Chalkley. **1968** H. HARRIS *Nucleus & Cytoplasm* p. vii, The object of this book..is to provide an introduction to some of the salient problems in the field of nucleo-cytoplasmic relationships. **1952** *Industr. & Engin. Chem.* June 1276/1 One of the more practical results of the theory of nucleogenesis is the explanation and the guidance..it has offered in preparing monodisperse colloids. **1955** *Nature* 16 July 130/2 If the assumptions..are valid,..all the radioactive elements with half-lives short compared to 4×10^8 yr. would have decayed in the time interval between nucleogenesis and the formation of the Earth. **1974** *Physics Bull.* Oct. 464/3 Nucleogenesis in stars. **1895** *Jrnl. Chem. Soc.* LXVIII. II. 52 The active agent in [blood] coagulation is regarded as a nucleo-albuminous substance, named nucleo-histon. **1914** *Chem. Abstr.* VIII. 714 There is no reason to assume that nucleohistones contain any other but the genuine nucleic acid. **1964** G. H. HAGGIS et al. *Introd. Molecular Biol.* ix. 236 Nucleic acids carry a large net negative charge, and the protein and nucleic acid components of nucleoprotamines and nucleohistones are held together largely by electrostatic forces. **1929** *Chem. Abstr.* XXIII. 4724 (*heading*) The behavior of nucleoprotamine and its components in animal metabolism. **1956** *Nature* 31 Mar. 603/1 The X-ray data indicate that the molecule [of DNA] has two grooves of unequal depths, and that in the nucleoprotamines the polypeptide chains lie inside these grooves. **1971** D. M. P. PHILLIPS *Histones & Nucleohistones* iii. 121 A conformation similar to the extended-chain form of protamine in nucleoprotamine could be present. **1886** *Jrnl. Chem. Soc.* L. 1051 The author [*sc.* E. Merck] calls 'nucleo-proteïds' substances which, when boiled with water under pressure or treated with acids, alkalis, or ferments, are resolved into nucleïn and albumin. **1894** Nucleoproteid [in Dict.]. **1914** M. DRUMMOND tr. *Haberlandt's Physiol. Plant Anat.* viii. 415 The reserve proteins include the various globulins, vitellins..and albumoses, also certain nucleoproteids. **1960** WASSERBURG, FOWLER, & HOYLE in *Physical Rev. Lett.* IV. 113/1 There is considerable uncertainty as to the exact time dependence of stellar evolution and nucleosynthesis in the Galaxy. **1960** FOWLER & HOYLE in *Ann. Physics* X. 281 Type I supernovae were considered to be the only events rapid enough for nucleosynthesis. [*Note*] We use the term *nucleosynthesis* rather than *nucleogenesis* for good reason. We refer..to the synthesis of the elements beyond hydrogen from..the proton, and the neutron... We reserve genesis for the creation of matter-energy. **1963** E. ANDERS in Middlehurst & Kuiper *Moon, Meteorites &*

Comets xiii. 458 A second model, involving continuous nucleosynthesis throughout the Galaxy, must be considered. **1965** *Ann. Rev. Astron. & Astrophysics* III. 227 Reynold's discovery was first interpreted as indicating a surprisingly short time-interval between the end of nucleosynthesis and the formation of the solar system. **1971** *Nature* 3 Sept. 39/2 It is now clear that while this effect is operating, a large amount of nucleosynthesis takes place early in the life of a galaxy. **1960** *Physical Rev. Lett.* IV. 113/1 The nucleosynthetic processes during which iodine was made were instantaneous. **1973** *Physics Bull.* Nov. 652/1 This high percentage of helium apparently could not have been produced by the kind of nucleosynthetic processes currently occurring in stars.

nucleoid, *a.* Add: (Further example.)

1889 *Jrnl. R. Microsc. Soc.* 429 (*heading*) Nucleus or nucleoid bodies of schizomycetes.

B. *sb.* † **a.** [a. G. *nucleoïd* (M. Lavdowsky 1893, in *Zeitschr. für wiss. Mikrosk.* X. 8).] (See quots.) *Obs.*

Arnold (*Virchows Arch. für path. Anat. u. Physiol.* (1896) CXLV. 22) took over the term from Lavdowsky.

1905 Gould *Dict. New Med. Terms* 383/2 *Nucleoid*, a term used by Arnold to designate the substance in the red corpuscles formed from the original nucleus. It is finely granular or fibrillar and is surrounded by a substance which Arnold calls paraplasm. **1913** O. C. Gruner *Biol. Blood-Cells* 361 *Nucleoid*. Syn.: *nuclear rests, inclusion-body.* (*a*) A precipitation effect of hæmoglobin; (*b*) if basic, a special appearance of the basophile cell membrane. **1928** E. B. Krumbhaar in E. V. Cowdry *Special Cytol.* I. x. 307 In addition to the several bodies just mentioned, various artefacts can be produced [in erythrocytes] by standing, poor fixation, non-isotonic solutions, etc., termed 'nucleoids'.

b. [a. G. *nucleoid* (coined independently in this sense by G. Piekarski 1937, in *Arch. für Mikrobiol.* VIII. 438).] An organelle in bacteria and viruses functionally analogous to the cell nucleus of higher organisms.

1938 *Biol. Abstr.* XII. 1407/2 The author's [*sc.* G. Piekarski's] studies seem to show that the nucleoids which he observed in bacteria and sarcina are equivalent to cell nuclei. **1965** *Bacteriol. Rev.* XXIX. 277/1 The genetic material in bacterial cells forms structures which are called nucleoids... Although from the very beginning there was no doubt that these structures are nuclei with respect to their function.., their simple architecture and morphological appearance, which distinguish them from the type of nucleus present in higher organisms..make a special term desirable. **1970** *Nature* 31 Oct. 410/2 The RNA dependent activity resides in the nucleoid. **1971** *Ibid.* 30 Apr. 568 (*caption*) Cell from culture of *B[acillus] subtilis*... Two chromosomes appear as tightly packed 'nucleoids'. **1972** *Sci. Amer.* Jan. 29/2 The virion of the Rous sarcoma virus consists of a lipid-containing envelope.., an inner membrane and a nucleoid, or core, that contains the viral RNA and certain proteins.

nucleoid, var. *nucloid.

nucleolar, *a.* Add: Also with pronunc. (niūkli,ōᵘ·lăr).

nucleolonema (niū:kliolonī·mă). *Cytology.* Pl. **-nemas, -nemata.** [a. Sp. *nucleolonema* (Estable & Sotelo 1951, in *Publicaciones Inst. de Invest. de Ciencias Biol.* I. 105), f. Nucleolo- + Gr. νῆμα thread.] (See quot. 1968.)

Quot. 1951 is from the authors' English translation of the summary of their Sp. paper.

[**1951** Estable & Sotelo in *Publicaciones Instituto de Investigación de Ciencias Biol.* I. 123 Every true.. nucleolus is made up of two different parts... The first one is always the most important, and on account of its filamentous structure we shall call it nucleoloneme. *Ibid.*, No cell having a nucleus lacks a nucleoloneme.] **1952** —— in *Stain Technol.* XXVII. 307 In a recent paper the authors have shown filamentous structures within the nucleolus of all cells. This structure was named the nucleolonema. **1955** *Jrnl. Biophysical & Biochem. Cytol.* I. 185 (*heading*) Note on nucleolonemata in human cultured cells. **1968** R. Rieger et al. *Gloss. Genetics & Cytogenetics* 316 As far as the ultrastructure of the n[ucleolus] is concerned, the early work was interpreted as indicating the presence of a coiled filament called the 'nucleolonema' (diameter 90–180 nm). Later this nucleolonema was found to consist of coarse granules of the size of ribosomes (diameter about 150 Å). **1973** *Jrnl. Invertebrate Path.* XXII. 405/2 The nucleolus was compact, without nucleolonema, and was completely surrounded by an electron-dense material, apparently chromatin.

nucleolus. Add: also with pronunc. (niūkli,ōᵘ·lǒs).

† **nucleon**¹ (niū·kliǫn). *Biochem. Obs.* [a. G. *nucleon* (M. Siegfried 1895, in *Ber. d. Deut. Chem. Ges.* XXVIII. 518), f. *nucle-ïn* (now *nuklein*) Nuclein + *pept-on* Peptone.] (See quots.)

1895 *Jrnl. Chem. Soc.* LXVIII. i. 314 The term *nucleon* is suggested for compounds, such as phosphorcarnic acid, which are allied to the nucleïns but contain peptone instead of albumin. **1905** W. H. Howell *Text-bk. Physiol.* ii. 60 The discoverer of nucleon has attributed to it a very great physiological importance, as a source of energy to the muscle, and as an efficient means of transportation of iron, calcium, [etc.]... It must be stated, however, that there still remains some doubt as to the chemical individuality of the nucleon or the nucleons. **1921** *Physiol. Abstr.* VI. 477 Nucleon is a mixture of which the chief constituent is denatured protein.

nucleon² (niū·kliǫn). *Nuclear Physics.* [f. Nucle(us *sb.* + *-on¹.] † **a.** = *proton 2. *Obs. rare.*

1923 D. Ll. Hammick tr. *Perrin's Atoms* (ed. 2) 223 If we represent the hydrogen nucleus or positive protoatom by *h* and the corpuscle or negative protoatom by *β* we may say that all matter is made up of protoatoms *h* and *β*... The negative protoatom may be called the corpuscle and the positive protoatom the nucleon. [*Note*] Suggested by P. Auger. *Proton* has also been proposed.

b. A proton or neutron; a sub-atomic particle of which these may be regarded as two distinct states, differing in the third component of isospin. [Orig. formed as *nuclon* (see quot. 1941).]

1939 F. J. Belinfante *Theory of Heavy Quanta* (Leiden Univ., thesis) 40 The interaction of the heavy quanta with the heavy particles (the proton-neutron, or 'nuclon', as we shall call it briefly). **1940** Pauli & Belinfante in *Physica* VII. 179 The particle that is a proton in its charged state and a neutron in its neutral state, we have called a nuclon. **1940** C. Møller in *Physical Rev.* LVIII. 1118/1 The strength of the couplings between the nuclons and the 'vector' and 'pseudoscalar' meson fields. [*Note*] Following the proposal of Belinfante..we use the word nuclon as a common name for the nuclear constituents, the protons and neutrons. **1941** —— in *Ibid.* LIX. 323/2 Following the original proposal of Belinfante, the writer has..used the word 'nuclon' as a common notation for..neutrons and protons. In the meantime, however, it has been pointed out to me that, since the root of the word nucleus is 'nucle', the notation 'nucleon' would from a philological point of view be more appropriate. **1952** *Sci. News* XXIII. 28 It seems that each nucleon (a general name for either proton or neutron) cannot interact with all the other particles in the nucleus, but only with its neighbours. **1968** M. S. Livingston *Particle Physics* v. 97 With both protons bombarding a high-Z target, to create a nucleon–antinucleon pair.., the threshold kinetic energy must be 5·4 GeV. **1971** *New Scientist* 17 June 695/2 The questions arise why cosmic-ray nucleons or X-rays or ultraviolet photons should be produced in the centres of Seyfert galaxies.

nucleonic (niūkliǫ·nik), *a.* [Partly f. prec. + -ic, partly a back-formation from next.] Of or pertaining to the nucleon or nucleonics.

1946 *Proc. Amer. Philos. Soc.* XC. 42/2 A second class of transformation..comprises the nucleonic changes which occur in the atmosphere under cosmic-ray bombardment. **1947** *Nucleonics* Sept. 1/1 Nucleonic physics..has come to be understood as the science of those changes in which there occurs a rearrangement, but no change, in the total number of nucleons present. Radioactivity, nuclear disintegration, nuclear fission, and nuclear synthesis are the processes comprehended by this science. **1947** *Electronics* Dec. 84/1 An important tool of nucleonic research is the mass spectrograph. **1955** J. A. Wheeler in W. Pauli *Niels Bohr* 163 Nuclear division calls forth a uniquely drastic kind of nucleonic re-arrangement. **1957** *Financial Times Ann. Rev. Brit. Industry* 35/5 Industrial applications..developed in conjunction with the nucleonic instrument manufacturers. **1974** *Physics Bull.* Dec. 579/3 We have been aware for many years of the inadequacy of the neutrons and protons only approach for the simplest systems because there we have had good enough nucleonic wavefunctions to show up the deficiency of the nucleons only approach.

nucleonics (niūkliǫ·niks), *sb. pl.* (const. as *sing.*). [Blend of *nucleon² + *electronics.] The branch of science and technology concerned with nucleons and the atomic nucleus, esp. with the practical applications of nuclear phenomena and associated techniques.

1945 *Nature* 10 Nov. 549/1 If science is to be controlled on a national level, the Association [of Oak Ridge Scientists] believes that the inevitable armament competition will prevent science, especially 'nucleonics', from ever being free again. **1946** Z. Jeffries in *Chem. & Engin. News* 25 Jan. 186 'Nucleonics' is the generic name used to some extent within the Atomic Energy Project during the war and its use is now gaining in popularity... Since released atomic energy and certain other phenomena [are] derived from the nuclei of atoms and thus from the nucleons, it seems appropriate that the generic name should be 'nucleonics'. **1950** Glasstone *Sourcebk. Atomic Energy* iv. 94 The use of the word 'nucleonics'.. was proposed by Z. Jeffries in July 1944. **1952** *Electronic Engin.* XXIV. 533 The newer science of nucleonics is gradually leaving the nuclear physics research laboratory and finding applications aimed at producing greater productivity of our industrial processes. **1955** J. A. Wheeler in W. Pauli *Niels Bohr* 164 Looking back, one sees in nucleonics as in so many other parts of physics how much progress can be made on the basis of simple principles. **1959** *Times* 2 Jan. 2 Developments will range from high voltage transmission systems to nucleonics and computer design. **1966** *New Scientist* 15 Dec. 623/1 Nucleonics—Soldering in place the printed circuit of a geiger counter kit, designed to patent specification of the UK Atomic Energy Authority.

nucleophile (niū·kliŏfəil). *Chem.* [f. Nucleo- + -phile.] A nucleophilic reagent.

1953 C. K. Ingold *Struct. & Mech. Org. Chem.* v. 201 All bases are nucleophiles. **1959** Cram & Hammond *Org. Chem.* xvii. 395 Nucleophiles such as RS^-, which owe much of their reactivity to high polarizability, tend to bring about substitution rather than elimination. **1971** *Nature* 5 Nov. 42/1 Any agent which..can therefore react with nucleophiles in the cell, is a potential carcinogen.

nucleophilic (niūkliŏfi·lik), *a. Chem.* [f. Nucleo- + *-philic.] **a.** Having an affinity for atomic nuclei, and so reacting at an electron-deficient bond or atom in a substrate; anionoid.

1933 C. K. Ingold in *Jrnl. Chem. Soc.* 1121 The terms *electrophilic* (electron-seeking) and *nucleophilic* (nucleus-seeking) are suggested in place of the adjectives anionoid and cationoid introduced by Lapworth. **1946** *Nature* 20 July 94/1 Those bimolecular and unimolecular substitutions in which a nucleophilic reagent displaces halogen as halide ion from an alkyl halide. **1968** R. O. C. Norman *Princ. Org. Synthesis* iv. 127 A thiol anion, RS^-, although less basic than its oxygen analogue, RO^-, is more strongly nucleophilic.

b. Of a reaction: brought about by a nucleophilic reagent.

1935 Hughes & Ingold in *Jrnl. Chem. Soc.* 245 According as this [*sc.* the substituting agent] is nucleophilic..or electrophilic.., the reaction may be termed a 'nucleophilic' or 'electrophilic' substitution. **1946** *Nature* 20 July 94/1 That the polar effect is not absent in general from bimolecular nucleophilic substitutions is consistent with the result of exchanging the electron-releasing methyl substituents for electron-attracting groups. **1969** T. C. Thorstensen *Pract. Leather Technol.* vi. 91 Windus and Showell have reported the explanation of mechanism of unhairing as a nucleophilic displacement.

Hence **nucleophi·lically** *adv.*, after the manner of a nucleophile; **nu:cleophili·city,** nucleophilic character.

1953 C. K. Ingold *Struct. & Mech. Org. Chem.* v. 201 Basicity..is a special manifestation of nucleophilic character, or nucleophilicity, that is, affinity for atomic nuclei in general. **1970** J. E. Gearin in A. Burger *Medicinal Chem.* (ed. 3) II. xlvii. 1302/2 This group must be capable of attacking nucleophilically the carbon atom of the ester group of acetylcholine. **1971** C. J. Gray *Enzyme-catalysed Reactions* i. 21 The nucleophilicity of the small fluoride ion is higher in non-hydroxyl solvents where the solvation is less effective.

nucleoprotein (niūkliŏprōᵘ·tīn). *Biochem.* [a. G. *nucleoproteïn* (E. Merck 1885, in *Patentschrift 35,724*), which was formerly rendered in Eng. as *nucleoproteid* (s.v. *nucleo-): see Protein.] A combination of a protein and a nucleic acid such as occurs in living organisms.

1907 *Practitioner* Oct. 588 From the nuclein and nucleoprotein, the purin bodies, are produced, such as hypoxanthin, xanthin, adenin, and uric acid. **1938** *Ann. Reg. 1937* 352 Tobacco mosaic virus is a nucleoprotein of special character. **1944** *Adv. Protein Chem.* I. 258 The simplest and perhaps best available definition of a nucleoprotein would be to designate as such any protein with which nucleic acid is associated. **1959** *Times* 12 June 15/6 Both genes..and viruses are nucleo-proteins. **1970** *Sci. Amer.* Feb. 102 The constituents of the chromosomes—deoxyribonucleic acid (DNA) and nucleoproteins—do not absorb visible light readily.

nucleoside (niū·kliŏsəid). *Biochem.* [ad. G. *nucleosid* (Levene & Jacobs 1909, in *Ber. d. Deut. Chem. Ges.* XLII. 2475), f. after *glucosid* Glucoside: see Nucleo-.] Any compound in which a sugar (usu. ribose or deoxyribose) is linked glycosidically to a purine or pyrimidine base; *spec.* such a compound derived from a nucleic acid by hydrolysis. (See quot. 1973.)

1911 [see *nucleotide]. **1911** [see *adenosine]. **1931** Levene & Bass *Nucleic Acids* vi. 126 The name 'nucleoside' was assigned to the substances of this group for the reason that..they contain sugar in a glucosidic union, and..the substances linked to the sugars are nuclein bases. **1946** *Nature* 24 Aug. 275/2 Miss Mejbaum has found.. that the pentose contained in pyrimidine nucleotides (uridylic acid and cydidylic [*read* cytidylic] acid) and nucleosides (uridine) are not determined by her method. **1969** *New Scientist* 10 July 65/2 A nucleoside like adenosine or inosine. **1973** [see *nucleotide].

Hence **nu·cleosidase** [*-ase], any enzyme which catalyses the hydrolysis of a nucleoside into its constituent base and sugar, or the reaction between a nucleoside and phosphate to yield a base and a sugar phosphate.

1911 Levene & Medigreceanu in *Jrnl. Biol. Chem.* IX. 396 Under the influence of mineral acids nucleosides are readily hydrolyzed into their components. The same cleavage can be brought about by the action of enzymes present in the plasma of most of the organs tested in that direction... Since this reaction is brought about by an enzyme different from the other nucleolytic enzymes, it may be proper to refer to it under the name of *Nucleosidase.* **1935** *Biochem. Jrnl.* XXIX. 1100 If adenine nucleosidase is present it must therefore be only in relatively small amounts. **1955** Chargaff & Davidson *Nucleic Acids* I. xv. 600 The enzymic cleavage of *N*-glycoside bonds of nucleic acid derivatives was first observed in nucleosides, and the term 'nucleosidases'..is still used. In the current literature this name tends to be replaced by the designations 'nucleoside phosphorylases' and 'nucleoside hydrolases'.

nucleotide (niū·kliŏtəid). *Biochem.* [ad. G. *nucleotid* (Levene & Mandel 1908, in *Ber. d. Deut. Chem. Ges.* XLI. 1907): see Nucleo- and

*-IDE.] Any compound in which a phosphate group is linked to the sugar of a nucleoside; *spec.* any of the compounds of this type obtained by the partial hydrolysis of a nucleic acid, which are the individual monomers of which such acids are composed. (See quot. 1973.)

1908 *Jrnl. Chem. Soc.* XCIV. I. 587 It is suggested that the nucleic acids are composed of simpler complexes, the nucleotides, each formed of phosphoric acid, a carbohydrate, and a base. **1911** *Jrnl. Biol. Chem.* IX. 66 It was demonstrated that the molecule of the complex nucleic acids is composed of nucleotides and these of phosphoric acid, carbohydrate and base linked to one another in the order here given... It is possible to detach from the complex either phosphoric acid alone, giving rise to a nucleoside, or a complex of carbohydrate and base. **1937** *Nature* 30 Oct. 745/2 The co-ferments now described as phosphopyridine nucleotides, the nature of which has been at last worked out. **1952** *Sci. News* XXIV. 33 The complete nucleic acid molecules are generally considered as being built up of nucleotides, linked through the hydroxyl (OH) groups of the sugar and the acid groups of the phosphoric acid. **1957** *Times* 1 Nov. 10/3 The award to Sir Alexander Todd..of the Nobel prize for chemistry ..for his work on nucleotides and nucleotide enzymes. **1968** *Observer* (Colour Suppl.) 10 Mar. 15/1 The DNA molecule..is a two-stranded helix. Each strand is built up of smaller molecules called nucleotides. *Ibid.* 15/2 There are only four kinds of nucleotide, each with a different chemical base. These bases are adenine, thymine, guanine and cytosine. **1971** J. Z. YOUNG *Introd. Study Man* iii. 47 The symbols of the genetic code..are the nucleotides arranged in the helical DNA molecules. **1973** HENDERSON & PATERSON *Nucleotide Metabolism* p. xiv, The terms 'nucleoside' and 'nucleotide' in the strictest sense refer to N-glycosides and phosphorylated N-glycosides, respectively, derived from nucleic acids. The term is now used, however, in several broader ways. Thus, adenosine triphosphate (ATP) is not derived from nucleic acids, but is quite legitimately a nucleotide through its relation to adenosine monophosphate (AMP), which is so derived. Other N-ribosides, such as nicotinamide mononucleotide (NMN), are called nucleotides only by extension and analogy, and nicotinamide-adenine dinucleotide (NAD^+), nicotinamide-adenine dinucleotide phosphate ($NADP^+$), etc., are called dinucleotides only by a similar process. Flavin mononucleotide (FMN) is a step still further removed, as it contains ribitol instead of ribose, and flavin-adenine dinucleotide similarly extends the meaning of dinucleotide. N-glycosides such as orotidylate (OMP) and adenylosuccinate are called nucleotides through their close relationship to the 'true' nucleotides. *Ibid.* i. 10 In animal cells, a few nucleotides with sugars other than ribose and deoxyribose are known.

Hence **nu·cleotidase** [*-ASE], any enzyme which catalyses the hydrolysis of a nucleotide to a nucleoside and phosphate.

1911 LEVENE & MEDIGRECEANU in *Jrnl. Biol. Chem.* IX. 395 The enzymes performing this cleavage [of nucleotides to phosphoric acid and carbohydrate-base complex] may be referred to as Nucleotidases. **1932** *Jrnl. Biol. Chem.* XCVI. 462 The optimal activity of the nucleotidase is at a pH > 11. **1970** R. W. MCGILVERY *Biochem.* xx. 481 The phosphate group of nucleotides is liberated by hydrolysis, catalyzed by nucleotidases.

nucleus, *sb.* Add: **I. 1. b.** *Astr.* A more condensed, usu. brighter, central part of a galaxy or nebula.

1784 W. HERSCHEL in *Phil. Trans. R. Soc.* LXXIV. 442, I have seen double and treble nebulæ, variously arranged; large ones with small, seeming attendants;.. others of the cometic shape, with a seeming nucleus in the center. **1849** J. F. W. HERSCHEL *Outlines Astron.* xvii. 601 The nebula in Andromeda is visible to the naked eye... Mr. G. P. Bond, assistant at the observatory of Cambridge, U.S., describes and figures it as..very suddenly condensed at the nucleus almost to the semblance of a star. **1898** A. M. CLERKE et al. *Concise Knowledge Astron.* IV. vi. 534 The photograph shows both nuclei of the nebula to be stellar. **1955** *Sci. Amer.* May 48/3 Because of heavy dust clouds this nucleus [of the Milky Way] has not been observed visually or photographically; it was discovered by radio astronomy. **1970** *Sci. Jrnl.* Feb. 61/1 The emission line spectrum of a Seyfert nucleus is rather like that from typical hot clouds of gas such as the Orion Nebula.

3. b. (Further *attrib.* examples.)

1905 *Fortn. Rev.* 2 Jan. 15 The officers and men withdrawn..from distant squadrons will be utilised as nucleus crews in the Reserve ships. **1914** C. F. TWENEY *Dict. Naval & Mil. Terms* 163 *Nucleus crew*, the essential members of a ship's crew, such as petty officers, gunners, etc., the crew being raised to full strength in case of mobilisation. **1926** in Fowler *Mod. Eng. Usage* 713/2 Ships with nucleus crews were not so efficient as ships fully manned. **1965** M. MORSE *Unattached* i. 57 The mood of each rehearsal..depended very much on the attitude of the nucleus group.

II. 6. c. Substitute for def.: Any discrete mass of grey matter in the central nervous system. (Earlier and later examples.)

The term is used in numerous English and mod.L. combs. distinguishing the various different nuclei.

1828 J. QUAIN *Elem. Anat.* x. 622 If a vertical section be made of one of the lobes of the cerebellum, in such a way as that two-thirds of its breadth shall lie external to the incision, an oval nucleus of grey substance (*corpus dentatum*, vel *rhomboideum*) will be exposed. **1856** *Ibid.* (ed. 6) II. 493 Another division passes directly up, its fibres embracing the olivary nucleus. **1875** *Encycl. Brit.* I. 878/1 The upper mass of grey matter projects into the lateral ventricle, and is called the intra-ventricular portion or nucleus caudatus. **1899** [see *HYPOTHALAMUS]. **1968** PASSMORE & ROBSON *Compan. Med. Stud.* I. xix. 12/1 Masses of grey matter are called nuclei, some of which, e.g. the basal nuclei, are large and embedded in the depths of the brain. **1972** *Sci. Amer.* Dec. 73/1 A sensory pathway consists of peripheral sense organs and several clusters of nerve cells called nuclei. Sensory information is processed in several stages, so that each nucleus receives input from the preceding one, processes the input and sends an output to the next nucleus.

7. *Biol.* A cell organelle present in most of the cells of all organisms except the most primitive, usu. as a single subspherical structure, and consisting (except when undergoing division) of a membrane enclosing a ground substance (the nuclear sap) in which lie the chromosomes, one or more nucleoli, etc., and functioning as the repository of genetic information and as the director of metabolic and synthetic activity of the cell. Hence, by extension, applied by some writers to an organelle in some of the more primitive organisms, esp. bacteria, which is analogous in function but structurally simpler (cf. *NUCLEOID *a.* B. b).

The definition is intended to embrace and replace those of senses 5 d and 6 a. The distinction implied in the Dict. between the nuclei of plant and animal cells was artificial and modern knowledge has confirmed their essential similarity.

1831, etc. [in Dict., senses 5 d and 6 a]. **1889** [see *NUCLEOID *a.*]. **1962** *Brit. Med. Bull.* XVIII. 31/1 (*heading*) Morphology of the bacterial nucleus. **1965** [see *NUCLEOID *sb.* b]. **1968** PASSMORE & ROBSON *Compan. Med. Stud.* I. xxvi. 2/1 The mature red [blood] cell..appears as a biconcave disc with no nucleus. **1970** AMBROSE & EASTY *Cell Biol.* v. 163 This may also explain how acridine dyes penetrate the nucleus without staining the cytoplasm.

8. *Chem.* An arrangement of atoms, esp. a ring structure, characteristic of a number of organic compounds.

1845 W. GREGORY *Outl. Chem.: Org. Chem.* 512 Laurent considers benzole as in some measure the fundamental compound, or nucleus, and calls it phene. **1886** E. F. SMITH tr. *V. von Richter's Chem. Carbon Compounds* 465 The azo-group, N=N, decomposes, each nitrogen atom remaining attached as NH_2 to a benzene nucleus. **1932** *Jrnl. Chem. Soc.* 1132 Table III summarises the effect of varying the nature of the side-chain halogen in the compounds with an unsubstituted phenyl nucleus. **1951** I. L. FINAR *Org. Chem.* x. 185 If *one* acetic acid nucleus is blocked off, the fragment required is ethyl chloroacetate. **1971** *Nature* 7 May 25/1 Many psychotomimetic substances possess an indole nucleus.

9. A particle on which crystals, droplets, or bubbles can form in a fluid.

1857 [in Dict., sense 3 a]. **1886** *Proc. R. Soc. Edin.* XIII. 79 If this were the case, no nucleus would be *absolutely* requisite for the formation either of liquid from vapour or of vapour from liquid. **1906** [see *NUCLEATION]. **1939** *Q. Jrnl. R. Meteorol. Soc.* LXV. 411 If supersaturation is attained the fogs may thicken considerably owing to the deposition of water on the sea-salt nuclei. **1952** *Industr. & Engin. Chem.* June 1273/1 A nucleus in water-fog formation consists of about 80 water molecules. **1957** G. E. HUTCHINSON *Treat. Limnol.* I. ix. 583 In a free volume of water containing no minute masses of gas that can act as nuclei, an enormous excess tension is needed for bubble formation. **1967** [see *NUCLEATION].

10. A small group of bees, including a queen, used as the foundation of a new colony.

1886 F. R. CHESHIRE *Bees & Bee-Keeping* II. vii. 306 These small nuclei will sustain themselves, in average seasons. **1915** E. F. PHILLIPS *Beekeeping* iii. 39 A mere handful of bees (perhaps 200) may constitute a small colony (usually called a nucleus). **1952** H. MACE *Bee-Keeper's Handbk.* xxxiii. 154 Nucleus hives can be purchased or made, either to hold a single nucleus up to four combs, or two or more separate nuclei, separated by partitions. **1963** F. G. SMITH *Beekeeping* vii. 60 A nucleus is a very small colony of bees. It consists of a queen and up to four or six frames of brood and food, well covered with bees.

11. *Physics.* The positively charged central constituent of the atom, comprising nearly all its mass but occupying only a very small part of its volume and now known to be composed of protons and neutrons.

In Rutherford's 1911 paper called merely a 'central charge'. In the examples in the first paragraph *nucleus* is used for various speculative notions concerning the atom.

[**1844** FARADAY in *Phil. Mag.* XXIV. 141 If, in the ordinary view of atoms, we call the particle of matter away from the powers *a*, and the system of powers or forces in and around it *m*, then in Boscovitch's theory *a* disappears, or is a mere mathematical point... To my mind..the *a* or nucleus vanishes, and the substance consists of the powers or *m*. **1851** W. J. M. RANKINE in *Phil. Mag.* I. 443 The fundamental suppositions of the hypothesis of molecular vortices are the following:—*First*. That each atom of matter consists of a nucleus or central physical point enveloped by an elastic atmosphere, which is retained around it by attraction. *Ibid.*, If an indefinitely extended vibrating medium..consist of a system of atomic nuclei. **1900** *Rep. Brit. Assoc. Adv. Sci. 1900* 619 The material atom must be some kind of permanent nucleus that retains around itself an æthereal field of physical influence. *Ibid.*, If..the distances at which they [*sc.* atoms] are kept apart are large compared with the diameters of the atomic nuclei. **1903** O. LODGE *Mod. Views on Matter* 5 If the charge of electricity usually associated with a single monad atom of matter were concentrated on to a spherical nucleus one hundred-thousandth of an atom's dimension in diameter, it would thereby possess a mass about one-thousandth of that of the lightest atom known... Such a hypothetical concentrated unit of electricity it has become customary to call an 'electron'.]

1912 E. RUTHERFORD in *Phil. Mag.* XXIV. 461 In a previous paper [sc. *Phil. Mag.* (1911) XXI. 669] I have given reasons for believing that the atom consists of a positively charged nucleus of very small dimensions, surrounded by a distribution of electrons in rapid motion, possibly of rings of electrons rotating in one plane. **1919** *Conquest* I. 1. 36/2 An atom is a sort of solar system in miniature, and comprises a central core or nucleus..and a number of particles, called corpuscles, circulating round the nucleus. **1942** J. D. STRANATHAN *'Particles' of Mod. Physics* xi. 417 The nucleus must be very small, not larger than 10^{-12} cm. **1955** C. G. DARWIN in W. Pauli *Niels Bohr* 6 In 1911 he [*sc.* Rutherford] tried the idea of a heavy central electric charge repelling the α-particle—it was I think several months before it was called the nucleus —and at once the whole theory of the nuclear atom emerged. **1962** H. D. BUSH *Atomic & Nuclear Physics* iii. 62 The hypothesis that every nucleus consisted of protons and neutrons, was first suggested by Heisenberg (1932).

12. a. *Phonetics.* The syllable of a word (spoken in isolation) that bears the primary accent; in an utterance, the syllable or syllables given particular emphasis.

1922 H. E. PALMER *English Intonation* ii. 7 Each Tone-Group contains a Nucleus, which is the stressed syllable of the most prominent word in the Tone-Group. The nucleus corresponds to what is usually called sentence-stress. *Ibid.* 8 In Southern English there are four characteristic Nucleus Tones. **1924** —— *Gram. Spoken Eng.* 6 If..tonetic transcription is used, the syllable ['] will be replaced by the appropriate nucleus-symbol. *Ibid.* 14 Instead of the rise taking place in the nucleus-syllable itself, it is distributed over the nucleus and tail. **1941** *Language* XVII. 224 The present study..will deal with junctures, stresses, and consonants only in summary, and then devote itself to the syllabic nuclei. **1942** *English Studies* XXIV. 157 In combinations of noun + adjective (like French master, black bird) the marking of the nucleus tone (i.e. the point at which the pitch begins to rise or fall) is an excellent device to bring home to students the two meanings such combinations may express. **1962** A. C. GIMSON *Introd. Pronunc. Eng.* x. 244 The primary accent (or accents) in a sentence is shown by initiating a change of pitch direction, with the nucleus (falling, rising, or a combination of the two) on the appropriate syllable of the word (or words) on which attention is particularly to be concentrated. **1962** S. STUBELIUS in F. Behre *Contrib. Eng. Syntax* 151 The main features of intonation, particularly whether the sentences studied had a falling or a rising end intonation (nucleus). **1973** *Archivum Linguisticum* IV. 21 Tonality, tonicity, and tone, which refer to the number of tone-groups, the location of the tonic, or nucleus, and the choice of tone used, respectively.

b. *Linguistics.* The main word or words in a combination, phrase, or sentence; also = *KERNEL *sb.*[1] 8 b.

1934 [see *DETERMINANT *a.* and *sb.* B. 2 c]. **1949** E. A. NIDA *Morphol.* (ed. 2) 83 The nucleus of a morphological construction consists of (1) a root or (2) a combination of roots... The nonnucleus is made up of nonroots. In the construction *boyishness* the element *boy* is the nucleus and *-ishness* constitutes the nonnucleus. **1961** R. B. LONG *Sentence & its Parts* i. 20 Isolates sometimes take adjunct modifiers, much as nucleuses do. *Ibid.* 497 *Nucleuses*, minimal sequences made up of subjects, predicators, and complements, or of such of these as occur... In *come in!* the nucleus is made up of the predicator *come* and the complement *in*. **1961** Y. OLSSON *Syntax Eng. Verb* iv. 77 The relationship between a group of nuclei (like *London*, etc.) and equivalent members of the paradigms based on them (like *London-er*, etc.) give rise to an expectancy which may or may not be met in the same way. **1968** J. LYONS *Introd. Theoretical Linguistics* viii. 334 The subject and the predicate together form the nucleus of the sentence.

nuclide (niū·klɔid). *Nuclear Physics.* [f. NUCL(EUS *sb.* + *-ide* (f. Gr. εἶδος form, kind).] A particular kind of atom, as defined by the number of protons and the number of neutrons in the nucleus.

Synonymous with *ISOTOPE in its broader sense, which the introduction of *nuclide* was intended to discourage in favour of the original stricter meaning of that word.

1947 T. P. KOHMAN in *Amer. Jrnl. Physics* XV. 356/2 There is at present no word in the English language to express the concept of a particular species of atom, differing from all others in the constitution of its nucleus... *Nuclear species* and the German *Kernsorte*..refer to nuclei rather than to atoms... In recent years the word *isotope* has come into use for this purpose, less by design than by default... Evidently a new word is required, and *nuclide* is proposed... The new word and its derivatives should be used in such expressions as 'stable nuclides' ..and 'nuclidic weight'. **1955** R. D. EVANS *Atomic Nucleus* xvi. 522 Because it is the only naturally occurring nuclide which undergoes fission by slow neutrons, U^{235} has attained international fame even in lay circles. **1957** *Technology* June 139/3 β and γ ionization chambers for secondary standardisation of radioactive nuclides have been designed. **1961** G. R. CHOPPIN *Exper. Nuclear Chem.* 215 Na^{22}, Na^{23}, and Na^{24} are all isotopes of sodium... Na^{22} and C^{14} are nuclides but are not isotopic to each other. **1967** *Guardian* 17 May 3/2 There was less Strontium-90 and Caesium-137 in milk last year... Levels of both nuclides were lower than at any time since 1962. **1971** *Daily Colonist* (Victoria, B.C.) 9 July 9/3 The nuclear explosive was designed to reduce the amount of residual tritium, a radioactive nuclide.

Hence **nuclidic** (-i·dik) *a.*

1947 [see above]. **1955** R. D. EVANS *Atomic Nucleus* xvi. 519 In order to identify the new artificial nuclides, it

was logical and essential to utilize the usual nuclidic notation, for example, $_{83}Bi^{213}$. **1962** *Nature* 19 May 621/2 Modern methods make possible much more exact measurements of nuclidic masses. *Ibid.*, The atomic physicist is usually concerned with individual nuclidic species—the differences in their nuclear characteristics and the nuclear, as opposed to chemical, changes they undergo. **1973** J. YARWOOD *Atomic & Nuclear Physics* xv. 429 A useful method of correlating data about the nuclides is to plot a nuclidic chart of *N*, the number of neutrons in the nucleus, against *Z*, the atomic number.

nucloid (niū·kloid). Also **nucleoid.** [f. NUCLEUS *sb.* + -OID.] (See quot. 1962.)

1908 *Westm. Gaz.* 31 July 1/3 (*heading*) 'Nucleoids' in naval manœuvres. *Ibid.* 2/2 The balance is still all on the side of the 'nucleoid' as against the newly commissioned ship. **1917** 'TAFFRAIL' *Sub* vii. 176 About June, came the summer manœuvres, when the crews of all the 'nucloids' were brought up to full strength. **1962** W. GRANVILLE *Dict. Sailors' Slang* 82/2 *Nucloid*, ship of the Reserve Fleet in peacetime, carrying a nucleus crew.

nuclon: see *NUCLEON² b.

nude, *a.* and *sb.* Add: **A.** *adj.* **3.** (Further examples.)

1926 E. O'NEILL *Great God Brown* I. iii. 46, I am thy shorn, bald, nude sheep! **1928** *Oxford Poetry* 3 The pale, nude flowers That I Picked for you. **1952** E. O'NEILL *Moon for Misbegotten* I. 38 It is full of nude rocks. **1964** D. VARADAY *Gara-Yaka* xii. 102 (*caption*) Vultures like baubles on a nude tree.

b. (Earlier and later examples.)

1845 *Punch* VIII. 247 A regret that Etty should content himself with merely painting from *'the nude Academy model'*. **1974** *Publishers Weekly* 26 Aug. 250/3 A novel about a nude model who longs for true love.

c. Of a revue, show, photograph, etc.: involving or portraying nude, or lightly clad, figures (usu. female).

In quot. 1870 the actresses referred to were clothed in flesh-coloured tights.

1870 O. LOGAN *Before Footlights & Behind Scenes* xv. 128 Bringing upon stage that hideous disgrace known as the 'nude drama', which took its rise with the flimsy absurdity called the 'Black Crook'. **1947** *Amer. Speech* XXII. 171 America enthusiastically adopted the word.. *nude drama.* **1957** J. OSBORNE *Entertainer* xiii. 86 Nude tableau, behind first act gauze. **1959** *Sunday Times* 16 Aug. 10/4 It is the later nude revue days of Collins's Music Hall. **1959** *Listener* 15 Jan. 132/3 The night-clubs in Calvin's city put on nude shows. *Ibid.* 6 Aug. 195/2 There are packed houses at nude revues. **1972** *Daily Tel.* 27 Nov. 17/6 An Italian magazine published nine pages of nude photographs of her last week.

4. As a colour, esp. of stockings, flesh-coloured.

1922 *Daily Mail* 18 Dec. 2 (Advt.), Ladies' Hose... Black, white,.. taupe, navy, nude, and all shades. **1926** GALSWORTHY *Silver Spoon* II. xii. 216 'Blue-stockings.' 'No, sir; they nearly all wear "nude".' **1931** M. DE LA ROCHE *Finch's Fortune* ix. 156 She had on.. 'nude' stockings. **1947** *Sun* (Baltimore) 10 Sept. 5 Nude and white in sizes 33 to 40. Corset Shop, third floor. **1973** *Philadelphia Inquirer* (Today Suppl.) 14 Oct. 17/3 (Advt.), Choose black, brown, navy or nude calfskin.

5. *Med.* Of a mouse: homozygous for a mutant gene which produces apparent hairlessness and (in most cases) a grossly hypoplastic thymus gland.

1966 S. P. FLANAGAN in *Genetical Res.* VIII. 295 [The hairless mutant was found by Dr. N. R. Grist of the Virus Laboratory, Ruchill Hospital, Glasgow... The name 'nude', symbol *nu*, has been adopted.] *Ibid.* 308 The majority of nude mice die of general body weakness within 2 weeks. **1974** *Nature* 20 Sept. 184/2 Nude mice have spread through the immunological world at a remarkable pace... The thymus abnormality leads to a marked deficiency in thymus-derived (T) lymphocytes and nude mice are rapidly replacing thymectomised mice as models of T cell deprivation and as a source of relatively pure B lymphocytes for *in vitro* studies. **1975** *Ibid.* 13 Mar. 140/2 (*heading*) Nude mice with normal thymus.

B. *sb.* **3.** *Med.* A nude mouse.

1968 *Nature* 27 Jan. 371/1 (*heading*) Section of liver of an adult homozygote nude. **1974** *Ibid.* 20 Sept. 184/2 The T cell deficiency in nudes make them highly susceptible to infection (but apparently not to cancer) and they survive poorly in conventional animal houses.

nudey, var. *NUDIE.

nudge, *sb.* Add: Also *fig.*

1922 JOYCE *Ulysses* 631 Hynes wrote it with a nudge from Corny. **1950** *Sun* (Baltimore) 20 June 21/4 Didn't you like the comeback of Cardinal Manager Eddie Dyer when given a slight nudge over his club's loss of three straight. **1953** A. HUXLEY *Let.* 19 July (1969) 679 Your publishers..would send me proofs as soon as they became available. I have heard nothing... Would you be kind enough to give them a little nudge?

nudge, *v.* Add: **1.** *fig.* (Further examples.) Also *transf.*

1877 G. H. LEWES *Let.* 27 Feb. in *Geo. Eliot's Lett.* (1956) VI. 345 He might still be induced to resume that idea if you thought fit to nudge his elbow a little. **1922** JOYCE *Ulysses* 63 Nudging the door open with his knee he carried the tray in. **1925** H. V. MORTON *Heart of London* (1926) 75 Watch the way a press of omnibuses.. will edge and nudge a way with a mere inch between their mudguards. **1936** DYLAN THOMAS *Twenty-Five Poems* 9 Half The dear, daft time I take to nudge the sentence. **1971** *Times* 28 Aug. 10/1 A smarter, cleaner place undergoing the upheaval of architectural surgery, being nudged by bulldozers and demolition gangs from one century into the next. **1973** *Guardian* 10 Mar. 1/7 Governments would use their reserves..and nudge the price if it tended to drift out of line. **1975** *Physics Bull.* Apr. 162/1 The Science Research Council's attempts to nudge university research into areas more relevant to social and economic needs are meeting some resistance.

2. Also const. *up*, to move up by pushing.

1940 DYLAN THOMAS *Portrait of Artist as Young Dog* 7 The bar was full; two fat women in bright dresses sat near the door, one with a small, dark child on her knee; they saw Uncle Jim and nudged up on the bench.

Hence **nu·dging** *pres. pple.* and *ppl. a.*, approaching, nearing, close to (used e.g. of someone's age).

1949 E. E. CUMMINGS *Let.* 23 Aug. (1969) 193 Now et comment The quote Oxford unquote Press registers alarm nudging horror. **1961** *Sunday Times* 30 Apr. 13/6 Nudging forty..Secombe knows where his ultimate responsibility lies. **1969** D. BARRON *Man who was There* ii. 30 Hughes was tough and nudging fifty. **1971** D. LEES *Rainbow Conspiracy* i. 17 The Manchester circulation is nudging the one and a half million a day mark. **1972** A. MACVICAR *Golden Venus Affair* i. 9, I was big, nudging six feet two. **1974** *Country Life* 25 Apr. 1012/2 A fuel gauge nudging zero.

nudger (nʌ·dʒəɹ). [f. NUDGE *v.* + -ER¹.] **a.** One who nudges another or others.

1910 H. G. WELLS *Hist. Mr. Polly* vi. 177 A sprinkling of girls in gay hats from Miriam's place of business appeared in church, great nudgers all of them. *Ibid.* 178 A murmer from the nudgers announced the arrival of the bridal party. **1960** S. PLATH *Colossus* 35 Nudgers and shovers In spite of ourselves Our kind multiplies.

b. *dial.* A hat.

1903 *Eng. Dial. Dict.* IV. 309/2 *Nudger*,..a hat. **1966** *Sun* 10 June 4/2 He was the only one wearing a bowler, called a 'nudger'.

nudging, *vbl. sb.* (Earlier example.)

1854 THOREAU *Walden* 97 We are not awakened by our Genius, but by the mechanical nudgings of some servitor.

nudie (niū·di). Also **nudey.** [f. NUDE *a.* and *sb.* + -IE.] A nude show; a nude person; a film, photograph, or magazine featuring nudity. Also *attrib.* or as *adj.*

1935 *Amer. Mercury* June 230/1 *Nudie*, nude show. **1939** *Amer. Speech* XIV. 4 A 'nudie' (nudist picture)..is 'cinemerotic'. **1942** BERREY & VAN DEN BARK *Amer. Thes. Slang* §509/24 *'Strip-tease'*,..nudie. *Ibid.* §583/31 *'Strip-teaser'*,..nudie. *Ibid.* §590/9 *Burlesque show*,..nudie. *Ibid.* §608/1 Bare skinema, nudie, nudie pic,..a nudist picture. **1964** *New Statesman* 21 Feb. 306/3 Trying to break away from nudies and naughties. **1967** *Punch* 4 Oct. 506/2 He had..submitted Furd's photograph to several nudie magazines. **1968** *Wall St. Jrnl.* 24 Apr., Russ Meyer is king of the 'nudies'. But his influence on American moviemaking is not inconsiderable. **1970** K. PLATT *Pushbutton Butterfly* xiv. 161, I riffled the chromos. Nudies of Janet Sanders. **1971** R. PETRIE *Thorne in Flesh* vi. 84 Desmond Morris's 'Naked Ape'. Another case of a nudey dust-jacket selling a serious book. **1971** *Petticoat* 17 July 7/3 The nudie stills appear in sex magazines all over the world. **1972** *Guardian* 16 Feb. 13/1 Male nudie pin-ups. **1974** P. GZOWSKI *This Country* 197/1 That the nudies have such phenomenal mass-market circulations says something about our sexuality.

nu·dified, *a. rare.* [See NUDI- and -FY.] Made or become bare.

1883 H. JAMES *Let.* 11 Jan. in R. B. Perry *Tht. & Char. of W. James* (1935) I. xxii. 388 This morning I went out to poor *nudified* and staring Cambridge [Massachusetts].

nudism (niū·diz'm). [f. NUDE *a.* and *sb.* + -ISM.] The cult and practice of going unclothed.

1929 *Time* 1 July 23/1 Made in Germany, imported to France, is the cult of Nudism, a mulligan stew of vegetarianism, physical culture and pagan worship. **1931** F. & M. MERRILL *Among Nudists* xv. 221 The Doctors Durville..insist that France is not ready for nudism as is Germany. *Ibid.* xvi. 233 In spite of their [*sc.* the French bourgeoisie's] modesty on the subject, nudism is growing in France. **1935** *Punch* 19 June 721/1 'A real tent... Think of the saving. Hotel bills, nothing. Meals, practically nothing. Clothes, nothing whatever.' 'Pamela,' I said imploringly, 'not Nudism.' **1944** B. MALINOWSKI *Sci. Theory of Culture* v. 44 If we were to examine from this point of view any movement, such as ..fundamentalism or nudism..we would see that in one and all we can register a certain agreement on the statement of a common purpose as between the members of the movement. **1973** *Guardian* 28 June 6/1 The principles of nudism.

nudist (niū·dist). [f. NUDE *a.* and *sb.* + -IST.] An adherent of the cult of the nude; a person who advocates or practises going unclothed. Also *attrib.*

1929 *Time* 1 July 23/1 Much publicity has been given the Nudist colony on an island in the Seine near Paris. *Ibid.*, A U.S. parallel would be if elegant Editor Frank Crowninshield of *Vanity Fair* should suddenly appear as a vegetable-eating, hairy-chested Nudist. **1931** *John o' London's* 8 Aug. 620/2 The other members of the nudist colony were..entirely normal people. *Ibid.* 620/3 The nudists of France are pursued by the police, by the clergy, by the wit of Parisian cartoonists. **1932** *Daily Express* 28 June 1/7 Nudist camps have sprung up all over England in the past fortnight, in which happy families disport themselves in the warm sunshine. **1938** L. MACNEICE *I crossed Minch* I. vi. 85 The Devil's business fell as flat As a nudist camp or an opera hat. **1960** *Guardian* 6 Jan. 1/7 One father..regularly went off and joined a nudist colony. **1966** J. BALL *Cool Cottontail* iii. 22 Have you ever been in a nudist park before, doctor? **1973** G. MITCHELL *Murder of Busy Lizzie* xiii. 146 'Did you know..that there is a nudist colony on the island?'.. 'If nudists excite you, you're welcome to them.'

‖**nudnik** (nu·dnik). *U.S.* Also **nudnick.** [Yiddish *nudnik*, f. Russ. *núdnyĭ* tedious, boring; see *-NIK.] Someone who pesters, nags, or irritates; a bore. Also *attrib.*

1947 *New Republic* 14 Apr. 42 The patrons of New York's Ruban Bleu are as boorish a collection of *nudnicks* as ever assembled in a public place. **1949** *Amer. Fabrics* No. 9. 108 *Nudnick*, a bothersome customer. **1950** *Commentary* 10 Dec. 558/2 It makes no difference to me if these *nudniks* happen to be atheists. **1955** T. STURGEON in E. Crispin *Best SF Two* (1956) 141 You are a nowhere type, a *nudnick* type, *nothing*! **1961** *John o' London's* 28 Sept. 345/2 What a pair of nudniks they are. **1964** W. MARKFIELD *To Early Grave* (1965) i. 12 'Worrier. Pest. *Nudnick*.' She lashed out at him. **1968** P. DURST *Badge of Infamy* v. 39 Nudnik is a kind of insulting endearment—a sort of lovable nitwit. **1968** L. ROSTEN *Joys of Yiddish* 265 A *nudnik* is someone who *nudzhes* or pesters. **1972** *New York* 8 May 70/1 Too many of our nudnik moviegoers..dread the prospect of sharing their pleasures with the plain folks.

‖**nuée ardente** (nüe ardɑ̃t). *Geol.* Pl. **nuées ardentes.** [Fr., lit. 'burning cloud'.

Introduced by A. Lacroix 1903, in *Compt. Rend.* CXXXVI. 874. In *La Montagne Pelée et ses Eruptions* (1904) 170 Lacroix says that he has since realised that the expression had earlier been used by the inhabitants of San Jorge in the Azores. He also says that by *ardent* he implies *brulant* 'burning' rather than *incandescent* 'glowing'. However the expression *nuée ardente* is usually rendered into English as 'glowing cloud' rather than 'burning cloud'.]

A hot, dense cloud of ash and fragmented lava suspended in a mass of gas, which typically is ejected laterally from the side of the dome of certain volcanoes (as Mount Pelée) and flows downhill at great speed like an avalanche. Also ellipt. **nuée.**

1904 A. HEILPRIN *Tower of Pelée* iv. 47 Professor Lacroix..refers to a number of discharges of the *nuée ardente* breaking out laterally from the base of the obelisk surmounting the crater-cone. **1912** *Amer. Jrnl. Sci.* CLXXXIV. 413 The highly viscous lavas of andesitic and trachytic nature might explode subaërially..into gas and divided solid material, causing such effects as the 'Nuées Ardentes' of Mt. Pelée. **1935** *Publ. Carnegie Inst. Washington* No. 458. 85 They witnessed the series of three rapidly succeeding *nuées* of July 9, 1902. *Ibid.* 89 The ejections followed one another at such brief intervals as to form an unbroken procession of *nuées ardentes.* **1966** *Earth-Sci. Rev.* I. 158 Large acid sheets might have a nuée origin. **1969** *Nature* 29 Nov. 864/1 Natural terrestrial examples of fluidized systems include certain quicksands ..and the volcanic eruptions known as *nuées ardentes.* **1969** BENNISON & WRIGHT *Geol. Hist. Brit. Isles* v. 94 The ignimbrites..are the product of nuées ardentes—the fiery cloud of lava and gas which occurs when lavas are silica rich and viscous. **1972** G. A. MACDONALD *Volcanoes* viii. 146 The cloud was the conspicuous feature and led Lacroix to give the name 'nuée ardente' (glowing cloud)... The name 'glowing cloud' seems, therefore, to give too much emphasis to a relatively minor feature, and many volcanologists today prefer to call the phenomenon a glowing avalanche.

Nuer (nū·əɹ). [Native name.] Name of an African people living in the south-eastern area of the Sudan; a member of this people; also, their language. Also *attrib.* or as *adj.*

1861 J. PETHERICK *Egypt, Soudan & Central Africa* xx. 362 We..made fast under two villages, which we found were inhabited by the Nouaer. **1873** E. E. FREWER tr. *Schweinfurth's Heart of Africa* I. iii. 118 We made a stop, and did some bartering with the Nueir... Here, in the heart of the Nueir population, in a district called Nyeng, we fixed our quarters. **1894** A. LEFÈVRE *Race & Lang.* v. 162 From the lakes of the Upper Nile to the Atlantic, the Negro dialects, properly so called, prevail: (1.) The Dinka group (Bari, Bongo, Chillouk, Nouer, etc.), the poorest of all, hardly issued from the monosyllabic stage. **1923** C. H. STIGAND (*title*) A Nuer-English vocabulary. **1932** C. G. & B. Z. SELIGMAN *Pagan Tribes Nilotic Sudan* i. 13 The Nuer..are tall, long-headed, very dark-skinned, and woolly-haired. *Ibid.* vi. 222 Every Nuer has a name given to him at birth by his father or other member of his family. **1940** E. E. EVANS-PRITCHARD *Nuer* iv. 184 Arab merchants..generally speak Nuer well. **1949** tr. *L. Homburger's Negro-African Langs.* iv. 89 In Nuer *ko* is used for 'we' distinct from *nè* 'I and thou' and *ne* 'we and you'. **1955** J. H. GREENBERG *Studies in African Linguistic Classification* 65 It is.. probable that the *ti* plural demonstrative and relative of Nuer..is cognate with the *ti* possessive and relative of Bari. **1964** E. A. NIDA *Toward Sci. Transl.* iii. 51 The Nuers of the Sudan have a very highly specialized vocabulary relating to cattle.

nuff (nʌf). *colloq.* (orig. *U.S.*). Also **nuf,** **'nuff.** [colloq. and dial. abbrev. of ENOUGH *a.*, *sb.*, and *adv.*; cf. *'NOUGH.] **1. a. nuff said,** an indication that nothing more need be said on a particular topic. Also *nuf(f) ced*, *nuf(f) sed*, abbrev. *N.C.*, *N.S.*

1840 *Ninawah* (Peru, Ill.) *Gaz.* 20 June 2/3 'N.S. (Nuff said,)' whispered Mr. Fox. **1841** *Spirit of Times* 30 Oct.

409/1 'N.S., nuf sed', and up went *the soap*. **1873** HOTTEN *Slang Dict.* 235 *N.C.*, 'enough said', being the initials of *Nuf ced*. A certain theatrical manager spells, it is said, in this style. **1882** *Sydney Slang Dict.* 6/2 *N.C.*, '*Nuff Ced*', enough said. Thea. origin. **1892** J. C. DUVAL *Young Explorers* 151 'Nuf ced,' says Bill, 'you jess take care of your own har, and I'll see arter mine.' **1909** J. R. WARE *Passing Eng.* 184 *Nuf ced* (*From America*). Contraction of 'enough said'—absurdly spelt. Warning to say no more. Used in Liverpool chiefly. **1912** *Pedagogical Seminary* XIX. 97 [Expressions of] Negation and denial..'nuff said. **1942** N. BALCHIN *Darkness falls from Air* xiv. 234 'All right,' he said. ''Nuff said.' **1958** *Spectator* 30 May 677/2 Mr. Randall is one of the newer members; 'nuff said. **1965** M. SPARK *Mandelbaum Gate* vi. 164, I hope the food..is not unwholesome. How well I remember those weeks following your return from Spain... 'Nuff said'! **1971** J. AITKEN *Nightly Deadshade* v. 49 'He and Steinherz knew one another at university before they were here.' 'Nuff said, I suppose.

b. sure 'nuff, sho' nuff, sure enough; often used as an intensive or to give emphasis to a point. (This sense chiefly *U.S.*, esp. in representations of Black English.)

1880 J. C. HARRIS *Uncle Remus* (1881) vi. 31 Den Brer Fox grit his toof sho' nuff; he did, en he look mighty dumpy. **1887** C. W. CHESNUTT in *Atlantic Monthly* Aug. 257/1 Sho nuff, it rain de nex' day. **1898** J. D. BRAYSHAW *Slum Silhouettes* 150 An' sure 'nuff the nex' night arter, bang-bang comes a posty's knock at the door. **1921** E. O'NEILL *Emperor Jones* (1953) ii. 168 I'se done up sho' 'nuff. *Ibid.* 170 I'se gone lost de place sho' 'nuff. **1935** Z. N. HURSTON *Mules & Men* I. i. 26 Ole Massa begin to figger dat John musta seen somethin' sho nuff because John never had disobeyed him before. **1942** S. KENNEDY in B. A. Botkin *Treas. S. Folklore* (1949) III. ii. 511 Sho nuff there was the preacher's buggy. **1971** J. D. CARR *Deadly Hall* xvii. 200 He's sho' nuff in good shape and ought to thank you.

2. Various other uses (see quots.).

1890 BARRÈRE & LELAND *Dict. Slang* II. 91/2 *Nuff* (soldiers): to have one's *nuff*, means to have had more drink than is good for one, *i.e.*, enough. **1923** J. MANCHON *Le Slang* 208 *Nuff*,..abr. *enough*; *to have one's nuff*,.. être plein, ivre. **1967** C. HIMES *Black on Black* (1973) 133 Go on, baby, you can be back in an hour with 'nuff bread so we can scoff. **1972** T. KENRICK *Tough One to Lose* xxi. 167 'Nuff outa you guys,' the big man called.

Nuffield (nʌ·fīld). The name of William Richard Morris, 1st Viscount *Nuffield* (1877–1963), founder of Morris Motors Ltd., used *attrib.* in **Nuffield Foundation**, a charitable trust set up by him to finance various schemes and organizations; hence *spec.* in *Educ.*, used *attrib.* and *absol.* in connection with the teaching methods and syllabuses advocated by the Nuffield Foundation since 1964, designed esp. for primary school level in mathematics, science, and French with the object of stimulating interest and individual thinking.

1943 *Times* 13 Feb. 4/4 Lord Nuffield has intimated his intention of founding forthwith a charitable trust, which will be known as 'The Nuffield Foundation'. **1946** *Nuffield Foundation First Report* 9 Early in 1943 Lord Nuffield established the Nuffield Foundation as a charitable trust and endowed it with Ordinary Stock Units in Morris Motors Ltd., to the value of £10,000,000. **1947** *Rep. Survey Comm. Old People* i. 1 The trustees of the Nuffield Foundation. **1952** C. P. BLACKER *Eugenics* 307 Some voluntary organizations, such as those embodied in the Nuffield Foundation, have performed semi-official functions, such as the regional hospital surveys conducted for the Ministry of Health during the war. **1964** *Times Educ. Suppl.* 21 Aug. 249/4 If we do get new syllabuses for our nationwide school examinations they will probably be Nuffield ones. *Ibid.* 20 Nov. 932/5 Members of the Nuffield teams will act as examiners. **1971** *Where* Nov. 332/1 The sort of problem, taken from the Nuffield materials, young secondary children would soon get to work on. **1972** E. ELIAS *Learning & Playing* v. 81 Your child's teacher may well be using the Nuffield 'guides', a series of booklets stressing..*how* to teach. *Ibid.* vii. 128 Like Nuffield maths..Nuffield science is being introduced into more and more junior schools. *Ibid.* 129 Nuffield French has spread to schools all over the country. **1975** *Physics Bull.* Dec. 532/3 When a school starts taking Nuffield (other than Nuffield physical science) it never appears to give up doing so.

nuffieldite (nʌ·fīldəit). *Min.* [f. the name of E. W. *Nuffield* (b. 1914), Canadian geologist + -ITE[1].] A sulphide of copper, lead, and bismuth, $Cu_4Pb_{10}Bi_{10}S_{27}$, found as steel-grey orthorhombic crystals at Lime Creek, British Columbia, Canada.

1968 P. W. KINGSTON in *Canad. Mineralogist* IX. 439 A second new sulphosalt mineral was discovered by R. M. Thompson... The new species is named nuffieldite in honour of E. W. Nuffield, who has made outstanding contributions to the understanding of many of the less well-known sulphosalt minerals. **1969** *Ibid.* X. 93 Because of the close similarity in physical properties of neyite, cosalite, aikinite, and nuffieldite, it was necessary to make numerous *x*-ray powder photographs to confirm the identity of the material used for analysis.

nuffin (nʌ·fin). Also **nuffink.** [Repr. a colloq. or dial. pronunc. of NOTHING.] = NOTHING *sb.* and *adv.* in var. senses.

1877 GEO. ELIOT *Let.* 23 Nov. (1956) VI. 426 We have never seen Saturn's ring, nor Jupiter's moons—'nor nuffin'. **1897** [see *DRIFT *sb.* 9]. **1898** J. D. BRAYSHAW *Slum Silhouettes* 1 If anyfink's wrong, yer won't get nuffink aht o' me. **1910** H. G. WELLS *Hist. Mr. Polly* ix. 316, I don't stick at nuffin. **1922** 'R. CROMPTON' *More William* (1924) i. 24, I can't do nuffink with the mincing machine gone. **1951** 'J. WYNDHAM' *Day of Triffids* (1956) ii. 46 On its [*sc.* the triffid's] origins the Russians, true to type, lay low and said nuffin. **1957** *Economist* 28 Sept. 1002/1 It is..very nearly impossible for an Opposition to lie low and say nuffin at a time like this. **1958** J. TOWNSEND *Young Devils* ii. 20 'Don't learn nuffin' in this school,' sneered another boy. **1971** G. SIMS *Deadhand* II. ii. 88 Albert Chevalier's adage: 'Wot's the good of hanyfink?—Why—nuffink!' **1974** 'A. GILBERT' *Nice Little Killing* ix. 119 We don't know nuffin about the dear departed.

nugæ. Add: *spec.* in phr. **nugæ difficiles** *Philos.*, matters of trifling importance over which a disproportionate amount of time may be taken owing to their difficulty.

1710 BERKELEY *Princ. Human Knowl.* 170 We may perhaps..look on all Inquiries about Numbers, only as so many *difficiles nugæ*, so far as they are not subservient to practise. **1867** MILL *Inaug. Addr.* 39, I am often tempted to ask the favourites of nature and fortune, whether all the serious and important work of the world is done, that their time and energy can be spared for these *nugae difficiles*? **1890** W. JAMES *Princ. Psychol.* II. xxviii. 662 Such painstaking attempts..to prove all necessary judgments to be analytic..seem accordingly but *nugae difficiles*, and little better than wastes of ink and paper.

nugget, *sb.* Add: **1.** *transf.* (Earlier example.)

*a*1859 T. DE QUINCEY *Coll. Writings* (1889) I. 412 The secret truth, that rarest of all 'nuggets'.

3. Substitute for def.: A small, compact, stocky animal or person; also, a runt. (Further examples.)

1919 W. H. DOWNING *Digger Dial.* 36 *Nugget*, a short soldier. **1941** BAKER *Dict. Austral. Slang* 50 *Nugget*, a small, weedy horse or other animal. (2) A small stocky man.

nugget(t)y, *a.* Add: **3.** Used also of other animals, and of persons. Also *N.Z.*

1874 C. DE BOOS *Congewoi Correspondence* 141 He's just oner them short, square-built, nuggetty kinder fellers. **1887** *Daily News* 9 Apr. 5/4 The typical volunteer is gradually framing himself into a medium-sized, somewhat thickset, sturdy style of fellow, with a good chest measurement, firm on the pins, with the stamp on him of strength and hardihood—the sort of man..the Australians style 'nuggetty'. **1926** 'J. DOONE' *Timely Tips for New Australians* (Gloss.) *Nuggetty*, short and sturdy. **1941** I. L. IDRIESS *Great Boomerang* vii. 52 Scowler was a square-faced, nuggety man, with a set scowl under a shock of hair. **1946** F. SARGESON *That Summer* 66 He wasn't a rangy specimen like me, no, he was nuggety. **1953** O. E. MIDDLETON in C. K. Stead *N.Z. Short Stories* (1966) 187 Belle was..more nuggetty, but still powerful. She was short-haired..but had less white on the throat. **1969** O. WHITE *Under Iron Rainbow* 107 He was a nuggety little bloke and moved as if he could handle himself in a blue. **1971** *Sunday Times* (Johannesburg) 28 Mar. 21/1 The nuggety young Wits University scrumhalf will be in the Springbok team to tour Australia. **1971** *N.Z. Listener* 19 Apr. 56/5 One was a nuggety bloke in a sou'-wester, oilskin slicker, and bowyangs.

nuisance. Add: **2. f.** In phr. *to commit a nuisance.*

1863 *Harper's Mag.* Dec. 24/1 Commit no Nuisance. *a*1922 T. S. ELIOT *Waste Land Drafts* (1971) 5 We'd just gone up the alley, a fly cop came along, Looking for trouble; committing a nuisance, he said. **1942** PARTRIDGE *Usage & Abusage* 122/1 Euphemism may be obtained by using an extremely vague phrase, as in *commit a nuisance*.

3. *attrib.* and *Comb.*, as *nuisance action, aspect, candidate, tactics, tax*; **nuisance ground** *Canad.*, a rubbish dump; **nuisance raid,** a wartime bomb attack intended only to inconvenience or disrupt the enemy; also **nuisance-bombing, -raider; nuisance value,** the value or importance of a person or thing arising from a capacity to be a nuisance.

1964 C. CHAPLIN *Autobiogr.* xxix. 499 It's nothing but a nuisance action, Charlie; all the same I want you to keep from being served a summons. **1941** *Scrutiny* X. 80 There is a certain savage heightening of his nuisance-aspect towards the end. **1940** *Times Weekly* 27 Nov. 6 The change in the enemy's air tactics from general nuisance bombing to concentrated attacks on more restricted targets. **1968** *Globe & Mail* (Toronto) 13 Feb. 7/6 The only apple carts that Mr. Trudeau could not upset are those of..the three nuisance candidates. **1889** in *Herald Mag.* (Calgary) (1961) 11 Jan. 8/6 A well-grounded complaint has been made..in reference to dumping of filth in to the old cellar holes along the main road..instead of taking it to the nuisance ground. **1970** J. H. GRAY *Boy from Winnipeg* 72 He had hauling contracts with the city that included carrying the manure from the city stables to the nuisance grounds. **1972** *Maclean's Mag.* (Toronto) Dec. 23/3 The town dump was known as the *nuisance grounds*, a phrase fraught with weird connotations, as though the effluvia of our lives was beneath contempt but at the same time was subtly threatening to the determined and sometimes hysterical propriety of our ways. **1942** *Hutchinson's Pict. Hist. of War* 18 Mar.–9 June 110 Some of the raids into enemy territory are merely nuisance raids to upset enemy nerves. **1943** *R.A.F. Jrnl.* Aug. 34 Cases of..nuisance raids by single rodents had been reported. **1944** *Ann. Reg. 1943* 341 The Germans..began a series of nuisance raids. **1944** *Daily Tel.* 11 July 1 German radio early to-day reported several nuisance raiders over the Berlin area. **1952** *Ann. Reg. 1951* 325 Government workers, forbidden..to strike, resorted to go-slow, work to rule, and other nuisance tactics. **1933** *Sun* (Baltimore) 4 July 6/6 (*heading*) Nuisance taxes help careerists. *Ibid.*, Authorities on taxation recently persuaded the State Legislature to abolish this tax as a nuisance, although its nuisance value was the chief reason for its existence. **1937** *Harper's Mag.* Jan. 846 If Hitler has a high nuisance value to France and England. **1958** A. HOCKING *Epitaph for Nurse* v. 82 To add to her other nuisance-values, Geraldine complained and made trouble from morning to night. **1961** P. W. BROOKS *Mod. Airliner* i. 22 'Nuisance value' of the aircraft to the general public on the ground (defined as the external overall noise level at climbing power at 650 ft.). **1972** *Guardian* 5 Jan. 4/6 Muskie's aides dismiss them airily as being no threat at all except for the nuisance value they may have in primaries.

‖**nuit blanche** (nwi blaŋʃ). [Fr., lit. 'white night'.] A sleepless night. Also *fig.*

1853 C. BRONTË *Villette* III. xli. 296 Leaving the radiant park and well-lit Haute-Ville (still well-lit, for this it seems was to be a 'nuit blanche' in Villette), I sought the dim lower quarter. **1904** W. STEVENS *Let.* 14 Feb. (1967) 69, I do *not* want my dreams—my castles, my hunts, my *nuits blanches*. **1923** D. H. LAWRENCE *Ladybird* 81 She had gone to sleep from the *nuit blanche* of her days. **1964** L. MEYNELL *More Deadly than Male* xiv. 244 He lay awake for the rest of the night. A *nuit blanche*.

Nuits (St. George(s (nwi sæ̃n ʒǭɹʒ). [The name of the capital town of the Côte de Nuits, in the department of Côte d'Or, France.] A red wine of Burgundy, produced in the district of Nuits St. Georges.

1841 THACKERAY in *Fraser's Mag.* June 715/1 We had ..A bottle of nuits with the beef. **1875** [see *BEAUNE]. **1914** G. K. CHESTERTON *Flying Inn* xvii. 196 A strictly vegetarian beverage which bears the noble and starry name of Nuits. **1946** G. MILLAR *Horned Pigeon* xvi. 236 We found Eugène and his wife celebrating..with a bottle of Nuits St. Georges. **1966** B. E. WALLACE *Murder in Touraine* vi. 56 Rocky swirled his Nuits St. George slowly round the glass. **1967** A. LICHINE *Encycl. Wines* 383/2 Bouquet is also a Nuits characteristic, and the wines are sometimes quite pungent.

Nujol (niū·dʒǭl). The proprietary name of a paraffin oil used as an emulsifying agent in pharmacy and for making mulls in infra-red spectroscopy.

1916 *Trade Marks Jrnl.* 16 Feb. 153 Nujol... Medicinal and curative preparations..all being for human use. Standard Oil Company.., Bayonne, Hudson County, New Jersey, United States of America; manufacturers. **1923** W. CLAYTON *Theory of Emulsions* ii. 30 If a solution of KI be added to an emulsion of 'Nujol' in sodium oleate solution, prismatic colours are secured. **1943, 1948** [see *MULL *v.*[1] 1 b]. **1956** [see *MULL *sb.*[1] 2]. **1971** ROSENBLATT & DAVIS *Course in Org. Chem.* iii. 71 Nujol is only useful in regions not involving carbon–hydrogen vibrations. **1975** D. H. BURRIN in Williams & Wilson *Biologist's Guide to Princ. & Techniques Pract. Biochem.* v. 151 A Nujol mull, consisting of a fine paste of sample in liquid paraffin may be prepared.

nuke (niūk, U.S. nūk), *sb.*[2] *slang* (chiefly *U.S.*). Abbrev. of 'nuclear bomb, weapon,' etc.

1959 *N.Y. Times Mag.* 1 Feb. 46/3 Soon there may be 5-inch nuclear shells and portable Davy Crockett 'nukes' for the infantryman. **1960** *Time* 4 July 52/1 But the nuclear submarines—called 'nukes'—can cruise underwater for weeks at top speed. **1969** *Life* 29 Sept. 23/2 Once communities vied for nuclear power plants ('nukes') as passports to prosperity. **1971** J. BALL *First Team* (1972) xv. 224 'What is nukes?' the man asked. 'Nuclear specialists; no one else can handle this stuff.' **1973** *Publishers' Weekly* 14 May 44/1 They hijack a liner at sea and sink it with a baby nuke... He is given the job of detonating the big nuke.

Hence as *v. trans.*, to use nuclear weapons against; **nu·king** *vbl. sb.*

1967 *Look* 11 July 25, I remember in Saigon how disturbed General Westmoreland was after talking to a group of American editors..who told him they favored 'nuking' (A-bombing) China. **1970** *New Yorker* 4 July 52 We have to get ready to nuke 'em to kingdom come. **1972** *S. China Morning Post* (Hong Kong) 29 Sept. 2/3 Dr. Strangelove nuked the Russians on his own authority. **1972** *Japan Times Weekly* 23 Dec. 4/2, I asked how he could be sure that the Soviet Union would nuke us if we nuked China. **1973** *Daily Tel.* (Colour Suppl.) 13 Apr. 40/1 'Nuked', for those unfamiliar with modern war-parlance, means to let off a nuclear bomb.

null, *sb.*[1] Delete †*Obs. rare* and add: **b.** *Cryptography.* (See quot. 1961.)

1915 J. BUCHAN *39 Steps* iii. 72 It was a numerical cypher, and by an elaborate system of experiments I had pretty well discovered what were the nulls and stops. **1961** SHULMAN & WEINTRAUB *Gloss. Cryptography*, *Null cipher*, a form of concealment in which most of the letters used in a text are nulls. *Nulls*, meaningless letters or numbers used in cryptograms for various purposes. **1968** 'S. JAY' *Sleepers can Kill* iv. 47 A very simple cypher, Mr. Connor, but it can of course be broken by frequency analysis... Don't forget to reverse and arrange in five letter groups, of course, with nulls to make the numbers up. **1972** *Sci. Amer.* Nov. 114/2 If this is intercepted and a translation demanded of the sender, he strikes out the symbols of the true text, explaining that they are what

cryptographers today call 'nulls', meaningless symbols inserted only to make the cipher harder to break.

c. *Linguistics.* (See quots.)

The *attrib.* example properly belongs in sense 4 of the *adj.*

1964 E. Bach *Introd. Transformational Gram.* v. 110 Since Y and Z (as usual) include the possibility of null, the transformation will have the desired effect of producing all permutations of the terminal elements. **1968** *Amer. Speech* XLIII. 277 In treating *few* in 'few people' and *much* in 'much money' as pre-article forms, Roberts assumes the existence of an unarticulated determiner he calls *null*. **1968** R. T. Harms *Introd. Phonological Theory* v. 44 If two obstruents occur initially, the first one is deleted. (Instead of 'null', the symbol 'ϕ' is sometimes used.) **1972** R. A. Palmatier *Gloss. Eng. Transformational Gram.* 111 *Null*, lacking status as a morpheme or formative—that is, having no overt representation on any level of the grammar... *Null string*, an empty string—that is, no string at all.

null, *a.* Add: Also **nul.** **4.** (Further examples.) Also more widely, esp. in *Math.*, with the sense: having, being, or associated with the value zero. *null space*, a space composed of all quantities that are transformed into zero by some given transformation.

1835 W. R. Hamilton *Conjugate Functions* 23 The transition may be said to be null, or a null step, as producing no real alteration in the moment from which it is made. *Ibid.* 31 The standard or zero-moment A itself may be denoted by the complex symbol 0 + A, because it may be conceived as generated from itself by applying the null step 0. *Ibid.* 35 The null cardinal (or number none). **1884** A. Buchheim in *Phil. Mag.* XVIII. 459 A linear space of (α–1) dimensions will be called an α-point... A matrix A of order *n* is considered as operating on the coordinates of the points of an *n*-point... If A is of nullity α, the equation $A(x_1 \ldots x_n) = 0$ is satisfied by all the points of a certain α-point, and conversely. I call this α-point the null space of A. **1885** *Proc. London Math. Soc.* XVI. 78 A point *x*, such that $\phi x = 0$, is called a null-point of [the matrix] ϕ. **1898** A. N. Whitehead *Universal Algebra* I. ii. iii. 25 Since in combination with any other element the null element 0 disappears, the symbolism may be rendered more convenient by writing $-a$ for $0-a$. **1922** E. H. Neville *Prolegomena to Analytical Geom.* v. v. 303 An ordinary circle of radius zero is called a nul circle. **1926** H. Bagchi *Course of Geom. Anal.* v. 263 The theorem..prescribes a null value for a determinant having two coincident rows or columns. **1930** J. W. Young *Projective Geom.* ix. 158 If *A* and *B* coincide, the vector *A B* is called the null vector and is denoted by 0. **1941** Birkhoff & MacLane *Surv. Mod. Algebra* x. 268 The null-space of a linear transformation *T* is the set of all vectors ξ such that $\xi T = O$. The null-space of a matrix *A* is the set of all row matrices *X* which satisfy the homogeneous linear equations $XA = O$. **1954** H. Griffin *Elem. Theory of Numbers* i. 8 A null element is an integer that divides only itself. *Ibid.*, Zero is the null element of the rational integers. **1956** R. H. Atkin *Math. & Wave Mech.* iii. 76 As in all algebras we find it convenient to introduce two identity operators. These are called the unit operator (idem factor) and the nul operator (zero). **1961** Seifert & Brown *Ballistic Missile & Space Vehicle Systems* xvii. 404 They [*sc.* gyroscopes]..operate as angular error detectors over a very small range around their reference or null positions. **1962** C. Wexler *Analytic Geom.* v. 141 The plane cuts the cone merely in a point (the vertex), resulting in a null circle or a null ellipse. **1964** E. Bach *Introd. Transformational Gram.* ii. 14 Among the elements assumed to be available for each grammar..there is one which plays a special role, namely, the null (unit or identity) element. It functions in the mathematical system underlying the representations of a grammatical theory as does zero in ordinary addition, or the digit 1 in ordinary multiplication. **1971** L. T. Agger *Introd. Electricity* xviii. 326 Balance occurs with null, or zero, deflection of the pointer. **1971** C. W. Curtis in Powell & Higman *Finite Simple Groups* iii. 171 *f* vanishes on the nullspace of α. **1971** J. Z. Young *Introd. Study Man* xvi. 201 This ingeniously establishes the change in growth power by a nul method.

b. Mech. and Geom. *null point* [tr. G. *nullpunkt* (A. F. Möbius *Lehrb. d. Statik* (1837) I. vi. 144)], the point of intersection of all the null lines of a given wrench that lie in a given plane; *null line*, a line about which the moment of a given wrench is zero; *null plane* [tr. G. *nullebene* (A. F. Möbius, *loc. cit.*)], the plane containing all the null lines of a given wrench that pass through a given point; *null system*, a system of null points and their corresponding null planes.

1903 C. M. Jessop *Treat. Line Complex* iii. 45 The distinction between the two spaces Σ and Σ' has now disappeared and we have a (1, 1) correspondence between the points and planes of space in which each point lies in its corresponding plane... Such a correspondence is called a null-system. The corresponding points and planes are called 'null-points' and 'null-planes'. **1911** *Encycl. Brit.* XVII. 967/1 In the 'Null-System' of A. F. Möbius (1790–1868), a line such that the moment of a given wrench about it is zero is called a null-line. **1942** Synge & Griffith *Princ. Mech.* x. 301 A rigid body is acted on by a force **F** at *O* and a couple **G**. *P* is an assigned point, with position vector **r** relative to *O*. Show that there is a single infinity of lines through *P* about which the force system has no moment; show that these lines lie in a plane... (The lines are called null lines, and the plane a null plane.) **1964** C. E. Springer *Geom. & Anal. Projective Spaces* x. 273 In a polar correlation with a skew-symmetric matrix, every point is incident with its corresponding plane. This type of correlation is called a null system, a designation used in the theory of statics as developed by Möbius.

c. *Math.* and *Logic.* Of a class or set: having no members. Of a propositional function or relation: always false; having the null class as its range.

1903 B. Russell *Princ. Math.* ii. 22 A propositional function is said to be null when it is false for all values of *x*; and the class of *x*'s satisfying the function is called the null-class, being in fact a class of no terms. **1906** W. H. & G. C. Young *Theory of Sets of Points* 288 The null-set..contains no point. **1932** Lewis & Langford *Symbolic Logic* vii. 208 The universal function is expressible as $p \vee \sim p$. The null-function is the negative of this. **1941** O. Helmer tr. *Tarski's Introd. Logic* v. 90 We have..in the calculus of relations two special relations, the universal relation V and the null relation Λ, the first of which holds between any two individuals, and the second between none. **1948** Ambrose & Lazerowitz *Fund. Symbolic Logic* x. 215 To say that a class is null, or empty, is the same as saying that there are no values satisfying its defining function. **1955** [see *domain *sb.* 4 f]. **1956** A. Church *Introd. Math. Logic* (rev. ed.) I. 31 If the range is given,..there is only one null class. But, e.g., the range of the null class associated with the form $\sin x = 2$ and the range of the null class associated with the form $\varepsilon < 0$ are not the same... We shall speak respectively of the 'null class of real numbers' and of the 'null class of positive real numbers'. **1966** S. Beer *Decision & Control* vi. 107 This does not matter; it simply means that the complementary set has no elements—and this is called a null set.

d. *Physics.* Existing between or joining points in space-time between which the interval is zero; *null cone* = *light cone* s.v. *light *sb.* 16.

1928 *Phil. Mag.* V. 242 A null-surface is defined as an envelope of null-cones,..while the characteristic lines on a null-surface prove to be geodesic null-lines. *Ibid.*, The history of a light wave in space-time is a null-surface. **1942** Synge & Griffith *Princ. Mech.* xvi. 475 A null line represents the history of a flash of light traveling along the axis *Ox* of a Galilean frame. **1959** J. Aharoni *Special Theory of Relativity* i. 25 An interval *ds* between two events can be either real, zero, or imaginary... In the first case the interval is called space-like, in the second case a null-interval, and in the third case time-like. **1968** T. C. Bradbury *Theoret. Mech.* xiii. 589 If the four-vector joins *O* and *C*, then $r^2 - c^2t^2 = r'^2 - c^2t'^2 = 0$. Such a vector is a null vector. Events separated by null vectors can be joined by light signals; in fact, the light cone is frequently called the null cone. **1972** J. Ehlers et al. in L. O'Raifeartaigh *Gen. Relativity* iv. 75 In a normal hyperbolic Riemannian manifold, the distinction between the interior and exterior of the null cone N_p of a point *p* can locally be defined by means of the sign of the world function $\Omega(p, q)$, for *q* near *p*.

e. Statistics. *null hypothesis*, a hypothesis that is the subject of a significance test, esp. the hypothesis that there is no difference between specified populations (any apparent difference being due to sampling or experimental error).

1935 R. A. Fisher *Design of Experiments* ii. 19 The two classes of results which are distinguished by our test of significance are..those which show a significant discrepancy from a certain hypothesis; namely, in this case, the hypothesis that the judgments given are in no way influenced by the order in which the ingredients have been added; and..results which show no significant discrepancy from this hypothesis. This hypothesis..is again characteristic of all experimentation... We may speak of this hypothesis as the 'null hypothesis', and it should be noted that the null hypothesis is never proved or established, but is possibly disproved, in the course of experimentation. **1973** *Jrnl. Genetic Psychol.* CXXIII. 86 The specific null hypotheses tested were as follows: 1. There were no differences in hostile press (fear of failure) score decreases between self-reinforcement, group therapy, and control groups. 2. Hostile press scores do not decrease significantly during the self-reinforcement condition. [Etc.] **1975** *Nature* 20 Feb. 607/1 The evidence ..for positive selection directing the evolution of early vertebrate haemoglobin is supported by a χ^2 test, performed to test the null hypothesis that sites where mutations produced acquired crucial functions did not evolve at a different rate from all other sites.

5. Passing into *sb.*: A condition of no signal; also, a direction in which no radiation is detected or emitted. Freq. *attrib.*

1926 *Bell Syst. Techn. Jrnl.* V. 295 The number of lobes is, of course, equal to the number of null directions. **1931** *Proc. IRE* XXXI. 1426 The nulls and maxima.. have been plotted in Fig. 16 for an element length of four wavelengths. *Ibid.* 1427 Figs. 15 and 16..give the null points. These are seen to be 0, 30, and 90 degrees in Fig. 15. **1931** Moyer & Wostrel *Radio Handbk.* xii. 601 A direct-current galvanometer, protected by a suitable shunt, is used as a null indicator. **1958** Condon & Odishaw *Handbk. Physics* iv. v. 66/2 Null determinations in d-c measurements are almost invariably made with a D'Arsonval-type galvanometer. **1962** *Newnes Conc. Encycl. Electr. Engin.* 94/2 The precision of a bridge measurement depends on the sensitivity of the null detector. **1968** M. Woodhouse *Rock Baby* xv. 150, I set up the loop of the D.F. set and plugged in the headset. When the signal came..I got a clear null a little west of due south. **1973** J. Hulbert *All About Navigating* vii. 96 It is much easier to pick out the softest point than the loudest point and so a null is used for direction finding. **1975** *Gramophone* Oct. 734/3 The many nulls and lobes beyond these angles are not too important, and are due to the interaction of the radiator with its housing and the corners of the cabinet.

null, *v.*[1] Add: **3.** (Further examples.) Also with *out*.

1957 *Electronics* 1 Mar. 163 The receiver uses a shielded-loop antenna to null out main powerline noise. *Ibid.*, The atmospherics..are greater in amplitude than most of the peaks of the background hash after nulling the main source of powerline noise. **1971** *Sci. Amer.* Aug. 65/2 The harmonic signal is electronically processed and sent through the feedback winding to 'null out', or cancel, the ambient field within the sensor.

null, *v.*[2] Add: Hence **nu·lling** *vbl. sb.*, the making of knurls; knurled work.

1851 C. Cist *Sk. Cincinnati* xiii. 245 All kinds of turning used by cabinet makers, including nulling of every pattern, furnished at the shortest notice. **1914** Eberlein & McClure *Pract. Bk. Period Furnit.* 63 Nulling, made up chiefly of beading, cabling and hollows, is often used to ornament the bulbous legs of Jacobean furniture. **1934** J. Gloag *Eng. Furnit.* v. 86 The edges of tables and desks were scalloped with nulling, heavily gilded. **1936** C. H. Hayward *Eng. Period Furnit.* ii. 33 The carved flutes partly filled with nullings are a feature that was used considerably in Elizabethan times. **1966** M. M. Pegler *Dict. Interior Design* 307 *Nulling*, a Jacobean wood-carving technique which produced an effect similar to repoussé or chased metalwork. The patterns were created by a series of small projections or recessions from the surface (like a boss or bead) of the wood.

nullah. Add: Also **nala.** (Further examples.)

1920 *Blackw. Mag.* Jan. 117/1 You feel him..open out again to his stride, or drop out into a sudden nala without a peck. **1933** *Discovery* June 204/1 The nalas and river beds were parched, awaiting the flood. **1963** T. Tullett *Inside Interpol* xiv. 184 After twenty minutes of careful tracking it led him to a *nala* (ditch) where he found the impression of the sole of a heavy boot. **1964** R. Perry *World of Tiger* i. 10 The tigers he shot were living in nullahs close to villages. **1972** I. Baker *Grave Doubt* vii. 90 Could it be because it was England and not some god-forsaken Afghan nullah?

nullification. **2. b.** (Earlier examples.)

1798 T. Jefferson *Writings* (1905) XVII. 386 Where powers are assumed which have not been delegated, a nullification of the act is the rightful remedy. **1830** *Massachusetts Spy* 22 Sept. (Th.), Nullification nullified.

nullify, *v.* **1.** (Earlier absol. example.)

1832 J. P. Kennedy *Swallow Barn* I. xviii. 186 I'd be glad to know if we couldn't nullify.

nulliplex (nɒ·lipleks), *a.* *Genetics.* [f. L. *nulli-*, *nullus* no + *-plex* as in Simplex, Duplex *adjs.* etc.] Of a polyploid individual: having the dominant allele of any particular gene not represented.

1921 A. F. Blakeslee in *Amer. Naturalist* LV. 257 A Poinsettia plant may, to speak in terms of the dominant factor, be considered nulliplex with no dominant genes, or simplex, duplex or triplex with, respectively, 1, 2, or 3 dominant factors. **1929** *Jrnl. Genetics* XXI. 141 From previous results it has been assumed that 14/26 is triplex for *Y* and heterozygous for *I*, and that 'White Star' is nulliplex for *Y* and heterozygous for *I*. **1963** Lewis & John *Chromosome Marker* iv. iii. 327 On selfing, a tetraploid of this kind [*sc.* AAaa] will give not three types of offspring but five, namely AAAA (quadruplex), AAAa (triplex), AAaa (duplex), Aaaa (simplex) and aaaa (nulliplex). *Ibid.* 328 Thus, with chromatid segregation a triplex can produce nulliplex offspring.

‖ **nulli secundus** (nɒ·li sĭkɒ·ndŭs), *adj. phr.* Also (applied to things) **nulli secundum.** [L.] Second to none.

1869 S. R. Hole *Bk. about Roses* iv. 55 If Mr. Shirley Hibberd..can grow good Roses within four miles of the General Post-Office..it is quite certain that he would be *nulli secundus* with the full advantage of situation and soil. **1935** G. K. Zipf *Psycho-Biol. Lang.* (1966) 75 The conventional Sanskrit alphabet is an amazingly accurate phonetic alphabet, practically *nulli secundum*. **1963** *Brewer's Dict. Phr. & Fable* 649/2 *Nulli secundus*,.. the motto of the Coldstream Guards, which regiment is hence sometimes spoken of as the *Nulli Secundus Club*.

nullisome (nɒ·lisōᵘm). *Cytology.* [f. L. *nulli-*, *nullus* no + *-some[4].] A pair of homologous chromosomes lacking from a diploid chromosome complement; also, a nullisomic individual.

1944 *Genetics* XXIX. 233 Speltoidy..has been shown.. frequently to be due to the effects of a particular monosome or its corresponding nullisome. *Ibid.* 234 Seventeen of the possible 21 different nullisomes in *Triticum vulgare* have now been obtained. **1968** [see next]. **1973** G. S. Khush *Cytogenetics Aneuploids* ix. 221 In wheat, a successful method was the test of the ability of a particular tetrasome to compensate for a particular nullisome.

nullisomic (nɒlisōᵘ·mik), *a.* (*sb.*) *Cytology.* Also † **nullosomic.** [f. as prec. + *-somic*, after *monosomic *a.* (*sb.*), etc.] Having or being a diploid chromosome complement in which one or more than one pair of homologous chromosomes is lacking. Hence as *sb.*, a nullisomic individual.

1932 *Genetics* XVII. 694 In the hybrid population the nullosomics were readily recognized. **1939** *Ibid.* XXIV. 510 Neither of the nullosomic plants set seeds. **1941** *Ibid.* XXVI. 167 (*heading*) Nullisomics in *Triticum vulgare*. **1944** *Ibid.* XXIX. 233 Some of these have been nullisomic types. **1968** R. Rieger et al. *Gloss. Genetics & Cytogenetics* 319 Normally, nullisomics (or nullisomes) cannot

survive in diploids. **1973** G. S. KHUSH *Cytogenetics Aneuploids* i. 3 Kihara (1924) and Winge (1924) were the first to report the nullisomic plants of wheat. *Ibid.* viii. 186 Some nullisomics of *Avena* may have normal viability.

nullity. Add: **6.** *Math.* The number of columns of a matrix minus its rank; the dimension of the null space of a matrix or linear transformation (equal to the dimension of its domain minus that of its range).

1884 J. J. SYLVESTER in *Amer. Jrnl. Math.* VI. 274 The absolute zero for matrices of any order is the matrix all of whose elements are zero. It possesses so far as regards multiplication..the distinguishing property of the zero, viz. that when entering into composition with any other matrix..the product..is itself over again... This is the highest degree of nullity which any matrix can possess, and (regarded as an integer) will be called ω, the order of the matrix... In general.., if all the minors of order $\omega-i+1$ vanish, but the minors of order $\omega-i$ do not all vanish, the nullity will be said to be i. **1941** BIRKHOFF & MACLANE *Survey Mod. Algebra* x. 268 Rank + nullity = Dimension of Domain. **1972** A. G. HOWSON *Handbk. Terms Algebra & Anal.* ix. 47 In the case of a homogeneous system, $Ax=0$, the inverse image of 0, i.e. the set of solutions, is $\mathrm{Ker}(t)$..which is a subspace of F^n..of dimension $n-r$, a number known as the nullity of t (or A).

nullness (nɒ·lnės). [f. NULL *a.* + -NESS.] The property or state of being null.

1949 E. BOWEN *Heat of Day* xvii. 301 The coming of winter to a stop had been most felt in the absolute nullness of night. **1959** *Proc. R. Soc.* A. CCLI. 521 The wave-like character will appear in the intrinsically *null* properties of these metrics... The nullness will become apparent from the physical properties of the metrics. **1967** *Punch* 22 Nov. 795/2 This feeling of organic injury is caused by..an utter nullness of non-taste, a denatured, defused..triviality.

nullo. Add: **2.** A type of bridge in which the object is to lose rather than gain tricks, or one in which tricks gained count against a player. Also *attrib.*

1914 *London Opinion* 7 Feb. 231/1 The new 'nullo' call at auction bridge is catching on... The Editor of the *Strand Magazine* intends publishing an article about 'nullos' in the March number. **1929** M. C. WORK *Compl. Contract Bridge* 241 *Nullos*, an unauthorized, and now obsolete, form of the game in which points were scored for losing instead of winning tricks. **1945** A. A. OSTROW *Compl. Card Player* 620 *Null* (*Nullo*): this is a declaration in which the bidder contracts not to win a single trick. **1972** H. PHILLIPS *Pop. Bk. Card Games* 373 Nullos is a form of Bridge for two which I have long recommended. *Ibid.* 375 Nullos with Contract scoring is an improvement on the original game, where the scoring and conditions are based on Auction.

‖ **nullus** (nɒ·lɒ̆s), *sb. rare*$^{-1}$. [L.] No one, nobody.

1929 D. H. LAWRENCE *Pansies* 100 My whole consciousness is cliché And I am null; I exist as an organism And a nullus.

nully (nɒ·li). *slang.* [? f. NULL *a.*; cf. *nullion* (Sc. Nat. Dict.) a stupid fellow.] A fool, a stupid person.

1973 BOYD & PARKES *Dark Number* iv. 45 You'll be a right nully if you don't mistrust all *polis* on sight. *Ibid.* vii. 78 He's a nully, a cipher. He contributes nothing. **1973** R. PARKES *Guardians* ii. 48 He's a sick, junked-up, pathetic old nully.

num, var. *YUM. Cf. *NUMMY-NUMMY.

1899 R. WHITEING *No. 5 John St.* ix. 86 Her handkerchief perfumes the whole room..to which Covey's frequent 'Num! num! num!' calls embarrassing attention. **1924** *Dialect Notes* V. 274 *Num, num, nummy, num* (humming or joy). **1961** W. SANSOM *Last Hours of Sandra Lee* vi. 112 Mouths ooed and nummed noises of appreciation.

numb, *a.* Add: **1. a.** Also *transf.*

1874 [see *DOBBER[2]]. **1892** P. H. EMERSON *Son of Fens* xxxii. 349 My old head fare as numb as a beetle. **1958** [see *FEEL *sb.* 5]. **1970** H. E. ROBERTS *Third Ear* 10/2 *Numb*, dumb; stupid.

numbat (nɒ·mbæt). *Austral.* [Aboriginal name.] The banded anteater, *Myrmecobius fasciatus*, a small, rare marsupial native to south-western Australia.

1923 F. WOOD JONES *Mammals of South Australia* I. 123 To the aboriginals..it is known as the Numbat, and this name will be adopted here. **1942** C. BARRETT *On Wallaby* iii. 38, I trailed the numbat, in South-western Australia, taking the first photograph..of that little-known animal. **1962** *Times* 22 Nov. 24/2 The numbat, once thought to be extinct, cannot be kept in captivity. **1965** *Sunday Mail Mag.* (Brisbane) 4 Apr. 14/1 The numbat, or banded anteater, of South-west Australia..is about the size of a large rat with a coat of coarse, reddish brown fur... It also has a long bushy tail, something like the fox's brush. On the upper part of its body it has white or cream bands. *Ibid.* 14/2 Ants are ripped out of the wood with a flick of the numbat's long tongue... When eating the numbat makes a noise which sounds like 'Tut-tut'. If interrupted it makes a sound more like 'Chur-rr!'.

number, *sb.* Add: **3. e.** *U.S. slang.* Usu. in *pl.* An illegal form of gambling in which bets are taken on the occurrence of numbers in a lottery or in the financial columns of a newspaper. Esp. in phr. *to play the numbers.* Also called **numbers game, racket.** Cf. POLICY *sb.*[2] 1 c. Freq. *attrib.* and *Comb.*, as *number(s)-man*; **numbers drop**, a session of such betting; **number(s)-runner**, one who collects the bets of those playing the numbers.

1897 ADE *Pink Marsh* 170 She tell Belle 'at she heah I like gin an' roll'e bones an' play numbehs. **1926** C. VAN VECHTEN *Nigger Heaven* 286 *Numbers*, a gambling game highly popular in contemporary Harlem. The winning numbers each day are derived from the New York Clearing House bank exchanges and balances..published in the newspapers. **1934** *Sun* (Baltimore) 25 Aug. 1/2 Hawkins..identified himself as a 'pay-off man' in the 'numbers business'. **1935** *Time* 21 Jan. 45/1 In Danville, Va., operators of a 'numbers' game were bankrupt. **1949** E. E. BLANCHE *You can't Win* 70 The 'numbers' racket is known by different names in various sections of the country—The Numbers Policy, Clearing House, Butter and Eggs, and the Bug. **1950** H. E. GOLDIN *Dict. Amer. Underworld Lingo* 146 Number-man, anyone engaged in the policy numbers racket. **1958** S. ELLIN *Eighth Circle* (1959) II. v. 65 He was saying something about the numbers game... The *bolita.* **1958** R. ELLISON in A. Dundes *Mother Wit* (1973) 63/1 As a numbers runner he is a bringer of manna and a worker of miracles. **1959** *Times Lit. Suppl.* 16 Jan. 29/3 The 'numbers' do for Harlem what the pools do for Notting Hill Gate—and for that matter Knightsbridge as well—provide unsustaining nourishment for dreams. **1959** *Listener* 28 May 924/2, I wonder how many people now remember that prominent feature of American life in the 'thirties—the numbers racket. **1964** O. HARRINGTON in J. H. Clarke *Harlem* 90 One of the local numbers runners dug my cartoon and.. nobody covers as much Harlem territory as the numbers man. **1965** 'MALCOLM X' *Autobiogr.* 52 Betting my dollar a day on the numbers. **1968** P. OLIVER *Screening Blues* iv. 134 The policy writers and numbers runners who took the bet by a rapid code of signals in the street or at the 'numbers drop' would urge them to play other numbers and at higher stakes. **1970** L. MERIWETHER *Daddy was Number Runner* 21 Mother played the numbers like everyone else in Harlem but she was scared about Daddy being a number runner. **1973** *Black Panther* 22 Sept. 8/3 A panel of prominent lawyers recommended last week that the District of Columbia legalize 'the numbers' racket. **1975** *New Yorker* 29 Sept. 54/3 She had met Delgado while she was selling numbers on the streets of the lower East Side.

f. *Austral.* and *N.Z.* Elementary arithmetic taught to children in primary school.

1922 *N.Z. Education Gaz.* 1 Dec. 137/1 Miss Caldwell has published a book entitled 'The Simplicity of Number', a copy of which, along with the apparatus, can..be obtained from her by teachers. **1963** B. PEARSON *Coal Flat* iv. 63 You'd best make sure of his reading and his number and see if he's good enough for this class.

4. a. (Further examples.)

1898 G. B. SHAW *Philanderer* in *Plays Unpleasant* III. 135 *Julia*... What is Dr Paramore's number in Savile Row? *Charteris.* Seventy-nine. **1908** E. F. BENSON *Blotting Bk.* i. 16, I saw one policeman trying to take my number. **1973** R. LEWIS *Blood Money* iv. 47 'Could it be the number of the hire-car he used?'..'It's a Leeds number.'

b. (*a*) (Further examples.) In later use also *transf.* in phr. *to make one's number*, to report one's arrival, to report for duty, to pay a duty or courtesy call, to make oneself known, to make oneself acquainted. *colloq.*

1861 J. LAMONT *Seasons with Sea-Horses* xviii. 293 We found that the 'Anna Louise' had only made her number twelve hours before us. **1897** P. E. STEVENSON *Deep-Water Voyage* 29 We made our number, where from, where bound, and 'all well' to the steamer, which hoisted her pennant immediately. **1927** B. M. CHAMBERS *Salt Junk* xxx. 256 Almost every ship on her way to and from South America makes her number to the island [Fernando Noronha]. **1937** C. S. FORESTER *Happy Return* xxiv. 281 The *Lydia* made her number, and the sound of the salutes began to roll slowly round the bay. **1942** PARTRIDGE in *New Statesman* 1 Aug. 75/1 'To *make one's number*' is still slang; it may be used absolutely, as in 'As soon as I join my unit I must make my number at Brigade', or in reference to a person, as in 'I must lose no time in making my number with one of the Staff Officers at Division'—in short, to *contact* him... By the way, one 'makes one's number' with one's *opposite number*, a phrase taken over from civil life. **1945** 'N. SHUTE' *Most Secret* ix. 211 Captain (D.) was there to see them off; I made my number with him as representing V.A.C.O. and we stood chatting for a time. **1951** H. JORDAN *Islander* II. vii. 92 Jim brought his ketch..alongside the *Islander* soon after breakfast and made his number to the master. **1955** E. WAUGH *Officers & Gentlemen* I. vi. 56 You go ahead and make your number with your CO. **1958** M. DICKENS *Man Overboard* xii. 192 Ben saw himself on Speech Day, making his number with mothers in garden-party hats. **1963** P. MCCUTCHAN *Man from Moscow* ix. 87 On arrival in Moscow..Shaw made his number at the W.I.O.C.A. office. **1965** B. SWEET-ESCOTT *Baker Street Irregular* vii. 224 We turned back and made our number with the navy there. **1974** D. SEAMAN *Bomb that could Lip-Read* xviii. 177 'Will you go to the conference site today?' 'Might as well make my number with the R.U.C.'

d. With reference to a lottery number, or some other number by or with which one may be identified, as an army number, esp. in fig. phr. *one's number is* (or *has gone*) *up*, one is doomed (to die), one's time is come, one is 'done for'; *one's number is on* (something, esp. a bullet or shell), one is doomed (to die, or to a particular destiny). Cf. *NAME *sb.* 1 g.

1806 C. LAMB *Let.* 25 Jan. in *Works* (1870) II. 89 Though this is a lottery to which none but G. Barnett would choose to trust his all, there is no harm just to call in at Despair's office for a friend, and see if *his* number is come up. **1899** C. ROOK *Hooligan Nights* iv. 56 You couldn't tallygraft to Billy no more. His number's up awright, wiv no error. **1914** *London Opinion* XL. 231/2 The late Patsey Cadogan, who left £100,000 when his number went up. **1915** 'BARTIMEUS' *Tall Ship* i. 11, I think our number's up, old thing. **1922** WODEHOUSE *Girl on Boat* xi. 181 Fate had dealt him a knock-out blow; his number was up. **1925** FRASER & GIBBONS *Soldier & Sailor Words* 163 *Name* (or *number*) *on, to have one's*, said of a bullet that hit a man; *i.e.*, that it was destined for him. **1929** *Mercury Story Bk.* 98 It was about midday that I first realised that his number was up. **1937** V. BARTLETT *This is my Life* xi. 188 The Director-General said that he would nevertheless like me to broadcast a short talk under my own name... My number was up. **1965** BROPHY & PARTRIDGE *Long Trail* 154 *Number on.* A fatalistic but consolatory superstition insisted that no man need fear any bullet or shell, however close it came, unless it *had his regimental number* (or his name and number) engraved on it. **1965** F. SARGESON *Memoirs of Peon* vi. 138 She was forgiven for insisting upon her husband's undertaking the labour which had unfortunately sent his number up. **1966** *Listener* 23 June 923/2 The endless stream of cars and lorries swept on, only momentarily slowed down when the number of one of them came up... It was the arbitrariness of accident. **1974** C. FREMLIN *By Horror Haunted* 15 I'm as safe here as..any where..if it's got your number on it, you'll get it, no matter *where* you are! **1975** J. AIKEN *Voices in Empty House* xviii. 331 He'd got leukaemia. He knew his number was up.

e. In *fig.* use in phr. *to get* (*take, have*) *someone's number*, to make a correct appraisal of someone's character, motives or intentions, to size someone up.

1853 DICKENS *Bleak Ho.* lvii. 550 Whenever a person proclaims to you 'In worldly matters I'm a child,'..that person is only a crying off from being held accountable, and..you have got that person's number, and it's Number One. **1889** 'MARK TWAIN' *Yankee* xxxiv. 405 Let him go, for the present; I took his number, so to speak. *Ibid.* xxxv. 414 That was the sort of master we had. I took *his* number. **1912** C. MATHEWSON *Pitching in a Pinch* i. 4 'I've got your number now, Matty!' he shouted at me as he drew up at second base. **1920** W. HARD *Raymond Robins' Own Story* 190 To hurt Bolshevism you need at least to get its number. **1921** R. D. PAINE *Comr. Rolling Ocean* viii. 129 Do you remember the day before when he made that crack at you in front of Miss Crozier? I had his number right then. **1934** J. M. CAIN *Postman always rings Twice* ii. 15 She knew what I meant, and she knew I had her number. **1939** I. BAIRD *Waste Heritage* vi. 74 'Never mind who I am,' Matt said, 'I got your number anyway.' **1956** W. GRAHAM *Sleeping Partner* xiii. 111, I was trying to think of a verse all last night... I can't think who wrote it, but he rather got my number. **1970** G. JACKSON *Let.* 29 May in *Soledad Brother* (1971) 265 Big Brother. He is rather transparent. I have his number. **1975** *Times Lit. Suppl.* 21 Mar. 332/4 Field-Marshal Lord Montgomery..had [Augustus] John's number right away. 'Who is this chap?' he demanded to know. 'He drinks, he's dirty, and I know there are women in the background!'

f. A number assigned to a particular telephone (or group of telephones) which corresponds to the terminals of its line at the exchange and in modern systems is dialled by a caller in order to establish a connection with it and cause it to ring; *number-unobtainable signal* or *tone*, a sound indicating to a caller that the number dialled is unobtainable for a reason other than its being engaged; similarly *number-engaged signal*; *wrong number*, a number obtained other than the one required by the caller.

1879 *Times* 8 Sept. 12/1 The person at No. 2 calls the attention of the attendant at the exchange by means of an electric bell. At the same moment a shutter on the switchboard falls and discloses the number of the applicant. *Ibid.*, So with any other numbers; they can be instantly connected or disconnected. **1884** *List of Subscribers* (London & Globe Telephone Co.) 4 Take telephones from hooks and speak at once, giving number of subscriber wanted. **1891** [see *ENGAGED *ppl. a.* 3]. **1911** W. J. LOCKE *Glory of Clementina Wing* 334 She..took up the telephone and gave a number. **1930** WODEHOUSE *Very Good, Jeeves!* vi. 169 A woman has tossed my heart lightly away, but what of it?.. The voice of Love seemed to call to me, but it was a wrong number. **1930** *Gloss. Terms Telegraphs & Telephones* (*B.S.I.*) 47/1 Number-unobtainable tone. **1932** E. BOWEN *To North* vi. 63 Markie, too well advised to encounter Cecilia over the wire, soon traced Emmeline to her number at Woburn Place. **1942** A. CHRISTIE *Body in Library* i. 12 Miss Marple's telephone rang... 'It must be,' Miss Marple decided, 'a wrong number.' **1959** H. HOBSON *Mission House Murder* xiv. 92 The phone..has been giving the number-engaged signal for over half an hour. **1965** MRS. L. B. JOHNSON *White House Diary* 3 June (1970) 283, I tried to reach him, or rather his wife, to no avail. The number didn't answer. **1969** 'D. RUTHERFORD' *Gilt-Edged Cockpit* viii. 148 He listened..to the high whine of the 'number unobtainable' signal, knowing that she had left the receiver off. **1972** H. MACINNES *Message from Málaga* xii. 183 The telephone will ring... I shall.. apologize for speaking to a wrong number. **1972** 'W. HAGGARD' *Protectors* iii. 38 Phone me at once... You know the number.

g. *to lose one's number*, to make a gaffe, to lose stock. *rare.*

a **1936** KIPLING *Something of Myself* (1937) iv. 86 He produced a bottle of real Tokay, which I tasted, and lost

my number badly by saying that it reminded me of some medicinal wine.

5. (Further examples.)

1930 E. H. Young *Miss Mole* ix. 79 She sometimes saw No. 16 [*sc.* the person living at that house] trundling towards the back gate, she sometimes heard him calling in the cats at night. **1938** S. Beckett *Murphy* v. 95 A staple recreation..had been to wait at Walham Green for a nice number eleven [bus] and take it through the evening rush to Liverpool Street and back. **1970** Y. Carter *Mr. Campion's Falcon* xii. 91 A shabby row of houses..[with] Queen Anne porches... Number Seven.. had an intricate semi-circular fanlight.

c. *number ones*, ellipt. form of 'No. 1 dress', 'No. 1 suit' (also used), a best dress uniform worn esp. in the Navy.

1829 F. Marryat *F. Mildmay* II. 132 Each was dressed out in our No. 1 suits, in most exact and unquizzable uniform. **1914** 'Bartimeus' *Naval Occasions* xviii. 157 The 'Rig of the Day' was 'Number Ones'. **1947** *Landfall* I. 287 Hughes unpacked his kit to find his number ones badly crushed, and cursing, he went in search of an iron. **1950** A. P. Herbert *Independent Member* lxi. 359 The queer-looking spectacled P.O., 'sculling about' in his No. 1's astern of the Field-Marshal. **1955** [see *doll *v.*[2]]. **1968** J. Lock *Lady Policeman* ix. 78 The PCs in their quaint, high-buttoned 'number one' uniforms look as though they have stepped out of a jaded print. **1972** *Police Rev.* 17 Nov. 1489/2 (*caption*) Probably the last Policemen ever to wear their 'number ones', the ceremonial dress of the Force which is probably being phased out at the end of the year.

d. colloq. number one, the finest quality, the best obtainable. As *attrib.* or *adj. phr.*, first-rate, 'tip-top'; leading, principal.

1839 *Spirit of Times* 29 June 195/1 He is the sole owner of the estate upon which the [race] track is located, and will, no doubt, do all he can to make it 'a number one' concern. **1843** F. Marryat *Trav. M. Violet* II. xi. 231 After having drained half-a-dozen cups of 'stiff, true, downright Yankee No. 1', we all of us took our blankets. **1846** *Swell's Night Guide* 40 This *sanctum-sanctorum* is.. the number one of cribberies. **1848** J. T. Fields *Let.* 15 Aug. in *R. W. Griswold's Corresp.* (1898) 242, I have some beautiful poems by me by Mrs. Barnes... They are No. 1, full of passionate feeling and eminently worthy of a place. **1855** *Trans. Mich. Agric. Soc.* VI. 495 Wheat first-rate, peas, also, oats number one. **1871** E. Eggleston *Hoosier Schoolmaster* (1872) xv. 125 Seems to me it would be number one to have God help you. **1872** —— *End of World* xi. 78 This walk seems the shortest, when I'm in superfine, number-one comp'ny. *c* **1882** in R. Pearsall *Worm in Bud* (1969) ii. 43 Awfully rollicking, fearfully frollicking, Number one Masher of all. **1897** G. B. Shaw *Let.* 16 Apr. in *Ellen Terry & Shaw* (1931) 186, I have *all* the British rights of Arms and all but eleven No. 1 towns for You Never Can Tell. **1904** —— *Let.* 9 Sept. in *Ibid.* 414 The tour is on the cheapest scale.. and the towns by no means all Number Ones. **1933** P. Godfrey *Back-Stage* xvi. 199 The No. 1 dates, such as Birmingham, Manchester, Liverpool, Glasgow, and Edinburgh, get the best companies. *Ibid.* 200 Actors on the No. 1's are the best paid. **1942** E. Paul *Narrow St.* xxiv. 212 The sluggish public began to scent the No. 1 scandal of the century. **1943** Koestler *Arrival & Departure* iv. 148, I could even point to a number of similarities between your No. 1 and our No. 1. **1944** *Living off Land* iv. 62 (*heading*) Panic as Enemy No. 1. **1955** W. Gaddis *Recognitions* III. ii. 752 Look, what did Schmuck's number-one boy want over there, when you stopped and talked to them. **1957** A. Grimble *Return to Islands* iii. 58 He turned out to be a number-one boat-builder. **1968** *Globe & Mail* (Toronto) 3 Feb. 51/3 One small folded letter on blue paper bearing a 12-pence stamp will be the number one feature. **1969** C. Burke *God is Beautiful, Man* (1970) 80 And it don't really make no difference if you're one or two. 'Cause with God, you're always number one. **1971** *Flying* Apr. S7/1 Pilot briefing is the number-one item in the present FSS system. **1974** *Plain Dealer* (Cleveland, Ohio) 26 Oct. 3-D/1 Officials here expect a crowd of only 35,000 for the No. 1 team in the nation.

e. *Number ten*, also *No. 10*, in full No. 10 Downing Street, the London residence of the Prime Minister. Hence used allusively to denote the influence or opinions of the Prime Minister. Also *transf.*, as quot. 1972.

1880 *Leisure Hour* 383/2 Doubtless 'oblivious forgetfulness' would occur to any one who, having been created a peer of Parliament by a late occupant of No. 10, should happen to be seen by the fallen Minister. **1905** [see *No., N°.]. **1934** *Punch* 28 Mar. 345/1 The Muse at No. 10. 'It is rare to find a Prime Minister who is also a poet.'—*Press.* **1939** *Ibid.* 13 Sept. 284/2 The mystery deepened when the man did not enter No. 10 at all. **1958** L. Durrell *Mountolive* iv. 86 Even in the rain there was the usual little cluster of tourists and loungers outside the gates of Number Ten. **1961** I. Jefferies *It wasn't Me!* iii. 36 If academic opinion differs from that at No. 10 we go our own way. **1969** 'W. Haggard' *Doubtful Disciple* i. 1 The summons to Number Ten had knocked him flat. Under-Secretaries weren't called to the Prime Minister's house. **1972** *Guardian* 14 June 12/1 Now that Mr Suto is on the brink of retirement..his wife feels she can lift the curtain on life at Japan's No. 10. **1974** *Daily Mail* 9/3 It was this which ..put Edward Heath into Number 10.

f. *number one*, a children's word or euphemism for 'urine'; similarly *number two* for 'fæces'.

1902 Farmer & Henley *Slang* V. 75/2 *Number one*,.. (nursery). Urination; also a chamber-pot. *Ibid.*, *Number two*,..(nursery). Evacuation. **1923** J. Manchon *Le Slang* 212 *I want to do number one*, je veux faire pipi. **1937** A. S. Neill *That Dreadful School* vii. 118 Our juniors have an interest in the Old English word for faeces. They use it a lot—the ones from polite homes do, I mean homes that talk of No. 2 and 'going to the House of Commons' (how appropriate a name!). **1938** I. Goldberg *Wonder of Words* vi. 108 The child is early taught to refer to his needs as 'number one' and 'number two'. **1949** F. Sargeson *I saw in my Dream* 15 You felt sick and told mother, and she felt your forehead and asked how long it was since you did number two. **1959** I. & P. Opie *Lore & Lang. Schoolch.* vi. 96 Dirty kangaroo, Sitting on the dustbin Doing his 'Number Two'. **1963** G. Greene *Sense of Reality* 47 'I want to do number one.' I blurted out... He called to Maria, 'The boy wants to piss. Fetch him the golden po.' **1967** A. Wilson *No Laughing Matter* II. 70 This little ginger [kitten] is going to do a number one if we're not careful. **1971** M. McCarthy *Birds of America* 145 When I had done Number Two, you always washed them out yourself before sending them to the diaper service.

g. *number two*: colloq. phr. (freq. attrib.), a provincial town (in contexts one not noted for its appreciation of the theatre); also, a person second in importance or rank to a head of a department, etc., a second in command.

1908 G. B. Shaw *Let.* 11 Aug. in *Lett. to G. Barker* (1956) 134 You might let her begin on a number two tour of it [*sc.* a play]. **1920** —— *Let.* 22 Dec. in *B. Shaw & Mrs. Campbell* (1952) 215 You yourself have held up the six big cities and kept poor Macdona wandering in the number twos. **1934** R. Ferguson *Celebrated Sequels* 180 My elocution..*has* been admired in such Number Two towns as Wigan. **1952** 'M. Innes' *Private View* xiv. 214 This fellow, Cadover, is your husband's Number Two? **1968** M. Woodhouse *Rock Baby* vii. 76 I'll introduce you to your Number Two... You'll need some help. **1970** *Guardian Weekly* 25 Apr. 17 Russia feels the understandable necessity to catch up in the arms race... It just does not pay to be number two. **1973** W. Fairchild *Swiss Arrangement* xiii. 173 'Lisa Kestler was in charge of the whole operation—right?' 'Right..Gray was her number two.' **1975** S. Johnson *Urbane Guerilla* II. 103 Usually we don't bother with the no. 2 man.

h. Naval. *number one*, a first lieutenant, esp. one who is second in command to the captain of a ship. Freq. as a form of address.

1909 J. R. Ware *Passing English* 184/2 *Number one*.., strictly naval for first lieutenant. **1916** 'Taffrail' *Stand By!* 120 'I'm sorry for him,' said No. One, lifting his glass with a grin. **1948** Partridge *Dict. Forces' Slang* 129 *Number one.* The sergeant in charge of a gun. (Army.) (2) The First Lieutenant. (Ward-room).

i. Forces' slang. *number nine*, an aperient pill freq. prescribed as a cure-all for minor illnesses or doubtful symptoms (see quot. 1925).

1916 *Anzac Book* 110 And should my health appear to fail And appetite grow fine, My doctor hands me—not a bill, But just a Number 9. **1925** Fraser & Gibbons *Soldier & Sailor Words* 211 *Number nine...* The popular name for the Service aperient dose or pill. From its listed number, No. 9, in the Field Hospital Case of drugs. Being the Medical Officer's stock remedy in case of doubtful ailments, or suspected malingering, in the war the expression 'A No. 9' came to be used in all kinds of applications, more or less in jest. **1926** N. Lucas *London & its Criminals* xv. 181 They have one medicine in prison for all ills—from toothache to broken limbs, this is known to all old-timers as 'white mixture' and it corresponds to the 'number nines' of the Army. **1930** Brophy & Partridge *Songs & Slang Brit. Soldier* 161 The regimental Medical Officer.. invariably gave him a standardized purgative pill, known as Number 9, and marked him down as *M.D.* i.e. medicine and duty.

6. e. An item in a programme of musical entertainment. Also, more loosely, any song or tune. Cf. senses 6 c and d in Dict.

1885 G. B. Shaw *How to become Musical Critic* (1960) 80 To tap their feet and wag their heads to the seductive swing of his numbers. **1900** E. E. Peake *Darlingtons* i. 2 After a rattling number by the band, a brief address by the Mayor, and another rattling number by the band, a neatly dressed, handsome man..advanced to the front of the platform. **1913** *Confessions of Dancing Girl* vi. 109 We had worked all the variety halls and cafés..and we had no novel 'numbers'. **1920** Wodehouse *Jill the Reckless* (1922) xi. 161 He's put over any amount of shows which would have flopped like dogs without him to stage the numbers. **1927** T. S. Eliot in *Newton's Seneca* (Tudor Translations) p. x, But the characters in a play of Seneca behave more like members of a minstrel troupe..rising in turn each to do his 'number'. **1933** P. Godfrey *Back-Stage* xiv. 173 A 'number' is any song or musical item in the programme, so named because every such item is numbered in rotation in the musical director's copy, and is always referred to by its cypher. **1948** *Penguin Music Mag.* Feb. 25 The B.B.C. could start..by putting some kind of check on the manner and matter of their inane songs—'numbers' I think they call them. **1958** *Publ. Amer. Dial. Soc.* xxx. 41 Words deeply engrained in the speech of the jazzman... Any tune is a 'number'. **1962** *Movie* Oct. 36/2 The garnish of musical numbers. **1973** J. Wainwright *Pride of Pigs* 175 It was a fine intro to a fine number. The style was traditional jazz.

f. *colloq.* A person or thing, esp. (i) an article of apparel.

1894 Somerville & 'Ross' *Real Charlotte* I. iii. 22 The shop windows..had progressed..to straw hats, tennis shoes, and coloured Summer Numbers. *c* **1900** in M. Johnson *Amer. Advertising* (1960), Indian panama horse hat. Last year our sales on this number were enormous, showing that this hat is no longer a fad. **1935** *Ladies' Home Jrnl.* Apr. 19/3 Deedee had swathed herself in an afternoon number and was happily emptying the last of my..perfume down her front. **1953** M. Steen *Anna Fitzalan* viii. 211 Petula Wimbleby's solution turned out to be an exquisite but throat-high 'little number' redeemed by lumps of jade. **1959** P. Bull *I know Face* ix. 149 The camel-hair number suffered most, as the majority of my friends wished to wear it. **1969** *Daily Tel.* 17 Jan. 17 Two of Mattli's best numbers were in impeccable white: a coat..and a wool suit.

(ii) A person, frequently with qualifying word; more usually, a woman. Cf. *article *sb.* 14 b.

1919 *Dialect Notes* V. 70 *Hot one, hot number*, used as a term of disgust. 'You're a hot one I must say.' New Mexico. **1924** H. C. Witwer in *Cosmopolitan* Apr. 70/1 Oh, she's beautiful enough!.. She's a snappy number with the skin you love to touch. **1936** L. C. Douglas *White Banners* xvi. 343 She's an odd number... I rather fancy she wears a hair shirt herself. **1938** R. C. Sherwood *Idiot's Delight* (ed. 2) 12 Bebe is a hard, harsh little number who shimmies. **1944** Auden *For Time Being* (1945) 10 And every gorgeous number may Be laid by anyone. **1950** R. Chandler *Trouble is my Business* i. 8 A girl. A red-headed number with bedroom eyes. **1955** W. Gaddis *Recognitions* II. vii. 627 Have you seen a little blond number named Adeline? **1960** C. Watson *Bump in Night* xii. 122 The fellow was rather a dull number when you get down to a straight life story. **1968** J. Sangster *Touchfeather* ii. 17, I make do with three [men]..my home number is just a nice guy who sells motor cars.

(iii) An occupation, job, assignment.

1948 Partridge *Dict. Forces' Slang* 129 *Number, quiet*, an easy job at sea or ashore. **1959** *N.Z. Listener* 24 July 5/1 A navigator's yeoman who had the cushy number of rubbing out old minefields and putting in new ones. **1968** *Listener* 19 Sept. 370/2 Transferred to what was described as a 'cushy number' with the Commandos. **1975** J. Wainwright *Square Dance* 187 He silently congratulated himself. It was a soft number, sitting here.

g. = *denier[3] 4. Cf. *count *sb.*[1] 2 b.

1923 G. G. Denny *Fabrics* I. 31 Yarn count—a number given to yarn indicating its fineness, based upon number of yards per pound, more correctly called 'yarn number'. **1927** M. H. Avram *Rayon Industry* 516 There are many systems by which the 'number', 'size', or 'count' of yarns is expressed. *Ibid.*, The number..is..the weight of a standard unit skein or hank. **1928** V. Hottenroth *Artificial Silk* ix. 160 Before the silk is ready for sale or for treatment in the dye works, it must be sorted according to quality and number (that is, thickness of thread). **1931** D. L. Pellatt *Viscose Rayon Production* xi. 97 For 150-denier yarn..the number has risen from 18 to 21, 24, 27.

19. *attrib.* and *Comb.*, as (sense 1) *number-word, -work*; (sense 3) *number continuum, series, system*; (sense 6 a) *number book, -carrier, man*; (sense 6 d) *number opera*; **number-average** *Chem.*, an average of some parameter of the molecules of a mixture calculated as an arithmetic mean with each individual molecule contributing equally, regardless of size; **number board,** a board on which numbers are displayed; **number-cloth,** the cloth bearing a horse's number in a race; **number-cruncher** *colloq.*, a machine (or occas. a person) with the capacity for performing arithmetical operations of great complexity or length; so **number-crunching**; **number-form,** the shapes into which series of numbers are formed in the mental imagery of some people; **number line,** a graduated line used to illustrate simple numerical concepts and operations; **number-plate,** a plate bearing a number, esp. that on a registered vehicle; **number six,** (*a*) *U.S. colloq.*, a household medicinal remedy, so called from its place on the pharmaceutical list of its inventor, Samuel Thomson; (*b*) a curl having the shape of the figure six which is dressed on to the forehead; cf. *figure-six* adj. (Figure *sb.* 26); **number six nose,** a large fleshy nose, supposed to be similar in shape to the figure six; **number theory,** the branch of mathematics dealing with the properties and relationships of numbers, esp. the positive integers (cf. Theory[1] 4 c); so **number-theoretic, -theoretical** *adjs.*; **number-theoretically** *adv.*; **number theorist.**

1935 Kraemer & Lansing in *Jrnl. Physical Chem.* XXXIX. 165 For heterogeneous materials, different methods for determining molecular weights give different 'average' values. Thus, it may be shown that freezing point, osmotic pressure, and end-group methods, when applied properly to an ideal mixture, result in an average value defined by the expression $M_n = 1/\Sigma(f_i/M_i)$ where f_i is the fractional weight of the constituent of molecular weight M_i in the mixture, and the summation is to be applied to all constituents present. This average may be designated as a 'number-average molecular weight'. **1955** *Jrnl. Polymer Sci.* XVII. 263 Number average degrees of polymerization are used to calculate the rates of initiation and transfer in vinyl polymerizations, and the extent of reaction in polycondensations. **1974** Allen & Patrick *Kinetics & Mechanisms Polymerization Reactions* vii. 419 Until recent years determination of number-average molecular weights was a most imprecise measurement. **1938** G. H. Sewell *Amateur Film-Making* v. 54 That [*sc.* numbering each shot] is done by exposing before each shot a Number Board. **1961** K. Reisz *Technique Film Editing* (ed. 9) 281 Number board, board momentarily held before the camera and photographed at the beginning of a take, recording the title of the film, number of the take and scene, in order to facilitate identification for the editor. **1969** D. Francis *Enquiry* I. i. 14 The Oxford Stewards had been elected for social reasons only..one of them couldn't read a number board at five paces. **1960** G. A. Glaister *Gloss. Bk.* 278 *Number books*, books published serially... Each part consisted of two or more sheets stitched together within blue-paper covers. **1963** *English Studies* XLIV. 149 But the kind of serialisation.. (often called 'number books' or 'subscription books') was

really the issue and sale of a book in separate fascicules.. so that the purchaser could..collect the entire work and have it..bound if he so wished. **1919** M. Beer *Hist. Brit. Socialism* I. II. ii. 108 He was successively a number-carrier, street bookseller, and editor of a democratic periodical. **1924** E. Wallace *Educated Evans* vi. 131 Catskin was the one horse..that Educated Evans would have recognized without colours and number-cloth. **1975** D. Francis *High Stakes* i. 5 People..carrying out saddles and number cloths for the next steeplechase. **1903** Number-continuum [see *continuum]. **1966** *New Scientist* 29 Sept. 729/1 The Flowers report recommended the setting up of some 'regional centres' each with a large 'number-cruncher' to take the bulk-computing load off more local machines. **1971** *Ibid.* 3 June 572/3 Tools ranging from the slide rule to the number-cruncher. **1971** A. Sampson *New Anat. Britain* v. xxvi. 497 Kenneth Keith, a brusque number-cruncher who had come into banking from accountancy. **1971** *Sci. Amer.* Aug. 100 (Advt.), Here's a calculator that speaks your language. You can customize its keyboard, memory size, display, programs and peripherals to suit your number-crunching tasks. **1883** F. Galton *Inquiries into Human Faculty* 124 The character of the forms under which historical dates are visualised contrast strongly with the ordinary Number-Forms. **1903** G. M. Stratton *Experimental Psychol.* xiii. 253 A peculiarity of this same number-form ..is that with the higher numbers the person changes his point of view. **1936** *Brit. Jrnl. Educ. Psychol.* VI. 60 The main object of the investigation..was to find if the presence of number forms is correlated to any significant degree with arithmetical ability. **1963** *Listener* 28 Mar. 547/1 Some people, whenever they think about numbers, picture them in a spatial arrangement... The experiences are called number forms. **1964** E. J. Swenson *Teaching Arithm. to Children* v. 99/1 When number lines are introduced to children, they should come in as a representation of a problem situation. **1968** Murphy & Kempf *New Math. made Simple* ii. 36 Since addition and subtraction are inverse operations, we expect subtraction to be associated with moving to the left on a number line. **1866** J. Blackwood *Let.* 21 Dec. in *Geo. Eliot's Lett.* (1956) IV. 321 The 'Number Men', i.e. men who sell the weekly and monthly publications in large numbers. **1947** A. Einstein *Music in Romantic Era* x. 117 Even a musician so retrospective as Louis Spohr could not help abandoning the number-opera towards the end of his career. **1958** *Listener* 24 July 141/3 'Die Zaubergeige', for example, is a 'number opera' whose folkish tunes stem from popular Bavarian art. **1869** *Good Words* 1 Mar. 170/2 The white porcelain number-plates upon the doors. **1901** *Motor-Car World* Apr. 74/1 We greatly fear that the number-plate is coming. **1911** *Chambers's Jrnl.* Dec. 831/1 White light to illumine the number-plate. **1973** P. Evans *Bodyguard Man* viii. 67 He..scooped up a handful of dirt from the roadside and rubbed it on to the rear number-plate until it became nearly illegible. **1975** *Drive* New Year 98/1 Numberplate collecting has always been a popular hobby in the USA. **1890** W. James *Princ. Psychol.* II. xxviii. 653 Little by little in our minds the number-series is formed. **1822** S. Thomson *Narr. Life* 63, I began with him by giving medicine to correct and strengthen the system; bathed the wound with my rhumatic drops, or No. 6. **1842** C. M. Kirkland *Forest Life* I. 71 We stick to thoroughwort,—balmony,—soot tea,—'number six',—and the like. **1909** *Bull. of Lloyd Library of Botany, Pharmacy & Materia Medica* 15 Thomson's *Compound Tincture of Myrrh and Capsicum* became celebrated as 'Number 6'. **1923** J. Manchon *Le Slang* 271 *Number sixes*,..des accroche-cœur. **1966** J. S. Cox *Illustr. Dict. Hairdressing & Wigmaking* 104/1 *Number sixes*, curls dressed onto the forehead. **1923** G. B. Shaw *Matter with Ireland* (1962) 260 Whereas my Irish nationality was formerly a valuable asset to me in England, I am now expected to apologize for it by men with wooly heads or number six noses. **1932** —— *Adventures of Black Girl* 18 A dark man with wavy black hair, and a number six nose. **1924** R. M. Ogden tr. *Koffka's Growth of Mind* v. 332 Max Wertheimer has investigated the kind of ideas employed by men who do not possess our developed number-system, in tasks where we would use numbers. **1914** *Q. Jrnl. Pure & Applied Math.* XLV. 373 We begin by listing the analogues of the algebraic invariants and then supplement these with the necessary invariants peculiar to the number-theoretic case. **1966** J. H. Cadwell *Topics Recr. Math.* xii. 133 The well-known ratio 22/7 shows that rational approximations have their uses. They are of considerable importance from a number-theoretic standpoint. **1968** A. M. Tropper tr. *H. Meschkowski's Introd. Mod. Math.* viii. 178 There are still many unsolved number theoretical problems. **1950** *Math. Tables & Other Aids to Computation* IV. 110 Something number-theoretically significant may be occurring. **1929** *Bull. Amer. Math. Soc.* XXXV. 779 There is no number-theorist who has not heard of 'Farey's series'. **1971** *Sci. Amer.* June 56/2 The pattern of occurrence of Mersenne numbers, Mersenne primes and perfect numbers continues to mystify number theorists. [**1798** A. M. Le Gendre *(title)* Essai sur la théorie des nombres. **1811** P. Barlow *(title)* An elementary investigation of the theory of numbers.] **1912** *Bull. Amer. Math. Soc.* XVIII. 335 The theory of determinants ..in the nineteenth century came to permeate all branches of number theory, algebra, [etc.]. **1939** Uspensky & Heaslet *Elem. Number Theory* p. v, Instruction in elementary number theory is given in an ever-increasing number of American universities and colleges. **1948** O. Ore *Number Theory & its Hist.* v. 76 The study of these laws in the distribution of the primes falls in the field of analytic number theory. This particular domain of number theory..is considered to be technically one of the most difficult fields of mathematics. **1964** M. McLuhan *Understanding Media* (1967) xxxiii. 370 Arithmetic in grade three or nine, when taught in terms of number theory, symbolic logic, and cultural history, ceases to be mere practice in problems. **1924** R. M. Ogden tr. *Koffka's Growth of Mind* v. 334 Many peoples use other number-words in counting than the ones they use in naming sums. **1911** S. S. Colvin *Learning Process* iii. 51 Much of it might function equally well for the reading habit, or the number-work habit. **1962** *Listener* 15 Mar. 469/2 Earlier attempts to teach 'number work' are premature and cannot lead beyond the learning of meaningless rules.

numbered, *ppl. a.* Add: **2.** *Comb.*, as **numbered account**, an account at a bank, esp. a Swiss bank, which is identified only by a number and does not bear the owner's name.

1963 'Han Suyin' *Four Faces* 31 He..had money salted away in a numbered account in Switzerland. **1968** J. Blackburn *Young Man from Lima* vi. 61 Numbered accounts in Swiss banks tell no tales. **1972** W. Davis *Money Talks* 136 Italian businessmen, who appreciate this more than most, often enter Switzerland with suitcases full of banknotes and open numbered accounts on the spot.

numbhead (nʌ·mhed). *U.S. colloq.* Also **numhead.** [f. Numb *a.* + Head *sb.*, after Numskull.] = Numskull. So **nu·mbheaded** *a.*

a **1852** F. M. Whitcher *Widow Bedott Papers* (1856) x. 98 The old coot was so awful numbheaded I couldent beat anythin' into him. **1876** *Rep. Vermont Board Agric.* III. 624 The opinion too generally prevails that almost any numhead will do for a farm laborer. **1960** Wentworth & Flexner *Dict. Amer. Slang* 359/2 *Numb-head*, a stupid or dull person.

numerable, *a.* Add: Hence also **numerabi·lity,** the quality of being numerable.

1943 [see *abstractable *a.*].

numeracy (niū·mĕrăsi). [f. *numerate *a.*, after *literacy*.] The quality or state of being numerate; ability with or knowledge of numbers.

1959 *15 to 18: Rep. Cent. Advisory Council for Educ. (Eng.)* (Ministry of Educ.) I. xxv. 270 When we say that a scientist is 'illiterate', we mean that he is not well enough read to be able to communicate effectively with those who have had a literary education. When we say that a historian or a linguist is 'innumerate' we mean that he cannot even begin to understand what scientists and mathematicians are talking about... It is perhaps possible to distinguish two different aspects of numeracy that should concern the Sixth Former. **1960** *English* XIII. 44 A certain lack of 'numeracy' on the part of those trained in the Arts can make them a little purblind to the implications of figures such as these. **1960** *Rep. Proc. Conf. Univ. U.K.* 23 If scientific barbarians are to be given a veneer of literacy, and literary barbarians a veneer of numeracy, I suggest the proper apparatus for it is a lot of deep armchairs in an open access library. **1966** *Economist* 22 Jan. 310/2 The need for numeracy today is enormous. Business requires..people who..have grasped the principles of reducing a chaos of information to some kind of order. **1970** *Sci. Jrnl.* Feb. 73/2 The scientist does, however, possess the advantage of numeracy and can usually acquire quite easily the statistical and theoretical background to modern management techniques. **1972** *Daily Tel.* 22 Jan. 2/5 The plan must be welcomed for introducing pre-school children to reading, writing and numeracy.

numeraire (niū·mĕrēᵊɹ). *Econ.* Also **numéraire.** [ad. F. *numéraire*.] The function of money as a measure of value or unit of account; a standard for currency exchange rates.

1964 Gould & Kolb *Dict. Soc. Sci.* 532/2 In a primitive society two knives might exchange for one calf. Often one good is singled out to serve as a *numeraire* or common measure for other goods, thus precious metals serve both as a good wanted for particular purposes and as a unit of value and exchange. **1965** J. L. Hanson *Dict. Econ. & Commerce* 302/1 *Numeraire*, a term sometimes used of the function of money as a measure of value. **1971** *New Yorker* 23 Oct. 118 The Bretton Woods agreement.. established the dollar as the *numéraire*, or measuring rod, against which the value of other currencies was set. **1972** *National Westminster Bank Quarterly Rev.* May 21 Three points constitute the core of the Barber proposals [at the last IMF meetings]: a) That SDRs 'become the numeraire in terms of which parities are expressed and in relation to which currencies are revalued or devalued'. **1972** *Times* 27 Sept. 21/2 The use of Special Drawing Rights rather than the dollar as the effective numeraire in the new system is widely acceptable. **1973** *Times* 26 Jan. 17/6 It is the European currencies which have been adjusted against the dollar—the numeraire in the exchange system.

numerate (niū·mĕrĕt). Restrict †*Obs.* to sense in Dict. and add: As *adj.* [f. L. *numerus* number + -ate², after *literate*.] Acquainted with the basic principles of mathematics and science.

1959 *15 to 18: Rep. Cent. Advisory Council for Educ. (Eng.)* (Ministry of Educ.) I. xxv. 269 Little is done to make science specialists more 'literate' than they were when they left the Fifth Form and nothing to make arts specialists more 'numerate', if we may coin a word to represent the mirror image of literacy. **1960** [see *art *sb.* 7]. **1966** A. Battersby *Math. in Management* i. 21 The aim of a good Sixth Form should be to send out into the world men and women who are both literate and numerate. **1967** *Times Rev. Industry* Mar. 103/2 (Advt.), Lecturer..in Management Science... Applicants should have a good honours degree..in a 'numerate' subject (e.g., engineering, mathematics, mathematical economics, physics, statistics). **1967** C. Berners-Lee in Wills & Yearsley *Handbk. Management Technol.* 1 It has become a commonplace of the day that we must all be numerate as well as literate. *Ibid.* 8 The ability to communicate easily with a computer is one which is greatly prized by all numerate professionals in the larger commercial and industrial organizations and in the universities. **1971** *Country Life* 20 May 1264/2 It has been my impression.. that..children are much less literate and numerate than ever before.

numeric, *a.* Add: **2.** = Numerical *a.* (and *sb.*) 1, esp. 1 e.

1949 E. C. Berkeley *Giant Brains* iv. 54 It will be reasonable to use numeric codes 0 to 9 in each column.. because..numeric codes can be sorted faster than alphabetic codes. **1955** [see *alpha-numeric *a.*]. **1967** D. Wilson in Wills & Yearsley *Handbk. Management Technol.* 45 In addition to the usual numeric and alphabetic characters, a range of special characters can normally be included. **1972** *Computer Jrnl.* XV. 209/1 A monotonically increasing numeric value is associated with each partition or level of the tree. **1973** *Sci. Amer.* June 65/2 Instruments that make rapid, high-precision measurements demand numeric readouts, since analogue presentations cannot display the results in any simple way.

numerical, *a.* (and *sb.*). Add: **1. g.** Special collocations: *numerical analysis*: the branch of mathematics that deals with the development and use of numerical methods for solving problems (usu. ones too complicated for analytic methods); so *numerical analyst*; *numerical aperture*: a measure of the resolving power of a microscope objective (for a given wavelength), equal to the product of the refractive index of the medium in front of it and the sine of the semi-angle of the cone it subtends at the centre of the object; *numerical control*: the use of numerical data stored on tape or punched cards to control automatically the movement and operations of machine tools and work-pieces.

[**1930** J. B. Scarborough *(title)* Numerical mathematical analysis.] **1946** *Ann. Computation Lab. Harvard Univ.* I. 338 *(heading)* Bibliography of numerical analysis. **1947** *Sci. News Let.* 27 Sept. 201/2 The National Bureau of Standards' new Institute of Numerical Analysis will feature high-speed electronic calculators. **1952** D. R. Hartree *Numerical Anal.* i. 2 The methods of numerical analysis..have that degree of generality which entitles them to be considered part of mathematics. **1974** *Encycl. Brit. Macropædia* XIII. 390/1 The numerical solution of ordinary differential equations is one of the most important branches of numerical analysis because many physical problems lead to ordinary differential equations that cannot be solved analytically. **1956** F. B. Hildebrand *Introd. Numerical Anal.* i. 1 Generally the numerical analyst does not strive for exactness. **1878** *Jrnl. R. Microsc. Soc.* I. 19 The inner scale shows the air-angle, the outer scale the 'numerical aperture'. *Ibid.* 21 This quantity α, which Professor Abbe calls 'numerical aperture', gives an absolute definition of aperture..by which lenses of every kind are directly comparable. **1952** R. W. Ditchburn *Light* viii. 253 With a dry lens, the maximum value of the numerical aperture is 1·0, and values up to 0·95 have been obtained. Oil-immersion objectives with numerical apertures up to 1·65 have been constructed. *Ibid.*, Higher magnifications have been obtained using electron microscopes... The effective wavelength may be of the order of 0·1 Å., but the numerical aperture of models so far available is very low, being only of the order of 0·01. **1969** S. G. & H. Lipson *Optical Physics* ix. 278 The limit of resolution of the microscope.. is equal to λ/numerical aperture. **1952** *Final Rep. Construction & Operation of Numerically Controlled Milling Machine* (Mass. Inst. Technol. Servomechanisms Lab.) 30 July 1 (AD 22241). Summary 1 A new technique of automatic machine-tool control..promises to simplify some of the manufacturing problems of medium and small run production often encountered in the aircraft industry. Called numerical control, this technique has been applied by M.I.T...to a milling machine controlled by a numerical code punched on paper tape. **1955** *IRE Trans. Industr. Electronics* II. 3 *(heading)* Numerical control of machine tools. *Ibid.* 5/1 The numerical control for this turret punch press uses the Remington-Rand 45 column tabulating card. **1966** *Economist* 2 July 56/1 What the two companies are claiming is that..numerical control is now suitable for mass production. *Ibid.* 57/1 There are 25 British companies producing machine tools for numerical control. **1971** H. C. Town *Design & Construction Machine Tools* vii. 159 With numerical control the instructions for the various phases of a cycle are transmitted by punched or magnetic tape inserted in a reader unit.

‖ **numéro** (nümero). [Fr.] Number. Also *transf.*

Quots. 1944 and 1958 reflect the Fr. sense 'une personne bizarre'.

1944 Auden *For Time Being* (1945) 118 George, you old numero, How did you get in the Army? **1958** L. Durrell *Mountolive* v. 107 Well, you can see what a *numéro* he is. **1961** *House & Garden* May 20/2 The chair he has designed... This heavy *numéro* seems very different from the essays in lightness with which Saarinen's name has hitherto been associated. **1973** *Sunday Times* 26 Aug. Katharine Schofield opens the second act with a *numéro* of great panache.

numerology (niūmĕrǫ·lŏdʒi). [f. L. *numer(us* number + -ology.] Divination by numbers; the study of the esoteric meaning of numbers.

1911 'Sepharial' *Kabala of Numbers* I. iii. 25 A general consideration of the principles involved in the science of numerology. **1926** K. Adams *Numerology Up-to-Date* i. 11 In the science of Numerology each letter of the alphabet has a given number and each number has its special significance. **1935** *Punch* 21 Aug. 207/1 Next we come to numerology. One of the most vital factors in your life is

the Science of Numbers. **1937** M. COVARRUBIAS *Island of Bali* (1972) ix. 312 For special occasions an offering, to be effective, must conform to certain specifications based on the influences that rule the day; the calendar, the cardinal directions, numerology and so forth. **1960** AUDEN *Homage to Clio* 30 The burly slave of ritual and a martyr To Numerology. **1962** *Times* 23 Feb. 5/1 Numerology is ..a term of superiority or near-abuse applied by physicists to those of their colleagues, who, by playing with numbers hope to arrive at physical understanding. **1971** *Times Lit. Suppl.* 1 Oct. 1179/1 Numerology has even had some impact on poetry in its 'concrete' forms.

Hence **numerolo·gical** *a.*, **numerolo·gically** *adv.*; **numero·logist**, one who studies or is expert in numerology.

1923 C. W. CHEASLEY *Numerology* (rev. ed.) vi. 67 The final digit of the whole name—the Expression..has the greatest influence of all... When Numerologists use the term 'a number 2 person', 'a number 6 person', etc., it is this Expression number that should be implied. **1926** K. ADAMS *Numerology Up-to-Date* ix. 79 What are the numerological properties of 1? *Ibid.* viii. 74 Cities, numerologically speaking, are a most fascinating study. **1932** *Discovery* June 204/1 It is not only the number seven that possesses a peculiar significance for numerologists. **1952** G. SARTON *Hist. Sci.* I. xvii. 439 The regular solids.. must each have some definite meaning... Plato bethought himself of the four elements; the fifth solid would then represent the whole universe. This patching up of the theory, plus the finding of a meaning for the superfluous solid, is typical of the analogies invented by numerologists and other mystical mathematicians. **1972** *Sci. Amer.* Feb. 101/1 Mel Stover, a Winnipeg numerologist, has pointed out that in Roman numerals 9 changes to 11 when turned over, but 9 in the binary system—1001—doesn't change at all. **1973** *Nature* 12 Oct. 313/1 Several dependent and independent numerological relations have been proposed. Dirac noticed that the ratio between the age of the Universe and the natural unit of time..is approximately equal to the ratio between the electrostatic and the gravitational force acting between two electrons. **1974** *Sci. Amer.* June 118/3 Anything numerologically interesting about Nixon and Watergate?

‖ **numero uno** (nū·mero ū·no). [It.] 'Number one', the best or most important (person). (Cf. *NUMBER *sb.* 5 d.)

1973 *Publishers Weekly* 25 June 71/1 Fred Carr, *numero uno* in the mutual fund game. **1973** *Philadelphia Inquirer* (Today Suppl.) 14 Oct. 24/1 (*caption*) 'Fat Rob'.. may be *numero uno* in his neighborhood, but he doesn't have anything that compares with the paneled office of Reuben Maldonado, president of the Royal Javelins in New York's South Bronx. **1975** *Publishers Weekly* 14 Apr. 55/1 The sex goddess of the moment, who stays aloof from filmland's numero uno stud only to be misused by an intellectual French director.

‖ **numerus clausus** (niū·mĕrŏs klau·sŏs). [L., lit. 'closed, or restricted, number'.] A fixed maximum number of entrants admissible to an academic institution.

1925 *Nation* (N.Y.) 8 Apr. 374 The *numerus clausus*, driven out of Russia, still keeps eager Jewish youth from the learning they crave in Poland, Hungary, and Rumania. **1959** D. D. RUNES *Conc. Dict. Judaism* 178 *Numerus clausus* (Latin), limited number of Jews admitted to schools of higher education; still operative in Soviet Union. **1960** *Encounter* June 46 Owing to the *numerus clausus* imposed in Russian universities, a very large number of the students present were Jews, compelled to come West in order to graduate. **1963** *Higher Educ.* (Cmnd. 2154) v. 38 Shortage of accommodation may effectively impose a *numerus clausus* in some disciplines.

numhead, var. *NUMBHEAD.

Numidian (niūmi·diăn), *sb.* and *a.* [f. L. *Numidia* the former name of a country in North Africa + -AN.] **a.** *sb.* A native or inhabitant of Numidia. **b.** *adj.* Of or belonging to Numidia. *spec.* **Numidian crane**, a grey and black crane, *Anthropoides virgo*, found in southern Europe, north Africa, and parts of Asia; = DEMOISELLE 2 a.

1600 HOLLAND tr. *Livy's Romane Hist.* XXIX. 731 Then the kingdome fell by descent, according to the custome and manner of the Numidians, unto Desalces the late kings brother. *Ibid.* XXX. 752 They would enlarge and set at libertie all the Numidian captives that lay in prison at Rome. **1614** A. GORGES tr. *Lucans Pharsalia* IV. 156 The vagrant fierce Numidæans. **1697** DRYDEN *Æneid* IV. 57 And fierce Numidians there your Frontiers bound. **1757** A. BUTLER *Lives Saints* III. 3 Certain false Numidian zealots. *Ibid.* 4 Seventy bishops, chiefly Numidians. **1766** [see DEMOISELLE 2 a]. **1836** N. ISAACS *Trav. E. Afr.* II. xvii. 324 The wild sort [of birds] are easily obtained... The Crane (Numidion [*sic*] or Demoiselle), Baleari or Crowned Crane..are common. *c* **1876** E. DICKINSON *Poems* (1955) III. 956 The Butterfly's Numidian Gown With spots of Burnish roasted on Is proof against the Sun. **1893** A. NEWTON *Dict. Birds* 111 In Europe, besides the *G[rus] communis* already mentioned, we have as an inhabitant that which is generally known as the Numidian Crane or Demoiselle..distinguished from every other by its long white ear-tufts. **1905** T. HODGKIN in L. Creighton *Life & Lett. T. Hodgkin* (1917) xi. 229, I wish I had come to this Numidian land when I was younger... Our Numidians long held Rome at bay. **1906** KIPLING *Puck of Pook's Hill* 147 'Was your nurse a—a Romaness too?' 'No, a Numidian... A dear, fat, brown thing.' **1921** *Edin. Rev.* July 105 A Numidian, riding bareback and stirrupless, is throwing a lasso at a wild ass. **1957** *Encycl. Brit.* XVI. 615/1 Numidians were divided into two great tribes, the Massyli on the east, and the Massaesyli on the west... At the end of the [second Punic] war,..the Numidian kingdom surrounded Carthage except towards the sea.

numinal, *a.* For † *Obs. rare*$^{-1}$ read *rare* and add later example.

1927 *Contemp. Rev.* Mar. 352 Rudolf Otto in his *Idea of the Holy*, accords to music a place upon the 'wholly other' or 'numinal' of religion.

‖ **numinosum** (niūminōu·zŏm). [ad. G. *numinose* the numinous.] = *NUMINOUS *sb.*

1938 C. G. JUNG *Psychol. & Relig.* i. 4 Religion, as the Latin word denotes, is a careful and scrupulous observation of what Rudolf Otto aptly termed the 'numinosum'. **1950** *Brit. Jrnl. Psychol.* XL. 235 Modern psychology, with its exploration of complexes, has touched upon a taboo laid by ego-consciousness on the psychic 'numinosum' and 'tremendum'. **1973** J. SINGER *Boundaries of Soul* v. 123 Many religious practices and performances seem to be carried out for the sole purpose of calling forth the power of the *numinosum* at will by invocation, incantation, sacrifice [etc.].

numinous, *a.* Delete † and add: Revived in senses: of or pertaining to a numen; divine, spiritual, revealing or suggesting the presence of a god; inspiring awe and reverence. Also *absol.* or as *sb.*

1864 R. S. HAWKER *Quest of Sangraal* 17 An Orient Cruse, Fulfill'd, and running o'er, with Numynous Light. **1923** J. W. HARVEY tr. *R. Otto's Idea of Holy* ii. 6 For this purpose I adopt a word coined from the Latin *numen*. *Omen* has given us *ominous*, and there is no reason why from *numen* we should not similarly form a word '*numinous*'. I shall speak..of a unique 'numinous' category of value and of a definitely 'numinous' state of mind. *Ibid.* iii. 11 The numinous is thus felt as objective and outside the self. **1934** W. TEMPLE *Nature, Man & God* i. 23 What Otto speaks of as the '*Mysterium tremendum*', the quality in the object of religion which he describes as 'Numinous', is just that before which we do not reason but bow. **1941** G. G. SCHOLEM *Major Trends in Jewish Mysticism* 59 The key-word of the numinous, the *Kedushah*, the trishagion from Isaiah VI, 3, in which the ecstasy of the mystic culminates: holy, holy, holy is the Lord of Hosts. **1951** J. L. ADAMS tr. *Tillich's Protestant Era* p. xxxix, Protestants..often are unaware of the numinous power inherent in genuine symbols. **1957** *Times Lit. Suppl.* 11 Oct. 602/5 He now urges us..to transfer finally our more numinous speculations from the altar to the earth, to the observable universe and to all its children. **1962** *Listener* 17 May, Simple English exchanges that caught the suburban yet numinous quality of the original French. **1967** G. STEINER *Lang. & Silence* 62, I want to draw attention to..the recurrent acknowledgement by poets..that music *is* the deeper, more numinous code, that language.. aspires to the condition of music. **1969** *New Scientist* 17 Apr. 114/1 There is a growing revolt of young people against what they call materialism..because they want to take seriously the experience of the inner life—in particular, experience of the 'numinous' and of 'immortal longings'. **1972** *Times Lit. Suppl.* 31 Mar. 365/4 Homer reveals the world of gods as well as the world of men, both in epic verse, and this difference from later, more numinous writers has many consequences. **1972** S. W. SYKES in Cox & Dyson *20th-Cent. Mind* II. vi. 154 [Rudolf] Otto defined numinous as the non-rational mystery behind religion, which is both awesome and fascinating. It is, he asserted, the permanent and essential feature of all religion, including Christianity.

Hence **numino·sity**, **nu·minousness**, the condition or state of being numinous.

1932 R. A. KNOX *Broadcast Minds* iv. 70 What is the proper object around which the idea of 'numinousness' ought to cling? **1936** *Essays & Stud.* XXI. 132 The poet's own religious fervour, mysticism, or (if you will) poetic 'numinosity'. **1951** *Theology* LIV. 233 Somehow he manages again and again to take from the Gospel its fascination, its haunting power over the imagination, its numinosity. **1962** *Listener* 29 Nov. 940/1 Nelly, the hag, the witch, the personification of Corvey's incipient madness, lost some of her numinousness in being acted out. **1963** *Times* 29 May 11/5 If the Church is to be preserved from degenerating into a nondescript club of nebulous numinosity. **1969** E. C. WHITMONT *Symbolic Quest* vii. 126 The energy which is withdrawn from the external world remains focussed exclusively upon the unconscious primitive image with its archaic numinosity.

nummion (nū·miọn) Usu. in pl. **nummia** (-iă). [ad. Gr. νουμ(μ)ίον, dim. of νοῦμμος coin.] A Byzantine copper coin, equal to one fortieth of a *FOLLIS.

1908, 1962 [see *FOLLIS]. **1970** *Ashmolean Mus. Rep. Visitors 1969* 40 The earliest in a series of Byzantine accessions is a scarce 33-nummia coin of Justinian I. **1973** P. D. WHITTING *Byzantine Coins* vii. 89 The copper nummia in their thousands were too small to have any recognizable value in themselves and could only circulate on a basis of public confidence.

nu·mmy-nu·mmy. An exclamation of pleasure; = *YUMMY-YUMMY. Cf. *NUM.

1929 E. BOWEN *Last September* vi. 62 'Nummy-nummy,' she said, pointing out the raspberries.

num-num (numnu·m). *S. Afr.* Also **nam-nam, noem-noem.** [Afrikaans, perh. f. Hottentot or Nama name.] A spiny, evergreen shrub or small tree of the genus *Carissa*, belonging to the family Apocynaceæ and bearing fragrant white flowers; also, the edible red or purple fruit of a plant of this kind. Cf. *Natal plum* (*NATAL *sb.*^{2} 2).

1822 W. J. BURCHELL *Trav. Interior S. Afr.* I. x. 192 The Hottentots call this shrub 'Num'num (or Noomnoom, agreeably to English orthography), each syllable preceded by a guttural clap of the tongue. **1897** S. J. DU TOIT *Rhodesia* iv. 32 Various kinds of sweet-grass and small shrubs, varied with very good large bush and trees, as..'noem noem', 'quarri', [etc.]. **1926** O. SCHREINER *From Man to Man* iii. 113 The nam-nams and jasmine shrubs made a thick wall on either side. [*Note*] A shrub with a small edible berry (also 'num-num'). **1951** R. CAMPBELL *Light on Dark Horse* ix. 127 It was the sort of scrub which reminds one of an enormous roll of vegetable barbed wire, composed chiefly of num-num and wait-a-bit thorn. **1972** PALMER & PITMAN *Trees S. Afr.* III. 1899 The species [of *Carissa*] are usually known as num-nums. *Ibid.* 1903 Although the Karoo num-num is most often a bush it can grow into a small tree 3·5 m high with a round, much-branched, immensely dense and twiggy evergreen crown.

numori, var. *NOMOLI.

nunatak. Add: Also applied to similar mountains in other regions. (Earlier and later examples.)

1877 *Q. Jrnl. Geol. Soc.* XXXIII. 145 At Kangerdlugssuak, where the mountains are lofty and the sides of the fjords steep, there are three Nunataks..equalling the height of the neighbouring land; but above the Inland Ice of Disko..the Nunataks are lower Knolls. **1921** E. R. G. R. EVANS *South with Scott* xiv. 190 Mount Hope is a nunatak of granite, about 2,800 feet in height. **1959** *Times* 9 Jan. 11/6 *Antarctic Findings*...At Shackleton Base..we lacked..solid ground. Some nunataks could be seen over 20 miles away to the east, near Vahsel Bay. **1963** 'G. CARR' *Lewker in Norway* vi. 129 The only light.. had turned snow-hummocks into far-off mountains and ricky *nunataks* into boulders.

nunc, nunk, nunks, varr. NUNCLE.

1841 *Comic Almanack* Dec. 48 Come, nunks, one game at Blindman's-buff. **1876** GEO. ELIOT *Dan. Der.* I. II. xvi. 311 His uncle or 'Nunc', as Sir Hugo had taught him to say. **1884** C. M. YONGE *Armourer's Prentices* I. 142 Should you know this nunks of yours? **1915** A. BENNETT *These Twain* (1916) II. xiii. 259 'Here's Nunks!' exclaimed George. **1919** C. ORR *Glorious Things* xxiii. 279 The very night old Nunk was away.

‖ **nunchaku** (nuntʃa·ku). [Jap., f. Okinawa dialect.] Esp. in *pl.*, two hardwood sticks joined together by a strap, etc., as a defensive weapon.

1970 *Guardian Weekly* 2 May 11 The radical taste tends ..to nunchakus, which go back more than 500 years. They were..invented by Japanese peasants for self-defence when metal weapons were forbidden to all but the Samurai. **1973** *Express* (Trinidad & Tobago) 27 Apr. 31/3 The experts will give exhibitions in kobudo (weaponery) displaying their martial skill with the sai, nunchaku stick, bow, sword and daggers. **1975** *Globe & Mail* (Toronto) 17 Jan. 4/1 The proper name is nunchaku sticks. They are made of two sticks of hardwood joined together at one end by a chain, leather or rope.

‖ **nunc stans.** [L. *nunc* now + *stans* pres. pple. of *stāre* to stand.] The eternal timeless 'now' presumed, as an attribute of God, to be co-existent with Time.

1651 HOBBES *Leviathan* xlvi. 374 But they will teach us that Eternity is the Standing still of the Present Time, a *Nunc-stans* (as the Schools call it;) which neither they, nor any else understand. **1678** CUDWORTH *Intell. Syst.* 645 *Nunc-stans*, or a Standing Now of Eternity. **1733** A. BAXTER *Enquiry Human Soul* viii. 376 The distinction of past and future vanishes with respect to such a Mind; and the expression *nunc stans* will appear to have propriety. **1854** H. L. MANSEL *Lett.* (1873) 119 Augustine, and the Schoolmen after him,..speaking of Eternity as a *nunc stans*. **1896** W. CALDWELL *Schopenhauer's System* viii. 393 In willing the world is at once an eternal process and an eternal stationary thing—a *nunc stans*—at the same time. **1946** J. LAIRD *Philos. Incursions Eng. Lit.* vi. 96 On a few occasions..Wordsworth described the specious *nunc stans* of mystical ecstasy; its apparent arrest of time itself .**1958** E. HELLER *Ironic German* vi. 241 Thomas Mann was..well prepared for 'the mystery of the revolving sphere' by Schopenhauer's philosophy of the eternal *nunc stans* which resides at the centre of the illusory motion of Time. **1967** P. MERLAN in *Cambr. Hist. Later Greek & Early Medieval Philos.* 100 A supreme god..lives in the *aiōn* which can also be characterized as a *nunc stans*.

nunky. Add: (Later examples.) Also **nunkie.**

1969 'A. GILBERT' *Missing from Home* vi. 86 We don't even know she had an uncle... And if it was seven o'clock ..she was running it pretty fine if she was going for a drive with Nunkie. **1973** *Times Lit. Suppl.* 30 Nov. 1472/2 She was A. J. Balfour's favourite niece... 'Nunky' died in 1930.

2. *slang.* A pawnbroker. Cf. UNCLE *sb.* 3.

1921 *Daily Colonist* (Victoria, B.C.) 5 Apr. 13/5 If you happen to want a ten-dollar bill and trot round the corner to 'nunky'; why, that's really not quite done, my dear fellow. **1937** in PARTRIDGE *Dict. Slang*.

nunny bag (nʌ·ni bæg). *Newfoundland.* Also **nonny bag.** [f. Eng. dial. *noony* meal at noon + BAG *sb.*] A kind of haversack, often made of sealskin.

1842 J. B. JUKES *Excursions in Newfoundland* II. 146 Having determined to return, we hung up in the tilt a 'nunny bag' full of bread. **1895** *Dialect Notes* I. 380 *Nunny bag*, lunch bag; usually made of a piece of sealskin, and used by sealers when they go off for a day. **1919**

W. T. GRENFELL *Labrador Doctor* 90 Our sealers carry dry oatmeal and sugar in their 'nonny bags', which, mixed with snow, assuage their thirst and hunger as well. **1925** *Dialect Notes* V. 337 *Nonny bag*, a small knapsack to carry out on the ice; ditty bag. **1944** H. WENTWORTH *Amer. Dial. Dict.* 419/1 *Nunny bag*, a lunch bag, usually of sealskin. **1961** *Maclean's Mag.* 28 Jan. 47/2 He clawed through his nunny-bag till he found a bit of oatmeal.

‖ **nuoc mam** (nwǫk mām). [Vietnamese.] A spicy Vietnamese fish sauce.

1919 *Experiment Station Record* (U.S. Dept. Agric.) July 66 Analyses of nuoc-mam (a product similar to soy sauce) and other sauces are reported. **1920** *Ibid.* Oct. 458 Nuoc-mam. the Indochinese fish sauce.., has been successfully condensed for transportation and use by the Indochinese soldiers in France. **1935** M. MORPHY *Recipes of All Nations* 782 A small teaspoon of nuoc-man, a typically Annamese condiment which is used in practically all their dishes. **1969** I. KEMP *Brit. G.I. in Vietnam* iv. 77 The staple Vietnamese diet of rice with fish and *nuoc mam* —'Vietnamese national sauce', they would explain, chuckling among themselves—made from rotten fish and sea water. **1970** *Harper's Mag.* July 83 Bits of rice and *nuoc-mam* are what they're used to. **1972** *Times* 25 Mar. 11 There is nothing in either Chinese or French cooking that exactly corresponds with the Vietnamese thin sauce or relish called nuóc mam formed..from the liquor of decomposing fish.

Nupe (nū·pe), *a.* and *sb.* Also 9 **Nufi, Nupé, Nyffee.** [f. the name of a former kingdom at the junction of the Niger and Benue rivers in West Africa.] **A.** *adj.* Of, pertaining to, or designating a Negro people of central Nigeria, or their language. **B.** *sb.* **a.** The Nupe people; a member of this people. **b.** The language of this people, which belongs to the Kura division of the Sudanic language family.

1829 H. CLAPPERTON *Jrnl. 2nd Exped. to Interior of Afr.* i. 25 He hoped that we should settle the war with the Nyffee people and the Fellatah. **1841** J. F. SCHÖN *Jrnl.* 14 Sept. (1842) 119 The Nufi Language is spoken to a considerable distance, even beyond Rabba. **1883** R. N. CUST *Sk. Mod. Lang. Afr.* I. xi. 228 At Lokója, at the confluence, Nupé is the principal language, though others are spoken. **1885** J. S. KINGSLEY *Standard Nat. Hist.* VI. 320 We meet the Ibo language on the lower course of the Niger, and the Nupe from the Benne up. *Ibid.* 321 The Nupe..are genuine negroes in complexion and form of face, and indisputably one of the best-formed tribes in Africa. **1888** G. T. BETTANY *World's Inhabitants* vi. 614 Gando..includes the territory of the Nupe negroes. **1892** A. F. MOCKLER-FERRYMAN *Up Niger* xiii. 151 The Mohammedan Nupe lives the life of a man-about-town. **1932** J. CARY *Aissa Saved* iv. 24 The new town on the waterside, inhabited by Hausas, Nupes, Yorubas, the mixed population of a harbour. **1942** S. F. NADEL *Black Byzantium* iii. 27 The Nupe have only one word for kinship, *dengi*, which defines relationship in the widest as well as in a more restricted sense. *Ibid.* vi. 70 The people in the capital regard the Nupe spoken in the districts and on the borders of the country as an inferior brand. **1974** *African Encycl.* 375/2 The Nupe people live in valleys of the middle Niger and Kaduna rivers in Nigeria... They are famous for their work in glass, silver, bronze, and brass.

nuplex (niū·pleks). [f. NU(CLEAR *a.* + COM)PLEX *sb.*] A combined agricultural and industrial complex built around a nuclear reactor as the source of all power and providing employment for a large number of people.

1968 *Courier-Mail* (Brisbane) 27 Aug. 4/1 Mr. Seaborg [Chairman of the U.S. Atomic Energy Commission] defined the 'nuplex' as 'a giant agro-industrial complex built around nuclear reactors'. **1970** *New Scientist* 8 Oct. 89/3 One such investigation is into nuclear farms for the Middle East: half-million-acre 'nuplexes' with a reactor desalinating seawater for irrigation.. and manufacturing fertilizer on the spot.

nuppence (nʌ·pěns). *slang.* [Modelled on *tuppence.*] No money.

1886 *Longman's Mag.* VII. 551 The Americans can get our books, and do get them, and republish them and give us nothing—that awful minus quantity, nuppence! **1964** *Observer* 20 Sept. 27/7 Living on nuppence. **1973** *Times Lit. Suppl.* 30 Mar. 347/4 For the appreciation of the novel, this information matters little more than nuppence.

nuptiality. Add: **4.** The frequency or incidence of marriage within a population.

1902 *Encycl. Brit.* XXXI. 839/1 Nuptiality and Fecundity.—In connexion with the subject of natural increase may be mentioned the tendency of a people towards marriage, and the average fertility of each union. **1949** *Population Studies* II. 356 The relations between male and female nuptiality in general. **1966** E. A. WRIGLEY *Introd. Eng. Hist. Demogr.* iv. 111 The demographic mechanisms which produced changes in population totals—the interplay of nuptiality, fertility and mortality. **1973** *Times* 12 Dec. 2/3 Although nuptiality was higher than ever, mean family size for couples..had dropped.

Nuremberg (niū·rěmbəɹg). Also (erron.) **-burg.** [*G. Nürnberg.*] The name of a city in southern Germany. **1.** Used *attrib.* to designate a type of porcelain manufactured in Nuremberg.

1617 F. MORYSON *Itinerary* III. II. iii. 80 The Germans export..*Nurnberg* wares (so they call small wares.) **1863** W. CHAFFERS *Marks Pott. & Porc.* 105 *Nuremburg*, there are two plates of the XVIIIth Century in the Sèvres Museum; one in imitation of Faenza, the other an allegory of Luther. **1925** B. RACKHAM tr. *Hannover's Pott. & Porc.* I. iv. 355 Chinese motives..are not wanting in Nuremberg faïence in the first and best period. But at an early stage they give way to plant ornament, in which a feather-like leaf..is a constantly-recurring element. **1960** R. G. HAGGAR *Conc. Encycl. Cont. Pott. & Porc.* 331/1 Two personalities are connected with Nuremberg *faïence* in the sixteenth century, Oswald Reinhard, and Augustin Hirsvogel. **1974** *Country Life* 6 June 1411/3 The architectural detail is executed in scagliola and the walls are clad in Nuremburg tiles.

b. *Nuremberg egg*, a type of watch (see quot. 1960).

[**1895** H. L. NELTHROPP *Catal. Collection of Clocks* 2 Nuremberg egg-shaped watch, metal and silver case.] **1960** H. HAYWARD *Antique Coll.* 201/1 *Nuremberg egg*, a misnomer applied to early South German watches. Arose from the misreading and mistranslation of 'Uhrlein' into 'Eierlein' (little clocks into little eggs). These early watches were usually drum shaped.

2. Used *attrib.* to designate a connection with the German National Socialist Party with which the city was associated, as **Nuremberg Laws**, laws promulgated in 1935 barring Jews from German citizenship and forbidding intermarriage between 'Aryans' and Jews; **Nuremberg rally**, one of the mass meetings of the German National Socialist Party which were held annually at Nuremberg from 1933 to 1938; **Nuremberg trial**(s), a series of trials of former Nazi leaders for alleged war crimes and crimes against humanity presided over by an International Military Tribunal formed from the victorious Allied Powers and held in Nuremberg in 1945–6 (also ellipt. as *Nuremberg*).

1937 JANOWSKY & FAGEN *Internat. Aspects German Racial Policies* ii. 106 Even the official commentary on the Nuremberg laws..concluded that the German Jews were a racial (voelkische), though not a national minority. **1945** H. NICOLSON *Diary* 4 June (1968) III. 64 Smuts recalled the decision... 'It..shows..the value of Nuremberg. Had we shot Jodl at sight, that precious piece of evidence would never have been obtained.' **1945** *Daily Mail* 19 Nov. 2/3 All day today Lord Justice Lawrence and Mr. Justice Birkett have been discussing..the arguments for and against postponement of the Nuremberg trials. **1946** M. BELGION *Epitaph on Nuremberg* 12 The argument rested on the plea..that justice was going to be done. Of this argument the official explanation of the Nuremberg trial consisted. **1952** A. BULLOCK *Hitler* II. vii. 347 The Nuremberg rallies held every year in September were masterpieces of theatrical art, with the most carefully devised effects. **1963** *Guardian* 25 Feb. 8/1 Towards the end of the Stalin era a Soviet brand of anti-Semitism had undoubtedly reached very dangerous proportions..even if it was never codified in a Soviet version of the 'Nuremberg Laws'. **1969** W. CARR *Hist. of Germany 1815–1945* xiv. 405 Hitler's violent speech at the Nuremburg party rally. **1970** *Guardian* 20 Nov. 12/6 Ever since Vietnam got big, Nuremberg has been injected into the national argument... The Nuremberg precedents demand that..American high commanders ought to be tried for war crimes. **1971** M. MCCARTHY *Birds of America* 110 Under the Nuremberg Laws, he would have counted as a Jew, while in Israel he would count as a Christian, since what mattered to them was your mother. **1974** *Times* 14 Feb. 16/7 Thank heavens we don't do it like the Tories. Their adulation is reminiscent of a Nuremberg rally.

Nuremberger (niū·rěmbəɹgəɹ). [f. *NUREMBERG + -ER[1].] A native or inhabitant of Nuremberg, Germany.

1673 J. RAY *Observations Journey Low-Countries* 112 Aldtdorf, a little walled Town and an University belonging to the Nurenbergers. **1894** S. WEYMAN *My Lady Rotha* xxxi. 349 Deserting a friend because the Nurembergers frowned upon him. **1946** H. NICOLSON *Diary* 1 May (1968) III. 62 If I were a Nuremberger I should feel nothing but undying hatred for those who had destroyed my lovely city.

nurse, *sb.*[1] Add: **3. b.** Prefixed as a title to the name of one qualified to nurse, esp. in a hospital; used as a mode of address to such a person.

1702 J. MORDAUNT *Let.* in E. Hamilton *Mordaunts* (1965) ii. 33, I did not doubt but that you would have great trouble in parting wth Nurse Lucas. **1791** F. BURNEY *Let.* 12 Sept. (1972) I. 65 Less than an hour compleated the whole business without any help excepting Nurse Whittons. **1874** [see SOUL *sb.* 13 a]. **1940** A. CHRISTIE *Sad Cypress* I. i. 21 'Do you think she's really good-looking, Nurse?' Nurse Hopkins said: 'Difficult to tell what these girls really look like under their make-up!' **1955** 'A. GILBERT' *Is she Dead Too?* vi. 116 I'll be sending Nurse Wilson along. **1975** P. D. JAMES *Black Tower* iv. 100 They made the bed together, Nurse Rainer flicking the sheets into place and neatly mitring each corner.

c. Without article in reference to the nurse in charge of a patient.

1766 [see *home-baked* (*HOME *sb.*[1] 14 i)]. **1914** G. B. SHAW *Misalliance* 68 Is anything the matter, John? Nurse says she heard you calling me a quarter of an hour ago. **1937** J. BETJEMAN *Continual Dew* 25 Nurse looked at the silent bedstead.

4. (Later examples.)

1966 *Times* 21 Apr. 16/6 Scots pines were commonly planted as nurses to oak. **1973** *Country Life* 6 Dec. 1928/1 Larch has been..used..as a nurse with hardwoods and alone.

8. *nurse-companion, -girl* (earlier and later examples), *-secretary*; **nurse-cell,** any cell whose function appears to be to assist another cell, esp. an ovum, in some way; **nurse cloth,** a plain-weave cotton fabric used for nurses' uniforms; **nurse-crop, -tree** = sense 4 in Dict. and Suppl.

1896 E. B. WILSON *Cell* iii. 114 In all these cases it is doubtful whether the nurse-cells are sister-cells of the egg which have sacrificed their own development for the sake of their companions, or whether they have had a distinct origin from a very early period. **1964** BISHOP & SURGENOR *Red Blood Cell* viii. 324 These authors present electron micrographs which depict erythroblastic islands in the bone marrow, in which a central reticulum cell (nurse cell) is surrounded by a ring of erythroblasts. **1967** *Jrnl. Cell Sci.* II. 613 Extensive nuclear fusion has been described in the trophocytes (nurse cells) in the ovaries of the milkweed bug *Oncopeltus*. **1907** *Harrods Catal.* 1407 Cotton dresses, in good quality Nurse Cloth. **1932** D. C. MINTER *Mod. Needlecraft* 248/2 *Book Carrier*..Blue nurse cloth, hessian or heavy Russian crash. **1908** B. HARRADEN *Interplay* 210 Dr. Edgar can no doubt find you a nurse-companion. **1973** A. CHRISTIE *Postern of Fate* III. ii. 132 She was a kind of nurse-companion with Mrs Beddingfield. **1938** *U.S. Dept. Agric. Yearbk.* 409 Wheat is a good nurse crop for the clover and grass. **1955** *Archit. Rev.* CXVII. 249 Even in hardwood country they [*sc.* conifers] are often required as nurse-crops to the deciduous trees. **1971** *Country Life* 4 Nov. 1237/1 Shall it [*sc.* seeding] be in spring or mid-August, under a nurse crop or without? **1847** C. BRONTË *Jane Eyre* III. iii. 98, I will be a servant, a nurse-girl, if I can be no better. **1953** D. LESSING *Five* i. 16 There was a little black nurse-girl seated on one of the logs, under a big tree, with a white child in her arms. **1950** Nurse-secretary [see *APPOINTMENT 4]. **1902** B. E. FERNOW *Economics of Forestry* vii. 175 When the latter [*sc.* the young crop] has come up, the nurse trees are gradually removed to give the young seedlings the required light. **1953** H. L. EDLIN *Forester's Handbk.* v. 75 Frost-tender trees should never be planted in frost-hollows without the protection of a hardier nurse-tree. **1971** E. HYAMS *Capability Brown* I. v. 49 He [*sc.* Brown] used some conifers as nurse trees.

nurse, *sb.*[2] Add: **b.** *nurse-hound*, a name used for several dog-fish, esp. the large-spotted dog-fish, *Scyliorhinus stellaris.* (Later examples.)

1921 *Nature* 29 Dec. 585/1 The spur-dog and nurse-hound are viviparous. **1922** *Ibid.* 12 Jan. 55/2 Mr. E. Ford writes to inform us that the term 'nurse-hound' is applied at Plymouth to *Scyliorhinus stellaris*, which is not viviparous. We understand from the writer of our article that confusion has arisen from the fact that the name 'nurse-hound' is also used by fishermen in his district to refer to *Mustelus vulgaris*, which is viviparous. **1959** A. HARDY *Fish & Fisheries* ix. 179 The rough hound and the nurse hound are both spotted with dark spots..upon a lighter ground. **1967** [see *HUSS *sb.*]. **1969** A. WHEELER *Fishes Brit. Is. & NW. Europe* 44/1 The nurse hound is most common on rough, even rocky ground and it may be found within the algal zone close inshore, although it is most common in deeper water. **1972** [see *HUSS *sb.*].

nurse, *v.* Add: **1. c.** (Earlier and later examples and examples with animal as subject.)

1893 DAVIS & KEATING *Mother & Child* xxiii. 74 A sore or cracked nipple may bleed when the infant nurses. **1938** M. K. RAWLINGS *Yearling* xi. 98 The fawn nuzzled her full udders and began to nurse. **1946** M. C. SELF *Horseman's Encycl.* 289 It is important that the foal nurse as soon as he is strong enough to stand. **1963** M. MCCARTHY *Group* x. 223 If they gave him a second drink of water, he might not nurse properly when feeding time finally came. **1972** *Sci. Amer.* Dec. 18/2 After the fifth week..the kittens are able to pursue her around the cage until they can get hold of a nipple, after which the mother allows them to nurse.

3. e. (Later examples.)

1933 P. GODFREY *Back-Stage* ix. 131 A good play which does not catch on at once may sometimes be 'nursed' to genuine success. **1936** *Discovery* May 164/1 If two climbers can be 'nursed' to that height the victory [over Everest] may at last be won. **1942** *Tee Emm* (Air Ministry) II. 72 The instructor is, therefore, less able to..nurse each individual into efficiency.

5. b. (Earlier example.) Also with an injury as object.

1778 F. BURNEY *Evelina* I. xix. 129 She had a bad cold, and chose to nurse it. **1951** *N. Y. Times* 11 Dec., The.. pilot was safely at his home..nursing only a slight scratch on his nose.

6. d. With a drink as object: to consume slowly, holding the glass in the hand between sips.

1942 *Sun* (Baltimore) 5 Oct. 13/4 They buy several drinks in the bar, then they come in to catch the floor show, and nurse one drink along. **1962** K. ORVIS *Damned & Destroyed* xiii. 88 'Don't nurse this—drink it!' I said. She gulped the straight whisky gratefully. **1964** B. MALAMUD *Idiots First* 70 Cronin, pretty much contented, had had one drink to her two, and he was nursing his first when she asked for a third. **1974** R. B. PARKER *God save Child* (1975) xix. 134 A thin black man..was nursing a brandy glass at..the bar.

nurse-maid. Add: **b.** *slang.* (See quot.)

1943 C. H. WARD-JACKSON *Piece of Cake* 44 *Nursemaid*, a long-distance fighter escort for bombers.

Hence **nu·rse-maid** *v.*, to tend and care for (a person) as a nurse-maid does her charge.

Also with non-personal object. Hence **nu·rse-maiding** *vbl. sb.*

1921 *Glasgow Herald* 19 Apr. 8 He had to be nurse-maided and chaperoned to his meals, his bath, and his bed. **1924** 'J. Sutherland' *Circle of Stars* iv. 40 'I really don't need the nurse-maiding you think I ought to have,' Gloria said impatiently. **1935** C. S. Forester *African Queen* iv. 87 That engine..was greased and cleaned and nurse-maided. **1960** *Times* 5 Apr. 14/6 The kroomen from the African mainland who nursemaided us. **1967** *Economist* 27 May 896/1 By..telling the UN force it could stop nursemaiding his country, President Nasser had scored a clear political success in the Arab world. **1973** 'A. York' *Captivator* ii. 32 Nursemaiding princesses..is not really in my line.

nursery. Add: **3. d.** An establishment for training promising young players of a particular sport.

1950 W. Hammond *Cricketers' School* viii. 80 Yorkshire does not run the usual cricket Nursery that a team like Middlesex maintains. **1954** F. C. Avis *Boxing Ref. Dict.* 76 *Nursery*, a club in which boxing talent is developed. **1961** —— *Sportsman's Gloss.* 36/1 *Nursery*, a junior club taken under the wing of a bigger club to which talented nursery players graduate. **1962** G. Scott in B. Glanville *Footballer's Compan.* 447 It seemed that lads who had been taken from the 'nursery' clubs by the slag heaps and the pits had weak heads for success.

8. a. *nursery bathroom, bedroom, -book* (earlier example), *chair, child, fender, food, -governess* (earlier example), *meal, -rhyme* (earlier and later examples), *-song, story, supper, -tale* (earlier example), *tea*; **nursery-girl**, a nursery-maid; **nursery language**, a stylized form of language used in addressing small children; **nursery word**, a non-standard word used by a child or by an adult to address a child.

1949 'J. Tey' *Brat Farrar* xii. 94 You can have the nursery bathroom all to yourself, but *do* go slow on the hot water, will you? **1941** T. S. Eliot *Dry Salvages* i. 7 His [*sc.* the river's] rhythm was present in the nursery bedroom. **1818** Keats *Let.* 23 Jan. (1958) I. 210, I was at Hunt's the other day, and he surprised me with a real authenticated Lock of *Milton's Hair*. I know you would like what I wrote thereon—so here it is—*as they say of a Sheep in a Nursery Book*. **1869** C. L. Eastlake *Hints on Household Taste* (ed. 2) viii. 191 The rush-bottomed 'nursery' chairs, of which the wood-work is stained black, with low seats and high backs..are still to be bought in the East of London. **1896** *Heal & Son Catal.* 153 Nursery Chair, low cane seat and high back. **1817** Jane Austen *Let.* 13 Mar. (1952) 484 When Caroline was sent to School some years, *Miss Bell* was still retained, though the others were then mere Nursery Children. **1973** *Guardian* 22 May 13/1 Nanny's pride, the nursery child, ringletted, smocked and sashed, is no more. **1907** *Yesterday's Shopping* (1969) 177/1 Nursery Fenders... Brass top, japanned diamond wire work, black bottom plate. **1913** C. Mackenzie *Sinister St.* I. i. i. 10 Round the fire was a nursery fender on which hung perpetually various cloths and clothes and blankets and sheets. **1926–7** *Army & Navy Stores Catal.* 275/2 Nursery fender, with..brass top. ⅜ in. mesh..30 in. high with 12 in. return ends. **1949** A. Christie *Crooked House* v. 29 Proper wholesome nursery food—not those queer spiced rice dishes. **1965** D. Francis *Odds Against* vi. 84 A tiny service lift used long ago to take nursery food to top floor children. **1861** C. M. Yonge *Stokesley Secret* xii. 193 She..suspected Rhoda, the little nursery-girl, who was quite a child, and had not long been in the house. **1873** —— *Pillars of House* I. v. 96 Why, you might as well turn nursery-girl at once. **1820** M. Wilmot *Let.* 4 May (1935) 60 The loss of a most valuable little french Nursery Governess. **1845** F. A. Kemble *Let.* 8 Dec. in *Rec. Later Life* (1882) III. 95 In nursery language, I *peacified* the good old lady to the best of my ability. **1925** O. Jespersen *Mankind, Nation & Individual* vii. 145 Another dialect used with regard to the person addressed is that more or less affected nursery-language which many mothers and nurses..use with small children—where 'stomach' is 'tum-tum', 'horse' is 'gee-gee', 'thank-you' is 'ta' etc. **1968** *Trans. Philol. Soc.* 107 The special structures and lexical items employed by adults when talking to young children, which we can conveniently group together under the label of *Nursery Language*. **1942** M. B. Lowndes *Let.* 15 Apr. (1971) 229 Many people..live in their country houses with relations, children, and so on. I know of one where there are three sets of nursery meals! **1953** H. Nicolson *Diary* 6 May (1968) III. 240 Dull nursery meals—beef, mutton and milk-puddings. **1832** A. Fonblanque *England under Seven Admins.* (1837) II. 304 The man of Thessaly, famed for wondrous wisdom in nursery rhymes, who, having scratched his eyes out by jumping into one hedge, jumped into another to scratch them in again. **1972** (*title*) The bedtime book of 365 nursery rhymes. *c* **1820** Nursery-song [in Dict.]. **1927** W. E. Collinson *Contemporary Eng.* 9, I mention these nursery-songs. **1971** A. Mizener *Saddest Story* xxvi. 358 Ford led them in a round dance on the [Avignon] bridge to the tune of the nursery song. **1834** G. Crabbe Jr. *Life of Rev. George Crabbe* in *Poetical Works & Life of Crabbe* I. x. 304 Little tales, as nearly resembling those which had delighted his own infancy as modern systems permit..the German Nursery Stories. **1848** Thackeray *Van. Fair* xxv. 219 It was as in the old nursery-story, when the stick forgot to beat the dog. **1966** B. Ireson (*title*) The Faber book of nursery stories. **1857** C. M. Yonge *Dynevor Terrace* II. xii. 186 She often comes down after our dinner to find something for the nursery supper. **1971** J. Drummond *Farewell Party* xxi. 117, I was given a huge nursery supper by old Bertha. **1741** Richardson *Pamela* IV. lxiv. 451 You desired me to send you a little Specimen of my *Nursery Tales* and *Stories*, with which..I entertain..my little Boys. **1888** Kipling *Story of Gadsbys* 4 *Miss T*... Won't you have some eggs? *Captain G*... Eggs! (*Aside.*) Oh Hades! She must have a nursery-tea at this hour. **1939** T. S. Eliot *Family Reunion* i. i. 17 Harry must often have remembered Wishwood—The nursery tea, the school holiday. **1958** M. Stewart *Nine Coaches Waiting* iii. 33 A little pantry with an electric stove for making nursery tea. **1933** L. Bloomfield *Language* ix. 157 In English almost any doubled syllable may be used, in almost any meaning, as a nursery-word. **1957** R. W. Zandvoort *Handbk. Eng. Gram.* ix. i. 287 Many of them are nursery words... *Georgy-Porgy, piggie-wiggie, tootsy-wootsies* (feet), etc.

c. In sense 3, as *nursery education*; **nursery class**, a class attached to a primary or other school for the education of children usu. between the ages of three and five years; **nursery nurse**, a person trained to care for babies and young children; so **nursery nursing**; **nursery school**, a school for children usu. between the ages of two and five years; also *attrib.* and *fig.*; so **nursery schooling**; **nursery slope** *Skiing*, a gentle slope considered most suitable for beginners; also in extended uses (see quots.).

1921 *Act* 11 & 12 *Geo. V* c. 51 § 21 Supplying.. nursery schools (which expression shall include nursery classes) for children over two or under five years of age. **1943** *Educational Reconstruction* 5 A certain number of children enter..nursery classes attached to infants' schools, at an earlier age on a voluntary basis. **1970** J. & P. Kent *Nursery Schools for All* ii. iv. 94 Nursery classes are..defined..as 'a class mainly for children who have attained the age of three years but not the age of five years', and which is part of a primary school for infants or juniors. **1938** P. E. Cusden *English Nursery School* xvii. 257 The general provision of facilities for nursery education. **1969** *Guardian* 17 Jan. 9/2 Under the new Urban Aid Scheme £3 million are promised for more nursery education. **1974** *Ibid.* 24 Jan. 13/2 Mrs Thatcher has announced a programme of expanding nursery education. **1947** A. B. Meering *Handbk. for Nursery Nurses* 1 The Nursery Nurse who prefers the care of individual children ..may become a nanny in a private family. **1967** V. C. Jones in P. J. Cunningham *Nursery Nursing* 13 Nursery nurses..care for the young child in its earliest and most impressionable years. **1972** *Guardian* 30 Aug. 11/3 The nanny or nursery nurse of today is trained in child care... Norland..describes nursery nursing as a growing profession. **1973** E. Lemarchand *Let or Hindrance* ii. 16 She was in training as a nursery nurse, and had one more year to go. **1835** D. W. Webber *Let.* in I. Butler *Eldest Brother* (1973) i. ii. 29 It was..in the year 1765 that Lord Wellesley was brought to school... It was quite a nursery school... As a kind of Preparatory School it was in great Fashion. **1891** Michaelis & Moore tr. *Froebel's Lett.* 30 He [*sc.* Froebel] thinks of christening it 'Nursery School for Little Children' or 'Self-teaching Institution'. **1918** *Act* 8 & 9 *Geo. V.* c. 39 The Board shall have regard to the adequacy of the provision of nursery schools for the area. **1958** *Economist* 24 Oct. 303/1 His [*sc.* Gaitskell's] backbenchers still belong to the nursery school of political manœuvre. **1967** O. Wynd *Walk Softly* iii. 33 A nursery-school teacher who has happily dedicated a whole life to very young minds. **1970** J. & P. Kent *Nursery Schools for All* i. i. 28 From that time the nursery school problem assumed the distinctive character which it still has today. **1974** *Times* 14 Oct. 4/1 Nursery school grants rejected by councils. Mrs Thatcher introduced a £34m programme in 1971..to make nursery schooling available to half the three to five age group by 1980. **1924** K. Furse *Ski-Running* p. vi, Every beginner should be content to devote two or three of his first days to the Nursery slopes. **1924** W. Le Queux *Crystal Claw* i. 21 She had been three times before to winter sports, and had long passed the period when she practised her 'telemarks' and 'stemmings' on the 'nursery slopes'. **1943** Hunt & Pringle *Service Slang* 47 *Nursery slopes*, the easy targets allotted to beginners on bombing tests. **1959** *Daily Mail* 14 Oct. 12/6 If you do not limber up before you go [skiing] you may find your second or third day on the nursery slopes surprisingly painful. **1972** M. Yorke *Silent Witness* ii. 12 The lifts, and even the cable-car.., had stopped... Only the two short drags on the nursery slopes were working. **1975** *Daily Tel.* 15 Jan. 13 (*caption*) An early flight [in hang-gliding] lasting about 45 seconds down a nursery slope, straight into wind.

nursey. Add: (Further examples.) Also nursie.

1860 G. H. Lewes *Let.* 17 Mar. in *Geo. Eliot's Lett.* (1954) III. 274, I went to see Nursie, who will 'keep house' while I am away. **1918** A. Bennett *Roll-Call* ii. i. 220 Nursey's sunshade was undiscoverable. **1968** 'D. Shannon' *Kill with Kindness* xiii. 210 He was nursie's favorite—he could coax money out of her. **1973** R. Adams *Watership Down* (ed. 2) xvii. 94 You risk the life of one of the best rabbits we've got, just to play nursey while you go wandering about like a moon-struck field-mouse.

nursing, *vbl. sb.* Add: **1. b.** The profession of a nurse (Nurse *sb.*[1] 3); the duties of a nurse.

1860 F. Nightingale *Notes on Nursing* 6, I use the word nursing for want of a better. *Ibid.* 72 She [*sc.* the writer]..honestly believes that the perfection of surgical nursing may be seen practised by the old-fashioned 'sister' of a London hospital. **1889** O'Neill & Barnett *Our Nurses* i. 2 It is commonly and justly coming to be held that nursing in all its branches is a career for educated women. **1937** E. C. Pearce (*title*) A general textbook of nursing. **1955** *Oxf. Jun. Encycl.* XI. 333/2 Florence Nightingale was the real founder of the modern profession of nursing. **1970** K. K. Guinée *Professional Nurse* i. 6 The teacher of nursing carefully selects learning experiences in the clinical area.

2. *nursing-bottle, -chair* (further examples); (sense *1 b) *nursing-training*.

1861 Mrs. Beeton *Bk. Househ. Managem.* 1041 Many kinds of nursing-bottles have been lately invented, and some mounted with India-rubber nipples. **1944** A. Seton *Dragonwyck* i. 4 She unbuttoned her bodice, snatched up the hungry baby, and settled on the low nursing chair. **1971** *Country Life* 22 July (Suppl.) 32b/2 (Advt.), A Wm. IV nursing chair of hammock shape upholstered in deeply buttoned Havana brown leather. **1914** W. Owen *Let.* 29 Oct. (1967) 291 The Nursing Training is capital for you.

b. Designating garments designed to facilitate the breast-feeding of a baby, as *nursing basque, bra, brassière, corset.*

1939 M. B. Picken *Lang. Fashion* 104/3 *Nursing basque*, basque with buttoned closings, one on each side of the front. **1969** *Sears, Roebuck Catal.* Spring/Summer 362/2 Finest nylon lace nursing bra... Easy-open clasp lets you hold baby as you open cups. **1950** Heaton & Daynes *Feeding Mothers & Babies* ii. 55 A nursing brassière.. should have a waterproof lining. **1895** *Montgomery Ward Catal.* 309/2 Dr. Strong's Tricora Nursing Corset has proved a great comfort to mothers.

c. Special Combs., as **nursing home**, (*a*) a small, private institution where the sick are cared for; also *attrib.*; (*b*) a place where certain qualities are nurtured.

1896 [in Dict., sense 2]. **1938** L. P. Smith *Unforgotten Years* vi. 149 Her barrister husband insisted..that I should be transferred without delay to what was, in his opinion, the only nursing home of reasonable thought and noble ambition—in fact, to Balliol College. **1951** [see *clinic *sb.*[2] 2]. **1959** T. S. Eliot *Elder Statesman* ii. 45 We've studied to avoid Anything like a nursing-home atmosphere.

nursing, *ppl. a.* Add: **1. b.** *nursing mother* (*b*) a woman who is breast-feeding her own baby.

1806 D. Wordsworth *Let.* 23 July in *Lett. William & Dorothy Wordsworth* (1969) II. 60 She thinks herself quite well, but *I* do not think she is as yet as strong as she ought to be for a nursing mother. **1897** G. Tucker *Mother, Baby & Nursery* 96 It becomes the first duty of the nursing mother to take care of herself. **1926** 'Eliza-beth' *Introd. to Sally* ix. 154 Good job I ain't a nursin' mother..or the lady'd turn my milk sour. **1950** E. Pantin *Mod. Mothercraft* i. 19 The health of a nursing mother affects the quality of her milk. **1970** J. de Bairacli-Levy *Natural Rearing of Children* iii. 28 It is an error to say that a nursing mother must take milk from animals to increase her own milk. **1974** A. Huxley *Plant & Planet* xxviii. 328 Nursing mothers in the United States have so much DDT in their milk that, to quote a scientific humorist, 'in strict terms of federal law, it is illegal for them to carry their busts..across one state line to another'.

nurtural (nɒ̄·ɹtiŭrăl), *a.* [f. Nurtur(e *sb.* + -al.] Of, belonging to, or due to nurture; usually designating characteristics, etc., which can be attributed to training, environment, or the like, and are not natural or inherited.

1889 *Jrnl. Anthrop. Inst.* XIX. 78 The problem of determining purely 'racial characteristics' will be considerably simplified if we can in this way determine what may be described in contradistinction as 'nurtural characteristics'. **1922** W. R. Inge *Outspoken Ess.* 2nd Ser. 257 Professor Pearson has tabulated a long list of natural characters, and another long list of nurtural characters. **1922** *Edin. Rev.* July 47 Religion is the strongest of nurtural influences.

nurturance (nɒ̄·ɹtiŭrăns). *Psychol.* [f. Nurtur(e *v.* + -ance.] Emotional and physical nourishment and care.

1938 H. A. Murray *Explorations in Personality* ii. 83 *Nurturance*,..to nourish, aid or protect... To express sympathy. To 'mother' a child. **1957** E. R. Hilgard *Introd. Psychol.* (ed. 2) vi. 134/2 Scales were designed to get at nurturance (i.e., the mother's care in feeding). **1964** Cofer & Appley *Motivation* xiv. 719 Someone else may help or sympathize with him, that is, he may receive nurturance from another. **1973** *Jrnl. Genetic Psychol.* June 185 A wide spectrum of 15 personality dimensions (e.g. need achievement, nurturance, dominance, aggression). **1974** *Nature* 9 Aug. 466/1 Warm and outgoing students (high on nurturance) also display a more favourable attitude.

nurturant (nɒ̄·ɹtiŭrănt), *a.* *Psychol.* [f. as prec. + -ant[1].] Caring or nourishing (emotionally or physically); exhibiting or pertaining to nurturance.

1938 H. A. Murray *Explorations in Personality* iii. 181 The succorance drive seeks a nurturant O and the nurturant drive seeks a succorant O. **1951** R. R. Sears in Parsons & Shils *Toward General Theory of Action* 471 The nurturant mother. **1973** *Jrnl. Genetic Psychol.* Mar. 37 Psychopaths..saw their fathers as having been less nurturant toward them and as having given them less praise. **1973** S. Fisher *Fem. Orgasm* iv. 108 Femininity is associated with being nurturant and 'nice'.

Nusranee, Nusrani: see *Nasrani.

Nusselt (nu·sělt). [the name of E. K. Wilhelm *Nusselt* (1882–1957), German engineer.] *Nusselt number*, a dimensionless parameter used in calculations of the heat transfer between a moving fluid and a solid, equivalent to hD/k, where h is the rate of heat loss per unit area per degree difference in temperature between the body and its surroundings, D is a characteristic length of the body, and k is the thermal conductivity of the fluid.

1933 W. H. McAdams *Heat Transmission* iv. 96 *hD/k*.. Nusselt number. 1958 Condon & Odishaw *Handbk. Physics* III. ii. 35/1 For low speeds the Nusselt number is a function of the Reynolds number, the Prandtl (or Péclet) number, and the Grashof number... In the case of forced convection, for which gravitational effects are insignificant, the Nusselt number is a function only of the Reynolds number and of the Prandtl number. In natural (free) convection the Nusselt number is a function only of the Grashof number and of the Prandtl number. 1974 J. R. Welty *Engin. Heat Transfer* v. 265 Heat Transfer for Cylinders in Crossflow... At higher Reynolds numbers.. the Nusselt number experiences two sudden increases, one at the separation point and one where the boundary layer undergoes a transition from laminar to turbulent flow.

nustaleek, var. *Nastalik.

nut, *sb.*[1] Add: **I. 1. f.** Pl. *vulg.* The testicles. Also in various vulgar phrases.

1915 *Dialect Notes* IV. 186 *Nut*, in *pl.* testicles. 1922 Joyce *Ulysses* 467 How's the nuts?..Off side. Curiously they are on the right. Heavier I suppose. 1955 W. Gaddis *Recognitions* II. vii. 630 The lady lost her nuts, Anselm said to no one. He mumbled,—That's the world we live in, the ladies wear the nuts. 1969 B. Malcolm in A. Chapman *New Black Voices* (1972) 385 Easy way out To hate the white man..for Kicking my papa in the nuts. 1970 C. Major *Dict. Afro-Amer. Slang* 58 *Get (one's) nuts off*, sexual release, implies ejaculation more than orgasm. 1970 E. Bullins *Theme is Blackness* (1973) 167 Screwin' my best white friend's black wife makes me feel even better. Makes me get my nuts off. 1973 R. Busby *Pattern of Violence* v. 79 Russell got a boot in the nuts. 1974 J. Wainwright *Evidence I shall Give* xxi. 102 He was working his nuts off.

3. Phr. *for nuts*, in neg. contexts: at all.

1895 W. Pett Ridge *Minor Dialogues* 82 An' the eldest gal *she* thinks she can play, and, if you'll believe me, she carn't play for nuts. 1899 [in Dict.]. 1934 A. Thirkell *Wild Strawberries* xi. 237 That Miss Stevenson can't play for nuts.

6. Also const. *about*.

1920 S. Lewis *Main Street* xxiii. 280 Carrie's nuts about this Russian revolution. 1945 E. Waugh *Brideshead Revisited* I. vii. 177, I was still nuts about Rex. 1975 *New Yorker* 21 Apr. 39/1 You're nuts about me, right?

7. a. (Earlier examples.)

1846 *Swell's Night Guide* 76 Why, she's getting groggy on her pins, and if you don't pipe rumbo, she'll go prat over nut (head over heels). 1852 J. Labern *Pop. Comic Song Bk.* 76 But vun chap flung a bunch of turnips, which nearly split Dick's nut in two.

c. *Pl.* (as *adj.*): insane, crazy, 'off one's head'.

1846 *Swell's Night Guide* 75 Vhy, Owen..you knows it's no use of me being nuts, ven the donna's only nut crackers. 1914 Jackson & Hellyer *Vocab. Criminal Slang* 62 Nuts,.. As an adjective and adverb it signifies daft, mentally deranged. 1928 C. Sandburg in *Amer. Mercury* Oct. 154 There was a screw loose somewhere in him, he had a kink and he was a Crank, he was nuts and belonged in a booby hatch. 1953 [see *gee *int.*[2]]. 1969 I. & P. Opie *Children's Games* ii. 76 The person was..looney, nuts, a nit.

d. Phr. *to do one's* (or *the*) *nut*, to become angry, lose one's head; to be worked up about something; to be crazy.

1919 W. H. Downing *Digger Dialects* 20 *Do the nut*, lose one's head. 1936 J. Curtis *Gilt Kid* 231 The jane'd be bound to think he had done his nut. 1956 [see *choked *ppl. a.* 2]. 1957 J. Osborne *Entertainer* xiii. 86 I'm doing me nut up here. 1958 F. Norman *Bang to Rights* III. 92 The twirl would do his nut and give up. 1959 P. Bull *I know Face* xi. 199, I would be doing my 'nut' and my probable swansong for Auntie BBC. 1960 *News Chron.* 16 Feb. 6/5 Been doing his nut about little Barbara for months, he had. 1961 J. Stroud *Touch & Go* xv. 155 He's nearly done his nut over this daughter of his. 1972 J. Brown *Chancer* v. 68, I thought what Grace would say, that she'd do her nut maybe. But she didn't blink an eyelid.

e. *Pl.* Used as a derisive retort: nonsense, rubbish; I defy you. Freq. const. *to*.

1931 M. E. Gilman *Sob Sister* 267 Nuts! You'll forget Nick the minute you smell your freedom. 1934 J. O'Hara *Appointment in Samarra* iv. 86 'Nuts to you, sister,' he said. 1936 *New Yorker* 18 Jan. 20 With a hay-nonny-nonny and a nuts to you. 1938 J. Curtis *They drive by Night* ix. 109 A feather shopping bag lay on a table. He stepped across towards it. As he stepped his golf-clubs rattled. Aw, nuts to that dog barking. 1946 Wodehouse *Joy in Morning* II. xii. 91 'If you think I've got the force of character to come back with a *nolle prosequi*—' 'With a what?' 'One of Jeeves' gags. It means roughly "Nuts to you!"' 1974 D. Francis *Knock Down* ii. 25 'I'll give you a hundred.' 'Nuts.' 'A hundred and fifty.'

f. *the nuts*, an excellent person or thing. *U.S. slang*.

1932 *Amer. Speech* VII. 334 *The nuts*, denotes superlative quality. 1949 W. Stevens *Let.* 9 Sept. (1967) 647 At the Museum of Modern Art they cultivate the idea that everything is the nuts. 1955 W. Gaddis *Recognitions* II. vii. 634 Get a little cross with mirrors in it, that would be the nuts if you want to suffer your way.

8. c. A madman; a crank. *slang* (orig. *U.S.*).

1903 R. L. McCardell *Conversat. of Chorus Girl* 15 'Circus Joe'..worked the nuts on the edge of the crowd. 1914 Jackson & Hellyer *Vocab. Criminal Slang* 62 *Nut*, commonly current in all circles when the meaning is 'loco'. 1919 [see *bughouse *sb.* 1]. 1931 D. Runyon *Guys & Dolls* (1932) 213, I am commencing to think this Count Saro is some kind of a nut, and is only speaking through his hat. 1936 K. Mackenzie *Living Rough* xv. 216 We're sure a pair of nuts riding the outside over the hump this time of the year. 1960 H. Pinter *Room* 118 You're not only a nut, you're a blind nut and you can get out the way you came. 1966 T. Pynchon *Crying of Lot 49* v. 107 Why worry, she worried; Nefastis is a nut, forget it, a sincere nut. 1973 *Nation Rev.* (Melbourne) 31 Aug. 1444/1 The Worker Student Alliance, a bunch of nuts in Melbourne.

8*. *slang.* A fashionable or showy young man of affected elegance; a 'young blood', fop, or masher. Cf. Nutty *a.* 4 and *knut.

1904 in *N. & Q.* (1913) 26 July 78/1 I'm one of the nuts, one of the nibs. 1913 *Punch* 12 Feb. 115/1 Spring socks will be black and Spring ties a quiet blue. A strike of nuts is expected at any moment. 1915 Kipling in *Nash's & Pall Mall Mag.* Oct. 131/2 Winchmore, the youngest, was more on the lines of a conventional nut. 1920 W. J. Locke *House of Baltazar* xvii. 205 I've a jolly good mind to set him up regardless, like a pre-war nut—with solid silver boot-trees and the rest to correspond. 1920 R. Macaulay *Potterism* I. iv. 44 He always looked the same, calm, unruffled, tidy, the exquisite nut. 1923 *Other Lands* Oct. 3/3 The last named continue to be marks of the 'nut'.

11. a. Also *fig.*

1911 *Rep. Labour & Social Conditions in Germany* (Tariff Reform League) III. 39 When we get our nuts screwed a little tighter we shall be able to look after our own industries and mind our own business. 1973 'J. Patrick' *Glasgow Gang Observed* x. 88 Asked why so few boys over twenty remained in the Fleet [gang], Tim replied: 'They used tae be in it but they've screwed the nut.' *Ibid.* 235 *Screw*, as in '*screw the nut*', to become sensible, to 'get wise' to oneself, to pull oneself together.

d. *fig.* in phr. (*the*) *nuts and bolts*, the practical, basic elements, or the mechanics, of a situation or thing. Freq. *attrib.*

1960 *Times* 9 Feb. 11/4 When we talk about technicians —the 'nuts-and-bolts boys'—we are all right there. 1967 *Observer* 30 Apr. 11/8 A..keen-eyed Army colonel..talks to you about 'the nuts and bolts' of the programme. 1971 *Times* 10 June 16/6 His preference was for journalism. He learnt the nuts and bolts of his profession with the Montreal *Gazette*. 1972 *Guardian* 10 June 11/7 Most of some hundreds of recommendations in the action plan and its annexe, where the nuts and bolts are, will go through. 1973 T. Allbeury *Choice of Enemies* xvii. 83 There are two kinds of security that we cover... A bit of cigarette ash on a magnetic tape could screw up a whole pay-roll..but..that's pretty well a nuts and bolts area for us. We know it inside out. 1974 *Times* 22 Feb. 14 The electors are not to be despised for this conspicuous lack of interest in the nuts and bolts of politics. 1974 *Socialist Worker* 7 Dec. 9/6 There was also a tendency to go very easy on replies to those delegates who urged the conference to adopt a fuller and finer programme rather than discuss the nuts and bolts of trying to build in the real world.

18*. *U.S. slang.* The amount of money required for a venture; overhead costs. Hence *transf.*, any sum of money.

1912 A. H. Lewis *Apaches N.Y.* 201 Every day I'm open puts me fifty dollars on th' nut. 1914 Jackson & Hellyer *Vocab. Criminal Slang* 62 *Nut*,.. used by grafters whose operations involve an investment to signify an expense incurred in connection with a venture. 1933 *Sun* (Baltimore) 28 Jan. 16/4 The difficulty of 'making the nut', the term applied to accumulating the rental charge due each night to the owner of the cab. 1935 *Amer. Mercury* June 230/1 *Nut*, concession charges for booking a joint; expenses. 1936 *Amer. Speech* XI. 219 He [*sc.* the producer] decides that in order to open the show a certain amount of money will be necessary. This amount is the production *nut*. 1948 *Sun* (Baltimore) 7 Aug. 9/2 In any event the 'nut' will be close to $400,000, counting fighters, rent and promotional expenses. 1955 *Publ. Amer. Dial. Soc.* xxiv. 37 Recreation, such as gambling..and other cultural pursuits dear to the hearts of pickpockets, will cost extra... All this is counted as *nut*..and anything they make over and above this they consider income. 1956 H. Gold *Man who was not with It* (1965) xviii. 159, I was getting a nut of cash, and it felt good. 1962 J. B. Priestley *Margin Released* vi. 202 In the Thirties, when we could produce *Laburnum Grove*..for about £800..the weekly running costs—the 'get-out' or 'nut'—were round about the same figure, theatre and all. 1970 *Daily Tel.* 27 Apr. 3 New York police have their own secret slang to deal with their illegal business... 'Nut' is a cash bribe. 1972 *Publishers' Weekly* 14 Feb. 60/1 He submitted a strong script that led Fox to substitute color film and wide screen for black-and-white and the conventional small-screen ratio, and to raise the nut to $400,000.

19. a. (sense *8 c), as *nut alley*, *-doctor*, *-farm*.

1935 A. J. Pollock *Underworld Speaks* 81/2 *Nut alley*, prison insane ward. 1955 A. Huxley *Let.* 7 May (1969) 742 Next week..I go to Atlantic City to attend the Psychiatrists' Assn. meeting... I shall arrange to meet the boys on my return from the nut-doctors. *a* 1940 F. Scott Fitzgerald *Last Tycoon* (1949) i. 12 Some mystic ..spouting tripe that'd land him on a nut-farm anywhere outside of California.

20. *nut-bearing*, *-questing*.

1877 L. H. Morgan *Anc. Society* (1907) I. ii. 20 In fruit and nut-bearing forests under a tropical sun, we are accustomed..to regard our progenitors as having commenced their existence. 1952 A. G. L. Hellyer *Sanders' Encycl. Gardening* (ed. 22) 130 Corylus (Cob-nut; Filbert)... Hardy deciduous nut-bearing shrubs. 1922 Joyce *Ulysses* 535 Who left his nutquesting classmates to seek our shade?

21. nut-butter, a substitute for butter obtained from the oil of nuts; **nut (milk) chocolate,** (milk) chocolate containing nuts; **nut college** *U.S. slang*, = *nut-house* (below); **nut cutlet,** a portion of meat-substitute made from nuts and various other ingredients and shaped like a cutlet; **nut factory** *U.S. slang*, = *nut-house* (below); **nut food,** food prepared from nuts; so **nut-fooder; nut-house** *slang*, a mental hospital; **nut-meat,** the kernel of a nut; **nut-pine,** substitute for def.: one of several species of pine producing edible seeds, native to south-western North America and the Rocky Mountains; (earlier and later examples); **nut runner,** a power tool for tightening nuts; **nut-steak,** a portion of meat-substitute made from nuts and shaped like a steak.

1907 Nut-butter [see s.v. Nucoline]. 1908 *Westm. Gaz.* 5 Aug. 2/3 Vegetarians cannot expect to be allowed to call their butter-substitute 'nut butter' when other people's butter-substitutes are called 'margarine'. 1918 C. A. Mitchell *Edible Oils & Fats* ix. 117 Deodorised coconut oil is used in the preparation of both margarine and 'nut butter'. 1961 C. Loewenfeld tr. *Bircher's Eating your Way to Health* II. iii. 246 Nut butter is a good and easily digested substitute for those who do not like, or should not have, butter. 1971 J. Hewitt *N. Y. Times Natural Foods* xv. 393 *Nut butter spread*... Place the nuts, sunflower seeds, kernels and seeds in an electric blender and blend until fine. 1975 *Times* 14 Feb. 9/7 They bake daily... They also make various nut butters. 1926–7 *Army & Navy Stores Catal.* 54/1 Chocolate..Nut (¼ lb. pkts.). 1936 'J. Tey' *Shilling for Candles* xi. 128 'Nut or plain?' 'What?' 'The chocolate.' 1955 M. Allingham *Beckoning Lady* xvi. 228 Offering Westy half a bar of nut chocolate. 1931 *Amer. Speech* VII. 111 *Nut college*, an insane asylum. 1951 in Wentworth & Flexner *Dict. Amer. Slang* (1960) 360/2 He has been recalled by the nut college to join Napoleon..and Shakespeare, inventing paper dolls! 1908 F. A. George *Vegetarian Cookery* ix. 113 *Nut cutlets*... Make into cutlet shapes. Egg and crumb. Fry in deep fat. 1925 D. H. Lawrence *Let.* ?17 Dec. (1962) II. 871 So Sonya will never cook us another goose, only marmite pie and nut-cutlet. 1959 'M. Innes' *Hare sitting Up* II. vi. 112 Didn't I say something about Burgundy? Capital with nut cutlets. 1965 J. B. Priestley *Lost Empires* II. ii. 115 Mr Foster-Jones makes Health Foods... He's probably brought a case of date sandwiches and nut cutlets with him. 1973 *Times* 10 Apr. 14/1 You can no longer get nut cutlets... What you get instead now are nut rissoles. 1915 *Recruiter's Bull.* (U.S. Marine Corps., N.Y.) Oct. 15/1 It would have been impossible to have found a man any other place than a 'nut-factory' who would voluntarily have told the commanding officer that he was a deserter. 1929 J. Callahan *Man's Grim Justice* xiii. 156 They should have been in the 'nut factory'..the insane department. 1939 J. H. Chase *No Orchids for Miss Blandish* i. 33 Johnnie was a rummy... Drink had rotted him, and he was only two jumps ahead of the nut-factory. 1905 *Vegetarian Messenger* Apr. 105, I will send any readers who wish for it an address where nut-foods can be had guaranteed free of pea-nuts. 1917 N. Douglas *South Wind* x. 142 He will be an anti-vivisectionist, a nut-fooder, costume-maniac.., or a spiritualist into the bargain. 1929 *Amer. Speech* IV. 343 *Nut House*, an insane asylum. 1936 'P. Quentin' *Puzzle for Fools* i. 6 It wasn't a sanatorium really. It was just an expensive nuthouse for people like me who had lost control. 1953 W. Burroughs *Junkie* (1972) 10, I decided I was not going to like the Army and copped out on my nut-house record... The nut-house doctors had never heard of Van Gogh. 1958 'N. Blake' *Penknife in my Heart* iii. 42 Miriam drives you into the nut-house. 1973 'H. Howard' *Highway to Murder* xi. 141 Supposing the plan succeeded and his wife got stuck away in a nut-house? 1974 *Radio Times* 24 Oct. 11/2 Clothing for the Government, prisons and nut-'ouses—what is it they call 'em now? 1913 A. B. Emerson *R. Fielding at Snow Camp* 102 The three boys stuck to their work..until there was a great bowl of nutmeats. 1967 *Economist* 9 Sept. 892/1 Kukui nut-meat burning gently in a shell. 1974 *Aiken* (S. Carolina) *Standard* 22 Apr. 8-A/5 The Viennese desserts called Torten are sometimes made with finely ground nut-meats without the inclusion of any flour. 1918–19 *T. Eaton & Co. Catal.* Fall & Winter 385/2 Eaton's Nut Milk Chocolate... Each bar made from fine chocolate, milk and nuts. 1932 R. Lehmann *Invitation to Waltz* III. vi. 215, I preferred to spend the afternoon on the schoolroom sofa reading *East Lynne* and eating nut-milk chocolate. 1960 *Sunday Express* 25 Dec. 13/3 When nut milk chocolate was 2d. a bar. 1845 J. C. Frémont *Rep. Expl. Exped. Rocky Mountains* 221 A pine tree..which Dr. Torrey has described as a new species, under the name of *pinus monophyllus*; in popular language, it might be called the nut pine. 1896 C. H. Shinn *Story of the Mine* 63 The nut-pine trees were soon cut down. 1949 Collingwood & Brush *Knowing your Trees* 18/1 This is one of four nut pines of the Southwest. 1969 T. H. Everett *Living Trees of World* 50/2 The piñon or Mexican stone pine (*P. cembroides*) is small and spreading and, like its variety *P. c. edulis*, the nut pine, produces delicious edible seeds or 'nuts'. Both are natives of the southwestern United States and Mexico, the nut pine extending north to Wyoming. 1958 R. M. Barnes *Motion & Time Study* (ed. 4) xvii. 288 The multiple-spindle air-operated nut runner..is used to tighten all five wheel nuts at once. 1966 *Engineers' Digest* Dec. 97/2 Suitable for light duties and often employed with power screwdrivers and nutrunners, another type of torque limiting device utilizes a spring-loaded steel ball. 1908 *Daily Chron.* 2 Sept. 3/4 High thinking is still nourished upon the banana and the nut-steak. 1922 Joyce *Ulysses* 163 Why do they call that thing they gave me nutsteak? Nutarians, Fruitarians. To give you the idea you are eating rumpsteak. 1966 K. Giles *Provenance of Death* iv. 103 The man..is a vegetarian... He had a nut steak.

22. Passing into *adj.* Stupid, insane (cf. senses 7, 8, and *19 a).

1919 *Sci. Amer.* 23 Aug. 184/1 Other ideas, no more revolutionary and no more absurd from the standpoint of entrenched orthodoxy, never graduate from the 'nut' class. 1922 U. Sinclair *They call me Carpenter* xix. 66, I just want to know where he got his nut ideas. 1922

S. LEWIS *Babbitt* ii. 17 Ever since somebody slipped up and let you out of college..you been pulling these nut conversations about what-nots and so-on-and-so-forths. **1966** T. PYNCHON *Crying of Lot 49* iii. 48 'You one of these right-wing nut outfits?' inquired the diplomatic Metzger.

nut, *v.* Add: **3.** *slang.* **a.** To think, to use one's head. Freq. const. *out,* also *up.* (Cf. NUT *sb.*¹ 7.)

1919 W. H. DOWNING *Digger Dialects* 36 *Nut it out,* think it out. **1925** FRASER & GIBBONS *Soldier & Sailor Words* 213 *Nut out, to,* to think over. Consider. To use one's head. **1951** D. STIVENS *Jimmy Brockett* 168, I did a bit of hard nutting over my plans for trotting. **1953** K. TENNANT *Joyful Condemned* iv. 38 Just nut that out. **1962** A. UPFIELD *Will of Tribe* xix. 180, I asked him how he nutted up the idea. **1965** M. SHADBOLT *Among Cinders* xiii. 112, I haven't nutted out what I'm going to say about the poultry. **1971** R. DENTRY *Encounter at Kharmel* (1973) v. 81 I've been nutting the whole thing out... There's no future in it for you.

b. To butt with the head; to hit a blow on the head. Also **nu·tting** *vbl. sb.*

1937 PARTRIDGE *Dict. Slang* 575/1 *Nut,*..to punch on the head. **1963** T. & P. MORRIS *Pentonville* xi. 241 Few prison fights are conducted in accordance with Queensberry Rules; fists, heads (for the painful infliction of injury to the opponent's nose by 'nutting'), teeth and nails may be used at any time. **1966** D. SKIRROW *It won't get you Anywhere* xiv. 61, I shot my head backwards in time to miss the nutting that was coming... The tearaway special nowadays is to hug tight, rupture his kidneys and nut him hard. **1971** J. MANDELKAU *Buttons* xiii. 145 He took it off and as I was getting out of mine he nutted me in the head.

Nut, var. *NAT¹.

nutarian (nɒtēə·riăn). [f. after *vegetarian.*] A vegetarian whose diet is based on nut products.

1914 *Chambers's Eng. Dict.* Suppl. 1281/2 *Nutarian,* one who lives on nuts.—Also adj. (From *Nut,* in imitation of *Vegetarian.*) **1922** [see *nut-steak* s.v. *NUT *sb.*¹ 21].

nutate, *v.* Delete *rare* and substitute for def.: To undergo or exhibit nutation. (Further examples of vb. and ppl. adj.)

1898 S. H. VIVES *Elem. Text-bk. Bot.* iii. 211 All growing members nutate in a more or less marked manner. **1921** J. SMALL *Textbk. Bot.* xvii. 221 In the mature plant the top three internodes of the stem turn or nutate in a circle. **1943** R. C. BINDER *Fluid Mech.* viii. 107 The nutating-disk meter or wobble-plate meter..is frequently used to meter the water supply for domestic use. **1948** C. E. INGALLS in S. N. Van Voorhis *Microwave Receivers* xv. 380 Tracking in azimuth and elevation is made possible by the use of a nutating antenna. A fixed paraboloidal reflector is combined with a dipole, which is caused to move in a small circular orbit about the focus of the reflector, to give a radiation pattern in the form of a beam that traces out a small cone. **1950** H. GOLDSTEIN *Class. Mech.* v. 168 It is not the regular precession encountered in force-free motion, for as the figure axis goes around it nods up and down..—the top nutates. **1965** BELL & COOMBE tr. *Strasburger's Textbk. Bot.* 390 A nutating shoot. **1969** R. SKINNER *Mech.* iv. 469 The top continues to spin about its axis of symmetry, while this axis rotates, or precesses, about a vertical axis. All the while, this axis [of symmetry] nods up and down, or nutates, as it precesses.

nutation. Add: **2. c.** Movement (as of a beam or aerial) by which an axis is made to describe a cone. (Analogous to the precession of a spinning top rather than its nutation.)

1947 *Bell Syst. Techn. Jrnl.* XXVI. 307 The axis of the beam was rotated in an orbit by 'nutation' about the mechanical axis of the antenna. **1966** *McGraw-Hill Encycl. Sci. & Technol.* XI. 204/2 Either the feed or the reflector whirls rapidly in a manner that causes the beam axis to describe a circular cone; this motion of the beam axis is called nutation.

nutational (niutē·ʃənăl), *a.* [f. NUTATION + -AL.] Of or pertaining to nutation.

1881 W. D. HAY *300 Years Hence* viii. 152 The precessional and nutational movements of the earth. **1959** VAN LEAR & LASSEN in Puckett & Ramo *Guided Missile Engin.* x. 275 If the gyro is started up with the inner gimbal initially inclined to the plane perpendicular to the outer gimbal, there is first a transitory nutational bobbing around. **1965** BELL & COOMBE tr. *Strasburger's Textbk. Bot.* 361 In both kinds of movement the mechanical cause may be either a difference in growth rates on the two sides of an organ (nutational movements) or differential changes in the turgor of the cells (variational movements).

nu·tburger. Also nutberger. [f. NUT *sb.*¹ 1 + *BURGER.] A meat-substitute made from nuts, formed into a cake, and usu. served between the two halves of a toasted bun; also, a hamburger topped with nuts. Also *attrib.*

1934 M. WESEEN *Dict. Amer. Slang* XIX. 291 *Nutberger,* a hamburger sprinkled with nuts. **1939** A. HUXLEY *After Many a Summer* I. i. 6 Drive In For Nutbergers—whatever they were. **1942** *Amer. Speech* XVII. 132/2 *Nutburgers* are on sale in California. **1948** E. WAUGH *Loved One* 120 Dennis..followed her to a nutburger counter. *Ibid.,* D'you know, this is the first time I've ever eaten a nutburger? **1959** *Listener* 24 Sept. 497/2 It is ready to try anything, from Mormonism to nutburgers. **1973** *Guardian* 17 Mar. 13/1 Thrifty high-protein meat substitutes..soyabeanburgers and nutburgers and fishwiches.

nu·t-cake. [NUT *sb.*¹ 1.] **a.** *U.S.* A dough-nut or fried cake. **b.** A cake containing nuts.

a **1800** *Spirit of Farmer's Museum* (1801) 235 Heap the nut-cakes, fried in butter. **1823** [in Dict. s.v. NUT *sb.*¹ 19]. **1844** *Knickerbocker* XXIV. 483 Reflection..was interrupted by the appearance..of 'nut-cakes and cider'. **1857** *Quinland* I. II. ii. 34 By the way, Hepsy, make us some 'nut-cakes', and bring us the cider. **1873** M. HOLLEY *My Opinions* (1891) 251 Where is the rich happy woman that wouldn't give a nutcake to a sick beggar? **1889** R. T. COOKE *Steadfast* xviii. 198 Who ever heard tell of puttin' a reason and a bit of citron into the middle of a riz nut-cake before 'twas fried? **1957** G. MANN *Bk. Cakes* 157 *Nut Cake...* Put into a shallow greased tin and spread the nut covering over the cake. **1966** W. I. KAUFMAN *Nut Cookery Bk.* 65 *Nut cake...* Fold in walnuts, stirring as little as possible... Bake in a moderate oven.

nu·t-case. *colloq.* [f. NUT *sb.*¹ (cf. *8 c) + CASE *sb.*²] A crazy person; a madman.

1959 *Punch* 21 Oct. 337/2, I couldn't get anyone to talk about it openly. The way they clammed up you'd have thought I was a spy or a nut-case. **1965** A. PRIOR *Interrogators* iii. 28 He knew the nut-cases, the convicted sexual offenders. **1969** *Listener* 24 Apr. 586/2 You nut-case, you ought to be locked up. **1973** BOYD & PARKES *Dark Number* v. 57 They were all shams... She was a nutcase really.

nut-cracker. Add: **5. Nutcracker Man,** a nickname for the fossil hominid, *Australopithecus robustus* (or *A. boisei*), the maker of the oldest stone tools known, esp. the specimen discovered by L. S. B. and M. D. Leakey at Olduvai, Tanzania, in 1959; similar remains, including the characteristic large premolar teeth, have also been found in South Africa.

1959 *Times* 4 Sept. 8/4 He [*sc.* L. S. B. Leakey] has named the species *Zinjanthropus Boisei...* The nickname given by Dr. Leakey to the world's oldest man is 'Nutcracker Man' because of the tremendously developed teeth. **1961** *New Scientist* 26 Oct. 221 Not only is *Zinjanthropus* or Nutcracker Man 'unquestionably' human but some of his fairly distant ancestors were human as well. **1962** *Listener* 5 Apr. 589/1 Dr. Leakey's famous 'nutcracker man' Zinjanthropus (which has now been dated as having lived over 1,000,000 years ago). **1972** S. CUPITT tr. *Wendt's From Ape to Adam* iv. 228 He [*sc.* Robert Broom] found the remains of an australopithecine equipped with a particularly powerful jaw and truly nutcracker-like teeth... These 'Nutcracker men' even had a small sagittal crest on their skulls. *Ibid.* 232 At first Leakey thought that this ancient Oldowan ancestor of ours was very different from the South African 'Nutcracker man', despite his powerful back teeth. **1974** WASHBURN & MOORE *Ape into Man* iv. 107 The huge molars..could have cracked nuts, and the Leakeys sometimes liked to call their discovery 'nutcracker man'.

nu·t-cut, *a. India.* [Hind. *naṭkhaṭ.*] Roguish. Also as *sb.,* a rogue, rascal.

1848 J. H. STOCQUELER *Oriental Interpreter* 175/2 *Nut-cut,* roguish, mischievous. A term of reproach, good-naturedly applied in India to *vauriens.* **1901** KIPLING *Kim* iv. 107 'That is a *nut-cut* (rogue),' she said. 'All police-constables are *nut-cuts*; but the police-wallahs are the worst.'

nut-grass. Substitute for def.: A small sedge of the genus *Cyperus,* esp. *C. rotundus,* whose roots form small nut-like tubers. (Earlier and later examples.)

1775 B. ROMANS *Conc. Nat. Hist. Florida* 129 In Carolina it [sc. *herbe au cheval*] is called nutt grass from a nutt found at its root. **1894** J. M. COULTER *Bot. W. Texas* III. 463 *Cyperus rotundus...* From the South Atlantic and Gulf States to the Texan coast... Often called 'nut grass'. **1903** 'S. RUDD' *Our New Selection* iv. 36 Nothing but burr and thistle and nut-grass grew. **1944** *Living off Land* ii. 42 The little bulbs of the onion weed (or nut grass). **1965** *Austral. Encycl.* VIII. 68/1 The latter species [sc. *Cyperus rotundus*], known as 'nut grass', is widely spread in warmer parts of the world (including Australia) and is a serious weed pest—probably the worst in areas where rice is extensively cultivated.

nuthin (nɒ·þin). Repr. of a colloq. pronunc. of NOTHING *sb.*

1925 E. O'NEILL *Desire under Elms* I. 69 Oceans o' trouble an' nuthin' but wuk fur reward. **1968** R. CLAPPERTON *No News on Monday* vi. 73 Course I never said nuthin'. **1968** A. DIMENT *Bang Bang Birds* x. 181 Don't you cats know nuthin' about acid? **1971** *Black World* Oct. 64/2 So I don't say nuthin'. **1973** 'J. PATRICK' *Glasgow Gang Observed* v. 51 Ah *hate* somewan in a company who disnae say nuthin'.

nutmeg. Add: **3.** (Example.)

1822 J. WOODS *2 Yrs. Res. Eng. Prairie Illinois* 307 There are many sorts of sweet melons... I have only noticed musk, of a large size; and nutmeg, a smaller one.

5. nutmeg hickory, a species of hickory, *Carya myristicæformis,* bearing a fruit resembling a nutmeg and found in southern North America.

1810 F. A. MICHAUX *Hist. Arbres Forestiers de l'Amérique Septentrionale* I. 21 Nutmeg hickory nut.., nom donné par moi. **1832** D. J. BROWNE *Sylva Amer.* 177 This species..bears the name of Nutmeg Hickory from the resemblance of its fruits to that of the nutmeg. **1901** C. T. MOHR *Plant Life Alabama* 101 The nutmeg hickory, when full grown, resembles the shagbark hickory in its pale, shreddy bark. **1951** *Dict. Gardening* (R. Hort. Soc.) I. 404/2 Nutmeg Hickory. Tree 80 to 100 ft., shoots covered with yellowish, glossy scales... Nut ovoid, sweet, its shell hard and furrowed like a nutmeg.

nutmeggy, *a.* (Further examples.)

1928 *Daily Express* 17 Feb. 4 Luscious prunes with a creamy, nutmeggy rice pudding. **1971** *Daily Tel.* 17 Apr. 7 A large proportion of the bed could be occupied by.. Cherry Pic, which has a warm nutty, almost 'nutmeggy' scent, spicy and yet sweet.

nutria. Add: Hence also, a mid-brown colour such as that of the nutria fur.

1897 *Sears, Roebuck Catal.* 234/1 Ranch Hats... Colors, light nutria or tan. **1923** *Daily Mail* 26 Mar. 6 Colours: Gold, Grey,..Nutria, Putty. **1949** *Brit. Colour Council Dict. Colours Int. Decoration* III. 19/1 *Nutria,* a colour selected in consultation with expert furriers and standardized by B.C.C. in 1934.

nutriceptor (niŭ·triseptǫɹ). *Immunol.* [f. *nutri-* (in *nutrient, nutrition,* etc., or L. *nūtrīment-um,* etc.) + RE)CEPTOR.] (See quot. 1926.)

1911 *Jrnl. Amer. Med. Assoc.* 7 Oct. 1210/2 According to Ehrlich's view, when a parasite becomes refractory to an immune serum it does so by developing new groups of receptors..these receptors being the same receptors as combine with the food materials, and hence called 'nutriceptors'. **1926** R. J. E. SCOTT *Gould's Med. Dict.* 907/2 *Nutriceptors,* Ehrlich's name for receptors which react with foodstuffs more or less exclusively, and which therefore serve the nutrition of the cell. **1932** [see *CHEMOCEPTOR].

nutrient, *a.* and *sb.* Add: **B.** *sb.* (Further examples.)

1899 *Bull. Div. Veg. Physiol. & Path.* (U.S. Dept. Agric.) XVIII. 6 We can accept it as an indisputable fact that mineral matters found in plants also are real nutrients for them. **1903** H. SNYDER *Chem. Plant & Anima Life* xxxvi. 344 A balanced ration is one which contains a sufficient amount of nutrients from a variety of foods to meet the requirements of the animal. **1924** *Bot. Gaz.* LXXVII. 121 (*heading*) Absorption of nutrients from subsoil in relation to crop yield. **1974** *Encycl. Brit. Macropædia* XIII. 403/2 Carbon dioxide (CO_2) and water (H_2O) ..are important nutrients for all organisms. *Ibid.* 407/2 Lists of nutrients—both organic and inorganic—required by plants and animals. *Ibid.,* Essential nutrients include many amino acids, some fatty acids, many vitamins, and some minerals and trace elements.

2. Comb. *nutrient-poor, -rich* adjs.

1946 *Nature* 21 Sept. 421/2 In the nutrient-rich waters of the Thames type, a burst of algal growth may sometimes cease before any serious depletion of the mineral nutrient in the water has apparently taken place. **1955** *New Biol.* XVIII. 115 *N. alba* occupies a wide range of waters in the British Isles, from the oligotrophic, or nutrient-poor, peat-bottomed moorland lakes in Scotland and Ireland, to the eutrophic, or nutrient-rich, fen-lodes and broads of East Anglia. **1967** *Oceanogr. & Marine Biol.* V. 108 Massive upward displacement of nutrient-rich water on to the shelf may occur a few times in a century.

nutrition. Add: Hence also **nutri·tionally** *adv.*

1890 *Cent. Dict.,* Nutritionally. **1922** *Sci. Amer.* July 42/3 A diet may furnish a sufficient amount of protein, fat, carbohydrates, salts and vitamins and yet fail to promote growth or sustain well-being unless the quality of protein is nutritionally adequate. **1949** M. MEAD *Male & Female* x. 215 Foods all of which are suitable nutritionally. **1972** *Which?* Sept. 263/2 Nutritionally, there is not much difference between dairy and non-dairy [ice cream].

nutritionalist (niutri·ʃənălist). [f. NUTRITIONAL *a.* + -IST.] = next.

1956 *Nature* 24 Mar. 565/2 The importance of close co-operation between chemists, pharmacologists, biochemists and nutritionalists in this field cannot be overemphasized. **1971** *Islander* (Victoria, B.C.) 9 May 14/3 Steers a clear course through conflicting nutritionalists' claims to a reasonable assessment of the nation's dietary practices.

nutritionist (niutri·ʃənist). [f. NUTRITION + -IST.] One who studies, or is knowledgeable about, food and nutrition, esp. of humans.

1926 *University of State of N.Y. Bull. to Schools* June 261/2 Dentists, dental hygienists and nutritionists, when employed, are required to assist the medical inspector. **1936** *Nature* 31 Oct. 744/2 That highly trained specialist, the nutritionist—who, to be competent, must needs use the methods not only of chemistry and physics but also those of the various biological sciences. **1959** *New Biol.* XXX. 106 Animal nutritionists also have considered the possibility that traces of boron may be required in the vertebrate diet. **1969** *Daily Tel.* 21 Nov. 17/1 Until recently, nutritionists and health experts focused their attention on expectant mothers, babies and adolescents. **1973** *Nature* 27 Apr. 593/2 Few nutritionists are interested in the problems of old age.

nutshell, *v.* (Earlier example.)

1883 'MARK TWAIN' *Life on Mississippi* lviii. 570 The clerk nut-shelled the contrast between the former time and the present.

nutsy (nɒ·tsi), *a. colloq.* Also **nutsey.** [f. *nuts* (*NUT *sb.*[1] 7 c) + -Y[1].] Crazy, insane.
a **1941** F. SCOTT FITZGERALD *Tender is Night* (rev. ed., 1953) III. viii. 175 A boy..she thought was pretty nutsey. **1942** BERREY & VAN DEN BARK *Amer. Thes. Slang* §152/5 *Insane; crazy*,..nutsy. **1962** *Guardian* 27 Aug. 5/3 Gee, it was nutsy. **1964** W. MARKFIELD *To Early Grave* (1965) x. 169 Take a train, you nutsy you!

Nu·tter[2]. Also **nutter.** [f. NUT *sb.*[1] 1 + BUT)TER *sb.*[1]] The proprietary name of a substitute for butter made from the oil of nuts; nut-butter.
1906 *Westm. Gaz.* 18 May 4/2 'Nutter', 'Nucoline', and 'Nuttene'—all representing butter made from nuts. **1909** H. G. WELLS *Ann Veronica* vii. §3 Fruitarian refreshments—chestnut sandwiches buttered with nutter, and so forth. **1915** BARNETT *Let.* 2 May (1915) 127 One [*sc.* a trench mortar].. fires a cylindrical thing like a *Nutter* tin. **1920** *Trade Marks Jrnl.* 19 May 971 Nutter... Fats used in cooking. Mapleton's Nut Food Company, Limited,..Liverpool; food manufacturers. **1926–7** *Army & Navy Stores Catal.* 67/1 Nutter—the ideal cooking fat. **1958** *Catal. County Stores* (Taunton) June 29 Vegetarian foods..Cooking Fat, Nutter lb. 2/1. **1974** R. B. PARKER *God save Child* (1975) xi. 81 Dolly Bartlett got a package of Nutter Butter cookies from the cabinet.

nu·tter[3]. *slang.* [f. *NUT *sb.*[1] 8 c + -ER[1].] An insane person; a violent and deranged person. Occas. used in weaker sense: an eccentric person.
1958 F. NORMAN *Bang to Rights* I. 36 The reason for this is to find out wether [*sic*] or not you are a nutter. **1960** *Observer* 24 July 24/7 Sally is, at first sight, one of those romantic schizoids, a near nutter. **1963** 'A. GARVE' *Sea Monks* ii. 66 Reckon we'd be nutters to try it now. *Ibid.* v. 135, I reckon Chris was right, Rosie—King's a nutter. I reckon he'll go on killin' till there ain't no one left. **1963** [see *BARM *sb.*[2] 3]. **1965** A. PRIOR *Interrogators* xi. 200 A lot of 'em are nutters, I reckon. **1968** J. LOCK *Lady Policeman* v. 43 The term 'nutter' was invariably used though not meant unkindly and included all types from the eccentric (a bit of a nutter) to the raving lunatic (a right nutter). **1972** R. QUILTY *Tenth Session* 7 You could make out on the tipping lark—all those rich nutters.

nuttery. Add: **1.** (Later *attrib.* example.)
1932 H. NICOLSON *Diary* 20 Mar. (1966) 113 What would be good..would be to put the end of the main nuttery walk at the end of a main vista.
3. *slang.* A mental hospital.
1931 'D. STIFF' *Milk & Honey Route* vi. 62 Should the sociotechnic social worker be convinced that you are not normal she will have you bound for a nuttery before sunset. **1950** H. E. GOLDIN *Dict. Amer. Underworld Lingo* 147/2 *Nuttery*, an institution for the criminally insane or for mentally defective delinquents.

nuttiness (nɒ·tinės). [f. NUTTY *a.* + -NESS.] The quality or state of being nutty (in various senses).
1865 R. D. BLACKMORE *Cradock Nowell* (1866) xv. 137 In the height of summer, [his colour was] a dappled bay; towards the autumnal equinox, a tendency to nuttiness. **1884** *Sat. Rev.* 8 Mar. 321/2 The six essays..have the 'nuttiness' of age about them. **1916** E. V. LUCAS *Vermilion Box* 27 All his nuttiness has gone. You remember how his hair used to be swept right back from his forehead with lovely comb marks in it. **1926** E. O'NEILL *Great God Brown* 20 And I know damn well, underneath your nuttiness, you're gone on her. **1965** H. GOLD *Man who was not with It* xv. 128 It's the nuttiness of the mark and his fist in his palm. **1965** *Listener* 24 June 951/2 Scientists ..regard these same assumptions as 'nuttiness from an amateur'.

nu·ttish, *a.*[2] [f. *NUT *sb.*[1] 8 c.] Characteristic or suggestive of a crank or a crazy person.
1909 *Punch* 24 Mar. 208/3 He indulged in a variety of eccentricities. I can imagine nothing more nuttish.

nutty, *a.* Add: **2. d. nutty slack,** coal slack in small lumps or nuts (see NUT *sb.*[1] 17). Also *fig.*
1953 *New Yorker* 31 Jan. 58/2 The low-grade small coal appetizingly known as 'nutty slack',..gives off far less appetizing fumes and dirt. **1953** *Truth* 13 Feb. 165 Durham Dilemma. We can't buy Nutty Slack. **1959** I. & P. OPIE *Lore & Lang. Schoolch.* ix. 163 Stew, a not infrequent component of school dinners, is..in Croydon, 'nutty slack'. After an inapt term coined by the Ministry of Fuel (1952) for a poor quality coal, obtainable off the ration. The nuts were few and far between.
3. b. (Earlier and later examples.) Also in phr. *nutty as a fruit-cake.*
1898 S. CRANE in *Cosmopolitan* Dec. 169/1 'What's the matter with that feller?' asked Martin. 'Nutty,' said the man. **1935** G. & S. LORIMER *Heart Specialist* vi. 163 'Listen, Alix, you're as nutty as a fruitcake,' I said.. 'If I were you I'd have more sense.' **1955** P. WILDEBLOOD *Against Law* 104 He's as nutty as a fruit-cake. **1960** H. PINTER *Caretaker* III. 77 He's nutty, he's half way gone. **1963** *Daily Mirror* 6 Nov. 2/3 You have to be a real sour square not to love the nutty, noisy, happy, handsome Beatles. **1967** WODEHOUSE *Company for Henry* v. 84 'He doesn't strike me as unbalanced.' 'On his special subject he's as nutty as a fruit cake.' **1972** C. WESTON *Poor, Poor Ophelia* (1973) xxxii. 207 Jesus, you and your nutty imagination! **1974** *Author* Spring 26 Yeats was a great poet and a fascinating critic, but if he had been hired to give a year's course of lectures on the development of English poetry his performance would have been extremely nutty.
c. Of jazz or popular music: see quots.
1955 L. FEATHER *Encycl. Jazz* x. 347 *Nutty*,..great, exceptional. **1959** 'F. NEWTON' *Jazz Scene* 290 The modern..fashion of using terms taken from mental derangement for praise (*crazy, insane, nutty*).

nyala (nyā·lă). [Native name in Tsonga and Venda languages.] A large, gregarious antelope, *Tragelaphus angasi*, or the closely related species, *T. buxtoni*, occurring in parts of southern Africa; the male is greyish-brown with several white stripes and spiral, black horns, the female is reddish-brown and hornless; = INYALA. Also *attrib.*
1899 [see *HARNESSED *ppl. a.* 4]. **1915** *Chambers's Jrnl.* Nov. 702/1 The horns of this antelope..approximate more to those of the nyala, one of the largest of the bushbucks. **1931** *Discovery* Feb. 61/1 It [*sc.* the nyala] is one of the few forest-frequenting antelopes, and there cannot be many hundreds left in the jungles of Zululand and Southern Nyasaland. **1947** J. STEVENSON-HAMILTON *Wild Life S. Afr.* xv. 109 Along the Pafuri River in the nyala bush they have become accustomed to motor traffic. **1964** *Punch* 2 Sept. 359/3 Shooting a nyala. **1975** *Country Life* 20 Feb. 444/3 A visit to..these [South African] reserves is always rewarded with views of zebra, nyala, impala, duiker, waterbuck.

nyam, *sb.* and *v.* Also **nyam-nyam.** See *YAM *sb.* and *v.*

Nyanja (nya·ndʒă), *sb.* and *a.* Also **Manganja, Anyanja.** [f. Bantu *nyanja* lake + *ma-* tribal prefix, or *a-* plural prefix.] **A.** *sb.* **a.** The name of a Bantu people found in Malawi. **b.** A member of this people. **c.** The Bantu language spoken by this people. **B.** *attrib.* or as *adj.* Of or pertaining to the Nyanja people or their language.
1865 D. & C. LIVINGSTONE *Narr. Expedition Zambesi* v. 108 The Manganja generally live in villages, each of which has its own headman. *Ibid.* 123 The practice of bathing..we afterwards found to be common in other parts of the Manganja country. **1892** D. C. SCOTT (*title*) A cyclopaedic dictionary of the Mang'anja Language spoken in British Central Africa. **1902** H. BARNES *Nyanja-English Vocab.* p. ii, The vocabulary is primarily intended to help people to understand the Nyanja that they hear or read, and not to make up Nyanja to inflict on wandering natives. **1914** J. B. KEBLE in *Oxf. Survey Brit. Empire* III. x. 243 The Anyanja are a large and important group... They inhabit the western and south-western shores of Lake Nyasa and the Shiré Highlands. **1924** A. WERNER in G. Lagden *Native Races of Empire* iii. 88 A Nyanja man, if addressed in Yao or Konde, would probably not understand... But a Nyanja and a Tumbuka might understand each other. **1930** A. HETHERWICK *Dict. Nyanja Lang.* p. v, Not only in Nyasaland itself, but also in Northern and Southern Rhodesia.. Mang'anja, or, as it is now called, Nyanja, has come to occupy the place of a lingua franca. **1966** C. G. SELIGMAN *Races of Africa* (ed. 4) ix. 148 The spirits of dead Nyanja chiefs..are specially appealed to for rain. **1974** *Encycl. Brit. Macropædia* XI. 361/2 Nine main groups are historically associated with modern Malawi—the Chewa, Nyanja, Lomwe, Yao, Tumbuka, Sena, Tonga, Ngone, and Ngonde.

Nyassa (nəiæ·să, ny-). Also **Nyasa. a.** Name of a people in Malawi. **b.** A member of this people. Also *attrib.* or as *adj.*
1849 C. PICKERING *Races of Man* ix. 197 The *N'yasa*, who inhabit the islands and perhaps the further shores of the Great Lake, seemed to be the most distant tribe known at Zanzibar. **1883** R. N. CUST *Sk. Mod. Lang. Afr.* II. xii. 330 Rebman..employed..a slave, whom he imagined to be a Swahili, but he overheard him speaking a totally different language, and upon inquiry he proved to be a Wa-Nyassa. **1887** A. C. MADAN *Kiungani* ii. 30 We had never seen a single European in my time... They are called in the Nyasa language 'wan'tu oyela' meaning 'white man'. **1912** C. T. DOMINGO *Let.* 17 Mar. in Shepperson & Price *Independent African* (1958) Plate 11 (betw. pp. 158 and 159) It may take sometimes [*sic*] to possess jewels of Independance [*sic*] among *we* [*sic*] the Nyassas. Yours, lovely. For Africa. **1959** *Listener* 24 Sept. 471/1 A Nyasa is hardly thought to be a man until he has gone off to work for some years in the Johannesburg gold-mines.

nychthemeral (nikþī·mĕrăl), *a.* Also **nycthemeral.** [f. NYCHTHEMER(ON + -AL.] Occurring with a variation that matches that of night and day.
1907 *Nature* 17 Jan. 287/2 The regulation of the nychthemeral cycle of temperature and its inversion in the aged. **1967** *Oceanogr. & Marine Biol.* V. 495 These nycthemeral changes of the gas tension in the different levels of water. **1974** *Nature* 13 Sept. 143/2 These animals have a nychthemeral variation of less than 2° C.

nyctinastic (niktinæ·stik), *a. Bot.* [a. G. *nyctinastisch* (W. Pfeffer *Pflanzenphysiologie* (ed. 2, 1904) II. xii. 476): see NYCTI- and *NASTIC *a.*] Of the movements of flowers or leaves, caused by a regular cycle of changes in light and temperature. So **nyctina·stism, ny·ctinasty,** movement of this kind. Cf. NYCTITROPIC *a.*, NYCTITROPISM.
1906 A. J. EWART tr. *Pfeffer's Physiol. Plants* III. ii. 97 Since the term 'tropism' is reserved for curvatures produced by unilateral stimuli, it becomes necessary to change the term 'nyctitropic' used by Darwin..into that of 'nyctinastic'. *Ibid.* 101 There is no reason for restricting the term nyctinastic to pronounced sleep-movements. **1921** J. SMALL *Textbk. Bot.* xxvi. 378 Nyctitropism or Nyctinastism includes the opening and closing of flowers.., also the rising and falling of leaves.. in response to the stimulation of changes in temperature and light. **1936** J. B. HILL et al. *Botany* ix. 228 Certain leaves as well as flowers may fold up at night. These so-called 'sleep movements' of plants, brought about by the alternation of night and day, are the most common nasties and are termed nyctinasties. **1968** *New Scientist* 26 Dec. 717/1 The closing of the leaves..in fact, happens after the transfer of the plants to darkness—a so-called nyctinastic or 'sleep' movement.

nyctograph (ni·ktŏgrɑf). [f. NYCTO- + -GRAPH.] A device invented by 'Lewis Carroll' with which one can record one's ideas at night, in the dark, or when not fully awake.
1891 'L. CARROLL' *Diary* 24 Sept. (1953) II. xiv. 486 To-day I conceived the idea of having a series of *squares*, cut out in card, and devising an alphabet, of which each letter could be made of lines along the edges of the squares, and dots at the corners... I shall call it 'The Typhlograph'. (24/10/91. Instead of 'typhlograph' I have adopted 'Nyctograph' at the suggestion of Warner). **1898** S. D. COLLINGWOOD *Life & Lett. L. Carroll* vii. 295 In 1891 he conceived the device..and he named it the 'Typhlograph', but, at the suggestion of one of his brother-students, this was subsequently changed into 'Nyctograph'. **1930** W. DE LA MARE *Eighteen-Eighties* 236 He invented..poetical acrostics and the nyctograph. **1959** R. THOMSON *Psychol. Thinking* x. 198 Lewis Carroll derived so much from this source [*sc.* hypnagogic imagery] that he invented a peculiar instrument, the 'nyctograph', to enable him to jot down ideas without fully waking up.

Nylex (nəi·leks). A proprietary name of nylon.
1957 *Official Gazette* (U.S. Patent Office) 3 Sept. TM 3/2 Polymers, Inc...*Nylex* for extruded synthetic fibres, particularly adapted for use as brush bristles. **1967** E. A. GOLLSCHEWSKY in *Coast to Coast 1965–66* 88 She sank into a patio chair of plaited nylex. **1969** *Guardian* 7 Jan. 7/2 For dinghy sailors, showerproof clothes in Nylex, lightweight and very strong, are..sufficient.

nylon (nəi·lǫn). Also **Nylon.** [Invented word, with *-on* suggested by *rayon, cotton.*
There is no evidence to support the derivations freq. given for this word in popular sources. Cf. the following quot.: **1940** *Women's Wear Daily* 9 Feb. 22 The du Pont letter, written by John W. Eckelberry, covers the general status of nylon as follows: 'The word is a generic word coined by the du Pont Co. It is not a registered name or trademark... We wish to emphasize the following additional points: First, that the letters n-y-l-o-n have absolutely no significance, etymologically or otherwise... Because the names of two textile fibers in common use—namely 'cotton' and 'rayon', end with letters 'on'..it was felt that a word ending in 'on' might be desirable. A number of words..were rejected because it was found they were not sufficiently distinct from words found in the dictionary, or in lists of classified trademarks. After much deliberation, the term 'nylon' was finally adopted.']
1. Any of the thermoplastics that are wholly synthetic polyamides with a straight-chain molecular structure, many of which are tough, lightweight, and resistant to heat and chemicals, may be produced as filaments, bristles, or sheets and as moulded objects, and are widely used for textile fabrics and industrially; *esp.* nylon 66, made from adipic acid and hexamethylenediamine.
1938 *N.Y. Times* 28 Oct. 34/3 'Nylon' is a generic name, coined by the du Pont chemists, to designate all materials defined scientifically as 'synthetic fiber-forming polymeric amides having a protein-like chemical structure; derivable from coal, air and water, or other substances, and characterized by extreme toughness and strength and the peculiar ability to be formed into fibers and into various shapes, such as bristles and sheets'. **1940** *Times* 21 Mar. 5/5 Imperial Chemical Industries, Limited, announce that progress is being made in the erection of three factories for the manufacture of nylon in England. **1942** *Industr. & Engin. Chem.* Jan. 56/2 After polymerization, the molten nylon is extruded as a ribbon onto a chilled roll. **1943** *Chem. Abstr.* XXXVII. 3947 A description of the manuf. of No. 66 Nylon (as the most important nylon). **1950** R. W. MONCRIEFF *Artificial Fibres* xvii. 206 '610' nylon may be preferred to '66', for use as bristles. **1955** *Sci. News Let.* 2 Apr. 217/2 The new, tempered form of nylon, named Nylon 8 by the Du Pont Co., is a liquid. It can be molded into fuel tanks, pipes, gaskets and seals. **1958** D. E. FLOYD *Polyamide Resins* i. 4 Nylon-6,10 means that the diamine contained 6 carbon atoms and the dibasic acid contained 10 carbon atoms. **1963** H. R. CLAUSER *Encycl. Engin. Materials* 451/1 Nylons resist electrolytic corrosion, hydrolysis, fungi, bacteria and most chemicals. **1964** *Which?* Aug. 253/2 There are a number of different nylons used in textiles. *Ibid.*, Fabrics made from nylon tend to attract dirt. **1964** N. G. CLARK *Mod. Org. Chem.* xvii. 361 The most famous example of this is nylon 66 (popularly known as Nylon), which is straight chain polyamide constructed from two six-carbon components. **1972** J. WREN-LEWIS in Cox & Dyson *20th-Cent. Mind* II. ix. 279 In modern chemical jargon the term 'nylon' refers, not to any one specific material but to any macromolecular material made by interacting dibasic acids with diamines: such materials are sometimes also called polyamides. **1973** *Sci. Amer.* July 42/3 Today the matrix in glass-

reinforced composites may be either a thermoset plastic, such as polyester,..or any of a number of thermoplastic resins, such as nylon, polyethylene or polystyrene.

2. *pl.* Nylon stockings.

1940 *Woman* (U.S.) V. II. 68 Dunk your nylons in rich suds of neutral soap. **1948** *Daily Mail* 21 Apr. 1/2 The two cases were opened by Customs officers. Both were full of nylons and powder compacts. **1951** M. McLuhan *Mech. Bride* (1967) 33/1 Food and nylons..are consumed and promoted with moral fervor. **1957** J. Braine *Room at Top* vii. 72 High heels and nylons. **1965** *N.Y. Times* 16 May VI. 80/2 By 1964, silk and rayon stockings were almost unknown in the United States, while production of nylons had risen to 83,900,000 dozen pairs. **1966** J. Betjeman *High & Low* 67 Encase your legs in nylons, Bestride your hills with pylons, O age without a soul.

3. Fabric or cloth made from nylon yarn.

1940 *Jrnl. R. Aeronaut. Soc.* XLIV. 312 Possible use of synthetic textile Nylon as a parachute material. **1945** *Times* 6 Nov. 4/4 Arrangements are being made for the conversion into clothing and other goods of 26,000,000 yards of nylon, cotton and celanese which will become available from finished parachutes surrendered by the services as surplus. **1958** *Woman's Own* 5 Feb. 37/3 (Advt.), Nighties, blouses, slips, underwear in silk, nylon, rayon, 'Terylene', chiffon..keep their soft sheen and filmy finery. **1967** E. Short *Embroidery & Fabric Collage* iii. 81 Appliqué in more net, or in nylon, organdie, etc., would give weight and definition to the design.

II. 4. *attrib.* or as *adj.* Made or consisting of nylon.

1939 *Industrial Fibres Rev.* III. 167/1 The first considerable use of 'Nylon' yarn will be in the full-fashioned hose trade where silk is at present the raw material. **1941** *Jrnl. R. Aeronaut. Soc.* XLV. 219 Fabrics manufactured of Nylon artificial fibre, a coal derivative.., has [*sic*] been..compared with pure silk, as a possible substitute for the latter, for use in the manufacture of parachutes. **1941** *Jrnl. Amer. Med. Assoc.* 4 Oct. 1221/1 One of the principal reasons why Nylon stockings have achieved popularity is the fact that they are more 'sheer' than silk stockings. **1951** *Good Housek. Home Encycl.* 29/2 Nylon brushes are available in a variety of colours. **1958** *New Statesman* 28 June 831/1 Men who had nylon shirts and terylene suits before those fabrics got into Marks and Spencer's. **1958** L. van der Post *Lost World of Kalahari* ix. 209 We had to make our home under a nylon tarpaulin stretched taut between our Land-Rovers. **1961** *Lancet* 22 July 206/2 Nylon film as a wrapping material for sterilisation. **1968** *Bodl. Libr. Rec.* VIII. 61 It runs on four 4-inch nylon wheels fitted with roller bearings. **1973** 'E. Peters' *City of Gold & Shadows* iv. 65 In a nylon jersey house-gown..she could not possibly be anyone but Mrs. Paviour.

b. (See quots.)

1955 *Caribbean Q.* IV. II. 103 Nylon, pronounced 'nilô' or 'dilô' has come to signify anything new, different, and better. The new ice house in Soufriere advertises 'nylon' ice, and nylon starch and nylon peanuts can be had, the latter being candies shaped like peanuts. **1967** Cassidy & Le Page *Dict. Jamaican Eng.* 326/2 *Nylon road*, any new very smooth asphalt-surfaced road—much smoother than the average Jamaican road. (From about 1958, FGC.)

5. General attrib.

1942 *Industr. & Engin. Chem.* Jan. 58/2 The nylon industry is only in its infancy. **1951** *Economist* 22 Sept. 686/1 Nylon output is now running at an annual rate of 100 million pounds. **1953** K. H. Inderfurth *Nylon Technol.* 11 Du Pont's third nylon plant. **1963** H. R. Clauser *Encycl. Engin. Materials* 452/1 Tubing and rod stock manufacture, plus the coating of wire and cable, are the major forms of nylon extrusion.

6. *Comb.* **a.** Instrumental, as *nylon-covered, -faced* adjs. **b.** Parasynthetic, as *nylon-bristled, -geared, -legged, -tipped* adjs.

1954 H. R. Mauersberger in *Matthews's Textile Fibers* (ed. 6) xviii. 946 Nylon-bristled toothbrushes. **1960** *Farmer & Stockbreeder* 29 Mar. 75/3 The pump..incorporates nylon-covered steel rollers to push the milk round. **1967** *Jane's Surface Skimmer Systems 1967–68* 25/1 Propulsion fans are driven by nylon-faced toothed rubber timing belts. **1961** *Listener* 5 Oct. 498/2 Nylon-geared egg beaters. **1954** J. Betjeman *Few Late Chrysanthemums* 74 And country girls with lips and nails vermilion Wait, nylon-legged, to straddle on the pillion. **1966** *Melody Maker* 23 July 10/4 His [drum] sticks are..Autocrat nylon-tipped and Japanese Star 7a.

7. Special comb.: **nylon (stocking) dermatitis,** dermatitis caused by the dye of nylon stockings; **nylon salt,** a salt formed by the reaction of hexamethylenediamine (or another diamine) with adipic acid (or another dibasic acid), which is polymerized to give nylon.

1954 H. R. Mauersberger in *Matthews's Textile Fibers* (ed. 6) xviii. 961 Any references to 'nylon dermatitis'..are distinct misnomers. **1964** *Listener* 26 Mar. 520/1 Nylon dermatitis and bunions are related to fashions of dress. **1945** *Industr. Fibres & By-Products* VII. 53/2 The nylon salt solution is..ready to be made into new nylon polymer. **1958** D. E. Floyd *Polyamide Resins* iv. 54 Nylon salts may be formed in water or aqueous alcohol solution and are crystallized from aqueous alcohol or alcohol itself. They are usually soluble in water, but insoluble in alcohol, acetone, ether, or hydrocarbons. **1964** J. G. Cook *Your Guide to Plastics* 239 Hexamethylene diamine and adipic acid are reacted together to form a salt, hexamethylene diammonium adipate, or 'nylon salt'. *Ibid.* 240 Hexamethylene diamine and sebacic acid are combined to form nylon 6:10 salt, or hexamethylene diammonium sebacate. **1947** *Jrnl. Investigative Dermatol.* IX. 207 All the subjects suffering from nylon stocking dermatitis were hypersensitive to azodyes used in the manufacture of the stockings. **1957** *Year Bk. Dermatol. & Syphilol.* 117 Nylon stocking dermatitis results from sensitivity to the dye.

nyloned (nəi·lǫnd), *a.* [f. prec. + -ED².] Clad in nylons.

1952 B. Malamud *Natural* (1963) 16 Her nyloned legs made Roy's pulses dance. **1959** *Times Lit. Suppl.* 9 Oct. 573/3 Also making the voyage are a group of American girls..normal, nyloned, streamlined, wide-eyed, cynical and destructive. **1962** *Economist* 31 Mar. 1240/1 The men are well shod, the women well nyloned. **1963** G. Freeman *Campaign* iv. 69 Lady Andover's knees emerging, pinkly nyloned, from under her black coat. **1975** I. Murdoch *Word Child* 195, I looked down, inspecting a nyloned ankle and a smart..high-heeled shoe.

nymph, *sb.* Add: **2. b.** (Further examples.)

1833 W. Tolmie *Jrnl.* 28 Mar. (1963) 133 Nymphs of the pavé numerous (in Honolulu). **1902** Farmer & Henley *Slang* V. 81 *Nymph of darkness* (or *the pavement*), ..a prostitute. **1942** Berrey & Van den Bark *Amer. Thes. Slang* §507/2 Prostitute... Nymph du pave. **1964** 'W. Haggard' *Antagonists* vii. 71 Counsellor of Embassy living with fellow-travelling nymph.... They'd do most things to muffle that one. **1965** 'S. Harvester' *Assassins Road* xvii. 180 He had been pretty sure she was a nymph. **1968** R. Stout *Father Hunt* (1969) xiii. 157 She was a nymph. She was a goddam tart.

3. b. A fishing fly made in imitation of the aquatic larval form of may-flies, insects of the order Ephemeroptera.

1910 G. E. M. Skues *Minor Tactics of Chalk Stream* iv. 32, I had tied some nymphs of appropriate colour of body. **1922** R. C. Bridgett *Dry-fly Fishing* i. 17 The place of honour [as a lure] is occupied by the artificial nymph. **1973** *Shooting Times & Country Mag.* 7 July 13/3 There were virtually no rising fish to be seen and I decided to plod on with the nymph.

6. *nymph-fishing, -song; nymph-haunted, -less* adjs.

1932 *Times Lit. Suppl.* 5 May 374/2 The delicate art of nymph-fishing. **1972** *Shooting Times & Country Mag.* 1 July 15/2 The Club rules permit only dry fly and nymph fishing until the end of July. **1881** O. Wilde *Poems* 69 Blue nymph-haunted seas. **1939** W. B. Yeats *On Boiler* 28 Nymph-haunted or Fury-haunted wood. **1948** C. Day Lewis *Poems 1943–47* 19 Otherwise the forest was silent: birdless; nymphless. **1930** E. Blunden *Summer's Fancy* 15 When nymph-songs echoed on the blossomed breeze.

nymph (nimf), *v.* [f. the sb., sense 3.] Of fish, esp. trout: to feed upon insect larvæ near the surface of the water. So **ny·mphing** *ppl. a.*

1963 O. Kite in C. F. Walker *Compl. Fly-fisher* iv. 140 A nymphing trout..can be seen making little movements, lifting slightly in the water from time to time. **1972** *Shooting Times & Country Mag.* 24 June 15/2 In the sheltered bay we saw the odd fish nymphing.

Nymphenburg (ni·mfənbɜ̄ɹg). The name of a former village in Bavaria, now a suburb of Munich, used *attrib.* to designate pottery manufactured there from 1761.

1863 W. Chaffers *Marks Pott. & Porc.* 183 Nymphenburg. Another form of the arms of Bavaria, also impressed on the ware. **1869** C. Schreiber *Jrnl.* 4 & 5 July (1911) I. 26 A small Nymphenburg vase mounted, £1. **1881** *Ibid.* 16 Nov. II. 374 Our only purchase was a Nymphenburg shell piece..signed and dated C.H.Z. 1771. **1882** 'Ouida' *Bimbi* 50 A little pale-faced chit of a damsel in white Nymphenburg china. **1910** *Encycl. Brit.* V. 751/1 His Nymphenburg figures are as highly esteemed as those he modelled at Höchst. **1960** *House & Garden* Oct. 112/1 A collection of Nymphenburg equestrian statuettes. **1971** L. A. Boger *Dict. World Pott. & Porc.* 247 (*caption*) Nymphenburg figure.

nymphet. Add: **b.** A nymph-like or sexually attractive young girl.

1955 V. Nabokov *Lolita* (1959) I. v. 18 Between the age limits of nine and fourteen there occur maidens who, to certain bewitched travellers, twice or many times older than they, reveal their true nature which is not human, but nymphic (that is, demoniac); and these chosen creatures I propose to designate as 'nymphets'. **1959** *Listener* 8 Jan. 63/2 A whole chorus of what the author of *Lolita* calls 'nymphets'. **1959** *Daily Mail* 31 Jan. 4/4 He is in the thick of an affair with an idealised nymphet of 20. **1963** *Spectator* 15 Feb. 199 Two nymphets visit him together, he orders them both into his bed. **1971** *Southerly* XXXI. 12 She is..at her first appearance a shameless nymphet of thirteen already *indifferent* to the number of boys who have enjoyed her favours. **1973** J. Di Mona *Last Man at Arlington* (1974) 51 Most of the 'sales executives' had turned out to be eighteen- and nineteen-year-old nymphets.

c. *attrib.* and *Comb.* in sense *b.

1959 *Spectator* 25 Sept. 406/1 Their 'baby doll' outfits had the nymphet look which has been in fashion this summer. **1960** *Spectator* 3 June 804/1 Seems to have convinced herself that..every nymphet gesture..can be repeated again and again with ever-increasing success. **1960** *Encounter* June 86/2 The hero..bails out a nymphet-loving painter. **1971** *Daily Tel.* 27 May 8/4 Mother, a randy alcoholic; father, a seedy, nymphet-chasing Peter Pan.

nympho (ni·mfo), colloq. abbrev. of Nymphomaniac *a.* and *sb.*

1935 [see *dipso]. **1954** D. Schwartz in *Avon Bk. Mod. Writing* II. 129 Some girls at school said that Phoebe was a nympho. **1958** A. Wilson *Middle Age of Mrs Eliot* 232 'That Cynthia Robertson's a bit nympho,' he announced in worldly tones. **1959** 'J. Bell' *Easy Prey* x. 106 Red-haired bitch... Distinctly nympho. **1960** 'R. East' *Kingston Black* xiv. 140 Tim Askew, degenerate turkey farmer, had pulled the trigger on the Danish nympho. **1973** 'E. Peters' *City of Gold & Shadows* xiii. 208 She was a sex-nut-case, a virgin nympho who couldn't stand being mauled but couldn't help asking for it.

nympholepsy. (Later examples.)

1955 V. Nabokov *Lolita* (1958) I. 174 The science of nympholepsy is a precise science. Actual contact would do it in one second flat. An interspace of a millimeter would do it in ten. **1974** *Times Lit. Suppl.* 8 Feb. 122/3 His congenital nympholepsy for slender girls with thin arms.

nymphology. Add: Hence **nympholo·gical** *a. rare.*

1953 R. Graves *Poems* 4 Confess, what elegant square or lumpish hamlet Lives free from nymphological disquiet?

nymphomania. Add: (Earlier and later examples.)

1775 E. S. Wilmot tr. de Bienville (*title*) Nymphomania, or, a dissertation concerning the furor uterinus. **1905** Moussu & Dollar *Dis. Cattle* VII. iv. 562 Nymphomania may be considered as almost invariably the result of a genital lesion. **1962** C. Allen *Textbk. Psychosexual Disorders* v. xvi. 306 Since writers..have become fascinated with the concept of nymphomania..it might be as well here to state that it is clinically very rare. **1967** L. W. van den Heever tr. *Heidrich & Renk's Dis. Mammary Glands Domestic Anim.* v. 48/1 In nymphomania the cysts should be ruptured when possible and chorionic gonadotropin..administered subcutaneously or intracystally to prevent recrudescence.

nymphomaniac *a.* and *sb.* (later examples); hence also **nymphomani·acal** *a.*

1906 J. Joyce *Let.* 13 Nov. (1966) II. 193 Cosgrave [was sure] that I would become a nymphomaniac. **1923** *Physiol. Rev.* III. 338 The writer has examined a section..of an ovary of a nymphomaniac cow. **1923** A. Huxley *Antic Hay* xx. 287 When I call my lover a nymphomaniacal dog, she runs the penknife into my arm. **1932** Gaiger & Davies *Vet. Pathol. & Bacteriol.* III. xxxv. 513 The presence of nymphomaniac cysts is always accompanied by sterility, even though the cysts are confined to one ovary. **1949** 'J. Tey' *Brat Farrar* xxiii. 208 Pawning his life to a nymphomaniacal moron. **1967** L. W. van den Heever tr. *Heidrich & Renk's Dis. Mammary Glands Domestic Anim.* iii. 34/2 Protracted nymphomaniacal estrus associated with relaxation of the pelvic ligaments, vaginal prolapse, nervousness and aggressiveness is commonly encountered. **1969** C. Allen *Textbk. Psychosexual Disorders* (ed. 2) v. xvi. 356 Nymphomaniacs who have a compulsion due to brain lesions, hormonal imbalance or other physical abnormalities. **1973** R. Hayes *Hungarian Game* viii. 59 From different sources I'd heard that she was nymphomaniacal or homosexual or frigid.

Nynorsk (niū·nǭɹsk). Also **nynorsk, Ny Norsk.** [Norw., f. *ny* new + *norsk* Norwegian.] The official name by which Landsmål is now known. Cf. *Landsmål.

1937 E. I. Haugen *Beginning Norwegian* 5 Ivar Aasen (1813–1896) conceived the idea that if one studied the most 'genuine' native dialects..one might create a form of Norwegian equivalent to what the national language would have been had Norway never been united with Denmark... He called it *landsmål*, a name by which it is still commonly known (though *nynorsk* is now official). **1952** B. Berulfsen in *Norseman* X. 187 In 1929 official action changed the names Landsmål to *Nynorsk* and Riksmål to *Bokmål*. **1966** E. I. Haugen *Lang. Conflict & Lang. Planning* vi. 257 The choice given in the proposed ballot was between 'natural Riksmål, Nynorsk, and official Bokmål'. **1971** *Computers & Humanities* V. 205 The data bank of the project, which covers both *bokmaal* and *nynorsk*, is intended to assist various types of linguistic projects in the future. **1975** *Scottish Rev.* I. 22 The 'Landsmaal', the distinctively Norwegian language that in the 70s of last century a group of writers were endeavouring to institute as the literary language of Norway as distinct from the usual Dano-Norwegian, an attempt which has developed into the 'Ny Norsk' (New Norwegian), in which a number of works are written now.

Nyon (nī·ǭn). The name of a commune in Switzerland, used *attrib.* and *absol.* to designate pottery manufactured there from *c* 1780.

1869 C. Schreiber *Jrnl.* 10 May (1911) I. 2 A very fine service of Nyon, dinner and dessert. **1910** E. Dillon *Porcelain & how to collect It* xii. 181 The only distinctive mark of Nyon is a fish painted in blue under the glaze. **1960** H. Hayward *Antique Coll.* 202/1 *Nyon porcelain*, a factory was founded at Nyon, near Geneva in 1780... Current French fashions were closely adhered to and many of the wares bear floral decoration.

nyssa (ni·să). [mod.L. (J. F. Gronovius in Linnæus *Systema Naturæ* (1735)), f. *Nysa* the name of a water nymph, in allusion to the swamp habitat of some species.] A deciduous tree of the genus so called, belonging to the family Nyssaceæ and native to North America and Asia, esp. the American species *Nyssa sylvatica*, the tupelo.

1886 G. Nicholson *Illustr. Dict. Gardening* II. 461/1 Nyssas thrive best in low, damp, moist situations, such as peat swamps. **1901** L. H. Bailey *Cycl. Amer. Hort.* III. 1109/2 Nyssas are trees or shrubs with petiolate, usually entire leaves and small flowers borne in short racemes or dense heads. **1961** *Amateur Gardening* 23 Sept. 3/3 The tulip tree..and the nyssa in the Long Walk to the Pagoda ..are among the tallest trees in the Garden [at Kew]. **1962** *Times* 24 Dec. 11/1 No exotics means..no *Nyssas*.

nystatin (nəi·stătin). *Pharm.* [f. the name of *New York State*, U.S.A., where it was developed + -IN[1].] A yellow antifungal substance, $C_{46}H_{77}NO_{19}$, that is produced by the growth of the bacterium *Streptomyces noursei* and is used locally in the treatment of moniliasis, esp. when caused by *Candida albicans*, and of anal and vaginal infections.

1952 *Arch. Pediatrics* LXIX. 414 Hazen et al. have shown that an antibiotic called fungicidin, Nystatin®, has inhibited coccidioides immitis spherules at 6·25 micrograms per milliliter. [*The name* Nystatin *is not in fact registered as a trade mark at the U.S. Patent Office.*] **1953** *Science* 29 May 609/2 The senior authors [*sc.* Brown & Hazen] have given the name Nystatin to their product fungicidin. It is being manufactured by E. R. Squibb and Sons under this name. **1962** E. O. MORRIS in Hawthorn & Leitch *Recent Adv. Food Sci.* I. 33 Yeasts appear to be particularly troublesome and it has been suggested that these organisms may be inhibited by the use of nystatin. **1974** R. N. RICHARDS *Venereal Dis.* 104/1 The diagnosis of monilia was made and she responded well to the insertion of nystatin tablets in her vagina twice daily.

nyuck, var. *YU(C)K.

nyumyum (nyŭ·myŭ·m). *rare*⁻¹. = *YUM-YUM.

1922 JOYCE *Ulysses* 159 O, that's nyumyum.

Nzima (n₁zĭ·mă). Also **Nsima**, **Nzema**. The name of an African language spoken in Ghana.

1911 F. W. H. MIGEOD *Lang. W. Afr.* I. vii. 179 In Nsima (Zema) there is also a suffix, but it appears that there exists also initial change, the same as in Twi. **1945** I. C. WARD *Rep. Investigation Gold Coast Lang. Probl.* 61 Nzema..appears to be a strong admixture of two language groups, the Fante branch of the Akan language and some other group lying to the west. **1971** L. A. BOADI in J. Spencer *Eng. Lang. W. Afr.* 49 The indigenous languages [of the Gold Coast],..are still used and are, in many cases, deliberately cultivated; no less than six of them—Akan, Gã, Ewe, Nzima, Dagbani and Hausa—are regularly heard on the radio. **1975** *Archivum Linguisticum* VI. 2 In certain environments Nzema and Ahanta *k* alternates with *g*.